2002
Britannica Book of the Year

Encyclopædia Britannica, Inc.
Chicago · London · New Delhi · Paris · Seoul · Sydney · Taipei · Tokyo

2002 Britannica Book of the Year

Editorial and design-production services provided by Proof Positive/Farrowlyne Associates, Inc., Evanston, IL.

Library of Congress Catalog Card Number: 38-12082
International Standard Book Number: 0-85229-812-9
International Standard Serial Number: 0068-1156

BRITANNICA BOOK OF THE YEAR

Britannica.com may be accessed on the Internet at http://www.britannica.com.

(Trademark Reg. U.S. Pat. Off.) Printed in U.S.A.

Foreword

It is the task of the editors of Britannica's yearbooks to get acquainted intimately with each calendar year, to discern each year's special "personality." We look for themes, or leitmotivs, and try to knit them all together into a coherent whole. The task of sorting out 2001 was both easier and more difficult in that, three-quarters of the way through, it suddenly became a one-story year—and 2001 was turned into one of the most remarkable years ever. The events of September 11 and its aftermath immediately swept other stories to the sidelines.

Our keynote article, written by the *Washington Post*'s Robert G. Kaiser, bears as its title a date, "9-11," and is placed at the head of the section of the book that examines the chronology of the year. Kaiser writes thoughtfully of the changes in the United States and the world after that date, pointing out that the events confirm the concept of the world as a "global village." As the hundreds of contributions to this yearbook began to arrive, the editors were amazed at how many of them referred to the terrorist attacks and the aftermath.

- **Health and Disease** "A few hours after the World Trade Center's twin towers collapsed, five designated city hospitals were prepared for the worst. Triage centres were set up within a few blocks of 'ground zero,' fully staffed and equipped to treat any possible injury and perform lifesaving surgery."
- **Environment** "[A]crid smoke, soot, and ash from tons of pulverized debris complicated the recovery in New York City."
- **Business** "Any hopes that the boom years of the 1990s would extend into the next decade ended for good after the September 11 terrorist attacks."
- **Fashion** "Prominent American buyers . . . refrained from traveling to see the European collections."
- **Museums** "A number of museums sought to upgrade their insurance policies and implement damage-control measures."
- **Architecture** "Architects and others debated the long-term impact of the disaster. Would the world stop building skyscrapers?"
- **International Law** "[B]ecause Osama bin Laden . . . was not the representative of any state, charges against him could not be brought in the [International Court of Justice]." "Were the attacks an act of war? Was a declaration of war required in order to respond with military force?"
- **Media and Publishing** "The September attacks forced first one and later a second postponement of the Emmys, as well as the delay of the TV season's debut by one week. . . . 'The 11th' hastened the decline of an industry already suffering lowered revenues and resulted in the closure of some well-known magazines."
- **Religion** "The [attacks] spurred a worldwide examination of Islamic doctrine. . . . Muslim scholars pointed out . . . that terrorist violence is an interpretation of Islam that most adherents of the faith reject."

Many country articles, such as Afghanistan and Pakistan, were heavily devoted to these events, of course, but other countries were affected as well:

- **Germany** "[Chancellor Gerhard] Schröder jumped ahead even of the U.S. in defining what had happened as a "conflict of cultures" and a "declaration of war on the free world."
- **U.K.** "[Prime Minister] Tony Blair . . . [won] overwhelming political and public support for his international role in the fight against terrorism."
- **Iraq** "Pres. Saddam publicly opposed the U.S.-led war on terrorism and called on other Islamic countries to help defeat it. He also decried the military action in Afghanistan, calling it a spark that could set 'the world on fire.'"
- **Egypt** "[Pres. Hosni] Mubarak . . . spoke of Egypt's need to coordinate actions with Western countries to combat terrorism."
- **Venezuela** "[Pres. Hugo] Chávez equated civilian casualties from the bombing with the deaths caused by terrorists on September 11."

Of course, there were other important events in 2001. Topping Britannica's list would be the economic downturn, both in the U.S. and around the globe; worldwide protests against globalization; the continuing AIDS epidemic in this the 20th year since it was first identified; foot-and-mouth disease and "mad cow" disease, both of which continued to affect agriculture, diets, and personal freedoms in the U.K. and continental Europe; the improvement in the prospects for peace in Northern Ireland but the deterioration in the Israel/Palestine and Pakistan/ India relationships; and the furor over the death penalty evoked by the execution in June of American terrorist Timothy McVeigh.

Both the Philippines and Indonesia got rid of old, corrupt leaders, and interesting new figures were elected in Israel, Bulgaria, Moldova, Peru, and Japan. Nine members of the Nepali royal family were massacred. Kofi Annan was whisked in for a second term as secretary-general of the United Nations, and the man and the organization shared the Nobel Prize for Peace. Apart from the business turndown, the Microsoft trial and the demise of Enron Corp. were probably the biggest business headlines. Scientific firsts in 2001 included evidence from Australia that Africa may not have been the only location where the human species arose; a spacecraft landed on an asteroid; and an artificial heart was implanted. Disastrous earthquakes shook India, El Salvador, and Chile.

The year's top names in sports included golfer Tiger Woods, baseball slugger Barry Bonds, the formidable Michael Jordan, race-car driver Jeff Gordon, and Jacques Rogge, the Belgian tapped to head the International Olympic Committee. In the realm of culture, Tony Kushner returned to the stage with a play about—do you believe it?—Afghanistan, while *The Producers* made records on Broadway and young Harry Potter performed his wizardry on movie theatre box offices.

All this, plus biographies, obituaries, a day-by-day calendar of events—and much, much more—awaits you in the pages that follow.

Editor

Contents

2002

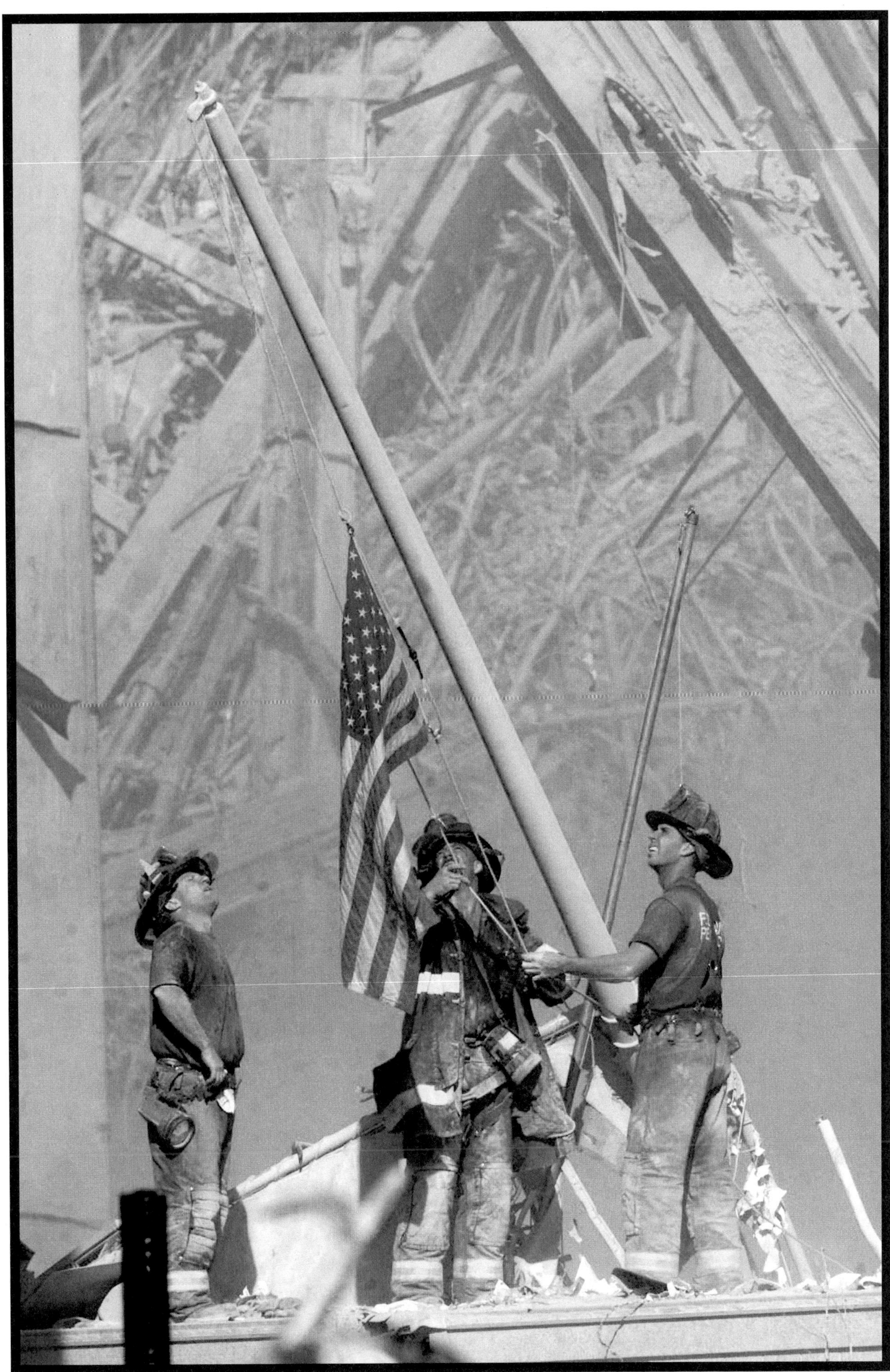

Dates of 2001

The September 11 terrorist attacks in the U.S. changed forever the contours of the world and affected the ways we all interact with one another.

Kathy Cacicedo

SPECIAL REPORT

9-11

Robert G. Kaiser

For years we said we lived in a global village. On Sept. 11, 2001, terrorists bent on wreaking havoc in New York City and Washington, D.C., proved that this was so. Never before had the world so intimately shared the same tragic disaster. Because the attacks occurred in the morning on the U.S. East Coast, perhaps 90% of the Earth's population was awake when two airplanes flew into the World Trade Center and another crashed into the Pentagon. Transported to New York by some of the most powerful images ever conveyed by television, billions of people vicariously experienced the horror.

Rare are the events that jolt the entire globe. In truth, there may never have been another that had the impact of September 11. The detonation of the first atomic bomb or the bringing down of the Berlin Wall may have been more important historical events, but neither had an audience as big or as raptly attentive as that on September 11. In part because nearly everyone was jolted, we will need a long time to grasp the true import of that date. It became a cliché almost immediately afterward that "everything has changed." Giving that phrase real content will take years.

Some of the things that changed were quickly obvious. The United States lost its innocence and its isolation, becoming in just a few days a different kind of global power. For 56 years after World War II, Americans had policed the globe as beneficent gendarmes, trying to keep the world safe for democracy and capitalism. Suddenly on September 11 the mission changed. The goal became to keep America itself safe.

For the first time, other nations rushed to America's side, offering condolences and active assistance. The North Atlantic Treaty Organization invoked Article 5 of its founding treaty, declaring that the terrorist actions constituted an attack against all NATO members, which would

The Pentagon from the southwest.

September 9

Suicide bombers attack Ahmed Shah Masoud, head of the anti-Taliban opposition

September 11

7:59 A.M. American Airlines Flight 11 takes off from Logan International Airport in Boston, bound for Los Angeles.

8:14 A.M. United Airlines Flight 175 takes off from Logan International Airport in Boston, bound for Los Angeles.

8:20 A.M. American Airlines Flight 77 takes off from Washington Dulles International Airport in Washington, D.C., bound for Los Angeles.

Jim LoScalzo for USN&WR

8:42 A.M. United Airlines Flight 93 takes off from Newark International Airport in Newark, N.J., bound for San Francisco.

8:48 A.M. American Airlines Flight 11 crashes into World Trade Center north tower in New York City.

9:03 A.M. United Airlines Flight 175 crashes into World Trade Center south tower in New York City.

9:40 A.M. American Airlines Flight 77 crashes into Pentagon.

9:45 A.M. Federal Aviation Authority orders all flights grounded.

9:59 A.M. South tower of World Trade Center collapses.

10:10 A.M. United Airlines Flight 93 crashes near Shanksville, Pa.

10:28 A.M. North tower of World Trade Center collapses.

5:25 P.M. A third building, 7 World Trade Center, 47 stories tall, collapses.

10:30 P.M. President Bush addresses the nation from the White House.

The World Trade Center collapses. AP/Wide World Photos

respond—as required by the treaty—as if they had been attacked themselves. Article 5 had never before been invoked. In Moscow the young president of Russia phoned the young U.S. president aboard Air Force One and pledged his country's cooperation for a war against terrorism. Vladimir Putin's call was the first the administration of George W. Bush received from a foreign leader. On September 19 the Organization of American States agreed by acclamation to invoke the Rio Treaty, a mutual defense pact. One after another the countries of the world lined up with the United States. Most did so without evident hesitation, a few because Bush made it so clear, in his speech to Congress on September 20, that the U.S. expected their support: "Every nation in every region now has a decision to make: Either you are with us or you are with the terrorists."

Ultimately, only Iraq offered sympathy to the terrorists; no other government would take their side. This was a huge change. The nations of the world had never before been so united on an important global issue. The collapse of international factions into a united front against terrorism signaled powerfully that, as U.S. Secretary of State Colin Powell put it in a speech in Shanghai on October 18, "not only is the Cold War over, the post-Cold War period is also over." Suddenly the world had a new cause and a new sense of shared challenge. Old alignments seemed to disappear.

But that near unanimity among political leaders was not so evident on the streets of the world's cities, towns, and villages. Within hours of the September 11 attacks, cameras caught Palestinians on the West Bank exulting over the terrorists' successes. Posters carrying the likeness of Osama bin Laden blossomed throughout the Muslim world. Public opinion polls and questioning reporters found that citizens of many lands felt sympathy for the terrorists and antipathy for the United States.

In China government officials had to censor Internet discussions, which included much cheering for a blow struck against American arrogance. A poll taken in Bolivia found that Bin Laden was the most admired man in that Andean nation. In Muslim countries certain myths took hold: that it was not the Arabs on board who hijacked the aircraft and flew them into the Pentagon and the WTC but, in fact, Israeli intelligence agents who were responsible for the attacks; that the Americans had no proof that Bin Laden was behind what had happened. One of the ugliest myths, written and repeated time and again in the Arab world, was that several thousand Jews who ordinarily worked in the World Trade Center did not show up for work on September 11—an implication that they had been warned of the attacks. In fact, many of the nearly 3,000 victims in the World Trade Center were Jewish.

These expressions of hostility toward the United States and sympathy for those who killed so many innocent people shocked and alarmed many Americans, who wondered how foreigners could wish them ill. Americans hold their country in a high regard, and many did not realize how ambivalent others could be in their attitudes toward the world's only superpower. Anti-Americanism was nothing new, of course, but this latest strain had special characteristics related to America's overwhelming power and the way it had been used and perceived through the 1990s.

Before September 11, Americans had clearly grown comfortable with their cushy position, above the world's frays. Americans liked being richer than the rest and well insulated from their tribulations. In 2001 the new U.S. administration was becoming famous for a go-it-alone approach to international affairs, infuriating allies and rivals by its unilateral policies and decisions and by its reluctance to join other nations in collective action. One example was the international effort to do something about global warming. On September 11 the international community was preparing for a conference that would complete a final agreement on emissions controls, but the U.S., the producer of one-fourth of the world's greenhouse gases, had opted not to participate.

On those occasions when the United States did play an active part in world affairs and did join other countries in some collaborative efforts, it was usually on its own terms. Many Americans considered this reasonable and appropriate. Why should they give others any influence over matters they wanted to, and could, control themselves?

September 11 created a new reality. Beginning with that communication from Russian Pres. Vladimir Putin, President Bush spent most of the first days

September 12

NATO, for the first time in its history, invokes Article 5, which states that an attack against one is an attack against all.

Osama bin Laden is identified by U.S. officials as likely to be connected with the bombings.

September 14

Congress authorizes President Bush to use all necessary force to retaliate against those responsible for the attacks.

Most U.S. airports are reopened.

Secretary of State confirms Bin Laden as top suspect.

September 17

The New York Stock Exchange reopens.

Major league baseball games are resumed.

September 19

The Organization of American States invokes the Rio Treaty, a mutual-defense pact.

FBI investigators scour the crash site of United Airlines Flight 93 in rural Pennsylvania. AP/Wide World Photos

after the attacks speaking and meeting with foreign leaders, building what he called a new global coalition against terrorism. "We will rally the world," Bush said, and he did just that. A president regarded warily by many world leaders as a unilateralist and a bit of a cowboy was suddenly courting support from every conceivable precinct. On September 24 the House of Representatives voted to release $582 million of the $819 million in back dues to the United Nations. Concerns that just before September 11 dominated American policy suddenly disappeared. So, for example, Uzbekistan, with its corrupt and authoritarian regime that had been held at arm's length by the United States before September 11, became an important ally and a base for American military operations soon afterward.

"Working well with others" became a category on school report cards in the U.S. in the last generation, but globally, this had not been an American value. George Washington, the founding father, offered his countrymen the vision of a United States totally insulated from foreign entanglements in his famous Farewell Address 205 years before September 11, and that remained a tantalizing goal for many Americans. Washington, of course, could not have imagined the technological changes that would shrink the world in our time. Even Americans who experienced those changes remained reluctant to accept their true implications.

September 11 ended the dream of "fortress America." The 19 Arab terrorists who hijacked four airliners that day obviously were not restrained by any sense that the United States enjoyed special protection from hostile foreign forces. The shock that went through the American population after September 11, all but eliminating air travel and tourism for weeks, also marked a turning point for the American experiment, though it was impossible to explain just how. That might take years to clarify.

The horror planned for September 11 was supposed to be worse, and very nearly was. The fourth hijacked airplane was evidently aimed at the Capitol or the White House in Washington—we may never know its target for certain. A direct hit on either would have been symbolically devastating, adding enormously to the impact of the attacks. But a group of brave and resourceful passengers on United Airlines Flight 93 prevented its hijackers from fulfilling their mission, forcing the plane down in a Pennsylvania farm field, where the lives of everyone on board ended.

The fate of Flight 93 was a demonstration of how the modern global village can function. Passengers on board the flight, who thought they were flying from Newark, N.J., to San Francisco, made calls to relatives on the ground with cellular telephones and learned that a hijacked plane already had been flown into the World Trade Center in New York. One of them was Jeremy Glick, 31, sales manager for a technology firm, who told his wife to "have a good life" and promised to go down fighting against the terrorists. Glick and several other passengers, all apparently held in the galley at the rear of the Boeing 757, were plotting to rush the cockpit of the plane, 110 feet forward of the galley, to disrupt whatever

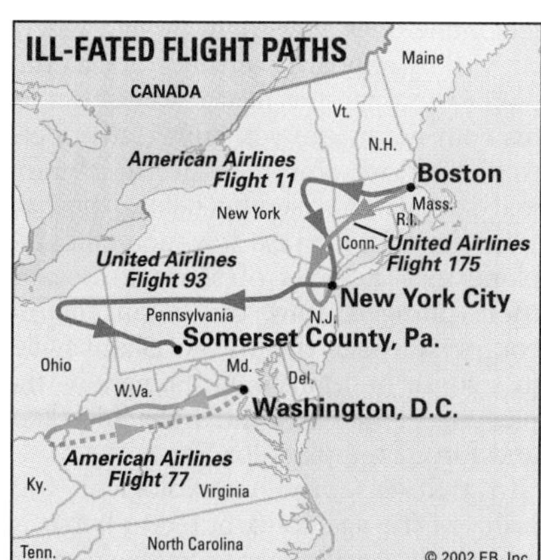

September 20

President Bush, in a televised speech to the nation, announces the creation of the Office of Homeland Security.

September 24

The U.S. freezes assets of organizations that are connected with the Taliban or Osama bin Laden.

September 26

President Bush authorizes two Air Force generals to order threatening commercial airliners shot down.

September 28

The UN Security Council adopts a resolution requiring all UN members to take steps to eliminate terrorism.

After the World Trade Center collapse.

James Nachtwey/VII for Time

plan their hijackers had in mind. One of the other plotters, Todd Beamer, told a telephone operator whom he had reached via an onboard "airfone" about this plan. The operator heard him shout to his comrades, "Are you guys ready? Let's roll!" The operator then heard screams and sounds of a scuffle before the line went dead. In the next few moments, the plane took a series of sharp turns and then plunged into the Pennsylvania countryside near the town of Shanksville, just south of Johnstown. Somehow, the passengers had disrupted the hijackers and forced the plane to Earth.

In that case the technological wizardry of the age contributed to heroism and a self-sacrifice that may have saved many lives in Washington. This was one example of how the events of September 11 were made possible by modern technology or modern styles of life. Other examples of the same phenomenon were not so uplifting.

Eerily, the terrorists, avowed enemies of secular modernity, were able to have the enormous impact they had by mastering skills and technologies that were part of what they claimed to detest. Their ability to move freely between their countries of origin, principally Saudi Arabia and Egypt, and the flying schools and Internet cafés of the United States they so ardently hated, and then into the cockpits of those four Boeing jetliners, was perhaps the most powerful symbol of what September 11 really represented—on one hand, angry young Arabs who belonged to a movement dedicated to antimodernism and an anti-American crusade; on the other hand, a hypermodern America open to the world, open even to these fanatics who were determined to inflict great harm on the United States. In an age of irony, this ultimate irony: the terrorists could do the damage they did only by acquiring skills from American flying schools, exploiting America's porous airport-security arrangements, and mastering the arts of hiding in plain sight in a society they abhorred. In the real global village of 2001, we were all startled to discover, such trickery was amazingly simple. On

October 7

The U.S. begins air strikes in Afghanistan and also begins dropping food packets.

October 11

The FBI issues another warning that there may be more terrorist attacks in the next few days.

October 19

U.S. ground troops begin operations in Afghanistan.

October 26

President Bush signs Anti-Terrorism Act into law.

September 10, it soon became clear, we had not understood the world we lived in; a month later we understood it a lot better, though far from thoroughly.

The easy, comforting notion of a global village implies that all the world's peoples are intimate neighbours, sharing more than they do not share. But this is not the global village that September 11 revealed so starkly.

In the real modern world, different peoples have taken what are sometimes radically different paths and reached very different destinations. In Europe and North America, where technology, education, and tradition produced the greatest wealth, the failure of the Muslim world to match this prosperity was just a fact of modern life, little remarked upon before September 11. Most Muslims lived in relative poverty; some were rich from oil; and almost none, rich or poor, occupied the most modern precincts of the global village. The most modern and successful nation in the Middle East, the centre of the Muslim world, was not Muslim at all: Israel. But Israel was a hated symbol to many of its Arab neighbours.

The gulf that divides Muslim, mostly Arab peoples from Europeans and Americans, and also Asians, may be the most significant dividing line in the 21st century world. Put simply, the secular global economy created by the richer countries gave great benefit to many and was a model to be emulated for many more. South Koreans, Chinese, Cypriots, and Chileans all subscribed to the same broad propositions that animated Americans, Germans, and Japanese: technological progress is good; wealth earned from global trade is desirable; consumerism and the democratization of wealth are goals to be pursued. For most of the adherents of this loose creed, political democracy was also part of the formula—democratic governments, most agreed, were most likely to achieve the prosperity so many were seeking.

Many Muslims and Arabs embraced the rich world's ideals—this is evident from the fact that millions of them have found ways to establish residency in rich countries and pursue new lives in them. The governments and especially the religious establishments of the Arab world, however, were not part of the fledgling consensus joined by so many other nations. No Arab government was a democracy, and no Arab nation was a full participant in the technological revolution of the age. Only a few oil-rich autocracies even took a stab at participation.

The Muslim world has never experienced anything comparable to the enlightenment of the 17th and 18th centuries that prepared the Christian nations of Europe for the Industrial Revolution and modernity. For Muslim fundamentalists—for example, the Wahhabi sect that dominates the religious life of Saudi Arabia—nonparticipation in the modern world is seen as a good thing, a way to avoid pollution of Muslim values by infidels. But such fundamentalists are surrounded by the temptations of the wealthy world, and often by neighbours in their own countries who do not share their disdain for modernity. Tens of thousands of well-to-do Saudis, for example, own houses or apartments in Europe or the United States and happily partake of modern pleasures when visiting those places. Yet at home they support a system that denies such pleasures to most of their countrymen and provides few opportunities for citizens to express themselves or influence their government.

The Arab world differs from the modernized West and Asia in another important respect. When countries get rich, their birthrates decline. Birthrates are so low in the developed European nations that they are all facing shrinkage of their native populations. Japan is in a similar position. Conversely, the Arab countries are experiencing rapid population growth. Saudi Arabia is growing more than 3% a year; Egypt, about 2%. Burgeoning populations aggravate tensions in these societies, none of which is creating opportunities for young people sufficient to satisfy the growing number of working-age citizens.

All of these factors are related to the success Bin Laden and his allies have had in building the al-Qaeda terrorist movement that shook the world on September 11. Obviously, only a tiny fraction of the young men of the Arab and Muslim worlds joined al-Qaeda and other like-minded groups. Might there be many more in the future? The possibility could not be dismissed.

Americans took comfort from their own response to September 11. The country found many heroes to thank, from those passengers on Flight 93 to the fire fighters and police officers of New York City, so many of whom gave their lives that day in service to their country and community. Americans poured hundreds of millions of dollars into charities to support the victims' families and stoically put up with the practical consequences of the attacks, which included a sharp economic downturn, closures and postponements of various meetings and events, and total disruption of domestic airline travel in the United States. Countless Americans remarked on a new mood in the country, a new spirit of cooperation and sharing, and a new recognition, as many put it, of what "really matters" in their lives.

The World Trade Center area: the shaded buildings were lost or damaged.

At year's end it was still too early to know the more profound impact of September 11 and its aftermath. Would Americans' lost innocence be translated into a real commitment to confronting the underlying problems confronting the global village? Or would a quick war on terrorism be followed by a relapse into American exceptionalism and another retreat from international engagement? The terrorists of September 11 challenged the United States to confront the fact that it overwhelms all other nations in its wealth, power, and influence and to accept the responsibilities that accompany such preponderance. The terrorists succeeded in making America the target. Americans would have to choose a response to that new status.

Robert G. Kaiser is an associate editor of the Washington Post, *coauthor (with Leonard Downie, Jr.) of* The News About the News: American Journalism in Peril *(forthcoming in 2002), and author of several other books on international affairs.*

November 13

Anti-Taliban forces overrun Kabul, the capital of Afghanistan.

December 7

Kandahar, the Taliban's capital, falls to Northern Alliance troops after allied bombings.

December 22

A new government, backed by the allies, is installed in Afghanistan.

December 31

The Taliban has been routed and the al-Qaeda terrorist network put on the defensive; Bin Laden and Taliban leader Mullah Omar are still at large, however.

January

America has never been united by blood or birth or soil. We are bound by ideals that move us beyond our backgrounds, lift us above our interests and teach us what it means to be citizens. Every child must be taught these principles. Every citizen must uphold them. And every immigrant, by embracing these ideals, makes our country more, not less, American.

George W. Bush, in his inaugural address, January 20

1 In a mass to celebrate the World Day of Peace, Pope John Paul II enjoins people of different cultures to treat one another with respect.

•

Fifteen people parachute from the top of the Petronas Towers in Malaysia to celebrate the arrival of the new millennium. (Photo right.)

•

Tyson Foods, Inc., agrees to acquire IBP, inc., in an agreement that will create the world's largest meat company.

•

El Salvador becomes the third Latin American nation (after Panama and Ecuador) to replace its national currency with the U.S. dollar.

AP/Wide World Photos

2 Two tourist boats, one from Quemoy Island and one from Matsu Island, become the first to travel legally from Taiwanese territory to mainland China.

•

Cambodia's legislature agrees to create a special tribunal in concert with the United Nations to try Khmer Rouge leaders who carried out a massacre in the 1970s; critics are dubious that this arrangement can be effective.

•

Women enlisting in the German armed forces become the first females eligible for combat duty in Germany; the exclusion of women in units of the military is illegal for all members of the European Union.

3 Hillary Rodham Clinton is sworn in as a senator from New York; it is the first time in U.S. history that a sitting first lady has held a political office.

•

International Paper Co. agrees to sell for $10.5 million three tracts of land totaling 10,725 ha (26,500 ac) in the Adirondacks in northern New York to the Nature Conservancy, an organization concerned with environmental preservation.

4 The Chief Rabbinate Council in Israel declares that Jewish law forbids allowing any but Jewish sovereignty over the Temple Mount in Jerusalem; earlier the mufti of Jerusalem had said that Islamic law prohibits any but Muslim sovereignty over the same area.

•

Sawt al-Shaab appears on newsstands in Syria; it is the first newspaper not published by the government or ruling party to be permitted in Syria since 1963.

•

The publisher of *George* announces that the quasi-political magazine founded in 1995 by John F. Kennedy, Jr., who died in 1999, will close with its March issue.

5 Australia bans the importation of beef and beef products from 30 European countries to prevent "mad cow" disease from entering the country. (*See* January 13.)

•

U.S. Pres. Bill Clinton signs an order banning logging and the building of roads in more than 23.5 million ha (58 million ac) of national forest land.

6 Elections are held in Thailand; the opposition Thai Rak Thai Party appears to win a majority of the 500 parliamentary seats.

•

Undeterred by bitterly cold weather, Muslim pilgrims from throughout the world gather in Bangladesh to celebrate the festival of Biswa Ijtema.

•

South Africa calls for assistance from the World Health Organization in attempting to contain a cholera outbreak that has struck more than 15,000 people in KwaZulu/Natal state.

7 John Kufuor is inaugurated as president of Ghana in that nation's first peaceful transition from one elected government to another.

•

Groups of soldiers attack the office of broadcast media during an attempted coup in Côte d'Ivoire.

•

In a referendum in Senegal a new constitution is approved by a margin of more than 92%.

8 The UN's World Food Programme releases a report and map detailing the incidence of undernourishment in the world; one-third of the population of sub-Saharan Africa, including 73% of Somalia's people, is chronically hungry, according to the report.

•

The French-based construction concern Lafarge Group announces that it will acquire the British company Blue Circle Industries to create the world's biggest cement company.

•

India's biggest film financier, Bharat Shah, is arrested on suspicion of having colluded with organized crime figures to extort money from the Bollywood film industry, the largest in the world.

9 At a meeting of the American Astronomical Society, Geoffrey W. Marcy announces that his team has found two planetary systems that call into question everything known about such systems; one has anomalous orbits, and the other has planets of seemingly impossible size.

•

Australian scientists say that analysis of DNA taken from human remains that are about 60,000 years old shows no links with human ancestors from Africa; this suggests that Africa is not the only site of the genesis of the human species.

•

Sen. Jesse Helms of North Carolina says that he will stop blocking U.S. payment of back dues to the United Nations; the UN estimates that the United States is close to $1.6 billion in arrears. (*See* September 24.)

•

The president of the Philadelphia Orchestra announces that Christoph Eschenbach will become the orchestra's seventh director in 2003 when Wolfgang Sawallisch retires.

10 American Airlines agrees to buy Trans World Airlines and, in a separate transaction, reveals plans to acquire 20% of US Airways. (*See* April 9.)

•

Actress Jeanne Moreau is inducted into the French Academy of Fine Arts; she is the first woman to be so honoured.

•

A controversial statue depicting Franklin Delano Roosevelt, the 32nd president of the U.S., seated in a wheelchair is unveiled in Washington, D.C.

•

An Asian gaur (an endangered species), cloned and implanted in the womb of a cow in Iowa, dies of dysentery two days after being born.

11 The U.S. Federal Communications Commission approves the megamerger of America Online and Time Warner, which has been in the works for a full year; the new company, AOL Time Warner, begins trading the next morning.

•

Yoichiro Kaizaki resigns as president and CEO of the Bridgestone Corp., the parent of Bridgestone/Firestone; he denies that he is doing so in order to accept responsibility for the massive tire recall in 2000, although that is how it is interpreted in Japan.

12 Anson Chan, the head of civil service and second-ranked official in Hong Kong, unexpectedly resigns; she had been appointed to her post by the British, and it was felt that her departure did not bode well for Hong Kong's continued autonomy under China.

•

In a study published in *Science,* scientists report that they inserted a jellyfish gene into the ovum of a rhesus monkey, and the resultant monkey, born in October 2000, carries the gene; it is the first transgenic primate.

13 A magnitude-7.6 earthquake strikes El Salvador; felt in Honduras and Nicaragua and even as far away as Mexico City, the quake shuts down the capital, San Salvador, and sets off landslides that bury the middle-class Las Colinas neighbourhood in Santa Tecla. (*See* February 13.)

•

A cow that appears to have "mad cow" disease is found in a slaughterhouse in Italy;

it is the first time the disease has been reported in an Italian-born cow. (*See* January 5 and January 30.)

•

In the worst public transportation accident in Swaziland's history, an overloaded bus crashes, killing 30 people.

14 Jorge Sampaio is reelected president of Portugal in a landslide; the voter turnout, the lowest in the nation's history, is attributed to the perception by many that the popular Sampaio is unbeatable.

15 The East African Community, an economic organization consisting of Kenya, Tanzania, and Uganda, is formally inaugurated; it replaces an organization of the same name and members that had ceased to exist in 1977.

•

Motorola, Inc., announces that it is closing the Harvard, Ill., plant, its only cellular phone manufacturing facility in the U.S., and laying off 2,500 workers.

•

In the field of children's literature, the Newbery Medal is awarded to Richard Peck for *A Year Down Yonder,* and David Small wins the Caldecott Medal for his illustration of *So You Want to Be President?* by Judith St. George.

•

A trilateral partnership for cooperation and research is announced by the Solomon R. Guggenheim Museum in New York City, the State Hermitage Museum in St. Petersburg, and the Kunsthistorisches Museum in Vienna.

•

Kim Jong Il, leader of North Korea, makes a sudden and secret visit to Shanghai; it is only the second time in 18 years that he has been known to travel outside his country.

16 Swiss food giant Nestlé SA agrees to acquire Ralston Purina Co., the St. Louis, Mo.-based manufacturer of pet foods, for $10.1 billion and create a company called Nestlé Purina Pet Care.

•

Luther and Johnny Htoo, the twin teenage leaders of the rebel Karen group in Myanmar (Burma) known as God's Army, surrender to Thai authorities at the border, together with 12 followers, mostly children or teenagers.

•

Dave Winfield, a power hitter who played with several teams and is the only athlete in history to have been drafted in football and basketball as well as baseball, and Kirby Puckett, who led the Minnesota Twins to two World Series championships, are elected to the National Baseball Hall of Fame. (*See* March 6.)

17 Two teams of scientists working in Cambridge, Mass., report that they have brought a beam of light to a full stop and then restarted it; the achievement means that it may be possible to store light.

•

California's beleaguered electrical power companies institute a series of rolling blackouts, in which blocks of customers are denied power for up to 90 minutes, in order to save power.

•

The British House of Commons overwhelmingly passes a bill to outlaw fox hunting with hounds; the ban is rejected by the House of Lords on March 26, however.

•

The School of the Americas, run by the U.S. Army and famous for having trained authoritarian Latin American leaders, including Panama's Manuel Noriega and Nicaragua's Anastasio Somoza, reopens (it had closed in December 2000) with the new name Western Hemisphere Institute for Security Cooperation.

18 The government of the Democratic Republic of the Congo acknowledges that Pres. Laurent Kabila has died, two days after reports that he had been assassinated circulated throughout the world. (*See* January 26.)

•

U.S. civil rights leader Jesse Jackson publicly acknowledges that he fathered and is providing financial support for an out-of-wedlock child born in May 1999.

19 The Ecuadoran oil tanker *Jessica,* which ran aground on a reef in the Galápagos Islands on January 16, suffers a crack in its cargo hold and begins leaking diesel fuel, threatening the fragile and unique ecosystem with disaster.

•

The man believed to be the head of the Sinaloa drug cartel, Joaquín Guzmán Loera, escapes from a maximum security prison near Guadalajara, Mex.

20 George W. Bush is inaugurated as the 43rd president of the United States; thousands of people who believe that he gained the office through illegitimate or unfair means protest. (*See* January 23.)

•

Faced with huge demonstrations against him and with the withdrawal of military support, Joseph Estrada resigns the presidency of the

Alain Rossignol/KTM Sportmotorcycle AG Motorsport

Philippines, and his vice president, Gloria Macapagal Arroyo, is sworn in to replace him. (*See* April 25.)

•

Michelle Kwan wins her fifth U.S. national figure-skating championship.

21 Pope John Paul II names a record 37 men to the Sacred College of Cardinals, 10 of them from Latin America; on January 28 he adds 7 more, bringing the number of voting cardinals to 135, a new high.

•

The annual Paris–Dakar Rally comes to a successful conclusion as threatened interference in Western Sahara fails to materialize; winners are Jutta Kleinschmidt, in a Mitsubishi Pajero; Fabrizio Meoni, on a KTM 660 LC4 motorcycle (photo left); and Karel Loprais, in a Tatra T815 ZER truck.

•

At the Golden Globe Awards in Hollywood, *Gladiator* and *Almost Famous* take home best picture honours; best director is Ang Lee for *Crouching Tiger, Hidden Dragon,* and best screenplay goes to Stephen Gaghan for *Traffic.*

22 Pakistan closes all of Afghanistan's Islamic Taliban's offices in the country and freezes the assets of suspected terrorist Osama bin Laden.

•

Akebono, the first non-Japanese *yokozuna* (grand champion sumo wrestler), announces his retirement at the age of 31, because of chronic knee pain.

23 Matthew Kneale wins the 2000 Whitbread Book of the Year Award for his novel *English Passengers;* the previous four prizes, awarded for books published in the U.K., had gone to collections of poetry.

•

The Florida State Association of Supervisors of Elections votes on a single standard for conducting recounts and asks the state legislature for uniform statewide voting technology. (*See* January 20.)

•

On the eve of the Chinese New Year, five Falun Gong followers set themselves on fire in Tiananmen Square in Beijing.

24 The year 4699, Year of the Snake, begins and is celebrated by Chinese throughout the world.

•

On the most auspicious day of the Kumbh Mela festival (which began on January 9 and ends on February 21), tens of millions of pilgrims bathe at the confluence of the Ganges, Yamuna, and mythical Saraswati rivers at Allahabad, India.

•

Marine archaeologists announce that they have completed the first archaeological survey of an offshore region in sub-Saharan Africa and have found four sunken ships and submerged Swahili villages off Kenya's coast.

25 The World Economic Forum opens in Davos, Switz.; in response to past criticism, delegates from unions and nongovernmental organizations will be included as well as government officials, and there will be live Internet broadcasts of some sessions.

•

In the ongoing "banana war," Chiquita Brands International sues the European Commission, contending that banana import quotas have nearly bankrupted the company. (*See* November 28.)

26 An earthquake of magnitude 7.9 strikes Gujarat state in India; the commercial city of Bhuj, with a population of 150,000, is largely destroyed, and several cities experience damage in the quake, which shakes the entire subcontinent.

•

Joseph Kabila is inaugurated as the president of the Democratic Republic of the Congo. (*See* January 18.)

27 At least 17 people die on the Tanzanian island of Zanzibar when police clash with opposition demonstrators demanding that new elections be held and the results of previous elections annulled.

•

Jennifer Capriati defeats Martina Hingis 6–4, 6–3 to win the Australian Open tennis tournament in the former Olympic champion's first Grand Slam win; on January 28 Andre Agassi beats Arnaud Clement in straight sets in the men's competition to win his seventh Grand Slam title.

28 The Baltimore Ravens, a franchise that has been playing in Baltimore, Md., only since 1996, defeats the New York Giants 34–7 to win Super Bowl XXXV. (*See* January 31.)

•

Kuwait's entire cabinet, including the premier, Crown Prince Sheikh Saad al-Abdullah as-Salim as-Sabah, resigns.

29 The Chrysler division of DaimlerChrysler announces plans to eliminate 26,000 jobs worldwide over the next three years; on the same day, the Xerox Corp. says it will eliminate 4,000 jobs to cut costs.

•

The New York Philharmonic announces that Lorin Maazel will replace Kurt Masur as music director to start the 2002–03 season.

30 Tiznow, which won the Breeders' Cup Classic race in November 2000, is named Horse of the Year for 2000.

•

Daron Rahlves becomes the first American male skier since 1982 to win a gold medal at the world Alpine championships when he stuns onlookers by winning the supergiant slalom in Sankt Anton, Austria.

•

The U.S. Food and Drug Administration says that it has quarantined 1,222 Texas cattle that have eaten feed containing animal by-products, which creates a risk for "mad cow" disease. (*See* January 13.)

31 A Scottish court convicts Libyan 'Abd al-Baset al-Megrahi of the 1988 bombing of Pan Am Flight 103 and acquits his countryman Lamin Khalifa Fhimah. (*See* February 3.)

•

Reports surface that law-enforcement officials in Tampa, Fla., photographed the face of every spectator at the Super Bowl in order to find out if any of them were wanted on charges by any agency. (*See* January 28.)

•

The new state flag is flown over the Georgia statehouse; approved by the lower house of the legislature on January 24, it features five historical flags and relegates the formerly prominent Confederate battle flag to a small banner near the bottom.

February

All the statues in the country should be destroyed because these statues have been used as idols and deities by the nonbelievers before.

Decree of the Islamic Taliban
in Afghanistan, February 26

1 The major European steelmaker Corus Group announces that it will cut one-fifth of its workforce, more than 6,000 jobs, mostly in depressed regions of Great Britain.

•

Edward Albee attends the opening of his new play, *The Play About the Baby,* in New York City; the playwright is known for not attending his openings.

2 BellSouth, the telephone company that serves the southeastern United States, announces that it will eliminate all its pay phones by the end of 2002, citing loss of revenue due to competition from cell phones.

•

A plan to reintroduce elk to the Great Smoky Mountains, from where they disappeared at least 150 years ago, gets under way with the arrival of 25 elk at a 1.2-ha (3-ac) pen in North Carolina.

3 During government-organized protests against the verdict in the case concerning the 1988 terrorist acts against Pan Am Flight 103 over Lockerbie, Scot., four Libyan students stab themselves in Tripoli. (*See* January 31.)

•

The XFL, a new professional football league founded by Vince McMahon and owned by World Wrestling Federation Entertainment and NBC, opens its season with the Las Vegas (Nev.) Outlaws against the New York/New Jersey Hitmen and the Orlando (Fla.) Rage against the Chicago Enforcers. (*See* May 10.)

4 An official of the Tibetan government in exile says that India has granted refugee status to the teenage Karmapa Lama, number three in the Tibetan Buddhist hierarchy, who had fled to India in January 2000.

•

At a pole-vault meet named for him in Donetsk, Ukraine, Sergey Bubka, who broke 35 world records in his career and who is widely held to be the best pole-vaulter ever, announces his retirement.

5 The Halifax Group, the largest mortgage bank in the U.K., agrees to buy out the Equitable Life Assurance Society for about $1.5 billion and rename the joint company Halifax Equitable.

•

The Internet toy retailer eToys announces that it will go out of business on April 6.

•

The Holy Land Experience, a new theme park that purports to re-create the Jerusalem of biblical times, opens in Orlando; the Jewish Defense League, which believes the park has an evangelical Christian bias, protests. (*See* February 8.)

6 Ariel Sharon defeats Ehud Barak in elections to become prime minister of Israel; his margin of victory is unprecedentedly large, and the voter turnout is unprecedentedly low. (*See* March 7.)

•

Thousands of people march in Kiev, Ukraine, to demand the resignation of Pres. Leonid Kuchma, who has been implicated in a variety of scandals.

•

Cipla Ltd., an Indian company that makes generic drugs, announces a plan to sell the drugs used to combat AIDS to Doctors Without Borders at a price substantially lower than that charged by the world's major pharmaceutical manufacturers.

•

The American household appliances manufacturer Sunbeam Corp. files for bankruptcy protection.

7 Jean-Bertrand Aristide is sworn in as president of Haiti; opposition parties set up what they call a parallel government, arguing that Aristide's election is not legitimate.

•

Alfred Sirven, a prominent figure in the complex and far-reaching Elf Aquitaine corruption scandal in France, presents himself for trial in Paris after four years in hiding. (*See* May 30.)

•

The Eagles (Aguilas Cibaeñas), representing the Dominican Republic, win baseball's Caribbean Series with a 4–2 record.

US Coast Guard/AFP Worldwide

8 Former German chancellor Helmut Kohl reaches a plea agreement with prosecutors investigating a fund-raising scandal in which criminal charges against him will be dropped and he will pay a fine; the investigation into Christian Democratic Union practices continues, however.

•

Disney's California Adventure, a new theme park based on the attractions of the Golden State, opens in Anaheim, Calif. (*See* February 5.)

9 ***The USS* Greeneville, *a U.S. submarine conducting exercises for a group of VIP tourists, strikes and sinks the* Ehime Maru, *a Japanese fishing boat, after surfacing rapidly near Hawaii; nine people, many of them vocational-high-school students, are killed in spite of the efforts of the U.S. Coast Guard, which arrives on the scene about 30 minutes after the collision. (Photo above.)***

•

Thaksin Shinawatra takes office as prime minister of Thailand.

•

On the eve of the anniversary of Iran's Islamic revolution, a demonstration in Tehran demanding freedom of expression is violently dispersed by police.

10 Members of an Islamic rebel group slaughter 27 people, mostly women and children, in a shantytown near Berrouaghia, Alg.

•

Astronauts Marsha S. Ivins, Robert L. Curbeam, Jr., and Thomas D. Jones install Destiny, the first of five planned scientific research laboratories, on the International Space Station.

11 In accordance with the peace treaty signed in 2000, Ethiopia begins withdrawing its troops from Eritrea.

•

Tens of thousands of nationalists demand early elections in Croatia, opposing the policy of Prime Minister Ivica Racan of cooperating with the UN in investigating possible Croatian war crimes against Serbs.

•

Ellen MacArthur breaks the women's solo around-the-world sailing record when she completes the Vendee Globe race in 94 days 4 hr 25 min; the previous record, 140 days, was set by Catherine Chabaud in 1997.

12 Omar Hassan al-Bashir is sworn in for a second five-year term as president of The Sudan after elections in December 2000.

•

In Dnipropetrovsk, Ukraine, Russian Pres. Vladimir Putin and Ukrainian Pres. Leonid Kuchma sign an agreement to cooperate in aviation and space research and to reconnect their power grids.

•

The spacecraft NEAR Shoemaker lands on the near-Earth asteroid Eros; the landing, planned at the last minute, is the first time a spacecraft has landed on an asteroid.

•

At a joint news conference, scientists from Celera Genomics and the Human Genome Project say it appears that there are only about 30,000 human genes, far fewer than the 100,000 that had long been assumed.

13 El Salvador is hit with its second earthquake in as many months when a magnitude-6.6 temblor strikes towns to the east of San Salvador, killing 402 (*see* January 13); on February 14 a magnitude-7.3 earthquake with its epicentre in the ocean shakes the island of Sumatra in Indonesia. (*See* February 28.)

•

The Indianapolis (Ind.) Baptist Temple, which denies that the U.S. government has jurisdiction over it, is seized by Internal Revenue Service agents to satisfy a debt of $6 million in unpaid taxes.

14 The European Parliament approves stringent standards governing all aspects of genetically modified foods and seed in hopes of ending an unofficial three-year moratorium on such items.

•

In Trinidad and Tobago, after a 55-day standoff, seven people who had lost elections to the House of Representatives and then had been nominated to the Senate by Prime Minister Basdeo Panday are appointed to the House by Pres. Arthur Robinson; Robinson and Panday had accused each other of undermining the constitution.

•

The Kansas State Board of Education reverses a 1999 decision and restores the teaching of the theory of evolution to the state science curriculum.

•

Violent protests by Hindu nationalist elements against the celebration of Valentine's Day, popular among the younger, more Westernized population, take place in cities throughout India.

•

A bichon frise named Special Times Just Right! wins best in show at the Westminster Kennel Club Dog Show; it is the first time the top prize at the premier American dog show has gone to this breed.

15 Voters in Bahrain approve a measure that changes the form of government to a constitutional monarchy, restores the parliament (which was abolished in 1975), and gives women the right to vote.

•

An official Russian state commission investigating the sinking of the submarine *Kursk* in August 2000 confirms that a torpedo exploded aboard the sub. (*See* October 8.)

•

A court in Frankfurt, Ger., sentences former terrorist Hans-Joachim Klein to nine years in prison for his participation in the 1975 attack on an OPEC conference in Vienna in which three persons were killed.

•

Nature magazine publishes a report that scientists have found two recently active volcanoes on the Gakkel ridge, under the Arctic Ocean off Greenland; the find is surprising because it was thought that such volcanic activity would not occur in slow-spreading seafloor sites.

16 Comoros and the breakaway island of Anjouan sign an agreement that provides for national elections and the adoption of a new constitution.

•

The New China News Agency says that an unusually severe winter has led to the deaths of 38 newborn babies and several expectant mothers in northern China near the Mongolian border; temperatures in this region have dipped to –51.7 °C (–61 °F).

•

Imelda Marcos opens the Marikina City Footwear Museum near Manila; the exhibits include hundreds of pairs of shoes donated by the former first lady and other local celebrities.

17 An aged, rusting freighter carrying 908 Kurdish men, women, and children runs aground on the French Riviera; the captain and crew have disappeared by the time authorities arrive to rescue the would-be immigrants.

•

The Welsh rock band Manic Street Preachers becomes the first English-language musical group to play in Havana since 1979; their song "Baby Elián" is particularly warmly received.

18 Violence between indigenous Dayak and Madurese migrants from other parts of Indonesia breaks out in Borneo; by the end of the week, well over 200 people are dead and ships are being sent to evacuate thousands of refugees.

•

Riots break out in 18 prisons across the state of São Paulo, Braz., and hundreds of people, most of them visiting family members, are taken hostage.

•

Celebrated stock-car racing star Dale Earnhardt, Sr., is killed in a crash near the end of the Daytona 500 race; Michael Waltrip goes on to win the race.

19 In a $3.1 billion deal, the Luxembourg company Arbed, Usinor of France, and Aceralia of Spain announce plans to merge to become the world's largest steel company; annual production of the new company is expected to be 46 million metric tons, while the current leader, Nippon Steel of Japan, produced 28 million metric tons in 2000.

•

Lieut. Gen. Tin Oo, a member of Myanmar's (Burma's) ruling junta, is killed in a helicopter crash together with a cabinet minister, seven government officials, and five others.

20 The U.S. Federal Bureau of Investigation acknowledges that one of its top experts on Russian counterintelligence, Robert Philip Hanssen, has been one of Russia's most valuable spies for 15 years.

•

Scientists report that DNA testing of the skeletons of children confirms that there was a major malaria epidemic in the 5th century AD in Rome; the epidemic may have contributed to Rome's decline and may have persuaded Attila to bypass the city.

•

An exhibit of erotic art by Pablo Picasso, featuring work he did from age 13 to age 92, opens at the Musée du Jeu de Paume in Paris.

21 Great Britain suspends all exports of animals and animal products and sets up quarantine areas in an attempt to contain an outbreak of foot-and-mouth disease; another outbreak, in Argentina, causes Brazil to issue a ban on Argentine beef.

•

In a Grammy Awards ceremony at which most of the attention is given to controversial rap artist Eminem, Song of the Year honours go to U2's "Beautiful Day," and Album of the Year is won by Steely Dan's *Two Against Nature*.

•

Francisco Xabier García Gaztelu, believed to be the top military leader of the Basque separatist group ETA, is arrested in Anglet, France.

•

The foreign ministers of Nigeria and São Tomé and Príncipe sign a treaty allowing the two countries to explore jointly for minerals in the region lying between them in the Gulf of Guinea.

22 For the first time, a non-nationalist government is elected in Bosnia and Herzegovina.

•

Finland wins the men's relay at the world Nordic skiing championships; four days later the result is annulled after several Finnish skiers fail their drug tests.

•

The Society of Stage Directors and Choreographers announces that its nine-year strike against Radio City Music Hall in New York City has been settled.

•

British fashion designer Alexander McQueen closes a deal in which he is selling a majority stake of his design label to the Italian luxury goods maker Gucci Group; the influential couturier served three years as head designer of the Givenchy fashion house.

23 In Moscow a judge rules that the Jehovah's Witnesses have not violated a law prohibiting religious sects that incite violence and thus are permitted to practice their religion freely in Russia.

•

A U.S. Court of Appeals rules that government agencies must give Native Americans a complete tally of how much money should be in their accounts; the accounts have been so badly mismanaged since they were started in 1887 that the Indians bringing suit believe more than $10 billion has been lost.

•

Laurence Olivier Awards are presented in London to, among others, actors Julie Walters, Samantha Spiro, Conleth Hill, and Daniel Evans; the best new play is *Blue/Orange* by Joe Penhall.

•

Concerto for Cello and Orchestra: In Memoriam F.D.R., a new piece by Peter Schickele commissioned by New Heritage Music, is performed by Paul Tobias and the Chamber Symphony of the Manhattan School of Music.

AP/Wide World Photos

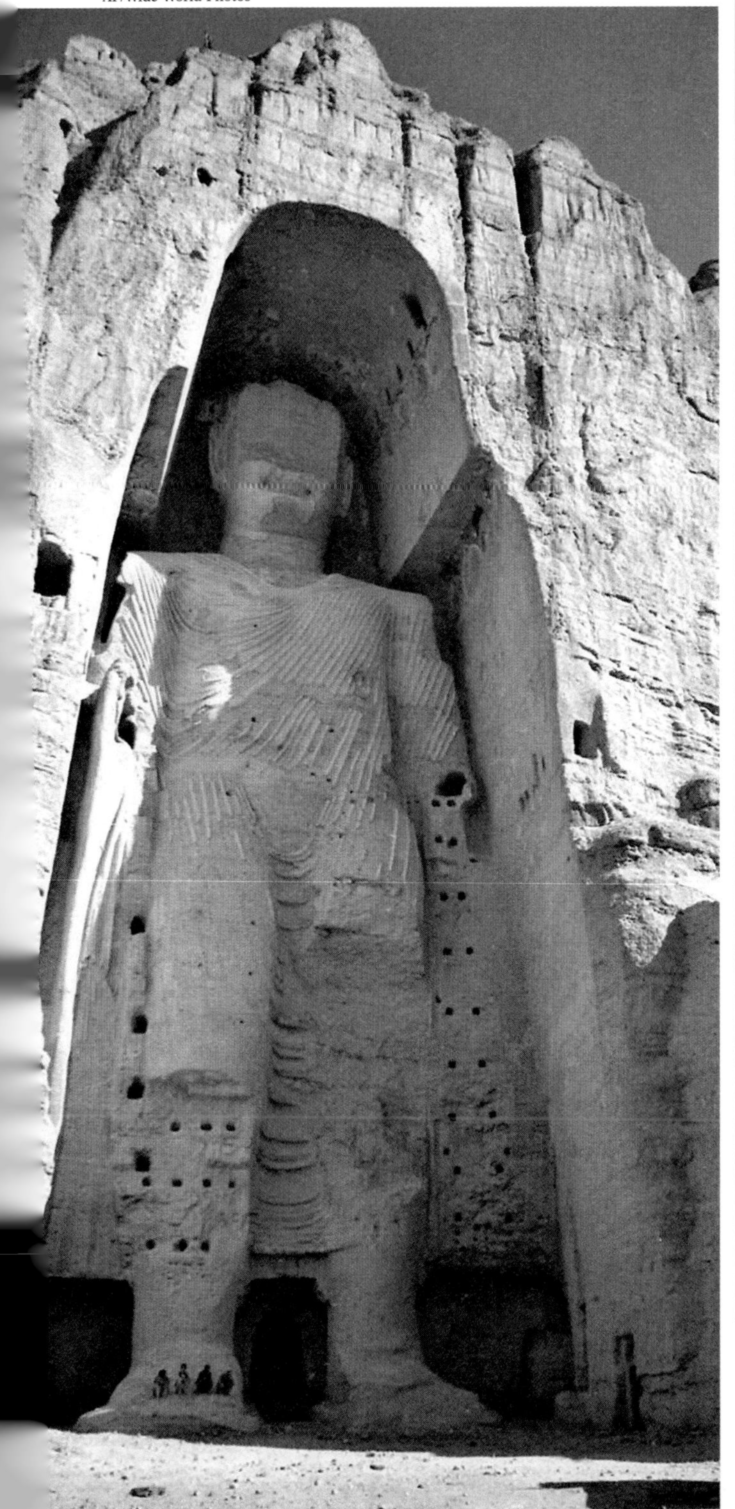

24 Violent storms hit the eastern half of the United States, with tornadoes in Mississippi and Arkansas, flooding in Kansas and Missouri, and heavy snowfall in Nebraska and Minnesota.

•

Zapatista leaders begin a 15-day march from Chiapas to Mexico City to demand greater rights and more autonomy for Indians in Mexico.

25 For the first time since independence, the Communist Party is returned to power in legislative elections in Moldova.

•

In runoff presidential elections held in Cape Verde, PAICV candidate Pedro Pires wins with a margin of 1%.

•

The British Academy of Film and Television Arts presents four awards each to *Gladiator* and *Crouching Tiger, Hidden Dragon.*

26 ***The Taliban rulers in Afghanistan order the destruction of all statues, including exquisite ancient statues of Buddha; the world community reacts with horror, but to no avail. (Photo left.)***

•

A U.S. federal judge orders the income-tax-preparation firm H&R Block to stop advertising its high-interest loans against expected tax refunds as "rapid refunds."

27 Nineteen foreign ministers representing the member states of NATO meet in Brussels to discuss solutions to, among other problems, growing conflict along the Kosovo border in Yugoslavia.

•

The Polisario Front celebrates the 25th anniversary of its declaration of an independent republic of the Western Sahara; the territory was annexed by Morocco in 1979.

•

The U.S. National Academy of Sciences publishes a report saying scientists at the Johnson Space Center in Houston, Texas, have found a crystal in a meteorite from Mars that resembles Earth crystals formed by bacteria, a finding that points toward the possibility of life on the red planet; many scientists are skeptical, however.

28 France defies the European Union and offers financial aid to farmers suffering from the collapse of beef prices caused by the outbreak of mad-cow disease, throwing into doubt the future ability of the EU to maintain a common agricultural policy among all its members.

•

Rwanda and Uganda begin withdrawing troops from the Democratic Republic of the Congo in accordance with a UN plan to bring peace to the area.

•

The Pacific Northwest is hit by an earthquake of magnitude 6.7 that lasts for 40 seconds, with the most damage occurring in Seattle, Wash.; no deaths are reported and injuries are few, at least in part because the epicentre is some 50 km (30 mi) underground. (*See* February 13.)

•

A panel in Oklahoma City, Okla., recommends the payment of reparations to the survivors and descendants of the victims of the Tulsa race riot of 1921, one of the nation's worst.

March

Our country made a great contribution in space, and we are not ashamed. But now our place will be a little smaller, and we have lost our independence.

Russian cosmonaut Aleksandr I. Lazutkin, on the destruction of *Mir,* March 23

1 Seven foreign oil workers—four Americans, an Argentine, a Chilean, and a New Zealander—who had been kidnapped in October 2000 in Ecuador are freed after a ransom of some $13 million is paid.

•

China ceremonially begins construction of what is to be the world's first commercial maglev (magnetic levitation) train, to run from Shanghai's financial district to one of its airports and begin operations in 2003.

•

A report in the journal *Nature* describes findings that a common compound, magnesium boride, is superconductive at temperatures 16 °C (29 °F) higher than any other simple metallic compound.

2 Jean-Marie Cherestal is sworn in as prime minister of Haiti, as is his cabinet, which includes members of opposition parties.

•

The U.S. Navy halts bombing exercises on Vieques Island, off Puerto Rico, pending talks with the Puerto Rican government. (*See* April 26.)

•

U.S. Pres. George W. Bush grants "temporary protected status" to 150,000 illegal immigrants from El Salvador; Salvadoran Pres. Francisco Flores has said that remittances from these immigrants are vital to El Salvador's recovery from the earthquakes that had shaken the country earlier in the year.

3 A supposed bomb placed in the cargo hold under the seat that Thai Prime Minister Thaksin Shinawatra was to occupy explodes, destroying the jet at Bangkok International Airport 35 minutes before its scheduled takeoff.

•

Senegalese Pres. Abdoulaye Wade replaces Prime Minister Moustapha Niasse; the new prime minister, Madior Boyé, is Senegal's first woman prime minister.

•

John Ruiz defeats Evander Holyfield in Las Vegas, Nev., to take the World Boxing Association title and become the first Hispanic heavyweight champion.

4 In a referendum, voters in Switzerland resoundingly reject a proposition to begin negotiations toward entering the European Union.

•

In the village of Castelo de Paiva, Port., a 116-year-old bridge collapses and two cars and a double-decker bus fall into the Douro River, killing about 70 people; it is the worst road accident in the history of Portugal.

5 A fire in a dormitory at a girls' secondary school in Gindiri, Nigeria, kills at least 23 girls; the dormitory had been locked for the night because of the proximity of a boys' school.

•

A freshman at Santana High School in Santee, Calif., opens fire at school, killing 2 other students and wounding 13.

6 An explosion kills 41 people, mostly children, at an elementary school in Wanzi county in China, and officials blame a lone terrorist; the children were reportedly being made to assemble fireworks by their teachers.

•

Bill Mazeroski, a second baseman famous for hitting the winning home run in the 1960 World Series, and Negro leagues pitcher Hilton Smith are elected to the National Baseball Hall of Fame. (*See* January 16.)

•

Russian Pres. Vladimir Putin takes part in a 40-minute live Internet conversation moderated and broadcast over the World Wide Web by the BBC.

7 Ariel Sharon takes office as the prime minister of Israel (*see* February 6); meanwhile, the Knesset (parliament) votes to return to the parliamentary system, whereby the prime minister is elected by legislators.

•

The government of Fiji is declared illegal by a court and resigns.

8 Bernard Landry, who has expressed aggressively separatist opinions, is sworn in as the pre-

George Serras/National Museum of Australia 2001

mier of Quebec, succeeding Lucien Bouchard.

•

Indictments for massive fraud in eBay art auctions on the Internet are brought against three men, none of whom has been arrested and one of whom has not even been located.

9 Flooding caused by snowmelt in Ukraine raises the Tisza River to its highest point in over a century; it is measured at 7.6 m (25 ft) in the Hungarian village of Zahony.

•

In Fort Lauderdale, Fla., Lionel Tate, age 14, who was convicted in January of having killed a six-year-old girl when he was 12, is sentenced to life in prison without parole.

10 German Gunda Niemann-Stirnemann breaks her own world record in speed skating in the 5,000-m race at the world championships in Salt Lake City, Utah.

•

The Nuu-chah-nulth Tribal Council, representing some 6,500 members of 12 First Nations of Canada, agrees to a treaty with the province of British Columbia and with the federal government that grants it a measure of autonomy and financial benefits in return for cessation of exemption from payment of federal taxes.

11 ***Prime Minister John Howard officially opens the National Museum of Australia in Canberra; the innovative museum, devoted to the history of Australia and its peoples, is immediately and immensely popular. (Photo above.)***

•

American astronauts James S. Voss and Susan J. Helms undertake the longest space walk since the shuttle program began, 8 hours 56 minutes; their task is to help move a docking port on the International Space Station.

•

Former secretary of the treasury Lawrence H. Summers is named to replace Neil L. Rudenstine as president of Harvard University.

12 Yoweri Museveni is reelected president of Uganda in a bitterly fought election.

•

In a military training exercise in Kuwait, a U.S. Navy jet mistakenly drops three bombs on an observation post, killing five U.S. military personnel and a New Zealand army major.

•

The largest transatlantic financial services deal to date takes place when Prudential PLC in Great Britain agrees to buy the American insurance company American General Corp. for some $26.5 billion; the merger creates the world's sixth largest insurance group.

•

In the London hotel where he was born, Crown Prince Alexander Karadjordjevic of Yugoslavia is presented with papers officially reinstating his Yugoslavian citizenship.

13 The first outbreak of foot-and-mouth disease in continental Europe is confirmed by the French Ministry of Agriculture; the disease has been found on a farm at Mayenne.

•

The Japanese stock market falls to its lowest level since 1985 amid political uncertainty and opposition to Prime Minister Yoshiro Mori.

•

The Australian dollar falls to 50.48 U.S. cents, its lowest level in history.

•

The Indian Internet news service Tehelka.com begins showing videotapes of government bribe taking over a defense contract; the exposé throws the government into chaos.

14 The first Albany Medical Center Prize in Medicine and Biomedical Research is awarded to Arnold J. Levine for his discovery of and work on the *p53* gene, which, when mutated, is a major cause of cancer.

•

Bristol-Myers Squibb announces that it no longer opposes other drugmakers' producing low-cost versions of its anti-AIDS drug Zerit for sale in Africa.

•

The Iditarod Trail Sled Dog Race is won for the third year in a row, and the fourth time overall, by Doug Swingley, who completes the 1,770-km (1,100-mi) trip in 9 days 19 hours 55 minutes.

•

A life-size bronze statue of Mother Teresa is unveiled at the Mother House, the headquarters of the Missionaries of Charity order that she founded, in Kolkata (Calcutta).

15 Uganda, Rwanda, Zimbabwe, and the Democratic Republic of the Congo all begin pulling their troops back from the front lines of the battle in the Congo, as required by an agreement made under the auspices of the United Nations.

•

A boat carrying some 60 would-be refugees who had left the Dominican Republic bound for Puerto Rico 24 days earlier crashes on a coral reef off Haiti; 57 occupants are feared dead.

•

A forensics expert confirms that the skeletons found on a ranch 145 km (90 mi) west of San Antonio, Texas, are those of atheist leader Madalyn Murray O'Hair and her son and granddaughter, who disappeared in 1995.

•

Two antiques dealers are charged with having faked appraisals (by arranging for friends to submit Civil War swords the dealers had given them previously) on the popular television show *Antiques Roadshow.*

16 In a ruling accepted by both disputants, the World Court divides territories long contested between Bahrain and Qatar; Bahrain gets the Hawar Islands and Qit'at Jaradah Island, while Qatar gets the islands of Janan and Hadd Janan and Fasht ad-Dibal reef as well as the coastal area of Zubara.

•

Explosions rip through four different apartment buildings owned by state cotton mills in Shijiazhuang, the capital of Hebei province, China; authorities blame a single former worker and say that only 108 people were killed, though many find both these claims implausible.

•

In Phoenix, Ariz., Swedish golfer Annika Sörenstam sets a new Ladies Professional Golf Association record when she shoots a 59; 59 is also the men's Professional Golfers' Association of America record.

17 In Cornwall, Eng., the Eden Project, the largest botanical garden in the world, opens; it bills itself as "the living theatre of plants and people" and expects to attract 750,000 visitors a day.

•

On the Greek island of Kalymnos, nine marble statues believed to be from the Hellenistic period and more than 2,000 years old are discovered; shepherds unearthed the ancient statues while digging holes for fence posts.

18 Bertrand Delanoë becomes the first elected Socialist mayor of Paris since the 19th century.

•

Aventis CropScience reports that the genetically modified StarLink corn (maize) has accidentally found its way into more than 430 million bushels of corn in the U.S. (*See* June 13.)

19 In a racially charged atmosphere and amid rioting, elections held in Guyana return Pres. Bharrat Jagdeo to power with 53% of the vote for his third consecutive term; he is sworn in on March 24.

•

The Interpublic Group of Companies, based in New York City, announces plans to buy Chicago's True North Communications for some $2.1 billion; the acquisition of True North will make the Interpublic Group of Companies the largest advertising company in the world.

•

The Australian mining concern BHP Co. Ltd. announces plans to merge with Billiton PLC, based in Great Britain, in what is expected to be the largest corporate merger in Australia's history; the value of the new firm, BHP Billiton Ltd., in late June when the merger is completed is U.S. $38 billion.

•

Mary Robinson, possibly the most successful high commissioner for human rights since the UN Commission on Human Rights was established in 1946, unexpectedly says she will leave the office when her term ends in September; she changes her mind on April 2, however.

•

The Rock and Roll Hall of Fame inducts, among others, Solomon Burke, Michael Jackson, Paul Simon, and Ritchie Valens and the bands Aerosmith, Queen, Steely Dan, and the Flamingos.

20 ***The largest offshore oil platform in the world, which is owned by the Brazilian company Petrobrás, sinks off the coast of Rio de Janeiro five days after explosions on the platform killed 10 workers. (Photo below.)***

•

The editor and owner of *Al-Majales* magazine, Hedayet Sultan as-Salem, one of the first women journalists in Kuwait, is shot dead in her car in Kuwait City.

•

The U.S. National Imagery and Mapping Agency says that it believes it has located the Mars Polar Lander in images of Mars; the spacecraft disappeared in December 1999.

21 The Boeing Co. announces that it will move its headquarters from Seattle, Wash., to either Dallas, Texas; Denver, Colo.; or Chicago, setting off shock waves in Seattle and a race to attract the company in the other three cities; on May 10 Boeing announces that it has picked Chicago.

•

The U.S. Department of Agriculture seizes two flocks of sheep, some 370 animals

AP/Wide World Photos

in all, in Vermont because of fears that the sheep, imported from Belgium and The Netherlands in 1996, may carry "mad cow" disease.

•

Ali Ahmeti, the political representative of the National Liberation Army, an Albanian rebel group in Macedonia, announces a unilateral cease-fire, saying his group wants to negotiate with the Macedonian government.

22 South Korean Pres. Kim Dae Jung opens Incheon International Airport, which will replace Seoul's Gimpo Airport as the gateway to South Korea; the facility has the capacity to become a major hub in northeastern Asia.

•

Pres. Mathieu Kérékou easily wins reelection as president of Benin in the second round of voting; there are allegations of election fraud, however.

•

The journal *Nature* publishes a report by paleontologist Maeve G. Leakey on a 3.5-million-year-old hominid skull she found in Kenya in 1999; Leakey believes it is a new genus and species, which she has named *Kenyanthropus platyops,* and it suggests that humans are not necessarily descended from *Australopithicus.*

23 The Russian space station *Mir,* after 5,511 days in space and 86,330 orbits of Earth, splashes down to its final resting place in the South Pacific Ocean.

•

The trust representing the heirs of Margaret Mitchell, author of *Gone with the Wind,* asks a federal judge to issue an injunction stopping the publication of *The Wind Done Gone,* a takeoff on Mitchell's work by Alice Randall. (*See* May 25.)

24 Michelle Kwan wins the world figure skating championship, her fourth, in Vancouver, B.C.; two days earlier Yevgeny Plushchenko had won the men's championship.

•

A magnitude-6.4 earthquake strikes Hiroshima, Japan, killing at least two people and destroying more than 500 homes.

25 Comedian Steve Martin hosts the annual Academy Awards extravaganza; top winners include *Gladiator,* director Steven Soderbergh, and actors Russell Crowe, Julia Roberts, Benicio Del Toro, and Marcia Gay Harden.

•

In Mariucci Arena in Minneapolis, Minn., the Minnesota-Duluth Bulldogs defeat the St. Lawrence Saints to win the first National Collegiate Athletic Association women's hockey title.

•

Local officials say that they have found more than 200 bodies in mass graves in Kinama, a suburb of Bujumbura, Burundi, that government forces have recently retaken from rebel guerrilla forces.

26 Kazakh Prime Minister Kasymzhomart Tokayev ceremonially opens a 1,580-km (900-mi)-long oil pipeline that will carry hundreds of thousands of barrels of oil daily from the Tengiz oil field in western Kazakhstan to Novorossiysk, a Russian port on the Black Sea.

•

An arson fire in a dormitory of a boys' secondary school in Machakos, Kenya, kills 67 of the students who were sleeping there; one of the exits from the building had been locked.

•

Great Britain calls out its army to bury the carcasses of animals that have been slaughtered to try to contain the spread of foot-and-mouth disease; the animals are being slaughtered too quickly to allow for the burning of the carcasses.

27 The Wellington Arch in London, built in 1828 to commemorate the British victory over Napoleon at Waterloo, is ceremonially reopened after a two-year restoration.

•

California's Public Utilities Commission approves electricity rate hikes of close to 50%, the highest increases in the state's history.

•

The Avery Fisher Career Grants are awarded to violinist Timothy Fain, cellists Daniel Lee and Hai-Ye Ni, and flutist Tara Helen O'Connor.

•

The United States casts its fifth UN Security Council veto since 1990; the issue is the creation of a UN observer force to be deployed in Israeli-occupied Palestinian territories.

28 The White House announces that U.S. Pres. George W. Bush opposes the Kyoto Protocol on greenhouse emissions; while not unexpected, the statement appalls the other signatories of the treaty. (*See* June 12.)

•

The first commercial flight lands at Eleftherios Venizelos Airport, the new facility outside Athens.

•

Henri Loyrette, head of the Orsay Museum in Paris, is chosen to succeed Pierre Rosenberg as director of the Louvre; Rosenberg will retire in April after 39 years at the Louvre.

29 The San Francisco Bay Bridge is lifted 1.3 cm (0.5 in) so that engineers can insert ball-bearing suspension devices under the bridge supports; the devices are meant to ensure that the bridge would survive an earthquake.

•

NorthPoint Communications becomes the first major digital subscriber line company to go bankrupt as its nationwide network of fast Internet access goes dark.

•

The Czech brewery Budejovicky Budvar announces its introduction to the United States of a lager beer that it is calling Czechvar, in order to avoid trademark problems with Anheuser-Busch, makers of Budweiser.

30 U.S. Pres. George W. Bush announces plans to build a small baseball field for the playing of T-ball on the south lawn of the White House.

31 The United Nations announces that 1996 Nobel Peace laureate José Ramos-Horta will become the head of the interim governing council in East Timor.

•

Ukrainian authorities rearrest Yuliya Tymoshenko, an opponent of Pres. Leonid Kuchma, who had been accused of corruption but had been released when a court ruled there were no grounds to keep her in custody while she awaited trial; a higher court overruled the decision.

April

It was not a military victory. It was a tragedy. . . . Though it could be justified militarily, I could never make my own peace with what happened that night.

Former U.S. senator Bob Kerrey, in a speech at Virginia Military Institute, acknowledging his role in a massacre of civilians in the Vietnam War, April 18

1 An international incident is created when a U.S. spy plane collides with a Chinese fighter jet that was tailing it in the South China Sea; the Chinese pilot is killed, but the American plane lands safely on Hainan Island, China, where the crew is held. (*See* April 12.)

•

After lengthy negotiations during which he threatens to kill himself and his family, former Yugoslav president Slobodan Milosevic is arrested without incident shortly after midnight; Milosevic is charged with corruption and abuse of power, including looting large sums from the government.

•

The National Collegiate Athletic Association championship in women's basketball is won by the University of Notre Dame, which defeats Purdue University 68–66; on April 2 Duke University defeats the University of Arizona 82–72 in the men's championship.

2 The Swiss architects Jacques Herzog and Pierre de Meuron, designers of London's Tate Modern museum, are announced as the winners of the 2001 Pritzker Architecture Prize; the prize will be awarded in a ceremony on May 7.

•

NASA scientists announce that a photograph of a supernova explosion 11 billion years ago snapped by the Hubble Space Telescope in 1997 confirms a theory that Einstein formulated, then repudiated, of the existence of dark energy, or negative gravity, as a force permeating the universe. (*See* April 24.)

3 Gao Zhan, a Chinese-born American scholar who has been detained in China for 51 days, is formally charged with espionage; her husband and five-year-old son, who were taken into custody with her, had been allowed to return to the U.S. on March 8. (*See* July 26.)

•

Japan approves the use of a new middle-school textbook that critics from South Korea and China say distorts Japan's role in World War II, downplaying atrocities and justifying invasions.

4 A Communist, Vladimir Voronin, is elected president of Moldova by an overwhelming margin in Parliament.

•

The toy manufacturer Mattel Inc. announces that it will close its last American manufacturing plant over the next two years and relocate production to Mexico; the plant, in Murray, Ky., makes Fisher-Price toys.

•

Astronomers at the Whipple Observatory in Arizona announce that they have observed the third and fourth known "extreme" galaxies; extreme galaxies, the first of which was discovered in 1996, emit very great amounts of gamma radiation.

5 Turkmen Pres. Saparmurad Niyazov orders the closing of the opera and ballet house in Ashgabat, the Turkmenistan capital, saying that these art forms are foreign to Turkmen culture.

•

The *Far Eastern Economic Review* reports that restoration work is almost complete on a huge reclining Buddha statue made of stone and dating to about the 5th century; the statue, which was unearthed in 1966 near the Afghanistan border in southern Tajikistan and kept out of public view since, will be featured in the Museum of National Antiquities, due to open in Dushanbe, the Tajik capital, in August 2001.

6 Pakistan's Supreme Court vacates the corruption conviction of former prime minister Benazir Bhutto but then orders a new trial; she has been in voluntary exile since 1999.

•

Pacific Gas and Electric, California's biggest investor-owned utility, files for bankruptcy protection.

7 NASA successfully launches the 2001 Mars Odyssey, which is expected to reach the "red planet" in October, orbit it for two and a half years, and send back data on chemical elements and minerals.

•

A helicopter carrying among its 16 passengers and crew 7

AP/Wide World Photos

Americans searching for those still listed as missing in action from the Vietnam War (1955–75) crashes into a mountain in central Vietnam; all aboard the aircraft are killed.

8 Victorious in the Masters golf tournament at Augusta, Ga., Tiger Woods becomes the first person in the history of golf to win four consecutive major professional tournaments.

•

In presidential elections held in Peru, Alejandro Toledo bests candidates Alan García and Lourdes Flores; but he wins less than 50% of the vote and therefore must contest a runoff election with second-place finisher García. (*See* June 3.)

•

Sophie, countess of Wessex, wife of Great Britain's Prince Edward, resigns as chairman of her public relations firm after the publication of some indiscreet remarks she made to undercover reporters.

9 American Airlines, having negotiated an agreement with the pilots' union, closes on the acquisition of TWA; American is now the world's largest airline. (*See* January 10 and July 27.)

10 The States-General in The Netherlands passes a bill permitting euthanasia; it is the first such national law in the world.

•

An agreement is reached on how to divide the gold reserves of former Yugoslavia, totaling some $440 million, which have been held in the Bank for International Settlements in Basel, Switz., since 1991: 36.5% to the present Yugoslavia, 28.5% to Croatia, 16.4% to Slovenia, 13.2% to Bosnia and Herzegovina, and 5.4% to Macedonia.

Bulgarian Foreign Minister Nadezhda Mihailova walks across the border to Greece to celebrate the European Union's lifting of visa restrictions on Bulgarians; it is the first time Bulgarians have been allowed to travel freely into Western Europe since World War II.

11 In a stampede at the beginning of an association football (soccer) match at Ellis Park, a stadium in Johannesburg, S.Af., at least 43 people are trampled to death.

•

China executes 89 convicted criminals as part of a crackdown on organized crime.

12 ***The crew of the American spy plane that had made an emergency landing in China after colliding with a Chinese fighter jet is released and flown to Guam after days of diplomatic wrangling. (See April 1 and August 11.) (Photo above.)***

•

After three nights of rioting following the fatal shooting of an unarmed African American man by police, Cincinnati, Ohio, Mayor Charlie Luken declares a state of emergency and a citywide curfew.

•

The National Basketball Association approves a series of bold rule changes designed to increase viewer interest: henceforth in professional basketball the zone defense will be allowed; defenders may remain in the lane for only three seconds unless they can reach an opponent; and the 10-second rule will become the 8-second rule.

13 Edward Natapei is elected prime minister of Vanuatu, succeeding Barak Sope, who had lost a no-confidence vote brought in the wake of corruption charges.

•

Workers from five trade unions return to work at Guinness plants after only one day of a strike that had raised fears of a shortage of stout in Ireland over Easter weekend.

14 A conference in the Republic of the Congo chaired by Gabonese Pres. Omar Bongo is brought to a close after adopting a draft constitution.

•

After a gun battle in Pinheiros jail in São Paulo, Braz., 150 prisoners break out and then hijack cars to make good their escape.

15 Rioting breaks out in the ethnically diverse neighbourhood of Lidget Green in Bradford, Eng.; two pubs are firebombed and a drugstore burned before calm is restored seven hours after the melee began. (*See* June 24.)

16 In New York City the winners of the 2001 Pulitzer Prizes are announced: journalism awards go to *The Oregonian,* the *Miami Herald,* the *Chicago Tribune,* and the *New York Times;* arts and letters winners include Michael Chabon for fiction and Joseph J. Ellis for history.

•

The 105th Boston Marathon is won by Lee Bong Ju of South Korea, with a time of 2 hr 9 min 43 sec; Catherine Ndereba of Kenya (2 hr 23 min 53 sec) is the women's winner for the second straight year.

•

The Miho Museum in Japan returns ownership of a rare 6th-century boddhisattva to China after acknowledging that the statue had been stolen from China, which in turn agrees to loan the statue to the Japanese museum until 2007.

17 Mississippi votes overwhelmingly to retain its state flag, which features the Confederate battle flag in its canton; opinions had been voiced that the inclusion of the Confederate flag is racially offensive.

•

A Web site that permits users to trace their ancestry through U.S. immigration records from Ellis Island debuts; by the following day the new site is logging 97 million hits per hour.

•

A frantic international search for the Nigerian-registered ship *MV Etireno* ends when the ship docks in Cotonou, Benin; it was believed to be carrying 180 slave children but proves to have only a few apparently enslaved children.

18 India for the first time successfully launches a rocket capable of placing a satellite into orbit; it is the sixth country to demonstrate that capacity.

•

In a speech at the Virginia Military Institute, former U.S. senator and Nebraska governor Bob Kerrey for the first time publicly acknowledges and expresses his pain over his role in a U.S. military raid that he led on Feb. 25, 1969, in the Mekong delta in Vietnam in which a number of unarmed women and children were massacred.

•

The UN announces that a 26-km (16-m)-wide buffer zone has been established between Ethiopia and Eritrea, where fighting over an ill-defined boundary had broken out in 1998.

•

Spain declines to extradite Vladimir A. Gusinsky to Russia, on the basis that he has done nothing that is illegal in Spain; one of the new breed of Russian oligarchs, Gusinsky is an outspoken critic of the government in Moscow.

•

The *Journal of the American Medical Association* publishes a study showing that, in the first large-scale trial of St. John's wort, the herbal remedy did nothing to alleviate major depression.

19 A lawsuit by 39 major pharmaceutical firms that had sought to block a law allowing South Africa to manufacture or import low-priced versions of anti-AIDS drugs is dropped.

•

Prime Minister Sani Lakatani of Niue complains that, since the grounding of Royal Tonga Airlines, the Pacific island has no access to the outside world and is in economic crisis; he appeals for help from New Zealand.

20 The Peruvian air force shoots down a small plane carrying missionaries, killing American Veronica Bowers and her infant daughter, Charity; the tragedy apparently occurred because of language difficulties between the Peruvians and American CIA personnel working together in a drug-interdiction program.

•

Thirty-four heads of state and government begin three days of meetings in Quebec for the third Summit of the Americas; thousands of protesters demonstrate energetically in the streets.

•

The day after it opens in New York City, the musical *The Producers* breaks a Broadway box-office record, selling $3 million worth of tickets in a single day; the previous record, set in 1997, was held by *The Lion King.*

21 China, Vietnam, Malaysia, Brunei, and the Philippines, all of which claim the Spratly Islands in the South China Sea, believed to be rich in oil, agree not to establish new settlements there.

•

Fernando da Costa, who had escaped from a Brazilian prison where he had been serving a term for trafficking in cocaine in 1996 and who is reputed to be a top drug lord, is arrested in Colombia after a concentrated two-month manhunt.

22 The elevation of Nong Duc Manh as the new leader of the Vietnamese Communist Party, replacing Le Kha Phieu, is announced; Manh is widely rumoured to be the illegitimate son of Ho Chi Minh.

•

Chris A. Hadfield becomes the first Canadian astronaut to walk in space when he and American astronaut Scott E. Parazynski attach a Canadian-made robot arm to the International Space Station.

•

In an astonishing upset, virtual unknown Hasim Rahman of the U.S. knocks out favourite Lennox Lewis of the U.K. in the fifth round in Brakpan, S.Af., winning the International Boxing Federation and World Boxing Council heavyweight championships.

•

The London Marathon is won by Abdelkader El Mouaziz of Morocco, in 2 hr 7 min 11 sec, and Deratu Tulu of Ethiopia, in 2 hr 23 min 57 sec; it is the best time El Mouaziz, winner of the New York Marathon, has ever posted, and it is the first marathon that Olympic 10,000-m champion Tulu has ever won.

23 The Goldman Environmental Prize, the largest prize for grassroots environmentalism, is awarded to American journalists Jane Akre and Steve Wilson, Rwandan conservationist Eugene Rutagarama, Bolivian activist Oscar

Olivera, Yosepha Alomang of Papua New Guinea, Greek biologists Myrsini Malakou and Giorgos Catsadorakis, and reef protector Bruno Van Peteghem of New Caledonia.

•

About 120 guests and staff of the luxury Swissôtel in Istanbul, Turkey, are released unharmed about 10 hours after being taken hostage by armed men; the terrorists are protesting Russian military presence in Chechnya.

•

A U.S. Global Hawk spy plane named the *Southern Cross II* becomes the first unmanned aircraft to fly across the Pacific Ocean when it touches down at an air force base near Adelaide, Australia, a day and a half after taking off from Edwards Air Force Base, California.

24 The running of the 94-year-old TT motorcycle road races in the Isle of Man is canceled in an effort to keep the island free of foot-and-mouth disease.

•

The flooding Mississippi River crests in Davenport, Iowa, as an army of volunteers works to hold the river back.

•

The 11th anniversary of the launching of the Hubble Space Telescope is celebrated by pointing it at a target selected by amateur astronomers voting on the Internet—the Horsehead Nebula. (See April 2.) (Photo below.)

25 Former Philippine president Joseph Estrada is arrested on a charge of plunder, the most serious of the charges that have yet been brought against him. (*See* January 20 and May 1.)

•

On a 3-1 pitch Rickey Henderson takes his 2,063rd career walk, breaking the record set by Babe Ruth; his team, the San Diego Padres, loses the game nonetheless.

26 Two days after the resignation of Yoshiro Mori, Junichiro Koizumi becomes Japan's prime minister.

•

In San Juan, P.R., 6,000 people turn out to protest the planned resumption of training exercises by the U.S. Navy on the island of Vieques; the exercises begin the following day. (*See* March 2 and June 14.)

•

American poet Yusuf Komunyakaa is announced as the winner of the Ruth Lilly Poetry Prize; the honour, given for lifetime achievement, includes a cash award of $100,000.

•

American singer and actress Jennifer Lopez introduces her own line of casual clothes, J. Lo by Jennifer Lopez; the brand will be carried by top-tier department and specialty stores.

27 A report in *Science* magazine details studies on the archaeological site of Caral in Peru; these studies show that it flourished for five centuries beginning about 2600 BC, which makes it by far the oldest city yet discovered in the Americas and indicates that a civilization began there much earlier than previously believed.

•

The same issue of *Science* reports that researchers at IBM have created transistors made of carbon nanotubes that are only a few molecules in width; the discovery may enable the creation of vastly smaller and more powerful computers.

•

John Tobin, an American postgraduate student at Voronezh State University in Russia who had initially been accused of espionage, is sentenced to 37 months in a penal colony for marijuana possession; Tobin contends the drugs were planted.

28 The first antigovernment rally in its 35-year history as an independent state takes place in Singapore as 2,000 people gather in support of Joshua Jeyaretnam, one of only three opposition representatives in the 93-member Parliament.

•

A Russian Soyuz booster rocket takes off from the Baikonur Cosmodrome in Kazakhstan, carrying two Russian cosmonauts in addition to the first space tourist, American millionaire Dennis Tito, to visit the International Space Station; NASA had finally dropped its objections to Tito's presence on April 20.

29 John Carlstrom, head of the Degree Angular Scale Interferometer team at the Centre of Astrophysical Research in Antarctica, presents findings that support the theory that tiny distortions in matter from the Big Bang led to the formation of the large structures in the universe; the findings also support the theory of dark matter and the idea that the universe is flat rather than curved.

•

The inaugural Firehawk 600 race at the Texas Motor Speedway in Fort Worth is canceled when drivers refuse to participate; the speedway's track allows speeds of over 370 km/h (230 mph) and thereby subjects drivers to dangerously high G-forces.

30 Pres. Frederick Chiluba is nominated for a third term as president by his party, although Zambia's constitution forbids presidents to serve more than two terms; on May 4 Chiluba agrees not to run for another term.

•

Germany proposes a plan to remodel the European Union into a centralized federal system similar to that of Germany's government; while there is general agreement that the present government of the EU is too unwieldy, other members fear loss of autonomy and domination by Germany.

•

Sweet Basil, a popular jazz club in the Greenwich Village section of New York City, closes.

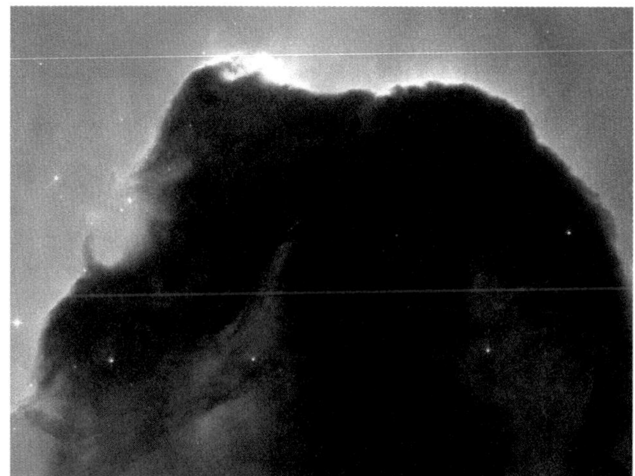

AFP Worldwide

May

Looking ahead, I can see more and more instances where I will disagree with the president on very fundamental issues.

U.S. Sen. James M. Jeffords in a speech on May 24 in Burlington, Vt., announcing he is leaving the Republican Party

1 In a speech at the National Defense University in Washington, D.C., U.S. Pres. George W. Bush proposes a new defense plan for the country that would include a network of defensive missiles; the initiative is seen by experts to contravene the Anti-Ballistic Missile Treaty signed by the U.S. and the Soviet Union in 1972.

•

Following an attack on Malacañang, the presidential palace, by supporters of ousted former president Joseph Estrada, Philippine Pres. Gloria Macapagal Arroyo declares a "state of rebellion" in Manila; she lifts the order on May 6.

•

Louis J. Freeh, the director of the U.S. Federal Bureau of Investigation, announces that he plans to retire in June; the FBI has been under pressure in recent months following the exposure of one of its agents, Robert P. Hanssen, as a long-time spy for the Russians.

•

Thomas E. Blanton, Jr., formerly a member of the Ku Klux Klan, is convicted of having murdered four African American girls in the bombing of the 16th Street Baptist Church in Birmingham, Ala., in 1963.

2 Novartis Pharmaceuticals, the Swiss drug company, announces that it will make its antimalaria medicine, Riamet, available to the World Health Organization for delivery to Africa for $2 a dose—about one-tenth the price normally charged in the West. (*See* May 7.)

•

The former heads of two leading auction houses, Sotheby's and Christie's, are indicted in New York City on antitrust charges for having fixed commission fees charged to customers over a six-year period.

•

Stanford University is the recipient of the largest gift ever made to an institution of higher learning in the United States (and possibly in the world) when the William and Flora Hewlett Foundation pledges $400 million to the university.

3 In a secret tally among the members of the United Nations Economic and Social Council, the United States is voted off the UN Human Rights Commission for the first time since it was created in 1947; the vote is seen as an expression of growing exasperation with U.S. conduct in international organizations.

•

Leaders of the Florida House of Representatives and Senate agree on a program of election reforms for the state, including the banning of punch-card ballot machinery and the requiring of hand recounts in particularly close elections; the outcome of the 2000 U.S. presidential election was delayed for weeks because of irregularities in balloting procedures in Florida.

4 Pope John Paul II begins a six-day trip to areas of the Mediterranean region associated with Saint Paul, including Syria and Malta, with a highly controversial visit to Greece; he is the first pope to visit Greece in close to 13 centuries. (*See* May 6.)

•

After learning that an American Hindu is suing McDonald's, alleging that the fast-food chain uses beef fat in making its french fries, hundreds of people riot against McDonald's outlets in India; the company maintains that, though it does flavour its fries with beef extract in the U.S., it uses no beef product in India.

5 In the 127th running of the Kentucky Derby, Monarchos, a horse not considered a contender, wins in the second fastest time in the history of the race.

6 After becoming the first pope ever to visit Syria, John Paul II becomes the first ever to set foot in a mosque when he visits the Great Mosque of Damascus. (*See* May 4.)

•

The first space tourist, American businessman Dennis Tito, returns to Earth in Kazakhstan.

7 The Antonov-225, the largest airplane in the world, successfully completes a short test flight in Ukraine; the airplane, reworked from a plane designed to carry the *Buran* space shuttle, has a wingspan of 88.4 m (290 ft).

•

Novartis Pharmaceuticals announces that it has bought a 20% stake in Roche Holding; market observers are surprised and speculate that it means the two Switzerland-based pharmaceutical corporations plan to merge. (*See* May 2.)

8 The World Trade Organization approves Moldova's application for admission; Moldova becomes the organization's 142nd member on July 26.

9 Police fire tear gas into the crowd at a soccer match in Accra, Ghana, when fans of the losing team begin throwing debris onto the field, triggering a panic in which more than 120 people are trampled to death; it is Africa's worst sports-related disaster ever.

•

American Susan Sontag receives the biennial Jerusalem Prize for Literature, awarded to writers whose work deals with the freedom of the individual within society; in her fiery acceptance speech, Sontag expresses strong disagreement with Israeli government policy in the Arab settlements.

•

In a concert at New York City's Carnegie Hall, Peter Wiley ceremonially replaces David Soyer as cellist for the Guarneri String Quartet; Wiley is the first new member to join the quartet since it started 37 years ago.

10 The U.S. Congress approves a budget plan that allows the first major tax cut in 20 years; final approval comes on May 26. (*See* July 22.)

•

President Bush nominates John P. Walters as director of the Office of National Drug Control Policy; Walters is viewed as being in favour of punishment rather than treatment for drug users.

•

Nature publishes a report by Carnegie Institute of Washington researchers who applied 25 million psi of pressure and transformed a nitrogen sample into a solid with semiconducting properties; moreover, if low temperatures are maintained, the nitrogen retains its new properties after the release of the pressure.

•

NBC and World Wrestling Federation Entertainment announce the demise of the XFL football league after one unprofitable and unpopular season. (*See* February 3.)

11 U.S. Attorney General John Ashcroft orders that the execution of Oklahoma City bomber Timothy McVeigh, originally set for May 16, be postponed until June 11 because McVeigh's defense counsel was improperly not given access to large quantities of FBI files before his trial. (*See* June 11.)

•

Cautious reductions in Germany's pension system are approved by the legislature; the very generous benefits have been strained by demographic changes, and gaining approval for the changes represents a great political victory for Chancellor Gerhard Schröder.

•

The* Toronto Globe and Mail *publishes a report saying that a Canadian man owns a portrait said to be of William Shakespeare, painted in 1603 and passed down for 12 generations in his family; it has been authenticated as being from the right time, but scholars are divided on whether the painting does, in fact, portray Shakespeare. (Photo below.)

12 Kinfe Gebremedhin, the head of the Ethiopian Federal Security and Immigration Authority (the intelligence service), is assassinated as he leaves an officer's club in Addis Ababa.

•

With their song "Everybody," the Estonian duet of Tanel Padar and Dave Benton (a native of Aruba) are the surprise winners of the 46th Eurovision Song Contest, held in Copenhagen.

•

The 2001 PEN/Faulkner Award for Fiction is presented to Philip Roth for *The Human Stain.* (*See* May 16.)

•

At New York City's Madison Square Garden, the undefeated Félix Trinidad wins a championship in his third weight class when he defeats World Boxing Association middleweight champion William Joppy (the fight actually ends shortly after midnight). (*See* September 29.)

•

More than 50 people riot in Paris to protest the popular reality TV series *LoftStory*.

13 Media tycoon Silvio Berlusconi wins election as prime minister of Italy for the second time.

•

Elections held in the Basque region of Spain are won by the moderate Basque Nationalist Party.

•

In Hannover, Ger., the Czech Republic wins its third consecutive International Ice Hockey Federation world championship, defeating Finland 3–2.

14 The sixth International IMPAC Dublin Literary Award is given to Canadian author Alistair MacLeod for his novel *No Great Mischief.*

•

The U.S. Supreme Court rules that under federal law there is no acceptable medical use for marijuana.

15 Japan's Imperial Household Agency confirms that, as long rumoured, Crown Princess Masako is pregnant; Masako, married to Crown Prince Naruhito since 1993, has had no children and suffered a miscarriage in 2000.

•

Acting Gov. Jane Swift of Massachusetts gives birth to twin girls; she had been hospitalized since May 8 but had continued to conduct state business by telephone.

•

Allen Iverson, a guard for the Philadelphia 76ers, is named the National Basketball Association's Most Valuable Player.

16 Richard Serra is awarded the annual Gold Medal for Sculpture by the American Academy of Arts and Letters, while the Gold Medal for Fiction, given every six years, is given to Philip Roth (*see* May 12); 14 new members, including Amiri Baraka and Garrison Keillor, are inducted into the academy.

•

The restored dome of the Choral Synagogue, the most important Jewish temple in Moscow, is officially unveiled amid great celebration; the dome features a large gilded Star of David.

17 Off the coast of Somaliland, a derelict ship is discovered on which more than 86 of 150 persons aboard perished; the ship reportedly developed engine trouble, and the officers forced the Somali passengers, bound for Yemen, to jump into the sea at gunpoint before the crew itself fled the vessel.

•

The American banking giant Citigroup says it will purchase the second largest bank in Mexico, Grupo Financiero Banamex-Accival.

18 France launches its first new aircraft carrier in nearly 40 years, the *Charles de Gaulle.*

•

Hong Kong orders the slaughter of more than one-third of the territory's poultry—1.2 million birds—and the cessation of imports from mainland China in an effort to stop the spread of a fatal avian influenza.

•

UNESCO inaugurates a new category for its historical preservation role, Masterpieces of Oral and Intangible Heritage, and names 19 cultural spaces and expressions to the list.

19 Point Given, the losing favourite at the Kentucky Derby, returns to form at the 126th running of the Preakness Stakes and is ridden to victory by Gary Stevens. (*See* June 9.)

20 Natsagiyn Bagabandi is reelected president of Mongolia; his party, the former ruling communist party, won control of the Great Hural in 2000.

•

As the Cannes International Film Festival closes, Italian director Nanni Moretti's *The Son's Room* wins the Palme d'Or; the Grand Prix goes to director Michael Haneke for *The Piano Teacher,* and its stars, Isabelle Huppert and Benoit Magimel, take home acting honours.

•

The media company Vivendi Universal agrees to acquire the on-line music-distribution company MP3.com less than one year after settling a copyright-infringement suit with MP3.

•

In Ireland the three-day St. Patrick's Day celebrations, postponed because of the outbreak of foot-and-mouth disease, conclude with the traditional parade in Dublin. (Photo below.)

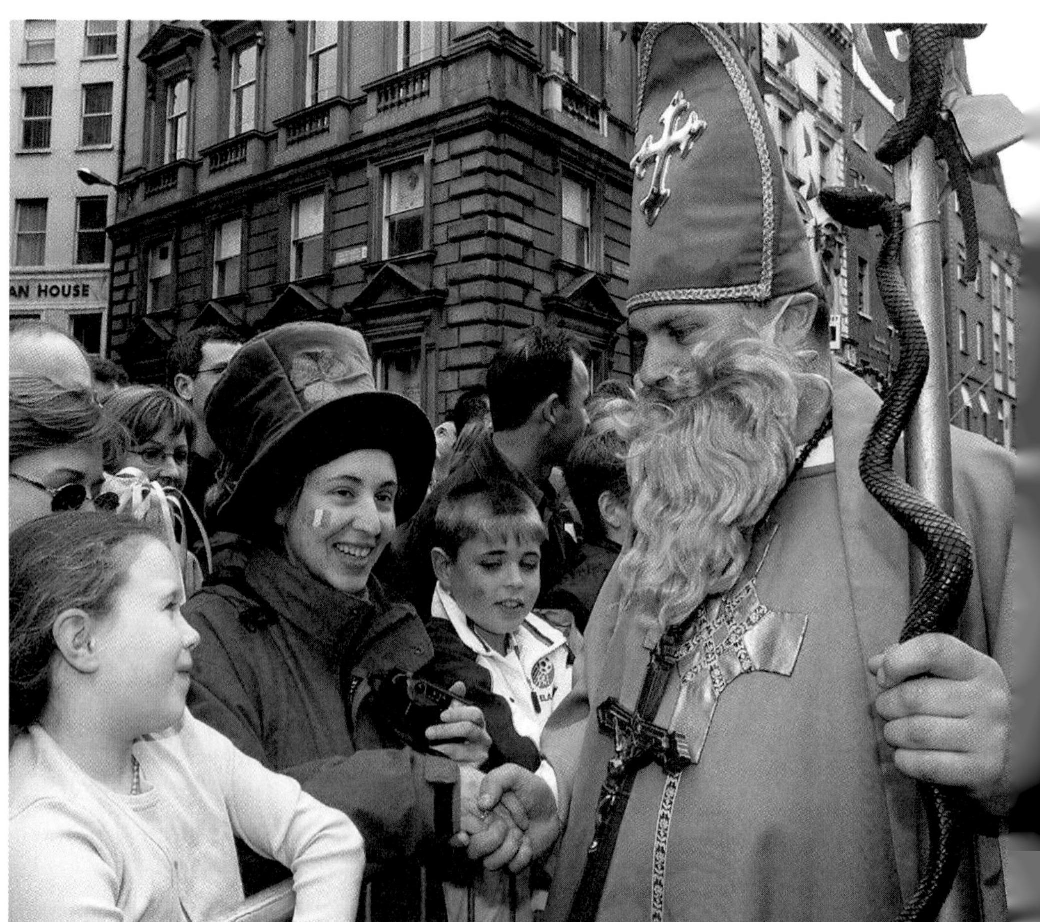

AP/Wide World Photos

21 Procter & Gamble agrees to buy the hair-products company Clairol from Bristol-Myers Squibb in a move that should give it nearly half the U.S. market.

•

Saad ad-Din Ibrahim, a sociology professor and prominent Egyptian human rights activist, is found guilty of antigovernment activities and sentenced to seven years in prison.

22 Reports indicate that the Taliban rulers of Afghanistan have set forth a plan to require non-Muslims in the country (primarily Hindus and Sikhs) to wear an identifying badge.

•

The Ford Motor Co. says that it plans to replace 13 million Firestone Wilderness AT tires, most of them on Ford Explorer sport-utility vehicles, with tires made by other manufacturers.

•

Embattled Ukrainian Pres. Leonid Kuchma nominates an ally, industrialist Anatoly Kinakh, to replace Viktor Yushchenko as prime minister.

•

The original manuscript of Jack Kerouac's *On the Road* is bought at auction for $2,430,000, a world record price.

23 India ends its six-month-long cease-fire in Kashmir but at the same time says it will invite the head of Pakistan's government, Gen. Pervez Musharraf, to go to New Delhi to discuss the action; the following day Pakistan grudgingly says it will accept the invitation.

•

Canada becomes the first country to ratify the Stockholm Convention, which bans the nonessential use of persistent organic pollutants; this category of chemicals is particularly troublesome in the Arctic, as they tend to accumulate and persist in colder climates.

•

U.S. Secretary of State Colin Powell begins a one-week tour of Africa with a meeting at the presidential palace in Bamako with Alpha Oumar Konaré, the president of Mali.

24 A three-story reception hall in Jerusalem hosting a wedding reception with more than 600 guests collapses, killing at least 25 and injuring hundreds.

•

Vermont Sen. James M. Jeffords announces that he feels the Republican Party is far more conservative than he is and that he is therefore abandoning his party affiliation to become an independent; this throws the balance of power in the evenly split Senate to the Democrats.

•

Horse breeders in central Kentucky are informed that the reason more than 500 thoroughbred foals and fetuses have died in the past few months is that the mares are somehow ingesting naturally occurring cyanide from black cherry trees; scientists suspect fecal matter from Eastern tent caterpillars may be the transmission source.

25 Pres. Chen Shui-bian of Taiwan meets in San Salvador, El Salvador, with leaders of eight Latin American nations that support Taiwan; the Latin American leaders sign a declaration recognizing Taiwan's democracy, a move Chen hopes will bolster Taiwan's efforts to join the UN.

•

The U.S. Court of Appeals for the 11th Circuit overturns an injunction preventing publication of *The Wind Done Gone,* Alice Randall's parody of *Gone with the Wind,* Margaret Mitchell's 1936 bestseller. (*See* March 23.)

26 Racial strife breaks out in Oldham, Eng., near Manchester, when a group of white youths attacks a home in a South Indian neighbourhood and residents respond by attacking a pub with a largely white clientele; sporadic fighting continues for the next three days.

•

Laurance S. Rockefeller donates his 448-ha (1,106-ac) JY Ranch in Wyoming to Grand Teton National Park; his father, John D. Rockefeller, Jr., had donated most of the land that makes up the park.

27 Brazilian Helio Castroneves, driving for Team Penske in the Indianapolis 500, takes the lead at lap 149 and, in spite of a 16-minute rain delay, holds on to win the auto race.

•

Czech athlete Roman Sebrle sets a new world record for the decathlon of 9,026 points, surpassing the record of 8,944 points set by Tomas Dvorak, also of the Czech Republic, in 1999.

28 In a coup attempt, supporters of André Kolingba fire on the home of Pres. Ange-Félix Patassé in Bangui, Central African Republic; the action sparks 10 days of fighting, but by June 7 the government has regained control.

•

The Women's College World Series of fast-pitch softball is won by the University of Arizona Wildcats when they defeat the UCLA Bruins 1–0; Arizona pitcher Jennie Finch wins the shutout.

29 In a federal courtroom in New York City, the four men on trial for having conspired with accused terrorist leader Osama bin Laden to bomb the American embassies in Kenya and Tanzania in 1998 are found guilty on all 302 charges.

•

Thai Prime Minister Thaksin Shinawatra removes the head of the Bank of Thailand, Chatumongkol Sonakul, for failing to heed his instructions to raise interest rates.

•

The U.S. Supreme Court rules that the Professional Golfers' Association of America tour must permit disabled golfer Casey Martin to use a golf cart when he competes, finding that walking is not fundamental to the game.

30 In the Elf Aquitaine corruption case, which has engulfed the government of France, former foreign minister Roland Dumas is found guilty of having received bribes from Elf and is sentenced to six months in prison. (*See* February 7.)

•

The General Motors Corp. formally offers to take over troubled South Korean car manufacturer Daewoo Motor Co.

31 The Scripps Howard National Spelling Bee, held in Washington, D.C., is won by 13-year-old Sean Conley, an eighth-grader at Minnesota Renaissance School in Anoka, Minn.; he wins the final round by correctly spelling *succedaneum.*

June

We have to ask for the opinions of experts on what we should do about the collapse of a safe society.

Japanese Prime Minister Junichiro Koizumi, responding to the Ikeda school killings, June 8

1 In Kathmandu, Nepal, Crown Prince Dipendra opens fire at a family party, killing King Birendra, Queen Aiswarya, and seven other members of the royal family before turning the gun on himself.

•

A Palestinian suicide bomber sets off his explosives in the midst of a crowd of teenagers outside a discotheque in Tel Aviv, Israel, killing 22 and injuring scores more.

•

Papua New Guinea's secessionist province of Bougainville ends a decade-long war when final terms for peace with Papua New Guinea are negotiated; the island is to have statelike autonomy and the option of total independence by the years 2011–16.

2 A woman taking part in a medical experiment at Johns Hopkins University, Baltimore, Md., becomes the first research subject to die in the university's history; the experiment was intended to help reveal how the human body fights asthma and involved a drug that produced an asthmalike reaction in healthy subjects.

3 Alejandro Toledo wins a runoff presidential election in Peru, defeating Alan García Pérez. (*See* April 8.)

•

The 55th annual Tony Awards are presented at Radio City Music Hall in New York City; winners include the plays *Proof, The Producers* (which wins 12 Tonys, a record number), *One Flew over the Cuckoo's Nest,* and *42nd Street* and the actors Richard Easton, Mary-Louise Parker, Nathan Lane, and Christine Ebersole.

•

Australian Karrie Webb wins the U.S. Women's Open golf tournament in Southern Pines, N.C., for the second year in a row. (*See* June 24.)

4 Utah Gov. Michael Leavitt declares a state of agricultural emergency resulting from what many call the worst infestation of Mormon crickets in 40 years; the insects, which are also bedeviling Nevada, are causing millions of dollars in crop damage, endangering vehicles on the road, and keeping residents indoors.

•

The state legislature of Nevada passes a law that allows regulators to permit casinos to offer Internet gambling.

5 Prosecutors representing the crown in Canada file charges against Inderjit Singh Reyat relating to the bombing of an Air-India flight in 1985; Reyat is serving time for murder in a bombing at Narita International Airport in Japan, and the filing of new charges in such a case is unprecedented.

•

James K. Hahn is elected mayor of Los Angeles over Antonio Villaraigosa in a closely watched runoff election, though in the April election that necessitated the runoff, Villaraigosa had come in ahead of Hahn.

•

A jury in Los Angeles awards over $3 billion to a man who was diagnosed with lung cancer after 40 years of smoking Marlboro cigarettes; Philip Morris Companies Inc. plans to appeal, though it does not deny that its product caused the cancer.

6 The State Duma of Russia votes to allow nuclear waste to be imported and stored in Russia; the bill is opposed by the general public in Russia and by environmentalists elsewhere because of Russia's poor record of nuclear safety.

•

The Democratic Party formally takes control of the U.S. Senate, and Tom Daschle succeeds Trent Lott as majority leader.

7 Prime Minister Tony Blair and the Labour Party coast to an expected victory in elections in the U.K.

•

Former Argentine president Carlos Saúl Menem is arrested in an investigation of his suspected involvement in arms smuggling to Croatia and Ecuador in 1991–95 during his tenure in office.

•

Ireland rejects the Treaty of Nice, which sets forth procedures for admitting new members to the European Union and requires ratification by all members.

8 A man armed with a knife invades an elementary school in Ikeda, Japan, stabs to death

AP/Wide World Photos

seven second-grade girls and one first-grade boy, and also seriously wounds six other students and a teacher, shocking the entire nation.

•

After a week of pounding southeastern Texas, Tropical Storm Allison hits Houston with renewed strength, causing massive flooding that cuts off power and access to most hospitals and forces more than 10,000 residents from their homes. (Photo above.)

•

In elections in Iran reformist Pres. Mohammad Khatami is reelected with 77% of the vote.

•

The 1,700th anniversary of the founding of the Armenian church by St. Gregory the Illuminator is celebrated at the church of St. Gregory in Kayseri, Turkey, by about 300 people, half of whom are Americans of Armenian descent.

9 American Jennifer Capriati defeats Kim Clijsters of Belgium in a hard-fought battle to win the women's French Open tennis title; the following day Brazilian Gustavo Kuerten defeats Alex Corretja of Spain to win the men's competition for the third time.

•

The Colorado Avalanche defeats the defending National Hockey League champions, the New Jersey Devils, 4 games to 3, to win the Stanley Cup.

•

Preakness winner Point Given runs to a commanding victory in the Belmont Stakes, the last of the U.S. Triple Crown horse races. (*See* May 19.)

10 The 49th Venice Biennale opens to the public; it is in the form of a Plateau of Humankind and has exhibitions of visual arts, film, theatre, poetry, and dance.

•

Gilberto Simoni wins the 84th Giro d'Italia bicycle race; one stage of the race had been canceled on June 7 after a dramatic drug raid on the cyclists' hotel rooms during the night.

•

In Switzerland a referendum to allow Swiss members of UN and NATO peacekeeping forces to carry arms passes in a very close vote.

11 In the first federal execution in the U.S. since 1963, Timothy McVeigh is put to death in Terre Haute, Ind., for having carried out what was at the time the worst terrorist attack in U.S. history, the 1995 Oklahoma City bombing. (*See* May 11.)

•

Mud slides caused by heavy rain fall into a road near Quito, Ecuador, killing 38 people.

•

The British pound sterling falls to its lowest point against the U.S. dollar in 16 years, apparently because of fears that the recent Labour electoral victory means that Britain is likely to abandon the pound in favour of the euro.

12 In his first overseas trip as president of the United States, George W. Bush arrives in Spain, where he reiterates his opposition to the Anti-Ballistic Missile Treaty and the Kyoto Protocol. (*See* March 28 and July 23.)

•

The Coalition to Stop the Use of Child Soldiers releases a report saying that at least 300,000 children under the age of 18, some as young as 7 years old, are fighting as soldiers in 41 countries.

•

The International Organization for Migration reports that an increasing number of teenagers from Eastern Europe, Africa, and Asia are being smuggled into Western Europe, most often to work in the sex industry.

13 Israeli Prime Minister Ariel Sharon and Palestinian leader Yasir Arafat reluctantly agree to an American-proposed cease-fire plan.

•

The U.S. Centers for Disease Control and Prevention announces that it has found no evidence that consumption of corn products tainted with genetically modified StarLink corn produced allergic reactions or illness of any sort. (*See* March 18.)

14 In a startling reversal of position, Pres. George W. Bush announces that the U.S. Navy will end its military exercises on Vieques Island, Puerto Rico, by May 2003. (*See* April 26 and July 29.)

•

Hundreds of thousands of ethnic Berbers and opposition party supporters march in Algiers, many rioting; Berber unrest has led to many days of rioting and demonstrations since April.

15 The Los Angeles Lakers defeat the Philadelphia 76ers 108–96 to win the National Basketball Association (NBA) championship for the second year in a row; also for the second time, Shaquille O'Neal is named Most Valuable Player of the finals.

•

In Göteborg, Swed., where a summit meeting of European Union leaders is taking place, thousands of antiglobalization demonstrators engage in 12 hours of sustained rioting.

•

A new international grouping, the Shanghai Cooperation Organization—made up of China, Kazakhstan, Kyrgyzstan, Russia, Tajikistan, and Uzbekistan—holds its inaugural meeting; delegates criticize the missile defense plan put forth by the U.S. and discuss joint action to counter Muslim separatists.

16 A bomb explodes in Narayanganj, Bangladesh, at a meeting of the Awami League, the country's ruling party, killing 22 people.

•

The Leaning Tower of Pisa opens for the first time since 1990 as work to keep it from falling over is completed; it now leans only 4.1 m (13.5 ft) off perpendicular, 44 cm (17 in) less than its previous lean. (Photo above.)

17 The party of former king Simeon II wins the parliamentary elections in Bulgaria; the king waits until July 12 to accept the post of prime minister.

•

Chelsea Clinton, the daughter of former U.S. president Bill Clinton and Sen. Hillary Rodham Clinton, graduates summa cum laude from Stanford University.

18 The Taliban agrees to let the UN World Food Programme employ women to conduct interviews in Afghanistan to determine where and how food should be apportioned; because women are forbidden to speak to men outside their family, the survey cannot be carried out effectively without women as interviewers.

•

In Tulsa, Okla., Retief Goosen of South Africa defeats American Mark Brooks by two strokes in an 18-hole play-off to win the U.S. Open golf tournament.

19 Authorities in Yemen say they have arrested eight men who they believe were plotting to bomb the U.S. embassy in San'a'; the men are said to have fought with Osama bin Laden against Soviet forces in Afghanistan in the 1980s.

•

Baltimore Orioles third baseman Cal Ripken, Jr., who played in 2,632 successive games between 1982 and 1998, announces that he will retire at the end of the baseball season.

20 Pervez Musharraf appoints himself president of Pakistan while maintaining that the nation will return to democratic rule after elections in October 2002; Musharraf came to power in a coup in October 1999.

•

American Lori Berenson is convicted of treason and sentenced to 20 years in prison in open court in Peru; she was convicted and sentenced to life in prison by a closed military court in 1996, but the decision was overturned and a new trial ordered in August 2000.

•

Billy Collins is named the next poet laureate of the U.S.; Collins will replace Stanley Kunitz in the post in October.

21 U.S. federal indictments are brought against 14 men, none of them in custody in the U.S., in the 1996 bombing of the Khobar Towers in Saudi Arabia, in which 19 American airmen were killed; though the men indicted are Saudi Arabian and Lebanese, U.S. officials believe Iran is behind the act.

•

Russia, Azerbaijan, and Kazakhstan agree in Paris to stop fishing sturgeon for the rest of the year to give dwindling stocks a chance to regenerate; 90% of the world's caviar is produced by sturgeon in the Caspian Sea, which these countries border.

22 A 120-year-old bridge over the Kadalundi River in Kerala, India, collapses as a passenger train is crossing it; three cars fall into the river, killing 59 passengers.

•

The Sara Lee Corp. pleads guilty in court to having produced and distributed meat that was infected with listeria in 1998; it is believed that 15 people died as a result of eating the contaminated meat.

•

The Constitutional Court of Turkey votes to ban the Virtue Party, the main opposition party; the pro-Islamic party has 102 deputies in the legislature.

23 A magnitude-7.9 earthquake strikes southern Peru, causing great damage in both Arequipa and Moquegua and killing at least 31 people.

•

Vladimiro Montesinos, the former head of the Peruvian spy agency and right-hand man to Peru's ousted president Alberto Fujimori, is captured in Venezuela; he was wanted on charges of gun running and collaborating with drug traffickers.

•

The Unitarian Universalist Association elects William Sinkford as its president; he is the first African American to lead the largely white church.

24 Three days of small skirmishes escalate into a race riot in the economically depressed town of Burnley in northern England; about 7% of Burnley's population is of South Asian background. (*See* April 15.)

•

Karrie Webb wins the Ladies Professional Golf Association championship and becomes the youngest woman golfer (age 26) ever to complete a career grand slam. (*See* June 3.)

•

Mayon Volcano in the Philippines erupts, forcing over 30,000 people to evacuate their homes.

•

A privately funded peace memorial is dedicated near the site of the Battle of the Little Bighorn, which took place 125 years earlier on June 25; speakers call for peace between whites and Native Americans.

25 The General Assembly of New York passes a law banning the use of a hand-held telephone while driving a motor vehicle; it is the first state in the U.S. to enact such a ban.

•

IBM announces that it has developed the world's fastest silicon-based transistor; the company expects that the chip will find applications in fibre-optic communications and in cellular telephones.

•

During the pontiff's visit to Kiev, Pope John Paul II and the chief rabbi of Ukraine, Yaakov Dov Bleich, visit the memorial honouring those who were killed by the Nazis in 1941–43 at Baby Yar.

•

A never-before-published novelette by Mark Twain appears in *The Atlantic Monthly;* "A Murder, a Mystery, and a Marriage" was written in 1876 as an entry for a contest Twain proposed to the magazine, but no one else agreed to take part in the contest.

26 In a light heavyweight professional boxing bout taking place aboard the Intrepid Sea-Air-Space Museum in the Hudson River in New York City, Beethavean Scottland suffers severe head injuries in the fight with the undefeated George Khalid Jones; Scottland dies of his injuries on July 2.

27 The United Nations approves the Declaration of Commitment, which treats AIDS as a political and economic threat and sets a goal of a 25% reduction in HIV infections in the worst-affected nations by 2005.

•

The tire manufacturer Bridgestone/Firestone announces plans to close its plant in Decatur, Ill., which produces 10% of the company's output.

•

In the NBA draft, for the first time ever, the first pick (by the Washington Wizards) is a high-school student, Kwame Brown, a 19-year-old senior from Brunswick, Ga.

28 Former Yugoslav president Slobodan Milosevic is extradited to The Hague to face war-crime charges before the UN tribunal; the following day Zoran Zizic, the prime minister of Yugoslavia, resigns in protest. (*See* July 17.)

•

A U.S. Court of Appeals, while upholding the finding of District Court Judge Thomas Penfield Jackson that Microsoft Corp. is a monopoly, voids the order that the computer company be broken up and bars Jackson from further involvement in the case.

29 Kofi Annan is elected with almost no opposition to a second term as secretary-general of the United Nations and swears himself in to the new five-year term. (*See* October 12.)

•

The National Japanese American Memorial is officially opened a few hundred metres north of the Capitol in Washington, D.C.

•

The first of four Russian military bases in Georgia, left over from the Soviet era, is turned over to the government of Georgia; a 1999 treaty gives Russia a deadline of July 1 for completing the transfer of all four bases.

30 The BBC's World Service discontinues its venerable shortwave radio service; its digital satellite radio and Internet service are supplanting it.

•

A rocket carrying the Microwave Anisotropy Probe, which will photograph so-called fossil light in the universe to show what the universe looked like immediately after the big bang, is launched from Cape Canaveral, Florida.

July

One hundred thousand people don't get upset unless there is a problem in their hearts and spirits.

French Pres. Jacques Chirac, speaking about antiglobalization protesters, in Genoa, Italy, July 20

1 David Trimble resigns his position as first minister of Northern Ireland, citing as his reason the failure of the Irish Republican Army to disarm; Gerry Adams, head of Sinn Fein, says the failure to disarm is a result of the British inability to produce an acceptable replacement for the Royal Ulster Constabulary. (*See* August 11.)

•

A U.S. law creating a 233-sq-km (90-sq-mi) zone called Tortugas North, for tourists, and a 158-sq-km (61-sq-mi) zone called Tortugas South, for scientists, underwater off the Dry Tortugas National Park, Florida, goes into effect; together called the Tortugas Ecological Reserve, it is the largest area of U.S. coastal waters that is off-limits for fishing.

2 Despite assurances by the Taliban ambassador to Pakistan to the U.S. ambassador to Pakistan that the Taliban would not permit Osama bin Laden to attack U.S. interests, U.S. Pres. George W. Bush signs an executive order to continue economic sanctions against the Taliban for harbouring Bin Laden, whom the U.S. blames for the 1998 bombings of the U.S. embassies in Tanzania and Kenya. (*See* July 30.)

•

The first completely implantable artificial heart, the AbioCor, is placed into a patient on the brink of death; the patient, later revealed to be Robert Tools, age 58, suffers a stroke in November and dies later that month.

•

In a surprise move, Mexican Pres. Vicente Fox Quesada marries his spokesperson, Martha Sahagún, putting an end to gossip about their relationship.

3 In Russia's worst airline disaster since 1996, a Russian passenger airliner flying between Yekaterinburg and Vladivostok crashes on its approach to an intermediate stop, Irkutsk, killing all 143 aboard.

•

Australia and East Timor agree on a plan to share the oil and gas reserves in the Timor Sea between the two countries; the plan will give 90% of the revenues to East Timor.

•

Two weeks after the collapse of the ruling coalition, the head of the Lithuanian Social Democratic Party, Algirdas Brazauskas, becomes prime minister; Brazauskas was Lithuania's president from 1992 to 1998.

4 Scientists from the U.S. and Vietnam meeting in Hanoi agree to work cooperatively on a study examining environmental damage caused by the use of the herbicide Agent Orange by U.S. forces during the Vietnam War.

•

Farmers in Klamath Falls, Ore., open irrigation gates that had been closed in April by order of the federal government to protect the endangered suckerfish; the disappearance of the irrigation water, together with a severe drought, has enraged local farmers.

5 The government of Macedonia signs a cease-fire agreement with leaders of the ethnic Albanian rebels who have been fighting in the northwestern part of the country.

•

In the first of several highly publicized shark attacks in U.S. coastal waters this summer, an eight-year-old boy, Jessie Arbogast, has his right arm bitten off by a 2-m (7-ft) bull shark; the boy's arm is rescued from the shark's mouth and later reattached by surgeons.

•

Susan P. Schoelwer, the curator of the Connecticut Historical Society, tells the press that a flag discovered in the society's storage area in 1998 has been authenticated as one of the five flags that were in the theatre box occupied by U.S. Pres. Abraham Lincoln on the night he was assassinated.

•

Hannelore Kohl, the wife of former German chancellor Helmut Kohl, in despair over the rare, painful, and untreatable allergy to sunlight that she had developed, commits suicide.

6 Scientists at the Stanford (Calif.) Linear Accelerator Center announce that they have found CP violation in the decay of B mesons, confirming results seen only once before, with another particle, the K meson, in 1964; CP violation is an inequality in certain basic processes of particle physics and may explain why vastly more matter than antimatter resulted from the big bang.

7 Maoist insurgents in Nepal kill 39 police officers at various security posts throughout the country, the highest one-day total since the insurgency began five years ago. (*See* July 19.)

•

Violence breaks out in Kingston, the capital of Jamaica, in the wake of a police raid for illegal weapons; when calm is restored three days later, at least 25 people have died.

•

Portugal decriminalizes the possession of recreational drugs for personal use, joining Spain and Italy in treating drug use as a medical rather than a criminal matter. (*See* July 30.)

•

Six people are gored in the first day of an unusually dangerous running of the bulls in Pamplona, Spain.

8 Great Britain's fourth race riot, the worst so far this year, rages for nine hours in the northern town of Bradford.

•

Officials in Bosnia and Herzegovina say they have found a mass grave containing at least 200 bodies in the village of Liplje.

•

American tennis star Venus Williams defeats Belgian Justine Henin to win her second consecutive Wimbledon title; a day later Goran Ivanisevic of Croatia becomes the first wild-card entrant to win a major tournament when he defeats Australian Patrick Rafter.

AP/Wide World Photos

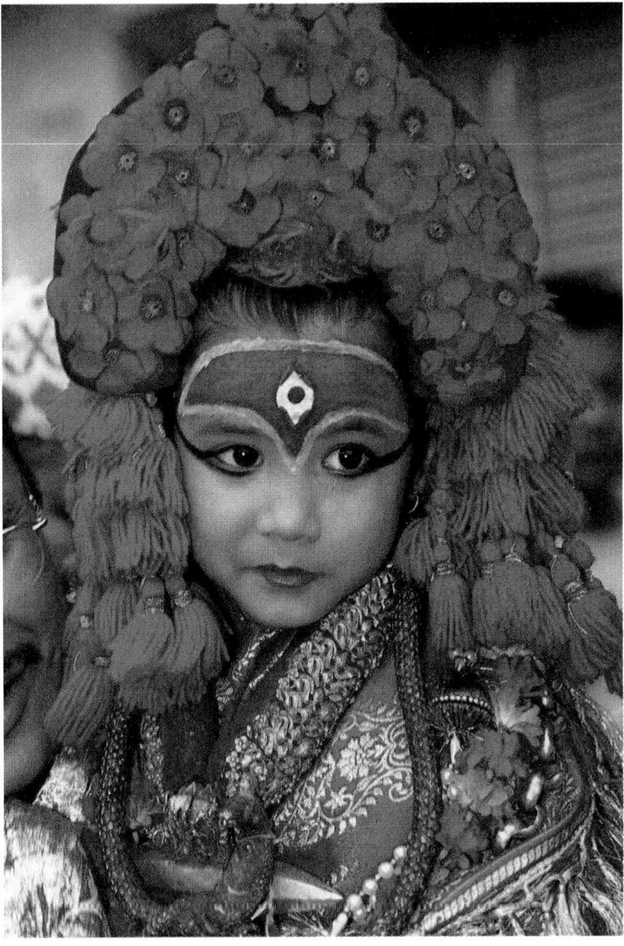

•

The Israeli conductor Daniel Barenboim creates an uproar in Israel when, at the conclusion of a program for the Israel Festival from which a planned piece by Richard Wagner, whom many consider an anti-Semite, had been excised, Barenboim asks the audience whether they would like a Wagner piece as an encore; after a half-hour debate a number of people leave, and the overture to Wagner's *Tristan und Isolde* is performed.

9 An appeals court in Chile rules that Augusto Pinochet Ugarte is too ill to stand trial; this effectively puts an end to efforts to bring him up on charges of human rights abuses during his 17-year tenure as ruler of Chile.

10 Sri Lankan Pres. Chandrika Kumaratunga orders Parliament suspended for two months and calls for a referendum on a proposed new constitution that would give more rights to Tamils.

•

Preeti Shakya, age four, is enthroned as Kumari, the virgin goddess who brings peace and prosperity to Nepal; she will lead a sequestered life, dressed in red, until her menarche causes her to lose her divinity and a new Kumari must be found. (Photo above.)

•

Zlatko Lagumdzija, a Bosnian Muslim and foreign minister, is appointed prime minister of Bosnia and Herzegovina, replacing Bozidar Matic, a Bosnian Croat who had resigned on June 22.

11 On the last day of its summit meeting in Lusaka, Zambia, the Organization of African Unity decides to dissolve the organization after 38 years of existence and transform itself into the African Union, modeled on the European Union.

•

Police in Washington, D.C., search the apartment of U.S. Rep. Gary Condit of California, looking for clues in the disappearance of Chandra Levy, a Washington intern who was last seen on April 30; Condit's personal life has come under increasingly heavy scrutiny throughout the summer. (*See* August 23.)

•

Four firefighters die in the deadliest wildfire in the U.S. since 1994; the blaze, in the Okanogan National Forest in Washington, explodes from 40 to 1,012 ha (100 to 2,500 ac).

12 A report issued by Human Rights Watch charges that the human rights record of the opposition to the Taliban in Afghanistan is as bad as that of the Taliban and that the countries supporting the opposition are doing so for their own self-interest.

•

France orders the extradition of former high-profile antiwar activist Ira Einhorn to the U.S., whence he fled in 1981 to avoid being tried for the 1977 murder of his girlfriend, Holly Maddux; on July 20 Einhorn arrives in the U.S., where he is immediately imprisoned.

13 Beijing is selected to host the 2008 Olympic Games, winning out over Toronto,

Paris, Istanbul, and Osaka; China responds with joy.

14 Pres. Pervez Musharraf of Pakistan arrives in India for a summit meeting with Indian Prime Minister Atal Bihari Vajpayee to discuss the Kashmir dispute; two days later the talks abruptly break off, however. (*See* October 1.)

•

The last original episode of the *Bozo's Circus* television show in the U.S. is broadcast in Chicago; at the height of its popularity in the 1960s, there were about 180 Bozos on the air throughout the nation.

15 Using a Canadian-supplied mechanical arm, the astronauts aboard the International Space Station install a new entryway onto the space station; the new airlock is compatible with NASA spacesuits as well as the Russian spacesuits that the other airlock is able to accommodate.

16 In Moscow Russian Pres. Vladimir Putin and Chinese Pres. Jiang Zemin sign a mutual friendship treaty, the first between the two countries in more than 50 years.

•

Jacques Rogge, a Belgian surgeon and former world champion yachtsman, is elected president of the International Olympic Committee; chosen partly for his personal integrity in the recent IOC scandals, he replaces Juan António Samaranch of Spain.

•

Germany asks the Czech Republic to close down the Temelin nuclear power plant near the border between the countries, contending that the plant is not safe.

•

The 50th anniversary of the publication of *The Catcher in the Rye* by J.D. Salinger is noted; in celebration the online bookseller Amazon.com sells the book at the 1951 price—$3.

•

Fifteen sea lions in Ecuador's Galápagos National Park are discovered butchered on the beach on San Cristóbal Island; the sea lions' sex organs are in demand in Asia, where they are used for folk medicinal purposes.

17 Dragisa Pesic is named by Pres. Vojislav Kostunica to replace Zoran Zizic as prime minister of Yugoslavia. (*See* June 28.)

18 A 60-car train carrying hazardous materials derails in a tunnel under Baltimore, Md., and catches fire, melting fibre-optic cables and slowing Internet and rail traffic throughout the Middle Atlantic region; five days later the tunnel is finally cleared.

•

A special train arrives in Vladivostok, Russia, from Moscow as part of a celebration of the centenary of the 9,267-km (5,758-mi)-long Trans-Siberian Railroad, still the longest railway in the world.

19 Indonesia passes a bill granting increased autonomy to the rebellious province of Aceh.

•

Faced with an ultimatum from his party, the Nepali Congress Party, as well as a burgeoning Maoist insurgency, Prime Minister Girija Prasad Koirala of Nepal resigns; on July 22 King Gyanendra appoints Sher Bahadur Deuba to replace him. (*See* July 7.)

•

Nearly two-thirds of Argentina's workers participate in a one-day strike, effectively shutting down the country, to protest recently announced austerity measures.

20 Outside the Group of Eight meeting in Genoa, Italy, Carlo Giuliani, one of tens of thousands of protesters, is killed by police; his is the first death among antiglobalization activists.

•

The London Stock Exchange goes public; its shares are traded—on its own exchange—for the first time.

•

A public uproar greets a media report about a study commissioned by the Philip Morris tobacco company in the Czech Republic that spells out the savings to public finances brought about by smokers' dying earlier than nonsmokers.

21 The United Nations Conference on the Illicit Trade in Small Arms and Light Weapons in All Its Aspects approves an agreement, much weakened by the demands of the U.S., to reduce trafficking in small arms.

•

Doctors in Murcia, Spain, report the largest-known outbreak of Legionnaires disease; more than 300 became ill with the disease, which they contracted from cooling towers in six different buildings.

22 David Duval of the U.S. wins his first major golf tournament when he finishes three strokes ahead of Niclas Fasth of Sweden at the 130th British Open.

•

The first of the tax-rebate checks authorized in the new U.S. budget are mailed out to American taxpayers; 91.6 million people are scheduled to receive such a check. (*See* May 10.)

23 A day after the military ignored Indonesian Pres. Abdurrahman Wahid's orders to shut down the People's Consultative Assembly (the legislature), the assembly votes unanimously to oust Wahid in favour of his vice president, Megawati Sukarnoputri.

•

In Bonn, Ger., 178 nations, not including the U.S., reach an agreement on the Kyoto Protocol after three days of marathon bargaining; under the agreement 38 nations must reduce their greenhouse gas emissions to 5.2% below 1990 levels by 2012. (*See* June 12.)

•

Burundi Pres. Pierre Buyoya signs an agreement with Hutu politicians to lead the first transitional government under the Arusha accords, designed to end the civil war in Burundi, as an attempted coup fanned by fears of the power-sharing arrangement is put down.

24 The Liberation Tigers of Tamil Eelam attack Sri Lanka's international airport at Colombo, destroying or disabling 14 commercial and military aircraft and leaving 20 dead.

•

A court in Seoul, S.Kor., finds seven former executives of the Daewoo Corp. guilty of accounting fraud and sentences them to as much as seven years in prison.

•

Phase I of the largest rat eradication program in the world is completed on the 106-sq-km (41-sq-mi) sub-Antarctic Campbell Island, believed to be infested with as many as 200,000 Norway rats.

25 The U.S. rejects an international protocol for compliance with the 1972 treaty banning germ warfare, objecting to provisions that it believes would be detrimental to the business community.

•

Louis G. Spisto, the executive director in New York of the American Ballet Theatre, quits abruptly; his two-year tenure has nearly torn the dance company apart.

26 The Chinese government says that it has released U.S. residents Gao Zhan and Qin Guangguang to the U.S. two days after having sentenced them both to 10 years' imprisonment for spying; U.S. Secretary of State Colin Powell is due to arrive in Beijing on July 28. (*See* April 3.)

•

Congressional Gold Medals are awarded to the 29 Navajo code talkers (only 5 of whom are still living) who were instrumental in the Allied victory over Japan in World War II by relaying military information coded in the Navajo language, which is spoken by only a handful of non-Navajos.

27 Scientists at California's Lawrence Berkeley National Laboratory retract a claim they made in 1999 that they had created a 118th element; with results that could not be reproduced, the researchers reexamined the original data and found they did not support the claim.

•

A judge in Bogotá, Colom., orders a halt to spraying intended to destroy the coca crop; local farmers contend that the herbicide used, glycophosate, is causing health problems and damaging legal crops.

•

United Airlines and US Airways call off their proposed merger as the U.S. Department of Justice threatens to sue to prevent it from taking place. (*See* April 9.)

28 The National Academy of Public Administration finds that the Smithsonian Institution needs about $1.5 billion worth of repairs and renovations and blames management problems for much of the deterioration.

29 American Lance Armstrong wins his third consecutive Tour de France bicycle race.

•

In a nonbinding referendum on the Puerto Rican island of Vieques, 68% of balloters vote for an immediate end to U.S. Navy exercises on the island. (*See* June 14.)

30 New rules go into effect in Canada that permit anyone who is terminally ill or suffers from certain specified chronic illnesses to grow and smoke marijuana for pain relief, provided they have a medical certificate verifying their condition. (*See* July 7.)

•

The UN Security Council approves a plan to appoint experts to monitor and help enforce an arms embargo against the Taliban in Afghanistan; the embargo is intended to press the Taliban into surrendering Osama bin Laden. (*See* July 2.)

31 Prime Minister Atal Bihari Vajpayee, frustrated by work involved in holding his coalition together, shocks the government of India when he offers to resign; he is immediately persuaded to stay on.

•

Lava from Mt. Etna in Sicily, Italy, which has been erupting for two weeks, threatens two villages and forces the closing of tourist and scientific facilities. (Photo below.)

AP/Wide World Photos

August

According to the second paragraph of Article 7, I have the right to speak the Albanian language.

Arben Xhaferi, ethnic Albanian leader, surprising participants at the signing of a peace agreement in Macedonia by addressing them in Albanian, August 13

1 The first book is ceremonially placed in the new Bibliotheca Alexandrina in Egypt, located approximately on the site of the ancient Library at Alexandria; included among the first volumes are a handwritten 7th-century Qur'an, a Bible, and the Microsoft Excel 2000 handbook.

•

Azerbaijan gives up Cyrillic and adopts the Latin alphabet (in a variant similar to Turkish) for its national language, Azerbaijani; the change, made for nationalist reasons, causes substantial confusion, especially because of a lack of computer fonts and keyboards.

•

In Germany, for the first time, homosexual couples exchange rings and vows as a new law permitting same-sex partnerships goes into effect; the law permits registered partners to inherit from one another and to share a surname but not to adopt children.

2 Former Bosnian Serb general Radislav Krstic is found guilty of genocide by the UN war crimes tribunal in The Hague and is sentenced to 46 years in prison; the following day three Bosnian Muslim officers are transferred to The Hague to face the tribunal.

•

Robert S. Mueller III is confirmed as the new FBI director, replacing Louis J. Freeh; on the same day, Mueller successfully undergoes an operation for prostate cancer.

3 Scientists from the Sloan Digital Sky Survey say they believe they have seen the beginning of the formation of stars; it is believed that, as stars began to form, clouds of hydrogen atoms were floating throughout the universe, and the Sloan scientists think they have seen the shadow of one of these clouds on a quasar.

•

Thailand's high court for the first time overturns an indictment by the anticorruption commission when it acquits Prime Minister Thaksin Shinawatra of financial irregularities.

4 North Korean leader Kim Jong Il and Russian Pres. Vladimir Putin issue a joint statement in Moscow in which they pledge to combat international terrorism, among other things; this is Kim's first visit to a noncommunist state.

•

In a ceremony in Canton, Ohio, players Lynn Swann, Nick Buoniconti, Mike Munchak, Jackie Slater, Ron Yary, and Jack Youngblood, as well as coach Marv Levy, are inducted into the Pro Football Hall of Fame.

•

Hundreds of First Nations people gather in Montreal in an encampment to reenact the Great Peace of 1701, a treaty signed between the French and the Iroquois, and to celebrate its 300th anniversary. (Photo right.)

5 Officers from the Taliban's Ministry for the Promotion of Virtue and the Prevention of Vice close the Kabul offices of Shelter Now, a Christian relief agency, and arrest 24 of its workers, accusing them of attempting to spread Christianity, which is forbidden in the Taliban-run areas of Afghanistan.

•

Pak Se Ri of South Korea wins her third major golf tournament when she outplays Australian Karrie Webb to win the Women's British Open in Sunningdale, Eng.

•

In Edmonton, Alta., American runner Maurice Greene wins the world championship 100-m sprint for the third consecutive time with a time of 9.82 sec; on the following day American sprinter Marion Jones loses her first 100-m race since 1997 to Zhanna Pintusevich-Block of Ukraine, and on August 8 Ethiopian runner Haile Gebrselassie, who had won every 10,000-m event that he had entered since 1993, finishes behind Charles Kamathi of Kenya.

6 The Irish Republican Army agrees to a method for putting its weapons beyond use as a deadline approaches for an agreement to prevent the shutdown of the Northern Ireland Assembly.

•

The publishing company Alfred A. Knopf, Inc., agrees to pay former U.S. president Bill Clinton an advance of

René Fortin/1701-2001 Corporation des fêtes du Tricentenaire de la Grande Paix de Montréal

$10 million to write his memoirs; it is the biggest publishing advance ever paid.

7 Pres. Hugo Bánzer Suárez of Bolivia hands the presidency over to his vice president, Jorge Quiroga Ramírez, because of ill health.

•

In Nairobi, Kenya, on the former site of the U.S. embassy, the August 7 Memorial Park is opened to commemorate the victims (207 Kenyans and 12 Americans) of the terrorist bombing that destroyed the building on Aug. 7, 1998.

8 Bayer AG withdraws its anticholesterol drug, Baycol, from the world market after 31 deaths are linked to it.

•

Kyrgyzstan announces plans to charge Kazakhstan, Tajikistan, and Uzbekistan for using water in rivers that originate in Kyrgyzstan, saying that it requires money for the upkeep of reservoirs that provide water for its neighbours.

9 After weeks of well-publicized ruminating, U.S. Pres. George W. Bush announces that the U.S. will support stem-cell research, provided the research is done only on the 60 existing stem-cell lines; it is unclear, however, whether these lines are in fact viable and available to American researchers.

•

The U.S. and Mexico reach an agreement in principle to expand a temporary worker program that will allow many undocumented Mexicans living and working in the U.S. to gain permits and work toward permanent legal residency.

•

Soldiers overthrow the secessionist government of Said Abeid Abderemanein on Anjouan Island; Anjouan had declared independence from Comoros in 1997 but signed a reconciliation agreement in 2000.

10 A passenger train strikes a land mine near Zenza do Itombe, Angola, and more than 250 passengers are killed; UNITA rebels claim responsibility, saying that the train was also carrying military supplies.

•

Cambodia's King Norodom Sihanouk signs a law to create a UN-assisted tribunal to try former Khmer Rouge leaders for war crimes.

11 Home rule is restored in Northern Ireland after a one-day suspension; the pause allows British authorities to wait another six weeks before calling new elections in the wake of David Trimble's resignation as first minister. (*See* July 1 and November 6.)

•

China refuses an offer of $34,576 from the U.S. to defray China's costs from the incident wherein a U.S. spy plane and Chinese fighter jet crashed; China had sought $1 million. (*See* April 12.)

12 Two days of heavy rains cause flash flooding and mud slides in northeastern Iran, killing at least 114 people, destroying crops, and leaving thousands homeless; on August 14 New Delhi suffers its heaviest rainfall in 40 years.

•

The space shuttle *Discovery* delivers a new three-member

crew to the International Space Station for a four-month stay; this crew is the space station's third.

13 Government and ethnic Albanian leaders sign a political deal in Macedonia that gives more representation to ethnic Albanians and recognizes Albanian as an official language. (*See* August 17.)

•

Japanese Prime Minister Junichiro Koizumi visits the Yasukuni shrine, a Shinto memorial to those who died during World War II; the visit excites a storm of protest in China and South Korea, where 20 young men chop off the tips of their little fingers to demonstrate their distress.

14 Leaders of the 11 African countries with a stake in Air Afrique agree to a restructuring plan whereby the airline will be dissolved and then recreated, with Air France holding a majority stake in return for significant financial support; African heads of state hail the plan, which has saved the airline from going out of business.

•

In spite of Pres. Daniel arap Moi's support, a bill that would have created the Kenya Anticorruption Authority is defeated in that country's parliament; continued financial aid to Kenya from the International Monetary Fund is contingent upon the creation of the authority.

•

Emmanuel Milingo, the Roman Catholic archbishop of Zambia—who had risked excommunication to marry Maria Sung of South Korea in a mass wedding in May presided over by the Rev. Sun Myung Moon of the Unification Church—renounces his wife and reconciles with the Roman Catholic Church.

15 A law to give Indian groups in Mexico greater rights goes into effect; in the five years since the law was drafted to satisfy demands of Zapatista rebels in Chiapas state, however, it has lost support among Indians throughout the country.

•

A new civil code granting women equal legal rights with men is passed in Brazil; the code was first proposed 26 years ago.

16 A six-day auction of the assets of the Amedeo Development Corp., Prince Jefri Bolkiah's defunct construction company, in Brunei comes to a close with total sales of $7.8 million, a fraction of the $15 billion the former finance minister had lost.

•

The Industry Standard, a respected financial magazine that focused on the dot-com economy, suspends publication.

17 The first of the NATO peacekeeping troops arrive in Macedonia; two days earlier NATO had decided to send only 400 British troops initially and to wait to see if the combatants held to their cease-fire before sending in the full contingent of 3,500 from 12 countries. (*See* August 13.)

•

Prime Minister Percival Patterson of Jamaica agrees with opposition leader Edward Seaga to create a strategy to reduce violence in the inner city; the following day 7 people are murdered in Kingston, bringing the death total since May to 71.

•

Because of bad weather, American balloonist Steve Fossett halts his fifth attempt to become the first person to circumnavigate the globe solo in a balloon; he lands in a field in Brazil after making it just past the halfway mark.

18 A hotel in Quezon City, Phil., burns down, killing 73; security bars on windows and inaccessible fire escapes contribute to the death toll.

•

Danny Almonte, playing for the Bronx, N.Y., Rolando Paulino All-Stars, pitches the first perfect game in the Little League World Series since 1957; it is later proved that Almonte is 14 years old, however, and his team's entire season is struck from the record books because he is two years too old to be eligible to play Little League baseball. (*See* August 26.)

•

The 10-day consecration of the Great Stupa of Dharmakaya is completed at Red Feather Lakes, Colo.; the stupa, built to honour the teacher Chogyam Trungpa Rinpoche, who died in 1987, attracted 2,000 Buddhists from around the world to the dedication ceremonies.

19 Three days of performances, parades, and fireworks celebrating the 800th anniversary of the city of Riga, the capital of Latvia, come to a close.

•

American David Toms wins the Professional Golfers' Association of America championship, simultaneously setting a new scoring record for a major tournament championship with a score of 265, breaking the record of 267 set by Greg Norman in 1993.

20 In Gaborone, Botswana, government officials from the Democratic Republic of the Congo, opposition politicians, and rebel leaders begin talks to try to settle the civil war in the country.

•

An orderly march of 100,000 persons calling for greater recognition of the Berber language and culture takes place in Kabylie, a region in northeastern Algeria considered to be the centre of Berber culture. (*See* October 3.)

21 Two hundred yachts race in the America's Cup Jubilee regatta over the course of the race in which the schooner *America* triumphed 150 years ago, an 80-km (50-mi) course circling the Isle of Wight; the winner is Gianni Agnelli's *Stealth.*

•

The 14th-century Orthodox monastery at Lesok, Macedonia, is destroyed by an explosion, apparently the work of ethnic Albanian terrorists; the incident is unusual, however, because cultural and religious monuments have not previously been targeted during the current civil strife in Macedonia.

22 Jesse Helms, the ultraconservative Republican senator from North Carolina, announces that he will retire at the end of his term in 2003; Helms turns 80 in October.

•

The Bush administration releases figures showing that the large projected U.S. budget surplus for the next several years has dwindled to a negligible amount.

•

New Scientist magazine publishes a report that Hans Beekman of Belgium's Royal Museum for Central Africa found banana fossils in Cameroon dating to 500 BC; experts had believed that bananas did not reach Cameroon until the 10th century AD.

23 Speaking at an elementary school in Crawford, Texas, Pres. George W. Bush says definitively that the U.S. will pull out of the Anti-Ballistic Missile Treaty, though he says the timing of the withdrawal has not been determined.

•

For the first time, an official of the government of China acknowledges that the country is facing an AIDS epidemic and discloses that HIV infections in China rose 67.4% in the first six months of 2001 compared with the first six months of 2000.

•

Beleaguered U.S. Rep. Gary Condit of California appears on a prime-time television interview with ABC News investigator Connie Chung; the program is the most-watched show in the summer of 2001, with an estimated audience of 24 million people. (*See* July 11.)

24 An article in *Science* magazine by geneticists for the Mpala Research Centre in Kenya and the U.S. National Cancer Institute reports their findings that forest elephants and savanna elephants in Africa are in fact two different species, which brings to three the number of living elephant species.

•

Tom Green is sentenced in Provo, Utah, to five years in prison for bigamy and nonsupport, in spite of the pleas of his five wives. (Photo right.)

25 Crown Prince Haakon of Norway marries Mette-Marit Tjessem Høiby, a commoner with a colourful past.

•

The hero of East Timor's independence struggle, José Alexandre Gusmão, bows to public pressure and announces that he will run for president when elections are held in 2002. (*See* August 30.)

•

The Women's United Soccer Association holds its first championship game, in Foxboro, Mass.; the Bay Area CyberRays defeat the Atlanta Beat 4–2 to win the Founders Cup.

26 In Williamsport, Pa., Kitasuna of Tokyo, Japan, becomes the 55th world champion Little League team when it beats the nine from Apopka, Fla., 2–1. (*See* August 18.)

•

Sammy Sosa of the Chicago Cubs becomes the third player in major league baseball history to have four 50-home-run seasons (the other two are Babe Ruth and Mark McGwire); by season's end he has 64.

27 *Physical Review Letters* publishes a study that suggests that the fine structure constant has increased slightly over the life of the universe; if confirmed, the finding would have astonishing inferences for other constants, such as the speed of light.

•

A parade in Chisinau marks the 10th anniversary of Moldova's independence; Ukraine and Belarus also celebrate the 10th anniversaries of their independence in August.

•

At the Tonga National Museum in the capital, Nuku'alofa, Prime Minister Prince 'Ulukalala Lavaka Ata officially opens the island country's first major exhibition of prehistoric artifacts, most dating to the Lapita era, about 3,000 years ago.

28 The computer manufacturer and retailer Gateway announces plans to lay off one-quarter of its workforce, eliminate most of its overseas operations, and close one factory and four support centres in the U.S.

•

Cuba's central bank says that U.S. coins will not be accepted as currency after October 15; the U.S. dollar has been accepted as currency on a temporary basis in Cuba since 1993.

29 Australian troops seize an overcrowded Norwegian container vessel off Christmas Island to prevent it from landing on Australian territory; four days earlier the ship had rescued 434 Afghan, Sri Lankan, and Pakistani asylum seekers from a sinking Indonesian ferry. (*See* September 19.)

•

Thirty Nigerian families file suit against the pharmaceutical company Pfizer, Inc. in U.S. federal court, contending that the drug company illegally experimented upon their children during a 1996 meningitis outbreak.

•

The National Black Sports and Entertainment Hall of Fame inducts its first 24 members in New York City; among the honorees are Muhammad Ali, Louis Armstrong, Ella Fitzgerald, and Wilma Rudolph.

30 Voters in East Timor go to the polls for their first free election, to select the assembly that will write the constitution for the new nation; the turnout is estimated at better than 90%. (*See* August 25.)

•

For the first time, the general public in India may gaze upon the astonishing wealth of jewelry that was accumulated by the Nizams of Hyderabad as the collection goes on exhibit in the National Museum in New Delhi.

31 Papua New Guinea signs a peace agreement with rebels in Bougainville after a decade-long civil war.

•

The International Labour Organization releases a report showing that Americans worked the longest hours of any country in the world between 1990 and 2000 and increased the hours spent on the job per year by nearly 40 over the course of the decade.

George Frey/AFP Worldwide

September

As for those that carried out these attacks, there are no adequate words of condemnation. Their barbarism will stand as their shame for all eternity.

British Prime Minister Tony Blair,
in his address to his nation, September 11

1 The Los Angeles Sparks overwhelm the Charlotte Sting to win the Women's National Basketball Association championship, and the team's centre, Lisa Leslie, is named Most Valuable Player.

•

A fire breaks out in a mah-jongg parlour in Tokyo's most famous red-light district; the death toll, at 44, makes it Tokyo's deadliest fire since 1982.

2 The Hewlett-Packard Co. announces that it will buy the Compaq Computer Corp.; they are the second and third largest personal computer manufacturers, respectively, in the U.S.

3 Israel and the U.S. abandon the UN World Conference Against Racism in Durban, S.Af., objecting that the proposed declaration unfairly singles out Israel as an offender. (*See* September 8.)

•

Fradique de Menezes is inaugurated as the new president of São Tomé and Príncipe; on September 25 he appoints Evaristo de Carvalho to replace Guilherme Posser da Costa as prime minister.

4 Disney opens its newest theme park, Tokyo DisneySea, which has an aquatic theme, in Japan; in spite of the straitened economy in Japan, theme parks remain popular.

•

An arson fire starting at the Straw Market engulfs the market, the offices of the Ministry of Tourism, an office complex, and a complex of shops and restaurants at the heart of the tourist strip in Nassau, Bahamas.

•

The *Proceedings of the National Academy of Sciences* publishes a report by researchers at the University of Wisconsin at Madison describing how they induced human embryonic stem cells to become blood-making cells.

5 Elections are held in Nagorno-Karabakh, which has declared itself independent; Azerbaijan maintains that the elections are illegal.

•

At a scientific conference in Washington, D.C., scientists describe an observation by the Chandra X-Ray Observatory of energy flares that provide strong evidence of the theorized black hole at the centre of the Milky Way Galaxy.

6 After a summer of media attention devoted to shark attacks on swimmers, the Florida Fish and Wildlife Conservation Commission bans the practice of using bait to attract sharks so tourists can swim with them.

•

The ABC television network announces that it will join CBS in broadcasting most of its offerings in the HDTV (high-definition television) format.

7 Surgeons at Mount Sinai Medical Center in New York City remove a diseased gall bladder from a woman in Strasbourg, France, through the use of robotics and computer imaging; it is the first transoceanic instance of what has come to be called telesurgery.

•

Counting of last week's ballots reveals that Laisenia Qarase has been elected prime minister of Fiji; he had been installed as interim prime minister by the military in July 2000 following the coup in May.

8 Tajikistan's minister of culture, Abdurahim Rahimov, is murdered by a gunman outside his home in Dushanbe.

•

The UN World Conference Against Racism in Durban, S.Af., finally succeeds in hammering out a declaration that the attending nations can agree to, though many are still somewhat dissatisfied; the declaration condemns slavery and discrimination against ethnic minorities, refugees, and women. (*See* September 3.)

•

At the U.S. Open women's tennis finals, telecast in prime time, American Venus Williams defeats her younger sister, Serena, to take her second straight U.S. Open title; the next day Australian Lleyton Hewitt defeats Pete Sampras of the U.S. for the men's title.

Patrick Witty

•

Monsoon Wedding, a film by Indian director Mira Nair, wins the Golden Lion award at the Venice Film Festival.

9 Suicide bombers attack Ahmad Shah Masoud, the leader of the anti-Taliban opposition in Afghanistan; it is initially unclear whether the assassination attempt is successful, but a spokesman finally confirms his death on September 15.

•

In presidential elections held in Belarus, Pres. Alyaksandr Lukashenka declares victory hours before the first returns are in.

•

The Jewish Museum Berlin, designed by Polish-born architect Daniel Libeskind, is opened with a gala attended by 800 dignitaries.

10 Tokyo's benchmark Nikkei Stock Average closes at its lowest point since 1984, while the *Financial Times* Stock Exchange 100 index in London closes below 5,000 for the first time since 1998.

•

A general election in Norway results in the Labour Party's worst showing since 1924. (*See* October 17.)

11 ***In a coordinated terrorist attack, two hijacked airliners strike the twin towers of the World Trade Center in New York City, which subsequently collapse (photo above), another strikes the Pentagon near Washington, D.C., and a fourth crashes in rural Pennsylvania, apparently short of its intended goal; the total death toll is in the vicinity of 3,100.***

•

For the first time ever, the U.S. government closes the airspace over the United States, as well as all airports, to commercial traffic in an attempt to prevent any possible further planned terrorist strikes from taking place.

•

An exceptionally violent typhoon kills five people in Tokyo and causes great damage to roads and rail.

12 The North Atlantic Council, the governing council of NATO, agrees to allow the U.S. to invoke Article 5 of the NATO charter, which declares that an attack against any NATO member is to be regarded as an attack against all members; it is the first time in the alliance's 52-year history that Article 5 has been invoked. (*See* October 2.)

•

U.S. authorities say that they have evidence that the hijackers in the September 11 terrorist attacks were followers of Osama bin Laden and also that they have identified accomplices in a number of cities.

•

The Federal Aviation Administration announces that henceforward knives and other cutting implements will not be allowed on U.S. airline flights; evidently the weapons used to hijack airliners on September 11 were of this previously permitted category.

13 U.S. Attorney General John Ashcroft says that federal investigators have identified 18 men who were hijackers in the September 11 terrorist attacks, and the following day the names of the 19 total number of hijackers are released; all were ticketed passengers aboard the airliners that they hijacked.

•

Bond markets in the U.S. resume trading for the first time since September 11; interest rates plummet.

•

The Federal Aviation Administration allows all airports in the U.S. except Logan International Airport in Boston, where two of September 11's hijacked flights originated, and Ronald Reagan Washington National Airport to reopen; few flights take off, however, and most of those are airplanes that had been diverted on September 11 and are returning to hub airports and their original destinations.

•

The government of Nigeria promises to step in to stop

the violence after three days of fighting between Muslims and Christians in the city of Jos leave hundreds dead; violence first broke out in this historically peaceful city on September 7.

•

The New England Journal of Medicine publishes findings that the bacterium that causes stomach ulcers, *Heliobacter pylori,* is also responsible for the vast majority of stomach cancers.

14 Tropical Storm Gabrielle makes landfall in Florida, causing extensive damage and flooding throughout central Florida.

•

Musicians who had gathered (and become stranded) in Los Angeles for the Latin Grammy Awards, scheduled for September 11 and canceled, hold an impromptu benefit concert for the Red Cross and the New York Disaster Relief Fund.

15 Pres. Pervez Musharraf pledges Pakistan's support for U.S. efforts to punish those responsible for the September 11 terrorist attacks; Pakistan borders Afghanistan, and its support is seen as crucial.

•

A barge collides with a piling of the Queen Isabella Causeway in Texas a few hours after midnight, causing two adjacent 24-m (80-ft) segments of the bridge to fall into the Laguna Madre channel and a number of vehicles to drive off the edge in the dark.

16 The Professional Golfers' Association of America announces that the Ryder Cup golf tournament, scheduled for later this month in Sutton Coldfield, Eng., will be postponed until next year in the wake of the September 11 terrorist attacks.

17 The New York Stock Exchange opens for the first time since it closed the morning of September 11.

•

After a week in abeyance, major league baseball resumes playing games; it is the first major sport to return to the arena.

•

The World Bank and the International Monetary Fund cancel their annual meetings, scheduled for September 29–30 in Washington, D.C.; it is the first time the institutions have ever called off a meeting.

•

The government of Macedonia reluctantly agrees to accept a small NATO security force to help keep the peace after the conclusion of the 30-day weapons-collection effort.

•

The General Motors Corp. agrees to buy about two-thirds of South Korea's bankrupt Daewoo Motor Co. from its creditors.

18 For the second straight day, Typhoon Nari pounds Taiwan with record rainfalls, causing massive flooding and killing 79 people.

•

Two days of talks between cabinet-level negotiators from North and South Korea end with a number of agreements, including plans for a new round of family visits and work to complete a rail link between the countries.

19 The Organization of American States agrees by acclamation to invoke the Rio Treaty, a hemispheric mutual-defense pact.

•

United Airlines announces plans to cut 20% of its workforce; since September 11 several airlines and Boeing have announced job cuts as a result of losses caused by the grounding of all flights and subsequent decreased demand layered onto problems caused by a softening economy.

•

Indonesian Pres. Megawati Sukarnoputri meets with U.S. Pres. George W. Bush in Washington, D.C.; Megawati does not pledge to crack down on Muslim extremists in her fragmented country.

•

The first of the 434 largely Afghan refugees turned away from Australia in late August land in Nauru, where they will be processed by officials from the United Nations High Commissioner for Refugees. (*See* August 29.)

20 In his first formal televised address to the nation since his inauguration, U.S. Pres. George W. Bush announces plans to create a new cabinet-level office to be called the Office of Homeland Security and to be headed by Tom Ridge, currently the governor of Pennsylvania.

•

Fans at an exhibition ice hockey game between the New York Rangers and the Philadelphia Flyers in Philadelphia's First Union Center insist on watching U.S. Pres. George W. Bush's address to the nation rather than the final period of the game.

•

Rwanda adopts a new national anthem, "Rwanda Nziza," replacing "Rwanda Rwacu," which was felt to have ethnically divisive lyrics.

21 *America: A Tribute to Heroes,* a two-hour benefit show to raise money for relief work in New York City and Washington, D.C., that was put together in less than a week, is broadcast on more than 30 cable and broadcast TV stations in the U.S. and in 200 other countries as well.

•

After the Riigikogu (legislature) fails to decide on a new president, a special assembly chooses Arnold Ruutel to replace Lennart Meri as president of Estonia.

•

The Lasker Awards for medical research are presented in a ceremony in New York City to Robert Edwards for clinical research; to Mario Capecchi, Martin Evans, and Oliver Smithies for basic medical research; and to William Foege for public service.

22 Deep Space 1, a NASA probe whose primary mission ended in September 1999, surprises scientists by successfully passing within 2,250 km (1,400 mi) of the nucleus of Comet Borrelly and transmitting pictures and other data that will greatly add to scientific understanding of comets.

23 In general elections in Poland, there is a lower-than-usual turnout, and the winning party is the Democratic Left Alliance, the former communist party; Solidarity not only is ousted from power but also receives too few votes to win seats in the National Assembly.

•

The leftist Social Democratic Party, which has governed the German city-state of Hamburg for the past 44 years, is voted out; the gains made by the conservative Christian Democratic Union and the new rightist Law and Order Party are seen as a reaction to the discovery that the terrorist attacks in the U.S. were apparently planned in Hamburg.

•

The worst U.S. coal mine disaster since 1984 takes place in Brookwood, Ala., when a pair of methane gas explosions kill 3 miners outright as well as 10 other miners who were attempting to rescue them.

24 Pres. George W. Bush announces that all assets of suspected terrorists will be frozen, and he threatens foreign banks that fail to follow suit or cooperate with U.S. efforts with measures that would make it impossible for them to do business in the U.S.

•

The U.S. House of Representatives votes to release $582 million of the $819 million in back dues that the U.S. owes to the United Nations. (*See* January 9.)

25 Saudi Arabia severs relations with the Taliban rulers of Afghanistan, three days after the United Arab Emirates did so; now only Pakistan recognizes the Taliban as the legitimate government of Afghanistan.

•

Basketball legend Michael Jordan announces his second comeback from retirement, declaring that he will sign a two-year contract with the Washington Wizards, sell his ownership stake in the team, and donate his salary for the season to the relief efforts in New York City and Washington, D.C.

•

General Motors announces that the 2002 model year will be the last in which the Chevrolet Camaro and the Pontiac Firebird are produced; four million Camaros have been sold since the model's debut in 1967, but sales of sports cars have fallen 53% since 1990, the company reports.

26 Pres. George W. Bush authorizes two air force generals to order, on their own authority, the shooting down of commercial airplanes that appear to be threatening U.S. cities.

•

A pro-Taliban mob burns down the long-abandoned U.S. embassy building in Kabul, Afg.

27 In Zug, Switz., an unhinged man armed with a standard Swiss army-issue assault rifle bursts into a cantonal parliament meeting and opens fire, killing 14 legislators; it is the worst mass murder in Switzerland's history.

•

Ali Ahmeti, political representative of the ethnic Albanian National Liberation Army in Macedonia, gives the rebel force orders to disband as part of the peace process.

28 The UN Security Council unanimously adopts a resolution requiring all UN members to take steps to eliminate terrorism, including cooperating in any international campaign against terrorists.

•

The Commonwealth cancels its biennial summit, scheduled for October 6–9 in Brisbane, Australia; in the wake of the September 11 terrorist attacks, leaders of the 54 member nations did not want to leave their countries.

•

In spite of a 10-day-old truce, a flare-up of violence in Palestinian areas in the Middle East marks the first anniversary of the new *intifadah.*

29 Members of the Free Papua Movement, a separatist organization, occupy the city of Ilaga, capital of the Central Highlands district in Irian Jaya, in spite of the fact that Indonesia recently granted Irian Jaya autonomy.

•

In a stunning upset, American Bernard Hopkins becomes the first unified middleweight champion in 14 years when he knocks out Félix Trinidad of Puerto Rico in the 12th round in front of a capacity crowd of more than 19,000 fans at Madison Square Garden in New York City.

30 Pres. George W. Bush approves the disbursement of funds for the covert support of the opponents of the Taliban in Afghanistan.

•

Japanese runner Naoko Takahashi sets a new world record for women in the Berlin Marathon, running 42.2 km (26.2 mi) in 2 hr 19 min 46 sec, nearly a full minute faster than the previous record, set in 1999 in Berlin by Kenyan Tegla Loroupe. (*See* October 7.)

•

A free concert of remembrance in New York City's Carnegie Hall features, among others, conductor James Levine and soprano Leontyne Price, who comes out of retirement for the event. (Photo below.)

AP/Wide World Photos

October

You can not stop us. We have this anthrax. You die now. Are you afraid? Death to America. Death to Israel. Allah is great.

Text of anthrax-laden letter sent to
U.S. Sen. Tom Daschle and opened on October 15

1 The Swissair Group files for bankruptcy protection for most of its operations; the following day the group grounds all its flights, but the Swiss government steps in, and Swissair begins flying an abbreviated schedule on October 4.

•

A car bomb explodes in the Legislative Assembly building in Srinagar, the summer capital of the Indian state of Jammu and Kashmir, and a gunfight ensues; 38 people are killed in the incident, for which a militant Pakistani group called Jaish-e-Muhammad claims responsibility. (*See* July 14.)

•

Italy's highest court acquits Prime Minister Silvio Berlusconi of having falsified documents while acquiring a film company in 1987; he had been convicted and sentenced to prison on that charge in 1997.

•

FOMA, the world's first third-generation (3G) high-speed cellular phone service, is launched in Japan.

•

Condé Nast announces that the November issue of *Mademoiselle,* a fashion magazine for young women that had been published for 66 years, will be the last.

2 NATO says that the U.S. has proved to its satisfaction that Osama bin Laden and al-Qaeda are responsible for the September 11 terrorist attacks in the U.S. and that it is therefore prepared to support the U.S. in retaliating against them. (*See* September 12.)

•

Russia and Iran sign a military accord under which Russia will sell missiles and other weapons to Iran; Russia had stopped selling arms to Iran six years earlier under pressure from the U.S.

•

U.S. Pres. George W. Bush expresses explicit support for the creation of a Palestinian state.

3 A deranged passenger on a Greyhound bus traveling through Tennessee attacks the bus driver; in the ensuing struggle the bus flips over, and six passengers, including the assailant, are killed.

•

The pharmaceutical giant GlaxoSmithKlein announces a new national discount program for low-income senior citizens whose health insurance coverage does not include a prescription-drug benefit.

•

A meeting takes place between Algerian Prime Minister Ali Benflis and Berber leaders in which Algeria agrees to give Tamazight, the Berber language, national recognition and promises to punish police brutality against Berbers. (*See* August 20.)

4 A Russian airliner explodes and crashes into the Black Sea, and all 76 aboard die; the cause proves to be an errant Ukrainian surface-to-air missile that went awry during training exercises.

•

Health officials report that a man in Florida has been hospitalized with the first case of pulmonary anthrax to have occurred in the U.S. since 1976, but they stress that there is no cause for alarm; the man, Robert Stevens, a photo editor for the supermarket tabloid *Sun,* dies the following day.

•

Parliamentary elections in Bangladesh, believed to be free and fair in spite of a high level of violence throughout the campaign, return a victory to the party of Khaleda Zia, who goes about forming a new government.

•

San Diego Padres outfielder Rickey Henderson, batting against the Los Angeles Dodgers, hits a home run and scores his 2,246th career run, breaking the record held by Ty Cobb since 1928.

•

The World Health Organization issues a report urging national governments to devote more resources to mental health; the dearth of such resources is particularly acute in the poorest countries, and the response in this area to the events of September 11 in the U.S. is singled out for praise.

5 The day after Israeli Prime Minister Ariel Sharon shocked the U.S. administration by implicitly comparing its attempts to discourage Israeli reprisals against

Palestinian attacks to former British prime minister Neville Chamberlain's policy of appeasement toward Nazi Germany, Pres. George W. Bush calls Sharon's remarks "unacceptable," an unusually strong rebuke.

•

Philippine authorities announce that Mustapha Ting Emmo, a key leader of the militant Muslim group Abu Sayyaf, has surrendered.

•

Barry Bonds, batting for the San Francisco Giants against the Los Angeles Dodgers, breaks Mark McGwire's single-season home-run record when he hits his 71st and 72nd home runs; he finishes the season with 73.

6 In an outdoor stadium in East Lansing, Mich., a record 72,554 people watch a tie ice hockey game between Michigan State University and the University of Michigan; the previous hockey attendance record, 55,000, was set in 1957 in Moscow.

7 U.S. and British forces launch air strikes against Taliban positions in Afghanistan; at the same time, U.S. forces begin dropping food packets in remote and poverty-stricken areas of Afghanistan.

•

A referendum to turn a number of responsibilities over to regional governments passes in Italy; the decentralizing legislation is the first poll on constitutional change in Italy in close to half a century.

•

Railtrack, the company that owns the railroad tracks in the U.K., undergoes bankruptcy reorganization in order to keep the nation's railway system from financial collapse.

•

Kenyan runner Catherine Ndereba sets a new world record in the women's marathon of 2 hr 18 min 47 sec at the Chicago Marathon (*see* September 30); the men's winner is Ben Kimondiu of Kenya.

8 It is discovered that a co-worker of Robert Stevens has been exposed to anthrax, and spores are found on Stevens's computer keyboard.

•

Girma Wolde-Giorgis is elected by the parliament as the second federal president of Ethiopia, succeeding Negasso Gidada.

•

The Nobel Prize for Physiology or Medicine is awarded to Leland H. Hartwell, R. Timothy Hunt, and Paul M. Nurse for their work in discovering the mechanisms regulating cell multiplication.

•

In Italy's worst civilian air disaster in nearly 30 years, a Cessna takes a wrong turn on a taxiway in Milan and crashes into an SAS airliner about to take off, which explodes; 118 people, including 4 airport workers, are killed.

9 In accordance with the terms of the peace pact worked out earlier this year, Macedonia grants amnesty to all ethnic Albanian rebels who have disarmed.

•

The Nobel Prize for Physics is awarded to Carl E. Wieman, Eric A. Cornell, and Wolfgang Ketterle for their production of the Bose-Einstein condensate; the Nobel Prize for Chemistry goes to William S. Knowles, Ryoji Noyori, and K. Barry Sharpless; and the Nobel Prize for Economic Sciences is awarded to Americans Joseph E. Stiglitz, George A. Akerlof, and A. Michael Spence.

•

The United Service Organization appoints entertainer Wayne Newton its official celebrity front man, replacing Bob Hope, who had served in that capacity since the early 1950s.

10 In order to avoid a no-confidence vote, Sri Lankan Pres. Chandrika Kumaratunga dissolves the government and calls for new elections. (*See* December 5.)

•

The five major American television news organizations agree to censor tapes of Osama bin Laden to remove inflammatory propaganda and possibly prevent the airing of clandestine signals to operatives.

11 The Nobel Prize for Literature is awarded to V.S. Naipaul, a Trinidadian-born British writer.

•

The broadcasting system NBC agrees to buy Telemundo Communications Group, the second biggest Spanish-language broadcaster in the U.S.

12 The centennial Nobel Prize for Peace is awarded jointly to the United Nations and its secretary-general, Ghanaian Kofi Annan.

•

The day after a warning from the FBI that more terrorist attacks may occur in the U.S. in the next few days, U.S. government officials say they have received more credible threats of a possible attack in the next two days; citizens are instructed to be calm but wary.

•

Erin M. O'Connor, an assistant to NBC newsman Tom Brokaw, is diagnosed with cutaneous anthrax in New York City; as was the case in Florida, the anthrax spores apparently came in the mail.

•

The Polaroid Corp. files for bankruptcy protection; its core business of instant photographs was decimated by competition from computer imaging.

13 Company officials at American Media, Inc. (owner of the *Sun* tabloid) say that blood tests have shown that five more employees, in addition to the man who died and two others who were infected with anthrax, have been exposed to anthrax.

•

After negotiations between the U.S. Department of Justice and the Microsoft Corp. fail to reach an agreement by a court-imposed deadline, U.S. District Court Judge Colleen Kollar-Kotelly appoints Eric D. Green, a specialist in dispute resolution, to mediate between the parties.

14 Ireland holds a state funeral for 10 Irish Republican Army volunteers who were hanged by British authorities in 1920 and 1921.

•

A large monument to nationalist leader Stepan Bandera is unveiled in Drohobych, Ukraine; Bandera had cooperated with Nazi Germany, believing that German victories would lead to independence for Ukraine.

15 An anthrax-laden letter addressed to Senate Majority Leader Tom Daschle is opened by one of his assistants, and the baby son of an ABC news producer in New York City is diagnosed with cutaneous anthrax; the following day it is revealed that the anthrax is of exceptionally high quality and that the anthrax-laden letters addressed to Daschle and to Tom Brokaw appear to have been sent by the same person.

•

The venerable Bethlehem Steel Corp. files for bankruptcy protection.

•

Brill's Content, a magazine about the media, suspends publication; the previous day *Lingua Franca,* a journal chronicling academic life, had stopped publication.

•

New York City Mayor Rudolph Giuliani is named a Knight Commander of the Most Excellent Order of the British Empire by Queen Elizabeth II for his support to British families affected by the September 11 terrorist attacks. (*See* December 23.)

•

Comedian Whoopi Goldberg receives the Mark Twain Prize of the John F. Kennedy Center for the Performing Arts in Washington, D.C.; the award is given annually for contributions to American humour.

16 The German pharmaceutical company Bayer AG announces that it will triple its production of Cipro, which is the primary antibiotic used to fight anthrax; on October 24 Bayer agrees to sell Cipro to the U.S. government for half the price it had been charging.

•

Peace talks to end the war in the Democratic Republic of the Congo begin in Addis Ababa, Eth.

17 Rechavam Ze'evi, the Israeli minister of tourism and a right-wing politician, is assassinated by members of the Popular Front for the Liberation of Palestine. (*See* October 23.)

•

Norwegian Prime Minister Jens Stoltenberg submits the Labour Party government's resignation after a poor showing in elections on September 10; a centre-right coalition led by the Christian People's Party under Kjell Magne Bondevik takes over on October 19.

•

In London the Booker Prize for literature is awarded to Australian author Peter Carey for *True History of the Kelly Gang.*

•

Daniel S. Goldin announces that he will resign as head of NASA, an agency he has led since 1992.

18 The men who were convicted in May of having conspired with Osama bin Laden to bomb the U.S. embassies in Kenya and Tanzania in 1998 are sentenced to life in prison without parole.

•

Japan's legislature approves a measure that will allow Japanese troops to go overseas to provide logistic and humanitarian support to U.S. troops fighting in Afghanistan; the Japanese constitution forbids the use of troops in a combat situation, however.

AP/Wide World Photos

19 U.S. ground forces for the first time enter the war in Afghanistan.

•

Leszek Miller of the Democratic Left Alliance is inaugurated as prime minister of Poland.

•

A wooden fishing boat carrying at least 400 refugees from the Middle East sinks in the Java Sea off Indonesia; only 44 survive.

20 ***Investigators say that a day after an anthrax-laden letter addressed to "the Editor of the New York Post" was found, anthrax spores have been found in the mail room of the U.S. House of Representatives. (Photo above.)***

•

In an address at the annual summit meeting of the Asian-Pacific Economic Cooperation forum in Shanghai, Pres. George W. Bush declares that the September 11 terrorist attacks in the U.S. were intended to disrupt the world economy.

21 The San Jose Earthquakes defeat the Los Angeles Galaxy in overtime to win the Major League Soccer championship in Columbus, Ohio; Dwayne DeRosario, who scored the winning goal, is voted Most Valuable Player of the game.

•

After a long and fractious search, the U.S. Olympic Committee elects Lloyd Ward its new CEO; Ward is the first African American to head the USOC.

22 Two postal workers in Washington, D.C., die of pulmonary anthrax, and two others are hospitalized with the same disease; a fifth postal worker, who works at a different facility from the previous four, is diagnosed with pulmonary anthrax on October 25.

•

East Timor's new constituent assembly requests that the United Nations, which is administering the territory, grant it independence on May 20, 2002.

23 In an effort to save the peace process in Northern Ireland, the Irish Republican Army begins putting its weapons verifiably beyond use.

•

Israel turns down a U.S. request that Israeli forces be withdrawn from Palestinian-controlled areas of the West Bank, maintaining that the forces will remain until the Palestinian Authority has arrested those responsible for the murder of Rechavam Ze'evi. (*See* October 17.)

•

A UN appeals court overturns the conviction of three Bosnian Croats whom the international war crimes tribunal had found guilty of persecution, saying there was insufficient evidence to convict; it is the first time a ruling by the war crimes tribunal has been reversed.

24 An accident caused by a truck swerving into the path of another truck in a tunnel 17 km (10.6 mi) long in Bellinzona, Switz., results in a conflagration that kills 11 people and closes the heavily used tunnel to all traffic for several weeks.

•

Pope John Paul II apologizes to China for what he calls errors by Roman Catholic missions; relations between China and the Holy See have been particularly tense since the canonization as martyrs on Oct. 1, 2000, of 120 Chinese whom Beijing regards as criminals.

25 The U.S. Congress passes an antiterrorism bill that grants the government expanded right to use electronic surveillance and expands its ability to detain immigrants without charges.

•

The Microsoft Corp. releases the newest version of its personal computer operating system, Windows XP.

26 South Africa and Burundi sign an agreement to allow South African peacekeeping troops to protect the transitional government due to be established in Burundi.

•

Bernadine Healy, the high-profile president of the American Red Cross, suddenly resigns; disagreements between Healy and the board of governors had come to a head over her handling of the September 11 disaster fund.

•

Abdul Haq, an ethnic Pashtun anti-Taliban leader, is executed by the Taliban days after he sneaked into Afghanistan from exile in Pakistan in hopes of putting together a Pashtun-based opposition to the Taliban.

27 A cofounder of the Intel Corp., Gordon Moore, and his wife, Betty Moore, donate $600 million to the California Institute of Technology in the single largest gift ever given to an American university.

•

The Democratic Alliance, a merger of the two majority-white parties, the New National Party and the Democratic Party in South Africa, collapses when former New National Party members pull out.

•

In the Breeders' Cup Classic race at Belmont Park in Elmont, N.Y., Tiznow, ridden by Chris McCarron, becomes the first horse in 18 years to win the event two years in a row.

28 Gunmen enter a Christian church in Bahawalpur, Pak., during services and mow down the worshipers, killing 16; it is assumed that the act is a reaction to the U.S. bombing in Afghanistan.

29 Once again, the U.S. government warns the general public that it has credible information that there may be some sort of terrorist attack against the U.S. in the next few days.

•

The U.S. Supreme Court hears cases outside the Supreme Court building, for the first time since 1935, while the courthouse is searched for evidence of anthrax; no workers are found to have been exposed.

30 Jacques Nasser resigns as chief executive of the Ford Motor Co.; he is replaced by William Clay Ford, Jr.

•

Nelson O. Oduber is sworn in as prime minister of Aruba.

31 A hospital worker in New York City, Kathy T. Nguyen, dies of pulmonary anthrax; investigators are baffled as to where she was exposed to it.

•

Five women who had been hanged as witches in Salem, Mass., more than 300 years earlier are officially exonerated.

•

A bridge designed by Leonardo da Vinci in 1502 to cross the Golden Horn inlet in Istanbul opens near Oslo; while Leonardo's design was for a bridge 352 m (1,155 ft) long, this bridge, over a highway, is 67 m (220 ft) long and proves that the design works. (Photo below.)

Siv Helene Kristensen

November

In hindsight, we made some very bad investments in noncore businesses that performed worse than we ever could have conceived.

Enron CEO Kenneth Lay, to investment analysts, two weeks before the company's financial collapse on November 28

1 The U.S. recalls its ambassador from Caracas after Venezuelan Pres. Hugo Chávez Frías criticizes the U.S. war in Afghanistan.

•

A transitional power-sharing government, headed by Pierre Buyoya, a Tutsi, is inaugurated in Bujumbura, Burundi; the majority of the population of Burundi is Hutu.

2 The U.S. government and Microsoft Corp. announce that they have reached an agreement to settle the long-running antitrust lawsuit; on November 6, 9 of the 18 states that had joined the lawsuit and the District of Columbia indicate they will not sign the deal.

•

The last issue of the daily newspaper the *Atlanta* (Ga.) *Journal* is published; it is absorbed by the *Atlanta Constitution,* which will henceforward be published as the *Atlanta Journal-Constitution.*

•

King Muhammad VI of Morocco completes a two-day trip to Western Sahara to emphasize his country's claim to the disputed area.

3 The ruling People's Action Party wins its ninth consecutive election in Singapore in elections in which only 29 of the 84 seats were contested.

•

For the first time since it was painted in 1931, the original of the Norman Rockwell painting *The Barefoot Boy,* commissioned by the Coca-Cola Co., is placed on view to the public, in the exhibition "Norman Rockwell: Pictures for the American People" at the Solomon R. Guggenheim Museum in New York City.

4 The Arizona Diamondbacks unexpectedly come from behind in the bottom of the ninth inning of game seven of the World Series to defeat the New York Yankees 3–2 and win the major league baseball championship in Phoenix, Ariz.

•

After being delayed twice, first by the September 11 terrorist attacks and then by the beginning of the war in Afghanistan, the television Emmy Awards are finally presented in Los Angeles; winners include the HBO comedy series *Sex and the City* and the NBC drama *The West Wing.*

•

The much-anticipated film version of J.K. Rowling's best-selling novel *Harry Potter and the Philosopher's Stone* premieres in London; the film, released as *Harry Potter and the Sorcerer's Stone* in the U.S. on November 14, breaks box-office records in both countries.

•

The New York City Marathon is won by Tesfaye Jifar of Ethiopia with a time of 2 hr 7 min 43 sec; Margaret Okayo of Kenya, with a time of 2 hr 24 min 21 sec, is the first woman across the finish line.

•

Hurricane Michelle makes landfall on Cuba's south coast, killing five people and causing great damage to the sugar-producing area; it is the worst storm to hit Cuba in 50 years.

•

In presidential elections held in Nicaragua, Enrique Bolaños Geyer of the Constitutionalist Liberal Party wins a surprisingly large victory over Daniel Ortega Saavedra of the Sandinista National Liberation Front.

5 IBM announces that it is placing a number of its software tools in the public domain as the first step toward creating a new open-source organization to be called Eclipse.

6 After losing in the first ballot on November 2, David Trimble wins reelection as the head of a renewed power-sharing government in Northern Ireland. (*See* August 11.)

•

The Belgian airline Sabena is declared bankrupt, and its final scheduled flight, from Benin, lands at Brussels International Airport.

•

Republican Michael R. Bloomberg is elected to succeed Rudolph Giuliani as mayor of New York City; it is the first time in New York's history that two consecutive Republicans have become mayor.

7 A federal appeals court in the U.S. vacates the $5.3 billion award Exxon was ordered to pay in 1994 for the *Exxon Valdez* oil spill in 1989, and the case is sent back to the Alaska district court for a reassessment of damages.

•

For the first time since the crash of the Concorde outside Paris in July 2000, the supersonic passenger craft flies again on a commercial flight, from Paris to New York City.

•

Taiwan for the first time in more than 50 years allows direct trade with and investment in China.

•

Registration begins for the new Internet domain designation .biz.

•

John Ashbery is named winner of the Wallace Stevens Award, a lifetime achievement award, by the Academy of American Poets.

8 First Minister Henry McLeish of Scotland resigns in the face of revelations of undeclared income that he realized by subletting his office; Jack McConnell is appointed to replace him on November 22.

•

A U.S. federal judge issues an order to temporarily stop the Department of Justice's plans to revoke the medical license of any Oregon doctor who prescribes lethal medications to terminally ill patients under Oregon's Death with Dignity Act, which has been in effect since 1997.

9 Representatives from some 140 countries gather in Doha, Qatar, for the fourth ministerial conference of the World Trade Organization.

•

With its stock price in free fall, Enron Corp. agrees to be acquired by its rival Dynegy Inc. (*See* November 28.)

10 After 15 years of negotiations, China becomes a member of the World Trade Organization; the following day Taiwan becomes the organization's 144th member.

•

U.S. Pres. George W. Bush makes his first speech to the General Assembly of the United Nations; he emphasizes the responsibility of all UN members to fight terrorism and reminds them that Osama bin Laden has condemned the organization.

•

After several days of battle, anti-Taliban forces capture the northern Afghanistan stronghold of Mazar-e Sharif.

•

Australian Prime Minister John Howard is elected to a third term of office.

11 Canada 3000, Canada's second largest airline company, goes bankrupt and abruptly ceases operations.

•

St. Louis Cardinals slugger Mark McGwire, who broke Roger Maris's single-season home-run record in 1998 only to see his own record broken in 2001 by Barry Bonds, announces his retirement from major league baseball. (*See* November 19.)

12 ***American Airlines Flight 587, en route from New York City to Santo Domingo, Dom.Rep., crashes shortly after takeoff into the Rockaway neighbourhood of the New York City borough of Queens, killing 260 people on the airplane and several people on the ground. (Photo right.)***

•

The immense underground neutrino-detection apparatus known as the Super-Kamiokande at the Kamioka Neutrino Observatory in Japan is nearly destroyed by an accident in which thousands of photomultipliers implode in a chain reaction.

•

A list compiled by the Heritage Foundation and *The Wall Street Journal* finds for the eighth year in a row that Hong Kong has the freest economy in the world.

13 Pres. George W. Bush signs an executive order permitting foreign nationals suspected of terrorism to be tried by military tribunals, with fewer rights than defendants in U.S. civil courts enjoy. (*See* November 23.)

•

Taliban fighters withdraw from Kabul, the capital of Afghanistan, and, though the U.S. government asks that the anti-Taliban forces not occupy the city until a new government has been agreed upon, the forces move in and take control.

•

The U.S. Conference of Catholic Bishops elects Wilton D. Gregory of the diocese of Belleville, Ill., as its new president; he is the first African American to be elected to this position.

14 Unification talks between North and South Korea break off abruptly; at issue is South Korea's maintenance of a military state of alert that began with the start of the war in Afghanistan.

•

The aid workers from Shelter Now who had been arrested on August 5 on charges of proselytizing for Christianity are abandoned

AP/Wide World Photos

by their Taliban captors outside Kabul and are rescued by U.S. military forces.

•

The National Book Awards are presented to Jonathan Franzen for his fiction work *The Corrections,* Andrew Solomon for his nonfiction book *The Noonday Demon: An Atlas of Depression,* Alan Dugan for his poetry collection *Poems Seven: New and Complete Poetry,* and Virginia Euwer Wolff for her young-adult book *True Believer;* playwright Arthur Miller is given a medal for distinguished contribution to American letters.

15 The U.S. Congress agrees on an aviation security bill that will see the federal government take over airport security screening within a year and provide training for the workers; the bill is signed into law on November 20.

•

Philip Morris, which owns Kraft Foods and the Miller Brewing Co. as well as the two major tobacco companies Philip Morris U.S.A. and Philip Morris International, announces that it will change its name next year to the Altria Group; it hopes that the new name will not be associated solely with tobacco products in the public's mind.

•

Roger Clemens, a pitcher for the New York Yankees, wins his sixth Cy Young Award.

16 Investigators sifting through impounded mail sent to Capitol Hill discover an anthrax-laden envelope addressed to Sen. Patrick Leahy that is similar to those sent to Sen. Tom Daschle and newsman Tom Brokaw; evidently, the letter was initially misdirected to the State Department, spreading anthrax spores wherever it went.

AP/Wide World Photos

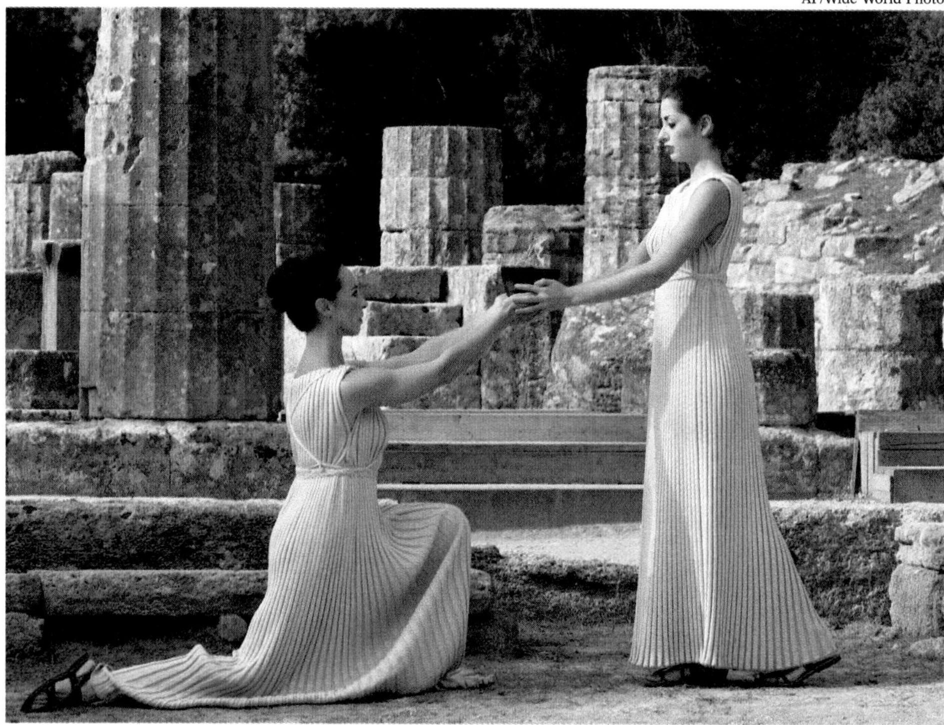

•

German Chancellor Gerhard Schröder narrowly wins a vote to allow German troops to be deployed in the war against terrorism; it would be the first use of German troops outside Europe in a combat role since 1945.

•

Macedonia adopts 15 constitutional amendments to give civil rights to ethnic Albanians.

•

Miss Nigeria, Agbani Darego, is crowned Miss World in Sun City, S.Af.; she is the first black African winner.

17 In Yugoslavia the Serbian province of Kosovo holds its first democratic legislative election; the majority of the seats go to the party of ethnic Albanian nationalist Ibrahim Rugova.

•

After a week of torrential rains causes flooding that kills nine people, the rains in Austin, Texas, ease up.

•

Lennox Lewis defeats Hasim Rahman in Las Vegas, Nev., to retake the World Boxing Council and International Boxing Federation heavyweight titles.

18 The oil companies Conoco Inc. and Phillips Petroleum Co. announce plans to merge into a company to be known as ConocoPhillips.

•

Georgi Parvanov of the Socialist Party is the victor over incumbent Pres. Petar Stoyanov in runoff presidential elections in Bulgaria.

19 ***The Olympic torch is lit in a ceremony at Mt. Olympus in Greece; it will be flown to the U.S. and carried throughout the country until it reaches Salt Lake City, Utah, to open the Winter Games in February 2002. (Photo above.)***

•

Barry Bonds is named the National League Most Valuable Player for a record fourth time; the next day Seattle Mariners outfielder Ichiro Suzuki is named the American League's MVP, a week after being voted Rookie of the Year. (*See* November 11.)

20 Danish Prime Minister Poul Nyrup Rasmussen's Social Democratic Party in legislative elections loses to the Liberal Party, which promises to limit immigration to the country; Anders Fogh Rasmussen is appointed prime minister on November 27.

•

The insurgent Moro National Liberation Front announces it is abrogating a 1996 peace agreement with the Philippine government after making a surprise attack on an army base; it is unclear how many former MNLF fighters will heed the renewed call to arms.

21 Ottilie Lundgren, an elderly woman living alone in rural Connecticut, becomes the fifth person in the U.S. to die of pulmonary anthrax; as in the earlier case of Kathy Nguyen, experts have no idea how Lundgren might have been exposed to the disease.

•

The British cruise line P&O Princess Cruises and the Miami, Fla.-based Royal Caribbean Cruises announce that they will merge; the new company, tentatively named RCP Cruise Lines, will surpass Carnival as the world's largest cruise ship company.

•

Four American food companies sign deals with Cuba to sell it food to help make up for the stocks that were destroyed by Hurricane Michelle; they are the first trade deals made by American companies with Cuba since the U.S. trade embargo was established in 1959.

22 Scientists at the American biotechnology company Advanced Cell Technology, Inc., say they have created 24 completely normal cow clones. (*See* November 25.)

•

A landslide kills approximately 80 people illegally working a closed open-pit gold mine in Filadelfia, Colom.

•

The first official papal e-mail is sent by Pope John Paul II from a laptop in his office in the Vatican; the message transmits a document that includes an apology for past injustices to South Pacific islanders committed by Roman Catholic missionaries.

•

Pakistan closes the Taliban embassy in Islamabad.

23 Officials in Spain tell U.S. officials that Spain will not extradite the eight men it has charged with complicity in the September 11 terrorist attacks without a guarantee that they will be tried in a civilian court rather than the military tribunal that Pres. George. W. Bush has said he would implement for trying suspected terrorists. (*See* November 13.)

•

Marks & Spencer announces that it is selling clothing retailer Brooks Brothers to Retail Brand Alliance Inc., which owns, among other brands, Casual Corner.

24 The Grand National Assembly of Turkey ratifies changes to the country's legal code that make women equal to men before the law and no longer subject to their husbands; the new code will become effective on Jan. 1, 2002.

•

Taliban soldiers surrender their last stronghold in northern Afghanistan, the city of Kunduz.

•

A Crossair jet crashes while coming in to land at the airport in Zürich, Switz., killing 24 of the 32 people aboard; Crossair is the designated successor airline to the defunct Swissair.

25 Taliban prisoners of war being held in a prison outside Mazar-e Sharif, Afg., revolt; by the time the revolt is crushed on November 27, 450 persons are dead, including one CIA operative from the U.S.

•

Advanced Cell Technology, Inc., announces that it has successfully cloned a human embryo; its purpose is to acquire embryonic stem cells for research into cures for various conditions, among them the neurodegenerative diseases. (*See* November 22.)

•

In presidential elections in Honduras, Ricardo Maduro, of the National Party, defeats the ruling Liberal Party's candidate, Rafael Pineda; Maduro had run on an anticrime platform.

26 The National Bureau of Economic Research declares that the U.S. economy officially entered a recession in March, ending a decade of expansion, the longest in history.

•

An AIDS advocacy group goes to court in South Africa to force the government to make a drug widely available that reduces by 50% the chance of transmission of HIV from an infected mother to her newborn baby.

•

A court in Russia orders the closure of TV-6, the last major independent television station in Russia.

27 The Nepalese army launches an air and ground offensive against Maoist insurgents who seek to topple the government; following a weekend of rebel attacks, King Gyanendra declares a state of emergency. (*See* July 19.)

•

The Cayman Islands, known as a haven for tax evaders, signs an agreement with the U.S. to share information that will make it possible for the U.S. to uncover tax violators and money laundering.

28 As the stock prices of the energy giant Enron collapse, Dynegy backs out of the deal it had made to buy the company, saying that Enron failed to disclose the depth of its financial problems. (*See* November 9.)

•

Chiquita Brands International (formerly known as the United Fruit Co.), a major global producer of bananas and other fruit, files a plan for bankruptcy protection. (*See* January 25.)

•

The World Health Organization releases a report saying that 40 million people in the world have either HIV or AIDS; 28 million live in sub-Saharan Africa, but the highest rates of increase occurred in Eastern Europe and Central Asia.

29 In Gaborone, Botswana, representatives of 30 countries plus the diamond industry agree on a certification process for the diamond trade intended to prevent diamond profits from supporting armed conflict in Africa.

•

Officials in Nigeria disclose that a cholera outbreak has killed at least 700 people in the northern part of the country.

•

Owing to a precipitous decline in advertising revenue, the publisher of *Asiaweek* magazine, based in Hong Kong, announces that it is ceasing publication.

•

Former Beatle George Harrison dies of cancer in Los Angeles.

30 Daniel arap Moi of Kenya, Benjamin Mkapa of Tanzania, and Yoweri Museveni of Uganda ceremoniously reestablish the East African Community in Arusha, Tanz.; the East African Community was originally established in 1967, but it ceased to exist in 1977.

•

The Apartheid Museum, which traces the history of the apartheid system and gives visitors a sense of what it was like to live under South Africa's former policy of racial segregation, opens in Johannesburg.

•

The *Caribbean Journal of Science* publishes a report of the discovery off the coast of the Dominican Republic of a dwarf gecko that is 1.9 cm (0.75 in) long; it is the world's smallest reptile.

December

It's not enough to choose a president. Argentina is insolvent.

Eduardo Camaño, acting president of Argentina, in a television interview on December 31

1 Legislative elections in Taiwan give Pres. Chen Shui-bian's Democratic Progressive Party a majority of the seats in the parliament as it supplants the Kuomintang as the ruling party.

•

Japanese Crown Prince Naruhito and his wife, Princess Masako, become the parents of a baby girl; on December 7 she is ceremonially named Princess Aiko.

•

Argentine Pres. Fernando de la Rúa issues an order that no one may withdraw more than $250 a week from a bank account; the previous days had seen bank runs as panicky citizens sought to protect themselves in a collapsing economy.

AP/Wide World Photos

2 In the largest corporate bankruptcy filing in U.S. history, the Enron Corp. asks for bankruptcy protection, at the same time filing a lawsuit against Dynegy Inc. for backing out of a buyout agreement. (*See* December 5.)

•

The annual John F. Kennedy Center for the Performing Arts Honors Gala celebrates the artistic achievements of actor and singer Julie Andrews, actor Jack Nicholson, pianist Van Cliburn, tenor Luciano Pavarotti, and composer Quincy Jones.

•

France defeats Australia to win its ninth Davis Cup in tennis competition in Melbourne, Australia.

•

Voters in Switzerland overwhelmingly reject a proposal to disband its citizen army.

3 It is revealed that one of the last 80 Taliban prisoners who surrendered on December 1 after an uprising in Mazar-e Sharif, Afg., is an American citizen, John Walker.

•

The long-awaited invention from Dean Kamen that has been variously code-named "It" or "Ginger" and has been touted as being epochal is unveiled; the Segway Human Transporter is a two-wheeled battery-powered gyroscopic scooter with a top speed of about 25 km/h (15 mph). (Photo above.)

•

A prototype antimissile weapon destroys a dummy warhead in a second consecutive successful test of technology for the proposed U.S. national missile-defense shield.

4 In a breakthrough, Turkish Cypriot leader Rauf Denktash and Greek Cypriot leader Glafcos Clerides agree to hold face-to-face negotiations in an attempt to bring peace to the divided island. (*See* December 29.)

•

U.S. Pres. George W. Bush freezes the assets of the Holy Land Foundation for Relief and Development, the largest Muslim charity in the U.S., saying it supports the Palestinian organization Hamas, which has claimed responsibility for suicide bombings in Jerusalem over the past few days.

•

The first bridge over the Mekong River opens to traffic, connecting eastern and western Cambodia by road for the first time.

5 Four Afghan factions, shepherded by a UN envoy and diplomats from the U.S., Great Britain, France, Germany, India, Iran, Pakistan, and Russia, agree to an interim government for Afghanistan. (*See* December 22.)

•

An Enron spokesman confirms that it paid out $55 million in bonuses to top employees shortly before filing for bankruptcy protection; separately, the U.S. Department of Labor announces that it is investigating the management of Enron employees' 401(k) retirement accounts. (*See* December 2.)

•

The opposition United National Party wins legislative elections in Sri Lanka; Ranil Wickremesinghe is sworn in to replace Ratnasiri Wickramanayake as prime minister on December 9. (*See* December 24.)

•

The televangelist Pat Robertson resigns as president of the Christian Coalition, a rightist American political organization.

•

The principal owner and former CEO of Sotheby's auction house, A. Alfred Taubman, is convicted in a U.S. federal court of having conspired to fix fees charged to sellers.

6 The name of the Canadian province of Newfoundland is officially changed to Newfoundland and Labrador.

•

Chivas Regal, representing Scotland, defeats the Tigresses, representing the U.S., to win the 20th annual World Elephant Polo Association championship in Chitwan, Nepal.

7 The Taliban abandons its last stronghold in Afghanistan, Kandahar, though U.S. forces are unable to locate either the head of the Taliban government in Afghanistan, Mohammad Omar, or Osama bin Laden.

•

A dance commissioned for the Olympic Arts Festival in Salt Lake City, Utah, in February 2002, *Here . . . Now,* a tribute to runner Florence Griffith Joyner choreographed by Judith Jamison, has its premiere by the Alvin Ailey Dance Theater in New York City.

•

The Right Livelihood Awards are presented in Stockholm to Uri and Rachel Avnery, Israeli peace activists; Angie Zelter, Ellen Moxley, and Ulla Roder, campaigners against Britain's Trident nuclear submarines; Leonardo Boff, a Brazilian who was an originator of "liberation theology"; and José Antonio Abreu, a Venezuelan founder of children's and youth orchestras.

8 After a week of rioting over rents charged in a slum on the outskirts of Nairobi, Kenya, that has left 15 people dead, leaders and residents of various ethnic groups hold a peace rally; the tenants are mainly Luo and Luya, and the landlords are mostly Nubians.

9 The World Health Organization confirms that there is an outbreak of Ebola fever in Gabon near the border with the Democratic Republic of the Congo; the Red Cross warns on December 14 that the disease is spreading quickly.

10 Accusations of corruption and political defections force new elections in Trinidad and Tobago less than one year after the last election; the legislative seats are divided equally between the ruling United National Congress and the opposition People's National Movement. (*See* December 24.)

•

A one-day strike to protest the economic policies of Pres. Hugo Chávez virtually shuts down Venezuela.

•

The 2001 Nobel Prizes are presented in ceremonies in Stockholm and Oslo.

11 The U.S. government brings its first indictment resulting from the September 11 terrorist attacks against Zacarias Moussaoui, a French citizen whom U.S. officials suspect of originally having been part of the group of airline hijackers; he will be tried in federal court.

•

The Science and Technology Foundation of Japan announces the winners of the Japan Prize: Timothy Berners-Lee, for inventing the World Wide Web, and Anne McLaren and Andrzej K. Tarkowski, for their work on mammalian embryonic development.

•

U.S. Attorney General John Ashcroft says that the U.S. has broken up the largest commercial operation to smuggle illegal immigrants in history; the investigation focused on a bus company called Golden State Transportation.

12 Chinese Pres. Jiang Zemin arrives in Myanmar (Burma) for a three-day visit to discuss transportation and trade ties; it is the first visit by a Chinese president since the Myanmar junta came to power in 1988.

•

The centennial of the first transatlantic telegraph signal is celebrated in a reenactment when, 100 years to the minute after the original, Guglielmo Marconi Giovanelli, the grandson of Guglielmo Marconi, sends a signal from Poldhu in Cornwall, Eng., which is received on Signal Hill in St. John's, Newfoundland and Labrador.

•

The last jai alai game is played in Connecticut; the first fronton had opened in 1972 as a way to bring gambling revenues to the state.

13 Five armed men attack the Parliament House in New Delhi, and, in a gun battle outside, they are killed before gaining entrance; five police officers, a driver, and a gardener are also killed, and two more people die later. (*See* December 21.)

•

Israel announces that it is breaking off contact with Palestinian leader Yasir Arafat, characterizing him as "irrelevant."

•

Pres. George W. Bush formally announces the U.S. withdrawal from the 1972 Anti-Ballistic Missile Treaty.

•

The U.S. releases an amateur videotape that government officials believe was made on November 9; the tape shows Osama bin Laden gloating about the September 11 terrorist attacks in the U.S.

14 An emergency antiterrorism bill passes both houses of Parliament to become law in Great Britain.

•

A high court judge in South Africa rules that the government must make available to HIV-positive pregnant women a low-cost drug that will reduce the risk of transferring the infection to their babies. (*See* November 26.)

•

Koloa Talake becomes the new prime minister of Tuvalu after Faimalaga Luka loses a no-confidence vote on December 7.

15 European Union leaders agree to set up a constitutional convention to revisit its institutions; the convention, to be headed by former French president Valéry Giscard d'Estaing, is to begin work in March 2002.

•

Throughout the U.S., 7,500 high-school seniors retake the SAT tests; their original exams were quarantined during the anthrax scare and never reached the Educational Testing Service in New Jersey for scoring.

•

Ethnic clashes break out in the provincial capital of Mendi in Papua New Guinea and continue for the next five days; some 25 people are killed in the fighting.

16 ***The beginning of the three-day Eid al-Fitr festival is celebrated in Kabul, Afg., as residents enjoy freedoms and pleasures forbidden to them under Taliban rule. (Photo below.)***

•

The first commercial shipment of food from the U.S. in almost 40 years arrives in Cuba; the consignment consists of frozen chicken thighs sold to the island by Archer Daniels Midland Co. (*See* November 21.)

•

The Philadelphia Orchestra plays its first program in its new home, Verizon Hall in the Kimmel Center for the Performing Arts; the project to build the new hall, first proposed in 1908, got under way in 1986.

•

Champion calf roper Cody Ohl wins the all-around world championship of the Professional Rodeo Cowboys Association in the National Finals Rodeo in Las Vegas, Nev.

17 Armed men storm the National Palace in Port-au-Prince, Haiti, in an apparent coup attempt against Pres. Jean-Bertrand Aristide; they are unsuccessful.

•

Vivendi Universal of France announces that it will buy the television and film units of USA Networks Inc.

•

Portuguese Prime Minister António Guterres announces his resignation after candidates from the opposition Social Democrats are victorious in local elections.

•

The parliament that was elected on December 5 in the first democratic elections in the Solomon Islands since the June 2000 coup selects Sir Allan Kemakeza as the new prime minister.

•

Portuguese association football (soccer) player Luis Figo, of the Real Madrid team, is named FIFA World Player of the Year; American Mia Hamm becomes the first player to win the newly established award for women.

18 A federal judge overturns the death sentence of celebrated black activist Mumia Abu-Jamal, who was convicted in 1982 of having killed a police officer in 1981; the judge lets the conviction stand, however.

•

The Parliament of France approves a bill to give a bit more autonomy to Corsica.

Ruth Fremson/NYT Pictures

•

The World Meteorological Organization says that 2001 will have been the second warmest year on record, with an average surface temperature of 14.42 °C (57.96 °F); the warmest year on record is 1998.

19 The U.S. federal government indicts Tyson Foods, Inc., the largest meat producer in the U.S., for smuggling illegal immigrants from Mexico to work in its meat-processing plants.

•

AT&T agrees to sell its cable television business to Comcast Corp.

•

Newsmagazine star Katie Couric and the NBC network sign a television news contract for the biggest amount ever—about $60 million over five years.

•

A botanist in Australia says that he has rediscovered a shrub, *Asterolasia buxifolia,* that for 130 years was believed extinct.

20 After several days of rioting and looting throughout Argentina, Pres. Fernando de la Rúa resigns.

•

The UN authorizes a security force, to be led by Great Britain, to assist in the transition to a new government in Afghanistan.

•

A series of wildfires, many of them set by teenagers, begin burning in New South Wales, Australia; at year's end the fires are continuing to destroy houses and land around Sydney.

•

Fire department officials in New York City declare that the fires from the World Trade Center disaster on September 11 have finally been extinguished.

21 In reaction to the raid on its Parliament House (*see* December 13), India recalls its ambassador to Pakistan and cuts off transportation ties between the countries.

•

Hamas announces that it is suspending the use of suicide attacks in Israel.

•

Science magazine documents sightings of a previously unknown squid, unlike known species in many ways, that has been seen on several occasions near the seafloor in many of the world's oceans.

•

The world's fastest roller-coaster, the Dodonpa, opens at the Fujikyu Highlands amusement park in Japan; it reaches speeds of up to 170 km/h (107 mph).

22 Hamid Karzai is sworn in as head of the interim government in Afghanistan; the ceremonies celebrate the cultural diversity of the country, and two rival leaders, Rashid Dostum and Ismail Khan, attend, which bodes well for the future. (*See* December 5.)

•

An American Airlines flight from Paris to Miami, Fla., makes an emergency landing in Boston after passengers and crew subdue a British man, Richard Reid, who was attempting to ignite the soles of his shoes, which were filled with powerful explosives.

23 In the biggest debt default in history, after Adolfo Rodríguez Saá is sworn in as interim president he immediately announces the suspension of payments on Argentina's external debt.

24 A truce agreed to by the new government of Sri Lanka and the Liberation Tigers of Tamil Eelam goes into effect. (*See* December 5.)

•

Patrick Manning takes office as prime minister of Trinidad and Tobago after having been selected by the president. (*See* December 10.)

•

The Adolph Coors Co. announces that it will acquire the Carling operations of Bass Brewers from Interbrew; Carling is the most popular beer in Britain.

25 In his annual Christmas address, Pope John Paul II enjoins the faithful to save the children of the world, as the hope of humanity rests on the children.

26 The Qatar-based television network Al-Jazeera broadcasts excerpts from a videotaped speech by Osama bin Laden; Bin Laden says that he is speaking three months after the September 11 terrorist attacks and looks rather gaunt and pale.

27 Presidential elections are held in Zambia; the winner, from a field of 11 candidates, is Levy Mwanawasa, but international observers cast doubts on the vote-counting process.

28 The Um-Kalthoum Museum, dedicated to the life and career of the great Egyptian singing star from the 1920s through the 1960s, opens in Cairo.

•

Bill Cartwright, who played as the centre on the Chicago Bulls championship teams in 1991, 1992, and 1993, is named head coach of the professional basketball team.

29 Nearly 300 people are killed when a firecracker ignites fireworks stands lining narrow streets in Lima, Peru.

•

For the first time since the Turkish invasion of Cyprus in 1974, Turkish Cypriot leader Rauf Denktash enters the Greek area to have dinner at the home of Pres. Glafcos Clerides in Nicosia; on December 5 Clerides had dined in the home of Denktash. (*See* December 4.)

•

The city of Buffalo, N.Y., begins digging out after a snowstorm that began on December 24 dumped 206 cm (82.3 in) of snow on the city in five days and thereby made this by far the snowiest December in the city's history.

30 Adolfo Rodríguez Saá resigns as interim president of Argentina; Ramón Puerta declines to resume the position.

•

In an effort to head off an imminent war with India, Pakistan arrests Hafiz Muhammad Saeed, founder of one of the militant Muslim groups believed to be behind the attack on India's Parliament House.

31 Eduardo Camaño takes the post of interim president of Argentina.

•

La Scala, Milan's famous opera house, closes for renovation; it is scheduled to reopen in 2004.

Disasters

The following list records the **MAJOR DISASTERS** that occurred in 2001. Events included in this feature involved the loss of **15 OR MORE LIVES** and/or **SIGNIFICANT DAMAGE** to property.

Aviation

January 25, Ciudad Bolívar, Venez. A DC-3 propeller airplane en route to Margarita Island in the Caribbean Sea crashed into a shantytown shortly after takeoff and burst into flames; all 24 persons aboard were killed, and 3 persons on the ground were injured.

March 3, Unadilla, Ga. A military transport plane en route from Florida to Virginia crashed in a field during heavy rain, killing all 21 national guardsmen aboard the craft.

March 24, On the island of Saint-Barthélemy, French overseas *département* of Guadeloupe. An airplane transporting passengers from Saint Martin to Saint-Barthélemy crashed into a house while preparing to land; all 19 persons aboard the plane and 2 persons on the ground were killed. It was the worst aviation disaster in the Caribbean in nearly 20 years.

March 29, Aspen, Colo. A private jet slammed into a hillside while attempting to land in snowy weather; 18 persons died.

April 4, Adaryel, The Sudan. A military plane crashed while attempting to land during a sandstorm; 15 persons were killed, including the Sudanese deputy defense minister, Col. Ibrahim Shams Eddin.

April 7, Quang Binh province, Vietnam. A helicopter carrying a team searching for the remains of U.S. soldiers missing in action from the Vietnam War slammed into a mountainside in hazy weather; all 16 persons aboard were killed.

May 16, Near Akcadag, Turkey. A military plane en route from Diyarbakir to Ankara crashed in a field, apparently after an engine malfunction; all 37 persons aboard the plane were killed.

May 17, Northern Iran. A plane encountered heavy rain and crashed in a mountainous area between the cities of Gorgan and Shahrud; 29 persons died, including Iranian Transport Minister Rahman Dadman and six members of the parliament.

July 3, Near Irkutsk, Russia. An airliner en route from Yekaterinburg in the Ural Mountains to the eastern port city of Vladivostok with 145 persons aboard went down in a Siberian forest; the disaster was blamed on pilot error; there were no survivors.

September 12, Mérida, Mex. A charter plane carrying tourists from a cruise ship to see ancient Mayan ruins crashed shortly after takeoff; 19 persons died, including 16 Americans.

October 4, Over the Black Sea. A Russian airliner en route from Tel Aviv, Israel, to Novosibirsk, Russia, exploded in midair and crashed in the Black Sea, killing all 78 persons aboard the craft. Initial suspicions of terrorism were discounted; the Ukrainian government later acknowledged that a stray surface-to-air missile fired during a Ukrainian air defense exercise had caused the explosion. Ukrainian Defense Minister Oleksandr Kuzmuk resigned over the incident.

October 8, Milan. A Scandinavian Airlines System passenger jet taking off for Copenhagen from Milan's Linate Airport collided with a small private plane in heavy fog and exploded; 118 persons were killed, including all 114 persons aboard the two planes and 4 airport workers. Investigators blamed the absence of ground-level radar at the airport in part. It was Italy's worst aviation disaster.

November 12, New York City. American Airlines Flight 587 crashed on takeoff from John F. Kennedy International Airport; the plane, which was headed to Santo Domingo, Dom.Rep., lost its tail in midair and went down in the borough of Queens, striking several buildings; 260 persons died, including all 255 persons aboard the plane and 5 on the ground. Although no evidence pointed to terrorism, investigators at year's end were still trying to determine why the tail sheared off the plane.

November 24, Near Zürich, Switz. A Swiss airplane en route from Berlin to Zürich crashed in a wooded area after encountering some rain and snow as it made its approach to land; 24 of the 32 persons aboard the plane died.

December 2, Near Okhotsk, Russia. A cargo plane crashed following a fire aboard the aircraft; as many as 18 persons were feared killed.

December 8, Near Taloqan, Afg. Bad weather conditions were blamed in the crash of a helicopter carrying Northern Alliance commandos and captured Taliban fighters; 21 persons aboard the craft died.

December 16, Near Medellín, Colom. A small plane carrying 16 persons crashed in a mountainous area shortly after taking off in rainy weather; there were no survivors.

Fires and Explosions

March 5, Gindiri, Nigeria. A fire, which began when a kerosene lantern overturned, swept through a dormitory of a government high school for girls; at least 23 girls died; rescue efforts were hampered because the dormitory doors had been locked and chained to prevent students from sneaking out or in.

March 6, Jiangxi province, China. An explosion flattened a two-story rural elementary-school building; the blast was believed to have been caused by an illegal fireworks factory located inside the school. According to the Xinhua news agency, 41 persons died, including 37 children and 4 teachers, and 27 persons were injured.

May 20, Northern Chile. An electrical fault in the Iquique penitentiary ignited a blaze that claimed the lives of 26 prisoners.

August 6, Erwady, India. A fire at a mental asylum killed at least 26 persons, many of whom had reportedly been chained to their beds; it was unclear to investigators what had started the blaze.

August 16, Katpadi, India. An accidental explosion at a government-run dynamite factory claimed the lives of at least 25 persons and seriously injured 3.

August 18, Quezon City, Phil. Fire swept through a six-story hotel, killing at least 73 persons, many of whom had been trapped by security bars on the windows of their rooms; 51 persons were injured. The fire was caused by a short circuit in the ceiling of a stockroom; the hotel's owner, who had been cited for safety violations, was later charged with reckless endangerment.

September 1, Tokyo. An explosion and fire in a nightclub in the Kabukicho entertainment district claimed the lives of 44 persons.

September 4–5, Kruger National Park, S.Af. A bush fire of unknown origins swept through the park, killing 15 villagers and 4 game rangers who were trying to rescue them.

September 21, Toulouse, France. A massive explosion at an industrial plant left a 15-m (50-ft) crater at the site and claimed the lives of at least 29 persons and injured some 2,000; officials stated that the blast was likely an accident.

December 17, Southern Italy. A state-run home for the disabled in a remote area of the Apennine Mountains was destroyed in a blaze started by an electrical short circuit; 19 patients were killed; authorities later acknowledged that the home had been constructed of flammable material and should have been torn down.

December 29, Lima, Peru. An explosion at a fireworks shop ignited a blaze that swept through a crowded commercial centre in Lima's historic district; the explosion was thought to have been caused by a fireworks demonstration that went out of control; at least 290 persons were killed.

December 30, Jiangxi province, China. An explosion at a fireworks factory destroyed a warehouse and 10 workshops; more than 40 persons died.

Marine

January 1, Off the coast of Mayaya, Sierra Leone. An overloaded boat en route to Freetown from Rokupr capsized in the Atlantic Ocean, killing some 60 persons.

January 1, Off the coast of Kemer, Turkey. A cargo ship filled with migrants from the Middle East and Asia broke apart in a storm during an attempt to immigrate illegally to Greece; at least 16 persons were confirmed dead, and 30 were missing. Most of the victims had apparently been locked in the cargo area of the ship.

January 23, Off the coast of the Dominican Republic. A motorboat—carrying a group of Dominicans intending to enter Puerto Rico illegally—overturned in rough seas; at least 50 persons were missing and presumed drowned.

January 26, Black Sea. A Ukrainian cargo and passenger ship en route to Yevpatoriya, Ukraine, sank during a storm; 14 persons were confirmed dead, and 5 were missing.

January 29, Off the coast of Karachi, Pak. A fishing boat returning to shore overturned in a storm, killing 35 persons.

March 3, Off the southeastern coast of Haiti. A ship capsized in rough seas; 6 persons were killed, and 17 were missing.

March 15, Off the island of Ile-à-Vache, southwestern Haiti. A boat loaded with Dominicans migrating illegally to Puerto Rico crashed on a coral reef after having drifted off course for 24 days; at least 50 persons died.

April 11, Off the coast of southwestern Japan. A South Korean-registered oil freighter went missing; although no distress signals were received, an oil slick believed to be from the freighter was sighted; 28 persons were feared dead.

April 15, Off the coast of Sulawesi Island, Indonesia. An overloaded boat sank after its engine failed; at least 21 persons drowned.

May 3, Goma, Democratic Republic of the Congo. A ferry sank in Goma harbour on Lake Kivu, apparently after scores of people rushed onto the vessel seeking shelter from a sudden cloudburst; more than 100 persons drowned.

May 12, Off the western coast of Madagascar. A passenger boat sank, claiming the lives of at least 26 persons, most of them members of a local football team.

July 21, Near Katoka, Democratic Republic of the Congo. An overcrowded ferry capsized in a whirlpool on the Kasai River; some 60 persons drowned; the accident occurred at night, and the boat captain who was piloting the craft reportedly was drunk.

July 22, Off the coast of Karachi, Pak. A boat described as old and in poor condition capsized on the Arabian Sea; 19 family members died.

October 19, Java Sea. An overcrowded fishing boat en route from the Indonesian island of Sumatra to Australia with some 400 illegal immigrants aboard broke apart and sank; only 44 persons were rescued.

November 16–17, Florida Straits. A twin-engine speedboat carrying some 30 Cubans intent on illegally entering the U.S. capsized; the U.S. Coast Guard later recovered the boat but no bodies.

November 18, Lake Tanganyika, Democratic Republic of the Congo. A collision between two boats as one was preparing to leave shore and another to dock claimed the lives of at least 19 persons.

November 29, Near Bhola, Bangladesh. A ferryboat sank on the Tetulia River after colliding with a larger vessel; around 90 persons were missing and feared drowned.

Mining and Construction

February 2, Bihar state, India. Water suddenly filled a coal mine, trapping many workers; 38 miners were feared dead.

February 5, Heilongjiang province, China. A gas explosion claimed the lives of 37 miners.

February 22–23, Xinjiang and Hunan provinces, China. Poisonous gas and high temperatures were blamed for the deaths of 11 miners at a coal mine in Xinjiang on February 22. In a separate incident on the following day, a gas explosion was believed to have killed 21 miners in Hunan.

March 4, Entre-os-Rios, Port. A bridge collapsed after one of its support pillars gave way, and a double-decker bus and three cars that were passing over the bridge at the time plunged into the Douro River; 59 persons died.

April 21, Shaanxi province, China. A gas explosion in a coal mine claimed the lives of 47 miners and injured 4.

May 8, Hegang, China. A gas explosion ripped through a coal mine; 54 miners were feared dead.

Mid-May, Urumqi, China. A brick wall surrounding a construction site collapsed onto a bazaar; 19 persons died, and over 30 were injured.

May 18, Sichuan province, China. Water pipes burst in a prison-run coal mine and flooded a shaft; 39 prison labourers were presumed dead.

May 24, West Jerusalem. A three-story banquet hall collapsed while some 700 people were celebrating a wedding; at least 23 persons died; the collapse was attributed to structural failure.

July 17, Shanghai. A massive crane toppled over at a shipbuilding plant; at least 36 persons were killed.

July 22, Xuzhou, China. An explosion occurred at a coal mine that had reopened illegally after having been shut down only a month before; 92 miners died.

August 19, Donetsk, Ukraine. A methane gas explosion ripped through the Zasyadko coal mine, igniting a raging fire and trapping workers; at least 47 miners died, and 44 were injured.

November 22, Filadelfia, Colom. A landslide buried a group of gold miners digging illegally at a condemned mine; about 80 persons were killed, and dozens more were missing and feared dead.

Natural

January, Inner Mongolia, China. A three-day-long blizzard that began on December 31 was followed by freezing temperatures in the region throughout January; of the estimated 1,640,000 persons affected by the storm and cold front, at least 39 lost their lives; more than 200,000 head of livestock also perished during the cold spell.

January 13 and February 13, El Salvador. A magnitude-7.7 earthquake, whose epicentre was off El Salvador's Pacific coast, jolted the country on January 13, leaving some 200,000 persons homeless. On February 13 a second earthquake struck with a magnitude of 6.6 and an onshore epicentre southeast of the capital, San Salvador. At least 1,259 persons died in the two quakes.

January 18, Western Tanzania. A landslide brought on by heavy rains destroyed 30 homes in a fishing village on Lake Tanganyika; at least 15 persons were missing and feared dead.

January 20, North Sulawesi province, Indon. A series of three landslides and the magnitude-5.8 earthquake that followed wreaked havoc on the islands; at least 33 persons died, and numerous houses and two bridges were destroyed.

January 20–late March, Southern Africa. Heavy rains in Zambia, Zimbabwe, and Malawi swelled the Zambezi River watershed, resulting in severe flooding in these countries and along the river in Mozambique. Hundreds of thousands of persons were displaced in Mozambique, where there were more than 80 confirmed deaths by March 28.

January 26, Gujarat state, India. A powerful earthquake of magnitude 7.7 devastated the state. In what was described as the worst earthquake to hit India in a half century, more than 300,000 houses were destroyed, and a further 751,086 homes were damaged, according to official government figures. The quake affected more than 15,000,000 persons and left at least 14,000 dead and more than 166,000 injured. The disaster caused at least $2.3 billion in damage.

January 30, Western Iran. Snow as deep as two metres (six feet) fell in Khuzistan province, burying many villages; 28 persons who had ventured from their homes in search of food and supplies were missing and feared dead in the drifts.

Early February, West Java province, Indon. Heavy rains triggered landslides and extensive flooding; at least 94 persons perished, including 62 in the district of Lebak.

Early February, Western Afghanistan. Frigid temperatures claimed the lives of more than 500 persons in refugee camps in Herat province; since June 2000 thousands of Afghans had been displaced from their homes by severe drought conditions.

May 1, Southwestern China. A landslide that occurred after days of heavy rain caused a nine-story apartment building to collapse, killing at least 65 persons.

May 6–7, Tazeh-Qalel, Iran. Torrential rains triggered floods that killed at least 32 persons and injured 50; 2,500 head of cattle also died in the downpour.

May 9, Bihar state, India. A powerful storm claimed the lives of at least 17 persons, including 9 who died when uprooted trees smashed into their home.

May 11, Bangladesh. A series of storms and landslides caused damage throughout the country; at least 31 persons died, and some 500 were injured.

Mid-May, Haiti. Heavy rains and flooding claimed the lives of at least 21 persons, including 12 killed in a shantytown in Pétionville, a suburb of Port-au-Prince.

A man in Gujarat state, India, combs through the wreckage of a home destroyed by the magnitude-7.7 earthquake that struck on January 26.
AP/Wide World Photos

June 6–17, Southern and eastern U.S. Tropical Storm Allison left a broad swath of destruction in her wake. The hardest-hit area was Houston, Texas, where the storm killed at least 20 persons and damaged up to 27,000 houses, bridges, and other structures. The death toll also included at least 2 persons in Louisiana, 9 in Florida, 9 in North Carolina, 1 in Virginia, and 6 in Pennsylvania.

June 12, Papallacta, Ecuador. Motorists who had been stranded by a landslide and had taken refuge in a mountain hut were buried when a second avalanche swept down on them; at least 36 persons died.

June 23, Southern Peru. An 8.1-magnitude earthquake, whose epicentre was located off the Peruvian coast, jolted the southern Andean region of the country; hardest hit were the cities of Arequipa and Moquegua; at least 102 persons died, 53 were missing, and 1,368 were injured.

June 23–24, Taiwan and Fujian province, China. Typhoon Chebi claimed the lives of 9 persons in Taiwan before sweeping across the Taiwan Strait and striking Fujian, where at least 73 persons died and 87 were missing and feared dead.

June 27, Limbe, Cameroon. Heavy flooding claimed the lives of at least 30 persons.

Early July, Southern Taiwan, northern Philippines, and Guangdong province, China. Typhoon Utor wreaked havoc in lands touching the South China Sea. The storm killed 1 person in Taiwan, at least 121 persons in the Philippines, and 23 persons in Guangdong.

July 15, South Korea. A tropical storm—described as the worst to have hit the country in 37 years—swept across South Korea, setting off landslides and flooding that left at least 40 persons dead and 14 missing. Some 34,000 homes were flooded in Seoul and the surrounding area.

July 23, Mansehra, Swat, and Buner districts, Pak. Monsoonal rains triggered a series of flash floods that claimed the lives of at least 150 persons and washed away hundreds of houses.

Late July, Southeastern Poland. Heavy flooding and thunderstorms devastated the region. By July 26, when the Vistula River overflowed its banks, at least 26 persons had died.

July 30, Hua-lien and Nan-t'ou counties, Taiwan. Typhoon Toraji ripped through the area, bringing heavy rains that set off landslides and flash floods; by the time the storm receded, 77 persons had been killed, and 133 were missing and presumed dead.

August 1, Nias Island, Indonesia. Massive landslides and floods struck the island following days of torrential rains; more than 70 persons were confirmed dead, and at least 100 were missing.

August 10–12, Northeastern Iran. The worst flooding in the region in 200 years inflicted widespread damage. According to figures announced on state television, 181 persons were known to have died, and at least 168 were missing. Some 10,000 persons were displaced by the disaster, which caused an estimated $25 million in damage.

August 11, Northern Thailand. Flash floods in the mountains of Phetchabun province followed heavy rains and killed about 86 persons.

Late August, Nepal. Heavy rains brought on flash floods and landslides across the country; at least 28 persons lost their lives.

September 16–19, Taiwan. Typhoon Nari pummeled the north of the island; flooding, mud slides, and power outages resulted; at least 94 persons died, including 25 in Taipei.

October 8–9, Southern Belize. Hurricane Iris—described as the worst storm to hit the country in 40 years—devastated much of the southern region; 22 persons died, at least 3,000 houses were destroyed, and some 12,000 persons were left homeless.

October 17, Southern India. A strong storm pummeled towns along the coast, killing at least 31 persons, including 16 in Kurnool.

November 7, Southern and central Philippines. Tropical Storm Lingling battered the regions, triggering flash floods and uprooting trees with winds as strong as 90 km/h (56 mph); particularly hard hit was the island of Camiguin, where hundreds were forced to flee their homes; at least 68 persons were killed, and dozens were missing.

November 9, Kerala state, India. A landslide in the village of Amboori claimed the lives of approximately 50 persons.

November 9–17, Northern Algeria. Torrential rain produced heavy flooding in the region; the official death toll was 750 persons, most of whom died in the Bab el Oued neighbourhood of Algiers; some 24,000 persons were left homeless, and at least 1,500 houses were destroyed in the capital alone.

Late December, Rio de Janeiro state, Braz. Torrential rains and mud slides claimed the lives of at least 52 persons; more than 30 were missing, and some 2,000 were forced to abandon their homes.

Railroad

January 10, Near Mvoungouti, Republic of the Congo. A train en route from Pointe-Noire to Brazzaville reportedly experienced engine problems before colliding with another train that had stopped at the Mvoungouti station; though both were freight trains, they were also carrying passengers; at least 45 persons died, and 98 were injured.

May 23, Near Ovrazhnoye, Russia. A train slammed into a passenger bus that had run a red light and driven onto the tracks at a railroad crossing; at least 14 persons were killed and 18 injured.

May 30, Lucknow, India. A train was struck by an overcrowded bus at a railroad crossing, killing 31 persons and injuring 49.

June 22, Near Kozhikode, India. Several cars of a passenger train en route from Mangalore to Chennai (Madras) derailed as the train was crossing a bridge and plunged more than 30 m (100 ft) into the rain-swollen Kadalundi River; at least 52 persons were killed, and some 230 were injured.

August 16, Ujani, India. An express train bound for Mumbai (Bombay) struck and killed 15 persons between stations at Bodhwad and Achaigaon.

December 25, Brebes, Indon. A head-on collision between two passenger trains crowded with holiday travelers claimed the lives of at least 42 persons; the driver of one of the trains reportedly had fallen asleep and sped past a stop signal.

Traffic

January 15, Mbabane, Swaziland. Two tires on an overloaded bus burst, causing the driver to lose control of the vehicle and crash; at least 28 persons were killed.

January 22, Southern Morocco. A passenger bus overturned on a highway between the cities of Marrakesh and Asni; 29 persons died, and 27 were seriously injured.

January 26, Punjab province, Pak. A collision between two passenger buses near the town of Pattoki claimed the lives of 38 persons and injured 52.

February 12, Zhejiang province, China. A bus fell into Thousand Islands Lake after a landslide struck the area; 10 deaths were confirmed, and 6 persons were missing and feared dead.

March 10, Near Ataye, Eth. A bus plummeted into a ravine after colliding with another vehicle; 22 persons aboard died, and 30 were injured.

April 1, Malindi, Kenya. Two passenger buses collided, and both then fell from a bridge into the rain-swollen Sabaki River; at least 34 persons were killed.

April 4, Tamil Nadu state, India. A head-on collision between a bus and an oil tanker truck claimed the lives of at least 40 persons.

April 7, Songwe, Tanz. A minibus hit a bull that had strayed onto a road; the driver lost control of the vehicle and collided with another bus, and all 32 persons in the minibus died.

April 11, Between Franklin and Kokstad, S.Af. An overloaded bus plummeted 64 m (210 ft) down an embankment after the driver lost control of the vehicle; at least 29 persons died.

April 12, Near N'Djamena, Chad. A trailer truck loaded with passengers, grain, and livestock crashed through the guardrail of a bridge and plunged into the Chari River; at least 40 persons lost their lives.

April 30, Northern India. A bus carrying Hindu pilgrims from the city of Hardwaru to the Badrinath temple plunged into the Alaknanda River; at least 45 persons were feared dead.

June 26, Near St. Louis du Sud, Haiti. A bus crashed in a ditch after its driver swerved to avoid hitting an abandoned truck; at least 41 persons were killed.

July 24, Near Jinju, S.Kor. A tourist bus struck a telephone pole and plunged down a steep hill; 18 persons were killed, and 25 were injured in the crash.

July 24, Punjab state, India. A bus toppled from a road into an irrigation canal after its brakes failed to work; at least 22 persons were feared dead.

August 12, Eastern Zambia. A crowded bus overturned and crashed into a ditch, killing at least 38 persons.

August 15, Near Nairobi, Kenya. An overloaded minibus swerved from a road to avoid hitting another vehicle and plunged into the Mwania River; 23 persons died.

August 18, Southern Iran. A head-on collision between a bus and a truck on a highway between Kerman and Sirjan claimed the lives of 30 persons and injured at least 20.

August 21, Near San Nicolas de los Arroyos, Arg. Some 20 persons lost their lives when a bus slammed into the back of a truck, reportedly after the driver of the bus fell asleep at the wheel.

August 26, Northern Nigeria. A speeding bus blew a tire and careened off a bridge into a river; 49 persons perished.

September 29, Northern Iran. A bus collided head-on with another bus and plummeted into an Alborz mountain valley; 20 persons died.

October 10, Near Calama, Chile. A bus carrying workers to a copper mine collided head-on with a truck, killing 22 persons and injuring 21; a plane carrying investigators to the site also crashed, killing 6.

Late October, Buenavista, Phil. A bus slammed into a house where mourners had gathered for a vigil; at least 21 persons died.

Early November, Karnataka state, India. A head-on collision between two trucks claimed the lives of at least 22 persons and injured 37.

November 14, Near Huelva, Spain. A bus carrying retirees on an excursion to caves in the area crashed after the driver lost control of the vehicle while trying to maneuver a curve in the road; 19 persons died, and 14 were injured.

November 18, Angash, Peru. A bus fell from a mountain road in the central Andes 183 m (600 ft) into a ravine; at least 25 persons died, and 20 were injured.

December 14, Southern Jordan. A bus loaded with Muslim worshipers returning home from a pilgrimage to Mecca crashed through the fence of a truck depot, slammed into other vehicles, and exploded into flames; the driver apparently had lost control of the vehicle after a brake failure; all 52 persons aboard the bus died.

December 31, Mpumalanga, S.Af. A truck carrying more than 100 family members on an annual pilgrimage to their ancestral burial ground overturned on a steep gravel road; at least 48 persons died.

Residents of the Bab el Oued neighbourhood of Algiers attempt to move a car in their search for victims following days of torrential rain in November that produced heavy flooding and mudslides.

Hocine/AFP Worldwide

Miscellaneous

March 5, Mina, Saudi Arabia. At least 35 persons died in a stampede on the first day of the hajj, the annual pilgrimage to Mecca; the stampede occurred as thousands of Muslims made their way across a bridge to perform the sacred rite known as "stoning the devil."

March 31, Pakpattan, Pak. A stampede at the gate of a Muslim shrine claimed the lives of at least 35 persons and injured some 125.

April 11, Johannesburg, S.Af. A stampede occurred at an association football (soccer) match between two local teams when thousands of fans who were locked outside Ellis Park stormed into the stadium; 43 persons were killed.

May 9, Accra, Ghana. In what was described as the worst tragedy at a sporting event in Africa's history, at least 130 persons were killed in a stampede toward locked stadium gates at an association football (soccer) match between Accra's Hearts of Oak and Kumasi's Asante Kotoko after Kotoko fans threw debris onto the playing field, and police fired tear gas into the crowd; in addition to the deaths, dozens of people were injured.

August 9, Dhaka, Bangladesh. A faulty fire alarm at a garment factory triggered a stampede; 16 workers, most of them women, were crushed to death in a stairwell as they tried to flee; 50 were injured.

Late August, Near Yamoussoukro, Côte d'Ivoire. At least 27 persons died after drinking corn broth contaminated with rat poison; the woman who sold the broth was detained by authorities and could face manslaughter charges, but officials described the poisoning as accidental.

Mid-September, Southern Estonia. About 60 persons died after drinking illegally brewed vodka—contaminated with methyl alcohol—that had been sold in the resort city of Parnu.

Late November, Sulawesi Utara province, Indon. At least 27 persons died and at least 4 were hospitalized after they drank contaminated homemade liquor.

Late November–early December, Tamil Nadu state, India. At least 50 persons had died by December 1 from drinking contaminated homemade liquor.

AP/Wide World Photos

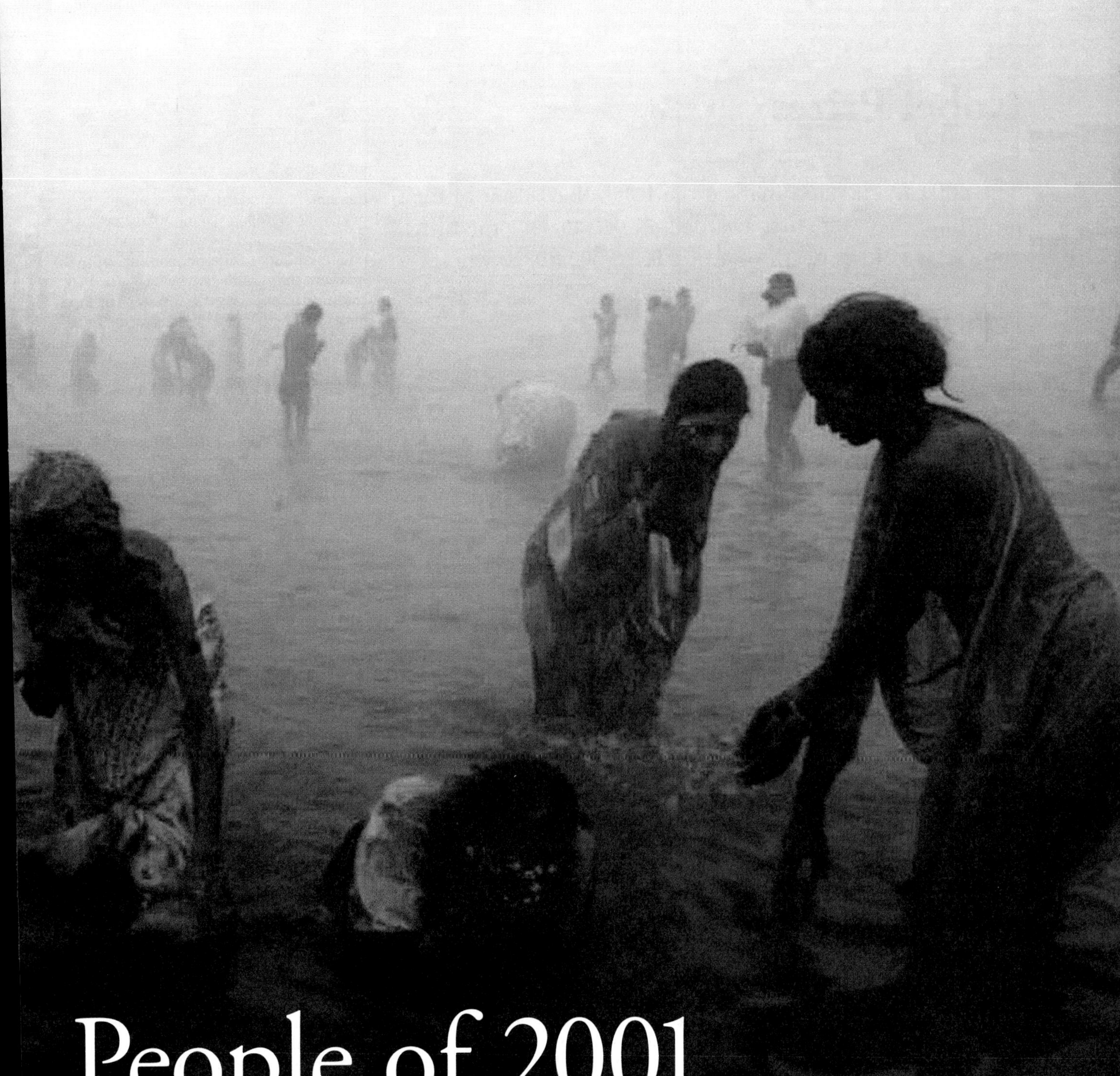

People of 2001

The portraits varied widely—Kumbh Mela pilgrims, refugees, rescue workers, world statesmen, Nobel Prize winners, and terrorists. These were only a few of the indelible images of the people of the year.

Nobel Prizes

The 2001 **NOBEL PRIZES** marked the **100th ANNIVERSARY** of their founding; they were first awarded on **DEC. 10, 1901**, the fifth anniversary of the death of **ALFRED BERNHARD NOBEL**, whose **WILL** had instructed the establishment of **FIVE PRIZES** (the Prize for **ECONOMICS** was added in 1969).

PRIZE FOR PEACE

The 2001 Nobel Prize for Peace was awarded to the United Nations (UN) and to its secretary-general, Kofi Annan. In announcing the prize in its centenary year, the Norwegian Nobel Committee said of the UN, "Today the organization is at the forefront of efforts to achieve peace and security in the world." Annan, who took office on Jan. 1, 1997, and who in 2001 was elected to a second term, was praised both for carrying out administrative reforms and for promoting the goals of the UN.

The UN charter came into effect on Oct. 24, 1945, in San Francisco. With its headquarters in New York City, the UN and its agencies and affiliates made up a worldwide organization of more than 50,000 employees involved not only in the settlement of disputes but also in promoting advances in fields such as health, social welfare, and finance. Through the 1980s the UN often was the victim of Cold War politics, particularly between the U.S. and the U.S.S.R. Nonetheless, it sometimes played an important role in armed conflicts, as in the Korean War (1950–53), and served as an important forum in confrontations, as with the Cuban missile crisis of 1962. During the 1990s the UN expanded its role in helping to settle regional wars, particularly in the Balkans, in East Timor, and in parts of Africa. Although this was the first Nobel Prize for Peace awarded to the UN, several of its agencies had received the honour: the Office of the United Nations High Commissioner for Refugees in 1954 and 1981; the United Nations Children's Fund (UNICEF) in 1965; and United Nations peacekeeping forces in 1988. The International Labour Organization, an affiliated agency, won the prize in 1969.

Annan was praised by the Nobel Committee as being "pre-eminent in bringing new life" to the UN. He was born on April 18, 1938, in Kumasi, Gold Coast (now Ghana), and was educated largely in Kumasi and in the U.S. He earned a degree in economics from Macalester College, St. Paul, Minn., in 1961 and a master's degree in management from the Massachusetts Institute of Technology in 1972. He began working for the UN in 1962 as a budget officer at the World Health Organization in Geneva and, except for the years 1974–76, made his career with the UN. During the 1990s he was an assistant and then an undersecretary-general, performing duties that included overseeing peacekeeping operations in Bosnia and Herzegovina.

Annan was elected secretary-general, the first to come from the ranks of the staff, with a mandate to streamline the UN bureaucracy. He also forcefully promoted human rights and programs to combat AIDS and terrorism. He took an active role in negotiations when necessary but also was forthright in criticizing members when he felt it his duty to do so. Annan was the second UN secretary-general to win the Nobel Prize for Peace. Dag Hammarskjöld was awarded the prize posthumously in 1961, after he had died in a plane crash earlier in the year.

(ROBERT RAUCH)

PRIZE FOR ECONOMICS

The Nobel Memorial Prize in Economic Sciences was awarded in 2001 to Americans George A. Akerlof, A. Michael Spence, and Joseph E. Stiglitz, whose research and analyses had laid the foundations for the theory of markets with asymmetrical information. Their analysis of markets in which one side had better information than the other was fundamental to modern microeconomic theory and changed economists' perceptions of how markets work. It enabled an understanding of the phenomena in real markets that could not be explained by traditional neoclassical theory. The application of the models was wide ranging—from economic development and labour markets to traditional agricultural and modern financial markets. These models were also used to explain the existence of certain economic and social institutions and the introduction of contracts to limit the negative effect of information asymmetries.

Akerlof received the Nobel for his exposition on markets with asymmetrical information, in which sellers of a product have more information than buyers about the product's quality. He demonstrated that this could lead to "adverse selection" of poor-quality products such as—in his well-cited example of a secondhand-car market—a defective car known as a "lemon." In his 1970 seminal work "The Market for Lemons: Quality Uncertainty and the Market Mechanism," Akerlof explained how private or asymmetrical information prevents markets from functioning efficiently and examined the consequences of this. Akerlof suggested that many economic institutions had emerged in the market in order to protect themselves from the consequences of adverse selection, including secondhand-car dealers who offered guarantees to increase consumer confidence. In the context of less-developed countries, Akerlof's analysis explained that interest rates were often excessive because moneylenders lacked adequate information on the borrower's creditworthiness.

Spence developed the theory of "signaling" to demonstrate how the better informed in the market communicate their information to the less-well-informed to avoid the problems associated with adverse selection. In his 1973 seminal paper "Job Market Signaling," Spence demonstrated how education was used as a signal in the labour market. While an employer could not observe the productivity of a potential employee, he could assume that the cost of achieving a freely available educational standard—in terms of effort, expense, or time—was less for a productive than an unproductive person. For signaling to work, its cost had to differ widely between the various job candidates.

Stiglitz concentrated on what could be done by ill-informed individuals and operators to improve their position in a market with asymmetrical information. He found that they could extract information indirectly through screening and self-selection. "Equilibrium in Competitive Insurance Markets: An Essay on the Economics of Imperfect Information," a classic 1976 article on adverse selection written by Stiglitz with Michael Rothschild, examined the insurance market in which the (uninformed) companies lacked information on the individual risk situation of their (informed) customers. The analysis showed that by offering incentives to policyholders to disclose information, insurance companies were able to divide them into different risk classes. The use of a screening process enabled companies to issue a choice of policy contracts in which lower premiums could be exchanged for higher deductibles.

Akerlof was born on June 17, 1940, in New Haven, Conn., and was educated at Yale University (B.A., 1962) and the Massachusetts Institute of Technology (Ph.D., 1966). In 1966 he joined the faculty of the University of California, Berkeley, where he served as Goldman Professor of Economics from 1980. In 2000 the University of Zürich, Switz., awarded him an honorary doctorate.

Spence was born in 1943 in Montclair, N.J., and was educated at Princeton University (B.A., 1966), the University of Oxford (B.A., M.A., 1968), and Harvard University (Ph.D., 1972). He taught economics at Harvard and at Stanford University, where in 1990 he became the Philip H. Knight Professor and dean of the Graduate School of Business.

Stiglitz was born on Feb. 9, 1943, in Gary, Ind., and was educated at Amherst (Mass.) College (B.A., 1964) and the Massachusetts Institute of Technology (Ph.D., 1967), where he began his teaching career in 1966. He later became a professor at Yale, Oxford, Stanford, and Princeton. From 2001 he was professor of economics, business, and international affairs at Columbia University, New York City. Stiglitz was an active member of Pres. Bill Clinton's economic team; a member of the U.S. Council of Economic Advisers (1993–97), of which he became chairman in June 1995; and senior vice president and chief economist of the World Bank (1997–2000).

(JANET H. CLARK)

PRIZE FOR LITERATURE

Trinidadian-born British writer V.S. Naipaul—who merged fiction and reminiscence as well as memoir and reportage to create a compelling oeuvre that reflected his intimate journey through memory and experience toward the realization of self-discovery and truth—was awarded the 2001 Nobel Prize for Literature. The author of more than 25 volumes of fiction, history, travelogue, and journalism, Naipaul was an astute and often condescending observer of a world he perceived to be governed by class consciousness, prejudice, and political injustice. His penetrating, nihilistic vision of contemporary society encompassed both the dark and often brutal realities of colonial imperialism and postcolonial chaos and diaspora. His was an uncompromising voice for the oppressed, disenfranchised, and stateless, who, like himself, migrated from place to place in search of purpose and acceptance in what he deemed "borrowed cultures."

A descendant of Hindu immigrants from northern India whose Brahmin grandfather immigrated to the Caribbean as an indentured labourer, Vidiadhar Surajprasad Naipaul was born Aug. 17, 1932, in Chaguanas, Trinidad. His father, affectionately portrayed in the highly acclaimed *A House for Mr. Biswas* (1961), was a local journalist with literary aspirations of his own and instilled in both Naipaul and his younger brother Shiva, also a celebrated writer, an appreciation for literature and respect for the expressiveness and eloquence of language. Educated in Chaguanas and later in Port of Spain, Naipaul at the age of 18 left Trinidad for Great Britain to continue his studies at University College, Oxford. After graduating with honours in English, he became a freelance journalist with the BBC in London. In 1955 Naipaul married, and in the following year he returned briefly to Trinidad before settling permanently in England, first in London and then in Salisbury, Wiltshire, near Stonehenge.

Early in his career, Naipaul was identified with the emerging generation of politicized West Indian authors—among them Edgar Mittelhölzer, Samuel Selvon, George Lamming, and Derek Walcott—who sought to create a decolonization of English literature. Naipaul's first published novel, *The Mystic Masseur* (1957), was awarded the John Llewellyn Rhys Memorial Prize and combined ethnic humour and layered cynicism to create a satiric composite of Trinidadian society. The condition of the marginalized West Indian also informed both his second novel, *The Suffrage of Elvira* (1958), and *Miguel Street* (1959), a collection of interrelated stories about life in Port of Spain. Naipaul first gained critical recognition with *A House for Mr. Biswas,*

© Reuters/Chris Ison/POOL DC

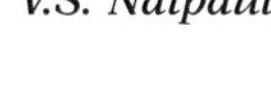
V.S. Naipaul

which reflected the struggle of a modern-day West Indian Everyman forced to endure the humiliation and anguish of servitude and exploitation while desperately searching for both self-preservation and identity.

In 1962 Naipaul released his first work of nonfiction, *The Middle Passage,* which provided an acerbic and often insolent assessment of European colonialism in the West Indies and South America. The following year *Mr. Stone and the Knights Companion,* the first of his novels with an English setting, was published. These were followed by the publication of *An Area of Darkness* (1964), the first volume in his so-called "India" trilogy, which also includes *India: A Wounded Civilization* (1977) and *India: A Million Mutinies Now* (1990). Naipaul broadened his literary perspective of cultural dislocation with *The Mimic Men* (1967), which was followed by one of his best-known fictional works—the Booker Prize-winning *In a Free State* (1971), an experimental novel merging several genres to examine the pervasive decay of postcolonial disorder and disillusionment. The destructive and grim reality of postindependence upheaval was further explored in *Guerrillas* (1975), the first of his works to receive widespread attention in the U.S., and in *A Bend in the River* (1979). Naipaul continued to delve into the boundaries between fiction and autobiography with *The Enigma of Arrival* (1987), a personal reflection on the condition of colonialism and the postcolonial experience.

After being knighted in 1990, Naipaul received the first David Cohen British Literature Prize in 1993 for "lifetime achievement by a living British writer." He remained productive throughout the 1990s, enhancing his reputation with the publication in 1994 of the meditative novel *A Way in the World* and the controversial account of Islamic fundamentalism *Beyond Belief: Islamic Excursions Among the Converted Peoples* (1998). Following the death in 1996 of his first wife, Naipaul remarried that year. In his latest work, *Half a Life* (2001), Naipaul returned to the themes of his earlier fiction—the postcolonial legacy of displacement and exile.

(STEVEN R. SERAFIN)

PRIZE FOR CHEMISTRY

The syntheses of many important chemicals rely on catalysts, substances that speed up reactions without being consumed themselves. The 2001 Nobel Prize for Chemistry went to three scientists who developed the first chiral catalysts, which drive chemical reactions toward just one of two possible outcomes. Their catalysts found almost immediate use, most significantly in the manufacture of new drugs but also in the production of flavouring agents, insecticides, and other industrial products. One-half of the $943,000 prize was shared by William S. Knowles, formerly of the Monsanto Co., St. Louis, Mo., and Ryoji Noyori of Nagoya (Japan) University. The other half of the prize was awarded to K. Barry Sharpless of the Scripps Research Institute, La Jolla, Calif.

Knowles was born on June 1, 1917, in Taunton, Mass. He received a Ph.D. from Columbia University, New York City, in 1942, after which he conducted research at Monsanto until his retirement in 1986. Noyori was born on Sept. 3, 1938, in Kobe, Japan. He took a Ph.D. from Kyoto University (1967) and in 1968 joined the faculty of Nagoya University. In 2000 he assumed directorship of the university's Research Center for Materials Science. Sharpless was born on April 28, 1941, in Philadelphia. He received a Ph.D. from Stanford University (1968) and, after postdoctoral work, joined the Massachusetts Institute of Technology (MIT) in 1970. In 1990 he became W.M. Keck Professor of Chemistry at Scripps.

Many molecules are chiral—they exist in two structural forms (enantiomers) that are nonsuperimposable mirror images, like a pair of human hands. In humans and other living things, one chiral form of a molecule often predominates in the biochemical activities inside cells. For instance, natural sugars, which are the building blocks of carbohydrates, are almost exclusively right-handed. Natural amino acids, the building blocks of proteins, are almost all left-handed. Likewise, the receptors, enzymes, and other cellular components made from these molecules are chiral and tend to interact selectively with only one of two enantiomers of a given substance. For many drugs, however, traditional laboratory synthesis results in a mixture of enantiomers. One form usually has the desired effect, binding with a cellular receptor or interacting in some other way. The other form may be inactive or cause undesirable side effects. The latter happened with the drug thalidomide, prescribed to pregnant women for nausea beginning in the late 1950s. One enantiomer relieved nausea, whereas the other caused birth defects.

Traditional syntheses for thalidomide and other drugs are symmetrical in the sense that they produce equal amounts of both enantiomers. For decades chemists had tried to develop asymmetrical methods that would yield more of one enantiomer or even one enantiomer exclusively. The three Nobel laureates developed asymmetrical catalysts for two important classes of reactions in organic chemistry, hydrogenations and oxidations.

In the early 1960s scientists did not know if catalytic asymmetrical hydrogenation even was possible. In many important syntheses, hydrogenation involves the addition of hydrogen to two atoms that are joined by a double bond in a molecular structure. An asymmetrical hydrogenation reaction would do so in a way that produced more of one enantiomer than the other. The breakthrough came in 1968 when Knowles, working at Monsanto, developed the first chiral catalyst for an asymmetrical hydrogenation reaction. Knowles was seeking an industrial synthesis for the drug L-dopa, which later became a mainstay for treating Parkinson disease. Variations of the new catalyst found almost immediate application in producing very pure preparations of the desired L-dopa enantiomer.

Beginning in the 1980s Noyori, working at Nagoya University, developed more general asymmetrical hydrogen catalysts. They had broader applications, could produce larger proportions of the desired enantiomer, and were suitable for large-scale industrial applications. Noyori's catalysts found wide use in the synthesis of antibiotics and advanced materials.

Sharpless addressed the great need for chiral catalysts for oxidations, another broad family of chemical reactions. Atoms, ions, or molecules that undergo oxidation in reactions lose electrons and, in so doing, increase their functionality, or capacity to form chemical bonds. In 1980, working at MIT, Sharpless carried out key experiments that led to a practical method based on catalytic asymmetrical oxidation for producing epoxide compounds, used in the synthesis of heart medicines such as beta blockers and other products. As was expressed by the Royal Swedish Academy of Sciences, which awarded the chemistry prize to Knowles, Noyori, and Sharpless, "Many scientists have identified Sharpless' epoxidation as the most important discovery in the field of synthesis during the past few decades."

(MICHAEL WOODS)

AP/Wide World Photos

Wolfgang Ketterle (centre), flanked by associates at the Massachusetts Institute of Technology

PRIZE FOR PHYSICS

Three scientists who first created a new ultracold state of matter that Albert Einstein had predicted more than 70 years earlier won the 2001 Nobel Prize for Physics. Eric A. Cornell of the U.S. National Institute of Standards and Technology (NIST), Carl E. Wieman of the University of Colorado at Boulder, and Wolfgang Ketterle of the Massachusetts Institute of Technology (MIT) shared the $943,000 prize for their production in 1995 of the so-called Bose-Einstein condensate (BEC).

Cornell was born on Dec. 19, 1961, in Palo Alto., Calif. He earned a Ph.D. from MIT (1990) and, after postdoctoral work, joined the faculty of the University of Colorado in 1992. That same year he became a staff scientist at NIST. Wieman was born on March 26, 1951, in Corvallis, Ore. After earning a Ph.D. from Stanford University (1977), he taught and conducted research at the University of Michigan at Ann Arbor until 1984, when he moved to the University of Colorado. Both Cornell and Wieman held positions as fellows of the Joint Institute for Laboratory Astrophysics (JILA), a research and teaching centre operated by NIST and the University of Colorado. Ketterle was born on Oct. 21, 1957, in Heidelberg, Ger. He received a Ph.D. from the University of Munich and the Max Planck Institute for Quantum Optics, Garching (1986). After postdoctoral work he joined the faculty at MIT in 1993. He also served as a principal investigator with the Center for Ultracold Atoms, a joint research institution sponsored by MIT, Harvard University, and the National Science Foundation. Ketterle was a German citizen with permanent residency in the U.S.

Generations of physicists had dreamed of creating a BEC since the concept for this exotic state of matter first emerged in the 1920s. In 1924 the Indian physicist Satyendra Bose made important theoretical calculations about the nature of light particles, or photons. Physicists already had recognized that the propagation of light can be thought to consist of discrete packets of energy traveling through space. Bose presented an alternative derivation of a law about the behaviour of photons that had been developed earlier by the German physicist Max Planck. The kinds of particles that fitted Bose's description eventually were named bosons in his honour. Bosons have a property that allows them to congregate without number, occupying the same quantum state at the same time.

Einstein translated Bose's work into German, submitted it for publication to a physics journal, and started working on the concept himself. Bose's work focused on particles, such as photons, that have no rest mass. Einstein extended it to particles that have mass, such as the atoms in a dilute gas. He predicted that if a sufficient number of such atoms get close enough together and move slowly enough, they will undergo a phase transition into a new state. That new state of matter became known as a Bose-Einstein condensate.

Physicists recognized the keys to achieving a BEC. The major challenge was to make the gas very cold, about a tenth of a millionth of a degree of absolute zero (–273.15 °C, or –459.67 °F), to slow down the motion of the atoms without causing them to condense to a liquid. Atoms in gases usually move about in an uncoordinated way, ricocheting off each other and nearby objects. Under the specific conditions described by Einstein, however, the atoms "sense" one another and transform from a mass of uncoordinated individuals to a coherent group that acts like a single giant atom.

Cornell and Wieman, working at the University of Colorado in 1995, used a combination of laser and magnetic techniques to slow, trap, and cool about 2,000 rubidium atoms to form a BEC. Ketterle, working independently at MIT, created a BEC from sodium atoms. Ketterle's BEC, which comprised a much larger sample of atoms, was used to carry out additional studies of the condensate, including an interference experiment that provided the first direct evidence of the coherent nature of a BEC. Those first successes led to a flurry of experiments in other laboratories in which physicists expanded the roster of BEC-forming gases and used BECs to produce "atom lasers" that emit coherent beams of matter rather than light.

In 2001 about 20 groups were conducting BEC experiments, which were providing new insights into the laws of physics and pointing to possible practical uses of BECs. (*See* MATHEMATICS AND PHYSICAL SCIENCES: *Physics*.) As the Swedish Academy observed, "Revolutionary applications of BEC in lithography, nanotechnology, and holography appear to be just round the corner."

(MICHAEL WOODS)

PRIZE FOR PHYSIOLOGY OR MEDICINE

Three researchers shared the 2001 Nobel Prize for Physiology or Medicine for their pioneering discoveries about one of life's most basic processes. Working independently, Leland H. Hartwell of the Fred Hutchinson Cancer Research Center, Seattle, Wash., and Paul M. Nurse and R. Timothy Hunt of the Imperial Cancer Research Fund (ICRF), London, illuminated the common mechanisms that regulate the cycle of growth and division in cells ranging from yeast to human beings. As was acknowledged by the Nobel Assembly at the Karolinska Institute in Stockholm, which awarded the $943,000 medicine prize, these findings greatly expanded scientific understanding of cancer and other diseases that occur when the machinery of the cell cycle goes awry.

Hartwell was born on Oct. 30, 1939, in Los Angeles. After earning a Ph.D. from the Massachusetts Institute of Technology (1964), he served on the faculty of the University of California, Irvine, from 1965 until 1968, when he moved to the University of Washington. In 1997 he assumed the duties of president and director of the Hutchinson Center. Nurse was born on Jan. 25, 1949, in Great Britain. He received a Ph.D. from the University of East Anglia, Norwich, Eng. (1973), later headed the ICRF Cell Cycle Laboratory (1984–87), and served on the faculty of the University of Oxford (1987–93). In 1996 he became director general of the ICRF and, once again, head of its Cell Cycle Laboratory. Hunt, born on Feb. 19, 1943, in Great Britain, earned a Ph.D. from the University of Cambridge (1968) and later served on its faculty (1981–90). In 1990 he joined the ICRF, rising to principal scientist.

The cell cycle comprises a carefully orchestrated series of events that unfolds countless times each day in the human body. An adult human has about 100 trillion cells, all of which originate from the division of a single fertilized egg cell. Even after a human is fully grown, cells continue to divide to replace those that die. In the first phase of the cell cycle, the cell enlarges. On reaching a certain size, it enters the second phase, in which DNA synthesis occurs—the cell duplicates its genetic material and creates a copy of each chromosome. In the next phase, the cell checks to ensure that DNA replication is accurate and prepares for cell division. In the fourth phase, the chromosomes separate into two sets, and the cell divides into two daughter cells, each with one set of chromosomes. The daughter cells then return to the first phase of the cell cycle.

AP/Wide World Photos

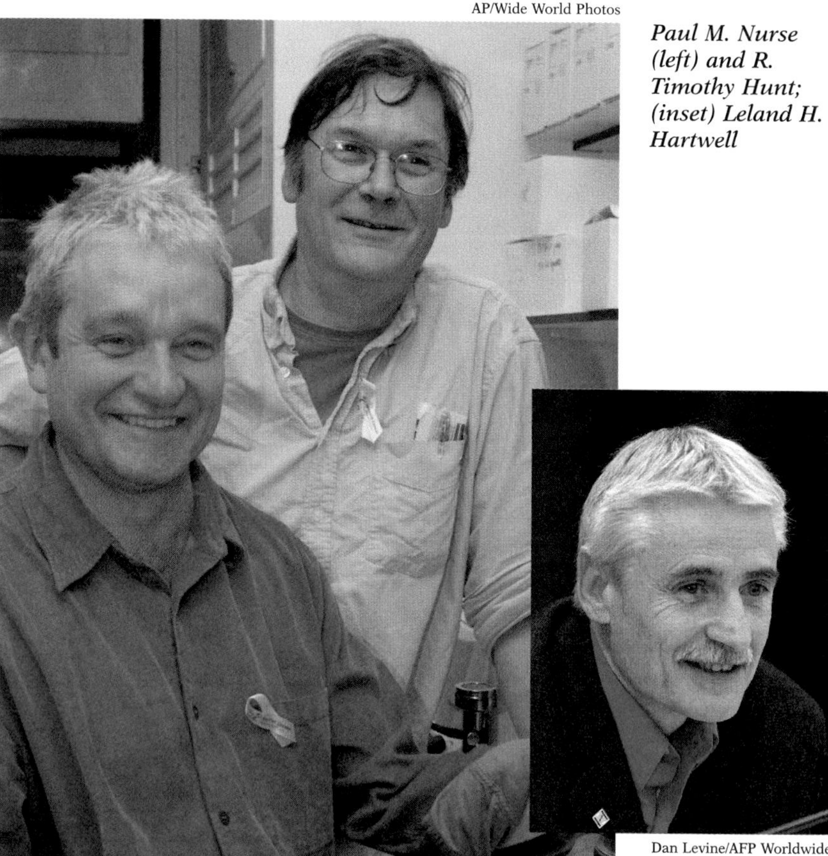

Dan Levine/AFP Worldwide

Paul M. Nurse (left) and R. Timothy Hunt; (inset) Leland H. Hartwell

The phases of the cycle must be coordinated with great precision. Each must occur in its proper order and be completed before the next phase begins. Errors in this orchestration may lead to chromosomal abnormalities—for example, chromosomes that have missing or rearranged parts or that are distributed unevenly between the daughter cells. Such abnormalities often occur in cancer cells, which have escaped the normal controls on the cell cycle and multiply in unrestrained fashion. The three Nobel laureates discovered key molecular regulators of the cell cycle, including proteins called cyclins and enzymes called cyclin-dependent kinases.

Hartwell started work in the late 1960s, using baker's yeast as a model organism to study the cell cycle with genetic methods. He identified more than 100 genes, termed cell-division-cycle (CDC) genes, involved in cell-cycle control. For instance, one—named *cdc28*—controls the first phase and so became known as "start." Hartwell also found that the cycle includes optional pauses, called checkpoints, that allow time for repair of damaged DNA.

Nurse used another type of yeast as his model organism. In the mid-1970s he discovered a gene called *cdc2,* which works as a master switch to regulate the timing of different cell-cycle events. In 1987 Nurse isolated the corresponding gene in humans, which was named cyclin-dependent kinase 1 (*cdk1*). The gene codes for a protein that belongs to a family of key enzymes, the cyclin-dependent kinases (CDKs), that participate in many cell functions. About a half dozen other CDKs were identified in humans.

Hunt isolated the first cyclin in the early 1980s from sea urchins. Cyclins are proteins formed and broken down during each cell cycle. Hunt discovered that cyclin binds to the CDK molecules discovered by Nurse, functioning as a biochemical enabling agent to activate the CDKs. Hunt also showed that the periodic degradation of cyclin is an important general regulatory mechanism in the cell cycle. By 2001 about 10 cyclins had been identified.

(MICHAEL WOODS)

Biographies

The SUBJECTS of these biographies are the people who in the editors' opinions captured the IMAGINATION of the world in 2001—the most INTERESTING and/or IMPORTANT PERSONALITIES of the year.

Aerosmith

The year 2001 was one of the highest peaks in the roller-coaster career of hard-rock survivors Aerosmith; the group was inducted into the Rock and Roll Hall of Fame and enjoyed the runaway success of its first self-produced album, *Just Push Play.* Overcoming the legendary excess that had brought its career to a screeching halt in the early 1980s, Aerosmith returned with even greater popularity than it had enjoyed as one of the biggest arena rockers of the '70s. In the process the group passed the 50-million mark in album sales to become the 10th best-selling act in recording history.

Aerosmith was formed in 1970 in New Hampshire by vocalist-drummer-harmonicist Steven Tyler (born Steven Tallarico on March 26, 1948, in New York City), guitar wizard Joe Perry (born Sept. 10, 1950, in Boston), and bassist Tom Hamilton (born Dec. 31, 1951, in Colorado Springs, Colo.). After the addition of guitarist Brad Whitford (born Feb. 23, 1952, in Winchester, Mass.) and drummer Joey Kramer (born June 21, 1950, in New York City), Tyler became a full-time front man. Relocating to Boston, Aerosmith honed its mixture of blues-based heavy metal and Rolling Stones-styled rock before signing with Columbia Records in 1972.

Touring nearly nonstop in support of its first two albums, *Aerosmith* (1973) and *Get Your Wings* (1974), the band won an enthusiastic following before releasing the multimillion-selling *Toys in the Attic* (1975)—featuring "Walk This Way" and "Sweet Emotion"—and *Rocks* (1976). The band's rerelease of "Dream On" in 1976 also became a huge hit, one of rock's first power ballads. In leotards and flowing scarves, Tyler, who resembled the Stones' Mick Jagger, exuded sex both in the band's raucous live shows and in the clever, libidinous lyrics that earned him the nickname the "Shakespeare of the salacious." The group's sex-and-drugs lifestyle took a heavy toll, however; alcohol, cocaine, and barbiturate abuse—and ultimately the heroin addiction of the "toxic twins" (Tyler and Perry)—resulted in rapidly declining creativity and erratic live shows. Perry went solo in 1979, following the release of the uninspired *Night in Ruts,* and Whitford followed. The band pushed on with new guitarists, but by the time *Rock in a Hard Place* (1982) appeared, Tyler was passing out onstage.

Hard-rock survivors Steven Tyler (right) and Joe Perry of Aerosmith

In 1984, however, the original members regrouped, and in 1986 Perry and Tyler guested on Run DMC's hip-hop remake of "Walk This Way." Soon after, the band committed to sobriety. As daily workouts replaced all-night parties, Aerosmith found a new generation of fans on MTV with a series of suggestive music videos, charting singles, and hit albums. Hit songs included "Dude (Looks like a Lady)" from *Permanent Vacation* (1987), "Janie's Got a Gun" from *Pump* (1989), and "Cryin'" from *Get a Grip* (1994); the latter album, like the follow-up *Nine Lives* (1997), reached number one. The group garnered Grammy Awards in 1990, 1993, and 1994. (JEFF WALLENFELDT)

Antinori, Severino

On Jan. 25, 2001, Severino Antinori, an Italian physician and research scientist specializing in human fertility, announced that he planned to begin work on a project to clone humans and that he had already found 10 couples who were willing to participate. Joining him as his future partner was American fertility specialist Panayiotis Zavos, who said that he and Antinori expected to produce a viable human embryo within 18 months. On March 9 at a conference in Rome, they stated that the number of volunteers had increased to more than 600 infertile couples.

In order to produce the clones, Antinori and Zavos planned to impregnate women with embryos made with the DNA of the child's intended father. The children would, therefore, be the genetic twins of their fathers, which would thus allow infertile men to pass their genes on to the next generation. Antinori, however, claimed that the babies would have a small amount of the DNA of their mothers and consequently would not be exact clones. Many throughout the world quickly expressed strong opposition to the project. Some objected on moral and religious grounds, while others cited the many miscarriages, stillbirths, and abnormal offspring that had resulted from the efforts to clone large mammals. In regard to the second criticism, Antinori and Zavos claimed that their long experience with in vitro fertilization and other types of assisted pregnancy would greatly increase their chances for success.

Antinori was born about 1945 in Rome. He studied medicine at the University of Rome, graduating in 1972, and then continued to work at the university, specializing in gastroenterology in 1973–74. Later in the 1970s he shifted his specialty to obstetrics and gynecology, working at various hospitals and institutions in Italy and eventually establishing his own clinic in

Rome. Antinori first gained international attention in 1993, when a 59-year-old British woman gave birth to twins as a result of treatment in his fertility clinic; eggs from a young Italian woman had been donated, fertilized with sperm from the British woman's husband, and then implanted in her. A year later, after undergoing the same procedure, a 62-year-old Italian woman gave birth to a son; she was believed to be the oldest woman ever to have given birth. Throughout 2001 Antinori continued to defend himself against those who opposed his cloning project. To his many critics he declared, "I can guarantee at 99% that I will not give birth to any monsters." (DAVID R. CALHOUN)

Arroyo, Gloria Macapagal

On Jan. 20, 2001, after angry protesters had driven Philippines Pres. Joseph Estrada from the presidential residence, Malacañang Palace, in Manila, the country's vice president, Gloria Macapagal Arroyo, assumed power. The demonstrations had been sparked by the Senate's halting of Estrada's impeachment trial on corruption charges. The armed forces withdrew support from Estrada; the Supreme Court unanimously declared the presidency to be vacant; and Arroyo was officially sworn in as his successor. Estrada later claimed that he had not relinquished the presidency, but the Supreme Court ruled her government legitimate.

Born on April 5, 1947, in San Juan, a suburb of Manila, Arroyo lived at Malacañang as a teenager when her father, Diosdado P. Macapagal, was president of the Philippines from 1961 to 1965. She was valedictorian of her high-school class and studied economics at Georgetown University, Washington, D.C., where she began a lasting friendship with classmate and future U.S. president Bill Clinton. After returning to the Philippines and graduating magna cum laude from Assumption College, Manila, in 1968, Arroyo earned a master's degree in economics from Ateneo de Manila University in 1978 and a doctorate of economics from the University of the Philippines, Quezon City, in 1986.

Arroyo was a university professor when Pres. Corazon Aquino appointed her undersecretary of trade and industry in 1986. She won a seat in the Senate in 1992 and was reelected in 1995 by a record 16 million votes. Arroyo, who wrote 55 laws on economic and social reform, was named several times by the media as the country's outstanding senator. The 13 million votes she garnered in her successful bid for the vice presidency in 1998 was the largest mandate ever in a Philippines presidential or vice presidential race, while Estrada, running separately, won the presidency with fewer votes.

Estrada named Arroyo secretary of social welfare and development, an unusual second job for a vice president. As scandal began to envelop Estrada, she resigned the cabinet post on Oct. 12, 2000, to rally opposition against him.

Arroyo brought an unprecedented academic and administrative background to the Philippines presidency. Even so, she enlisted experienced officials to help her tackle national problems, especially poverty. A member of the wealthy elite, she sought to win over the masses who had supported the charismatic Estrada, adopting a more informal style on visits to poor areas. Unusual for Philippines politics, she had not been known by a nickname, but her publicists encouraged the use of Ate Glo ("Big Sister Gloria"). Although Arroyo tried to be folksy, she showed a steely side by taking a tougher line than Estrada on combating rebellion in the southern Philippines. (HENRY S. BRADSHER)

Gloria Macapagal Arroyo walks tall as she reviews troops in Manila

Romeo Gacad/AFP Worldwide

Bachchan, Amitabh

By far the biggest draw on Indian television in 2001 was *Kaun Banega Crorepati,* the Hindi version of *Who Wants to Be a Millionaire.* The show captured the imagination of millions, and fueling its popularity was *Kaun Banega Crorepati*'s charismatic host, Amitabh Bachchan. The television assignment was a decided departure for Bachchan, a former film star who was once regarded as "the king of Indian cinema."

Born on Oct. 11, 1942, in Allahabad, India, Bachchan was the son of a noted Hindi poet, Harivansh Bachchan. He was educated at Sherwood College, Nainital, and the University of Delhi. After working for a time as a business executive in Calcutta (now Kolkata) and performing in theatre, Bachchan began a long career in film. His screen debut, *Saat Hindustani* (1969; "Seven Indians"), flopped. Initially, Indian audiences found it hard to accept Bachchan's gangly physique and "angry young man" persona. Four years later, however, he tasted his first commercial success with *Zanjeer* (1973; "Chain"). A string of hit action films followed, including *Deewar* (1975; "Wall"), *Sholay* (1975; "Embers"), and *Don* (1978). Bachchan's oeuvre was not confined to action alone, however; his comic flair was showcased in breezier fare such as *Chupke Chupke* (1975) and *Mr. Natwarlal* (1979).

An accident on the set of the film *Coolie* in 1982 left Bachchan comatose, but he eventually made a full recovery. His subsequent films did poorly at the box office, however. Motivated by his friend Indian Prime Minister Rajiv Gandhi, Bachchan entered politics and was elected to Parliament from Allahabad by an overwhelming majority. His stint in politics proved to be short-lived. In 1989, after being implicated in the bribery scandal that toppled Gandhi's government, Bachchan was forced to resign his post. Returning to film, he won the National Award for his portrayal of a mafia don in *Agneepath* (1990; "Path of Fire").

In 1992 Bachchan took another hiatus from moviemaking, and when he reappeared three years later, it was as head of his own entertainment venture, Amitabh Bachchan Corp. Ltd. (ABCL). The business, which specialized in film production and event management, brought the Miss World beauty pageant to India in 1996 but quickly ran into deep financial trouble. The actor was forced to explore other options. *Kaun Banega Crorepati* first aired in July 2000. Taking a role on the small screen was perceived as a move that Bachchan was forced to make in order to pay off ABCL creditors. The transition was a successful one, however. Bachchan's fluent Hindustani and easygoing charm helped put contestants at ease and *Kaun Banega Crorepati* on top of the ratings chart. His annual salary of $3.2 million made him Indian television's highest-paid star. (SHALAKA PARADKAR)

Barber, Patricia

She rose from Chicago cult performer to international jazz star, but Patricia Barber's rise was slow and far from steady. On one opening night in 1984 at a small club on the city's fashionable Gold Coast, only two people showed up. "A year later there were lines of people around the block waiting to get in," says Barber, and that six-nights-a-week gig stretched into eight years. Her audience grew in the 1990s when she began performing her own subtle, sophisticated songs and her arrangements of modern pop tunes; she also recorded four albums showcasing her originals. For her sixth album, *Nightclub,* Barber returned to interpreting familiar standard songs in her intimate yet dramatic style. The compact disc became a jazz best-seller, spending eight weeks among *Billboard*'s top five jazz albums in

2001. Barber expanded her fame with months of touring clubs, concerts, and jazz festivals in North America, Europe, and Israel.

Barber, the daughter of two musicians, was born on Nov. 8, 1955, in Lisle, Ill. She began taking classical piano lessons when she was six years old. She grew up in Illinois and Iowa, majored in classical music and psychology at the University of Iowa, and initially resisted becoming a jazz musician as "a stupid thing to do for a smart woman."

Jimmy Katz

Patricia Barber's modern cool

But jazz proved an irresistible lure, and in 1979, a year after graduation, she migrated to Chicago, where she scuffled for work for five years, sometimes surviving on a hot-dog diet. Her break came with that 1984 booking at the Gold Star Sardine Bar, where the club owner insisted that Barber sing and play only standards. The intimate quality of her music became evident, as she often chose slow tempos for the familiar songs that she sang quietly, over her lyrical, Bill Evans-influenced piano playing. She continually added new material to her repertoire. She also borrowed money from her sister to record her first album, which she sold from the bandstand.

With her early 1990s move to the Green Mill, a jazz club in a former Chicago speakeasy, she began expanding her horizons, adding unusual selections, from 11th-century Gregorian chants to Santana and Joni Mitchell. Barber began writing songs too, setting poems of E.E. Cummings and Maya Angelou to music and also writing her own lyrics. Songs of hers, including "Touch of Trash" and "Postmodern Blues," revealed veins of ironic humour, melancholy, and whimsy; she began expressing her own worried vision of today's "materialistic" society in song. Dissatisfied with the way a major label handled her second album, Barber began producing her own recordings, using her own loyal musicians, for a small local label. Against all odds, Barber's discs *Café Blue* (1994), *Modern Cool* (1998), and *Companion* (1999) spread her reputation beyond Chicago. When a major label began distributing her albums, sales shot up. Despite the hit status of *Nightclub* and her increased time on the road, Barber remained based in Chicago and still sang regularly at the Green Mill. (JOHN LITWEILER)

Beckham, David and Victoria

Even for a country as obsessed with celebrity status as Great Britain, the phenomenon of David and Victoria Beckham grew in 2001 into something remarkable. When David, the captain of England's association football (soccer) team and a key midfielder on Manchester United (England's, and arguably the world's, most famous football club), and Victoria, "Posh Spice" of the Spice Girls pop group, moved into their vast new home in Hertfordshire, north of London, the house quickly acquired the sobriquet "Beckingham Palace," an ironic reference to Buckingham Palace, the London home of Queen Elizabeth II. Yet despite the glitz of stardom, "Posh" and "Becks" gained many admirers beyond the normal ranks of pop music and sports fans, not least for the obvious delight they took in raising their baby son, Brooklyn. Coming from two different popular cultures, both widely associated with rowdy behaviour and personal excess, the couple offered young people gentler and healthier role models.

David Beckham was born on May 2, 1975, in Leytonstone, east London. He joined Manchester United as a trainee in 1991 and first distinguished himself as a special talent in a televised league match in August 1996, when he scored a goal from the halfway line (a feat roughly equivalent to a golfer's hole in one). From 1998 he played regularly for England, and he was made captain of the national team for its 2001 qualifying matches, ahead of the 2002 World Cup. Beckham's autobiography, *David Beckham: My World*, was an immediate best-seller upon publication in 2000. His glamour status was so high that his regular changes of hairstyle caused consternation among hairdressers throughout Britain, who would be flooded with demands from their regular customers to copy Becks's new look.

Posh was born Victoria Caroline Adams on April 17, 1974, in Hertfordshire. In 1994 she was one of the five young women selected to form the Spice Girls. The Spice Girls was the first group to reach number one in the British pop music charts with each of its first four singles, and the five members—both together and individually—became a cultural phenomenon. When Adams met Beckham, their relationship was widely expected to be very short-lived—a view that was not greatly disturbed by the birth of Brooklyn in March 1999. In July of that year, however, the couple married in an ostentatious ceremony at a castle outside Dublin. Conducted by the bishop of Cork, the wedding was reputed to have cost £500,000 (about $750,000). The couple still made a profit, though; they sold photographic rights to the celebrity magazine *OK!* for £1 million (about $1.5 million), including pictures of the bride and groom sitting on red velvet thrones under crown-shaped chandeliers.

Despite criticism for the "vulgarity" of their nuptials, the Beckhams gradually silenced the doubters by presenting themselves as model, if unusual, parents. David would often take Brooklyn to Manchester United matches. Victoria, who did some fashion modeling and started to make solo records, showed that motherhood could be combined with a successful career. In the fall of 2001, she released her first solo album and her own autobiography, *Learning to Fly.* Few people would hazard a guess as to how long their joint celebrity status would last, but back in 1998 not that many had expected the Posh and Becks show to be still going strong in 2001. (PETER KELLNER)

Berlusconi, Silvio

On June 11, 2001, Italian media magnate Silvio Berlusconi, a tycoon with an estimated fortune of over $10 billion, was sworn in as the country's new prime minister after his centre-right alliance, the House of Freedoms, scored a resounding victory in the May 13 general elections. His installation followed more than six years of leading the opposition. Though Berlusconi was an articulate and dynamic figure, controversy surrounded him; his numerous entanglements with the judiciary were coupled with the seeming incompatibility of his roles as both a leading politician and Italy's most powerful

AP/Wide World Photos

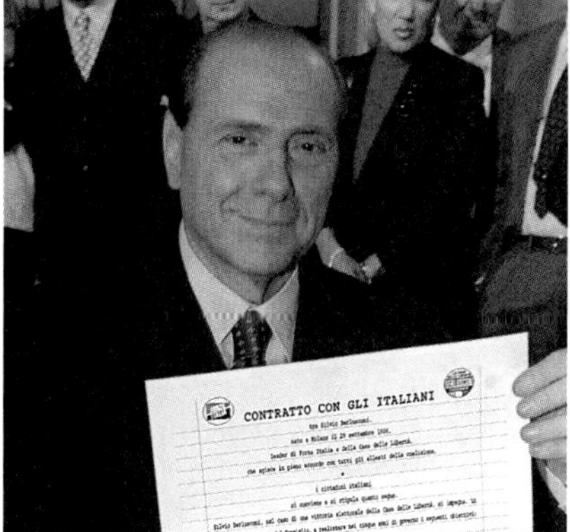

Silvio Berlusconi and his contract with the Italian people

media magnate. Once in office, he pledged swift action to regulate such "potential conflicts of interest." Following the September 11 attacks, he was quick to offer support to the U.S., but he courted controversy again when in a speech given in Berlin he asserted that Western civilization was superior to the Islamic world. He later said his remarks, which were denounced by European Union and Muslim leaders, were taken out of context.

Berlusconi was born on Sept. 29, 1936, in Milan. As a youth he engaged in moneymaking ventures by putting on puppet shows and then by charging for "ghosting" homework assignments for his classmates. As a law student at the University of Milan, he paid for his tuition by selling vacuum cleaners and by crooning (backed by his own band) on summer cruises. After obtaining a loan from the bank that employed his father, he launched a successful real-estate-development concern in Milan, reportedly with the help of local socialist politicians. The bulk of his fortune, however, was made in television. In 1978 he circumvented a law that guaranteed the national monopoly of RAI, the state TV network, and set up rival TV stations. Then, aided by the socialist government (1983–87) of Bettino Craxi, a friend from university, Berlusconi acquired three national TV channels. They formed the foundation of his media empire.

Berlusconi launched into politics in 1993. Exploiting a gap left by a corruption scandal that wiped out the old political order, he founded the conservative populist Forza Italia ("Go, Italy") movement to fight off a growing challenge from the left wing. After relinquishing his positions in the Fininvest Group, his giant holding company, Berlusconi led the right-wing Freedom Alliance, headed by Forza Italia, to a landslide election triumph in 1994. His government fell after seven months, however, when a vital coalition ally defected amid charges of corruption in Berlusconi's business empire. Since 1994 Berlusconi had been involved in some nine court cases for financial misdeeds ranging from bribing judges to tax evasion. Though proceedings were dropped in four cases, near year's end five cases were still pending, one of them in Spain. Berlusconi, however, rejected all charges, claiming they sprang from a political conspiracy against him by the left wing. (DEREK WILSON)

bin Laden, Osama

Almost as soon as Americans grasped the reality of the Sept. 11, 2001, terrorist attacks, their attention began to focus on the figure of Osama bin Laden. The vehemence of his anti-Americanism, the scope of his resources, and the refinement of planning already exhibited in Bin Laden's previous terrorist attacks had advertised his readiness to resort to such breathtaking brutality. Subsequent investigation confirmed Bin Laden's involvement.

Bin Laden was born on March 10, 1957, in Riyadh, Saudi Arabia, the son of a wealthy contractor with ties to the Saudi royal family. He attended King Abdul Aziz University in Riyadh, where he took a degree in 1981. In 1980 Bin Laden traveled to Peshawar, Pak., and became active in recruiting "Arab Afghans," Muslims from various countries who went to fight with the Afghan mujahideen against the Soviet army. Through associations with these militant Islamists, he began to devote himself to the cause of international jihad. He established al-Qaeda, an organization that was establishing camps inside Afghanistan for the purpose of training Arab Afghans to fight in other countries.

After the Soviet withdrawal from Afghanistan in 1989, Bin Laden returned home to Saudi Arabia, where he opposed the government over the stationing of U.S. troops in the country at the time of Iraq's occupation of Kuwait. In 1991 he was expelled, and three years later his Saudi citizenship was revoked. Meanwhile, the jihad in Afghanistan had lost its focus, and Bin Laden settled in The Sudan, where he invested in several commercial enterprises as support and cover for al-Qaeda. From there he allied himself with other militant Islamist organizations. After 18 U.S. soldiers were killed in Somalia in October 1993—for which Bin Laden later took credit—the U.S. withdrew its forces, which confirmed for Bin Laden the weakness of American resolve.

Forced to leave The Sudan in May 1996, he moved once more to Afghanistan, where the Taliban was now in a position to offer him protection. Early in 1998 al-Qaeda joined militants from other countries in an international jihad against Jews and "Crusaders"—it was announced that every Muslim had the duty to kill or fight Americans and their allies, whether civilian or military. Responsibility for the August 1998 bombing of U.S. embassies in Kenya and Tanzania was laid on Bin Laden, and in response the U.S. launched cruise missiles against targets in The Sudan and Afghanistan. Surviving the attacks and harboured by the Taliban in Afghanistan, Bin Laden became a world figure, as admired in the Muslim world as he was reviled in the U.S.

Despite repeated demands from the West, the Taliban refused to surrender Bin Laden to any form of international justice. After the September 11 attacks, however, the Taliban themselves became the target of U.S. reaction. Bin Laden, meanwhile, demonstrated his mastery of another Western technology—the media—by releasing a series of videotaped interviews to the Qatar-based satellite network Al-Jazeera in which he taunted the U.S. and its allies. At year's end, as allied troops mopped up the remains of Taliban resistance, Bin Laden had still not been apprehended.

(STEPHEN SEGO)

Bloomberg, Michael

In 2001, after 20 successful years of leading the financial information firm he founded, Michael Bloomberg was ready to lead something new. For his next challenge he entered the race for mayor of New York City. The formal announcement of his candidacy in early June sparked two types of speculation: what effect Bloomberg's election as mayor might have on New York City and what effect his absence as CEO might have on his company, Bloomberg LP.

Michael Rubens Bloomberg was born in Medford, Mass., on Feb. 14, 1942. His father was a bookkeeper and his mother a secretary. After earning a bachelor's degree in engineering from Johns Hopkins University, Baltimore, Md., in 1964, he attended Harvard University (M.B.A., 1966) and then took an entry-level job with Salomon Brothers investment bank. Within 15 years he had achieved the level of partner and was leading the firm's block trading operations. A political shake-up at Salomon in 1981 left him without a job, but with his $10 million partnership buyout, he created Innovative Market Systems. By 2001 the renamed Bloomberg LP employed more than 7,000 people around the world. Central to the company's success was the Bloomberg computer terminal, a comprehensive financial news and information source that was leased to users at a price of $1,285 per month. The company's other holdings included the Bloomberg Business News wire service, news radio station WBBR in New York City, Bloomberg Television, and specialty magazines.

While the firm's customers were among the wealthiest people in the world, and Bloomberg—being one of them—operated in a fairly narrow spectrum of privilege and influence, he was generous with his money. Over the years he had donated or pledged roughly $100 million to Johns Hopkins University. He also served on the boards of leading cultural institutions, including the Metropolitan Museum, Lincoln Center, the Central Park Conservancy, and the Jewish Museum. Reportedly worth about $4.5 billion, Bloomberg funded much of his mayoral campaign himself, spending more than $68 million from his personal fortune. His campaign themes focused on issues of great concern to New Yorkers: improvements in traffic and transit, housing, and education. What helped him most, however, was the endorsement of outgoing New York City Mayor Rudolph Giuliani, whose leadership following the September 11 terrorist attacks was universally praised. After trailing badly in the polls just weeks before the November 6 election, Bloomberg went on to win the mayor's race, defeating Democrat Mark Green by a narrow margin.

Certainly Bloomberg's political and business strategies had been made in tandem. Perhaps to reveal his own concerns about his company's future growth, Bloomberg had chosen the head of Bloomberg's European sales force, Lex Fenwick, to manage the firm's day-to-day business operations during the campaign. As mayor, Bloomberg knew that his old firm would have to fight to retain customers while attracting new ones. (SARAH FORBES ORWIG)

Blunkett, David

Following the U.K.'s 2001 general election, Prime Minister Tony Blair appointed David Blunkett to be home secretary, one of the most senior cabinet positions. Blunkett's sterling reputation amply justified this promotion; it also raised the possibility that Blunkett might eventually succeed Blair as leader of Great Britain's Labour Party. What made this prospect remarkable was the fact that Blunkett had managed to establish himself as one of the U.K.'s leading politicians without ever having been able to see.

Blunkett, who was blind from birth, was born on June 6, 1947, in the northern England city of Sheffield and was brought up in poverty after his father died in an industrial accident at work. He was educated at schools for the blind, but he turned down a course in training to be a piano tuner and insisted on a wider education. He studied part time at a technical college and did well enough on his exams to win a place at the University of Sheffield, where he studied politics. His passion for politics led him at the age of 22 to become the youngest-ever councillor on Sheffield's city council, and he rose to become the council's leader in 1980. Blunkett belonged to Labour's left wing, a position that helped in his election to the party's national executive in 1982.

At that time Labour, having lost power nationally in 1979, was badly divided. In the 1980s these divisions came to a head when party leader Neil Kinnock sought to expel a group of hard-line left-wingers. Blunkett sided with Kinnock on this and on a wider strategy for modernizing the party. In 1987 Blunkett was elected MP for the safe Labour constituency of Sheffield Brightside. In 1994 Labour's new leader, Tony Blair, appointed him the party's shadow minister, or spokesman, on education. It was a key appointment, as Blair announced that on becoming prime minister he would make his three top priorities "education, education, education."

When Labour won the 1997 general election, Blunkett became education secretary, with the task of raising school standards to match those of other prosperous countries. Blunkett introduced a number of reforms, including requiring schools to provide children up to the age of 11 with a daily "literacy hour" and a "numeracy hour" in order to improve basic skills. Blunkett frequently cited his own disability and impoverished background to argue that all children had the potential to succeed and that no school should be allowed to use the fact that its children came from deprived or broken families as an excuse for bad results. Blunkett's tough strategy was widely praised, although he was not always popular with teachers unions. His promotion to home secretary on June 8, 2001—with a brief to be equally tough in tackling crime, disorder, and threats to internal security—was his reward for having been one of the most successful cabinet ministers during Blair's first term in office. After the terrorist attacks in the U.S. on September 11, however, Blunkett's job looked to be an even bigger challenge.

(PETER KELLNER)

Bonds, Barry

On Oct. 5, 2001, Barry Bonds, the left fielder of the San Francisco Giants, set a single-season major league baseball record by hitting his 71st and 72nd home runs, erasing the previous mark of 70 set by Mark McGwire of the St. Louis Cardinals in 1998. Two days later, in the last game of the season, Bonds raised his total to 73. Along with his home runs, he also finished the season with an .863 slugging percentage, breaking the record of .847 set by Babe Ruth in 1920. Bonds surpassed another Ruth mark by walking 177 times, seven more than Ruth had done in 1923. Bonds hit a home run in every 6.52 times at bat, breaking McGwire's 1998 record of 7.27. His efforts were rewarded after the season ended when he was voted the National League's Most Valuable Player (MVP), the fourth time he had earned that honour.

Barry Lamar Bonds was born on July 24, 1964, in Riverside, Calif. He was the son of Bobby Bonds, an All-Star player for the Giants and the Yankees who also played for several other teams. After showing outstanding talent as a centre fielder in high school, Bonds was drafted by the Giants in 1982. Instead, he chose to attend college at Arizona State University, where he won all-conference honours for three straight years. In 1985 the Pittsburgh Pirates drafted Bonds in the first round. In his first major league season in 1986, he led all National League rookies with 16 home runs, 48 runs batted in, and 36 stolen bases in 113 games. In 1990 he hit .301 with 33 home runs and led the Pirates to a division championship. After the season he was voted the league's MVP.

In 1991 Bonds batted .292 and hit 25 home runs and won a second MVP award. In December 1992 he left Pittsburgh as a free agent and signed a six-year, $43,750,000 contract with the Giants, which at that time was the highest pay for any major league player. Bonds enjoyed a remarkable debut season with San Francisco; he hit a career-high .336 with 46 home runs and collected his third MVP award. During the next four years, Bonds hit 37, 33, 42, and 40 home runs, and he helped his team reach the play-offs in 1997. In 2000 he smacked 49 home runs—his highest single-season total until 2001—but as in several previous years, he struggled in the play-offs, gaining only three hits in 17 at-bats against the New York Mets. Although overshadowed by his hitting, Bonds's fielding prowess also earned him several Gold Glove awards.

As for the future, Bonds expressed a desire to continue playing for the Giants. After nine years with San Francisco, however, he was eligible for free agency, and there was some doubt that the Giants would be able to afford his salary demands. (DAVID R. CALHOUN)

Bush, George W.

The presidency of George W. Bush, which began on an uncertain note, was transformed by the terrorist attacks in the U.S. on Sept. 11, 2001. He had come into office in January after having lost the popular vote but with a five-vote margin in the electoral college. Although he had campaigned as a "uniter, not a divider," a number of his appointments and policies had a clear right-wing bias. He quickly moved through Congress a huge tax cut favouring those with high incomes, though other proposals—including an education reform bill and a so-called faith-based initiative that would funnel money to religious groups for social services—were significantly altered or simply languished. Nonetheless, the president pushed ahead with his agenda; he rolled back several environmental policies and appointed a study panel that favoured the partial privatization of Social Security. In foreign affairs the administration took a unilateral, even isolationist, approach, adopting a hard line toward China, vowing to abandon the 1972 Anti-Ballistic Missile Treaty in order to conduct tests for a missile defense system, and withdrawing from work on treaties dealing with matters such as global warming and bioterrorism. The Bush approach did not appear to be playing well, for at midyear barely 50% of Americans approved of the president's performance.

The terrorist attacks dramatically changed the situation. The American people rallied around the president, and a poll taken shortly afterward gave Bush no less than a 90% approval rating. The focus of the administration shifted to what came to be called the "war on terrorism." Abandoning previous policies, the president consulted with governments throughout the world to develop a coalition and support for military action against the Taliban government in Afghanistan, which harboured Osama bin Laden—the apparent mastermind of the attacks—and he won promises of cooperation even from Russia and China. Although the administration had earlier taken a hands-off approach to the Israeli-Palestinian conflict, it now pressured the two sides to settle their dispute. It reversed its stance on the bioterrorism treaty. While bombing Taliban targets, the administration began making plans for a new government in Afghanistan, even though Bush had earlier disdained such "nation building." A critic of big government, Bush now pushed for expanded powers. He created a cabinet-level Office of Homeland Security under Pennsylvania Gov. Thomas Ridge (*q.v.*) and won a vast expansion of intelligence-gathering powers. Abandoning strict free-market policies, Bush supported the intervention of the government in support of the U.S. economy, including a bailout of airlines. In November he signed legislation authorizing the federal takeover of airport security within one year.

AP/Wide World Photos

George W. Bush at Ground Zero with New York City Mayor Rudolph Guiliani and Fire Commissioner Thomas Van Essen

Bush was born on July 6, 1946, in New Haven, Conn. He graduated from Yale University (B.A., 1968) and Harvard Business School (M.B.A., 1975) and then worked in the oil business in Texas. He was an adviser to his father, George H.W. Bush, in the late 1980s, and after his father was elected to the presidency in 1988, he returned to Texas. He was managing partner of the Texas Rangers baseball team before being elected governor of Texas in 1994 and winning reelection in 1998.

(ROBERT RAUCH)

Calderón, Sila María

On Jan. 2, 2001, Sila María Calderón, who had served as mayor of San Juan from 1997 to 2000, became Puerto Rico's first female governor. Heading the Popular Democratic Party (PPD) ticket, she narrowly defeated the New Progressive Party candidate Carlos Pesquera by a margin of 48.5% to 45.7% in the November 2000 election. Her victory was viewed as a setback for proponents of Puerto Rican statehood; though Calderón pledged to work for greater Puerto Rican autonomy, she supported its status as a commonwealth with the United States.

Calderón was born in San Juan on Sept. 23, 1942, and was influenced by her father, who was a strong supporter of the PPD. Following a conventional upbringing, Calderón was educated at Manhattanville College, Purchase, N.Y., where she earned a bachelor's degree in political science in 1964; she later gained a master's degree in public administration from the University of Puerto Rico. When Luis Silva Recio, a former professor of Calderón's, was chosen as Puerto Rico's secretary of labour in 1973, she became his executive assistant.

Calderón gained valuable experience in both the public and the private sectors in Puerto Rico. In 1984 she served as the special assistant to Gov. Rafael Hernández Colón. The following year Colón appointed her chief of staff, and she then served as secretary of the interior before becoming secretary of state in 1988. During her private-sector career, she served as a vice president of Citibank and as president of the Commonwealth Investment Co., Inc. In 1996 Calderón was elected mayor of San Juan with just over 50% of the vote and was later chosen as head of the PPD. In the 1998 referendum on Puerto Rican statehood organized by pro-statehood governor Pedro Rosselló, she led the pro-commonwealth campaign; her efforts were rewarded when the majority of votes were cast in favour of Puerto Rico's seeking commonwealth status.

In running for governor in 2000, Calderón promised to end corruption and the U.S. Navy's bombing exercises on Vieques, a large island off the east coast of the main island of Puerto Rico that had been used for naval exercises since 1941. Calderón's strong antibombing stance, plus the killing of a security officer by an errant bomb in 1999 and the island's alarmingly high cancer rate (which many attributed to the exercises), catapulted her to victory.

Despite U.S. Pres. Bill Clinton's offer to hold a referendum on the bombings in Vieques in 2001, Calderón vowed immediately after her inauguration that she would step up efforts to end the military use of the island. On April 24 Calderón launched legal action against the U.S. government, basing the lawsuit on the Noise Control Act of 1972. Although U.S. Pres. George W. Bush had initially resisted ending the exercises, in June his administration announced that the bombings would be permanently halted in 2003, and in a nonbinding referendum in July more than two-thirds of the island's residents voted to end the exercises immediately, significant victories for the very visible governor. In September she announced plans to conduct a binding referendum, allowing voters to choose either to halt the exercises in 2003 or to accept a $50 million aid package with continued bombings.

(MICHAEL I. LEVY)

Capriati, Jennifer

In 2001 American tennis player Jennifer Capriati served up one of the greatest comeback stories in sports as she won her first Grand Slam singles titles, the Australian Open and the French Open. Though such success had once been predicted for the former child prodigy, personal problems, including burnout and alleged drug use, had seemingly ended her career.

Jennifer Maria Capriati was born on March 29, 1976, in New York City and lived in Spain until the age of four, when her family moved to Florida so that she could pursue a tennis career. Capriati quickly attracted attention with her innate talent and bubbly personality. By the time she turned professional in 1990, she had earned more than $6 million in endorsements. During her first year on the Women's Tennis Association (WTA) tour, Capriati set a number of records, including becoming the youngest player to reach the semifinals at a Grand Slam event (the French Open) and to win a match at Wimbledon. In late 1990 she won her first professional title, the Puerto Rico Open, and she finished the year ranked in the WTA top 10—the youngest player ever to do so. With powerful strokes and incredible consistency, Capriati continued to impress in 1991, reaching the semifinals at Wimbledon and the U.S. Open. In 1992 she defeated Steffi Graf to capture the gold medal at the Summer Olympics in Barcelona, Spain.

AP/Wide World Photos

American tennis ace Jennifer Capriati on a comeback

The pressures of professional play and her parents' divorce, however, began to take their toll on Capriati. After an unexpected first-round loss at the U.S. Open in 1993, she took a break from the tour. Her troubles continued, however, as she was arrested for shoplifting and later for possession of marijuana; she was not convicted in either case. Though she returned to the tour in 1994, she lacked commitment and fitness and faced intense media scrutiny. Playing well only sporadically, Capriati managed to win just one match at a Grand Slam tournament between 1994 and 1998.

In 1999 Capriati regained her focus. Dedicating herself to getting into shape, she lost some 14 kg (30 lbs) and that year claimed her first title since 1993. She finished 1999 ranked number 23 in the world, and the following year, with her father as her coach, Capriati climbed in the rankings to number 14. At the 2001 Australian Open, in her first Grand Slam final, she upset top-seeded Martina Hingis 6–4, 6–3. With the victory, Capriati entered the top 10 for the first time in seven years. Her astonishing comeback continued at the French Open. Two points from defeat, she rallied to overcome Kim Clijsters in a three-set thriller (1–6, 6–4, 12–10) to take the title. Her bid for a Grand Slam (winning all four major events in one year), however, ended with a semifinal loss at Wimbledon.

(AMY TIKKANEN)

Carabias Lillo, Julia

In January 2001 the World Wildlife Fund (WWF) awarded its 23rd annual J. Paul Getty Wildlife Conservation Prize to Mexican environmental scientist Julia Carabias Lillo. The WWF commended Carabias for her efforts to promote public participation in the development of environmental policy. During her term as Mexico's secretary of the environment, natural resources, and fisheries, she doubled the size of the nation's protected-area system to more than 6% of the total area of the country and thereby safeguarded such species as the gray whales and pronghorn antelope of Baja California and the manatees and jaguars of Yucatán.

Carabias was born in 1954 in Mexico City. She gained both undergraduate and master's degrees from the science department at the National Autonomous University of Mexico (UNAM) in Mexico City. In 1977 she began teaching at UNAM, and in 1981 she became a full professor of science there, concentrating her research on such subjects as rain forest regeneration, environmental restoration, and the use of natural resources. She served as a member of UNAM's University Council from 1989 to 1993. Among the works she coauthored were *Manejo de recursos naturales y pobreza rural* (1994), *Areas naturales prioritarias para la conservación en la región* (1997), and *Desarrollo sustentable* (1999). She coauthored *For Earth's Sake* for the UN Conference on Environment and Development, held in Brazil in 1992. Carabias entered government service in early 1994 as president of Mexico's National Institute of Ecology. She was a member of the advisory council for the National Conservation Fund and in late 1994 became secretary of the environment, natural resources, and fisheries, a position she held until late 2000.

In June 2000 she arranged a meeting of officials from Mexico and the U.S. to work on the problem of restoring natural water flows to the Rio Grande, and she also helped create an international task force to deal with a water crisis on the middle section of that river. In addition, she played an important role in enforcing the environmental provisions of the North American Free Trade Agreement. After receiving the WWF prize, Carabias donated the $100,000 cash portion of it to the protection of the Chajul region of southern Mexico's Lacandon forests. (DAVID R. CALHOUN)

Cavallo, Domingo

When Domingo Cavallo was appointed economy minister on March 20, 2001, Argentines hailed him as a reformer who could rescue the economy from its dire straits. It was the second time in a decade that he had been appointed to the position, and he was the third person to hold it within a month. The Argentine economy, the second largest in South America, had been in recession for nearly three years, with an unemployment rate of 15% and large budget deficits. The government had been unable to meet targets set by the International Monetary Fund (IMF), and there was widespread fear that it would default on loans. Thus, the task before Cavallo, both to invigorate the economy and to restore confidence, was enormous.

Cavallo was born on July 21, 1946, in San Francisco, Córdoba province. He was trained as a certified public accountant (1966) and earned master's (1968) and doctoral (1969) degrees in economics from the National University of Córdoba. In 1977 he earned a Ph.D. in economics from Harvard University. He taught at the National University of Córdoba (1969–84), Catholic University of Córdoba (1970–74), and New York University (1996–97). He was the author of a number of books and articles and the publisher of *Forbes Global* in 1998–99. In addition, he received many awards and prizes, as well as a number of honorary degrees.

Cavallo was the head of Argentina's central bank in 1982, minister of foreign affairs from 1989 to 1991, and economy minister from 1991 to 1996. In the early 1990s the Argentine economy was suffering from runaway inflation, which Cavallo controlled by pegging the value of the peso to the U.S. dollar. He also instituted an extensive privatization plan. The economy revived, but in 1996 Cavallo left the government of Pres. Carlos Menem, which was charged with widespread corruption. The following year Cavallo founded the Action for the Republic (AR), a centre-right party, and won his first term to the Chamber of Deputies. He was unsuccessful in a bid for the presidency in 1999 and was defeated in a run for mayor of Buenos Aires in 2000.

Upon his appointment as economy minister by Pres. Fernando de la Rúa in 2001, Cavallo acted quickly. His program called for increased tax revenues coupled with spending cuts, and he took steps to stimulate investment. These measures, however, failed to pull the Argentine economy out of its slump, and public confidence in the government tanked. After a $400 million bank run on November 30, Cavallo limited cash withdrawals to $250 per week—a move that in part triggered the massive street protests that erupted in Buenos Aires in December. Argentina could not avoid defaulting on its $132 billion foreign debt, and both Cavallo and de la Rúa resigned office on December 20. (ROBERT RAUCH)

Corigliano, John

Premieres during the 2000–01 season of new works by the American composer John Corigliano, including his *Symphony No. 2*, continued his reputation as a prolific writer whose compositions were regularly heard in concert halls. Corigliano did not write in a particular style but rather drew from eclectic influences that varied from work to work. Many of his compositions were virtuosic, tailored to the performers who commissioned them. His music was generally tonal and accessible and was often highly expressive. He wrote in many forms, including works for orchestra, solo instruments, and chamber groups, as well as operas, choral works, and film scores.

Corigliano was born on Feb. 16, 1938, in New York City. His father was concertmaster of the New York Philharmonic from 1943 to 1966, and his mother was a well-known piano teacher. He tried many instruments but had only sporadic lessons. In his teens he began analyzing the scores of compositions while listening to recordings, and he demonstrated an ability to transpose and harmonize. He studied at Columbia University, graduating cum laude in 1959, and also studied at the Manhattan School of Music. He then worked for radio stations, assisted Leonard Bernstein in the production of his Young People's Concerts, produced recordings, and did orchestrations for pop albums. In 1964 his *Sonata for Violin and Piano* won first prize in the chamber music competition at the Festival of Two Worlds in Spoleto, Italy. It received its premiere two years later at Carnegie Hall, and his career as a composer was launched.

Among the best known of Corigliano's compositions were *Concerto for Clarinet and Orchestra* (1977), a favourite that remained in the repertoire; *Pied Piper Fantasy* (1982), a work for flute and orchestra commissioned by James Galway; and *A Dylan Thomas Trilogy* (1999), for three male voices with two choruses and orchestras. *Symphony No. 1*, completed when he was composer in residence with the Chicago Symphony Orchestra from 1987 to 1990, was a response to the AIDS epidemic. Its recording by the orchestra received two Grammys, as the best new composition and the best orchestral performance. *String Quartet* (1995), commissioned for the Cleveland Quartet's final tour, also won two Grammys, for best new composition and best performance. It was the first time two recordings of a composer's works had been so honoured. His opera *The Ghosts of Versailles*, commissioned by the Metropolitan Opera and premiered in 1991, was performed throughout the world. *The Red Violin*, his third film score, won an Academy Award in 2000.

Corigliano taught at institutions in New York City, including the Juilliard School. He received numerous prizes and awards. In 1991 the versatile and prolific composer became a member of the American Academy of Arts and Letters. (ROBERT RAUCH)

Crowe, Russell

All hailed Russell Crowe in 2001 as the New Zealand-born actor captured a best actor Academy Award for his portrayal of Maximus, a general turned gladiator in ancient Rome. His commanding performance, which combined brutal fight scenes with emotional longing, also helped *Gladiator* win an Oscar for best picture and made the epic one of the highest-grossing films of 2000. The role of a warrior was not unfamiliar to Crowe, whose commitment and intensity had led to his reputation for being combative on film sets and during interviews. Such uncompromising behaviour, however, combined with charisma, dry humour, and rugged good looks, made Crowe one of Hollywood's most sought-after and talked-about performers.

Jaap Buitendijk/Getty Images

Russell Crowe as Maximus the gladiator

Four years after his birth, April 7, 1964, in Wellington, N.Z., Russell Ira Crowe moved with his family to Australia. He was the son of film- and television-set caterers, and he made his acting debut at the age of six on the television series *Spyforce.* After returning to New Zealand in the late 1970s, Crowe cofounded the rock band Roman Antix, serving as songwriter, guitarist, and lead singer; the group later reformed as 30 Odd Foot of Grunts, and in 2001 it released its second full-length compact disc, *Bastard Life or Clarity.* In the mid-1980s Crowe began performing in musicals, and from 1986 to 1988 he toured with *The Rocky Horror Picture Show* as the cross-dressing Dr. Frank N. Furter. In 1990 he moved to the big screen, appearing in *Prisoners of the Sun* and *The Crossing.* Crowe displayed an innate ability to inhabit the characters he portrayed and for his next film, *Proof* (1991), received a best supporting actor award from the Australian Film Institute (AFI). With the controversial *Romper Stomper* (1992), his career reached a turning point. As a menacing neo-Nazi, Crowe earned an AFI best actor award and attracted the attention of Hollywood. In 1995 he appeared in his first American film, *The Quick and the Dead.* The western, however, had little success at the box office, nor did the series of films that followed, including the cyberthriller *Virtuosity* (1995).

Crowe's breakthrough came as the brutish but vulnerable policeman Bud White in the 1950s crime drama *L.A. Confidential* (1997). His complex performance helped make the film a commercial and critical hit and put Crowe on the Hollywood map. After learning to ice-skate for *Mystery, Alaska* (1999), he gained some 18 kg (40 lb) and 20 years to portray a tobacco-industry whistle-blower in *The Insider* (1999). Crowe immersed himself in the role and earned an Academy Award nomination for best actor. After his star-making turn in *Gladiator,* he appeared as a hostage negotiator opposite Meg Ryan in *Proof of Life* (2000). The film, however, attracted more attention for the offscreen relationship that developed between the two costars than for the onscreen action. For his next project, *A Beautiful Mind,* Crowe transformed himself once again, playing John Forbes Nash, a Nobel Prize-winning mathematician suffering from schizophrenia. It was a predictable choice for the unpredictable actor. (AMY TIKKANEN)

Daschle, Tom

On June 6, 2001, the U.S. Senate passed from Republican to Democratic control, and Tom Daschle of South Dakota became the new majority leader. The shift occurred without a single change in membership when Sen. James Jeffords of Vermont left the Republican Party to become an independent, which gave the Democrats a 50–49 majority. The Democrats under Daschle thus suddenly found themselves with greater power to determine the legislative agenda and to pass judgment on the appointments and judicial nominees of Pres. George W. Bush.

Thomas Andrew Daschle was born on Dec. 9, 1947, in Aberdeen, S.D. The first member of his family to attend college, he graduated from South Dakota State University in 1969 with a B.A. in political science. From 1969 to 1972 he served in intelligence in the Air Force Strategic Air Command. For five years, from 1972 to 1977, he was a congressional aid to U.S. Sen. James Abourezk, and in 1978 he won the first of four terms in the House of Representatives. In 1986 Daschle defeated the incumbent to win election to the Senate, and he was reelected overwhelmingly in 1992 and 1998. He became a member of the powerful Finance Committee while still a freshman senator and in 1988 was appointed cochair of the Democratic Policy Committee. Other legislative interests of Daschle included agriculture and veterans' and Indian affairs. He compiled a record that was generally liberal on economic matters and moderate on social issues. Daschle gained a reputation for looking out for the interests of his constituents, and every year he drove himself throughout South Dakota to visit each of its 66 counties and to talk to voters.

In 1994 Daschle won the position of Democratic leader by one vote, and he became minority leader in the Senate at the beginning of the 1995 session. A soft-spoken man, he had a reputation for being fair and inclusive, but he was a skillful tactician and could be tough when needed. He opposed the tax-cut bill of President Bush on the grounds that it was fiscally irresponsible and that it unduly benefited the wealthy. As he took control of the Senate, he declared that parts of the Bush legislative program, including drilling for oil in the Arctic National Wildlife Refuge and quick deployment of a missile defense system, would not pass the Senate. In the first three weeks under Daschle's leadership, a patients' bill of rights, guaranteeing certain protections to those who were covered under managed-care health insurance, cleared the Senate despite the president's threat to veto it. Later in the year Daschle took the lead in blaming the Bush tax cut for the disappearance of the budget surplus. (ROBERT RAUCH)

Alex Wong/Getty Images

Tom Daschle on the summit of Capitol Hill

Delanoë, Bertrand

When on March 18, 2001, Bertrand Delanoë became the first Socialist mayor of Paris since 1871 he entered the history books. On a shorter time scale, Delanoë's victory was also noteworthy for having ended nearly a quarter of a century of domination of the City of Light by the former mayor, French Pres. Jacques Chirac, and his neo-Gaullist party, the Rally for the Republic (RPR).

That domination—and the way it finally crumbled into scandals of corruption and internecine warfare among Chirac's political heirs—eventually contributed heavily to Delanoë's victory. Delanoë's avowed homosexuality proved to be a nonissue, and his low-key style and persistence eventually came to be preferred by Parisians to the higher-profile Socialist rivals who at several points looked certain to eclipse him. He was helped mightily by the split in the RPR ranks between Philippe Séguin, the official RPR candidate, who polled 25.7% of the vote in the March 11 first round of balloting, and Jean Tiberi, the incumbent RPR mayor, who had split with his party but still scored 13.9%. Had these two candidates combined, they would have surpassed Delanoë's 31.4%. Delanoë, however, was able to secure backing from the Greens, who made a strong showing, and he won fairly easily in the final round of voting on March 18.

Delanoë was born on May 30, 1950, in Tunis, Tun. After his early years in North Africa, he went to France and finished his education in Toulouse. He plunged into politics, becoming secretary of the Socialist Federation of Aveyron *département* at the age of 23. His potential was spotted by François Mitterrand, the Socialist Party leader, and he rose fast, becoming a Paris city councillor. Delanoë was elected a deputy to the National Assembly in 1981, and in 1983 he became head of the Socialist Party's national federations. At 33 he was effectively number three in the ruling Socialist Party.

In 1986 Delanoë lost his National Assembly seat, though he kept his seat on the Paris city council. He founded a public relations business, mainly on behalf of institutional clients, including teacher and student associations. He returned to prominence when he became leader of the Socialist group on the city council in 1993, and he led it into the 1995 election with modest success, taking 6 of the 20 arrondissements from the right. That same year saw Chirac end his 18 years as mayor of Paris when he became president. The system of government that Chirac had installed in Paris came under growing criticism and judicial investigation for possible "kickbacks." In a campaign manifesto, Delanoë complained that during Chirac's long time as mayor, he had "progressively transformed the capital into an island outside the law."

After becoming mayor in March, Delanoë had his biggest and most controversial impact in 2001 on the city's traffic system. Elected with Green support, he embarked on a series of controversial measures to discriminate against cars in favour of other forms of transport. These included closing the Seine riverbank motorway from mid-July to mid-August, adding new bus lanes on main boulevards, and establishing studies on the reintroduction of trams and more use of the Seine to carry cargo. (DAVID BUCHAN)

bottom: AP/Wide World Photos

Duncan Smith, Iain

On Sept. 13, 2001, in the wake of its second successive crushing general election defeat, the U.K.'s Conservative Party elected as its leader a right-wing MP whose most distinctive policy was hostility to closer links between the U.K. and the European Union (EU). Iain Duncan Smith's victory was all the more remarkable for the fact that, of the five candidates who sought the Tory leadership, he was alone in never having served before as a government minister.

George Iain Duncan Smith was born on April 9, 1954, in Edinburgh. His father had been a Royal Air Force pilot during World War II and had been credited with shooting down 19 German aircraft. Duncan Smith was educated privately, including a period at HMS Conway, a school in Wales where the sons of officers were brought up in spartan conditions. In 1975 he entered army training at the Royal Military Academy, Sandhurst, and he was subsequently commissioned into the Scots Guards, rising to the rank of captain in 1979. In 1981 he decided that his future lay in civilian life and joined the defense electronics company GEC-Marconi as a sales and marketing executive—a role that took him frequently to the U.S., where he forged links with Pentagon officials and Republican politicians. In 1982 he married the Hon. Elizabeth Wynne Fremantle, daughter of the 5th Baron Cottesloe.

In 1992 Duncan Smith entered the House of Commons as MP for Chingford and Woodford Green, strongly Conservative middle-class suburbs on the outskirts of London. He quickly established himself as a member of the anti-EU "awkward squad" of Conservative backbench MPs who attacked their own party's government for signing the EU's Maastricht Treaty and who frequently voted against the government on European issues. He also established himself as a right-winger on other issues, most notably by arguing that the role of the state should be curbed significantly and that taxes should be sharply reduced.

When the Conservatives lost power in 1997, the party's new leader, William Hague, appointed Duncan Smith to his shadow cabinet, first as the party's official spokesman on social security. He became shadow defense secretary in 1999, but he continued to be best known for his uncompromising views on Europe. When Hague resigned following the party's disastrous performance in the general election held on June 7, 2001, Duncan Smith stood for the party leadership, promising that he would "never" support the entry of Britain into the EU's single currency. In the final runoff against his pro-European (and far more experienced) rival, Kenneth Clarke, Duncan Smith's views proved to be far more in tune with the party membership, and he won 61% of the votes cast. (PETER KELLNER)

Ellroy, James

American author James Ellroy, long regarded as a master of the crime-fiction genre, continued his move into the realm of general fiction with the publication of his novel *The Cold Six Thousand* in May 2001. The book, which covered the turbulent years between the assassination of U.S. Pres. John F. Kennedy in 1963 and that of his brother Robert in 1968, was the sequel to Ellroy's best-selling 1995 novel *American Tabloid.* As in his earlier crime novels, themes of violence and corruption were still prominently featured, but *The Cold Six Thousand* and *American Tabloid* aimed for a much broader scope; together they represented the author's expressed ambition to "recreate 20th-century American history through fiction."

Lee Earle Ellroy was born on March 4, 1948, in Los Angeles. His parents were divorced in 1954, and Ellroy moved with his mother to El Monte, Calif., a suburb of Los Angeles. In 1958 his mother was murdered there, a crime that was never solved; in his autobiographical *My Dark Places* (1996), Ellroy wrote about the crime and its effect on his life. After his mother's death Ellroy lived with his father. He attended high school in Fairfax, a predominantly Jewish section of Los Angeles, but was expelled before graduation for "ranting about Nazism" in his English class. He then enlisted in the army but soon decided that he did not belong there and convinced an army psychiatrist that he was not mentally fit for combat. After three months he received a dishonourable discharge. Soon afterward his father died, and after a brief stay with a friend of his father, Ellroy landed on the streets of Los Angeles. From the age of 18 he lived in parks and vacant apartments; he spent most of his time drinking, taking drugs, and reading crime novels. After being jailed for breaking into a vacant apartment, Ellroy got a job at a bookstore. Meanwhile, he had become addicted to Benzedrex, a sinus inhaler that he swallowed to gain a euphoric high. With his health deteriorating and fearing for his sanity, Ellroy joined Alcoholics Anonymous and found steady work as a golf caddy. At the age of 30 he wrote and sold his first novel, *Brown's Requiem* (1981).

Most of Ellroy's books dealt with crime and corruption. Among the best known were four novels that constituted the "L.A. Quartet" series: *Black Dahlia* (1987); *The Big Nowhere* (1988); *L.A. Confidential* (1990), made into an acclaimed movie of the same title in 1997; and *White Jazz* (1992).

After publishing *White Jazz,* Ellroy produced *American Tabloid* and *The Cold Six Thousand.* In 2001 Ellroy fans were happy to hear that a cable television miniseries, entitled *James Ellroy's Los Angeles,* was set to air in September 2002 and that a film adaptation of *My Dark Places* was also in the works. (DAVID R. CALHOUN)

Grant, Hugh

Although in real life British film actor Hugh Grant could occasionally be a scoundrel—witness his 1995 arrest with a prostitute and his resultant "I did a bad thing" apology tour of American television talk shows—in "reel" life he was generally known to the public as the boyishly appealing leading man who finally got the girl. That was not the case in 2001, however, when in *Bridget Jones's Diary* he portrayed the womanizing boss and scheming sometime lover of the film's leading character. According to Grant, his character was closer to his off-screen personality than most of the roles he previously had played. In most people's minds, however, he was not a cad but rather an endearing, stammering, bumbling, and funny love interest—much like the one they had taken to in Grant's first big hit, *Four Weddings and a Funeral* (1994).

Hugh John Mungo Grant was born on Sept. 9, 1960, in London. It was not until his senior year at the University of Oxford, where he was studying English literature, that he became involved in acting. He appeared in a student film, *Privileged* (1982), and joined the Oxford University Dramatic Society. Following graduation (1982), Grant wrote and occasionally performed in radio commercials and attempted to write a novel before turning once again to acting. His stage debut came at the Nottingham (Eng.) Playhouse in 1985. He went from there to London, where he formed the Jockeys of Norfolk comedy troupe, for which he wrote, directed, and performed in revues. He began his professional film career with the James Ivory–Ismail Merchant film *Maurice* (1987), for which he won a best actor award at the Venice Film Festival, and added numerous films and television productions to his credits, including *White Mischief* (1988), *Impromptu* (1991), *The Remains of the Day* (1993), and *Sirens* (1994). It was his charming performance in *Four Weddings and a Funeral,* however, that brought him to the attention of the general public; he also won the Golden Globe best actor award and was named best actor by the British Academy of Film and Television Arts. Grant quickly followed up with *An Awfully Big Adventure, The Englishman Who Went up a Hill but Came down a Mountain, Restoration, Nine Months,* and *Sense and Sensibility,* all of which were released in 1995. He took on a more serious role in *Extreme Measures* (1996) but returned to romantic comedy in *Notting Hill* (1999), *Mickey Blue Eyes* (1999), and *Small Time Crooks* (2000).

Given that one of Grant's most commented-upon physical attributes was his unruly mop of hair, audiences for his forthcoming film, *About a Boy,* were in for another surprise. In addition to playing another irresponsible womanizer—though this time one who wises up—he would be sporting a much shorter and more conventional haircut.

(BARBARA WHITNEY)

Graves, Michael

In a ceremony on Feb. 16, 2001, American architect Michael Graves was honoured with what many in his field considered the ultimate compliment—recognition of excellence by one's own peers—when he was presented with the 2001 Gold Medal of the American Institute of Architects, the AIA's lifetime achievement award. Graves's designs had ranged from large multiuse buildings, office interiors, and hotels to private domestic commissions and a host of consumer products.

Graves was born on July 9, 1934, in Indianapolis, Ind. He earned degrees in architecture from the University of Cincinnati, Ohio, and

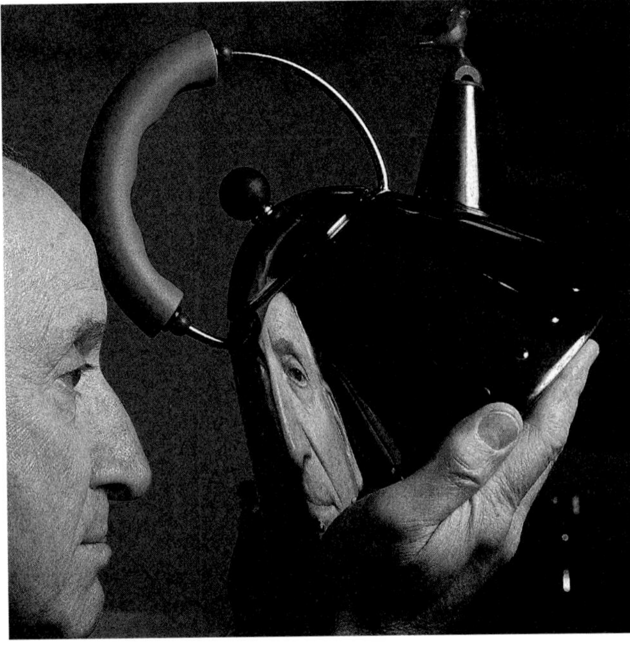

Michael Graves reflects on his designs (the Alessi teakettle)
Steve Simon

Harvard University in 1958 and 1959, respectively. In 1960 he attended the American Academy in Rome. The influence of Italian architecture and design was clearly present in his work, as were the colours that reflected the mood of Tuscany and the Mediterranean—warm terra-cotta tones, azures, and reds—and that figured prominently in the overall conception of his projects.

Influential as a theorist as well as a practicing architect and designer, Graves had taught at Princeton University in the school of architecture since 1962; the offices of his firm were also located in the town of Princeton. Though some described Graves as a "Postmodern classicist," he resisted such a categorization. His style was marked by a synthesis of classical elements, strong geometric shapes, and frequent playful touches. In the Renaissance-inspired facade for his design of the Walt Disney Corp. headquarters, figures of the Seven Dwarfs were positioned across the entablature in place of ordinary columns. Some of his other well-known projects included the Swan and Dolphin hotels at Disney World in Orlando, Fla., and the Humana Building in Louisville, Ky.—a 27-story high-rise with a dramatic glass pyramid over its entrance and an open porch area on the 25th floor. Graves's projects were purposefully geared toward capturing public attention. In late 1998 and for the following year and a half, visitors to Washington, D.C., saw his inventive interpretation of scaffolding enshrouding the Washington Memorial during its renovation. Public reactions to Graves's solution were mixed; the nearly 58 km (36 mi) of aluminum scaffolding covered with a layer of blue mesh took four months to erect. The scaffolding was intended to perform on both functional and aesthetic levels, protecting workers while maintaining a certain visual interest during the restoration.

The extra-architectural nature of this project pointed to the breadth of Graves's interests and the range of his endeavours. In addition to buildings and interior spaces, he designed small accessories and household objects that bore his personal stamp, including lamps, salt and pepper shakers, bookends, watches, picture frames, and, most famously, the Alessi stainless-steel teakettle with instantly recognizable bird spout and blue handle. His design-friendly products were also featured at discount chain Target Corp. stores. Despite the scale or purpose, Graves approached each project with the same humanist philosophy of design that he had worked to refine for nearly 40 years. (MEGHAN DAILEY)

Gusinsky, Vladimir

Media tycoon Vladimir Gusinsky was the first Russian businessman to recognize the political and financial benefits of the mass media. His holdings included television, radio, newspapers, and magazines known both for their professionalism and for the critical stance they often adopted toward Kremlin policies. In 2001 Gusinsky lost control of his media empire at the end of what some observers depicted as a Kremlin-inspired campaign to destroy him.

Vladimir Aleksandrovich Gusinsky was born into a Jewish family in Moscow on Oct. 6, 1952. He studied at a petrochemical institute and began his career as a theatre actor and director in the provincial city of Tula. In the late 1980s, however, he took advantage of a new mood of economic liberalization to establish himself in private business. Gusinsky differed from the majority of those who made their fortunes at that time by exploiting privileged backgrounds to strip the assets of the Soviet state. In cooperation with an American partner, Gusinsky by contrast set up a consulting company that facilitated joint ventures between Soviet and Western firms. In 1989 he established Most Bank, which soon became one of the most active and innovative commercial banking groups in Russia. In 1993 Most began to handle the accounts of the Moscow city government and the vast amounts of money passing through them. In turn, Mayor Yury Luzhkov's administration reportedly helped Most acquire some of the choicest development plots in Moscow's booming real-estate market. This made Gusinsky many enemies, while the Kremlin suspected him of financing Luzhkov's presidential ambitions. Gusinsky was one of seven "oligarchs" who, alarmed by the prospect of a Communist victory in Russia's presidential election in 1996, bankrolled Pres. Boris Yeltsin's reelection campaign.

In 1992 Gusinsky founded the newspaper *Segodnya* and the independent television channel NTV. Later he acquired the Ekho Moskvy radio station, and in 1996 he launched a weekly political magazine, *Itogi,* a joint venture with *Newsweek.* NTV raised Kremlin hackles both through its critical coverage of Russia's 1994–96 war in Chechnya and through its merciless satirizing of the foibles of Russia's leaders. In 1997 Gusinsky left his post at Most Bank to concentrate on his media interests, run by the private holding company Media-Most.

Following Russia's 1998 financial crash, advertising revenues dried up. To keep his publications afloat, Gusinsky was obliged to borrow large sums of money. He turned for funding to the natural gas monopoly Gazprom. This put him heavily in debt to a company seen by many as an arm of the Russian state. Russia's new president, Vladimir Putin, came to power in 2000 vowing to strip the "oligarchs"—Russia's richest businessmen—of their privileged access to political power. Within weeks of Putin's inauguration, Gusinsky had been jailed on embezzlement charges. Then Gazprom began to demand repayment of its loans. After a bitter court battle, Gusinsky was forced unwillingly to relinquish control of his media holdings and left the country for exile in the Spanish resort of Sotogrande. NTV was placed under new management; *Itogi* and *Segodnya* were closed down. The Russian government demanded Gusinsky's extradition, but the Spanish courts refused.

Gusinsky and his supporters depicted him as a champion of media freedom and victim of Kremlin persecution. The Russian authorities countered that the case was a matter simply of property rights and the repayment of loans. Many felt that the truth contained elements of both interpretations and lay somewhere in between. (EDITOR)

Haakon, Crown Prince, and Crown Princess Mette-Marit

On Aug. 25, 2001, Crown Prince Haakon of Norway married Mette-Marit Tjessem Høiby, who was not only a commoner but also a single mother when they began dating in 1999. Even in permissive Norway—where in 1998 almost 50% of firstborn children were born to unmarried women—the prince's choice of bride raised eyebrows.

The objection, however, seemed to be less the issue of descent—her four-year-old son,

Mette-Marit, Marius, and Haakon

Marius, could never be king—than the people with whom the new crown princess had associated in her former life. Less than a week before they tied the knot, the crown prince and his bride-to-be held a press conference in which she apologized for her former life and made her statement serve as both a plea and an object lesson. She hoped to curtail future questions about her past and, without admitting she had used drugs, used the occasion to condemn them. For that was the issue Norwegians cared most about; her former boyfriend (and the father of her son) had been sentenced to prison for assault and possession of cocaine. Crown Prince Haakon, who acknowledged in mid-May 2000 that Mette-Merit was his girlfriend, was completely supportive of her, as were his parents, King Harald V and Queen Sonja. The king did not stand in the way of the marriage, perhaps because he had had to wait nine years before his father, King Olav V, and the Norwegian Parliament approved his marrying commoner Sonja Haraldsen.

The crown prince was born on July 20, 1973, in Oslo. Though he had an older sister, Märtha Louise, Haakon Magnus was the only son of then crown prince Harald and crown princess Sonja, and as such he was from birth heir to the throne. (The succession law was changed in the 1990s.) He had a happy childhood, mostly out of the limelight. After four years of service in the navy, including time at the Naval Academy in Bergen, he broke with Norwegian tradition to attend the University of California, Berkeley, where he obtained (1999) a B.A. in political science. Thereafter he enrolled at the University of Oslo to study law and social science. On Dec. 1, 2000, he introduced his fiancée, with whom he was already sharing an apartment, to the public.

Mette-Marit Tjessem Høiby was born on Aug. 19, 1973, in Kristiansand, Nor., and grew up under quite different circumstances, with an ordinary middle-class upbringing. She was an exchange student in Wangaratta, Australia, during six months of her high-school years. Thereafter she experienced what she called a "youth rebellion" that resulted in her "wild life." That life came to an end for her in an almost fairy-tale manner when she met, and ultimately married, a prince.

(KATHLEEN KUIPER)

Handler, Daniel

Capitalizing on the unsentimental tastes of legions of 10–13-year-old readers, American storyteller Daniel Handler (a.k.a. Lemony Snicket) captured the imagination of his youthful audiences with *A Series of Unfortunate Events.* These unhappy morality tales—featuring titillating alliterative titles such as *The Reptile Room* (1999), *The Austere Academy* (2000), and *The Miserable Mill* (2000)—had sold more than one million copies by 2001.

Handler was born on Feb. 28, 1970, in San Francisco. After earning a B.A. in 1992 from Wesleyan University, Middletown, Conn., he received an Olin fellowship to write a novel, which he discarded upon finishing. He returned to his hometown, worked as an administrative assistant and a writer for a radio program, and, in the meantime, wrote another novel before moving to New York City, where he began reviewing movies and reading manuscripts for a literary agent. His novel was rejected so many times that he began hosting a reading series called "Great Writers Who Can't Get Published." Shortly thereafter, he appeared on the literary scene with *The Basic Eight* (1999), a critically acclaimed novel about a high-school student bludgeoned with a croquet mallet wielded by a classmate. *Watch Your Mouth* (2000), written in the form of an opera, was a satiric work centred on the theme of incest.

Remembering his youth, Handler had railed against the number of novels devoted to sports or fantasy themes. When urged to turn his hand to creating the kind of books that he would have enjoyed, Handler resurrected Lemony Snicket—a name he had invented when requesting materials from a right-wing organization for a book project—as the doleful narrator and author of the series. *The Bad Beginning* (1999), which introduced the travails of three orphaned siblings (and also introduced his habit of naming some characters after past literary luminaries, in this case Klaus, Sunny, and Violet Baudelaire), launched the series and established an aura of mystery around Snicket. He was typically featured on the back of the hardcover books as a shadowy figure—his image appearing out of focus or away from the camera.

Handler deftly served as Snicket's representative at book events, regaling his listeners with the travails of Snicket as well as entertaining them with accordion music and dire tales about danger lurking in the most unlikely places. A favourite story recounted how a bug had bitten Snicket in his armpit and prevented him from appearing. Handler also warned readers not to read or purchase the Snicket books, which typically feature unhappy

Daniel Handler a.k.a. Lemony Snicket

left: AP/Wide World Photos; right: Meredith Heuer

beginnings, middles, and endings. Notwithstanding, his fans waited with eager anticipation for each new offering in the projected 13-book series. The latest installments of Snicket's imagination—*The Ersatz Elevator, The Vile Village, The Hostile Hospital*—all appeared in 2001. (KAREN J. SPARKS)

Harvey, Paul

In 2001 American broadcaster Paul Harvey was off the air for part of the year after damaging a vocal cord. His vastly popular radio programs, however, passed major milestones: *The Rest of the Story,* heard Mondays through Saturdays, turned 25 in May, while *Paul Harvey News and Comment,* on the air twice each weekday, celebrated 50 years of syndication. Harvey's mix of current events news, human-interest anecdotes, and common-sense editorials reached some 24 million listeners via 1,600 radio stations daily. His staccato pacing, bouncing intonation, and signature hooks ("Stand by . . . for news!"; "Paul Harvey . . . good day!") helped make his voice one of the most recognizable in the history of radio.

Paul Harvey Aurandt was born on Sept. 4, 1918, in Tulsa, Okla. He was descended from five generations of Baptist preachers. His mother raised him and his sister alone after their father was shot to death. At 14 he landed a job at KVOO radio in Tulsa, and he was soon doing voice work there. He studied briefly at the University of Tulsa but quit to work full-time in radio; by age 25 he had gained experience at stations across the plains and the Midwest and had covered the activities of the U.S. military for the Office of War Information. In 1940 he married Lynne ("Angel") Cooper, who afterward took control of his business affairs. Following a medical discharge from the Army Air Corps in 1944, he shortened his name to Paul Harvey and began broadcasting for Chicago radio station WENR. *Paul Harvey News and Comment* proved immediately popular in Chicago and was nationally syndicated by the American Broadcasting Company in 1951. In 1976 the program spun off *The Rest of the Story,* whose brief biographical narratives were written by the Harveys' only child, Paul Harvey Aurandt, Jr.

Harvey often opined on rising taxes, bloated government, and the decay of American values. He called his particular conservative cast "political fundamentalism." Though he was associated with prominent figures of the American right—he once hosted Sen. Joseph McCarthy at his home and was short-listed among George C. Wallace's potential vice presidential running mates in 1968—Harvey resisted identification with any ideology but his own. He publicly urged Pres. Richard Nixon to abandon the Vietnam War in 1970, and in the 1980s he decried several of Pres. Ronald Reagan's conservative positions.

Apart from his radio work, Harvey regularly appeared as a television and newspaper commentator and published several books, including *Remember These Things* (1952), *Autumn of Liberty* (1954), and *You Said It, Paul Harvey* (1970). In 2001 his son and actor David Hartman split Harvey's broadcasting duties while he recovered from surgery in May to repair his vocal cord, and he returned to the airwaves in late August. (COLIN J. MURPHY)

Hau, Lene Vestergaard

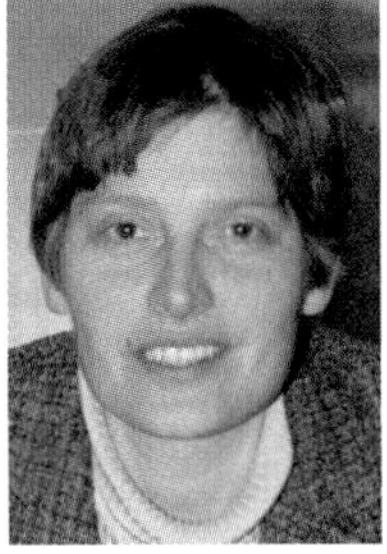

In 2001 Danish scientist Lene Vestergaard Hau became one of the all-time most prominent women physicists when the journal *Nature* published a paper in which Hau and a team of physicists at the Rowland Institute for Science in Cambridge, Mass., described how they had sent a pulse of laser light into a tiny cloud of extremely cold gas, halted the light, stored it for a fraction of a second, and then released it. Though Hau's team was not the only one to achieve this feat, the latest research related to altering the speed of light had its roots in an experiment conducted by Hau in 1999. In that experiment Hau and her colleagues at the Rowland Institute shone lasers through a cloud of ultracold sodium atoms—known as a Bose-Einstein condensate—which effectively slowed light from its normal speed of about 299,792 km (186,282 mi) per second to 61 km (38 mi) per hour. It was believed that these advances could translate into practical applications that would substantially improve telecommunications and computers.

Hau was born on Nov. 13, 1959, in Vejle, Den. From an early age she enjoyed mathematics, and she excelled at school, skipping the 10th grade. She entered Aarhus University, where she was drawn to studying physics owing to an interest in mathematics and quantum mechanics. She earned a B.S. degree in mathematics in 1984, an M.S. in physics in 1986, and a Ph.D. in physics in 1991, all from Aarhus University. Her studies included seven months at CERN in Geneva. She accepted a postdoctoral position on the faculty at Harvard University, where she later became the Gordon McKay Professor of Applied Physics. Hau also took a position at the Rowland Institute, serving as principal investigator for the Atom Cooling Group. In 1994, working with Jene A. Golovchenko at the Rowland Institute, Hau developed one of the first elements that led to the slowing of light. Called a "candlestick," the device wicks sodium atoms out of molten sodium metal and projects them into a cooling apparatus that, by using lasers, cools the atoms to a temperature 50 billionths of a degree above absolute zero.

Hau attributed her success in a field dominated by men to her upbringing and her homeland. Her parents, she said, encouraged her in her studies just as much as they did her brother. In addition, in Denmark laypeople and other scientists regarded physicists highly, and research was sometimes funded by private interests. Hau herself had studied for a year on a scholarship subsidized by Carlsberg brewers. (ANTHONY G. CRAINE)

Herzog, Jacques, and de Meuron, Pierre

The 2001 Pritzker Architecture Prize was awarded to Jacques Herzog and Pierre de Meuron, a pair of Swiss architects whose modernist designs were characterized by a reliance on established architectural principles coupled with imaginative new techniques suited to each individual project. A prime example of this meeting of tradition and innovation was the Dominus Winery in Napa, Calif. Essentially a long, low-slung rectangular box, the building had a facade constructed of local stone held together with wire rather than mortar. Some portions of the stone walls were packed tightly enough to provide insulation from heat and cold, while other sections were stacked loosely enough to allow air and light to penetrate where needed.

Both men were born in Basel, Switz., in 1950, Herzog on April 19 and de Meuron on May 8. Friends and schoolmates during childhood, the two began at an early age to work together on drawings and models. When it came time to attend college, neither chose to study architecture initially. Herzog first studied commercial design before attending the University of Basel to study biology and chemistry. With an interest in drawing and math, de Meuron pursued a degree in civil engineering. Unsatisfied after a year of school, both decided to study architecture, first at the Swiss Federal Institute of Technology at Lausanne, then at the institute's Zürich campus, where they received their degrees in 1975. Among their instructors was Aldo Rossi, who would receive the Pritzker Prize in 1990. After three years as professor's assistants, Herzog and de Meuron established their own architecture firm in Basel. Herzog took the post of visiting professor at Cornell University, Ithaca, N.Y., in 1983, and both men became visiting professors at Harvard University in 1989. Their firm, meanwhile, grew to 120 employees in offices in Basel; London; Munich, Ger.; and San Francisco.

Their most prominent project was the Tate Gallery of Modern Art in London. To create the museum, Herzog and de Meuron converted a former power plant on the South Bank of the River Thames. Incorporating traditional elements with Art Deco and modernism, the architects created what they described as a "building of the 21st century." Upon opening to the public in May 2000, the new Tate Modern received critical acclaim and served as a catalyst for the revitalization of its South Bank neighbourhood. Other high-profile projects included the nearly transparent headquarters of a cough drop manufacturer in Laufen, Switz., in which glass panels made up much of the facade; a railroad utility building in Basel that was sheathed in copper strips; and the Rudin House in Leymen, France—a cartoonish-looking residence that, perched on a platform, appeared to float above the landscape.

Herzog likened the pair's body of work to that of Pop artist Andy Warhol, who used common, recognizable forms and objects and attempted to create something new from them. "We love to destroy the clichés of architecture," Herzog said. (ANTHONY G. CRAINE)

MaryAnn Nilsson/Rowland Institute

Hill, Faith

Though American Faith Hill did not release a new album or embark on a concert tour in 2001, the country and pop singer sustained her star status. Besides contributing a song, "There You'll Be," to the sound track for the movie *Pearl Harbor,* she won three Grammy Awards in country categories, including one she shared with her husband, country singer Tim McGraw; she appeared on Barbara Walters's annual Academy Award-night special on ABC; and she performed in the landmark *America: A Tribute to Heroes,* a cross-network TV benefit for victims and rescue workers in the September 11 terrorist attacks in the U.S.

Audrey Faith Perry was born on Sept. 21, 1967, in Jackson, Miss., and was the adopted daughter of Pat and Edna Perry. The family later moved to the nearby town of Star, Miss. Influenced by Elvis Presley, Reba McEntire, and Tammy Wynette, Hill left home at the age of 19 to pursue a career as a professional singer in Nashville, Tenn.

In 1993 she released her first album, *Take Me as I Am,* which included two country chart-topping singles, "Wild One" and "Piece of My Heart." Her second album, *It Matters to Me,* appeared in 1995 and produced a number one single of the same title. It was her third album *Faith* issued in 1998, that propelled Hill to major stardom; helped by the crossover success of "This Kiss," a romantic up-tempo song, the album sold five million copies. In the fall of 1998 Hill began appearing as a headliner, and in April 1999 she launched her first major tour as a solo artist. Her four-month This Kiss tour traveled to 50 cities.

Hill's fourth album, *Breathe,* appeared in November 1999 and set the stage for a spectacular run of media exposure, touring, and industry awards. It debuted at the number one spot on the *Billboard* country album chart and on the *Billboard* 200 chart, which measured all music genres. During 2000 Hill sang the national anthem at Super Bowl XXXIV, and she performed at the Academy Awards, during which Pepsi premiered a commercial featuring her. *People* magazine named Hill one of the 50 most beautiful people of 2000, and she served as a celebrity spokesperson for Cover Girl cosmetics and Pepsi.

Hill also starred in the *VH1 Divas 2000,* together with Diana Ross, Mariah Carey, and Donna Summer. Hill's first network TV special, *Faith!,* aired Thanksgiving Day 2000 on CBS, and her recording of "Where Are You Christmas" was featured in the film *How the Grinch Stole Christmas* (2000). When Hill and McGraw combined talents for their Soul 2 Soul Tour 2000, more than one million fans turned out for more than 60 shows. Both the Los Angeles-based Academy of Country Music and the Nashville-based Country Music Association named Hill top female vocalist for 2000. She had reportedly sold more than 20 million albums worldwide, including more than 7 million copies of *Breathe.* (JAY ORR)

Iverson, Allen

With his remarkable play during the 2000–01 National Basketball Association (NBA) regular season and a gritty, determined performance during the play-offs, Allen Iverson, a guard for the Philadelphia 76ers, forced the NBA and its fans to accept him as one of the league's elite players. Previously known primarily as a talented but difficult player with a checkered past, Iverson won the league scoring title, earned Most Valuable Player honours, and led his team to the NBA finals, all during a season in which he improved relations with his coach and developed a new reputation as a team player.

Allen Ezail Iverson was born on June 7, 1975, in Hampton, Va. Growing up in poverty with his mother and two sisters, Iverson attended Bethel High School, where he led the school's football and basketball teams to state championships his junior year. At age 17 Iverson was jailed after being accused of starting a racially charged brawl in a bowling alley, but his conviction was later overturned owing to lack of evidence. He was offered a scholarship to Georgetown University, Washington, D.C., where in two years he averaged 23 points per game and won two Big East Conference Defensive Player of the Year awards before making the decision to leave school to play professionally. Iverson was chosen first overall in the 1996 NBA draft by the 76ers.

Despite being one of the smallest players in the league (1.8 m, 75 kg [6 ft, 165 lb]), Iverson made a big splash immediately, scoring 30 points in his first game and, late in the 1996–97 season, stringing together five consecutive games of 40 points or more. He led his team with a 23.5 scoring average and won Rookie of the Year honours. His quickness and his signature crossover dribble often left even the best defenders helpless. His refusal to conform to a conservative off-the-court persona, however, such as that of Michael Jordan, made Iverson an outcast. His hip-hop-styled clothing, flashy jewelry, and braided hair were not part of the image the league wanted to promote. One NBA publication even went so far as to obscure Iverson's tattoos in a photo. An arrest after his rookie year (all charges were later dropped) tarnished his reputation further.

Iverson led his team in scoring and steals in each of his first five seasons, winning the league scoring title in 1998–99 and being named to the All-NBA first team. During his first several years in the league, however, his clashes with 76ers coach Larry Brown over late arrivals to practice and other issues became as well known as his scoring prowess. He was portrayed by the media as a selfish, disruptive player. At the beginning of the 2000 season, Iverson released a controversial rap song from his upcoming album that contained derogatory lyrics about women and homosexuals, which further cast a negative light. As the season progressed, however, Iverson began to show a new side. He worked harder in practice, praised his teammates in public, and mended his relationship with Brown. The NBA, meanwhile, began to recognize that Iverson had a huge following of young fans who identified with his rebellious image.

During the 2001 play-offs, Iverson staged one brilliant effort after another, averaging 32.9 points despite nagging injuries. During game four of the Eastern Conference finals against the Milwaukee Bucks, Iverson was elbowed in the mouth and knocked to the floor. He went on to score 28 points in a 76ers win, later admitting that he had swallowed the blood from his wound as he ran the court so that the referees would not force him to leave the game to be treated. The moment typified Iverson's season and helped to define a new image for one of the game's most talked-about players.

(ANTHONY G. CRAINE)

M. David Leeds/Allsport

Hoops marvel Allen Iverson

Jo, Sumi

In 2001 South Korean soprano Sumi Jo continued to grace the stages of major opera houses and concert halls throughout the world; she also released a critically acclaimed compact disc (CD), *Prayers,* which featured her renditions of religious songs ranging from Franz Schubert's "Ave Maria" to the hymn "Amazing Grace." *Prayers* followed Jo's release of another highly praised CD, *Only Love* (2000), a collection of songs from Broadway musicals.

Soo Kyong Jo was born in Seoul, S.Kor., on Nov. 22, 1962. She began studying music at an early age. She entered the music school of Seoul National University but left in her second year

above: Chris Weeks/Getty Images

to attend the Accademia di Santa Cecilia in Rome. There, beginning in 1983, she studied keyboard and vocal music. After graduating in 1985, she came to the attention of Austrian conductor Herbert von Karajan, who praised the beauty of Jo's voice, and on his recommendation she appeared at the Salzburg (Austria) Festival in 1986. In the same year, she made her operatic debut as Gilda in Guiseppe Verdi's *Rigoletto,* and in 1988 she appeared as Oscar in that composer's *Un ballo in maschera,* with Karajan conducting. She recorded the work with Karajan and counted Oscar among her favourite roles. During the late 1980s Jo took first place in a number of international competitions. By the end of the decade her career had been established, and she was on her way to becoming an international star.

Thierry Cohen, Paris, France/Warner Classics International

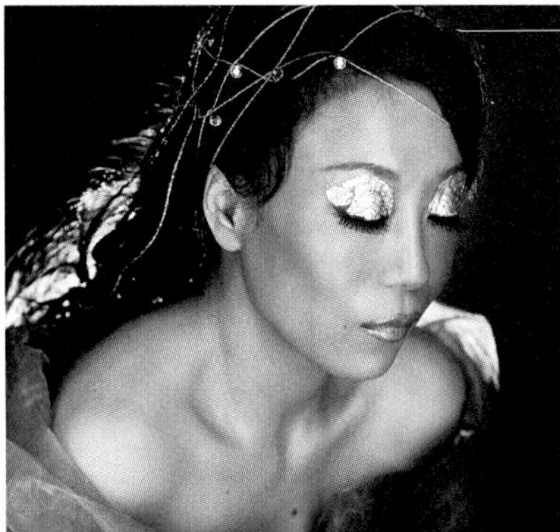

Korean coloratura Sumi Jo

Jo's light, expressive voice made her well suited for the major coloratura roles of the operatic repertoire. She was particularly noted for her portrayal of the Queen of the Night in Mozart's *Die Zauberflöte* and for her title role in Donizetti's *Lucia di Lammermoor.* Among the operas of Richard Strauss, she sang Sophia in *Der Rosenkavalier* and Zerbinetta in *Ariadne auf Naxos.* In the 1992 Grammy Award-winning recording of Strauss's *Die Frau ohne Schatten* by the Vienna Philharmonic, conducted by Georg Solti, Jo was the Voice of the Falcon. She also recorded a number of collections of arias as well as CDs that had crossover appeal to popular music audiences.

In 1993 Jo was named the best soprano of the year at the sixth La Siola Doro in Forli, Italy. She found herself in demand by the leading opera companies of the world. Among European houses, she sang at La Scala (Milan), Covent Garden (London), and the Vienna Staatsoper. In the U.S. she performed at the Metropolitan Opera in New York City and at Lyric Opera of Chicago. Her résumé also included engagements in South America, Australia, and Asia. (ROBERT RAUCH)

Jung, Andrea

Though Avon Products, Inc., the world's largest direct-selling company, had built its reputation selling women's cosmetics door-to-door, its 115-year-old sales strategy was being revamped to draw on Avon CEO Andrea Jung's background in department store retailing. In 2001 Avon announced plans to sell beauty and lifestyle products through retail stores while maintaining the three million Avon sales representatives in more than 130 countries. The company chose to focus on American department stores with the planned September launch of a new beComing line in 125 Sears and 75 J.C. Penney stores. Before the products were launched, however, Sears canceled its plan to participate, and J.C. Penney was left as the sole retailer opening exclusive Avon boutiques.

Jung was born in 1959 in Toronto but moved to Wellesley, Mass., with her family when she was a young child. Her parents (her father was an architect, and her mother was a chemical engineer) were Chinese immigrants who had high expectations for their daughter. She took piano lessons and was schooled in Mandarin Chinese. After graduating magna cum laude (1979) from Princeton University, Jung followed her interest in fashion and retailing by joining Bloomingdale's executive training program. Her career choice might have shocked her parents—at least until Jung achieved increasingly important positions at I. Magnin (senior vice president and general merchandise manager) and Neiman Marcus (executive vice president).

When she joined Avon in 1993—she began as a consultant but was quickly promoted to president of product marketing for American operations—Jung opposed the company's move into retailing. She saw that the products and the people were not ready to expand beyond the company's traditional direct-selling approach. By the time she was named president in 1998 and CEO in 1999, she and others had already been studying new sales approaches that might take advantage of traditional retailing and Internet marketing while maintaining productive relationships with the company's sales representatives worldwide.

Jung was known for making informed decisions. As an attractive Asian American (Mattel made an Andrea Jung Barbie doll for her), she promoted a glamorous image for the company and served as a role model for customers, company representatives, and rising executives who took cues from her example. She was also a figurehead for the company's commitment to diversity.

Foremost, Avon was a company for and about women, and Jung epitomized the successful woman. Under her leadership Avon continued to prosper—exceeding $5 billion in annual sales—even as it sought new opportunities. In addition, her dedication to women's health was recognized in 2000 when she was named the recipient of the Award for Distinguished Service from the Columbia-Presbyterian Medical Center; the Avon Worldwide Fund for Women's Health had sustained programs in more than 30 countries and provided more than $100 million. Jung pledged to increase that amount to $200 million by the end of 2002. (SARAH FORBES ORWIG)

Kabila, Joseph

On Jan. 26, 2001, Joseph Kabila was inaugurated as the president of the Democratic Republic of the Congo (DRC). He was the eldest son of the former president, Laurent Kabila, who had been shot by a bodyguard and apparently killed on January 16, although the death was not announced until two days later. (*See* OBITUARIES.) The son—named interim president on January 17 and subsequently chosen to succeed his father—inherited a country that, for the most part, was without a functioning government or basic services and whose economy had largely been ruined during two and a half years of civil war. Almost nothing was known about the new president either inside or outside the country, and the first assessment was that his father's advisers had chosen him as a figurehead. During the following months, however, the son surprised many people by taking the initiative and turning the policies of the government in a different direction.

Kabila was born on June 4, 1971, in Sud-Kivu province and grew up and was educated in Tanzania. He came to speak primarily English and Swahili but was not fluent in French, which along with English was an official language of the DRC. When his father deposed Pres. Mobutu Sese Seko in 1997, the son followed him to Kinshasa. In 1998 he was sent to Rwanda and then to China for military training. Upon his return, he became head of the country's armed forces, with the rank of major general.

Less than a week after being sworn in, Kabila made his first trip abroad as president. He conferred with government leaders in France and Belgium and also traveled to the U.S., where he met with Secretary of State Colin Powell (*q.v.*) and with officials of the World Bank, the International Monetary Fund, and the United Nations. While in the U.S., he also met with Paul Kagame, head of Rwanda, who had been one of his father's principal opponents. In a meeting in Zambia later in February, the new president agreed to begin the implementation of a cease-fire agreement that had been signed in Lusaka in July 1999 but that his father had refused to honour. As part of the agreement, he held talks with rebel groups, and the governments of five neighbouring countries—Rwanda, Uganda, Zimbabwe, Angola, and Namibia—that had troops in the country agreed to begin their withdrawal. UN peacekeepers arrived at the end of March to monitor the cease-fire and the pullback of troops. On April 14 Kabila, having dismissed the cabinet that had been held over from his father's administration, named his own group of ministers. (ROBERT RAUCH)

Karzai, Hamid

The U.S. bombing of Afghanistan, launched in October 2001, produced dramatic military results before a political framework for reconstructing the country could be established. By

above: Matt Campbell/AFP Worldwide

mid-November the Taliban regime had collapsed, and there were fears that a destructive power struggle might break out among Afghanistan's conflicting ethnic, religious, and political communities. Talks were hastily arranged in Bonn, Ger., under the auspices of the United Nations; they were to include representatives of the non-Pashtun Northern Alliance as well as factions still loyal to the former Afghan king, Zahir Shah. Agreement was reached on December 5 that Hamid Karzai should chair an interim administration for six months, until a Loya Jirga, a traditional Afghan assembly, could be convened. Karzai was a tribal leader (but not a warlord), educated, fluent in Western and Eastern languages, and, above all, known and trusted in the U.S.

Karzai was born on Dec. 24, 1957, in Kandahar, Afg., son of the chief of the Popalzai Pashtuns. Both his father and his grandfather had served the government of Zahir Shah from the 1930s until he was overthrown in 1973. Under the Soviet-imposed regime in the 1980s, the Karzai family left Afghanistan and settled in Pakistan. Karzai attended university in India, and during the Soviet occupation he worked in Pakistan with the Liberation Front of Sibgatullah Mojaddedi. When the communist government of Mohammad Najibullah fell in April 1992, the mujahideen established a coalition government under Mojaddedi's presidency, and Karzai served as deputy foreign minister. He continued in this position when Burhanuddin Rabbani became president. At this point the mujahideen turned on one another, causing tens of thousands of deaths and countrywide turmoil. In 1994 Karzai again left the country.

Like most Afghans, Karzai was at first optimistic when the Taliban appeared and brought a kind of order to Afghanistan. The Taliban, although they were mostly ethnic Pashtun, had no sympathy for the traditional social and political institutions to which Karzai remained faithful, however. For his part, Karzai opposed the influence that the Pakistanis and other foreigners exerted over the Taliban. Karzai blamed the Taliban when his father was assassinated in July 1999 near the family home in Quetta, Pak. The leadership of the Popalzai now fell to him.

As the U.S. began bombing, Karzai entered southern Afghanistan to rally support against the Taliban. Then he received the call from Germany. He immediately began negotiating the surrender of Kandahar with local Taliban leaders and moved into the compound formerly occupied by Taliban supreme leader Mullah Mohammad Omar.

At ceremonies in late December in Kabul, attended by the Iranian and Pakistani foreign ministers, Karzai and his cabinet were sworn in before a gathering of representatives from most of Afghanistan's ethnic and tribal groups. In his address Karzai spoke in both Pashtu and Dari and wore an Uzbek robe. Behind the platform hung an enormous portrait of the late Tajik leader Ahmad Shah Masoud. The few women present—including two cabinet members—wore head scarfs, not burqas. A smiling Rabbani embraced Karzai and wished him success. (STEPHEN SEGO)

Koizumi, Junichiro

In 2001 the Liberal Democratic Party (LDP), which had dominated Japan's politics since 1955, experienced an intraparty revolt. Unpopular Prime Minister Yoshiro Mori had been selected by backroom party barons, and LDP members and local legislators demanded that the next party president be chosen by the rank and file. Under pressure, Mori resigned on April 6. The candidate favoured to succeed him was 59-year-old Junichiro Koizumi, who was a longtime member of the Diet (parliament) but had only limited cabinet experience and national exposure as a politician. In fact, Koizumi ranked second in most public opinion polls behind a popular woman, Makiko Tanaka (*q.v.*), who eventually withdrew as a candidate.

Koizumi subsequently opened a whirlwind campaign. With his mop of gray-flecked hair and trendy wardrobe, the new candidate was an interesting and charismatic presence on television and one who proved especially appealing to women. He spoke in a positive fashion. His campaign slogan, "Saa! kaeyo . . . " ("Well! Let's go back . . . [to prosperity]"), was seen on posters all over the country. Among other proposals, Koizumi advocated economic reform as a means of solving Japan's towering debt. He urged that pressure be applied to banks, whose nonperforming loans had risen by 15% during the previous year. He did relatively well in his appeals to voters in urban areas, where the LDP had traditionally managed only slim support.

In the party primaries, Koizumi won significant majorities. On April 24 he was elected president of the LDP by a sizable margin. Two days later he was confirmed by the Diet as the nation's 87th prime minister.

Koizumi was born on Jan. 8, 1942, in Yokosuka, Kanagawa prefecture, Japan. He was a member of an established political family; both his father and grandfather served in the Diet. Koizumi graduated from Keio University, Tokyo, with a degree in economics. While he was a graduate student at the London School of Economics, his father died; Koizumi returned to Japan and ran for the Diet himself but lost. He ran again three years later, however, and was successful, and he thereafter was reelected to the Diet 10 consecutive times.

Since Koizumi's confirmation by the Diet as prime minister was made possible by a strategic alliance between the LDP and a number of smaller parties, the new prime minister's cabinet was quite unusual. It included members of the alliance parties but relatively few representatives of the powerful factions that had long dominated the LDP. For the first time in Japan's history, five women were given portfolios, including Tanaka, who became the first woman to be named foreign minister. (ARDATH W. BURKS)

Koons, Jeff

In the summer of 2001, the completed paintings from American artist Jeff Koons's much-anticipated and ongoing series of works were exhibited to great acclaim at the Kunsthaus in Bregenz, Austria. They represented his most ambitious project, *Celebration,* an extensive series of large-scale paintings and sculptures that had occupied him since 1993 and that included canvases and sculptural works depicting popular recognizable imagery, notably children's

An exuberant Jeff Koons

Reinhard Kaufhold/Berliner Verlag

toys, snack foods, or a colourful pile of Play-Doh set against a Mylar-silver background.

Koons was born on Jan. 21, 1955, in York, Pa. After studying at the Art Institute of Chicago and the Maryland Institute College of Art, he moved to New York City in 1976. His career as a commodities trader on Wall Street helped fund his artistic endeavours, which in the beginning involved the purchase of consumer goods and the repositioning of them as art objects. Perhaps more than any of his contemporaries in the New York art world of the 1980s, Koons and his art embodied the flashy materialism and technique of appropriation that were associated with that period; for Koons, however, it was a matter of context. One of his first series consisted of brand-new vacuum cleaners placed in glass cases, lit by fluorescent lights, and showcased like precious objects or cultural specimens.

He followed with *Equilibrium Tanks*—ordinary aquariums filled with water in which basketballs were suspended. Many visitors to his exhibits, in addition to critics, dismissed Koons as a fraud, declaring him and his work facile at best and insincere, talentless, and totally corrupt at worst. These opinions were fostered in part because of the atelier of assistants and fabricators who performed much of the labour involved in making a "Jeff Koons." Koons, however, viewed his work in an almost moral dimension; as he explained in a 1997 interview, "I have the need to maintain a spiritual trust in the work, so if somebody is viewing it they will never feel let down."

The provocative nature of his work reached its high point when Koons first showed his controversial *Made in Heaven* series at the Venice Biennale in 1990. This group of works included small glass sculptures and numerous photographic tableaux of Koons and Ilona Staller, the Italian porn star better known as Cicciolina, engaging in sexual acts. A combination of kitsch, theatricality, and explicit sexuality, the works were intended by the artist to celebrate his love for Cicciolina, whom he married in 1991. The couple produced a son, Ludwig, but separated in 1992.

Koons's work was also playful at times, conveying an almost childlike innocence. After *Made in Heaven,* he created a series of three-dimensional brightly painted ceramic figures of dogs and cats and porcelain bouquets of flowers. His monumental sculpture *Puppy* was an example of his desire to create archetypal images that would be understood by everyone. The 12-m (40-ft)-high puppy covered with many thousands of live flowering plants was unveiled in 1992 in Arolsen, Ger., and was later shown in Bilbao, Spain, and it most recently was displayed at Rockefeller Center, New York City, in 2000. *Celebration* signaled that a new, mature phase was under way in Koons's career. (MEGHAN DAILEY)

Kufuor, John

On Jan. 7, 2001, Ghanaian politician John Kufuor of the New Patriotic Party (NPP) began his first term as president of Ghana. His inauguration marked the first peaceful transfer of power between democratically elected governments since Ghanaian independence in 1957.

John Kofi Agyekum Kufuor was born on Dec. 8, 1938, in Kumasi, Ghana's second largest city and the traditional capital of the Asante people. He was the 7th of 10 children and the son of Nana Kwadwo Agyekum, an Asante royal, and Nana Ama Dapaah, a queen mother. Kufuor was educated at Prempeh College, Kumasi, and in Great Britain. He was called to the bar in 1961 at Lincoln's Inn, London, and then studied at the University of Oxford, where he earned (1964) a master's degree in philosophy, politics, and economics.

After completing his education, Kufuor returned to Ghana and launched his political career. In 1967 he became chief legal officer and town clerk for the city of Kumasi. By 1969 he was a member of Parliament and deputy foreign minister in the government of Kofi Busia. After Busia was overthrown in 1972, Kufuor spent several years as a businessman in the private sector. During Ghana's transition back to democracy in 1979, Kufuor returned to public life. He was a member of the assembly that drafted the constitution of the third republic, and he was elected to Parliament in 1979, serving as deputy minority parliamentary leader. After Jerry Rawlings overthrew the government in late 1981, Kufuor stayed on as Rawlings's secretary for local government. He resigned less than a year later, however, expressing his disappointment with the Rawlings regime.

Kufuor spent the rest of the decade as a private citizen until Ghana returned to democratic politics in 1992. He helped found the NPP and in 1996 became the party's candidate for president. Though Kufuor lost to Rawlings in the national elections that year, the NPP nominated him again to stand for the 2000 elections. Running on a platform that emphasized improving the Ghanaian economy and educational system and capitalizing on the mood of voters who were ready for a change in leadership, Kufuor won the election by capturing 57% of the vote in a runoff.

He spent his first year in office concentrating his efforts on the national economy. Though unemployment and inflation remained high, the national currency stabilized, and investment in the country increased. (AMY SETTERGREN)

Landry, Bernard

Bernard Landry was sworn in as Quebec's 28th prime minister (premier) on March 8, 2001. Changes in the leadership of the separatist Parti Québécois (PQ) following the defeat of the province's 1995 referendum on sovereignty had helped bring Landry to the head of the government. The new prime minister's goals for Quebec were clear and uncompromising: independence combined with an economic union with the rest of Canada. Landry asserted that Quebec was more than a "distinct society" within Canada; it was a nation that deserved to be recognized as a state. Only statehood, he believed, would allow Quebec to fulfill its destiny as a French-language community in North America.

Landry was born on March 9, 1937, near Joliette, Que. He studied law and economics in Montreal and Paris. In the 1970s he joined the PQ, a movement committed to winning independence for Quebec. The PQ came to power in the province in 1976, and Landry was elected to the legislature. He rose rapidly through a number of cabinet posts to become Quebec's minister of finance.

In 1985 the PQ—and Landry—lost office, but nine years later the party was returned to power, and Landry resumed his former position as minister of finance. He was also appointed deputy prime minister, a post that made him second in command of the provincial administration. He threw himself into the important task of reviving the Quebec economy, which had been weakened by years of political uncertainty. He also saw the need to restore a sound basis to Quebec's public finances. Both these tasks were essential, he argued, to give credibility to Quebec's claims of statehood. His efforts were crowned with success when he balanced the books of the provincial government in 1999 for the first time in many years.

Observers expected Landry to face some tough challenges in his mission to secure an independent Quebec. In particular, he had to contend with the province's English-speaking residents and immigrants, who were strongly opposed to separation. Overall popular support for independence had been falling steadily since the 1995 referendum and by 2001 stood at about 40%. Landry had also developed a reputation for being short-tempered and outspoken. Whether he could placate his opponents and revive a flagging Quebec nationalism was open to question. Another referendum would have to be held in order to win the right to negotiate independence, and Landry made it clear that a vote would take place only when conditions were ripe for the referendum's success. By year's end it was still too early to assess whether Landry would become the first head of an independent Quebec. (DAVID M.L. FARR)

Lane, Nathan

American actor Nathan Lane, no stranger to plaudits for his abilities as a performer, reaped new praise in 2001 for his masterfully hilarious turn as con man Max Bialystock in Mel Brooks's blockbuster Broadway musical comedy *The Producers.* For his indefatigable effort he was rewarded with his second Tony Award for best performance by a leading actor in a musical. Brooks said he considered Lane "God's gift to Broadway."

Lane, born Joseph Lane on Feb. 3, 1956, in Jersey City, N.J., discovered his flair for musical comedy when he appeared in a high-school production of *No, No, Nanette,* and following graduation he embarked on a career in theatre. Among his early productions was a dinner-theatre staging of *Guys and Dolls,* in which he played Nathan Detroit, and when he was about to join Actors' Equity and learned that there was already a Joe Lane in the membership, he named himself after that character. He moved to New York City in the late 1970s, appeared in some Off-Broadway

AP/Wide World Photos

productions, and—in addition to taking odd jobs to help support himself—put together a comedy act with another actor, Patrick Stark. Sent to Los Angeles, the team, known as Stark and Lane, spent about two and a half years performing in nightclubs and as the opening act at concerts before Lane returned to New York. He then had a part in a short-lived 1982 television sitcom, *One of the Boys,* and shortly thereafter was cast in a Broadway production of *Present Laughter.* Such plays as *Love* and *She Stoops to Conquer* (both in 1984) followed, and in 1987 Lane made his motion picture debut in *Ironweed.* An Off-Broadway role in *The Lisbon Traviata* (1989) attracted critical praise, as did his performance in *Lips Together, Teeth Apart* (1991) and the film *Frankie and Johnny* (1991). In 1992 he reprised his role in *Guys and Dolls,* this time in a dream-fulfilling run on Broadway. The following year Lane's performance in *Laughter on the 23rd Floor* was singled out as exceptional, and he further charmed audiences with his voicing of the meerkat Timon in the animated film *The Lion King* (1994), his performance in the play *Love! Valour! Compassion!* (1994), and his role as the drag queen Albert in the movie *The Birdcage* (1996). Lane then went on to play the lead character Pseudolus in a Broadway revival of *A Funny Thing Happened on the Way to the Forum* (1996), a performance that garnered him his first Tony Award. In 1999 he starred in the TV series *George and Martha,* and in 2000 he appeared onstage in *The Man Who Came to Dinner* as well as in TV productions of that play and of *Laughter on the 23rd Floor.* (BARBARA WHITNEY)

Lewis, Ray

A year that began with two weeks in jail on a charge of murder ended in triumph for Baltimore Ravens middle linebacker Ray Lewis, who on Jan. 28, 2001, led his team to a convincing 34–7 victory over the New York Giants in Super Bowl XXXV in Tampa, Fla. Lewis was named the game's Most Valuable Player and was also voted the National Football League's (NFL's) Defensive Player of the Year.

One year earlier, on Jan. 31, 2000, Lewis and several friends attended a post-Super Bowl party at a nightclub in Atlanta, Ga., and as the party was breaking up, a fight erupted outside the club. When it was over, two men, Richard Lollar and Jacinth Baker, had been stabbed to death. Lewis was seen driving away from the fight, and he and two companions, Joseph Sweeting and Reginald Oakley, were charged with the murders. During a four-week trial in the spring of 2000, the charge was dropped against Lewis, who pleaded guilty to misdemeanour obstruction of justice and testified against Sweeting and Oakley. The NFL later fined Lewis $250,000; Sweeting and Oakley were subsequently acquitted of the murder charges.

Ray Anthony Lewis was born on May 15, 1975, in Bartow, Fla. After starring in several sports in high school, he enrolled at the University of Miami, Fla., where he became a middle linebacker and was named to the Freshman All-America team. In his junior year, his last at the university, Lewis finished the season with a team-high 160 tackles and earned first-string All-America honours. After his first season with the Ravens in 1996, he gained recognition as a member of the NFL's all-rookie team. In 1997 he led the league in tackles with 210 and played in the Pro Bowl. Lewis again competed in the Pro Bowl in 1998, and in 1999 he led the NFL with 198 tackles.

In the days leading up to Super Bowl XXXV, Lewis bristled at relentless questions from reporters about the brawl in which Lollar and Baker were killed, and he vowed to take his frustrations out on the field. Spearheading a defense that forced five turnovers and held the Giants to a mere 152 yd on offense, Lewis solidified his reputation as one of the league's best middle linebackers by making three solo tackles and deflecting four passes in the game. He also helped convince many observers that the Baltimore defense was one of the best in NFL history. (DAVID R. CALHOUN)

Lopez, Jennifer

In early 2001 American superstar Jennifer Lopez was burning up multiple entertainment charts with a number one album (*J.Lo*) and a hit movie at the box office (*The Wedding Planner*) in the same week. The multitalented Lopez was known as much for her acting and singing as for her voluptuous curves, revealing evening gowns, highly publicized romance and subsequent breakup during the year with rapper and producer Sean ("Puffy" or "P. Diddy") Combs, and later surprise marriage to dancer Cris Judd. Lopez was the highest-paid Latina actress in the history of Hollywood; she reportedly was negotiating for a fee of over $10 million for her role in the upcoming thriller *Taking Lives.*

Lopez was born on July 24, 1970, in the Bronx, New York City, to a family of Puerto Rican descent. She took dance lessons throughout her childhood and performed internationally with stage musicals, and at age 16 she made her film debut with a small role in *My Little Girl* (1986). Her television break came in 1990 when she was cast as one of the "Fly Girls," dancers who appeared on the comedy show *In Living Color.* After she left the show, she turned her focus to acting, first in a couple of short-lived television series, then in movie roles. Film success came quickly, and by 1995 she was appearing with such big-name stars as Wesley Snipes and Woody Harrelson (*Money Train*), Robin Williams (*Jack;* 1996), and Jack Nicholson (*Blood and Wine;* 1997). Lopez still remained somewhat in the periphery of the public vision, however, until she landed the lead role in *Selena* (1997), a biopic of the murdered Tejana singer. She went on to star in a number of thrillers and action dramas, including *Anaconda* and *U Turn* (both 1997), *Out of Sight* (1998), and *The Cell* (2000), and she gained widespread praise for *The Wedding Planner,* her successful first attempt at romantic comedy. That release was quickly followed by the romantic drama *Angel Eyes* in the middle of the year.

Ambitious, driven, and a self-admitted perfectionist, Lopez was not one to rest on her laurels; in 1999 she added pop artist to her list of titles with the release of her debut album *On the 6.* To the surprise of many critics, the album quickly went platinum and subsequently sold

Jeremy Piper/Getty Images

J.Lo

over eight million copies worldwide. Two years later her second album, *J.Lo,* sold more than 272,000 copies in its first week. By mid-2001 Lopez had a number of films in the works, and there were plans for her to star in and produce specials for television and to develop a sitcom. She also announced that she would launch a clothing line with the help of Andy Hilfiger, which would be available in retail stores by the year's end. (SANDRA LANGENECKERT)

Loyrette, Henri

On March 28, 2001, the French government announced the appointment of Henri Loyrette, head of the Orsay Museum, to be the new director of the Louvre Museum. The 48-year-old arts administrator and historian thus moved across the Seine River on April 14 to take on the responsibility of running the national museum of France, the largest in the country and one of the largest and most important in Europe. He replaced the retiring Pierre Rosenberg, who had been associated with the Louvre for nearly 40 years and who had been its director since 1994. Not only was Loyrette one of the youngest persons ever to head the Louvre, but it was also notable that he had not risen through the ranks at the institution, which was the normal path of advancement to the top.

Loyrette was born on May 31, 1952, in Neuilly-sur-Seine, a suburb of Paris. He received a university degree in history and in 1975–77 studied in Rome at the Academy of France. Upon his return to France in 1978, he was appointed curator at the Orsay, where he remained for 23 years, becoming director in 1994. The Orsay boasted the largest collection of 19th-century art of any French museum, and Loyrette, whose specialties were 19th-century painting and architecture, organized a number of successful exhibitions there. These included exhibitions on Edgar Degas, on whom Loyrette was an expert, on the caricaturist Honoré Daumier, and on the still lifes of Édouard Manet, as well as on lesser-known European artists. Loyrette also organized exhibitions on the origins of Impressionism and on the relation of Impressionism and Art Nouveau, in addition to the 1987–88 exhibition "Chicago, Birth of a Metropolis." Loyrette's writings included three books on Degas, as well as works on a number of other 19th-century artists, on Gustave Eiffel, and on Marcel Proust's views on modern art.

Loyrette held important positions in several French cultural organizations, and he had been widely honoured. He served as secretary-general of the French Committee on Art History and was a member of the board of directors of a number of institutions, including the National Graduate School of Decorative Arts and the Cité de la Musique, an interactive museum in Paris. When he was elected to the Académie des Beaux-Arts in 1997, he was its youngest member.

As the new director of the Louvre, Loyrette faced the kinds of problems museums throughout the world were grappling with, including ensuring sources of adequate funding. This was particularly acute at the Louvre, where the large numbers of visitors put enormous demands on the staff and physical plant. Nonetheless, Loyrette, with his distinguished background and experience, appeared to be a natural fit for the position. (ROBERT RAUCH)

MacLeod, Alistair

For his long-awaited first novel, *No Great Mischief* (2000), Canadian author Alistair MacLeod won the 2001 International IMPAC Dublin Literary Award; a superbly crafted work, the book chronicled the lives of several generations of Scottish immigrants on Cape Breton Island in northeastern Nova Scotia. MacLeod, a meticulous stylist who wrote *No Great Mischief* over the course of 13 years, was the first Canadian writer to receive the $172,000 award, the world's richest literary prize for fiction. Until the award was announced, MacLeod was largely unknown outside his native country, despite his having earlier published two critically acclaimed short-story collections. Fellow Canadian author Michael Ondaatje once called him "one of the great undiscovered writers of our time." Following the publication of *No Great Mischief*, the *Toronto Globe and Mail* went farther, describing MacLeod as "the greatest living Canadian writer."

MacLeod was born in North Battleford, Sask., on July 20, 1936. His parents were natives of Cape Breton, and when MacLeod was 10 years old, he returned with his family to the island. He worked as a miner and logger before earning a teacher's certificate from Nova Scotia Teachers College. He went on to obtain his B.A. and B.Ed. from St. Francis Xavier University, Antigonish, N.S., in 1960, his M.A. from the University of New Brunswick at Saint John, in 1961, and his Ph.D. from the University of Notre Dame in 1968. He taught at Indiana University at Fort Wayne from 1966 to 1969, then returned to Canada as a professor of English and creative writing at the University of Windsor, Ont. For many years MacLeod also taught writing at the Banff (Alta.) Centre for Continuing Education. He was named professor emeritus at the University of Windsor in 2000.

MacLeod's writing career began in 1968 with the publication of his short story "The Boat," which was included in the 1969 anthology *The Best American Short Stories*. Many critics acknowledged him as a master of the short-story form after the appearance of his first collection, *The Lost Salt Gift of Blood*, in 1976, and a second volume of stories, *As Birds Bring Forth the Sun* (1986), further solidified his reputation. MacLeod's fiction dwelled mostly on the working people of Cape Breton—miners, loggers, fishermen, and small farmers—and sensitively explored family relationships as well as examining the relationship of the islanders to their Celtic past.

MacLeod's literary oeuvre was notable for its smallness. Together, *The Lost Salt Gift of Blood* and *As Birds Bring Forth the Sun* included only 16 stories, and each book took some 10 years to write. His lean output might be explained by his admitted perfectionism; MacLeod revised constantly and read each of his sentences aloud in his belief that "the ear is a good editor." In part to satisfy the growing numbers of admirers of his work, he followed up *No Great Mischief* with *Island* (2000), which collected all of his previously published stories and included one new one. (SHERMAN HOLLAR)

Mami, Cheb

In 2001 internationally renowned Algerian *rai* singer Cheb Mami continued his efforts to cultivate an American fan base. Before his 1999 collaboration with British pop singer Sting on the smash-hit single "Desert Rose," Mami, a popular figure in Europe and North Africa, had been virtually unknown in the U.S. The success of "Desert Rose," however, propelled Mami into the spotlight; he was a guest on *The Tonight Show* and *The Late Show with David Letterman*, performed with Sting at the 2000 Grammy Awards, and saw his celebrated song used in a Jaguar television commercial. In 2001 Mami performed with Sting at the Super Bowl and embarked on a seven-city U.S. tour following the July release of *Dellali*, his seventh album.

The performer known as the "prince of *rai*" was born Khelifati Muhammad on July 11, 1966, in Saida, Alg. He initially followed in the occupational footsteps of his father and took a job as a welder. At the age of 12, Mami began singing in the streets and at weddings. In 1982 he placed second in a radio talent contest and was approached by record producers. Under a local record label, the newly discovered Cheb Mami (Arabic for "the young mourner") released cassettes that sold well but made little money. In 1985 he performed in the nearby port city of Oran (the birthplace of *rai* music) at a festival that had been organized by Khaled, the "king of *rai*." The frank, often racy lyrics of *rai* music coupled with what some believed were undertones of political protest made *rai* a controversial art form amid the growing volatility of the Algerian political scene during the 1980s. As a result, many of the genre's artists began to leave the country in fear for their lives. Like many others, Mami moved to France, where he found an enthusiastic audience among the second-generation North Africans living there.

In the years following the move, Mami became a French club favourite before emerging as an international star. Though his style was an eclectic fusion of reggae, funk, salsa, hip-hop, and North African rhythms, *rai*'s distinct flavour was apparent. Mami's first album, *Prince of Raï*, was released in 1989 and was followed by *Let Me Raï* (1990), *Saida* (1995), *Let Me Cry* (1998), *Douni el Bladi* (1998), *Meli Meli* (1999), and *Dellali*. (SHANDA SILER)

McCartney, Stella

When Stella McCartney was asked by a London fashion critic why the clothes she designed for French fashion label Chloé held so much appeal for young women, she quipped, "I know what makes chicks tick." McCartney's words were validated in April 2001 when, after protracted negotiations with the Gucci Group, Gucci chairman Domenico de Sole announced that the Italian luxury goods conglomerate would provide at least 51% of the funds to back a new design label produced under McCartney's name.

McCartney, born in 1972 in London, was the daughter of Sir Paul McCartney (a former Beatle) and Linda McCartney, a noted photographer and animal rights activist. She graduated (1995) from Central Saint Martin's College of Art and Design, London, and rose quickly to the forefront of the international fashion world. She was hired in 1997 by the Vendome Group to revitalize its 47-year-old design label, Chloé. McCartney replaced legendary designer Karl Lagerfeld, who expressed skepticism about her design skill. "I think they should have taken a big name," he said. "They did, but in music, not fashion." Indeed, McCartney's design experience had been limited. Prior to her formal schooling, she worked for a time at the French couture house Christian Lacroix and as an intern at

Mary McCartney Donald

Stella McCartney—knows what makes chicks tick

British *Vogue*. Though she produced a blockbuster graduation show that featured supermodel Naomi Campbell, one of McCartney's tutors admitted that she was "a very hardworking girl, but she did not really stand out in her year."

McCartney did, however, succeed in establishing Chloé as a desirable brand; its sales reportedly increased fivefold. Her first collection, featuring lacy petticoat skirts and dainty camisoles, silenced critics, and her 2001 Paris romantic offerings—sexy silk pants set off by midriff-baring tops, signature body-hugging jeans paired with showier tunic tops or jackets, and fake-fur coats and vests splashed with jeweled appliqués—cemented her reputation. McCartney also built the brand a celebrity cult following. This in part was due to her high-profile customers and friends, notably Madonna (for whom she designed a wedding dress), Kate Hudson (whom McCartney outfitted for the 2001 Academy Award ceremonies), actresses Liv Tyler and Gwyneth Paltrow, and model Kate Moss.

Rumours that McCartney had met with Tom Ford, the Gucci Group's design director, began circulating early in 2000. Some suspected that she would take over design at Gucci, because Ford had been named design director of Yves Saint Laurent. McCartney's position as a staunch animal rights activist (shortly after her mother's death, she made a video supporting animal rights for People for the Ethical Treatment of Animals) prevented her from signing a deal, however. She refused to work with leather or fur—both central design elements for Gucci. In hiring McCartney, Gucci both acquired the design talent that it had long sought and, it seemed, concluded that an animal-friendly label could potentially turn a profit. (BRONWYN COSGRAVE)

Middelhoff, Thomas

Could signal success in publishing be translated into the music business as well? In 2001 Thomas Middelhoff, the dynamic chairman and CEO of Bertelsmann AG, the German global media giant, was betting that it would.

Middelhoff was born in Düsseldorf, Ger., on May 11, 1953. He earned an MBA (Westphalian Wilhelm University of Münster) and studied marketing before joining his family's textile business in 1984. He took his first position with a Bertelsmann subsidiary in 1986 and moved up the corporate ranks quickly.

Renowned for his high-tech savvy, Middelhoff met America Online (AOL) founder Steve Case in 1994 and was so impressed with the Internet service provider that he urged his company to invest millions in AOL and its European counterpart. The value of that investment soared, as did Middelhoff's standing with Bertelsmann. These and other successes propelled Middelhoff, then aged 45, into Bertelsmann's CEO position in 1998. Shortly thereafter, Bertelsmann sold its interests in AOL and AOL Europe for nearly $9 billion and turned to investing in other on-line technologies, specifically the Internet file-sharing company Napster, Inc.

At the same time Middelhoff was making a name for himself, Bertelsmann was accelerating its global strategy to acquire publishing houses and other media assets throughout the world. Key subsidiaries included newspaper and magazine publisher Gruner+Jahr, American book publishers Bantam Doubleday Dell and Random House, science and business publisher BertelsmannSpringer, and BMG Entertainment (which owned more than 200 record labels in more than 50 countries, including Arista and RCA in the United States). In February 2001 the firm gained a controlling interest in the Luxembourg-based RTL Group, Europe's largest producer of radio, television, and movie content and operator of 18 radio and 24 TV stations across the continent. Still, American markets accounted for much of the company's international growth, and Bertelsmann chose New York City—where Middelhoff spent roughly half his time—as the seat of its book-publishing operations in 1999. In mid-2001 Bertelsmann enjoyed annual revenues of €16.5 billion (about $15 billion).

As CEO, Middelhoff set out to shed unprofitable businesses (such as AOL and pay television), reinvigorate traditional ones (European book clubs), and, principally, make Bertelsmann a leading provider of content. Middelhoff's Napster gamble surprised many observers. Napster provided software that allowed individuals to swap electronic music files without paying for them, and the service spent much of 2000 mired in legal battles brought on by music companies. To the chagrin of Bertelsmann executives, however, Middelhoff came down in support of Napster, assuming that users would be willing to pay for the legal acquisition of music files over the Internet. In July Konrad Hilbers, a Bertelsmann executive, was named CEO of Napster. Middelhoff showed his commitment to the agreement by anteing up $50 million intended to help Napster comply with copyright laws. Early signs, however, suggested that Napster's customers might not be willing to pay the price of copyrights, and they turned to competing companies such as FastTrack, Gnutella, and Audiogalaxy. At year's end the chips were still out on Middelhoff's bet. (SARAH FORBES ORWIG)

Morris, Mark

American dancer-choreographer Mark Morris had special reason to celebrate the 20th anniversary season of his company, the Mark Morris Dance Group, in 2001—the opening of the troupe's first permanent American home, the Mark Morris Dance Center in Brooklyn, N.Y. The $6 million building, conveniently across the street from the company's usual home performing venue, the Brooklyn Academy of Music (BAM), included such amenities as offices, kitchens, dressing rooms and showers, and rehearsal studios that could double as performance spaces for smaller, more experimental works. Having such a sumptuous home was a unique accomplishment in the world of American modern dance.

Morris was born on Aug. 29, 1956, in Seattle, Wash., and at age eight, after attending a performance by the José Greco flamenco company, decided to become a Spanish dancer. He took classes, began performing professionally at age 11, joined the Koleda Folk Ensemble at 13, and began choreographing professionally at 14. He spent part of 1974 studying in Spain and in 1976 moved to New York City, where he danced in the companies of such choreographers as Eliot Feld, Lar Lubovitch, Laura Dean, and Hannah Kahn. In 1980 Morris launched his company when he and 10 fellow dancers presented a concert of five of his works, and its reputation was solidified at BAM's 1984 Next Wave Festival. Only two years later Morris won a Guggenheim fellowship, was choreographing for major ballet companies, began taking his company on tour, and was the subject of an hour-long public television special. In 1988 Morris accepted an invitation to become the resident choreographer of the Théâtre Royal de la Monnaie in Brussels, expanded the membership of the company, and renamed it the Monnaie Dance Group/Mark Morris. Even at home many considered him the "bad boy of modern dance" and especially did not appreciate or understand his outrageous humour or his more innovative works, and the Belgians, not accustomed to his style of dance, were even less receptive. Nonetheless, during his three years in Belgium, Morris choreographed some of his most acclaimed and enduring creations, including *L'Allegro, il penseroso ed il moderato* (1988), his first full-evening work and the subject of a photo and essay book by that name in 2001; *Dido and Aeneas* (1989), a dance version of the opera, in which Morris danced the parts of both Dido and the Sorceress; and *The Hard Nut* (1991), his version of *The Nutcracker.* He was awarded a MacArthur fellowship in 1991. While Morris was out of the U.S., Mikhail Baryshnikov and the White Oak Dance Project kept Morris's works before the American public.

Following the company's return to the U.S. in 1991, Morris created an average of five or six new works each year for his company—including *Beautiful Day* (1992), *The Office* (1994), *Somebody's Coming to See Me Tonight* (1995), and *Four Saints in Three Acts* (2000), his version of the Gertrude Stein–Virgil Thomson opera—and by 2001 had choreographed more than 100 numbers. Noted for his musicality, he also created classical ballets for numerous companies, including the American Ballet Theatre, the San Francisco Ballet, and Les Grands Ballets Canadiens. The onetime enfant terrible of modern dance had become a setter of standards and a solid member of the dance establishment. (BARBARA WHITNEY)

Mueller, Robert

Just days after taking the oath of office (Sept. 4, 2001) as director of the Federal Bureau of Investigation, Robert Mueller was confronted with the daunting task of assigning some 4,000 FBI agents to pursue thousands of leads and gather intelligence relating to the activities and identities of the perpetrators behind the September 11 terrorist attacks in the U.S. In the wake of the national crisis, Mueller sent agents to at least 30 countries, but it soon became clear that more investigators fluent in

Emilie Sommer/AFP Worldwide

Arabic, Farsi, and Pashtu were needed by the FBI; he appealed to the general population to contact the agency via a hotline if anyone was fluent in any of these languages. Mueller had little time to recover from the major surgery he had undergone in early August.

In his years investigating everything from street-corner crimes to terrorist bombings and bank fraud, Mueller had established himself as a top-notch law enforcer who emphasized the government's responsibility "to protect its citizens from criminal harm within the framework of the Constitution." Pres. George W. Bush characterized him as a man of "fidelity, bravery, and integrity." The nation's top crime-fighting organization was sorely in need of such a leader; after years of critical missteps, the FBI had come to be identified by its failures rather than its successes. These included the disappearance of computer laptops and firearms, the tardiness in identifying FBI agent Robert Hanssen as a Russian spy, and the mishandling of evidence in the Oklahoma City bombing case that came to light only days before convicted bomber Timothy McVeigh was to be put to death.

Robert Swan Mueller III was born Aug. 7, 1944, in New York City and was raised in Philadelphia. He earned some ribbing among fellow law enforcers, who—because of the "III" after his name—called him "Bobby Three Sticks." After attending St. Paul's, a private school in Concord, N.H., Mueller studied at Princeton University (B.A., 1966). He served as a Marine Corps officer for three years, including one year in Vietnam, and was awarded the Bronze Star, the Purple Heart, and the Vietnamese Cross of Gallantry. He next pursued a master's degree in international studies from New York University and earned his law degree from the University of Virginia School of Law.

Though Mueller had worked in private law practices in San Francisco, Boston, and Washington, D.C., he left each position for work in public law enforcement. As the assistant attorney general for the criminal division of the Department of Justice (1990–93), he supervised the investigation of the Pan Am Flight 103 bombing. Among his various other appointments, he served as U.S. attorney in two regions: the District of Massachusetts (Boston, 1986–87) and the Northern District of California (San Francisco, 1998–2001). In San Francisco Mueller improved performance by reassigning supervisors, implementing tough new rules, and emphasizing productivity. Despite the fact that he sometimes stepped on toes, California's leading politicians were impressed. Though his no-nonsense style was unlike the star-quality public persona the White House sought for its new FBI director, Mueller was catapulted to the centre of international affairs following the September terrorist attacks. (SARAH FORBES ORWIG)

Newton, Helmut

A larger-than-life nude photograph of a statuesque female model overshadowed the entrance to the spring show at the Barbican Gallery in London in 2001. It was one of 200 images by German-born fashion photographer Helmut Newton, shown on the occasion of his 80th birthday, and it loomed large over visitors to the exhibit, which had previously been mounted at the New National Gallery in Berlin. Similarly, the retrospective proved that Newton himself loomed large; he had cast a shadow over the field of fashion photography since the 1960s and had influenced scores of camera buffs and advertising campaigns with his provocative photos, which explored the eroticism of glamour. Sex and power were constant themes in his work, with hints of violence and fetish that earned his cold, sophisticated photos the label "porno-chic."

Newton was born on Oct. 31, 1920, in Berlin to well-to-do Jewish parents. He came of age during the bourgeois decadence of Berlin society in the 1930s. As a teenager, Newton took up photography and set up homemade fashion shoots. Dropping out of school at age 16, he became apprenticed to the fashion photographer Yva (Else Simon). In 1938, when his family fled the Nazi regime and moved to South America, Newton went his separate way, eventually settling in Australia, where in 1947 he became a citizen. The following year he married June Browne, who later would also find success as a photographer under the name Alice Springs. Initially, Newton struggled as a freelance in Melbourne, but by the late 1950s he was working primarily for high-fashion magazines in Paris, where he lived from 1961 to 1981.

Newton made his name on the pages of *Vogue, Elle, Marie-Claire, Jardin des modes, Stern,* and *Nova,* with carefully composed voyeuristic images known for their staged fin de siècle settings and sexually charged content. The shock of a heart attack in 1971 caused him to reassess his career, and from that point forward he began exercising greater creative control over his shoots, helping to establish French *Vogue* as the height of fashion photography in the 1970s. Sometimes controversial, his sensationalistic images prompted attacks from feminists as well as from disparaging art critics when his work began appearing in museums. In 1981 he moved to Monte-Carlo and began photographing nudes; his oversized images appeared in the book *Big Nudes* (1982). Newton was also sought after for his celebrity poses, which were collected in *Portraits* (1987). Other published works included *White Women* (1976), *Sleepless Nights* (1978), *World Without Men* (1984), and *SUMO* (2000), a massive 480-page tome, which at 50 × 70 cm (20 × 27.5 in) and 30 kg (66 lb) was less a coffee-table book than a coffee table itself. (TOM MICHAEL)

Obaid, Thoraya

On Jan. 1, 2001, Thoraya Ahmed Obaid became the executive director of the United Nations Population Fund (UNFPA) and the first Saudi national to head a UN agency. The UNFPA, the largest internationally funded source of population assistance, actively promoted equality between the sexes and universal education and health care, especially better reproductive health care for women. Its campaigns to battle AIDS, expand the availability of reproductive information and services for adolescents, and end violence against women, including female genital mutilation, met with resistance in many conservative areas of the world, especially those that were reluctant to address such concomitant issues as homosexuality, teen sexuality, and women's rights. It was believed that Obaid, a Muslim woman (like her predecessor, Nafis Sadik of Pakistan), would be sensitive to Muslim concerns and serve as a role model in Muslim countries where the status of women was still low. In Saudi Arabia, for example, where women could not appear in public unless covered from head to toe, were not permitted to drive, and could not travel without written permission from male relatives, Obaid's success and visibility contributed to changes in government policy, including an agreement by the government to sign the Convention on the Elimination of All Forms of Discrimination Against Women. Indeed, the Saudi government fully supported Obaid's candidacy for the UNFPA position. Obaid herself had expressed the hope that she could, from her own personal experience, tell less-developed countries, especially in Muslim societies, that educating women, allowing them to work, and enabling them to make choices about their lives were Islamic rather than un-Islamic in nature.

Obaid was born on March 2, 1945, in Baghdad, Iraq. Her parents were devout Muslims, and they took as a literal command the instruction in the Qur'an's very first *surah*—"Read." They believed in educating their daughter as well as their sons and enrolled her in an Islamic school in Mecca, Saudi Arabia, when she was three. Because education for girls was limited in Saudi Arabia at the time, Obaid was sent in 1951 to the American College for Girls in Cairo. She later became the first Saudi woman to receive a government scholarship to study in the United States. She earned a B.A. (1966) in English literature from Mills College, Oakland, Calif., and M.A. (1968) and Ph.D. (1974) degrees from Wayne State University, Detroit. In 1975 Obaid began working for the UN Economic and Social Commission for Western Asia, and she became that agency's deputy executive secretary in 1993. In 1998 she was appointed director of the UNFPA's Division for Arab States and Europe. Her 25 years of experience at the UN and her demonstrated commitment to empowering women moved UN Secretary-General Kofi Annan to describe her as "the ideal candidate" to head the UNFPA. (AMY R. TAO)

Parker, Sarah Jessica

Although Sarah Jessica Parker struggled to define the rules of dating as Carrie Bradshaw on *Sex and the City,* the American actress knew the secrets to a successful relationship with television viewers: sex, friends, and fashion. In 2001 Parker returned for the highly anticipated fourth season of *Sex and the City,* and millions tuned in for the candid look at four friends—Bradshaw, Miranda (played by Cynthia Nixon), Samantha (Kim Cattrall), and

Trendsetter Sarah Jessica Parker
Craig Blankenhorn/Getty Images

Charlotte (Kristin Davis)—searching for Mr. Right in New York City. Broadcast on the cable channel HBO, the series offered an uncensored, humorous, and, at times, risqué look at the lives of thirtysomethings. Swearing, nudity, and graphic discussions about sex were common features, as were the cosmopolitan cocktail, Manolo Blahnik high heels, and designer fashions. At the centre was Parker, who combined comedy, sensuality, and compassion to create a character to whom single women could relate. Critics also applauded her performance, and in 2001 she won her second Golden Globe Award for best actress in a television comedy or musical series.

Parker was born on March 25, 1965, in Nelsonville, Ohio. Although her family was far from wealthy, young Sarah was encouraged to participate in the arts and took ballet and acting classes as a child. At the age of 11, Parker moved with her family to New York City so that she and her siblings could pursue careers in entertainment.

In 1978 she landed the lead role in Broadway's *Annie,* and she stayed with the musical for some three years. Other stage work followed, and in 1979 she made her film debut in *Rich Kids.* In 1982 Parker portrayed a high-school nerd in the television series *Square Pegs.* Although the show lasted only one season, it developed a cultlike following and led to several film offers for Parker, including *Footloose* (1984) and *Girls Just Want to Have Fun* (1985). Parker continued her work in the theatre, appearing in *The Heidi Chronicles* (1989), *The Substance of Fire* (1991), *Sylvia* (1995), for which she earned critical praise for her portrayal of a dog, and *How to Succeed in Business Without Really Trying* (1996), in which she appeared with her longtime boyfriend, Matthew Broderick; the couple married the following year.

In 1991 Parker's film career received a boost with her performance opposite Steve Martin as the bouncy SanDeE* in *L.A. Story.* Other movies quickly followed, notably *Honeymoon in Vegas* (1992), *Ed Wood* (1994), and *The First Wives Club* (1996), but the roles failed to establish Parker as a leading lady. That changed, however, with *Sex and the City.* Premiering in 1998, the series, inspired by the best-selling book by Candace Bushnell, brought Parker unprecedented attention. The show, however, was not without its detractors. In addition to complaints concerning the ribald nature of the show, some charged that it objectified men—Carrie's former boyfriend, for example, is known only as Mr. Big. Quite a few others, however, believed that such a role reversal in American television was long overdue. (AMY TIKKANEN)

Parsons, Timothy

Capping a career of more than 40 years in which he had established himself among the world's leading marine biologists, Canadian Timothy Parsons was named a winner of the Japan Prize in 2001. The award recognized Parsons's pioneering exploration of the complex relationships between fish and the physical, chemical, and biological aspects of their environment and the application of that new understanding to reversing the decline in fishery resources. In contrast to the traditional population-dynamics approach to fishery management, Parsons's work concentrated on the entire marine ecosystem and led to methods for nurturing the environment to help increase fish populations that had become depleted owing to overfishing and pollution. His advances helped create an alternative, holistic approach to marine conservation and management and influenced a new school of oceanographers and fishery managers. Parsons also conducted important research on the effects of pollution on the marine environment through the innovative use of mesocosms—large floating tubes of water that simulated natural ecosystems—and computer modeling.

Timothy Richard Parsons was born on Nov. 1, 1932, in Colombo, Ceylon (now Sri Lanka). He attended McGill University, Montreal, where he earned a bachelor's degree (1953), a master's degree (1955), and a doctorate (1958). He took a position as a research scientist at the Fisheries Research Board of Canada but left in 1962 for a post in the Office of Oceanography at UNESCO in Paris; he returned to the Fisheries Research Board in 1964. In 1971 Parsons joined the faculty at the University of British Columbia, where he remained until he retired to the post of professor emeritus in 1992. He also served as honorary scientist emeritus at the Institute of Ocean Sciences in Sidney, B.C.

During his career Parsons served as president of the International Association of Biological Oceanography (1976–82), won numerous awards and honours, including a fellowship of the Royal Society of Canada (1979), the Oceanographic Society of Japan Prize (1988), and the Killam Research Prize (1990). He published more than 150 works, including three textbooks.

Parsons was the first Canadian recipient of the Japan Prize, given by the Science and Technology Foundation of Japan; the award was considered comparable in stature to a Nobel Prize. (ANTHONY G. CRAINE)

Paterno, Joe

On a cool autumn day, in a small American town called State College, Pa., in an area called Happy Valley, a group of young men in plain uniforms gathered to play amateur football. This game was no small affair, especially for a bespectacled old man on the sidelines in cuffed khaki pants. That man was coach Joe Paterno of Pennsylvania State University. On that day, Oct. 27, 2001, he became the winningest football coach in major college history, and he did it in front of a jubilant home crowd in the nation's second largest college stadium. Both the size of the stadium and the success of the football program were testimony to Paterno's brilliant reign as head coach of the Penn State Nittany Lions. In the final quarter of the game, the Nittany Lions roared back from an 18-point deficit to hand Ohio State University a 29–27 loss and to give their coach his 324th career win, surpassing the record held by Paul ("Bear") Bryant of the University of Alabama.

Paterno finished the year with 327 total wins over 36 seasons. His long career sparkled with highlights, including two national championships (1982, 1986), five undefeated seasons, and five seasons with only one loss. There were also 20 victories in bowl games, 20 top-10 finishes, and 34 shutouts. The Nittany Lions were especially dominant in the 1990s, during which the team joined the Big Ten Conference and posted 97 wins with only 26 losses. Paterno saw 250 of his players advance to playing in the professional National Football League. Known for his conservative, brass-tacks approach to the game, Paterno excelled at developing first-rate linebackers, some of whom were among his 31 players named to the All-America first team.

In January 2002 Paterno became the first active coach in 20 years to receive the Amos Alonzo Stagg Award, the highest honour given by the American Football Coaches Association. A four-time winner of the association's Coach of the Year award, he was also the first coach to be named Sportsman of the Year by *Sports Illustrated* magazine (1986). Not content only to build the football program, Paterno was an advocate for academic integrity and donated millions to build up the nonsporting programs of the university.

Joseph Vincent Paterno was born on Dec. 21, 1926, in Brooklyn, N.Y., where he attended Catholic schools and played football. He served in the U.S. Army in the final year of World War II before accepting an athletic scholarship to Brown University, Providence, R.I., where he studied English literature and led the team as quarterback. Upon graduation in 1950 he intended to enroll in law school at Boston University but was lured away when his former coach at Brown, Charles ("Rip") Engle, became head coach at Penn State. After 16 years as Engle's assistant, Paterno succeeded him in 1966. (TOM MICHAEL)

Peacocke, the Rev. Canon Arthur Robert

The winner of the 2001 Templeton Prize for Progress in Religion was the Rev. Arthur Peacocke, a biochemist, theologian, and Anglican priest who had spent most of his career encouraging cooperation between science and religion. Peacocke was the sixth scientist, and the third in a row, to receive the lucrative ($1 million in 2001) award created to serve as the equivalent of a Nobel Prize for religion. Peacocke, who took part in some of the earliest work on the DNA molecule, compared the relationship between science and religion to that of the two helical strands that make up DNA. The search for intelligibility and the search for meaning, he said, are necessary, complementary approaches to answering the same questions about how things came to be. Most scientists dismissed attempts to integrate faith and science because of a lack of proof of a supreme being, but Peacocke countered that theologians had successfully used supporting evidence for their claims in the same fashion that scientists did for theirs.

Peacocke was born Nov. 29, 1924 in Watford, Eng. He received a doctorate in physical biochemistry from the University of Oxford in 1948 and during the 1950s, while working at the virus laboratory at the University of California, was part of a team that identified properties of the recently discovered DNA molecule. A self-described mild agnostic during his college years, Peacocke found himself searching for answers to questions he considered too broad for science alone to answer. He began theology studies and received a bachelor of divinity degree from the University of Birmingham, Eng., in 1971, when he was also ordained a priest in the Church of England. He took a post teaching biochemistry and theology at the University of Cambridge before returning to Oxford, where he served two terms (1985–88 and 1995–99) as director of the Ian Ramsey Centre, which promoted teaching and research in science and religion. He also founded the Science and Religion Forum (1972) and the Society of Ordained Scientists (1985). In 1993 Peacocke was made an MBE. He was the author of a number of books that examined the ties between science and religion, including *Theology for a Scientific Age* (1990) and *Paths from Science Towards God: The End of All Our Exploring* (2001).

An early adherent to the anthropic principle—the notion that the universe contains conditions ideal for the development of living beings—Peacocke concluded that a likely explanation for the existence of life was the existence of a supreme being. Advances in astronomy were shedding new light on what scientists knew about the creation of the universe; advances in genetics were forcing scientists to grapple with new ethical considerations. Peacocke maintained that it was time for science and theology to work together to draw meaning and guidance from what was being learned. (ANTHONY G. CRAINE)

Powell, Colin

On Jan. 20, 2001, the engaging former chairman of the U.S. Joint Chiefs of Staff Colin Powell—whose leadership role in the 1991 Persian Gulf War had brought him to the attention of the American public—was sworn in as U.S. secretary of state.

Born on April 5, 1937, in New York City, Colin Luther Powell was the son of Jamaican immigrants. While attending the City College of New York, Powell joined the Reserve Officers' Training Corps program and rose to become commander of the college's Army ROTC unit. After graduation in 1958, Powell was commissioned a second lieutenant in the U.S. Army, and he served two separate tours (1962–63; 1968–69) in Vietnam. He earned an M.B.A. from George Washington University in Washington, D.C., in 1971, after which he became an assistant to Frank Carlucci, the deputy director of the Office of Management and Budget. Powell later served as a battalion commander in South Korea (1973–74) and in positions at the Pentagon (1974–75). In 1975 he was promoted to the rank of colonel, and in the early 1980s he became a major general and the senior military assistant to the secretary of defense.

In 1986 Powell was appointed deputy director of the National Security Council under Carlucci, who was then Pres. Ronald Reagan's national security affairs assistant. The following year Powell succeeded Carlucci, and in early 1989 he assumed command of the Army Forces Command. In April of that year he was elevated to the rank of four-star general, and in August he was appointed chairman of the Joint Chiefs of Staff, the first African American and at age 52 the youngest person to occupy the highest post in the military.

After retiring from the army in 1993, Powell remained active in politics, helping to broker a compromise in which Haiti's military regime ceded power to elected Pres. Jean-Bertrand Aristide. Popular with broad segments of the electorate, Powell was lobbied by both the Democratic and Republican parties to run for national office. Although polls in 1995 showed Powell a formidable contender for president, he declined to run. Nonetheless, he publicly declared himself a Republican, despite his support for abortion rights and affirmative action—two issues that put him outside the Republican Party's mainstream.

As secretary of state Powell spent the early months of 2001 attempting to broker an end to hostilities between Israel and the Palestinians and to gain support for loosening the UN-imposed trade sanctions against Iraq. In June he attended a UN AIDS conference and pledged U.S. financial support for an international fund to combat the disease. Though he was scheduled to attend the UN World Conference Against Racism, which began on August 31, Powell led a U.S. boycott in response to Arab efforts to single out Israel as racist. In the wake of the September 11 terrorist attacks in the U.S., Powell focused on building international support for U.S. actions against the Taliban to force it to cease harbouring Osama bin Laden (*q.v.*), whom the U.S. blamed for the attacks. (MICHAEL I. LEVY)

Redstone, Sumner

"The words *step down,* the word *retire* . . . is not in my dictionary. I love what I'm doing. I know I'm at the top of my game." These sentiments were expressed in June 2001 by Sumner Redstone, the 78-year-old chief executive officer and chairman of the board of Viacom Inc., a media conglomerate whose holdings included, among others, Paramount Pictures, CBS, Blockbuster, Simon & Schuster, and MTV. Also in 2001, along with his executive duties, Redstone published his autobiography, *A Passion to Win,* written with Peter Knobler.

Redstone was born Sumner Rothstein on May 27, 1923, in Boston. He graduated with a B.A. degree from Harvard University in 1944. Because he had become fluent in Japanese, he was chosen to join a U.S. Army team charged

Statesman Colin Powell, in Mali

AP/Wide World Photos

with cracking secret Japanese military and diplomatic communication codes during the remainder of World War II. After the war he entered Harvard Law School, from which he graduated in 1947. During the next few years, he worked for the U.S. Court of Appeals and served as an instructor at the University of San Francisco and as special assistant to U.S. Attorney General Tom Clark. In 1951 he became a partner in the Washington, D.C., law firm of Ford, Bergson, Adams, Borkland, & Redstone.

Stating that "litigation is generally offensive to me," Redstone in 1954 returned to Boston and began working for Northeast Theater Corp., a motion picture-exhibition business that his father had established. By 1964 he had expanded Northeast Theater to 59 screens in the Boston area, and three years later he became president and chief executive officer of the firm, which was renamed National Amusements. During the next few years, he continued to increase the company's number of movie theatres. Although prosperous and successful, he concluded that the real money and power in the movie business was in Hollywood. After seeing the film *Star Wars* in 1977, he began buying shares in Twentieth Century Fox, the movie's producer, and he later sold them at a large profit.

In 1979 Redstone suffered severe burns in a hotel fire in Boston. At the time, he had increased the number of National Amusements theatres to 180. With time to reflect during his recovery, he began to think, however, that his ambitions had been too limited. In 1987 he purchased Viacom, which was then a somewhat obscure television company. With that acquisition he became the largest producer of programs for cable television subscribers, owning Showtime, the Movie Channel, MTV, five network-affiliated TV stations, and syndication rights to *The Cosby Show*, one of the most popular programs on television; at the same time, his movie-theatre chain had expanded to 1,300 screens.

In 1994 Redstone added to his empire by winning hard-fought battles to acquire Paramount Communications and Blockbuster, and in 2000 he merged Viacom with CBS to create the second largest media company in the world, behind only AOL Time Warner.

(DAVID R. CALHOUN)

Reza, Yasmina

During the 2000–01 theatre season, French playwright and actress Yasmina Reza seemed to be everywhere. Her hit plays were being staged throughout the world, and she herself took a role in a Paris production. Though best known for *Art*, she was enjoying renewed attention for her latest stage work, *Trois versions de la vie*. It had its premiere in Vienna in October 2000 and opened the following month in Paris, with the author in the cast, and in December in London under the title *Life × 3*. The work showed a ticklish situation—a couple arriving a day early for a dinner party—working itself out in three ways.

Reza, born on May 1, 1959, in Paris, was the daughter of Jewish parents who had immigrated to France. Her father was an Iranian born in Moscow, and her mother was from Budapest. The father was an engineer and businessman who was also a pianist, and her mother was a violinist. The daughter studied at the University of Paris X, Nanterre, and at the drama school of Jacques Lecoq before working as an actress. Her first plays, both winners of a Molière Award, were *Conversations After a Burial* (1987), involving death and sex, and *Winter Crossing* (1990). It was *Art*, however, which premiered in 1994, that brought her wide notice. In the play three friends quarrel over a work of modern art and thereby show just how fragile friendship can be. The play was in production on major stages worldwide virtually continuously after its opening. It won Molière Awards for best author, play, and production, Olivier and *Evening Standard* awards in London, and a Tony Award in New York as best play. Another hit, *The Unexpected Man* (1995), was a two-hander set on a train. Following long monologues by a male author and his female seatmate and fan, the play ends with a brief dialogue between the two that centres on people's need for one another.

Included in Reza's other writings was *Hammerklavier*, novelized vignettes of memories of her father, published in 1997. She did a French translation of an adaptation of Franz Kafka's *Metamorphosis* for the filmmaker Roman Polanski and wrote two screenplays, including *Le Pique-nique de Lulu Kreutz* for a film directed by her companion, Didier Martigny. Returning to her first profession, she took part in the filming of *Loin* (also known as *Terminus des anges*), directed by André Téchiné, in 2000.

Critics said that not since Jean Anouilh in the 1950s had a French playwright been so exportable. Reza's brief dramas with small casts, written in a spare, witty language, offered satire in the tradition of Molière. At the same time, the playwright spoke to contemporary anxieties, and critics compared her to Harold Pinter and Edward Albee.

(ROBERT RAUCH)

Ridge, Tom

In response to the Sept. 11, 2001, terrorist attacks in the U.S., Pres. George W. Bush created by executive order a new department to counter future domestic threats—the Office of Homeland Security—and on September 20 selected his friend Tom Ridge to head it. Taking the post required Ridge to step down as governor of Pennsylvania. No sooner had he been sworn in on October 8 than he found himself reacting to widespread public fear and outrage over bioterrorism in the form of anonymous letters mailed to public figures carrying lethal amounts of anthrax, an infectious disease, that resulted in several deaths. Ridge hit the ground running, developing a program of antiterrorist training, preventive technologies, and emergency responses. One outcome was the mobilization of the National Guard to augment security at the nation's airports. His new cabinet-level position put him squarely in the national spotlight as he issued general alerts of suspected future threats, however vague, with a public wary of any new acts of terror. Despite his high profile, there was concern in Washington that, even with high-level council members, a 100-member staff, a $25 million start-up budget, and the executive backing of the president, Ridge would be unable to coordinate the myriad activities of some 46 different state and federal agencies related to his chain of command.

A popular two-term governor who had been due to leave office in 2003, Ridge was a leading figure in the Republican Party. He had been considered as a running mate for presidential candidates in 1996 and 2000, despite being pro-choice on the volatile issue of abortion. In office he was a moderate Republican, fiscally conservative with a streak of independence, known for his hard-working, pleasant demeanour.

Thomas Joseph Ridge was born on Aug. 26, 1945, to Slovak-Irish-Cherokee parents in a blue-collar family in Erie, Pa. Educated at private schools, he earned a scholarship to Harvard University (B.S., 1967). In 1969, after his first year at Dickinson School of Law, Carlisle, Pa., he was drafted to serve in the Vietnam War, becoming a staff sergeant in the army and winning the Bronze Star for Valor, among other decorations. After returning to complete his J.D. (1972) at Dickinson, he practiced law in Erie and in 1982 narrowly won election to the U.S. Congress. Ridge steadily improved his margins of victory in succeeding elections and served a total of six terms in Congress.

A long shot in the 1994 gubernatorial elections, Ridge defeated the incumbent lieutenant governor but stumbled in his first years in office, with failed attempts to institute school vouchers and privatize liquor stores. Soon afterward, though, buoyed by a strong economy and budget surplus, Ridge found his footing and launched his programs with success. When on September 11 one of the four hijacked planes crashed in the countryside of his home state, Ridge was at the site within hours.

(TOM MICHAEL)

Tom Ridge: on his shoulders, America's security

Rogge, Jacques

As a former Olympic yachtsman, Belgian Jacques Rogge was no stranger to rough waters, but he faced a flood of problems when he took over the helm of the International Olympic Committee (IOC) in July 2001, succeeding outgoing president Juan António Samaranch of Spain, a figure who became nearly synonymous with the triumphs and excesses of the modern Olympic movement. Rogge was elected in the hope that he would clear away the aura of scandal that had imperiled the IOC in recent years, particularly the high-profile resignations and felony charges of bribery that grew out of the successful bid by Salt Lake City, Utah, for the 2002 Winter Games. Rogge, a medical doctor who served on the board of the World Anti-Doping Agency, was chosen to cleanse the public image of the IOC and bring some down-to-earth governance to what had become the most opulent sports organization in the world.

Rogge won election to the eight-year post (with a possible four-year extension) over rivals Kim Un Yong of South Korea, Dick Pound of Canada, and Pal Schmitt of Hungary. His first challenge prior to the Olympic Games at Salt Lake City was to maintain calm and tighten security in the wake of the terrorist attacks in the United States on September 11. Though Rogge was granted emergency powers to cancel the Games without the vote of the full committee, he had no intention of backing out. Voicing his confidence in the safety of the event, he declared that he would take lodging in the Olympic Village dormitories along with the athletes, rather than in a hotel.

Rogge was born on May 2, 1942, in Ghent, Belg. In Great Britain he studied sports medicine and earned his medical degree before returning to Belgium to work as an orthopedic surgeon in Deinze, where he performed as many as 800 operations a year. He also lectured at Free University in Brussels and the University of Ghent. A successful athlete, he was a 16-time national champion in rugby and one-time yachting world champion. He competed in the Finn class of sailing at the Summer Games in 1968, 1972, and 1976 before he left competition but not the Olympic movement. As the head official of Belgium's Olympic team in 1980, he refused to join the U.S.-led boycott of the Moscow Summer Games protesting the Soviet invasion of Afghanistan. Despite intense pressure on Rogge, Belgian athletes competed in Moscow. "This was a milestone in my life," Rogge declared later. "We thought it was our duty to participate in the Olympic Games."

In 1989 he became president of the European Olympic Committee, and in 1991 he joined the IOC; he became a member of various IOC commissions, including the medical committee, and in 1998 he joined the IOC executive board. Rogge was instrumental in coordinating the successful 2000 Summer Games in Sydney, Australia, and in helping to formulate the 2004 Games in Athens. The new IOC president—the eighth in the 107-year history of the organization—planned to leave his medical practice and take up residence in Lausanne, Switz., home to the IOC headquarters. (TOM MICHAEL)

Sa'd ad-Din Ibrahim

On May 21, 2001, less than two hours after the defense lawyers had completed their summation, Egypt's High Security Court found Sa'd ad-Din Ibrahim, a respected university professor, guilty of having accepted money from overseas without government approval, embezzled grant funds, and defamed Egypt abroad. Sentenced together with 27 co-defendants, Ibrahim received seven years' imprisonment at hard labour, despite the fact that he was 62 years old and in poor health.

Ibrahim was born on Dec. 3, 1938, in Mansurah, a city in Egypt's Nile Delta. He graduated from Cairo University (B.A., 1960) and was awarded a government scholarship to study sociology at the University of Washington (Ph.D., 1968). He took U.S. citizenship and, while teaching at DePauw University, Greencastle, Ind., met his future wife, Barbara Lethem. In 1975, however, Ibrahim returned to Cairo, where he won a tenured position at the American University. He performed pioneering research on militant Islamic movements in Egypt. In 1988 he founded the Ibn Khaldun Center for Development Studies, which soon became a leading institution in the Muslim world for the study of human rights, civil society, and minority rights.

On June 30, 2000, Ibrahim was arrested and imprisoned by the authorities. Two of the charges against him were related to a $250,000 European Commission grant Ibrahim had won to make a documentary about voting rights in Egypt. The charge that he had received funds from foreign organizations without government approval was considered suspect by many because the Ibn Khaldun Center was a registered organization that paid Egyptian taxes and therefore was entitled to make such transactions. Similarly, the embezzlement charge was shaky because Ibrahim's handling of the grant money had been properly audited. The third accusation—that Ibrahim had defamed Egypt's reputation abroad—stemmed from his participation in seminars on the plight of Christian Copts, who had suffered widespread discrimination at the hands of the Egyptian authorities, and from his studies on parliamentary elections that proved unflattering to the Mubarak regime. On Aug. 10, 2000, Ibrahim was released on bail, and his trial opened in Cairo some three months later, on November 18.

At the end of 2001, many Egyptian people felt themselves squeezed between the authoritarian Mubarak regime and the radical Islamists. The possibility of a third alternative—a country in which the citizens enjoyed democracy and the rule of law as well as their Islamic faith—seemed quite distant as long as men like Ibrahim languished in prison.

(MARIUS K. DEEB)

Sade

The year 2001 witnessed the reunion of a beloved pop icon and an adoring fan base as Nigerian-born British singer Sade emerged from an almost decade-long hiatus to embark on a world tour with new material from her latest album, *Lovers Rock* (2000). The singer renowned for her sensual voice and exotic looks had lapsed into silence after the release in 1992 of the wildly successful *Love Deluxe* and a subsequent tour.

Helen Folasade Adu was born to a Nigerian economics professor and an English nurse on

AP/Wide World Photos

Sade returns to the stage

Jan. 16, 1959, in Ibadan. Because people in the community refused to address her by her English first name, her parents began calling her Sade, a shortened form of her Yoruba middle name. When she was four years old, her parents separated, and she moved with her mother and younger brother to Essex, Eng. At 17 Sade began a three-year program in fashion and design at Central St. Martin's College of Art and Design in London. After graduating, she worked as a menswear designer and did some modeling. Her foray into music was the result of her agreement to fill in temporarily as lead singer for Arriva, a funk band that had been put together by her friends. Sade later sang with another funk band, Pride, before breaking away with fellow Pride members Stuart Matthewman, Andrew Hale, and Paul Spencer Denman to form the band that would eventually bear her own name.

Sade's music was a sophisticated blend of soul, funk, jazz, and Afro-Cuban rhythms that defied easy categorization. The sound was exemplified by the songs "Your Love Is King" and "Smooth Operator," both tracks from Sade's Grammy Award-winning debut album *Diamond Life* (1984). A second album, *Promise* (1985), enjoyed similar popularity and was followed by a world tour. The album featured the hit song "The Sweetest Taboo," which stayed on the American pop charts for six months. In 1988 Sade embarked on a second world tour to coincide with the release of a third album, *Stronger than Pride*.

After *Love Deluxe,* Sade enjoyed life away from the limelight. She became a mother, while other members of her band recorded separately as Sweetback. They reunited to produce the long-awaited *Lovers Rock,* and Sade completed her comeback with a triumphant return to the concert stage. Fans were so overjoyed that tickets to many of her performances sold out within an hour. (SHANDA SILER)

Saxecoburggotski, Simeon

On July 24, 2001, Simeon Saxecoburggotski became prime minister of Bulgaria. The new head of government had ruled the country as King Simeon II from 1943 to 1945. In early April 2001 he formed a party that, in the elections held in June, won exactly half of the seats in the National Assembly. He then formed a coalition government dedicated to economic reform and to ending corruption.

The future tsar was born on June 16, 1937, in Sofia. His father, Tsar Boris III, died suddenly on Aug. 28, 1943, and at the age of six the boy ascended the throne as Simeon II. By late 1944 the Red Army had occupied Bulgaria, and regents ruling in the boy's name were executed in 1945. A referendum in September 1946 ended the monarchy, and Simeon II and his mother were forced into exile. They lived first in Egypt, where the boy studied in Alexandria at Victoria College (1946–51), and then went to Spain. He graduated from the Lycée Français in Madrid in 1957, attended the Valley Forge Military Academy in Wayne, Pa., in 1958–59, and became a successful businessman in Madrid. In 1962 he married the daughter of a Spanish banking family. He first returned to Bulgaria as a visitor in 1996, and most of the royal property was later returned to him.

In April 2001 he announced the formation of the National Movement for Simeon II to field candidates in the national legislative elections scheduled for June 17. When the courts ruled that the party had not met all of the requirements for registration, two minor parties allowed the movement to join them in a coalition, which allowed it to participate in the election. Although the former tsar was not himself a candidate, he campaigned for those running under the party banner. The party won 120 of the 240 seats and formed a coalition with the Movement for Rights and Freedoms, which represented the country's Turkish minority.

Upon taking office, the new prime minister took as his surname Saxecoburggotski, the Bulgarian form of the name of his royal house, Saxe-Coburg-Gotha. His cabinet was notable for including a large number of professionals, particularly people trained in finance and economics, and for its youth. Few members had previous political experience, and none had ever been a member of a cabinet; two of the positions went to Turks. The new prime minister announced an 800-day reform plan that called for lower taxes, a balanced budget, increased investment, and improved living standards, and he stressed the importance of preparing Bulgaria for membership in the European Union and NATO. He brushed aside charges from opponents that his ultimate aim was to restore the monarchy. (ROBERT RAUCH)

Schumacher, Michael

On Oct. 14, 2001, German racing car driver Michael Schumacher completed a record-breaking year by winning the Japan Grand Prix, the final event of the Formula One automobile racing season. The victory was Schumacher's ninth in the season's 17 Grand Prix races, a tally he had achieved twice before, in 1995 and 2000. Briton Nigel Mansell (in 1992) was the only other driver to win nine races in one season. Even more noteworthy for Schumacher, however, was his season-ending career total of 53 Grand Prix triumphs, the most ever by a Formula One driver and two more than the previous record of 51 held by retired French driver Alain Prost. His achievements also won for Schumacher his fourth drivers' world title. Only Juan Manuel Fangio of Argentina, with five championships in the 1950s, had won more.

Schumacher was born Jan. 3, 1969, in Hürth-Hermülhein, W.Ger. As a young boy he became interested in go-kart racing, an enthusiasm that was supported by his father's management of a go-kart track in the town of Kerpen. In 1984 and 1985 Schumacher won the German junior karting championship, and in 1987 he gained the German and European karting titles. The next year, at the age of 19, he left karting and became a driver of Formula Three cars, vehicles that were less powerful than the Formula One racers. Two years later, in 1990, he won the German Formula Three championship.

In 1991 Schumacher moved up to Formula One competition as a driver for the Jordan team. He switched to Benetton the following year and won the drivers' world championship for that team in 1994 and 1995. Before the 1996 season he moved to the Ferrari team, though many thought that he might have won a third consecutive world title if he had remained with Benetton. When questioned about that possibility, Schumacher commented, "I've always been more interested in the way I achieve victories rather than just to achieve them. I had won two championships, so I needed something different." His younger brother, Ralf, joined him on the Grand Prix circuit in 1997.

In the 1999 British Grand Prix at Silverstone, Michael Schumacher veered off the track at Stowe corner, plowed through a wall of tires at 160 km/h (100 mph), and crashed into a concrete wall. With ambulances and medical teams rushing to the ruined Ferrari, many in the crowd feared that Schumacher would not survive the accident. He emerged from the car, however, with nothing worse than a broken leg. He recovered from this setback to win the drivers' championship in 2000, Ferrari's first drivers' title since 1979. The triumphs of 2001 followed. In May it was announced that Schumacher had signed a contract to drive for Ferrari until 2004. In October, two weeks after completing his triumphant Grand Prix season, he returned to Kerpen and finished second in the karting world championship.

(DAVID R. CALHOUN)

Sharon, Ariel

In elections in Israel on Feb. 6, 2001, Ariel ("Arik") Sharon, leader of the right-wing Likud, defeated Ehud Barak of the Labor Party by a margin of 62.4% to 37.6%. After assembling a broad-based coalition government, Sharon took office as the country's 11th prime minister on March 7. Ironically, it was Sharon's visit to Jerusalem's Temple Mount in September 2000 that sparked the Palestinian uprising that in turn discredited Barak's peace policies and paved the way for Sharon's landslide victory.

As prime minister, Sharon set up a national unity government with Labor and announced two major policy changes—there would be no negotiations with the Palestinians as long as violence continued, and interim, rather than final, arrangements would be made when the shooting stopped.

Ariel Sheinerman was born on Feb. 26, 1928, in Kfar Malal, a small farming village north of Tel Aviv, Palestine. The village often came under Arab attack, and from the age of 13, Sharon, armed with a club and dagger, helped patrol the fields at night. In Israel's 1948 War of Independence, he made a name for himself as a fearless young officer, and in 1953 he was handpicked to set up a commando unit to retaliate against relentless Arab incursions. The unit, known as 101, did more than carry out reprisal raids; it transformed the Israel Defense

Thomas Coex/AFP Worldwide

Electee Ariel Sharon's show of hands at the Western Wall in Jerusalem

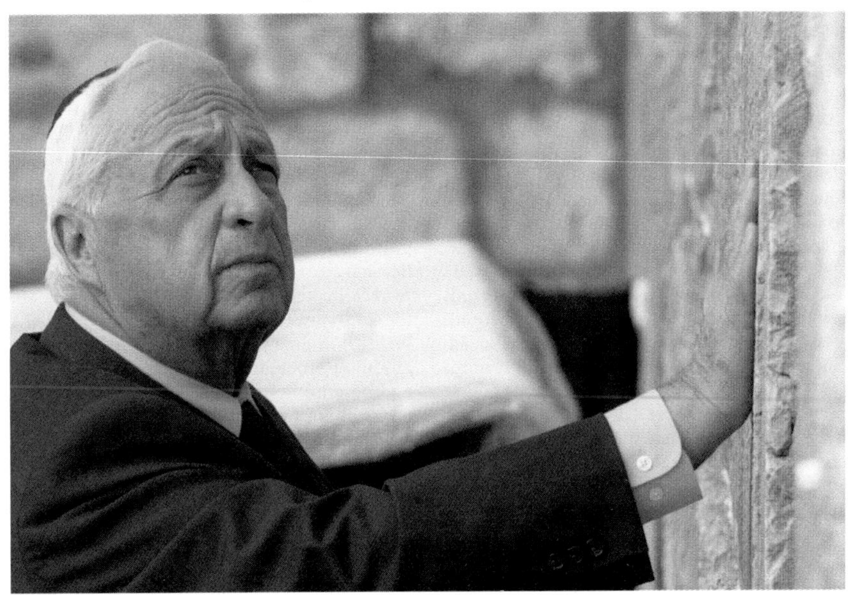

Forces' ethos, with a strategy that emphasized taking the attack to the enemy.

His command of Unit 101 highlighted failings that would dog Sharon in later life: his headstrong belief in his own better judgment and his penchant for exceeding orders. The most blatant case was a 1953 raid on the West Bank village of Qibya, where Sharon's men blew up more than 40 houses and left 69 civilians dead.

Sharon's brilliance as a field commander was never in question. He led one of three lightning armour thrusts into Sinai in the 1967 Six-Day War and in 1971, as head of Southern Command, crushed Palestinian terror in Gaza. When he was denied the post of chief of staff, however, he left the army in 1973, and within months unified political forces on the right to form the present-day Likud. Recalled to service in the 1973 Yom Kippur War, he made a daring crossing of the Suez Canal that turned the tide and made him a national hero.

His star waned when, as defense minister in 1982, he masterminded Israel's ill-fated invasion of Lebanon and was forced to resign after a commission of inquiry found him indirectly responsible for a massacre by Israel's Christian allies in the Sabra and Shatila Palestinian refugee camps.

Sharon, however, continued to serve in Likud-led governments, incurring U.S. wrath for persistent promotion of Jewish settlement activity in occupied territory. In 1998 he became foreign minister, a platform from which he took over as party leader when Benjamin Netanyahu lost the premiership to Barak in 1999. With elections looming, Netanyahu launched a comeback in November 2000 and seemed set to recapture the leadership. He withdrew, however, at the 11th hour, paving the way for what months before had seemed a highly improbable victory for Sharon at the polls. (LESLIE D. SUSSER)

Soderbergh, Steven

Onetime independent film prodigy Steven Soderbergh had two films competing against one another in two categories at the 2001 Academy Awards. Both his David-versus-Goliath tale *Erin Brockovich* (2000) and his drug-trade pseudodocumentary *Traffic* (2000) vied for best picture and best director awards. Critics feared that the double nominations would cause a split vote in the Academy and ultimately result in both films' defeat. In the end both movies won laurels—Julia Roberts won the best actress award for *Brockovich,* and Soderbergh won the best director award for *Traffic,* which took three other awards but lost out to *Gladiator* for best picture.

Steven Andrew Soderbergh was born on Jan. 14, 1963, in Atlanta, Ga. When he was 13, his family relocated to Baton Rouge, La., where his father assumed the post of professor and administrator at Louisiana State University. Soderbergh enrolled in a film animation course at the university while still a high-school student, and it was then that he began making short films. After graduating from high school, he moved to Hollywood to pursue a career as a screenwriter, but his efforts were met with rejection. A year later he returned to Baton Rouge, where he worked at a video arcade while continuing to write and shoot low-budget short pieces. His change of fortune came in 1986 when he was asked to develop one such project into a full-length promotional film for the rock band Yes. This relatively small beginning emboldened Soderbergh to set out for Hollywood once more. He then completed the celebrated *sex, lies, and videotape* (1989), which explored the complexities of modern relationships. The film was a surprise hit at the Cannes International Film Festival that year, picking up three awards, including the Palme d'Or, and catapulting the 26-year-old Soderbergh to fame. *Kafka* (1991), *King of the Hill* (1993), *Underneath* (1995), *Gray's Anatomy* (1996), and *Schizopolis* (1996) followed, but they were not as well received. At the height of his return to obscurity, a shunned Soderbergh was forced to make a living as a freelance, but he persisted in making films. He again found commercial and critical success with *Out of Sight* (1998), the story of a bank heist and unlikely romance between the lead characters, played by George Clooney and Jennifer Lopez (*q.v.*). *The Limey* (1999), a gritty gangster's tale, enjoyed similar kudos. That year he published the memoir *Getting Away with It: or, The Further Adventures of the Luckiest Bastard You Ever Saw.* Soderbergh continued to explore crime and its implications in *Brockovich* and *Traffic.* After the excitement of the 2001 Oscars, Soderbergh began work on *Ocean's Eleven*—a star-studded remake of the 1960 classic—which was released in December. (SHANDA SILER)

Sontag, Susan

American essayist, cultural and literary critic, and novelist Susan Sontag had been honoured with numerous awards for her work, but when she was named the recipient of the Jerusalem Prize for the Freedom of the Individual in Society, there was an outcry among those who felt that she should not accept the prize. Sontag was reluctant to refuse, however, an action she deemed would be "boorish, unconvivial, pretentious."

At the award ceremony, she was disinclined to voice opinions on the situation in Israel, but she spoke against "the doctrine of collective responsibility as a rationale for collective punishment." She decried "the use of disproportionate firepower" and other military actions against civilian Palestinians. She called for the dismantling of Jewish settlements. In the end, however, she gratefully accepted the prize "in the name of peace and the reconciliation of injured and fearful communities" and because it "honours, above all, the international republic of letters."

Sontag seemed destined for life as a public intellectual. She was born on Jan. 16, 1933, in New York City and reared there, until age five, by her grandparents. When her father, who was a fur trader working mostly in China, died, her mother returned home. The family ultimately settled in Los Angeles. Sontag started school at age six and was quickly advanced to the third grade. At 15 she entered the University of California, Berkeley, and a year later she transferred to the University of Chicago. She married intellectual Philip Rieff in her sophomore year (they divorced in the late 1950s) and graduated with a B.A. (philosophy) in 1951. She took master's degrees in English literature (1954) and philosophy (1955) at Harvard University and taught before publishing her first novel in 1963.

Sontag first came to national attention in 1964 with an essay entitled "Notes on 'Camp'," in which she discussed the attributes of taste in gay culture. This and other essays were some of the earliest to treat modern culture in a serious philosophical manner. She wrote on theatre and film, as well as on 20th-century cultural figures such as writer Nathalie Sarraute, director Robert Bresson, and painter Francis Bacon, among others. Many of the essays and reviews collected in early volumes were first published in *The New York Review of Books, Commentary,* and *Partisan Review.* Her later critical works included the award-winning *On Photography* (1977), *Illness as Metaphor* (1977), and *AIDS and Its Metaphors* (1988). Her most popular novel was *The Volcano Lover* (1992), a postmodern romance about the life of Sir William Hamilton. *In America* (2000), a work of fiction based on the life of actress Helena Modjeska, won a National Book Award in 2000. (KATHLEEN KUIPER)

Sörenstam, Annika

Swedish golfer Annika Sörenstam reestablished herself in 2001 as the top player on the Ladies Professional Golf Association (LPGA) tour. Although she had led all LPGA golfers by winning 18 tournaments during the 1990s, Sörenstam had watched Australian Karrie Webb grab all the headlines and dominate the tour in 1999 and 2000. Sörenstam played well in 2000, winning five tournaments. Though her victory at the Welch's/Circle K Championship in Tucson, Ariz., qualified her for the Hall of Fame, her season went largely unnoticed, owing to the attention Webb received. This did not sit well with the notoriously competitive Sörenstam. Determined to recapture the number one spot on the tour, she spent the off-season working on a new physical fitness regimen and concentrating on her short game and her putting. The result was a resurgence that at times caught even Sörenstam herself by surprise. A prime example was her record-setting 10-stroke comeback victory in the last round of the Office Depot tournament in Los Angeles, which broke the previous last-round comeback record of eight strokes. She characterized the amazing performance as "more than a miracle"; it gave Sörenstam her fourth win in a row and made her one of only four women golfers ever to string together that many victories. During that stretch she also became the first woman golfer to break 60 when she shot a 59 in the second round of the Standard Register Ping tournament in Phoenix, Ariz. At the same tournament, she set a new 72-hole mark with her 27-under-par performance.

Sörenstam was born Oct. 9, 1970, in Stockholm. She began playing golf at the age of 12,

Nitzan Shorer/AFP Worldwide

and she was a member of the Swedish national team from 1987 to 1992. She attended the University of Arizona, where she won a National Collegiate Athletic Association title in 1991 and earned All-America honours in 1991 and 1992. In 1992 she won the world amateur championship, finished second at the U.S. women's amateur championship, and posted the second lowest score among amateurs at the U.S. Women's Open. She was the European tour's Rookie of the Year in 1993 and with three top-10 finishes on the LPGA tour the following year, including one tie for second, was named that tour's Rookie of the Year. In 1995 she posted her first LPGA tour victory at the U.S. Women's Open and went on to win Player of the Year honours while capturing the Vare Trophy for lowest scoring average (71.0). She also became the first player to lead the LPGA tour and the European tour in winnings in the same season. In 1996 she successfully defended her title at the U.S. Women's Open and won the Vare Trophy (70.47) again. Six titles in 1997 earned her Player of the Year laurels for a second time, then she repeated as Player of the Year in 1998, when she became the first player on the LPGA tour to finish the season with a scoring average below 70 (69.99).

Other highlights of 2001 included a victory with Tiger Woods in a made-for-TV match-play event against Webb and David Duval. By the end of her remarkable season, Sörenstam had won her first major title (the Nabisco Championship) since 1996, led the tour in earnings for the year, and become the first woman golfer to break the $7 million mark for career earnings. (ANTHONY G. CRAINE)

Stella, Frank

After keeping a low profile throughout the 1990s, American artist Frank Stella returned to the limelight in a big way, with large public sculptures. In 2001 the 65-year-old completed work on *The Prince of Homburg,* a massive mostly metal sculpture for the plaza outside the National Gallery of Art in Washington, D.C. The 9,100-kg (20,000-lb) piece followed on the heels of public art murals for the Princess of Wales Theatre in Toronto (1992–93), designs for a museum addition in Dresden, Ger., and a bandshell in Miami, Fla. A pioneer of Minimalism in the 1960s, Stella traced a gradual arc from the stark flatness of his first paintings, through three-dimensional constructions, and finally to architecture. All the while, though, he continued to sharpen the cutting edge of modern art with innovative work upheld by sound theories.

Stella was born on May 12, 1936, in Malden, Mass. He was educated at Phillips Academy, Andover, Mass., and at Princeton University (B.A., 1958), where he was taught appreciation for the reigning New York school of Abstract Expressionism by Stephen Greene and William Seitz. After graduation Stella moved to New York City and became an instant sensation when his paintings appeared in a group show at the Museum of Modern Art in 1959–60. His "black paintings" were shockingly two dimensional: cruciform stripes of common black house paint bordered by narrow strips of raw canvas. Inspired by the object-oriented work of Jasper Johns and troubled by what he saw as growing ambiguity in Abstract Expressionism, Stella promoted a Gestalt theory of "What you see is what you see" that became the credo for Minimalism, which rejected illusionism, narrative, and symbolism, and he concentrated on fundamental shapes of primary colours. In exhibits at the influential Leo Castelli Gallery, Stella helped minimalism eclipse Action painting to become (along with Pop art) the driving force of the New York school by the mid-1960s.

Stella furthered his nonobjective aesthetic by achieving greater flatness through the use of aluminum paints and by notching his rectangular canvases so that no negative space appeared. He was one of the first artists to use shaped canvases. He explored colour and shape with the *Benjamin Moore* series (1961), *Concentric Square* series (1963), and *Irregular Polygon* series (1966), culminating with the *Protractor* series (1967–69). Never bound by the movement he helped launch, Stella shifted to a larger colour field with *Irregular Polygons* (1966–67) and *Polish Village* (1971–73). He edged toward sculpture with the "maximalist" protrusive relief series of the 1970s: *Brazilian* (1974–75), *Exotic Bird* (1976–80), and *Indian Bird* (1977–79). This period also introduced the French curve into Stella's art, a dominant feature in his later work.

While visiting Rome in 1982–83, Stella was taken with the historical Baroque response to the decline of Renaissance art, particularly through artists such as Caravaggio, and he sought to revive abstract art in the same manner. He gave a series of lectures at Harvard University, later published as *Working Space* (1986), and created a group of Baroque-influenced abstract paintings called *Circuit and Shards* (1983), which was followed by the *Cones and Pillars* series (1987); the latter showed Stella toying with illusionism and spatial dynamics. He was the subject of two retrospectives by the Museum of Modern Art (1970, 1987) and was the only American to mount a solo show in 2000 at the Royal Academy of Arts in London. (TOM MICHAEL)

Jim McHugh, February 1993

Frank Stella in the limelight

Stroman, Susan

Of the record-breaking 12 Tony Awards won by the musical comedy *The Producers* in 2001, two went to Susan Stroman, the show's innovative director and choreographer. No stranger to honours, she had previously amassed three other Tonys, as well as multiple Outer Critics Circle, Drama Desk, and Laurence Olivier awards.

"Stro," as she was known, was born on Oct. 17, 1954, in Wilmington, Del., and grew up in a home in which music was prized. She loved watching Fred Astaire movies and later admitted that, even when she was very young, she visualized dance when she heard music. She began dance classes at age five and learned to play musical instruments. Stroman got some choreographing experience in local theatres during her student years in high school and at the University of Delaware, and in 1977, a year after graduation, she headed for New York City. Knowing that she would need to have some performing credentials before she could break into choreographing professionally, Stroman secured work in several shows and in 1980 became assistant director, assistant choreographer, and dance captain of a little-known show, *Musical Chairs.* In 1987, after spending several years at small choreographing jobs, she and a member of that show's cast, Scott Ellis, collaborated on an Off-Broadway revival of *Flora, the Red Menace.* It became a cult success and helped them make some important connections, which led to further work on such shows as the New York City Opera's *Don Giovanni* (1989) and the John Kander and Fred Ebb revue *And the World Goes 'Round* (1991). For the latter, Stroman won her first Outer Critics Circle Award for choreography. In 1992, her inventiveness was showcased to great success when she choreographed *Crazy for You* and took Broadway by storm, winning Tony, Drama Desk, Outer Critics Circle, and later—for the London production—Olivier awards. Among shows that followed were *Show Boat* (1994), for which she was honoured with another Outer Critics Circle Award, *Big* (1996), *Steel Pier* (1997), and the London revival of *Oklahoma!* (1998), which won her another Olivier Award. Stroman's imagination took a different direction for *Contact* (1999), telling three separate stories almost entirely through dance; among that show's awards were Tonys for both choreography and best new musical. Another award-winning musical was the revival of *The Music Man* in 2000. Stroman also choreographed for film and television and counted such ballets as *But Not for Me* for the Martha Graham Company in 1998 and *Blossom Got Kissed* for the New York City Ballet in 1999 among her credits.

Originally, Stroman's husband since 1995, *Crazy for You* director Mike Ockrent, was to have been director of *The Producers,* with Stroman as choreographer, but after he died in 1999, Stroman took over the directorship as well. In October 2001 yet another of her efforts as director-choreographer opened in New York City—*Thou Shalt Not,* a musical version of Émile Zola's *Thérèse Raquin. Oklahoma!,* with Stroman's London choreography, was scheduled to open in New York in March 2002, Broadway's first production of that play without the original Agnes de Mille choreography. (BARBARA WHITNEY)

Tanaka, Makiko

Dubbed "the Lady with the Big Mouth" by *Time* magazine, Japanese Foreign Minister Makiko Tanaka made headlines in 2001 for her outspoken comments and her skirmishes with Japan's senior political bureaucrats. She was criticized by members of the Diet, Japan's parliament, which did not permit her to represent Japan at the United Nations General Assembly in November, and officials of her own Liberal Democratic Party (LDP) for, among other comments, suggesting that the best way former prime minister Yoshiro Mori could help Japan was by putting a big adhesive bandage over his mouth; characterizing most party elections as "like a garage sale full of senior politicians who've been in office too long," some of whom she said should be strapped to satellites; and making decisions and expressing opinions that veered from the official government policy. Her supporters, however, praised her as a reformer who spoke only the truth and provided a much-needed shake-up of the old scandal-ridden system.

Many observers found it ironic that Tanaka was challenging the LDP old guard, since her father, former prime minister Kakuei Tanaka, had been instrumental in establishing the powerful political machine. Some analysts attributed her motives to the belief that her father had been betrayed when Noboru Takeshita (who later became prime minister) took over the ruling LDP faction that Kakuei Tanaka had helped found.

Maki, as she was affectionately known, was born on Jan. 14, 1944. She attended high school in the United States before graduating from the School of Commerce at Waseda University in 1968. She frequently served as an unofficial first lady during her father's prime ministership (1972–74). In 1983 she campaigned for her husband, Naoki Tanaka, who was elected to the Diet, but she retreated from the public eye to care for her father when he suffered a stroke in 1985. In 1993 Tanaka was elected to the Diet, and she served as head of the Science and Technology Agency from 1994 to 1995. She was reelected in 1996 and 2000, and by 2001 her relaxed, informal personal style and sharp wit had made her one of the most popular political figures in Japan. Her active support of reformist candidate Junichiro Koizumi (*q.v.*) contributed to his election as prime minister in April 2001, and he promptly appointed her Japan's first female foreign minister. She just as promptly began making waves, describing traditional Japanese diplomacy as "an exercise in telling nothing with as many words as possible." In contrast, she remarked, "I usually like to say what's on my mind. I think that's what diplomacy is about." She proved her point in the following months, even criticizing several of Koizumi's decisions, but the controversies served only to boost Tanaka's popularity with the public. (AMY R. TAO)

Thaksin Shinawatra

Though he came late to politics after spectacular successes in the telecommunications industry, Thaksin Shinawatra, one of Thailand's richest men, captured the imagination of voters with his promises of a fresh approach to politics and led his newly created Thai Rak Thai Party to a convincing win in national elections on Jan. 6, 2001. He was appointed prime minister by King Bhumibol Adulyadej on February 9. Thaksin's tenure in office, however, came perilously close to an abrupt end when the independent National Countercorruption Commission prosecuted him on April 3 before the Constitutional Court on charges of having concealed assets in a mandatory declaration of wealth. Acquitted by a vote of 8–7 on August 3, Thaksin was left free to pursue his populist political platform.

Thaksin was born on July 26, 1949, in the northern Thailand city of Chiang Mai. He was a descendant of Chinese merchants who had settled in the area before World War I. Although his father was a politician, Thaksin originally planned for a career in the police force. He graduated from the Police Cadet Academy in 1973, winning a scholarship to study criminal justice at Eastern Kentucky University. On his return to Thailand, Thaksin first taught at the Police Academy before being tapped for special duties in the office of Prime Minister Seni Pramoj. In 1978 Thaksin completed a doctorate at Sam Houston (Texas) State University. Back in Thailand, he worked in police planning and public relations positions and became adept in computer technology. After having attained the rank of lieutenant colonel in the police force, he left the force in 1987 to run his business in the computer field alongside his wife, Potjaman.

Pornchai Kittiwongsakul/AFP Worldwide

Thaksin Shinawatra: saluting or giving thanks?

It was an era when business fortunes were inextricably linked with political influence. After a brush with bankruptcy, Thaksin eventually obtained a monopoly on satellite communications and a cell phone concession, and he rapidly translated these into a vast fortune. In 1994 he was asked to be foreign minister; he served three months until the fall of the government. The following year he assumed leadership of the Palang Dharma Party, and on the party's entrance into Prime Minister Banharn Silpa-archa's government coalition in 1995, he served as deputy prime minister. Thaksin served as deputy prime minister a second time under Chavalit Yongchaiyudh in 1997.

In his new position as prime minister, Thaksin injected a corporate CEO-style of leadership, brushing aside the objections of bureaucrats and implementing a "workshop" approach to problem solving. His platform had great popular appeal. Thaksin promised the creation of a new bank for small businesses, a three-year debt moratorium for delinquent farmers, and a development fund for each of Thailand's 70,000 villages. (ROBERT WOODROW)

Thomson, James

On Aug. 9, 2001, U.S. Pres. George W. Bush (*q.v.*) announced that the federal government would support research on the approximately 60 existing lines (self-sustaining colonies) of human embryonic stem cells, microscopically tiny undifferentiated cells that have the potential capability of growing into any one of the approximately 200 cell types that compose

left: Koichi Kamoshida/Getty Images

a human. Because of this capability, scientists believed that stem cells could be used as replacement cells in transplantation therapies in humans to treat such ailments as Parkinson disease, diabetes, spinal-cord injuries, and Alzheimer disease.

President Bush's decision was the culmination of a series of developments that began in 1998 when James Thomson, a biologist at the University of Wisconsin at Madison, became the first person to isolate stem cells from human embryos. For Thomson this achievement was the result of a long process of research and experimentation that began when he was an undergraduate at the University of Illinois at Urbana-Champaign.

Thomson was born in Chicago on Dec. 20, 1958, and grew up in the Chicago suburb of Oak Park. At the University of Illinois, he was encouraged to work in the biology laboratories, where he became interested in the process of early development—the explosive surge of biological activity that occurs when a fertilized egg implants itself in a womb and then begins to divide and form the specialized cells that eventually become the great variety of tissues in the body. Continuing his education and research at the University of Pennsylvania, where he gained a Ph.D. in molecular biology, Thomson learned that biologists in 1980 had succeeded in extracting embryonic stem cells from mice. Because embryonic development in mice differs considerably from that in humans, Thomson then decided to conduct stem cell research on a species much more similar to humans; he chose the rhesus monkey.

In 1991 Thomson moved to the University of Wisconsin, where he continued his research at the primate centre. After many months of painstaking work, he succeeded in isolating the rhesus monkey embryonic stem cells in 1995. The obvious next step, to Thomson, was to try to extract stem cells from human embryos. This, however, confronted him with a moral dilemma, because such an extraction kills the embryo. After consulting with bioethicists at the university, Thomson decided that continued research was "the better ethical choice" as long as the embryos, created by couples who no longer wanted them in order to have children, would otherwise be destroyed.

After he succeeded in isolating the human embryonic stem cells, Thomson assigned the patent for his discovery to the Wisconsin Alumni Research Foundation; the patent covered both the method of isolating the cells and the cells themselves. Consequently, the National Institutes of Health, the agency responsible for implementing President Bush's decision, planned to negotiate with the foundation in order to gain access to the stem cells. As for Thomson, he commented that he was somewhat disappointed that the Bush edict would restrict the creation of new cell lines, but he was generally pleased that the research would go forward. (DAVID R. CALHOUN)

Thorpe, Ian

In July 2001 at the world swimming championships in Fukuoka, Japan, Australian freestyler Ian Thorpe added to his already formidable reputation by winning six gold medals, setting four world records, and leading his nation to a team victory. Living up to his nickname of "the Thorpedo," he set individual world marks of 1 min 44.06 sec in the 200-m freestyle, 3 min 40.17 sec in the 400-m freestyle, and 7 min 39.16 sec in the 800-m freestyle. He was also a member of the 4 × 200-m freestyle relay team, which set a world record of 7 min 4.66 sec. Thorpe's additional gold medals were won in the 4 × 100-m freestyle relay and the 4 × 100-m medley relay. Named both best male and best performer of the meet, he credited his coach, Doug Frost, with playing a major role in his success.

Thorpe first attracted widespread international attention at the Olympic Games in September 2000 before a hometown crowd in Sydney. In that competition he won gold medals and achieved world records in the 400-m freestyle, the 4 × 100-m freestyle relay, and the 4 × 200-m freestyle relay. His only defeat was a second-place finish in the 200-m freestyle.

Thorpe was born on Oct. 13, 1982, in the Paddington district of Sydney. Inspired by the success in the pool of his older sister, Christina, he began swimming competitively at the age of eight under coach Jenny McAdam. He later commented that as a young boy he had felt like a "fish out of water" at other sports, including cricket, at which his father had gained recognition. A high-school classmate described him as having "no coordination at all on land." At the age of 13, Thorpe broke 10 national age-group records in one meet, and one year later he became the youngest swimmer to make Australia's national team. At the 1998 world championships, he became at the age of 15 the youngest world swimming champion with his world-record victory in the 400-m freestyle. At the Pan Pacific championships in August 1999, Thorpe, (now 2 m [6 ft 4 in] tall and taking full advantage of his extraordinarily large feet, which some compared to flippers), set world long-course records in the 200-m and 400-m freestyle events. Remarking on his subsequent celebrity status, he said, "Nothing can really prepare you for this." According to 1984 Olympic swimming champion Rowdy Gaines, Thorpe has "revolutionized freestyle. He is doing the 400 free with a six beat [per arm cycle] kick the whole way. The only other people doing that are sprinters." In addition, his stroke length of 2.7 m (8 ft 8.5 in) is longer than that of his competitors.

Thorpe also became notable for his generosity. After setting his first world record at the Pan Pacific championships, he donated his $25,000 prize money to two charities, and for several years he spent much time helping a childhood friend through a difficult bout with cancer. (DAVID R. CALHOUN)

Toledo, Alejandro

On July 28, 2001, nearly five centuries after Europeans conquered the Incas—and after two years of campaigning—Alejandro Toledo was sworn in as Peru's first democratically elected president of Quechua ethnicity. Although easily half of Peruvians were Amerindians, the white and mestizo minorities had held the key to economic, scholastic, and political power since colonial times. Excepting the dictatorship of "El Indio" ("the Indian"), Juan Velasco Alvarado (1968–75), Peru's first president to break the colour barrier was Alberto Fujimori (1990–2000), who quickly became known as "El Chino" ("the Chinaman"), although he was of Japanese ancestry. Toledo accepted the moniker "El Cholo" (also "the Indian") with pride. He spent his last campaign day in Cuzco, the former Inca capital, and, a day after taking office, the shoeshine-boy-turned-economist paid homage to his ancestors and the Andean mountain *apus* (gods, or spirits) at the ruins of Machu Picchu.

Alejandro Toledo Manrique, the son of peasant farmers, was born on March 28, 1946, in Cabana, Ancash department, and grew up on the northern coast at Chimbote. An academic scholarship took him to the United States and the University of San Francisco (B.S., 1970). After earning a Ph.D. (1976) in economics of human resources from Stanford University, he worked in international economics at the United Nations (1976–78, 1989), the World Bank (1979–81), and Harvard's Institute for International Development (1991–94). In 1998 he became director of international affairs at the Graduate School of Business Administration (ESAN) in Lima.

The smear tactics used by the Fujimori camp against the other candidates unwittingly paved the way for Toledo, who led the centrist Perú Posible party in the 2000 presidential race. Toledo withdrew from the runoff in protest and launched a series of popular demonstrations against Fujimori's victory. After a bribery scandal toppled Fujimori's government, Toledo led the pack of new candidates for the April 2001 elections and won 36.5% of the vote in the first round.

Alejandro Toledo takes the measure of his land at Machu Picchu

Toledo's image was marred somewhat by allegations of infidelity, immoral behaviour, and cocaine use. He also had a falling out with campaign chief Álvaro Vargas Llosa (son of the novelist Mario Vargas Llosa, who lost the 1990 presidential race to Fujimori), who began to advocate blank ballots to protest the candidacies of both Toledo and former president Alan García Pérez. On the positive side, Toledo was aided by his daughter and his wife, the anthropologist Eliane Karp, who gave campaign speeches in Quechua. In the second round of voting, on June 3, Toledo took 53.1% of the ballots. Fewer than 3% of votes were blank. In his inaugural speech, Toledo promised to create new jobs, partly by increasing tourism, and to fight corruption, narcotraffic, and human rights abuses—in short, "to be the president of all Peruvians and of all races."
(STEPHEN P. DAVIS)

Whitman, Meg
During a year when many Internet ventures had either failed or were struggling to survive, the on-line auction firm eBay Inc. continued to flourish in 2001. At the head of this thriving enterprise was president and CEO Meg Whitman. Under her leadership, revenues in 2000 totaled more than $430 million, an increase of 92% over 1999, and the percentage of sales that came from international business doubled between 2000 and 2001. Visitors to the firm's Internet site could find an array of offerings in more than 4,500 categories, ranging from automobiles to clothing, jewelry, books, and dolls.

When a corporate headhunter first approached her for the position in 1998, Whitman, then an executive with toy and game manufacturer Hasbro, Inc., was not interested. A visit to eBay's headquarters and the testimonies of many enthusiastic users impressed her, however, and she accepted the offer to lead the company. Whitman later commented that she quickly realized that eBay's strength lay in the fact that its services could not be duplicated by old-economy brick-and-mortar concerns because its job was to connect people rather than to sell them things.

Margaret Whitman was born in 1957 and grew up in Cold Spring Harbor, N.Y., on Long Island. She earned her undergraduate degree from Princeton University in 1977 and a master's degree in business administration from Harvard University in 1979. From 1979 to 1981 she worked in brand management for Procter & Gamble in Cincinnati, Ohio. After moving with her husband to California in 1981, she joined the consulting firm Bain & Co. as a vice president and remained there until 1989. From 1989 to 1992 Whitman served as senior vice president of marketing at the Consumer Products Division of Walt Disney Co., where she played a major role in Disney's acquisition of *Discover* magazine. Again moving with her husband, this time to Boston in 1992, she became president of the children's shoe manufacturer Stride Rite, a division of Stride Rite Corp. Leaving Stride Rite in 1995, she accepted an offer to become CEO of Florists Transworld Delivery (FTD), a federation of commercial florists. There Whitman encountered opposition from staff members and member florists, who strongly objected to FTD's transformation into a privately held firm. She resigned from FTD in 1997 and became general manager of the Playskool division of Hasbro.

One of Whitman's first responsibilities at eBay was to prepare the company for its initial public offering (IPO) in September 1998. She brightened the design of eBay's Web pages and walled off all firearm and pornography auctions into separate age-restricted sites; eBay later banned auctions of firearms and prohibited sales of tobacco, drugs, alcohol, animals, and body parts. At the IPO 3.5 million shares of eBay were offered at $18 per share; at the end of the first day, each share was valued at $47.1875. Whitman was described as "relentlessly optimistic," and those who worked with her said that her ability to stay focused and positive set her apart from most executives. (DAVID R. CALHOUN)

Wirtz, Jacques
Even after a 50-year career in which he had designed more than 100 gardens, Belgian landscape architect Jacques Wirtz was far from considering retirement; in fact, he seemed to be hitting his stride in 2001. A decade earlier Wirtz's work was not well known outside Belgium, but during the 1990s he took on more high-profile projects, including gardens at the Louvre in Paris, the headquarters of the Bank of Luxembourg, and gardens for celebrities, notably one for actress Catherine Deneuve. His work became internationally known, and he was hailed as one of the most talented and influential landscape designers in Europe. During the year Wirtz continued to work in England on one of his larger projects, a $20-million commission by the duchess of Northumberland to redesign the 5-ha (12-ac) walled garden at Alnwick Castle, a spectacular undertaking that would feature waterfalls and Wirtz's famous (and often duplicated) mass plantings of geometric-shaped hedges of beech, box, hornbeam, and yew. Some of his hedges were carefully sculpted and pruned for years in order to achieve the desired effect.

Wirtz was born in 1924 in Antwerp; his family moved to the environs outside the city when he was 12, and he was influenced by the natural beauty of the countryside. He studied landscape architecture at a horticultural college in Vilvoorde before starting his own business growing and selling flowers and maintaining local gardens. In 1950 Wirtz designed his first complete garden; the majority of his creations were for private residences. His style was inspired by gardens of his childhood as well as those seen on visits to other European countries and Japan. He came to be known for designs that served to complement rather than conceal the natural surroundings, and he favoured flowering plants, grasses, clipped trees and hedges, and water, rather than the harsh man-made materials that adorned many other modern gardens.

His career received a boost in the 1970s when he won a competition to design the garden for Belgium's pavilion at the International Exhibition in Osaka, Japan. During this time he also designed the campus of the University of Antwerp, a plan that featured an ivy ground cover and an abundance of flowering trees. Wirtz gained wider recognition in the early '90s when he won a contest to redesign the Carrousel Garden, which connected the Louvre with the 25-ha (63-ac) Tuileries Gardens, redesigned in 1664 by celebrated French landscape architect André Le Nôtre. At the end of the year, Wirtz and his two sons, who shared in his business, had a number of projects in the works, including a garden at Canary Wharf in London, a small Jewish cemetery in Switzerland, and gardens around a law court in Italy, all scheduled for completion by 2003 or 2004. He was also poised to begin his first work in the U.S., designing private gardens in Los Angeles, Chicago, and Florida. (SANDRA LANGENECKERT)

Yang Yang
Chinese short-track speed skater Yang Yang—known as Yang Yang (A)—confirmed her dominance on the ice in 2001 by winning her fifth consecutive world championship overall title. During three days of competition in Chonju, S.Kor., Yang reached the finals of all five women's events, taking gold in the 1,000-, 1,500-, and 3,000-m individual races and the 3,000-m relay and silver in the 500-m race. Her decisive win came as little surprise. After a season in which she had reached the finals in 14 of the 17 events she competed in and had tallied eight individual wins, she entered the world championships as the top-ranked woman on the World Cup circuit. The letter A often appended to Yang's name stood for her birth month of August and distinguished her from teammate Yang Yang (S), who was born in September and with whom Yang often shared the medalists' podium. The written distinction between Yang Yangs (A) and (S) was for the benefit of non-Chinese speakers, because their names were pronounced differently in Chinese.

Yang was born on Aug. 24, 1976, in the northeastern Chinese province of Heilongjiang, near the Russian border. She began skating in 1984, and by age 13 she had reached the finals of an International Skating Union test competition. Yang qualified for the Chinese short-track team in 1995, but she overtrained for the 1996 world championships and achieved only mediocre results. By the next season she had perfected her training, and at the 1997 world championships she split an overall win with two-time world champion Chun Lee Kyung of South Korea. In doing so she became China's first world short-track champion.

Yang had a mixed showing at the 1998 Winter Olympics in Nagano, Japan, where she failed to win any individual medals. She was strong in early heats and, in fact, set a world record (1 min 31.991 sec) in the 1,000-m quarterfinal. In the 1,000-m final, she again met Chun, the defending Olympic champion, whom she led for most of the race. The two tangled arms at the finish, however, and Chun kicked forward to win by centimetres before falling to the ice. Compounding the loss, judges then disqualified Yang for interference.

Kim Jae-Hwan/AFP Worldwide

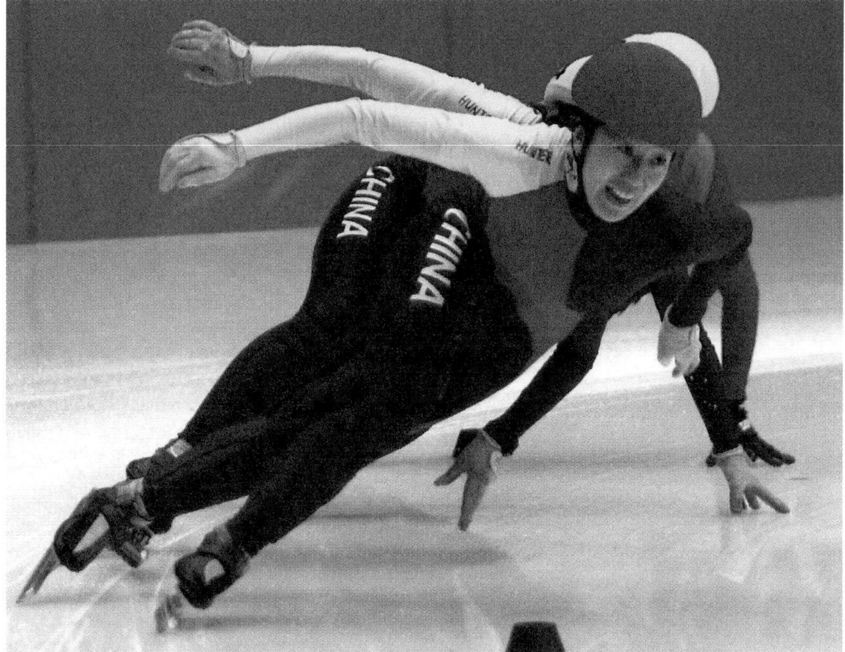

Yang Yang roars ahead

The only medal Yang took home from Nagano was a silver for the 3,000-m relay. She blamed poor mental preparation for the results. Later in 1998, however, Yang won her second world championship—this one hers alone—and she thereafter dominated the World Cup circuit and the world championships. After the 2001 win, her hopes settled on the 2002 Winter Olympics in Salt Lake City, Utah, where she promised to be a strong contender to capture China's first-ever winter gold.

(COLIN J. MURPHY)

Yoshimoto, Banana

"Banana mania" was not an enthusiasm triggered by potassium deprivation but rather the way journalists around the world referred in 2001 to the wild popularity of Japanese writer Banana Yoshimoto. Her stories were light, their action slight, and their characters unusual. They were not entirely evanescent; they briefly budded, flowered, and faded, leaving behind a lingering scent of great beauty and loss.

Born in Tokyo on July 24, 1964, Mahoko Yoshimoto appeared to have a genetic predilection for both writing and nonconformity; her father, Takaaki ("Ryumei") Yoshimoto, was an intellectual, critic, and leader in the radical student movement in the late 1960s. Reared in a much freer environment than that of most Japanese children, Yoshimoto entered the College of Art at Nihon University, Tokyo. There her graduation story, *Moonlight Shadow* (1986), was an immediate hit and earned her the Izumi Kyoka Prize from the faculty. About this time, by her own account, she chose the pen name Banana Yoshimoto because it was both cute and androgynous. While working as a waitress, she wrote the novella *Kitchin* (*Kitchen*), published in 1988. Two more books—*Kanashii yokan* ("Sad Foreboding") and *Utakata/Sankuchuari* ("Bubble/Sanctuary")—were published in Japan that year. Yoshimoto never looked back.

The Chinese were the first to catch Banana mania, translating and publishing *Kitchin* in 1989. A translation of *Tsugumi* (1989) appeared the following year in South Korea. Her first English-language book, which contained both *Moonlight Shadow* and *Kitchen,* was published as *Kitchen* in 1993, and her reputation spread to readers throughout the United States and England. Soon her work had also been translated into German, Hebrew, Spanish, Italian, and Albanian. Two Japanese directors, Jun Ishikawa (*Tsugumi,* 1990) and Yoshimitsu Morita (*Kitchin,* 1990), adapted her novels to the large screen, and in 1997 Hong Kong director Ho Yim made a Cantonese-language version of *Kitchin.* While her name spread, Yoshimoto continued to write, producing the novels *NP* (1990; *N.P.*) and *Amurita* (1994; *Amrita*) and several volumes of essays (*Painatsupurin* [1989; "Pinenuts Pudding"], *Songs from Banana Note* [1991], *Yume ni tsuite* [1994; "About a Dream"], and *Painappuru heddo* [1995; "Pineapple Head"]) and short stories (*Shirakawa yofune* [1989; *Asleep*] and *Tokage* [1993; *Lizard*]). In 2000–01 a one-volume author's selection came out, and four volumes of collected works were published. Yoshimoto was just 36.

Her Japanese fans continued to respond to elements in her writing that were both old and new. Though her characters, settings, and titles were modern and influenced by American culture, they were unmistakably Japanese at the core. Some cited the Japanese sensibility known as *mono no aware,* usually translated as "the pathos of things," as the essence of her style. The phenomenal appeal of her work was not always evident to English-language critics, some of whom called her writing superficial and simplistic and her characters unbelievable. Her appeal appeared to lie deep in her identity and her personal response to life, in a biography that was as quirky as her writing.

(KATHLEEN KUIPER)

Zöggeler, Armin

After having closed out the 2000 international luge racing season with victories in three of the final four events and clinching the year's World Cup overall luge championship, Armin Zöggeler of Italy barely skipped a beat to kick off the 2001 season. Zöggeler defeated defending Olympic champion Georg Hackl of Germany in the two-track European championships in January. He finished third in a subsequent race in Austria but returned to the top of the medalists' podium in Altenberg, Ger., by posting a time of 1 min 49.685 sec. In early February the luge circuit moved on to Nagano, Japan, where Zöggeler finished second behind Germany's Wilfried Huber. Two weeks later, in Park City, Utah, Zöggeler was victorious once again as he recorded the year's fastest time, 1 min 29.391 sec.

Zöggeler capped off a tremendous 2001 season in Calgary, Alta., by capturing his third world championship with a time of 1 min 30.139 sec. In the process, he again defeated Hackl as well as nine-time overall World Cup champion Markus Prock, who placed second and third, respectively. Zöggeler also led his Italian squad to a fourth-place finish in the team event in Calgary.

Zöggeler was born on Jan. 4, 1974, in Merano, in Italy's South Tirol region. He broke onto the luge racing scene as a 15-year-old in 1989; his 14th-place finish in an international competition was a sure sign of things to come. He joined the Italian national team that year. In 1994, competing as a 20-year-old in the Lillehammer (Nor.) Olympic Games, he finished third behind Hackl and Prock. In 1995 he returned to Lillehammer and captured his first world championship and took second place in the overall World Cup standings. In 1997 he moved his performances up a notch and was able to claim the World Cup title. One year later, in the 1998 Winter Olympics in Nagano, he lost to Hackl and took the silver medal. Later that year Zöggeler's Italian team won the silver in the European championships in Oberhof, Ger. From that point on, Zöggeler dominated the world luging scene. In 1999 he captured five of the seven races he entered on his way to taking his second World Cup championship.

By the close of the 2001 season, Zöggeler, who lived and trained in Völlan, Italy, where he supported himself and his family by working as a police officer, was looking to the future. With silver and bronze medals already in his Olympic collection, he vowed to go for the gold in the 2002 Winter Games in Salt Lake City, Utah.

(BILL BRADLEY)

bottom: The Yomiuri Shimbun

Obituaries

In 2001 **THE WORLD LOST** many leaders, **PATHFINDERS,** news-makers, **HEROES,** cultural icons, and **ROGUES.** The pages below **RECAPTURE** the **LIVES** and accomplishments of those we **REMEMBER** best.

Aaliyah (Aaliyah Dana Haughton), American rhythm and blues singer and actress (b. Jan. 16, 1979, Brooklyn, N.Y.—d. Aug. 25, 2001, Abaco Islands, The Bahamas), was considered on the verge of superstardom after the success of her first two albums—*Age Ain't Nothing but a Number* (1994), with its hit singles "Back and Forth" and "At Your Best (You Are Love)," and *One in a Million* (1996)—and her Grammy nominations for her singles "Are You That Somebody?" (1998) and "Try Again" (2000), as well as her starring role in the movie *Romeo Must Die* (2000); she recently had released a third album, *Aaliyah*, had finished work on the film *Queen of the Damned*, and was beginning two sequels to the movie *The Matrix* (1999) when she was killed in a plane crash as she was leaving The Bahamas after filming a music video.

Rising star Aaliyah

AP/ Wide World Photos

Abu Ali Mustafa (Mustafa az-Zibri), Palestinian nationalist (b. 1938, Arabeh, Palestine—d. Aug. 27, 2001, Ram Allah, West Bank), was a cofounder and, from July 2000, secretary-general of the Popular Front for the Liberation of Palestine (PFLP), a radical faction of the Palestine Liberation Organization (PLO). He was born Mustafa az-Zibri and later took the nom de guerre Abu Ali Mustafa. As a young man he joined George Habash's Arab National Movement, and in 1967 he and Habash formed the Marxist-oriented PFLP, based in Damascus, Syria. The PFLP, which staunchly rejected PLO peace talks with Israel, was believed to have been responsible for several terrorist attacks and hijackings. Mustafa eventually acknowledged the Palestinian Authority, however, and in September 1999 he unexpectedly returned to the West Bank. He was killed in an Israeli rocket attack on his offices.

Adams, Douglas Noël, British novelist (b. March 11, 1952, Cambridge, Eng.—d. May 11, 2001, Santa Barbara, Calif.), was the creator of the satiric science-fiction whimsy *The Hitchhiker's Guide to the Galaxy,* which first saw life as a radio series and then became a book, a television series, a play, record albums, comic books, and a computer game, gaining cult status along the way. The book and its sequels feature British suburbanite Arthur Dent, who—after being rescued by Ford Prefect, a visitor from the planet Betelgeuse, just before Earth is destroyed to clear the way for a hyperspace freeway—encounters such characters as the two-headed alien Zaphod Beeblebrox and learns that the secret of the universe is the number 42. More than 14 million copies of the books were sold worldwide. Adams was educated at St. John's College, Cambridge, earning an M.A. in English literature in 1974. At Cambridge he wrote comedy sketches for the Footlights revue, and following graduation he occasionally worked on writing projects while making his living at a series of odd jobs, including serving as a bodyguard for the Qatari royal family. From 1978 to 1980 Adams wrote scripts for the BBC and worked as a script editor for the *Dr. Who* TV series. In 1978 *The Hitchhiker's Guide,* the culmination of an idea he had had while hitchhiking in Europe in 1971, began on BBC radio. It quickly gained a huge following, and a stage version was produced in 1979. Adams turned it into a novel that same year, and it became a TV series in 1981. The first book was joined by four sequels—*The Restaurant at the End of the Universe* (1980), *Life, the Universe and Everything* (1982), *So Long, and Thanks for All the Fish* (1985), and *Mostly Harmless* (1992)—to become what Adams called his five-part trilogy. Adams also wrote such books as *The Meaning of Liff* (with John Lloyd; 1983) and two detective-story satires—*Dirk Gently's Holistic Detective Agency* (1987) and *The Long Dark Tea-Time of the Soul* (1988)—as well as the nonfiction *Last Chance to See* (with Mark Carwardine; 1990), which reflected his interest in ecology and his concerns about endangered species. He also formed (1996) a multimedia company, the Digital Village, and shortly before his death finished writing the script for a Hollywood film version of *The Hitchhiker's Guide to the Galaxy.* The day before Adams died, his main character achieved immortality when asteroid 18610 was named Arthurdent.

Adler, Lawrence Cecil ("Larry"), American musician, composer, writer, and entertainer (b. Feb. 10, 1914, Baltimore, Md.—d. Aug. 6, 2001, London, Eng.), played classical music on the harmonica, which he insisted on calling a "mouth organ"; he then enjoyed a long career as a humorist, telling stories of his encounters with celebrity friends and British royalty. Though the harmonica had previously been associated only with folk music, in his hands it became a highly versatile and expressive instrument. At age 10 Adler became the youngest cantor in Baltimore, and the following year he ordered an expensive piano, which he then persuaded his parents to accept; he also began playing the harmonica. In 1927 he won the Maryland Harmonica Championship by playing a Beethoven minuet. The next year, at 14, Adler left home for New York City and played harmonica on the streets, then in nightclubs; by age 17 he was performing with Fred Astaire on Broadway in *Smiles*. He also appeared in

AP/Wide World Photos

Harmonica virtuoso Larry Adler

small film roles and became a favourite of New York City and Hollywood stars before playing his first of many concerts with symphony orchestras in Sydney, Australia, in 1939. Adler learned music by listening and memorizing; he did not learn to read music until 1940, when French composer Jean Berger wrote a concerto for him. Among others who composed music for him were Ralph Vaughan Williams and Darius Milhaud; William Walton called him a "genius," and George Gershwin praised his performance of *Rhapsody in Blue*. A liberal who entertained American troops during World War II and the Korean War and in Israel during its 1967 and 1973 wars, Adler opposed the House Committee on Un-American Activities; as a result, he was blacklisted in the U.S., and in 1949 he moved to England, where he had long been popular. There he composed for the stage, films, and television, and he performed as a stand-up comedian-storyteller as well as a musician in nightclubs, in theatres, and on the air. At age 80 Adler issued the disc *The Glory of Gershwin* with guest stars that included Elvis Costello and Elton John; it made him the oldest performer to have placed an album on the British hit record charts. In later life Adler also became a successful book, film, and restaurant critic, as well as the author of *Jokes and How to Tell Them* (1963) and the autobiography *It Ain't Necessarily So* (1984).

Adler, Mortimer Jerome, American educator, philosopher, editor, and writer (b. Dec. 28, 1902, New York, N.Y.—d. June 28, 2001, San Mateo, Calif.), influenced by the ideas espoused by his heroes, Aristotle and St. Thomas Aquinas, championed the notion that a liberal education—the study of the great literature of the Western world—could provide the foundation of education for all people and lead to an understanding of the human condition. To that end he, along with Robert Maynard Hutchins, created (1947) the Great Books Foundation, which led members of the public in reading and meeting to discuss classic works. He was a cofounder and regular lecturer at the Aspen (Colo.) Institute. He also had a long association with Encyclopædia Britannica, during which he counted the compilation of the 54-volume *Great Books of the Western World* (1952) and its *Syntopicon*, a two-volume index based on 102 great ideas, and the restructuring of the *Encyclopædia Britannica* for its 15th edition (1974) among the numerous projects he guided; he served on the board of editors from its inception in 1948 and was its chairman from 1974 until 1995, when he retired. Adler dropped out of high school at age 15 and was working for the *New York Sun* when he determined that he would become a philosopher and enrolled in Columbia University, New York City. Although he completed the course work in three years, his refusal to take a required swimming test kept him from graduating (his bachelor's degree was, however, finally awarded in 1983). Nevertheless, he became (1923) a psychology instructor there, and in 1928 he was awarded a Ph.D. In 1930 Hutchins created the position of associate professor of the philosophy of law for Adler at the University of Chicago, and in 1942 Adler became a full professor. He left the university in 1952 and founded the Institute for Philosophical Research in San Francisco. Among the works created there was the two-volume *The Idea of Freedom* (1958 and 1961). The institute was moved to Chicago in 1963, and Adler then edited the 10-volume *Gateway to the Great Books* (1963) and the 20-volume *Annals of America* (1968) for Encyclopædia Britannica. In the early 1980s he conceived the Paideia Project, a plan for a humanist education in the elementary and secondary grades, which he put forth in the books *The Paideia Proposal: An Educational Manifesto* (1982), *Paideia Problems and Possibilities* (1983), and *The Paideia Program: An Educational Syllabus* (1984). Among the dozens of Adler's other books were *How to Read a Book* (1940; rev. ed., 1972), *The Difference of Man and the Difference It Makes* (1967), *How to Think About God* (1980), and *Six Great Ideas* (1981). Adler served (1988–91) as a professor at the University of North Carolina at Chapel Hill and was a cofounder (1990) of the Center for the Study of Great Ideas in Chicago. His memoirs were published in *Philosopher at Large: An Intellectual Autobiography* (1977) and *A Second Look in the Rearview Mirror* (1992).

Akesson, Birgit, Swedish dancer and choreographer (b. March 24, 1908, Malmö, Swed.—d. March 24, 2001, Stockholm, Swed.), sought to replace conventional expressionistic modern dance techniques with a new idiom of dance as pure nonrepresentational form. As a dancer she created stark solos that relied on slow movement and almost sculptural abstract shapes, often performed without music. In 1963 she founded the Choreographic Institute in Stockholm (later the State Dance School), where she headed the choreography department after her retirement as a dancer in 1965. Akesson, who later studied dance forms in Africa and East Asia, was awarded the title of professor by the Swedish government in 1992.

Alboreto, Michele, Italian race-car driver (b. Dec. 23, 1956, Milan, Italy—d. April 25, 2001, Klettwitz, Ger.), was one of Italy's most popular and successful Formula One (F1) drivers in the early 1980s. After being the European Formula Three champion in 1980, Alboreto won five F1 Grand Prix races, including three during his years driving for Ferrari (1984–88). He finished second to Alain Prost in the 1985 F1 drivers' championship, but thereafter he was plagued with mechanical failures. After leaving F1 racing in 1994 and switching to sports-car racing, Alboreto, with co-drivers Stefan Johansson and Tom Kristensen, won the 1997 24-hour Le Mans Grand Prix d'Endurance. He died in a crash at the Lausitzring circuit while test-driving a new Audi in preparation for the 2001 Le Mans race.

Alekan, Henri, French cinematographer (b. Feb. 10, 1909, Paris, France—d. June 15, 2001, Auxerre, France), was one of the most accomplished filmmakers of the 20th century. After working for a time as a puppeteer, Alekan broke into the film industry as an assistant camera operator in 1927. His career was interrupted by the German occupation of France during World War II. After the war Alekan became a director of photography. He worked with film director René Clément to create *La Bataille du rail* (1946) and *Les Maudits* (1947) and with poet Jean Cocteau to create the film *La Belle et la bête* (1946). In 1953, under director William Wyler, Alekan shot his first American film, *Roman Holiday*, for which he received an Academy Award nomination. He remained in demand throughout the rest of the 1950s and early '60s; however, interest in his work waned thereafter until German film director Wim Wenders drafted Alekan to handle the photography for *The State of Things* (1982) and *Wings of Desire* (1987).

Amado, Jorge, Brazilian novelist (b. Aug. 10, 1912, Ferradas, near Ilhéus, Braz.—d. Aug. 6, 2001, Salvador, Braz.), was the literary patriarch of his country. The first half of his career was characterized by ideological works and the second by humorous, often ribald, novels of Brazilian life. The publication of Amado's second novel, in 1933, led to his being briefly detained, the first of many harassments by the government. This book was followed by others dealing with the exploitation of plantation workers and with the brutality of life in Brazil. He was forced into exile from 1938 to 1942. The masterpiece of his first period was *Terras do sem fim* (1942; *The Violent Land*, 1965), an epic novel about the struggles of workers. In 1946 he was elected to Congress as a member of the Communist Party, but two years later the party was banned, and he was again forced into exile. After returning to Brazil in 1952, Amado began to write the novels that made him famous. He became known particularly for his celebration of the Afro-Brazilian culture, including the candomblé religion, of his native Bahia state. He was called the author of "whores and tramps," a title he embraced. The best known of his later works were *Gabriela, cravo e canela* (1958; *Gabriela, Clove and Cinnamon*, 1962) and *Dona Flor e seus dois maridos* (1966; *Dona Flor and Her Two Husbands*, 1969). Both were made into films and adapted as soap operas for Brazilian television. To charges that he had abandoned his earlier views, he replied that it was important to portray the dreams of the poor. In all, he published 32 books, which were translated into some 50 languages and sold 20 million copies. Among his many honours were France's Legion of Honor and the Graça Aranha Prize of the Brazilian Academy of Letters.

Ammons, A(rchie) R(andolph), American poet and scholar (b. Feb. 18, 1926, near Whiteville, N.C.—d. Feb. 25, 2001, Ithaca, N.Y.), won almost every major American poetry award during a career that spanned nearly half a century. Regarded as a 20th-century Transcendentalist poet, Ammons explored the relationship between man, nature, and the self through free verse. In his work, which also often dealt with the quotidian, he skillfully maintained a philosophical yet conversational tone. Ammons, who grew up on a farm during the Depression, joined the U.S. Naval Reserve at the age of 18, at the height of World War II. It was during his service aboard a navy destroyer in the Pacific that he began writing poetry. After the war Ammons earned a degree in biology (1949) from Wake Forest College (now Wake Forest University), Winston-Salem, N.C., and attended graduate school at the University of California, Berkeley. He worked as an elementary school principal, a real-estate agent, and a sales executive at a New Jersey glass company before publishing his first volume of poetry, *Ommateum: With Doxology* (1955). It was followed by *Expressions of Sea Level* (1963) and *Tape for the Turn of the Year* (1965; written on adding-machine tape), which was published the year after he became a teacher of creative writing at Cornell University, Ithaca, where he spent the rest of his career. Ammons published nearly 30 books, including *Uplands* (1970), *A Coast of Trees* (1981; winner of the National Book Critics Circle Award), and National Book Award winner *Garbage* (1993), a book-length poem about a huge pile of decomposing trash he spotted near Interstate 95 in Florida. *Glare,* his last volume, appeared in 1997.

Anderson, Maceo, American tap dancer (b. Sept. 3, 1910, Charleston, S.C.—d. July 4, 2001, Los Angeles, Calif.), was a founding member of the Four Step Brothers, a widely popular tap-dance act. Anderson danced from the age of three. In his early teens he formed a trio of dancers that eventually began performing at the famed Cotton Club in New York City in the mid-1920s. The group became a quartet in the mid-1930s. By the 1940s the Four Step Brothers were the best-known tap-dance act in the nation. Anderson and his fellow dancers regularly appeared at Radio City Music Hall and the Roxy and Paramount theatres in New York City and on *The Ed Sullivan Show* until they disbanded in the late 1960s. Anderson later taught at his own dance school in Las Vegas, Nev.

Anderson, Poul William, American science-fiction writer (b. Nov. 25, 1926, Bristol, Pa.—d. July 31, 2001, Orinda, Calif.), was the prolific author of more than 100 books of science fiction and fantasy. Over a period of about half a century, he tapped his knowledge of both science and Scandinavian folklore and mythology to create powerfully imaginative depictions of the future, writing in such varied styles as farce, adventure tales, romantic and heroic fantasy, mystery, sociopolitical drama, and serious science fiction. Anderson lived in Denmark for a short time when he was a child and there developed the interest in and acquaintance with Scandinavian mythology that would inform his later fiction, as would his bachelor's degree in physics from the University of Minnesota. In 1947, a year before graduation—during the time known as the golden age of science fiction—he had his first story, "Tomorrow's Children," published in *Astounding Science Fiction* magazine. Following graduation, Anderson began his career as a freelance and had his stories published in a number of pulp magazines. His first novel, *Vault of the Ages,* was published in 1952, and in 1954 his first successful novel, *Brain Wave,* appeared. The latter reflected one of Anderson's primary interests—how people draw on their resources of courage in the face of challenges. Considered his best novel was *Tau Zero* (1970); its theme was the life and death of the universe. Other notable novels included *A Midsummer Tempest* (1974), in which William Shakespeare's works come true; *The Boat of a Million Years* (1989), which addresses immortality; and *Genesis* (2000), which deals with the intelligence of machines and which won the John W. Campbell Memorial Award. Anderson also counted numerous Hugo and Nebula awards among his many honours; served as president of the Science Fiction Writers of America (1972–73), which presented him its Grand Master Award in 1997; and was inducted into the Science Fiction and Fantasy Hall of Fame in 2000.

Anscombe, G(ertrude) E(lizabeth) M(argaret), British philosopher (b. March 18, 1919, Limerick, Ire.—d. Jan. 5, 2001, Cambridge, Eng.), was a close associate of Ludwig Wittgenstein and served as one of the executors of his literary estate; in addition, she was an important philosopher in her own right. Anscombe attended Sydenham School, London, and St. Hugh's College, Oxford. While working in the early 1940s as a research fellow at Newnham College, Cambridge, she met Wittgenstein, to whom she became philosophically and personally close. She translated his late masterwork *Bemerkungen über die Grundlagen der Mathematik* (1956; *Remarks on the Foundations of Mathematics*) and his *Philosophische Untersuchungen* (1953; *Philosophical Investigations*). Anscombe explicated the development of his philosophy in *An Introduction to Wittgenstein's Tractatus* (1959). Her own work centred on questions of the philosophy of action and ethics. *Intention* (1957) stressed reasons rather than causes in the analysis of action. In the "Modern Moral Philosophy" (1958), she argued for a return to an Aristotelian notion of virtue over modern consequentialism. Anscombe converted to Roman Catholicism in 1940 and was an advocate of many of the church's philosophical and moral teachings. She condemned contraception in *Contraception and Chastity* (1975) and defended the ontological argument for the existence of God. Her acceptance of the Catholic notion of just war led her to criticize British entry into World War II and to oppose an honorary Oxford degree for former U.S. president Harry Truman in 1956. Anscombe was a research fellow of Somerville College, Oxford (1946–64), and she taught at the University of Chicago. In 1970 she was called to the chair of philosophy at Cambridge, where Wittgenstein had taught. Anscombe, who wore a tunic and trousers at a time when trousers were not completely acceptable for women, also sported a monocle and smoked cigars. She married (1941) philosopher Peter Geach, with whom she had seven children.

Anthony, Earl, American bowler (b. April 27, 1938, Kent, Wash.—found dead Aug. 14, 2001, New Berlin, Wis.), was the winningest player in the history of the Professional Bowlers Association (PBA); he also became the first bowler to earn $1 million in his career. Anthony, whose childhood dream of becoming a major league baseball player was derailed by an ankle injury, joined the PBA Tour in 1963. After a slow start he went on to dominate professional bowling during the 1970s and early '80s. He won a record 41 PBA tournaments from 1970 to 1983, including 10 major titles. During this time professional bowling was regularly broadcast on television, and Anthony achieved widespread fame. He was named PBA Player of the Year six times and was the tour scoring leader five times. He retired from the sport in 1984 but made a brief comeback in 1987 and a year later joined the PBA Senior Tour, on which he won seven senior titles. He garnered a career total of $1,441,061 in prize money. Anthony was inducted into the PBA Hall of Fame in 1981. In later years he worked in television as a commentator on bowling broadcasts. He died from head trauma after falling down a flight of stairs.

Asahina, Takashi, Japanese conductor (b. July 9, 1908, Tokyo, Japan—d. Dec. 29, 2001, Kobe, Japan), was credited with popularizing the Austro-German repertoire—especially Bruckner, Beethoven, and Mahler—in Japan and had one of the longest careers of any conductor, remaining professionally active virtually right up until his death at the age of 93. A self-taught violinist, Asahina abandoned a legal career and worked as a department-store clerk and a railroad engineer before apprenticing himself to Russian conductor Emmanuel Metter in the early 1930s. Asahina made his conducting debut in 1939 and founded the Kansai Symphony Orchestra (now the Osaka Philharmonic Orchestra) in 1947. He became widely known internationally after conducting the Berlin Philharmonic in 1956. Asahina conducted more than 60 orchestras in 15 countries and in 1994 was awarded the Japanese Order of Culture in recognition of his achievements in the arts.

Ash, Mary Kay (Mary Kathlyn Wagner), American entrepreneur (b. May 12, 1918, Hot

Ed Lallo/Getty Images

Cosmetics queen Mary Kay Ash in her pink cadillac

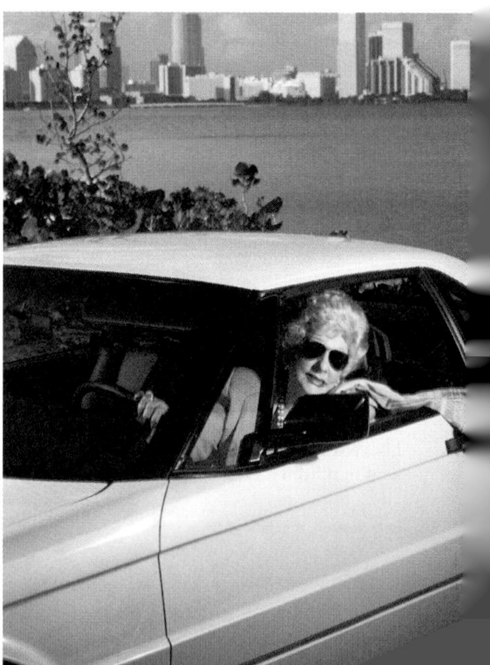

Wells, Texas—d. Nov. 22, 2001, Dallas, Texas), was the founder of cosmetics giant Mary Kay Inc. and one of the most famous businesswomen in the world. Ash had held relatively modest jobs in direct sales before establishing her own business in 1963. Mary Kay Cosmetics (as the company was originally known) was an almost instant success, recording nearly $1 million in sales by 1965. By 2000 the company's wholesale revenue was estimated at $1.2 billion. Ash cultivated a flashy image as an executive and was known for lavishly rewarding productive employees with such gifts as diamonds, minks, and pink Cadillacs. She wrote a number of best-selling books, including *Mary Kay: You Can Have It All* (1995).

Astafyev, Viktor Petrovich, Soviet-Russian novelist (b. May 1, 1924, Ovsyanka, Krasnoyarsk *kray,* Russia—d. Nov. 29, 2001, Krasnoyarsk, Krasnoyarsk *kray*), drew on his experiences living in a rural village as well as his stint as a volunteer in the front lines during World War II to pen novels that chronicled the bleakness and despair of life in Siberia and the madness and horror of war. As one of the *derevenshchiki* ("village writers"), Astafyev was renowned for the stark realism of his narratives, which centred on rural people who were removed from Communist Party discipline. Among his most acclaimed works were *Tsar-ryba* (1980; *Queen Fish* [1982]), an epic tale about the threat of ecological destruction in Siberia; *Pechalny detektiv* (1986; "The Sad Detective Story"), a gruesome look at the alcoholism, violence, and animosity among Soviet people; and *Proklyaty i ubity* (1993; "The Damned and the Dead"), considered one of the most authentic yet disturbing depictions of the effect of World War II on Russian villages. Astafyev's collected works were published by Molodaya Gvardiya in four volumes in 1979–81. He was the recipient of the Hero of Socialist Labour (1989).

Aston, Kenneth George, British association football (soccer) referee (b. Sept. 1, 1915, Colchester, Essex, Eng.—d. Oct. 23, 2001, Ilford, Essex), invented the yellow (caution) and red (ejection) disciplinary cards, which were first employed during play at the 1970 World Cup finals and were quickly introduced around the world. Aston qualified as a referee in 1936. In 1962, having worked successfully for the Football Association in England, he was invited to officiate at the World Cup finals in Chile. He replaced the designated referee for the contentious first-round game between Chile and Italy, but the players resisted all attempts to control violent play, and the match deteriorated into a brawl that came to be known as "the Battle of Santiago." Although he never officiated another World Cup match, Aston supervised all officials at the 1966 and 1970 World Cups. In 1970 he introduced the red and yellow cards (inspired, he said, by the colours used in traffic lights) to help referees clarify disciplinary actions on the field. He was made MBE in 1997.

Astor, Francis David Langhorne, British newspaper editor (b. March 5, 1912, London, Eng.—d. Dec. 7, 2001, London), as editor of *The Observer* from 1948 to 1975, was largely responsible for turning the paper's viewpoint from a conservative, establishment-supporting one to espousal of a number of liberal causes, including anticolonialism, human rights, and prison reform. He came to be considered one of the most outstanding and influential 20th-century editors.

AP/Wide World Photos

Fingerpicker extraordinaire Chet Atkins

Atef, Muhammad (Sobhi Abu Sitta), Egyptian-born Islamist militant (b. 1944?, Egypt—d. Nov. 14/15, 2001, near Kabul, Afg.), was believed to have been a close associate of Osama bin Laden (in early 2001 his daughter married Bin Laden's son) and chief military strategist for the Islamic terrorist organization al-Qaeda. He reportedly trained as a police officer before joining the radical Egyptian Islamic Jihad, members of which assassinated Pres. Anwar as-Sadat in 1981. Atef, whose other suspected noms de guerre included Abu Hafs al-Misri and Abu Khadijah, fled to Afghanistan in the 1980s. In 1999 he was one of more than 100 defendants convicted of subversion in Egypt and sentenced to prison in absentia. Intelligence sources indicated that Atef was involved in terrorist attacks on Americans in Somalia as well as the 1998 bombings of the U.S. embassies in Kenya and Tanzania and the terrorist attacks in the U.S. on Sept. 11, 2001. The U.S. government placed him on the FBI's list of "most wanted terrorists" and offered a $5 million reward for his capture. He was reported to have been killed in a bombing raid on an al-Qaeda stronghold outside Kabul.

Atkins, Chet (Chester Burton Atkins), American guitarist and record producer (b. June 20, 1924, Luttrell, Tenn.—d. June 30, 2001, Nashville, Tenn.), was a major figure in country music. Atkins shone as a guitarist, talent scout, and record producer who created the "Nashville sound" of the 1960s; Don Gibson, Dolly Parton, Charley Pride, Waylon Jennings, Willie Nelson, Elvis Presley, and Perry Como *(q.v.)* were among the stars he produced or discovered for RCA Records. Atkins played fiddle and guitar with country bands on several Southern and Midwestern radio stations before making his first records as a singer-guitarist in 1946 (he later tried to destroy the master recordings on which he sang). After appearances on the Grand Ole Opry and hit guitar solos, including "Galloping on the Guitar" (1949), he played at many recording sessions with Hank Williams and others. Atkins became an assistant producer in 1952 and urged RCA to sign Presley, which led to the latter's rise to stardom; in 1957 Atkins became manager of RCA's Nashville recording operations. He then championed a modern country music sound that abandoned banjos, fiddles, and steel guitars in favour of string sections and vocal choruses. Atkins became an RCA vice president in 1967 but soon began to perform more actively. He made over 100 albums under his own name, playing the guitar in his signature fingerpicking style that he had adapted from that of Merle Travis. Atkins won a total of 14 Grammy Awards during his career and costarred on albums with guitar legends Travis, Les Paul, Doc Watson, Jerry Reed, and Mark Knopfler as well as his Nashville cronies Boots Randolph, Floyd Cramer, Danny Davis, and the Nashville String Band, among others. He toured the world playing country music, pop, and jazz and was sometimes featured with symphony orchestras. In the 1980s Atkins left RCA to record for Columbia. The guitarmaker Gretsch introduced its Chet Atkins Country Gentleman model in the 1960s. Atkins was inducted into the Country Music Hall of Fame in 1973.

Aumont, Jean-Pierre (Jean-Pierre Philippe Salomons), French actor (b. Jan. 5, 1911, Paris, France—d. Jan. 30, 2001, St. Tropez,

France), employed his suave good looks and Gallic charm in more than 60 French and American motion pictures during a 70-year stage and screen career. Although Aumont was often cast in B-grade movies, his films included Marcel Carné's *Hôtel du Nord* (1938), François Truffaut's *La Nuit américaine* (1972; *Day for Night*), and Claude Lelouch's *Le Chat et la souris* (1975; *Cat and Mouse*). He also starred in the original stage production of Jean Cocteau's *La Machine infernale* (1934; *The Infernal Machine*) and the 1963 Broadway musical *Tovarich* opposite British actress Vivien Leigh; on television Aumont appeared in such miniseries as *A Tale of Two Cities* (1989) and *Le Comte de Monte Cristo* (1998; *The Count of Monte Cristo*). In 1991 he received an honorary César (French Oscar) for lifetime achievement.

Loomis Dean/TimePix

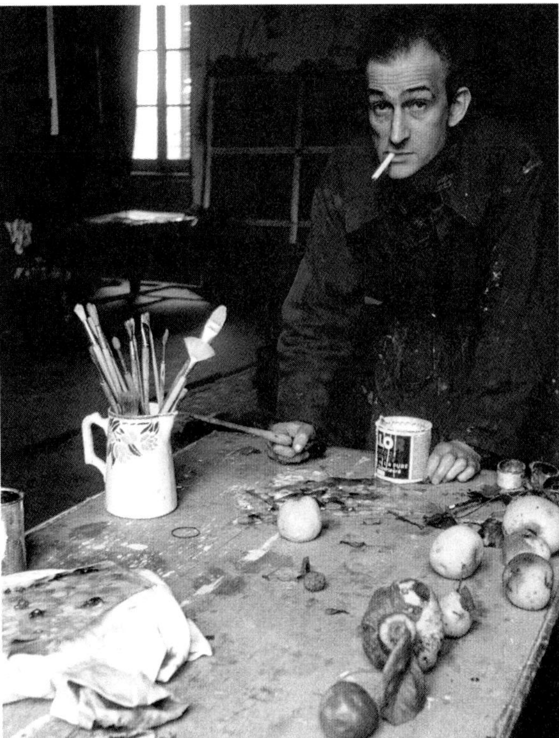

Figurative painting master Balthus

Babu Chhiri Sherpa, Nepalese mountaineer (b. June 22, 1965, Taksindu, Nepal—d. April 29, 2001, Mt. Everest), was a legendary guide who reached the summit of Mt. Everest 10 times and set two records on the world's tallest peak; in May 1999 he survived for more than 21 hours without bottled oxygen while "camping" overnight on the 8,850-m (29,035-ft) summit, and in May 2000 he ascended from Base Camp (about 5,350 m [17,600 ft]) to the summit in an astounding 16 hours 56 minutes. Babu Chhiri reportedly fell into a crevasse while taking photographs near Camp II at about 6,500 m (21,300 ft).

Balthus (Balthazar Klossowski), French artist (b. Feb. 29, 1908, Paris, France—d. Feb. 18, 2001, Rossinière, Switz.), was one of the greatest figurative painters of the 20th century. His works included street scenes, portraits of fellow artists, and provocative depictions of young girls, who were often shown with cats. Balthus was largely self-taught and had a strong sense of tradition, with Piero della Francesca and Nicolas Poussin among his important influences. He was the son of Polish artists and grew up in Paris, Berlin, and Switzerland. In 1921, when he was 16, he published *Mitsou*, a series of drawings depicting his cat, with a preface by Rainer Maria Rilke. In 1924 Balthus went to Paris to study, and early in his career he supported himself by painting portraits and working as a stage designer and illustrator. Balthus had his first one-man show in Paris in 1934, and he subsequently became well known in the U.S., with eight exhibitions at the Pierre Matisse Gallery in New York City from 1938 to 1977. From 1961 to 1977 he was director of the French Academy in Rome, and it was during this period that he began to paint the Japanese model Setsuko Ideta, who in 1967 became his second wife. Balthus had a number of retrospectives, including exhibitions at museums in Paris, New York City, London, and Venice. Although he was reclusive and shunned publicity about his personal life, he collaborated with Nicholas Fox Weber on a biography, *Balthus* (1999). Among his paintings were *Guitar Lesson* (1934), depicting a young girl spread over the knees of an older woman and described variously as an erotic portrait of lesbianism or as a pietà; *The Mountain* (1937), one of his best-known landscapes, combining realistic detail with a sense of fantasy; and *Therese* (1938), one of his many suggestive portraits featuring a young girl.

Barnard, Christiaan Neethling, South African surgeon (b. Nov. 8, 1922, Beaufort West, S.Af.—d. Sept. 2, 2001, Paphos, Cyprus), performed the first transplant of a heart from one human to another (1967), the first "piggyback" heart transplant, in which a second heart was inserted in order to aid the patient's own weak one (1974), the first transplantation of an animal's heart into a human, again to assist the patient's heart and give it time to heal (1977), and the first heart-lung transplant (1981). His early transplants were daring and controversial, in part because they set a precedent for the consideration of brain death as acceptable for the harvesting of organs for transplant and in part because he flouted the racial barriers of apartheid. They also gained the handsome and charismatic doctor instant fame both professionally and socially, and he became an international celebrity and member of the jet set. Barnard graduated from the University of Cape Town in 1946, spent some time in private practice, and then returned to the university to conduct research. He earned his M.D. degree in 1953, became a surgeon at Groote Schuur Hospital in Cape Town, and in 1956–58 studied at the University of Minnesota, earning a Ph.D. There Barnard developed his interest and expertise in open-heart surgery, and when he returned (1958) to South Africa, he took a U.S. government-donated heart-lung machine with him. At Groote Schuur he formed one of the world's finest heart-surgery units, where he had especially good results with valve surgery and with correcting children's congenital cardiac problems and where he also began experimenting with heart transplantation, generally in dogs. Although Barnard's first heart-transplant patient died of double pneumonia 18 days after surgery because his dosage of immunosuppressant drugs was too high, his second patient lived more than 19 months. More experience and the development of better antirejection drugs eventually made heart transplant surgery standard, and some 100,000 such operations had been performed by late 2001. Barnard suffered from rheumatoid arthritis and in 1983 was forced to retire from the practice of surgery. He thereafter included conducting research in Oklahoma, running his farm in South Africa, and writing a weekly newspaper column among his activities. In addition to the autobiography *One Life* (1969; with Curtis Bill Pepper)—whose royalties were donated to the Chris Barnard Foundation, which supported research and made it possible for children from all over the world to travel to South Africa for heart surgery—Barnard also wrote papers for scholarly journals and a number of other books, including another autobiography, *The Second Life* (1993), such works on health topics as *Heart*

South African transplant surgeon Christiaan Barnard

Attack: You Don't Have to Die (1971), *The Arthritis Handbook* (1984), and *50 Ways to a Healthy Heart* (2001), and several novels.

Basov, Nikolay Gennadiyevich, Soviet physicist (b. Dec. 14, 1922, Usman, near Voronezh, Russia—d. July 1, 2001, Moscow, Russia), was corecipient of the Nobel Prize for Physics in 1964 with Aleksandr M. Prokhorov, his colleague at the P.N. Lebedev Physical Institute in Moscow, and Charles H. Townes of the United States. The award was given for fundamental research in quantum electronics that led to the development of the maser and the laser, which produce parallel monochromatic coherent beams of microwaves and light, respectively. Basov studied theoretical and experimental physics at the Moscow Engineering Physics Institute, graduating in 1950. From 1952 he did postgraduate work in quantum radiophysics under Prokhorov at the Lebedev Institute. By 1954 Basov and Prokhorov had developed the concept for a device that would emit microwave radiation of a single wavelength. The next year they learned that Townes's team at Columbia University, New York City, had already built such a device, which they called a maser (microwave amplification by stimulated emission of radiation). Basov and Prokhorov soon constructed a maser, and by 1958 other teams had applied the maser principle to the optical spectrum to lay the groundwork for the laser (light amplification by stimulated emission of radiation), the first of which was built in 1960. Basov served as deputy director (1958–73) and director (1973–89) of the Lebedev Institute and as director (1989–2001) of its Institute of Quantum Radiophysics. He was a deputy in the Supreme Soviet (1974–89) and a member of the Presidium (1982–89). In 1982 Basov was among 97 Nobel laureates to call for an international freeze on nuclear weapons.

Beame, Abraham David (Abraham David Birnbaum), British-born American politician (b. March 20, 1906, London, Eng.—d. Feb. 10, 2001, New York, N.Y.), served as mayor of New York City from 1974 to 1977; he was the city's first Jewish mayor. An accountant by profession, Beame worked in the city's budget office from 1946 to 1961, when he was elected city comptroller. He failed in his first mayoral bid in 1965, and he later served another term as comptroller. Beame was successful in his second campaign for mayor, though the outgoing administration left him to contend with severe financial problems. The ensuing fiscal crisis dominated Beame's one term in office and drove the city to the brink of bankruptcy in 1975. Beame's solutions, which included raising taxes, cutting services, and reducing the municipal workforce by 65,000, proved unpopular, and he was defeated in his reelection bid.

Bebey, Francis, Cameroonian-born writer, composer, and musician (b. July 15, 1929, Douala, Cameroon—d. May 28, 2001, Paris, France), achieved international kudos both as a novelist and poet and as an influential "Afropop" musical performer. Bebey was educated in literature and musicology at the Sorbonne and at New York University. He experimented with jazz and classical guitar before expanding his eclectic musical repertoire with traditional African rhythms and instruments, notably the *sanza* (thumb piano) and *ndewhoo* (a one-note pygmy flute). He recorded and performed worldwide, singing in English, French, and Douala. Bebey's first novel, *Le Fils d'Agatha Moudio* (1967; *Agatha Moudio's Son,* 1971), won the Grand Literary Prize of Black Africa in 1968. His wide-ranging literary output also included musicology studies, such as *Musique de l'Afrique* (1969; *African Music,* 1975); poetry, such as *Nouvelle saison des fruits* (1980); and fiction, notably *Le Roi Albert d'Effidi* (1973; *King Albert,* 1981).

Bécaud, Gilbert (François Gilbert Silly), French singer-songwriter (b. Oct. 24, 1927, Toulon, France—d. Dec. 18, 2001, Paris, France), composed "chansons françaises," romantic melodies that became pop hits for him as well as for many other French- and English-language performers. Bécaud, who earned the nickname "Monsieur 100,000 volts" for his dynamic stage presence, wrote more than 400 songs, most notably "Et Maintenant" ("What Now, My Love"), "Je t'appartiens" ("Let It Be Me"), "L'Important c'est la rose" ("What's Important Is the Rose"), and "Seul sur son étoile" ("It Must Be Him").

Beti, Mongo (Alexandre Biyidi), Cameroonian novelist and political writer (b. June 30, 1932, Mbalmayo, Cameroon—d. Oct. 8, 2001, Douala, Cameroon), was a critic of colonialism, which he believed destroyed traditional African society, and of the authoritarian regime that ruled Cameroon after independence in 1960. He was widely translated and gained an international reputation. He was the son of the owner of a cocoa plantation and was educated in Cameroon before going to France in 1951 to study at the Sorbonne. In the late 1950s he took a position teaching literature at the Lycée Corneille in Rouen, France, where he remained for 30 years. He published his first novel, *Ville cruelle* (1954), on the exploitation of peasants, under the pseudonym Ezra Boto. His second novel, *Le Pauve Christ de Bomba* (1956), appeared under the name Mongo Beti, which he used thereafter. Considered his most important work, the book was a satire on the influence of Roman Catholic missionaries in Africa. *Mission terminée* (1957), published in the U.K. as *Mission to Kala* and in the U.S. as *Mission Accomplished,* was an attack on French colonial policy. *Maine basse sur le Cameroun* (1972) was banned in both France and Cameroon. Other novels included *Remember Ruben* (1974) and its sequel, *La Ruine presque cocasse d'un polichinelle* (1979), which told of revolutionaries who defeated a French-backed regime in their native country. Later novels, such as *Les Deux Mères de Guillaume Ismaël Dzewatama, futur camionneur* (1982), dealt with mixed marriages. In 1978, with his French-born wife, he founded *Peuples Noirs/Peuples Africains,* a journal opposing neocolonialism in Africa. He returned to Cameroon in the 1990s.

Bibby, (Thomas) Geoffrey, British archaeologist (b. Oct. 14, 1917, Heversham, Cumbria, Eng.—d. Feb. 6, 2001, Odder, near Århus, Den.), unearthed, with his Danish colleague Peter Vilhelm Glob, the 4,000-year-old remnants of the ancient kingdom of Dilmun beneath the modern city of Manama, Bahrain. The excavations, which began in 1953 and eventually extended over several countries, verified that the legendary Dilmun was a real trading centre and confirmed the Persian Gulf region's historic significance. Bibby's books included *Testimony of the Spade* (1956), *Four Thousand Years Ago* (1961), and *Looking for Dilmun* (1969).

Birendra Bir Bikram Shah Dev, Nepalese royal (b. Dec. 28, 1945, Kathmandu, Nepal—d. June 1, 2001, Kathmandu), was king of Nepal for 29 years. Educated at St. Joseph's School, Darjeeling, India, Eton (Eng.) College, the University of Tokyo, and Harvard University, he was the first Nepalese royal to study abroad. Upon the death of his father, King Mahendra, on Jan. 31, 1972, Birendra acceded to the throne. He was a popular, though autocratic, ruler. During his reign he opened up Nepal to extensive tourism and managed to maintain the country's independence despite political pressure from India, China, and the Soviet Union. In November 1990 he approved a new constitution that, while preserving his status as monarch, restored the multiparty democracy that his father had abolished. Along with his wife, Queen Aishwarya, and six other royal family members, Birendra was shot and killed at the Royal Palace; the massacre was carried out by Birendra's eldest son, Crown Prince Dipendra, who afterward turned the gun on himself and died three days later. Dipendra reportedly had been enraged by his mother's opposition to his choice of bride.

Black, Charles Lund, Jr., American legal scholar and educator (b. Sept. 22, 1915, Austin, Texas—d. May 5, 2001, New York, N.Y.), was a renowned authority on constitutional law; his 1974 book *Impeachment: A Handbook* was widely studied during the Watergate Scandal and was reissued during the impeachment proceedings against Pres. Bill Clinton in 1999. Black, who held a law degree from Yale University, taught at Columbia University, New York City, from 1947 to 1956, at Yale from 1956 to 1986, and again at Columbia from 1986 to 1999. A noted champion of civil rights, he helped write the legal brief for the plaintiff in the landmark *Brown v. Board of Education of Topeka* (Kan.), the 1954 case in which the U.S. Supreme Court ruled that racial segregation in public schools violated the 14th Amendment to the Constitution.

Blake, Sir Peter James, New Zealand yachtsman and explorer (b. Oct. 1, 1948, Auckland, N.Z.—d. Dec. 6, 2001, off Macapá, Braz.), was the winner of the two most important yachting competitions—the Whitbread Round the World Race (1989–90) and the America's Cup (1995 and 2000)—and in 1994 in the *ENZA New Zealand* won the Jules Verne Trophy when he set a nonstop circumnavigation world record of 74 days 22 hours 17 minutes 22 seconds, which went unbroken for three years. He later combined his enthusiasm for sailing with

America's Cup winner Sir Peter Blake

© Nigel Marple/Reuters 2000

his environmental interests and investigated pollution and global warming in Antarctica and South America. Blake began sailing when he was a young boy and at age 16 participated in his first long ocean race. In 1973–74 he served as a crew member in the first Whitbread race—and the first of the five in which he sailed—and when he finally won, in *Steinlager 2,* he did it by being the first competitor ever to win all six of the race's legs. Blake made an unsuccessful effort to win the America's Cup for New Zealand in 1992 but saw victory on board the *Black Magic* in the next challenge three years later. For his success in winning the cup, Blake, who had been created MBE in 1983 and OBE in 1991, was rewarded with a knighthood in 1995. He went on to manage *Black Magic*'s victorious defense in 2000, but he also had already begun his environmental activities. He served as head of the Jacques Cousteau Society, formed his own company, blakexpeditions, to promote interest in the oceans' ecology, and was appointed special envoy of the UN Environment Program. Blake, on a pollution-monitoring exploration of the Amazon River and the Rio Negro in Brazil, was murdered when robbers boarded his boat and he rushed on deck to try to protect the vessel and its crew.

Boetticher, Budd (Oscar Boetticher, Jr.), American film director and screenwriter (b. July 29, 1916, Chicago, Ill.—d. Nov. 29, 2001, Ramona, Calif.), was a professional matador in Mexico before becoming a leading director of classic western movies. Much of his reputation was based on seven films he directed from 1956 to 1960, including *Seven Men from Now, The Tall T,* and *Decision at Sundown;* they starred Randolph Scott as a lonely but resolute cowpoke hero confronted by villains, and Boetticher called them "morality plays." He was also acclaimed for directing *Bullfighter and the Lady* (1951), a story based on his own experiences; he directed his last feature film, *A Time for Dying,* in 1971.

Bonfá, Luiz Floriano, Brazilian guitarist and songwriter (b. Oct. 17, 1922, Rio de Janeiro, Braz.—d. Jan. 12, 2001, Rio de Janeiro), was one of the originators of bossa nova, a musical style that blended samba and jazz. In the late 1940s and early '50s, Bonfá played with a popular Brazilian band called the Quitandinha Serenaders, but he left the group to concentrate on songwriting. He achieved international fame after performing on the sound track of the 1958 film *Orfeu negro* (*Black Orpheus*). In 1962 he was a featured performer at a widely publicized bossa nova concert held at Carnegie Hall in New York City. Several Bonfá recordings became hits and pop/jazz standards, including "Manhã de Carnaval" and "Samba de Orfeu."

Bosch Gaviño, Juan, Dominican writer and politician (b. June 30, 1909, La Vega, Dom. Rep.—d. Nov. 1, 2001, Santo Domingo, Dom. Rep.), was the country's first democratically elected president. Serving only seven months in 1963 before being deposed, he nonetheless remained a power in Dominican politics. He left secondary school at the end of his third year. A foe of dictator Rafael Trujillo, he went into exile in the late 1930s. In 1939 he founded the Dominican Revolutionary Party (PRD), the country first political party. After Trujillo's assassination in 1961, Bosch returned and ran for president in the election of Dec. 20, 1962. With the support of the poor, the middle class, and intellectuals, he won almost two-thirds of the votes. Bosch took office on Feb. 27, 1963, with a program of land reform, nationalization of certain businesses, and curbs on the power of the military; a new constitution was adopted in April. Although he was a cautious reformer, he earned the enmity of landowners, businessmen, and the military, as well as of the Roman Catholic Church and of the U.S., which saw him as a leftist. On Sept. 25, 1963, he was overthrown in a military coup, which was followed by civil war and, in April 1965, an invasion by U.S. troops. He returned from exile to run in the election of 1966 but lost. In 1973 he split with the PRD to form the Dominican Liberation Party. Although he ran for president another five times, he never regained power. A charismatic orator, he also was a prolific writer and published essays, novels and short stories, biographies of Pablo Duarte and Simón Bolívar, and historical works that included a history of the Caribbean.

Dominican political and literary lion Juan Bosch

AP/Wide World Photos

Boudreau, Louis ("Lou"), American baseball player and manager (b. July 17, 1917, Harvey, Ill.—d. Aug. 10, 2001, Olympia Fields, Ill.), began his professional career as a dazzling defensive shortstop, became the second youngest manager in major league history, and went on to lead the American League in batting and manage the Cleveland Indians to their last world championship; he then managed three more teams and broadcast major league games for nearly three decades. Boudreau signed a baseball contract with the Cleveland Indians in 1938. By 1940 he was playing in the All-Star Game, and the following year he nominated himself to become the next player-manager of the Indians. Team president Alva Bradley surprised everyone by naming the 24-year-old Boudreau to the post; his fellow players responded by winning 728 games for him, the most victories for any Cleveland manager, during the next nine seasons. He was noted for inspiring self-confidence in his players. His most famous innovation was the "Williams shift," in which he moved all defensive players except the left fielder to the right side of the field, to stymie the Boston Red Sox's power-hitting Ted Williams. On offense as well as defense, he was his own best player, hitting over .300 four times; his .327 was best in the league in 1944, and his lifetime batting average was .295. He was a favourite among fans as well as fellow players, and when new team owner Bill Veeck threatened to replace him in 1947, Cleveland fans held pro-Boudreau rallies to protest. The next year, after his team had added the league's first African American players—slugging outfielder Larry Doby and pitcher Satchel Paige—Boudreau hit .355, with 18 homers and 106 runs batted in, and led the Indians to their first World Series victory in 28 years. After Boudreau's playing career ended, he managed the Red Sox (1952–54) and the Kansas City Athletics (1955–57) and then became the Chicago Cubs radio announcer in 1958. Apart from a season off, during which he managed the Cubs to a seventh-place finish in 1960, he remained the team's radio voice until 1987. He was elected to the National Baseball Hall of Fame in 1970.

Boulting, Roy, British filmmaker (b. Nov. 21, 1913, Bray, Berkshire, Eng.—d. Nov. 5, 2001, Eynsham, Oxfordshire, Eng.), created, in partnership with his twin brother, John, some of Great Britain's most popular motion pictures of the 1940s and '50s. In 1937 the Boultings founded Charter Film Productions Ltd. and began making movies, usually with one brother serving as producer of the films that the other directed. During World War II Roy directed documentaries for the Army Film and Photographic Unit, notably the Academy Award-winning *Desert Victory* (1943). After the war the Boultings reteamed and made films ranging from the thriller *Brighton Rock* (1947) to social dramas such as *Fame Is the Spur* (1946), *The Guinea Pig* (1948), and *Seven Days to Noon* (1950). They were best known for their satiric comedies, including *Private's Progress* (1956), *Lucky Jim* (1957), and *I'm All Right, Jack* (1959), many of which served as star vehicles for Ian Carmichael and Peter Sellers. Roy Boulting's final films included *The Family Way* (1966), *Twisted Nerve* (1968), and *There's a Girl in My Soup* (1970). John Boulting died in 1985.

Legendary batsman Sir Donald Bradman

Allsport Hulton/Archive/Allsport

Bradman, Sir Donald George ("the Don"), Australian cricketer (b. Aug. 27, 1908, Cootamundra, N.S.W., Australia—d. Feb. 25, 2001, Adelaide, Australia), was the most effective batsman in the history of the game and one of the most celebrated Australians of the 20th century. Bradman's achievements far surpassed those of any other cricket batsman. His career averages of 99.94 in Tests and 95.14 in first-class matches were well ahead of those in second place: R.G. Pollock (60.97) in Tests and V.M. Merchant (71.22) in first-class matches. He made a world-record 37 scores of 200 or greater in a total of 338 first-class innings, compared with runner-up W. Hammond (36 in 634 innings), and scored his hundredth first-class hundred in his 295th innings, while the next-fastest, D.C.S. Compton, needed 552 innings. Bradman's 452 not out, against Queensland in 1930, remained the highest first-class score for almost 30 years, and his 334 against England in 1930 (309 in one day) was the highest Test score at the time. In 234 first-class matches for New South Wales, South Australia, and Australia, he made 28,067 runs, including 117 hundreds and six scores of 300 or more runs (another world record), with one score of more than 400. In 52 Tests he scored 6,996 runs, with 29 hundreds, including 2 triple and 10 double centuries. After playing for Bowral Cricket Club, Bradman was invited (1927) to play for New South Wales, scoring 118 not out in his first match. His Test debut came the next year against England at Brisbane. He batted poorly and was dropped, but he soon was recalled and batted 79 and 112. The Australian tour of England in 1930, in which he scored 974 runs in the Test series (average 139.14), established him as the game's dominant batsman. He continued his high scoring against the West Indies (1930–31) and South Africa (1931–32). To counter Bradman's devastating batting, England captain D.R. Jardine devised the infamous "bodyline" bowling for the 1932–33 tour of Australia. In a bitterly contentious atmosphere, England won the series and "contained" Bradman to an average of 56.57 for the Test series, with only one century. After bodyline was condemned and outlawed, Bradman resumed his assault on the bowlers and never averaged less than 84.16 for any season until World War II interrupted his career in 1940. Bradman, who had been named captain in 1936, was well into his 30s and plagued with health problems when cricket resumed after the war. Nevertheless, he led Australia to victory in four Test series (15 wins, 3 losses, and 6 draws). Although only 1.7 m (5 ft 7 in) tall, Bradman had deft footwork and strong wrists and forearms, combined with intense powers of concentration and an insatiable appetite for runs. After retiring in 1948, he served as a selector, and he was twice chairman of the Australian Board of Control. He was knighted in 1949 and appointed Companion of the Order of Australia in 1979. The Bradman Museum was opened in Bowral in 1989. The 2000 *Wisden Cricketers' Almanack* named Bradman the top cricketer of the 20th century.

Braun, Victor, Canadian opera singer (b. Aug. 4, 1935, Windsor, Ont.—d. Jan. 6, 2001, Ulm, Ger.), was an internationally renowned baritone. After studying opera at the Royal Conservatory of Music, Toronto, he made his professional debut in a 1957 Canadian Opera Company production of Puccini's *Tosca.* He was the grand prize winner of the International Mozart Competition in 1963. Braun joined the Bavarian State Opera in Munich, Ger., in 1968, and a year later he debuted at Covent Garden in London in the title role of Humphrey Searle's *Hamlet.* His repertory included more than 100 roles, most notably the title roles of Verdi's *Falstaff* and Tchaikovsky's *Eugene Onegin.*

Brown, Lester Raymond ("Les"), American bandleader (b. March 14, 1912, Reinerton, Penn.—d. Jan. 4, 2001, Pacific Palisades, Calif.), led a top swing-era dance band that went on to long-term Hollywood and television success and spent 40 years accompanying comedian Bob Hope's stage and broadcast shows. Excellent arrangers and musicians contributed to the Brown band, notably singer Doris Day, who joined when she was 17 years old. While the dance-band business was collapsing in the late 1940s, Brown's band thrived by appearing on Hope's weekly radio programs, and it was featured on television with Hope, Steve Allen, and Dean Martin. Brown began playing soprano saxophone in boyhood; he later attended Duke University, Durham, N.C., where he led the student dance band. The big band he formed in 1938 won popular success, especially after Day joined in 1940, and made a musical breakthrough with its 1941 hit "Joltin' Joe Dimaggio." Brown's arrangers, influenced by the Jimmie Lunceford, Count Basie, Woody Herman, and other top jazz bands, crafted a modern swing style; Brown's musicians, including his brother, trombonist Clyde ("Stumpy") Brown, played with singular precision and technical skill. The band scored a number of hit records, including "Mexican Hat Dance," "I've Got My Love to Keep Me Warm," and, most famously, "Sentimental Journey," a number one song in 1945 featuring Day's vocals. Two years later the Brown band first appeared with Hope; it made 18 overseas Christmas tours with him to entertain troops, including 7 trips to wartime Vietnam, and appeared in over 800 shows with Hope. Brown led his band at inauguration balls for Presidents Richard Nixon and Ronald Reagan, as well as for the U.K.'s Queen Elizabeth. The band—often introduced as "Les Brown and His Band of Renown"—continued to perform at concerts and dances and record throughout the rock era, although in 1990, a decade before his retirement, he maintained, "There won't be much demand for big bands soon."

Callaway, Ely Reeves, American golf-equipment manufacturer (b. June 3, 1919, La Grange, Ga.—d. July 5, 2001, Rancho Santa Fe, Calif.), founded the Callaway Golf Co. in 1982; under his leadership the company became the world's leading manufacturer of golf equipment. His most popular golf club, the oversized "Big Bertha" driver, introduced in 1991, was credited with revolutionizing the sport by making the driver one of the easiest golf clubs to use. Another Callaway driver, the ERC, was banned by the U.S. Golf Association for allegedly propelling the golf ball too far. Callaway had been president of a textile company and a vineyard owner before launching his golf company.

Campanelli, Pauline Eblé, American artist (b. Jan. 25, 1943, Bronx, N.Y.—d. Nov. 29, 2001, Pohatcong township, N.J.), painted superrealist still lifes that, while never of much interest to prestigious, expensive galleries and art museums, sold by the thousands through catalogs, furniture stores, and print and poster shops, rivaling only Andrew Wyeth in sales by a living artist. Purchases of prints of her most popular picture, *Wild Rose Berries,* topped 600,000.

Carver, Richard Michael Power Carver, Baron, British field marshal (b. April 24, 1915, Bletchingley, Surrey, Eng.—d. Dec. 9, 2001, Fareham, Hampshire, Eng.), rose steadily through the military ranks from 1935, when he graduated from Sandhurst and was commissioned into the Royal Tank Corps, until he was promoted to field marshal and made chief of the defense staff in 1973. During the intervening years he saw action in the World War II campaigns in North Africa and Europe and held a series of prominent military posts, notably chief of staff (1955) in Kenya during the Mau Mau uprising, head (1964) of the UN peacekeeping forces on Cyprus, and commander (1967–69) of all British troops in the Far East. After retiring in 1976, Carver spent a year (1977–78) in Rhodesia (later Zimbabwe) as the British resident commissioner. Having been knighted in 1966, he was made a life peer in 1977 and served in the House of Lords, where he was openly critical of NATO and the concept of nuclear deterrence. Carver also wrote a dozen books, including several volumes on military strategy and an autobiography, *Out of Step* (1989).

Cavagnoud, Régine, French skier (b. June 27, 1970, La Clusaz, France—d. Oct. 31, 2001, Vienna, Austria), was one of France's finest young Alpine skiers and a top prospect for the 2002 Winter Olympic Games. Cavagnoud first qualified for the World Cup circuit in December 1994. Despite recurrent injuries, she steadily improved, eventually winning eight World Cup races and representing France at three Winter Olympics. In January 2001 she won the gold medal in the supergiant slalom (super G) at the world championships in St. Anton, Austria; a month later she clinched her first super G title in the 2000–01 World Cup and finished third for the overall title. Cavagnoud died from severe brain injuries she sustained when she collided with a German ski coach during a high-speed training run on October 28.

Chang Hsüeh-liang, Chinese warlord (b. June 3, 1901, Haicheng, China—d. Oct. 14, 2001, Honolulu, Hawaii), kidnapped Nationalist leader Chiang Kai-shek in 1936 in an attempt to force him to fight the Japanese rather than the Communists. His action had a decisive effect on subsequent Chinese history. Chang was the son of the warlord Chang Tso-lin, who dominated Manchuria. The son took military training, joined his father's army at age 19, and soon became a general commanding his own troops. When the Japanese murdered his father in 1928, Chang assumed power, proving to be an able ruler and forming an alliance with Chiang. In 1931, however, the Japanese invaded Manchuria, forcing Chang and his troops to the south. He was cured of an opium addiction and then traveled throughout Europe. Chang returned to China in 1934, and in 1935–36 Chiang used his troops against Communist forces. Chang was intent on persuading Chiang to form an alliance with the Communists to fight the Japanese invaders, and in 1936 the Nationalist leader went to Sian to meet with him. Chang took Chiang hostage and held him for two weeks, until he agreed to Chang's demand. This so-called Sian Incident temporarily took pressure off the Communists, who had been pushed to northwestern China at the end of their Long March, and allowed them to rebuild. The Nationalists later court-martialed Chang, and he was put under house arrest. When the Nationalists fled to Taiwan in 1949, they took Chang with them, and he remained under arrest until 1990, gaining the distinction of becoming the world's longest-serving political prisoner. In 1991 he was allowed to visit his children in the U.S., and three years later he settled there. At his death he was honoured by the presidents of both China and Taiwan.

Chavis, Wilson Anthony ("Boozoo"), American singer and accordion player (b. Oct. 23, 1930, Dog Hill, Lake Charles, La.—d. May 5, 2001, Austin, Texas), helped popularize zydeco music with such hits as "Paper in My Shoe" (1954). Chavis made numerous recordings in the 1950s but, after a dispute with his record company, gave up performing for more than two decades. He launched a successful comeback in the 1980s, touring widely and releasing a string of new albums, including *Louisiana Zydeco Music* (1986) and *Zydeco Homebrew* (1988). Chavis, who by the 1990s had earned the nickname "king of Zydeco," was especially noted for his mastery of the diatonic button accordion.

Chelimo, Richard, Kenyan athlete (b. Feb. 24, 1972?, Marakwet region, Kenya—d. Aug. 15, 2001, Eldoret, Kenya), was one of his country's top long-distance runners in the early 1990s, but his many achievements were marred by controversy and disappointment. Chelimo captured the world junior 10,000-m title in 1990. The next year he won a silver medal at that distance at the world championships in Tokyo after having yielded the lead on the last lap to his teammate Moses Tanui. At the 1992 Olympic Games in Barcelona, Spain, Chelimo was awarded the gold medal in the 10,000 m when the winner, Khalid Skah, was disqualified because a fellow Moroccan had cheated on his behalf, but the decision was reversed controversially on appeal. In 1993 Chelimo set a world record of 27 min 7.91 sec for the 10,000-m event only to watch it fall to his Kenyan compatriot Yobes Ondieki less than a week later.

Christensen, Willam (William Farr Christensen), American ballet company director (b. Aug. 27, 1902, Brigham City, Utah—d. Oct. 14, 2001, Salt Lake City, Utah), began dancing at a time when men could not expect to have a career in ballet in the U.S. and, with his brothers Harold and Lew, was instrumental in establishing important companies in the country. He also staged the first full-length American productions of the ballet classics *Coppélia* (1939), *Swan Lake* (1940), and *The Nutcracker* (1944). Christensen and his brothers received a thorough education in music and classical dance, primarily from their relatives, and toured in vaudeville in the late 1920s and early '30s. In 1932 Christensen moved to Portland, Ore., where he taught ballet and started a company. He became a soloist with the San Francisco Opera Ballet in 1937, and the following year he was named director of the company. Although programs composed of several short works were customary in the U.S. at that time, Christensen introduced evening-length ballets in addition to choreographing a number of shorter works, including *In Vienna* (1938), *Winter Carnival* (1942), and *Nothin' Doin' Bar* (1950). In 1951 Christensen left the company, which by then had become the San Francisco Ballet, and moved to Salt Lake City to serve as professor of theatre ballet at the University of Utah. There he developed a department of ballet and choreography and in 1952 founded a company, the Utah Ballet. That company became professional in 1963 and in 1968 took the name Ballet West. Christensen remained with Ballet West until 1978, and from that time until he was in his late 90s, he ran his Christensen Ballet Academy.

Chukhrai, Grigory Naumovich, Soviet motion picture director (b. May 23, 1921, Melitopol, Ukraine, Soviet Russia—d. Oct. 28, 2001, Moscow, Russia), broke away from the restrictions of hagiographic Socialist Realism during the relatively censorship-free late 1950s to create poignant films about simple people in wartime. His finest work included *The Forty-First* (1956), which won the special jury prize at the Cannes Film Festival; *Ballad of a Soldier* (1959), which won major awards at film festivals in San Francisco, Cannes, London, and other cities and earned its director the Lenin Prize; and *Clear Skies* (1961), which won first prize at the Moscow Film Festival. In 1963 Chukhrai was barred from traveling abroad when he spurned orders to withhold the Moscow Film Festival's top prize from Frederico Fellini's *8 1/2;* his later films suffered after official censorship was reintroduced.

Chung Ju Yung, South Korean businessman (b. Nov. 25, 1915, Tongchon, Korea—d. March 21, 2001, Seoul, S.Kor.), was the founder of the Hyundai Group, one of the world's largest business conglomerates. He was credited with having played a leading role in the revival of the South Korean economy in the aftermath of the Korean War. Born into a poor farming family, Chung got his start in business as the owner of an auto repair shop. He poured his earnings into other ventures and established Hyundai Engineering and Construction in 1947. Chung was awarded lucrative contracts by South Korean leader Park Chung Hee and was eventually able to acquire the Hyundai Motor Co. and the Hyundai Electronics Industries Co., among other firms, as part of his business empire. He ran unsuccessfully for president in 1992. Although Hyundai's overall sales approached $80 billion per year in the 1990s, the conglomerate fell heavily into debt and was forced to accept government mandates to downsize its global operations. In later years Chung helped South Korean Pres. Kim Dae Jung in his efforts to engage North Korea in dialogue; Chung donated cattle and corn (maize) to the North in 1998 and sponsored a tourism project in the North's Mt. Kumgang region. He officially retired from Hyundai in 2000.

Coca, Imogene Fernandez de, American actress and comedian (b. Nov. 18, 1908, Philadelphia, Pa.—d. June 2, 2001, Westport, Conn.), employed her expressive, elastic face—enhanced by saucer eyes and a huge smile—as well as her energetic physicality and improvisational abilities to great effect, most notably in skits with comedian Sid Caesar on live television during American TV's Golden Age. For the five years from 1949 to 1954, their acts—lampooning everything from opera, ballet, and movies to everyday life and marriage (via their husband-and-wife team "The Hickenloopers")—brought 90 minutes of hilarity weekly to the Saturday-night viewing public and set the standard for TV comedy. The daughter of professional performers, Coca began piano lessons at age 5, singing lessons at 6, and dance lessons at 7, and by the time she was 11, she was working in vaudeville. Her Broadway debut came in 1925 in the chorus of the short-run *When You Smile,* and after appearances in a variety of shows, she got her lucky break. While rehearsing in a cold theatre, Coca donned a massively oversized coat and began to clown around with some other cast members. The producer added her bit to the show, *New Faces of 1934,* and Coca caught the attention of both the critics and the public. Performances at summer vacation resorts and in such Broadway shows as *New Faces of 1936* and *The Straw Hat Revue* (1939) followed, but it was 10 years later, when she was paired with Caesar on the TV show *Admiral Broadway Revue,* that she finally achieved stardom. The pairing lasted through 160 editions of the show that succeeded it, *Your Show of Shows.* Coca won the Emmy Award in 1951 for her work on that program. She later starred in her own half-hour TV show, *The Imogene Coca Show,* for a season and appeared in nightclubs, TV specials, films, including *Under the Yum Yum Tree* (1963), and Broadway plays, including *On the Twentieth Century* (1979).

Durable comedian Imogene Coca

Como, Perry (Pierino Roland Como), American singer and entertainer (b. May 18, 1912, Canonsburg, Pa.—d. May 12, 2001, Jupiter, Fla.), had a mellow baritone voice and a relaxed, easygoing manner—typified by his trademark cardigan sweaters that made him an audience favourite during a career that lasted over six decades and in which he sold more than 100 million records. For 15 years (1948–63) he hosted weekly television variety shows, winning Emmy Awards in 1954, 1955, 1956, and 1959, and his annual Christmas TV shows became a staple of the holiday season. Como began sweeping up in a barber shop when he was about 10 years old, and by the time he was in his mid-teens, he was the owner of his own shop, where he sang while he worked. Encouraged by his customers and his family, he became a singer with Freddy Carlone's band in 1933, and in 1936 he was signed by Ted Weems to sing with his orchestra. Como recorded and broadcast with Weems until 1942 and was about to give up singing for a return to barbering when in 1943 he accepted a contract to record and appear on radio. His first single, "Goodbye Sue," was released later that year. In 1944 Como had his first hit record, "Long Ago and Far Away," and the first of his over a dozen million-selling hits, "Till the End of Time," followed in 1945. Among his other popular recordings of the 1940s and '50s were "If I Loved You," "I'm Always Chasing Rainbows," "Hot," "Temptation," "Don't Let the Stars Get in Your Eyes," which was the first of his 14 number one records, and "Catch a Falling Star," for which he won a Grammy Award in 1958. Between 1944 and 1950 Como starred in his own NBC radio show, *The Chesterfield Supper Club,* which from 1948 was also televised. *The Perry Como Show* began broadcasting on CBS in 1950 and from 1955 to 1959 appeared on NBC, where the show opened with the theme "Dream Along with Me" and included the popular "Letters, we get letters" segment. Beginning in 1959 Como served as host of the *Kraft Music Hall*; he ended his weekly TV appearances in 1963 and thereafter, until 1992, headlined occasional specials. During the later years of his career, he kept his name on the charts with such hits as "It's Impossible," "And I Love You So," and "For the Good Times." Como was awarded a Kennedy Center Honor in 1987.

Cooper, Malcolm, British marksman (b. Dec. 20, 1947, Camberley, Surrey, Eng.—d. June 9, 2001, Eastergate, West Sussex, Eng.), won consecutive Olympic gold medals in rifle shooting; he claimed his first gold in the small-bore rifle event at the 1984 Summer Olympic Games in Los Angeles and successfully defended the title at the 1988 Olympics in Seoul, S.Kor. Cooper was the first shooter ever to win consecutive gold medals in the event and the first British athlete since 1908 to win a rifle-shooting gold. Throughout the 1980s he dominated the sport; his achievements included winning individual gold medals in all five shooting events at the 1985 European championships in Zürich, Switz. A naval architect by profession, Cooper retired from competition in 1991 to concentrate on designing weapons for the British army.

Corso, Gregory Nunzio, American poet, playwright, and novelist (b. March 26, 1930, New York, N.Y.—d. Jan. 17, 2001, Robbinsdale, Minn.), was along with Allen Ginsberg and Jack Kerouac—at the centre of the bohemian Beat literary and social movement from its beginning in the mid-1950s and was the last of that movement's original leading members. His poetry, with its unconventional spontaneity, could be candid and inelegant while at the same time inspiring and influential, and his public poetry readings were equally unconventional. Corso had a troubled childhood, living in a succession of orphanages and foster homes and having run-ins with the law, and at age 16 he began a three-year prison term for theft. During his imprisonment he began to read classic poetry and literature voraciously and then to write his own poetry. In 1950 Corso met Ginsberg in a bar in New York City's Greenwich Village, and Ginsberg—seeing promise in Corso's writing—took him into his circle and guided him in writing in a more experimental style. Corso later spent some time in the Boston area. His works were first published in the *Harvard Advocate* in 1954, and in 1955 his play *In This Hung-Up Age* was performed by Harvard University students. Students at Harvard and nearby Radcliffe College also financed his first book, *The Vestal Lady on Brattle, and Other Poems* (1955). The following year, soon after the famous public reading in San Francisco that included Ginsberg's "Howl" and that marked the rise of the Beats, Corso moved there and became recognized as one of the major figures of the movement. *Gasoline,* his first major book of poems, was published in 1958. Corso also wrote one of his most famous poems, "Bomb," in 1958; when printed, it was typed in the shape of a mushroom cloud. It was included in the volume of poetry *The Happy Birthday of Death* (1960). Other notable works included the novel *The American Express* (1961) and the poetry volumes *Long Live Man* (1962), *The Mutation of the Spirit* (1964), *Elegiac Feelings American* (1970), *Earth Egg* (1974), *Herald of the Autochthonic Spirit* (1981), and *Mindfield* (1989).

Costa Gomes, Francisco da, Portuguese military leader (b. June 30, 1914, Chaves, Port.—d. July 31, 2001, Lisbon, Port.), was the president of Portugal's ruling military junta from 1974 to 1976. Costa Gomes was chief of staff of Portugal's armed forces from 1972 until March 1974, when he reportedly was dismissed because of his support for decolonization. In April of that year, army officers overthrew Prime Minister Marcelo Caetano in a bloodless coup that came to be known as the Revolution of the Carnations. Costa Gomes took power when the junta's interim president, Gen. António de Spínola, went into self-exile in September. As head of state, Costa Gomes presided over the granting of independence to Portuguese colonies in Africa and Asia. After guiding Portugal through two attempted countercoups and parliamentary elections, he relinquished power in June 1976 to Gen. António dos Santos Ramalho Eanes, the newly elected president. In 1981 Costa Gomes was promoted to marshall, Portugal's highest military rank.

Counts, Ira Wilmer, Jr. ("Will"), American photographer (b. Aug. 24, 1931, Little Rock, Ark.—d. Oct. 6, 2001, Bloomington, Ind.), was on the staff of the *Arkansas Democrat* when he took his most famous photos, which captured the turmoil that attended the integration of Little Rock Central High School in 1957. In his best-known image, an African American student is being jeered as she makes her way past a white mob. Another, of a black journalist being kicked by a white man wielding a brick, was said to have led Pres. Dwight D. Eisenhower to send federal troops to Little Rock. Counts went on to work for the Associated Press in Chicago and Indianapolis, Ind., and later spent 32 years (1963–95) on the faculty of Indiana University.

Covas, Mário, Brazilian politician (b. April 21, 1930, Santos, Braz.—d. March 6, 2001, São Paulo, Braz.), was one of Brazil's most influential and respected politicians and a founder of the Brazilian Social Democratic Party. Covas served two terms in Congress before being appointed mayor of São Paulo in 1983. He later served as senator for São Paulo from 1986 to 1994 and as governor of São Paulo state from 1995 to 2001. A close ally of Pres. Fernando Henrique Cardoso, Covas had been planning a presidential campaign for 2002 when he succumbed to cancer.

Craighead, Frank Cooper, Jr., American naturalist (b. Aug. 14, 1916, Washington, D.C.—d. Oct. 21, 2001, Jackson, Wyo.), with his identical twin, John, spent 12 years studying grizzly bears in the Yellowstone National Park area, elucidating details about their lives and habits and demonstrating their importance to the ecosystem. The Craigheads' work helped prevent the extinction of grizzlies.

Cram, Donald James, American chemist (b. April 22, 1919, Chester, Vt.—d. June 17, 2001, Palm Desert, Calif.), was awarded the 1987 Nobel Prize for Chemistry for his development of ways to build molecules that could mimic the functioning of molecules in living organisms; he shared the prize with Charles J. Pedersen and Jean-Marie Lehn. After earning his bachelor's degree from Rollins College, Winter Park, Fla., and his master's degree from the University of Nebraska, Cram received a Ph.D. in organic chemistry from Harvard University in 1947. That same year he joined the faculty of the University of California, Los Angeles. He was appointed a full professor at UCLA in 1956 and became professor emeritus in 1997. Working independently from Pedersen and Lehn, Cram helped pioneer the field of host-guest chemistry. He synthesized an array of large organic molecules that—because of their differently shaped three-dimensional structures—could interact selectively with other, smaller molecules in a process analogous to the interactions between enzymes and other biological molecules. Molecules of the type developed by Cram were later widely used in sensors and electrodes. Cram was a renowned teacher and author of more than 400 research papers and seven books, including *Organic Chemistry* (1959, with George Hammond), a standard college textbook.

Curnow, (Thomas) Allen Monro, New Zealand poet and writer (b. June 17, 1911, Timaru, N.Z.—d. Sept. 23, 2001, Auckland, N.Z.), gained an international reputation for his verse. He was also known as the editor of two anthologies of New Zealand poetry. Curnow's father was an Anglican clergyman and an amateur poet. Curnow also studied for the ministry from 1931 to 1933 but then turned to journalism, working for the *Christchurch Press* from 1935 to 1948. The first of 20 volumes of poems appeared in 1933, and in 1938 he received a B.A. degree from the University of Canterbury, Christchurch. In 1948 he worked as a journalist in London. In 1951 Curnow joined the faculty of the English department at the University of Auckland, where he remained until his retirement in 1976. Much of his early poetry consisted of social and political satire; this was followed by a period in which he focused on the history of New Zealand and on national identity. Later he wrote of the Auckland landscape as well as on universal and metaphysical themes. Among major collections were *Trees, Effigies, Moving Objects: A Sequence of Poems* (1972), *You Will Know When You Get There: Poems 1979–81* (1982), and *Early Days Yet: New and Collected Poems 1941–1997* (1997). He was the editor of *A Book of New Zealand Verse 1923–45* (1945), considered to be the first serious study of poetry in New Zealand. He also edited *The Penguin Book of New Zealand Verse* (1960), an anthology that generated intense controversy, partly because of his selection of those to be included. Curnow received six New Zealand Book Awards, the Commonwealth Poetry Prize (1988), and the Queen's Gold Medal for Poetry (1989). He was made a Companion of the Order of the British Empire (1986) and was a member of the Order of New Zealand (1990).

Nigel Gardiner

Poetic powerhouse Allen Curnow

Dagmar (Virginia Ruth Egnor), American comic actress (b. Nov. 29, 1921, Logan, W.Va.—d. Oct. 9, 2001, Ceredo, W.Va.), portrayed a stereotypical sexy dumb blonde in early 1950s television, most notably on the late-night talk show *Broadway Open House,* the prototype for *The Tonight Show* and similar programs. With a repertoire of silly poetry and mangled-language lectures—which she dubbed treasises—Dagmar became an overnight sensation.

Davidsen, Arthur, American astrophysicist (b. May 26, 1944, Freeport, N.Y.—d. July 19, 2001, Baltimore, Md.), was a leading researcher in the fields of high-energy astrophysics and ultraviolet space astronomy. After service in the U.S. Navy during the Vietnam War, Davidsen earned a Ph.D. in astronomy from the University of California, Berkeley, in 1975. That year he joined the faculty of Johns Hopkins University, Baltimore, where he spent the rest of his career. Davidsen oversaw the construction of the Hopkins Ultraviolet Telescope (HUT), a project he began in 1979 to study intergalactic space. HUT was carried aboard the space shuttle *Columbia* in 1990 and the space shuttle *Endeavour* in 1995. Davidsen served (1985–88) as the founding director of the Center for Astrophysical Sciences at Johns Hopkins.

Dawson, John Myrick, American physicist (b. Sept. 30, 1930, Champaign, Ill.—d. Nov. 17, 2001, Los Angeles, Calif.), was one of the world's foremost authorities on plasma physics. Dawson was known for his development of the so-called particle-in-cell computer model, a technique for simulating plasmas on computers; he was also the first to suggest using plasma in particle accelerators in order to make them more powerful without increasing their size. Dawson was a research physicist at Princeton University from 1956 to 1962 and a professor of physics at the University of California, Los Angeles, from 1973 until his death. Dawson, who published more than 300 papers on plasma physics, was elected to the National Academy of Sciences in 1977.

Dertouzos, Michael Leonidas, Greek-born computer scientist (b. Nov. 5, 1936, Athens, Greece—d. Aug. 27, 2001, Boston, Mass.), as director of the Massachusetts Institute of Technology's computer science laboratory from 1974, provided valuable support that helped enable the World Wide Web Consortium to develop the standards that made the Internet accessible to individual users throughout the world.

Desio, Ardito, Italian geologist and explorer (b. April. 18, 1897, Palmanova, Italy—d. Dec. 12, 2001, Rome, Italy), led the first successful expedition to scale K2, the world's second tallest mountain; he did not make the final assault to the peak, however, owing to his age. The 1954 feat was largely attributed to his meticulous planning and disciplined military strategy. During World War I Desio served as lieutenant of the Alpine Troops. He later attended the University of Florence, where he studied natural sciences; he then began what became a lifetime post as a professor at the University of Milan. Desio was the author of more than 400 geologic publications. He served as president (1966–73) of the Italian Geological Committee and was the recipient of numerous honours related to the 1954 climb. Desio traveled extensively; he led scientific expeditions in Africa, the Middle and Near East, and Antarctica. He was credited with the discovery of the first deposits of natural oil and gas in Libya (1939) and with having been the first Italian to reach the South Pole (1962). His book *Ascent of K2* (1955) was translated into 11 languages.

de Valois, Dame Ninette (Edris Stannus), Irish-born British dancer and choreographer (b. June 6, 1898, Baltiboys, Blessington, County Wicklow, Ire.—d. March 8, 2001, London, Eng.), was the founder and first director of what became England's Royal Ballet and its renowned school. One of the most influential and highly revered individuals in the arts world in the 20th century—she was generally referred to simply as Madam—she guided the development of a British ballet style and tradition and led the company to international repute. Her family had moved to England when she was a child, and when she was a young teenager, she began her performing career, as one of Lila Field's Wonder Children, and studied dance with such noted teachers as Enrico Cecchetti. In 1923 de Valois began dancing with Sergey Diaghilev's Ballets Russes, but in 1926, having discovered that she was suffering the aftereffects of a childhood case of polio that had gone undiagnosed, she gave up performing and founded a school in London, the Academy of Choreographic Art. She also worked with Dublin's Abbey Theatre and Cambridge's Festival Theatre and began an association with Lilian Baylis at the Old Vic theatre. Baylis had another theatre, the Sadler's Wells, where in 1931 de Valois's dancers presented their first full-length program. This marked the launch of the Vic-Wells Ballet Company. With Frederick Ashton as chief choreographer and Constant Lambert as musical director, the company, later called the Sadler's Wells Ballet, grew in size and stature, and in 1946 it moved to the Royal Opera House at Covent Garden. It was granted a royal charter in 1956 and became the Royal Ballet. De Valois in the meantime had formed a second company, the Sadler's Wells Theatre Ballet, which later became one of England's top regional dance companies, the Birmingham Royal Ballet. She retired as the Royal Ballet's director in 1963 but continued leading the school until 1972. De Valois choreographed such works as *La Création du monde* (1931), *Job* (1931), *The Haunted Ballroom* (1934), *The Rake's Progress* (1935), and *Checkmate* (1937; with Arthur Bliss) and wrote three books. She was made a Chevalier of the Legion of Honour in 1950, Dame of the British Empire in 1951, and a Companion of Honour in 1982, and in 1992 she was awarded the Order of Merit.

Hulton/Archive/Getty Images

Dame Ninette de Valois, doyenne of British ballet

Devi, Phoolan, Indian bandit and politician (b. Aug. 10, 1963, Uttar Pradesh state, India—d. July 25, 2001, New Delhi, India), was the notorious "Bandit Queen" who became legendary for both her acts of revenge on those who had abused her and her Robin Hood-like activities to aid the lower castes. After being imprisoned, however, she became a member of the Lok Sabha, the lower house of Parliament, where she continued as a champion of the poor and oppressed. Devi's life story was a mixture of fact and legend, beginning with her arranged marriage at age 11 to a man three times her age. A year later, having been brutalized by him, she returned home, an act her family considered disgraceful. By the time she was in her early 20s, she had joined (or been kidnapped into) a gang of *dacoits* (bandits), been sexually assaulted numerous times—once by upper-caste landowners, Thakurs, in the village of Behmai—and left barren, and become the mistress of a *dacoit* leader. On Feb. 14, 1981, Devi led a notorious act of revenge known as the Saint Valentine's Day massacre; some 20 of Behmai's Thakurs were rounded up and shot in retribution for her gang rape. This act intensified both her status in modern folklore and the police search for her. In 1983, in poor health and exhausted by the struggle to stay hidden, Devi negotiated her surrender to avoid a death sentence. Although she agreed to 8 years' imprisonment, she ended up being jailed for 11 years, without trial, and gained release only through the efforts of the lower-caste chief minister of Uttar Pradesh. In 1994, shortly before her release, she was the subject of the Bollywood film *Bandit Queen.* In 1996, Devi took advantage of her cult status and, as a member of the Samajwadi Party, won election to Parliament. She lost her seat two years later but regained it in 1999. Devi was killed when masked assassins opened fire on her outside her home.

Diamond, John, British journalist (b. May 10, 1953, London, Eng.—d. March 2, 2001, London), chronicled his four years with cancer with unflinching honesty, humour, and unsentimental insight through his weekly column in *The Sunday Times* magazine and the best-selling book *C: Because Cowards Get Cancer Too* (1998). Diamond was already a successful consumer writer, newspaper columnist, television presenter, and frequent talk-show guest when he was diagnosed with throat cancer in 1997. Diamond continued to write about the daily minutiae of life with cancer until his death.

Dickson, Gordon Rupert, Canadian-born American science-fiction writer (b. Nov. 1, 1923, Edmonton, Alta.—d. Jan. 31, 2001,

right: Getty Images

Minneapolis, Minn.), was one of the world's most prominent science-fiction writers; he published more than 80 novels and some 200 short stories. Among Dickson's best-known science-fiction works were *Dorsai!* (1960), *Soldier, Ask Not* (1967), and *Tactics of Mistake* (1971). He also excelled in the fantasy genre; his 1976 novel *The Dragon and the George* won the British Fantasy Society's August Derleth Award.

Didi (Waldir Pereira), Brazilian association football (soccer) player (b. Oct. 8, 1928/29, Campos, Braz.—d. May 12, 2001, Rio de Janeiro, Braz.), was a key inside-right midfielder on the Brazilian national team from 1952 until 1962, scoring 31 goals in 85 international matches. On the field Didi was a masterful playmaking strategist and ball handler, but he was most admired for his devastating *folha seca* ("dry leaf") free kicks. He played for Brazil in the 1954 World Cup and was captain of the teams that won the World Cup in 1958 (when he was named Most Valuable Player) and 1962. Except for a brief, unsatisfactory stint in Spain (1959–60) with Real Madrid and Valencia, Didi played professionally in Brazil. In 1950 he signed with Fluminense, which won the Rio League title the next year; in 1956 he transferred to Botafogo, which won the title in 1961 and 1962. After retiring in 1965 he coached club teams in Brazil and other countries and in 1970 led Peru to the World Cup quarterfinals. Didi was inducted into the International Football Hall of Champions in 2000.

Dionne, Yvonne, Canadian personality (b. May 28, 1934, Callander, Ont.—d. June 23, 2001, Montreal, Que.), was one of the celebrated Dionne quintuplets, whose birth was hailed as a medical miracle; the five identical sisters were the first documented set of quintuplets to have survived more than a few days. In 1935, after the Ontario government deemed the parents of the quintuplets unfit to care for them, the five were placed in a compound called Quintland, where tourists were allowed to view them through one-way glass; during the 1930s up to 6,000 tourists per day visited Quintland. The sisters also appeared in films and advertisements. The Dionne parents regained custody of the girls in 1941. Years later the quintuplets successfully sued the Ontario government for having separated them from their family and put them on display. Yvonne eventually became a librarian and an activist on behalf of Canadian orphans. With her two surviving sisters, Annette and Cécile, she published a book, *Family Secrets: The Dionne Quintuplets' Autobiography,* in 1994.

Donahue, Troy (Merle Johnson, Jr.), American actor (b. Jan. 27, 1936, New York, N.Y.—d. Sept. 2, 2001, Santa Monica, Calif.), was a teen heartthrob in the late 1950s and early '60s, with starring roles in movies, including *A Summer Place* (1959), *Parrish* (1961), *Rome Adventure* (1962), and *Palm Springs Weekend* (1963), and the television series *Surfside Six* (1960–62) and *Hawaiian Eye* (1962); after overcoming substance-abuse problems in the early 1980s, he appeared in some two dozen more movies, including *Cry-Baby* (1990).

Downey, (Sean) Morton, Jr., American television talk-show host (b. Dec. 9, 1933, New York, N.Y.—d. March 12, 2001, Los Angeles, Calif.), pioneered tabloid-style television as the abrasive host of *The Morton Downey Jr. Show,* which aired from 1987 to 1989. Downey worked as an actor, singer-songwriter, and record producer before breaking into radio as a talk-show host in the 1980s. His show became an instant, albeit controversial, hit after moving to television. Known as "Mort the Mouth," Downey frequently insulted his guests, and his outbursts sometimes provoked raucous arguments and fistfights.

Drobny, Jaroslav, Czechoslovak-born sportsman (b. Oct. 12, 1921, Prague, Czechoslovakia—d. Sept. 13, 2001, London, Eng.), during the 1940s was one of his country's finest tennis players and a key member of the national ice hockey team, but he achieved his greatest success on the tennis court after his defection to the West in 1950. Drobny played at Wimbledon in 1938 (representing Czechoslovakia) and in 1939 (representing "Bohemia-Moravia," that part of Czechoslovakia not then under German occupation). After working in a munitions factory during World War II, he led Czechoslovakia to victory in the European zone of the 1947 and 1948 Davis Cup tennis tournaments. At the same time, he guided the Czechoslovak national ice hockey team to a gold medal at the 1947 world championships and a silver at the 1948 Winter Olympic Games. After his defection Drobny played tennis on an Egyptian passport and won the French (1951 and 1952) and Italian (1950, 1951, and 1953) championships. He lost in the final at Wimbledon in 1949 and 1952, but in 1954 he finally captured the All-England title in a thrilling four-set final against Ken Rosewall. In 1960 Drobny took British citizenship and retired from elite-level tennis, although he continued to compete for Britain in veterans' events. In 1983 he was inducted into the International Tennis Hall of Fame.

Dudek, Louis, Canadian poet (b. Feb. 6, 1918, Montreal, Que.—d. March 22, 2001, Montreal), was one of Canada's most influential poets; he was particularly noted for his book-length poems, including *Europe* (1955), *En México* (1958), and *Atlantis* (1967). Dudek was a professor at McGill University, Montreal, from 1951 until the time of his death. In 1952 he helped launch Contact Press, which published leading Canadian poets of the 1950s and '60s. Dudek also published his own literary journal, *Delta,* from 1957 to 1966. He was named a member of the Order of Canada in 1984. His last book, *Surface of Time,* appeared in 2000.

Dudley, Jane, American dancer, choreographer, and teacher (b. April 3, 1912, New York, N.Y.—d. Sept. 19, 2001, London, Eng.), was influential in the development of modern dance in three countries. In the U.S. she danced with Martha Graham's company from 1937 to 1944 and frequently thereafter as a guest artist, as well as teaching for Graham and at colleges and universities and dancing with and choreographing for the New Dance Group and the Dudley-Maslow-Bales Trio. In 1968 she went to Tel Aviv, Israel, as artistic director of the Batsheva Dance Company, and in 1970 she moved to England to join the staff of the London Contemporary Dance School. Dudley left the post of director of contemporary dance studies in 1990 but remained affiliated with the school until 1998.

Duong Van Minh ("Big Minh"), South Vietnamese general (b. Feb. 16, 1916, Long An province, French Indochina—d. Aug. 6, 2001, Pasadena, Calif.), was a key member of the military coup that overthrew South Vietnamese Pres. Ngo Dinh Diem in November 1963; in April 1975 he succeeded Nguyen Van Thieu (*q.v.*) as president just days before North Vietnamese forces captured Saigon. Minh was a French-educated officer in the colonial army before the bifurcation of newly independent Vietnam in 1954. Although he was credited with having authorized the execution of Diem and Diem's brother Ngo Dinh Nhu in 1963, Minh proved to be a cautious and ineffectual leader. After officially surrendering Saigon, Minh was placed in detention, but he was allowed to emigrate in 1983.

Earnhardt, (Ralph) Dale, Sr., American race-car driver (b. April 29, 1951, Kannapolis, N.C.—d. Feb. 18, 2001, Daytona Beach, Fla.), was one of the most successful stock-car racing drivers in history. He won a total of 76 races in his career, and he captured the National Association for Stock Car Auto Racing's (NASCAR's) Winston Cup season points championship seven times—a feat equaled by only one other driver, racing legend Richard Petty. Earnhardt also won NASCAR's American Driver of the Year award twice, in 1987 and 1994. Earnhardt, who began racing at the age of 19 on dirt tracks, claimed his first NASCAR victory in 1979. His aggressive driving style earned him the nickname "the Intimidator" and also helped to make him one of the most

Brian Cleary/AFP Worldwide

"The Intimidator" Dale Earnhardt

popular drivers of his era. He won NASCAR's 1979 Rookie of the Year award. In 1980 he took his first Winston Cup title and, with $588,926 in earnings that year, established a new single-season earnings record. He won back-to-back Winston Cup championships in 1986–87, 1990–91, and 1993–94. His earnings of $3,083,056 in 1990 made him the first NASCAR driver to top the $3 million mark. In 1996 Earnhardt became only the third driver in NASCAR history to start 500 consecutive Winston Cup races, and the following year he became the first driver to earn more than $30 million. His victory in the Daytona 500 in 1998, after 19 unsuccessful bids to win the event, was another major milestone for Earnhardt. His last victory came in October 2000 when he triumphed in the Winston 500 in Talladega, Ala. He was killed on the last turn of the last lap of the Daytona 500 in a crash that involved cars driven by Sterling Marlin and Ken Schrader. At the time of his death, Earnhardt had amassed $41,742,384 in career earnings—an all-time record.

Egan, Msgr. John Joseph, American clergyman (b. Oct. 9, 1916, New York, N.Y.—d. May 19, 2001, Chicago, Ill.), was a Roman Catholic priest who became a noted social activist. Egan was ordained in 1943. As director of the Chicago Archdiocese Office of Urban Affairs from 1958 to 1969, he attracted attention by championing racial integration and criticizing the effects of urban-renewal projects on the poor. Egan was among the clergymen who joined the Rev. Martin Luther King, Jr., on his historic 1965 protest march from Selma to Montgomery, Ala. Egan served as director of the Institute for Pastoral and Social Ministry at the University of Notre Dame from 1970 to 1983. From 1987 until his death, he was head of the Office of Community Affairs at DePaul University, Chicago. In 2001 he again attracted headlines by calling for the Roman Catholic Church to ordain women and married men. An acclaimed biography of Egan, *An Alley in Chicago: The Ministry of a City Priest,* by Margery Frisbie, appeared in 1991.

Enebish, Lhamsurengiyn, Mongolian politician (b. 1947, Mogod Sum, Mong.—d. Sept. 29, 2001, Ulaanbaatar, Mong.), was secretary-general (from 1996) of the Mongolian People's Revolutionary Party (MPRP) and speaker (from July 19, 2000) of the country's Great Hural (parliament). Enebish studied engineering at Mongolian National University and after graduation worked as an engineer (1970–75) and as director of the engineering and architecture bureau in Ulaanbaatar (1975–77). After serving (1980–83) as an economic adviser at the Mongolian embassy in Moscow, he returned to Ulaanbaatar, where he was deputy mayor (1983–90) and mayor (1990–92). Enebish became Mongolia's first deputy prime minister in 1993. He was elected speaker after the MPRP won an overwhelming majority in the July 2000 parliamentary elections.

Evans, Dale (Frances Octavia Smith), American actress, singer, songwriter, and writer (b. Oct. 31, 1912, Uvalde, Texas—d. Feb. 7, 2001, Apple Valley, Calif.), reigned as "queen of the West" alongside her "king of the cowboys" husband, Roy Rogers, in films in the 1940s and early '50s and on television in the 1950s and '60s. These shows featured lavish costumes for the stars, straightforward story lines, and wholesome family values. The couple also recorded some 400 songs together, among them their theme song, "Happy Trails," one of the about 25 that she wrote. Evans was working as a stenographer when, at the suggestion of her boss, she sang on a local radio program. This led to further radio appearances, including a stint as a regular vocalist on a CBS network show, *News and Rhythm,* in addition to employment as a nightclub vocalist. Evans's first notable motion picture appearance was in 1943 in the John Wayne film *In Old Oklahoma* (later titled *The War of the Wildcats*), and the following year found her cast opposite Rogers for the first time, in *The Cowboy and the Señorita.* Besides leading to their marriage (1947), the pairing also was a hit with the public, and they made more than two dozen westerns together. From 1951 to 1957 Evans and Rogers starred in a television series, *The Roy Rogers Show,* and they returned in 1962 for *The Roy Rogers and Dale Evans Show. Happy Trails Theatre* (1986–89) brought their films to the TV audience on cable television's Nashville Network. The deeply religious Evans also wrote more than 20 inspirational books. In the best known of her works, *Angel Unaware* (1953), she told the story of Robin, the only child born to the couple, who had Down syndrome and heart problems and died shortly before her second birthday. Evans and Rogers opened the Roy Rogers–Dale Evans Museum in Victorville, Calif., in 1964 and featured in it much of their career memorabilia, including the preserved bodies of their horses, Buttermilk and Trigger. They were inducted into the National Cowboy Hall of Fame, Oklahoma City, Okla., in 1976. Rogers died in 1998 after nearly 51 years of marriage to Evans.

Evans, Rowland, American journalist (b. April 28, 1921, Whitemarsh, Pa.—d. March 23, 2001, Washington, D.C.), advocated conservative causes as a prominent newspaper columnist and television host. With journalist Robert Novak, Evans published a syndicated column, called "Inside Report," from 1963 to 1993. From 1980 the pair served as cohosts of Cable News Network's political talk show *Evans & Novak,* which was renamed *Evans, Novak, Hunt & Shields* in 1998 after fellow pundits Al Hunt and Mark Shields joined the program. In his columns Evans correctly predicted that Barry Goldwater would win the Republican presidential nomination in 1964 and celebrated the demise of the Soviet Union. With Novak he wrote several books, including *Nixon in the White House: The Frustration of Power* (1971) and *The Reagan Revolution* (1981).

Fahey, John Aloysius, American guitarist (b. Feb. 28, 1939, Takoma Park, Md.—d. Feb. 22, 2001, Salem, Ore.), created extended, serene guitar compositions that fused American folk, country music, and rural blues traditions on noted underground albums of the 1960s; his style, which he called "American primitive guitar," made him a major influence on 1980s New Age music, an idiom that he disliked.

Fano, Ugo, Italian-born American physicist (b. July 28, 1912, Turin, Italy—d. Feb. 13, 2001, Chicago, Ill.), was a pioneering nuclear physicist who helped identify the hazards of radioactivity for humans and whose research provided the groundwork for the development of the gas laser, among other inventions. In 1939, after studying under Enrico Fermi, Fano left Italy for the U.S. in order to escape fascism. Working for the National Bureau of Standards in the 1940s and '50s, he led research into the effects of radiation on biological systems. Fano joined the University of Chicago as a professor in 1966, became chairman of the university's physics department in 1972, and was named professor emeritus in 1982. Among the numerous honours he received was the U.S. Department of Energy's Enrico Fermi Award for lifetime achievement (1995).

Fariña, Mimi (Mimi Margharita Baez), American folk singer and social activist (b. April 30, 1945, Stanford, Calif.—d. July 18, 2001, Mill Valley, Calif.), was the younger sister of folk singer Joan Baez and was also a well-known performer in her own right. With her first husband, Richard Fariña, she made two popular albums in the mid-1960s, *Reflections in a Crystal Wind* and *Celebrations for a Grey Day.* After her husband's death in a motorcycle accident in 1966, she continued to make recordings, including *Take Heart* (1971), a duo album with Tom Jans. Fariña was also known as the founder of Bread & Roses, a charity that organized musical shows for audiences in nursing homes, hospitals, homeless and drug rehabilitation centres, and correctional facilities.

Finster, the Rev. Howard, American artist and preacher (b. Dec. 2, 1916, Valley Head, Ala.—d. Oct. 22, 2001, Rome, Ga.), with his simple colourful works that combined his evangelistic messages with pop culture icons, became one of the most noted folk artists of the 20th century. He was best known for Paradise Garden in Pennville, Ga., which he concocted from items he retrieved from a dump, and his designs also appeared on album covers for such rock groups as R.E.M. and the Talking Heads.

Flanagan, Tommy Lee, American jazz pianist (b. March 16, 1930, Detroit, Mich.—d. Nov. 16, 2001, New York, N.Y.), improvised fluent melodies with swing, harmonic ingenuity, and a light touch. A sensitive accompanist, he made his first recording with Miles Davis; played on classic modern albums, notably Sonny Rollins's *Saxophone Colossus* (1956) and John Coltrane's *Giant Steps* (1959); and toured with tenor saxophonist Coleman Hawkins, singer Tony Bennett, and especially Ella Fitzgerald (1963–65, 1968–78) before becoming leader of his own trio.

Fock, Jeno, Hungarian politician (b. May 17, 1916, Budapest, Austria-Hungary—d. May 23, 2001, Budapest, Hung.), was a moderate communist who tried to institute economic reforms during his service as Hungarian deputy prime minister (1961–67) and prime minister (1967–75). His efforts were blocked by the Soviet Union, however, and he was pushed out of office in 1975. Fock continued to criticize General Secretary Janos Kadar's hard-line regime from within the Politburo for another five years, and he was considered a moderating influence on the Central Committee until he was retired in 1989.

Francis, Arlene (Arlene Francis Kazanjian), American actress and television personality (b. Oct. 20, 1907, Boston, Mass.—d. May 31, 2001, San Francisco, Calif.), enjoyed widespread popularity as a regular panelist on the long-running television quiz show *What's My Line?* and as host of the variety show *Talent Patrol*. She was also a cohost of the television morning show *Home*. Francis appeared on Broadway from 1936 and starred in the hit play *The Doughgirls* in 1942. Work in film and television followed. She appeared on *What's My Line?* from 1950 to 1975.

Freeman, Kathleen, American character actress (b. Feb. 17, 1919, Chicago, Ill.—d. Aug. 23, 2001, New York, N.Y.), appeared in some 100 films, including nearly a dozen Jerry Lewis movies and, most memorably, in the role of vocal coach Phoebe Dinsmore in *Singin' in the Rain* (1952); in her last movie role, she was the voice of an old woman in the animated *Shrek* (2001). In addition to showing up in most of the popular television sitcoms from the late 1950s on, she also had a notable stage career that included tours as Miss Hannigan in *Annie* and Helga Ten Dorp in *Deathtrap* and the role of sassy piano player Jeanette Burmeister in the Broadway production *The Full Monty,* for which she received a Tony nomination and which she played until five days before her death.

Furnas, J(oseph) C(hamberlain), American author and social historian (b. Nov. 24, 1905, Indianapolis, Ind.—d. June 3, 2001, Stanton, N.J.), published a noted social history of the U.S. The three-volume work included *The Americans: A Social History of the United States, 1587–1914* (1969), *Great Times: An Informal Social History of the United States, 1914–1929* (1974), and *Stormy Weather* (1977), covering the years 1929–45. Furnas, a prolific contributor to newspapers and magazines, wrote one of the most widely circulated articles in history, ". . . And Sudden Death," about driving fatalities and the need for automobile safety; some eight million reprints were issued after the article was originally published in *Reader's Digest* in August 1935. Furnas's autobiography, *My Life in Writing: Memoirs of a Maverick,* appeared in 1989.

Futch, Edward ("Eddie"), American boxing trainer (b. Aug. 9, 1911, Hillsboro, Miss.—d. Oct. 10, 2001, Las Vegas, Nev.), was dubbed "the professor of pugilism" for the sharp observation, compassion, and determination that he used to coach more than 20 world champions, including heavyweights Joe Frazier, Ken Norton, Trevor Berbick, Larry Holmes, Michael Spinks, and Riddick Bowe; light heavyweights Bob Foster and Montell Griffin; and welterweights Don Jordan and Marion Starling. Futch's observation that heavyweight champion Muhammad Ali was vulnerable to left-handed punches helped Frazier become the first boxer to defeat Ali, in 1971; two years later Futch trained Norton, only the second to defeat Ali. Futch became controversial in 1975 while handling Frazier in the boxer's historic 15-round Manila bout with Ali ("the Thrilla in Manila"). Blinded and wounded after 14 three-minute rounds of Ali's brutal blows, Frazier wanted to continue, but Futch withdrew his man from the match. He grew up in Detroit, where he won a local Golden Gloves lightweight title in 1933; altogether he won 37 fights and lost 3 before a heart murmur finished him as an amateur boxer. For a time he was Joe Louis's sparring partner; Futch went on to work for four decades in factories, in a post office, in a restaurant, and as a labourer while training boxers in Detroit and Los Angeles. The first boxer whom he transformed into a world champion was welterweight Jordan in 1958, but Futch did not become a major figure in boxing until he began training Frazier in 1971. Sometimes he had to train under difficult conditions, notably when he was hired in 1981 to train Michael Spinks just two hours before the boxer won an important light heavyweight bout. Often he had to train difficult-to-handle fighters such as Bowe, his last heavyweight champion (1992–93). Futch entered boxing's International Hall of Fame in 1994.

Ganesan, Sivaji (Villupuram Chiniah Pillai Ganesan), Indian actor (b. Oct. 1, 1927, Tamil Nadu, India—d. July 21, 2001, Chennai [Madras], India), was a legendary star in southern India's Tamil film industry, employing his expressive face and eloquent voice in some 300 motion pictures over nearly 50 years. Ganesan began his stage career as a child and achieved almost instant fame with his screen debut in *Parasakthi* (1952). He took his professional name from the 17th-century Maratha warrior king Sivaji, whom he portrayed onstage and later in a 1956 film. Ganesan brought an intense screen presence to scores of historical and dramatic films, notably *Navarathri,* in which he portrayed nine roles. In the 1980s he had a brief unsuccessful political career in Tamil Nadu. In 1995 Ganesan was presented with the French government's highest civilian award, the Chevalier of the Order of Arts and Letters; in 1997 he received the Dada Saheb Phalke from the Indian government for his lifetime contribution to Indian cinema.

Gascoyne, David Emery, British poet (b. Oct. 10, 1916, Harrow, Middlesex, Eng.—d. Nov. 25, 2001, Newport, Isle of Wight, Eng.), introduced French Surrealism to Great Britain. He was acquainted with many of the leading intellectual and artistic figures in England and France and became a noted translator and critic. Unusual among British poets of the time, he was not university educated. He published his first book of poems, *Roman Balcony,* in 1932 at the age of 16 and his only full-length novel, *Opening Day,* the following year. Influenced by writers such as André Breton and Paul Éluard, he published *A Short Survey of Surrealism,* the first such work in English, in 1935. This was followed by *Man's Life Is This Meat* (1935), a volume of Surrealist verse, as well as by a translation of Breton's *What Is Surrealism?* His years in Paris during the 1930s were recorded in two works published much later: *Paris Journal 1937–1939* (1978) and *Journal 1936–1937* (1980). Although he had at first been interested primarily in the visionary and mystical elements of Surrealism, he later became more interested in its religious aspects. *Poems 1937–42,* which was published in 1943, was his first book of religious verse. *Night Thoughts,* written for the radio, was performed in 1955 and published in 1956. *Collected Poems* appeared in 1965. Addicted to amphetamines and afflicted with depression, he suffered a breakdown in the early 1960s and in 1964 went to live in his father's house on the Isle of Wight, where he remained to the end of his life. He published little poetry after the 1950s, although a number of collections continued to appear.

Surrealist poet David Gascoyne

Gebel-Williams, Gunther, German-born American circus animal trainer (b. Sept. 12, 1934, Schweidnitz, Ger. [now Swidnica, Pol.]—d. July 19, 2001, Venice, Fla.), was one of the most celebrated circus entertainers in history. As animal trainer for the Ringling Brothers and Barnum & Bailey Circus, he was particularly known for his work with big cats; among other feats, he trained lions to ride on the backs of elephants, taught leopards and tigers to jump through flaming hoops, and wrapped panthers around his neck and shoulders. His act also included horses, zebras, camels, and llamas. After beginning his career in a Munich-based circus, Gebel-Williams made his American debut in 1969. The star performer of the Ringling Brothers and Barnum & Bailey Circus for the following 22 years, he appeared in some 12,000 shows. An autobiography, *Untamed,* was published in 1991.

Gierek, Edward, Polish politician (b. Jan. 6, 1913, Porabka, Pol., Austria-Hungary—d. July

29, 2001, Cieszyn, Pol.), as the first secretary of the Polish Communist Party for almost a decade (1970–80), sought to modernize Poland's economy and introduce social reforms, but his attempts ultimately led to financial insolvency and political unrest. After Gierek's father died (1923) in a coal-mining accident, his mother moved the family to France, where Gierek worked as a coal miner and joined the Communist Party (1931). He fought with the Belgian Resistance during World War II. In 1948 he returned to Upper Silesia, Poland's most industrialized region, and within three years he had risen to local party leader. He succeeded Wladyslaw Gomulka as first secretary in December 1970 after price increases had led to major strikes and civil unrest. Gierek eased foreign travel restrictions and allowed greater intellectual freedom. He tried to raise living standards through expanded industrialization and Western-style consumerism, financed by massive foreign investment and loans. Instead, mismanagement, corruption, and a deepening international recession left Poland with crushing national debts. Strikes in 1976 and again in 1980 led to the formation of the powerful new trade union Solidarity. Gierek was replaced as first secretary in September 1980 and was expelled from the party the next year.

Gilbreth, Frank Bunker, Jr., American novelist and journalist (b. March 17, 1911, Plainfield, N.J.—d. Feb. 18, 2001, Charleston, S.C.), drew on his madcap experiences as one of 12 children in a household run by parents who were engineers and efficiency experts to co-write (with his sister Ernestine Gilbreth Carey) the best-selling memoir *Cheaper by the Dozen* (1948; filmed 1950) and its popular sequel, *Belles on Their Toes* (1950; filmed 1952). He was also the longtime writer (1947–93), under the name Ashley Cooper, of the "Doing the Charleston" column for the *News and Courier* (now the *Post and Courier*) newspaper in Charleston.

Gombrich, Sir Ernst Hans Josef, Austrian-born art historian (b. March 30, 1909, Vienna, Austria-Hungary—d. Nov. 3, 2001, London, Eng.), as one of the field's greatest popularizers, introduced millions of people to art through his best-known book, *The Story of Art* (1950; 16th rev. ed. 1995), a clearly written, accessible work that was originally intended for young people but eventually sold millions of copies in more than 20 languages. Gombrich eschewed aesthetics and art criticism, which he considered too deeply rooted in personal emotions, preferring to focus on iconography and innovations in technique, taste, and form as demonstrated in specific works by individual artists. He had little use for modernism, which he derided as overly commercial and too often bent on novelty for its own sake. Gombrich studied art history under Julius von Schlosser at Vienna University and in 1936 moved to London, where he joined the staff at the Warburg Institute. During World War II he translated German-language radio broadcasts for the BBC, which greatly improved his English. Gombrich's first book, *Weltgeschichte für Kinder* (1936), led to the idea of an art book for children, and the eventual result was *The Story of Art.* His later books included *Art and Illusion* (1960), *Meditations on a Hobby Horse, and Other Essays on the Theory of Art* (1963), *The Sense of Order* (1979), and *The Image and the Eye* (1981). Gombrich served as director of the Warburg Institute from 1959 until his retirement in 1976; he also held appointments at the Universities of Oxford, London, and Cambridge, as well as at Harvard and Cornell universities in the U.S. He was elected a fellow of the British Academy in 1960, made CBE in 1966, knighted in 1972, and appointed a member of the Order of Merit in 1988.

Graham, Katharine Meyer, American newspaper executive (b. June 16, 1917, New York, N.Y.—d. July 17, 2001, Boise, Idaho), took over the leadership position at the *Washington Post* following the death of her publisher husband and guided it to a position of new success, influence, and respect. Among her most important actions were the decisions to publish the Pentagon Papers—secret government documents concerning decisions about the conduct of the Vietnam War—and to allow two of the paper's reporters, Bob Woodward and Carl Bernstein, to investigate what became known as the Watergate scandal and led to the resignation of Pres. Richard M. Nixon. She was the first woman to serve as the head of a *Fortune* 500 company and was considered the most powerful woman in the U.S. Graham attended Vassar College, Poughkeepsie, N.Y., from 1934 to 1936 and then transferred to the University of Chicago, from which she graduated in 1938. After working as a reporter for the *San Francisco News,* she went (1939) to the *Washington Post,* where her father was editor and publisher. In 1940 she married Philip L. Graham and moved with him to Florida. In 1946 they returned to Washington when, at his father-in-law's behest, he became associate publisher and then publisher of the *Post.* Her husband became increasingly troubled by mental illness, however, and in 1963 committed suicide; Graham became sole owner of the paper and took over its presidency. Though she initially was uneasy about running the company, which by then included *Newsweek* magazine, other publications, and a number of television stations, she persevered and, with the addition of Benjamin Bradlee, whom she hired as executive editor in 1965, the paper thrived. Graham became publisher in 1969. In 1971 the *Post* gained new prominence when it published the Pentagon Papers after the *New York Times,* which had begun publishing them, was stopped by a federal restraining order. When the Supreme Court sided with the newspapers, freedom of the press prevailed. The next year, following a break-in at Democratic National Committee headquarters in the Watergate complex in Washington, D.C., the *Post* relentlessly investigated the action and its connection to the Nixon reelection campaign. The paper was awarded the 1973 Pulitzer Prize for public service. Graham became CEO and chairman of the board in 1973 and served in those capacities until 1991 and 1993, respectively. In 1979 she turned over the post of publisher to her son, Donald E. Graham, and he also succeeded her when she left her other positions. Graham won her own Pulitzer in 1998—for her autobiography, *Personal History* (1997).

Granz, Norman, American concert and record producer (b. Aug. 6, 1918, Los Angeles, Calif.—d. Nov. 22, 2001, Geneva, Switz.), presented top musicians in Jazz at the Philharmonic (JATP) concerts around the world and documented them on records for over four decades. At JATP shows, soloists won wild applause for frantic honking-horn "battles," but they also created music of lasting merit. Virtually every major black swing-era musician played and recorded for him—among them the Duke Ellington and Count Basie bands, pianist Art Tatum, saxophonists Lester Young, Coleman Hawkins, and Benny Carter, and singers Billie Holiday and Louis Armstrong—as did modernists such as Dizzy Gillespie (trumpet), Charlie Parker, Stan Getz, John Coltrane (saxophones), and Bud Powell (piano). Pianist Oscar Peterson was his favourite JATP accompanist and by far his most prolific recording artist; Granz also produced Ella Fitzgerald's concerts and her popular series of *Songbook* albums. Though Granz lost revenue when he refused to present concerts before racially segregated audiences, his enterprises were valued at $5 million by the mid-1950s. After service in the U.S. Army Air Force, Granz became an MGM film editor and produced the Academy Award-nominated short film *Jammin' the Blues* (1944). That year he produced the concert that began his globe-trotting career of staged jam sessions. He founded Clef Records in 1946 and Norgran Records in 1953 and combined them into Verve Records in 1956; in 1973 he formed Pablo Records, but he sold it in 1987.

Graves, Morris Cole, American artist (b. Aug. 28, 1910, Fox Valley, Ore.—d. May 5, 2001, Loleta, Calif.), was a self-taught painter whose works expressed a deeply felt connection with nature. After dropping out of high school, Graves became a seaman and, between 1928 and 1930, made three trips to China and Japan, where he developed an interest in East Asian art and religion, especially Zen Buddhism. He worked for the Federal Art Project in the early 1930s, and in 1936 at the Seattle (Wash.) Art Museum, he held his first one-man show. Living as a recluse on an island in Puget Sound, Graves completed some of his best-known paintings, including *Blind Bird* (1940) and *Little Known Bird of the Inner Eye* (1941). In his early works he frequently painted birds, insects, and other woodland animals. A number of his paintings were included in "Americans 1942: 18 Artists from 9 States," a show at the Museum of Modern Art in New York City that attracted widespread attention. A pacifist, Graves was confined to a military jail for 11 months during World War II and settled in Dublin after his release. In 1954–56 he painted the birds and animals of Ireland. Graves eventually returned

Diana Walker/Getty Images

to the U.S., where he turned his attention to creating floral paintings rather than depictions of animals.

Greenberg, Joseph Harold, American anthropologist and linguist (b. May 28, 1915, New York, N.Y.—d. May 7, 2001, Stanford, Calif.), proposed influential theories regarding relationships between the world's languages. After receiving a Ph.D. in anthropology from Northwestern University, Evanston, Ill., in 1940 and serving in the Army Signal Intelligence Service during World War II, Greenberg embarked on an academic career. He was a professor of anthropology and linguistics at Columbia University, New York City, from 1948 to 1962 and at Stanford University from 1962 until 1985. He was primarily interested in language universals. In *The Languages of Africa* (1955; rev. 1963), Greenberg grouped African languages into four families: Niger-Kordofanian, Afroasiatic, Nilo-Saharan, and Khoisan. He later argued that most of the world's languages could be categorized into 12 "superfamilies." Among his other notable works were *Language in the Americas* (1987) and *Indo-European and Its Closest Relatives: The Eurasiatic Language Family* (2000). He also edited *Universals of Language* (1963) and *Universals of Human Language,* 4 vol. (1978).

Greer, Jane (Bettejane Greer), American actress (b. Sept. 9, 1924, Washington, D.C.—d. Aug. 24, 2001, Los Angeles, Calif.), made only a few notable motion pictures but secured her image as a femme fatale with her portrayal of Kathie Moffat, the quintessential film noir temptress, in the classic *Out of the Past* (1947); when the movie was remade in 1984—as *Against All Odds*—she appeared as that character's mother.

Hailsham of St. Marylebone, Quintin McGarel Hogg, Baron, British politician (b. Oct. 9, 1907, London, Eng.—d. Oct. 12, 2001, London), between 1938 and 1987 served six Conservative governments in a variety of posts, most notably 12 years (1970–74, 1979–87) as lord high chancellor (head of the British judiciary), a position his father, Viscount Hailsham, had held in the 1920s. Hogg was educated at Eton and Christ Church, Oxford, called to the bar in 1932, and took silk in 1953. He was elected to the House of Commons in 1938 but was forced to move to the House of Lords on his father's death (1950). A passionate and often eccentric politician, he was finally allowed in 1963 to relinquish the title 2nd Viscount Hailsham, which he had never wanted. He lost in his bid for Conservative Party leader that year but was reelected to the Commons. In 1970 he was granted his own peerage and returned to the Lords. When he retired in 1987, he was the longest-serving lord chancellor of the 20th century.

Hamburger, Viktor, German-born American embryologist (b. July 9, 1900, Landeshut, Ger. [now Kamienna Gora, Pol.]—d. June 12, 2001, St. Louis, Mo.), was a pioneer in the field of neuroembryology; he was noted for having defined and classified the different stages of embryonic development and for having helped identify a chemical substance called nerve growth factor, which stimulates the growth of nerve cells and promotes the development of the nervous system. While earning his Ph.D. from the University of Freiburg, Ger., he performed research under experimental embryologist Hans Spemann. Hamburger received a fellowship to study at the University of Chicago in 1932. Because of his Jewish ancestry, he was not allowed to return to Germany after the Nazis took power in 1933. In 1935 Hamburger joined the faculty of Washington University, St. Louis. Within six years he had advanced to full professor. He served as chairman of the university's biology department from 1941 to 1966 and assumed emeritus status in 1969. Among numerous honours for his contributions to the field of neuroembryology, Hamburger was elected to the U.S. National Academy of Sciences in 1953 and to the American Academy of Arts and Sciences in 1959. He was awarded a National Medal of Science in 1989.

Hank González, Carlos, Mexican politician (b. Aug. 28, 1927, Santiago Tianguistenco, Mex.—d. Aug. 11, 2001, Santiago Tianguistenco), was a highly influential member of Mexico's long-ruling Institutional Revolutionary Party and held public office almost continuously from 1955 to 1994. During his career he served as the mayor of Mexico City, the governor of Mexico state, and agriculture secretary, among other posts. He was also a successful businessman, with a fortune estimated at $1.3 billion in 1993.

Hanna, William Denby, American animator (b. July 14, 1910, Melrose, N.M.—d. March 22, 2001, Los Angeles, Calif.), in his more than 50-year collaboration with Joseph Barbera, created such popular cartoon characters as Tom and Jerry, Yogi and Boo Boo Bear, Huckleberry Hound, and the Flintstones; Fred Flintstone's frequent exclamation "yabba dabba doo" became part of the contemporary vocabulary. The Hanna-Barbera team produced 113 Tom and Jerry cartoons and over 3,000 half-hour shows for 150 television cartoon series, and they won seven Academy Awards and eight Emmy Awards, including the Governors Award of the Academy of Television Arts and Sciences (1988). Hanna dropped out of college and was working as a construction engineer, but when he lost his job during the Depression, he took a job at Pacific Art and Title, which produced cartoons. In 1930 he moved to another cartoon-production company, Harman-Ising Studios, the home of the Looney Tunes and Merrie Melodies series. Metro-Goldwyn-Mayer hired the company to produce some cartoons, for which Hanna, besides inking and painting, created songs and lyrics. When MGM added its own cartoon section in 1937, Hanna became a director there. He soon discovered that the gag-writing and sketching talents of another new employee, Barbera, were a perfect complement to his sense of timing and knack for story construction. They teamed up, and when their first cartoon, "Puss Gets the Boot" (1940), was nominated for an Academy Award, MGM allowed them to develop its cat-and-mouse theme. Fifteen years' worth of Tom and Jerry cartoons were the result, including the innovative teaming of cartoon and live action when Jerry danced with Gene Kelly in *Anchors Aweigh* (1944) and both characters swam with Esther Williams in *Dangerous When Wet* (1953). MGM, however, closed its animation department in 1957, whereupon the two men formed their own company, Hanna-Barbera Productions, and began creating cartoons for television. Because of TV's budget limitations, Hanna and Barbera developed a "limited animation" technique that allowed them to produce cartoons much more cheaply by stressing character and witty dialogue instead of the action that had highlighted the Tom and Jerry cartoons. Their first TV show, *The Ruff and Reddy Show* (1957), was followed by *Huckleberry Hound* (1958), the first animated series to be awarded an Emmy. In 1960 *The Flintstones,* a Stone Age parody of the hit television series *The Honeymooners,* made its appearance. Equally appealing to children and adults, it was the first half-hour animated situation comedy and came to be considered Hanna-Barbera's greatest hit. A Space Age version, *The Jetsons,* debuted in 1962, and series featuring numerous other characters, including Magilla Gorilla and Scooby Doo, followed. In 1996 Warner Brothers bought Hanna-Barbera, but Hanna continued working.

Hulton/Archive/Getty Images

Animator William Hanna (right) with Joseph Barbera and friends

Haq, Abdul (Humayoun Arsala), Afghan resistance leader (b. 1957/58, Nangarhar province, Afg.—d. Oct. 26, 2001, Kabul, Afg.), was an audacious guerrilla commander in Afghanistan's war against the Soviet Union and later became an internationally known English-language spokesman for the anti-Taliban resistance. In 1977 he joined the fight against the Soviets, eventually taking the nom de guerre Abdul Haq. He was a strong supporter of Afghanistan's exiled king, Mohammad Zahir Shah, and served in Prime Minister Gulbuddin Hekmatyar's interim government in the mid-1990s. When war again broke out among the Afghan warlords, Haq left the country and became a successful businessman in Pakistan and the United Arab Emirates. In September 2001, after the assassination of Northern Alliance leader Ahmad Shah Masood (*q.v.*), a political and military rival, and the terrorist attacks in the U.S., Haq tried to dissuade the Western allies from bombing Afghanistan. He reportedly was attempting to negotiate with anti-Taliban supporters when he was captured by Taliban forces and, within hours, executed as a spy.

Harris, Marvin, American anthropologist and theoretician (b. Aug. 18, 1927, New York, N.Y.—d. Oct. 25, 2001, Gainesville, Fla.), was a prominent anthropologist known for his research on cultural materialism, which led him to pose a number of controversial theories, including that warfare was a means of reducing population numbers when protein became scarce and that cannibalism among the Aztecs arose from a need for protein sufficiency. From 1952 to 1980 Harris taught at Columbia University, New York City, where he earned a Ph.D. in 1953. From 1980 to 2000 he was a research professor at the University of Florida. Harris conducted extensive fieldwork in Brazil and Mozambique. Drawing parallels between functionalism in the social sciences with adaptation in biology, he came to see the social life of humans as shaped by practical problems of existence. He expressed his views in such works as *The Rise of Anthropological Theory* (1968), *Cannibals and Kings: The Origins of Cultures* (1977), *Cultural Materialism: The Struggle for a Science of Culture* (1979), and *Cultural Anthropology* (1983).

AP/Wide World Photos

Rock and roll icon George Harrison

Harrison, George, British musician, singer, and songwriter (b. Feb. 25, 1943, Liverpool, Eng.—d. Nov. 29, 2001, Los Angeles, Calif.), was the lead guitarist of the Beatles, who infused rock and roll with new depth and sophistication and became one of the most important and influential bands in the history of rock music; he later also achieved singular success as a songwriter and performer. Harrison was the youngest of the "Fab Four" and was known as the "quiet Beatle," and though he had wanted to be successful, he never became comfortable with fame. He met fellow Beatle Paul McCartney when the two were grammar-school students at the Liverpool Institute. McCartney and John Lennon had formed a rock band, the Quarrymen—which changed its name to Johnny and the Moondogs and then the Silver Beatles before it became the Beatles—and eventually invited Harrison and later Ringo Starr to join. Although Lennon and McCartney wrote most of the songs the Beatles performed, Harrison contributed some of their finest ones, including "While My Guitar Gently Weeps," "Here Comes the Sun," and "Something"—the latter eventually recorded by some 150 other artists, second only to "Yesterday" among Beatles tunes covered. In 1965 Harrison, having become intrigued with the sound of the sitar, studied with Ravi Shankar so that sitar music could be used in Beatles songs. After it was heard in "Norwegian Wood" (1965), musicians in other groups also began featuring it. Harrison was also becoming increasingly interested in Eastern religions and culture, and in 1968 he and the Beatles, as well as a number of other celebrities, explored transcendental meditation with the Maharishi Mahesh Yogi in India. This trip helped bring Eastern religion to the attention of the West and influenced dozens of subsequent Beatles songs, but Harrison was the only Beatle to actually make these religious principles part of his life. Following the breakup of the Beatles in 1970, Harrison released the first of his many post-Beatles recordings, the highly successful triple album *All Things Must Pass* (1970); in 1971 he staged two concerts to raise money to fight starvation in Bangladesh—the prototype for later star-studded fund-raising events; and in 1979 he ventured into a new field, film production, as a founder of Handmade Films. Among the company's efforts were the Monty Python film *Life of Brian* (1979), *Time Bandits* (1981), and *Mona Lisa* (1986). In 1987 Harrison scored one of his biggest solo successes with the album *Cloud Nine.* Some of his most memorable songs as a solo artist included "My Sweet Lord," "Give Me Love (Give Me Peace on Earth)," and "I Got My Mind Set on You." Although Harrison spent much of his time in near seclusion with his family following the murder of Lennon in 1980, in the late 1980s he recorded and performed with the Traveling Wilburys, which also included Bob Dylan, Roy Orbison, Tom Petty, and Jeff Lynne, and in the mid-1990s he took part in the Beatles anthology project. The last years of Harrison's life were difficult. In 1997 he was treated for throat cancer, and in late 1999 he was attacked in his home by a deranged intruder and suffered multiple stab wounds. The cancer recurred in mid-2001, and treatments were unsuccessful.

Hartford, John, American musician and singer-songwriter (b. Dec. 30, 1937, New York, N.Y.—d. June 4, 2001, Madison, Tenn.), was a virtuoso banjoist, fiddler, and guitarist whose best-known song, "Gentle on My Mind" (1967), earned two Grammy Awards; the song was later recorded by Glen Campbell, Elvis Presley, Dean Martin, and others. A passionate performer, Hartford became a popular attraction on the bluegrass circuit after his debut album, *John Hartford Looks at Life,* appeared in 1966. He went on to record some 40 albums, including *The Love Album* (1968), *Aereo-Plain* (1971), and *Morning Bugle* (1972). He recorded his final album, *Good Old Boys,* in 1999, and two of his songs, "Man of Constant Sorrow" and "Indian War Whoop," were included on the sound track for the 2000 film *O Brother, Where Art Thou?*

Hartwell of Peterborough Court in the City of London, William Michael Berry, Baron, British newspaper magnate (b. May 18, 1911, Merthyr Tydfil, Wales—d. April 2, 2001, London, Eng.), was chairman and editor in chief of the *Daily Telegraph* for more than 30 years, from when he inherited the newspaper from his father, Viscount Camrose, in 1954 until his retirement in 1987. He built the *Daily Telegraph* into one of Britain's most admired quality newspapers and launched the equally successful *Sunday Telegraph* in 1960. Lord Hartwell was slow to modernize, however, and lost financial control to Canadian entrepreneur Conrad Black in 1985. He was granted a life peerage in 1968 and inherited the viscountcy, which he disclaimed for life, on the death of his older brother in 1995.

Hawthorne, Sir Nigel Barnard, British actor (b. April 5, 1929, Coventry, Eng.—d. Dec. 26, 2001, Baldock, Hertfordshire, Eng.), displayed his versatility in roles both comic and classic during a half-century-long career that saw him gain his first real fame only after some 30 years in the profession, when he was in his 50s and costarred as the quintessential civil servant Sir Humphrey Appleby in the satiric BBC series *Yes, Minister* (1980–83, 1985–86) and its sequel, *Yes, Prime Minister* (1986–87), a role that won him four British Academy of Film and Television Arts Awards. His reputation grew even more with his Oscar-nominated role as the title character in *The Madness of King George* (1994). Hawthorne made his professional stage debut in 1950 in *The Shop at Sly Corner.* The following year he moved to England and, although he appeared on the London stage in *You Can't Take It with You* in 1951, he had little other success and moved back to South Africa. There Hawthorne performed a number of leading roles, and in 1961 he toured in *Beyond the Fringe.* Upon returning to London in 1962, he made his West End debut in *Talking to You,* and besides touring as Field Marshal Haig in *Oh! What a Lovely War,* played Major Flack in *Privates on Parade* (1977). That role led to his being cast in *Yes, Minister.* Hawthorne went on to stage triumphs in *Shadowlands* in London (1989) and on Broadway (1990), where he won a Tony Award, and then *The Madness of George III* (1991) in London, for which he won an Olivier Award. The lead role in the film adaptation of the latter followed. Hawthorne was created CBE in 1987 and was knighted in 1999. Also in 1999 came his final stage role, the title character in the Royal Shakespeare Company's *King Lear.* Although Hawthorne had been undergoing treatment for cancer for some 18 months, he died of a heart attack in the home he shared with his longtime partner, screenwriter Trevor Bentham.

Heckart, (Anna) Eileen, American actress (b. March 29, 1919, Columbus, Ohio—d. Dec. 31, 2001, Norwalk, Conn.), took advantage of her lanky stature, smoky voice, and winning smile to enjoy a long career on the stage, in film, and on television, often playing eccentric characters. Besides her Oscar-winning role as an overbearing mother in *Butterflies Are Free* (1972)—a role she also had filled on Broadway (1969)—and her Emmy Award-winning roles in *Save Me a Place at Forest Lawn* (1966) and an episode of *Love & War* (1994), she was especially remembered for performances on Broadway in *Picnic* (1953), *Barefoot in the Park* (1965), and *The Waverly Gallery* (2000) and on television as Mary Richards's Aunt Flo on *The Mary Tyler Moore Show* (1975 and 1976). Heckart was presented with a special Tony Award for Excellence in Theatre in 2000, which honoured her body of theatre work.

Hélou, Charles Alexandre, Lebanese politician (b. Dec. 25, 1912, Beirut, Lebanon—d. Jan. 7, 2001, Beirut), served as president of Lebanon from 1964 to 1970. After receiving a law degree, Hélou edited two French-language newspapers, *L'Eclair du Nord* in 1932 and *Le Jour* in 1935–46. He was ambassador to the Vatican in 1947 and later held several cabinet posts, including minister of justice and health (1954–55) and minister of education (1964). Hélou earned the support of Pres. Fuad Chehab and became his successor when Chehab retired in 1964. Not long after his inauguration as president, Hélou agreed at an Arab summit meeting to Arab sponsorship of the Palestine Liberation Organization (PLO), but he refused to allow the stationing of PLO bases in Lebanon, an issue that grew increasingly explosive during the course of his term. In 1968–69 a pattern emerged in which Hélou—a Christian—and the army command opposed the stationing of Palestinian guerrillas in Lebanon, while the Muslim prime minister, Rashid Karami, favoured it. Under great pressure from Arab nations and from Lebanese Muslims, Hélou in 1969 moved to avert a crisis by accepting Karami's proposed policy of coordination between the PLO and the Lebanese army, whereby the PLO secured the right to establish armed units in Lebanese refugee camps. After leaving office in 1970, Hélou had little involvement in public affairs, though he served briefly as minister of state in 1979.

Henderson, Joseph A. ("Joe"), American jazz tenor saxophonist (b. April 24, 1937, Lima, Ohio—d. June 30, 2001, San Francisco, Calif.), was among the handful of important saxophonists from the heyday of hard bop who remained active at the end of the 20th century. Henderson first won acclaim for solos on 1960s hard-bop hits (Lee Morgan's "The Sidewinder" and Horace Silver's "Song for My Father"), and he played in avant-garde and jazz-rock settings before achieving his greatest success in the 1990s by playing the standard repertoire. The phrasing of modern tenor sax giants Sonny Rollins and John Coltrane influenced his less-vivid style; Henderson was notable for high harmonic sophistication, complex lines, abstract forms, and, especially in later years, lyricism. He attended Kentucky State College (now University) briefly, then while studying at Wayne State University, he soon became active in Detroit's lively modern jazz scene. Following two years in the army, he settled in New York City in 1962 and worked in Kenny Dorham's and Horace Silver's combos. Henderson also recorded often for Blue Note, adapting to Andrew Hill's experiments in harmony and form as readily as he adapted to Morgan's and Silver's blues-oriented pieces. Later he played for a time in the popular rock-jazz band Blood, Sweat and Tears and with the Herbie Hancock sextet and pianist Chick Corea. From 1963 he also recorded his own albums, which eventually totaled 34, and he included his own tunes such as "Recordame" and "Isotope." Henderson's greatest success began in 1985 with his live trio album, *The State of the Tenor;* it was followed by compact disc tributes to Billy Strayhorn, Miles Davis, and Antônio Carlos Jobim; a big-band collection; and the album *Porgy and Bess,* with an all-star band and singers Chaka Khan and Sting. With these he became a best-selling recording artist; Henderson went on to win four Grammy Awards.

Herblock (Herbert Lawrence Block), American political cartoonist (b. Oct. 13, 1909, Chicago, Ill.—d. Oct. 7, 2001, Washington, D.C.), had a 72-year-long career, through the terms of 13 presidents, during which his drawings, syndicated in hundreds of newspapers throughout the U.S. and in several other countries, simply and clearly spotlighted his support of civil liberties and civil rights and his view of the political issues of the day. He was awarded three Pulitzer Prizes (1942, 1954, and 1979—the last for his entire body of cartoon work) and shared a fourth (1973) with the *Washington Post.* Herblock's talent was apparent early, and at age 11 he began classes at the Art Institute of Chicago, which the following year awarded him a scholarship. He attended Lake Forest (Ill.) College for two years but dropped out (1929) to work for the *Chicago Daily News.* Before long, his cartoons were being syndicated. Herblock was employed by the Newspaper Enterprise Association in Cleveland, Ohio, from 1933 to 1943, during which his work focused attention on the dangers of the rise of fascism in Europe. Following World War II army service (1943–46), Herblock joined the *Washington Post* and began producing six cartoons a week; only late in life did he cut back to five a week. An early target was Sen. Joseph McCarthy and his communist witch-hunts, and it was Herblock who coined the term *McCarthyism.* Another favourite target was Richard M. Nixon, whom Herblock's cartoons always showed sporting a five o'clock shadow until he became president, at which time Herblock desisted out of respect for the office. Besides his cartoon work, Herblock wrote 12 books, including *Herblock: A Cartoonist's Life* (1993). He was awarded the Presidential Medal of Freedom in 1994, and his final cartoon appeared on Aug. 26, 2001.

Hewlett, William Redington, American engineer and businessman (b. May 20, 1913, Ann Arbor, Mich.—d. Jan. 12, 2001, Palo Alto, Calif.), was the cofounder of the Hewlett-Packard Co. (HP), the electronics and computer giant credited with pioneering California's Silicon Valley and thus the computer age. He and his partner, David Packard, promoted an innovative management style that stressed creativity, flexibility, openness, and teamwork, and they both became noted philanthropists. Hewlett's interest in science and electronics began when he was a child,

Hewlett-Packard/Getty Images

Computer pioneer William Hewlett (standing) with David Packard

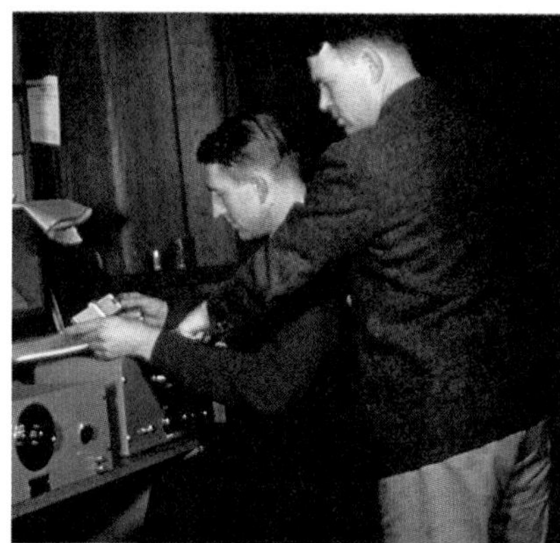

and in 1930 he began studying engineering at Stanford University. It was there that he met Packard, and the two became lifelong friends. After graduation (1934) Hewlett earned (1936) a master's degree at the Massachusetts Institute of Technology and then returned to Stanford for further study. On Jan. 1, 1939, at the suggestion of engineering professor Frederick Terman and with start-up funds of $538, Hewlett and Packard set up a small electronics business in a rented garage in Palo Alto. That garage was later (1989) designated a California historical landmark. One of HP's products, an audio oscillator, brought the company its first success when Walt Disney Productions purchased eight of the devices to test sound equipment for the animated film *Fantasia* (1940). Following service in the U.S. Army Signal Corps during World War II, Hewlett returned to HP (1947) and was made a vice president, and in 1964 he became president, a position he retained until 1977. The company expanded rapidly and in 1968 produced the first desktop scientific calculator. The pocket scientific calculator followed in 1972, rendering slide rules largely obsolete. HP became even better known in 1984 with its laserjet printer. The company eventually became the second largest computer maker and Hewlett became one of the 50 wealthiest Americans. Hewlett served as HP's CEO (1969–78), chairman of the executive committee (1977–83), vice chairman of the board (1983– 87), and director emeritus (from 1987). In 1966 he and his first wife, Flora, established the William and Flora Hewlett Foundation. In 1985 Hewlett was honoured with the National Medal of Science, the highest scientific award in the U.S.

Heym, Stefan (Helmut Flieg), German writer and political activist (b. April 10, 1913, Chemnitz, Ger.—d. Dec. 16, 2001, Jerusalem, Israel), as the author of over a dozen novels, including *The Crusaders (*1948), provoked controversy with his dissident writings. Although he was an avowed Marxist-Leninist, he was a steady critic of East Germany's government throughout that regime's existence, and when German reunification came, he held out hope for socialism to prevail. To that end, he ran for election to the Bundestag (second house of parliament) in 1994, served for a year, and thereafter continued in his activist dissent.

Hibbler, Albert ("Al"), American singer (b. Aug. 16, 1915, Tyro, Miss.—d. April 24, 2001, Chicago, Ill.), rose to fame with the Duke Ellington band (1943–51), singing some of composer Ellington's most enduring songs—"I'm Just a Lucky So and So," "Don't Get Around Much Anymore," and "Do Nothin' Till You Hear from Me"—in a low baritone voice and with eccentric vocal effects. On his own the blind performer recorded his biggest hit, the ballad "Unchained Melody" (1955), followed by "After the Lights Go Down Low." During the civil rights movement, Hibbler was arrested twice during protest marches; he continued to perform regularly into the 1970s.

Higgins, Billy, American drummer (b. Oct. 11, 1936, Los Angeles, Calif.—d. May 3, 2001, Inglewood, Calif.), helped create the free jazz idiom while a member of Ornette Coleman's classic 1950s groups and later became the busiest drummer in jazz; he played on dozens of Blue Note albums and accompanied top jazz artists from Thelonious Monk, Cecil Taylor, and John Coltrane in the early 1960s to latter-day young lions Joshua Redman and Roy Hargrove. Higgins's drumming was characterized by his enthusiastic swing, very precise beat, and crisp-sounding, stimulating, often complex interplay with soloists. In his teens Higgins began playing drums with trumpeter Don Cherry and other Los Angeles bop musicians; by 1957 Coleman was teaching Higgins and Cherry to play his new kind of jazz, with improvisations based on melodies rather than on traditional harmonic patterns. The Coleman quartet created a sensation when it debuted in New York City in November 1959, but Higgins left the group in 1960. He played with Sonny Rollins's quartet, then became a top hard bop drummer and recorded prolifically with masters such as Lee Morgan, Hank Mobley, Dexter Gordon, Jackie McLean, Herbie Hancock, and Cedar Walton. Higgins seldom led groups but was constantly in demand, even after he moved back to Los Angeles in 1978. Besides participating in international tours with the Timeless All Stars and reunions with Coleman and Cherry, he played and acted in Bertrand Tavernier's 1986 jazz film *Round Midnight.* He then cofounded the World Stage, a Los Angeles storefront arts centre where he enticed noted jazz musicians to perform and teach; he also taught at the University of California, Los Angeles. Though liver disease curtailed his career in the 1990s, he resumed performing after a liver transplant in 1995. Two years later Higgins received a Jazz Master Award from the National Endowment for the Humanities. In 2000 liver failure again halted his playing.

Effervescent drummer Billy Higgins

Hlavsa, Milan (Mejla Hlavsa), Czech musician (b. March 6, 1951, Prague, Czech. [now Czech Rep.]—d. Jan. 5, 2001, Prague), founded (1968) and served as songwriter and bass guitarist for the underground rock and roll band Plastic People of the Universe, which became a symbol of political unrest in communist Czechoslovakia. Plastic People, which sang in English until the early 1970s, was banned by the Czech government in 1970. The band continued to perform, however, and to make recordings, which were surreptitiously distributed and smuggled out of the country to the West. The arrest of Hlavsa and other rock musicians in 1976 helped to galvanize the formation of the Czech human rights movement Charter 77.

Hohenemser, Kurt, German-born American aerospace engineer (b. Jan. 3, 1906, Berlin, Ger.—d. April 7, 2001, St. Louis, Mo.), was a pioneer in the field of helicopter design. During World War II, Hohenemser worked in Germany for inventor Anton Flettner, helping Flettner build the Fl 282 Kolibri, one of the first helicopters used in combat. Hohenemser relocated to the U.S. in 1947. Working as an engineer for the McDonnell Aircraft Corp., he designed, among other helicopters, the XV-1, a precursor of the Osprey military aircraft. From 1966 until his retirement in 1975, he was a professor of aerospace engineering at Washington University, St. Louis.

Hooker, John Lee, American blues artist (b. Aug. 22, 1917, Clarksdale, Miss.—d. June 21, 2001, Los Altos, Calif.), sang and played guitar with a passionately intense feeling that made him one of the most emotionally compelling of all bluesmen. His voice was a big strong baritone; he shouted fast blues over simple, repeated, driving boogie guitar, and he sang bleak slow blues, often muffling the lyrics, over stark guitar chords; he wore dark glasses when singing because, he said, the blues often moved him to tears. Hooker was one of 11 children in a Mississippi sharecropping family; he learned to play guitar from his stepfather and became interested in gospel music and blues in boyhood. In 1943 he moved to Detroit, where he made his first recordings, including "Boogie Chillen," "Crawling King Snake," and "Weeping Willow" (1948–49), hit singles notable for the

Emotive bluesman John Lee Hooker

raw power of his singing, accompanied only by his riveting guitar. Though his unrhyming lines, pentatonic melodies, and one-chord modal harmonic structures sounded primitive, his swinging energy and his electric guitar, which was just becoming popular among blues audiences, marked him as an urban blues performer with a unique sound. In later hits such as "Dimples" (1956) and "Boom Boom" (1962), he was accompanied by bands. One of the most prolific blues recording artists, he recorded for many labels, often using pseudonyms such as John Lee Booker, John Lee Cooker, Texas Slim, and Birmingham Sam and his Magic Guitar. As the black blues audience dwindled, Hooker gradually became popular with white listeners, first playing unamplified guitar and singing traditional blues in folk music venues and recordings; he eventually sang with rock stars Bonnie Raitt, Van Morrison, and Canned Heat. Hooker toured widely for most of his career and appeared in the films *The Blues Brothers* (1980) and *The Color Purple* (1985). He was inducted into the Rock and Roll Hall of Fame in 1991.

Horwich, Frances Rappaport, American educator and television host (b. July 16, 1908, Ottawa, Ohio—d. July 25, 2001, Scottsdale, Ariz.), was host of the popular children's educational television show *Ding Dong School* from 1952 to 1967. Horwich earned a Ph.D. in education from Northwestern University, Evanston, Ill., in 1942. Before her career in television, she worked as a primary-school teacher, kindergarten director, and college professor. *Ding Dong School* was an immediate hit and helped pave the way for later educational shows aimed at children, including *Sesame Street* and *Mister Rogers' Neighborhood.* Horwich received a George Foster Peabody Award in 1953. After leaving television she worked as an educational consultant.

Hoyle, Sir Fred, British astrophysicist (b. June 24, 1915, Bingley, Yorkshire, Eng.—d. Aug. 20, 2001, Bournemouth, Dorset, Eng.), was the foremost promoter of the "steady-state theory," which holds that the universe is always expanding and that new matter is being continuously created to maintain a constant mean density in space. To his great consternation, however, Hoyle was forever associated with the term *big bang,* which he coined in the early 1950s as a term of derision to denigrate the opposing cosmological theory that the universe began in a sudden explosive expansion of matter and energy from a highly compressed primordial state. Hoyle never accepted the growing evidence in favour of the big-bang model, but in *A Different Approach to Cosmology* (2000), he submitted a modified "quasi-steady state" model in which an infinite universe expands and contracts over time. Hoyle studied mathematics at Emmanuel College, Cambridge, and, after working on military radar development during World War II, returned to Cambridge, where he was a mathematics lecturer (1945–58), Plumian Professor of Astronomy (1958–72), and founding director (1967– 73) of the Institute of Theoretical Astronomy. In 1948 Hoyle formulated the steady-state model in collaboration with mathematician Hermann Bondi and astronomer Thomas Gold. During the 1950s he turned to research on the chemical composition of stars. In 1957 Hoyle, William Fowler, and Geoffrey and Margaret Burbridge jointly published the breakthrough paper "Synthesis of the Elements in Stars," in which they explained how all but the lightest chemical elements were created through nuclear reactions within the interiors of stars or during stellar explosions known as supernovas. In 1983 Fowler won the Nobel Prize for Physics for this work, while a disappointed Hoyle eventually was awarded the Royal Swedish Academy of Science's Crafoord Prize (1997). Hoyle was equally well known for his other theories, including his belief that life on Earth evolved from biological material formed in outer space and that some diseases are caused by viruses that originated in space. A prolific science writer and successful popularizer of difficult scientific concepts, Hoyle also wrote several science-fiction novels, notably *The Black Cloud* (1957), *A for Andromeda* (1962), and *October the First Is Too Late* (1966). Hoyle was elected a fellow of the Royal Society in 1957 and served (1971–73) as president of the Royal Astronomical Society. He was knighted in 1972.

Hubley, Faith Elliott, American film animator (b. Sept. 16, 1924, New York, N.Y.—d. Dec. 7, 2001, New Haven, Conn.), made films that combined music, magic, and myth in their celebration of life and humanity. Of the many animated works on which she collaborated with her husband, John Hubley, three won Academy Awards—in 1959, 1962, and 1966.

Hughes, Glenn, American singer (b. July 18, 1950, New York, N.Y.—d. March 4, 2001, New York), performed as a leather-clad biker in the flamboyant disco band the Village People. Hughes had been working as a toll collector before successfully auditioning for the openly gay band in 1977. The Village People went on to record a string of international hits, including "Macho Man" (1978), "Y.M.C.A." (1978), and "In the Navy" (1979). Hughes sang with the group until 1996. At his own request, he was buried in his leather biker's outfit.

Hume, Paul Chandler, American music critic (b. Dec. 13, 1915, Chicago, Ill.—d. Nov. 26, 2001, Baltimore, Md.), wrote highly esteemed reviews for the *Washington Post* for 35 years (from 1947), taught music history at Georgetown University, Washington, D.C. (1950–77), and served as a visiting professor at Yale University (1975–83). In 1950, in a review that brought him to the attention of the general public, he infuriated Pres. Harry Truman when he expressed a less-than-complimentary opinion of a voice recital given by the president's daughter, Margaret Truman.

Hunter, Maxwell White, American aeronautical engineer (b. March 11, 1922, Hollidaysburg, Pa.—d. Nov. 10, 2001, Los Angeles, Calif.), was a leading rocket scientist who was influential in the development of the U.S. space program. After earning a Ph.D. from the Massachusetts Institute of Technology in 1944, Hunter went to work for Douglas Aircraft. While at Douglas he designed early versions of the B-42 and B-43 bombers, rockets for the Apollo Moon-landing program, Nike antiaircraft missiles, and an intermediate-range ballistic missile known as Thor. In the 1960s he served as space policy adviser to Presidents John F. Kennedy and Lyndon B. Johnson. From 1965 to 1987 Hunter worked for the Lockheed Missiles and Space Co. He reportedly helped sell the administration of Pres. Ronald Reagan on the idea for the U.S. Strategic Defense Initiative, known as "Star Wars." In later years Hunter established a consulting firm, SpaceGuild Inc., and worked on designs for a reusable launch vehicle to replace the space shuttle.

Hunzvi, Chenjerai ("Hitler"), Zimbabwean political activist (b. Oct. 23, 1949, Chikomba district, Southern Rhodesia—d. June 4, 2001, Harare, Zimb.), as chairman (from 1996) of the War Veterans' Association of Zimbabwe, built that formerly small organization into a huge political force; during the last months of his life, he engineered increasingly violent attacks on government opponents as well as the forcible occupation of hundreds of white-owned farms by malcontent Zimbabwean black "veterans." Hunzvi, who took the nom de guerre Hitler during the guerrilla war against white-minority rule in Rhodesia, pursued medical studies in Poland before returning to his homeland in 1990 to practice medicine. Despite reports that he had never fought in the war, Hunzvi proclaimed himself a lifelong freedom fighter, and his successful demands to Pres. Robert Mugabe on behalf of government-funded veterans' pensions earned him a considerable power base. He was elected to the Zimbabwean parliament in 2000.

Husseini, Faisal ibn ʿAbd al-Qadir al-, Palestinian political leader (b. July 17, 1940, Baghdad, Iraq—d. May 31, 2001, Kuwait City, Kuwait), was the most senior Palestine Liberation Organization (PLO) official in Jerusalem and a pragmatic but persistent spokesman for Palestinian claims to East Jerusalem. Much of Husseini's influence within the Palestinian community was due to respect for his illustrious family. His father was a Palestinian military hero who died in battle against Zionist forces outside Jerusalem in 1948; a more distant relative, Amin al-Husayni, had been the grand mufti of Jerusalem (1921–48). Husseini studied science in Egypt and military tactics in Syria and joined Yasir Arafat's Fatah movement in 1961 and the PLO in 1965. When most other PLO leaders left Israel, Husseini remained in Jerusalem. He was repeatedly arrested by Israeli authorities and learned Hebrew while in prison. In later years he joined other moderates on both sides in support of U.S.-mediated peace negotiations, and he was often invited to represent the Palestinian point of view on Israeli radio and television. Husseini's home, Orient House, served as the unofficial PLO headquarters in East Jerusalem. He died of a heart attack while on a PLO peace mission to Kuwait.

Ingstad, Helge Marcus, Norwegian writer and adventurer (b. Dec. 30, 1899, Meraaker, Nor.—d. March 29, 2001, Oslo, Nor.), proved the long-debated theory that Vikings established a settlement in North America in about AD 1000. From the early 1950s Ingstad and his wife, archaeologist Anne Stine, explored the sites of known Viking settlements in Greenland and, using information garnered from Norse histories and sagas, began searching for the legendary "Vinland." In 1960 the pair unearthed ruins of an ancient village near L'Anse aux Meadows on the north coast of Newfoundland. By 1964 excavations on the site had revealed Norse artifacts and had provided conclusive evidence of a 1,000-year-old Viking settlement. In 1978 L'Anse aux Meadows was made a UNESCO World Heritage site. Ingstad, who trained as a lawyer in Norway before becoming a fur trapper and explorer in Canada, published several books on his adventures, notably *Landet under Leidarstjernen* (1959; *Land Under the Pole Star*, 1965) and *Vestervej til Vinland* (1965; *Westward to Vinland*, 1969).

Ireland, George, American basketball coach (b. June 15, 1913, Madison, Wis.—d. Sept. 14, 2001, Addison, Ill.), served at Loyola University (Chicago) for 24 seasons beginning in 1951 and retired with a 321–255 record. His most famous victory came in 1963, when the Loyola Ramblers won the National Collegiate Athletic Association championship, defeating the defending champion University of Cincinnati (Ohio) team 60–58 in overtime after having been 15 points behind in the second half of the game.

Jansson, Tove Marika, Finnish author and artist (b. Aug. 9, 1914, Helsinki, Fin., Russian Empire—d. June 27, 2001, Helsinki, Fin.), was the author-illustrator of the popular series of children's books that recounted the adventures of the Moomins, a family of hippopotamus-like trolls that spent much of its time sleeping when not coping with floodwaters, comets, and other, less-perilous situations. Following the publication of her first book, *Småtrollen och den stora översvämningen* (1945; "The Small Trolls and the Large Flood"), Jansson released *Kometjakten* (1946; *Comet in Moominland*, 1951). She produced several more Moomintroll books, more than 2,000 other Moomin products—plush toys, wallpaper, pens, jewelry, candles—and a comic strip, *Moomins*, which appeared (1953–60) in the *Evening News* (London). Jansson's books were written in Swedish, the language that she spoke with her parents; her juvenile works, however, were translated into more than 30 languages. Among her other works were plays for children, short stories, adult fiction, and an autobiography, *Bildhuggarens dotter* (1968; *Sculptors' Daughter*, 1969).

AP/Wide World Photos

Moomin creator Tove Jansson

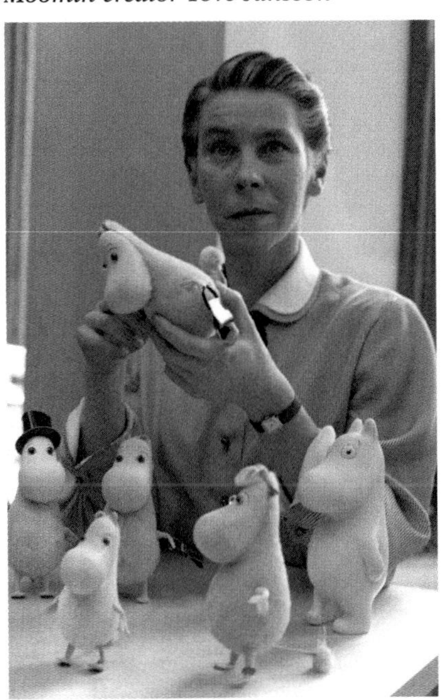

Jennings, Elizabeth Joan, British poet (b. July 18, 1926, Boston, Lincolnshire, Eng.—d. Oct. 26, 2001, Bampton, Oxfordshire, Eng.), wrote traditional verse that was both intensely personal and universal. Her poetry was direct and understated, and it reflected her devout Roman Catholicism. She read English at St. Anne's College, Oxford, where her friends included Kingsley Amis and Philip Larkin. From 1950 to 1958 she worked at the Oxford City Library and then briefly for a publisher. Beginning in 1960 she supported herself by writing and reviewing. *Poems*, which appeared in 1953, won the first of her three Arts Council Awards, and *A Way of Looking* (1955) won the Somerset Maugham Award. Robert Conquest selected her work for his 1956 anthology *New Lines*, which also included poems by Amis and Larkin, among others, and which led to her being grouped with the Movement poets. Unlike the other members of this group, however, she was not an ironist. After a trip to Italy she published *A Sense of the World* (1958), expressing her passion for that country. *Song for a Birth or a Death* (1961), which suggested a somewhat fierce view of love, led critics to call her a confessional poet, a label she firmly rejected. She suffered a breakdown in the early 1960s, and a number of subsequent poems, as in *Recoveries* (1964), reflected on her illness. Later volumes such as *Growing-Points* (1975) and *Extending the Territory* (1985) showed an expansion of technique. Major collections included *Collected Poems 1967* (1967), *Selected Poems* (1979), and *Collected Poems 1953–1985* (1986), which won the W.H. Smith Award. *The Sonnets of Michelangelo*, published in 1961 and revised in 1969, came to be considered the standard translation. She also published criticism, a biography of Robert Frost, and poetry for children. She was made CBE in 1992.

Jia Lanpo, Chinese archaeologist (b. Nov. 25, 1908, Hebei province, China—d. July 8, 2001, Beijing, China), was internationally known for his work as director of the Peking man excavation at the Zhoukoudian cave complex near Beijing. In 1929, while still a graduate student, Jia was named interim overseer of the excavation; he became director in 1935. At the site, Jia helped unearth the first Chinese hominid fossils ever discovered; the Peking man fossils, which were about 900,000 to 130,000 years old and belonged to the Middle Pleistocene Era, included 14 skullcaps, several mandibles, facial and limb bones, and the teeth of about 40 individuals. Though many of the fossils were lost during World War II, Jia had made casts of all of them and had taken some 2,000 photographs of the excavation site. He later directed excavations at other Pleistocene sites in China. A prolific writer, Jia published more than 180 scientific articles as well as two highly regarded books, *Chinese Homo Erectus* (1950) and *Early Man in China* (1980).

Johnson, J.J. (James Louis Johnson), American jazz musician and composer (b. Jan. 22, 1924, Indianapolis, Ind.—d. Feb. 4, 2001, Indianapolis), was the first trombonist to improvise in the fast, complex phrases of bebop, and he was considered by many the most important modern jazz artist on his instrument. The Johnson style was dominant during the 1950s and '60s; virtually all other bop-era and modal trombonists based their styles on his lyric art. He played

AP/Wide World Photos

Improvisational trombonist J.J. Johnson

in the Benny Carter and Count Basie big bands before becoming active in 1945 in New York-centred bebop circles and working and recording with Charlie Parker, Miles Davis, Illinois Jacquet, Sonny Stitt, and others. In addition, Johnson led his own groups. By then his sound was smooth in all ranges of his horn, and he played fast melodic phrases, full of short, staccato notes, with great ease. Remarkably, he developed his virtuoso technique on the slide trombone, a singularly unwieldy horn; hearing his early recordings, many listeners assumed he was playing the valve trombone, a far easier instrument to manipulate. For a time Johnson also worked as a blueprint inspector, but the popularity of the unusual Jay and Kai Quintet (1954–56), which included fellow trombonist Kai Winding, enabled him to concentrate on music full-time. The middle and late 1950s were the height of Johnson's career as a soloist; he led his own groups, toured and recorded often, and appeared on noted albums, including *Stan Getz and J.J. Johnson at the Opera House* (1957) and ones for Miles Davis and Sonny Rollins. He also began composing large-scale works, including *Poem for Brass* (1956), *El Camino Real* (1959), *Sketch for Trombone and Orchestra*

(1959), and the suite *Perceptions* (1961). During 1967–87 he concentrated on composing and arranging for commercials, films (*Cleopatra Jones*, *Barefoot in the Park*, and *Shaft*), and television (*That Girl*, *The Mod Squad*, and *Starsky and Hutch*). When Johnson returned to the limelight (1987–97), his jazz improvisations recaptured the vigour and mastery of his early work.

Johnson, Nkosi (Xolani Nkosi), South African activist (b. Feb. 4, 1989, Daveytown, S.Af.—d. June 1, 2001, Johannesburg, S.Af.), became the human face of AIDS in South Africa and an iconic figure in the campaign to raise money and public awareness about the disease. Johnson, who was born HIV-positive, was abandoned by his birth mother (who later died of AIDS) and was reared by a white foster mother. At the age of seven he was identified as his country's longest-surviving AIDS baby. Later his foster mother went to court to force the local primary school to enroll him as a pupil. Johnson attracted international attention in July 2000 when he made an impassioned speech at the opening ceremony of the XIII International AIDS Conference in Durban, S.Af., in which he called for compassion and improved medical treatment for AIDS sufferers, especially children and pregnant women, and implicitly criticized official South African government policy.

Jovanovich, William (Vladimir Jovanovich), American publisher (b. Feb. 6, 1920, Louisville, Colo.—d. Dec. 4, 2001, San Diego, Calif.), joined the Harcourt Brace and Co. publishing company as a college textbook salesman in 1947 and by 1954 was president. Under his leadership the company—renamed Harcourt Brace Jovanovich in 1970—incorporated such innovations as the use of colourful illustrations and detailed teachers' guides and grew to be one of the largest textbook publishers. He also published his own works, including *The World's Last Night* (1990).

Kabila, Laurent-Désiré, Congolese political leader (b. Nov. 27, 1939, Jadotville, Katanga province, Belgian Congo—confirmed dead on Jan. 18, 2001, Kinshasa, Democratic Republic of the Congo [DRC; formerly Zaire]), was president of the DRC from 1997 until his death. In 1960, after studying in France and Tanzania, Kabila became a youth leader in a political party allied to Congo's first postindependence prime minister, Marxist-Maoist Patrice Lumumba. Lumumba was deposed in 1961 by Mobutu Sese Seko and later killed. Assisted for a time in 1964 by guerrilla leader Che Guevara, Kabila helped Lumumba supporters lead a revolt, but it was eventually suppressed in 1965 by the Congolese army led by Mobutu. Kabila then founded (1967) the People's Revolutionary Party, which established a Marxist territory in the Kivu region of eastern Zaire and managed to sustain itself through gold mining and ivory trading. When that enterprise came to an end during the 1980s, he ran a business selling gold in Dar es Salaam, Tanz., until he resurfaced in Zaire in 1996 as leader of the newly formed Alliance of Democratic Forces for the Liberation of Congo-Zaire. Supported by a nation outraged by the dictatorial leadership of Mobutu,

AP/Wide World Photos

Assassin's target Laurent Kabila

Kabila rallied forces consisting mostly of Tutsi from eastern Zaire. Marching west toward the capital city of Kinshasa, Kabila's troops forced Mobutu to flee the country before their arrival. On May 17, 1997, Kabila installed himself as head of state. He also rejected the name Zaire, which Mobutu had given the country in 1971, and reverted its name to the DRC. Kabila was able to secure regional support, and his plan to revive the economy was welcomed both internationally and at home. Humanitarian organizations, however, soon voiced reservations. Reportedly, Kabila's troops had been responsible for the murder of thousands of Hutu refugees who had fled Rwanda into Zaire in 1994; Kabila ignored UN demands for an inquiry into the massacre. Resorting to many of the same dictatorial methods as his predecessor, Kabila refused to hold new elections, banned political parties, imprisoned journalists and human rights workers, and invited members of his family into the government. His years in office were largely consumed by a fierce conflict in the eastern part of the country between government forces and rebels backed by Uganda and Rwanda. Kabila was shot dead in the presidential mansion, allegedly by one of his bodyguards.

Kael, Pauline, American film critic (b. June 19, 1919, Petaluma, Calif.—d. Sept. 3, 2001, Great Barrington, Mass.), was an outspoken reviewer for *The New Yorker* magazine from 1968 to 1979 and 1980 to 1991, wielding untold influence among film fans and perhaps even moviemakers themselves. Celebrated as much for the provocative style of her writing as for the content, she honed a swordlike sharpness that would eviscerate a faulty work as deftly as it would crown a new piece of art. Thoughtful and high-minded, she nonetheless was wary of overintellectualizing the cinematic experience and encouraged her readers and imitators, known as "Paulettes," to trust their emotions. As such, she became a keen observer of popular culture and championed her favourite actors with fervour. She supported many filmmakers who came to prominence in the 1970s, including Francis Ford Coppola, Martin Scorsese, and Robert Altman. Fans and detractors alike found her pans as quotable and opinionated as her praises. "In love" with movies, as she defined it, from childhood, Kael attended the University of California, Berkeley, and began working as a critic in her mid-30s for *City Lights* magazine in San Francisco. She had begun to appear frequently in film journals and on the radio by the time she first published her reviews in the best-selling collection *I Lost It at the Movies* (1965). Thereafter she was a regular contributor to such mainstream titles as *Life*, *McCall's*, and *The New Republic*, and her work at these publications eventually earned her a spot at *The New Yorker*. During her hiatus from *The New Yorker* in 1979–80, she worked for the motion picture industry. Her other collections included *Kiss Kiss Bang Bang* (1968), *Deeper into Movies* (1973), *When the Lights Go Down* (1980), *Taking It All In* (1984), *Hooked* (1989), and *For Keeps* (1994).

Kato, Shizue Hirota, Japanese feminist and political leader (b. March 2, 1897, Tokyo, Japan—d. Dec. 22, 2001, Tokyo), began in the 1920s to campaign for women's rights and was the first woman to promote family planning in Japan. When women received the vote in 1946, she became one of the first to be elected to the Diet (parliament), serving first in the lower house (1946–50) and then in the upper (1950–74). In 1988, in recognition of her work in less-developed countries, she was given the UN Population Award, the first Japanese person to be so honoured.

Kazantzidis, Stelios, Greek folk singer (b. Aug. 29, 1931, Athens, Greece—d. Sept. 14, 2001, Athens), used his expressive vocal interpretations to capture the joys as well as the melancholy longings of Greeks everywhere, especially those in the working class and emigrants in the Greek diaspora. Kazantzidis had little formal education and began singing professionally in 1950. Although he made scores of recordings in his career, he did not fare well during the military junta (1967–74) and made no recordings between 1975 and 1987. Kazantzidis made a comeback to a new generation of fans in the 1990s.

Keïta, Seydou, Malian photographer (b. 1921/23?, French Sudan—d. Nov. 21, 2001, Paris, France), fashioned insightful studio portraits of ordinary Malian people, usually posed with intriguing combinations of African and Western clothing and props that he provided. Keïta, who was entirely self-trained, founded a small photography studio in the city of Bamako in 1948 and quickly gained a reputation for formal portraiture. He was designated the Republic of Mali's official photographer in 1962 and closed his studio to concentrate on his new duties, but he carefully preserved and stored thousands of black-and-white images. He retired

bottom: AP/Wide World Photos

AP/Wide World Photos

Ken Kesey, a Merry Prankster

from government service in 1977. In the late 1990s Keïta's early work was discovered by André Magnin of the Contemporary African Art Collection in Paris. Thereafter, Keïta's portraits were exhibited in Paris and across the U.S. A book dedicated to his photography was published in 1997, and in early 2001 the Seydou Keïta Foundation was established in Bamako to preserve his work and to support young African artists.

Kepes, Gyorgy, Hungarian-born American artist and theorist (b. Oct. 4, 1906, Selyp, Hung.—d. Dec. 29, 2001, Cambridge, Mass.), experimented with new technologies for art through design, photography, and painting. He headed the Light and Color Department at the New Bauhaus in Chicago (later renamed the Chicago Institute of Design) from 1937 until 1945, when he began teaching at the School of Architecture and Planning of the Massachusetts Institute of Technology. There he founded (1967) the Center for Advanced Visual Studies, a collective that fostered the marriage between art and science and art and modernity. His books included *The Language of Vision* (1944) and *The New Landscape in Art and Science* (1956).

Kesey, Ken Elton, American writer (b. Sept. 17, 1935, La Junta, Colo.—d. Nov. 10, 2001, Eugene, Ore.), became an icon of the counterculture with both his first book, *One Flew over the Cuckoo's Nest* (1962), and his hippie lifestyle as he and a group of friends—the Merry Pranksters—made a cross-country school-bus trip, along the way staging LSD-inspired "happenings." That trip, which helped bring the antiestablishment's antics into the public eye, was chronicled in Tom Wolfe's *The Electric Kool-Aid Acid Test* (1968). While a student at the University of Oregon, Kesey performed in some student productions, and following graduation (1957) he did some acting in Hollywood. His chief interest was in writing, however, so he spent a year in the graduate program at Stanford University. In 1959 Kesey became a subject of mind-altering-drug experiments at a veterans hospital, and when the tests ended, he remained at the hospital as an orderly in the mental ward. These experiences gave him the basis for *One Flew over the Cuckoo's Nest,* which achieved both critical and popular acclaim. A stage version was produced on Broadway in 1963–64, and a film version was released in 1975; the movie won five Academy Awards, including best picture. To prepare for his next book, *Sometimes a Great Notion* (1964)—a saga about a logging family—Kesey returned to Oregon and worked as a logger. That book also was filmed (1971). Following his school-bus trip with the Merry Pranksters and some trouble with the law, Kesey returned once again to Oregon and settled on his farm. Over the next several years, he wrote short fiction, children's books, and magazine articles; published two collections of his writings, *Kesey's Garage Sale* (1973) and *Demon Box* (1986); founded (1973) and published an underground magazine, *Spit in the Ocean;* and taught writing at the University of Oregon. In 1992 Kesey published another major novel, *Sailor Song,* and in 1994, in collaboration with fellow Prankster Ken Babbs, he published his final novel, *Last Go Round.*

Ketcham, Henry King ("Hank"), American cartoonist (b. March 14, 1920, Seattle, Wash.—d. June 1, 2001, Pebble Beach, Calif.), was the creator of the *Dennis the Menace* comic strip, which daily chronicled the antics and misadventures of a blond, freckle-faced scamp perpetually "five-ana-half" years old. The 50-year-old strip appeared in some 1,000 newspapers in 48 countries and 19 languages. Ketcham discovered his desire to become a cartoonist when he was six years old; after watching a family friend draw some comic-strip characters, he asked to borrow the man's "magic pencil." He attended the University of Washington but dropped out in order to pursue his career. Ketcham worked as an animator first for Woody Woodpecker creator Walter Lantz and then for Walt Disney. At Disney he worked on animated films, including *Fantasia* (1940), *Pinocchio* (1940), and *Bambi* (1942). During World War II Ketcham served in the navy, where he drew cartoons to be used on posters and in material for training and war-bond-sales purposes, and following the war he became a freelance cartoonist. Ketcham's inspiration for the character of Dennis came (1950) from his rambunctious son of the same name; the child's mother—complaining that when Dennis was supposed to be taking a nap, he instead wrecked his room—exclaimed to Ketcham, "Your son is a menace!" Within five months the strip was running in 16 newspapers, and by 1953 it was being enjoyed by 30 million readers of 193 newspapers in the U.S. and 52 abroad. Cartoon books, a television series (1959–63), a musical, films, games, and toys followed. Ketcham ceased drawing the Sunday strips himself in the mid-1980s and in 1994 turned the daily strips over to a team of artists and writers. He thereupon devoted his artistic skills to oil and watercolour painting.

Kharibian, Leo, American-born dancer, choreographer, and director (b. April 27, 1927, Boston, Mass.—d. Aug. 23, 2001, Leicestershire, Eng.?), helped change the face of musical theatre choreography in Great Britain by incorporating American jazz dance movement in works for the stage, film, and television. He was best known for the "We're Knights of the Round Table" number in the movie *Monty Python and the Holy Grail* (1975).

Kiam, Victor Kermit, II, American businessman (b. Dec. 7, 1926, New Orleans, La.—d. May 27, 2001, Stamford, Conn.), was the innovative owner of Remington Products, a company that specialized in selling electric shavers; he became widely known after appearing in a series of television advertisements in which he proclaimed, "I liked the shaver so much, I bought the company." After receiving a master's of business administration degree from Harvard University, Kiam worked from 1951 to 1955 in the sales and marketing divisions of Lever Bros., maker of Pepsodent toothpaste, among other products. He was an executive at Playtex for the following 13 years before buying his first company, watchmaker Wells-Benrus, in 1968. He acquired a failing Remington from the Sperry Rand Corp. in 1979 and made the company profitable within a year, in part through his unique approach to advertising. Kiam was the majority owner (1988–92) of the New England Patriots of the National Football League.

Kilburn, Tom, British computer engineer (b. Aug. 11, 1921, Dewsbury, Yorkshire, Eng.—d. Jan. 17, 2001, Manchester, Eng.), was a key member of Frederic (later Sir Frederic) Williams's team that designed the first cathode-ray-tube memory system (known as the Williams tube) and built the first working stored-program electronic digital computer. Kilburn, who trained as a mathematician, wrote the original software program, which was successfully tested at the University of Manchester in June 1948. Kilburn was named the university's first professor of computer science in 1964, was made a fellow of the Royal Society in 1965, and was appointed CBE in 1973.

Klaus, Josef, Austrian politician (b. Aug. 15, 1910, Mauthen, Austria, Austria-Hungary—d. July 26, 2001, Vienna, Austria), as chairman of the centre-right People's Party (ÖVP), was Austria's chancellor in an uneasy coalition with the Socialist Party for two years (1964–66); after the ÖVP won a narrow parliamentary majority in 1966, he served at the head of the country's first post-World War II noncoalition, single-party government (1966–70). Klaus, who had been finance minister (1961–64), was admired for his financial reforms and for forging improved ties with Western European nations, but his unwillingness to pursue former Nazis was widely criticized.

Knapp, (Geoffrey Goodman) James ("Jimmy"), British labour leader (b. Sept. 29, 1940, Hurlford, Ayrshire, Scot.—d. Aug. 13, 2001), was, from 1983, general secretary of the U.K.'s largest railway workers' federation, the National Union of Railwaymen (NUR), and its successor, the Rail, Maritime and Transport Union (RMT). A lifelong socialist, Knapp supported the contentious miners' strike of 1984 and successfully managed a series of one-day railway stoppages in 1989 as well as a 15-week signalmen's strike in 1994. He was unable to sustain the union's power amid privatization and increasing globalization, however, and membership declined, even after the NUR merged with the seamen's union in 1990 to form the RMT.

Knowles, John, American writer (b. Sept. 16, 1926, Fairmont, W.Va.—d. Nov. 29, 2001, near Fort Lauderdale, Fla.), won instant acclaim for his first novel, *A Separate Peace* (1959), which sold more than eight million copies. The enduring classic became a part of the syllabus of high-school English classes throughout the U.S. In 1942, at the age of 15, Knowles entered Phillips Exeter (N.H.) Academy. Following graduation in 1945, he received training as a pilot in the U.S. Army Air Corps. In 1946 he entered Yale University, from which he graduated in 1949 with a B.A., and from 1950 to 1952 he worked as a reporter and drama critic for the *Hartford* (Conn.) *Courant.* He then went to Europe, where he was befriended by Thornton Wilder, who encouraged Knowles to write about his experiences. Returning to New York City in 1955, he worked as associate editor of *Holiday* magazine from 1957 to 1960. *A Separate Peace,* a story of the inner conflicts of adolescents, dealt with questions of loyalty and betrayal among boys at a New England boarding school. The novel won the Rosenthal Award of the National Institute of Arts and Letters and the William Faulkner Foundation Award. It was made into a film in 1972. In a 1998 poll of students at Radcliffe College, Cambridge, Mass., it was named the 67th best novel ever written in English. Neither a sequel, *Peace Breaks Out* (1981), nor his other books, including seven additional novels and a book of short stories, enjoyed much success, however. During the 1960s he was writer in residence at the University of North Carolina at Chapel Hill and at Princeton University, and in the 1990s he taught creative writing at Florida Atlantic University.

Kohl, Hannelore Renner, German political wife (b. March 7, 1933, Berlin, Ger.—d. July 5, 2001, Ludwigshafen, Ger.), as the wife of Helmut Kohl (from 1960), was the de facto first lady during his 16 years as chancellor of West Germany (1982–90) and reunified Germany (1990–98). Trained as an interpreter in French and English, she used superb language skills as well as her personal warmth and charm to enhance the traditional role of political wife. Kohl elicited sympathetic public support as she stood by her husband during the difficult period before and after West German reunification with East Germany, the hard-fought national election he lost in 1998, and the financial scandal that engulfed him after he left office. In 1993 she was stricken with photodermatitis, a rare allergy to sunlight, and the escalating isolation and physical pain she experienced eventually led her to take her own life.

AP/Wide World Photos

Germany's "first lady" Hannelore Kohl

Koner, Pauline, American dancer and choreographer (b. 1912, New York, N.Y.—d. Feb. 8, 2001, New York), created works for stage shows at New York City's Roxy Theater, for ice shows, and for television programs and from 1946 to 1960 performed with the José Limón Dance Company. She worked closely with modern dance pioneer Doris Humphrey and choreographed her best-known piece, *The Farewell* (1962), to honour Humphrey's memory. Koner also led the Pauline Koner Dance Consort (1976–82) and at a number of schools taught a course, Elements of Performing, that gained her additional fame.

Korda, Alberto (Alberto Díaz Gutiérrez), Cuban photographer (b. Sept. 14, 1928, Havana, Cuba—d. May 25, 2001, Paris, France), took one of the most famous photographs of the 20th century—a 1960 image of guerrilla leader Che Guevara that was widely reproduced on posters, cards, and T-shirts. Korda had been a prominent fashion photographer in the 1950s before deciding to chronicle the lives of Cuba's revolutionary leaders, including Guevara and Fidel Castro. Exhibits of his photographs were later staged in France and the U.S., among other countries. In the 1990s Korda waged a legal battle against the commercial reproduction of his iconic portrait of Guevara.

Kramer, Stanley Earl, American film producer and director (b. Sept. 29, 1913, New York, N.Y.—d. Feb. 19, 2001, Woodland Hills, Calif.), created unconventional, socially conscious works on a variety of issues not usually addressed in mainstream Hollywood fare, including racial prejudice (e.g., *The Defiant Ones* [1958]), nuclear annihilation (*On the Beach* [1959]), and war crimes (*Judgment at Nuremberg* [1961]), and in tackling such themes acquired a reputation as a maker of "message" pictures, a label he disliked. He also showed support for blacklisted writers by hiring those who could not secure work under their own names following the communist witch-hunts. His nearly three dozen films were nominated for some 80 Academy Awards and won 16, and three—*High Noon* (1952), *Guess Who's Coming to Dinner* (1967), and *It's a Mad Mad Mad Mad World* (1963)—were placed on the American Film Institute's list of the 100 all-time best movies. Kramer graduated from high school at age 15 and earned a bachelor's degree in business administration from New York University in 1933. Soon thereafter, he moved to Hollywood and entered the film industry, working first in such capacities as researcher, editor, and writer, and during World War II service with the Army Signal Corps, he made training and orientation films. Following the war Kramer established an independent production company, and in 1948 its first motion picture, *So This Is New York,* was released. Kramer's first success, *Champion,* followed in 1949 and, in dealing with the ruthlessness of an ambitious prizefighter and the corruption in the fight profession, established the moral tone his best-known future films would reflect. It also sparked the career of Kirk Douglas. The next year he launched Marlon Brando's film career with *The Men,* which explored the challenges faced by disabled war veterans. Later notable films either produced or produced and directed by Kramer included *Cyrano de Bergerac* (1950), *Death of a Salesman* (1951), *The Member of the Wedding* (1952), *The Wild One* (1954), *The Caine Mutiny* (1954), *Inherit the Wind* (1960), and *Ship of Fools* (1965). Kramer was honoured with the Academy of Motion Picture Arts and Sciences' Irving G. Thalberg Memorial Award in 1962. Such later films as *R.P.M.* (1970), *The Domino Principle* (1977), and *The Runner Stumbles* (1979) were not successful. He retired from filmmaking in 1980.

Kumar, Ashok (Kumadlal Kunjilal Ganguly), Indian actor (b. Oct. 13, 1911, Bhagalpur, Bihar, India—d. Dec. 10, 2001, Mumbai [Bombay], India), became one of the most popular, best-loved, and longest-lasting stars of India's "Bollywood" motion picture industry in a career that spanned more than 60 years and some 300 films. He had a natural style of acting that allowed him to be effective and believable in a variety of characters that included both romantic leading men and roguish antiheroes, and he set a style—especially for cigarette smoking—that was copied by young men all across the country. Kumar studied law but was more interested in the direction and technical aspects of film. He was hired (1934) as a laboratory technician trainee and camera assistant at Bombay Talkies, but in 1936, when a replacement was needed for the star of *Jeevan naya* ("New Life"), Kumar was tapped for the role. That same year his next film, *Achhut kanya* ("Untouchable Girl"), made him a star. Among his most notable and most successful films—and one that brought him even greater fame—was *Kismet* ("Fate"; 1943), in which he portrayed a lovable pickpocket and made criminal behaviour appear glamorous. It set box-office longevity records that held for some three decades. Among later films were *Jewel Thief* (1967) and two for which his performances won him the Filmfare Award, India's equivalent of the Academy Award, for best actor: *Raakhi* ("Filial Bond"; 1962) and *Ashirwad* ("Blessings"; 1968). Kumar was also honoured with India's highest cinema prize, the Dada Saheb Phalke Award (1989), and the Filmfare Lifetime Achievement Award (1996).

Kushida, Fuki, Japanese peace and women's rights activist (b. Feb. 17, 1899, Yamaguchi prefecture, Japan—d. Feb. 5, 2001, Tokyo, Japan), was a noted campaigner for world peace and the advancement of women. She became the first secretary-general of the Women's Democratic Club, a feminist and peace organization, in 1946 and worked with feminist writer Yuriko Miyamoto. Kushida was elected president of the Federation of Japanese Women's Organizations in 1958. In 2000 the centenarian attracted attention as the leader of demonstrations against U.S. military bases on Okinawa.

Kuwa Mekki, Yousif, Sudanese resistance leader (b. August 1945, Al-Akhwal, The Sudan—d. March 31, 2001, Norwich, Eng.), as the charismatic commander of the Sudan People's Liberation Army (SPLA), led a guerrilla rebellion on behalf of non-Muslim blacks in southern Sudan against the Islamic fundamentalist rulers based in the Arab north of the country. Kuwa was a member of the Miri tribe, an ethnic subgroup of the Nuba people, and was reared as a Muslim with little knowledge of his ethnic heritage. He studied political science and Nuba history at the University of Khartoum, qualified as a teacher, and was elected (1981) to the regional assembly. As The Sudan slipped into civil war between the north and the south, Kuwa abandoned his teaching career to join the SPLA in 1984.

Lachmon, Jaggernath, Surinamese politician (b. Sept. 21, 1916, Nieuw Nickerie, Dutch Guiana [now Suriname]—d. Oct. 19, 2001, Amsterdam, Neth.), was a prominent figure in Surinamese politics for over half a century. He helped found two political parties, was an MP from 1949 (except during the 1980–87 military dictatorship), and served for many years (1964–67, 1969–73, and 1988–2001) as speaker of the National Assembly.

Lal, (Chaudhuri) Devi, Indian politician (b. Sept. 25, 1914, Chautala, Punjab [now in Haryana state], India—d. April 6, 2001, New Delhi, India), served (1989–91) as India's deputy prime minister under two prime ministers. Lal was appointed deputy prime minister in Prime Minister V.P. Singh's National Front government in 1989; after being dismissed in August 1990, Lal helped engineer Singh's ouster by Chandra Shekhar, who reappointed him to the post. Lal, a vigorous champion of the interests of peasant farmers, was also a longtime member of the Haryana legislature and was Haryana's chief minister (1977–80 and 1987–89); his son Om Prakash Chautala later became chief minister.

Lapidus, Morris, Russian-born American architect (b. Nov. 25, 1902, Odessa, Russia [now Ukraine]—d. Jan. 18, 2001, Miami Beach, Fla.), designed some 1,200 buildings, including 250 hotels; his flamboyant style was long scorned by critics but gained a measure of respect late in his career. Lapidus, who graduated from Columbia University, New York City, with a degree in architecture in 1927, designed retail spaces for 20 years before turning his attention to buildings. He was best known for his glitzy Miami Beach hotels, such as the Fontainebleau (1954), the Eden Roc (1955), and the Americana (1956; now the Sheraton Bal Harbour). His designs were always popular with the general public, but it was not until the 1980s and '90s that critics began to appreciate his work. In 2000 Lapidus received a National Design Award from the Smithsonian Institution's Cooper-Hewitt, National Design Museum. His autobiography, *Too Much Is Never Enough,* appeared in 1996.

Lechín Oquendo, Juan, Bolivian trade union leader and revolutionary politician (b. May 19, 1914, Corocoro, Bol.—d. Aug. 27, 2001, La Paz, Bol.), was the key founder (1946) and longtime leader of the Trade Union Confederation and as such was commander of a workers' uprising that, with its triumph in 1952 and the reforms it brought, began what became known as a "golden decade"; during that decade he served as minister of mines and petroleum (1952–56), senator (1956–60), and vice president (1960–62). Though the government was soon thereafter ousted in a military coup, Lechín remained prominent in Bolivian politics—as the radical opposition—until the mid-1980s.

Lemmon, Jack (John Uhler Lemmon III), American actor (b. Feb. 8, 1925, Boston, Mass.—d. June 27, 2001, Los Angeles, Calif.), excelled in both comic and dramatic character roles, especially in portrayals of a beleaguered everyman beset by the quirks and trials of everyday life; his career was especially defined by two partnerships—with Billy Wilder, who directed him in 7 films, and with his good friend and fellow actor Walter Matthau, with whom he costarred in 10 films and who preceded him in death by almost exactly a year. Lemmon first discovered his passion for acting when he was a young boy, participated in amateur theatre during his years as a student at Harvard University, and, following navy service toward the end of World War II and graduation from Harvard (1947), moved to New York City to pursue a performing career. Having earlier taught himself to play the piano by ear, he supported himself by supplying the music for silent films in a beer hall as he began getting roles on radio and in the live television series *Robert Montgomery Presents, Danger, Studio One,* and *Suspense.* Lemmon's Off-Broadway debut came in *Power of Darkness* in 1947, and in 1953 he made his Broadway debut in a revival of *Room Service.* That performance caught the attention of a film talent scout, and the following year Lemmon was cast opposite Judy Holliday in *It Should Happen to You.* A year later he played Ensign Pulver in *Mr. Roberts,* for which he won the best supporting actor Oscar. *Some Like It Hot* (1959), Lemmon's first movie with Wilder, and *The Apartment* (1960), his second, provided two of his definitive performances, and another Wilder film, *The Fortune Cookie* (1966), introduced his partnership with Matthau. That collaboration was highlighted by the two friends' performances as a neat freak (Lemmon, as Felix Unger) and a slob (Matthau, as Oscar Madison) attempting to survive each other as roommates in Neil Simon's *The Odd Couple* (1968). Late in their careers their teaming found them in *Grumpy Old Men* (1993) and its sequel (1995), *Out to Sea* (1997), and *The Odd Couple II* (1998). In addition, Lemmon excelled in dramatic films—including *Days of Wine and Roses* (1962), *Save the Tiger* (1973), for which he won a best actor Oscar, *The China Syndrome* (1979), *Missing* (1982), and *Glengarry Glen Ross* (1992)—and throughout his career he also returned to the stage, notably in *Tribute* (1978) and *Long Day's*

Getty Images

Versatile actor Jack Lemmon

Journey into Night (1986). He was last seen in the TV production *Tuesdays with Morrie* (1999), for which he won an Emmy. Among Lemmon's many other honours were the American Film Institute's Life Achievement Award in 1988, the Screen Actors Guild's Life Achievement Award in 1990, and a Kennedy Center Honor in 1996.

Leone, Giovanni, Italian politician (b. Nov. 3, 1908, Pomigliano d'Arco, Italy—d. Nov. 9, 2001, Rome, Italy), was a respected member of the Christian Democratic Party, a practicing attorney and professor of criminal law (from 1933), a longtime member of the Italian parliament (1948–67), a life senator (from 1967), and twice interim prime minister (1963 and 1968). In 1971 he was a compromise choice for president, but his term as Italy's head of state came during a tumultuous period of terrorist attacks and political scandal. Despite his reputation for honesty, Leone was forced to resign in 1978 amid allegations that he had taken bribes from the American firm Lockheed Aircraft Corp. Years later Leone's accusers admitted that they had had no proof against him and apologized.

Léotard, (Ange-)Philippe, French actor, poet, and chansonnier (b. Aug. 28, 1940, Nice, France—d. Aug. 25, 2001, Paris, France), appeared in more than 70 French- and English-language films, including *French Connection II* (1975), *Les Misérables* (1995), and *La Balance* (1982; *The Nark*), for which he won a César, France's highest cinema award, as best actor. He also cofounded the avant-garde Théâtre de Soleil, recorded several albums of "chansons française," and published poetry, notably the collection *Pas un jour sans une ligne* (1992; *Not a Day Without a Line*). In his 1997 autobiography Léotard detailed his long struggle with alcoholism and drug abuse.

Lewis, David Kellogg, American philosopher (b. Sept. 28, 1941, Oberlin, Ohio—d. Oct. 14, 2001, Princeton, N.J.), created the theory of "modal realism," which considered possible worlds—that is, all conceivable states of affairs that do not involve logical contradictions—as actually existing rather than as mere heuristic devices. Lewis's actuality of other possible worlds was comparable to that of previous times in this world. For an analytic philosopher, Lewis was systematic in his approach to philosophical problems. He employed a principle he called "Humean supervenience," according to which the world is composed of a "vast mosaic" of local physical facts, upon which all other states of affairs depend. Lewis was educated at Swarthmore (Pa.) College, the University of Oxford, and Harvard University. He taught at the University of California, Los Angeles, from 1966 to 1970 and at Princeton University from 1970 until his death. His paper "Convention: A Philosophical Study" (1969) was awarded the Matchette Prize in philosophy for scholars under 40. Among his other publications were *Counterfactuals* (1973) and *On the Plurality of Worlds* (1986).

Lewis, John Aaron, American composer and pianist (b. May 3, 1920, La Grange, Ill.—d. March 29, 2001, New York, N.Y.), brought elegance and charm to jazz while leading the Modern Jazz Quartet (MJQ) to musical and popular success for over four decades. He played piano in a spare, graceful style, and his compositions included sophisticated modern melodies as well as breaks, ostinatos, riffs, and other devices from the early jazz and swing eras. Lewis, inspired by bebop and Bach, was especially noted for creating forms derived from classical music; he joined Baroque canons and fugues to modern improvisation. Lewis grew up in Albuquerque, N.M., and studied music and anthropology at the University of New Mexico; later he attended New York City's Manhattan School of Music (M.A., 1953). After army service during World War II, he became a vital figure in the bebop avant-garde, playing in and composing ("Two Bass Hit" and "Emanon") for Dizzy Gillespie's big band and accompanying Charlie Parker in classic recordings; Lewis also helped create the cool jazz idiom by composing for Miles Davis's 1948 *Birth of the Cool* nonet. In 1952 Lewis began leading the MJQ, one of the longest-lived of all jazz groups. It featured Lewis's piano interplay with the great vibraphone soloist Milt Jackson, accompanied sensitively by Percy Heath, bass, and Connie Kay, drums, and it was active until the late 1990s, apart from a 1975–80 hiatus. Lewis's compositions for the MJQ included songs (his most famed was "Django"), fugues ("Concorde" and "Vendome"), extended works (*The Comedy* and *A Day in Dubrovnik*), and film scores (*Sait-on jamais?* [*No Sun in Venice*] and *Odds Against Tomorrow*). Apart from the MJQ, the versatile Lewis encouraged Third Stream music, which united jazz and classical elements, by composing for orchestras and small ensembles and by coleading Orchestra U.S.A. (1962–65). He was musical director of the Monterey (Calif.) Jazz Festival (1958–82) and of the American Jazz Orchestra (1985–92), a repertory big band. Meanwhile, he also played his intimate style of piano in a variety of jazz combos; in his last major concert (New York City, January 2001), he played unaccompanied solos and directed the Lincoln Center Jazz Orchestra.

Modern Jazz Quartet pianist John Lewis

Li Kwoh-ting, Chinese-born Taiwanese economist and government official (b. Jan. 28, 1910, Nanjing, China—d. May 31, 2001, Taipei, Taiwan), helped spearhead the effort to transform Taiwan's economy from a relatively poor, agrarian-based system into one of the world's leading producers of information and telecommunications technology. Li, a Nationalist Party member who fled from China to Taiwan in 1949, served as the country's economics minister from 1965 to 1969 and as finance minister from 1969 to 1976. As a minister without portfolio from 1976 to 1988, he remained an influential policy maker in those fields. In 1979 Li created a large industrial park in the port city of Hsinchu that came to be known as Taiwan's "Silicon Valley." In later years he served as an adviser to Pres. Lee Teng-hui and to Lee's successor, Chen Shui-bian.

Lilburn, Douglas Gordon, New Zealand composer (b. Nov. 2, 1915, Wanganui, N.Z.—d. June 6, 2001, Wellington, N.Z.), was one of New Zealand's most distinctive composers, fusing European musical traditions with inspirations from the literature, landscape, and culture of his native land. Lilburn studied journalism, history, and music at Canterbury University College. After winning (1936) the Grainger Prize for his symphonic tone poem *In the Forest,* he was sent to study under Ralph Vaughan Williams at the Royal College of Music in London. He returned to New Zealand in 1940. Lilburn's powerful earlier compositions, most notably his three symphonies, demonstrated strong influence from such contemporary composers as Vaughan Williams, Jean Sibelius, Igor Stravinsky, Bela Bartok, Arnold Schoenberg, and Aaron Copland. Later, however, he experimented with electronic music. Lilburn was on the music faculty (1947–79) of Victoria University in Wellington and was the founding director (1966–79) of the university's Electronic Music Studio. In addition to his many chamber orchestra and symphonic works, he also composed film, television, theatre, and ballet music. He was awarded the Order of New Zealand in 1983.

Lindbergh, Anne Spencer Morrow, American writer and aviator (b. June 22, 1906, Englewood, N.J.—d. Feb. 7, 2001, Passumpsic, Vt.), was perhaps best known as the wife of Charles ("Lucky Lindy") Lindbergh—the pilot who had made (1927) the first solo transatlantic flight—and the mother of the 20-month-old baby whose kidnapping and subsequent murder in 1932 was sensationalized in the press and labeled the "crime of the century." In her own right, however, she was a renowned pilot and the author of a number of popular books of fiction, diaries, and poetry. Her best-known work, *Gift from the Sea* (1955)—a series of meditative essays on the struggle, especially by women, to achieve balance and serenity in life—sold more than five million copies in its first 20 years in print. Lindbergh met her husband when he was her family's guest during the Christmas 1927 season. She graduated from Smith College, Northampton, Mass., in 1928, and the couple was married the following year. Lindbergh took up flying herself and in 1930 became the first woman in the U.S. to be granted a glider pilot's license. She became her husband's co-pilot, navigator, and radio operator and in 1930 helped him set a new transcontinental speed record of 14 hours 45 minutes from Los Angeles to New York City. In 1931 they made a three-month-long journey to survey air routes over Canada and Alaska to East Asia, and that trip later became the subject of Lindbergh's first book, *North to the Orient* (1935), which was an instant success. Lindbergh solidified her reputation with her second book, *Listen! The Wind* (1938), which recounted a 1933–34 survey of transatlantic air routes. The excessive attention surrounding their first son's kidnap-murder and the trial and death sentence of accused killer Bruno Hauptmann, as well as threats made on the life of their second son, had prompted the family to move to England in 1935, and they remained in Europe until the eve of World War II. Lindbergh's controversial next book, *The Wave of the Future, a Confession of Faith* (1940), supported the isolationist stance her husband was taking and diminished her popularity for a time, but her first novel, *The Steep Ascent* (1944), was well received, and *Gift from the Sea* spent many weeks on the best-seller list. Later works included *The Unicorn, and Other Poems, 1935–1955* (1956) and her five volumes of diaries covering the years 1922–44: *Bring Me a Unicorn* (1972), *Hour of Gold, Hour of Lead* (1973), *Locked Rooms and Open Doors* (1974), *The Flower and the Nettle* (1976), and *War Within and Without* (1980).

Bettmann/Corbis

Aviatrix Anne Morrow Lindbergh, with son Charles Jr.

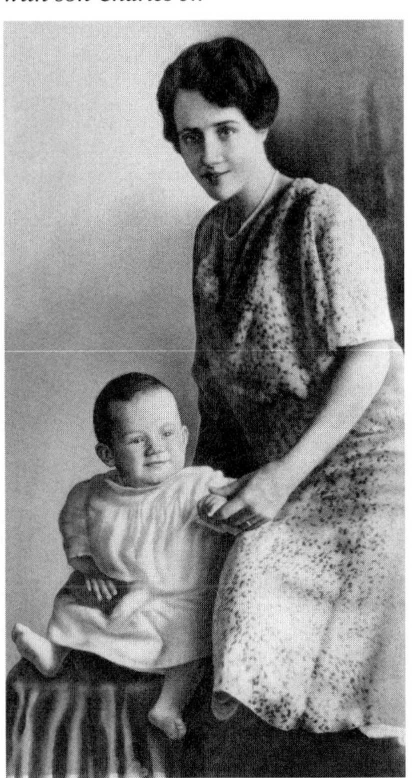

Lindon, Jérôme, French publisher (b. June 9, 1925, Paris, France—d. April 9, 2001, Paris), took control of the small independent publishing house Les Éditions de Minuit in 1948, at age 23, and thereafter was a central figure in the *nouveau roman* ("new novel," or antinovel) literary movement of the 1950s and '60s. Lindon personally oversaw the publication of significant works by Nathalie Sarraute, Alain Robbe-Grillet, Marguerite Duras, Michel Butor, Claude Simon, and, especially, Samuel Beckett. Other prizewinning novelists followed, notably Jean Rouaud and Jean Échenoz in the 1990s. Lindon also published the literary review *Critique,* several nonfiction books critical of French involvement in Algeria, and works by such prominent philosophers as Pierre Bourdieu, Michel Serres, and Jacques Derrida.

Lions, Jacques-Louis, French mathematician (b. May 2, 1928, Grasse, France—d. May 17, 2001, Paris, France), as a leading figure in the field of applied mathematics, was remarkably proficient at developing and systematizing methods for analyzing nonlinear partial differential equations and thereby increasing the potential scientific and industrial applications. A mathematics professor from 1954 until his retirement in 1986, Lions was an early proponent of the use of computer simulations to assist in nonlinear analysis. He was elected to the French Academy of Sciences in 1973 (president 1996–98) and was president of the National Centre for Space Study (1984–92) and the International Mathematical Union (1991–94). Lions also won numerous international prizes in mathematics, held scientific and industrial advisory posts, and published some 500 scientific papers and more than 20 books. His son, Pierre-Louis, won the Fields Medal in 1994 for his own work in nonlinear partial differential equations.

Livingston, Jay Harold, American songwriter (b. March 28, 1915, McDonald, Pa.—d. Oct. 17, 2001, Los Angeles, Calif.), in collaboration with Ray Evans, created songs for some 80 motion pictures, including three songs that won Academy Awards—"Buttons and Bows" from the Bob Hope western comedy *The Paleface* (1948); "Mona Lisa" from *Captain Carey, U.S.A.* (1950) and later made famous by Nat ("King") Cole; and "Que Sera, Sera," sung by Doris Day in *The Man Who Knew Too Much* (1956). Among their numerous other popular movie songs was "Silver Bells" from another Hope feature, *The Lemon Drop Kid* (1951); it became a Christmas standard and sold over 140 million records. The team also wrote television theme music for such shows as *Bonanza* and *Mr. Ed,* and it was Livingston's voice that was heard singing the latter.

Longford, Francis Aungier Pakenham, 7th earl of, British politician and social reformer (b. Dec. 5, 1905, London, Eng.—d. Aug. 3, 2001, London), was admired as an active, though sometimes eccentric, social reformer in a long political career as a government minister in the 1940s and '50s and later as an outspoken member of the House of Lords, of which he was leader 1964–68. The son of the 5th earl of Longford, he was educated at Eton College and New College, Oxford, where he specialized in banking. During the 1930s he converted from Anglo-Irish Protestantism to Roman Catholicism and from the Conservative Party to the socialist Labour Party. He held a variety of ministerial posts under Prime Minister Clement Attlee, notably undersecretary of state for war (1946–47), chancellor of the duchy of Lancaster overseeing the British zone in occupied Germany (1947–48), minister of civil aviation (1948–51), and first lord of the admiralty (1951). He was created Baron Pakenham in 1945, succeeded to the earldom on the death of his older brother in 1961, and was made a knight of the garter in 1971. As a member of the House of Lords for 40 years, Longford was most often associated with his vigorous campaigns against pornography and for prison reform. Longford was also chairman (1955–63) of the National Bank in London, chairman (1970–80) and director (1980–85) of the publishing house Sidgwick and Jackson, and the author of a score of books.

Lowe, Jacques, German-born American photographer (b. Jan. 24, 1930, Cologne, Ger.—d. May 12, 2001, New York, N.Y.), served as Pres. John F. Kennedy's campaign and personal photographer. Lowe took more than 40,000 photographs of Kennedy and his family, many of them touching candid shots that helped create the image of the Kennedy White House as "Camelot." Lowe collected his photographs in several books, including *JFK Remembered: An Intimate Portrait by His Personal Photographer* (1993), and in a 1996 traveling exhibition.

Ludlum, Robert, American writer (b. May 25, 1927, New York, N.Y.—d. March 12, 2001, Naples, Fla.), was a best-selling author of suspense novels; his books sold more than 220 million copies in some 40 countries. After working as an actor and theatrical producer for 20 years, Ludlum wrote his first novel, *The Scarlatti Inheritance* (1971), which was an instant commercial hit. The book was followed by several more equally successful thrillers, including *The Osterman Weekend* (1972), *The Bourne Identity* (1980), *The Icarus Agenda* (1988), and *The Prometheus Deception* (2000). Three novels by Ludlum were scheduled to be published posthumously.

Maas, Peter, American writer (b. June 27, 1929, New York, N.Y.—d. Aug. 23, 2001, New York), had a half-century-long career during which he published over a dozen books as well as numerous magazine articles. He counted among his works such fact-based investigative best-sellers as *The Valachi Papers* (1969) and *Underboss* (1997), both of which detailed Mafia life and secrets, and *Serpico* (1972; filmed 1973), a whistleblower's revelation of New York City police corruption.

MacNeish, Richard Stockton ("Scotty"), American agricultural archaeologist (b. April 29, 1918, New York, N.Y.—d. Jan. 16, Belize City, Belize), conducted fieldwork investigating the origins of corn (maize) and rice under the auspices of the Andover (Mass.) Foundation for Archaeologic Research and stirred controversy with some of his interpretations derived from his work. His most notable discovery came during the 1960s when he found tiny ears of corn in a cave in the Tehuacán Valley in Mexico; these forebears of modern corn at first were believed to be as much as 7,000 years old but later were dated at 5,500 years old. During the 1990s MacNeish found remnants of cultivated rice paddies that were 9,000 years old along the Chang Jiang (Yangtze River) basin. MacNeish's 1992 discovery in New Mexico of human fingerprints on human-made hearths that were believed as old as 38,000 years led him to discredit a widely held theory that humans first set foot in the Americas about 12,000 years ago by crossing the Bering land bridge from Asia, a hypothesis that raised the hackles of proponents of that theory. MacNeish was killed when he crashed after losing control of his car while driving between two archaeological sites.

MacStiofain, Sean (John Edward Drayton Stephenson), British-born Irish militant (b. Feb. 17, 1928, London, Eng.—d. May 17, 2001, Navan, County Meath, Ire.), was the first chief of staff of the Provisional Irish Republican Army after the hard-line militarist wing's split from the Official IRA in 1969. Originally drawn to the Irish republican cause by his Belfast, N.Ire.-born mother, he joined the IRA in his 20s and later changed his name. As the leader of the Provos, he advocated implacable violent resistance to British rule in Northern Ireland and was credited with waging a terrorist campaign, including at least one fatal bombing. In 1973, however, after an unsuccessful hunger strike while in prison, he was ousted from his post. MacStiofain, who published *Memoirs of a Revolutionary* in 1975, never fully recovered from a stroke he suffered in the mid-1980s.

Magloire, Paul, Haitian military ruler (b. July 19, 1907, Cap-Haitien, Haiti—d. July 12, 2001, Port-au-Prince, Haiti), ruled Haiti from 1950 to 1956. The son of a general, Magloire rose through the ranks of the Haitian army to become a general himself by the late 1940s. He orchestrated the overthrow of Pres. Dumarsais Estimé in 1950 and installed himself as ruler. During his reign Magloire developed tourism, started an ambitious program of modernization, and cultivated good relations with the Dominican Republic and the U.S. Corruption scandals and the severe economic problems that followed Hurricane Hazel in 1954, however, eventually turned the public against Magloire. He was ousted by the military in 1956 and went into exile in New York. After the reign of Jean-Claude Duvalier ended in 1986, Magloire returned to Haiti.

Majali, Habes al-, Jordanian field marshall (b. 1913?—d. April 22, 2001, Amman, Jordan), was one of Jordan's most successful military leaders. Majali joined the army in 1932 and in 1948 led an Arab force that defeated Israeli troops near Latrun. He was placed in charge of the personal guard for Jordan's King Abdullah in 1949, though he failed to prevent the king's assassination two years later. This failure did not destroy his career, however, and in 1957 King Hussein named him armed forces chief of staff. Majali served Hussein as defense minister from June 1967 until 1970, when he was reappointed commander of the army in order to crush a Palestinian uprising. He also commanded troops in the 1973 Yom Kippur War. After retiring from the army, Majali was appointed to the upper house of the parliament.

Mansfield, Michael Joseph ("Mike"), American politician and diplomat (b. March 16, 1903, New York, N.Y.—d. Oct. 5, 2001, Washington, D.C.), served as majority leader of the U.S. Senate from 1961 to 1977 under four presidents—the longest anyone had held that post. During that time he was instrumental in guiding a number of vital acts of legislation to passage, among them the Civil Rights Act of 1964, the Voting Rights Act of 1965, legislation that paved the way to ratification of the 26th Amendment, which lowered the voting age to 18 (1971), and the War Powers Act (1973). Mansfield was reared by an aunt and uncle in Montana, and when he was not yet 15, he joined the navy just before the U.S. entered World War I. Because he had lied about his age, he was discharged after 19 months, whereupon he joined the army, served for a year, and then joined the marines. Service in East Asia ignited a lifelong interest in that area. After returning to Montana, Mansfield worked in the copper mines and then, at the urging of his future wife, resumed his education, studying at the Montana State School of Mines, earning a high-school diploma through a correspondence course, and in 1930 entering the University of Montana. He received a bachelor's degree in 1933, joined the university's faculty, and the following year was awarded a master's. A growing interest in politics led Mansfield to seek the Democratic nomination for Montana's seat in the House of Representatives in the 1940 primary election, and though unsuccessful, he ran again in 1942 and won. He served in Congress for 10 years and in 1952 won election to the Senate, despite the anticommunist, red-baiting tactics of Sen. Joseph McCarthy, who campaigned for his opponent. Mansfield served on the Foreign Relations Committee, was named assistant majority leader in 1957, and in 1961, when Lyndon B. Johnson became vice president, moved up to majority leader. He remained in that position—guiding the increasing opposition to U.S. involvement in the Vietnam War and being a leading voice against the Richard M. Nixon administration during the Watergate scandal—until he retired from the Senate in 1977. Mansfield then was appointed ambassador to Japan, a post he held for 10 years, and upon his return to the U.S. in 1988, he became a senior adviser at the investment banking firm Goldman Sachs.

Maria José of Savoy, Queen (Maria José Charlotte Henrietta Gabriella of Saxe-Coburg), Belgian-born Italian royal (b. Aug. 4, 1906, Ostend, Belg.—d. Jan. 27, 2001, Geneva, Switz.), was the last queen of Italy for 27 days, from May 9, 1946, when her husband succeeded his father as King Umberto II, until the Italian electorate voted to abolish the monarchy on June 2. While living in forced exile in Switzerland, Maria José, the daughter of King Albert I of Belgium, wrote books on Italian and Belgian royals. Although the Italian constitution banished all members of the royal House of Savoy, after her husband's death (1983) she was allowed (1988) to visit Italy as a private citizen.

Masoud, Ahmad Shah, Afghan resistance leader and politician (b. 1953, Bazarak, Afg.—death reported on Sept. 15, 2001, Takhar, Afg.), was a military leader in the Afghan mujahideen, first against the Soviets and the Soviet-backed Afghan government (1978–89) and then against the Taliban (from 1992). Masoud, an ethnic Tajik, studied engineering before the Soviet intervention in Afghanistan and then moved to Pakistan for military training. A clever and persistent guerrilla leader, he earned the sobriquet "the lion of Panjshir." Masoud briefly served as defense minister during the mujahideen interim government set up in 1989. After the Taliban took control of most of Afghanistan, including the capital, in 1996, he was the chief commander of the anti-Taliban forces that came to be known as the Northern Alliance. Masoud died of wounds suffered during an attack by two suicide bombers on September 9, two days before the September 11 terrorist attacks in the U.S.

Masters, William Howell, American gynecologist (b. Dec. 27, 1915, Cleveland, Ohio—d. Feb. 16, 2001, Tucson, Ariz.), was a pioneer in the field of human sexuality research and therapy. With partner Virginia Johnson, who later (1971) became his wife, he founded what was known as the Masters & Johnson Institute and conducted hundreds of interviews and observations in extensive—and controversial—investigations of the physiological aspects of sexual activity; they published their findings in a series of best-selling books. Masters graduated from Hamilton College, Clinton, N.Y., in 1938 and received his medical degree from the University of Rochester (N.Y.) School of Medicine and Dentistry in 1943. After further study, including an internship in obstetrics and gynecology at the St. Louis (Mo.) Maternity Hospital and Barnes Hospital in St. Louis, he took (1947) a faculty position at the Washington University School of Medicine, also in St. Louis. His first work there was on hormone-replacement therapy. In 1954 Masters began the research that would bring him renown, and two years later he hired Johnson. During their studies they observed volunteers performing a vast range of sexual acts, and they often employed electronic monitors to note physiological changes their subjects experienced. Masters and Johnson's first book, *Human Sexual Response* (1966), reported the results of these studies. Although it was written in a clinical manner and was intended mainly for medical professionals, it

Robert Nickelsberg/TimePix

Researcher William Masters, with his colleague Virginia Johnson
© Bettmann/Corbis

became a best-seller. With the information they garnered from their research, Masters and Johnson devised new methods of treating sexual dysfunction. Especially controversial was their use of prostitutes as sexual surrogates to work with people suffering from sexual performance and enjoyment difficulties; this practice was later dropped, and "ordinary people" volunteers were used. The book *Human Sexual Inadequacy* (1970) described results of their therapeutic methods. As they continued their work, Masters and Johnson published such further books as *The Pleasure Bond* (1975; with Robert J. Levin); *Homosexuality in Perspective* (1979), in which they claimed the ability to change homosexuals' sexual orientation; *Human Sexuality* (1982; with Robert C. Kolodny); and *Crisis: Heterosexual Behavior in the Age of AIDS* (1988; with Kolodny). Masters and Johnson divorced in 1992 but continued working together until Masters closed the institute in 1994.

Mathews, Edwin Lee ("Eddie"), American professional baseball player (b. Oct. 13, 1931, Texarkana, Texas—d. Feb. 18, 2001, San Diego, Calif.), was one of major league baseball's most prolific hitters, with 512 home runs and 2,315 hits in his 17-year career, and was widely regarded as the best third baseman of the 1950s and early '60s. Mathews made his major league debut with the Boston Braves in 1952 and remained with the franchise when it moved to Milwaukee, Wis., in 1953 and to Atlanta, Ga., in 1966; he was the only person to play with the Braves in all three cities. He helped Milwaukee win the World Series in 1957. In Atlanta, Mathews and Hank Aaron established the all-time home-run record for teammates, with 863 between 1954 and 1966. Mathews played in 10 All-Star Games, and he was inducted into the Baseball Hall of Fame in 1978.

Maxim, Joey (Giuseppe Antonio Berardinelli), American boxer (b. March 28, 1922, Cleveland, Ohio—d. June 2, 2001, West Palm Beach, Fla.), was the world light heavyweight champion from 1950 to 1952. On Jan. 24, 1950, Maxim knocked out heavily favoured Englishman Freddie Mills in London to win the world light heavyweight title. In one of the most memorable boxing matches in history, Maxim defended his title against Sugar Ray Robinson on June 25, 1952, at Yankee Stadium in New York City. The fight took place before a crowd of 48,000 spectators and with the temperature above 38 °C (100 °F). Late in the bout Robinson, who was ahead on the scorecards, began to suffer from fatigue and dehydration and failed to answer the bell for the 14th round. Maxim was awarded the victory by technical knockout. He lost the light heavyweight crown to Archie Moore later that year. Maxim was inducted into the International Boxing Hall of Fame in 1994.

Maximos V (Georges Hakim), Egyptian cleric (b. May 18, 1908, Tanta, Egypt—d. June 29, 2001, Beirut, Lebanon), was spiritual leader of the Greek Catholic Church from 1967 to 2000; his formal title was patriarch of Antioch and all the East and Alexandria and Jerusalem. He was ordained in 1930 and served as archbishop of Acre, Haifa, Nazareth and all Galilee from 1943 until his elevation to patriarch. Maximos V was regarded as a popular and politically shrewd leader to more than one million Greek Catholics. He was known for advocating closer ties with the Eastern Orthodox Church, and he was successful in cultivating good relations with leaders in the predominantly Muslim countries of Syria, Egypt, and Lebanon, where most of his followers lived.

Mayer, Hans Heinrich, German literary scholar (b. March 19, 1907, Cologne, Ger.—d. May 18, 2001, Tübingen, Ger.), was a distinguished academic and critic who sought to achieve a greater understanding of German literature and culture through the application of Marxist-socialist analysis. Mayer, a member of the German Jewish bourgeoisie, trained as a lawyer. He left Germany for France shortly after Hitler's rise to power in 1933 and spent most of World War II in Switzerland, returning to Frankfurt in the U.S.-occupied zone after the war. In 1948 he joined the faculty of the University of Leipzig (in the Soviet-controlled zone), where he was professor of cultural history (1948–50) and of German literature (1950–64). Increasingly dismayed by the restrictions of East Germany's officially sanctioned socialist realism, he defected to West Germany, where he was professor of German language and literature at the Polytechnical University in Hannover (1965–73). Mayer's authoritative works included studies on Georg Büchner, Bertolt Brecht, Thomas Mann, Johann Wolfgang von Goethe, Martin Luther, Friedrich Dürrenmatt, Richard Wagner, and Friedrich von Schiller.

Mbeki, Govan Archibald Mvuyelwa, South African nationalist (b. July 9, 1910, Nqamakwe, S.Af.—d. Aug. 30, 2001, Port Elizabeth, S.Af.), as a teacher, writer, labour organizer, and editor of the leftist newspaper *New Age,* was in the vanguard of the antiapartheid struggle against the South African government. Mbeki joined the African National Congress (ANC) in 1935 and rose to become national chairman in 1956. Arrested in 1963 for plotting to overthrow the government, he was one of the eight ANC leaders tried in the celebrated Rivonia Trial and sentenced to life imprisonment on Robben Island. His best-known book, *South Africa: The Peasants' Revolt,* reportedly was written on toilet paper in jail and smuggled to London, where it was published in 1964. Mbeki was released from prison in 1987. He won a seat in the country's first all-race Parliament in 1994 and five years later watched as his son, Thabo Mbeki, was sworn in as president.

McCorkle, Susannah, American jazz singer (b. Jan. 4, 1946, Berkeley, Calif.—d. May 19, 2001, New York, N.Y.), brought fresh meaning to popular songs through subtle inflections, rhythmic wit, and a sense of dramatic nuance; she sang in an unforced, smoky voice, and her swing made her a success in jazz clubs as well as cabarets. McCorkle's extensive repertoire ranged widely from Broadway to bop to contemporary jazz and pop material. She also wrote magazine articles about classic jazz singers; authored short stories, notably "Ramona by the Sea," which won a 1973 O. Henry Award; and conducted interactive music workshops for children. McCorkle, who reportedly suffered from depression, took her own life.

McGuire, Alfred James ("Al"), American basketball coach and broadcaster (b. Sept. 7, 1928, New York, N.Y.—d. Jan. 26, 2001, Milwaukee, Wis.), was one of college basketball's most talented and innovative coaches, and he enjoyed a second career as a popular television broadcaster for collegiate games. McGuire played guard on the basketball teams at St. John's Preparatory School and St. John's University, both in Brooklyn, N.Y. He went on to play in the professional National Basketball Association, with the New York Knickerbockers (1951–54) and the Baltimore Bullets (1954–55), before coaching at Dartmouth College, Hanover,

N.H., from 1955 to 1957 and at Belmont (N.C.) Abbey College from 1957 to 1964. In 1965 he became basketball coach at Marquette University, Milwaukee, where he also served as athletic director from 1971 until his retirement in 1977. His career record was 404 games won and 114 lost. At Marquette his teams won 295 games and lost 80 and appeared in 11 postseason tournaments; McGuire led Marquette to the National Collegiate Athletic Association championship in 1977. He was a master of tactics in the final minutes of games. His penchant for drawing technical fouls from officials was viewed as a weakness by his critics and as a psychological ploy by his admirers. After 1977 he worked briefly as a sports equipment manufacturing executive before embarking on a highly successful 23-year broadcasting career. He was inducted into the Basketball Hall of Fame in 1992.

McGuire, Dorothy Hackett, American actress (b. June 14, 1918, Omaha, Neb.—d. Sept. 14, 2001, Santa Monica, Calif.), had a long stage and screen career in which she specialized in portraying gentle, warm, and intelligent women.

Kobal Collection/Powolny, Frank

Dorothy McGuire: integrity and strength

The qualities she projected—kindness, integrity, and inner strength—did not rely on glamour, and she was thus able to make a smooth transition into motherly roles in her later years. By age 13 McGuire had made her stage debut, opposite Henry Fonda in an Omaha Community Playhouse production of *A Kiss for Cinderella.* After moving to New York City, she acted on radio in a soap opera and in 1938 became an understudy in *Our Town,* taking over the character of Emily—and thus making her Broadway debut—when Martha Scott left the show. Three years later McGuire landed the lead in *Claudia;* she made her film debut in that role in 1943. She portrayed leading roles in numerous films, including *A Tree Grows in Brooklyn* and *The Enchanted Cottage* (both 1945); *The Spiral Staircase* (1946); *Gentlemen's Agreement* (1947), for which she was nominated for an Academy Award; and *Three Coins in the Fountain* (1954). McGuire also continued performing onstage, with a tour in *Summer and Smoke* (1950) and a Broadway appearance in *Legend of Lovers* (1951) among her credits. Her transition to motherly roles began with *Friendly Persuasion* (1956) and continued in *Old Yeller* (1957), *The Remarkable Mr. Pennypacker* (1959), *Swiss Family Robinson* (1960), *The Dark at the Top of the Stairs* (1960), and, most notably, *The Greatest Story Ever Told* (1965), in which she portrayed the Virgin Mary.

McKay, (George Cadogan) Gardner, American actor, playwright, and novelist (b. June 10, 1932, New York, N.Y.—d. Nov. 21, 2001, Honolulu, Hawaii), achieved fame as the star of the popular television series *Adventures in Paradise,* which aired from 1959 to 1962. McKay abruptly abandoned his acting career when the series ended. After a number of years spent traveling around the world, he returned to the U.S. and became a playwright. One of his many plays, *Sea Marks* (1983), won the Los Angeles Drama Critics Circle Award. From 1977 to 1982 McKay was the drama critic for the *Los Angeles Herald-Examiner.* A novel, *Toyer,* appeared in 1999.

McKay, John Harvey, American football coach (b. July 5, 1923, Everettsville, W.Va.—d. June 10, 2001, Tampa, Fla.), guided the University of Southern California football team to four national titles—in 1962, 1967, 1972, and 1974. McKay also led the team to five Rose Bowl victories and was voted the national collegiate Coach of the Year in 1962 and 1972. From 1976 to 1984 he coached the Tampa Bay Buccaneers of the National Football League, but he achieved only a lacklustre record—44 victories, 88 losses, and 1 draw. McKay was elected to the College Football Hall of Fame in 1988.

McTaggart, David Fraser, Canadian environmental activist (b. June 24, 1932, Vancouver, B.C.—d. March 23, 2001, Perugia, Italy), as chairman of Greenpeace International from 1979 to 1991, was responsible for leading the environmental organization to worldwide prominence. McTaggart's involvement with Greenpeace began in 1972, when he sailed a yacht to Mururoa—an isolated atoll in the South Pacific—as part of a protest against the French government's nuclear testing in the area. He later organized other demonstrations against nuclear testing as well as campaigns to save whales, to protect Antarctica from mineral exploitation, and to end the practice of dumping nuclear waste at sea.

McVeigh, Timothy James, American terrorist (b. April 23, 1968, Pendleton, N.Y.—d. June 11, 2001, Terre Haute, Ind.), was put to death after having been convicted of bombing the Alfred P. Murrah Federal Building in Oklahoma City, Okla., on April 19, 1995; 168 persons died in the blast. McVeigh was the first federal prisoner to be executed since 1963.

Mérieux, Charles, French virologist (b. Jan. 9, 1907, Lyon, France—d. Jan. 18, 2001, Lyon), devised an efficient industrial technique for mass producing vaccines to fight such human and veterinary viruses as those for polio, rabies, meningitis, diphtheria, tetanus, and foot-and-mouth disease. During World War II he expanded operations at the microbiological laboratory set up by his father, a protégé of Louis Pasteur, distributing blood plasma to members of the Resistance and a serum to help malnourished children. In 1947 Mérieux founded the French Institute of Foot-and-Mouth Disease (later renamed the Mérieux Institute), which fought an outbreak of that virus in the 1960s and stopped a 1974 outbreak of meningitis in Brazil by producing enough vaccine to inoculate some 90 million people. The Mériuex Institute later formed joint ventures with the Pasteur Institute and the pharmaceutical company Rhône-Poulenc. Mérieux also established foundations to train public health technicians, an epidemiological teaching centre, and a laboratory in Lyon to study hemorrhagic fever.

Metlitzki, Dorothee, American literary scholar, educator, and Jewish activist (b. July 27, 1914, Königsberg, East Prussia [now Kaliningrad, Russia]—d. April 14, 2001, Hamden, Conn.), was a noted scholar of medieval English and Arabic literature and of the works of Herman Melville. After completing her education at the University of London, Metlitzki moved to Jerusalem, where she helped found the English department at Hebrew University and, after the establishment of Israel in 1948, mustered support for the country while traveling around the world. She settled in the U.S. in 1954. Metlitzki taught at Yale University from 1964 until her retirement in 1984. In 1977 she published a major work in comparative literature, *The Matter of Araby in Medieval England.*

Meyer, Harry Martin, Jr., American pediatric virologist (b. Nov. 25, 1928, Palestine, Texas—d. Aug. 19, 2001, Kenmore, Wash.), was co-developer of the first vaccine against rubella (German measles), refinement of which resulted in the MMR (measles, mumps, and rubella) vaccine; he contributed to textbooks, published over 100 scientific papers, and achieved worldwide acclaim for his research on infectious diseases and vaccines to protect against them.

Mishin, Vasily Pavlovich, Soviet rocket scientist (b. Jan. 18, 1917, Orekhovo-Zuyevo, Russia—d. Oct. 10, 2001, Moscow, Russia), was named the chief designer of the Soviet lunar program when Sergey P. Korolyov died in 1966. Despite his accomplishments as an engineer on the Sputnik satellite program, Mishin lacked his charismatic predecessor's knack of maneuvering within the political bureaucracy. Faced with insufficient funding and a stifling level of secrecy imposed upon the Soviet space agency, Mishin's team failed to beat the U.S. in the race to the Moon. Mishin was removed from his post in 1974, but he reemerged in the 1980s.

Modjadji V, South African tribal ruler (b. 1936/37, Ga-Modjadji, Northern province, S.Af.—d. June 28, 2001, Pietersburg, S.Af.), was the revered Rain Queen of the Bantu-speaking Lovedu tribe, the latest representative of a 400-year-old matriarchal dynasty believed to have magical rainmaking powers, and South Africa's only reigning queen. As Rain Queen, Modjadji V served as the secular and religious leader of her people, although her brother handled most administrative details because of the seclusion her position traditionally required. Modjadji V was initiated into the dynasty's rainmaking secrets after her mother, Queen Modjadji IV, succeeded to the crown in 1960, and she gained the throne upon the latter's death in 1982. In recent years she was seldom called on to make rain, but Modjadji V, like her predecessors, was respected and consulted by tribes throughout the region as well as by national leaders, including former president Nelson Mandela. Her great-grandmother, Queen Modjadji II, was the inspiration for H. Rider Haggard's 1887 novel *She.*

Moore, Francis Daniels, American surgeon (b. April 17, 1913, Evanston, Ill.—d. Nov. 24, 2001, Westwood, Mass.), was the chief surgeon at Peter Bent Brigham Hospital in Boston when in 1954 a team under his direction performed the first successful human organ transplant—a kidney transplant between identical twins. Moore graduated from Harvard University in 1935 and from Harvard Medical School in 1939. After an internship and residency at Massachusetts General Hospital, he worked at Brigham Hospital from 1948 to 1976. He also served as professor of surgery at Harvard Medical School until his retirement in 1981. In addition, Moore helped develop procedures for the care of postoperative patients. His memoirs, *A Miracle & a Privilege: Recounting a Half Century of Surgical Advance,* appeared in 1995.

Muhlstock, Louis, Polish-born Canadian painter (b. April 23, 1904, Narajow, Pol.—d. Aug. 26, 2001, Montreal, Que.), was celebrated for his artistic depictions of the Great Depression. Muhlstock emigrated with his family to Montreal in 1911. He studied art in Paris from 1928 to 1931, then returned to Montreal to become a full-time painter. Many of his works, rendered in a modernist style, portrayed street scenes and unemployed workers in Montreal. Muhlstock was a founding member of the Contemporary Art Society of Montreal and of the Federation of Canadian Artists. He was made an Officer of the Order of Canada in 1990.

Muñoz, Juan, Spanish sculptor (b. June 17, 1953, Madrid, Spain—d. Aug. 28, 2001, Ibiza, Spain), created moody and challenging installation artworks, most of which featured monochromatic human figures placed amid unnerving architectural spaces and often incorporating animatronics and sound. In 2000 Muñoz received Spain's highest cultural award, the Premio Nacional de Belles Artes. His last completed significant work, which was installed in London's Tate Modern in June 2001, was "Double Bind," a vast structure that filled half the museum's grand turbine hall with a false suspended floor, a working elevator, and sculpted figures seemingly frozen in time. A retrospective of Muñoz's work opened at the Smithsonian Institution's Hirshhorn Museum in Washington, D.C., on October 18.

Narayan, R.K. (Rasipuram Krishnaswami Narayanswami), Indian novelist, short-story writer, and essayist (b. Oct. 10, 1906, Madras [now Chennai], India—d. May 13, 2001, Chennai), was a spellbinding storyteller whose fictional creation, the small town of Malgudi, enchanted readers around the world with its dusty milieu and endearingly eccentric inhabitants; his gentle prose and wry humour brought small-town India alive. Narayan, the third of eight children born into a liberal Tamil family, spent an idyllic childhood in his grandmother's Madras house. He was schooled at Maharaja's College, Mysore, and after graduation (1930) briefly worked as a schoolteacher and a newspaper reporter before turning to writing full time. In September 1935 Malgudi, a town bearing the palimpsests of both Mysore and Madras but smaller than either, debuted in *Swami and Friends*. Narayan's first novel suffered several rejections before Graham Greene recommended it to Hamish Hamilton, who published the work. Greene also shortened Narayanswami's last name to Narayan. (Their correspondence lasted until Greene's death in 1991, and they met once, in 1956.) Narayan's next books, *The Bachelor of Arts* (1937) and *The Dark Room* (1938), also won critical praise: Disregarding the tradition of arranged matches, Narayan fell in love with and married Rajam in 1933. Her death in 1939 plunged him into desolate literary sterility, broken by the autobiographical *The English Teacher* (1945). Narayan never remarried, and he raised his daughter, Hema, alone. *Mr. Sampath* (1949), *The Financial Expert* (1952), and *Waiting for the Mahatma* (1955) were followed by his finest work, *The Guide* (1958). The latter—about a conman turned swami who discovers sanctity through self-sacrifice—was filmed in Hindi. *The Vendor of Sweets* (1967), *The Painter of Signs* (1976), and *A Tiger for Malgudi* (1983) also visited Malgudi and its characters. Besides 15 novels, Narayan published the short-story collections *Lawley Road* (1956) and *Under the Banyan Tree and Other Stories* (1985), as well as a 1974 memoir, *My Days*. He was awarded the Padma Bhushan and membership to the upper house of Parliament, and he was also short-listed twice for the Nobel Prize. Later novels included *Talkative Man* (1986), *The World of Nagaraj* (1990), and *Grandmother's Tale* (1992), his last and the only one not set in Malgudi. His works were widely translated.

Nguyen Van Thieu, Vietnamese military leader and politician (b. April 5, 1923, Tri Thuy, French Indochina [now in Vietnam]—d. Sept. 29, 2001, Boston, Mass.), was president of the Republic of Vietnam (South Vietnam) from 1967 to 1975. Although he had U.S. support, he eventually blamed American policies for the collapse of South Vietnam. In 1945 Thieu, the son of a small landowner, joined the Viet Minh against the French. He soon left the Viet Minh, however, because of its communist orientation. In 1947 he entered the National Military Academy in Da Lat, and in 1949 he was commissioned as an officer in the army organized by the French. Thieu later undertook military studies in France, in the U.S., and elsewhere, and for four years beginning in 1954, he was head of the National Military Academy. In 1963 he helped organize a coup, undertaken with U.S. approval, against South Vietnamese Pres. Ngo Dinh Diem. Thieu emerged as chief of state in 1965. In 1967 he won election as president, and he was reelected without opposition in 1971. He headed the government during the period of the major U.S. intervention in the war against the Viet Cong and North Vietnam. An authoritarian president, he was at the same time generally considered to be a weak and indecisive political and military leader. He opposed the Paris peace agreements of 1973 but was forced to accept a cease-fire and the withdrawal of U.S. troops, with the promise that other military assistance would continue. By early 1975 North Vietnamese troops had overrun the northern and central provinces of South Vietnam. On April 21, 1975, only days before the fall of the capital, Saigon, he fled the country, leaving his successor, Duong Van Minh (*q.v.*), to surrender. Thieu lived at first in London and then in the U.S., where he remained almost entirely out of public view.

Noble, Maurice, American animator (b. May 1, 1910, Spooner, Minn.—d. May 18, 2001, La Crescenta, Calif.), helped create some of the most famous animated features in entertainment history. Noble's career began at Walt Disney Productions, where he worked on such classic films as *Snow White and the Seven Dwarfs* (1937), *Fantasia* (1940), *Dumbo* (1941), and *Bambi* (1942). He later worked for Warner Bros. and Metro-Goldwyn-Mayer. With Chuck Jones, Noble designed highly popular animated versions of several Dr. Seuss books, including *How the Grinch Stole Christmas!* (1966) and *The Cat in the Hat* (1971).

Nygaard, Jens, American pianist and conductor (b. Oct. 26, 1931, Stephens, Ark.—d. Sept. 24, 2001, New York, N.Y.), was the maverick founder and director of the Jupiter Symphony, which for more than two decades offered concerts of rare and unusual classical music in New York City. Nygaard was noted for conducting obscure works by early 19th-century composers—among them, Louis Spohr, Carl Reinecke, and Carl Czerny—and for finding forgotten works by Wolfgang and Leopold Mozart, among others. As his Jupiter Symphony staggered from one financial crisis to the next, Nygaard was criticized for overworking and underpaying his young musicians—after one concert he could afford to pay each of them only subway tokens and a book of Shakespeare's sonnets. Nonetheless, he ensured that the orchestra played a third of its concerts for charities. Nygaard's mother gave him his first piano lessons, and his father had played clarinet in John Philip Sousa's band; Nygaard himself could play most orchestra instruments by the time he entered Louisiana State University on a clarinet scholarship. He received his bachelor's (1957) and master's (1958) degrees from the

AP/Wide World Photos

Juilliard School of Music in New York City. After suffering a mental breakdown in 1959, he endured a period of homelessness. During the 1960s and '70s, he made his reputation for wide-ranging musical tastes by leading orchestras, sometimes featuring himself as piano soloist, in and around New York. In 1979 he formed the Jupiter Symphony, named for Wolfgang Mozart's last symphony, and the Rockefeller Foundation contributed a $35,000 grant, but the iconoclastic Nygaard refused further Rockefeller aid rather than establish a conventional orchestra board.

Oakes, John Bertram, American newspaper editor (b. April 23, 1913, Elkins Park, Pa.—d. April 5, 2001, New York, N.Y.), was the editorial-page editor for the *New York Times* from 1961 to 1976; he was credited with devising the modern op-ed page format by including opinion articles written by both the newspaper's own columnists and outside writers. Oakes worked as a reporter for the *Washington Post* and served in the U.S. Army during World War II before joining the *Times* in 1946. Until 1961 the paper's editorial page was largely viewed as impartial, but under Oakes's guidance, it began to champion liberal causes. Oakes was a contributing columnist at the *Times* from 1978 into the early 1990s. He received a George Polk Award for lifetime achievement in the field of journalism in 2001.

O'Connor, Carroll, American character actor (b. Aug. 2, 1924, New York, N.Y.—d. June 21, 2001, Culver City, Calif.), was classically trained and appeared in scores of movies and television programs, but to the majority of the viewing public, he was the irascible but lovable bigot Archie Bunker, the lead character in the groundbreaking sitcom *All in the Family* (1971–79) and its sequel *Archie Bunker's Place* (1979–83). Although Bunker was outspoken in his beliefs in ethnic and gender stereotypes, O'Connor brought out the character's humanity and made sympathetic his bewilderment at the rapidly changing society he was attempting to cope with. O'Connor served in the merchant marine during World War II and afterward attended the University of Montana and then the National University of Ireland in Dublin (B.A., 1952). He appeared in productions presented by the Gate Theatre in Dublin and also toured other European cities, but after returning to the U.S. (1954), he found it difficult to find acting jobs and instead earned a master's degree (University of Montana, 1956) and became a teacher. In 1958, however, O'Connor was cast in an Off-Broadway production of *Ulysses in Nighttown*, and his success in that show led to another Off-Broadway role, in *The Big Knife* (1959). He also amassed numerous TV and movie credits, including roles in the films *Lonely Are the Brave* (1962), *Cleopatra* (1963), and *What Did You Do in the War, Daddy?* (1966), but he was still relatively unknown when he was cast as Bunker in *All in the Family*, an adaptation of the edgier BBC series *Till Death Us Do Part*. Although the character initially stirred up enormous controversy with the outrageous closed-mindedness that Archie Bunker spouted at every opportunity—views that were the exact opposite of those held by O'Connor himself—the show grew in popularity as most of the audience came to recognize that it was the evident absurdity of Bunker's beliefs that was the target of the humour. The show spent five years in the number one spot, at its peak counting some 50 million weekly viewers, and O'Connor's performance as Bunker won him four best actor Emmy Awards. In 1989 he won a fifth Emmy for another successful series, *In the Heat of the Night* (1987–94). Following the 1995 suicide of his son, who had been struggling with alcohol and drug addiction, O'Connor dedicated much of his time to a crusade against drug abuse. His last film role was in *Return to Me* (2000).

Carroll O'Connor (centre) as curmudgeon Archie Bunker

Okawa, Isao, Japanese businessman (b. 1926, Osaka, Japan—d. March 16, 2001, Tokyo, Japan), was chairman of the Sega Corp. from 1984 until his death. Okawa was involved with a number of Japanese technology companies. He founded CSK Corp., a computer services company that was Sega's largest shareholder, and served on the boards of several other companies, including the ASCII Corp. and Bellsystem 24, Inc. As chairman of Sega he became responsible for shifting the company's emphasis away from the production of video games and toward software development.

Parker, Eddie ("Fast Eddie"), American billiards player (b. June 2, 1931, Springfield, Mo.—d. Feb. 2, 2001, Brownsville, Texas), was a legendary pool player whose exploits reportedly inspired the critically acclaimed 1961 film *The Hustler*. Parker played the game from the age of nine and, after a stint in the U.S. Navy in the early 1950s, toured extensively as a money player. In 1959 Walter Tevis, a young pool hall worker whom Parker had befriended, published a novel entitled *The Hustler*, on which the hit film was based. Actor Paul Newman portrayed the Parker-like character "Fast Eddie" Felson in the movie and reprised the role in the film's 1986 sequel, *The Color of Money*. In later years Parker made appearances at billiards tournaments, gave exhibitions, and created instructional videotapes and books.

Paz Estenssoro, Víctor, Bolivian statesman (b. Oct. 2, 1907, Tarija, Bol.—d. June 7, 2001, Tarija), was elected president of Bolivia a record four times and was a founder of the Nationalist Revolutionary Movement (MNR) in 1941. During the course of his political career, Paz Estenssoro moved from leftist to free-market policies. He earned a law degree (1927) from the University of San Andrés in La Paz, where he later (1939–41) taught economics. Beginning in the late 1920s, he held a number of government positions, and in 1932–35 he fought in the Chaco War against Paraguay. In 1938 and 1940 Paz Estenssoro was elected to the Chamber of Deputies, and in 1951 he was elected president. A military junta prevented his taking office until, after three days of fighting, the MNR seized power in 1952. As president Paz Estenssoro instituted radical changes, expropriating and nationalizing foreign-owned tin mines, extending suffrage to the 80% of Bolivians who had never voted before, and beginning a land-reform program. In 1956 he became ambassador to Britain, and in 1960 he was elected to a second term as president. Paz Estenssoro then began to turn rightward, but he was reelected in 1964 with 70% of the vote. Three months later, however, he was ousted in a military coup. He went into exile in Peru, where he taught economics at the University of Lima until, in 1971, he returned to Bolivia to become an adviser in the military government of Gen. Hugo Banzer Suárez. In 1979 he ran unsuccessfully for president, and in the election of 1985 he ran again. He finished second to Banzer in the popular vote in 1985, but neither had a majority. Congress chose Paz Estenssoro as president, and during his last term he reversed a number of earlier policies. He shut unprofitable tin mines and privatized others, instituted austerity measures to reduce the country's hyperinflation, and introduced a number of financial reforms. In 1989 he resigned as leader of the MNR.

Popular Bolivian Pres. Víctor Paz Estenssoro

Pérez Jiménez, Marcos, Venezuelan military dictator (b. April 25, 1914, Michelena, Venez.—d. Sept. 20, 2001, Madrid, Spain), headed a regime (1952–58) that was defined by its brutal suppression of dissent, ambitious public-works schemes, and widespread corruption. Pérez Jiménez attended the Venezuelan Military Academy from 1931 to 1934, graduating as a second lieutenant. In 1939–40 he studied at the Superior War School in Peru. He held a number of powerful positions in the military, including chief of the army staff (1945), chairman of the joint chiefs of staff (1946), and minister of defense (1946–52). Pérez Jiménez took part in a military coup in 1945 that ousted the dictator Gen. Isaias Medina Angarita and installed the democratic government of Rómulo Gallegos. In 1948 he was part of a three-man junta that overthrew Gallegos and then ruled until 1952. In 1952 Pérez Jiménez was declared president, and his appointment was confirmed by the parliament in 1953. Using his dreaded National Security police, he repressed all opposition—jailing and torturing critics—and censored the press, abolished labour unions, closed the national university, and earned the enmity of the Roman Catholic Church. His public-works projects included tunneling a highway from Caracas through the mountains to the Caribbean Sea. His regime was corrupt, and the country suffered high inflation. Nonetheless, as an anticommunist who controlled major oil supplies, he was supported by the U.S. In a plebiscite in 1957, Pérez Jiménez was confirmed for a second five-year term, but increasing unrest, which culminated in a general strike, forced him to flee the country on Jan. 23, 1958. He went to the Dominican Republic and then to the U.S. He was extradited in 1963 to stand trial for embezzlement but was freed in 1968 and went to live in Madrid.

Phillips, James Frederick ("the Fox"), American environmentalist (b. Nov. 20, 1930, Aurora, Ill.—d. Oct. 3, 2001, Aurora), employed a number of creative means of demonstrating his displeasure with pollution, especially that caused by corporations, and he acknowledged his efforts by leaving a note signed "the Fox," with a fox's face drawn in the *o*. Among his methods were the dumping of sewage in the reception room of the company that had released it into Lake Michigan and the placement of skunks on the doorsteps of executives of companies that polluted. In 1986 he started the Fox River Conservation Foundation.

Phillips, John Edmund Andrew, American singer and songwriter (b. Aug. 30, 1935, Parris Island, S.C.—d. March 18, 2001, Los Angeles, Calif.), was the guiding force behind the Mamas and the Papas, the folk-pop-rock group that in only about two years in the mid-1960s had six numbers in the top 10 and worldwide sales in the millions. They came to epitomize the hippy "flower power" era in the U.S. In the mid-1960s Phillips and his second wife, Michelle (Holly Michelle Gilliam), teamed up with Dennis Doherty and later Cass Elliot, moved to Los Angeles, and named themselves the Mamas and the Papas. Their first single, "California Dreamin'" (1965), reached the number four spot on the charts, and their next, "Monday, Monday" (1966), reached number one and won a Grammy Award. Eleven other hit singles followed. The group disbanded in 1968, reuniting only briefly in 1971. Phillips released a solo album, *John Phillips: The Wolfking of L.A.,* in 1970, and although he struggled with alcohol- and drug-abuse problems in the 1970s, he wrote music for films. In 1982 he toured with a new lineup of the Mamas and the Papas that included one of his daughters as well as Doherty. Phillips's autobiography, *Papa John,* was published in 1986, and in 1998 the Mamas and the Papas were inducted into the Rock and Roll Hall of Fame. Phillips had recently completed a new solo album.

Plumb, Sir John Harold, British historian and academic (b. Aug. 20, 1911, Leicester, Eng.—d. Oct. 21, 2001, Cambridge, Eng.), was a prolific author and a noted expert on the social and political history of 18th-century England, but he was almost as well-known for his sumptuous epicurean lifestyle, acerbic tongue, and reputation as a cantankerous eccentric. Plumb came from a working-class background and was educated at the University of Leicester before studying under historian G.M. Trevelyan at the University of Cambridge. In 1946 Plumb became a fellow at Christ's College, Cambridge, where he held numerous positions during his long academic career, including chairman of the history faculty (1966–68) and master of Christ's (1978–82). His learned and elegantly written books included *England in the Eighteenth Century* (1950), two biographical volumes on Sir Robert Walpole (1956 and 1960), and the text for the *Royal Heritage* television series (1977). Plumb was knighted in 1982.

Porter, Nyree Dawn (Ngaire Dawn Porter), New Zealand-born British actress (b. Jan. 22, 1940, Napier, N.Z.—d. April 10, 2001, London, Eng.), became one of British television's first romantic sex symbols for her portrayal of the mistreated beauty Irene Forsyte in *The Forsyte Saga,* the BBC's 26-part adaptation of John Galsworthy's novel sequence. The series, which was first broadcast in 1967, achieved equal success in the U.S. and numerous other countries and brought Porter international fame. Although she starred in the TV series *The Protectors* in the 1970s and had a successful stage and screen career, she never fully escaped the image of Irene. Porter was appointed OBE in 1970.

Pusey, Nathan Marsh, American educator (b. April 4, 1907, Council Bluffs, Iowa—d. Nov. 14, 2001, New York, N.Y.), was president of Harvard University from 1953 to 1971. Despite his success in revitalizing the university, he left the post embittered by confrontations with antiwar protesters in the late 1960s. He was educated at Harvard and earned a B.A. (1928), an M.A. (1932), and a Ph.D. (1937); his field was ancient history. In 1935 Pusey undertook the development of a great books program at Lawrence College, Appleton, Wis., and he later taught briefly at Scripps College, Claremont, Calif. Beginning in 1940 he taught at Wesleyan University, Middletown, Conn., and in 1944 he returned to Lawrence College as its president.

Verner Reed/TimePix

Harvard humanities booster Nathan Pusey

After becoming president of Harvard in 1953, Pusey led the university in a program of expansion, increasing the endowment, building new facilities, and hiring additional faculty, including many women. The university once again came to emphasize the humanities. Under his leadership the university adopted a "need blind" policy, admitting qualified students irrespective of their ability to pay. As a result of his policies, Harvard became a much more diverse university. In the 1950s Pusey defended the university against attacks by Sen. Joseph McCarthy that the faculty harboured members of the Communist Party. In the late 1960s he opposed equally strongly the tactics of antiwar protesters. When they took over the administration building in 1969, the president called in state and local police, and violence ensued. After leaving Harvard, he was president of the Andrew W. Mellon Foundation (1971–75) and of the United Board for Christian Higher Education in Asia (1979–80). Among his writings was the book *American Higher Education, 1945–70* (1978).

Quinn, Anthony Rudolph Oaxaca, Mexican-born American actor (b. April 21, 1915, Chihuahua, Mex.—d. June 3, 2001, Boston, Mass.), appeared in more than 150 films but was universally identified with one role especially—the earthy full-of-life title character in *Zorba the Greek* (1964), whom he inhabited so completely and comfortably that many of his later parts seemed also to be infused with that character's spirit. He embraced his offscreen life with the same gusto, a fact that was evidenced in part by the fact that his 13th child was born when he was in his 80s. Quinn had a variety of jobs—prizefighter, painter, and musician and preacher for an evangelist among them—and, besides studying for the priesthood, considered becoming an architect. To aid him in the latter, he began taking acting lessons after Frank Lloyd Wright suggested that he improve his speech, and before long he had been cast in the play *Clean Beds.* In 1936 Quinn appeared in a small part in the movie *Parole,* and he thereafter garnered a number of roles of various ethnic

bottom: Getty Images

and/or outlaw characters in the films *They Died with Their Boots On* (1941), *The Ox-Bow Incident* (1943), *Guadalcanal Diary* (1943), and *Back to Bataan* (1945). His first lead role came in 1947 in *Black Gold.* That same year Quinn went to New York City and made his Broadway debut in *The Gentleman from Athens.* He followed that with touring as Stanley Kowalski in *A Streetcar Named Desire,* returning to New York in 1950 to replace Marlon Brando in that role, and then touring in *Born Yesterday* and *Let Me Hear the Melody.* He also appeared in a number of live television programs. Returning to Hollywood, Quinn had roles in *The Brave Bulls* (1951) and *Viva Zapata!* (1952), for which he won the first of his two Academy Awards for best supporting actor. He then made a few films in Italy, the most notable of which was Federico Fellini's *La Strada* (1954), in which he gave one of his finest performances. Quinn won his second Oscar for *Lust for Life* (1956) and went on to roles in the memorable motion pictures *Wild Is the Wind* (1957), *The Savage Innocents* (1959), *The Guns of Navarone* (1961), *Requiem for a Heavyweight* (1962), and *Lawrence of Arabia* (1962). Quinn returned to the stage in 1982 to tour with and appear on Broadway in a revival of the musical version of *Zorba,* and he also became a successful artist and sculptor. His final movie role was in the not-yet-released *Avenging Angelo.*

Rabal Valera, Francisco ("Paco"), Spanish actor (b. March 8, 1925, Aguilas, Spain—d. Aug. 29, 2001, Bordeaux, France), during his nearly 60-year stage and screen career, evolved from a handsome leading man into an impressive character actor, notably in films directed by Luis Buñuel—including *Nazarín* (1958), *Viridiana* (1961), and *Belle de jour* (1967)—and in Pedro Almodóvar's *¡Átame!* (1990; *Tie Me Up! Tie Me Down!*). Rabal was named best actor at the 1984 Cannes Film Festival for *Los santos inocentes (The Holy Innocents)* and at the 1991 Montreal Film Festival for *L'Homme qui a perdu son ombre (The Man Who Lost His Shadow).* In 2000 he won the Goya, Spain's highest acting award, for his leading role in *Goya* (1999; *Goya in Bordeaux*). Rabal had just been given a lifetime prize at the Montreal Festival and was flying back to Spain, where he was to receive the Donostia Lifetime Achievement Award at the San Sebastián Film Festival, when he suddenly was taken ill.

Rabbani, Mullah Mohammad, Afghan Muslim cleric (b. 1956?, Kandahar province, Afg.—d. April 16, 2001, Rawalpindi, Pak.), was the second most powerful man in Afghanistan's Taliban regime and the de facto chairman of the Taliban Council of Ministers (the equivalent of a prime minister). Rabbani attended an Islamic seminary before joining the jihad against the communist government installed after the Soviet Union's military intervention in Afghanistan in 1979. During the ensuing civil war, he was a founding member of the fundamentalist Muslim Taliban, originally a religious students' militia. It was widely reported that Rabbani had ordered the execution of former president Mohammad Najibullah after Taliban forces captured the capital, Kabul, in 1996.

Ramone, Joey (Jeffrey Hyman), American rock singer (b. May 19, 1951, New York, N.Y.—d. April 15, 2001, New York), was the lead singer for the influential punk rock band the Ramones. Founded in 1974, the Ramones created a new style of vigorous, thrashing music that became the foundation of punk rock; the first of the band's 21 albums, *Ramones,* appeared in 1976. A tall, gangly man with limited singing ability, Ramone was an unlikely rock star. Nevertheless, his feverish live performances helped the band develop a loyal following, and he was credited with sparking a fashion trend by always wearing torn jeans, black leather, and tinted sunglasses. The band's tour of England in 1976 proved a major inspiration for the punk movement in Great Britain, where the Ramones enjoyed greater commercial success than at home. With a shifting lineup, the group continued to record and perform into the 1990s before disbanding in 1996.

Rascher, Sigurd, German-born Scandinavian saxophonist (b. May 15, 1907, Elberfeld [now Wuppertal], Ger.—d. Feb. 25, 2001, Shushan, N.Y.), was a virtuoso performer who established the saxophone as a classical instrument and expanded its range to four octaves. A number of composers created works for him, and during his career he appeared with virtually all major orchestras in Europe and the U.S. From 1933 to 1938 he taught at the Royal Danish Conservatory in Copenhagen and at the Conservatory of Music in Malmö, Swed.

Raven, Simon Arthur Noël, British writer (b. Dec. 28, 1927, Leicester, Leicestershire, Eng.—d. May 12, 2001, London, Eng.), was a prolific author whose sardonic wit was showcased in the 10-novel sequence *Alms for Oblivion.* Raven's education in the classics influenced his moral outlook, and as a satirist he was often compared to Evelyn Waugh. He attended Charterhouse in Godalming, Surrey, but was expelled in 1945 for homosexual activity. Raven then joined the National Service and was stationed in India. In 1948 he won a scholarship to King's College, Cambridge, but he left in 1952 without finishing his work. He joined the army and served in Africa before resigning in 1956 to avoid a court-martial for gambling debts. Raven wrote essays and reviews for periodicals, including *The Spectator,* and his first published novel, *The Feathers of Death,* on homosexuality in the army, appeared in 1959. In 1961 Raven's publisher subsidized his move to Deal, Kent, to help him avoid the temptations of London, and he lived there for more than 30 years. *Alms for Oblivion,* a portrait of the upper classes from the end of World War II to the mid-1970s, began appearing in 1964. The novels were romans à clef, with the central character, Fielding Gray, loosely modeled on the author and other characters on classmates and friends, some of whom became prominent in British public life. A seven-volume sequel, *The First-Born of Egypt* (1984–92), was less successful. Raven had both artistic and financial success with his adaptations for television, including Aldous Huxley's *Point Counter Point* (1968), Anthony Trollope's *The Way We Live Now* (1969) and *The Pallisers* (1974), and *Edward and Mrs. Simpson* (1978). Among his nonfiction was the collection of essays *The English Gentleman* (1961) and the memoir *Shadows on the Grass* (1982). Raven was a cricketer and an accomplished writer on the sport.

Reagan, Maureen, American political activist (b. Jan. 4, 1941, Los Angeles, Calif.—d. Aug. 8, 2001, Granite Bay, Calif.), was the daughter of former president Ronald Reagan and his first wife, Jane Wyman; a lifelong Republican, she was nevertheless an outspoken advocate of feminism and abortion rights—positions that clashed with her father's conservative views. After a brief career in film, television, and radio, Reagan devoted herself to political causes. Between 1985 and 1992 she directed a political action committee that supported more than 100 women candidates across the country. She twice ran unsuccessfully for office herself, losing bids for the U.S. Senate in 1982 and for the U.S. House of Representatives in 1992. She served (1987–89) as cochair of the Republican National Committee. After her father was diagnosed with Alzheimer disease in 1994, Reagan became a spokeswoman for the Alzheimer's Association. She published a best-selling memoir, *First Father, First Daughter,* in 1989.

AP/Wide World Photos

Activist "first daughter" Maureen Reagan

Reynolds, Peter John, British archaeologist (b. June 11, 1939, Shifnal, Shropshire, Eng.—d. Sept. 26, 2001, Kemer, Turkey), was one of the world's experts on the Iron Age and a pioneer in the field of experimental archaeology. Reynolds refused to accept theories about pre-Roman Iron Age life without practical testing, and he reconstructed Iron Age technologies, agricultural techniques, and building construction as authentically as possible. His work was most fully expressed at Butser

Ancient Farm, an open-air laboratory in Hampshire, which was established in 1972 as a replica of a working British farming settlement from about 300 BC.

Rhodes, James Allen, American politician (b. Sept. 13, 1909, Coalton, Ohio—d. March 4, 2001, Columbus, Ohio), was Ohio's longest-serving governor; although he was credited with improving his state's economy, infrastructure, and educational system, his career was overshadowed by his decision to quell an antiwar protest by sending National Guard troops to Kent (Ohio) State University—an action that led to the shooting deaths of four students on May 4, 1970. Rhodes worked his way up through the local ranks of the Republican Party to become mayor of Columbus at the age of 33. He lost his first bid for the governorship in 1954 but was elected eight years later; he held the post from 1962 to 1970. The day after the Kent State shootings, Rhodes lost the Republican primary for the U.S. Senate, but four years later he was reelected governor. He stepped down in 1982 and lost a bid for a fifth term as governor in 1986.

Richler, Mordecai, Canadian writer (b. Jan. 27, 1931, Montreal, Que.—d. July 3, 2001, Montreal), was celebrated for his vivid, boldly satiric portraits of the haves and have-nots of his native Quebec. His wickedly acerbic novels and essays often garnered outrage from offended parties (of which there were many) while consistently earning him critical acclaim. Born the son of a Jewish scrap-metal merchant in the largely Francophone province of Quebec, Richler considered himself "a minority within a minority" and continually returned to the examination of his experiences as such in his writings. After two years of study at Sir George Williams University in Montreal, Richler abandoned school to cultivate his dream of becoming a novelist and moved to Paris. His first novel, *The Acrobats* (1954), told the story of disillusioned expatriates in Spain à la Ernest Hemingway; Richler subsequently disowned this book owing to its lack of maturity. He spent the next several years in London, where he continued to produce novels. His first major recognition came with the publication of *The Apprenticeship of Duddy Kravitz* (1959), a coming-of-age story of a shrewd, street-smart young Jewish man making a way for himself in postwar Montreal; a literary success before it became a commercial one, the novel was made into a major motion picture in 1974. The film's screenplay (written by Richler) was nominated for an Academy Award. His next book to win critical acclaim was *Cocksure* (1968), a racy portrait of life in 1960s London; though banned in some places, it won the Canadian Governor General's Award. Richler won that award a second time for *St. Urbain's Horseman* (1971). That book was also short-listed for the Booker Prize, as was a later book, *Solomon Gursky Was Here* (1989). In 1972 Richler moved back to Montreal with a wife and children in tow; his popular children's books chronicling the adventures of Jacob Two-Two developed out of the stories Richler made up to entertain his own children. Richler remained primarily in Montreal for the rest of his life, continuing simultaneously to delight and dismay in fiction and in fact. He contributed essays on various political concerns to leading publications and was most notably a stringent opponent of Quebec's anti-English language laws. His last book of fiction, *Barney's Version,* appeared in 1997, and *Mordecai Richler on Snooker* was published posthumously.

Ridler, Anne Barbara Bradby, British poet (b. July 30, 1912, Rugby, Warwickshire, Eng.—d. Oct. 15, 2001, Oxford, Eng.), wrote verse that was devotional and meditative, reflecting her Christian faith, and that dealt with domestic concerns such as marriage and motherhood. Her Elizabethan sense of form and her use of complex metaphors led critics to compare her to the 17th-century Metaphysical poets, particularly George Herbert and Thomas Traherne. She also wrote verse dramas, wrote and translated opera librettos, and served as the editor of a number of anthologies and collections. Ridler's father, a poet, was headmaster of Rugby School, and her mother was a children's writer. Members on both sides of the family were distinguished in literary, artistic, and clerical circles. She earned a degree from King's College, London, in 1932. From 1935 to 1940 she worked for Faber and Faber, part of this time as secretary to T.S. Eliot and as an assistant in publishing *The Criterion.* In 1938 she married Vivian Ridler, who later (1958–78) was printer to the University of Oxford. He published *Poems,* her first volume, in 1939. Other volumes included *Some Time After and Other Poems* (1972), *New and Selected Poems* (1988), and *Collected Poems* (1994; rev. ed. 1997). Verse dramas included *Cain* (1943) and *The Trial of Thomas Cranmer* (1956). She collaborated with composers as a librettist and did highly regarded performing translations of the librettos of operas by Cavalli, Monteverdi, and Mozart. *The Little Book of Modern Verse* (1941) and the *Faber Book of Modern Verse* (1951; rev. ed. 1960) were among the anthologies she edited. She also edited the poems of Traherne and the writings of Charles Williams, an early influence. In 1998 she received the Cholmondeley Prize for Poetry, and in 2001 she was appointed OBE.

Ridley, Sir (Nicholas) Harold Lloyd, British ophthalmologist (b. July 10, 1906, Kibworth Harcourt, Leicestershire, Eng.—d. May 25, 2001, Salisbury, Wiltshire, Eng.), devised the first successful artificial intraocular lens (IOL) transplant surgery for cataract patients. During World War II, Ridley observed that, when splinters of Perspex from cockpit canopies became lodged in the eyes of wounded pilots, they did not trigger immune reactions. Traditionally, following surgical removal of cataracts, patients were fitted with thick-lensed eyeglasses, but Ridley, on the basis of his wartime observations, developed IOL implants. The British medical community rejected the procedure as too risky, so in 1949 Ridley conducted his first implant operation in secret. Despite some initial problems with complications, by the 1970s improved instrumentation and microsurgical techniques had made the procedure the most common treatment for cataracts in the U.S. British doctors eventually followed suit, and in 1986, some 15 years after his retirement from medical practice, Ridley was elected to the Fellowship of the Royal Society. He was knighted in 2000.

Riegner, Gerhart Moritz, German-born lawyer and human rights activist (b. Sept. 12, 1911, Berlin, Ger.—d. Dec. 3, 2001, Geneva, Switz.), was the first to warn government officials in London and Washington, D.C. (in August 1942, in what came to be known as the "Riegner telegram"), that the Nazis had made the decision to exterminate the Jews in Europe and had begun putting their plans in motion. To Riegner's horror, however, only in December did the Allies condemn the plan, and not until January 1944 did U.S. Pres. Franklin D. Roosevelt create the War Refugee Board to aid the Jews.

Ripley, S(idney) Dillon, II, American museum director, educator, and author (b. Sept. 20, 1913, New York, N.Y.—d. March 12, 2001, Washington, D.C.), was secretary of the Smithsonian Institution in Washington, D.C., from 1964 to 1984 and was responsible for greatly expanding the museum complex's activities and popularity. Ripley earned a Ph.D. from Harvard University in 1943 and served in the Office of Strategic Services during World War II. He joined the Yale University faculty as a professor of zoology and biology in 1946, and from 1959 to 1964 he was director of the university's Peabody Museum. During Ripley's tenure at the Smithsonian, the number of annual visitors to the complex rose from 10.8 million to more than 30 million. He added eight new museums to the institution, began television programs, and launched *Smithsonian* magazine.

Rogers, William Pierce, American lawyer and politician (b. June 23, 1913, Norfolk, N.Y.—d. Jan. 2, 2001, Bethesda, Md.), served as U.S. deputy attorney general (1953–57) and then attorney general (1957–61) during the administration of Pres. Dwight D. Eisenhower and was secretary of state (1969–73) under Pres. Richard M. Nixon. Though he had long been a close and loyal friend to Nixon, he was greatly overshadowed and rendered largely ineffectual by Nixon's national security adviser, Henry Kissinger, and was replaced by him early in Nixon's second term. Rogers was educated at Colgate University, Hamilton, N.Y., and Cornell University Law School, Ithaca, N.Y., and then became an assistant district attorney in New York City. Following World War II navy service, he returned to that office, and in 1947 he moved to Washington, D.C., and went to work on Capitol Hill. Rogers became friends with Nixon when he assisted Nixon in the House Committee on Un-American Activities investigation of the Alger Hiss case—the case that made Nixon's reputation. Rogers again came to Nixon's aid by first supporting him when, as Eisenhower's vice presidential candidate, Nixon was accused of

Reuters/TimePix

having benefited from a political slush fund and then by helping him prepare his famous "Checkers" speech. While serving as attorney general, Rogers was central to the drafting of the Civil Rights Act of 1957 and to the establishment of the Justice Department's Civil Rights Division. Rogers returned to private law practice in 1961, and in 1964 he played a prominent role in a landmark Supreme Court case that further defined libel law and increased protection for journalists. While serving as Nixon's secretary of state, Rogers was generally kept in the dark about most foreign policy concerns, though he did get involved in seeking peace in the Middle East. After leaving office, untainted by the Watergate scandal, he once again went into private practice. In 1986 he served as chair of the commission that investigated the explosion of the space shuttle *Challenger.*

Ross, Herbert David, American dancer, choreographer, and film director (b. May 13, 1927, Brooklyn, N.Y.—d. Oct. 9, 2001, New York, N.Y.), had a career as a dancer on Broadway and choreographed for ballet companies, the stage, and motion pictures before turning to film directing. Among his numerous popular movies were five Neil Simon comedies—*The Sunshine Boys* (1975), *The Goodbye Girl* (1977), *California Suite* (1978), *I Ought to Be in Pictures* (1982), and *Max Dugan Returns* (1983)—and a drama that tapped his knowledge of the dance world, *The Turning Point* (1977); one of the main characters in the latter was modeled on his first wife, ballerina Nora Kaye. Ross dropped out of high school to pursue a performing career in New York City, where he danced in the choruses of several shows. While attending an exhibition of artworks by Francisco de Goya, he was especially impressed by the series "Los caprichos" and decided to choreograph a ballet inspired by them. *Caprichos* (1950) was so successful in a workshop that American Ballet Theatre included it in its 10th anniversary season. Ross created more ballets for the company during the following several years, most notably *The Maids* (1957), as well as choreographing for television and supper-club acts; he also did the choreography for a number of Broadway hits, including *A Tree Grows in Brooklyn* (1951), *I Can Get It for You Wholesale* (1962), which launched Barbra Streisand's career, *Anyone Can Whistle* (1964), and *On a Clear Day You Can See Forever* (1965), as well as such films as *Carmen Jones* (1954) and *Funny Girl* (1968). Ross made his film-directing debut with the musical version of *Goodbye Mr. Chips* (1969), and his hit movies included *The Owl and the Pussycat* (1970), *Play It Again, Sam* (1972), *The Last of Sheila* (1973), *Footloose* (1984), and *Steel Magnolias* (1989).

Roy, Pankaj Khirod, Indian cricketer (b. May 31, 1928, Calcutta [Kolkata], India—d. Feb. 4, 2001, Kolkata), was a solid opening batsman for Bengal (1946–68) and India (1951–60), scoring 11,868 first-class runs (average 42.38), including 2,442 runs in 43 Tests (average 32.56). Although Roy's highest individual first-class score was 202 not out, in 1955 he made 173 runs in a world-record 413 opening stand with Vinoo Mankad against New Zealand. Their record for a first-wicket Test partnership still stood at the time of Roy's death.

Saddler, Joseph ("Sandy"), American boxer (b. June 23, 1926, Boston, Mass.—d. Sept. 18, 2001, Bronx, N.Y.), won 144 of his 162 professional fights, was world junior lightweight champion in 1949–51, and was world featherweight champion in 1948–49 and 1950–57. He was known as one of the hardest-punching small men in boxing, a reputation he most notably lived up to in his four extremely brutal title bouts with Willie Pep, three of which he won. Saddler was voted into the International Boxing Hall of Fame in 1990.

Salahuddin Abdul Aziz Shah (Tuanku Salahuddin Abdul Aziz Shah ibni al-Marhum Sultan Hisamuddin Alam Shah), Malaysian monarch (b. March 8, 1926, Klang, Malaya—d. Nov. 21, 2001, Kuala Lumpur, Malaysia), was the ceremonial head of state, or *yang dipertuan agong* (paramount ruler), of Malaysia from April 26, 1999. Salahuddin was educated in Malaya and at the University of London. In 1960 he succeeded his father as sultan of Selangor, and in 1999 he assumed the throne as independent Malaysia's 11th king (*agong*), in a constitutional monarchy that rotated among the sultans of the country's nine constituent states. Although he occasionally clashed with the prime minister, Salahuddin was particularly popular among the common people. In 1974 he declared that a great mosque should be built in the capital, Kuala Lumpur, which was located under his jurisdiction in Selangor; some 14 years later Southeast Asia's largest mosque was completed and named after Salahuddin.

Salem, Hidaya Sultan as-, Kuwaiti journalist and social activist (b. 1936, Ash-Shuwaykh, Kuwait—d. March 20, 2001, Kuwait City, Kuwait), campaigned against official corruption and for women's suffrage in Kuwait. Salem, one of her country's first female teachers and journalists, was a founding member (1964) of the Kuwaiti Literary League, a board member of the Kuwait Journalists Association, owner and editor in chief of *Al-Majalis* magazine, and the author of several books, notably *Women in the Koran.* She was assassinated on her way to a conference.

Sampson, Nikos (Nikos Georghiades), Greek Cypriot journalist and militant nationalist (b. Dec. 16, 1934, Famagusta, Cyprus—d. May 9, 2001, Nicosia, Cyprus), was president of Cyprus for eight days in 1974, but the coup of which he was a part led directly to the Turkish invasion that resulted in the island nation's division into two antagonistic parts. Sampson, a member of the EOKA guerrilla movement, was sentenced to death in 1957 for having assassinated British servicemen stationed in Cyprus, but he was released from prison when the island gained its independence in 1960. On July 15, 1974, when military forces under the direction of Greek officers overthrew the Cypriot government under Archbishop Makarios III, Sampson was named president. Turkish forces landed on Cyprus on July 20, and three days later Sampson resigned in favour of Glafkos Clerides. In 1977 Sampson was the only participant in the coup to face trial. He was sentenced to 20 years' imprisonment, but in 1979 he was permitted to go to France for medical treatment. He returned to prison in 1990, but he was freed again because of his continuing poor health.

Sawaki, Kin'ichi, Japanese haiku poet (b. Oct. 6, 1919, Toyama, Japan—d. Nov. 5, 2001, Tokyo, Japan), was one of the preeminent Japanese *haijin* during the second half of the 20th century; he served as president of the Haiku Poets Association from 1987 to 1993. Sawaki founded *Kaze* ("Wind"), an influential journal for new-style haiku, in 1946. His last haiku collection was *Ayako no te* (2000; "Ayako's Hand"). *Hakucho* (1995; "White Swan") won the 1996 Iida Dakotsu Prize, and his book of essays, *Showa haiku no seishun* (1996; "Springtime of Showa Era Haiku"), received the Haiku Poets Association Criticism Prize in the same year.

Schaap, Richard Jay ("Dick"), American journalist, biographer, and talk-show host (b. Sept. 27, 1934, Brooklyn, N.Y.—d. Dec. 21, 2001, New York, N.Y.), zestfully documented the inner workings of public figures, notably sports heroes. He came to notice in the 1960s alongside New York City newspapermen such as Jimmy Breslin, Pete Hamill, and Tom Wolfe—creators of a forceful, emotive style known as New Journalism. Genial and prolific, Schaap traveled easily among celebrities, penning best-selling autobiographies for sporting legends. He was an editor at *Newsweek*, the *New York Herald Tribune*, and *Sport Magazine*, and he won six Emmy Awards for his radio and television work, which included stints on NBC, ABC, and ESPN. His autobiography, *Flashing Before My Eyes*, appeared in 2001.

Schach, Rabbi Eliezer Menachem, Lithuanian-born Israeli Orthodox Jewish scholar and political leader (b. 1896?, Wabolnick [now Vabalninkas], Lithuania, Russian Empire—d. Nov. 2, 2001, Tel Aviv, Israel), as the spiritual leader of Israel's non-Zionist ultra-Orthodox political parties—Agudat Yisrael, Shas, and Degel Hatorah—wielded great influence on Israeli government policies. In 1940 Schach emigrated from Lithuania to British Palestine, where he was a revered scholar at the Ponevezh Yeshiva in Bnei Brak, near Tel Aviv. In 1984 he sided with Sephardic Jews who broke away from the predominantly Ashkenazic Agudat Yisrael to form Shas. Four years later he founded Degel Hatorah, which in 1992 joined with Agudat Yisrael in a new political bloc, United Torah Judaism. Schach preached moderation in Arab-Israeli relations, opposed Jewish settlements in the occupied territories, and supported trading land for peace, but his fierce contempt for the

The Yomiuri Shimbun

liberal secularism of the Labor Party led him to support right-wing governments.

Schindler, Emilie Pelzl, German-born industrialist (b. Oct. 22, 1907, Alt Moletein, Sudetenland, Austria-Hungary [now Czech Republic]—d. Oct. 5, 2001, Strausberg, Ger.), was the wife of Oskar Schindler, whom she helped in saving some 1,300 Jews during World War II. She married Schindler in 1928 and worked closely with her industrialist husband throughout the war, scrounging on the black market for food and other supplies for the Jews in their employ, as well as personally protecting them and caring for those too ill to work. In 1949 the bankrupt Schindlers moved to Argentina, where Emilie lived in poverty after her husband returned to Germany in 1957. She eventually was granted a small pension. She received Israel's Righteous Among the Nations award in 1993, and two years later Argentina bestowed its highest honour for foreigners, the Order of May. She delineated her wartime efforts in her 1997 memoir, *Where Light and Shadow Meet.*

Schultes, Richard Evans, American scientist (b. Jan. 12, 1915, Boston, Mass.—d. April 10, 2001, Boston), pioneered the field of ethnobotany, the study of indigenous peoples and their uses of hallucinogenic and medicinal plants. Schultes spent extensive time among native tribes in South America and collected more than 24,000 plant specimens from the Amazon region. Although his books on hallucinogenic plants were widely read by drug experimenters during the 1960s, he dismissed the notion of "mind expansion" espoused by counterculture figures such as Timothy Leary and maintained that such plants should be studied for their medicinal value. Schultes had a long association with Harvard University, where he earned a Ph.D. in biology in 1941 and worked as a curator, lecturer, and professor from 1954 to 1985. Among Schultes's numerous awards were the Tyler Prize for Environmental Achievement in 1987 and the Linnean Society Gold Medal in 1992.

Scindia, Madhavrao, Indian Hindu prince and politician (b. March 10, 1945, Bombay [now Mumbai], India—d. Sept. 30, 2001, Mainpur, India), succeeded (1961) his father as maharaja of the ancient princely state of Gwalior (which was absorbed by independent India in 1948 and incorporated into the modern state of Madhya Pradesh in 1956); after the government abolished Indian royalty, he went into national politics. Scindia was educated in England at Winchester College and New College, Oxford. He was first elected to Parliament in 1971 as a member of the Hindu nationalist party Jan Sangh (later the Bharatiya Janata Party), cofounded by his mother, Vijayraje Scindia. Later in the decade he switched to the Congress (I) Party. The charismatic and popular "commoner-king" was reelected eight times, regardless of his party affiliation. The switch, however, generated a permanent rift with his mother (who had been imprisoned briefly by the government in 1975) and led to years of legal battles between the two over the family estates. Before Vijayraje died in January 2001, she disinherited her son; her will indicated that he should not have the honour of lighting her funeral pyre—a public ritual he undertook all the same. Scindia held several cabinet ministries in the 1980s and '90s and was deputy leader of Congress (I) at the time of his death. A sports enthusiast, he served as president (1990–93) of the Indian Cricket Control Board and had a cricket trophy named after him. Scindia was killed when the small plane in which he was a passenger crashed.

Sebald, Winifred Georg, German-born novelist and scholar (b. May 18, 1944, Wertach im Allgäu, Ger.—d. Dec. 14, 2001, Norwich, Eng.), entranced casual readers and critics alike with his haunting, richly imaginative, nonchronologically constructed stories. His work often explored themes of memory as they related to the Holocaust. Sebald's novels included *Schwindel, Gefühle* (1990; *Vertigo,* 1999), *Die Ausgewanderten* (1992; *The Emigrants,* 1996), *Die Ringe des Saturn* (1995; *The Rings of Saturn,* 1998), and *Austerlitz* (2001, in German and English).

Secombe, Sir Harry Donald, British comedian, actor, and writer (b. Sept. 8, 1921, Swansea, Wales—d. April 11, 2001, Guildford, Surrey, Eng.), starred as the gullible Neddie Seagoon in the revolutionary 1950s radio program *The Goon Show,* a zany, satiric, anarchic series that became a cult favourite and paved the way for such shows as the TV cult hit *Monty Python's Flying Circus.* Secombe left school at age 15 and worked as a clerk before joining the army during World War II. After the war he appeared as a comic at the Windmill Theatre in London's Soho district, in provincial variety theatres, and on such radio programs as *Variety Bandbox* and *Welsh Rarebit.* He also began gathering with Peter Sellers, Spike Milligan, and Michael Bentine in the Grafton Arms pub, where they shaped their jokes and banter into radio scripts. The quartet's work was accepted by BBC radio, and they began presenting *Crazy People* in 1951. It was renamed *The Goon Show* in 1952 and continued until early 1960 (without Bentine after the second season); a reunion, "The Last Goon Show of All," was broadcast in April 1972 to honour the BBC's 50th anniversary. Secombe's most notable stage appearances were in the musical *Pickwick* (1963)—which featured "If I Ruled the World," a song he made famous—and *The Four Musketeers* (1967); his best-known film was *Oliver!* (1968), in which he played Mr. Bumble. He also contributed to *Punch* magazine and published the novels *Twice Brightly* (1974) and *Welsh Fargo* (1981), as well as two autobiographical works, short stories, and children's books. From 1983 to 1993 he was host of the Sunday evening religious TV program *Highway,* and from 1995 he presented another religious program, *Songs of Praise.* Secombe was made CBE in 1963 and was knighted in 1981.

Senghor, Léopold Sédar, Senegalese poet, philosopher, politician, and statesman (b. Oct. 9, 1906, Joal, Senegal, French West Africa—d. Dec. 20, 2001, Verson, Normandy, France), straddled the literary and political spheres in his dual roles—as Senegal's first president from 1960 until he voluntarily stepped down 20 years later and as one of Africa's most distinguished French-language poets and the leading figure of the "Négritude" movement, which reassessed African culture in the 1930s and '40s and affirmed the literary and artistic expression of the black African experience. Senghor studied at the Sorbonne in Paris and taught school in France until he was drafted into the military in 1939. Captured by German forces in 1940, he composed what later were acknowledged as some of his finest poems while being held in a prison camp. He was released in 1942 and joined the French Resistance. After the war he entered politics and represented his native land in the French National Assembly as the head of the Senegalese Democratic Bloc. Back home Senghor founded the socialist Senegalese Progressive Union (later the Socialist Party) and advocated a confederacy of former French colonies in West Africa. When the so-called Mali Federation broke apart and Senegal was granted separate independence, Senghor was unanimously elected president. Throughout his five terms in office, he worked to modernize his country, fight official corruption, and enhance international cooperation. In 1975 he

Kobal Collection/Columbia

Harry Secombe as Mr. Bumble in Oliver!

authorized the formation of two opposition parties; five years later he was the first black African leader to hand over the reins of office in a peaceful transfer of power. As an acclaimed poet, Senghor's literary contributions included *Chants d'ombre* (1945), *Hosties noires* (1948), *Ethiopiques* (1956), *Nocturnes* (1961; Eng. trans. 1969), and *Oeuvre poétique* (1990), and he also edited a 1948 French-language verse anthology. In addition, he wrote numerous philosophical treatises on Négritude and published critical essays under the pseudonyms Silmang Diamano and Patrice Maguilene Kaymor. Senghor received scores of international awards, and in 1984 he became the first black member of the French Academy.

Shaffer, Anthony Joshua, British playwright and screenwriter (b. May 15, 1926, Liverpool, Eng.—d. Nov. 6, 2001, London, Eng.), delighted audiences with his ingenious comic thriller *Sleuth,* which played 2,359 performances in London's West End and more than 2,000 performances on Broadway, where it won the Tony Award for best play of 1970. He went on to write the screenplay for the 1972 Oscar-nominated film version. Shaffer devised several additional plays, notably *Murderer* (1975). He had far greater success, however, with his many other screenplays, including Alfred Hitchcock's *Frenzy* (1972), *The Wicker Man* (1973), *Sommersby* (1993), and three Agatha Christie adaptations, *Death on the Nile* (1978), *Evil Under the Sun* (1983), and *Appointment with Death* (1988). Shaffer also wrote novels in collaboration with his twin brother, Sir Peter Shaffer, playwright of *Equus* and *Amadeus.*

Shakhnazarov, Georgy Khosroevich, Armenian-born Soviet political analyst (b. Oct. 4, 1924, Baku, Transcaucasia, U.S.S.R. [now Baku, Azerbaijan]—d. May 15, 2001, Tula, Russia), as an advocate of glasnost and other political and social reforms, was one of Soviet Pres. Mikhail S. Gorbachev's most loyal and trusted political advisers. Shakhnazarov studied law at Azerbaijan State University and earned a doctorate in political science and philosophy from the Moscow Institute of Law. He worked as a writer and editor for the political publisher Politizdat and later for an international communist magazine based in Prague, where he quietly endorsed the unsuccessful reform movement. A senior official in the Central Committee, Shakhnazarov was responsible (1972–88) for guiding Moscow's relations with its Eastern European allies. In 1988, however, he was invited to join Gorbachev's personal staff. After the president's departure from office in 1991, Shakhnazarov devoted himself to analyzing globalization issues for the Gorbachev Foundation.

Shanahan, Eileen, American journalist (b. Feb. 29, 1924, Washington, D.C.—d. Nov. 2, 2001, Washington), was a pioneering journalist at the *New York Times* and, from 1977 to 1979, a spokeswoman for the administration of U.S. Pres. Jimmy Carter. Shanahan was hired to work in the Washington bureau of the *Times* in 1962. She covered national economic policy and was the first female reporter at the bureau to handle an assignment other than coverage of presidential wives. Shanahan attracted widespread attention in 1974 when she and six other female employees at the *Times* successfully sued the newspaper for sex discrimination; the case was the subject of a 1992 book, *The Girls in the Balcony,* by one of Shanahan's fellow plaintiffs, Nan Robertson. After her service in the Carter administration, Shanahan worked as an assistant managing editor at the *Washington Star* and the *Pittsburgh* (Pa.) *Post-Gazette.* In 1987 she also helped found a magazine, *Governing,* devoted to covering developments in state and local governments.

Shannon, Claude Elwood, American mathematician and computer scientist (b. April 30, 1916, Petoskey, Mich.—d. Feb. 24, 2001, Medford, Mass.), laid the theoretical foundations for modern mass communications and came to be regarded as the "father of the information age." After graduating from the University of Michigan at Ann Arbor in 1936, he earned (1940) both a master's degree in electrical engineering and a Ph.D. in mathematics from the Massachusetts Institute of Technology (MIT). He joined the mathematics department at Bell Labs in 1941, where he contributed to work on antiaircraft missile control systems. He remained affiliated with Bell Labs until 1972. Shannon became a visiting professor at MIT in 1956, a permanent member of the faculty in 1958, and professor emeritus in 1978. Shannon's master's thesis, "A Symbolic Analysis of Relay and Switching Circuits" (1940), used Boolean algebra to establish the theoretical underpinnings of digital circuits, which became fundamental to the operation of modern computers and telecommunications equipment. In 1948 Shannon published a paper entitled "A Mathematical Theory of Communication," which established basic tenets of information theory and contained the first published use of the term *bit* to designate a single binary digit. His formulation of information theory was an immediate success with communications engineers and continued to prove useful to later researchers. It also inspired many attempts to apply information theory in other areas, such as cognition, biology, linguistics, psychology, economics, and physics. Aside from producing many provocative and influential articles on information theory, cryptography, and chess-playing computers, Shannon also designed various mechanical devices, including an electromechanical mouse—one of the first experiments in artificial intelligence.

Hulton/Archive/Getty Images

Mathematician Claude Shannon with his electronic mouse

Sherlock, Dame Sheila Patricia Violet, British hepatologist (b. March 18, 1918, Dublin, Ire.—d. Dec. 30, 2001, London, Eng.), was one of the world's leading authorities on diseases of the liver and served as professor of medicine (1959–83) at London's Royal Free Hospital School of Medicine, where the distinguished liver clinic and research centre was named in her honour. Sherlock received (1941) her medical degree from the University of Edinburgh. During her long career she did breakthrough research on different forms of hepatitis, cirrhosis, and liver cancer. She published hundreds of papers; edited several periodicals, notably the *European Journal of Hepatology* and the journal of the British Society of Gastroenterology, of which she was president; and wrote the classic textbook *Diseases of the Liver and Biliary System* (1955; 11th ed., 2001). Sherlock was appointed DBE in 1978 and was made a fellow of the Royal Society in 2001.

Shull, Clifford Glenwood, American physicist (b. Sept. 23, 1915, Pittsburgh, Pa.—d. March 31, 2001, Medford, Mass.), shared the 1994 Nobel Prize for Physics for his development of neutron-scattering techniques—in particular, neutron diffraction, a process that enabled scientists to better explore the atomic structure of matter. He shared the prize with Canadian physicist Bertram N. Brockhouse, who conducted separate but concurrent work in the field. After graduating from New York University with a Ph.D. in 1941, Shull began a career as a research physicist. His award-winning work was completed at Oak Ridge (Tenn.) National Laboratory from 1946 to 1955. In Shull's technique of neutron diffraction, a beam of single-wavelength neutrons was passed through the solid or liquid material under study. Neutrons interacting with atoms of the target material were scattered into a pattern that, when recorded on photographic film, yielded information about the relative positions of atoms in the material. Shull was also one of the first to demonstrate a way to use neutron scattering to study the structure of magnetic materials. From 1955 until his retirement in 1986, he was a professor at the Massachusetts Institute of Technology.

Sieff of Brimpton, Marcus Joseph Sieff, Baron, British businessman (b. July 2, 1913, Manchester, Eng.—d. Feb. 23, 2001, London, Eng.), succeeded his father, Baron Sieff, and uncle, Simon Marks, in the family business—retailer Marks and Spencer, which was founded by his maternal grandfather, Michael Marks, in 1884. Under Sieff's stewardship—as assistant managing director (1963–65), vice chairman (1965–67), joint managing director (1967–83), deputy chairman (1971), chairman (1972–84), president (1984–85), and honorary president (1985–2001)—the company, popularly known as M&S or "Marks & Sparks," grew into Britain's most profitable retailer and an international concern with outlets in several countries. Sieff was also a prominent fund-raiser for Zionist causes and the nonexecutive chairman (1986–93) of *The Independent* newspaper. In 1980 he became the first son of a life peer to be awarded his own life peerage.

Silva, Adhemar Ferreira da, Brazilian track star (b. Sept. 29, 1927, São Paulo, Braz.—d. Jan. 12, 2001, São Paulo), broke the triple-jump world record seven times and won two Olympic gold medals in the event. Between 1950 and 1956 Silva won 60 consecutive triple jumps. At the 1952 Olympics in Helsinki, Fin., he captured his first gold with a world-record jump of 16.22 m (53 ft 2$^{3}/_{4}$ in). He broke the world record for a final time in 1955 with a jump of 16.56 m (54 ft 4 in) at the Pan American Games in Mexico City. A year later, at the Olympics in Melbourne, Australia, he won his second gold with a jump of 16.35 m (53 ft 8 in), an Olympic record. Silva was Brazil's cultural attaché to Nigeria from 1964 to 1966 and later worked as a film actor.

Silverstein, Abe, American aerospace engineer and researcher (b. Sept. 15, 1908, Terre Haute, Ind.—d. June 1, 2001, Fairview Park, Ohio), was an early space researcher who coined the name Apollo for the missions that resulted in placing the first human on the Moon's surface in 1969. Silverstein began his career with the National Advisory Committee for Aeronautics (NACA), the forerunner of the National Aeronautics and Space Administration (NASA). At NACA he helped create and direct the efforts leading to the Mercury series of manned spaceflights. From 1961 until his retirement in 1969, Silverstein was director of the NASA Lewis Research Center, Cleveland, Ohio.

Simon, Herbert Alexander, American social scientist (b. June 15, 1916, Milwaukee, Wis.—d. Feb. 9, 2001, Pittsburgh, Pa.), was awarded the 1978 Nobel Prize for Economics for his theory regarding decision-making processes in economic organizations. Simon studied political science at the University of Chicago, where he received a B.A. in 1936 and a Ph.D. in 1943. After holding various administrative posts, he was appointed (1949) a professor at Carnegie Mellon University, Pittsburgh, where he helped form several departments and schools, including the Graduate School of Industrial Administration and the School of Computer Science. He was best known for a theory of corporate decision making known as behaviourism. In his book *Administrative Behavior* (1947), he sought to replace the highly simplified classical approach to economic modeling and its concept of the single decision-making, profit-maximizing entrepreneur with an approach to decision making that recognized a multiplicity of factors. According to Simon, this framework provided a more satisfactory theoretical approach for a world in which decision-making units were large enough for each one to have significant effects on prices and outputs. Crucial to this theory was the concept of satisfying behaviour—the achievement of acceptable levels of economic variables while keeping complications and risks at a minimum—as contrasted with the traditional emphasis on the achievement of maximum profits as the primary motivating factor. Simon's theory thus attempted to consider the psychological factors involved in decision making that classical economists tended not to take into account. Later in his career, Simon increasingly became involved in an attempt to create artificial intelligence by computer technology. He was the author of 27 books, including *Models of My Life* (1991), an autobiography.

Courtesy of Carnegie-Mellon

Sinopoli, Giuseppe, Italian conductor and composer (b. Nov. 2, 1946, Venice, Italy—d. April 20, 2001, Berlin, Ger.), performed with an intensity and daring that made him one of Europe's most controversial orchestra leaders. Sinopoli simultaneously studied medicine, psychiatry, and anthropology at the University of Padua, Italy (M.D., 1971), and composition at the Venice Conservatory, whose faculty he joined in 1972. He founded the Bruno Maderna Ensemble for contemporary music in 1975. Sinopoli was principal conductor and music director of London's Philharmonia Orchestra (1984–94) and principal conductor of the Dresden (Ger.) State Opera (from 1991), as well as a frequent guest conductor throughout Europe. Known for his use of extreme tempos and psychological interpretations of the Romantic opera repertory, Sinopoli also conducted his own avant-garde compositions, notably his two-act opera *Lou Salomé* (1981). He recorded extensively for the Deutsche Grammophon label. Sinopoli died of a heart attack he suffered while conducting a performance of Verdi's *Aida* at the Berlin Opera House.

Slaughter, Frank Gill, American author and physician (b. Feb. 25, 1908, Washington, D.C.—d. May 17, 2001, Jacksonville, Fla.), was a surgeon-turned-writer who wrote some 56 best-selling novels, many of which dealt with medical issues. After earning a medical degree from Johns Hopkins University, Baltimore, Md., Slaughter worked as a surgeon in Florida from 1934 to 1942. He published his first novel, *That None Should Die,* a book about socialized medicine, in 1941, and after service in the U.S. Army during World War II, he devoted himself to writing full-time. Other novels with medical themes included *Doctors' Wives* (1967) and *No Greater Love* (1985). He was also noted for his historical novels, including *Constantine: The Miracle of the Flaming Cross* (1965), about the Roman emperor. Slaughter's books sold more than 60 million copies worldwide.

Söderbaum, Kristina, Swedish-born German film actress (b. Sept. 5, 1912, Stockholm, Swed.—d. Feb. 12, 2001, Hitzacker, Ger.), portrayed the Aryan ideal heroine in a series of films in the 1930s and '40s, particularly those directed by her husband, Veit Harlan, under the aegis of Nazi propaganda minister Joseph Goebbels. The blonde, blue-eyed star's credits included *Jugend* (1938), *Die Reise nach Tilsit* (1939), and *Der Grosse König* (1942). Most controversial were her lead roles in the blatantly anti-Semitic propaganda film *Jud Süss* (1940; *Jew Süss*) and *Kolberg* (1943), said to be Goebbels's imitation of the American epic *Gone with the Wind.* After World War II Harlan was indicted for war crimes several times, but he was never convicted; he died in 1964. Söderbaum too was unapologetic for her role in Nazi filmmaking. She spent the postwar years photographing other film stars and occasionally acting in films and television programs.

Sørensen, Villy, Danish writer and philosopher (b. Jan. 13, 1929, Copenhagen, Den.—d. Dec. 16, 2001, Copenhagen), became one of the most influential Danish intellectuals of his generation. A prominent literary critic after World War II, he began his career writing modernist short stories whose subjects often drew upon the rich allegorical traditions of myth and religion and whose themes earned the writer comparisons to Hans Christian Andersen and Franz Kafka. These themes, which later were expanded in Sørensen's philosophical writings, dealt with notions of the extraordinary in the everyday and with the isolation of the self in society. His first short-story collection, *Sære historier* (1953; *Tiger in the Kitchen and Other Strange Stories,* 1957) was followed by *Ufarlige historier* (1955; *Harmless Tales,* 1991). His philosophical texts included *Digtere og dæmoner* (1959) and *Hverken-eller* (1961), which were both published during the period in which he was coeditor of *Vindrosen,* the leading Danish modernist journal of its time. During the 1960s he edited Karl Marx's *Økonomi of filosofi* (1962) and translated Kafka's short stories and works on Friedrich Nietzsche and Arthur Schopenhauer. Along with Niels I. Meyer and K. Helveg Petersen, Sørensen wrote *Oprør fra midten* (1978), a widely discussed treatise that put forth a nonpartisan, utopian vision of the future. Other notable works by Sørensen included *Formynderfortællinger* (1964; *Tutelary Tales,* 1988), *Ragnarok* (1982), and *Apollons oprør* (1989).

Sothern, Ann (Harriette Lake), American actress (b. Jan. 22, 1909, Valley City, N.D.—d. March 15, 2001, Ketchum, Idaho), achieved fame with her roles in films that included *Maisie* (1939) and *Lady Be Good* (1941) and as the star of the 1950s television series *Private Secretary.* Sothern began her film career after performing in Broadway musicals. Her success in the title role of *Maisie* led to a series of films that included *Maisie Was a Lady* (1941) and *Undercover Maisie* (1947). *Private Secretary* aired from 1953 to 1957, and another television series, *The Ann Sothern Show,* ran from 1958 to 1961. Sothern was nominated for an Academy Award for best supporting actress for her performance in the 1987 film *The Whales of August.*

Southern, Sir Richard William, British historian (b. Feb. 8, 1912, Newcastle upon Tyne, Eng.—d. Feb. 6, 2001, Oxford, Eng.), brought his love of medieval European history to an international audience with the publication of his first book, *The Making of the Middle Ages* (1953), which was later translated into more than two dozen languages. Southern, who spent his entire professional career (1933–81) at the University of Oxford, was knighted in 1974. His other books included *Western Views of Islam in the Middle Ages* (1962), *Saint Anselm and His Biographer* (1963), and *Scholastic Humanism and the Unification of Europe* (vol. 1, 1995; vol. 2, 2000).

Spedding, Sir David Rolland, British intelligence agent and administrator (b. March 7, 1943—d. June 13, 2001, London, Eng.), was from 1994 to 1999 chief of the Secret Intelligence Service (MI-6), the branch of the British government responsible for foreign intelligence and espionage activities. Under the traditional code name "C," Spedding, an Arabist who studied at Hertford College, Oxford, and the Middle East Centre for Arabic Studies, reorganized the post-Cold War MI-6 into a modern operation dealing with such international crimes as drug trafficking, money laundering, and terrorism. Although Spedding's appointment was officially announced in 1994, he never appeared in public, and no photographs of him were published until after his death. He was knighted in 1996.

Stanley, Kim (Patricia Beth Reid), American actress (b. Feb. 11, 1925, Tularosa, N.M.—d. Aug. 20, 2001, Santa Fe, N.M.), achieved renown on the Broadway stage in roles that ranged from the tomboyish Millie in *Picnic* (1953) to the nightclub singer Cherie in *Bus Stop* (1955) and to Masha in *The Three Sisters* (1964), attracting both critical and popular acclaim. She won Emmy Awards for two of her numerous television performances, in an episode of *Ben Casey* (1963) and as Big Mama in *Cat on a Hot Tin Roof* (1984), and although she acted in only five films, she garnered Academy Award nominations for two of her roles, a scheming medium in *Séance on a Wet Afternoon* (1964) and actress Frances Farmer's overpowering mother in *Frances* (1982).

Stargell, Wilver Dornel ("Willie"; "Pops"), American professional baseball player (b. March 6, 1940, Earlsboro, Okla.—d. April 9, 2001, Wilmington, N.C.), was one of the greatest hitters in the history of baseball; he led the Pittsburgh Pirates to two World Series championships, in 1971 and 1979. He spent his entire major-league career with the Pirates, playing with the team from 1962 until his retirement in 1982. Stargell was a powerful and prolific hitter known for his ability to knock long home runs; he once held longest-home-run records in nearly half of the National League ballparks. Stargell swatted a total of 475 home runs, 2,232 hits, and 1,540 runs batted in. His career batting average was .282. After retiring as a player, Stargell coached briefly for the Pirates and, later, for the Atlanta Braves. He was inducted into the Baseball Hall of Fame in 1988. Stargell died of a stroke only two days after the Pirates unveiled a 3.65-m (12-ft) bronze statue of him in front of the team's new home in Pittsburgh, PNC Park.

Powerful Pirate Willie Stargell

Stassen, Harold Edward, American politician (b. April 13, 1907, West St. Paul, Minn.—d. March 4, 2001, Bloomington, Minn.), was the youngest governor of Minnesota, though his early political triumphs were overshadowed by his nine unsuccessful presidential campaigns. Stassen was elected Dakota county attorney at the age of 23 and governor at the age of 31; he served in the latter office from 1938 to 1943. He made his first bid to capture the Republican presidential nomination in 1948 and his last in 1992. Stassen was a delegate to the 1945 San Francisco Conference, which created the United Nations charter. He served as president of the University of Pennsylvania from 1948 to 1953 and later as a disarmament adviser in the Dwight D. Eisenhower administration.

Stern, Isaac, American violinist (b. July 21, 1920, Kremenets, Ukraine—d. Sept. 22, 2001, New York, N.Y.), was one of the 20th century's best-known musicians and an influential teacher and advocate for the arts. His parents immigrated to the U.S. in 1921, and he grew up in San Francisco, where he began violin studies at the age of eight. Stern made his Carnegie Hall, New York City, debut in 1943 and performed there more than 200 times during his life. His repertoire ranged from Bach to 20th-century composers and included contemporary music. With pianist Eugene Istomin and cellist Leonard Rose, he formed one of the greatest of modern piano trios, which performed from the 1960s until Rose's death in 1984. He made more than 100 recordings, and in 1995 Sony Classical issued the 44-compact disc set *Isaac Stern: A Life in Music.* He performed on a number of Hollywood sound tracks, and the documentary *From Mao to Mozart: Isaac Stern in China,* based on a 1979 tour, won an Academy Award in 1981. He promoted the careers of a number of younger musicians, including the violinists Itzhak Perlman and Pinchas Zukerman and the cellist Yo-Yo Ma. In 1960 Stern organized a campaign to save Carnegie Hall from demolition, and he served as chairman of the Carnegie Hall Corp. until his death. He oversaw the hall's restoration in 1986 and the celebration of its centenary in 1991. Stern, active in political causes, took a role in the creation of the U.S. National Endowment for the Arts in the 1960s and became chairman of the America-Israel Cultural Foundation in 1964. A supporter of Israel, he refused to perform in Germany. His autobiography, *My First 79 Years,* written with novelist Chaim Potok, was published in 1999. Among his many honours was the first Albert Schweitzer Music Award (1975).

Carnegie Hall hero Isaac Stern

Stix, Thomas Howard, American physicist (b. July 12, 1924, St. Louis, Mo.—d. April 16, 2001, Princeton, N.J.), was a pioneer in the field of plasma physics. After serving (1943–46) as a radio technician in the U.S. Army, Stix earned a B.A. from the California Institute of Technology and a Ph.D. from Princeton University. In 1953 he was recruited to join Project Matterhorn, an effort by scientists at Princeton to induce a controlled thermonuclear fusion reaction in a confined plasma, or electrified gas, in order to generate energy. Stix developed an antenna—later known as a Stix coil—that generated microwaves to heat plasma to the high temperatures necessary for fusion. Much of his later research involved refining the process of heating plasma with waves. Stix published an influential book, *The Theory of Plasma Waves,* in 1962. He was also responsible for establishing a graduate program in plasma physics at Princeton—the first of its kind. He received the Maxwell Prize, the highest award in plasma physics, in 1980.

Straight, Beatrice Whitney, American actress (b. Aug. 2, 1914, Old Westbury, N.Y.—d. April 7, 2001, Los Angeles, Calif.), won an Academy Award for best supporting actress in 1976 for her portrayal of a spurned wife in the motion picture *Network.* In 1953 she also earned a Tony Award for best supporting actress for her performance in Arthur Miller's play *The Crucible,* in which she portrayed a Puritan woman accused of witchcraft. Straight was a versatile actress whose career onstage, in films, and on television spanned more than half a century. She made her Broadway debut in *Bitter Oleander* in 1935 and appeared in her last film, *Deceived,* in 1991.

Sucksdorff, Arne, Swedish motion-picture director and cinematographer (b. Feb. 3, 1917, Stockholm, Swed.—d. May 4, 2001, Stockholm), was a noted documentary filmmaker and nature photographer. Sucksdorff studied painting and natural history before becoming a still photographer. He made his first documentary in 1939, and in 1949 his impressionistic study of Stockholm, *Människor i stad* (1946; "The Rhythm of the City"), won an Academy Award for best short subject. His feature-length films included *Det stora äventyret* (1953; *The Great Adventure*), a lyrical story of two boys and a wild otter, which captured the same beauty and love of nature as his nonfiction works. In the early 1950s he directed two films in India. Sucksdorff lived in Brazil for some 30 years, working with children and teaching documentary filmmaking for UNESCO. He made only one film while in Brazil, *Mitt hem är Copacabana* (1965; *My Home Is Copacabana*). In the 1990s Sucksdorff returned to Sweden, where he received a lifetime achievement award from the Göteborg Film Festival in 1997.

Sullivan, Leon Howard, American clergyman and civil rights leader (b. Oct. 16, 1922, Charleston, W.Va.—d. April 24, 2001, Scottsdale, Ariz.), was instrumental in helping to end apartheid in South Africa, in part by developing the "Sullivan Principles," a code of conduct for companies operating in that country. After graduating from West Virginia State College, Sullivan studied theology at Union Theological Seminary, New York City, and sociology at Columbia University, New York City. In 1950 he became pastor of the Mt. Zion Baptist Church in Philadelphia, a post he held until 1988. In 1964 Sullivan founded the Opportunities Industrialization Center, a job-training program for minorities. In 1977, six years after being named the first African American board member of General Motors Corp., he drew up the Sullivan Principles, which called for, among other things, equal pay and training opportunities for South African workers, regardless of race. In the mid-1980s Sullivan called for a multinational boycott of South Africa and persuaded many companies to pull out of the country. After Nelson Mandela was freed from prison in 1990, Sullivan worked with him to encourage companies to return to South Africa. Sullivan was awarded the U.S. Presidential Medal of Freedom in 1992.

Sylvester, (Anthony) David Bernard, British art critic and exhibition curator (b. Sept. 21, 1924, London, Eng.—d. June 19, 2001, London), was a towering figure in the British art world and a champion of Modernism, most notably the works of Francis Bacon, Henry Moore, Alberto Giacometti, and René Magritte. Although he had no formal training, Sylvester discovered an interest in art at age 17, unsuccessfully tried his hand at painting, and began writing art reviews in 1942 for the socialist weekly *Tribune*, of which George Orwell was literary editor. In 1945 Sylvester's last article for the magazine, a review of a book on Moore, attracted the notice of the artist, who hired him as a part-time assistant. Sylvester curated his first exhibition, a Moore retrospective, at the Tate Gallery in 1951. By the 1960s Sylvester had gained tremendous influence through his lectures and exhibitions, as well as his pithy reviews, articles, and catalog essays. He also had broadened his zeal to include nonfigurative artists, such as Jackson Pollock (whose work he had initially disparaged) and Willem de Kooning (he organized a de Kooning exhibition at the Serpentine Gallery in 1977), and Pop art. Sylvester appeared on the 1964 BBC television series *Ten Modern Artists* and at various times served on the Arts Council, the British Film Institute production board, the board of trustees for the Tate and Serpentine galleries, and the acquisitions board of the National Museum of Modern Art in Paris. His books included *Henry Moore* (1968), *Magritte: The Silence of the World* (1992), *About Modern Art: Critical Essays, 1948–1996* (1996), and the five-volume Magritte catalogue raisonné, which took him 25 years to complete. Sylvester was made CBE in 1983.

Szulc, Tadeusz Witold ("Tad"), Polish-born American journalist and author (b. July 25, 1926, Warsaw, Pol.—d. May 21, 2001, Washington, D.C.), was working as a foreign correspondent for the *New York Times* when he broke the story of the abortive 1961 invasion of Cuba by U.S.-financed Cuban exiles at the Bay of Pigs (Bahía de los Cochinos). Szulc later wrote at greater length about the incident in *The Cuban Invasion: The Chronicle of a Disaster* (1962) and published a biography of Fidel Castro, entitled *Fidel: A Critical Portrait*, in 1986. Szulc worked at the *Times* from 1953 to 1972, when he left to become a freelance writer. Among his other books were *Pope John Paul II: The Biography* (1995) and *Chopin in Paris* (1998).

Taglioni, Fabio, Italian engineer and motorcycle designer (b. Sept. 10, 1920, Lugo di Romagna, Italy—d. July 18, 2001, Bologna, Italy), during his 35-year career as the chief engineer for the state-owned Ducati (1954–89), transformed that company's motorcycles from cheap, low-powered scooters that were little more than motorized bicycles into high-priced, high-performance road-racing cycles. Taglioni was responsible for both the elegant appearance and the state-of-the-art engines for a series of Ducati motorcycles that won plaudits for their quality, styling, and speed and quickly came to dominate the world Superbike championships.

Tate, Buddy (George Holmes Tate), American tenor saxophonist (b. Feb. 22, 1915, Sherman, Texas—d. Feb. 10, 2001, Chandler, Ariz.), played with a big, rich tone and fluent melodic imagination, first with traveling swing bands in the Midwest. As a featured soloist with Count Basie (1939–48), he incorporated some of Lester Young's innovative melodic and harmonic concepts; he then led a popular band at the Celebrity Club in New York City (1953–74), toured internationally with all-star swing revival groups, and occasionally played lyric clarinet.

Teshigahara, Hiroshi, Japanese film director and flower arranger (b. Jan. 28, 1927, Tokyo, Japan—d. April 14, 2001, Tokyo), was a leading avant-garde film director who achieved worldwide fame with the release of *Suna no onna* (1964; *Woman in the Dunes*). Teshigahara made his directorial debut with *Otoshiana* in 1962. He was nominated for an Academy Award for best director for *Suna no onna,* which also won a Special Jury Prize at the Cannes International Film Festival and was nominated for an Academy Award for best film. After directing *Natsu no heitai* (1972; *Summer Soldiers*), Teshigahara turned his attention to flower arrangement and in 1980 he became grand master of the prominent Sogetsu School of Ikebana. He returned to directing films with *Rikyu* (1989). Teshigahara's last film was *Gohime* (1992; *Basara: The Princess Goh*).

Thérond, Roger Jean, French photojournalist and editor (b. Oct. 24, 1924, Sète, France—d. June 23, 2001, Paris, France), transformed *Paris-Match* from a conventional news weekly into one of Europe's most controversial and popular tabloids. Thérond joined *Paris-Match* in 1949; he was named senior editor the next year and editor in chief in 1962. After having left the magazine to work for a rival weekly, *L'Express,* in 1968, he returned in 1976. Thereafter he boosted flagging sales by switching to a steady diet of sensational news scoops, candid photographs (most of which he personally selected), and juicy gossip about public figures. *Paris-Match* often triggered international outrage and lawsuits, most notably when it published embarrassing snapshots of Monaco's royal family; Britain's Diana, princess of Wales; and former president François Mitterrand on his deathbed. Thérond, however, claimed that the peoples' right to know made all news coverage equally valid. Shortly before his death Thérond was honoured with an award from the International Center of Photography in New York City for his role in shaping European photojournalism.

Tjio, Joe Hin, Indonesian-born American geneticist (b. Nov. 2, 1919, Java, Indon.—d. Nov. 27, 2001, Gaithersburg, Md.), dispelled a 50-year-held belief that the number of chromosomes in the human cell was 48 when he established that the majority of human cells contain 46 chromosomes, arranged in 23 pairs. While working in 1955 at the Institute of Genetics in Lund, Swed., Tjio used a newly discovered technique to separate chromosomes from the nucleus of a cell; he helped establish modern cytogenetics—the study of the relationship between the structure and activities of chromosomes and the mechanisms of heredity—as a major branch of genetics. His work led to the discovery in 1959 that those people afflicted with Down syndrome have an additional chromosome in their cells. Tjio's early education was in strict Dutch schools in Indonesia, and he also became a student of photography (his father was a professional portrait photographer). After earning a degree in agriculture from the School of Agronomy in Bogor, he conducted research to develop hybrid plants that would be resistant to disease. His photographic skills were instrumental in preparing slide samples. Following a three-year imprisonment in a Japanese prison camp during World War II, he traveled to The Netherlands, where he secured a fellowship to study in Europe. He relaunched his studies on plant and insect cytogenetics and became a noted expert in the field. The government of Spain invited him to conduct studies on a plant-improvement program, and he spent 11 years in Zaragoza. During holidays, however, he carried out research at the Institute of Genetics, where he turned his attention to mammalian tissue. When Tjio published his findings about the correct number of chromosomes in the Scandinavian journal *Hereditas* in 1956, he created a stir because he failed to cite Albert Levan, the head of the Institute of Genetics, as first author of the paper, a long-standing European convention. Tjio threatened to throw the work away unless he was named first author. In the interests of scientific advancement, Levan relented. During the last 37 years of his career, Tjio worked in the U.S. at the National Institutes of Health, Washington, D.C., where he compiled a remarkable collection of scientific photographs that documented his work.

Tjupurrula, Johnny Warrangkula, Australian Aboriginal artist (b. 1925?, Minjilpiri, N.Terr., Australia—d. Feb. 12, 2001, Papunya, N.Terr.), was a pioneer of modern Aboriginal abstract art; his innovative works, which combined intricate calligraphic lines and tiny dots, drew international praise and defined the Aboriginal style known as "dot painting." In the 1960s Tjupurrula was transported with other nomadic Aboriginals from their tribal lands to Papunya, a bleak government settlement west of Alice Springs. There, encouraged by a local white schoolteacher, many residents began painting acrylic artwork and decorated trinkets. In 1997 one of Tjupurrula's early paintings, *Water Dreaming at Kalipinya* (1972), sold for a record price for Aboriginal art, A$206,000 (U.S. $263,145); the painting set another record three years later when it sold for more than double that price. Tjupurrula, however, who originally sold the painting for A$150 (about U.S. $75), struggled for years with alcoholism and poor health and died in poverty.

Trenet, Charles (Louis Charles Augustin Claude Trenet), French singer and songwriter (b. May 18, 1913, Narbonne, France—d. Feb. 19, 2001, Créteil, France), was for more than 60 years one of the most celebrated practitioners of the French chanson, a form of cabaret ballad distinguished by catchy tunes and sophisticated, witty lyrics. Trenet's exuberant stage presence and signature rumpled fedora helped earn him the nickname "la Fou chantant" ("the Singing Fool"). He composed more than 1,000 songs, most notably "Douce France" ("Sweet France"), "Que reste-t-il de nos amour?" ("I Wish You Love"), and "La Mer." The latter reportedly had some 4,000 recordings, the best known of which was Bobby Darin's "Beyond the Sea." Trenet, who also painted and wrote several novels, was made a member of the Legion of Honour in 1998.

Trigano, Gilbert, French businessman (b. July 28, 1920, St.-Maurice, Val-de-Marne, France—d. Feb. 4, 2001, Paris, France), was cofounder (1950), with his Belgian partner, Gérard Blitz, of Club Méditeranée, which introduced a revolutionary style of all-inclusive, cash-free holiday "villages." By the early 1980s there were more than 100 Club Med resorts, offering club "members" sun-drenched locations, group activities that included sports under the direction of attractive young "organizers," and a relaxed social environment that was conducive to sexual freedom. Trigano, a member of the Legion of Honour, retired as CEO in 1993 in favour of his son; in 1997 Club Méditeranée was reorganized under new ownership. In the 1980s Trigano also supervised an ambitious government program to install computers in French schools.

Trinh Cong Son, Vietnamese singer and songwriter (b. 1939, Dac Lac province, Vietnam, French Indochina—d. April 1, 2001, Ho Chi Minh City, Vietnam), composed more than 600 songs, but he was dubbed the "Bob Dylan of Vietnam" in the West for his poignant antiwar songs during the 1960s and '70s. After his first hit, "Uot Mi" ("Crying Eyes"), in 1957, Son became one of South Vietnam's best-known singer-songwriters. He was often under pressure from the government, which was disturbed by the pacifist lyrics of such songs as "Ngu Di Con" ("Lullaby," about a mother grieving for her soldier son). After the reunification of Vietnam in 1975, the new communist government sentenced Son to "reeducation" in a labour camp. In later years, however, his often melancholy songs about love and postwar reconciliation gained new acceptance and popularity.

Tupolev, Aleksey Andreyevich, Russian aircraft designer (b. May 20, 1925, Moscow, U.S.S.R.—d. May 12, 2001, Moscow, Russia), designed many of the Soviet Union's most successful jet airplanes, including the Tu-104 (the country's first commercial jetliner), the Tu-134, and the Tu-154, as well as the Tu-26 medium-range bomber and the Tu-160 swing-wing long-range strategic bomber; however, his most ambitious enterprise, the world's first supersonic passenger jet, the Tu-144, ended in failure. Tupolev became chief designer at Tupolev Design Bureau in 1963 and succeeded his father, the celebrated aircraft designer Andrey N. Tupolev, as chief of the design bureau in 1972. The Tu-144 had its first test flight in 1968, two months before the Concorde, and flew more than 100 scheduled flights within the Soviet Union, but fatal crashes in 1973 and 1977 spelled the project's end.

Tutin, Dame Dorothy, British actress (b. April 8, 1931, London, Eng.—d. Aug. 6, 2001, London), was one of the British theatre's most accomplished leading ladies during a 50-year stage career. Tutin's varied repertoire included most of the leading female characters in Shakespeare, Chekhov, and Ibsen, as well as Sally Bowles in the original 1954 London production of *I Am a Camera* and modern plays by John Osborne, Tom Stoppard, and Harold Pinter. Although Tutin concentrated on the theatre, she occasionally appeared on television and in motion pictures, notably as Cecily Cardew in her first film, *The Importance of Being Earnest* (1952), and as Polly Peachum in *The Beggar's Opera* (1953). Tutin was made CBE in 1967 and was elevated to DBE in 2000.

Uhse, Beate (Beate Köstlin Rotermund-Uhse), German entrepreneur (b. Oct. 25, 1919, Wargenau, German East Prussia [now in Poland]—d. July 16, 2001, Switzerland), revolutionized sexual attitudes in post-World War II Germany as the founder of Beate Uhse AG, Europe's largest chain of shops selling erotic products and the first sex-related company to be listed (1999) on the Frankfurt stock exchange. She obtained her pilot's license at age 18 and, after qualifying as a Luftwaffe fighter pilot, ferried planes to the front during the war. After her pilot husband was killed in action, Uhse settled in Flensburg, W.Ger., where she began printing and distributing advice on sex and contraceptive information, which was at that time illegal. Although often faced with official writs and public condemnation, Uhse was admired by many for her honest, even humorous, approach to sex. By the time her company went public, she controlled a mail-order catalog, a Web site, a chain of adult cinemas, an erotica museum, and boutiques throughout Germany that sold everything from contraceptive devices to lingerie to adult videos and sex toys.

Uslar Pietri, Arturo, Venezuelan novelist, journalist, and politician (b. May 16, 1906, Caracas, Venez.—d. Feb. 26, 2001, Caracas), was one of the world's leading Spanish-language writers and a fierce critic of political corruption in Venezuela. His novels included, most notably, *Las lanzas coloradas* (1931), *El camino de El Dorado* (1947), and *La isla de Robinson* (1981). In his fiction Uslar Pietri often used magic realism, and he was one of the first Latin American writers to employ that technique. He edited the Venezuelan daily newspaper *El Nacional* from 1969 to 1974. He also served as a senator from 1958 to 1973 and ran unsuccessfully for president in 1963. Uslar Pietri was outspoken in his belief that Venezuela's lucrative oil business had a corrupting influence on the country in general and on the government of Hugo Chávez Frías in particular.

Utaemon VI, Nakamura (Fujio Kawamura), Japanese actor (b. Jan. 20, 1917, Tokyo, Japan—d. March 31, 2001, Tokyo), was regarded as the preeminent performer of Japan's traditional kabuki theatre during his lifetime. Born into a family of kabuki actors, Utaemon VI made his theatrical debut in 1921. He specialized in *onnagata* (female) roles, considered the most demanding in the highly stylized art form. During his career he played more than 500 different roles. In the 1960s Utaemon VI toured the U.S., Europe, and the Soviet Union. He attempted to preserve the classical style, and to this end he encouraged novelist Mishima Yukio and others to write new kabuki plays in a style that conformed to traditional practices. He also helped revive old plays that were seldom performed. In 1968 the Japanese government designated Utaemon VI a Living National Treasure.

Uzaemon XVII, Ichimura (Bandô Mamoru), Japanese actor (b. 1916, Tokyo, Japan—d. July 8, 2001, Tokyo), was one of the greatest *tachiyaku* (male-role) actors in the traditional kabuki theatre of Japan. Ichimura was the nephew of Kikugoro Onoe VI, one of the foremost interpreters of kabuki plays. After debuting at the Imperial Theatre in Tokyo at the age of five, Ichimura went on to star in numerous dramas, one of the most memorable of which was an elaborately staged performance of the play *Shibaraku* ("Wait!") during the Tokyo Olympics in 1964. In 1990 the Japanese government designated him a Living National Treasure.

Vanden Boeynants, Paul, Belgian politician (b. May 22, 1919, Brussels, Belg.—d. Jan. 9, 2001, Aalst, Belg.), was a longtime member of Parliament (1952–85), the French-speaking leader of the centrist Social Christian Party (from 1961), defense minister (1972–79), and twice prime minister of Belgium (1966–68 and 1978–79). Although he was criticized for his handling of Belgium's 1968 language crisis and for his drastic policy of urban renewal in Brussels, it was a conviction for fraud and corruption in 1986 (and a subsequent three-year suspended sentence) that ended his career. In 1989 Vanden Boeynants returned to the headlines when he was kidnapped by a left-wing group; he was released a month later after payment of the 60 million Belgian franc (over $2 million) ransom.

Verdet, Ilie, Romanian politician (b. May 10, 1925, Comanesti, Rom.—d. March 20, 2001, Bucharest, Rom.), as the brother-in-law of Romanian dictator Nicolae Ceausescu, held a variety of government posts, including first deputy prime minster (1966–74) and prime minister (1979–82). After Ceausescu's overthrow and execution (1989), Verdet declared himself head of a provisional government that lasted about 20 minutes. In 1990 Verdet cofounded the opposition Socialist Labour Party.

Verey, Rosemary Isabel Baird Sandilands, British garden designer and writer (b. Dec. 21, 1918, Chatham, Kent, Eng.—d. May 31, 2001, London, Eng.), inspired horticulturists and amateur gardeners alike through her books and the award-winning 1.6-ha (4-ac) English garden at her home, Barnsley House. Verey was particularly known for her attention to detail and historical perspective and for her inspired use of textures, ornamental vegetables, and a year-round colour scheme. She studied mathematics and economics at University College, London, and married architectural historian David Verey in 1939. In 1951 her husband's parents ceded control of the family home, a 17th-century former rectory near Cirencester, Gloucestershire. In 1970 she opened the house's redesigned gardens to the public, and by the 1990s Barnsley House was welcoming up to 30,000 visitors a year. Verey lectured widely and appeared on the BBC television series *The English Country Garden* in the 1990s. She also designed plans for clients and friends, notably for the gardens at Highgrove for Charles, prince of Wales. Her books included *Classic Garden Design* (1984), *The Garden in Winter* (1988), and *Rosemary Verey's Making of a Garden* (1995). Verey was made OBE in 1996 and in 1999 received both the Victoria Medal of Honour from the Royal Horticultural Society and a special award from the Massachusetts Horticultural Society.

Vicente, Esteban, Spanish-born American painter (b. Jan. 20, 1903, Turégano, Spain—d. Jan. 10, 2001, Bridgehampton, N.Y.), was a first-generation member of the avant-garde New York school of painting, which flourished from the 1940s to the '80s and established New York City as the epicentre of the international art world. In 1929, after training at the Royal Academy of Fine Arts of San Fernando in Madrid, Vicente moved to Paris, where he met Pablo Picasso. Vicente divided his time between Paris, Madrid, and Barcelona until 1936, when he relocated to New York City. During the 1940s Vicente began to create abstract paintings. He contributed to the highly publicized "Talent 1950" exhibition at the Kootz Gallery, which showcased paintings by New York school artists, and for awhile he shared a studio with Willem de Kooning. From 1964 until the mid-1980s, Vicente taught art at a number of universities, including Black Mountain (N.C.) College, New York University, and Yale University. In 1998 the Spanish government opened the Esteban Vicente Contemporary Art Museum in Segovia.

Wade, Henry Menasco, American attorney and prosecutor (b. Nov. 11, 1914, Rockwall, Texas—d. March 1, 2001, Dallas, Texas), served as district attorney of Dallas county from 1951 to 1987; he attracted national attention for his prosecution of Jack Ruby and for his role in the landmark abortion case *Roe v. Wade*. After Ruby shot and killed Lee Harvey Oswald, John F. Kennedy's assassin, in 1963, Wade successfully led the prosecution of Ruby the following year. In 1970 Wade was sued by Jane Roe (a fictional name used to protect the identity of Norma McCorvey), who sought to keep him from enforcing a state law that prohibited abortion; Wade's office defended the law, which the U.S. Supreme Court ultimately, in 1973, declared unconstitutional. Wade served as counsel to a Dallas law firm after stepping down as district attorney in 1987.

Walker, Arthur Bertram Cuthbert, II, American physicist and educator (b. Aug. 24, 1936, Cleveland, Ohio—d. April 29, 2001, Stanford, Calif.), helped develop solar telescopes used in 1987 to capture the first detailed images of the Sun's outermost atmosphere. Walker, a professor of physics at Stanford University from 1974 until his death, encouraged minorities and women to pursue careers in science, and among his students was Sally Ride, the first American woman to fly into outer space. Walker was appointed by Pres. Ronald Reagan to serve on the commission that investigated the causes of the 1986 space shuttle *Challenger* disaster.

Walker, David Mathieson, American astronaut (b. May 20, 1944, Columbus, Ga.—d. April 23, 2001, Houston, Texas), was the pilot of the space shuttle *Discovery* in 1984 and the commander of three later space shuttle missions. After graduating from the U.S. Naval Academy, Annapolis, Md., in 1966, Walker became one of the navy's "top gun" fighter pilots; he earned six Navy Air Medals for combat duty during the Vietnam War. NASA selected him to become an astronaut in 1978. As pilot of the *Discovery* shuttle, he played an integral part in the first space salvage mission in history; the crew successfully retrieved two communications satellites that had been stranded in the wrong orbits. Walker later served as mission commander of the *Atlantis* shuttle in 1989, *Discovery* in 1992, and *Endeavour* in 1995.

AP/Wide World Photos

Space shuttle pilot David Walker

Walston, Ray, American actor (b. Nov. 22, 1914?, New Orleans, La.—d. Jan. 1, 2001, Beverly Hills, Calif.), had a long career filled with quirky, endearingly cranky characters on the stage, in movies, and on television but was especially popular as the extraterrestrial masquerading as Bill Bixby's earthling Uncle Martin in the TV series *My Favorite Martian* in the mid-1960s. Indeed, his portrayal of the antennaed alien was so successful that he thereafter had trouble shaking that image. Walston began his professional acting career in the late 1930s in Houston, Texas, and in 1943 went to the Cleveland (Ohio) Play House. He made his Broadway debut in 1945 in a small part in Maurice Evans's production of *Hamlet*. Appearances followed in such shows as *Summer and Smoke* (1948), for which he won the Clarence Derwent Award, and *The Rat Race* (1949), and in 1950 he began touring in *South Pacific* in the role of Luther Billis, a part he also played in the film version (1958). In 1955 Walston opened in his breakthrough role, Mr. Applegate—the devil—in *Damn Yankees,* for which he won a Tony Award and which he also repeated in the film version (1958). Walston went on to roles in such films as *The Apartment* (1960), *Paint Your Wagon* (1969), *The Sting* (1973), *Silver Streak* (1976), *Popeye* (1980), and *Fast Times at Ridgemont High* (1982). He appeared on TV series, most notably *Picket Fences* (1992–96). Walston's portrayal of the irascible Judge Henry Bone won him Emmy Awards in 1995 and 1996.

Warmerdam, Cornelius Anthony ("Dutch"), American pole-vaulter (b. June 22, 1915, Long Beach, Calif.—d. Nov. 13, 2001, Fresno, Calif.), was the first in his sport to clear 4.57 m (15 ft), which he attained on April 13, 1940, with a bamboo pole, and he went on to break the outdoor record another six times. His outdoor record of 4.77 m (15 ft 7¾ in), set in 1942, and indoor record of 4.79 m (15 ft 8½ in), set in 1943, were not broken until 1957 and 1959, respectively, and the men who broke them used more flexible aluminum poles.

Waugh, Auberon Alexander, British writer and satirist (b. Nov. 17, 1939, Dulverton, Somerset, Eng.—d. Jan. 16, 2001, Combe Florey, near Taunton, Somerset), simultaneously delighted and outraged readers with acerbic wit and conservative snobbery in his pointed, pithy, and cruelly funny commentaries on British politics and society. The eldest son of novelist Evelyn Waugh, "Bron" published five novels, beginning in 1960, but in 1972 he renounced fiction for journalism. Thereafter, his often vitriolic columns appeared in such publications as *The Independent, Daily Telegraph, Daily Mirror, New Statesman, Spectator, Evening Standard,* and *Private Eye,* for which he wrote a regular column from 1970 to 1986. As editor (1986–2000) and editor in chief (2000–01) of *Literary Review,* Waugh annually bestowed the good-humoured Bad Sex Award, granted to the novel containing the year's worst prose describing sex. Waugh published several collections of his writings and an autobiography, *Will This Do?* (1991).

Waxman, Albert Samuel ("Al"), Canadian actor (b. March 2, 1935, Toronto, Ont.—d. Jan. 17, 2001, Toronto), achieved fame with his roles on the television series *The King of Kensington* and *Cagney & Lacey.* Waxman studied acting at the Playhouse Theatre in New York City and appeared in a number of films, including *The War Lover* (1962) and *Vengeance Is Mine* (1974), before turning to television. In his most memorable role, he played shopkeeper Larry King on the Canadian Broadcasting Corp. sitcom *The King of Kensington* from 1975 to 1980. From 1981 to 1988 he portrayed Lieut. Bert Samuels on the popular police drama *Cagney & Lacey.* Among later roles, Waxman played a prison warden in the critically acclaimed motion picture *The Hurricane* (1999).

Welty, Eudora Alice, American short-story writer and novelist (b. April 13, 1909, Jackson, Miss.—d. July 23, 2001, Jackson), was known for the lyricism, perception, wit, and humanity that infused her works. Although she wrote primarily about the inhabitants of her native Deep South and their everyday lives, her characters and stories had an appealing universality in their depictions of human emotions and relationships, and her stories were included in numerous anthologies. Welty was educated at Mississippi State College (now University) for Women (1926–27), the University of Wisconsin (B.A., 1929), and the Columbia University Graduate School of Business (1930–31), New York City, but returned home when her father died in 1931. In 1933 she began traveling throughout Mississippi as a publicity agent for the Works Progress Administration (WPA), interviewing and photographing people of all classes and writing stories. Welty had her first story, "Death of a Traveling Salesman," published in 1936 in *Manuscript,* a small literary magazine, and more stories appeared in such publications as the *Southern Review, The Atlantic Monthly,* and *The New Yorker.* One of these, "Why I Live at the P.O.," became a classic, and Welty was especially pleased that it inspired Steven Dorner to name the Eudora e-mail program after her. For another story, "A Worn Path," she won the first of her six O. Henry Awards. A collection of short stories, *A Curtain of Green* (1941), was Welty's first book. Among those that followed were the novella *The Robber Bridegroom* (1942), which was later adapted for the musical stage; *Delta Wedding* (1946), her first full-length novel; *The Ponder Heart* (1954), an adaptation of which became a Broadway hit; and the autobiographical *The Optimist's Daughter* (1972), for which she received a Pulitzer Prize. Welty was also noted for her photographs, which reflected the dignity and humanity of their subjects. A collection of pictures she took while with the WPA was exhibited in New York City in 1936 and years later achieved greater acclaim; 100 of the photos were published in *One Time, One Place: Mississippi in the Depression* in 1971, and many were included in a book of more than 200 pictures, *Eudora Welty Photographs* (1989). Another book of images, *Country Churchyards* (2000), was her last published work. Welty counted among her many awards the Presidential Medal of Freedom (1980) and the French Legion of Honour (1996), and she became (1998) the first living writer to be included in the Library of America series.

Southern novelist Eudora Welty

Whitehouse, Mary Hutcheson, British schoolteacher and campaigner (b. June 13, 1910, Nuneaton, Warwickshire, Eng.—d. Nov. 23, 2001, Colchester, Eng.), was a founder (1964) and president of the Clean Up TV Campaign (later [1965] the National Viewers' and Listeners' Association and then [1994] Mediawatch) and for some three decades pursued her goal of removing sexual and violent content from television, stage, and film. Although she did not achieve most of her goals, she came to be considered a national institution and had a few victories, such as the Indecent Displays Act (1981). She was made CBE in 1980.

Wildenstein, Daniel Leopold, French-born art historian, art dealer, and thoroughbred race horse owner (b. Sept. 11, 1917, Verrières-le-Buisson, France—d. Oct. 23, 2001, Paris, France), was the head of Wildenstein & Co., a secretive and tightly controlled billion-dollar art dynasty that was founded in the 1870s by his grandfather and later moved to New York City by his father. The family company, which Daniel Wildenstein joined in New York in 1940, owned a vast collection of valuable art (including many works by the French Impressionists), as well as art galleries in Japan and New York. Wildenstein, a respected art historian, compiled the catalogues raisonnés for Monet, Manet, and Gauguin. As the owner of a major horse-racing stable in France, Wildenstein was named Owner of the Year six times; his horses won the Prix l'Arc de Triomphe, France's most prestigious race, on four occasions.

Williams, Harrison Arlington, Jr., American politician (b. Dec. 10, 1919, Plainfield, N.J.—d. Nov. 17, 2001, Denville, N.J.), was a prominent Democrat who later served time in federal prison after being convicted of bribery and conspiracy in the Abscam scandal. An advocate of liberal policies, Williams served in the U.S. House of Representatives from 1953 to 1957 and in the U.S. Senate from 1959 to 1982. Williams was one of a number of politicians implicated in Abscam, a sting operation carried out by federal agents who posed as wealthy Middle Eastern businessmen and offered bribes in exchange for political favours. After his conviction on May 1, 1981, Williams resigned from office and eventually served three years in prison. Pres. Bill Clinton refused his request for a pardon in 2000.

Winning, Thomas Joseph Cardinal, Scottish cleric (b. June 3, 1925, Wishaw, Scot.—d. June 17, 2001, Glasgow, Scot.), was the spiritual leader of Roman Catholics in Scotland; his service as archbishop of Glasgow from 1974 until his death—cardinal from 1994—was marked by his unflinching defense of Catholic views on abortion and homosexuality. He supported the Pro-Life Initiative, a program that gave money and other aid to women who agreed not to have abortions, and forcefully argued against equating homosexual relationships with traditional marriage. He was also a notable advocate of public efforts to combat poverty and homelessness. Winning studied at the Pontifical Scots College in Rome. He was ordained in 1948, and became a bishop in 1971, three years before his elevation to archbishop.

Withers, (Elizabeth) Audrey, British journalist (b. March 28, 1905, Hale, Cheshire, Eng.—d. Oct. 26, 2001), was appointed editor of *Vogue* in 1940 and over the following two decades increased both the magazine's size and its subscription base through her transformation and modernization of its content. She was made OBE in 1953, and she published two books: *The Palaces of Leningrad* (1973), in collaboration with her second husband, Victor Kennett, and her autobiography, *Lifespan* (1994).

Woodcock, Leonard Freel, American labour leader and diplomat (b. Feb. 15, 1911, Providence, R.I.—d. Jan. 16, 2001, Ann Arbor, Mich.), served as president of the United Automobile Workers (UAW) from 1970 to 1977. Woodcock dropped out of Detroit City College for financial reasons in 1933 and went to work as a machine assembler; he later joined a small union that eventually became affiliated with the UAW. Woodcock served as an international representative for the UAW from 1940 to 1946 and held a number of posts within the union before being elected its vice president in 1955. He was elevated to president in 1970 and in that year led the union through a highly publicized strike against General Motors Corp., which ended after General Motors agreed to significant wage increases and cost-of-living protection for employees. Woodcock was chosen by Pres. Jimmy Carter to serve as an envoy to China in 1977 and succeeded in negotiating the reestablishment of U.S.-Chinese diplomatic relations. Woodcock served as ambassador to China in 1979–80, after which he worked as an adjunct professor of political science at the University of Michigan at Ann Arbor.

Woods, Donald, South African journalist and antiapartheid campaigner (b. Dec. 15, 1933, Elliotdale, S.Af.—d. Aug. 19, 2001, Sutton, Surrey, Eng.), captured the attention of the world in 1977 with an exposé on the death while in police custody of his friend Steve Biko, a prominent young black activist and founder of the Black Consciousness Movement. Woods, who trained as a lawyer, was a veteran editor (from 1965) of the liberal white *Daily Dispatch* newspaper in East London, S.Af., and was arrested repeatedly by the government for his antiapartheid activities. When he published details regarding Biko's death at the hands of the South African police, Woods was banned and the newspaper was shut down. He escaped to Lesotho and then to the U.K., where he wrote and campaigned for international sanctions against the racist South African government. Woods's book *Biko* (1978) and his personal experiences as described in his autobiography, *Asking for Trouble* (1981), inspired the 1987 film *Cry Freedom*. In 1978 he was the first private citizen invited to address the UN Security Council. Woods was made CBE in 2000, shortly before *Rainbow Nation Revisited* was published.

Wright, L(aurali) R(ose) ("Bunny"), Canadian novelist (b. 1939, Saskatoon, Sask.—d. Feb. 25, 2001, Vancouver, B.C.), was internationally known for her crime novels, many of which featured detective Karl Alberg of the Royal Canadian Mounted Police, Wright's most popular character. Her first novel, *Neighbours* (1979), won the Alberta Best First Novel Award. The first title in her Karl Alberg series, *The Suspect* (1985), was awarded the Mystery Writers of America's Edgar Allen Poe Award for best crime novel. Two later Alberg mysteries, *A Chill Rain in January* (1990) and *Mother Love* (1995), received the Crime Writers of Canada's Arthur Ellis Award. Wright's final novel, *Menace*, was published posthumously.

Xenakis, Iannis, Romanian-born Greek-French composer and architect (b. May 29, 1922, Braila, Rom.—d. Feb. 4, 2001, Paris, France), based his music on mathematical principles, particularly theories of probability. Although his music was generated by the rigorous application of nonmusical ideas, the results were often powerful and moving. He created orchestral, ensemble, and solo works for traditional instruments and also used electronically generated sounds. He studied music as a child, but he was trained principally as an engineer and architect, entering the Polytechnic School in Athens in 1940. A member of the Greek resistance during World War II, he was wounded in 1945 and lost sight in one eye. He received a degree in 1947 but, under a sentence of death for his political activities, fled to Paris. From 1947 to 1959 he worked at the studio of Swiss architect Le Corbusier; there Xenakis was involved in the design of projects that included the Philips Pavilion at the 1958 Brussels World's Fair. During this time he also studied with a number of prominent French musicians, including Olivier Messiaen, and in 1953–54 he completed *Metastasis*, a work for orchestra and his first to gain widespread attention. Other early works included *Pithoprakta*, for trombones, percussion, and strings, which George Balanchine later combined with *Metastasis* to form a ballet. *Concerto PH*, using the amplified sound of burning charcoal, was created for the Philips Pavilion. Xenakis also produced electronic music to accompany laser projections, as at the site of ancient Persepolis, now in Iran, in 1971. He created a number of works for solo percussion, as well as *Pleiades* for percussion sextet, along with works using literary texts. In 1966 he formed a centre for the study of mathematical music. He taught at Indiana University at Bloomington (1967–72) and at the Sorbonne (1973–89).

Musical innovator Iannis Xenakis

Hulton-Deutsch Collection/Corbis

Yardley, John Finley, American aeronautical engineer (b. Feb. 1, 1925, St. Louis, Mo.—d. June 26, 2001, Chesterfield, Mo.), was responsible for helping to coordinate the first manned spaceflights conducted by the U.S. Yardley began his career as a structural and aeronautical engineer at McDonnell Aircraft Corp. in 1946. He was recruited as a project engineer in the U.S. space program in 1958. After managing the launching operations for the Mercury series of manned spaceflights from 1961 to 1963, he served as technical director of the Gemini program from 1964 to 1967. As an associate administrator for spaceflights for NASA from 1974 to 1981, he helped develop the space shuttle program and oversaw the launch in 1981 of *Columbia*, the first reusable rocket-launched space vehicle. That same year he returned to work at McDonnell Douglas; he retired from the company as senior vice president in 1989.

Ze'evi, Rechavam, Israeli soldier and politician (b. Aug. 20, 1926, Jerusalem, Palestine—d. Oct. 17, 2001, Jerusalem, Israel), pursued hard-line ultranationalist policies, most notably in support of his outspoken belief that all Palestinians should be removed from the Israel-occupied territories in Gaza and the West Bank and transferred to Arab countries and his claim that the kingdom of Jordan should belong to Israel. Ze'evi joined the fight for an independent Israel at age 18 and rose through the army ranks to become military commander in the West Bank. After retiring as a major general in 1974, he served (1974–77) as an antiterrorism adviser to Prime Minister Yitzhak Rabin. In 1988 Ze'evi, who often drew criticism for his inflammatory remarks, entered politics at the head of the tiny ultranationalist Moledet (Homeland) party. Two days after he resigned as minister for tourism, Ze'evi was shot dead, reportedly by the militant Popular Front for the Liberation of Palestine in retaliation for the Israeli assassination of PFLP leader Abu Ali Mustafa (*q.v.*).

Zubkovskaya, Inna (Inna Borisovna Izraelyeva), Russian ballerina and teacher (b. Nov. 29, 1923, Moscow, U.S.S.R.—d. Feb. 5, 2001, St. Petersburg, Russia), as a member of the Kirov (now Mariinsky) Ballet from 1941 to 1970, distinguished herself in most of the leading roles in the classic ballets, including Phrygia in *Spartacus*, one of the roles created on her. She continued to teach and coach until her death.

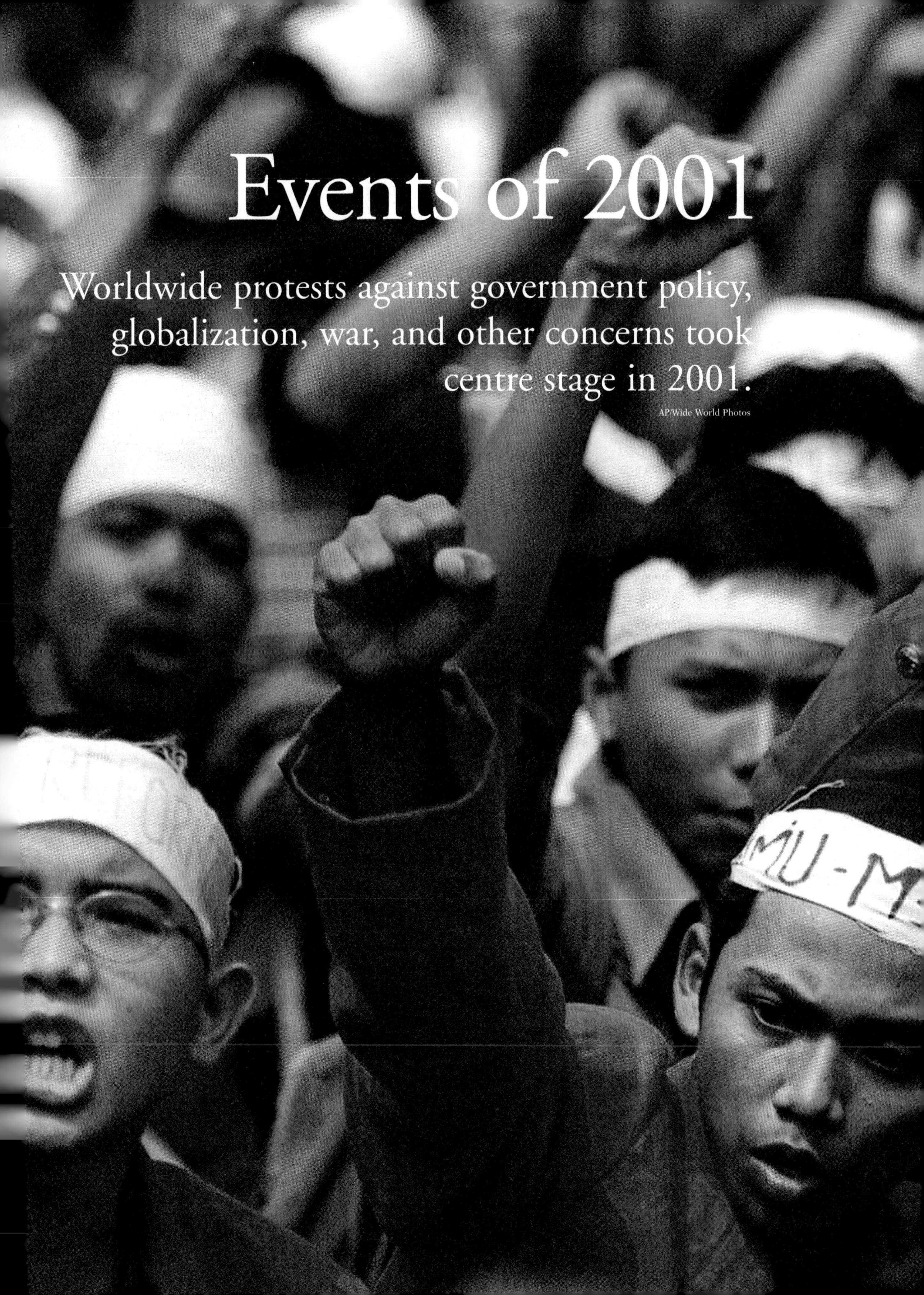

Events of 2001

Worldwide protests against government policy, globalization, war, and other concerns took centre stage in 2001.

AP/Wide World Photos

Agriculture and Food Supplies

Food **SUPPLIES** in 2001 were plentiful, and **PRICES** remained low. The **WTO** adjudicated trade **DISPUTES** between the U.S. and Europe, while many Europeans stopped eating **BEEF** because of livestock **DISEASES**. Agriculture felt the tugs of a **DECLINING** world **ECONOMY**.

NATIONAL AND INTERNATIONAL ISSUES

Food Production. Total agricultural and food production increased slightly in 2001, while global per capita food production was 1.1% lower. (*See* TABLE I.) Taken together, less-developed countries increased output, while production in developed countries was slightly lower; per capita food production in both regions fell.

Two regions had persistently weak production compared with the 1989–91 period. Transitional countries in the former Soviet Union and Eastern Europe continued to have agricultural and food production at levels 70% of those for 1989–91, and little recovery was evident in 2001. These countries faced agricultural bottlenecks due to poor infrastructure, weak credit markets, underdeveloped input and land markets, weak macroeconomic performance, and incomplete privatization. Moreover, reduced agricultural production in some of these economies may have been affected by market forces. Production difficulties experienced by sub-Saharan Africa during the 1990s also continued into the new millennium. Some African countries expanded total output but saw declining per capita output, primarily because of quickly rising populations. Other countries experienced total and per capita output declines owing to environmental degradation and war. In the Democratic Republic of the Congo, per capita food output was 37% lower than in 1989–91. Ethiopia experienced a substantial fall in per capita output beginning in 1997 as a result of drought and its war with Eritrea.

Food Aid. International food aid continued to be critical for several countries. (*See* TABLE II.) Shipments of cereal grains for aid in 2000–01 declined sharply from the previous year, largely owing to reduced contributions from the United States. The U.S. remained the largest international donor, but American shipments fell by 35%. Meanwhile, Japan moved past the European Union (EU) to become the second largest donor.

The main aid recipients were largely the same as in previous years. Somalia

Table I. Selected Indexes of World Agricultural and Food Production (1989–91 = 100)

	Total agricultural production					Total food production					Per capita food production				
Region and country	**1997**	**1998**	**1999**	**2000**	**2001**	**1997**	**1998**	**1999**	**2000**	**2001**	**1997**	**1998**	**1999**	**2000**	**2001**
Developed countries	**98.9**	**98.1**	**99.8**	**100.7**	**99.9**	**99.6**	**99.0**	**100.7**	**101.7**	**100.6**	**96.1**	**95.2**	**96.5**	**97.1**	**95.9**
Australia	118.3	123.5	131.5	131.2	132.6	129.6	136.8	147.4	146.1	146.8	118.2	123.4	131.4	128.9	128.2
Canada	116.2	124.0	131.7	132.6	120.2	116.1	123.7	131.7	133.2	120.5	107.4	113.4	119.7	120.0	107.6
European Union	102.2	102.5	104.9	105.0	103.4	102.2	102.4	104.7	104.9	103.3	99.6	99.6	101.7	101.7	100.0
Japan	95.2	91.0	92.3	91.7	91.0	95.6	91.5	92.8	92.2	91.6	93.6	89.4	90.4	89.6	88.8
South Africa	100.8	95.8	101.8	105.6	99.3	103.6	98.2	104.2	108.9	102.2	90.9	84.7	88.6	91.4	84.8
Transition countries	72.5	67.6	68.0	67.9	70.8	73.7	68.6	69.0	69.0	71.6	73.3	68.3	68.8	68.8	71.6
United States	118.7	119.5	120.9	123.6	120.6	118.6	120.7	121.6	124.6	121.4	110.0	110.8	110.4	112.0	108.2
Less-developed countries	**131.0**	**134.8**	**138.9**	**141.2**	**142.7**	**132.8**	**137.2**	**141.8**	**144.0**	**145.5**	**117.5**	**119.5**	**121.4**	**121.5**	**120.8**
Argentina	122.4	131.7	134.8	134.1	139.1	125.0	135.0	139.1	139.1	144.4	114.1	121.6	123.8	122.3	125.4
Bangladesh	111.6	114.4	127.0	130.4	129.1	111.3	115.2	129.0	132.4	130.9	94.9	96.1	105.4	106.0	102.6
Brazil	126.5	128.8	139.2	145.0	148.7	130.1	131.4	142.1	147.3	151.6	117.4	117.1	124.9	127.9	129.9
China	153.9	159.8	164.1	169.5	173.5	157.2	165.4	170.6	175.7	179.5	146.1	152.4	155.8	159.1	161.3
Congo, Dem. Rep. of the	93.7	93.4	90.4	87.8	87.8	94.5	94.6	91.8	89.6	89.6	74.1	72.4	68.6	65.1	63.2
Egypt	141.8	140.5	149.0	152.2	152.2	143.5	144.2	153.2	156.7	156.7	125.5	123.8	129.2	129.8	127.6
Ethiopia	124.8	115.7	122.5	118.6	118.6	126.1	116.2	123.4	119.4	119.4	102.6	92.2	95.6	90.2	88.1
India	121.1	122.0	127.3	126.8	125.3	121.7	122.2	127.8	127.8	126.0	107.1	105.8	108.7	107.0	103.8
Indonesia	119.4	117.2	119.5	121.4	122.4	119.8	117.2	120.1	122.2	123.4	107.4	103.6	104.7	105.1	104.8
Malaysia	121.2	119.2	124.6	127.4	131.8	131.2	130.1	138.7	142.8	148.4	112.0	108.8	113.6	114.7	117.1
Mexico	121.8	122.9	128.2	131.8	134.8	122.7	123.8	130.1	134.4	137.4	108.4	107.5	111.3	113.2	114.0
Nigeria	142.8	149.2	153.3	157.2	157.2	143.2	149.7	153.8	157.8	157.8	117.4	119.4	119.4	119.2	116.1
Philippines	122.3	112.5	123.7	126.6	126.5	123.9	113.8	125.8	129.0	128.6	106.1	95.5	103.5	104.1	101.8
Turkey	108.5	116.4	110.4	109.6	108.4	107.7	116.0	110.1	109.2	107.9	95.0	100.7	94.0	91.9	89.5
Venezuela	117.7	113.2	117.5	115.2	115.4	119.3	114.9	119.7	117.8	117.5	102.1	96.4	98.4	95.0	93.0
Vietnam	143.5	150.7	162.0	170.2	167.3	138.8	146.2	155.9	160.3	155.8	122.1	126.9	133.5	135.5	130.0
World	**116.5**	**118.2**	**121.2**	**122.9**	**123.3**	**117.5**	**119.6**	**122.8**	**124.5**	**124.8**	**106.1**	**106.5**	**107.9**	**108.0**	**106.9**

Source: World Wide Web site for UN Food and Agriculture Organization: <http://apps.fao.org> (Dec. 14, 2001).

faced drought and war and was a major target of aid programs. Although North Korea's harvest improved in 2001, that country continued to be short of food and sought assistance through the UN's World Food Programme. When Hurricane Michelle damaged Cuban agriculture, U.S. producers sold food to Cuba despite the trade embargo that had been in effect since the early 1960s. Fighting in Afghanistan and a huge refugee population created a food emergency, for which the U.S. and other donor countries provided supplies. At the time the U.S. bombing began, food-aid packets were also delivered by air drop, but ground fighting disrupted the delivery of food and other aid to civilians.

World Trade Organization. The members of the World Trade Organization (WTO) met in Qatar in November and launched a new round of global trade liberalization negotiations. China and Taiwan were both accepted for WTO membership. Problem areas in agricultural trade negotiations were discussed, including further limits on export subsidies.

During 2001 the WTO heard a number of international trade disputes. The U.S. complained about Mexico's adoption of tariff measures against the U.S., Canadian dairy policy, and South Korean beef-import rules. Argentina and the EU quarreled over import barriers on bovine hides, while the EU and the U.S. confronted each other over wheat gluten and continued their long-running dispute over the EU ban on hormone-treated beef. The U.S. had filed a case in the WTO against the EU banana-import policy that relied on import quotas for various countries. The WTO had ruled in favour of the U.S., but the EU had not complied. In April the parties agreed that the EU would adopt a tariff-only import regime effective Jan. 1, 2006, and until then would institute a system of licensing based on historical trade levels, with increased quotas for Latin American bananas.

In July 1999 the U.S. had introduced import barriers against lamb meat to protect its domestic industry. Australia and New Zealand filed complaints that were upheld by the WTO, and in November the U.S. restrictions were removed.

Agricultural Policy. U.S. farm-support regulations, which were to expire in 2002, had been adopted in 1996 when global agricultural markets were tight and farm prices were strong. Since 1998, however, Congress had been obligated to provide special annual supplemental assistance and spend far more than anticipated to maintain adequate levels of farm income. New legislation passed by the House of Representatives in October 2001 formalized this supplemental spending and made a 10-year commitment to continue substantial government subsidies to farming. Another concern in the U.S. was the granting of trade-promotion authority. The U.S. was finding itself at a disadvantage when it participated in WTO talks to liberalize agricultural trade. Other countries were reluctant to negotiate with the executive branch when it was Congress that enjoyed the authority of final approval of trade agreements. Pres. George W. Bush sought the renewal of presidential authority for "fast-track" trade negotiation, which had lapsed in the mid-1990s, but the measure was controversial and opposed by groups that opposed liberalizing trade. On December 6 the House approved trade-promotion authority by a one-vote margin, but by year's end the Senate had yet to consider the matter.

Agricultural policy was proving a significant obstacle to the ongoing negotiations to enlarge the EU to embrace Central and Eastern European countries. EU farm-support policies were quite generous to farmers but were costly, consuming about half of the EU's annual budget. A number of the countries that were seeking admission had large agricultural sectors, and some, such as Poland, had numerous small farms. If the existing EU farm policy was expanded to take in those countries, cost would rise steeply. Farm policy reform was unpopular with EU farmers, but farmers in countries applying for membership wanted equal treatment, even while fearing competition with highly efficient, highly subsidized Western European agriculture.

Livestock Diseases. Foot-and-mouth disease (FMD) outbreaks occurred in many countries, including Great Britain and Argentina, beginning in late February. (*See* Special Report.) Measures were quickly undertaken to restrict the spread of the disease. Infected animals in Britain were placed in quarantine and slaughtered. Britain destroyed over four million animals, or about 8% of its animal inventory. Movements of products in rural areas were restricted or banned, and tourists were prohibited from visiting certain areas; large economic losses resulted. Fresh meat exports from countries with the infection were banned, and travelers faced increased security. Although FMD is rarely transmissible to humans, the outbreaks following the experience with bovine spongiform encephalopathy (BSE) caused a reduction in European meat consumption. By late summer the disease appeared to have been contained, and few new cases were being reported.

In late September BSE, which does seem to be transmissible to humans, appeared in Japan. Demand for beef in Japan plummeted; wholesale beef prices fell by 50%; and other countries prohibited beef imports from Japan. Although Japan was a large net importer of beef, it exported some specialty beef products.

Hong Kong experienced an outbreak of influenza in poultry, and about one million birds were eradicated. Trade in poultry meat through Hong Kong was disrupted as China tightened inspections on poultry originating in Hong Kong and on frozen poultry from other countries transported through Hong Kong. South Korea, the Philippines, and Japan banned poultry imports from Hong Kong, and Taiwan introduced tighter screening of travelers.

(continued on page 156)

Table II. Shipment of Food Aid in Cereals[1] (in 000,000 metric tons)

	1997–98	1998–99	1999–2000	2000–01
Shipments from				
United States	2,787	6,403	7,247	4,697
Canada	384	332	421	192
European Union	890	1,557	1,387	707
Norway	45	65	63	58
Switzerland	42	37	47	25
Australia	296	267	264	240
Japan	356	1,149	331	720
Others	1,441	1,440	1,408	1,825
Total	**6,241**	**11,250**	**11,168**	**8,464**
Shipments to				
To LIFDC[2]	5,480	8,404	7,561	7,399
Sub-Saharan Africa	*2,172*	*2,530*	*2,853*	*2,733*
To other countries	761	2,876	3,607	1,065

[1]July–June years. [2]Low-income food-deficit countries.
Source: World Wide Web site for UN Food and Agriculture Organization: <http://apps.fao.org> (Dec. 14, 2001).

Trouble on the Hoof: Disease Outbreaks in Europe

by Brian J. Ford

Farmers rarely celebrate good fortune in the modern world, but British agriculture seemed to be emerging from a period of darkness as 2001 began. The scourge of "mad cow" disease was in retreat.

After mad cow disease (bovine spongiform encephalopathy [BSE]) had first been causally related to a human brain illness in March 1996, British beef farming had plunged into crisis. It was evident that eating infected beef in Great Britain had led to a newly recognized fatal illness in humans, initially dubbed new variant Creutzfeldt-Jakob disease ($_{nv}$CJD) and later shortened to variant CJD (vCJD).

Sufferers of vCJD have an average age of around 30. When stricken, they become depressed and apprehensive, and they suffer delusions of being attacked and persecuted by others. They lose the ability to walk and howl like animals as they wither. No cure has been found and little treatment is available.

The causative agent of vCJD is a prion, a form of infectious protein devoid of any genetic material, that causes malformation of brain cells. There are other theories, including one that posits that organophosphate pesticides have given rise to vCJD, but these pesticides are in use elsewhere around the world, and yet vCJD is confined to Britain. Only in the U.K. has the processing of animal feed dramatically changed. Since the early 1980s lower processing temperatures have been authorized, and it is claimed that this allows infectious prions to spread. The incidence of vCJD in Britons rose to a total of about 90 cases at the start of 2001, but it was still showing no signs of the widely forecast dramatic increase. The prions seemed, to humans, to be mercifully uninfectious.

The annual cases of BSE in British cattle rose from 447 by the end of 1987 to 37,280 in 1992. From that date the incidence fell until by the start of 2001 the annual figure was down to 1,537 cases. The figure continued to fall. In the final week of March—five years since the link between BSE and disease in humans had been announced—there were only five new cases of BSE reported. By June, however, the unthinkable had happened: there were 214 new cases of BSE in Britain, while mainland Europe, which had remained largely free of BSE and had placed severe restrictions on the U.K. meat producers ever since the epidemic emerged, now had more confirmed cases—313—than the U.K.

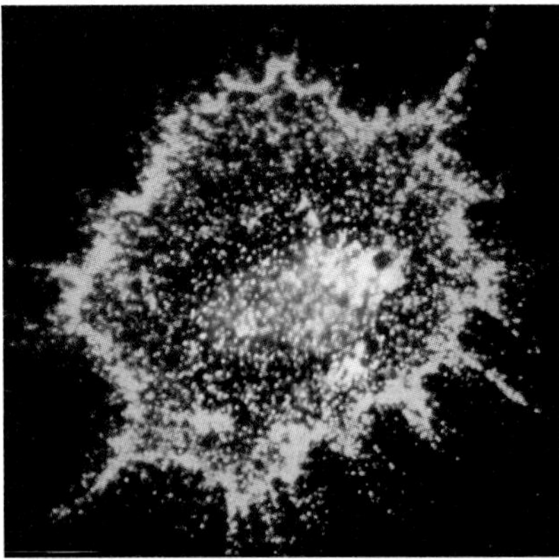

Prions (shown in gold) are thought to be the pathogenic agents of diseases such as variant Creutzfeldt-Jakob disease.

James King-Holmes/Institute of Animal Health/Science Photo Library, Photo Researchers

In the meantime, the hopes prevailing early in the year had already been dashed by a devastating outbreak of foot-and-mouth disease (also known as hoof-and-mouth disease in the U.S.). According to the Northumberland (Eng.) County Council, a farmer had been illegally feeding unprocessed kitchen waste to his pigs. Among the scraps was meat from a restaurant that had illicitly imported supplies of produce from East Asia, and some of this was infected with the virus.

Council officials who were prosecuting the farmer stated that he had noticed symptoms among his pigs but did not report them. As his animals were moved from farm to marketplace, the virus spread, and within weeks Britain was in the throes of the outbreak. British agriculture was crippled once again.

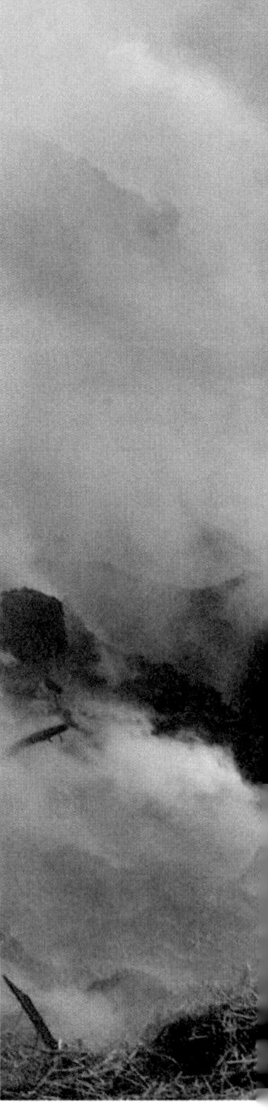

A government ban on the movement of livestock meant that newborn lambs were left to die in the wet mud of open ground instead of being returned to the warmth and safety of the lambing shed. Slaughtermen at infected farms killed all the animals they found. Thousands of decomposing carcasses were left piled high in farmyards. In July the government canceled the sterilization of infected farms because of the high cost involved. A ban on exports meant that British farmers once more had no access to the open market.

Foot-and-mouth disease had last caused a major outbreak in the U.S. in 1929. It was one of the illnesses most feared by farmers. Infected animals dribble saliva and develop sores on hooves and around the mouth. Curiously, the disease is rarely fatal. Tropical animals carry the virus as a matter of course, and in water buffaloes it produces few effects. The worldwide extent of the virus means that there will be no end to it in the foreseeable future.

For months the story was featured in the media, but eventually the press coverage diminished. Many people imagined that the disease outbreak had been controlled, yet figures from the U.K.'s new Department for Environment, Food and Rural Affairs—which replaced the Ministry of Agriculture,

Hundreds of slaughtered cows are burned near Elonby, Eng., in April to help prevent the spread of foot-and-mouth disease.

AP/Wide World Photos

Fisheries and Food following the British general election in June 2001—showed that there were between three and five new outbreaks in some parts of the U.K. every day. Among those were 12 new cases in Cumbria and 17 in Yorkshire.

In July sheep grazing free on the Brecon Beacons in Wales were corralled together and tested for the virus; 10% of them showed positive results. The rural affairs minister for Wales, Carwyn Jones, announced that the unfenced sheep would be slaughtered. The survival of the British landscape depends on grazing animals. From the sweeping grandeur of the Lake District to the rugged headlands of Cornwall and the wild Welsh hills, grazing sheep and cattle are the principal agents of land management.

By midyear almost five million animals had been slaughtered. Stories circulated of farmers' buying infected sheep in order to claim compensation. Fears of a resurgence in the fall, when animals were brought down from the hills, proved to be unfounded, and by mid-January 2002 the British farm herds were declared officially free of infection.

Nations around the world adopted antivirus measures, with disinfecting hand washes and shoe mats imposed upon tourists. Most governments in areas normally free from the virus relied on a policy of slaughtering infected herds whenever there was an outbreak. This method worked when outbreaks were rare, but many observers expected that the practice of vaccination might become necessary in the future. Meanwhile, the global reach of the Internet has given people the chance to import exotic meats from around the world—free of import restrictions and usually falsely labeled. This fact leads to speculation that local diseases could become global epidemics in the new millennium.

The effect of foot-and-mouth disease on tourism is severe, despite the fact that there are very few cases of the disease infecting people, and the human illness is fleeting and mild. The tourism industry has lost millions, and for all the promises of financial assistance offered by the British government, little benefit was reported by rural communities themselves. Some apparently unrelated businesses also face extinction. Hot-air balloon companies, for example, have been unable to operate, and thousands of employees have been laid off. The Institute of Directors claimed that the total cost of the epidemic would be £20 billion (about $30 billion).

Nearing year's end, the number of victims of vCJD rose beyond 100. They were not the only people to die. After watching in utter despair as their livestock were shot, more than 100 British farmers turned their shotguns on themselves.

Brian J. Ford is a biologist and the author of many books, including BSE: The Facts *(1996) and* The Future of Food *(2000).*

(continued from page 153)

Global Economic Developments. Agricultural trade was adversely affected by global economic developments in 2001, notably the spread of recession. Consumption of agricultural products is linked to income. As incomes fall, demand for agricultural goods declines and trade shrinks. In 2001 every major economy experienced weaker economic activity, and a recession began in the United States in March. The terrorist attacks in September further weakened both the U.S. and the world economies. Japan continued to have a poor economic performance, and European economies saw lower growth rates. Reduced U.S. imports of technology lowered growth in Pacific Rim countries. Argentina was mired in a multiyear recession and by the end of the year was facing a default on $132 billion in international debt obligations.

Currency values affect international trade for agricultural products. Most trade occurs in U.S. dollars, and a strong U.S. dollar weakens the purchasing power of countries importing U.S. agricultural goods. While the U.S. dollar weakened during much of the year, it remained high by historical standards and strengthened against the currencies of rival exporting countries, which thus reduced the competitiveness abroad of U.S. agricultural products.

Mormon crickets like this one—which was found in a barley field in Idaho—caused millions of dollars of crop damage in Utah and Nevada during 2001.

Agricultural Research Service, USDA

GLOBAL MARKETS IN 2001

Grains, Oilseeds, and Livestock. Global production of grains and oilseed was higher in 2001, and prices for farm commodities remained weak. World grain production in the 2001 crop year rose from 1,836,000,000 tons to 1,843,000,000 tons (tons here and throughout are metric tons). Coarse grains output was 2% higher. Coarse grain production in the U.S. fell 11 million tons, or 1%, from the large 2000 crop. Major exporters had smaller coarse grains crops, but several key importing countries harvested larger crops. Russia, Ukraine, and other Eastern European countries had significantly larger harvests. China recovered from a drought, and 2001 production was up by two million tons. World rice production dropped 1.1%. This was the second year of smaller global rice production and marked a break with the steadily rising harvests experienced in the 1990s. World wheat production fell nearly 1% to 577 million tons, dragged down by the decline in the U.S. The U.S. had been experiencing a long-run decline in area planted in wheat because farmers found other crops more attractive. Improved wheat crops were recorded by Eastern Europe, North Africa, Russia, and Kazakhstan. Chinese wheat production decreased from 100 million tons to 94 million tons. India and Pakistan saw output declines of 10%. World coarse grains trade fell 4%. Rice trade remained 24 million tons. With reduced global production, world wheat trade was 4% higher. With global wheat consumption greater than production, global stocks fell to the lowest level since 1995–96. Even with a larger global coarse grains crop, expanded consumption in 2001–02 reduced stocks. For rice, growing use combined with lower output caused a stock reduction. The tightening global supply and use balance caused higher wheat and coarse grains prices; however, price levels remained low.

World oilseed production had continuously increased since 1991, and production expanded by 3.6% in 2001, a new record. The U.S. harvested a huge soybean crop, 4.8% above even the large 2000 crop. Soybean outputs in Argentina and Brazil were also large. Oilseed trade rose 5.6%, and ending stocks were 1.9% lower. Oilseed meal and vegetable oil outputs rose with trade increasing owing to expansion of meal and oil use. Prices remained low.

Global meat production expanded in 2001. Beef and pork output rose by nearly 1% to 133.1 million tons. That rise was not matched by increased demand, however, and trade in meat dropped from 9.1 million tons to 8.8 million tons. Both global production and trade of poultry meat expanded. Output increased 2.8%, and trade was 3% higher, which resulted in a 3% increase in consumption. Worldwide output of dairy products grew; cow's milk output was greater in 2001 at 378.5 million tons, compared with 377.1 million tons in 2000. Production declines in the U.S. and the EU were offset by increased production in Oceania. The U.S. and the EU saw butter production decline because of low prices relative to other dairy products, but trade in butter remained unchanged. Cheese production grew 2%, but total world exports were unchanged because increases from Oceania were offset by reduced EU trade. Nonfat dry milk production was 5% below the 2000 level owing to lower milk and stable cheese output in the U.S. and the EU and to expectations that prospects for nonfat dry milk were not as favourable as those for cheese.

Tropical Products. World sugar production for 2001–02 was down 2% from the previous year. Brazilian output, down sharply in 2000–01, recovered by 8.1% in 2001–02, while EU sugar production during the year fell 12.5% below the 2000–01 level. At 34.2 million tons, global sugar trade was down by 2 million tons. Brazilian exports rose 23%, but exports from the EU dropped 44%. World sugar consumption in 2001–02 rose by 1.5%. Owing to the tighter global supply, prices that had been low for two years strengthened somewhat.

Coffee production in 2001–02 rose slightly above the level of the previous year. This, added to the large beginning stock, meant that total supply was 4% greater. Brazilian coffee output was 1% lower, but large stocks permitted a 16% increase in exports. These large supplies put downward pressure on coffee prices worldwide. In September 2000 the Association of Coffee Producing Countries agreed to reduce export supplies by 20% in order to boost prices, but one year later, with prices at new lows, the attempt was abandoned. Some members could not bear the costs of withholding coffee exports as nonmembers expanded their exports to take up the slack.

(PHILIP L. PAARLBERG)

FISHERIES

Production trends for the top ten catching nations, 1990–99 (in metric tons)

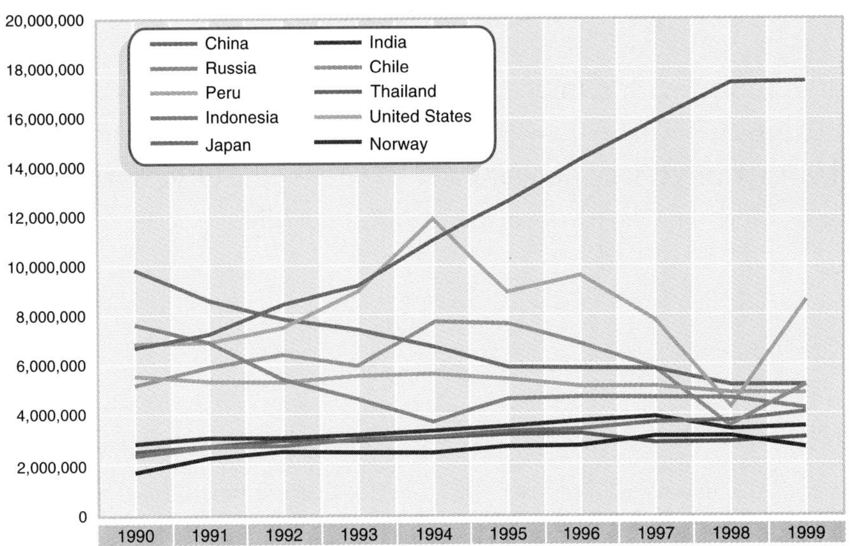

Catch trends for the top five caught fish species, 1990–99 (in metric tons)

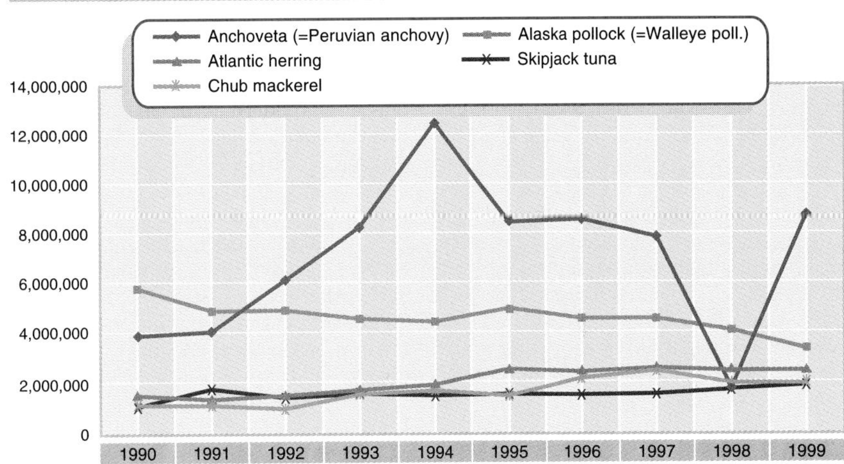

Total world production (aquaculture and capture fisheries) (in metric tons)

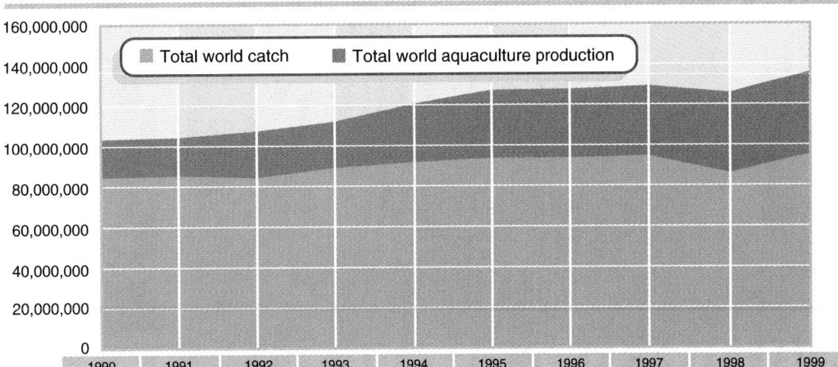

Total world fish-catch figures for 1999, the latest year for which figures were available in 2001, were finalized by the UN Food and Agriculture Organization and showed a recovery from the disastrous effects of the El Niño weather patterns the previous year to reach 92,866,600 metric tons. The total catch of fish, crustaceans, and mollusks from marine and inland waters rose 7% over the 1998 figure of 86,933,100 metric tons. (*See* GRAPH.)

The leading fishing nation in 1999 again was China, with a figure of 17,240,000 metric tons. (*See* GRAPH.) This total was similar to the 1998 figure and was expected to remain relatively constant while the country's main focus remained the continued growth in farmed production. There was also an increase in China's farmed production to a massive 22,790,000 metric tons.

Peru recovered second position in the world catch league in 1999 with a haul of 8,430,000 metric tons, a staggering 94% increase over the previous year, when El Niño decimated the anchoveta stocks off the Pacific coast of South America. (*See* GRAPH.) While the recovery was welcome for the Peruvian fishing fleet and fishmeal industry, it would go only a short way to offset the debts incurred by the industry when El Niño's warm waters devastated the fish catch.

Chile, which was also affected by the decline in anchoveta resources, recorded a large recovery with a 55% rise to 5,050,528 from 3,265,383 metric tons in 1998. Despite this, there was continued serious concern over the country's jack mackerel stocks, which registered a 30% decrease in catch from 2,060,000 metric tons in 1998 to 1,420,000 metric tons in 1999. Tight fishing controls on the jack mackerel fishery were in place.

The U.S. managed only a 2% increase in its catch of 4,749,645 metric tons. Russia, which was dependent on its Alaska pollock catch, reported a 7% decrease to 4,141,157 metric tons. The Russian fishing industry was finding the going tough, and unless it could reverse the trend, it was likely to find itself below 4,000,000 metric tons. A change in economic policy by the Russian Central Fisheries Committee had left the industry having to cope with high fuel prices and bid for its fishing quotas against foreign fishing interests in government-organized auctions.

Morocco, in 25th place with a relatively modest catch of 750,000 metric tons, was growing in importance. In 2001 the European Union failed to agree on the renewal of a third-party access agreement with Morocco that would allow significant access to Spanish and Portuguese vessels. Morocco was therefore preparing to see its own landings rise significantly in the coming years.

(MARTIN GILL)

Anthropology and Archaeology

The multiregional theory of human **ORIGINS** gained support during the year. A new exhibition commemorated the 100th anniversary of **MARGARET MEAD**'s birth. Discoveries also shed new light on ancient **MAYA CULTURE**.

ANTHROPOLOGY

Physical Anthropology. The year 2001 turned out to be an extraordinary period for the study of human origins. An Australian research team published a molecular analysis of mitochondrial DNA (mtDNA) extracted from 10 southeastern Australian skeletal remains dating from approximately 2,000 to 60,000 years before the present (BP). Six specimens came from Kow Swamp, while four were from Lake Mungo in the Willandra Lakes region. The Lake Mungo 3 individual yielded a consensus date of 62,000 (±6,000) years BP and was considered to be the oldest accurately dated anatomically modern human from which DNA had been successfully recovered. The key finding was that the Lake Mungo 3 mtDNA differed greatly from the mtDNA of all living humans as well as from all other fossil mtDNA sequences, including those from three recently analyzed Neanderthal individuals from Germany, Russia, and Croatia. Unexpectedly, the Lake Mungo 3 mtDNA fragment did survive as a geographically widespread remnant inserted on chromosome 11 in the modern human nuclear genome. Although the four Lake Mungo individuals spanned the entire aforementioned time range, they all displayed a modern (gracile) form, while the anatomically more robust Kow Swamp people lived from approximately 8,000 to 15,000 years ago. Five of the six Kow Swamp specimens and the other three Lake Mungo specimens had mtDNA closely related to the mtDNA of living Aboriginal Australians.

The authors proposed that the aberrant Lake Mungo 3 mtDNA lineage probably diverged before the most recent common ancestor of all contemporary mtDNA. Thus, the earliest known human mtDNA lineage occurred in Australia, rather than in Africa, as had been inferred from studies of mtDNA from living populations. Even though this finding did not prove that modern humans originated in Australia, according to one of the authors it provided support for the multiregional theory of human origins rather than for the more widely held out-of-Africa replacement theory.

Also during the year, two new genera of African hominins (a taxonomic grouping that includes modern humans and fossil species more closely related to *Homo sapiens* than to any other living species) were proposed, and additional, older specimens of a previously named genus (*Ardipithecus*) were described. First, a joint French and Kenyan research team published a report based on 13 fossils representing at least five individuals from the Lukeino formation in the Tugen Hills region of Kenya. An isolated molar was described in 1975. Newly discovered fossils found in October and November 2000 included two mandibular fragments (containing a total of three molars), five isolated teeth, three partial femora, the shaft of a humerus, and a finger bone. Volcanic tuffs in the Lukeino formation were radiometrically dated at 5.9 (±0.3) million years, which made these remains the

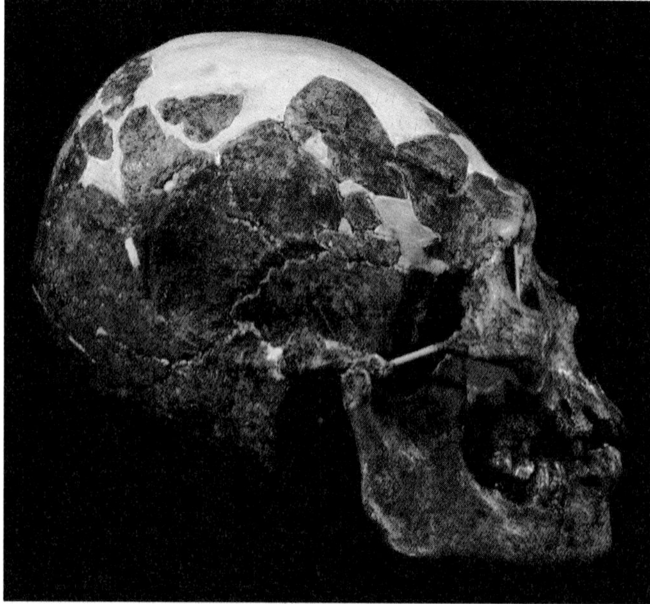

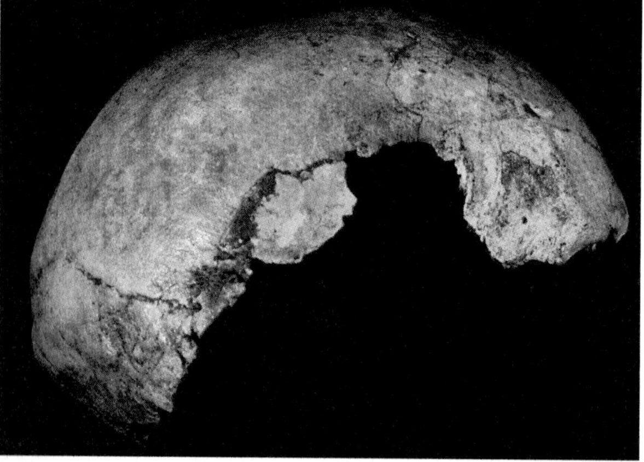

(Left) The age of this skull and mandible specimen from Kow Swamp in southeastern Australia was estimated to be 13,000 years. (Above) The calvarium of the Lake Mungo 3 skeleton.

oldest-known reputed hominins in the fossil record. They were named *Orrorin tugenensis* ("original man" from Tugen). The femora indicated that *Orrorin* was about the size of a female chimpanzee and walked bipedally when on the ground; however, the humerus and finger bone suggested arboreal adaptations and good climbing ability as well. The teeth exhibited a complex mixture of humanlike, apelike, and intermediate characteristics. The small, thickly enameled molars confirmed that this condition was an archaic feature for the lineage that eventually led to *H. sapiens* and implied that the vast majority of the large-molared australopithecines did not have a direct ancestral-descendant relationship with the genus *Homo*.

The second new African hominin taxon was named *Kenyanthropus platyops* ("flat-faced man" from Kenya). An almost complete, though distorted, cranium (WT 40000) was found at Lomekwi on the western side of Lake Turkana. Although more than 30 skull and dental fragments were discovered in 1998 and 1999 at various Lomekwi localities by an international team of researchers, only this 3.5-million-year-old cranium and a 3.3-million-year-old mandibular fragment (WT 38350) were placed in the new taxon. The cranium exhibited derived facial and primitive craniodental features unlike those of its only hominin contemporary, *Australopithecus afarensis*, or of any earlier hominin. The transverse facial contour was flat below the nasal bones, which resulted in a comparatively flat face with only moderate subnasal prognathism. The malar (cheek) region was particularly tall, and there were no large depressions behind the brow ridges. On the other hand, WT 40000 possessed a small chimpanzee-sized brain and had a small, thickly enameled molar, reminiscent of the primitive condition found in *Orrorin*. Of all the subsequent hominin specimens, WT 40000 most closely approximated the overall facial morphology of ER 1470, the 1,870,000-year-old East Turkana specimen currently placed in the taxon *H. rudolfensis*. The authors suggested that in light of the new *Kenyanthropus* material, *Homo rudolfensis* should now be named *Kenyapithecus rudolfensis*.

Eleven new specimens (representing at least five individuals) of *Ardipithecus* from 5.2 million to 5.8 million years BP were discovered between 1997 and 2001 in the Middle Awash area of Ethiopia. This material was associated with a wet woodland paleoenvironment and was thought to represent a new bipedal hominin subspecies, *Ardipithecus ramidus kadabba*. The chief evolutionary lesson provided by the new *Ardipithecus* specimens combined with the discovery of *Orrorin* and *Kenyanthropus* was that the substantial hominin taxonomic diversity characteristic of the time period from 1.5 million to 3 million years ago might also extend back to just after the time that human and chimpanzee lineages diverged, which thereby made the drawing of clear-cut evolutionary connections within the 6-million-year-old hominin lineage an even more difficult endeavour. (*See also* LIFE SCIENCES: *Zoology*.)

(STEPHEN L. ZEGURA)

AP/Wide World Photos

American anthropologist Margaret Mead is pictured on a field trip to Bali in 1957; the year 2001 marked the 100th anniversary of Mead's birth.

Cultural Anthropology. The year 2001 was significant for U.S. anthropology, as it marked both the 100th anniversary of the birth of Margaret Mead and the 100th annual meeting of the American Anthropological Association (AAA), November 28–December 2 in Washington, D.C. To commemorate both, an exhibition entitled "Margaret Mead: Human Nature and the Power of Culture" was organized at the Library of Congress to document Mead's life and works and the events that shaped them. Exhibit curators selected some of the letters, photographs, artworks, films by and about Mead, and field notes to convey to the wider public the scope of Mead's accomplishments and insights. The exhibit was scheduled to run until May 2002. Numerous other exhibits and programs were organized around the world to remember Mead, the best-known and most-engaged and public American anthropologist of the 20th century.

The AAA recognized Laura Nader, a social and cultural anthropologist from the University of California, Berkeley, with its highest honour by inviting her to deliver the Distinguished Lecture at its November 2000 meeting. Nader gave an overview of anthropology by discussing issues concerning ethics, ethnography, and fieldwork. This emphasis continued the effort to redirect American anthropology to its empirical foundations as well as to public and world issues.

In June 2001 a conference was held in Agrigento, Italy, on "Children and Young People in a Changing World: A Holistic Approach." The meeting was cosponsored by the International Union of Anthropological and Ethnographical Studies and the University of Florence's International Institute for the Study of Man, which produces the *International Journal of Anthropology*. The Agrigento conference discussed the effects on children and young people of such developments as the rise of new nationalisms and cultural diversity. Some stressed the environments in which children are raised, focusing on such subjects as high stress levels among single mothers in Australia, adolescent children of divorced parents in Mexico, and women in the U.S. caught between raising children and caring for aging parents. One study compared children's stages of physical development in New Guinea and in the U.S. and challenged claims that child development is the same everywhere. For example, despite claims by some physicians and researchers, this study argued, an infant's crawling stage is not universal.

Overall, presentations warned against hegemony of models from a few countries or international organizations and the imposition of social programs without prior careful studies that take into account local practices and knowledge. It was strongly recommended that youths be involved in social programs intended for them. From Egypt a visual ethnographic study of a birth ceremony showed how the family functions as the locus of identity and as the basis of the cultural construction of childhood through which the transmission of values and ideals takes place.

A different situation was presented regarding postcommunist southeastern Europe as well as postapartheid South Africa. Remedies for the social crisis in southeastern Europe are not readily available, since key cultural institutions lay dormant for many years under communism. In what could be described as a transitional situation there, children had to work because of low family incomes, so the social structure changed from children-oriented to non-children-oriented. Consequently, children spent more time in the streets and exhibited new patterns of aggression, including sexual abuse and other dysfunctional behaviours, such as involvement in the male sex industry and the trafficking of young women and drugs. A shift in the Balkan countries from coexistence of ethnicities to nationalism and a new focus on homogeneity of ethnic groups had implications for inclusion and exclusion in societies, presenting conflict for people with local identities and displaced children.

In New York City in September, the 54th Annual DPI/NGO Conference for nongovernmental organizations associated with the United Nations Department of Public Information heard an anthropological paper on "Roots of Volunteerism in Arabo-Islamic Society & Culture: Insights from the Bottom Up," read by Fadwa El Guindi. She made the point that the notion of "civil society," which had been adopted by international institutions, was merely a new name for age-old practices in traditional societies and that the notion of "diversity" must be accompanied by the established fact of "a common humanity." In their work UN organizations and committees could and should benefit from voluntary participation of local citizens already part of their traditional practices—i.e., establish volunteerism from the bottom up.

Renewed scholarly energy—and a resurgence of old concerns—in visual anthropology was manifest in the increase in book-length publications and in a recent international conference. "Beyond Picturing Culture: A Critique of a Critique," published in the *American Anthropologist* in June, included all prominent founders and theorists in the field of visual anthropology and practitioners of ethnographic film and photography worldwide. Discussions ranged from personal narratives, to the role of ethnographic film, to photography as a research tool. Plans were made to publish the proceedings of this seminal meeting. (FADWA EL GUINDI)

ARCHAEOLOGY

Eastern Hemisphere. The dawn of the new millennium proved bountiful for Old World archaeology. Nauticos, a deep-ocean exploration firm hired to recover an Israeli submarine that had sunk in the eastern Mediterranean, found instead the remains of a 2,300-year-old shipwreck that had foundered in 3,000 m (1 m=3.28 ft) of water. Located between Alexandria, Egypt, and the Greek island of Rhodes, the ship, an estimated 26 m long and 16 m wide, challenged a long-held assumption that ancient mariners lacked the navigational skills necessary to sail great distances over open water and were thus restricted to coastal sailing.

Neolithic rock paintings and carvings found on the Greek island of Andros showed a level of Stone Age art previously unknown in the Aegean. The petroglyphs, believed to date to between 4500 and 3300 BC, included images of six ships, measuring between 20 and 30 cm (7.8 and 11.8 in), geometric shapes that may represent the Aegean, and 17 animals, including deer. Archaeologists believed they collectively constituted a larger composition, the earliest complex rendering ever found in the Cyclades. A 5th-century BC gold wreath was discovered by a farmer plowing his fields in Apollonia, near Thessaloniki, Greece. Composed of 30 hammered gold ivy leaves and two bunches of molded berries, the well-preserved wreath was similar to two gold wreaths previously discovered in the region.

A memo signed by the Egyptian queen Cleopatra VII was discovered among hundreds of documents recycled for use in the construction of a mummy case found by a German expedition at Abusir in 1904. Now in the collection of Berlin's Ägyptisches Museum und Papyrussammlung, the two-column text was dated to Feb. 23, 33 BC.

The excavation of some 3,000 mid-2nd-century BC bullae, or clay document seals, within an administrative building that was destroyed by fire in c. 145 BC at Tel Kadesh in Israel's northern Galilee suggested that the Phoenicians had continued to exercise their cultural and religious authority in the region much longer than previously thought.

In Great Britain a number of Roman finds came to light, including two waterwheels dating to between AD 63 and 108, which were unearthed within ancient wells in London and were the first of their kind to be discovered in the U.K. The waterwheels apparently had been powered by slaves walking on treadmills. More recently, a contractor outside the village of Lopen happened upon a Roman mosaic; it measured 6 × 10 m and featured a dolphin, wine urns, and twining vines. The floor had apparently been made by craftsmen based at Cirencester in the late 4th century AD. This area previously had borne no hint of Roman occupation. Exploration of a medieval manor complex at Wetwang, east Yorkshire, revealed a chariot burial dating from the 3rd or 4th century BC, the earliest Iron Age burial of its kind ever discovered in England. This was the seventh chariot burial found in the area, thought to have been a tribal centre of a Celtic people—known by the Romans as the Parisi.

Among the most ancient relics discovered recently were stone tools, animal bones, and an incised mammoth tusk unearthed at a 40,000-year-old campsite at Mamontovaya Kurya, Russia, near the Arctic Ocean. The finds predated the oldest documented evidence for human activity in the far north by more than 20,000 years. Researchers believed that the date of the site implied either that Neanderthals had expanded much farther north than previously thought or that modern humans were present in the Arctic only a few thousand years after their appearance in Europe. If the toolmakers were modern humans, the timing was significant; the period corresponded to the transition from the Middle to the Upper Paleolithic, a turning point in the history of human evolution in Europe heralded by the arrival of the rich culture associated specifically with modern humans.

Mammoths, rhinoceroses, deer, horses, bison, birds, and unknown animals with elongated muzzles and open mouths were among the more than 200 newly discovered Upper Paleolithic engravings found in Cussac Cave in southern France. Also depicted were line drawings of women and schematic vulvas. Most of the figures appeared to have been engraved with stone tools; there were no paintings. The archaic nature of the figures, some of which were more than four metres in height, suggested that they were done during the Gravettian period (c. 26,000–20,000 BC). Hundreds of fine ceramic vessels used for drinking, feasting, and fertility rites—possibly of an orgiastic nature—were discovered along with a phallic-shaped stalagmite in a cave near the abandoned village of Nakovana, Croatia, on the Adriatic Sea. According to site excavators Tim Kaiser of the Royal Ontario Museum and Staso Forenbaher of the Institute for Anthropological Research in Zagreb, Croatia, the cult site should clarify previously hazy theories about the religious beliefs of the Illyrians, warriors and neighbours of the Greeks, who lived in the area during the 1st and 2nd centuries BC.

A number of important finds were unearthed in China, including 20 carts and the remains of dozens of horses found during rescue excavations at a Zhou dynasty (770 BC–AD 221) site in the central Chinese city of Xicheng. Within a tomb belonging to the Yangshao culture (c. 5000–3000 BC) in northwestern Shaanxi province, archaeologists found the remains of numerous adults and children, who had been buried separately. A large site thought to have been used by the royal family for sacrificial rituals 3,000 years ago was discovered in Yanshi, onetime capital of the Shang dynasty (1600–1046 BC) in western Henan province. The sacred site lay within one of the largest Shang sites discovered to date.

After toiling for more than a year, Chinese archaeologists discovered a large pit adjacent to that containing the well-known terra-cotta warriors and horses buried with Qin Shihuangdi, China's first emperor (reigned 221–210 BC). Rather than warriors, however, the newfound pit contained terra-cotta statues representing civilians.

A nine-year excavation at the site of Dholavira in the western Indian state of Gujarat yielded a walled Indus Valley city dated to the middle of the 3rd millennium BC and covering nearly 50.6 ha (125 ac). The Archaeological Survey of India team uncovered a sophisticated water-management system with a series of giant reservoirs—the largest 80 × 12 m wide and 7 m deep—used to conserve rainwater.

For all of the richness of these new discoveries, the field of archaeology had suffered setbacks in terms of site destruction, mainly through flooding. Emerging nations—e.g., Turkey, India, and China—needed to balance their requirement for hydroelectric power with heritage management. Conflict was running a close second in destroying the collective heritage, particularly in Afghanistan, as witnessed by the deliberate destruction of the Bamiyan Buddhas in

Archaeological Survey of India

During the year an ancient walled city was uncovered at the Dholavira site in Gujarat state, India.

the spring of 2001. In addition, much of that country's heritage was in peril from the pillaging of sites; many ancient objects had already appeared on the art market. (ANGELA M.H. SCHUSTER)

Western Hemisphere. Recent discoveries shed new light on ancient Maya civilization. Arthur Demarest and Tomás Barrientos excavated and surveyed an important Maya centre named Cancuén, the "Place of Serpents," in a remote area of Guatemala. Cancuén was first located in 1905 by Harvard University archaeologist Teobert Maler, but it was largely forgotten until Demarest deciphered Maya glyphs at the nearby Dos Pilas site that told of a great lord's conquest of Cancuén. Demarest and his colleagues mapped approximately 13 sq km (5 sq mi) of the site, identifying a three-story limestone palace with 170 rooms grouped around 11 courtyards. The ruling dynasty of Cancuén dates back to the 2nd or 3rd century BC. Its lords flourished by forming alliances with other states such as Teotihuacán on the Mexican highlands and the Maya cities of Calakmul, Dos Pilas, and Tikal. Cancuén boasted a palace close in size to that in Tikal, surrounded by workshops where artisans laboured on jade plaques, pyrite mirrors, and obsidian artifacts. A nearby and still unexplored cave complex may have been the ritual centre for Cancuén. This important site would fill major gaps in the understanding of Maya history.

Archaeologist Norman Hammond of Boston University uncovered a 2,900-year-old sweat house at Cuello in northern Belize. Cuello was the oldest Maya settlement in the lowlands, with occupation beginning perhaps as early as 2000 BC and continuing for 16 centuries. Elite residences or public buildings surrounded a courtyard enclosed on three sides. When the excavators investigated the fourth side, they unearthed a structure, about 2.4 × 2.5 m (8 × 9 ft), that had a domed roof and an outside firebox chamber. Hot embers and stones were pushed down a channel into the house through an opening in the wall. As many as six bathers could sit on benches with their feet stretched above the channel. Hammond compared the Cuello sweat house to the elaborate royal bathhouses at Tikal and other later Maya cities.

A Mayan burial vase was one of the artifacts unearthed at the Cancuén excavation site in Guatemala.

© Christopher Talbot/AFP Worldwide

Archaeology continued to make important discoveries concerning more recent American history. Tainter Cave near La Crosse, Wis., yielded the most comprehensive set of Native American rock paintings in the Upper Midwest. Found by an amateur archaeologist in 1998 but announced only in 2001, the paintings included images of birds, humans, deer, and numerous geometric shapes. There were also scenes of an infant bound to a cradle board and nine hunters with bows taking six or seven deer in late winter. This panel lay below a group of birds, bird feet, and feathers, representing the classic Native American separation of earth and sky. Rolled birchbark torches and a 500-year-old moccasin fragment lay on the cave floor. One of the drawings was radiocarbon-dated to AD 900, but some could be earlier. The style of the paintings linked them to the Late Woodland Effigy Mound Culture.

In 1863 an African American named William A.G. Brown went to Virginia City, Nev., hoping to profit from the gold and silver boom at the nearby Comstock Lode. He opened the Boston Saloon, which catered to the small black population in the region, and operated it until 1875. The saloon burned to the ground soon after he closed shop. In mid-2000 a team of archaeologists excavated portions of the Boston Saloon. They recovered thousands of artifacts, including bottle fragments, crystal and glassware, and clay pipes. This was the fourth bar to be excavated in Virginia City, among them Piper's Old Corner Bar, which catered to an upscale clientele. Virginia City was reasonably well integrated for the day, but its black population nonetheless lived under severe social constraints. A preliminary examination of the Boston Saloon artifacts suggested, however, that the African Americans were drinking the same drinks and using similar glassware to what passed over the counters at the upscale Piper's bar.

In 1864 a group of Confederate volunteers under Lieut. George Dixon manned the submarine *H.L. Hunley* and torpedoed the Union sloop USS *Housatonic* off Charleston (S.C.) harbour. The missile hit the sloop's torpedo magazine, and the ship exploded with a massive roar. The *H.L. Hunley* never returned to port and sank 6.4 km (4 mi) offshore. In 1995 a dive team located the sunken vessel with sonar and global positioning technology. The submarine was finally raised on Aug. 8, 2000. An intricate structure of suction piles and nylon slings combined with a polyurethane foam cushion protected the fragile hull during its eight-hour journey to the surface. The archaeologists then attempted to X-ray the steel plates, but sediment blocked the radiation. Eventually they excavated the hull by removing individual steel plates. By late 2001 the partial skeletal remains of eight crew members had been found.

Dos Cabezas ("Two Heads"), a 32-m (105-ft)-high Moche pyramid, lies in Peru's lower Jequetepeque Valley, close to the Pacific Ocean. Three richly decorated tombs of nobles dating to AD 450–550 were excavated from the south side of the pyramid. The three men were remarkable for their exceptional stature. Average Moche males stood between about 1.5 m (4 ft 10 in) and 1.7 m (5 ft 6 in) in height. The Dos Cabezas men, however, towered between 1.75 m (5 ft 9 in) and 1.8 m (6 ft) and died between the ages of 18 and 22 years. Biological anthropologists suspected that they may have suffered from a chronic genetic disorder such as Marfan syndrome, which causes thin, elongated bones. The three appeared to have died within a few weeks of one another. The most important of them lay in Tomb 2, cocooned in clay and wrapped in textiles with his ceremonial possessions. The man had a copper funerary mask with shell eyes, golden eyebrows and nose ornament, and beardlike bangles. He wore a tunic adorned with a cloth human figure with gilded head, hands, and feet. He was buried with an exquisite ceramic bat (an animal sacred to the Moche), a headdress adorned with gilded copper bats, and a nose ornament of solid gold—also a bat. The lord held metalworking chisels and lay with a funerary bundle crammed with war clubs, spear throwers, and gold-plated shields. Sacrificial offerings, a llama and a young woman, lay at a slightly higher level. The excavators believed that the three men were related to one another, but their exact role in early Moche society remained a mystery. (BRIAN FAGAN)

Architecture and Civil Engineering

STAR architects designed a number of **EYE-POPPING** buildings that were stars in themselves, but their **CREATIVITY** was overshadowed by the collapse of the **TWIN TOWERS** of the World Trade Center in September.

ARCHITECTURE

The top architectural story in 2001 was the collapse of the World Trade Center towers in New York City following the September 11 terrorist attacks. Architects and others debated the long-term impact of the disaster. Would the world stop building skyscrapers? Would the threat of terrorism lead people to abandon cities? A number of groups in New York City, including the American Institute of Architects (AIA), the Regional Plan Association, and the Municipal Art Society, joined with city planners and business leaders in informal task-force groups to formulate a redevelopment plan for the site. Proposals ranged from reconstructing the towers exactly as they were to leaving the entire 6.5-ha (16-ac) site as an open-space memorial. Some businesses left the area in fear of further attacks. As a result, a preservation group, the World Monuments Fund, added "Historic Lower Manhattan" to its list of Most Endangered Sites in the world. The twin collapse was scrutinized by engineers, who noted that the intense fire and heat—(upwards of 1,093 °C [2,000 °F]) generated by the explosion of jet fuel aboard the two jetliners that slammed into the towers—had weakened the towers' steel supports and thus caused them to buckle and the floors to cascade nearly straight down. The towers, capable of withstanding hurricane-force winds and ordinary fires, had not been built to withstand an assault of this magnitude. Though they had never been widely admired as works of architecture, the towers' departure was viewed as a human tragedy, an economic disaster, and a blow to Manhattan's great architectural skyline.

Awards. The world's most coveted architectural honour, the $100,000 Pritzker Architecture Prize, was awarded to the Swiss partnership of Jacques Herzog and Pierre de Meuron. (*See* BIOGRAPHIES.) They were also the architects of a proposed addition to the de Young Museum in San Francisco's Golden Gate Park, a design some thought a bit too imposing for the site; it had not been approved by year's end.

Jean Nouvel of France received the Praemium Imperiale of the Japan Art Association for lifetime achievement. He also was the recipient of the Gold Medal of the Royal Institute of British Architects. Nouvel was best known for his transparent all-glass buildings, such as the Arab Institute and Cartier Foundation, both in Paris. Japanese architect Tadao Ando was the winner of the Gold Medal of the American Institute of Architects. Ando's Pulitzer Foundation for the Arts, housing a collection of modern art, opened in St. Louis, Mo., in October. Like such Ando works as the Naoshima Contemporary Art Museum and the Church on the Water in Japan, it was an elegant, minimal building of pale concrete.

The AIA 25-Year Award, for a building that had proved its merit over time, went to the Weyerhaeuser Headquarters (1971) near Tacoma, Wash.; it was designed by Skidmore, Owings & Merrill and landscape architect Peter Walker. The AIA also announced 14 recipients of its annual architecture Honor Awards. Among the more notable were Antunovich Associates and McClier's restoration and recycling of the Burnham Hotel (named after its original architect, Daniel Burnham) in Chicago; Fox & Fowle Architects' exterior design of the Condé Nast Building office tower in Times Square, New York City; and Tod Williams Billie Tsien & Associates' design of the Williams Natatorium, a skylighted pool at Cranbrook Academy of Art in Bloomfield Hills, Mich. Among the 12 recipients for interior spaces were Skidmore, Owings & Merrill's Jin Mao Tower in Shanghai and Hardy Holzman Pfeiffer Associates' restoration of Radio City Music Hall in New York City. "A Civic Vision for Turnpike Air Rights in Boston," an urban-design plan by Goody, Clancy & Associates in collaboration with neighbourhood groups, claimed one of the four awards for urban design.

The Aga Khan Award for Architecture, given every three years for architecture in the Islamic world, was presented as scheduled in Aleppo, Syria, on November 6. Among the world's most respected prizes, the Aga Khan Awards dealt with social as well as purely architectural issues. Among the nine project winners were "New Life for Old Structures," a program to restore buildings in Iran; Barefoot Architects, a rural self-help group in Tilonia, India; and the Nubia Museum, Aswan, Egypt, which housed the culture of Nubia ("Land of Gold"), an ancient area that was partly submerged by the Aswan High Dam in 1971.

Civic and Cultural Buildings. Perhaps the most notable new building of 2001 was the Bibliotheca Alexandrina, the new library located on the harbour in Alexandria, Egypt, designed by the firm Snøhetta of Oslo. Snøhetta's members were unknown in 1989 when their design was selected in a competition that received 524 entries from 77 countries. The library's outstanding feature was a circular reading room with floors that terraced down under a dramatic sloped roof; as one critic described, "A huge inclined silver disk appears to be rising over the sea." The round reading room was undoubtedly influenced by the famous 1857 reading room in the British Museum in London. (*See* LIBRARIES AND MUSEUMS: *Sidebar.*) A notable renovation was that of a courtyard around the reading room of the British Museum. In British architect Sir Norman Foster's design, the courtyard was roofed in a delicate glass structure that curved like a hanging fabric, creating a memorable space that was renamed the Queen Elizabeth II Great Court.

The vast new chancellery building designed by architects Axel Schultes and Charlotte Frank opened near Foster's glass-domed Reichstag in Berlin. The new structure was criticized by some as being bombastic and inefficient. In Sendai, Japan, architect Toyo Ito created a new arts centre called the Sendai Mediatheque. Though the transparent glass structure looked like a watery aquarium from the outside—its seven floors were held up by clusters of slanting columns meant to look like seaweed swaying underwater—inside it housed a great variety of art and media centres for public use.

In Wisconsin Spanish architect and engineer Santiago Calatrava created a new entrance wing for the Milwaukee Art Museum. Its outstanding feature was a 66-m (217-ft)-wide sunshade, which was intended to open and close like a bird's wings over the glass roof of the entry pavilion. The museum hoped that the spectacular building would put the city on the world tourist map and thus do for Milwaukee what architect Frank Gehry's Guggenheim Museum in Bilbao, Spain, did for that city. In that regard, Milwaukee typified the recent rush by cities and institutions to hire one of the 20 or 30 world "star" architects who, like Gehry, were capable of producing memorably sculptural buildings.

Two small chapels in Japan were also notable. Ando's Komyo-ji, a temple for a Buddhist sect in Saijo, was a symphony of elaborately interlocking wood columns and beams, a type of architectural forest.

Adrian D. Smith of Skidmore, Owings & Merrill LLP.
© Hedrich Blessing

The interior of Skidmore, Owings & Merrill's 88-story Jin Mao Tower in Shanghai, the tallest building in China, won an AIA Honor Award in 2001.

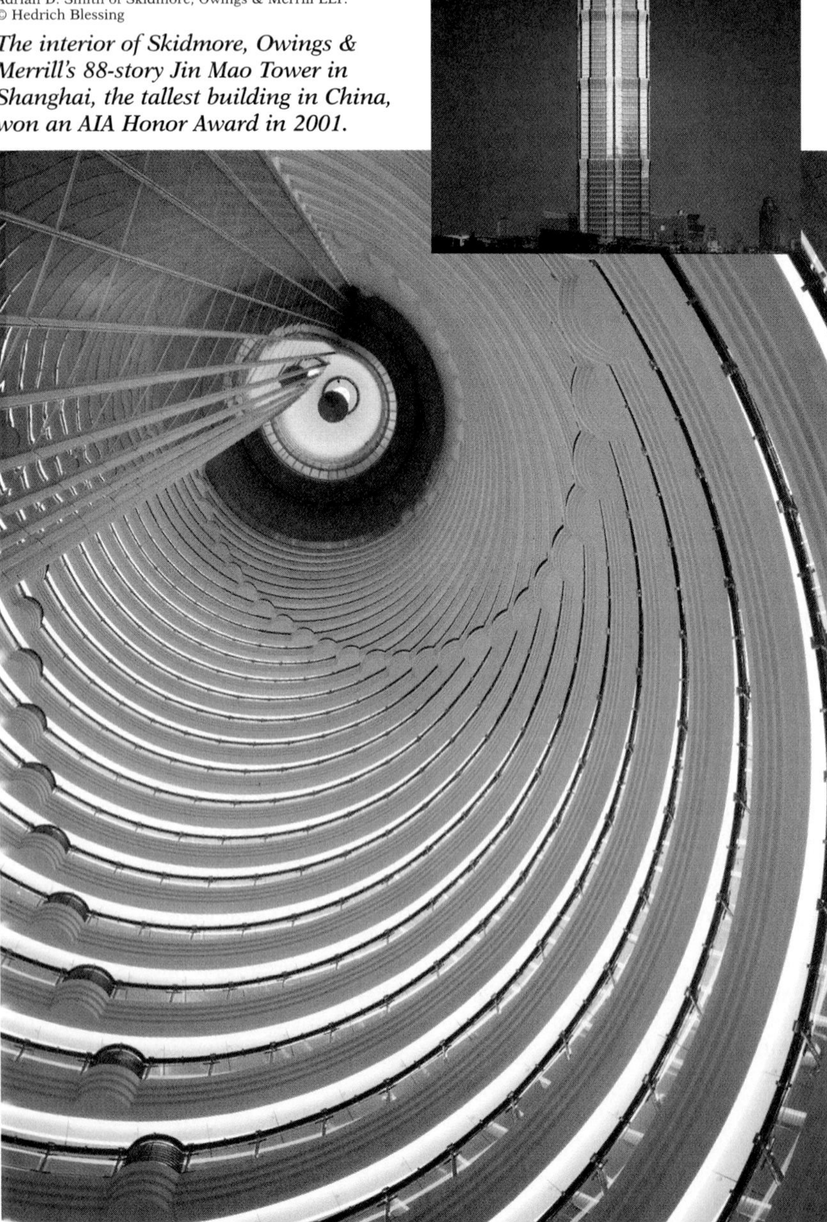

Takashi Yamaguchi's White Temple near Kyoto, by contrast, was a tiny one-room box, pure white both inside and out, bathed in mysterious light that made it feel as if it were floating.

Commercial Buildings. One of the most amazing efforts to date of American architect Frank Gehry was the DG Bank in Berlin, located on the Pariser Platz near the Brandenburg Gate. The building's exterior was straitjacketed by rigid rules that were established by the city of Berlin in an effort to make new buildings on the famous square look compatible with one another. Gehry responded by designing a simple, elegant limestone building on the outside, but he broke loose in the interior with a dramatic atrium. The atrium had a delicate glass floor and roof, both warped into improbable shapes, and in its middle, seeming to float in the space, was a conference room sheathed in stainless steel and shaped like a horse's head.

Though the Austrian firm Coop Himmelblau, led by Wolf Dieter Prix and Helmut Swiczinsky, had long been known for its radically modern, or "deconstructivist," buildings that were so pitched that they seemed to be frozen at the moment before they collapsed—its SEG Apartment Tower in Vienna was less unconventional than some of its other designs. The publicly funded "social housing" development tilted in a way that reminded some of the Leaning Tower of Pisa in Italy, but it also contained a 14-story "climate lobby" that helped the building ventilate itself naturally. In Sydney, Australia, Italian Renzo Piano designed Aurora Place, a 41-story office tower with an 18-story apartment building next to it. Sail-like glass shapes rose from the top of the tower, recalling the shapes of the Sydney Opera House nearby. In New York City high-fashion French architect Philippe Starck converted a 1920s brick women's residence into a super elegant hotel called Hudson, which featured inventively theatrical indoor and outdoor lobby spaces.

Exhibitions. The year's most remarkable exhibitions were all in New York City. "Frank Gehry, Architect" filled the great spiral of Frank Lloyd Wright's Guggenheim Museum. On display were 40 projects by the master Los Angeles architect rendered in photos, drawings, and hundreds of models. Among the projects shown was a design for a new branch of the Guggenheim, to be built over the water in New York's East River, which would be 10 times the size of Wright's Guggenheim. By year's end, however, a downturn in the American economy had

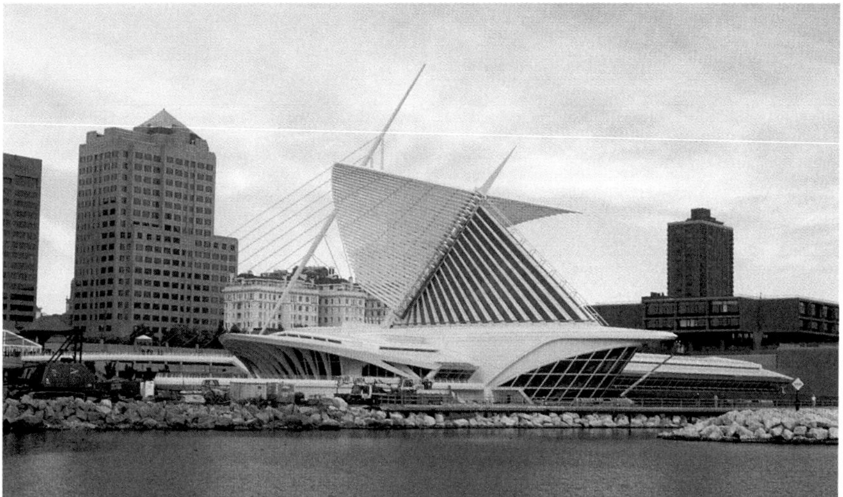

The Milwaukee (Wis.) Art Museum, with a new entrance wing by Santiago Calatrava, features an immense, movable sunshade.

dampened enthusiasm for the proposal. A double exhibit on the modernist Ludwig Mies van der Rohe opened simultaneously at the Whitney Museum of American Art and the Museum of Modern Art (MoMA). "Mies in Berlin" at MoMA showcased his early work in Europe, including such masterpieces as the Barcelona Pavilion and Tugendhat House. The exhibit also explored Mies's early development and the sources from which he learned. "Mies in America" at the Whitney focused on his later work after he immigrated to the United States, including such icons as the Seagram Building in Manhattan and the Farnsworth House in Plano, Ill. The latter had been a concern to preservationists, but during the year it was purchased from a private owner by the state of Illinois, which would maintain it and open it to the public. "Exploring the City: The Norman Foster Studio" filled a large space in the British Museum, next door to the architect's new Queen Elizabeth II Great Court. The exhibit included detailed models of projects from all over the world as well as some of the 900 sketchbooks the architect had filled over the years. "The Architecture of R.M. Schindler," at the Los Angeles Museum of Contemporary Art, showcased the work of the visionary early California modernist. "Albert Kahn: Inspiration for the Modern," at the University of Michigan at Ann Arbor, displayed the work of the designer of such industrial giants as the Ford River Rouge Plant. "Out of the Ordinary: The Architecture and Design of Robert Venturi, Denise Scott Brown & Associates," at the Philadelphia Museum of Art, was a summary of the life work of the influential firm, whose members espoused the virtues of ordinary vernacular and commercial architecture. "Frank Lloyd Wright and the Art of Japan: The Architect's Other Passion," at the Japan Society in New York City, explored the architect's secondary career as a collector and dealer in Japanese prints.

Preservation. The Leaning Tower of Pisa was at last stabilized by the simple method of removing earth from its high side so that side would settle. The tower was slowly straightened by one degree to restore it to its tilting angle of 163 years earlier, considered safe. The Kaufmann Conference Center, a Manhattan interior that was one of only four American works by the great Finnish architect Alvar Aalto, was withdrawn from a proposed sale and was to be preserved. Preservationists in New York were also concerned about the fate of the TWA Terminal at John F. Kennedy International Airport (1962) by Eero Saarinen. The owner wished to remove part of the building and convert the remainder into a restaurant or another use. The National Trust for Historic Preservation released its annual "Eleven Most Endangered Places" in the U.S. Among them was another modern building—the CIGNA Campus in Bloomfield, Conn., a classic example of "corporate modernism" designed in 1957 (as the Connecticut General Life Insurance headquarters) by Gordon Bunshaft—which was slated to become a golf course. Others on the list were Ford Island at Pearl Harbor, Hawaii, threatened by redevelopment, and Los Caminos del Rio, a 322-km (200-mi) stretch of land along the lower Rio Grande in Texas, home to Hispanic and Anglo historic sites. At Yale University it was announced that the landmark Art and Architecture Building (1963) by Paul Rudolph would be restored by New York architect David Childs of Skidmore, Owings & Merrill.

Controversies and Future Buildings. The World War II Memorial, on the Mall in Washington, D.C., was under construction at year's end after having survived a court challenge by its critics, who hoped to overturn a law passed by Congress in May that cleared the way for the project. The designer, whose proposal won a national competition, was Friedrich St. Florian of Providence, R.I. Meanwhile, a federal task force published a Memorials and Museums Master Plan, which suggested that future memorials in Washington be sited elsewhere than on the Mall. In San Francisco the city's planning board approved—over the objection of its staff—a design by Pritzker Prize winner Rem Koolhaas of The Netherlands for a new headquarters for Italian clothier Prada, but the company later delayed the project. In New York City hotelier Ian Schrager nixed plans for a new hotel by Koolhaas and Herzog & de Meuron that would have featured a differently shaped window for each room. A design for a presidential library in Arkansas for former president Bill Clinton was unveiled by architect James Stewart Polshek of New York, but the project was delayed by cost problems and by an owner who sued to prevent the city from taking the land. Polshek's design, in a park by the Arkansas River, included a wing that cantilevered out over the water. In Chicago a new lakefront Millennium Park, including a band shell by Frank Gehry, was also troubled by cost overruns. Diller + Scofidio of New York City, a partnership long known for its art installations, was chosen for its first major architectural job, a new Institute of Contemporary Art in Boston. A slowing economy also put this project in jeopardy.

Deaths. Among the notable architects who died during the year were Morris Lapidus, famed for the gaudy hotels he built in Miami, Fla., notably the Fontainebleau and Eden Roc (*see* OBITUARIES); Ian McHarg, considered by many the founder of modern landscape architecture and planning in the U.S. and the author of the seminal book *Design with Nature* (1969); and Steven Izenour, a longtime partner in Venturi, Scott Brown and Associates and coauthor of *Learning from Las Vegas* (1972).

(ROBERT CAMPBELL)

Notable Civil Engineering Projects (in work or completed, 2001)

Name	Location		Year of completion	Notes
Airports		**Terminal area (sq m)**		
Incheon International (new airport)	Incheon (Inchon), South Korea (near Seoul)	369,000	2001	Landfill between islands; opened March 22
Guangzhou Int'l (new replacement airport)	Guangzhou (Canton), China	300,000	2002	
Pearson International	Toronto, Ont., Canada	332,000	2003	New horseshoe-shaped terminal at Canada's busiest airport
Athens International (new airport)	Spata, Greece	209,000	2001	Europe's biggest airport project; opened March 28
JFK Int'l (new Terminal 4)	Queens, New York City, N.Y.	139,000	2001	Connected by 13-km light rail to Manhattan by 2003; opened May 24
Nong Ngu Hao (new int'l airport)	Bangkok, Thailand	?	2004	Construction began December 2001
Aqueduct		**Length (m)**		
Great Man-Made River (phase 2)	Libyan interior to Tripoli area	1,650,000	2001	Phase 1 to Benghazi area (1983–93); phase 2 begun 1990
Bridges		**Length (main span; m)**		
Carquinez (#3)	Crockett, Calif.–Vallejo, Calif.	728	2003	Begun 2000; first major U.S. suspension bridge since 1965
Rion Antirion	Patrai, Greece (across Gulf of Corinth)	560	2004	Multicable-stayed; complex deepwater foundations
San Francisco–Oakland Bay (East Span)	Yerba Buena Is., Calif.–Oakland, Calif.	385	2006	2-km causeway + world's largest suspension bridge hung from single tower
William Natcher	Owensboro, Ky.–near Rockport, Ind.	366	2002	To be longest cable-stayed bridge over U.S. inland waterway
Rosario–Victoria	Rosario to Victoria, Argentina	350	2002	Bridges/viaducts across 59-km wide Paraná wetlands
Millau Viaduct	Tarn Gorge, west of Millau, France	342	2004	8 cable-stayed spans; world's highest (285 m) road viaduct
Leonard P. Zakim Bunker Hill	Boston, Mass.	227	2002	Widest (56 m) cable-stayed bridge in world (*see* **Urban Developments**)
Maria Valeria (cross-Danube link)	Esztergom, Hungary–Sturovo, Slovakia	119	2001	Replication of 106-year-old bridge destroyed in 1944; opened Oct. 11
Kizuna	Mekong River, near Kampong Cham, Cambodia	?	2001	First bridge across Mekong in Cambodia; opened December 4
Buildings		**Height (m)**		
Lotte World Tower	Busan (Pusan), South Korea	464.5	2005	Begun December 2000; will be world's tallest
Taipei Financial Center	Taipei, Taiwan	448	2003	Begun 1999; will be world's second tallest to rooftop (with spire, 508 m)
Two International Finance Centre	Hong Kong, China	412	2003	Begun 2000; to be world's fourth tallest building
Plaza Rakyat	Kuala Lumpur, Malaysia	382	2002	Will be tallest reinforced-concrete complex; seventh tallest overall
Migdal (Tower) Egged	Tel Aviv, Israel	326	2006	Begun 2001
Trump World Tower	New York City, N.Y.	262	2001	Tallest residential development in the world
Torre Generali	Panama City, Panama	250	2003	Begun mid-2000; will be Latin America's tallest building
City Tower	Birmingham, England	245	2004	Will be tallest building in the U.K.
Torre Mayor	Mexico City, Mexico	225	2003	Will be tallest building in Mexico
Canal		**Length (m)**		
Sheikh Zayed	into bedrock of Lake Nasser, Egypt	72,000	2002	Feeds irrigation system for central Egypt oases
Dams		**Crest length (m)**		
Birecik Dam	Euphrates River, Turkey	2,507	2001	First major hydroelectric plant in Turkey
Three Gorges	west of Yichang, China	1,983	2009	World's largest hydroelectric project; begun 1993
San Roque Multipurpose	Agno River, Luzon, Philippines	1,100	2003	Irrigation and flood control; tallest earth-and-rock fill dam in Asia
Mohale (Lesotho Highlands Water Project, phase 1B)	Senqunyane River, 100 km east of Maseru	700	2002	First transfer of water to South Africa in 1998, second transfer in 2003
Sardar Sarovar Project	Narmada River, Madhya Pradesh, India	?	?	Construction halted 1995, resumed 2000
Alqueva Dam	Guadiana River, 180 km SE of Lisbon, Portugal	?	2002	Will create Europe's largest (250 sq km) reservoir; extends into Spain
Bakun Dam	Balui River, Sarawak, Borneo, Malaysia	?	2006	Hydroelectricity to peninsular Malaysia via world's longest submarine cable
Highways		**Length (km)**		
Indus Highway	Karachi–Peshawar, Pakistan	1,265	?	59% complete as of September 2001
Beijing–Shanghai Expressway or "Jinghu"	Beijing–Shanghai, China	1,262	2000	Opened late December; construction began in 1987
Egnatia Motorway	Igoumenitsa–Thessaloniki, Greece	687	2006	First Greek highway at modern int'l standards; 70 tunnels
Railways (Heavy)		**Length (km)**		
Qinghai–Tibet	Golmud, Qinghai, China–Lhasa, Tibet, China	1,118	2007	Highest world rail (5,072 m at summit); half across permafrost
Guangdong–Hainan	Zhangjiang, China–northern tip of Hainan at Haikou	568	2001	Rail with container ship to Hainan
Panama Canal	Cristóbal–Balboa, Panama	89	2001	Rebuilt railroad for transcontinental container traffic
Kyongui (51-year-old reconnection)	Munsan, S.Kor.–Kaesong, N.Kor.	24	2002?	6.8 km South Korean part complete as of September 2001
Railways (High Speed)		**Length (km)**		
Spanish High Speed (second line)	Madrid–Barcelona, Spain	760	2004	Madrid–Lleida to be completed by 2002
Kyongbu	Seoul–Busan (Pusan), South Korea	323	2003	Connects largest and third largest cities
TGV Méditerranée	Valence–Marseille, France (branch to Montpellier)	249	2001	Completes high-speed rail across France ("Calais to Marseille")
German High Speed (third line)	Frankfurt–Cologne, Germany	226	2002	Connects Ruhr to Frankfurt International Airport
Italian High Speed (second line)	Rome–Naples, Italy	222	2004	Begun 1994; part of planned 1,300-km high-speed network
Shanghai maglev ("magnetic levitation")	Pudong Int'l airport–metro line 2, Shanghai, China	29.9	2003	World's first maglev train for public use; 430 km/h
Subways/Metros/Light Rails		**Length (km)**		
Oporto Light Rail	Oporto, Portugal	70.0	2003	Europe's largest total rail system project; first line opened in 2001
Hong Kong Railway (West Rail, phase 1)	Western New Territories to Kowloon, Hong Kong	30.3	2003	5,500-m tunnel and viaduct
Los Angeles Metro (Blue Line ext.)	L.A. Union Station to Pasadena, Calif.	22.0	2003	
Copenhagen Metro	Copenhagen, Denmark	21.0	2002–05	Line 1: 2002; most extensive driverless system in world
Tren Urbano (phase 1)	San Juan, P.R.	17.2	2003	Bayamón (western suburbs) to north San Juan; 60% elevated
Istanbul Metro (phase 2)	Istanbul, Turkey	5.4	2001	Bridge link across Golden Horn; extends under historic city centre
Tunnels		**Length (m)**		
Apennine Range tunnels (9)	Bologna–Florence, Italy (high-speed railway)	66,000	2006	Begun 1996; longest tunnel, 18.6 km; tunnels to cover 90% of railway
Qinling	between Xi'an and Ankang, China	18,457	2001	World's ninth largest railway tunnel
A86 Ring Road	around Paris, France	17,700	2008	Two tunnels (to east [10,100 m], to west [7,600 m])
Södra Länken	part of Stockholm, Sweden, ring road	16,600	2004	Complex underground interchanges
Pinglin Highway	near Taipei, Taiwan	12,900	2003	Twin tunnels under Sheuhshan Range; Taipei-I-lan expressway link
Westerschelde	Terneuzen to Ellewoutsdijk, Neth.	6,600	2003	Longest world tunnel in "bored weak soil"
Vestmannasund Subsea Tunnel	Streym (Streymoy) and Vágar islands, Faroe Is.	4,700	2002	First subsea tunnel in the Faroe Islands
Urban Developments		**Area (ha)**		
Putrajaya	25 km south of Kuala Lumpur, Malaysia	4,581	2012	Planned national capital begun 1996; first staff moved in June 1999
Central Artery/Tunnel	Boston, Mass.	–	2004	Complex highway/tunnel/bridge project begun in 1991

1 m=3.28 ft; 1 km=0.62 mi; 1 ha=2.47 ac

Art, Antiques, and Collections

In 2001 the **VENICE BIENALE** and other exhibitions featured **NONTRADITIONAL** mediums—notably video, film, and sculpture-as-architecture—as well as **SNAPSHOTS** of New York City after September 11. A **LEONARDO** drawing and a **JACK KEROUAC** manuscript fetched record auction prices.

PAINTING AND SCULPTURE

At the 49th Venice Biennale, directed for the second time (his first was in 1999) by Harald Szeemann, the international art world gathered to experience what was considered the most significant show of the new and important. Painting and sculpture were not as well represented as other mediums, particularly video and film, which were high in quantity but not always quality. Painting and sculpture were not entirely absent, however. One of the iconic works in Venice was the Australian-born British artist Ron Mueck's 4.8-m (16-ft)-high fibreglass sculpture of a crouching boy, which greeted visitors as they entered one of the Biennale's main exhibition spaces. The piece was a gesture toward a kind of monumental figuration, and it was as immediately imposing as one of Richard Serra's steel-torqued ellipses shown nearby. Subtler were the works by Robert Gober, who used bronze to interpret the light and porous quality of Styrofoam. Gober also presented one of his vaguely anatomic forms cast in wax and set into a wicker basket.

One alternative to the massive scale and unmet goals of the Biennale was Site Santa Fe. "Beau Monde: Toward a Redeemed Cosmopolitanism," curated by Las Vegas, Nev.-based critic Dave Hickey, was the fourth installment of this biannual exhibition. "Beau Monde" featured many established names—notably Ed Ruscha, Jo Baer, Ellsworth Kelly, and Bridget Riley—among emerging and trendier artists. One of these was Japan's Takashi Murakami, who received attention for his two solo exhibitions and his installation in New York City's Grand Central Station. Murakami's signature "superflat" mode of painting featured smiley-faced flowers set against silver backgrounds; he also made sculptures inspired by Japanese comics and animation. An important venue featuring emerging talent was New York City's Studio Museum in Harlem, which mounted "Freestyle," a show of young black artists curated by Thelma Golden. Some standouts included Eric Wesley's full-scale sculpture of a donkey kicking through a gallery wall and Kori Newkirk's paintings made from plastic beads, artificial hair, and hair pomade, which was applied directly to the museum wall to create one work.

Several artists explored the familiar dialectic of sculpture-as-architecture, and vice versa. Gregor Schneider's *Dead House ur* (created for the German pavilion at the Venice Biennale) was an extension of a project that had occupied him for several years. This reconstruction of his family home, a standard tenement construction in Rheydt, Ger., was an elaborately conceived interior within an interior. The pathos of the domestic also fascinated British artist Rachel Whiteread, who made monumental casts of two architectural spaces: a basement staircase and the entire interior space of a small apartment, both of which were created from spaces in her new home, a former London synagogue. Whiteread, whose Holocaust Memorial in Vienna was completed at the end of 2000 to great critical success, followed up with a smaller public commission. Known for making casts of ordinary objects using plaster or synthetic resin, Whiteread most recently cast a replica of a plinth in clear resin. The piece, entitled *Monument,* was installed in June atop an actual stone plinth in Trafalgar Square, London; it was scheduled to remain there until sometime in 2002. An interest in architecture also informed the work of Brooklyn,

Ron Mueck's **Untitled (Big Man)** *(2000) was emblematic of his oversized sculptures of human figures; the work was acquired by the Smithsonian Institution's Hirshhorn Museum and Sculpture Garden in 2001.*

Lee Stalsworth/Hirshhorn Museum and Sculpture Garden, Smithsonian Institution, Joseph H. Hirshhorn Bequest Fund, 2001

N.Y.-based Ricci Albenda, who used building materials such as drywall and metal sheeting to construct "spaces within spaces," including a large cube suspended nearly a metre from the floor that almost entirely filled the space of a gallery, giving onlookers only a narrow area of space in which to move between the piece and the wall.

Tate Britain's Turner Prize, worth £20,000 (about $29,000) in 2001, triggered even more controversy than usual when it was awarded to Martin Creed in December for "The Lights Going On and Off," which consisted of an empty gallery with a pair of ceiling lights that flashed on and off.

Combining performance with sculptural and installation elements in a collaborative practice that defied easy definition, the Austrian collective known as Gelatin sparked critical interest. For a large-scale installation called *Total Osmosis,* they transformed an outdoor area into a swampy, toxic backyard. Abandoned toys and other refuse filled a pungent muddy area that was traversable only via narrow wooden planks. Another project involved stuffed animals, semipornographic photo collages, and a series of "lectures," during which, in a disorienting mix of fact and fiction, the artists described their previous projects while executing a wall drawing to illustrate the given topic, ranging from "Hawaii" to "Autopsy."

Italian artist Maurizio Cattelan constructed a larger-than-scale replica of the Hollywood sign and installed it in Sicily in the hills above Palermo, near a garbage dump. Cattelan, known as a provocateur in the art world, deliberately chose this particular location, an action that raised the curiosity—and the hackles—of the local population. In another provocative move, Wim Delvoye pushed the boundaries of good taste with his machine-sculpture entitled *Cloaca.* His contraption, essentially a defecation machine, employed mechanisms that were controlled by computer to duplicate the human digestive process. *Cloaca* traveled in Europe and was scheduled to arrive in New York City in 2002.

There was plenty of painting by both established figures and relative newcomers. James Rosenquist, best known for his mural-sized Pop art works that depicted the motifs of consumerism and mass production, exhibited a new group of works that were studies in dynamism—large canvases filled with shiny geometric shapes that appeared to change and morph when viewed. The works also reflected Rosenquist's movement forward as an artist; he had succeeded in creating a formidable body of work late in his career. New paintings by Cy Twombly, another artist who had emerged in the 1960s, continued his very recognizable style of calligraphic drips executed in springlike colours. Like a small-scale warm-up for his upcoming 2002 major retrospective at the Museum of Modern Art in New York City, Gerhard Richter showed a group of new, mostly abstract paintings, many of which were executed by means of his "squeegee" method; the squeegee was dragged across a freshly painted canvas, and the layers of wet pigment were smeared into an entirely different composition that was both random and controlled. American sculptor-artist Jeff Koons (*see* BIOGRAPHIES) unveiled some new works, the completed paintings from his *Celebration* series. Also back on the scene in a big way was artist Frank Stella (*see* BIOGRAPHIES), who completed work on his monumental metal sculpture, *The Prince of Homburg,* for the plaza outside the National Gallery of Art in Washington, D.C.

Abstraction, newly interpreted, was seen in many galleries. Charline von Heyl's large-scale abstractions were distinguished from similar works by virtue of her tangible confidence as a painter as well as of the works' compositional strength and unusual colour choices. Another artist who made sophisticated, formally oriented work was Jacqueline Humphries, who exhibited a group of new paintings that worked within the boundaries of the medium—paint and canvas—while incorporating extra-painterly considerations, including the kind of light emitted from computer screens. The intersection of art and technology (or the limits of such an exchange) was on the minds of many artists, and the traditional methods of art making—painting, photography, and sculpture—continued to be expanded or even replaced by new methods. Though Jeremy Blake's "moving paintings," as he called them, were actually animated digital video discs that mobilized the language of painting and made many historical art references, his colour-saturated works emphatically pointed toward the future.

(MEGHAN DAILEY)

Courtesy: Marian Goodman Gallery, New York

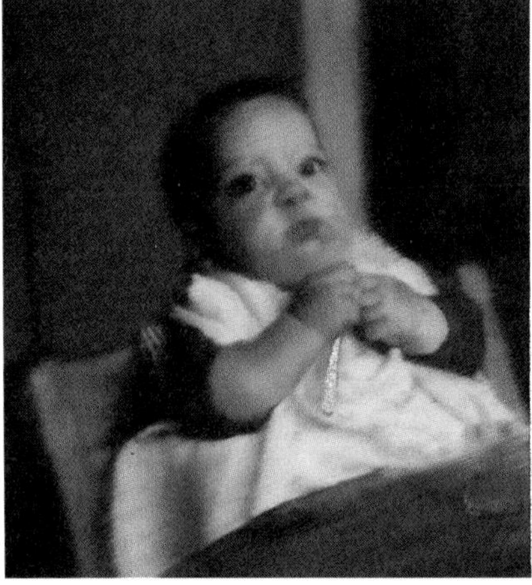

Gerhard Richter's Moritz *(2000) was among the paintings featured in a show of the German artist's works at the Marian Goodman Gallery in New York City.*

ART EXHIBITIONS

Several important architecture shows were among the critical and popular successes of 2001. Preeminent modernist Ludwig Mies van der Rohe had two distinct phases in his long career: his early years in his native Berlin and those after his 1938 arrival in the U.S. Together, "Mies in Berlin" (at the Museum of Modern Art [MoMA] in New York City and Altes Museum, Berlin) and "Mies in America" (at the Whitney Museum of American Art, New York City, and then the Canadian Centre for Architecture, Montreal) explored the rationality of Mies's International Style of architecture as well as his more expressionistic bent in the years before he coined the dictum "Less is more." In the 1920s Vienna-born architect R.M. Schindler made his home in Los Angeles and captured its casual elegance in domestic dwellings that were perfectly integrated into the landscape. The Museum of Contemporary Art, Los Angeles, mounted the largest show to date covering Schindler's career. Another architect synonymous with Los Angeles was Frank Gehry, whose projects were marked by his signature use of unusual materials and strong, undulating forms. A major exhibition spanning his 40-year career was held at the Solomon R. Guggenheim Museum, New York City, and also traveled to the museum's outpost in Bilbao, Spain, which Gehry himself designed.

Three cultural institutions in Chicago (where the ethnic Polish population numbered second only to Warsaw) hosted the ambitious "In Between: Art from Poland, 1945–2000." The Museum of Contemporary Art, the Renaissance

Society, and the Chicago Cultural Center presented surveys of the work of nearly 40 avant-garde and contemporary artists in addition to projects commissioned especially for the occasion.

The 500th anniversary of the European discovery of Brazil sparked several important exhibitions in the U.S. that celebrated the dynamic range of Brazil's art and culture. With about 350 objects, "Brazil: Body & Soul," which opened at the Guggenheim Museum, New York City, on October 19, was the largest of these. The centrepiece of the show was a large gilded 18th-century altar that filled the museum's rotunda. At El Museo del Barrio in New York City, "O Fio da Trama/The Thread Unraveled" focused on recent Brazilian art that used fabric and weaving as metaphors for social and personal narratives. Several Brazilian-born contemporary artists had solo exhibitions, including Beatriz Milhazes at the Birmingham (Ala.) Museum of Art, and the influential work of Hélio Oiticica was featured at the Wexner Center, Columbus, Ohio. Organized by the Museum of Contemporary Art in San Diego, Calif. (and also shown at the Museum of Modern Art, San Francisco), "Ultrabaroque: Aspects of Post-Latin American Art" featured 16 artists whose work reconsidered the use of the "baroque" as a metaphor for contemporary experience. Twenty-five contemporary artists considered the contentious dynamics between colonizer and colonized in Brazil in "Virgin Territory" at the National Museum of Women in the Arts, Washington, D.C.

At other Washington museums the focus was on American artists. Jacob Lawrence was the subject of a retrospective at the Phillips Collection that was also scheduled to travel extensively. More than 200 works from Lawrence's long career were shown, among them works from his seminal "Migration" series, which tells the story of the northern exodus of African Americans and what was experienced during and after that epic journey. At the Hirshhorn Museum 39 of Clyfford Still's large colour field paintings were presented, with many related works shown together for the first time. From high abstraction to 19th-century American Realism, Thomas Eakins's masterful figurative works (portraits, photographs, sculpture, and drawing) were presented in several venues in his native Philadelphia, including the Pennsylvania Academy of Fine Arts, where Eakins taught in the 1870s and '80s.

Interestingly, an exhibition of one of the most influential American artists of the past 30 years did not have a venue in the U.S. Conceptual art maverick Dan Graham's important retrospective opened at the Museu de Arte Contemporânea de Serralves, Pôrto, Port., and continued on to museums in Paris; Helsinki, Fin.; and Otterlo, Neth. The influence of Graham's practice, particularly his use of seriality in photography, was clearly visible in the work of German photographer Andreas Gursky—the subject of an exhibition at the MoMA. Gursky had garnered international attention for his images of contemporary scenes: global exchange markets, hotel interiors, airports, drab apartment-block facades, crowded sports or music events, often on a monumental scale—with some as large as 4.8 m (16 ft) wide.

The styles that constituted what was known as early Modernism were as diverse and varied as the artists who created them, as several important international exhibitions revealed. Henri Rousseau was a self-taught painter whose "naive" style drew the admiration of artists Pablo Picasso and Paul Gauguin, poet Guillaume Appolinaire, and others. The Kunsthalle in Tübingen, Ger., showed a number of important and lesser-known paintings by Rousseau as well as a selection of works that demonstrated his influence over others, among them Fernand Léger, Franz Marc, and Wassily Kandinsky. Though often overshadowed by his contemporary Georges Seurat, Paul Signac was nonetheless an important figure for early Modernism. The Grand Palais, Paris, was the first venue for a large-scale retrospective (the first of the artist's work in 40 years) that included Signac's well-known Pointillist paintings as well as works dating to the end of his life in 1935. Decorative, sumptuous, and often fraught with psychological tension, Gustav Klimt's Art Nouveau embodies the spirit of fin de siècle Vienna. The National Gallery of Canada, Ottawa, presented the first major retrospective of Klimt's work at a North American venue, including 35 paintings and nearly 90 drawings. The Jewish Museum, New York City, showed an unprecedented selection of early works by Marc Chagall culled from Russian collections, including some never before exhibited in the West. Chagall's influence on early 20th-century art was often considered minor, an assumption that this show meant to call into question.

In Paris the Centre Georges Pompidou organized a retrospective of Raymond Hains, a founding member of the Nouveaux Réalistes. The group emerged in France in the late 1950s

The altar of the Monastery of São Bento in Olinda, Braz., was the centrepiece of "Brazil: Body & Soul" at the Guggenheim Museum in New York City.

Juan J. Real/Notimex

and reacted against the refinement of Abstract Expressionism by using found objects to make their work. The Nouveaux Réalistes were included in another exhibition at the Pompidou, the blockbuster "Les Années Pop"—which presented a distinctively European perspective on Pop art, so often labeled a quintessential American style—a showcase of the broad and varied range and meaning of Pop and the breadth of work created beyond American shores. A movement that emerged in Italy in the years after the triumph of Pop, Arte Povera emphasized the tactile, physical qualities of the work of art and the use of "poor" or common materials—concrete, twigs, discarded newspapers, or rags. London's Tate Gallery presented 140 works in "Zero to Infinity: Arte Povera 1962–1972." Elsewhere in London, at the National Gallery, "Vermeer and the Delft School," co-organized by the Metropolitan Museum of Art in New York City, featured paintings by Vermeer and Pieter de Hooch, both of whom helped establish Delft as one of the most significant 17th-century artistic centres, as well as some 50 works by other artists of the period. An enormous selection of Romantic poet and artist William Blake's many paintings, watercolours, and illustrated books was presented at the Tate Britain, and a smaller version of the exhibition traveled to New York's Metropolitan Museum, where visitors could partake of Blake's imaginative world, in which poetry, dream life, and the imaginary become reality. (MEGHAN DAILEY)

AP/Wide World Photos

Hiroshi Sugimoto's photograph of a wax likeness of Napoleon Bonaparte was included in the exhibition "Sugimoto: Portraits" in the Guggenheim Museum SoHo.

PHOTOGRAPHY

As scenes of carnage and destruction were repeatedly aired and published following the September 11 terrorist acts in the U.S., people around the world compulsively gaped in horror and disbelief at the images that had been captured on film and magnetic media. From snapshots grabbed with cheap single-use cameras to images made with the most expensive professional video equipment, photography once again demonstrated its shattering power as eyewitness. Hundreds of these photographs gained a life-affirming purpose in late September with the opening of "Here Is New York." At this busy SoHo storefront show, professional and amateur pictures of the World Trade Center attacks and their aftermath could be bought for $25 each, with the proceeds going to aid the children of the victims.

During 2001 Walker Evans received superstar treatment with two major exhibitions. "Walker Evans & Company," a loan exhibition put together by the Museum of Modern Art (MoMA) in New York City, displayed some 60 photographs by Evans himself plus nearly 200 images from other photographers, painters, sculptors, and graphic artists strongly influenced by his penetrating vision and powerful personality. Complementing the MoMA exhibition was "The American Tradition & Walker Evans," which featured more than 100 images from the collection of the J. Paul Getty Museum in Los Angeles. The show explored how American photographers such as Carlton Watkins, Lewis Hine, Paul Strand, and Dorothea Lange were shaped by Evans's seminal insights into the American character and the power of a straight documentary esthetic to illuminate it.

The busy Getty Museum dipped into its collection of work by the German documentary portraitist August Sander to mount an important retrospective, "August Sander: German Portraits, 1918–1933." During those hectic years of the Weimar Republic and Adolf Hitler's rise to power, Sander worked on an ambitious visual document, "Man in the Twentieth Century." His goal was to make "simple, natural portraits that portray the subject in an environment corresponding to their own individuality" while "simultaneously revealing the social and cultural dimensions of a highly stratified society." To accomplish this, he photographed an "arc" of subjects ranging from artists, intellectuals, business executives, teachers, skilled workmen, and common labourers to the unemployed and the handicapped. When the Nazis came to power, their opposition to his broad, humanistic view of German life forced him to discontinue the project, but, fortunately, both Sander and a representative fraction of his thousands of pre-World War II photographs survived the war.

During the year ink-jet printing technology achieved stunning new levels of photographic reality and exhibition-quality reproduction. Ink-jet printing involved the spraying of minuscule dots of ink onto paper or other absorbent material to form graphic images, which could be derived from digitally recorded photographs or conventional photographs that had been digitized. In particular, recently developed ink products from Iris Graphics and printing equipment from Epson were used to create giant photographic prints with hyperrealistic detail and flamboyant colour. Among highly praised examples were 40 prints exhibited by Stephen Wilkes. This collection, of which the largest print measured about 2½ × 1 m (8 × 3 ft), included a splendid "Horse in Meadow, Belle Fourche, S.D."

The questions "What is a photograph?" and "What are its dimensions as visual reality when the subject is itself a representation?" were explored by conceptual artist Hiroshi Sugimoto with eerie twice-life-size black-and-white "portraits" of waxwork figures. His photographs of the wax effigies of 20th-century celebrities including Yasir Arafat, Salvador Dalí, and Diana, princess of Wales, were briefly displayed at New York City's Sonnabend Gallery. Scheduled for a longer engagement at New York's Guggenheim Museum SoHo was a collection that also included historical figures such as Napoleon, Voltaire, and Henry VIII and his six wives. Sugimoto used only conventional photographic and printing techniques to achieve effects that some found confusing or unsettling. As he commented, "People think these are photos of a painting, or an actor posed in a historical costume."

Spring sales at major photographic auction houses such as Sotheby's, Swann, and Phillips were affected by the continuing economic slowdown in the U.S. Significant numbers of lots up for auction went unsold, and some individual images that had been expected to command top prices failed to do so. Prints of "Chairs, The Medici Fountain, Paris," by André Kertész, which had been expected to fetch $100,000–$150,000, and of Diane Arbus's classic "Identical Twins, Roselle, N.J.," which had been estimated to bring $120,000–$180,000, were both withdrawn after they failed to meet their reserve prices. A signed photogravure of Alfred Stieglitz's "Gossip, Katwyck," about the size of a credit card, exceeded its high estimate, however, and sold for $29,900 at Swann in February.

A definite chill settled in as the year wore on toward the critical autumn photo auctions, and it was not for lack of attractive, valuable photographs. Well before the terrorist attacks, there was concern in the art world because of conditions closely linked to what seemed to be a failing economy and loss of consumer confidence. After the traumatic events of September 11, many art dealers and collectors became pessimistic. Nevertheless, as the year ended, other collectors such as Donald Rubell remained enthusiastic. "I'm like one of those overeaters who can't stop," he commented. "There's not a time when I don't feel like buying art."

The 2001 Pulitzer Prize for breaking news photography went to Alan Diaz of the Associated Press for his photograph of U.S. federal agents removing six-year-old Elián González from his relatives' Miami, Fla., home. Matt Rainey of the *Newark* (N.J.) *Star-Ledger* took the Pulitzer for feature photography for his sensitive photographs documenting the care and recovery of two students critically burned in a dormitory fire at Seton Hall University, South Orange, N.J. At the 58th Annual Pictures of the Year competition, sponsored by the National Press Photographers Association and the University of Missouri School of Journalism, Scott Strazzante of the *Herald News*/Copley Chicago Newspapers and CITY 2000 (Chicago in the Year 2000) photo project won the award for Newspaper Photographer of the Year, while Jon Lowenstein of CITY 2000 was named Magazine Photographer of the Year.

Notable people in the photographic field who died during the year included American photojournalist Will Counts, Cuban photographer Alberto Korda, German-born American photographer Jacques Lowe, French photojournalist and editor Roger-Jean Thérond, and Malian photographer Seydou Keïta. (*See* OBITUARIES.) Another loss was Jack Manning, veteran freelance photographer for the *New York Times* who was particularly well-known for his candid portraits of Cuban leader Fidel Castro. (ARTHUR GOLDSMITH)

ART AUCTIONS AND SALES

The art market continued to thrive in 2001 despite consumer reticence in some markets, and Christie's and Sotheby's continued to sustain challenges for domination from competitors. The two auction houses once again battled for the privilege of offering some of the most coveted art collections in the world, and both managed to secure strong art- and antique-related sales. In December Sotheby's co-owner and former CEO A. Alfred Taubman was convicted in a New York court of conspiring with London-based Christie's chairman Sir Anthony Tennant to fix sellers' fees and other illegal business practices between 1993 and 1999. The auction houses already had settled a related civil suit, but the scandal had little or no effect on sale prices.

Sotheby's Old Master paintings sale held in New York City once again attained impressive results—$32,320,475—and included *Hare in the Forest,* a work by Hans Hoffman that was purchased by the J. Paul Getty Museum for $2,645,750. Sotheby's then offered a selection of Old Master and Modern drawings and prints from the Franz Koenigs collection, which brought $4,895,900; the highlight of that sale was Hans Bol's *Cycle of the Twelve Months,* which hammered at $1,800,000.

Leonardo da Vinci's **Horse and Rider** *was auctioned at Christie's London in July.*

In January Christie's New York offered an extraordinary collection that totaled $26,276,500. At Christie's London in July, a rare drawing—a masterpiece by Leonardo da Vinci, *Horse and Rider*—sold for a resounding £8,143,750 (about $11,533,000), a record for a Leonardo.

The most notable sales in the art world, the spring series of Impressionist and Modern Art and Contemporary Art, registered record sales at both auction houses. In May at Sotheby's New York, the totals for these sales outdid all of the competition and reached a staggering $222.3 million, led by the works in the collection of Stanley J. Seeger. Top lots from the Seeger collection were Francis Bacon's triptych *Study of the Human Body,* which sold for the world-record price of $8,585,750, and Joan Miró's *Nocturne,* which brought $5,615,750, a record for works on paper by the artist. Also offered in the Impressionist series was Claude Monet's *Le Parlement,* a piece that fetched $14,580,750, and *Self Portrait with Horn,* a haunting painting by Max Beckmann, which made a record $22,555,750. An innovative porcelain sculptural work by American artist Jeff Koons (*see* BIOGRAPHIES), *Michael Jackson and Bubbles,* reached a record $5,615,750.

Christie's New York May sale of Impressionist and Modern Art also achieved exciting results, especially when *Nymphéas,* a work by Monet, sold for $9,906,000. In the same evening, Christie's New York also offered three important Picassos from the estate of Patricia A. Withofs; they brought $16,628,000. The unquestionable standout of the trio, *Figure,* a surrealistic depiction of Marie Thérèse Walter, fetched $7,156,000.

In its Masters of the Post-War sale, Christie's sold more than 10 works for more than $1 million each. The focal point of the sale was Andy Warhol's *Large Flowers,* which set a record as the second highest price for the artist at auction—$8,476,000.

Sales remained robust across the Atlantic as well. At Sotheby's London in June, the Impressionist and Modern Art sales totaled some $47 million, with Monet's *Haystacks, Last Rays of the Sun* contributing to the total $14,286,620, an auction record for a work from his iconic series. Another Monet, *Au parc,* which had been forcibly sold in Nazi Germany in 1935, sold for $5,282,950. The painting was offered under an agreement between the current owners and the original heirs.

Christie's Impressionist and Modern June sales in London were equally strong and totaled a decade-high total of $47,241,190. Maurice de Vlaminck's *Peniche sur la Seine* went for $6,698,256. That evening Juan Gris's *Le Gueridon* achieved $6,231,306, a world auction record for the artist.

Also in fine form were the sales of Contemporary and 20th-century art in London. Sotheby's London sale brought the highest total in 10 years—$16,728,841. Attention centred on a colour chart painted by Gerard Richter, which made $2,582,360, a world record for colour charts.

Christie's American Paintings sale in New York in May reached $31,607,175, the second highest total for this category in the auction house's history. Accenting the sale was Georgia O'Keeffe's *Calla Lillies with Red Anemone,* which sold for $6,166,000. Maurice Brazil Prendergast's painting *The Stony Beach* brought $3,526,000. In May Sotheby's American paintings, drawings, and sculpture sale in New York commanded $20,511,125. The apex of the sale was John Singer Sargent's *Rosina-Capri,* which fetched $5,395,750.

Latin American art enjoyed another successful year. In May at Sotheby's New York the sale totaled $7,189,075 and was once again led by an exceptional Frida Kahlo, *Portrait of Christina, My Sister,* which topped the auction at $1,655,750. The May sale at Christie's New York of Latin American paintings achieved $5,753,057, including a $556,000 tag for Rufino Tamayo's *Madre Feliz.*

Both Christie's and Sotheby's celebrated continued success in the jewelry market. In April, Property of a Lady, Christie's New York sale of magnificent jewels, totaled $6,956,477; the real dazzler in the sale was a diamond ring by Bulgari, which realized $3,636,000. Shortly thereafter, Christie's New York offered important jewels from the house of Harry Winston, which brought $1,145,566. Christie's Geneva boasted the highest sales of the spring series, approximately $22 million. The April sale of jewelry at Sotheby's New York brought $11,154,665; an emerald-cut diamond ring fetched $709,750. At Sotheby's spring jewelry sale in Geneva, which totaled $17,018,001, a heart-shaped diamond pendant went for $1,588,230.

In April the front-runner of Sotheby's New York sale of photographs was the single-owner collection from the archives of the Museum of Modern Art, New York City, which totaled a record $4 million. The top lot of this landmark sale was Walker Evans's *Penny Picture Display, Savannah,* which brought $181,750 and established a world auction record for the artist. Christie's New York also offered some rare Brassaï photographs in a sale totaling $2,539,175.

A new world auction record for a literary manuscript was set when the original 36.6-m (120-ft) scroll of *On the Road* (1957), Jack Kerouac's Beat classic that was written in three weeks, fetched a staggering $2,430,000 at Christie's New York in May. In January in New York, Sotheby's offered the scientific library of Joseph A. Freilich, which realized $10,675,080; an intense battle for a first edition of Aristotle's *Opera* ended with a winning bid of $583,250. In a private Christie's sale in June, a fragment of an unfinished work by Mozart sold for a record £355,750 (about $510,600).

At Sotheby's in June the three-day sale of fine art, fashion drawings, and furnishings from the collection of Gianni Versace achieved $10,177,340.

(AMY TODD MIDDLETON)

ANTIQUES AND COLLECTIBLES

Like the economy, the collectibles market in 2001 showed signs of softening. Collectibles that were offered on the Internet sold for about 30% less than they had a year earlier, and fewer items sold at major auctions. Both serious and novice collectors learned more about the value or popularity of items as a result of various reports on trends as well as the plethora of television shows devoted to antiques and collectibles. (*See* Sidebar.)

Among the standout items that sold at auction were a Philadelphia Chippendale card table, which commanded $1,320,000 at a regional auction house in Northfield, Mass., and brought the second highest auction price ever for a card table; a plain beaker-shaped 17th-century silver wine cup (c. 1660) by Hull and Sanderson of Boston, which sold for $775,750 at an international auction house in New York City; and a Southern California American Indian olla (basket), which brought $145,875 in San Francisco.

Costume jewelry, Danish silver jewelry, and theme pieces, including Christmas tree pins or flag pendants, sold as well as in 2000. Bakelite jewelry, perhaps because of the many reproductions, dropped almost 20% in price for all but the greatest rarities. Average California and Czech pottery pieces went for under $200, but prices began rising, especially in the West.

Courtesy of Swann Galleries Inc.

This ski poster fetched a record price for poster art when it was auctioned in New York City in February.

The most newsworthy sale of the year was the auction in Waterville, Maine, of the Buddy "L" Corp.'s toy archives. The Buddy "L" Express truck brought $33,000; the Insurance Patrol truck with box fetched $40,700; and the 1930s International truck-mounted steam shovel with box went for $35,200. Though all toys continued to sell well, robots, cars, and mechanical banks were especially popular.

Rare 19th-century bottles also commanded record-setting prices, including $46,200 for a Corn for the World purple quart flask, $11,200 for a Double Eagle half-pint amethyst flask, and $55,000 for a Masonic-Eagle flask; an aquamarine and milk glass Mason fruit jar sold for $21,280.

Though Arts and Crafts decorative objects sold well, the only record was $195,500 for a Gustav Stickley music cabinet designed by Harvey Ellis. Other furniture records included $36,400 for a carved walnut hat rack (c. 1868) by Mitchell & Rammelsberg of Cincinnati, Ohio, and $138,000 for an 18th-century American sack-back Windsor armchair. Collectors favouring expensive formal 18th-century furniture began substituting moderately priced good reproductions made in the 1930s. Large old dining-room sets were in demand, and prices for them had doubled in the past few years. Tramp art and unrestored rustic and country furniture continued to sell well.

Late 19th- and 20th-century art pottery remained a best-seller at shows, at auctions, and on the Internet. A 23-cm (1 cm = 0.39 in) Grueby tile decorated with geese sold for a record $11,500, and a Marblehead Pottery vase decorated with Ipswich marsh scenes brought $108,640. As prices rose for Roseville—the most popular of American potteries—Grueby, Rookwood, and Weller, collectors turned to Hull, Shawnee, and other less-famous wares. Late 19th-century majolica remained popular and expensive. Mochaware, an early 1800s ware, set records when a 23-cm jug with twig designs and blue and rust bands sold for $14,950; that record was surpassed a few weeks later when a 14.6-cm mug decorated with lime green and rust-coloured bands brought $19,250.

Swann Auction Galleries in New York City sold a ski poster titled "Yosemite Winter Sports," for a record $6,325. A major poster auction in Ohio set a number of records—$4,312 for Eric Von Stroheim's poster for the 1925 film *Greed;* $3,910 for a lobby card advertising the 1920 movie *Terror Island,* starring Harry Houdini; and $2,185 for a 1920 Tom Mix six-sheet *Days of Daring* movie poster. The Academy Award statuette won by Bette Davis for *Jezebel* (1938) went for $578,000.

Some sports memorabilia also set records. An astounding $577,610 was paid via an Internet auction for "Shoeless" Joe Jackson's baseball bat, Black Betsy, and $275,000 was paid in a private sale for a Mickey Mantle mint 1952 Topps card. The press book for the 1920 sports movie *Play Ball with Babe Ruth* sold for $2,415.

Other interesting record sales for the year included an 1880 Edison Spectacle phonograph, $49,500; a 1946 Phantom camera, $220,000; a Remington claw & ball gun cane (c. 1859), $16,240; an 1880 occupational shaving mug decorated with a lunch wagon, $42,550; a 1950 George Lawrence fishing creel of split willow with leather trim, $9,020; and a cobalt blue glass whale-oil lamp, $26,795. (RALPH AND TERRY KOVEL)

Antiquing for the Ages: The Search for Hidden Treasures

The promise of huge payoffs sent droves of treasure seekers to attics, basements, yard sales, and trash piles in 2001. Fueling the antique mania was the popularity and high visibility of television shows, including *Antiques Road Show, Treasures in Your Attic,* and *Appraisal Fair,* featuring experts who revealed in a number of instances that items thought to be worthless relics were priceless antiques.

Author and appraiser Helaine Fendelman stated that as the new millennium dawned, Americans became more aware that objects they owned might have monetary value. At the same time, the Internet drew more and more individuals on-line, and Internet auctioneers eBay and Antique Networking brought additional attention to the antiques market.

Americans began to wonder about the real value of their own possessions. Unless one was careful, someone more knowledgeable might scoop up castoffs and sell them in turn for a profit. As a result, would-be fortune seekers were sent scrambling to learn everything they could about their family heirlooms and attic treasures. They read trade papers, notably *Collectors News* and *Maine Antique Digest,* listened to radio shows (*Whatcha Got,* hosted by Harry L. Rinker), and watched special TV spots shown on *Martha Stewart Living* and ABC's *PrimeTime.*

It was the television programs devoted to appraisals, however, that spurred the antiquing phenomenon of the 21st century. Antiques experts were virtually transported into the average American living room, where they discussed common misconceptions about antiques, told the difference between an antique and a reproduction, assessed the values of antiques, and exposed unscrupulous practices in the industry. Appraisers shared the history and lore of items and their status as collectibles, whereas owners shared their own personal stories.

Noncollectors were finding that they owned valuable treasures and that the value of the objects increased if they remained in their original condition. An old Depression glass pitcher, found in a box at a flea market, was revealed to be a sought-after piece in the Cameo pattern valued at $1,500–$2,000. Great-grandfather's old railroad conductor's lantern, dating from the 1860s, was assessed at $700–$900. A table lamp, handed down in the family, turned out to be signed by Tiffany Studios and worth $10,000–$12,000.

During these "at-home" courses on collecting, hopefuls also learned the hard reality that not everything "old" was collectible and worth substantial amounts of money. Though a number of items were preserved, owners found in many cases that their keepsakes' only value was sentimental.

Nonetheless, the dream of being one of the lucky owners of a precious possession could not be dampened. It was that dream that brought hundreds of collectibles to the surface and that would continue to send Americans on a search for hidden treasures.

(LINDA M. KRUGER)

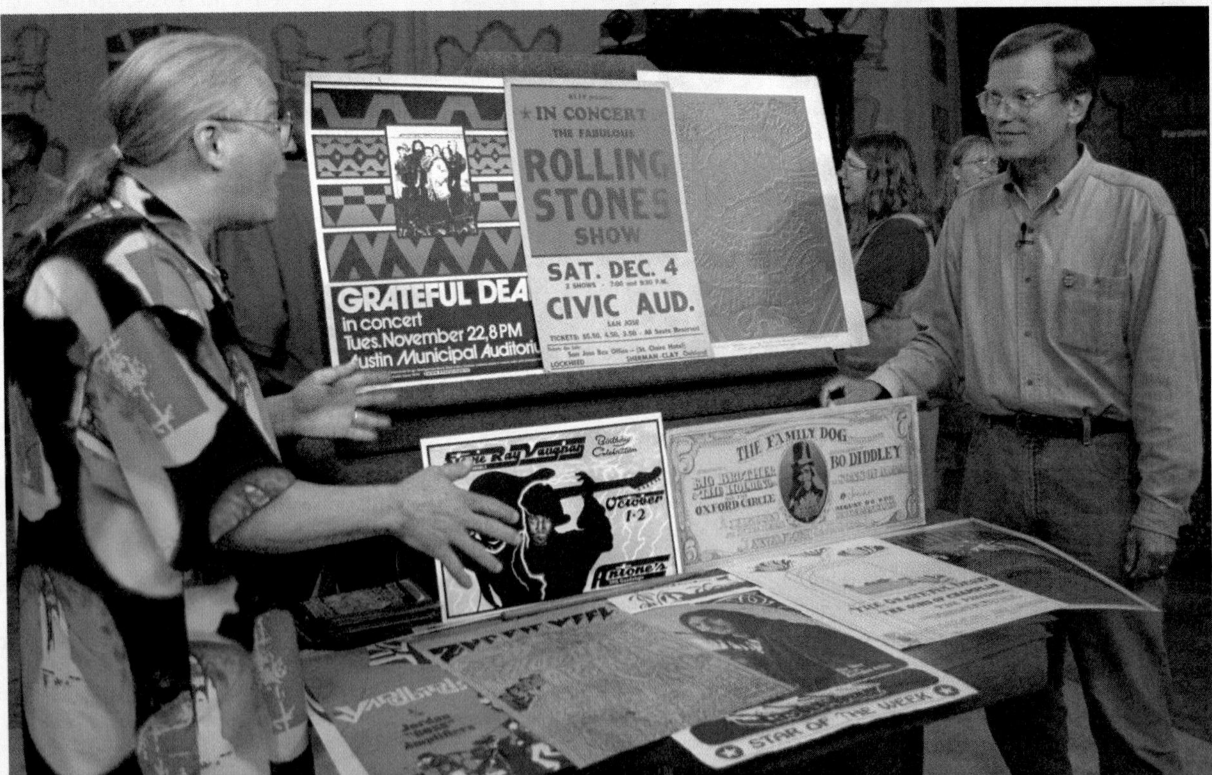

On a February 19 episode of Antiques Road Show, *antiques dealer Gary Sohmers (left) appraises a collection of concert posters and other rock-and-roll memorabilia from the 1960s and '70s at $15,000.*

Jeff Dunn for WGBH

Computers and Information Systems

Corporate **CUTBACKS, LAYOFFS, AND MERGERS** dominated information systems sectors in 2001 as the U.S. recession pushed high-tech stocks even lower; **MICROSOFT** released Windows XP and reached a tentative settlement in its widely followed court case; the first **THIRD-GENERATION (3G) CELLULAR PHONE** service was introduced in Japan.

The recession year 2001 hit the computers and information systems sector hard. Already reeling from the collapse of dot-com companies a year earlier, the industry had to deal with reduced demand for its products and services. That in turn produced a steady stream of corporate cutbacks and layoffs. The terrorist attacks in the U.S. on September 11, which stunned the world and sent the U.S. stock market tumbling, dealt the troubled technology sector yet another blow.

The computer industry laid off tens of thousands of workers in 2001 as a slowing U.S. economy combined with fallout from the previous year's meltdown of high-tech dot-com companies to reduce demand for information technology products. Cisco Systems, reporting its first quarterly loss in its 11-year history in May, took more than $3 billion in charges against earnings. The charges were mainly related to inventory Cisco believed it might never sell because of the downturn in demand. Layoffs were announced at dozens of computer-related companies, including AOL Time Warner, Inc., Dell Computer Corp., IBM Corp., Sun Microsystems, Inc., Oracle Corp., Texas Instruments, Inc., Siemens AG of Germany, and the Japanese companies Fujitsu, Ltd., Hitachi, Ltd., and Toshiba Corp.

Yet out of the decline a new industry was taking shape. The Hewlett-Packard Co. said it would purchase competitor Compaq Computer Corp., combining two major competitors in the personal computer (PC) market. In the long-running Microsoft Corp. antitrust trial, an appeals court freed Microsoft from the threat of a breakup, and the Department of Justice (DOJ), under the new Republican administration of Pres. George W. Bush, indicated that it would not pursue the software-bundling issues that had been the heart of the original lawsuit.

The Internet became less competitive. The contracting economy left even strong electronic-commerce (e-commerce) companies struggling with losses, and brick-and-mortar companies began to see their e-commerce operations less as profit centres and more as strategic efforts. The huge declines in the value of technology stocks and the dearth of new capital for technology companies resulted in the collapse of alternative high-speed digital subscriber line (DSL) Internet access providers.

The music industry won its battle against Napster but not the war against free Internet music. Napster, the renegade World Wide Web site that stood accused of aiding copyright infringement by allowing consumers to trade music files for free, was shut down by court order, but other file-sharing Web sites rose up to take its place.

Attitudes toward computer security changed in the wake of the September 11 terrorist attacks. Personal privacy on the Internet seemed likely to decline as the government gained additional freedom to track e-mail, instant messaging, and Web surfing. Several devastating attacks by malicious Internet software resulted in coordinated government and business efforts to prevent future threats.

Microsoft. The Microsoft antitrust case ended the year without a resolution, but the year was a busy one in the ongoing battle over Microsoft's behaviour. The company appeared to have avoided being broken up, but it still faced court penalties for violating antitrust laws.

A federal court previously had found that Microsoft violated federal antitrust laws through actions intended to maintain Microsoft's monopoly on PC operating system (OS) software. That finding was confirmed in June by a seven-judge panel from the U.S. Court of Appeals for the District of Columbia Circuit, which held that Microsoft had violated antitrust laws repeatedly.

The appeals court judges vacated, or nullified, the breakup of Microsoft imposed the previous year by U.S. District Judge Thomas Penfield Jackson, who had put his ruling on hold pending appeals. At the same time, the appeals court removed Jackson from the case, an unusual action, and criticized him for comments about the case he had made outside the courtroom. A newly appointed federal judge, Colleen Kollar-Kotelly, ordered settlement talks. In October the U.S. Supreme Court declined to hear Microsoft's appeal, which requested that the high court dismiss the lower court's findings against the company on the basis of the appeal courts reprimand of Judge Jackson. It was a setback for Microsoft, but one that many who followed the case had expected.

The Bush administration signaled late in the year that it did not have as much enthusiasm for pursuing the Microsoft case as former president Bill Clinton's administration had. The DOJ said in September that it had decided not to seek a breakup of Microsoft or to insist that Microsoft's bundling, or inclusion, of its Internet Explorer browser with the Windows OS was illegal. Instead, the DOJ said it would pursue limitations on Microsoft's business conduct similar to those Jackson previously ordered. Those restrictions included requiring Microsoft to share Windows technical information with other software companies, to offer PC manufacturers "unbundled" versions of Windows that did not include extra Microsoft software, and to sell Windows to all PC makers at the same price. Microsoft previously had resisted efforts to place any restrictions on what it could bundle into its operating system. Some legal experts said that at least part of the government's announcement was a practical move—a breakup of Microsoft was unlikely to occur because the federal appeals court had already vacated Jackson's initial breakup order.

In early November Microsoft and the DOJ reached a tentative settlement, but half of the 18 states that had joined the federal government in the case appeared unwilling to compromise. Some of the states threatened to carry on their antitrust cases independently if the DOJ settled with Microsoft on terms the states considered too easy. Nine states—California, Connecticut, Florida, Iowa, Kansas, Massachusetts, Minnesota, Utah, and West Virginia, plus the District of Columbia—rejected the federal government's settlement with Microsoft because they said it let the company off too easily, and planned to continue the antitrust suit. California, one of the largest states in the group, was expected to pay much of the cost involved. It appeared that a hearing on what action the federal court should take against Microsoft would occur in March 2002.

The states wanted rules to prevent Microsoft from combining or "bundling" with Windows any additional free software features—a move that worked to the disadvantage of Microsoft's competitors. In addition, states wanted the court to prevent Microsoft from offering incentives to PC manufacturers to put Microsoft applications software on new PCs instead of applications from competitors. (The states said the federal settlement would only prevent Microsoft from penalizing PC makers for not using its software.) The states also wanted competitors to have better access to underlying Windows software code than required under the proposed federal settlement.

The states also continued to be concerned about recent Microsoft behaviour not directly related to the antitrust case: Microsoft's new Windows XP operating system, which bundled new technologies—such as streaming video and instant messaging—that could adversely affect Microsoft's competitors. Windows XP went on sale on October 25, but details of what it contained had been disclosed by Microsoft months earlier. In a separate class-action suit, Microsoft offered a settlement that would include donating computer equipment and software to schools. Opponents, led by Apple Computer Corp., objected that this action would effectively expand Microsoft's inroads into education, where it did not yet have a monopoly.

Personal Computers. The PC industry was in decline in 2001 as demand dropped, and a price war broke out between PC manufacturers. It was a sharp reversal for a traditional growth industry. When worldwide PC shipments dropped 1.9% in the second quarter, it was the first decline since 1986.

A revised outlook issued in early September by market research firm IDC predicted that PC shipments worldwide would decline 1.6% in 2001, to about 130 million units. That was in sharp contrast to IDC's June prediction that shipments would grow 5.8% and far less than IDC's earlier prediction that shipments would grow 10.3% for the year. The consumer portion of the PC market declined even more than the overall market; unit shipments were expected to drop 9.6% worldwide.

The slack demand resulted in a price war between manufacturers that was expected to lower revenues for the PC industry. IDC predicted a 10.8% drop in worldwide PC revenue for the year. Some PC companies decided they had had enough. Micron Electronics dropped out of the PC business and laid off 400 people who worked in that business unit.

It was unclear how the IDC projections would be affected by the September 11 terrorist attacks, which shook consumer confidence and rattled the U.S. economy. Merrill Lynch & Co. said in late September that the struggling PC market had been hurt further by the attacks as well as by a likely global recession and that a recovery from the decline in PC unit shipments, revenues, and average sale prices was not expected for at least a year.

In the first quarter of 2001, Dell replaced Compaq as the world's largest PC maker. It was the first change in the top position in several years. Later in the year Dell aggressively courted additional customers by continuing the price war it had begun in 2000. The company said its goal was to increase its mid-2001 global market share of 13% to 40% over several years.

Windows XP was considered by many to be the PC industry's best hope to boost demand. Because many older PCs lacked the processing power and memory required for running XP, industry observers expected the product launch to increase sales of new PCs. Windows XP featured higher reliability than earlier versions of Windows, plus new features dealing with instant messaging, digital photography, and security (in the form of a "personal firewall" to block Internet intruders). While some feared that the ongoing Microsoft antitrust case might lead government regulators to try to block the introduction of XP or force it to be altered, that did not happen, and the product was launched as expected.

By the time Windows XP was introduced in October, many industry watchers were predicting that it would not make a significant difference in 2001 PC sales, both because of concerns about the economy and because XP did not offer enough incremental benefits to boost sales of PCs that came equipped with the new operating system.

Another potential roadblock to the XP introduction did not have much impact. Some privacy advocates asked the Federal Trade Commission to take action against Microsoft based on their contention that Windows XP facilitated the collection of too much personal information about consumers through the sign-up for Microsoft's on-line e-commerce services.

Microsoft made some changes to Windows XP on its own in response to industry complaints. In June the company removed XP's "smart tags," which could link any word on any Web page to another Web site selected by Microsoft. The implication was that Microsoft would be able to use XP to divert e-commerce customers to its own Web sites. Another controversial XP technology, called product activation, remained. To prevent customers from installing one copy of XP on multiple computers, the software took the "electronic fingerprint" of the PC on which it was installed. Substantial changes in that computer would cause XP to deactivate, on the theory that the operating system had been installed on a different machine. Some industry watchers said merely upgrading a computer could cause the deactivation; Microsoft said the changes to the machine would have to be more elaborate than that but did not provide details.

Apple's rival operating system, Mac OS X, which was released for public beta testing in 2000, began shipping in early 2001. A much-anticipated upgrade, OS X version 10.1, followed in the autumn. During the year Apple opened the first of a series of company-owned retail stores in high-traffic shopping malls, veering away from its strategy of selling strictly through independent resellers, large electronics retailers, and its own Web site. The firm hoped to attract some current users of Windows-based PCs at a time when Apple's share of the PC market was about 4.5%. The company's independent dealers believed the new stores were a necessary evil that would take some sales away from dealers but would ultimately help Apple compete against the market domination of Windows-based PCs. Apple also discontinued its Power Mac G4 Cube, a small cube-shaped computer introduced a year earlier, blaming lower-than-expected sales. The company, in a move to remain competitive with Windows-based PC prices, brought back a $799 iMac desktop computer that had been replaced by higher-priced models.

A father and son try out a Flower Power iMac during the grand opening of an Apple retail store in McLean, Va., on May 19.

AP/Wide World Photos

In October Apple introduced iPod, a pocket-sized portable music player that could download and play up to 10 hours of music in the popular MP3 format. A Windows version was expected to follow.

PCs got faster, but as the price of chips came down, they debuted at lower prices than previous top-of-the-line models. In August PCs installed with Intel Corp.'s 2-GHz (gigahertz) Pentium 4 chips (operating at two billion computing cycles per second) arrived. Their beginning prices were as low as $1,500, a switch from the previous generation of new computers; less than a year and a half earlier, a low-end 1-GHz PC had cost $3,000. In large part the price declines were related to lower selling prices for microprocessor chips.

Another kind of PC, the handheld personal digital assistant (PDA), continued to make inroads with consumers and business customers, although sales growth slowed and manufacturers cut prices in response. The best-known PDA brands from Palm, Inc., and Handspring were more than handheld organizers but less than laptop computers. They had date and address books, to-do lists, and memo pads and used handwriting-recognition software. Handspring licensed the Palm OS, but more capable and expensive devices running the Microsoft Pocket PC operating system were being positioned to compete in the business market.

Acquisitions and Mergers. The biggest industry deal of the year was announced in September. Hewlett-Packard, the third largest PC maker, said it would buy Compaq, the second largest, for $25 billion in stock. The merged firm would control about 70% of the retail PC market and would rank second in sales to IBM, with $87.4 billion. To realize cost savings, the two firms would need to cut some 15,000 jobs, leaving the combined company with about 135,000 workers. Carly Fiorina, chairman and chief executive of Hewlett-Packard, was to retain those positions in the combined company, and Michael Capellas, chairman and CEO of Compaq, would be president. The acquisition was not viewed positively by Wall Street. Between the September announcement and mid-October, when a shareholder group voiced opposition to the combination, Hewlett-Packard shares fell 22% and Compaq shares fell 20%. Analysts said one concern was that there was too much overlap between the operations of the two firms. Shareholder opposition to the deal grew as members of the Hewlett and Packard families, who held 18% of the company's shares, publicly opposed the merger. Should shareholders vote against the merger, it was widely believed that Fiorina would lose her top post at Hewlett-Packard. A shareholder vote on the deal was expected in early 2002.

In January Ariba, Inc., a business transaction software company, announced plans to acquire Agile Software Corp., which helped manufacturing companies collaborate on the Internet, for $2,550,000,000 in stock. LSI Logic Corp., which manufactured communications and storage chips, bought C-Cube Microsystems, Inc., for $878 million in stock. TMP Worldwide Inc., the parent company of Internet jobs Web site Monster.com, tried to acquire HotJobs.com, its biggest competitor, but was outbid by Yahoo! Inc., which agreed to pay $436 million.

Jupiter Media Metrix, Inc., which measured the popularity of top Web sites and advised companies on Internet use, was acquired by NetRatings, another Web audience-measurement firm, for $71.2 million. Computer Associates International, Inc., successfully resisted an effort to take over its board of directors, turning back a bid by investor Sam Wyly to replace four directors, including the company's founder and chairman.

On-Line Music. On-line music downloading continued to blossom, despite the music industry's efforts to stop unauthorized free distribution of copyrighted music and the industry's own slowly unfolding plan to sell music over the Internet.

There was a major development in the Recording Industry Association of America's lawsuit against Napster, the high-profile Web service that popularized free music downloads. A federal judge in July ordered Napster to halt its music-file-sharing service until it could show that it had taken all possible steps to prevent the free exchange of copyrighted music. Napster was later allowed to resume Internet operations but chose not to in order to prepare for the 2002 launch of its new membership service. In addition, Napster settled separate copyright-infringement suits filed against it by the heavy-metal band Metallica and the rap artist Dr. Dre, although settlement terms were not disclosed.

Other free file-sharing services took Napster's place, and one, Fast Track, even exceeded the volume that Napster had had at its peak. In October some 30 music and film studios filed suit in federal court against three Internet music Web sites—MusicCity.com, Grokster Ltd., and Consumer Empowerment BV—alleging that they improperly allowed the exchange of music, images, and movies that were copyrighted.

The new free music services on the Internet presented the music industry with vexing legal problems. Court injunctions might be unable to shut down the new services, which allowed music sharing directly between PCs instead of relying on a centralized corporate Web site, as Napster did. Shutting down the Web sites might not end the file sharing among users.

The music industry announced plans to offer, by year's end, two for-pay subscription services for on-line music. Sony Music Entertainment Inc. and Universal Music Group cooperated on a service to be called Pressplay, while EMI Group PLC, AOL Time Warner, Bertelsmann AG's BMG, and RealNetworks, Inc., were behind a competing service to be called MusicNet. Other, similar services were likely to emerge. The exact nature of the music offerings was not disclosed, but the industry's licensing arrangements with music publishers and songwriters covered streaming music—a technique that would let customers listen to music but not record it—and music file downloads that would be limited by how much or how long they could be used. The music industry's efforts to move into for-pay on-line music distribution prompted the DOJ to launch an antitrust investigation aimed at determining whether the music industry was attempting to dominate Internet music illegally. It also was uncertain how successful the initially limited for-pay offerings would be against the free file-sharing services.

The Internet. Despite growing demand for high-speed Internet service, the declining economy effectively reduced the number of competitors, and the DSL service was left largely in the hands of the former regional Bell telephone companies. Several independent companies that provided DSL either failed or were in serious trouble. NorthPoint Communications Group, Inc., and Rhythms NetConnections Inc. shut down. DSL firm Covad Communications Co., which sought protection from creditors in bankruptcy court, said it hoped to attract $200 million in cash investments that would make it profitable again by the end of 2003.

The cable modem service offered by cable TV system operators, which was DSL's chief competitor for high-speed Internet access, had fewer spectacular declines, but even there business failure occurred. At Home Corp. (which did business as Excite@Home), a provider of high-speed Internet access to about four million subscribers through various cable TV systems, filed for bankruptcy protection in September but continued to serve its customers. A month earlier Excite@Home's auditing firm, which had already been slated to be fired, had raised doubts about the company's ability to continue in business. These doubts were confirmed in early December as hundreds of thousands of AT&T Broadband subscribers were left temporarily without Internet access when Excite@Home canceled its contract with AT&T and cut off their service. Excite@Home said it would cease operations in February 2002.

Wireless high-speed networking companies also ran into trouble. Metricom, Inc., which offered wireless Internet access for notebook computer users in several cities, filed for bankruptcy in July and began selling its assets. MobileStar Network Corp., which provided high-speed wireless Internet access to Starbucks Corp.'s coffee outlets and to several hotels, laid off its workforce and planned to sell its assets.

The world's largest Internet access provider raised prices for its dial-up modem service. America Online, a part of AOL Time Warner, boosted its popular unlimited-use plan by about 9%, to $23.90 a month. AOL justified its first price increase in three years by saying usage of its service by customers had increased more than 50% in that time. AOL remained the market leader in U.S. Internet access. At the time of the price increase, AOL had about 30 million subscribers, MSN (Microsoft Network) was second with about 5 million, and EarthLink, Inc., was third with about 4.8 million. Freeserve remained the most widely used provider in the U.K., with AOL second.

Late in the year President Bush signed legislation that extended a moratorium on Internet-related taxes for two years, at least temporarily preventing states from levying their own Internet taxes on billions of dollars in e-commerce sales as well as on the sale of Internet access services. There had been fears that Internet taxation by states might contribute to the nation's economic problems.

The virtual world of the Internet proved to be vulnerable to natural disasters in the real world. In July a fire in a Baltimore, Md., train tunnel burned fibre-optic telecommunications cables. Rerouting Internet traffic to other cables resulted in slowdowns in Internet traffic. Damage to undersea cables near China, probably caused by cargo ships dragging their anchors, disrupted Internet traffic between Asia and the U.S. in September.

The U.S. Census Bureau reported in 2001 that 51% of the households in the nation had one or more personal computers in 2000 and that more than 40% of households were connected to the Internet. The results were based on a survey of about 50,000 U.S. households in August 2000.

An Internet-oriented product, the Web appliance, began to disappear from the market owing to lack of demand. Web appliances were intended to offer consumers an easier way to browse the Web and often were less complex than a PC. They were not much less expensive than a PC, however, and never sold in significant numbers. Sony, 3Com Corp., and Gateway, Inc., dropped Web appliance products in 2001.

E-Commerce. E-commerce continued the downward slide that had begun in early 2000. In the first half of 2001, U.S. Internet advertising revenues declined 7.8% from the same period a year earlier. The on-line ad sales decline compared with revenue growth of 78% in 2000 and marked the end of several years of substantial growth in on-line ad revenues. The Interactive Advertising Bureau, a trade group, said the decline in Internet advertising had come at a time when traditional TV, radio, and newspaper advertising revenues also had dropped.

Many smaller e-commerce players dropped out of the market, and even top players such as Yahoo! were troubled. A 44% decline in revenue caused a third-quarter net loss at Yahoo! and led the company to warn that difficult times and layoffs lay just ahead. Amazon.com, another big player, eliminated 1,300 jobs on January 30, 450 of them by shutting down a distribution centre in McDonough, Ga. One of the few Internet ventures to buck the downward trend was the on-line auction firm eBay Inc., which was flourishing under its president and CEO, Meg Whitman. (*See* BIOGRAPHIES.)

For big corporations e-commerce took on a different tone. On-line business units of brick-and-mortar retailers were valued less as profit centres and more as on-line testing grounds for measuring the appeal of new products and identifying customer buying patterns. In addition, the automobile industry, which knew that consumers were inclined to do their car-buying research on the Web, concentrated on using the Internet as a means to draw people into traditional showrooms rather than as a way to sell cars directly.

E-commerce companies, which relied heavily on credit card purchases, became concerned about increasing credit card fraud. Some claimed that Web fraud expanded after credit card companies ruled that sellers would be liable for disputed card purchases unless the seller had a copy of the buyer's credit card or of the buyer's signature. E-commerce marketers who did business over the Web usually did not have those copies and as a result found themselves stuck for purchases that buyers said they did not make.

In tough times new, unorthodox methods of competition arose. When customers visited some e-commerce sites, free software that ran in the background of a customer's computer would flash ads for competing services on the PC's screen. This software, typically downloaded for free from sites such as Gator.com, offered to make Web browsing easier. In another unusual move, many search engine Web sites, unable to make enough money with advertising, sold listings. This essentially guaranteed that a paid customer would show up near the top of search query results on a particular topic. Web sites that did not sell listings in their searches were able to differentiate themselves from the competition.

Microsoft was undeterred by the e-commerce downturn and introduced its new .NET strategy for selling more services on-line to consumers and businesses. Microsoft said its .NET My Services would sell subscription-based Internet services revolving around online content, banking, shopping, and entertainment.

Crime, Security, and Law. After a year in which malicious attacks by creators of Internet viruses and worms made headlines for weeks, it was the U.S. government's actions following the September 11 terrorist attacks that had the greatest potential impact. In October President Bush signed into law the USA PATRIOT Act, which gave law-enforcement officials greater ability to tap telephones and track Internet users.

The new law expanded the use of a federal government Internet spying technology formerly called Carnivore. Carnivore allowed the government to collect, through an Internet service provider (ISP) network, a person's e-mail, instant messaging, and Web surfing activities. The law also expanded the way information was shared between government agencies and made it easier for government investigators to obtain wiretapping permission for Internet activity. In addition, ISPs would be required to make it easier for the government to install wiretaps on their systems. Unlike some other parts of the new law that would not expire, the Internet surveillance portion would expire at the end of 2005.

Meg Whitman, president and CEO of eBay Inc., shakes hands with Microsoft CEO Steve Ballmer after the announcement on March 12 of a new strategic alliance between the two companies.

AP/Wide World Photos

Privacy advocates criticized the new law as a hasty action that unnecessarily expanded the governments surveillance powers, particularly when there was not much evidence that greater surveillance would have warned of the September 11 terrorist attacks.

Some observers worried that another wave of terrorist attacks could be made against "infrastructure" computer systems, including those that ran the electric power grid. Utilities, telecommunications plants, and factories that ran process-control equipment at remote locations by using the Internet were considered potentially vulnerable. The Internet Corporation for Assigned Names and Numbers planned to review the security of the Internet's domain name system.

Computerized disaster-recovery services, originally envisioned to help corporations recover data lost in natural disasters such as fires or storms, got more attention as corporations and Wall Street firms recovered from the terrorist attacks. Disaster-recovery firms provided crucial computer network repairs, temporary data-processing centres, and replacement computers.

Following the terrorist attacks, there was much discussion of increased security. Microsoft said it would increase internal security after six employees in its Reno, Nev., office were exposed to life-threatening anthrax spores sent by mail from Malaysia. Elaborate computer security schemes for airports were discussed, including facial-recognition systems that would pick out people whose features matched those of suspected terrorists. Fear of flying also produced a surge of interest in videoconferencing, which enabled businesspeople to meet face-to-face even though they were hundreds or thousands of kilometres apart.

The CERT (originally the computer emergency response team) Coordination Center, a government-funded group that monitored computer security threats, estimated that the number of Internet attacks could double in 2001 compared with 2000, when there were nearly 22,000 recorded attacks, each representing a report filed by a company or an organization. The projected increase was attributed to growth in the Internet as well as to an increase in the number of attackers.

The Code Red worm attracted national attention when it struck in July and reappeared in August. (A "worm" is a malicious Internet program that reproduces itself. Unlike a virus, which tricks a computer user into starting it, a worm acts without human intervention and thus spreads rapidly.) Code Red attempted to attack the White House Web page in mid-July by first infecting an estimated 225,000 Internet Web server computers worldwide. It did so by taking advantage of a well-known Microsoft server software flaw, for which Microsoft had issued a software "patch." Many companies operating these Web servers had not put the patch in place. Code Red then used those servers to launch a "denial of service attack," in which the infected computers tried to overload the White House Web page by sending thousands of simultaneous requests for information. Some 350,000 computers were ultimately infected.

Code Red provoked major concern about the Internet's ability to withstand the attack. The FBI's National Infrastructure Protection Center called Code Red a significant threat that could "degrade services running on the Internet." Those fears were heightened when a second version of Code Red appeared in early August; that version of the worm left open a "back door" on a server that would allow a hacker to gain access to the server. The Internet as a whole never was seriously affected by Code Red. Other high-profile attacks included the "SirCam" virus, which arrived as an e-mail attachment and could delete or e-mail files from infected PCs, and the Nimda worm, which infected both Web server computers and PCs and caused damage by overwriting computer files.

There were some high-profile computer-related crimes and court cases during 2001. Dmitry Sklyarov, a Russian cryptographer, was one of the first people to be prosecuted for allegedly violating the Digital Millennium Copyright Act, a 1998 law that limited unauthorized copying of digital material. Sklyarov was arrested after he gave a presentation at a hacker convention on how to decode software used to protect electronic books. About 100 people were arrested in August for what federal officials said was participation in a global Internet child pornography ring. The investigation revolved around Landslide Productions Inc. of Fort Worth, Texas, which offered subscribers access to foreign-based Web sites containing child pornography.

The FBI and the DOJ said 90 individuals and companies were charged as part of an Internet fraud investigation called "Operation Cyber Loss." Based on losses by thousands of people totaling $117 million, the unnamed defendants faced federal and state charges that included wire fraud, mail fraud, bank fraud, money laundering, and violation of intellectual property rights. The charges revolved around on-line auction fraud, nondelivery of products bought on-line, bank fraud, and pyramid schemes.

The Securities and Exchange Commission (SEC) accused two former top executives at software company AremisSoft Corp. of having defrauded investors of at least $200 million. In a civil suit the SEC said the two had used untrue financial statements in order to sell millions of shares of company stock at inflated prices.

The U.S. Supreme Court ruled in favour of a group of freelance writers who had sued newspaper and magazine publishers for infringing on the writers' copyrights. The suit claimed the publications had infringed by not obtaining permission to make articles available in computer databases following publication. (*See* MEDIA AND PUBLISHING: *Newspapers*.) Another case scheduled to go before the court was a challenge to the 1996 Child Pornography Prevention Act, which had widened the definition of child pornography. The law extended a ban on images of real children engaging in sexual acts to cover computer-generated images that did not involve real children. Civil libertarians argued that the law set a dangerous precedent by punishing creators of computer-generated pictures; proponents of the law said the wider definition was needed to protect children from pedophiles who wanted such images.

At Lawrence Livermore National Laboratory near San Francisco, a Unix system administrator opens the back door of a node of ASCI White, the world's most powerful computer.

AP/Wide World Photos

Other Developments. Lernout & Hauspie Speech Products NV, the Belgian firm that was Europes largest developer of speech-recognition and translation software, was declared insolvent, and a court ordered its assets liquidated. The firm had sought protection under the bankruptcy laws of Belgium and the U.S. in late 2000 after a $100 million cash shortfall was discovered in its South Korean unit and an investigation showed that the company's questionable accounting practices had overstated overall company sales by $373 million from 1998 to 2000.

IBM designed the world's most powerful supercomputer for the U.S. government's Lawrence Livermore National Laboratory, Livermore, Calif. The supercomputer was to be used to simulate nuclear weapons explosions. It was funded by the Accelerated Strategic Computing Initiative, which paid computer manufacturers to build supercomputers from ordinary computer components.

IBM also said it had found a way to speed up computer chips by using conventional chip-manufacturing technologies to reduce electrical resistance in chips, which resulted in processing speeds up to 35% faster. Meanwhile, scientists believed that nanotubes, cylinder-shaped molecules 1.4 nanometres (billionths of a metre) in diameter, held out the promise of improving future computer chip designs. Researchers from Michigan State University and IBM said the molecules could help chips run cooler by conducting heat away and might be used as structurally stronger replacements for the tiny metal wires connecting transistors on a chip.

Computer chip manufacturers also were seeking higher chip performance by switching from aluminum to copper (which conducts electricity better than aluminum) for the tiny wires on a chip. In addition, Intel said it was considering using strands of fibre-optic material in place of aluminum and copper wires inside computers. Initially that would mean connecting separate computer components with fibre optics, but eventually the technology could be used on computer chips too. The fibre-optic technology could help boost chip performance because it required less power than wires.

Bell Labs, the research unit of Lucent Technologies Inc., said it had created a tiny organic transistor by assembling carbon molecules. Scientists said the technology might one day be used to make computer chips that were faster, smaller, and easier to manufacture.

Video game enthusiasts had a good year in 2001. Nintendo Co., Ltd., introduced its new Game Boy Advance handheld game machine, and in November two next-generation game console machines, the Microsoft Xbox and the Nintendo GameCube, were introduced. Xbox and GameCube competed with the Sony PlayStation 2. Another competitor, Sega Enterprises Ltd., ended production of its game console, the Dreamcast.

The game industry was attacked in a study from Japan's Tohoku University that said video games might adversely affect brain development in children. A game industry group, the European Leisure Software Publishers Association, claimed that the Japanese research had only a "very limited focus" and that game playing developed several skills.

Gordon Moore, cofounder and retired chairman of Intel, and his wife, Betty, donated $600 million to the California Institute of Technology, from which Moore had graduated with a Ph.D. in chemistry in 1954. It was believed to be the biggest gift ever received by an individual American school. Moore, age 72, was CEO of Intel from 1975 to 1987 and was chairman until 1997.

(STEVE ALEXANDER)

MICROELECTRONICS

In 2001 the global semiconductor industry suffered its worst-ever decline, with projected worldwide sales of semiconductors down 31% to $141 billion, according to the U.S.-based Semiconductor Industry Association (SIA). The association predicted, however, that sales of personal computers (PCs), wireless communications solutions, and consumer products would enable the global semiconductor industry to recover from the inventory buildup that occurred in 2000 and the weak demand for end-market equipment in 2001. After the beginnings of recovery in the fourth quarter of 2001, the industry was expected to continue with slow growth of 6% to $150 billion in 2002 and then return to a traditional growth pattern with 21% increases in sales to $181 billion in 2003 and $218 billion in 2004.

Sales of flash memory decreased 27% to $7.8 billion in 2001 after having grown 133% in 2000. The SIA predicted that demand for flash-memory devices, led by cellular deployment, digital photography, and automotive applications, would bring growth of 5% to $8.1 billion in 2002. Advances of 23% in 2003 and 25% in 2004 to $12 billion would make flash memory one of the fastest-growing semiconductor sectors. Digital signal processors (DSPs) were another fast-growing sector, for which the SIA expected the key drivers to be wireless and wired communications, emerging digital consumer applications, and portable information devices. Despite having declined 34% to $4 billion in 2001, sales of DSPs were predicted to grow 16% in 2002, 33% in 2003, and 29% in 2004 to $8 billion. The dynamic random access memory sector decreased 60% to $12 billion in 2001, but the SIA expected it to increase 16% in 2002, 44% in 2003, and 54% in 2004 to $29 billion. The microcontroller market declined 17% in 2001 to $10 billion, but it was predicted to rise to $16 billion by 2004. The market for programmable logic devices, which included display drivers for flat-panel displays, declined 28% in 2001 to $25 billion but was expected to grow 6% in 2002, 21% in 2003, and 19% in 2004 to $38 billion. The microprocessors found in PCs, servers, and embedded applications decreased 28% in 2001 to $23 billion. Growth of 7% in 2002, 16% in 2003, and 10% in 2004 to $31 billion was predicted by the SIA, however. The optical storage market was expected to be driven by a rapid shift to compact disc-read/read and write (CD-R/RW) and digital versatile (or video) disc-read only memory (DVD-ROM), especially as more CD-R/RW and DVD-ROM drives were being preinstalled in PCs. In 2001 the optoelectronics market declined 22% to $7.6 billion, but it was predicted to grow 0.1% in 2002, 15% in 2003, and 20% in 2004 to $11 billion.

Although all four major world markets decreased in 2001, the Asia-Pacific market declined least (23% to $39 billion) and therefore took over from the Americas as the world's biggest semiconductor market. The SIA predicted that Asia-Pacific would be the fastest-growing region over the next three years and was likely to reach $67 billion in 2004. The Americas market declined 43% in 2001 to $36 billion, but it was expected to grow to $56 billion in 2004. The market in Japan, which declined 26% in 2001 to $35 billion, was projected to reach $52 billion in sales by 2004. The European market (down 29% in 2001 to $30 billion) was predicted to rise to $44 billion.

In July 2001 U.S. integrated circuit analyst IC Insights listed the worldwide top 10 semiconductor suppliers (on the basis of sales in the first half of the year). U.S.-based Intel Corp. remained at the top, followed by Toshiba Corp. (Japan), NEC Corp. (Japan), STMicroelectronics (France), Texas Instruments Inc. (U.S.), Samsung Electronics Co., Ltd. (South Korea), Hitachi, Ltd. (Japan), Motorola, Inc. (U.S.), Infineon Technologies AG (spun off from Siemens AG of Germany), and Mitsubishi Electric Corp. (Japan). The top three positions were unchanged from 2000.

On August 27 Intel introduced the world's first 2 GHz (gigahertz) microprocessor in the form of the latest version of its Pentium 4 chip. The company also demonstrated a Pentium 4 running at 3.5 GHz, noting that the chip's microarchitecture was expected to scale to 10 GHz eventually. In September Intel introduced its 845 chipset for Pentium 4-based PCs. Microsoft Corp.'s Windows XP operating system, released on October 25, was optimized for the Pentium 4 for processor-intensive applications. In August Intel demonstrated a new technology called hyper-threading, which enabled microprocessors to handle more information concurrently by sharing resources more efficiently. This was achieved through multiprocessing on a single chip, which the company intended to bring to market in its Xeon processor family in 2002. The company also disclosed details of its forthcoming Banias mobile processor architecture, which would deploy new low-power circuitry and design techniques.

In August Advanced Micro Devices, Inc., the world's second largest microprocessor supplier (with around 22% of the market; Intel was first with 77%), marked the second anniversary of its Athlon processor by announcing that its new 1.2 GHz mobile Athlon 4 processor would be used by Compaq Computer Corp. in its Presario notebook computers and introducing its Windows XP-compatible 1.6 GHz Athlon 1900+.

(ALAN STEWART)

TELECOMMUNICATIONS

In 2001 telecommunications companies around the world experienced a year of tumbling stock prices and huge job losses. By September the stock market valuation of the world's telecom carriers and suppliers had declined by $3.8 trillion from a peak of $6.3 trillion in March 2000. More than a quarter of a million jobs were lost throughout the world in the second quarter of 2001 alone. The major equipment manufacturers—Motorola, Inc., Lucent Technologies, Inc., and Cisco Systems (U.S.), Marconi Corp. PLC (U.K.), Siemens AG (Germany), Ericsson (Sweden), and Nokia Corp. (Finland)—all announced job cuts both in their home countries and in subsidiaries around the world. Some of the biggest losses were announced by the Canadian supplier Nortel Networks Ltd., which shed 50% of its workforce (almost 50,000 jobs). In France equipment manufacturer Alcatel cut 33,000 jobs—almost a third of its employees.

On October 1 FOMA, the world's first third-generation (3G) cellular phone service, was launched in Japan on a fully commercialized basis by NTT DoCoMo, Inc., the wireless operator in which Nippon Telegraph & Telephone (NTT) had a 64% holding. A pilot version of the service had been running since May 30. FOMA (which stood for Freedom Of Mobile multimedia Access) was initially available in the Tokyo area only, but it was to be extended to other major cities in late 2001 and early 2002. As well as a voice service, the 3G handset also provided 64-Kbps (kilobits-per-second) digital communication for a videophone service and a maximum 384-Kbps data downlink for DoCoMo's i-mode mobile Internet service. On November 19 DoCoMo introduced i-motion, a video-clip distribution service using FOMA at speeds of up to 384 Kbps. Movie trailers, news highlights, and music tracks were provided by 28 content providers from 37 i-motion sites accessed via DoCoMo's official i-mode portal. Full video- and music-distribution services were planned to begin in the spring of 2002.

In October Motorola forecast that mobile phone sales would fall for the first time ever in 2001, predicting global sales of 380 million–400 million, compared with around 400 million in 2000. To counter this trend, rival Nokia unveiled an "entertainment phone," featuring a full keyboard, digital music player, FM radio, five games, and advanced messaging capabilities. In April Ericsson and Sony Corp. of Japan announced that they were setting up a joint venture, based in London, to combine the two companies' cellular handset manufacturing businesses. Bell Labs, the research and development arm of Lucent Technologies, introduced the first high-capacity all-optical router.

AP/Wide World Photos

An NTT DoCoMo, Inc., employee poses while a colleague videotapes her with a FOMA handset, which featured videophone and mobile Internet service.

Bermuda-based international carrier Global Crossing Ltd. was the first customer for the technology, deploying the router on its global fibre-optic network.

During 2001 much of the telecom industry was dominated by spin-offs, mergers, and acquisitions. AT&T Corp. and British Telecommunications PLC (BT) implemented restructuring plans announced in late 2000, which included demerging their wireless businesses. AT&T Wireless became an independent company on July 9. In October AT&T Wireless Services, Inc., which held a 23% stake in American wireless provider TeleCorp PCS, Inc., acquired the rest of that company for $4.7 billion. AT&T had paid $135 million in March for the assets of the bankrupt American digital subscriber line provider NorthPoint Communications Group, Inc. In October AT&T and BT decided to unwind their loss-making international joint venture Concert, set up in 1998, and return its assets to the parent companies in the first half of 2002. In December Comcast Corp. agreed to pay $72 billion to acquire AT&T's cable television business, AT&T Broadband, to form a new company to be called AT&T Comcast Corp. The transaction was subject to regulatory and shareholder approval.

In January BT confirmed that it would buy 45% of VIAG Interkom from German energy conglomerate E.ON AG for €7,250,000,000 (about $6.5 billion), giving it complete ownership of the German fixed and mobile operator. BT took full ownership of Irish mobile operator Esat Digifone in February, acquiring the 49.5% stake held by Norwegian carrier Telenor ASA for $1,240,000,000. As of March 31, BT's debt stood at £27.9 billion (£1=about $1.42). Calls from shareholders for changes at the top led to the departure of Sir Iain Vallance as chairman in April, to be replaced by Sir Christopher Bland, chairman of the BBC. During the summer the new management seemed to reverse course. BT sold to Vodafone Group PLC, the U.K.'s largest wireless operator, its 17% stake in the Spanish mobile operator Airtel Móvil, SA, for £1.1 billion, as well as its interests in Japan Telecom and J-Phone Co., Ltd., for £3.7 billion, and announced that it had agreed to sell its interest in Rogers Wireless Communications Inc. in Canada to AT&T Wireless for £269 million. In October it was announced that Sir Peter Bonfield would stand down at the end of January 2002 after six years as BT's chief executive. BT Wireless (which had been renamed mmO2 in September) became independent on November 19.

The main French carrier, France Telecom, in June relaunched its Itineris wireless network (which had a 48% market share) under the Orange brand. In 2000 Vodafone had acquired U.K. rival Orange plc as part of its purchase of German wireless network Mannesmann AG and had then sold Orange to France Telecom, the majority of whose wireless interests were merged with Orange's to become the Orange SA group. On June 12 BT Wireless and T-Mobile International, the wireless business of Germany's main carrier, Deutsche Telekom AG, announced that they would cooperate on the rollout of 3G networks by their subsidiaries in the U.K. and in Germany.

A similar agreement was announced in October by two of the largest American wireless communications companies. VoiceStream Wireless Corp. (which was acquired by Deutsche Telekom in May) and Cingular Wireless (a joint venture between SBC Communications Inc. and BellSouth Corp.) agreed to share their networks in New York City, California, and Nevada. In November the U.S. Federal Communications Commission voted to relax rules imposing a cap of 45 MHz on ownership of wireless spectrum capacity in cities. The spectrum cap was raised to the rural level of 55 MHz immediately and was to be abolished completely as of Jan. 1, 2003.

(ALAN STEWART)

Earth Sciences

Scientists in 2001 reported finding an **ASTONISHING** field of white **CARBONATE TOWERS** on the Atlantic **SEAFLOOR**; data from a space probe orbiting **MARS** showed images of **SEDIMENTARY FORMATIONS.** Climatologists projected 2001 to be the **SECOND WARMEST** year on record.

GEOLOGY AND GEOCHEMISTRY

In June 2001 geology and geochemistry were successfully merged in Edinburgh at the novel Earth System Processes: A Global Meeting (June 24–28, 2001), coconvened by the Geological Society of America and the Geological Society of London (cosponsored by the Edinburgh Geological Society, University of Edinburgh, and Geological Surveys of the U.S. and the U.K.). The concept was that the plate tectonics revolution of the 1960s was only a first step in understanding the whole Earth system. In order to understand the dynamic whole, interdisciplinary studies of interactions between its component parts are required. The sessions were designed to emphasize the linkages between geologic, chemical, physical, and biological processes, along with their social and economic implications.

The linkages between geology, geochemistry, and the biosphere are clearly displayed by the submarine hydrothermal vents that spew hot water and deposit minerals that form chimneys. A report from a project of the University of Washington and the American Museum of Natural History, New York City, to characterize a suite of large sulfide chimneys from the Juan de Fuca Ridge was published during the year by John Delaney and Deborah Kelley of the University of Washington and seven coauthors. Using a centimetre-scale navigation-control system, optical- and sonar-imaging sensors, and real-time navigation techniques, the researchers produced the highest-quality fine-scale map of a complex with more than 13 chimneys ranging in height from 8.5 to 23 m (1 m=3.28 ft). Water venting from the chimneys reached 300 °C (570 °F). Dense clusters of tubeworms, snails, crabs, and microbial communities covered the structures. In a remarkable feat of remote engineering in water 2,250 m deep, the team sawed off and recovered four samples of chimneys about two metres in length. These were digitally imaged, cored, split, and immediately subjected to geochemical and microbiological examination. The research team discovered complex vertical zones of minerals, networks of flow channels lined with sulfides, and microorganisms distributed within well-defined mineral zones. The proportions of specific bacteria varied from the hot interior to the cooler exterior of the chimneys and were clearly related to, and perhaps even modifiers of, the geochemistry of their local environment.

The largest submarine hydrothermal towers yet discovered were described and explained in 2001 by Kelley, Donna Blackman (Scripps Institution of Oceanography), and many coauthors from the U.S. and Europe. The submersible research vessel *Alvin* revealed to its three astonished crew members a large field of white towers at a water depth of 700–800 m. This "Lost City Hydrothermal Field" extends across a terrace on the steep southern wall of the Atlantis Massif, about 15 km (1 km=0.62 mi) west of the Mid-Atlantic Ridge near 30° N. It consists of about 30 pinnacle-like chimney structures, the largest reaching 60 m in height and more than 10 m in diameter. In contrast to the black, high-temperature, sulfide-rich chimneys associated with the volcanically active oceanic ridge axes, these white towers vent relatively cool water of less than 70 °C (160 °F); the water precipitates carbonates and hydrated minerals, and there is no evidence for recent volcanism. The mineralogy of the carbonate chimneys and the fluid composition are consistent with reactions occurring between percolating seawater and the mantle rock that underlies the Atlantis Massif. The water is heated by the chemical reactions that convert the peridotite rock to serpentinite. Although few mobile creatures were found around these structures, there are abundant, dense microbial communities. These low-temperature carbonate chimneys may be widespread on older oceanic crust, supporting chemosynthetic microbial populations in environments similar to those in early Earth systems when life first evolved.

There was a new claim for the oldest rock on Earth, arising from the geochemistry of tiny minerals, zircons, in Western Australia. Igneous gneisses there are about 3,750,000,000 years old. The zircons, collected from a series of sedimentary rocks formed in a large delta, had previously been dated at 4,276,000,000 years. Detailed investigations by two teams from Australia, the U.S., and Scotland (Simon Wilde and three coauthors, and Stephen Mojzsis and two coauthors), however, yielded an age of 4,404,000,000 years, closer by 128,000,000 years to the formation of the Earth. Measurements of isotope concentrations were made on the sliced zircons by means of a precise ion microprobe that bombards the mineral in tiny spots, releasing atoms that are then weighed in a mass spectrometer. Both groups also measured the oxygen isotope ratios in the zircons and concluded that the minerals were derived from preexisting igneous rocks that had been involved with water at near-surface conditions. The existence of liquid water within 150,000,000 years of the Earth's formation 4,550,000,000 years ago was unexpected, given the intense bombardment of the Earth by asteroids at the time. Perhaps there was early formation of oceans and primitive life-forms, which were periodically destroyed on a global scale and then reformed through an interval of about 400,000,000 years earlier than life on Earth is currently thought to have begun.

Insight into the periodic disruptions caused more recently by asteroid impacts was provided by the study of helium in a sequence of limestones deposited in deep seas between 75 million and 40 million years ago. Graduate student Sujoy Mukhopadhyay, working with Kenneth Farley at the California Institute of Technology, and Alessandro

Montanari of the Geological Observatory, Apiro, Italy, studied the limestones near Gubbio in Italy. This series of limestones, composed predominantly of the calcite skeletons of plankton, includes a finger-thick clay layer at the boundary between the Cretaceous and Tertiary periods corresponding in time to the extinction 65 million years ago of 75% of all living species, including the dinosaurs. The sharp boundary at the top of the Cretaceous limestones indicates an abrupt reduction in productivity of plankton, which then rather suddenly increased above the clay layer with different plankton species forming more limestones. Analyses of the rare element iridium in the clay layer, reported in the early 1980s, had provided the first evidence that the mass extinction was caused by the impact of an extraterrestrial body, accompanied by a huge explosion and the global distribution of dust through the stratosphere. The new analyses of isotopes of helium confirmed that no comet shower had passed near the Earth at that time, and a single large extraterrestrial body was thus left as the destructive agent. The analyses also permitted calculations of rates of sedimentation, which led to the conclusion that, following the impact and destruction of global life, the food chain became reestablished in only 10,000 years. Repopulation of the ocean was then achieved within a short time interval. This rapid turnover contrasts with the longer time interval recognized by many paleontologists for the progressive extinction of larger land animals, such as the dinosaurs.

The "Lost City Hydrothermal Field" discovered below the North Atlantic Ocean includes this white carbonate chimney more than 9 m (30 ft) tall. In contrast to the high-temperature, sulfide-rich chimneys associated with volcanism at seafloor spreading centres, the spires of the Lost City field expel comparatively cool water that precipitates carbonates and hydrated minerals.

University of Washington/ Woods Hole Oceanographic Institution

Some significant steps for the parallel development of experiment and theory were achieved during 2001 in defining the framework of phase relationships that control the geology and geochemistry of rock-melt reactions. Two publications by Tim Holland (University of Cambridge), Roger Powell, and R.W. White (both of the University of Melbourne, Australia) presented a comprehensive thermodynamic model for granitic melts in a synthetic system with eight oxide components, including water. The internally consistent dataset with software Thermo-Calc makes possible calculation of the melting relationships for many rocks through the entire thickness of the continental crust. Manipulations of the complex phase diagrams permit the evaluation of processes, including the extent of melt loss during high-temperature metamorphism.

The continuing dependence of thermodynamic databases on new experiments at higher pressures and with additional components was demonstrated by Robert Luth (University of Alberta). The nature of the melting reaction in the Earth's upper mantle under conditions in which carbon dioxide is present is significantly affected by the position of a particular reaction among calcium-magnesium carbonates. Earlier experimental measurements for this reaction at pressures up to 55 kilobars (1 kilobar=1,000 atmospheres) and a temperature of 600 °C (1,100 °F) had been extrapolated by calculations using Thermo-Calc, yielding the result that dolomite (calcium magnesium carbonate) would not be involved in mantle melting at pressures greater than 60 kilobars, corresponding to a depth of 180 km. When Luth measured the reaction experimentally, however, he determined that dolomite does persist as the carbonate relevant for melting reactions in the upper mantle. The presence of dolomitic carbonate-rich melts in mantle rocks beneath an island off the coast of Brazil was demonstrated in 2001 by Lia Kogarko (Vernadsky Institute, Moscow), Gero Kurat (Natural History Museum, Vienna), and Theodoros Ntaflos (University of Vienna). Textures indicated the formation of immiscible (incapable of being mixed) carbonate, sulfide, and silicate liquids.

Experiments by Roland Stalder, Peter Ulmer, A.B. Thompson, and Detlef Günther of the Swiss Federal Institute of Technology, Zürich, on the effect of water on the conditions for melting in the Earth's mantle provided convincing evidence for the occurrence of a critical endpoint on the melting reaction, at a temperature of 1,150 °C (2,100 °F) and a pressure (130 kilobars) corresponding to a depth of about 400 km. At that point the melt and the coexisting aqueous fluid phase become identical in composition and properties. Despite the advances in thermodynamic calculations, experimental data were still insufficient to calculate the high-pressure behaviour of aqueous fluids under those conditions. (PETER J. WYLLIE)

GEOPHYSICS

An intraplate earthquake of magnitude 7.7 (moment magnitude) shook the Indian state of Gujarat on the morning of Jan. 26, 2001, India's Republic Day. Called the Bhuj earthquake, it was one of the deadliest ever recorded in the country. At least 20,000 people were killed, 166,000 injured, and 600,000 displaced. More than 350,000 houses were destroyed; property damage and economic losses were estimated in the billions of dollars.

The Bhuj earthquake occurred on a fault system adjacent to one on which a major shock (moment magnitude 7.8) took place in the Great Rann of Kachchh in 1819. Its focus was determined to be as deep as 23 km (1 km=about 0.62 mi). In a review of geophysical data from seismology, geology, and tectonics, Roger Bilham and Peter Molnar of the University of Colorado at Boulder and Vinod K. Gaur of the Indian Institute of Astrophysics, Bangalore, demonstrated how this earthquake was triggered by the release of elastic strain energy generated and replenished by the stress resulting from the ongoing collision of the Indian plate with the Asian plate, which began between 40 million and 50 million years ago. In this scenario the top surface (basement rock) of the Indian plate south of the Himalayas flexes and slides under the Himalayas in an uneven, lurching manner, similar to the behaviour observed in rapidly converging lithospheric plates beneath the ocean.

The researchers also showed, on the basis of Global Positioning System (GPS) satellite measurements, that India and southern Tibet were converging at a rate of 20 mm (about 0.8 in) per year, consistent with the rate deduced from concurrent field observations. Moreover, they pointed out that the convergence region along the Himalayas held an increased hazard for earthquakes and that 60% of the Himalayas were overdue for a great earthquake. The Bhuj earthquake did not occur along the Himalayan arc and so did nothing to relieve the accumulating strain on the arc. An earthquake of magnitude 8 would be catastrophic for the densely populated region in the Ganges Plain to the south.

In addition to the Bhuj earthquake, major earthquakes (magnitude 7 and greater) with high casualties occurred on January 13 in El Salvador (magnitude 7.7, with more than 800 people killed and 100,000 homes destroyed) and June 23 off coastal Peru (magnitude 8.4, with at least 100 people killed—many by tsunami—and 150,000 homes destroyed).

Sicily's Mt. Etna, Europe's largest and most active volcano, erupted on July 17 in a dramatic display that continued into August. The flow of molten magma, which emerged from fissures along Etna's southeastern slopes, caused tremendous damage to the tourist complex of Rifugio Sapienza and set fire to a cable-car base station. The July–August event, which was the first flank eruption of the volcano since 1993, aroused wide interest from both the scientific community and emergency managers. It occurred from five short vent segments over a linear distance of six kilometres at an elevation of 2,950–2,100 m (9,680–6,890 ft) and discharged 30 million cu m (1.1 billion cu ft) of new magma. Significant losses were avoided when the lava stopped a few kilometres short of the first major mountain community, Nicolosi. Interest for scientists lay in the simultaneous eruption of two magma types, of contrasting chemistry and residence time in the volcano, and in the wide diversity of eruption intensities observed over short distance and time scales.

The economically crippling eruption of Soufrière Hills volcano on the Caribbean island of Montserrat continued through the growth and collapse of the lava dome in 2001. This long-lived (since 1995) and complex event prompted the publication of a major analytic memoir by the Geological Society of London. The even more protracted eruption of Kilauea volcano in Hawaii, which began in 1983, also carried on unabated throughout the year.

Christopher G. Fox of Oregon State University and colleagues reported on the first detailed observation of the eruption of a submarine volcano—Axial volcano on the Juan de Fuca Ridge off the Oregon coast—by a seafloor instrument serendipitously positioned very close to the event. The instrument, a Volcanic System Monitor, carried several sensors, including one for measuring bottom pressure, which served as an indicator for vertical deformation of the seafloor associated with magma movements. Although the instrument was overrun by a lava flow, the scientific data were retrieved.

The mantle, that part of Earth that lies beneath the crust and above the central core, constitutes 82% of Earth's volume and 65% of its weight. Progress was being made in the use of seismic tomography to infer temperature anomalies associated with thermal convection in the mantle. Analogous to the use of X-rays in medical tomography, seismic tomography yielded accurate maps of variations in the velocities of seismic waves produced by earthquakes. By combining this information with a knowledge of the elastic properties (wave-propagation velocities) of various mantle mineral phases as a function of pressure and temperature, scientists could make accurate estimates of the temperature distribution in Earth's mantle. Such velocity data for a number of mantle mineral phases, for example, (Mg, Fe)SiO_3 (perovskite) and $(Mg, Fe)_2SiO_4$ (ringwoodite), were being obtained in various laboratories.

Surface geophysical data (e.g., geodetic measurements and observed tectonic plate motions) and global seismic tomographic models were together providing useful information on the flow and thermochemical structure in the deep mantle. In this respect, A.M. Forte of the University of Western Ontario and J.X. Mitrovica of the University of Toronto suggested the existence of a very high effective viscosity near 2,000 km depth, which would suppress flow-induced deformation and convective mixing in the deep mantle.

Leonid Dubrovinsky of Uppsala (Swed.) University and associates suggested that the observed heterogeneity in composition, density, and thermal state (revealed by seismological data) at Earth's core-mantle boundary and in the inner core could plausibly be explained by chemical interaction. They based their reasoning on experimental data on the chemical interaction of iron and aluminum oxide (Al_2O_3) with $MgSiO_3$ (perovskite phase) under simulated conditions of pressure and temperature at the core.

High-resolution images gathered by the Mars Global Surveyor (MGS), which began orbiting the planet in 1997, yielded exciting views of massive layered outcrops of sedimentary rock, as thick as four kilometres, as reported by Michael C. Malin and Kenneth S. Edgett of Malin Space Science Systems, San Diego, Calif. Although the age relationships of these erosional landforms and the processes of deposition and transport that created them, including the possible role of liquid water, remained to be ascertained, their discovery provided some initial clues to the previously unknown geologic and atmospheric history of Mars.

Mars currently lacks a global dipole magnetic field like that of Earth, but the detection of strongly magnetized ancient crust on Mars by the MGS spacecraft was indicative of the presence of a liquid core and an active magnetic dynamo early in the planet's history. Building on this information, David J. Stevenson of the California Institute of Technology reported important new interpretations and insights about the Martian interior—the nature and history of the iron-rich Martian core and the influence of the core on the early climate and possible life on Mars. According to Stevenson, heat flow from the Martian core also appeared to have contributed to volcanic activity and feeding of mantle plumes, as in the case of Earth's core.

(MURLI H. MANGHNANI)

METEOROLOGY AND CLIMATE

A revived La Niña—the condition of below-normal sea-surface temperatures dominating the central and eastern equatorial Pacific—influenced the weather over parts of the Earth early in 2001. By April equatorial temperatures had returned to normal, which suggested that La Niña, which had begun in 1998, had finally ended.

The upward trend in global surface temperatures continued, while NASA estimates from land and ocean data for the first ten months of 2001 had the year on track to be the second warmest on record. In contrast, lower tropospheric temperatures as measured by satellite averaged close to the 1979–98 mean, suggesting no significant recent warming trend above the surface. La Niña played a role in aggravating long-term drought over the southeastern United States, particularly Florida, where the 12-month period that ended in April was the third driest in 107 years. Drought also developed over the northwestern U.S. during the 2000–01 winter as blocking high pressure aloft steered storms to the north and south. November–April precipitation in the region was the second lowest since records began in 1895.

The layered floor of Mars's western Candor Chasma is revealed in a high-resolution image taken by the Mars Global Surveyor spacecraft. On Earth such a pattern is evidence of sediment deposited at the bottom of a lake or stream.

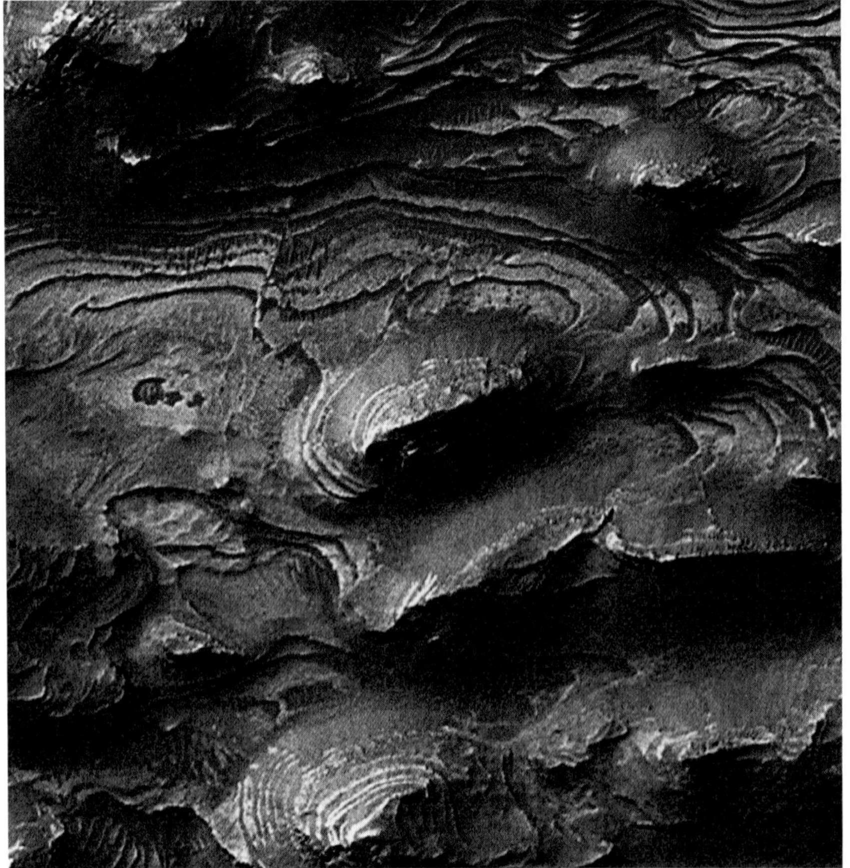

NASA/JPL/Malin Space Science Systems

For other parts of the U.S., winter brought abundant snowfall, especially in the Northeast and the Great Plains. Major winter storms struck the Northeast in February and March, with a particularly severe storm burying New England and the northern mid-Atlantic region on March 4–5. A wet and stormy April in the upper Midwest led to serious flooding and considerable property damage along the upper reaches of the Mississippi and other rivers.

The first tropical storm in the Atlantic basin, Allison, made landfall June 5 on Galveston Island, Texas. Although the storm was relatively weak, its historic two-week odyssey across the South and up the mid-Atlantic coast cost about $5 billion and left 50 dead. The storm, which turned Houston's streets into raging rivers after depositing up to 890 mm (1 mm=0.04 in) of rain, ended up as the costliest tropical storm in U.S. history.

In central and western Texas a persistent high-pressure system aloft brought drought to the region for the second consecutive summer. Rainfall totaled well under 50% of normal in both June and July, and temperatures above 37.8 °C (100 °F) worsened the dryness. Rains exceeding 300 mm in late August and early September ended dryness in eastern Texas but triggered flooding.

Over the central U.S., the high-pressure ridge responsible for the heat and dryness in the southern plains expanded northward in late July and early August, bringing dangerous heat to the upper Midwest. The ridge further broadened, which resulted in a nearly coast-to-coast heat wave August 6–9. Nationwide, widespread heat during June–August resulted in the fifth warmest summer on record for the U.S., while above-normal temperatures during September–November across all but the Southeast caused autumn to rank as the fourth warmest on record. Drought intensified along the

Shimmering colours of the aurora borealis paint the sky over Rockford, Mich., in early November. Beginning in late September, a series of coronal mass ejections from the Sun triggered unusually vivid and far-reaching auroral displays, to the delight of sky watchers worldwide.

Eastern Seaboard in autumn as rainfall totaled under 50% of normal from North Carolina to Massachusetts. In contrast, a series of Pacific storms in November and December eased drought in the West.

The Atlantic tropical storm season was active, with 15 named storms of which 9 became hurricanes. The bulk of activity occurred in the last three months of the season—September to November—during which 11 of the named storms formed. For the second consecutive year, no hurricanes made U.S. landfall. Two storms, Barry and Gabrielle, brought some flooding to Florida but also relieved its long-term drought.

In Central America drought in June and July damaged crops from Nicaragua to Guatemala. Hurricane Iris, a category 4 storm packing winds of 233 km (145 mi) per hour, caused severe damage to southern Belize on October 8. The tropical depression that later became Hurricane Michelle brought extremely heavy rains to portions of Nicaragua and Honduras at the end of October. On November 4, Michelle slammed into the coastal islands of Cuba as a category 4 hurricane and into the main island as a category 3 hurricane. Michelle was the strongest hurricane to hit Cuba since 1952.

Across the Middle East and south-central Asia, another dry winter and spring resulted in countries from Syria to Pakistan enduring a third consecutive year of drought. Much of the region experienced four straight months (January–April) with precipitation below half of normal. The drought slashed crop production and depleted rivers and reservoirs. In Algeria, an intense storm struck the north coast on November 9–11. Up to 260 mm of rain led to catastrophic floods and mud slides in Algiers, leaving more than 700 people dead.

Crops dependent on rain failed almost totally in Afghanistan again in 2001. Major drought during the first half of the year also affected northern China and North and South Korea. March–May rainfall in Beijing totaled about one-third of normal. The opposite extreme prevailed in southern China, where torrential June rains exceeding 800 mm killed hundreds of people. An active storm season also affected the region, with Taiwan enduring damage from Typhoons Chebi in June, Toraji in July, and Nari and Lekima in September. Other storms hit the Philippines, China, and Japan, with two typhoons, Pabuk and Danas, striking the Tokyo area within one month of each other (August 21 and September 10). In the Philippines, Typhoon Utor left more than 150 dead in July, and Tropical Storm Lingling caused at least 180 deaths in early November. Monsoon flooding hit South and Southeast Asia, although on a smaller scale than in 2000. India suffered severely again as floodwaters affected millions during July and August. (DOUGLAS LE COMTE)

Economic Affairs

Even before the **TERRORIST ATTACKS** in the U.S. on Sept. 11, 2001, the world economy was **SLOWING DOWN** faster than expected. By the end of the year, most world **STOCK MARKETS** were down, numerous companies were implementing **LAYOFFS** or filing for **BANKRUPTCY**, and there were fears of a global **RECESSION**.

Expectations of an economic slowdown at the start of 2001 proved to be well founded, and as the year drew to a close, fears of a global recession were being expressed. In the year 2000 the global economy had grown by 4.7%, its fastest rate in a decade and a half. In November the International Monetary Fund (IMF) revised down its projection for 2001 to 2.4%, but by year's end this looked too optimistic. Growth in the 30 industrialized countries of the Organisation for Economic Co-operation and Development (OECD), which accounted for most world output, was not expected to exceed 1%, which in turn constrained growth of the less-developed countries (LDCs).

The slowdown in the first half of 2001 was more severe than had been expected. The world's stock markets were already falling, and interest rates were being steadily lowered in the U.S. and the European Union (EU) to stimulate economic activity. While several factors had contributed to the global slowdown, the various regions and countries were differently affected. A key factor was a stronger-than-predicted fall in demand for information technology (IT) products. This particularly affected the producer countries in Asia, which were heavily dependent on technology exports.

In Western Europe and other industrialized areas, growth slowed more than expected—partly because of the effects of tighter monetary policies and the need to adapt to higher oil prices—and corporate profits were falling. The Japanese economy was still bordering on recession, but its imports continued to rise strongly. China's economy remained buoyant, with strong domestic demand and a stable currency in terms of the U.S. dollar. In the first half of the year, China's trade was slowing, but it was still recording double-digit growth in imports and a 9% increase in exports.

While the slowdown had been more severe than expected, it was the unprecedented terrorist attacks in the U.S. that really shook world confidence. While the initial impact was felt in the U.S., where there was a huge loss of life and the physical destruction of much of the business infrastructure of lower Manhattan, the attacks created fear and uncertainty across the world. The economic might of the U.S., which had been a driving force behind much of the world's economic growth, was seriously undermined. The insurance cost of the damage was likely to reach $50 billion, according to early estimates by the U.S. Bureau of Economic Analysis. This was well in excess of the $19 billion in damage caused when Hurricane Andrew hit Louisiana and Florida in 1992, previously the largest claim to date.

The loss of confidence was quickly reflected in the world's leading financial markets, and acceleration in corporate failures and job losses; major European firms laid off 97,000 workers in October alone, almost twice as many as in September. At the end of November, one of the world's largest conglomerates, the energy trader Enron Corp., filed for Chapter 11 protection in what would be

Table I. Real Gross Domestic Products of Selected OECD Countries
% annual change

Country	1997	1998	1999	2000	2001[1]
United States	4.4	4.3	4.1	4.1	1.3
Japan	1.9	−1.1	0.8	1.5	−0.5
Germany	1.4	2.0	1.8	3.0	0.8
France	1.9	3.5	3.0	3.4	2.0
Italy	2.0	1.8	1.6	2.9	1.8
United Kingdom	3.5	2.6	2.3	3.1	2.0
Canada	4.3	3.9	5.1	4.4	2.0
All developed countries	3.5	2.7	3.4	3.8	1.3
Seven major countries above	3.2	2.8	3.0	3.4	1.1
European Union	2.6	2.9	2.7	3.4	1.8

[1]Estimated.
Note: Seasonally adjusted at annual rates.
Source: International Monetary Fund, *World Economic Outlook*, October 2001.

Table II. Standardized Unemployment Rates in Selected Developed Countries
% of total labour force

Country	1997	1998	1999	2000	2001[1]
United States	4.9	4.5	4.2	4.0	4.8
Japan	3.4	4.1	4.7	4.7	5.0
Germany	9.5	9.3	8.6	7.9	8.1
France	12.2	11.8	11.2	9.5	8.9
Italy	11.8	11.8	11.4	10.5	10.0
United Kingdom	6.5	6.3	6.1	5.5	5.1
Canada	9.1	8.3	7.6	6.8	7.3
All developed countries	6.8	7.1	6.8	6.4	6.5
Seven major countries above	6.4	6.4	6.1	5.7	—
European Union	11.4	9.9	9.1	8.2	8.5

[1]Projected.
Source: OECD, *Economic Outlook*, November 2001.

the world's biggest-ever bankruptcy. Possibly the most lasting impact was on transport and world travel and tourism. Within weeks once-strong national airlines Swissair and Belgium's Sabena were being declared bankrupt as a result of the slump in demand for air travel. The number of international tourist arrivals in 2000 reached 699 million and generated $476 billion. Before the terrorist attacks international tourism in 2001 was on track for a 3–4% increase; in November the World Tourism Organization lowered its forecast to 1%.

On a more positive note, despite the critics of trade liberalization, the World Trade Organization (WTO) meeting in Doha, Qatar, on November 11–14 went ahead as planned, and a new agreement was reached. Most countries were continuing to make efforts to participate in globalization by attracting foreign investment. Of the 150 regulatory chan-ges in investment conditions made by 69 countries in 2000, 147 were more favourable. As a result, foreign direct investment (FDI) continued to be a major influence on economic development, increasing at a much faster rate than world trade or production. In 2000 world FDI reached a record $4,270,000,000,000, 18% up on the previous year and well in excess of forecasts. Sales of the over 800,000 affiliates of transnational corporations also rose by 18% to reach $15,680,000,000,000, while the number of employees, which had doubled over the previous decade, reached 45,600,000. In 2001, however, the slackening in merger and acquisition (M&A) activity was expected to result in a decline in overall FDI.

Against the overall trend, FDI into the LDCs of Asia rose 44% to a record $143 billion in 2000. This was due to an investment boom in Hong Kong associated with China's forthcoming membership in the WTO. At $643 billion in 2000, Hong Kong's share of the total inflow into Asia rose to 45% and overtook that of China. Nevertheless, China was making policy changes in advance of joining the WTO, and it received 12% more FDI in the first four months of 2001 than in the same 2000 period. Southeast Asia's share fell to 10% in 2000, mainly because of divestments in Indonesia. In South Asia, India continued to be the largest recipient, with $2.3 billion.

Outward investment from Asia doubled to a record $85 billion, led by Hong Kong but with increasing flows from China and India. Investment in Latin America and the Caribbean declined from the particularly high level of 1999.

NATIONAL ECONOMIC POLICIES

The revised IMF growth forecast for output in the advanced countries was 1% (in November), compared with the 3.8% achieved in 2000. By the middle of the year, economic activity in many of the advanced countries was, at best, stagnating. The effects of the terrorist attacks in the U.S. in September led to output falls in the final months of the year, for the first time in 20 years.

United States. The longest period of continuous expansion since the National Bureau of Economic Research (NBER) began keeping records in 1854 came to an abrupt halt in 2001, just 10 years after it began. Following expansion of 4.1% in both 1999 and 2000, it was doubtful whether the U.S. economy would grow by the revised IMF economic forecast of 1%. From being the dynamo of world growth, the U.S. suddenly became the generator of a serious global slowdown. After lengthy deliberations the NBER concluded on November 28 that the U.S. had slid into recession in March.

The slowdown in the economy had begun in the second half of 2000 when demand for information and communications equipment began to slump, bringing an 80% drop in high-tech company share prices. It gathered momentum in 2001 as the loss of confidence in high-tech companies, which then had to meet the higher costs of investment, and in the "new economy" was followed by a general deterioration in business and consumer confidence. An easing of monetary policy from the start of 2001 contributed, however, to continuing strong investment in housing as the cost of mortgages fell. Household spending remained buoyant, with retail sales in April and May up 3.9% on year-earlier levels.

The downturn in demand led companies to reduce output to lower stock levels. As a consequence, manufacturing activity in May reached a 10-year low. Job losses pushed unemployment to 4.9% by August, and reductions in overtime led to shorter workweeks. Nevertheless, by historic standards the unemployment level remained compatible with "full employment" conditions. An easing of the tight labour market was desirable insofar as it brought some stability to employee compensation, which had been spiraling out of control. While rises in average earnings slowed down, however, there was an acceleration in unit labour costs. Company profits fell 13% in the year to the second quarter, with a bigger decline in the year to the third quarter.

By midyear there were mixed signals and some speculation that economic growth would resume by the end of the year. Consumer spending, which accounted for more than two-thirds of U.S. gross domestic product (GDP), was expected to accelerate in the second half of the year as a result of tax cuts and repeated reductions in interest rates.

Inflation Rate
(percentage change from December to December)

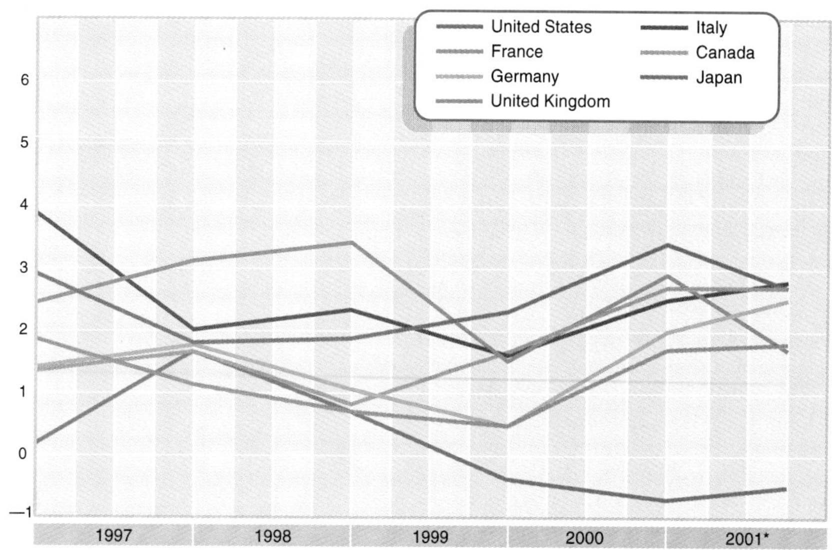

*Percentage change from third quarter average 2000 to third quarter average 2001.
Source: International Monetary Fund, *International Financial Statistics*.

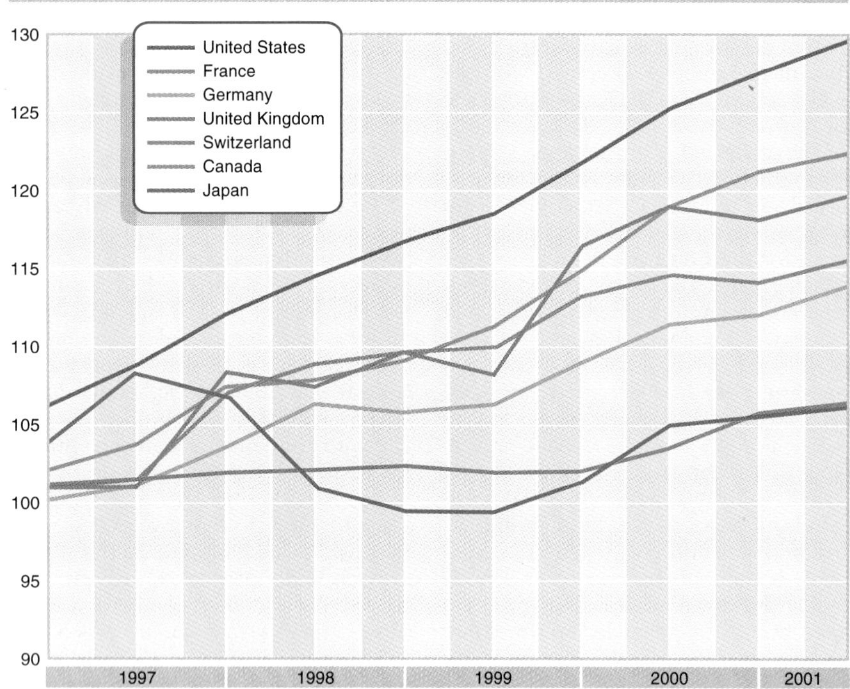

After the September 11 terrorist attacks, however, the downside risks to the economy were intensified. The U.S. was making the hard landing that had been the subject of speculation and fear just a year earlier, when there had been no suggestion that the country could be the target of such terrorism. In October industrial output fell (–1.1%) for the 13th consecutive month, which made it the longest unbroken decline since 1932. There were glimmers of hope, with consumer confidence rising in November for the second straight month. At the same time, new claims for unemployment benefits, at 427,000, fell for the fourth consecutive month. In December it was reported that unemployment had risen to 5.8%, the highest in more than six years.

In the weeks following the attacks, Pres. George W. Bush was given authority to spend $40 billion to respond. Another $15 billion of support was granted to help the American airline companies, many of which had been in trouble before September 11. A further package of $75 billion was being planned to stimulate the economy. This was beginning to reverse the trend in fiscal policy established in the previous seven years, during which the large federal budget deficit had been eliminated and replaced with a healthy surplus. A return to a federal deficit was likely in 2002. On November 6 the Federal Reserve (Fed) cut the federal funds rate for the 10th time in 2001, by half a percentage point to 2%, which brought it to a 40-year low and nearly 70% below the end-of-2000 level. Another cut in December brought the rate down to 1.75%.

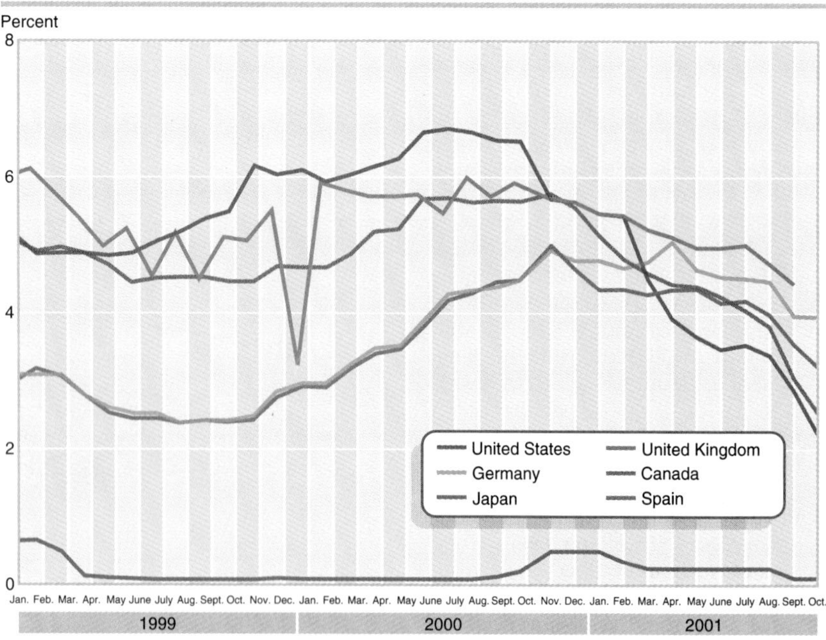

United Kingdom. During the year the U.K. had one of the most resilient economies among the major advanced countries. The growth in output was forecast at 2–2.25%, compared with 3.1% in 2000, which made it the fastest of the industrialized Group of Seven (G-7) countries.

While economic growth had been strong since the summer of 2000, this was largely because of global factors. The collapse of the information and communications technology sector, the U.S. recession, and a general slowdown in overseas demand constrained exports of goods and services, which were expected to rise only 3–4%, compared with 10.6% in 2000.

On the domestic front, however, the combination of a foot-and-mouth epidemic and poor weather conditions proved disastrous for much of the agricultural sector and the tourism industry. In theory, the relative strength of sterling against the euro was eroding the competitiveness of U.K. goods and services, especially in continental European markets. At the same time, however, it was prompting industry to take measures to increase efficiency, particularly in manufacturing.

The main stimulus to the British economy once again came from domestic demand, which increased by 3.7% in 2000 and was expected to rise in 2001. Household spending rose 1.2% in the first quarter and gathered momentum in the second, when it rose 3.7% above the year-earlier level—the biggest increase in more than a year—and underpinned increased retail sales. Buoyant conditions continued through the third quarter. In September retail sales rose 5.9% over the same year-earlier period, which made the third-quarter year-on-year growth the fastest in 13 years. Prospects for the retail sector remained positive, with a Confederation of British Industry survey showing the strongest outlook for the sector since October 1966. By contrast, survey results for the services sector indicated a weaker outlook, with signs that contracts had been deferred because of the September 11 attacks.

A strong influence on consumer confidence was the high level of employment. In September unemployment was 5.1% (5.4% a year before), compared with an average 8.3% in the euro zone. The number of jobless increased in October and again in November, however, the first time since 1992 unemployment had increased for two straight months. On a claimant-count basis, it was the lowest in 26 years. As a result, wage pressure remained strong and was reflected in higher average earnings, which nevertheless eased back to 4.4% in September, year on year. Unusually, public-sector earnings were rising faster than those in the private sector, a reflection of the priority the government was giving to the public services.

Japan. During the year the Japanese economy deteriorated sharply, and output was estimated to have fallen by 0.9%. The modest recovery in 2000, when the economy grew 1.5%, was due mainly to the strong growth in capital investment and was not sustainable. The 2001 recession was the fourth in 10 years and was predictable, given the decline in technology-related demand in Asia. The harsher-than-expected slowdown in the global IT industry was particularly damaging to Japan, and this had implications for the region. Although Japan's economic role in the Asia-Pacific region had diminished over recent years, it remained important. Reciprocal trade with East Asia in particular was badly affected by the downturn.

First-quarter economic indicators reflected the economic stagnation, which was to continue unabated. Capital-goods shipments were falling, industrial production was down, household incomes were deteriorating, and unemployment was continuing to rise. Real GDP shrank by 0.2% and was followed by a 2% drop in the second quarter. The

Interest Rates: Long-term

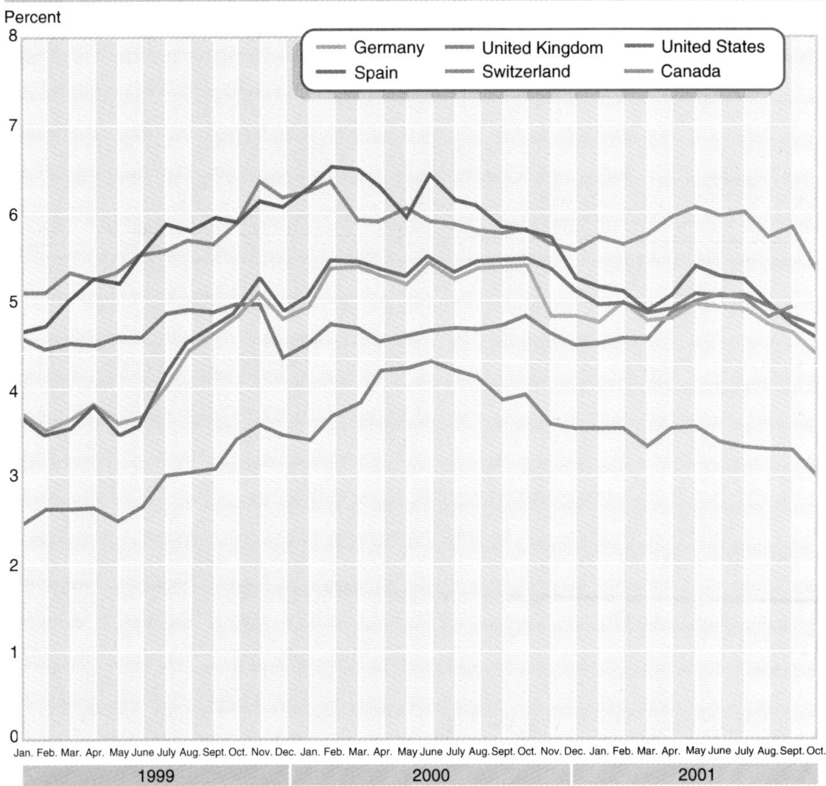

Source: International Monetary Fund, *International Financial Statistics.*

AP/Wide World Photos

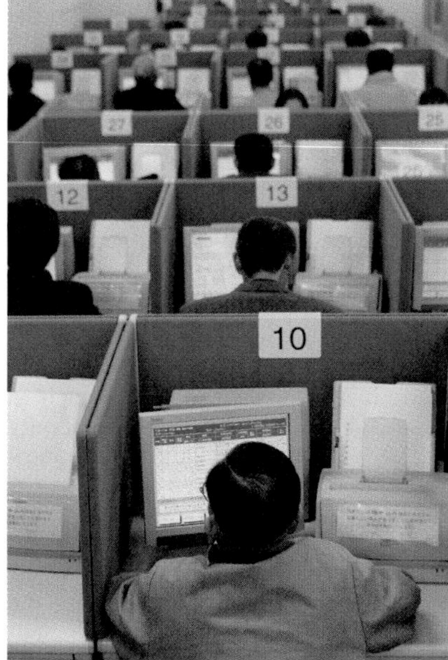

Unemployed workers in Tokyo check job advertisements at Hello Work, a government-run placement centre, on November 30.

outlook deteriorated further in the wake of the September 11 terrorist attacks in the U.S., and in that month industrial output fell 12.7% (from a year earlier). Retail sales continued to decline, not helped by declines in average earnings because of reductions in overtime. Consumer prices continued to fall and in September were 0.8% lower than one year earlier.

Unemployment was becoming a growing problem. Although the rate had dipped temporarily in 2000, reflecting the improvement in the economy, the trend had been generally upward. From just over 3% in early 1997, the rate had climbed to a record high of 5.3% by September 2001, and it continued to rise in October (5.4%) and November (5.5%). Of particular concern was the mismatch in the labour market.

The emergency economic package unveiled by the Japanese government in April 2001 aimed to stimulate employment through measures that included deregulation, provision of child care, and vocational training. This was in marked contrast to previous policies, which were directed toward preventing layoffs through subsidies, but it was unlikely to produce an early solution to the mismatch problem.

Euro Zone. The belief among many euro-zone policy makers that somehow the region would be, at worst, only marginally affected by a global downturn (which in turn depended on what happened in the U.S.) gradually became discredited. GDP growth in the euro zone increasingly weakened as the year progressed. Sluggish trade and a stagnation in business investment were exacerbated by the September 11 attacks. Nevertheless, the European Commission at the end of November optimistically estimated that euro-zone growth would outpace that of the U.S. at 1.6% in 2001 and 1.3% in 2002. This was in sharp contrast to the record growth of 3.5% in 2000, when many of the smaller countries, such as Ireland (11.5% growth) and Luxembourg (8.5%), outperformed, making a contribution to output that was disproportionate to their size.

The final outcome was heavily dependent on Germany, the zone's largest economy and the country leading the downturn. Economic indicators suggested that there would be no early upturn. In the third quarter, GDP contracted by 0.6% (annual rate), industrial output was down 2.6%, and retail sales fell 2.1%. Unemployment, at 9.5% in October, was marginally higher than a year earlier. France, Germany's largest European neighbour, proved more resilient to the downturn in the first half of the year, being supported by tax cuts and employment growth.

Across the euro zone the improvement in the labour market had come to a halt, and unemployment was a cause of growing concern. It remained intractably high in several countries, led by Spain (13% according to national statistics), Belgium (11.7%), Germany (9.5%), Italy (9.4%), and France (8.9%), but it was not an issue in Luxembourg or The Netherlands.

The rate of inflation was rising for much of the year. The initial problem was the euro's weakness against the dollar and then the rapid rise of commodity prices, particularly of oil. In the second half of the year, however, the effect of lower energy prices brought the consumer price rise to 2.7% in the September quarter over the year before. Food prices, which accounted for about 20% of the index, escalated for much of the year as a result of the foot-and-mouth and "mad cow" diseases. Unprocessed-food prices were running at 7.8% up on the year earlier in August and September, having peaked at 9.1% in June.

The Former Centrally Planned Economies. The former centrally planned economies (also called the countries in transition) saw an increase in output for the third year in succession. Nevertheless, at around 2% the rate represented a considerable decline from the record 6.3% growth in 2000 and a bigger fall in output growth than that sustained by any other region. Several factors contributed to the decline, including the slowdown in the world economy and the uncertainty created by the attacks on September 11. More specifically, export growth fell sharply from 12% in 2000 to around 5% in 2001, largely as a result of the reduction in import demand from Western Europe, which accounted for half the region's exports.

The fall in economic activity was most marked in the Commonwealth of Independent States (CIS), where output was expected to rise at around half the rate of increase of 7.8% achieved in 2000. Growth was constrained in 2001 by a slowdown in Russia, where output growth was unlikely to exceed 4% following on from an exceptional 8.3% rise in 2000 that was largely the result of increased oil revenues. Output in Central and Eastern Europe also moderated from a 3.8% increase in 2000, but steep declines were averted by a strengthening of domestic demand in many member countries.

Rates of inflation were contained in most countries, and over the region the rate was expected to fall for the third consecutive year to around 15% (20% in 2000), with rates much lower in Central and Eastern Europe (around 9%). Inflation in Russia continued to be a problem, with the annual rate running at around 20%, as in the previous year.

Less-Developed Countries. The weaker-than-expected global economy led to adjustments in output forecasts. The IMF projection for LDCs of 4% for 2001 was, if achieved, the same as the 1999 outcome but well below the 5.8% growth in 2000. The wide regional disparities, which had long been a characteristic of the less-developed world, narrowed considerably in 2000 but were expected to reemerge in 2001, with conditions in Latin America and the Middle East deteriorating more sharply than expected at the start of the year. Within regions, too, wide disparities persisted.

Asia, excluding the newly industrializing countries (NICs) such as South Korea, Taiwan, and Singapore, continued to drive growth in the LDCs, although the 5.6% IMF projection appeared overly optimistic, given the dramatic falloff in trade, on which many Asian countries depended. While some countries, including China and Malaysia, increased fiscal spending to mitigate the effects, for most this could be only a short-term solution because of concerns about raising the level of public debt. In Indonesia and the Philippines, for example, this was already too high. The increase in China's GDP was expected to fall to 7–7.5% from 8% in 2000.

South Asia, which remained one of the world's poorest regions, relied less on trade. Output in this area was expected to fall from 4.9% in 2000 to 4.5%. Because of the military response in Afghanistan to the September 11 at-

Table III. Changes in Output in Less-Developed Countries
% annual change in real gross domestic product

Area	1997	1998	1999	2000	2001[1]
All less-developed countries	5.8	3.5	3.9	5.8	4.3
Regional groups					
Africa	3.1	3.3	2.5	2.8	3.8
Asia	6.5	4.0	6.1	6.8	5.8
Middle East, Europe, Malta, & Turkey	5.1	4.1	1.0	6.0	2.3
Western Hemisphere	5.3	2.3	0.2	4.2	1.7
Countries in transition	1.6	–0.8	3.6	6.3	4.0

[1]Projected.
Source: International Monetary Fund, *World Economic Outlook*, October 2001.

Table IV. Changes in Consumer Prices in Less-Developed Countries
% change from preceding year

Area	1997	1998	1999	2000	2001[1]
All less-developed countries	9.7	10.5	6.8	6.0	5.9
Regional groups					
Africa	14.2	10.8	11.5	13.6	12.6
Asia	4.8	7.7	2.5	1.9	2.8
Middle East, Europe, Malta, & Turkey	27.7	27.6	23.2	19.2	18.9
Western Hemisphere	12.9	9.9	8.8	8.1	6.2

[1]Projected.
Source: International Monetary Fund, *World Economic Outlook*, October 2001.

tacks, the region faced special risks. Pakistan was most affected, with its trade being severely disrupted. That country reduced its fiscal deficit to 5.2% of GDP, but its external debt was a large $38 billion and its reserves were low. India was more insulated from the global slowdown because of its relatively closed economy. By contrast, in neighbouring Bangladesh agricultural output was well up after the flood-induced 2000 slowdown, and tax revenue increased strongly.

In Africa output accelerated from 2.8% in 2000 to 3.5%. Improvements in the Mahgreb countries (Algeria, Morocco, and Tunisia), where output was projected to more than double over the year before, made a major contribution to overall growth.

In sub-Saharan Africa output growth declined (from 3% to 2.7%) because of the global slowdown. Nevertheless, in many countries, including Kenya, Ethiopia, and Mozambique, agriculture and, hence, household incomes were helped by better weather. Political instability continued to hamper growth in several countries, including Angola and The Sudan, while the politico-economic crisis in Zimbabwe intensified as elections due in early 2002 approached. In South Africa, the region's largest economy, sound macroeconomic policies reduced the country's vulnerability to external shocks.

Output in Latin America rose by 1% at most, following on from the strong 4.2% export-driven growth of 2000. The largest three countries, Argentina, Brazil, and Mexico, were worst affected by the global and U.S. slowdown, and lower interest rates did little to help. Political and financial problems in Argentina led to a dramatic decrease in confidence, and output was declining.

Middle East output was not likely to exceed half the 5.5% advance in 2000. The reduction in oil quotas and lower oil prices, combined with lowered global demand for goods and services, constrained economic activity.

INTERNATIONAL TRADE, EXCHANGE, AND PAYMENTS

International Trade and Payments. The increase in the volume of world trade in 2001 was expected to be just 1% in 2001, following a record 13.3% in 2000. The contraction created a new and unfamiliar situation in which the growth in world output exceeded the volume of world trade. For at least two decades, annual rises in world output had exceeded export growth. During the 1990s the annual rise in the volume of merchandise exports had outpaced the growth of GDP by three to one, and in each major region exports increased faster than domestic demand. Trade in services, too, had expanded rapidly over the previous decade and accounted for a quarter of all cross-border trade.

In 2001, in contrast to the year before, when all regions had participated in the upsurge in trade, there were many individual country and regional losers in the downturn. The volume of exports from the advanced countries had risen 11.5% in 2000 and by 16.1% (25% in U.S. dollar value) from LDCs. In 2001 the simultaneous slowdown in the U.S., Europe, and Japan meant that any increase in exports of either group would be close to negligible. Even before September 11 it was evident that the world slowdown, which centred on the recession in the high-tech sector, was deeper than expected.

The most affected was the East Asia–Pacific region, which relied on the U.S. and Japanese markets for around 40% of its exports. Exports in the first half of the year were already running at levels well below the year earlier, by up to 25% in Taiwan, South Korea, Malaysia, Singapore, and the Philippines. South Asia was expecting to see a modest increase, as some countries had depreciated their currencies to increase their competitiveness. In Latin America little growth could be expected. In the first half of the year, Mexico's export growth rate fell from 23% in 2000 to zero. Like many other countries in the region, its exports were mainly destined for the U.S. market. The severe slowdown in the EU was affecting many of the former centrally planned economies, and few would see any increases.

The overall current account of the balance of payments in the advanced economies remained in deficit for the third straight year after six years of surplus. It was expected to fall to $223 billion, from a higher-than-expected $248 billion in 2000. The U.S. deficit once again exceeded the total surplus but at $407 billion had fallen from the year before ($445 billion). Among the major G-7 countries, the U.S. and the U.K., as usual, had substantial deficits. The euro zone moved from a deficit in 2000 to a $16 billion surplus, with member countries Germany and Spain each sustaining $14 billion surpluses. The U.K. deficit, at $23 billion, was little changed from the year before. By contrast, Japan's traditional surplus fell quite heavily, from $117 billion to $89 billion. Of the other advanced countries, only Portugal and Australia had significant deficits—$10 billion and $11 billion, respectively. All four of the Asian NICs remained in surplus, with a total of $48 billion, just slightly down on the year before.

After many years of deficits, the LDCs had a surplus for the second year running. It fell sharply, however, from $60 billion to $20 billion owing to a halving of the Asian LDCs' surplus to $22 billion and an increase in Latin America's deficit to $58 billion. Indebtedness of the LDCs eased up slightly to $2,155,400,000,000.

Globalization. Events during the year demonstrated the extent to which world trade and financial markets had become interlinked and global. The synchronized downturn by the Triad (the U.S., Europe, and Japan) could not have occurred even a decade before. Nevertheless, the debate on whether the continued liberalization of world trade was desirable continued. There was no evidence to show that imports led to a widening of the gap between rich and poor. On the contrary, research published in 2001 showed that a representative sample of LDCs that had globalized since 1980 had benefited strongly from rising incomes and a reduction of poverty.

The annual meeting of WTO international trade ministers in Seattle, Wash., in 2000 had been disrupted by violent protests against the perceived capitalist ambitions behind any attempts to increase globalization. The 2001 meeting to expand and extend the multilateral trading system was held in Qatar at a time of increased uncertainty fueled by the sharp downturn in world trade and the terrorist attacks in the U.S. It took place amid the highest security, which limited access of antiglobalization protesters, and most nongovernmental organizations were too busy to protest.

The meeting was successfully concluded. Of great international significance (because of its massive market and trading potential) was the November 11 ratification of membership for China, which became the 143rd member of the WTO a month later. China's membership followed drawn-out preliminary negotiations on various issues dating back to 1986, when it first applied to join the General Agreement on Tariffs and Trade, the WTO's predecessor. In 2001 these issues included a China-U.S. agreement reached on June 8. This limited the amount of support and export subsidies the Chinese government could give to its agricultural sector, as well as easing and clarifying the conditions on various aspects of foreign investment. On the day after China's ratification, membership for Taiwan was approved. To satisfy Beijing (which considered Taiwan part of its sovereign territory), the newest member was designated "a separate customs territory" of Taiwan and its offshore islands of P'eng-hu, Quemoy, and Matsu. The two countries were committed to opening their markets and gradually liberalizing sectors in which the government was involved. China would also have more export opportunities, which many other countries feared would erode their competitiveness.

Exchange and Interest Rates. The global slowdown in 2001 and the September 11 attacks were the major influences on interest and exchange rates during the year. The U.S. started cutting interest rates in January, and Canada quickly followed suit. As the year got under way, most central banks in the industrialized countries outside the euro zone were cutting interest rates, and fiscal policy was being directed toward boosting confidence at household, corporate, and market levels to prevent outright recession. In March these included Australia, Canada, New Zealand, and Switzerland.

The U.S. wasted no time in cutting rates to prevent the "hard landing" that much of the world had been fearing since the middle of 2000. Weak data over the Christmas 2000 period, as well as low business and consumer-confidence indicators, prompted Fed Chairman Alan Greenspan to take early action. On January 3 the Fed cut its Fed funds interest-rate target from 6.5% to 6%. The move came before formal meetings and was on a scale that surprised many observers. It was intended to boost confidence but was not enough, and it was quickly followed by a second cut on January 31 and then a third on March 20, bringing the target down to 5%. Markets reacted positively, and the dollar remained firm against sterling, the euro, and the yen. Further cuts brought the Fed rate to 3.75% in June, down 275 basis points since the start of the year. In the wake of the terrorist attacks on September 11, more reductions were made. By early November the Fed rate was down to 2%, its lowest since 1961. At the start of December, there were positive signs that some sectors of the economy were growing again; equity prices were rallying, and long-term bond yields were up.

Daniel Janin/AFP Worldwide

Euros are coined on this assembly line in Sérifontaine, France, in October.

Despite this, interest rates were cut again, for the 11th time, to 1.75%.

In the U.K. interest rates moved almost in tandem with the U.S. through most of the year. To reduce vulnerability to the effects of the global slowdown, the Bank of England steadily cut the interest rates from February 8. By August 2 the rate had been reduced four times, by 100 basis points, to 5%. After September 11 raised more recession concerns, three more reductions were made. The last, on November 8, was the most aggressive at half a percentage point and brought the rate to 4%, the lowest in nearly 40 years. The Bank of England, which took the view that inflationary pressures were continuing to ease and the global slowdown might last longer than previously thought, did not cut rates again in December.

The euro zone was widened on January 2 to include Greece, which was relinquishing its drachma in favour of the euro and became the 12th EU member to join the euro system. The European Central Bank (ECB) was slow to experience and recognize the extent of the global slowdown. Its economic output accelerated slightly in the fourth quarter of 2000 over the previous three months, and going into 2001 consumer confidence was higher because of falling oil prices, tax cuts, and lower unemployment. Over the three months to the end of January 2001, the euro appreciated by 15% against the dollar and 8% against sterling. By mid-March, however, there were clear signs of a serious economic downturn, and sentiment turned against the euro. The ECB was widely criticized for not cutting interest rates. The ECB justified its inaction on the grounds that inflation was too high and that growth over the year would exceed 2.25%, a view not shared by the market.

In the following weeks all sectors of the economy were affected by falling demand, and the euro continued to weaken against the dollar and even the yen, despite the ailing Japan. Finally, on May 10 the ECB cut its interest rates by 25 basis points to 4.5%, which was seen as too little too late. It was not until August 30, after the euro had softened against most major currencies, that the ECB cut the rate again, by a meagre 25 basis points to 4.25%. The events of September 11 prompted a final and more decisive cut of 50 basis points to 3.75%. By the end of November, compared with a year earlier, the euro was trading slightly less than a percentage point lower.

A major preoccupation of consumers, businesses, and banks as the year drew to a close was the likely effect of the arrival and circulation of some 10 billion euro notes and several hundred thousand metric tons of coins on Jan. 1, 2002. These were to replace the 12 national currencies in the euro zone. The Deutsche Mark was to cease to be legal tender in Germany on January 1, while most other currencies had until the end of February.

In Japan nominal interest rates had been below 1% since the mid-1990s, underlying inflation was negative, and land

and stock prices were declining, which left little room for maneuver on interest rates. The year 2001 started on a gloomy note as fears rose that the economic recovery in the second half of 2000 was not as strong as expected, despite large injections of capital. There was speculation that the Bank of Japan (BOJ) would reverse the interest-rate increase implemented in August 2000. This had followed an 18-month zero-interest-rate policy. Growing doubts about the recovery led to a weakening of the yen against the dollar, and by March 8 the exchange rate had reached ¥120 to the dollar for the first time in 20 months.

On March 21 the BOJ announced a further easing of its monetary policy, increasing liquidity and effectively reinstating zero rates. The yen had reached a new two-and-a-half-year low at ¥126 to the dollar on April 6 when the government announced an emergency package that included a proposal to force the banking sector to deal with its bad-debt problems.

In mid-May it briefly rose to ¥118 to the dollar before returning to the ¥121–¥124 range, in which it remained until September 11. The BOJ intervened in the market with large-scale yen selling. This steadied the yen, which remained around ¥120 to the dollar for a while—just half its value of a year earlier—before sliding again to end the year at around ¥131. (IEIS)

STOCK EXCHANGES

Globalization works both ways: just as the internationalization of financial markets can power worldwide growth, it can equally throw the development into reverse. By the end of 2001, all the signs of impending global contraction were in place. The United States, usually the driver of international growth, had entered recession, dragging most of Asia with it and forcing Europe almost to a standstill.

The third-quarter 0.4% drop in gross domestic product (GDP) signaled that the recession had started in the U.S. in March, following the longest period of expansion in U.S. history—121 months, compared with the earlier record of 106 months between 1961 and 1970. Long before the terrorist attacks in the U.S. on September 11 and their aftermath, the year had produced a succession of bleak facts for the record books.

As early as midyear, operating earnings per share in the U.S. were recorded to be down nearly 40% overall, the worst performance since the Great Depression of the 1930s. Consumers, the backbone of the stock markets' long bull run, had been nervous months before the terrorist attacks, and after September 11 they all but stopped spending. Business investment fell 11.9% that month, and by year's end the Federal Reserve (Fed) had cut the base interest rate for the 11th time in the year to just 1.75%.

For more than a year, investors had been grappling with a seemingly endless succession of bad news about company

Table V. Selected Major World Stock Market Indexes[1]

Country and Index	2001 range[2] High	2001 range[2] Low	Year-end close	Percent change from 12/31/00
Australia, Sydney All Ordinaries	3425	2867	3360	6
Belgium, Brussels BEL20	3030	2323	2782	–8
Brazil, Bovespa	17,889	10,006	13,578	–11
Canada, Toronto Composite	9348	6513	7688	–14
Denmark, KFX	348	236	272	–13
Finland, HEX General	12,872	5584	8805	–32
France, Paris CAC 40	5998	3653	4625	–22
Germany, Frankfurt Xextra DAX	6795	3787	5160	–20
Hong Kong, Hang Seng	16,164	8934	11,397	–25
Ireland, ISEQ Overall	6458	4650	5673	–1
Italy, Milan Banca Commerciale Italiana	1948	1083	1433	–25
Japan, Nikkei Average	14,529	9504	10,543	–24
Mexico, IPC	6869	5082	6372	13
Netherlands, The, CBS All Share	906	557	708	–21
Philippines, Manila Composite	1712	979	1168	–22
Singapore, SES All-Singapore	515	335	426	–15
South Africa, Johannesburg Industrials	8720	6155	7764	–4
South Korea, Composite Index	705	469	694	37
Spain, Madrid Stock Exchange	964	649	824	–6
Switzerland, SBC General	5604	3547	4383	–22
Taiwan, Weighted Price	6104	3446	5551	17
Thailand, Bangkok SET	343	265	304	13
United Kingdom, FT-SE 100	6335	4434	5217	–16
United States, Dow Jones Industrials	11,338	8236	10,022	–7
World, MS Capital International	1249	854	1009	–17

[1]Index numbers are rounded. [2]Based on daily closing price.
Source: *Financial Times*.

Financial Times **Industrial Ordinary Share Index**
annual averages, 1978–2001

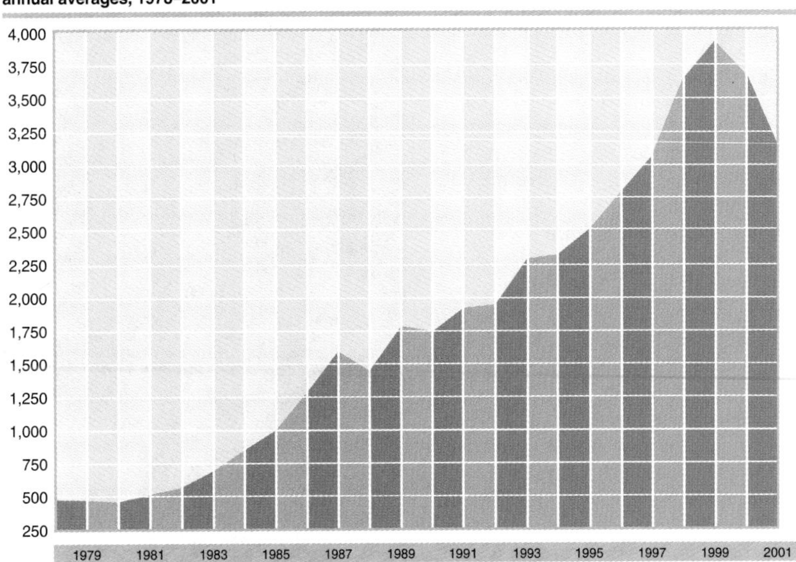

Source: *Financial Times*.

earnings, not only in the high-technology sectors devastated by the bursting of the dot-com bubble but also increasingly across all sectors. In summer the corporate news had looked far worse than the economic fundamentals: by October the whole picture had darkened, even though stock markets soon recovered to pre-September 11 levels. The rout when markets reopened after the attacks was only partly the result of the deep uncertainty the events induced.

According to the Organisation for Economic Co-operation and Development (OECD), the industrial world had contracted for the first time in 20 years. It was, said the organization, the cumulative effect of the collapse of the high-tech sector and a slump in equity values generally, reduction in inventories, rises in the price of oil, which tripled in 1999–2000, and the rise in interest rates over the same period.

The extent of the slowdown elsewhere varied in severity according to countries' trading links with the U.S. Although Europe was undergoing a less-severe contraction, forecasts for the region were revised down. Much of Asia was hard hit, and Japan, suffering a fourth recession in 10 years, was expected to contract more in the coming year.

It was perhaps not surprising that the year ended with nearly all the major developed country stock exchange indexes well down on the year before, in both local currency and U.S. dollar terms. Austria was an exception (up 11.7% in dollar terms), while Japan's Nikkei index declined 23.5%. Germany, France, The Netherlands, and Italy all suffered market falls in excess of 20% over the year. In the U.K. the *Financial Times* Stock Exchange 100 (FTSE 100) index was down 16.2% and was closer to the Morgan Stanley Capital International (MSCI) World Index drop of 16.9%. In the less-developed countries, stock market performances were more mixed, but by December 31 most were sharply down on year-end 2000, with the Hong Kong Hang Seng index slumping 24.5%. The major exceptions were South Korea, Taiwan, Mexico, and Russia, all of which were up for the year. (IEIS)

United States. Falling corporate profits, recession, and the continuing decline of the Internet sector combined to make 2001 a down year for stocks. The technology-driven plunge in stock prices from the heights of the previous year persisted and broadened to create a bear market affecting nearly all sectors. It was the second year in a row that stock prices had declined after a nearly decade-long bull market. The Fed cut the federal funds rate a record 11 times throughout the year, motivated by a manufacturing-led downturn that had evolved into a recession by March. The terrorist attacks on September 11 shocked the markets and the nation, forcing the longest closure of the U.S. stock exchanges since the Great Depression. Stocks rallied at year's end but did not make up for earlier losses.

All three of the major indexes were down for the second year in a row. The Dow Jones Industrial Average (DJIA) of 30 blue-chip stocks fell 7.10% on the year; the broader Standard & Poor's index of 500 large-company stocks (S&P 500) slid 13.04%; and the National Association of Securities Dealers automated quotation (Nasdaq) composite index, made up largely of technology stocks, suffered the worst, dropping 21.05%. The Russell 2000 index of small market-capitalization (small-cap) stocks fared better, eking out a 1% increase, while the broadest market measure, the Wilshire 5000 index, fell 12.06%.

The DJIA began the year at 10,786.85 and showed no major movement through January and February. The index fell more than a thousand points in March but largely recovered in April, rallying to its yearlong peak of 11,337.92 on May 21. This was followed by a steady decline that progressed largely uninterrupted through the summer months.

The Nasdaq began the year at 2470.52 and showed respectable gains through January, briefly reaching a yearlong peak of 2859.15 on January 24. A decline through February and March cost the index more than a thousand points; some of that loss was recovered in an April rally that gave way to a long, slow decline lasting through the summer.

The S&P 500 index began at 1320.28 and roughly mirrored the Nasdaq's path, pointing to the relatively new prominence of technology stocks in the overall stock market. The S&P 500 hit its yearlong peak of 1373.73 on January 30. On November 30 the S&P 500 had an estimated price-to-earnings (P/E) ratio of 30.97, up from 24.59 at the year's beginning, which reflected a sharp decrease in earnings.

The terrorist attacks on the World Trade Center towers crippled the financial district of New York City. The New York Stock Exchange (NYSE), the Nasdaq stock market, and the American Stock Exchange (Amex) remained closed until September 17, the longest the NYSE had been closed since 1933 and the longest closure ever for the other exchanges. In the first week of trading following the attack, the DJIA fell 14.26%, the Nasdaq was down 16.05%, and the S&P 500 slid 11.6%. Each of these three indexes hit its yearlong low on September 21, with the DJIA falling to 8235.81, the Nasdaq at

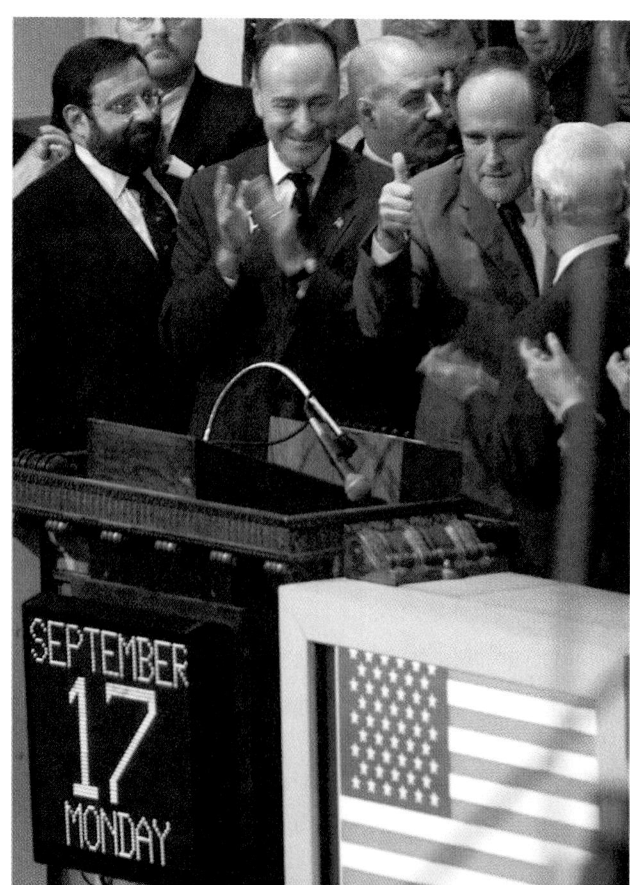

New York City Mayor Rudolph Giuliani gives a thumbs up to traders at the reopening of the New York Stock Exchange on September 17.

AP/Wide World Photos

1423.19, and the S&P 500 at 965.80. The energy-heavy Amex reached its yearlong low, 780.46, on September 25.

Markets then embarked on a rally lasting through year's end, fueled by expectations of economic recovery. The major stock indexes' decline reflected the influential role of technology stocks. JDS Uniphase went from single-digit value in 1999 to over $100 per share in early 2000, gained entrance to the S&P 500 in 2000, and fell back down to single-digits in 2001. Cisco Systems, the leading Internet networking company, fell by more than 50% over the course of 2001. Dramatic price declines were also seen in the stocks of other Internet-related companies such as Amazon.com and Yahoo! and in a wide range of technology firms, including Oracle, Compaq, Advanced Micro Devices, and Vitesse Semiconductor, all of which had risen dramatically in recent years.

Stock prices largely followed expectations about the state of the economy. The year began with an economic downturn centred in the manufacturing sector and marked by excess inventories. By February this slump had broadened, affecting many sectors, including media, telecommunications, and pharmaceuticals. Stock prices plunged in February and March, and the economy entered recession.

Corporate profits, already declining, fell sharply in the first three quarters, as did businesses' capital spending. Third-quarter profits were 22.1% lower than a year before, marking the largest 12-month drop in the 47 years that the government had tracked these statistics. The National Association of Purchasing Management's PMI index showed reduced manufacturing activity in every month through November. In mid-November 4,420,000 people were collecting or had filed for unemployment insurance, the largest such number since 1982. By the end of the month, firms had announced 1,795,000 layoffs, according to outplacement firm Challenger, Gray & Christmas. At the same time, the unemployment rate had climbed to 5.7%, already its highest level in six years; it rose again in December to 5.8%.

Investors' enthusiasm for stocks waned in 2001. According to the Investment Company Institute, through October a net of only $14.9 billion had entered stock funds in 2001, down from $292.8 billion for the same period in 2000. The two largest stock mutual funds, Fidelity's Magellan Fund and Vanguard's 500 Index Fund, both large-cap blend funds, were down 11.7% and 12%, respectively, for the year, while the average large-cap blend fund declined 12.9%. By the end of November, four out of five U.S. stock mutual funds were down on the year.

Caution and pessimism dominated the investment landscape. Venture capital investment, which had topped $20 billion in every quarter of 2000, was at $12 billion in the first quarter of 2001 and declined to $7.7 billion in the third quarter, matching the level of the first quarter of 1999. Through September there were

Table VI. Selected U.S. Stock Market Indexes[1]

	2001 range[2] High	2001 range[2] Low	Year-end close	Percent change from 12/31/00
Dow Jones Averages				
30 Industrials	11,338	8236	10,022	–7
20 Transportation	3146	2034	2640	–10
15 Utilities	399	275	294	–29
65 Composite	3392	2489	2892	–13
Standard & Poor's				
500 Index	1374	966	1148	–13
Industrials	1613	1113	1334	–13
Utilities	342	219	237	–32
Others				
NYSE Composite	667	504	590	–10
Nasdaq Composite	2859	1423	1950	–21
Amex Composite	959	780	848	–6
Russell 2000	517	379	489	1

[1]Index numbers are rounded. [2]Based on daily closing price.
Sources: *Financial Times; The Wall Street Journal.*

New York Stock Exchange Composite Index, 2001 stock prices (Dec. 31, 1965 = 100)

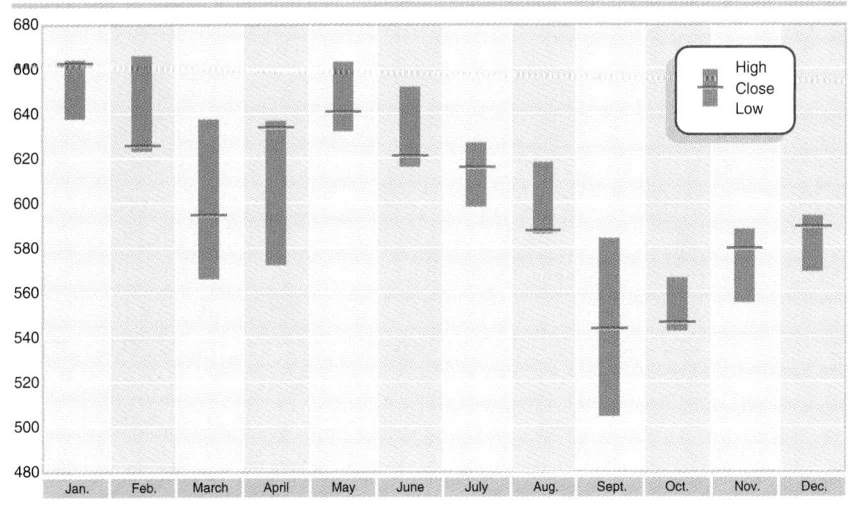

Average daily share volume in thousands of shares

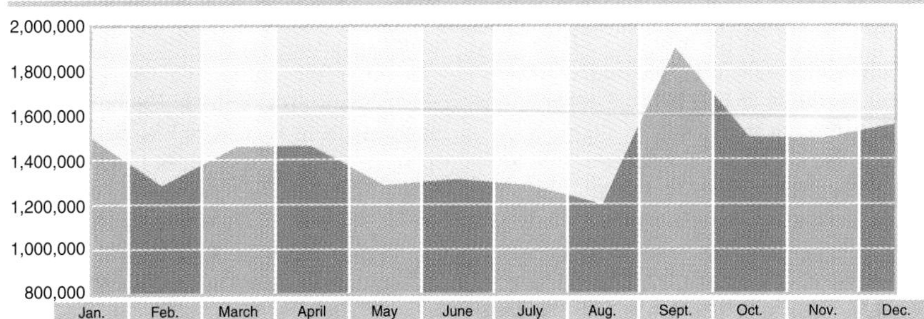

Sources: *Barron's National Business and Financial Weekly; The Wall Street Journal.*

New York Stock Exchange Common Stock Index Closing Prices
stock prices (Dec. 31, 1965 = 50)

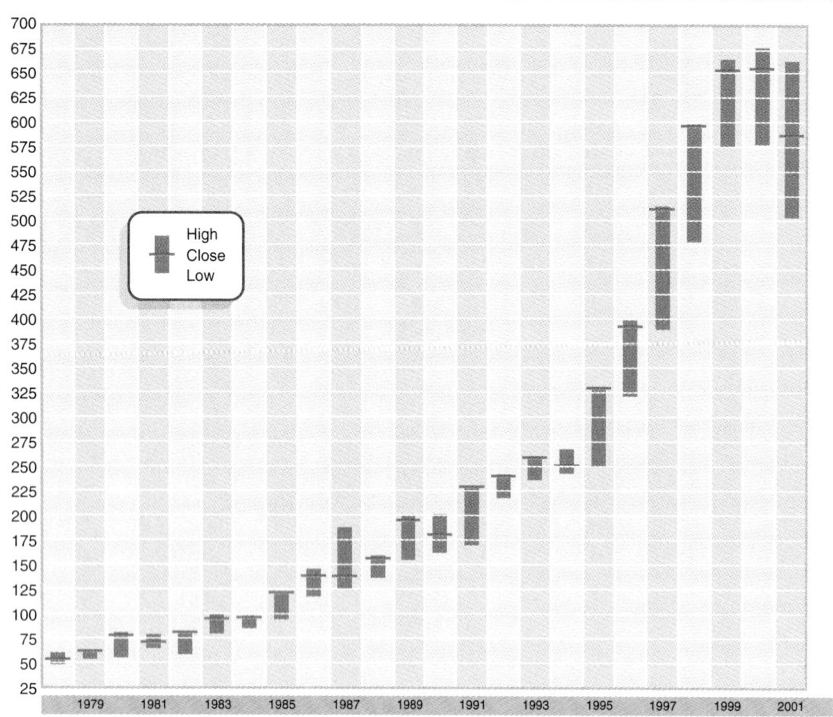

Number of shares sold
In billions of shares

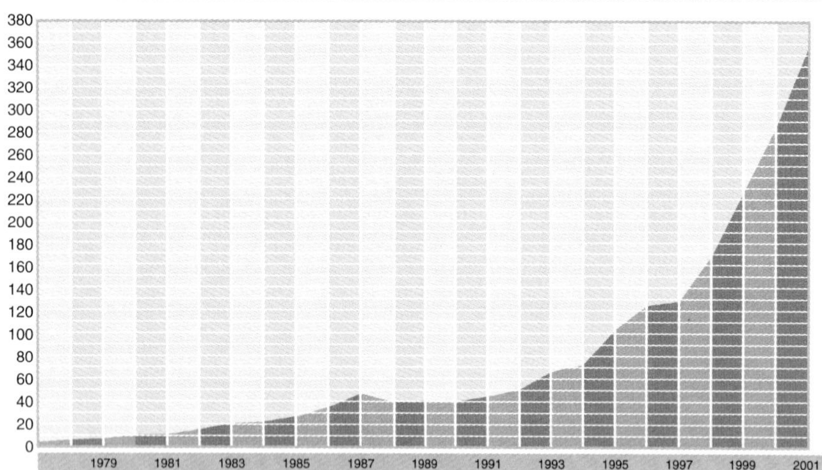

Sources: *Barron's National Business and Financial Weekly; The Wall Street Journal.*

only 65 initial public offerings (IPOs) in U.S. markets, with another 32 IPOs between October and December, down from a total of 451 in 2000. Mergers and acquisitions activity was at about $99.9 million a month on average, a 30% decline from the 2000 average monthly activity, according to Thomson Financial. The risky practice of margin borrowing fell sharply; in June margin debt stood at $157.9 billion, down from its peak of $299.9 billion in March 2000. Short selling—wherein investors bet that a stock would decline—was up.

Through November 12 short interest on the New York Stock Exchange had increased to a record 6.3 billion shares, up from 4.9 billion shares in December 2000. Through October investors filed 5,690 arbitration claims with NASD Dispute Resolution Inc. (a unit of the National Association of Securities Dealers), up from 4,646 for the same period in 2000.

NYSE average daily trading through October was 1,240,000,000 shares, up slightly from the previous year. Dollar volume was $42.6 billion, down slightly. Of the 3,973 equities traded on the NYSE, 2,370 advanced on the year, 1,569 declined, and 34 ended the year unchanged. The most actively traded stocks on the exchange were Lucent Technologies (6.4 billion shares traded), General Electric, EMC Corp., Enron Corp., AOL Time Warner, and Nortel Networks. Enron, which traded 4.4 billion shares, peaked above $84 before collapsing to end the year at 60 cents.

On January 29 the NYSE completed its conversion mandated by the Securities and Exchange Commission (SEC) to a system of decimalized trading, wherein stocks were traded in dollars and cents rather than in the traditional sixteenths of a dollar. Preliminary evidence suggested that decimalization had reduced bid-ask spreads by 37%, according to SEC staff analysis, which resulted in lower transaction costs. This particularly benefited small investors and active traders and improved trading capacity and transparency. A seat on the NYSE sold for $2,200,000 on October 29, down from its peak of $2,650,000 on Aug. 23, 1999.

Average daily trading on the Nasdaq stock market was 1.9 billion shares, up slightly from 2000; dollar volume, however, was $46.6 billion, down sharply from $88.3 billion in 2000, reflecting the lower average price per share. Some Nasdaq stocks began a slow recovery, and at year's end advancers led decliners 2,690 to 2,450, with 32 unchanged. The most active shares traded on the Nasdaq were all high-tech companies—Cisco, Intel, Sun Microsystems, Microsoft, JDS Uniphase, and Dell Computer.

The Nasdaq completed its decimalization on April 9. The SEC reported that bid-ask spreads had been reduced by 50%. The Nasdaq temporarily loosened its continued listing requirements to accommodate stocks hit by the market drop in the week following the September 11 attacks. The $1 minimum bid and public float requirements were suspended until Jan. 2, 2002.

The Amex composite reached a yearlong high of 958.75 in mid-May and slid thereafter to close at 849.92, down 5.59% for the year. Advancers narrowly led decliners 550 to 539, and only 9 issues were unchanged. Surprisingly, the most actively traded issue was the Nasdaq 100.

In 2001 the Chicago Mercantile Exchange for the first time became the largest futures exchange in the U.S., surpassing its annual trading record in August. This record volume was attributed to continuous interest-rate adjustments by the Fed and stock market uncertainty. In November the Chicago Board of Trade recorded the highest monthly trading volume in its history, at 30,009,125 contracts, reflecting a positive shift in market sentiment. Volume was up 10.3% on the year. On September 14 the New York Mercantile Exchange introduced its Internet-based version of NYMEX ACCESS, which led to heavier-than-normal volume.

The Commodity Futures Trading Commission, which regulated the U.S. futures and options markets, issued a warning to the public to be wary of companies promising profits from commodity futures and options trading based on information relating to the September terrorist attacks.

Electronic communications networks (ECNs)—computerized systems used to match buyers and sellers of securities without using the traditional trading venues—continued to grow in importance. During October the nine registered ECNs accounted for 34.5% of the reported share volume in Nasdaq trading, up from 26.8% a year earlier. In January the SEC approved Nasdaq's SuperMontage, a redesign of the market's stock-trading platform intended to provide a range of improvements, including better access to price information and simpler order executions in the Nasdaq market.

It was a good year for bonds as investors avoided stocks. Bond prices rose for most of the year, falling only during the stock rallies in January, April, and May, before dropping sharply in November and December as stocks recovered. High bond returns coincided with the slowing of the economy. The Lehman Brothers U.S. Aggregate Bond Index showed a return of 3.03% in the first quarter, 0.56% in the second, and 4.61% in the third, well down from 2000 figures.

The Fed's repeated rate cuts resulted in a steep yield curve for Treasuries. In December the spread, or difference, between 2-year Treasury notes and 30-year Treasury bonds was 2.3%. In October the U.S. Treasury announced that it would no longer issue its 30-year bond; this prompted an immediate 30-basis-point drop in yields. Many bond experts saw this discontinuation as an attempt to drive down long-term interest rates. The spread between the yields of high-yield corporate, or junk, bonds and 7-year Treasuries rose sharply, nearing 10%, a level last seen in 1990. This spread reflected concern over the risk of default among troubled firms, driven by several high-profile bankruptcies, notably Pacific Gas & Electric, which was caught up in California's energy crisis, and Enron.

In 2001 the SEC cracked down on accounting fraud, investigating between 240 and 260 cases. The first antifraud injunction against a Big Five accounting firm in more than 20 years was entered against Arthur Andersen, which agreed to a settlement of $7 million, the largest civil penalty ever imposed on a major accounting firm. In June the SEC issued an alert to investors, urging them not to rely solely on analyst recommendations. The SEC reported widespread conflicts of interest among analysts who covered stocks underwritten by their firms or those they personally owned.

The fortunes of traditional blue-chip stocks were mixed. Philip Morris gained 4.2% and Procter and Gamble 0.9%, while General Motors lost 4.6% and Minnesota Mining & Manufacturing lost 1.9%. Media giant Disney lost 28.4%, and pharmaceutical company Merck & Co. lost 37.2%.

In November, after more than three years of litigation, the Microsoft Corp. reached a settlement with the Department of Justice and 9 of the 18 states that had joined the suit. This settlement was widely seen as a victory for Microsoft, despite the fact that the nine other states had refused to sign on. The software giant's stock ended the year up by about 53%. Personal computer manufacturer Dell was up some 55%, and technology blue chip IBM rose by roughly 42% on the year.

At year's end 8 of the 10 stock sectors tracked by Dow Jones were down on the year, with only consumer cyclicals (+0.18) and noncyclicals (+1.12) in positive territory. The best-performing individual industries were consumer services (+57.12%), office equipment (+50.38%), toys (+38.89%), and water utilities (+37.07%), while the worst were gas utilities (–71.60%), communications technology (–56.58%), advanced industrial equipment (–46.85%), nonferrous metals (–39.85%), and airlines (–34.13%).

Profits and payrolls at many brokerage firms tumbled. Discount broker Charles Schwab reduced its staff by 17% through the third quarter of 2001 as its new assets fell from $31 billion in the first quarter to $11 billion in the second and $18 billion in the third. Merrill Lynch, the largest full-service broker, saw new assets drop from $35 billion in the first quarter of 2001 to only $5 billion in the second and $13 billion in the third.

Canada. The Canadian stock market declined considerably in 2001. The primary measure of the Canadian market, the Toronto Stock Exchange (TSE) 300, fell by 13.94% over the year. The Dow Jones Global Index for Canada fell by about 20% in U.S. dollar terms.

Through October the TSE reported average daily trading of 147.3 million shares, 11.4% lower than the same period in the previous year, and dollar volume of $2.9 billion, 23.7% lower than the same period of 2000. A total of 1,322 companies were listed on the exchange, down from 1,430. IPOs were roughly steady at 42, compared with 43 for the same period of 2000.

Nortel Networks, the largest TSE stock by market capitalization, lost more than 75% of its value on the year and closed at Can$11.90 (Can$1 = about U.S. $0.63) from its yearly high of Can$61.10. The next largest, Thomson Corp., lost 16% of its value and ended the year at Can$48.35, down from a high of Can$57.85. Canada 3000, the country's second biggest airline, received bankruptcy protection in November.

The two-year-old Canadian Venture Stock Exchange (CDNX) was up 8.7% through December 7, though it was down 11.1% from its peak of June 8. On December 10, the main CDNX index was replaced by the new S&P/CDNX Composite index, introduced as a broad indicator of the venture capital market in Canada. Through September, 113 IPOs were completed on the CDNX, up from 101 in the same period of 2000. Average market capitalization was down to $3,820,000 on September 30, from $5,740,000 at the end of the previous year. The TSE and CDNX merged on August 1, but the exchanges continued to operate separately under joint ownership.

The terrorist attacks in the U.S. on September 11 caused a 294-point drop in the TSE 300, and trading was halted. The exchange reopened on September 13, but interlisted American companies were not traded until September 17, the day the major U.S. markets reopened.

On November 14 the Securities Industry Committee on Analyst Standards issued a report recommending that securities firms require their analysts to disclose conflicts of interest and prohibit certain activities.

Foreign investment in Canadian shares plummeted. Through July foreign investors made net investments of only $3.8 billion in Canadian stocks, compared with $36 billion in the same period of the previous year. Canadians made net withdrawals of $26.8 billion from foreign stock markets, continuing the trend from the previous year. The Canadian brokerage industry reported an operating profit of $1.4 billion through July, 31% below the same period of the previous year. Mergers and acquisitions totaled $71 billion in the first six months, less than half the $149 billion of the same period of 2000.

The Canadian central bank, the Bank of Canada, followed the Fed for much of the year and reduced its overnight interest rate nine times, from 5.75% to 2.25%. The Canadian unemployment rate was 7.5% in November, the highest since mid-1999. (BETH KOBLINER)

Western Europe. Early in the year most investors judged the European Union to be the only relatively safe place for their money as problems mounted in Japan and in the United States. Yet as early as March—and despite the confidence of many in the region that the euro zone would continue to grow—European equity funds suffered their first overall outflows in six years. Investors sold two billion in fund holdings. By year's end many more were disappointed.

Europe's main stock markets approached the winter holiday season firmly in negative territory. Most had lost around a quarter of their value, with the German Xetra DAX down 25%, France's CAC 40 down 27.4%, and Italy down 28.6% (all in U.S. dollar terms). The U.K.'s FTSE 100 fared a little better, recording a sterling loss of 17.7% (20.4% in dollars). Dollar investors who lost least were those invested in the constituents of Spain's Madrid Stock Exchange, down 8.9% late in the year. The newest entrant to the euro zone, Greece, continued to perform poorly. Early in the year a 3.7% drop in the level of the Athens index dashed hopes that investors would pile in when interest rates fell to euro-zone levels. Within a month of the country's May 31 upgrading by the MSCI index series from an emerging to a developed market, investors fled, sending the market down by 12%. Emerging market investment funds reportedly had pulled out an estimated $1 billion.

Markets had reacted positively to the surge in U.S. markets that followed the surprise New Year's cut in the federal funds interest rate by the Fed. The European Central Bank (ECB) left interest rates unchanged in January, concerned that inflation was above the bank's target ceiling of 2%, and through the year the continued reluctance of the ECB to cut rates made investors increasingly nervous.

By midyear short-term prospects had deteriorated further with a spike in oil prices. Manufacturing activity declined as big exporting companies in Germany, France, Italy, and Spain faced slowing demand from the U.S. and Japan. Industrial production fell sharply in the second quarter, down 1.4% in July alone. Europe's slowdown was exacerbated by the effects of the sharp tightening of monetary policy by the ECB between the end of 1999 and October 2000, weakening retail sales. Inflation, however, rose well above the central bank's 2% target to 2.9%, again choking off any likelihood of rate cuts.

In June additional signs of global weakness disappointed investors awaiting a second-quarter revival. Little progress could be made in markets dominated by concerns over corporate weakness and the ECB's failure to deliver rate cuts as expected. It was August before the bank made a quarter-point base-rate cut to 4.25%. By contrast the Fed had, between January and June, cut its rate by 2.5 percentage points. In November the U.S. rate was 2%, compared with the euro-zone rate of 3.25%. Profit warnings, especially from Finnish mobile phone company Nokia, sent the Helsinki exchange down 16.7% in June and undermined the position of other technology stocks, especially when U.S. high-tech companies also reduced their profit forecasts. Pessimism was deepened by falling demand for factory goods, inducing greater declines in activity in Europe and the U.S. Amid anxiety over the slowdown in the U.S. and Japan and another spike in oil prices, euro-zone GDP growth dropped to 2.5%, against 2.9% achieved in the last quarter of 2000.

As the summer wore on, European investors' sentiment increasingly matched that of U.S. investors as prospects for euro-zone growth deteriorated. They were concerned about the continued weakness of the euro and the ECB's resistance to calls for rate cuts. Manufacturing activity declined more than expected, and unemployment rose sharply. Germany's influential Ifo Business Climate Index fell to a five-year low, and the U.K. manufacturing sector entered recession, output having fallen for a second successive quarter.

Other Countries. While all eyes were on the United States, most of Asia became engulfed by a deeper and possibly more dangerous downturn. In Japan, which set the pattern for the region, the recession continued unabated, and the market was volatile. The fall in the yen and tumbling share prices raised fears of a credit crisis. The level of prices had fallen in five of the past six years and was forecast to fall further. As the year began, Japan's retail sales slumped 0.9% year-on-year as household spending fell and retail sales were down for a fourth successive year. Unemployment hit 5% at the end of November, outstripping a post-World War II record high of 4.9%, and ended the year at an estimated 5.4%. Consumer prices had registered their steepest drop in 30 years during 2000, and by January 2001 foreign investors were deserting the market in droves, forcing share prices down.

Nevertheless, the Japanese market enjoyed a brief respite in January 2001 when the unexpected rate cut by the U.S. Fed lifted sentiment. Soon after, equity markets sank, weighed down by reports of weak corporate earnings. The election of a new Japanese prime minister on April 24 triggered a 6% rise in the Topix index, but again this was short lived. In July the market fell when the Tankan survey showed a further weakening of the economy, only to rise again in August on news that the Bank of Japan would boost the money supply. It reverted to a downward trend when it became clear that the earnings of Japan's healthiest companies were set to decline.

The contraction of Singapore's and Taiwan's economies—5.6% and 4.2% of GDP, respectively—was unprecedented. By the end of November, output was stagnating in Malaysia, Hong Kong, and Thailand, and export growth was slowing sharply in China, although domestic demand was helping to sustain output. Despite this, a lack of confidence in the global economy pushed the China market down by more than 20%.

Argentina was the focus of attention in South American markets. Early in the year the U.S. interest-rate cuts briefly lifted investor confidence, but on July 10 the failure of an Argentine government bond auction precipitated another financial crisis. In September the International Monetary Fund agreed to increase its loan to $22 billion. In November, however, the Argentine government announced that it would restructure its debts through exchanging loans, which involved both local and international investors. The proposal was seen by many as debt default, and the country quickly moved into a deeper crisis, with the markets ending down 29% in dollar terms. The problem in Argentina had a contagious effect on Brazil, which was already suffering an energy crisis. The Brazilian currency depreciated 28% in the first 10 months of the year, and although it recovered slightly, the Brazilian stock market ended the year down almost 24% in dollar terms.

According to the investment bank Morgan Stanley Dean Witter, the risk of global deflation was higher at the end of 2001 than at any time in the previous 70 years. Yet in the final quarter of 2001, there was consensus among professional investors in global equities that the "bear" market had hit bottom on September 21. The attacks on September 11, they judged, might have helped to resolve more quickly the problem of past overinvesting by prompting faster rate cuts and reducing capacity in the travel and leisure sectors.

Commodity Prices. Commodity prices were expected to weaken generally as global growth slowed. Amid the general gloom, however, there were a few winners. Cocoa prices rose during October and November by around 30% to reach a three-year high. The market expected production to fall by around 200,000 metric tons over the year to September 2002, mainly because of disease and poor farm maintenance in Côte d'Ivoire, the chief producer. Another more marginal winner was gold. Even before September 11, sentiment for the yellow metal was positive. As the year drew to a close, it had regained some of its attraction as a store of value to reach a price of more than $278 an ounce, a three-year high. Demand had eroded over the previous few years to make a high level of precautionary investment necessary to offset that erosion.

The prices of other metals had fallen steadily despite lower levels of stock, which indicated low expectation of demand. Aluminum fell 11% between April and August and was expected to slide further in the short term. Copper, however, which followed a similar pattern, was always the metal to watch. Traditionally, copper was the first metal to recover from a stock market correction, as the liquidity that results when investors cash in their stock market holdings usually lifts construction activity. (Historically, the price of copper shows a statistical feature known as an "absorbing state." When the price reaches a certain level, it tends to remain there until an unexpected event jars it and sends it back to its long-term average price of around 91 cents a pound. Absorbing states arise from the tendency of each phase of the economic cycle to linger.) Copper entered an absorbing state in July 2001 at below 70 cents a pound and ended the year at 67 cents; analysts were not expecting an early "breakout."

The price of oil had been highly volatile, and the outlook remained deeply uncertain by the end of the year. In 2000 production cuts, low stocks, and high demand driven by global growth had pushed prices well above the target price range of $22–$28 dollars a barrel set by OPEC. By the third quarter of 2001, demand from the U.S., the world's biggest oil consumer, was 300,000 bbl a day lower than in the third quarter of 2000. The slowdown and the need to sell oil caused producers outside OPEC to be less inclined to cooperate in cutting production, and it was thought that their need to keep up production and sales could keep prices, which ended 2001 below $20 a barrel, depressed. Any extension of the war in Afghanistan, though, could cause interruptions to supply that would force prices up in 2002. (IEIS)

BANKING

The September 11 attacks in the United States and the resulting international efforts to cut off the source of terrorist funding gave rise to sweeping new legislative and other measures that brought the global banking and financial services industry to the front lines of the war on terrorism in 2001.

On October 26, U.S. Pres. George W. Bush signed into law the U.S.A. Patriot Act, which granted the government broad new investigative and surveillance powers and provided for a significant expansion of anti-money-laundering requirements applicable to banks and other financial institutions. The U.S. measures were part of an intensive global campaign against terrorist-funding sources. International groups such as the Financial Action Task Force (FATF), the anti-money-laundering arm of the Organisation for Economic Co-operation and Development, were deeply involved in the global war against terrorism.

Even before the September 11 attacks, actions had been taken or were under consideration in a number of countries to combat money laundering. Particularly notable were the actions taken by countries identified in the June 2000 report by the FATF as jurisdictions where existing measures to combat money laundering were deemed to be inadequate. The Cayman Islands and Panama instituted a number of remedial actions in response to the FATF report, and in June 2001 they were removed from the FATF list. Israel for the first time enacted an anti-money-laundering law, an action recognized by the FATF as "welcome" progress.

In other places, including Bermuda and Luxembourg, legislation was enacted expanding the coverage of anti-money-laundering laws. The European Union (EU) had under consideration revisions to its 1991 directive in order to expand its scope. Actions to enhance the effectiveness of reporting on suspicious activity were instituted in Argentina and Canada. Italy adopted guidelines (commonly known as the "Ten Commandments") that provided for significant enhancements to anti-money-laundering practices.

There were also widespread efforts in 2001 to adapt existing laws and regulatory structures to the requirements of an increasingly globalized and integrated financial system. A number of countries continued to grapple with the problem of how to modernize their financial services laws to permit their domestic institutions to meet the challenges presented by advances in information and

World's 25 Largest Banks[1]

	Bank	Assets (in U.S. $000,000)
1	Mizuho Holdings (Japan)	1,428,928
2	Sumitomo Mitsui Banking (Japan)	991,791
3	Citigroup (U.S.)	902,210
4	Deutsche Bank (Germany)	885,135
5	Allianz (Germany)	869,561
6	United Financial of Japan	844,692
7	Mitsubishi Tokyo Financial Group	817,280
8	J.P. Morgan Chase (U.S.)	715,348
9	HypoVereinsbank (Germany)	674,670
10	UBS (Switzerland)	673,876
11	HSBC Holdings (U.K.)	673,312
12	BNP Paribas (France)	653,505
13	Bank of America	642,191
14	Credit Suisse (Switzerland)	613,084
15	ING Group (Netherlands)	612,202
16	ABN Amro (Netherlands)	511,448
17	Royal Bank of Scotland (U.K.)	477,903
18	Barclays (U.K.)	472,207
19	AXA (France)	446,899
20	Commerzbank (Germany)	432,818
21	Société Générale de France	429,258
22	Morgan Stanley (U.S.)	426,794
23	Fortis Group (Belgium/Netherlands)	412,499
24	HBOS (U.K.)	401,175
25	Grupo Santander Central Hispano (Spain)	328,551

[1]Ranked by asset size as of Dec. 31, 2000.
Source: *The Wall Street Journal*, Oct. 1, 2001.

communications technology that make possible the delivery of a broad array of financial services and intensify the competitive pressures on those institutions to provide their customers with banking, investment, insurance, and other financial services on an integrated basis. Canada passed Bill C-8, which revised the policy framework for its financial services sector and for the first time provided bank financial groups the option of organiz-ing their business activities in Canada under a holding company structure. Equally significant changes were under way in Denmark, which passed the Act on Financial Undertakings unifying in a single legislative act provisions relating to banking, investment, insurance, and mortgage activities.

Similarly, reform of domestic regulatory systems to enable them to meet the challenges presented by the formation of complex financial groups engaged in a diverse array of activities both at home and abroad was high on the legislative agenda in many countries. In Austria a Financial Market Supervisory Authority Bill was introduced. It would provide for the devolution of banking supervision from the Ministry of Finance while also creating a central supervisory authority for financial services. Germany had under consideration legislation that would significantly revise the financial supervisory system by combining the three supervisory offices for banking, insurance, and securities activities into a single organization. This Federal Agency for Financial Service and Financial Market Supervision would be affiliated with the German Ministry of Finance.

Ireland contemplated legislation that would provide for a new structure for the regulation of financial services. It proposed that the Central Bank of Ireland be restructured and called the Central Bank of Ireland and Financial Services Authority, which would consist of two functional divisions, one responsible for prudential regulation of all financial services (the Irish Financial Services Regulatory Authority) and the other charged with the management of external reserves and the country's participation in the European System of Central Banks (the Irish Monetary Authority). Portugal adopted legislation creating a National Council of Financial Supervisors to promote coordination between the three existing financial supervisors responsible for oversight of the banking, securities, and insurance industries.

Reviews of existing regulatory and supervisory relationships were under way in other countries. In Finland the government assigned a special advisory body the task of preparing a proposal on how to integrate insurance companies into the financial markets' supervisory structure. South Africa continued to debate whether to follow the route taken by Australia and the U.K. and establish a single financial regulator outside the central bank, while in Switzerland debate centred on a recommendation that the Swiss Federal Banking Commission and the Federal Office of Private Insurance be melded into a single integrated financial-market supervisory authority.

The global trend clearly continued to be in the direction of some form of consolidated oversight, but there was as yet no international consensus in 2001 on what kind of governmental authority should exercise this responsibility.

Another important development in 2001 was the pending transition to the euro in the 12 euro-zone countries and the ultimate disappearance of their local currencies in favour of euro banknotes and coins as legal tender for cash transactions. This was scheduled to occur on Jan. 1, 2002, and extensive efforts were under way to ensure that the changeover occurred with minimal disruption. The possible shortage of euro cash in the first weeks of 2002 and the logistic and security challenges of moving euro and legacy currencies at the end of the transition phase were the two major concerns of this gigantic project. In some countries special security arrangements were instituted to protect the new euro banknotes and coins as they were shipped to banks for distribution.

Daniel Janin/AFP Worldwide

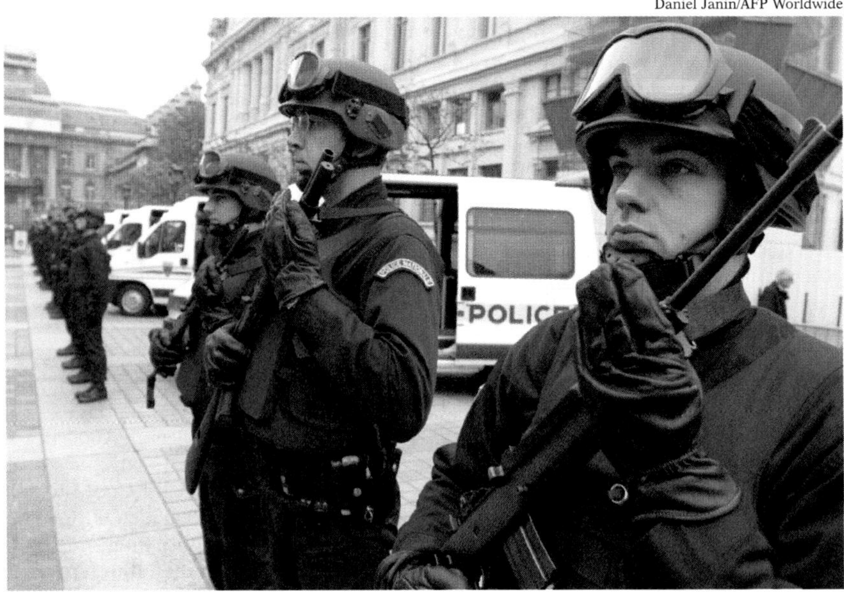

A special police unit in Paris guards the arrival of new euro bank notes at the Bank of France on November 20.

There was also extensive debate surrounding the changes to the Basel Capital Accord proposed in January 2001 by the Basel Committee on Banking Supervision. Key issues in these debates included the use of an "internal ratings-based approach" to setting risk-based capital standards and whether (and how) to incorporate measurements of operational risk into the standards. Another important issue was the role of home and host country authorities in the supervisory review process contemplated under Pillar 2 of the proposal as well as in connection with the application of disclosure standards contemplated under the market discipline principles set forth in Pillar 3.

Deposit insurance schemes were introduced or strengthened in several countries, including Luxembourg, South Africa, and Turkey, while in South Korea deposit insurance coverage was reduced. In the U.S., reform of deposit insurance coverage was the subject of heightened scrutiny by Congress, which considered several proposals to raise coverage limits as well as premium payments. This issue drew public attention in late July when the U.S. Federal Deposit Insurance Corp. seized Illinois-based Superior Bank FSB in a bailout that analysts suggested could cost as much as $500 million. Important revisions to bank-liquidation procedures, including enhancements to depositor protection, also were under consideration in Switzerland.

A number of countries, including India, Pakistan, and Panama, implemented changes to enhance their banks' practices regarding classification of assets and loan loss provisions. In this connection an initiative was undertaken in Spain, where an "insolvency statistical coverage fund" was created. The idea behind the fund was to accumulate additional resources during healthy economic periods to be used in the worst periods of the cycle.

Corporate governance issues also received increasing attention in several jurisdictions, notably Singapore, where a Corporate Governance Code was introduced, and Germany, where consideration was given to a Corporate Governance "Best Practices" Code.

In addition, there were extensive efforts to adapt legal and regulatory systems to the changing world of electronic banking and commerce. Luxembourg adopted a law on electronic commerce, and several countries, including Belgium, Italy, and Sweden, adopted measures to establish the legal framework for electronic signatures. Germany and Singapore undertook efforts to promote Internet payment systems and virtual banking. Legislation on electronic funds transfers (EFT) was adopted in Belgium, while Australia adopted an EFT Code of Conduct.

Privatization of banks continued in a number of countries, including the Czech Republic and Romania. Pressures for cross-industry consolidation resulted in several large mergers. In Germany Allianz AG took control of Dresdner Bank in a $21 billion deal that created the world's sixth largest financial services institution. (*See* TABLE.) Kookmin Bank and Housing & Commercial Bank combined under the Kookmin name to create South Korea's largest commercial bank, with some $121 billion in assets. In the U.S. two North Carolina-based institutions, First Union and Wachovia, joined forces to create the nation's fourth largest bank holding company, with assets estimated at $322 billion.

Cross-border merger activity also continued, as witnessed by the ongoing integration occurring within the Nordic region. BNP Paribas of France increased its presence in the U.S. market by purchasing 55% of BancWest in early 2001 and then acquiring United California Bank from UFJ Holding of Japan in a $2.4 billion buyout. Several countries, notably Israel and Poland, took measures to promote an expanded foreign bank presence in their domestic markets, while in Japan such actions focused on the rescue of failed institutions. Japan was also notable in that it permitted nonfinancial enterprises to establish commercial banking operations. At year's end the regional Ishikawa Bank became the first middle-level Japanese bank to file for bankruptcy since 1999.

(LAWRENCE R. UHLICK)

BUSINESS OVERVIEW

It was a new, unstable era in 2001. Any hopes that the boom years of the 1990s would extend into the next decade ended for good after the September 11 terrorist attacks that destroyed the World Trade Center, launched the United States into war, and sent the business world into chaos.

The U.S. economy was skirting the edge of recession before the attacks; afterward it tumbled. Already-suffering industry sectors begged for government bailouts, and what had been known as the "new economy" of technology companies and Internet-based start-ups—the stars of the 1990s boom—fell further into disrepair. (*See* COMPUTERS AND INFORMATION SYSTEMS.)

The stock market had been deflating in value throughout the year, equally reducing valuations of traditional companies such as the ExxonMobil Corp. and new economy titans such as Yahoo! Inc. By year's end all signs of a recession were in place. Real gross domestic product (GDP) growth in the U.S. fell at a 0.4% annual rate in third-quarter 2001, the biggest drop since the 1991 first quarter, and real GDP was expected to fall by 1% in the fourth quarter, compared with an annual growth rate of 5% for full-year 2000. In October the Consumer Confidence Index hit 85.5, its lowest standing in seven years, while manufacturing activity fell to its lowest level since February 1991.

For many industries the havoc caused by the terrorist attacks was more toxic than a typical recession. The worst affected were those sectors connected to travel, in particular the airlines, which were rattled to the point of near collapse. Analysts expected the U.S. airline industry to have an after-tax loss of $5.6 billion in 2001.

The airlines already had been in fragile financial health for most of 2001—the result of years of price wars and rising fuel costs. The U.S. government's freeze on air travel for two days in September, combined with the public's overall fear of flying in the weeks after the hijackings, pushed many airlines to the brink of bankruptcy. U.S. airlines lobbied for a government bailout to help compensate for the loss of revenues and ultimately came away with a $15 billion package that, while enormous, still was not enough to prevent most leading airlines from posting severe losses. Almost all the major U.S. and foreign airlines cut staff by the thousands and slowed production drastically in the last few months of 2001. In mid-October, UAL Chairman James Goodwin warned that the airline could "perish" in the next year; soon afterward he was forced to resign and was replaced by UAL board member John W. Creighton.

European airlines, faced with the economic downturn and a drop in passenger traffic to North America, also registered massive losses. In early October Swissair briefly grounded all flights as it sought an infusion of cash. Sabena, jointly owned by Swissair and the Belgian government, was formally declared bankrupt in November. Out of the ashes of Sabena, Belgian investors created a successor of sorts, former Sabena unit Delta Air Transport, which seemed likely to merge with Virgin Express in early 2002. Air France announced staff cuts and reorganization plans for troubled Air Afrique, which it had acquired in August after the 11 African countries that shared ownership relinquished control of the airline.

Aircraft manufacturers were in equally rough shape. The Boeing Co., which moved its headquarters to Chicago in 2001, planned to cut up to 30,000 employees by the end of 2002 and slashed its airplane deliveries for 2001 to roughly 500, down from an expected 538. That

Air travelers stranded in Brussels on November 6 wait at a Sabena baggage claim that was closed due to demonstrations by employees of the debt-ridden Belgian airline.

Jacques Collet/AFP Worldwide

total was anticipated to fall to about 350 deliveries in 2002. Boeing's chief rival, European manufacturer Airbus, announced plans to deliver 320 aircraft in 2001 but acknowledged that cutbacks by airlines would reduce future orders. On a positive note, the Anglo-French Concorde aircraft, grounded since a fatal accident in July 2000, officially returned to the air in November.

Other industries linked to travel suffered as well. The lodging industry's profits for the year were expected to decline to between $18 billion and $20 billion, compared with 2000's record profit of $23.5 billion; revenue per available room was expected to fall by as much as 5% in 2001, the worst performance in 33 years. Industry occupancy rates were anticipated to fall to 60% of capacity, the lowest since the Persian Gulf War. The damage was such that some analysts predicted 6–10 hotel-chain bankruptcies by early 2002.

In the American automotive sector, sales were weakened by a reduction in rental car usage as well as consumer wariness about making large purchases. After September 11 all of the Big Three auto manufacturers initiated layoffs and began reducing production. The Ford Motor Co. planned to reduce its output by 13%, or up to 120,000 units, and stop production at five North American assembly plants. Ford posted a $692 million loss in the third quarter, and its worldwide automotive revenues fell by 12.4% in the quarter. Ford's woes were compounded by the expenses incurred because of the Firestone tire recall in 2000 and what critics termed a costly acquisition spree. By year's end Ford Chairman Jacques Nasser had been ousted in favour of William Clay Ford, Jr., the great-grandson of company founder Henry Ford. The General Motors Corp., although it posted a loss for the third quarter of $368 million, seemed to be in better shape. Sales of GM pickup trucks and sports utility vehicles shot up by 10% in the otherwise grim month of September. On September 21 GM revealed an agreement to buy the bankrupt South Korean Daewoo Motor and its international subsidiaries. DaimlerChrysler AG, which saw net income fall by 69% in the third quarter, was shaking out its operations to improve productivity. The company planned to slash more than 2,700 jobs and close three plants to get its troubled Freightliner LLC truck subsidiary to profitability by 2003.

As of September, 1,560,000 import cars had been sold year-to-date in the U.S., compared with 1,550,000 in the 2000 period. Imported light-vehicle sales rose to an estimated 2.2 million cars, compared with 2.1 million in 2000. It was good news for Japan's Nissan Motor Co., which said it would post $2.7 billion in profits for its fiscal year ending in March 2002. In November German carmaker BMW AG reported strong international sales and higher-than-expected revenue, with net profits (before taxes) up 63.3% for the first nine months of 2001.

The overall market volatility also had an impact on the energy sector, which was coming off one of its best years in recent history. As many analysts had predicted, the spike in oil prices that had helped deliver record revenues to oil and gas companies in 2000 began to abate in mid-2001. Where oil had been in the $30-per-barrel range for much of 2000, prices cooled down to roughly $24 per barrel by August. With jet-fuel usage dramatically down in the third quarter owing to reduced flight loads, many oil players lost revenues.

The oil market continued to tier into the ranks of global superpowers—The ExxonMobil Corp., The ChevronTexaco Corp., BP PLC (formerly BP Amoco), and the Royal Dutch/Shell Group—and lesser, regional players. Many of the latter went on acquisition binges to increase their meagre market shares. The Canadian oil and gas market was ripe for American companies looking for acquisitions, and some observers predicted that the Canadian energy market would no longer be independent by mid-2002. American energy players that bought Canadian energy companies included the Anadarko Petroleum Corp., the Duke Energy Corp., and Conoco Inc. There were signs that some companies had grown overextended during the energy boom of 1999–2000. The most prominent case was the fall of Enron Corp. After a string of accounting irregularities came to light in late 2001, Enron's stock value collapsed to pennies per share, as the company faced charges of massively defrauding its shareholders and formally declared bankruptcy in December. Controversy over ties between Pres. George W. Bush's administration and the ruined company was expected to be a major political issue in 2002.

Heightened demand for electricity also fueled a rebirth in the coal industry, which grew at a rate of about 4.5%, more than double the average growth rate. Spot prices for western coal soared from $5 a ton to as much as $14 a ton. The Peabody Energy Corp., the largest coal company in the U.S., beat analyst expectations when it posted $4.1 million in net income for third-quarter 2001.

The chemicals industry was hammered by continued high oil and gas prices and declines in business and consumer demand for plastics and other products. Earnings eroded across the board. Market leader E.I. DuPont de Nemours and Co. continued to struggle; total revenues fell by 11% in the first half of 2001. DuPont, which already had sold its oil subsidiary, Conoco, in 1999, pulled out of the pharmaceuticals sector by selling its pharmaceuticals subsidiary to the Bristol-Myers Squibb Co. for $7.8 billion. The Dow Chemical Co. started the year by completing a $10 billion acquisition of the Union Carbide Corp. but wound up posting severe declines in revenues and net income by year's end. A host of smaller chemical manufacturers had declining earnings, including the Cambrex Corp., the Crompton Corp., Cytec Industries Inc., the PolyOne Corp., and Praxair Technology, Inc.

Few sectors were as hard-pressed as the U.S. steel industry, which appeared to be on the verge of collapse throughout the year. When Bethlehem Steel Corp. filed for Chapter 11 bankruptcy protection in October, it was the 25th domestic steel company to have done so since 1998. Other steel companies filing for bankruptcy in 2001 included the Riverview Steel Corp., Edgewater Steel Ltd., GS Industries, Inc., the LTV Corp., and CSC Ltd. The industry was reeling with losses in 2001, recording a $1.4 billion loss in the third quarter alone. Steel manufacturers pointed to high energy costs and, most emphatically, extremely low import prices as the causes of their industry's troubles. The steel manufacturers that managed to avoid bankruptcy often took drastic measures to keep afloat. Top steelmaker USX Corp., which owned the U.S. Steel Group and the energy company Marathon Group, decided to separate the two companies to give them more flexibility to expand through acquisitions. U.S. Steel, which posted an $18 million net loss in third-quarter 2001, was spun off in October into a publicly traded company called United States Steel Corp. The merger of three European companies—Usinor of France, Aceralia of Spain, and Luxembourg's Arbed—was announced in February. The deal would create the world's largest steel group.

Other metals industries were also on the decline. In aluminum, year-to-date shipments as of August were down 14.4%, in part because of the slowdown

Exchange rates of major currencies to U.S.$, 2001

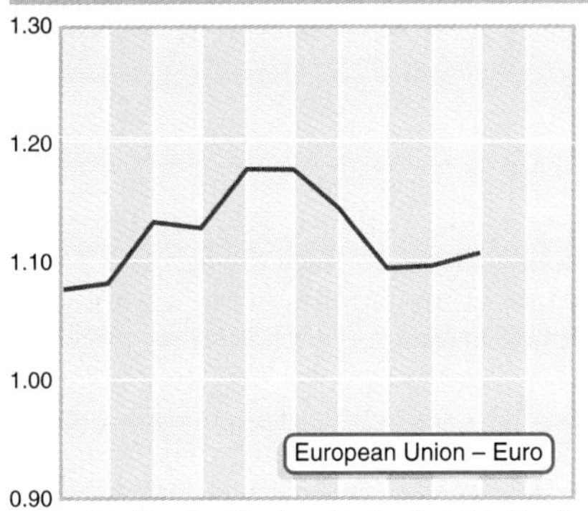

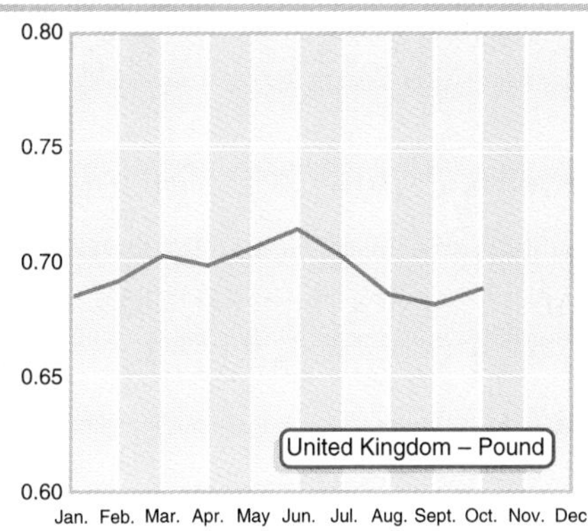

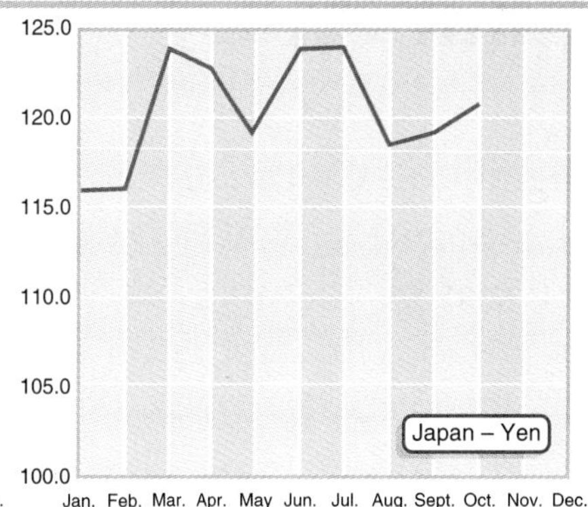

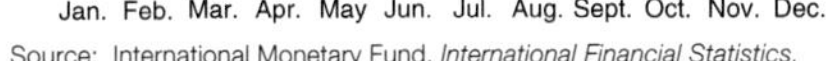
Source: International Monetary Fund, *International Financial Statistics.*

in automobile production. American exports of aluminum ingot and mill products were 725.8 million kg (1.6 billion lb) year-to-date as of August, down from 861.8 million kg (1.9 billion lb) in the same period in 2000, while imports were down 11.7% for the year. The leading worldwide aluminum producer, Alcoa Inc., remained strong, however, with revenues of $17.7 billion for the first three quarters, up from $16.4 billion in the comparable 2000 period. The company's health was in part due to an intensive cost-cutting initiative designed to offset falling demand. In November Alcoa reported that it was buying an 8% stake in China's largest aluminum producer.

Gold demand held up fairly well against signs of a growing worldwide economic slowdown. After a 17-month low of about $260 per ounce in February, gold prices rebounded to the $270–$290-per-ounce range for much of the year, and prices shot up after September 11, as investors poured into the market for security. Top worldwide gold producer AngloGold Ltd., based in Johannesburg, S.Af., bought Normandy Mining Ltd. of Australia for $2.3 billion in September. This followed an earlier $2.3 billion merger of Canada's Barrick Gold Corp. and its American rival, the Homestake Mining Co., which had created the world's second largest gold producer. Analysts approved of the mergers, hoping that less competition and production would improve the market's overall health.

The forest-products industry foundered owing to overall industry volatility, declining prices, and collapsing markets. The U.S. imposed higher duties on Canadian softwood lumber, which it claimed had been dumped on the American market at artificially low prices. (*See* WORLD AFFAIRS: *Canada.*) In 2000 there had been a divide between rising pulp prices and falling lumber prices, which provided many manufacturers with steady earnings, but in 2001 all paper markets suffered.

Top paper manufacturers such as the Weyerhaeuser Co. and Bowater Inc. reported serious declines in business for the year. Weyerhaeuser reported a 54% drop in quarterly profits in third-quarter 2001, and its net earnings were $369 million for the first nine months of 2001, compared with $646 million in the same period in 2000. The International Paper Co. posted a $632 million net loss for the first nine months of 2001, and the Georgia-Pacific Corp. had a $289 million loss from continuing operations in the same period.

Home building had enough ballast from yearlong low mortgage rates to withstand a declining economy. Total new houses sold were 8.1 million through September, up slightly from the 8 million in the same period in 2000. Total construction starts for 2001 were estimated to be worth $481.4 billion. Commercial space construction, however, was expected to fall by 16% in 2001 and by 9% in 2002, with the steepest declines hailing from the industries most afflicted by the September 11 attacks, including hotels and office spaces. The weaker economy also caused banks, which had seen their earnings erode in 2001, to be more stringent with funds for commercial development, and this caused some projects to be delayed or canceled. Other sectors were expected to improve, including public-works projects, health care facilities, and multifamily housing.

The tobacco industry was healthy overall, in good part owing to rising product prices.

The pharmaceutical industry was resilient for much of the year, and top players were thriving. Market leader Pfizer Inc. had a 153% increase in net income for the first nine months of 2001, driven by worldwide sales increases for its key products, including a 13% increase for Viagra and a 37% increase for Lipitor, its cholesterol-reducing drug that in 2001 became the largest-selling pharmaceutical in the world. Heightened competition between generic and patent drug manufacturers threatened to erode revenues for top pharmaceuticals. About $50 billion in drug patents were scheduled to expire in the next five years, and already generic players were profiting at the expense of patent manufacturers. Eli Lilly and Co. lost about 80% of its market share in Prozac once Barr Laboratories, Inc.'s generic reached the shelves.

Drug companies, faced with criticism of high drug prices and the threat of competition from cheaper generics, reached agreements to provide drugs to combat AIDS in several less-developed countries at a fraction of the Western prices, but demands for cheaper drugs continued. When mailborne anthrax hit newsrooms and government offices in September and October, the German pharmaceutical company Bayer AG faced intense pressure from the U.S. government to either reduce the price of its antibiotic Cipro or face the loss of its patent. Waiting in the wings with their generic versions of Cipro were manufacturers, including Barr, that offered their products free or at a steep discount to the government for its stockpiles. While Bayer managed to hold onto its patent by agreeing to reduce Cipro prices, the continuing threat of chemical and biological war ensured that the rivalry between generics and patent drug manufacturers had taken on new, unknowable connotations.

(CHRISTOPHER O'LEARY)

Education

Significant educational developments during 2001 included the expansion of **ACHIEVEMENT-TESTING** programs, educational alternatives to public schools, controversies over **RELIGION** in schools, limitations on freedom of inquiry, and **ETHNIC QUOTAS** in college admission policies.

PRIMARY AND SECONDARY EDUCATION

Newly inaugurated U.S. Pres. George W. Bush made the improvement of education a central goal of his administration. He began the year by appointing Houston (Texas) superintendent of schools Roderick R. Paige the nation's secretary of education. The president adopted the motto "No child left behind" and sent Congress proposed legislation featuring his four pillars of comprehensive educational reform: accountability, local control and flexibility, expanded parental choice, and a focus on what works. Whereas Congress endorsed such key provisions of the bill as nationwide achievement testing and money for poor schools, the legislators eliminated Bush's voucher plan that would have provided public funds for parents to send their children to any school of their choice, including private schools administered by religious groups.

Around the world the rapidly growing popularity of nationwide achievement testing was accompanied by several vexing problems. In the U.S. the nation's largest teachers union, the National Education Association (NEA), passed resolutions denouncing high-stakes testing. Parents' and students' rejection of "test-driven education" led to student boycotts of state achievement testing in several school districts. (*See* Special Report.) When school systems in Florida paid bonuses to schools whose students scored above average on the state achievement test, critics charged that such rewards placed undue emphasis on test passing in contrast to gaining a well-rounded education. Officials in states, notably New York, that already had ambitious testing requirements questioned why more exams, imposed by the federal government, were necessary. An expanded national testing program in Great Britain for students 14 years old and above drew complaints from teachers and parents and motivated the minister of education and skills, Estelle Morris, to order a review of the recently revised curriculum, which had produced what was described as an examination logjam. At the same time, the Labour government's proposal that private companies take over the operation of underperforming public schools met strong opposition from teachers unions.

Tax-supported alternatives to regular public schools continued to increase in the U.S. The Bush legislation included additional money for charter schools, which were established by private groups financed by tax funds and were permitted to offer a curriculum different from that of public schools. About 518,000 (1%) of the country's 50 million schoolchildren attended charter schools. The NEA announced its endorsement of charter schools that hired certified teachers, were subject to the same student-assessment measures as other public schools, honoured teachers' collective-bargaining rights, and had initial construction funds that did not rely heavily on tax revenue. As a further educational option, 850,000 (1.7%) American schoolchildren studied at home under parental guidance. About 18% of homeschoolers were also enrolled in regular schools part-time; 11% used books or materials from a public school; and 8% followed a public-school curriculum. A newly established Patrick Henry College opened in Virginia specifically for youths who had been homeschooled and who chose to pursue higher education in a Christian-based institution.

Private-school enrollments increased in Canada, rising over a 10-year period from 4.6% to 5.6% of all school-age children. Contrary to the impression that only wealthy families sent their children to private institutions, a survey reported that 29% of children enrolled in private schools across Canada came from families with incomes below Can$50,000 (about U.S. $32,000); that percentage rose to 46.1% in the western provinces of Manitoba, Saskatchewan, Alberta, and British Columbia.

Delegates from nine countries' ministries of education met in Beijing to outline steps they would take to upgrade schooling, especially to slash the rate of school dropouts and to turn around low school enrollment and poor classroom performance. The plan was signed by Bangladesh, Brazil, China, Egypt, India, Indonesia, Mexico, Nigeria, and Pakistan.

The South Korean government intended to improve the standard of education in the nation by limiting the number of students per class to 35 by 2004; the head count was currently 35.7 in elementary schools, 38 in middle schools, and 42.7 in high schools. To facilitate the program the government expected to hire 23,600 additional teachers and open 1,208 new schools with a total of 14,494 classrooms.

The Anglican Church of Canada faced the threat of bankruptcy as the result of lawsuits filed by native peoples (American Indians and Inuits) for mistreatment they allegedly had suffered in residential schools that were operated for more than a century by Anglicans, Roman Catholics, Presbyterians, and the United Church of Canada and were financed by the Canadian government. Between 1998 and 2001 more than 7,000 suits were registered, charging sexual-physical abuse and cultural damage to native inhabitants, with by far the largest number of claims focusing on cultural damage. The only cases accepted in the courts by the end of 2001 concerned sexual-physical abuse.

Efforts to curb violence and improve discipline in schools appeared in Israel, Japan, and the U.S. In an effort to reduce the number of incidents of youth violence, which had quadrupled over the past decade, Israel's Education Ministry permitted teachers to search pupils' bags for weapons and toughened legislation that barred the sale of alcohol to minors. Violence-prevention teams composed of teachers, parents, and students were authorized at every school to monitor incidents of hostility.

Japan's central legislative body, the Diet, sought to protect students' "right to learn" by means of a bill empowering school personnel to suspend students who disrupted classes, damaged school property, or attacked fellow students or teachers or caused them psychological distress. In early June a knife-wielding man on a stabbing rampage killed 8 children and injured 13 others at Ikeda Elementary School in Osaka prefecture. The school's children were so traumatized by the setting in which the stabbings took place that the Ministry of Education ordered the construction of a prefabricated building on a nearby site to serve the 680 pupils until the original building could be razed and replaced by a new permanent structure. In response to the incident, other schools introduced such safety measures as the distribution of personal alarms to teachers and the establishment of telephone hot lines between schools and police.

In the U.S. steps to make schools safer included assigning more police to schools as resource officers, instituting "red-code drills" in which students practiced protecting themselves against armed attacks, training teachers to identify potentially dangerous students, and having the courts assign stricter prison sentences to weapon-carrying teenagers. In addition, more schools were installing video surveillance systems, providing hot lines for reporting incidents of violence, encouraging students to take greater responsibility for maintaining a secure school environment, and engaging parents in safe-schooling campaigns. California's Supreme Court strengthened the authority of school personnel by ruling that schools could detain students without first having to prove "reasonable suspicion" of wrongdoing.

Countries differed in the adequacy of their present and future supplies of teachers. In England and Wales a survey revealed 10,000 unfilled permanent jobs in secondary schools; this represented the most serious teacher shortage in 36 years. The British government attempted to lure college graduates into teaching with attractive salaries during their training period, accelerated promotion schemes, and cheaper mortgages, but the incentives had limited success. The booming economy and tight labour market were blamed for the teacher shortage, since graduates, especially women, could easily find better-paid careers. To fill the shortages teacher-placement agencies continued to search abroad, particularly in New Zealand, Australia, South Africa, and Canada, which had furnished the United Kingdom with more than 25,000 teachers over the previous decade.

An investigative team was appointed in Australia to determine the reasons why 1,700 men had dropped out of the nation's corps of teachers since 1990. By 2001 males made up only 17.1% of all teachers in state primary schools and 48.7% in high schools.

Scotland's declining population of school-age children was expected to result in an overabundance of teachers in the coming decade. According to government predictions, the number of pupils in state primary schools would fall from the 2001 level of 425,200 to 368,600 in 2011, a 13% decrease. Students in state secondary schools would decrease from 319,000 to 286,500 by 2011, 10% fewer than in 2001. As a result, the number of full-time secondary teachers would drop to 22,900 in 2011, 7% fewer than in 2001.

Russian Pres. Vladimir Putin announced that in 2002, for the first time, the country planned to spend more on education than on defense. Putin also pledged to double teachers' salaries, which in 2001 averaged about $35 a month.

In India's Punjab province education officials in mid-August sought to fill 7,230 public-school teaching vacancies and 1,200 lecturerships in colleges. The AIDS epidemic in Africa seriously damaged many of the continent's education systems. Delegates at an Education International conference learned that HIV/AIDS had a greater effect on teaching than on any other profession and might nearly wipe out the supply of teachers in Africa within 10 years. An estimated 35–40% of secondary-school teachers in Botswana were reported to carry HIV, and the incidence of HIV infection also was high among teachers in Zimbabwe, South Africa, Swaziland, Malawi, and Zambia. Hadino Hishongwa, deputy minister of higher education for Namibia, reported that 25% of Namibians had tested positive for HIV/AIDS, a level he attributed partly to a lack of sufficient AIDS education for youths, who made up 72% of the country's population.

For the first time in the history of schooling in the U.S., an entire state's public schools were shut down by teachers striking for higher pay. Throughout the state of Hawaii, 13,000 teachers and 3,100 university faculty members abandoned their classrooms in early April in an effort to force legislators to authorize a salary increase, which the teachers union claimed was necessary to keep up with the rising cost of living. The walkout affected 180,000 students.

Controversies continued in India and the U.S. over allowing religious doctrine and practices in public schools. Opponents of India's ruling Bharatiya Janata Party accused the government of attempting to "saffronize" the nation's public-education system by fostering Hindu religious beliefs in schools, a

(continued on page 210)

AP/Wide World Photos

During a rally in Seoul on July 16, South Korean students wear traditional masks to protest Japanese textbooks that play down the aggressive role of the Japanese in their invasions of Asian countries during World War II.

Does Testing Deserve a Passing Grade?

by Charles D. Claiborn

High-Stakes Testing. As the term suggests, high-stakes testing is the use of educational and psychological tests to make decisions of often considerable consequence to individuals and institutions. Some tests assess the achievement or competencies of students at specific grade levels to determine whether they should be advanced to the next grade or, upon completing the secondary-school curriculum, be awarded a high-school diploma. Results of these tests additionally may be taken as an indicator of how well particular schools are educating their students and may in turn be used in allocating resources to schools or determining whether changes in their governance are warranted. Other tests assess the aptitude of applicants to be successful in college or graduate school and are used to make admissions decisions that dramatically affect the educational and professional futures of individuals. The differential impact these tests have on various racial, ethnic, and socioeconomic groups makes high-stakes-testing practices highly controversial.

Characteristics of High-Stakes Tests. According to some, high-stakes tests are "cognitively loaded" in that they measure the primarily cognitive constructs of knowledge and skill and, in some cases, potential or aptitude for gaining further knowledge and skill. The tests are also standardized—developed according to accepted practices of test development, such as those put forth jointly in 1999 by the American Educational Research Association, the American Psychological Association, and the National Council on Measurement in Education—and have thus been validated for their intended purpose and normed for populations with which they will be used. The psychometric adequacy of a test depends on the extent to which these practices have been followed.

The validity of a test is the adequacy of the test to perform a specific function. The types of validity that should be established for high-stakes tests thus vary according to the function of the test. For competency tests, such as minimum-competency tests used for grade advancement or graduation decisions, content validity is of particular concern, since it is important for the test to represent a designated domain of knowledge and skill adequately. A content-valid test of 10th-grade mathematics knowledge and skills, for example, is one that fairly and representatively reflects the range of mathematics topics and problems learned in the 10th grade, as determined by professionals in the area and, in some cases, the public at large. Different interest groups—a teachers union and a state legislature, for example—may naturally have different ideas about what a particular test should contain and who should determine that content. Content validity of competency tests can clearly be a source of controversy.

A second type of validity, criterion-related validity, is important for tests used in the selection of students. The value of a college entrance examination, notably the ACT (American College Testing Program) or SAT (Scholastic Assessment Test), depends on its ability to predict academic performance, which is the criterion of interest. The usefulness of any test for screening or selecting applicants for a position is based on the test's ability to predict job performance, the criterion in this case. It would be highly problematic, scientifically and legally, if a test used for selection or screening of applicants measured something that was not clearly related to criteria of school performance. The test-criterion relationship is the very heart of validity for this sort of test. It would also be problematic if the relationship between test scores and performance differed for different groups within the population, such as ethnic minority groups. The use of a test in such circumstances would constitute bias, though some experts have indicated that standardized tests used in selection do not generally suffer from this sort of distortion.

High-Stakes Testing in Selection—the Diversity Dilemma. Even when high-stakes tests have established validity, they are still open to controversy, especially with respect to issues involving ethnic diversity. In a recent review it was argued that the weight of the scientific evidence supports the validity of high-stakes tests used in selection. Standardized tests of knowledge and skill are indeed effective in predicting performance, at least within the cognitive domain. However, the authors of the review and others have also noted the well-established findings that African Americans and Latinos consistently score lower than whites on such tests and that Asian Americans score higher than whites on measures of quantitative ability and lower than whites on measures of verbal ability. Such ethnic-group differences are typically confounded with socioeconomic status, with members of lower socioeconomic groups typically scoring lower on such tests than members of higher socioeconomic groups. Nevertheless, such findings present a dilemma, that of choosing between the goal of using the most valid tests—those making the best predictions of performance—and the goal of having a more diverse student body or workforce. Several ways of resolving this dilemma have been proposed, though none has been researched thoroughly enough to merit recommendation.

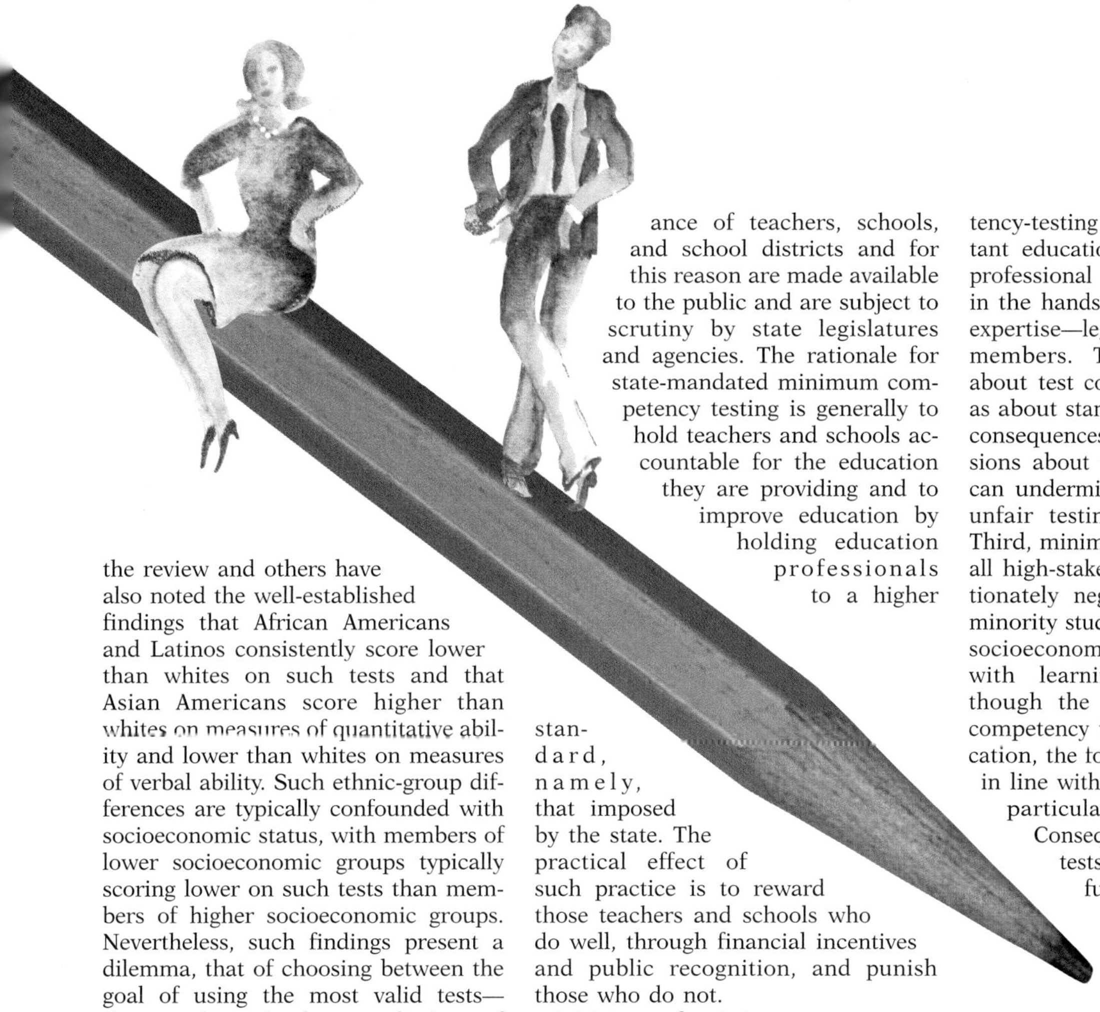

Competency Assessment in Education. The widespread and growing use of competency assessment in schools brings high-stakes testing into the public and political spotlight. Minimum-competency tests are now used in some 23 states to determine grade advancement and graduation. In December the U.S. Senate passed a landmark education bill that would require mandatory annual state math and reading tests for all students in grades three through eight. In addition, the results of such tests are used to assess the performance of teachers, schools, and school districts and for this reason are made available to the public and are subject to scrutiny by state legislatures and agencies. The rationale for state-mandated minimum competency testing is generally to hold teachers and schools accountable for the education they are providing and to improve education by holding education professionals to a higher standard, namely, that imposed by the state. The practical effect of such practice is to reward those teachers and schools who do well, through financial incentives and public recognition, and punish those who do not.

Criticism of minimum-competency testing as a means to improve education has been considerable. First, there is little evidence to suggest that such testing really improves education. A 1990 report found that the use of minimum-competency tests is associated with higher dropout rates, though the reason for this is unclear. A number of researchers have documented the negative effects of minimum-competency testing on the curriculum and instruction. These include narrowing the curriculum to what is covered on the test ("teaching to the test"), taking time away from instruction in order to prepare students for the test, and limiting instruction to the types of knowledge and problem solving required by the test format (for example, emphasizing the recognition of information as emphasized on multiple-choice tests). Second, minimum-competency-testing policies often take important educational decisions away from professional educators and place them in the hands of those with little or no expertise—legislators or school-board members. These include decisions about test content and format as well as about standards for passing and the consequences of failure. Inexpert decisions about test development and use can undermine test validity and make unfair testing practices more likely. Third, minimum-competency tests, like all high-stakes tests, have a disproportionately negative impact on ethnic-minority students, students from lower socioeconomic groups, and students with learning disabilities. Finally, though the rationale for minimum-competency testing is to improve education, the focus of testing is often not in line with the instructional goals of particular teachers and schools. Consequently, the results of such tests are not particularly useful as feedback regarding how well teachers and schools are meeting the goals they set for themselves and their students. Though the use of minimum-competency testing has considerable public relations value by appearing to provide hard data on how well or how poorly schools are doing—with an accompanying set of high standards to which students, teachers, and schools are held—the reality of such testing falls short, in regard to both the flawed tests themselves and the often unhelpful, even hurtful, use to which the test results are put.

Charles D. Claiborn is professor of psychology in education at Arizona State University. He is the author of more than 60 articles and book chapters on psychotherapy process, including "Feedback" in Psychotherapy Relationships That Work: Therapists' Relational Contributions to Effective Psychotherapy.

Anna Mycek-Wodecki

(continued from page 207)
violation of the secular status of public schools prescribed in the nation's constitution. Saffron was the colour of the flag flown by the Rashtriya Swayamsevak Sangh, a Hindu-supremacist organization that administered 14,000 schools. Practices that drew the critics' complaints included government subsidies to universities that offered astrology or ancient Vedic mathematics in the curriculum and practiced Vedic rituals, including the chanting of the Saraswati Vandana hymn to the Hindu goddess of education at the beginning of all educational events.

In the U.S., although the Oregon Senate voted to prohibit posting the biblical Ten Commandments in public schools, the North Carolina Senate voted to permit it. The Hawaii state board of education struck down a proposal that would have permitted the Judeo-Christian biblical version of the world's creation to be taught in science classes as a proper theory of human beginnings along with Darwin's theory of evolution. The U.S. Supreme Court, in a 6–3 decision, ruled that church-sponsored groups, including Christian youth clubs, could use public-school buildings for after-school meetings along with other nonschool clubs. Observers speculated that the court's action could give impetus to the Bush administration's effort to furnish government funds to finance religious groups' programs for assisting people in poverty.

All but a handful of Japanese junior high schools rejected a controversial new history textbook, *Atarashii rekishi kyokasho,* which critics said glossed over Japan's wartime atrocities. The book, compiled by the nationalistic Japanese Society for History Textbook Reform, was scheduled for use beginning in April 2002.

Newly appointed U.S. Secretary of Education Roderick R. Paige speaks to students, teachers, and parents at an elementary school in Portland, Maine, on April 12.

AP/Wide World Photos

HIGHER EDUCATION

Eight nations that bordered the Arctic Circle launched a University of the Arctic that was designed to offer circumpolar studies and prepare students to help maintain the quality of life in the polar region against destructive intrusions by global-development forces. The cooperating nations included Canada, Denmark (with its territories of Greenland and the Faroe Islands), Finland, Iceland, Norway, Russia, Sweden, and the U.S. Courses were offered via the Internet and on existing campuses of the eight nations. Students were required to spend at least one semester of study in a circumpolar neighbour institution before graduating.

The Chinese government, as a means of promoting the progress of universities in the nation's less-developed western regions, paired 13 western universities with advanced institutions in the east, including Beijing University, Xinjiang Shihezi University, and Tsinghua University. The partnerships, funded by loans from commercial banks and world financial organizations, were designed to develop key universities in the west, particularly by training over 1,000 teachers and administrators for the western institutions over a three-year period.

New restrictions on freedom of inquiry appeared in Russia, Egypt, and Cuba. The Russian Academy of Sciences instructed its hundreds of affiliated institutions to curtail the nation's 53,000 researchers by requiring them to report any attempt by scholars to apply for foreign grants. The academy also required institutions to report all visits by foreigners and to submit articles for inspection before they were published abroad. Egypt's premier Islamic higher-learning institution—Al-Azhar University, Cairo—instituted a policy of outlawing any publication that, according to university president Ahmad Omar Hashem, lacked "respect for God, His Prophet [Muhammad], and all religious values." After Cuban Pres. Fidel Castro had announced in 1998 that "in Cuba there are no prohibited books," economist Berta Mexidor started a system of independent libraries that stocked publications formerly banned in the country. By 2001 the network had grown to 65 small private libraries. Some claimed that the arrest of four leaders of the movement on various charges was politically motivated, while government officials asserted that the "libraries" were created to promote the views of antigovernment parties (with aid from abroad) and denied that the detentions represented an attempt to curb intellectual freedom.

Problems arising from basing college admissions on ethnic quotas continued in Malaysia and the U.S. Malaysia's education minister, Musa Mohamed, announced that the nation's existing laws favouring Malay applicants over citizens of Chinese and Indian heritage in public universities would likely be extended to private institutions as well. At the same time, statistics released by the Ministry of Education showed that 7,168 university places were unfilled because not enough Malay students had applied and that 560 Chinese Malaysians who had scored at the highest levels on university entrance tests had been denied a place at a public institution. The government, however, approved the long-stalled plans by the Malaysian Chinese Association to establish a university to be governed by the association and, according to association spokespersons, to be open to all ethnic groups. In the U.S. advocates of affirmative-action programs that gave preferential admissions treatment to blacks and Hispanics argued that such programs increased the racial diversity on campuses and thereby had the educational benefit of helping all students develop enlightened attitudes and learn to work with people of different cultural backgrounds. Opponents of such programs contended that the research needed to adequately support the diversity argument had not been forthcoming and that special admissions opportunities for selected minorities not only violated the principle of basing admissions on academic merit but also placed other minorities at an unfair disadvantage.

Students' use of illegal drugs drew attention in Great Britain and the U.S. A survey of colleges in the U.K. reported a recent fivefold increase in the number of students using cocaine, which made the drug the second favourite narcotic, after cannabis. Investigators attributed much of the growing popularity of cocaine to its dramatic drop in price. As a result of a law in the United States that denied government financial aid to students with drug convictions, an estimated 34,000 students were denied loans and grants in 2001, more than triple the number in 2000.

The autonomy of higher-education institutions was challenged in Taiwan when a college student, after having been dismissed from Shih Hsin University, Taipei, for failing half his courses during a single semester, filed a lawsuit against the university, contending that the institution's dismissal policy violated his right to continue his education. A national debate was sparked when the Administrative High Court supported the student's claim by ruling that individual universities lacked the authority to oust students for weak academic performance. Although such authority had been awarded to institutions by a Ministry of Education directive, representatives of the Taiwan Association for Human Rights argued that decisions about dismissals would need to be based on regulations passed by the Taiwan legislature, which would thereby ensure uniform practice nationwide.

The Korean Council for University Education initiated an international internship plan to further student-exchange programs and to address problems arising from the fast rise in the number of South Korean students studying abroad. Under the program, about 2,000 students from 63 South Korean universities would travel overseas in 2002. The council currently had exchange agreements with 30 U.S. universities and intended to forge bonds with institutions in Australia, New Zealand, Japan, China, and Europe. Recent reforms of the education system in Greece failed to stem the flow of youths seeking higher education in other nations. Over 55,000 Greek students entered foreign universities in 2001, 65% more than in 1998.

As an effort to revitalize the traditional influence of French culture in Egypt, leaders of the Egypt-based French University Friends' Association announced the establishment of a new French University in Cairo, scheduled to accept students in 2002.

(R. MURRAY THOMAS)

The Environment

The adoption of **ALTERNATIVE ENERGY** methods, talks leading to agreement on the **KYOTO PROTOCOL**, and demonstrations over the transportation of spent **NUCLEAR FUEL** were among 2001's environmental issues. **ARTIFICIAL INSEMINATION** of zoo animals topped **CONSERVATION EFFORTS**, and measures to save the **ANIMALS** at the **KABUL ZOO** were implemented.

INTERNATIONAL ACTIVITIES

On June 5, 2001, World Environment Day, UN Secretary-General Kofi Annan announced a $21-million, four-year study of the condition of the global environment. With the participation of 1,500 scientists and many organizations, the Millennium Ecosystem Assessment would be the first comprehensive assessment of this kind ever attempted.

At a meeting held in Johannesburg, S.Af., Dec. 4–9, 2000, representatives from 122 governments had finalized an international treaty to reduce or eliminate the production and use of the persistent organic pollutants aldrin, chlordane, dieldrin, endrin, heptachlor, mirex, toxaphene, and hexachlorobenzene. Tropical countries were allowed to continue using DDT for malaria control until a suitable substitute became available. The phasing out of polychlorinated biphenyls would be gradual so that equipment containing them could remain in use until 2025. The treaty was opened for signature in Stockholm in May 2001 and would come into force once 50 countries had ratified it.

Eight people shared the $750,000 Goldman Environmental Prize at a presentation in San Francisco on April 23. The winners were Eugène Rutagarama of Rwanda, who worked to save his country's last mountain gorillas; Yosepha Alomang of Indonesia for helping to reverse some of the damage caused by mining in Irian Jaya; Oscar Olivera of Brazil, who helped reverse the privatization of the Brazilian water industry that had led to sharp increases in water prices; Bruno Van Peteghem of New Caledonia for his opposition to nickel mining in the New Caledonia coral reef; Myrsini Malakou and Giorgos Catsadorakis of Greece, who helped establish the Prespa Park conservation zone in wetlands with the friendly collaboration of Albania, Macedonia, and Greece; and American journalists Jane Akre and Steve Wilson for their investigation into health risks from the agricultural use of recombinant bovine growth hormone.

On September 7 the European Union (EU) formally approved a directive on renewable energy. This required member states to ensure that 12% of gross internal energy consumption and 22.1% of electricity consumption would come from renewable sources by 2010.

NATIONAL DEVELOPMENTS

Germany. On June 11 the federal government and leading energy companies signed a formal agreement to phase out nuclear power. The core of the agreement was a limit on the amount of power each of Germany's nuclear power plants would be permitted to produce. On the basis of an average life of 32 years for each reactor, this would mean the newest reactor would have to close in about 2021. The government published a draft of the necessary legislation on July 9, and after a period for consultation, the cabinet approved it on September 5. As well as setting a limit to the life span of existing nuclear plants, the law required power generators to provide intermediate storage

AP/Wide World Photos

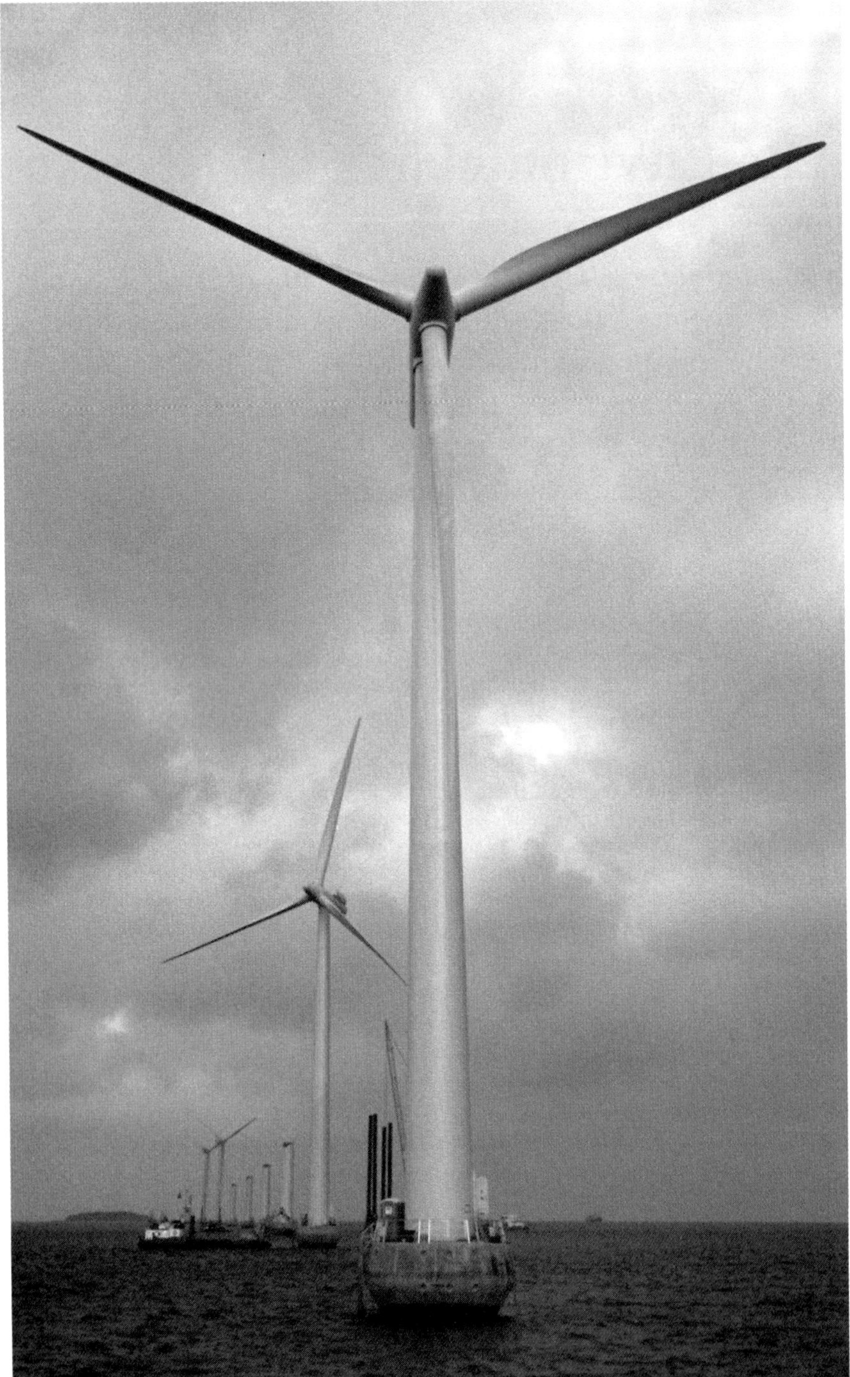

Middelgrunden, a wind park off the coast of Copenhagen that included the world's largest windmill, began producing energy on May 6.

facilities close to their plants for spent fuel and banned all shipments of waste for reprocessing from 2005.

On June 6 Environment Minister Jürgen Trittin announced that the government planned a major expansion of offshore wind-power generation. By 2030 offshore wind parks, using 4,000 generators, would be generating between 75 and 80 terawatts of power annually. Two North Sea areas had been identified as suitable because they were clear of all marine- and bird-conservation areas. The required investment would be made possible by the German renewable energy support law, which guaranteed a price of €0.09 (about $0.08) per kilowatt-hour for wind power.

Spain. On September 5 Boliden Ltd., the Swedish-Canadian company operating the Los Frailes iron pyrite mine at Aznalcóllar in Andalusia, said production at the mine would cease immediately. The mine was the source of the 1998 leakage of waste upstream of the Coto Doñana National Park. The cost of cleaning up the leakage was estimated at €180 million (about $165 million), and compensation also would have to be paid. The company, which filed for bankruptcy in 2000, said these costs were a significant factor in the closure.

United Kingdom. On July 18 the British government announced that there would be no further reprocessing of nuclear fuel at the Dounreay plant in Caithness, Scot. Reprocessing at Dounreay had been suspended in 1996 owing to an equipment failure, and almost 25 metric tons of spent fuel remained on-site. This would either be stored at Dounreay or be transported to Sellafield, Eng., for reprocessing.

Ukraine. On Dec. 15, 2000, the last of the four Chernobyl reactors was closed down permanently. In fact, reactor 3 had closed some weeks earlier for technical reasons and had to be restarted in order to be shut down formally. Pres. Leonid Kuchma had issued the command through a television link from the Ukraina Palace in Kiev. On April 26, 2001, the 15th anniversary of the accident at Chernobyl, Kuchma led a memorial service in Kiev. Meanwhile, scientists continued to study the long-term effects of low-level radiation released in the accident.

United States. In its annual *Toxic Release Inventory,* published in April, the Environmental Protection Agency (EPA) reported that two-thirds of the over 3.5 billion kg (1 kg=2.2 lb) of toxic chemicals released into the U.S. environment in 1999 came from hard-rock mining companies and operators of electric power plants. The highest releases were from Nevada and Utah, with nearly 530 million kg and 527 million kg, respectively; Arizona, 437 million kg; and Alaska, 196 million kg. Hard-rock mining companies released some 1.8 billion kg of chemicals into the air, land, and water, and electricity utilities released more than 527 million kg, mostly from stack emissions from coal-burning plants.

On April 25 the Senate unanimously passed legislation authorizing an annual expenditure of $200 million for cleaning up more than 500,000 abandoned industrial sites. On June 7 a

Republican-led subcommittee of the House of Representatives rejected Pres. George W. Bush's request for $2 million for preparatory studies on oil drilling in the Alaskan Arctic National Wildlife Refuge (AANW). Though on August 2 the House passed the energy bill by 240 votes to 189, complete with its provision allowing oil exploration and drilling in the refuge, on December 3 the Senate roundly rejected a bill (94–1) that would allow drilling in the AANW.

In the wake of the September 11 terrorist attacks in the U.S., acrid smoke, soot, and ash from tons of pulverized debris complicated the recovery in New York City. The EPA reported that asbestos levels did not appear to be dangerous, but doctors recommended that people use special air filters and masks to avoid inhaling particulate matter even during the smallest clean-up operations.

AP/Wide World Photos

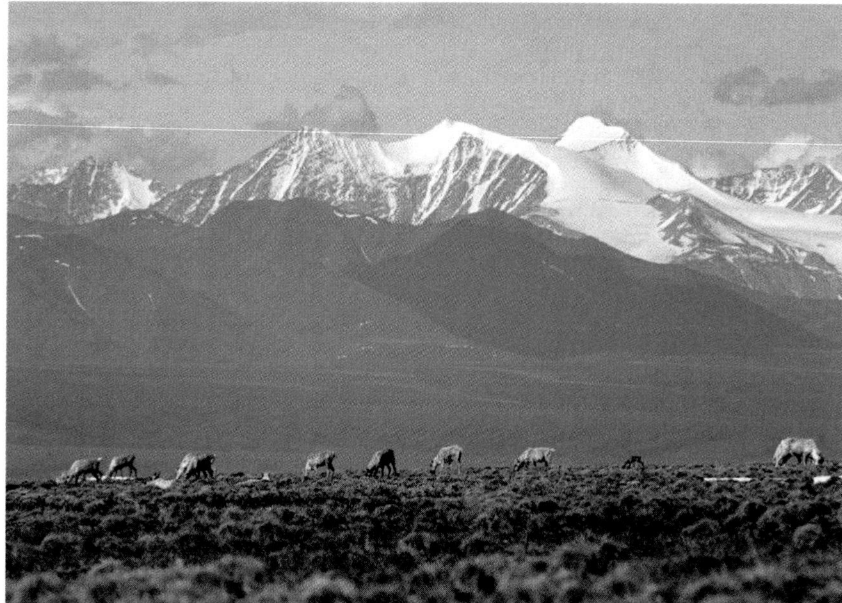

Caribou graze in the Alaskan Arctic National Wildlife Refuge. Whether or not to allow oil exploration and drilling in the refuge was the subject of debate in the U.S. House of Representatives during the year.

ENVIRONMENTAL ISSUES

Climate Change. The sixth conference of parties to the 1992 UN Convention on Climate Change was held at The Hague in November 2000. There was disagreement over the issues of carbon sinks and nuclear power. The umbrella group of countries, led by the U.S. and including Australia, Austria, Canada, Japan, New Zealand, Norway, Russia, Switzerland, and Ukraine, opposed any restriction on the means used to meet the cost of implementing the Kyoto Protocol. In particular, the group wanted forests (including forests planted long ago), as well as agricultural land, to be counted as sinks that absorb carbon dioxide. Although the EU agreed in the course of negotiations to limit the amount of carbon dioxide counted in this way, EU members rejected the offer on the ground that it would allow countries to claim reductions in greenhouse gas emissions without taking actual steps to reduce them. Negotiations continued during the winter.

On March 13, 2001, however, in a letter to four senior politicians, newly inaugurated President Bush said he would not accept mandatory controls on emissions of carbon dioxide because this would force utilities to switch from coal to gas, which was more expensive and would raise electricity prices. EPA administrator Christine Whitman confirmed the U.S. position on the protocol on March 27, though on March 29 Bush said he would remain open-minded on ways to address the problem of global warming. The EU sent a delegation to Washington to try to persuade Bush to change his mind. They met Whitman and other EPA officials on April 3, but the effort failed.

The conference of parties resumed in Bonn, Ger., on July 16 and concluded on July 27. Detailed rules for attaining Kyoto targets were finally accepted on July 23 by 178 countries (including Japan but not the U.S.) after the EU had made major concessions over carbon sinks. In another round of talks that was held in Marrakesh, Mor., and ended in November after two weeks of bargaining, negotiators reached agreement on the details of the treaty and hammered out a compliance scheme to insure that pollution levels were met. Some 40 industrialized countries would be required to reduce emissions of carbon dioxide and other greenhouse gases by an average of 5% below 1990 levels by 2012. Before the Kyoto Protocol could come into force, however, the pact needed to be ratified by 55 countries.

The 2,600-page latest report from the Intergovernmental Panel on Climate Change was published on July 12. It estimated that temperatures might rise 1.4–5.8 °C (2.5–10.4 °F) by 2100 and assumed that carbon dioxide levels would reach 540–970 parts per million by that year. The report also concluded that the burning of fossil fuels and the emission of man-made chemicals "have contributed substantially to the observed warming over the last 50 years."

Air Pollution. Figures published on June 5 by the German electricity-supply industry showed that sulfur dioxide emissions from power plants fell 92% between 1991 and 2000. Most of the improvement resulted from retrofitting desulfurization equipment in former East Germany and closing plants that could not be retrofitted economically.

The Norwegian Pollution Control Authority reported in August that acid-rain precipitation increased in 2000 over the southern and eastern parts of the country. In some areas heavy rain and snowfall increased sulfur deposition to levels comparable to those of the late 1980s, causing damage rated from "marked" to "severe."

In September the Mexican Metropolitan Environmental Commission unveiled a 10-year plan to improve air quality. This replaced a five-year program that had ended in 2000. Claudia Sheinbaum, Mexico City's environment secretary, said the aim was to reduce levels of ozone and fine particulate matter.

Freshwater Pollution. In January thousands of fish were killed by cyanide that had spilled into the Siret River near the town of Lespezi, Rom., 340 km (210 mi) northeast of Bucharest, and nearly 60 people required hospital treatment after eating the contaminated fish. The cyanide level in the Siret and one of its tributaries peaked at 128 times acceptable levels. The spill was thought to have originated at a chemical factory owned by Metadet, and the company was immediately fined. The authorities released additional water into the rivers, and the cyanide concentration was quickly reduced.

On July 27 the U.S. House of Representatives voted to maintain the limits for arsenic in drinking water set by former president Bill Clinton's administration. These reduced permitted levels from 50 to 10 parts per billion (ppb). The Bush administration asked a National Academy of Sciences panel to review the risks. Their report, *Arsenic in Drinking Water: 2001 Update*, was released in September. The panel found that the dangers were higher than had been supposed and concluded the proposed 10-ppb limit, based on a study done in southwestern Taiwan, had underestimated risks. The previous study had estimated 0.8 extra cancer cases per 1,000 people, whereas the new panel estimated 1.3–3.7 extra cases, depending on whether it used the background cancer rate in Taiwan or the rate in the U.S. In October the EPA adopted the Clinton arsenic standard.

The Austrian Environment Ministry announced in August that testing for 100 pollutants at 2,000 sites showed that streams and rivers were becoming cleaner. Nitrates in groundwater continued to cause concern, with levels having risen at 13% of measuring stations.

Marine Pollution. On January 16 the Ecuadorian-registered cargo ship *Jessica* ran aground in a bay close to the harbour on San Cristóbal in the Galápagos Islands, spilling about 700,000 litres (1 litre=about 0.26 gal) of diesel and bunker fuel oil from its cargo of about 920,000 litres. About 200,000 litres were removed from the ship safely, and U.S. Coast Guard vessels arrived quickly to help in the effort to contain and recover the oil. The spilled oil formed a slick that reached the islands of Santa Cruz and Santa Fe but caused little harm. Attempts to remove the ship, lying at an angle of about 45° some 800 m (2,600 ft) from the shore, were defeated by heavy seas, and it was decided to make the wreck into an artificial reef.

The Helsinki Commission (Helcom) announced on August 24 that the amount of 47 hazardous substances entering the Baltic Sea had been halved since the late 1980s and that it would aim for discharges to be phased out completely by 2020. At a Helcom meeting in Copenhagen on September 10, transport and environment ministers from countries bordering the Baltic agreed on tighter rules to prevent oil spills. The need for new rules arose following a collision on March 28 between a cargo ship and a tanker that released about 2,700 metric tons of heavy fuel oil into the southwestern Baltic, causing the worst oil spill in the region in at least six years.

A meeting of parties to the Ospar Convention, held in Valencia, Spain, in late June, finalized an agreement on the discharge of oil into the northeast Atlantic. The oil content of produced water (a by-product of oil pumping) would be reduced by about 15%, calculated from a 2000 deadline. The meeting also added neodecanoic acid, ethenyl ester, and triphenyl phosphine to the list of substances to be phased out as a priority, bringing the total of such substances to 29.

Radioactive Waste. On March 29 the first shipment since 1997 of nuclear waste from the Cogema reprocessing facility at Cap de la Hague, France, arrived at a temporary storage site at Gorleben, Ger. The three-day journey was marked by antinuclear protests, and over 15,000 police were employed to guard the six armoured containers. On May 17 the second shipment, of about 54 spent fuel rods from Germany to Cap de la Hague, was halted for more than an hour by about 20 protesters who blocked the train at Amiens, France. About 15 protesters also blocked the rail track near Caen, France, and on May 16 some 40 protesters threw red smoke generators at the train near Strasbourg, France. Another such incident occurred in November when about 100 protesters attempted to block the motion of a train carrying nuclear waste from Cap de la Hague to Gorleben; they chained themselves to signal boxes and trees along the 600-km (375-mi) route.

Twelve Greenpeace protesters chained themselves to the track beneath an empty wagon at a railhead in Mannheim, Ger., on April 23 to demonstrate against the first shipment in three years of nuclear waste to Sellafield.

Genetically Modified Food. The first meeting of the intergovernmental committee for the Cartagena Protocol took place in Montpellier, France, in December 2000. Representatives from more than 80 countries began developing detailed rules to govern the international movement of live genetically modified organisms (GMOs). The discussions covered information sharing, traceability of GMOs, packaging, handling and transport, national capacity building, and the formation of an expert advisory group. It was agreed to establish a pilot biosafety clearinghouse to give countries access to up-to-date lists of GMOs and information about national policies and regulations.

The UN Codex Alimentarius Commission agreed in July to require exporters of GM foods to undertake risk assessments, primarily of the foods' allergenicity, before placing them on the market. Findings by the Royal Commission on Genetic Modification in New Zealand were published on July 30. The commission recommended that GM agriculture be introduced "selectively with appropriate care" and rejected outright the idea of a GM-free New Zealand as incompatible with the modern world and the nation's future.

A report published on September 10 found that windborne pollen from corn (maize) plants genetically modified to express *Bacillus turingiensis* toxins posed a negligible risk to monarch butterflies. The study was prepared for the National Academy of Sciences by researchers at the University of Illinois at Urbana-Champaign, Iowa State University, the University of Minnesota, and private biotech companies.

Pesticides. An integrated crop production (ICP) plan announced on July 6 by Dutch Agriculture Minister Laurens Jan Brinkhorst aimed to reduce pesticide use in The Netherlands dramatically. Farmers would be required to adopt such measures as choosing pest-resistant crop varieties and growing "companion" plants. Farmers would be allowed to use pesticides only as a last resort, and in 2003 a tax would be imposed on pesticides. It was hoped that farmers would adopt the ICP plan voluntarily, but unless 90% of farmers had gained ICP certification by 2004, non-certified farms would be forbidden to use any pesticides.

On May 9 a report from the UN Food and Agriculture Organization (FAO) called on leading pesticide manufacturers to help pay for the safe destruction of an estimated 500,000 metric tons of obsolete pesticides that had been dumped in various parts of the world. The FAO reminded the Global Crop Protection Federation (GCPF) of its past commitment to pay up to $1 per litre or kilogram for safe destruction. Chris Waller, coordinator of the GCPF obsolete stocks team, said the industry was waiting for the FAO to devise a scheme that would ensure that money was used to deal only with products made or distributed by the companies contributing to the fund.

Electromagnetic Fields. It was reported in March that a study had found that 0.5% of children exposed to electromagnetic fields of 0.4 microteslas or more could double their risk of contracting leukemia before age 15, from 1 in 1,400 to 1 in 700. The study, commissioned by the U.K. National Radiological Protection Board, analyzed 3,247 childhood leukemia cases in Europe, North America, and New Zealand. Epidemiologist Sir Richard Doll of the Cancer Studies Unit at the University of Oxford said that taken by themselves these results might be due to chance, but there was a possibility that intense and prolonged exposure to magnetic fields could increase the risk of leukemia in children.

On September 11 the results of a study by researchers led by Tom Sorahan at the University of Birmingham, Eng., was published in *Occupational and Environmental Medicine*. The study found that workers in the electricity industry were no more likely to develop brain tumours than the general population. The study looked at the causes of death of some 84,000 electricity workers in England and Wales and found the death rate from brain cancer similar to that for the general population. (MICHAEL ALLABY)

WILDLIFE CONSERVATION

In January 2001 Mexico's former environment secretary Julia Carabias Lillo received the J. Paul Getty Wildlife Conservation Prize from the World Wildlife Fund (WWF). Carabias Lillo (*see* BIOGRAPHIES) was credited with doubling the protected-habitat system in Mexico. Thirty years of conservation effort were rewarded in March when the birth of a male golden tamarin (*Leontopithecus rosalia*) took the number living in the wild to 1,000. The native habitat of the species was in the lowland coastal forest in the Brazilian state of Rio de Janeiro, where habitat destruction had reduced numbers to 200 by the early 1970s.

A celebrated discovery of a new mammal in 1993 was reported as a fake in February. The wild ox *Pseudonovibos spiralis* was described from unusual-shaped horns collected from markets in Vietnam and Cambodia. Local hunters claimed it came from a mysterious beast in the forest, but genetic and morphological tests revealed that the horns were of the domestic cow. The horns had been twisted and carved by local people in a long-standing folk industry.

A report in *Science* in January indicated that Arctic species were suffering as Arctic ice continued to decline, covering 15% less area than it had in 1978. A long-term study indicated that emperor penguins (*Aptenodytes forsteri*) in the Antarctic were highly susceptible to climate change and that their numbers were declining markedly in warm periods with reduced sea ice.

While concern continued over the effects of global climate change on wild species and habitats, some scientists thought that demand for food by a wealthier and larger human population would be the major driver of environmental change in the next 50 years, causing unprecedented ecosystem simplification, loss of ecosystem services, and species extinctions. In May the UN Environment Programme launched the Great Apes Survival Project because poaching and habitat loss could drive the apes of Africa and Southeast Asia to extinction in 5–10 years. The project would help police forests, link patches of habitat, encourage ecotourism, and educate local people. Harvard University biologist Edward O. Wilson argued that large-scale private investment was needed to augment government protection for lands of high value for biodiversity. He said that an investment of $28 billion would protect up to 70% of the species on Earth.

The ornithological literature reported several new birds, including two new flycatchers: the Mishana tyrannulet (*Zimmerius villarejoi*) from the white-sand forest near Iquitos, Peru, where an ongoing study had revealed the presence of at least four bird species new to science, and the Chapada flycatcher (*Suiriri islerorum*) from the Cerrado region of Brazil and adjacent eastern Bolivia. A new species of petrel, the Vanuatu petrel (*Pterodroma occulta*), was described from specimens collected at sea. It was presumed to breed in the Banks Islands or elsewhere in northern Vanuatu. The chestnut-eared laughing thrush (*Garrulax konkakinhensis*) was identified from a narrow altitudinal range on Mount Kon Ka Kinh in central Vietnam. There were plans to extend an existing reserve to include the sites where it had been found.

Populations of some seabirds hit by the *Exxon Valdez* oil spill in Alaska in 1989 had still to show signs of recovery, according to scientists in Anchorage, who believed that food species in the intertidal zone were still contaminated with oil. The wreck of the oil tanker *Jessica* in the Galápagos Islands (see *Marine Pollution*, above) highlighted the fragility of the islands and the inadequacy of conservation legislation. On July 16, 15 sea lions in the Galápagos National Park were butchered on the beach on San Cristóbal for their sex organs, which were in demand in Asia for use as aphrodisiacs. Suspicion rested on foreign fishermen harvesting sea cucumbers in the area.

Many wild species used traditionally as human food were in decline because of increased commercial use, including sharks captured for shark fin soup and sturgeon killed for caviar. The U.S. and Australia had banned the capture of sharks for their fins, and there were calls for other nations to follow. Three caviar-producing states (Russia, Kazakhstan, and Azerbaijan) bordering the Caspian Sea (source of 90% of the world's caviar) halted sturgeon fishing on June 21 in response to plummeting stocks. India gave legal protection to whale sharks (*Rhinocodon typus*) on May 28 because trade threatened them with extinction. A workshop convened by the World Conservation Union (IUCN), the UN Food and Agriculture Organization, and TRAFFIC (the joint wildlife trade monitoring program of the IUCN and the WWF) was held in Cameroon in September. More than 40 representatives from 18 organizations met to find solutions to the problems of declining populations of wild animals used traditionally for human food.

Only six Bali starlings (*Leucopsar rothschildi*) remained in the wild, all in Indonesia's Bali Barat National Park, where relentless trapping for the pet trade threatened them. Saving species created problems for some people. Wolves brought back from the brink of extinction in northern Italy were reported to be hunting farmers' livestock, and legally protected wild boars in Germany caused problems for Berliners by digging up gardens, raiding trash cans, and attacking dogs. In Norway wolves were culled despite court action brought by conservationists.

The 834 species of the mainly insectivorous bats in the order Microchiroptera faced numerous threats from human activities; some species had experienced precipitous declines. The publication of *Microchiropteran Bats: Global Status Survey and Conservation Action Plan* in May aimed to stimulate conservation action for these mammals, which occurred in every continent except in the polar regions and constituted a quarter of all known mammal species.

In September participants in the British Association Festival of Science

African elephants wander in Great Limpopo Transfrontier Park in Mozambique on October 4 after having been moved from Kruger National Park in South Africa.

AP/Wide World Photos

were warned that coral reefs would disappear in 30–50 years because global warming would cause widespread coral bleaching (a condition in which high water temperatures kill the algal partners of coral). Experiments also showed, however, that corals can evict their algae as an adaptation to warmer seas and may be recolonized by partners better suited to higher temperatures.

New molecular evidence showed that forest and savanna elephants, heretofore classified as a single species, *Loxodonta africana,* merited separate taxonomic status. This had implications for conservation, since one-third of the 500,000 elephants in Africa were forest dwellers. On October 4 South Africa announced that the first 40 of a total of 1,000 African elephants were to be moved from Kruger National Park to Mozambique as part of a plan to establish the world's biggest reserve and to reopen natural migratory routes. (JACQUI M. MORRIS)

ZOOS

Zoos and aquariums continued to be immensely popular in 2001, attracting some 130 million visitors in the U.S. alone. On May 3 officials at the National Zoo in Washington, D.C., welcomed the one millionth person to see the giant pandas Tian Tian and Mei Xiang since the pair went on display on January 10. The pandas, which arrived in the U.S. in December 2000, were on loan from the China Research and Conservation Center for the Giant Panda in Wolong, Sichuan province. In return for the loan of the pandas for research and exhibit purposes, the Smithsonian Institution, which operated the National Zoo, agreed to donate $10 million to support China's panda preservation and research projects.

Throughout the year Chinese officials relayed exciting news from Wolong; by the end of October five giant pandas at the centre had given birth to healthy twins, and it was reported that there were several more giant pandas waiting to give birth. The practice of artificially inseminating zoo animals, especially those belonging to threatened or endangered species, was followed elsewhere. At the Colchester (Eng.) Zoo in March, an African elephant named Tanya became the first elephant in the country to become pregnant through artificial insemination. German scientists from the Berlin Institute of Wildlife Medicine and Research performed the procedure.

Animals at the Kabul Zoo were found to be in poor condition after the Taliban was routed from Afghanistan in December. Overseas zoos and well-wishers raised thousands of dollars in pledges to care for the starving animals.

Public interest in aquatic environments helped drive a rapid expansion of aquariums. In the past decade new aquariums were opened in Charleston, S.C.; Denver, Colo.; Newport, Ky.; Myrtle Beach, S.C.; Gatlinburg, Tenn.; Pittsburgh, Pa.; Columbus, Ohio; and Long Beach, Calif. Several smaller aquatic facilities within American zoos also opened. In addition, by 2001 major expansions and renovations were under way in almost every major public aquarium in the country.

The John G. Shedd Aquarium in Chicago undertook a five-year, $85 million renovation and expansion program. Its "Amazon Rising" exhibit, which opened in 2000, was recognized by both the American Zoo and Aquarium Association and the American Association of

Museums as the best new exhibit of the year. The Shedd was constructing a 1,860-sq-m (20,000-sq-ft) addition to house a new exhibit portraying the coral reefs of the Philippines. This exhibit promised to give visitors the sensation of walking on the ocean floor as they moved through a series of marine habitats featuring living corals and the many species that depended on reefs for food and shelter. One of the exhibit's highlights was to be a 1,890,000-litre (500,000-gal) shark habitat, which would give the Shedd an opportunity to exhibit larger sharks for the first time.

North Carolina's three state aquariums —all located along the coast—also were undergoing major expansion and rebuilding projects. The aquarium-building boom even prompted a name change by one of the country's major zoological institutions. The venerable Columbus (Ohio) Zoo, which opened in 1927, was renamed the Columbus Zoo and Aquarium as a result of the new aquatic facility built on its grounds. One of its most popular features was a new manatee exhibit. The Cincinnati (Ohio) Zoo and Botanical Garden also opened a "Manatee Springs" exhibit. Both of these facilities supported manatee-conservation programs in collaboration with the state of Florida.

New aquariums were planned for or under construction in Cleveland, Ohio; Atlanta, Ga.; West Palm Beach, Fla.; Portland, Maine; New Bedford, Mass.; and several other areas. In addition, new aquariums were set to open in several European locations, including Rotterdam, Neth.; Lisbon, Port.; Hirtshals, Den.; and Plymouth, Eng., and in Japan.

Aquariums offered research scientists opportunities to observe marine species, especially cetaceans, in ways that would be impossible from research vessels. Sea World in Orlando, Fla.; the Mystic and Shedd aquariums; and facilities in Vancouver, B.C., and New York state were all participating in and contributing to the research and husbandry of beluga whales as well as cetaceans and other marine mammals.

Also increasing in popularity were butterfly gardens, which offered visitors something new and pleasing to the eyes while raising awareness of the importance of invertebrates, especially pollinators, and the need for habitat-conservation measures to protect these often-overlooked animals. Zoological institutions that had expanded their collections with butterflies included the Bronx (N.Y.) Zoo, the Cincinnati Zoo, and the St. Louis (Mo.) Zoo.

(TED A. BEATTIE)

The "Amazon Rising" exhibit at the John G. Shedd Aquarium in Chicago was recognized as a top new exhibit during the year.

© Jan Kanter/John G. Shedd Aquarium

GARDENING

Recent trends in gardening continued unabated in 2001. In the horticultural industry, buying patterns moved farther away from seed toward plants and from mail order to garden centres and mass-market retailers. Consumer interest in heirloom and "organic" seed increased, but commercial growers of flowers and vegetables chose cultivars bred for high yield, disease resistance, and long shelf life, characteristics that were important to their production and distribution methods.

Foster and Gallagher, which in 2000 claimed that it was the largest horticultural retailer in the United States, filed for bankruptcy protection and ceased operations at its subsidiaries, some of which, including Stark Brothers, Breck's, and Spring Hill Nurseries, were among the most well-established horticultural enterprises in the U.S. The 125-year-old W. Atlee Burpee & Co. also filed for bankruptcy protection; it had acquired some of the assets of the defunct on-line marketer GARDEN.COM, purchased the renowned West Coast Heronswood Nursery, and failed in an attempt to enter the retail sector with a chain of garden stores. Operations were expected to continue under new ownership.

The European association Fleuroselect chose 34 cultivars for recognition in the upcoming 2002 season, including three that won a Gold Medal. *Dianthus barbatus* Noverna Purple won for its ability to bloom without vernalization—exposure to a cold period—a first for the species known to generations of gardeners as Sweet William. The 40-cm (1 cm=0.4 in) diploid hybrid bloomed only 80–100 days from sowing and bore light purple 1.5-cm single flowers arranged in 7–10-cm clusters.

A new colour in the Wave series of cascading or spreading petunias also received a Gold Medal. *Petunia hybrida* Lavender Wave produced large numbers of 5.5-cm light lavender single blooms on plants that, though they reached 10 cm in height, spread to 120 cm, which made them ideal for baskets and containers. Good weather tolerance also made Lavender Wave useful for groundcover applications in sunny locations.

The final Gold Medal was given to *Viola X wittrockiana* Ultima Morpho for its uniquely coloured flowers. The small (5-cm) blossoms had a gradient of blue to white above a lemon-yellow ray petal at the bottom, with radial black markings. Plants of this tetraploid hybrid were a compact 15 cm high and across and bloomed for three to four months in the spring and fall.

All-America Rose Selections presented two awards. The hybrid tea rose Love & Peace—bred by Jerry Twomey and Ping Lim and introduced by Bailey Nurseries in St. Paul, Minn.—was created by crossing the famous Peace rose with an unnamed seedling. Disease-resistant and upright, with glossy dark green foliage, Love & Peace grew in height to 120–150 cm and had a diameter of 90 cm; it produced 12.5-cm-diameter spiraform golden-yellow blooms that had a pink edge and a fruity scent.

Shrub rose Starry Night was recognized for its wide adaptability and pure white dogwoodlike blossoms. Bred by Pierre Orard of Feyzin, France, by combining the cultivar Anisley Dickson with the species *Rosa wichurianna* and introduced by Edmunds' Roses of Wilsonville, Ore., Starry Night had a height and width of 90 cm in cool climates but a height and width of 180 cm in mild-to-warm climates. The pure white five-petaled single blossoms, 6–8 cm in diameter, contrasted well with the glossy medium green foliage.

All-America Selections (AAS) did not award a Gold Medal in either the vegetable or the flower category for the 2002 season. Fleuroselect Gold Medal winners *Petunia* Lavender Wave and *Viola* Ultima Morpho received the lesser designation of flower award, along with *Petunia hybrida* Tidal Wave Silver, chosen for its tall plant habit and unique colouring; *Cleome spinosa* Sparkler Blush, chosen for its dwarf habit and because it was the first commercial hybrid cleome; *Pelargonium zonale* Black Magic Rose, selected for its strongly contrasting foliage and flowers; *Rudbeckia hirta* Cherokee Sunset, recognized for its unique colour range of double and semidouble flowers; and *Catharanthus roseus* (Vinca) Jaio Scarlet Eye, acknowledged for its single bicolour rose and scarlet blooms. In addition, ornamental pepper (*Capsicum annum*) Chilly Chili won a flower award for its decorative fruits, which, unlike others of its class, were nonpungent and thus made it suitable as a potted plant in homes with small children.

AAS vegetable awards were given to basil Magical Michael for its attractive flowers with purple calices and white corollas and to Diva—a cucumber bred by Janika Eckert of Johnny's Selected Seeds—for its superior yields of high-quality seedless fruits. Two pumpkins were honoured: Sorcerer for its uniformity in the 6.8–9.9-kg (15–22-lb) jack-o'-lantern class and Orange Smoothie for its compact plant habit, high resistance to disease, small 1.8–3.2-kg (4–7-lb) size, and exceptionally smooth skin, which made it ideal for painting rather than carving. Finally, AAS granted a vegetable award to winter squash Cornell's Bush Delicata for its compact plant habit, improved flavour, and exceptional disease resistance.

Belgian landscape architect Jacques Wirtz's redesign for the walled garden at Alnwick Castle, Northumberland, Eng., featured waterfalls and geometric-shaped hedges of beech, box, hornbeam, and yew.

The Perennial Plant Association in the U.S. chose as its Perennial Plant of the Year *Calamagrostis xacutiflora* Karl Foerster, a natural hybrid of *Calamagrostis epigejos* and *Calamagrostis arundinacea;* the long-blooming grass was first found in the Hamburg (Ger.) Botanical Garden collection and was introduced to the nursery trade by Karl Foerster in his 1957 book *Einzug der Gräser und Farne in die Gärten*.

In England Belgian landscape architect Jacques Wirtz (*see* BIOGRAPHIES) continued work on the 5-ha (12-ac) walled garden at Alnwick Castle; he was commissioned by the duchess of Northumberland to redesign the enclosure. Wirtz's garden designs, featuring mass plantings of geometric-shaped hedges, were much in demand in Europe.

On the lighter side, the ubiquitous garden gnome—a fixture in British lawns and gardens for more than 100 years—fell out of favour during the year. Gnome ownership declined from about 5 million in 1990 to 3.8 million in 2001. In France matters were taken a step or two further; the self-styled Liberation Front for Garden Gnomes took hundreds of the figures from suburban residences and "returned" them to woodland settings.

(SHEPHERD OGDEN)

Fashions

Black-and-white **CONFECTIONS** and looks that featured nautical, opulent, and **TRAILER-TRASH** themes edged out the **MILITARY-INSPIRED** creations that were featured prominently prior to the September 11 terrorist attacks in the U.S.

The international fashion industry, already suffering from early signs of recession, found its gloomy outlook compounded following the Sept. 11, 2001, terrorist attacks in the U.S. Prior to the attacks, the Gap, an American retail giant, had laid off 800 employees and reported that company earnings had decreased by 22%. Luxury goods companies LVMH Moët Hennessy Louis Vuitton and the Gucci Group revised their strategies in the wake of the attacks and admitted that earnings would slow and that they were preparing for a "prolonged slowdown." Wolfgang Ley, chief executive of the German fashion empire Escada, confirmed that his company's American sales had dropped by half following September 11.

The attacks in New York City coincided with 7th on Sixth, the Council of Fashion Designers of America's (CFDA) spring-summer 2002 shows. Though the international fashion community had gathered in the city to celebrate, critique, and acquire merchandise for the upcoming season, business ground to a halt as the disaster unfolded. The CFDA canceled the runway shows. A week or two later several New York designers presented their collections in their showrooms. Prominent American buyers, frightened

A dramatic catwalk setting dramatized the staging in Milan of Antonio Marras's fall-winter collection, which featured styles ranging from military overcoats adorned with medals to frothy ensembles.

AP/Wide World Photos

by the prospect of more terrorist hijackings and aware of the lean financial times ahead, refrained from traveling to see the European collections.

That fashion reflected the change in society was a point that became apparent when the U.S. and Great Britain declared war on terrorism in October. The trappings of battle—military-inspired clothing and camouflage print as well as a range of urban-guerrilla graffiti art—had dominated the international spring-summer catwalks. To the sound of a coronet and battle drums, Miguel Adrover offered suits modeled on 1940s army uniforms and trousers based on army fatigues. Miuccia Prada wore a belted military jacket and platform shoes to the unveiling of her collection—plain gray, navy, and black cotton skirts and sweaters that were reminiscent of the drab Mao uniform. In Paris camouflage was seen at Comme des Garçons, Jean-Charles de Castelbajac, and Christian Dior; at Celine, Michael Kors accessorized bikini bottoms, hot pants, and mesh tank-top dresses with bullet-studded belts. Marc Jacobs at Louis Vuitton featured jackets with epaulets. The onset of war, however, forced the fashion industry to reconsider its direction. Violent imagery and terrorist-chic styling were reappraised.

At the autumn-winter 2001 collections—shown in the summer—designers explored the Middle East. Heads were wrapped and faces were hidden behind scarves at Raf Simons's menswear show. Adrover looked to Egypt for inspiration; his collection made its debut in a nomad's tent, where a female model wore a white headdress and a djellaba, a male model donned harem pants, and pantsuits were layered over tunics and kaftans. Though Gucci showed harem pants for spring-summer 2002, the look failed to take off on the street.

Luella Bartley and Jacobs's punkish sensibility was shared by designers Donatella Versace, Balenciaga, Anna Sui, and Junya Watanabe, who for inspiration also looked to the New Wave scene that dominated popular music in the early 1980s. Prom dresses, cocktail sheaths, full 1950s-style skirts (which were favoured in the '80s), minis, pedal pushers, leather jackets worn over slips, fur stoles, and rhinestones showed up on their catwalks. For spring-summer, playful trends were plentiful. Modern floral prints—roses, hydrangeas, and wildflowers that had been digitally enhanced by computer technology—looked more abstract than realistic after the images were transferred onto skirts and dresses designed by Cacharel (which presented its first collection in Paris designed by the London duo Clements Ribeiro), Louis Vuitton, Dries Van Noten, Dolce & Gabbana, Eley Kishimoto, Marni, and Jean-Paul Gaultier. A nautical look—interpreted as striped shirts—appeared at Prada and Marni, and a trailer-trash look—handbags inspired by 1950s Cadillacs and chiffon dresses featuring silver YKK zippers and strips of denim—was the theme behind John Galliano's collection for his own line as well as Christian Dior. Nicolas Ghesquiere's collection for Callaghan, which included draped jersey dresses, revealed a Grecian influence. At their spring-summer shows, John Bartlett, Kors, Gucci, and Chanel introduced the white shirt as a new staple. Both seasons also signified a return to black dressing. Karan's and Ralph Lauren's spring-summer shows were composed of black and white (Lauren also included chocolate-brown pieces). Tom Ford's much-anticipated debut collection for Yves Saint Laurent ready-to-wear, almost entirely composed of black and white clothes, disappointed critics who were waiting for something more spectacular. The focal point of the collection was Saint Laurent's iconic 1960s tuxedo suit, Le Smoking.

Emblematic of the colours favoured by top designers during the year was this frilly black and white gown for Frank Sorbier's spring-summer collection.

Pierre Verdy/ AFP Worldwide

Opulence was a theme at autumn-winter shows. Designer Ford presented satin clothes in deep purple at Yves Saint Laurent and hot pink at Gucci. The Versace and Valentino shows were laden with fur, and Milanese designer Roberto Cavalli incorporated ostrich feathers into his collection; he also lined distressed denim dresses with fur and encrusted silk blousons with semiprecious jewels. Amid the fun and frivolity, sensible styles prevailed.

Basic black and white did not disappoint critics at the autumn-winter 2001 collections. Particular standouts were Nicolas Ghesquiere's work for Balenciaga, which included items ranging from reworked Victorian corset tops to biker jackets and combat trousers made from oiled cotton; "little black dresses" featured by Jacobs and Diane von Furstenberg; Gucci baby dolls; Viktor & Rolf's entirely black collection; Fendi's white Courrèges-style Mod look—composed of white boots, handbags, and patent coats—and Jacobs's Doctor Zhivago-themed collection for Louis Vuitton; it featured black-and-white fur hats, black lace-up boots, and structured, Cossack-inspired black coats that were trimmed with white mink.

Women also responded to the black-and-white theme. Socialites and celebrities at high-profile parties wore ensembles composed of a solid shade of either colour or a combination of both. Black dresses proved to be the chic choices on Oscar night—Julia Roberts looked refined in a silver-trimmed black 1982 Valentino couture gown; Catherine Zeta-Jones chose a black strapless Versace dress; and Sarah Jessica Parker (*see* BIOGRAPHIES) appeared in a chic black mini dress.

Parker's eclectic wardrobe for her role as Carrie Bradshaw in the hit show *Sex & the City* was talked about as much as the show's plotline. Discussion about shoes designed by Manolo Blahnik figured prominently in the script, and designs by Marni, Fendi, Prada, Chanel, Dolce & Gabbana, Givenchy, and Dior were just some of the labels that Carrie and her fellow characters—Samantha, Charlotte, and Miranda—could be seen in each week. The show also launched trends—including a craze for the fabric corsages Carrie frequently wore as accessories—and designers who supplied clothes for the show saw incredible returns; Timmy Woods, a Beverly Hills, Calif.–based designer, reported taking 1,000 orders for a horse-head purse that appeared on the show for only two seconds.

On the street, however, young women embraced "reality dressing," a casual chic uniform that was composed of three essential pieces: designer jeans, a deconstructed T-shirt, and high heels or athletic shoes. This style emerged in response to the popularity of reality TV programs. (*See* MEDIA AND PUBLISHING: *Sidebar.*)

American designer Sean "P. Diddy" Combs's Sean Jean line for fall featured a suede shearling wrap coat that partially concealed a white thermal crewneck pullover and wool pinstriped five-pocket pants.

AP/Wide World Photos

Throngs of celebrities appeared at the spring-summer and autumn-winter shows. Tickets for the presentation of rap star Sean ("P. Diddy") Combs's label, Sean John, were in great demand; the event occurred in the midst of his trial on weapons and bribery charges. The CFDA's decision in February to sell 7th on Sixth to the International Management Group, an agency that represented athletes and entertainers, heightened the sense that fashion was increasingly becoming part of the entertainment industry. Further proof was evidenced in the launch of more fashion brands by celebrity and personality designers, including the jeans line J. Lo by Jennifer Lopez (*see* BIOGRAPHIES); Intimates, a line of lingerie by model Elle MacPherson; and Marie-Chantal, upscale baby clothes labels designed by Princess Marie-Chantal Miller of Greece. Reinvigorated brands appeared on the retail frontier. Under the direction of its new designer in chief Scott Fellows, Bally of Switzerland debuted on Milan catwalks clothing lines for men and women as well as its more fashion-forward line of bags and shoes. At Burberry, CEO Rose Marie Bravo appointed Christopher Bailey, who had worked with Tom Ford at Gucci, to the position of designer. In March, Narciso Rodríguez announced his departure from Spanish leather-goods house LVMH. Loewe and LVMH appointed Julien MacDonald design director of Givenchy, where he replaced Alexander McQueen, who in December 2000 had sold 51% of his company to the Gucci Group. In April, Gucci announced that, in a similar joint venture, it would back Stella McCartney (*see* BIOGRAPHIES), Chloé's former designer, in establishing her own design label. Phoebe Philo became Chloé's new creative director. Gucci also acquired Balenciaga and Bottega Veneta. Asprey & Garrard announced that it would split into two labels with two distinct retail operations. Jade Jagger and Hussein Chalayan were asked to form an in-house design team that would create a new luxury label.

In the realm of modeling, Karolina Kurkova, a 17-year-old Czech model, became the new face of glamour; Brazilian supermodel Gisele Bündchen announced her retirement from runway shows; Elizabeth Jagger—the daughter of Mick Jagger and Jerry Hall—launched her modeling career; and Carolyn Murphy replaced actress Elizabeth Hurley as the new face of Estée Lauder.

(BRONWYN COSGRAVE)

Health and Disease

The deliberate mailing of **ANTHRAX**-tainted letters in the U.S. in October resulted in deadly **OUTBREAKS** of the disease on the East Coast and heightened fears of **BIOTERRORISM**. During the year researchers took the first steps toward **CLONING** human embryos, and several critically ill patients received a new type of implantable **ARTIFICIAL HEART**.

The medical response to the havoc wreaked by four jetliner crashes on September 11 due to terrorist activity was massive and rapid at all three impact sites: Lower Manhattan, the Pentagon in Virginia, and rural Shanksville, Pa. It was in New York City, however, that the need for an unprecedented level of trauma care seemed likely, at least at first. A few hours after the World Trade Center's twin towers collapsed, five designated city hospitals were prepared for the worst. Triage centres were set up within a few blocks of "ground zero," fully staffed and equipped to treat any possible injury and perform lifesaving surgery. To be sure, about 600 people were treated on September 11, about 150 of whom were critically injured, but as the day wore on, the numbers of new patients dwindled, and the anticipated deluge never materialized.

It soon became obvious that far more people had perished than had survived with injuries. It was the rescue crews, not medical personnel, who had their work cut out for them—digging through the rubble day and night in a mostly vain search for the still living, at significant risk to themselves. In fact, the need was greater for specially trained rescue dogs than for doctors to aid in the on-site search and recovery.

Fears of bioterrorism in the wake of the September 11 terrorist attacks led the U.S. government to evaluate its supply of vaccines against anthrax and smallpox. The available anthrax vaccine was of questionable potency and had safety risks. Whereas new vaccines were in development, they were not available when in early October a smattering of anonymous letters carrying spores of *Bacillus anthracis* began arriving in the mailboxes of broadcast and print media on the East Coast and federal offices in Washington, D.C. Dissemination of the spores as the letters were processed through postal machinery and handled at their destinations was believed responsible for nearly 20 confirmed cases of cutaneous and inhalation (pulmonary) anthrax and several deaths from the rapidly fatal inhalation form.

Because anthrax was preventable and treatable with antibiotics, the U.S. government's strategy was not to vaccinate but to treat everyone who may have been exposed to the bacterium with the antibiotic ciprofloxacin (Cipro). The Food and Drug Administration (FDA) took action to approve two other widely available generic antibiotics, doxycycline and penicillin, for treatment of inhalation anthrax in the event of a large-scale terrorist attack. Anthrax could not be spread by infected individuals, which rendered many of the usual communicable-disease-prevention measures unnecessary. Various actions, including widespread testing of suspected locations for the presence of spores and decontamination of spore-tainted buildings, offices, and mail-sorting equipment, were taken in an attempt to limit further dispersal. Mail from contaminated postal facilities was impounded for several weeks until it could be sanitized by irradiation and returned to the mail stream for delivery. Government authorities also moved to install equipment in post offices that would kill anthrax spores during regular mail processing.

Smallpox, unlike anthrax, was highly contagious, and an estimated 80% of the U.S. population was thought to be susceptible. The devastating viral disease was effectively eradicated from the world in 1977, but samples of the virus still existed and could get into the hands of terrorists. Consequently, the federal government sought to increase its relatively meagre supply of vaccine, 15.4 million doses. Medical scientists at several universities were exploring the possibility of diluting the existing supply to increase the number of doses. At the same time, the government arranged to acquire new smallpox vaccine from several pharmaceutical companies—up to the 300 million doses needed to protect everyone in the U.S.

Stem Cell Research and Human Cloning. Although the tragedy of September 11 and the threat of bioterrorism overshadowed so many events of the year, there were myriad noteworthy developments in health and disease. The field that probably generated the most excitement, and the most heated political debate, was research on human stem cells. These unspecialized cells have the potential to become specific cells—i.e., cells of almost any organ or tissue—and their ideal source was considered to be a five-day-old human embryo, comprising about 200–250 cells. (Stem cells from adults appeared to have less therapeutic promise.)

A long-awaited pronouncement on embryonic stem cell research in the U.S. came on August 9. In a television address Pres. George W. Bush said that he would allow federal support of such research, but only on cell lines that already had been derived from "leftover" embryos grown in infertility clinics. Many research scientists considered the decision severely limiting, and in September the Institute of Medicine (IOM) issued a report concluding that new cell lines would still be needed down the road, in part because existing lines were likely to accumulate genetic mutations.

In November a private Massachusetts biotechnology firm, Advanced Cell Technology, provoked much sound and fury when it announced that it had taken the first steps toward cloning human embryos. According to the company, the goal was not to clone a human being but to produce stem cells for treating disease. In fact, most of the embryos died before reaching even an eight-cell stage, without producing the desired stem cells. President Bush, religious and political leaders, and many scientists condemned the work as immoral and a dangerous move in the wrong direction.

Desirey Minkoh/AFP Worldwide

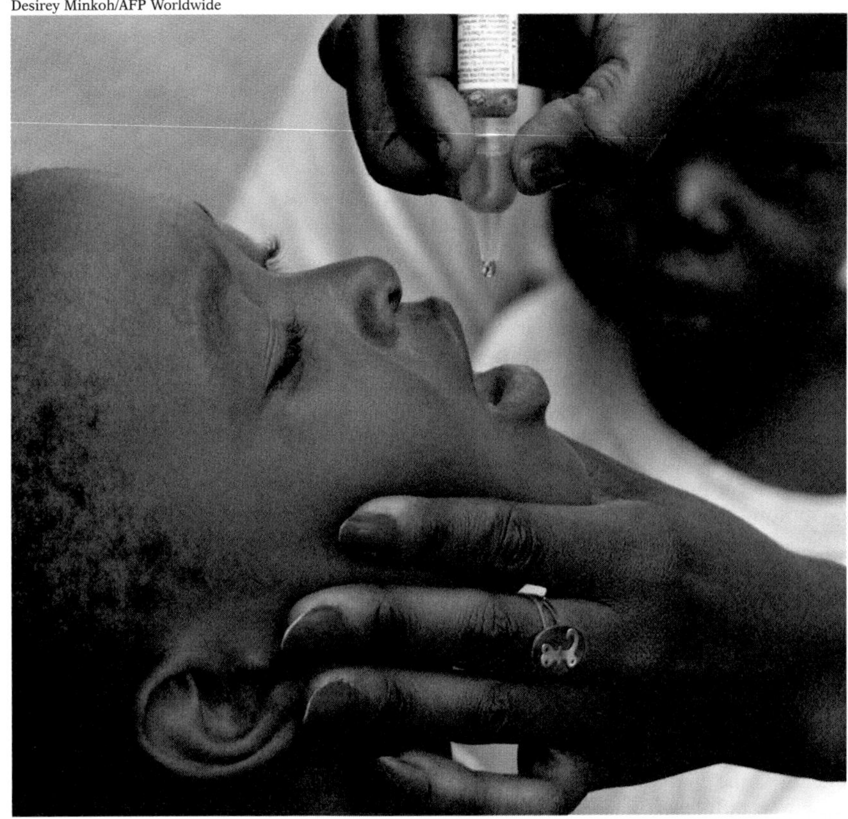

A medical worker in Gabon vaccinates a child against polio on August 12.

Infectious Disease. The World Health Organization's (WHO) Communicable Disease Surveillance and Response service, which tracked major infectious diseases worldwide, reported a number of major outbreaks. They included cholera in West Africa, Chad, Tanzania, South Africa, Pakistan, and India; Ebola hemorrhagic fever in Uganda; measles in South Korea; yellow fever in Brazil, Peru, Côte d'Ivoire, Liberia, and Guinea; plague in Zambia; dengue fever in Venezuela; meningococcal disease in Angola, Ethiopia, the Democratic Republic of the Congo, and the "African meningitis belt," an area that extended across the middle of the continent and included all or part of at least 15 countries between Senegal and Ethiopia; Crimean-Congo hemorrhagic fever in Pakistan and the Kosovo province of Yugoslavia; legionellosis in Spain and Norway; and an illness described as a "highly lethal variant of measles" in India.

One of the greatest scourges of all time, poliomyelitis, came closer to being a thing of the past, thanks to a massive global eradication effort coordinated by WHO, UNICEF, Rotary International, and the U.S. Centers for Disease Control and Prevention (CDC). From 1999 to 2000 the number of polio cases in the world was cut in half to 3,500, and the number of endemic countries (those with naturally occurring poliovirus) dropped from 50 to 20. As of mid-2001, India, which once bore the world's greatest polio burden, had only 10 confirmed cases. The target date for global eradication was 2005, but completion of the task would require an all-out vaccination effort in Southeast Asia, the eastern Mediterranean, and Africa, at a cost of $400 million.

Although childhood vaccines had saved millions of youngsters the world over from infectious disease, deformity, and death, their safety continued to be a source of controversy. Studies published during the year demonstrated that some alleged risks of vaccine use were not real. Combination vaccines against diphtheria, pertussis, and tetanus (DPT) and measles, mumps, and rubella (MMR) were shown not to be associated with long-term risks of seizures or other neurological problems in children. Furthermore, no evidence was found that hepatitis B vaccine caused or aggravated multiple sclerosis. Public health professionals hoped these and other "negative results" would alleviate some of the public's fears.

HIV and AIDS. The year 2001 was the 20th anniversary of the initial reports of a mysterious deadly immune-system disorder that came to be known as AIDS. The medical community, international AIDS organizations, and especially the media saw the occasion as a time to reflect upon the relentless epidemic that had killed more than 21 million people on every continent and from every walk of life. In 2001 an estimated 36 million people were living with HIV infection.

The long-held hope for an AIDS vaccine continued to be pursued. Although as many as 80 potential vaccines had been tried in humans, only one had reached large-scale human trials. About 8,000 volunteers at high risk for HIV in North America, The Netherlands, and Thailand had received either an experimental preventive vaccine developed by the California-based firm VaxGen or a placebo. Periodically they were being tested for HIV. The trials would continue until 2002–03.

At the 8th Conference on Retroviruses and Opportunistic Infections, held in Chicago in February, HIV/AIDS treatment specialists voiced a loud cry for newer and safer drugs and pointed out that the highly lauded combination-drug therapies, also known as AIDS "drug cocktails," were not working for thousands of patients. Clinicians reported a range of adverse effects associated with the life-prolonging drugs, including high cholesterol, diabetes, fat accumulations in the neck and abdomen, weakened bones, and nerve damage in the extremities. Among the many experimental drugs that were described at the conference, perhaps most promising was a new class called entry inhibitors, which blocked the binding of HIV to key receptors on the cell surface.

Excitement about new treatments, however, had little relevance for the millions of people in less-developed countries living with HIV, many of whom had no access to treatment. The high cost of existing drugs and their unavailability to the vast majority of HIV/AIDS sufferers had aroused considerable ire among government officials and others trying to combat AIDS in less-developed countries. To make treatment more accessible, a handful of pharmaceutical companies in India, Thailand, and other countries began producing cheaper generic versions of the patented agents used in drug cocktails, a move vigorously opposed by the multinational companies holding the patents. As sentiments against the drug giants mounted, however, several conceded to pressure and slashed their prices on AIDS drugs for less-developed countries, and a few waived their patent rights. Some 39 major companies that manufactured AIDS drugs had sued South Africa in 1998 in an effort to bar the country from importing cheaper drugs. In April 2001 the companies dropped their case.

UN Secretary-General Kofi Annan called the battle against AIDS one of his personal priorities when he initiated a global fund to allot between $7 billion and $10 billion annually to combat a trio of diseases that continued to ravage the Third World—AIDS, tuberculosis, and malaria. Addressing the delegates to the first UN summit on AIDS, held in New York City in June, Annan said, "This year we have seen a turning point. AIDS can no longer do its deadly work in the dark. The world has started to wake up."

China was one country that "woke up" to its AIDS crisis. In August its deputy health minister, Yin Dakui, admitted that the country was "facing a very serious epidemic of HIV/AIDS" and that the government had "not effectively stemmed the epidemic." An estimated 70% of China's cases were among intravenous drug users. The Chinese government claimed that about 600,000 citizens were infected with HIV, whereas the UN estimated the number at more than one million.

In the U.S. the incidence of new HIV infections among homosexual African American men aged 23 to 29 was called "explosive." CDC surveys found that 30% of men in this group were HIV-positive.

Cancer. Rarely do research scientists become unmitigatedly exuberant over a new treatment. Nevertheless, this was the overwhelming sentiment among cancer specialists about a new drug, imatinib (marketed as Gleevec in the U.S. and Glivec in Europe). Imatinib was one of a new class of anticancer agents known as growth-factor inhibitors, which targeted cancer cells by recognizing their unique molecular defects. The FDA approved imatinib in record time after tests showed that it had induced remissions in 53 of 54 patients with chronic myelogenous leukemia (CML). Less than a month after publication of the CML results, scientists reported that 60% of nearly 200 patients with gastrointestinal stromal cancer (GIST) treated with imatinib had became symptom-free. GIST is a rare intestinal malignancy for which there had been no known treatment.

An IOM report issued in June put some of the fanfare about new cancer treatments in perspective. "The reality is that half of all patients diagnosed with cancer will die of their disease within a few years," the report stated. The expert panel that prepared the report was highly critical of the "almost single-minded focus on attempts to cure every patient at every stage of disease." It found that at least half of dying cancer patients suffered symptoms for which they received little or no treatment; these included pain, difficulty breathing, emotional distress, nausea, and confusion. The report called for a vastly stepped-up program to ensure that suffering cancer patients received palliative (symptom-abating) treatments.

Diabetes. Diabetes was fast becoming one of the most worrisome epidemics of the 21st century. In 2001 more than 135 million people worldwide were affected, and the number was expected to reach 300 million by 2025. The vast majority had type 2, or non-insulin-dependent, diabetes. With globalization, less-developed countries were experiencing some of the steepest increases. A survey published in September indicated that during the decade of the 1990s the proportion of Americans with diabetes increased 49%. Duly alarmed, CDC Director Jeffrey Koplan said, "If we continue on this course for the next decade, the public health implications in terms of both disease and health care costs will be staggering."

As a counterpoint to these dire predictions, a study carried out in Finland found that overweight middle-aged women and men who increased their activity level and ate a low-fat, high-fibre diet were unlikely to develop diabetes, even if their weight loss was minimal. In August a similar study in the U.S. was cut short when it became clear that lifestyle changes were overwhelmingly effective at staving off diabetes in those at high risk.

Three studies reported during the year showed that a common class of drugs for high blood pressure, angiotensin II receptor blockers, could significantly delay inexorable deterioration of the kidneys in people with diabetes. Commenting on these results, one of the investigators said, "For pennies . . . we can prevent a lot of disease and ultimately save billions of dollars in treatment."

A novel antidiabetes drug, nateglinide (Starlix), which became available in a number of countries, offered a new option for people with poorly controlled blood sugar. Studies found that when taken just before a meal, nateglinide triggered an immediate release of insulin by the pancreas. The insulin prevented spikes in postmeal glucose levels; such spikes were associated with blood vessel damage.

Cardiovascular Disease. Balloon angioplasty was among the most frequently performed procedures for restoring blood flow to partially obstructed coro-

On July 2 surgeons in Louisville, Ky., prepare to implant a self-contained artificial heart in the chest of Robert Tools.

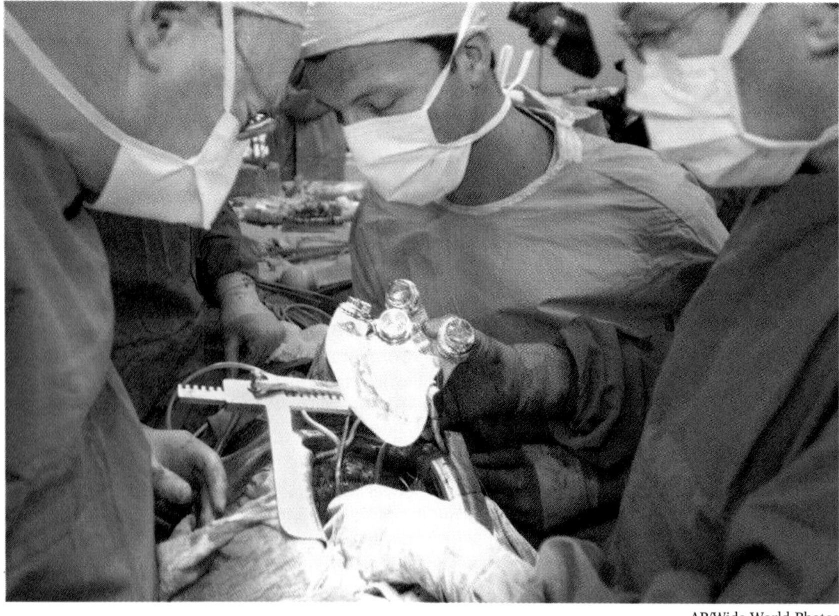

AP/Wide World Photos

Alzheimer Disease: Clues from Convents

An ongoing study of a highly cooperative group of long-lived nuns has been shedding considerable light on aging and Alzheimer disease. The Nun Study, led by neurologist David Snowdon of the University of Kentucky, began in 1986 and has focused on 678 American members of the School Sisters of Notre Dame, a Roman Catholic religious congregation. When the study began, the sisters ranged in age from 75 to 102 years. All agreed to undergo yearly physical and cognitive-function exams and to donate their brains for study at death.

As a piece of scientific research, the Nun Study has obvious limitations—the outcomes cannot always be generalized to the population at large. On the other hand, because the nuns share so many key lifestyle factors—e.g., ethnicity (Caucasian), reproductive history, occupation, and access to health care—the conclusions drawn about their aging processes are less likely to be confounded by differences in individual experiences.

Another singular aspect of the Nun Study is the researchers' access to the convent archives, ranging from birth certificates to socioeconomic, educational, residential, social, and occupational data. The data that have excited Snowdon the most, however, are those acquired in face-to-face interviews. Recalling his first meeting with residents of a Minnesota convent, Snowdon said, "It shattered all my stereotypes of how 80- and 90-year-old people are supposed to behave."

The insights that scientists have gleaned from this distinctive group are varied. For example, results of studies published in 2001 noted a connection between the nuns' outlook early in life and their longevity. Investigators analyzed autobiographies composed by 180 sisters at the time they took their vows (between ages 18 and 32). Although the majority of this group lived to a ripe old age, those who revealed positive emotions in young adulthood lived about seven years longer—to a median age of 93½—than their more negative-thinking counterparts.

Snowdon's team also found links in the nuns' autobiographies to changes in their cognitive abilities with age. Sisters who showed "low linguistic ability" as young adults were found more likely to experience declines in language facility as they aged and to develop dementia in later life. In postmortem studies the brains of nuns whose linguistic ability had been rated low had clear pathological evidence of Alzheimer disease. The researchers surmised that less-than-optimal brain development might have predisposed those nuns to the disease.

Although these and other results from the Nun Study are highly intriguing and suggestive, they are not yet conclusive. As Snowdon and his team gather more data on their subjects, they will undoubtedly establish clearer cause-and-effect relationships.

(ELLEN BERNSTEIN)

nary arteries. In 90% of angioplasties, after a catheter-delivered balloon had been inflated to widen the artery, a tiny mesh coil (stent) was inserted to help keep the artery open. In as many as 20% of cases, however, the artery renarrowed at the site of treatment within six months as a result of scar formation, a process called restenosis. During the year an experimental technique for preventing restenosis after angioplasty was hailed as a "major breakthrough" by the American Heart Association. The approach used stents that were coated with an antibiotic and designed to release the medication slowly over a one-month period to prevent local scar-tissue formation. In a European trial more than 100 patients who received antibiotic-coated stents had no incidence of restenosis seven months after angioplasty.

In July the first of a new type of artificial heart, developed by the Massachusetts-based firm Abiomed, Inc., was implanted in Robert Tools, aged 58, at Jewish Hospital in Louisville, Ky. Tools had diabetes and end-stage heart disease and was far too sick to be considered for a heart transplant. After removing most of his diseased heart, the surgical team attached the grapefruit-sized device, made mostly of titanium and plastic, to the remains of the two upper heart chambers and aorta. A battery pack worn outside the body transmitted power to the implanted device with no skin penetration. By contrast, the first artificial heart, the Jarvik-7, which had been given to a few deathly ill patients in the early 1980s, had tubes leading from an internal pump to external compressors and consoles. Tools's recovery exceeded his surgeons' expectations over the first four months, but in November his condition worsened, and he died from severe abdominal bleeding associated with his pre-implant illness. Four subsequent patients successfully received artificial hearts during the year. The goal of these first implants was to enable the severely ill recipients to live an extra six months with a satisfactory quality of life. Abiomed expressed the hope that later generations of its device would be suitable for a broader group of patients, who would gain five or more years of life.

Alzheimer Disease. The Alzheimer's Association estimated that about 4 million people in the U.S. had Alzheimer disease (AD) at the start of the 21st century and predicted that by 2050 the number would jump to 14 million. WHO estimated that there were 37 million people worldwide with dementia, the large majority of whom had AD. As of 2001, there was still no cure or treatment that could significantly halt the progression of the disease.

During the year about three dozen clinical trials were either under way or in the recruitment stage to test potential AD treatments. At the University of California, San Diego, medical researchers began testing the first gene therapy procedure for AD. Their first volunteer was a 60-year-old woman with early-stage disease. Initially, skin cells were taken from the woman and genetically modified to produce large amounts of nerve growth factor. Then, in an 11-hour operation, neurosurgeons implanted the cells into diseased tissue in her brain. The primary goal was to see if the treatment was safe. The researchers hoped that ultimately the therapy would prevent the death of specific nerve cells that are affected by AD and enhance the function of others, which would thereby delay the onset of major symptoms.

An optimistic report published in the March 13 *Proceedings of the National Academy of Sciences* found that people who were physically and mentally active in early adulthood and middle age had an excellent chance of avoiding AD. Similar findings were emerging from a unique ongoing investigation known as the Nun Study. (*See* Sidebar.)

(ELLEN BERNSTEIN)

Law, Crime, and Law Enforcement

The prosecution of **TERRORISTS** and those charged with war crimes, the federal **EXECUTION** of American terrorist Timothy **McVEIGH,** and the move toward the abolition of the **DEATH PENALTY** in a number of countries were among the **LEGAL MATTERS** that captured the headlines during 2001.

INTERNATIONAL LAW

Throughout 2001 countries continued to work toward a common understanding of international law, particularly on the issue of "universal jurisdiction," the concept that war criminals may be punished anywhere regardless of where or against whom they committed their crimes. The September terrorist attacks in the United States raised critical questions for international law, including how terrorists should be punished and what the rules were for taking action against countries alleged to have harboured those responsible.

Peru continued to seek the extradition of former president Alberto Fujimori, who was living in exile in Japan. Fujimori was accused of abandonment of his office, dereliction of duty in the wake of corruption scandals, and failure to appear for court hearings. Japan refused to extradite Fujimori and said the case would be handled according to Japanese domestic law. Chile's former dictator Gen. Augusto Pinochet Ugarte, who faced allegations of war crimes committed during his tenure, was found medically unfit to stand trial.

The collision of a Chinese fighter jet with an American surveillance jet caused the American plane to land on Chinese soil in distress, while the Chinese aircraft was lost at sea. The U.S. questioned whether the Chinese had the right to board the downed American plane, hold its crew, and remove equipment from the plane, all of which the Chinese did. Although there was no international law directly applicable to such a situation, the U.S. raised two legal points: first, the U.S. plane had not overflown China's 19-km (12-mi) recognized territorial seas and therefore did not violate China's sovereignty or break international law, and, second, customary international law recognizes that a ship in distress can enter a harbour unannounced; furthermore, a foreign military ship in port is not subject to the jurisdiction of the port state. These laws could be interpreted to cover aircraft as well as ships. Chinese authorities claimed that since the aircraft had no right to be on Chinese territory, it was not immune to being searched.

The International Court of Justice. In July the International Court of Justice (ICJ) found that the U.S. had breached its obligations to Germany under Article 36 of the Vienna Convention on Consular Relations. Walter LaGrand, a German national, was sentenced to death for his involvement in a 1982 murder in Arizona. The night before the execution, Germany brought suit in the ICJ. Germany argued that LaGrand had not been informed of his rights under the Vienna Convention, under which he could have notified the German consulate of his arrest and incarceration. Despite the ICJ's issuance of a "provisional measure of protection," LaGrand was executed as scheduled. The court held that the U.S. violated the convention's requirements. It determined that individual rights in one's nation of origin might be invoked in the World Court when the individual was being detained in another country.

The principality of Liechtenstein brought suit in the ICJ against Germany, claiming that Germany had improperly disposed of property belonging to Liechtenstein. After World War II, Czechoslovakia, one of the Allies, seized property without compensation in defeated Germany, including some objects owned by Liechtensteiners. Subsequently, in 1952 Germany and Liechtenstein agreed that although Germany had given up the right to pursue the recovery of its own goods, those objects belonging to Liechtenstein had been illegally taken by Czechoslovakia. When in 1991 a Czechoslovak museum sent to Germany on loan a painting that was among those claimed by Liechtenstein, that principality's leader, Prince Hans Adam II, sued the Germans, claiming that the painting had been illegally seized in 1945 and that Germany should relinquish it. The German courts disagreed, finding that the painting was properly seized German property; it was later returned to the Czech Republic. The ICJ had not reached a decision as of year's end.

Universal Jurisdiction. In June a Belgian jury sentenced two nuns and two men to jail terms from 12 to 20 years for crimes committed during the 1994 genocide in Rwanda. A 1993 Belgian law gave its courts jurisdiction over violations of the Geneva Conventions regardless of where the crimes were committed, by whom, or against whom. The Geneva Conventions call for the humane treatment of noncombatants, and they prohibit murder, mutilation, and cruel or degrading treatment. This was the first jury trial to address violations of international humanitarian law that occurred in another country. A Belgian court delayed until November a preliminary hearing to determine whether that country had jurisdiction to bring charges against Israeli Prime Minister Ariel Sharon (*see* BIOGRAPHIES) for his role in a 1982 Palestinian massacre. The court's decision to hear arguments on the case prompted outrage from some countries and caused the Belgian government to consider exempting sitting prime ministers and presidents from the reach of the 1993 law. In a similar case, Senegal's high court ruled that it did not have jurisdiction over Chad's exiled president Hissène Habré for crimes he committed while in Chad. Habré's victims spoke of seeking his extradition to Belgium instead. Similarly, a Cuban American group threatened to file suit in Belgian court against Cuban leader Fidel Castro, alleging crimes against humanity.

International Criminal Tribunal for the Former Yugoslavia. There were several landmark decisions from the International Criminal Tribunal for the Former Yugoslavia (ICTY). Three eth-

AP/Wide World Photos

Former Yugoslav president Slobodan Milosevic is escorted by a security guard into the courtroom of the International Criminal Tribunal for the Former Yugoslavia on July 3 in The Hague.

nic Serbs were convicted on charges of rape and torture for their abuse in 1992 of women in a "rape camp" in Bosnia and Herzegovina. This was the first case to issue convictions for rape as a crime against humanity. In June Serbia surrendered former Yugoslav president Slobodan Milosevic to the ICTY. He would be the first former head of state to stand trial at an international tribunal. Article 7 of the ICTY specifically denies immunity to heads of state. Milosevic was indicted in 1999 on charges of crimes against humanity and war crimes for the killings of ethnic Albanians in Kosovo. He was indicted in October for crimes in Croatia in 1991–92 and in November for crimes in Bosnia in 1992–96. Gen. Radislav Krstic was sentenced to 46 years in prison for his role in the execution of 7,000 unarmed Muslim men and boys near the Bosnian town of Srebrenica in 1995. According to the verdict issued in the case, "ethnic cleansing became genocide." Former Bosnian Serb leader Radovan Karadzic and his top general, Ratko Mladic, indicted by the tribunal on charges of genocide and crimes against humanity, were still fugitives, as were many others. In October, after six years of refusing to cooperate, the Bosnian Serb parliament passed a law supporting the ICTY and calling for the arrest of war-crimes suspects living in Republika Srpska (Serb Republic).

Terrorism. A Scottish court found a Libyan, 'Abd al-Baset al-Megrahi, guilty of the bombing of Pan Am Flight 103 over Lockerbie, Scot., in 1988. A second Libyan was acquitted, and al-Megrahi planned to appeal. The court placed responsibility for the bombing on Libya but did not specify who might have been involved. An American federal grand jury indicted 14 men (13 Saudi nationals) in connection with the 1996 bombing of the U.S. military barracks in Saudi Arabia. Saudi Arabia protested, claiming that the U.S. did not have the jurisdiction to prosecute a crime that occurred on Saudi territory, nor did it have the right to prosecute Saudi nationals. Although universal jurisdiction had been recognized for war crimes and genocide, it was less accepted for acts of terrorism. The September 11 terrorist attacks in the U.S. could cause that to change, however. On September 28 the UN Security Council adopted Resolution 1373, which was legally binding on all members and called for states to take measures to combat terrorism, including bringing terrorists to justice.

Most international law concerned interstate disputes and had little to do with individuals. Thus, because Osama bin Laden, the prime suspect in the terrorist attacks, was not the representative of any state, charges against him could not be brought in the ICJ. The proper forum would have been the International Criminal Court, but the act enabling the ICC had not been ratified by the requisite number of countries—the U.S. being among the nonratifiers. What constituted a legal response to the September attacks was also moot. Were the attacks an act of war? Was a declaration of war required in order to respond with military force?

On October 18 a New York judge handed down life sentences to three foreigners and a naturalized American found guilty of involvement in the 1998 attacks on the U.S. embassies in Kenya and Tanzania. Bin Laden was linked to these attacks as well, but he and 12 others indicted for the bombings remained at large. (VICTORIA C. WILLIAMS)

COURT DECISIONS

Between Oct. 2, 2000, and June 28, 2001, the United States Supreme Court decided 79 cases. While the term would be forever remembered for *Bush* v. *Gore,* a number of other significant cases also attracted attention. Statistically, if not rhetorically, the term ranked as the most divisive since the current composition of the court was established in 1994. In one-third of the cases, the court ruled 5–4; in the area of civil rights, the "faction-fraction" rose to two-thirds. Not surprisingly, many of the most divisive cases raised salient constitutional questions, and the court's answers to them clarified not only the tenuous status of individual rights but patterns of judicial decision making as well. This was especially true in the fields of civil rights, civil liberties, and criminal law.

The cases of *Alexander* v. *Sandoval, Board of Trustees of the University of Alabama* v. *Garrett,* and *Easley* (formerly *Hunt*) v. *Cromartie* exemplified the dividing line in civil rights jurisprudence. In the first pair of cases, the philosophical split was identical: Justices

William Rehnquist, Antonin Scalia, Anthony Kennedy, Sandra Day O'Connor, and Clarence Thomas formed the conservative majority, with the more liberal Stephen Breyer, Ruth Bader Ginsburg, John Paul Stevens, and David Souter constituting the minority.

Alexander v. *Sandoval* involved a challenge to Alabama's English-only driver's license examinations. Arguing that Title VI of the Civil Rights Act of 1964 and related federal regulations prohibiting discrimination in federally funded programs were never intended to permit or award lawsuits filed by private individuals, Scalia held that there is no private cause of action to enforce such regulations. In the second Alabama-based case, the court ruled that the states are immune from lawsuits claiming discrimination under the Americans with Disabilities Act. Just as the former case limited the application of federal law owing to a narrow interpretation of congressional intent, the latter restricted congressional authority in the area of equal protection, reaffirming a stellar commitment to a state-centred theory of federalism. The notable exception to this trend was established in the case of *PGA Tour, Inc.* v. *Martin.* By a vote of 7–2, the court ruled that Casey Martin, a professional golfer with diminished ambulatory ability, had a legal right under the Disabilities Act to use a golf cart during the Professional Golfers' Association of America (PGA) tour. Despite the PGA's insistence that such a decision would give Martin an unfair advantage, the court ruled that the use of a cart constituted a reasonable accommodation of the petitioner's disability.

In the area where civil rights, civil liberties, and electoral politics converged, the Supreme Court addressed two important cases. In *Easley* v. *Cromartie,* the minority in *Alexander* and *University of Alabama* gained the support of Justice O'Connor, producing the one-vote margin necessary to uphold the configuration of North Carolina's 12th Congressional District. In ruling that the district, which was 47% black, was crafted through a bipartisan effort and not according to racial identity, the level of suspicion historically associated with apparently race-based districts was relaxed enough to facilitate a judicial inclusion of intent and method, rather than simply racial composition. The inclusion of O'Connor in this case indicated a unique flexibility in terms of both the law and the justice's own position. Since her appointment O'Connor had been an opponent of presumably race-based districting, and the cases were decided along those relatively rigid lines. By taking into consideration other variables—the source, method, and motives of redistricting—a new jurisprudential flexibility emerged.

In the related field of campaign finance, the same majority upheld limitations on coordinated campaign expenditures. The court held in *Federal Election Commission* v. *Colorado Republican Federal Campaign Committee* that party expenditures were substantively different from individual expenditures and therefore ineligible for the full First Amendment protection offered to citizens. Also, by rejecting party exemptions, the court avoided setting a standard that could conceivably have facilitated the circumvention of other campaign finance rules and regulations.

Although political parties were limited in the expression of support they may give, the speech and actions of attorneys employed by a government corporation may not be subjected to congressional restrictions. Compatible with its philosophy of limited congressional authority, the court ruled in the consolidated cases of *Legal Services Corporation* v. *Velazquez* and *United States* v. *Velazquez* that a 1996 provision limiting various modes of conduct including, but not limited to, lobbying, class-action litigation, immigrant representation, and welfare reform violated the First Amendment rights of the attorneys and their clients.

In *Good News Club* v. *Milford Central School,* the court revisited the controversial issue of speech rights and religious liberty in public schools. Arguing that the school's attempt to deny Christian groups access to facilities for religious instruction amounted to viewpoint discrimination, the court held that public schools must provide the same after-hours privileges for religious organizations as they do for nonreligious organizations. Because the school itself was not sponsoring or requiring religious instruction, the establishment clause was not violated.

In the area of criminal law, the court decided at least four major Fourth Amendment cases: *Illinois* v. *McArthur, Atwater* v. *City of Lago Vista, Kyllo* v. *United States,* and *Ferguson* v. *City of Charleston.* The *Illinois* and *Atwater* cases were similar in that they involved police conduct relating to the execution of warrants and arrests. In *Illinois* v. *McArthur,* the court ruled that the Fourth Amendment was not violated when police, while awaiting a warrant

David Maxwell/AFP Worldwide

Disabled golfer Casey Martin rides down a fairway at Quail Hollow Country Club in Concord, Ohio, on June 14 following the U.S. Supreme Court's decision that he had a legal right to use a golf cart during PGA competition.

to search property for evidence of a controlled dangerous substance, prohibited a man from entering his home. Because police had probable cause to believe the home contained evidence of a crime, because of the reasonable suspicion that such evidence would be destroyed by the suspect if he was allowed to enter the home, and because there was a minimal intrusion into the man's personal privacy, the warrantless seizure was considered constitutionally permissible.

Atwater v. *City of Lago Vista* involved the related question of warrantless arrests. Writing for the court, Justice Souter argued that the Fourth Amendment does not forbid warrantless arrests for minor criminal offenses. The offense in this case was the failure of an adult driver to secure herself and her children with safety belts while in an automobile. Despite competing claims regarding the applicability of common-law traditions and the presumed severity of the penalty, there simply is no constitutional prohibition of the legal action in question.

Kyllo v. *United States* and *Ferguson* v. *City of Charleston* both involved questions of illegal searches—the former involving a home, the latter involving a person. In *Kyllo* v. *United States*, the court ruled that police use of thermal imaging devices aimed at a private residence constituted an unconstitutional search of private property. According to Justice Scalia, using the device to detect heat and light necessary for growing marijuana amounted to a search under the Fourth Amendment, which would have required a warrant. In the *Ferguson* case, the court was asked to determine whether a hospital's policy of testing for drug use and providing such results to police in order to deter pregnant women from using cocaine violated the generally recognized prohibition of warrantless nonconsensual searches. Striking down the law, Stevens wrote that the policy, which emanated from a program designed at the height of the "crack babies" epidemic and ultimately resulted in the use of medical procedures to alert police to criminal conduct, was unconstitutional.

In *Whitman* v. *American Trucking Associations, Inc.*, which was proclaimed by the *New York Times* to be "the most important regulatory ruling" of the term, the court unanimously defended the Clean Air Act against a legal challenge by the ATA. The legal challenge was two-pronged: to argue that the Environmental Protection Agency's power was derived from an unconstitutional delegation of legislative authority to an administrative agency and that cost-benefit analysis should be part of the calculus for developing environmental standards. The court rejected both claims, finding that public-health matters should constitute the sole determinant of new clean-air standards.

The court's 2001–02 term could well be remembered for the manner in which the institution began its session in October: with the unprecedented necessity of acknowledging the impact of terrorism on American soil in the wake of the September 11 attacks and, for the first time since the completion of the Supreme Court building, holding its session outside the historic structure. The dramatic events relating to war and conflict had an immediate impact on the operation, if not the judgment, of the court—so much so, in fact, that one of the court's first orders of business, upholding the prohibition of former president Bill Clinton's privilege of practicing law before the bench, went largely unnoticed. (BRIAN SMENTKOWSKI)

CRIME

Terrorism. On Sept. 11, 2001, terrorist attacks of unprecedented savagery and destruction were launched against the United States. In a coordinated assault terrorists simultaneously hijacked four commercial airliners flying from Newark, N.J.; Boston, Mass.; and Washington, D.C. Two of the planes were then flown into the twin towers of the World Trade Center (WTC) in New York City, while a third plowed into the country's military nerve centre, the Pentagon, outside Washington, D.C. The fourth aircraft crashed into a field in Pennsylvania, apparently after passengers struggled to overpower the hijackers following news received over their cell phones of what had just occurred in New York. This aircraft was believed to have been targeted to fly into either the White House or the U.S. Capitol building in Washington. (*See* Special Report, pp. 8–13.)

More than 3,000 persons were thought to have perished during the course of these attacks, most having been buried amid the rubble of the WTC towers, which collapsed about one hour after being struck. The death toll made this the deadliest single day of violent action against the U.S. since the American Civil War, exceeding the 2,403 deaths in Japan's attack on Pearl Harbor in 1941. In the wake of the September 11 attacks, Pres. George W. Bush declared the U.S. to be "at war" with international terrorism and readied the nation for military retaliation against the perpetrators of the assault. While no terrorist group made immediate claim to have assisted the 19 hijackers identified by the FBI as having been aboard the doomed flights, a massive criminal investigation garnered compelling evidence that the attacks were the work of al-Qaeda ("the Base"), a network of Islamic terrorist organizations led by Saudi-born Osama bin Laden. (*See* BIOGRAPHIES.) Al-Qaeda, according to extensive testimony given at a number of highly publicized terrorist trials in the U.S. during recent years, was a well-organized and sophisticated body that acted as a facilitator and coordinator of terrorist activities in many countries. Al-Qaeda was known to support at least four elite training camps in Afghanistan for its adherents, where instruction was given in bomb making, sabotage, intelligence gathering, abduction, hijacking, and related terrorist activities. When conducting an operation like the attacks upon two U.S. embassies in East Africa in August 1998, al-Qaeda used teams composed of long-term "sleepers," who had been resident in a country for years, as well as "cleanskins," who had never been involved in an operation before. It was believed that Bin Laden and his aides adopted a similar strategy when planning and executing the September 11 assault from their shadowy base within Afghanistan, where they continued to be given sanctuary by that nation's extremist Islamic regime, the Taliban. Despite the imposition upon Afghanistan of severe international sanctions and armed intervention by the U.S. and its allies, the Taliban refused to meet demands that they cease their support for al-Qaeda and hand over Bin Laden and his associates to face justice.

The level of international support and assistance offered to the U.S. in responding to the events of September 11 was demonstrated by NATO, which declared that the attacks were against the alliance as a whole. On October 7 U.S.-led military strikes commenced against a range of targets within Afghanistan, including suspected terrorist bases. Shortly after the attacks began, a prerecorded message from Bin Laden, speaking from an undisclosed location, was broadcast by the Qatar-based satellite TV network al-Jazeera to millions of television screens around the world. During the broadcast Bin Laden implicitly admitted his involvement in the September 11 assault, called upon Muslims to engage in a holy war against the U.S., and suggested that his actions were in part a response to Israeli reprisals against Palestinians.

Drug Trafficking. As required under U.S. law, President Bush delivered to Congress in March a report certifying which governments of the major drug-producing countries and drug-transit countries had cooperated fully with the U.S., or taken adequate steps on their own, to curb drug use and trafficking. Failure to gain certification made a government ineligible for most forms of U.S. assistance. U.S. drug-enforcement officials claimed that the certification process resulted in certain countries eradicating drug crops, capturing seemingly elusive drug barons, and taking other actions to ensure that they met the deadline set each year to receive a favourable presidential ruling. Two countries, Afghanistan and Myanmar (Burma), were denied certification in 2001. U.S. officials observed that during 2000 the cultivation of the opium poppy in Afghanistan increased by 25% and that the country accounted for about 72% of the global supply. Earlier in the year, however, there had been credible reports of decreased poppy cultivation in Taliban-controlled areas. Large opiate stockpiles remained in the country, and drug trafficking continued unabated from Afghanistan to Europe and other regions of the world.

On April 20 an American missionary, Veronica Bowers, and her seven-month-old daughter were killed when the light aircraft in which they were flying was shot down by a Peruvian air force fighter plane in the mistaken belief that it was engaged in a drug-trafficking operation. The incident prompted an extensive examination by the U.S. Senate Select Committee on Intelligence of a six-year-old agreement between the U.S. and Peru under which U.S. assistance was provided in tracking drug smugglers. At the time of the shooting down of the missionaries' aircraft, it was under the surveillance of a U.S. tracking plane flown under CIA contract. As a result of the mistaken attack, the U.S. suspended all of its drug-surveillance flights in Central and South America while officials reassessed the rules and procedures they followed.

Murder and Other Violence. Preliminary figures released in May from the FBI's nationwide Uniform Crime Reporting Program indicated that in 2000 the Crime Index, comprising murder, forcible rape, robbery, aggravated assault, burglary, larceny, theft, and motor-vehicle theft, remained relatively unchanged from 1999. This was the first time in eight years that a decline had not been reported in the number of serious crimes in the U.S. Experts and law-enforcement officials had long cautioned that the crime rate could not drop indefinitely, and this FBI report tended to confirm that the trend had run its course. In the past a large increase or decrease in homicide, or in crime in the biggest cities, had tended to predict significant fluctuations in general rates of serious crime. No indicators of this type were contained in the 2000 figures.

On March 5, in a tragic repeat of school shootings in the past several years that had traumatized rural and suburban communities in the U.S., a 15-year-old high-school freshman, Charles Andrew Williams, killed two fellow students and wounded 13 others at Santana High School in Santee, a suburb of San Diego, Calif. The shooting was the worst episode of school violence since the mass slayings in April 1999 at Columbine High School in Littleton, Colo.

On June 8, in an incident that shocked the entire nation of Japan, a knife-wielding man burst into an elementary school in Ikeda and stabbed to death eight children—seven second-grade girls and one first-grade boy—and also seriously wounded six more students and a teacher. Police arrested Mamoru Takuma, a 37-year-old who had a history of mental illness.

War Crimes. Slobodan Milosevic, the past president of Yugoslavia, became the first former head of state to sit in a defendant's dock facing charges of war crimes and crimes against humanity. On July 3 Milosevic made his initial appearance before the International Criminal Tribunal for the Former Yugoslavia in The Hague following his dramatic nighttime transfer from a Belgrade prison on June 28. Milosevic, who had been placed under arrest by the Yugoslav government on April 1 on unrelated corruption charges, remained defiant before the international tribunal and challenged its legitimacy to place him on trial. Experts predicted that the proceedings against Milosevic could last for years and that his testimony could embarrass a number of Western leaders who had negotiated and dealt with him for much of his period in office. By surrendering Milosevic to the international tribunal, the Yugoslav government received immediate pledges of substantial aid from the U.S. and other nations to assist in rebuilding its shattered economy.

White-Collar Crime, Corruption, and Fraud. "A worldwide corruption crisis" was identified by Transparency International (TI), a Berlin-based nongovernmental organization established to expose and prevent corruption. Releasing its annual Corruption Perceptions Index in June, TI ranked 91 countries on a 10-point scale. A high score, indicating very low levels of perceived corruption, was obtained by some of the world's richest nations—Finland, Denmark, New Zealand, Iceland, Singapore, and Sweden. In contrast, low scores were recorded by some of the world's poorest countries, with Azerbaijan, Bolivia, Cameroon, Kenya, Indonesia, Uganda, Nigeria, and Bangladesh ranked at the bottom of the list. TI's chairman said that the index illustrated once more "the vicious circle of poverty and corruption" as vast amounts of public funds were squandered and stolen by corrupt governments and their officials.

In the Philippines in January, a wave of public anger against corruption forced Pres. Joseph Estrada from office in a bloodless coup. In April Estrada became the first Philippine president to be jailed on suspicion of corruption. Prosecutors alleged that he had pocketed more than $76 million in tax money and illegal gambling receipts during his two and a half years in office. If convicted of plunder, the most serious charge against him, Estrada faced the possibility of a death sentence or life imprisonment.

Law Enforcement. The FBI came under sustained scrutiny during the year as a result of a number of well-publicized incidents that suggested that failures had occurred in its management and information network. The most damaging and embarrassing revelation came in February when it was announced that a veteran FBI counterintelligence agent, Robert Philip Hanssen, had been arrested and charged with committing espionage by providing highly classified national security information to Russia and the former Soviet Union. At the time of his arrest at a park in Vienna, Va., Hanssen was clandestinely placing a garbage bag containing secret information at a prearranged "dead drop" for pickup by his Russian handlers. Hanssen had previously received large sums of money from the Russians for the information he disclosed to them. In July Hanssen pleaded guilty to 15 counts of having spied for Moscow since 1979. As part of a plea deal, Hanssen was given a sentence of life imprisonment rather than death after he agreed to participate in extensive debriefing with government agents and cooperated truthfully and fully with them. Prosecutors said that Hanssen betrayed nine double agents, including two who were later executed. He also provided Moscow with details of several top-secret communication programs, U.S. nuclear war preparations, and a listening tunnel underneath the Soviet embassy in Washington, D.C. A few weeks before this plea bargain, U.S. Attorney General John Ashcroft stated that a review would be conducted of the FBI's security program to try to ensure that the lapses that allowed Hanssen to operate as a spy would not happen again.

(DUNCAN CHAPPELL)

PRISONS AND PENOLOGY

In 2001 the prison population throughout the world continued to exceed the eight-million mark. Accounting for a quarter of this total, the U.S. held more of its inhabitants in prison (702 per 100,000 inhabitants) than any other country. Elsewhere, prison population rates declined in Russia and South Africa to 465 and 385, respectively, while the rate for China remained stable at 112. In Europe the prison population rate for England and Wales rose to 128, which made it the highest of any country in the European Union; Portugal's rate remained at 127, while Finland (52), Northern Ireland (60), and Denmark (61) had the lowest rates.

Various countries announced measures intended to reduce prison numbers. The ruler of Bahrain announced an amnesty for some 400 political prisoners jailed for crimes during the 1990s. Malawi Pres. Bakili Muluzi released 880 prisoners to celebrate nationhood, and 40,000 prisoners were released in Kazakhstan to honour the 10th anniversary of the nation's independence. In Kyrgyzstan an amnesty involving at least 5,000 prisoners was agreed upon. The Russian State Duma approved legislation intended to reduce the prison population by 300,000 through the wider use of bail and settlement colonies.

Violence, death, and disease continued to surface in prisons around the globe. The most serious disturbances in Brazil's penal history occurred in the state of São Paulo's prison system, with prisoners at 29 institutions across the state taking some 8,000 prisoners, prison guards, and visitors hostage as part of a protest against the removal of gang leaders from one of the prisons. Twenty prisoners were reported killed as paramilitary police secured the release of the hostages and regained control of the prisons. In Chile 26 inmates serving sentences in the Iquique penitentiary were killed in a fire caused by an electrical fault. (*See* DISASTERS.) In Mexico a prison governor was shot dead, apparently as a reprisal for a security clampdown recently ordered at his prison. Serious overcrowding and health problems continued to blight many prisons across Africa. In Morocco it was reported that prison regimes were immersed in corruption, violence, and the sexual abuse of children. In Malawi overcrowding and lack of proper sanitation facilities reportedly led to a dramatic rise in the spread of infectious diseases, including scabies and tuberculosis. Eighty-three prisoners died of suffocation, hunger, and thirst in November 2000 in a Mozambique prison where 120 prisoners were held in a cell measuring 21 sq m (226 sq ft). In South Africa poor hygiene and water facilities were cited as the cause of a cholera outbreak that infected 600 prisoners. Problems caused by overcrowding and poor conditions were also experienced in various European countries. In Russia, where some 100,000 prisoners were suffering from tuberculosis, the World Bank announced a $50 million credit to combat the disease and to assist HIV-positive prisoners. In Turkey some 250 prisoners joined a hunger strike (resulting in more than 30 deaths of prisoners and their supporters) to protest the transfer of inmates to new prisons where, it was claimed, conditions breached international standards.

AP/Wide World Photos

Timothy McVeigh, convicted of the bombing of the federal building in Oklahoma City in 1995, was executed by lethal injection on June 11 at the U.S. Penitentiary in Terre Haute, Ind.

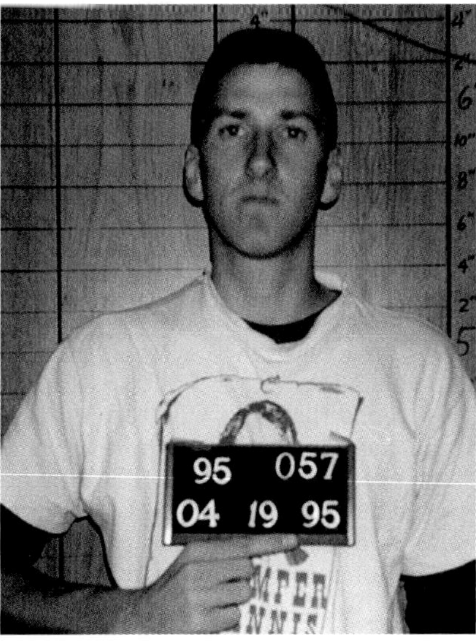

DEATH PENALTY

A gradual movement toward abolition of capital punishment continued in 2001. Chile, where the last execution took place in 1985, enacted legislation to abolish the death penalty for peacetime offenses. The Lebanese parliament repealed legislation that had sought to expand the scope of the death penalty by abolishing judicial discretion to consider mitigating factors. In Russia, despite renewed calls for the death penalty from many quarters, Pres. Vladimir Putin stated that he favoured abolition and urged upholding a five-year-old moratorium on the practice. Elsewhere, judicial decisions sought to reduce the scope of the death penalty. In a number of eastern Caribbean countries, including Antigua and Barbuda, Dominica, and Grenada, mandatory death sentences were declared unconstitutional.

Against this global trend, executions took place for the first time in 17 years in Guinea, 6 years in Indonesia, and 3 years in Bangladesh. The Council of Europe found the treatment of prisoners awaiting execution in Japan to be "inhumane" and drew particular attention to the practice of the condemned persons' being given only one hour's notice of their impending deaths. Japan had, however, refused to abandon executions on the grounds that 80% of its population found the practice to be useful. In April the Chinese government embarked upon a "Strike Hard" anticrime campaign during which hundreds of prisoners were paraded at public rallies prior to their executions. A Western diplomat recorded 801 deaths in China in the final three weeks of April, while Amnesty International reported that 89 people had been executed during a single day. In the U.S. 66 prisoners were put to death during the year—a sharp reduction from the 85 executions that took place in 2000. Those put to death included Timothy McVeigh (*see* OBITUARIES), who had been convicted of having placed a bomb in the federal building in Oklahoma City, Okla., that killed 168 people; he was the first federal prisoner executed in the U.S. in 38 years.

(ANDREW RUTHERFORD)

Libraries and Museums

Egypt's Bibliotheca **ALEXANDRINA** and the **JEWISH** Museum Berlin were among the new libraries and museums completed in 2001; many other facilities faced **LEGAL** challenges, natural **DISASTERS**, and abrupt changes in **DIRECTORSHIP**.

LIBRARIES

Though in recent years the most newsworthy events pertaining to libraries worldwide had involved war damage, fires, floods, earthquakes, and other tragedies, there were fewer such disasters in 2001 and proportionally more instances that demonstrated the synergies between networked computing and the traditional library functions of organizing knowledge and making it accessible.

Images and information on 20,000 magnificent pre-Columbian textiles created by the Incas and other indigenous cultures were mounted on the Internet—<http://textiles.perucultural.org.pe>—by the National Museum of Archaeology, Anthropology and History, Lima, Peru, with financial support from Fundación Telefónica. In Cambridge, Mass., Genomics Collaborative, Inc. (GCI), began building the world's largest library of genetic material—human tissue and blood. Samples were being collected from around the country, classified, and stored. GCI believed that the collection would be invaluable in developing new drugs to treat cancer, diabetes, and many other diseases. The government of South Australia established the Digital Library of Indigenous Australia to collect and disseminate information about Aboriginal Australians: <http://www.dosaa.sa.gov.au>.

A host of new and unique libraries opened. In France a government-financed automotive research centre began building a compact-disc library of automobile noises that would be available to engineers in pursuit of sweet sounds, including the desirable resonance made by the solid sound of a door closing on a BMW 7-Series sedan. In October the Bibliotheca Alexandrina was completed. (*See* Sidebar.)

New public libraries offered hope to residents of war-torn or impoverished areas. The first large-scale public library opened in Beirut, Lebanon. In Rwanda the design for the country's first-ever public library, in Kigali, was finalized. It was hoped that the library, scheduled to open in 2002, would help raise the country's literacy rate, which at 47% was one of the lowest in the world. The Jaffna Public Library in Sri Lanka, which had been the repository of the history and culture of the island's minority Tamil people, was in the process of rebuilding, 20 years after it had been incinerated by Sinhalese police officers.

In the U.S., technology brought not only new services and capabilities but also conflict and legislation that threatened to alter basic tenets of the library ethos. In 2001 a federal law took effect that mandated the installation of Internet-filtering software in all libraries that received federal funding. Suits filed by the American Library Association (ALA) and the American Civil Liberties Union challenged the law's constitutionality. ALA president Nancy Kranich maintained that "blocking technologies come between librarians and their mission—to connect people with a broad range of information." The ALA position of resisting any action that might keep information from anyone drew fierce censure from socially conservative critics, including radio host Laura Schlessinger and *The Wall Street Journal.* On the other hand, a librarian at the Chicago Public Library sued her employer on the grounds that the pornography viewed by library users created a hostile workplace for library workers.

American libraries also found their missions endangered by other legislative initiatives and legal challenges that surrounded information technology. Provisions of the federal Digital Millennium Copyright Act (DMCA), passed in 1998, markedly restricted the "fair use" policies of former copyright laws, on which libraries and educators had long relied to permit the copying of documents for educational purposes. In 2001, however, some relief was in the offing, as an amendment to the DMCA was under consideration.

Not all library travails, however, arose from technology. Novelist Nicholson Baker's *Double Fold* offered a scathing indictment of library preservation policies, particularly in regard to the practice of discarding newspapers after they were microfilmed. Baker was well remembered by librarians for his similarly vituperative attack in the April 1994 issue of *The New Yorker,* in which he scorned libraries' abandonment of the venerable card catalog in favour of automated versions. Though libraries traditionally landed "below the radar" of august publications, critically acclaimed authors, and outspoken radio talk-show hosts, their importance in contemporary society might be gauged by the quality of their critics. Conversely, it might also be measured by the behaviour of ordinary citizens. In 2001 the Australian Bureau of Statistics reported that more Australians visited libraries than went to the movies.

Shelving was torqued in academic, public, and special libraries, and hundreds of thousands of volumes were launched onto the floor when an earthquake hit western Washington. One public library in the region suffered structural damage from the magnitude-6.8 temblor that struck in February. A month earlier a 7.6–7.9 quake shattered libraries in El Salvador. The Biblioteca Gallardo, a private 80,000-volume library that housed rare manuscripts, art works, and other materials dating back to the 16th century, was virtually destroyed. The country's national library, which never fully recovered from a 1986 quake, was also further damaged. Plans for a June renovation financed by Spain were postponed while the new damage was assessed.

Floods ravaged libraries in West Virginia, where some eight libraries sustained varying degrees of damage in one of the worst disasters to hit the state in decades. In Houston, Texas, Tropical Storm Allison dumped nearly 0.9 m (3 ft) of rain in July, causing billions of dollars of damage. Numerous

Bibliotheca Alexandrina

In a sense, all libraries serve a totemic function. They symbolize man's efforts to preserve knowledge, culture, and wisdom and transmit it to future generations. Large national libraries and university libraries are especially powerful symbols.

No other library, however, has the totemic power of the lost ancient Library of Alexandria, Egypt. Though little is known with certainty about this wonder of the classical world, it has come to be viewed as a kind of scholarly Camelot. Sometime in the 3rd century BC, the library's founder, probably Ptolemy I Soter, began to collect all the written information from throughout the known world. In time, the library held 500,000—or as many as 700,000—papyrus documents, mainly in Greek, including the works of Plato, Socrates, Thucydides, Euclid, Hippocrates, and Sophocles. The library at Alexandria was the world's first think tank, providing a home for many of the greatest minds of the time. Euclid completed his seminal *Elements* there; Eratosthenes accurately calculated the circumference of the Earth.

The circumstances of the library's destruction are still a mystery. Scholarly guesses on the date of its loss range from 48 BC to AD 600. Despite—or because of—the many unknowns, fascination with the institution has persisted for nearly two millennia.

In Alexandria, Egypt, construction was completed during the year on the Bibliotheca Alexandrina, which opened its doors to the public in October.

Snohetta/Hamza Consortium courtesy of the Bibliotheca Alexandrina

In 2001 construction was completed on a new Library of Alexandria, officially known as the Bibliotheca Alexandrina. Scholars around the world are transfixed by the dramatic architecture and the hope that the $200 million structure will recapture the glory of the original. The design has drawn worldwide praise. Essentially, it is a massive cylinder, emerging from the ground at a shallow angle only about 40 m (130 ft) from the sea. The disk-shaped roof suggests the sun rising over the Mediterranean, and the roof pattern of aluminum and glass panels resembles a microchip. One outer wall of the structure is made up of some 6,400 granite panels bearing characters from all the known alphabets. The symbolism of these elements seems ideal.

The Bibliotheca will ultimately house four million volumes on seven cascading levels. The collection will be shelved with the oldest materials on the lowest level, forming a metaphoric foundation for later works. In addition, the library will house a planetarium, a school of library and information science, facilities for the digital preservation of rare books and manuscripts, and a conference centre. The new library will be the most modern facility in the region and will surely become a key node in the expanding Internet.

Despite the allure of the library's revival, critics point to difficulties that may compromise the institution's success. The greatest concern is inadequate funding for maintenance and collections. An architect from the Norwegian firm that designed the library has questioned the lack of funding for upkeep of the spectacular structure. The library will open with a collection of some 400,000 books, many donated but some inappropriate to the library's interests. Moreover, during 2001 the Egyptian government banned some publications that Islamic fundamentalists found objectionable. It remains to be seen if potential difficulties such as these will undermine either the reality or the symbolism of the library. The official inauguration of the Bibliotheca Alexandrina is set for April 23, 2002.

(THOMAS M. GAUGHAN)

branch libraries of the Houston Public Library and the libraries of Houston Academy of Medicine–Texas Medical Center and the Houston Symphony all suffered extensive damage to collections, furnishings, and equipment.

(THOMAS M. GAUGHAN)

MUSEUMS

Following the Sept. 11, 2001, terrorist attacks in the United States, the role of museums as custodians and guardians of cultural heritage was underscored worldwide. In an effort to safeguard the value of their collections, a number of museums sought to upgrade their insurance policies and implement damage-control measures.

Earlier in the year the International Council of Museums, along with the Canadian Museum Association and the United Nations Security Council, publicly condemned the Taliban's destruction in Bamian, Afg., of two several-centuries-old giant Buddha statues that had been carved into a cliff. The Taliban claimed that these priceless treasures were idolatrous symbols.

A number of new museums as well as additions to existing structures appeared during the year. In Germany the Jewish Museum Berlin, designed by Polish-born American architect Daniel Libeskind, opened its doors on September 9. The $60 million zinc-clad structure, meant to symbolize a deconstructed Star of David, was the first Jewish museum in the city in 60 years; the Nazis had destroyed the previous museum in 1938. The centrepiece of the new museum—which chronicled Jewish history from Roman times—was the Holocaust Tower, where visitors found themselves enclosed in a dimly lit concrete chamber after a door slammed closed behind them.

When the new National Museum of Australia (NMA) debuted in March in Canberra following 20 years of planning, it opened to mixed reviews. Though some praised architect Howard Raggatt's design as a "masterpiece," others deemed the design plagiarized from the Jewish Museum Berlin, which, though it opened in September, had been completed two years earlier. Aerial photographs comparing the two museums had disclosed a disturbingly similar zigzag shape. The director of the NMA, Dawn Casey, maintained that the design was "brilliant," and she downplayed the similarity of the roof designs. The NMA was the first museum devoted exclusively to the country's social history and would house five permanent exhibitions—Nation, Horizons, Eternity,

Tangled Destinies, and the First Australians Gallery. For its opening the NMA featured the temporary blockbuster exhibit "Gold and Civilisation."

On February 15, Singapore opened a new war museum, which chronicled the experiences of the people held at the Changi prison camp in that city during the Japanese World War II occupation. The museum courtyard featured a replica of a chapel built by prisoners of war. After 10 years of planning, Ronald S. Lauder, chairman of Estée Lauder International, opened the Neue Galerie in New York City in November. The museum was devoted exclusively to German and Austrian fine and decorative arts.

In Johannesburg, S.Af., the Apartheid Museum opened in November. The privately financed museum was the first of several planned exhibits to examine the history of apartheid. Upon entering the new museum all visitors were arbitrarily assigned a racial classification ("white" or "nonwhite") and then directed down separate hallways with appropriate "white" and "nonwhite" displays before being allowed to mingle in the final rooms.

Beginning on January 1 the M.H. de Young Memorial Museum in San Francisco's Golden Gate Park, which featured collections of American, African, and Oceanic art, among other objets d'art, shuttered its doors. A new museum—expected to open on the site in the spring of 2005—would showcase the design of Swiss architects Jacques Herzog and Pierre de Meuron. (*See* BIOGRAPHIES.)

A few institutions made significant additions to their structures, notably the British Museum in London, where architect Sir Norman Foster redesigned the central courtyard, which opened in December 2000. In May 2001 the museum unveiled a priceless 17th-century Indian jewel collection that had been looted by Iraq from Kuwait during the Persian Gulf War but later returned. The collection—many of the pieces had never before been seen in the West—was on loan from the Kuwaiti government. Kuwait was rebuilding its museum, which Iraq had burned to the ground during the war. In Wisconsin the Milwaukee Art Museum on October 11 unveiled its gigantic $75 million movable sunshade, designed by Spanish architect Santiago Calatrava. (*See* ARCHITECTURE.)

A number of museums saw changes in directorship. The Victoria and Albert (V&A) Museum, London, announced in February that Mark Jones would succeed Alan Borg. Jones had spent 15 years at the British Museum before becoming founding director of the new National Museum in Edinburgh. On May 2, the day after starting his new job, Jones announced that the V&A would take the lead in abolishing all entrance fees, beginning in November. The Natural History Museum and the Imperial War Museum would be the only top London museums to continue to charge admission.

Following the announcement of Smithsonian Institution secretary Lawrence M. Small's "new strategic direction for science," Robert Fri, director of the National Museum of Natural History, Washington, D.C., tendered his resignation. Fri cited his lack of enthusiasm for the new personnel structure, which would have left control of the scientists to J. Dennis O'Connor, the undersecretary for science. Small had also raised the ire of Smithsonian officials, curators there and at other museums, and Washington lawmakers when he announced the closure of the Smithsonian's wildlife conservation centre in Virginia; he later retracted that decision. Spencer Crew, the director of the Smithsonian Institution's National Museum of American History, Washington, D.C., also departed.

In Venezuela, Pres. Hugo Chávez Frías purged the leadership at 36 government cultural institutions in his effort to rid the country of a "rancid oligarchy." Art critic Sofía Imber, the founding director in 1971 of the Caracas Museum of Contemporary Art (which was later given her name), was one of the most prominent figures to have been removed.

In a surprise move David A. Ross, director of the San Francisco Museum of Modern Art, announced his resignation after three years. During his tenure he had boosted membership from 24,000 to 44,000 and had spent $140 million to enhance the museum's collection. Henri Loyrette, head of the Orsay Museum in Paris, was named the new director of the Louvre. (*See* BIOGRAPHIES.)

The Internet continued to play a major role in museums. The Solomon R. Guggenheim Foundation launched Guggenheim.com, a premium arts centre site, and the U.S. federal government awarded $1.4 million to 6 of 32 applicants—the Exploratorium in San Francisco; the Illinois State Museum Society; the Lowell Observatory, Flagstaff, Ariz.; the North Carolina Zoological Society, Asheboro; the Skyscraper Museum, New York City; and the Wildlife Conservation Society/Bronx Zoo, New York City—in the second year of its Museums Online grant program. (KAREN J. SPARKS)

Visitors at the National Museum of Emerging Science and Innovation in Tokyo walk past a new exhibit called GEO-COSMOS, a huge sphere equipped with 951,040 light-emitting diodes that can display, for instance, real-time weather conditions and carbon monoxide density around the world.

Toru Yamanaka/AFP Worldwide

Life Sciences

Scientists in 2001 announced the **COMPLETE SEQUENCING** of the **RICE GENOME** and reported **INSIGHTS** into the genetics of congenital **HEARING AND VISION** impairments. The value of a primary **CONSERVATION** strategy was challenged by results of a study of a **PANDA** reserve in China. A new look at filamentous structures in **DINOSAUR** fossils fueled debate over the origin of bird **FEATHERS**.

ZOOLOGY

Zoological researchers in 2001 continued to assess the effectiveness of the protection mechanisms that animals use against predators. Such knowledge was fundamental to the understanding of certain aspects of population dynamics—the ways in which the size and composition of a population change over time and the factors that influence those changes. A basic principle of Batesian mimicry is that an edible prey species, the mimic, is afforded some level of protection from predators when it closely resembles a venomous or distasteful species, the model. By definition such protection should be less effective or absent in regions where the mimic, but not the model, is present. David W. Pfennig and William R. Harcombe of the University of North Carolina at Chapel Hill and Karin S. Pfennig of the University of Texas at Austin conducted field experiments to test whether the close likeness between nonvenomous king snakes and venomous coral snakes should be regarded as a case of Batesian mimicry.

The investigators used three-coloured snake-shaped replicas made of plasticine (a nontoxic modeling substance) that duplicated the conspicuous red, black, and yellow-to-white ringed pattern of either scarlet king snakes (*Lampropeltis triangulum elapsoides*) or Sonoran mountain king snakes (*L. pyromelana*). The patterns of these nonvenomous snakes are similar to the ringed patterns of the eastern coral snake (*Micrurus fulvius*) and western, or Arizona, coral snake (*Micruroides euryxanthus*), respectively. Regional predators avoid the venomous coral snakes, which are presumed to be the models that the king snakes mimic. The investigators placed their king snake replicas at a series of eastern sites in North Carolina and South Carolina and at western sites in Arizona in tests to determine whether predators would avoid them. Two other kinds of snake replicas, one plain brown and one with conspicuous longitudinal stripes, were placed within 2 m (6.6 ft) of the ringed replicas as controls. Tests were conducted using 480 replicas at 16 eastern sites where scarlet king snakes occurred—at 8 sites where they occupied the same range as coral snakes and at 8 sites where they were outside the coral snake's range. In Arizona 720 replicas were used at 14 sites where king snakes and coral snakes occurred together and at 10 sites where only king snakes occurred. The replicas were removed from the eastern sites after four weeks and from the western sites after two weeks.

Studies of bite and gouge marks left in the replicas revealed that predators had attacked the king snake replicas significantly more often at sites outside the coral snakes' ranges than at sites where king snakes and coral snakes coexisted. Furthermore, outside the coral snakes' ranges, the three types of replicas were attacked indiscriminately, whereas in the coral snakes' ranges, king snake replicas were attacked significantly less often than the others. The results supported the premise of Batesian mimicry that the benefit of being a mimic depends on the model's being present in the same area.

A universal challenge in investigations of the demography and population dynamics of animals has been to deter-

Field experiments reported during the year used replicas of venomous coral snakes and nonvenomous king snakes to study Batesian mimicry. A coral snake (left) and a king snake (right) are shown below.

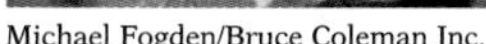

Michael Fogden/Bruce Coleman Inc.

mine how different factors influence the sometimes large fluctuations in population size that are observed in some species over time. Distinctive regulators of population size include those that depend on population density (the population size in a given area) and those, resulting from environmental effects, that are independent of density. To determine the relative influence of various factors on population dynamics, Tim Coulson of the Zoological Society of London and colleagues studied the effects of age, sex, density, and winter weather over more than a decade on fluctuations in the population of Soay sheep (*Ovis aries*) on the island of Hirta, northwest of Scotland. One objective was to quantify how interactions between different variables affected the population fluctuations. Since the 1950s the Soay sheep population has varied in size from fewer than 600 individuals to more than 2,000, with the proportion of various sex and age categories (e.g., numbers of male and female lambs, prime adults, and old adults) varying independently of population density.

The severity of winter weather can differentially affect survivorship in the various age and sex categories; through such interaction with the population demography, it can increase or decrease the total size of the population. For example, during periods of high population density, lambs and old females were observed to fare worse at survival than female yearlings and prime adults. On the other hand, in response to winter weather, survival rates for lambs and males were negatively affected by bad weather throughout the winter, whereas those for yearlings and prime adult females were negatively affected primarily by heavier rainfall at the end of winter. Thus, the dynamics of a population of large mammals can take dramatically different courses depending on differences in the age structure and sex-ratio pattern of the population and in the weather conditions that it experiences. The investigators concluded that management and conservation models that rely on predictions of population size must incorporate the effects of demographic variations and their interaction with climate.

Although all species respond to natural threats to individuals through either evolution or extinction, the current decline in biodiversity observed in terrestrial, freshwater, and marine habitats as a consequence of human activities was causing alarm on a global scale. Understanding the natural processes that regulate species diversity and abundance was seen as an important step toward developing conservation and management approaches that address the human-based causes of species loss. David R. Bellwood and Terry P. Hughes of James Cook University, Townsville, Australia, studied the distribution patterns of species of fish and corals in Indo-Pacific waters to determine what factors influence the variation in species composition in coral reefs, which are highly diverse habitats. Of four major variables that were examined because of their potential to explain such variation, the available area of shallow-water habitat was found to be the most influential. Two other variables, latitude and longitude, were of minor significance in explaining the species diversity of fish and corals. The fourth variable, reef type, was found to be of little importance. The investigators concluded that suitable habitat had to be protected on a regional scale if the diversity of coral reef assemblages was to remain intact in the Indo-Australian archipelago—a principle that presumably would be applicable globally.

Setting aside protected areas for wildlife is traditionally accepted as a primary conservation strategy to guard against the detrimental effects of human activity. Jianguo Liu of Michigan State University and colleagues, however, challenged the effectiveness of the approach at the Wolong Nature Reserve for giant pandas (*Ailuropoda melanoleuca*) in Sichuan province, China. The investigators used Landsat and declassified spy-satellite data collected before and after establishment (1975) of the 200,000-ha (500,000-ac) reserve to assess the rates of change in giant panda habitat. In addition to forest cover, the slope of the terrain and elevation are also important habitat variables that affect pandas. Two key observations were made in the analysis of habitat changes from 1965 to 1997. First, panda habitat within the reserve continued to decrease in quality and quantity and became even more fragmented after 1975. Second, the habitat areas most severely affected were those deemed to be of high quality for pandas. The direct cause of the ecological degradation was attributed to the presence and rapid increase in numbers of humans living within the reserve, most of whom were minority ethnic groups that were exempt from China's one-child-per-family policy. A variety of socioeconomic activities, including tourism, collection of wood for fuel, and road construction all contributed to habitat loss. One conclusion of the study was that the development of effective conservation policies for protected lands required the integration of ecological principles with human demography, behaviour, and socioeconomics.

Further insights into the ancestry of humans were provided during the year through the use of molecular techniques. Li Jin of Fudan University, Shanghai, and the University of Texas at Houston and colleagues sampled genetic material from 163 populations of living humans in 13 geographic regions in Asia, ranging from India to Siberia, to test competing hypotheses of the origin of modern humans. The so-called out-of-Africa hypothesis maintained that the ancestors of present-day humans originated in Africa approximately 100,000 years ago and totally replaced all other hominids, such as Neanderthals (an early form of *Homo sapiens*), during their dispersal to other regions. The alternative view was that some genetic mixing occurred between dispersing Africans and other hominids, such as Peking man and Java man (*H. erectus*), in Asia. The investigators tested for genetic markers on the Y chromosome of more than 12,000 human males to determine if all carried one of three chromosome polymorphisms (distinct genetic variations) characteristic of an African origin. Without exception, all of the individuals sampled had genetic markers of African derivation; this supported the hypothesis that hominids dispersing onto the Asian continent from Africa displaced all other hominids already present. (*See also* ANTHROPOLOGY AND ARCHAEOLOGY: *Physical Anthropology.*)

(J. WHITFIELD GIBBONS)

BOTANY

Among milestones in plant science that became widely acknowledged in 2001 was the mapping of the genomes of two plants. The entire DNA blueprint of thale cress (*Arabidopsis thaliana*), a weed related to cabbage and mustard and long a favourite laboratory organism in plant research, was published at the end of 2000. The sequencing of its more than 115 million pairs of chemical bases, the molecular building blocks of DNA and the basis of the genetic code, was the culmination of a six-year, $70 million project involving 300 scientists worldwide. The achievement, the first for a plant genome, promised new types of genetically modified crop plants and a better understanding of the process of evolution.

Early in 2001 scientists announced completion of the sequence of the larger genome of the rice plant (*Oryza sativa*), which comprises 430 million base pairs representing some 50,000 genes. It was anticipated that, as the functions of many of these genes were worked out, the information could lead to significant improvements in the major cereal crops, which are all closely related to rice. Unraveling of the rice genome by the Swiss agribusiness firm Syngenta International AG and the American firm Myriad Genetics, Inc., beat the efforts of a publicly funded international team to map the same genome. The two companies indicated that they would make the rice genome data publicly available through collaboration agreements.

Research into the evolution of plants also made great progress during the year. The Deep Green project, which had been established to investigate the ancestry of green land plants, was completed after five years' work involving more than 200 scientists worldwide. Data were integrated from morphology, biochemistry, and fossil sources to construct the most complete "tree of life" for any group of living things on Earth. Results indicated that green algae and land plants form the plant kingdom, clearly separated from other algae such as red algae, brown algae, diatoms, and dinoflagellates. It was also revealed that the first plants to grow on land were members of a class of freshwater green algae called Charophyceae; this overturned the idea that seawater algae spearheaded the land-plant invasion. Another surprise from the project was that the Charophyceae are the ancestors of all green land plants now alive. Although some other plant groups established themselves on land, they later died out for reasons not yet understood. In the animal kingdom, by contrast, many different groups made the jump from water to land successfully.

Another mystery of plant evolution came one step closer to being understood—the sudden appearance of flowering plants around 130 million years ago. Biologists at the University of California, San Diego, led by Martin Yanofsky, converted leaves of *Arabidopsis* plants into petals by activating five different genes involved in the formation of flower organs lying dormant in leaves. This achievement indicated that flowers evolved from modified leaves. It also could lead to the development of interesting genetically modified plants, such as ornamental flowering varieties that have colourful petals growing along their stems.

*An intriguing study of the flower movements of the Arctic gentian (*Gentiana algida*) appeared in 2001.*

One of the most significant genetic-engineering breakthroughs of the year was the creation of a tomato plant that thrives in salty water, even seawater. A gene for salt tolerance, discovered in *Arabidopsis* in the late 1990s by plant biologists at the University of California, Davis, and the University of Toronto, was introduced into tomato plants. The gene protects the plants from salt damage by coding for a protein that pumps salt into sealed compartments inside leaf cells; the tomato fruit produced was claimed to have no salty taste. Salty water blights 40% of the world's irrigated land, and engineering salt tolerance into crops could exploit huge tracts of this poisoned land. In addition, the modified tomato plants soaked up so much salt that they could be used to help clean up salty water supplies. Field trials were needed to make sure that the gene would not cross to other plants to create salt-tolerant weeds.

The possibility of unintentional transfer of genes from genetically modified crops was spotlighted in November when researchers from the University of California, Berkeley, reported detection of transgenic DNA in native maize (corn) from remote regions of Mexico, despite a ban in that country on planting genetically modified maize since 1998. Native maize and other ancestors of crop plants were considered a vital genetic resource for crop-breeding programs, and their contamination with foreign genes could threaten global food security.

Many plant roots form partnerships with fungi that live in the soil. Typically the fungi supply phosphorus from the soil to the plant in exchange for carbohydrates and other nutrients. John Klironomos and Miranda Hart of the University of Guelph, Ont., revealed that the roots of the eastern white pine (*Pinus strobus*) support a carnivorous fungus that kills and devours small insects in the soil. Radioactively labeled nitrogen was used to track nutrients as they were absorbed from the animal bodies into the fungus, which then passed them into the tree. Klironomos speculated that, because similar root fungi are nearly ubiquitous among trees, the relationship could be very common and that scientists might have to rethink their ideas about how woodland ecosystems work.

In a rare example of research on flower movements, Michael Bynum of the University of Wyoming and William Smith of Wake Forest University, Winston-Salem, N.C., made a fascinating study of the flowers of the Arctic gentian (*Gentiana algida*) at several field sites in Wyoming. The plant blooms in August, the peak month for thunderstorms in the region. As rain approaches, the flower pinches its petal tube shut and reopens after the rain has passed. The investigators determined that these movements protect the pollen and nectar from being ruined by rain, which in turn helps both pollination and seed set. The movements are a response to the drop in air temperature that often precedes a storm.

The importance of biodiversity was highlighted by scientists at the Imperial College of Science, Technology and Medicine, London, and the École Normale Supérieure, Paris. They found that communities of plants are more productive when they consist of "teams" of different species that specialize in roles that are complementary to one another. It may mean that some plants, and therefore their entire ecosystems, grow more poorly when team members become extinct. This finding gave support to conservationists campaigning to preserve natural environments in their totality.

Scientists were heartened when a tree species, *Trochetia parviflora*, thought to have gone extinct in 1863 on the island of Mauritius, was rediscovered. Vincent Florens and Jean-Claude Svathian of the Mauritius Herbarium recognized the tree from old herbarium specimens. The scientists collected cuttings and seeds to try to propagate the species in hopes of boosting the remaining wild population. (PAUL SIMONS)

MOLECULAR BIOLOGY

A Bucket Brigade for Copper. Soluble copper—copper in its +2 oxidation state [written Cu(II)]—is an effective and nonspecific catalyst of oxidation. As such, it can facilitate the oxidation of many biologically essential molecules such as ascorbic acid, glutathione, and polyunsaturated lipids and thereby prevent them from participating in vital reactions. For this reason, free Cu(II) cannot be tolerated by living cells and is considered a poison. Nevertheless, Cu(II) is found at the active sites of several enzymes and is essential for their catalytic functions. One such enzyme present in cells is superoxide dismutase, a protein that contains both Cu(II) and zinc at its active site. The enzyme catalyzes the elimination of the dangerously reactive superoxide radical produced as a by-product of respiration and thus serves as a defense against oxygen toxicity. Without such defense, aerobic life would not be sustainable.

One intriguing question that life scientists had posed about superoxide dismutase was how Cu(II) is delivered to the enzyme during its synthesis in the cell without harming the cell. In 1997 a team of researchers from three U.S. universities reported that they had discovered part of the answer. Working with the yeast *Saccharomyces cerevisiae,* they found a protein that serves to deliver Cu(II) specifically to the active site of newly synthesized superoxide dismutase. They named it copper chaperone for superoxide dismutase (CCS). In 2001 the structure of CCS bound to superoxide dismutase was determined by X-ray crystallography, and that structure illuminated how CCS works. CCS contains two distinct structural parts, or domains. One domain has the same structure as a protein called Atx1, which was known to pick up Cu(II) ions from a transmembrane Cu(II) transporter, a protein embedded in the cell membrane that brings Cu(II) into the cell. The second domain of CCS is strikingly similar in structure to one-half of the mature form of superoxide dismutase, which is a homodimer, a molecule made of two identical subunits (monomers).

The scenario that emerged from the most recent findings resembles a bucket brigade for passing Cu(II) ions from the outside of the cell to the superoxide dismutase without "spilling" them—i.e., without ever allowing the Cu(II) the freedom to catalyze unwanted oxidations. First, a Cu(II) ion outside the cell is bound by the transmembrane transporter, which moves it to the inside of the cell. Next, using its Atx1-like domain, CCS picks up the Cu(II) from the transporter and diffuses with it to a newly synthesized superoxide dismutase monomer, to which, using its superoxide dismutase domain, CCS then transiently binds and delivers the Cu(II). After receiving the Cu(II), the superoxide dismutase monomer binds with a second monomer (dimerizes) to form the stable and active mature enzyme.

An analog of the yeast CCS was found in human cells, an indication that this type of Cu(II) delivery system is likely widespread in living species. If CCS is needed to deliver Cu(II) to superoxide dismutase in the cell, then a mutant organism that lacks functional CCS should also lack superoxide dismutase activity. This was demonstrated to be the case in mice. Importantly, the mutant mice were normal with respect to the activities of other Cu(II)-containing enzymes. This was evidence for the existence of additional chaperones for delivering Cu(II) to other copper-containing enzymes. In 2001 these other chaperones were under investigation.

Progress in DNA Vaccines. Immunization of humans and other animals is traditionally accomplished by injecting a heat-killed bacterium or virus, or a component protein of it. The administered proteins are recognized as foreign by cells of the immune system, which respond by producing antibodies that circulate in the blood plasma and bind to the foreign proteins with great specificity and affinity. If the protein is from the surface of a bacterium or virus, the elicited antibody binds to and inactivates the bacterium or virus. To partially circumvent this defense, pathogens frequently mutate their surface proteins so that antibodies elicited against one variety cannot recognize and bind to a future variety.

Another aspect of immunity involves the generation of specialized white blood cells, called T cells, that can recognize foreign proteins, or parts of them, displayed on the surface of cells and then kill those cells. Many virus-infected cells, within which virus proteins are being made for the assembly of new virus particles, will display fragments of those proteins on their surface. The killing of these infected cells by T cells sensitized to the foreign proteins serves to abort the infection. A problem with conventional heat-killed or protein-based vaccines, however, is that they do not cause foreign proteins to display on cell surfaces and thus do not elicit sensitized T cells.

A relatively new approach to vaccines has focused on preparations of foreign DNA rather than foreign protein. The DNA is in the form of small circular molecules, called plasmids, that can be taken into cells and cause the cells to produce those proteins encoded by the plasmid. One might anticipate that a plasmid encoding a foreign protein or protein fragment would elicit both specific soluble antibodies and sensitized T cells and thus give rise to effective and long-lasting immunity.

This approach was first tested in chickens, mice, and other animals, where it was found to work spectacularly well even against pathogens hard to target by traditional means. Unfortunately, when tested in humans, DNA vaccines proved disappointing in that much higher doses of the plasmid DNA were found to be required than had been anticipated from the prior studies with animals. These high doses would make the DNA vaccines prohibitively expensive.

Because an essential step in the immune response occurs in lymphoid tissue, it seemed possible that the response to DNA vaccines could be increased if they were administered directly into lymph nodes, rather than into the skin or muscle tissue. During the year Thomas M. Kündig of Zürich (Switz.) University Hospital and his associates tried this approach and reported a 100–1,000-fold gain in response after injecting the vaccine into the peripheral lymph nodes of mice. If tests in humans proved successful, medical science could see the development of DNA vaccines vastly superior to the classic vaccines.

An Antimicrobial Peptide. All multicellular organisms have evolved a constellation of natural defenses to ward off infection from myriad disease-causing agents. One such defense is the production of peptides (molecules structurally like proteins but smaller) with antimicrobial properties. Families of cationic, cystine-rich antimicrobial peptides are found in plants (thionins and plant defensins), insects (heliomycin, thanatin, and insect defensins), mollusks (mytilin and myticin), and mammals (protegrins and alpha and beta defensins).

During the year Tomas Ganz and coworkers at the Harbor-UCLA Medical Center, Torrance, Calif., reported the isolation of a defensin-type antimicrobial peptide from human urine and named it hepcidin because it is made in the liver. It is apparently common to vertebrates because the DNA sequence coding for hepcidin was identified in pigs, rats, and flounder. Hepcidin is antifungal as well as antibacterial, and it also inhibits the germination of fungal spores. In keeping with a defensive function, the synthesis of hepcidin in the liver is stimulated by specific molecules, called lipopolysaccharides, present on the surface of bacteria. The peptide could someday prove useful as an antibiotic or antifungal agent.

(IRWIN FRIDOVICH)

Genetics of the Senses. Humans, like all other species on Earth, have myriad systems for acquiring information about their surroundings. For humans and other mammals, these systems include the senses of sight, hearing, touch, smell, and taste. Humans and many other animals also have a sense of balance, which enables them to move and orient their bodies with reference to Earth's gravitational field. Some species, although not necessarily humans, even have a sense of direction based on the presence of tiny magnetic deposits in their bodies, which allows them to sense Earth's magnetic field.

Although many species share a given sense, the exact range of that sense can vary between species according to need. For example, whereas the typical frequency range of human hearing is 20–20,000 Hz, dogs can hear sounds at much higher frequencies, and whales and elephants can hear sounds at much lower frequencies. Similarly, human vision responds to colours of light that range from 400 nm (nanometres; violet) to 700 nm (red), the so-called visible wavelengths. Bees and other pollinating insects, by contrast, can see into the ultraviolet range.

Research by a number of teams has begun to reveal the genetics underlying the human senses, helping to explain how these complex systems work and enabling better diagnosis and intervention for those with genetic impairments of these systems. Results and implications of this effort were summarized in several papers published during the year. Some highlights regarding hearing and vision are discussed below, as well as legal and ethical dilemmas that have surfaced as a consequence.

Congenital Hearing Loss. Optimal human hearing requires not only proper structure and function of the outer, middle, and inner ears but also proper reception and interpretation of the electrical signals sent along the auditory nerve to the brain. Compromise at any level, due to gene defects or other causes, can result in impaired hearing. At least one in 10 adults aged 65 years or older experiences significant hearing loss, and about one in every 1,000 infants demonstrates profound congenital hearing loss.

Most hearing loss, especially among older adults, is not considered genetic in origin but is typically the result of accumulated damage from trauma or infection. On the other hand, a majority of the cases of isolated hearing loss—hearing loss unaccompanied by other symptoms (such as blindness)—seen in young infants are genetic. Recent studies show that hearing loss in these infants is the result of mutations in one or more of an extraordinary number of different genes. Identification of the relevant genes and mutations has given powerful insight into the broad range of gene products that must function together to achieve normal hearing. They include intracellular motor proteins, ion channels and pumps, transcription factors that regulate the expression of other genes, and extracellular matrix proteins that help to form the tectorial membrane of the inner ear. More will likely be identified in the years to come. Perhaps the mutated genes seen most often in these patients, however, are those that code for the connexins. Connexins are gap junction proteins—proteins spanning the cell membrane that control the passage of small molecules directly from the interior of one cell to that of another. These gap junction proteins contribute to the communication between supporting, nonsensory cells of the inner ear. Mutations in the gene *CX26*, which codes for the protein connexin 26, account for almost half of all cases of isolated congenital deafness in Caucasian populations.

In 2001 knowledge of the identities and functions of these genes and their products was leading to improved early diagnosis, which in turn was offering improved options for intervention, including cochlear implants. Early diagnosis followed by prompt intervention is important because the auditory regions of the brains of infants born with profound hearing loss will not develop properly unless hearing is restored quickly. Partly in recognition of this urgency, congenital hearing loss joined the list of other, mostly metabolic, impairments for which newborn screening procedures were mandated in some U.S. states and other parts of the world.

Colour Blindness. Like hearing, human vision involves the function and interaction of a multitude of gene products that together make up the sensing organ—the eye—as well as the proper transmission, reception, and interpretation of the electrical signals sent by the eye to the appropriate regions of the brain. Also like hearing, visual impairment is extremely common and complex, involving the interplay of genetic and environmental influences, including normal processes of aging. The underlying cause of late adult-onset farsightedness, for example, is generally considered to be a natural loss of flexibility of the lens with age. Late adult-onset cataracts are believed to result from progressive processes that alter the chemical properties of the lens.

In contrast, hereditary loss of vision generally appears much earlier in life (childhood to early adulthood) and can be either accompanied by other symptoms (syndromic) or isolated. Examples range from albinism, a syndrome that includes severe visual impairment, to such isolated conditions as congenital glaucoma, progressive retinitis pigmentosa, and myopia (nearsightedness). Perhaps one of the best understood of the isolated hereditary causes of vision loss is colour blindness, a fairly common congenital inability to see or distinguish specific colours.

Black-and-white vision is mediated by rhodopsin, a protein located in specialized cells, called rods, in the retina at the back of each eye. Three independent but related proteins, expressed individually in the cone cells of the retina, are responsible for normal human trichromatic colour vision. The gene coding for the protein most sensitive to blue light is located on chromosome 7, whereas the genes coding for the red-sensitive and green-sensitive proteins are both located on the X chromosome. This physical proximity, coupled with a close resemblance in the sequences of the red and green genes, results in a high frequency of unequal recombination events (regrouping of maternal and paternal genes during the formation of sex cells) involving these genes. This, in turn, can lead to either deletion or duplication of one or both genes on the resulting chromosomes. Because the chromosome involved is the X, females who inherit a deleted gene on one X chromosome will most likely carry a compensating normal copy on their other X chromosome, and so they will not experience visual impairment. In contrast, males, who carry only one X (and one Y) chromosome, will have no compensating copy, and so they will experience a form of colour blindness corresponding to the specific gene deletion inherited—either red or green. Indeed, in some studies close to 8% of all males demonstrated some form of colour blindness, generally characterized as red-green colour confusion.

Although treatments for colour blindness were still lacking, studies to elucidate its genetic basis were leading to improved diagnosis and prognosis. In addition, the results of those studies were helping scientists and physicians gain a better understanding of the normal functioning of the human eye and thus of other, in some cases more debilitating, forms of visual impairment.

Legal and Ethical Issues. The recent gains in understanding the genetic basis of sensory impairments in humans have raised moral and legal questions, in large part because of the possibilities presented for prenatal diagnosis of these impairments and for their early diagnosis and intervention after birth. Issues that must be considered include, for example, whether the option of terminating a pregnancy should be offered to "hearing" parents of a child who will be born deaf or to deaf parents of a child who will be born "hearing." Similarly, mandated newborn screening for profound hearing impairment, with the clear intent to encourage early intervention, has been taken by some members of the deaf community as a threat to the continued existence of the well-established deaf language and culture. Clearly, these issues emerge from differing opinions of what is a disease and what is simply a trait. In 2001 such dilemmas over sensory impairment remained but the tip of the iceberg with regard to human genetics. How individuals and societies handled these specific questions would set a precedent for the many similar problems that lay ahead.

(JUDITH L. FRIDOVICH-KEIL)

PALEONTOLOGY

The most primitive plants in the fossil record lack both seeds and leaves. In 2001 a study of the main lineages of living land plants, which considered both genetic and morphological features, concluded that horsetails and ferns belong to a monophyletic group (group with a single common ancestor) that includes the closest living relatives to modern seed-bearing plants. This finding refuted the prevailing view that horsetails and ferns, both of which are spore-bearing plants, represent transitional evolutionary steps from which seed plants eventually were derived. A second plant study suggested that the origin of leaves was caused by falling levels of carbon dioxide in the atmosphere during the Devonian Period (417 million to 354 million years ago), which drove plants to evolve structures for gas exchange and photosynthesis that were more efficient than simple green stems.

For many years paleontologists had assumed that the complex tribosphenic molars typical of marsupial and placental mammals had a single origin in some fossil mammal group from one of the northern continents. A U.S.-Polish study published during the year suggested that fossil tribosphenic mammals recently discovered from Gondwana, the ancient landmass that included all of the present southern continents and India, might have had a separate origin from their northern counterparts more than 100 million years ago. The investigators in the study speculated that this southern lineage gave rise to the monotremes, represented today by the egg-laying platypus and echidna, while the northern lineage produced all other modern mammals, both marsupials and placentals.

Madagascar continued to yield fossils of unusual new Cretaceous dinosaurs. One report described a large sauropod belonging to the Titanosauria, the only group of sauropods that survived until the end of the Cretaceous Period, 65 million years ago. While most titanosaur material was very fragmentary, the new Madagascar genus, *Rapetosaurus,* was the most complete titanosaur skeleton found to date. A phylogenetic study that included this specimen confirmed that titanosaurs were closely related to brachiosaurs. Another new titanosaur, *Paralititan,* was discovered in Egypt's Bahariya Formation of the Late Cretaceous (99 million to 65 million years ago). With a length of nearly 1.7 m (5.6 ft), its humerus (upper forelimb bone) was the largest of any known Cretaceous sauropod. *Paralititan* was the first tetrapod reported from the Bahariya Formation since 1935.

A second new dinosaur from Madagascar, *Masiakasaurus,* was shown to belong to the unusual group of Gondwana theropods called abelisauroids. Measuring 1.8 m (5.9 ft) long, it was unique in being the only theropod known with heterodont dentition (different teeth specialized for different functions). Whereas other theropods (and most other dinosaurs) were homodont (all teeth similar in shape), *Masiakasaurus* had distinctly differently shaped teeth in the lower jaw.

A report by Chinese and American paleontologists revisited the controversial topic of the origin of feathers. Previous studies had suggested that some filamentous covering structures observed in the fossils of several theropod dinosaurs represent primitive feathers. Other analyses, however, had disputed the relationship between these structures and feathers. Moreover, two genera that had been described as having true feathers (*Caudipteryx* and *Protarchaeopteryx*) may have been flightless birds rather than theropods. The new study examined the filamentous covering structures in fossils of *Sinornithosaurus*, a basal dromaeosaurid dinosaur first described in 1999. The investigators concluded that the structures are composed of multiple filaments and show types of branching structure that are unique to bird feathers. If confirmed, this finding would substantiate the theropod origin of bird feathers.

A recent reexamination of skulls of the ornithomimids *Gallimimus* and *Ornithomimus* showed that these toothless dinosaurs may have had keratinized beaks—i.e., beaks made of the fibrous protein keratin, the chemical basis of horny tissue. These animals appear to have had a comblike keratinized plate in the mouth, somewhat similar to the jaw comb of a duck. The researchers involved in the study speculated that the animals may have used their beaks to filter small invertebrates from the water and sediment—certainly a new idea about the diets of toothless theropods.

A study combining medical scanning techniques and engineering analytic methodology analyzed the bite of the well-known theropod dinosaur *Allosaurus* of the Late Jurassic (159 million to 144 million years ago). While conventional wisdom assigned *Allosaurus* a very powerful bite, this research concluded that its bite force was quite low, similar to that of smaller living carnivorous mammals such as wolves and leopards and a sixth of the bite force calculated for *Tyrannosaurus*. The investigators suggested that, because of its comparatively weak bite, *Allosaurus* had to be discriminating in how and where it attacked its prey.

Late Cretaceous sediments in Mongolia yielded *Apsaravis*, a new fossil bird. According to a description published during the year, the specimen was one of the best ever found of a group of birds known as ornithurines. The new genus appeared to fill an important gap in avian evolution. *Apsaravis* also indicated that the Mesozoic relatives of modern birds were not restricted to nearshore and marine environments, as previously speculated, and it provided new insight into the evolution of flight following its appearance.

Canadian paleontologists unearthed the world's largest recorded trilobite fossil in late 2000.

Manitoba Museum of Man and Nature

A mass of juvenile bird bones reported from the Early Cretaceous of Spain (144 million to 99 million years ago) appeared to represent a regurgitated pellet. The mass contained bones from four individuals and provided the first positive evidence that Mesozoic birds were prey for other animals. Whereas the predator may have been an early mammal, lizard, crocodile, pterosaur, theropod dinosaur, or another bird, mammals and crocodiles typically do not regurgitate bones in pellets, and the lizards and birds found at the same site appeared too small to have been the predators. That means that either a nonavian theropod dinosaur or a pterosaur most likely produced the pellet.

In October 2000 a group of Canadian invertebrate paleontologists reported finding the world's largest recorded trilobite in rocks of Late Ordovician age (458 million to 443 million years ago) near Manitoba. At more than 70 cm (28 in) long, the specimen was 70% larger than the previous record-sized trilobite. Another invertebrate study addressed the origin of modern corals. The primary reef-forming corals belong to the order Scleractinia, the stony corals. It had been postulated that the scleractinians may have evolved from a group of Paleozoic corals called rugosids (rugose corals). One problem with the theory was that the rugosids disappear from the fossil record at the end of the Permian Period (248 million years ago), whereas the scleractinians do not appear until some 14 million years later. The new study suggested that skeletons in corals may be ephemeral—that is, they are produced only when ocean chemistry is favourable for the precipitation of calcium carbonate. This idea would account for the gap in fossil evidence for the origin of modern corals from Paleozoic forms if conditions in the Early Triassic were unfavourable for skeleton formation.

The Herefordshire Lagerstätte is a Silurian deposit in England of about 425 million years in age that has yielded marine invertebrate fossils in exceptional three-dimensional detail. A wormlike mollusk from this collection was described during the year as a plated aplacophoran. The Aplacophora, along with the chitons, are considered to be the most primitive living mollusks, but up until this discovery they had been unknown from the fossil record. (WILLIAM R. HAMMER)

Literature

V.S. NAIPAUL netted the Nobel, while Peter Carey took his second **BOOKER. PHILIP ROTH** and **J.G. BALLARD** mused on the end of literature. Novelists in many countries wrote about the **PAST,** while **SOCIAL** and **POLITICAL** themes attracted the talents of others. **OBSCENITIES,** eroticism, and **PROMISCUITY** also crept into literary works.

ENGLISH

United Kingdom. The Booker Prize chairman of judges, Lord Kenneth Baker, reported that the many entries he had read during 2001 proved that the novel was thriving and keeping abreast of developments within British life. Displacement, often depicted through the uprooted feelings of émigrés or refugees, was a strong presence in many novels considered by the panel. Though historical themes remained popular, World War I was less in evidence as a subject. Instead, writers moved on to World War II and the years leading up to and spanning the 1970s, decades that, though conjuring up a sense of difference, were within living memory. Lord Baker also praised many of the year's novelists for their vivid and unsentimental treatment of childhood. Stories were told from the point of view of children with unusual and forceful personalities, and romanticization was successfully avoided, as evidenced in Philip Pullman's *The Amber Spyglass* (2000), which narrowly missed the Booker shortlist but marked the first time that a children's book read widely by adults had made the long list.

The six titles short-listed included Rachel Seiffert's assured literary debut, *The Dark Room,* a Holocaust story from the German perspective that *The Observer* newspaper praised as a "simply phrased and understated" book that "shatters prejudices"; Andrew Miller's *Oxygen,* an intricate story about a Hungarian writer and his play of the same name, which was tipped as third favourite to win; David Mitchell's fast-paced Postmodern *number9dream,* an ambitious and complex tour de force about a young man's search for his father in a brash futuristic Tokyo; Ali Smith's *Hotel World,* which was also nominated for the Orange Prize and featured a cinematic blend of five different female narratives; and Ian McEwan's best-selling *Atonement,* which opens in 1935 and follows its protagonists to the century's end. McEwan's handling of time, memory, and revisionism was hailed as "impressive, engrossing, deep, and surprising" by *The Observer.* McEwan had won the Booker in 1998 for his last novel, *Amsterdam.*

The 6–4 favourite, *True History of the Kelly Gang* (2000) by Australian Peter Carey, was named the prizewinner. Carey, who had also won the Booker for his *Oscar & Lucinda* (1988), declared that he was "wildly excited and exhilarated" and that, as a result of a private bet between him and McEwan, he owed the latter a sumptuous dinner. Lord Baker observed that both Carey's and McEwan's offerings were their best books ever. In Carey's "magnificent story of the early settler days in Australia," he re-created the character of the outlaw Ned Kelly, sometimes described as an Australian Robin Hood. Carey admitted that were Kelly alive today he might not recognize himself in the book's narrator. A piece of literary ventriloquism, the work was inspired by a 56-page letter Kelly once wrote in justification of a bank robbery.

The Orange Prize for Fiction, awarded annually to a woman writer, was also won by an Australian. Kate Grenville's *The Idea of Perfection* (1999) was acclaimed for its touching and humorous depiction of love between two unlikely rustics in a farming community in the outback. It beat, among other strong contenders, Smith's *Hotel World* and Margaret Atwood's odds-on favourite *The Blind Assassin* (2000). A male panel of judges, set up as a research project in tandem with the actual female panel, sharply criticized the shortlist. Novelist Paul Bailey, who admitted that he did not approve of the prize because "sexes should not be separated like this in art," said the women judges had gone "soft when it came to the crunch" and had chosen big names and dull, soppy stories instead of seeking out grittier stories by lesser-known writers. Despite his objections, his male "shadow panel" admitted that Grenville's book, which had hitherto been little known in Great Britain, was the one worthy contender on the shortlist.

The other major literary award, the 2000 Whitbread Book of the Year—in which novels, volumes of poetry, and nonfiction vied for the prize—was won by novelist Matthew Kneale. This was the first time in five years that the award had not been given to a volume of poetry. Kneale's *English Passengers* (2000), a story of an 1857 expedition to Tasmania, was praised by jury chairman Sir Tim Rice for the way several of its characters, both English and Aboriginal, came together "to tell a story which is at times hilarious and at times tragic." A close contender was Lorna Sage's *Bad Blood* (2000), a forthright memoir of teenage pregnancy and family tensions in postwar Britain. The panel of 10 judges had been evenly divided, and Rice had been obliged to cast the deciding vote. Unexpectedly, Sage died 13 days before the award was announced in January. Her agent, Faith Evans, divulged that the book had been the result of 15 years' work.

The David Cohen British Literature Prize for lifetime achievement went to 81-year-old veteran Doris Lessing. The award, administered by the Arts Council, was given every two years to a writer who had significantly contributed to literature. Arts Council Chairman Gerry Robinson characterized Lessing's novels as "an accumulation of excellence—a body of work that has in its unique and determined way shaped the literary landscape." Meanwhile, a previous recipient of the David Cohen Prize, Trinidadian-born V.S. Naipaul, was awarded the Nobel Prize for Literature. (*See* NOBEL PRIZES.) Both he and Lessing published novels (*Half a Life* and *The Sweetest Dream,* respectively) in a year in which reviewers found strong elements of nonfiction.

WORLD LITERARY PRIZES 2001

All prizes are annual and were awarded in 2001 unless otherwise stated

Nobel Prize for Literature

Awarded since 1901; included in the behest of Alfred Nobel, who specified a prize for those who "shall have produced in the field of literature the most outstanding work in an ideal direction." The prizewinners are selected in October by the Swedish Academy and receive the award on December 10 in Stockholm. Prize: a gold medal and an award that varies from year to year; in 2001 the award was SKr 10,000,000 (about $943,000).

V.S. Naipaul (British, born in Trinidad)

International IMPAC Dublin Literary Award

Awarded since 1996; the largest and most international prize of its kind and is open to books written in any language, the Award is a joint initiative of Dublin Corporation, the Municipal Government of Dublin City, and the productivity improvement company IMPAC. It is administered by Dublin Corporation Public Libraries. Prize: £Ir 100,000 (about $110,000) of which 25% goes to the translator. The awards are given at Dublin Castle by the president of Ireland in June.

No Great Mischief by Alistair MacLeod (Canada)

Neustadt International Prize for Literature

Established in 1969 and awarded biennially by the University of Oklahoma and *World Literature Today.* Novelists, poets, and dramatists are equally eligible. Prize: $50,000, a replica of an eagle feather cast in silver, and a certificate. Last awarded in 2000.

David Malouf (Australia)

Commonwealth Writers Prize

Established in 1987 by the Commonwealth Foundation. In 2001 there was one award of £10,000 (about $14,500) for the best book submitted and an award of £3,000 (about $4,360) for the best first book. In each of the four regions of the Commonwealth two prizes of £1,000 (about $1,450) are awarded: one for the best book and one for the best first book.

Best Book	*True History of the Kelly Gang* by Peter Carey (Australia)
Best First Book	*White Teeth* by Zadie Smith (U.K.)
Regional winners—Best Book	
Africa	*The Heart of Redness* by Zakes Mda (South Africa)
Caribbean & Canada	*The Hero's Walk* by Anita Rau Badami (Canada)
Eurasia	*Super-Cannes* by J.G. Ballard (U.K.)
South East Asia & South Pacific	*True History of the Kelly Gang* by Peter Carey (Australia)

Booker Prize

Established in 1969, sponsored by Booker McConnell Ltd., and administered by the National Book League in the U.K. Awarded to the best full-length novel written by a citizen of the U.K., Ireland, Pakistan, South Africa, or the Commonwealth and published in the U.K. during the 12 months ending September 30. Prize: £20,000 (about $28,500).

True History of the Kelly Gang by Peter Carey (Australia)

Whitbread Book of the Year

Established in 1971. The winners of the Whitbread Book Awards for Poetry, Biography, Novel, and First Novel as well as the Whitbread Children's Book of the Year are eligible for the £25,000 Whitbread Book of the Year prize.

English Passengers by Matthew Kneale (2000 award)

Orange Prize for Fiction

Established in 1996. Awarded to a work of published fiction written by a woman in English and published in the U.K. during the 12 months ending March 31. Prize: £30,000 (about $42,800).

The Idea of Perfection by Kate Grenville

PEN/Faulkner Award

The PEN/Faulkner Foundation each year recognizes the best published works of fiction by contemporary American writers. Named for William Faulkner, the PEN/Faulkner Award was founded by writers in 1980 to honour their peers and is now the largest juried award for fiction in the United States. Prize: $15,000.

The Human Stain by Philip Roth

Pulitzer Prizes in Letters and Drama

Begun in 1917 and awarded by Columbia University, New York City, on the recommendation of the Pulitzer Prize Board for books published in the previous year. Five categories in Letters are honored with prizes: Fiction, Biography, and General Non-Fiction (authors of works in these categories must be American citizens); History (the subject must be American history); and Poetry (for original verse by an American author). The Drama prize is for "a distinguished play by an American author, preferably original in its source and dealing with American life." Prize: $7,500 in each category.

Fiction	*The Amazing Adventures of Kavalier & Clay* by Michael Chabon
Biography	*W.E.B. Du Bois: The Fight for Equality and the American Century, 1919–1963* by David Levering Lewis
Poetry	*Different Hours* by Stephen Dunn
History	*Founding Brothers: The Revolutionary Generation* by Joseph J. Ellis
General Non-Fiction	*Hirohito and the Making of Modern Japan* by Herbert P. Bix
Drama	*Proof* by David Auburn

National Book Awards

Awarded since 1950 by the National Book Foundation, a consortium of American publishing groups. Categories have varied, beginning with three—Fiction, Nonfiction, and Poetry—swelling to 22 awards in 1983, and returning to four (the initial three plus Young People's Literature) in 2001. Prize: $10,000 and a crystal sculpture.

Fiction *The Corrections* by Jonathan Franzen

Nonfiction *The Noonday Demon: An Atlas of Depression* by Andrew Solomon

Poetry *Poems Seven: New and Complete Poetry* by Alan Dugan

Frost Medal

Awarded annually since 1930 by the Poetry Society of America for distinguished lifetime service to American poetry.

Sonia Sanchez

Governor-General's Literary Awards

Canada's premier literary awards. Prizes are given in 14 categories altogether: Fiction, Poetry, Drama, Translation, Nonfiction, and Children's Literature (Text and Illustration), each in English and French. Established in 1937. Prize: Can$15,000 (about U.S. $9,540).

Fiction (English)	*Clara Callan* by Richard B. Wright
Fiction (French)	*Le Ravissement* by Andrée A. Michaud
Poetry (English)	*Execution Poems* by George Elliott Clarke
Poetry (French)	*Des ombres portées* by Paul Chanel Malenfant

Griffin Poetry Award

Established in 2001 and administered by the Griffin Trust for Excellence in Poetry. Prize: Can$40,000 (about U.S. $25,300) each for the two awards.

Canadian Award	*Men in the Off Hours* by Anne Carson
International Award	*Glottal Stop: 101 Poems by Paul Celan* translated by Heather McHugh and Nikolai Popov (United States)

Büchner Prize

Georg-Büchner Preis. Awarded for a body of literary work in the German language. First awarded in 1923; now administered by the German Academy for Language and Literature. Prize: DM 60,000 (about $27,700).

Friederike Mayröcker (Austria)

Hooft Prize

P.C. Hooftprijs. The Dutch national prize for literature, established in 1947. Prize: f. 75,000 (about $31,000).

Gerrit Krol, for his prose works

Nordic Council Literary Prize

Established in 1961. Selections are made by a 10-member jury from among original works first published in Danish, Norwegian, or Swedish during the past two years or other Nordic languages (Finnish, Faroese, Sami, etc.) during the past four years. Prize: DKr 350,000 (about $42,000)

Oppdageren (1999) by Jan Kjærstad (Norway)

Prix Goncourt

Prix de l'Académie Goncourt. First awarded in 1903 from the estate of French literary figure Edmond Huot de Goncourt to memorialize him and his brother, Jules. Prize: F 50 (about $6.75).

Rouge Brésil by Jean-Christophe Rufin

Prix Femina

Established in 1904. The awards for works "of imagination" are announced by an all-woman jury in the categories of French fiction, fiction in translation, and nonfiction. Announced in October together with the Prix Médicis. Prize: F 5,000 (about $690).

French Fiction	*Rosie Carpe* by Marie Ndiaye

Cervantes Prize for Hispanic Literature

Premio Cervantes. Established in 1976 and awarded for a body of work in the Spanish language. Announced in December and awarded the following April. Prize: €90,000 (about $80,000).

Álvaro Mutis (Colombia)

Planeta Prize

Premio Planeta de Novela. Established in 1951 by the Planeta Publishing House for the best unpublished, original novel in Spanish. Awarded in Barcelona in October. Prize: Ptas 100 million (about $550,000) and publication by Planeta.

La canción de Dorotea by Rosa Regás

Camões Prize

Premio Luis de Camões da Literatura. Established in 1988 by the governments of Portugal and Brazil to honor a "representative" author writing in the Portuguese language. Prize: $100,000.

Eugénio de Andrade (Portugal)

Smirnoff Russian Booker Prize

Awarded since 1992; sponsored principally since 1997 by Guinness UDV's Smirnoff brand. Prize: $12,500 for the winner; $1,000 for each finalist.

Kazus Kukotskogo ("Kukotsky's Case") by Lyudmila Ulitskaya

Naguib Mahfouz Medal for Literature

Established in 1996 and awarded for the best contemporary novel published in Arabic. The winning work is translated into English and published in Cairo, London, and New York. Prize: a silver medal and $1,000.

Awrāq an-narjis ("Narcissus Leaves") by Sumayya Ramadān

Jun'ichirō Tanizaki Prize

Tanizaki Jun'ichirō Shō. Established in 1965 to honor the memory of novelist Jun'ichirō Tanizaki. Awarded annually to a Japanese author for an exemplary literary work. Prize: ¥1,000,000 (about $8,170) and a trophy.

Hiromi Kawakami, for her novel *Sensei no kaban* ("The Teacher's Briefcase")

Ryūnosuke Akutagawa Prize

Akutagawa Ryūnosuke Shō. Established in 1935 and awarded semiannually for the best serious work of fiction by a promising new Japanese writer. Short stories or novellas win the prize more frequently than do full-length novels.

"Kuma no shikiishi" ("The Bear's Pavement") by Toshiyuki Horie

"Seisui" ("Holy Water") by Yūichi Seirai

"Chūin no hana" ("The Mourning Flower") by Sōkyū Gen'yū

Mao Dun Literary Award

Established in 1981 to honour contemporary Chinese novels and named after novelist Shen Yanbing (1896–1981), whose nom de plume was Mao Dun; awarded every four years. Latest awards were announced on October 19, 2000.

Jueze ("Hard Choice") by Zhang Ping

Chang hen ge (1996; "Song of Everlasting Sorrow") by Wang Anyi

Chen'ai luo ding (1999; "When the Dust Settles") by Ah Lai

Nanfang you jiamu ("Fine Tree Possessed in Southland") and *Buye zhi hou* ("Delightful Marquis to Break Drowsiness"), from *Charen sanbuqu* ("Trilogy of Tea Men") by Wang Xufeng

Visibly missing from the Booker shortlist was Beryl Bainbridge. Her *According to Queeney,* described by *The Literary Review* as "the grimmest but also the funniest book Bainbridge has written," was an unflinching treatment of the subject of death. Other prominent novelists whose offerings similarly failed to attract enthusiasm from the judges included Salman Rushdie, whose *Fury* was coolly received by critics, and Pat Barker, whose *Border Crossing* was much praised. Hanif Kureishi's *Gabriel's Gift*—a quirky, stalwart tale about a 15-year-old boy whose parents split up—was another lacuna, as was Jonathan Coe's *The Rotters' Club,* an artful comedy, with moving interludes set in 1970s Britain. Elaine Feinstein's *Dark Inheritance* (2000) was an elegant evocation of an academic woman's unhealthy fascination with Rome.

The children's book market remained buoyant. South African-born writer Beverley Naidoo was a surprise winner of the Carnegie Medal. Her story for children aged 10 and up, *The Other Side of Truth* (2000), addressed the sensitive issue of asylum seekers and beat tough competition from David Almond, Melvyn Burgess, and Philip Pullman. Naidoo hoped that her book would "encourage readers to make leaps of imagination, heart and mind as they explore our common humanity."

Claims that the novel was dead had been made since the 1950s, and the author J.G. Ballard, on publication of what he termed his "complete" short stories, claimed that these too were "heading for extinction" because people had "lost the knack of reading them" and there was almost "nowhere to publish them."

The memoir, however, enjoyed continued popularity. Paul Arnott's *A Good Likeness: A Personal Story of Adoption* (2000) described the author's sometimes hilarious quest for his natural parents and was greeted by *The Literary Review* as a "wonderful, multifaceted voyage of discovery." Also praised was Penelope Lively's *A House Unlocked,* an ingenious depiction of nine decades of family history woven around her grandmother's Edwardian home in Somerset.

There were a number of notable biographies, including Adrian Tinniswood's *His Invention So Fertile: A Life of Christopher Wren,* a vivid portrait of an era that had been dubbed the "Wrenaissance" and a versatile accolade to Wren's scientific and architectural achievement. Antonia Fraser's *Marie Antoinette: The Journey* was an intelligent consideration of a much-misunderstood life. Susan Watkins tackled another legend in *Mary, Queen of Scots* and achieved a succinct story of an intelligent woman whose Achilles heel was a lack of discrimination in her love life. At 674 pages, Alison Weir's *Henry VIII: King and Court* was a well-paced, ambitious retelling of this larger-than-life monarch; his queens and counselors were vividly drawn alongside an analysis of his political legacy. The witty, urbane, and sometimes pompous Roman writer was the deftly handled subject of Anthony Everitt's biography *Cicero: A Turbulent Life.* One of the last Republicans in a time of civil discord, Cicero enjoyed telling jokes—a predilection that Everitt demonstrated proved part of his undoing.

History painted across large canvases appeared in three notable books. Barry W. Cunliffe's 600-page *Facing the Ocean: The Atlantic and Its Peoples, 8000 BC–AD 1500* was a confident and erudite charting of developments across nearly 10 millennia in the Atlantic world, based largely on archaeological evidence. John E. Wills attempted a lateral approach with his *1688: A Global History.* He mined historical sources from a time of global change in such diverse parts of the world as Bolivia, Japan, China, Africa, and Europe. Niall Ferguson presented a 300-year consideration of whether economics alone drove world events with his *The Cash Nexus: Money and Power in the Modern World 1700–2000;* he concluded that the explanation of global change could be attributed only partly to the traffic of money and that people, with their often irrational actions, also affected the course of history.

An immense and impressive historical offering was Hew Strachan's 1,190-page *The First World War, Volume 1: To Arms.* The first of three planned volumes, the book examined the war's origins and its launch, demonstrating that the conflict was doomed to be global in its extent from the start. This work was complemented by Margaret MacMillan's probe of the ensuing peace agreement, *Peacemakers: The Paris Conference of 1919 and Its Attempt to End War,* which argued that the decisions made that year, and subsequently, made World War II inevitable. Meanwhile, the British mandate in Palestine came under the unbiased eye of Israeli journalist Tom Segev. His *One Palestine, Complete: Jews and Arabs Under the Mandate* (2000) explored new research resources and reached a verdict—that the British were chiefly pro-Zionist, not pro-Arab. Moving on through the postwar era, the culture of spies as it waxed and waned was the arena of Richard Aldrich's fascinating *The Hidden Hand: Britain, America and Cold War Secret Intelligence.*

Two notable edited collections were a volume of Bertrand Russell's letters—presented with helpful commentary by Nicholas Griffin to portray a long life of intensity and brilliance—and *The Oxford Dictionary of Phrase and Fable* (2000), a 1,223-page treasury assembled by Elizabeth Knowles containing apocrypha, outré stories, and unusual turns of phrase.

Among the literary deaths during the year were those of novelist, book reviewer, and editor of *The Literary Review* Auberon Waugh, who admitted in later life that he was overshadowed by his father, Evelyn Waugh; Douglas Adams, the creator of the quirky and original tale of Arthur Dent's trip around the universe, *The Hitchhiker's Guide to the Galaxy,* which was first broadcast on radio in 1978 and spawned an industry of TV shows, stage adaptations, books, and a huge following of fans; poet and dramatist Anne Ridler, whose devotional verse evoked that of T.S. Eliot; writer Simon Raven, whose 10-novel sequence *Alms for Oblivion* highlighted his sardonic wit; and poet Elizabeth Jennings, whose verse reflected her devout Roman Catholicism and her love of Italy. (*See* OBITUARIES.)

(SIOBHAN DOWD)

United States. In a talk in August 2001, novelist Philip Roth put forward the proposition that in 25 years literature as it had been known to the present time would be relegated to the dust. Roth argued that the popularity of the screen and the image, currently riding high, would ride even higher in the future.

One might wonder, however, if David Kepesh, the main character in a number of other Roth novels and now an aging professor-journalist with a sex drive still rampant, would agree. Kepesh stands as the main figure in Roth's brilliant short novel *The Dying Animal,* an erotically charged story that reads as a kind of satyr play following the novelist's prizewinning *The Human Stain.* The metaphor-making power of *The Dying Animal* rivaled anything that Henry Miller had written on the sexual encounter and made pornographic images look pallid by comparison. ("You feel it and you get a sense of this other-world fauna, something from the sea. As though it were related to the oyster or the octopus or the squid, a creature from miles down and eons back. . . . The secret ecstatically exposed.")

Literature dying? *Après moi, pas de deluge,* Roth seemed to be arguing.

Writers would say almost anything, however, to gain public attention. Speaking rather immodestly as someone who probably still would be around and writing in 25 years, novelist Jonathan Franzen, author of the much-touted best-selling (and National-Book-Award-winning) novel *The Corrections,* gave an interview to *The New York Times Magazine* in which he suggested that his own work was going to turn contemporary fiction on its head. He also won the distinction of having his book chosen for Oprah Winfrey's book club—then un-chosen.

The rest of the American writers who came out with new publications let the works speak for themselves. Unsurprisingly, the results were mixed. Veteran fiction writer James Salter revised his 1961 novel *The Arm of Flesh* and in late 2000 published it as *Cassada,* a moody and brilliant homage to fighter pilots between wars, in which his evocative lyric prose worked heroically to evoke landscape or, in this case, skyscape. ("[The sun] was in the last quarter of its elevation, the light flat. The white of the clouds had faded like an old wall. Everything seemed silent and still. . . . There was a strange, lost feeling, as though they were in an empty house, in rooms without furniture, looking through windows that had no glass.") Paul Theroux signed in with *Hotel Honolulu,* in which the prose was flat but the linked stories about the inhabitants of a downtown Honolulu tourist spot led the reader on and on. Amy Tan's *The Bonesetter's Daughter* was a successful reworking of the pattern that Tan used in her biggest hit, *The Joy Luck Club*—the reader was taken from contemporary San Francisco to historical China and back again.

Santa Cruz novelist James Houston, the uncrowned laureate of contemporary California fiction, turned to the 19th century and the material of the Donner party and a few of its members for *Snow Mountain Passage,* a solid hit. In *Carry Me Across the Water,* Ethan Canin, a Californian living half the year in self-imposed exile in Iowa, went from the Pacific theatre in World War II to the present for his quiet, lyrical study of a Jewish-American man assessing his life. Reginald McKnight sent his anthropologist hero to Africa for an engaging study of a black man abroad in *He Sleeps.* Percival Everett stayed home to parody black middle-class culture and the American publishing industry in *Erasure.*

With mixed success octogenarian novelist Mary Lee Settle turned to America's colonial past for her novel *I, Roger Williams,* and William T. Vollmann, her junior by more than 40 years, added *Argall,* another huge—flawed—volume, to his already gargantuan "Seven Dreams" series, this one taking up the matter of the colonization of Virginia. At least Vollmann had a sense of humour; he reviewed his own book in the *Los Angeles Times Book Review* and basically dismissed it. Puerto Rican novelist Rosario Ferré worked on the story of Russian ballerina Anna Pavlova and her sojourn in the Caribbean in the slow-moving *Flight of the Swan.* The accomplished Louise Erdrich created an engaging epic out of the material of the lonely North Dakota landscape and its inhabitants, European and Native American, in *The Last Report on the Miracles at Little No Horse.* The talented young African American writer Colson Whitehead made variations out of myth and history in *John Henry Days.* Gifted Brooklyn, N.Y., writer Jonathan Lethem amused his fans with a 55-page novella he called *This Shape We're In.*

After years of writing for television, fiction writer Michael Malone returned to the novel with a wonderfully entertaining murder mystery set in North Carolina called *First Lady.* Novelist Chaim Potok came out with a collection of three linked novellas in *Old Men at Midnight,* and novelist and short-story writer Ward Just turned to the one-act play and published *Lowell Limpett,* along with two previously unpublished stories with a Washington, D.C., setting. Published posthumously was a nearly 600-page novel by Tennessee writer Richard Marius, *An Affair of Honor,* a bulky old-fashioned and splendid story about a double murder in rural Tennessee. ("Saturday night, August 8, 1953. It had been miserably hot. The temperature broke slightly when the sun sank in the west, turning off the fire that baked the world. The round thermometer with the needle and the dial over the door of Kelly Parmalee's clothing store on the square showed ninety-four degrees.")

Chuck Kinder and Peggy Rambach turned their associations with writers Raymond Carver and Andre Dubus into gossipy romans à clef, titled *Honeymooners* and *Fighting Gravity,* respectively. The two best first novels of the year also took historical material as their subjects, often in highly charged prose, as in David Anthony Durham's *Gabriel's Story,* about a young black cowboy on a quest from Kansas across the Southwest ("The mountains before them rose like sand blankets draped around skeletons of rock . . . ancient carcasses of some giant creatures—backbones, ribs, limbs and digits stretched out and decaying beneath a godawful sun."), and the Armenian genocide in Micheline Aharonian Marcom's intensely lyrical *Three Apples Fell from Heaven* ("In the desert, the Mesopotamian beetles drink blood and soup. There is a lake that overflows its bounds, transshapen by flesh.").

A couple of volumes of collected stories, both by influential stylists, deserved serious notice: a more than 440-page volume from Saul Bellow and the posthumously published *The Collected Stories of Richard Yates.* Also published posthumously was *Meteor in the Madhouse,* several novellas by Leon Forrest, an African American writer from Chicago. From established story writers came *Faithless* by Joyce Carol Oates, *Perfect Recall* by Ann Beattie, *Drinking with the Cook* by Laura Furman, *Zigzagging down a Wild Trail* by Bobbie Ann Mason, and *Bargains in the Real World* by Elizabeth Cox. Chitra Banerjee Divakaruni focused on Asian American transplants in *The Unknown Errors of Our Lives,* and Rick Moody jazzed the usually more placid melodies of Anglo-Americans in *Demonology.* Extremely promising, if somewhat uneven, first books of stories came from Baltimore, Md., writer Christine Lincoln—*Sap Rising*—and Vermont-based writer Arthur Bradford —*Dogwalker.*

Poetry became more prosaic as Billy Collins, the new U.S. poet laureate, pub-

AP/Wide World Photos

U.S. Poet Laureate Billy Collins

lished his low-key, sometimes even trivial verses in *Sailing Alone Around the Room.* J.D. McClatchy and Stephen Yenser edited the *Collected Poems* of the late James Merrill. Louise Glück presented *The Seven Ages.* ("In my first dream the world appeared/ the salt, the bitter, the forbidden, the sweet/ In my second I descended// I was human, I couldn't just see a thing/ beast that I am/ I had to touch.") The subtle nuances of familiar emotions packed the pages of Jane Hirschfield's lyrical collection *Given Sugar, Given Salt.* ("It is foolish/ to let a young redwood/ grow next to a house.// Even in this/ one lifetime,/ you will have to choose.// That great calm being,/ this clutter of soup pots and books—// Already the first branch-tips brush at the window./ Softly, calmly, immensity taps at your life.")

Al Young, in *The Sound of Dreams Remembered,* rhymed "sixties" and "striptease." *The Darkness and the Light* came from Washington, D.C., poet Anthony Hecht, and *Poems Seven: New and Complete Poetry* was released by Alan Dugan. Old hand Robert Bly issued *The Night Abraham Called to the Stars,* and younger poets Forrest Gander and Mark Doty signed in with *Torn Awake* and *Source,* respectively. Novelist John Updike produced a collection of occasional verse titled *Americana.*

Some fine translations by American poets were released, among them Brooks Haxton's *Fragments: The Collected Wisdom of Heraclitus* ("The river/ where you set/ your foot just now/ is gone—those waters/ giving way to this,/ now this.") and Arthur Sze's translations from a number of classical Chinese poets in *The Silk Dragon* (including this gem from the 8th-century poet Wang Wei—"Sir, you come from my native home/ and should know the affairs there./ The day you left, beside the silk-paned window—/ did the cold plum sprout flowers or not?").

A number of fiction writers and poets turned to autobiography and memoir. John Edgar Wideman explained the importance of basketball in his life in *Hoop Roots;* Horton Foote told of his early life in the theatre in *Beginnings;* Jimmy Santiago Baca chronicled his emergence as a poet in *A Place to Stand;* Deborah Digges described her relationship with her difficult son in *The Stardust Lounge;* Tess Gallagher detailed her relationship with Raymond Carver in *Soul Barnacles;* and novelist and essayist Edward Hoagland recounted his descent into blindness in *Compass Points: How I Lived.*

A number of fiction writers published essay collections, criticism, and journalism. The first essay in Tom Wolfe's *Hooking Up* (2000) was his attempt to sum up "What Life Was Like at the Turn of the Century." In *Political Fictions,* Joan Didion collected her columns from the *New York Review of Books.* Native American writer Louis Owens weighed in with *I Hear the Train: Reflections, Inventions, Refractions;* Alan Cheuse produced *Listening to the Page: Adventures in Reading and Writing;* and Clarence Major collected a number of essays and reviews in *Necessary Distance.* Adrienne Rich offered *Arts of the Possible: Essays and Conversations.* Farther afield, if not entirely trivial was Jay McInerny's wine book *Bacchus & Me* (2000). A much more interesting example of a novelist writing on a subject other than literature was Nicholas Delbanco's short history of a Niccolò Paganini cello in *The Countess of Stanlein Restored.* An example of a nonfiction writer working with the imagination of a novelist was *Red,* Terry Tempest Williams's evocative book about the Utah desert. In *Halls of Fame,* essayist John D'Agata explodes the form of the nonfiction collection as he explores the various Americana exhibitions around the nation, ranging from ones devoted to bowling to those honouring modern dance. ("Woman in black [Clytemnestra] enters empty stage from right flanked by two attendants who carry red cloth. Clytemnestra moves stage left & sits on throne. Man dressed in gold [Agamemnon] enters from stage right on litter.")

Various artists served as the subject for some interesting biographies. Nancy Milford's *Savage Beauty: The Life of Edna St. Vincent Millay* won a lot of praise among reviewers. Less well noticed were *Isadora: A Sensational Life* by Peter Kurth and *Norman Rockwell* by Laura Claridge. Biographer Alfred Habegger released *My Wars Are Laid Away in Books: The Life of Emily Dickinson,* and crime-fiction writer James Sallis worked on *Chester Himes.* African American scholar Emily Bernard edited *Remember Me to Harlem: The Letters of Langston Hughes and Carl Van Vechten, 1925–1964.* In the political realm, Tom Wells recounted the life and times of Daniel Ellsberg in *Wild Man.* In the world of therapy, Charles B. Strozier concentrated on *Heinz Kohut: The Making of a Psychoanalyst.* The most widely read biography of the year was David McCullough's *John Adams.*

Roth captured the PEN/Faulkner Award for Fiction for *The Human Stain,* and the PEN/Malamud Award for Excellence in the Short Story went to Richard Ford and Sherman Alexie. Chabon won the Pulitzer Prize for fiction for *The Amazing Adventures of Kavalier & Clay,* and Stephen Dunn took the Pulitzer in poetry for *Different Hours.* The latest volume in David Levering Lewis's biography of W.E.B. Du Bois—*W.E.B. Du Bois: The Fight for Equality and the American Century, 1919–1963*—won the Pulitzer for biography. The Pulitzer for history was captured by Joseph Ellis for *Founding Brothers: The Revolutionary Generation.*

Among the literary luminaries who died during the year were poet A.R. Ammons, poet, playwright, and novelist Gregory Corso, novelists Frank Gilbreth, Jr., Ken Kesey, and John Knowles, suspense writer Robert Ludlum, crime novelist Peter Maas, and short-story writer and novelist Eudora Welty. (*See* OBITUARIES.) (ALAN CHEUSE)

Canada. The past—personal, historical, and imaginary—was the chosen ground for many Canadian novels in 2001, ranging from Nega Mezlekia's exploration of precolonial Africa from a postcolonial perspective in *The God Who Begat a Jackal* to Robert Hough's 20th-century circus saga about a tiger-taming woman, *The Final Confession of Mabel Stark,* and including along the way the globe-encompassing 18th-century quest for the infinite book in Thomas Wharton's *Salamander.* In addition, early 19th-century Newfoundland was powerfully evoked in Michael Crummey's *River Thieves;* prerevolutionary Russia and beyond, where the focus was on the trials of Mennonite families, were explored in both Sandra Birdsell's *The Russlander* and Rudy Wiebe's *Sweeter than All the World;* and World War I Ontario and France were the disparate locales of Jane Urquhart's *The Stone Carvers,* which revealed the complex relations between workers, immigrants, and other nomads. Richard B. Wright's *Clara Callan* and her sister survive the Depression in their separate ways, and the postwar Hiroshima of *The Ash Garden* was thoroughly cultivated by Dennis Bock.

More contemporary times were reflected in myriad facets in Nancy Huston's *Dolce Agonia,* a town-and-gown tale set in New England; Timothy Taylor's *Stanley Park,* in which a young chef and his father meet on the cutting edge of experience and self-knowledge; Kelli Deeth's *The Girl Without Anyone,* exploring the search for self through self-imposed exile; poet Michael Redhill's first novel, *Martin Sloane,* an excursion

Rudy Wiebe—chronicler of the Mennonites

© Todd Korol

through minutia to obsession; Kelly Watt's *Mad Dog,* depicting a chaos of characters crazy as foxes; and Diane Schoemperlen's *Our Lady of the Lost and Found,* in which some of the many apparitions of Mary are chronicled during the Lady's weeklong retreat in the author's home. Yann Martel's *Life of Pi* seemed to occur in no time at all.

The fact that single acts could have far-reaching consequences was apparent in a number of works. In Kenneth Radu's *Flesh and Blood,* falling in love with someone of a different race liberates and confounds both lovers in unexpected ways; in *Critical Injuries,* Joan Barfoot dissected the long-term consequences—good, bad, and ambivalent—of a happenstance encounter between a middle-aged woman and a teenager ripe for trouble; and in *Spadework,* Timothy Findley played with the interlocking fates of people whose lives are disrupted by a single stroke of a gardener's spade.

Short fiction as usual ranged widely in theme and content. In *Hateship, Friendship, Courtship, Loveship, Marriage,* Alice Munro framed her latest collection of stories in the vagaries of a childhood game; in *The Path of Totality,* Audrey Thomas observed the darkness, metaphoric and personal, of those blinded by the light of a sun studied too closely. P.K. Page's *A Kind of Fiction* was an odd assortment of tales drawn from a poet's point of view by a prosaic pen, while the *Simple Recipes* of Madeleine Thien combined the shifting alliances of family relationships in bold new flavours of character and intrigue. Joseph Boyden's *Born with a Tooth* traced the paths of those caught between two worlds, native and white, while Adam Lewis Schroeder's *Kingdom of Monkeys* took the reader into the jungles of Southeast Asia and the human heart.

Poetry is founded in the ever-present tension between senses and meaning, exemplified in George Elliott Clarke's *Execution Poems* or the communion of romance and reality that distinguished *This Tremor Love Is* by Daphne Marlatt. Robert Kroetsch elucidated the mysteries of passion in *The Hornbooks of Rita K.;* Zoë Landale ventured with brave foolishness into the conundrums of parenthood in *Blue in This Country;* David Zieroth examined the conflicting claims and alliances of the spirit and the flesh in *Crows Do Not Have Retirement;* Rhea Tregebov tested the connections between grief and joy in *The Strength of Materials;* and David Helwig presented four epic poems in *Telling Stories.*

New voices included those of Billie Livingston in *The Chick at the Back of the Church,* singing the sad, triumphant songs of a survivor, and Shani Mootoo in a mouthwatering concoction of native-English vocabulary and syntax, *The Predicament of Or.* Voices that became silent included those of poet Louis Dudek, essayist and novelist Mordecai Richler, and crime novelist L.R. Wright. (*See* OBITUARIES.)

(ELIZABETH WOODS)

Other Literature in English. Australia, New Zealand, and South Africa continued to provide critically acclaimed and commercially successful literary works in English in 2001. Australian Peter Carey became only the second two-time winner of Great Britain's Booker Prize. His fictional treatment of 19th-century Australian folk hero and outlaw Ned Kelly in *True History of the Kelly Gang* (2000) also garnered the author his second top Commonwealth Writers Prize and eclipsed much notice of Carey's other published work of the year, *30 Days in Sydney: A Wildly Distorted Account.* Another Australian, Arabella Edge, won the South East Asia and South Pacific regional Commonwealth Writers Prize for Best First Book with her historical novel *The Company: The Story of a Murderer* (2000), which was set in 17th-century Amsterdam. Frank Moorhouse won the 2001 Miles Franklin Award for *Dark Palace* (2000), and Hannie Rayson's *Life After George* (2000) represented the first time in the award's history that a play had been short-listed. Tim Winton drew praise

© Michael Crabtree/Reuters 2001

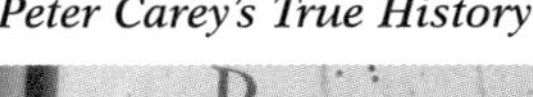

Peter Carey's True History

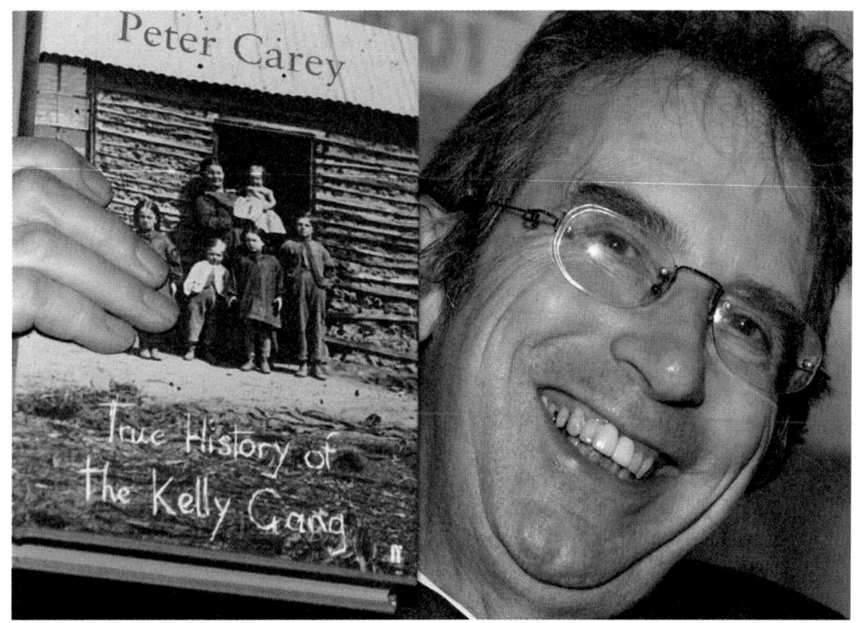

for his *Dirt Music,* a novel that explored the complexities of existence and of marginal relationships. Anna Rutherford—Australian editor, publisher, and scholar of Commonwealth literature—died in February.

Literary highlights in nearby New Zealand were dominated by poets and included the publication of the inaugural poet laureate Bill Manhire's *Collected Poems;* Ian Wedde's long-awaited collection inspired by Horace, *The Commonplace Odes;* the final and posthumously published verse collection *Late Song* (2000) by much-loved poet Lauris Edmond; and the latest collection by veteran Allen Curnow, *The Bells of Saint Babel's: Poems 1997–2001,* his first book in four years. Before his death in September, Curnow had been revered by many as the country's greatest living poet. (*See* OBITUARIES.)

South Africa offered its usual fare of outstanding works and award-winning authors. The much-heralded novelist J.M. Coetzee brought out *Stranger Shores: Literary Essays 1986–1999,* a selection of 26 pieces on literature and writing, and Nobel laureate Nadine Gordimer released her 13th novel, *The Pickup,* the story of a provocative and complex relationship between a wealthy white woman and an Arab mechanic. Countrymen Zakes Mda (*The Heart of Redness* [2000]) and K. Sello Duiker (*Thirteen Cents* [2000]) were honoured as the African regional winners of the Commonwealth Writers Prize for Best Book and Best First Book, respectively.

Also of note was Tanzanian Abdulrazak Gurnah's latest novel, *By the Sea,* which focused on immigrants and exiles in its depiction of two very different refugees who both left the same seaside town in Zanzibar to be reunited many years later in Great Britain. Elsewhere, internationally acclaimed Somalian-born novelist and essayist Nuruddin Farah received the 2001 Fonlon-Nichols Award, conferred by the African Literature Association. (DAVID DRAPER CLARK)

GERMANIC

German. In his 2001 novel *Rot,* Uwe Timm sought to come to terms with the experiences of the generation of so-called 68ers, people who went through the cultural and political turmoil of the 1960s and '70s in West Germany. The protagonist of *Rot* is Thomas Linde, a 68er who makes his living as a eulogist at burials, a profession that becomes a metaphor for the death of the utopian dreams for social and political renewal of an entire generation—one that now holds the reins of political power in both Germany and the United States. In the end the protagonist dies, and the novel was, in a sense, a eulogy for him and his generation.

Bodo Kirchhoff's novel *Parlando* dealt with the experiences of the children born to the 68ers. The novel's main character, Karl Faller, is in his mid-30s and is a screenwriter for television; he attempts to free himself from the influence of an oppressive father who was once, like so many other 68ers, a social revolutionary and is now a cynic. Like many of Kirchhoff's other works, *Parlando* was also an erotic journey.

In his novel *Die Vertreibung aus der Hölle,* Austrian writer Robert Menasse wove together two stories, one from contemporary Europe and the other from the Europe of the 17th century. The contemporary story deals with a semiautobiographical 68er who experiences the political turmoil of the late 1960s and early '70s, and the other story chronicles the life of a distant ancestor of the contemporary Central European, a Jewish philosopher who must contend with Christian anti-Semitism. Although the novel suggested parallels between the two life stories, the fundamental differences between the kinds of persecution that the two protagonists endure suggested that there is such a thing as progress in human history. In his novel *Fräulein Stark,* Swiss author Thomas Hürlimann told an autobiographical story about a teenager coming of age in provincial Switzerland in a devout Roman Catholic milieu.

© Jerry Bauer

Erotic journeyman Bodo Kirchhoff

Friedrich Christian Delius also combined contemporary narrative and historical fiction in his novel *Der Königsmacher,* which told the story of Minna —the illegitimate daughter of William of Orange and Marie Hoffmann—a working-class girl in Berlin, and on another level followed the life of the fictional novelist Albert Rusch, Minna's descendent and biographer. *Der Königsmacher* was also a satire of contemporary literary life in Germany, notably the tendency to turn certain authors into pop stars. Martin Walser's *Der Lebenslauf der Liebe* told the pathetic story of Susi Gern, a woman who rises from humble beginnings to riches following her marriage but then falls into degradation and despair.

Juli Zeh's first novel, *Adler und Engel,* was a serious political and crime thriller that offered a devastating critique of contemporary European society. Its protagonist, Max, finds himself mixed up in criminality through his relationship with Jessie, the daughter of a wealthy businessman who happens to be a major drug dealer. In the end the novel told the story of Max's disillusionment and, like Bertolt Brecht's *Die Dreigroschenoper* (1928), suggested an identity between capitalism on the one hand and criminality on the other. In his novel *1979,* Christian Kracht explored the tensions between the European world and Islamic fundamentalism at the time of the 1978–79 Iranian revolution. Both of these novels by young authors produced strong evidence that the much-discussed younger generation of German writers was by no means ready to banish politics completely from their thinking.

Ursula Krechel's novel *Der Übergriff* told a far less overtly political story of loneliness and aging. Its protagonist is a middle-aged woman who must gradually learn to assert herself and to overcome her tendency toward self-deprecation. Norman Ohler's novel *Mitte,* set in the lively Berlin neighbourhood of the novel's title, showed a colourful counterculture coexisting uneasily with Germany's government. The protagonist moves into one of the many old apartment buildings in the centre of Berlin, where he makes a number of mysterious discoveries that lead him to an understanding of the haunted nature of the German capital. Georg Klein's *Barbar Rosa* was set in early 1990s Berlin at the time of German reunification.

Ralf Rothmann's short-story collection *Ein Winter unter Hirschen* explored the miracles of everyday life and the possibility that a book with a Christian theme could find an audience in contemporary Germany. Thomas Hettche's novel *Der Fall Arbogast* was a postmodern thriller exploring the relationship between sex and death in the story of a coroner on the trail of an erroneous verdict handed down many years earlier.

On May 18 Germany lost its most distinguished literary critic, Hans Mayer, who during his 94 years had experienced six states and political systems as well as their writers. Stefan Heym, one of the former German Democratic Republic's most respected dissident writers, died on December 16. (*See* OBITUARIES.) (STEPHEN BROCKMANN)

Netherlandic. In 2001 well-known novelist and essayist Louis Ferron was awarded the Dutch national Constantijn Huygens Prijs for his uncompromisingly singular and "completely unfashionable and contrary" body of work. The Libris Literatuur Prijs went to Tomas Lieske for his novel *Franklin* (2000), which showcased his brilliant style and bold wit.

Jeroen Brouwers's novel *Geheime Kamers* (2000) was awarded three literary prizes—the Gouden Uil, the Multuli Prijs, and the AKO Literatuur Prijs, the most lucrative award for Dutch literature. The work was lauded as a great novel that "sounds like a symphony and is constructed like a cathedral"; it featured a complex plot in which all the narrative lines connected in the end, grounded in the dark underworld of myth, forgotten fears, and suppressed needs and desires. In his acceptance speech for the Gouden Uil, Brouwers criticized the practice of making the presentation of the AKO Literatuur Prijs in a televised ceremony (as Arnon Grunberg had also done the previous year), and he declined to attend the ceremony. Brouwers maintained that the "circus" surrounding literary prizes debased the literature itself and fostered an inappropriate sense of competition between authors.

In his novel *De mensheid zij geprezen*, Grunberg radically questioned Erasmus's humanist legacy—the lawyer who defends humankind's offenses (hatred, opportunism, lies, and war) sports great rhetorical skill. Harry Mulisch published *Siegfried*, a novel that takes on the relationships between fiction, imagination, and reality in a story about a writer who decides to undo Adolf Hitler by way of fiction. In *Als op de eerste dag* Stefan Hertmans explored the sublime and the sinister potential of fantasy. A younger writer, Floor Haakman, also considered thoughts of fantasy in *Oneetbaar brood*, a suspenseful philosophical novel.

More Dutch works were also being published in English, notably Oscar van den Boogaard's novel *Love's Death*, translated by Ina Rilke, and Grunberg's *Silent Extras* (2000), translated by Sam Garrett. *Love's Death*, written in a fluid and virtuoso style, told a compelling story in a narrative that revealed surprises and complicated motives.

(JOLANDA VANDERWAL TAYLOR)

Danish. Danish writers cast reality to the wind and explored "surreality" in 2001. Per Højholt's novel *Auricula* described a universal silence that is followed by the marvelous conception of actual ears that witness pivotal events of the 20th century; gossip with artists, philosophers, and politicians; and serve as "ear witnesses to history." Søren Jessen's novel *Zambesi* focused on odd characters whose Kafkaesque lives conclude at Café Zambesi, the place where everyone meets and reality unravels. Grete Roulund's *Kvinden fra Sáez* was a tale of intrigue and crime close to home. Hans-Otto Jørgensen's novel *Molly—historien om en engel* (2000) focused on a Juttish farmer, Jens Thorstensen, and the missing moments in his life. The novellas in Jens-Martin Eriksen's *Jonatan Svidts forbyrdelse. Nye beretninger* (2000) depicted ominous outsiders who wreak havoc on serene villages.

In *Fiske i livets flod* (2000), Merete Pryds Helle created a wonderful palimpsest of stories dealing with the written word. Nina Belling and Nina Bolt recaptured other times and places in their works. Belling's *Til en fremmed* (2000) concerned a young Florentine illuminator whose inheritance proves very dangerous. *Spejlmageren* (2000), Bolt's novel of early Renaissance Venice, focused on Bartolomeo, a Murano glassmaker searching for perfection, and on a company of players whose dramas both reflect and transform life. Maria Helleberg's historical novel *Rigets frue* concerned Danish Queen Margrethe I.

In *Til sidst* Asger Baunsbak-Jensen offered a poignant look at the final days of a sadly forgotten and very ill office executive. Jens Christian Grøndahl's *Virginia* (2000) traced wartime love between a 16-year-old girl and an English pilot, as witnessed by a 14-year-old boy. A problematic love lasting through time was the subject of *Bonsai* (2000), Kirsten Thorup's first novel in six years. Anne Strandvad's *Hvor er svalerne om vinteren?* (2000) focused on young Karina's meeting with love and death—and with dire consequences. Kirsten Hammann's *Bruger De ord i kaffen?* conjoined a novel about a novelist with "poetics," discussions on writing. In *Sjælen marineret* Benny Andersen combined a suite from younger days, surrealistic lyrics, and cityscape poems. Christian Yde Frostholm's poems in *Mellem stationerne* (2000) dealt with urban rhythms, personal journeys, and loves. The Children's Book of the Year Prize went to Henrik Einspor for *Med døden i hælene*, and Joakim Garff garnered both the Georg Brandes Prize and *Weekendavisen's* Literary Prize for *SAK*, his biography of Søren Kierkegaard. Kirsten Thorup claimed the Annual Award of the Danish Academy. Essayist and short-story writer Villy Sørensen died in December. (*See* OBITUARIES.)

(LANAE HJORTSVANG ISAACSON)

Norwegian. The year 2001 was a successful one for established authors in Norway. The 2001 Nordic Council Literature Prize was awarded to Jan Kjærstad for *Oppdageren* (1999). Lars Saabye Christensen won acclaim for his gigantic novel *Halvbroren*, which chronicled three generations in Oslo; it was awarded the Brage Prize and Bokhandlerprisen and was nominated for the 2002 Nordic Council Literature Prize. Ingvar Ambjørnsen released *Dukken i taket*, which portrayed the psychological perversity of revenge, and he was awarded a Tabuprisen for his openness about angst. In *Om bare* Vigdis Hjorth returned to the tangles of love, a theme she excelled in exploring.

Hans Herbjørnsrud's short-story collection *Vi vet så mye* investigated the tension between the unexpected and the familiar; it was also nominated for the 2002 Nordic Council Literature Prize. Frode Grytten received rave reviews for *Popsongar*, which spun each story around a pop song. *Svømmetak*, by acclained short-story writer Laila Stien, followed the everyday life of women.

In addition, several young authors made their debuts during the year. Many of their works were inspired by the dirty realism launched by cult figure Ari Behn in 1999 and rebelled against the authority of well-established social realism. *The Cocka Hola Company—Skandinavisk misantropi* by Abo Rasul (Matias Faldbakken's pseudonym) instigated controversy with its obscenities. Grethe Nestor's *Kryp* turned the popular genre of the urban single woman à la Bridget Jones into a disturbing tale of venereal disease and crawling insects. Espen Dennis Kristoffersen's *Hvit* was a Lolita-like story, told from the girl's perspective, that was loaded with swearing.

Mystery novels concerned with contemporary issues flourished, notably Jon Michelet's *Den frosne kvinnen* and Fredrik Skagen's *Blitz*. Tom Kristensen's and Jon Lyng's debuts *En Kule* and *Valgets kval*, respectively, described Oslo's financial and political circles.

Annie Riis was awarded the Brage Prize for poetry for *Himmel av stål*, which was praised for its thematic scope and imagery. Veteran poet Cecilie Løveid's *Split* delighted with its cheerfulness and confident language. Endre Ruset's promising debut, *Ribbeinas Vingespenn*, plumbed the possibilities of transgressing physical limits in language and content.

Numerous biographies were welcomed. Sven Kærup Bjørneboe used humour and melancholy in the revealing portrayal of his uncle Jens Bjørneboe. With *Jæger* Ketil Bjørnstad completed his work on the Christiania Bohemians. (ANNE G. SABO)

Swedish. A feeling of lost control and an urge to use language to beseech a present and a past that had gone out of hand served as a rough summary of preferred themes in Swedish literature in 2001. Per Olov Enquist's *Lewis resa* portrayed revivalist Lewi Pethrus, the founding father of the Swedish branch of the Pentecostal Movement. The 600-page factual novel told the story not only of the man but of the time, and it was also discussed as a biography and 20th-century document.

One observed an inclination for the subjective and a biographical turn, explicit in Lisbeth Larsson's *Sanning och konsekvens*, a study of the art of biographical narration. Using personal experience, many writers found ways to formulate a growing feeling of social estrangement, notably Stig Claesson in *Det lyckliga Europa*, Theodor Kallifatides in *Ett nytt land utanför mitt fönster*, and Bodil Malmsten in *Priset på vatten i Finistère*.

The inspired preacher, a patriarch lost or abandoned, turned out to be somewhat of an icon in Kerstin Norborg's well-written first novel, *Min faders hus*, in senior poet Ragnar Thoursie's first prose book, *Ditt ord är ljus*, and in lyrical form in Jesper Svenbro's *Pastorn, min far.* The murdered prime minister Olof Palme turned up as a lost secular father figure in Lars Åke Augustsson's *Sveavägen*. In Ellen Mattson's impressive short novel *Snö*, the ambivalence surfaced in a bravely unheroic historical version of the theme staged at the death of King Charles XII in 1718. History—convincingly studied and deliberately animated—acted as a possible mirror for the present in Maja Lundgren's novel *Pompeji*.

Ulla Montan

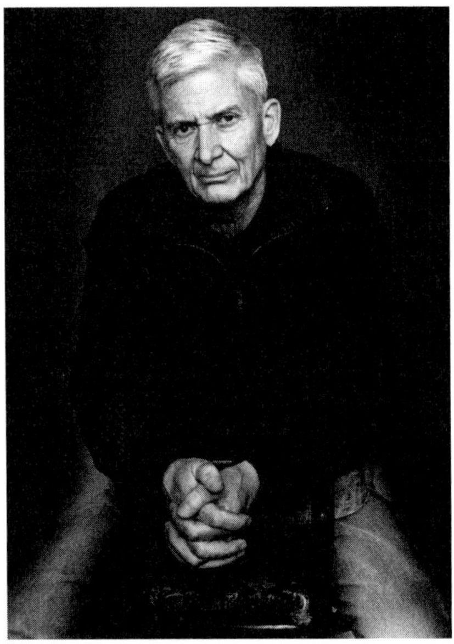

Per Olov Enquist—purveyor of documentary-style fiction

As for genre, short—often hybridic—forms were frequent. Along with the explicit subjective focus, there was an opposing trend that brought out a marked impersonal attitude. Interesting examples, including Magnus Florin's *Cirkulation* and Lotta Lotass's *Aerodynamiska tal*, left realism behind, whereas Mare Kandre's *Hetta och vitt*, Mats Kempe's *Saknar dig sällan så mycket som nu*, Mats Kolmisoppi's *Jag menar nu*, and Alejandro Leiva Wenger's *Till vår ära* used other techniques to estrange everyday life, often by focusing on the effects of migration on identity and language. (IMMI LUNDIN)

FRENCH

France. In 2001 French literature's marked inclination toward gloom continued unabated as it had for over a decade, leaving no permutation of familial misery. Death in the family was a favourite topic, and Laure Adler's *À ce soir* described the death of her son and the subsequent guilt that has consumed her for the past 20 years. François Bon's autobiographical *Mécanique* traced childhood memories of an existence surrounded by cars, recollections that were stirred by the death of his father, a Citroën car dealer. In *Des phrases courtes, ma chérie*, Pierrette Fleutiaux chronicled a voyage of self-discovery that a daughter took as she accompanied her mother during her final months, while conversely, Isabelle Hausser's *La Table des enfants* depicted the death of a daughter and a distraught mother's attempt to dispel the shroud of mystery concealing the person she was. Marie Darrieussecq covered mourning from several angles at once in *Bref séjour chez les vivants*, in which she examined the devastation wreaked upon a family member one at a time by the drowning of Pierre, their youngest son and brother. Though Anne Sibran's *Ma vie en l'air* did not revolve around death, it did relate the young heroine's insane delusions of flying, which stemmed from incestuous sexual abuse.

Amid the horrors of family life, cracks appeared in the monolithic depressiveness with novels noteworthy for the strategies they used to overcome bleakness. In the undisputed literary event of the year, Michel Houellebecq's *Plateforme* fully recognized and even wallowed in the ills of directionless Western life but reversed conventional values by seemingly singing the praises of Europeans' sexual tourism to poor countries such as Thailand, a twist that aroused a storm of controversy even before the novel was released. In *La Vie sexuelle de Catherine M.*, Catherine Millet also overturned sexual taboos to make promiscuity a banner of individual freedom by describing in explicit, even scandalous, detail her encounters with men of every stripe and perversion. Eric-Emmanuel Schmitt's strategy was even more original; in his *La Part de l'autre*—in contrast to a utopia, or place that never existed—he created a *uchronia*, or time that never existed, to invent the happy 20th century that would have been if only young Adolf Hilter had been accepted into the Viennese art school to which he applied in 1908.

Though dealing with death, Jean d'Ormesson's *Voyez comme on danse*, which began at a funeral, used the normally mournful occasion to resurrect the joy of a man whose love of life and women blazed through the nightmares of Nazism and Stalinism from the Greek Mediterranean to the war zone of Algeria. In *Paulette et Roger*, the ever-sunny Daniel Picouly avoided the blandness of the present by tenderly and lovingly reconstructing what his parents' life as a couple must have been before children came along. Eric Chevillard sidestepped the real world altogether with perhaps the most original work of the year, *Les Absences du Capitaine Cook,* a feast of the absurd in which the usual unities of character and plot were abandoned in favour of a series of insane episodes strung together by far-fetched analogies, word games, and proverbs taken literally that served to reaffirm the author's reputation as one of the most dazzling writers on the literary scene.

Two perennial favourites also published new works; Nobel laureate Claude Simon's *Le Tramway* reconstructed the world of the author's childhood by the freewheeling analogies of memory as one thought resurrected another with the connecting thread of the trolley rides Simon had taken as a youth. Alain Robbe-Grillet returned to fiction after a long foray into autobiography and a nine-year silence with *La Reprise,* which, in a style familiar to readers of his earlier experimental works, used the trappings of a conventional spy novel to present the story of a secret agent sent in 1949 to bombed-out Berlin to carry out a mission about which he himself knows nothing, a mystery only deepened by the strange memories the city seems to awaken in him.

Michel Houellebecq—directionless in France

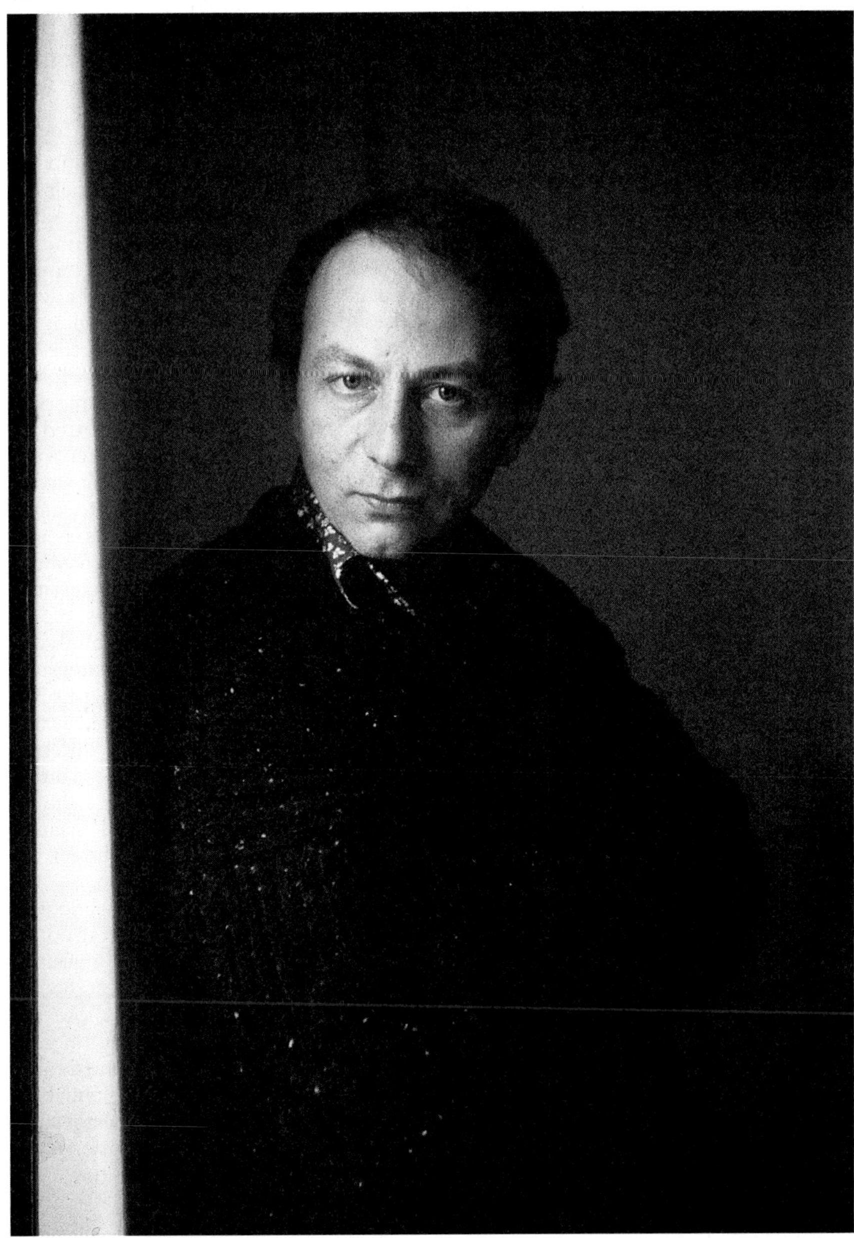

The Prix Femina went to Marie Ndiaye's *Rosie Carpe,* in which the protagonist and her brother, adrift in the world and on the run from themselves, progressively decline into misery as they reproduce upon their own children the same loveless environment their parents had inflicted on them. The Prix Médicis was awarded to Benoît Duteurtre's *Le Voyage en France,* which presented modern-day France as seen through the disillusioned and shocked eyes of a young man, the illegitimate son of an American woman and a French father he never knew. After years of idealizing the country from afar, the protagonist at last decides to take the trip from New York to see Paris for himself. Martine Le Coz won the Prix Renaudot for *Céleste,* the story of the love between a white woman and a black doctor in cholera-stricken 1830s Paris, a love threatened by the incestuous passion of her uncle, who rages with the jealousy of one forbidden love for another. The Prix Goncourt went to Jean-Christophe Rufin's *Rouge Brésil,* a tale of bitingly ironic wit set against the backdrop of the 16th-century French conquest of Brazil, in which the Europeans' religious fury contrasts with the native Indians' pristine simplicity. (VINCENT AURORA)

Canada. Though the French literary community in Canada viewed itself as a society distinct from the rest of the country, its tastes remained entirely global in 2001. The third installation of Pierre Godin's ongoing biography about the late René Lévesque, the popular provincial politician, attracted attention among parliamentarians and ordinary citizens alike, but readers also were captivated by the adventures of Harry Potter and anything that would shed light on Afghanistan following the September 11 terrorist attacks in the U.S. Nothing, however, could match the outpouring of love for Marie Laberge, the author of several best-selling works of romantic fiction. Her popularity—always strong—was unstoppable, especially with the completion of her trilogy *Le Goût du bonheur* (2000). Another female voice that had fallen by the wayside reemerged with new strength—that of Acadian novelist Antonine Maillet, who in 1979 had become the first non-French person to win France's Prix Goncourt. Her new novel was *Madame Perfecta.*

Another worldwide trend, pornography written by women, was evidenced in Quebec-born writer Nelly Arcan's *Putain,* the story of a girl who engages in the world's oldest profession and who makes her confession to a nameless psychiatrist. The question of whether the author actually experienced the scenarios described in the book occupied many readers' minds. Madness among women continued to be a favourite topic in French Canada, and writer Andrée A. Michaud produced *Le Ravissement;* her efforts were recognized with the Governor-General's Award, Canada's premier French-language fiction prize. Though plays were rarely published for their literary merit, Normand Chaurette's *Le Petit Köchel* was an exception; it picked up the Governor-General's Award for French-language drama.

One positive trend in publishing was the solidifying of the so-called outlaw small presses, including Les Intouchables, Planète Rebelle, and Trait d'Union, which relied on daring and worked at poverty wages to give younger writers a forum for their works. Though writers in English-speaking markets faced a crisis with the downfall of Chapters, the country's largest retail bookstore chain, French-Canadian authors were largely unaffected by the closure, owing to the strength of independent bookstores in French-speaking Canada.

(DAVID HOMEL)

Pierre Longtin

Pushing the envelope in French Canadian literature—Nelly Arcan

ITALIAN

The most distinctive feature of Italian literature in 2001 was the publication of several novels whose settings in the recent past served as a framework for a reflection on history. Davide Longo's *Un mattino a Irgalem* takes place during the Italian colonization of Ethiopia, a topic traditionally neglected by historians and creative writers. In the action a short and failed investigation into the crimes of a bloodthirsty sergeant unveils the brutality of colonialism, as well as the dilemmas facing those who are not willing to justify it on ideological grounds. Antonio Franchini's *L'abusivo* focused on more recent history and on the parallel lives of Giancarlo Siani—a young journalist killed by the camorra in 1985 for his reportage on organized crime—and the author-narrator, a former colleague of Siani's, who left journalism and Naples for literature and Northern Italy and tried to reconstruct the dramatic events that led to Siani's death.

Bruno Arpaia, Laura Pariani, and Massimiliano Melilli also looked to the past and anchored their fiction in the biographies of three philosophers: Walter Benjamin, Friedrich Nietzsche, and Antonio Gramsci, respectively. In *L'angelo della storia,* Arpaia alternated scenes from Benjamin's life with those of Laureano Mahojo, a republican fighter in the Spanish Civil War (1936–39). Reflection and action and different perspectives and narrative rhythms run parallel until the two protagonists meet at Port Bou, where Benjamin tragically ends his life. More introspective and lyrical was Pariani's *La foto di Orta,* centred on an 1882 photo of Nietzsche with Lou Salomé and the glimpse at love and happiness it symbolized in the eyes of the philosopher, bound to loneliness and insanity. Largely based on Gramsci's letters and notebooks, Melilli's *Punta Galera* reconstructed the 43 days the antifascist intellectual spent in confinement on the island of Ustica before being sent to prison on the Italian mainland. Melilli re-created Gramsci's relationship with the other exiles and paid special attention to a school of science and humanities they established for the island community. What emerged was the portrayal of a curious, active, and generous man, determined to defy the infamous sentence pronounced at the 1928 trial by the Fascist tribunal that sought "to prevent Gramsci's mind from functioning for twenty years."

Andrea Camilleri confirmed his success with a new adventure for his hero, police inspector Montalbano. More than for its plot, *L'odore della notte* was remarkable for the protagonist's evolution: the inspector, just over 50, longs for human warmth and love and views globalization and the new economy with bitter irony. Antonio Tabucchi ingeniously played with the conventions of the epistolary genre in his *Si sta facendo sempre più tardi,* where the perturbing letters sent by 17 men to their beloved ones (be they real or imaginary, dead or alive) are answered by a single, pointed female response.

Writing outside current trends, Paola Mastrocola and Niccolò Ammaniti received widespread public acclaim. Mastrocola's *Palline di pane* treated with lightness and humour the uneasiness of family life, whereas Ammaniti's *Io non ho paura* chronicled the adventures of Michele, a boy struggling to save a newly found friend, in the incomprehensible world of grown-ups.

Strong theatrical features marked Claudio Magris's *La mostra,* centred on the life of Vito Timmel, a painter from Trieste who died in 1949 in a psychiatric hospital. The title alludes to an exhibit organized after Timmel's death, but it could also be interpreted as a reference to the structural characteristics of the text, in which a life is reconstructed through the fragmented discussions of friends, fellow inmates, and hospital personnel as well as through the visionary monologue of the artist himself. Alternating between different chronological periods and voices, Magris developed an analysis of the relationship between sanity and insanity and explored madness as a refuge from the persecution of life.

Some of the most relevant poetic production of the year was written not in Italian but in dialect, notably in *Rimis te sachete,* Flavio Santi's latest collection. The 28-year-old Santi chose the dialect of the Friuli region for poems that allude to international music and cinema (from rock star Jimi Hendrix to film director David Cronenberg) without losing sight of the dramatic recent history of the area (from the 1976 earthquake to Pier Paolo Pasolini's death). Andrea Zanzotto also employed some dialect in *Sovrimpressioni,* in which the poet revisited the natural landscape he had celebrated in *Dietro il paesaggio* (1951); 40 years later that environment was almost unrecognizable, altered by pollution and cement and devastated by consumerism.

Following the disappearance and death of Geno Pampaloni (1918–2001) —a scholar as well as a militant critic and the author of hundreds of articles for newspapers and magazines—Giuseppe Leonelli edited a collection of Pampaloni's selected essays, *Il critico giornaliero,* which paid tribute to the activity of this intellectual of subtle irony and masterful synthetic precision.

(LAURA BENEDETTI)

SPANISH

Spain. Readers looking for novels with a historical base, for novels presenting stories about real people, for history books, or for poetry about the passage of time, would find many possibilities in the literature published in 2001 in Spain.

Juan Marsé won the National Prize for Narrative with *Rabos de lagartija* (2000), another of his works set in the postwar years of the Spanish Civil War (1936–39). The novel centred on David, an adolescent who had a love-hate relationship with his parents; his father was an anarchist sought by the police, and his mother had an ambiguous relationship with the officer looking for her husband. Antonio Muñoz Molina's *Sefarad* was an account of the history of the 20th century through the voices of the persecuted and forgotten. The novel contained thousands of stories, some true and some fictionalized, that recalled cruel episodes in history, including the Holocaust and the communist repression. In Juan Manuel de Prada's most recent work, *Desgarrados y excéntricos,* he rescued from oblivion 15 frustrated 20th-century Spanish writers. Each portrait was the result of a meticulous investigation about the writers, all of whom were ignored in the literary canon. The Planeta Prize, which awarded approximately $550,000 on its 50th anniversary, was given to Rosa Regás's *La canción de Dorotea,* a story of mystery and intrigue involving a woman hired to take care of an ailing man in a country house.

In *El oro del rey,* the fourth and final volume of Arturo Pérez-Reverte's series of adventure novels about the mysterious Capitán Alatriste, the captain and his partner become involved in a mission concerning the smuggling of gold aboard Spanish galleons arriving from the Indies. One of the most applauded novels of the year was Eduardo Mendoza's *El tocador de señoras,* a funny, clever, and satiric X-ray of certain guilds (politicians and journalists) as well as several members of the Catalonian bourgeoisie. Lucía Etxebarria published her fourth novel, *De todo lo visible y lo invisible,* which began with the second suicide attempt of Ruth, a film director; Ruth meets Juan, a poet who has just arrived in Madrid to write a novel, and these two narcissistic and insecure characters develop a passionate dependence that degenerates into a terribly destructive relationship. Enrique Vila-Matas was the winner of the Rómulo Gallegos Prize of Venezuela for *El viaje vertical* (1999), his traveling book framed in the Spanish Civil War. Promising young author Javier Lucini weighed in with *La canción del mal amado, y otras desmitologías,* a collection of short stories based on Greek mythologies.

Antonio Muñoz Molina, spokesman for the persecuted and forgotten

A year after his death, José Ángel Valente was awarded the National Prize for Poetry for *Fragmentos de un libro futuro* (2000), which appeared posthumously and encompassed more than 90 poems and some brief prose pieces. The coveted Cervantes Prize, the highest distinction in Spanish letters, went to Colombian Álvaro Mutis. After nine years of silence, Ángel González published *Otoños y otras luces,* which explored the endless autumn, the extinguishing life, and the silence discovered by the poetic creation.

(VERÓNICA ESTEBAN)

Latin America. In 2001 many works explored Latin America's past and present social and political realities as well as offering variations on the theme of love. From Mexico, writer Carlos Fuentes returned to fantastic literature and to the theme of love's difficulties in *Instinto de Inez.* In *La piel del cielo,* Elena Poniatowska, winner of the 2001 Alfaguara Prize, offered an overview of science in Mexico as well as a political social history of that country's past 70 years as seen through the eyes of an astronomer. Laura Esquivel brought indigenous and Spanish-speaking cultures together in *Tan veloz como el deseo,* a tale in which love is the redeeming force in the difficult years following the Mexican Revolution. In *El espía del aire,* Ignacio Solares returned to the charged atmosphere of Mexico in the late 1960s. Other fiction from Mexico included Federico Campbell's novella *La clave Morse,* the story of an alcoholic telegraph operator and amateur writer told through the eyes of his daughters; Ana García Bergua's *Púrpura* (1999), which presented another vision of 20th-century Mexico and the political transformations of that country; and Álvaro Uribe's *Por su nombre,* a tale of obsessive love. In the realm of awards, novelist Juan García Ponce won the Juan Rulfo Prize, and the poet José Emilio Pacheco was awarded the first José Donoso Prize for his extensive body of work, which spanned over four decades. The literary world was saddened by the death of Juan José Arreola, author of a small but brilliant narrative corpus.

Sergio Ramírez of Nicaragua released *Catalina y Catalina,* a collection of stories that presented his country's harsh social and political realities. Rey Rosa of Guatemala published the short novel *Piedras encantadas,* which told the story of children in the streets of Guatemala City and the mysterious death of an adopted boy. *Milagro en Miami* by Zoé Valdés of Cuba explored the theme of exile involving a girl kidnapped from the island to become a supermodel in Milan. More than 10 years after the death of Reinaldo Arenas of Cuba, Alfaguara published his *El palacio de las blanquísimas mofetas,* the story of a boy growing up in rural poverty during the last years of the Fulgencio Batista regime. In *La fábula de José,* Eliseo Alberto of Cuba chronicled the life of a 33-year-old Cuban who arrives during the 1960s in Florida on a raft; he is given a choice of staying in jail or being exhibited in a zoo.

From Colombia, Álvaro Mutis's seven novels dealing with the popular protagonist Gaviero were republished in a volume entitled *Empresas y tribulaciones de Maqroll el Gaviero.* In December Mutis was named the recipient of the Cervantes Prize. Héctor Abad Faciolince published *Basura,* which explored the relationship between reading and writing. Medardo Arias Satizábal wrote *Que es un soplo la vida* about Carlos Gardel's death and the transporting of his body across Colombia. Making significant international literary news was the widely anticipated auction of the galleys of Gabriel García Márquez's *Cien años de soledad,* but the minimum opening bid of $530,000 was not met.

Chilean novelist Antonio Skármeta released *La chica del trombón,* a story of a young girl looking for her identity in the days prior to the election of Salvador Allende. Marcela Serrano's novel *Antigua vida mía,* a finalist for the Planeta Prize, was a narrative about a depressed woman who travels with a friend to Chiapas after the death of her son. Chilean poet Raúl Zurita won the national literature prize, awarded in August 2001.

From Argentina came Federico Andahazi's political novel *El principe,* which chronicled the rise to power of the son of a diabolical and fantastic father. Juan Forn published *Puras mentiras,* the tale of a man who finds his life unraveling and ends up traveling anonymously to a small coastal village. Marcelo Birmajer published *Tres mosqueteros,* a novel in which a Jewish man returns to Argentina on an unknown mission after having lived 20 years in Israel and is kidnapped in the airport. Tulio Stella's novel *La familia Fortuna,* in the tradition of Julio Cortázar's *Rayuela,* allows the reader to freely combine the seven "novels" in the text. Juan Gelman, one of Argentina's leading poets, published *Valer la pena,* a collection of 149 poems he wrote between 1966 and 2000.

Uruguayan authors had a banner year. Hugo Burel won the Lengua de Trapo Prize for Narrative for *El guerrero del crepúsculo,* about an encyclopaedia salesman who leaves the hospital after a brain operation only to enter a comic Kafkaesque world and end up in a house of prostitution, and Rafael Courtoisie showcased his narrative talent with the stories in *Tajos* (1999). In Hugo Fontana's *Veneno,* a friend from childhood narrates the story of a man who is condemned to death in the U.S. for alleged arson of a hotel frequented by gays. Mario Benedetti received the José Martí Iberoamerican Prize for his vast contributions to literature over almost 50 years. (JOHN BARRY)

PORTUGUESE

Portugal. The Association of Portuguese Writers awarded its 2001 Great Prize for Fiction to Maria Velho da Costa for her novel *Irene ou o contrato social* (2000). Velho da Costa, who first gained international acclaim with the publication in 1972 of *Novas cartas portuguesas,* turned to the subject of euthanasia in her latest prizewinning novel, in which a contract is made between a female patient and a male friend who helps her to die. The story was told in a complex and tangled way, challenging the reader to decipher literary allusions and echoes and associations with characters from her previous novels.

Short-listed for the same prize was Helder Macedo's novel *Vícios e virtudes,* a story about a fiction writer whose reputation is on the rise. Macedo used the literary technique of a narrative within a narrative to tell the story of an intriguing woman who is having an affair with a friend, who in turn is writing his own novel based on her. The interplay of situations and affections, the suspicions that assail the narrator, the ambiguities of language that prevail, changing everything into its opposite, confuse the narrator in the pursuit of the obscure object of his own desire. This most entertaining novel, written in an elegant and witty style, possessed a depth of thought that was never sacrificed to literary effect. Vices could become virtues, and virtues could masquerade as vices, depending on the way in which the cards were played.

Concern with language was pursued with great rigour and discipline by Gastão Cruz in his book of poems *Crateras* (2000), which was awarded the D. Dinis Prize for Literature. The sound of the word and the music of the verse served as the essence of his poetry, and meaning was subordinate to them. A simple description of a place had to convey its presence in the tone and colour of the word.

The Camões Prize was awarded to Eugénio de Andrade for his exceptional body of work. His poems breathed the air of nature and reflected an intense contemplation of nature-related objects, including leaves, seeds, roots, water, and birds. They all combined in a symphony of the four elements. In his *O sal da língua* (1995), the complexity of thought was matched by simplicity of expression. (L.S. REBELO)

Brazil. Brazilians mourned the death in August 2001 of Jorge Amado (*see* OBITUARIES), who for some 70 years was the country's most distinguished writer. In the 1930s and '40s he produced a body of Social Realist fiction that was totally committed to an ideal of communism, a factor that led to periods of his enforced exile from Brazil. From the mid-1950s he developed a unique style of "utopian realism," in which social dilemmas were dealt with from a more comical perspective. Amado claimed that his favourite among his works was *The Violent Land* (1942), which presented the cacao land struggles in his native state of Bahia. It was with his later group of works—including *Gabriela, Clove and Cinnamon* (1958) and *Dona Flor and Her Two Husbands* (1966)—and their adaptation to film, stage, and television that he earned international fame. These and other later novels were notable for highlighting the lives of blacks in Brazilian society and for their sympathetic portrayal of female characters in a traditionally macho society, approaches that caused these works to be praised and detested at the same time.

Fabrício Carpi Nejar published a new poetry collection, *Um terno de pássaros do Sul,* and the *Complete Poetical Works* of the symbolist poet Alphonsus de Guimaraens was published by his son and his grandson, both poets, Alphonsus Filho and Afonso Henriques da Costa Guimarães, respectively. The Guimaraens family continued its long tradition in Brazilian letters—dating back to 19th-century poet and novelist Bernardo Guimaraens—with the publication of Alphonsus Filho's own volume of poems, *O tecelão do assombro.*

Notable works of fiction included Joyce Cavalcante's novel *O cão chupando manga* and new short fiction by Luci Collin, *Precioso Impreciso.*

Two quite insightful volumes of cultural criticism appeared in late 2000. The essays in *Brasil, país do passado?,* edited by Lígia Chiappini, Antônio Dimas, and Berthold Zilly, took Stefan Zweig's classic *Brasil, país do futuro* (1941) as the starting point for a reevaluation of the concept of past, present, and future within the Brazilian

© Jerry Bauer

Brazilian literary giant Jorge Amado died during the year.

context. Fiction and essays by many of Brazil's leading militant intellectuals of the past 50 years, including Antônio Callado, Darcy Ribeiro, Paulo Freire, Paulo Francis, and Herbert José de Souza ("Betinho"), were analyzed to decipher the significance of the national past and what might occur in the future. An interdisciplinary study of the social role of Brazilian soap operas appeared in English: *Living with the Rubbish Queen: Telenovelas, Culture and Modernity in Brazil* by Thomas Tufte. In addition to analyzing the relevance of their themes and contents, the author sought to determine the impact of soap operas on the typical Brazilian viewer—the low-income urban woman. (IRWIN STERN)

RUSSIAN

The year 2001 was one of losses and gains for Russian literature. Several leading figures died, among them Viktor Krivulin, a major poet, critic, and organizational force in Russia's 1970s "underground"; Vadim Kozhonov—critic, literary scholar, and an intellectual leader of the "populist" wing of Russian literature; and Viktor Golyavkin, a prose writer in the absurdist vein who was a prominent figure in the 1960s. The suicide of 27-year-old Yekaterinburg poet Boris Rizhy received considerable attention in literary circles, especially after the news that he had been posthumously awarded the Northern Palmyra Prize.

Skirmishes continued between the two major literary "parties." The first, led by critics Pavel Basinsky and Andrey Nemzer, stood for values associated with the best traditions of Soviet literature—"humanness," "emotionality," and the "accurate depiction of the realities of daily life." Much of the success of poets Rizhy and Vera Pavlova, winner in 2001 of the Apollon Grigoryev Prize, was attributed to their appeal to this segment of the Russian reading public. Pavlova's poetry was especially interesting in this regard, combining traditional Soviet poetic devices with explicit eroticism.

The opposing literary party, whose primary bastions were the journal of literary criticism *Novaya russkaya kniga* ("The New Russian Book") and the Andrey Bely literary prizes, looked upon the literary Conceptualists (Dmitry Prigov, Lev Rubinshteyn, Vladimir Sorokin, and other postmodernists) as the driving force of contemporary literature. Yaroslav Mogutin was awarded the Andrey Bely Prize for poetry for his militantly homosexual verse, and the prize for prose went to Aleksandr Pyatigorsky for his postmodern combination of scholarship and play in *Vspomnish strannogo cheloveka* (1999; "You Remember That Strange Man"). At the same time, postmodern and avant-garde writing sought a wider audience through publishing ventures (the Amfora Publishing House in St. Petersburg was a typical example) and new literary prizes, including the National Best-Seller. This prize, which attempted to merge serious and escapist literature, was awarded to Leonid Yuzefovich for *Knyaz vetr* ("The Wind King"), an intellectual mystery that took place at the end of the 19th century in Russia and Mongolia. None of the nominated books, however, could be called true best-sellers; the only real crossover author continued to be Boris Akunin, whose novels—like those of Yuzefovich—combined history, fantasy, and the mystery genre.

The nominees for the Russian Booker Prize in 2001 included Tatyana Tolstaya's anti-utopian novel *Kys;* Lyudmila Ulitskaya's *Kazus Kukotskogo* ("Kukotsky's Case"); Alan Cherchesov's *Venok na mogilu vetra* (2000; "A Wreath on the Wind's Grave"), written in the magic realism style; Sergey Nosov's postmodern *Khozyayku istorii* (2000; "To the Master of History"); and two fictionalized memoirs, Anatoly Nayman's *Ser* ("Sir"), about Isaiah Berlin, and Aleksandr Chudakov's *Lozhitsya mgla na staryye stupeni* ("Darkness Falls on the Old Stairs"). The winner was Ulitskaya's *Kazus Kukotskogo*.

© Jerry Bauer

Anti-utopian Tatyana Tolstaya, short-listed for the Russian Booker

Some more aesthetically daring works were published, including a volume of short stories from Nikolay Kononov, nonfiction from essayist Kirill Kobrin, and a novel from Oleg Yuryev, *Poluostrov zhidyatin* ("Jews' Peninsula"), which described the encounter of a group of descendants of 15th-century Jewish heretics with contemporary assimilated Jews.

The most important poetry publications were Yelena Shvarts's *Dikopis poslednego vremeni* ("A Nonsense of Recent Times") and the four volumes released by *Novoye literaturnoye obozreniye* ("New Literary Review") of the 2000 Andrey Bely Prize for poetry finalists: Yelena Fanaylova (who won the award), Sergey Stratanovsky, Mikhail Ayzenberg, and Aleksandra Petrova. Soon after Krivulin's death, a powerful last book appeared, *Stikhi posle stikhov* ("Verse After Verse"). Viktor Sosnora also published a new book, as did his less-well-known contemporary Sergey Volf. Other notable volumes were released by Prigov, Dmitry Vodennikov, Aleksandr Levin, and Kirill Reshetnikov (who also wrote under the pseudonym Shish Bryansky). The work of the 24-year-old Reshetnikov, very much characteristic of his generation, was marked by a combination of exalted lyricism, weary sarcasm, and provocative vulgarity.

In criticism Olga Slavnikova and Nikita Yeliseyev were singled out for the quality and variety of their publications. Two works of the typically Russian genre of *publitsistika* (social and political commentary) were also superior: Aleksandr Solzhenitsyn's examination of the "Jewish question" in Russia, *Dvesti let vmeste, 1795–1995* ("Two Centuries Together"), and Mikhail Epshteyn's rather different but no less lively futurological study *Debut de siècle.*

The role of the "thick journals" continued to diminish, and all attempted to compensate for lower print runs (each now below 10,000 copies) with an Internet version, sometimes in tandem with their journals, but sometimes—like *Text Only*—as stand-alone Web sites. Finally, the Little Booker Prize was awarded to the Yuratin Foundation from the city of Perm for its publishing and literary activities. Following that award the Little Booker ceased to exist; part of the rationale for eliminating the prize was the optimistic view that contemporary Russian literature was ready to stand on its own feet and no longer needed external support.

(VALERY SHUBINSKY)

JEWISH

Hebrew. The quantitative prosperity of Hebrew fiction in 2001 produced mixed results. The few impressive achievements included Gabriela Avigur-Rotem's *Hamsin vetziporim meshuga'ot* ("Heatwave and Crazy Birds"), Yoel Hoffmann's *The Shunra and the Schmetterling* ("The Cat and the Butterfly"), Daniella Carmi's *Lesha'hrer pil* ("To Free an Elephant"), and Reuven Miran's *Shalosh sigariot bema'afera* ("Three Cigarettes in an Ashtray"). A noticeable improvement was marked by the new collection of short stories of Gafi Amir (*Dash mine'ura'yich* ["Regards from Your Youth"]) and the new novel of Yael Ichilov (*Zman ptsiot* ["Overtime"]).

A.B. Yehoshua published his most pretentious work by far, *Hakala ha-mesh'hreret* ("The Liberating Bride"), which sums up his canon by implicit allusions to his stories and novels and on the other hand copes with the difficulties of understanding the Palestinians and their culture from a Jewish-Israeli point of view. The novel, however, did not match Yehoshua's previous literary achievements. Several other works by veteran writers failed to match previous accomplishments. Among them were Joshua Kenaz's *Nof im shlosha etzim* (2000; "Landscape with Three Trees"), Avram Heffner's *Kemo Abelar, Kemo Elu'yiz* ("Like Abelard, Like Héloïse"), Yoram Kaniuk's *Hamalka ve'ani* ("The Queen and I"), and Sammi Michael's *Ma'yim noshkim lema'yim* ("Water Kissing Water"). First novels were penned by Rachel Talshir (*Ha'ahava mesha'hreret* ["Liebe Macht Frei"]) and Marina Groslerner (*Lalya*). Ronit Matalon published a spellbinding collection of autobiographical essays along with articles about art and literature (*Kro ukhtov* ["Read and Write"]).

Louis Monier

A.B. Yehoshua looks at Palestinian culture

Perhaps the best collection of poetry was *Isha shemitamenet belih'yot* ("A Woman Who Practices How to Live") by Shin Shifra. Other notable books of poetry included Aryeh Sivan's *Eravon*

("Pledge"), Dory Manor's *Mi'ut* (2000; "Minority"), Ronny Someck's *Hametofef shel hamahapekha* ("The Revolution Drummer"), Maya Bejerano's *Ha'yofi hu ka'as* ("Beauty Is Rage"), Yohai Openhaimer's *Beshesh a'hrei hatzohora'yim* (2000; "At Six in the Afternoon"), Dalia Kaveh's *Geshem* ("Rain"), and Ariel Rathaus's *Sefer hazikhronot* ("The Memories' Book").

The most intriguing work of literary scholarship was Dan Miron's *Parpar min hatola'at* ("From the Worm a Butterfly Emerges"), which studied the life and work of young Nathan Alterman. Hannan Hever examined nationality and violence in Hebrew poetry of the 1940s (*Pitom mar'e hamilhama* ["Suddenly, the Sight of War"]); Hillel Barzel published the fifth volume of the *History of Hebrew Poetry,* which deals with the poetry of Abraham Shlonsky, Nathan Alterman, and Lea Goldberg; and Aharon Komem discussed David Vogel's poetry and fiction in *Ha'ofel vehapele* ("Darkness and Wonder").

(AVRAHAM BALABAN)

Yiddish. The year 2001 was a stellar one for Yiddish poetry, but only a few other Yiddish works were noteworthy.

Baym rand fun kholem ("At the Edge of a Dream"), by master of the short novella Tsvi Ayznman, was a family chronicle of tales and sketches that traced a life journey from Poland to the Soviet Union, with sojourns in the Czech lands, Italy, and Cyprus. After finally settling in Israel, an Auschwitz survivor finds a terrorist on his doorstep whose appearance, in the wake of a bloody outrage, presents the protagonist with a series of moral dilemmas.

Another notable work was Ite Taub's authoritative reminiscence in rich Ukrainian Yiddish, *Ikh gedenk* ("I Remember"). Her narrative began with a retelling of childhood memories in the shtetl of Stidenitse, Ukraine, and provided incisive commentary about the pre- and post-October Revolution years and the political currents that had an impact on the Jewish communities of that republic.

Azarya Dobrushkes's ambitious three-volume miscellany, *Shpeter shnit* ("Late Harvest"), included vignettes about pre-World War II Vilna together with essays on a variety of literary themes.

Dvoyre Kosman's *Yidish: heymish, geshmak* ("The Yiddish Language: Native and Tasty") was a capacious anthology of prose and poetry. Eli Beyder's *Fun bolshevistishn "gan-eydn" in emesn heymland* ("From the Bolshevik 'Paradise' to My Real Homeland") portrayed a hegira in verse and provided a stinging indictment and eyewitness account of Soviet attitudes toward the national minorities.

In the thought-provoking volume *Velfisher nign* ("Lupine Melody"), author Velvl Chernin, a recent arrival from Russia, explored the life, people, and history of Jerusalem; the book's title was a pun on the author's name. Chernin employed Hebrew chapter titles and found biblical resonances in the perennial political tensions of his adopted country. Gele Shveyd Fishman's *In shtile shoen* ("In Quiet Hours") was an inspirational collection of lyric poetry. Beyle Schaechter-Gottesman's *Mume Blume di makhsheyfe* ("Aunt Blume the Witch") was a charming fairy tale in verse that featured animal protagonists and richly embellished colour illustrations by Adam Whiteman.

(THOMAS E. BIRD)

TURKISH

The Turkish literary field proved fertile in 2001. Many impressive works of fiction with wide-ranging themes and topics appeared, including Ahmet Altan's *İsyan günlerinde aşk* ("Love in Days of Rebellion"), about an early 20th-century fundamentalist uprising; Buket Uzuner's *Uzun beyaz bulut—Gelibolu* ("Tall White Cloud—Gallipoli"); Ayla Kutlu's *Zehir zıkkım hikâyeler* ("Bitter Stories"); Ömer Zülfü Livaneli's *Bir kedi, bir adam, bir ölüm* ("A Cat, a Man, a Death"), winner of the Yunus Nadi Award; Yashar Kemal's *Tanyeri horozları* ("Roosters of the East"); Erhan Bener's *Sonbahar yaprakları* ("Leaves of Autumn"); Hasan Ali Toptaş's chilling neosurrealistic *Ölü zaman gezginleri* ("Planets of Dead Times"); Oya Baydar's *Sicak külleri kaldı* (2000; "Hot Ashes Remain"), which won the Orhan Kemal Prize; and Hıfzı Topuz's *Gazi ve fikriye,* a semifictionalized account of Kemal Atatürk's love affair and its tragic end.

A new genre appeared—book-length interviews dubbed *"nehir söyleşileri"* ("interview *fleuves*"). The first two books in the series featured two major novelists, Adalet Ağaoğlu and Tahsin Yücel. A welcome event was the publication, in 13 volumes, of the complete short stories of the late satirist Aziz Nesin. A succès d'estime was Emre Kongar's *Kızlarıma mektuplar,* his collection of letters written to his twin daughters. In other literary news, eminent poet Fazıl Hüsnü Dağlarca was awarded an honorary doctorate by Mersin University, UNESCO designated 2002 as "the Year of Nazim Hikmet" in honour of the centennial of Hikmet's birth, and Orhan Pamuk's *My Name Is Red* (translation from Turkish by Erdağ Göknar) was featured on the September 2 cover of the *New York Times* Book Review. In addition, a number of important collections of poetry appeared, including those by Hilmi Yavuz, Küçük İskender, and Lale Müldür, among others. The publication of critic Mehmet H. Doğan's anthology of modern poetry generated controversy after numerous omissions were noted.

It was a banner year for essays and criticism, with impressive collections published by Melih Cevdet Anday, Enis Batur, Memet Fuad, Erendiz Atasü, Doğan Hızlan, and Ahmet Oktay. Memoirs and autobiographies attracting wide attention included those by Ayfer Tunç, Abidin Dino, Vedat Türkali, Hilmi Yavuz, and Uğur Kökden.

(TALAT S. HALMAN)

PERSIAN

By all accounts, 2001 was an eventful year for Persian literature, both in revisiting the achievements of the previous century from fresh perspectives and in providing glimpses into new literary experiments. Two important international conferences examined the literature of the 20th century, one by focusing on M.T. Bahār (1880–1951) and the other by surveying the entire literary canon of the Persian-speaking world. In the United States, Harvard Film Archive published the bilingual edition of *Hamrāh bā bād.* Titled *Walking with the Wind,* the collection featured haikulike poems by renowned Iranian filmmaker Abbas Kiarostami, who was prevented from participating in scheduled appearances and readings in several American cities following the terrorist attacks in September.

In Iran the granting of several literary awards by private cultural organizations signaled further loosening of state-imposed restrictions on creative writing and greater attention to literary works produced by secular writers. The foundation named for novelist Hūshang Gulshīrī awarded prizes to two newly published novels, Abū Turāb Khusravī's *Asfār-i kātibān* ("Books of the Scribes") and Khusraw Hamzavī's *Shahrī kih zīr-i dirākhtān-i sidr murd* ("The Kingdom That Died Beneath the Cedar Trees"). The foundation's lifetime achievement award went to Aḥmad Maḥmūd. The Kārnāmah Cultural Association awarded its poetry prize to Ali Āmūkhtah-nijād's *Yak panjshanbah, yak piādahrow* ("One Thursday, One Sidewalk").

The most notable literary event of the Iranian diaspora was the publication in Sweden of the original Persian version of Gulshīrī's *Shāh-i siyāh Pūshān,* a haunting narrative of a prison encounter between a secular poet and a turncoat political activist. Though Abbas Milani's 1990 *King of the Benighted,* the English translation of Gulshīrī's novella, had already been recognized as a notable work, Gulshīrī's original work was not released for publication until after his death in 2000. 'Izzat Gūshahgīr's collection of short stories . . . *Va nāgahān palang guft: zan* (". . . And Suddenly the Panther Cried: Woman!") contributed to an emerging and significant trend in writing by Iranian women, audacious articulations of gender relations in narratives of deep psychological insight. The most significant work by a Tajik author was Askar Hakim's long poem *Sang-i man almās ast* ("My Stone Is Diamond").

(AHMAD KARIMI-HAKKAK)

ARABIC

The predominant theme of 2001 was literature that chronicled the ordeals of political prisoners in a number of Arab countries. Works defined as "prison literature" were authored by freed political prisoners motivated to speak out by the relative freedom in the past two years in their countries. Writing in French, Moroccan Ahmad Marzouki published *Tazmamart, cellule 10* (2000), and Jaouad Mdidech followed with *La Chambre noire; ou, Derb Moulay Chérif* (2000), with a preface by another freed prisoner, Abraham Serfaty. Moroccan Tahar Ben Jelloun fictionalized the experience of a prisoner in Tazmamart in his novel *Cette aveuglante absence de lumière.* Before his death in April, Egyptian 'Ali ash-Shūbāshī published *Madrasat al-thūwār* ("The School of Revolutionaries"), in which he recounted his prison experience between 1950 and 1964.

Though modern Arabic literature was increasingly targeted by conservative religious groups, a number of Arab writers addressed the issue of fanaticism critically in an effort to protect the freedom of expression in their societies. Egyptian critic Jābir 'Aṣfūr published *Ḍidd al-ta'assub* ("Against Fanaticism"), and Moroccan Zuhūr Guerrām wrote *Fī ḍiyāfat al-Riqābah* ("A Guest of the Censor") in support of Kuwaiti writer Laylā al-'Uthmān, who was fined and condemned with 'Āliyā Shu'ayb to a two-month suspended prison sentence; they were accused of producing texts damaging to religion and morality.

The Arab intellectuals' preoccupation with the threatening spectre of globalization continued. Writers again analyzed the damaging effects of globalization on the economy and culture of the region. Two Moroccan critics sounded the alarm, Sa'īd Yaqṭīn in *Al-adab waal-mu'assasuah* (2000; "Literature and the Institution") and Mahdī al-Manjara in *Intifāḍāt fī zamān al-dhuluqrāṭiyyah* ("Upheavals in the Era of Disgrace"). They deplored increased government control and interference in everyday life, the stifling of creativity, and the deterioration of intellectual thinking. Al-Manjara viewed globalization as a cultural war on Arab-Islamic values.

Ironically, the author who had recently attracted the critics' attention and praise was Leila Aboulela, a veiled Sudanese woman who wrote in English and was inspired by her Islamic faith. Her novel, *The Translator* (1999), was hailed by critics, and her collection of short stories, *Coloured Lights,* showcased her creativity and the harmonious coexistence of Islamic and Western values.

The short story made a noticeable comeback. Two important collections were published in Egypt. Ibrāhīm 'Abd al-Majīd's *Sufun qadīmah* ("Old Boats") portrayed aspects of social and psychological disorientation in Alexandria, and Idwār al-Kharrāt's *Raqṣat al-ashwāq* ("The Dance of Longing") was a collection of previously published short stories. Prolific Moroccan novelist Muḥammad 'Izz ad-Dīn at-Tāzī published *Shams sawdā'* (2000; "A Black Sun"), which reflected the melancholic mood of his society. The regular publication of a number of reputable literary journals, including *Al-Ādāb* in Lebanon, *Manārāt* in Morocco, *Aqwās* in the West Bank city of Rām Allāh, and *Al-Hilāl* in Egypt, provided a platform for a new generation of young writers who, in the absence of government-subsidized presses, would find it difficult to publish their work independently.

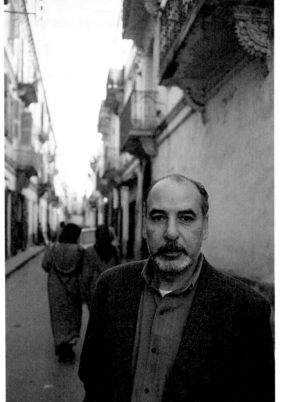

Moroccan novelist, poet, and dramatist Tahar Ben Jelloun

Poetry, on the other hand, found the Internet a suitable outlet. A Web site dedicated to *intifāḍah* poetry featured verse by established writers, notably Maḥmūd Darwīsh's *Muḥammad,* following the tragic killing of Muḥammad ad-Durrah in 2000; Ḥanān 'Ashrāwī's *Hadīl's Song;* Fadwā Tūqān's *Martyrs of the Intifada;* and Naomi Shihab Nye's *For the 500th Dead Palestinian Ibtisām Bozieh.* Noteworthy printed collections included those of two Moroccan female poets, Malīkah al-'Āṣimī's *Dimā' al-shams* ("The Blood of the Sun"), a daring thematic and artistic work; and Thurayyā Mājdūlīn's second collection, *Al-mut'abūn* (2000; "The Weary"). Another woman, Egyptian Sumayya Ramadān, received the 2001 Naguib Mahfouz Medal for her novel *Awrāq an-narjis* ("Narcissus Leaves").

Departing from his usual interest in social issues, Egyptian Bahā' Ṭāhir portrayed characters striving to fill a spiritual void in their lives in his novel *Nuqṭat al-nūr* ("The Point of Light"). Al-Kharrāt, on the other hand, focused on his Coptic roots and his Upper Egyptian traditions in his novel *Ṣukhūr al-samā'* ("The Rocks of the Sky"). Morocco lost a great writer when Muḥammad Zifzāf died in July; Egyptian short-story writer Jādibiyya Sidqī died in December.

(AIDA A. BAMIA)

CHINESE

Three novels were particularly eye-catching to the Chinese literati in 2001. The first was You Fengwei's *Zhongguo 1957* ("China 1957"). Written in the first person, the novel told a series of tragic stories about the victims—mostly university students and teachers—of the antirightist campaign of 1957 in which more than 550,000 Chinese were subjected to severe criticism and, in some cases, retribution by the Communist government. The book detailed the hardships that followed for some of the victims, including imprisionment, forced labour, and public humiliation. The novel was considered one of the most important literary works to address this dark chapter in Chinese history.

The second novel was Wang Anyi's *Fuping.* It told the story of a young girl, Fuping, from a rural area who settles in 1950s Shanghai in hopes of making a better life for herself. The book offered a vivid description of the city, with a wonderful presentation of the various styles and customs of everyday life in Shanghai at the time.

Photo courtesy of Mo Yan

Mo Yan: the headsman and the rebel

The third novel was Mo Yan's *Tanxiang xing* ("Penalty of Sandalwood"). On display were the author's active imagination and his characteristic use of inflated language and satire, but this story was darker than his previous works. It was a portrait of a royal executioner at the beginning of the 20th century and gave a very detailed description of how he did his job; the executioner's story is intertwined with that of a peasant rebel who becomes the target of the headsman after his revolt against German merchants and soldiers fails. The novel contained so many cultural and political hints about contemporary conditions in China that it drew great attention when it was published.

In the field of Chinese poetry only one important work appeared, *Mengchao shuibi* ("Writing in Dream-Nest") by dissident poet Huang Xiang, who was living in the U.S. and whose works had been banned by the Chinese government. *Mengchao shuibi,* which included both poetry and prose, was published in Taipei, Taiwan. Huang's unrestrained imagination and unyielding spirit made the book attractive.

So-called Internet literature continued to appear in 2001, with more literary Web sites emerging in China, Taiwan, and Hong Kong. The largest Web site featuring Chinese literature was Rongshu.com, which boasted some 1,600,000 registered users and more than 600,000 manuscripts in its database. The site reportedly received more than 6,000 literary submissions per day. Although the boundary between electronic and print literature was becoming indistinct, with an increasing number of writers publishing their works on the Internet, many highly touted e-books failed to find a good market during the year. It seemed that Chinese readers still paid most attention to traditional writers such as Wang Anyi and Mo Yan.

(WANG XIAOMING)

JAPANESE

In the first half of 2001, the Akutagawa Prize, awarded semiannually to the most promising new Japanese writers of fiction, went to Toshiyuki Horie for his story "Kuma no shikiishi" ("The Bear's Pavement," published in the December 2000 issue of *Gunzō*), and to Yūichi Seirai for his story "Seisui" ("Holy Water," from the December 2000 *Bungakukai*). In Horie's work a Japanese narrator visits an old friend, a Frenchman of Jewish descent, in the Normandy countryside. During the visit the friend tells the narrator the harrowing story of his family's experiences during the Holocaust. On one level the work explored the relationship between two friends from vastly different cultures; on a broader level it critiqued the Japanese reaction to events in modern European history.

Seirai's "Seisui" told the story of a son and his dying father. Although alienated by conflicting beliefs and desires (the father is a fervent Christian who wants his son to take over the family business; the son is a religious skeptic who has his own plans for the future), the two attempt to resolve their differences before the father's death. Such themes as family loyalty and the nature of faith were sensitively addressed in "Seisui."

In the second half of the year, the Akutagawa Prize went to Sōkyū Gen'yū for his story "Chūin no hana" ("The Mourning Flower," from *Bungakukai,* May 2001). Gen'yū, a Buddhist priest, used the story as a means to expound a profound vision of life and death.

One of Japan's most prominent—and prolific—writers, Banana Yoshimoto, continued to attract attention. (*See* BIOGRAPHIES.) Her best-selling collection of novellas, *Asleep,* first published in Japanese in 1989, appeared in English during the year, earning her an even wider international audience. A new English translation of *Genji monogatari* (*The Tale of Genji*) was wel-

In Celebration of the World's First Novel

One thousand years ago in Heian Japan, a woman of whom little is known was widowed. But for her personal loss, that woman, known as Murasaki Shikibu, might never have written *Genji monogatari* (c. 1010; *The Tale of Genji*), which is considered the greatest work of Japanese literature and the world's first novel.

The details of the author's life are sketchy. Even her actual name is unknown; Murasaki Shikibu was assigned by scholars—who used the name of the book's dominant female character (Murasaki) and the author's father's position (Shikibu) at the Bureau of Rites to identify her. Born into a lesser branch of the noble and highly influential Fujiwara family, she had been well educated, learning Chinese (generally the exclusive sphere of males). She had married a much older distant cousin and borne a daughter by him, and after two years of marriage, he had died. It is not known how, four years later, she came to be summoned to the court. In any case, her new position within what was then a leading literary centre enabled her to produce a diary, a collection of poetry, and, most famously, the classic romance *Genji monogatari.*

Because Chinese was the scholarly language of the Japanese court, works written in Japanese (the literary language used by women) were not taken very seriously. Nor was prose considered the equal of poetry. What made Lady Murasaki's work different is this: although it is prose, it is clearly informed by a comprehensive knowledge of Chinese and Japanese poetry; it is a graceful work of imaginative fiction, not a personal account of life at court; it incorporates some 800 *waka,* courtly poems purported to be the writing of the main character; and its supple narrative sustains the story through 54 chapters of one character and his legacy.

At its most basic, *Genji* is an absorbing introduction to the culture of the aristocracy in early Heian Japan, its forms of entertainment, its manner of dress, its daily life, and its moral code. The era is exquisitely re-created by the author through the story of Genji, the handsome, sensitive, gifted courtier, an excellent lover, and a worthy friend.

Eminent British sinologist Arthur Waley was the first to translate *Genji monogatari* into English, completing the last of six volumes in 1933. Waley's was a beautiful and inspiring translation, but it was also very free and proved disappointing to serious students. Edward Seidensticker's 1976 translation was true to the original in both content and tone, but its notes and reader aids were very sparse, an assessment not lost on *Genji*'s third translator, American scholar Royall Tyler of Australian National University. The publication of Tyler's version in 2001—nearly a millennium after *Genji monogatari* was written—attests to a continuing fascination with early Japanese culture and the durability of one remarkable woman's literary achievement.

(KATHLEEN KUIPER)

The Art Archive/Private Collection/Paris/Dagli Orti

Murasaki Shikibu as depicted in a screen painting by 17th-century Japanese artist Ogata Korin

comed as the world's first novel approached its 1,000th anniversary. (*See* Sidebar.)

A more recent classic, *Kuroi ame* (1966; "Black Rain") by Masuji Ibuse, who died in 1993, was again the subject of literary discussion. Ibuse's book chronicled, in diary and documentary form, the effects of the atomic bomb on the people of Hiroshima and especially on a young girl, Yasuko, who could not marry because of her exposure to radiation. Readers had assumed that the diary in the novel was the product of Ibuse's imagination, but critic Naoki Inose pointed out in his work *Pikaresuku* (2000; "Picaresque") that there actually existed a real diary on which the novel was based, and he claimed that in some instances Ibuse had copied directly from this text. The controversy intensified after the diary, entitled *Shigematsu nikki* ("Shigematsu's Diary"), was published in 2001. Comparing the two works, however, most critics were reluctant to suggest plagiarism and agreed that the device of the diary simply shed light on Ibuse's fictional technique.

The Tanizaki Prize went to Hiromi Kawakami for her novel *Sensei no kaban* ("The Teacher's Briefcase"), a love story about a teacher and a student. The Yomiuri Prize for Literature was awarded to Naoyuki Ii's short-story collection *Nigotta gekiryū ni kakaru hashi* (2000; "A Bridge over a Muddy Torrent"), which portrayed the lives of rural Japanese, and Eimi Yamada's *A2Z* (2000; "A to Z"). Best-selling literary works that appeared during the year included Haruki Murakami's essay on the Sydney Olympic Games, *Shidoni!* ("Sydney!"), Randy Taguchi's novel *Mozaiku* ("Mosaic"), and Yasutaka Tsutsui's *Daimajin* ("Daimajin, the Stone Samurai").

(YOSHIHIKO KAZAMARU)

Mathematics and Physical Sciences

The **LANDING** of a spacecraft on an **ASTEROID**, an incisive **CRITIQUE** of various **ELECTORAL SYSTEMS**, and the report of an **EXPERIMENT** that **STOPPED A LIGHT PULSE** and **STARTED IT AGAIN** were among the scientific and mathematical headliners of 2001.

MATHEMATICS

The closeness of the 2000 U.S. presidential election highlighted the unusual characteristics of the American electoral system, such as the electoral college, in which all but a few states assign electoral votes on a winner-take-all basis, and simple plurality elections, in which the leading candidate wins without having a runoff election to establish a majority winner. Mathematicians and others had investigated voting systems in the past, and this contentious election inspired further research and discoveries in 2001. (*See* WORLD AFFAIRS: *United States:* Sidebar.)

When there are only two candidates, the situation is very simple. In 1952 the American mathematician Kenneth May proved that there is only one voting system that treats all voters equally, that treats both candidates equally, and where the winning candidate would still win if he or she received more votes. That system is majority rule.

When there are more than two candidates, as was the case in the 2000 presidential election, the situation is most unsatisfactory. Two notable voting systems have been proposed as better for multicandidate races. The first is commonly attributed to the 18th-century French mathematician Jean-Charles, chevalier de Borda. Borda's method requires each voter to rank the candidates, with the lowest candidate getting 1 point, the next lowest candidate 2 points, and so forth, up to the highest candidate, who gets as many points as there are candidates. The points from all voters are added, and the candidate with the most points wins. This system was actually first described in 1433 by Nicholas of Cusa, a German cardinal who was concerned with how to elect German kings. Today it is used in the United States to rank collegiate football and basketball teams.

Borda believed that his system was better than the one devised by his French contemporary Marie-Jean-Antoine-Nicolas de Caritat, marquis de Condorcet. Condorcet felt that the winner should be able to defeat every other candidate in a one-on-one contest. Unfortunately, not every election has a Condorcet winner. In the 2000 presidential election, however, polls indicated that Al Gore would have been a Condorcet winner, since—with the help of supporters of Ralph Nader—he would have beaten George W. Bush in a one-on-one contest (or in a runoff election).

Like the Borda system, the Condorcet system had already been proposed for ecclesiastical elections; it was first described in the 13th century by the Catalan philosopher and missionary Ramon Llull, who was interested in how to elect the abbess of a convent. Nicholas of Cusa made a copy of one of Llull's manuscripts before deciding he could do better, by devising the Borda system. Another of Llull's manuscripts, with a more complete description of his voting system, was discovered and published in 2001, by Friedrich Pukelsheim and others at the University of Augsberg, Germany.

Part of the reason for the great controversy between Borda and Condorcet was that neither of their systems was ideal. In fact, the American Nobel Prize-winning economist Kenneth Arrow showed in 1951 that no voting system for multicandidate elections can be both decisive (produce a Condorcet winner) and completely fair (candidates change position only with a change in their rankings). Nevertheless, after the 2000 presidential election, Americans Donald Saari and Steven Brams argued persuasively for modifying the U.S. system.

Saari used geometry in order to reveal hidden assumptions in voting methods. He favoured the Borda system, which he believed more accurately reflects the true sentiment of voters, as well as having a tendency to produce more centrist winners than the plurality method. In practice, ranking all the candidates can be onerous, and the "broadly supported" winner may just be everybody's third or fourth choice.

Another criticism of the Borda system is that the electorate may vote strategically, rather than sincerely, in order to manipulate the election. Such strategic voting takes place under the current system; in the 2000 presidential election, many voters who preferred Nader voted for Gore out of fear of giving the election to Bush.

Brams favoured approval voting, which is used by some professional societies; Venetians first used it in the 13th century to help elect their magistrates. Under approval voting, voters cast one vote for every candidate they regard as acceptable; the winner is the candidate with the most votes. Approval voting has several attractive features, such as the winner always having the broadest approval and voters never having to choose between two favoured candidates.

Saari and Brams both agreed that the plurality method, together with the winner-take-all feature of the electoral college, has fundamentally flawed the American electoral process, preventing the election of candidates with broad support and frustrating the will of the electorate. (PAUL J. CAMPBELL)

CHEMISTRY

Carbon Chemistry. In 2001 Hendrik Schön and associates of Lucent Technologies' Bell Laboratories, Murray Hill, N.J., announced the production of buckminsterfullerene crystals that become superconducting at substantially warmer temperatures than previously possible. Superconductors conduct electric current without losses due to resistance when they are cooled below a certain critical temperature. In 1991 a Bell Labs team first showed that buckminsterfullerene molecules (C_{60}), which are spherical hollow-cage structures made of 60 carbon atoms each, can act as superconductors at very low temperatures when doped with potassium atoms.

Schön's group mixed C_{60} with chloroform ($CHCl_3$) or its bromine analogue, bromoform, to create "stretched" C_{60} crystals. In the modified crystal structure, chloroform or bromoform molecules were wedged between C_{60} spheres, moving them farther apart. The altered spacing between neighbouring C_{60} molecules, coupled with the experimenters' use of a setup that took advantage of transistor-like effects, raised the critical temperature of the material. Tests showed that C_{60} mixed with bromoform became superconducting below 117 K (–249 °F), which is more than double the previous temperature record of 52 K (–366 °F) for a C_{60}-based material set the previous year.

Although still very cold, the record-breaking temperature was warm enough for the C_{60} superconductor to function while cooled by liquid nitrogen (boiling point 77 K [–321 °F]), instead of the lower-boiling and much more expensive liquid helium. The only other superconductors that operate at higher temperatures are copper oxide ceramic superconductors. These materials were used in powerful magnets, superconductive wires for power-transmission systems, and other applications, but they were expensive and had other drawbacks. Schön speculated that C_{60} superconductors could turn out to be cheaper. He also believed that increasing the spacing between C_{60} spheres in the crystal by just a small percentage could boost the critical temperature even more.

Physical Chemistry. Water can flow uphill, as chemical engineer Manoj K. Chaudhury demonstrated in a notable 1992 experiment that delighted and perplexed the public. Chaudhury, then at Dow Corning Corp., and George M. Whitesides of Harvard University coaxed microlitre-sized droplets of water to run uphill on the surface of a polished silicon wafer at a rate of about one millimetre per second. The secret involved the creation of a surface tension gradient—a swath of continually decreasing hydrophobicity, or tendency to repel water—across the silicon wafer. The wafer was then tilted from the horizontal so that the most hydrophobic end was lower than the least hydrophobic end. Water droplets deposited at the low end were propelled across the surface against gravity by the imbalance of surface tension forces between the uphill and downhill ends of the drop.

In a report published during the year, Chaudhury and co-workers at Lehigh

Susan Daniel and Manoj K. Chaudhury

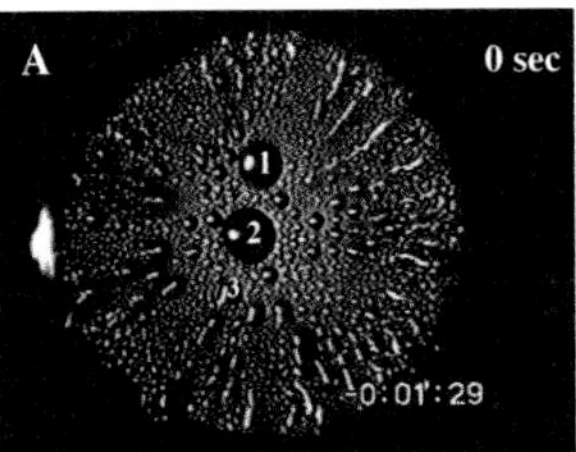

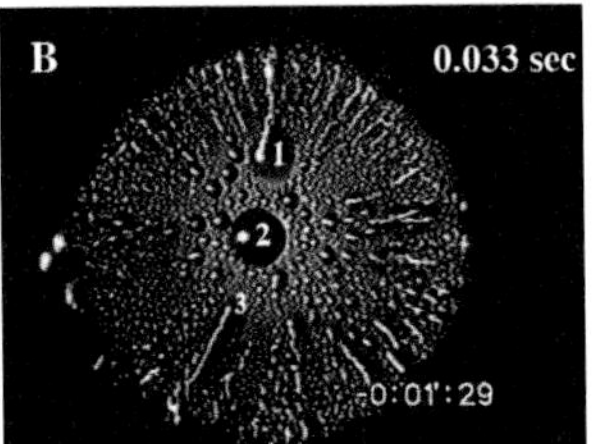

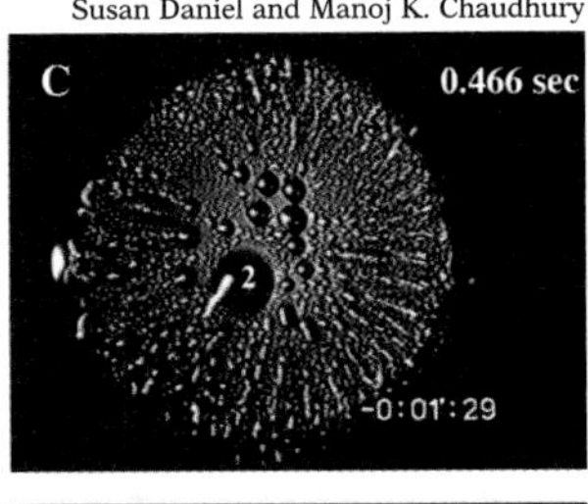

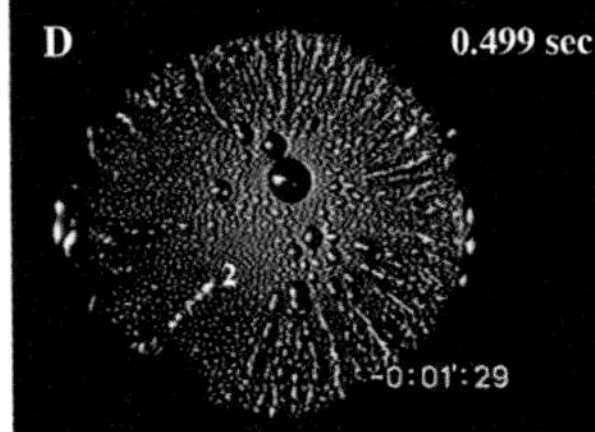

Water drops condense on a level silicon surface given a radial surface tension gradient and then merge and travel rapidly from centre to edge in this image sequence (A–D) taken from a video covering a half-second period. The labels 1, 2, and 3 identify individual drops and their trails after movement.

University, Bethlehem, Pa., described a technique for making water droplets move across a silicon surface hundreds of times faster than in the previous experiment, at rates of centimetres to a metre or more per second. The speeds were achieved by passing saturated steam over a relatively cool silicon surface possessing a surface tension gradient. In this case the gradient was applied radially, with the wafer's surface being most hydrophobic at the centre and least so at the circumference. As water droplets condensed on the surface from the steam, they first moved slowly outward but then rapidly accelerated as they merged with neighbouring drops. The energy that was released during drop coalescence and directionally channeled by the surface tension gradient accounted for the increased speed of the drops. Chaudhury suggested that the phenomenon could be put to practical use in heat exchangers and other heat-transfer applications and in microfabricated devices where tiny amounts of fluid need to be pumped from one component to another.

Analytic Chemistry. Nuclear magnetic resonance (NMR) spectroscopy was among the chemist's most important tools for studying the physical and chemical properties of plastics, glasses and ceramics, catalysts, DNA and proteins, and myriad other materials. Spectroscopy is the study of interactions between electromagnetic radiation and matter. NMR spectroscopy is based on a phenomenon that occurs when atoms of certain elements are immersed in a strong static magnetic field and exposed to radio-frequency waves. In response, the atomic nuclei emit their own radio signals that can be detected and used to understand a material's properties.

Researchers from the U.S., France, and Denmark reported a technique for obtaining more precise NMR information about a material's atomic structure. The group, headed by Philip Grandinetti of Ohio State University at Columbus, found that spinning samples at speeds as high as 30,000 cycles per second can often boost the NMR signal strength by 10-fold or more. They termed the new technique FASTER (for "fast spinning gives transfer enhancement at rotary resonance"). Spinning materials during NMR was not new. A technique known as magic-angle spinning rotated materials at a certain angle in relation to the NMR's static magnetic field. Unfortunately, magic-angle spinning did not work well for about 70% of the chemical elements, including the common elements oxygen, aluminum, and sodium. Analysis required the averaging of weeks of test results and the use of expensive high-power amplifiers. FASTER could produce results in hours with a much less costly low-power amplifier, according to Grandinetti.

Organic Chemistry. French chemist Louis Pasteur, who established the basics of stereochemistry in the 1840s, tried unsuccessfully to influence biological and chemical processes toward a preference for molecules with a right-handed or a left-handed structure. For example, Pasteur rotated growing plants in an effort to change the handedness of their naturally produced chemical compounds, and he performed chemical reactions while spinning the reactants in centrifuges. Over the next century and a half, chemists tried other ways of producing an excess of either left- or right-handed chiral molecules from achiral precursors, a process termed absolute asymmetric synthesis. (Molecules that exist in right- and left-handed versions, like a pair of gloves, are said to be chiral. Molecules lacking such handedness are said to be achiral.) To date, the only acknowledged successes had come with sophisticated approaches such as the induction of reactions with circularly polarized light and chiral selection based on the electroweak force, a fundamental interaction of nature that has asymmetric characteristics. Scientists had uniformly dismissed reports of asymmetric synthesis by simple stirring—clockwise or counterclockwise rotation during the chemical conversion of an achiral compound.

During the year Josep M. Ribó and associates of the University of Barcelona, Spain, reported convincing evidence that chiral assemblies of molecules can be produced by stirring. They used achiral porphyrins, large disk-shaped molecules made of connected organic rings. The porphyrins had a zwitterionic structure—each molecule contained both positively and negatively charged regions—which allowed them to aggregate through electrostatic interactions and hydrogen bonding. Individual porphyrin disks can assemble linearly into left-handed or right-handed helices, and when left undisturbed they formed equal amounts of each kind. Ribó showed that stirring caused the formation of chiral assemblies, with the chirality controlled by the direction of the stirring.

The findings could shed light on the mystery of homochirality in biological systems on Earth—why the essential molecules in living things are single-handed. Natural sugars, for example, are almost exclusively right-handed; natural amino acids, left-handed. Ribó's work suggested that vortex action during early stages of chemical evolution could be the explanation.

Nuclear Chemistry. During the year scientists at Lawrence Berkeley National Laboratory (LBNL), Berkeley, Calif., retracted their two-year-old claim for the synthesis of the superheavy element 118. The original announcement in 1999 had gained worldwide attention because element 118 was considered to be the heaviest chemical element ever produced and was regarded as evidence for existence of the so-called island of stability, a region of the periodic table consisting of superheavy elements with half-lives significantly longer than their slightly lighter superheavy neighbours on the table.

The retraction came after confirmation experiments at LBNL and in Japan, Germany, and France had failed to reproduce the earlier results. In addition, after reviewing the original data using different analytic software, an LBNL committee of experts found no evidence for the decay chains that pointed to the existence of element 118. The LBNL researchers in 1999 had not directly observed the element. Rather, after bombarding a target of lead-208 with high-energy krypton-86 ions at LBNL's 224-cm (88-in) cyclotron, they inferred the production of three atoms of element 118 from data that they interpreted as characteristic of the way that the atoms decayed into a series of lighter elements.

(MICHAEL WOODS)

PHYSICS

Particle Physics. In the field of neutrino physics, years of work by large teams of researchers worldwide finally bore fruit in 2001. Of the fundamental particles that make up the standard model of the universe, neutrinos are the most enigmatic. Their existence was postulated in 1930 to explain a mysterious loss of energy seen in the nuclear beta-decay process. Because neutrinos interact so weakly with matter, however, they are extraordinarily difficult to observe, and experimental confirmation of their existence came only a quarter century later. Three types of neutrinos were known—electron, muon, and tau neutrinos. They were generally assumed to be massless, but the question remained open until 1998 when a team at Super-Kamiokande, a mammoth neutrino detector located in a Japanese zinc mine, found the strongest evidence to that time that neutrinos indeed possess a tiny mass.

During the year, this work was extended to solve a major puzzle concerning solar physics. The accepted physical model for the nuclear reactions taking place in the Sun required the emission of a large number of electron neutrinos, but decades of experimental measurement had shown only a third of the expected number arriving at Earth. Physicists working at the Sudbury Neutrino Observatory, a neutrino detector built in a Canadian nickel mine, combined their data with complementary data from Super-Kamiokande to produce direct evidence for the remaining two-thirds. Their results confirmed the theory that electron neutrinos oscillate, or transform, among the three types as they travel through space from the Sun, which explained why earlier work had found a shortfall of two-thirds from that predicted. For neutrinos to oscillate, they must have a finite mass, which was consistent with the 1998 finding from Super-Kamiokande.

The new results enabled the theoretical model of the Sun's nuclear reactions to be confirmed with great accuracy. The number of emitted neutrinos depends very sensitively on the Sun's central temperature, giving this as 15.7 million K, precise to 1%. At the same time, the oscillation between neutrino types would enable a better estimate for the neutrino mass, which had implications for cosmology. (See *Astronomy,* below.)

Another result from particle physics that affected an understanding of the universe as a whole came from work on a phenomenon known as CP violation. In the standard model every matter particle has an antiparticle with the same mass but with properties such as electric charge and spin reversed—for example, electrons and their positron counterparts. When a particle meets its antiparticle, mutual annihilation takes place with the release of energy. Conversely, a particle and its antiparticle can be created from energy. When the formation of particles and antiparticles in the hot early universe is modeled, a difficulty arises. If particles and antiparticles are identical, an equal number of both sorts should now exist. Because particles vastly outnumber antiparticles in the observable universe, however, there must be some kind of asymmetry in properties between the two types of matter. In present theories a very small asymmetry would do the job, and CP violation appeared to be a possible explanation.

Until the 1950s it was assumed that nature is symmetrical in a number of ways. One example is parity—any reaction involving particles must be identical to the equivalent antiparticle reaction viewed in a mirror. In 1957 it was discovered that nuclear beta decay violated this symmetry. It was assumed, however, that symmetry in particle reactions involving both a change of parity (P) and a change of charge sign (C)—for example, the exchange of a negatively charged electron for a positively charged positron—was not violated. This conservation of charge and parity considered together is called CP symmetry. In 1964 decays of K mesons were found to violate CP symmetry. During 2001 independent teams of physicists at the Stanford Linear Accelerator Center and the High Energy Accelerator Research Organization, Tsukuba, Japan, reported evidence for CP violation in the decay of another particle, the B meson. The experimental results also yielded a numerical value representing the amount of CP violation, which turned out to be about half of the required value predicted by the standard model to produce the known universe. The work was preliminary, however, and further refinement was needed to determine whether the standard model as currently formulated was an accurate picture of nature.

Lasers and Light. Two achievements reported during the year could be said to span the speed range of research in optical physics. Harm Geert Muller of the FOM Institute for Atomic and Molecular Physics, Amsterdam, and collaborators produced the shortest light pulses ever measured—just 220 attoseconds (billionths of a billionth of a second, or 10^{-18} second) in duration. The investigators focused an intense pulse of infrared laser light on a jet of dilute argon gas, which converted some of the light into a collection of higher harmonics (multiples of the original frequency) in the ultraviolet range. The relative phases of the harmonics were such that the frequencies interfered in a special way, canceling each other except for very brief time intervals when they all added constructively. The result was a train of extremely short light spikes. Pulses this short could enable the study of a range of very fast phenomena and perhaps even follow electron motion around atomic nuclei.

In 1999, working at the other end of the speed range, a group led by Lene Vestergaard Hau (*see* BIOGRAPHIES) of Harvard University and the Rowland Institute for Science had demonstrated techniques for slowing a light pulse in a cloud of extremely cold gas from its normal speed of about 300,000 km (186,000 mi) per second to roughly the speed of urban automobile traffic. In 2001 Hau and her colleagues reported on a technique to halt a light pulse in a cold gas and release it at a later time. They first prepared a gas of ultracold sodium atoms and treated it with light from a so-called coupling laser, which altered the optical characteristics of the gas. They then fired a probe pulse from a second laser into the gas. Switching off the coupling beam while the probe pulse was traversing the gas brought the light to a stop and allowed all the information about it to be imprinted on the sodium atoms as a "quantum coherence pattern." Switching on the coupling laser again regenerated a perfect copy of the original pulse. This technique could have applications for controlling and storing information in optical computers.

Condensed-Matter Physics. In 1995 researchers first produced a new state of matter in the laboratory—an achievement that was recognized with the 2001 Nobel Prize for Physics. (*See* NOBEL PRIZES.) Called a Bose-Einstein condensate, it comprises a collection of gaseous atoms at a temperature just above absolute zero (–273.15 °C, or –459.67 °F) locked together in a single quantum state—as uniform and coherent as a single atom. Until 2001 condensates of elements such as rubidium, lithium, and sodium had been prepared by cooling a dilute gas of atoms in their ground states. During the year separate research groups at the University of Paris XI, Orsay, and the École Normale Supérieure, Paris, succeeded in making a condensate from a gas of excited helium atoms. Because no existing lasers operated in the far-ultraviolet wavelength needed to excite helium from the ground state, the researchers used an electrical discharge to supply the excitation energy.

Although each helium atom possessed an excitation energy of 20 eV (which was more than 100 billion times its thermal energy in the condensate), the atoms within the condensate were stabilized against release of this energy by polarization (alignment) of their spins, which greatly reduced the probability that excited atoms would collide. When the condensate came into contact with some other atom, however, all the excitation energy in its atoms was released together. This suggested the possibility of a new kind of laser that emits in the far ultraviolet.

Practical devices based on such advanced techniques of atomic and optical physics were coming closer to realization. During the year a team led by Scott Diddams of the U.S. National Institute of Standards and Technology, Boulder, Colo., used the interaction between a single cooled mercury atom and a laser beam to produce the world's most stable clock, with a precision of about one second in 100 million years. Such precision could well be needed in future high-speed data transmission.

(DAVID G.C. JONES)

ASTRONOMY

Solar System. On Feb. 12, 2001, the unmanned spacecraft NEAR (Near Earth Asteroid Rendezvous) Shoemaker gently touched down on asteroid 433 Eros. NEAR had spent the previous 12 months in orbit about the potato-shaped object, photographing its surface features. After it landed, its onboard gamma-ray spectrometer showed that Eros has a low abundance of iron and aluminum relative to magnesium. Such proportions are found in the Sun and in meteorites called chondrites, thought to be among the oldest objects in the solar system. The observations suggested that Eros was formed some 4.5 billion years ago and did not undergo significant chemical changes after that time. In another postlanding study, a magnetometer aboard NEAR confirmed the lack of a detectable magnetic field on Eros. This finding suggested that magnetized meteorites (which constitute the majority of meteorites found on Earth) may be fragments knocked from other types of asteroids or that they acquired their magnetization on their journey to Earth.

On September 22 another spacecraft, Deep Space 1, successfully navigated its way past Comet Borrelly, providing the best view ever of the ice particles, dust, and gas leaving comets. The spacecraft came within 2,200 km (1,360 mi) of the roughly 8 × 4-km (5 × 2.5-mi) cometary nucleus. It sent back images that showed a rough surface terrain, with rolling plains and deep fractures—a hint that the comet may have formed as a collection of icy and stony rubble rather than as a coherent solid object. From the amount of reflected light—only about 4%—the surface appeared to be composed of very dark matter. Cosmochemists proposed that the surface was most likely covered with carbon and substances rich in organic compounds.

In mid-2001 an international group of astronomers using 11 different telescopes around the world reported the discovery of 12 new moons of Saturn. This brought the total to 30, the largest number so far detected for any planet in the solar system. The moons range in diameter from 6 to 32 km (4 to 20 mi). Saturn previously had been known to have six large moons, Titan being the largest, and 12 small ones, all but one of which were classified as regular moons because they move in circular orbits in the planet's orbital plane. All of the new moons move in highly eccentric orbits, which suggested that they are remnants of larger objects that were captured into orbit around Saturn early in its history and subsequently broken up by collisions.

Stars. One of the most perplexing problems in modern astrophysics, an observed shortage in the predicted number of neutrinos emanating from the Sun, appeared to be finally resolved during the year. Detailed theoretical studies of nuclear reactions in the Sun's core had predicted that energy is released in the form of gamma rays, thermal energy, and neutrinos. The gamma rays and thermal energy slowly diffuse to the solar surface and are eventually observed as visible light and other electromagnetic radiation. Neutrinos are electrically neutral particles that travel almost

NASA, J. Bell (Cornell University), M. Wolff (SSI), and the Hubble Heritage Team (STScI/AURA)

Two strikingly different visages of Mars appear in Hubble Space Telescope images made in late June and less than three months later, when a global dust storm—the biggest in decades—obscured all surface features.

unaffected through the Sun and interplanetary space on their way to Earth. Beginning in the late 1960s, scientists sought to detect these elusive particles directly. Because neutrinos interact so weakly with matter, detectors containing enormous quantities of mass were built to detect them. These were placed deep underground to allow neutrinos originating in the Sun to be distinguished from background galactic cosmic rays. Despite many experiments employing a variety of detectors, scientists consistently had observed only about a third of the predicted neutrino flux.

Neutrinos come in three varieties, or flavours—electron, muon, and tau. Because nuclear fusion in the Sun's core should produce only electron neutrinos, most of the earlier experiments had been designed to detect only that flavour. The Sudbury Neutrino Observatory (SNO), sited deep inside a Canadian nickel mine, was built to have enhanced sensitivity to muon and tau neutrinos. It used as its detector a 1,000-ton sphere of extremely pure heavy water (water molecules in which the two hydrogen atoms are replaced with deuterium, one of hydrogen's heavier isotopes). A second facility, called Super-Kamiokande and located in a zinc mine in Japan, employed a tank of 50,000 tons of ultrapure ordinary water to detect electron and muon neutrinos. In 2001 the international collaboration running SNO, headed by Art McDonald of Queen's University at Kingston, Ont., reported evidence derived from SNO and Super-Kamiokande data for the detection of the missing two-thirds of the neutrino flux. The results confirmed the theory that electron neutrinos transform, or oscillate, among the three possible flavours on their journey to Earth. Oscillation also implied that neutrinos have a tiny but finite mass and thus make a contribution to the nonluminous, unobserved "dark matter" in the universe. (See *Physics,* above.)

The detection of planets orbiting other stars was first announced in 1995. By the beginning of 2001 about 50 extrasolar planets had been reported, and by year's end the number had risen to more than 70. Most of the planets found to date are quite different from those in Earth's solar system. Many are large (as much as 20 times the mass of Jupiter) and often move in elliptical orbits quite close to their parent stars.

During the year, for the first time, a planetary system remarkably similar to Earth's solar system was detected. Geoffrey Marcy of the University of California, Berkeley, Paul Butler of the Carnegie Institution of Washington, D.C., and their collaborators reported that a star visible to the naked eye, 47 Ursae Majoris, is orbited by at least two planets. The presence of one planet had been known since 1996, but the discovery of the second companion changed astronomers' picture of the system in important ways. One planet has a mass at least three-fourths that of Jupiter, and the other has at least two and a half times Jupiter's mass. Interestingly, the ratio of their masses is close to the ratio of the masses of Saturn and Jupiter. Both extrasolar planets move in nearly circular orbits, a property that was thought to increase the odds that the system contains Earth-like planets as well.

Galaxies and Cosmology. Over the past 75 years, observations and theory have combined to produce a consistent model of the origin and evolution of the universe, beginning with a big-bang explosion some 10 billion to 20 billion years ago. Left behind and detectable today as a relic of this hot event is a highly uniform flux of cosmic microwave background radiation. Because the matter that is observed filling the universe attracts other matter gravitationally, the expansion rate of the universe should be slowing down. Nevertheless, observations in 1998 of the brightness of fairly distant exploding stars called Type Ia supernovas suggested that the expansion is currently accelerating. The findings were interpreted as evidence for the existence throughout space of a kind of cosmic repulsion force first hypothesized by Albert Einstein in 1917 and represented by a term, the cosmological constant, in his equations of general relativity. The supernovas observed in the studies were found to be dimmer than expected, which implied that they were farther away than a decelerating universe could account for.

During the year Adam G. Riess of the Space Telescope Science Institute, Baltimore, Md., and collaborators reported new studies of the most distant supernova yet found, designated SN 1997ff. Their analysis of observations of the supernova, which were made with the Hubble Space Telescope, indicated that the expansion rate of the universe was slower at the time of the supernova explosion billions of years ago than it is now. Their results also refuted the possibility that intervening dust or other astrophysical effects could be an explanation for the unexpectedly dim supernovas seen in the earlier studies. SN 1997ff provided the best evidence to date that the expansion of the universe is indeed accelerating.

The existence of galaxies and their current distribution in space to form clusters, filaments, and voids indicated that large-scale fluctuations in the density of matter were present in the very early universe, and theoretical studies indicated that the cosmic background radiation should also carry an imprint of those fluctuations in the form of slight variations in brightness across the sky. In 2001 the combined findings of three recent experiments designed to study the cosmic background radiation provided dramatic evidence for this prediction. First reported on in 2000, two of the experiments—Maxima (Millimeter Anisotropy Experiment Imaging Array) and

Boomerang (Balloon Observations of Millimetric Extragalactic Radiation and Geophysics)—used balloons to carry detectors high above most of Earth's atmosphere. The third experiment—DASI (Degree Angular Scale Interferometer)—was a ground-based interferometer located at the South Pole. All three measured fluctuations in the intensity of the cosmic background radiation on various angular scales across the sky and with an accuracy of one part in 100,000. Taken together, their results implied that more than 95% of the material content of the universe is made up of at least two kinds of dark exotic matter that has gravitational effects on the observed matter. Furthermore, the studies reinforced the idea that about two-thirds of the energy content of the universe exists in the form of the repulsive gravitational force represented by the cosmological constant or some equivalent. (KENNETH BRECHER)

Earth Perihelion and Aphelion, 2002

Jan. 2	Perihelion, 147,098,130 km (91,402,370 mi) from the Sun
July 6	Aphelion, 152,094,370 km (94,506,880 mi) from the Sun

Equinoxes and Solstices, 2002

March 20	Vernal equinox, 19:16[1]
June 21	Summer solstice, 13:24[1]
Sept. 23	Autumnal equinox, 04:55[1]
Dec. 22	Winter solstice, 01:14[1]

Eclipses, 2002

May 26	Moon, penumbral (begins 10:12[1]), the beginning visible in North America (except the northeast), Central America, western South America, eastern Asia, the Pacific Ocean, the southeastern Indian Ocean; the end visible in southwestern Alaska, Asia (except the far north), Australia, the eastern Indian Ocean, the Pacific Ocean.
June 10–11	Sun, annular (begins 23:48[1]), the beginning visible in western Indonesia, southwestern Asia, northern Australia, the western Pacific Ocean; the end visible in North America (except northeastern Canada), the eastern Pacific Ocean, the Caribbean Sea.
June 24	Moon, penumbral (begins 20:18[1]), the beginning visible in Australia, southern and western Asia, Europe, Africa, eastern South America, the eastern and southern Atlantic Ocean, the southwestern Pacific Ocean; the end visible in Africa, Europe, South America (except the northwest), western Australia, the southeastern Pacific Ocean.
Nov. 19–20	Moon, penumbral (begins 23:32[1]), the beginning visible in Africa, Europe, North America (except the west), Central and South America, extreme western Asia, the Atlantic Ocean, the western Indian Ocean; the end visible in North, Central, and South America, Greenland, Europe, northwestern Russia, western Africa, the Atlantic Ocean, the eastern Pacific Ocean.
Dec. 4	Sun, total (begins 07:38[1]), the beginning visible in central and southern Africa, the eastern South Atlantic Ocean, the extreme southern Indian Ocean; the end visible in Australia, southern New Zealand, southern Indonesia, the southern Indian Ocean.

[1] Universal time.
Source: The Astronomical Almanac for the Year 2002 (2001).

SPACE EXPLORATION

Manned Spaceflight. Human activity in space faced an uncertain future as the International Space Station (ISS) encountered massive cost overruns and as cuts in general space spending were anticipated in response to the Sept. 11, 2001, terrorist attacks.

Following the start of full-time manned operations in late 2000, the ISS underwent rapid expansion with the addition of several key elements. First to arrive was the U.S.-built Destiny laboratory module, taken into orbit February 7 by the space shuttle *Atlantis*. Destiny, about the size of a bus, was designed to hold 24 standard payload racks, about half of them housing equipment for research into human adaptation to space travel, materials fabrication, and the behaviour of fluids and fires in microgravity. Because of weight limitations on shuttle cargos, the module was only partially outfitted inside and out at launch. The next mission, conducted in March by the shuttle *Discovery*, took up the Leonardo Multi-Purpose Logistics Module. Contributed by the Italian Space Agency as a reusable cargo carrier, Leonardo carried supplies and equipment for the station and transported trash back to Earth. Astronauts also conducted space walks to prepare the ISS for attachment of the Canadian-built robot arm. Three of *Discovery*'s crew stayed aboard the station as the Expedition Two crew, while the original Expedition One crew, which had occupied the ISS since Nov. 2, 2000, returned to Earth on the shuttle.

A month later the shuttle *Endeavour* took up the Canadarm2 robot arm and Raffaello, another Italian-built logistics module. Addition of the arm (derived from the earlier Canadarm carried on the shuttle since 1981) would let the ISS crew position new modules as they arrived. Because Canadarm2 could relocate itself along rails on the ISS exterior, it could reach virtually any location where work had to be done. More capability was added in July when *Atlantis* took up the Joint Airlock (called Quest), which allowed the ISS crew to conduct space walks independent of the shuttle. Further outfitting was conducted in August by the crew of *Discovery*, which delivered Leonardo to the ISS a second time. The mission also took the Expedition Three crew to relieve the Expedition Two crew. In September, using an expendable launcher, Russia sent up a Docking Compartment; the module carried an additional docking port for Soyuz and Progress spacecraft and an airlock for space walks. Previously the ISS had only two Soyuz/Progress-style ports, which had necessitated some juggling when new craft arrived. On December 5, after a six-day delay caused by an ISS docking problem with a Progress cargo ferry, *Endeavour* lifted off for the space station to carry out another crew exchange and deliver cargo in Raffaello once again.

The future of the ISS became clouded with the revelation in early 2001 that budget estimates were running $4 billion over plan. In response, NASA moved to cancel the U.S. habitat module and Crew Return Vehicle, or lifeboat, that would allow the station to house a crew of seven. With the crew restricted to three, virtually no crew time would be left for research, and the station would effectively be crippled as a science tool. At year's end NASA was negotiating with its European partners to have them pick up the responsibilities for finishing the habitat and lifeboat.

Russia's aging space station, Mir, was deliberately destroyed when mission controllers remotely commanded a docked Progress tanker to fire rockets and lower the station into Earth's atmosphere, where it burned up on March 23. Mir, whose core module was launched in 1986 and served as the nucleus of an eventual six-module complex, had operated long beyond its planned five-year lifetime.

China continued development of a human spaceflight capability with the second unmanned flight test of its Shenzhou ("Divine Ship" or "Magic Vessel") spacecraft in early January. The Shenzhou design was derived from Russia's Soyuz craft. The descent module returned to Earth after a week in orbit, but the little news that was released afterward raised doubts about its success. Analysts disagreed on when China would conduct its first manned space mission but expected it to happen within a few years.

Space Probes. The high point of the year occurred on February 12 when the Near

Earth Asteroid Rendezvous spacecraft (NEAR; officially, NEAR Shoemaker) touched down on asteroid 433 Eros, becoming the first spacecraft to land on a small body. NEAR had been orbiting Eros since Feb. 14, 2000, while taking thousands of video images and laser rangefinder readings to map the asteroid in detail. As the spacecraft ran low on fuel, controllers moved it into a lower orbit that let it collide gently with the surface of the rotating rock—a "soft" hard landing, a task for which it was not designed—and gather data on the surface. (See *Astronomy,* above.)

NASA launched the 2001 Mars Odyssey spacecraft on April 7 on a mission to study Mars from orbit and serve as a communications relay for U.S. and international landers scheduled to arrive in 2003 and 2004. On October 23 Mars Odyssey entered into a Mars orbit, where it spent the next several weeks using the Martian atmosphere as a brake to reshape its orbit for a 917-day mapping mission. Visible-light, infrared, and other instruments would collect data on the mineral content of the surface, including possible water locations, and the radiation hazards in the orbital environment.

The Cassini mission to Saturn, which carried the European-built Huygens probe designed to explore Saturn's moon Titan, continued toward its goal following a trajectory-assist flyby of Jupiter in late 2000 and early 2001 and returned images in conjunction with the Galileo spacecraft orbiting Jupiter. Cassini was to arrive at Saturn in 2004. Although finished with its official primary and extended missions, Galileo continued to operate during the year with additional flybys of Jupiter's moons Callisto and Io.

NASA's Microwave Anisotropy Probe (MAP) was launched on June 30 into a temporary Earth orbit and later moved to its permanent station in space about 1.5 million km (930,000 mi) from Earth, where it would use a pair of thermally isolated microwave telescopes to map small variations in the background radiation of the universe. These irregularities, discovered by the Cosmic Background Explorer (launched 1989), were believed to correspond to density differences in the early universe that gave rise to today's galaxies. NASA launched the Genesis probe on August 8 to gather 10–20 micrograms of particles of the solar wind. The material would be captured on ultrapure collector arrays exposed for more than two years in space and then returned to Earth for analysis in 2004. The collected particles could provide clues to the composition of the nebula that formed the solar system.

Launches in support of human spaceflight, 2001

Country	Flight	Crew[1]	Dates	Mission/payload
China	Shenzhou 2	—	January 9	second test flight of manned spacecraft
U.S.	STS-98, *Atlantis*	Kenneth Cockrell Mark Polansky Robert Curbeam Thomas Jones Marsha Ivins	February 7–20	delivery of Destiny laboratory module to ISS
Russia	Progress	—	February 26	ISS supplies
U.S.	STS-102, *Discovery*	James Wetherbee James Kelly Andy Thomas Paul Richards Yury Usachyov (u) Susan Helms (u) James Voss (u) William Shepherd (d) Yury Gidzenko (d) Sergey Krikalyov (d)	March 8–21	delivery of Leonardo logistics module to ISS; station crew exchange
U.S.	STS-100, *Endeavour*	Kent Rominger Jeffrey Ashby Chris Hadfield Scott Parazynski John Phillips Umberto Guidoni Yury Lonchakov	April 19–May 1	delivery of Canadarm2 and Raffaello logistics module to ISS
Russia	Soyuz-TM 32	Talgat Musabayev Yury Baturin Dennis Tito[2]	April 28–May 6	exchange of Soyuz return craft for ISS crew (TM 31 with TM 32)
Russia	Progress	—	May 20	ISS supplies
U.S.	STS-104, *Atlantis*	Steven Lindsey Charles Hobaugh Michael Gernhardt James Reilly Janet Kavandi	July 12–24	delivery of Joint Airlock to ISS
U.S.	STS-105, *Discovery*	Scott Horowitz Rick Sturckow Daniel Barry Patrick Forrester Frank Culbertson (u) Vladimir Dezhurov (u) Mikhail Tyurin (u) Yury Usachyov (d) Susan Helms (d) James Voss (d)	August 10–22	delivery of Leonardo logistics module to ISS; station crew exchange
Russia	Progress	—	August 21	ISS supplies
Russia	Progress-type	—	September 15	delivery of Docking Compartment-1 to ISS
Russia	Soyuz-TM 33	Viktor Afanasyev Konstantin Kozeyev Claudie Haigneré	October 21–30	exchange of Soyuz return craft for ISS crew (TM 32 with TM 33)
Russia	Progress	—	November 26	ISS supplies
U.S.	STS-108, *Endeavour*	Dominic Gorie Mark Kelly Linda Godwin Daniel Tani Frank Culbertson (d) Vladimir Dezhurov (d) Mikhail Tyurin (d) Yury Onufriyenko (u) Daniel Bursch (u) Carl Walz (u)	December 5–17	delivery of Raffaello logistics module to ISS; station crew exchange

[1] Commander and pilot (or flight engineer for Soyuz) are listed first.
[2] Flew as paying passenger.
u = ISS crew member carried up to station (ISS commander listed first).
d = ISS crew member returned to Earth (ISS commander listed first).

Unmanned Satellites. On February 20 Russia launched Sweden's Odin satellite, which carried a 1.1-m (43-in) radio telescope as its main instrument. Using two separate operating modes, the dual-mission craft was designed to observe radiation from a variety of molecular species to elucidate ozone-depletion mechanisms in Earth's atmosphere and star-formation processes in deep space. The Ukrainian-built Coronas-F satellite, launched by Russia on July 31, carried X-ray, radio, and particle instruments to study solar activity.

Other launches included the Geosynchronous Lightweight Technology

Experiment (GeoLITE; May 18), an advanced technology demonstration satellite carrying experimental and operational communications equipment for the U.S. military, and a twin payload (December 7) comprising Jason-1, a French-U.S. ocean-surface topography satellite designed as a follow-on to the highly successful TOPEX/Poseidon satellite launched in 1992, and the Thermosphere-Ionosphere-Mesosphere Energetics and Dynamics (TIMED) satellite, which would study the effects of the Sun and human activity on Earth's middle and upper atmosphere.

Launch Vehicles. NASA's plans to reduce the cost of getting payloads to orbit were set back by the cancellation of two high-profile reusable launch vehicle (RLV) projects. The X-33 subscale test craft was to have been a technology demonstrator for a larger single-stage-to-orbit VentureStar RLV. The aircraft-launched X-34 RLV test rocket would have demonstrated technologies for low-cost orbiting of smaller payloads. Both projects ran into technical problems that led NASA to decide that further investment would not save either project. In their place NASA set up the Space Launch Initiative to focus on advancing individual technologies rather than complete systems while continuing to pursue a next-generation RLV.

Boeing's new Delta IV launcher moved toward its maiden flight in 2002 with the delivery in 2001 of the first common booster core to Cape Canaveral, Florida, and successful ground tests of its new RS-68 hydrogen-oxygen liquid-fueled engine. The Delta IV family would be able to boost payloads of 8,000–23,000 kg (17,600–50,600 lb) into low Earth orbit. India successfully launched its Geosynchronous Satellite Launch Vehicle on April 18 and thereby took an important step closer to entering the commercial space market. On August 29 Japan's National Space Development Agency launched its first H-2A rocket, a revamped version of the troubled H-2 that was intended to compete with Europe's Ariane launcher and support Japan's partnership in the ISS. The H-2 family used a liquid-hydrogen–fueled first stage and twin solid rocket boosters. On September 29 NASA and the state of Alaska inaugurated a new launch complex on Kodiak Island with the launch of the Kodiak Star payload (comprising four small satellites) by an Athena I launcher. The Kodiak location, which faced south across the open Pacific Ocean, was ideal for launching satellites into a variety of polar (north-south) orbits.

(DAVE DOOLING)

Milestones in Spaceflight

April 12, 2001, marked the anniversaries of two landmark events in space travel: the 40th anniversary of the first human spaceflight—U.S.S.R. cosmonaut Yury Gagarin's single orbit of Earth in 1961—and the 20th anniversary of the U.S. launch of the first space shuttle, *Columbia,* in 1981. Gagarin's feat and the subsequent goading by Soviet leadership sparked a chain of events that started on May 25, 1961, when U.S. Pres. John F. Kennedy petitioned Congress to commit the nation to landing a man on the Moon "before this decade is out." Though that goal was achieved on July 20, 1969, when the Apollo 11 Lunar Module carried astronauts Neil Armstrong and Edwin ("Buzz") Aldrin to the surface of the Moon, aspirations for space travel continued to expand.

Ironically, the manned space race that had started between the U.S. and the U.S.S.R. 40 years earlier was replaced by a spirit of co-operation in 2001; the former competitors worked together to build the International Space Station (ISS) with other nations that became space farers in the 1960s, '70s, and '80s. On a more sombre note, the year also marked the 30th anniversary (April 19, 1971) of the first space station, the U.S.S.R.'s Salyut 1, and the death of its first three-man crew on their return to Earth (June 30, 1971); it was also the 15th anniversary (Jan. 28, 1986) of the explosion of the space shuttle *Challenger,* which killed seven astronauts.

The year 2001 also evoked the bolder vision of space activity painted by Stanley Kubrick and Arthur C. Clarke in their 1968 motion picture *2001: A Space Odyssey.* Not only was the ISS far smaller than its movie counterpart, it was likely to be even less than what had been planned; budget overruns threatened to reduce its crew size and science facilities. Exploration beyond the immediate vicinity of Earth was by automated spacecraft. No plans were in sight for large-scale lunar exploration as depicted in the film. The first government-industry venture to develop a reusable space liner, somewhat similar to its film version, faltered amid technical and financial problems.

These endeavours highlighted the technical, economic, and political challenges facing space explorers. For instance, descendants of the R-7 rocket that launched Gagarin continued to launch the three-man Soyuz and other spacecraft for Russia. The 20-year-old *Columbia* remained operational along with three other shuttles, and all four were expected to remain in service at least through 2020.

Nevertheless, humans continued to push at the frontier. American businessman Dennis Tito became the first space tourist when he rode a Russian Soyuz to the ISS in May 2001. In addition, Russia was considering more tourist flights, and several private American ventures were trying to develop affordable space tourism as a business.

(DAVE DOOLING)

Russian State Archive for Scientific-Technical Documentation (RGANTD)

Media and Publishing

Consolidation and **MERGERS** continued in the broadcast and publishing industries, while the **TERRORIST** and **ANTHRAX** attacks brought a new **SERIOUSNESS** as well as new challenges for all media content. **SATELLITE** and **CABLE TV** dominated even as **INTERACTIVE TV** and **STREAMING** media carved out niches for themselves.

TELEVISION

Organization. By 2001 the late 1990s rush to complete megamergers seemed to have ended in the United States, as each of the six leading American broadcast networks had aligned with a much larger entertainment/business company. With the smoke cleared and regulatory approval granted, ABC was part of the Disney empire, NBC was part of General Electric, CBS and UPN belonged to Viacom, WB was primarily part of AOL Time Warner, and Fox had been taken over by Rupert Murdoch's News Corp. Such alignments provided vital protection for the business model of network television, still the nation's most powerful aggregator of audiences for advertisers but increasingly seen by analysts as outdated for having only one revenue stream—advertising—which was vulnerable to economic fluctuations.

The year's major deal involving a network saw NBC in October making a nearly $2 billion acquisition of Telemundo Communications, the Spanish-language network with a 20% share of the Hispanic audience. The move was significant because of the booming U.S. Hispanic population. (*See* WORLD AFFAIRS: *United States:* Special Report.) NBC outbid Viacom for Telemundo, owned by Sony Pictures and Liberty Media Corp., and said the companies were planning to combine advertising sales efforts and offices and share some news resources. NBC's costly Olympic telecasts would have an additional outlet, and Telemundo could draw on NBC expertise to develop comedy series. Meanwhile, Univision, which reached 80% of Hispanic viewers, was moving forward with plans to launch Telefutura, a Spanish-language network targeting younger viewers, in early 2002.

News Corp. had long been considered the leading suitor of Hughes Electronics, owner of the top American satellite television service, DIRECTV. In October, however, General Motors Corp., the controlling shareholder of Hughes, accepted a surprise $25.8 billion bid by DIRECTV's major rival in consumer satellite programming, EchoStar Communications. If granted regulatory approval, the merger would make the new company the country's largest provider of television subscriptions, with 16.7 million customers totaling 17% of the pay-TV market, compared with cable operator AT&T's 14 million. Analysts and legislators expressed doubt that the merger would pass muster because it effectively killed competition in rural areas not served by cable.

In December the French company Vivendi Universal announced it was picking up USA Networks Inc's TV and film production units, including the USA and Sci-fi cable networks—as well as executive Barry Diller—for some $10.3 billion (*see* Book Publishing, *below*). Cable TV tycoon John C. Malone strengthened Liberty Media's German holdings by adding six cable systems, including those servicing Berlin, Hamburg, and Bavaria, for $5 billion. Meanwhile, AOL Time Warner became the first foreign broadcaster licensed by China. Its Hong Kong-based China Entertainment Television (CETV) broadcast a Chinese-language channel over cable systems in Guangdong. In exchange, Time Warner Cable carried China Central Television's (CCTV's) English-language channel in New York City, Los Angeles, and Houston, Texas. Having obtained 29% of China's Sun Television Cybernetworks, the Chinese-language online network SINA.com became the company's largest shareholder. Sun TV, a major satellite TV broadcaster and cable TV program syndicator, owned restricted land rights to operate two satellite TV channels in China. Phoenix satellite TV, which broadcast from Hong Kong in Mandarin Chinese, also received rights to transmit, but only in the Pearl River Delta area of southern China, where foreign broadcasts were allowed. Phoenix was partly owned by News Corp.'s satellite TV network, STAR. Murdoch reported a 15% drop in News Corp.'s fiscal-third-quarter revenue, while losses in film, magazine, and newspaper sectors were somewhat offset by gains in cable network programming and TV businesses. Chief executive Mark Schneider of Europe's cable operator United Pan-Europe Communications NV resigned after reporting huge losses beginning the second quarter.

New York cosmetics heir and owner of Central European Media Enterprises (CME) Ronald S. Lauder won his complaint against the government of the Czech Republic, which failed to protect CME from being squeezed out of TV Nova, the Czechs' most popular TV station. An international arbitration panel in Stockholm ordered the government to pay CME some $500 million.

Germany's second-largest TV network, Zweites Deutsches Fernsehen (ZDF), signed an agreement to cooperate with T-Online International AG as a way of getting around new regulations banning advertising on the news and information Web sites of public institutions (such as ZDF) funded by TV license fees. T-Online's parent company, Deutsche Telekom, proposed to team with the Kirch Group, Europe's largest producer of entertainment, sports, and news content, to develop hardware and software platforms for TV set-top boxes, but the deal fell through. RTL New Media took over Bertelsmann AG's interactive-TV and broadband division for $12 million. Bertelsmann then started BeBroadband for its e-commerce activities with a "preferred partner" relationship with RTL.

American Programming. The September 11 terrorist attacks in the United States dramatically altered the American television ratings picture. Before that date NBC was riding high, having finished first among young adults during the 2000–01 television season completed in May. CBS was looking forward to a ratings bonanza from the third edition of the reality game show *Survivor,* scheduled for October. The annual Emmy

Reuters/TimePix

The October 3 episode of The West Wing *dealt with issues of the September 11 terrorist attacks.*

Awards, announced in September, would recognize top prime-time achievers and give the networks a promotional boost going into the new season. The networks and other television producers were also feeling happy to have averted potential disaster in the spring of 2001 by reaching contract agreements with actors and writers unions, which had seemed poised to go out on strike. Some networks had prepared for a walkout by stockpiling new series episodes, but most admitted that if it had occurred, they would have had to fill their most popular hours, prime time, with reruns, reality series, and newsmagazines.

The September attacks forced first one and later a second postponement of the Emmys, as well as the delay of the TV season's debut by one week. When things finally got started, it seemed that the television order had changed. Television news organizations drew plaudits for selflessness in the immediate aftermath of the terrorist attacks. In addition to agreeing to share video, they provided nonstop commercial-free coverage from the attacks on the World Trade Center and the Pentagon beginning on Tuesday morning until Saturday, September 15. In the process all three of the old-line networks—ABC, CBS, and NBC—broke their previous records for continuous coverage, established during the first Moon walk and after the assassination of Pres. John F. Kennedy. In the first three days, CBS anchor Dan Rather and ABC counterpart Peter Jennings each put in 44 on-air hours.

High ratings continued for cable news provider CNN, which earlier in the year had modernized its format and brought in new anchors in response to growing competition from the likes of Murdoch's Fox News Channel. In the first three weeks after the attacks, CNN's ratings were up 500% from what they had been during the first eight months of 2001.

The prime-time landscape was also altered by the terrorist attacks. Viewers were now drawn to established quality series, which resulted in record ratings for such shows as CBS's *Everybody Loves Raymond* and NBC's *Friends, Law & Order,* and *The West Wing.* The producers of *The West Wing,* a dramatic series about a fictional but realistic White House, even hustled to put together a special episode directly responding to the acts of terrorism; it drew the series' highest ratings ever. Meanwhile, reality series other than *Survivor* drew very few viewers. This type of programming, so popular in 2000, had succeeded in stanching the steady loss of network audience share to cable. In September and October it was flailing, however. People coping with dramatic realities in their own lives had no patience for the ersatz danger in "reality" shows, which typically staged grueling competitions amid harsh living conditions for their nonactor participants. Even *Survivor,* while still drawing top-10 ratings, saw its popularity shrink considerably from the previous winter's edition, which had led the series to first place in the 2000–01 season ratings race.

On top of all of this, the decline in the American economy hit advertising-dependent television networks particularly hard even before September 11 and the several days without advertising that ensued. Afterward, the economy reeled, ad spending dropped even further, and the networks were talking openly about the need for major changes. The top four broadcast networks—ABC, CBS, Fox, and NBC—had increased their ad revenue by an average of almost 7% a year for five years straight, building up to a total of more than $16 billion during 2000. According to the *Los Angeles Times,* however, what analysts had projected to be a 2% drop during 2001 looked after September to be more like a 6% drop, a decline the paper called "unprecedented." This blow to the networks came against a backdrop of escalating production costs and loss of market share to cable. In response the networks vowed to slash costs, develop fewer new series, and possibly even eliminate Saturday-night prime-time programming altogether—a very drastic move.

When the *Primetime Emmy Awards* ceremony finally was held in early November, the networks got another bit of bad news. For the first time, one of the coveted best series Emmys went to a show made for cable television, the HBO look at "30-something" single women in New York, *Sex and the City* (series star Sarah Jessica Parker [*see* BIOGRAPHIES] was herself an Emmy nominee). Another HBO series, the critically acclaimed *The Sopranos,* saw two of its actors take two of the other top honours, best actor in a drama (James Gandolfini) and best actress in a drama (Edie Falco). *The West Wing* otherwise held off *The Sopranos* to win the best drama Emmy for the second year in a row. Best comedy actress went to repeat winner Patricia Heaton of *Everybody Loves Raymond,* and best comedy actor went to first-timer Eric McCormack of NBC's *Will & Grace.*

International Programming. When the private Independent Television (NTV) network was taken over by Russian government-owned Gazprom in April, after a protracted struggle with its cofounder and original owner, tycoon Vladimir Gusinsky (*see* BIOGRAPHIES), a majority of the news team (including general director Yevgeny Kiselyov) transferred to TV6. That station later faced court-mandated liquidation, however, in the wake of a lawsuit by energy giant Lukoil, whose daughter company, Lukoil-Garant, was a 15% shareholder. Boris Berezovsky, another of Russia's "oligarchs," who was now living in exile and who controlled 75% of TV6, had offered to buy out Lukoil-Garant, which then countered with an offer to buy out Berezovsky.

TV—Too Big a Dose of Reality?

Strictly speaking, reality programming—unscripted and unrehearsed programs in the form of sporting events, talk shows, documentaries, *Candid Camera,* and the like—had been part of the television landscape from the earliest days of broadcasting. Later, in 1973, it became more deliberate when, on PBS's *An American Family,* the innermost secrets of the William C. Loud family unfolded before the TV audience in 12 hour-long segments culled from 300 hours of footage shot in the family's home. Then, beginning in 1992, the American cable station MTV scored a hit by having seven young people, strangers to each other, live together for several months in a house under constant camera scrutiny, with the highlights broadcast weekly. Nevertheless, it was not until the American television network CBS in 2000 peopled an island with a band of castaways and had them vote to expel one member each week until the last person claimed a million-dollar prize that the world took notice. *Survivor,* CBS's version of a Swedish TV success, set summer viewership records, and television executives everywhere rushed to launch their own offerings. CBS itself followed later in the summer by isolating 10 persons in a house and having the audience vote them out until only one was left in *Big Brother,* its version of a Dutch hit. Not only did this type of show grab audience attention, but it was relatively cheap to produce because it did not depend on professional screenwriters and actors but instead used ordinary people. A second (and later a third) version of *Survivor* and a second *Big Brother* appeared in 2001, along with such shows as ABC's *The Mole,* in which a group facing various challenges had a saboteur in its midst, and Fox's *Temptation Island,* in which unmarried couples were separated and their fidelity was tested. PBS broadcast the British *The 1900 House,* in which a family lived for three months with no modern amenities.

The concept emerged worldwide. Great Britain, which already in 2000 had presented *Castaway,* recounting the experiences of a group that created a community for a year on a Scottish island, launched *Castaway 2001.* In addition, France had *Loft Story;* Canada offered *Pioneer Quest;* at least 18 countries had a version of *Big Brother;* and more than 20 countries had shown or were considering their own *Survivor* series.

Perhaps inevitably, with all this popularity came controversy. Accusations were made that some scenes were staged, edited, shown out of sequence, or reenacted with body doubles, that voting was rigged or influenced by show officials, that copyrights were infringed, or that the backgrounds of some participants were not checked carefully enough. Even though such shows as NBC's *Fear Factor,* with contestants subjected to stunts involving whatever scared them, and *Spy TV,* where the staged situations often were designed to evoke terror, were very popular, their mean-spiritedness also drew many complaints. Nonetheless, reality shows continued to proliferate worldwide, and there was no sign that they would disappear soon.

(BARBARA WHITNEY)

Winners of the French reality-TV show Loft Story, *Christophe and Loana, leave their studio lot near Paris on July 5.*

Olivier Morin/AFP Worldwide

"Canada's Own" CBC Television, launched its new season with theme nights accompanied by on-air hosts, as well as new branding that tied together drama, comedy, news, and sports programming on both the main network and CBC Newsworld. Hockey Night in Canada provided leaguewide coverage, including highlights, features, and analysis. Australian rugby fans in 300 households participated in a four-month interactive-TV trial by Cable & Wireless Optus beginning in August. Viewers of Seven Network's Bledisloe Cup broadcast chose match data they wanted displayed and participated in live polls. Nine Network unveiled plans to elevate Friday nights in its programming with headline matches of the Australian Football League (AFL). Seven lost its 45-year association with the AFL earlier in the year.

Seven Network could expect significant cost savings once its new $40 million broadcast centre in Melbourne—the first such digital facility in the country—began operations by the end the year. The capacious centre had 100-hour video servers and on-line storage that could contain one full year's programming.

France's first reality-TV show, *Loft Story,* garnered 5.2 million viewers daily, most between 15 and 25 years old, since it aired early in the year. Its creators, Holland-based Endemol Entertainment, had been told that *telepoubelle,* or "garbage TV," would never catch on in France. Earlier, *Big Brother* had hit it big all over Europe except France. *Loft Story* was *Big Brother* with a twist; five women and six men, in their 20s, agreed to live in a loft for 10 weeks and be filmed around-the-clock. TV watchers voted by telephone each week to eliminate one of two participants. The lone woman and lone man who remained by July won a $416,000 Parisian apartment—but had to live together in it for the next six months. (*See* Sidebar.)

India's state-owned Doordarshan television network aired before a live audience the country's first matchmaking TV show, *Swayamvar* ("Own Groom"). The program, based on a common practice in northern India in which princes vie for the most beautiful princesses, gave women participants the prerogative to choose their own men. The program featured 26 women, one per episode, from cities across India. The biggest hit on Indian TV, however, was the Hindi-language version of *Who Wants to Be a Millionaire,* starring the popular film star Amitabh Bachchan. (*See* BIOGRAPHIES.)

In other media news, Fernando Dutra Pinto, wanted for the kidnapping of Patricia Abravanel, the 24-year-old daughter of Brazilian TV baron Silvio Santos, broke into the magnate's mansion and held the 70-year-old Santos hostage for

Media Voices of the Muslim World

The terrorist attacks of Sept. 11, 2001, and the military actions against Osama bin Laden, the alleged mastermind of the operation, brought increased visibility and international attention to the news media in the Middle East and Central Asia. This was especially true of the satellite television network Al-Jazeera, which was perceived as Bin Laden's media voice when it broadcast taped interviews with him and others of the al-Qaeda terrorist group. Al-Jazeera also became the major supplier to Western media of TV footage from inside Afghanistan. Questions were raised in the U.S., however, about the propriety of the media's giving terrorists a soapbox from which to argue their views, as well as about the assertions of objectivity by Al-Jazeera and others of Al-Jazeera's reporting on Middle East issues. Al-Jazeera was founded in 1996 by Sheikh Hamad ibn Khalifah ath-Thani, the emir of Qatar, and symbolized his desire to modernize the country. Based in Doha, Qatar, Al-Jazeera was by far the most international of the Arabic-language broadcasters, reaching 35 million viewers in 20 countries. Although the staff claimed adherence to the journalistic values of free speech and fair play—and indeed they were most likely among regional broadcasters to present non-Islamic points of view—there was never any question about where the network's sympathies lay. Still, the tone of Al-Jazeera's independent reporting of the Palestinian *intifadah* in 2000, for example, contrasted significantly with that of government-controlled Arab networks.

Hezbollah-owned Lebanon-based Al-Manar TV was established in 1997 to promote the Palestinian *intifadah* and highlight the plight of Palestinians. It proudly expanded its mission in 2001, denouncing what in its broadcasts it tagged "The American Aggression on Afghanistan." Program intermission snippets, which showed the U.S. A-bomb attacks in Japan and military actions in Vietnam, Iraq, and Lebanon, were billed as "Terrorism Without Borders." In May Palestinian TV came under scrutiny when it ran commercials asking children to drop their toys, pick up rocks, and do battle with Israel. Actors re-created the well-publicized and shocking death of 12-year-old Muhammad Dura in his father's arms during crossfire between Israelis and Palestinians and showed the boy in paradise, urging other children to follow.

An Osama bin Laden videotape airs on the Al-Jazeera television network on December 26.

AP/Wide World Photos

Opposition TV channels Pars TV and National Iranian Television (NITv), beamed from Los Angeles, encouraged Iranian viewers to step up reform efforts. The Iranian government confiscated satellite dishes receiving these broadcasts and apparently jammed NITv signals in October 2000. The opposition Iraqi National Congress opened a new front with a daily hour-long broadcast via satellite of Television Hurriah (Liberty TV). Funded by the U.S. but beamed from London, Liberty TV brought news, political profiles, music videos, and even call-in shows. In early October a bill was introduced in the U.S. Congress to create a Radio Free Afghanistan to join Radio Free Europe, Radio Liberty, Radio Martí, and other "surrogate" stations. Few remembered that there once had been a Radio Free Afghanistan but that it was discontinued by the U.S. government in 1992.

(RAMONA MONETTE SARGAN FLORES)

seven hours (telecast live) before surrendering to the police.

Kim Ahyun, who complained that she was not allowed to cover "male" subjects such as politics and business, quit her job on South Korean TV. She founded Fasonaki, a company that shot and sold footage of international fashion shows to local TV and cable companies. Sally Wu, Phoenix news anchor in Hong Kong, was praised as a model journalist by Chinese Premier Zhu Rongji. Her company, five-year-old Hong Kong broadcaster Phoenix (through its parent company Fox News), was first in its live coverage and Chinese translation of September 11 in New York City, by going on air within minutes of the attack.

Technology. New television sets in the U.S. were equipped with secondary audio programming technology that, when activated by the remote control, allowed Spanish-speaking viewers to hear TV dialogue in Spanish. The system could also provide auditory assistance to the visually impaired by describing what was happening on the screen. The U.S. Federal Communications Commission required American broadcasters to provide descriptive video service (DVS) for the blind, equivalent to closed-captioning for the deaf. DVS allowed for a second audio track in which a narrator describes visual action. Pioneered by public TV station WGBH in Boston, DVS was commercially available only on the Turner Classic Movies channel on cable TV.

It was reported that V-chip technology—which allowed the blocking of program material and had been standard equipment on all television sets manufactured since January 2000—was being used by only 7% of American parents to regulate children's viewing habits.

In December flat-panel TVs from Sharp's new Aquos line in 76-cm (1 cm=0.39 in) and 56-cm liquid crystal display (LCD) panels were introduced. Sharp also unveiled its first consumer plasma display panel (PDP) TV prototypes in 109-cm and 127-cm models.

Hitachi and Sanyo had earlier exhibited high-definition 107-cm PDP TVs, while Toshiba rolled out its 107-cm and 127-cm PDP TVs in November. Sony offered rear-projection LCD "Grand Wega" TVs, including a 152-cm prototype. HDNet, the world's first high-definition national TV network, debuted with a major league baseball game. Sports and entertainment programming was seen as the key to increasing sales of digital high-definition TV.

Microsoft Corp.'s long-delayed Interactive TV software debuted in June on Portugal's TV Cabo. Interactive TV subscribers received e-mail, banked, shopped, placed bets, and played games on TV, using a set-top box. ReplayTV technology was to be integrated in Motorola set tops for its DigiCable business. ReplayTV enabled users to record 60 hours of television on a hard drive and eliminate commercials with a 30-second skip button. TiVo won patents for its digital video recording (DVR) technology, which AOL Time Warner planned to include in next-generation set-top boxes to be developed and marketed jointly with Samsung Electronics. Japan launched its e-platform, and a startup company to broadcast data services for it, at the CEATEC consumer show in October. Japan's ep Corp. promised the first service in the world that would seamlessly combine digital broadcasting, Internet access, and data storage in a hard-disk drive. Princeton Graphic System's high-definition TV receiver and Channel 1's companion service enabled Web surfing without a set-top box, using Internet hardware that was built into the set. The 91-cm HDTV-ready AI3.6HD display supplied connections for every TV service and device.

A report from Scarborough Research found that almost one-quarter of adult Americans were watching less TV since they started using the Internet. On the other hand, Nielsen//NetRatings found that heavy Internet users were big consumers of all media and might not necessarily have decreased time spent watching TV or reading newspapers. Scarborough's findings showed that Americans had increased radio listening since going on-line.

RADIO

The dominant news in American radio was the potentially debilitating ailments suffered by two of the medium's biggest stars. Paul Harvey (*see* BIOGRAPHIES), fresh off a 10-year contract to continue his lucrative work with ABC Radio Networks, was off the air for about four months in midyear after an apparent viral infection cost him the temporary use of his voice. Harvey's daily news reports and commentary were heard on more than 1,200 stations. More shocking, conservative talk host Rush Limbaugh revealed in October that he had gone virtually deaf because of a rare autoimmune disease that attacks the inner ear, and there was little chance of recovery. A few listeners thought they detected a change in the rhythm and timbre of Limbaugh's talk. During the summer the popular Limbaugh had signed a contract with Premiere Radio Networks reportedly paying him $250 million through 2009, and he vowed to continue with his work, using technological aids to help him hear listeners or read what they had said—or simply to stop taking calls and do his daily show as a monologue. "Nothing's stopped me from talking, and that's what I get paid to do," he told the Associated Press. "Nobody's paying me to listen."

Recent years' consolidation waves in the radio business seemed to have ebbed, perhaps because there was little left to consolidate. Like other advertiser-dependent businesses during 2001, Clear Channel Communications Inc., which had emerged as the largest American radio broadcaster, with 1,180 stations, was undergoing a rough year, posting a large third-quarter loss. Toward year's end Radio One Inc., with 65 stations the largest owner and operator of urban radio stations, and ABC Radio Networks, with 163 urban affiliates the largest urban programmer, combined forces in a partnership creating the leading African American radio service.

The most intriguing radio story of the year, however, might have been the first stirrings of Internet-based radio as a force. The technology awaited cheap and ubiquitous Internet access to really come into its own, but some experts believed there was a huge potential audience of disaffected local radio listeners, troubled by ever-narrowing formats and ever-increasing commercial time. An executive with Arbitron Webcast Services, which rated Internet radio stations' popularity, told *Time* magazine that the proportion of Americans who had listened to Web radio had grown to 20% from 6% in just two years. A competing company, MeasureCast, reported that listening to the stations whose Internet broadcasts it measured had more than tripled during 2001.

In the latest incident in press crackdowns by authoritarian African regimes, Zambia's popular private station Radio Phoenix was shut down for having allegedly defamed Pres. Frederick Chiluba. Many silenced journalists flocked to the Internet, which was relatively safe from censorship.

Following a federal parliamentary inquiry, the Australian government was tasked with funding a "black-spots" scheme to improve radio services in certain areas. The inquiry also highlighted concerns about a lack of local content due to networked or syndicated programs.

(RAMONA MONETTE SARGAN FLORES; STEVE JOHNSON)

The future of popular radio talk show host Rush Limbaugh was cast in doubt during the year after an illness left him virtually deaf.

NEWSPAPERS

A severe advertising recession that forewarned a global economic downturn overtook newspapers in 2001, even as the September 11 attacks in the United States produced some of the most dramatic news coverage by the press in more than a half century.

Advertising sectors—notably employment advertising and so-called dot-com advertising—were exposed to economic whims after having led the newspaper-industry revenue surge in the late 1990s, and their vulnerability served as an early-warning system for the overall economy. In the first half of 2001, newspaper employment advertising in the U.S. plunged 25%. Dot-com advertising, which had begun declining after the April 2000 crash of Internet stocks, was virtually nonexistent in newspapers.

Sharp contractions in classified, retail, and national advertising began in February in the U.S. and continued to decline throughout the year—a pattern repeated in Europe and the Asia-Pacific area later in the year. In some non-U.S. regions, national advertising was the first recessed sector as media buyers in global economic capitals, already reeling from an economic contraction, began pulling back advertising plans. In Latin America the already-poor economic situation from the previous four years was made worse by sinking economies in Brazil and Argentina, and the Western downturn made matters even worse.

Meanwhile, newspapers worldwide chafed at the unpredictability of newsprint prices, which made up 20–30% of the total cost of the publishing business. After successive price hikes in 2000, newspapers entered 2001 with projections of a 10–20% rise in prices, a sharp increase coming from a paper-manufacturing industry that had rapidly consolidated during the previous four years. The price increases did not materialize, however, at least not to predicted levels; the advertising recession, combined with the threat of higher newsprint prices, forced newspapers to reduce print consumption sharply.

Overall, the combination of an advertising pullback and the unpredictability of newsprint prices produced a sharp decrease in financial performance by newspapers. In the first half of 2001, American publicly traded newspaper companies saw revenues decline 4.7%, operating profits drop 30%, and profit margins contract nearly seven percentage points to 16.6%—albeit from record highs in 2000.

Throughout the year newspapers responded to the economic distress with layoffs, employee buyouts, a cutback in the number of pages printed, and the elimination of sections no longer supported by advertising. The trend toward small physical page widths, which had begun in the late 1990s as a cost-saving measure, continued in 2001. Critics noted that while all economy-exposed media were undergoing turbulent times, the defensive nature of the newspaper response was similar to how newspapers responded to the previous economic recession in 1990–91. After that recession, newspapers lost advertising market share to targeted and measurable media such as direct mail, cable television, and local radio.

In the U.S. the immediate cutbacks by newspaper companies provoked cries of corporate greed from quarters within the journalism community, notably by the publisher of the *San Jose Mercury News;* he resigned his prominent position within the industry instead of following through on cutbacks made by corporate giant Knight Ridder.

It was against this backdrop that newspapers responded immediately to the September terrorist attacks in the U.S. Many newspapers in the Americas published extra editions in the afternoon of the attacks, some for the first time since the Japanese attack on Pearl Harbor in 1941. Newspapers worldwide published among the most memorable newspapers of all time the day after the attacks and subsequently boosted circulation. Newspapers also mobilized their large staffs in editorial, circulation, production, and marketing departments to produce unique print newspapers, Web-site updates, instant-message alerts, e-mail newsletters, and other ways to deliver the news. Newspaper Web sites, like other Internet ventures, saw record hit counts in the immediate aftermath of September 11.

With the exception of Japan, leading industrialized countries saw a 1% annual decrease in paid daily circulation during much of the past decade. Analysts suggested that this downward trend might end because young people had become intensely interested in the news events, and they drove up circulation sales.

Though newspapers reported record circulation sales in the aftermath of the terrorist attacks, the same could not be said of advertising. Historically, advertisers pulled back media commitments in such situations for fear of being associated with negative news events. The pullback after September 11, however, was more severe because the economic foundation was already in place to encourage lower marketing expenditures.

Meanwhile, traditional publishers continued to face a third consecutive year of rapid expansion from the newest publishing sector—free commuter newspapers. As Stockholm-based Modern Times Group (MTG) launched new editions of its advertiser-supported free newspapers aimed at subway and bus-system customers, traditional publishers launched competing products, with varying degrees of success. Europe remained the focal point of MTG strategy and subsequent countermeasures by traditional publishers, though expansions were also seen in Canada, the U.S., Argentina, and Singapore.

"Convergence" remained a hot topic among newspaper executives in 2001, even if definitions varied. Though American newspapers struggled to get regulatory officials to abandon local cross-media ownership rules, newspapers in countries where such rules were nonexistent or less stringent began toying seriously with notions of re-positioning themselves as "information mills" with different distribution platforms—print newspapers, Web sites, e-mail, instant messaging, and even television, radio, and other venues. Publishers eyed the possibilities of future cost savings in news gathering as well as cross-media advertising packages. The allure of such future convergence was among the driving forces behind multimedia giant Tribune Co.'s purchase of Times Mirror properties in the United States and cable operator CanWest's purchase of Hollinger properties in Canada in 2000.

Over a 20-year period, the newspaper ownership landscape in Australia, Canada, New Zealand, the United Kingdom, and the U.S. changed dramatically, with similar trends—far fewer owners and far more public ownership of a constitutionally and legally protected industry. The daily newspaper markets for Australia and New Zealand, for example, were now dominated by two companies; those in Canada, by four companies. The U.K., with clear distinctions between regional newspapers and national newspapers, continued to see sharp contraction in ownership. In the United States 20% of the country's 1,500 newspapers, including almost all metropolitan dailies, were owned by publicly traded companies.

In a challenging economic environment, newspapers continued to seek a more immediate return on investment from the high level of Internet activities started in the late 1990s. With the sharp downturn in the advertising market not supportive of Web-site profitability, newspaper managements turned to the more difficult issue of the degree to which readers should pay subscription fees. In early 2001 anecdotal evidence was mounting that providing free content on-line while charging for the same content in print was beginning to hurt print circulation. Two alternative models emerged—one required an individual to register for continued free access to content, another allowing free access to online content only to paid subscribers of the print newspaper. Many newspapers charged for access to archived materials.

In late 2001 American newspaper offices were gripped by fear of anthrax attacks. After two *New York Post* employees tested positive for anthrax and several newspapers reported anthrax scares, many newspapers changed mail-handling procedures.

The issue of copyright in the digital age challenged newspapers during the year. In a landmark decision the United States Supreme Court ruled that newspaper and magazine publishers broke copyright law when they failed to secure freelance writers' permission to include their works in digital databases—a decision that affected hundreds of thousands of articles stored in electronic archives as well as those republished in CD-ROM and other digital formats. In response to the decision and subsequent lawsuits by freelances, newspapers such as the *New York Times* and the *San Diego Union-Tribune* removed from their archives materials subject to review in light of the court ruling. Similar copyright issues faced newspaper publishers in Europe. In Germany the Bundestag (lower house of parliament) considered a European payment standard of between 10% and 30% for electronic reusage, outraging newspaper publishers.

Though commercial concerns overwhelmed newspapers in 2001, other pub-

AP/Wide World Photos

Outside the News Corp. building in New York City on October 20, an electronic sign announces that anthrax had been found in the offices of the New York Post.

lishers struggled to maintain an environment in which they could publish. In South Korea the government of Pres. Kim Dae Jung charged and jailed three opposition newspaper owners on tax-evasion and embezzlement charges, which observers charged was a heavy-handed attempt to silence government critics. New press restrictions were adopted in Chile, Sri Lanka, Venezuela, Argentina, Malaysia, Mongolia, and Vietnam. According to the Committee to Protect Journalists, Iran, Liberia, and China remained the most oppressive enemies of a free press. Meanwhile, journalists working within Russia reported that a corrupt general environment, combined with actions by the government of Pres. Vladimir Putin, had created an atmosphere of deteriorating press freedom.

Two prominent figures in the American newspaper industry died during the year, Katherine Graham, owner of the *Washington Post,* and John Bertram Oakes, an editorial-page editor for the *New York Times.* (*See* OBITUARIES.)

(EARL J. WILKINSON)

MAGAZINES

The magazine industry faced a bad year that got worse after the Sept. 11, 2001, terrorist attacks in the U.S. "The 11th" hastened the decline of an industry already suffering lowered revenues and resulted in the closure of some well-known magazines. During the first nine months of 2001, total ad pages declined about 10%, and revenue slipped slightly more than 1%.

The good news for 2001 was that 2000 was an unusually healthy year (U.S. and worldwide advertising revenue rose by 13.5% and 4%, respectively), which meant that the decline in 2001 was probably not as precipitous as it appeared.

The only winners were the newsweeklies. *Newsweek* increased its newsstand sales sixfold after the terrorist attacks, and *Time* and *U.S. News & World Report* tripled theirs. All three published special advertisement-free editions within days of the attacks. *Fire Engineering* was most directly affected by the tragedies. The 125-year-old magazine lost 10 of its contributors, nine New York City firefighters and one Port Authority officer, who had served as both writers and trainers at the magazine's fire department instruction conferences. Among the dead was Ray Downey, the battalion chief of the New York Fire Department special operations command and a key member of the magazine's advisory board.

The implications of the attacks reverberated throughout the magazine industry, and several trade magazines, including *Pit & Quarry, Convenience Store News,* and *Cheese Market News,* covered the events and how their industries were affected. Later in the year, magazines were also involved in the anthrax scare. In early October Iowa police called Thomas Ryder, chief executive of Reader's Digest Association, Inc., after an Iowa subscriber notified police about a white powdery substance on her magazine. The residue was cornstarch, commonly used in the printing process to help ink dry faster and reduce static cling. A series of similar false alarms elsewhere forced some magazine printers, including R.R. Donnelley & Sons, to search for a substitute to cornstarch.

The Magazine Publishers of America (MPA) and the American Society of Magazine Editors moved their annual American Magazine Conference, scheduled for late October, from Phoenix, Ariz., to New York City. MPA president Nina Link explained that "many of our member attendees as well as speakers expressed their reluctance to leave their New York-based offices during such challenging times."

The most notable closure of the year was that of 66-year-old *Mademoiselle,* which ended its run with the November 2001 issue; subscribers were sent *Glamour* in its place. Condé Nast closed the 1.1-million-circulation magazine, stating, "Current economic conditions have produced a situation where . . . the magazine is no longer viable." Other closures included *Brill's Content, George, Working Woman, Expedia Travels, Family PC, Mode, Nova, Individual Investor, Lingua Franca, Asiaweek, Golf & Travel, Maximum Golf, The Industry Standard, Silicon Alley Reporter,* and *Woman's Realm. McCall's,* a venerable title among the women's magazines, published its last issue in March, but its publisher, Gruner+Jahr USA Publishing, successfully relaunched it a month later as *Rosie;* by the end of June, it ranked 12th in total circulation. A prominent Russian news magazine, *Itogi,* was a casualty of the struggle between the new government of Vladimir Putin and oligarch Vladimir Gusinsky. (*See* BIOGRAPHIES.) After corporate shareholders aligned with Putin fired the editor in chief, Sergey Parkhomenko, most of the staff departed and *Newsweek* severed its partnership with the magazine; its last issue was dated April 17.

O: The Oprah Magazine, launched in May 2000, became one of the most successful magazine launches in history. After two press runs the initial May–June issue sold out of 1.6 million copies on newsstands. By the end of June 2001, the average paid circulation reached 2.7 million—20th among all magazines.

Making the rounds at *The Nation,* the most venerable left-leaning political magazine in the U.S., was a joke about its increase in circulation: "What's bad for the country is good for *The Nation.*" After George W. Bush became president, the magazine's circulation rose 4%. *Mother Jones,* another liberal magazine, increased its circulation by 6%, and two smaller left-leaning magazines, *American*

Prospect and *In These Times,* also registered healthy increases. Likewise, conservative magazines had profited from the election of Bill Clinton in the 1990s. *The American Spectator* had experienced a sevenfold circulation jump and *National Review* had increased its readership by 66% during the Clinton years.

Internet publishing was another bright spot for publishers. On-line advertising grew faster than that in any other medium and continued to increase during times of recession, according to Danny Meadows-Klue, chairman of the Interactive Advertising Bureau. At an October conference in Geneva, Meadows-Klue reported that sustained growth had more than doubled each year for three years.

Magazine covers following September 11 reflect the impact of the terrorist attacks.

AP/Wide World Photos

Hubert Burda, president of the Association of German Magazine Publishers, received the annual Freedom of Commercial Speech medal from the European Association of Communication Agencies at its October conference in Berlin. Burda had been a prominent champion of advertising and press freedom in Europe. (DAVID E. SUMNER)

BOOK PUBLISHING

United States. The American book-publishing industry was profoundly affected by the Sept. 11, 2001, terrorist attacks in the U.S. In the immediate aftermath local bookstores reported that they had become "de facto" community centres crowded with people seeking information, connection, and whatever comfort might be found. There was a surge in sales of books about Islam, including the Qur'an, as well as such topics as religious fundamentalism, terrorism, the Taliban, the Middle East, and biological and chemical warfare. Rutgers University Press, publisher of a pictorial history of the World Trade Center, was overwhelmed with orders for the book. Plans for stepped-up media exposure for upcoming books and their authors were derailed. Some books slated for fall publication had their publication dates pushed back until 2002, and a number of publishers used their Web sites (chat rooms, audio readings, and pictures) in an attempt to compensate for the lost face-to-face contact between authors and their audience.

Even before the terrorist attacks, some publishing segments failed to live up to expectations, especially the electronic-book (e-book) market. Though a 2000 study had projected that under the right conditions the electronic publishing market for consumer books could reach $2.3 billion–$3.4 billion by 2005, accounting for 10% of all book sales, the e-book market was slowed by ongoing technical issues, including the lack of "interoperability." The Association of American Publishers took the lead to develop open standards for the e-book marketplace in an effort to provide authors, publishers, retailers, and consumers with the widest possible array of choices in developing, selling, and utilizing information in digital form. Standards were developed in the areas of metadata and numbering, along with recommendations on digital-rights management standards. In April 2001 an agency was selected (Content Directions, Inc.) to register digital object identifiers, or DOIs, a system used by book publishers to identify and exchange electronic content.

The issue of copyright protection, especially as it applied to digital information, remained paramount for publishers; two important copyright cases dealt with electronic rights. In June in *New York Times Co.* v. *Tasini,* the Supreme Court ruled 7–2 in favour of a group of freelance journalists who had sued newspaper and magazine publishers for copyright infringement. The plaintiffs objected to the defendants' reproduction and distribution in a database of their previously published print articles. The court found that the articles in an electronic database "as presented to and perceptible by" a database user could not be considered a permissible part of a "revision of a collective work," as claimed by the defendants, because the articles were reproduced in the database "clear of the context" provided either by the original periodical editions or any revision of them.

In *Random House* v. *RosettaBooks,* the plaintiff publisher sought to enjoin the defendant publisher from issuing e-book versions of works previously published by the plaintiff under contracts to "print, publish, and sell the work in book form." The federal district court, however, denied the injunction request, finding that the contract language did not convey electronic rights to the plaintiff for the works at issue.

Two of the industry's highest priorities—the protection of intellectual property and the defense of intellectual freedom—met head-on in a highly publicized court case. In May the U.S. Court of Appeals for the 11th Circuit overturned a preliminary injunction that had banned the publication of *The Wind Done Gone* by Alice Randall. The case began in April when trustees of the Margaret Mitchell estate brought a copyright and trademark infringement action against the Houghton Mifflin Co. The complaint sought to enjoin publication of that book, which it claimed used elements of *Gone with the Wind* and was therefore a misappropriation of a copyrighted work. Randall and Houghton Mifflin maintained that the book, told from the point of view of a former slave, was a work of social commentary and parody protected by the First Amendment and allowable under copyright law. In the wake of the appellate court ruling, the book was published in June. (PATRICIA S. SCHROEDER)

Fan Fiction—TV Viewers Have It Their Way

Television shows had long captivated audiences and provided a temporary escape from reality for viewers who could vicariously live another life. Some devoted viewers would often discuss their favourite dramas and begin to play out "what-if" scenarios: What if Agent Mulder never returned to *The X-Files* and Agent Scully began having an affair with Assistant Director Walter Skinner? What if Captain Kirk of *Star Trek* had never met Spock? What if the title character of *Buffy the Vampire Slayer* found true love in a demon?

When surfing on the Internet became popular in the 1990s, fans began taking their fantasies on-line and publishing "fan fiction" or "fanfic," a practice that had started with "fanzines" (magazines or books created by fans). The year 2001 saw a burgeoning of Web sites devoted to tale-tellers who spun their imaginations and transported TV characters into a different universe. The Internet had become their vanity press.

Henry Jenkins, author of *Textual Poachers: Television Fans & Participatory Culture* (1992), had kept a watchful eye on the fan community for a number of years. He found that though there was initial anxiety and resistance to digital media, "even those who were actively . . . resistant to moving on-line five years ago are now not only putting new stuff on-line, but are archiving stories going back 20 years."

The Internet was a powerful tool; a fan could instantly enter fandom with a couple of clicks. Those looking for *Star Trek* stories could surf to trekiverse.org; prose focusing on *Star Wars* could be found at FanfiX.com. The free site Fanfiction.net was a clearinghouse for all fan-based fiction, and monthly it boasted 1.2 million authors and readers, all digesting or sharing stories—both short stories and novel-length works—based on preexisting characters.

Though many purists believed that "real" fiction came completely from the imagination, Jenkins disagreed: "What would Shakespeare have done without dealing with preexisting characters? All of his stories were based on characters that already existed." Jenkins believed that fan fiction was another way of continuing the folk process that dominated the storytelling tradition long before "we began to think of stories as legal property of individuals or companies rather than the shared property of a culture."

For producers, fan fiction was viewed as a compliment, not a threat. *The X-Files* executive producer Frank Spotnitz remarked, "Somebody said to [creator Chris Carter] early on . . . when he first started to see fan fiction about Mulder and Scully on the Internet, 'You know you've got a hit because the characters have taken hold in the imagination of the audience.'" (NANCY SCHULZ)

Europe, Asia, Australia. In the European book-publishing industry, consolidation was the byword in 2001. Bertelsmann AG, the giant German publishing company headed by Thomas Middelhoff (*see* BIOGRAPHIES), announced in May that in an effort to compete with Amazon.com, it would integrate BOL.com, its on-line bookstore in 16 European countries, into its multichannel book club division.

In August Vivendi Universal acquired Houghton Mifflin for about $2.2 billion, which included Houghton Mifflin's $500 million debt. The purchase greatly strengthened Vivendi's position in the English-language markets and propelled the company to the number two position (behind Pearson PLC) in worldwide educational publishing. (See *Television*, above.) Although Macmillan Publishers Ltd. of the U.K. bought from Pearson Education the right to use the Macmillan name in the U.S., it would continue to use Palgrave as its global academic imprint.

AP/Wide World Photos

Alice Randall, author of The Wind Done Gone, *and her husband unpack copies of her novel at a bookstore in Nashville, Tenn., after an injunction that had banned the release of the* Gone with the Wind *parody was overturned.*

The traditional balance of power between publishers and booksellers was threatened after a survey of 291 publishers in France revealed that although only 30% of titles originated from the top six publishers, these accounted for nearly 70% of total turnover. In response the 10-year-old Cahart agreements between French publishers and booksellers were revamped to give the latter more control over the number of books received and to include mass-market paperbacks in the formula for determining discounts.

In May public sentiment was squashed when the Swedish Riksdag (parliament) refused to cut the value-added tax (VAT) on books from 25% to 6%. Elsewhere in Europe there was concern that e-books, which were not subject to sales tax in the U.S., would be treated as services rather than goods (printed versions were treated as goods) and attract VAT.

The abolition of price-fixing on new editions and reprints began to show results in Denmark, where publishing houses Gyldendal and Cicero launched popular novels at half the customary price and the Dansk Supermarked sold low-priced versions of remaindered books under its own label. In Switzerland the royalty payment mechanism (rpm) was verging on collapse after it had been declared illegal by the antitrust authorities. Europe, nevertheless, remained as divided as ever on the virtues of rpm; Italy reimposed it in February but permitted discounts of up to 10% for trade books, and Belgium considered whether to follow suit.

Copyright remained a vexing issue in a wide variety of contexts. In January police raids to stem rampant book piracy in India revealed the existence of modern, well-stocked bookshops in which not one single title was found to be original. In Australia the Copyright Amendment (Parallel Importation) Bill 2001 amended the 1968 law and allowed the "parallel importing of books, periodicals and sheet music in both electronic and print form." Meanwhile, agreement was reached on the wording of the European Union (EU) digital copyright directive, which sought to balance the rights of copyright owners with those of users. The directive harmonized the reproduction, distribution, and communication of digitally stored material as well as the legal protection of anticopying devices, including encryption. Copying by individuals for educational or private purposes remained legal. EU member states had only 18 months to convert the directive into national law. (PETER CURWEN)

Military Affairs

The **ATTACKS** on Sept. 11, 2001, opened a **NEW CHAPTER** in the history of warfare. A coalition of forces toppled the regime of the **TALIBAN** in Afghanistan. New **ANTITERRORISM** legislation was passed, and countries increased their defense **BUDGETS.**

The devastating aerial attacks by terrorists in the United States on Sept. 11, 2001, caused untold chaos and horror and initiated a flood of events that affected all aspects of life in all corners of the world. The United States declared a "war on terrorism" and promptly focused on the international al-Qaeda group and its Taliban protectors in Afghanistan. The antiterrorist coalition included contributions from Germany and Japan, countries that were largely able to overcome their post-World War II angst about deploying armed forces abroad.

SEPTEMBER 11 AND AFTERWARD

Within days of the attacks on the World Trade Center and the Pentagon, NATO, for the first time in its history, invoked Article 5 of its charter, declaring that the atrocities were an attack on the alliance. As a demonstration of support, Australia invoked the ANZUS Pact, putting elements of its armed forces on a higher state of readiness in case they were called upon to assist the U.S. On September 19 the Organization of American States agreed by acclamation to invoke the Rio Treaty, also a mutual-defense pact.

The week after the attacks was a period of shock and rage for most Americans, but there was also a feeling of helplessness because of great uncertainty about who exactly had attacked, where precisely in the world they could be found, and how they could be punished. On September 19 the U.S. dispatched more than 100 combat and support aircraft to various bases in the Middle East and the Indian Ocean. A large naval task force was sent to join what was first called Operation Infinite Justice but later, after complaints were received from Muslims, was renamed Operation Enduring Freedom. Japan sent three warships to support the effort, although they were restricted to a noncombat role according to the terms of Japan's pacifist constitution.

Allied air strikes in Afghanistan began on October 7. Later U.S. special forces, including Delta Force and Rangers, launched ground raids inside the country. The U.S. enlisted as an ally the anti-Taliban Northern Alliance, the principal remaining opposition to the Taliban takeover of Afghanistan, relying on them to provide the bulk of ground troops for the campaign. The northern city of Mazar-e Sharif fell a month later, and on November 13 the Northern Alliance entered Kabul as Taliban forces fled the capital. On December 9, with the fall of the Taliban's principal city of Kandahar imminent, American B-52s began carpet bombing a network of caves in the Tora Bora mountains of eastern Afghanistan, the last stronghold of forces loyal to Osama bin Laden and the Taliban. On December 15 anti-Taliban Afghan troops, backed by British and American commandos, surrounded a cave where they thought Bin Laden and a dwindling force of al-Qaeda fighters were hiding, but he was not found. His whereabouts were still unknown at year's end.

Smoke pours from a Taliban-controlled village in Afghanistan after a bombing raid by U.S. aircraft on November 9.

AP/Wide World Photos

OTHER CONFLICTS AND CONFRONTATIONS

The U.S. and China. A U.S. Navy surveillance aircraft made an emergency landing in China after colliding with a Chinese fighter jet on April 1 and thereby initiated a diplomatic confrontation. The aircraft and its crew of 24 were detained on Hainan Island until April 11. The aircraft was not returned until July, after the United States, in a carefully worded diplomatic note, said it was "very sorry" that the pilot of the Chinese jet had died. At the height of the dispute, U.S. Pres. George W. Bush announced that the U.S. would sell Taiwan up to eight diesel submarines, four *Kidd*-class destroyers, and 12 antisubmarine aircraft to bolster its defenses against China. The $4 billion weapons package was the most expensive sale to Taiwan since 1992.

The Balkans. In March tension increased along the border between Macedonia and the Serbian province of Kosovo following a series of armed clashes between Macedonian security forces and ethnic Albanian gunmen. The situation prompted the deployment of international peacekeeping soldiers from the NATO-led Kosovo Force (KFOR). The fighting spread round the country, however, including in and around Macedonia's capital, Skopje. After a peace agreement was brokered in August, NATO was given a one-month mandate in Macedonia to collect and destroy more than 3,000 weapons that the ethnic Albanian guerrillas of the National Liberation Army had agreed to surrender. Sporadic violence continued for the remainder of the year.

Russia. The Russian army's war against Chechen secessionists remained at a stalemate in 2001. Tens of thousands of Russian troops stationed in the mountainous republic were unable to eliminate the rebels, whose sporadic attacks against Russian forces and pro-Russian Chechens resulted in a steady flow of fatalities. Moscow claimed that the Chechen rebels had links to Afghanistan's Taliban regime and Bin Laden, which made it all the more palatable for Russian Pres. Vladimir Putin to pledge support for U.S. President Bush's call for a war on global terrorism. In December Russia stepped up military operations in response to Chechen raids on its forces.

Middle East. The situation in Israel and the Palestinian Autonomous Areas devolved into a war in all but name. Palestinian militants used small arms, mortars, and suicide bombers, mostly against civilian targets. The Israeli military used weapons ranging from F-16 fighter jets and missile-equipped attack helicopters to tank-fired flechette rounds, which contained thousands of 5-cm (2-in)-long steel darts. Also, both sides used assassination as a weapon; for example, Palestinian gunmen shot Israel's tourism minister, Rechavam Ze'evi, dead in October in retaliation for the death of Palestinian nationalist Abu Ali Mustafa (*see* OBITUARIES) in a rocket attack in August, and an Israeli helicopter gunship destroyed a car carrying Mahmoud Abu Hanoud, a Hamas leader, and two others on November 24.

During the year U.S. and British war planes attacked numerous sites in southern Iraq to prevent Iraqi Pres. Saddam Hussein from reconstituting his air defenses. According to the U.K. Royal Air Force, there were nearly 400 incidents of Iraqi surface-to-air-missile and antiaircraft fire against U.S. and British aircraft operating over the southern no-fly zone during the first eight months of 2001. German and U.S. intelligence agencies reported that since the 1990–91 Persian Gulf War, Iraq had been able to reconstruct a significant number of its production facilities for weapons of mass destruction. The U.S. also believed that Iraq was continuing work on a ballistic missile with a range of 3,000 km (1 km=about 0.62 mi) that could be operational as early as 2005.

South Asia. The long-festering dispute over Kashmir continued to poison relations between India and Pakistan, and the two nuclear-armed countries were virtually at war at the end of 2001. India blamed Kashmiri separatists for an assault on the Indian Parliament in December in which five attackers killed eight people with guns and grenades before being killed themselves. India accused Pakistan's secret service of having assisted the attackers. In retribution India considered punitive military strikes on what they said were militant training camps in Pakistan. Pakistan denounced India's test launch of an Agni-2 ballistic missile in January. The Agni-2 was capable of carrying a nuclear warhead, and its 2,000-km range meant it could reach targets anywhere in Pakistan or deep inside China.

King Gyanendra of Nepal declared a state of emergency after the worst violence in the nearly six years the Himalayan nation had been contending with a Maoist insurgency. The Maoists had stepped up their campaign in the months following the June 1 massacre of King Birendra (*see* OBITUARIES) and other members of the Nepalese royal family.

Since 1983 the Liberation Tigers of Tamil Eelam (LTTE) had fought for an independent homeland for Sri Lanka's Tamil population. In April the Sri Lankan military launched a major assault on guerrilla positions south of the Jaffna Peninsula after the collapse of a four-month-old cease-fire. More than 300 government soldiers were killed or reported missing in action, however, and the assault was terminated after only three days. In July the LTTE attacked the country's only international airport and a nearby military base, leaving at least 18 dead and destroying several aircraft. Following the election of a new prime minister in Sri Lanka on December 5, talks with the LTTE resumed, yielding a truce agreement that entered into effect on December 24.

Southeast Asia. A new military operation began in Aceh province on the Indonesian island of Sumatra and resulted in an intensification of the conflict. There were reports of many civilians' being killed by security forces and the Gerakan Aceh Merdeka. Despite a cease-fire agreement by Indonesia and the separatist organization signed on May 12, the violence by both sides continued throughout the year. (*See* WORLD AFFAIRS: *Indonesia:* Special Report.)

Philippine Pres. Gloria Macapagal Arroyo (*see* BIOGRAPHIES) declared all-out war on Muslim extremists in April. Fighting in the southern island of Jolo pitted thousands of army troops against guerrillas loyal to a rebellious Muslim governor and head of the Moro National Liberation Front, and more than 100 people were left dead.

Sub-Saharan Africa. In 2001 the government of Burundi agreed to direct cease-fire talks with the main ethnic Hutu rebel group, Forces for the Defense of Democracy, in an attempt to end seven years of civil war. The talks, brokered by South African statesman Nelson Mandela, led to the installation of a transitional power-sharing government backed by a South African peacekeeping force under a UN mandate. The Burundian army gained control of the whole of the capital, Bujumbura, after two weeks of heavy fighting in April.

In the neighbouring Democratic Republic of the Congo (DRC), a cease-fire monitored by the UN Mission in the Democratic Republic of the Congo (MONUC) largely held during the year, although there was intermittent violence. The South African National Defence Force contributed several dozen specialist support personnel to MONUC. This was the South African force's first substantial deployment in a UN operation since the Korean War. By September approximately 15,000 guerrillas had turned in their weapons as part of a cash-for-arms scheme. The conflict was called "Africa's First World War," because Zimbabwe, Angola, and Namibia had sent troops to fight on the side of the DRC government while soldiers from Rwanda and Uganda supported the rebels. In the autumn Uganda and Rwanda began pulling their troops out of the country, and troops from Zimbabwe followed suit. None of the belligerents fully respected their commitments under the 1999 Lusaka cease-fire agreement, however. By December renewed killings and the redeployment of Ugandan troops in parts of the DRC were heightening fears of escalating violence.

Underage soldiers were a growing concern in many countries of the world; the Congolese government released a first group of child soldiers into the care of the United Nations in December. The 235 youths, aged 15 to 19, had spent up to five years in the Congolese army.

The United Nations Mission in Sierra Leone peacekeeping force deployed 17,500 troops across the country. At least 26,000 insurgents were said to have given up their weapons following a peace accord signed in May between the government, the rebels, and the UN to end the civil war, which began in 1991.

Peace talks held in Nairobi, Kenya, in June failed to make any progress toward resolving the 18-year civil war in The Sudan, but a short-lived cease-fire allowed some food aid to be delivered in the country for the first time in a decade.

In order to allow for the deployment of the UN Mission to Ethiopia and Eritrea (UNMEE) peacekeeping force established in June 2000, both sides agreed to the creation of a 25-km-wide security zone in February 2001. Delays prevented this from occurring until mid-April, however. The UNMEE included the first-ever deployment of the UN's Standing High-Readiness Brigade—a multinational unit that had been under development since 1995. Despite accusations about preparations for war, both countries had respected the 2000 Algiers agreement, but tension between the two countries remained high through the end of the year.

MILITARY TECHNOLOGY

Under the most lucrative defense contract ever awarded, the Pentagon selected the Lockheed Martin Corp. to build the Joint Strike Fighter (JSF). The contract had a potential total value of over $200 billion during the life of the program. The U.S. planned to buy nearly 3,000 JSFs for its air force, navy, and Marine Corps, while the U.K. was expected to procure up to 150.

At the beginning of the new millennium, the era of ray guns was fast approaching. A laser device designed to destroy ballistic missiles as they were boosted on their flight produced its first test beam. The Airborne Laser (ABL) was designed to patrol near the borders of hostile countries. Tests of a weapon designed to heat a person's skin with a microwave beam showed that it can disperse crowds. The U.S. Air Force Research Laboratory finished testing the system on human volunteers. It wanted to use this Active Denial Technology, which was claimed to be nonlethal, for peacekeeping or riot control.

After nearly 24 hours of flight, a Global Hawk unmanned aerial vehicle (UAV) landed successfully in South Australia after having taken off from its base in California, over 13,000 km away. This was the first nonstop flight across the Pacific Ocean by a UAV. The jet-powered Global Hawk was designed for surveillance of enemy territory. Its sensor package included a synthetic aperture radar, which can provide detailed photographs even through cloud cover. Although still in development, the Global Hawk was used during operations over Afghanistan. Also reportedly used in that conflict was a prototype armed version of the U.S.'s propeller-driven RQ-1 Predator UAV. It was said to have fired Hellfire antitank missiles at enemy positions. If true, this was the first time a UAV had fired a weapon against a target in war.

The British test ship RV *Triton,* the world's largest powered trimaran, completed its first transatlantic crossing in September. The 90-m (295-ft)-long *Triton* was launched in 2000 to prove the triple-hull concept on a full-size ship. It was being evaluated by the Royal Navy and was attracting the attention of other navies. Trimarans offer greater speed and stability over conventional hull designs, especially in rough seas.

Traditional military technologies also made news in 2001. The Belgian small arms manufacturer FN Herstal launched its new 5.56-mm-calibre F2000 rifle. This modular assault rifle included a 40-mm low-velocity grenade launcher and a computerized fire-control system with a laser rangefinder.

The list of countries producing their own advanced weapons continued to grow. Iran announced that it had successfully flight-tested an indigenously produced solid-fuel short-range ballistic missile named Fateh 110. Solid propellants are harder to manufacture than liquid fuels but offer advantages in terms of superior storage, safety in handling, and faster launch times. According to Israeli and U.S. officials, Iran began serial production of its Shahab-3 liquid-fueled ballistic missile, which had a range of 1,300 km. Taiwan deployed the Tien Chi, a new ballistic missile capable of reaching China. It was believed that as many as 50 could already be in service.

The RV Triton *sails on its first transatlantic voyage, which it completed in September.*

ARMS CONTROL AND DISARMAMENT

In December 2001 President Bush announced that the United States would withdraw from the 1972 Anti-Ballistic Missile Treaty with Russia. Bush considered the treaty a roadblock to building the National Missile Defense (NMD) system and an anachronism from the Cold War that allowed so-called rogue states to develop long-range ballistic missiles. Despite months of negotiations, Russia and the U.S. failed to agree on how to amend the treaty or move beyond it. At a meeting in Texas in November, Bush and Russian President Putin agreed to reduce their nuclear arsenals by up to two-thirds over the next decade. Bush met NATO leaders in June to try to win endorsement for the NMD. Spain, Hungary, Italy, Poland, the Czech Republic, and the U.K. offered support, but France, Germany, and others were opposed, arguing that American defense needs would be better served by strengthening existing arms-control agreements.

Meeting in New York City in July, the UN Conference on the Illicit Trade in Small Arms and Light Weapons failed to agree on a treaty to curb the spread of such weapons following U.S. opposition. The U.S. argued that a distinction had to be made between firearms used for traditional and cultural reasons and those that were traded illegally and led to or fueled wars. The U.S. also dropped its support for a protocol intended to include verification powers in the 1972 Biological and Toxin Weapons Convention. The document, already accepted by more than 50 other countries, would require member states to permit international inspection of sites that could be used for the development of biological weapons.

Under a revised agreement with the U.S., South Korea was given the go-ahead to develop ballistic missiles capable of hitting targets in most of North Korea. Seoul would also be permitted to develop civilian rockets for research and commercial purposes. A 1979 agreement with the U.S. limited the range of South Korea's missiles to 180 km. Also, South Korea joined the Missile Technology Control Regime, which bars its members from providing any other country with technology to build missiles with a range over 300 km.

A gratifying example of how arms-control treaties can work occurred when Turkey agreed to join the 1997 Ottawa Convention banning antipersonnel land mines, and in response the Greek Parliament dropped its opposition to ratifying the convention. Greece and Turkey also agreed to clear mines along their border. On January 29 Turkey and Georgia had agreed to remove land mines along their common border.

Although it received little attention from news media, the last inspection under the 1987 Intermediate-Range Nuclear Forces Treaty (INF) took place in Russia. Under the treaty, signed by the Soviet Union and the United States during the height of the Cold War, an entire class of nuclear missiles and related equipment was eliminated. During 13 years of inspections (540 by the United States and 311 by the Soviet Union and its successor states), the INF established a new standard for openness in arms control by including short-notice inspections and around-the-clock monitoring of missile-assembly plants.

Defense ministers from 10 of 14 Southern African Development Community countries in late July approved a draft of a mutual-defense pact that aimed to prevent conflict in the region and establish a collective approach to security.

MILITARY AND SOCIETY

A growing number of countries were looking abroad to fill in the ranks of their armed forces. The British army was recruiting foreign Commonwealth citizens in an attempt to reduce a shortage. South Africans, Australians, Canadians, and West Indians helped bring the strength of the army back up to 108,000 from 100,000. Spain actively recruited in Latin America to help make up for a shortfall in recruits resulting from the phasing out of conscription, and more than 300 Argentines and Uruguayans traveled there to enlist in the Spanish armed forces. France announced that it would end conscription in 2001, 18 months ahead of schedule.

The German government bowed to an order by the European Court of Justice and henceforth would allow women to serve in combat units of its armed forces. The court ruled on January 11 that the German ban on women in combat violated the principles enshrined in the 1976 guidelines on sexual equality adopted by the European Union (EU). The Canadian armed forces lifted restrictions barring women from serving aboard submarines. An Australian Defence Force study recommended that women be allowed to serve in ground combat units. Women already served aboard Australian warships and were allowed to pilot combat aircraft.

ARMED FORCES, POLITICS, AND THE ENVIRONMENT

The movement against live-fire military training gained momentum during the year. President Bush announced that the U.S. Navy would cease using the island of Vieques, off the coast of Puerto Rico, for bombing exercises by 2003. A group of islanders had filed a $100 million lawsuit claiming that the bombing caused significant damage to the environment and public health. The U.S. Navy maintained that it would not be able to find a suitable alternative site for amphibious warfare training. Protesters in Seoul called on the U.S. to close a bombing range it operated along the coast of South Korea. The protesters argued that the range was noisy and dangerous to local citizens. Opposition to foreign military training also surfaced in Kenya, where lawyers attempted to bring legal action against the British army over its use of two training areas. The complainants said that people had been injured and livestock killed as a result of unexploded munitions left by the British forces.

The year was also one of contrasts. While Turkey announced the establishment of a National Space Agency to help develop policy for the military and civilian uses of space, New Zealand said it would scrap its air-combat capability by retiring its aging A-4K Skyhawk fighters and give priority to the army's ability to participate in peacekeeping operations. As a sign of growing European integration and independence from NATO, the EU Military Staff, formed to provide military analysis and advice, was declared operational. Nonaligned Austria hosted armed troops from several NATO countries on its soil for the first time for a Partnership for Peace exercise.

Previous wars also continued to haunt the planet. Russian soldiers discovered several thousand German artillery shells dating from World War II buried at a military base in Kaliningrad. The stockpile was found next to chemical warfare warehouses belonging to the Russian Baltic Fleet.

After years of negotiations the U.S. and Vietnam agreed to research jointly the effects of the chemical defoliant Agent Orange. Vietnam alleged that the health of up to one million people had been severely damaged by Agent Orange, which was used by U.S. forces in Vietnam between 1962 and 1971. Some U.S. veterans groups also believed that their members suffered from exposure to dioxin, a known carcinogen found in Agent Orange. (PETER SARACINO)

Performing Arts

CONTROVERSIES dominated the performing arts in 2001. A **WAGNER** performance caused a furor in Israel. A **STORM OF CRITICISM** swirled around a landmark TV documentary on **JAZZ.** Violent **RAP LYRICS** provoked outrage. Nevertheless, after **SEPTEMBER 11,** artists of all stripes demonstrated their capacity to respond to **TRAGEDY.**

MUSIC

Classical Music. More than a century after his death in 1883, German composer Richard Wagner continued to generate controversy. In Bayreuth, Ger., at the opera festival Wagner established to preserve and promote his music, the composer's descendants were engaged in a bitter struggle for power. In Israel a performance of a piece by Wagner revealed deep divisions among the nation's music lovers.

Wagner was notoriously anti-Semitic, the author of a diatribe against "Jewishness" in music that was largely an attack on his operatic rival, Giacomo Meyerbeer. This attitude, as well as his German chauvinism and his ideas on "racial purity," endeared him to Adolf Hitler and the Nazi regime. In Israel, on the other hand, an unofficial ban on live performances of Wagner's music had been loosely in effect for more than half a century, though recordings were readily available. Feelings on the subject ran deep, as Zubin Mehta, conductor of the Israel Philharmonic, had been shown at a concert in 1981 when, as he was about to lead the orchestra in a Wagner selection, a concentration camp survivor rushed on stage and stopped the proceedings, displaying Nazi-inflicted wounds he had suffered. No Wagner was played on that occasion.

Israel's traditional ban on Wagner performance was shattered in July by pianist and conductor Daniel Barenboim, a citizen of Israel who led orchestras in Berlin and Chicago. During a concert given on tour in Jerusalem by the Berlin Staatskapelle (orchestra), Barenboim conducted the Prelude to Wagner's *Tristan und Isolde* as an encore, creating a furor. Barenboim, a vigorous advocate of Wagner's music, said he was hopeful that "this opens the door a little bit." Mehta, a close friend of Barenboim, expressed "100 percent" support.

Meanwhile, the Bayreuth Festival, which had been inaugurated in 1876, observed its 125th anniversary very quietly. Wolfgang Wagner, a grandson of the composer, ran the festival for half a century, originally in partnership with his brother Wieland, who died in 1966. Though he was 81 years old and obviously near the end of his tenure, Wolfgang Wagner steadfastly refused to name any successor except for his second wife, Gudrun, and their daughter, Katharina. Pressure was building in the family, the German government, and the news media to open up the possibility of new leadership for the Bayreuth Festival.

During a concert in Jerusalem, conductor Daniel Barenboim looks on while a man in the audience tries to calm protesters who objected to Barenboim's decision to perform a work by Richard Wagner.

Varda Polak-Sahm

A particularly vigorous campaign was launched by Nike Wagner, daughter of Wieland and author of a book that criticized many family traditions, *The Wagners: The Dramas of a Musical Dynasty.* Among the changes Nike Wagner proposed for the festival was an enlarged repertoire, which was traditionally limited to the 10 operas of Richard Wagner's maturity. Under the direction of Nike Wagner, the festival might expand to include not only such early operas as *Rienzi* but even the work of other composers, such as Meyerbeer. In any case, significant changes in the Bayreuth Festival were postponed by Wolfgang Wagner, who announced his plans for the next five years at a press conference. Those plans included contracting Danish film director Lars von Trier to direct a new production of the *Ring* cycle, to be conducted by Christian Thielemann, beginning in 2006.

Meanwhile, other major festivals were going through transitions; at Salzburg, Austria, Gerard Mortier concluded a stormy decade as festival director with a bitter prediction that after his departure the festival would revert to "Strauss waltzes and yodeling contests." In London, for the first time in history, an American—Leonard Slatkin—conducted the popular *Last Night at the Proms.* In the wake of the terrorist attacks on the World Trade Center and the Pentagon, Slatkin omitted the traditional sing-along of "Land of Hope and Glory" and "Rule, Britannia" that customarily concluded *Proms* programs and substituted Samuel Barber's *Adagio for Strings* and a selection of spirituals. In Australia another American, Peter Sellars, was forced to resign as artistic director of the Adelaide Festival of the Arts. He was replaced by former Melbourne Festival director Sue Nattrass. The board had asked Sellars to broaden his program for the upcoming year, but he refused. "I have made my share of mistakes since coming to Adelaide two and a half years ago, but I deeply believe in the principles for which this festival stands," he said in a statement issued in Paris. Marin Alsop, yet another American, was the first woman to become principal conductor of a British symphony when she was named to that post at the Bournemouth Symphony Orchestra in June.

The September 11 terrorist attacks in the U.S. climaxed a series of financial crises in the performing arts. Travel plans were disrupted, concerts were canceled, ticket sales plummeted, and various bankruptcies and reorganizations were announced. The San Jose (Calif.) Symphony and the Toronto Symphony Orchestra were the latest additions to the list of financially troubled North American orchestras. In the past 20 years a dozen orchestras—including those in Denver, Colo., Birmingham, Ala., and the California cities of Oakland, Sacramento, and San Diego—had confronted serious money problems. The Toronto Symphony players, faced with the need to cut expenses, agreed to a 15% salary reduction.

Alberto Vilar, a Cuban emigré who had become enormously wealthy investing in technology stocks, gave $25 million to the Berlin Philharmonic's musician-training program. The German orchestra was only one of many musical organizations that benefited from Vilar's largesse at a rate of more than $1 million; others included the Metropolitan Opera in New York City, the Vienna State Opera, the Royal Opera House at Covent Garden in London, the Mozart Festival in Salzburg, the Kirov Opera in St. Petersburg, and the Los Angeles and Washington, D.C., opera companies. Besides the Vilar contribution, the Berlin Philharmonic was reluctantly given $11.7 million, half of its annual operating budget, by the Berlin city government. The contribution, which would help to increase the players' salaries, was demanded by Sir Simon Rattle before he signed a 10-year contract as the orchestra's music director to begin in 2002.

In New York City the Lincoln Center for the Performing Arts launched a billion-dollar renovation program that promptly disintegrated into bickering between the constituent organizations. The Metropolitan Opera, geographically but not administratively part of the complex, was conducting its own redevelopment program. James Levine, artistic administrator of the Met, planned to keep that position while he succeeded Seiji Ozawa as music director of the Boston Symphony Orchestra. Ozawa was to become director of the Vienna State Opera. Tony Hall, a BBC executive, was named to replace Michael Kaiser as director of the Royal Opera House in London; Kaiser was slated to head the John F. Kennedy Center for the Performing Arts in Washington, D.C. Other major personnel changes included Raymond Leppard's retirement as music director of the Indianapolis (Ind.) Symphony Orchestra, Jesús López-Cobos's departure as music director of the Cincinnati (Ohio) Symphony Orchestra, Christopher Hogwood's retirement as music director of the Handel and Haydn Society of Boston, and Lotfi Mansouri's leaving the general directorship of the San Francisco Opera. In January the New York Philharmonic announced that Lorin Maazel would replace Kurt Masur (who was ill and awaiting an organ transplant at year's end) as music director beginning with the 2002–03 season, and in May the Minnesota Orchestra announced that the Finnish conductor Osmo Vanska would replace Eiji Oue as its music director in 2003. In September American conductor James Conlon announced that he would not renew his contract with the Paris Opera; the contract was to end in 2004.

Popular Korean soprano Sumi Jo (*see* BIOGRAPHIES) broadened her audience, singing half Broadway songs and half works for the operatic repertory in her Carnegie Hall concert in February.

World premieres included three cello concertos. Elliott Carter's second concerto (the first had been written some 30 years earlier), written for and played by Yo-Yo Ma, was premiered by Barenboim and the Chicago Symphony Orchestra in September as part of the conductor's Wagner and Modernism series. The second, *Concerto for Cello and Orchestra,* was written by Philip Glass for Julian Lloyd Webber and had its premiere in Beijing in October. The third was *Concerto for Cello and Orchestra: In Memoriam F.D.R.* by Peter Schickele, commissioned by New Heritage Music and performed in February by Paul Tobias and the Chamber Symphony of the Manhattan School of Music. Hans Werner Henze's *L'Heure bleue,* a serenade for 16 players, received its first performance in Frankfurt, Ger., in September. Sir Peter Maxwell Davies's *Antarctic Symphony (Symphony No. 8)* was premiered by the Philharmonia Orchestra at the 50th anniversary celebration of the Royal Festival Hall in London on May 6. The Philharmonia Orchestra had also commissioned and performed Ralph Vaughn Williams's *Sinfonia Antarctica* for the sound track to the 1948 film *Scott of the Antarctic.* (*See* WORLD AFFAIRS: *Antarctica.*) On a less-serious note, British comedian and composer Richard Thomas and his Kombat Opera Company altered the musical landscape with *Jerry Springer: The Opera,* a musical setting of material from a popular television show often punctuated with outbreaks of violence. The most unusual musical event of the year, and perhaps of the century, however, took place in Halberstadt, Ger.—the preparations for a performance of John Cage's *Organ 2/ASLSP.* It was to be played, in accordance with the instruction "as slow as possible," at the ultraslow rate of two notes per year, and estimates were that the piece, which would have its first notes played in January 2003, would be finished in 639 years.

John Corigliano (*see* BIOGRAPHIES) was honoured with the 2001 Pulitzer Prize in Music for his *Symphony No. 2 for String Orchestra;* the work had first been performed by the Boston Symphony Orchestra in November 2000. The gold medalists in the 11th Van Cliburn International Piano Competition (May 25–June 10, 2001) were Stanislav Ioudenitch from Uzbekistan and Olga Kern of Russia. In New York City the Avery Fisher Career Grants were awarded in March to violinist Timothy Fain, cellists Daniel Lee and Hai-Ye Ni, and flutist Tara Helen O'Connor.

Violinist Isaac Stern, who was generally credited with saving Carnegie Hall from demolition, died in September of heart failure. Giuseppe Sinopoli died on the podium in April while conducting *Aïda* at the Berlin Opera House. Japanese conductor Takashi Asahina died on December 29. Among other musicians who died in 2001 were composers Iannis Xenakis and Douglas Gordon Lilburn, pianist Yaltah Menuhin, harmonica virtuoso Larry Adler, and Canadian operatic baritone Victor Braun. (*See* OBITUARIES.)

(JOSEPH MCLELLAN)

Jazz. The precarious condition of jazz in 2001 was best dramatized by the extended uproar surrounding Ken Burns's documentary *Jazz,* which aired on the PBS television network in January. Ten episodes long—each episode lasted nearly two hours—and costing a reported $13 million to produce, *Jazz* attempted to portray the art form's development from its beginnings early in the 20th century. Burns used a wealth of historic film clips and photos, many of them rare, and the sources of most of the series music were recordings, many of them classic. Over half of *Jazz* was devoted to the quarter century between World Wars I and II, when jazz was one of the U.S.'s most popular styles of music among black and white audiences. An important nonmusical theme was the changing relations between black and white Americans. The lives of Louis Armstrong and Duke Ellington, two of the greatest jazz musicians, provided recurring story lines throughout the series; commentators, especially musician Wynton Marsalis and critics Stanley Crouch and Gary Giddins, offered frequent perspectives.

Praise for Burns's *Jazz* centred on the quality of the music and illustrations, including the historic dance styles exhibited; on the fact that many singers, musicians, and bands were profiled in each episode; and especially on the very fact that the documentary was broadcast at all—jazz had all but disappeared from American television networks, apart from cable's Black Entertainment Television. As with any history of jazz, criticism centred on the important figures and events that were omitted. Many of the omissions followed a pattern; the influence of Europe and European music on jazz was downgraded, as were white performers, especially after World War II. In addition, cool and West Coast jazz played very minor roles in Burns's history. A storm of criticism swirled around the only episode devoted to jazz of the past 40 years. In that episode later idiomatic developments, including free jazz and fusion music, played only a secondary role. Instead, Burns profiled older musicians and the revival of older styles by Marsalis and other younger musicians. After viewing Burns's grand documentary, viewers were left with a sense that jazz was something historic—such as French Impressionist painting or epic poetry—an art form that at best now only lingered on long after its natural life span.

Was it true? Was jazz a vanishing art? At one point early in 2001, according to *Billboard* magazine, of the 25 best-selling jazz albums, only 7 were current releases. In the course of the year, *Down Beat*'s usually effusive reviewers awarded five stars to only two jazz albums, *Black Dahlia* by arranger Bob Belden and *Not for Nothin'* by the Dave Holland Quintet. Although jazz still accounted for only about 3% of all U.S. compact-disc (CD) sales, the flood of new recordings continued, the vast majority of them from independent labels. The public appetite for live jazz, at least, remained high. Younger generations of listeners predominated in nightclub audiences in cities with busy jazz scenes. Jazz festivals thrived in the Americas, Europe, Asia, and Australia—*JazzTimes* listed 422 festivals that featured jazz and blues in 2001.

Roger Viollet/Liaison

Louis Armstrong—one of the central figures depicted in Ken Burns's 2001 TV documentary Jazz*—is surrounded by (from left to right) Mezz Mezzrow, Claude Luter, and Duke Ellington in a 1960 photo.*

In a generally uneventful year, 23-year-old singer Jane Monheit, an Ella Fitzgerald devotee, sparked attention with her CD *Come Dream with Me.* Chicago's cult favourite Patricia Barber (*see* BIOGRAPHIES) sang standards on her hit sixth album, *Nightclub* (2000). While revivalism and eclecticism prevailed among younger musicians, urgent personal statements could be heard in albums by tenor saxophonist Mark Turner (*Dharma Days*) and trumpeter Dave Douglas, whose *Witness* was devoted to songs of freedom and nonviolent protest. Turner, torn between cool and hard bop styles, also played on veteran altoist Lee Konitz's *Parallels.* Other outstanding albums were the Italian Instabile Orchestra's *Litania Sibilante*, the freely improvising Boston trio of Maneri-Morris-Maneri in *Out Right Now*, and the *Yet Can Spring* duets by pianist-composer Myra Melford and clarinetist-saxophonist Marty Ehrlich. A growing phenomenon was the release of albums of long-ago concerts by important artists, including woodwind improviser Anthony Braxton's *Quintet (Basel) 1977*, tenorist Fred Anderson's *Dark Day: Live in Verona 1979*, and Chris McGregor's Brotherhood of Breath big band, comprising English and South African exile musicians, in *Travelling Somewhere* from 1973. Albums began appearing from Sunday jam sessions produced by the Left Bank Jazz Society (Baltimore, Md.) during 1965–80; the first four were by Stan Getz, Sonny Stitt, Cedar Walton, and Al Cohn and Zoot Sims.

While outstanding new albums were few, there were some extraordinary reissues. A singular project was the discovery of a major composer's rarest recordings, Charles ("Baron") Mingus's *West Coast 1945–49* (2000). *The Complete in a Silent Way Sessions*, from Miles Davis's first fusion music project, was the latest of Columbia's many Davis collections. From 1919 came *Lieut. Jim Europe's 369th U.S. Infantry "Hell Fighters" Band: The Complete Recordings* (1996), a historic African American big ragtime band at the very border of early jazz. Art Pepper's *The Hollywood All-Star Sessions*, released as Japanese albums in the early 1980s, at last appeared in the U.S. as a boxed set. Two of the finest swing-era singers had their finest recordings collected. *Lady Day: The Complete Billie Holiday on Columbia (1933–1944)* was a 10-CD boxed set gathering 230 of her joy-infused early recordings. *The Complete Columbia Recordings of Mildred Bailey* was offered by Mosaic, the busy mail-order outfit that also released boxed sets of 1950s Max Roach and 1960s Gerald Wilson big band in 2001.

The year's death toll included pianist-composer John Lewis, who during the year had released the concert album *Evolution II*, trombonist J.J. Johnson, swing bandleader Les Brown, pianist Tommy Flanagan, singers Al Hibbler and Susannah McCorkle, drummer Billy Higgins, saxophonists Joe Henderson and Buddy Tate and impresario Norman Granz. (*See* OBITUARIES.) Other notable deaths included those of trumpeter Conte Candoli, saxophonists Harold Land, Billy Mitchell, Ken McIntyre, and Flip Phillips, popular Canadian flutist Moe Koffman, Latin jazz arranger Chico O'Farrill, arranger Manny Albam, record producer Milt Gabler, and author Helen Oakley Dance. (JOHN LITWEILER)

Popular. The fortunes of American popular music in 2001 were in a decline even before the terrorist attacks of September 11. In the first half of the year, overall music sales were reportedly down 5.4%, and concert ticket sales dropped 15.5%, compared with the same period in 2000.

Pop artists responded to the tragedy with performances dedicated to remembering victims and helping survivors. *America: A Tribute to Heroes* aired without commercial interruption on radio and television in more than 210 countries. The tribute was filmed on soundstages in Los Angeles, New York, and London and featured performances by Bruce Springsteen, Neil Young, Céline Dion, and Faith Hill (*see* BIOGRAPHIES), among others; it generated $150 million in pledges and a two-CD set. Paul McCartney helped organize the Concert for New York City at Madison Square Garden. The Who, Eric Clapton, Mick Jagger, Keith Richards, James Taylor, Macy Gray, and many other artists performed before an audience that included 5,000 rescue workers. George Strait, Hank Williams Jr., Tim McGraw, and Alan Jackson were part of the Country Freedom Concert in Nashville, Tenn.

The Grammy nomination of rapper Eminem's *The Marshall Mathers LP* for Album of the Year sparked a huge controversy owing to its violent content. Though the award went to rock veterans Steely Dan for *Two Against Nature,* Eminem performed a duet with Elton John on the awards show and won three Grammys in rap categories.

The most popular band in the U.S., *NSYNC, sold 1,880,000 copies of its fourth album, *Celebrity,* during its first week of release. Many believed that the quintet had adopted a more mature attitude with its latest release. Since the automated tracking of sales was established in 1991, only the band's previous album, *No Strings Attached,* had sold more during its first week—2.4 million copies in March 2000. The Backstreet Boys postponed a national tour when a member of the group sought help for alcohol abuse and depression. On her third album, *Britney,* 19-year-old Britney Spears sent mixed messages as she lingered between teen innocence and womanhood.

Alicia Keys, a 20-year-old native of New York City, sold three million copies of her debut album, *Songs in A Minor,* spurred by the hit single "Fallin'." Keys's music mixed hip-hop, soul, and classical styles. The precocious singer and actress Aaliyah, 22, released her third album, *Aaliyah,* just weeks before her death in an airplane crash in The Bahamas. (*See* OBITUARIES.) Destiny's Child—Beyonce Knowles, Kelly Rowland, and Michelle Williams—cemented their status as major pop stars with *Survivor,* which sold more than three million copies by year's end. Rock band Staind connected with disaffected youth on its dark album *Break the Cycle;* System of a Down explored political stances on *Toxicity;* and Christian rap-metal band P.O.D. found an audience with *Satellite.*

Michael Jackson returned to the top of the pop-album chart with *Invincible,* his first release in six years. Though his first single, "You Rock My World," performed poorly, peaking at number 10, the album sold 366,000 copies during its first week of release. Jackson staged two New York City concerts, titled "The Thirtieth Anniversary Celebration," at Madison Square Garden and combined them in a network TV special. Pop icon Bob Dylan turned 60 and issued *Love and Theft,* his 43rd album, to critical acclaim.

A sound-track album, *O Brother, Where Art Thou?,* with a large musical cast that included Emmylou Harris, Ralph Stanley, John Hartford (*see* OBITUARIES), Gillian Welch, and Chris Thomas King, dominated the country album chart and shipped three million copies. The Country Music Association and the International Bluegrass Music Association both named *O Brother, Where Art Thou?* Album of the Year.

After having announced his retirement at a 2000 press conference, Garth Brooks, country's biggest all-time seller, released *Scarecrow,* his first album of new material in four years. To boost sales of the new release, Brooks appeared for three consecutive weeks in hour-long network TV specials.

A new Country Music Hall of Fame and Museum opened in Nashville and inducted a large class of members, including Bill Anderson, the Delmore Brothers, the Everly Brothers, Don Gibson, Homer & Jethro, Waylon Jennings, the Jordanaires, Don Law, the Louvin Brothers, Ken Nelson, Webb Pierce, and Sam Phillips.

The Latin Grammys were moved and then postponed. The awards ceremony was moved in August from Miami, Fla., to Los Angeles when security problems arose, stemming from anti-Fidel Castro demonstrators protesting the appearance of Cuban artists, but planned to keep its scheduled date of September 11. The terrorist attacks on that day forced a postponement, however, and the awards were finally presented in late October. The big winners were Spanish pop star Alejandro Sanz, who picked up four awards, including Record of the Year and Song of the Year, and Colombian singer Juanes, a newcomer who won three awards, including best new artist. "Queen of Salsa" singer Celia Cruz captured the award for best traditional tropical album for *Siempre Viviré.*

The Rock and Roll Hall of Fame welcomed Aerosmith (*see* BIOGRAPHIES), Solomon Burke, the Flamingos, Michael Jackson, Queen, Paul Simon, Steely Dan, and Ritchie Valens.

The popular music of North Africa continued to attract a wider global audience, thanks partly to the work of the fiery and highly political Algerian exile Rachid Taha. He was influenced by British punk, French chanson, and even Jamaican reggae, and his album *Made in Medina,* which was recorded in both Paris and New Orleans, was a rousing blend of Arabic and Western styles that had much of the wild fervour of punk or early rock and roll. This sense of danger and the unexpected was repeated in Taha's exuberant live shows.

Thanks to the North African immigrant community, Paris had developed into a world music centre and home for both Taha and Khaled, who was the best-known exponent of Algerian *rai.* Another such exile, Cheb Mami (*see* BIOGRAPHIES), developed a considerable

James Taylor (second from left), Melissa Etheridge (centre), and Bon Jovi band member Richie Sambora (right) are joined by other singers for a final number during the Concert for New York City at Madison Square Garden on October 20.

AP/Wide World Photos

audience across Europe, North Africa, and elsewhere with his more easygoing commercial blend of *rai* and Western pop. His album *Dellali* and his collaboration with British star Sting, with whom he toured and recorded "Desert Rose," increased his audience. Senegalese singer Baaba Maal released a classic new album, *Missing You (Mi Yeewnii)*. After having mixed West African styles with experimental Western pop in his recent work, Maal returned to the acoustic music he had popularized earlier in his career with his *Djam Leelii* album, but with more subtle and sophisticated treatment. Recorded in a village in Senegal by the British producer John Leckie (best known for his work with Radiohead), the album made use of the *kora* (the West African lute) and acoustic guitar work from Maal's longtime friend and musical associate Mansour Seck, the blind griot, or hereditary singer.

The move back to delicate easygoing songs was also reflected in Senegal with the return of Orchestra Baobab, a band that had pioneered the fusion of African and Cuban styles two decades earlier and had enormous influence on the subsequent development of West African music. The group also rereleased its celebrated album *Pirate's Choice*—recorded in 1982 but not released until 1989—which still sounded as mellow and as fresh as ever. In the war-torn Democratic Republic of the Congo, there was a similar development with the emergence of Kekele, a fine semiacoustic band that included such veteran guitarists as Papa Noel and Syran Mbenza, famous for their work in the classic era of Congolese rumba back in the 1960s and '70s. Mbenza also toured with Sam Mangwana, a celebrated singer from that era. From Zimbabwe, another crisis-torn African state, there were fine performances from the soulful vocalist Oliver Mtukudzi, the star of the year's WOMAD festival in the U.K., and from the veteran guitar band the Bhundu Boys, who released *The Shed Sessions*, an anthology of early recordings.

In the Caribbean and Latin America, the fashion for Cuban music sparked by the success of the Buena Vista Social Club had eased a little, though there was one outstanding spin-off album; *Cachaito*, a solo set from the bass player Orlando ("Cachaito") López, was a brave and experimental mixture of Latin, jazz, and even Jamaican dub influences. Though Brazil—traditionally a powerhouse of Latin music—had been somewhat overshadowed by the fashion for Cuba in recent years, it made a comeback, thanks partly to a new work from the long-established singer Gilberto Gil, who provided the sound track for the much-praised Brazilian feature film *Me, You, Them*, which featured songs of Luiz Gonzaga, his boyhood hero. The more experimental side of the new Brazilian scene was shown by Andrea Marquee, who mixed Latin and contemporary Western pop styles in her rousing, adventurous album *Zumbi*.

The Beatles' newest album, *1* (2000), a compilation of its greatest hits, broke an unofficial record when it topped the charts in 34 countries early in 2001. The death in November of George Harrison, known to many as the quiet Beatle, saddened the music world after he succumbed to a long battle with cancer. (*See* OBITUARIES.)

The Irish band U2 posted yet another classic year; the group embarked on a world tour in support of its album *All That You Can't Leave Behind*, which marked a return to the grand soulful ballads of its early years. One of the most promising newcomers in the U.K. was Susheela Raman, whose album *Salt Rain* was a cool, soulful blend of jazz and North African and Indian styles. Raman was nominated for the U.K.'s Mercury Music Prize, but the award was won by the more emotional female singer P.J. Harvey with her compelling album *Stories from the City, Stories from the Sea*.

Iranian pop diva Googoosh, banned from her homeland following the 1979 Islamic revolution, embarked in March on what she called a "homecoming tour"; she performed in March in Dubayy, U.A.E., before a crowd of some 30,000 people, most of whom flew there from Iran. In 2000, after a 20-year absence from the stage, she had performed to appreciative audiences in Canada and the U.S.

Those fleeing the war in Afghanistan reported that the Taliban government's extremist policies included a ban on the country's once-celebrated popular songs. Anyone found listening to a cassette was fined in proportion to the length of the offending tape and was forced to confess in public. In a climate such as this, it was little surprise that the country's best-known performers, Nashenas and Naghma, had fled abroad.

Among the other major music figures who died during the year were Joey Ramone, John Phillips (of the Mamas and the Papas), Chet Atkins, and John Lee Hooker. (*See* OBITUARIES.)

(ROBIN DENSELOW; JAY ORR)

DANCE

North America. In June the innocently titled *Free to Dance*—a selective, three-hour documentary chronicling African American influences in modern dance—was telecast nationally in the U.S. on the Public Broadcasting System. Once the terror events of September came and went, the chronicle's simply stated focus on freedom and dancing began to resonate throughout dance in general and suggest more complicated dimensions.

The big ballet troupes lived through both status-quo activity and stressful times. Early in 2001 New York City Ballet (NYCB) unveiled a new work by Eliot Feld. Called *Organon*, the 63-dancer work proved overly grandiose and, many thought, a large-scale waste of the company's time and personnel. Ballet master in chief Peter Martins's new ballet, *Burleske*, was as inconsequential as Feld's was awful.

Happily, Christopher Wheeldon, who recently had retired as an NYCB dancer and turned full time to choreography, gave the repertory a plummy new work called *Polyphonia*, and by the summer, shortly before the premiere of another engaging new work of his called *Variations Sérieuses*, he had been named the troupe's first-ever "resident choreographer." American Ballet Theatre (ABT) began the year by unveiling at the John F. Kennedy Center for the Performing Arts in Washington, D.C., Paul Taylor's savvy Depression-era suite, *Black Tuesday*.

In its lengthier New York City season, the company offered another modern dance-based work, the somewhat dry *Gong* by Mark Morris. (*See* BIOGRAPHIES.) Though David Parsons's *The Pied Piper* arrived with great hoopla, because of its technologically advanced digitally worked decor and modernist trappings, it turned out to be a dud. More successfully, the company also unveiled its first staging of John Cranko's *Onegin*, which showcased a good number of ABT's stellar dancers. By the summer, however, trouble was unsettling the administration, and executive director Louis Spisto resigned under pressure, partly in the wake of the *Pied Piper* fiasco. The smaller fall season featured a revival of Antony Tudor's *Dim Lustre* and the premiere of Stanton Welch's *Clear*.

Similar shifts and uncertainty befell Boston Ballet (BB) when early in the year Maina Gielgud, though due to take over from departing artistic director Anna-Marie Holmes in July, quit her post even before she started. Later,

Jeffrey Babcock left his general director's post with BB for a position at Boston University. By September Mikko Nissinen, artistic director of Canada's Alberta Ballet, had been hired as BB artistic director and was due to commence full duties in July 2002. Prior to his appointment Nissinen actively participated in a Balanchine celebration at the Banff (Alta.) Arts Festival, possibly a preview of the vision he would bring to Boston. Houston (Texas) Ballet (HB) also suffered some natural and artistic disasters.

After presenting James Kudelka's lavish *Firebird* (from the National Ballet of Canada), the HB sustained damage to a good deal of its scenery and costumes as a result of heavy flooding in Houston. In addition, long-standing director Ben Stevenson resigned but then returned to artistic direction in a more limited capacity. The company's English tour to Stevenson's homeland, however, was not much of an artistic success.

Dance Theatre of Harlem performed in June at New York City's famous Apollo Theatre and in the fall for two weeks at New York's City Center, followed by a later stint at the Kennedy Center. Miami (Fla.) City Ballet added a ballet by Sir Frederick Ashton to its repertory but had to cancel planned additions of Balanchine and Jerome Robbins ballets owing to financial cutbacks. Nonetheless, artistic director Edward Villella was able to make progress toward a full-evening creation with the first two parts of a four-act work in progress celebrating *The Neighborhood Ballroom.* Kansas City (Mo.) Ballet (KCB) held a Stravinsky Festival that showcased a reconstruction of Balanchine's *Renard,* put together by octogenarian Todd Bolender, former KCB director.

The Joffrey Ballet of Chicago led off its fall season with an all-Nijinsky ballet bill, including the American premiere of the recently reconstituted *Jeux,* which the company billed as *Games.* Carolina Ballet presented the world premiere of Lynne Taylor-Corbett's *Carmina Burana.* Pacific Northwest Ballet, which relocated to the Mercer Arts Arena during renovations at the Seattle (Wash.) Opera House, marked the 20th anniversary of favourite company ballerina Patricia Barker. San Francisco Ballet got *A Garden,* the newest freelance ballet from Morris.

Morris, who moved into a specially renovated headquarters (replete with classrooms, rehearsal studios, and other amenities) near the Brooklyn (N.Y.) Academy of Music (BAM), celebrated his 20th anniversary at BAM with an ambitious three-week season, capped by glorious performances of his present-day classic, *L'Allegro, il penseroso, ed il moderato.* Twyla Tharp, who had previously announced that she too would relocate and set up a company and school in Brooklyn not far from Morris's building, later pulled out of the project. The Merce Cunningham Dance Company gave New York City a world premiere of the master iconoclast's *Way Station* in a run that also featured Cunningham's most recent collaboration with Robert Rauschenberg, *Interscape.* During the year Paul Taylor presented two new works, *Dandelion Wine* and *Fiends Angelical.*

A contingent of 10 French modern dance groups presented a festival called "France Moves" throughout New York City. The American Dance Festival commissioned modern works from John Jasperse, Ronald K. Brown, Shen Wei, Meredith Monk, and Garth Fagan, who also received the festival's Scripps Award. Brown also worked again for the Alvin Ailey American Dance Theatre; its winter season also featured a premiere by company director Judith Jamison. Mikhail Baryshnikov's White Oak Dance Project (WODP) took its *PASTForward* program of works by postmodern dance innovators from the 1960s and '70s on tour nationally and internationally. BAM's annual Next Wave Festival included a concentration of performance groups from Australia, as well as offerings that included the work of such leading lights of European dance as Anne Teresa De Keersmaeker, Pina Bausch, and William Forsythe. Though the Martha Graham Dance Company was still in "suspended operations" owing to legal battles between the Martha Graham Center for Contemporary Dance and Ron Protas, head of the trust overseeing the staging of Graham's work, the school reopened in January

Carolina Ballet's Timour Bourtasenkov and Melissa Podcasy in the world premiere of Lynne Taylor-Corbett's Carmina Burana.

Nina Alovert (201) 615-1780

even as legal wrangling over the use of Graham's copyrighted name continued. In August a court ruling favoured the Graham Center and ruled against the trust's claim to exclusive rights to Graham's name.

England's Royal Ballet (RB) played both the Kennedy Center and Boston, marking the engagements as a kind of "farewell tour" for its retiring director Anthony Dowell. (ABT's gifted Ethan Stiefel performed with the RB as a guest artist.) With ambitious new ideas for the Kennedy Center, newly arrived head Michael Kaiser planned a high-profile season for his first year at the helm, notably buoyed by financial support from arts patron Alberto Vilar. In addition to presenting both the National Ballet of Cuba, which also toured elsewhere, Kaiser backed plans to expand the number of dancers and performances for the Suzanne Farrell Ballet, which began an East Coast tour with two weeks of offerings at the Kennedy Center.

In other touring ventures, the Paris Opéra Ballet played San Francisco and Orange county, Calif., and La Scala Ballet performed as part of Lincoln Center Festival 2001, with Sylvie Guillem's staging of *Giselle* proving a big draw in New York City after having gained similar attention in its Orange county season. Starting in St. Paul, Minn., Matthew Bourne's Adventures in Motion Pictures presented a run of *The Car Man,* the British choreographer's take on Georges Bizet's *Carmen.*

National Ballet of Canada launched its 50th anniversary with a repertory headed by director James Kudelka's *The Contract,* a work partly based on *The Pied Piper of Hamelin.* Les Grands Ballets Canadiens de Montréal added to its store of Balanchine works by mounting *Episodes* and reviving *Concerto Barocco.* The 10th outing of the Festival International de Nouvelle Danse offered a total of 32 productions and works by Boris Charmatz, Cunningham, Trisha Brown, and WODP. A number of events that had been scheduled for presentation in New York City during September and October had to be canceled, notably many offerings of the Québec New York 2001 festival.

Changeovers included the departure from Fort Worth (Texas) Ballet (FWB) of Benjamin Houk and the assumption by Paul Mejia, formerly with FWB, of the executive directorship of Ballet Arlington (Texas). After years of relocation in temporary quarters, the New York Public Library for the Performing Arts moved back to its fully renovated site at Lincoln Center, with the Jerome Robbins Dance Division one of its brightest jewels, holding a king's ransom of written and visual records, including countless moving-picture items.

Deaths during the year included those of dancers Pauline Koner (*see* OBITUARIES), Willam Christensen (*see* OBITUARIES), Sonia Arova, Maria Karnilova, Mario Delamo, Jamake Highwater, Barton Mumaw, Laura Foreman, Nicholas Orloff, Robert Pagent, and Jane Dudley; choreographer and director Herbert Ross (*see* OBITUARIES); writer Robert Garis; lighting designer Nananne Porcher; and costumer Barbara Matera.

(ROBERT GRESKOVIC)

Europe. The most noticeable feature of the year 2001 in Europe was the number of directorship changes among the leading companies. Some were carefully planned, but several others resulted from artistic differences between the current director and company boards or funding bodies.

In London the Royal Ballet's final season under the direction of Sir Anthony Dowell showed many ballets closely associated with his distinguished career as a dancer. The final program had four pieces created by Sir Frederick Ashton for Dowell, including perhaps his most famous role, Oberon in *The Dream.* In the absence of Darcy Bussell and Sylvie Guillem (due to pregnancy and injury, respectively), attention focused on less-well-known dancers, one of whom, 19-year-old Romanian Alina Cojocaru, was promoted to principal dancer after her debut performances in *Giselle.* The new artistic director, Ross Stretton, made his first mark on the company by replacing the existing production of *Don Quixote,* by Mikhail Baryshnikov, with the Rudolf Nureyev version; his second innovation was the company premiere of John Cranko's *Onegin.*

The Birmingham Royal Ballet, touring more than planned while awaiting the reopening of its home theatre, presented the second part of director David Bintley's *Arthur,* which completed the story of the legendary king. English National Ballet's retiring director, Derek Deane, made a new version of *Swan Lake* for his last production; described originally as a staged adaptation of his in-the-round choreography, it was in fact largely new, closely resembling the Royal Ballet's former readings except in the last act, which was Deane's own. It was very well received. Incoming director Matz Skoog was faced with the company's ongoing financial problems.

The Rambert Dance Company, the oldest company in Great Britain, celebrated its 75th anniversary with a number of specially devised programs. Northern Ballet Theatre was another company that saw a change of director; David Nixon moved from BalletMet in Columbus, Ohio. Its first new production of the year, Massimo Moricone's *Jekyll and Hyde,* was a failure with both critics and the public, and it was withdrawn during the company's spring tour. A new company, George Piper Dances, was formed by Michael Nunn and William Trevitt—two of the dancers who had left the Royal Ballet to join Tetsuya Kumakawa's K-Ballet Company—and they made a successful debut with programs featuring contemporary ballets. Michael Clark, once the "bad boy" of British dance, reformed his company after a three-year absence and introduced a program that contrasted his older style with new work.

Scottish Ballet announced that the contract of director Robert North would not be renewed and that the company would make a major change of direction in the upcoming season, moving away from classical works toward a more contemporary style. The change would make audiences for traditional ballet dependent on visits from companies from south of the border, and there were many protests.

London had visits from both major Russian companies. The Bolshoi Ballet, represented by a group of 50 dancers, presented programs that each contained one ballet and a selection of pas de deux and solos; the performances were greeted by very sparse houses. The Mariinsky Ballet, at Covent Garden for a four-week season, also initially played to smaller audiences than expected, but enthusiasm built up during the season. The San Francisco Ballet, a London favourite, made a welcome return visit; New York City Ballet appeared at the Edinburgh International Festival, bringing three programs containing only recent works, with nothing by George Balanchine.

Elsewhere in Europe, both the Dutch National Ballet and the Stuttgart (Ger.) Ballet celebrated 40th anniversaries. The Dutch company marked the occasion with a program that included works new to the company by William Forsythe and Toer van Schayk, as well as one of the company's own signature works, Rudi van Dantzig's *Four Last Songs.* Earlier in the year the company premiered *Kurt Weill* by choreographer Krzysztof Pastor, and revivals included

The Paris Opéra Ballet dancers perform Pierre Lacotte's Paquita.

Léonide Massine's 1933 masterwork *Choreartium* and Ashton's *Cinderella.* The Stuttgart company focused mainly on new work, but its season also included a fresh production of *Don Quixote* by dancer Maximiliano Guerra; it was the first new full-length ballet it had staged in five years.

In Russia the Bolshoi Ballet, rebuilding after its leadership problems in 2000, invited Roland Petit to make a new ballet based on Aleksandr Pushkin's *Queen of Spades.* Entitled *Three Cards,* it played in repertoire alongside Tchaikovsky's opera on the same subject. The Bolshoi Theatre celebrated its 225th anniversary, but there was grave concern about the physical state of the building, and much effort was concentrated on raising money for a reconstruction fund. In St. Petersburg in February, the Mariinsky Ballet hosted the first International Ballet Festival, which included a program of excerpts of ballets from the Soviet era and a controversial new version of *The Nutcracker,* with choreography by company soloist Kyrill Simonov; the work was masterminded by conductor Valery Gergiev and designer Mihail Chemyakin. Much of the year was taken up by extensive foreign tours.

Another change of management saw the Finnish National Ballet replacing director Jorma Uotinen, after 10 years, with the Dane Dinna Bjørn; the company mounted a ballet based on British novelist J.R.R. Tolkien's *The Hobbit.* In Sweden ballerina Natalia Makarova staged a new version of *Giselle* for the Royal Swedish Opera Ballet; later in the year that company also mounted *Swan Lake* in the Peter Wright–Galina Samsova production originally made for the Birmingham Royal Ballet. Aage Thordal-Christensen resigned his position as director of the Royal Danish Ballet after only two years; he was replaced by Frank Andersen, who had directed the company from 1985 to 1994. At the same time, American Lloyd Riggins, a former company dancer, was appointed first guest instructor. Thordal-Christensen mounted his own new version of *The Nutcracker* in December. The company of Peter Schaufuss devoted an entire evening to the Danish storyteller Hans Christian Andersen.

The Paris Opéra Ballet started the year with a major new production by Pierre Lacotte of the 19th-century classic *Paquita,* using the fragments that remained of Marius Petipa's original but with much additional choreography by Lacotte. The ballet provided many striking roles for the company's dancers and was greeted with much acclaim. Later in the season the company added a new work by Jiri Kylian to its repertory and also gave the world premiere of Jean-Claude Gallotta's *Nosferatu,* a ballet inspired by Friedrich Wilhelm Murnau's classic film *Nosferatu, eine Symphonie des Gravens.* Under the Opéra's rules, a number of étoiles reached compulsory retirement at the age of 40; Isabelle Guerin, Fanny Gaida, and Carole Arbo gave their last performances. In the new season the company took part in a mixed opera and ballet bill, including Balanchine's *Prodigal Son,* paying homage to librettist Boris Kochno, and showed a program that contained both Vaslav Nijinsky's *L'Après-midi d'un faune* and Jerome Robbins's version of the same ballet, *Afternoon of a Faun.*

New technology began to play a part in the dance world; the annual competition for young dancers, the Prix de Lausanne, was transmitted live on the Internet for the first time.

British ballet mourned the death of Dame Ninette de Valois (*see* OBITUARIES), founder of the Royal Ballet. Other deaths included Kirov ballerina, teacher, and coach Inna Zubkovskaya (*see* OBITUARIES), longtime Royal Ballet dancer Leslie Edwards, dancer and choreographer Terry Gilbert, and critic and writer Richard Buckle.

(JANE SIMPSON)

World Dance. African war dances and the hoarse pleading and staccato heel rhythms of Spanish gypsies in the flamenco passion were emblematic themes of the world dance scene in 2001, primarily in New York City, Chicago, London, and Paris. There was also renewed interest in Irish dance, made popular by the *Riverdance* extravaganza, an engagement of which played in New York City in the summer.

The small Trinity Irish Dance Company (trained and directed by Mark Howard) outshone all competitors at the National Irish Dance Competition in Toronto; it won five gold, two silver, and four bronze medals. At competitions and in the traditional dances of the repertoire, the Trinity dancers performed in the classic Irish dance style—arms motionless and held straight at the sides—but in noncompetitive performances they freely used their arms. For the troupe's touring repertoire, Howard choreographed dances on modern subjects, notably the plight of Irish miners in Pennsylvania in the 19th century.

The intricate movements and flashy speed of the Argentine tango found renewed interest in the U.S., where TangoDanza drew crowds in the Midwest. The company consisted of three couples and one additional woman; the latter was needed when an additional character appeared in narrative works. The leading couple, Leandro Palou and Andrea Missé, performed double duty; Palou was the company's choreographer, and Missé designed the many elegant costumes. In addition to the traditional tango, they introduced the playful milonga and the valsa criolla, the latter danced in the light romantic mood of the waltz.

In London, Manuel Santiago Maya, known as Manolete, directed a Spanish dance company that presented innovative Spanish dance, classical dance, and the expected flamenco. Choreographer-dancer Joaquín Cortés presented his troupe in a piece titled *Pura Pasión*, which London critics called "a cacophony of wailing." In New York, Pilar Rioja headed her flamenco group in several appearances. Spanish dance was highly visible at the Noche Flamenca at Jacob's Pillow, the annual summer dance festival in Becket, Mass., and at the New World Flamenco Festival in Irvine, Calif.

The Ballet Folklórico de México, founded and directed for many years by Amalia Hernández, was prominent on world stages throughout the season despite the death of Hernández in 2000. The Ballet Fiesta Mexicana de Yloy Ybarra was a colourful folkloric show that performed primarily in American locales populated with Mexican immigrants.

Choreographer-educator Chuck Davis, who delved into the African American search for roots, established Dance-Africa festivals in Chicago and New York (at the Brooklyn Academy of Music [BAM]). Sabar Ak Ru Afriq ("Dream and Spirit of Africa"), a New York-based troupe directed by African American Obara Wali Rahman Ndiaye and his wife, presented Senegalese dances at BAM. Forces of Nature, another New York-based group, and Ndere Troupe, from Uganda, also performed at BAM. Lincoln Center in New York City hosted *Africa Out Loud*, which presented groups from the Democratic Republic of the Congo, Mali, Senegal, and South Africa.

The Muntu Dance Theatre of Chicago toured the U.S. and made an especially successful appearance at Lincoln Center Out of Doors. Directed by choreographer Aboulaye Camara, Muntu presented *Ancestral Memories*, dances of Mali, Guinea, and Senegal. Compagnie Käfig, a French-based hip-hop group of seven dancers of North African descent, appeared at Jacob's Pillow. Their combined break dance and poetry with scenic elements was presented to North African melodies.

Tibetan monks living in exile in Paris explained their threatened culture in sacred ritual dances that were forbidden in China. In addition to the ethnic rites and tribal folklore of its modern polyglot population, the Bayanihan Philippine National Dance Company presented the preserved Spanish-influenced dances of a past era.

The dances of India were a staple in Chicago. The Kalapriya Center for Indian Performing Arts regularly presented visiting and immigrant dancers, and the Dance Center of Columbia College presented Bharatanatyan in the Diaspora, a series of programs that illustrated several Indian dance forms.

The 10th annual Chicago Human Rhythm Project, conceived and directed by tap artist Lane Alexander, showcased leading American tap dancers, notably Broadway star Savion Glover. At that gala opening the Israeli Sheketak troupe—consisting of three highly trained dancers and two musicians—produced percussive sounds on their bodies, on the floor, and on a hanging line of pots and pans. They won standing ovations and ecstatic newspaper reviews.

In an effort to resurrect the dances of the Khmer, the New England Foundation for the Arts, in partnership with the Asia Society, sponsored a Cambodian group, which toured 12 cities.

(ANN BARZEL)

Amampondo, a South African-based percussion and dance ensemble, performs during the Africa Out Loud *series at Lincoln Center in New York City on July 13.*

THEATRE

Great Britain and Ireland. Upheaval was the byword behind the scenes at the Royal Shakespeare Company (RSC), where artistic director Adrian Noble announced far-reaching changes that affected the structure and ambitions of the company in 2001. The RSC withdrew from its residency at the Barbican Centre and initiated short seasons in other London venues. Confusion reigned among the public, which was uncertain when the Stratford-upon-Avon seasons would begin or end, and resentments grew among the company over layoffs in the technical "plant" in Stratford.

The RSC had a fine new Hamlet in Samuel West, who led a lively full-text production by Steven Pimlott. The company also debuted a remarkable new play, Martin McDonagh's *The Lieutenant of Inishmore,* in which IRA terrorist activity was the stuff of black and very bloody comedy. The RSC, however, once again played second fiddle to the Royal National Theatre (RNT).

The big RNT talking point was an impeccable revival of *My Fair Lady,* directed by Trevor Nunn, starring the pop singer Martine McCutcheon as Eliza. McCutcheon was afflicted with a severe throat infection and missed so many performances that her understudy, 18-year-old Alexandra Jay, became a new star in her own right. When Jay herself became indisposed, the show's Professor Higgins, Jonathan Pryce, while announcing another actress in the role, asked that night's audience if anyone out there fancied giving it a go. Still, the show was a resounding success and transferred to the Theatre Royal, Drury Lane, under the auspices of the producer Sir Cameron Mackintosh.

The RNT announced that Nicholas Hytner, the director of *Miss Saigon, Carousel,* and the award-winning movie *The Madness of King George,* would succeed Trevor Nunn in April 2003. Hytner clinched his appointment with two outstanding productions, Shakespeare's *The Winter's Tale* and Mark Ravenhill's *Mother Clap's Molly House.*

Though both plays were highly polished, there was evidence that Hytner took some risks, one of his trademarks. *The Winter's Tale* featured a modern dysfunctional royal marriage at the court of Leontes (Alex Jennings) and a sheep-shearing festival in Bohemia presented as a hippie-style rock concert. Ravenhill's play was an outrageous attempt to mix a bawdy, Restoration comedy of sexual party time in an 18th-century male brothel with a contemporary gay scenario. Nunn himself directed Alex Jennings as Lord Foppington in a generous, colourful revival of *The Relapse* by Sir John Vanbrugh. John Caird directed one of the best plays of the year, *Humble Boy* by Charlotte Jones; it was a modern shadow play inspired by the RNT's 2000 production of *Hamlet,* with Simon Russell Beale and Cathryn Bradshaw playing contemporary equivalents of their own Hamlet and Ophelia. Russell Beale portrayed Felix Humble, a university research fellow, and Bradshaw was cast as a former girlfriend who arrives to arouse him in the long grass of a gorgeous garden deep in the English countryside. Bees and flowers figured large, as did the superstrand theory of universal matter. Dame Diana Rigg and Denis Quilley played, respectively, Felix's mother and her long-standing lover. The play had fine acting from leading players, lots of good jokes, a gloriously seductive design (by Tim Hatley), and an abundance of strong, poetic writing.

Another RNT new play, *Howard Katz*—from Patrick Marber, author of *Closer* (1999)—was a disappointing tale of a nasty show business agent's rise and fall, meticulously charted in Ron Cook's mesmerizing performance. The experience was like watching *Death of a Salesman* rewritten as *King Lear,* but the final effect was strangely unsatisfying.

The Royal Court Theatre, viewed by many as the home of new British playwriting, had another poor year. Kevin Elyot's *Mouth to Mouth* sustained an impression of poetic virtue. On transferring to the West End, however, the tragicomedy of lost love and misdirected passion—in a tangled domestic drama played backward to the point of crisis, then forward again (like a theatrical palindrome)—seemed paper thin, despite the acting talents of Lindsay Duncan and Michael Maloney.

The Royal Court presented a retrospective season of the work of Sarah Kane, who had committed suicide in 1999, but her notorious *Blasted* was drained of impact in a cool, dispassionate production. Though playwright Leo Butler premiered *Redundant,* his work about dead-end life in a northern town had none of the vitality of similar, more groundbreaking Royal Court plays of the 1960s. This was enclosed, self-indulgent drama, unexcitingly staged until, almost gratuitously, at the end the ceiling rose slowly into the flying area. Why?

No such doubts surrounded American playwright Neil LaBute's *The Shape of Things* at the Almeida Theatre, temporarily rehoused in an abandoned bus depot in the King's Cross district while the home base underwent an overhaul. This world premiere was for many the play of the year, a brilliant dissection of the exploitation of trust in the cause of art and a Frankenstein morality for our media-savvy age. LaBute himself directed a quartet of hot young actors—Rachel Weisz, Gretchen Mol, Paul Rudd, and Frederick Weller—in a dozen pungent scenes punctuated by the blaring rock music of Smashing Pumpkins.

The Almeida also presented an ambitious but finally disappointing revival of Frank Wedekind's *Lulu,* with Anna Friel as a sexy but spiritually underpowered heroine, and a stunning new version by Sir David Hare of Anton Chekhov's unwieldy apprentice piece *Platonov.* Jonathan Kent's production of a play best known in recent years as *Wild Honey* in Michael Frayn's rewrite was extravagant and filmic. The vast stage area contained a revolving dacha, a forest of silver birches, another of head-high sunflowers, and a long canal that concealed the railway line. Aidan Gillen played Chekhov's feckless hero, a 27-year-old wastrel teacher who attracted women like a magnet does iron filings. It was a magnificent, panoramic evening, with superb performances from Gillen, Helen McCrory, Jhodi May, and Adrian Scarborough, among many others.

It was a mightily subdued first-night audience—the play opened on September 11, the day of the terrorist attacks in the United States. In addition, the Almeida's co-directors, Jonathan Kent and Ian McDiarmid, had previously announced that they would leave their posts in 2002, after 12 years.

The other London powerhouse, the Donmar Warehouse, had a quiet year in comparison. David Mamet's *Boston Marriage* proved a slight, though beautifully written, letdown, even if Zoë Wanamaker and Anna Chancellor acted their socks off. Sam Shepard's *A Lie of the Mind,* a demanding and convulsively depressing play, was given the works by a fine cast led by Sinéad Cusack and Catherine McCormack. It failed to attract the usual Donmar crowds. Christopher Hampton's *Tales from Hollywood* was another revival from the 1980s. The writing shimmered with sharp dialogue and wit as the European intellectual émigrés in the lotusland of Los Angeles formed a metaphor of artistic homelessness. The play seemed cramped, however, in the small theatre.

Feelgood by Alistair Beaton was a stinging satire on British Prime Minister

Tony Blair's government, with Henry Goodman in electrifying form as a devious spin doctor trying to keep the troops "on message" as the prime minister prepares a conference speech. His job is complicated by the revelation that one of the prime minister's inner circle, a hapless life peer—played with glorious deadpan by Nigel Planer—was responsible for the inadvertent introduction of genetically modified hops grown on his family estate that produced beer with a strange side effect on male drinkers all over Europe—they began to grow large breasts.

Feelgood originated at the Hampstead Theatre but quickly moved to the West End. Other commercial highlights were *Caught in the Net* by Ray Cooney, a hilarious, if old-fashioned, farce starring Russ Abbot and Eric Sykes; *Japes* by Simon Gray, a strong comedy of sibling rivalry across the decades, with powerful performances by Toby Stephens and Jasper Britton; and a sensationally costumed revival by Philip Prowse of Sir Noël Coward's *Semi-Monde* (1926), a forgotten play about the sexual misdemeanours and wholesale bitchiness that takes place in the foyer of a hotel; it was the second time that Prowse had rescued the play from oblivion—the first time having been 25 years earlier in Glasgow.

The classics made surprisingly big inroads on Shaftesbury Avenue. Fiona Shaw was ferocious, pitiless, and extraordinary in the title role in *Medea,* a stunning modern-dress version of the Euripides tragedy directed by Deborah Warner. Dawn French, the very large and popular television comedienne, played Bottom in a mildly daring gender-bending *A Midsummer Night's Dream.* Hollywood stars Brendan Fraser and Frances O'Connor headlined in Tennessee Williams's *Cat on a Hot Tin Roof,* with Ned Beatty as a ferocious Big Daddy. Ian Holm was an electrifying Max in Harold Pinter's *The Homecoming.* Alan Rickman and Lindsay Duncan teamed languidly in Coward's *Private Lives.*

There were no new musicals to speak of apart from *Peggy Sue Got Married,* a lively-enough stage version of the Francis Ford Coppola movie, with new music by Bob Gaudio and a vibrant Ruthie Henshall in the title role; she was sensational while traveling in time from 1980s torch songs to '50s jive and jitterbug. Playwright Jonathan Harvey's *Closer to Heaven,* at the newly refurbished Arts Theatre, was a nonevent aimed at a gay niche market, and it was inefficiently molded around a few trite numbers by the Pet Shop Boys.

AP/Wide World Photos

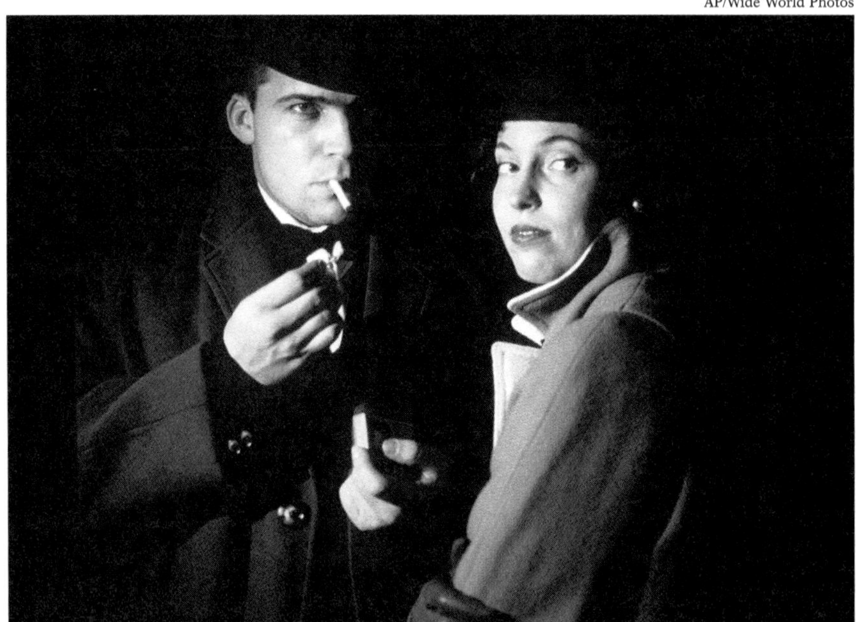

Ryan Philpott and Emma Powell perform in one of the Agathie Christie plays staged at the Palace Theatre in Westcliff, Eng., during the year.

The ever-popular open-air Globe at Southwark gave a solid showing of *Macbeth* in tuxedos and *King Lear.* The Open Air Theatre in Regent's Park scored with a truly magical *Love's Labour's Lost,* directed by Rachel Kavanaugh, and an irresistible revival of *Where's Charley?,* the 1948 Broadway version of the 1892 farce *Charley's Aunt.* The other summer musical treat was *My One and Only,* with Janie Dee and Tim Flavin tapping and sloshing (there was water on the stage) their way to happiness in the 1983 romantic hybrid of Ira Gershwin songs.

Other notable productions beyond London included Christopher Marlowe's *Edward II* at the Sheffield Crucible, starring Joseph Fiennes; a long summer season of Dame Agatha Christie plays—all of them—were at the Palace Theatre, Westcliff; *King Lear,* directed by Terry Hands and featuring Nicol Williamson as an erratic but gloriously compelling Lear at the Theatre Clwyd, Mold, Flintshire, north Wales; a brilliant cut-up job of Shakespeare's *Henry VI* trilogy—set in an abattoir—directed by Edward Hall (Sir Peter's son) at the Watermill, Newbury; and *Uncle Vanya,* featuring Tom Courtenay in manic mode in the title role in the 25th-anniversary season of the Royal Exchange, Manchester.

A strong candidate for best production of the year was Aleksandr Pushkin's great epic play *Boris Godunov,* performed in Russian by an ad-hoc company of Russian actors, directed by Declan Donnellan, at the Brighton Festival and the Riverside Studios in London.

Notable new plays premiered at the Traverse Theatre during the Edinburgh International Festival included Gregory Burke's *Gagarin Way,* a tense thriller set in a factory storeroom where a kidnapping went wrong, and Iain Heggie's *Wiping My Mother's Arse,* a bright and funny comedy about the problems of old age in a nursing home, with more than a touch of Joe Orton.

The Dublin Theatre Festival also concentrated on new work, with a trilogy of short plays by Brian Friel, Conor McPherson, and filmmaker Neil Jordan and a first stage play by novelist Roddy Doyle loosely inspired by the movie *Guess Who's Coming to Dinner?* The Abbey Theatre presented a season of works by Tom Murphy ranging from his first success, *A Whistle in the Dark,* to his denser, more knotted and poetic plays *The Gigli Concert* and *The Sanctuary Lamp.* (MICHAEL COVENEY)

U.S. and Canada. The most startling and talked-about event of the American theatre year was the premiere in mid-December 2001 of Tony Kushner's new play *Homebody/Kabul,* which debuted at Off-Broadway's New York Theatre Workshop. The ballyhoo was not so much related to Kushner's return to the New York stage with a major work nearly 10 years after his Pulitzer Prize-winning *Angels in America* AIDS epic had catapulted him into the ranks of the nation's literary elite—making him as close to a household name as American dramatists ever get to be—but to the play's setting and its subject—Afghanistan.

In fact, it was more coincidence than calculation that Kushner's three-and-a-half-hour drama about the West's contemporary and historic relationship to Afghanistan arrived onstage a scant two months after the U.S. had all but declared war on that country. A writer with an ongoing interest in international affairs (wartime Germany in *A Bright Room Called Day* and corruption in the Soviet Union in *Slavs!*), Kushner had long indulged a fascination with Afghanistan and its geopolitical plight, and he had finished the initial version of *Homebody/Kabul* the previous winter. Nevertheless, the play's events—it follows the journey of a British woman who disappears into the chaos of Afghan life—seemed eerily prescient, and director Declan Donnellan's Off-Broadway production generated avid international attention.

As in other sectors of American life, the September 11 terrorist attacks reverberated throughout the nation's theatre community. Performances were postponed, canceled, modified, and reexamined as theatres in New York and Washington, D.C., struggled with logistic problems, and those in other parts of the country deferred to the mood of a shocked and mourning public. Some plays no longer seemed appropriate—a Broadway revival of Stephen Sondheim's dark musical *Assassins* was delayed, for example—and others took on surprising new resonances. In the wake of widespread uncertainty, one thing seemed certain: the economic consequences for theatre would be severe. The New York City commercial theatre, which suffered disastrously during the first weeks after the attack, continued to post below-average ticket sales through the end of the year, and the not-for-profit theatre prepared to bear the brunt of a vastly diminished pool of resources available for the arts.

In some locales existing prosperity compensated for worries about future want. California's Berkeley Repertory Theatre opened a new $20 million, 600-seat second theatre with a grand-scale two-part production of *The Oresteia,* co-directed by artistic director Tony Taccone and opera specialist Stephen Wadsworth (who said he viewed the Aeschylus tragedy as a "totemic dysfunctional family saga"). Outsized productions of the Greeks were also de rigueur in Washington, D.C., where Arena Stage artistic director Molly Smith put her lightly feminist brand on a new compilation of classic texts called *Agamemnon and His Daughters,* and Shakespeare Theatre artistic director Michael Kahn staged *The Oedipus Plays* in an African mode, with the gifted Avery Brooks in the title role.

A number of established playwrights debuted important works. Edward Albee had a success d'estime with his esoteric and literate theatrical fable *The Play About the Baby,* directed by David Esbjornson in an Off-Broadway production that made glorious use of the turn-on-a-dime talents of veteran actors Marian Seldes and Brian Murray. Suzan-Lori Parks, best known for poetic abstraction in works such as *The America Play,* favourably surprised critics with an ostensibly realistic comedy-drama *Topdog/Underdog,* in which a pair of down-and-out brothers fret and feud. (George C. Wolfe's taut Public Theater production was expected to return for a Broadway run during the next season.) Historian-turned-playwright Charles L. Mee made "love" the operative word in a trilogy of dissimilar plays—*Big Love, First Love,* and *True Love*—that alternately engaged and puzzled audiences across the country with their collagelike texts and juggled time frames.

AP/Wide World Photos

Playwright Tony Kushner stands in front of the set (still under construction) of his new play, **Homebody/Kabul,** *at the New York Theatre Workshop in November.*

Playwright Richard Nelson would mark 2001 as a prime year. He debuted a new play, *Madame Melville,* in London and New York, featuring Macaulay Culkin, the former child movie star, in the role of a 15-year-old American lad seduced by his Parisian teacher, and wooed audiences with his book and lyrics for the unusual musical play *James Joyce's The Dead,* which was widely produced across the country and on national tour.

Much attention was also paid to a national tour of *The Tragedy of Hamlet,* auteur British director Peter Brook's elegant condensation of Shakespeare's expansive tragedy, pared down to two and a half intermissionless hours and rendered with passionate restraint by a mere eight actors. Audiences in Seattle, Wash., New York City, and Chicago debated the merits of Brook's agenda, but there was general agreement that the agile black actor Adrian Lester was a thrilling prince of Denmark.

The sensation of the commercial theatre season—and the only show to take the September 11 slump in box-office stride—was comedian Mel Brooks's deliriously tasteless musicalization of his own 1967 cult film *The Producers.* The sure-fire casting of Nathan Lane (*see* BIOGRAPHIES) as the hard-luck showman Max Bialystock and Matthew Broderick as his nebbishy accountant Leo Bloom (roles played in the film by Zero Mostel and Gene Wilder), abetted by a dazzling supporting cast and Brooks's own silly-sophisticated songs and lyrics, proved irresistible to ticket buyers, who lined up around the block from the St. James Theatre and jammed Ticketmaster phone lines. Among the records broken were the biggest advance sale ever ($33 million), the most Tony nominations (15), and the most Tonys won (12). Of the 12 awards won, 2 went to Susan Stroman, its director and choreographer. (*See* BIOGRAPHIES.)

David Auburn's Pulitzer-confirmed drama *Proof,* produced by Manhattan Theatre Club, was the second most honoured Broadway show of the season, with Tonys for best play, best director (Daniel Sullivan), and best actress (Mary-Louise Parker). The actors that played the old and young British poet A.E. Housman in Tom Stoppard's *The*

Invention of Love, Richard Easton and Robert Sean Leonard, respectively, also won acting awards, as did Viola Davis of August Wilson's wordy but well-received drama *King Hedley II.*

The post-Tony arrival of an unlikely but high-spirited musical, Mark Hollmann's and Greg Kotis's savvy Bertolt Brecht–Kurt Weill parody *Urinetown,* enlivened the theatre year, as did a crowd-pleasing, all-star New York City staging in Central Park's Delacorte Theatre of Anton Chekhov's *The Seagull,* directed by Mike Nichols and reuniting long-ago stage confederates Meryl Streep and Kevin Kline. On the West Coast a revival of the tuneful 1958 Rodgers and Hammerstein musical *Flower Drum Song,* politically revamped via David Henry Hwang's rewritten book, earned high marks at the Mark Taper Forum.

In Canada, southern Ontario's Stratford Festival continued its economic and artistic upswing under the artistic direction of former actor Richard Monette. Although on the financial ropes 10 years earlier (Monette said he almost closed one of Stratford's three theatres), now—thanks in part thanks to an endowment campaign that had topped $10 million—the festival was opening a fourth theatre and planning an ambitious 50th anniversary season in 2002, with Christopher Plummer signed to star in *King Lear.* Just 90 minutes away in Toronto, the four-year-old Soulpepper Theatre Company, founded by a cluster of Canada's best-known actors, tapped ever more successfully into the depth of the city's audience for serious theatre. A September run of two Eugène Ionesco plays, *The Bald Soprano* and *The Lesson,* for example, was a sellout.

Among the losses to the theatre community in 2001 were stage and film actress Kim Stanley, famous for her roles in *Bus Stop* and *Picnic,* and rubber-faced comedienne Imogene Coca. (*See* OBITUARIES.) Other notable deaths included actress Gloria Foster, known for her expertise in classic and contemporary roles, and producer Arthur Cantor, who in the course of a long career presented more than 50 productions in New York, London, and Paris. (JIM O'QUINN)

MOTION PICTURES

United States. It seemed the sign of troubled times that in 2001 the world film-going public seized hungrily upon two adaptations of children's books of mythical tales about the conflict of Good and Evil. *Harry Potter and the Sorcerer's Stone* ("Philosopher's Stone" in the international release), directed by Chris Columbus with an all-British cast, faithfully translated into images the story and the visions of J.K. Rowling's 1997 best-seller. The film of J.R.R. Tolkien's trilogy *The Lord of the Rings*—first published in 1954–55 and adapted in 1978 as an animated film—was directed by the once-maverick New Zealand director Peter Jackson. The first installment, *The Fellowship of the Ring,* was released in 2001; the other two parts, already filmed, were scheduled for Christmas release in 2002 and 2003. The spirit of childhood legend also imbued the future-world science fiction of Steven Spielberg's *Artificial Intelligence: AI,* a quasi-collaboration based on a longtime idea of the late filmmaker Stanley Kubrick.

Another outstanding success of mixed national progeny was *Bridget Jones's Diary,* directed by Sharon Maguire from Helen Fielding's original newspaper column. The 30ish heroine found a response on both sides of the Atlantic, and the film offered a change-of-pace role for Hugh Grant. (*See* BIOGRAPHIES.) The sequel to 1991's *The Silence of the Lambs, Hannibal,* directed by Ridley Scott, was a predictable box-office winner. The Australian director

The Kobal Collection/Warner Bros/Mountain, Peter

A scene from the hit film Harry Potter and the Sorcerer's Stone *("Philosopher's Stone" in the international release).*

Baz Luhrmann excelled his own previous tours de force with his Parisian musical fantasy *Moulin Rouge.* Veteran Woody Allen directed a modest tribute to cinema of the 1940s, *The Curse of the Jade Scorpion,* while Robert Altman's *Gosford Park* resembled an old-style Agatha Christie whodunit, with a murder at a 1930 country house whose divided society Altman observed with pleasure but not much depth. Lasse Hallström brought E. Annie Proulx's novel *The Shipping News* to the screen.

The Coen brothers, Joel and Ethan, attempted, with only mixed success, a pastiche of 1940s film noir with *The Man Who Wasn't There.* David Lynch's *Mulholland Dr.,* developed out of a rejected TV series pilot, was a characteristic assembly of offbeat characters and enigmatic incidents, set in Los Angeles. Satire was healthily in evidence in Peter Howitt's *AntiTrust,* in which Tim Robbins patently based his performance as a computer supermogul on Bill Gates. After two Oscar-nominated dramas in 2000 (and an Oscar for one, *Traffic*), director Steven Soderbergh returned with the lively crime caper *Ocean's Eleven.* (*See* BIOGRAPHIES.)

Two sober and distinguished biopics were Michael Mann's *Ali,* with Will Smith in the role of Cassius Clay/Muhammad Ali, and Ron Howard's *A Beautiful Mind,* with Russell Crowe (*see* BIOGRAPHIES) as John Nash, the mathematical genius who conquered schizophrenia to become a Nobel Prize winner in 1994. The most spectacular critical failure of the year was the costly but banal three-hour spectacle *Pearl Harbor.*

A few interesting works appeared from the independent sector of production. Actor Todd Field made a distinguished directing debut with *In the Bedroom,* a sensitive and expansive study of the effect of a family tragedy. The off-Broadway success *Hedwig and the Angry Inch,* the musical saga of a transsexual entertainer, was brought to the screen by its writer-star creator John Cameron Mitchell.

Shrek, the outstanding animated story of a reluctantly kindly ogre directed by Andrew Adamson and Vicky Jenson, was aimed at adult as well as infant audiences and, with the year's other animated hit, *Monsters, Inc.,* confirmed the current thirst for myth and fairy tale.

In 2001 Hollywood said farewell to legendary director Stanley Kramer, as well as two double Oscar-winning actors, Jack Lemmon and Anthony Quinn, actress Dorothy McGuire, and director-choreographer Herbert Ross, among others. (*See* OBITUARIES.)

British Isles. The first apparent effect of the "New Labour" administration's initiative to centralize film activities under a Film Council was overproduction; of a total of more than 100 feature films, a substantial proportion were undeniably lamentable. British directors favoured character comedy, with Mel Smith's crime farce *High Heels and Low Lifes,* Jez Butterworth's *Birthday Girl,* about a prim bank teller who acquires a mail-order bride from Russia, and Steve Barron's *Mike Bassett: England Manager,* a self-deprecatory comedy about a disastrous English international football (soccer) team. Alan Taylor's *The Emperor's New Clothes* was a witty and likable speculation about an imagined incident in the life of Napoleon; the film offered a rewarding dual role to Ian Holm. Ken Loach made one of his most brilliant works of social criticism, *The Navigators,* describing with rich comedy the effect on the lives of a little group of workers of the disastrous degeneration of Britain's railway system after privatization.

John Boorman's *The Tailor of Panama* was a stylish adaptation of John le Carré's 1996 novel. Other successful literary adaptations were Fred Schepisi's *Last Orders,* from Brian Swift's prize-winning novel; and Michael Apted's thriller *Enigma,* adapted by the dramatist Tom Stoppard from a novel by Robert Harris, set in the wartime code-breaking headquarters at Bletchley Park. The British taste for biopics brought Richard Eyre's study of the novelist Iris Murdoch, *Iris.*

In Ireland the gifted Yugoslav director Goran Paskaljevic made *How Harry Became a Tree,* a tale of neighbour hate in 1920s Ireland that was an open metaphor for the Bosnian conflict.

Canada. One of the year's greatest surprises was *Atanarjuat, the Fast Runner,* the first film to be made in the Inuktitut language, directed by Zacharias Kunuk. Drawing upon legend and the ancient Inuit storytelling tradition, the film vividly presented an integral culture, beautifully filmed (on digital video) against the Arctic landscapes of an island in the north Baffin region.

Australia. In a lean year Ray Lawrence's *Lantana* brought to the screen Andrew Bovell's play *Speaking in Tongues,* which shrewdly probed the frustrations of 10 middle-class people. Robert Connolly's *The Bank* mined a currently popular theme—ordinary people's battle with corporate villainy. David Caesar's *Mullet* looked at a small-town community in an increasingly unfriendly world, seen through the eyes of a young man returning home after life in Sydney. Australia's hit hero of the 1980s, Crocodile Dundee, made a somewhat weary comeback in Simon Wincer's *Crocodile Dundee in Los Angeles.*

France. Among world filmmakers France remained a leader in terms of variety, invention, and craftsmanship. Jean-Pierre Jeunet's *Le Fabuleux Destin d'Amélie Poulain* (*Amélie*), an exquisitely visualized story of a young woman driven to adjust the reality of her Montmartre neighbours, enjoyed international success. One of the more controversial productions, Patrice Chéreau's English-language *Intimacy* (2000; called *Intimité* in the 2001 French release) was an uneasy combination of frank sex and overly artificial dialogue. Claude Miller triumphantly translated Ruth Rendell's 1984 novel *The Tree of Hands* to a French setting, as *Betty Fisher et autres histoires* (*Betty Fisher and Other Stories*). Another of the year's most talented films was Anne Fontaine's *Comment j'ai tué mon père,* about the disruption of a bourgeois family by the return of their prodigal paterfamilias. Of the veterans of the 1960s nouvelle vague, Jean-Luc Godard made a characteristic essay on history, politics, and, unusually, love, in *Éloge de l'amour* (*In Praise of Love*). The 81-year-old Eric Rohmer made a charming and elegant costume picture, *L'Anglaise et le duc* (*The Lady and the Duke*). The veteran Jacques Rivette returned to direction with *Va savoir* (*Go Figure,* or *Who Knows?*), an ensemble piece set in the context of a theatrical production.

Germany. Among the few outstanding films of the year was Hungarian director István Szabó's Franco-German (but English-language) production *Taking Sides,* adapting Ronald Harwood's 1995 play about the postwar investigations of conductor Wilhelm Furtwängler's relations with the Nazi elite. Roland Suso Richter's *Der Tunnel,* reconstructing one of the biggest escape attempts from East to West Berlin in Cold War days, successfully made the transition from television miniseries to theatrical release. Franziska Buch's new adaptation revealed the perennial attractions of Erich Kastner's often-filmed children's book *Emil und die Detektive.*

Italy. Nanni Moretti's *La stanza del figlio* (*The Son's Room*), a very human story about the private grief of a couple at the death of their teenage son, won

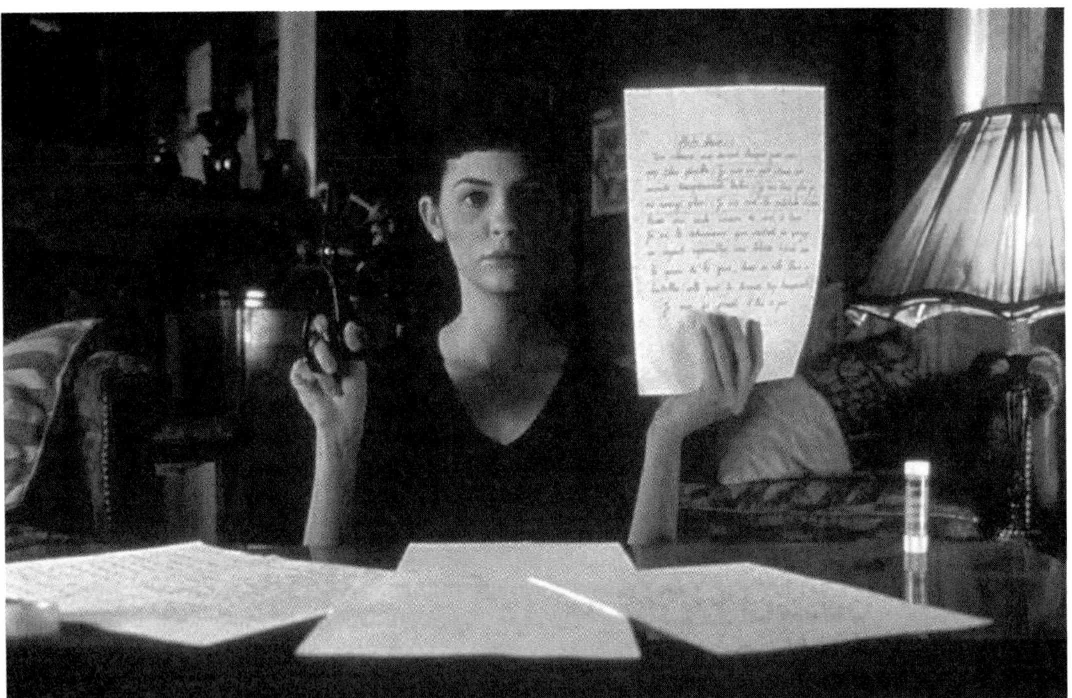

French actress Audrey Tautou plays the lead character in Jean-Pierre Jeunet's Le Fabuleux Destin d'Amélie Poulain *(*Amélie*).*

AP/Wide World Photos

for Italy the Cannes Festival Palme d'Or. Other, senior filmmakers turned to remote history. Pupi Avati's *I cavalieri che fecero l'impresa* (*The Knights of the Quest*) followed the adventures of five young 13th-century Crusaders in search of the Holy Shroud. Ermanno Olmi's *Il mestiere delle armi* (2000; *Profession of Arms*) recounted the final days and death, in 1521, of Giovanni de' Medici.

Comedy flourished. A major commercial success in the home market was *Chiedimi se sono felice* (2000; *Ask Me if I'm Happy*), directed, written, and performed by the popular comedy trio Aldo, Giovanni, and Giacomo; while the idiosyncratic Maurizio Nichetti made intelligent use of digital facilities and multilingual dialogue (with most of the comedy being visual) for his comedy about the tribulations of a Milanese office worker, *Honolulu Baby* (2000).

Iberia. Spanish films had rarely tackled contemporary social issues, so Javier Balaguer's *Sólo mía* (*Only Mine*, or *Mine Alone*), a forthright drama about domestic violence, was exceptional. The talented Joaquín Oristrell's *Sin vergüenza* (*No Shame*) explored the ambitions and relationships of an acting school.

Two Catalan directors made notable films; Ventura Pons's *Anita no perd el tren* (*Anita Takes a Chance*) related a romantic middle-aged woman's discovery of love, while Marc Recha, using a minimalist style, directed a sensitive and positive study of the effect of a death upon a family, *Pau i el seu germà* (*Pau and His Brother*).

The nonagenarian Manoel de Oliveira produced another surprise and change of direction with a French co-production, *Je rentre à la maison*, featuring a majestic performance by Michel Piccoli as an aged actor.

Nordic Countries. A major box-office hit for Sweden was Josef Fares's *Jalla! Jalla!* (2000), relating the stories of two friends, an immigrant from Lebanon striving to evade a family-arranged marriage and his Swedish friend suffering a bad attack of impotence. The expatriate Briton Colin Nutley made an elaborate comedy about the human maneuverings in the entertainment business, *Gossip* (2000).

Denmark had an international success with Lone Scherfig's *Italiensk for begyndere* (2000; *Italian for Beginners*, 2001), showing six lonely working-class people in a Copenhagen suburb learning an emotional language along with the verbal one in their evening Italian courses.

Two notable Danish-Swedish co-productions were Bille August's delicate adaptation of Ulla Isaksson's novel *En sång för Martin* (*A Song for Martin*), about a late love affair that endures through the perils and problems of life, and Jan Troell's *Så vit som en snö* (*As White as in Snow*), which re-creates the story of Sweden's first aviatrix, Elsa Andersson.

Russia. The lawlessness of contemporary Russian urban life was featured in Andrey Nekrasov's *Lyubov i drugiye koshmary* (2000; *Lubov and Other Nightmares*), which centred on a transvestite professional assassin, and Sergey Bodrov's effective drama *Syostry* (*Sisters*), about two women on the run from the mob enemies of their gangster father. In a lighter vein, Karen Shakhnazarov's comedy *Yady, ili vsemirnaya istoriya otravleniy* (*Poisons, or the World History of Poisoning*) described a modest would-be wife killer who seeks the aid of some of the great poisoners of history.

Eastern Europe. In a generally weak year for Hungarian production, one outstanding film was Árpád Sopsits's *Torzók* (*Abandoned*), a largely autobiographical account of a small boy's sufferings in a Cold War-era orphanage.

In the Czech production *Tmavomodrý svet* (*Dark Blue World*), the gifted Jan Sverák looked back, with a very human mixture of humour and sadness, at the experience of Czech pilots in Britain in World War II and their subsequent sufferings under communism.

The Romanian director Lucian Pintilie revisited the dark days of the Ceaușescu regime with *L'Après-midi d'un tortionnaire* (*The Afternoon of a Torturer*), based on the true confessions of a man formerly implicated in torturing political prisoners. The debutant Cristi Puiu's *Marfa și banii* (*Stuff and Dough*) provided an object lesson for filmmakers in all economically depressed national cinema industries—a film made on a minimal budget but triumphing by imagination, invention, verve, and craftsmanship. This road movie was the story of a young would-be entrepreneur undertaking a delivery to Bucharest and discovering too late that he is in thrall to petty mafiosi.

Albanian films are few in number and rarely seen abroad. Gjergj Xhuvani's *Slogans,* a tragicomedy ridiculing official postures in the late days of communist rule, and Fatmir Koçi's apocalyptic portrayal of Albanian society in the late 1990s, *Tirana, année zéro* (*Tirana Year Zero*), were welcome exceptions.

Greece. Among debutant feature writer-directors, Christos Demas's *I akrovates tou kipou* (*The Cistern*) offered an inventive rite-of-passage story of five 11-year-old boys in the fateful summer of 1974, while Christos Georgiou's *Kato apo ta asteria* (*Under the Stars*) was a road movie set in the aftermath of the division of Cyprus following the Turkish invasion of 1974. Of films by established directors, the most notable were Constantine Giannaris's *Dekapentaugoustos* (2000; *One Day in August*) and Andrea Pantzis's *To tama* (2000; *Word of Honor*). Giannaris's film was a virtuoso and occasionally visionary interweaving of the four stories of a disturbed young burglar and the absent occupants of the three apartments he devastates. Pantzis's epic was a Cypriot *Pilgrim's Progress,* set in the 1940s—the story of a devout man who encounters every kind of temptation on his journey to give thanks at the shrine of Saint Andreas for the birth of his son.

Turkey and Iran. The Turkish writer-director Kasım Öz created an epitome of the Kurdish tragedy in *Fotograf* (*The Photograph*), the story of the encounter and brief friendship on a bus journey of two young men, unaware that they will soon find themselves on opposing sides of a war. Yılmaz Erdoğan and Ömer Faruk Sorak made an auspicious debut with *Vizontele,* a comedy about the arrival of television in a back-of-beyond township.

A marked new phase in Iranian cinema was the appearance of films of open social criticism. Maziar Miri's *Qateh-ye natamam* (*The Unfinished Song*) ironically portrayed an ethnomusicologist's efforts to record the songs of peasant women when Islamic law makes it a crime for women to sing or dance in public. Rakhshan Bani-Etemad's *Zir-e poost-e shahr* (2000; *Under the Skin of the City*) was a ranging examination of social conditions in contemporary Tehran, seen through the daily problems of neighbouring families and concluding with a remarkable interrogation of the role of cinema in Iran as the tormented woman protagonist turns on the cameraman and asks him why he is making this film. Seyyed Reza Mir-Karimi's *Zir-e noor-e maah* (*Under the Moonlight*) told the story of a young student mullah who accidentally finds himself with a group of homeless people and discovers greater fulfilment in this human contact than in the religious life. Film director and reform parliamentarian Behrooz Afkhami directed an intelligent dramatic examination of the custom of "temporary marriage" in Islamic society, *Shokaran* (*Hemlock*). Comedy is not a common commodity in Iranian cinema, but Babak Payami's *Raye makhfi* (*Void Votes,* or *Secret Ballot*) found fun in the first unaccustomed exercise of democracy. The Afghan troubles figured in several films. Mohsen Makhmalbaf's *Safar e Ghandehar* (*Kandahar*) exposed, with a remarkable poetic atmosphere, the sufferings of the Afghan people under Taliban oppression. Majid Majidi's gentle bittersweet fable *Baran* related the love story of an Iranian boy and a young Afghan girl who disguises herself as a boy to find meanly paid work on a building site. Abolfazl Jalili applied his meticulous film craft to the story of an Afghan child refugee in *Delbaran.*

Israel. An exceptionally accomplished debut film, Joseph Cedar's *Ha-Hesder* (2000; *Time of Favor*) used a personal drama about a good rabbi and his child and followers to explore troubling philosophical divisions. Dover Kosashvili's *Hatuna meuheret* (*Late Marriage*) offered a wry comedy of manners about a conventional Jewish family's desperation to marry off their 32-year-old son, who has other ideas than the "suitable" virgins they propose.

East and Southeast Asia. In Japan the major theatrical sensation of the year was 70-year-old Kinji Fukasaku's *Battle Royale* (2000), based on a best-selling novel by Koshun Takami. Its violent story of a high-school project in which pupils are compelled to kill one another led to political calls for restraints on violent films. Less controversially, another veteran, Shohei Imamura, adapted a novel by Henmi Yo, *Akai hashi no shita no nurui mizu* (*Warm Water Under a Red Bridge*), about a beautiful young woman whose body is stimulated by sex to release a magical spring gushing forth streaks of water. In a comparable vein, Gō Rijū's *Chloe* effectively and touchingly orientalized Boris Vian's novel *L'Écume des jours,* about a young women who discovers a flower bud growing in her lung.

Few films of international interest emerged from China, where the production of propaganda-loaded feature films had moved into a new and more sophisticated stage. The country's finest director, Zhang Yimou, produced an endearing character comedy, *Xingfu shiguang* (2000; *Happy Times*), which told of a dyed-in-the wool con man whose heart is moved by the young blind daughter of the woman whose hand and cash he is striving to win.

Artists in the new Hong Kong could still make films on political themes. Herman Yau's *From the Queen to the Chief Executive* (2000) argued the case of a real-life young offender who had spent 12 years detained "at Her Majesty's pleasure" and who now faced further imprisonment at the pleasure of the chief executive. Stanley Kwan's *Lan Yu* was also controversial for the new Hong Kong, depicting a homosexual love affair between the son of a communist official and a lad from the country. The biggest box-office successes of the year, however, were a Jackie Chan action thriller, *Te wu mi cheng* (*The Accidental Spy*), directed by Teddy Chan, and Johnnie To's costume comedy *Wu Yen.*

From Taiwan, Hsiao Ya-chuan's *Ming dai ahui zhu* (2000; *Mirror Image*) was essentially no more than a sketch, loosely constructed but full of wit and promise in its observation of the comings and goings of the clients of a pawnbroker's shop, left in charge of the sick proprietor's odd son.

In South Korea, Kwak Kyung-Taek drew on often painful personal memories for *Chin goo* (*Friend*), tracing the histories of four young men from boyhood in the 1970s to the present. The film proved the country's all-time box-office winner.

Thailand's runaway box-office successes were period stories dealing with Thai-Burmese conflicts of the 18th century, Thanit Jitnukul's *Bangrajan* (2000) and Chatrichalerm Yukoi's *Suriyothai.*

India. The Indian commercial cinema styled "Bollywood" broke significantly into the international market thanks to Ashutosh Gowariker's remarkable *Lagaan* (*Land Tax*). Using indigenous conventions, this skillfully related story of a group of Indian peasants challenged to compete at cricket with the arrogant British military establishment provided gripping and intelligent entertainment at any level. More limited international acceptance was earned by Santosh Sivan's Bollywood epic *Asoka* (*Ashoka*

(continued on page 299)

INTERNATIONAL FILM AWARDS 2001

Golden Globes, awarded in Beverly Hills, Calif., in January 2001

Best motion picture drama	*Gladiator* (U.K./U.S.; director, Ridley Scott)
Best musical or comedy	*Almost Famous* (U.S.; director, Cameron Crowe)
Best director	Ang Lee (*Wo hu zang lon* [*Crouching Tiger, Hidden Dragon*], China/Hong Kong/Taiwan/U.S.)
Best actress, drama	Julia Roberts (*Erin Brockovich,* U.S.)
Best actor, drama	Tom Hanks (*Cast Away,* U.S.)
Best actress, musical or comedy	Renée Zellweger (*Nurse Betty,* Germany/U.S.)
Best actor, musical or comedy	George Clooney (*O Brother, Where Art Thou?,* U.K./France/U.S.)
Best foreign-language film	*Wo hu zang lon* (*Crouching Tiger, Hidden Dragon*) (China/Hong Kong/Taiwan/U.S.; director, Ang Lee)

Sundance Film Festival, awarded in Park City, Utah, in January 2001

Grand Jury Prize, dramatic film	*The Believer* (U.S.; director, Henry Bean)
Grand Jury Prize, documentary	*Southern Comfort* (U.S.; director, Kate Davis)
Audience Award, dramatic film	*Hedwig and the Angry Inch* (U.S.; director, John Cameron Mitchell)
Audience Award, documentary	*Dogtown and Z-Boys* (U.S.; director, Stacy Peralta); *Scout's Honor* (U.S.; director, Tom Shepard)
Audience Award, world cinema	*Wode fuqin muqin* (*The Road Home*) (China; director, Zhang Yimou)
Best director, dramatic film	John Cameron Mitchell (*Hedwig and the Angry Inch,* U.S.)
Best director, documentary	Stacy Peralta (*Dogtown and Z-Boys,* U.S.)
Special Jury Prize, dramatic film	*In the Bedroom* (U.S.; director, Todd Field)
Special Jury Prize, documentary	*Children Underground* (U.S.; director, Edet Belzberg)

Berlin International Film Festival, awarded in February 2001

Golden Bear	*Intimacy* (*Intimité*) (France/U.K./Germany/Spain; director, Patrice Chéreau)
Silver Bear, Grand Jury Prize	*Shiqi sui de dan che* (*Beijing Bicycle*) (China/Taiwan/ France; director, Wang Xiaoshuai)
Silver Bear, Jury Prize	*Italiensk for begyndere* (*Italian for Beginners*) (Denmark; director, Lone Scherfig)
Best director	Lin Cheng-sheng (*Ai ni ai wo* [*Betelnut Beauty*], Taiwan/France)
Best actress	Kerry Fox (*Intimacy* [*Intimité*], France/U.K./Germany/ Spain)
Best actor	Benicio Del Toro (*Traffic,* Germany/U.S.)

Césars (France), awarded in February 2001

Best film	*Le Goût des autres* (France; director, Agnès Jaoui)
Best director	Dominik Moll (*Harry, un ami qui vous veut du bien* [*Harry, He's Here to Help*], France)
Best actress	Dominique Blanc (*Stand-by,* France)
Best actor	Sergi López (*Harry, un ami qui vous veut du bien* [*Harry, He's Here to Help*], France)
Best new director of a feature film	Laurent Cantet (*Ressources humaines* [*Human Resources*], France/U.K.)

British Academy of Film and Television Arts, awarded in London in February 2001

Best film	*Gladiator* (U.K./U.S.; director, Ridley Scott)
Best director	Ang Lee (*Wo hu zang lon* [*Crouching Tiger, Hidden Dragon*], China/Hong Kong/Taiwan/U.S.)
Best actress	Julia Roberts (*Erin Brockovich,* U.S.)
Best actor	Jamie Bell (*Billy Elliot,* U.K./France)
Best supporting actress	Julie Walters (*Billy Elliot,* U.K./France)
Best supporting actor	Benicio Del Toro (*Traffic,* Germany/U.S.)
Outstanding British film	*Billy Elliot* (U.K./France; director, Stephen Daldry)
Best foreign-language film	*Wo hu zang lon* (*Crouching Tiger, Hidden Dragon*) (China/Hong Kong/Taiwan/U.S.; director, Ang Lee)

Academy of Motion Picture Arts and Sciences (Oscars, U.S.), awarded in Los Angeles in March 2001

Best film	*Gladiator* (U.K./U.S.; director, Ridley Scott)
Best director	Steven Soderbergh (*Traffic,* Germany/U.S.)
Best actress	Julia Roberts (*Erin Brockovich,* U.S.)
Best actor	Russell Crowe (*Gladiator,* U.K./U.S.)
Best supporting actress	Marcia Gay Harden (*Pollock,* U.S.)
Best supporting actor	Benicio Del Toro (*Traffic,* Germany/U.S.)
Best foreign-language film	*Wo hu zang lon* (*Crouching Tiger, Hidden Dragon*) (China/Hong Kong/Taiwan/U.S.; director, Ang Lee)

Cannes International Film Festival, France, awarded in May 2001

Palme d'Or	*La stanza del figlio* (*The Son's Room*) (Italy/France; director, Nanni Moretti)
Grand Jury Prize	*La Pianiste* (*The Piano Teacher*) (Austria/France; director, Michael Haneke)
Best director	David Lynch (*Mulholland Dr.,* France/U.S.); Joel Coen (*The Man Who Wasn't There,* U.S.)
Best screenplay	Danis Tanovic (*No Man's Land,* Belgium/Bosnia and Herzegovina/France/Italy/Slovenia/U.K.)
Best actress	Isabelle Huppert (*La Pianiste* [*The Piano Teacher*], Austria/France)
Best actor	Benoît Magimel (*La Pianiste* [*The Piano Teacher*], Austria/France)
Caméra d'Or	*Atanarjuat, the Fast Runner* (Canada; director, Zacharias Kunuk)

Locarno International Film Festival, Switzerland, awarded in August 2001

Golden Leopard	*Alla rivoluzione sulla due cavalli* (Italy; director, Maurizio Sciarra)
Special Jury Prize	*Delbaran* (Iran/Japan; director, Abolfazl Jalili)
Silver Leopard	*L'Afrance* (France/Senegal; director, Alain Gomis); *Love the Hard Way* (Germany/U.S.; director, Peter Sehr)
Best actress	Kim Ho Jung (*Nabi* [*The Butterfly*], South Korea)
Best actor	Andoni Gracia (*Alla rivoluzione sulla due cavalli,* Italy)
Audience Award	*Lagaan* (*Land Tax*) (India; director, Ashutosh Gowariker)

Montreal World Film Festival, awarded in September 2001

Best film (Grand Prix of the Americas)	*Baran* (Iran; director, Majid Majidi); *Torzók* (*Abandoned*) (Hungary; director, Árpád Sopsits)
Best actress	Sandrine Kiberlain, Nicole Garcia, and Mathilde Seigner (*Betty Fisher et autres histoires* [*Betty Fisher and Other Stories*], France/Canada)
Best actor	Robert Stadlober (*Engel & Joe,* Germany)
Best director	Oliver Hirschbiegel (*Das Experiment* [*The Experiment*], Germany)
Grand Prix of the Jury	*El hijo de la novia* (*The Son of the Bride*) (Argentina; director, Juan José Campanella)
Best screenplay	*Mariage* (Canada; writer, Catherine Martin)
International Critics' Award	*Betty Fisher et autres histoires* (*Betty Fisher and Other Stories*) (France/Canada; director, Claude Miller)

Toronto International Film Festival, awarded in September 2001

Best Canadian feature film	*Atanarjuat, the Fast Runner* (director, Zacharias Kunuk)
Best Canadian first feature	*Inertia* (director, Sean Garrity)
Best Canadian short film	*Film(dzama)* (director, Deco Dawson)
Discovery award	*Chicken Rice War* (Singapore; director, Chee Kong Cheah)
International Critics' Award	*Inch'Allah dimanche* (France; director, Yamina Benguigui)
People's Choice Award	*Le Fabuleux Destin d'Amélie Poulain* (*Amélie*) (France/Germany; director, Jean-Pierre Jeunet)

Venice Film Festival, awarded in September 2001

Golden Lion	*Monsoon Wedding* (India; director, Mira Nair)
Grand Jury Prize	*Hundstage* (*Dog Days*) (Austria; director, Ulrich Seidl)
Special Jury Prize	*Raye Makhfi* (*Secret Ballot,* or *Void Votes*) (Canada/Iran/ Italy/ Switzerland; director, Babak Payami)
Volpi Cup, best actress	Sandra Ceccarelli (*Luci dei miei occhi,* Italy)
Volpi Cup, best actor	Luigi Lo Cascio (*Luci dei miei occhi,* Italy)

San Sebastián International Film Festival, Spain, awarded in September 2001

Best film	*Taxi para 3* (*A Cab for Three*) (Chile; director, Orlando Lubbert)
Special Jury Prize	*En construcción* (*Work in Progress*) (Spain; director, José Luis Guerín)
Best director	Jean-Pierre Améris (*C'est la vie,* France)
Best actress	Pilar López de Ayala (*Juana la Loca,* Spain)
Best actor	Düzgün Ayhan (*Escape to Paradise,* Switzerland)
Best photography	Roman Osin (*The Warrior,* U.K.)
New Directors Prize	Gerardo Tort (*De la calle* [*Streeters*], Mexico)
International Critics' Award	*En construcción* (*Work in Progress*) (Spain; director, José Luis Guerín)

Chicago International Film Festival, awarded in October 2001

Best feature film	*À ma soeur!* (*For My Sister,* or *Fat Girl*) (France/ Italy/Spain; director, Catherine Breillat)
Grand Jury Prize	*Ni neibian jidian* (*What Time Is It There?*) (Taiwan/ France; director, Tsai Ming-Liang)
Best director	Tsai Ming-Liang (*Ni neibian jidian* [*What Time Is It There?*], Taiwan/France)
Best actress	Sandrine Kiberlain and Nicole Garcia (*Betty Fisher et autres histoires* [*Betty Fisher and Other Stories*], France/Canada)
Best actor	Koji Yakusho (*Akai hashi no shita no nurui mizu* [*Warm Water Under a Red Bridge*], Japan/France)
Silver Hugo	*Qianxi manbo* (*Millennium Mambo*) (Taiwan/France; director, Hou Hsiao-hsien)
International Critics' Award	*Anyangde guer* (*The Orphan of Anyang*) (China; director, Wang Chao)

Vancouver International Film Festival, Canada, awarded in October 2001

Federal Express Award for Most Popular Canadian Film	*Obaachan's Garden* (director, Linda Ohama)
Air Canada Award for Most Popular Film	*Promises* (U.S./Israel; directors, B.Z. Goldberg, Justine Shapiro, and Carlos Bolado)
NFB Award (documentary feature)	*Jung* (*War*)*: In the Land of the Mujaheddin* (Italy/Afghanistan; directors, Alberto Vendemmiati and Fabrizio Lazzaretti)
Telefilm Canada Award for Best Western Canadian Feature	*Turning Paige* (director, Robert Cuffley)
Telefilm Canada Award for Best Western Canadian Short Film	*10-Speed* (directors, Jeff Cunningham and Adam Locke-Norton)
Dragons and Tigers Award for Young Cinema	*Ming dai ahui zhu* (*Mirror Image*) (Taiwan; director, Hsiao Ya-chuan)

Tokyo International Film Festival, awarded in November 2001

Grand Prize	*Slogans* (Albania/France; director, Gjergi Xhuvani)
Special Jury Prize	*Zir-e noor-e maah* (*Under the Moonlight*) (Iran; director, Sayed Reza Mir-Karimi)

European Film Awards, awarded in Berlin, December 2001

Best European film	*Le Fabuleux Destin d'Amélie Poulain* (*Amélie*) (France; director, Jean-Pierre Jeunet)
Best actress	Isabelle Huppert (*La Pianiste* [*The Piano Teacher*]), France/Austria)
Best actor	Ben Kingsley (*Sexy Beast,* U.K./Spain)

(continued from page 297)
the Great), the story of a historical hero of the 3rd century BC. Contemporary subjects were treated in Digvijay Singh's *Maya*, a shocking tale of child abuse sanctified as religious ceremony; in Rituparno Ghosh's *Utsab* (2000; "The Festival"), which chronicled the family crises brought to a pitch in the course of an annual festive reunion; and in the Bengali Nabyendu Chatterjee's *Mansur mian aur ghora* (*The Last Ride*), the touching story of an old man forced to give up his horse-drawn cab under pressure from his limo chauffeur son. Mira Nair's *Monsoon Wedding* was a perceptive, witty, fast-moving ensemble work about the romantic problems of a large Punjab family assembled for a wedding. Two of India's most enduring film stars died during the year: Ashok Kumar, one of Bollywood's best-loved actors for more than 60 years, and Sivaji Ganesan, a legendary star in southern India's Tamil movie industry. (*See* OBITUARIES.)

Latin America. Gerardo Tort's unsparing picture of street children in Mexico City, *De la calle* (*Streeters*), was based on a play by Jesús González Dávila. Marysa Sistach's *Perfuma de violetas, nadie te oye* (*Violet Perfume: Nobody Hears You*) dealt intelligently with rape in working-class Mexico City. Guillermo del Toro's Spanish co-production *El espinazo del diablo* (*The Devil's Backbone*) ingeniously combined a story of the perils of the Civil War and a ghost story.

Argentine cinema was seeing a marked revival with the appearance of a generation of new and distinctive filmmakers. Ana Poliak's *La fé del volcán (The Faith of the Volcano)* looked at the effects of the country's recent history through the friendship of two social outcasts, a 12-year-old cleaning girl and a middle-aged knife grinder. Sergio Bizzio's *Animalada* was the startling tale of a bourgeois gentleman who abandons his wife for a pretty young sheep. The biggest box-office hit in more than a decade, writer-director Fabián Bielinsky's *Nueve reinas* (*Nine Queens*), combined a brilliantly structured script and fine characterization in its depiction of small-time con men.

Brazil enjoyed its biggest-ever box-office success with Gurel Arraes's *O auto da compadecida* (2000; *A Dog's Will*), a comedy adapted from a stage success and veering between surreality and traditions of picaresque in its tale of an amiable rogue drifting through society. In *Abril despedaçado* (*Behind the Sun*), Walter Salles, director of *Central Station*, brought the weight of classical tragedy to a story of deathly feuding, based on a novel by the Albanian writer Ismail Kadare. (DAVID ROBINSON)

Nontheatrical Films. *Clive Alive*, directed by Anders Envall and produced by the Swedish company Dockhouse Film & Television AB, creatively depicted the thorough safety testing of Volvo cars. The film, which starred a test dummy named Clive, beat out nine other nominees to earn the 2001 Best of Festival award at the U.S. International Film and Video Festival in Chicago. This was the third time since 1995 that Dockhouse had garnered the Best of Fest. *Clive Alive* also took the Grand Prize at three other festivals, one in Sweden and two in Germany. Swedish documentary filmmaker Arne Sucksdorff died in May at age 84. (*See* OBITUARIES.)

A young Jewish baseball player who challenged Babe Ruth's home-run record and became an American hero was chronicled in *The Life and Times of Hank Greenberg* (2000), a documentary produced by Aviva Kempner. The film was named best overall at the Columbus (Ohio) International Film & Video Festival. Film critics in Chicago, Las Vegas, Nev., New York City, and Florida voted it best documentary of the year.

Bean Cake, a 12-minute student film by David Greenspan of the University of Southern California, won high praise during the year. The film, which featured Japanese narration with English subtitles, earned the Palme d'Or for short film at the Cannes (France) International Film Festival in addition to a College Emmy and numerous other awards.

The Pigeon Murders, produced by Sean Fine for *National Geographic*, departed from the style and subject matter of traditional environmental films. The documentary depicted a detective's hunt to find out who was poisoning pigeons by the thousands in New York City. *The Pigeon Murders* won the CINE Golden Eagle, two Emmys, and numerous wildlife awards in England and the U.S. (THOMAS W. HOPE)

The life of Detroit Tiger star Hank Greenberg, shown here with legendary New York Yankee Lou Gehrig, was the subject of a celebrated documentary.

Greenberg Family Collection

Religion

Relations between **MUSLIMS** and members of other faiths dominated the world of religion during 2001. Churches continued to tackle controversies over **ORDINATION** of homosexuals and sexual **ABUSE** by clergy, and some religious organizations found themselves examining basic beliefs on such matters as **CREATION** and **SALVATION.**

The Teachings of Islam. The September 11 terrorist attacks in the United States spurred a worldwide examination of Islamic doctrine, particularly after the FBI discovered a document left behind by a key organizer of the airplane hijackers that cited Islamic teachings in urging them to ask God for help and assuring them that by dying for the faith they would be assured entry into paradise. Muslim scholars pointed out, however, that terrorist violence is an interpretation of Islam that most adherents of the faith reject.

Attention soon focused on Afghanistan, where Osama bin Laden, the Saudi Arabian businessman and alleged mastermind of the attacks, was receiving asylum. Afghanistan's fundamentalist Islamic Taliban government had stirred controversy throughout the year because of its policies toward non-Muslims. In January Taliban leader Mullah Mohammad Omar warned that any Muslim who converted to another faith and any non-Muslim trying to win converts would face the death penalty.

In August authorities detained eight aid workers on charges of preaching Christianity and notified all Western aid organizations and the United Nations that they would be carefully watched for evidence of proselytizing. The foreign aid workers were airlifted out of the country after the Taliban fled Kabul. In March the Taliban announced that it had destroyed as idols all Buddha statues in Afghanistan, including a 53.3-m (175-ft)-high statue above the Bamian Valley that was believed to be the world's largest Buddha statue. Two months later the government said all non-Muslims had to wear distinctive marks on their clothing to set them apart from the country's Muslims, who formed an overwhelming majority. Although the ruling seemed to be especially directed against Afghanistan's largest religious minority, the tiny Hindu community, the Taliban said it was intended to protect Hindus from religious police who enforce Islamic law.

Fighting between Christians and Muslims in September in the northern Nigerian city of Jos took more than 500 lives and reportedly destroyed tens of thousands of churches, mosques, homes, and shops. Pres. Olusegun Obasanjo called out the army to restore order and declared that true believers in God must not start killing other human beings. The Catholic Bishops Conference of Nigeria said the introduction of Islamic law in some states violated the human rights of non-Muslims and was a threat to peace in the country. In June Pakistan's military ruler, Gen. Pervez Musharraf, denounced radical Islamic groups for misappropriating money collected in the name of jihad, or holy war. Addressing a gathering of Muslim leaders to mark the birthday of the Prophet Muhammad, he urged them to stop issuing "irresponsible statements" calling for holy war against the U.S. and Russia.

Interfaith Relations. Pope John Paul II became the first pope to enter a mosque when he toured a 1,300-year-old Islamic house of worship in May in Damascus, Syria. He was greeted at the Umayyad Mosque by Mufti Ahmed Kuftaro, Syria's top Muslim cleric, and the pontiff urged joint forgiveness by Christians and Muslims for all the times they had offended one another. In September the pope arrived in Kazakhstan, a predominantly Muslim state in Central Asia, with a message of good wishes for Islamic leaders. Dato Seri Mahathir bin Mohamad, the Muslim prime minister of Malaysia, told 600 Christian leaders from 82 nations attending the 11th General Assembly of the World Evangelical Fellowship in Kuala Lumpur that "we should be careful that we don't propagate religions at the cost of conflicts and violence."

Christian-Jewish relations suffered in July when a commission of Catholic and Jewish historians suspended its study of the church's actions during the Holocaust because the Vatican had not released all of its archives from the era. The Rev. Peter Gumpel, speaking for the Vatican, subsequently said that some Jewish historians on the commission had helped mount a "slanderous campaign" against the Roman Catholic Church and that the panel's work had failed because of "irresponsible" actions by some of its members. Discussions at a meeting of Christians and Muslims in Rome organized in October by the liberal lay Catholic Community of Sant'Egidio turned raw as concord was sought over recent events in the Middle East and offended Jews (who were not represented) with talk of "arrogant Zionists."

Poland's Roman Catholic bishops apologized in May for a 1941 massacre of Jews in northeastern Poland and for wrongs committed by Polish Catholics against Jews during World War II. In *Constantine's Sword,* a book on the history of Christian anti-Semitism, however, former Catholic priest James Carroll suggested that such apologies failed to grapple with how Christian teaching created a climate that led to mob violence against Jews. The Israeli army's occupation of part of the premises of the Evangelical Lutheran Church of the Reformation in August in the West Bank town of Beit Jala was denounced by the Lutheran World Federation. The federation's general secretary, the Rev. Ishmael Noko, said the troops had invaded "one of the holy places of the Christian community."

The Israeli government came into conflict with Greek Orthodox leaders in July when Prime Minister Ariel Sharon tried to disqualify 5 of the 15 candidates vying to succeed the late Diodoros I as Greek Orthodox patriarch of Jerusalem. Although Sharon cited a centuries-old church law that allowed governmental authorities to disqualify candidates for the position, the church subsequently elected Irineos I, one of the five the Israeli leader had rejected.

AP/Wide World Photos

Pope John Paul II (left) embraces Catholicos Karekin II, patriarch of the Armenian Apostolic Church, at the church's seat, Ejmiadzin, on September 25.

The opening of the Holy Land Experience, a Christian theme park in Orlando, Fla., stirred concern among some Jewish leaders, who saw it as an attempt to convert Jews to Christianity. The founder of the $16 million theme park, Marvin Rosenthal, was a Baptist minister who was raised Jewish and became a Christian as a teenager.

Pope John Paul II won praise from Greek Orthodox leaders when, during a visit to Athens in May, he apologized for Roman Catholic sins of "action or omission" against Orthodox Christians. He specifically offered "deep regret" for the sacking by Catholic crusaders of Constantinople, now Istanbul, in 1204. A spokesman for Greek Orthodox Archbishop Christodoulos said the pope's words would "help heal one thousand years of mistrust between the two churches and create the possibility for new dialogue."

The pope's visit to Ukraine in June, however, drew fire from Russian Orthodox Patriarch Alexey II and Metropolitan Volodymyr of the Ukrainian Orthodox Church. They warned that John Paul's embrace of Ukraine's five million members of the Greek Catholic Church would hinder ecumenical relations. In Ukraine the number of Orthodox parishes outnumbered Catholic parishes by about three to one, but the Orthodox churches were divided into three denominations, of which the largest was loyal to Moscow. Alexey also rebuked the pope for his later visit to Kazakhstan, saying the Catholic leader should have asked his permission before making the trip.

After leaving Kazakhstan, John Paul visited Armenia and made ecumenical history by celebrating mass at the altar of an Orthodox church for the first time. The outdoor mass was held at Ejmiadzin (Echmiadzin), the seat of the Armenian Apostolic Church, an independent Oriental Orthodox church that was celebrating the 1,700th anniversary of Christianity's becoming the country's state religion.

Pope John Paul II made a number of other formal apologies during the year as well. In October he acknowledged "errors" by historical Roman Catholic missions to China (relations between China and the Holy See had been particularly tense since October 2000, when the Roman Catholic Church canonized as martyrs 120 Chinese people whom China regarded as criminals), and a month later the pontiff transmitted a document (by means of the first official papal e-mail—from a laptop computer in the pope's office in the Vatican) to dioceses around the world, which included an apology for past injustices to South Pacific islanders committed by Catholic missionaries.

Ecumenism. Representatives of Catholic, Lutheran, and Reformed churches met in Rome in February to exchange views on indulgences, the Catholic practice of remitting punishment for sins in exchange for prayer and repentance. The Vatican said it was the first ecumenical consultation on the subject since the Protestant Reformation. In March representatives of the Presbyterian Church (U.S.A.) met with Vatican officials and issued a joint statement pledging to work toward agreement on the doctrine of justification, mutual recognition of baptisms, and the removal of mutual condemnations that went back to the Reformation. Also in March the Church of England's House of Bishops issued a statement criticizing the Catholic Church's ban on receiving communion in Anglican churches as "an ecumenical, theological and pastoral affront." A bishop of the Evangelical Lutheran Church in America (ELCA) and his Episcopal counterpart presided in June at joint ordinations of each's churches in Chicago for the first time since their two denominations joined in a full communion agreement in 2000. The Anglican Church of Canada and the Evangelical Lutheran Church in Canada approved a similar accord in July. The ELCA's national convention in August in Indianapolis, Ind., modified the agreement, however, by voting to allow clergy to be ordained by pastors rather than bishops on grounds of conscience. The Lutheran Church–Missouri Synod declared at its national convention in July in St. Louis, Mo., that it could not consider the ELCA to be "an orthodox Lutheran body" because of its full communion agreements with non-Lutheran churches. Two pastors filed charges against the president of the Missouri Synod in November for joining with ECLA clergy in worship and supporting an interfaith prayer service. Representatives of the Mennonite Church and the General Conference Mennonite Church agreed to a merger in July, forming a denomination of about 125,000 members in 1,100 congregations. The merging groups resolved differences on standards for membership by leaving such questions up to individual congregations in consultation with their local conferences.

Ministry and Membership. The General Assembly of the Presbyterian Church (U.S.A.) voted in June in Louisville, Ky., in favour of repealing a five-year-old ban on ordination of homosexuals to the ministry. The resolution was then sent to the denomination's 173 regional presbyteries for approval, in the wake of their failure to ratify a ban on same-sex unions that had been passed by the 2000 assembly. The ELCA began a four-year study of whether to ordain active homosexuals and bless same-sex unions, and an Anglican catechism commissioned by Archbishop David Hope of York said homosexuality might have "divinely ordered and positive qualities." Four bishops defied church law in the ELCA in April when they joined in the ordination of Anita C. Hill, a lesbian. One of the four, Paul W. Egertson, subsequently resigned as bishop of the Southern California (West) Synod over what he described as his "act of ecclesiastical disobedience." In June in Denver, Colo., two Anglican archbishops defied Archbishop George Carey of Canterbury in consecrating as bishops four American priests who opposed the Episcopal Church's positions on homosexuality and biblical authority. Gwynne Guibord, chief ecumenical officer of the predominantly homosexual Universal Fellowship of Metropolitan Community Churches, became the first openly gay person to head a state ecumenical council in the United States when she was appointed president of the California Council of Churches in January. The Reform Jewish movement in the United

Worldwide Adherents of All Religions by Six Continental Areas, Mid-2001

	Africa	Asia	Europe	Latin America	Northern America	Oceania	World	%	Number of Countries
Christians	368,244,000	317,759,000	559,359,000	486,591,000	261,752,000	25,343,000	2,019,052,000	32.9	238
Affiliated Christians	342,819,000	312,182,000	536,588,000	481,132,000	213,038,000	21,600,000	1,907,363,000	31.1	238
Roman Catholics	123,467,000	112,086,000	285,554,000	466,226,000	71,391,000	8,327,000	1,067,053,000	17.4	235
Protestants	90,989,000	50,718,000	77,497,000	49,008,000	70,164,000	7,478,000	345,855,000	5.6	232
Orthodox	36,038,000	14,219,000	158,375,000	564,000	6,400,000	718,000	216,314,000	3.5	134
Anglicans	43,524,000	735,000	26,628,000	1,098,000	3,231,000	5,428,000	80,644,000	1.3	163
Independents	85,476,000	157,605,000	25,850,000	40,357,000	81,032,000	1,536,000	391,856,000	6.4	221
Marginal Christians	2,502,000	2,521,000	3,606,000	6,779,000	10,747,000	468,000	26,623,000	0.4	215
Unaffiliated Christians	25,425,000	5,577,000	22,771,000	5,459,000	48,714,000	3,743,000	111,689,000	1.8	232
Baha'is	1,779,000	3,538,000	132,000	893,000	799,000	113,000	7,254,000	0.1	218
Buddhists	139,000	356,533,000	1,570,000	660,000	2,777,000	307,000	361,985,000	5.9	126
Chinese folk religionists	33,100	385,758,000	258,000	197,000	857,000	64,200	387,167,000	6.3	89
Confucianists	250	6,277,000	10,800	450	0	24,000	6,313,000	0.1	15
Ethnic religionists	97,762,000	129,005,000	1,258,000	1,288,000	446,000	267,000	230,026,000	3.8	140
Hindus	2,384,000	813,396,000	1,425,000	775,000	1,350,000	359,000	819,689,000	13.4	114
Jains	66,900	4,207,000	0	0	7,000	0	4,281,000	0.1	10
Jews	215,000	4,476,000	2,506,000	1,145,000	6,045,000	97,600	14,484,000	0.2	134
Muslims	323,556,000	845,341,000	31,724,000	1,702,000	4,518,000	307,000	1,207,148,000	19.7	204
New-Religionists	28,900	101,065,000	160,000	633,000	847,000	66,900	102,801,000	1.7	60
Shintoists	0	2,669,000	0	6,900	56,700	0	2,732,000	0.0	8
Sikhs	54,400	22,689,000	241,000	0	535,000	18,500	23,538,000	0.4	34
Spiritists	2,600	2,000	134,000	12,169,000	152,000	7,100	12,466,000	0.2	55
Taoists	0	2,658,000	0	0	11,200	0	2,670,000	0.0	5
Zoroastrians	910	2,519,000	670	0	79,100	1,400	2,601,000	0.0	22
Other religionists	67,300	63,100	238,000	99,600	605,000	9,500	1,082,000	0.0	78
Nonreligious	5,170,000	611,876,000	105,742,000	16,214,000	28,994,000	3,349,000	771,345,000	12.6	236
Atheists	432,000	122,408,000	22,555,000	2,787,000	1,700,000	369,000	150,252,000	2.5	161
Total population	**802,150,000**	**3,730,168,000**	**728,270,000**	**525,878,000**	**311,877,000**	**30,164,000**	**6,128,512,000**	**100.0**	**238**

Continents. These follow current UN demographic terminology, which now divides the world into the six major areas shown above. See United Nations, *World Population Prospects: The 1998 Revision* (New York: UN, 1999), with populations of all continents, regions, and countries covering the period 1950–2050. Note that "Asia" includes the former Soviet Central Asian states and "Europe" includes all of Russia extending eastward to Vladivostok, the Sea of Japan, and the Bering Strait.

Countries. The last column enumerates sovereign and nonsovereign countries in which each religion or religious grouping has a numerically significant and organized following.

Adherents. As defined in the 1948 Universal Declaration of Human Rights, a person's religion is what he or she says it is. Totals are enumerated for each of the world's 238 countries following the methodology of the *World Christian Encyclopedia*, 2nd ed. (2001), using recent censuses, polls, surveys, reports, Web sites, literature, and other data.

Christians. Followers of Jesus Christ affiliated with churches (church members, including children: 1,907,363,000, shown divided among the six standardized ecclesiastical megablocs), plus persons professing in censuses or polls to be Christians though not so affiliated. Figures for the subgroups of Christians do not add up to the totals in the first line because some Christians adhere to more than one denomination.

Independents. This term here denotes members of churches and networks that regard themselves as postdenominationalist and neo-apostolic and thus independent of historic, organized, institutionalized, denominationalist Christianity.

Marginal Christians. Members of denominations on the margins of organized mainstream Christianity (e.g., Church of Jesus Christ of Latter-day Saints, Jehovah's Witnesses, and Christian Science).

Buddhists. 56% Mahayana, 38% Theravada (Hinayana), 6% Tantrayana (Lamaism).

Chinese folk religionists. Followers of traditional Chinese religion (local deities, ancestor veneration, Confucian ethics, universism, divination, and some Buddhist and Taoist elements).

Confucianists. Non-Chinese followers of Confucius and Confucianism, mostly Koreans in Korea.

Ethnic religionists. Followers of local, tribal, animistic, or shamanistic religions, with members restricted to one ethnic group.

Hindus. 70% Vaishnavites, 25% Shaivites, 2% neo-Hindus and reform Hindus.

Jews. Adherents of Judaism. For detailed data on "core" Jewish population, see the annual "World Jewish Populations" article in the American Jewish Committee's *American Jewish Year Book*.

Muslims. 83% Sunnites, 16% Shi'ites, 1% other schools. Until 1990 the Muslims in the former U.S.S.R. who had embraced communism were not included as Muslims in this table. After the collapse of communism in 1990–91, these Muslims were once again enumerated as Muslims if they had returned to Islamic profession and practice.

New-Religionists. Followers of Asian 20th-century New Religions, New Religious movements, radical new crisis religions, and non-Christian syncretistic mass religions, all founded since 1800 and most since 1945.

Other religionists. Including a handful of religions, quasi-religions, pseudoreligions, parareligions, religious or mystic systems, and religious and semireligious brotherhoods of numerous varieties.

Nonreligious. Persons professing no religion, nonbelievers, agnostics, freethinkers, uninterested, or dereligionized secularists indifferent to all religion but not militantly so.

Atheists. Persons professing atheism, skepticism, disbelief, or irreligion, including the militantly antireligious (opposed to all religion).

Total population. UN medium variant figures for mid-2001, as given in *World Population Prospects: The 1998 Revision*.

States urged families and synagogues to sever ties with the Boy Scouts of America in January to protest the scouts' ban on homosexuals in leadership positions.

The General Council of the Assemblies of God voted in August in Springfield, Mo., to permit divorced people to be ordained to the ministry if they were divorced before becoming Christians.

The Rev. William Sinkford of Cambridge, Mass., became the first African American person to win the presidency of the Unitarian Universalist Association when he was elected in June at its General Assembly in Cleveland, Ohio. In November, Bishop Wilton Gregory of Belleville, Ill., became the first black elected to lead the U.S. Conference of Catholic Bishops.

A French court sentenced Catholic Bishop Pierre Pican of Bayeux-Lisieux to a three-month suspended prison term in September for having concealed information that a priest was sexually abusing children. The Vatican said in March that it was investigating allegations that some priests had regularly forced nuns to have sex with them. A report commissioned by the Catholic

Religious Adherents in the United States of America, AD 1900–2000

	Year 1900	%	mid-1970	%	mid-1990	%	Annual Change, 1990–2000 Natural	Conversion	Total	Rate (%)	mid-1995	%	mid-2000	%
Christians	**73,270,000**	**96.4**	**191,182,000**	**91.0**	**217,719,000**	**85.7**	**2,081,000**	**−278,000**	**1,802,000**	**0.80**	**227,586,000**	**85.2**	**235,742,000**	**84.7**
Affiliated Christians	54,425,000	71.6	153,299,000	73.0	175,820,000	69.2	1,680,000	−79,500	1,601,000	0.88	184,244,000	69.0	191,828,000	68.9
Protestants	35,000,000	46.1	58,568,000	27.9	60,216,000	23.7	575,000	−140,000	435,000	0.70	62,525,000	23.4	64,570,000	23.2
Roman Catholics	10,775,000	14.2	48,305,000	23.0	56,500,000	22.2	540,000	−390,000	150,000	0.26	56,715,000	21.2	58,000,000	20.8
Anglicans	1,600,000	2.1	3,196,000	1.5	2,450,000	1.0	23,400	−28,400	−5,000	−0.21	2,445,000	0.9	2,400,000	0.9
Orthodox	400,000	0.5	4,163,000	2.0	5,150,000	2.0	49,200	12,000	61,200	1.13	5,472,000	2.1	5,762,000	2.1
Multiple affiliation	0	0.0	−2,704,000	−1.3	−24,336,000	−9.6	−233,000	−87,300	−320,000	1.24	−25,360,000	−9.5	−27,534,000	−9.9
Independents	5,850,000	7.7	35,645,000	17.0	66,900,000	26.3	639,000	526,000	1,165,000	1.62	72,943,000	27.3	78,550,000	28.2
Marginal Christians	800,000	1.1	6,126,000	2.9	8,940,000	3.5	85,400	28,600	114,000	1.21	9,502,000	3.6	10,080,000	3.6
Evangelicals	*32,068,000*	*42.2*	*31,516,000*	*15.0*	*37,349,000*	*14.7*	*357,000*	*−27,800*	*329,000*	*0.85*	*39,314,000*	*14.7*	*40,640,000*	*14.6*
evangelicals	*11,000,000*	*14.5*	*45,500,000*	*21.7*	*87,656,000*	*34.5*	*838,000*	*263,000*	*1,101,000*	*1.19*	*93,457,000*	*35.0*	*98,662,000*	*35.4*
Unaffiliated Christians	18,845,000	24.8	37,883,000	18.0	41,899,000	16.5	400,000	−199,000	202,000	0.47	43,342,000	16.2	43,914,000	15.8
Baha'is	2,800	0.0	138,000	0.1	600,000	0.2	5,700	9,600	15,300	2.30	682,000	0.3	753,000	0.3
Buddhists	30,000	0.0	200,000	0.1	1,880,000	0.7	18,000	39,000	57,000	2.68	2,150,000	0.8	2,450,000	0.9
Chinese folk religionists	70,000	0.1	90,000	0.0	76,000	0.0	730	−480	250	0.32	77,000	0.0	78,500	0.0
Ethnic religionists	100,000	0.1	70,000	0.0	280,000	0.1	2,700	12,800	15,500	4.50	387,000	0.1	435,000	0.2
Hindus	1,000	0.0	100,000	0.1	750,000	0.3	7,200	21,000	28,200	3.24	930,000	0.4	1,032,000	0.4
Jains	0	0.0	0	0.0	5,000	0.0	48	150	200	3.36	6,000	0.0	7,000	0.0
Jews	1,500,000	2.0	6,700,000	3.2	5,535,000	2.2	52,900	−44,300	8,600	0.15	5,600,000	2.1	5,621,000	2.0
Muslims	10,000	0.0	800,000	0.4	3,560,000	1.4	34,000	23,200	57,200	1.50	3,825,000	1.4	4,132,000	1.5
Black Muslims	0	0.0	200,000	0.1	1,250,000	0.5	12,700	17,300	30,000	2.29	1,400,000	0.5	1,650,000	0.6
New-Religionists	0	0.0	110,000	0.1	575,000	0.2	5,500	18,100	23,600	3.50	690,000	0.3	811,000	0.3
Shintoists	0	0.0	0	0.0	50,000	0.0	480	140	620	1.18	53,900	0.0	56,200	0.0
Sikhs	0	0.0	1,000	0.0	160,000	0.1	1,500	5,900	7,400	3.87	192,000	0.1	234,000	0.1
Spiritists	0	0.0	0	0.0	120,000	0.1	1,100	690	1,800	1.44	133,000	0.1	138,000	0.1
Taoists	0	0.0	0	0.0	10,000	0.0	96	17	110	1.08	10,600	0.0	11,100	0.0
Zoroastrians	0	0.0	0	0.0	42,400	0.0	410	630	1,000	2.20	47,500	0.0	52,700	0.0
Other religionists	10,000	0.0	450,000	0.2	530,000	0.2	5,100	−390	4,700	0.85	550,000	0.2	577,000	0.2
Nonreligious	1,000,000	1.3	10,070,000	4.8	21,414,000	8.4	205,000	162,000	366,000	1.59	23,150,000	8.7	25,078,000	9.0
Atheists	1,000	0.0	200,000	0.1	770,000	0.3	7,400	30,600	37,900	4.09	950,000	0.4	1,149,000	0.4
Total population	**75,995,000**	**100.0**	**210,111,000**	**100.0**	**254,076,000**	**100.0**	**2,428,000**	**0**	**2,428,000**	**0.92**	**267,020,000**	**100.0**	**278,357,000**	**100.0**

Methodology. This table extracts and analyzes a microcosm of the world religion table. It depicts the United States, the country with the largest number of adherents to Christianity, the world's largest religion. Statistics at five points in time across the 20th century are presented. Each religion's *Annual Change* for 1990–2000 is also analyzed by *Natural* increase (births minus deaths, plus immigrants minus emigrants) per year and *Conversion* increase (new converts minus new defectors) per year, which together constitute the *Total* increase per year. *Rate* increase is then computed as percentage per year.

Structure. Vertically the table lists 30 major religious categories. The major religions (including nonreligion) in the U.S. are listed with largest (Christians) first. Indented names of groups in the "Adherents" column are subcategories of the groups above them and are also counted in these unindented totals, so they should not be added twice into the column total. Figures in italics draw adherents from all categories of Christians above and so cannot be added together with them. Figures for Christians are built upon detailed head counts by churches, often to the last digit. Totals are then rounded to the nearest 1,000. Because of rounding, the corresponding percentage figures may sometimes not total exactly 100%.

Christians. All persons who profess publicly to follow Jesus Christ as Lord and Saviour. This category is subdivided into **Affiliated Christians** (church members) and **Unaffiliated** (nominal) **Christians** (professing Christians not affiliated with any church). *See also* the note on Christians to the world religion table.

Evangelicals/evangelicals. These two designations—italicized and enumerated separately here—cut across all of the six Christian traditions or ecclesiastical megablocs listed above and should be considered separately from them. **Evangelicals** are mainly Protestant churches, agencies, and individuals that call themselves by this term (for example, members of the National Association of Evangelicals); they usually emphasize 5 or more of 7, 9, or 21 fundamental doctrines (salvation by faith, personal acceptance, verbal inspiration of Scripture, depravity of man, Virgin Birth, miracles of Christ, atonement, evangelism, Second Advent, et al). The **evangelicals** are Christians of evangelical conviction from all traditions who are committed to the evangel (gospel) and involved in personal witness and mission in the world; alternatively termed Great Commission Christians.

Jews. Core Jewish population relating to Judaism, excluding Jewish persons professing a different religion.

Other categories. Definitions are as given under the world religion table.

(DAVID B. BARRETT; TODD M. JOHNSON)

Church in England and Wales recommended that all clergy, staff, and volunteers be subject to police checks to stamp out sexual abuse of children. A consortium of eight missionary organizations reported that nearly 7% of more than 600 former missionary children said they had been sexually abused during their elementary school years.

Doctrine. Two Presbyterian denominations debated matters of biblical interpretation during 2001. The General Assembly of the 2.5-million-member Presbyterian Church (U.S.A.) adopted a statement affirming salvation through Jesus Christ but leaving unanswered the eternal destiny of non-Christians. In another resolution the PCUSA said the theology of the popular Left Behind fiction series "is not in accord with our Reformed understanding" of the biblical book of Revelation. The General Assembly of the 300,000-member Presbyterian Church in America, meeting in Dallas, Texas, in June, rejected an attempt to require members to view the six days of biblical creation as literal 24-hour days. Reflecting a growing interest in tradition, the rabbinical arm of Judaism's liberal Reform movement adopted voluntary guidelines on conversion in June in Monterey, Calif. In taking the action, the Central Conference of American Rabbis urged that converts be immersed in ritual baths and affiliated with synagogues. The Conservative movement of Judaism adopted its first official Torah commentary, a 1,560-page volume that was designed to replace a commentary written in 1937 by Rabbi J.H. Hertz.

Personalities. Zambian Catholic Archbishop Emmanuel Milingo broke his celibacy vow in May in marrying a Korean woman in a group wedding in New York City conducted by the Rev. Sun Myung Moon of the Unification Church. Threatened with excommunication, however, Milingo announced three months later that he was ending the marriage. The Rev. Paul Collins of Australia resigned from the Catholic priesthood in March after having been under investigation for three years by the Vatican's Congregation for the Doctrine of the Faith. His resignation coincided with his publication of a book titled *From Inquisition to Freedom*, a critical examination of the Vatican agency with chapters written by six other prominent Catholics who had been investigated by the congregation. The Rev. Kevin Mannoia resigned the presidency of the (U.S.) National Association of Evangelicals (NAE) in June over what the organization's board described as "divergent perspectives about certain operational and fiscal matters." Mannoia, a bishop emeritus in the Free Methodist Church, said a bylaw change allowing denominations affiliated with the more liberal National Council of Churches to affiliate with the NAE had stirred controversy among some of the NAE's 50 denominational and 250 ministry affiliates. In February the board of National Religious Broadcasters voted unanimously in Dallas to end its 57-year relationship with the NAE.

The North American convention of the Antiochian Orthodox Christian Church voted in July in Los Angeles to ask its mother church in Syria for autonomy. Archbishop Philip Saliba, the church's North American primate, declared that the United States and Canada represent "the new Antioch,"

AP/Wide World Photos

At the Baha'i Shrine of the Bab in Haifa, Israel, 19 terraces with gardens, waterfalls, and staircases were dedicated in May, marking the completion of a project that began in the 1930s.

referring to the ancient city (located in present-day Turkey) in which followers of Christ were first called Christians.

The Rev. Arthur Peacocke, an English biochemist and Anglican priest, received the $1 million Templeton Prize for Progress in Religion for his work exploring the relationship between science and theology. (*See* BIOGRAPHIES.) In July officials in Nepal installed Preeti Shakya, a four-year-old girl from Kathmandu, as the new Kumari, a virgin goddess revered by both Hindus and Buddhists.

Preserving Religious Heritage. The UN General Assembly adopted a resolution in May calling on governments to "exert their utmost efforts to ensure that religious sites are fully respected and protected" through initiatives including national legislation. Earlier during May representatives of the Vatican and an umbrella organization of Jewish groups issued a similar appeal, in which they said, "We are all the more disturbed when members of our own religious communities have been the offenders" against religious freedom.

The dedication in May of the Baha'i faith's 19 terraced shrine gardens in Haifa, Israel, drew about 4,500 people from 200 countries. The $250 million project began in the 1930s and was designed to represent the 19th-century religious leader known as the Bab and his first 18 followers. The Jewish Museum Berlin was officially opened in September with an exhibition emphasizing Jewish contributions to German culture. In August Tibetan Buddhist monks dedicated a 33-m (108-ft)-tall stupa, a commemorative shrine, in a Rocky Mountain valley in Colorado. It contained the ashes of Chogyam Trungpa Rinpoche, a Tibetan exile who took Buddhist teachings to the West, and was the largest religious project undertaken by native-born Americans who had embraced Buddhism.

Church and State. Reports from international monitoring groups indicated that Chinese authorities had forced thousands of Tibetan Buddhist monks and nuns to leave a religious study centre in Sichuan province in June because of what an official of the Sichuan Religious Affairs Bureau called "concerns about social stability." A Belgian court sentenced two Catholic nuns in June to 12 and 15 years in prison for complicity in the genocide in Rwanda in 1994 in which 800,000 people were killed. In Guatemala in June three military officers and a priest were convicted of the 1998 murder of Catholic Bishop Juan Gerardi, who headed the church's human rights office in that country.

Shoko Asahara, the leader of Japan's AUM Shinrikyo (Supreme Truth) sect, was ordered in July to pay $3.7 million in compensation to the families of four people killed in a 1994 nerve gas attack in the town of Matsumoto. The attack had been perpetrated by Asahara's group, which was also behind a better-known attack the following year in the Tokyo subway system in which 12 people were killed.

Catholic bishops in the Philippines issued a statement in June supporting what they called "the government's all-out war policy against lawless elements" of the Abu Sayyaf, a radical Islamic movement that attacked churches and clergy. Jagjit Singh Chauhan, a Sikh separatist, returned to India in June after 21 years of self-imposed exile in London and said he would continue to work for Khalistan, a homeland for Sikhs.

In the United States, federal officials took control of the Indianapolis Baptist Temple in February to satisfy a $6 million tax debt in what was believed to be the first time the federal government had seized a church. The independent congregation had stopped withholding federal income taxes and Social Security deductions from employee paychecks in 1984, claiming that it was not a legal entity and therefore not subject to taxation. Pres. George W. Bush proposed allowing religious organizations to receive government grants and contracts for social services. The proposal was approved by the House of Representatives in July but was stalled in the Senate. More than 250 leaders of faith-based groups organized a Progressive Religious Partnership in April in Washington, D.C., saying they wanted "to restore a progressive religious presence to its rightful place in the public square." The U.S. Supreme Court ruled 6–3 in June that public schools could not discriminate against student religious clubs on the basis of religion. In March a federal appeals court in Cincinnati ruled 9–4 that the Ohio state motto, "With God, all things are possible," was constitutionally acceptable if the state did not attribute the words to their biblical source.

(continued on page 308)

At the Rocky Mountain Shambhala Center near Red Feather Lakes, Colo., a Buddhist stupa, or commemorative shrine, was dedicated in August.

AP/Wide World Photos

SPECIAL REPORT

Christianity's Newest Converts

by Kenneth L. Woodward

Though 2001 will undoubtedly be remembered as the year that the terrorist attacks in the U.S. were attributed to Islamic radicals, that action reminded Christians in the U.S. and other Western countries that Islam claims the allegiance of 1.2 billion people worldwide, second only to Christianity itself, which claims some 2 billion devotees. During the year there was another significant revelation—that Christianity itself is now an essentially non-Western religion. In 1900, at the dawn of what American Protestants imagined would be "the Christian century," 80% of Christians were either European or North American. In 2000 statistics showed that 60% of Christians were citizens of the "two-thirds world"—Africa, Asia, and Latin America.

Specific comparisons demonstrate some of the dimensions of this demographic shift. In Nigeria alone, for example, there are seven times as many Anglicans as there are Episcopalians in the U.S. South Korea boasts a population of Presbyterians four times that of the U.S., and as of 2001 it was the first Asian country since the Philippines to have become majority Christian. In the past 10 years, the Assemblies of God have gained 438,000 new American members, but in Africa alone this Pentecostal denomination quadrupled its size, adding nearly 7,000,000 converts. More than 90% of Seventh-day Adventists, a 150-year-old millenarian movement that began in New York, now live outside North America, most of them in Brazil and sub-Saharan Africa.

As Christianity prospers in the less-developed world, it is shrinking in the West. Northern Europe is essentially post-Christian, a society in which religious affiliation functions essentially as an identity tag, and church attendance is declining in once staunchly Catholic Spain. In Scotland fewer than 10% of Christians attend church regularly, but in the Philippines the figure is nearly 70%. Even in the U.S., still the most religious of the world's advanced industrial societies, most of the growth in Christianity is attributed to immigration from Latin America and various non-Western countries. Within the Presbyterian Church (U.S.A.), for instance, the only growth has come through immigrants from South Korea. The effects on American Catholicism are especially pronounced. One in six priests serving in U.S. Catholic parishes in 2000 was imported from abroad, and among native-born Catholic seminarians, a disproportionate number were Asian Americans. Though the U.S. was once the primary source of new recruits for the Jesuits, India now reigns as the largest supplier of Jesuit seminarians.

In short, the map of world Christianity has been redrawn. For the first time in history, the majority of Christians can be found mainly among the poor, the marginalized, the powerless, and—in parts of Asia and the Middle East—the oppressed. The face of Christianity has also changed—it is no longer the white man's religion. As a result of this massive demographic shift, areas that were once considered Christian homelands have become the mission territories of the new millennium. Evangelists from Latin America, Asia, and Africa now hold crusades in cities such as London and Berlin. Aware that the future of the church lies in part in Africa, Pope John Paul II has made 10 pastoral visits to various countries there, more than to any other continent outside Europe. On February 21 the pope expanded the Sacred College of Cardinals to a record 184 members. Of the 135 cardinals eligible to elect the next pope, 41% hail from non-Western nations.

The changing face of the church was also manifest in shifting spheres of influence within mainline American Protestant denominations. In early 2001 the presiding bishops of the worldwide Anglican Communion met in North Carolina amid a rift between

the liberal Anglican churches of the West, notably the Episcopal Church, U.S.A., and the more conservative Anglican churches of Asia and Africa, over issues that included the ordination of women and homosexuals and the blessing of same-sex marriages. Unless a resolution is reached, there could be a major split within the Communion. The liberal Presbyterian Church (U.S.A.) was also feeling a rightward pull from its Korean American faithful, who also opposed the ordination of homosexuals.

The emergence of Christianity as a predominantly non-Western religion had many causes. In Latin America, Christianity arrived with the conquistadors in the 16th century and has continued to expand in part because of population explosion. Though South America is the largest Catholic continent in the world, in recent decades evangel-

Children at the Sacred Heart Roman Catholic Church in New Delhi light candles during Good Friday services on April 13.

AP/Wide World Photos

ical and Pentecostal Protestantism have made impressive inroads there. In India the spread of Christianity is mainly among the outcasts, who find in Christianity hope and dignity denied them by the caste system. In China, Christianity answers problems of meaning that Marxism fails to address. In Africa, where Christianity is growing faster than at any time or place in history, the faith originally introduced by missionaries has boomed following the collapse of European colonialism. Since then, sub-Saharan Africa has seen a wild proliferation of indigenous Christian churches and cults, many of them inspired by personal visions and prophesies. According to the *World Christian Encyclopedia,* there are now 33,800 different Christian denominations, the fastest growing of which are independent churches that have no ties to the historic Catholic and Protestant churches. Wherever it spreads, Christianity is also seen as the religion of the successful West—a spiritual way of life that is compatible with higher education, technology, and globalization.

From its very beginning, Christianity has always been a migratory religion, seeking to plant the gospel at the centre of whatever alien culture its missionaries could penetrate. In the process the gospel has been not only transplanted but also repeatedly reinterpreted according to the previously existing religious understandings. The same process exists today. In officially Roman Catholic Brazil, for instance, many church members still appease the old tribal deities brought over from Africa by slaves. In other parts of Latin America, Christians practice a hybrid form of piety that includes elements of native religions the Spaniards never really extinguished. Many Christians in China include veneration of their deceased but "living" ancestors as part of the worship services at certain times of the year. In India, where sin is traditionally identified with bad karma in this and previous lives, many converts interpret the cross to mean that Jesus's self-sacrifice removes their own karmic deficiencies and thus liberates their souls from future rebirths. Millions of Christians in Africa still turn to rituals of their tribal religions in time of crisis, especially toward warding off evil spirits. There, as in many other parts of the "two-thirds world," the fastest-growing form of Christianity is Pentecostalism, which offers exorcisms and other forms of healing, though in this case they are done in the name of Jesus Christ and against the native religions themselves. Conversely, many Christians who migrate from Asian countries where they were persecuted find American Christianity too secular, individualistic, and accepting of secular mores—especially the sexual variety—for their taste. In sum, Christianity for the first time in its history is truly a global religion—but it is also becoming increasingly diverse. The problem for the pope and other church leaders in the West is how to decide which elements of Western thought and culture are essential to the faith. Put differently, the question remains how far Christianity can bend toward accepting non-Western world views without compromising its own traditional doctrines about the nature of God and the uniqueness of Jesus Christ as Savior.

Kenneth L. Woodward, the religion editor of Newsweek *magazine, is also the author of* The Book of Miracles: The Meaning of the Miracle Stories in Christianity, Judaism, Buddhism, Hinduism, and Islam *(2000). This report is adapted from his article "The Changing Face of the Church," which first appeared in* Newsweek.

(continued from page 305)

Gatherings. The Maha Kumbh Mela, or "Great Pitcher Festival," drew some 110 million people to the city of Prayagraj (Allahabad), India, over 42 days in January and February. (*See* Sidebar.) The Hindu festival, held every 12 years, was also attended by the Dalai Lama, spiritual leader of Tibetan Buddhists, who joined the Shankaracharya of Kanchi, one of India's top four Hindu religious leaders, in a prayer on the banks of the Ganges River. The Dalai Lama also met with leaders of the World Hindu Council and criticized efforts to persuade adherents of one religious faith to convert to another. "I always believe it's safer and better and reasonable to keep one's own tradition or belief," he said. More than 150 cardinals from around the world assembled at the Vatican in May in the largest such gathering in history, during which several called for more power sharing and frank debate on important issues.

Demographics. Christianity remained the world's largest religion, claiming over two billion followers—nearly 33% of the Earth's population—in mid-2001. The most dramatic growth in Christianity in recent years had been registered in Asia, Africa, and Latin America. (*See* Special Report.)

In September Cardinal Cormac Murphy-O'Connor told a gathering of priests in Leeds, Eng., that Christianity had "almost been vanquished" as a backdrop for people's lives in Great Britain. A World Council of Churches delegation to the Middle East reported in August that violence in the region was leading Christians to emigrate, spurring fears that "the holy sites of Christianity will become museums." The American Jewish Identity Survey found that the number of American Jews who identified with another religion had more than doubled in the past decade, to 1.4 million, while an additional 1.4 million American Jews said they are secular or have no religion at all, leaving just 51% of American Jews who say they are Jewish by religion.

(DARRELL J. TURNER)

Maha Kumbh Mela

Millions of pilgrims, many of whom had traveled for days to participate in the Maha Kumbh Mela—"Great Pitcher Festival"—walked to the various camps set up on the sandy plains along the Ganges River. About 110 million people, including more than 65,000 foreigners, gathered for the Hindu festival; this was believed to be the largest-ever congregation of people on the planet for a single purpose. The pilgrims went to the city of Allahabad (newly renamed Prayagraj), where the holy rivers Ganges, Yamuna, and the invisible, mythical Saraswati converge, to wash away their sins. A dip in the river, Hindus believe, ensures *moksha,* liberation from the cycle of life, death, and rebirth. According to Hindu mythology, gods and demons fought a battle in the sky over a pot containing the nectar of immortality. During the battle four drops of nectar fell at four different sites. Accordingly, Maha Kumbh Mela is held, on a rotation basis, every three years in one of four different cities (Nasik, Ujjain, Haridwar, and Allahabad) and thus returns to the same city every 12 years. The Allahabad festival is considered the holiest, and the 2001 event was considered especially propitious because of an unusual alignment of the Sun, Moon, and Jupiter that occurred only every 144 years. (SHANTHA UDDIN)

AP/Wide World Photos

Social Protection

The economic **SLOWDOWN** and September 11 terrorist attacks delayed anticipated **REFORMS** for welfare, Social Security, and Medicare in the U.S.; human rights **TRIBUNALS** pursued cross-nation **PROSECUTIONS**; and refugees, particularly those from **AFGHANISTAN**, strained international resources.

BENEFITS AND PROGRAMS

The financial viability of social protection programs continued to be a matter of worldwide concern. In 2001 many countries restructured their various schemes with a view to ensuring their long-term stability. In the process the pros and cons of private elements in public social protection programs were debated as well as the question of what was the "right" public-private mix for each scheme. Governments and social security administrators also strove to improve the delivery of social services and to give more people access to benefits.

North America. As with so many other areas of life, social protection was deeply affected by the terrorist attacks in the United States on September 11 and by the nation's prolonged economic downturn. High-priority legislation to provide prescription drug assistance for Medicare patients and federal support for faith-based charities was relegated, at least temporarily, to a back burner. Pledges that the Social Security Trust Fund would not be used to finance other needs were broken. Greater stress was put on the welfare system by an explosion of jobless workers. For the most part, as the federal government turned to more immediate concerns, social welfare activity was limited to debate, studies, and postponed action.

The two giant social programs for the elderly, Social Security and Medicare, had received good news early in the year when the funds' trustees reported that both would be solvent longer than previously predicted—until 2038 for Social Security, a year longer than had been forecast earlier, and 2029 for Medicare, four years longer. Nevertheless, concerns about the financial health of Social Security, which in 2001 covered some 45,526,000 retired and disabled persons, continued because of the approaching retirement of approximately 77,000,000 baby boomers and the increasing life span of beneficiaries. In 2001 three to four workers supported one retiree; that ratio was expected to be just two to one by about 2030. Past strategies for dealing with the developing demographic problems centred mainly on such "tune-ups" as reducing benefits, increasing payroll taxes, and raising the retirement age (already slated to rise gradually from 65 to 67).

U.S. Pres. George W. Bush favoured a plan for totally overhauling the system by partially privatizing it and allowing individual workers to invest a percentage of their payroll taxes in personal accounts. These, it was argued, would earn greater returns than the Trust Fund's more conservative investments. Opponents of that idea contended that it would deplete the Trust Fund more quickly and could be disastrous for individuals if stock values collapsed.

Bush appointed a 16-member bipartisan commission in May to explore the issue and recommend solutions. Although it was a bipartisan group, critics charged that it was stacked with proponents of privatization. The commission announced in December that it had agreed unanimously on three options, all of which would rely on personal retirement investment accounts, reduce traditional benefits for retirees, and require further actions for long-term sustainability.

The government announced a cost-of-living increase of 2.6% in Social Security benefits starting in January 2002. The average retiree would get $874 a month, up $22 from the $852 in 2001, and the average couple would receive $1,458 a month, an increase of $36. By law, annual increases in Social Security payments must equal increases in the consumer price index.

Disagreement also flared over a cornerstone of the president's "compassionate conservatism," his faith-based initiative for dealing with social problems. The administration wanted to extend federal financing for the charitable work of religious groups and make it easier for individuals to contribute to them. Proponents of the plan argued that religious organizations could reach some individuals with food, housing, job training, and additional assistance when many other types of social initiatives could not. Critics voiced concerns about violating First Amendment guarantees of separation of church and state. They raised the possibility that the plan would permit religious organizations to hire only members of their own faith and would exempt them from state and local laws that forbid discrimination in hiring based on sexual orientation.

In a delicate constitutional balancing act, the U.S. House of Representatives narrowly approved a watered-down version of the Bush plan. It would allow faith-based groups to use federal aid for religious activities if they received it indirectly (through vouchers, for example) and if they kept religious activities separate from social services and allowed those they helped to refrain from religious observances. The measure also allowed tax deductions for small donations for taxpayers who did not itemize their deductions. Late in 2001, faced with strong Democratic opposition in the Senate and pressures from the war on terrorism, Bush dropped the most controversial aspects of his proposal.

The upbeat report on Medicare's financial condition was tempered by studies showing that dramatic increases in the cost of prescription drugs could create serious problems. One study by a nonprofit, nonpartisan group found that spending on these drugs had risen 18.8% in 2000 to $131.9 billion. With large budget surpluses forecast early in 2001, both political parties backed legislation to add some kind of prescription drug coverage for the 40 million elderly and disabled Americans who had Medicare, but they disagreed on how to do it. Democrats generally favoured working through Medicare, while the administration looked to private insurers. By the end of the year, however, the window of opportunity that was open earlier had been closed by the recession and the costs of fighting terrorism. No action was taken, and hopes faded for any in 2002, which was a midterm election year.

In addition, the administration pushed to increase enrollment of Medicare recipients in health maintenance organizations (HMOs). In 2001 slightly more than 14% of Medicare beneficiaries were already enrolled. A potential setback to greater participation occurred when 58 HMOs serving 536,000 people announced that they would withdraw from the Medicare program in 2002.

As efforts bogged down at the federal level, states began setting up programs of their own to help low-income Medicare recipients buy prescription drugs. For example, Pennsylvania paid part of the cost of each prescription, while California and Florida put caps on how much pharmacies could charge elderly customers. By the end of the year, more than half of the states had taken steps to help with drug costs.

Welfare moved back into the spotlight in the U.S. Massive layoffs of workers following the terrorist attacks created unexpected problems for the social protection system just as Congress began to gear up for reauthorization of the 1996 welfare reform act in 2002. Pulled by the booming job market and pushed by tighter laws that limited their eligibility for welfare, nearly seven million people had left welfare rolls since 1996. Meanwhile, the U.S. Census Bureau reported that the number of people in the nation living in poverty fell in 1999 for the fourth consecutive year—to 11.8%, compared with 13.7% in 1996.

Despite those encouraging numbers and even before the terrorist impact, critics of the new welfare system had questioned how well it could withstand a weakening of the national economy. Moreover, they argued, people still on welfare rolls were those who had the most serious problems and needed as much, or more, federal spending to help them escape. There was also concern about many of those who had left welfare. The Urban Institute in Washington, D.C., reported that one-third of former recipients had to skip meals or eat less and that 46% had not been able to pay their rent or utility bills during the previous year. Supporters of the 1996 overhaul, on the other hand, claimed that the new safety net was the strongest ever and pointed out that welfare rolls continued to decline in some states even as unemployment there rose.

In September Health and Human Services Secretary Tommy G. Thompson announced a series of national "listening and discussion" sessions to air issues and ideas about the coming welfare reauthorization. One of those issues was poverty among the young. Although conditions had improved since 1993, when child poverty reached its peak, children under 18 continued to have a higher poverty rate than any other age group. Democrats pressed for action in areas such as affordability and availability of day care, restoration of cuts in food stamps and Medicaid for immigrants, and an increase in the minimum wage, which had not been raised since 1997.

A senior citizen purchases drugs at a pharmacy in Springfield, Ill., in May; how to add prescription drug coverage for the 40 million elderly and disabled Americans who had Medicare was the subject of debate during the year.

AP/Wide World Photos

Republicans generally favoured tax credits and more money for policies that emphasized work and reductions in single-parent families.

Welfare reform also was a major issue in Canada, where Ontario, the most populous province, announced plans to impose the toughest rules ever in Canada for welfare recipients. Persons would be required to pass a literacy test before they could receive public assistance, and benefits would be cut off to those who had drug or alcohol problems and had refused treatment for them. Anyone who failed the literacy test would be required to enroll in a workfare program.

Critics labeled the measure mean-spirited and overly harsh and said it was a possible violation of Ontario's human rights code. Officials responded that those receiving assistance needed to be pushed toward independence. They said that welfare rolls in Ontario had been cut by 60% in six years, but those who remained on them were the toughest cases.

In other action the Canadian government raised the maximum pensionable earnings for 2001 under the Canada Pension Plan by Can$700 (Can$1 = about U.S. $0.63) to Can$38,300. The contribution rate was increased to 4.3% for employees and 3.9% for employers, which brought the maximum employee contribution, after a basic Can$3,500 exemption, to Can$1,496.40 per year.

Europe. Portugal endowed itself with a new framework law on social protection, which came into force in February. France modernized its social protection system by introducing new benefits, such as a "parental attendance allowance," to allow the parents of seriously ill children to take time off from work. In Romania the social protection system was adapted to new socioeconomic realities in that survivors' pensions were now also granted not only to widows but also to widowers.

In Poland a discussion was under way to reform agricultural social insurance in order to build in mechanisms for structural reform based on solutions used in the European Union. The Netherlands took another step toward integrating the special system for civil servants into the general system for employee benefits when special unemployment regulations for employees in public service were abolished. Earlier, civil servants had been covered under the general Disability Benefits Act.

Ireland took measures to reduce long-term costs related to disability benefits. The government encouraged disabled

AP/Wide World Photos

An elderly opponent of a proposed pension-reform program in Russia attempts to tear a banner from the hands of pension-reform supporters in front of the State Duma in Moscow on July 5.

people to return to work by allowing them to retain part of their benefits during the first few years of employment after having been on government disability benefits. Beginning in April social security contributions in Italy were waived for those employees eligible for a seniority pension who postponed their retirement.

In Russia a pension-reform program that would create a three-pillar system was brought before the State Duma (parliament) in the summer and was expected to come into force in 2002. Latvia made progress in the construction of its three-pillar pension program. The law on funded state pensions went into force in July, establishing the legal basis for a capital-funded second pillar of the system that, together with the first pay-as-you-go pillar, formed the compulsory government scheme.

In the United Kingdom "stakeholder pensions" became a reality in April. The stakeholder pension was initially foreseen as a low-cost supplement to the basic government pension for people without an occupational pension or other form of privately funded pension arrangements, but its scope was broadened to allow the inclusion of people who either had personal pensions or were members of occupational programs.

In Germany pension-reform legislation was enacted in May, providing for government support for supplementary pensions in the form of cash subsidies or tax relief. At the same time, it was decided to reduce slightly and gradually the main (first) pillar of the system, essentially by introducing changes in the pension adjustment so that the replacement rate would decline from 70% to 67% of average net wages by 2030. Low-income pensioners were granted entitlement to a minimum income equal to 115% of the social assistance payment to a head of household. Workers were given the right to have a percentage of their wages paid into an occupational pension scheme. Vesting rights were modified, with employer-financed benefits becoming legally vested after five years and benefits from deferred remuneration becoming vested immediately. Earlier, one had to work for a company for 10 years to qualify for a pension.

To cut health care costs, Switzerland developed a new payment model for medicines; beginning in January advisory services provided by pharmacists and dispensing physicians were to be refunded by the social sickness insurance separately from the preparation and sales element of the costs of medicines in order to eliminate mechanisms that made it advantageous to dispense large quantities or particularly expensive medications. Austria restricted access to illness benefits as of January. Earlier, an employee's partner who was not covered in his or her own right by social sickness insurance automatically received coverage through the working partner. This coverage was now restricted to people with children. The European Court of Justice declared during the year that medical services fell within the freedom to provide services, one of the four basic freedoms in the Maastricht Treaty.

Industrialized Asia and the Pacific. In June Australia passed legislation that provided for the split of superannuation (mandatory occupational pension) entitlements upon the breakdown of a marriage, whether by agreement or court order. Either a new account would be created in the superannuation fund for the nonmember spouse, or the nonmember's interest would be rolled over into a savings account or similar regulated product.

Thailand's Securities and Exchange Commission formally approved the framework for a new system of individual retirement mutual funds, and the Revenue Department made it known that it would grant tax deductions for personal contributions to those funds. In Singapore the health minister announced the creation of a voluntary long-term-care program based on insurance underwriting principles, which the government would subsidize.

In Japan the Ministry of Health and Welfare and the Ministry of Labour were merged in January to create a more transparent administration with more effective political leadership. Also in January the Medical Care Insurance Reform Act went into force. It was designed to cope with rising health care expenditures, essentially by revising the co-payment system. A new cost-sharing system for patients over the age of 70 was introduced, moving from flat-rate to percentage contributions; the "high-cost medical benefits scheme" was also revised, with people now having to self-finance larger shares of medical expenses before receiving a benefit.

South Korea's government proposed to introduce a system of individual medical savings accounts. It would be possible to withdraw funds from the account, up to a specified limit, to pay for medical expenses. The public health care system would cover amounts exceeding that limit. Hong Kong's Social Welfare Department made a similar proposal in relation to medical expenses after retirement.

Emerging and Less-Developed Countries. Many social protection systems in less-developed countries in Africa and Asia continued to suffer from financial imbalances stemming from unfavourable economic conditions. Nonetheless, efforts were made to extend coverage, provide better benefits and services, and proceed to structural reform.

Uganda worked on implementing legislation adopted in 2000 to transform the National Social Security Fund, established in 1967 as a provident fund, into a social insurance pension scheme. In order to be able to finance future unemployment benefits in addition to existing retirement benefits, the Board of the Nigeria Social Insurance Trust Fund approved a new broader basis for calculating members' contributions, setting higher contribution rates and a new ceiling on insurable earnings.

A health insurance program for civil servants was established in Rwanda and became operational in March. The program was designed to provide protection for the whole family; in cases where both spouses were civil servants, only one was required to contribute. In Tunisia a major reform of health insurance was under way. At the end of the process, Tunisia would possess a basic unified compulsory scheme (covering both public and private sectors) that would guarantee coverage for the most prevalent forms of sickness and an optional complementary program whose management would be open to both social security funds and private insurance companies.

The Indonesian government announced that it would abolish the rules that prevented a pension fund from investing more than 20% of its assets in securities of any single issuer, a move essentially aimed at stimulating pension fund investment in government bonds. To speed up administrative procedures and increase client satisfaction, the Social Security Organization of Iran worked on a database that would cover all of the people that it insured, an exercise concerning approximately 26 million employees.

Several Caribbean nations were able to improve their social benefits and services. In Belize a package to modernize social security was introduced. The access to a number of benefits was eased in the British Virgin Islands, and in the Netherlands Antilles the Law on Medical Insurance was amended so as to extend its coverage to retired workers and their family members aged 60 and over.

In Latin America the trend continued for countries to introduce private elements into government-operated social protection programs. In Ecuador the pros and cons of such a mixed system for retirement pensions were discussed throughout the year. In Venezuela a presidential commission tabled a proposal that provided for a substantial proportion of a person's social security contribution to go into funded personal pension accounts that would be managed by the pension fund administrator of the individual's choice.

(CHRISTIANE KUPTSCH; DAVID M. MAZIE)

HUMAN RIGHTS

Special attention was given during 2001 to racial discrimination, efforts to end the impunity of major human rights abusers, the expansion of the ethnic conflicts in southeastern Europe to Macedonia, and problems associated with the rapidly growing number of refugees in the world community. In addition, for the first time, major economic and health issues took their place as the focus of international human rights attention. Concerns about economic globalization and the HIV/AIDS pandemic and its treatment received long-overdue recognition as major human rights issues. Finally, the September 11 attacks in the United States and their aftermath raised a number of major issues of human rights concern related to terrorism and to resulting antiterrorism efforts.

Racial and Ethnic Discrimination. The United Nations targeted racial and ethnic discrimination as an issue deserving special attention through the convening of a World Conference Against Racism in Durban, S.Af., in August. A major controversy arose at the conference and in the regional preparatory meetings that preceded it over language proposed for inclusion in the conference report that sought to equate Zionism with racism and also that called for financial reparations for the practice of slavery, particularly in the context of the transatlantic slave trade in the 16th through the early 19th century.

Compromise language finally was adopted that deleted mention of Zionism but did condemn the treatment of the Palestinians by Israel in the first instance and, in the second, that replaced references to monetary compensation for the practice of slavery with demands for debt forgiveness, greater access to markets, and poverty relief for countries in Africa and the less-developed world that were targets of the slave trade. That settlement was not reached, however, until after U.S. and Israeli government representatives withdrew from the conference in protest. Many other government delegates and nongovernmental organization participants also expressed concern that the emphasis given to the Zionism and reparations issues tended to undercut efforts to give attention to a broader range of problems associated with ongoing practices of racism, including the treatment of indigenous peoples.

Human Rights Abusers. The broadening application of criminal sanctions to major human rights abuses represented an important emerging trend in the international community. In addition to indictments and trials by the tribunals for former Yugoslavia and Rwanda established by the UN Security Council, a number of individual nations, such as Belgium and Spain, instituted criminal prosecutions under legislation that provided for the exercise of universal jurisdiction over torture and other major human rights violations by every nation in the world. The principles of criminal accountability and universal jurisdiction established by the tribunals for former Yugoslavia and Rwanda and by the case in the U.K. of former Chilean dictator Augusto Pinochet Ugarte resulted in the conviction by a Belgian court of four individuals accused of participation in the 1994 genocide of the Tutsi in Rwanda, the arrest and trial of former Yugoslav president Slobodan Milosevic by the International Criminal Tribunal for the Former Yugoslavia (ICTY), and the sentencing by the ICTY of Gen. Radislav Krstic, the most senior Bosnian Serb military official prosecuted thus far, to 46 years in prison for genocide and crimes against humanity associated with mass ethnic executions at Srebrenica. The extradition of Milosevic by Yugoslavia to the ICTY in The Netherlands and the initial hearings in his case marked the first time that a former head of state had been subjected to criminal trial for violation of international human rights standards. Milosevic was charged with having authorized and supervised the massacre and forced displacement and deportation of thousands of ethnic Albanians in Kosovo by Serbian forces acting under his control and direction as part of a campaign of terror and violence that included shelling and destruction of homes and villages and mass executions of unarmed civilians. The stakes were raised even further when he was charged with genocide during the 1992–95 war in Bosnia and Herzegovina. This was the first time that a head of state had been prosecuted for genocide violations. By the end of 2001, the former Yugoslavia and Rwanda tribunals had indicted 101 and 51 individuals, respectively.

Military action erupted in Macedonia in February when the frustrations of ethnic Albanians, who constituted over 22% of the population, bubbled over and both sides resorted to military means. An agreement brokered by NATO in August called for the ethnic Albanians to surrender their arms in return for a more substantial political role and greater rights to use their own language, especially in education. The Macedonian legislature began consideration of constitutional amendments guaranteeing minority rights.

An investigation of Israeli Prime Minister Ariel Sharon for massacres at Palestinian refugee camps in Lebanon was instituted by Belgian courts under the very broad criminal prosecution statute adopted in that country. Ricardo Miguel Cavallo, a naval officer during the period of the "dirty war" in Argentina, was ordered extradited from Mexico to Spain to stand trial for kidnapping and torture violations. Mexico was believed to be the first country in Latin America to have applied the doctrine of universal jurisdiction. (*See* LAW, CRIME, AND LAW ENFORCEMENT: *International Law*.)

Efforts were also under way to establish special courts to try individuals suspected of massive human rights crimes in Cambodia, East Timor, and Sierra Leone and to constitute a permanent international tribunal, the International Criminal Court, that would have ongoing jurisdiction to apply criminal sanctions to a wide variety of international crimes wherever they might occur. Cambodia's National Assembly, after months of negotiation, approved the creation of a special court with both international and domestic judges to prosecute top members of that country's Khmer Rouge regime who supervised the extermination of an estimated 1.7 million people in the 1970s.

Economic and Social Rights. Increased recognition of economic and social rights as part of the human rights equation was observed throughout the year. Health needs associated with HIV and AIDS received attention as a result of a series of meetings in Africa following the XIII International AIDS Conference, held in South Africa in 2000. Several countries challenged pharmaceutical companies to make HIV medications more readily available in the less-developed world by permitting the manufacture of those medications in generic form. This would substantially reduce the cost of the treatments and make them more accessible to very-low-income populations, particularly in Africa, where the incidence of HIV/AIDS exceeded 25% of the population in many countries. Cipla Ltd., an Indian company that made generic drugs, announced just such a plan in February, and in April a lawsuit brought by 39 major pharmaceutical firms that had sought to block a law allowing South Africa to manufacture or import low-priced versions of anti-AIDS drugs was dropped.

Large-scale antiglobalization demonstrations took place in a number of cities, including Washington, D.C.; Quebec City; and Genoa, Italy, targeting major international trade and banking institutions such as the World Trade Organization (WTO), the World Bank,

The rising incidence of human trafficking in Western Europe led Britain during the year to install X-ray scanners in ports around the country that could detect passengers hidden inside trucks.

AFP Worldwide

and the International Monetary Fund. The demonstrators sought improved trade and credit policies for countries in the less-developed world and a greater voice by poor nations in determining international credit and development assistance policies. The demonstrators in Quebec City in April objected to consideration at the third Summit of the Americas of a proposed Free Trade Area of the Americas that would strengthen protections for foreign investments and patents and thereby make it more difficult for poor nations to secure loans and provide social services for their citizens. In July Italian police were accused of having used particularly brutal tactics against demonstrators at the Group of Eight economic summit meeting in Genoa. One protester was fatally shot; more than 200 were reported injured; and nearly 300 were arrested. Similar disruptions were threatened for the WTO meetings that began November 9 in Doha, Qatar, particularly in light of the terrorism concerns in that part of the world raised as a result of the international bombing campaign in Afghanistan, but massive security preparations kept protests to a minimum in Qatar.

Terrorism. The September 11 terrorist attacks in the U.S. and the American reaction to them generated a number of human rights concerns. The extensive aerial bombardment of Afghanistan raised fears about deaths and injury to civilians caused by "collateral damage," possibly in violation of the humanitarian protections of the Geneva Conventions. Within the U.S. there were a number of incidents of harassment, hate crimes, and discriminatory treatment aimed at those of Middle Eastern or South Asian appearance. The concern with increased security in airports, government offices, postal facilities, and public buildings was also accompanied by questions of freedom of access, individual rights in cases of searches of persons or property, and racial and ethnic profiling. Large-scale detention of suspected terrorists and a presidential order authorizing the use of military tribunals to prosecute aliens, including those residing in the U.S., drew wide criticism from Congress and civil liberties groups. In November a proposed UN treaty designed to combat terrorism was blocked by the demand of the 57-member Organization of the Islamic Conference that anti-Israeli militants and other national liberation groups be exempted from the pact's provisions.

(MORTON SKLAR)

REFUGEES AND INTERNATIONAL MIGRATION

At the beginning of 2001, the worldwide number of refugees and persons of concern to the Office of the United Nations High Commissioner for Refugees (UNHCR) decreased slightly, from 22,300,000 in 1999 to 21,800,000 in 2000. The latter figure included some 12,000,000 recognized refugees, 786,000 returnees, 914,000 asylum seekers, and about 8,000,000 other persons requiring protection or assistance.

During the year a process was launched to revitalize the international protection regime; Global Consultations on International Protection coincided with the 50th anniversary of the 1951 Convention Relating to the Status of Refugees. These wide-ranging consultations involved states, legal experts, nongovernmental organizations, regional bodies, and refugees themselves.

The challenges facing humanitarian responses to refugee and international migration issues continued to be spread across the globe. The main durable solutions for refugees—i.e., repatriation and local integration and resettlement—were consistently pursued. Encouragingly, there were many successful resolutions of the dilemmas facing exiled or displaced persons, such as in East Timor (a former Portuguese colony that had been invaded by Indonesia in 1975) and in the Balkans. In other instances the desire to return to the country of origin—the preferred solution for many—was dashed by persistent or new outbreaks of conflict or political and economic disruption.

In Africa the areas of particular concern remained Guinea, Sierra Leone, and Liberia, where ongoing conflict plagued the northern area, particularly in Lofa county. Violence and insecurity along Guinea's border with Sierra Leone posed considerable challenges. The issues of "safe access" to refugees for humanitarian workers and "safe passage" for the displaced were priorities for all concerned. Since early 2001 UNHCR, working together with governmental and fellow agency partners, had successfully relocated 58,000 Sierra Leonean refugees to new and more secure sites away from the border and had facilitated the repatriation of another 27,000 Sierra Leonean refugees by boat.

In the Democratic Republic of the Congo (DRC), war displaced an estimated 1,800,000 people internally and forced another 350,000 refugees to seek sanctuary in neighbouring countries. Following Joseph Kabila's installation in January as president of the DRC (*see* BIOGRAPHIES), the international community hoped for continued progress in the implementation of the Lusaka cease-fire agreement. An accord would help pave the way for reinforced humanitarian protection and assistance to refugees from neighbouring countries who had sought safe haven within the DRC as well as for the commencement of a repatriation operation for hundreds of thousands of Congolese nationals who had fled the conflict in the DRC.

The Arusha peace process in Burundi continued to move forward, but many obstacles remained. When conditions became settled, UNHCR, with the support of the governments of Burundi and Tanzania, would work toward the voluntary repatriation of 567,000 Burundian refugees, most of whom were in Tanzania.

Other long-standing conflicts, however, showed fewer signs of progress. The civil war in The Sudan dragged on—leaving some 443,000 refugees in exile and huge numbers internally displaced. Peace initiatives showed limited progress. Angola presented one of the continent's most acute humanitarian crises, with an estimated four million displaced and war-affected people. Nearly 350,000 Angolan refugees were outside their country, mainly in the DRC and Zambia.

Afghanistan continued to be the source of one of the largest, most complex, and intractable humanitarian situations ever known. More than 20 years after the first exodus to Iran and Pakistan—and even after the repatriation of more than four million people—Afghans constituted the world's largest refugee population. By late October 2001, an estimated 1.2 million or more people were displaced within the country, and approximately 7.5 million Afghans required assistance, protection, or both. Even before the international military strikes began in Afghanistan in October, Afghans were on the move. Beginning in late August the Australian government triggered an international furor when it refused entry to boatloads of asylum seekers, mainly Afghans, who had sailed from Indonesia in an attempt to reach Australian territory, and forcibly transferred them to refugee camps in other South Pacific countries. (*See* WORLD AFFAIRS: *Australia.*) Afghan refugees were uprooted by myriad factors, including the cumulative pressures of an endless war; the lack of respect for basic human rights, particularly for women; the most severe drought in decades; and the lack of ready

Some of the more than 400 refugees who were rescued from a stranded Indonesian ferry in the Indian Ocean gather on the deck of a Norwegian cargo ship off the coast of Christmas Island on August 27.

AP/Wide World Photos

sources of income. Prior to September acute asylum and donor fatigue had compounded the challenges facing humanitarian efforts to address these needs. The first priority was to provide immediate assistance for the coming winter months. At the same time, future needs were being assessed in the event that the conflict was resolved; a return movement would likely be large-scale and require the mobilization of huge resources to ensure sustainable return, reintegration, and stability.

In Southeast Asia UNHCR completed its shelter program in East Timor and began phasing down activities during the second half of the year. After the murder of UNHCR staff in Atambua in September 2000, West Timor remained for many months under UN security Phase V, which precluded any permanent UN presence. In mid-2001 UNHCR, working together with other concerned parties, reviewed its position in light of the changing security situation and the peaceful Timorese elections in August. Given the increased postelection interest in voluntary repatriation among the refugees in West Timor and cooperation by the Indonesian government, many believed that the remaining refugees would return home by mid-2002.

The Balkans continued to cause serious concern. By August the conflict in Macedonia between the government and ethnic Albanians had already displaced more than 140,000 people, including some 81,000 persons to neighbouring Kosovo (a province of Serbia, Yugos.), 12,000 others to the south of Serbia, and more than 50,000 who were internally displaced. The cease-fire agreement negotiated by NATO in mid-August was enforced over the next few months, and as a result, by late 2001 some 57,000 refugees had been able to return from Kosovo and southern Serbia. The processes of democratic change in Yugoslavia and Croatia raised new hopes of achieving durable solutions for the 1.2 million people still displaced from their homes in these countries and in Bosnia and Herzegovina. UNHCR anticipated that of the 700,000 refugees and displaced people in Serbia, most would not return home. National reconstruction and development programs gave priority to the integration needs of these people. Nevertheless, ongoing efforts to make return a real option were also essential in order to consolidate peace in the region.

The return of displaced persons, notably the Serb minority, to Kosovo was a more problematic issue. Tensions remained extremely high between ethnic Albanians and non-Albanians, particularly with the small remaining Serb community. UNHCR and its partners had to strike a balance between upholding the fundamental right of people to go home and the need to ensure their safety. A limited number of Serb returns to safe areas in Kosovo raised hopes for the reestablishment of multiethnic collaboration and reintegration.

In Western Europe an alarming growth was noted in the number of asylum seekers and the extent and nature of irregular migration issues, including human smuggling and trafficking. These trends indicated further evidence of a continuing cycle of violence, persecution, and ethnic conflict. Even stringent controls failed to dissuade desperate people from using desperate means—including employing the services of human smugglers—in an attempt to reach safety. There was a pressing need for consultation and collaboration in developing high-quality asylum systems among the European nations.

The major concern in the Americas during the first part of the year was the worsening conflict in Colombia, which resulted in escalating levels of violence and an increase in forced displacement. Struggles for territorial control in strategically important border areas intensified, which increased concerns in neighbouring countries over national security and possible mass influxes of refugees. The number of individual Colombians recognized as refugees continued to rise. From January to August, 121,115 persons left the country permanently by air, compared with approximately 125,000 during all of 2000. In addition, in Europe and North America, Colombians constituted the 12th largest group of asylum seekers, whereas in 2000 they had ranked only 21st.

Following the terrorist attacks in the United States, the U.S. government announced new rules that would allow its Immigration and Naturalization Service to detain immigrants suspected of committing crimes for 48 hours without filing charges against them and to deport terrorist suspects without submitting any evidence. Another new antiterrorist law granted the U.S. attorney general authority to certify and detain the spouses and children of asylum seekers who were found inadmissible on terrorism-related grounds. These measures were likely to have a far-reaching effect on the asylum process, both in the U.S. and elsewhere, with a risk of increased xenophobia and racist reactions. (UNHCR)

Sports and Games

In 2001 the year in sports was **DIVIDED** into two—the events held **PRIOR** to the September 11 terrorist **ATTACKS** in the U.S. and those that occurred afterward, many of which were **POSTPONED** or went on without **AMERICAN** athletes.

In the wake of the Sept. 11, 2001, terrorist attacks in the U.S., the sporting world paused momentarily to pay its respects. Stadiums across North America stood empty and silent as professional football, ice hockey, and baseball and college games were postponed or canceled. The National Association for Stock Car Auto Racing's (NASCAR's) mighty race cars were similarly silenced, and Major League Soccer's regular season came to a premature close. The Ryder Cup in golf was postponed until 2002, and though the world archery championships took place as scheduled in Beijing, the Americans stayed home.

At the start of the year, football fans witnessed a blowout in the Super Bowl, the National Football League championship, held in Tampa Bay, Fla., on Jan. 28, 2001. Quarterback Trent Dilfer, aided by standout middle linebacker Ray Lewis (*see* BIOGRAPHIES), led the American Football Conference champion Baltimore Ravens to a 34–7 romp over the National Football Conference New York Giants.

Auto-racing fans mourned the death in February of seven-time NASCAR Winston Cup champion Dale Earnhardt, Sr., who perished in a fatal car accident in the final moments of the Daytona 500. (*See* OBITUARIES.)

American tennis player Jennifer Capriati made an impressive comeback, winning the Australian Open and the French Open, her first Grand Slam singles titles (*see* BIOGRAPHIES), and National Basketball Association superstar Michael Jordan made headlines in October when he abandoned retirement to play for the Washington Wizards.

In baseball the final game of the World Series drew the largest viewership in years as the New York Yankees faced the Arizona Diamondbacks, who won their first World Series in a thrilling seven-game finish and ended the Yankees' streak of three straight titles. San Francisco Giants slugger Barry Bonds (*see* BIOGRAPHIES) notched 73 home runs to break the record set just three seasons earlier by Mark McGwire of the St. Louis Cardinals.

An outbreak of foot-and-mouth disease in Europe led to the postponement in April of the last games of the Rugby Union Six Nations championship, which was finally won by England in October. In steeplechasing the disease forced the cancellation of numerous races in Great Britain and Ireland.

Preparations continued for the 2002 Winter Olympic Games in Salt Lake City, Utah, under new International Olympic Committee (IOC) chairman Jacques Rogge of Belgium. (*See* BIOGRAPHIES.) Meanwhile, China rejoiced when the IOC awarded Beijing the 2008 Summer Games, the country's first-ever Olympics. In association football (soccer), 32 nations qualified for the upcoming World Cup finals in 2002.

(GAVIN FORBES EHRINGER)

ARCHERY

In world archery competition, U.S. senior teams won two gold and two silver medals at the Fédération Internationale de Tir à l'Arc (FITA) world indoor target championships in Florence in March 2001. The U.S. junior teams held their own by winning two gold and one silver.

The senior men's recurve team of Richard ("Butch") Johnson, Joseph McGlyn, and Vic Wunderle defeated Russia in the gold medal round. The senior women's team took the silver medal in the recurve, behind the victorious Russians. The junior women's recurve team also earned the silver, losing to Ukraine in the final.

In the compound bow division, the senior women's team of Ashley Kamuf, Michelle Ragsdale, and Mary Zorn (who also won gold in the individual competition) edged France in the final. The Italians prevailed over the Americans to take the men's compound gold. The U.S. junior teams both won gold in the compound division.

The FITA world outdoor championships, held in Beijing, were not so kind to the U.S. team. Team members were scheduled to fly to China on the morning of September 11 but found themselves grounded after the terrorist attacks on the East Coast. The competition went on as scheduled on September 16–22, but without the Americans. Dejan Sitar of Slovenia won the men's individual compound title, and Ulrika Sjöwall of Sweden captured the women's. In the recurve championships, South Koreans showed the way, with Yeon Jung Ki and Park Sung Hyun winning the men's and women's divisions, respectively. Team gold medals went to Norway in the men's compound division and France in the women's compound. The South Korean men won the recurve gold, while in an upset the Chinese women gained the recurve team title for the host country.

At the U.S. National Field Archery Association (NFAA) indoor championships March 31–April 1, Ragsdale and George Ryals each won a shoot-off to break ties for the champions bowls in the professional freestyle competition. At the NFAA outdoor championships in July, Ragsdale made it a clean sweep, and the men's champions bowl went to Michael Anderson in a shoot-off.

(LARRY WISE)

AUTOMOBILE RACING

Grand Prix Racing. Grand Prix racing sustained its globally televised momentum throughout the 2001 season, although there was precious little evidence that this high-profile international sport could remain insulated from the turbulent events in the wider world over the next few years.

Sponsors and investors who bankrolled the high-technology sport in the belief that its global reach equated to something close to a commercial bargain in terms of TV viewership were nevertheless understandably nervous about committing sums that could approach an annual $70 million for title sponsorship of one of the top teams.

Second-guessing the future was a fruitless task, of course. As for the immediate past, in Formula One (F1) terms, 2001 was another season of decisive domination for the remarkable Michael Schumacher at the wheel of his scarlet Italian Ferrari. (*See* BIOGRAPHIES.) The 32-year-old German racked up another nine Grand Prix wins out of 17 races, memorably breaking Alain Prost's all-time career record of 51 wins.

By the end of the season, Schumacher had 53 race wins to his credit, in addition to a record number of Grand Prix Championship points scored. The only remaining barrier to be cleared was matching—and exceeding—the five world championships won by the legendary Juan Manuel Fangio of Argentina between 1951 and 1957. Few would doubt that Schumacher was on course to break that record.

Scottish driver David Coulthard drove his best season ever but was let down by uncharacteristic unreliability on the part of his machinery. His McLaren-Mercedes teammate Mika Hakkinen had a patchy year and decided to take a sabbatical in 2002. Both men won two races apiece, although it certainly should have been more.

By contrast, the Williams-BMW squad was on the rise. Ralf Schumacher won three races and his dynamic new teammate Juan Pablo Montoya just one. Montoya, nevertheless, was probably the most exciting new talent to emerge on the F1 scene since Michael Schumacher himself in 1991.

A telling index of the generally unremarkable performances delivered by most of the teams could be gauged from the fact that the Sauber-Petronas squad finished fourth in the Constructors' Championship behind Ferrari, McLaren, and Williams. Sauber, a staid and normally somewhat average team, had benefitted from a decent chassis and two motivated young drivers in Kimi Raikkonen and Nick Heidfeld.

By the end of the season, the chill winds of financial reality seemed to be blowing through the ranks of the F1 teams. Prost Grand Prix finished the season on the commercial ropes, battling for its very survival. Toyota might have been looming large on the horizon for 2002, but even the top team principals conceded there could be bumpy times ahead.

The 2001 season was also marked by the reintroduction of electronic control systems, most notably traction control. Ferrari had raised its rivals' suspicions by insisting that the reintroduction of such systems be deferred until the fifth race of the season in Spain.

When it came to it, nothing changed in terms of F1's status quo, and it was clear that Ferrari had no problems adapting to the new rules. Its rivals' hoped-for advantage under this new technical initiative simply did not materialize.

Grand Prix racing's popularity was challenged in Europe by the advent of two U.S.-style oval track races held at the Lausitzring in Germany and at Rockingham in Great Britain. Both were purpose-built brand-new facilities specifically catering to Championship Auto Racing Teams (CART) single-seaters, and both races were hugely well received. Sadly, a terrible accident in the German race ended the career of popular former Williams F1 driver Alex Zanardi, who had to have both legs amputated as a result of a high-speed collision with another competitor.

Although the standard of CART racing was of a very high quality, the American domestic series finished the year under a cloud of commercial and economic uncertainty. The economic consequences of the September 11 terrorist attacks formed only part of the downside. The split five years earlier between CART and the Indy Racing League (IRL), headed by Indianapolis (Ind.) Motor Speedway president Tony George, inevitably diluted both categories, but with Penske—American racing's blue-ribbon team and the U.S. equivalent of Ferrari—poised to desert CART to join the IRL full-time in 2002, CART faced a bleak future.

The one man who won, of course, was George. Not only would his Indianapolis 500 continue to thrive in the future, but the track also now played host to the U.S. Grand Prix, which was held in the immediate aftermath of the terrorist attacks. The race was won superbly by Hakkinen in the McLaren-Mercedes, but not before Montoya challenged at the front of the field.

Montoya had been the winner of the 2000 Indianapolis 500, so the crowds knew him and could identify with him. That in itself gave F1 a long-overdue boost in the U.S. Signs were that the American fans had reignited their interest in F1 for the first time since the late 1980s. It certainly seemed a promising development for the sport as a whole.

(ALAN HENRY)

U.S. Auto Racing. Tragedy and off-track turmoil notwithstanding, U.S. auto racing's major organizations posted another stirring—if less profitable—season. The death of Dale Earnhardt, Sr. (*see* OBITUARIES), a quarter of a mile from the finish of the Daytona 500—which was won by Chevrolet stablemate Michael Waltrip, with Earnhardt's son, Dale, Jr., second and Ford's Rusty Wallace third—began a season that

Michael Schumacher of Germany leaves the pit after refueling during the French Formula One Grand Prix on July 1.

AP/Wide World Photos

Increasing Safety in Auto Racing: A Winning Formula?

Automobile racing aficionados had never denied that part of the attraction of their favourite sport was the element of perceived danger. The skill of the drivers, the talent of the car constructors, and the rules of auto racing's sanctioning bodies were designed to balance the danger and thus maintain the element of exciting competition.

In 2000–01 that balance was sorely tested by four deaths within nine months in National Association for Stock Car Auto Racing (NASCAR) events; among those killed was Dale Earnhardt, Sr.—one of the icons of the sport—during the Daytona 500, an annual classic watched by millions via television. (*See* OBITUARIES.) Adding to the problem was the postponement at Texas Motor Speedway of an entire Championship Auto Racing Teams (CART) event because the drivers said they could not stand gravity loads at speeds in excess of 370 km/h (230 mph). The race had been scheduled despite a CART official's warning that the speedway's tight corners and high banks were unsuitable for CART vehicles.

AP/Wide World Photos

What proved to be a fatal collision occurred on the last lap of the Daytona 500: Dale Earnhardt, Sr.'s car (3) is hit by one driven by Ken Schrader.

In truth, NASCAR, CART, the Indy Racing League, and Grand Prix (Formula One) racing organizations had been keenly aware of the thin boundary between excitement and mortality for years. Money and racing's own success had altered the equation, however. Auto racing had become desirable entertainment for vast television audiences and filled racetracks accommodating crowds in excess of 100,000. The fan base reached far beyond the original cadre of enthusiasts. NASCAR, for instance, negotiated an eight-year contract for $212 million with NBC-TV and Fox TV. The races regularly won weekend ratings battles.

Drivers in the top series, who could earn more in one afternoon than the president of the U.S. did annually, remained the most frangible components of the man-machine combinations that provided the excitement and the dollars. The challenge facing auto-racing organizers was to find ways to enhance driver protection without lessening the sport's entertainment value.

To accomplish this, the sanctioning bodies continually refined rules prescribing vehicle construction, driver attire, the manner of racing, and the conditions on the track. In Earnhardt's accident, however—as well as in other crashes that had claimed the lives of NASCAR drivers Adam Petty and Kenny Irwin—the forces generated on the vehicle and other safety equipment upon impact were not survivable. Among the solutions floated for increasing driver safety were construction of "softer" walls at racetracks, but the idea that had attracted the most attention was the HANS (head and neck support) device. Now mandated for CART and its subsidiary series, the device was developed in the early 1980s by engineer Robert Hubbard and former sports car champion Jim Downing. The device, a collar-and-yoke system worn around the driver's neck and down the front of the shoulders, permitted normal movement of the head and neck but limited the extreme front-to-back and side-to-side movements that could make a crash fatal. Downing stated that his company equipped over 800 drivers from all series with the HANS device in the months immediately following Earnhardt's death. NASCAR made HANS-type devices voluntary, but most drivers, including Dale Earnhardt, Jr., and other stars, utilized it. NASCAR also announced the establishment of a research facility at Hickory, N.C., to develop new technology for race cars and driver equipment.

(ROBERT J. FENDELL)

changed the National Association for Stock Car Auto Racing (NASCAR) forever. It dragged the most uniquely American sanctioning body into major actions to increase driver safety. (*See* Sidebar.) Waltrip won $1,331,185 of the $9,291,741 Daytona 500 purse as 14 drivers shared 49 lead changes; the victory margin was a scant 0.124 sec.

The tragedy overshadowed the return after a 16-year absence of Dodge, which fielded three cars that finished in the Daytona top 10. Chevrolet's Jeff Gordon, the eventual Winston Cup season champion, went out 88 km (55 mi) from the finish. Gordon became a four-time season champ; he collected victories in the Brickyard 400 at the Indianapolis (Ind.) Motor Speedway, the second richest NASCAR event, and five other races. Gordon won nearly $11 million for the season.

CART pilots again invaded the IRL's domain and won the 85th Indianapolis 500. They swept the first six places. Brazilian Helio Castroneves, driving a Marlboro Team Penske Dallara Oldsmobile, beat teammate Gil de Ferran by 1.74 sec, followed by Michael Andretti, Jimmy Vasser, Bruno Junqueira, and NASCAR regular Tony Stewart. The first IRL finisher, a lap back, was Eliseo Salazar. IRL's Greg Ray led at the halfway point but completed only 192 of the 200 laps, and pole sitter Scott Sharp spun on the first lap. Castroneves took home $1,270,475 of the $9,610,325 purse. For Penske this was the 11th Indy 500 victory in 28 attempts; to become eligible to compete, he and the other two CART car owners, Chip Ganassi and Barry Green, had had to acquire IRL-conforming vehicles.

De Ferran in a Marlboro Team Penske Reynard Honda defended his CART season championship after a 21-event battle with ex-IRL champion Kenny Brack in a Team Rahal Lola Ford-Cosworth. Andretti, the lone American in the top 10, finished third in a Reynard Honda for Team Motorola.

Brack won four of CART's oval-track races, significant because major CART sponsor Marlboro announced that it would shift to the rival IRL, which competed only on ovals. CART was facing the ultimate loss of all three of its engine suppliers, angered over a late-season switch from a turbocharged to a normally aspirated formula for 2003. Honda and Ford said they could not produce such an engine so quickly. Toyota already had announced a shift to the IRL. During the season CART canceled two scheduled races, one in Brazil because of local politics and the other—which allegedly cost it a settlement in excess of $3.5 million—at the Texas Motor Speedway.

While the lure of the Indy 500 to sponsors and carmakers alike strengthened the IRL, the 13-race series for normally aspirated single-seaters continued to develop exciting new drivers. One of them, 22-year-old Sam Hornish, Jr., of Ohio, won the season championship for Panther Racing in a Pennzoil Dallara Oldsmobile. His closest competitor was Buddy Lazier; Sharp was third.

NASCAR's Busch Series, usually the Saturday feature at Winston Cup weekends, crowned Chevrolet's Kevin Harvick as champion. The Craftsman Truck title was won by Jack Sprague of Chevrolet over Ted Musgrave and Joe Ruttman, both in Dodges. (ROBERT J. FENDELL)

Rallies and Other Races. In the world rally championship circuit, Finnish driver Tommi Mäkinen (Mitsubishi) won his third straight Rally of Monte Carlo in January 2001. Mäkinen became the first driver to win the rally three years in a row since German Walter Rohrl accomplished the feat in 1984.

In late November British driver Richard Burns (Subaru), winner of the Rally New Zealand earlier in the year, became World Rally champion for the season. The schism in professional road racing in the U.S. continued with two distinct series. The Rolex 24 Hours of Daytona, a Grand American Road Racing Association event, was plagued by bad weather and the inability of the allegedly fastest SportsRacing Prototypes (SRPs) to survive that length of time. Instead, the winner came from the Grand Touring Super class, a Chevrolet Corvette driven by Ron Fellows, Chris Kneifel, Franck Freon, and Johnny O'Connell. Second was a Porsche-supported GT3R. The first SRP was 11th overall.

The rival American Le Mans Series watched Audi factory R8s dominate, beginning with the 12 Hours at Sebring and ending with the 1,611-km (1,001-mi) Petit Le Mans at Road Atlanta. Audi's Emanuele Pirro won the driver crown.

(ROBERT J. FENDELL; EDITOR)

BADMINTON

In 2001, for the first time in 21 years, a badminton player from India captured the prestigious All-England Championships. Pullela Gopichand defeated world number one Peter Gade of Denmark 17–14, 17–15 in a thrilling semifinal and Chinese national champion Chen Hong 15–12, 15–6 in the final. Gong Zhichao of China easily dismissed her teammate Zhou Mi for the women's singles crown, and in an all-Indonesian men's doubles final, Halim Haryanto and Tony Gunawan topped Sigit Budiarto and Chandra Wijaya. The championships also featured Chinese winners in women's doubles and mixed doubles.

The Sudirman Cup, a best-of-five-match mixed-team competition held every other year, was contested in Seville, Spain, on May 28–June 2. In the semifinals, China edged Denmark 3–2 in a match that included Gong Zhichao's demolition of reigning world champion Camilla Martin of Denmark 11–1, 11–0. China faced Indonesia in the final and, after losing the opening men's doubles match, won three matches in a row to capture the title 3–1.

The world championships were staged in Seville immediately after the Sudirman Cup. In the men's singles semifinals, Taufik Hidayat of Indonesia was leading his teammate Hendrawan until a groin injury forced him to retire. Hendrawan then defeated Gade for his first world championship title. In the men's doubles competition, Gunawan and Haryanto conquered defending champions Kim Dong Moon and Ha Tae Kwan of South Korea. When Martin fell victim to an early-round upset, Gong Zhichao became the favourite but lost to teammate and eventual women's champion Gong Ruina in the semifinals. Chinese players accounted for the remaining two titles as Gao Ling and Huang Sui won the women's doubles and Zhang Jun and Gao Ling took the mixed doubles.

At the World Grand Prix Finals held in Brunei in August, Xia Xuaneze became the first Chinese man to win a major badminton title in 2001 with a final-round victory over Indonesia's Marleve Mainaky. Gong Zhichao lost to Zhou Mi in the women's singles final. Gunawan and Wijaya successfully defended their doubles title, and Huang Nanyan and Yang Wei of China took the women's doubles. The only European winners were the Danish mixed-doubles team of Jens Eriksen and Mette Schjoldager.

(DONN GOBBIE)

BASEBALL

The eventful 2001 major league baseball season, delayed one week by the attacks on September 11, extended into November for the first time in history and featured a new home-run record by the San Francisco Giants' Barry Bonds (*see* BIOGRAPHIES) and a new World Series champion—the National League (NL) Arizona Diamondbacks, who ended the three-year reign of the American League (AL) New York Yankees in a dramatic seven-game series.

Bonds hit 73 home runs to shatter the mark of the St. Louis Cardinals' Mark McGwire, who hit 70 in 1998. At the same time, however, major league offensive totals decreased. Runs per game fell from 10.28 in 2000 to 9.55 in 2001, and only 12 players hit 40 or more home runs, 4 fewer than the previous season. Despite the debut of new stadiums in Milwaukee, Wis., and Pittsburgh, Pa., overall attendance was up only slightly, to an average of just over 30,000 per game.

World Series. The Diamondbacks scored two runs in the bottom of the ninth inning of game seven at home to defeat the Yankees 3–2 and win the World Series four games to three. By doing so, the Arizona team, which debuted in 1998, staged the quickest trip to a title of any franchise in major league history. The previous mark of five years to a championship was established by the Florida Marlins in 1997.

In the Series opener in Phoenix on October 27, the Diamondbacks routed the Yankees 9–1 before a record home crowd of 49,646. Curt Schilling, the team's star right-handed pitcher, worked seven strong innings for Arizona, while the Diamondbacks collected five runs off New York starter Mike Mussina in three innings. Craig Counsell and Luis Gonzalez hit home runs for the Diamondbacks.

In game two pitcher Randy Johnson, the left-handed ace for Arizona, authored a 4–0 shutout, yielding just three hits and striking out 11 in a complete-game performance. The Diamondbacks held a slim 1–0 lead into the seventh inning when Matt Williams clubbed a three-run home run off the Yankees' starter and loser, Andy Pettitte.

On October 30 the Series moved to Yankee Stadium, where Pres. George W. Bush tossed out the first pitch before an emotional crowd of 55,820 and Mariano Rivera threw the last pitch in a 2–1 game-three victory for the Yankees. New York's Roger Clemens pitched seven innings, by which time the Yankees had broken a 1–1 tie on a single by Scott Brosius. Earlier, Jorge Posada had hit a homer for the Yankees against Arizona's Brian Anderson.

The Diamondbacks were one out away from winning game four in Yankee Stadium on October 31 when Tino Martinez clubbed a two-out, two-run home run in the bottom of the ninth inning. In the bottom of the 10th, Derek Jeter hit a home run to provide the Yankees a dramatic 4–3 triumph that tied the Series at two games each. Both home runs came against Arizona's star relief pitcher, Byung-Hyun Kim, who came on in the eighth inning trying to protect a 3–1 lead for Schilling.

The Yankees accomplished another remarkable comeback in game five at Yankee Stadium the next night, which was the first time a World Series game ever had been played in November. Home runs by Steve Finley and Rod Barajas off Mussina staked Arizona to a 2–0 lead in the fifth inning. The Yankees, for the second consecutive night, were down by two runs with two outs in the ninth inning when Brosius hit a game-tying two-run home run off Kim. By the time the defending champions achieved a 3–2 triumph in 12 innings, it was, in fact, early the next morning. Few fans had departed, however, when Alfonso Soriano slashed a single to right field to score the winning run from second base and provide the Yankees a three-games-to-two lead.

When the Diamondbacks returned home for game six before a record Bank One Ballpark crowd of 49,707, they demolished the Yankees 15–2 to square the Series at three games each. The Diamondbacks knocked out Pettitte in two-plus innings and mounted a 12–0 margin by the third for Johnson, who cruised to his second Series victory with a seven-inning stint. The Diamondbacks' 22 hits broke a single-game Series record of 20, and the 13-run margin of victory was the second largest in Series history.

To win the final game on November 4, the Diamondbacks had to mount a rally against Rivera, one of the most accomplished relief pitchers in history. Arizona had fallen behind by 2–1 on an eighth-inning home run by Soriano. Tony Womack doubled-in one run to forge a 2–2 tie, and then Gonzalez hit a bases-loaded bloop single to score the winning run for the Diamondbacks. Johnson was credited with the victory, his third of the Series, by pitching 1⅓ innings of relief one night after he had hurled the Diamondbacks to victory in game six. In game seven he finished for Schilling, who had made his third start of the series. Johnson and Schilling shared Most Valuable Player (MVP) honours for the Series.

Play-offs. The Diamondbacks won the NL pennant by defeating the Atlanta Braves four games to one. Arizona clinched the pennant in Atlanta's Turner Field on October 21 by winning 3–2 on a two-run pinch home run by Erubiel Durazo and strong pitching by Johnson, who worked seven innings before giving way to Kim. Counsell was voted MVP of the National League Championship Series.

The Yankees claimed their 38th pennant one night later by routing the Seattle Mariners 12–3 at home to win the American League Championship Series (ALCS) four games to one. Paul O'Neill, Bernie Williams, and Martinez hit home runs for the Yankees, and Pettitte pitched 6⅓ innings to register his second victory of the ALCS, for which he was named series MVP.

The Diamondbacks won the first round of the NL play-offs, defeating the Cardinals three games to two, while the Braves advanced by sweeping the Houston Astros. In the AL the Yankees defeated the Oakland Athletics (A's) three games to two, despite losing the first two games at home, the first time a team had won a best-of-five series in that fashion. After losing game three 17–2, the Mariners had to win the last two games of their series against the Cleveland Indians to prevail three games to two.

The Mariners posted a regular-season record of 116–46 to win the AL West division by 14 games over the A's, who had the second best record in the major leagues (102–60) and qualified as the AL wild-card team. The 116 victories by Seattle tied the 1906 Chicago Cubs for the most ever. The Yankees romped in the AL East by 13½ games, and Cleveland won the AL Central by six games.

The Diamondbacks won the NL West division with a mark of 92–70, two games better than the Giants. The Braves won an unprecedented 10th consecutive division title by finishing first in the NL East. The Astros and Cardinals tied for first in the NL Central at 93–69. The Astros were crowned champions by virtue of winning the season series against the Cardinals, who earned a wild-card berth.

Individual Accomplishments. Ichiro Suzuki, a 28-year-old rookie from Japan, won the AL batting title for the Mariners by amassing 242 hits for a .350 average. Seattle's Bret Boone led the league with 141 runs batted in, and Alex Rodriguez of the Texas Rangers hit the most home runs, 52. Mark Mulder of Oakland led AL pitchers with 21 victories, though two others won 20 games, Seattle's Jamie Moyer and Clemens. Clemens won 16 straight decisions at one point, tying an AL record. Rivera of the Yankees led relief pitchers with 50 saves.

Larry Walker of the Colorado Rockies led the NL with a .350 batting average. Sammy Sosa of the Chicago Cubs batted in 160 runs and 64 home runs in his fourth straight season of 50 or more homers. Schilling and Matt Morris of the Cardinals each posted 22 victories; Johnson had 21; and Chicago's Jon Lieber had 20. Robb Nen of the Giants led NL relief pitchers with 45 saves. In an achievement that rivaled Bonds's, Rickey Henderson of San Diego broke Ty Cobb's all-time runs record by scoring his 2,246th; he finished the season with 2,248.

Pitchers Randy Johnson (left) and Curt Schilling of the Arizona Diamondbacks hold aloft the World Series Most Valuable Player trophy.

Jed Jacobsohn/Allsport

In postseason honours Suzuki was voted MVP and Rookie of the Year in the AL, a feat accomplished by only one other player—Fred Lynn of the Boston Red Sox in 1975. Albert Pujols of St. Louis was the NL Rookie of the Year. Bonds earned MVP honours in the NL for a record fourth time. Clemens won a record sixth Cy Young Award in the AL; Johnson earned his third straight NL Cy Young Award. Lou Piniella of Seattle and Larry Bowa of the Philadelphia Phillies were voted Manager of the Year in the AL and NL, respectively. Cal Ripken, Jr., of the Baltimore Orioles, Tony Gwynn of the Padres, and McGwire, each a decorated veteran, retired after the 2001 season.

Atsushi Mochizuki of Tokyo delivers a pitch against the Apopka, Fla., team en route to a 2–1 victory in the Little League World Series final game on August 26.

AP/Wide World Photos

Little League World Series. The Tokyo-Kitasuna team scored two runs in the sixth and final inning to beat Apopka, Fla., 2–1 on August 26 in South Williamsport, Pa., and win the Little League World Series title. Nobuhisa Baba delivered the winning hit as Japan won its fifth Little League championship. Tokyo-Kitasuna had advanced by beating Curaçao, Netherlands Antilles, 2–1; Apopka had advanced by whipping the Bronx, N.Y., team 8–2 for the U.S. championship. Earlier in the tournament, Florida had been victimized by a perfect game thrown by Danny Almonte of the Bronx, the first in the Little League World Series since 1957. After the conclusion of the tournament, it was discovered that Almonte was 14, an infraction of the Little League rules requiring players to turn 13 no earlier than August 1 in the season they are competing. Little League Baseball declared that the Bronx team had to forfeit all victories for the season as well as the team's third-place finish in the World Series. Rolando Paulino, the team's founder, and Felipe de Jesus Almonte, father of the pitcher, were banned for life from any further involvement in Little League.

(BOB VERDI)

Latin America. The 2001 Caribbean Series was held in Culiacán, Mex., on February 2–8. The Cibao Eagles (Aguilas Cibaeñas), representing the Dominican Republic, compiled a 4–2 record and won their third title. Mexico (Hermosillo Orangegrowers [Naranjeros]) and Venezuela (Lara Cardinals [Cardenales]) tied for second with 3–3 marks, while Puerto Rico (Caguas Creoles [Criollos]) was last with a 2–4 record.

Santiago de Cuba won its third consecutive Cuban championship. It defeated Granma in the quarterfinals, beat Camagüey in the semifinal round, and took four out of five games from Pinar del Río in the finals to win the title. Maels Rodríguez, a pitcher from the Sancti Spiritus team, set the Cuban all-time single-season record for strikeouts with 263. In addition to leading the league in strikeouts, Rodríguez also had the best earned run average (1.77) and was tied for the most victories (15).

Nelson Barrera, player-manager with Oaxaca, broke the Mexican League all-time home-run record held by Hector Espino when he hit his 454th homer. Barrera, aged 43, had played 25 years in the league. The Mexico City Tigers defeated the Mexico City Red Devils four games to two in the league's championship series. It was the Tigers' eighth—and second consecutive—league title.

During March, Major League Baseball sponsored exhibition games between big league teams in Valencia, Venez., and three Mexican cities (Culiacán, Hermosillo, and Mexico City) as part of its "Month of the Americas." The event was capped off by a regular-season opening series featuring the Toronto Blue Jays and Texas Rangers in San Juan, P.R.

(MILTON JAMAIL)

Japan. The Yakult Swallows beat the Osaka Kintetsu Buffaloes four games to one in the 2001 Japan Series. The Swallows claimed their fifth Japan Series title and their fourth in nine years. Swallows catcher Atsuya Furuta was named series Most Valuable Player (MVP) after having hit .500 with seven hits and one home run. He also finished second in the Central League's (CL's) 140-game regular season with a batting average of .324, behind the Yomiuri Giants' Hideki Matsui, who had a .333 average. The Swallows finished the regular season with 76 wins, one more than the defending champion Giants, who came close late in the season before suffering four straight losses at the very end. The Swallows' Roberto Petagine, leading the league with 39 home runs and 127 runs batted in, was named CL regular-season MVP. Left-handed starting pitcher Shugo Fujii and closer Shingo Takatsu led the league with 14 wins and 37 saves, respectively, for the team.

In the Pacific League (PL) the Buffaloes won their first crown since 1989 after having finished last in 1999 and 2000. The hard-hitting team ended the regular season two and a half games ahead of the Fukuoka Daiei Hawks. Buffaloes outfielder Karl ("Tuffy") Rhodes, who was named the PL's MVP, blasted 55 home runs to tie the all-time single-season Japanese record set by home-run king Sadaharu Oh in 1964. The biggest news for Japanese baseball in 2001 was Shigeo Nagashima's retirement as Giants manager. Nagashima had been extremely popular both as a player and as a manager.

(HIROKI NODA)

BASKETBALL

United States. *Professional.* In 2001 the Los Angeles Lakers continued to dominate the National Basketball Association (NBA). Head coach Phil Jackson at times during the season had to serve as both mediator and conciliator while trying to defuse the animosity between his superstars, Shaquille O'Neal and Kobe Bryant. Well before the 2001 play-offs opened, however, the Lakers again were functioning like a finely tuned machine, winning their last eight regular-season games.

The Lakers breezed through the Western Conference play-offs; the team won 11 straight games to reach the NBA finals unscathed. Heavily favoured over Eastern Conference representative Philadelphia, the Lakers were expected to sweep the 76ers in the best-of-seven series and repeat as NBA champions with a 15–0 record in postseason play. That would have made Jackson's team the first in NBA history to go unbeaten in every play-off round. The grand plan got derailed, however, by a 107–101 overtime loss to the inspired 76ers in game one.

Although the 2.16-m (7-ft 1-in), 143-kg (315-lb) O'Neal towered over him, 1.8-m (6-ft), 75-kg (165-lb) 76ers point guard Allen Iverson (*see* BIOGRAPHIES) was virtually unstoppable in the play-offs, as he had been all season. Iverson outscored O'Neal 48–44 in the opener, but injuries and fierce Los Angeles defensive pressure prevented the superquick guard from carrying his team to another victory. The next four games went to the Lakers, who wrapped up the title with a 108–96 victory in Philadelphia on June 15.

The NBA's youth movement accelerated sharply in the 2001 draft. The search to find another Michael Jordan dipped more deeply into the high-school ranks even while Jordan, who had become president of the Washington Wizards, made his second comeback as a player at age 38, also bringing back sellout crowds to see him. Of the first eight players drafted, four were making the jump directly from high school to the pros. They included the top two picks, Kwame Brown and Tyson Chandler, along with the fourth and eighth picks, Eddy Curry and DeSagana Diop, respectively.

The NBA also brought its Developmental League (NBDL) plans to fruition. Eight teams, with players at least 20 years old, opened a 56-game inaugural season in November. The NBDL play-offs were set for March 2002.

In the Women's National Basketball Association (WNBA), the Los Angeles Sparks swept to their first championship, defeating the Charlotte (N.C.) Sting in the finals. The Sparks' victory ended the Houston (Tex.) Comets' domination in each of the WNBA's first four seasons.

College. Duke University basketball coach Mike Krzyzewski and his Blue Devils were the consensus favourites to win the 2001 National Collegiate Athletic Association (NCAA) championship, but sentimental fans and media alike were pulling for the Arizona Wildcats and their coach, Lute Olson. The death of Olson's wife, Bobbi, on January 1 had brought an outpouring of sympathy from across the country.

After Bobbi's death, Olson's top assistant, Jim Rosborough, had taken over the reins temporarily, but Olson soon discovered that returning to work was therapy for grief. When he went back to the team, the Wildcats went on an emotional winning streak that launched them into the Final Four. That gave Olson—at 66 years and six months—a chance to become the oldest coach to capture an NCAA title; legendary Kansas coach Phog Allen was two months younger when he steered the Jayhawks to the 1952 crown.

It was not to be. Olson, whose Wildcats had won the title in 1997, was denied his second national championship when Arizona and Duke met on April 2 in the Minneapolis (Minn.) Metrodome. Duke was led by swingman Mike Dunleavy, who hit three straight three-point baskets in a second-half spree. After hitting just one basket in six attempts in the opening half, Dunleavy found the mark for 18 of his 21 points after the intermission. That sort of clutch shooting made the difference in the game. Dunleavy totaled five three-pointers in the championship showdown, and Blue Devil team captain Shane Battier played a critical role at the end of the game. The senior scored the needed baskets to help the Blue Devils survive repeated Arizona rallies and go on to clinch the final 82–72.

Jed Jacobsohn/Allsport

Lisa Leslie of the Los Angeles Sparks drives past Yolanda Griffith of the Sacramento Monarchs in the first game of the WNBA Western Conference finals.

Battier became only the fourth player in college basketball history to compile over 1,500 career points, 500 rebounds, 200 assists, 200 steals, and 200 blocked shots. Along with the retirement of his jersey by Duke, Battier was named the outstanding player of the 2001 NCAA Final Four. The unanimous first-team All-American also swept other major honours, including the Wooden and Naismith Player of the Year awards. His accomplishments reflected the way Krzyzewski had been able to recruit athletes who excelled on the court as well as in the classroom. The 54-year-old Krzyzewski had taken the Blue Devils to the Final Four 9 times in 21 years. The victory over Arizona was the third national championship of his career.

Bobby Knight largely avoided the media in the aftermath of his controversial departure from Indiana University. He did, however, accept another coaching position, becoming the new head basketball coach at Texas Tech. Soft-spoken Mike Davis, a former assistant to Knight at Indiana, stepped successfully into the position vacated by his mentor. After leading the Hoosiers to a stunning 59–58 upset of top-ranked Michigan State on January 7 and steering the team into the NCAA tournament at the close of the season, Davis was rewarded with a four-year contract.

In the women's ranks, it was Notre Dame's year. The Fighting Irish captured their first NCAA championship by prevailing over Purdue in a 68–66 thriller in St. Louis, Mo. Fittingly, Notre Dame star senior Ruth Riley hit the decisive free throws in the final seconds of the game. Riley's 28 points and 13 rebounds fueled her team's run to the title. Perennial powerhouse Connecticut had beaten the Irish 11 straight times in previous years but lost to them twice during the 2000–01 season. A major factor in that turnabout was Riley, who also earned NCAA Player of the Year honours. (ROBERT G. LOGAN)

International. In 2001 the Fédération Internationale de Basket (FIBA) was unable to reach an agreement with the Union des Ligues Européenes de Basketball (ULEB), which had organized a European league apart from the FIBA, resulting in competition between the ULEB's Euroleague and the FIBA's SuproLeague. In November the FIBA announced its reorganization into five continental zones beneath the umbrella FIBA-World group.

The focus of international basketball in 2001 was on the continental championships, which were qualifying tournaments for the 2002 world championships in Indianapolis, Ind. The hotly contested 2001 European championship yielded five qualifiers for the world championships: Yugoslavia, Turkey, Spain, Germany, and Russia, in that order. In the African championship Angola and Algeria qualified. In the Americas competition Venezuela, Brazil, Argentina, Puerto Rico, and Canada advanced to the worlds; the U.S., as host country of the 2002 event, automatically qualified, despite placing last in the region. In the Asian championship Lebanon mounted a spectacular 75–72 semifinal upset of South Korea to advance to its first world championships, despite losing in the final game to the other Asian qualifier, China. In the Oceania region New Zealand advanced at the cost of Australia, which it defeated in the best-of-three tournament.

Automatic qualifiers for the women's 2002 world championships were the host country, China, and the 2000 Olympic champion, the U.S. The qualifiers from the European championship were France, Russia, Spain, Lithuania, and Yugoslavia, while Brazil, Cuba, and Argentina advanced from the Americas. China dominated the Asian tournament, with distant contenders Japan, South Korea, and Taiwan also qualifying for the event. Australia bested New Zealand for the qualifying spot in the Oceania championship.

Shane Battier of Duke University slams home two points in the NCAA championship game against Arizona on April 2.

Brian Bahr/Allsport

In August Yugoslavia captured the gold medal in the men's World University Games, defeating China in the final game. For the bronze Germany was bested by the U.S., which had earned a medal in every biennial tournament since 1965, six years after the games were founded in 1959. On the women's side the U.S. won handily, despite an early tournament loss to Canada. China and the Czech Republic took home the silver and bronze medals, respectively.

The FIBA world championship for young men was hosted in August by Japan, where the U.S. captured the gold with a victory over Croatia. Argentina won the bronze medal game over the Dominican Republic. The world championship for junior women, held in the Czech Republic, was won by the host country in the final seconds over Russia. In the semifinals the Czech Republic had defeated the U.S., which later wrested the bronze medal from Australia. With National Basketball Association pros playing, the U.S. dominated the Goodwill Games in Australia in September, with a gold-medal win over Argentina.

In club play Maccabi Tel Aviv of Israel won its first European title in 20 years, defeating Panathinaikos BSA of Greece for the SuproLeague championship in May. The Maccabi coach was asked to step down in July after making racial slurs. In the British Basketball League (BBL), the Chester Jets claimed the 2001 trophy over the Newcastle Eagles, while in the BBL championship finals, the Leicester Riders defeated the Sheffield Sharks, who shortly afterward lost their franchise. In the ULEB's Euroleague finals Kinder Bologna of Italy defeated TAU Cerámica of Spain in the five-game series. (TOM MICHAEL)

BILLIARD GAMES

Carom Billiards. Swedish carom billiards star Torbjörn Blomdahl defeated American Pedro Piedrabuena in the International Dutch Open, held in Barendrecht, Neth., on January 12–14, 2001. The champion compiled an average of 1.794, with a high run of 12.

On February 4 South Korean-born Sang Chun Lee of New York City captured his 12th consecutive U.S. Billiard Association three-cushion championship. Lee finished the tournament with a 9–0 record and a high run of 12 and averaged 2.667 in the final game against American runner-up Carlos Hallon.

The first event of the 2001 Carom Corner Tour was held in Peabody, Mass., in March, with Dick Jaspers of The Netherlands defeating Piedrabuena for the title. Jaspers had a high run of 15, scoring 4.286 in his best game.

Greece played host to the three-cushion stars in February. Semih Sayginer of Turkey beat a strong field for the title. At the Billiards Worldcup Association tournament in Bogotá, Colom., in May, Sayginer won for the second straight year, prevailing over Jaspers in the final.

In June Frédéric Caudron of Belgium captured the title at the St. Willebrord (Neth.) Invitational, with Blomdahl taking second. The Monte Carlo Crystal Kelly tournament also was held in June. Jaspers avenged his earlier loss to Sayginer for the win.

In July Las Vegas, Nev., hosted the Carl Conlon Memorial Worldcup. It was the largest three-cushion event ever held in the U.S., with 152 competitors representing 21 countries. Blomdahl defeated Jaspers 3–1 for the title and posted an impressive grand average of 2.039 with a high run of 14. Legendary Belgian three-cushion star Raymond Ceulemans, who lost to Blomdahl in the second round, was inducted into the Billiard Congress of America (BCA) Hall of Fame just days earlier. Ceulemans had captured over 100 international titles in his 40-year career and was the first non-U.S. player to enter the hall since Alfredo de Oro of Spain was inducted in 1967.

Pocket Billiards. The 2001 pool season kicked off in January with Shannon Daulton defeating former U.S. Open champion Johnny Archer in the Music City Open in Nashville, Tenn. In the Derby City Classic, held in Louisville, Ky., later that month, Jose Parica took the nine-ball banks title, Buddy Hall the one-pocket crown, and Daulton both the nine-ball title and the all-around championship. At the Lexington (Ky.) All Star Championships, Jeremy Jones defeated Corey Deuel and Parica for the nine-ball crown, while John Brumback captured the nine-ball banks title.

Efren Reyes of the Philippines pocketed $20,000 for his 13–9 victory over Earl Strickland in the Masters Nine-Ball Championships in Chesapeake, Va., in April. One week later Reyes lost to fellow Filipino Francisco Bustamante in the finals of the Turning Stone Classic in Verona, N.Y. May saw the players head for the desert and the BCA nine-ball event in Las Vegas. Rising star Deuel knocked off Parica 7–5 in the final. Eight invited players descended on Uncasville, Conn., during July 11–12 for the International Challenge of Champions. Chao Fong-pang of Taiwan brushed aside Bustamante in a one-game sudden-death final.

At the World Pool–Billiard Association (WPA) men's world championships, held July 14–22 in Cardiff, Wales, Mika Immonen of Finland defeated Ralf Souquet of Germany 17–10 in the final to take home $65,000.

Back in Chesapeake in September, Deuel crushed Immonen 11–0 to capture the U.S. Open nine-ball championship. At season's end Deuel was the highest-ranked man in points, but Reyes, with more than $230,000 in winnings, topped the money list.

The Women's Professional Billiard Association (WPBA) seemed like a two-woman show in 2001 as Karen Corr, originally from Northern Ireland, and England's Allison Fisher between them won nearly everything in sight. The tour kicked off in March with Corr capturing the Players Championship in Valley Forge, Pa. She followed with another title a month later in the Spring Classic in Alpine, Calif., where she defeated Taiwan's Jennifer Chen for the second consecutive event.

Taiwan hosted the Amway Cup in early April, with Fisher pocketing $20,000 and the title. At the BCA championship in Las Vegas in May, American Jeanette Lee relegated Corr to a second-place finish with a 7–5 victory in the final. It was the year's only major women's event that neither Fisher (who finished third) nor Corr won.

In a battle of former snooker professionals, Corr defeated Fisher 7–3 at the Cuetec Cues Carolina Classic in Charlotte, N.C., in June. With this victory, Corr's third of the season, she overtook Fisher atop the WPBA rankings. Fisher had held the number one spot since September 1996. By season's end Corr had swept the WPBA tour, winning all six official events. Fisher, however, captured the $25,000 prize at the International Tournament of Champions in Uncasville on November 8 and then bested Corr 11–8 in the final of the WPA world nine-ball championship in Quebec two weeks later. Though Corr held onto her number one ranking in points, Fisher outearned her on the year's money list.

Snooker. England's Ronnie O'Sullivan capped off a sensational season in May 2001 by defeating former champion John Higgins of Scotland 18–14 to capture his first world professional snooker championship. O'Sullivan's title was his fifth of the season and added £250,000 (about $350,000) to push his season earnings to nearly £700,000 (almost $1 million). O'Sullivan, described by many observers as the greatest natural talent ever to play the game, climbed to number two in the world rankings, just ahead of Higgins. Though defending champion Mark Williams of Wales had crashed out in the second round, he retained his number one ranking for the 2001–02 season. In January Higgins, with teammates Stephen Hendry and Alan McManus, defeated a team from Ireland 6–2 to win the 2001 Nations Cup for Scotland.

Canadian Cliff Thorburn, who remained the only overseas player to have won the world snooker championship (1980), celebrated his return to the amateur snooker ranks with a dramatic 4–3 last-ball victory over another former professional, Tom Finstad, to capture the Canadian amateur snooker championship. (BILL BRADLEY)

BOBSLEDDING AND LUGE

Bobsledding. The top story of the 2000–01 bobsled season was the success of Jean Racine (and her brakeman, Jennifer Davidson) of the U.S. The duo combined to win six gold medals out of seven World Cup races, and for the second year in a row, Racine won the women's World Cup season title. Sandra Prokoff of Germany was second, and American Bonny Warner finished third. At the 2001 world championships, held in Calgary, Alta., in February, Racine and Davidson were edged out, however, losing by only 0.02 sec to Switzerland's Françoise Burdet and Katharina Sutter. Susi Erdmann and Tanja Hees of Germany placed third.

In men's bobsled action, the World Cup tour had seven stops throughout Europe and the U.S. Germany's André Lange won both the four-man title and the combined season title. In four-man season standings, Sandis Prusis of Latvia took second, with Matthias Benesch of Germany finishing in third. Martin Annen of Switzerland won the two-man season title, followed by Germans René Spies and Lange. Christoph Langen of Germany dominated the men's world championship in St. Moritz, Switz., winning his fifth two-man world title (with brakeman Marco Jakobs) and the four-man gold medal.

Skeleton. American Lincoln DeWitt and Alex Coomber of Great Britain won the men's and women's skeleton World Cup season titles, respectively, after they both won the World Cup finals at Utah Olympic Park. On the men's side, Kazuhiro Koshi of Japan placed second, and American Jim Shea, Jr., won the bronze. Steffi Hanzlik of Germany finished second in the women's World Cup standings, with Switzerland's Maya Pedersen in third. At the world championships in Calgary, Austria's Martin Rettl took the crown by 0.88 sec over Jeff Pain of Canada. DeWitt finished third. Pedersen rallied to gain the women's crown, while Coomber finished second and Tricia Stumpf of the U.S. placed third.

Luge. Throughout the 2000–01 luge season, Italy's Armin Zöggeler (*see* BIOGRAPHIES) controlled the men's singles action, winning his third men's singles luge world championship title and the overall World Cup title. Georg Hackl of Germany finished second in both the world championships and the World Cup standings. Austrian Marcus Prock finished third in the World Cup.

In women's singles, Germany grabbed the top two positions in the overall World Cup standings with their duo of Silke Kraushaar and Sylke Otto. Otto also successfully defended her world championship title, while Kraushaar secured second place. Austria's Angelika Neuner finished third in the World Cup.

André Florschütz and Torsten Wustlich of Germany captured the doubles title at the 35th luge world championships. Fellow Germans Steffen Skel and Steffen Wöller raced to a silver-medal finish. Markus Schiegl and Tobias Schiegl of Austria finished in the bronze-medal position—only 0.268 sec back. In the overall World Cup standings, Germany swept the top three positions, led by Skel and Wöller. Florschütz and Wustlich took second, while Patric Leitner and Alexander Resch finished third.

In the team competition of the world championships, Germany I, comprising Hackl, Kraushaar, and the duo of Leitner and Resch, raced to the gold medal. Germany II, consisting of Karsten Albert, Otto, and the pair of Skel and Wöller, won the silver. The U.S., which came in third, captured its first non-Olympic team medal. The American team comprised Tony Benshoof, Becky Wilczak, and the duo of Mark Grimmette and Brian Martin. (JULIE URBANSKY)

BOWLING

World Tenpins. In June 2001 the Fédération Internationale des Quilleurs (FIQ), the world governing body for the sport of tenpin bowling, reported at its biennial congress, held in Ålborg, Den., that 123 national member federations, with close to 15 million individual members, were affiliated with the FIQ. Traditionally, the FIQ was formed by three geographic zones—American, Asian, and European. The forming of a new African zone was under consideration, however, because the number of tenpin countries on that continent had reached 15.

In October 2000, at the beginning of the 2000–01 season, the 36th AMF Bowling World Cup took place in Lisbon. The field included 67 female and 88 male national qualifiers from as many countries. Mel Isaac of Wales and Tomas Leandersson of Sweden won the women's and men's titles, respectively.

The world youth championships, held in Santo Domingo, Dom.Rep., ended on Nov. 4, 2000. The American team took home 12 of the 21 medals awarded (5 gold, 5 silver, and 2 bronze). Kelly Kulick of the U.S. won the girls' singles and all-events titles, finished second to teammate Diandra Hyman in the masters, and teamed with Hyman to take silver behind England in the doubles. South Korea's Kim Jae Hoon captured gold in the boys' singles, all-events, and doubles (with partner Kong Sun Jong).

After two postponements the FIQ's 24 top-ranked men and women gathered in Abu Dhabi, U.A.E., in mid-April 2001 to determine the world's best amateur bowlers. Jesmine Ho of Singapore and Sunny Hui of Hong Kong won the women's and men's titles, respectively. At the European championships in June, Finland captured the most medals (12), while England won the most gold (5). Top bowlers Kirsten Penny of England and Mika Luoto of Finland each won four golds and a bronze. Women competitors broke 14 tournament records, while the men broke 9.

In 2001, for the first time, the national coaches elected an International Bowler of the Year—Clara Juliana Guerrero of Colombia. (YRJÖ SARAHETE)

U.S. Tenpins. In July 2001 the new owners of the Professional Bowlers Association (PBA) presented a 20-tournament schedule for the 2001–02 season, with all of the events to be carried on ESPN cable television as part of a three-year contract. In March 2000 the troubled PBA had been purchased by a trio of former computer software executives, Chris Peters, Mike Slade, and Rob Glaser. In the process the nonprofit PBA was converted into a for-profit corporation.

ESPN guaranteed a set time for the 10-tournament first half of the season, to be broadcast on Tuesday evenings from September to December with only a few variations. The second half of the season would be shown on Sunday afternoons, beginning on Jan. 6, 2002, and concluding with the "Battle of Little Creek" in Norfolk, Va., on March 17. The finals of the PBA world championship, with a top prize of $120,000, would be televised March 3.

To attract bowlers who had withdrawn from competition because of insufficient incentive, the PBA boosted the prize fund from $1.8 million in 2000–01 to approximately $4 million in 2001–02. Ian Hamilton, the new PBA commissioner, who previously had directed the Nike global tennis program for 14 years, said that the TV finals of the PBA tournaments would have a completely different look "without affecting the integrity of the sport." Spectators would be seated on both sides of the tournament lanes and would be encouraged to participate vocally at all times. An indefinite number of summer events would be scheduled.

During the year a joint task force began to explore the feasibility of combining five American governing bodies—the men's American Bowling Congress, the Women's International Bowling Congress, the Young American Bowling Alliance, Bowling, Inc., and USA Bowling—into one single-membership organization for amateur bowling.

In August Earl Anthony, the PBA's most prolific champion and six-time Player of the Year, died at age 63. (*See* OBITUARIES.) (JOHN J. ARCHIBALD)

Matthew Stockman/Allsport

Jean Racine and Jennifer Davidson of the U.S. compete in the women's bobsled event at the Park City (Utah) World Cup in February.

BOXING

In 2001 Lennox Lewis (U.K.) brought a measure of continuity to a year filled with unexpected results when he regained the World Boxing Council (WBC) and International Boxing Federation (IBF) heavyweight titles by knocking out Hasim Rahman (U.S.) in the fourth round of their November 17 rematch in Las Vegas, Nev. Lewis ended the fight with a single right hand to the jaw that floored Rahman for the 10 count. The unheralded Rahman had sprung a stunning upset on April 22, knocking out Lewis in the fifth round of a bout held in Johannesburg, S.Af., to win the WBC and IBF belts.

John Ruiz (U.S.) became the first boxer of Latino heritage to win a heavyweight title when he annexed the World Boxing Association (WBA) title with a 12-round decision over Evander Holyfield (U.S.) on March 3 in Las Vegas. A rematch in Mashantucket, Conn., on December 17 ended in a draw. Former heavyweight champion Mike Tyson (U.S.) fought only once during the year, scoring a seventh-round knockout of Brian Nielsen (Den.) on October 13 in Copenhagen. The victory ensured Tyson a title bout in 2002.

Timothy A. Clary/AFP Worldwide

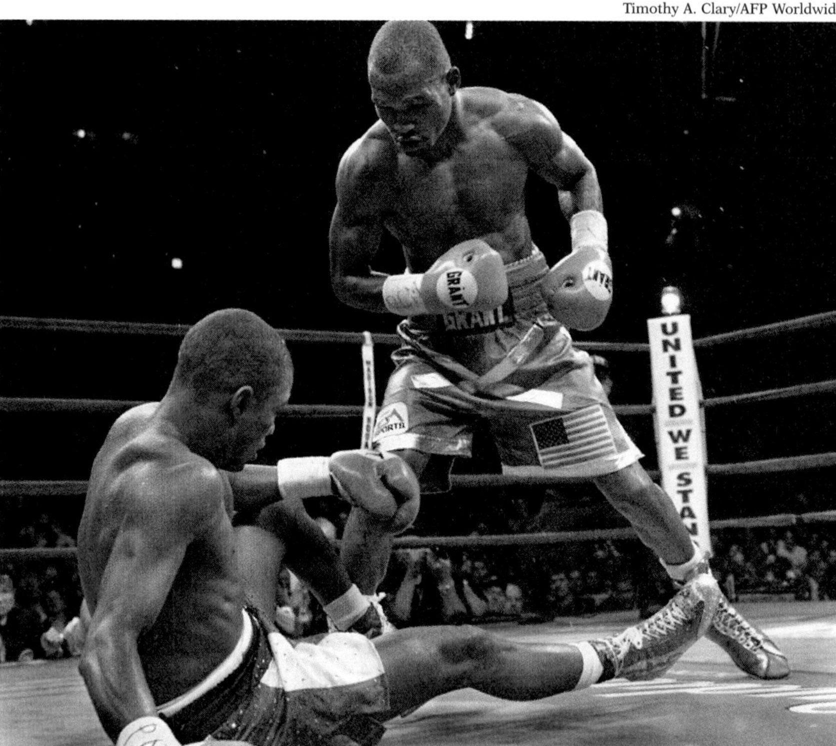

Bernard Hopkins of the U.S. knocks down Félix Trinidad of Puerto Rico en route to unifying the middleweight titles on September 29.

In another stunning upset, Bernard Hopkins (U.S.) became the first unified middleweight champion in 14 years when he knocked out Félix Trinidad (P.R.) in the 12th round on September 29 in front of a capacity crowd of more than 19,000 fans at Madison Square Garden in New York City. The match was the final bout in a middleweight championship tournament promoted by Don King. In the first bout of the tournament, IBF middleweight champion Hopkins added the WBC title by winning a 12-round decision over Keith Holmes (U.S.) on April 14 at Madison Square Garden. In the next round of the tournament, Trinidad won the WBA middleweight title with a fifth-round knockout of William Joppy (U.S.) on May 12 at the Garden. Trinidad was heavily favoured to win the finale, but the bout was dominated by Hopkins, who gave one of the finest performances in middleweight history. Approximately 475,000 households purchased the Hopkins-Trinidad television pay-per-view, making it the largest pay-per-view sale of the year. It was Trinidad's first loss in 41 professional bouts and left Hopkins in possession of all three major middleweight titles—IBF, WBA, and WBC.

Undisputed light heavyweight champion Roy Jones, Jr. (U.S.), defended his WBA, WBC, and IBF titles twice in 2001. Jones scored a 10th-round knockout of Derrick Harmon (U.S.) on February 24 in Tampa, Fla., then tallied a 12-round decision over Julio Gonzalez (U.S.) on July 28 in Los Angeles. Despite these two relatively easy victories, Jones lost prestige owing to the mediocre quality of his challengers.

Box-office attraction Oscar de la Hoya (U.S.), who had been without a world title since June 17, 2000, when he lost the WBC welterweight title to Shane Mosley (U.S.), moved up to the super welterweight (junior middleweight) class, where he won the WBC title with a 12-round decision over Francisco Castillejo (Spain) on June 23 in Las Vegas. The undefeated Mosley enhanced his standing as one of the sport's finest practitioners by making two defenses of the WBC welterweight title. Mosley scored a fifth-round knockout of Shannon Taylor (Australia) on March 10 in Las Vegas, then followed with a third-round knockout of Adrian Stone (U.K.) on July 21 in Las Vegas.

The first major upset of the year came on April 7 when featherweight Marco Antonio Barrera (Mex.) won a 12-round decision over previously undefeated Naseem Hamed (U.K.) in Las Vegas. Hamed, known for his outspoken personality and extravagant ring entrances, was exposed as a one-dimensional fighter by Barrera's clever boxing and accurate punching. The bout drew 12,847 live spectators, and close to 250,000 homes purchased the pay-per-view program, which made it the largest-grossing featherweight bout in history. Barrera followed up with a sixth-round knockout of Enrique Sánchez (Mex.) on September 8 in Reno, Nev., to further establish his credentials as the world's foremost featherweight.

The theme of unification and upsets continued when WBA/WBC 140-lb titleholder Kostya Tszyu (Australia) became the first undisputed junior welterweight champion since Nicolino Locche, in 1968, by stopping favoured IBF champion Zab Judah (U.S.) in the second round of a bout held on November 3 in Las Vegas. After the fight was halted, an enraged Judah shoved his glove under referee Jay Nady's chin and threw a stool. In a disciplinary action, the Nevada State Athletic Commission suspended Judah's boxing license for six months and fined him $75,000.

In a bizarre match between the offspring of two famous rivals, Laila Ali (U.S.), the daughter of former heavyweight champion Muhammad Ali, won a spirited eight-round decision over Jacqui Frazier-Lyde (U.S.), the daughter of former heavyweight champion, Joe Frazier, on June 8 in Verona, N.Y. Although panned by the media beforehand, the pay-per-view event was sold to approximately 100,000 households, which made the surprisingly entertaining contest the richest women's boxing match in history.

(NIGEL COLLINS)

CHESS

The chess world settled down to a threefold division of influence in 2001—Vladimir Kramnik was considered world champion by many after his match victory over fellow Russian Garry Kasparov, while Viswanathan Anand was the official world champion, authorized by the world ruling body Fédération Internationale des Échecs after the Indian was successful in the knockout contest organized by FIDE in New Delhi and Tehran in late 2000. Meanwhile, there was Kasparov himself, still recognized by many as the strongest player in the world and certainly the undisputed leader of the international rating list.

Kasparov's aspirations for a return match against Kramnik foundered early in the year when the contractual obligations of the two players to the Brain Games Network private company came to an end. BGN planned instead an eight-game match between Kramnik and the Fritz computer program to be held in Bahrain in October. After the September 11 terrorist attacks in the U.S., the match was postponed until 2002.

Judit Polgar of Hungary contemplates a move in her match against Vladimir Kramnik of Russia during the City of Dos Hermanas (Spain) chess tournament in April.

Emilio Morenatti/AFP Worldwide

Tension between the players on the international circuit and FIDE intensified after the introduction of a new faster time limit for the top tournaments. "Classical chess" had traditionally been played at the rate of 40 moves in two and a half hours, a rate introduced by José Raúl Capablanca in the 1920s. This had given way in the 1990s to the slightly quicker rate of 40 moves in two hours, then 20 moves in an hour plus half an hour to finish the game. Such standard rates naturally involved playing only one game a day, so that top tournaments and matches lasted several weeks or even longer.

The initial proposal by FIDE was for the 2001 world championship cycle to be run at the rate of 40 moves in 40 minutes plus 20 minutes to finish or, with the new digital clocks, at 40/40 and a 30-second bonus for every move made. This was eased somewhat in the face of protests, but those events that had been run on this modified basis had been replete with complaints by the players that the standard of the games was very disappointing. Too many games had had farcical finishes for true lovers of chess to be satisfied with the innovation.

It was assumed that the long-term plan was to have two games a day and generally reduce the costs of contests. FIDE argued that shorter games would stand a better chance of gaining television coverage. Attempts continued to have chess admitted to the Olympic Games, with the first step being the admission of chess as an exhibition sport in the 2002 Winter Olympics.

Another bone of contention arose between FIDE and traditional organizers in Western Europe when the former tried to incorporate their events in a new World Chess Grand Prix. The "Big Three" of the tournament circuit—Wijk aan Zee, Neth.; Linares, Spain; and Dortmund, Ger.—rejected the overtures and in a joint statement indicated their intention to remain independent and preserve the character of their events. This rebuff was met by threats of FIDE's running parallel spoiler contests at the usual times in the calendar for the traditional events.

At the Wijk aan Zee event, held January 13–28, the top scores were Kasparov (9 points out of 13), Anand (8.5), Kramnik and Vasily Ivanchuk of Ukraine (both 8), and Michael Adams of England, Russian Aleksandr Morozevich, and Aleksey Shirov representing Spain (all 7.5). At the Linares tournament, which took place from February 23 to March 6, Kasparov (7.5 out of 10) scored an overwhelming victory in a double-round contest, followed by a unique tie for second-to-last place between Judit Polgar of Hungary, Anatoly Karpov of Russia, Shirov, Peter Leko of Hungary, and the new teenage Russian star Aleksandr Grischuk (all 4.5). The Dortmund Sparkassen Chess Meeting, on July 12–22, was also a double rounder and ended with Kramnik and Veselin Topalov of Bulgaria tied at 6.5 out of 10, followed by Leko (5.5), Morozevich (5), Adams (3.5), and Anand (3).

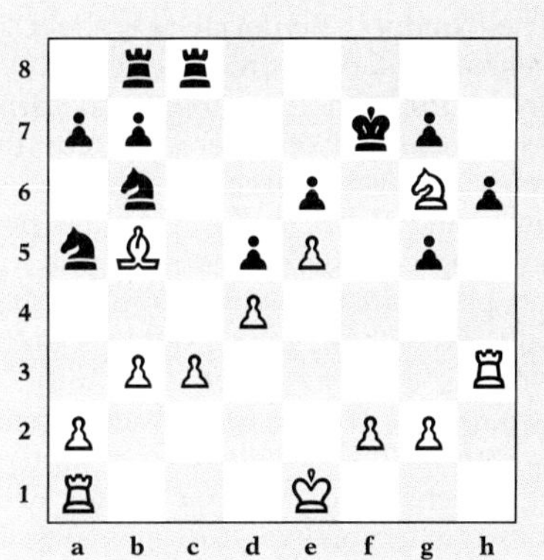

In a rapid-play tournament at Zürich, Switz., in late April 2001, Garry Kasparov showed up well. Here is a position in which he defeated the great veteran Viktor Korchnoi. Korchnoi, Black, appears to have won the loose knight at g6, but Kasparov continued: 1 Rf3+ Kxg6 (or 1 . . . Kg8 2 Ne7+ and 3 Nxc8) 2 Bd3+ Kh5 3 Rh3+ Kg4 4 f3+ Kf4 5 Kf2 g4 6 g3+ and Black resigned in view of 6 . . . Kg5 7 f4 mate.

Anand's failure to win a single game and his lowly placing somewhat undermined the credibility of his FIDE title. The other significant result was Kasparov's first place at the six-man tournament in Astana, Kazakhstan, to celebrate the 10th anniversary of the independence of that Central Asian country. This was played as yet another double rounder and was won by Kasparov (7 points out of 10), followed by Kramnik (6.5), Boris Gelfand of Israel (5.5), Shirov and Morozevich (both 4.5), and Darmen Sadvakasov of Kazakhstan (2).

Kasparov also played a short match at odds in London, conceding two pawns to the English businessman Terry Chapman in a reversion to 19th-century practice. The Russian won 2.5–1.5. A sign of the times came in mid-March in Seattle, Wash., when China beat the U.S. 21–19 in a four-round, 10-board match, with the Chinese junior players clinching the victory.

The Najdorf Memorial was held in Buenos Aires, Arg., on September 4–13. For the first time in a top tournament, two female players were invited: the women's world champion, Xie Jun of China, and Polgar, a former child prodigy long considered the strongest woman player in the world. Both finished mid-table with 4.5 points out of 9 in the 10-player contest, which was won by Karpov (6.5). He had recently celebrated his 50th birthday, and the event marked his comeback to the world elite. Even more remarkable was the age range in the joint second-place finishers with 6 points—70-year-old Viktor Korchnoi of Switzerland and 14-year-old Teimur Radjabov of Azerbaijan, who thereby gave notice that he could be the world's best player within the next few years.

The chess world lost two significant figures late in the year. On November 12 Anthony John ("Tony") Miles died in his native Birmingham, Eng., at age 46, two years after being diagnosed with diabetes. Miles became the first English grandmaster at over the board play in 1976, after winning the junior world championship in 1974. His 10-year run of success against top players such as Karpov helped England to rise from a mediocre position in the international chess rankings to challenge the mighty Soviet Union. John W. ("Jack") Collins, a respected American chess teacher whose students had included former world champion Bobby Fischer, died on December 2 at age 89.

(BERNARD CAFFERTY)

CONTRACT BRIDGE

The two major 2001 world championships for contract bridge, the Bermuda Bowl and, for women, the Venice Cup, were originally scheduled to be played in Bali, Indonesia. Following the September 11 attacks in the United States, however, the tournaments were transferred to Paris. In the Bermuda Bowl, contested October 21 through November 3, the final was a dramatic match between Norway, which had defeated cofavourite Italy in the semifinals, and USA-2; cofavourite USA-1 had lost to Italy in the quarterfinals. With 16 deals remaining, Norway led by two points. In the final session Norway bid a small slam that went down only when both the opposing cards were distributed unfavourably and Peter Weichsel found the killing trump lead. Consequently, USA-2 won 286–265. An outstanding feature of the competition was that Rose Meltzer became the first woman to play on a victorious Bermuda Bowl team. The USA-2 team consisted of Meltzer–Kyle Larsen, Chip Martel– Lew Stansby, and Alan Sontag–Peter Weichsel, with Jan Martel the nonplaying captain.

The final of the Venice Cup was even more closely contested than the Bermuda Bowl. After trailing by 46.5 points with 16 deals remaining, Germany defeated France 218–215.5. The winning players were Sabine Auken–Daniela von Arnim and Pony Nehmert–Andrea Rauscheid, with Christoph Kemmer the nonplaying captain. (Katrin Farwig and Barbara Hackett were also on the team but did not play in the final round.)

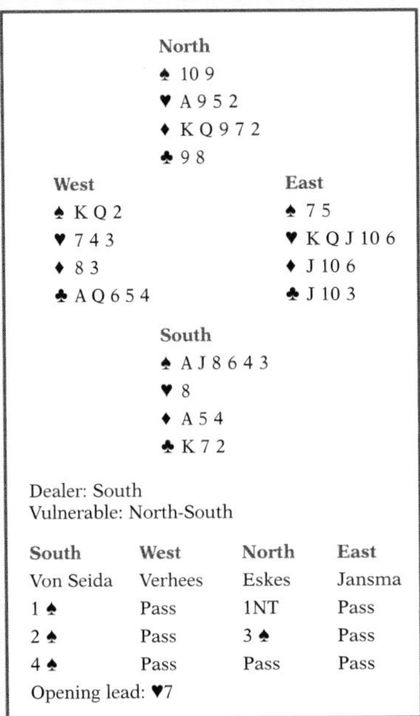

North
♠ 10 9
♥ A 9 5 2
♦ K Q 9 7 2
♣ 9 8

West
♠ K Q 2
♥ 7 4 3
♦ 8 3
♣ A Q 6 5 4

East
♠ 7 5
♥ K Q J 10 6
♦ J 10 6
♣ J 10 3

South
♠ A J 8 6 4 3
♥ 8
♦ A 5 4
♣ K 7 2

Dealer: South
Vulnerable: North-South

South	West	North	East
Von Seida	Verhees	Eskes	Jansma
1 ♠	Pass	1NT	Pass
2 ♠	Pass	3 ♠	Pass
4 ♠	Pass	Pass	Pass

Opening lead: ♥7

West, Louk Verhees from The Netherlands, opened with a heart. South called for dummy's ace, and East signaled with the king to show his king-queen-jack sequence. South ran dummy's ♠10 to West's queen. What did Verhees lead next? (Erik Kirchhoff found the same play.)

For his raise to game, South was marked with the ♦A and ♣K. And as his two-spade rebid guaranteed at least a six-card suit, declarer was threatening to score 10 tricks via four spades, one heart, and five diamonds. It was tempting to lead another heart, expecting East to win the trick and to shift to a club through declarer's king. Verhees, however, judged that to accept his partner's game-invitational raise with a minimum point count, South was more likely to have 6=1=3=3 distribution than 6=2=3=2 or 6=2=2=3. And if that was true, there was only one hope: that his partner had the ♣J. Consequently, there was only one correct card to lead: the ♣Q.

What could South do after winning with the ♣K? If he returned a low club, East would win and push through a trump. If South cashed the ♠A and tried to get a discard on the fourth round of diamonds, West would ruff the third diamond, cash the ♣A, and lead a low club to his partner's jack. Similarly, if South played a diamond to dummy and took another spade finesse, Verhees would win, take the ♣A, and play another club. In all cases, the defense wins two spades and two clubs. Yes, a shift to a low club works here, but not if declarer has ♣K-10-x. If that is the situation, declarer wins East's ♣J with his king and continues with the ♠10, forcing West to win the trick. Then South either ruffs his last club in the dummy (and loses only two spades and one club) or holds his trump losers to one (if West returns a spade to stop that club ruff).

From July 6 to 8 the world junior pairs tournament took place in Stargard Szczecinski, Pol. The winners were Andreas Gloyer and Martin Schifko of Austria with a score of 15,132 points. Finishing second was the Dutch pair of Sjoert Brink and Bas Drijver with a score of 14,821. Fabio Lo Presti and Francesco Mazzadi of Italy placed third with 14,266. Gloyer completed an impressive double, having won in 1999 with Bernd Saurer.

The world youth team championship was contested in Mangaratiba, Braz., August 6–15. In the final USA-1 defeated Israel 262–156. The USA-1 team consisted of Brad Campbell, Joe Grue, John Hurd, John Kranyak, Kent Mignocchi, and Joel Wooldridge, with Robert Rosen as nonplaying captain and Dennis McGarry as coach. To qualify for both of these tournaments, a player had to be born after Dec. 31, 1974. (PHILLIP ALDER)

CRICKET

On Feb. 25, 2001, cricket lost its most famous player. Sir Don Bradman, who was recognized throughout the world as the supreme batsman in the game, died at the age of 92, and Australia mourned. Had Bradman not been out for 0 in the very last of his 80 Test innings, he might have stretched his final average of 99.94 beyond 100. (*See* OBITUARIES.)

The morning following the news, the Australian team, led by Steve Waugh, stood to observe a minute's silence before the first Test against India in Mumbai (Bombay). The match proved to be the last in a record-breaking sequence of 16 straight Australian victories stretching back almost two years. Australia's only series defeat of the 2000–01 season came after a remarkable turnaround in the second Test in Kolkata (Calcutta), in which V.V.S. Laxman's innings of 281 allowed the home team to become only the third in Test history to win after following on its first innings. The decisive Test in Chennai (Madras) was as dramatic a game of cricket as any in the year as India scrambled home to victory by two wickets. The young Indian off spinner Harbhajan Singh took 15 wickets in the match and 32 in the series, including a hat trick.

The standard of Australia's cricket helped to divert attention away from the issue of match fixing, which continued to dog the sport. The dismissed Pakistan coach, Javed Miandad, openly hinted that his players had fixed matches during the one-day series against New Zealand, and the Pakistan Cricket Board appointed a judge to look into allegations that Pakistan fixed a defeat against Bangladesh in the 1999 World Cup. An interim report of the independent commission chaired by Sir Paul Condon, the former chief commissioner of the Metropolitan Police in London and the recently appointed head of the International Cricket Council's Anti-Corruption Unit, highlighted the difficulty in proving allegations against individuals and teams. The report suggested that the proliferation of one-day internationals, particularly in neutral venues such as Ash-Shariqah, U.A.E., had encouraged a more relaxed attitude to betting and match fixing. It also touched on possible links to organized crime and referred to a kidnapping and a murder linked to match fixing. The report was widely criticized for lacking proper jurisdiction or authority and for not being thorough enough in interviewing players accused of taking money from bookmakers. The commission's recommendations included more stringent contracts for players, better security (including fewer mobile phones in dressing rooms), and wider powers for the Anti-Corruption Unit. In October a court in South Africa upheld the lifetime ban imposed on Wessel Johannes ("Hansie") Cronje, the former South African captain, whose admission that he had taken money from an Indian bookmaker in April 2000 initially pitched the game into crisis.

At the Oval in London on August 24, Steve Waugh bats for the Australian team in a Test match against England.

William West/AFP Worldwide

England won its Test series in both Pakistan and Sri Lanka, showing a resilience and organization under captain Nasser Hussain that augured well for the Ashes against Australia, cricket's oldest and most prestigious rivalry. Australia once again proved too strong, however, as leg spinner Shane Warne recovered his form and passed 400 career Test wickets during the five-Test series and Glenn McGrath proved to be an equally potent bowler. The pattern was set in the opening Test at Edgbaston, Birmingham, Eng., when England was bowled out twice cheaply, while Waugh, Damien Martyn, and Adam Gilchrist all made centuries for Australia. Only three times in 10 innings did England's batsmen score more than 300; four times in the first six innings they were bowled out for less than 200. England salvaged some vestige of pride in the fourth Test when, with the Ashes already lost once again, Mark Butcher scored an unbeaten 173 in the fourth innings to lead England to an unlikely target (315). Waugh, who was denied the right to take home the original 19th-century Ashes urn by the authorities at Lord's cricket ground in London, unsuccessfully tried to burn a bail so that the Australians could return home with an urn containing some ashes.

Bangladesh became the 10th Test-playing nation in November 2000, marking its debut with a defeat to India. Aminul Islam made the country's first Test century. Zimbabwe produced two record-breaking batsmen in a busy year. Just 11 days before his 18th birthday, Hamilton Masakadza became the youngest debutant to score a Test century—119 against the West Indies in Harare, Zimb. Andrew Flower totaled 1,324 runs for the year, including a double century, three centuries, and seven 50s in 15 innings. Masakadza's record was later beaten by Mohammad Ashraful of Bangladesh, who scored 114 at the age of 17 years and 63 days against Sri Lanka in Colombo.

The West Indies endured a depressing year, losing 5–0 to Australia and 2–1 to South Africa. Courtney Walsh, the great West Indian fast bowler, bowed out on his home ground in Jamaica, finishing with a record 519 Test wickets in his career. Former England captain Michael Atherton also retired from first-class cricket.

Pressure continued to grow for cricket to use more television technology to aid in making decisions on the field. Pakistan's defeat of England at Old Trafford, Manchester, Eng., was marred by the subsequent discovery that at least three of England's wickets had fallen to no balls shown clearly by TV. Television replays were used only for run-outs, but it was argued that they could also be used by umpires to judge catches close to the wicket or even lbws.

In domestic cricket, Yorkshire won the county championship in England for the first time in 33 years, and Somerset captured the one-day C&G Cup. Other four-day champions were Western Province (South Africa), Queensland (Australia), and Wellington (New Zealand). KwaZulu/Natal in South Africa and New South Wales in Australia won one-day trophies, and the Western Warriors from Perth, Australia, won the inaugural Champions Cup for the one-day champions of the Southern Hemisphere. New Zealand triumphed in the women's World Cup, beating Australia by four runs in the final.

(ANDREW LONGMORE)

CURLING

Peter Lindholm of Sweden finally regained his international curling crown in 2001 after having made it to the men's final in four of the past five world championships. Playing in Lausanne, Switz., the 1997 world champion and 1989 world junior winner defeated Swiss skip Andreas Schwaller 6–3 in the men's final on April 8. Lindholm had finished second at the worlds in 2000 and 1998. The silver medal for Schwaller was significant in that it qualified Switzerland for the 2002 Winter Olympic Games in Salt Lake City, Utah. Norway finished third in the men's competition, pushing fourth-place Canada out of the men's medals for only the fifth time in 30 years at the worlds. Rounding out the top 10 were Finland, France, Germany, the U.S., New Zealand, and Denmark.

Colleen Jones of Halifax, N.S., earned Canada its second consecutive women's world title by defeating Anette Norberg of Sweden 5–2 in the final. Jones had first made it to the worlds in 1982 and returned in 1999, finishing fifth in both those attempts. Denmark won the bronze medal by defeating Scotland. The other women's finishers, in order, were Germany, the U.S., Japan, Norway, Russia, and Switzerland.

In June Finland announced it had pulled its women's curling entry from the 2002 Olympics because of the country's poor international results. Finnish women failed to qualify for either the 2000 or 2001 world championships but still held the 10th Olympic qualifying berth. Finland was to be replaced on the women's side in Salt Lake City by Russia, which had qualified 11th after a ninth-place finish in Lausanne—the country's first appearance at the world curling championships.

The 2001 world junior curling championships took place in March at the 2002 Olympic curling venue in Ogden, Utah. Brad Gushue of Canada defeated Casper Bossen of Denmark for the men's championship, while the U.S. defeated Scotland for the bronze. The women's junior title was won by Canada's Suzanne Gaudet, who defeated Matilda Mattsson of Sweden in the final. Switzerland won bronze, relegating Japan to fourth place. (BRUCE CHEADLE)

CYCLING

Riding in the Pyrenees, American cyclist Lance Armstrong leads the pack during the 14th stage of the Tour de France on July 22.

Pascal Rondeau/Allsport

In 2001 American rider Lance Armstrong sealed his place in cycling history when he became the fifth man to win the Tour de France, the sport's premier event, in at least three successive years, joining Louison Bobet (1953–55), Jacques Anquetil (1961–64), Eddy Merckx (1969–72), and Miguel Indurain (1991–95). The Texan finished 6 min 44 sec ahead of Germany's Jan Ullrich after 3,454 km (about 2,146 mi) of racing, establishing his superiority with a commanding display of strength on the mountain stages. Armstrong won successive road-race and time-trial legs in the Alps before taking the overall lead for the first time three days later in the Pyrenees. A fourth win followed in the last time-trial stage, two days before the event finished in Paris. Erik Zabel of Germany won the points competition, based on daily finishing positions over the 20 stages and intermediate sprints, for a record sixth time.

The sport's governing body, the Union Cycliste Internationale (UCI), in April introduced a new "health check" in the quest to eradicate the use of the human hormone erythropoietin (EPO). The UCI required any rider whose blood test showed a hematocrit level—the functional level of red blood cells as a percentage of total blood plasma—above the considered-safe level of 50% to submit to a urine test. Italy's Fabiano Fontanelli was the first rider to be excluded from a race, the Tour of Flanders on April 8, for an overly high hematocrit reading and to then take a urine test, which did not reveal any trace of EPO.

At the Tour of Italy (Giro d'Italia), second in importance to the Tour de France, police and customs officials mounted raids on hotels where riders were staying after the June 6 stage in San Remo. The riders refused to race the following day, in protest against their treatment, which led to the cancellation of stage 18 between Imperia and San Anna di Vinadio. Italy's Dario Frigo, who was in second place overall, was dismissed by his team and left the race after doping products were found in his room. After an analysis of substances taken away in the raid, 86 people, including doctors and team managers, were later placed under investigation.

The world track championships were held at the indoor Sportpaleis velodrome in Antwerp, Belg., in September. Arnaud Tournant of France won the individual kilometre time trial for the fourth successive year and gained gold medals in the individual sprint and three-man-team Olympic sprint. Nancy Contreras Reyes won Mexico's first-ever senior world title, in the women's 500-m time trial. In October Tournant became the first rider to beat one minute for a standing-start kilometre, covering the distance in 58.875 sec with an average speed of 61.146 km/h (about 38 mph) on the La Paz, Bol., track, which had an altitude of 3,417 m (11,211 ft). (JOHN R. WILKINSON)

EQUESTRIAN SPORTS

Thoroughbred Racing. *United States.* The thoroughbred breeding industry in the United States was dealt a severe setback in the spring of 2001 when Kentucky farms were ravaged with an outbreak of mare reproductive loss syndrome. Several thousand late-term foals and early-term fetuses, including thoroughbreds and other equine breeds, were lost. Long-term damage to the thoroughbred breeding industry was estimated at about $350 million. Speculation among veterinarians and other equine experts was that Eastern tent caterpillars had transferred cyanide from wild black cherry trees to grass, which was then ingested by the pregnant mares. Unusual spring weather conditions were thought to have caused a high production of cyanogenic material by the trees, which were common in central Kentucky.

Louisiana Downs in Bossier City, La., received permission from the state gaming board on March 19 to open an on-track casino. Another casino was planned at Delta Downs in Vinton, La. Other states that had previously legalized on-track casinos included West Virginia, Iowa, Delaware, New Mexico, and Minnesota. In October the New York legislature voted overwhelmingly to allow video lottery terminals (slot machines) at two of the state's thoroughbred tracks, Aqueduct and Finger Lakes, as well as at three of the state's harness tracks.

California became the 12th state to allow account wagering on horse racing when Gov. Gray Davis signed a bill approving it on August 13. Attached to the bill was a provision that would allow grooms, exercise riders, and hot walkers to unionize. Earlier that month, New York City Mayor Rudy Giuliani had awarded the right to buy a majority interest in the New York City Off-Track Betting Corp. to a group led by Magna Entertainment Corp. The group was selected over the New York Racing Association.

The National Thoroughbred Racing Association (NTRA) and Breeders' Cup Ltd., which had merged in 2000, announced on June 26 that the title World Thoroughbred Championships would be a permanent addition to the name of the Breeders' Cup. It was also announced that the Bessemer Trust, one of the country's leading investment banking companies, had signed on as title sponsor of the Breeders' Cup Juvenile and a new series for two-year-olds on the CNBC financial television network.

Racetracks across the country ceased operation for at least a day after the September 11 terrorist attacks, while Belmont Park in Elmont, N.Y., and the Meadowlands in East Rutherford, N.J. (the track closest to the New York City attack site), shut down for a week. The Breeders' Cup races, however, went on as planned at Belmont on October 27. Jockeys, trainers, and owners who participated in the event donated $2,760,000 of the money they earned to the New York Heroes Fund, which was established by the NTRA.

Racetrack attrition continued with the closing and planned demolition of historic Garden State Park in Cherry Hill, N.J. Opened in 1942, it was destroyed by fire in April 1977 and reopened as "the racetrack of the 21st Century" eight years later. The site was to be redeveloped into a residential and commercial complex.

The Racing Network (TRN) ceased operation abruptly on July 30, citing a lack of an adequate number of subscribers. TRN was a 24-hour multichannel satellite-based network that carried horse and dog races on a subscription basis.

Monarchos, who captured the 2001 Kentucky Derby, was sidelined in July when a hairline fracture was discovered in his right knee. He was expected to resume his racing career as a four-year-old. Point Given, winner of the Preakness and Belmont stakes, was retired on August 31 with a strained tendon in his left front leg. Tiznow, the reigning Horse of the Year and three-year-old colt champion, became the first two-time Breeders' Cup Classic winner by successfully defending his title in the $4 million, 1¼-mi event. Battling between horses, he surged in the final strides to defeat Sakhee by a nose following a stretch-long battle.

Pat Day, age 47, became only the third jockey in American racing history to win 8,000 races; his landmark victory came on May 31. Only Laffit Pincay, Jr., still active with more than 9,100 career wins, and the retired Bill Shoemaker (8,833) had more victories. Russell Baze reached career win number 7,500 on September 15, and Chris McCarron captured his 7,000th victory on April 28. Jerry D. Bailey became the first jockey in history to surpass $20 million in purse earnings in a single year.

Earlie Fires, the leading apprentice jockey in the United States in 1965 and still active with more than 6,150 victories, and West Coast-based trainer Richard Mandella were inducted into the Racing Hall of Fame on August 6. Also entering the Hall was the 1994 Horse of the Year, Holy Bull.

Hall of Famer Horace Allyn ("Jimmy") Jones, trainer of 1948 Triple Crown champion Citation and 53 other stakes winners and the son of the great trainer Ben Jones, died at age 94 on September 2. Affirmed, America's 11th and most recent Triple Crown champion, was euthanized at age 26 on January 12. Nureyev, one of thoroughbred racing's most successful sires, died on October 29 at age 24. (JOHN G. BROKOPP)

Point Given, ridden by Gary Stevens, crosses the finish line in first place to win the Preakness Stakes on May 19.

Matthew Stockman/Allsport

Thoroughbred Racing. *International.* Two stables—the Ireland-based racing division of Coolmore Stud, the world's largest owners of stallions, and Godolphin, which deployed the pick of the horses owned by the Maktoum family—divided the European 2000–01 thoroughbred racing season between them. Godolphin, which spent the months from late October to late April in Dubayy, U.A.E., before returning to Newmarket in England, appeared to hold an advantage after a rainy winter and spring. Their luck ran out, however. Dubai Millennium, winner of the 2000 Dubayy World Cup and Godolphin's best-ever horse, died of grass sickness on April 29, halfway through his first season at stud, and their three-year-olds were disappointing. Noverre, Godolphin's only classic winner, was disqualified two months after his victory in the French Poule d'Essai des Poulains because he tested positive for methylprednisolone.

Aidan O'Brien, who trained the Coolmore horses, dominated the classics and ended the season with 23 Group 1 victories in Europe, including 7 of the 15 English, French, or Irish classics. Galileo, who easily won the Epsom and Irish Derbys, was his best horse. The three-year-old colt went on to defeat Godolphin's Fantastic Light in the King George VI and Queen Elizabeth Diamond Stakes. The Godolphin five-year-old turned the tables in the Irish Champion Stakes, however; Fantastic Light was too good for Galileo in the two-furlong-shorter race and held on by a head. Two-year-old racing also was dominated by O'Brien, whose horses won 9 of the 10 European Group 1 races open to juvenile colts. O'Brien became the first British champion trainer since 1977 to be based abroad.

Among four- and five-year-old horses, the pendulum swung to Godolphin. Sakhee had won the Juddmonte International by seven lengths 18 days before the Irish Champion Stakes, and he went on to win the Prix de l'Arc de Triomphe in Paris by six lengths. Kutub followed a hat trick of Group 1 victories in Germany and Italy by winning the Singapore Gold Cup. Slickly was a

Group 1 winner in France and Italy. Hatha Anna gave the stable its first success in Australia in the Group 2 Queen Elizabeth II Stakes, while Give the Slip led until the final 50 yards of the Melbourne Cup before losing to Ethereal by three-quarters of a length.

Irish prize money rose by 18% in 2000 and was projected to increase again in 2001 with government help. The British government attempted similar help by abolishing the off-course betting tax (on-course betting had been tax-free since 1987) and by replacing the betting levy. Negotiations on a new system to contribute extra finance proved difficult, however, and were nowhere near a solution at the end of the season.

Betting turnover increased in Great Britain, Ireland, and France, but French racing had other problems. It had allowed most Group race prizes to fall behind British ones, while a protest by pari-mutuel workers caused the postponement of the Grand Prix de Paris meeting. It was run two days later but without betting. André Fabre was the champion trainer in France for the 15th consecutive year, helped by two Group 1 disqualifications from each of which Vahorimix was the beneficiary. Italy enjoyed a better season, with prizes the highest since 1997.

German racing, which suffered from low betting turnover and static prize money, had a champion horse in Silvano, which won the Singapore Cup in March, the Queen Elizabeth II Cup in Hong Kong in April, and the Arlington Million in the U.S. in August. Silvano also was placed in other rich prizes in Dubayy, the U.S., and Australia. He was third to the Japanese-trained Stay Gold in the Dubayy Sheema Classic, on a race day that challenged the claim of the U.S.-based Breeders' Cup to be the "World Thoroughbred Championships."

Captain Steve from the U.S. beat rivals from Japan and France in the 2001 Dubayy World Cup, while Jim and Tonic, from France, bested Fairy King Prawn from Hong Kong and Sunline from New Zealand in a thrilling finish to the Dubayy Duty Free. Caller One in the Dubayy Golden Shaheen was another American winner at the most international meeting to date.

Three horses divided the 2001 Canadian Triple Crown. Dancethruthedawn, whose dam, Dance Smartly, had won the series in 1991, defeated Win City by half a length in the Queen's Plate Stakes in June, then lost to her rival by the same distance in the Prince of Wales Stakes in July. Both horses skipped the third jewel, the Breeders' Stakes, which was won easily by Sweetest Thing.

Ethereal, who gave New Zealand-bred horses their 12th Melbourne Cup win in 20 years, earlier had triumphed in the Caulfield Cup. The four-year-old mare was the 11th horse to complete the double and the first Melbourne Cup winner to be trained by a woman, Sheila Laxon. Northerly won the Cox Plate just ahead of Sunline, with Silvano fourth.

(ROBERT W. CARTER)

Harness Racing. Two European trotters went to North America in 2001 and in just four races beat the U.S.'s best and took more than a million dollars back to the continent.

The Italian sensation Varenne won the $1 million Breeders Crown at the Meadowlands in New Jersey on July 28. Driver Giampaolo Minnucci raced his champion with the utmost confidence, reaching the wire 4½ lengths ahead of his closest pursuer. Verenne's time of 1:51⅕ was the fastest race-mile ever trotted. Earlier in the 2001 season the six-year-old trotter had won the Prix d'Amerique in France, the Lotteria in his native Italy, and the Elitlopp in Sweden. No horse had swept those events in a single year in many decades. Varenne returned to Europe after winning the Breeders Crown, then traveled back to North America for the Can$500,000 (about U.S. $320,000) Trot Mondial at the Hippodrome in Montreal in September. He again prevailed over North America's finest and sealed his claim as the greatest trotter in the world. In his two starts in North America, Varenne earned U.S. $750,000.

On the same day that Varenne won the Breeders Crown, a photographer-turned-horseman from Sweden named Stefan Melander started his colt Scarlet Knight in a qualifying heat for the $1 million Hambletonian. Scarlet Knight won the heat and thus earned a chance to compete for the biggest prize for three-year-old trotters. Melander had purchased Scarlet Knight in 1999 at an auction in Pennsylvania, then returned to Sweden. The colt showed remarkable ability, and Melander began to dream of winning the Hambletonian. No horse had ever come from Europe to win the Hambletonian, but Melander's dream came true on August 4. Banker Hall stole off to a huge early lead but began to tire. Melander guided Scarlet Knight to the outside and past Banker Hall in the stretch, raising his whip in jubilation as he crossed the finish line first. In his two starts at the Meadowlands, Scarlet Knight earned $535,000.

A pair of American three-year-old fillies also enjoyed impressive seasons. The trotter Syrinx Hanover cruised through the season unbeaten; her victories included the Hambletonian Oaks and the Breeders Crown. She was raced sparingly, however, as her owner wanted to conserve her for future years. The popular three-year-old pacing filly Bunny Lake used her base in New York as a springboard to success, winning major races in New Jersey, Kentucky, Ontario, and Pennsylvania.

Bettor's Delight and Real Desire gave racing fans thrills whenever they battled in the classic events for three-year-old pacers. Bettor's Delight won the North America Cup in June, but Real Desire rebounded to victory in a hard-fought stretch duel in the Meadowlands Pace in July. In September Bettor's Delight won a two-heat victory in the Little Brown Jug over Real Desire, but Real Desire got revenge when he led all the way to take the Breeders Crown in October.

Although Scarlet Knight won the Hambletonian, the king of the three-year-old trotters was a colt named SJ's Caviar. He had been so sick as a two-year-old that his owner wondered if the colt would survive an early illness, but he blossomed into the best of his class in 2001. The trotter's owners had dropped his Hambletonian eligibility when he was deemed too sick to compete, but SJ's Caviar still earned over $1.2 million in 2001.

(DEAN A. HOFFMAN)

Steeplechasing. Foot-and-mouth disease led to the cancellation of British racing for 10 days in March 2001 and the loss of many other meetings, including the Cheltenham Festival. There was no racing in Ireland between February 25 and April 16, and only three Irish horses were permitted to race in Great Britain in the Grand National, which was won by Red Marauder. Only 2 out of 40 entries completed that race without mishap, but 2 horses, Blowing Wind and 2000 National winner Papillon, were remounted and finished. Free traffic across the Irish Sea resumed in early May.

French-trained First Gold won the King George VI Chase and Martell Cup Chase but was only fifth in the Grand Steeplechase de Paris behind Kotkijet, winning his sixth consecutive race. Kotkijet was one of many champion horses owned by Daniel Wildenstein. (*See* OBITUARIES.) The New Zealand-trained Rand won the inaugural Pegasus Jump Stakes at Nakayama, Japan, in March but then was brought down in the Nakayama Grand Jump won by Gokai three weeks later.

(ROBERT W. CARTER)

Show Jumping and Dressage. Ludger Beerbaum of Germany rode Gladdy's S to victory in the European individual show jumping championship at Arnhem, Neth., in July 2001, and ended the season as undisputed world number one in the Fédération Equestre Internationale/Gandini world riders rankings. The pair lost, however, to Brazilian Rodrigo Pessoa on Gandini Lianos in the Nortel Networks Grand Prix, the world's richest show jumping prize, at Calgary, Alta., in September. Ireland's team of four won the Nations Cup at both Arnhem and Calgary.

The U.K. surpassed France and Italy to win the European three-day event championship at Pau, France, in October. The U.K.'s Pippa Funnell captured the individual gold medal on Supreme Rock. Riders from Germany and Spain took silver and bronze.

Ulla Salzgeber of Germany rode the Russian-bred Rusty to win both the World Cup and European championship dressage. The pair were also part of the winning German team in the Nations Cup at Aachen, Ger., in June and at Verden, Ger., in August.

(ROBERT W. CARTER)

Polo. In the 2001 U.S. high-handicap season, held in Palm Beach, Fla., from January to April, Outback, led by Argentine Adolfo Cambiaso, prevailed at the U.S. Open for the third straight year, and Boca Polo triumphed in the Gold Cup in Boca Raton, Fla. Peter Brant's White Birch, led by Mariano Aguerre and Carlos Gracida, won the Sterling Cup and the Gold Cup of the Americas. In the summer season, held in Long Island, N.Y., White Birch won the Hampton Butler Handicap Cup.

In the English high-handicap season, Cambiaso conducted Dubai to three victories in a row. With his teammates—patron Ali Abwardy of Saudi Arabia, Bartolomé ("Lolo") Castagnola, and Ryan Pemble—the polo star captured the Indian Empire Shield, the Warwickshire Cup, and the Gold Cup. The Queen's Cup was suspended as a consequence of the outbreak of foot-and-mouth disease.

In Australia, Brazil outclassed the local quartet 10–9 in the final of the low-handicap (14 goals) world championship. Château La Cardonne was the winner of the French Open, held in Chantilly, France. In Sotogrande, Spain, Talandracas, led by Milo Fernández Araujo, was the champion of the Gold Cup for the first time. Prior to this tournament, Sebastián Merlos and Santiago Chavanne, who also stood out in the U.S. season as Cambiaso's Outback teammate, were the key for Geebung to reach victory in the Silver Cup.

In a rainy season in Argentina, La Dolfina (Cambiaso, Castagnola, and brothers Sebastián and Juan Ignacio Merlos) won the Hurlingham Open. The quartet was beaten 17–16 in the final of the Argentine Open, however, by Indios Chapaleufú I. The champions (Aguerre and brothers Bautista, Marcos, and Horacio Heguy) won the Open, the world's most important polo tournament, for the sixth time after a six-year losing streak.

(JORGE ADRIÁN ANDRADES)

FENCING

Proposed rule changes to foil were debated within the Fédération Internationale d'Escrime (FIE) during 2001. Since the foil target was restricted to the trunk, a white light traditionally had been used in the scoring apparatus to indicate an off-target nonvalid hit. As with an on-target hit, this resulted in a pause in play, leading to confusion for spectators and irritation for the media, especially television. The FIE sought to make the sport more media- and spectator-friendly, and the "white light" problem in foil had proved to be among the most difficult to resolve. Many experts believed that removing the white light and allowing play to continue after nonvalid hits would transform foil. Others thought this would destroy the essence of foil and that other measures, such as altering the blade flexibility and the pressure needed to register a hit, would prove equally effective. In December the FIE congress decided to establish a working committee to examine the "white light" issue, with a brief report to the General Assembly due in April 2002.

The special commission formed in 2000 finally authorized transparent masks from three European manufacturers. The masks were passed as safe and technically satisfactory in all three weapons (foil, épée, and sabre) but were not made compulsory, and many fencers still would not accept them. The other continuing major concern, wireless scoring equipment, made further progress with the approval of apparatus for sabre developed by Ukrainian engineers and manufactured by the German company Allstar/Uhlmann.

While the countries traditionally strong in fencing maintained their dominant positions through the year, others, especially China, South Korea, and the U.S., continued to challenge. The U.S. particularly showed strength in women's and men's junior sabre. The 2001 senior world championships were held on October 26–November 1 in Nîmes, France, inside the covered Roman amphitheatre and amid tight security. France, Italy, Germany, and Russia took most of the glory, but encouragingly the U.S. and Sweden also won medals.

In July Gian Carlo Brusati of Italy, one of the grand old men of fencing, died at age 91. Brusati won épée team gold at the 1936 Olympic Games and was FIE president in 1981–84.

(GRAHAM MORRISON)

Paolo Milanoli of Italy (right), having scored a hit against Basil Hoffman of Switzerland, moves to evade his opponent en route to winning the mens' épée final at the world fencing championships in Nîmes, France, on October 29.

Dominique Faget/AFP Worldwide

FIELD HOCKEY

On April 21, 2001, Els van Breda Vriesman of The Netherlands became the first woman president of the Fédération Internationale de Hockey (FIH). At the FIH congress in Brussels, the first round of voting, against Alain Danet of France, ended 40–40. In the second round the majority opted for van Breda Vriesman, who had been named the first woman secretary-general in 1994. Australian Peter Cohen was unanimously elected secretary-general. Van Breda Vriesman took the reins of the FIH's restructured 21-member Executive Board. She was elected to the International Olympic Committee in July.

On the field it was an eventful year, highlighted by the World Cup qualifying competitions for men and women and the World Cup finals for juniors (under 21). South Korea stunned many by winning the junior women's competition in May against host team Argentina in a tiebreaker (4–3) after being 2–2 at the end of regulation time. The 16-team, four-pool system introduced in Argentina continued for the men's junior event in Hobart, Australia, in October. India won the cup for the first time, beating Argentina 6–1. Germany defeated England 5–1 to gain the bronze.

Seven countries (Argentina, Belgium, India, Japan, New Zealand, Poland, and Spain) qualified for the 2002 World Cup from the men's championship, held in Edinburgh in July. The women's qualifier, held in Amiens and Abbeville, France, in September, concluded with England taking the top spot, followed by Russia, Ukraine, Japan, and Scotland. Ireland was declared the winner for the sixth place after Lithuania was disqualified for refusing to participate in a replayed tiebreaker. The U.S. missed the event as a result of the disrupted flight schedules after the September 11 terrorist attacks in the U.S. The FIH gave the American women a chance to fight for the seventh spot in a three-Test series against India. On an appeal from Lithuania, the disciplinary commission of the FIH recommended the four countries—Ireland, Lithuania, India, and the U.S.—play in the Challenge Cup in Randburg, S.Af., to determine the sixth and seventh qualifiers.

Argentina defeated The Netherlands 3–2 to claim the women's Champions Trophy at Amstelveen, Neth., in August. The men's competition was shifted to Rotterdam, Neth., from Lahore, Pak., in the wake of the September 11 attacks. Two goals by Florian Kunz, the top scorer with 10 goals, helped Germany regain the Champions Trophy against Australia (2–1). The Netherlands beat Pakistan 5–2 for the bronze.

Stephan Veen of The Netherlands and Alyson Annan of Australia were named the Players of the Year for the second straight year. (S. THYAGARAJAN)

FOOTBALL

Association Football (Soccer). *Europe.* In 2001 the majority of European national association football (soccer) teams concerned themselves with qualifying matches for the 2002 Fédération Internationale de Football Association (FIFA) World Cup, to be held in Japan and South Korea. Nine European nations qualified for the World Cup finals by winning their respective Union des Associations Européennes de Football (UEFA) groups: Croatia, Denmark, England, Italy, Poland, Portugal, Russia, Spain, and Sweden. By year's end five second-place teams also had qualified: Belgium, Germany, Ireland, Slovenia, and Turkey. The prospects for England, led by captain David Beckham (*see* BIOGRAPHIES), had improved with the appointment of a Swede, Sven-Goran Eriksson, as its first foreign coach. France, the defending champion and therefore exempt from the preliminaries, was able to add another trophy to its 1998 World Cup and Euro 2000 titles by winning the FIFA 2001 Confederations Cup for area champions, which also was staged in Japan and South Korea. The triumphant French beat Japan 1–0 in the final on June 10. In September young players representing France defeated Nigeria 3–0 to capture the under-17 world championship.

At club level, despite moves toward more freedom of contract, the scramble for first-class players continued to escalate transfer fees. In July the Spanish club Real Madrid paid some $64 million to Italy's Juventus for French forward Zinedine Zidane, the reigning FIFA World Player of the Year. England, with eight current French internationals playing in its Premier League, saw champions Manchester United pay £19 million (about $28.1 million) for Dutch striker Ruud Van Nistelrooy from PSV Eindhoven and a British-record fee of £28.1 million (about $41.6 million) for Argentine midfield player Juan Sebastián Verón from Italy's Lazio, Eriksson's former club.

Manchester United's record third championship in succession—and its

David Beckham of England scores on a free kick in a World Cup qualifying match against Greece.

Gary M. Prior/Allsport

seventh in the nine years of Premier League football—produced an average crowd attendance of 67,544, the highest ever achieved in 112 years of professional football in the country.

United's league title achievement was overshadowed by the three cup victories of Liverpool, which had also managed twice to beat United in league games. Under the tutelage of French coach Gerard Houllier, Liverpool annexed the League Cup, the Football Association (FA) Cup, and the UEFA Cup for a unique treble. In August it defeated Manchester United 2–1 in the annual Charity Shield match between FA league and cup winners and then added the European Super Cup to its list of honours, beating Germany's Bayern Munich 3–2.

By the conclusion of its UEFA Cup venture, Liverpool had completed 63 competitive games during the season. The UEFA final in Dortmund, Ger., on May 16 against the Spanish finalist, Alavés, was an absorbing encounter full of goals.

For Alavés, only six years out of the third division, it was a fairy-tale scenario, but when the team found itself a goal down in three minutes to Liverpool's first serious attack, the Spanish players' prospects seemed poor. Scotsman Gary McAllister's free kick was headed in for Liverpool by Germany's Markus Babbel, and worse followed for the team from Spain's Basque region. Liverpool's other German international, Dietmar Hamann, combined with Michael Owen after 17 minutes to produce a goal for Steven Gerrard to make the score 2–0.

Rather than lapse into free fall, Alavés shrugged off these early setbacks. Coach José Manuel Esnal ("Mané") brought on striker Iván Alonso for defender Dan Eggen and switched from a 4-5-1 formation to an attacking 3-5-2 system. In the 27th minute the substitute headed in Cosmin Contra's cross to reduce the deficit to one. Alavés goalkeeper Martín Herrera then tripped Owen, and McAllister restored Liverpool's two-goal advantage at 3–1 from the resulting penalty kick in the 41st minute. Surprisingly, Herrera received only a yellow card for his indiscretion.

By the 51st minute Alavés had evened the score at 3–3 through two goals by Javi Moreno early in the second half. In the 48th minute he headed in Contra's centre and then converted a free kick for his second successful effort. Houllier then changed tactics, bringing on Vladimir Smicer in midfield for defender Stephane Henchoz, shuffling the team around, and replacing Emile Heskey with Robbie Fowler up front. Mané's response was to withdraw Moreno, a move that arguably cost them the chance of taking the initiative. In the 73rd minute Fowler ran through to make it 4–3 for Liverpool, only to have Alavés tie the score in the dying seconds of normal time. From a corner kick from Pablo Gómez, Jordi Cruyff headed in to force the game into overtime.

Alas, the Spaniards then fell apart. Magno Mócelin of Brazil was shown the red card for a foul on Babbel in the 99th minute. Captain Antonio Karmona, already on a yellow card, was cautioned again for pulling back Smicer in the 117th minute, and Alavés was left with only nine players. From McAllister's resulting free kick, the ball clipped the head of defender Delfí Geli and found the corner of the net to give Liverpool a 5–4 sudden-death victory.

In contrast, the European Champions League final a week later between Bayern Munich and Valencia of Spain in Milan's San Siro Stadium was dominated by penalties and caution, although there was a similar 5–4 score from the final shoot-out. The Spaniards took a dramatic lead in the second minute when Swedish international defender Patrik Andersson was adjudged to have handled the ball in a scramble at the mouth of the goal. Gaizka Mendieta drove the penalty kick past goalkeeper Oliver Kahn's right hand. Four minutes later Bayern had the opportunity to level the score with a penalty of its own. Jocelyn Angloma tripped Stefan Effenberg, and although Mehmet Scholl's penalty kick was on target, the ball hit Valencia goalkeeper Santiago Cañizares's legs and rebounded over the crossbar.

Both teams made second-half changes, and Bayern equalized from the game's third penalty award in the 50th minute. Amedeo Carboni handled the ball in a panic, and Effenberg put the teams into a tie at 1–1. Neither team seemed ambitious enough to take undue risks from then on as the game drifted toward the end of 90 minutes. It was only in overtime that the Bayern players stirred themselves more than the opposition, who seemed content to await the fate of the inevitable shoot-out. Paulo Sergio missed for Bayern with the first penalty attempt, but the Germans emerged 5–4 victors after Mauricio Pellegrino's effort was saved by Kahn with what was the 17th penalty kick of the match.

In purely domestic terms Bayern had won the German Bundesliga on the last day of the season. The team needed at least a draw at Hamburg to prevent Schalke 04 from overtaking it, and it did so 1–1. It was Bayern's 17th championship and its third in succession.

In Azerbaijan there was a closer contest, which had to be determined by a play-off in which Shamkir beat Neftchi Baku after both teams had finished level on goal difference. Boavista became only the fifth different team in 66 years to win the title in Portugal, while the French first division club Toulouse was relegated to the third division when it was unable to make adequate financial guarantees. French cup winner Strasbourg also suffered relegation to the second division. Europe's ace marksman was Swedish international striker Henrik Larsson of Scotland's Celtic. He scored 35 league goals and 52 in all competitions as the Glasgow club won all three domestic trophies. Cypriot champion Omonia Nicosia saw its German striker Rainer Rufmann head the leading scorers for the fourth season in succession.

(JACK ROLLIN)

The Americas. There were some significant changes in association football (soccer) in Latin America during 2001. While Argentina easily won the South American World Cup qualifying group, Brazil—which lost its number one spot in the FIFA ranking for the first time in years—struggled all the way and managed to make sure of a top-four automatic qualifying place only at the end. Uruguay, the other usual powerhouse, reached the finals only after a play-off against Oceania winner Australia. Ecuador made the finals for the first time ever.

The South American championship, the Copa América, held in Colombia in July, lost stature when it was canceled owing to local terrorist activity and then reinstated with six days to go (owing to pressure from television-rights holders). By that time Argentina, the favourite, had disbanded its squad and withdrawn, and guest nations and most other countries sent weak squads. Colombia took the cup for the first time, winning all six of its games with no goals against, but there were plans to revitalize the tournament, which was next scheduled for Peru in 2003.

Argentina's Boca Juniors retained the South American club championship, the Libertadores de América Cup, beating Mexico's Cruz Azul on penalties in the two-legged final, which finished with a 1–1 aggregate score. The Argentine team could not retain the Intercontinental Cup against the European champions, however, and lost 1–0 to Germany's Bayern Munich.

The made-for-TV Mercosur and Merconorte cups were played for the fourth and last time. In spite of lucrative prizes, rising from $200,000 per home match in the first round to $3 million for the final winner, many clubs fielded virtual teams, and crowds were small at most games—only six tickets were sold for one match—in spite of reduced admission prices. All four Merconorte tournaments were won by Colombian clubs, with Bogotá's Millonarios crowned in 2001. The Mercosur Cup, which had been won by Brazilian clubs on the three previous occasions, could not be completed in 2001. Flamengo (Brazil) and San Lorenzo (Argentina) drew the first leg 0–0 in Rio de Janeiro. The second leg in Buenos Aires was scheduled on the day an uprising started that brought down the Argentine government. The match was postponed until January 2002.

In domestic leagues it was the year of the small club. Atlético Paranense took the Brazilian title for the first time, beating another small club, São Caetano, in the final. In Chile the Wanderers triumphed for the first time in 33 years. While Nacional retained the Uruguayan championship, it had to face modest opening-tournament winner Danubio in the final. Alianza Lima took the Peruvian title after winning the opening tournament and then beating Cienciano of Cusco, which won the closing tournament. Both clubs were celebrating their 100th anniversary.

Though popular Racing Club was one of Argentina's big clubs, its opening-tournament title, without established stars, was its first success in 35 years. Racing Club was Argentina's only top-division club run by a company; other Argentine clubs, as well as some in Brazil and other South American countries, were close to bankruptcy through bad management, in spite of the continued sale of star players to European clubs.

In the Confederation of North, Central American and Caribbean Association Football (CONCACAF), Costa Rica, Mexico, and the U.S. qualified for the 2002 World Cup finals. On October 21 the San Jose Earthquakes won their first Major League Soccer (MLS) Cup, scoring a sudden-death overtime goal to defeat the Los Angeles Galaxy 2–1. There were reports, however, that two MLS teams—possibly the Tampa Bay Mutiny and Miami Fusion—could soon be eliminated. The eight-team professional Women's United Soccer Association finished its first year of play, with the Atlanta Beat defeating the Bay Area CyberRays on penalty kicks in the final on August 25. (ERIC WEIL)

U.S. Football. *College.* The University of Miami (Fla.) won its fifth national championship of college football by defeating the University of Nebraska 37–14 in the Rose Bowl at Pasadena, Calif., on Jan. 3, 2002. This was the first Rose Bowl contest since 1946 that did not match the Big Ten and Pacific conference winners. Big East champion Miami (12–0) had the only undefeated record in Division I-A of the National Collegiate Athletic Association (NCAA), which it led with 45 turnovers on defense and the lowest regular-season defensive yields: 9.4 points per game and a 75.6 passing-efficiency rating.

Although Miami was the fourth undisputed champion in four years of the Bowl Championship Series (BCS), Nebraska's inclusion in the title game generated the third controversy in identifying the two finalists. The BCS computer formula ranked Nebraska (11–2) second, but both the media reporters' and coaches' regular-season polls ranked it behind Pacific-10 champion Oregon (11–1) and Colorado (10–3), which had defeated Nebraska 62–36 during the season and won the Big 12 championship before losing to Oregon 38–16 in the Fiesta Bowl.

With Miami's victory, its third in four national championship games against Nebraska, both final polls ranked Oregon, Orange Bowl winner Florida (10–2), Tennessee (11–2), Texas (11–2), and Cotton Bowl champion Oklahoma (11–2) next in the top six. The media's Associated Press poll followed in order with Southeastern Conference champion Louisiana State (10–3), Nebraska, Colorado, Washington State (10–2), Atlantic Coast champ Maryland (10–2), and Big Ten winner Illinois (10–2), which lost to Louisiana State in the Sugar Bowl. The coaches' *USA Today*-ESPN poll flipped two pairs of those rankings with higher positions for Nebraska and Maryland; Maryland's Ralph Friedgen was the consensus Coach of the Year. Other I-A conference winners were Louisville (11–2) in Conference USA, Toledo (11–2) in the Mid-American, Brigham Young (12–2) in the Mountain West, and Louisiana Tech (7–5) in the Western Athletic, while North Texas (5–7) and Middle Tennessee State (8–3) shared the Sun Belt title.

Quarterbacks for Miami and Nebraska each won Player of the Year honours, with the Maxwell Award going to Miami's Ken Dorsey and Nebraska's Eric Crouch winning the Heisman Trophy, the Walter Camp Award, and the Davy O'Brien Award for quarterbacks. Nebraska also led Division I-A with 314.7 yd rushing per game. Oregon's 11 turnovers lost were the fewest. Miami offensive tackle Bryant McKinnie won the Outland Trophy for interior linemen.

Florida and Brigham Young were the top offensive teams. Florida passed for 405.2 yd per game behind quarterback Rex Grossman, the leader with 9.9 yd per pass attempt, 354.9 yd total offense per game, and an efficiency rating of 170.8. Brigham Young averaged 542.8 yd and 46.8 points per game, with a division-high 28 touchdowns by Luke Staley, the Doak Walker Award-winning running back.

Fresno State quarterback David Carr's 42 touchdown passes and 4,299 yd passing were best, as was Wes Counts's .726 completion percentage for Middle Tennessee State. The receiving leaders were Hawaii's Ashley Lelie with 19 touchdowns, Utah State's Kevin Curtis with 100 catches, and Fred Biletnikoff Award winner Josh Reed with 1,740 yd for Louisiana State. Nevada freshman Chance Kretschmer's 1,732 yd rushing and Levron Williams's 200.1 all-purpose yards per game for Indiana also were tops.

North Carolina defensive end Julius Peppers won the Chuck Bednarik Award for best defender and the Vince Lombardi Award for linemen. Oklahoma teammates Rocky Calmus and Roy Williams, respectively, won the Dick Butkus Award for linebackers and the Jim Thorpe Award for defensive backs. Miami's Edward Reed led with nine interceptions, and Texas allowed the fewest yards per game, 236.2.

Ray Guy Award winner Travis Dorsch of Purdue led punters with a 48.4-yd average. New Mexico's Vladimir Borombozin had the best field-goal percentage, .944 on 17-for-18, just ahead of Lou Groza Award winner Seth Marler's 15-for-16 for Tulane.

Among schools with smaller football budgets, 15–1 Montana defeated 12–3 Furman for the Division I-AA championship, 14–1 North Dakota won the Division II championship game over 12–1 Grand Valley State (Mich.), 14–0 Mount Union (Ohio) won its fifth Division III title in six years (and its 82nd game out of 83) by beating Bridgewater (Va.), and 14–0 Georgetown (Ky.) won its second straight National Association of Intercollegiate Athletics (NAIA) championship game against 12–2 Sioux Falls (S.D.). The Walter Payton and Buck Buchanan awards for Division I-AA recognized Villanova running back Brian Westbrook and James Madison linebacker Derrick Lloyd, respectively, as the top overall and

Harry How/Getty Images/Allsport

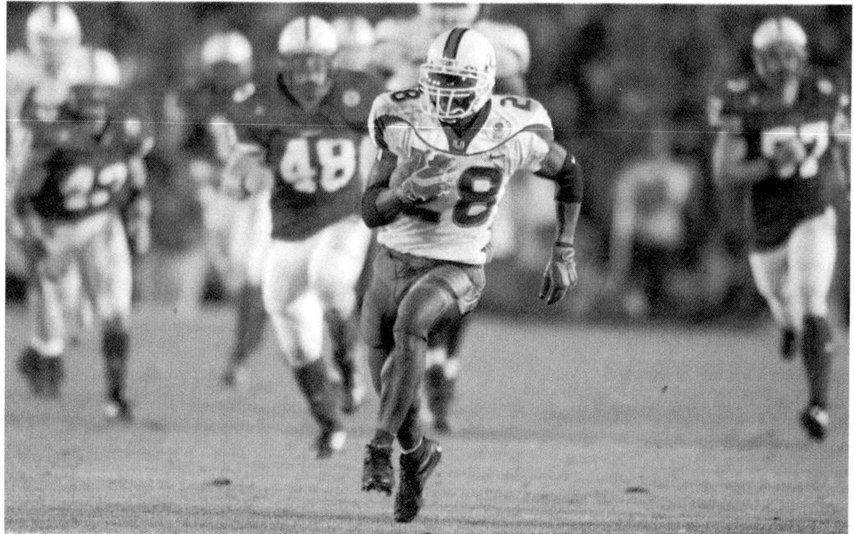

Clinton Portis of the University of Miami outsprints Nebraska defenders in the Rose Bowl on January 3.

defensive players. Valdosta State (Ga.) quarterback Dusty Bonner won his second Harlon Hill Trophy for Division II; Mount Union running back Chuck Moore received the John Gagliardi Trophy for Division III; and Georgetown quarterback Eddie Eviston won his third NAIA Player of the Year award.

Professional. On Feb. 3, 2002, in a surprisingly thrilling Super Bowl XXXVI, the American Football Conference (AFC) New England Patriots upset the heavily favoured National Football Conference (NFC) St. Louis Rams 20–17 before a crowd of 72,922 in the New Orleans Superdome. New England started with a 47-yd interception touchdown by Ty Law and unexpectedly led 14–3 at the half; St. Louis came back in the fourth quarter to tie the game at 17. Then Adam Vinatieri kicked a 48-yd field goal in the final seconds to give New England its first National Football League (NFL) championship in the franchise's 42-year history. Most Valuable Player (MVP) honours went to the Patriots' 24-year-old quarterback Tom Brady. During the play-offs, the Patriots had upset Oakland 16–13 with a game-ending 45-yd field goal and then beat Pittsburgh 24–17 with veteran Drew Bledsoe filling in for an injured Brady. St. Louis crushed Green Bay 45–17 and then defeated Philadelphia 29–24 to reach the final matchup.

In regular-season play NFC West champion St. Louis had the league's best offense with per-game averages of 31.4 points, 418.1 yd, and 306.4 yd passing. That was more than five points and 35 yd ahead of Indianapolis, the AFC leader in each category. AFC Central winner Pittsburgh ran for the most yards on offense with 173.4 per game, allowed the fewest yards on defense with 258.6 per game total and 74.7 on the ground, ranked second to NFC Central champion Chicago's league-low yield of 12.7 points per game, and led the NFL with 55 sacks. Dallas's top-ranked pass defense allowed 188.7 yd per game. Other NFC defensive leaders were St. Louis in total yards and Chicago in rushing yards.

Other division winners were Philadelphia in the NFC East, New England in the AFC East, and Oakland in the AFC West, which repeated as division champion. Of the five other division winners in 2000, only Miami made the play-offs as a "wild-card" team, as did defending champion Baltimore and the New York Jets in the AFC, along with San Francisco, Green Bay, and Tampa Bay in the NFC. Miami's five consecutive play-off appearances led the league. Chicago won its division for the first time since 1990 with a league-best improvement of eight games, and Philadelphia won its first since 1988. Like Chicago, New England improved from last place to first, matching San Francisco's improvement of six games, and all three were among the six play-off teams that had missed the tournament in 2000–01, joining Green Bay, Pittsburgh, and the New York Jets.

New York Giants defensive end Michael Strahan set an NFL record with 22.5 sacks. Other records included Emmitt Smith's 11th season with at least 1,000 yd rushing for Dallas and Marshall Faulk's fourth with at least 2,000 yd from scrimmage. Faulk was 22 yd behind that category's leader, Kansas City's Priest Holmes, who gained 2,169 yd from scrimmage and also led the NFL with 1,555 yd rushing. Faulk had the best average gain with 5.3 yd per rush and led the league with 21 touchdowns and 128 points, one more than teammate and top-scoring kicker Jeff Wilkins. San Francisco's Terrell Owens and Seattle's Shaun Alexander had league highs of 16 touchdowns receiving and 14 rushing, respectively.

Kurt Warner of St. Louis, the regular-season MVP, led most passing categories with a 101.4 efficiency rating, 4,830 yd, 8.85 yd per attempt, and 36 touchdowns with an .066 touchdown percentage. Oakland's Rich Gannon's nine interceptions were the fewest, as was his .016 percentage. The receiving leaders were Denver's Rod Smith with 113 catches and Arizona's David Boston with 1,598 yd. Tampa Bay's Ronde Barber and Cleveland's Anthony Henry shared the interception lead with 10 apiece.

The league's top kick returners were Ronney Jenkins of San Diego with 26.6 yd per kickoff return and Troy Brown of New England with 14.2 yd per punt return. Todd Sauerbrun of Carolina had the best punting averages, 47.5 yd gross and 38.9 yd net. Jason Elam's 31 field goals for Denver were the NFL's most, while Miami's Olindo Mare had the best percentage, .905 on 19 for 21.

In spring and summer leagues, the Grand Rapids Rampage defeated the Nashville Kats 64–42 for the 15th Arena Football League championship, and the Berlin Thunder won the NFL's developmental NFL Europe championship by beating the Barcelona Dragons 24–17. The XFL, a winter-spring league standing for extreme football, folded after its only season, which included the lowest-rated prime-time telecast in network history. (KEVIN M. LAMB)

Canadian Football. The Calgary Stampeders won the 2001 Canadian Football League (CFL) championship by upsetting the favoured Winnipeg Blue Bombers 27–19 in the Grey Cup on November 25 at Montreal. Calgary's championship was its second in four years and the second in a row by a team with a losing regular-season record, something that never had happened in the cup's previous 87 years. Calgary, with a won-lost record of 8–10, overpowered West Division champion Edmonton (9–9) by 34–16 for the division title before beating East Division winner Winnipeg (14–4) in the cup final.

Calgary led the league with 136.9 yd rushing per game, and Grey Cup Most Outstanding Player Marcus Crandell led the quarterback field with 61.9% pass completions. Winnipeg led CFL defenses with per-game yields of 336 yd, 83.8 yd rushing, and 21.3 points. The Blue Bombers also had four top-ranked players: quarterback Khari Jones, the league's Most Outstanding Player, had CFL passing highs of 4,545 yd and 30 touchdowns, as well as an 87.8 efficiency rating; Milt Stegall led the league with 14 touchdown catches; tackle Dave Mudge was the Most Outstanding Offensive Lineman; and defensive lineman Doug Brown was Most Outstanding Canadian.

Other league award winners included Most Outstanding Defensive Player Joe Montford of Hamilton with 19 sacks and Most Outstanding Rookie Barrin Simpson of British Columbia with 115 tackles. (KEVIN M. LAMB)

Brisbane and Essendon players vie for the ball during the Australian Football League Grand Final match.

Mark Dadswell/Allsport

Australian Football. In 2001 the Brisbane Lions ended a historic year by winning the Australian Football League (AFL) premiership for the first time. Once the Cinderella club of the AFL and the worst-performing club in a 16-team competition as late as 1998, the Lions beat 2000 titleholder Essendon 15.18 (108) to 12.10 (82) in the Grand Final at the Melbourne Cricket Ground on September 29 before a crowd of 91,482. The win also brought much joy to the former Fitzroy supporters, whose club had dropped from the competition after the 1996 season and merged with the former Brisbane Bears to form the Lions in 1997.

The Grand Final victory was the Lions' 16th successive win, easily breaking the previous club record of 10. Five days earlier Brisbane had also been on centre stage when it was announced that team member Jason Akermanis was the upset winner of the Brownlow Medal, awarded to the fairest and best player in the 22 home-and-away rounds as adjudged by the field umpires.

Essendon started the Grand Final a slight favourite, but it could not withstand the pressure. The defending champions opened up an early lead, but the Lions produced a sizzling third quarter of 6.2 to 1.2 that virtually won it the match. Shaun Hart, the Brisbane onballer, was voted best man on the ground and won the Norm Smith Medal.

(GREG HOBBS)

Rugby Football. Australia's global domination of Rugby Union continued in 2001, as it again won the Tri-Nations Championship and gained the first series victory over the Lions (a team comprising the best players from England, Scotland, Ireland, and Wales) in its history. The Lions—in Australia with Rugby League convert Jason Robinson as one of their stars—opened the series with a stunning 29–13 win in Brisbane, only to fall to Australia in Melbourne (35–14) and Sydney (29–23) as the Wallabies took the series 2–1.

The Lions tour was unfortunately marred by a number of players' open criticism of the management—headed by Graham Henry and Donal Lenihan—and one player's launch of a tirade against the Australian side. These outbursts led to two English players, Austin Healey and Matt Dawson, being fined. Australia's victory in the Tri-Nations was confirmed with a dramatic 29–26 win over New Zealand on September 1. The triumph was sealed with a last-minute try from Toutai Kefu in a game that was legendary captain John Eales's last match. Eales ended his career as possibly the most successful Rugby Union captain of all time, with two World Cups (1991 and 1999), the Tri-Nations title, and a series victory over the Lions.

England's failure to win a Six Nations (formerly Five Nations) grand slam (a clean sweep of all five wins) continued, as it suffered its only loss on the final day of the championship for the third successive season. In 2001 it was Ireland that exposed England's inability to win under pressure, and the Irish won a pulsating encounter 20–14. England still walked off with the Six Nations title, but it was scant reward for its efforts. The championship—usually staged between February and April—was finished in October owing to the foot-and-mouth crisis, which caused the postponement of three Ireland matches.

In domestic competition the ACT Brumbies struck a big blow for Australia in the Super 12 championship (contested by the best sides in New Zealand, Australia, and South Africa), winning the final against the South African Sharks 36–6. Most of the previous competitions had been dominated by sides from New Zealand, but this time none of the Kiwi teams made the semifinals. The Leicester Tigers won the championship in England for a third successive year and lifted the Heineken (European) Cup in an exciting 34–30 win over Stade Français in Paris, with centre Leon Lloyd scoring two tries. Newcastle took the Tetley's Bitter Cup in England, beating Harlequins 30–27. Swansea was confirmed as the Welsh champion, winning the title over Cardiff by six points, while Newport lifted the Principality Cup. In Scotland Hawick was champion, and in Ireland it was Dungannon. In France Christian Califano said goodbye to Toulouse—before he moved to Auckland—by delivering the French championship in a 34–22 final win over Montferrand in Paris.

In Rugby League's Super League, the Bradford Bulls defeated the Wigan Warriors 37–6 to be crowned English champions. In Australia the Newcastle Knights won the National Rugby League premiership in front of a sellout crowd of more than 90,000 at Stadium Australia, beating the Parramatta Eels 30–24. (PAUL MORGAN)

GOLF

In the immediate aftermath of the Sept. 11, 2001, terrorist attacks in the U.S., at a time of national mourning, American players collectively decided not to travel to England. The Ryder Cup was postponed until September 2002.

In April Eldrick ("Tiger") Woods became the first player in the sport's history to hold all four of the modern major championships—the Masters, the U.S. Open, the British Open, and the Professional Golfers' Association of America (PGA) Championship—at the same time. The Masters, always held at the Augusta (Ga.) National Golf Club, was the only one of the four that Woods did not have in his possession at the start of the year.

Woods set the stage perfectly by winning his two preceding events. In Augusta his opening round of 70, two under par, left him five strokes behind fellow American Chris DiMarco. A second-round 66 heightened the excitement going into the weekend and brought the 25-year-old Woods into a share of second place, only two behind DiMarco. When he added a 68 on the third day, Woods moved into a one-stroke lead. Four years earlier the first major title of his career had come by a record 12-shot margin and with a record 18-under-par aggregate of 270, but completing his "Tiger Slam" was to prove much more difficult. A bogey on the first hole of the final round dropped Woods level with American Phil Mickelson, and David Duval, also of the U.S., made four successive birdies from the fifth hole and another birdie at the 10th to tie for the lead.

With three holes to play, Woods and Duval were 15 under par and Mickelson 14 under. Both Duval and Mickelson bogeyed the short 16th, and Duval missed a 1.5-m (5-ft) birdie chance on the final green. A drive and pitch to within 5.6 m (18 ft) of the final hole left Woods with two putts needed for victory. He holed for a birdie and finished at 16 under par for a two-stroke win over Duval.

The next opportunity came with the U.S. Open, at Southern Hills Country Club in Tulsa, Okla., in June. Woods had won the event in 2000 by a major championship record margin of 15 strokes, but his title defense was to be the start of a disappointing summer. An opening round of 74, four over par, left him eight behind the surprise leader, Retief Goosen. The 32-year-old South African, a member of the European circuit, had missed the halfway cut in seven of his previous nine majors in the U.S., but although he was caught on the second day by Americans Mark Brooks and J.L. Lewis, he dug his heels in.

With a round to go, Goosen shared the lead with American Stewart Cink, and with one hole to play, the two were locked together with Brooks, who had not won a tournament since he captured the PGA championship in 1996. What followed ensured that the event would be remembered for more than the simple fact that Woods did not win (he was joint 12th). Brooks three-putted for a bogey five, and Cink then took a double-bogey six. Goosen had hit his second shot to within 3.7 m (12 ft) and had two putts with which to become champion. His first went past the hole, and to the astonishment of the millions watching on television, he missed the next putt as well. This left Goosen and Brooks tied on the four-under-par total of 276 and meant that the pair faced an 18-hole play-off the next day. Not having to go into sudden death gave Goosen the opportunity to regroup, and he did so superbly, winning by two strokes with a par 70 to become only the sixth overseas player to take the title since 1927.

Much less of a surprise was Duval's victory in the British Open, held at Royal Lytham and St. Annes in Lancashire, Eng., in July. Coming into the event he had had eight top-10 finishes in the space of 13 majors. Scotland's Colin Montgomerie led for the first two days, and at the halfway point Duval was seven shots behind. On the third day the American shot a 65, good enough to bring him into a four-way tie as Montgomerie and others fell back, and with a final-round 67 the 29-year-old Duval triumphed by three with a 10-under-par total of 274.

The final day of the British Open, however, had another extraordinary story. On the second tee Wales's Ian Woosnam, joint leader after a birdie at the first hole, was told by his caddie that he had 15 clubs in his bag, one more than the rules permitted. A driver with which Woosnam had been practicing, but which he had decided not to use, was still in the bag. A two-stroke penalty was imposed, and the former world number one player, mortified and furious, finished joint third. The blunder was calculated to have cost him more than $312,000—and a place on Europe's Ryder Cup team. Two weeks later the same caddie was late in arriving for a round at the Scandinavian Masters in Malmö, Swed.—forcing Woosnam to find a last-minute replacement—and was fired.

The final major of the year, the PGA championship, held at the Atlanta Athletic Club in Duluth, Ga., in August, had no such incident, but it did include a record-breaking performance. Mickelson shot one stroke under the previous lowest aggregate in major history with a 14-under-par 266, but fellow American David Toms's closing pitch and 3-m (10-ft) putt for par, after a calculated decision not to go for the green in two at the par four, lowered that one more to a 15-under-par 265 and gave Toms, like Goosen and Duval, his first major title.

The win also qualified Toms for a Ryder Cup debut, but that had to be put on hold after September 11. Discussions

Annika Sörenstam chips onto the green on her way to shooting a record 59 (13-under-par) in March.

Scott Halleran/Allsport

eventually led to the decision that the match between the U.S. and Europe would be put back 12 months. Subsequent matches were changed to even-numbered years to restore the two-year cycle, with the Presidents Cup matches (the U.S. versus an international side comprising all countries outside Europe) switching to odd-numbered years starting in 2003.

The loss of three of his major titles did not stop Woods from maintaining a commanding lead in the world rankings to the end of the year or from topping the PGA Tour money list for the third successive season and the fourth time in five years, with a final total of $5,687,777. Goosen was the leading money winner on the European tour at £1,779,975 (about $2,537,000).

If Woods's victory in the Masters was the performance of the year, the round of the year was surely that by Sweden's Annika Sörenstam (*see* BIOGRAPHIES) during the Standard Register Ping tournament at the Moon Valley Country Club in Phoenix, Ariz, in March. Sörenstam became the first woman to break 60 in an official event. Not surprisingly, she went on to win the tournament and did so with a Ladies Professional Golf Association (LPGA) record total of 261, 27 under par.

The Swedish player won the Nabisco Championship, the first women's major of the season, by three shots the following week at Missions Hills Country Club in Rancho Mirage, Calif., and regained the world's number one position from Australian Karrie Webb before Webb hit back with an eight-stroke win in the U.S. Women's Open, held in June at the Pine Needles Lodge and Golf Club in Southern Pines, N.C. Three weeks later Webb gained a two-stroke victory at the McDonald's LPGA championship at the DuPont Country Club in Wilmington, Del.

That gave Webb her fifth victory in eight majors and made her at 26 the youngest woman golfer to record a career Grand Slam. The fourth and final major, the Weetabix Women's British Open held at Sunningdale, Eng., in August, resulted in a South Korean one-two finish. Pak Se Ri, who won both the U.S. Women's Open and the LPGA championship in 1998, beat Kim Mi Hyun by two strokes. Despite the tough competition, Sörenstam finished the season as the LPGA's top money winner with a record $2,105,868.

The high spot of the amateur season was the Walker Cup, which matched the U.S. against Great Britain and Ireland at the Ocean Forest course in Sea Island, Ga. The home side led by a point after the first day, but just as they had been at Nairn, Scot., in 1999, the Americans were totally outplayed on the second day and again lost 15–9. It was Britain and Ireland's first-ever successful defense of the trophy and only their second away win. (MARK GARROD)

GYMNASTICS

The 2001 artistic gymnastics world championships were held in Ghent, Belg., on October 27–November 4. The Belarus men's team won its first world championship title with a score of 169.622, rounding out its collection of medals, which included a team silver medal in 1997 and a team bronze in 1999. The U.S. earned its first men's team medal since 1979, winning the silver; Ukraine took the bronze. China's 16-year-old Feng Jing, competing in his first world championship event, won the all-around title with a score of 56.211. Belarusian Ivan Ivankov, a two-time world and European all-around champion, had to settle for the silver, followed by Bulgaria's Jordan Jovtchev with the bronze.

Jovtchev and Romania's Marian Dragulescu tied for the gold medal on the floor exercise with a pair of 9.550 scores. Dragulescu also won gold on the vault (9.668), and Jovtchev secured the title on the still rings (9.775). Marius Urzica, the 2000 Olympic gold medalist, repeated his success on the pommel horse (9.800). U.S. national champion Sean Townsend claimed top honours on the parallel bars (9.70). Vlasios Maras of Greece won gold on the horizontal bar (9.737) in his first world championship.

On the women's side, Romania, with a score of 110.209, won its sixth team title, followed by Russia and the U.S. Russia's Svetlana Khorkina, the 1997 world champion and two-time Olympic gold medalist, won yet another all-around title at the 2001 worlds, scoring 37.617. Her teammate Nataliya Ziganshina took second. Romania's Andreea Raducan—who was initially declared the all-around gold medalist at the 2000 Olympic Games but then was disqualified for having a positive drug test—finished third in Ghent.

Khorkina went on to win two individual events in addition to the all-around title, scoring a 9.412 on the vault and a

Chinese phenomenon Feng Jing competes at the artistic gymnastics world championships.

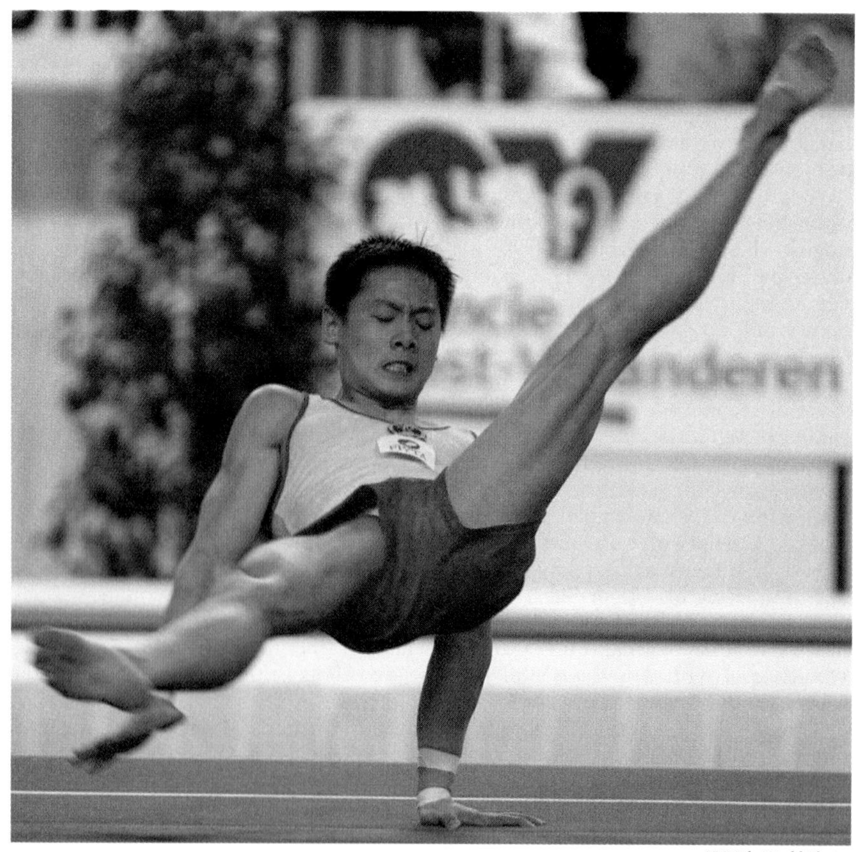

AP/Wide World Photos

9.437 on the uneven bars. Raducan grabbed the gold medals on the balance beam and the floor exercise, with scores of 9.662 and 9.550, respectively.

The rhythmic world championships took place on October 18–21 in Madrid. Former Soviet countries earned all three team medals. Russia dominated the team competition, scoring 275.900, more than 16 points over its nearest competitor, Ukraine, which claimed the silver. Belarus captured the bronze. Russia's Alina Kabayeva won her second world all-around title, with a score of 113.025, followed by her teammate Irina Chashina and Ukraine's Tamara Yerofeyeva. (LUAN PESZEK)

ICE HOCKEY

North America. The National Hockey League (NHL) delivered one of the most heartwarming human interest stories of the 2000–01 season when the Colorado Avalanche dethroned the New Jersey Devils on June 9, 2001, at Denver, Colo., in a historic showdown for the Stanley Cup. The championship series went to a seventh game for only the third time in 30 seasons as Colorado clinched the Stanley Cup for the second time since 1996 with a 3–1 victory. The Avalanche thus became the first NHL team since the 1971 Montreal Canadiens to overcome a three-games-to-two deficit in the final series.

The biggest story of the play-offs was 40-year-old Colorado defenseman Ray Bourque. The captain of the winning team usually skates around the rink with the Cup in his grasp, but Colorado's Joe Sakic ignored tradition and immediately handed it to Bourque as the sellout crowd of 18,007 cheered ecstatically. This marked the first time in a career that spanned a record 1,826 games that Bourque, who spent almost 21 seasons with Boston before he went to Colorado in a trade in March 2000, had celebrated victory in the final game of the season. It was also the last game of Bourque's career, as he announced his retirement 17 days later.

Of the 30 teams that contested the 82-game regular season prior to the play-offs, Colorado led the NHL in victories (52) and points (118) to capture its division by a huge 25-point margin over Edmonton. Detroit and New Jersey (111 points each), Ottawa (109), Dallas (106), and Washington (96) were the other division champions that advanced to the 16-team play-offs. Colorado advanced to the Stanley Cup finals by routing Vancouver in four straight games and beating Los Angeles four games to three before taking the Western Conference title over St. Louis four games to one. New Jersey reached the Stanley Cup finals for the second straight season by beating Carolina four games to two, Toronto four games to three, and Pittsburgh four games to one for the Eastern Conference title.

In addition to the motivation the Avalanche players had in trying to bring Bourque his first Stanley Cup, their title quest was greatly energized by Sakic, the high-scoring centre, and Patrick Roy, their accomplished goaltender. Sakic won both the Hart Trophy as the league's Most Valuable Player (MVP) and the Lady Byng Trophy for good sportsmanship, having been penalized only 30 minutes during the regular season. Roy finished the season as the first three-time winner of the Conn Smythe Trophy awarded to the MVP of the play-offs. Roy also reached an enviable milestone on Oct. 17, 2000, when he led Colorado to a 4–3 overtime win at Washington to become the NHL all-time leader in regular-season victories. It was Roy's 448th victory in his 847th game. Terry Sawchuck of Detroit had set the former record in 1970, achieving his 447th victory in his 968th game.

The 51st NHL All-Star game, played in Denver on February 4, produced more goals than any previous All-Star match when the North Americans defeated the World team 14–12. The American trio of Bill Guerin, Tony Amonte, and Doug Weight combined for six goals and seven assists to raise North America's record to three games to one under the game format adopted in 1998. In his first All-Star game appearance, Guerin scored three goals and had two assists to win MVP honours.

Mario Lemieux of Pittsburgh ran Bourque a close second on the human-interest front during the season, reentering the NHL on Dec. 27, 2000, after a 3½-year retirement dictated by a long recovery from serious back injuries and Hodgkin disease. Lemieux proved that the layoff hardly had diminished his skills by scoring 35 goals and posting 41 assists in only 43 games.

Off the ice, controlling interest in the storied Montreal Canadiens was sold to George Gillett, Jr., an American businessman and ski-resort developer, for Can$275 million ($183 million). The franchise had received no offers from any Canadian buyer.

International. Taking another step toward dynasty status, the men's team from the Czech Republic and the Canadian women's team dominated their respective international ice hockey rivals once again in 2001. Each team graced its season by winning a world championship in what was a familiar achievement for both organizations.

The Czech men captured their third straight world ice hockey championship at Hannover, Ger., with a 3–2 overtime victory against Finland on May 13. David Moravec scored the game-winning goal on a backhand shot that flew past Pasi Nurminen, the Finland goalie, after 10 minutes 38 seconds of overtime. Finland goals by Juha Lind and Juha Ylonen left the Czechs trailing 2–0 after the first two periods, but Martin Prochazka and Jiri Dopita beat Nurminen to square the score in the third period and send the game into overtime. That set the stage for Moravec, a Czech League journeyman whose NHL career consisted of one game with the Buffalo Sabres.

He scored off a pass from Pavel Patera. Moments later the crowd of 10,513 at Hannover's Preussag Arena roared its approval while Moravec and Czech goalie Milan Hnilicka were joyously mobbed by their teammates. It marked the sixth time in nine world tournament games that the resilient Czechs had overcome a deficit score to win. With the victory the Czech Republic became the first team to win three world titles in succession since the Soviet Union dominated from 1981 through 1983. Moravec was named MVP of the 2001 world championships.

The Finns, who similarly suffered an overtime loss to the Czechs in 1999, went home with their third silver medal in four years. Sweden took the bronze medal with a 3–2 victory over the United States.

Team Canada showed even greater domination in capturing the women's world championship for the seventh time in a row at Minneapolis, Minn., on April 8. The Canadian women claimed the world title with a 3–2 victory over the U.S. at the University of Minnesota's Marriucci Arena. In their fifth meeting of the season, the U.S. women outshot their rivals 35–18, but that barrage was not enough to beat Kim St. Pierre, the Canadian goalkeeper. She stopped 33 shots and stymied a U.S. power play in the second period when she blocked three shots and saw two others bounce off the pipes of her goalie cage.

The Canadian offense was led by Tammy Shewchuck and Jennifer Botterill, a pair of Harvard University teammates. Shewchuck scored the go-ahead goal with 9 minutes 45 seconds left in the second period after Canada's Dana Antal and Carisa Zaban of the U.S. matched goals in the first. Botterill, the world tournament MVP, gave Canada a two-goal lead when she tipped in a shot by Theresa Brisson with 3 minutes 45 seconds to go. The U.S. got its second goal from A.J. Mleczko with 79 seconds remaining after pulling its goalie, but the Americans failed to score again.

The victory was Canada's 100th in international play, raising the team's record to 35–0 in world championship games, and it demonstrated Canada's superior depth in women's ice hockey. The U.S. team had lived and trained together at Lake Placid, N.Y., for seven months preceding the world championships; the Canadian team was assembled only a week before the tournament began. The North American rivals had met 14 times since the U.S. beat Canada for the women's hockey gold medal at the 1998 Winter Olympic Games in Nagano, Japan. Including the 2001 world championship, the Canadians raised their record in the rivalry to 10–4.

(RON REID)

ICE SKATING

Figure Skating. Michelle Kwan of the U.S. and Yevgeny Plushchenko of Russia celebrated an extraordinary figure-skating season during 2001, a year in which each once again captured a world championship.

Kwan, aged 21, gave an indication of what she would achieve on January 20 in Boston, where she won her fourth straight U.S. women's championship and the fifth of her career. Kwan's remarkable free-skating performance earned a total of nine perfect 6.0 marks from the judges. She tied her record of seven 6.0s for her short program and added two more in the longer free skate to become the first woman to win four consecutive U.S. titles since Linda Fratianne (1977–80).

Plushchenko, aged 18, also got off to a superb start by winning the men's title for the second straight year at the European championships in Bratislava, Slovakia, on January 25. Plushchenko skated a bold program that included an extremely difficult quadruple toe loop and seven superbly executed triple jumps to win an emotional rivalry with fellow Russian Aleksey Yagudin, who also landed two quads and seven triple jumps. The intensity of the Russians' competition was so close that two judges gave first place to Yagudin. The European women's title went to Irina Slutskaya for the fourth time, even though the Russian champion, who had beaten Kwan twice earlier in the year, hardly looked in top form as she struggled with the flu. Russia made it a clean sweep in the women's competition for the third consecutive year when Mariya Butyrskaya won the silver medal, despite two falls, and Viktoriya Volchkova took the bronze.

Doug Pensinger/Allsport

Yevgeny Plushchenko skates his way to a world title in March.

With her victory in the world championships at Vancouver, B.C., on March 24, Kwan was hailed as the dominant skater in her sport. She started the final night in second place, trailing Slutskaya, and responded with one of the greatest performances of her career. It brought Kwan her fourth world title (her second in a row). While Slutskaya managed the first triple Salchow/triple loop/double toe combination ever witnessed in a ladies' world championship, she finished as the silver medalist for the second straight year. Sarah Hughes, the runner-up to Kwan at the U.S. championships, rallied from fourth place after her short program to capture the bronze medal; Angela Nikodinov took fifth.

Plushchenko picked off the men's title that had eluded him the previous two seasons. He landed a quadruple jump during a strong free-skating program that included eight triple and two double jumps to leave Yagudin, a three-time world champion, as a runner-up once again. Todd Eldredge, the 1996 world champion and five-time U.S. champion, captured the bronze medal. At 29 he became the oldest man to medal since Roger Turner took the silver in 1931 three days short of his 30th birthday.

The pairs title went to hometown favorites Jamie Salé and David Pelletier, the first Canadian duo to win the gold since 1993. Barbara Fusar Poli and Maurizio Margaglio of Italy, the ice-dancing gold medalists of the European championships, took their first world title in what was the first-ever world figure-skating medal for their nation.

Speed Skating. Rintje Ritsma of The Netherlands captured the men's all-around title at the 2001 world speed-skating championships contested February 9–11 in Budapest. A second-place finish in the 10,000-m race on the final day of competition enabled Ritsma to move past his countryman Ids Postma to secure the fourth world title of his career. Anni Friesinger of Germany took the women's all-around championship, holding off teammate Claudia Pechstein. Friesinger increased her first-day point total by winning the woman's 1,500-m final in 2 min 3.38 sec as a prelude to a sixth-place finish in the 5,000 m for a final total of 169.690 points. Pechstein finished second for the fifth time in her career by a centimetre or so, with 169.791 points. The women's competition might have evolved more predictably had Gunda Niemann-Stirnemann, the European all-around champion and eight-time world champion from Germany, not been disqualified in the 3,000 m for an inexplicable lane-change mistake.

Pechstein rebounded in a big way on March 2 in Calgary, Alta., where she won a World Cup 3,000-m race in 3 min 59.27 sec—a world record. Canada's Michael Ireland set another world record on the same track one day later when he covered 1,000 m in 1 min 8.34 sec. Ireland's Canadian teammate Jeremy Wotherspoon finished second by one one-hundredth of a second in what may have been the most exciting race of the year. Chris Witty of the U.S. lowered the women's world record for 1,000 m to 1 min 14.58 sec later that day.

Chinese athletes dominated the world short-track speed-skating championships at Chonju, S.Kor., during the final week of March. Yang Yang (A) topped the women's final standing for the fifth straight year, winning the 1,500-, 1,000-, and 3,000-m finals, in that order. (*See* BIOGRAPHIES.) Li Jiajun took the men's overall title for the second time since 1999, winning the 500-m and 1,000-m finals.

(RON REID)

JUDO

The world judo championships, held July 26–29 in Munich, Ger., was the standout judo event of 2001. Shinichi Shinohara of Japan emerged as the heavy favourite in the men's over-100-kg competition when David Douillet of France—who had faced Shinohara in the finals at the 2000 Olympic Games in Sydney, Australia—retired after winning gold in that event. In a stunning upset in the quarterfinals, however, Aleksandr Mikhaylin of Russia took only 12 seconds to score an *ippon* (full-point) victory over Shinohara, the defending world champion. Mikhaylin proceeded to beat Fashandi Miran of Iran and Selim Tataroglu of Turkey to claim the world title and then went on to victory in the open-weights event. Kosei Inoue of Japan became the only man to win gold at both the Sydney Olympics and the 2001 world championships when he successfully defended his under-100-kg world title at Munich. Olympic champion Ryoko Tamura of Japan continued her dominance in women's judo, winning her fifth straight world title in the under-48-kg event. In the overall medal count, the Japanese team placed first with 10 medals, including 4 golds, followed by Cuba (8 medals) and South Korea (5).

The 2001 Individual Grand Prix was held on October 13 in Moscow for men and on November 24 in Seville, Spain, for women. Mikhaylin placed second behind fellow Russian Tameryan Tmenov in the over-100-kg competition, and Nicolas Gill of Canada claimed the under-100-kg title. Tamura sat out the tournament, but another Japanese woman, Kayo Kitada, took the under-48-kg title.

(EDITOR)

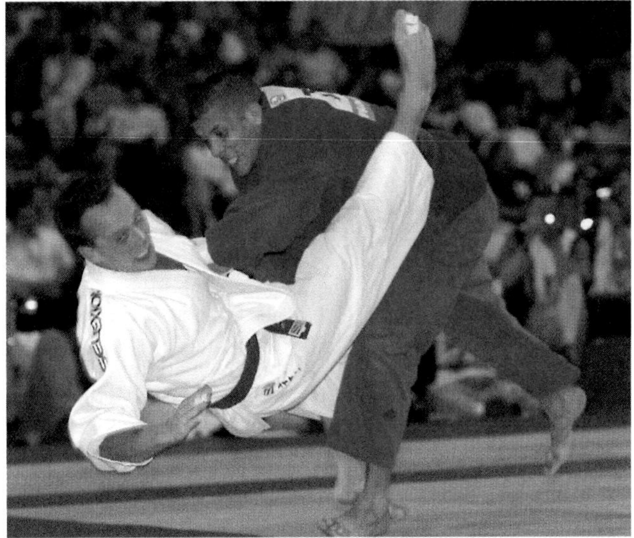

Anis Lounifi of Tunisia throws Cedric Taymans of Belgium in their world judo championships final match on July 29.

Peter Kneffel/AFP Worldwide

RODEO

In 2001 the Professional Rodeo Cowboys Association's Wrangler Pro Rodeo Tour wrapped up its second year with a sold-out concert-rodeo at the new American Airlines Center in Dallas, Texas. Billed as the Texas Stampede, the finale to the pro tour season featured $700,000 in prize money, second only to the world-championship-deciding Wrangler National Finals Rodeo (NFR), which was held December 7–16 in Las Vegas, Nev.

The NFR featured a $4.6 million purse, the largest in the event's 42-year history. Topping the list of competitors was Cody Ohl of Stephenville, Texas, who earned $296,419 in three events to claim the all-around world title. In addition, Ohl claimed the third calf-roping world title of his career with $222,026 in earnings. In the ninth round of the NFR, however, the cowboy tore ligaments in his right knee, an injury that was expected to keep him out of competition for at least six months. Ohl did not anticipate a title defense in 2002; world championships in professional rodeo were based on prize money won over the yearlong rodeo season as well as the money made at the season-ending NFR. In addition to the all-around—awarded to the cowboy who won the most money in a combination of events—individual event world championships were bestowed in bareback riding, steer wrestling, team roping (heading and heeling), saddle-bronc riding, calf roping, bull riding, and women's barrel racing.

In the steer-wrestling world title race, Rope Myers of Van, Texas, rose from 14th place to first after racking up $117,774 at the 10-round NFR, bringing his total season earnings to $176,584. Bareback rider Lan LaJeunesse of Morgan, Utah, earned his second world championship (his first was in 1999), defeating newcomer Bobby Mote in the final round. His earnings for the year totaled $185,556. Saddle-bronc rider Tom Reeves of Stephenville, Texas, collected his first world championship while competing at his 17th straight NFR; he topped the field with $204,008.

Janet Stover of Rusk, Texas, rode a horse owned by former NFR competitor Peyton Rainey to the barrel racing title after her own horse, Gotowin Bo, was sidelined with a leg injury. Stover won $126,934 at the finals, the most in a single event, to finish the year with $186,812. (GAVIN FORBES EHRINGER)

ROWING

The preparation cycle for the 2004 Olympic Games in Athens began by extending the World Cup series in 2001, with a new opening round in the U.S. in April. The Fédération Internationale des Sociétés d'Aviron (FISA) international rowing congress also took a step along the road to championship status for student rowing by renaming the Nations Cup the "World Under 23 Regatta." A new regulation was introduced for the automatic removal of a boat class from the world championship program if there were fewer than seven starters for three consecutive years. A Cuban proposal to give the FISA executive discretion in sentencing first-time doping offenders was overwhelmingly rejected. FISA, almost alone among international sports federations, imposed an automatic life ban for serious doping offenses.

Germany, winner of the team title, and Great Britain were the most successful of the 10 nations that won gold medals at the FISA world championships in Lucerne, Switz., in August. In men's events Romania captured the eights by 0.99 sec over Croatia, while France and Great Britain won the coxed and coxless fours, respectively. The German men's sole victory was in quadruple sculls. Hungary finished just 0.13 sec ahead of France in double sculls, and Olaf Tufte became Norway's first world single sculls champion by only 0.32 sec. Germany won the three sculling titles in the women's events, while Australia triumphed in eights and coxless fours, with Romania taking the coxless pairs. Ireland had triple winners in the lightweight events, with Italy claiming two titles. The remainder of the 24 gold medals at stake were won by Australia, Austria, France, Germany, and Great Britain.

The biggest drama of the championships was provided by Great Britain's second bid for a golden double in men's coxed and coxless pairs. This had never been achieved, and Britain's previous attempt with Steven (later Sir Steven) Redgrave in the 1988 Olympic Games had only narrowly failed. James Cracknell and Matthew Pinsent—two members of Redgrave's 2000 Olympic gold medal coxless fours—had already won coxless pairs in the 2001 World Cup convincingly enough to be persuaded to go for the elusive double at the world championships. With an interval of only two hours for physical recovery between finals, it was a risky challenge. The British pair led all the way to win the coxed event by 0.42 sec, but in the coxless final they were never ahead until the last stroke, where a photo finish gave them the verdict and a unique world record by 0.02 sec.

At the 152nd Henley Royal Regatta in England, Redgrave won the Queen Mother Challenge Cup (quadruple sculls) for his 20th Henley medal. Overseas entries from seven countries, led by Australia, harvested 11 trophies. Duncan Free of Australia took the Diamond Challenge Sculls; Australia also captured the Princess Elizabeth Challenge Cup (eights), Henley Prize (eights), and Fawley Cup (quaduple sculls). The U.S. won twice in eights in the Ladies' Challenge Plate and the Temple Challenge Cup. The Grand Challenge Cup (eights) went to H.A.V.K. Miladost and V.K. Croatia of Croatia, while Belgium won the Thames Cup (eights). Two-time world champions Tomasz Kucharski and Robert Scez of Poland won the Double Sculls Cup. Champion women scullers included Germany in Quadruple Sculls and Yekaterina Karsten of Belarus in the Princess Royal Cup (single sculls).

In the 147th University Boat Race, Cambridge avenged Oxford's interruption in 2000 of Cambridge's seven straight wins. After 20 strokes the race was stopped for the first time since 1829 before Cambridge won by $2^1/_2$ lengths to bring its overall lead in the series to 77–69. (KEITH L. OSBORNE)

SAILING (YACHTING)

Technology was central to sailing in 2001, with dramatic effect on the sport. At the upper end a relative handful of professionals sailed boats built to aircraft specifications and using space-age materials, most of them financed by commercial sponsors that gained display platforms for their logos. In September the 2001–02 Volvo Ocean Race (formerly the Whitbread Round-the-World Race) started eight entries, all 18.3-m (60-ft) water-ballasted boats built for the event and financed by sponsorship. The Vendee Globe Race, for 18.3-m (60-ft) boats built to a different but similar rule, fielded 24 starters for a nonstop circumnavigation. Fifteen of the boats finished, and Michel Desjoyeaux established a new record, completing the voyage in 93 days 3 hr 57 min. An even faster time occurred in a new event, titled simply "the Race." Six giant catamarans, limited in size only by the availability of sponsorship funds, started this nonstop "Around" race; five entries finished. The winning *Club Med* required only 62 days 6 hr 56 min for the circumnavigation. By year's end 10 challengers had registered to contest New Zealand's hold on the America's Cup in late 2002. The America's Cup had always been a technological contest, and teams were already on New Zealand's Hauraki Gulf testing boats and sails. A successful challenge was expected to cost at least $80 million.

The official report on the storm-ravaged 1998 Australian Sydney–Hobart race was issued in the spring and suggested that the race management team had "abdicated its responsibility at the time of crisis." A long series of recommendations was included in the report, which was being studied worldwide for its legal implications. In the Sydney–Hobart race that ended at the beginning of January 2001, the racing fleet again met challenging conditions, and 24 of the 82 starters were forced to retire. Four crew were swept overboard in the race, but they were recovered successfully. *Nicorette* and *SAP Ausmaid* (both sponsored boats) won the line honours and the overall race, respectively.

In 2001 World Sailor of the Year Ellen MacArthur became the fastest—and youngest—woman to sail around the world.

Gerry Penny/AFP Worldwide

On the administrative front the International Sailing Federation (ISAF) took the Offshore Racing Council under its wing and began providing oversight for all sail racing in the world. A controversial decision dropped the men's three-man (spinnaker) keelboat from the Olympic program and added a women's keelboat fleet racing event. This left the men without a spinnaker keelboat—when even the Olympic catamaran employed these colorful and powerful sails—and denied women the match-racing venue many of them had sought. The French youth team won the ISAF world championship for the fourth consecutive year. The ISAF's World Sailors of the Year were Ellen MacArthur of Great Britain and Robert Scheidt of Brazil.

Two notable speed records were established by Steve Fossett's giant catamaran, *Playstation*. Sailing ahead of a strong weather front, the boat logged 687 nautical miles in 24 hours and completed a transatlantic crossing in 4 days 17 hr 28 min at an average speed of 25.86 knots. (JOHN B. BONDS)

SKIING

Alpine Skiing. In 2000–01, for the second straight season, Austrian icon Hermann ("the Herminator") Maier won four World Cup titles—overall, downhill, supergiant slalom (super G), and giant slalom (GS). Although he did not win any gold medals at the 2001 Alpine world championships in St. Anton, Austria, the Herminator did not miss much else. He finished more than 740 points ahead of teammate Stephan Eberharter for the overall title, collecting a record-tying 13 World Cup victories. In August Maier broke his leg seriously in a motorcycle accident, and it was uncertain if he would compete in the 2002 Winter Olympics in Salt Lake City, Utah.

On the women's side, Croatian teenager Janica Kostelic earned her first two

World Cup titles, despite having injured ligaments in her left knee in the final month of the season. Austrian Renate Götschl fell in several races and failed to defend her overall crown. Kostelic, who later underwent three knee surgeries, had won the first eight World Cup slaloms and cruised to the slalom title before edging Götschl in overall points. Isolde Kostner of Italy won the women's downhill title; France's Régine Cavagnoud was the super G champion; and Sonja Nef of Switzerland captured the GS title.

The world championships started with heavy snowstorms and a surprise gold medal in the men's super G for American Daron Rahlves. Austria dominated, collecting 14 medals though only 3 golds. Michaela Dorfmeister led an Austrian medals sweep in the women's downhill; "local boy" Mario Matt took the men's slalom championship on the final day; and Hannes Trinkl won the men's downhill title. Swiss great Michael von Grünigen won the GS. Martina Ertl of Germany sparkled in the combined, despite having injured her right knee a month earlier. Cavagnoud won the super G gold medal, and Nef claimed the GS title. The world champion in slalom was Sweden's Anja Paerson. In October the outlook for the 2002 Olympics changed again when Cavagnoud was killed. (*See* OBITUARIES.)

Nordic Skiing. The overriding story for the 2000–01 Nordic season was the doping scandal at the world championships in Lahti, Fin. Six Finns—including national icons Mika Myllylä and Harri Kirvesniemi—were caught using a banned drug, hydroxyethyl starch, a blood thinner that could boost endurance and could mask other illegal drugs. Myllylä and Kirvesniemi retired; Jari Isometsä and Janne Immonen received two-year suspensions. Virpi Kuitunen, who had won the "pursuit" gold medal at the championships, and Milla Jauho received three-month suspensions when an arbitrator ruled that they may have been innocent victims of coaches and doctors. The Fédération Internationale de Ski (FIS) had caught Isometsä and Immonen in routine postrace drug tests. The World Anti-Doping Agency (WADA) had uncovered the other four in a surprise test after the relays.

In the last two weeks of the season, Russian Yuliya Chepalova overtook two-time champion Bente Skari (formerly Martinsen) of Norway for the women's World Cup cross-country title. Per Elofsson, despite a month off to prepare for the world championships, gave Sweden its first men's crown since the great Gunde Svan's win in 1989.

Freestyle Skiing. American aerialist Eric Bergoust, who already had won everything else in his sport, won the first two World Cup events and edged teammate Joe Pack by four points for his first World Cup title. Jacqui Cooper of Australia breezed to her third straight women's aerials crown. At the world championships at Blackcomb, B.C., Canadian Veronika Bauer won the women's aerials championship; Belarusian Aleksey Grishin collected the men's title.

Norwegian Kari Traa secured a unique trifecta: the World Cup moguls title plus world championship gold in moguls and dual moguls. Mikko Ronkainen made it three straight World Cup titles for Finnish men, winning both the World Cup and the world championship title.

Karine Ruby speeds to victory in the women's parallel slalom during the World Cup snowboarding finals on January 11.

Laurent Gillieron/AFP Worldwide

Snowboarding. The many-prismed world of snowboarding featured World Cup tours run by the FIS and the International Snowboard Federation (ISF) plus the U.S. Open and a variety of non-Cup contests. As a result, some athletes rode both World Cup circuits, some rode just one, and others stayed in the U.S. and competed in non-World Cup events.

On the FIS tour Karine Ruby of France, the most dominant woman rider for years, won two gold medals at the world championships plus the World Cup overall, GS, and snowboardcross titles; Canadian Jasey Jay Anderson was the World Cup overall champion and gold medalist in the GS at the worlds. On the ISF tour Olympic champion Gian Simmen of Switzerland was the men's halfpipe titleholder. Norway's Stine Brun Kjeldaas won the first three FIS women's halfpipes (en route to finishing second for the season), then switched to the ISF tour and easily won that halfpipe title.

(PAUL ROBBINS)

SQUASH

Australian David Palmer started 2001 ranked eighth in the world and ended it as number one. Another Australian, Sarah Fitz-Gerald, returned to the top 10 and finished at number one.

The British Open in June was indicative of how the year would go for the erstwhile top two men, Peter Nicol of Scotland and Canadian Jonathon Power. Both disappeared early in the tournament, and it was left to English veteran Chris Walker to celebrate reaching 34 years of age and reaching the final. There—tired after having played in the qualification rounds—he succumbed to the 24-year-old Palmer.

Power struggled as ever with a series of leg and back injuries in 2001, but Nicol's loss of edge emanated from a different quarter. The defending world champion surprised the squash world in February by announcing a change of allegiance from Scotland to England (based on residential qualification) in a bid to benefit from more favourable National Lottery funding. The furor seemed to affect his form, but as the year closed, wins in Cairo and Qatar took Nicol to the brink of regaining the number one spot.

After losing in the semifinals of the women's World Open in November 2000, Fitz-Gerald was beaten only once in the next 14 months—by New Zealander Leilani Joyce in the semifinals of the Hong Kong Open in August. In June Fitz-Gerald won the British Open, the only title that had threatened to elude her, and by early October she was back at number one. Later that month she traveled home to Melbourne, where she cruised to victory over Joyce in the final to win her fourth World Open title.

Australia beat defending champion Egypt 3–0 in the final of the men's team World Open after the young Egyptian side had swept past Scotland and Canada in earlier rounds. The men's World Open, due to be staged in Mumbai (Bombay), India, in December, was postponed owing to economic difficulties.

(ANDREW SHELLEY)

Michael Klim competes in a 50-m butterfly heat at the world swimming championships in Fukuoka, Japan.

AP/Wide World Photos

SWIMMING

As 2001 dawned—three months after the Sydney, Australia, Olympic Games, with 14 world records and historic performances by Inge de Bruijn and Pieter van den Hoogenband of The Netherlands and Australian phenomenon Ian Thorpe—many assumed that the new year would be anticlimactic. "The Thorpedo," however, repeatedly obliterated his already mind-boggling world records. (*See* BIOGRAPHIES.)

At the Australian national championships in Hobart, Tas., in March, Thorpe and Grant Hackett engaged in a stroke-for-stroke duel for the first 700 m of the 800-m freestyle. Then Thorpe left Hackett in his wake. When he touched the wall, Thorpe had clocked 7 min 41.59 sec, almost four and a half seconds under Kieren Perkins's seven-year-old mark. Hackett also finished well under the old standard. The next night Thorpe regained the 200-m world mark he had lost to van den Hoogenband in Sydney, lopping an extraordinary 0.66 sec off "Hoogie's" world record.

Meanwhile, at the U.S. national championships, 15-year-old Michael Phelps became the youngest man ever to set a world swimming record when he clocked 1 min 54.92 sec in the 200-m butterfly. Ed Moses took the 100-m breaststroke standard away from Russia's Roman Sludnov, touching in 1 min 00.29 sec. Anthony Robinson lowered the 50-m breaststroke record to 27.49 sec, but it lasted only two days until Moses reduced it again to 27.39 sec.

At the Russian national championships in June, Sludnov responded to Moses's challenge, first reducing the American's record in the 100-m breaststroke by three-hundredths of a second and then breaking the one-minute barrier with a historic 59.97-sec performance. On April 13 China's Qi Hui took the global mark in the women's 200-m breaststroke to 2 min 22.99 sec; it was the year's only women's record set in a 50-m pool.

The Fédération Internationale de Natation Amateur (FINA) world championships, held on July 16–29 in Fukuoka, Japan, saw eight men's world records broken, four by Thorpe. He lowered his own world record in the 400-m freestyle to 3 min 40.17 sec, beating Hackett, whose 3-min 42.51-sec finish made him the second fastest man in history. In the 800-m freestyle the result was the same, with both men again under the old record. In the 200-m freestyle Thorpe exacted his revenge for his Olympic upset loss to van den Hoogenband, thrashing his Dutch rival and taking the world mark down to 1 min 44.06 sec.

The next day Thorpe, Hackett, Michael Klim, and William Kirby cut two seconds off Australia's 4 × 200-m freestyle relay record set in Sydney. Thorpe also swam legs on Australia's gold-medal-winning 4 × 100-m freestyle and medley relay teams. Not surprisingly, at year's end *Swimming World* magazine named him World Swimmer of the Year.

There were three other world-record swims in Fukuoka. Hackett took a phenomenal seven seconds off Perkins's 1994 global standard in the 1,500-m freestyle. Phelps destroyed the strongest 200-m butterfly field in history, taking his own mark down to 1 min 54.58 sec. Sludnov easily defeated Moses, as well as Olympic champion Domenico Fioravanti of Italy, in the 100-m breaststroke. American Anthony Ervin was the only man besides Thorpe to win more than one individual event, sweeping the 50-m and 100-m freestyle sprints.

In women's events de Bruijn won the 50-m and 100-m freestyle and the 50-m butterfly. Ukraine's Yana Klochkova, Germany's Hannah Stockbauer, China's Luo Xuejuan, and Australia's Petria Thomas were double winners in individual events, with Thomas adding a third gold medal in the medley relay. In the women's 4 × 200-m freestyle, both the Australians and the Americans were disqualified, leaving the third-place British quartet as the gold medalists.

An amazing 16 new world records were set in short-course (25-m pool) competition during 2001, with five falling during the FINA World Cup series early in the year. Although she set no new records, Slovakia's Martina Moravcova was easily the most dominant swimmer on the World Cup circuit, winning 29 of 34 races and taking second in the other five.

Five world records were erased at the Australian short-course championships in Perth, only a week after the world championships. Hackett took nine seconds off Perkins's 800-m freestyle mark and lowered his own 1,500-m freestyle standard with astonishing times of 7 min 25.28 sec and 14 min 10.10 sec, respectively. An hour after setting the 1,500-m record, Hackett teamed with Thorpe, Klim, and Kirby to clock 6 min 56.41 sec in the 4 × 200-m freestyle relay, almost five full seconds under the old mark held by the U.S. Three more global standards fell at the European Short Course Championships in December, while Natalie Coughlin (U.S.) lowered the 100- and 200-m backstroke marks in the FINA World Cup series in November.

Diving. China extended its decade-long dominance in diving in 2001 and won 8 of the 10 events contested at the world swimming championships in Fukuoka. Only Russian Olympic champion Dmitry Sautin and Canadian Blythe Hartley could dent the Chinese machine. The Russian won his specialty, the men's 3-m springboard, narrowly defeating China's Wang Tianling and Japan's Ken Terauchi. A "shocked" Hartley eked out a three-point win on the women's 1-m springboard over China's Wu Minxia.

China's Wang Feng took the men's 1-m title, with teammate Wang Tianling 11 points behind. Tian Liang was an 18-point victor in the 10-m platform. The men's 3-m synchronized diving title fell to Bo Peng and Wang Kenan. The 10-m synchro crown went to China's Tian and Hu Jia.

Guo Jingjing and Wu Minxia of China teamed up to take the women's 3-m synchro crown, and Guo followed up by breezing to a 44-point victory in the women's 3-m springboard, with Olympian Irina Lashko, a Russian-turned-Australian, second. Fourteen-year-old Xu Mian of China won the 10-m platform over her fellow 14-year-old teammate Duan Qing, and Duan and Sang Xue, age 17, added the 10-m synchro title with little difficulty.

Synchronized Swimming. The year's focus for synchronized swimming was also in Fukuoka. Olga Brusnikina breezed to the solo gold medal to go with her 2000 Olympic duet title. The 22-year-old Russian scored 99.434 points, well ahead of France's Virginie Dedieu (98.287), who also had finished second, to Olga Sedakova of Russia, at the 1998 world championships. Japan's Miya Tachibana was third (97.870).

Tachibana and Miho Takeda combined to win the duet title. The victory marked the first time Japan had ever won gold at a world championship level in any aquatic discipline.

In 2000 Russia had won the Olympic gold in the team competition using an experienced team. In 2001, in a daring move, the Russians fielded a team of juniors who performed to the same music. The result, however, was the same; Russia won with 98.917 points. Japan was second, and Canada finished third.

(PHILLIP WHITTEN)

TABLE TENNIS

At the 2001 table tennis world championships held April 23–May 6 in Osaka, Japan, the Chinese were totally dominant. They scored easy victories in the team events—the men defeated Belgium (which had upset defending champion Sweden in the semifinals), and the women topped North Korea. Pro Tour grand final winner Wang Liqin won the men's singles and, with his partner from the 2000 Olympic Games, Yan Sen, captured the men's doubles. Olympic gold medalist Wang Nan won the women's singles and, with her Olympic partner, Li Ju, secured the women's doubles. Qin Zhijian and Yang Ying took the mixed title. World Cup winners were Belarus's Vladimir Samsonov and China's Pro Tour grand final women's champion Zhang Yining. The Europe Top 12 men's and women's champions were Samsonov and Hungary's Csilla Batorfi, respectively.

On September 1 the International Table Tennis Federation (ITTF) changed the scoring in its tournaments from the traditional 21-point game to an 11-point game and increased match play to best three-out-of-five or four-out-of-seven games. As of Sept. 1, 2002, a new service rule would ensure that the receiver sees the server make contact with the ball—that is, the server would not be permitted to interpose part of his or her body to hide, and so delay the receiver from seeing, the spin applied to the ball. It was likely that the ITTF's 186 member countries would observe these new rules in their domestic competitions.

(TIM BOGGAN)

TENNIS

Although the men produced four different champions at the illustrious Grand Slam events in 2001, the "man of the year" label was worn deservedly by a pugnacious 20-year-old from Australia named Lleyton Hewitt. He captured the first major title of his career at the U.S. Open; recorded an impressive six tournament triumphs, including the season-ending Tennis Masters Cup at Sydney, Australia, in November; and became the youngest man ever to conclude a year as the number one ranked player in the world. American Andre Agassi continued his late-career exploits by claiming the Australian Open crown for the second year in a row. Brazil's Gustavo Kuerten came through at the French Open for the third time. The enigmatic Croatian Goran Ivanisevic ruled at Wimbledon.

The women, meanwhile, garnered more than their share of the public's imagination, particularly a trio of prominent Americans. Venus Williams replicated her immense feat of 2000, sweeping to triumphs at both Wimbledon and the U.S. Open. Lindsay Davenport collected seven tournament titles and finished a year ranked number one for the second time. Arguably the year's most inspiring player in the game—man or woman—was Jennifer Capriati, who completed an astounding career comeback at 25 and surged to Australian Open and French Open triumphs in a sterling 2001 campaign. (*See* BIOGRAPHIES.) Capriati earned a number two status on the official Women's Tennis Association computer, but she was rewarded by an International Tennis Federation panel as "world champion" because no one else could match her consistency in the major championships. Kuerten was the men's leader in prize money for the second straight year with $4,091,004, while Williams earned top prize money for the women at $2,662,610.

Australian Open. In an unprecedented personal feat, Switzerland's wily Martina Hingis toppled both Venus and Serena Williams in the same tournament. She upended Serena in a spirited quarterfinal clash 6–2, 3–6, 8–6 after Williams built a 4–1, two service-break lead in the final set. Then Hingis crushed Venus Williams 6–1, 6–1 to set up a final-round appointment with the number 12 seed, Capriati. Capriati had ousted four-time former champion Monica Seles of the U.S. and defending champion Davenport to reach the title match. Capriati's weight of shot was too much for Hingis as the American overcame her Swiss adversary for the first time, majestically casting aside the favourite 6–4, 6–3.

Agassi was seeded sixth in his bid to rule "Down Under" for the third time, but three months before he turned 31 the American performed with the panache of a man much younger. In the semifinals he prevailed in a magnificent five-set collision with Australia's Patrick Rafter. Agassi obliterated Frenchman Arnaud Clement 6–4, 6–2, 6–2 with meticulous ground-stroke execution to win the seventh Grand Slam tournament title of his uneven yet estimable career.

French Open. In the middle of his bid for a second consecutive crown on the slow red-clay courts of Roland Garros, Kuerten found himself on the edge of elimination. Facing American qualifier Michael Russell, the 24-year-old Brazilian was match point down before recouping to win 3–6, 4–6, 7–6 (7–5), 6–3, 6–1 in a pivotal fourth-round showdown. Revitalized, Kuerten soared to the title, cutting down Russian Yevgeny Kafelnikov and two Spaniards, Juan Carlos Ferrero and Alex Corretja. The resourceful Corretja picked an uneasy Kuerten apart in the first set with a brisk wind blowing. As the weather conditions became calmer, however, Kuerten's slow court artistry took over and carried him to a 6–7 (3–7), 7–5, 6–2, 6–0 victory.

Capriati was pushed to her physical and emotional limits in a spectacular final against Belgium's rapidly improving Kim Clijsters. After holding back Serena Williams in a three-set quarterfinal and Hingis in a straight-set semifinal, Capriati came into the title-round confrontation with immense confidence. The number four seed from the U.S. was the heavy favourite, but Clijsters, who turned 18 the day before the match, was undaunted in her first major final. Her big-hitting, free-wheeling style of play unsettled the American. In the final set of an uncommonly suspenseful struggle, Capriati was two points away from defeat four times before she prevailed 1–6, 6–4, 12–10.

Wimbledon. At the All-England Club, all eyes were focused on Capriati. In the semifinals she took on number eight seed Justine Henin of Belgium. The American was blazing off both sides at the beginning but in the end Henin's exquisite one-handed backhand enabled the 19-year-old to move past Capriati 2–6, 6–4, 6–2 and into the final. Henin gave Venus Williams sporadic problems during the final, but the number two seed retained her title with a convincing 6–1, 3–6, 6–0 victory.

Ivanisevic was greatly relieved when he was given a wildcard into the main draw. The three-time former finalist had suffered from severe shoulder problems the previous year and had fallen in the qualifying rounds at the Australian Open in January. The towering left-hander had one of the biggest serves ever, however, and over the Wimbledon fortnight his shoulder pain was minimal. Breaking a record he had set in 1992, Ivanisevic released an amazing 212 aces in his seven-match run past (among others) defending U.S. Open champion Marat Safin of Russia, Briton Tim Henman, and Rafter. American Pete Sampras, the victor for seven of the previous eight years, was beaten in five sets by the gifted Roger Federer of Switzerland in the fourth round. Rafter and Ivanisevic confronted each other in a rare Monday final after rain disrupted the schedule. Two points from defeat at 6–7 in the fifth set, Ivanisevic emerged with a 6–3, 3–6, 6–3, 2–6, 9–7 win.

U.S. Open. Sampras had struggled all year long to find his customary drive and inspiration, but with the American crowds boosting him vociferously, the 30-year-old put on some dazzling displays in New York City. Sampras knocked out three former champions in a row to reach the final—Rafter, Agassi in a classic 6–7 (7–9), 7–6 (7–2), 7–6 (7–2), 7–6 (7–5) quarterfinal, and Safin in a straight-set semifinal. Sampras lost his chance to become the first man to win at least one major title for nine consecutive years when he fell 7–6 (7–4), 6–1, 6–1 to Hewitt in a disappointing final.

The women's event did not sparkle as promised. Venus Williams overpowered her younger sister, Serena, 6–2, 6–4 in a battle between the 2000 and 1999 champions, respectively. It was the first time since 1884 that two sisters had clashed in the final of a major championship. In one-sided semifinals Venus had defeated Capriati 6–4, 6–2, and Serena had routed Hingis 6–3, 6–2.

Other Events. Hewitt took the Tennis Masters Cup. In this eight-player round-robin tournament, Hewitt did not lose a match, defeating Sebastien Grosjean of France in straight sets in the final. Serena Williams was victorious at the women's season-ending Sanex Championships, which was moved from New York City to Munich, Ger. Davenport suffered a knee injury during her semifinal win over Clijsters and was forced to default the title match to Williams.

France upset Australia in Melbourne 3–2 to take the Davis Cup for the ninth time. Belgium defeated Russia 2–1 to capture the Fed Cup.

Off the court the story of the year was that of Agassi and Germany's Steffi Graf, who were married in Las Vegas, Nev., on October 22, four days before the birth of their son. Between them, Agassi and Graf had secured 29 major singles titles.

(STEVE FLINK)

Alex Livesey/Allsport

Viva Guga! Gustavo Kuerten triumphs in the French Open.

TRACK AND FIELD SPORTS (ATHLETICS)

The year 2001 was highlighted by both indoor and outdoor world championships, as well as high-profile world records. A Czech decathlete, Roman Sebrle, took the global standard in track and field's "jack-of-all-trades" event from his countryman Tomas Dvorak; American Stacy Dragila, the reigning queen of the women's pole vault, rewrote the record books eight times; and a single autumn week saw the first two women's marathon clockings under 2 hours 20 minutes. The year also saw the farewell tour of Michael Johnson, the American world-record holder at 200 m and 400 m and history's most successful championship long sprinter.

World Indoor Championships. At the International Association of Athletics Federation (IAAF) world indoor championships, held in Lisbon on March 9–11, Cuban long jumper Iván Pedroso jumped 8.43 m (27 ft 8 in) to become the first athlete to win five world indoor golds in a career. Only two other champions from the 2000 Olympic Games in Sydney, Australia—Mozambican Maria Mutola in the women's 800 m and Tereza Marinova of Bulgaria in the women's triple jump—won titles in Lisbon.

Hicham El Guerrouj of Morocco, dominant in the 1,500-m and mile runs since 1997 (with the exception of his loss at the Sydney Olympics), set his eye on the 3,000 m. He had run the second fastest indoor two-mile in history, 8 min 9.89 sec, just two weeks before. In Lisbon he made winning look easy again with a time of 7 min 37.74 sec. Hoping to defend her 3,000-m title on the heels of a women's world record 8 min 32.88 sec three weeks earlier, Romania's Gabriela Szabo wound up more than two seconds behind Russian Olga Yegorova's final-lap burst of speed.

World Outdoor Championships. On August 3–12 Edmonton, Alta., hosted the first world outdoor championships held in North America. In the men's and women's 100-m sprints, two Americans sought to extend their winning streaks in world and Olympic dashes. Maurice Greene succeeded, hobbling the last 15 m as his left thigh muscles cramped painfully. His 9.82-sec clocking into a minor headwind (–0.2 m/sec) was the third fastest in history, inferior only to two of his own times, and it led a U.S. medal sweep in the men's event.

Marion Jones had won 42 consecutive 100-m finals dating back to a loss in September 1997. In Edmonton, however, Zhanna Pintusevich-Block, a Ukrainian whose training was guided by her American husband in Johnson City, Tenn., bested Jones by 0.03 second, at 10.82 sec. Pintusevich-Block had celebrated what she at first thought was a victory over Jones before, at the 1997 world championships in Athens, only to learn when official times were posted that the American had edged her by 0.02 second. After that disappointment, Pintusevich-Block had gone on to win the world 200-m title in Athens. This time, as Pintusevich-Block limited herself to the 100 m, Jones won the 200-m gold in 22.39 sec and ran the anchor leg on the victorious U.S. 4 × 100-m relay.

American John Godina, the outdoor world shot-put champion in 1995 and 1997, scored a third gold, throwing 21.87 m (71 ft 9 in). German discus thrower Lars Riedel picked up his fifth world title. The 34-year-old Riedel stood fourth after the third round, in which 2000 Olympic champion Virgilijus Alekna of Lithuania had thrown a meet record 69.40 m (227 ft 8 in). In rounds four and five, though, Riedel whirled off throws of 69.50 m (228 ft) and 69.72 m (228 ft 9 in), the longest marks ever in world championships or Olympic competition. Javelin world-record holder Jan Zelezny of the Czech Republic showed the form that had won him two previous world titles and three Olympic golds since 1992. Finnish rival Aki Parviainen opened with a meet record, 91.31 m (299 ft 7 in), but Zelezny answered with an arching throw of 92.80 m (304 ft 6 in) to win his third world gold at age 35.

In a tense women's pole vault, Dragila cleared 4.75 m (15 ft 7 in), higher than any woman other than herself had ever gone, and then watched as Russian Svetlana Feofanova matched her. Dragila won the gold on the basis of fewer misses.

Men's 10,000-m world-record holder Haile Gebrselassie of Ethiopia had not raced in more than 10 months since Sydney, and 23-year-old Kenyan policeman Charles Kamathi outsprinted him to gold in 27 min 53.25 sec. Gebrselassie took bronze for his first 10,000-m loss in eight seasons and his first defeat at any distance above 1,500 m since 1996. Pedroso, on the other hand, kept his streak going and won the long jump for his fourth outdoor world title.

Drug-testing controversies enveloped the men's and women's 5,000-m races but not men's winner Richard Limo. Limo and his Kenyan teammates used team tactics to blunt the finishing speed of opponents, and Limo took gold in 13 min 0.77 sec. Ali Saïdi Sief, the 2000 Olympic silver medalist, finished second, but later came word that the Algerian had tested positive for the banned steroid nandrolone. Pending an appeals process likely to take months, Saïdi Sief faced disqualification.

Yegorova arrived for the women's 5,000 m under the cloud of a positive test for banned synthetic erythropoietin (EPO) following a win at the Paris Golden League meet. French drug testers, however, had failed to administer a required blood test along with the urinalysis, and the IAAF exonerated her on that basis. Among others in the final, Yegorova met 1,500-m winner and defending 5,000-m champion Szabo, who at one point threatened to withdraw if the Russian competed. Szabo, looking fatigued, faded to eighth place. Yegorova sprinted to victory in 15 min 3.39 sec as jeers rained down from the stands. Regarding the question of EPO use, she maintained her innocence in a postrace press conference.

Men's International Competition. The decathlon world record had belonged to a Czech since Dvorak scored 8,994 points in 1999. At Götzis, Austria, in May, Sebrle outdid Dvorak, scoring 9,026 as the first decathlete in history to surpass 9,000 points. The new champion produced personal bests in the long jump, discus, and javelin and equaled his fastest-ever 100-m time; no decathlete had ever matched his 8.11 m (26 ft 7¼-in) with legal wind. A groin injury hampered Sebrle at the world championships, however, and he placed 10th as Dvorak defended his world title and Olympic gold medalist Erki Nool of Estonia finished second.

Moroccan Brahim Boulami finished 10th in the steeplechase at the world championships, but he followed up at Grand Prix events in Zürich, Switz., and Brussels with wins in 7 min 58.50 sec and a world-record 7 min 55.28 sec, respectively. El Guerrouj assuaged in part his Olympic disappointment with an undefeated year. Briton Jonathan Edwards, the triple-jump world-record holder, won 13 straight meets between June 17 and September 9, including European Cup and world championships victories.

Swiss runner André Bucher, victor in the overall men's IAAF Grand Prix worth $150,000, won 11 of 12 outdoor meets at 800 m and 1,000 m, including the 800-m world title. Russian Yury Borzakovsky had to run the fifth fastest 800 m in history (1 min 42.47 sec) to hand Bucher his only defeat in Brussels. Bucher and El Guerrouj, along with American hurdler Allen Johnson, each garnered one-fifth shares in the Golden League series jackpot of 50 kg (110 lb) of gold.

Women's International Competition. For consistent excellence Dragila, with 25 meets and just three losses, stood out. She matched four indoor world records with four outdoors, topped by a 4.81-m (15-ft 9¼-in) vault in Palo Alto, Calif., in June. From May through the season-ending Grand Prix final in Melbourne, Australia, she never lost.

Yegorova went undefeated at 5,000 m, with just one 3,000-m loss. Her one championship failing was to lose the European Cup 1,500-m final to Romanian Violeta Szekely, herself the past recipient of a drug ban. Szekely won 11 of 12 outdoor 1,500-m races and the women's overall Grand Prix title. She and Yegorova each earned a one-fifth share of the Golden League gold. Jones, supreme star of the three preceding seasons, went undefeated except for her world championships loss, compiling 14 wins in 15 finals at 100 m and 200 m.

Cross Country and Marathon Running. In Berlin on September 30, Olympic champion Naoko Takahashi of Japan became the first woman to break 2 hr 20 min in the women's marathon, knocking 57 seconds from the previous world record. The 2-hour 20-minute barrier had loomed ever since Norwegian Grete Waitz broke 2 hours 30 minutes in 1979, but Takahashi held the record for just a week before Catherine Ndereba of Kenya ran 2 hr 18 min 47 sec at the Chicago Marathon. So strong was Ndereba's finish that she ran from 40 km (24.9 mi) to the finish faster than the top male finishers, Kenyans Benedict Kimondiu and Paul Tergat.

Tergat drew attention with his marathon debut in April, when he ran 2 hr 8 min 15 sec to place second in London. In Chicago Kimondiu, in the race as a pacemaker, elected to finish and defeated Tergat by 4 seconds in 2 hr 8 min 52 sec.

At the world cross country championships in Ostend, Belg., Kenya won four of six team titles, and Ethiopia captured the other two. Belgian Mohamed Mourhit repeated as men's long-course champion. Radcliffe won the women's long-course race over Ethiopian Gete Wami, with positions reversed and Wami defeating Radcliffe in the short-course race. (SIEG LINDSTROM)

VOLLEYBALL

The U.S. women's volleyball team made a large step toward reestablishing itself as a world power with a victory in the ninth World Grand Prix, held in Macau, China, in August 2001. It defeated the host country 3–1 in the final. The U.S. had won the team title in 1995 and had not returned to the final since. Russia, which swept Cuba to capture the bronze medal, finished among the top three for the sixth consecutive World Grand Prix season. In the semifinals the Americans had upset Russia, and China beat defending champion Cuba. Danielle Scott of the U.S. was named the best scorer and blocker; teammates Stacy Sykora and Robyn Ah Mow were tabbed the best digger and best setter, respectively.

In the men's $15 million World League finals, held in Katowice, Pol., in June, Brazil captured its first team title since 1993 as it dethroned Italy 3–0. Italy had won the previous two titles and 8 of the 11 championships. Russia downed Yugoslavia to garner the bronze medal, its fifth World League medal in six campaigns. The 2001 campaign also marked the largest field of nations (16) competing in the World League since its inception in 1990. Yugoslavia's Ivan Milijkovic was named the best scorer, and Mauricio Lima of Brazil was tabbed the best setter.

In beach volleyball the Brazilian duo of Adriana Behar and Shelda won their second straight world title. Mariano Baracetti and Martin Conde of Argentina defeated Brazilians Ricardo and Loiola to win the men's world championship.

(RICHARD S. WANNINGER)

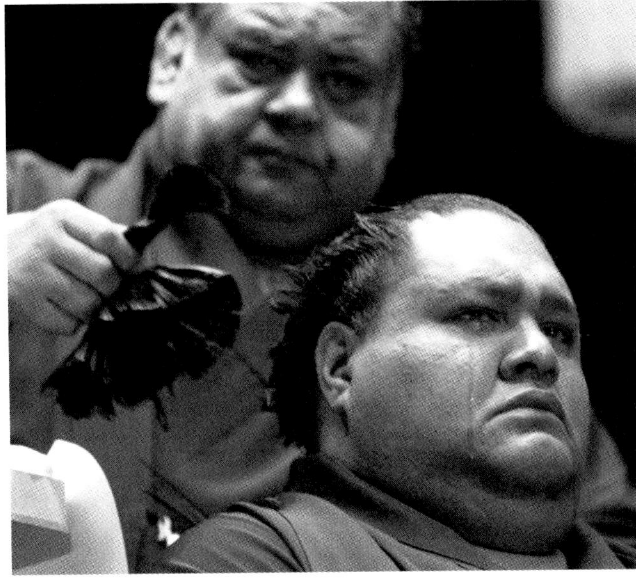

Akebono sheds a tear as his stable master chops off his topknot on September 29.

AP/Wide World Photos

WEIGHT LIFTING

The 2001 International Weightlifting Federation world championships were held in Antalya, Turkey, on November 3–11. A total of 265 athletes entered the competition: 151 men representing 47 countries in eight body-weight classes and 114 women representing 34 countries in seven body-weight classes.

In the men's division Turkey topped the medal rankings with 8 (5 gold, 2 silver, and 1 bronze), followed by Qatar (6 medals, 5 of them gold), Bulgaria (5), Russia (10), and Georgia (3). Superheavyweight Saeed Salem Jaber of Qatar won the overall world champion title with a 460-kg (1,012-lb) overall total. Two-time Olympic superheavyweight champion Andrey Chemerkin of Russia finished third. Henadzy Aliyashchuk of Belarus, Vladimir Smorchkov of Russia, and Halil Mutlu of Turkey each broke one world record.

Russia topped the women's rankings with 9 medals (6 gold, 2 silver, and 1 bronze), followed by China (14, including 5 gold), Poland (8), Hungary (7), and Taiwan (10). Albina Khomitch of Russia won the superheavyweight class with a 282.5-kg (622.8-lb) overall total. Agatha Wrobel of Poland was second.

(DRAGOMIR CIOROSLAN)

WRESTLING

Freestyle and Greco-Roman. In 2001 the world wrestling championships attracted most of the attention in freestyle and Greco-Roman wrestling. The joint event was originally scheduled for New York City's Madison Square Garden on September 26–29, but it was canceled after the terrorist attacks on September 11. The freestyle championships for men and women were later held simultaneously in Sofia, Bulg., on November 22–25. In the men's division Russia won the team race with 51 points. Second place went to host country Bulgaria (46 points); Iran came in third (37 points). In the women's division China won the team title with 36 points. Close behind for second and third places were Japan and Ukraine, both with 33 points. Japan broke the tie and took second place by having more gold medals than Ukraine.

The Greco-Roman championships were held in Patras, Greece, on December 6–9. Cuba pulled a big upset by ousting Russia for the team title with 54 points to Russia's 38. Third place went to the United States, the first time in history the U.S. had won a team medal. This bronze-medal performance was made possible by the efforts of reigning Olympic superheavyweight (130-kg [286-lb]) champion Rulon Gardner, 1996 Olympic 54-kg (119-lb) silver medalist Brandon Paulson, and 2000 Olympic 85-kg (187-lb) silver medalist Matt Lindland, who won gold, silver, and silver, respectively, in Patras. (JOHN HOKE)

Sumo. Professional sumo's popularity in Japan continued to slip in 2001. The slump was partially attributed to the country's faltering economy and the resultant decline in domestic consumption. The aging of the popular top *rikishi* of the 1990s, however, and the inability of a new generation of *rikishi* to advance to the higher ranks also contributed to reduced popularity.

The most dramatic event in sumo in 2001 was the abrupt retirement of American-born *yokozuna* (grand champion) Akebono after missing the New Year's tournament (Hatsu Basho) in January. Akebono retired at a topknot-cutting ceremony in September with an impressive career record of 566 wins, 198 losses, and 181 days absent in the *makuuchi* division.

Takanohana, the strongest *yokozuna* of the 1990s, won the Hatsu and Natsu (summer) bashos, but he suffered a severe kneecap injury on the next-to-last day of the May tournament and was unable to compete for the rest of the year. *Ozeki* (champion) Kaio won the Haru Basho in March and the Nagoya Basho in July, but he was unable to move up to *yokozuna* because of back trouble.

(CLYDE NEWTON)

Sporting Record

ARCHERY

FITA Outdoor World Target Archery Championships*

Year	Men's individual Winner	Points	Men's team Winner	Points
1997	Kim Kyung Ho (S.Kor.)	108	South Korea	254
1999	Hong Sung Chil (S.Kor.)	115	Italy	252
2001	**Yeon Jung Ki (S.Kor.)**	**115**	**South Korea**	**247**

Year	Women's individual Winner	Points	Women's team Winner	Points
1997	Kim Du Ri (S.Kor.)	105	South Korea	242
1999	Lee Eun Kyung (S.Kor.)	115	Italy	240
2001	**Park Sung Hyun (S.Kor.)**	**111**	**China**	**232**

*Olympic (recurve) division.

Tommi Mäkinen after winning the Monte-Carlo Rally on January 21.

AP/Wide World Photos

AUTOMOBILE RACING

Formula One Grand Prix Race Results, 2001

Race	Driver	Winner's time (hr:min:sec)
Australian GP	M. Schumacher	1:38:26.533
Malaysian GP	M. Schumacher	1:47:34.801
Brazilian GP	D. Coulthard	1:39:00.384
San Marino GP	R. Schumacher	1:30:44.817
Spanish GP	M. Schumacher	1:31:03.305
Austrian GP	D. Coulthard	1:27:45.927
Monaco GP	M. Schumacher	1:47:22.561
Canadian GP	R. Schumacher	1:34:31.522
European GP	M. Schumacher	1:29:42.724
French GP	M. Schumacher	1:33:35.636
British GP	M. Hakkinen	1:25:33.770
German GP	R. Schumacher	1:18:17.873
Hungarian GP	M. Schumacher	1:41:49.675
Belgian GP	M. Schumacher	1:08:05.002
Italian GP	J. Montoya	1:16:58.493
United States GP	M. Hakkinen	1:32:42.840
Japanese GP	M. Schumacher	1:27:33.298

WORLD DRIVERS' CHAMPIONSHIP: M. Schumacher 123 points, Coulthard 65 points, Barrichello 56 points. CONSTRUCTORS' CHAMPIONSHIP: Ferrari 179 points, McLaren/Mercedes 102 points, Williams/BMW 80 points.

International Cup for Formula One Manufacturers

Year	Car	Year	Car
1996	Williams/Renault	1999	Ferrari
1997	Williams/Renault	2000	Ferrari
1998	McLaren/Mercedes	**2001**	**Ferrari**

World Championship of Drivers

Year	Winner	Car
1999	M. Hakkinen (Fin.)	McLaren/Mercedes
2000	M. Schumacher (Ger.)	Ferrari
2001	**M. Schumacher (Ger.)**	**Ferrari**

National Association for Stock Car Auto Racing (NASCAR) Winston Cup Champions

Year	Winner
1999	D. Jarrett
2000	B. Labonte
2001	**J. Gordon**

Indy Car Champions*

Year	Driver
1999	J. Montoya
2000	G. de Ferran
2001	**G. de Ferran**

*CART champion.

Indianapolis 500

Year	Winner	Avg. speed in mph
1999	K. Brack	153.176
2000	J. Montoya	167.607
2001	**H. Castroneves**	**153.601**

Le Mans 24-Hour Grand Prix d'Endurance

Year	Car	Drivers
1999	BMW V12 LMR	Y. Dalmas, P. Martini, J. Winkelhock
2000	Audi R8	F. Biela, T. Kristensen, E. Pirro
2001	**Audi R8**	**F. Biela, T. Kristensen, E. Pirro**

Monte-Carlo Rally

Year	Car	Driver
1999	Mitsubishi Lancer	T. Mäkinen (Fin.)
2000	Mitsubishi Lancer	T. Mäkinen (Fin.)
2001	**Mitsubishi Lancer**	**T. Mäkinen (Fin.)**

BADMINTON

All-England Championships—Singles

Year	Men	Women
1999	P. Gade Christensen (Den.)	Ye Zhaoying (China)
2000	Xia Xuanze (China)	Gong Zhichao (China)
2001	**P. Gopichand (India)**	**Gong Zhichao (China)**

Uber Cup (women)

Year	Winner	Runner-up
1995–96	Indonesia	China
1997–98	China	Indonesia
1999–2000	China	Denmark

Thomas Cup (men)

Year	Winner	Runner-up
1995–96	Indonesia	Denmark
1997–98	Indonesia	Malaysia
1999–2000	Indonesia	China

World Badminton Championships

Year	Men's singles	Women's singles	Men's doubles	Women's doubles
1997	P. Rasmussen (Den.)	Ye Zhaoying (China)	B. Sigit, C. Wijaya (Indon.)	Ge Fei, Gu Jun (China)
1999	Sun Jun (China)	C. Martin (Den.)	Kim Dong Moon, Ha Tae Kwon (S.Kor.)	Ge Fei, Gu Jun (China)
2001	**Hendrawan (Indon.)**	**Gong Ruina (China)**	**T. Gunawan, H. Haryanto (Indon.)**	**Gao Ling, Huang Sui (China)**

BASEBALL

Final Major League Standings, 2001

AMERICAN LEAGUE

East Division				Central Division				West Division			
Club	W.	L.	G.B.	Club	W.	L.	G.B.	Club	W.	L.	G.B.
*New York	95	65	—	*Cleveland	91	71	—	*Seattle	116	46	—
Boston	82	79	13½	Minnesota	85	77	6	*Oakland	102	60	14
Toronto	80	82	16	Chicago	83	79	8	Anaheim	75	87	41
Baltimore	63	98	32½	Detroit	66	96	25	Texas	73	89	43
Tampa Bay	62	100	34	Kansas City	65	97	26				

NATIONAL LEAGUE

East Division				Central Division				West Division			
Club	W.	L.	G.B.	Club	W.	L.	G.B.	Club	W.	L.	G.B.
*Atlanta	88	74	—	*Houston	93	69	—	*Arizona	92	70	—
Philadelphia	86	76	2	*St. Louis	93	69	—	San Francisco	90	72	2
New York	82	80	6	Chicago	88	74	5	Los Angeles	86	76	6
Florida	76	86	12	Milwaukee	68	94	25	San Diego	79	83	13
Montreal	68	94	20	Cincinnati	66	96	27	Colorado	73	89	19
				Pittsburgh	62	100	31				

*Gained play-off berth.

Caribbean Series

Year	Winning team	Country
1999	Licey Tigers	Dominican Republic
2000	Santurce Crabbers	Puerto Rico
2001	**Cibao Eagles**	**Dominican Republic**

World Series*

Year	Winning team	Losing team	Results
1999	New York Yankees (AL)	Atlanta Braves (NL)	4–0
2000	New York Yankees (AL)	New York Mets (NL)	4–1
2001	**Arizona Diamondbacks (NL)**	**New York Yankees (AL)**	**4–3**

*AL—American League; NL—National League.

Japan Series*

Year	Winning team	Losing team	Results
1999	Fukuoka Daiei Hawks (PL)	Chunichi Dragons (CL)	4–1
2000	Yomiuri Giants (CL)	Fukuoka Daiei Hawks (PL)	4–2
2001	**Yakult Swallows (CL)**	**Osaka Kintetsu Buffaloes**	**4–1**

*CL—Central League; PL—Pacific League.

BASKETBALL

NBA Final Standings, 2000–01

EASTERN CONFERENCE

Team	Won	Lost	Team	Won	Lost
Atlantic Division			Central Division		
*Philadelphia	56	26	*Milwaukee	52	30
*Miami	50	32	*Toronto	47	35
*New York	48	34	*Charlotte	46	36
*Orlando	43	39	*Indiana	41	41
Boston	36	46	Detroit	32	50
New Jersey	26	56	Cleveland	30	52
Washington	19	63	Atlanta	25	57
			Chicago	15	67

WESTERN CONFERENCE

Team	Won	Lost	Team	Won	Lost
Midwest Division			Pacific Division		
*San Antonio	58	24	*L.A. Lakers	56	26
*Utah	53	29	*Sacramento	55	27
*Dallas	53	29	*Phoenix	51	31
*Minnesota	47	35	*Portland	50	32
Houston	45	37	Seattle	44	38
Denver	40	42	L.A. Clippers	31	51
Vancouver	23	59	Golden State	17	65

*Gained play-off berth.

National Basketball Association (NBA) Championship

Season	Winner	Runner-up	Results
1998–99	San Antonio Spurs	New York Knicks	4–1
1999–2000	Los Angeles Lakers	Indiana Pacers	4–2
2000–01	**Los Angeles Lakers**	**Philadelphia 76ers**	**4–1**

Women's National Basketball Association (WNBA) Championship

Season	Winner	Runner-up	Results
1999	Houston Comets	New York Liberty	2–1
2000	Houston Comets	New York Liberty	2–0
2001	**Los Angeles Sparks**	**Charlotte Sting**	**2–0**

Division I National Collegiate Athletic Association (NCAA) Championship—Men

Year	Winner	Runner-up	Score
1999	Connecticut	Duke	77–74
2000	Michigan State	Florida	89–76
2001	**Duke**	**Arizona**	**82–72**

Division I National Collegiate Athletic Association (NCAA) Championship—Women

Year	Winner	Runner-up	Score
1999	Purdue	Duke	62–45
2000	Connecticut	Tennessee	71–52
2001	**Notre Dame**	**Purdue**	**68–66**

National Invitation Tournament (NIT) Championship

Year	Winner	Runner-up	Score
1999	California	Clemson	61–60
2000	Wake Forest	Notre Dame	71–61
2001	**Tulsa**	**Alabama**	**79–60**

World Basketball Championship—Men

Year	Winner	Runner-up
1996	United States	Yugoslavia
1998	Yugoslavia	Russia
2000	United States	France

World Basketball Championship—Women

Year	Winner	Runner-up
1996	United States	Brazil
1998	United States	Russia
2000	United States	Australia

BILLIARD GAMES

WPA World Nine-Ball Championships

Year	Men's champion	Year	Women's champion
1999*	N. Varner (U.S.) E. Reyes (Phil.)	1999	Lu Shin-Mei (Taiwan)
2000	Fong Pang Chao (Taiwan)	2000	J. Kelly (Ire.)
2001	**M. Immonen (Fin.)**	**2001**	**A. Fisher (U.K.)**

*1999 men's tournament played twice.

World Professional Snooker Championship

Year	Winner	Year	Winner
1996	S. Hendry	1999	S. Hendry
1997	K. Doherty	2000	M. Williams
1998	J. Higgins	**2001**	**R. O'Sullivan**

BOWLING

ABC Bowling Championships—Regular Divisions

Year	Singles	Score	All-events	Score
1999	D. Winter	825	T. Jones	2,158
2000	G. Hein	811	R. Daniels	2,181
2001	**N. Hoagland**	**798**	**D.J. Archer**	**2,219**

WIBC Bowling Championships—Classic Division

Year	Singles	Score	All-events	Score
1999	N. Gianulias	746	H. Mizobuchi	2,065
2000	C. Krasner	729	C. Dorin-Ballard	2,147
2001	**L. Wagner**	**756**	**J. Armon**	**2,044**

Professional Bowlers Association (PBA) Tournament of Champions

Year	Champion	Year	Champion
1996	D. D'Entremont	1999	J. Couch
1997	J. Gant	2000	J. Couch
1998	B. Goebel	**2001**	**not held**

FIQ World Bowling Championships—Men

Year	Singles	Pairs	Triples	Team (fives)
1991	Ying Chieh Ma (Taiwan)	United States	United States	Taiwan
1995	M. Doi (Can.)	Sweden	Netherlands	Netherlands
1999	G. Verbruggen (Belg.)	Sweden	Finland	Sweden

FIQ World Bowling Championships—Women

Year	Singles	Pairs	Triples	Team (fives)
1991	M. Beckel (Ger.)	Japan	Canada	South Korea
1995	D. Ship (Can.)	Thailand	Australia	Finland
1999	K. Kulick (U.S.)	Australia	South Korea	South Korea

BOXING

World Heavyweight Champions No Weight Limit

WBA

Lennox Lewis (U.K.; 11/13/99)
stripped of title in 2000
Evander Holyfield (U.S.; 8/12/00)
John Ruiz (U.S.; 3/3/01)

WBC

Lennox Lewis (U.K.; 2/7/97)
Hasim Rahman (U.S.; 4/22/01)
Lennox Lewis (U.K.; 11/17/01)

IBF

Lennox Lewis (U.K.; 11/13/99)
Hasim Rahman (U.S.; 4/22/01)
Lennox Lewis (U.K.; 11/17/01)

World Cruiserweight Champions Top Weight 195 Pounds

WBA

Virgil Hill (U.S.; 12/9/00)

WBC

Juan Carlos Gómez (Ger.; 2/21/98)

IBF

Vassily Jirov (Kazakh.; 6/5/99)

World Light Heavyweight Champions Top Weight 175 Pounds

WBA

Roy Jones, Jr. (U.S.; 7/18/98)
declared super champion in 2001
Bruno Girard (Fr.; 12/22/01)

WBC

Roy Jones, Jr. (U.S.; 8/7/97)

IBF

Roy Jones, Jr. (U.S.; 6/5/99)

World Super Middleweight Champions Top Weight 168 Pounds

WBA

Bruno Girard (Fr.; 4/8/00)
stripped of title in 2001
Byron Mitchell (U.S.; 3/3/01)

WBC

Davey Hilton (Can.; 12/15/00)
stripped of title in 2001
Eric Lucas (Can.; 7/10/01)

IBF

Sven Ottke (Ger.; 10/24/98)

World Middleweight Champions Top Weight 160 Pounds

WBA

William Joppy (U.S.; 1/31/98)
Félix Trinidad (P.R.; 5/12/01)
Bernard Hopkins (U.S.; 9/29/01)
declared super champion in 2001
William Joppy (U.S.; 11/17/01)

WBC

Keith Holmes (U.S.; 4/24/99)
Bernard Hopkins (U.S.; 4/14/01)

IBF

Bernard Hopkins (U.S.; 4/29/95)

World Junior Middleweight Champions Top Weight 154 Pounds

(also called super welterweight)

WBA

Félix Trinidad (P.R.; 3/3/00)
gave up title in 2001
Fernando Vargas (U.S.; 9/22/01)

WBC

Javier Castillejo (Spain; 1/29/99)
Oscar de la Hoya (U.S.; 6/23/01)

IBF

Félix Trinidad (P.R.; 12/2/00)
gave up title in 2001
Ronald Wright (U.S.; 10/12/01)

BOXING (continued)

World Welterweight Champions Top Weight 147 Pounds

WBA

James Page (U.S.; 10/10/98)
stripped of title in 2000
Andrew Lewis (Guyana; 2/17/01)

WBC

Shane Mosley (U.S.; 6/17/00)

IBF

Félix Trinidad (P.R.; 6/19/93)
gave up title in 2000
Vernon Forrest (U.S.; 5/12/01)
stripped of title in 2001

World Junior Welterweight Champions Top Weight 140 Pounds
(also called super lightweight)

WBA

Sharmba Mitchell (U.S.; 10/10/98)
Kostya Tszyu (Austl.; 2/3/01)
declared super champion in 2001

WBC

Kostya Tszyu (Austl.; 8/21/99)

IBF

Zab Judah (U.S.; 2/12/00)
Kostya Tszyu (Austl.; 11/3/01)

World Lightweight Champions Top Weight 135 Pounds

WBA

Takanori Hatakeyama (Japan; 6/11/00)
Julien Lorcy (Fr.; 7/1/01)
Raul Balbi (Arg.; 10/8/01)

WBC

José Luis Castillo (Mex.; 6/17/00)

IBF

Paul Spadafora (U.S.; 8/20/99)

World Junior Lightweight Champions Top Weight 130 Pounds
(also called super featherweight)

WBA

Joel Casamayor (Cuba; 5/21/00)

WBC

Floyd Mayweather, Jr. (U.S.; 10/3/98)

IBF

Steve Forbes (U.S.; 12/3/00)

World Featherweight Champions Top Weight 126 Pounds

WBA

Derrick Gainer (U.S.; 9/9/00)

WBC

Gustavo Espadas (Mex.; 4/14/00)
Erik Morales (Mex.; 2/17/01)

IBF

Mbulelo Botile (S.Af.; 12/16/00)
Frankie Toledo (U.S.; 4/6/01)
Manuel Medina (Mex.; 11/16/01)

Lennox Lewis jabs at Hasim Rahman en route to regaining the WBC and IBF heavyweight championship belts on November 17 in Las Vegas, Nev.
Matthew Stockman/Allsport

World Junior Featherweight Champions Top Weight 122 Pounds
(also called super bantamweight)

WBA

Clarence Adams (U.S.; 3/4/00)
stripped of title in 2001
Yober Ortega (Venez.; 11/17/01)

WBC

Willie Jorrin (U.S.; 9/9/00)

IBF

Lehlohonolo Ledwaba (S.Af.; 5/29/99)
Manny Pacquiao (Phil.; 6/23/01)

World Bantamweight Champions Top Weight 118 Pounds

WBA

Paulie Ayala (U.S.; 6/26/99)
stripped of title in 2001
Eidy Moya (Venez.; 10/14/01)

WBC

Veeraphol Sahaprom (Thai.; 12/29/98)

IBF

Tim Austin (U.S.; 7/19/97)

World Junior Bantamweight Champions Top Weight 115 Pounds
(also called super flyweight)

WBA

Leo Gámez (Venez.; 10/9/00)
Shoji Kobayashi (Japan; 3/11/01)

WBC

Masanori Tokuyama (Japan; 8/27/00)

IBF

Félix Machado (Venez.; 7/22/00)

World Flyweight Champions Top Weight 112 Pounds

WBA

Eric Morel (U.S.; 8/5/00)

WBC

Malcolm Tunacao (Phil.; 5/19/00)
Pongsaklek Wongjongkam (Thai.; 3/2/01)

IBF

Irene Pacheco (Colom.; 4/10/99)

World Junior Flyweight Champions Top Weight 108 Pounds

WBA

Bebis Mendoza (Colom.; 8/12/00)
Rosendo Alvarez (Nic.; 3/3/01)

WBC

Choi Yo Sam (S.Kor.; 10/17/99)

IBF

Ricardo López (Mex.; 10/2/99)

World Mini-flyweight Champions Top Weight 105 Pounds
(also called strawweight)

WBA

Keitaro Hoshino (Japan; 12/6/00)
Chana Porpaoin (Thai.; 4/16/01)
Yutaka Niida (Japan; 8/25/01)
gave up title in 2001

WBC

José Antonio Aguirre (Mex.; 2/11/00)

IBF

Zolani Petelo (S.Af.; 12/27/97)
gave up title in 2000
Roberto Leyva (Mex.; 4/29/01)

CHESS

FIDE Chess Championship—Men

Year	Winner	Runner-up
1998	A. Karpov (Russia)	V. Anand (India)
1999	A. Khalifman (Russia)	V. Akopyan (Arm.)
2000	V. Anand (India)	A. Shirov (Spain)

FIDE Chess Championship—Women

Year	Winner	Runner-up
1996	Z. Polgar (Hung.)*	Xie Jun (China)
1999	Xie Jun (China)	A. Galyamova (Russia)
2000	Xie Jun (China)	Qin Karying (China)

*Stripped of title in 1999.

FIDE Olympiad—Men

Year	Winner	Runner-up
1996	Russia	Ukraine
1998	Russia	United States
2000	Russia	Germany

FIDE Olympiad—Women

Year	Winner	Runner-up
1996	Georgia	China
1998	China	Russia
2000	China	Georgia

CONTRACT BRIDGE

World Team Olympiad

Year	Open winner	Open runner-up	Women's winner	Women's runner-up
1992	France	United States	Austria	United Kingdom
1996	France	Indonesia	United States	China
2000	Italy	Poland	United States	Canada

World Contract Bridge Pair Championship

Year	Open winners	Women's winners	Mixed winners
1994	Marcin Lesniewski, Marek Szymanowski (Pol.)	Carla Arnolds, Bep Vriend (Neth.)	Danuta Hocheker, Apolinare Kowalski (Pol.)
1998	Michal Kwiecien, Jacek Pszczola (Pol.)	Jill Meyers, Shawn Quinn (U.S.)	Enza Rossano, Antonio Vivaldi (Italy)

Bermuda Bowl

Year	Winner	Runner-up
1997	France	United States
2000	United States	Brazil
2001	**United States**	**Norway**

CRICKET

Cricket World Cup

Year	Result			
1992	Pakistan	249–6	England	227
1996	Sri Lanka	245–3	Australia	241
1999	Australia	133–2	Pakistan	132

All-Time First-Class Test Cricket Standings (as of Sept. 30, 2001)

	England			Australia			South Africa			West Indies			New Zealand		
	Wins	Draws	Losses	W	D	L	W	D	L	W	D	L	W	D	L
England v.	—	—	—	94	86	121	50	47	23	31	43*	52	37	39	6
Australia v.	121	86	94	—	—	—	34	17	14	42	22†	31	18	12	7
South Africa v.	23	47	50	14	17	34	—	—	—	7	2	2	15	9	3
West Indies v.	52	43*	31	31	22†	42	2	2	7	—	—	—	10	14	6
New Zealand v.	6	39	37	7	12	18	3	9	15	6	14	10	—	—	—
India v.	14	38	32	13	18†	29	2	4	6	7	35	28	14	20*	7
Pakistan v.	10	34	16	11	17	18	1	1	2	10	14	13	19	17	6
Sri Lanka v.	3	1	5	1	5	7	1	4	6	0	2	1	4	7	7
Zimbabwe v.	0	3	1	0	0	1	0	1	4	0	1	3	0	6	5
Bangladesh v.	‡	‡	‡	‡	‡	‡	‡	‡	‡	‡	‡	‡	‡	‡	‡

	India			Pakistan			Sri Lanka			Zimbabwe			Bangladesh		
	W	D	L	W	D	L	W	D	L	W	D	L	W	D	L
England v.	32	38	14	16	34	10	5	1	3	1	3	0	‡	‡	‡
Australia v.	29	18†	13	18	17	11	7	5	1	1	0	0	‡	‡	‡
South Africa v.	6	4	2	2	1	1	6	4	1	4	1	0	‡	‡	‡
West Indies v.	28	35	7	13	14	10	1	2	0	3	1	0	‡	‡	‡
New Zealand v.	7	20*	14	6	17	19	7	7	4	5	6	0	‡	‡	‡
India v.	—	—	—	5	33	9	8	12	3	3	2	2	1	0	0
Pakistan v.	9	33	5	—	—	—	13	9*	5	6	5*	2	1	0	0
Sri Lanka v.	3	12	8	5	9*	13	—	—	—	5	5	0	1	0	0
Zimbabwe v.	2	2	3	2	5*	6	0	5	5	—	—	—	2	0	0
Bangladesh v.	0	0	1	0	0	1	0	0	1	0	0	2	—	—	—

*Including one match abandoned. †Including one tie. ‡No matches.

Mufty Munir/AFP Worldwide

Bangladeshi wicket keeper Khaled Masood (right) during a match against Pakistan. Bangladesh became a Test nation in 2001.

CRICKET (continued)

Test Match Results, October 2000–September 2001

Host/Ground	Date	Scores	Result
Bangladesh/Dhaka	Nov. 10–13	Bangl. 400 and 91; India 429 and 64 for 1	India won by 9 wickets
Pakistan/Lahore	Nov. 15–19	Eng. 480 for 8 dec and 77 for 4 dec; Pak. 401	Match drawn
Pakistan/Faisalabad	Nov. 29–Dec. 3	Pak. 316 and 269 for 3 dec; Eng. 342 and 125 for 5	Match drawn
Pakistan/Karachi	Dec. 7–11	Pak. 405 and 158; Eng. 388 and 176 for 4	Eng. won by 6 wickets; Eng. won series 1–0
South Africa/Bloemfontein	Nov. 17–21	S.Af. 471 for 9 dec and 103 for 5; N.Z. 229 and 342	S.Af. won by 5 wickets
South Africa/Port Elizabeth	Nov. 30–Dec. 4	N.Z. 298 and 148; S.Af. 361 and 89 for 3	S.Af. won by 7 wickets
South Africa/Johannesburg	Dec. 8–12	N.Z. 200; S.Af. 261 for 3 dec	Match drawn; S.Af. won series 2–0
India/Delhi	Nov. 18–22	Zimb. 422 for 9 dec and 225; India 458 for 4 dec and 190 for 3	India won by 7 wickets
India/Nagpur	Nov. 25–29	India 609 for 6 dec; Zimb. 382 and 503 for 6	Match drawn; India won series 1–0
Australia/Brisbane	Nov. 23–25	W.Ind. 82 and 124; Austl. 332	Austl. won by an innings and 126 runs
Australia/Perth	Dec. 1–3	W.Ind. 196 and 173; Austl. 396 for 8 dec	Austl. won by an innings and 27 runs
Australia/Adelaide	Dec. 15–19	W.Ind. 391 and 141; Austl. 403 and 130 for 5	Austl. won by 5 wickets
Australia/Melbourne	Dec. 26–29	Austl. 364 and 262 for 5 dec; W.Ind. 165 and 109	Austl. won by 352 runs
Australia/Sydney	Jan. 2–6	W.Ind. 272 and 352; Austl. 452 and 174 for 4	Austl. won by 6 wickets; Austl. won series 5–0
New Zealand/Wellington	Dec. 26–30	N.Z. 487 for 7 dec and 153 for 4 dec; Zimb. 340 for 6 dec and 60 for 2	Match drawn
South Africa/Durban	Dec. 26–30	S.Af. 420 and 140 for 7 dec; SriL. 216 and 149 for 6	Match drawn
South Africa/Cape Town	Jan. 2–4	SriL. 95 and 180; S.Af. 504 for 7 dec	S.Af. won by an innings and 229 runs
South Africa/Centurion	Jan. 20–22	S.Af. 378; SriL. 119 and 252	S.Af. won by an innings and 7 runs; S.Af. won series 2–0
Sri Lanka/Galle	Feb. 22–26	SriL. 470 for 5 dec; Eng. 253 and 189	SriL. won by an innings and 28 runs
Sri Lanka/Kandy	March 7–11	SriL. 297 and 250; Eng. 387 and 161 for 7	Eng. won by 3 wickets
Sri Lanka/Colombo	March 15–17	SriL. 241 and 81; Eng. 249 and 74 for 6	Eng. won by 4 wickets; Eng. won series 2–1
India/Mumbai	Feb. 27–March 1	India 176 and 219; Austl. 349 and 47 for 0	Austl. won by 10 wickets
India/Kolkata	March 11–15	Austl. 445 and 212; India 171 and 657 for 7 dec	India won by 171 runs
India/Chennai	March 18–22	Austl. 391 and 264; India 501 and 155 for 8	India won by 2 wickets; India won series 2–1
New Zealand/Auckland	March 8–12	Pak. 346 and 336 for 5 dec; N.Z. 252 and 131	Pak. won by 299 runs
New Zealand/Christchurch	March 15–19	N.Z. 476 and 196 for 1 dec; Pak. 571 for 8 dec	Match drawn
New Zealand/Hamilton	March 27–30	Pak. 104 and 118; N.Z. 407 for 4 dec	N.Z. won by an innings and 185 runs; Series drawn 1–1
West Indies/Guyana	March 9–13	W.Ind. 304 and 333 for 7 dec; S.Af. 332 and 142 for 2	Match drawn
West Indies/Trinidad	March 17–21	S.Af. 286 and 287; W.Ind. 342 and 162	S.Af. won by 69 runs
West Indies/Barbados	March 29–April 2	S.Af. 454 and 197 for 9 dec; W.Ind. 387 and 88 for 7	Match drawn
West Indies/Antigua	April 6–10	S.Af. 247 and 215 for 7 dec; W.Ind. 140 and 240	S.Af. won by 82 runs
West Indies/Jamaica	April 19–23	W.Ind. 225 and 301; S.Af. 141 and 255	W.Ind. won by 130 runs; S.Af. won series 2–1
Zimbabwe/Bulawayo	April 19–22	Bangl. 257 and 168; Zimb. 457	Zimb. won by an innings and 32 runs
Zimbabwe/Harare	April 26–30	Bangl. 254 and 266; Zimb. 421 for 9 dec and 100 for 2	Zimb. won by 8 wickets; Zimb. won series 2–0
England/London (Lord's)	May 17–20	Eng. 391; Pak. 203 and 179	Eng. won by an innings and 9 runs
England/Manchester	May 31–June 4	Pak. 403 and 323; Eng. 357 and 261	Pak. won by 108 runs; Series drawn 1–1
Zimbabwe/Bulawayo	June 7–10	Zimb. 173 and 328; India 318 and 184 for 2	India won by 8 wickets
Zimbabwe/Harare	June 15–18	India 237 and 234; Zimb. 315 and 157 for 6	Zimb. won by 4 wickets; Series drawn 1–1
England/Birmingham	July 5–8	Eng. 294 and 164; Austl. 576	Austl. won by an innings and 118 runs
England/London (Lord's)	July 19–22	Eng. 187 and 227; Austl. 401 and 14 for 2	Austl. won by 8 wickets
England/Nottingham	Aug. 2–4	Eng. 185 and 162; Austl. 190 and 158 for 3	Austl. won by 7 wickets
England/Leeds	Aug. 16–20	Austl. 447 and 176 for 4 dec; Eng. 309 and 315 for 4	Eng. won by 6 wickets
England/London (The Oval)	Aug. 23–27	Austl. 641 for 4 dec; Eng. 432 and 184	Austl. won by an innings and 25 runs; Austl. won series 4–1
Zimbabwe/Bulawayo	July 19–22	Zimb. 155 and 228; W.Ind. 559 for 6 dec	W.Ind. won by an innings and 176 runs
Zimbabwe/Harare	July 27–31	Zimb. 131 and 563 for 9 dec; W.Ind. 347 and 98 for 1	Match drawn; W.Ind. won series 1–0
Sri Lanka/Galle	Aug. 14–17	India 187 and 180; SriL. 362 and 6 for 0	SriL. won by 10 wickets
Sri Lanka/Kandy	Aug. 22–25	SriL. 274 and 221; India 232 and 264 for 3	India won by 7 wickets
Sri Lanka/Colombo	Aug. 29–Sept. 2	India 234 and 299; SriL. 610 for 6 dec	SriL. won by an innings and 77 runs; SriL. won series 2–1
Pakistan/Multan	Aug. 29–31	Bangl. 134 and 148; Pak. 546 for 3 dec	Pak. won by an innings and 264 runs
Sri Lanka/Colombo	Sept. 6–8	Bangl. 90 and 328; SriL. 555 for 5 dec	SriL. won by an innings and 137 runs
Zimbabwe/Harare	Sept. 7–11	S.Af. 600 for 3 dec and 79 for 1; Zimb. 286 and 391	S.Af. won by 9 wickets
Zimbabwe/Bulawayo	Sept. 14–18	Zimb. 419 for 9 dec and 96 for 3; S.Af. 519 for 8 dec	Match drawn; S.Af. won series 1–0

CURLING

World Curling Championship—Men

Year	Winner	Runner-up
1999	Scotland	Canada
2000	Canada	Sweden
2001	**Sweden**	**Switzerland**

World Curling Championship—Women

Year	Winner	Runner-up
1999	Sweden	United States
2000	Canada	Switzerland
2001	**Canada**	**Sweden**

CYCLING

Cycling Champions, 2001

Event	Winner	Country
WORLD CHAMPIONS—TRACK		
Men		
Sprint	A. Tournant	France
Individual pursuit	A. Symonenko	Ukraine
Kilometre time trial	A. Tournant	France
40-km points	B. Risi	Switzerland
Team pursuit	S. Chernyavsky, O. Fedenko, A. Symonenko, L. Polotayko	Ukraine
Keirin	R. Bayley	Australia
Olympic sprint	L. Gane, F. Rousseau, A. Tournant	France
60-km Madison	J. Neuville, R. Sassone	France
Women		
Sprint	S. Grankovskaya	Russia
Individual pursuit	L. Zijlaard-Van Moorsel	Netherlands
500-m time trial	N. Contreras Reyes	Mexico
25-km points	O. Slyusareva	Russia
WORLD CHAMPIONS—ROAD		
Men		
Individual road race	O. Freire Gomez	Spain
Individual time trial	J. Ullrich	Germany
Women		
Individual road race	R. Polikeviciute	Lithuania
Individual time trial	J. Longo-Ciprelli	France
WORLD CHAMPION—CYCLO-CROSS		
Men	E. Vervecken	Belgium
Women	H. Kupfernagel	Germany

Event	Winner	Country
WORLD CHAMPIONS—MOUNTAIN BIKES		
Men		
Cross-country	R. Green	Canada
Downhill	N. Vouilloz	France
Women		
Cross-country	A. Dunlap	United States
Downhill	A.-C. Chausson	France
MAJOR ELITE ROAD-RACE WINNERS		
Tour de France	L. Armstrong	United States
Tour of Italy	G. Simoni	Italy
Tour of Spain	A. Casero Moreno	Spain
Tour of Switzerland	L. Armstrong	United States
Milan–San Remo	E. Zabel	Germany
Tour of Flanders	G. Bortolami	Italy
Paris–Roubaix	S. Knaven	Netherlands
Liège–Bastogne–Liège	O. Camenzind	Switzerland
Amstel Gold	E. Dekker	Netherlands
San Sebastian Classic	L. Jalabert	France
HEW–Cyclassics Cup	E. Zabel	Germany
Zurich Championship	P. Bettini	Italy
Paris–Tours	R. Virenque	France
Tour of Lombardy	D. Di Luca	Italy
Paris–Nice	D. Frigo	Italy
Ghent–Wevelgem	G. Hincapie	United States
Flèche Wallonne	R. Verbrugghe	Belgium
Tour of Romandie	D. Frigo	Italy
Dauphiné Libéré	C. Moreau	France
Tirreno–Adriatico	D. Rebellin	Italy

Tour de France

Year	Winner	Kilometres
1999	L. Armstrong (U.S.)	3,687
2000	L. Armstrong (U.S.)	3,663
2001	**L. Armstrong (U.S.)**	**3,454**

EQUESTRIAN SPORTS

The Kentucky Derby

Year	Horse	Jockey
1999	Charismatic	C. Antley
2000	Fusaichi Pegasus	K. Desormeaux
2001	**Monarchos**	**J. Chavez**

The Preakness Stakes

Year	Horse	Jockey
1999	Charismatic	C. Antley
2000	Red Bullet	J. Bailey
2001	**Point Given**	**G. Stevens**

The Belmont Stakes

Year	Horse	Jockey
1999	Lemon Drop Kid	J. Santos
2000	Commendable	P. Day
2001	**Point Given**	**G. Stevens**

2,000 Guineas

Year	Horse	Jockey
1999	Island Sands	L. Dettori
2000	King's Best	K. Fallon
2001	**Golan**	**K. Fallon**

The Derby

Year	Horse	Jockey
1999	Oath	K. Fallon
2000	Sinndar	J. Murtagh
2001	**Galileo**	**M. Kinane**

The St. Leger

Year	Horse	Jockey
1999	Mutafaweq	R. Hills
2000	Millenary	R. Quinn
2001	**Milan**	**M. Kinane**

EQUESTRIAN SPORTS (continued)

Triple Crown Champions—U.S.

Year	Horse
1973	Secretariat
1977	Seattle Slew
1978	Affirmed

Triple Crown Champions—British

Year	Winner
1918	Gainsborough
1935	Bahram
1970	Nijinsky

Melbourne Cup

Year	Horse	Jockey
1999	Rogan Josh	J. Marshall
2000	Brew	K. McEvoy
2001	**Ethereal**	**S. Seamer**

The Hambletonian Trot

Year	Horse	Driver
1999	Self Possessed	M. Lachance
2000	Yankee Paco	T. Ritchie
2001	**Scarlet Knight**	**S. Melander**

Major Thoroughbred Race Winners, 2001

Race	Won by	Jockey
United States		
Acorn	Forest Secrets	C. McCarron
Alabama Stakes	Flute	E. Prado
Apple Blossom	Gourmet Girl	C. Borel
Arlington Million	Silvano	A. Suborics
Ashland Stakes	Fleet Renee	J. Velazquez
Beldame	Exogenous	J. Castellano
Belmont	Point Given	G. Stevens
Beverly D.	England's Legend	C. Nakatani
Blue Grass Stakes	Millennium Wind	L. Pincay, Jr.
Breeders' Cup Juvenile	Johannesburg	M. Kinane
Breeders' Cup Juvenile Fillies	Tempera	D. Romero Flores
Breeders' Cup Sprint	Squirtle Squirt	J. Bailey
Breeders' Cup Mile	Val Royal	J. Valdivia, Jr.
Breeders' Cup Distaff	Unbridled Elaine	P. Day
Breeders' Cup Turf	Fantastic Light	L. Dettori
Breeders' Cup Filly and Mare Turf	Banks Hill	O. Peslier
Breeders' Cup Classic	Tiznow	C. McCarron
Champagne	Officer	V. Espinosa
Charles Whittingham Handicap	Bienamado	C. McCarron
Cigar Mile Handicap	Left Bank	J. Velazquez
Coaching Club American Oaks	Tweedside	J. Velazquez
Donn Handicap	Captain Steve	J. Bailey
Eddie Read	Redattore	A. Solis
Florida Derby	Monarchos	J. Chavez
Flower Bowl Invitational	Lailani	J. Bailey
Fountain of Youth	Songandaprayer	E. Prado
Gulfstream Park Handicap	Sir Bear	E. Coa
Haskell Invitational	Point Given	G. Stevens
Hollywood Derby	Denon	C. McCarron
Hollywood Futurity	Siphonic	J. Bailey
Hollywood Gold Cup	Aptitude	L. Pincay, Jr.
Hollywood Starlet	Habibti	V. Espinoza
Hollywood Turf Cup	Super Quercus	A. Solis
Hopeful Stakes	Came Home	C. McCarron
Jim Dandy Stakes	Scorpion	J. Bailey
Jockey Club Gold Cup	Aptitude	J. Bailey
Kentucky Derby	Monarchos	J. Chavez
Kentucky Oaks	Flute	J. Bailey
Man o' War	With Anticipation	P. Day
Matriarch Stakes	Starine	J. Velazquez
Metropolitan	Exciting Story	P. Husbands
Mother Goose	Fleet Renee	J. Velazquez
Oaklawn Handicap	Traditionally	P. Day
Pacific Classic	Skimming	G. Gomez
Pimlico Special	Include	J. Bailey
Preakness	Point Given	G. Stevens
Queen Elizabeth II Challenge Cup	Affluent	E. Delahoussaye
Santa Anita Derby	Point Given	G. Stevens
Santa Anita Handicap	Tiznow	C. McCarron
Secretariat Stakes	Startac	A. Solis
Spinaway Stakes	Cashier's Dream	D. Meche
Spinster	Miss Linda	R. Migliore
Super Derby	Outofthebox	L. Meche
Swaps Stakes	Congaree	G. Stevens
Travers	Point Given	G. Stevens
Turf Classic Invitational	Timboroa	E. Prado
United Nations Handicap	Senure	R. Davis
Whitney	Lido Palace	J. Bailey
Woodward	Lido Palace	J. Bailey
Yellow Ribbon Stakes	Janet	D. Romero Flores
England		
One Thousand Guineas	Ameerat	P. Robinson
Two Thousand Guineas	Golan	K. Fallon
Derby	Galileo	M. Kinane
Oaks	Imagine	M. Kinane
St. Leger	Milan	M. Kinane
Coronation Cup	Mutafaweq	L. Dettori
Ascot Gold Cup	Royal Rebel	J. Murtagh
Coral-Eclipse Stakes	Medicean	K. Fallon
King George VI and Queen Elizabeth Diamond Stakes	Galileo	M. Kinane
Sussex Stakes	Noverre	L. Dettori
Juddmonte International Stakes	Sakhee	L. Dettori
Dubayy Champion Stakes	Nayef	R. Hills
France		
Poule d'Essai des Poulains	Vahorimix	C. Soumillon
Poule d'Essai des Pouliches	Rose Gypsy	M. Kinane
Prix du Jockey-Club	Anabaa Blue	C. Soumillon
Prix de Diane	Aquarelliste	D. Boeuf
Prix Royal-Oak	Vinnie Roe	P. Smullen
Prix Ganay	Golden Snake	P. Eddery
Prix Jacques Le Marois	Vahorimix	O. Peslier
Grand Prix de Paris	Chichicastenango	A. Junk
Grand Prix de Saint-Cloud	Mirio	C. Soumillon
Prix Vermeille	Aquarelliste	D. Boeuf
Prix de l'Arc de Triomphe	Sakhee	L. Dettori
Grand Criterium	Rock of Gibraltar	M. Kinane
Ireland		
Irish Two Thousand Guineas	Black Minnaloushe	J. Murtagh
Irish One Thousand Guineas	Imagine	S. Heffernan
Irish Derby	Galileo	M. Kinane
Irish Oaks	Lailani	L. Dettori
Irish St. Leger	Vinnie Roe	P. Smullen
Irish Champion Stakes	Fantastic Light	L. Dettori
Italy		
Derby Italiano	Morshdi	P. Robinson
Gran Premio del Jockey Club	Kutub	L. Dettori
Germany		
Deutsches Derby	Boreal	J. Reid
Grosser Preis von Baden	Morshdi	P. Robinson
Europa Preis	Kutub	L. Dettori
Australia		
Melbourne Cup	Ethereal	S. Seamer
Cox Plate	Northerly	D. Oliver
Caulfield Cup	Ethereal	S. Seamer
United Arab Emirates		
Dubayy World Cup	Captain Steve	J. Bailey
Japan		
Japan Cup	Jungle Pocket	O. Peslier
Canada		
Queen's Plate Stakes	Dancethruthedawn	G. Boulanger
Prince of Wales Stakes	Win City	C. Montpellier
Breeders Stakes	Sweetest Thing	J. McAleney

FENCING

World Fencing Championships—Men

Year	Individual			Team		
	Foil	Épée	Sabre	Foil	Épée	Sabre
1999	S. Golubitsky (Ukr.)	A. Schmitt (Ger.)	D. Touya (Fr.)	France	France	France
2000	Kim Young Ho (S.Kor.)	P. Kolobkov (Russia)	M.C. Covaliu (Rom.)	France	Italy	Russia
2001	**S. Sanzo (Italy)**	**P. Milanoli (Italy)**	**S. Pozdnyakov (Russia)**	**France**	**Hungary**	**Russia**

World Fencing Championships—Women

Year	Individual			Team		
	Foil	Épée	Sabre	Foil	Épée	Sabre
1999	V. Vezzali (Italy)	L. Flessel-Colovic (Fr.)	E. Jemaeva (Azer.)	Germany	Hungary	Italy
2000	V. Vezzali (Italy)	T. Nagy (Hung.)	E. Jemaeva (Azer.)	Italy	Russia	United States
2001	**V. Vezzali (Italy)**	**C. Bokel (Ger.)**	**A.-L. Touya (Fr.)**	**Italy**	**Russia**	**Russia**

FIELD HOCKEY

World Cup Field Hockey Championship—Men

Year	Winner	Runner-up
1990	Netherlands	Pakistan
1994	Pakistan	Netherlands
1998	Netherlands	Spain

World Cup Field Hockey Championship—Women

Year	Winner	Runner-up
1990	Netherlands	Australia
1994	Australia	Argentina
1998	Australia	Netherlands

FOOTBALL

FIFA World Cup—Men

Year	Result			
1990	West Germany	1	Argentina	0
1994	Brazil*	0	Italy	0
1998	France	3	Brazil	0

*Won on penalty kicks.

FIFA World Cup—Women

Year	Result			
1991	United States	2	Norway	1
1995	Norway	2	Germany	0
1999	United States*	0	China	0

*Won on penalty kicks.

Association Football National Champions, 2001

Nation	League Champions	Cup Winners
Albania	Vllaznia	SK Tirana
Andorra	Santa Coloma	Santa Coloma
Argentina	San Lorenzo	
Armenia	Araks	Mika
Austria	Tirol Innsbruck	Kärnten
Azerbaijan	Shamkir	Shafa
Belarus	Slavia	Belshina
Belgium	Anderlecht	Westerlo
Bolivia	Oriente Petrolero	
Bosnia	Zeljeznicar	Zeljeznicar
Brazil	Atlético Paranaense	Gremio
Bulgaria	Levski	Liteks
Chile	Santiago Wanderers	
Colombia	América Cali	
Croatia	Hajduk Split	Dynamo Zagreb
Cyprus	Omonia	Apollon
Czech Republic	Sparta Prague	Viktoria Zizkov
Denmark	FC Copenhagen	Silkeborg
Ecuador	Emelec	
England	Manchester United	Liverpool
Estonia	Levadia	Trans Narva
Faroe Islands	VB Vagur	GI Gøtu
Finland	Haka	HJK Helsinki
France	Nantes	Strasbourg
Georgia	Torpedo Kutaisi	Torpedo Kutaisi
Germany	Bayern Munich	Schalke
Greece	Olympiakos	PAOK Salonika
Hungary	Ferencvaros	Debrecen
Iceland	KR Reykjavik	IA Akranes
Ireland	Bohemians	Bohemians
Israel	Maccabi Haifa	Maccabi Tel Aviv
Italy	Roma	Fiorentina
Latvia	Skonto Riga	Skonto Riga
Liechtenstein	(no league)	Vaduz
Lithuania	Kaunas	Atlantas
Luxembourg	Dudelange	Etzella
Macedonia	Sloga	Pelister
Malta	Valletta	Valletta
Moldova	Serif Tiraspol	Serif Tiraspol
Netherlands	PSV Eindhoven	Twente
Northern Ireland	Linfield	Glentoran
Norway	Rosenborg	Odd Grenland
Paraguay	Cerro Porteño	
Peru	Alianza Lima	
Poland	Wisla	Polonia
Portugal	Boavista	Porto
Romania	Steaua	Dinamo Bucharest
Russia	Spartak Moscow	Lokomotiv Moscow
San Marino	Cosmos	Domagnano
Scotland	Celtic	Celtic
Slovakia	Inter	Inter
Slovenia	Maribor	Gorica
Spain	Real Madrid	Zaragoza
Sweden	Halmstads	Elfsborg
Switzerland	Grasshoppers	Servette
Turkey	Fenerbahce	Genclerbirligi
Ukraine	Dynamo Kiev	Shakhtar Donetsk
Uruguay	Nacional	
Venezuela	Estudiantes	
Wales	Barry Town	Caersws
Yugoslavia	Red Star Belgrade	Partizan Belgrade

FOOTBALL (continued)

Libertadores de América Cup

Year	Winner (country)	Runner-up (country)	Scores
1999	Palmeiras (Braz.)	Deportiva Cali (Colom.)	0–1, 2–1, 4–3*
2000	Boca Juniors (Arg.)	Palmeiras (Braz.)	2–2, 0–0, 4–2*
2001	**Boca Juniors (Arg.)**	**Cruz Azul (Mex.)**	**1–0, 0–1, 3–1***

*Winner determined in penalty shootout.

European Cup of Champion Clubs

Season	Result			
1998–99	Manchester United (Eng.)	2	Bayern Munich (Ger.)	1
1999–2000	Real Madrid (Spain)	3	Valencia (Spain)	0
2000–01	**Bayern Munich (Ger.)***	**1**	**Valencia (Spain)**	**1**

*Won on penalty kicks.

U.S. College Football National Champions

Season	Champion
1999–2000	Florida State
2000–01	Oklahoma
2001–02	**Miami**

Fiesta Bowl

Season	Result			
1999–2000	Nebraska	31	Tennessee	21
2000–01	Oregon State	41	Notre Dame	9
2001–02	**Oregon**	**38**	**Colorado**	**16**

Rose Bowl

Season	Result			
1999–2000	Wisconsin	17	Stanford	9
2000–01	Washington	34	Purdue	24
2001–02	**Miami**	**37**	**Nebraska**	**14**

Orange Bowl

Season	Result			
1999–2000	Michigan	35	Alabama	34
2000–01	Oklahoma	13	Florida State	2
2001–02	**Florida**	**56**	**Maryland**	**23**

Cotton Bowl

Season	Result			
1999–2000	Arkansas	27	Texas	6
2000–01	Kansas State	35	Tennessee	21
2001–02	**Oklahoma**	**10**	**Arkansas**	**3**

Sugar Bowl

Season	Result			
1999–2000	Florida State	46	Virginia Tech	29
2000–01	Miami	37	Florida	20
2001–02	**Louisiana State**	**47**	**Illinois**	**34**

NFL Final Standings, 2001–02

AMERICAN CONFERENCE

Eastern Division

	W	L	T
*New England	11	5	0
*Miami	11	5	0
*New York Jets	10	6	0
Indianapolis	6	10	0
Buffalo	3	13	0

Central Division

	W	L	T
*Pittsburgh	13	3	0
*Baltimore	10	6	0
Cleveland	7	9	0
Tennessee	7	9	0
Jacksonville	6	10	0
Cincinnati	6	10	0

Western Division

	W	L	T
*Oakland	10	6	0
Seattle	9	7	0
Denver	8	8	0
Kansas City	6	10	0
San Diego	5	11	0

NATIONAL CONFERENCE

Eastern Division

	W	L	T
*Philadelphia	11	5	0
Washington	8	8	0
New York Giants	7	9	0
Arizona	7	9	0
Dallas	5	11	0

Central Division

	W	L	T
*Chicago	13	3	0
*Green Bay	12	4	0
*Tampa Bay	9	7	0
Minnesota	5	11	0
Detroit	2	14	0

Western Division

	W	L	T
*St. Louis	14	2	0
*San Francisco	12	4	0
New Orleans	7	9	0
Atlanta	7	9	0
Carolina	1	15	0

*Qualified for play-offs.

Super Bowl

	Season	Result			
XXXIV	1999–2000	St. Louis Rams (NFC)	23	Tennessee Titans (AFC)	16
XXXV	2000–01	Baltimore Ravens (AFC)	34	New York Giants (NFC)	7
XXXVI	**2001–02**	**New England Patriots (AFC)**	**20**	**St. Louis Rams (NFC)**	**17**

Grey Cup*

Year	Result			
1999	Hamilton Tiger-Cats (ED)	32	Calgary Stampeders (WD)	21
2000	British Columbia Lions (WD)	28	Montreal Alouettes (ED)	26
2001	**Calgary Stampeders (WD)**	**27**	**Winnipeg Blue Bombers (ED)**	**19**

*ED—Eastern Division; WD—Western Division.

AFL Final Standings, 2001 (League ladder after round 22)

Team*	W	L	D	Points
Essendon	17	5	0	68
Brisbane	17	5	0	68
Port Adelaide	16	6	0	64
Richmond	15	7	0	60
Carlton	14	8	0	56
Hawthorn	13	9	0	52
Sydney	12	10	0	48
Adelaide	12	10	0	48

*Teams that qualified for play-offs.

FOOTBALL (continued)

Record of International Rugby Union Test Matches 1871 to Oct. 31, 2001

	England			Scotland			Ireland			Wales			British Isles*		
	Wins	Draws	Losses	Wins	Draws	Losses	Wins	Draws	Losses	Wins	Draws	Losses	Wins	Draws	Losses
England *v.*	—	—	—	61	17	40	67	8	39	46	12	49	—	—	—
Scotland *v.*	40	17	61	—	—	—	61	5	46	45	3	57	—	—	—
Ireland *v.*	39	8	67	46	5	61	—	—	—	39	6	60	—	—	—
Wales *v.*	49	12	46	57	3	45	60	6	39	—	—	—	—	—	—
British Isles* *v.*	—	—	—	—	—	—	—	—	—	—	—	—	—	—	—
South Africa *v.*	12	1	7	9	0	3	12	1	1	12	1	1	19	4	10
New Zealand *v.*	18	1	4	21	2	0	13	1	0	14	0	3	23	2	6
Australia *v.*	16	1	8	12	0	7	14	0	6	12	0	8	4	0	9
France *v.*	28	7	43	37	3	33	43	5	27	33	3	41	†	†	†

	South Africa			New Zealand			Australia			France		
	Wins	Draws	Losses	Wins	Draws	Losses	Wins	Draws	Losses	Wins	Draws	Losses
England *v.*	7	1	12	4	1	18	8	1	16	43	7	28
Scotland *v.*	3	0	9	0	2	21	7	0	12	33	3	37
Ireland *v.*	1	1	12	0	1	13	6	0	14	27	5	43
Wales *v.*	1	1	12	3	0	14	8	0	12	41	3	33
British Isles* *v.*	10	4	19	6	2	23	9	0	4	†	†	†
South Africa *v.*	—	—	—	25	3	25	27	1	14	19	5	6
New Zealand *v.*	25	3	25	—	—	—	71	5	33	26	0	9
Australia *v.*	14	1	27	33	5	71	—	—	—	11	2	13
France *v.*	6	5	19	9	0	26	13	2	11	—	—	—

*The British Isles ("British Lions") is a combined team from the four "Home Unions" (England, Ireland, Scotland, and Wales). †No matches.

Rugby League World Cup

Year	Result			
1992	Australia	10	Great Britain	6
1995	Australia	16	England	8
2000	Australia	40	New Zealand	12

Rugby Union World Cup

Year	Result			
1991	Australia	12	England	6
1995	South Africa	15	New Zealand	12
1999	Australia	35	France	12

Six Nations Championship*

Year	Result
1999	Scotland
2000	England
2001	**England**

*Five Nations until 2000.

GOLF

Masters Tournament

Year	Winner
1999	J.-M. Olazábal (Spain)
2000	V. Singh (Fiji)
2001	**T. Woods (U.S.)**

United States Open Championship (men)

Year	Winner
1999	P. Stewart (U.S.)
2000	T. Woods (U.S.)
2001	**R. Goosen (S.Af.)**

British Open Tournament (men)

Year	Winner
1999	P. Lawrie (Scot.)
2000	T. Woods (U.S.)
2001	**D. Duval (U.S.)**

U.S. Professional Golfers' Association (PGA) Championship

Year	Winner
1999	T. Woods (U.S.)
2000	T. Woods (U.S.)
2001	**D. Toms (U.S.)**

United States Amateur Championship (men)

Year	Winner
1999	D. Gossett (U.S.)
2000	J. Quinney (U.S.)
2001	**B. Dickerson (U.S.)**

British Amateur Championship (men)

Year	Winner
1999	G. Storm (U.K.)
2000	M. Ilonen (Fin.)
2001	**M. Hoey (Ire.)**

United States Women's Open Championship

Year	Winner
1999	J. Inkster (U.S.)
2000	K. Webb (Austl.)
2001	**K. Webb (Austl.)**

Women's British Open Championship

Year	Winner
1999	S. Steinhauer (U.S.)
2000	S. Gustafson (Swed.)
2001	**Pak Se Ri (S.Kor.)**

Ladies Professional Golf Association (LPGA) Championship

Year	Winner
1999	J. Inkster (U.S.)
2000	J. Inkster (U.S.)
2001	**K. Webb (Austl.)**

United States Women's Amateur Championship

Year	Winner
1999	D. Delasin (U.S.)
2000	M. Newton (U.S.)
2001	**M. Duncan (U.S.)**

Ladies' British Amateur Championship

Year	Winner
1999	M. Monnet (Fr.)
2000	R. Hudson (U.K.)
2001	**M. Prieto (Spain)**

Walker Cup (men; amateur)

Year	Result
1997	United States 18, Britain and Ireland 6
1999	Britain and Ireland 15, United States 9
2001	**Britain and Ireland 15, United States 9**

David Duval shows off his winning form in the British Open.

Harry How/Allsport

GOLF (continued)

World Cup (men; professional)

Year	Winner
1999	United States (T. Woods and M. O'Meara)
2000	United States (T. Woods and D. Duval)
2001	**South Africa (E. Els and R. Goosen)**

Ryder Cup (men; professional)

Year	Result
1997	Europe 14½, United States 13½
1999	United States 14½, Europe 13½
2001	**postponed until 2002**

Curtis Cup (women; amateur)

Year	Result
1996	Britain and Ireland 11½, United States 6½
1998	United States 10, Britain and Ireland 8
2000	United States 10, Britain and Ireland 8

GYMNASTICS

World Gymnastics Championships—Men

Year	All-around team	All-around individual	Horizontal bar	Parallel bars
1999	China	N. Krukov (Russia)	J. Carballo (Spain)	Lee Joo Hyung (S.Kor.)
2000	China	A. Nemov (Russia)	A. Nemov (Russia)	Li Xiaopeng (China)
2001	**Belarus**	**Feng Jing (China)**	**V. Maras (Greece)**	**S. Townsend (U.S.)**

Year	Pommel horse	Rings	Vault	Floor exercise
1999	A. Nemov (Russia)	Dong Zhen (China)	Li Xiaopeng (China)	A. Nemov (Russia)
2000	M. Urzica (Rom.)	S. Csollany (Hung.)	G. Deferr (Spain)	I. Vihrons (Latvia)
2001	**M. Urzica (Rom.)**	**J. Jovtchev (Bulg.)**	**M. Dragulescu (Rom.)**	**J. Jovtchev (Bulg.)* M. Dragulescu (Rom.)***

* Tied.

World Gymnastics Championships—Women

Year	All-around team	All-around individual	Balance beam
1999	Romania	M. Olaru (Rom.)	Ling Jie (China)
2000	Romania	S. Amanar (Rom.)	Liu Xuan (China)
2001	**Romania**	**S. Khorkina (Russia)**	**A. Raducan (Rom.)**

Year	Uneven parallel bars	Vault	Floor exercise
1999	S. Khorkina (Russia)	Ye. Zamolodchikova (Russia)	A. Raducan (Rom.)
2000	S. Khorkina (Russia)	Ye. Zamolodchikova (Russia)	Ye. Zamolodchikova (Russia)
2001	**S. Khorkina (Russia)**	**S. Khorkina (Russia)**	**A. Raducan (Rom.)**

AP/Wide World Photos

Svetlana Khorkina acknowledges the crowd after winning the all-around individual gold medal at the world gymnastics championships in Brussels on November 2.

ICE HOCKEY

NHL Final Standings, 2001

EASTERN CONFERENCE

Northeast Division	W	L	T	OTL*
†Ottawa	48	21	9	4
†Buffalo	46	30	5	1
†Toronto	37	29	11	5
Boston	36	30	8	8
Montreal	28	40	8	6

Atlantic Division	W	L	T	OTL*
†New Jersey	48	19	12	3
†Philadelphia	43	25	11	3
†Pittsburgh	42	28	9	3
New York Rangers	33	43	5	1
New York Islanders	21	51	7	3

Southeast Division	W	L	T	OTL*
†Washington	41	27	10	4
†Carolina	38	32	9	3
Florida	22	38	13	9
Atlanta	23	45	12	2
Tampa Bay	24	47	6	5

WESTERN CONFERENCE

Central Division	W	L	T	OTL*
†Detroit	49	20	9	4
†St. Louis	43	22	12	5
Nashville	34	36	9	3
Chicago	29	40	8	5
Columbus	28	39	9	6

Northwest Division	W	L	T	OTL*
†Colorado	52	16	10	4
†Edmonton	39	28	12	3
†Vancouver	36	28	11	7
Calgary	27	36	15	4
Minnesota	25	39	13	5

Pacific Division	W	L	T	OTL*
†Dallas	48	24	8	2
†San Jose	40	27	12	3
†Los Angeles	38	28	13	3
Phoenix	35	27	17	3
Anaheim	25	41	11	5

*Overtime losses, worth one point. †Qualified for play-offs.

The Stanley Cup

Season	Winner	Runner-up	Games
1998–99	Dallas Stars	Buffalo Sabres	4–2
1999–2000	New Jersey Devils	Dallas Stars	4–2
2000–01	**Colorado Avalanche**	**New Jersey Devils**	**4–3**

World Ice Hockey Championship—Men

Year	Winner
1999	Czech Republic
2000	Czech Republic
2001	**Czech Republic**

World Ice Hockey Championship—Women

Year	Winner
1999	Canada
2000	Canada
2001	**Canada**

ICE SKATING

World Figure Skating Champions—Men

Year	Winner
1999	A. Yagudin (Russia)
2000	A. Yagudin (Russia)
2001	**Ye. Plushchenko (Russia)**

World Figure Skating Champions—Women

Year	Winner
1999	M. Butyrskaya (Russia)
2000	M. Kwan (U.S.)
2001	**M. Kwan (U.S.)**

World Figure Skating Champions—Pairs

Year	Winners
1999	Ye. Berezhnaya, A. Sikharulidze (Russia)
2000	M. Petrova, A. Tikhonov (Russia)
2001	**J. Salé, D. Pelletier (Can.)**

World Ice Dancing Champions

Year	Winners
1999	A. Krylova, O. Ovsyannikov (Russia)
2000	M. Anissina, G. Peizarat (Fr.)
2001	**B. Fusar Poli, M. Margaglio (Italy)**

World Ice Speed-Skating Records Set in 2001 on Major Tracks*

Event	Name	Country	Time
MEN			
500 m	Hiroyasu Shimizu	Japan	34.32 sec
1,000 m	Michael Ireland	Canada	1 min 8.34 sec
	Jeremy Wotherspoon	Canada	1 min 8.28 sec
	Jeremy Wotherspoon	Canada	1 min 7.72 sec
1,500 m	Lee Kyu Hyuk	South Korea	1 min 45.20 sec
WOMEN			
500 m	Catriona LeMay-Doan	Canada	37.40 sec
	Catriona LeMay-Doan	Canada	37.29 sec
	Catriona LeMay-Doan	Canada	37.22 sec
1,000 m	Christine Witty	United States	1 min 14.58 sec
	Monique Garbrecht-Enfeldt	Germany	1 min 14.13 sec
	Sabine Völker	Germany	1 min 14.06 sec
1,500 m	Anna Friesinger	Germany	1 min 54.38 sec
3,000 m	Gunda Niemann-Stirnemann	Germany	4 min 0.26 sec
	Claudia Pechstein	Germany	3 min 59.26 sec
5,000 m	Gunda Niemann-Stirnemann	Germany	6 min 52.44 sec

*Subject to ISU ratification.

World Ice Speed-Skating Records Set in 2001 on Short Tracks*

Event	Name	Country	Time
MEN			
500 m	Jeffrey Scholten	Canada	41.514 sec
1,000 m	Steve Robillard	Canada	1 min 25.985 sec
1,500 m	Eric Bédard	Canada	2 min 15.393 sec
	Steve Robillard	Canada	2 min 15.383 sec
	Fabio Carta	Italy	2 min 13.533 sec
5,000-m relay	Canada National Team	Canada	6 min 43.730 sec
WOMEN			
500 m	Evgenia Radanova	Bulgaria	43.671 sec
1,000 m	Yang Yang (A)	China	1 min 31.871 sec
3,000-m relay	China National Team	China	4 min 13.541 sec

*Subject to ISU ratification.

World Speed-Skating Sprint Championships

Year	Men	Women
1999	J. Wotherspoon (Can.)	M. Garbrecht (Ger.)
2000	J. Wotherspoon (Can.)	M. Garbrecht (Ger.)
2001	**M. Ireland (Can.)**	**M. Garbrecht-Enfeldt (Ger.)**

World All-Around Speed-Skating Champions—Men

Year	Winner
1999	R. Ritsma (Neth.)
2000	G. Romme (Neth.)
2001	**R. Ritsma (Neth.)**

World All-Around Speed-Skating Champions—Women

Year	Winner
1999	G. Niemann-Stirnemann (Ger.)
2000	C. Pechstein (Ger.)
2001	**A. Friesinger (Ger.)**

World Short-Track Speed-Skating Championships—Overall Winners

Year	Men	Women
1999	Li Jianjun (China)	Yang Yang (A) (China)
2000	Ryoung Min (S.Kor.)	Yang Yang (A) (China)
2001	**Li Jianjun (China)**	**Yang Yang (A) (China)**

JUDO

World Judo Championships—Men*

Year	Open weights	60 kg	65 kg (66 kg)	71 kg (73 kg)
1997	R. Kubacki (Pol.)	T. Nomura (Japan)	Kim Hyuk (S.Kor.)	K. Nakamura (Japan)
1999	S. Shinohara (Japan)	M. Poulot (Cuba)	L. Benboudaoud (Fr.)	J. Pedro (U.S.)
2001	**A. Mikhaylin (Russia)**	**A. Lounifi (Tun.)**	**A. Miresmaeili (Iran)**	**V. Makarov (Russia)**
Year	**78 kg (81 kg)**	**86 kg (90 kg)**	**95 kg (100 kg)**	**+95 kg (+100 kg)**
1997	Cho In Chul (S.Kor.)	Jeon Ki Young (S.Kor.)	P. Nastula (Pol.)	D. Douillet (Fr.)
1999	G. Randall (U.K.)	H. Yoshida (Japan)	K. Inoue (Japan)	S. Shinohara (Japan)
2001	**Cho In Chul (S.Kor.)**	**F. Demontfaucon (Fr.)**	**K. Inoue (Japan)**	**A. Mikhaylin (Russia)**

*Figures in parentheses represent new weight classes established in 1999.

World Judo Championships—Women*

Year	Open weights	48 kg	52 kg	56 kg (57 kg)
1997	D. Beltran (Cuba)	R. Tamura (Japan)	M.-C. Restoux (Fr.)	I. Fernández (Spain)
1999	D. Beltran (Cuba)	R. Tamura (Japan)	N. Narasaki (Japan)	D. González (Cuba)
2001	**C. Lebrun (Fr.)**	**R. Tamura (Japan)**	**Kye Sun Hui (N.Kor.)**	**Y. Lupetry (Cuba)**
Year	**61 kg (63 kg)**	**66 kg (70 kg)**	**72 kg (78 kg)**	**+72 kg (+78 kg)**
1997	S. Vandenhende (Fr.)	K. Howey (U.K.)	N. Anno (Japan)	C. Cicot (Fr.)
1999	K. Maeda (Japan)	S. Veranes (Cuba)	N. Anno (Japan)	B. Maksymow (Pol.)
2001	**G. Vandecaveye (Belg.)**	**M. Ueno (Japan)**	**N. Anno (Japan)**	**Yuan Hua (China)**

*Figures in parentheses represent new weight classes established in 1999.

RODEO

Men's World All-Around Rodeo Championship

Year	Winner	Year	Winner
1996	J. Beaver	1999	F. Whitfield
1997	D. Mortensen	2000	J. Beaver
1998	T. Murray	**2001**	**C. Ohl**

ROWING

World Rowing Championships—Men

Year	Single sculls	Min:sec	Double sculls	Min:sec	Quadruple sculls	Min:sec	Coxed pairs	Min:sec
1999	R. Waddell (N.Z.)	6:36.68	L. Spik, I. Cop (Slvn.)	6:04.37	Germany	6:24.37	J. Neil, P. Henry (U.S.)	6:48.56
2000	R. Waddell (N.Z.)	6:48.90	L. Spik, I. Cop (Slvn.)	6:16.63	Italy	5:45.56	K. Borcherding, M. Guerrieri (U.S.)	7:07.15
2001	**O. Tufte (Nor.)**	**6:43.04**	**A. Haller, T. Peto (Hung.)**	**6:14.16**	**Germany**	**5:40.89**	**J. Cracknell, M. Pinsent (Gr.Brit.)**	**6:49.33**

Year	Coxless pairs	Min:sec	Coxed fours	Min:sec	Coxless fours	Min:sec	Eights	Min:sec
1999	D. Ginn, J. Tomkins (Austl.)	6:19.00	United States	6:38.31	Great Britain	5:48.57	United States	6:01.58
2000	M. Andrieux, J.-C. Rolland (Fr.)	6:32.97	Great Britain	6:16.82	Great Britain	5:56.24	Great Britain	5:33.08
2001	**J. Cracknell, M. Pinsent (Gr.Brit.)**	**6:27.57**	**France**	**6:08.25**	**Great Britain**	**5:48.98**	**Romania**	**5:27.48**

World Rowing Championships—Women

Year	Single sculls	Min:sec	Double sculls	Min:sec	Quadruple sculls	Min:sec
1999	Ye. Karsten (Bela.)	7:11.68	J. Thieme, K. Boron (Ger.)	6:41.98	Germany	7:06.53
2000	Ye. Karsten (Bela.)	7:28.14	J. Thieme, K. Boron (Ger.)	6:55.44	Germany	6:19.58
2001	**K. Rutschow-Stomporowski (Ger.)**	**7:19.25**	**K. Boron, K. Kowalski (Ger.)**	**6:50.20**	**Germany**	**6:12.95**

Year	Coxless pairs	Min:sec	Coxless fours	Min:sec	Eights	Min:sec
1999	E. Robinson, T. Luke (Can.)	7:00.85	Belarus	6:26.25	Romania	6:47.66
2000	G. Damian, D. Ignat (Rom.)	7:11.00	Belarus	6:44.90	Romania	6:06.44
2001	**G. Damian, V. Susanu (Rom.)**	**7:01.27**	**Australia**	**6:27.23**	**Australia**	**6:03.66**

James Cracknell and Matthew Pinsent compete in the world rowing championships in Lucerne, Switz., on August 19.

Jamie McDonald/Allsport

The Diamond Challenge Sculls

Year	Winner	Min:sec
1999	M. Hacker (Ger.)	7:59
2000	A.H. Abdullah (U.S.)	8:12
2001	**D.S. Free (Austl.)**	**8:18**

Grand Challenge Cup

Year	Winner	Min:sec
1999	Hansa Dortmund and Berlin, Ger.	6:15
2000	Institute of Sport, Australia	6:19
2001	**H.A.V.K. Mladost and V.K. Croatia, Croatia**	**6:29**

SAILING (YACHTING)

America's Cup

Year	Winning yacht	Owner	Skipper	Losing yacht	Owner
1992	*America*[3] (U.S.)	America[3] Foundation	B. Koch	*Il Moro di Venezia* (Italy)	Compagnia della Vela di Venezia
1995	*Black Magic* (N.Z.)	P. Blake and Team New Zealand	R. Coutts	*Young America*	Pact 95 syndicate
2000	*Black Magic* (N.Z.)	Team New Zealand	R. Coutts	*Luna Rossa* (Italy)	Prada Challenge

World Class Boat Champions, 2001

Class	Winner	Country
Etchells 22	S. Childerley	Great Britain
Europe	S. Multala	Finland
Finn	S. Godefroid	Belgium
2.4 Metre	H. Kroger	Germany
470 (men)	Y. Braslavets/I. Matviyenko	Ukraine
470 (women)	S. Bekatorou/E. Tsoulfa	Greece
49er	J. McKee/C. McKee	United States
Laser	R. Scheidt	Brazil
Mistral (men)	N. Kaklamanakis	Greece
Mistral (women)	Lee Lai Shan	Hong Kong
J/24	K. Hyodo	Japan
Optimist	L. Calabrese	Argentina
Star	F. Lööf/C. Finnsgård	Sweden
Tornado	D. Bundock/J. Forbes	Australia
Yngling	C. Skolaut	Austria

Admiral's Cup

Year	Winning team
1997	United States
1999	Netherlands
2001	**canceled**

Bermuda Race

Year	Winning yacht	Owner
1996	*Boomerang*	G. Coumantaros
1998	*Kodiak*	L. Ecclestone
2000	*Restless*	E. Crawford

Transpacific Race

Year	Winning yacht	Owner
1997	*Ralphie*	J. Montgomery
1999	*Grand Illusion*	J. McDowell
2001	***Bull***	**S. Radow**

SKIING

World Alpine Skiing Championships—Slalom

Year	Men's slalom	Men's giant slalom	Men's supergiant	Women's slalom	Women's giant slalom	Women's supergiant
1998	H.-P. Buraas (Nor.)	H. Maier (Austria)	H. Maier (Austria)	H. Gerg (Ger.)	D. Compagnoni (Italy)	P. Street (U.S.)
1999	K. Palander (Fin.)	L. Kjus (Nor.)	L. Kjus (Nor.)* H. Maier (Austria)*	Z. Steggall (Austl.)	A. Meissnitzer (Austria)	A. Meissnitzer (Austria)
2001	**M. Matt (Austria)**	**M. von Grünigen (Switz.)**	**D. Rahlves (U.S.)**	**A. Paerson (Swed.)**	**S. Nef (Switz.)**	**R. Cavagnoud (Fr.)**

*Tie.

World Alpine Skiing Championships—Downhill

Year	Men	Women
1998	J.-L. Cretier (Fr.)	K. Seizinger (Ger.)
1999	H. Maier (Austria)	R. Götschl (Austria)
2001	**H. Trinkl (Austria)**	**M. Dorfmeister (Austria)**

World Alpine Skiing Championships—Combined

Year	Men	Women
1998	M. Reiter (Austria)	K. Seizinger (Ger.)
1999	K.A. Aamodt (Nor.)	P. Wiberg (Swed.)
2001	**K.A. Aamodt (Nor.)**	**M. Ertl (Ger.)**

Alpine World Cup

Year	Men	Women
1999	L. Kjus (Nor.)	A. Meissnitzer (Austria)
2000	H. Maier (Austria)	R. Götschl (Austria)
2001	**H. Maier (Austria)**	**J. Kostelic (Cro.)**

World Nordic Skiing Championships—Men

Year	Sprint	10-km	15-km	30-km	50-km	Relay
1998		B. Dæhlie (Nor.)	T. Alsgaard (Nor.)	M. Myllylä (Fin.)	B. Dæhlie (Nor.)	Norway
1999		M. Myllylä (Fin.)	T. Alsgaard (Nor.)	M. Myllylä (Fin.)	M. Myllylä (Fin.)	Austria
2001	**T.A. Hetland (Nor.)**	**P. Elofsson (Swed.)**	**P. Elofsson (Swed.)**	**A. Veerpalu (Est.)**	**J. Mühlegg (Spain)**	**Norway**

World Nordic Skiing Championships—Women

Year	Sprint	5-km	10-km	15-km	30-km	Relay
1998		L. Lazutina (Russia)	L. Lazutina (Russia)	O. Danilova (Russia)	Yu. Chepalova (Russia)	Russia
1999		B. Martinsen (Nor.)	S. Belmondo (Italy)	S. Belmondo (Italy)	L. Lazutina (Russia)	Russia
2001	**P. Manninen (Fin.)**	**V. Kuitunen (Fin.)**	**B. Skari Martinsen (Nor.)**	**B. Skari Martinsen (Nor.)**	**canceled**	**Russia**

World Nordic Skiing Championships—Ski Jump

Year	Normal hill*	Large hill†	Team jump (normal hill)	Team jump (large hill)	Combined (7.5-km)	Combined (15-km)	Team combined
1998	J. Soininen (Fin.)	K. Funaki (Japan)		Japan		B.E. Vik (Nor.)	Norway
1999	K. Funaki (Japan)	M. Schmitt (Ger.)		Germany	B.E. Vik (Nor.)	B.E. Vik (Nor.)	Finland
2001	**A. Malysz (Pol.)**	**M. Schmitt (Ger.)**	**Austria**	**Germany**	**M. Baacke (Ger.)**	**B.E. Vik (Nor.)**	**Norway**

*90-m. †120-m through 1999, 116-m in 2001.

Nordic World Cup

Year	Men	Women
1999	B. Dæhlie (Nor.)	B. Martinsen (Nor.)
2000	J. Mühlegg (Spain)	B. Martinsen (Nor.)
2001	**P. Elofsson (Swed.)**	**Yu. Chepalova (Russia)**

Zoom Sports/Allsport

Sonja Nef races to a first-place finish in the women's giant slalom event at the world alpine skiing championships in February.

SQUASH

British Open Championship—Men

Year	Winner
1998–99	J. Power (Can.)
1999–2000	D. Evans (Wales)
2000–01	**D. Palmer (Austl.)**

British Open Championship—Women

Year	Winner
1998–99	L. Joyce (N.Z.)
1999–2000	L. Joyce (N.Z.)
2000–01	**S. Fitz-Gerald (Austl.)**

World Open Championship—Men

Year	Winner
1999	P. Nicol (Scot.)
2000	not held
2001	**canceled**

World Open Championship—Women

Year	Winner
1999	C. Campion (Eng.)
2000	C. Owens (Austl.)
2001	**S. Fitz-Gerald (Austl.)**

SWIMMING

World Swimming Records Set in 2001 in 25-m Pools

Event	Name	Country	Time
MEN			
50-m freestyle	Mark Foster	United Kingdom	21.13 sec
800-m freestyle	Grant Hackett	Australia	7 min 25.28 sec
1,500-m freestyle	Grant Hackett	Australia	14 min 10.10 sec
50-m breaststroke	Roman Sludnov	Russia	29.90 sec
50-m butterfly	Mark Foster	United Kingdom	22.87 sec
	Geoff Huegill	Australia	22.84 sec
100-m butterfly	Thomas Rupprath	Germany	50.26 sec
200-m butterfly	Franck Esposito	France	1 min 51.58 sec
	Thomas Rupprath	Germany	1 min 51.21 sec
4 × 50-m medley relay	German National Team	Germany	1 min 35.14 sec
	German National Team	Germany	1 min 34.78 sec
4 × 200-m freestyle relay	Australia National Team	Australia	6 min 56.41 sec
WOMEN			
800-m freestyle	Chen Hua	China	8 min 15.15 sec
1,500-m freestyle	Rebecca Cooke	United Kingdom	15 min 52.97 sec
50-m backstroke	Li Hui	China	26.83 sec
100-m backstroke	Mai Nakamura	Japan	58.45 sec
	Natalie Coughlin	United States	57.08 sec
200-m backstroke	Sarah Price	United Kingdom	2 min 4.44 sec
	Natalie Coughlin	United States	2 min 3.62 sec
50-m breaststroke	Li Wei*	China	30.56 sec
	Luo Xuejuan*	China	30.56 sec
200-m breaststroke	Qi Hui	China	2 min 19.25 sec
50-m butterfly	Anna-Karin Kammerling	Sweden	25.36 sec
4 × 200-m freestyle relay	British National Team	United Kingdom	7 min 58.69 sec

*Tied.

World Swimming Records Set in 2001 in 50-m Pools

Event	Name	Country	Time
MEN			
200-m freestyle	Ian Thorpe	Australia	1 min 44.69 sec
	Ian Thorpe	Australia	1 min 44.06 sec
400-m freestyle	Ian Thorpe	Australia	3 min 40.17 sec
800-m freestyle	Ian Thorpe	Australia	7 min 41.59 sec
	Ian Thorpe	Australia	7 min 39.16 sec
1,500-m freestyle	Grant Hackett	Australia	14 min 34.56 sec
50-m breaststroke	Anthony Robinson	United States	27.49 sec
	Ed Moses	United States	27.39 sec
100-m breaststroke	Ed Moses	United States	1 min 0.29 sec
	Roman Sludnov	Russia	1 min 0.26 sec
	Roman Sludnov	Russia	59.97 sec
	Roman Sludnov	Russia	59.94 sec
50-m butterfly	Geoff Huegill	Australia	23.44 sec
200-m butterfly	Michael Phelps	United States	1 min 54.92 sec
	Michael Phelps	United States	1 min 54.58 sec
4 × 200-m freestyle relay	Australia Olympic Team	Australia	7 min 4.66 sec
WOMEN			
200-m breaststroke	Qi Hui	China	2 min 22.99 sec

World Swimming and Diving Championships—Men

	Freestyle					
Year	50 m	100 m	200 m	400 m	800 m	1,500 m
1994	A. Popov (Russia)	A. Popov (Russia)	A. Kasvio (Fin.)	K. Perkins (Austl.)		K. Perkins (Austl.)
1998	B. Pilczuk (U.S.)	A. Popov (Russia)	M. Klim (Austl.)	I. Thorpe (Austl.)		G. Hackett (Austl.)
2001	**A. Ervin (U.S.)**	**A. Ervin (U.S.)**	**I. Thorpe (Austl.)**	**I. Thorpe (Austl.)**	**I. Thorpe (Austl.)**	**G. Hackett (Austl.)**

	Backstroke			Breaststroke		
	50 m	100 m	200 m	50 m	100 m	200 m
1994		M. López Zubero (Spain)	V. Selkov (Russia)		N. Rozsa (Hung.)	N. Rozsa (Hung.)
1998		L. Krayzelburg (U.S.)	L. Krayzelburg (U.S.)		F. De Burghgraeve (Belg.)	K. Grote (U.S.)
2001	**R. Bal (U.S.)**	**M. Welsh (Austl.)**	**A. Piersol (U.S.)**	**O. Lisogor (Ukr.)**	**R. Sludnov (Russia)**	**B. Hansen (U.S.)**

	Butterfly			Individual medley		Team relays
	50 m	100 m	200 m	200 m	400 m	4 × 100-m freestyle
1994		R. Szukala (Pol.)	D. Pankratov (Russia)	J. Sievinen (Fin.)	T. Dolan (U.S.)	United States
1998		M. Klim (Austl.)	D. Silantyev (Ukr.)	M. Wouda (Neth.)	T. Dolan (U.S.)	United States
2001	**G. Huegill (Austl.)**	**L. Frölander (Swed.)**	**M. Phelps (U.S.)**	**M. Rosolino (Italy)**	**A. Boggiatto (Italy)**	**Australia**

			Diving				
	4 × 200-m freestyle	4 × 100-m medley	1-m springboard	3-m springboard	Platform	3-m synchronized	10-m synchronized
1994	Sweden	United States	E. Stewart (Zimb.)	Yu Zhuocheng (China)	D. Sautin (Russia)		
1998	Australia	Australia	Yu Zhuocheng (China)	D. Sautin (Russia)	D. Sautin (Russia)	China	China
2001	**Australia**	**Australia**	**Wang Feng (China)**	**D. Sautin (Russia)**	**Tian Liang (China)**	**China**	**China**

SWIMMING (continued)

World Swimming and Diving Championships—Women

	Freestyle					
Year	**50 m**	**100 m**	**200 m**	**400 m**	**800 m**	**1,500 m**
1994	Le Jingyi (China)	Le Jingyi (China)	F. van Almsick (Ger.)	Yang Aihua (China)	J. Evans (U.S.)	
1998	A. Van Dyken (U.S.)	J. Thompson (U.S.)	C. Poll (C.Rica)	Chen Yan (China)	B. Bennett (U.S.)	
2001	**I. de Bruijn (Neth.)**	**I. de Bruijn (Neth.)**	**G. Rooney (Austl.)**	**Ya. Klochkova (Ukr.)**	**H. Stockbauer (Ger.)**	**H. Stockbauer (Ger.)**

	Backstroke			Breaststroke		
	50 m	**100 m**	**200 m**	**50 m**	**100 m**	**200 m**
1994		He Cihong (China)	He Cihong (China)		S. Riley (Austl.)	S. Riley (Austl.)
1998		L. Maurer (U.S.)	R. Maracineanu (Fr.)		K. Kowal (U.S.)	A. Kovacs (Hung.)
2001	**H. Cope (U.S.)**	**N. Coughlin (U.S.)**	**D. Mocanu (Rom.)**	**Luo Xuejuan (China)**	**Luo Xuejuan (China)**	**A. Kovacs (Hung.)**

	Butterfly			Individual medley		Team relays
	50 m	**100 m**	**200 m**	**200 m**	**400 m**	**4 × 100-m freestyle**
1994		Liu Limin (China)	Liu Limin (China)	Lu Bin (China)	Dai Guohong (China)	China
1998		J. Thompson (U.S.)	S. O'Neill (Austl.)	Wu Yanyan (China)	Chen Yan (China)	United States
2001	**I. de Bruijn (Neth.)**	**P. Thomas (Austl.)**	**P. Thomas (Austl.)**	**M. Bowen (U.S.)**	**Ya. Klochkova (Ukr.)**	**Germany**

			Diving				
	4 × 200-m freestyle	**4 × 100-m medley**	**1-m springboard**	**3-m springboard**	**Platform**	**3-m synchronized**	**10-m synchronized**
1994	China	China	Chen Lixia (China)	Tan Shuping (China)	Fu Mingxia (China)		
1998	Germany	United States	I. Lashko (Russia)	Y. Pakhalina (Russia)	O. Zhupina (Ukr.)	Russia	Ukraine
2001	**United Kingdom**	**Australia**	**B. Hartley (Can.)**	**Guo Jingjing (China)**	**Xu Mian (China)**	**China**	**China**

TABLE TENNIS

World Table Tennis Championships—Men

Year	St. Bride's Vase (singles)	Iran Cup (doubles)	Swaythling Cup (team)
1999	Liu Guoliang (China)	Kong Linghui, Liu Guoliang (China)	not held
2000	not held	not held	Sweden
2001	**Wang Liqin (China)**	**Wang Liqin, Yan Sen (China)**	**China**

World Table Tennis Championships—Women

Year	G. Geist Prize (singles)	W.J. Pope Trophy (doubles)	Corbillon Cup (team)
1999	Wang Nan (China)	Wang Nan, Li Ju (China)	not held
2000	not held	not held	China
2001	**Wang Nan (China)**	**Wang Nan, Li Ju (China)**	**China**

World Table Tennis Championships—Mixed

Year	Heydusek Prize
1997	Liu Guoliang, Wu Na (China)
1999	Ma Lin, Zhang Yingying (China)
2001	**Qin Zhijian, Yang Ying (China)**

2001 Table Tennis World Rankings*

Men	Women
1. Wang Liqin (China)	1. Wang Nan (China)
2. Liu Guozheng (China)	2. Zhang Yining (China)
3. Kong Linghui (China)	3. Li Ju (China)
4. Ma Lin (China)	4. Mihaela Steff (Rom.)
5. Chiang Peng-Lung (Taiwan)	5. Tamara Boros (Cro.)

*ITTF ranking as of September 2001.

Table Tennis World Cup

Year	Men
1999	V. Samsonov (Bela.)
2000	Ma Lin (China)
2001	**V. Samsonov (Bela.)**

Year	Women
1999	Wang Nan (China)
2000	Li Ju (China)
2001	**Zhang Yining (China)**

TENNIS

Australian Open Tennis Championships—Singles

Year	Men	Women
1999	Ye. Kafelnikov (Russia)	M. Hingis (Switz.)
2000	A. Agassi (U.S.)	L. Davenport (U.S.)
2001	**A. Agassi (U.S.)**	**J. Capriati (U.S.)**

Australian Open Tennis Championships—Doubles

Year	Men	Women
1999	J. Bjorkman, P. Rafter	M. Hingis, A. Kournikova
2000	E. Ferreira, R. Leach	L. Raymond, R. Stubbs
2001	**J. Bjorkman, T. Woodbridge**	**S. Williams, V. Williams**

TENNIS (continued)

French Open Tennis Championships—Singles

Year	Men	Women
1999	A. Agassi (U.S.)	S. Graf (Ger.)
2000	G. Kuerten (Braz.)	M. Pierce (Fr.)
2001	**G. Kuerten (Braz.)**	**J. Capriati (U.S.)**

All-England (Wimbledon) Tennis Championships—Singles

Year	Men	Women
1999	P. Sampras (U.S.)	L. Davenport (U.S.)
2000	P. Sampras (U.S.)	V. Williams (U.S.)
2001	**G. Ivanisevic (Cro.)**	**V. Williams (U.S.)**

United States Open Tennis Championships—Singles

Year	Men	Women
1999	A. Agassi (U.S.)	S. Williams (U.S.)
2000	M. Safin (Russia)	V. Williams (U.S.)
2001	**L. Hewitt (Austl.)**	**V. Williams (U.S.)**

Davis Cup (men)

Year	Winner	Runner-up	Results
1999	Australia	France	3–2
2000	Spain	Australia	3–1
2001	**France**	**Australia**	**3–2**

Fed Cup (women)

Year	Winner	Runner-up	Results
1999	United States	Russia	4–1
2000	United States	Spain	5–0
2001	**Belgium**	**Russia**	**2–1**

French Open Tennis Championships—Doubles

Year	Men	Women
1999	M. Bhupathi, L. Paes	S. Williams, V. Williams
2000	T. Woodbridge, M. Woodforde	M. Hingis, M. Pierce
2001	**M. Bhupathi, L. Paes**	**V. Ruano Pascual, P. Suarez**

All-England (Wimbledon) Tennis Championships—Doubles

Year	Men	Women
1999	M. Bhupathi, L. Paes	L. Davenport, C. Morariu
2000	T. Woodbridge, M. Woodforde	S. Williams, V. Williams
2001	**D. Johnson, J. Palmer**	**L. Raymond, R. Stubbs**

United States Open Tennis Championships—Doubles

Year	Men	Women
1999	S. Lareau, A. O'Brien	S. Williams, V. Williams
2000	L. Hewitt, M. Mirnyi	J. Halard Decugis, A. Sugiyama
2001	**W. Black, K. Ullyet**	**L. Raymond, R. Stubbs**

TRACK AND FIELD SPORTS (ATHLETICS)

World Track and Field Championships—Men

Event	1999	2001
100 m	M. Greene (U.S.)	M. Greene (U.S.)
200 m	M. Greene (U.S.)	K. Kederis (Greece)
400 m	M. Johnson (U.S.)	A. Moncur (Bahamas)
800 m	W. Kipketer (Den.)	A. Bucher (Switz.)
1,500 m	H. El Guerrouj (Mor.)	H. El Guerrouj (Mor.)
5,000 m	S. Hissou (Mor.)	R. Limo (Kenya)
10,000 m	H. Gebrselassie (Eth.)	C. Kamathi (Kenya)
steeplechase	C. Koskei (Kenya)	R. Kosgei (Kenya)
110-m hurdles	C. Jackson (U.K.)	A. Johnson (U.S.)
400-m hurdles	F. Mori (Italy)	F. Sánchez (Dom.Rep.)
marathon	A. Antón (Spain)	G. Abera (Eth.)
20-km walk	I. Markov (Russia)	R. Rasskazov (Russia)
50-km walk	G. Skurygin (Russia)	R. Korzeniowski (Pol.)
4 × 100-m relay	United States (J. Drummond, T. Montgomery, B. Lewis, M. Greene)	United States (M. Grimes, B. Williams, D. Mitchell, T. Montgomery)
4 × 400-m relay	United States (J. Davis, A. Pettigrew, A. Taylor, M. Johnson)	United States (L. Byrd, A. Pettigrew, D. Brew, A. Taylor)
high jump	V. Voronin (Russia)	M. Buss (Ger.)
pole vault	M. Tarasov (Russia)	D. Markov (Austl.)
long jump	I. Pedroso (Cuba)	I. Pedroso (Cuba)
triple jump	C.M. Friedek (Ger.)	J. Edwards (U.K.)
shot put	C.J. Hunter (U.S.)	J. Godina (U.S.)
discus throw	A. Washington (U.S.)	L. Riedel (Ger.)
hammer throw	K. Kobs (Ger.)	S. Ziolkowski (Pol.)
javelin throw	A. Parviainen (Fin.)	J. Zelezny (Cz.Rep.)
decathlon	T. Dvorak (Cz.Rep.)	T. Dvorak (Cz.Rep.)

World Track and Field Championships—Women

Event	1999	2001
100 m	M. Jones (U.S.)	Z. Pintusevich-Block (Ukr.)
200 m	I. Miller (U.S.)	M. Jones (U.S.)
400 m	C. Freeman (Austl.)	A. Mbacke Thiam (Senegal)
800 m	L. Formanova (Cz.Rep.)	M. Mutola (Mozam.)
1,500 m	S. Masterkova (Russia)	G. Szabo (Rom.)
5,000 m	G. Szabo (Rom.)	O. Yegorova (Russia)
10,000 m	G. Wami (Eth.)	D. Tulu (Eth.)
100-m hurdles	G. Devers (U.S.)	A. Kirkland (U.S.)
400-m hurdles	D. Pernía (Cuba)	N. Bidouane (Mor.)
marathon	Jong Song Ok (N.Kor.)	L. Simon (Rom.)
20-km walk	Liu Hongyu (China)	O. Ivanova (Russia)
4 × 100-m relay	Bahamas (S. Fynes, C. Sturrup, P. Davis, D. Ferguson)	United States (K. White, C. Gaines, I. Miller, M. Jones)
4 × 400-m relay	Russia (T. Chebykina, S. Goncharenko, O. Kotlyarova, N. Nazarova)	Jamaica (S. Richards, C. Scott, D.-A. Parris, L. Fenton)
high jump	I. Babakova (Ukr.)	H. Cloete (S.Afr.)
pole vault	S. Dragila (U.S.)	S. Dragila (U.S.)
long jump	N. Montalvo (Spain)	F. May (Italy)
triple jump	P. Tsiamita (Greece)	T. Lebedeva (Russia)
shot put	A. Kumbernuss (Ger.)	Y. Korolchik (Bela.)
discus throw	F. Dietzsch (Ger.)	N. Sadova (Russia)
hammer throw	M. Melinte (Rom.)	Y. Moreno (Cuba)
javelin throw	M. Tzelili (Greece)	O. Menéndez (Cuba)
heptathlon	E. Barber (Fr.)	Ye. Prokhorova (Russia)

TRACK AND FIELD SPORTS (ATHLETICS) (continued)

2001 World Indoor Records—Men

Event	Competitor and country	Performance
60 m	Maurice Greene (U.S.)	6.39 sec*
3,000-m walk†	Andreas Erm (Ger.)	10 min 31.42 sec

*Equaled existing world record. †Not an officially ratified event; best performance on record.

2001 World Indoor Records—Women

Event	Competitor and country	Performance
3,000 m	Gabriella Szabo (Rom.)	8 min 32.88 sec
Pole vault	Stacy Dragila (U.S.)	4.63 m (15 ft 2¼ in)
	Stacy Dragila (U.S.)	4.65 m (15 ft 3 in)
	Stacy Dragila (U.S.)	4.66 m (15 ft 3½ in)
	Stacy Dragila (U.S.)	4.70 m (15 ft 5 in)

2001 World Outdoor Records—Men

Event	Competitor and country	Performance
Steeplechase	Brahim Boulami (Mor.)	7 min 55.28 sec
Decathlon	Roman Sebrle (Cz.Rep.)	9,026 pts

2001 World Outdoor Records—Women

Event	Competitor and country	Performance
Steeplechase	Justyna Bak (Pol.)	9 min 25.31 sec
20-km walk	Susana Feitor (Port.)	1 hr 29 min 36.4 sec
	Olimpiada Ivanova (Russia)	1 hr 26 min 52.3 sec
Half-marathon*	Susan Chepkemei (Kenya)	1 hr 5 min 44 sec
Marathon*	Naoko Takashi (Japan)	2 hr 19 min 46 sec
	Catherine Ndereba (Kenya)	2 hr 18 min 47 sec
Pole vault	Stacy Dragila (U.S.)	4.65 m (15 ft 3 in)
	Stacy Dragila (U.S.)	4.70 m (15 ft 5 in)
	Stacy Dragila (U.S.)	4.71 m (15 ft 5½ in)
	Stacy Dragila (U.S.)	4.81 m (15 ft 9¼ in)
Javelin throw	Osleidys Menéndez (Cuba)	71.54 m (234 ft 8 in)

*Not an officially ratified event; best performance on record.

Maurice Greene celebrates his victory in the 100-m event at the world track and field championships on August 5.

Don Emmert/AFP Worldwide

IAAF World Cup—Men

	100 metre	200 metre	400 metre	800 metre	1,500 metre
1992	L. Christie (Gr.Brit.)	R. Caetano da Silva (Amer.)	S. Bada (Africa)	D. Sharpe (U.K.)	M. Suleiman (Asia)
1994	L. Christie (Gr.Brit.)	J. Regis (Gr.Brit.)	A. Pettigrew (U.S.)	M. Everett (U.S.)	N. Morceli (Africa)
1998	O. Thompson (Amer.)	F. Fredericks (Africa)	I. Thomas (Gr.Brit.)	N. Schumann (Ger.)	L. Rotich (Africa)

	3,000 metre	5,000 metre	10,000 metre	Steeplechase	110-m hurdles
1992	—	F. Bayesa (Africa)	A. Abebe (Africa)	P. Barkutwo (Africa)	C. Jackson (U.K.)
1994	—	B. Lahlafi (Africa)	K. Skah (Africa)	M. Kiptanui (Africa)	T. Jarrett (Gr.Brit.)
1998	D. Baumann (Ger.)	D. Komen (Africa)	—	D. Kallabis (Ger.)	F. Balzer (Ger.)

	400-m hurdles	4 × 100-m relays	4 × 400-m relays	Triple jump	High jump
1992	S. Matete (Africa)	United States	Africa	J. Edwards (U.K.)	Y. Sergeyenko (UT)
1994	S. Matete (Africa)	Great Britain	Great Britain	Y. Quesada (Amer.)	J. Sotomayor (Amer.)
1998	S. Matete (Africa)	Great Britain	United States	C. Friedek (Ger.)	C. Austin (U.S.)

	Pole vault	Long jump	Shot put	Discus throw	Hammer throw
1992	I. Potapovich (UT)	I. Pedroso (Amer.)	M. Stulce (U.S.)	T. Washington (U.S.)	T. Gecsek (Europe)
1994	O. Brits (Africa)	F. Salle (Gr.Brit.)	C.J. Hunter (U.S.)	V. Dubrovshchik (Europe)	A. Abduvaliyev (Asia)
1998	M. Tarasov (Europe)	I. Pedroso (Amer.)	J. Godina (U.S.)	V. Alekna (Europe)	T. Gecsek (Europe)

	Javelin throw	Team
1992	J. Zelezny (Europe)	Africa
1994	S. Backley (Gr.Brit.)	Africa
1998	S. Backley (Gr.Brit.)	—

TRACK AND FIELD SPORTS (ATHLETICS) (continued)

IAAF World Cup—Women

	100 metre	200 metre	400 metre	800 metre	1,500 metre
1992	N. Voronova (UT)	M.-J. Pérec (Europe)	J. Miles (U.S.)	M. Mutola (Africa)	Y. Podkopayeva (UT)
1994	I. Privalova (Europe)	M. Ottey (Amer.)	I. Privalova (Europe)	M. Mutola (Africa)	H. Boulmerka (Africa)
1998	M. Jones (U.S.)	M. Jones (U.S.)	F. Ogunkoya (Africa)	M. Mutola (Africa)	S. Masterkova (Russia)

	3,000 metre	5,000 metre	10,000 metre	100-m hurdles	400-m hurdles
1992	D. Tulu (Africa)	—	D. Tulu (Africa)	A. López (Amer.)	S. Farmer-Patrick (U.S.)
1994	Y. Murray (Gr.Brit.)	—	E. Meyer (Africa)	A. López (Amer.)	S. Gunnell (Gr.Brit.)
1998	G. Szabo (Europe)	S. O'Sullivan (Europe)	—	G. Alozie (Africa)	N. Bidouane (Africa)

	4 × 100-m relays	4 × 400-m relays	Triple jump	High jump	Long jump
1992	Asia	Americas	—	I. Quintero (Amer.)	H. Drechsler (Ger.)
1994	Africa	Great Britain	A. Biryukova (Europe)	B. Bilac (Europe)	I. Kravets (Europe)
1998	United States	Germany	O. Vasdeki (Europe)	M. Iagar-Dinescu (Europe)	H. Drechsler (Ger.)

	Shot put	Discus throw	Javelin throw	Team
1992	B. Laza (Amer.)	M. Marten (Amer.)	T. Sanderson (U.K.)	Unified Team
1994	Zhihong Huang (Asia)	I. Wyludda (Europe)	T. Hattestad (Europe)	Europe
1998	V. Pavlysh (Europe)	F. Dietzsch (Ger.)	J. Stone (Oceania)	—

World Cross Country Championships—Men

Year	Individual	Team
1999	P. Tergat (Kenya)	Kenya
2000	M. Mourhit (Belg.)	Kenya
2001	**M. Mourhit (Belg.)**	**Kenya**

World Cross Country Championships—Women

Year	Individual	Team
1999	G. Wami (Eth.)	Ethiopia
2000	D. Tulu (Eth.)	Ethiopia
2001	**P. Radcliffe (U.K.)**	**Kenya**

Boston Marathon

Year	Men	h:min:s
1999	J. Chebet (Kenya)	2:09:52
2000	E. Lagat (Kenya)	2:09:47
2001	**Lee Bong Ju (S.Kor.)**	**2:09:43**

Year	Women	h:min:s
1999	F. Roba (Eth.)	2:23:25
2000	C. Ndereba (Kenya)	2:26:11
2001	**C. Ndereba (Kenya)**	**2:23:53**

New York City Marathon

Year	Men	h:min:s
1999	J. Chebet (Kenya)	2:09:14
2000	A. El Mouaziz (Mor.)	2:10:09
2001	**T. Jifar (Eth.)**	**2:07:43**

Year	Women	h:min:s
1999	A. Fernández (Mex.)	2:25:06
2000	L. Petrova (Russia)	2:25:45
2001	**M. Okayo (Kenya)**	**2:24:21**

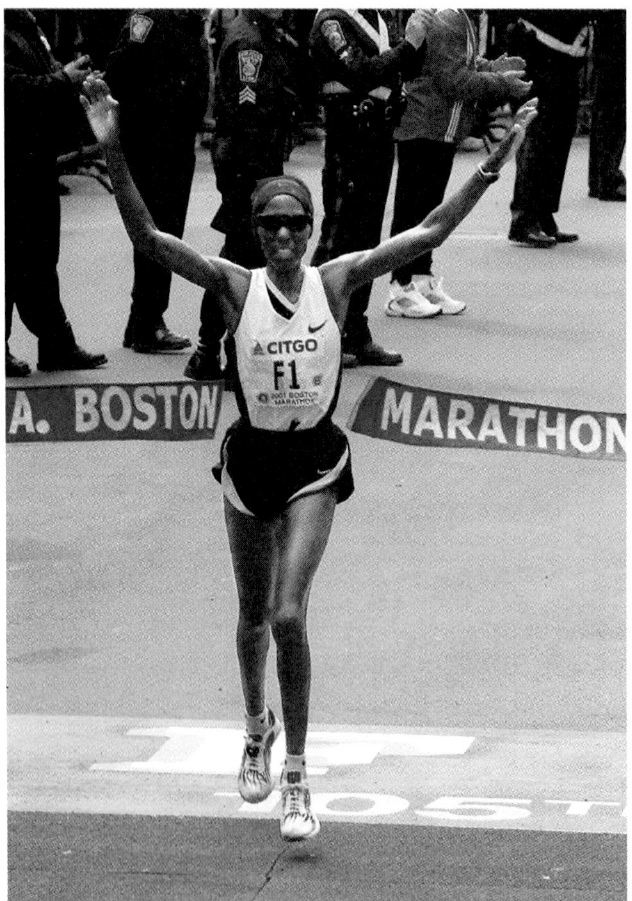

Catherine Ndereba wins the Boston Marathon on April 16.

VOLLEYBALL

World Volleyball Championships

Year	Men	Women
1996	Netherlands	Cuba
1998	Italy	Cuba
2000	Yugoslavia	Cuba

WEIGHT LIFTING

World Weight Lifting Champions, 2001

MEN

Weight class	Winner and country	Performance
56 kg (123 lb)	Halil Mutlu (Turkey)	300 kg (660 lb)
62 kg (136.5 lb)	Henadzy Aliyashchuk (Bela.)	317.5 kg (698.5 lb)
69 kg (152 lb)	Galabin Boevski (Bulg.)	340 kg (748 lb)
77 kg (169.5 lb)	Abbas Nader (Qatar)	365 kg (803 lb)
85 kg (187 lb)	George Asanidze (Georgia)	390 kg (861.9 lb)
94 kg (207 lb)	Kouroush Bagheri (Iran)	407.5 kg (896.5 lb)
105 kg (231 lb)	Vladimir Smorchkov (Russia)	422.5 kg (929.5 lb)
+105 kg (+231 lb)	Saeed Salem Jaber (Qatar)	460 kg (1,012 lb)

WOMEN

Weight class	Winner and country	Performance
48 kg (105.5 lb)	Wei Gao (China)	190 kg (418 lb)
53 kg (116.5 lb)	Li Feng-ying (Taiwan)	210 kg (462 lb)
58 kg (127.5 lb)	Aleksandra Klejnowska (Pol.)	215 kg (473 lb)
63 kg (138.5 lb)	Xiao Ying (China)	230 kg (506 lb)
69 kg (152 lb)	Valentina Popova (Russia)	257.5 kg (566.5 lb)
75 kg (165 lb)	Gyorgy Likerecz (Hung.)	255 kg (561 lb)
+75 kg (+165 lb)	Albina Khomitch (Russia)	282.5 kg (621.5 lb)

Valentina Popova hoists 142 kg (314 lb) in the clean-and-jerk en route to a first-place finish in her weight class at the world weight lifting championships in November.

AP/Wide World Photos

WRESTLING

World Wrestling Championships—Freestyle

Year	54 kg	58 kg	63 kg	69 kg
1999	Kim Woo Yong (S.Kor.)	H. Dogan (Tur.)	E. Tedeyev (Ukr.)	D. Igali (Can.)
2000	N. Abdullayev (Azer.)	A.R. Dabier (Iran)	M. Umakhanov (Russia)	D. Igali (Can.)
2001	**H. Kantoyeu (Bela.)**	**G. Sissaouri (Can.)**	**S. Barzakov (Bulg.)**	**N. Paslar (Bulg.)**
Year	**76 kg**	**85 kg**	**97 kg**	**130 kg**
1999	A. Saytyev (Russia)	Y. Romero (Cuba)	S. Murtasaliyev (Russia)	S. Neal (U.S.)
2000	B. Slay (U.S.)	A. Saytyev (Russia)	S. Murtasaliyev (Russia)	D. Musulbes (Russia)
2001	**B. Saytyev (Russia)**	**K. Magomedov (Russia)**	**G. Gogchelidze (Russia)**	**D. Musulbes (Russia)**

World Wrestling Championships—Greco-Roman Style

Year	54 kg	58 kg	63 kg	69 kg
1999	L. Rivas (Cuba)	Kim In Sub (S.Kor.)	M. Manukyan (Kazakh.)	Son Sang Pil (S.Kor.)
2000	Sim Kwon Ho (S.Kor.)	A. Nazaryan (Bulg.)	V. Samurgashev (Russia)	F. Azcuy (Cuba)
2001	**H. Rangraz (Iran)**	**D. Aripov (Uzbek.)**	**V. Galustyan (Arm.)**	**F. Azcuy (Cuba)**
Year	**76 kg**	**85 kg**	**97 kg**	**130 kg**
1999	N. Avluca (Tur.)	L. Méndez (Cuba)	G. Koguashvili (Russia)	A. Karelin (Russia)
2000	M. Kardanov (Russia)	H. Yerlikaya (Tur.)	M. Ljungberg (Swed.)	R. Gardner (U.S.)
2001	**A. Abrahamian (Swed.)**	**M. Vakhrangadze (Georgia)**	**A. Bezruchkin (Russia)**	**R. Gardner (U.S.)**

2001 Sumo Tournament Champions

Tournament	Location	Winner	Winner's record
Hatsu Basho (New Year's tournament)	Tokyo	Takanohana	14–1
Haru Basho (spring tournament)	Osaka	Kaio	13–2
Natsu Basho (summer tournament)	Tokyo	Takanohana	13–2
Nagoya Basho (Nagoya tournament)	Nagoya	Kaio	13–2
Aki Basho (autumn tournament)	Tokyo	Kotomitsuki	13–2
Kyushu Basho (Kyushu tournament)	Fukuoka	Musashimaru	13–2

AP/Wide World Photos

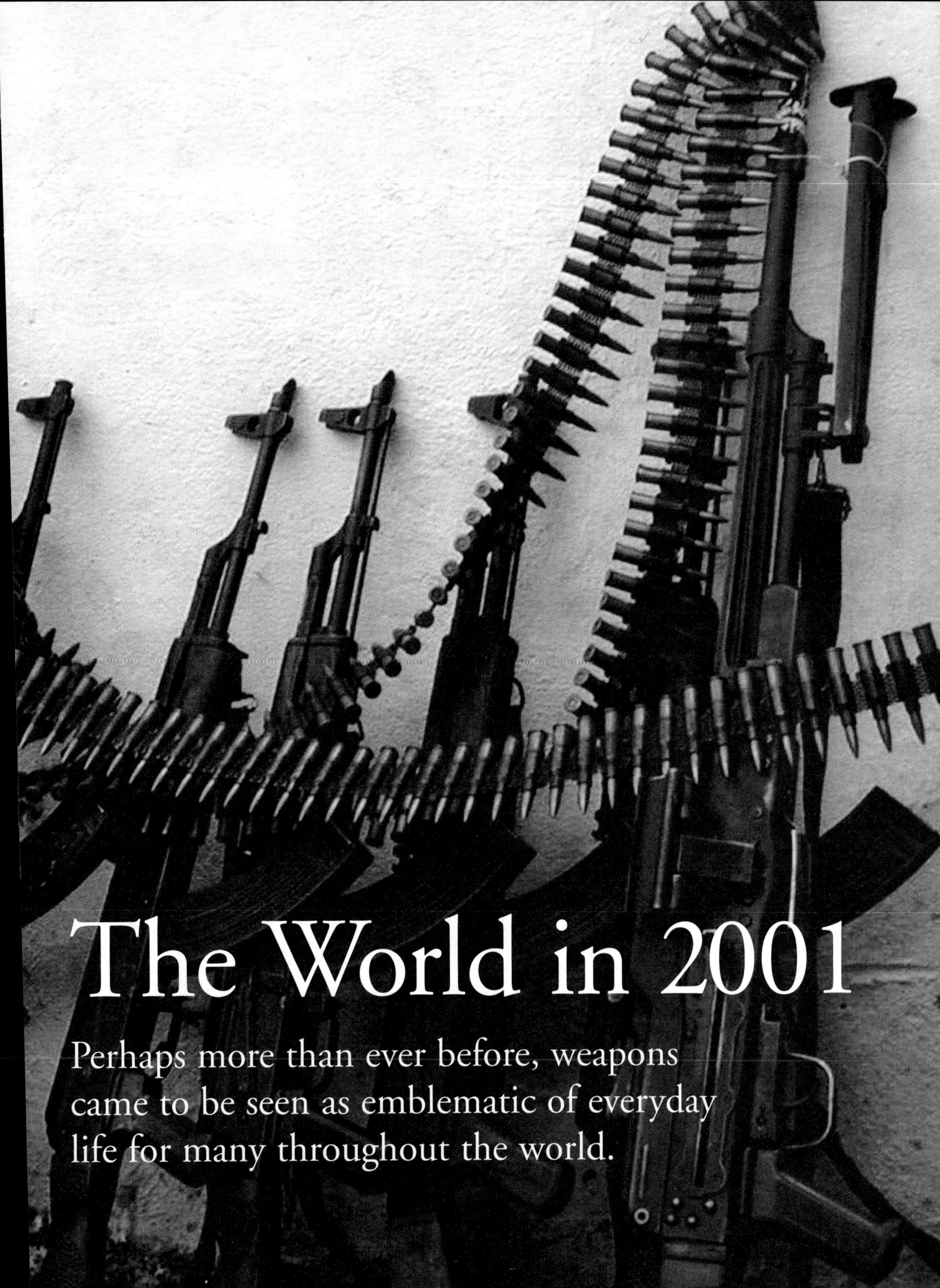

The World in 2001

Perhaps more than ever before, weapons came to be seen as emblematic of everyday life for many throughout the world.

World Affairs

WAR in Afghanistan; possible **PEACE** in Northern Ireland and Sri Lanka; **CRISIS** in Argentina, Israel/Palestine, and India/Pakistan; **NEW LEADERS** in Japan, Peru, Italy, Bulgaria, and the U.S.—these were a few of the highlights of 2001.

UNITED NATIONS

Though UN Secretary-General Kofi Annan's term was scheduled to end on Dec. 31, 2001, he announced on March 22 his availability for five more years. UN delegates credited him with having strengthened internal management, gained control over the organization's budget, and improved ties with the U.S., and they reelected him by acclamation on June 29. He was praised for his levelheadedness, clarity of vision, modesty, talent for listening, and negotiating ability.

At 5 AM on October 12, Annan received a telephone call, and he knew from experience that such an early-morning summons usually meant "something disastrous." This time, however, he learned that he and the UN had been awarded the Nobel Prize for Peace. The citation lauded Annan for "bringing new life to the organization," for moving beyond the UN's traditional responsibility for peace and security to emphasize its obligations to promote human rights, for assuming new challenges such as fighting HIV/AIDS and international terrorism, and for using the UN's "modest resources" more efficiently. The prize committee observed that the end of the Cold War "has at last made it possible for the United Nations to perform more fully the part it was originally intended to play." (*See* NOBEL PRIZES.)

War Crimes. For the first time, the UN War Crimes Tribunal in The Hague defined rape as a war crime. On June 28 former Yugoslav head of state Slobodan Milosevic was brought to trial on charges of genocide and crimes against humanity in Bosnia and Herzegovina, Croatia, and Kosovo. In September the UN Security Council ended the three-year-old arms embargo against Yugoslavia because it had satisfied the conditions for terminating the ban.

Refugees. Ruud Lubbers, former prime minister of The Netherlands, succeeded Sadako Ogata of Japan as UN High Commissioner for Refugees on January 3. He immediately tried to provide a "safe corridor" for tens of thousands of refugees from border fighting between Sierra Leone and Liberia who had sought shelter in dense rain forests and were trapped there. At year's end he faced a growing crisis in Afghanistan, where refugees, fleeing the effects of U.S. bombing, massed on the Pakistani border, joining thousands who had previously attempted to escape the country's drought. In December the World Food Programme delivered an unprecedented 114,000 metric tons of food to Afghanistan, enough to feed six million displaced persons for two months. The UN Children's Fund was also providing food and water to help an estimated 1.5 million children survive the effects of conflict, drought, disease, and displacement.

Lubbers reduced his staff by 800, following a more than $100 million budget cut, and he chided Europeans for reducing their contributions to refugees. A pledging conference in Geneva on December 3 left a shortfall of $100 million for the next fiscal year. (*See* SOCIAL PROTECTION: *Refugees and International Migration.*)

Afghanistan. On several occasions during the year, the UN rebuked Afghanistan's ruling Taliban. Annan and Koichiro Matsuura, director general of UNESCO, pointed out that the Taliban interpreted Islam in a way that no one else recognized. When the government proposed to require non-Muslims to wear yellow badges in an effort to "protect" Sikhs and Hindus from being subject to strict Islamic rules enforced by "religious police," Annan called the measure reminiscent of "some of the most deplorable acts of discrimination in history." In August, when the Taliban detained eight foreign aid workers for the capital offense of propagating Christianity, Annan deplored the authorities' failure to allow the detainees consular access and legal representation and warned them that their act could have "severe consequences on critical human-

Shortly after learning that he and the UN had been awarded the Nobel Prize for Peace, UN Secretary-General Kofi Annan appears at a news conference.

AP/Wide World Photos

itarian assistance." The Taliban said that they intended to try the detainees, but in November, as they retreated before attacks by the Northern Alliance, U.S. helicopters rescued the detainees and ferried them to Pakistan. On September 18 the Security Council president called on the Taliban to surrender Osama bin Laden for his alleged connections to the August 1998 bombings of U.S. embassies in Africa and to the attacks in the U.S. on September 11.

When the Taliban fled Kabul after ground attacks by the Northern Alliance and air attacks by the U.S., Lakhdar Brahimi, UN special representative for Afghanistan, proposed that the Security Council convene a meeting of Afghan representatives to devise a provisional administration and to deploy an international security presence in the capital. That meeting opened on November 27 in Bonn, Ger., and on December 5 the delegates agreed to create a broad-based Governing Council that they hoped would end more than 20 years of internal warfare. The Security Council endorsed the agreement on December 6, and the Governing Council, led by Hamid Karzai, a Pashtun tribal leader who previously fought the Taliban in southern Afghanistan, took power on December 22. Britain offered on December 19 to take the lead in organizing and commanding an International Security Assistance Force for six months, and the Security Council accepted the offer on December 20, the same day the first British Marines arrived in Kabul to maintain it as a neutral zone.

Health. On June 25 the General Assembly opened a special three-day session on HIV/AIDS and invited pledges to a "global superfund" of $7 billion–$10 billion that Annan proposed to fight the disease. By year's end the pledges amounted to $1.6 billion. UN estimates indicated that 25 million people were infected with HIV in sub-Saharan Africa, 4.8 million needed treatment, and all but 30,000 of them could expect to die without drugs commonly prescribed in the West. (*See* HEALTH AND DISEASE.)

Human Rights. China on February 28 ratified the International Convention on Economic, Social and Cultural Rights one day after UN High Commissioner for Human Rights Mary Robinson visited the country. In ratifying the measure the government seemed to hedge its support of workers rights to form and join free labour unions. China recognized just one union; the state-sanctioned All China Federation of Trade Unions forbade the formation of independent groups and did not recognize the right to strike. Nevertheless, on May 17 China agreed to work with the International Labour Organization to promote workers' rights and well-being.

In elections on May 3 for the UN Commission on Human Rights, the U.S. lost a seat it had held since the UN was founded in 1945. The defeat was attributed to the growing strength of less-developed states opposed to U.S. policies, the U.S. failure to lobby for the seat, widespread dismay at U.S. failure to support important international treaties, and U.S. resistance to plans to allow poor countries to make generic versions of anti-AIDS drugs. Members were also upset by a perceived U.S. inattention to the UN after Pres. George W. Bush (*see* BIOGRAPHIES) took office in January and did not at once appoint an ambassador to the UN. Not until September 13, when the Senate approved the nomination of John D. Negroponte, was the U.S. represented by an ambassador at the UN.

The UN World Conference Against Racism, held in Durban, S.Af., from August 31 to September 7, declared that slavery and the slave trade were "a crime against humanity and should always have been so" and called on states to reverse the lasting consequences of slavery, apartheid, and genocide. It expressed concern "about the plight of the Palestinian people under foreign occupation" and recognized their right to self-determination and to establishment of an independent state; the conference also called for governments to ensure that Roma (Gypsies) received equal access to education, to guarantee religious freedom to minorities, to ensure access to services for people with AIDS, and to see that police did not engage in racial or ethnic profiling. The conferees asked the UN to appoint a panel of five experts to help countries carry out these objectives and to review progress.

Budget. On December 24 the General Assembly approved an increase of nearly 4% in the UN budget for the next two years to finance a modest increase in peacekeepers. It was the first increase in eight years apart from inflation adjustments. The budget authorized spending $2,625,000,000 for regular operations through 2003, an increase of $92 million over the current two-year budget of $2,533,000,000. The UN collected $4.2 billion in current and overdue payments by December 31.

Climate. On December 18 the World Meteorological Organization confirmed that Earth's temperature in 2001 was the second highest in the 140 years of record-keeping. Temperatures were getting hotter faster than ever before and causing more storms, droughts, and other weather extremes.

East Timor. On September 10 the UN certified the results of East Timor's first democratic election, and a newly chosen constituent assembly started drafting a constitution as a step toward full independence. (See *Dependent States:* Indian Ocean and Southern Asia, below.)

Iraq. On November 29 the Security Council unanimously extended the "oil for food" program in Iraq for six months on the understanding that Russia would agree before May 30, 2002, to a new list of goods requiring UN review before being shipped to Iraq and that the U.S. would comply with Russia's demand to specify steps leading to the lifting of the embargo on the condition that Iraq allowed UN weapons inspectors to resume their work. Earlier in the year the Council had failed to devise a "smart sanctions plan" for Iraq that might do more to help civilians and restrict the military, and the proposals were dropped on July 2.

UN officials revealed on March 6 that some Iraqi officials were demanding kickbacks on contracts for food, medicine, and other essential civilian goods bought from foreign companies under the UN oil for food program and that Saddam Hussein was diverting money intended to help the civilian population into a slush fund for himself and his associates and possibly for his weapons program. Profiting from a UN-supervised program was illegal, and Annan warned Iraq and buyers of crude oil that surcharges were not permitted and that they should pay nothing to non-UN accounts.

Palestine/Israel. During a visit to the UN on March 21, Israeli Prime Minister Ariel Sharon (*see* BIOGRAPHIES) warned the Security Council against sending an observer force to the Middle East lest its presence increase violence in the West Bank and Gaza. Annan urged Sharon to reduce restrictions on Palestinians working in Israel, and Sharon replied that he was prepared to do so. On March 27 the U.S. vetoed a Security Council resolution requested by the Palestinians, calling for a UN observer force in Israeli-occupied territories. In a speech to the General Assembly in November, Israeli Foreign Minister Shimon Peres called creating an independent Palestinian state "the best bet" for settling the problems of the Middle East. On December 15 the U.S. vetoed a draft resolution in the Security Council that would have demanded an immediate end to all acts of violence, provocation, and destruction in the area and would have required the parties to return to the positions existing before September 2000. The draft asked the two sides to implement the recommendations in the Mitchell report for building confidence measures and to establish a monitoring mechanism to help the parties implement the recommendations. The U.S. objected to the resolution's not condemning recent acts of terrorism against Israel. On December 20 the General Assembly adopted the text of the rejected resolution by a vote of 124–6 with 25 abstentions.

Biological Weapons. Negotiations in Geneva in May aimed at establishing a verification scheme for the 1972 Biological Weapons Convention were jarred by U.S. statements that the treaty's verification measures could not detect cheating and might allow foreign governments to try to steal U.S. secrets. On July 25 the U.S. confirmed that it would not sign the draft protocol. The proposals, 10 years in the making and already signed by 140 countries, were designed to strengthen the convention outlawing germ warfare. They would oblige signatories to allow inspectors into sites that could be used to manufacture biological weapons. On November 18 the U.S. stated that Iran, Iraq, Libya, North Korea, and Syria were all developing germ weapons and violating the 1972 treaty. On the last day of a three-week review of the treaty in Geneva that opened on November 19, the U.S. proposed ending negotiations. The delegates then chose to adjourn until Nov. 11, 2002, rather than admit failure.

International Law. A two-week conference in New York City opened on July 9 to consider drafting a pact curtailing the international flow of illegal small arms. At the opening session the U.S. backed away from the conference objective, saying that "the responsible use of firearms is a legitimate aspect of national life" and that it intended to retain its "cultural tradition of hunting and sport shooting." China, India, and Russia, all of which had large arms industries, supported the U.S. UN officials insisted that the conference would in no way contradict the Second Amendment to the U.S. Constitution and that it was not about taking guns away from Americans but about keeping an estimated 500 million weapons, 40–60% of which had been acquired illegally, out of the hands of child soldiers and pickup armies, often in the poorest countries.

Terrorism. Annan said on September 11 that there was no doubt that the attacks in the U.S. that day were "deliberate acts of terrorism, carefully planned and coordinated," and he condemned them "utterly." The next day both the Security Council and the General Assembly condemned the terrorist acts, and the Assembly expressed its "condolences and solidarity with the people and government of the U.S." The Security Council called on "all states to work together," stressed that "those responsible for aiding, supporting, or harbouring the perpetrators, organizers and sponsors of these acts will be held accountable," and expressed its readiness to take all necessary steps to respond to the terrorist attacks. On September 21 Annan offered the UN as a forum for building a universal coalition against terrorism and for ensuring global legitimacy for the long-term response to terrorism. A week later the Security Council unanimously adopted a U.S.-sponsored resolution obliging all UN members to freeze bank accounts of suspected terrorists, to provide them with no training, to monitor their movements, and to cooperate in any campaign against them, including one involving the use of force. The resolution marked an enhanced U.S. appreciation of the importance of the UN. On November 30 the Security Council Counter-Terrorism Committee began receiving reports from member states on their antiterrorism measures. On December 19 the secretary-general cautioned against expanding the war against terrorism into Iraq lest it lead to a major escalation in the region.

Armaments. On December 13 President Bush served notice that in six months the U.S. would withdraw from the Anti-Ballistic Missile Treaty, generally regarded as a cornerstone of global arms control since 1972. He had concluded that the treaty hindered his government's ability to protect the U.S. from "future terrorist or rogue-state missile attacks." The announcement met with scarcely concealed dismay around the world.

On December 21 arms control experts from nearly 90 countries met in Geneva and agreed to take the first steps to reduce civilian casualties caused by explosives long after conflicts end. They established an expert group to report back in 2002 on whether to open negotiations on the subject. (RICHARD N. SWIFT)

COMMONWEALTH OF NATIONS

The Sept. 11, 2001, terrorist attacks in the U.S. profoundly disrupted the Commonwealth. An immediate consequence was the cancellation of its finance ministers' meeting, which had been about to convene in St. Lucia. Much more serious was the postponement, for the first time in its long history, of the Commonwealth Heads of Government Meeting (CHOGM). These meetings, the longest running of all international summits and rooted in the late 19th-century imperial conferences, had been held biennially since 1969. The 2001 CHOGM had been planned for October 6–9 in Brisbane, Australia. When it became evident that many heads could not attend because of the world crisis, the gathering of an expected 52 leaders was rescheduled for 2002.

Tens of millions of Muslims lived in Commonwealth countries, most notably in India, Pakistan, and Bangladesh. Other members, such as Nigeria, Malaysia, and Brunei, contained large Muslim communities. Politically embarrassing circumstances for the Commonwealth developed when Pakistan emerged as a critical player in the war against terrorism. In its drive to secure democracy in all member countries, the Commonwealth had succeeded over the years in eliminating military rule. A setback had come in 1999 when Gen. Pervez Musharraf seized power in Pakistan. The Commonwealth had suspended Pakistan from its councils, barring its attendance at official meetings until democracy was restored. After two years it faced expulsion.

Musharraf vowed to end army rule by 2002 and held local elections during 2001. This looked set to secure agreement at the Brisbane summit to give Pakistan a year's grace. As a vital member of the alliance against terrorism, however, Musharraf came centre stage globally, with British Prime Minister Tony Blair and others needing to buttress him in power rather than persuade him to restore civilian rule.

Another consequence of the global concentration on Afghanistan was to distract international attention from the deteriorating situation in Zimbabwe. Farm seizures and a breakdown in law and order there violated Commonwealth principles, but when the eight-member Commonwealth Ministerial Action Group tried to send three ministers to Zimbabwe, Pres. Robert Mugabe refused to let them in.

Threatened stability of the southern African region increasingly worried Commonwealth African governments. After months of diplomacy Pres. Olusegun Obasanjo of Nigeria convened a meeting in Abuja of nine Commonwealth ministers, including the foreign minister of Zimbabwe, on September 6. Zimbabwe agreed to restore order and to

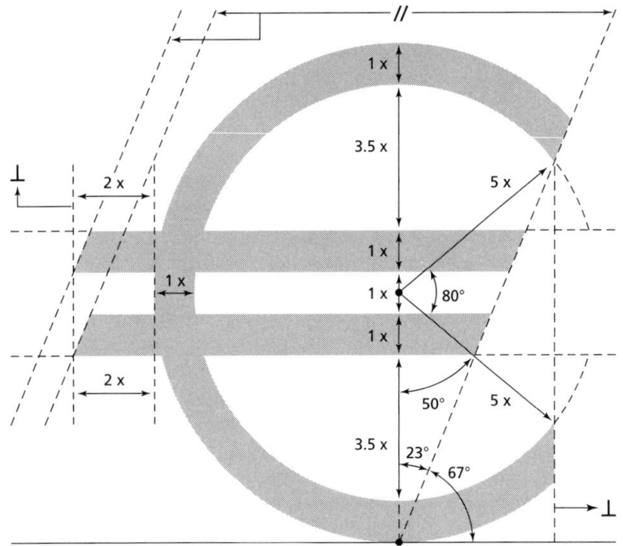

The graphic symbol for the euro was inspired by the Greek letter epsilon and refers to the cradle of European civilization and to the first letter of the word **Europe.**

European Central Bank

implement a sustainable, transparent, and just program of land reform, in return for British and UN funding.

Nevertheless, the Abuja meeting changed nothing. Farm takeovers and violence continued. The Brisbane postponement meant the leaders lost the opportunity to confront Mugabe personally. Part of the Abuja deal had been the dispatch of seven Commonwealth ministers to Zimbabwe. This happened on October 25–27. The result was disappointing. Mugabe berated the ministers, and they left fearing little would change. It did not.

Despite the leaders' absence, the rest of Brisbane's Commonwealth program went ahead. An elaborate People's Festival, intended to take place alongside the summit, showcased the huge range of work of the nongovernmental organizations and the arts. A meeting of 250 business leaders in Melbourne had to be canceled.

Continuing disputes between Commonwealth countries and the Organisation for Economic Co-operation and Development (OECD) over tax havens led to a stormy conference in Barbados chaired by Prime Minister Owen Arthur, at which the OECD backed down on a Memorandum of Understanding imposing new tax procedures on small states.

(DEREK INGRAM)

EUROPEAN UNION

As 2001 began, the European Union (EU) looked forward to a solid 12 months of steady progress on the road toward a united continent. Europe's leaders had much to do as they prepared to expand membership into Eastern Europe and introduce euro notes and coins in 12 member states in 2002. Preparations for these historic developments, however, were eclipsed by unexpected events. Unforeseen tensions, pressures, and disasters on a global scale stole the headlines and overshadowed the EU's internal work. Alarmingly for the pro-EU lobby, antiglobalization protests that caused havoc at summits exposed how much the EU still had to do to win broad-based public support. In addition, the diplomatic fallout from the September 11 terrorist attacks in the U.S. exposed how far the EU was from being taken seriously as a key player in foreign policy and global diplomacy.

In January the focus was on how to restructure the EU's institutions if new member states were admitted from former communist Eastern Europe, as well as Cyprus, Malta, and Turkey. The worry was that an overly large EU would slow down decision making even more and take government too far from the citizen. How could Europe expand, how could the goal of creating a wider market and area of peace be achieved while making its ever-expanding institutions more democratic at the same time?

Early in the year there was also an undercurrent of concern about the euro's sickly performance. Its price against the dollar did not bode well. Would the public refuse to accept a weak new currency in exchange for strong ones, such as the Deutsche Mark, that had served them so well? During its first two years as a noncash currency, the euro had lost over 30% of its value against the dollar. The hope was that the launch of notes and coins on Jan. 1, 2002—the thrill of handling the new money and the realization of the convenience it would bring—would lift confidence in the euro on the markets and among a skeptical public.

German Chancellor Gerhard Schröder was the first to offer his vision for a new Europe. In a speech made in the spring, he called for the creation of a European government that would involve the transformation of the European Commission (EC) into a strong executive, a reform of the Council of Ministers to make it a chamber of European states, and the drafting of an EU constitution. Germany, which had been a strong proponent of greater political integration, had already sunk the rock-steady Deutsche Mark into the euro and was looking to its partners—primarily France—to deliver their side of the bargain—political union. Schröder's "federal" vision for the EU won swift support from the leaders of Belgium, Finland, and Luxembourg, and it was in keeping with the ideas of EC Pres. Romano Prodi of Italy. Schröder's recommendations, however, did not chime with the messages coming from London and Paris, where the British and French prime ministers, Tony Blair and Lionel Jospin, respectively, were quick to reject the German vision. Presenting his own ideas for a revitalized Europe, Jospin put the emphasis on strong ties between the national governments under which power remained firmly vested with the member states.

While European leaders were busy pondering the future architecture of Europe, the message dominating headlines was that the EU was losing touch with its 376 million citizens. The first wake-up call came when on June 8 Ireland voted in a referendum to reject (by 54%) the Treaty of Nice, an agreement that had been made in 2000 by the 15 heads of state to begin a reform of the EU's decision-making procedures to allow it to enlarge. Voters, fearing that enlargement would weaken Ireland's influence in the EU and that participation in peacekeeping forces could threaten the country's military neutrality, rejected the treaty. The shock was all the more stark coming from Ireland, traditionally one of the EU's most loyal and pro-European members.

A few days later the EU was shaken once again, this time by riots at its summit in Göteborg, Swed., during which one antiglobalization protester was seriously injured by police. Important agreements concerning enlargement and the environment were utterly overshadowed by the violent protests that cast strong doubts over the viability of holding such summits in the future. Ironically, the outcome of the summit was in tune with what many of the peaceful demonstrators there were demanding—a commitment to sustainable development, including measures on climate change and energy conservation. Together with the Irish "no" vote, the episode graphically underscored the growing sense of disconnection between the EU's institutions and its citizens and the need for its leaders to explain their objectives better.

As a result, EU leaders and the Brussels commission initiated a debate on the need to make the EU more relevant to its people. In early September foreign ministers agreed that in 2002 a convention should start preparing a large-scale reform of the EU's responsibilities and institutions to allow it to connect better with its citizens and cope with enlargement.

Such issues, however, were totally eclipsed by the September terrorist attacks in the U.S. As the horror of the events sank in, EU leaders took the opportunity to emphasize that such global crises demanded a global response. The need for EU member nations to work together on cross-border crime, intelligence sharing, and immigration was given a new urgency. In the 10 days that followed, the outraged member states broke new ground in foreign policy and dropped long-held taboos in the areas of justice and home affairs. Agreements that would normally have taken months, even years, to conclude were swiftly adopted. Though the political will to work together was strong, the EU's clumsy instruments for making policy, particularly on foreign and defense issues, were quickly exposed as inadequate. It soon became clear that in the short term the EU would be unable to make an effective collective contribution to the war against terrorism.

This fact was underscored by the flow of EU leaders to Washington, D.C. Though Javier Solana had been an energetic "high representative" of the EU's common foreign and security policy, it was Blair, Schröder, and French Pres. Jacques Chirac who set the pace in bilateral discussions with U.S. Pres. George W. Bush.

In addition, leaders of the 15 member states circumvented the EU institutions in their dealings with one other. Amid the frantic diplomacy, new tensions between the large and small member states arose. Many of the smaller countries felt sidelined by the efforts of the more powerful member states that were committed to making military contributions to the war against terrorism. They were particularly incensed by Blair's decision, four weeks into the war, to abandon the usual EU summit formula in favour of a meeting in London to which only certain member states were invited.

Among those most angered by developments was Prodi, who was furious at the way Brussels was being ignored. A series of gaffes earlier in the year, however, had put Prodi on weak ground, and many were losing faith in his effectiveness as a leader. He barely figured in the headline-grabbing initiatives that followed September 11. Earlier, following the Irish "no" vote on the Treaty of Nice, Prodi had infuriated the Irish government and forced the EC into a damage-control mode when he stated that EU enlargement could continue in spite of the Irish vote—a remark that left EU leaders even more open to charges of being detached from the electorate. More questions about his political judgment were raised when he refused to appear at a press conference in October with Belgian Prime Minister Guy Verhofstadt, one of the few EU leaders who could still be considered his supporter. Prodi's office issued a statement saying he had stayed away because he could not compete with Verhofstadt's verbose accounts of events in Dutch and French.

Amid the uncertainty created by the war against terrorism, preparations for the introduction of euro notes and coins continued on schedule. While plans for deploying troops to help distribute the new currency were finalized, retailers protested that the first few days would be chaotic because of the European Central Bank's refusal to authorize the distribution of notes, as well as coins, ahead of January 1. A sense of unease about the impending switchover (and a fear that people were not focusing on the task at hand) was exacerbated by the euro's persistent failure to strengthen against the dollar even after the terrorist attacks and as the U.S. economy slipped into recession.

Optimistic talk earlier in the year that Europe would somehow be able to insulate itself from an economic downturn in the U.S. was also proving to be unfounded. Throughout the year Germany revised growth forecasts downward to the point where, by the autumn, there were fears that the country was entering a recession.

By year's end the expected publicity campaign about the introduction of the euro and the excitement generated by its imminent arrival unexpectedly failed to dominate the news. Even though this was to be the biggest peacetime operation of any kind in Europe since 1945, like everyone else the EU was thinking more about its role in the post-September 11 world. (EMMA TUCKER)

MULTINATIONAL AND REGIONAL ORGANIZATIONS

March 26, 2001, marked the 10th anniversary of Mercosur, the Southern Cone Common Market (Argentina, Brazil, Paraguay, and Uruguay). The group was the world's third largest market, with production reaching more than $1 trillion annually.

From April 20 to 22, the third Summit of the Americas met in Quebec City to discuss a Free Trade Area of the Americas that would reduce or eliminate tariffs and encourage trade from the Canadian Arctic to southern Argentina. Hemispheric leaders adopted an "action plan" to strengthen democratic foundations in the Americas and to prepare for free trade. An Organization of American States fact-finding mission arrived in Haiti on May 10 to meet with Pres. Jean-Bertrand Aristide and other local leaders and to investigate the state of democracy there.

Another organization that marked its 10th anniversary during the year was the Commonwealth of Independent States (CIS). At its November 30 summit meeting, the organization, which comprised 12 of the 15 republics of the former U.S.S.R., reiterated "the common quest of its member states for stable socioeconomic development and dignified integration into the world community." The CIS also urged improved cooperation between the members' security agencies in an effort to provide unified support for the CIS antiterror centre.

China, Russia, Kazakhstan, Kyrgyzstan, Tajikistan, and Uzbekistan formed the Shanghai Cooperation Organization on June 15. Formerly called the Shanghai Five, the group changed its name to accommodate the inclusion of Uzbekistan into the organization. Its general aim was to safeguard regional security and to fight Islamic terrorism. On December 25 China called for the foreign ministers of Russia and Central Asian countries to meet with the organization on Jan. 7, 2002, to discuss Afghanistan's future, the struggle against religious extremism, and separatism and terrorism in each country.

After 38 years the Organization of African Unity (OAU) met on July 9 in Lusaka, Zambia, for its last session before starting a one-year transition period into the African Union. The AU would be modeled on the EU, with its own parliament, executive committee, court, currency, and laws. Former Côte d'Ivoire foreign minister Amara Essy was elected secretary-general on July 10 to take responsibility for steering the OAU during its critical transition period. In late November Kenya, Tanzania, and Uganda reestablished the East African Community, a group that was founded in 1967 but dismantled in 1977 owing to regional strife. The main goal of the revived group was to reduce trade barriers and stimulate economic growth in the region.

The 10 countries along the Nile River that formed the Nile Basin Initiative (Burundi, the Democratic Republic of the Congo, Egypt, Eritrea, Ethiopia, Kenya, Rwanda, The Sudan, Tanzania, and Uganda) continued to promote the sustainable development of the river and safeguard its future. The two-year-old program was aimed at bolstering hydropower and food production; improving transportation, industry, and trade; and conserving Lake Victoria and the vast wetlands of the Sudd. In June the members called a meeting of donors and development agencies in Geneva to launch an international consortium to raise funds for the initiative.

At a July 23–27 meeting in Hanoi, the Association of Southeast Asian Nations (ASEAN) faced problems arising out of a sense that the region's security and political arrangements were in flux owing to political feuding in Indonesia, its largest member; the members feared that the fighting there might lead to a breakup of the country and cause instability elsewhere. (See *Indonesia:* Special Report, below.) The members were also concerned over tensions between the U.S. and China, U.S. plans to build missile defenses, and the growing ties between the U.S. and Japan. The ASEAN Regional Forum held its annual meeting at the ministerial level on July 25. The group still hoped to launch a Southeast Asian free-trade zone by 2003 in an effort to make its countries more attractive to investors. At ASEAN's November meeting held in Brunei, talks between Chinese Prime Minister Zhu Rongji and the 10 leaders of ASEAN ended in approval for the establishment of the world's largest free-trade area within 10 years; the area would encompass about two billion people.

In March at the Arab League's summit in Amman, Jordan, the 22-member group appointed former Egyptian foreign minister Amr Moussa as its new secretary-general and agreed to support the Palestinian uprising against Israel but failed to issue a statement on the decade-long estrangement between Kuwait and Iraq. In November Moussa renounced Osama bin Laden's latest call for a holy war but urged that a Palestinian state be established.

The Organization of the Islamic Conference met on August 27–28 in Tehran, and delegates from 22 Muslim nations agreed to encourage tourism among member countries and to facilitate residents' travel to other member countries. They met again in an emergency meeting in Doha, Qatar, on October 10 to reject "the targeting of any Islamic or Arab state under the pretext of fighting terrorism." They also stated that the terrorist attacks in the U.S. on September 11 contradicted "the teaching of all religions and human and moral values." Some delegates called for an internationally led campaign against terrorism in preference to the one led by the U.S.

The six-nation Gulf Cooperation Council (Bahrain, Kuwait, Oman, Qatar, Saudi Arabia, and the United Arab Emirates) signed an agreement on December 31 paving the way to establish joint customs tariffs in 2003 and a single market and currency by 2010. The European Union pressed for the decision as a precondition of a free trade agreement that the two organizations have discussed for 13 years. (RICHARD N. SWIFT)

DEPENDENT STATES

Europe and the Atlantic. On May 7, 2001, the British nuclear submarine HMS *Tireless,* which had been stranded in Gibraltar for repairs for nearly a year, finally set sail. The crippled *Tireless* had limped into Gibraltar, the nearest port, on May 19, 2000, with a leak in the nuclear reactor's coolant system; repairs took far longer than anticipated. Concern over possible radiation leaks had triggered months of demonstrations by environmental activists in Gibraltar and in nearby Spain, as well as formal protests from Madrid. In November, Gibraltar Chief Minister Peter Caruana boycotted new talks between the U.K. and Spain on the territory's future status. London and Madrid declared that an agreement on Gibraltar would be reached by mid-2002, but Caruana reiterated that no settlement could be valid unless it was approved by Gibraltarians, who would never accept Spanish sovereignty.

In the South Atlantic a fire inadvertently started by British troops on tiny South Jason Island seriously damaged a major seabird nesting site in January; it was feared that hundreds of black-browed albatross and rockhopper penguin chicks might have perished. In March the last British troops were withdrawn from the island of South Georgia to make way for the new British Antarctic Survey base. Future security for the island would be provided by troops based in the Falkland Islands/Islas Malvinas. A month earlier 59 young reindeer, part of a herd introduced in the early 19th century, had been transferred to the Falklands from South Georgia. After the remote island of Tristan da Cunha sustained severe hurricane damage in May, Falkland Islanders sent more than £9,000 (about $13,000) in disaster aid.

Faroe Islands Prime Minister Anfinn Kallsberg in March announced that the semiautonomous territory's referendum on independence from Denmark, scheduled for May, would be postponed indefinitely.

Caribbean and Bermuda. Sila María Calderón of the Popular Democratic Party was sworn in as governor of Puerto Rico on January 2. (*See* BIOGRAPHIES.) Although Calderón supported Puerto Rico's status as a commonwealth with the U.S., she pledged in July to hold another referendum in 2002 on whether the territory's 3.8 million people wished to retain their present status, become a full-fledged state of the U.S., or opt for independence. In the last such vote, in 1998,

Dependent States[1]

Australia	United Kingdom
Christmas Island	Anguilla
Cocos (Keeling) Islands	Bermuda
Norfolk Island	British Virgin Islands
Denmark	Cayman Islands
Faroe Islands	Falkland Islands
Greenland	Gibraltar
France	Guernsey
French Guiana	Isle of Man
French Polynesia	Jersey
Guadeloupe	Montserrat
Martinique	Pitcairn Island
Mayotte	Saint Helena Tristan da Cunha
New Caledonia	Turks and Caicos Islands
Réunion	**United Nations**
Saint Pierre and Miquelon	East Timor
Wallis and Futuna	**United States**
Netherlands, The	American Samoa
Aruba	Guam
Netherlands Antilles	Northern Mariana Islands
New Zealand	Puerto Rico
Cook Islands	Virgin Islands (of the U.S.)
Niue	
Tokelau	

[1]Excludes territories (1) to which Antarctic Treaty is applicable in whole or in part, (2) without permanent civilian population, (3) without internationally recognized civilian government (Western Sahara), or (4) representing unadjudicated unilateral or multilateral territorial claims.

the majority came out strongly for maintaining the commonwealth relationship.

The antibombing lobby in Puerto Rico prevailed against the U.S. government in June when Washington announced it would cease using Vieques Island for target practice by navy pilots from May 2003. Opposition to the bombing policy had been increasing since 1999, when one civilian was killed and four persons were injured. The White House had previously insisted that Vieques was critical to maintaining U.S. military readiness. This position might still cause the deadline to be pushed back, however, especially in light of the war against terrorism following the September 11 terrorist attacks in the U.S.

Seven policemen were injured during violent protests in Pointe-à-Pitre, Guadeloupe, in June. The situation was triggered by the refusal of shop owners to observe May 27 as the anniversary of the abolition of slavery on the island. The union had urged businessmen to shut up shop on that day and reacted strongly against those who did not. The arrest of a union leader sparked the demonstrations.

As a sign of the gradual disappearance of the artificial barriers that had long existed between Caribbean territories with different colonial histories, Saba, a Dutch Antillean territory with a population of only 2,000, indicated in August its keen interest in joining the English-speaking Organization of Eastern Caribbean States.

The self-governing Dutch territory of Aruba was commended by the International Monetary Fund in September for having improved surveillance and detection procedures relating to its growing offshore-banking sector. The opposition People's Electoral Movement (MEP) emerged victorious in the September election, taking 12 of the 21 seats in the Aruba legislature. MEP leader Nelson Oduber became prime minister.

The New People's Liberation Movement, led by former chief minister John Osborne, won the April general election in the volcano-ravaged island of Montserrat, taking seven seats in the nine-seat legislature. The National Progressive Party obtained the other two. The new government said it would concentrate on restoring jobs lost as a result of the still-active Soufrière Hills volcano, which erupted again in July following a partial collapse of the lava dome.

In June the Cayman Islands was removed by the Paris-based Financial Action Task Force (FATF) from the "blacklist" of states said to be lax in tackling money laundering in the Caribbean region. Inclusion on the list had affected the Caymans' reputation as a respectable offshore tax haven. The FATF commended the Caymanian authorities for having made "significant improvements" to anti-money-laundering systems. In Bermuda former prime minister Pamela Gordon resigned as leader of the opposition in October.

Pacific. In May elections in French Polynesia, the pro-autonomy Tahoeraa Huiaatira (TH) party was again successful, winning 28 of 49 seats; the leading pro-independence party secured 13 seats. Gaston Flosse of the TH was returned as territorial president by the assembly, which for the first time was chaired by a woman, Lucette Taero, a former minister of employment with responsibility for women's affairs. The new government placed a high priority on economic development, with special emphasis on tourism, pearl farming, fisheries, and agriculture. Earlier in the year the government had introduced financial incentives for tourism investment, but in the wake of the terrorist attacks in the U.S. on September 11, tourist numbers fell by nearly one-quarter. Flosse advocated an expansion of local responsibilities under the constitutional arrangements with France, as well as increased formal representation in the French government through the Senate.

In New Caledonia rivalries within the pro-independence movement created a degree of political uncertainty. In April Pierre Frogier was elected president of the territory's government. Tourism development struggled, with a continuing decline in air services from France and, as a consequence, fewer tourists from Europe. There were further difficulties in the latter part of the year arising from the impact of international terrorism on major airlines and related tourism activity. Potential for growth in the nickel industry was confirmed with major new investments proposed for nickel and cobalt deposits in both the northern and the southern regions.

Both the Cook Islands and Niue were warned by the Organisation for Economic Co-operation and Development that continuing failure to ensure tighter controls on money laundering would give rise to sanctions. Niue's prime minister, Sani Lakatani, called for small Pacific nations to stand together against bullying from large and powerful countries. Tourism in Niue had been affected in March, and some resorts closed when the airline responsible for most international links was grounded for safety reasons. Subsequent negotiations with other airlines were affected by the events of September 11, which added to—but did not originally cause—difficulties faced by other regional carriers. In the Cook Islands, where tourism accounted for half of gross domestic product, the economy also suffered a serious downturn resulting from the fall in tourist travel and other airline difficulties after September 11. In an attempt to stimulate economic growth and address rising inflation, the government had earlier approved the introduction of a consumption tax.

The terrorist attacks on September 11 had a major impact on U.S. dependencies in the Pacific. Andersen Air Force Base in Guam assumed greater importance for both staging and training, while the bombing range on the uninhabited Farallon de Mendinilla in the Northern Mariana Islands was put to greater use. Tourism was seriously affected in all dependencies but particularly in Micronesia, which depended on tourists from Japan, South Korea, and Taiwan. The U.S. Office of the Inspector General criticized the Guam Economic Development Authority for unauthorized tax rebates and abatements that affected tax revenues for the territory. In October Guam experienced a magnitude-7 earthquake, which caused only minor damage to buildings but disrupted power and water supplies.

In American Samoa, Gov. Tauese Sunia expressed concern over the possible implications for the territory of tax cuts proposed by U.S. Pres. George W. Bush, and legislation to prevent flow-on of any such measures was introduced. The government also attempted to tighten immigration controls by deporting those who were discovered after a brief amnesty to have overstayed their visas and proposing to hold the passports of visitors. It also adjusted employment laws to facilitate employment in the fish-canning and garment-manufacturing industries.

Indian Ocean and Southern Asia. In July 2001 Mayotte officially became a French dependent collectivity. The change to a full French departmental collectivity would take place over 10 years, with the administrative and political systems adapting to a basically Muslim society. Although French since 1841, the island had historic links to the Comoros. Illegal immigration to Mayotte (about 2,000 people annually) persisted in 2001, especially from the island of Anjouan, where a secessionist movement continued to disrupt life. (See *Comoros*, below.)

In Réunion local elections in March gave a large victory to the right, which

AP/Wide World Photos

East Timorese residents, with their identity cards in hand, crowd a polling station in Dili on August 30 to vote for a Constituent Assembly.

was generally hostile to the island's being divided into two separate departments. The government withdrew the bill proposed in 2000. Administrative reforms were not the population's first concern, however; high unemployment and the rapidly expanding population were the root causes of the island's social problems.

In October Diego Garcia, the largest atoll in the Chagos Archipelago, or British Indian Ocean Territory (BIOT), once again became a strategically important military base, as it had been in 1991 during the Gulf War. Diego Garcia was the main American naval and air backup base in the war in Afghanistan. In November, exactly a year after a U.K. High Court ruling in their favour, the Ilois, the BIOT's former population, continued to demand the right to return to the 65-island group.

Christmas Island was in the news several times during the year. Australia in June announced plans to build a space launch centre on the island. In August the Norwegian cargo ship *Tampa,* having picked up a boatload of illegal immigrants in distress, was refused permission by Australia to disembark them on Christmas Island. (See *Australia,* below.) An Australian military ship eventually transported the immigrants to Nauru and New Zealand, which had accepted them temporarily. By mid-November, however, several hundred other asylum seekers had been placed in a detention centre on Christmas Island.

In East Timor the UN mandate ended in 2001 and prepared the way for independence. Indonesian Pres. Megawati Sukarnoputri recognized the island's sovereignty by making the first official visit to the capital, Dili, in September. The Timorese voted in August by universal suffrage for a Constituent Assembly of 88 members, who within three months were to prepare the first constitution of the new state. Of the 16 rival parties, the Revolutionary Front of an Independent East Timor (Fretilin), the former movement for national independence, won a comfortable majority. Fretilin's charismatic leader, Xanana Gusmão, was expected to win the presidential elections in April 2002, and East Timor was scheduled to gain independence a month later.

(CHARLES CADOUX; BARRIE MACDONALD; DAVID RENWICK; MELINDA C. SHEPHERD)

ANTARCTICA

Ice averaging 2,160 m (7,085 ft) in thickness covers more than about 98% of the continent of Antarctica, which has an area of 14 million sq km (5.4 million sq mi). There is no indigenous human population, and there is no land-based industry. Human activity consists mainly of scientific research. The 45-nation Antarctic Treaty is the managerial mechanism for the region south of latitude 60° S, which includes all of Antarctica. The treaty reserves the area for peaceful purposes, encourages cooperation in science, prescribes environmental protection, allows inspections to verify adherence, and defers the issue of territorial sovereignty.

Conferences in Australia and the U.K. in 2001 commemorated the 40th anniversary of the Antarctic Treaty. The treaty, which entered into force on June 23, 1961, with 12 member nations, in late 2001 had 45 signatories, including Estonia, which joined in 2001. Of the 45 nations, 27 pursued programs of Antarctic scientific research. Some 8,000 scientists and supporting personnel in these national programs were in Antarctica and aboard ship in the adjacent Southern Ocean. They operated 38 year-round stations and additional temporary research camps. The austral summer continental population peaked at around 4,000; the isolated wintering crews in 2001 numbered about 1,000. In an unprecedented winter rescue mission, a Canadian aircraft landed at the U.S. Amundsen-Scott research station in April to evacuate Ronald Shemenski, who was seriously ill, and to deliver a replacement physician.

In September, Russian Prime Minister Mikhail Kasyanov called for an assessment of the country's polar research—apparently shelving a decision whether to invest more in the program or shut it down. The Soviet Union was one of the original 12 members of the Antarctic Treaty, and Western observers doubted a shutdown. The Czech Republic announced that it would establish its first science program in Antarctica, relying on Poland for help in building a station. Chile said that by 2003–04 it would scale up Antarctic tourism by expanding its landing strip on King George Island and would expand research, transferring the Chilean polar institute from Santiago to the University of Magallanes in the country's far south.

France and Italy continued to build a new research station, Concordia, on Dome C, far inland on the continental ice sheet at an altitude of 3,200 m (1 m=3.28 ft). The site was regarded as exceptionally clear for astronomy because of its high altitude, absence of humidity, and mild winds. The station was to be ready in 2003. Science already under way included ice-core drilling to 1,458 m by an international team funded by the European Union; the goal of 3,250 m in two more drilling seasons would enable study of the evolution of climate back to 500,000 BP. At the British Antarctic Survey station Rothera, fire destroyed the biology laboratory in September; a replacement was planned.

Tourism decreased from the 1999–2000 season, which had had 14,762 tourists, of whom 14,402 were shipborne. For the period November 2000 to March 2001, 12,248 persons traveled to the Antarctic on privately organized expeditions, comprising 11,997 passengers aboard 21 commercial vessels, 112 persons on chartered yachts, and 139 land-based visitors. American, German, and British visitors accounted for over two-thirds of the tourists.

The krill catch in the Southern Ocean around Antarctica in the 2000–01 season was 98,209 metric tons, down slightly from the previous season's 101,286 metric tons. Catches of other species (finfish, sharks and rays, crustaceans, and squid) totaled 14,725 metric tons. Of this, the Patagonian toothfish and the Antarctic toothfish totaled 12,733 and 626 metric tons, respectively. Illegal, unreported, and unregulated fishing took, by one estimate, 8,376 metric tons of the two toothfish species—nearing the amount of the legal take and up a thousand metric tons from the previous year.

Scientists found that the eastern Pacific Ocean warming known as El Niño and its counterpart, La Niña, appeared to be behind the periodic advance and retreat of Antarctic sea ice. The finding had implications for global climate because sea ice reflects solar energy; when there is less sea ice, the ocean absorbs the sun's heat and warming is amplified. French researchers linked a 50% reduction in some emperor penguin numbers to reduced sea ice in the 1970s, calling their find the first identification of consequences of major oceanic changes in an Antarctic large predator.

American cosmologists released new findings based on data collected from a ground-based instrument operating at the South Pole and a high-altitude balloon. The data provided the strongest evidence to date for the theory of inflation, the leading model for the formation of the universe, and supported the model that the universe experienced a tremendous spurt of growth shortly after the big bang. Another U.S. observatory, with 677 photodetectors buried deep in ice beneath the South Pole to create one of the world's largest particle detectors, became the first in the world to detect high-energy neutrinos, subatomic particles created by cataclysmic collisions.

An iceberg designated B-15A, which had calved from the Ross Ice Shelf in early 2000, drifted to the western Ross Sea, where it went aground, enabling a buildup of sea ice between it and Victoria Land that could jeopardize ship access to the U.S.'s McMurdo station, Antarctica's largest settlement, and threatened penguin populations that depend on open water for food. The Russian icebreaker *Kapitan Khlebnikov* entered the Bay of Whales, where the berg had calved, establishing a record southern latitude for a surface ship of 78° 37′ S. Satellite data showed that 31 cu km (7.4 cu mi) of ice was lost from the fast-flowing Pine Island Glacier, which demonstrated that this part of the Antarctic ice sheet was thinning and suggesting that Pine Island Glacier would be lost to the ocean within a few hundred years. Another satellite image revealed a crack 25 km (15.5 mi) long, which stretched more than two-thirds across the glacier. The crack had formed in less than five weeks, which led to the prediction that an iceberg might calve within 18 months.

An ice core from Siple Dome revealed the largest and most abrupt warming spike yet found in the Southern Hemisphere and provided evidence that climate change can be dramatically fast. The 4.5 °C (18 °F) hike over a few decades had come as the last ice age began to wane 19,000 years ago. The timing of the warming correlated with an abrupt sea-level rise and belied previous evidence that Antarctic warming events were much more gradual than Northern Hemisphere events.

Sir Peter Maxwell Davies's *Antarctic Symphony,* composed on a commission by the British Antarctic Survey after the British composer's visit south in 1997, was played for the first time by the Philharmonia Orchestra at the Royal Festival Hall in London on May 6. In addition to classical instruments, the score required pebbles, tuned brandy glasses (with water), a biscuit tin (filled with broken glass), and a plastic soap dish scraped across a tam tam. Inspiration for the work included sounds of ice breaking, the silence of the continent, and the lament of the wind. (GUY G. GUTHRIDGE)

ARCTIC REGIONS

The Arctic regions may be defined in physical terms (astronomical [north of the Arctic Circle, latitude 66° 30′ N], climatic [above the 10 °C (50 °F) July isotherm], or vegetational [above the northern limit of the tree line]) or in human terms (the territory inhabited by the circumpolar cultures—Inuit [Eskimo] and Aleut in North America and Russia, Sami [Lapp] in northern Scandinavia

NSF/U.S. Antarctic Program photo by Kristan Hutchison

An aerial photograph shows a section of the U.S.'s new elevated station in Antarctica (right); the finished arches for a garage, shop, cargo warehouse, and power plant (centre); and the silver dome of the old station (left).

and Russia, and 29 other peoples of the Russian North, Siberia, East Asia). No single national sovereignty or treaty regime governs the region, which includes portions of eight countries: Canada, the United States, Russia, Finland, Sweden, Norway, Iceland, and Greenland (part of Denmark). The Arctic Ocean, 14,090,000 sq km (5,440,000 sq mi) in area, constitutes about two-thirds of the region. The land area consists of permanent ice cap, tundra, or taiga. The population (2001 est.) of peoples belonging to the circumpolar cultures is about 375,000. International organizations concerned with the Arctic include the Arctic Council, institutions of the Barents Region, and the Indigenous Peoples' Secretariat. International scientific cooperation of the Arctic is the focus of the International Arctic Research Center of the University of Alaska at Fairbanks.

Although the Arctic was one of the most complicated and expensive areas in the world in which to operate, petroleum, mining, and transportation companies were aggressively exploring North America's last great frontier in 2001. From BP Exploration (Alaska) Inc.'s Northstar project in the Beaufort Sea to three large oil and gas fields discovered inside the 9.3-million-ha (23-million-ac) National Petroleum Reserve–Alaska, oil and gas exploration and development were surging. Throughout 2001 Alaskan and western Canadian Arctic natural gas producers went forward with government lobbying and with plans to build huge new pipeline projects to move northern natural gas reserves to U.S. markets. In a related development, U.S. Pres. George W. Bush proposed opening Alaska's Arctic National Wildlife Refuge to oil and gas exploration. There was also renewed interest in building a Canada-Alaska railway that would run parallel to one of the pipeline proposals and that could eventually be linked to Russia via a tunnel across the Bering Strait.

Early in the year a draft agreement was reached between the Canadian government, the Northwest Territories, and aboriginal groups to establish a one-stop regulatory process and streamline a review of two potential natural gas pipelines. One proposal was for a stand-alone pipeline that would only carry the estimated reserves of 254.8 billion cu m (1 cu m=about 35.3 cu ft) of Mackenzie (River) Delta Canadian natural gas. The other was for the so-called over-the-top Beaufort Sea route, in which gas from the much larger Prudhoe Bay gas fields in northern Alaska would be piped offshore along the northern coast of the Yukon Territory to the Mackenzie Delta in the Northwest Territories; from there it would be sent to southern markets with the Canadian gas.

During the summer doubt was cast on the Canadian pipeline because of the withdrawal of support by key native groups unless developers agreed to certain conditions, including resource revenue agreements and an equal role for native groups in monitoring the environmental impacts of the project. In June a proposal was endorsed by which native groups would own the pipeline while one of the competing pipeline companies, Arctic Resources Co., would manage it under a long-term contract. The native groups also considered a proposal from an ExxonMobil group that would have given them a one-third stake in a proposed $3 billion pipeline. It was possible that the massive project to take Alaska natural gas reserves—estimated to hold about 991 billion cu m of gas—to markets in the U.S. would hinge on a Canada-U.S. treaty signed in 1977. Foothills Pipe Lines Ltd. claimed that, on the basis of the treaty, they had sole authority to transport Alaska natural gas to market, using the land-based Alaska Highway pipeline route. A consortium of Alaska gas producers—a partnership of ExxonMobil, BP (formerly British Petroleum), and Phillips—initiated a $100 million study of all the alternative pipeline routes that they initially estimated would cost $15 billion–$20 billion.

In August the Alaska Gas Producers announced that their early analysis showed that none of the pipeline options was economically feasible. Their early conclusions were that costs would be too high—$15 billion if the pipeline ran through the Beaufort Sea to the Mackenzie Delta or $17.2 billion if the pipeline was routed along the Alaska Highway through the Yukon to the continental U.S. A separate feasibility study, begun in early 2000, on how to exploit natural gas reserves in the Mackenzie Delta was also expected by the end of the year.

In September the World Wildlife Fund called for the eight countries sharing the Arctic to set aside at least 20% of the region as nature preserves and protected areas by 2010. The conservation call came as pressure for industrial development in the North intensified. Canadian government analysts announced in January that they believed that the eastern Arctic territory of Nunavut had huge reserves of precious metals, including scarce platinum and palladium and diamonds. In Iceland there were proposals to develop major new hydroelectric facilities. Norilsk, Russia, had emerged as one of the most prosperous cities in the former Soviet Union, while achieving a reputation as the world's most polluted Arctic metropolis. Studies showed that traces of heavy metal from Norilsk's vast nickel, copper, and palladium smelters were among the leading sources of toxic pollutants in the Canadian North.

According to a two-decade study based on NASA satellite images, the northern part of the world—from Alaska to Canada and Russia—was becoming warmer and greener and the growing season was longer as global temperatures rose. The increased vegetation growth was especially pronounced in woodlands and forests, ranging from Central Europe to Siberia and the eastern edge of Russia. Average temperatures could increase about 2–6 °C (3.6–10.8 °F) over the next century, however, and plant life might not be able to adjust to such dramatic changes. *The Wall Street Journal* reported that the thawing of polar ice and the opening of the once unnavigable Northwest Passage in the Canadian Arctic was creating a potential boon for shipping and other commerce, but it also presented an increased security problem. Canadian defense facilities had detected undeclared foreign submarine activity in the Far North. According to a June report from the University of Alaska at Fairbanks, the warming trend had melted about 2,490,000 sq km (960,000 sq mi), or roughly 10% of the Arctic's sea ice. The resulting rise in sea level had forced some Alaskan communities to make plans to move their coastal villages inland to higher ground.

In September the journal *Nature* reported that stone tools, animal bones, and an incised mammoth tusk found at a site on the Usa River at the Arctic Circle in Russia had provided what a team of Russian and Norwegian researchers said was the first evidence that modern humans or Neanderthals lived in the Arctic more than 30,000 years ago. This was at least 15,000 years earlier than previously reported.

The Nunavik Commission, created in November 1999, presented its recommendations for a new form of government for the Arctic region of Quebec, which was largely populated by Inuit. Among the important recommendations was the creation of nonethnic public institutions for the region, such as a Nunavik Assembly, a Council of Elders, and a Court of Justice, as well as the recognition of English, French, and Inuktitut (Inuit) as Nunavik's official languages.

(KENNETH DE LA BARRE)

AFGHANISTAN

Area: 652,225 sq km (251,825 sq mi)
Population (2001 est.): 26,813,000 (including Afghan refugees estimated to number about 2,000,000 in Pakistan and about 2,000,000 in Iran)
Capital: Kabul
Chief of state: de facto Taliban Supreme Leader (Amir-ul-Momenin), Mullah Mohammad Omar; President Burhanuddin Rabbani from November 13 to December 22, and, from December 22, Chairman of the Interim Administration Hamid Karzai
Head of government: heads of the Supreme Council Mullah Mohammad Rabbani, and, acting from April 16 to November 13, Mawlawi Abdul Kabir

Northern Alliance soldiers advance toward Kunduz, Afg., on November 13.

Sion Touhig/Getty Images

Crippling drought and unending internal fighting characterized the first half of 2001 in Afghanistan, but the terrorist attacks of September 11 in the U.S. set off a chain reaction that reversed fortunes and produced Afghanistan's first peaceful change of government in decades. A year that saw the rigid control of the Taliban on the verge of total victory also witnessed its military defeat and political marginalization.

Though humanitarian aid continued to reach Afghanistan, Taliban attitudes toward the public role of women and sensitivity to foreign influences frustrated the work of aid agencies. Its unyielding policies also provoked international condemnation and economic sanctions. In May the U.S. announced increased assistance for Afghanistan, but in that same month the Taliban closed several UN political offices in the country. UN efforts to distribute food in Kabul were threatened in a dispute over the use of Afghan women in this work. In August eight foreign relief workers were detained on charges of promoting Christianity and threatened with the death penalty; after three months in custody, however, they were rescued by U.S. forces in November.

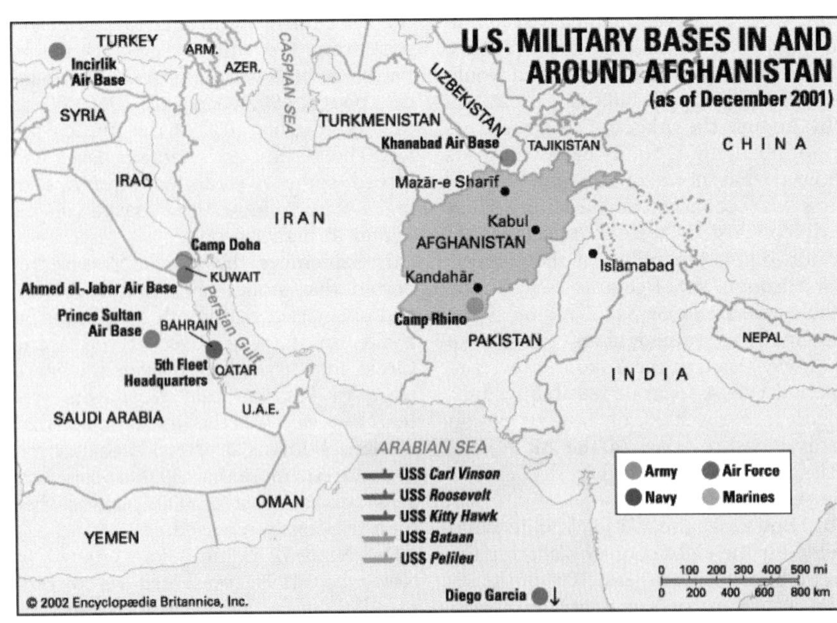

THE TALIBAN'S SHRINKING CONTROL

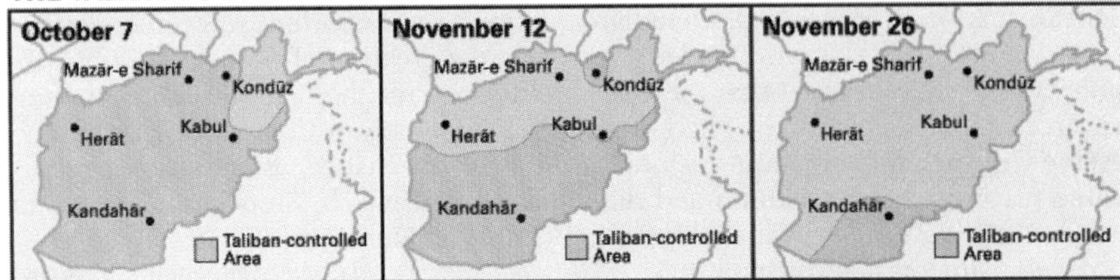

Farmers across Afghanistan were severely affected when the winter rains failed for the third consecutive year. It was estimated that half of Afghanistan's irrigated land was out of use and that livestock herds had been reduced by as much as 70%. Unable to sustain themselves on the land, large numbers of the rural population became refugees in Afghanistan's cities or fled to neighbouring countries.

UN Secretary-General Kofi Annan reported in August that the opium poppy had almost completely disappeared from Taliban-controlled areas. Though the international community welcomed the news, the hardship it brought to local farmers contributed to the flow of refugees, both internal and international.

After overcoming bitter resistance, the Taliban retook Bamiyan in central Afghanistan in February. In March Mullah Mohammad Omar ordered that two large statues of Buddha hewn from a cliff at Bamiyan be destroyed because they were offensive to Islam. Although there were almost no Buddhists in Afghanistan, the statues, dating from the 4th and 5th centuries, were esteemed throughout the world as cultural treasures. The colossal figures were destroyed with explosives, and Taliban officials expressed dismay that so much concern was given statues when Afghans themselves were in such want. Taliban second-in-command Mullah Mohammad Rabbani died of cancer in April. (*See* OBITUARIES.)

On September 9 Ahmad Shah Masoud (*see* OBITUARIES), military leader of the Northern Alliance and the most respected hero of Afghan resistance to Soviet invasion and Taliban advances, was killed by suicide bombers thought to have been sent by Osama bin Laden. (*See* BIOGRAPHIES.) This major setback to anti-Taliban resistance appeared to leave the Northern Alliance more vulnerable than ever.

Blaming Bin Laden for the September 11 attacks on New York City and Washington, D.C., the U.S. turned its military wrath against the Taliban for continuing to protect him. A bombing campaign begun by U.S. and British forces on October 7 was aimed at Taliban military targets and coordinated to support a Northern Alliance offensive. Later that month the Taliban executed Abdul Haq, a military commander and potential threat. (*See* OBITUARIES.)

Taliban fighters were pushed out of Mazar-e Sharif and Kunduz in the north with significant losses, and on November 12 they abandoned Kabul. Soon the Taliban seat of power in Kandahar had been surrendered, and many Taliban had disappeared into the countryside, fled to Pakistan, or shifted their allegiance. U.S. bombing continued in the mountainous Tora Bora area near the border with Pakistan, where Bin Laden and many of his al-Qaeda fighters were thought to have fled. At year's end neither Bin Laden nor Taliban leader Mohammad Omar had been located.

International moves to solve the resulting political crisis focused on avoiding the chaos and destruction that had followed the mujahideen takeover from the Communist government of Mohammad Najibullah in 1992. On November 27 a UN-sponsored conference in Bonn, Ger., convened to settle on an interim government to replace the Taliban. The largest share of delegates represented the Northern Alliance, whose political leader, Burhanuddin Rabbani, had retained international recognition even after being driven from Kabul in 1996. Supporters of former king Zahir Shah also participated. The result was an agreement that Hamid Karzai (*see* BIOGRAPHIES), a Pashtun tribal leader and supporter of the former king, would lead an interim administration for six months, when a Loya Jirga, a traditional Afghan assembly of notables, would choose a new government. On December 22 Karzai and a cabinet that included two women were installed in a peaceful ceremony joined by outgoing President Rabbani and most of the country's ethnic and political factions.

(STEPHEN SEGO)

ALBANIA

Area: 28,703 sq km (11,082 sq mi)
Population (2001 est.): 3,091,000 (not including Albanians living abroad)
Capital: Tirana
Chief of state: President Rexhep Meidani
Head of government: Prime Minister Ilir Meta

Relations with neighbouring Macedonia, where members of the large ethnic Albanian minority staged an armed rebellion in March, were of prime concern in Albania in 2001. Although Prime Minister Ilir Meta supported international peace negotiations, which led to a truce and a peace settlement in late August, there was evidence to suggest that Albanian border guards had at first failed to seal the border completely to arms smugglers supplying the rebels in Macedonia.

The focus of domestic politics was on the country's fourth democratic general elections, held June 24 and July 8. The Socialist Party (PS—the former Communists), with a reform-oriented program, gained an absolute majority in the parliament with 73 of the 140 seats. The opposition coalition Union for Victory (BpF), dominated by the Democratic Party (PD) of former president Sali Berisha, received only 46 seats. The opposition had been split since 2000, when the New Democrat Party split off from the PD. Its leader, Genc Pollo, charged Berisha with failing to offer convincing answers to the country's essential problems. His leadership appealed to many PD voters who were looking for a group among the opposition that could demonstrate some political competence. The new party won six seats in the new parliament. Berisha and PD legislators continued to boycott the parliament and called for early elections. In September the BpF itself launched a new boycott of the parliament, charging the government with having manipulated the elections. Observers from the Organization for Security and Cooperation in Europe dismissed suggestions, however, that irregularities during the voting had affected the overall outcome. It took the parliament nearly three months—until September 12—to give Prime Minister Meta's new coalition government a vote of confidence. The delays were due to vote recounts in some districts.

Within the governing coalition the PS controlled all key ministries. Arta Dade became the first woman in Albanian history to serve as foreign minister. Former prime minister Pandeli Majko became defense minister. The interior, justice, public economy, and finance portfolios all went to Socialists as well. The chairman of the Social Democratic Party, Skender Gjinushi, took charge of labour and social affairs, while another Social Democrat, former foreign minister Paskal Milo, became minister of Euro-Atlantic integration. Former justice minister Arben Imami became minister of local government and decentralization, pledging to focus on strengthening the role of cities and towns; Niko Kacalidha (of the Union Party, which represents many ethnic Greeks) was appointed to the new post of state minister for minorities and the diaspora. For his part, Prime Minister Meta pledged to upgrade power supplies, proceed with privatization, fight corruption and organized crime, improve ties with Western Europe and neighbours in the Balkan region, and promote free trade.

Albania's economy suffered a slight recession in 2001. The national statistical institute expected an inflation rate of 2–4% at the end of the year and 7.3% growth in gross domestic product, just slightly less than the 7.8% registered in 2000. Nonetheless, unemployment dropped from 17.1% in 1999 to 13.3% in 2001, thanks to a government-supported job-creation program that included infrastructure-development projects within the framework of the Stability Pact for South Eastern Europe.

(FABIAN SCHMIDT)

ALGERIA

Area: 2,381,741 sq km (919,595 sq mi)
Population (2001 est.): 30,821,000
Capital: Algiers
Chief of state: President Abdelaziz Bouteflika
Head of government: Prime Minister Ali Benflis

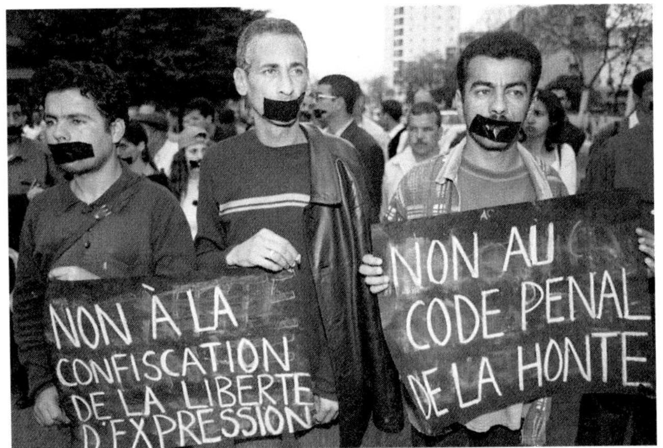

Wearing black tape over their mouths to protest government restrictions on freedom of the press and to express support for those killed in earlier riots, Algerian journalists march in the streets of Tizi Ouzou on May 23.

AP/Wide World Photos

In 2001 Algeria continued to suffer from the chronic and endemic violence of the past decade. Though the levels of violence had diminished from the peaks of 1998, the Armed Islamic Group and the Salafist Group for Preaching and Combat continued to attack civilians and military targets. Violence even returned to the hearts of the cities, including the capital, Algiers. In July car bombs exploded and an assassination was carried out in Zeralda, and a spate of attacks on civilians took place in Annaba.

More worrying for Pres. Abedelaziz Bouteflika was a protest in Kabylia in April on the 21st anniversary of the "Berber Spring" riots. This time the violence was triggered by the killing of a teenager in gendarmerie custody; the government claimed the death was accidental. In the aftermath in May and June, some 80 persons were killed and hundreds were injured. Massive demonstrations—more than 100,000 people protested in the provincial capital, Tizi Ouzou, in late May—spilled over into the capital. At the end of May, 300,000 Socialist Forces Front supporters demonstrated in Algiers, and more than one million people clogged the streets in mid-June. In the ensuing violence 4 persons died and 1,000 were injured. An independent commission established by the government reported in August that the gendarmerie was to blame for the teenager's death. In October the government reluctantly conceded that Berber languages should be given the status of "national languages," but all political demands were refused. By September Berber demonstrators had been cleared from the capital, but the government was then faced with continuing confrontations in Kabylia and a widening circle of mass protest. Algerians elsewhere in the country, particularly in the east, protested worsening economic and social conditions.

There was also growing discontent in the Council of the Nation, Algeria's upper house of the parliament, where one-third of the members were appointed by the president. The presidential choice for speaker was approved unanimously in April, but two members resigned in July, complaining of governmental indifference to the role of the parliament. In May the government lost one of its coalition partners; the Rally for Culture and Democracy, a Berber party, left over the conduct of the government during the riots in Kabylia. The army command—considered the country's power base—was faced with another problem when Gen. Khalid Nezzar was threatened with arrest for human rights abuses in France. The beleaguered president, at odds with the army command, visited the U.S. in July. Following the September terrorist attacks in the U.S., Algiers offered to hand over details of the Algerian nationals involved in the al-Qaeda movement. Though the economy benefited from high oil prices—foreign reserves rose to $15.4 billion in midyear—economic restructuring ensured that unemployment remained disturbingly high. In November massive flooding led to the deaths of some 700 persons. (GEORGE JOFFÉ)

ANDORRA

Area: 468 sq km (181 sq mi)
Population (2001 est.): 66,900
Capital: Andorra la Vella
Chiefs of state: Co-princes of Andorra, the president of France and the bishop of Urgell, Spain
Head of government: Chief Executive Marc Forné Molné

Led by Chief Executive Marc Forné Molné, the ruling Liberal Party of Andorra (PLA) swept to victory in parliamentary elections held on March 4, 2001. With a turnout of 81.6% of the electorate, the PLA won an absolute majority—15 of the 28 seats; the Social Democratic Party garnered 6 seats, the Democratic Party 5, and the Lauredian Union 2 seats. Forné had led Andorra since December 1994.

Smuggling in Andorra continued with a new wrinkle in 2001. Older, retired people who had stashed their money under the mattress to avoid paying tax on it were flocking to Andorra with their carefully hoarded stashes of pesetas, francs, marks, and lire. There they hoped to exchange their banknotes on the black market for goods before July 2002, when the introduction of the euro would make them for the most part valueless.

Andorra also began exploring the construction of a subway system to alleviate traffic congestion. (ANNE ROBY)

ANGOLA

Area: 1,246,700 sq km (481,354 sq mi)
Population (2001 est.): 10,366,000 (excluding about 300,000 refugees in the Democratic Republic of the Congo and Zambia)
Capital: Luanda
Chief of state and head of government: President José Eduardo dos Santos

With inflation for the 12-month period to Jan. 1, 2001, having reached 241% and with the currency showing every sign of continuing to depreciate rapidly,

Angola's annual budget, published on February 20, made depressing reading for a country with such ample resources of oil and minerals. Despite pledges given in the previous April to promote measures to alleviate poverty, the government felt it necessary to warn that there might have to be cuts in spending on health and education. Meanwhile, donors and aid agencies complained of corruption in government circles and of the diversion of money to military activities in the Democratic Republic of the Congo (DRC), as well as to the continuing struggle against the National Union for the Total Independence of Angola (UNITA) rebels at home.

The two military operations were, in fact, closely linked. Unlike most of the other countries involved in the Congo war, Angola did not aim to exploit the situation for its own financial gain but was trying to ensure that the UNITA rebels, who had devastated so much of their homeland, did not use the DRC as a secure base for their operations.

Accusations of official corruption were not so easily justified. In March ongoing investigations in France into corruption and illegal arms deals with Angola that had taken place in 1993–94 were reported to have uncovered documents demonstrating the existence of personal contacts between Angolan Pres. José Eduardo dos Santos and Charles Pasqua, one of those alleged to have been involved in illegal arms trafficking.

In April serious flooding in Benguela province rendered 13,000 families homeless, and in May the economy suffered a further unwelcome setback when De Beers Consolidated Mines, Ltd., suspended its investment and prospecting operations after having failed to agree to the revival of contracts with the Angolan government.

Nevertheless, it was the long-running war against UNITA rebels that mainly hampered the country's development. In January the president replaced his military chief of staff. Then early in June, in spite of a marked escalation of rebel activity in Uíge and Bengo provinces during the previous month, the government claimed that the civil war had virtually ended.

UNITA quickly challenged that assertion by shooting down a United Nations World Food Programme cargo plane. On August 10 UNITA forces attacked a railway train near Luanda, killing more than 250 people, and 14 days later 50 passengers in a bus were massacred in a rebel ambush. In the face of such evidence of the government's inability to contain the threat from UNITA, and with acute economic mismanagement causing tensions even among ruling-party loyalists, the president's announcement on the same day as the ambush that he would not stand in any future presidential elections gave rise to considerable speculation about his motives for making the statement. Opposition commentators suggested that, there being no obvious successor, it was a deliberate gamble aimed at reawakening support for himself and uniting the ruling party behind him, an opinion with which even some government loyalists were inclined to concur.

(KENNETH INGHAM)

ANTIGUA AND BARBUDA

Area: 442 sq km (171 sq mi)
Population (2001 est.): 71,500 (including evacuees from Montserrat)
Capital: Saint John's
Chief of state: Queen Elizabeth II, represented by Governor-General James Carlisle
Head of government: Prime Minister Lester Bird

Following a sharp rebuke by the International Monetary Fund (IMF) over what it said was a deficit of 12% of gross domestic product in public-sector finances during 2000, Prime Minister Lester Bird in March 2001 suspended ministerial traveling allowances and announced a variable cut in public servants' salaries. In April an IMF team visited the country to discuss aspects of "tax reform" designed to help the government bring its finances back into balance.

In May Bird fired both Attorney General Errol Cort and Minister of Health Bernard Percival for "a lapse of

Demonstrators in Luanda, Angola, stage a protest on August 18 against UNITA rebels, who one week earlier had attacked a train near the city and massacred more than 250 people.

Afonso Francisco/AFP Worldwide

good judgement" regarding the government's Medical Benefits Scheme. Though Bird initially had resisted a call for a commission of inquiry into the matter, he announced in June that one would occur "to maintain public confidence in the working of the scheme."

In July the U.K. government lifted its two-year-old financial advisory against Antigua and Barbuda, which had been under scrutiny by British financial institutions paying "special attention" to its transactions amid allegations of money laundering. The U.S. followed suit in August. (DAVID RENWICK)

ARGENTINA

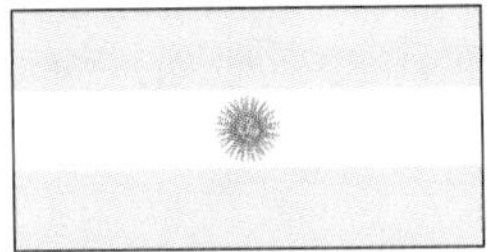

Area: 2,780,092 sq km (1,073,400 sq mi)
Population (2001 est.): 37,487,000
Capital: Buenos Aires
Head of state: Presidents Fernando de la Rúa (assisted by Ministerial Coordinator Chrystian Colombo), Ramón Puerta (acting) from December 21, Adolfo Rodríguez Saá (interim) from December 23 until December 30, and, acting from December 31, Eduardo Camaño

In 2001 the Argentine recession entered its fourth year, with the embattled government of Pres. Fernando de la Rúa under mounting political and social pressure. The country's gross domestic product shrank by 3%; consumer prices dropped 1%; and the unemployment rate increased from an already high 15% to 17%.

Owing to his inability to reverse the country's continued economic decline, Minister of Economy José Luis Machinea resigned in March. He was replaced by Ricardo López Murphy. López Murphy's economic reform plan, designed to reduce the fiscal deficit and restore economic growth, was, however, deemed too extreme (especially the spending cuts it entailed) by the moderate and progressive wings of the governing Alliance. López Murphy resigned after only two weeks in office.

De la Rúa replaced López Murphy with Domingo Cavallo. (*See* BIOGRAPHIES.) Cavallo was former president Carlos Saúl Menem's minister of economy between 1991 and 1996 and was, along with Menem (who in June was placed under house arrest owing to corruption charges but was freed in November), the co-architect of the country's impressive economic turnaround in the early 1990s. As a member of Menem's cabinet, Cavallo had been widely criticized, if not demonized, by a large majority of the members of the Alliance (then in the opposition). His reappointment by de la Rúa provoked considerable discontent among virtually all of the members of the Alliance's junior partner, the Front for a Country in Solidarity (Frepaso), as well as among a substantial portion of the Alliance's senior partner, the Radical Civic Union (UCR), the party of de la Rúa.

Once in office, Cavallo immediately launched a series of important, albeit piecemeal, economic reforms. These included implementing a tax on bank transactions, extending the value-added tax to previously exempt activities, and modifying the country's 1991 Convertibility Law. By July it was clear that Cavallo's reforms had been ineffective, with a lack of investor confidence pushing interest rates to such a level that the external credit market was, for all intents and purposes, closed to Argentina. In a move designed to restore investor confidence and obtain additional external financial support, principally from the International Monetary Fund, Cavallo introduced a "zero deficit law," which was approved by Congress in late July. The law stipulated that Argentine government expenditures equal government revenues, with deficit spending prohibited. As a result, the government had to reduce its expenditures to keep them in line with revenues. During the third quarter this adherence resulted in a 13% reduction in government employee salaries and pensions and a considerable cutback in government purchases of goods and services.

The combination of 39 months of recession and the fallout from the implementation of the zero deficit law did not augur well for de la Rúa and the Alliance in the October 14 midterm elections. In these elections the entire 72-member Senate (the first direct Senate election since 1973) was renewed along with one-half of the Chamber of Deputies. De la Rúa's UCR, the remnants of Frepaso, and a few minor parties presented a joint Alliance list of candidates in 16 provinces, while in the remaining 8 provinces the UCR and Frepaso ran separately. The Alliance-UCR and Frepaso received a strong rebuke at the polls, garnering a meager 23% of the popular vote in the Chamber election (down from 44% in 1999) and an equally scant 24% in the Senate election. The principal opposition Justicialist Party (PJ) won 37% (up from 32%) and 40% of the Chamber and Senate vote, respectively.

In spite of the Alliance's dismal showing in the popular vote, owing to a combination of the rules governing the direct election of senators (two for the plurality winner and one for the first runner-up in each province) and the previous mode of Senate election (by provincial legislatures), the Alliance increased its Senate representation from 23 to 26. Likewise, while its number of Chamber seats won (35) represented a considerable drop from 1999 (63), the Alliance still remained a substantial force in the Chamber with 88 seats total. The PJ retained its majority in the Senate, winning 40 seats, while improving its presence in the Chamber by winning 65 seats (up from 50 in 1999) for a total of 116.

In the fourth quarter the continuing economic decline sparked a political crisis. Antigovernment protesters rioted in the capital in late December, and Cavallo resigned on December 20. After President de la Rúa unsuccessfully attempted to patch up his shaky coalition by appealing to the opposition Peronist Party to join a government of national unity, he too resigned on the 20th. On December 23 Adolfo Rodríguez Saá was installed as interim president, and that same day he suspended payment on the country's $132 billion debt. The rioting continued, however, and Saá was forced to step down on December 30 after he was unable to secure political support from his party.

(MARK P. JONES)

ARMENIA

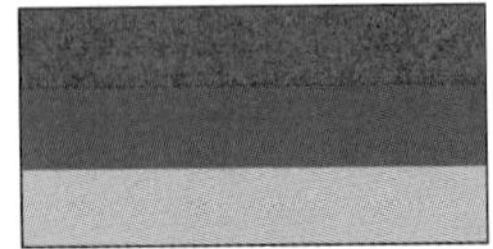

Area: 29,743 sq km (11,484 sq mi). Some 12–15% of neighbouring Azerbaijan (including the 4,400-sq-km [1,700-sq-mi] disputed region of Nagorno-Karabakh [Armenian: Artsakh]) has been under Armenian control since 1993.
Population (2001 est.): officially 3,807,000; actually about 3,000,000 (plus 100,000 in Nagorno-Karabakh)
Capital: Yerevan
Chief of state: President Robert Kocharyan
Head of government: Prime Minister Andranik Markaryan

The configuration of forces within the Armenian parliament underwent sweeping changes during 2001. In February former prime minister Aram Sarkisyan and several supporters quit the Republican Party of Armenia to form a new opposition party named Hayastan ("Armenia"). During the summer several deputies, including parliament speaker Armen Khachatryan and one of his deputies, Gagik Aslanyan, quit the People's Party of Armenia, the Republican Party's partner in the majority Unity bloc. Aslanyan founded the new People's Democratic Party. The Communist Party of Armenia expelled two of its senior leaders. Two leading members left Vazgen Manukyan's National Democratic Union and established rival parties.

On September 5 People's Party chairman Stepan Demirchyan officially declared the Unity bloc defunct, and two days later he, together with Sarkisyan and National Unity Party chairman Artashes Geghamyan, announced their shared intention to impeach Pres. Robert Kocharyan for violating the Armenian constitution, condoning terrorism, precipitating a crisis in the country, and thwarting the investigation into the October 1999 parliament shootings. (The trial of the five perpetrators of those murders began in February.) President Kocharyan announced on September 8 that he would seek a second presidential term in 2003. Members of his bodyguard were implicated in the death in a Yerevan cafe on September 25 of an ethnic Armenian from Georgia.

Armenia's economy performed quite well, with 9.1% gross domestic product growth during the first 11 months and an 11.5% increase in agricultural output. The World Bank warned in July, however, that economic growth had still not translated into an improvement in living and social conditions for the majority of the population. Visiting Yerevan in September, Russian Defense Minister Sergey Ivanov and Pres. Vladimir Putin both stressed the strategic significance of military cooperation with Armenia. The Russian government nonetheless insisted on Armenia's prompt repayment of debts for supplies of gas and nuclear fuel.

In January Armenia was accepted into full membership of the Council of Europe. President Kocharyan's visit to Iran in November reaffirmed the importance both countries attached to economic cooperation.

In late September Pope John Paul II traveled to Armenia to participate in celebrations to mark the 1,700th anniversary of the country's adoption of Christianity as the state religion.

(ELIZABETH FULLER)

AUSTRALIA

Area: 7,692,030 sq km (2,969,910 sq mi)
Population (2001 est.): 19,358,000
Capital: Canberra
Chief of state: Queen Elizabeth II, represented by Governors-General Sir William Deane and, from June 29, the Right Rev. Peter Hollingworth
Head of government: Prime Minister John Howard

Domestic Affairs. Australia celebrated the Centenary of Federation in 2001. Amid a year of festivities, a grand meeting of all the elected members of the state and commonwealth parliaments took place on May 9. The gala event was held in the Royal Exhibition Building in Melbourne, where 100 years earlier the Australian states had formally convened the first federal Parliament. On June 29 the Right Rev. Peter Hollingworth, the Anglican archbishop of Brisbane, replaced Sir William Deane as governor-general.

Prime Minister John Howard's government faced its biggest crisis in office when the Norwegian freighter *Tampa* picked up a boatload of more than 430 refugees on August 26 and sailed with them to Christmas Island, an Australian dependency. The mainly Afghan asylum seekers had sailed from Indonesia on August 24 in a decrepit Indonesian fishing boat, which was sinking. Howard took a hard line and declared that none of the refugees would be allowed to set foot on Australian soil. Despite international protests, Australian Special Air Service troops boarded the *Tampa* on September 3 and forcibly transferred its passengers to the troopship HMAS *Manoora* for transport to Nauru and New Zealand, which had agreed to hold these and other asylum seekers temporarily while their claims were being processed. On September 12 an Australian federal court ruled that the refugees were being illegally detained, but the government remained adamant and pushed through legislation that would tighten Australia's laws on refugees. The HMAS *Tobruk* later picked up and transported 260 additional "boat people" to Nauru, and more than 200 others were taken to Papua New Guinea for processing. A large number of Australian voters—around 75%—supported the prime minister's decision, which was perhaps the most popular act his government had ever made.

The dramatic turnaround in public opinion gave Howard the opportunity to buck the trend of normal politics and win an historic third term in office. With the strong assistance of Immigration Minister Philip Ruddock, Howard stood against world opinion, and his strong line on Australian sovereignty was endorsed by the electorate on November 10. The prime minister's decisive support of U.S. Pres. George W. Bush's administration, and his decision to commit Australian armed forces to the war against terrorism, also gained popular approval. Howard's coalition enjoyed a strong working majority after the election, which saw high-profile Australian Labor Party (ALP) frontbencher Cheryl Kernot lose her seat and led the ALP's Kim Beazley to resign as the leader of the opposition. The Greens' national vote was a record, and party leader Bob Brown was returned as a senator from Tasmania, while Pauline Hanson's One Nation party lost support.

Howard went into the federal election leading a divided and demoralized Liberal Party of Australia (LPA). Successive election losses in the states had left Australia with only one LPA premier, John Olsen of South Australia. Even in the Northern Territory, where the Country Liberal Party had governed for 26 years, Clare Martin defeated Denis Burke and formed the territory's first ALP government. To make matters worse, the LPA president, Shane Stone, in a leaked memorandum, described Howard's coalition government as mean, tricky, and out of touch.

The government faced continued problems with riots in its three refugee detention centres at Port Hedland, Curtin, and Woomera. In June, exactly a year after a mass breakout from the Woomera camp, asylum seekers who had been unsuccessful in their attempts to remain in Australia smashed windows and broke furniture; shortly afterward, seven Iranian refugees burrowed under perimeter fencing and escaped. In response to the criticism of the centres—which suffered from riots, allegations of child abuse, and remote desert locations—Ruddock proposed a Swedish-style improvement under which the women and children among the refugees could be released from detention and allowed to live in the wider community in Woomera. In December, in the worst violence in 18 months, asylum seekers shouting "visa, visa, visa" set fire to 15 buildings (5 were incinerated) at the Woomera facility. At year's end more than 100 bush fires, about half of which had been set deliberately by arsonists, threatened the largest city, Sydney, and destroyed about 150 homes.

Before the federal elections Australia's major political parties had faced a resurgence of the One Nation movement in 2001. The ALP in Western Australia swept to power on the back of One Nation. Senior Minister Bob Katter resigned from the National Party to stand as an independent, declaring it was time to stand up for the bush. In a major change in national politics, Sen. Natasha Stott Despoja was elected to lead Australia's third political force, the Australian Democrats. Sen. Aden Ridgeway became deputy leader; he was the first Aboriginal politician elected to a party leadership position in what the press described as the "Dream Team."

The Economy. In 2001 Treasurer Peter Costello produced a budget with increased spending on welfare, older Australians, and health care. To make it clear to the electorate that they should take the budget concessions into account when voting, the government launched a saturation television campaign to emphasize the budget's positive features, which were largely aimed at winning back voters unhappy with the goods and services tax introduced in 2000.

The Civil Aviation Safety Authority grounded Ansett Australia's fleet of Boeing 767 aircraft in April, saying that service documents for the aircraft had to be inspected. Once this was completed, Ansett resumed normal services, but it remained under a cloud caused by negotiations between Air New Zealand, Singapore Airlines, and Qantas Airways over how best to structure future international, Australian, and regional airline ownership. The managing director of Singapore Airlines revealed that Singapore Airlines had invested in Air New Zealand Ansett for the long term. Impulse Airlines, Flightwest Airlines, and Air Pacific, which operated under a franchise as Qantas New Zealand, all ceased to be viable and ended operations. Matters were further complicated by the successful entry of Richard Branson's Virgin Blue Airlines into Australian aviation.

Serious corporate collapses marred the overall improved Australian economic performance. The government was forced to rescue policy holders when the HIH Casualty and General Insurance company went bankrupt with debts of $A 4 billion ($A 1 = about U.S. $0.51). HIH underwrote compulsory third-party indemnity insurance in the building industry, and the government accordingly provided a $A 500 million bailout package to protect consumers who were in the process of building homes. Equally important was the liquidation of One.Tel, one of Australia's biggest telephone service providers. One.Tel went into voluntary liquidation in June with debts of more than $A 600 million.

Asylum seekers who had unsuccessfully attempted to enter Australia prepare for the day at a refugee camp on the island of Nauru in September.

AP/Wide World Photos

Foreign Affairs. Australia tried to improve relations with Indonesia in 2001. As part of the process, Indonesian Pres. Abdurrahman Wahid arrived in Australia on June 25. It was the first visit by an Indonesian leader to Australia in more than a quarter of a century. Howard hoped that the two countries could overcome Indonesian resentment of Australia's leadership role in peacekeeping during the East Timor crisis in 1999, and Wahid reassured Australia that Indonesia would find political stability in a short time. When Wahid was replaced by Megawati Sukarnoputri, however, relations took a step backward. The newly installed Indonesian president refused to negotiate over the refugee crisis or to accept any responsibility for the Afghan asylum seekers who had set sail from Indonesia.

Australia and Thailand began a new era in their relationship by exploring a free-trade deal in return for help from Thailand in overcoming Australia's exclusion from such key regional bodies as the Association of Southeast Asian Nations. Singapore and Australia improved economic cooperation when Canberra gave Singapore's government-controlled company SingTel permission to buy Australia's second largest telecommunications carrier, Cable & Wireless Optus.

Australia reinforced good relations with the U.S. during the year. U.S. Defense Secretary Donald Rumsfeld and Secretary of State Colin Powell were leaders of a distinguished team sent to Australia in August to thank the Howard government for its support of U.S. policy on missile defense and the Kyoto Protocol on global warming. After the September 11 terrorist attacks in the U.S., both Howard and Beazley affirmed their support for the U.S. and sought to reassure Indonesia, a predominantly Muslim country, that the U.S. and its allies were waging a fight against terrorism and not against Islam.

(A.R.G. GRIFFITHS)

AUSTRIA

Area: 83,858 sq km (32,378 sq mi)
Population: (2001 est.): 8,069,000
Capital: Vienna
Chief of state: President Thomas Klestil
Head of government: Chancellor Wolfgang Schüssel

Austria's right-of-centre coalition government, comprising the moderate People's Party (ÖVP) and the populist—and occasionally xenophobic—Freedom Party (FPÖ), completed its first full year in office in 2001. Allaying early fears that the inclusion of the FPÖ in government heralded a lurch to the reactionary right in Austria, the coalition's policies and actions remained on a moderate and largely uncontroversial course throughout the year. This was largely because the ÖVP continued to dominate the arrangement, remaining in almost complete control of the political and policy agenda, while the inexperienced FPÖ made an impact only occasionally.

This inability to make its mark contributed to a significant loss of support for the FPÖ and led to calls from within the party for a return to opposition. More moderate elements successfully resisted this, helped by an understanding among members and supporters that withdrawal from the government would likely precipitate an election in which the party would lose considerable ground. To add to its woes during 2001, the FPÖ was bedeviled by unsightly public squabbles, often over trivial personal rivalries.

Vienna was the only one of the nine federal provinces to go to the polls in 2001. As expected, the opposition Social Democrats (SPÖ) and the Green Party made gains at the expense of the FPÖ, while ÖVP support remained static. The result allowed the centre-left SPÖ to win outright control of the city's legislature and end its former coalition arrangement with the ÖVP.

The most fundamental change undertaken by the federal government was its continued efforts to limit the role of Austria's powerful social partnership, which had traditionally given trade unions, employers, and other interest groups an important role in the formulation of economic and social policies. Since coming to power in 2000, the government had sought to wrest from the SPÖ the leverage it had on policy (even while in opposition) via its close links with the trade union movement and to remove those individuals not affiliated with either the ÖVP or the FPÖ from positions of power in public institutions. The trade unions fought a rearguard action, however, and this resulted in the souring of the industrial relations climate and in occasional street demonstrations—unusual occurrences in socially stable Austria.

A government attempt to forge closer links with former communist countries attempting to join the European Union had little success, probably because those countries were sensitive to any appearance that Austria would take a leading role in the region. Meanwhile, the government moved closer to NATO. Although the country had been militarily neutral since 1955, both government parties had supported Austrian membership in NATO since the end of the Cold War in the early 1990s, arguing that neutrality no longer served Austria's security interests. Given public opposition, however, the government conceded that NATO membership would not be contemplated in the foreseeable future.

The rate of economic growth slowed throughout 2001. Despite this, unemployment remained below 5%—one of the lowest rates in the industrialized world. Inflation, though higher than in 2000, remained low and stable, easing back during the course of the year. Although some progress was made in reducing the deficit level in 2001, the slowdown in the economy depressed tax revenues and pushed expenditure above expected levels. (DAN O'BRIEN)

AZERBAIJAN

Area: 86,600 sq km (33,400 sq mi), including the 5,500-sq-km (2,100-sq-mi) exclave of Nakhichevan and the 4,400-sq-km (1,700-sq-mi) disputed region (with Armenia) of Nagorno-Karabakh
Population (2001 est.): 8,105,000
Capital: Baku
Head of state and government: President Heydar Aliyev, assisted by Prime Minister Artur Rasizade

Speculation over who would succeed 78-year-old Pres. Heydar Aliyev intensified in 2001. Media reports identified presidential administration chief Ramiz Mekhtiyev as a potential rival to Ilham Aliyev, the president's son and preferred successor. The authorities continued to suppress opposition activity, evicting the Azerbaijan National Independence Party from its headquarters and either closing or bringing libel proceedings against independent and opposition media outlets. Nine participants of a hunger strike in February by war invalids demanding an increase in their pensions that degenerated into fighting with police were tried and sentenced to up to six years' imprisonment. New restrictions were imposed on all religious organizations and communities. In late December President Aliyev proposed measures to loosen constraints on the media.

Four international consortia engaged in oil extraction in Azerbaijan's sector of the Caspian Sea reported that trial wells failed to yield hydrocarbons. Disagreements over transit tariffs delayed the planned signing of an agreement with Georgia on the export of natural gas to Turkey from late July to late September. Cooperation in the Caspian with international oil companies was called into question in July after Iranian military aircraft and gunboats threatened a prospecting vessel leased to British Petroleum, which promptly suspended operations. A long-proposed visit by President Aliyev to Iran was postponed yet again. Also postponed until early in 2002 was a visit by Aliyev to Moscow during which an agreement allowing Russia to continue using the Gabala radar facility was expected to be signed.

The unauthorized publication in February of confidential Organization for Security and Cooperation in Europe proposals for resolving the conflict over Azerbaijan's Armenian-populated breakaway Nagorno-Karabakh region triggered widespread demands for a military campaign to reconquer the region. Talks between Pres. Aliyev and his Armenian counterpart, Robert Kocharyan, in Paris in March and in Florida in early April were billed as heralding a formal agreement ending the conflict, but Aliyev subsequently denied that any agreement in principle had been reached. In January Azerbaijan was admitted to full membership of the Council of Europe.

As of August 1, Azerbaijan gave up the Cyrillic alphabet and adopted Latin letters (in a variant similar to Turkish) for the national language, Azeri. The changeover caused substantial confusion, especially because of a lack of computer fonts and keyboards. (ELIZABETH FULLER)

BAHAMAS, THE

Area: 13,939 sq km (5,382 sq mi)
Population (2001 est.): 298,000
Capital: Nassau
Chief of state: Queen Elizabeth II, represented by Governors-General Orville Turnquest and, from November 13, Ivy Dumont (acting)
Head of government: Prime Minister Hubert Ingraham

The Bahamian government moved smartly against dubious offshore banks in February 2001; it closed down two operations and revoked the licenses of five others following the publication of a U.S. Senate report that described them as conduits for money laundering. In June The Bahamas was removed from the Paris-based Financial Action Task Force list of countries with inadequate laws to fight money laundering. The government had launched several initiatives, including the banning of anonymous ownership of the more than 100,000 international business companies registered in the country.

In May the government announced budget spending of $1,035,000,000 designed to stimulate economic growth. The International Monetary Fund (IMF) had forecast growth of 3.5%, down from about 5% in 2000. The reduction was partly based on the sluggish U.S. economy. The Bahamas was dependent on the U.S. for tourists and property investors.

Tommy Turnquest, leader of the governing Free National Movement, was designated at an internal party poll in August to succeed Prime Minister Hubert Ingraham upon his forthcoming retirement. (DAVID RENWICK)

BAHRAIN

Area: 694 sq km (268 sq mi)
Population (2001 est.): 701,000
Capital: Manama
Chief of state: Emir Hamad ibn Isa al-Khalifah
Head of government: Prime Minister Khalifah ibn Sulman al-Khalifah

In 2001 Emir Hamad ibn Isa al-Khalifah accelerated the constitutional and political reforms that he had begun the previous year. On February 14–15 Bahrainis approved by referendum the National Action Charter by an overwhelming majority—98.4%. The charter, proposed by the government, promised democratic reforms, including parliamentary elections and a separation of powers. Subsequently, the emir released 900 political prisoners and allowed hundreds of exiled Bahrainis and their families to return from abroad. The emir also abolished the unpopular state security law and the state security court, both of which had given "exceptional powers" to the government. The government further promised a law to allow the establishment of professionals' and workers' unions.

Despite reforms, however, unemployment remained high—10% among men and much higher among women. It still constituted the main source of social tension in Bahrain. Political stability was essential, since Bahrain aimed to become a centre of trade and finance in the Persian Gulf.

On March 16 the International Court of Justice in The Hague reached its verdict on the Bahrain-Qatar border dispute. Since the 1930s the two countries had disputed ownership of several territories, chief among them the Hawar Islands, which were reputed to be a rich source of natural gas. The court ruled in favour of Bahrain on the Hawar Islands but awarded Qatar some smaller islands. Both Bahrain and Qatar welcomed the decision, and relations between the two countries improved to the point where they agreed to link their countries with a 45-km (28-mi) bridge. (LOUAY BAHRY)

BANGLADESH

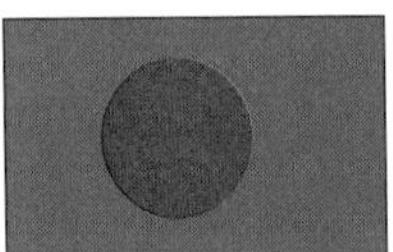

Area: 147,570 sq km (56,977 sq mi)
Population (2001 est.): 131,270,000
Capital: Dhaka
Chief of state: Presidents Shahabuddin Ahmed and, from November 14, A.Q.M. Badruddoza Chowdhury
Head of government: Prime Ministers Sheikh Hasina Wajed, Latifur Rahman from July 15, and, from October 10, Khaleda Zia

AP/Wide World Photos

Khaleda Zia of the Bangladesh Nationalist Party casts her vote—with help from her granddaughter—in Bangladesh's parliamentary elections on October 1.

In a stunning upset in the parliamentary elections held on Oct. 1, 2001, the four-party opposition alliance headed by the Bangladesh Nationalist Party (BNP) won a two-thirds majority, taking 214 of the 300 seats. The Awami League (AL), which had run the country since 1996, suffered its worst-ever defeat, securing only 62 seats. The BNP itself claimed 191 seats. In order to isolate the AL and capture the bloc votes of the religious parties, the BNP had allied with the Jamaat-e-Islami Party, which took 17 seats, the Jatiya Party (4 seats), and Islami Okiya Jote (2 seats). The election saw a massive voter turnout that was estimated at nearly 75%. Women turned out in heavy numbers and were thought to have had a decisive impact on the outcome. The AL rejected the election results, however, and declared that it would boycott Parliament and not cooperate with the future government.

During much of the rest of the year, violence dominated the news. The trouble began on January 20 when 4 people died and 50 were injured in a bomb blast in the capital, Dhaka, during a rally of the Communist Party of Bangladesh. Then on April 14 in Dhaka, a bomb killed at least 9 people and injured some 50. On June 16 an explosion in the AL party office in Narayanganj (on the outskirts of the capital) killed 22 people.

Just two days before presidential elections were to be held on November 14, independent candidate Mohammad

Raushan Ali withdrew from the race; running unopposed, Foreign Minister A.Q.M. Badruddoza Chowdhury was named president by the Election Commission.

Relations between Bangladesh and India took a totally unexpected turn on April 17 when Bangladesh's border security force suddenly took control of an outpost at Padua, which had been under Indian occupation for 30 years. In retaliation, Indian troops crossed into the Bangladesh territory on April 19 and tried to capture Boroibari, another border post. The clash resulted in the death of 16 Indian soldiers. A serious strain on relations with India followed, and Bangladesh returned Padua to Indian control. Signs of tension remained, however, with intermittent border incidents continuing throughout the year.

The news from the economic front was mixed. Bangladesh achieved a gross domestic product growth rate of 6.04%—its highest ever—while the inflation rate remained at an impressive low of 1.59%. Industry also grew at 9.1%. As in 2000, agriculture performed exceptionally well, and with another bumper crop, Bangladesh turned its food deficit into a food surplus. This was a significant change, with both economic and psychological implications. For the first half of the year, exports grew at an impressive 14% following a yearlong lean period, but they slowed down after July, triggering fears of recession. Throughout the year government borrowing remained at a high level, and the foreign-exchange reserve hit its lowest point ever at $1,050,000,000 in July.

(MAHFUZ ANAM)

BARBADOS

Area: 430 sq km (166 sq mi)
Population (2001 est.): 269,000
Capital: Bridgetown
Chief of state: Queen Elizabeth II, represented by Governor-General Sir Clifford Husbands
Head of government: Prime Minister Owen Arthur

The dangers posed to Caribbean exporters by drug traffickers were illustrated in April 2001 when Canadian garment manufacturer Gildan Activewear Inc. shut down its newly opened Barbados operation after marijuana was found in one of its export containers.

The 2001 sugar crop, the country's main export, was again a disappointment; only 49,796 metric tons were produced, well down from the 2000 level of 58,373 metric tons. Excessive dry weather was blamed for the poor showing. The diminished sugar crop and sluggish output in manufacturing had an impact on economic growth, which was expected to shrink to 1–1.5% from an average of 3% in the previous three years.

Prime Minister and Minister of Finance Owen Arthur, faced with increased unemployment of 10%, in August outlined measures to improve growth, including an "employment fund" to strengthen manufacturing, $10 million to promote the country's tourist attractions, and a 2.5% corporate tax cut for 2002. On September 28 government and public-sector officials met to discuss emergency measures to minimize fallout from the terrorist attacks in the U.S.

In August the Inter-American Development Bank moved to help Barbados modernize and reform its justice system by approving a $8,750,000 loan for that purpose.

(DAVID RENWICK)

BELARUS

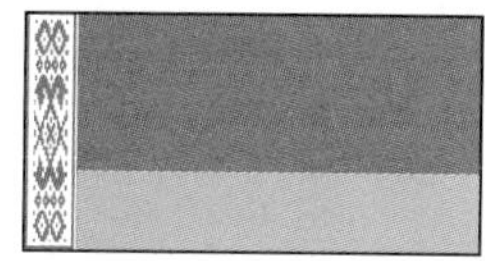

Area: 207,595 sq km (80,153 sq mi)
Population (2001 est.): 9,986,000
Capital: Minsk
Head of state and government: President Alyaksandr G. Lukashenka, assisted by Prime Ministers Uladzimir Yarmoshyn and, from March 14 (acting until October 10), Henadz Navitski

The year in Belarus was dominated by a controversial presidential election campaign and the vote on Sept. 9, 2001, which resulted in a victory for incumbent Pres. Alyaksandr Lukashenka. Initially 22 candidates filed applications, including prominent opposition leaders Zyanon Paznyak, exiled leader of the Conservative Christian Party of the Belarusian Popular Front; Mikhail Marinich, the Belarusian ambassador to Latvia, Estonia, and Finland; and Natalya Masherova, daughter of a former Communist Party leader. The Central Election Commission accepted

A Belarusian election official collects ballots in a farm field near the village of Osovo on September 9.

AP/Wide World Photos

only four candidates, but several political parties banded together to nominate a single opposition candidate, trade unionist Uladzimir Hancharyk.

Despite promises made to the Organization for Security and Cooperation in Europe (OSCE), the government did not allow a democratic election process. Opposition candidates were permitted two prerecorded 30-minute broadcasts on television but were otherwise deprived of a voice in the media. During the campaign Lukashenka threatened to expel the OSCE's chief observer and place restrictions on opposition rallies. About 15% of the electorate voted early, and government workers were threatened with dismissal unless they voted for the president. The results were predictable. With a reported turnout of 83.9%, 75.6% voted for Lukashenka, while Hancharyk was second with 15.6%. The OSCE refused to recognize the election as democratic, and the United States described it as "meaningless," although Russia accepted the results.

Russia continued to spend about $1 billion annually to support the Belarusian economy through debt relief, cheap supplies of oil and gas, and purchases of Belarusian goods that would be unlikely to find a market elsewhere. In the first half of 2001 Belarus reported a rise of 3% in gross domestic product and of 4.1% in industrial production. At the same time, although exports rose by 3.9% between January and July, imports decreased by 11.4%. In June the World Bank approved a loan of $22.6 million for Belarus to improve heating, lighting, and insulation in schools, hospitals, and orphanages, the first such loan in seven years.

Human and political rights continued to be a major concern in Belarus. The opposition Magic printing press was closed down on January 9. Notable incarcerations included that of 60-year-old parliamentary deputy and journalist Valery Shchukin, who was beaten by the police and imprisoned for three months for having attempted to attend a press conference. Two foreigners were accused, Cold War style, of espionage: German citizen Christopher Letz, who was sentenced to seven years in prison in July but was subsequently pardoned, and Angelo Antonio Piu, an Italian businessman, who was sentenced to four and a half years in a high-security prison in September along with a Belarusian "accomplice." Lukashenka's continuing dependence on the secret service was illustrated by the promotion of Ural Latypau, who had served as secretary of the State Security Council since November 2000, to the position of chief of staff in September. (DAVID R. MARPLES)

AP/Wide World Photos

Two nuns, Sister Gertrude and Sister Maria Kisito, appear in a court in Brussels on April 17 to face charges of complicity in genocide in Rwanda.

BELGIUM

Area: 30,528 sq km (11,787 sq mi)
Population (2001 est.): 10,268,000
Capital: Brussels
Chief of state: King Albert II
Head of government: Prime Minister Guy Verhofstadt

The Belgian Parliament approved a further decentralization of power to the country's three regions during 2001. After six months of intense negotiations between the major political parties, it was agreed in July that responsibility for agricultural policy, foreign trade, development cooperation, and control over communal and provincial councils would pass from the national to the regional level at the beginning of 2002. Regional governments in Flanders, Wallonia, and Brussels were also being given increased fiscal autonomy with the power to raise or lower tax rates by 6.7%—considerably more than the 3.25% leeway they previously enjoyed. Under the four-part agreement, the federal government would also increase funding to the Dutch- and French-speaking language communities, which were responsible for running the country's education system. Some estimates suggested that by 2020 this would mean the transfer of an extra BF 250 billion (about $5.7 billion). The final element of the package provided for increased representation for Dutch speakers in the Brussels region.

Belgium's Liberal-led coalition continued to implement its social agenda. It legalized the use of cannabis for those over 18 years old; passed legislation to allow gay and lesbian partners to marry, which made Belgium the second country, after The Netherlands, to do so; and was preparing to decriminalize euthanasia. The government also took the first step toward reducing the country's tax burden over the next five years. From 2003 the top two rates of 52.5% and 55% would be reduced to a maximum rate of 50%, and existing thresholds would also be raised. Despite these changes and the introduction of more generous tax allowances, Belgium would remain one of the most heavily taxed European countries.

Belgium's legal system broke new ground during 2001 with the trial of four Rwandans—two nuns, a factory manager, and a university professor. They were accused and found guilty of complicity in the genocide of 800,000 members of Rwanda's Tutsi minority in 1994. The judgment was the first time that powers granted by a 1993 act allowing Belgian courts to prosecute serious crimes against humanity had been used.

On the business front, it proved to be a good year for Belgian brewing giant Interbrew. The Leuven-based company, the world's second largest brewer, bought Germany's fourth largest brewer, Beck's, and thereby strengthened its position in the U.S. After months of negotiations Interbrew overcame the British government's concerns regarding the company's acquisition of Bass Brewers by preparing to sell off the latter's top brand, Carling. During the first six months of 2001,

Interbrew posted its best half-yearly results in 10 years. It was turbulent times, however, for another of Belgium's corporate flagships, Sabena. The airline, jointly owned by the Belgian state and Swissair, announced drastic plans in August to shed staff, dispose of larger planes and certain assets, and cut back on long-haul operations. On October 2 Swissair, faced with financial collapse, grounded all of its flights indefinitely. The next day Sabena filed for bankruptcy protection, which sent Swissair stock plummeting. Though the Belgian government vowed to work to save the national airline, in November the struggle became too great, and Sabena became the first European carrier to be declared bankrupt. The government and financial community moved quickly to support as its successor DAT (Delta Air Transport), formerly Sabena's regional subsidiary. By year's end, however, DAT itself was facing a battle for survival as it struggled to raise the finances necessary to guarantee its survival.

Belgium's presidency of the European Union in the second half of the year ensured the country and its leading politicians a place in the international limelight.

The country's premier sporting achiever was probably Jacques Rogge, who in July was elected the eighth president of the International Olympic Committee. (*See* BIOGRAPHIES.) Former prime minister Paul Vanden Boeynants died at age 81 in January. (*See* OBITUARIES.) At the end of October Princess Mathilde gave birth to a daughter, Elisabeth Thérèse Marie Hélène, who would be second in line to the throne after her father, Prince Philippe. (RORY WATSON)

BELIZE

Area: 22,965 sq km (8,867 sq mi)
Population (2001 est.): 247,000
Capital: Belmopan
Chief of state: Queen Elizabeth II, represented by Governor-General Colville Young
Head of government: Prime Minister Said Musa

In September 2001 Belize celebrated its 20th anniversary of independence in a relatively low-key fashion in the wake of the terrorist attacks in the U.S. In his state of the nation address, Prime Minister Said Musa highlighted the accomplishments of the People's United Party government during its three years of rule. These included a booming tourist industry, which had been a central force behind Belize's rapidly growing economy, and increased cocoa production, which showed promise of one day rivaling the citrus, banana, and sugar industries in terms of foreign-exchange earnings for Belize. Cocoa growers requested additional land in order to meet the European market requests for more cocoa. For the first time, a new public-private-sector model of patient-centred health care delivery got under way during the year. The emphasis was on preventive medicine. A pilot project was scheduled for a three-year period.

On October 8 Hurricane Iris struck southern Belize with winds as strong as 225 km/h (140 mph). The storm, which forced the evacuation of Belize City, pummeled coastal towns and left some 13,000 persons homeless. (*See* DISASTERS.) (INES PARKER)

BENIN

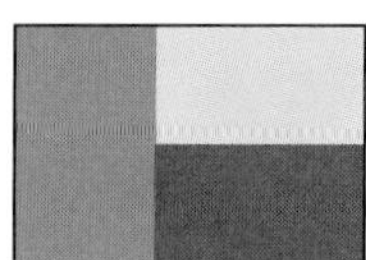

Area: 114,760 sq km (44,300 sq mi)
Population (2001 est.): 6,591,000
Capital: Porto-Novo (executive and ministerial offices remain in Cotonou)
Head of state and government: President Mathieu Kérékou

Incumbent Pres. Mathieu Kérékou won a plurality in the first round of the presidential elections that were held in Benin on March 4, 2001. His triumph in the second round was virtually ensured when two of the four candidates withdrew after citing the large number of votes that seemed to have disappeared. Kérékou took 84% of the vote in the second round of balloting on March 24, defeating the sole remaining candidate, cabinet minister Bruno Amoussou. There was, however, widespread criticism of the handling of the poll, and nine members of the national electoral commission resigned. Nonetheless, Kérékou was expected to maintain his grip upon a nation that he had ruled for all but five years since 1972. The National Assembly granted an amnesty on June 25 to all those arrested for allegedly having caused trouble during the election campaign.

Two separate reports of child trafficking from Benin into Gabon and Côte d'Ivoire were investigated by government authorities. On April 17 a number of children believed to have been destined for slavery were said to have been removed from a Nigerian ship then docked in Cotonou. On May 9, 10 adults were arrested and charged with having attempted to smuggle another 23 children by bus across the Benin frontier. On June 26 Japan donated nearly $1 million to Benin to combat poverty and child trafficking.

With at least one-third of the population living below the poverty line, much attention was focused in 2001 on boosting economic growth. Sixty experts from West African institutions met in Cotonou on May 15 to propose new development strategies. (NANCY ELLEN LAWLER)

BHUTAN

Area: 47,000 sq km (18,150 sq mi)
Population (2001 est.): 692,000 (excluding more than 100,000 refugees in Nepal)
Capital: Thimphu
Head of state: Druk Gyalpo (King) Jigme Singye Wangchuk
Head of government: Chairmen of Council of Ministers Lyonpo Yeshey Zimba and, from August 8, Lyonpo Khandu Wangchuk

The close working relationship between the king of Bhutan, the Council of Ministers (Lhengye Zhungtshog), and the National Assembly continued throughout 2001. On August 8 Lyonpo Khandu Wangchuk took over as chairman of the council from Lyonpo Yeshey Zimba, but most council ministers retained their posts. A Civil and Criminal Procedure Code, under which the powers of the judiciary were expanded and the judicial process defined, was passed on July 23 by the National Assembly.

Discussions with Nepal continued on the status of refugees from Bhutan in seven refugee camps in southeastern Nepal. Some headway was made with a verification process, but it was evident by midyear that it would take at least another year to complete the work. Little progress was made in persuading the Assamese militants in southeastern Bhutan to withdraw their forces back into India.

The economy continued to flourish in 2001, owing primarily to the expansion of hydropower resources. Much of the power generated was sold to India, and enough currency was earned to make Bhutan's economy self-supporting. Some economic problems emerged as the number of foreign tourists declined substantially after the September 11 terrorist attacks in the United States.

(LEO E. ROSE)

BOLIVIA

Area: 1,098,581 sq km (424,164 sq mi)
Population (2001 est.): 8,516,000
Capitals: La Paz (administrative) and Sucre (judicial)
Head of state and government: Presidents Hugo Bánzer Suárez and, from August 7, Jorge Quiroga Ramírez

In Bolivia the year 2001 was marked by renewed protests over economic and social grievances and by the illness and subsequent resignation of unpopular Pres. Hugo Bánzer Suárez. The 75-year-old Bánzer, a major figure in Bolivian public life for 30 years, was treated in the U.S. for lung and liver cancer and resigned for health reasons on August 6. Vice Pres. Jorge Quiroga Ramírez, a Texas-educated industrial engineer and former IBM executive, was sworn in as president the next day. Quiroga, aged 41 and considered a moderate in Bánzer's conservative National Democratic Action party, said he represented a new generation in Bolivian politics. He named 12 new cabinet ministers and kept only 4 from Bánzer's team.

Opposition leader Felipe Quispe Huanca organized protests against Bánzer's market-oriented economic policies. Quispe's supporters included street vendors in La Paz as well as trade unionists, teachers, health workers, and growers of coca, the raw material for cocaine. Most of the illegal coca crop had been forcibly eradicated in a U.S.-supported campaign, and farmers said they feared starvation as a result. The protests, which also included road blockades, were hampered by conflicts among the organizers. A truce was reached in August, and the government agreed to talks on land reform and other social issues. The protests indicated deep discontent with policies that attracted foreign investment but provided few jobs and little relief from economic hardship. The International Monetary Fund acknowledged that despite 15 years of adjustment programs under its supervision, nearly two-thirds of Bolivians lived in poverty.

Bánzer's political troubles continued after he stepped down. His former defense minister accused him of corruption, charging that Bánzer had inflated the amount paid for a government aircraft, and human rights campaigners threatened to prosecute him for abuses committed during his military dictatorship in the 1970s. Meanwhile, Bolivia pushed ahead with judicial reform, and the first "citizen judges" appointed under a new criminal procedure code began hearing cases in September.

Bolivian coca farmers stage a protest against the government on February 22 by scattering thousands of coca leaves along the main street of the city of Chimore.

AP/Wide World Photos

Quiroga hoped revenues from natural gas exports would replace economic losses from coca eradication and a crackdown on smuggling. Gas exports in the first six months of the year rose by 151% over 2000, but demand in Brazil, Bolivia's major customer, was lower than expected because of economic and regulatory difficulties there. Finance Minister Jacques Trigo Loubiere said in September that the economy would register no growth during 2001. Quiroga and gas producers promoted a scheme in which liquefied Bolivian gas would be exported to Mexico, converted back to gas, and piped to the energy-hungry United States. Quiroga also hoped to further capitalize on Bolivia's vast gas fields by producing petrochemicals and issuing bonds backed by future exports.

(PAUL KNOX)

BOSNIA AND HERZEGOVINA

Area: 51,129 sq km (19,741 sq mi)
Population (2001 est.): 3,922,000
Capital: Sarajevo
Heads of state: Tripartite presidency headed by Zivko Radisic and, from June 14, Jozo Krizanovic
Head of government: Prime Ministers Martin Raguz, Bozidar Matic from February 22, and, from July 18, Zlatko Lagumdzija

In 2001 Bosnia and Herzegovina began to stand on its own administratively without extensive international supervision. Moderate parties took over the leadership of the Bosniak (Muslim)-Croat Federation and won considerable influence in Republika Srpska (Serb Republic). Prime Minister Zlatko Lagumdzija advised the world that "the role of the international community is to help us, but not to work, think, and decide for us."

In January the reform-oriented 10-party Alliance for Change succeeded in getting its members appointed speaker, deputy speaker, and parliamentary secretary of the legislative assembly by narrowly outvoting the two dominant Croat and Muslim nationalist parties, the Croatian Democratic Union (HDZ) and the Party of Democratic Action (SDA). The House of Representatives also passed a bill that standardized procedures for all elected offices—though the nationalist Serb Democratic Party (SDS) and the HDZ boycotted the vote. Local organizations were beginning to take over from international organizations in monitoring voter education and human rights, but the nongovernment sector remained too weak to monitor elections and develop a civic society. Meanwhile, the three nationalist parties were cooperating closely in order to maintain their grip on power. In March Wolfgang Petritsch, head of the Office of the High Representative (OHR), sacked HDZ leader Ante Jelavic from the Bosnian tripartite presidency after Jelavic called for the formation of two predominantly Croat cantons; in October Jelavic was reelected HDZ president despite repeated warnings from the OHR. The OHR advised the federation government that more progress would be required in electoral laws before Bosnia and Herzegovina could be admitted to the Council of Europe.

The spurt of growth that came with postwar reconstruction faltered in 2001. Dissatisfied workers staged daily work stoppages, and much of the country's economic activity was forced underground owing to irrational tax codes and business regulations. Almost 50% of the active labour force was unemployed, in large part because of cutbacks in international aid and the lack of foreign capital investment.

In August the United Nations International Criminal Tribunal for the Former Yugoslavia (ICTY) released former Bosnian Serb president Biljana Plavsic from detention until the start of her trial. The same month, Gen. Radislav Krstic received a 46-year prison sentence for having planned, prepared, and carried out the killings of thousands of Muslim men at Srebrenica. In September Sefer Halilovic, the highest-ranking Bosnian Muslim to appear before the war crimes court, pleaded not guilty to charges of having failed to prevent the 1993 killings of Bosnian Croat civilians by his troops.

In the wake of the September 11 attacks in the U.S., Bosnia and Herzegovina found itself on a list of favourite destinations for terrorists. Interior Minister Muhamed Besic admitted that his country attracted terrorists—some with ties to Osama bin Laden—and that some had been granted Bosnian passports by militant elements of the former Sarajevo government. He denied the existence of terrorist training camps in the country, however.

(MILAN ANDREJEVICH)

BOTSWANA

Area: 581,730 sq km (224,607 sq mi)
Population (2001 est.): 1,586,000
Capital: Gaborone
Head of state and government: President Festus Mogae

Economic growth continued unabated in Botswana in 2001, with employment still expanding ahead of population growth. Government revenue from diamonds continued to rise, and new highways, administrative buildings, and large shopping malls were constructed. A challenge to the style of governmental paternalism established in the late colonial period was becoming evident, however.

In the annual Transparency International survey, Botswana was ranked the least-corrupt state in Africa (and 26th in the world), but there was increasing evidence of management laxity. An extensive north-south scheme of water articulation could not be commissioned because of defective piping. As many as 10,000 university students had to be sent to South Africa, Australia, Great Britain, and North America because the capacity of local universities had been overestimated. A complete census of households was held in August.

The death penalty made news in March when a white South African woman was hanged for having murdered her lover's wife. The most controversial issue, however, was that of ethnic minorities, whose representation in the upper house of Parliament was recommended by a report in March from the commission headed by Patrick Balopi, a former cabinet minister. Subsequent debate challenged established policies of national integration. In August Survival International, an organization devoted to the rights of tribal peoples, picketed the Botswana embassy in London over the San (Bushman) minority in the Kalahari. For 15 years the Botswana government had been inducing residents to leave the Central Kalahari Game Reserve, and wildlife officials harassed people who stayed.

In August former president Ketumile Masire started peace negotiations for the Democratic Republic of the Congo by bringing warring factions together in Gaborone, Botswana's capital.

(NEIL PARSONS)

BRAZIL

Area: 8,547,404 sq km (3,300,171 sq mi)
Population (2001 est.): 172,118,000
Capital: Brasília
Head of state and government: President Fernando Henrique Cardoso

Leadership elections in the Senate and the Chamber of Deputies in 2001 strained Brazilian Pres. Fernando Henrique Cardoso's fragile governing coalition, which included the Brazilian Social Democratic Party (PSDB), the Liberal Front Party (PFL), the Brazilian Democratic Movement Party (PMDB), and the Brazilian Progressive Party. The PMDB candidate for Senate president, Jader Barbalho of Pará state, won the election by a narrow majority (receiving 41 of 81 votes) on February 14 after having traded charges of corruption with his rival, the incumbent Senate president, Antônio Carlos Magalhães (PFL). Though the victory earned Barbalho the title of president of Congress, it exacerbated his feud with Magalhães, which carried on throughout the year and impeded progress relating to Cardoso's agenda. The Chamber of Deputies elected Aécio Neves (PSDB) of Minas Gerais state to head the lower house.

On January 25–30 Pôrto Alegre, the capital of Brazil's Rio Grande do Sul state, hosted the World Social Forum, an event that shadowed the annual World Economic Forum in Davos, Switz. The Pôrto Alegre conference attracted more than 10,000 people, including representatives of approximately 900 nongovernmental organizations from Europe, Africa, and Latin America. The forum criticized the policies of international multilateral financial institutions and called for international debt amnesty and a financial transactions tax levied on behalf of citizens.

On February 18 riots broke out in 29 state penitentiaries involving around 28,000 inmates and more than 5,000 visitors. Angered by the transfer of its leaders from São Paulo's Carandiru prison, a gang of convicts used mobile phones to order simultaneous riots during weekend visiting hours. By the time order was restored on February 19, at least 15 persons had been killed and 8 injured.

The federal government then sought to avoid a parliamentary commission of inquiry (CPI) into government corruption that would occupy Congress and the executive branch. Adding fuel to the opposition's call for a CPI, on February 22 Magalhães gave an interview to state prosecutors in which he hinted at corruption involving Cardoso, Barbalho, the PMDB, the PFL, and the Supreme Court. The interview, which was leaked to the press, prompted Cardoso to begin sacking government appointments linked to Magalhães.

With public opinion favouring investigation into allegations of government corruption, the opposition sought the votes of 27 senators and 171 federal deputies necessary to constitute a CPI. On May 8, after the opposition had apparently secured these votes, Barbalho canceled a joint session of Congress and thereby prevented the opposition from bringing the issue to the floor. Afterward, political maneuverings persuaded enough legislators to change their minds, and the CPI threat was ended. On May 16 Saturnino Braga, the rapporteur of the Senate Ethics Committee, concluded that Magalhães and the government leader in the Senate, José Roberto Arruda of the Federal District, were guilty of having violated secrecy rules in the June 2000 vote that expelled Federal District Sen. Luis Estevão from Congress. After damaging testimony from the director of the Senate data-processing system, who stated that she broke into the voting system under orders from Magalhães and Arruda, the Senate Ethics Committee recommended the impeachment of Magalhães and Arruda for having broken Senate decorum. Rather than risk impeachment and a loss of political rights for eight years, Arruda resigned on May 24; Magalhães followed suit on May 30.

An injured female prison guard is dragged away from the scene of rioting at São Paulo's Carandiru prison on February 19.

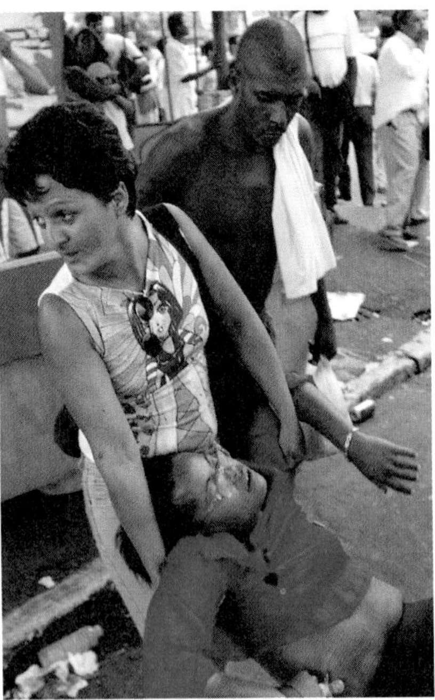

Mauricio Lima/AFP Worldwide

With Arruda and Magalhães out of office, Congress, at risk of becoming ineffectual, continued to be mired in scandal as more allegations of past corruption involving Barbalho surfaced. A growing number of investigations into fraud in the state Bank of Pará, the Superintendency for Development of the Amazon, and the National Land Reform Institute revealed the involvement of Barbalho when he was governor of Pará and minister of land reform. Barbalho took a leave of absence from his post as senate president on July 20. In the face of mounting evidence and the likelihood of impeachment, he resigned from the Senate on October 4, following the same path of Magalhães and Arruda. For Barbalho the loss of immunity opened up the possibility of indictment by federal police.

In late April and May, Brazil faced a looming energy crisis, which threatened to cause blackouts. The federal government formed an energy crisis task force chaired by the presidential chief of staff, Pedro Parente. On May 18 the energy crisis team introduced a rationing plan, which included incentives, surcharges, rate hikes, and the threat of disconnection to persuade households and businesses to curb power usage by approximately 20%. Among the factors contributing to the energy crisis were insufficient rainfall to sustain hydroelectric power generation, rising demand for energy, and weak transmission infrastructure. Plans to privatize the energy sector were temporarily halted as the government announced its short-term rationing plan with medium-term plans to increase capacity by auctioning hydroelectric-power-generation and gas-turbine units.

A breakdown of law and order ensued in June and July when armed police officers protesting low wages went on strike in the states of Tocantins, Alagoas, Pernambuco, and Bahia. On August 10 Cardoso issued temporary measures to tighten public security, permitting state governors to borrow police from neighbouring states during strikes and authorizing federal intervention of the armed forces.

On September 14 the International Monetary Fund approved a new agreement with Brazil, making more than $15 billion available through December 2002. The agreement was conditioned on the federal government's reaching primary budget surpluses of 3.35% of gross domestic product (GDP) in 2001 and 3.5% in 2002. By October the Brazilian census bureau was estimating that inflation for 2001 would reach 5.8% (±2%). Over the course of the year, the central bank raised the benchmark interest rate from 15.25% in January to 19% in October. By midyear Brazil's GDP had increased an estimated 3.12% from a year earlier. (JOHN CHARLES CUTTINO)

BRUNEI

Area: 5,765 sq km (2,226 sq mi)
Population (2001 est.): 344,000
Capital: Bandar Seri Begawan
Head of state and government: Sultan and Prime Minister Haji Hassanal Bolkiah Mu'izzaddin Waddaulah

The fallout from the scandal involving former finance minister Prince Jefri Bolkiah, the youngest brother of Hassanal Bolkiah, the sultan of Brunei Darussalam, continued in 2001. As finance minister the prince had been in charge of the Brunei Investment Agency (BIA), which was responsible for investing the nation's oil wealth, and of the Amedeo Development Corp., Brunei's largest private company. By 1998 Amedeo had collapsed under heavy debts, and reports surfaced that $15 billion in BIA funds had disappeared. The prince was sued by the state for having squandered the funds on Amedeo projects, including palaces and luxury hotels. Though an out-of-court settlement was reached in 2000, with the prince agreeing to hand over his remaining assets in exchange for a $300,000 monthly allowance, the royal family endured further embarrassment in August 2001 as 10,000 items once owned by Jefri Bolkiah were sold at a debtor's auction in Bandar Seri Begawan. Meanwhile, the prince faced a multimillion-dollar civil court action by his creditors.

New press laws went into effect on October 1 requiring newspapers in Brunei to obtain a publishing license each year from the government; under the new legislation, editors and journalists also faced jail terms if they were found guilty of publishing "false news." (EDITOR)

BULGARIA

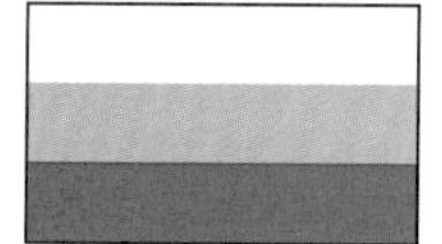

Area: 110,971 sq km (42,846 sq mi)
Population (2001 est.): 7,953,000
Capital: Sofia
Chief of state: President Petar Stoyanov
Head of government: Prime Ministers Ivan Kostov and, from July 24, Simeon Saxecoburggotski

On a campaign swing through the town of Blagoevgrad on June 13, Simeon II, Bulgaria's former king, accepts a gift of flowers from a child.

In the spring of 2001, the government of Ivan Kostov became the first post-communist administration in Bulgaria to run its full four-year course. It was not returned to power. Early in the year rumours had circulated that the former king, Simeon II, would return to Bulgaria and contest the presidential elections to be held in the fall. The constitution forbade this, however, and he decided to compete in the parliamentary campaign instead. In the elections of June 17, his National Movement for Simeon II, formed in April, secured 120 of the 240 seats. In July Simeon agreed to take the post of prime minister; Bulgaria thereby became the first country ever to elect its exiled king as head of government. Simeon henceforth officially used the surname Saxecoburggotski from his lineage in the royal house of Saxe-Coburg-Gotha, but he was universally known as "the King." (*See* BIOGRAPHIES.) His government's parliamentary majority was to be guaranteed by support from the Movement for Rights and Freedoms (MRF), a party representing primarily Bulgaria's ethnic Turkish minority.

The victory of the movement was based on Simeon's dramatic promise that his movement would restore the country to economic and political health within 800 days of taking office. This goal was to be accomplished by easing tax burdens on business, promoting enterprise, widening privatization, and reducing state involvement in the economy. Both economic and political health were to be gained by eliminating corruption. A reform program to promote these objectives was announced in August.

To spearhead the economic campaign, the prime minister appointed to key economic ministries young men who had spent time working in Western financial institutions. The foreign minister was from the small Jewish minority, and two ministers were ethnic Turks from the MRF. Surprisingly, Saxecoburggotski gave ministerial posts to two members of the Bulgarian Socialist Party, which did not support his government in the parliament.

In the second round of presidential elections held on November 18, Socialist Party leader Georgi Parvanov defeated centre-right Pres. Petar Stoyanov by capturing more than 50% of the vote. Parvanov would take office after Stoyanov's term expired on Jan. 22, 2002.

In foreign policy the new administration differed little from its predecessor in making admittance to NATO and the European Union its prime objectives. With its long historic association with Macedonia, Bulgaria could not be indifferent to the growing crisis in that country, but the Sofia government insisted that solutions had to be found by peaceful means. Unilateral action by Bulgaria was ruled out. The fate of six Bulgarian medics charged in Libya with having deliberately infected 393 children with HIV became a matter of great concern when the trial began on June 2. Though a decision was expected in late December, the hearing was postponed until Feb. 17, 2002. (RICHARD J. CRAMPTON)

BURKINA FASO

Area: 274,400 sq km (105,946 sq mi)
Population (2001 est.): 12,272,000
Capital: Ouagadougou
Chief of state: President Blaise Compaoré
Head of government: Prime Minister Ernest Paramanga Yonli

Tensions between Burkina Faso and Côte d'Ivoire continued throughout 2001 as thousands of Burkinabe citizens returned home, complaining of persistent harassment at the hands of Ivorian officials. On July 4, at a meeting brokered by Libyan leader Muammar al-Qaddafi, Pres. Blaise Compaoré and his Ivorian counterpart, Laurent Gbagbo, agreed to take steps to restore good relations between the two nations. Nonetheless, in August Côte d'Ivoire decided to send three extra battalions to safeguard its frontiers, and on September 6 Compaoré responded by deploying additional troops along Burkina's southern border.

On February 5 the government finally acted to resolve the uncertainty surrounding the death in 1998 of journalist Norbert Zongo when the former chief of the Presidential Guard was charged with the murder.

A severe meningitis epidemic struck the country, with over 7,000 cases reported by the beginning of April. There remained a crippling shortage of vaccine. In June international donors pledged $85 million for a five-year campaign against the spread of AIDS; more than 7% of Burkinabe adults were considered HIV-positive. In August grants for poverty alleviation totaling $45 million were approved by the World Bank and the International Monetary Fund. A $70 million water project for Ouagadougou was to be undertaken with further World Bank funding. (NANCY ELLEN LAWLER)

BURUNDI

Area: 27,816 sq km (10,740 sq mi)
Population (2001 est.): 6,224,000 (including 400,000 refugees in Tanzania)
Capital: Bujumbura
Head of state and government: President Pierre Buyoya

Widespread fighting between the government and rebel groups continued throughout 2001 amid efforts to implement the Arusha, Tanz., peace plan brokered in 2000 by former South African president Nelson Mandela. The peace process foundered, however, when the parties failed to agree on the composition of a transitional government.

On April 18 a group of junior army officers calling themselves the Patriotic Youth Front attempted to seize power in Bujumbura, but soldiers loyal to the government quickly suppressed the mutiny. Opposition leaders charged that Pres. Pierre Buyoya staged the uprising as a pretext for strengthening internal security measures.

A breakthrough came in July when Mandela announced a transition plan. Under the arrangement, Buyoya (a Tutsi) would continue as president for the first 18 months of a three-year transition period. Domitien Ndayizeye (a Hutu) would serve alongside him as vice president. During the second half of the transition, a Hutu would occupy the presidency, and a Tutsi would serve as vice president. The plan also called for the transitional government to include all 19 parties that signed the Arusha accord. It also required that the transitional government accept international peacekeeping forces and lift restrictions on political activity. The transition plan was endorsed by regional leaders and Burundian parties at a July 23 meeting in Arusha.

While Pres. Buyoya was attending a regional summit to endorse the transition, soldiers opposed to the Arusha process attempted a coup in Bujumbura. Though the uprising was quickly put down, many Burundians feared for the stability of the government. Armed rebel groups not party to the Arusha agreement vowed to continue fighting. Throughout the year government troops clashed with rebels of the National Forces of Liberation and the Forces for the Defense of the Democracy.

As a result of attacks on aid workers, humanitarian agencies frequently suspended their operations in parts of the country. An estimated 400,000 Burundian refugees were in Tanzania, and approximately 800,000 persons were displaced internally. Though Burundi and Tanzania agreed to a plan for the return of refugees, few were repatriated.

The transitional government was sworn in on November 1 amid continued fighting by Hutu rebels. The UN Security Council approved a 700-man international peacekeeping force to help protect the new government. The first contingent, 230 South African troops, was deployed just before the new government's inauguration.

(MATTHEW A. CENZER)

AP/Wide World Photos

A Burundian woman walks past a house in Bujumbura destroyed in fighting between government troops and armed rebel forces in April.

CAMBODIA

Area: 181,035 sq km (69,898 sq mi)
Population (2001 est.): 12,720,000
Capital: Phnom Penh
Chief of state: King Norodom Sihanouk
Head of government: Prime Minister Hun Sen

In 2001, with the problems of insurgency and political quarrels within the government under control, the administration of Cambodian Prime Minister Hun Sen was able to focus on helping the economy grow. At last the country seemed to be in a place where it could move beyond its turbulent and often bloody past and build a viable environment for business. Since 1999 gross domestic product growth had been healthy; in 2001 the GDP growth rate clocked in above 5%, with expectations of more than 6% for 2002. Although analysts still described Cambodia as a "predeveloped" country, at least certain industries were flourishing.

Some 80% of the population still worked in agriculture, a sector where inefficient farming methods and problematic distribution held back its growth and shrank its importance to the national coffers. Garment manufacturing became a star industry, growing by around 50% annually since 1998. In 2001 the kingdom exported $1 billion in clothes to the U.S. and Europe; the amount represented some 70% of Cambodia's exports. Factories were located mostly near the capital, Phnom Penh. The garment business boomed as Asian companies set up shop to subcontract for Western labels. With factory workers earning $45 a month, Cambodia owned a niche as a cheap-labour destination. Revelations of sweatshoplike conditions and certain instances of the use of child labour, however, prompted several international companies to withdraw from the market.

The other sector that enjoyed vigorous growth was tourism. Nearly 500,000 travelers visited Cambodia in 2001. The government hoped for one million arrivals by 2003. The travel and hospitality industry posted a record $200 million in annual earnings, half the government budget. The primary draw for travelers was Siem Reap province and its temples. To lure even more visitors, the government made it a new policy to welcome high-profile Hollywood film productions to Angkor Wat—the 1,000-year-old World Heritage monument Cambodians considered to be sacred ground—and other sites.

On the political front, after four years of wrangling and numerous postponements, King Norodom Sihanouk in August finally signed a law providing for some surviving Khmer Rouge leaders to be tried in court before foreign and local judges. When the likes of Nuon Chea, Pol Pot's second-in-command, and former Khmer Rouge head of state Khieu Samphan might actually face the justice process was uncertain. Both men made fresh public denials of responsibility for the deaths and suffering of millions during their rule in the 1970s, placing all the blame on Pol Pot. The international community, which funneled $500 million in aid annually into Cambodia, demanded that the trial—expected to cost upwards of $50 million—take place so that a dark chapter in history could be closed and the struggling nation could face its future in a new light.

(ALEXANDRIA A. SENO)

CAMEROON

Area: 475,442 sq km (183,569 sq mi)
Population (2001 est.): 15,803,000
Capital: Yaoundé
Chief of state: President Paul Biya
Head of government: Prime Minister Peter Mafany Musonge

Following an inquiry into a February 18 explosion and fire at Yaoundé's armory, Col. Jean-Paul Mengot, chief of the Presidential Guard, was dismissed on Feb. 23, 2001, and an unspecified number of soldiers were arrested. Fears that a military coup might be under way had created near panic in the city. On July 26, in an effort to defuse reports of growing discontent within the military, Pres. Paul Biya ordered a total reorganization of the nation's armed forces.

The disappearance of nine men arrested in Douala in January for theft caused widespread anger against the Operational Command (OC), a special paramilitary crime-fighting unit that had been created by presidential decree in February 2000. On April 7 President Biya fired the OC commander, Brig.-Gen. Philippe Mpay. Several other officers of the unit, which was suspected of having carried out hundreds of summary executions, were arrested on April 7–8. On June 15 the OC was disbanded.

Six men charged with high treason for membership in the Anglophone secessionist Southern Cameroon National Council were freed on March 20 after 14 months in prison, but authorities termed the releases temporary while investigations continued. Relations between the main opposition party, Ndi's Social Democratic Front (SDF), and the government deteriorated further when the SDF accused the state-controlled media of exercising partisan censorship over its broadcasts.

In February scientists from around the world began removing poisonous gases from Lake Nyos; emissions from the volcanic crater had killed several thousand people over the past 15 years.

The government took vigorous action to reduce its internal debt, and full payment of all outstanding salary arrears was made to civil servants.

(NANCY ELLEN LAWLER)

CANADA

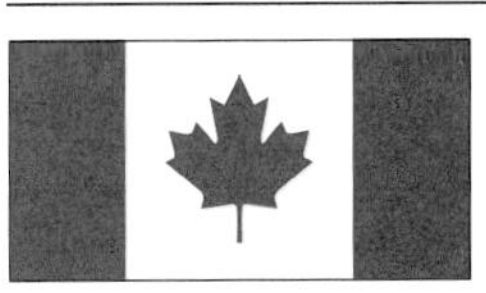

Area: 9,970,610 sq km (3,849,674 sq mi)
Population (2001 est.): 31,002,000
Capital: Ottawa
Chief of state: Queen Elizabeth II, represented by Governor-General Adrienne Clarkson
Head of government: Prime Minister Jean Chrétien

Domestic Affairs. After having won three elections in eight years, the Liberal Party government under Prime Minister Jean Chrétien dominated Canadian politics in 2001. Chrétien's grasp on power came from his long experience and unrivaled political skills. It was also helped by the fragmented nature of his opposition in Parliament.

In 2001, with the Liberals holding 172 of 301 seats in the House of Commons, this opposition seemed the weakest ever. During the previous year a determined effort had been made to unite the right around a Western protest movement, the Reform Party. The new grouping, the Canadian Alliance, had turned away from Reform's founder, Preston Manning, and chosen Stockwell Day as its leader. Day had served successfully as provincial treasurer of Alberta, but he was inexperienced in national politics. He led the Alliance to 66 seats in the November 2000 election and became official leader of the opposition.

Criticism of Day came forward soon after Parliament resumed sitting in the new year. Statements and actions by the Alliance leader raised questions about his political judgment. He was accused of disregarding the views of his caucus and being out of touch with the party membership. On April 24 Deborah Grey, deputy leader of the Alliance and its longest-serving member of Parliament, stated she no longer had confidence in Day. By July, amid rancorous quarreling, 11 other Alliance MPs had left the caucus, threatening to set up a new party. Some had been supporters of Manning.

The divisions within the Alliance damaged it seriously in the eyes of the public. Support dropped everywhere in Canada to a 6% approval rating in late June. By contrast, Liberal support rose to 60%. Some Alliance members talked of cooperating electorally with the rival Progressive Conservative Party (PCP), which had formed the government before Chrétien came to power in 1993.

By the end of the summer, Day had had enough. He delivered an ultimatum to the dissident Alliance members: return to the party caucus and accept his leadership by September 10, or be expelled. Four of the dissidents returned, while the other eight entered into a working coalition with the PCP, acknowledging PCP leader Joe Clark as head of the new grouping. It was the first opposition coalition in Canadian history.

If the Alliance was in disarray, the other opposition parties were also enfeebled. The separatist Bloc Québécois (BQ) held 38 seats but faced declining sentiment at home for Quebec's independence. The PCP was engaged in rebuilding itself as a national party but had still only 12 seats in the Commons. The socialist New Democratic Party (NDP), with 13 seats, appeared to be a victim of Canada's prosperity.

The BQ faced additional stress when Lucien Bouchard, the outspoken leader of the Parti Québécois and provincial premier in Quebec, abruptly announced his resignation on January 11. His successor, Bernard Landry, was sworn in on March 8 and promised to continue the fight for sovereignty. (*See* BIOGRAPHIES.)

The steadily rising costs of public health care brought about labour unrest in several provinces during the year. Nurses and health care providers engaged in noisy job action in Nova Scotia and British Columbia, while in New Brunswick physicians and nursing-home staffs went on strike to press demands for higher salaries. The federal government, eager to investigate possible changes to the system that would bring about greater efficiency, appointed Roy Romanow, the recently retired premier of Saskatchewan, to conduct a thorough probe.

In the meantime, other provinces, including Ontario, which spent 45% of its revenues on medical costs, argued that the federal government's share of health care funding was declining. Ottawa responded that in the previous year it had offered a Can$23.4 billion (Can$1=about U.S. $0.65) increase over five years in health and social transfers. Ontario pressed ahead with a demand for an immediate additional grant of Can$7 billion. This demand was endorsed by the other nine provinces in a meeting in Victoria, B.C., on August 2–3. Ottawa rejected the demand as "unrealistic."

Lucien Bouchard, provincial premier of Quebec, wipes his eyes before announcing his resignation on the floor of the Canadian province's National Assembly on January 11.

Marcos Townsend/AFP Worldwide

In December the federal government passed a constitutional amendment that officially changed the name of the province of Newfoundland to Newfoundland and Labrador.

The Economy. A strong Canadian economy faltered by midyear. Exports to the United States, Canada's principal market, were hurt by the downturn in the American economy. During the first quarter the Canadian gross domestic product, the total value of all goods and services produced in the country, expanded by 2%. Economic growth in the second quarter came virtually to a standstill at only 0.4%. The unemployment rate remained steady at 7% for the first half of the year but rose slightly in August.

A drought, perhaps the worst in Canadian history, gripped the country from coast to coast during the summer months. All sectors of agriculture were affected, with prairie wheat production expected to be cut by 20%.

The struggle against international terrorism led to a federal budget on December 10. Earlier, Finance Minister Paul Martin had seen no need for a 2001 budget, owing to the strong economic performance during the first half of the year, but September 11 dramatically changed the course of events both politically and economically.

The budget provided for new spending of more than $12 billion over the next five years, of which $7.7 billion would be devoted to strengthening Canada's security. Funds would be spent for tighter screening of passengers and baggage at Canada's airports, for armed undercover air marshals to man selected domestic and international flights, and for improved counterterrorism operations by the Royal Canadian Mounted Police and the military. Although there was no evidence that the terrorists who carried out the September hijackings had entered the U.S. through Canada, closer attention would be paid to immigrant and refugee screening. Procedures would be adopted for easing the massive flow of goods across the Canada-U.S. border, estimated to be worth $1.3 billion a day.

The 9.4% increase in government expenditures for the current year would eliminate the surplus that Martin had predicted earlier, but he insisted that the budget would be kept in balance over the next three years. Although the economy had languished in recession since midyear, Martin estimated a growth of 1.3% in gross domestic product during 2001.

Foreign Affairs. The historic old city of Quebec played host to the third Summit of the Americas, held April 20–22, with 34 countries taking part. Emphasizing the need for democratic government as the basis for hemispheric cooperation, the summit did not extend an invitation

AP/Wide World Photos

Anticapitalist demonstrators face police during the Summit of the Americas in Quebec on April 22.

to Cuba. In a "democratic clause" issued at the end of the meeting, the summit made it plain that only states with democratic institutions would be permitted to take part in the hemispheric movement for economic integration. Although elaborate precautions were taken to maintain order in Quebec, including the construction of a perimeter fence around the site of the meeting, more than 25,000 demonstrators converged on the city. Linking the expansion of free trade with the growth of capitalism, the protestors held parallel seminars and study sessions as well as marches and demonstrations.

The more serious protests that marred the Group of 8 (G-8) summit of industrialized nations at Genoa, Italy, in July influenced Chrétien's choice of a meeting place for the G-8 summit to be held in Canada in 2002. He chose the Rocky Mountain resort of Kananaskis, 100 km (62 mi) west of Calgary, Alta. The resort had been the site of the 1998 Winter Olympic Games. Isolated in the mountains and with limited hotel facilities, Kananaskis was expected to provide a more intimate atmosphere for the next meeting of the world's leaders. Its location would also discourage the gathering of protesters.

Canada did not follow the example of the U.S. in withdrawing from the Kyoto Protocol of 1997 for the reduction of carbon emissions. Instead, it worked with a group of like-minded states, including Scandinavian nations, Australia, and Japan, in urging that states find their own ways of achieving lower emission standards. In a conference in Bonn, Ger., in mid-July, Canada pressed for the freedom to carry out emission reductions in its own way. Its large forests constituted "sinks" that soaked up carbon gasses. Domestic reductions would also represent a large part of the Canadian program. Collectively, the states meeting in Bonn agreed to work toward a 5.2% cut in 1990 emission levels by 2010. Canada, which promised to achieve a 6% reduction over the same period, hoped to ratify the Kyoto agreement in 2002.

Canada sent a junior minister responsible for multiculturalism to the UN World Conference Against Racism held in Durban, S.Af., for nine days in early September. Although it assisted nongovernmental organizations (NGOs) in attending the meeting, Ottawa disassociated itself sharply from views expressed by some of the NGOs. In commenting on the final declaration approved by the conference, Canada took the "strongest objections" to mention of the Israeli-Arab conflict in the Middle East. Ottawa also had serious reservations regarding the assertion that 19th-century slavery constituted a crime against humanity. It did not approve of the proposal that compensation be paid for the wrongs of slavery. Behind the scenes the Canadian delegation at Durban worked to moderate the language of the conference's final text.

During 2001 Canada cautiously considered new directions in U.S. foreign policy. The new administration of U.S. Pres. George W. Bush immediately made it clear that it considered relations with Mexico a top priority. Within a decade, it was surmised, Mexico might become the U.S.'s largest trading partner. To Canada, which had occupied this position for many years, this was a sobering reassessment. Chrétien wasted no time in traveling to Washington, D.C., to meet with Bush on February 5, only 11 days before Bush visited his Mexican counterpart. Canadian spokesmen pointed out that Canada possessed a more substantial bilateral relationship with the U.S. than did Mexico. It was also a long-standing partner with the U.S. in important international organizations, including NATO.

Canada, as the junior partner in its links with the U.S., had always preferred to work with other countries in dealing with its giant neighbour. Canada was frustrated, therefore, when the Bush administration prepared to abandon international agreements, notably the 1972 Anti-Ballistic Missile Treaty, and pressed ahead with a missile defense system unpopular with America's allies. U.S. action or lack of action on multilateral agreements to discourage trafficking in small arms and on the creation of an international criminal court also worried Canada. It was apparent, therefore, that the Bush administration's preference for unilateral action in the international sphere would be a cause of concern in Canada in the immediate future.

An old trade dispute reemerged to trouble Canada-U.S. relations in 2001. Softwood lumber—pine, cedar, spruce—had long been a principal export, valued at $10 billion a year, of Canada to the U.S. This trade was not conducted under the North American Free Trade Agreement but was governed by a 1996 bilateral arrangement under which the U.S. applied a quota on Canadian lumber imports. This agreement expired on March 31, and on August 10 the U.S. Department of Commerce imposed a preliminary 19.3% duty on Canadian lumber imports from all but the four Atlantic provinces. The nub of the dispute was the price Canadian provinces charged for the right to cut timber on Crown (public) lands. The U.S. charged that this fee, called stumpage, was set below world market levels and thus constituted a subsidy to Canadian lumber exporters, allowing them to undercut American lumber producers. Canada vigorously rejected this claim, stating that there was no basis for it in fact or in law. The economic consequences were serious to both parties. Forestry was still the largest industry in Canada, with over 380,000 employees and 337 communities dependent on the sale of lumber. For the U.S., dependent on Canada for one-third of its lumber needs, the imposition of a duty, even though the proceeds were to be paid to American lumber producers, would result in higher costs to U.S. homebuilders.

(DAVID M.L. FARR)

CAPE VERDE

Area: 4,033 sq km (1,557 sq mi)
Population (2001 est.): 446,000
Capital: Praia
Chief of state: Presidents Antonio Mascarenhas Monteiro and, from March 22, Pedro Pires
Head of government: Prime Ministers António Gualberto do Rosário and, from February 1, José Maria Neves

The year 2001 marked the end of 10 years of rule by the Movement for Democracy and the return to power of the African Party for the Independence of Cape Verde (PAIVC). In legislative elections held in January, the PAIVC won the majority of seats, and its leader, José Maria Neves, became the new prime minister. In the second round of the presidential election, held in February, Pedro Pires, the PAIVC candidate and a former prime minister, emerged as the winner by a very narrow margin of votes.

For both major parties the chief issue was the archipelago's troubled economy. Though Neves underscored the need to reduce unemployment and tackle poverty, the means by which he intended to accomplish this remained far from clear. The economy, hard hit by drought, remained heavily reliant on agriculture and fishing. Cape Verde continued to depend on international aid, most notably from the European Union and Portugal. In July Cape Verde signed two financial agreements with Portugal aimed at strengthening the convertibility of the currency and promoting the restructuring of the economy and of the country's debt. (CHRISTOPHER SAUNDERS)

CENTRAL AFRICAN REPUBLIC

Area: 622,436 sq km (240,324 sq mi)
Population (2001 est.): 3,577,000
Capital: Bangui
Chief of state: President Ange-Félix Patassé
Head of government: Prime Ministers Anicet Georges Dologuélé and, from April 1, Martin Ziguélé

Army rebels loyal to former president André Kolingba attempted to overthrow the government on May 28, 2001. The mutineers, reportedly aided by several hundred Rwandan and Angolan mercenaries, attacked the Bangui palace of Pres. Ange-Félix Patassé; the assault resulted in at least 20 deaths. The government received swift military assistance from Libya, and reinforcements also arrived from Chad and the neighbouring Democratic Republic of the Congo (DRC); those from the latter were a group seeking to overthrow the DRC government. Fighting continued in the capital for more than a week, and unofficial estimates put the number of persons killed at between 250 and 300. Many rebel soldiers caught by government forces were thought to have been summarily executed. On June 7 the government claimed complete success at suppressing the coup, although sporadic outbreaks of violence continued. Kolingba and other suspected coup leaders remained at large. The government appealed for relief supplies to aid the nearly 80,000 people who had fled the fighting.

Kolingba's Central African Democratic Rally, once the sole legal political party, was ordered dissolved on June 22. Accused of implication in the coup attempt, Defense Minister Jean-Jacques Demafouth was dismissed on August 25. Two days later Kolingba's wife and children were abducted from the French embassy in Bangui, where they, along with an estimated 300 others, had taken refuge after the coup. Their fate was unknown. (NANCY ELLEN LAWLER)

CHAD

Area: 1,284,000 sq km (495,755 sq mi)
Population (2001 est.): 8,707,000
Capital: N'Djamena
Chief of state: President Lieut. Gen. Idriss Déby
Head of government: Prime Minister Nagoum Yamassoum

Chadian Pres. Idriss Déby won 63% of the vote in the May 2001 presidential election, securing for himself another five-year term, but this was only after many irregular electoral practices. Opposition members of the electoral commission resigned before the results

Cesaria Evora, whose sad, lilting mornas *have put Cape Verde on the world music map, performs at the Palace of Culture in Warsaw on May 26.*

were announced, maintaining that the election had been rigged. The opposition parties continued to refuse to accept the results, but their appeal to the constitutional court failed, protest meetings were banned, and demonstrations were broken up. Such actions cost Déby support, both within the country and in the international community. He postponed the legislative elections until 2002, and the opposition feared that in the interval he would use his patronage to strengthen his party, the Patriotic Salvation Movement.

By mid-2001 the Office of the UN High Commissioner for Refugees was approaching the end of the voluntary repatriation of thousands of people who had fled Chad for Cameroon in the 1980s. More than 40,000 Chadian refugees in Cameroon did not return to their homeland, however, in part because of the deteriorating political situation in northern Chad. The Movement for Democracy and Justice in Chad (MDJT) continued fighting in the Tibesti region in the northwest, close to the Libyan border, under Youssouf Togoimi, a former defense minister. In July the MDJT claimed to have captured the strategic town of Fada and opened a new front 900 km (560 mi) northeast of the capital, N'Djamena. President Déby suspected that Libyan leader Muammar al-Qaddafi was helping the rebels.

(CHRISTOPHER SAUNDERS)

AP/Wide World Photos

Police in Santiago, Chile, apprehend student demonstrators during a protest against a delay in the reduction of public transportation fares for students on April 20.

CHILE

Area: 756,626 sq km (292,135 sq mi)
Population (2001 est.): 15,402,000
Capitals: Santiago (national) and Valparaíso (legislative)
Head of state and government: President Ricardo Lagos Escobar

The year 2001 posed both economic and political challenges for Chile and for the government of Ricardo Lagos Escobar. The case of former Chilean president Gen. Augusto Pinochet Ugarte remained in the spotlight. Pinochet, who had been charged with human rights abuses, underwent a series of medical exams after his lawyers allowed them to go forward. Although the Chilean appeals courts decided that Pinochet was not fit to stand trial, the general was not out of the legal morass. Other actions continued against him in Chile and elsewhere. Judicial proceedings in France led to his indictment, along with six other senior Chilean military officers, including former intelligence chief Gen. Manuel Contreras, who had spent seven years incarcerated in Chile for the 1976 murder of Chilean diplomat Orlando Letelier in Washington, D.C.

On the political front, the Lagos government had to face a stronger political opposition—the activist mayor in Santiago, Joaquín Lavín Infante. Lavín, who narrowly lost to Lagos in 2000, continued to position himself to run again for the presidency. Much to the dismay of the Lagos government, Lavín had increased his popularity by focusing on issues such as public safety. Lavín's activities bore fruit in the December parliamentary elections when his right-wing Independent Democratic Union (UDI) party overtook the Christian Democratic Party (PDC) by winning more than 25% of the vote. The right-wing Alliance for Chile coalition, which included the UDI, won 44.3% of the vote, compared to the ruling Concertación coalition's 47.9%. As a result, the two political forces were tied in the Senate (24–24), and the Concertación's majority in the lower house was reduced to 63–57 from 70–50.

The PDC suffered an earlier embarrassment when it somehow missed the deadline for registering its candidates for the congressional elections. Although the situation was rectified via congressional action and PDC candidates were included in the Concertación electoral slate, the event demonstrated a shocking lack of internal organization and led to a shake-up within the party. There were also growing intracoalition conflicts between the PDC and its coalition ally, the Socialist Party (PS). These came to light when the PS announced that it had reached an agreement to share some of its electoral seats with the Communist Party, which was not a member of the coalition. The strongly anticommunist PDC was outraged by the agreement, which had been negotiated without the prior consent of coalition members.

In addition, the Lagos government faced difficulties on the economic front. Although Chile's economy continued to grow, the rate of growth was lower than had been originally predicted—3.5% instead of the 5% estimate. That was a much lower number than the vigorous 7% growth rates Chile had experienced prior to the 1997 Asian financial crisis, which negatively affected Chile's export-dependent economy. Unemployment remained stubbornly high, reaching 9.7% in Santiago by October. Prices for two major exports, copper and wood pulp, also sank to record lows. Although Chile tried to insulate itself from the severe economic problems across the Andes in Argentina, its peso was affected, dropping in value to an exchange rate of about 670 pesos to the dollar by December. On the plus side, Chile had virtually no foreign debt, which allowed it to offer for sale $650 million in government bonds.

(LOIS HECHT OPPENHEIM)

CHINA

Area: 9,572,900 sq km (3,696,100 sq mi), including Tibet and excluding Taiwan and the special autonomous regions of Hong Kong and Macau
Population (2001 est., excluding Taiwan, Hong Kong, and Macau): 1,274,915,000
Capital: Beijing
Chief of state: President Jiang Zemin
Head of government: Premier Zhu Rongji

Three external events diverted the attention of the Chinese government and people from their primary focus on domestic affairs in 2001. The first was a contretemps with the U.S. in April over the crash of a Chinese military jet after a midair collision with an American surveillance plane over the South China Sea. The second was the International Olympic Committee's decision in July to award the 2008 Summer Olympics to Beijing. The third was the cataclysmic September 11 terrorist attacks in the U.S. that presented China with an opportunity to get in step with the global campaign to combat terrorism. For the most part, however, China focused inward on the formidable task of maintaining domestic prosperity, the indispensable precondition for stability in a system perennially threatened by social divisions, ethnic fragmentation, endemic corruption, and political fatigue. As the global economy slowed even before September 11, China managed to sustain a still-impressive rate of economic growth, though it was lower than in previous years.

Politics and the Economy. The ruling Communist Party of China (CPC) continued to prepare for its 16th Congress in 2002, at which time Pres. Jiang Zemin, National People's Congress head Li Peng, and Premier Zhu Rongji were slated to retire from their party posts. The 75-year-old Jiang was almost certain to retain his chairmanship of the vital Central Military Commission, however, and to wield considerable behind-the-scenes influence over his designated successor, Hu Jintao, as long as he remained in good health. Meanwhile, Political Bureau member Li Ruihuan, a relative moderate who was several years younger than the members of the ruling troika, successfully resisted pressure from party conservatives to join Jiang, Li, and Zhu in retirement.

For 20 years, while brooking no organized political opposition, the CPC had struggled to regain the authority and prestige it once enjoyed. The party's internal corruption and the effects of rapid social and economic change in Chinese society had called into question the CPC's leading role and eroded its legitimacy. In order to bring in new blood, on July 1, the CPC's 80th anniversary, Jiang called on the party to open its ranks to the once-reviled capitalists, who had been responsible for most of China's economic growth since the mid-1980s. Old-guard party members, faithful to Karl Marx's dictum that communist parties were the political instrument of the proletariat (working class), gagged at this bold initiative to recruit members of the "class enemy," but Jiang brushed aside all objections and shut down an orthodox party theoretical journal that dared to question his decision. In September the Central Committee dutifully en-

On March 28, during a rally in support of China's bid to host the 2008 Summer Olympics, dragon dancers perform at the Great Wall of China near Beijing.

AP/Wide World Photos

dorsed Jiang's proposal to revise the party constitution and thereby opened the door for capitalists to enter the CPC.

Earlier in the year the first CPC Work Conference since 1988—attended by 2,000 top officials—endorsed the leadership's campaign to suppress the Falun Gong and reaffirmed once again the leadership's decision 12 years earlier to crush the spring 1989 student-led democracy movement. This may have been in response to the publication, first in English in the U.S. and later in Chinese in Hong Kong, of *The Tiananmen Papers*. Edited by American scholars Andrew J. Nathan and Perry Link, this documentary collection was the authenticated secret record of high-level CPC discussions that culminated in the decision to use lethal force against unarmed demonstrators on June 3–4, 1989 (the Tiananmen Square massacre). The book cast many of the party's old guard, including then premier Li Peng and paramount leader Deng Xiaoping, in a particularly unflattering light. Additional secret evidence concerning this still-controversial decision leaked out in the course of the year and fed Beijing's paranoia that Washington was trying to split the CPC and overturn communism in China.

After four years as a special administrative region of China, Hong Kong felt the collar of Chinese control tighten ever so slowly around its neck. Such at least was the perception among that section of Hong Kong public opinion concerned with defending the autonomy promised at the time of the handover in 1997. In July Hong Kong's Legislative Council, chosen in elections that favoured elite occupational groups over direct popular representation, voted by a 2–1 margin to give Beijing the right to fire the chief executive. This seemingly small action enhanced the power of Chinese central authorities responsible for selecting Chief Executive Tung Chee-hwa, who had proved to be a faithful, if locally unpopular, executor of Beijing's wishes.

Like an indelible stain on the fabric of Chinese society, the reality of Chinese human rights abuses continued to resist Beijing's detergent action. In late November 2000, during a visit by Mary Robinson, the UN High Commissioner for Human Rights, who was openly critical of China's human rights record, China signed an agreement providing for UN advice and assistance to upgrade its criminal justice system, including the police, legal procedures, courts, and prisons. The effects, if any, of this and similar prior expressions of China's intention to bring its human rights practices into conformity with international norms and practices were not evident during 2001. In February Amnesty International, the bellwether international human rights organization, issued a report alleging that China was stepping up its use of torture in police interrogations of dissidents, Tibetan nationalists, migrants, and other criminal defendants. As always, Chinese authorities rejected this report, as they did the U.S. State Department's annual review of human rights that said the human rights situation in China was getting worse. To deal with rising social discontent, Beijing instructed Chinese municipal authorities to beef up their antiriot police units, which, along with the million-strong People's Armed Police, were the instruments of first choice to deal with the contingency of urban riots, worker and student strikes, and other threats to public order. The police and paramilitary assault on the village of Yuntang in Jiangxi province demonstrated that such preparations were more than contingency planning. Villagers in Yuntang, unable to get relief from exorbitant taxes levied by local officials, seized and held control of their village until overwhelmed by lethal force from outside. Such popular indignation was widespread, and the default response of authorities was more likely to be the application of force than the satisfaction of grassroots demands for equity and social justice.

Sociologist Gao Zhan, accompanied by her husband, speaks to reporters in Detroit on July 26 after being expelled from China following her arrest and detention on charges of revealing state secrets to Taiwan.

For several years Beijing had targeted pervasive networks of corruption that linked venal local officials with unscrupulous entrepreneurs. Despite massive arrests and numerous well-publicized public executions, corruption persisted and exacted not only an economic cost but also a heavy toll on ordinary workers. For example, when safety inspectors ignored hazardous working conditions and failed to enforce safety standards in unsafe local mines, thousands of miners paid with their lives, as happened again in 2001. Children were also victimized. In a case that drew international attention and provoked some soul-searching on the part of Premier Zhu Rongji, 42 people, including 38 schoolchildren, were killed in an explosion in a Fanglin township (Jiangxi province) primary school whose pupils were forced to make fireworks as part of their regular activities. (*See* DISASTERS.)

In their ongoing campaign against Falun Gong, the eclectic Buddhist-influenced meditation and exercise association that was outlawed in 1999 as a supposed threat to public order, Chinese authorities added psychiatric internment to their familiar repertoire of arrests, beatings, incarceration, torture, and coercive reeducation. On June 20 at least 14 Falun Gong prisoners either hanged themselves or were tortured to death in a prison camp in northern Heilongjiang province. The apparent effect of President Jiang's quixotic but brutal campaign to destroy the Falun Gong had been to weaken the organization considerably and drive it underground.

The arrest and detention of American permanent resident Gao Zhan, a sociologist, and Li Shaomin, a naturalized American citizen teaching in Hong Kong, on charges of revealing state secrets indicated the bureaucratic power of China's Ministry of State Security. Their detention sent a chill through the large community of overseas Chinese students and scholars. Under pressure from the U.S. government and Western scholars, Gao and Li were expelled from China after being convicted in dubious trials. Less fortunate was Stanford research scholar Hua Di, who—though his 15-year prison sentence on similar charges was overturned—was retried and received a 10-year sentence.

Environmental concerns commanded the attention of policy makers and the public in a country whose huge population and rapid industrialization had pressed against the limits of natural resources, particularly water, wood, and air. China made some progress in curbing emissions of carbon dioxide, carbon monoxide, and nitrous oxide. The switchover from coal to natural gas and the ongoing conversion of Beijing's bus and taxi fleet from diesel fuel and gasoline to liquefied petroleum gas contributed to the amelioration of the air in the capital city. Beijing announced plans to address the severe water shortage affecting all of northern China by encouraging less-water-intensive agricultural practices, shutting factories that polluted groundwater and surface water, and constructing new sewage-treatment plants.

The determination of national and municipal officials to improve Beijing's environment was motivated in part by the desire to show the city's best face to the world. In July the International Olympic Committee announced that it was awarding the 2008 Summer Olympics to Beijing. Upon receiving the news, jubilant Communist Party and government leaders as well as ordinary citizens joined in a rare spontaneous mass celebration in Tiananmen Square. In this connection Beijing unveiled plans to invest $34 billion in new stadiums, parks, transportation systems, housing, and pollution-abatement measures.

According to official statistics, China's gross domestic product grew by 7.9% in the first half of the year, with domestic demand, accounting for fully 93% of growth, the primary engine of expansion. At the end of the third quarter, consumer prices had risen a modest 1%, and foreign exchange reserves stood at $195.8 billion. China's currency was stable, but its trade balance, while still positive, declined by $5.6 billion compared to the previous year at that point. Long-standing problems of liquidity and bad loans in the banking system and the mammoth task of converting state-owned enterprises into profitable firms remained mostly unresolved. However, these problems loomed ever larger as the World Trade Organization finally certified China for membership following 15 years of difficult multilateral negotiations that culminated in agreement in mid-September.

Foreign Relations. A decade earlier Chinese leaders had greatly valued the pragmatism of then U.S. president George H.W. Bush, who cooperated with them to stabilize Sino-American relations after the shock of Tiananmen. They were understandably leery, however, of the new U.S. president, George W. Bush. The younger Bush not only lacked foreign policy experience but also had surrounded himself with advisers who for the most part viewed China as a strategic adversary that threatened American interests and the U.S.'s friends in Asia, including Taiwan. An unfortunate aerial confrontation over the South China Sea on April 1 near China's southernmost province of Hainan sorely tested Sino-American relations just three months into the new Bush administration. While on a routine patrol over international waters off the South China coast, a lumbering, propeller-driven American EP-3 surveillance plane, crammed with sophisticated electronic eavesdropping equipment, collided with one of two Chinese jet fighters that were shadowing its flight. Washington claimed that the daredevil Chinese pilot had approached too closely and struck the American craft; Beijing countered that the U.S. plane had deliberately veered into the path of the Chinese fighter. Badly damaged, the EP-3 made an arguably unauthorized emergency landing at a Chinese military airfield on Hainan Island, where the 24-person crew was taken into custody by Chinese authorities. The Chinese F-8 jet involved in the collision crashed into the sea. The Chinese government and media immediately transformed the missing pilot, Wang Wei, into a national hero who had sacrificed his life for the motherland. As Chinese anti-American sentiment reached fever pitch, expressed, among other ways, in vituperative postings on Chinese Internet chat rooms, Beijing demanded that Washington admit responsibility for the incident and offer a public apology before it would release the sequestered crew members. American public opinion was equally incensed. After a shaky start, Chinese and American officials eventually agreed on a carefully worded official U.S. statement whose linguistic legerdemain enabled Beijing to claim it was an American apology and Washington to deny that it was anything of the sort. After 11 days of detention, the crew was released in good condition, and the disassembled U.S. plane, which Chinese intelligence officers had carefully examined, was eventually returned to its home base. Tempers abated, but many Chinese criticized their government for caving in to the Americans.

Later in April Beijing again had occasion to censure Washington for President Bush's decision to supply Taiwan with many, though not all, of the items on its high-tech military shopping list deemed necessary to preserve a rough military balance of power across the Taiwan Strait in the face of Beijing's military modernization and offensive ballistic-missile buildup. Speaking extemporaneously, President Bush said the U.S. "would do whatever it took" to defend Taiwan, although his advisers quickly asserted that there had been no change in the U.S. policy of strategic ambiguity regarding what Washington would do in the event of a Chinese attack on the island, which Beijing claimed as its inalienable territory. In an August interview with executives of the *New York Times,* President Jiang tried to defuse tension by speaking soothingly of the bright prospects for good relations with the U.S. Following the September 11 terrorist attacks, China expressed condolences and offered verbal support to the U.S.-led antiterrorist coalition. The reduction or elimination of Islamic fundamentalist terror networks in Central Asia would help ease Beijing's worries regarding the vast northwestern province of Xinjiang, where small groups of Uighur militants, supported from across the border, had challenged Chinese power.

These ups and downs in Sino-American relations bracketed a major Chinese effort to consolidate its relations with Russia. Beijing and Moscow shared a common strategic interest in containing the further extension of American power, and China was Russia's largest customer for high-performance Russian military aircraft and other equipment. At a summit meeting in Moscow in July, Jiang and Russian Pres. Vladimir Putin signed a new "strategic partnership" that fell well short of a military alliance but nevertheless enhanced cooperation between the two countries. Among other things, Russia agreed to sell China 38 SU-30 ground attack fighters worth $2 billion. (STEVEN I. LEVINE)

COLOMBIA

Area: 1,141,568 sq km (440,762 sq mi)
Population (2001 est.): 43,071,000
Capital: Santafé de Bogotá, D.C.
Head of state and government: President Andrés Pastrana Arango

During 2001 real change in Colombia appeared tantalizingly close on a variety of fronts, but in every instance only incremental gains were made or the prospects for progress vanished altogether. Observers gave the government of Pres. Andrés Pastrana Arango high marks on international relations, foreign commerce, and modernization of the armed forces. On the other hand, there were plenty of disappointments in the form of unproductive negotiations with guerrillas, government corruption, and weak economic performance. Political reform was dashed in Congress. The administration had pushed several ideas, including campaign finance reform, the use of roll-call votes in Congress (to increase transparency), the end to intraparty competition in general elections (to make party labels more meaningful), and tougher punishments for corruption. Opponents of reform watered down proposals until they were considered a waste of time.

The government continued to negotiate with the two major guerrilla groups, the Revolutionary Armed Forces of Colombia (FARC) and the National Liberation Army (ELN). One positive note was a prisoner exchange in June between the government and the FARC in which the guerrillas released a far larger number of police and soldiers than had been expected—363 in exchange for 15 guerrillas. The FARC, however, pointed out that the estimated 1,000–1,500 guerrillas who had been guarding these prisoners were now free to return to fighting. A disturbing development in the conflict was the increased use of urban bombings. Despite the prisoner release, talks between the government and the FARC moved very slowly. In addition, the likelihood for success of a proposed six-month cease-fire (part of a plan developed by a "commission of notables") seemed dim.

In August talks with the ELN broke down completely after the government refused to grant the group a demilitarized safe haven in the department of Bolívar (the FARC already had a far larger zone in the southeastern part of the country). The ELN's demand had been opposed vociferously by local residents who received prompting from right-wing paramilitary units, the United Self-Defense Forces of Colombia. The government's resolve was also bolstered by the belief in some circles of the military that the group could be defeated militarily. There was some speculation that shunning of the ELN's demand and the breakdown of talks would lead the group to step up its violent activities to reinforce the sense that it was a force with which to be reckoned.

Fits and starts on negotiations coincided with a series of indications that an escalation of combat was likely. The guerrillas showed no sign of getting out of the kidnapping business, and they displayed their resolve to use bombings to open up the urban front of their conflict. For its part, despite concerns that the way was being cleared for human rights abuses, the government adopted a Law of National Security and Defense that increased the military's power to adjudicate in issues surrounding the conflict and gave the president power to expedite an antiterrorism statute and regulation of the "theatres of operations." Implementation of Plan Colombia, a U.S.-supported effort to counteract the drug trade (and the guerrillas), got under way in earnest. Dusting of drug crops with weed killer was temporarily suspended, however, owing to legal challenges based on a lack of study regarding its unintended effects on humans, livestock, nondrug crops, and the environment generally.

After a recession in 1999, the modest growth achieved in 2000 was expected to continue in 2001 at a rate of 3% or less. Private investment was slow to recover after the recession, and the banking industry remained particularly weak. Oil and coal sectors looked strong, but they were dominated by foreign investors. Coffee, on the other hand, continued to struggle. (BRIAN F. CRISP)

A Colombian special forces policeman takes aim during a raid against guerrilla forces in the city of Barrancabermeja on March 3.

COMOROS

Area: 1,862 sq km (719 sq mi), excluding the 375-sq-km (145-sq-mi) island of Mayotte, a de facto dependency of France since 1976
Population (2001 est.): 566,000 (excluding 159,000 on Mayotte)
Capital: Moroni
Chief of state and head of government: Col. Azali Assoumani

The crisis brought about by the island of Anjouan's secession from the Comoros federation continued throughout 2001. Organization of African Unity (OAU) envoy José Francisco Madeira Caetano led intensive talks that produced a reconciliation agreement. Federal and Anjouan government officials, as well as opposition parties, signed the agreement on February 17. It provided greater autonomy for individual island governments but reserved defense and foreign policy for the national government. In March the reconciliation process stalled amid disputes over the composition of a committee to implement the agreement provisions. The OAU reaffirmed its commitment to ending the secession and vowed to maintain economic sanctions to this end.

On August 9 soldiers on Anjouan deposed the island's ruler, Lieut. Col. Said Abeid Abdermane. The three-member military committee that took power cited Abdermane's alleged corruption and the government's failure to pay soldiers and civil servants. By August 28 the coup leaders had nominated chief of the gendarmerie Cmdr. Mohamed Bacar as head of state. In early November Abdermane attempted to retake power but was defeated by forces loyal to Bacar. In a referendum on December 23, 77% of voters backed a new constitution that would grant increased autony to the three Indian Ocean states that made up the country but keep them part of the federation.

The economy continued to struggle despite the World Bank's approval of an $11.4 million credit in March for improving basic infrastructure.

(MATTHEW A. CENZER)

CONGO, DEMOCRATIC REPUBLIC OF THE

Area: 2,344,858 sq km (905,354 sq mi)
Population (2001 est.): 53,625,000 (including 1998–2001 war deaths approaching 3 million in eastern DRC [mostly from starvation, disease, and deprivation] and an unknown figure in the western DRC)
Capital: Kinshasa (executive and ministerial); Lubumbashi (legislative from August 2000)
Head of state and government: Presidents Laurent-Désiré Kabila and, from January 17 (acting until January 26), Joseph Kabila

On Jan. 16, 2001, Pres. Laurent-Désiré Kabila was shot and killed, reportedly by a bodyguard. (*See* OBITUARIES.) The circumstances of his death were unclear, but there were few signs of regret even among his political allies. A report released on May 23 by the chief state prosecutor concluded that the assassination was part of an attempted coup involving Uganda, Rwanda, and rebel Congolese—a claim immediately denied by all parties.

Officials quickly announced that Kabila's son, Joseph, would succeed his father. Joseph Kabila, who had been born and brought up in Tanzania, proved a successful guerrilla commander in the campaign that had brought his father to power, but he spoke neither French nor Lingala, the language of the inhabitants of Kinshasa and the surrounding region. (*See* BIOGRAPHIES.)

His first actions impressed Western observers. He had a cordial meeting with Pres. Paul Kagame of Rwanda and between January and March undertook a round of visits to Brussels, Paris, Berlin, London, and Washington, D.C. At a meeting of the signatories of the Lusaka Accord in the Zambian capital on February 15, he also expressed his willingness to negotiate directly with the rebels.

At home one of his first significant decisions was to pay the salary arrears of his army. On April 4 Kabila dismissed the corrupt cabinet members appointed by his father, replacing them 10 days later with men who appeared better qualified to direct the country's affairs. With inflation running at 500%, he also set about reorganizing the economy. He revoked a much-criticized monopoly awarded by his father to Israel's International Diamond Industries and renegotiated concessions to work some of the country's copper and cobalt resources. On May 27 Jean-Claude Masangu, governor of the central bank, announced that the currency would be allowed to float with an opening rate of 315 Congolese francs (FC) to the U.S. dollar instead of the hitherto official rate of FC 50. Masangu also removed price controls on fuel, allowing the cost to rise from the unrealistic FC 70 to FC 280 per litre.

Kabila had made an early promise of free elections, and on May 4 government representatives met with leaders of three main rebel groups in Lusaka and signed a declaration containing 14 principles that would form the basis for an Inter-Congolese National Dialogue. The opening phase of the dialogue took place in Botswana in August, and a full meeting was convened in the Ethiopian capital, Addis Ababa, on October 15. The meeting broke up after a week without any progress being made, but it was proposed that it should reassemble, probably in South Africa, on Jan. 28, 2002.

On the eastern front there were signs that Uganda and Rwanda were beginning to withdraw their troops. A UN Security Council resolution of June 15, while welcoming the apparent cease-fire in the region, called upon all foreign governments to accelerate the total withdrawal of their forces.

(KENNETH INGHAM)

Military officials escort the coffin of slain DRC president Laurent-Désiré Kabila from the People's Palace in Kinshasa on January 23.

AP/Wide World Photos

CONGO, REPUBLIC OF THE

Area: 342,000 sq km (132,047 sq mi)
Population (2001 est.): 2,894,000
Capital: Brazzaville
Head of state and government: President Denis Sassou-Nguesso

The search for national reconciliation continued during 2001 following the ravages of the 1997 civil war, in which an estimated 20,000 people perished. Nevertheless, opposition parties boycotted the first phase of inter-Congolese talks launched on March 22 by Pres. Denis Sassou-Nguesso and mediated by Gabonese Pres. Omar Bongo. The government announced four days later that regional assemblies had approved a draft constitution as a first step in the restoration of the democratic process. Representatives of political parties, including some opposition groups, community leaders, and members of the government, attended the second round of the peace conference, which opened on April 10. Although the conference ended with a symbolic burning of 800 rifles, its success was marred by the absence of deposed former president Pascal Lissouba and former prime minister Bernard Kolelas. The latter, sentenced to death in absentia in April 2000, was threatened with arrest if he returned to participate. Constitutional Minister Martin Mberi, in the cabinet since 1977 and a close associate of Lissouba, resigned on May 8; he criticized the draft constitution for placing too much personal power in the hands of the president. The parliament adopted the draft constitution on September 2, and the nation was expected to vote on it in January 2002. If the referendum was approved, presidential and legislative elections would follow. Sixty-four refugees from the civil war returned from Gabon to Brazzaville on August 7, but an estimated 14,000 people still remained in self-imposed exile there.

Despite an increase in public debt, fueled by loss of revenues through evasion of customs duties and poor management of oil revenues, the government achieved a level of economic growth. On May 18 the European Union (EU), citing its support for Congo's efforts to restore civil stability and democracy, resumed economic aid to the country. The EU granted Congo €41.3 million (about $37.1 million) for humanitarian and development projects. The World Bank announced on May 10 that Congo, having repaid all outstanding service charges on loans, would once again be eligible for development credits.

(NANCY ELLEN LAWLER)

COSTA RICA

Area: 51,100 sq km (19,730 sq mi)
Population (2001 est.): 3,936,000
Capital: San José
Head of state and government: President Miguel Ángel Rodríguez Echeverría

Because national elections were set to take place in early February 2002, both of the two main political parties in Costa Rica spent much of the first half of 2001 gearing up for what proved to be hotly contested primary elections. The National Liberation Party (PLN) held its primary on June 3, with some 250,000 party members casting their ballots. Rolando Araya Monge won handily over his opponents José Miguel Corrales Bolaños and Antonio Álvarez Desanti. Corrales, who was making his third run for the presidency and who had been the party's losing candidate in the 1998 presidential election, declared that this was his last attempt. Araya, a nephew of Luis Alberto Monge Álvarez, who had served as president of Costa Rica from 1982 to 1986, emerged from the core of the traditional PLN leadership and had the support of the party standard-bearer, former president and Nobel laureate Oscar Arias Sánchez.

On June 10 the Social Christian Unity Party nominated Abel Pacheco de la Espriella by an overwhelming margin. Pacheco hoped to continue his party's grip on the presidency, but he was well aware that there was a long tradition of alternation in power between the two leading parties. Thus, he would have to work very hard to prevail against Araya.

Of major concern to voters was the sharp decline in the growth rate, which was estimated to end in 2001 at about 3%. A growth spurt created by the opening of a large Intel computer-chip production plant in the late 1990s had increased exports but had not had the spillover into the larger economy that had been anticipated. One major drag on the economy was the decline in world coffee prices to their lowest level in seven years. Inflation had been running at 10% annually, among the highest in Latin America, but there was some good economic news as Costa Rica signed a trade pact with Canada in April.

(MITCHELL A. SELIGSON)

CÔTE D'IVOIRE

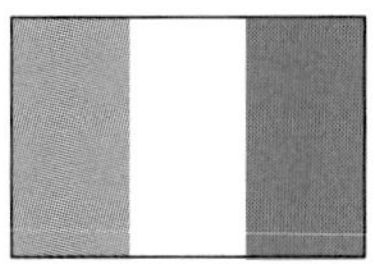

Area: 322,463 sq km (124,504 sq mi)
Population (2001 est.): 16,393,000
Seats of government: predominantly Abidjan; some ministries have relocated to Yamoussoukro
Chief of state: President Laurent Gbagbo
Head of government: Prime Minister Affi N'Guessan

Political turmoil continued throughout 2001 in a nation that had once been hailed as a model of stability and tolerance. On January 7 disaffected soldiers occupied radio and television stations in the capital as part of an apparent military coup. Troops loyal to the government, however, regained control of the city after a night of heavy fighting, in which an unknown number of people were killed. Migrant traders were attacked on January 10 following accusations by the government that unnamed bordering countries had backed the coup. Thousands of foreigners, who make up an estimated 40% of the Ivorian population, fled the city. Opposition leader Alassane Ouattara's Rally of Republicans (RDR) denied any part in the coup. The government's refusal, however, to allow the northern politician to run in the October 2000 presidential election or the January 2001 parliamentary elections (presumably over doubts about his Ivorian nationality) led to a series of protests in which more than 200 people lost their lives. In the parliamentary elections the ruling Ivorian Popular Front (FPI), aided by the electoral boycott by the RDR, won a majority of seats. On January 22, in what was seen as a gesture of reconciliation, the parliament elected former finance minister Mamadou Koulibaly, also a northerner, as its speaker. In regional elections held on March 24–25, Ouattara's RDR won control of 64 local councils, the former ruling Democratic Party (PDCI-RDA) another 60, and the FPI 34.

On August 3 eight policemen were acquitted of the massacre of 57 civilians in the aftermath of the 2000 presidential elections. President Gbagbo proposed broad-based reconciliation talks between Ivorian political leaders past and present but they were postponed from September. In November Quattara returned from a year in self-imposed exile to take part in the rescheduled forum.

On April 5 secondary-school teachers ended a three-day strike over pay and working conditions. The following day police closed all campuses of the University of Abidjan after battles between two rival student unions, one backing the RDR and the other the FPI, resulted in one death and many injuries. The prospect of yet another voided year for higher education impelled the two factions to sign an agreement on May 14; they pledged to discontinue all demonstrations on university grounds.

Abuses of migrant child labourers who were sold into virtual slavery to cocoa farmers in Côte d'Ivoire captured headlines around the world. Traffickers in children were arrested in Benin, Burkina Faso, and Gabon. It was estimated that more than 15,000 children from Mali alone were working on

Issouf Sanogo/AFP Worldwide

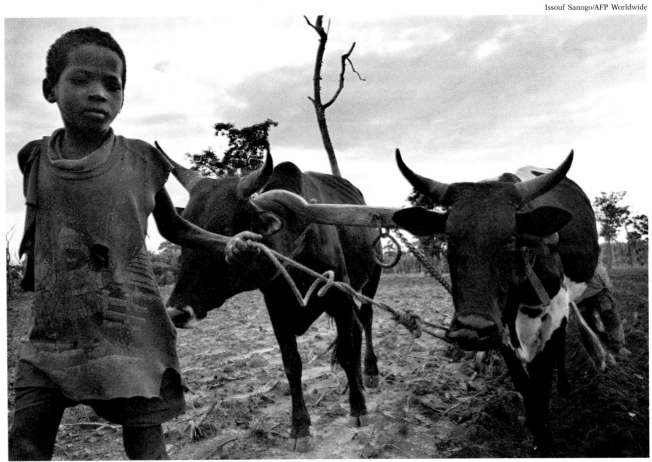

Child labour was an important issue throughout West Africa in 2001; here, a youngster works on a cocoa farm in Côte d'Ivoire on June 12.

Ivorian cocoa farms. On May 4 the government accused multinational chocolate companies of keeping cocoa prices low, a factor that would lead impoverished farmers to use slave labour.

(NANCY ELLEN LAWLER)

CROATIA

Area: 56,542 sq km (21,831 sq mi)
Population (2001 est.): 4,393,000
Capital: Zagreb
Chief of state: President Stipe Mesic
Head of government: Prime Minister Ivica Racan

Croatia's six-party governing coalition frayed in 2001, revealing deep division over both the country's role during the violent breakup of former Yugoslavia and the government's inability to invigorate a moribund economy.

On December 5 Parliament approved the Stabilization and Association Agreement, putting the country on track to possible future membership in the European Union. Croatia's relationship with the United Nations International Criminal Tribunal for the Former Yugoslavia dominated foreign policy, however. Two senior military officers, Gen. Ante Gotovina and Gen. Rahim Ademi, were indicted by the tribunal on June 8 for alleged crimes against ethnic Serbs committed during military campaigns in the mid-1990s to recover seized territories. The indictments sparked outrage among Croatian veteran groups, opposition parties, coalition members, and others who considered the officers war heroes. Prime Minister Ivica Racan, an advocate of cooperation with the court, criticized the indictment for its factual errors and reliance on indirect responsibility. In May Croatia had been the first Eastern European country to ratify the International Criminal Court Treaty.

The ensuing political fracas forced Racan to call an emergency session of the parliament. The government decision to deliver both generals to The Hague prompted Drazen Budisa, leader of the centre-right Croatian Social-Liberal Party (HSLS)—the Social Democratic Party of Croatia's junior ruling partner—to resign his post as party head. Though the coalition survived a no-confidence vote on July 15, Budisa's resignation emboldened local HSLS leaders to seek coalitions with the opposition Croatian Democratic Union (HDZ), the party displaced by the coalition two years earlier. Many considered this a prelude to a possible HSLS-HDZ-led centre-right bloc. The indictment in September of Serbian strongman Slobodan Milosevic for war crimes in Croatia and another against four Serbian senior military officers in October for the shelling of Dubrovnik did little to allay public distrust of the tribunal.

Nationwide local elections on May 20 revealed growing public dissatisfaction with government underperformance;

the country had an unemployment rate of 22% and an economy that was growing at a rate of only about 3%. Voter turnout was low, but the coalition won 15 of 20 county governments as well as the capital city, Zagreb. Voters gave more than a quarter of their votes to the nationalist HDZ, confirming it as still the country's largest party. On June 4 the regional Istrian Democratic Party left the coalition after it failed to gain coalition support for a controversial law that would make Italian the second official language in the province. On March 28 Parliament's lower house abolished the upper House of Counties.

Tourism revenues were one of the few economic bright spots, approaching prebreakup levels with $4 billion in revenues, a 14% increase. Deutsche Telekom purchased 16% of Croatian Telecom, giving it a 51% majority stake and bringing the Croatian government €500 million (about $425 million) in revenues. This deal was an exception to the general reluctance to sell even uneconomical parastatals to foreigners. With limited revenues from privatization and taxes, the government faced chronic budget deficits and was forced to make unpopular cuts in social spending and public-sector salaries and dismiss state employees. Reform of the bankrupt pension system stayed on track, however, as preparations went forward for the introduction of mandatory private pension funds.

Croatian sports figures helped counter the widespread national malaise. On March 11 Janica Kostelic took the World Cup in women's skiing. Tennis star Goran Ivanisevic received a hero's welcome from 100,000 fans in his hometown of Split after winning at Wimbledon. (MAX PRIMORAC)

CUBA

Area: 110,861 sq km (42,804 sq mi)
Population (2001 est.): 11,190,000
Capital: Havana
Head of state and government: President of the Council of State and President of the Council of Ministers Fidel Castro Ruz

In 2001 intense speculation about who would become Cuba's next head of state dominated both the domestic and international fronts after 74-year-old Pres. Fidel Castro Ruz suffered a fainting spell in late June. Though Cuban authorities claimed the aging ruler was in good health, there were some signs of planning for a post-Castro transition. Among the candidates who could take major roles in a new government were First Vice Pres. Gen. Raúl Castro Ruz, who was also Fidel's brother and his most likely successor; the Council of State vice president, Carlos Lage Dávila; and the president of the National Assembly, Ricardo Alarcón de Quesada.

Owing to its internal politics, Cuba remained isolated from important international events in 2001. It was the only country in the Americas not invited to the third Summit of the Americas in Quebec City. President Castro claimed the U.S. would use the Summit to co-opt its neighbours into signing a trade deal at unfavourable terms. He used his time at home for high-profile celebrations marking the 40th anniversary of the defeat of the Bay of Pigs invasion. Despite tense relations with most of Latin America, Cuba consolidated its friendship with Venezuelan Pres. Hugo Chávez Frías. After signing an oil accord at favourable terms for Cuba in October 2000, the two countries participated in a series of cultural, scientific, and academic exchanges.

The George W. Bush administration's nominations of anti-Castro exiles to high-level government posts led to increased friction between the two countries, despite the fact that Bush continued former president Bill Clinton's practice of waiving the controversial Title III of the 1996 Helms-Burton Act. The act would have allowed Americans to seek damages against foreign companies that benefited from confiscated property in Cuba. In July the Bush administration also oversaw new regulations that would allow limited agricultural sales to Cuba for the first time in the nearly 40-year embargo. In November four American companies signed deals to supply food to replenish Cuba's food stocks in the wake of Hurricane Michelle, which had killed five people earlier that month. The deals were made on a one-time basis only.

The Cuban economy grew for the seventh consecutive year despite high oil-import prices and a low sugar output. Real gross domestic product (GDP) growth for 2000 was 5.6%. Early estimates for GDP growth in 2001 varied from 3.5% to 5% for the year. A 13% decline in the 2000–01 sugar harvest due to economic inefficiencies as well as a severe drought, coupled with an increasing foreign-trade deficit, made it unlikely that the year's GDP would come close to the government's target of 5%. The government was also disappointed by the decision of Brazilian state oil company Petrobrás to pull out of oil exploration in Cuba after it discovered an offshore well that came up dry. Producing domestic oil was a major goal of the Cuban government, which now imported two-thirds of the island's energy needs.

Tourism, the main engine of the economy for the past five years and one of the biggest earners of hard currency (along with remittances), had trouble

AP/Wide World Photos

A new hotel in Havana nears completion on January 5.

earning double-digit growth in 2001. Though authorities expected a total of two million tourists, a strong dollar in the middle of the year made travel for Europeans more expensive. Finally, though the full effect had yet to be determined, the September 11 terrorist attacks in the U.S. were expected to affect tourism negatively in general, as people were more wary of airplane travel. Cuban authorities, recognizing that government regulation of the tourism industry had been inefficient, announced in 2001 that all new high-end hotels would be managed in partnership with foreign companies.

International human rights organizations as well as press-freedom organizations continued to condemn Cuba's record on free speech and harassment of dissidents. In its report for 2000, Amnesty International noted that hundreds of people remained imprisoned for political offenses and that critics of the government were subject to "short term detention, house arrest, threats and harassment." The government claimed that limited repression was justified to maintain national unity against the U.S. embargo. (SANDRA A. GROSSMAN)

Louisa Gouliamaki/AFP Worldwide

Escorted by Greek Pres. Konstantinos Stephanopoulos (far left), Cypriot Pres. Glafcos Clerides (centre, forefront) reviews an honour guard in Athens on May 2.

CYPRUS

Area: 9,251 sq km (3,572 sq mi) for the entire island; the area of the Turkish Republic of Northern Cyprus (TRNC), proclaimed unilaterally (1983) in the occupied northern third of the island, 3,355 sq km (1,295 sq mi)
Population (2001 est.): island 873,000; TRNC only, 198,000 (including recent Turkish settlers and Turkish military)
Capital: Lefkosia/Lefkosa (also known as Nicosia)
Head(s) of state and government: President Glafcos Clerides; of the TRNC, President Rauf Denktash

Greek Cyprus reported in 2001 that it had provisionally completed two-thirds of the accession requirements for European Union (EU) membership. Completion of the requirements was expected in 2002, with full membership in 2004. The EU planned to provide significant economic support for the transition. While the EU was prepared to accept Greek Cyprus despite partition, the issue added complication to the island's already-complex situation. In May parliamentary elections in the Greek sector, the socialist Progressive Party of the Working People (AKEL) secured the largest number of seats—20 of the 56 seats, up from 19. Pres. Glafcos Clerides's Democratic Rally dropped from 20 seats to 19.

While the island saw little violence in 2001, tension continued. In May the European Court of Human Rights found Turkey guilty of human rights violations when it invaded northern Cyprus in 1974, a finding rejected by both Turkey and Turkish Cyprus. After a pause lasting more than a year, Clerides and Turkish-Cypriot Pres. Rauf Denktash met on December 4 under UN auspices and agreed to resume negotiations in early 2002.

Moved by environmental and health concerns, about 1,000 Greek Cypriots protested construction of a 190-m (about 620-ft) radio antenna on the British Sovereign Base at Akrotiri. The incident left some 40 people injured and caused more than £300,000 (about $430,000) in damage. A later survey found that the antenna met EU standards, and the issue was somewhat defused.

Turkish Cypriot bank failures in 2000 were joined by a 2001 economic crisis in Turkey, resulting in serious inflation and currency devaluation. The per capita gross national product (GNP) of Turkish Cyprus was less than a third of that of the Greek sector. By contrast, the Greek Cypriot economy was solid, with 4.5% GNP growth and unemployment of approximately 3.3% expected in 2001. Tourist arrivals increased more than 5%. Perhaps more important, a second desalination plant opened, with removal of all restrictions on the water supply. (GEORGE H. KELLING)

CZECH REPUBLIC

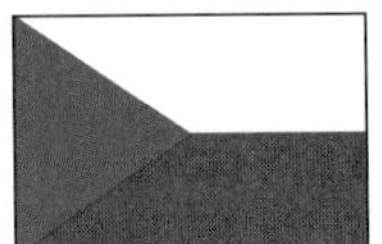

Area: 78,866 sq km (30,450 sq mi)
Population (2001 est.): 10,269,000
Capital: Prague
Chief of state: President Vaclav Havel
Head of government: Prime Minister Milos Zeman

Czech political life was not without conflict but was relatively stable in 2001, while the economy improved considerably. The country continued to be ruled by a minority Czech Social Democratic Party (CSSD) government, which had been in power since the June 1998 elections, thanks to that party's power-sharing "opposition agreement" with its rival, the Civic Democratic Party (ODS). The CSSD and ODS frequently bickered in public, but they often managed to agree in private.

Two government ministers left office in 2001; Finance Minister Pavel Mertlik was replaced by Jiri Rusnok in April, while Jaroslav Tvrdik took over from Vladimir Vetchy as defense minister in May. Mertlik resigned over his frustration at having failed to persuade the government to carry out his privatization and fiscal-reform plans. Vetchy was replaced because of alleged financial mismanagement, and Tvrdik set out to professionalize the army and abolish compulsory military service. Leadership changes also took place within several key parties. As expected, Vladimir Spidla was chosen CSSD chairman at the party's congress in early April, taking over from Prime Minister Milos Zeman. Changes also took place in the leadership of the opposition Quad Coalition (4K) as well as of the two major parties within that group, the Christian Democrat Union–Czech People's Party (KDU-CSL) and the Freedom Union (US). Cyril Svoboda was elected KDU-CSL chairman in May, while Hana Marvanova was chosen US leader in June, becoming the first woman to head a Czech parliamentary party.

In late January the Constitutional Court struck down elements of a controversial electoral reform bill that the CSSD and ODS had hoped would push small parties out of the parliament by raising the threshold. The court upheld a provision obliging coalitions to obtain at least 5% of the vote for each of its member parties, a requirement apparently aimed at the 4K. As a result, the extraparliamentary Democratic Union decided in early December to merge with the US as of January 1, 2002, thereby reducing the coalition's required vote from 20% to 15%.

The ruling parties started the year in a poor position as a wave of public protests continued over the appointment of Jiri Hodac as head of the state-owned Czech Television in December 2000. The resulting drop in support was especially apparent in the case of the ODS, the party with which Hodac was associated. Although the 4K topped popularity polls in the first months of 2001, internal squabbling over personnel and the coalition's future direction sent its public support down. Many polls later in the year put the 4K, CSSD, and ODS at approximately equal levels, with the Communists farther behind.

An issue that drew considerable attention in 2001 was the decision of British immigration officials in July to check passengers at Prague's Ruzyne airport before they boarded flights to London. That step was taken because Great Britain had faced an increasing inflow of Czech Roma (Gypsies) seeking asylum, and the CSSD viewed the immigration checks as preferable to the imposition of visas for Czech citizens. Critics argued that the Czech government was caving in to British demands and failing to defend the right of Czech citizens to travel abroad.

The biggest economic problem faced by the Czech Republic in 2001 related to fiscal reform, and the CSSD appeared unconcerned about the rising budget deficit and soaring public debt. Following Mertlik's departure, economic policy took a more leftist direction, led by Rusnok and Industry and Trade Minister Miroslav Gregr, who replaced Mertlik as deputy prime minister for economy. In July the cabinet approved a scaled-down version of Gregr's "big bang" plan; the new plan would devote more than $4 billion over two years to bail out of struggling industries and support transport and housing construction.

By early December the Czech Republic had closed 22 of 31 chapters of the *acquis communautaire*, the body of legislation needed for membership in the European Union. The country hoped to become a full EU member by early 2004. The Czechs were forced to compromise on the free movement of people chapter after Germany and Austria proposed a seven-year moratorium for new EU members, a move that was perceived by Czechs as an attempt to make their country a second-class member of the European Union. Tensions also mounted between the Czech Republic and Austria over the Temelin nuclear power plant near Ceske Budejovice. The two countries reached a historic agreement on November 29, however. While Prague vowed to introduce stricter safety measures, Vienna promised not to block Czech negotiations with the EU on the energy chapter of the *acquis communautaire*.

(SHARON FISHER)

DENMARK

Area: 43,096 sq km (16,639 sq mi)
Population (2001 est.): 5,358,000
Capital: Copenhagen
Chief of state: Queen Margrethe II
Head of government: Prime Ministers Poul Nyrup Rasmussen and, from November 27, Anders Fogh Rasmussen

The issue of immigration topped the agenda in Denmark in 2001. The country's impeccable record as a bastion of democracy, human rights, and egalitarianism was tarnished by a barrage of international criticism that cited racial intolerance and maltreatment of asylum seekers amid an atmosphere of growing xenophobia at home. Government plans, though later scrapped after much furor, to confine asylum seekers on remote islands while their applications were being processed, coupled with the revelation that many would-be immigrants were being housed in container homes (albeit well-appointed), further dented Denmark's reputation abroad. In addition, fewer than 5% of Denmark's population were foreigners, and most of that figure represented citizens from European Union (EU) states or the U.S.; there were only about 165,000 Muslims in the country.

The prevailing trepidation among many Danes about their country's becoming a multiethnic society and fears that their culture or "Danishness" were threatened helped anti-immigration groups gain a foothold, notably the xenophobic Danish People's Party (DF) led by Pia Kjaersgaard. The DF—campaigning on a direct anti-Muslim, anti-foreigner platform—made solid progress in opinion polls and forced other parties, including the ruling Social Democrats and the main opposition Liberals, to adopt tougher stances on immigration. Taxes and dwindling welfare services were the other main themes of a short and bitter campaign, which ended as predicted with a landslide victory for the Liberal Party of Anders Fogh Rasmussen. The Liberals, with the support of the Conservatives and centrist and rightist groups, won 98 seats in Folketing (parliament); the Social Democrats and the centre-left bloc garnered 77 seats, down from the 89 held in the previous parliament. On

© Stefan Lindblom HBG-BILD/Corbis Sygma

Anders Fogh Rasmussen and his wife, Anne-Mette, celebrate the victory of Rasmussen's Liberal Party in Denmark's national elections on November 20.

November 27 Anders Fogh Rasmussen announced that he would head a Liberal-Conservative minority-rightist coalition government, which called for a major tightening of immigration laws, cuts in overseas development aid, an income-tax freeze, improvements in hospital services and social welfare, tougher law-and-order provisions, and a reduction by half of Denmark's $70 billion gross public debt by 2002.

On the economic front, Denmark's historic "no" vote in 2000 to participation in the European Economic and Monetary Union did not have the predicted damaging effect—unemployment hit its lowest level in 25 years; inflation was moderate; the krone currency remained firm; and foreign trade and current account surpluses stayed buoyant. A draft budget for 2002 showed a surplus in state finances for the sixth consecutive year amid forecasts that Denmark would not be as hard hit by the world economic downturn as some of its neighbours.

Following the September terrorist attacks in the U.S., the Danish government pledged to take action to abolish Denmark's exemptions from joint defense and legal cooperation within the EU, citing the need for closer international efforts to fight terrorism.

Relations between Denmark and the Faroe Islands remained strained following the postponement in the spring of a planned local referendum on the issue of independence. Prime Minister Poul Nyrup Rasmussen had threatened to cut off Copenhagen's annual $120 million grant to the islands, about one-third of Faroese public expenditure. Undeterred by this development and the inconclusive results from the first test drillings for oil off the islands, the Faroese home-rule government announced plans to phase out Danish aid and influence gradually, starting in 2002. (CHRISTOPHER FOLLETT)

DJIBOUTI

Area: 23,200 sq km (8,950 sq mi)
Population (2001 est.): 461,000 (excluding an unknown number of refugees)
Capital: Djibouti
Chief of state and head of government: President Ismail Omar Guelleh, assisted by Prime Ministers Barkat Gourad Hamadou and, from March 4, Dileita Muhammad Dileita

In February 2001 Prime Minister Barkat Gourad Hamadou, who had served in the post since 1978, resigned for health reasons. On March 4 Pres. Ismael Omar Guelleh named Dileita Muhammad Dileita, a senior civil servant and Djibouti's ambassador to Ethiopia, as the new prime minister.

In May the government concluded a peace agreement with the radical wing of the Front for the Restoration of Unity and Democracy (FRUD). This group had battled on behalf of the Afar ethnic group after FRUD moderates had reached an accord with the government. Although details of the agreement were not announced, FRUD leader Ahmad Dini Ahmad talked about decentralization, the establishment of local governance councils, and recognition of more political parties. The disarmament of FRUD fighters and a ceremonial destruction of weapons followed in June. In July President Guelleh formed the second government of his six-year term. To the surprise of many observers, the 20-member cabinet omitted representatives from FRUD's radical wing.

Throughout the year Djibouti suffered from drought. In addition, by September Djibouti's towns had absorbed nearly 100,000 refugees, including migrants from neighbouring countries. The influx strained Djibouti's urban infrastructure. The UN World Food Programme announced a relief package, including 11,000 tons of supplies. To add to the country's woes, various missions from the International Monetary Fund and the European Union criticized the government for its growing debt.

In December the country hosted a high-level German delegation to discuss stationing German troops in Djibouti. These forces would support the U.S.-led campaign against terrorism.

(MATTHEW A. CENZER)

DOMINICA

Area: 750 sq km (290 sq mi)
Population (2001 est.): 71,700
Capital: Roseau
Chief of state: President Vernon Shaw
Head of government: Prime Minister Pierre Charles

Dominica Prime Minister Pierre Charles told the parliament in April 2001 that the preliminary findings of an inquiry into allegations of corruption against the former United Workers Party (UWP) government had shown "clear prima facie evidence" that the UWP had engaged in "illegal and unethical conduct" while in office. Opposition leader Edison James made no immediate response to the statement.

Acknowledging the uncertain long-term future of the country's main export crop, bananas, the government in May agreed to provide EC$4 million (about U.S. $1.4 million) in soft loans to help local farmers rehabilitate or replant their banana holdings. Banana production had fallen by 23.5% in 2000.

Dominica fell in line with the rest of the Caribbean in June when it stiffened its money-laundering legislation to permit more wide-ranging inspection by the supervisory authority. Despite these efforts, Dominica remained on the Paris-based Financial Action Task Force's list of "uncooperative" countries.

Dominica came under pressure in July from the International Monetary Fund to tighten government expenditure and find ways to boost revenues. The IMF proposed the introduction of a value-added tax, restraint in wage increases, and a hike in fuel prices; the government categorically rejected the latter measure. (DAVID RENWICK)

DOMINICAN REPUBLIC

Area: 48,671 sq km (18,792 sq mi)
Population (2001 est.): 8,693,000
Capital: Santo Domingo
Head of state and government: President Hipólito Mejía Dominguez

Within a few months of the inauguration of Pres. Hipólito Mejía Dominguez in August 2000, the relatively smooth waters upon which the Dominican Republic had been sailing turned choppy. After the start of 2001, gross domestic product growth projections dropped close to zero, reflecting the downturn in the U.S. economy, the temporary shutdown of the Falconbridge nickel plant, and softening tourism figures. The September 11 terrorist attacks in the U.S. inflicted further damage on the tourism industry, a principal source of foreign exchange and employment growth in the Dominican Republic. Partial recovery from the impact of the attacks suffered a setback with the November 12 crash in New York City of a Santo Domingo-bound passenger aircraft. (*See* DISASTERS.)

Disillusionment with Mejía's administration set in. His extravagant campaign promises looked hollow. No structured program for poverty reduction appeared, nor for problems of infant mortality and low literacy. The misery quotient in the traditional sugar-producing areas and the regions bordering Haiti remained acutely high. Mejía promised transparency in public administration but was unable to reconcile his commitment with the pent-up appetite for patronage by his Dominican Revolutionary Party supporters after 16 years out of power. The leading opposition contender, the Dominican Liberation Party, defeated by Mejía in 2000, positioned itself strongly for municipal and congressional elections scheduled for May 2002. Although good news for the government was sparse, patchwork progress was made toward solving the country's chronic power outages, a few holes in the porous income tax regime were filled, and falling oil prices provided some solace.

Recognizing that poverty and environmental degradation required Hispaniola-wide solutions, Mejía gave priority to improving relations with Haiti and asked international donors to examine the challenge through this lens. In November Juan Bosch died; he was the country's first democratically elected president. (*See* OBITUARIES.)

(JOHN W. GRAHAM)

ECUADOR

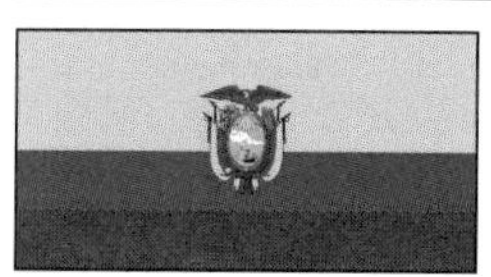

Area: 272,045 sq km (105,037 sq mi), including the 8,010-sq-km (3,093-sq-mi) Galápagos Islands
Population (2001 est.): 12,879,000 (Galápagos Islands, about 17,000)
Capital: Quito
Chief of state and head of government: President Gustavo Noboa Bejarano

Armed conflict in Colombia, Ecuador's northern neighbour, spilled across the border in 2001. The Ecuadoran army discovered several abandoned training camps set up by leftist Colombian guerrillas, as well as jungle laboratories for producing cocaine. In January right-wing Colombian paramilitary units forced hundreds of Indians in Sucumbios province to leave their homes. In June the army clashed in Carchi province with suspected members of the Colombian National Liberation Army. Thousands of Colombians fled to Ecuador to escape fighting and the U.S.-supported aerial spraying of illegal coca plantations. The government said the spraying had afected food crops in Ecuador and appealed to Colombia to stop fumigating areas close to the frontier.

There was speculation that former guerrillas had been responsible for kidnapping 10 foreign oil workers in Ecuador late in 2000. In February, after more than four months in captivity, seven of the hostages were released in exchange for a $13 million ransom. Two

AP/Wide World Photos

On July 4 Hipólito Mejía (second from left), president of the Dominican Republic, talks with a group of tourists in The Bahamas, where he later gave a speech on environmental degradation at the 22nd Conference of the Caribbean Heads of Government.

others had escaped earlier. One was shot dead in January to underscore the ransom demand. Fifty-two people, five of whom the U.S. sought to extradite, were later arrested in connection with the case.

U.S. military aircraft began flying anti-drug-trafficking surveillance missions from the air force base at Manta under a 10-year agreement. U.S. authorities said the base would not be used for operations against the Colombian guerrillas, but some Ecuadorans feared the agreement would draw them further into Colombia's conflicts.

The Colombia-related troubles overshadowed political and economic developments. The adoption of the U.S. dollar as Ecuador's currency in 2000 (see *El Salvador:* Special Report, below) and high oil prices helped stabilize the economy. Construction began on a second oil pipeline. The government made progress on fiscal reform but met heavy opposition from Congress and the Supreme Court. Pres. Gustavo Noboa responded by proposing political reforms, including a new electoral system and a second legislative chamber. Early in the year Indian protests forced the government to stabilize fuel prices and sign an agreement on indigenous rights. Hundreds of thousands of Ecuadorans continued to live outside the country, and the press devoted considerable attention to their difficulties.

Fears for the rare fauna of the Galápagos Islands were raised in January when a tanker ran aground and spilled 655,000 litres (173,000 gal) of fuel, but winds blew much of the slick out to sea.

(PAUL KNOX)

Peter Endig/AFP Worldwide

Egyptian Pres. Hosni Mubarak (left) is received in Berlin by German Pres. Johannes Rau on September 25 for discussions on world terrorism.

EGYPT

Area: 997,690 sq km (385,210 sq mi)
Population (2001 est.): 65,239,000
Capital: Cairo
Chief of state: President Hosni Mubarak
Head of government: Prime Minister Atef Ebeid

During 2001 Pres. Hosni Mubarak sought to play a mediatory role in the Middle East peace process. Palestinian leader Yasir Arafat made numerous visits to Egypt, but the violence that had begun when the Palestinian *intifadah* erupted and the subsequent election of Ariel Sharon (*see* BIOGRAPHIES) as prime minister of Israel rendered all Egyptian mediatory efforts futile.

Mubarak made his annual visit to the United States in early April. The deadlocked peace process and economic relations were uppermost on his agenda. Egypt's ties with the U.S. were vital if only for the continued $2 billion in military and economic aid Egypt received.

In late February Egypt hosted a summit of the Developing Eight Group, or D-8, which included Egypt, Nigeria, and six non-Arab Muslim Asian countries. The leaders called for greater cooperation in international communication and set guidelines for a doubling of trade between the member states. On June 25 Egypt and the European Union signed an association agreement to establish a free-trade area for manufactured goods, with trade barriers to be phased out over 12 years.

On February 5 a court in the town of Sawhaj in Upper Egypt convicted four Muslims and sentenced them to prison terms varying from one to 10 years for the execution-style killings in January 2000 of 21 Christian Copts. The lightness of the sentences was held up by many as an illustration of official discrimination against Christians—in this instance, by the Egyptian judiciary. In May Sa'd ad-Din Ibrahim, a professor at the American University in Cairo who had been arrested by the government in June 2000 for speaking out in seminars about this particular incident, was sentenced to seven years' hard labour by the Egyptian State Security Court. (*See* BIOGRAPHIES.)

The September 11 terrorist attacks in the United States led to a flurry of visits by Arab leaders to Egypt. These included Arafat, King Abdullah II of Jordan, and Syrian Pres. Bashar al-Assad. Mubarak's reaction to the acts of terrorism was to support the U.S.—but with reservations. He advised the U.S. to restrict its military actions against those accused of terrorism and not to extend terrorism to others. Egypt sought to shield its close allies, such as Libya and Syria, which had been known to sponsor terrorism in the past. Many Egyptians expressed their disbelief that Saudi Arabian-born businessman Osama bin Laden was behind the September 11 atrocities. (*See* BIOGRAPHIES.) The general lack of freedom of communication in Egypt and the anti-Western tirades that had been the hallmark of the Egyptian media, including the government-owned press, contributed during the year to the spread of anti-Jewish conspiracy theories in which Israel loomed large.

Following the September tragedy, President Mubarak embarked on a European tour, which included stops in France, Italy, and Germany. He spoke of Egypt's need to coordinate actions with Western countries to combat terrorism. The intelligence information provided by the Egyptian authorities might be very valuable indeed; many leading members of Bin Laden's al-Qaeda organization, including Ayman az-Zawahiri and Muhammad Atef (*see* OBITUARIES), were Egyptian.

(MARIUS K. DEEB)

EL SALVADOR

Area: 21,041 sq km (8,124 sq mi)
Population (2001 est.): 6,238,000
Capital: San Salvador
Head of state and government: President Francisco Flores Pérez

On Jan. 13, 2001, a major earthquake rocked much of El Salvador. (*See* DISASTERS.) Thousands of aftershocks and another major quake in February added to the destruction, which was especially heavy in the populous region around the capital, San Salvador. In addition to direct damage from the earthquakes, massive mud slides left hundreds of thousands homeless and disrupted communications, transportation, and public services. The quakes claimed the lives of 1,259 persons and caused an estimated $1.6 billion in damage. A massive international relief effort followed, but charges of corruption and misappropriation of funds clouded the relief effort.

The earthquake imperiled El Salvador's economy and added to the confusion that had begun on January 1 when the country adopted the U.S. dollar as its official currency. (*See* Special Report, below.) Confusion and difficulty in converting the Salvadoran colón accompanied dollarization, as many Salvadorans resisted the change. Polls reflected that up to 80% of the population expressed preference for the colón. By the middle of the year, only a third of the currency had been converted to dollars, and at least two lawsuits challenged the constitutionality of the new system in the courts. The government insisted that the new system was working and contributing to economic growth by lowering interest rates, checking inflation, expanding credit, increasing dollar remittances from the U.S.—which rose 13.3% during the first five months of dollarization—and increasing foreign investment. Labour and leftist groups especially opposed dollarization. High oil prices, low coffee prices, and a serious drought slowed economic progress. Agricultural interests complained that the government's emphasis on expanding manufacturing and foreign trade was responsible for a serious decline in agricultural production, with rising rural poverty and hunger the result.

Beginning on March 15, El Salvador joined with Guatemala and Honduras in a new free-trade agreement with Mexico, which promised new jobs and Mexican investment, but since it excluded the export to Mexico of coffee, sugar, or bananas, there was fear that the treaty benefitted Mexico much more than El Salvador. In April Pres. Francisco Flores Pérez argued that economic liberty was the key to saving democratic development in the region. While El Salvador made progress in improving its bleak human rights record during 2001, extrajudicial killings, kidnappings, and allegations of police abuse continued. A United Nations Development Programme report for 2001 ranked El Salvador 95th among 162 countries for human development on the basis of its poverty, low rate of tax collection, and meagre spending on social programs.

(RALPH LEE WOODWARD, JR.)

Triggered by a major earthquake in El Salvador on January 13, a mud slide rips through the town of Santa Tecla, near the country's capital, San Salvador.

AP/Wide World Photos

EQUATORIAL GUINEA

Area: 28,051 sq km (10,831 sq mi)
Population (2001 est.): 486,000
Capital: Malabo
Chief of state: President Brig. Gen. Teodoro Obiang Nguema Mbasogo
Head of government: Prime Ministers Ángel Serafín Seriche Dougan and, from March 4, Cándido Muatetema Rivas

At the end of February 2001, the government of Prime Minister Ángel Serafín Seriche Dougan, which had been accused by the ruling Democratic Party of Equatorial Guinea of corruption and mismanagement, resigned. Pres. Teodoro Obiang Nguema Mbasogo then appointed a new prime minister, Cándido Muatetema Rivas, and cabinet.

As President Nguema's health deteriorated in 2001, there was speculation about a contest for power between his two eldest sons. Teodorín Nguema Obiang Mangué spent much of his time abroad and was rarely seen in Malabo; his half brother, Gabriel Nguema Lima, had been an effective minister of mines and energy but lacked charisma. By mid-year the Nguema family, head of the dominant Mongomo clan, seemed to be looking to Gen. Agustín Ndong Ona, a conservative with close links to the president, as a possible successor.

Oil production increased to almost 200,000 bbl a day, with Exxon Mobil the main producer. Other companies invested millions of dollars in oil exploration offshore. Although Equatorial Guinea had the world's fastest-growing economy in 2001, few had reaped any benefits from the oil bonanza.

(CHRISTOPHER SAUNDERS)

SPECIAL REPORT

Dollarization

Is it worth it?

by Guillermo A. Calvo

By mid-2001 a number of Latin American countries had officially adopted the U.S. dollar as their currency. Ecuador replaced its sucre with the dollar in September 2000. On Jan. 1, 2001, El Salvador followed suit, and Guatemala elevated the dollar to equal status with its quetzal on May 1. Panama had been officially dollarized since the beginning of the 20th century. In 1999 Argentina had seriously considered adopting the dollar, but after much heated debate the proposal was dropped. Argentina had, however, already pegged its peso one-to-one with the U.S. dollar back in 1991. As Latin American countries continued to negotiate with the U.S. for a hemispheric trade agreement, the move to the dollar was expected only to accelerate.

Dollarization Costs. To many analysts the trend toward dollarization was unexpected, since adopting a new currency can be quite costly. One major expense is the loss of seigniorage, the profit that a country earns when it issues a currency. For example, the cost to the U.S. of printing its currency is estimated at less than 0.1% of the currency's face value, yet the notes are sold at face value to banks. If a foreign country dollarizes, it will no longer earn seigniorage and will have to buy the dollars—not an insubstantial budgetary consideration. In addition, a dollarized country will lack an independent monetary policy and, in particular, will not be capable of printing money to rescue banks in case of a liquidity crisis. Given these negatives, why would a country consider dollarization?

The Benefits. It is important to note that many countries in Latin America and elsewhere are already unofficially dollarized. In particular, countries that have experienced high and erratic inflation for long periods of time have tended to set prices in dollars (especially on big-ticket items like cars and real estate). Some governments have imposed controls on the use of the dollar, but they have proved to be very difficult to enforce. This phenomenon, where a local currency and the dollar circulate side by side, is called currency substitution. In places where currency substitution exists and the dollar is already legally recognized, conversion to a completely dollarized system will be relatively simple. Dollarized countries, in effect, import the monetary policy of the U.S. This usually results in the dropping of inflation rates toward U.S. levels. Already in Ecuador, for example, inflation has plummeted from more than 90% in 2000 to a projected rate of 30% in 2001. The drop in inflation rates and the elimination of the risk of devaluation, in turn, help boost domestic savings and attract foreign investment. Dollarization reduces interest-rate volatility as well. The monetary system stabilizes, and with less skittishness over possible devaluations, the risk of bank runs lessens—a situation common in economies that have exhibited poor monetary discipline.

Considerations for the U.S. Thus far the U.S. government has neither encouraged nor discouraged dollarization. The Federal Reserve has simply requested that it be notified in advance when a country plans such a move. Clearly, however, the more countries that use the U.S. dollar, the more the U.S. government stands to earn by gaining additional seigniorage revenue. Many experts have suggested that, in order to encourage dollarization, the U.S. could repay some of the seigniorage to countries that are officially dollarizing. This has the potential to create a "win-win" situation, with the U.S. benefiting from the expansion of the use of its currency and dollarized countries minimizing one of the biggest costs of replacing their currency. In 1999, in fact, U.S. Sen. Connie Mack put forward a proposal to share seigniorage with countries that adopt the dollar, but the bill did not pass out of committee.

To Dollarize or Not to Dollarize? The countries best suited for successful dollarization are those in which currency substitution already exists and that have ample international reserves. In many cases the reserves are so great that they would be sufficient to buy up the entire supply of domestic currency and thus dollarize.

Dollarization costs will vary from country to country and from period to period, depending in part on the interest rates prevailing in the U.S. Estimates show that in most cases the seigniorage cost is less than 1% of a country's gross domestic product. Another possible drawback, however, is that once dollarization has been adopted, it may be hard to undo—i.e., to "de-dollarize". In contrast, fixed exchange rates such as Argentina's can be modified at the stroke of a pen. There

are circumstances in which a devaluation could help restore international competitiveness, as when an economy is faced with a sharp deterioration in its trade terms. This relative advantage of fixed exchange rates is lost, however, in periods in which devaluation does not take place. This is so because the knowledge that a devaluation could happen at any time leads to what has been called the "peso problem"—that is, domestic-currency interest rates substantially higher than dollar interest rates. For example, in Argentina interest rates for the peso have exceeded dollar domestic interest rates by about 3% during tranquil periods (and reached astronomical numbers during periods of turmoil). Two other issues that countries must consider before dollarizing are, first, the likelihood that larger amounts of counterfeit currency will surface and, second, that time and effort will be required for overcoming the resistance of a population to the conversion. Therefore, the decision to dollarize is not trivial or even straightforward, and each country's currency structure needs to be assessed on its own terms.

The main experiment in currency replacement of modern times is the adoption of the euro simultaneously by several countries in the European Union (EU), a process that started in 1999 and will come to fruition in 2002 as euro bills and coins begin to circulate. The EU machinery provides for member countries to share seigniorage, and access to credit lines is available if a member state finds itself in a liquidity crunch. The several countries involved have agreed to coordinate banking regulations. It is too early to tell how the system will operate, but sharply lower interest rates have already been registered in Italy and Spain, countries that prior to the adoption of the euro suffered from the peso problem. Actually, lower interest rates account for much of the fiscal adjustment that Italy had to implement to comply with the Maastricht Treaty, which outlined the EU's economic unification. In contrast to the situation in the EU, dollarization is being considered in the less-developed world mostly by individual countries and is therefore more costly. The issue of dollarization is certain to resurface in connection with the negotiations for the Free Trade Area of the Americas, a scheme that will extend the North American Free Trade Agreement to the entire hemisphere. Countries that belong to a large free-trade area and share the same currency can be less concerned about the vagaries of the exchange rate. For them, dollarization will be attractive.

Guillermo A. Calvo is chief economist at the Inter-American Development Bank in Washington, D.C., and director of the Center for International Economics at the University of Maryland. Opinions are those of the author and do not necessarily represent those of the institutions with which he is affiliated.

left and right: Encyclopædia Britannica, Inc.

ERITREA

Area: 121,144 sq km (46,774 sq mi)
Population (2001 est.): 4,298,000
Capital: Asmara
Head of state and government: President Isaias Afwerki

On May 24, 2001, Eritrea celebrated the 10th anniversary of its effective independence from Ethiopia. Nevertheless, Eritrea's triumphal claims to exceptionalism from the African continent's postcolonial malaise of dictatorship were exposed to scrutiny during the year. In 2000 a group of reformists had emerged from within the ranks of the ruling People's Front for Democracy and Justice (PFDJ) and had demanded that the constitution (ratified in 1997) be implemented and that national elections be held in December 2001. In May 2001 the group published an *Open Letter to the PFDJ,* which exposed the absence of accountability and transparency in the regime led by Pres. Isaias Afwerki. The group, which was made up of 14 men and one woman and included several high-profile government officials, came to be known as the G-15. Among other demands, the G-15 called for establishing a pluralist system of government, amending laws governing the national economy, instituting a merit-based civil service system in lieu of existing patronage systems and tokenism, and preventing further degradation of women and ethnic and religious minorities.

Stung by the criticism, the ruling regime moved to crack down on the G-15. On September 18–19, 11 of the 15 were jailed without being charged. At the same time, the government announced that it was shutting down privately run newspapers in the country. In October international outcries against the crackdown irked the regime such that it expelled the European Union representative in Asmara and incarcerated local personnel at the U.S. embassy. Average Eritreans, who were unaccustomed to witnessing the airing of differences between their leaders, began to voice their concerns, which further threatened the hegemony of the PFDJ loyalists.

One member of the G-15, Mesfin Hagos, a former defense minister and a cofounder of the Eritrean People's Liberation Front, had been in the U.S. at the time his 11 fellow dissidents were jailed. Although his diplomatic passport was subsequently revoked by the regime, Hagos announced his intention to return to Eritrea—regardless of the threat of arrest—and publicly urged the Eritrean people to rise up against tyranny. In an interview on the Internet Hagos called Afwerki "an old-fashioned dictator, who reacts to any form of criticism with arbitrary, cruel and excessive measures." After 10 years of sovereignty Eritreans, too, joined postcolonial Africa's battle against home-grown dictatorship. (RUTH IYOB)

AP/Wide World Photos

Former Estonian president Lennart Meri (left) hangs the presidential regalia on his successor, Arnold Rüütel, during inaugural ceremonies in Tallinn on October 8.

ESTONIA

Area: 45,227 sq km (17,462 sq mi)
Population (2001 est.): 1,363,000
Capital: Tallinn
Chief of state: Presidents Lennart Meri and, from October 8, Arnold Rüütel
Head of government: Prime Minister Mart Laar

On Sept. 21, 2001, Arnold Rüütel, a leading former communist and candidate of the rural-oriented People's Union, was elected Estonia's second postcommunist president for a five-year term by gaining a bare majority (186 votes) in the 367-member electoral college, composed of the 101 members of the Riigikogu (parliament) and 266 representatives of local government assemblies. As in 1996, the initial attempt to elect a president in the parliament failed because no candidate achieved the required two-thirds majority. At age 73 the oldest candidate in the field, Rüütel had been presidential runner-up twice in the 1990s, but his election this time was a surprise, since he had trailed in nearly all opinion polls. He won because of the failure of the ruling national coalition to agree on a single candidate, the strong rural representation in the electoral college, and a protest vote against the policies of the current national government. On December 27 Rüütel began negotiations with chairmen of the Coalition Reform and Center Party Siim Kallas and Edgar Savisaar to form a new government.

Estonia's overall economic performance, as suggested by various macroeconomic indicators, remained strong during 2001, but growing unemployment and the highest rate of inflation in the Baltic States were cause for concern. Privatization of various branches of the economy had proceeded quite smoothly in previous years, but Prime Minister Mart Laar's centre-right coalition faced strong criticism for its handling of the privatization of a major railroad and the electrical energy industry, especially the lack of transparency in the latter case.

Rüütel's election did not signify any change in Estonia's strongly Western-oriented foreign policy. Although NATO's next summit meeting on expansion was not scheduled until November 2002, the three Baltic States moved closer to membership as various Western leaders, notably U.S. Pres. George W. Bush and French Pres. Jacques Chirac, offered the most explicit statements to date on Baltic inclusion. In the aftermath of the events of September 11, Russia also softened its opposition to NATO membership for the Baltic States. (TOIVO U. RAUN)

ETHIOPIA

Area: 1,133,882 sq km (437,794 sq mi)
Population (2001 est.): 65,892,000
Capital: Addis Ababa
Chief of state: Presidents Negasso Gidada and, from October 8, Girma Wolde-Giyorgis
Head of government: Prime Minister Meles Zenawi

Local elections were held across Ethiopia in February and March 2001. *Woreda* (county) elections in February resulted in the overwhelming victory of the ruling Ethiopian People's Revolutionary Democratic Front (EPRDF) coalition. Criticisms that the elections were not free and fair led to an opposition boycott of the March *kebele* (township) elections, which the EPRDF also won handily.

Beginning on April 18, student protests over the right to form a union and opposition to police presence on the Addis Ababa University campus led to one of the worst incidents of civil disturbance in Ethiopian history. In an effort to dispel the protesters, police stormed the university dormitories, killing between 30 and 41 students. There were hundreds of additional casualties, and 3,000 more students were detained in army camps for several weeks. The university was closed for several weeks and many students chose not to return when it reopened. Additionally, some university students sought refuge in Djibouti and Kenya.

Almost immediately following the riots, there was a critical split in the ruling Tigrayan People's Liberation Front (TPLF) faction within the EPRDF coalition. The split emerged over the government's anticorruption agenda as well as the capitalist path being taken by the government of Meles Zenawi—a sharp break from the previous Marxist-Leninist

Students at Addis Ababa University listen as one of their colleagues reads a list of demands during student protests in April.

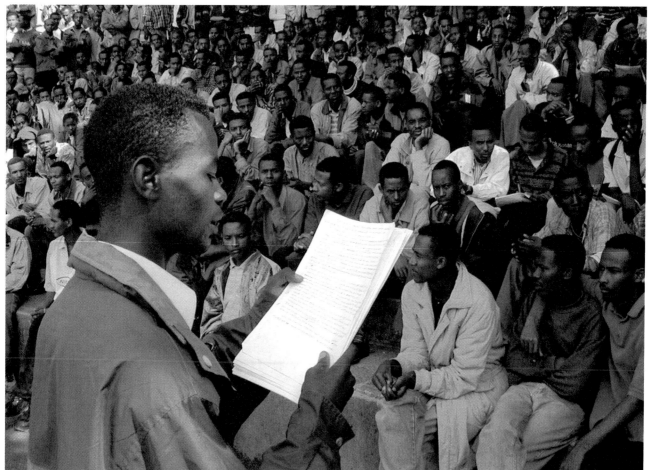

AP/Wide World Photos

ideology of the party. The 12 TPLF members who opposed the Meles regime were purged from the party and held under house arrest. Shortly thereafter, Kinfe Gebremedhin, the head of the Ethiopian Federal Security and Immigration Authority, was shot dead by a military officer as he walked out of an officers club in Addis Ababa. Kinfe had been a strong supporter of the Meles government.

In further fallout from the party split, Pres. Negasso Gidada aligned himself with the splinter group of the TPLF and was ousted from the leadership of his party, the Oromo People's Democratic Organization, though he maintained his position as federal president until his term was up in September. In October Girma Wolde-Giorgis was elected by the parliament as the second president. The year ended with a much-weakened EPRDF regime.

The economy grew at a brisk 6.5% in 2001, favoured by a good harvest and the end of the violent conflict with Eritrea, which was estimated to have cost the Ethiopian state $2.9 billion. International coffee prices remained low, however, and farmers in the south of the country were affected. Ethiopia benefited from a canceling of 67% of its $430 million debt to Paris Club countries under the World Bank's HIPC (Heavily Indebted Poor Countries) program.

Despite the end of active fighting, tensions with Eritrea remained high as both countries rejected the temporary security zone (TSZ) proposed by the United Nations in an attempt to demarcate the border between the two states. UN troops remained fully deployed in the TSZ, and the UN chose not to renew its arms embargo against Ethiopia. Ethiopian troops were involved in border skirmishes with both Kenya and Somalia. Relations with Djibouti remained good in spite of a significant increase in port fees for Ethiopian exports.

(SANDRA F. JOIREMAN)

FIJI

Area: 18,272 sq km (7,055 sq mi)
Population (2001 est.): 827,000
Capital: Suva
Chief of state: President (interim until March 15) Ratu Josefa Iloilo
Head of government: Prime Minister (interim until March 15) Laisenia Qarase

On Oct. 1, 2001—after more than a year of political instability stemming from a coup in May 2000, when Fiji's Parliament was stormed by ethnic-Fijian armed nationalists—newly elected lawmakers were sworn in amid tight security. Coup leader George Speight remained in prison on treason and firearms charges, but he was nonetheless elected to Parliament. His absence from proceedings, however, prompted the speaker of the house to vacate his seat.

Following general elections in August and September, in which Prime Minister Laisenia Qarase's nationalist United Fiji Party won 32 seats and 26% of the vote and the Indian-dominated Fiji Labour Party (FLP) of former prime minister Mahendra Chaudhry won 27 seats and 34.8% of the vote, Qarase refused to follow a constitutional provision requiring representation in the cabinet for all parties securing 10% of the vote. Chaudhry challenged the Qarase government in court and awaited a decision. In recognition of Fiji's return to democracy, the country was readmitted as a full member of the Commonwealth in December.

Fiji declined a request by Australia to establish a refugee-processing centre, owing to strong public sentiment against it. The gradual recovery of the economy, especially tourism, was challenged following the September terrorist attacks in the U.S. (BARRIE MACDONALD)

FINLAND

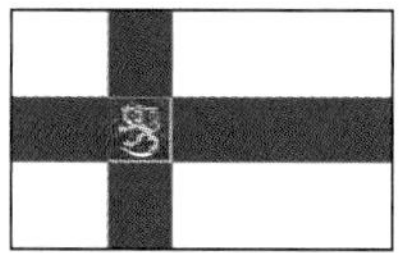

Area: 338,145 sq km (130,559 sq mi)
Population (2001 est.): 5,185,000
Capital: Helsinki
Chief of state: President Tarja Halonen
Head of government: Prime Minister Paavo Lipponen

Though other countries in the region made plans in 2001 to join NATO, Finland maintained its nonalliance stance but welcomed NATO's open-door policy and pledged to cooperate closely within NATO's Partnership for Peace.

During his visit in September, Russian Pres. Vladimir Putin remarked in Helsinki that he understood the feelings of Finns who demanded the restoration of Karelia, which was ceded to the Soviet Union after World War II, but he maintained that closer cross-border contacts would be a better way to address the issue. Though he saw no need for NATO enlargement, he understood that Estonia, Latvia, and Lithuania wished to join the organization; he pledged not to launch a hysterical campaign against their efforts.

Finnish Pres. Tarja Halonen became involved in a tiff with the Baltic States following her interview in the German

Finnish Pres. Tarja Halonen (right) shares a toast with Russian Pres. Vladimir Putin during his visit to Helsinki in September.

Martti Kainulainen/AFP Worldwide

press. Critics maintained that she had indicated that she was opposed to the Baltics' joining NATO. She denied taking that position, and her later talks with Baltic leaders evidently smoothed over the matter. Accession of Estonia, Latvia, and Lithuania would leave Finland as the sole nonallied country along the immediate sea approaches to St. Petersburg.

While visiting Finland, Putin laid a wreath at the tomb of Marshal of Finland C.G.E. Mannerheim, a courtesy that had not been observed by previous visiting leaders from the former Soviet Union. In a speech made while visiting St. Petersburg, Finnish Prime Minister Paavo Lipponen remarked that Putin's gesture could exemplify a new dimension in bilateral relations. Lipponen was also hoping to secure funds from the European Union to make railroad-track improvements, which could reduce to three hours the train journey between St. Petersburg and Helsinki.

Finnish Foreign Minister Erkki Tuomioja came under criticism after an interview in which he asserted that Israel's policy was to suppress, humiliate, and impoverish the Palestinians with the kind of treatment that the Nazis had meted out to Jews in the 1930s. He later denied any intention to compare Israelis to Nazis.

The Finnish economy surged early in 2001 before sliding toward zero growth. The governor of the central bank, Matti Vanhala, warned that a higher employment rate would be necessary if the welfare state was to be maintained. By year's end the threat of a prolonged recession made it likely that Finnish industry would remain weak.

(EDWARD SUMMERHILL)

FRANCE

Area: 543,965 sq km (210,026 sq mi)
Population (2001 est.): 59,090,000
Capital: Paris
Chief of state: President Jacques Chirac
Head of government: Prime Minister Lionel Jospin

The year 2001 was one of transition and transformation for France. Tensions arose inside the coalition government of Socialist Prime Minister Lionel Jospin as economic growth dipped below 3% for the first time in four years and as the 2002 presidential and parliamentary elections approached. Tension also naturally increased between the expected two main rivals for the presidency—Jospin and Gaullist Pres. Jacques Chirac. The 2001 municipal elections showed left and right evenly matched, and at the personal level the electoral impact of allegations of past corruption surrounding the president appeared to be offset by the downturn in the prime minister's popularity that accompanied a downturn in the economy.

The year marked the passing of two elements of French statehood—the franc, which was scheduled to give way to the euro in January 2002, and military conscription, which was finally phased out in December in favour of a smaller volunteer army. Both changes could be seen in the context of a France far more willing to cooperate—at least with its European neighbours—than it had been under Charles de Gaulle. The integration was obvious in the case of the euro, to be shared with 11 other countries in the European Union (EU), but it was also an element in France's acceptance that defense of its territory was better ensured by a smaller professional army working in close cooperation with allies than by a mass army maintained on its own.

Domestic Affairs. The only formal political contest of the year was in March for control of the country's 36,000 communes. It was essentially a draw. The first round of voting (which historically was the fullest measure of political parties' standing) gave the opposition Rally for the Republic (RPR) Gaullists and their centre-right Union for French Democracy allies 46.9% of the vote and the governing left-wing coalition of the Socialist, Green, and Communist parties 44.9%. The right won control of a majority of big towns but lost two of their historic strongholds, Lyon and Paris, where Bertrand Delanoë (*see* BIOGRAPHIES) became the first Socialist mayor since 1871. Several government ministers lost their mayoral seats.

Of all the parties, the Communists fared the worst. To compensate and to show their supporters that they could make a difference in the government coalition, Communist leaders subsequently pushed Jospin into toughening the law on layoffs. Laurent Fabius, the powerful finance minister and former prime minister who was in the right wing of the Socialist party, made little secret of his view that if the government raised the cost to companies of dismissing workers, then the companies would think twice about hiring.

Scandal, as usual in France, provided much of the year's political theatre. In March Chirac rejected a summons from a magistrate investigating allegations that contractors for the city of Paris had "kicked back" a portion of their proceeds into the coffers of the governing RPR party. The magistrate, Eric Halphen, said he had plausible evidence that Chirac had been involved with the kickbacks while he was mayor of Paris from 1977 to 1995. In rejecting the summons, Chirac relied on a recent Constitutional Court ruling that sitting presidents were immune from "ordinary" judicial action. The president gained further time when on September 4 senior judges took Halphen off the kickbacks case, which he had been investigating for seven years. The dossier was passed to a magistrate who earlier in the year had been given the job of investigating the origin of F 2.4 million (F 1 = about $0.14) that Chirac had spent on holiday travel for himself, his family, and his entourage in 1992–95. The president said the money came not from any kickbacks but rather from secret legal funds that as prime minister in 1986–88 he had controlled.

The left suffered its own public embarrassment, one that stemmed from the trial of Roland Dumas, the Socialist former foreign minister and president of

AP/Wide World Photos

Roland Dumas, a former French foreign minister, arrives for his trial on corruption charges at a court in Paris on February 5.

the Constitutional Court. Dumas, his mistress, Christine Deviers-Joncour, and five others were charged with having misused the funds of Elf Aquitaine in 1989–93. The trial started on January 22 but was adjourned on the dramatic news that Alfred Sirven, one of those who had been charged in absentia, had been arrested in the Philippines. When the trial resumed, Sirven, once a senior Elf employee, proved a disappointment to the press by refusing to testify; he claimed the whole process should have been restarted for him. For his silence Sirven was given the heaviest sentence—four years' imprisonment and a fine of F 2 million. Dumas received a 30-month jail term, of which 24 months was suspended, and a fine of F 1 million.

Of concern to all sides in French politics was the unsettled situation of Corsica, despite Jospin's moves to neutralize nationalist sentiment on the island by giving it more autonomy. The National Assembly in Paris voted to give Corsicans the right to amend tax, budget, environment, and tourist laws on an experimental basis. This amending right would be enshrined in the French constitution after the 2002 elections and would enter into force in 2004 if there was also an end to violence. The difficulty of meeting this precondition was brutally underlined, however, by continuing acts of violence, notably the assassination on August 17 of François Santoni, a Corsican nationalist leader. The suspects were other nationalists whom Santoni had accused of having Mafia connections. As a result, Jospin faced further criticism that he was playing into the hands of those who would never give up violence.

The Economy. After a buoyant start to the year, the government found itself steadily scaling back its growth estimates for 2001, from 3.3% to 2.3%. This still left France one of the fastest-growing European countries but meant that the government found itself with a rising budget deficit for the first time since 1993. Unemployment also was rising again as more companies, including Danone, Marks and Spencer, Moulinex, Alcatel, and Philips, announced layoffs.

The government moved not only to make layoffs more difficult but also to extend youth-employment programs, made all the more necessary by the ending of military conscription. The funding of these programs, as well as of the incentives accompanying the lowering of the standard workweek in France to 35 hours, became more difficult within the budgetary constraints of European monetary union. The government dragged its feet on structural economic reform of the pension system and energy markets. At the EU summit in Stockholm in March, Jospin led the successful opposition to the European Commission's plan to accelerate liberalization of the gas and electricity sectors.

Foreign Policy. In common with most EU states, France complained about the "unilateral" approach to foreign policy of U.S. Pres. George W. Bush's administration and its rejection of international arms and pollution-control treaties. Indeed, France was probably the most outspoken EU critic of Bush's rejection of the Kyoto climate-change protocol and of his plan to develop a "national missile defense" (NMD). As the U.S. made clear that whatever the objections of others, it would press ahead to build NMD, designed to protect the U.S. against missile threats from so-called rogue states, Paris moderated its criticism somewhat. In September Chirac was the first foreign head of state to meet with Bush after the terrorist attacks in the U.S. and the first to survey the devastation in New York City. Chirac pledged French solidarity with the U.S. in support of an international coalition against terrorism.

Within the EU, France made no progress toward restoring its former close relationship with Germany, despite a special meeting in January between Chirac and German Chancellor Gerhard Schröder. The meeting was designed to patch up their rift over EU reform at the December 2000 summit in Nice, France. Jospin subsequently came up with his vision of EU reform, which, in common with Chirac, favoured a strengthening of the intergovernmental Council of Ministers as distinct from supranational institutions such as the European Parliament preferred by Germany.

The year showed that some French were as resistant as ever to various aspects of economic globalization, despite—or perhaps because of—the fact that the country was one of the most successful in exporting its goods, services, and style around the world. In January Yahoo! said it would obey a landmark ruling by a French court on Internet access and would block French users' access to Web sites selling Nazi memorabilia banned by French law. In mid-March the first case of foot-and-mouth disease in continental Europe was recorded near Paris. An EU ban on French exports was immediately imposed, but it was lifted in April. The cause of the outbreak was almost certainly imports from the U.K., where the disease raged all year. (*See* AGRICULTURE: *Special Report.*) Nonetheless,

Antinuclear militants march toward the railway station of Mezidon-Canon in northeastern France on October 21 to protest the resumption of the transport of nuclear waste by rail from Germany.

radical farm groups were more excited by genetically modified organisms developed by multinational food companies, many of them American. The protesters ripped up plants in experimental plots.

The antiglobalization movement got some backing from the prime minister. Having had the luxury of not attending the riot-torn G-8 summit in Genoa, Italy, in July, Jospin surprised many by expressing sympathy for the antiglobalization protesters there. He recalled that France had always sought to instill order into trade and monetary policy, rather than leaving everything to the free market. Earlier in the year, Jospin admitted that he had retained far-left Trotskyist connections into the 1970s, but his support for taxing international capital flows seemed more a political ploy designed to rally the left for the 2002 elections. (DAVID BUCHAN)

GABON

Area: 267,667 sq km (103,347 sq mi)
Population (2001 est.): 1,221,000
Capital: Libreville
Chief of state: President Omar Bongo
Head of government: Prime Minister Jean-François Ntoutoume-Emane

Amid a rising wave of urban crime, on March 1, 2001, Gabon's minister of the interior suspended the import and sale of firearms. Prime Minister Jean-François Ntoutoume-Emane addressed the National Assembly on May 16 to answer deputies' concerns about public safety. Despite the creation during the year of a special crime squad, the incidents of armed robbery and other violent crimes continued to escalate.

On May 8 unemployed workers staged a peaceful demonstration in the nation's commercial capital, Port-Gentil. Although a special commission was established to hear their grievances, it apparently made little impact, because on June 20 police had to use tear gas to disperse youths who rioted. The authorities regained control on the next day, and it was announced that meetings between the unemployed and a government official would soon take place. In legislative elections held on December 9 and 23, the ruling Gabonese Democratic Party won 84 of the 120 seats in the legislature. In December there was also an outbreak of Ebola fever, which killed at least 11 persons.

Relations between Benin and Gabon cooled when the former accused Gabonese farmers of using thousands of underage Benin nationals in conditions of virtual slavery. Despite Gabon's adoption on June 16 of a new law imposing severe penalties on those exploiting children under age 16 as forced labour, the smuggling of children into the country appeared to continue unabated. (NANCY ELLEN LAWLER)

GAMBIA, THE

Area: 10,689 sq km (4,127 sq mi)
Population (2001 est.): 1,411,000
Capital: Banjul
Head of state and government: President Col. Yahya Jammeh

The Gambian government spent much of the first half of 2001 dealing with calls for the scrapping of Decree 89, which banned the former main parties—including Sir Dawda Jawara's People's Progressive Party, which Pres. Col. Yahya Jammeh had ousted from power in 1994—from participating in elections. Opposition parties also called for the repeal of the decrees muzzling the press and civil society. On July 22 President Jammeh finally lifted the restrictive Decree 89.

Former president Jawara, who was living in exile in London, was ineligible to stand for election because he was older than 65. Some of the opposition parties formed a coalition in August and chose a popular lawyer, Ousainou Darboe of the United Democratic Party, as their presidential candidate. Earlier in the year Darboe had been charged with murder in an attempt to disqualify him from running. In the election held on October 18, Jammeh captured 53% of the vote, compared with Darboe's 32%. Though the opposition claimed that a number of irregularities had occurred, including the registration of foreign nationals from Casamance, it accepted the election results, which was a significant victory for Jammeh, whose win in the 1996 election had been tainted by allegations of fraud. Legislative elections were planned for January 2002.

Jammeh had earlier rejected the findings of a commission of inquiry, led by a senior judge, into the fatal shooting in April 2000 of 14 demonstrators. Brushing aside the commission's criticisms of the interior minister and the police intelligence unit, the government pushed legislation through the National Assembly to indemnify those involved in the shooting. (CHRISTOPHER SAUNDERS)

GEORGIA

Area: 69,700 sq km (26,911 sq mi)
Population (2001 est.): 4,989,000
Capital: T'bilisi
Head of state and government: President Eduard Shevardnadze, assisted by Secretary of State Giorgi Arsenishvili

Reformist members of the majority Citizens' Union of Georgia (SMK) criticized Pres. Eduard Shevardnadze repeatedly during the first half of the year for failing to crack down on corruption within the government. In late August, after Shevardnadze rejected a bill drafted by Justice Minister Mikhail Saakashvili that would have required ministers to prove that their wealth was acquired legally, Parliament Chairman Zurab Zhvania warned Shevardnadze that the country was on the verge of a major crisis and demanded the dismissal of allegedly corrupt police and security officials. The SMK Parliament faction failed to support Zhvania's demand, however, and the faction collapsed, leaving Parliament without a majority.

On October 30 thousands of T'bilisi residents took to the streets to protest a raid by security officials on the TV station Rustavi-2. At an emergency Parliament session on November 1, Shevardnadze offered to step down if deputies demanded the resignation of Interior Minister Kakha Targamadze and Prosecutor General Gia Meparishvili, but after both they and Zhvania quit, Shevardnadze announced that he would not resign. Shevardnadze then fired the entire government, but he included most outgoing ministers in the new government. On November 10 Parliament elected as its new speaker the Foreign Relations Committee chair, Nino Burdzhanadze, and on December 21 it finally approved Avtandil Djorbenadze as minister of state.

Gross domestic product growth during the first half of the year amounted to 5.2%, but during the first seven months industrial production fell by 2.6% compared with 2000. In late October a large tax-revenue shortfall necessitated slashing projected budget spending by 15%.

In early October several hundred armed men advanced into the Kodori gorge on the territory of the unrecognized Republic of Abkhazia, but they retreated after two weeks of sporadic fighting with Abkhaz forces. During the incident more than 100 of the interlopers were killed, a helicopter belonging to the UN Observer Mission was shot down with the loss of nine lives, and unidentified aircraft bombed remote Georgian villages but inflicted no injuries. The alleged participation of Chechen fighters in that raid further soured the strained relations between Russia and Georgia, as did Moscow's failure to comply with its commitment to withdraw all personnel from its military base in Gudauta, Abkhazia, by July 1 and Russian air raids in October and November on uninhabited border areas.

On November 18 Lyudvig Chibirov failed to win reelection as president of the unrecognized Republic of South Ossetia. Moscow-based businessman Eduard Kokoyev was elected in a runoff ballot on December 6.

(ELIZABETH FULLER)

GERMANY

Area: 357,021 sq km (137,847 sq mi)
Population (2001 est.): 82,386,000
Capital: Berlin; some ministries remain in Bonn
Chief of state: President Johannes Rau
Head of government: Chancellor Gerhard Schröder

For Germany, 2001 was marked by increased involvement in world affairs but a slowdown in the pace of economic growth and reform. As the country's Social Democratic government entered the second half of its four-year term, Chancellor Gerhard Schröder lost the lustre that he had acquired as a market reformer. In some respects the year was more remarkable for what did not happen than for what Germany accomplished in its economic-reform process. The government passed an overhaul of the pension system but shied away from further reforms in an apparent effort to preserve the support of Germany's powerful trade unions for the 2002 election. Partly as a result, Germany's became the slowest-growing economy in Europe and job creation diminished, taking Schröder's personal approval ratings down with it. At the same time, the chancellor gained in stature as a statesman as Germany embarked on a more active and assertive foreign policy course after more than half a century of restraint. Throughout the year Europe's most populous nation assumed a greater leadership role in European affairs and grew more active in other international trouble spots such as Macedonia and the Middle East. In the wake of the terrorist attacks in the United States in September, Germany said it would support the American response with both diplomatic and military means if necessary. In the past the country had shirked military intervention, especially outside Europe.

Domestic Politics. An issue inherited from the previous year dominated the early days of 2001; bovine spongiform encephalopathy (BSE, or "mad cow" disease), an animal infection that could kill humans, occupied public and political attention. Millions of Germans stopped eating beef, which helped bring Europe's beef market to the brink of collapse. Mad cow disease also claimed political victims in Germany when in January the country's health and agriculture ministers stepped down amid accusations of having mishandled the crisis. BSE faded from the public limelight when another animal illness, foot-and-mouth disease, spread across Europe. The disease did not appear in Germany, but the meat crisis created an adverse political atmosphere as Chancellor Schröder's government, just past its midterm mark, acquired an aura of instability. (*See* AGRICULTURE AND FISHERIES: *Special Report.*)

Only a day before the cabinet resignations over mad cow disease, Schröder had been obliged to make a public statement in support of Foreign Minister Joschka Fischer, a member of the Green Party who was under fire for his militant past. A series of photographs published in the newsmagazine *Stern* in January showed Fischer using violence against a police officer during a political protest in the early 1970s. Fischer appeared before a special question period in the parliament and apologized for his actions. The affair lingered for weeks, even though Fischer was one of Germany's most popular politicians. Fischer was subsequently forced to testify in the terrorist trial of a former friend, and his court appearance then prompted a perjury probe to investigate whether he had given false testimony in the trial. The inquiry was eventually dropped, and the revelations about Fischer's past did not cloud his first meetings in Washington, D.C., in February with the new U.S. administration.

The government's midterm wobbles did not affect two key regional elections in Baden-Württemberg and Rhineland-Palatinate in March. Both of these prosperous regions in the western part of the country reelected their incumbent governments, run respectively by the conservative Christian Democratic Union

AP/Wide World Photos

German Foreign Minister Joschka Fischer (left) and Chancellor Gerhard Schröder in the Bundestag in August. Earlier in the year the chancellor had defended Fischer when his colourful past came under intense public scrutiny.

German army troops guard a convoy on August 28 in Baumholder, Ger., as part of their training for the NATO mission in Macedonia known as Operation Essential Harvest.

(CDU) and Chancellor Schröder's centre-left Social Democratic Party (SPD).

A principal reason for the government's strength despite political mismanagement, scandals, and a worsening economic outlook was the persistent weakness of the Christian Democratic Union–Christian Social Union (CSU) opposition. Throughout 2001, as for most of the year before, the CDU-CSU was haunted by the fallout of a major financing scandal that broke in late 1999 and led to the fall from grace of former chancellor Helmut Kohl, once one of Europe's most respected elder statesmen. In the spring Kohl agreed to pay a fine that closed the criminal case against him. It ended an important chapter in the affair, but the former leader's reputation and the party's fortunes did not fully recover.

The new postscandal party leadership spent much of 2001 involved in political infighting, which was dominated by the question of who would be the candidate to challenge Schröder in the 2002 election. The most prominent combatants were CDU chair Angela Merkel, a Protestant, childless, once-divorced woman from the former East Germany, and Edmund Stoiber, the Catholic, ultraconservative CSU chief and prime minister of Bavaria. Another competitor was Friedrich Merz, the CDU-CSU floor leader in the Bundestag (lower house of parliament) who clashed with Merkel over political strategy and claimed his own right to run for chancellor.

The Christian Democrats scored only one political victory, when they ousted the long-standing SPD government in the city-state of Hamburg in a September election. The real winner, however, was Ronald Schill, a former judge who campaigned on a law-and-order platform and won almost 20% of the vote for his own—newly founded—party. Otherwise, the strife within the opposition yielded Schröder several political victories, including the passage of his pension package and parliamentary approval for military participation in the autumn mission of NATO in Macedonia.

The federal government enacted several minor reforms in 2001. They included a new recycling law and a measure that improved the legal standing for same-sex couples, which resulted in a series of so-called gay marriages. Berlin also moved to attract talented foreign workers, proposing legislation that would allow it for the first time to compete with the U.S., Canada, and other industrialized nations for highly skilled professionals, scientists, and technicians from the less-developed world. Faced with a growing shortage of skilled labour and an aging workforce, Germany decided to move toward a radical break with past immigration policies. The new measures included the creation of the country's first-ever immigration law and the granting of permanent immigration status for qualified foreigners. Passage of the law was delayed past year's end, however, by a debate about a stricter security regime, notably for foreigners in Germany, after the terrorist attacks in the U.S.

Germany closed a chapter in the unending struggle with its own history. In May a fund created by several thousand large and small German companies said it would begin making payments to compensate slave labourers who worked in German factories under the Nazi regime. The announcement came after the companies felt they had sufficient protection against future lawsuits, especially from the U.S. Two years of haggling, much of it about legal details, had left many of the hopeful beneficiaries bitter and dissatisfied with what was originally intended to be a gesture of German goodwill and generosity.

The Economy. One of Germany's most pressing economic problems, a makeover of its overburdened 120-year-old pension system, was finally addressed in 2001. In May the parliament reformed the retirement law in an effort to deflect the demographic time bomb ticking in the country's pay-as-you-go pension scheme, where ever-fewer workers supported a rapidly rising number of pensioners. After years of bipartisan bickering and a last-minute protest by the trade unions, Germany introduced a dramatic change in its retirement regime. Under the new law the government would for the first time support private provisions while at the same time cutting state pension benefits. Economists and the business community welcomed the reform as an important step toward addressing the problems of Germany's graying population, stretched public finances, and high labour costs, but they warned that the reform had been so diluted by political compromise that it would not provide lasting relief for the state system. The Schröder government also abolished a restriction, dating from the time of Adolf Hitler, on retail store discounts and, under pressure from the conservative opposition, provided tax relief for small and medium-sized enterprises that tax reforms in 2000 had neglected.

Another item on Schröder's reform agenda gained prominence because it did not materialize—a renovation of the labour market. Burdened with rigid regulations and high labour costs, German companies were reluctant to hire new workers. As a result, few new jobs were being created, and Germany's unemployment rate was among the highest in Europe. The stubbornly high number of jobless presented a growing political problem for Schröder because he had explicitly tied his political future to job creation. Yet the government did little to make hiring easier or cheaper for businesses; in several respects it made it harder. Soon after entering office Schröder undid the reform efforts of the previous government by boosting sick pay and worker protection against layoffs. Later he imposed restrictions on employers trying to hire workers on fixed-term contracts. In 2001 he expanded labour's role in management and instituted a right to part-time work.

The new regulations were an apparent effort by Schröder to reconcile labour unions with pension reform and to court the traditionalist left wing of his SPD. His jockeying alienated German industry, however—especially small companies, which complained that the new labour laws added red tape and cost. The move dealt a major blow to Schröder's image as a market reformer and threatened one of his biggest political assets—the hard-won support of Germany's business community, which traditionally sided with the Christian Democrats or the small, pro-market Free Democrats. Another blow to Schröder's reform credentials came from his reluctance to reform Germany's expensive and inefficient health care system despite continually rising contributions to public health insurance.

The unsolved structural problems in the German economy became more visible with the economic slump that ended nearly a decade of unprecedented growth and productivity gains across the industrialized world. Heavily dependent on exports, Germany was hit hard by the slowdown, especially that in the U.S., one of its most important markets. The September terrorist attacks in the U.S. put additional strain on the world's third largest economy.

The outlook steadily worsened throughout 2001. The government and economists were forced into several downward adjustments of their growth forecasts for the year. By the fall Germany—already the slowest-growing economy in Europe—began to fear a recession. At the same time, inflation hit an eight-year high and unemployment continued to rise. In March Schröder promised to push the number of jobless to under three million Germans. One month later he adjusted that pledge to under 3.5 million. By the autumn that goal also appeared impossible to reach, and the chancellor merely said there would be fewer unemployed Germans than when he took office in 1998.

Schröder's perceived inaction yielded him lower approval ratings and negative newspaper headlines. "Do something, Chancellor," said *Bild,* Germany's leading tabloid, in a large summer headline. "For the first time in Schröder's term, voters feel like they're back in the paralyzing stagnation of the Kohl era," echoed the news magazine *Der Spiegel* in September. Schröder responded to the growing pressure by announcing a "calm hand" policy, free of short-term activism, fresh debt, and costly economic stimuli.

With his image as a reformer stained, Schröder was certain to face a tougher-than-hoped-for leap into the election year of 2002. Throughout 2001 he repeated well-worn and ambiguous campaign slogans, such as "Innovation and justice" and "Security in change." It was uncertain whether he could continue to walk a tightrope between needed reforms and reassurance of his left-leaning core clientele. The months to come also held another challenge for which Germany meticulously planned throughout 2001—the introduction of the euro, Europe's common currency, as legal tender in January 2002.

Foreign Relations. The government's weakening domestic performance was offset by Schröder's growing standing as a statesman in a newly self-confident Germany that took greater responsibility in world affairs than it had in decades past. Following the terrorist attacks in the United States in September, Schröder jumped ahead even of the U.S. in defining what had happened as a "conflict of cultures" and a "declaration of war on the free world." He announced an international coalition against terror and promised "the unlimited, I stress, the unlimited solidarity of Germany." That promise put a strain on the pacifist Greens, the junior member of Schröder's governing coalition, which had long opposed the use of military force. Leading Greens said they supported the military strikes against Afghanistan that began in October, but many more warned against military "adventures" and restrictions on civil liberties once domestic security was tightened to prevent terrorist activity on German soil. Germany had served as an operational base for several of the suspects in the raids on the U.S.

Tensions within the government grew so strong that in November, Schröder called a confidence vote in the parliament. He won the vote along with the freedom to assist as he saw fit the international coalition against terror. The terrorist attacks effectively ended the transatlantic tensions that had been simmering for months and came to the fore in the early months of the administration of George W. Bush. Like other Europeans, Germans were dismayed by the Americans' insistence on building a missile defense shield, the U.S. rejection of an international treaty against global warming, and other policies perceived as selfish and unilateralist. Even before the terrorist strikes, the German government had grown more active in international affairs. A long list of foreign visitors went to Berlin, and unlike in previous years, they went not only for money but also for German mediation, support, and political intervention. Schröder nurtured his close relations with Russian Pres.Vladimir Putin. Early in the year he celebrated Orthodox Christmas with the Russian leader, and he was the first to lobby him face-to-face for support in the battle against international terrorism.

Meanwhile, Foreign Minister Fischer became an active interlocutor in the struggling Middle East peace process. The government also scored a success when in August the parliament approved the participation of German troops in NATO's Macedonia mission. An hour after the vote, the first soldiers left their air base in Bavaria for Macedonia, and a few weeks later Germany took command of the NATO mission. The country's readiness to assume leadership in the Balkan conflict was another sign of its effort to expand its international responsibilities, both military and diplomatic.

Schröder also stepped up his involvement in the process of European integration. In April he presented a blueprint for the future of Europe that sketched out a restructuring of the European Union's (EU) governing institutions to advance political unity. He proposed to widen the executive role of the European Commission, strengthen the European Parliament by giving it full control over the EU finances—including the large agriculture budget—and make the secretive Council of Ministers more transparent. The ideas also served Germany's self-interest because they preserved the powers of its federal states and duplicated the structure of Germany's two-house parliament on a European level. Partly as a result, the German proposals met with a cool response from France and the U.K. (CECILIE ROHWEDDER)

Relatives of victims killed in a stampede at a soccer match on May 9 in Accra, Ghana, observe a moment of silence at a memorial service four days after the incident.

AP/Wide World Photos

GHANA

Area: 238,533 sq km (92,098 sq mi)
Population (2001 est.): 19,894,000
Capital: Accra
Head of state and government: Presidents Jerry John Rawlings and, from January 7, John Kofi Agyekum Kufuor

For Ghana 2001 began with the first peaceful transfer of power between democratically elected governments in the country's 44-year history. On January 7 John Kofi Agyekum Kufuor (*see* BIOGRAPHIES) commenced his first term as president. His New Patriotic Party also gained a majority in Parliament.

Kufuor's government immediately turned its attention to Ghana's economy, which in 2000 had struggled with high unemployment, inflation, and a major devaluation of the cedi, the national currency. Soon after his installation, Kufuor declared that the state of the economy was worse than expected. In spite of criticism from many Ghanaians, he announced that Ghana would join the Heavily Indebted Poor Countries program for debt relief, and he increased prices of petroleum and utilities. Kufuor's reforms had some success. The cedi stabilized, and investment in the country increased. Kufuor also instituted political reforms, setting up a National Reconciliation Committee to look into past corruption and abuses of power.

Tragedy struck during a May 9 soccer match in Accra. Accra's Hearts of Oak was beating its longtime rival, Kumasi's Asante Kotoko, 2–1 when Kotoko fans began throwing bottles and chairs onto the field. Police fired tear gas into the crowd, and a rush to the stadium's locked gates resulted. In the ensuing confusion and stampede, around 130 people died and dozens more were injured. It was the worst sporting disaster in Africa's history. President Kufuor canceled his engagements, declared a three-day period of national mourning, and announced a government investigation into the incident.

(AMY SETTERGREN)

GREECE

Area: 131,957 sq km (50,949 sq mi)
Population (2001 est.): 10,975,000
Capital: Athens
Chief of state: President Konstantinos Stephanopoulos
Head of government: Prime Minister Konstantinos Simitis

On April 6, 2001, the Greek Parliament adopted a thorough constitutional revision, which changed 78 articles of the country's basic law. Many amendments were passed jointly by the two biggest political parties, the ruling Panhellenic Socialist Movement (Pasok) and the centre-right New Democracy (ND). Changes to the constitution included better protection of citizens' private data, the constitutional guarantee of alternative service for conscientious objectors, and the abolition of the death penalty in times of peace. Another key amendment stipulated that changes to the electoral legislation would affect the next elections only if passed by a two-thirds majority. Previously, the ruling party had often changed the election law in order to bolster its majority or limit its defeat in upcoming elections. Parliament, however, failed to separate state and church completely and to change the provision that automatically triggered early parliamentary elections in the event that Parliament failed to elect a new head of state in three rounds of voting.

Another of the government's key projects, a reform of the pension system, triggered the strongest antigovernment protests in years. In particular, plans to raise the retirement age and reduce pensions were rejected by trade unions, opposition parties, and leading Pasok members. In the midst of a general strike on April 26 and massive antigovernment demonstrations on May 1, Prime Minister Konstantinos ("Kostas") Simitis announced that a dialogue "on everything and without preconditions" with relevant social groups would be initiated, but the reform was put on hold.

On October 13–15 Pasok held its sixth congress. Simitis was reelected Pasok president, and Environment and Public Works Minister Konstantinos Laliotis was named party secretary.

Simitis reshuffled his government extensively on October 23; he promoted so-called reformers at the expense of "traditionalists." Apostolos Tsochatzopoulos was moved from the Defense Ministry to the Development Ministry. He was succeeded by Yiannos Papantoniou, who was replaced as finance and economy minister by Nikolaos Christodoulakis, previously the development minister. Vasso Papandreou was moved from the Interior Ministry to the Environment and Public Works Ministry; Konstantinos Skandalidis, Pasok secretary until the congress, became interior minister. Foreign Minister Georgios Papandreou and Public

Order Minister Michalis Chrysochoidis retained their portfolios.

The main opposition ND held its regular congress on March 30–April 1. The congress strengthened the position of party leader Konstantinos ("Kostas") Karamanlis and welcomed the return of senior politicians who had left the party following disagreement with Karamanlis.

On March 6 Athens Mayor Dimitris Avramopoulos, who had left the ND the previous year, announced the establishment of a new political party, the Movement of Free Citizens (KEP). Although he maintained that the KEP was open for cooperation with other political forces, Avramopoulos ruled out any alliance with other parties in the next parliamentary elections, due by 2004.

The government's decision to remove any reference to religious affiliation from personal identity documents continued to strain relations between the government and the Greek Orthodox Church. The church collected more than three million signatures, which Archbishop of Athens and All Greece Christodoulos submitted to Pres. Konstantinos ("Kostis") Stephanopoulos on August 29. The president, however, rejected for constitutional reasons the church leader's request for a referendum on the issue.

On May 4–5 Pope John Paul II visited Greece. Despite protests by some Orthodox clerics and believers, the first visit by a pontiff since the Schism of 1054 was widely considered a success.

As the crisis in Macedonia unfolded, Greece made clear its support of the country's integrity, calling for a political settlement. Greece also contributed some 400 troops to the "Operation Essential Harvest." Though the dispute over Macedonia's name remained unsettled, UN-mediated talks continued in 2001. Relations with other neighbours remained largely unchanged, although there was further atmospheric improvement in relations with Turkey, witnessed by the signing of the first Greek-Turkish city partnership, by the government's support for plans to jointly host Euro 2008, the European association football (soccer) championships, and by the signing of a landmark treaty allowing Greece to return illegal immigrants to Turkey.

Preparations for the 2004 Olympic Games in Athens continued at a slow pace. International Olympic Committee representatives visited Greece repeatedly and urged Greek officials to speed up preparations. On March 27 the new Athens International Airport, one of the largest infrastructure projects in Greece in recent years, started operations. No solution was found for Olympic Airways, Greece's ailing national carrier. Deadlines for a privatization tender were extended repeatedly, but no buyer was identified. Meanwhile, Olympic Airways staff staged several strikes against the airline's privatization and inherent restructuring. Two private Greek airlines, Cronus Airlines and Aegean Airlines, announced their merger in March.

The Greek economy continued to grow. In the first half of 2001, gross domestic product grew by 4.9% over the same period in 2000; investments and exports also increased. Year-on-year inflation stood at 3.8% in August. The Athens Stock Exchange continued its downward slide, however; by the end of September, the index had lost two-thirds of its value compared with its all-time high in 1999.

On February 4 composer Iannis Xenakis died in Paris. (*See* OBITUARIES.)

(STEFAN KRAUSE)

GRENADA

Area: 344 sq km (133 sq mi)
Population (2001 est.): 102,000
Capital: Saint George's
Chief of state: Queen Elizabeth II, represented by Governor-General Daniel Williams
Head of government: Prime Minister Keith Mitchell

Grenada was as active as any other Caribbean state against undesirable offshore banks in 2001, closing down 17 in one day in March. They were all linked to the First International Bank of Grenada, which collapsed in October 2000, taking $150 million worth of mainly American depositors' money along with it. A U.S. Senate committee had described First International as "one of the most notorious rogue banks" in the Caribbean offshore industry. In June another six banks had their licenses to operate canceled.

Despite its actions against offshore banks, Grenada was added in September to the list of countries deemed by the Paris-based Financial Action Task Force (FATF) to have failed in cooperating with international efforts to stop money laundering. The FATF described Grenada's system for dealing with money laundering as having "serious deficiencies." The task force pointed out that regulators in Grenada did not have adequate access to customer account information and lacked the authority to cooperate with overseas counterparts. The government reacted angrily, calling the FATF decision "shocking."

Also in September Grenada's UN ambassador, Lamuel Stanislaus, urged the UN to restore Taiwan's membership in the world body, which had been revoked in 1971. In common with other small Caribbean countries, Grenada was a recipient of generous Taiwanese aid.

(DAVID RENWICK)

GUATEMALA

Area: 108,889 sq km (42,042 sq mi)
Population (2001 est.): 11,687,000
Capital: Guatemala City
Head of state and government: President Alfonso Portillo Cabrera

Scandals eroded support for the government of Alfonso Portillo Cabrera during 2001, beginning with the continuing legislative investigation known as "Guategate." The governing Guatemalan Republican Front sought to prevent the trial of 24 indicted members of its congressional delegation, including President of the Congress Efraín Rios Montt. In April a court exonerated Rios Montt, but controversy continued along with other charges of government corruption, financial mismanagement, and conflict of interest. Portillo's frequent foreign journeys and the high crime rate were further sources of criticism, and rumours spread of an impending coup d'état.

On the positive side, despite repeated death threats to judges and witnesses, a Guatemalan court on June 8 convicted and sentenced three military officers to 30 years in prison for the 1998 murder of human rights advocate Bishop Juan Gerardi Conedera. The murder on May 5, 2001, of a former investigator for Gerardi, Barbara Ann Ford, an American nun who had worked in Guatemala for two decades to promote social justice, prompted new outcries against human rights violations.

Declining coffee prices and high oil prices hurt the Guatemalan economy during the year, although increased banana exports helped offset lower banana prices. On March 15 Guatemala began a limited free-trade agreement with Mexico and other Central American states, but it excluded Guatemalan coffee and sugar. Free circulation of the dollar and other hard currencies began on May 1 in a measure designed to improve Guatemala's trading position. On August 1 the sales tax rose from 10% to 12%, accompanied by social improvements mandated by the 1996 peace accord, including a higher minimum wage and regulations to bring Guatemala into compliance with international labour standards. Mass protests resulted as opponents charged that these measures increased inflation and discouraged investment. Most employers ignored the minimum-wage increase. Many measures agreed to in the peace accord had yet to be implemented. The UN's 2001 Human Development Index, based on life expectancy, educational attainment, and per capita GDP, ranked Guatemala lower than any other country in the Americas except Haiti. (RALPH LEE WOODWARD, JR.)

GUINEA

Area: 245,857 sq km (94,926 sq mi)
Population (2001 est.): 7,614,000
Capital: Conakry
Head of state and government: President Gen. Lansana Conté, assisted by Prime Minister Lamine Sidimé

The conflicts in neighbouring Liberia and Sierra Leone, which had spilled over into Guinea at the end of 2000, led to a refugee problem in Guinea in 2001. In February the governments of Liberia and Sierra Leone agreed to cooperate with the UN in establishing safe corridors for any refugees who wished to return home. The various upheavals also led to the displacement of about 70,000 Guineans. Pres. Gen. Lansana Conté appealed for increased international aid to all the victims of the conflicts. The UN High Commissioner for Refugees twice suspended all deliveries of food as a result of the fighting. By May 27 the UN had nevertheless managed to complete the evacuation of 57,000 refugees from the Guinean border villages around an area in the southeast known as Parrot's Beak before closing down its operations there. Under pressure from other West African countries, defense and security ministers from Guinea, Liberia, and Sierra Leone met on September 26–28 in Monrovia, Liberia, to attempt to resolve the problems.

Political tensions mounted as President Conté's ruling party launched efforts to alter the constitution to enable a president to serve more than two terms. In late July members of three opposition parties flew to Paris in search of French support to discourage Conté's bid for a third term. Longtime opposition leader Alpha Conde, who had been arrested in December 1998 and found guilty of capital crimes at his trial in September 2000, was released from prison on May 18. He took up his seat in the parliament on September 25.

The economy experienced little growth during the year, largely because of the border conflicts. On May 7 the International Monetary Fund underwrote a three-year, $82 million aid package designed to finance antipoverty measures and accelerate economic development; on July 24 and 26 the World Bank approved $120 million in credits for education reforms and the alleviation of poverty; and on September 27 the African Development Fund announced that it would loan Guinea nearly $16 million for a new structural-adjustment program.

(NANCY ELLEN LAWLER)

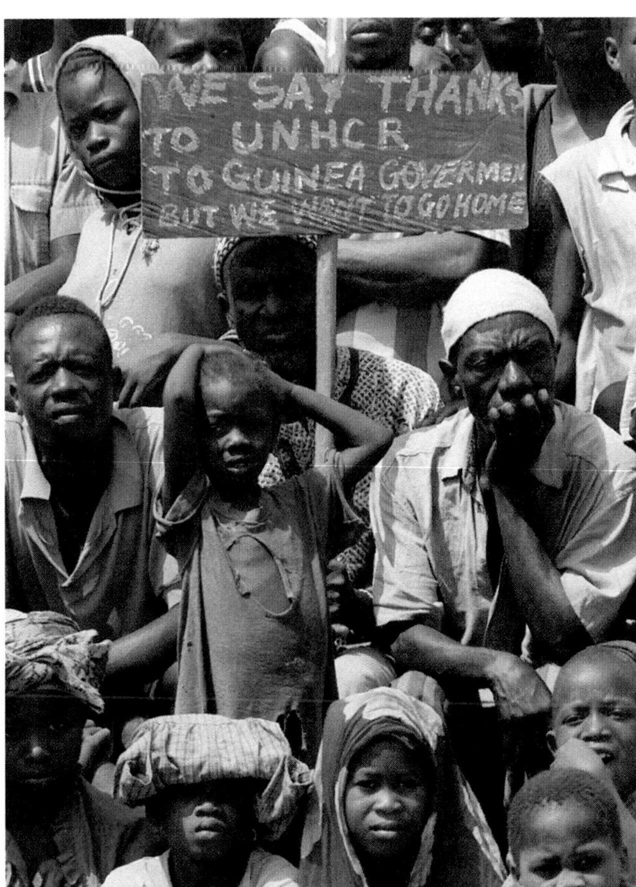

AP/Wide World Photos

At a camp in southwestern Guinea on February 11, refugees from Sierra Leone and Liberia wait to return home.

GUINEA-BISSAU

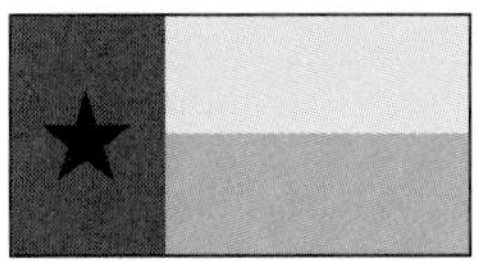

Area: 36,125 sq km (13,948 sq mi)
Population (2001 est.): 1,316,000
Capital: Bissau
Chief of state: President Kumba Ialá (Yalla)
Head of government: Prime Ministers Caetano N'Tchama, Faustino Imbali from March 21, and, from December 8, Alamara Nhassé

In January 2001 the coalition between the Guinea-Bissau Resistance–Bah Fatah Movement and the Party for Social Renewal collapsed. A period of uncertainty followed until Pres. Kumba Ialá appointed Faustino Imbali the new prime minister. The new government soon ran into trouble, however, when $15 million disappeared from the treasury, and the opposition called for its resignation.

After inquiries into the matter by Imbali and the National People's Assembly proved fruitless and the arrest of two Ministry of Finance employees by the attorney general's office outraged a parliamentary commission, calls for the government's resignation mounted. On December 8 Interior Minister Alamara Nhassé was appointed the new prime minister.

President Ialá was roundly criticized for suspending the activities of the Ahmadiyya Islamic group and deporting its leaders. He claimed that the Ahmadiyya was destabilizing the country's Muslim community, almost half the population. A Bissau court declared his decision unconstitutional, and both the judiciary and the parliament declared unconstitutional Ialá's dismissal of four Supreme Court judges and its president and the appointment of new ones. In August President Ialá dismissed Attorney General Rui Sanha and replaced him with former prime minister Caetano N'Tchama, who began threatening journalists from a private radio station. Meanwhile, public servants' salaries were not paid. An opposition forum warned that stability was threatened and demanded that municipal elections be held by March 2002. A rumour that Ialá wanted to replace Armed Forces Chief of Staff Verissimo Correia Seabra with Umberto Gomis led some officers to threaten war if Ialá carried out this plan.

(CHRISTOPHER SAUNDERS)

GUYANA

Area: 215,083 sq km (83,044 sq mi)
Population (2001 est.): 776,000
Capital: Georgetown
Chief of state: President Bharrat Jagdeo
Head of government: Prime Minister Sam Hinds

Guyana's ruling People's Progressive Party (PPP)/Civic alliance was returned to office in the general election held on March 19, 2001. The victory gave the alliance's leader, Bharrat Jagdeo, another five-year term as president and head of state. PPP/Civic, which took 209,031 of the 393,709 votes cast, secured 34 of the nation's 65 parliamentary seats. The opposition People's National Congress (PNC)/Reform Party won 164,074 votes and claimed 27 seats.

Sporadic violence and looting followed the announcement of the election results, and a 43-year-old woman lost her life after being shot by an unknown gunman. PNC/Reform filed a motion to prevent Jagdeo from taking office, but this was dismissed by the High Court. In an effort to prevent further violence, Jagdeo and PNC/Reform leader Desmond Hoyte met in April and several times thereafter. They agreed to the formation of six joint committees to deal with contentious issues, including local government reform and the distribution of public land and housing.

Guyana's long-standing border row with Venezuela—an issue both sides had previously relegated to the back burner—suddenly came alive in July when Venezuela's foreign minister visited the disputed Essequibo region and denounced the 1899 treaty that ceded it to Guyana, then a British colony. It was the first visit by a Venezuelan government minister to the border area in almost 20 years. That same month heads of government from Caribbean Community and Common Market countries had reiterated support for Guyana's "sovereignty" and "territorial integrity."

(DAVID RENWICK)

On March 22 police officers stand guard along a street in Buxton Village, near Georgetown, after riots erupted following the announcement of election results in Guyana.

AP/Wide World Photos

HAITI

Area: 27,700 sq km (10,695 sq mi)
Population (2001 est.): 6,965,000
Capital: Port-au-Prince
Chief of state and government: Presidents René Préval and, from February 7, Jean-Bertrand Aristide, assisted by Prime Ministers Jacques-Édouard Alexis and, from March 2, Jean-Marie Chérestal

The new government of Haitian Pres. Jean-Bertrand Aristide faced several political challenges in 2001. Leaders of 15 political organizations that had boy-

AP/World Wide Photos

A Haitian man stands in an alley between tin shacks in Port-au-Prince. Haiti, with a gross national income per capita of $480, remained one of the world's poorest countries in 2001.

cotted the November 2000 presidential election formed an alliance known as Convergence Démocratique and challenged his legitimacy by establishing an alternative national unity government headed by educator Gérard Gourgue as provisional president. Most of these organizations were quite small and had a very limited constituency within the country. Nevertheless, their leaders were articulate enough to gather broad international backing. The roots of the confrontation ran to the May 2000 legislative elections, when Aristide's Lavalas Family party swept more than 80% of about 7,000 elected posts but failed to hold a runoff for 10 disputed Senate seats. The U.S. and international financial organizations withheld more than $500 million in scheduled foreign aid and pressured Aristide and his prime minister, Jean-Marie Chérestal, to negotiate with the opposition. In July both sides agreed to hold new elections, but they had not set a date for them by year's end.

Meanwhile, on December 17, Haitian commandos stormed the presidential palace in an attempted coup, but they were subdued after battling the police for several hours.

The economy continued to decline in 2001. The World Bank listed Haiti's gross national income per capita as $480. About 80% of the rural Haitian population lived below the poverty line. The cost of living rose sharply with the price of gasoline, going up by 40%. The gourde, the local currency, barely recovered after losing half of its value, which made staples such as rice and beans much more expensive to the average Haitian. Macroeconomic and structural reforms successfully initiated since 1994 stagnated in 2001. Poor state management of Haiti's ports and road network and public utilities such as electricity, water, and telephones continued to discourage new private investment and limit employment opportunities. Earlier privatization efforts did not succeed because of a lack of political will to carry them out.

(JEAN-CLAUDE GARCIA-ZAMOR)

HONDURAS

Area: 112,492 sq km (43,433 sq mi)
Population (2000 est.): 6,490,000
Capital: Tegucigalpa
Head of state and government: President Carlos Roberto Flores Facussé

The national elections held on Nov. 25, 2001, were the sixth since 1981, marking an unprecedented two decades of democracy in Honduras. The presidential election was won by Ricardo Maduro of the National Party. The new government was scheduled to take office in January 2002. The campaign was marred by mutual accusations by the Liberal and National parties regarding the eligibility of front- running presidential aspirants. Conflict began in October 2000 when the National Elections Tribunal, dominated by the incumbent Liberals, claimed that Maduro was not a native Honduran and thus was ineligible to run for president. The dispute was finally resolved on Feb. 23, 2001, when the Congress reinterpreted the constitutional requirements for citizenship and allowed Maduro to run.

With reconstruction from the massive damage caused in October 1998 by Hurricane Mitch still ongoing in 2001, Honduras suffered an extensive drought that the UN World Food Programme called the worst natural disaster to hit Central America since Mitch. More than 316,000 people were severely affected, and some 128,000 were to receive food aid. The drought also caused severe water shortages in the capital.

Internationally several events were important. On February 21 the archbishop of Tegucigalpa, Oscar Rodríguez Maradiaga, became a cardinal. Rodríguez was the first Honduran, and only the third Central American, appointed to the Sacred College of Cardinals. On March 15 the free-trade agreement signed with Mexico, Guatemala, and El Salvador in 2000 took effect. In May the U.S. government renewed the Temporary Protected Status of 105,000 Hondurans living in the U.S. for an additional year (until July 2002) as part of continued U.S. efforts to help Honduras recover from the economic effects of Hurricane Mitch. Finally, the border disputes and economic sanctions that arose between Honduras and Nicaragua in 2000 continued during 2001.

(MICHELLE M. TAYLOR-ROBINSON)

HUNGARY

Area: 93,030 sq km (35,919 sq mi)
Population (2001 est.): 10,190,000
Capital: Budapest
Chief of state: President Ferenc Madl
Head of government: Prime Minister Viktor Orban

The Sept. 11, 2001, terrorist attacks in the U.S. did not have a major impact on Hungary's political or economic life. On the other hand, the numerous political scandals during the year led to a de facto, if not actual, breakup of the coalition that held power in Budapest. A bribery scandal in February triggered a wave of allegations against the Independent Smallholders' Party (FKGP), the junior coalition partner, although it did not affect the Federation of Young Democrats (Fidesz)–Hungarian Civic Party, the senior governing party. The affair resulted in the ousting of Jozsef Torgyan from both the FKGP presidency and the top position in the Ministry of Agriculture.

The level of public support for political parties generally stagnated, even with general elections anticipated in 2002. Fidesz and the former governing Hungarian Socialist Party ran neck and neck in opinion polls for most of the year, both attracting about 26% of the electorate. According to a September poll by the Gallup organization, however, support for a joint Fidesz–Hungarian Democratic Forum party list would enjoy the approval of 33% of the voters, with the Socialists drawing 28% and other opposition parties 3%. Meanwhile, public support for the FKGP plunged from 14% in 1998 to 1% in 2001. As many as 40% of the voters remained undecided, however. Although the Socialists had picked their candidate for prime minister—former finance minister Peter Medgyessy—the opposition largely remained at sixes and sevens, unable to attract political support in light of Fidesz's overwhelmingly professional political communication campaign. The Socialist Medgyessy seemed most likely to stand alone against Prime Minister Viktor Orban in the May 2002 elections.

Still, much could depend on the radical nationalist Hungarian Justice and Life Party (MIEP), whose parliamentary support for the government Orban had accepted, notwithstanding MIEP leader Istvan Csurka's fiercely anti-Semitic rhetoric. MIEP was in opposition, but it could not be ruled out that it could be kingmaker in 2002.

Hungary attracted international media attention during the year for its passage of a law that extended education and health benefits as well as employment rights to the estimated three-million-strong Magyar (ethnic Hungarian) minority in neighbouring countries. Governments in adjacent states, particularly Romania, were insulted by the so-called status law, which they saw as a direct interference in their domestic affairs. A report in March by the Brussels-based International Federation of Journalists criticized the Hungarian government for improper political influence in the media as the country's public service broadcaster teetered close to bankruptcy.

The year 2001 was one of economic downturn. The government continued to weather criticism for being nontransparent and for operating on an unprecedented two-year budget. Despite troubling macroeconomic indicators, the long budgetary term promoted excessive social spending, including augmented state pensions and higher minimum wages. Largely owing to the government's reversal of Hungary's traditionally liberal financial policy, trading on the Budapest stock exchange was weaker compared with 2000—so much so that in the autumn the government suggested merging the Central European stock exchanges in order to create a better environment for foreign, and particularly American, investors. The idea was turned down by exchange officials in other countries, however.

(ZSOFIA SZILAGYI)

A news broadcast airs on Hungarian television; the state media suffered from stiff financial and political pressures during the year.

Photo by MTI Katalin Sándor

ICELAND

Area: 102,819 sq km (39,699 sq mi)
Population (2001 est.): 284,000
Capital: Reykjavík
Chief of state: President Ólafur Ragnar Grímsson
Head of government: Prime Minister Davíd Oddsson

Iceland's economic growth slowed to 2% in 2001 after five years of more than 4.5% growth. The economy began overheating in 2000; inflation increased and a current account deficit widened. Economic activity, which had peaked late in 2000, began shrinking during 2001. Signs of recession emerged late in the year, though employment continued to be virtually full.

In December 2000 the Supreme Court ruled that the government had unconstitutionally reduced the disability benefits of individuals who were part of a married couple. In response, legislation was passed that increased disability benefits from $170 a month to $402, retroactive for four years.

The policy of managing fish stocks through fishing quotas came under increased scrutiny. Despite many years of quota management, the stocks of important fish species, such as cod and haddock, were shrinking, a factor that called into question this management method and initiated a debate about whether illegal fishing was at fault for the decline. On the other hand, the system of allocating fishing quotas for free, which in turn could be sold in the open market for a windfall profit, came under increased criticism. A government-appointed commission reported that fishing quotas should be subject to a modest charge, and the government promised to introduce legislation to that effect.

The plan to build a hydroelectric dam at Kárahnjúkar, in the northeast of the country, received a setback when it failed to pass environmental scrutiny. The power company appealed the verdict. As a result, the decision to build the dam and an aluminum plant at Reydarfjördur was postponed. Construction could not begin until 2003 at the earliest. (BJÖRN MATTHÍASSON)

INDIA

Area: 3,166,414 sq km (1,222,559 sq mi)
Population (2001 est.): 1,029,991,000
Capital: New Delhi
Chief of state: President Kocheril Raman Narayanan
Head of government: Prime Minister Atal Bihari Vajpayee

Deshakalyan Chowdhury/AFP Worldwide

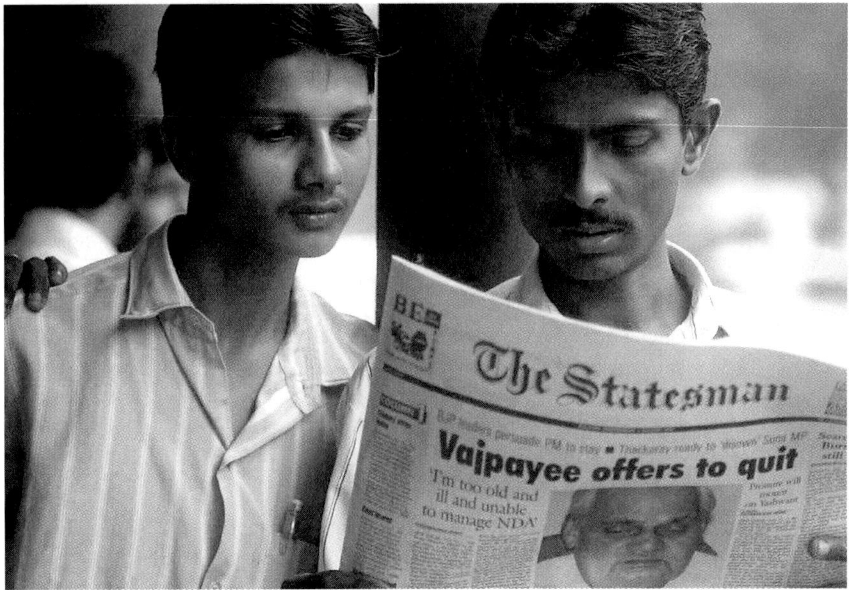

Young men in Kolkata (Calcutta) on August 1 read about Indian Prime Minister Atal Bihari Vajpayee's offer to step down, which was rejected by the ruling National Democratic Alliance.

In 2001 it was the year of the terrorist in India; secessionists and raiders from across the borders stepped up their activities in Jammu and Kashmir state, India's northeastern region, and the capital itself. On December 13 five terrorists, armed with automatic weapons and explosives, made a daring bid to enter Parliament House in New Delhi. Security guards prevented their entrance, and in the exchange of fire all five raiders and nine others were killed. India held two Pakistan-based organizations, Jaish-e-Mohammad and Lashkar-e-Taiba, responsible. Earlier, on October 1, a car-bomb attack on the Jammu and Kashmir Assembly killed 38 persons. Jaish-e-Mohammad claimed responsibility.

Early in the year the government made a serious attempt at peace by halting its antiterrorist drive and holding talks with militant organizations, especially those that it suspected were encouraged by Pakistan. The talks yielding no results, Prime Minister Atal Bihari Vajpayee made the bold decision to negotiate directly with the chief executive of Pakistan, Gen. Pervez Musharraf, and invited him to New Delhi. The general arrived on July 14. His discussions with Vajpayee, which were held in Agra over the next two days, remained deadlocked, with Pakistan maintaining that a political solution to the Kashmir issue should be found first and India insisting that cross-border terrorism should be first stopped.

India was deeply shaken by the events of September 11 and hastened to assure the U.S. of its full cooperation, as did Pakistan. Although Pakistan and India found themselves on the same side, there was no abatement in mutual rancour. One benefit that both derived by responding to the call to fight terrorism was that the U.S. ended the economic embargoes it had imposed after both countries carried out nuclear tests in 1998. India emphasized that it had long been pointing out the need for international action against cross-border terrorism. It handed over to the U.S. information about the Taliban's training camps in Afghanistan and Pakistan. Vajpayee went to Washington in November on invitation from Pres. George W. Bush for talks on the campaign against terrorism. Vajpayee also met Pres. Vladimir Putin in Russia on his way to the U.S. On his way back he had talks with Prime Minister Tony Blair in Britain. Blair had earlier paid a short visit to India. In December Vajpayee also visited Japan.

In the last week of September, India banned the Students Islamic Movement of India on the grounds that it had close links with the Taliban and arrested more than 200 of its leaders. In October a Prevention of Terrorism Ordinance was promulgated with one of its provisions enabling detention without trial for a period of six months, but the government was unable to secure parliamentary endorsement for it.

Domestic Affairs. On January 26, the western state of Gujarat suffered an earthquake of magnitude 7.9. (*See* DISASTERS.) Over 14,000 people died, and more than 166,000 were injured. Some 370,000 houses were totally destroyed. The coalition government set aside 2% of the nation's income tax revenue to meet the expenditures for relief.

A political earthquake was soon to hit the government itself. In March a Web site, Tehelka.com, issued an extensively documented report that included videotapes of senior officials and prominent members of the ruling National Democratic Alliance (NDA) accepting money in exchange for defense contracts. (*See* Sidebar.) Tehelka.com revealed later that its reporters had posed as representatives of nonexistent foreign arms dealers. Bangaru Laxman, president of the Bharatiya Janata Party (BJP), resigned from his post on March 13; Jaya Jaitly, president of the Samata Party, and George Fernandes, India's defense minister, followed suit two days later. The defense portfolio was assigned to Foreign Minister Jaswant Singh as an additional responsibility. Several other NDA officials were suspended. Fernandes was reappointed as minister of defense in October.

More discomfiture was in store for the ruling coalition. In elections for four state legislative assemblies and a union territory in May, the NDA could not win

The Tehelka Tapes

In 2001 a stunning exposé by a New Delhi news portal claimed the jobs of India's defense minister, senior party functionaries of the ruling coalition, and at least five high-ranking members of the armed forces. The exposé, which appeared on Tehelka.com in March, included videotapes showing senior government officials accepting money in exchange for defense contracts.

In Tehelka.com's sting operation, reporters posed as representatives of nonexistent foreign arms dealers. The reporters' modus operandi involved offering to sell thermal cameras and other equipment to the Indian army. The ensuing encounters—including kickbacks accepted by politicians and army officials—were filmed by hidden cameras. The investigation, which lasted more than six months, culminated in a press conference by Tehelka.com on March 13, during which the editor in chief, Tarun Tejpal, showed the footage assembled by his team.

The exposé came during a crucial budget session of Parliament and paralyzed the proceedings. Bangaru Laxman, president of the Bharatiya Janata Party, had to resign after being caught on camera accepting money. Defense Minister George Fernandes had to resign after his Samata Party colleague Jaya Jaitly was shown meeting arms brokers at his official residence. Three of the five implicated army officers faced a court martial, while another's services were terminated.

The government-appointed commission of inquiry probing the scandal consisted of a single member, Justice K. Venkataswami, a retired Supreme Court judge. Tehelka.com submitted all of its videotapes and transcripts to Venkataswami, who on October 12 ruled that the tapes were genuine and that they had not been doctored. The commission probe was still underway at year's end.

On August 22 the *Indian Express* reported that Tehelka.com had employed prostitutes as a "honey trap" to cement the arms deals, a fact not disclosed earlier by the portal. The encounters between defense personnel, middlemen, Tehelka reporters posing as arms dealers, and the women were also captured on camera. Subsequent reports revealed that Tehelka had filmed sexual encounters, allegedly without the consent of the prostitutes, a fact admitted by the portal. This revelation put Tehelka's credibility in question—the portal was accused of violating individuals' rights to privacy, selectively editing, and erroneously transcribing the tapes to suit the story. The government was quick to denounce Tehelka's investigative methods. Tejpal's defense was that his reporters, to maintain their cover, had to accede to demands for paid sex made by the army officers.

Tejpal's "end-justifies-the-means" argument found as many supporters as critics. For the latter, Tehelka's nondisclosure of having used prostitutes and then filming the sex was proof of mala fide intent. To Tehelka supporters the tactics that were employed represented a genuine effort not to let sleaze sidetrack the main issue of corruption and to protect the women on the tapes.

(SHALAKA PARADKAR)

even one. Three of the five new chief ministers belonged to the Congress (I) party—A.K. Anthony in Kerala, Tarun Gogoi in Assam, and P. Shanmugam in the union territory of Pondicherry. Shanmugam later made way for N. Rangaswamy. In West Bengal the Communist Party of India (Marxist) won for the sixth time. In Tamil Nadu the All-India Anna Dravida Munnetra Kazhakam swept the polls and its leader, J. Jayalalitha, was sworn in as chief minister. The Supreme Court, however, removed her from the post on the grounds that as a convicted person she should not have been allowed to contest the election in the first place. O. Panneerselvam took over as chief minister. Soon thereafter, Jayalalitha's appeal against her original conviction was upheld in the Madras High Court, clearing the way for her return.

Gujarat also had a new chief minister. Poor showings in by-elections forced the ruling BJP to replace Keshubhai Patel with Narendra Modi in October. In Manipur frequent party hopping on the part of legislators prompted the coalition government to place the state under president's rule. In September the Supreme Court ruled that Sonia Gandhi, opposition leader and president of Congress (I), was an Indian citizen and upheld her election to Parliament.

The Economy. A fall in exports slowed both agricultural and industrial production during the year. The International Monetary Fund in September placed India's growth rate in 2001 at 4.5%, compared with 6% the previous year. Owing to numerous instances of irregularities, all stock markets languished throughout the year in spite of several attempts to prop them up.

In February the finance minister presented the central budget, which provided several incentives for industries, including a 15-year tax holiday for software firms. The revenue receipts of the central government in 2001–02 were placed at about Rs 2.3 trillion (1 Rs = about $0.02) and revenue expenditure at some Rs 3.1 trillion, which left a revenue deficit of Rs 788.2 billion, or 3.2% of India's gross domestic product.

Disinvestment plans made slow progress. In the first nine months of 2001, only one public-sector company, the Bharat Aluminium Co., was privatized. The terms of sale gave rise to accusations of underevaluation and corruption, but Parliament approved the deal. In September the government declared its determination to go ahead with plans to allow private participation, wholly or partially, in 13 more companies, including the State Trading Corp., Videsh Sanchar Nigam (international telecommunications), and Maruti (automobile manufacturing). It reiterated its resolve to sell Air India and Indian Airlines. The government also decided to appoint a single regulatory authority to cover information technology, telecommunications, and broadcasting, merging the ministries.

(H.Y. SHARADA PRASAD)

INDONESIA

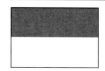

Area: 1,922,570 sq km (742,308 sq mi)
Population (2001 est.): 212,195,000
Capital: Jakarta
Head of state and government: Presidents Abdurrahman Wahid and, from July 23, Megawati Sukarnoputri

In Indonesia the year 2001 was dominated by politics. Abdurrahman Wahid was removed as president by Indonesia's supreme decision-making body, the People's Consultative Assembly (MPR), on July 23, which thereby ended months of political crisis over his tenure.

The drawn-out dismissal process was initiated early in the year when a parliamentary inquiry found circumstantial evidence that Wahid had been complicit in the misuse of some $4 million from the state logistics agency. The findings led to a constitutional showdown. Wahid denied the charges and disputed the authority of the parliament to sit in judgment of him. The parliament asserted its right to monitor the executive and triggered the dismissal proceedings in the MPR (the MPR comprised the 500 members of the parliament plus 195 regional and community group representatives). Facing certain defeat, and against the advice of most of his cabinet, Wahid declared a state of emergency in the early hours of July 23 and tried to suspend the MPR. Political leaders and the security services ignored his declaration, and the MPR met in emergency session and removed him later that day. Wahid claimed he had acted to defend the constitution, but most legal experts believed that he had acted unconstitutionally, a view supported by the Supreme Court.

Wahid's downfall was due more to disillusionment with his leadership style than to any alleged corruption. Upon his election in October 1999, he had attracted a diverse coalition of parties into his government, but he proved unable to maintain its unity. His idiosyncratic and often gratuitously provocative remarks and his removal of several powerful ministers undermined cabinet solidarity and alienated many of the parties that had supported his presidential bid. He also showed himself to be an inept manager of government business. His grasp of key policy areas such as economics, justice, and defense was weak, and his approach to policy making tended to be ad hoc and inconstant.

His replacement, Vice Pres. Megawati Sukarnoputri, came to the presidency with a strong popular mandate and a public expectation that she would restore a measure of stability after the turmoil of Wahid's term. Her party, the Indonesian Democratic Party of Struggle (PDI-P), had won 34% of the national vote at the 1999 general election, by far the largest of any party. Much of PDI-P's success was due to Megawati's own personal following. Her popularity derived not only from her status as the eldest daughter of Indonesia's founding president, Sukarno, but also from her image as a person of quiet integrity who had stoically resisted the manipulations of the Suharto regime in the mid-1990s. Her personality traits were atypical of a leading politician; she was reserved, cautious, and averse to confrontation and political deal making—characteristics that critics said were hindrances to successful leadership. Megawati's government comprised representatives from secular nationalist and Islamic parties as well as military officers and technocrats. Though ideologically nationalist, she pursued pragmatic policies during her first months in office.

AP/Wide World Photos

On September 8 Indonesian Pres. Megawati Sukarnoputri, wearing traditional Acehnese attire, arrives at the house of the governor of Aceh on her first official visit to the troubled province.

The political tumult surrounding the presidency had drawn attention away from more fundamental issues related to political, economic, and legal reform. This reform process, which had begun after the fall of Suharto's New Order in May 1998, had been fitful and uneven. The transition to democracy continued, though elements of the political culture had changed little from the Suharto era. Parties remained elite-dominated and driven by personalities and patronage rather than ideology or grassroots participation. The parliament provided close scrutiny of government activities, but it remained tardy in passing legislation and prone to graft. Constitutional reform was badly needed, particularly in defining the relationship between the legislature and the executive, but appeared in danger of stalling. Confidence in the judiciary and police was low, and this contributed to rising vigilantism by local communities against suspected wrongdoers. Civilian control over the military improved, but the armed forces continued to be an important, but not dominant, element in Indonesian politics. Corruption still permeated Indonesian life but was no longer as blatant or extreme as during the Suharto era. A range of government anticorruption measures helped to ensure greater transparency, and regular press exposure of improper practices raised the risks of engaging in corruption. On November 28 Tommy Suharto, the fugitive son of Suharto, was arrested after more than a year on the lam. He was facing an 18-month prison term for corruption when he fled.

One of the most radical reforms was that of decentralization. Under this program, which began in January 2001, extensive political and economic powers were being devolved to the second tier of regional government (i.e., regency or municipality). Within two years the central government was supposed to cede to the regions authority in all administrative areas except defense, justice, fiscal controls, religion, and matters relating to technical standards. So far, the devolution process had been surrounded by controversy and confusion. Poorly drafted legislation and complex, often contradictory enabling regulations had been core problems and had been compounded by a lack of central government supervision and local government disregard for existing national laws and administrative protocols. The Megawati government announced that it would revise the legislation in early 2002. The decentralization process was likely to strengthen democracy in the regions and ease re-

(continued on page 442)

SPECIAL REPORT

Resisting Disintegration in Post-Suharto Indonesia

by Greg Fealy

Since the fall of Suharto's authoritarian New Order regime in May 1998, Indonesia has undergone a number of dramatic changes. At the political level, there has been a rapid and rather chaotic transition to democracy, including a significant dismantling of state controls over social and political expression. At the same time, the level of communal violence and secessionist demands has risen sharply. Many observers have seen a link between the two processes and questioned whether a society as heterogeneous as Indonesia's can survive these fissiparous tendencies intact without a strong, even repressive, central government.

For much of its independent history, Indonesia has been seen as a nation at high risk of disintegration. It has one of the world's most ethnically, culturally, and religiously diverse populations. Among the groups dispersed across a sprawling archipelago of some 13,000 islands are the staunchly Muslim Acehnese in far-north Sumatra, Catholics of Flores and Timor in the east, the Hindu Balinese, and animists in Irian Jaya and Kalimantan. In the late 1940s and 1950s, regional rebellions broke out on Java, Sumatra, Sulawesi, and Ambon, most of which were put down militarily. Under Sukarno's Guided Democracy regime (1959–66) and Suharto's New Order (1967–98), tight central control was imposed over the regions and separatist tendencies were suppressed, often harshly.

The rise in communal conflict and secessionist pressures since Suharto's downfall has led to renewed speculation about Indonesia's possible breakup. The former Portuguese colony of East Timor, effectively annexed by Indonesia in 1975, seceded in 1999. Separatist activity in Aceh and Irian Jaya—both of which have had long-standing independence movements—has grown rapidly in scope and popular support, prompting a forceful response from Indonesian security services. Aceh has experienced by far the worst violence. Separatist rebels there have been conducting a bloody guerrilla war against Indonesian forces and by 2001 controlled large areas of the rural hinterland. It is estimated that since 1999 more than 2,000 people have died, victims not only of the fighting but also of brutality by the Indonesian police and army as well as by the rebels. Armed conflict in Irian Jaya is far more sporadic, but military intervention and intimidation of pro-independence groups are common. Secessionist calls have also emerged from several other provinces, including Riau, South Sulawesi, and Bali, but these are aimed at pressuring the central government and do not have serious separatist intent. Even so, the use of such appeals shows that the earlier taboo on separatist rhetoric no longer applies.

The most severe nonseparatist violence has taken place in the Maluku archipelago, where a virtual civil war has been waged between Christian and Muslim communities since early 1999. More than 5,000 people have lost their lives in this bitter conflict, and over 500,000 have been displaced. In Kalimantan, tensions between indigenous Dayaks and Madurese internal migrants have led to a series of massacres of Madurese since 1997. In a violent outbreak in February 2001, some 500 Madurese were killed and roughly 100,000 fled to other regions. In addition to this, there has been an upsurge in attacks on places of worship across the nation. During the New Order, an average of 14 churches were attacked each year; the figure since 1998 has been about 140 per annum, in addition to the damage inflicted on scores of mosques.

While these events represent a serious challenge to Indonesia's cohesion, there are strong grounds for arguing that the nation is not in imminent danger of breakup. Despite Indonesia's diverse population, commitment to national unity is strong across most regions and

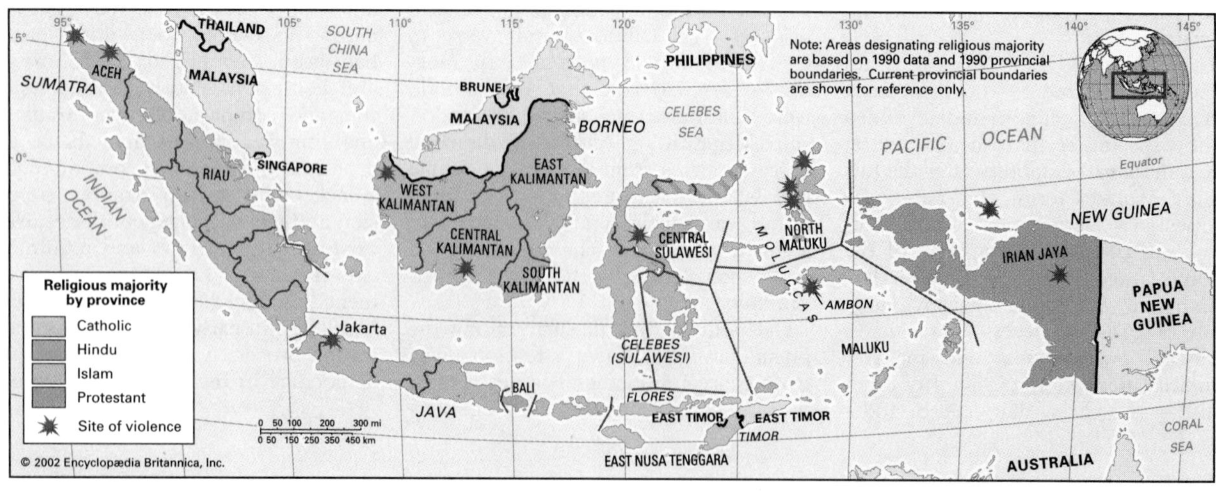

Rioters overturn a van during a massive labour demonstration outside the State Palace in Bandung, Indon., on June 13.

AP/Wide World Photos

sections of society, judging by responses to the loss of East Timor and separatist calls in Aceh and Irian Jaya.

Ethnic and religious animosities are clearly important factors in communal and separatist unrest, though closer examination of Indonesia's social composition and dynamics suggests that most Indonesians accept diversity as an essential element of their national character. Ethnographers disagree on exactly how many ethnic groups exist in Indonesia, but most estimates put the number at about 200. There are no accurate figures on the size of each ethnic group, though some indication of ethnicity can be gained from census statistics on the "mother tongue" of citizens. The most recent available census data (1995) suggest that the main ethnic groupings are Javanese (about 40% of the population), Sundanese (14%), Madurese (4%), and Batak, Bugis, Banjarese, and Balinese (each less than 2%). There are also diasporas of Chinese (3%) and Arabs, South Asians, and Europeans (each less than 1%). Javanese are the most widely dispersed and politically dominant group, with four of Indonesia's five presidents having been Javanese. The Chinese, though a small minority, are economically dominant and constitute the wealthiest ethnic group.

Indonesia has five "officially recognized" religions. Islam is by far the largest; according to the 1990 census, it was the faith of 87% of Indonesians. This makes Indonesia the world's largest Muslim nation. The minority religions are Catholicism (6%), Protestantism (3%), and Hinduism and Buddhism (each less than 1%). In addition, animism is widely practiced among more traditional communities.

Indonesia's dispersion of ethnic and religious groups is highly complex. There are few restrictions on internal migration, and Indonesians have proved highly mobile in pursuing career or commercial opportunities outside their home provinces. The large cities are especially heterogeneous. This has led to extensive intermarriage between ethnic groups and, to a much lesser extent, religious groups (strict rules apply to marriage between Muslims and non-Muslims). Most urban Indonesians live or work in environments that are ethnically and religiously mixed. Before the upsurge in communal violence, Indonesia enjoyed a reputation for tolerance and pluralism, and the great majority of the population still coexists in relative harmony.

Ethnic and religious tensions, although important elements in social conflict and separatism, are seldom the only factors. Often there are deep-seated social, economic, or political issues that take on an ethnic or religious expression. A key driver of divisive tendencies has been that of socioeconomic grievance. This has been most evident in Aceh and Irian Jaya, both of which are rich in natural resources but receive from the central government only a small percentage of the wealth extracted from their provinces. Infrastructure and government services and facilities are poor in both regions, and employment opportunities in local oil and mineral developments have been limited. New regional autonomy laws should result in a significant rise in the share of revenue going to these and other resource-rich provinces. The greater political autonomy flowing from these laws should also ease resentment toward Jakarta.

The violence in Maluku and Kalimantan also has an economic dimension. Malukan Christians have been angered by what they see as Muslim encroachment into traditionally Christian-dominated sectors of the economy and also by a perceived Islamization of local government. The Dayaks in Kalimantan have felt marginalized by Madurese settlers taking over their traditional lands and depriving them of positions in the local economy and bureaucracy.

Another important factor in provoking unrest and separatist demands has been large-scale human rights abuses by the security services. In both Aceh and Irian Jaya, police and military brutality has alienated large sections of the community against Jakarta's rule and played a major role in galvanizing support for the independence cause.

Indonesia's ethnic and religious complexities are not, in themselves, inherently destabilizing elements. They can, however, in combination with other grievances, add to the country's volatility. Appropriate government responses in addressing economic disparities, political disenfranchisement, and human rights abuses by military and police could do much to reduce regional and intracommunal tensions. Furthermore, there is no a priori reason why a democratizing and decentralizing Indonesia should be less stable than an authoritarian and centralizing one. In fact, many of Indonesia's current problems derive from the excesses of the Suharto regime.

Greg Fealy is a research fellow in Indonesian history at the Research School of Pacific and Asian Studies, Australian National University, Canberra.

(continued from page 439)
sentment toward Jakarta, but it would also increase the disparities of wealth between resource-rich, industrially developed regions and the poorer, less-developed areas.

Indonesia's economy continued its weak recovery from the 1997 Asian financial crisis, though it remained vulnerable to an international downturn. Although growth in 2000–01 was 3.5%, better than most of its Southeast Asian neighbours, this was due largely to increased output from small and medium-sized businesses. Many of Indonesia's corporations remained heavily indebted, and much of the financial sector was in need of restructuring. The budget deficit remained large at $4.2 billion, or 2.5% of the nation's gross domestic product, and the slow pace of privatizing state enterprises and selling assets of bankrupt banks was expected to put pressure on the government to take unpopular measures such as cutting fuel and transport subsidies. A return to the robust growth rates of the Suharto era was impossible without large-scale foreign investment, and this was unlikely to occur in the short term.

The Megawati government faced daunting challenges in restoring Indonesia's economic health and political stability as well as in improving internal security. It would be undertaking these tasks in an increasingly uncertain international environment. The world economy was facing a slowdown, and the U.S.-led war against terrorism had already aroused strong protests within Indonesia's majority Islamic community. If Megawati did not provide stable and effective government, public confidence in her leadership and in democratic government could be seriously undermined. (GREG FEALY)

IRAN

Area: 1,629,918 sq km (629,315 sq mi)
Population (2001 est.): 63,442,000 (excluding roughly 2,000,000 Afghan refugees and fewer than 400,000 Iraqi refugees)
Capital: Tehran
Supreme political and religious authority: *Rahbar* (Spiritual Leader) Ayatollah Sayyed Ali Khamenei
Head of state and government: President Mohammad Khatami

The two wings of the Iranian political establishment remained firmly at loggerheads in 2001. Liberals and reformists were inhibited in their programs of economic privatization and development of a more open social regime by hard-line Islamic conservatives' opposition to change. The judiciary in particular rigorously repressed free speech. On January 13 a Revolutionary Court gave prolonged jail terms or heavy fines to 10 Iranian reformists who had participated in a proscribed conference in Berlin. The aggressive crackdown on reform-oriented Islamic factions and student groups culminated in March and April in the arrest of more than 60 eminent political figures associated with the banned Iran Freedom Movement. In addition, many reformist journals were closed down and reporters silenced by judicial organs controlled by the right wing. During the year 60 reformers in the parliament had been called before the courts on a variety of charges. In December a pro-reform member of the parliament was sentenced to 13 months in jail for insulting the courts.

The hard-line offensive against the press and the reformists was part of a sustained campaign to frustrate Pres. Mohammad Khatami and his cabinet but was also a tactic used to weaken the pro-Khatami wing of the regime in advance of the presidential election that took place on June 8. The election, however, proved a major success for the Khatami camp. The president was returned to power with an overwhelming 77% of the votes—an outcome that rebutted the hard-line contention that Khatami and his followers had lost the support of the nation. Khatami's political platform was extremely modest, promising only that he would continue within a formula of extreme moderation to pursue reform and move Iran toward an Islamic democracy.

The new presidential term was expected to bring about significant strengthening of the reformist component within the Majlis (parliament). Khatami declined as a matter of policy to confront the hard-liners, and his postelection cabinet was little changed from his original group of ministers. Indeed, the entire tone of policy in the wake of the June election was one of continuity of deference to conservative clerics, even on issues such as the hard-liners' introduction of regulations in midyear for the public flogging of persons found guilty of social/religious offenses.

Opposition to and alienation from the Islamic government was apparent during the presidential election when almost a third of the electorate opted not to vote. Active dissent was manifest in sporadic urban unrest. Officially reported cases included demonstrations in north Tehran against press controls, student protests in Tehran against the hard-liners in January, and a major confrontation against the use of foreign labour at the Assaluyeh refinery in September. In April there was an intensive Iranian missile attack on Mujahedin-e Khalq Organization camps in Iraq, which indicated a continuing apprehension of MKO influence by the Iranian authorities.

Iran struggled to make headway in its key foreign policy aims, impeded by the domestic stalemate between the president and the conservatives. The U.S. renewed its Iran-Libyan Sanctions Act in mid-2001 for a period of five years. In June allegations were made in Washington that Iran had been involved in the 1996 bombing of the al-Khobar Towers in Saudi Arabia, which claimed the lives of 19 U.S. personnel. Although the Iranian leadership, notably President Khatami, was quick to condemn the September 11 terrorist attacks in the United States, hopes that the campaign against terrorism would offer some degree of rapprochement with the U.S. were dimmed in late September when the Iranian spiritual leader, Ali Khamenei, made a hard-line anti-American speech. In the speech Khamenei explicitly rejected, except under a UN banner, Iranian participation in any actions against the Taliban government in Afghanistan or in a global antiterrorist movement. Meanwhile, Iranian diplomatic relations with Central Asia, the Arabian peninsula, China, and the European Union were generally lukewarm. Arms purchases were negotiated with Russia in early October.

The economy enjoyed mixed fortunes. Oil revenues remained high at approximately $24 billion for the year ended March 2001, and foreign borrowing was estimated at a modest $12.8 billion. There were continuing difficulties, however, with real growth in the economy, which was estimated at 5.6%. Moreover, structural reform through privatization almost totally stalled, and price inflation was still running at 12.6%. Iran suffered its third straight year of severe drought in 2001; losses in agriculture were put at $2.6 billion. (KEITH S. MCLACHLAN)

IRAQ

Area: 435,052 sq km (167,975 sq mi)
Population (2001 est.): 23,332,000
Capital: Baghdad
Head of state and government: President and Prime Minister Saddam Hussein

In the wake of the terrorist attacks in the U.S. on Sept. 11, 2001, Iraq was virtually alone among countries in failing to offer official condolences to the U.S. In line with his adversarial relationship with the U.S., Pres. Saddam Hussein publicly opposed the U.S.-led war on terrorism and called on other Islamic countries to help defeat it. He also decried the military action in Afghanistan, calling it a spark that could set "the world on fire." In response, U.S. Secretary of State Colin Powell suggested that once the U.S. had concluded its campaign in Afghanistan, it would deal with Iraq's weapons program as part of its effort against terrorism. Meanwhile, the U.S. focused on persuading Russia to sign off on a "smart sanctions" package that would ease the restrictions on civilian goods imported into Iraq but tighten restrictions on military supplies. The package also included measures to prevent Iraq from smuggling oil to the outside world, as it continued to do. Pending action on new UN measures, in November the existing "oil for food" program was renewed, while the U.S. and its allies dealt with Afghanistan. Hussein reiterated that UN arms inspectors would not be allowed to return to Iraq unless international sanctions against the country were lifted.

U.S. and British airplanes continued to attack Iraqi radar installations and other military targets throughout the year. The Iraqis strengthened their military capacity and announced that they had downed three unmanned U.S. surveillance planes patrolling the no-fly zone in southern Iraq. The Pentagon confirmed in September that it had lost contact with the planes.

Iraq put major efforts into improving relations with its neighbours, with considerable success. Relations between Iraq and Syria warmed considerably during the year. Railroad links between the two countries were reestablished in May. In June Syria abolished visa requirements for Iraqis visiting Syria, and in August, accompanied by a huge delegation, Syrian Prime Minister Mustafa Mero made a three-day visit to Iraq. The two countries signed several trade agreements. Regular commercial air travel resumed between Damascus (Syria) and Baghdad and between Amman (Jordan) and Baghdad.

Relations between Turkey and Iraq also improved during the year despite continued Turkish military incursions into northern Iraq in pursuit of Turkey's Kurdish rebels. The two countries resumed railway links, and the first train to go from Turkey to Iraq in more than 20 years arrived in Baghdad in early May. In July the two countries agreed to open a second border crossing in northern Iraq, at a point yet to be determined. A new Turkish ambassador presented his credentials to Baghdad on January 19 and thereby upgraded diplomatic relations between the two countries.

Relations between Iraq and Iran remained strained, however. Each country accused the other of continuing to hold prisoners of war from the 1980–90 Iran-Iraq War, and each country harboured organized groups opposed to the other's regime.

The economic situation inside Iraq did not improve substantially during the year. There were increases in the basic monthly food rations, sold to the population at nominal prices, but other food items and most consumer goods remained beyond the reach of the general public because of high prices. Iraqis were paid very low salaries, and inflation remained high. The government made efforts to stimulate the economy. It announced loan programs for Iraqi businessmen to establish local industries and created free-trade zones with Syria and Egypt, which were designed to increase the flow of Egyptian and Syrian goods to Iraq. Smuggling operations of various kinds remained strong, providing Iraqi local markets with goods that were not allowed under the sanctions, such as electronics and computers. Smuggling of Iraqi archaeological treasures out of the country continued. The Iraqi government admitted the existence of such operations and announced severe measures to curb them.

Politically, the year saw the consolidation of power in the hands of Hussein's youngest son, Qusay. The 34-year-old Qusay headed elite units of army and security forces. On May 17 he was elected to membership of the Regional Command of the ruling Arab Socialist Ba'th Party, and on May 19 Hussein named him one of the two deputy commanders of the influential military branch of the Ba'th Party. The rise of Qusay's star strengthened the prospect that he would

A mosaic in central Baghdad depicts Iraqi leader Saddam Hussein on horseback (centre), flanked by his sons Uday (left) and Qusay.

AP/Wide World Photos

succeed his father. Previously, Hussein's eldest son, Uday, had been thought to be next in line, but his prospects dimmed after he was badly wounded in an assassination attempt in 1996.

(LOUAY BAHRY)

IRELAND

Area: 70,273 sq km (27,133 sq mi)
Population (2001 est.): 3,823,000
Capital: Dublin
Chief of state: President Mary McAleese
Head of government: Prime Minister Bertie Ahern

Voters in Dublin celebrate the rejection of a referendum to endorse the Treaty of Nice on June 8.

AP/Wide World Photos

The year 2001 saw expectations in Ireland adjusting sharply downward after five years of rapid growth. With the slide in the U.S. economy and in the aftermath of the September 11 terrorist attacks, leading analysts in Ireland estimated the country's economic growth for the year at about 6%.

Even before September the slowdown in the U.S. had begun to have an impact on Ireland. As Silicon Valley companies shrank operations, up to 10,000 job losses were predicted for Ireland's information-technology sector. Big-name closures such as Gateway sent a shock through the community and unsettled government planners.

The effects of September 11 were immediate. The state airline, Aer Lingus, announced a 25% cut in services and said it would drop 2,500 employees. The wider implications were signaled later when Waterford Crystal—one of the jewels of Irish industry—put its operation on a three-day workweek.

The factors that had facilitated Ireland's progress suddenly made it vulnerable. Ireland had had the best of both worlds—European Union (EU) support and American investment. By year's end, however, European transfers had all but ended. With no clarity as to when the U.S. economy might start to turn around, Ireland wondered whether it had yet to feel the full brunt of the downturn.

Domestic factors added to the Irish economic worries. Inflation ran ahead of EU averages at 5%. A series of strikes disrupted schools and rail and air services. On the positive side, unemployment remained below 4%.

The spread of bovine spongiform encephalopathy (BSE), or "mad cow" disease, in Great Britain was held at bay in Ireland but at the cost of closing the countryside. Tourism revenues and farm exports fell. Meanwhile, although cases of BSE had been few, exporters struggled to hold international markets. Some optimism emerged late in the year when the Egyptian beef market partially reopened. (*See* AGRICULTURE AND FISHERIES: *Special Report.*)

Public finances suffered. In September, for the third quarter in succession, the Department of Finance reduced its forecast for taxation revenues. At that point the government still hoped for a budget surplus of perhaps £Ir 1 billion (about $1.1 billion).

A general election was due by May 2002. The centre-right government was led by Prime Minister Bertie Ahern. His Fianna Fail party and its partners, the Progressive Democrats, were determined to complete their five-year term and to seek reelection after having jump-started the slowing economy. Even if they were successful on the economic front, other problems loomed. In particular, social services and infrastructure had not kept pace with the economic growth of the past few years. There was widespread concern over the health services, while problems of transport, housing, and the environment continued. The government planned a network of new motorways, an underground and light-rail system for Dublin, an overhaul of the health system, and a special pension fund for Ireland's future elderly.

Not all of these objectives could be met. The budget presented to the Dail (parliament) in December masterfully balanced spending against revenues without borrowing, but it seemed clear that future spending would involve some deficit budgeting. For Ireland, this prompted fearful recollections of the 1980s, when the national debt reached crisis proportions.

The economy was not the only disappointment. In June voters rejected a referendum to endorse the Treaty of Nice, which provided for EU expansion. The rejection signaled the end of Ireland's love affair with the EU. Paradoxically, the Economic and Monetary Union had given stability to the Irish economy, and the business community eagerly welcomed the advent of the euro in 2002.

Meanwhile, the future of the Belfast Agreement, which envisaged a lasting peace in Northern Ireland, appeared more secure after the illegal Irish Republican Army destroyed or "put beyond use" at least part of its armoury. Northern Ireland's elected assembly and administration was thus enabled to get down to the routine business of government.

Throughout 2001 a series of judicial tribunals continued to investigate allegations of corruption involving politicians and business figures. Central to these was the investigation of former prime minister Charles Haughey, who allegedly had received substantial sums of money from prominent businesspeople while he was in office.

In October the government announced plans for a referendum on the country's abortion laws. Abortions were illegal in Ireland unless giving birth threatened the life of the mother. Debate on this deeply divisive issue was gathering momentum as the year drew to a close. Simultaneously, the government sought a way forward after the electorate's rejection of the Treaty of Nice. Ahern established a forum in October to redefine policy on Europe. Notwithstanding encouraging sentiments from the government, Ireland found itself cast in the unwelcome role of obstructing EU expansion. (CONOR BRADY)

ISRAEL

Area: 21,671 sq km (8,367 sq mi), including the Golan Heights and disputed East Jerusalem, excluding the Emerging Palestinian Autonomous Areas
Population (2001 est.): 6,258,000
Capital: Jerusalem is the proclaimed capital of Israel (since Jan. 23, 1950) and the actual seat of government, but recognition has generally been withheld by the international community
Chief of state: President Moshe Katzav
Head of government: Prime Ministers Ehud Barak and, from March 7, Ariel Sharon

The Emerging Palestinian Autonomous Areas (the West Bank and the Gaza Strip)
Total area: West Bank 5,900 sq km (2,270 sq mi), of which (prior to September 2000) 342 sq km is under Palestinian administration, 3,369 sq km under Israeli administration, and 2,189 sq km under joint administration; Gaza Strip 363 sq km (140 sq mi), of which about 236 sq km is under Palestinian administration and about 127 sq km under Israeli administration
Population (2001 est.): West Bank 2,268,000, including 2,069,000 Arabs and 199,000 Jews; Gaza Strip 1,203,000, including 1,196,000 Arabs and 7,000 Jews
Principal administrative centres: Ram Allah and Gaza
Head of government: President Yasir Arafat

Following the Sept. 11, 2001, terrorist attacks in the U.S., Palestinian Authority leader Yasir Arafat declared a cease-fire in the yearlong Palestinian confrontation with Israel—known as the second *intifadah*—but the violence soon resumed, and it reached a crescendo in December.

On February 6 the hawkish Ariel Sharon (*see* BIOGRAPHIES), leader of the right-wing Likud, was elected prime minister, defeating Ehud Barak by 62.4% to 37.6%. The Israeli electorate swung dramatically to the right in the wake of the eruption of the September 2000 *intifadah.* Despite his sweeping victory, Sharon had only 19 Likud members in the 120-member Knesset (parliament), but he formed a broad-based coalition government supported by 77 Knesset members from seven political parties, including Labor.

The power-sharing arrangement with Labor in the "government of national unity" was reflected in the distribution of cabinet posts; Labor's Shimon Peres and Benjamin Ben-Eliezer secured the key foreign and defense portfolios, respectively. Another Labor Knesset member, Salah Tarif, of the minority Druze sect, became the first non-Jewish cabinet minister.

One of the new coalition's first acts was to amend the electoral law. The two-ballot system, in which Israelis cast one vote for prime minister and another for a party, was abolished. The system had been designed to create a more stable government, but it had strengthened small one-issue groupings at the expense of the two major national parties, Labor and Likud. It was replaced by a return to one-vote proportional representation, with the key addition of a constructive no-confidence mechanism, by which the opposition would have to muster 61 of the 120 Knesset votes and present an alternative candidate in order to oust a sitting prime minister.

Three days before Sharon took office on March 7, a Palestinian suicide bomber blew himself up in the seaside town of Netanya. The fundamentalist Hamas organization announced that the bomber was the first of 10 "martyrs" waiting to greet Sharon's new government. Other bombings followed in Hadera, Binyamina, Tel Aviv, Haifa, and Jerusalem. Israel responded with a policy of "targeted killings," arguing that the only way to preempt the bombers was to assassinate the men planning to send them. Palestinian ambushes and drive-by shootings, which took a heavy toll in Jewish settler lives in the occupied West Bank, prompted Israeli troops to seal off Palestinian towns and villages to restrict Palestinian movement, but the measures failed to curb the violence.

According to the Israeli army, there were about 8,000 "serious" Palestinian attacks during the first year of the *intifadah,* 84 of them inside Israel proper. A total of 176 Israelis lost their lives, and 1,742 were injured; the number of Palestinians killed was 604, and between 8,500 and 10,000 were injured.

After taking office, Sharon announced two major policy changes: no negotiations with the Palestinians as long as violence continued and interim rather than final arrangements when the shooting stopped. Two weeks later he visited the U.S. and persuaded the administration of Pres. George W. Bush to back his demand for a cease-fire as a precondition for talks with the Palestinians. Sharon's aim was to contain the *intifadah* through a combination of military action and international pressure on Arafat. The policy suffered from an inherent contradiction, however; the tougher the measures that Israel took, the less international support it got. In addition, the Israelis demanded an end to violence before new peace proposals would be put on the table, and the Palestinians insisted on some idea of the direction that a new peace process might lead before calling an end to the *intifadah;* as a result, the fighting continued.

On May 21 a fact-finding committee led by former U.S. senator George Mitchell presented its report on the causes of the violence, and both the Israelis and the Palestinians expressed readiness to accept Mitchell's call for a four-phase process leading to political reengagement: a cease-fire, a cooling-off period, confidence-building measures, and resumption of negotiations.

On June 1 a suicide bomber blew himself up outside a Tel Aviv discotheque, killing 20 Israeli teenagers. The outrage drew widespread international condemnation, and German Foreign Minister Joschka Fischer, who was in Tel Aviv near the scene of the carnage, pressured Arafat into calling a cease-fire. U.S. CIA Director George Tenet flew in to negotiate the terms, and on June 13 both sides announced a cease-fire designed to jump-start the Mitchell process; it failed to hold, however.

Achieving a durable cease-fire proved elusive. The Palestinians demanded international observers to oversee any truce, but Israel refused, agreeing only to reactivate the existing Supreme Security Coordination Committee, consisting of Israeli, Palestinian, and CIA officials. More important, the Palestinians sought reassurance that negotiation with the Sharon government would lead to a final settlement, at the very least along the lines of the understandings reached with the government of Ehud Barak in Taba, Egypt, in late January. Those discussions were based on the so-called "Clinton parameters," the bridging proposals announced by then U.S. president Bill Clinton in December 2000. The parameters allocated 94–96% of the West Bank to the Palestinians with an exchange of land in Israel proper to compensate for the remaining 4–6% and made equally far-reaching proposals on the core issues of Jerusalem and refugees. Sharon declared that he would be ready to discuss only a string of less-ambitious interim agreements, but he also said he would be ready to accept the establishment of a Palestinian state.

The ongoing *intifadah* led to an erosion of Israel's position in the Arab world and to widespread criticism of Israeli countermeasures by the international community. A wave of anti-Israel sentiment came to a head at the UN-sponsored World Conference Against Racism in Durban, S.Af., in early September. Arab and Muslim countries pressed for strong anti-Israel language in the final communiqué, including a statement equating Zionism with racism. The United States and Israel walked out.

On October 17 Tourism Minister Rehavam Ze'evi was assassinated in retaliation for the killing in August of Palestinian Popular Front leader Abu Ali Mustafa. (*See* OBITUARIES.) The action led Israeli forces to invade Bethlehem and five other West Bank cities. The violence escalated, and Sharon cut short a visit to the U.S. when 26 Israelis were killed and more than 270 injured in a string of suicide and car bombings in a crowded Jerusalem shopping mall late on the night of December 1 and on a bus in Haifa the following morning. By mid-December, under pressure from the United States and other countries, Arafat called for a halt to "terrorist activities," and he ordered the closure of about a dozen Hamas and Islamic Jihad offices.

The *intifadah* brought great hardship on the Palestinians, but it also hurt Israel's economy. In the third quarter of 2000, before the fighting erupted, there had been an economic upsurge, with a staggering 9.1% increase in gross domestic product; but in the fourth quarter GDP was down by 8%, and it continued to slide by a further 0.6% in the first half of 2001. Tourism slumped to unprecedented lows, and foreign investment fell by about 70%. As the economic slowdown deepened, unemployment topped the 9% mark.

The global downturn in high-tech activity also had a devastating economic effect. Exports were down by 26.5% in the first half of the year, owing mainly to the fall in high tech and in the diamond trade. In September, partly as a result of the slump in world money markets in the wake of the terrorist attacks in the U.S., the shekel lost about 6% of its value against the dollar. Inflation, however, remained under control, at an annual rate of about 1.5–2%.

(LESLIE D. SUSSER)

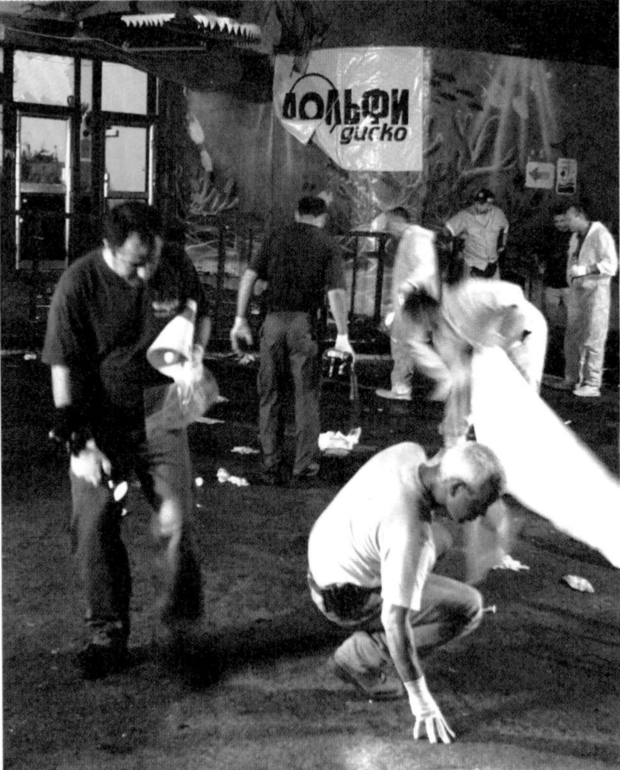

Israeli policemen search the scene outside a discotheque in Tel Aviv where a Palestinian suicide bomber blew himself up and killed 20 Israeli teenagers on June 1.

© Reinhard Krause/Reuters 2001

ITALY

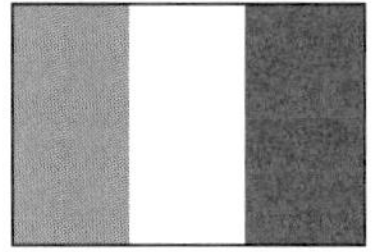

Area: 301,337 sq km (116,347 sq mi)
Population (2001 est.): 57,892,000
Capital: Rome
Chief of state: President Carlo Azeglio Ciampi
Head of government: Prime Ministers Giuliano Amato and, from June 11, Silvio Berlusconi

In Italy six and a half years of rule by centre-left governments came to an end in 2001 when elections swept into power a centre-right coalition led by media magnate Silvio Berlusconi, the richest man in the country. (*See* BIOGRAPHIES.) Shortly afterward, violence broke out in the northern port city of Genoa during antiglobalization protests staged while a Group of Eight (G-8) summit was being held in the city. What ultimately overshadowed these events, however, was a deep anxiety in Italy over possible repercussions from the U.S.-led war on terrorism.

The elections in May, with 630 seats at stake in the Chamber of Deputies and 315 in the Senate, were essentially a fight between two alliances—Berlusconi's House of Freedoms and the centre-left Olive Tree partnership led by Francesco Rutelli, a former mayor of Rome. The campaign centred on a highly personalized duel between the leaders of the two alliances, with Berlusconi branding his opponents "communists" and Rutelli applauding the British magazine *The Economist* for describing Berlusconi as "unfit to rule" in part because he had recently come under investigation for money laundering, tax evasion, and bribery, among other charges. Whereas Rutelli struggled to pull together partners split by chronic bickering, however, Berlusconi's alliance, led by his own Forza Italia party—the country's biggest—maintained unity. Commentators noted that superior financial resources also greatly helped Berlusconi's cause; for instance, he was able to send a biographical photo album of himself to every household in the country. In a television spot aired shortly before the elections, Berlusconi brandished a huge parchmentlike scroll bearing pledges that bound him—over five years—to lower taxes, create more than a million new jobs, embark on a major public-works program, and increase the minimum monthly pension to 1 million lire

Police in Genoa, Italy, surround an antiglobalization demonstrator during protests against the G-8 summit on July 20.

AP/Wide World Photos

(about $465). He called this his "contract" with Italians.

The outcome was a triumph for Berlusconi, who had already enjoyed seven months of premiership in 1994. The House of Freedoms scooped up 368 seats in the Chamber against the Olive Tree's 242, while in the smaller Senate the figures were 177 to 125, respectively. Forza Italia increased its share of the House's cake by 9%, while another alliance member, Umberto Bossi's Northern League—which championed more autonomy for the north of Italy—fared worse than predicted. It took Berlusconi a month to put together a 23-member cabinet, in which Bossi, after much haggling, became minister for devolution, while the foreign minister's post went to a nonpolitician, Renato Ruggiero. The new prime minister's team won a vote of confidence in June by 351–261. Before the vote Berlusconi had promised an unspecified solution to a much-aired issue, that of the "conflict of interest" he faced as a political leader involved in big business.

Trouble came in July when Genoa was for three days ravaged and turned into a virtual theatre of war during pitched battles between 19,000 police and tens of thousands of antiglobalization demonstrators besieging a summit of the G-8. One protester was killed when a police officer whom he had threatened with a fire extinguisher shot him. The reported number of persons injured in the mayhem amounted to more than 200, and about 280 arrests were made. Police met assaults, stone throwing, and molotov cocktails with baton charges and tear gas, but both protest organizers and the government ascribed most of the violence to black-clad intruders, including many non-Italians, who belonged to a group known as the Black Bloc; this was the same group that had first attracted headlines by rioting at a World Trade Organization summit in Seattle, Wash., in 1999. Accused of muscling in on a protest meant to be peaceful, the Black Bloc members were generally identified as the ones who set cars and rubbish bins ablaze in Genoa, vandalized banks, shops, and supermarkets, and attacked the local jail. Another incident during the Genoa protests contributed to nationwide dismay. Police conducted a midnight raid on a school housing scores of protesters, after which the Italian media showed pools and splashes of blood on the floors and walls of the school. Later the opposition noisily accused police of "brutal violence," but Interior Minister Claudio Scajola ignored cries for his resignation, claiming that the raid was justified because the school had harboured troublemakers. A parliamentary commission, under a Forza Italia chairman, eventually declared the summit "a success," ascribed police "excesses" to individuals, and charged that "peaceful protesters" were guilty of tolerating violent elements in their midst.

Fearing a repetition of violence at other planned international meetings in Italy, the government proposed changing the locations of a September NATO conference in Naples—which, as a result, was held in Brussels instead—and a November UN Food and Agriculture Organization (FAO) conference in Rome. After contemplating a switch to the Adriatic resort of Rimini, the FAO opted not to relocate its conference from Rome after all.

Uproar then broke out in Parliament when, in August and October, it passed legislation explained by the government as a step toward sweeping away obsolescence and helping business but denounced by an angry opposition as meant to serve the interests of the prime minister or his friends. One new law replaced a prison term for rendering false tax returns with a pecuniary penalty. A left-wing leader, Pierluigi Castagnetti, told Parliament that no country in the world would "pass a measure to solve its leader's problems with the law." At the time he spoke, Berlusconi faced penal proceedings for alleged financial misdeeds. Another new law, which dealt with rules of evidence, decreed as inadmissible documentation acquired from abroad if the procedure followed to obtain it differed from Italy's. The government refuted the charges against it, terming its opponents "guardians of lies."

The prime minister stuck to his pledge on pensions but urged followers to vote "no" in an October referendum on devolution called by the previous government. Nevertheless, Italians, by a margin of 64%–34%, voted "yes" to the referendum and thus approved proposed changes in the working of the Italian state. The central government would relinquish powers to the country's regions in, for example, the spheres of education and the environment. City councils would also be able to raise certain taxes.

Following the September 11 terrorist attacks in the U.S., Berlusconi was among the European leaders who lined up to pledge support for the U.S.-led war on terrorism. The prime minister put the country on heightened alert and promised that Italy was "by the side of the United States and all who are committed to the battle against terrorism." Italy offered troops as well as the use of its ports and airports, but many in the country were anxious over possible repercussions from the conflict. Berlusconi hardly helped allay these anxieties with his statement to reporters in late September that the West was "superior" to Islamic civilization because it provided wealth and guaranteed respect for human rights. While the prime minister maintained that his comments had been taken out of context, European Union leaders took pains to distance themselves from his remarks.

Disaster struck Italy in October at Milan's Linate airport when, in heavy fog, a Scandinavian airliner collided during takeoff with a small jet taxiing across its path, killing a total of 118 people. (*See* DISASTERS.) Terrorism was initially suspected, but aviation experts later ruled it out, putting part of the blame instead on the absence of a working ground-level radar at the airport. (DEREK WILSON)

JAMAICA

Area: 10,991 sq km (4,244 sq mi)
Population (2001 est.): 2,624,000
Capital: Kingston
Chief of state: Queen Elizabeth II, represented by Governor-General Sir Howard Cooke
Head of government: Prime Minister Percival J. Patterson

Tourism was dealt a severe blow when in March and April 2001 four cruise lines dropped Jamaica from their itineraries following complaints about visitor harassment. The reduction in tourist revenue was expected to amount to as much as $22 million. In May the government unveiled a $2 billion "master plan" for development of the tourist industry.

The electricity problems plaguing Jamaica and hampering development seemed on their way to being rectified in March when the government sold 80% of the Jamaica Public Service Co., the country's power generator and transmitter, to the American company Mirant, which promised to add another 385 MW of power to the existing 660 MW.

In a report issued in April by London-based Amnesty International, Jamaica's police service was sharply criticized for its violations of human rights. The report said that the police had unlawfully killed 140 people in 2000—a rate of about 5.4 per 100,000 persons, which, Amnesty said, was one of the highest in the world. The government described the report as "one-sided, false, and misleading."

Jamaica was bedeviled by spasmodic gang violence during much of the year, particularly in the West Kingston area, where in July at least 25 persons were killed in street violence. The government set up a commission of inquiry in September to look into gangs and links with the drug trade and organized crime.

(DAVID RENWICK)

JAPAN

Area: 377,837 sq km (145,884 sq mi)
Population (2001 est.): 127,100,000
Capital: Tokyo
Symbol of state: Emperor Akihito
Head of government: Prime Ministers Yoshiro Mori and, from April 26, Junichiro Koizumi

Domestic Affairs. For nearly five decades the Liberal-Democratic Party (LDP)—either alone or in coalition—had formed the government in Tokyo. Early in 2001, however, the party looked forward to the next national poll with unease. An election for 121 contested seats in the 247-seat (upper) House of Councillors was scheduled for the end of July. LDP leaders considered the real possibility of a loss in the vote.

In April 2000 Prime Minister Yoshiro Mori had been, as usual, selected in secret by LDP faction bosses. In 10 months of service, he had averaged one major blunder per month. On one occasion he referred to Japan as a "divine country," a phrase that called up memories of militarist rhetoric during the Pacific wars. In February 2001, after an American submarine collided with a Japanese trawler off the coast of Hawaii, with nine persons aboard the trawler missing, Mori continued to play golf for two hours after hearing about the accident.

A month later Mori bore a public approval rating of 6.5%, the lowest ever for a Japanese prime minister. On March 5 he survived a no-confidence vote in the (lower) House of Representatives, but rumours spread that he would soon step down. On April 6 Mori notified his cabinet that he would resign. In four days no fewer than five LDP leaders announced their candidacies for party president. At the head of popularity polls was Makiko Tanaka (*see* BIOGRAPHIES), the daughter of former prime minister Kakuei Tanaka. Her outspoken, often acerbic, comments on politics and politicians struck a responsive chord with the Japanese public. Tanaka once referred to her closest rival, Junichiro Koizumi, as a "crank." She eventually withdrew her candidacy and supported Koizumi, however.

A two-hour television debate on April 18 featured the four remaining candidates. Three veteran politicians faced off with Koizumi, the rising star. He seized the opportunity to air his platform. Instead of fiscal expenditures, which would result in additions to Japan's towering deficits, he urged economic reform and restraint. Koizumi was especially critical of Japan's debt-laden banking community; he also proposed privatization of the sacrosanct postal savings system.

In the LDP primaries, held on April 22–23, Koizumi took the first step toward power. He won a majority of votes (298 of 487) representing the 2.3 million party members and 346 LDP legislators. On April 24 he was elected president of the LDP. Two days later the Diet (parliament) confirmed him as prime minister. (*See* BIOGRAPHIES.)

Koizumi's victory, which was remarkable, considering he had denounced party factions, put him on a collision course with vested interests within the LDP itself. Faction bosses represented branches of the postal service, local construction firms, small retailers, and rice farmers all over Japan. In forming his administration, the new leader kept in mind the nature of his support. He led a three-party coalition that included the New Komeito (backed by the nation's largest Buddhist group) and the New Conservative Party. Only 6 of the 17 members of his cabinet came from the LDP's three main factions. An unprecedented number of women—five, including Tanaka, Japan's first female foreign minister—were given portfolios. For his minister of economic policy, Koizumi chose Heizo Takenaka, an economist from Keio University, Tokyo. In a surprise he named Masajuro Shiokawa finance minister. The 79-year-old Shiokawa had served in several governments but never as an adviser on finance matters.

The new regime enjoyed popular support, with surveys showing approval over the 80% level. At first Koizumi avoided controversial economic issues, concentrating instead on proposals attractive to the centre and the right. He called for a review of the so-called MacArthur constitution, imposed on Japan by the Allied powers in 1946. He advocated a more democratic system, including the direct election of the prime minister. Most important, Koizumi joined nationalists in urging that Japan allow its military forces to exercise a full-fledged (rather than only defensive) security policy. This last goal guaranteed opposition from a coalition ally, the pacifist New Komeito. Moreover, many Japanese, especially elders with grim wartime memories, were uneasy with the idea of increased military forces.

A preliminary but important endorsement of the new regime was received on June 24 in the Tokyo municipal poll. The coalition won a majority in an urban area where the LDP had always been weak. The next challenge was the scheduled upper house election set for July 29. Normally, Japanese political campaigns were mercifully short and discreet. In this case, however, there was an explosion of posters heralding Koizumi, as well as vigorous debates between local candidates. The LDP enjoyed its best victory since 1992; its coalition won 78 of the 121 contested seats.

On December 1 the royal family celebrated the birth of the first child—a daughter—to Crown Princess Masako and Crown Prince Naruhito; although the emperor traditionally would have decided the name, the couple themselves chose it—Princess Aiko.

The Economy. Japan's recession lingered during the year, with few signs that the country would emerge from it soon. The Finance Ministry announced that in December 2000 Japan's trade surplus had shrunk to $7 billion, the lowest monthly level since March 1997. Officials later identified the first two quarters of 2001 as marking the sharpest trade decline on record, with the surplus down 44% from the same two quarters of the previous year.

In similar fashion the current account surplus (the difference between income from foreign sources and payments on foreign obligations) for fiscal year 2000 fell 4.5%, the second consecutive annual decline. The month of July 2001 was the eighth straight in which this surplus fell, down 28% from a year earlier. Slowing global growth had reduced demand for Japan's exports.

Trade was by no means the only problem. On September 3 Tokyo stocks dove to a 17-year low, with the benchmark 225-issue Nikkei index down to 10,409.68—its worst showing since August 1984. On September 17, in the wake of the terrorist attacks in the U.S., the index sank to an 18-year low of 9,504.41. By October year-on-year industrial output had fallen by 11.9% to a 13-year low. Consumer spending, usually an engine of Japanese growth, was sluggish despite a deflation in retail prices.

Among the world's industrial powers, Japan traditionally expected low levels of unemployment. Corporations often provided lifetime employment to their workers. Therefore, one of the biggest shocks in the country's economic downturn had been the spread of unemployment. In October the unemployment rate reached 5.4%, a postwar high. Japan's demography, marked by an aging population and a sharply declining birthrate, exacerbated the problem.

The national census, released in October 2000, set Japan's population at 126,920,000 and cited only a 0.2% per annum rise in population from the prior count (1995). This was the smallest increase since World War II. Just as significant, the proportion of elderly Japanese (17.5% at age 65 and older) surpassed youngsters (14.5% at 15 or younger). The dilemma was that a shrinking number of working-age Japanese would be expected to support an exploding number of people at retirement age. Indeed, Japan had become the fastest-aging society among advanced industrial powers.

Foreign Affairs. With new executive leaders, Japan and the U.S. continued their discussions of familiar issues. U.S. Pres. George W. Bush (*see* BIOGRAPHIES), during his election campaign of 2000, had urged reinforcement of security ties with Japan. He recognized the problems generated by the presence of some 47,000 American troops based in Okinawa and promised adjustments. Before his election Bush had referred only indirectly to the economic downturns in both countries.

In fact, shortly after his inauguration Bush met with Koizumi's predecessor, Yoshiro Mori, already a lame duck. On March 18 the embattled Mori arrived in Washington, D.C., carrying a portfolio of problems. In January an American

On April 26, the day of his inauguration, Japanese Prime Minister Junichiro Koizumi (front row, centre) appears with his newly appointed cabinet.

AP/Wide World Photos

AP/Wide World Photos

On December 8 Crown Prince Naruhito and Crown Princess Masako leave the palace hospital in Tokyo with their infant daughter, Princess Aiko.

marine corporal stationed in Okinawa had harassed a local girl. The local assembly immediately issued a resolution calling for a reduction of American forces in the area. On January 23 the senior U.S. commander there, Lieut. Gen. Earl Hailston, fired off an e-mail to fellow officers, referring to the local officials as "nuts" and "wimps." When this was leaked to the press, Hailston apologized. The assembly nevertheless issued a demand for his dismissal on February 7. Local leaders insisted on a revised U.S.-Japan Status of Forces Agreement, and on February 22—for the first time—Okinawa Gov. Keiichi Inamine, who had hitherto supported the American military, joined the requests for an adjustment to the agreement.

Meanwhile, Washington and Tokyo faced another, more bizarre challenge. On February 9 the USS *Greeneville,* an American submarine, collided with the *Ehime-maru,* a Japanese fishing trawler, near Hawaii. The submarine, which had been executing a quick surface drill, sliced the Japanese vessel in half and helplessly watched as it sank. Teachers and students from a fisheries-vocation school in Japan were aboard the ship, and after the accident nine persons remained missing.

The next day the commander in chief of the U.S. Pacific fleet, Adm. Thomas Fargo, apologized to Tokyo, as did Secretary of State Colin Powell (*see* BIOGRAPHIES), who passed along President Bush's condolences. In presenting his formal farewell to Emperor Akihito, retiring Ambassador Thomas Foley also expressed regret. On February 28 the captain of the submarine, Comdr. Scott D. Waddle, sent a letter of regret to the victims' families through Japan's consulate in Hawaii.

On March 26 Bush named a former senator, Howard H. Baker, Jr., to be ambassador to Japan. Before Baker arrived, however, a range of new issues arose.

The April 1 incident involving a collision between an American reconnaissance plane and a Chinese fighter jet over the South China Sea seemed to some observers to have only marginal interest to the Japanese. The American plane had, however, taken off from the U.S. Air Force base at Kadena, Okinawa. After the collision—which caused the crash of the Chinese jet and the death of its pilot—the American plane made an emergency landing on Hainan Island. The plane's crew members, detained for a time by Chinese authorities, were eventually released. Japanese opinion was divided over the incident. For some it represented a warning about growing threats—posed not only by China but also by North Korea, which supported Beijing.

On May 8 U.S. Deputy Secretary of State Richard Armitage publicly urged Japan to form a strategic partnership like that between the U.S. and Great Britain. Some Japanese worried about the "overwhelming presence" of U.S. military forces already on Okinawa, and many were concerned about Tokyo's tacit support of a deliberately vague Washington policy toward Taiwan.

On June 30 Koizumi made his first visit as prime minister to the U.S., meeting President Bush at Camp David, Maryland. On the very eve of Koizumi's arrival, yet another incident involving U.S. military personnel based on Okinawa emerged to overshadow the summit. Japanese police picked up an American air force sergeant in a small village near Kadena. He was questioned about an encounter with a local woman but was released. After she claimed she was raped, local officials demanded that the man be returned to them. For only the second time, the U.S. released a serviceman on active duty for trial in a local court. The sergeant pleaded not guilty, and the trial dragged on.

Meanwhile, the Koizumi-Bush summit turned out to be somewhat of an anticlimax. A communiqué listed the topics informally discussed by the two leaders. These included continued security cooperation, economic partnership for growth, and cooperation on global change. The prime minister visited Washington again on September 25, when he promised the president help in logistics and intelligence in the U.S. campaign against terrorism.

The subject of textbooks came to dominate diplomatic relations between Japan, South Korea, Taiwan, and China. In Seoul on February 28—the day before the 82nd anniversary of a Korean uprising against Japanese rule—South Korean Foreign Minister Lee Joung Binn gave a warning to Ambassador Terusuke Terada of Japan, stating that Tokyo's approval of a textbook praising Imperial Japan's record as a colonial ruler of Korea and much of China would undermine relations. Some 19 groups demonstrated in front of the Japanese embassy in Seoul, and demonstrators in Pusan burned a Japanese flag and destroyed an effigy of a right-wing Japanese politician.

In Japan Foreign Minister Tanaka admitted that the textbook controversy was having a negative impact. Indeed, on May 8 Seoul canceled a scheduled joint military exercise with Japan. Koreans were particularly upset over the fact that Japan had never confessed to the mobilization of thousands of Koreans to be "comfort women" for Japanese troops. Koizumi nevertheless replied that Tokyo could not "revise again" textbooks approved by the Education Ministry. On June 11 hundreds of protesters—including Japanese, Chinese, Koreans, and Filipinos—surrounded the ministry and sang "We Shall Overcome."

To make matters worse, Koizumi remarked that he was considering a visit, as prime minister, to the Yasukuni Shrine in Tokyo on August 15, the anniversary of Japan's surrender at the end of World War II. The shrine memorialized the sacrifices of Japan's dead veterans, including several well-known convicted war criminals. This plan met the opposition of Tanaka, who had received warnings from Taiwan, China, and the Philippines. As it turned out, Koizumi retreated a bit but on August 13 did officially, though briefly, pay homage at the shrine. China and South Korea filed protests. On December 22 Japanese Coast Guard ships exchanged fire with and sank a vessel suspected of being a North Korean spy boat. Tokyo later announced that it planned to seek Beijing's permission to salvage the boat from waters claimed to be in China's economic zone.

In a telephone conversation on June 6, Tanaka and her Russian counterpart, Foreign Minister Igor S. Ivanov, agreed to resume talks toward signing a formal peace treaty. No such accord had been reached since 1945, when Russian forces occupied small islands—long claimed by Japan—between Hokkaido and the Russian-held Kuril Islands. Japan referred to these islets as the Northern Territories. In June, Voice of Russia radio announced that South Korean fishing vessels would be welcome to work in the area. Japan's Fisheries Ministry had threatened to bar Korean fishing in Japanese waters if the Korean vessels did fish there. By September tempers had cooled, and senior officials in Tokyo and Moscow predicted that they could settle the dispute. (ARDATH W. BURKS)

JORDAN

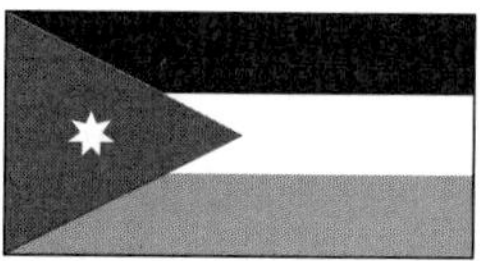

Area: 89,342 sq km (34,495 sq mi)
Population (2001 est.): 5,133,000 (including more than 1,500,000 Palestinian refugees, most of whom hold Jordanian citizenship)
Capital: Amman
Head of state and government: King Abdullah II, assisted by Prime Minister ʿAli Abu ar-Raghib

Jordan hosted the 13th ordinary session of the Arab League summit on March 27–28, 2001. The Arab leaders, who decided to meet annually, regarded this conference as a milestone to safeguarding "the vital interests of Arab countries within the context of achieving Arab accord and pan-Arab security."

On June 16 the Jordanian cabinet, headed by Prime Minister ʿAli Abu ar-Raghib, was reshuffled. Eleven cabinet ministers were replaced, but the total membership remained at 29. Among the newcomers were two independent Islamists.

On July 22 the State Security Court, in a retrial ordered in April, passed life sentences against nine defendants, all members of the radical Islamic Reform and Challenge organization, who had been accused of a series of car-park bombings in Amman in 1998. Amnesty International denounced the proceedings and called for a retrial by a criminal court.

King Abdullah II was the first Arab leader to visit the U.S. following the terroist attacks of September 11. In talks with Pres. George W. Bush, Abdullah fully supported the war against terrorism and pointed to Jordan's successful foiling of Osama bin Laden's terrorist operations in Jordan in 1999.

Although Palestinian leader Yasir Arafat, who made numerous visits to Amman, sought Abdullah's help to revive the Middle East peace process, Jordanian opposition parties headed by the Islamic Action Front had a different agenda. On September 28 these parties marked the first anniversary of the Palestinian *intifadah* by declaring "that the strategic option of peace with Israel is no longer valid." The Islamic Action Front, the political arm of the Muslim Brotherhood Movement, was the largest and most influential political group among Jordan's 25 registered parties.

On October 8, one day after U.S. air strikes began against Afghanistan, the Jordanian government adopted amendments to the penal code with restrictive measures against the press, including fines and prison sentences up to three years. The new law stipulated the permanent or temporary closure of publications that carried "false or libelous information that can undermine national unity or the country's reputation."

During the year Jordan further improved its excellent relations with Egypt, Syria, and Iraq. On March 14 King Abdullah, Egyptian Pres. Hosni Mubarak, and Syrian Pres. Bashar al-Assad inaugurated the Dair Ali power station, located at the Jordanian-Syrian border. The joint power grid linked the three countries. On June 5 Royal Jordanian Airlines resumed regular flights to Baghdad, Iraq, and in August a delegation headed by the Jordanian minister of industry and trade and four other members of the cabinet made an official visit to Iraq. (MARIUS K. DEEB)

KAZAKHSTAN

Area: 2,724,900 sq km (1,052,090 sq mi)
Population (2001 est.): 14,868,000
Capital: Astana
Head of state and government: President Nursultan Nazarbayev, assisted by Prime Minister Kasymzhomart Tokayev

In 2001 Kazakhstan's efforts to integrate into the international community beyond the Commonwealth of Independent States (CIS) were stymied by the country's worsening human rights record. In early March a delegation from the Parliamentary Assembly of the Council of Europe arrived in Almaty to examine the human rights and social situation in connection with Kazakhstan's application for observer status in the Council. Opposition activists publicly criticized the government for allowing only meetings with pro-government groups, which portrayed the progress of democratization in the country as far rosier than warranted by reality. Kazakhstan's application was subsequently denied by the Council.

The opposition and international observers were also critical of draft amendments to laws on the media and on religion. The latter included a provision for banning extremist sects and unauthorized missionary activity. In March the National Security Committee complained of an increase in Islamic religious and extremist activities in southern Kazakhstan. Shortly thereafter a group of adherents of the banned Muslim sect Hizb ut-Tahrir were put on trial for terrorism.

Leaders of the opposition Republican People's Party and members of seven other opposition groups told foreign contacts that they had been harassed by the authorities because of their objections to the revised media law. Kazakhstan's international reputation was further damaged when security officials prevented two opposition politicians from taking part in a congressional hearing in the United States in July, though the country's image received a boost at the end of that month when the abolition of exit visas for Kazakhstani citizens was announced.

Kazakhstan's economic outlook improved with the commissioning in March of the pipeline linking the Tengiz oil field in western Kazakhstan to the Russian Black Sea oil port of Novorossiysk. The pipeline, fully operational by December, significantly increased the amount of Kazakhstani oil that could be exported. An official proposal to raise money by accepting nuclear waste from abroad for burial in Kazakhstan set off protests by the country's influential environmental lobby.

In May Kazakhstan agreed with Russia, Kyrgyzstan, and Tajikistan to set up a rapid reaction force under the CIS Collective Security Treaty. In the wake of the September 11 attacks in the U.S., Kazakhstani Pres. Nursultan Nazarbayev ordered intensified security on Kazakhstan's borders and offered use of the country's airspace and ground facilities to the U.S.-led antiterrorism coalition. In a step that caused considerable friction within the region, Kazakhstan's borders were closed to citizens of Tajikistan. (BESS BROWN)

KENYA

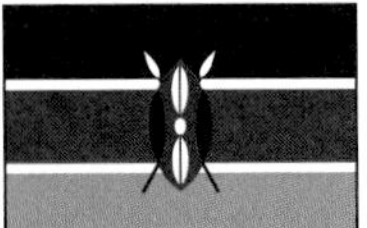

Area: 582,646 sq km (224,961 sq mi)
Population (2001 est.): 30,766,000
Capital: Nairobi
Head of state and government: President Daniel arap Moi

In January 2001 Kenyan Pres. Daniel arap Moi joined with the presidents of Tanzania and Uganda to launch a new East African Economic Community. Conditions at home were far from propitious for such a venture, however. The economy was shrinking; the value of the Kenyan shilling (K Sh) had declined and now stood at about 79 to the U.S. dollar; and the price of petroleum had risen to K Sh 56 per litre (about $2.68 per gallon). Meanwhile, the International Monetary Fund (IMF) and the World Bank continued to withhold aid because of the government's failure to control corruption.

Early in February hopes were raised when the government selected a consortium led by South Africa-based Econet Wireless to buy 49% of the state-owned telecommunications company, Telkom, which the IMF had insisted should be privatized. To the disgust of the World Bank, which blamed the Kenyan government, the deal fell through, but other donors had already warned that, even if the plan had materialized, aid would not be forthcoming until an effective anticorruption policy was in place.

The resignation as head of the Kenyan Civil Service on March 26 of Richard Leakey, who had been appointed to lead the campaign against corruption, was seen at first to have been another serious setback to the reform program. Leakey's campaign, however, had been faltering for some months because of the opposition of senior officials and other members of the government who feared for their own reputations. Leakey's own reputation was threatened when it became known that his resignation followed upon allegations by a British-born businessman that Leakey had written a letter to the attorney general of Kenya urging him to halt proceedings on a charge of fraud that the businessman had brought against a Dutch bank. Leakey, who was known to have close links with the Dutch royal family, had argued that the case would put a strain on Kenya's relations with The Netherlands. He was replaced as head of the civil service by Sally Kosgei, a highly respected civil servant and former high commissioner in London.

On June 17 President Moi began engineering a merger between the ruling Kenya African National Union and the National Development Party (NDP), Kenya's second largest opposition party. He then appointed Raila Odinga, the leader of the NDP, together with Adhu Owiti, another prominent figure in the party, to a reshuffled cabinet.

Opponents of the government were not slow to respond. On June 24 Charity Kaluki Ngilu, the Social Democratic Party's candidate in the 1997 presidential election, launched a new party, the National Party of Kenya, claiming that gender equality would feature prominently in the party's manifesto. More significantly, on August 14 opposition members in the National Assembly prevented the government from achieving the two-thirds majority needed to enact a bill ostensibly aimed at combating corruption. The opposition claimed that the bill was a sham, intended to deceive the IMF into renewing aid. The following day the IMF announced that it would remain in dialogue with the government but would be unable to resume aid payments. This meant that help from other sources would not be forthcoming. A few days later the government joined with six other eastern African countries to launch an African Trade Insurance Agency, to be based in Nairobi and intended to undercut the high premiums demanded from African companies by foreign insurance agencies, which regarded Africa as a high-risk area.

Early in December disturbances broke out in the most deprived locality in Nairobi, ostensibly in support of a demand for reduced rents, though there were suggestions that the violence had political undertones. Later that month the government agreed that U.S. and U.K. troops might use Kenya as a base for operations against alleged terrorist cells in Somalia.

(KENNETH INGHAM)

Japanese Prime Minister Yoshiro Mori and Kenyan Pres. Daniel arap Moi listen to the Japanese national anthem upon Mori's arrival in Nairobi on January 10.

AP/Wide World Photos

KIRIBATI

Area: 811 sq km (313 sq mi)
Population (2001 est.): 94,100
Capital: Bairiki, on Tarawa
Head of state and government: President Teburoro Tito

In Kiribati, with stability in domestic politics and the economy remaining largely dependent on foreign aid and trust investments derived from previous phosphate mining, the high points of 2001 had an international dimension. In October the government joined Australia in investigating the establishment of a processing centre for asylum-seeking refugees on Kanton (Canton), an island 1,900 km (about 1,200 mi) southeast of Tarawa. Kanton, a part of Kiribati formerly governed under a British-U.S. condominium, had been used for transpacific civil aviation from the 1930s and as a U.S. military base.

During the year Kiribati opened its first overseas diplomatic mission (in Fiji), while the U.K. reopened its mission in Kiribati. Early in the year Kiribati hosted a meeting on the implications of global warming for itself and other low-lying atoll nations facing the possibility of land loss and an increased frequency of cyclonic storms. The country was also one of the signatories to the Waigani Convention—a 1995 Pacific Islands initiative banning the importation of radioactive waste and placing controls on the shipment of hazardous materials; it finally went into effect in late 2001. Pres. Teburoro Tito announced plans for an airline with service links to neighbouring countries. (BARRIE MACDONALD)

KOREA, DEMOCRATIC PEOPLE'S REPUBLIC OF

Area: 122,762 sq km (47,399 sq mi)
Population (2001 est.): 21,968,000
Capital: Pyongyang
Chief of state: Chairman of the National Defense Commission Kim Jong Il
Head of government: Chairman of the Council of Ministers (Premier) Hong Sang Nam

AP/Wide World Photos

Work progresses toward reconnecting a railway across the border between North and South Korea on June 15.

Reclusive North Korean chief of state Kim Jong Il made several state visits to other countries in the year 2001. In January Kim visited Shanghai, China's financial capital, touring several companies and holding economic discussions. In late July–early August he made a 10-day trip to Russia, meeting with Russian Pres. Vladimir Putin. North Korea had been dismayed at the growing economic cooperation between Russia and South Korea; on the military front the two leaders spoke of limitations on North Korean missile testing. Kim pledged to continue a moratorium on missile testing until at least the year 2003. Western nations hoped that Putin would be able to persuade North Korea to become more open and more willing to contact Western countries directly.

Relations between North Korea and the U.S. had been developing through negotiations during the final years of Bill Clinton's administration, but all negotiations were put on hold after George W. Bush took office. The new Bush administration initially announced that it was going to review the relationship before proceeding. Secretary of State Colin Powell later called for resumed talks, but North Korea demanded to set the agenda before any meetings took place.

North Korea continued to struggle with a failing economy and agriculture shortfalls domestically. In mid-May at a UNICEF conference in Beijing, remarkable statistics revealing conditions inside North Korea were reported by Deputy Foreign Minister Choe Su Hon. The report indicated that life expectancy had fallen from 73.2 years in 1993 to 66.8 by 1999. Mortality rates for children under five rose during those years from 27 to 48 per 1,000. Infant mortality rose from 14 to 22.5 per 1,000 births. Per capita gross national product dropped from $991 per year to $457. The percentage of children getting vaccinations for diseases such as polio and measles fell from 90% to 50% between 1990 and 1997. The percentage of the population with access to safe water fell from 86% to just 53% between 1994 and 1996. The report at the UNICEF conference confirmed some of the worst fears the outside world had had of the situation inside the closed and secretive country. (MARK PETERSON)

KOREA, REPUBLIC OF

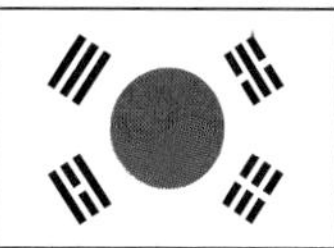

Area: 99,461 sq km (38,402 sq mi)
Population (2001 est.): 47,676,000
Capital: Seoul
Head of state and government: President Kim Dae Jung

In late 2000 South Korean Pres. Kim Dae Jung was awarded the Nobel Peace Prize for his efforts to bring peace to the peninsula by way of negotiations with North Korea. In early 2001, however, cold water was thrown on these efforts by none other than Korea's closest ally—the United States. Soon after his inauguration in January, U.S. Pres. George W. Bush announced that the U.S. wanted to review its policy toward North Korea. In March President Kim visited the Bush White House but was unable to persuade the Americans to again get on board his program for negotiations. The situation eventually improved, and Secretary of State Colin Powell announced at midyear that the U.S. would be interested in reopening discussions with North Korea.

South Korean–Russian relations took a step forward in February when Russian Pres. Vladimir Putin visited Seoul. The two countries agreed to increase economic cooperation, and South Korea joined Russia in expressions of opposition to American development of a missile-defense system. Within a few weeks, however, American protests had pushed the South Korean government into rethinking its position. By late March the confusion over foreign policy had led to a shuffle of the president's cabinet; among the changes were the office of foreign minister—Lee Joung Binn was replaced by Han Seung Soo, formerly trade minister and ambassador to the U.S.

South Korea opened a new airport in late March. Incheon International Airport, located outside Seoul and built at a cost of $5.5 billion, could handle 27 million passengers per year.

Relations with Japan took a turn for the worse when the textbook controversy again flared up. As in the past, Japan's officially sanctioned textbooks played down the aggressive role of the Japanese in their invasions of Asian countries during World War II. The controversy hit the press in April and in protest South Korea canceled a planned joint military exercise in May. The National Assembly passed a resolution condemning the Japanese action. The dispute had a peaceful resolution by the end of the year, when Japanese Prime Minister Junichiro Koizumi (*see* BIOGRAPHIES) visited Seoul and apologized for the errors.

There was both good news and bad news on the economic front. The best of the good news was that South Korea paid off the last of the loans from the International Monetary Fund (IMF) bailout. The economic disaster that hit the country in December 1997—and was thereafter referred to in South Korea as the "IMF period"—was officially over, although there were still many economic problems. In mid-August the government announced that 40 companies were going to collapse. By November the Central Bank and Finance Ministry announced that the economy would likely grow a meagre 2.5% during the year.

South Korea, though disappointed in the lack of progress in talks with North Korea and the U.S., pushed ahead with contacts with the North. Although Red Cross talks and family visits were suspended, South Korea continued its humanitarian aid to North Korea on the one hand and tourism to the special tourist zone in the Diamond Mountains on the other. Tourism was an important source of income for North Korea, and South Korean aid, together with aid from many other countries, had become essential to preventing even greater human suffering in the North.

(MARK PETERSON)

South Korean Pres. Kim Dae Jung (right) is greeted by Chinese Pres. Jiang Zemin at the Science and Technology Museum in Shanghai prior to an Asia-Pacific Economic Cooperation meeting on October 21.

AP/Wide World Photos

KUWAIT

Area: 17,818 sq km (6,880 sq mi)
Population (2001 est.): 2,275,000
Capital: Kuwait City
Head of state and government: Emir Sheikh Jabir al-Ahmad al-Jabir as-Sabah, assisted by Prime Minister Crown Prince Sheikh Saad al-Abdullah as-Salim as-Sabah

Prior to the terrorist attacks in New York City and Washington, D.C., on Sept. 11, 2001, strength in oil prices had led economic analysts to predict another year of prosperity for Kuwait. The strong oil market had boosted gross domestic product growth in the country for a second year in a row. Following September 11, however, slumping demand in Kuwait's principal markets, Asia and Europe, exposed the fragility of the economy. The one bright spot in the domestic sector was a boom in house construction. Government housing programs were so far behind demand that Kuwaitis increasingly had been availing themselves of interest-free loans and building homes on their own.

The stagnant economy reflected a deeper problem: government paralysis due to the age and debility of the nation's leaders. In late September Emir Sheikh Jabir al-Ahmad al-Jabir as-Sabah suffered a brain hemorrhage and was taken to London for medical treatment. The caretaker government—constrained from taking initiatives without the emir's backing—was thus stymied with regard to continued Islamist agitation, including fallout from the revelation following the September 11 attacks that a member of the inner circle of the al-Qaeda terrorist organization was a Kuwaiti.

A January 2001 request by Uday Hussein, son of Pres. Saddam Hussein, to the Iraqi parliament to revise the country's maps to include Kuwait within Iraq's borders served as a grim reminder that, despite having signed a treaty recognizing Kuwait as an independent state, Iraq remained a threat to its continued independence. Even so, the Kuwaiti government had backed down repeatedly in confrontations with Islamists. In a startling statement about government laxity in this regard, a former oil and information minister and member of the ruling family, Sheikh Saud Nasir as-Sabah, connected the government's tepid support for U.S. antiterrorism measures following September 11 to the successful "hijacking" of the government by Islamist militants. "We should remove the veil of secrecy that protects these groups and their financial and political activities in Kuwait and abroad," the sheikh declared.

(MARY ANN TÉTREAULT)

KYRGYZSTAN

Area: 199,900 sq km (77,200 sq mi)
Population (2001 est.): 4,883,000
Capital: Bishkek
Head of state and government: President Askar Akayev, assisted by Prime Minister Kurmanbek Bakiyev

In mid-January 2001 Kyrgyzstan's Defense Council concerned itself with repelling attacks by Muslim extremists.

Top priority was given to strengthening defense, and Kyrgyzstan joined the Central Asian rapid reaction force that was set up in Bishkek in August.

In July fighting was reported in the south between Kyrgyz troops and the Islamic Movement of Uzbekistan. Tajikistan, whence the militants were supposed to have come, questioned the accuracy of the reports, however, and the head of Kyrgyzstan's National Security Council asserted that the fighting had actually involved an armed gang of drug smugglers. Later reports emerged of an attempt by presumed militants to seize control of a television relay station in the mountains of Batken region.

There was also growing concern in Kyrgyzstan over the possibility that extremism would develop among the population in the southern part of the country, which had a large Uzbek component and had long felt itself neglected by the more developed north. In April Prime Minister Kurmanbek Bakiyev stated that many mosques had been built recently in the south and the government was intensifying its supervision of religion. The state commission on religious affairs was moved to Osh, the "southern capital," in an effort to counter extremist tendencies, including the growth of the banned Hizb ut-Tahrir sect. A number of persons in the south were put on trial for their membership in the sect, which was officially regarded in all Central Asian states as a terrorist organization, although its adherents insisted that they rejected violence and sought to set up an Islamic state through peaceful means.

Relations with Uzbekistan remained cool throughout the year, partly because of the Uzbek practice of shutting off the gas supply to Kyrgyzstan. A Kyrgyz proposal to exchange gas for water was rejected by Tashkent. In February the Kyrgyz government signed a secret memorandum that would give Uzbekistan easier access to an exclave in southern Kyrgyzstan, but the Kyrgyz parliament rejected the transfer of land that would be involved and sharply criticized the government for its secret dealings. Lawmakers also attacked the leadership for striking an agreement with China to settle a long-standing border dispute by handing over some mountainous territory. In September the parliament refused to ratify an agreement with Uzbekistan on fighting terrorism, demanding that the Uzbeks first remove their land mines from the common border. In December the parliament approved the use of the Manas Airport by the U.S.-led antiterrorist coalition. (BESS BROWN)

LAOS

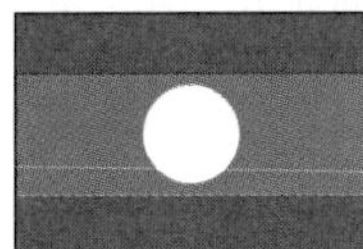

Area: 236,800 sq km (91,429 sq mi)
Population (2001 est.): 5,636,000
Capital: Vientiane (Viangchan)
Chief of state: President Khamtai Siphandon
Head of government: Prime Ministers Sisavath Keobounphanh and, from March 27, Boungnang Vorachith

The seventh congress of the Lao People's Revolutionary Party was opened on March 12, 2001, by Pres. Khamtai Siphandon, who, as anticipated, was unanimously reelected party chairman. Contrary to widespread predictions that Vientiane's increasingly market-oriented policies would lead to a more reform-minded leadership, most of the secretive political and military chiefs retained their positions. On March 27 the compliant National Assembly chose Finance Minister Boungnang Vorachith to replace Sisavath Keobounphanh as prime minister, but Sisavath kept his seat on the all-powerful Political Bureau. President Khamtai was uncharacteristically frank about the failure of the previous government to bring about increased prosperity and outlined an ambitious 20-year program for economic growth and better education, health, and living standards. Few impartial observers, including analysts at the international lending agencies, put much faith in the promised outcome, however, pointing out that Laos's dependence on foreign aid had doubled over the previous 15 years to about half of the annual budget in 2001. In April the International Monetary Fund approved a $40 million loan for financial stability.

Laos and Thailand signed an agreement in March to construct a second bridge over the Mekong River at Savannakhet, about 500 km (310 mi) downstream from the existing bridge near Vientiane. New roads were envisaged to promote trade with Vietnam. In August Laos and Cambodia approached Japan for financial backing for yet another Mekong bridge. Laos's largest source of foreign exchange—the income from selling hydroelectricity to Thailand—was dealt a blow when Bangkok, blaming an economic slowdown, reduced the number of purchases it promised to make. In June the problem of refugees was addressed at a UN-sponsored conference in Louangphrabang, the old royal capital. Human rights groups in the U.S. heavily criticized the continuing forced repatriation of refugees from Thailand. A simmering row over the detention of two Australian business executives for what Vientiane claimed to be fraud in a gem-mining business threatened to damage relations with one of the country's leading aid donors. Eventually the two were released to the Australian ambassador. During the course of this controversy, Vientiane introduced new controls over both local and foreign media.

(ROBERT WOODROW)

At a press conference in Brisbane on November 9, Kerry Danes and his wife, Kay—the two Australian business executives who had been accused of fraud in Laos—describe the relief they felt at being allowed to return home.

William West/AFP Worldwide

LATVIA

Area: 64,589 sq km (24,938 sq mi)
Population (2001 est.): 2,358,000
Capital: Riga
Chief of state: President Vaira Vike-Freiberga
Head of government: Prime Minister Andris Berzins

Latvians and foreign visitors joined to celebrate Riga's 800th anniversary in 2001; commemorative cultural events took place throughout the summer. Latvians were buoyant with optimism as the country neared membership in the European Union (EU) and NATO and generally enjoyed fine foreign relations. The economy had recovered, with predictions that the 6.6% growth rate in 2000 would even be exceeded in 2001. Politics, too, seemed to have stabilized, with Prime Minister Andris Berzins's government having held office since May 2000, which set some kind of Latvian record for longevity. The most popular leaders in the country represented the centre-right, but the local elections on March 11 demonstrated the vigour of the left as well.

In acknowledgment of Latvia's adherence to the principles of human rights and integration of its noncitizens (mostly ethnic Russians), the Council of Europe Parliamentary Assembly ended its monitoring procedures in the country, and the Organization for Security and Cooperation in Europe announced in December that it would close its mission in January 2002. Nonetheless, Russia continued to accuse Latvia of violating the rights of its Russian-speaking population. Latvian diplomatic missions in Russia were targeted for vandalism on the occasions of war-crimes trials against World War II Soviet officers and when young National Bolsheviks from Russia were sentenced for having tried to blow up a church in Riga in November 2000. The Latvian and Russian presidents met in Austria on February 10, but little progress was registered overall on substantive issues such as Russia's not signing the border accords with Latvia, which had been ready since 1997. Squabbling picked up again after Latvia's supportive response to the U.S. call for a worldwide campaign against terrorism. Russia claimed that Latvia was aiding Chechen terrorists, but Latvia countered that the Russians were simply trying to impede Latvia's membership in the EU and NATO. (DZINTRA BUNGS)

LEBANON

Area: 10,400 sq km (4,016 sq mi)
Population (2001 est.): 3,628,000 (excluding Palestinian refugees estimated to number about 330,000)
Capital: Beirut
Chief of state: President Gen. Émile Lahoud
Head of government: Prime Minister Rafiq al-Hariri

Before the events of Sept. 11, 2001, Lebanon was consumed to a large extent with its own internal affairs. In August state security forces, apparently with the approval of Pres. Émile Lahoud, conducted a wave of arrests of anti-Syrian activists, some of whom were accused of conspiring with Israel. Although most of them were released later, two journalists and a political adviser to Samir Geagea, the imprisoned leader of disbanded right-wing Lebanese forces, remained in custody because security forces said they had hard evidence linking them to Israel. The episode triggered a crisis between the Lebanese president and the prime minister, Rafiq al-Hariri, since the cabinet was not consulted and did not approve the steps taken by the security forces. Normalcy did not return to relations between Lahoud and al-Hariri until Syrian officials intervened and asked the two to put aside their differences. A year after the Israeli withdrawal from southern Lebanon, Hezbollah—Lebanon's main resistance force in the region—refused to consider that the country had regained its full sovereignty, since Israel still controlled the Sheba' farms enclave and had not released all Lebanese prisoners of war, and Israeli warplanes patrolled Lebanese skies at will. A military attack by Hezbollah in June on Israeli targets in the Sheba' farms region was countered by an Israeli attack on Syrian military targets in the Lebanese Al-Biqa' (Bekaa Valley). At the end of July, the UN Security Council voted unanimously to downgrade the UN interim force in southern Lebanon to an observer mission and cut its military personnel from 4,500 to 3,600.

In its first steps toward privatization, the government laid off all the employees of the official television network. It also laid off one-third of the employees of Middle East Airlines, the national carrier. Privatization was also being considered for other state-run utilities, such as electricity. Lebanon's mounting public debt was expected to reach 170% of the country's gross domestic product by the end of the year.

In the aftermath of the September 11 terrorist attacks in the U.S., Lebanon tried to walk a tightrope. Lebanese officials were at pains to stress their condemnation of the attacks against civilians, while at the same time, they emphasized the distinction between terrorism and the struggle for liberation. U.S. Pres. George W. Bush's statement in early October in support of establishing a Palestinian state was welcomed by Lebanese officials, who had been fearful of what they perceived as international pressure on them to naturalize about 330,000 Palestinian refugees living on Lebanese soil. The same officials were uneasy, however, about mixed signals from Washington over the possibility of targeting Hezbollah for attack as a terrorist organization. Although certain Lebanese sectors—particularly tourism—were negatively affected by the September 11 attacks and the U.S.-led retaliation on Afghanistan in October, some saw a glimmer of hope, since many Lebanese and Arabs living in the West felt unwelcome there and many were starting to transfer part of their liquid wealth to Lebanese banks, while Arab students who were targets of harassment were expected to transfer to Lebanese universities that followed Western educational systems. On a different note, and owing to the tense situation in the Middle East, the Francophone Summit that was scheduled to meet in Beirut in October 2001 was postponed to October 2002. (MAHMOUD HADDAD)

LESOTHO

Area: 30,355 sq km (11,720 sq mi)
Population (2001 est.): 2,177,000
Capital: Maseru
Chief of state: King Letsie III
Head of government: Prime Minister Bathuel Pakalitha Mosisili

AP/Wide World Photos

In Monrovia, Liberia, on September 10, men repair shoes beneath a billboard protesting UN-imposed sanctions against the West African country.

More than two years of wrangling over the way an election should be held was ended in February 2001 when the country's political parties endorsed a plan that was drawn up by the Independent Electoral Commission for the holding of elections. Preparations for voter registration were then made, and registration itself took place in August and September. An election was to be held in 2002.

A power struggle within the ruling Lesotho Congress for Democracy party, which had itself emerged as a breakaway from the Basotho Congress Party in 1997, began with the election of a new national executive committee in January. The election was disputed and referred to the Court of Appeal to settle. At the end of September, the deputy prime minister and minister of law, justice, and constitutional affairs, Kelebone Maope, resigned from the cabinet. He had long been a critic of Prime Minister Bathuel Pakalitha Mosisili, and in October he formed an opposition party, the Lesotho People's Congress.

There was much disillusion within the country about the political infighting, which distracted attention from the real issues of poverty and HIV/AIDS. One bright note was a grant of $15,240,000 by the World Bank to the governments of South Africa and Lesotho for a five-year Maloti-Drakensberg Transfrontier Conservation and Development Project. This was to protect an area on Lesotho's eastern border and develop small businesses involved with ecotourism. With further retrenchments in the South African mines causing unemployment in Lesotho to reach perhaps 50%, the government saw new foreign direct investment, especially in the textile sector, as one hope for the future.

(CHRISTOPHER SAUNDERS)

LIBERIA

Area: 97,754 sq km (37,743 sq mi)
Population (2001 est.): 3,226,000
Capital: Monrovia
Head of state and government: President Charles Taylor

In March 2001 the UN Security Council voted to impose sanctions on Liberia unless it stopped supporting Sierra Leone's Revolutionary United Front rebels. The sanctions, which included a worldwide ban on Liberian diamonds and travel restrictions on senior government officials, took effect in May despite Liberian claims of compliance with UN demands. Some humanitarian groups called for sanctions against Liberian timber, alleging that Pres. Charles Taylor was diverting timber profits to military use.

Beginning in April there was an increase in fighting between the army and antigovernment rebels in Lofa county in the north of the country. President Taylor claimed that Guinea and Sierra Leone supported the rebels and expelled those countries' ambassadors, although they were later allowed to return. In September defense ministers from the three countries met in an effort to find ways to end the conflict. Though rebels captured two towns in Gbarpolu county, northwest of Monrovia, in November, the government forces later retook the towns. Fighting remained heavy at year's end, and some humanitarian organizations withdrew from the worst areas. According to humanitarian sources, more than 40,000 people had fled this latest round of fighting. The UN World Food Programme reported feeding nearly 300,000 people in Liberia, including internally displaced persons and refugees from Sierra Leone.

The government imposed numerous restrictions on the press. Several newspapers were closed, and journalists were arrested after criticizing the government. In March security forces entered the University of Liberia and arrested students who were rallying in support of detained journalists. Students and faculty members reported being beaten.

In April former deputy information minister Milton Teahjay disappeared after trying to leave the country. Teahjay, a former opposition activist, had been taken into the government by President Taylor but was later dismissed for opposing logging activities in parts of the country. Human rights organizations and opposition groups alleged a government role in Teahjay's disappearance, and they demanded a full investigation into the matter. Also in April the sports minister, François Massaquoi, who was himself a former faction leader, was killed when rebels allegedly fired on his helicopter. President Taylor appointed a commission to investigate the killing, as some opposition figures charged that the government was involved.

(MATTHEW A. CENZER)

Muammar al-Qaddafi speaks to reporters in Tripoli on February 5 regarding the trial of two Libyan officials accused of the December 1988 downing of a Pan Am jetliner over Lockerbie, Scot.

LIBYA

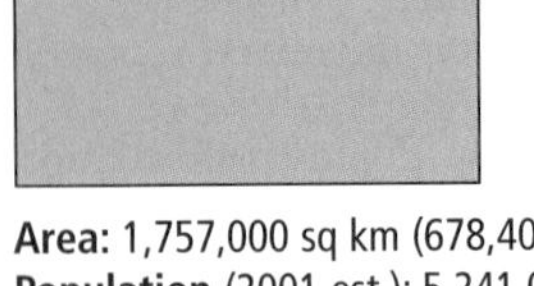

Area: 1,757,000 sq km (678,400 sq mi)
Population (2001 est.): 5,241,000
Capital: Tripoli (policy-making body and many secretariats intermittently meet in Surt)
Chief of state: (de facto) Col. Muammar al-Qaddafi; (nominal) Secretary of the General People's Congress Zentani Muhammad az-Zentani
Head of government: Secretary of the General People's Committee (Prime Minister) Mubarak Abdallah ash-Shamikh

In Libya January 2001 was dominated by the trial in The Netherlands of two Libyan officials charged with having downed Pan Am Flight 103 over Lockerbie, Scot., on Dec. 21, 1988. The trial, conducted under Scottish law, found Lamin Khalifa Fhimah not guilty, but ʿAbd al-Baset al-Megrahi was jailed for life. A preliminary administrative hearing of the appeal was held on October 15, and a full hearing was anticipated in January 2002. After 12 years of intense inquiry and an 84-day trial, the case ended abruptly when the defense failed to obtain evidence from the Syrian government. On March 14 the French high court exempted the Libyan leader, Col. Muammar al-Qaddafi, from prosecution in connection with the bombing of a French UTA DC-10 airliner that killed 170 people over Niger in 1989.

In March the U.S. and Great Britain conducted a closed-door meeting to discuss the requirements that Libya would have to meet before UN sanctions could be lifted. The U.S. refused to lift its own sanctions, although there was strong evidence that American companies were keen to gain access to the expanding Libyan market and, especially, to oil interests. On October 1 the head of Libya's national oil company met in Vienna with officials of the American oil companies Conoco, Marathon, Amerada Hess, and Occidental.

In late February Syrian Pres. Bashar al-Assad met with Qaddafi in Tripoli. Qaddafi later attended meetings in Africa, and his assistance to South Africa was rewarded by public statements of support by Nelson Mandela and Pres. Thabo Mbeki. At the Arab League summit in Amman, Jordan, in March, Qaddafi's speech shocked participants by calling on Arabs to "forget about Jerusalem and join Africa."

Libya's economy was strengthened by improved oil prices. Annual growth rates of 6.5% had fallen to about 5.5% in 2001, but it was sufficient as oil-exploration deals were struck with European and Asian interests. Commitment to the once-derided tourist sector was reinforced. Technical problems with the Great Man-Made River (GMMR) were overcome, as were the consequent embarrassing contractual relations with the project's bankrupt South Korean contractor. By 2000 desalination costs had fallen to below those of water delivered by the GMMR, however, and a fierce debate became public between the advocates of desalination and those backing the GMMR approach.

After the terrorist attacks of September 11, the U.S.-Libyan international discourse on terrorism shifted. In early October U.S. and British security officials met in London with a Libyan contingent headed by Musa Kusa, who had been implicated in the shooting of a London policewoman outside the Libyan embassy in 1984. (J.A. ALLAN)

LIECHTENSTEIN

Area: 160 sq km (62 sq mi)
Population (2001 est.): 33,000
Capital: Vaduz
Chief of state: Prince Hans Adam II
Head of government: Mario Frick and, from April 5, Otmar Hasler

In 2001, as Prince Hans Adam II reiterated his threat to "sell up" if constitutional changes vastly increasing his powers were not accepted, a survey found that 60% of the people favoured the status quo, only 20% wanted to give the prince more power, and 20% favoured less power. In parliamentary elections on February 9–11, the Progressive Citizens' Party (FBP), which had ignored the dispute during the campaign, won 13 of the 25 seats with 49.9% of the vote. The Fatherland Union (41.1%) won 11 seats, and the Free List party took the remaining seat. Otmar Hasler of the FBP was sworn in as the new head of government on April 5.

After two years of diplomatic maneuvering, on June 1 Liechtenstein filed a complaint against Germany at the International Court of Justice in The Hague demanding reparations for alleged violation of its sovereignty and property rights of its citizens. At issue was the confiscation of land, artwork, and other property of the prince's family by Czechoslovakia at the end of World War II to pay war debts to Germany. The Czechs had refused to negotiate, while Germany, which considered the property German-owned, had used the assets to pay war reparations. (*See* LAW, CRIME, AND LAW ENFORCEMENT: *International Law.*)

Liechtenstein faced new indictments for money laundering in July. Two financial advisers were charged with conspiracy to hide millions of dollars for the drug cartel based in Cali, Colom. (ANNE ROBY)

LITHUANIA

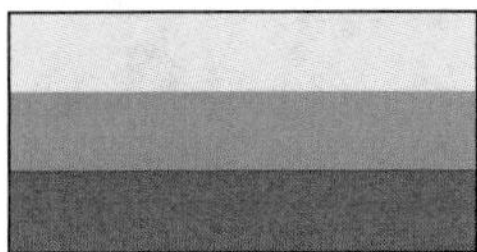

Area: 65,300 sq km (25,212 sq mi)
Population (2001 est.): 3,691,000
Capital: Vilnius
Chief of state: President Valdas Adamkus
Head of government: Prime Ministers Rolandas Paksas, Eugenijus Gentvilas (acting) from June 20, and, from July 3, Algirdas Brazauskas

Lithuania's Prime Minister Rolandas Paksas, the leader of the Liberal Union, resigned in June 2001, principally over disagreements with his coalition partners, the populist New Union (Social Liberals), over the supply of oil to the Mazeikui Nafta oil refinery, privatization of the state-owned natural gas monopoly, and tax and pension reforms. A new coalition between the Social Liberals and the Social Democratic Party was formed, with Algirdas Brazauskas, the Social Democrat leader (and former Communist) and former president of Lithuania, as head of government.

Despite election promises, the government failed to address social problems. Average annual wages remained at approximately $3,300, and the rate of unemployment topped 12%. The majority of pensioners and people in rural areas found themselves in particularly difficult straits. On the other hand, gross domestic product increased by nearly 5%. The volume of foreign trade in the first half of the year was $5.2 billion. The largest proportion of Lithuanian exports and imports was directed to and from European Union countries—49.4% and 42.5%, respectively; exports increased by 24% and imports by 15% over 2000 levels.

The NATO Parliamentary Assembly spring session, held in Vilnius on May 27–31, was the largest international event in Lithuania in a decade and the first such meeting held outside NATO territory. Some 270 parliamentarians from NATO and NATO-associated states gathered in the Lithuanian capital. The assembly approved a declaration on NATO enlargement, and Lithuania once again declared its commitment to join the organization during its 2002 summit in Prague. (DARIUS FURMONAVIČIUS)

Vytautas Landsbergis, head of the Homeland Union Party and former Lithuanian president, receives an award from the University of Wales, Cardiff.

Darius Furmonavičius

LUXEMBOURG

Area: 2,586 sq km (999 sq mi)
Population (2001 est.): 444,000
Capital: Luxembourg
Chief of state: Grand Duke Henri
Head of government: Prime Minister Jean-Claude Juncker

In 2001, his first year as head of state, Grand Duke Henri sought to make his own mark as leader of Luxembourg. In an emotional ceremony on June 21, he presented his father, Grand Duke Jean, with the Croix de la Résistance in honour of his father's service with the British army during World War II. Then on October 10, stating that he wished to underscore the importance of its work, Grand Duke Henri broke with tradition by officially opening the parliament in person. The last time the parliament had been opened by a royal was in 1877.

The parliament voted unanimously on June 28 to extend and upgrade the European Parliament complex. It planned to expand the conference centre, build new office blocks, and add a concert hall. Also in June, the head of Luxembourg's army proposed to increase its size, to purchase a military transport plane, and, with Belgium, to buy a transport ship. There were again proposals to establish a University of Luxembourg, but government officials felt a full university in the country would discourage its citizens from studying abroad and have a negative effect on their overall education.

In the wake of the September 11 terrorist attacks in the U.S., several Luxembourg banks acknowledged that some of their customers might have ties to Osama bin Laden (*see* BIOGRAPHIES), and the bank accounts of such depositers were placed under investigation. (ANNE ROBY)

MACEDONIA

Area: 25,713 sq km (9,928 sq mi)
Population (2001 est.): 2,046,000
Capital: Skopje
Chief of state: President Boris Trajkovski
Head of government: Prime Minister Ljubco Georgievski

In 2001 Macedonia's fragile interethnic balance collapsed. Fighting between government security forces and the self-styled ethnic Albanian National Liberation Army (UCK) brought the country to the verge of all-out civil war and cast doubts over its very future.

A bomb attack on a police station in the village of Tearce on January 22 was followed by armed clashes between government forces and UCK fighters near Tanusevci in February. Fighting soon erupted in and around Tetovo, the country's second largest city, with a largely ethnic Albanian population. Throughout the spring and summer, government forces and rebels were fighting around Tetovo, Skopje, and Kumanovo. More than 100 persons lost their lives, often indiscriminately, in the early months of the year, and large numbers of persons were displaced within the country as a result of the fights. Many Albanians also fled across the border to Kosovo. Anti-Albanian riots occurred in several towns.

Government threats throughout the spring to launch counteroffensives led only to short-lived cease-fires. Meanwhile, UCK demands for negotiations on

In Krivolak, Macedonia, on September 10, a metal worker cuts apart a machine gun surrendered to NATO forces by ethnic Albanian rebels.

AP/Wide World Photos

the future status of Macedonia were rejected by the government. The international community, which initially condemned the UCK attacks, later called on the government to address the problems of Macedonia's ethnic Albanian community.

On May 13 a government of national unity was formed that included all relevant parties from both ethnic groups. Negotiations between ethnic Macedonian and ethnic Albanian parties brought little result, nor was Western shuttle diplomacy between the government and the UCK eminently successful. July and August saw renewed fighting and killings of soldiers and civilians. Ethnic Macedonians stormed the parliament building on June 25, and one month later rioters attacked Western embassies, accusing the West of pro-Albanian bias. Finally, European Union (EU) and U.S. mediators assembled the leaders of the main political parties in Ohrid for peace talks. The Ohrid Agreement, signed on August 13, provided for constitutional amendments raising the status of the ethnic Albanian community, increased local self-government, the disarmament of ethnic Albanian rebels to be followed by an amnesty, and increased participation of ethnic Albanians in state structures, including the police. The parties also agreed on early parliamentary elections in January 2002.

In August the North Atlantic Council decided to deploy 3,500 troops to collect UCK weapons, and a month later NATO began "Amber Fox," the 1,000-troop-strong follow-up mission designed to protect Western monitors in Macedonia. While UCK weapons were being successfully collected, parliamentary debates on constitutional amendments were delayed repeatedly by legislators from both ethnic groups and were not concluded on schedule. Complaining that the Macedonian government and parliament had failed to meet their part of the peace plan, the EU twice cancelled a planned donors' conference. Finally, Parliament also decided to postpone holding early elections. On November 23, the Social Democrats and two smaller parties left the government, but Prime Minister Ljubco Georgievski managed to form a new cabinet.

The interethnic conflict severely hurt Macedonia's economy and resulted in a sharp drop of industrial output, agricultural production, and imports and exports; widening trade and budget deficits; and increasing unemployment.

(STEFAN KRAUSE)

MADAGASCAR

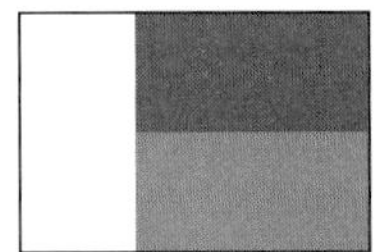

Area: 587,041 sq km (226,658 sq mi)
Population (2001 est.): 15,983,000
Capital: Antananarivo
Chief of state and head of government: President Didier Ratsiraka, assisted by Prime Minister Tantely Andrianarivo

At the beginning of May 2001, Pres. Didier Ratsiraka reinstated the country's Senate, which he had suspended after he came to power in 1975. The Senate was inaugurated in new $6 million premises in Antananarivo. The 90 senators elected a former director of the civil service as Senate leader. It remained to be seen what role the new body would play in checking executive power, for the president's Association for the Rebirth of Madagascar, with its allies, retained an overwhelming majority in the parliament. Though early results from the mid-December presidential elections suggested that Antananarivo Mayor Marc Ravalomanana had a slight lead over

President Ratsiraka, neither had a majority of votes and a second round of elections would be needed in February 2002.

One of the president's projects aimed at providing as many as possible of the almost 16 million people of the island with glasses to protect them against the solar eclipse in June. A special budget of 23 billion Malagasy francs (about $3.6 million) was established.

Bringing Madagascar some international attention during the year was the discovery of the 70-million-year-old remains of several specimens of dinosaurs. (CHRISTOPHER SAUNDERS)

MALAWI

Area: 118,484 sq km (45,747 sq mi)
Population (2001 est.): 10,491,000
Capital: Lilongwe (legislative, ministerial, and financial), Blantyre (executive and judicial)
Head of state and government: President Bakili Muluzi

In February 2001 Judge Edward Twea sentenced John Chikakwiya, mayor of Blantyre and a prominent member of the ruling United Democratic Front, together with three senior policemen, to two weeks in prison, suspended for 18 months. Chikakwiya had ordered the teargassing of a legal and peaceful gathering of the National Democratic Alliance, deliberately disregarding a court ruling that barred him from disrupting opposition party meetings.

On February 21 four government officials were arrested—followed by two more the following day—and charged with having embezzled funds from the Ministry of Education. Also on February 22 former cabinet member Cassim Chilumpha was arrested and charged with corrupt practices during the campaign that led up to the elections in June 1999. On March 26 six people were charged with treason as a result of their alleged involvement in a plot to overthrow the government.

After this internal cleansing the government took part in the replacement of the Organization of African Unity by a new African Union at a July meeting in Lusaka, Zambia. The following month Malawi joined with six other East African governments to create the African Trade Insurance Agency (ATI) in an attempt to counter the high premiums demanded by foreign companies that considered Africa a high-risk area. In December the ATI signed an agreement with Gerling, the world's third largest credit insurance group, which offered protection to companies trading to and within Africa against nonpayment by buyers. (KENNETH INGHAM)

MALAYSIA

Area: 329,845 sq km (127,354 sq mi)
Population (2001 est.): 22,602,000
Capital: Kuala Lumpur; head of government office in Putrajaya (the future planned capital) from 1999
Chief of state: *Yang di-Pertuan Agongs* (Paramount Rulers) Tuanku Salahuddin Abdul Aziz Shah ibni al-Marhum Sultan Hisamuddin Alam Shah, Tuanku Mizan Zainal Abidin ibni al-Marhum Sultan Mahmud (acting) from October 8 and (interim) from November 21, and, from December 13, Tuanku Syed Sirajuddin ibni al-Marhum Tuanku Syed Putra Jamalullail
Head of government: Prime Minister Datuk Seri Mahathir bin Mohamad

The ruling United Malays National Organization (UMNO), led by Prime Minister Datuk Seri Mahathir bin Mohamad, began the year 2001 under stress. A diverse new opposition coalition had emerged called the Alternative Front, which included many younger generation Malaysians and counted among its members both Malays and non-Malays as well as Muslims and non-Muslims. The UMNO was also under unprecedented scrutiny from the newly created Human Rights Commission for its recourse to harsh measures limiting the rights of assembly and freedom of speech. Elements within the judiciary had begun to reassert their independence from the executive, and Mahathir faced mounting criticism over the government's continuing protection of UMNO-connected corporations with close ties to Finance Minister Tun Daim Zainuddin and his protégés.

Although Mahathir's legitimacy among the nation's demographically and politically dominant Malay citizens was threatened by these issues and developments, by year's end he had turned the situation around decisively. He had accepted Tun Daim's resignation as finance minister and had further allayed public disquiet by removing from the personal grasp of Tun Daim's protégés the great national and party assets they controlled.

Mahathir also turned up the pressure on the Alternative Front coalition by exploiting the deep and unresolved tensions between the coalition's two largest partners: the Islamic Party of Malaysia (PAS), which wanted Malaysia to become a Shar'iah-based Islamic state, and

Malaysian Prime Minister Mahathir bin Mohamad warns in a radio address on July 6 of a possible crackdown on student activists in the country.

AP/Wide World Photos

the stridently anticlericalist Democratic Action Party (DAP), which held explicitly non-Malay-centric views of Malaysian society and identity. By September the Alternative Front had cracked.

To the UMNO's great advantage, Malaysian voters were once again likely to be faced in 2004 with the hardly attractive choice between the UMNO's crude regimen of statist authoritarianism and the PAS's increasingly assertive neotraditionalist Islamism.

Arrests and detentions ensued of young PAS activists and other Islamic militants allegedly involved in jihad-type actions throughout Southeast Asia. Initially greeted with skepticism, this government action was placed beyond questioning by the September 11 terrorist attacks in the U.S. If the PAS/DAP entente had not already been dead, this would have killed it.

Far from boasting of any vindication, Mahathir coolly asserted that the arrests were unconnected with the search for Osama bin Laden's associates and pointedly questioned U.S. strikes against Afghanistan. Mahathir's political enemies were suddenly tainted by association with deeds far exceeding the most lurid UMNO propaganda. Domestic criticism of his strong-handed government was discredited, and, as a prominent Muslim moderate, Mahathir could be confident that international—especially U.S.—criticism of his rule as repressive would end. (CLIVE S. KESSLER)

MALDIVES

Area: 298 sq km (115 sq mi)
Population (2001 est.): 275,000
Capital: Male
Head of state and government: President Maumoon Abdul Gayoom

Sustainable development remained the single most important objective of Maldives in 2001. In his address at the opening session of the Majlis (parliament) on February 22, Pres. Maumoon Abdul Gayoom listed poverty alleviation, rural development, and expansion and modernization of education as priority areas. Liberalization of the fishing industry and private-sector participation in development plans were also proposed. In August Gulf Craft Inc., a company based in the United Arab Emirates, was allowed to set up a boatbuilding and repair centre at Thilafushi in Male Atoll. Maldives decided to ratify an agreement establishing the Islamic Corporation for the Development of the Private Sector under the control of the Islamic Development Bank. Considering the importance of foreign investment in sustaining economic progress, the government promised to take steps to inspire confidence among investors.

Haveeru Daily/AFP Worldwide

Pres. Maumoon Abdul Gayoom (right) welcomes Chinese Premier Zhu Rongji to Maldives on May 16.

An important diplomatic event was the visit of Chinese Premier Zhu Rongji on May 16–17. An agreement on economic and technical cooperation was signed between Maldives and China. Population growth and environmental degradation were other areas of concern. On July 11—World Population Day—President Gayoom underlined the need to control the population growth in order to reduce pressure on trees, coastlines, and reefs. (PONMONI SAHADEVAN)

MALI

Area: 1,248,574 sq km (482,077 sq mi)
Population (2001 est.): 11,009,000
Capital: Bamako
Chief of state: President Alpha Oumar Konaré
Head of government: Prime Minister Mande Sidibe

Thousands of hunters from West Africa converged on Bamako on Jan. 27, 2001, carrying handmade shotguns and bows and arrows to celebrate the millennium of hunting. Their mission was to call attention to the role of hunters in the new global economy.

On May 7 Mali and Namibia became the first two member states of the Organization of African Union (OAU) to agree to join the Pan-African Parliament, which was established on May 26 and would form part of the new organization that would replace the OAU.

The annual meeting of foreign ministers from member countries of the Islamic Conference Organization opened in Bamako on June 25, and on July 11 Mali became the first country to sign a binding international agreement designed to halt the proliferation of small arms.

On August 9—pursuant to a law passed by the parliament on June 29 making those convicted of child trafficking subject to prison sentences of 5–20 years—the government enacted legislation that required all children under 18 years of age to carry travel passes. Pres. Alpha Oumar Konaré canceled a December 23 referendum that would give the president immunity from prosecution after critics decried the reform.

Ibrahim Bahanga, one of the last Tuareg rebel chiefs to defy the government after the official end of the uprising, announced on September 24 that he was laying down his arms for the good of the people of northern Mali.

(NANCY ELLEN LAWLER)

MALTA

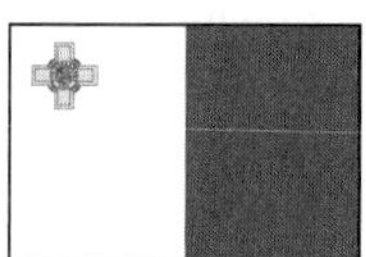

Area: 316 sq km (122 sq mi)
Population (2001 est.): 384,000
Capital: Valletta
Chief of state: President Guido de Marco
Head of government: Prime Minister Eddie Fenech Adami

Speaking in February 2001 on Malta's application to become a member of the European Union, Günter Verheugen, the EU commissioner for enlargement, remarked that the progress Malta had made in the previous two years was surprising. Though EU accession was the top foreign-policy priority for the government, the opposition Labour Party held that it was not in Malta's interest to join the EU. Nonetheless, negotiations were expected to be concluded by the end of 2002.

In May, after having visited Greece and Syria, Pope John Paul II arrived in Malta to beatify three persons—a nun, a priest, and a layman. They were the first-ever Maltese to be so honoured. He urged the Maltese to cherish their Christian vocation.

During his July 1–8 visit to China, Pres. Guido de Marco invited Chinese Pres. Jiang Zemin to Malta. Jiang readily accepted the offer and arrived for a state visit on July 23. The two leaders agreed to establish in Malta a Chinese cultural centre for the Mediterranean region, to maintain cultural cooperation between the two countries during 2001–03, and to list Malta as a tourist destination for Chinese citizens.

In April the neolithic temple at Mnajdra, a World Heritage site, was vandalized; about 60 megaliths were dislodged. The government condemned in the strongest terms the September terrorist attacks in the United States, and it pledged to cooperate fully in the effort to eradicate international terrorism.

(ALBERT GANADO)

MARSHALL ISLANDS

Area: 181 sq km (70 sq mi)
Population (2001 est.): 52,300
Capital: Majuro
Head of state and government: President Kessai Note

Having reestablished his position in January 2001 by defeating a motion of no-confidence brought by the supporters of former president Imata Kabua, Marshall Islands Pres. Kessai Note held his majority in the Nitijela (legislative assembly) throughout the year. Financial relations with the U.S. remained a priority with the Compact of Free Association between the two countries due to expire in 2001 and negotiations over the future relationship already in train. The U.S.—through direct allocations, funding under the compact, and special federal grants—contributed more than 53% of the total Marshall Islands government expenditure of $106.6 million. The government's financial administration, though improved over recent years, remained weak. The U.S. General Accounting Office criticized the government for its lack of compliance and accountability and for the misdirection of funds. The government also had a shortfall in social security funds against anticipated future drawing rights.

In February the Marshall Islands High Court rejected 10 of 11 charges brought by the government against major American tobacco companies to seek compensation for health costs related to smoking; this decision was upheld in a further hearing in June. The judge was critical of the government's legal team for its poor presentation of its client's case.

(BARRIE MACDONALD)

Spectators crowd the Floriana Granaries square in Valletta, Malta, for an open-air mass performed by Pope John Paul II on May 9.

AP/Wide World Photos

MAURITANIA

Area: 1,030,700 sq km (398,000 sq mi)
Population (2001 est.): 2,591,000
Capital: Nouakchott
Chief of state: President Col. Maaouya Ould Sidi Ahmad Taya
Head of government: Prime Minister Cheikh El Afia Ould Mohamed Khouna

On April 8, 2001, police arrested Mohamed Lemine Ch'Bih Ould Cheikh Melainine, leader of the Popular Front. Despite widespread criticism by opposition parties and international human rights organizations, he was brought to trial in Nouakchott on May 9 and charged with criminal conspiracy. Defense lawyers resigned in protest after the proceedings were abruptly moved to Aioun, near the Malian border, 800 km (500 mi) south of the capital. Though critics condemned the trial as nothing more than a show, Melainine was sentenced on June 14 to five years' imprisonment.

On August 4 an agreement on fishing rights was renewed between the government and the European Union. Despite the fears of environmentalists that increased fishing would further reduce the already sharply depleted stocks, the revised protocol nevertheless allowed for an increased number of European vessels to fish the area around the island of Agadir off the northern Mauritanian coast.

King Muhammad VI of Morocco began a three-day state visit to Mauritania on September 10. Ties had been strained between the two countries since 1975, when in a dispute over independence for Western Sahara, claimed by Morocco, Mauritania had actively supported the Western Saharan Polisario Front; Mauritania later shifted to neutrality, and the king's visit was seen as an indication of the importance that both countries attached to improving relations.

In the legislative and municipal elections held on October 19 and 26, the ruling Democratic and Social Republican Party garnered 51% of the vote and captured 64 of the 81 seats in the National Assembly. (NANCY ELLEN LAWLER)

MAURITIUS

Area: 2,040 sq km (788 sq mi)
Population (2001 est.): 1,195,000
Capital: Port Louis
Chief of state: President Cassam Uteem
Head of government: Prime Minister Sir Anerood Jugnauth

Throughout 2001 there were signs of rivalry between Prime Minister Sir Anerood Jugnauth of the Mauritian Socialist Movement and Deputy Prime Minister Paul Berenger of the Mauritian Militant Movement. Despite clashes over government appointments and other matters, however, their ruling coalition remained intact.

Mauritius made a concerted effort during the year to develop a high-technology economy. In January Berenger announced the creation of the Infocom Development Authority to manage growth in the information-technology sector. India agreed to provide Mauritius with a $100 million line of credit for the development of a "cybercity" technology-development centre. A number of Indian software companies also announced that they would invest in the project.

The Mauritian government offered a variety of tax incentives for Indian businesses to establish export operations on the island. While visiting India, Prime Minister Jugnauth noted that Mauritius had preferential access to the U.S. and European Union markets under, respectively, the Africa Growth and Opportunity Act and the Cotonou Agreement. The country's export earnings remained strong, with the Export Processing Zone increasing 7% over the previous year while the Mauritius Freeport registered 43% growth over a similar period. (MATTHEW A. CENZER)

MEXICO

Area: 1,964,375 sq km (758,449 sq mi)
Population (2001 est.): 99,969,000
Capital: Mexico City
Head of state and government: President Vicente Fox Quesada

The inauguration of Vicente Fox Quesada as president of Mexico on Dec. 1, 2000, ended 71 years of uninterrupted national rule by the Institutional Revolutionary Party and opened a new historical era. Although economic and political constraints slowed change in some areas, perhaps disappointing some domestic and foreign observers expecting a more rapid transformation, Fox's personal-approval ratings remained in the 60% range throughout 2001.

As the candidate of the opposition National Action Party (PAN), Fox had promised quick resolution of the long-simmering conflict in southern Chiapas state, and in his first months in office he devoted substantial political capital to seeking a peaceful resolution of the matter. In his inaugural address to the Mexican Congress, Fox announced his commitment to the restarting of negotiations with the rebel Zapatista National Liberation Army (EZLN), the withdrawal of army troops from several controversial postings in Chiapas, and the appointment of a cabinet-level indigenous rights coordinator. Fox also submitted to Congress a constitutional-reform initiative congruent with the terms of a peace accord that the EZLN and the federal government had reached in 1996. In July this initiative, known as the Law on Indigenous Rights and Culture, was ratified by the required number of state legislatures. The EZLN and its allies, however, harshly denounced the measure, claiming that it broke with the earlier peace accord by not creating an autonomous territorial base for the exercise of indigenous rights. Legislatures in states with some of Mexico's largest indigenous populations rejected the constitutional reform for this same reason.

The Fox administration's other major legislative initiative concerned fiscal reform. The proposal sought to stabilize (and make more transparent) the Mexican banking system and modify the federal budgetary-approval process in order to prevent executive-legislative political deadlock from threatening continued government operations at the end of each calendar year. The measure's most controversial components concerned taxes, however. The administration touted its proposal with the phrase "Because it is just" and underscored the importance of expanding the country's tax base for future social spending, education, infrastructure development, and the national savings rate. Nevertheless, the prospect of significant tax increases generated considerable opposition, much of it focusing on the proposal to eliminate value-added-tax exemptions for food and medicines. It appeared by year's end that there would be substantial modifications to the government's reform proposal before it won final congressional approval.

As a presidential candidate, Fox had also promised significant measures to reduce poverty, but during 2001 a sharp downturn in the Mexican economy constrained a number of social-policy initiatives. The downturn followed an economic slump in the U.S.—the market for approximately 90% of Mexico's exports. Fox had promised 7% economic growth on a sustained basis and the creation of 1,350,000 new formal-sector jobs each year, yet it was projected that inflation-adjusted growth in 2001 would be close to zero, and there was a loss of more than 600,000 jobs in the first eight months of the Fox administration. Most experts anticipated continued low inflation (4–6%) and moderate interest rates in 2002, but they also predicted a real increase in gross domestic product of only about 2%.

It was in the foreign-affairs arena that the Fox administration initially made most rapid progress. In a high-profile gesture of the signal importance that both leaders attached to Mexican-U.S. relations, Fox and U.S. Pres. George W. Bush met at Fox's ranch in the state of Guanajuato on February 16. The two recently inaugurated leaders agreed to closer bilateral cooperation in a num-

AP/Wide World Photos

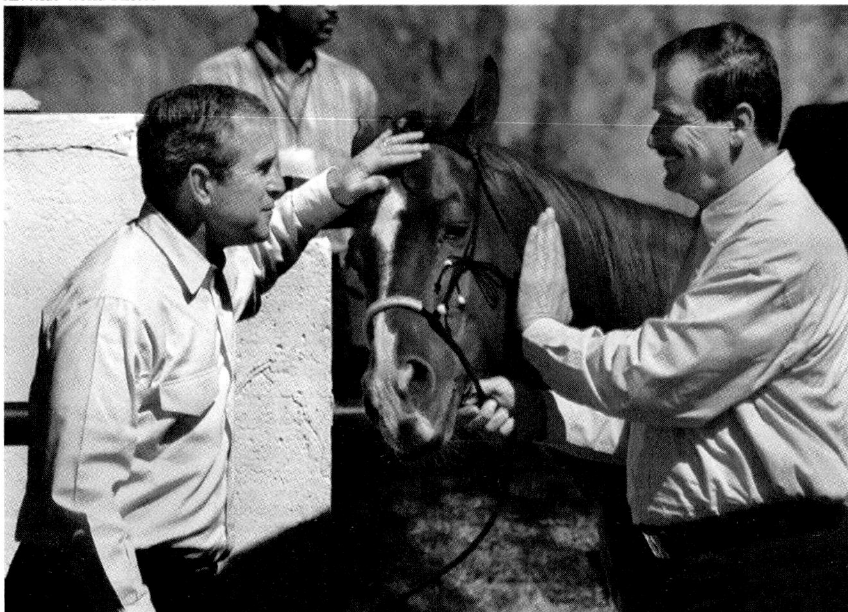

Mexican Pres. Vicente Fox and U.S. Pres. George W. Bush chat during Bush's visit to Fox's ranch in San Cristobal in February.

ber of areas, and in the months following the meeting, there was indeed evidence of more effective collaboration against drug traffickers and immigrant smugglers. Responding to Bush's commitment to reviewing U.S. drug-certification policy (in which the U.S. Congress required the executive branch to certify that countries were collaborating effectively with the U.S. in the battle against drug traffickers), Mexico broke with long-established precedent by extraditing suspected drug traffickers to the U.S. for trial. The two governments also made efforts to resolve long-standing disagreements concerning the sharing of Rio Grande water.

Immigration policy was the area in which the most novel developments occurred. The U.S. had vetoed consideration of immigration issues during negotiations of the North American Free Trade Agreement in the early 1990s, and when President-elect Fox traveled to Washington, D.C., in August 2000, his call for a more open border between Mexico and the U.S. was greeted with considerable skepticism. Nevertheless, Bush and Fox established a cabinet-level working group composed of senior officials from the U.S. Department of State and Department of Justice and the Mexican Ministry of Foreign Affairs and Ministry of the Interior. In the following months, discussions focused primarily on expanded visa quotas for temporary workers (especially in agriculture but also in construction, food processing, and the hotel and restaurant industries) and ways to normalize over time the status of the estimated 3.5 million undocumented Mexican migrants in the U.S. Bush and leading Republican strategists appeared eager both to consolidate a highly positive bilateral relationship with Mexico and the Fox administration and to win support from the increasingly influential Latino electorate while simultaneously reducing opposition from conservative forces adamantly opposed to the amnesty of illegal immigrants. When domestic political opposition in the U.S. threatened to stall negotiations, Fox used his state visit to Washington, D.C., on September 5–6 to highlight the importance of the issue.

In this area as well, unanticipated events intervened. The September 11 terrorist attacks in the U.S. immediately reordered American foreign-policy priorities, and relations with Mexico were forced onto the back burner. American attitudes toward border enforcement also shifted dramatically, accompanied by stringent new border and visa controls. Bush reassured Fox that he remained committed to changing immigration policy, and Fox attempted to regain momentum in this area by proposing a continentwide security area in which Mexico would actively combat cross-border terrorist activities. The prospects for rapid action on immigration issues dimmed considerably, however.

In October Fox's efforts to move Mexico away from an isolationist position were realized when Mexico won a seat on the UN Security Council; it was the first time in two decades that Mexico would serve on the council. The country attracted unfavourable headlines in late November when a National Human Rights Commission released a report that held the Mexican government responsible for the detention and torture of hundreds of those who "disappeared" in the 1970s in the "dirty war" against leftist groups. Fox acknowledged the government role and appointed a special prosecutor to investigate the cases.

(KEVIN J. MIDDLEBROOK)

MICRONESIA, FEDERATED STATES OF

Area: 701 sq km (271 sq mi)
Population (2001 est.): 118,000
Capital: Palikir, on Pohnpei
Head of state and government: President Leo A. Falcam

Negotiations for the renewal of the Federated States of Micronesia's (FSM) Compact of Free Association with the U.S. continued in 2001. The governments agreed that the FSM's defense and security relationship with the U.S. should remain, private enterprise should be strengthened, and greater financial accountability should be achieved. FSM negotiators sought an annual grant and an annual payment to the FSM Trust Fund, both inflation protected; the U.S. agreed to the payments in principle, but at a lower level and without inflation adjustment. Negotiations were ongoing. A special session of Congress was called in March to consider business pending from the previous session, including the establishment of a retirement plan and housing allocations.

Voters in the district of Faichuuk overwhelmingly passed a referendum to declare the district a separate state within the FSM. A proposal envisaged a transition phase of three years, although the FSM legislature had yet to decide on the matter. In March Pres. Leo A. Falcam made a state visit to Japan. In October he offered the U.S. use of FSM facilities for staging points in the U.S.-led "war on terrorism" following the September 11 attacks.

(BARRIE MACDONALD)

MOLDOVA

Area: 33,700 sq km (13,000 sq mi)
Population (2001 est.): 4,211,000 (including some 600,000 persons working abroad)
Capital: Chisinau
Chief of state: Presidents Petru Lucinschi and, from April 7, Vladimir Voronin
Head of government: Prime Ministers Dumitru Braghis and, from April 19, Vasile Tarlev

Following early general elections on Feb. 25, 2001, Moldova became the first former Soviet republic in which unreformed Communists returned to power. Playing on widespread dissatisfaction with the post-Communist transition, the Communist Party of the Republic of Moldova garnered 50.1% of the votes, taking 71 of the 101 seats in Parliament. The remaining seats were divided between the Braghis Alliance, a loose centre-left bloc led by incumbent Prime Minister Dumitru Braghis, and the right-wing Christian Democratic Popular Party. On April 4 Parliament elected Communist leader Vladimir Voronin as Moldova's president, and he set up a government of technocrats led by Vasile Tarlev, a 37-year-old manager. One main goal was to increase the role of the state in the economy. Another was the introduction of Russian as the country's second official language, but this evoked protests, especially among the intelligentsia.

As might be expected, the Communists advocated a reorientation toward Moscow and favoured joining the Russia-Belarus Union. On November 19 Voronin and Russian Pres. Vladimir Putin signed a basic bilateral treaty covering cooperation in many fields and favouring the special status of the Russian language in Moldova. The Moldova Parliament ratified the treaty on December 27. Moldova was admitted to the Stability Pact for South Eastern Europe in June, and in July it became a full member in the World Trade Organization. Neighbouring Romania introduced strict passport controls for Moldovan citizens effective July 1, and in October Romanian Prime Minister Adrian Nastase canceled an official visit to Chisinau following statements by Moldovan Justice Minister Ion Morei, who accused Romania of interference in Moldova's internal affairs and of "expansionism."

The Communists' pledge to find a firm resolution to the Transnistria conflict proved unrealistic. In September the breakaway heavily Slavic-populated region suspended negotiations with Moldovan authorities, whom it accused of imposing an economic blockade. In early October Putin disbanded the Russian State Commission for Transnistria, and in mid-November Russian officials announced that the withdrawal of heavy military equipment from the region had been completed.

(DAN IONESCU)

MONACO

Area: 1.95 sq km (0.75 sq mi)
Population (2001 est.): 31,800
Chief of state: Prince Rainier III
Head of government: Minister of State Patrick Leclercq

As health problems continued to sideline Prince Rainer III, his son, Prince Albert, took the spotlight in 2001, making a number of official trips abroad. In March Albert chaired a convention on air-pollution monitoring in Rabat, Morocco. In Cuba on a five-day visit in April, he attended a sports conference and, after meeting with Pres. Fidel Castro, opened Monaco's first consulate in Cuba. Albert also traveled to Moscow, where he met with Russian Prime Minister Mikhail Kasyanov to discuss cooperation in business, finance, culture, and sports. The July visit was the first by a prince of Monaco to Russia since 1913. In New York City in October, Albert attended a benefit in tribute to his late mother, Princess Grace, and gave Mayor Rudolph Giuliani a check for $710,000 to be contributed to the Twin Towers Fund.

An ambitious building program to attract more visitors to Monaco continued during the year. The new Grimaldi Forum provided conference facilities with space for such special events as trade fairs. Monte-Carlo announced its intention to develop more family-oriented activities, especially attractions for children. Government data showed that the number of people who spent at least one night in Monaco hit a record high of 300,185 in 2000.

(ANNE ROBY)

MONGOLIA

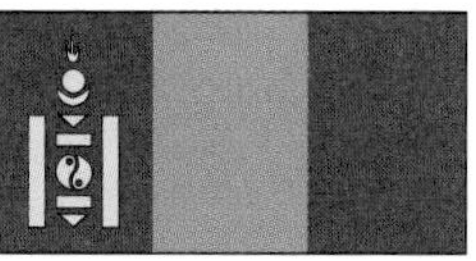

Area: 1,564,116 sq km (603,909 sq mi)
Population (2001 est.): 2,435,000
Capital: Ulaanbaatar
Chief of state: President Natsagiyn Bagabandi
Head of government: Prime Minister Nambaryn Enhbayar

Consolidating its victory in the July 2000 elections to the Great Hural (parliament), the reformed communist Mongolian People's Revolutionary Party (MPRP) won the May 2001 presidential elections. Standing for a second term, MPRP candidate Natsagiyn Bagabandi with 58.1% of the ballot easily beat the 36.5% gained by the Mongolian National Democratic Party's choice, Radnaasumbereliyn Gonchigdorj. After a two-year power struggle between presidency and legislature, President Bagabandi finally stamped his seal on the Great Hural's first

Newly reelected Mongolian Pres. Natsagiyn Bagabandi, standing before a portrait of Mongolian People's Revolutionary Party founder Sukhbaatar, welcomes members of the media to the Government House in Ulaanbaatar on May 22.

AP/Wide World Photos

amendments to the constitution. Prime Minister Nambaryn Enhbayar was unanimously reelected party chairman by the MPRP's 23rd congress in March. The 626 delegates approved a new Little Hural of 244 members, who elected a new 15-member Leadership Council. Chinese Foreign Minister Tang Jiaxuan, visiting Mongolia in July, expressed support for Mongolian membership in the Shanghai Cooperation Organization—China, Russia, Kazakhstan, Kyrgyzstan, Tajikistan, and Uzbekistan. The new group had just issued a declaration in Dushanbe, Tajikistan, opposing "international terrorism, religious extremism, and national separatism." The Ulaanbaatar Declaration, signed during the visit to Mongolia of Russian Pres. Vladimir Putin in November 2000, had pledged Mongolia and Russia not to allow their territory "to be used by any third state for purposes of aggression or other acts of violence" against the other.

The September 11 terrorist attacks in the U.S. were condemned by President Bagabandi and Prime Minister Enhbayar, who visited the U.S. embassy to express Mongolia's condolences. In a broadcast to the nation, Bagabandi called the attacks a crime against democracy, freedom, and humanity. A Great Hural resolution supported the "world community's fight against terrorism."

The Paris meeting in May of the Consultative Group on aid for Mongolia agreed to a new package worth $330 million for one year. A second successive autumn drought and hard winter had killed another 3.3 million head of livestock.

Lhamsurengiyn Enebish, the Great Hural speaker and secretary-general of the MPRP, died of a stroke on September 29. (*See* OBITUARIES.)

(ALAN J.K. SANDERS)

MOROCCO

Area: 710,850 sq km (274,461 sq mi), including the 252,120-sq-km (97,344-sq-mi) area of the disputed Western Sahara annexation
Population (2001 est.): 29,237,000, of which Western Sahara 251,000
Capital: Rabat
Head of state and government: King Muhammad VI, assisted by Prime Minister 'Abd ar-Rahman Youssoufi

Moroccans became worried during 2001 over a slowdown in political liberalization after the banning of three newspapers (*Le Journal, Demain,* and *Assahifa*) in December 2000 and the arrest of three French TV journalists. The newspapers had published information about a letter from a veteran opposition leader, Muhammad Basri, admitting links between the Socialist Union of Popular Forces (USFP) and the organizer of an unsuccessful coup in 1972. Though the USFP dominated the government coalition and vehemently objected to the accusation, the newspaper ban was lifted after international protest in January.

Anxiety over basic rights mounted with the arrest of Hannouda Taibi, a journalist on the USFP newspaper *Al-Ittihad al-Ishtiraki,* and the king's decision in January to cancel a planned meeting with the directors of the International Federation for Human Rights. In May 36 human rights activists from the Association Marocaine des Droits Humains—who had been arrested during a protest the previous December—were sentenced to three months in prison. Concerns were heightened when the interior minister was replaced in September by former businessman Driss Jettou in a move to reassert royal control.

The Moroccan government welcomed the appointment of Margaret Tutwiler as U.S. ambassador to Morocco; she had been a close associate of James Baker, the U.S. secretary of state under the former George H.W. Bush administration, and her appointment was seen as an expression of American confidence in King Muhammad VI. Baker, serving as special envoy for the UN secretary-general in resolving the 25-year-long territorial dispute between Morocco and the Polisario Front over the Western Sahara, put forward a new peace plan in June, just before the UN Security Council granted a five-month extension to the peacekeeping force there.

The plan envisioned limited autonomy for the region under Moroccan sovereignty for a five-year period, after which the promised referendum for self-determination could be held. Algeria, the Polisario Front's main backer, objected to the plan, and the Polisario Front rejected it. In the first visit of his reign, King Muhammad VI traveled to the Western Sahara in November to underscore Morocco's claim to the disputed area.

(GEORGE JOFFÉ)

MOZAMBIQUE

Area: 812,379 sq km (313,661 sq mi)
Population (2001 est.): 19,371,000
Capital: Maputo
Head of state and government: President Joaquim Chissano, assisted by Prime Minister Pascoal Mocumbi

When an interview given to a Portuguese newspaper by Afonso Dhlakama, leader of the Mozambique National Resistance (Renamo) opposition movement, was published on Jan. 2, 2001, it added fuel to the dispute between his party and the Mozambique Liberation Front (Frelimo) government that had flared up in the north of the country the previous November. In the interview Dhlakama accused the ruling party of orchestrating violence against opposition supporters.

The problem was immediately overshadowed when the Zambezi River on January 3 again burst its banks after a week of heavy rains; the downpour continued through February and March. As many as 180,000 people were reported to have been displaced, and the situation was made worse when the floodgates on the Cabora Bassa Dam were partially opened to reduce pressure on the wall and thereby added to the volume of water sweeping over the Zambezi plain.

Though help was quickly forthcoming from the South African air force, many farmers were reluctant to leave their homes in spite of exhortations, and even threats of arrest, from the government. Donor agencies in Germany, The Netherlands, Portugal, Sweden, the U.K., and the U.S. were quick to respond to the government's appeal for financial assistance, but Mozambique found it difficult to recover from such an overwhelming setback. The annual growth rate of the economy had dropped from 9% in the 1990s to 1.7% in 2000, and the estimated growth rate for 2001 was not expected to exceed 3%. The country was suffering from the general decline in investment in Africa, and though it received $700 million in aid in 2001 in addition to flood-relief payments, that sum represented 90% of all foreign investment in the country and accounted for 60% of government spending, a state of dependency that discouraged enterprise.

Midyear, Pres. Joaquim Chissano announced that he would not run for reelection in 2004. Under the terms of the constitution, he was entitled to be reelected twice, and since he had been first elected in 1994 and reelected in 1999, there was no reason why he should not run again in 2004. Because, however, he had already been president for eight years before the 1994 election, he considered that to campaign again would be contrary to the spirit, if not the letter, of the law. A final decision on the issue would not be made until the eighth party congress in 2002.

Mozambique's relations with South Africa were strengthened when the two countries signed a "protocol of cooperation" on December 6.

(KENNETH INGHAM)

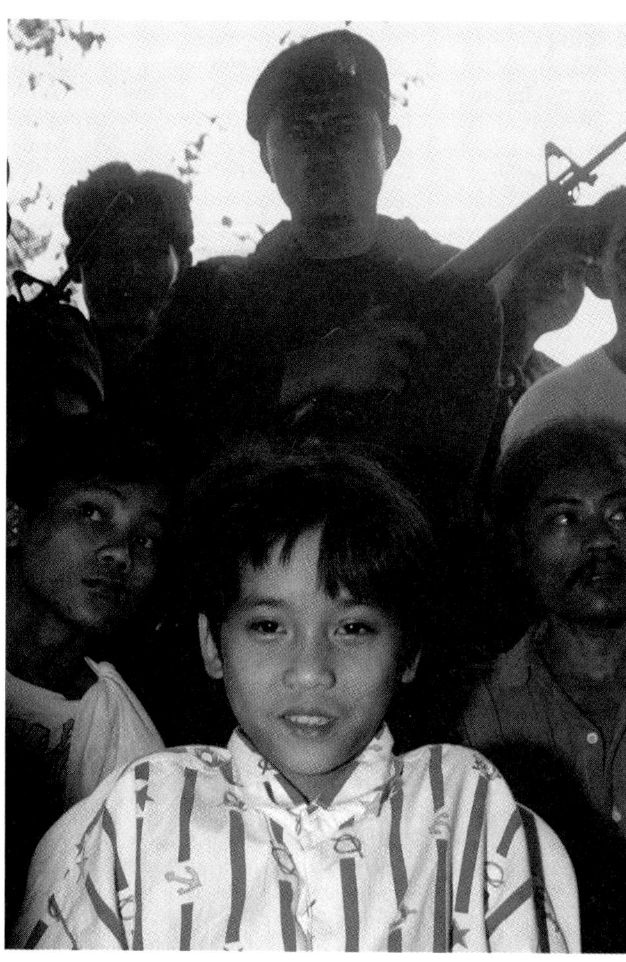

Along with some of his followers, 13-year-old Luther Htoo (centre)—who with his twin brother, Johnny, led the rebel group God's Army in Myanmar—is heavily guarded by police after laying down arms in Thailand.

AP/Wide World Photos

MYANMAR (BURMA)

Area: 676,577 sq km (261,228 sq mi)
Population (2001 est.): 41,995,000
Capital: Yangon (Rangoon)
Head of state and government: Chairman of the State Peace and Development Council Gen. Than Shwe

In Myanmar the year 2001 saw the continuation of the ruling military junta's talks aimed at resolving the 10-year standoff with opposition National League for Democracy (NLD) leader Daw Aung San Suu Kyi. Since talks began in October 2000, almost 200 political prisoners had been released (though about 1,500 still remained in detention), and the media's virulent attacks on the opposition had ceased. Frustrated with the slow pace of the talks, and with little hope of a breakthrough after 12 months, the NLD in September called for the immediate release of Suu Kyi from house detention and the recognition of the party's 1990 election victory.

Following a fact-finding team's visit to Myanmar in early 2001, the European Union (EU) renewed sanctions on the country for a further six months, citing human rights violations. The EU, however, increased humanitarian aid funding. Myanmar allowed access to an International Labor Organization delegation to evaluate progress on banning forced labour. Religious riots between Buddhists and Muslims claimed the lives of an unknown number of people in October.

The first half of the year saw a marked deterioration in Myanmar-Thai relations, with fierce border skirmishes taking place. After 19 years of being oriented toward Thailand's eastern border, Thai and U.S. Special Forces staged joint military exercises on Thailand's western border with Myanmar in May. Myanmar troops also exchanged fire in the west with Bangladeshi forces.

While China remained the main supplier of military hardware and economic aid to Myanmar, the junta also strengthened its ties with Russia, North Korea, Pakistan, and India. Yangon was reportedly purchasing a nuclear reactor and sophisticated MiG-29 fighters from Russia and conventional arms from North Korea. Pakistani chief executive Gen. Pervez Musharraf's visit on May 1–3 was preceded by calls by three Pakistani naval ships to Myanmar ports. India's external affairs minister visited Myanmar to strengthen economic ties and inaugurated an Indian-built highway. A joint Indo-Myanmar military offensive against rebel groups operating in India's northeast was also undertaken. On December 12–15 Chinese Pres. Jiang Zemin visited Myanmar, the first such trip by a Chinese chief of state since 1988.

Political uncertainty, high inflation, declining foreign investment, and sluggish agricultural growth worsened Myanmar's economic situation. The value of the kyat slipped more than 20% in mid-August, and tourism declined significantly. (MOHAN MALIK)

NAMIBIA

Area: 825,118 sq km (318,580 sq mi)
Population (2001 est.): 1,798,000
Capital: Windhoek
Chief of state and head of government: President Sam Nujoma, assisted by Prime Minister Hage Geingob

The security situation in northeastern Namibia remained tense in 2001 in the aftermath of Angolan attacks from Namibian soil on National Union for the Total Independence of Angola (UNITA) rebels and the failed secessionist attempt in the Caprivi Strip. Tourism, one of the country's main foreign-currency earners, was badly affected. In mid-October a dusk-to-dawn curfew was reimposed along a stretch of the border with Angola.

At the first cabinet meeting of the year, Pres. Sam Nujoma criticized unnecessary expenditure by top officials and instructed them to give up their Mercedes-Benz vehicles and limit their overseas trips. By August most of the Namibian troops in the Democratic Republic of the Congo had been withdrawn. The president and some of his ministers were criticized for using strong words against human rights organizations, foreigners, and homosexuals. In March President Nujoma announced that the police had orders to imprison and deport homosexuals. Some suggested that he was frustrated by the increase in AIDS deaths; at least one in five Namibian adults was infected with HIV.

Though legislation was introduced to establish an anticorruption commission with wide powers to investigate and uncover corruption in public and private bodies, the president was specifically excluded from its provisions. After sending out contradictory signals about his intention to stand for a fourth term in 2004, President Nujoma finally bowed to pressure and announced in late 2001 that he would not seek another term of office. (CHRISTOPHER SAUNDERS)

NAURU

Area: 21.2 sq km (8.2 sq mi)
Population (2001 est.): 12,100
Capital: Government offices in Yaren district
Head of state and government: Presidents Bernard Dowiyogo and, from March 30, Rene Harris

Rene Harris returned as president following a vote of no-confidence against Pres. Bernard Dowiyogo in Nauru's Parliament on March 29, 2001. Dowiyogo lost his job over international criticism of Nauru's financial system and in particular over allegations of money laundering for the Russian mafia. Russia's central bank claimed that about $70 billion had been lost in transactions processed through Nauru's 400 offshore banks. In December the Financial Action Task Force on Money Laundering announced that it would take countermeasures against Nauru's failure to meet a November 30 deadline to address the shortcomings of its laws against money laundering.

Relations with the U.S. proved difficult for Nauru in 2001. Nauru's ambassador to the UN, Vinci Clodumar, led regional opposition to a proposed U.S. missile-defense system. Clodumar said that the development of the system was not in the best interest of the Pacific region, as it could lead to radioactive fallout from missile intercepts landing on Pacific islands.

In September Nauru received UN approval to process several hundred refugees denied access to Australia and temporarily settled on Nauru. Under an agreement with Australia, Nauru would receive about $10 million in financial aid in exchange for processing the asylum seekers, most of whom were from Iraq or Afghanistan. (See *Australia*, above.) (A.R.G. GRIFFITHS)

NEPAL

Area: 147,181 sq km (56,827 sq mi)
Population (2001 est.): 25,284,000
Capital: Kathmandu
Head of state: Kings Birendra Bir Bikram Shah Dev and, from June 4, Gyanendra Bir Bikram Shah Dev
Head of government: Prime Ministers Girija Prasad Koirala and, from July 21, Sher Bahadur Deuba

Nepal seemed on the brink of political chaos and even disintegration in mid-2001. The assassination of King Birendra (*see* OBITUARIES) and eight other members of the royal family by Crown Prince Dipendra threatened the traditional monarchical system. Divisions within the ruling Nepali Congress Party led to changes in the prime ministership in July, and the Maoist insurgency in the western hill area posed a major challenge to the democratic parliamentary system of government. By October King Gyanendra, the late king's brother, was

The bodies of Nepalese King Birendra, Queen Aiswarya, and other relatives shot and killed by Birendra's eldest son, Crown Prince Dipendra, are cremated in Kathmandu on June 2.

AP/Wide World Photos

functioning effectively as a constitutional monarch, the Nepali Congress government was in control, and all the political parties, including the Maoists, were engaged in political dialogues. In late November, however, in the wake of renewed Maoist violence, the king and Prime Minister Sher Bahadur Deuba declared a state of emergency. The army and the Maoists were still battling at year's end.

Nepal's difficult but essential relationship with neighbouring India also caused major problems. Their vital 1996 trade treaty, due to expire in December 2001, was extended until March 2002 as negotiations continued to iron out a few basic differences between the two sides.

The economic-growth rate remained low, owing to a limited resource base, rapid population growth, environmental degradation, low levels of social development, and widespread poverty. Nepal's vast hydropower resources also were at an early stage of development—despite a variety of agreements with India and others on the subject—primarily because of political division within Nepal. In September Deuba's government announced major land-reform programs that could provide land to the large landless population.

(LEO E. ROSE)

NETHERLANDS, THE

Area: 41,526 sq km (16,033 sq mi)
Population (2001 est.): 15,968,000
Capital: Amsterdam; seat of government, The Hague
Chief of state: Queen Beatrix
Head of government: Prime Minister Wim Kok

The Dutch economy was strong in 2001—jobs were plentiful; incomes went up across the board; and the government continued to invest in public projects and in strengthening the economy. Though growth seemed to be slowing, the government planned to invest more than €3.5 billion (about $3.1 billion) in 2002 to improve health care, education, and safety. The government also planned to continue to pay down the national debt.

The year began with a catastrophic fire during New Year's celebrations in a café in Volendam, in which more than 180 people were hurt; at least 12 people eventually died of their injuries. The number of casualties was much higher than expected because proper safety precautions had been ignored. An estimated 2,000 individuals were traumatized to such an extent that they would need ongoing psychological treatment. In the aftermath—with memories still fresh from the explosions in a fireworks factory in Enschede the previous year—renewed interest surfaced in the enforcement of safety standards.

The agricultural sector suffered from an outbreak of foot-and-mouth disease, which dampened farmers' morale and had adverse effects on their income. Beyond the sphere of agriculture, travel restrictions interfered with commerce and led to the cancellation of some celebrations of the national holiday (Koninginnedag, or Queen's Day) and some World War II memorial events. Bovine spongiform encephalopathy (also referred to as "mad cow" disease) was also detected in The Netherlands.

Though the euro was about to become the only legal tender in January 2002, The Netherlands nonetheless celebrated its tradition of creating beautifully designed currency by issuing one "last" guilder coin in mid-June. One side was drawn by a 12-year-old boy, whose design, selected from more than 50,000 submissions, sported a cartoonish flag-waving "Dutch lion." Sixteen million copies of the popular coin were put into circulation.

The royal family turned its attention to matrimony. Prince Constantijn, the third son of Queen Beatrix, married Laurentien Brinkhorst. Crown Prince Willem-Alexander announced his engagement to Máxima Zorreguieta. The proposed marriage was approved by the States-General after skillful negotiation by Prime Minister Wim Kok. At issue was the fact that Zorreguieta's father had been the minister of agriculture in Argentina during the Jorge Rafaél Videla regime. Kok authorized an independent study to explore the extent of her father's involvement in human rights violations. Zorreguieta denied having known of any such violations by his government at the time and stated that he would not attend the nuptials, scheduled for Feb. 2, 2002. Máxima Zorreguieta publicly expressed regret that her father had "worked hard" for a regime that had engaged in unacceptable practices. The fact that she was able to make such statements in Dutch helped establish her credibility with the Dutch public.

The Netherlands made news around the world on April 1 when the first four gay and lesbian couples were legally married in Amsterdam. Almost 400 couples followed suit that month. Of those, 80% were already registered as domestic partners, an option that had been available since 1998.

(JOLANDA VANDERWAL TAYLOR)

Gay couples celebrate at City Hall in Amsterdam on April 1 after exchanging wedding vows under a new law allowing same-sex marriages.

AP/Wide World Photos

NEW ZEALAND

Area: 270,534 sq km (104,454 sq mi)
Population (2001 est.): 3,861,000
Capital: Wellington
Chief of state: Queen Elizabeth II, represented by Governors-General Sir Michael Hardie-Boys, Dame Sian Elias (acting) from March 22, and, from April 4, Dame Silvia Cartwright
Head of government: Prime Minister Helen Clark

In 2001, the Labour Party's second full year in power, Prime Minister Helen Clark continued to have the support of her coalition deputy, Jim Anderton of the liberal Alliance, and the less-reliable support of various fragmentary groupings, which came and went on different issues. Anderton's personal ambition to convert the national post office to a People's Bank came closer with his appointment of former National Party (NP) prime minister Jim Bolger as that project's leader. The mildly conservative NP provided a dull parliamentary opposition, and it was no surprise to insiders when NP leader Jenny Shipley paid the price. On October 8 her colleagues produced the numbers to persuade her it was time to step down. Deputy party leader Bill English, minister of health and then of finance in past NP governments, stepped up.

In the wake of the attacks in the United States on September 11, New Zealand offered deployment of its elite Special Air Service (SAS) to an antiterrorism operation coordinated and led by the U.S. The SAS force specialized in undercover long-range reconnaissance and counterterrorism missions, and a New Zealand government spokesman acknowledged that it might serve in Afghanistan. Anderton's support for New Zealand's involvement triggered some dissent within the Alliance. The situation also provoked some New Zealanders to recall the country's post-World War II treaty with the U.S. and Australia, the ANZUS Pact, which New Zealand had effectively jettisoned when it barred nuclear-age U.S. warships from its ports in the 1980s. In May the government had announced plans to scrap all of New Zealand's combat aircraft. A legal challenge to the decision was rejected by a High Court judge in November, and the squadrons were disbanded in December.

Pierre Vinet/New Line Cinema

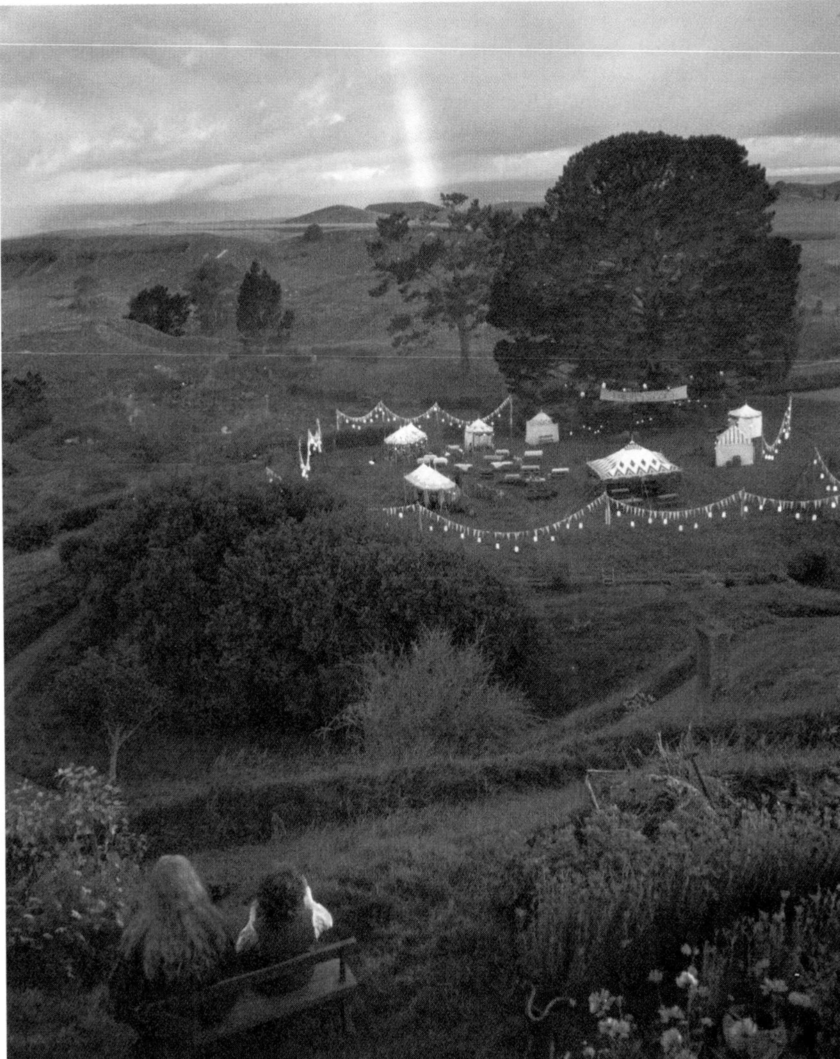

The spectacular landscape of New Zealand provided the backdrop for the popular 2001 film **The Fellowship of the Ring.**

In the second half of the year, the government passed initiatives to help Australia place Afghan and other refugees and also to save New Zealand's international airline. Beginning in late August Afghan "boat people" bearing down on northern and western Australia were refused permission to land. New Zealand agreed to accept a quota for settlement, and in late September more than 140 refugees were flown to Auckland from a transshipment centre on Nauru. At the same time, New Zealand Muslims announced plans to combat perceived harassment and met with a government-appointed race relations conciliator. Air New Zealand's (ANZ) crisis was partly attributable to world reaction against flying, as well as to a failed attempt to digest fully the Australian airline Ansett in a many-sided takeover operation. For the New Zealand government it meant returning to the business of running an airline 12 years after privatization. In early October it assumed control of ANZ, with a cost of NZ$885 million (about U.S. $366.5 million), 83% ownership, and a less-than-buoyant market. ANZ chief executive Gary Toomey immediately resigned. John Palmer replaced him in late November.

The engineering of genetically modified (GM) organisms became a tentative new issue with the release at the end of July of a Royal Commission report backing commercial use of GM products in New Zealand. One reviewer said the commission had balanced the need for progress with the need for robust safety controls. In October the government allowed a moratorium on GM research, including experimental field trials, to lapse, but it announced a new two-year moratorium on the commercial release of GM organisms under development.

In November yachtsman Sir Peter Blake was killed by bandits. (*See* OBITUARIES.) (JOHN A. KELLEHER)

NICARAGUA

Area: 130,373 sq km (50,337 sq mi)
Population (2001 est.): 4,918,000
Capital: Managua
Head of state and government: President Arnoldo Alemán Lacayo

In Nicaragua socioeconomic conditions worsened in 2001 as the world recession, poor commodity prices, administrative malfeasance and incompetence, bank failures, and drought caused economic growth to slow to an estimated 2.1%. Unemployment, poverty, and income inequality grew. At midyear starving peasants from the north erected protest encampments along major highways and in Managua. In acknowledgment of the country's dire conditions, the international donor community had finally admitted Nicaragua to the Heavily Indebted Poor Countries Initiative in December 2000 and canceled much of its foreign debt. The government was to make fiscal reforms and combat corruption, but medications donated by the international community to the government were soon found being distributed in ruling party campaign offices. The U.S. chose to deliver its food aid through nongovernmental organizations.

It was also an election year. The 1999 "pact" between Sandinista Daniel Ortega and Constitutionalist Liberal Arnoldo Alemán Lacayo had resulted in 2000 in the packing of the Supreme Electoral Council. Controlled by partisans, the council rejected all attempts by third parties to qualify to compete in the next presidential elections except that of the Conservative Party, whose bid was apparently saved by U.S. pressure. As the unofficial campaign heated up early in 2001, however, with Ortega seven points in the lead, the U.S. successfully pressured the Conservatives to withdraw in order not to split the anti-Sandinista vote.

Though the Conservatives later named new candidates, the contest narrowed to a tight two-way race. While the Liberal candidate, 73-year-old businessman Enrique Bolaños Geyer, sought to establish his concern for Nicaragua's impoverished majority, erstwhile revolutionary Ortega presented himself as a "new man" able to coexist with practically anyone. Unmoved, the Catholic hierarchy and various American officials—including Secretary of State Colin Powell—made strong anti-Sandinista declarations. Following the September 11 attacks in the U.S., Washington even drew connections between Ortega and world "terrorism," and one American official predicted a "vicious" U.S. response should an Ortega government be found to have links to terrorism. On November 4 Bolaños trounced Ortega 56.3%–42.3%, while the Conservatives claimed 1.4% of the vote. Hours before the election, former U.S. president Jimmy Carter, heading an observer team in Nicaragua, commented: "I personally disapprove of statements or actions by any country . . . to influence the vote . . . in another sovereign nation." In December, citing that the statute of limitations had run out, a judge dismissed charges of rape brought against Ortega by his stepdaughter.

(THOMAS W. WALKER)

NIGER

Area: 1,267,000 sq km (489,000 sq mi)
Population (2001 est.): 10,355,000
Capital: Niamey
Head of state and government: President Tandja Mamadou, assisted by Prime Minister Hama Amadou

Thousands of University of Niamey students, protesting against government plans to reduce their grants, clashed with security forces on Feb. 21, 2001. One policeman later died of head wounds received during the violence, and nearly 50 persons from both sides were injured. Sixteen students were arrested after the demonstration, and the university was closed. On March 24 the government easily defeated an opposition no-confidence vote over its handling of the unrest. The Niamey students rejected an agreement signed on March 28 between the government and their parent organization, the Union of Niger Students, that would have reopened the university and restored full financial support. They demanded the release of the arrested students as a precondition for negotiations. At a court appearance on April 3, however, only four were released; the remaining 12 were charged with murder. On April 28 the imprisoned students began a hunger strike, and in May 100 other students staged a sit-down strike outside the parliament building. The action was abandoned after 11 days, and students staged a peaceful demonstration through the streets of Niamey. The prisoners' hunger strike continued for several more days.

Niger's food crisis remained at critical levels throughout the summer, though the year's increased rainfall held promise of an improved harvest. On July 25 the UN World Food Programme launched an appeal for donors to give Niger $5 million for emergency purchases of grain. The government announced on August 15 that, in order to try to halt ongoing desertification, it would more than double the number of tree seedlings to be planted during the year. (NANCY ELLEN LAWLER)

AP/Wide World Photos

At a special forum on child slavery held during the World Conference Against Racism in Durban, S.Af., Mariama Oumarou tearfully recounts her experiences as a child slave in Niger.

NIGERIA

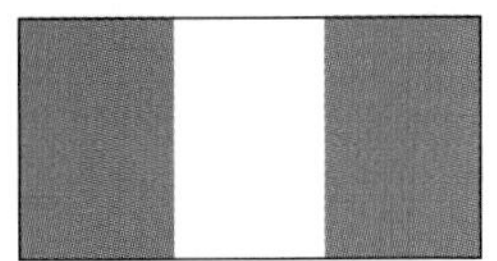

Area: 923,768 sq km (356,669 sq mi)
Population (2001 est.): 126,636,000
Capital: Abuja; judiciary and some ministries remain in Lagos, the former capital
Head of state and government: President Olusegun Obasanjo

Throughout 2001 Nigeria experienced ethnic and religious violence. In June and July battles between the Tiv minority and Hausa majority left approximately 50,000 people displaced in Nassarawa state. In August Christians and Muslims fought in Bauchi state over the state government's efforts to institute Shari'ah (Islamic law). Similar clashes in the central city of Jos claimed an estimated 1,000 lives in September. Violence flared in October between Muslims and Christians in Kano following Muslim protests against U.S.-led military action in Afghanistan. Official reports put the death toll at 18, though the unofficial tally reached more than 100.

The oil-producing Niger Delta region was again the site of environmental problems and political conflicts. A blown-out well in the Yorla oil field released crude oil for nine days before being capped. Residents fled several surrounding villages as their crops were destroyed and drinking water was poisoned by the oil. Shell Oil Co. officials charged that they were prevented from taking adequate safety precautions by the Movement for the Survival of Ogoni People (MOSOP), a group formed to protect the interests of the delta region's inhabitants. For its part MOSOP claimed that Shell failed to consult local people about the oil fields.

In January the federal government asked the Supreme Court to clarify a constitutional provision allowing state governments to keep a portion of profits from oil produced in their territory. The federal government claimed the proceeds of offshore oil production, money that oil-producing states had attempted to keep. In July the court sided with the federal government. As a result, oil-producing states received 7.8% of the national oil revenue rather than the 13% they had claimed.

In April Pres. Olusegun Obasanjo announced the simultaneous replacement of the heads of the army, navy, and air force. The move was widely interpreted as a result of Obasanjo's desire to remove Army Chief of Staff Lieut. Gen. Victor Malu from office. Malu caused controversy when he publicly criticized military training and cooperation arrangements between Nigeria and the U.S. The new top military men were Maj. Gen. Alexander Ogomudia (army), Air Vice Marshal James Wuyep (air force), and Rear Adm. Samuel Afolayan (navy).

George Esiri/TimePix

A burnt-out church in Kano, Nigeria, on October 17, attests to the Muslim-Christian fighting in the area that reportedly claimed more than 100 lives.

In March the police arrested Gilbert Okoye in connection with the murder of a politician in Anambra state. Okoye led the Anambra Vigilance Services, better known as the Bakassi Boys, a vigilante group that was revived in 2000 and supported by the Anambra government. That support ended amid criticism that the group killed suspected criminals instead of turning them over to the authorities. In April police in Lagos exchanged fire with members of the Oodua Peoples' Congress, a banned Yoruba militia.

In September serious flooding struck northern parts of the country. The Taura dam in Jigawa state overflowed following heavy rains, killing more than 100 people and leaving 40,000 homeless. Another 60 lives were lost and 10,000 people rendered homeless by floods in nearby Kano state. Late in the year a cholera outbreak claimed more than 700 lives.

The Human Rights Violation Investigation Commission (HRVIC) continued to look into alleged abuses by the country's former military governments. In July Justice Chukwudifu Oputa, chairman of the HRVIC, called on three former military rulers to appear before the commission. The three, Generals Muhammadu Buhari, Ibrahim Babangida, and Abdulsalam Abubakar, all refused and challenged the commission summons in court. President Obasanjo appeared before the commission in September to answer charges stemming from his tenure as a military ruler in 1978. In December gunmen assassinated Attorney General and Justice Minister Bola Ige. The attack was blamed on a power struggle between political factions in Ige's home state of Osun. (MATTHEW A. CENZER)

NORWAY

Area: 323,758 sq km (125,004 sq mi)
Population (2001 est.): 4,516,000
Capital: Oslo
Chief of state: King Harald V
Head of government: Prime Ministers Jens Stoltenberg and, from October 19, Kjell Magne Bondevik

Norway's long-dominant Labour Party lost much of its grip on power after a miserable showing in the general election held on Sept. 10, 2001. In its worst showing since 1924, the party won only 24.4% of the popular vote and managed to secure just 43 seats in the 165-member Storting (parliament), down from the 65 seats the party had won four years earlier. The big winners were the Conservatives and the Socialist Left Party. The Conservatives obtained 38 seats—a gain of 15 from 1997—while the Socialist Left Party increased its number of seats from 9 to 23. The Labour government chose to resign as a result of the elections. On October 17 a minority government was formed that included the Conservatives, the Christian People's Party (22 seats), and the Liberal Party (2 seats). Kjell Magne Bondevik of the Christian People's Party became prime minister for the second time in his career, and Conservative leader Jan Petersen was named foreign minister. The populist right-wing Progress Party (26 seats) pledged its support for the new government.

The marriage of Crown Prince Haakon to the beautiful, courageous, but controversial Mette-Marit Tjessem Høiby on August 25 in Oslo captured the nation's attention. (*See* BIOGRAPHIES.) The prince's choice of bride had raised eyebrows not only because she was a commoner but because she had a four-year-old son by a convicted drug dealer. Public opinion, however, began to swing in her favour after Mette-Marit held a news conference only days before the wedding to publicly apologize for aspects of her past and to condemn drug use. The hour-long wedding in Oslo Cathedral was relayed via a giant screen to thousands of people who had gathered outside the building. On December 13 the second heiress to the throne, Princess Märtha Louise, and author Ari Behn declared their engagement. At the end of the year support for the monarchy was strongly expressed in most of the press.

Prices in the global oil market continued to influence the Norwegian economy. Average daily oil production was an estimated three million barrels. Until October the average oil spot price per barrel of Brent Blend was $26. It then dropped to around $20. The negative effect from the oil price reductions that followed was counterbalanced by Norway's long-term contracts of gas deliveries by pipelines to the European market.

Surplus state income from the oil industry went into a Petroleum Fund that was set up in part to ensure pensions for the elderly. In March the government declared that future interest income from the fund should be used to cover state budget deficits.

Unemployment remained relatively low at about 3.6% during the year. The consumer price index rose by 4.3% in May but declined to 2.5% in July owing to tax cuts. In June the Bank of Norway decided to maintain the interest rate at 7% (the highest level in Western Europe) and even declared that it would raise the rate should inflation once more approach 4%. By the end of November the bank had reduced the rate by 0.25%.

(GUDMUND SANDVIK)

OMAN

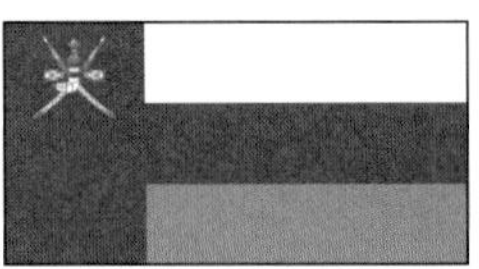

Area: 309,500 sq km (119,500 sq mi)
Population (2001 est.): 2,497,000
Capital: Muscat
Head of state and government: Sultan and Prime Minister Qabus ibn Sa'id

In the immediate aftermath of the terrorist attacks in the U.S. on Sept. 11, 2001, Oman, in fulfillment of preparations launched two and a half years earlier, hosted a joint military exercise with Great Britain. The presence of some 30,000 British troops in the sultanate facilitated the U.S.-led coalition's military campaign against the Taliban regime and al-Qaeda terrorist network in Afghanistan. Throughout the campaign Oman remained supportive of the coalition, allowing the deployment of American B-1 bombers to bases in the sultanate and agreeing to serve as a staging area for British and American special forces.

Sultan Qabus ibn Sa'id was more visible in 2001 than in previous years. He was among the regional leaders who met personally with U.S. Secretary of Defense Donald Rumsfeld during Rumsfeld's three-day swing through the Middle East in early October to garner international support for the war on terrorism. At the end of the year, the sultan was elected chairman of the Gulf Cooperation Council's (GCC's) Supreme Council for 2002. The GCC, established in 1981 and committed to enhancing economic, defense, and political cooperation between its six member states, had become one of the world's most prominent subregional organizations. The members—Bahrain, Kuwait, Oman, Qatar, Saudi Arabia, and the United Arab Emirates—possessed nearly half the planet's proven petroleum reserves.

Domestically, Oman continued along the path of its previous political reforms. In addition to the cabinet and government headed by the sultan, a 52-member State Council helped determine national development strategies. As part of a larger Oman Council, the State Council also rendered advice regarding the sultanate's economic and financial policies. The uncertain future of oil revenues continued to underpin the government's resolve to diversify the economy. This entailed further development of the country's liquefied natural gas industry, tourism, and the southernmost port of Salalah, one of the world's largest container terminals.

(JOHN DUKE ANTHONY)

PAKISTAN

Area: 796,095 sq km (307,374 sq mi), excluding the 84,159-sq-km Pakistani-administered portion of Jammu and Kashmir
Population (2001 est.): 144.6 million (excluding 4 million residents of Pakistani-administered Jammu and Kashmir as well as 2 million Afghan refugees)
Capital: Islamabad
Head of state and government: President and Chief Executive Gen. Pervez Musharraf

The leader of Pakistan's military regime, Gen. Pervez Musharraf, found himself walking a political tightrope in 2001. After having consolidated his grip on power by declaring himself president in June, Musharraf risked a highly unpopular move with his decision—in the wake of the terrorist attacks in the United States on September 11—to side with the U.S. in its war against the Taliban government in Afghanistan and the al-Qaeda terrorist network led by Saudi-born Osama bin Laden. (*See* BIOGRAPHIES.) Pakistan had been one of only three countries ever officially to recognize the Afghan Islamists, and the Taliban enjoyed the sympathies and support of many of Pakistan's 140 million Muslims. In the aftermath of September 11, Islamic militants staged protests in dozens of cities throughout

Pakistan, burning U.S. Pres. George W. Bush in effigy and promising a "holy war" against any American troops that set foot in the country. Some 10,000 Pakistanis were thought to have crossed the Suleman Mountains into Afghanistan to fight alongside the Taliban against the U.S.-led forces.

Musharraf appeared on nationwide television on September 19 to defend his decision to side with the U.S., and as time went on, he appeared more confident in his ability to restrain the vocal Muslim clerics and militant groups responsible for the rash of angry protests. In fact, Musharraf all but abandoned his initial calls for a political settlement to the conflict that had included uniting so-called moderate Taliban members with rival Afghan groups in a new government. Instead, he expressed support for removing the Taliban outright and, at home, went about purging Taliban-friendly officers in the Pakistani military. Moreover, he ordered a complete ban on any public gathering that included what he described as seditious conduct or language. By December these measures appeared to have had an impact. The militants had failed to ignite anything close to a real threat to Musharraf. As the military rout of the Taliban progressed, the Pakistani government began to devote considerable attention to the role it might play in the establishment of a post-Taliban government in Afghanistan. Islamabad clearly wanted to ensure that Pashtuns—who made up the largest ethnic group in Afghanistan and dominated Pakistani regions on the Afghan border—had a major voice in any future Kabul government.

Pakistan's dispute with India over Jammu and Kashmir state remained essentially unsettled despite several attempts at negotiation. Alarmed by an increase in secessionist violence in the region, Indian Prime Minister Atal Bihari Vajpayee invited Musharraf to India for talks on the matter. Musharraf accepted the invitation and arrived in New Delhi on July 14. Discussions were held in Agra over the following two days. India pushed for help in ending cross-border terrorism, but Pakistan continued to insist that a political solution to the Jammu and Kashmir issue needed to be reached before effective change could be brought about. While no final agreement was reached, Vajpayee accepted an invitation to visit Pakistan later in the year. A meeting scheduled for September in New York City was canceled owing to the terrorist attacks. After both countries had pledged their support for the U.S.-led war on terrorism following the events of September 11, the U.S. decided to end the economic embargoes it had imposed on Pakistan and India for carrying out nuclear tests in 1998. Pakistani and Indian relations deteriorated severely after India blamed two Pakistan-based organizations for the terrorist attack on Parliament House in New Delhi on December 13.

On the economic front, Pakistan's attempt to follow an International Monetary Fund reform program met with mixed results. Although recession continued and unemployment steadily climbed, Pakistan successfully secured loan guarantees from the World Bank, which promised to deliver $350 million for bank restructuring and a like amount to help reduce the country's current-account deficit. Gross domestic product growth, which had been targeted at 4.5% for 2001, was revised down to 3.8%. The government plans to privatize some 50 companies over the next two years were still intact, despite the fact that few investors had expressed interest in the state-owned banks and corporations slated for sale. (EDITOR)

Arif Ali/AFP Worldwide

Pakistani paramilitary troops check their ammunition while patrolling the Indian border near Wagah on December 28.

PALAU

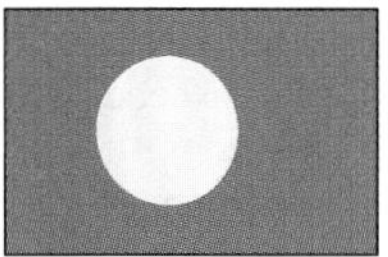

Area: 488 sq km (188 sq mi)
Population (2001 est.): 19,700
Provisional capital: Koror; a site on Babelthuap was designated to be the permanent capital
Head of state and government: Presidents Kuniwo Nakamura and, from January 19, Tommy Remengesau

Voters in Palau elected a new president. Tommy Remengesau began his four-year term on Jan. 19, 2001, and replaced Kuniwo Nakamura, who enthusiastically endorsed his successor. Remengesau moved quickly to strengthen economic relations with Taiwan, especially in the tourism industry, and Taiwan sent a delegation to attend his inauguration.

In April Palau and Saga University, Saga City, Japan, signed an agreement for technical cooperation in the implementation of a power-generation method developed by the university. Under the agreement, Palau would generate its electric power through ocean thermal energy conversion (OTEC). In the South Pacific region, water temperatures can differ by as much as 11 °C (20 °F) between the surface and depths of several hundred metres, a factor that was ideally suited to the environmentally friendly OTEC method using ocean temperature differentials.

(A.R.G. GRIFFITHS)

PANAMA

Area: 74,979 sq km (28,950 sq mi)
Population (2001 est.): 2,903,000
Capital: Panama City
Head of state and government: President Mireya Moscoso

The year 2001 marked the second anniversary of Panamanian Pres. Mireya Moscoso's administration. Four issues dominated the domestic agenda: the slowing economy, the reorganization of the state-owned water company, growing charges of corruption, and problems stemming from an effort to modernize public transportation.

Panama's economy continued a downward trend during the year. The finance minister was forced to admit that economic growth would not exceed 2%. Economists attributed the downturn in the economy to a slowdown in activity in the Colón Free Trade Zone and reduced foreign investment. In addition, the government announced that the September 11 terrorist attacks in the U.S. would depress Panama's tourism sector.

Throughout the year a battle ensued between the president and the Legislative Assembly over the reorganization of the state-owned water and sewer company IDAAN. During the presidential campaign, Moscoso had promised that she would never privatize IDAAN. Once in office, however, she was faced with the company's massive operating deficit. Initially, she sought to pump $150 million from the Fiduciary Fund into IDAAN. The opposition-controlled Congress refused to support the idea without a major overhaul of the way the company was run. Efforts to reach a compromise were under way.

The media and opposition party leaders highlighted charges of nepotism and misuse of public funds. A leading adviser to Moscoso quit the administration, alleging that "crooks disguised as businessmen" surrounded the president. Additional problems surfaced when Moscoso commuted the sentence of a known drug trafficker whose brother worked at the Ministry of the Presidency. Moscoso later rescinded the commutation.

Mass protests were sparked by a 67% transit hike that had been part of a government effort to modernize public transportation. The demonstrations, which blocked many key streets in Panama City, led the education minister to temporarily close down all public schools in the city and the adjoining district of San Miguelito. Under pressure, the government formed a negotiating commission and in the end backed away from the hike. (ORLANDO J. PÉREZ)

PAPUA NEW GUINEA

Area: 462,840 sq km (178,704 sq mi)
Population (2001 est.): 5,287,000
Capital: Port Moresby
Chief of state: Queen Elizabeth II, represented by Governor-General Silas Atopare
Head of government: Prime Minister Sir Mekere Morauta

Papua New Guinea's secessionist province of Bougainville ended a decade-long war when final terms for peace were negotiated on June 1, 2001. Under an agreement signed by the minister for Bougainville affairs, Moi Avei, on behalf of the national government, the island was to have statelike autonomy and the option of total independence by 2011–16.

Widespread breakdowns in law and order caused by difficult economic conditions and popular hostility to the Papua New Guinea Privatization Commission, the World Bank, and the International Monetary Fund posed serious problems in 2001. In the most serious incident, rebellious soldiers stole weapons from armouries in Port Morseby. The soldiers were angered by a Commonwealth Eminent Persons Group recommendation that the size of the army be halved and that the army headquarters be sold off as commercial real estate. To defuse the situation, Prime Minister Sir Mekere Morauta gave an unconditional amnesty to all those who took part in the uprising.

In Port Moresby four students died during protests against privatization. The government promised a commission of inquiry into the killings. Violent squabbling between rival tribes over potential royalties from an

AP/Wide World Photos

Alfred Kaibe, a member of Parliament in Papua New Guinea, wears traditional clothing from the Southern Highlands during a legislative session on July 25.

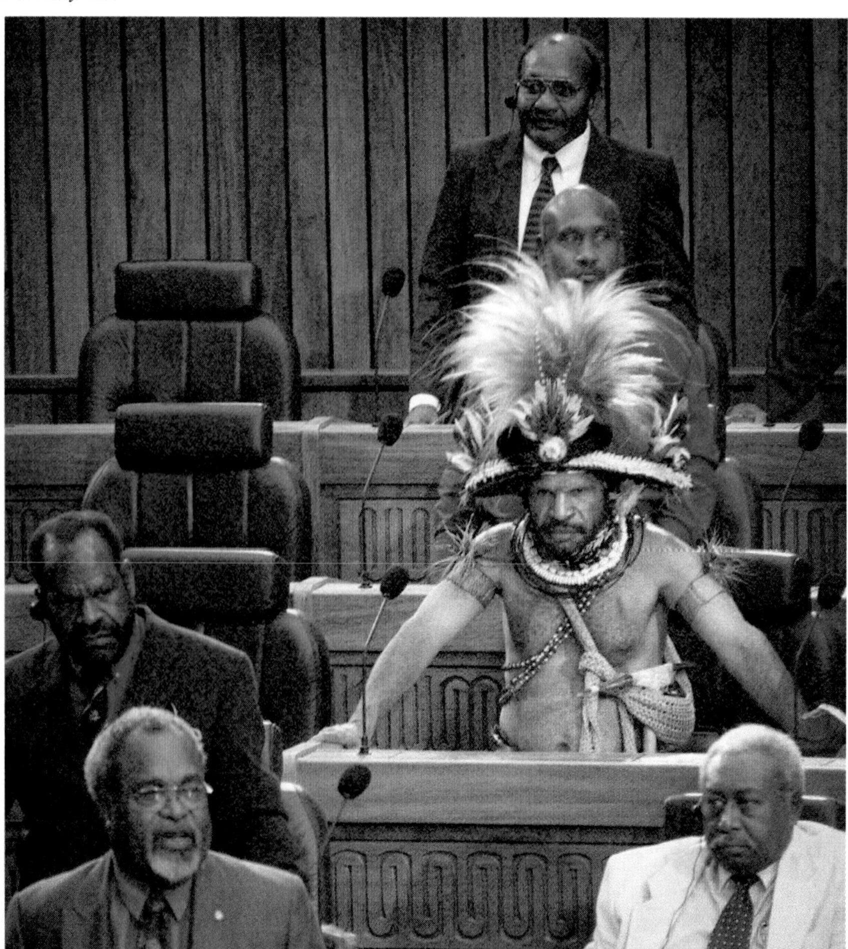

A$8,590,000,000 (U.S. $4,278,000,000) project worried possible investors in a gas consortium. At least 25 people died during tribal fighting sparked by land ownership claims along the projected route of the PNG-Queensland (Australia) gas pipeline. In December clashes near Mendi between the Ujimap and Tugumap tribesmen killed at least 36 persons. (A.R.G. GRIFFITHS)

PARAGUAY

Area: 406,752 sq km (157,048 sq mi)
Population (2001 est.): 5,636,000
Capital: Asunción
Head of state and government: President Luis Ángel González Macchi

During 2001 Paraguay faced a series of political and socioeconomic challenges—largely dealing with corruption scandals and ineffective economic policies—that threatened to overwhelm the country's weak democracy and fragile economic system. A general feeling of uncertainty and despair contributed to rumours of presidential resignation, coups, and social violence. In March, after the collapse of the National Unity government, unconfirmed rumours spread that Pres. Luis Ángel González Macchi had resigned in the face of demands from several labour groups and opposition parties that he "step down because of incompetence." Vice Pres. Julio César Franco and Miguel Abdon Saguier of the opposition Authentic Radical Liberal Party organized several protests and lobbied the legislature to have the president impeached and removed from office.

González was further weakened by a series of corruption scandals involving his family, including an allegation that the president's siblings were involved in the illegal diversion of offshore accounts of nearly $16 million in assets from two failed banks. Also, it was disclosed in March that the president's official car had been illegally imported after apparently having been stolen in Brazil.

The political crisis was exacerbated by a continued decline in economic and social conditions. Approximately a dozen strikes and roadblocks were staged during the year, most of them by landless peasants, teachers, labour unions, bus drivers, and owners of small businesses. The one thing that all of them had in common was a demand for a coherent and just economic policy and the resignation of González. Paraguay's economy grew by less than 1% during the year, while unemployment was expected to increase from 18% in 2000 to about 25% in 2001.

The domestic, political, and economic crisis overwhelmed the attention of the government and did not allow for many foreign-policy initiatives. Paraguay hosted the summit of the Southern Cone Common Market (Mercosur) members in Asunción June 21–22. During the summit Paraguay expressed concern about the consequences of exchange-rate adjustments in Argentina, demanding that a compensation mechanism be created to alleviate the negative effects on Paraguayan exports. After the September attacks in the U.S., Paraguay was one of only two countries in Latin America to consider offering troops in the U.S.-led effort to stamp out international terrorism. (FRANK O. MORA)

PERU

Area: 1,285,216 sq km (496,225 sq mi)
Population (2001 est.): 26,090,000
Capital: Lima
Head of state and government: Presidents Valentín Paniagua (interim) and, from July 28, Alejandro Toledo

The year 2001 finally brought some stability and order to Peru after a tumultuous period of political upheaval. In 2000 Pres. Alberto Fujimori had stood for a third election, in which he claimed victory despite universal outcries of fraud and ballot manipulation. Shortly after his apparent victory, however, a series of scandals involving him and Vladimiro Montesinos, his chief intelligence officer, brought about his downfall, which ended with Fujimori's faxing in his resignation as president from Japan, where he sought and received asylum.

Following Fujimori's fall from power, the Peruvian Congress had named Valentín Paniagua as interim president. He was able to bring a certain calm to Peru, stabilize a chaotic political situation, and shepherd elections through a first round in May 2001 and then a second round some weeks later. The first round saw Alejandro Toledo, an independent candidate from Peru's highlands, and former president Alan García Pérez finish first and second, respectively, but neither won the required simple majority. In the second round Toledo won a close (52–48%) race and was inaugurated on July 28. (*See* BIOGRAPHIES.)

Vladimiro Montesinos (in handcuffs), former Peruvian president Alberto Fujimori's chief intelligence officer, arrives for a criminal hearing at a naval base in Callao on September 7.

AFP Worldwide

In the meantime, Montesinos was finally captured after having fled Peru to Venezuela. He was returned to Lima, where he faced dozens of charges ranging from money laundering and drug smuggling to human rights abuses and murder. Several congressional committees as well as an independent investigator were overseeing the investigation, which was expected to take some years. Montesinos had made numerous videotapes that incriminated perhaps hundreds of high-ranking military officers, politicians, judges, businessmen, and others. At the same time, Peru was attempting to persuade Japan to extradite Fujimori, a first-generation Peruvian of Japanese descent, so that he could also face numerous charges, including murder and embezzlement. Whether Japan would accede to such requests was open to question.

As president, Toledo inherited a difficult political and economic situation. He did not have a majority in Congress, and since Peru's political party system was highly fluid, politics was largely a game of personalities—inherently unstable and dependent on shifting and uncertain coalitions. The centre-left American Popular Revolutionary Alliance (APRA) was probably the best organized party in the country, although nowhere near as strong as it had been in its past. APRA showed restraint as the major opposition early in Toledo's term, but how long such a truce could last was anyone's guess. In addition, the presidency was Toledo's first elected position; he had to learn a great deal quickly in order to be able to govern successfully. Following his first 100 days in office, critics began to scrutinize his work habits and private life unfavourably; as a result, Toledo slashed his pay by one-third—from $18,000 to $12,000 a month.

In any case, Toledo's presidency promised to be a departure from his predecessors; his ethnic background as an indigenous non-European made him distinctive and gave him a certain popularity among Peru's poor. His cabinet was nevertheless composed of well-known individuals, for the most part from Peru's economic, financial, and political establishment.

Economically, Peru was in the midst of a significant recession; new investment was low, meaning that job creation was scarce and unemployment and poverty levels were high. To add to the misery, a severe earthquake struck southern Peru on June 23 in and around the city of Arequipa, causing widespread damage to houses, highways, and other infrastructure. On December 29 a demonstration that went awry at a Lima fireworks shop caused an explosion that killed at least 290 persons. (*See* DISASTERS.)

(HENRY A. DIETZ)

PHILIPPINES

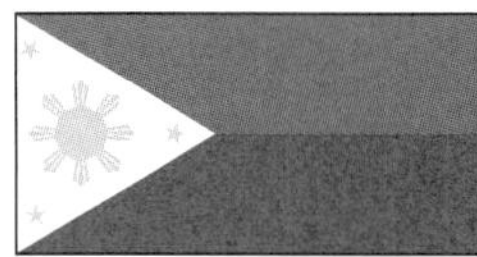

Area: 300,076 sq km (115,860 sq mi)
Population (2001 est.): 78,609,000
Capital: Quezon City (designated national government centre and the location of the lower house of the legislature and some ministries); many government offices are in Manila or other suburbs
Head of state and government: Presidents Joseph Estrada and, from January 20, Gloria Macapagal Arroyo

Angered by corruption charges against Philippines Pres. Joseph Estrada, demonstrators drove him from office on Jan. 20, 2001. That same day Vice Pres. Gloria Macapagal Arroyo was installed as president. (*See* BIOGRAPHIES.)

The Philippines Senate had begun trying Estrada on impeachment charges in late 2000. When the trial was abandoned because some senators blocked the admission of evidence, protesters poured into the streets of Manila. After four increasingly tense days, the army chief of staff, Gen. Angelo Reyes, informed Estrada on Jan. 19, 2001, that the military was "withdrawing its support" from him. Without troops to protect the presidential palace, Estrada fled that night. The Supreme Court declared the presidency to be vacant and swore Arroyo in as his successor.

Estrada later claimed that he had only temporarily vacated the presidency, not resigned, but the Supreme Court unanimously upheld Arroyo's succession. As accusations against Estrada piled up, Arroyo, vice president since 1998, distanced herself from him and became an opposition leader.

Using evidence from the impeachment proceedings, authorities arrested Estrada on April 25. In protest some 20,000 of his supporters marched on the presidential palace on May 1. Four people were

Jay Directo/AFP Worldwide

Life goes on for residents of a house in Jolo, Phil., damaged in an attack by Moro National Liberation Front rebels on November 21.

killed as riot police stopped them. Arroyo declared a "state of rebellion" that lasted five days.

More than 100 people were killed in the bloodiest congressional and local elections in more than a decade. In voting on May 14, Arroyo's supporters won 8 of the 13 open Senate seats, and the new president was given a Senate majority.

Estrada's trial on charges of plundering the country began in October. It could take years, during which he was to remain behind bars. The charges carried a possible death penalty, but few observers expected that sentence if he was convicted. Estrada's wife and son also faced charges.

Rumours of corruption involving Arroyo's husband, a wealthy businessman and lawyer, were denied by the president. She asked for official investigations to clear their names.

In her first state of the nation address, given on July 22, Arroyo tackled the issue of poverty. She announced plans to create at least one million jobs as part of agricultural modernization and to distribute 200,000 ha (494,000 ac) of land annually to landless farmers. Just 5% of Filipinos owned nearly 90% of all the land in the country.

On Basilan Island in the southern Philippines, 7,000 army troops fought a long jungle campaign against a bandit group known as Abu Sayyaf, which the U.S. government said had links to terrorist Osama bin Laden. The group, estimated at 1,000 strong, comprised former guerrillas who had fought for a separate Muslim state in the south and had turned to kidnapping. The troops stormed an Abu Sayyaf camp on nearby Jolo Island on April 12 and freed a kidnapped American, Jeffrey Schilling. On May 27 the bandits raided a resort off Palawan Island and abducted 20 people to Basilan, including three Americans. They later beheaded one of the Americans and raided villages, beheading 10 Filipino Christians.

On August 7 the government signed a cease-fire agreement with the main Muslim group still seeking independence in the south, the Moro Islamic Liberation Front. After at least 12 cease-fire violations, another agreement was signed on October 18. In November a rebel faction of the Moro National Liberation Front that was loyal to Nur Misuari—governor of the Autonomous Region of Muslim Mindanao—broke a five-year peace agreement and launched an attack on Jolo Island to prevent elections for Misuari's successor. (HENRY S. BRADSHER)

POLAND

Area: 312,685 sq km (120,728 sq mi)
Population (2001 est.): 38,647,000
Capital: Warsaw
Chief of state: President Aleksander Kwasniewski
Head of government: Prime Ministers Jerzy Buzek and, from October 19, Leszek Miller

The focal point in Poland during 2001 was the September 23 parliamentary election. In the spring and summer, a number of new right-wing parties began to coalesce, including the new Right-Wing Alliance in March and the centre-right pro-business party Civic Forum–Christian Democracy in July. A new election bill with a provision that would admit to the Sejm (lower house of the legislature) only parties that won at least 5% of the vote was adopted in April.

The elections attracted a low voter turnout (46%), but the left won a decisive victory. The big winner was the Democratic Left Alliance (SLD), led by former communist Leszek Miller, which took 216 of 460 seats. Second was the Civic Platform (65 seats), followed by Self Defense, a radical farmers group that opposed Poland's joining the European Union (EU), with 53, and the right-wing Law and Justice party (44). The incumbent Solidarity Electoral Action of the Right (AWSP) was routed, failing to meet the required threshold and therefore not able to claim a single Sejm seat. Despite its big win, the SLD found itself 15 seats short of a majority, and a coalition agreement was struck with the Polish Peasant Party (PSL), which had taken 8.9% of the vote. The same two parties had shared power uneasily from 1993 to 1997. Miller named his cabinet on October 10. SLD members took the key portfolios of finance (Marek Belka) and the economy (Jacek Piechota); PSL leader Jaroslaw Kalinowski was deputy prime minister and minister of agriculture. A new Infrastructure Ministry, embracing transportation, communications, and regional policy, was also created. At his inauguration Prime Minister Miller pledged continuity, "not to start or pursue any revolutions." An amendment to the civil service regulations passed by the Sejm in December raised eyebrows, as it seemed to open the way for more political appointments to administrative positions.

AWSP's big losses were principally chalked up to Poland's sinking economy. Prime Minister Jerzy Buzek was under severe pressure to trim the $20 billion budget deficit, and the government floundered throughout the spring and summer trying to do so. Shares in the state telecom company Telekomunikacja Polska had to be sold to raise cash in March. The government tried to raise the budget deficit by $2 billion in July. Finance Minister Jaroslaw Bauc was fired in late August, ostensibly for not having warned of the magnitude of the problem. In September the Sejm rejected Buzek's report on the budget. Picking up the struggle to balance the budget, the new government adopted a 20% tax on interest from savings and investments and froze income tax thresholds in order to postpone an expected loss of revenue from that quarter. On October 20 state expenditures were ordered cut by about $2 billion, and salaries of central administration employees were frozen. In the austerity draft budget for 2002, adopted on November 20, the deficit was limited to 5% of gross domestic product. Projected 2001 GDP growth figures of 2.3% were reduced to 1%; inflation figures were estimated at 4.5%, down from the 4.7–4.8% forecast earlier. By December unemployment had soared to 16.8%, a record for the postcommunist period.

Poland's foreign policy focused on trying to accelerate the process of joining the European Union. The new foreign minister, Wlodzimierz Cimoszewicz, ran into trouble with the Sejm in late November because of concessions he had made in EU negotiations earlier that month. Poland signed a gas deal with Denmark in July, trying to reduce the country's dependence on Russian energy supplies. Miller visited Russia on December 20 to discuss the imbalance of trade and a planned new oil pipeline from Russia through Poland to Western Europe.

The return of a leftist government was not the only reminder of Poland's past during the year. Former leader Gen. Wojciech Jaruzelski was placed on trial in May for having given orders, when he was defense minister in 1970, to shoot striking workers. In June the first checks from a German fund set up to reimburse workers from Nazi-occupied countries who had been impressed into slave labour were distributed in Poland. Meanwhile, public debate continued over the question of the proper apportionment—between the Nazi occupiers, the Polish Roman Catholic Church, and the local populations—of responsibility for a number of massacres of Polish Jews during World War II. On July 10 Pres. Aleksander Kwasniewski voiced a formal apology on behalf of the Polish people for one such massacre, in the village of Jedwabne, in 1941.

(EDITOR)

PORTUGAL

Area: 92,365 sq km (35,662 sq mi)
Population (2001 est.): 10,328,000
Capital: Lisbon
Chief of state: President Jorge Sampaio
Head of government: Prime Minister António Guterres

Against a backdrop of slowing growth, rising inflation, and growing public deficits, Portugal's government lost its popular appeal in 2001; opposition parties remained fragmented, however, and were unable to capitalize on the Socialist government's woes. Though the government won reelection in January, it looked particularly shaky in the first half of the year. Finance Minister Joaquim Pina Moura was forced to resign at the end of June after issuing a "corrective" supplementary budget to get the economy back on track. The reshuffle also brought changes at the Health, Economy, Defense, Education, and Culture ministries but did not—as some observers expected—spark snap elections.

The economic problems continued in the fall, exacerbated by global fallout from the September 11 terrorist attacks in the U.S. Drafts for the 2002 budget indicated that the government deficit would rise to 1.7% of gross domestic product by year's end. Along with other European Union (EU) partners, Portugal blamed the deficit slippage on the global economic troubles. The new finance minister, Guilherme de Oliveira Martins, stressed that the 2002 budget would cut back sharply on ministerial spending but would boost state investment in an attempt to make the economy grow. In addition, efforts to fight tax fraud and tax evasion would be stepped up. The Socialist government—which held 115 seats in the 230-seat Assembly of the Republic (parliament)—would once again be forced to forge a deal with at least one of the opposition parties in order to pass the 2002 budget.

In the December local and municipal elections, the main interest was the Lisbon mayoral race between Portuguese Socialist Party (PSP) incumbent João Soares—son of former president Mário Soares—and centre-right Social Democratic Party (PSD) candidate Pedro Santana Lopes. Though Lisbon had long been a Socialist stronghold, Santana Lopes had found support there for his urban-renewal platform, and he emerged victorious. The PSD also won elections in Porto and the Lisbon suburb of Sintra. After the PSD won control of 144 councils, compared to the 98 captured by the PSP, Prime Minister António Guterres took responsibility for the poor PSP showing and resigned. Pres. Jorge Sampaio dissolved the parliament and called a general election for March 17, 2002.

One of the country's deadliest accidents claimed the lives of 59 persons in March when a bridge spanning the northern Douro River collapsed while a bus and three cars were passing over it. The collapse was blamed on erosion and extensive sand dredging in the area, as well as on a stronger river current due to the unusually rainy winter. The incident spurred inspection of all the country's bridges, and, as a result, a handful of spans were either closed or reinforced.

Late in the year the government moved to tighten drunk-driving and speeding laws in hopes of reducing the country's troubling rate of road deaths, one of the highest in the EU. Vehicular accidents in Portugal annually killed about 240 of every million persons, compared with an EU average of about 110 per million population. Wine producers protested the new blood-alcohol limit of 0.2 g per litre from the previous 0.5 g per litre limit, complaining that it would severely cut consumption. In addition, professional truck drivers staged a one-day strike, saying that they had been unfairly targeted by the new laws.

Another legal change that drew criticism from a number of quarters was a decision to treat drug use as an illness rather than a crime. In July the parliament voted that drug users would not face jail sentences, a law that effectively decriminalized drugs and replaced prison time with counseling and monitoring of addicts. Though the changes focused mainly on heroin and Portugal's growing population of heroin users, other drugs such as cannabis and ecstasy were also covered. Trafficking and drug dealing remained a criminal offense punishable with jail time, but the changes brought a rash of foreign media coverage touting Portugal as a "paradise" for "drug tourism," an accusation swiftly and forcefully challenged by the government.

(ERIK T. BURNS)

AP/Wide World Photos

In northern Portugal a bridge collapsed and four vehicles plunged into the Douro River.

QATAR

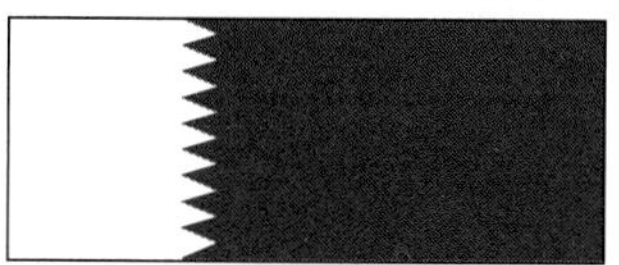

Area: 11,427 sq km (4,412 sq mi)
Population (2001 est.): 596,000
Capital: Doha
Head of state and government: Emir Sheikh Hamad ibn Khalifah ath-Thani, assisted by Prime Minister Sheikh Abdullah ibn Khalifah ath-Thani

In 2001 Qatar continued its increasingly prominent role in regional, interregional, and global affairs. In November 2000 Qatar had succeeded Iran as head of the 57-member-state Organization of the Islamic Conference. During its three-year term, Qatar would enjoy unprecedented standing among the world's 1.2 billion Muslims.

In addition, Qatar's Al-Jazeera television station remained the Arab world's most prominent media force in publicizing the al-Aqsa *intifadah* (Palestinian uprising). In the aftermath of the September 11 terrorist attacks in the U.S., Al-Jazeera became the leading source for news and analysis, with reports about Osama bin Laden and his al-Qaeda network. (*See* MEDIA AND PUBLISHING: *Television:* Sidebar.)

In November Qatar hosted the meeting of the World Trade Organization, the WTO's first summit since 1999 in Seattle, Wash. In December, at the annual heads of state summit in Muscat, Oman, Qatar was elected to head the Gulf Cooperation Council's Secretariat-General in Riyadh, Saudi Arabia. As a result, a Qatari would be the seniormost official responsible for the day-to-day administration of the six member-states' (Bahrain, Kuwait, Oman, Qatar, Saudi Arabia, and the United Arab Emirates) efforts to establish a common market and customs union by 2003.

In March the International Court of Justice resolved a long-standing territorial dispute between Qatar and Bahrain; Bahrain was awarded the Hawar Islands, and Qatar retained sovereignty over the Zubarah town and land strip in the northern part of the country. Qatar also continued to make progress in widening the base of its elected representatives and in developing its niche as the Gulf region's leading exporter of natural gas.

(JOHN DUKE ANTHONY)

ROMANIA

Area: 237,500 sq km (91,699 sq mi)
Population (2001 est.): 22,413,000
Capital: Bucharest
Chief of state: President Ion Iliescu
Head of government: Prime Minister Adrian Nastase

Stability returned to Romania in 2001 after a shock in the November 2000 presidential elections in which Corneliu Vadim Tudor, a populist demagogue with close links to a number of Middle Eastern radical regimes, won almost one-third of the vote. In October 2001 the ruling Social Democratic Party of Romania (PDSR) took steps to lift Vadim's parliamentary immunity after he made unsubstantiated claims that in 1995 members of the Palestinian extremist group Hamas had been given training in Romania by the security forces.

The Romanian economy grew by nearly 5%, and the privatization of Sidex, the country's largest steelmaker and biggest loss-making plant, was announced in July. Two-thirds of the economy was still state-owned, however, and overall production was still only 75% of its level in 1989. Foreign investors remained wary of Romania, but there was an increasing willingness by the government to reduce the multiple layers of bureaucracy that were discouraging investment. Membership in the European Union (EU) remained a key goal, which meant that the left-wing PDSR was prepared to accept many EU recommendations for moving away from a state-led economy.

Romania was also keen to join NATO. In 2001 spending on defense was boosted to 4% of gross domestic product in anticipation of the next phase of NATO expansion in 2002. Romania's NATO hopes may have been dented, however, by revelations about the continuing influence of the feared communist-era secret police, the Securitate, in business, politics, and no fewer than nine different intelligence services in the state structure.

The PDSR strengthened its credentials as moderate by being more receptive to the demands of the 1.6-million-strong ethnic Magyar (Hungarian) minority, whose parliamentarians helped sustain Adrian Nastase's minority government, and showing a new disinclination to flirt with extremist figures like Vadim, which it did for much of the 1990s. Nonetheless, relations with the Hungarian government were strained following the passage in the Hungarian parliament on June 19 of the Status Law. This law extended to Magyar minorities in neighbouring countries education, health, and employment rights that may not be available to other ethnic groups in these countries. On July 2 Pres. Ion Iliescu branded the Status Law "a diversionary, provocative, antidemocratic and discriminatory document."

Relations with Moldova (part of Romania from 1918 to 1940) were strained after the return to power there in February of the communists. Moldova resented the view, long held in Romania, that the majority of its population was ethnically Romanian. On October 3 Nastase canceled a visit to Chisinau following charges by the Moldovan minister of the interior of unwarranted interference by Romania in the affairs of his country.

One unexpected reconciliation occurred in the spring, however, between President Iliescu and former king Michael, whom the communists forced to abdicate in 1947. The 80-year-old former monarch was given back part of the royal family's property, and he decided to return to Romania to live.

(TOM GALLAGHER)

In 2001 former Romanian king Michael demanded the return of royal family property, including Peles Castle (above) in the mountain resort of Sinaia.

AP/Wide World Photos

RUSSIA

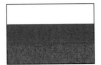

Area: 17,075,400 sq km (6,592,800 sq mi)
Population (2001 est.): 144,417,000
Capital: Moscow
Chief of state: President Vladimir Putin
Head of government: Prime Minister Mikhail Kasyanov

Domestic Affairs. Russian Pres. Vladimir Putin's popularity remained consistently high in 2001, and Russians drew renewed confidence from the fact that their country was headed by a young and vigorous leader. Putin's efforts to bring Russia's rebellious regions to heel were particularly successful. Central control was tightened over tax collection, the police, and the law courts. Regional governors were compensated for the loss of their seats in the Federation Council (upper house of the parliament) by the adoption in January of a law allowing the leaders of 69 of the country's 89 regions to stand for a third or even fourth term in office. In February Putin used his new power to remove regional governors to secure the resignation of the controversial governor of Primorsky *kray* in Russia's Far East. Regional legislatures gradually brought local laws into accord with federal legislation, though some of the larger republics, notably Tatarstan and Bashkortostan, continued to drag their feet in this respect.

Putin's strong support in the parliament enabled him to promote potentially far-reaching reforms. Promising to make the law apply equally to everyone, Putin in May announced a reform of the judicial system. Bills submitted to the State Duma (lower house of the parliament) sought to raise the status and powers of judges and defense lawyers and to enhance the rights of defendants. A revised Code of Criminal Procedure promised to transfer the right to issue arrest and search warrants from prosecutors to judges and to institute trial by jury nationwide. Educational reform was also promised.

Putin continued his campaign to wrest the mass media from the control of the "oligarchs." Tycoons Vladimir Gusinsky (*see* BIOGRAPHIES) and Boris Berezovsky were stripped of their electronic media holdings. Gusinsky lost control of the independent television network, NTV, the only major national electronic media outlet not controlled by the state, while Berezovsky was removed from his position of influence at Russian Public Television, Russia's most widely watched TV channel. Threatened with arrest on corruption charges, both men went into self-imposed exile. Legislation was passed to restrict foreign ownership of the Russian media.

In July a Kremlin-inspired law on political parties was adopted. Parties would be officially registered and permitted to compete in national elections only if they had a minimum of 10,000 members and registered offices in at least half of Russia's regions. Those that met the criteria would receive federal funding after the 2003 legislative elections. As many as 60% of Russia's existing 180 parties were not expected to meet the criteria and would therefore be forced to disband. The Kremlin argued that the law would prevent corrupt businessmen from funding pocket parties, but regional political movements were also expected to be hard hit. In October the pro-Kremlin Unity party merged with its erstwhile archrival, the Fatherland movement led by Moscow Mayor Yury Luzhkov. The merger was expected to produce Russia's dominant political organization.

Russian media tycoon Vladimir Gusinsky leaves the Valdemoro prison near Madrid on March 26.

AP/Wide World Photos

Economy. Economic growth continued in 2001, though at a reduced rate from that of 2000. Revised official data put gross domestic product (GDP) growth in 2000 at 8.3% above 1999. In the first half of 2001, the increase in output was about 5% up from the level of first-half 2000. The government revised its medium-term forecasts (through 2004) down to around 3.5–4% a year.

Growth revived somewhat in mid-2001, and the government remained bullish, maintaining that in the longer term (through 2010) output could be expected to grow at an average annual rate of 5%. Independent economists in Moscow were more skeptical, and there were good reasons to question the sustainability of rapid growth. The output recovery that followed the August 1998 financial crisis had been jump-started by the massive devaluation from 6 rubles to the dollar before the crisis to an average of 25 in 1999 and 28 in 2000. By the end of 2001 the rate was 30.5. With inflation still quite high (heading for a rise in consumer prices of some 18.6% in 2001), the leveling off of the exchange rate meant that Russian producers were gradually losing the competitive advantage they had gained from devaluation. Similarly, Russian external finances, company profits, and tax revenues had all benefited from the steep rise in international oil prices in 1999. A downturn in oil prices in late 2001 reduced those gains.

The state both of Russia's balance of payments and of public finances in 2000–01 reflected the combination of a devalued currency and a high oil price. Imports fell dramatically as their ruble prices inside Russia soared. Producers in the hitherto severely depressed manufacturing sector—especially in textiles, clothing, food processing, and engineering—suddenly found life much easier as competition from imports dried up. That, plus the higher oil and gas prices on world markets, had given Russia a current-account balance of payments surplus of over $46 billion in 2000—an extraordinary 17% of GDP. Gold and foreign exchange reserves grew to $35 billion by July 2001. That level, enough to finance almost nine months' imports, was far above what was needed on grounds of prudence.

The federal budget moved into surplus in 2000 and (with some fluctuations) in 2001. This enabled Moscow to service its external debt without significant new borrowing. Having paid off some of its external sovereign debt in 2000, Russia went on in 2001 to make debt-service payments (repayment of principal plus payment of interest) equivalent to 5% of GDP. Western governments and international financial institutions, faced with this revival in Russian fortunes, were less disposed than before to charitable giving. Until spring 2001 the Russian government had been counting on rolling over its inherited Soviet-era debt to Western governments while keeping current with its servicing of post-Soviet debt. Western governments, negotiating with Moscow in the framework of the Paris Club, began instead to insist on payment in full, and they got their way. The International Monetary Fund (IMF), negotiating with the Russian government over IMF approval (and associated loan facilities) for Russian economic policies, held out for a reform agenda that was quite demanding. Eventually, a compromise was reached: Russian reforms would be monitored by the Fund, without formal approval of them; Moscow would forgo new IMF loans.

The government and the central bank were pushed to pursue more liberal policies than they had perhaps wished at the beginning of 2001. Domestic critics (notably Putin's economic adviser Andrey Illarionov) and foreign governments wanted external-debt service in full and got it. They also wanted to see the implementation of structural reforms: tax reform, including a lowering of profits tax; land reform to allow a free market in all land; measures to strengthen corporate governance; the introduction of competition into the gas, electricity, and rail industries; banking reform; an easing of foreign exchange controls; and a general reduction in the bureaucratic (read "bribery") burden on producers.

Putin, most notably in a state of the nation address to the Russian parliament in April, espoused the cause of radical economic reform. Strikingly, he spoke of the precarious nature of Russia's economic recovery and the urgent need to improve the business environment. It appeared that, in his concern to see Russia strong again, he had become convinced that free-market reforms were needed to provide the economic sinew that a revived Russia would require—hence his resolve to back economic liberalization. Legislative progress was achieved in all the measures mentioned, though with concessions over land reform and banking reform.

In September the Duma gave its approval to a land code that would pave the way for the creation of a property market in Russia for the first time since the establishment of Soviet power. Communist and nationalist parliamentarians vehemently opposed the bill, warning that it would lead to the country's being bought up by foreigners and wealthy Russians, and the bill's first reading saw a punch-up among parliamentarians. The final version of the code was a compromise, setting rules for the sale only of commercial land in towns and cities (about 2% of the total) and leaving the vexing issue of farmland to the discretion of regional authorities.

Promising to introduce a wide-ranging restructuring of the natural gas industry, the Kremlin in May asserted control over Russia's state-controlled natural gas monopoly, Gazprom, by replacing veteran Rem Vyakhirev as chief executive with its own appointee, 39-year-old Aleksey Miller. Anatoly Chubais—chief executive of the state-controlled United Energy Systems (UES), which controlled Russia's electricity grid—launched a series of reforms aimed at separating the distribution of electricity from its generation and gradually privatizing the latter. Minority inves-tors expressed concern over some of Chubais's proposals to break up UES. Regional governors were also wary of the reforms, which would reduce the power hitherto enjoyed by local politicians to manipulate electricity prices.

Plans were accelerated to raise charges for the maintenance of urban housing and for the provision of electricity, gas, water, and sewerage to cost-recovery (that is, unsubsidized) levels by 2003. Low-income families would continue to receive housing subsidies, but others would be required to pay their own way.

Defense and Foreign Policy. In March a cabinet reshuffle saw Putin's close associate Sergey Ivanov shifted laterally from the post of Security Council secretary to head the Defense Ministry as its first civilian minister. Ivanov was expected to spearhead a long-awaited reform of the armed forces. In October Putin met with top military leaders and told them bluntly to speed up reform. He promised to increase defense spending in response to the terrorist attacks in the U.S. He also announced that Russia would close two relics of the Cold War—its electronic reconnaissance centre in Cuba and its last big overseas naval base at Cam Ranh Bay in Vietnam.

Russia's military campaign in the breakaway Chechen Republic dragged on. The rebels showed no sign of giving up the fight. Polling data suggested that the Russian population was growing unhappy with the failure to bring the conflict to a close. Optimists spied light at the end of the tunnel when, in June, Putin told a press conference that Chechnya's independence was not the issue; what was vital, he said, was to ensure that Chechen territory would never again be used as a bridgehead for an attack on Russia. In September Putin issued an "ultimatum" that was essentially a proposal to begin talks with those rebels prepared to lay down their arms. Although the offer expired without visible effect and the fighting continued, the two sides did begin to negotiate about negotiating. It seemed unlikely, however, that Chechnya's relatively moderate [resident, Aslan Maskhadov, would be able to negotiate on behalf of uncompromising rebel leaders who controlled their own armies and territory.

In October after a difficult three-month operation, the remains of the nuclear submarine *Kursk* were salvaged from the Barents Sea, where it had sunk after an explosion in August 2000.

During the year Putin maintained a busy program of foreign meetings and visits. In a speech in January, he defined Russia's major foreign policy objective as creating stable and secure conditions on Russia's borders to allow the government to concentrate on solving the country's social and economic problems. He identified Europe as an important partner for Russia.

Putin shifted Russia's relations with its closest allies, the Commonwealth of Independent States, from the multilateral focus that had characterized the years of Boris Yeltsin's presidency to highlight bilateral relations. Russian analysts interpreted this as a sign that Putin recognized that the close ties that had existed during the Soviet period could not be reestablished. Meanwhile, Russia maintained and in some cases strengthened ties with former allies and markets for Soviet and Russian arms—India, Iraq, Cuba, Libya, Vietnam, and North Korea. In July a 20-year friendship treaty was signed with China.

Relations with the new U.S. administration were initially strained. Missile defense (NMD), U.S. plans to abandon the 1972 Anti-Ballistic Missile (ABM) Treaty, and NATO's possible enlargement to include Estonia, Latvia, and Lithuania were the main bones of contention. Russia opposed U.S.-British plans for revised sanctions against Iraq. Russia planned too to continue arms sales to Iran and to finish construction work on the controversial Iranian nuclear power reactor at Bushehr in the Persian Gulf, identifying Iran as a key ally in the struggle against fundamentalist Islamic movements on Russia's southern borders.

Relations with the U.S. improved in May when Moscow responded positively to a call by U.S. Pres. George W. Bush for new nuclear arms reductions and for improved relations. A breakthrough occurred in June when the two presidents met in Slovenia for direct talks and established an immediate rapport.

The remains of the Russian nuclear submarine Kursk, *which sank after an explosion in 2000, are raised for examination in a dock at the port of Roslyakovo, near Murmansk.*
AP/Wide World Photos

The terrorist attacks of September 11 brought a further improvement in U.S.-Russian relations. Putin was the first world leader to call Bush after the attacks, pledging Russia's support and cooperation in the U.S.-led campaign against terrorism, and offering use of Russia's airspace for humanitarian deliveries and help in search and rescue operations. Overruling his defense minister, Putin said Russia would not object if the former Soviet republics of Central Asia made their airspace and military facilities available to the U.S. In October Putin became the first Russian leader to visit NATO headquarters in Brussels, where he spoke of "qualitatively new" relations between Russia and the alliance. Also in October Putin attended a Russia–European Union (EU) summit at which it was decided to hold monthly consultations on security issues. The European Commission said afterward that it and the U.S. would work to give fresh impetus to Russia's eight-year-old bid to join the World Trade Organization.

(ELIZABETH TEAGUE)

RWANDA

Area: 26,338 sq km (10,169 sq mi)
Population (2001 est.): 7,313,000
Capital: Kigali
Head of state and government: President Maj. Gen. Paul Kagame, assisted by Prime Minister Bernard Makuza

On March 6, 2001, Rwandans participated in the country's first-ever local elections. Voters chose 2,765 district representatives, and an electoral college selected 106 mayors and 424 district executives. The vote was a step toward political decentralization and part of the country's postgenocide reconstruction plan. Observers reported that the voting was generally free from irregularities, and nearly 90% of those eligible voted. Opposition groups charged that the National Electoral Commission unfairly favoured candidates from the ruling Rwandan Patriotic Front. During the year the government introduced a new flag and a new anthem that emphasized national unity.

After a two-year peaceful interval, elements of the extremist Hutu Interahamwe militia launched attacks in May near Ruhengeri in the northwest of the country. The clashes continued, and the army reported 150 rebels killed in a June battle. Security forces scored a major victory in July when they captured Pierre Habimana, the Interahamwe's chief of staff. The Rwandan government charged that the rebels were operating from bases in the Democratic Republic of the Congo (DRC). Though Rwanda had begun to withdraw its troops from the DRC in late February, it halted the withdrawal in June and demanded that the DRC stop aiding Rwandan rebels. Some progress was made toward easing tensions in September when the DRC announced that it would hand over 3,000 Rwandan rebels to UN observers.

Relations between Rwanda and Uganda soured in March when the Ugandan government listed its southern neighbour as a "hostile nation." In July Pres. Maj. Gen. Paul Kagame met his Ugandan counterpart in an effort to mend relations. Though their meeting was described as cordial, tensions persisted over both countries' military involvement in the DRC.

In May former president Pasteur Bizimungu planned the creation of a new political party, the Democratic Party for Renewal. Security forces interrupted the party's launch and placed Bizimungu under house arrest. Though he was quickly released, the new party remained outlawed.

In June the UN-sponsored International Criminal Tribunal for Rwanda issued its first acquittal, finding Ignace Bagilishema, the former mayor of Mabanza, innocent of genocide and crimes against humanity. In an attempt to clear the backlog of 115,000 genocide suspects awaiting trial, the government announced plans to establish courts according to the traditional justice system. The move would create 11,000 courts that could handle some genocide suspects, though the most serious offenders would continue to be tried in higher courts. In June a Belgian court found four Rwandans, including two Roman Catholic nuns, guilty of having committed war crimes during the 1994 genocide. In December the government reported that over one million people had died during the genocide and other violence between 1991 and 1994.

(MATTHEW A. CENZER)

SAINT KITTS AND NEVIS

Area: 269 sq km (104 sq mi)
Population (2001 est.): 38,800
Capital: Basseterre
Chief of state: Queen Elizabeth II, represented by Governor-General Cuthbert Sebastian
Head of government: Prime Minister Denzil Douglas

Prime Minister Denzil Douglas reshuffled his cabinet in August 2001 in an effort to instill new dynamism into government programs. He kept the key portfolios of finance and national security for himself.

St. Kitts and Nevis saw its hope of being removed from the Paris-based Fi-

Villagers in Ryinyo, Rwanda, sit in front of some of the arms and ammunition captured by government troops in a clash with Hutu rebels in May.
AP/Wide World Photos

nancial Action Task Force's (FATF's) list of states not doing enough to combat money laundering dashed when the task force met in September. St. Kitts and Nevis expected to be given a clean bill of health, but despite the country's establishment of a Financial Services Commission to oversee the offshore banking industry, the FATF was unsatisfied with the overall effort to identify tainted funds.

The Concerned Citizens Movement, led by Vance Amory, was returned to office in the September local elections in Nevis. The party had consistently been elected to run local affairs in Nevis since 1992. It won four of the five seats in the Island Assembly, with the Nevis Reformation Party retaining one.

Following the September 11 terrorist attacks in the U.S., Douglas extended to all New York City and Washington, D.C., firefighters, police officers, and emergency medical service workers the offer of a free one-week vacation in St. Kitts. More than 170,000 tourists had visited the islands in the first six months of 2001. (DAVID RENWICK)

SAINT LUCIA

Area: 617 sq km (238 sq mi)
Population (2001 est.): 158,000
Capital: Castries
Chief of state: Queen Elizabeth II, represented by Governor-General Pearlette Louisy
Head of government: Prime Minister Kenny Anthony

The opposition moved to shore up its forces in May when controversial left-winger George Odlum, who had been fired by Prime Minister Kenny Anthony from his St. Lucia Labour Party government, joined forces with former prime minister Sir John Compton and the United Workers' Party (UWP) to form the National Alliance. The partnership proved to be short-lived, however. In December elections to the House of Assembly, the Labour Party won 14 of the 17 seats. Morella Joseph resigned as UWP leader and was replaced by Marius Wilson.

Even before the events of September 11, tourism in St. Lucia was experiencing a downturn, mainly brought on by the weakening U.S. economy. August was described by the St. Lucia Hotel and Tourism Association as "extremely bad." Three hotels actually closed for the summer. The decrease in tourist revenue was predicted to be as much as 18% for the year, representing a loss of $35.5 million in national income.

In October Prime Minister Anthony came down firmly against any sale of St. Lucia bananas to Libya, as had been touted during a visit to the North African state by three Caribbean leaders in September. He insisted that St. Lucia could not "compromise" its long-standing trading relationships with other countries, particularly the U.K.

(DAVID RENWICK)

SAINT VINCENT AND THE GRENADINES

Area: 389 sq km (150 sq mi)
Population (2001 est.): 113,000
Capital: Kingstown
Chief of state: Queen Elizabeth II, represented by Governor-General Sir David Jack
Head of government: Prime Ministers Arnhim Eustace and, from March 29, Ralph Gonsalves

The Unity Labour Party, led by left-wing firebrand Ralph Gonsalves, won the general election in St. Vincent and the Grenadines in March 2001, grabbing 12 of the 15 seats in the parliament and decisively ousting the New Democratic Party (NDP) of Prime Minister Arnhim Eustace, who only narrowly held on to his own seat.

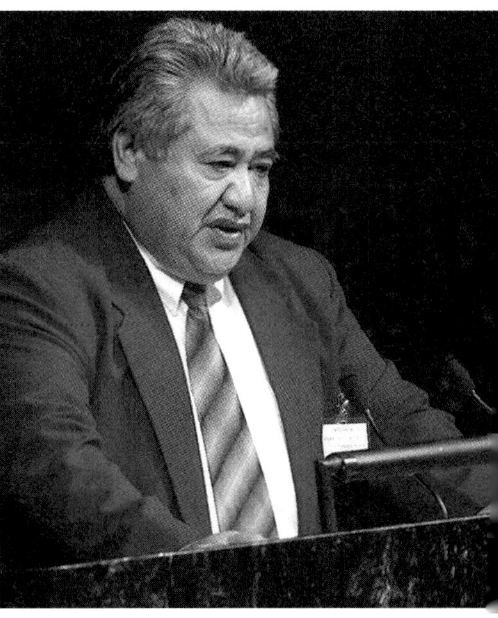

Samoan Prime Minister Tuila'epa Sa'ilele Malielegaoi addresses the UN General Assembly in New York City on November 11.

AP/Wide World Photos

The election had not been constitutionally due until 2003, but Eustace agreed to move it up following antigovernment protests. The NDP had been in office since 1984. Gonsalves assumed several portfolios, including finance, economic development, labour, and Grenadines Affairs, as well as the prime ministership.

The country's lack of strong legislative and supervisory systems for offshore financial institutions kept it on the Paris-based Financial Action Task Force's list of uncooperative states, even though the government promised to "rewrite" the entire package of laws governing offshore operations. The licenses of two offshore banks were revoked in June.

St. Vincent and the Grenadines signed a "comprehensive cooperation accord" with Cuba in September, covering matters such as health, tourism, trade, and language training, following an official visit to Havana by Gonsalves. The prime minister had earlier raised eyebrows by going to Libya on a controversial trip from which other Caribbean leaders had withdrawn.

(DAVID RENWICK)

SAMOA

Area: 2,831 sq km (1,093 sq mi)
Population (2001 est.): 179,000
Capital: Apia
Chief of state: *O le Ao o le Malo* (Head of State) Malietoa Tanumafili II
Head of government: Prime Minister Tuila'epa Sa'ilele Malielegaoi

Samoa's general election in March 2001 saw the return of the governing Human Rights Protection Party led by Prime Minister Tuila'epa Sa'ilele Malielegaoi, although the new government relied on the support of independent members for its majority. There was a strong emphasis on local issues and the record of the government in an election campaign that saw a number of members elected unopposed and, at the same time, petitions alleging election fraud in 10 of the 49 seats. Three women were elected to the new parliament. Longtime opposition leader Tuiatua Tupua Tamasese Efi gave way to Le Mamea Ropati.

In international affairs, Samoa was one of two South Pacific nations that did not support the establishment of a whale sanctuary. It denied allegations from Australia and New Zealand as well as environmental groups that this stance was related to the fact that Japan, Samoa's largest aid donor, sought to expand its whaling activity in South Pacific and Antarctic waters.

The economy remained heavily dependent on remittances from Samoans living overseas, tourism revenue, and agricultural production (which acounted for some 16% of the country's gross domestic product).

(BARRIE MACDONALD)

SAN MARINO

Area: 61.2 sq km (23.6 sq mi)
Population (2001 est.): 27,200
Capital: San Marino
Heads of state and government: The republic is governed by two *capitani reggenti,* or coregents, appointed every six months by a popularly elected Great and General Council.

The major focus in San Marino in 2001 was debate by opposition parties over the government's proposal to privatize the country's public utilities company, which was founded in 1981 to furnish electricity, gas, and drinking water. The opposition was concerned about the impact the action might have on San Marino's poorer population.

In the June 10 parliamentary elections the ruling Christian Democratic-Socialist coalition stayed in power, winning 40 of the 60 seats in the Great General Council.

Another area of sensitivity involved European Union plans to close up loopholes in European tax law to make it impossible for EU citizens to utilize San Marino as a tax haven for investments. San Marino believed that the new tax laws would unfairly penalize the 5,000 Italians who worked there. San Marino and Italy were both preparing to adopt the new euro, which would replace the Italian lira as the domestic currency in 2002.

On another front San Marino took measures to thwart a possible terrorist attack and created a special team to safeguard its mail system.

(GREGORY O. SMITH)

SÃO TOMÉ AND PRÍNCIPE

Area: 1,001 sq km (386 sq mi)
Population (2001 est.): 147,000
Capital: São Tomé
Chief of state: Presidents Miguel Trovoada and, from September 3, Fradique de Menezes
Head of government: Prime Ministers Guilherme Posser da Costa and, from September 26, Evaristo de Carvalho

Until September 2001 the country's two main parties, the Independent Democratic Action (ADI) and the Movement for the Liberation of São Tomé and Príncipe (MLSTP), had enjoyed seven years of cooperation. The ADI held the presidency, and the MLSTP, which had won the parliamentary elections of 1994 and 1999, claimed the prime ministership. Though Pres. Miguel Trovoada was barred from running for a third term in the July 2001 presidential election, the ADI's new candidate, businessman Fradique de Menezes, won with a considerable majority (56% to 39%) over former president Manuel Pinto da Costa in an election that was generally regarded as free and fair. After being sworn in as Trovoada's successor on September 3, de Menezes demanded a cabinet reshuffle. When Prime Minister Guilherme Posser da Costa refused to sack certain MLSTP ministers, he was himself dismissed and the cabinet dissolved.

A new government was then formed under Evaristo de Carvalho, whose 10-member cabinet was drawn exclusively from the two parties that had supported de Menezes in the presidential election. In December de Menezes dissolved parliament and announced that legislative elections would take place on March 3, 2002.

(CHRISTOPHER SAUNDERS)

SAUDI ARABIA

Area: 2,248,000 sq km (868,000 sq mi)
Population (2001 est.): 22,757,000
Capital: Riyadh
Head of state and government: King Fahd

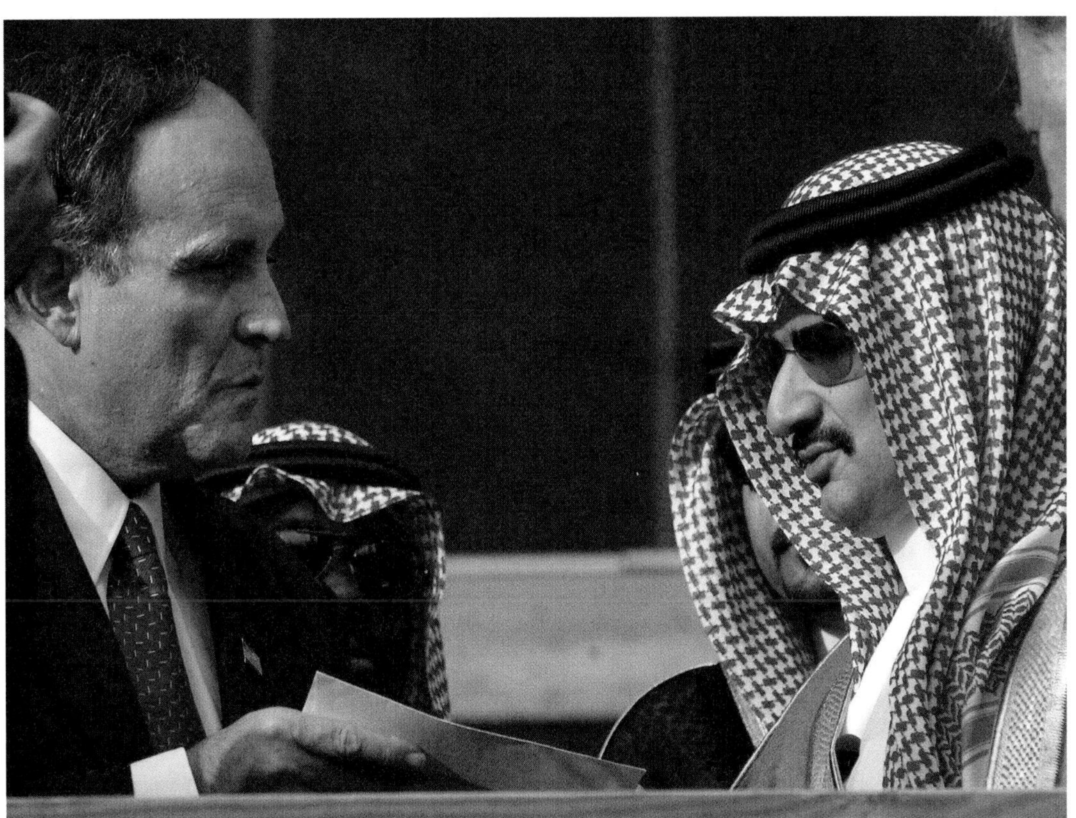

Saudi Prince Alwaleed bin Talal presents New York City Mayor Rudolph Giuliani with a $10 million check for relief efforts following September 11; Giuliani later returned the check after the prince said America's relationship with Israel was partly to blame for the attacks.

AP/Wide World Photos

In Saudi Arabia the year 2001 was dominated by security and regional political issues. During the year four British nationals, as well as a Canadian and a Belgian, confessed to involvement in a series of car bombings in what authorities described as a "Mafia war" between resident aliens who were illegally trafficking in alcohol. In late August Prince Turki al-Faisal, who headed the kingdom's General Intelligence Directorate, was replaced by Prince Nayif ibn ʿAbd al-ʿAziz. Relations with Washington were not at their best. On September 5, less than a week before the attacks by militant Islamists in the U.S., Prince Saud al-Faisal, Saudi Arabia's minister of foreign affairs, said that the peace process between the Palestinians and the Israelis had failed because of "the policies of Israel" and declared that it was "time especially for the U.S. to assume its own responsibility and prevent Israeli aggression against the Arab world."

The September 11 attacks had a profound impact on Saudi Arabia, since the primary suspect was Osama bin Laden, a wealthy Saudi national who had been stripped of his citizenship some years before. Saudi authorities were quick to condemn the attacks. The government was reluctant to permit U.S. warplanes to use Prince Sultan Airbase, the most sophisticated such installation south of Riyadh, to launch attacks on Afghanistan, but it played the role of "silent partner" in the American-led coalition against Afghanistan's Taliban government. At a summit meeting of foreign ministers of the countries attending the Organization of the Islamic Conference in Qatar on October 10, Saudi Arabia was instrumental in passing a resolution that condemned terrorism and the September 11 attacks but—in reference to the situation of the Palestinians in the West Bank and Gaza—drew a distinction between terrorism and what were labeled acts of self-defense. The organization warned against targeting any other Muslim or Arab country by the Western coalition under the pretext of fighting terrorism.

On the economic front, Saudi Arabia was still far from gaining admittance to the World Trade Organization, because the country had not fully liberalized its economy. Saudi reforms introduced in May 2000 that permitted total outside ownership in some sectors were, however, able to attract pledges of about $10 billion in foreign investment in 2001. There was every reason to believe that the country's gross domestic investment was keeping pace with the 21.3% of gross domestic product in nominal terms realized in 2000 before the fourth quarter, which witnessed a slowdown due to the fallout from the war in Afghanistan and the decrease in crude oil prices. Real GDP growth for 2001 was projected to be 1%. This figure was expected to rise to 2.5% in 2002 and 4.5% in 2005 on account of the returns from the $25 billion in investments made in gas projects. (MAHMOUD HADDAD)

SENEGAL

Area: 196,712 sq km (75,951 sq mi)
Population (2001 est.): 10,285,000
Capital: Dakar
Chief of state: President Abdoulaye Wade, assisted by Prime Ministers Moustapha Niasse and, from March 3, Mame Madior Boye

On April 29, 2001, Sopi ("Change")—a coalition of 40 parties, led by Pres. Abdoulaye Wade, won an overwhelming victory in the country's parliamentary elections, taking 89 of the National Assembly's 120 seats. The Alliance of Progressive Forces, led by former prime minister Moustapha Niasse, won 11 seats, while the former ruling Socialist Party managed to hold only 10. On May 12 the new prime minister, Mame Madior Boye, announced her 24-member cabinet, which was dominated by ministers from Wade's own Democratic Party. In January Wade also won a referendum on constitutional reforms.

Efforts to end 19 years of unrest in the Casamance region once again encountered setbacks. On February 16, rebels attacked a convoy of trucks north of Ziguinchor, killing at least 13 civilians. The Movement of Democratic Forces of Casamance (MFDC), the main separatist group, signed two peace agreements with the government on March 16 and 23, but several other rebel factions announced that they would continue the armed conflict. Despite this pact, the army renewed its efforts to crush the MFDC after April 6, when a second rebel attack on a convoy of cars near Ziguinchor took place. The government's offensive was suspended on May 25 in order to provide a more secure atmosphere for peace talks between the MFDC and hard-line rebel groups. After several postponements the three-day forum of the separatist groups was held in Banjul, Gambia, on August 7–9, but apparently no consensus was reached, and the scheduled closing ceremony was canceled. On August 10 Augustia Diamacoune, the MFDC's longtime leader, was replaced by Jean-Marie François Biagui.

Léopold Sédar Senghor—the first president of Senegal, the first African to be elected to the French Academy, and the first head of state in post-colonial Africa to relinquish power voluntarily—died on December 20 in his retirement home in Normandy, France. (*See* OBITUARIES.)

(NANCY ELLEN LAWLER)

SEYCHELLES

Area: 455 sq km (176 sq mi)
Population (2001 est.): 80,600
Capital: Victoria
Head of state and government: President France-Albert René

In September 2001, the Seychelles held its closest-fought presidential election since independence. Pres. France-Albert René, who had been in office since 1977, took 54% of the vote to win another five-year term. His opponent, Wavel Ramkalawan of the Seychelles National Party, took 45% of the vote. Approximately 50,000 of the islands' 60,000 registered voters decided a contest that had been dominated by economic issues.

An International Monetary Fund report published at the end of 2000 pointed to slow economic growth and falling foreign exchange reserves. The report also called on the government to remove exchange rate controls on the Seychelles rupee. Unofficial markets were trading foreign currencies with a 100% premium over the official rate.

In February the Seychelles reached an agreement with the Organisation for Economic Co-operation and Development (OECD) to reform its banking sector. The agreement provided greater regulation of accounts held by offshore companies. The Seychelles also agreed to cooperate with criminal and tax investigators from OECD member states.

Also in February the government announced it was considering membership in the Common Market for Eastern and Southern Africa, a free-trade zone. (MATTHEW A. CENZER)

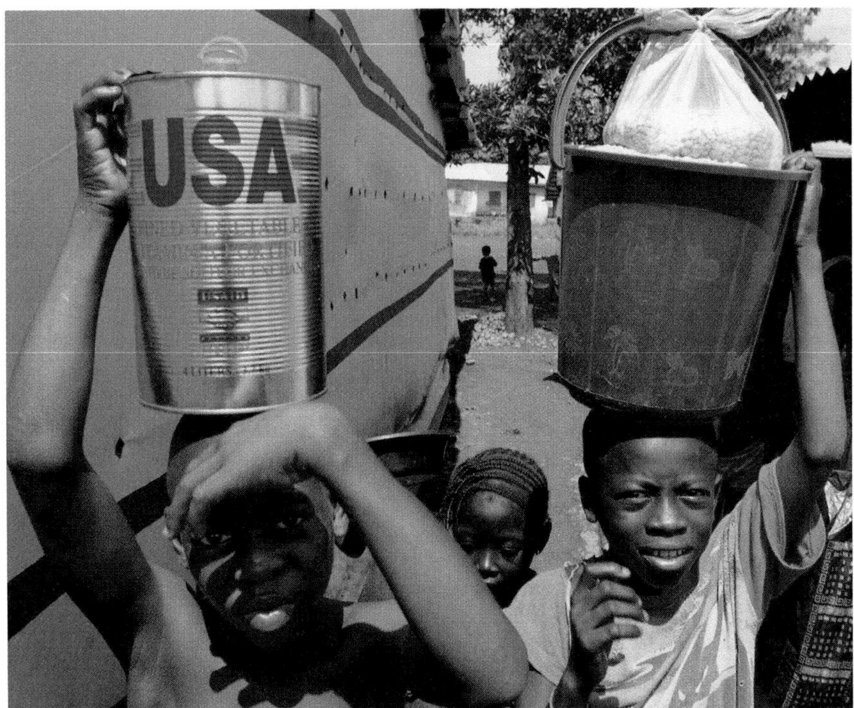

Children in Sierra Leone carry a can of oil and bucket of corn distributed by the World Food Programme in November.

Issouf Sanogo/AFP Worldwide

SIERRA LEONE

Area: 71,740 sq km (27,699 sq mi)
Population (2001 est.): 5,427,000 (including about 185,000 Sierra Leonean refugees temporarily residing in Guinea and other West African countries)
Capital: Freetown
Head of state and government: President Ahmad Tejan Kabbah

Throughout 2001 the United Nations Mission in Sierra Leone (UNAMSIL) attempted to implement a compromise peace based on the Lomé agreement. UNAMSIL had occasional success disarming Revolutionary United Front (RUF) rebels and the Civil Defense Force (CDF), a pro-government militia. During May some RUF and CDF fighters surrendered their weapons to the UN in Kambia and Port Loko, and other RUF forces disarmed in October. In March UNAMSIL forces occupied Lunsar, their first deployment into an area where the RUF had taken 500 UN troops hostage in 2000. In August UNAMSIL began deployment in the diamond-rich Kono district, an RUF stronghold. By year's end over 45,000 fighters had been disarmed.

The U.K. government ended its training program for Sierra Leone's army in September but pledged to continue assisting with the reintegration of former rebels into the army. In May the army had occupied formerly RUF-held areas around Kambia, north of Freetown.

Despite ongoing efforts, violence continued in parts of the country. In April RUF and CDF forces clashed near Tonga, a diamond-producing area in the east. In May the two groups agreed to a cease-fire, but this was broken within a week by fighting in the eastern town of Jagbwema. During July serious violence flared between the RUF and the CDF in the northern and eastern parts of the country. In one incident 22 civilians were reported killed when the RUF attacked the town of Henekuma.

Aid organizations continued efforts to remedy the damage caused by years of war. Humanitarian groups, including the Save the Children Fund, helped to secure the release of child soldiers and aid their reintegration into society. Donors announced a number of measures to help rebuild the country. In March the European Union pledged €11 million (about $10 million) in humanitarian aid, and the African Development Fund provided $13 million for economic recovery. The U.S. government pledged $14.5 million to support the reintegration of society.

In March, Pres. Ahmad Tejan Kabbah replaced five cabinet members, including the foreign and finance ministers. Citing the ongoing disarmament process, the National Electoral Commission announced that presidential voting slated for December would be postponed until May 2002. Despite a shortfall in funds, the UN proceeded with plans for the establishment of a tribunal for those accused of war crimes in Sierra Leone's civil war.

(MATTHEW A. CENZER)

SINGAPORE

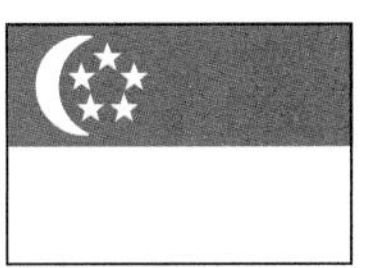

Area: 683 sq km (264 sq mi)
Population (2001 est.): 3,322,000 (excluding 808,000 newly arrived nonresidents)
Chief of state: President S.R. Nathan
Head of government: Prime Minister Goh Chok Tong

Pres. S.R. Nathan formally dissolved the Singaporean Parliament on Oct. 18, 2001, and called for new general elections to be held on November 3, well in advance of an August 2002 deadline. Most observers believed the elections were called early in anticipation of an economic downturn that was sure to reflect badly on the ruling People's Action Party (PAP). A new opposition coalition, made up of four previously unallied parties, emerged to challenge the PAP; among other measures, the Singapore Democratic Alliance (SDA) called for the establishment of a welfare system for the unemployed and a demonstration by the government of greater fiscal responsibility. The SDA proved unable to take advantage of public discontent over the deteriorating economy, however. On election night the PAP won a landslide victory, taking 82 of the 84 parliamentary seats. The opposition complained that tight government control of the media made it difficult, if not impossible, to make serious headway against the PAP. Nonetheless, despite the country's economic woes, Singapore still ranked as one of the wealthiest states in Southeast Asia, and few Singaporeans were willing to risk a change in leadership.

The country was hit hard by slumping worldwide demand for electronic products, which made up some 60% of Singapore's manufacturing output, and by a downturn in the economies of key trading partners such as the U.S. and Japan. Singapore officially entered a recession in the second quarter, which saw a steep 10% drop in growth figures. Before the election the government unveiled a $6.2 billion stimulus package intended to reactivate the flagging economy. The package allowed for an array of tax cuts and an increase in government spending; at year's end it was still too early to tell whether the measures had begun to have their intended effect.

Aside from the economy, government officials were alarmed at the country's rapidly declining birthrate, which had fallen to 1.5 children per woman. An estimated 2.5 children per woman were needed to maintain Singapore's current population level. (EDITOR)

SLOVAKIA

Area: 49,035 sq km (18,933 sq mi)
Population (2001 est.): 5,410,000
Capital: Bratislava
Chief of state: President Rudolf Schuster
Head of government: Prime Minister Mikulas Dzurinda

Although Slovakia continued to struggle with political uncertainty and economic difficulties in 2001, the country also made considerable progress in reforms. The ruling parties showed remarkable unity when necessary, which was demonstrated by the adoption in February of 85 constitutional amendments, the most important of which allowed for public administration reforms and the introduction of an ombudsman.

The parliament approved territorial and public administration reforms in July aimed at granting more power to municipalities. Slovakia's first regional elections were held on December 1 and 5. The centre-right ruling coalition parties won a clear majority in just three of the eight regions and obtained the post of regional leader in only two. The other regions went to former prime minister Vladimir Meciar's Movement for a Democratic Slovakia, sometimes in coalition with the left-wing ruling parties and the extra-parliamentary Smer ("Direction"). The turnout was disappointingly low, at just 26% in the first round and 23% in the second.

The government experienced two major upheavals in 2001. The first was a squabble on the centre-right in May over who would appoint a replacement for Interior Minister Ladislav Pittner. Prime Minister Mikulas Dzurinda eventually prevailed, putting forward his close ally Ivan Simko. In the summer the five-party ruling coalition faced collapse when the Party of the Hungarian Coalition (SMK) threatened to leave the government because of its disagreement over the territorial reforms. The parliament had voted to retain the 8 regions established by the previous government rather than switch to the 12-region model preferred by the SMK. However, the SMK finally decided to stay in the government after the parliament approved all the relevant laws on administrative reforms by early October, transferring approximately 300 powers from the central government to regions and municipalities.

On the economic front the government pushed forward quickly with privatization, completing the sales of the country's major banks and making significant headway into privatizing the energy sector. Nonetheless, economic growth continued to be slowed by weak household consumption, a sign that ordinary Slovaks had yet to benefit from the government's reforms.

Slovakia remained on the fast track for membership in NATO and the European Union (EU). Defense Minister Jozef Stank worked hard to push forward military reforms, and Slovakia was seen as one of the two favourites to receive an invitation to NATO in 2002. Slovakia caught up with the first-round countries in preparations for EU membership, closing 22 of 31 chapters of the *acquis communautaire,* the body of legislation that regulates the activities of EU member states. The one major setback was related to a scandal in May over the alleged misuse of EU PHARE funds, which led to the resignation of the deputy prime minister for European integration, Pavol Hamzik; he was replaced by Maria Kadlecikova. (SHARON FISHER)

SLOVENIA

Area: 20,273 sq km (7,827 sq mi)
Population (2001 est.): 1,991,000
Capital: Ljubljana
Chief of state: President Milan Kucan
Head of government: Prime Minister Janez Drnovsek

On June 16, 2001, Slovenia played host to the first meeting between U.S. Pres. George W. Bush and his Russian counterpart, Vladimir Putin. The two met at Brdo, a government-owned guest house northwest of Ljubljana.

The left-centre coalition government formed by Prime Minister Janez Drnovsek of the Liberal Democracy of Slovenia—by far the largest party in the parliament following the Oct. 15, 2000, election—was stable during 2001. In October Drnovsek confirmed the possible return of the cancer for which he had undergone successful surgery in 1999 but said he planned to run for president in late 2002.

Slovenia devoted much attention to improving relations with its immediate neighbours. On February 14 Italy's Parliament approved a law protecting its Slovene minority, alleviating a decades-long source of tension. On July 23 Drnovsek and Croatian Prime Minister Ivica Racan signed an agreement defining the sea and land border between the two countries, but opposition arose in Croatia, and by year's end it was clear that Croatia would not ratify the agreement. The impasse was likely to require international arbitration, which Slovenia opposed. On September 17 Slovenia opened an embassy in Belgrade and thus normalized relations with Yugoslavia; the latter reciprocated on November 2. Relations with Austria remained touchy, however, in large part because of Slovenia's concerns about treatment of the Slovene minority in the Austrian province of Kärnten.

Slow implementation of the nearly 10-year-old law on denationalization caused problems for Slovenia in its relations with the European Union (EU) and the United States. Government-approved decisions to return large tracts of land and major properties to the Catholic Church led to court appeals delaying the transfers, while Archbishop Franc Rode, head of the Slovene Church, spoke out against

AP/Wide World Photos

On June 16 in Ljubljana, Slovenia, U.S. Pres. George W. Bush and Russian Pres. Vladimir Putin share a laugh during the first meeting between the two heads of state.

what he viewed as the antireligious attitude of the predominantly leftist political establishment and mass media. Slovenia seemed to make progress in its effort to meet the conditions for membership in the EU. A similar effort continued with respect to gaining an invitation to join NATO in 2002, with less-obvious results. (RUDOLF M. SUSEL)

SOLOMON ISLANDS

Area: 28,370 sq km (10,954 sq mi)
Population (2001 est.): 480,000
Capital: Honiara
Chief of state: Queen Elizabeth II, represented by Governor-General John Lapli
Head of government: Prime Ministers Manasseh Sogavare and, from December 17, Sir Allan Kemakeza

Despite the peace agreement reached in 2000 that ended two years of ethnic conflict in the Solomon Islands, the government led by Prime Minister Manasseh Sogavare struggled to function in 2001. The economy remained in a state of near collapse, and the government was unable to meet its financial obligations or provide basic services. The power supply was irregular, civil servants went unpaid, businesses closed, and there were few exports in an economy where consumption was already heavily dependent on imports. The situation was exacerbated by the murder of a former commander of the Isatambu Freedom Movement and by violent attacks on politicians and government officials. In July the first $8 million tranche of a soft loan from Taiwan to compensate victims of ethnic violence led to disputes concerning distribution.

The government passed legislation granting amnesty to those who had taken part in ethnic violence since October 1998. A possible move from a provincial and national system of government to a federation of states remained under consideration. Despite concern over a lack of funds and administrative capacity, elections for the new 50-seat parliament took place on December 5. Former minister of foreign affairs Sir Allan Kemakeza was sworn in as prime minister. (BARRIE MACDONALD)

SOMALIA

Area: 637,000 sq km (246,000 sq mi, including the 176,000-sq-km [68,000-sq-mi] area of the unilaterally declared [in 1991] and unrecognized Republic of Somaliland)
Population (2001 est.): 7,489,000 (including Somaliland); about 300,000 refugees are registered in neighbouring countries
Capital: Mogadishu; Hargeysa is the capital of Somaliland
Head of state and government: Somalia's government under President Abdiqassim Salad Hassan was barely functioning in 2001, with opposition forces controlling parts of the country.

By the end of 2001 the economic situation of Somalia was critical. The failure of the main seasonal rains led to crop failure, and in December the UN Food and Agriculture Organization estimated that some 800,000 people were experiencing food difficulties, while 300,000, mainly in the southern regions, were threatened by starvation. The Gulf states still banned livestock from the region on health grounds, thus killing the country's main export. In February and April continued deliveries of unauthorized Somali shilling banknotes led to hyperinflation. Nevertheless, at the beginning of the year business thrived, supported largely by remittances from abroad. Financial and telephone services functioned well, and in April Mogadishu's first Internet cafe opened. A crippling blow was dealt in November when the U.S. authorities closed down Al Barakat, the company that handled most of the money-transfer and overseas telecommunications services, on the grounds that it supported terrorism.

The new Transitional National Government (TNG) under Pres. Abdiqassim Salad Hassan appeared from the outside to be working; it occupied Somalia's seat in the UN and was backed by the Organization of African Unity, the Arab League, and the European Union, which pledged aid. At home, however, it failed to control even the capital, Mogadishu, let alone the rest of the country.

In an effort to establish law and order in Mogadishu, the TNG began enrolling former gunmen into a new army and recalled former police officers, but most of the city remained in the hands of faction leaders; two deputies of the Transitional

National Assembly were assassinated, and spasmodic clan and faction fighting continued. In November the prime minister, Ali Khalif Ghalayr, was voted out of office by the Transitional National Assembly in a vote of no confidence; he was replaced by Hasan Abshir Farah.

Outside Mogadishu, clans divided into factions; some supported the TNG, but others opposed it. The breakaway regions of Somaliland in the northwest and Puntland in the northeast totally rejected the TNG, though it contained members from those regions and claimed to represent the whole country. (*See* Sidebar.) The result was the formation of a new alliance in opposition to the TNG, the Somalia Reconciliation and Restoration Council (SRRC), which was inaugurated in April at a meeting in Ethiopia and with the backing of the Ethiopian government. The TNG, backed by Egypt and Saudi Arabia, accused Ethiopia of sending troops to support the SRRC, though Ethiopia denied the charge. At the end of the year, reconciliation talks between the TNG and various factions opposed to it were held in Kenya, where a peace deal was signed on December 24. However, this was followed by fighting in Mogadishu between supporters and opponents of the deal.

In the southern port of Kismaayo, a new administration was organized by the pro-TNG Juba Valley Alliance. The area around Luuk and Bardera in the Gedo region remained under the control of al-Ittihad al-Islami, a hard-line Islamic group. (VIRGINIA LULING)

How Many Somali States?

For the past decade there has been one island of relative stability in the sea of clan warfare and political uncertainty that is the Horn of Africa. On May 18, 2001, the "Republic of Somaliland" celebrated its 10th anniversary. This territory in the northwest of Somalia comprises the former British Somaliland protectorate (which was independent for six days in 1960 before it amalgamated with the former Italian Somalia to form the Somali Republic). So far, however, it has failed to win international recognition.

In 1991, after the fall of Somalia's military dictator Muhammad Siad Barre, the victorious Somali National Movement unilaterally reasserted the independent status of the northwest area and claimed the old protectorate frontiers. The bustling capital, Hargeysa, was rebuilt after its destruction by Siad Barre's forces. Muhammad Ibrahim Egal (who had been Somalia's prime minister at the time of independence in 1960) was elected president in 1993 at a conference of traditional elders. In 2001 he was seeking a third term but faced strong opposition. In a referendum held on June 1, 97% of the eligible voters supported the new constitution, which affirmed the region's independence from the rest of Somalia.

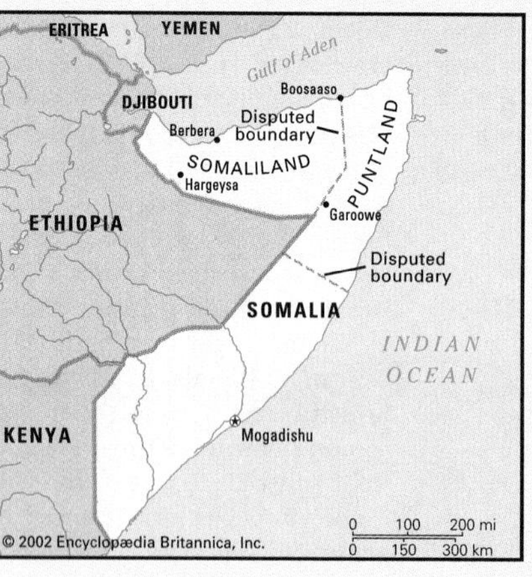

Women in Somaliland sing as they wait to cast their ballots in the constitutional referendum held on June 1.

Pedro Ugarte/AFP Widewide

In 1998 the northeastern area of Somalia also proclaimed itself the "autonomous region" of Puntland, but, unlike Somaliland, its stated goal was eventual incorporation into a federal Somali state. Puntland is governed by a house of representatives and a traditional elders' council. The inland town of Garoowe is the official capital, while the thriving port of Boosaaso is the commercial centre. Col. Abdullahi Yusuf was elected president by the elders' council. Yusuf's mandate was to have expired on June 30, 2001, but was extended for another three years by the elders' council and the house of representatives. Opposition leaders claimed, however, that the vote was manipulated. In July Chief Justice Yusuf Haji Nur issued a decree deposing him. A general conference called in November elected Col. Jama Ali Jama president; Yusuf and his supporters responded by attacking Garoowe, and a standoff ensued.

So far, beyond the creation of Eritrea from Ethiopia in 1993, the international community has not been willing to sanction the political fragmentation of the Horn by recognizing these secessionist states. As long as the jockeying and fighting between clan groups continues to paralyze government in Somalia, however, the delicate balance between multiple Somali states is likely to continue.

(VIRGINIA LULING)

SOUTH AFRICA

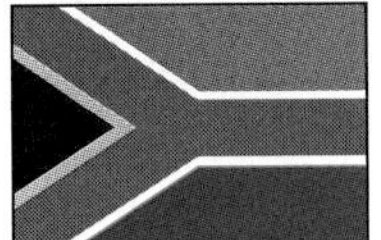

Area: 1,219,090 sq km (470,693 sq mi)
Population (2001 est.): 43,586,000
Capitals (de facto): Pretoria/Tshwane (executive); Bloemfontein/Mangaung (judicial); Cape Town (legislative)
Head of state and government: President Thabo Mbeki

Domestic Affairs. The key words in South Africa in 2001 were *privatization* and *corruption*. In his annual address to Parliament, Pres. Thabo Mbeki enumerated the improvements made in South Africa since the inception of democratic government in 1994: 1,129,612 houses had been or were being built, and nearly 7 million people had been furnished with clean water. During 2000 some 397,019 homes were connected to the electricity grid, 412,000 new telephones were installed, and 127 clinics were built. Mbeki planned to speed up delivery of services and to accelerate economic growth by lowering costs through a continued policy of privatization. He also stressed that he would combat corruption in the ruling African National Congress (ANC) government. For most of the year the main opposition party, the Democratic Alliance (DA), was making strides in becoming an important alternative to the ANC and hoped to win 30% of the vote by 2004, particularly by gaining support from blacks. DA leader Tony Leon stressed the country's need for strong leadership in the fight against crime and poverty and in the creation of jobs, and he demanded faster privatization. In October, however, a split occurred between the two components which had formed the DA, the New National Party (NNP) and the Democratic Party (DP). The catalyst for this was the expulsion from the DA of Cape Town Mayor Peter Marais. In April Marais had proposed that two principal streets in the city be renamed after former president Nelson Mandela and former president F.W. de Klerk. The proposal proved controversial, and fraud was detected in the final vote. Following the expulsion of Marais, Marthinus van Schalkwyk led much of the NNP out of the DA and into an alliance with the ANC.

Privatization threatened the alliance between the ANC, the Congress of South African Trade Unions (COSATU), and the South African Communist Party (SACP). In August COSATU and other trade unions, supported by ANC-aligned civic and student organizations, launched a two-day general strike against privatization. Nonetheless, the government severely criticized the strike and vowed that it would not change its policy. The COSATU president, Willie Madisha, cited a class struggle inside the alliance. In October the government narrowly averted a strike by public-sector workers over wages and retrenchment procedures.

The arms deal concluded in 1999, whose cost had escalated from R 30 billion (R 1=about $0.12) to more than R 60 billion due to the decline in value of the rand, continued to provoke controversy. After allegations of corruption, the government set up a joint investigating team into the deal which cleared government ministers of any wrongdoing. Opposition parties, however, believed that the investigation was compromised, and its mode of establishment had undermined the independence of parliament. Several people, including the ANC chief whip, Tony Yengeni, were charged with offenses related to the arms deal, such as corruption or fraud, perjury, and forgery. All of the major parties encountered severe internal tensions.

In April the ANC minister of safety and security provoked considerable incredulity when he claimed that three businessmen, ANC supporters, were involved in a plot to oust President Mbeki and that they were being investigated by police and national intelligence. COSATU called the statement "highly irresponsible." The government was accused of using state resources to thwart a possible political challenge to Mbeki. Though President Mbeki regretted that the businessmen had been named, he justified a police investigation on the grounds that there were also rumours circulating that he had been involved in the 1993 assassination of SACP leader Chris Hani.

In July thousands of people who had occupied land illegally in Gauteng—they had bought plots costing R 25 each from the Pan-Africanist Congress (PAC)—were forcibly evicted by the government. This led to tensions and disagreements within the PAC.

Controversy over HIV/AIDS continued. In March the DA and COSATU wanted the government to declare the AIDS epidemic a state of emergency. Such an action would permit the acquisition of less-costly medicines, but the government refused. In April the Pharmaceutical Manufacturers' Association, representing 39 manufacturers, withdrew its 1998 court case against the government, which had empowered itself to import generic drugs, including less-expensive anti-AIDS drugs, without the permission of the patent holder. The dropping of the suit was regarded as a victory for the government and the AIDS-activist organization, the Treatment Action Campaign. The health minister, however, said that the decision did not mean that the government would purchase large quantities of the drugs. In October a Medical Research Council report—which was leaked to the *Johannesburg Sunday Times* after the government had suppressed its contents—concluded that AIDS was the chief cause of death in the country and that unless measures were taken to curb the disease, it would claim the lives of between five million and seven million South Africans by 2010.

In a stampede for seats at a soccer match on April 11 at Ellis Park stadium in Johannesburg, 43 fans died and hundreds were injured. The stadium held 62,000 persons, but thousands more went to the contest. ANC stalwart and former Robben Island prisoner Govan Mbeki, father of President Mbeki, died in early August at the age of 91. Christiaan Barnard, the first surgeon to perform a successful heart transplant, succumbed in September. (*See* OBITUARIES.) On December 4 Marike de Klerk, F.W. de Klerk's ex-wife, was found murdered in her home near Cape Town. A 21-year-old security guard in her housing complex was arrested days later, though the motive for the crime was unclear.

The Economy. From a 3.1% growth rate in 2000, the economy slowed to an increase of 1.5% in the first quarter, 1.8% in the second quarter, and 1.2% in the third quarter of 2001. The slowdown was attributed to a decline in the growth of export volume. Gross domestic fixed investment, which increased by 1.5% in 2000, grew by 5.5% in the first half of 2001. The job sector remained problematic, however. Though employment estimates rose from 9.2 million in 1996 to 10.4 million in 1999, mainly in the informal sector, unemployment as of February 2000 was 26.7% on a narrow definition, which excluded people who had not actively sought work in the previous week, and 37.3% on a broader definition.

The budget for 2001–02 provided a tax-relief package of R 8.3 billion, and it also included an economic-stimulus package of R 7.8 billion, which would be spent on infrastructure; the R 600 million allocated as tax incentives for job creation was criticized as too little by COSATU. The increases in pensions and child-

AP/Wide World Photos

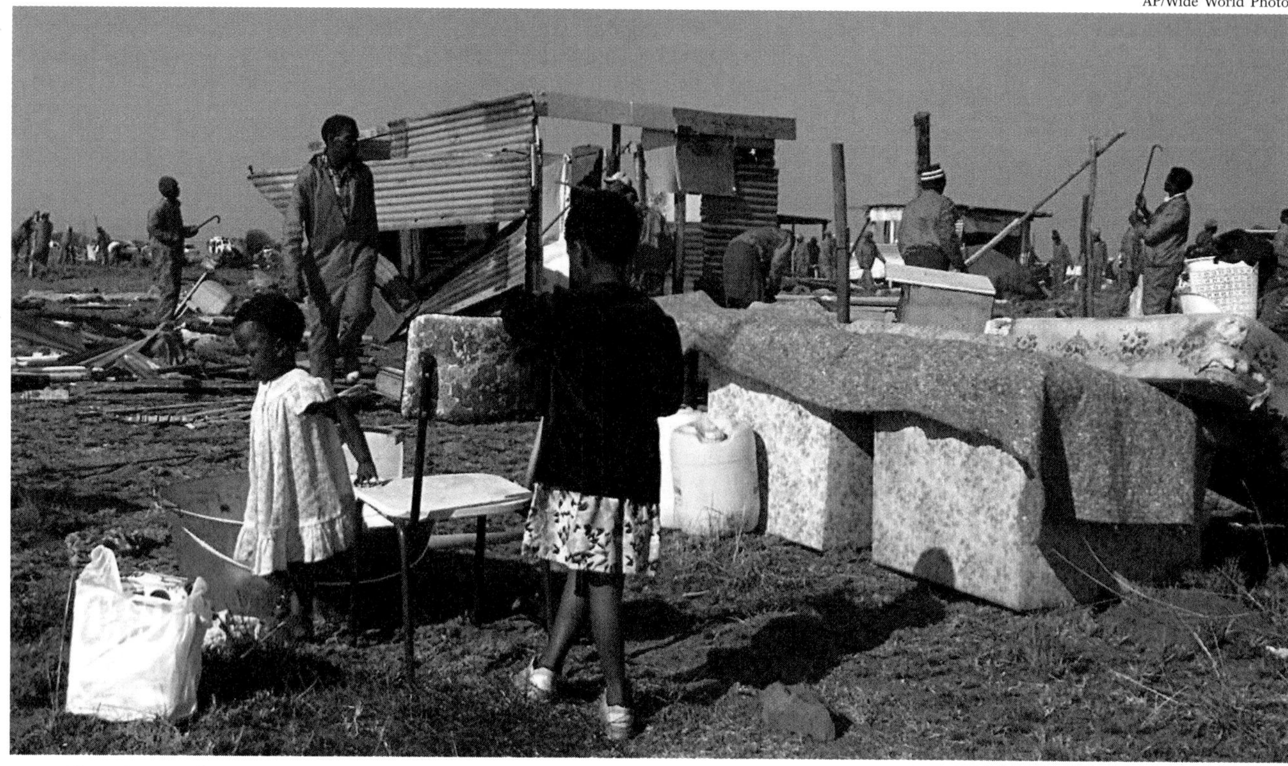

Outside Johannesburg, S.Afr., workers dismantle the shacks of squatter families on July 13.

support grants were criticized as insufficient. During the year the rand slumped by near 40% against the dollar.

Foreign Affairs. President Mbeki's Millennium Africa Recovery Program, which aimed to combat poverty through investment and trade, received a warm response from developed countries during the year. Mbeki and other African leaders first presented the plan in January at the World Economic Forum summit in Davos, Switz. He then emerged from the Organization of African Unity conference in July with Senegal's proposals for a New African Initiative. Mbeki went on to present the proposal to the Group of Eight industrialized nations in July, and the measure was expected to be finalized for the group in 2002. In August–September, South Africa hosted the UN's World Conference Against Racism, which provoked controversy when the U.S. withdrew in protest against attempts to equate Zionism with racism and demands for reparations for slavery and colonialism.

Mbeki's unilateral "quiet diplomacy" to deal with the land and law-and-order crisis in Zimbabwe was supplemented by multilateral pressure from the Commonwealth of Nations and the Southern African Development Community. In February Mbeki's international investment council expressed concern that the violence in the Zimbabwe land crisis would spill over into South Africa. South Africa's defense force assisted refugees from Mozambican floods in February, and a limited number of South African troops were deployed to the UN peacekeeping force in the Democratic Republic of the Congo. In October South Africa and Burundi signed an agreement that would deploy as many as 700 South African peacekeeping troops to monitor the installation in November of Burundi's transitional government. The first visit by a sitting Japanese prime minister to South Africa took place in January. President Mbeki visited Cuba in March; the U.K., the U.S., and Germany in June; and Japan in October.

(MARTIN LEGASSICK)

SPAIN

Area: 505,990 sq km (195,364 sq mi)
Population (2001 est.): 40,144,000
Capital: Madrid
Chief of state: King Juan Carlos I
Head of government: Prime Minister José María Aznar López

Spain was one of the fastest-growing economies in the European Union (EU) in 2001. Despite inflation nearing 4% and the clear signs of slowdown, the strong economy helped Prime Minister José María Aznar López through a rather troubled year for his centre-right Popular Party (PP) government.

The government's problems involved politics as much as policies. A number of issues were handled clumsily, including implementation of immigration legislation passed in January and a health scare over low-quality olive oil in July. Complaints that the government was steamrolling controversial university reforms through the parliament inflamed the opposition, and students all over the country joined in strikes, demonstrations, and sit-ins.

A number of senior officials were implicated in financial scandals during the year. In July Foreign Minister Joseph Piqué only narrowly escaped prosecution for his role in alleged irregularities committed in 1991 by the chemicals group Ercros, of which he was then a director. Just days later the collapse of the stockbroking house Gescartera with debts amounting to over $82 million spelled more trouble for the government. The junior finance minister, Enrique Giménez-Reyna, whose sister was managing director of Gescartera, and

Pilar Valiente, president of the stock market regulator, resigned amid accusations of official incompetence and favouritism. The PP's parliamentary majority ensured that the congressional inquiry exonerated the government from all responsibility in the case, but opposition parties called for the dismissal of the ministers of the economy and finance. These scandals also conjured up the spectre of corruption that had cost the previous government under the Spanish Socialist Workers' Party (PSOE) so dearly in the 1996 elections.

The PP's disappointing performance in the Basque regional elections on May 13 was another setback. Following the signing of an antiterrorist pact with the PSOE in December 2000, the two "constitutional" parties had fought the campaign hand-in-hand. Preelectoral polls suggested they might be able to oust the moderate Basque Nationalist Party (PNV) after 21 years in power, but the PNV won a resounding victory, taking 33 seats in the 75-seat parliament (up from 27). The main loser was Euskal Herritarrok (EH), the political wing of the Basque separatist organization Euskadi Ta Askatasuna (ETA), which apparently was punished by voters for having ended its unilateral cease-fire six months earlier.

These elections were widely seen as a personal triumph for Basque regional president Juan José Ibarretxe, as well as an endorsement for his demands for both greater regional autonomy and self-determination. The latter was rejected out of hand by the PP government, which accused the nationalist regional government—which the Basque federation of the left-wing United Left (IU) coalition joined in September—of being soft on terrorism.

ETA continued its campaign of street violence, arson, and assassination, undeterred by the evident electoral costs and successful police antiterrorist operations. The organization claimed 13 mortal victims in 2001, taking its death toll to well over 800 in just over three decades. Victims included bystanders as well as local politicians and members of the police, press, military, and judiciary. Late in the year José Javier Arizkurn Ruíz, who was believed to be the former military leader of the ETA, was extradited from France to face charges of plotting to kill King Juan Carlos I in 1995; Arizkurn also faced 12 murder charges.

Spain's domestic terrorist problem framed its response to the September 11 attacks in the U.S. Seeing an opportunity to consolidate ties with U.S. Pres. George W. Bush's administration as well as to secure closer international cooperation against ETA, Aznar immediately offered sympathy and full support to the U.S. Spanish bases and troops were put at the disposition of Washington, and on November 13 the Spanish police arrested 11 suspected members of the terrorist organization al-Qaeda. Spain also strongly supported initiatives to tighten the EU's antiterrorist legislation. With the exception of the IU, there was a broad consensus behind the government's response to the international crisis.

A number of long-running tensions between Spain and Morocco surfaced in 2001. Madrid's response to the events of September 11 included tightening entry controls in the North African enclaves of Ceuta and Melilla, which helped trigger a diplomatic crisis with Morocco in November. Moroccan resentment of Spanish occupation of these "colonies" was inflamed by signs of progress on Spain's claims to the British colony of Gibraltar. The collapse of talks between the EU and Morocco over European fishing rights in Moroccan waters in April was followed in September by suggestions from Madrid that Rabat could do more to stem the flow of illegal immigration into Spain across the Strait of Gibraltar. Press criticism of the pace of political reform in Morocco also irritated that country, as did Spain's perceived opposition to Rabat's plans for Western Sahara, the former Spanish colony occupied by Morocco in 1975. The tension came to a head on October 27, days before Moroccan King Muhammad VI began his first official visit to Western Sahara, when Rabat unexpectedly recalled its ambassador to Madrid and canceled a bilateral summit.

(JUSTIN BYRNE)

On May 14, a day after Juan José Ibarretxe's Basque Nationalist Party triumphed in the Basque regional elections, workers cover an election poster of one of his rivals, Jaime Mayor Oreja of the Popular Party.

Rafa Rivas/AFP Worldwide

SRI LANKA

Area: 65,610 sq km (25,332 sq mi)
Population (2001 est.): 19,399,000
Capitals: Sri Jayawardenepura Kotte (legislative and judicial); Colombo (executive)
Head of state and government: President Chandrika Kumaratunga, assisted by Prime Ministers Ratnasiri Wickramanayake and, from December 9, Ranil Wickremesinghe

Although in 2001 the Sri Lankan civil war entered its 19th year, and there was no end in view by year's end, there was new hope that a negotiated settlement might finally be attainable. In April the Liberation Tigers of Tamil Eelam (LTTE), who had long fought to establish an independent nation in the north and east of the nation, canceled the cease-fire they had unilaterally declared the previous December, blaming the government for not reciprocating. Norwegian-brokered efforts to initiate peace talks had foundered because the LTTE demanded that the political ban on its organization and economic embargo against it be lifted and a cease-fire declared by the government, which in turn insisted that peace talks proceed without preconditions.

Soon after the LTTE's cease-fire was canceled, the government launched an offensive in the area of Elephant Pass, which had been lost to rebel forces a year earlier. The offensive was repelled with heavy losses, and government troops retreated to their original lines. Sporadic fighting continued throughout the year, despite renewed efforts to start negotiations. The rebels scored a spectacular coup in July when they briefly seized Bandaranaike International Airport and its nearby air base, terrifying passengers and staff and destroying half of Air Lanka's Airbus fleet as well as military planes and an oil depot.

Meanwhile, a prolonged political crisis began in June with the withdrawal of the Sri Lanka Muslim Congress from Pres. Chandrika Kumaratunga's People's Alliance coalition. In an effort to survive, the president suspended Parliament and called for a national referendum, provoking further controversy. In August the crisis was temporarily relieved when the Marxist People's Liberation Front (JVP) agreed to support the government for one year in exchange for several concessions. In December, however, a general election returned control of Parliament to the opposition United National Party. The new government quickly declared a cease-fire, eased restrictions on internal movement, and took initial steps toward negotiations with the rebels.

Economic growth declined sharply from the 6.9% real gross domestic product growth achieved in 2000. Dampening factors included a severe drought, which caused electricity shortages, and the need to pay war-risk insurance premiums on imports and exports. Hope for economic recovery rose at the year's end, but that remained dependent on the success of the peace effort and faced severe resource depletion in any case.

(DONALD R. SNODGRASS)

SUDAN, THE

Area: 2,503,890 sq km (966,757 sq mi)
Population (2001 est.): 36,080,000
Capitals: Khartoum (executive and ministerial) and Omdurman (legislative)
Head of state and government: President and Prime Minister Lieut. Gen. Omar Hassan Ahmad al-Bashir

On Jan. 3, 2001, Pres. Omar Hassan Ahmad al-Bashir extended the existing state of emergency in The Sudan for an additional 12 months. He stressed, however, that this extension would not restrict religious freedom or freedom of speech among opposition parties. Late in February a former supporter of the president, Hassan al-Turabi, eager to reassert his authority, was arrested after signing a memorandum of understanding with the rebel Sudanese People's Liberation Army (SPLA). At about the same time, President Bashir began discussions with Sadiq al-Mahdi, leader of the opposition Ummah Party, who had returned to The Sudan from self-imposed exile the previous November.

During the year a number of disturbing contrasts emerged. The 25-year-old Kenana Sugar Co.—which employed some 16,000 people and provided education and health care for 100,000 others—announced record production in 2000–01. The harvest produced a large surplus that fully supplied the needs of the domestic and export markets. Meanwhile, the UN World Food Programme warned that three million people were threatened by hunger resulting from drought and civil war. Though the oil industry was earning approximately $1 million per day for the government, a report by the charity organization Christian Aid accused the government of driving hundreds of thousands of people from the land where the oil companies were operating and killing them and burning their villages if they resisted. The oil industry also funded the civil war, which continued unabated in spite of recurring disputes between the leaders of the SPLA. On the other hand, the government's military expenditures, which since 1998 had doubled, by 2001 equaled exactly its income from oil.

Nevertheless, the Sudanese government, which had been accused by the U.S. of sponsoring terrorists and which U.S. Pres. George W. Bush had described on May 3 as presiding over a country that was "a disaster area for all human rights," gave its immediate support to the antiterrorist campaign launched by the U.S. following the September terrorist attacks. In August diplomatic relations with Uganda were reestablished. In September the UN Security Council lifted sanctions imposed on The Sudan in 1996, and in November the U.S. sent an envoy with proposals to end the civil war in the country. (KENNETH INGHAM)

SURINAME

Area: 163,820 sq km (63,251 sq mi)
Population (2001 est.): 434,000
Capital: Paramaribo
Head of state and government: President Ronald Venetiaan

Into his second year of government in 2001, Pres. Ronald Venetiaan brought some improved fiscal and economic stability to Suriname, which was still recovering from the 1986–92 civil conflict that destructively polarized the coastal and interior cultures. He wrestled too with the chaotic economic legacy of his predecessor, Jules Wijdenbosch. Under Venetiaan's guidance, the currency had responded to corrective measures, inflation had been reduced, the armed forces had been largely depoliticized, and loans to underpin health, education, and social programs had been negotiated with The Netherlands and the Inter-American Development Bank. Disruptive frontier disputes with neighbouring Guyana had been positively addressed, while an expansion of oil production was anticipated.

Key to Venetiaan's modest success was his ability to keep his fragile New Front coalition of four political parties intact in the face of major challenges, notably a towering fiscal deficit, a robust informal economy of illegal mining and narcotics smuggling, a swollen and diet-resistant public service, and the accelerating global downturn on traditional export earnings, including bauxite and rice.

Although issues such as land rights and natural resources in the interior remained unresolved, in July in Paramaribo the country formally commemorated the successful eight-year Organization of American States mission to assist Suriname in finding "durable peace" and strengthening "institutions and democratic order." (JOHN W. GRAHAM)

Pres. Ronald Venetiaan of Suriname speaks at a press conference in Paramaribo on August 9.

Ranu Abhelakh/AFP Worldwide

SWAZILAND

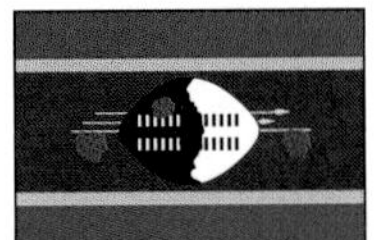

Area: 17,364 sq km (6,704 sq mi)
Population (2001 est.): 1,104,000
Capitals: Mbabane (administrative and judicial); Lozitha and Ludzidzini (royal); Lobamba (legislative)
Chief of state: King Mswati III, with much power shared by his mother, Queen Mother Ntombi Latfwala
Head of government: Prime Minister Barnabas Sibusiso Dlamini

The high point in Swazi politics during 2001 was reached when on August 10 the Constitutional Review Commission (CRC) submitted its report to King Mswati III. The entire nation was called to Ludzidzini to witness the king's receipt of the commission's report, which provided a constitutional framework for the legal experts who would write the country's constitution.

In April 1973 Sobhuza II, King Mswati III's father, had abolished the constitution that Great Britain bequeathed when colonial rule ended on Sept. 6, 1968. Although most parts of that constitution were restored in Swaziland after independence, the sections providing a bill of rights and allowing political parties to be formed were removed. The CRC reported that the majority of the Swazi population did not favour the formation of political parties.

Pro-democracy groups, however, continued to call for the establishment of such parties and for greater open participation in governance. The Swaziland government appeared to allow open political activities in October; for the first time, campaigns in the local government elections were promoted publicly.
(ACKSON M. KANDUZA)

SWEDEN

Area: 449,964 sq km (173,732 sq mi)
Population (2001 est.): 8,888,000
Capital: Stockholm
Chief of state: King Carl XVI Gustaf
Head of government: Prime Minister Göran Persson

The first six months of 2001 were dominated by Sweden's role as president of the European Union (EU), and while the country was criticized for lacking a grand vision for its time in charge, it was praised for the efficiency with which it ran the presidency.

For the Swedes the most obvious achievement was the injection of fresh impetus to the process of EU enlargement. At the end of the Göteborg summit in June, Prime Minister Göran Persson said he hoped the most advanced candidates would complete entry negotiations by the end of 2002 with the objective of participating in the 2004 European Parliamentary elections.

Sweden's term as president also marked some bold foreign initiatives for the EU. With the U.S. under Pres. George W. Bush appearing to disengage from some of the world's most intractable political disputes, it was left to Persson to visit the Middle East and North Korea. The EU also took the lead in attempting to prevent an all-out war in Macedonia.

For all the successes, most Swedes would remember the presidency not for the long line of foreign dignitaries who visited the country but for the bloody riots that marred the Göteborg summit as groups of antiglobalization protesters and police battled in the streets of the city.

Domestic politics got under way in the second half of the year but were overshadowed by the September 11 terrorist attacks in the U.S. Persson wholeheartedly supported the U.S.-led campaign against terrorism and the bombing in Afghanistan, a position that prompted sharp criticism from some members of his Social Democratic Labour Party (SAP).

Despite the dispute, Persson remained unchallenged as party leader and was set to take the SAP into the September 2002 general election. In opinion polls the SAP claimed about 35% of the support, with its ally the Left Party at around 12–13%. The environmental Green Party, which the SAP also relied upon for its legislative majority, might struggle to return to the Riksdag (parliament) after the election. If this happened, or if support for the Left and the SAP slipped further, then the way would be open for a nonsocialist four-party coalition to take power, headed by the conservative Moderate Party leader Bo Lundgren.

Economically, the bursting of the information technology bubble had as marked implications for Sweden as for other countries. Ericsson, the world's largest producer of mobile telecommunications equipment, shed thousands of jobs, as did the country's once fast-expanding Internet consulting firms and dot-com start-ups.

Gross domestic product growth of 3.6% in 2000 was expected to have fallen to around 1.5% in 2001, and only a minor recovery was forecast for 2002. The government was hoping that measures such as tax cuts, subsidies on child-care expenses, and wage increases would boost consumer confidence with real disposable income to increase by 5.4%. Exports were also expected to pick up in 2002, helped by the weakness of the Swedish krona, which hit record lows against both the dollar and the euro in 2001.

For the time being, Sweden had decided to remain outside the European single currency, and Persson was eager to ensure that membership did not become an issue in the general election. At the earliest a referendum on the matter could be held after the election, but there was little obvious enthusiasm for the monetary project among the general public.
(NICHOLAS GEORGE)

SWITZERLAND

Area: 41,284 sq km (15,940 sq mi)
Population (2001 est.): 7,222,000
Capitals: Bern (administrative) and Lausanne (judicial)
Head of state and government: President Moritz Leuenberger

In the worst accident of its kind that Switzerland had ever experienced, 11 people lost their lives on Oct. 24, 2001, in a head-on collision between two heavy trucks and the consequent fire in the 17-km (10.5-mi) St. Gotthard tunnel, hitherto considered as having "above-average security." Traffic in the tunnel, a main route through the Swiss Alps between Göschenen and Airolo on the way to Italy, had increased significantly since a fire that resulted in 39 deaths closed the Mont Blanc tunnel—the principal Alpine link between France and Italy—in 1999. By the end of 2001, the Mont Blanc tunnel had reopened initially for light traffic. The Gotthard tunnel reopened on December 21. In a further accident on November 24, a Crossair plane crashed as it was on the point of landing at Zürich airport; 24 people died. (*See* DISASTERS.)

The Swiss public was likewise traumatized by the mass killing on September 27 in the cantonal parliament of Zug. A man wearing what looked like a police uniform and armed with a grenade and an assault rifle burst into a joint session and opened fire, killing 14 people and wounding many more, before shooting himself.

After a fairly promising start to the year, the Swiss economy was shaken by successive restructuring, entailing thousands of layoffs and bringing unemployment up to almost 2%, though inflation was at its lowest since February 1999. This culminated in the downfall of the national airline, Swissair, which since its founding in 1931 had established itself as the hallmark of Swiss efficiency. Swissair had experienced serious financial difficulties in preceding years (at a stormy shareholders meeting in April, the management was severely criticized), which were compounded by repercussions from the September 11 terrorist attacks in the U.S. Swissair grounded its fleet of 73 planes for two days in early October when two of its jets were denied fuel replenishment at London's Heathrow Airport and the company was refused further credit. Thousands of passengers were stranded.

Difficult weeks followed, leading to the collapse of the SAirGroup. Its subsidiary, Crossair, emerged as the national airline, taking over 52 flights from Swissair, which was granted a six-month protection against bankruptcy proceedings. Financial support was pledged by government, banks, and the private sector, with UBS and Credit Suisse holding 70.5% of the share capital of Crossair.

In a March referendum voters followed the government's advice to postpone a decision on joining the European Union to allow more time for reflection. In June voters approved by a narrow majority government proposals that Swiss soldiers serving abroad be armed. The electorate also narrowly voted to permit military training in NATO countries or common exercises with NATO troops on Swiss soil. Action for an Independent and Neutral Switzerland and other opponents expressed fears that the country might otherwise lose its neutrality and be drawn into a military entanglement. At the same time, voters accepted the repeal of an article in the constitution by which the creation of new bishoprics needed the blessing of the political authorities. In December limitations on budgetary indebtedness were accepted, while abolishing the army was once more rejected, as were replacing the army by a peace service, imposing a tax on energy, and another tax on capital gains.

AP/Wide World Photos

A plane of the financially troubled Swissair—part of the SAirGroup—takes off in Zürich on November 18.

Continuing its reform "Army XXI," the Swiss cabinet decided that new military recruits would serve for 21 weeks, up from 15. Parliamentary approval of this change was taken for granted. It would apply from 2004, by which time the strength of the army would be reduced from 350,000 to 200,000, while the annual budget would remain at Sw F 4.3 billion (about $2.6 billion).

Although a massive majority in the National Council was in favour of joining the United Nations, the final decision still depended on a referendum to be held in March 2002. By the end of 2001, the Swiss political scene had moved slightly to the right, as the Swiss People's Party had gained representation in all cantonal parliaments.

The Federal Council opened the way to simplify the procedure for foreigners of the second and third generation to acquire Swiss nationality (subject to parliamentary approval and acceptance in a future referendum). Belgium was by the end of the year the last EU country to have ratified the bilateral agreements with Switzerland. After adjustments, due largely to some donators being unable to meet their pledges, the Swiss national exhibition, Expo02, was expected to open as scheduled. It was already a year late. (ALAN MCGREGOR)

SYRIA

Area: 185,180 sq km (71,498 sq mi)
Population (2001 est.): 16,729,000
Capital: Damascus
Head of state and government: President Bashar al-Assad, assisted by Prime Minister Muhammad Mustafa Mero

Political discussion groups blossomed throughout Syria as 2001 opened. In mid-January the reform movement published a Basic Document that called for a return to "constitutional legitimacy" and the rule of law. Immediately after this manifesto appeared, leftist reformers organized a Gathering for Democracy and Unity to encourage public debate and promote competitive parties. Influential liberals responded by forming the Social Peace Movement, committed to orderly dialogue between the regime and its critics and to opening the political arena to previously excluded viewpoints, especially those of the younger generation. At the end of

January, however, the minister of information warned that "any talk that undermines the unity of society is a threat to society as a whole" and equated the spread of Western conceptions of civil society with "neocolonialism."

Attacks on the reform movement by senior government officials and the state-run media escalated in February, and discussion forums were ordered to clear their agendas, speaker lists, and participants with the authorities in advance. By late summer outspoken dissidents were being accused of insulting the honour of the nation. The historic leader of the Syrian Communist Party, Riyad at-Turk, was arrested after he publicly criticized the Ba'th Party's economic policies and Syria's involvement in Lebanon. Prominent liberal activists were rounded up by the security services during September.

Economic and diplomatic relations with Iraq steadily improved during the year. An agreement to phase out tariffs on trade between the two countries was signed in January, and some 150,000 bbl of oil per day flowed through the long-abandoned pipeline linking northern Iraq to the docks at Baniyas. Rapprochement with Iraq accompanied heightened tensions with Israel. On April 16 and July 1, following Hezbollah operations against Israeli forces on the Golan Heights front, Israeli warplanes bombed Syrian military positions in eastern Lebanon.

Prime Minister Muhammad Mustafa Mero led a delegation of state officials and businesspeople to Baghdad, Iraq, in mid-August. The trip resulted in a mutual defense pact, along with treaties to expand bilateral commercial and technical exchanges. On September 10 the interior ministers of Syria and Turkey pledged to coordinate efforts to combat organized crime and terrorism. Foreign Minister Farouk ash-Shara' expressed regret over the attacks in the U.S. the next day, but he urged those set on eliminating international terrorism to focus their attention on Israeli policy toward the Palestinians and neighbouring states. In December the cabinet resigned, and Pres. Bashar al-Assad asked the prime minister to form a new government that could handle economic reform.

Pres. Bashar al-Assad announced on January 2 that the previous day he had married Asma Akhras, who was born in Syria and educated in the U.K. In May the couple traveled to Spain in Assad's first trip to Europe since being named president in July 2000.

(FRED H. LAWSON)

TAIWAN

Area: 36,188 sq km (13,972 sq mi)
Population (2001 est.): 22,340,000
Capital: Taipei
Chief of state: President Chen Shui-bian
Head of government: President of the Executive Yuan (Premier) Chang Chun-hsiung

Ripples from the global economic slowdown in 2001 produced a severe negative impact on Taiwan's economy and overshadowed the ongoing political turmoil that resulted from a divided government. The perennial threat from China evoked a variety of responses from within Taiwan, while the new U.S. administration of Pres. George W. Bush proved more sympathetic to Taiwan's security needs than the Bill Clinton administration had been in the preceding eight years.

Shrinking demand in the U.S. and Japan for Taiwan's high-tech exports, particularly computer chips, and the exodus of thousands of manufacturing plants to China, where labour costs were significantly lower, crippled the economy. Growth slowed from a robust 6.3% in 2000 to just over 1% in the first quarter of 2001, and the economy actually contracted by 2.35% in the second quarter compared with the previous year as the island entered recession for the first time since 1975. At midyear the unemployment rate, which had hovered around 2% for many years, shot up to 4.22%, the highest figure on record. Diminished bank credit added to the economic gloom. One of the few bright spots was that Taiwan's long-standing application to join the World Trade Organization was finally approved in mid-September, the day after China's bid to join the WTO was sealed.

The election in March 2000 of Democratic Progressive Party (DPP) presidential candidate Chen Shui-bian ended the Kuomintang's (KMT) half-century monopoly of that office, but the KMT

Taiwanese Pres. Chen Shui-bian speaks at the conclusion of economic meetings held in Taipei in late August.

Sam Yeh/AFP Worldwide

retained its majority in the Legislative Yuan pending the outcome of parliamentary elections scheduled for December 1. The inexperience of the new DPP administration combined with the determination of the KMT to make things difficult for its political nemesis made this unprecedented experiment in divided government a series of partisan political skirmishes. Former president Lee Teng-hui, who had resigned as head of the KMT after his handpicked candidate, Lien Chan, was crushed in the March 2000 election, threw his support to a new political party, the Taiwan Solidarity Union (TSU), which favoured the maintenance of Taiwan's de facto independence from China.

Meanwhile, the KMT endorsed the novel concept of confederation with China as a way out of the half-century impasse between the People's Republic and the Republic of China. In September the KMT expelled elder statesman Lee from its ranks, severing its ties with the man who had been the party's most important leader for the past dozen years. In the December 1 parliamentary elections, the KMT suffered a crushing defeat, dropping from 110 to 68 seats while its share of the vote plummeted from 46% to 31%. The DPP increased its seats from 66 to 87, and its vote share from 30% to 37%, making it the largest party in the 225-seat Legislative Yuan. The fledgling People First Party led by James Soong picked up 46 seats, and the TSU 13. Overall, these results gave the DPP and President Chen an unprecedented opportunity to create a reform-minded coalition with a small but workable majority.

In January the KMT-dominated Legislative Yuan voted to override Chen's decision to halt construction of Taiwan's fourth nuclear power plant, in fulfillment of a campaign promise, and the courts ruled that Chen had acted improperly. Over the objections of his DPP and environmentalist supporters who opposed nuclear power on principle, Chen bowed to opposition pressure and authorized resumption of construction on the contested power plant.

Taiwan's sole major power patron, the U.S., showed a more sympathetic face to the island under the new Republican Bush administration. In April Bush said he would do whatever it took to defend Taiwan. That same month, in response to Taiwan's annual request for defensive weaponry, Washington announced that it would provide Taiwan with four Kidd-class destroyers, 12 P-3C Orion surveillance aircraft, eight diesel submarines, minesweeping helicopters, surface- and submarine-launched torpedoes, and Avenger surface-to-air missiles, while it withheld approval of the advanced Aegis antimissile defense system that was Taiwan's most coveted item. The transfers were designed to bolster Taiwan's navy in the face of a steadily growing military imbalance across the Taiwan Strait. China, as usual, objected vociferously to U.S. support for Taiwan, since it hoped to intimidate the island into surrendering its de facto sovereignty. Washington also eased restrictions on Taiwan leaders visiting the U.S., another thing that China deemed objectionable. In May, en route to a tour of Latin American allies, President Chen stopped over in New York City and Houston, where he met with municipal officials and sympathetic congresspeople. (STEVEN I. LEVINE)

TAJIKISTAN

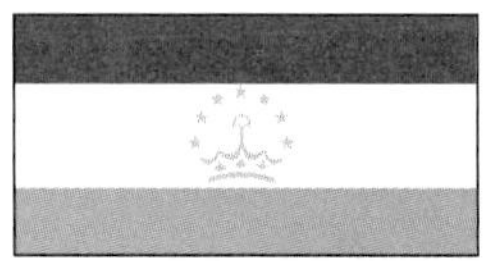

Area: 143,100 sq km (55,300 sq mi)
Population (2001 est.): 6,252,000
Capital: Dushanbe
Chief of state: President Imomali Rakhmonov
Head of government: Prime Minister Akil Akilov

Tajikistan continued to suffer the effects of the regionwide drought, which continued for a third year. International humanitarian assistance provided some relief, but the country's vital agricultural sector had little chance to start the process of recovery.

The post-civil war peace process was endangered by outbreaks of violence that lasted from April, when the deputy minister of internal affairs was assassinated in Dushanbe, through the summer as government troops battled two armed gangs that had formerly been part of the Islamic opposition. Members of the Islamic opposition who had become government officials stated that the cleanup operation was necessary because, since the end of the civil war, the two groups had engaged in criminal activities, including hostage taking. One former opposition official reported that the killing of civilians during the operations against the gangs had undermined the implementation of the peace process. In July the adviser to Pres. Imomali Rakhmonov was shot dead in Dushanbe. Politicians of various parties attributed the violence to unspecified forces that wanted to destabilize the country. The minister of culture was assassinated in September.

From the beginning of the year, Tajikistan was under pressure from international humanitarian-aid agencies to admit a group of several thousand Afghan refugees stranded on islands in the Amu Darya. The Tajik authorities refused to allow the refugees into Tajikistan on the grounds that there were armed men among them and in any case Tajikistan was unable to care for its own people. In April the mayor of Dushanbe ordered all Afghan refugees out of the capital.

In January the Tajik authorities began jailing adherents of the banned Islamic sect Hizb ut-Tahrir, which was particularly strong in northern Tajikistan. In early April Kyrgyz officials asserted that militants of the Islamic Movement of Uzbekistan had returned to Tajikistan, which in previous years they had used as a launching point for attacks on Kyrgyzstan. Tajik officials denied this charge and subsequent claims that leaders of the Afghanistan-based group had been sighted in Tajikistan.

Relations with neighbouring Uzbekistan remained tense; the Uzbeks had mined the border between the two countries, and numerous Tajik citizens were killed or maimed when they stepped on mines. The Tajik military spent the summer trying to remove as many mines as possible.

Tajikistan continued to depend on the Russian military presence to protect its borders with Afghanistan. In May it joined the NATO-sponsored Partnership for Peace program. After the terrorist attacks in the U.S. in September, Dushanbe was obliged to consult with Russia before agreeing to provide help to the international antiterrorist coalition.

(BESS BROWN)

TANZANIA

Area: 945,090 sq km (364,901 sq mi)
Population (2001 est.): 36,232,000 (including nearly 1,000,000 refugees, nearly all of whom are from Burundi)
De facto capital: Dar es Salaam; the legislature meets in Dodoma, the capital designate
Chief of state and head of government: President Benjamin William Mkapa, assisted by Prime Minister Frederick Tulway Sumaye

On January 26–27, 2001, police used tear gas and live ammunition to break up demonstrations called by the opposition Civic United Front (CUF) on the islands of Zanzibar and Pemba; the CUF demanded a rerun of the October 2000 parliamentary and presidential elections. Though CUF reports of the number of people killed during the demonstrations were exaggerated, the government's estimate of 20 dead was regarded by impartial observers as too low. The U.S. and several European countries condemned the killings, and Amnesty International criticized the excessive use of force by police and called on both the Tanzanian and Zanzibari governments to institute an impartial investigation. The simultaneous demonstrations that were planned on the mainland were apparently forestalled when officials and other supporters of the CUF were arrested. Foreign Minister Jakaya Kikwete visited London, Washington, Brussels, and Stockholm in a damage-control effort, even though there were no signs that donors were threatening to withhold aid.

Tanzania's continuing dependence on foreign aid was highlighted by the budget presented by Finance Minister Basil Mramba on June 14. Estimated income for the year 2001–02 amounted to markedly less than 60% of estimated expenditure, with something less than the about 40% remaining to come from external grants and loans. Nor was external aid uniformly successful in achieving its aims. Primary-school enrollment suffered a sharp decline; the Heavily Indebted Poor Countries debt-relief program, launched jointly by the World Bank and the International Monetary Fund (IMF), insisted that poor parents contribute a part of the cost of educating their children, a condition that few could meet. Moreover, in spite of the program, Tanzania was still spending 26% of its export earnings on debt servicing. After a March meeting with the members of an IMF–World Bank mission in Tanzania, leaders of southern and central African countries called for urgent steps to be taken to encourage African exports.

Against this backdrop, the news that the British government was contemplating issuing an export license that would authorize a British company to provide a sophisticated $40 million air traffic control system for Tanzania caused the World Bank and the IMF considerable consternation in August.

There were, however, some hopeful signs for the economy. Increased investor interest in gold mining raised Tanzania's hopes of becoming the third largest gold producer in the world by 2004; some 300 of the 400 companies that had been earmarked for privatization had achieved their aim. In addition, tourism, which in 1999 had accounted for 14% of gross domestic product, continued to expand. Telecommunications lagged well behind neighbouring countries, but the rapid growth in mobile phone ownership—more than 160,000 by midyear—meant that business development was not being held back. There was further good news on November 27 when the IMF and World Bank agreed to a reduction of $77 million in Tanzania's debt repayment for the year 2002. On the political front, however, the peace accord signed between the ruling party, Chama Cha Mapinduzi (CCM), and the CUF on October 10 ran into difficulties when the leadership of the CUF accused the CCM of lacking the will to implement it.

(KENNETH INGHAM)

THAILAND

Area: 513,115 sq km (198,115 sq mi)
Population (2001 est.): 61,251,000
Capital: Bangkok
Chief of state: King Bhumibol Adulyadej
Head of government: Prime Ministers Chuan Leekpai and, from February 9, Thaksin Shinawatra

Thailand's national elections on Jan. 6, 2001—the first held under the new code of conduct mandated by the 1997 constitution—delivered a resounding victory to Thaksin Shinawatra's newly formed Thai Rak Thai Party, which took 248 of the 500 parliamentary seats. This gave Thaksin an overwhelmingly powerful role under the country's coalition-dominated political traditions. The New Aspiration Party of former prime minister Chavalit Yongchaiyudh and the Chart Thai Party of former prime minister Banharn Silapa-archa joined with Thai Rak Thai, and the cabinet was sworn in by King Bhumibol Adulyadej on February 17. The delay was caused by the independent Election Commission, which disqualified 62 winners from various parties and ordered new elections for those seats on January 29. Chavalit was appointed minister of defense, but Banharn declined a portfolio. The powerful post of interior minister went to little-known Thaksin associate Purachai Piumsombun, who promptly declared his intention to curb the excesses of the kingdom's vibrant nightlife. Another close associate of Thaksin, Somkid Jatusripitak, was given the Finance Ministry.

Thaksin, a billionaire telecommunications tycoon (*see* BIOGRAPHIES), campaigned on a populist platform. He promised to create a development fund for each of the country's 70,000 villages. Farmers were to be given a three-year debt moratorium. Virtually free health care was to be offered at state hospitals. In addition, 1,350,000,000,000 baht ($30,000,000,000) in bad debts from state and private banks was to be bought up by a new agency. These measures were steered through the parliament but were fiercely opposed by the opposition Democrat Party amid doubts cast by economists. Minutes be-

AP/Wide World Photos

Thai soldiers use bamboo sticks to hack opium poppies near the Myanmar border on January 24.

fore Thaksin was to board a domestic flight at Bangkok's airport on March 3, an explosion destroyed the aircraft. Thaksin was unharmed. Attempted assassination was at first assumed, but the U.S. National Transportation Safety Board declared the blast to have been a fuel-tank accident.

The National Countercorruption Commission on April 3 brought a charge against Thaksin before the Constitutional Court, accusing him of having understated his wealth in a mandatory assets declaration. On August 3 the court ruled 8–7 in the prime minster's favour. Meanwhile, the Election Commission completed its probe of the 2000 Senate election and ousted 10 senators, including the speaker. In new elections on April 21, only two of the senators were reelected. Addiction to methamphetamine drugs became so rampant in Thailand that death penalties were handed down to large numbers of traffickers, and tensions mounted with Myanmar (Burma), where many illicit drug factories were located. Financial and sexual scandals involving leading Buddhist clergy, including a monk revered by Thaksin, led to calls for a thorough overhaul of the tradition-bound ecclesiastic hierarchy. After the September 11 terrorist attacks in the U.S., Thailand adopted a studied neutrality, fearful of unrest among the Malay-speaking Muslims in its southern border provinces.

(ROBERT WOODROW)

TOGO

Area: 56,785 sq km (21,925 sq mi)
Population (2001 est.): 5,153,000
Capital: Lomé
Chief of state: President Gen. Gnassingbé Eyadéma
Head of government: Prime Minister Gabriel Agbéyomé Kodjo

On Jan. 30, 2001, after months of negotiations, the government announced plans to hold new parliamentary elections on October 14. In 1999 opposition parties had charged the government with fraud (following the disputed 1998 presidential election) and boycotted the parliamentary elections. On February 23 the findings of a joint Organization of African Unity–UN report on the conduct of the 1998 presidential election revealed that the government had systematically violated human rights. Fearing that the newly announced elections would be postponed, thousands of supporters of the main opposition party, the Action Committee for Renewal (CAR), took to the streets of the capital the following day in protest. Police, using tear gas and truncheons, broke up the demonstration.

On June 5 senior journalist Lucien Messan was convicted of having published "falsehoods" about alleged killings that took place during the 1998 presidential election campaign. He was sentenced to 18 months' imprisonment.

Further controversy erupted in August when CAR leader Yawovi Agboyibo was sentenced to six months' imprisonment for having defamed Prime Minister Gabriel Abéyomé Kodjo. On August 11 riot police dispersed a large demonstration demanding Agboyibo's release. A proposed constitutional amendment that would enable President Eyadéma to stand for a third five-year term in 2003 brought new protests and threats of strong action from the opposition to prevent Africa's longest-serving leader (34 years) from extending his tenure. On August 31 Eyadéma announced that he would respect the constitution and step down at the end of his term. Nevertheless, on October 5 the electoral commission, citing insufficient time for preparation, announced that legislative elections would be postponed. The government seized issues of independent newspapers several times during the year.

(NANCY ELLEN LAWLER)

TONGA

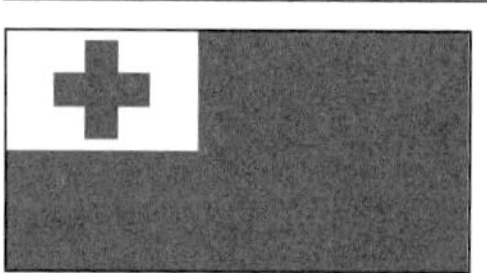

Area: 750 sq km (290 sq mi)
Population (2001 est.): 101,200
Capital: Nuku'alofa
Head of state and government: King Taufa'ahau Tupou IV, assisted by Prime Minister of Privy Council Prince 'Ulukalala Lavaka Ata

A major political and financial scandal brought Tonga to international attention in 2001. More than $20 million from Tonga's trust fund was lost following its investment in a Nevada-based "viatical" scam that involved, in effect, gambling on the death dates of 16 terminally ill patients in the U.S. The trust invested in the scheme on the advice of American speculator Jesse Bugdonoff, who had also persuaded Tonga's king to appoint him court jester. The lost funds were part of $30.7 million raised more than a decade earlier from the sale of passports and citizenship to foreign nationals—mostly Hong Kong Chinese but also former Philippine president Ferdinand Marcos and his family. The trustees responsible for the investment included then prime minister Baron Vaea, Deputy Prime Minister Tevita Tupou, and Minister of Education Tutoatasi Fakafanua. The latter two resigned in September at the request of the regent, Princess Pilolevu, who was acting for King Taufa'ahau Tupou IV. He was in Auckland, N.Z., for medical tests; the government denied news stories that the 82-year-old king was near death. Meanwhile, investigations into the investment scheme continued.

Air transport within Tonga and to major international links in Australia, New Zealand, and Fiji was disrupted by the grounding in March for safety reasons of Royal Tongan Airlines. In July consumer protection legislation was enacted. On New Year's Eve, Tonga, and the Vava'u group expecially, were struck by Cyclone Waka.

(BARRIE MACDONALD)

TRINIDAD AND TOBAGO

Area: 5,128 sq km (1,980 sq mi)
Population (2001 est.): 1,298,000
Capital: Port of Spain
Chief of state: President Arthur Napoleon Raymond Robinson
Head of government: Prime Minister Basdeo Panday

The unexpected outcome (an 18–18 parliamentary seat tie) of the general election called on Dec. 10, 2001, in Trinidad and Tobago after a United National Congress (UNC) government lost its majority in the House of Representatives created uncertainty for a period of time. The two party leaders, UNC's Basdeo Panday and the People's National Movement's (PNM's) Patrick Manning, agreed to let chief of state Pres. Arthur Robinson settle the issue. Robinson opted for Manning, a choice that did not go down well with Panday, who, at year's end, was calling loudly for a fresh election within six months.

AP/Wide World Photos

Dhanraj Singh (centre), former minister of the local government in Trinidad and Tobago, is escorted to court in Port of Spain on February 20 to answer charges for the 1999 murder of a former local government councillor.

In January 2001, for the first time since the Tobago House of Assembly (THA) was established in 1980, the PNM had wrested control of the THA from the National Alliance for Reconstruction (NAR). In February Dhanraj Singh, the former minister of local government, was charged with the murder of a former UNC local government councillor, Hansraj Sumairsingh. At year's end his trial was still under way.

Local Muslim leader Yasin Abu Bakr, who had led a short-lived insurrection in 1990, denied in September that he had any connection with wanted terrorist Osama bin Laden. As with other areas in the Caribbean, Trinidad and Tobago had been on heightened alert since the terrorist attacks in the U.S. on September 11. (DAVID RENWICK)

TUNISIA

Area: 164,150 sq km (63,378 sq mi)
Population (2001 est.): 9,828,000
Capital: Tunis
Chief of state: President Gen. Zine al-Abidine Ben Ali
Head of government: Prime Minister Mohamed Ghannouchi

Tunisia's human rights record was again the subject of international concern during 2001. In January veteran activist Moncef Marzouki, spokesman for the National Council for Liberties in Tunisia (CNLT), was imprisoned for one year. He had already been banned from foreign travel and had lost his professorship at the University of Sousse. His defense team walked out in protest over trial procedure—as did lawyers at proceedings in February against the Tunisian League for Human Rights after its leadership was suspended. Saida, the sister of Taoufik Ben Brik, and Sihem Ben Sédrine, CNLT spokesperson and editor of the on-line magazine *Kalima*, were arrested in June after allegedly having criticized the government during an appearance on the London-based Arab television station Al Mustaquilla; international pressure, however, ensured their speedy release.

In an open letter to Pres. Zine al-Abidine Ben Ali, Tunis judge Mokhtar Yahyaoui protested the harassment and official intimidation he had experienced. After international protest he was reinstated to the bench on August 2, but concerns over governmental judicial interference continued throughout the year. The president, in response to pressure from abroad, agreed to an early release from an eight-year sentence for veteran protester Nejib Hosni. President Ben Ali also promised to improve human rights observance, and a slightly more liberal press law was introduced in August. Human Rights Watch, however, continued to condemn the government for its human rights record; Tunisia had more than 1,000 political prisoners, and for the fourth year running, it was listed as one of the 10 countries most hostile to a free press.

Though the constitution limited the president to three terms in office, it seemed likely that it would be amended and that Ben Ali would run again in 2004, especially when the central committee of the governing Democratic Constitutional Rally called on him in September to run again. The cabinet was changed twice, in January and October, apparently to bring in younger talent, although veterans controlled the foreign affairs, defense, and interior portfolios. Foreign Minister Habib Ben Yahia visited London shortly after the September terrorist attacks in the U.S. to argue once again of the danger of Tunisian Islamist dissidents abroad and to call for the extradition of the an-Nahda ("Renaissance Party") leadership there.

Tunisia's economic progress continued unabated. Gross domestic product grew an estimated 6% in 2001 despite an ongoing drought. Tourism rose in 2000 by 3.5%, and direct foreign investment was up by 144% to $768 million. Unemployment, however, remained stubbornly high at 15.6%. The privatization program forged ahead; 35 of 41 firms completed privatization, with an average 5% improvement in their turnover. (GEORGE JOFFÉ)

TURKEY

Area: 779,452 sq km (300,948 sq mi)
Population (2001 est.): 66,229,000
Capital: Ankara
Chief of state: President Ahmet Necdet Sezer
Head of government: Prime Minister Bulent Ecevit

The financial crisis that struck Turkey in November 2000 worsened in 2001. Financial markets tumbled in February after Pres. Ahmet Necdet Sezer accused Prime Minister Bulent Ecevit of obstructing corruption inquiries involving government ministers. The Turkish lira, which had been pegged to targeted inflation under the program arranged with the International Monetary Fund (IMF) at the end of 1999, was allowed to float on February 22. By the end of the year, it had depreciated by 114% year-on-year. A number of banks failed and had to be taken over by the state. The gross national product dropped by 8% in the first nine months of the year; industrial production decreased by 14% by the end of November; imports were down by 25% (though exports rose 13%) by the end of October. Consumer prices surged 68% year-on-year by the end of December. Demonstrations by shopkeepers, tradesmen, and public employees over price rises and the sharp contraction in employment took place without incident. Calls by business associations for the government's resignation or for a change of economic policy also had little impact, and the draft budget for 2002 submitted to the parliament in October maintained a restrictionist stance by calling for a primary surplus of 6.5%.

On March 2 Kemal Dervis, vice president of the World Bank in charge of the Middle East and North Africa, was appointed minister of state in charge of the economy. He secured additional funding from the IMF for a revised program. Although some $19 billion was secured from international financial institutions, the government's ability to service its domestic debt, swollen by bank takeovers, continued to depend on foreign help. In mid-November, however, the IMF signaled that it would approve a rescue loan to bridge a $10 billion financing gap. As a result, market confidence increased at the end of the year.

The campaign against corruption and accusations of foot-dragging in implementing the IMF program led to the resignation of several ministers. Nonetheless, the ruling coalition—made up of Ecevit's Democratic Left Party, Devlet Bahceli's Nationalist Action Party, and Mesut Yilmaz's Motherland Party—retained a solid majority of seats (338) in the 550-member single-chamber Turkish Grand National Assembly. In June the Islamist Virtue Party (FP) was banned by the constitutional court, and 2 of its 101 MPs were disqualified for engaging in activities against the secular character of the state. The remaining Islamist deputies divided between two parties: the Felicity Party, headed by former FP leader Recai Kutan, and the Justice and Development Party, established in August by former Istanbul mayor Recep Tayyip Erdogan. The courts had yet to decide whether Erdogan's former conviction for antisecularist pronouncements barred him from political office, however.

Grounds for banning political parties were narrowed and wider freedoms recognized (including the freedom to use any language, and, therefore, the right to broadcast in Kurdish) under a package of constitutional amendments approved by the parliament in October. After a month of debate, the parliament ratified sweeping changes to a civil code dating to 1926. Women, who previously had not been given a voice concerning family life, including decisions about home or children, were granted equal roles in family matters. In addition, in the event of a divorce, women would be entitled under certain conditions to an equal division of marital property and assets, not just the properties that were in both names. The new code would be effective Jan. 1, 2002.

After the September 11 terrorist attacks in the U.S., Turkey—the only Muslim nation belonging to NATO—agreed immediately that Article 5 of the NATO alliance should be invoked; Turkey opened its air space to U.S. and other allied military aircraft and allowed the use of the U.S. air base at Incirlik (near Adana in southern Turkey) for antiterrorist opera-

Turkish Pres. Ahmet Nacdet Sezer reviews a Pakistani honour guard upon his arrival in Islamabad on October 25.

Saeed Khan/AFP Worldwide

tions. On October 9 the parliament authorized the dispatching of Turkish troops abroad and the stationing of foreign troops on Turkish soil at the government's discretion. Only the two Islamist parties voted against the measure. Turkish diplomacy, which had long sought to persuade Western governments to deny facilities to Kurdish, Marxist, and Islamic fundamentalist terrorists seeking to subvert the regime in Turkey, went into action in support of the coalition. President Sezer traveled to Pakistan to strengthen the hand of Pres. Pervez Musharraf, and Foreign Minister Ismail Cem sought to gain support for the initiative at the summit meeting of the Organization of the Islamic Conference in Doha, Qatar, and from the Turkic republics of the former Soviet Union, which he toured in October.

In early November Turkey and Greece signed a landmark agreement that provided for the return by Greece of illegal Turkish immigrants. The deal significantly improved relations between the two countries and lessened fears by Greece that it would face an increased influx of refugees in the wake of the U.S. bombings in Afghanistan.

Sabiha Gokcen, Turkey's first woman military pilot and the adopted daughter of the republic's founder, Mustafa Kemal Ataturk, died on March 22. A few months earlier, an airport named for her had opened on the Asian shore of Istanbul. (ANDREW MANGO)

TURKMENISTAN

Area: 488,100 sq km (188,500 sq mi)
Population (2001 est.): 4,462,000
Capital: Ashgabat
Head of state and government: President Saparmurad Niyazov

The rapid turnover of personnel in government posts in Turkmenistan that had begun in 2000 accelerated in 2001. Ministers of both foreign affairs and defense were replaced. By the end of the year, few persons in top positions had held their jobs for more than a year. One of the most significant changes was the concentration of power in the hands of the chairman of the National Security Committee (KNB), who was appointed deputy prime minister responsible for defense, law enforcement, and foreign affairs as well as the president's special adviser on legal matters. In January the KNB received a major infusion of new personnel from other law-enforcement agencies.

In February Pres. Saparmurad Niyazov presented the People's Council with a draft of the *Ruhnama,* which he intended as a sort of moral code for the Turkmen people. Its final version, with additional material on the ideal Turkmen family, was completed for the 10th anniversary of Turkmenistan's independence in October.

Official pressure continued on small unregistered religious congregations, primarily Protestant, to stop holding religious services in private homes, although such activities did not violate the law. A decree requiring that foreigners pay the state insurance company $50,000 in order to marry a citizen of Turkmenistan brought sharp international criticism. The Turkmen authorities attempted to defend the decree, saying that it was intended to prevent marriages of convenience that ended in the Turkmen partner's being abandoned without means of support.

The planned summit of heads of state of countries bordering the Caspian Sea was postponed several times in the course of the year. The summit was intended to settle the issue of the division of the Caspian seabed, which was in urgent need of resolution because the littoral states wanted to exploit the sea's natural resources, especially its oil. As discussions continued through the year, the Turkmen position shifted. A major dispute resumed with Azerbaijan in May over Azerbaijani work in oil fields claimed by Turkmenistan. Meetings of experts from the two countries were unable to resolve the dispute, and in June Turkmenistan withdrew its ambassador to Baku. Talks in Ashgabat in July ended in mutual recriminations, with each side accusing the other of unreasonableness.

The Turkmen authorities denied that the regionwide drought was having any effect on the country's agriculture, but the official claims of record wheat harvests were discounted by citizens and international observers alike.

As a neutral state, Turkmenistan refused to allow its airspace or military facilities to be used for attacks on Afghanistan, but the president's agreement to permit transit of international humanitarian aid to Afghanistan was quickly acted upon by UN and other agencies. (BESS BROWN)

TUVALU

Area: 25.6 sq km (9.9 sq mi)
Population (2001 est.): 11,000
Capital: Government offices in Vaiaku, Fongafale islet, of Funafuti atoll
Chief of state: Queen Elizabeth II, represented by Governor-General Sir Tomasi Puapua
Head of government: Prime Ministers Lagitupu Tuilimu (acting), Faimalaga Luka from February 24, and, from December 14, Koloa Talake

Following the death of Prime Minister Ionatana Ionatana in December 2000, Lagitupu Tuilimu served as acting prime minister until Faimalaga Luka, a former civil servant, was elected in February 2001 to lead the government, but he lost office in December after a parliamentary vote of no-confidence. He was replaced by Koloa Talake, a former public servant and minister of finance. A referendum on the country's future constitutional status was scheduled to be held in early 2002.

The government's commercialization of its Internet domain—.tv had generated revenue of some $30 million in less than two years. Some funds were invested and, with aid donors, the government embarked on major infrastructure projects, including roads, outer-island electrification, and airport development; the .tv Corp. also became a major shareholder in Air Fiji, which would have the exclusive right to provide air service to Tuvalu for five years.

Internationally, the government continued to express concern over the implications of global warming for low-lying states and criticized Australia for its unwillingness to develop a systematic relocation scheme for Tuvalu residents in the event that Tuvalu's islands became uninhabitable. Scientific evidence, however, suggested that Tuvalu had changed little in eight years.

Though Tuvalu was admitted as the 54th member of the British Commonwealth of Nations in 2000, its formal induction was deferred when the October 2001 Commonwealth Heads of Government Meeting planned for Brisbane, Australia, was canceled following the terrorist attacks in the U.S. Tuvalu established its mission at the United Nations in New York City.

(BARRIE MACDONALD)

UGANDA

Area: 241,038 sq km (93,065 sq mi)
Population (2001 est.): 23,986,000
Capital: Kampala
Head of state and government: President Yoweri Museveni, assisted by Prime Minister Apolo Nsibambi

The last victim of the Ebola virus, which had ravaged northern districts of Uganda in the previous year, recovered in January 2001. A month later the epidemic was officially declared to be at an end; of the 426 people infected, 224 of them had died.

A presidential election was held on March 12. Though there were six candidates, including Pres. Yoweri Museveni, only one, Kiiza Besigye, a founding member of Museveni's National Resistance Movement (NRM) and a former close associate of the president, appeared to offer a serious challenge. Prior to the election Besigye's supporters underwent considerable harassment, and independent observers reported numerous cases of irregularities in the conduct of the election. Nevertheless, they concluded that these instances did not have any significant impact on the election outcome. Museveni captured 69.3% of the votes to Besigye's 27.8%. Relations between Uganda and Rwanda, its former ally in the war in the Democratic Republic of the Congo (DRC), worsened after allegations were made that Besigye's campaign had been financed by Rwanda, an accusation that was vehemently denied.

On April 16 a UN panel appointed to inquire into the illegal exploitation of the DRC's natural resources called upon the UN Security Council to use "strong measures, including sanctions" against Uganda, Rwanda, and Burundi for looting the DRC's mineral reserves. These charges appeared to carry no weight with aid donors.

Approval of Uganda's campaign against HIV/AIDS was reflected in the decision to locate an international treatment and training centre in Kampala. The work there would be overseen by a coalition consisting of the Academic Alliance for AIDS Care and Prevention in Africa, Uganda's Makerere University, and the Infectious Diseases Society of America.

Minister of Finance Gerald Sendawula presented his budget on June 14. His aim was to remedy the decline in Uganda's economic growth rate, which in 2000 had fallen below the estimated 7% owing to a rise in oil prices and a fall in the price of coffee, Uganda's chief export earner. A timely boost to Uganda's economic prospects was provided by the announcement that a consortium known as Eagle Drill, led by Canada's Heritage Oil Corp., had carried out a four-year study of the Semliki River Valley on the western border and had found indications that significant reserves of oil were located there. The consortium planned to carry out tests until January 2002 and to start drilling in Lake Albert in March of that year.

On June 26 parliamentary elections were held. Once again, with all the resources of the government at its disposal and with opposition groups forbidden to operate as parties, Museveni's "no-party" NRM won an overwhelming victory, claiming 230 of the 292 seats, including those to which candidates were indirectly elected by the army, by women, and by other selected groups.

(KENNETH INGHAM)

UKRAINE

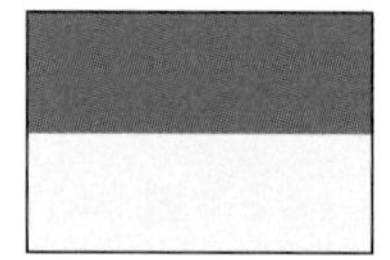

Area: 603,700 sq km (233,100 sq mi)
Population (2001 est.): 48,767,000
Capital: Kiev
Chief of state: President Leonid Kuchma
Head of government: Prime Ministers Viktor Yushchenko and, from May 29, Anatoly Kinakh

Ukraine in 2001 was marked by high-level political conflict and a notable improvement in economic performance but continuing social problems. On January 19 Pres. Leonid Kuchma dismissed Yuliya Tymoshenko, a deputy premier for the energy and fuel sector. Tymoshenko, a former colleague of disgraced former prime minister Pavlo Lazarenko, was arrested a month later and accused of having passed a bribe to Lazarenko. She was released on March 27, however, after a district court in Kiev annulled the original arrest warrant. Tymoshenko was widely regarded as a possible presidential contender when Kuchma's second term expired in 2004.

The president continued to face political fallout from the disappearance in September 2000 of dissident journalist Georgy Gongadze—who had been investigating Lazarenko—and from recordings that allegedly had captured Kuchma's voice sanctioning Gongadze's elimination. The tapes had been taken

Mikhailo Markiv/AFP Worldwide

Yuliya Tymoshenko, former deputy premier for the energy and fuel sector in Ukraine, receives flowers from well-wishers as she leaves prison in Kiev on March 27.

out of the country by a former presidential bodyguard and later made public. On January 10 officials stated that a headless corpse found outside Kiev in November 2000 was most likely that of the missing journalist. A protest movement arose, and tents pitched by activists on Kiev's main street had to be forcibly removed by the militia on March 1. The largest demonstration, on March 9—part of a new movement called Ukraine Without Kuchma—led to fierce clashes between demonstrators and the police close to the presidential administration building. By the summer the protests appeared to have died down somewhat. Several officials were dismissed in the aftermath of the Gongadze scandal, including Leonid Derkach, head of the Security Service, and Interior Minister Yury Kravchenko. In mid-April the U.S. granted political asylum to the bodyguard as well as to Gongadze's widow and two children.

The political turmoil continued when, on April 26, the parliament passed a vote of no-confidence in Prime Minister Viktor Yushchenko, probably the most pro-Western figure in Kuchma's cabinet. The parliamentary resolution, which was proposed by the Communist faction and passed 263–69, also accused the cabinet of having failed to ameliorate the economic situation. Yushchenko was replaced by Anatoly Kinakh, who subsequently formed an electoral bloc called Our Ukraine to contest the 2002 parliamentary elections. It remained unclear whether this bloc was opposed to the continuation of the Kuchma presidency.

Economic performance in Ukraine improved in the first half of 2001. Gross domestic product rose by 9% during 2001, following a growth figure of 6% for the year 2000. According to Prime Minister Kinakh, wages increased by almost 17% between January and July, and real income rose by 8.5%. Inflation remained at about 6%, and although the state debt had fallen, it continued to exceed the 50 billion hryvnia (about $9.4 billion) mark. The improved economic performance might be linked to the expansion of Russian business enterprises into Ukraine, but it had not yet offset the general decline in living standards that had characterized the independence period. By mid-August Ukraine had already surpassed its grain production target of 35 million metric tons for the 2001 harvest, which also added to the improved performance of the agricultural sector over the year 2000.

In early February Ukraine dismantled its last Tu-160 strategic bomber at a base near Kiev. The government accepted responsibility for the accidental downing of a Russian commercial airliner by a stray missile on October 4. The plane was flying from Israel to Russia but was hit while flying over the Black Sea. Defense Minister Oleksandr Kuzmuk resigned three weeks later over the incident, and he was replaced by Chief of Staff Volodymyr Shkidchenko on a temporary basis.

Pope John Paul II visited Ukraine in the summer and, in beatification ceremonies in the city of Lviv, paid tribute to some 27 Greek Catholic priests who were victims of the Soviet secret police in the early postwar years. The pontiff also tried to reconcile the Orthodox and Catholic factions in Ukraine. In the social sphere, Médicins sans Frontières (Doctors Without Borders) sponsored an AIDS-awareness campaign in March on the heels of an announcement that over 250,000 Ukrainians were HIV-positive, the highest rate per capita in the countries of the former U.S.S.R.

(DAVID R. MARPLES)

UNITED ARAB EMIRATES

Area: 83,600 sq km (32,280 sq mi)
Population (2001 est.): 3,108,000
Capital: Abu Dhabi
Chief of state: President Sheikh Zaid ibn Sultan an-Nahayan
Head of government: Prime Minister Sheikh Maktum ibn Rashid al-Maktum

On March 13, 2001, the U.A.E. Offsets Group, a government agency, signed a $3.5 billion agreement with Qatar to develop natural gas from Qatar's North Field and import it by a 350-km (217-mi) undersea pipeline to Abu Dhabi and Dubayy emirates. Though the American company Enron and the European firm TotalFinaElf were the original partners in this "Dolphin" project, Enron withdrew in May. Qatar's gas, which was expected to flow by 2004 or 2005, would meet important United Arab Emirates economic needs and help to solidify an already strong political relationship.

Meanwhile, the U.A.E. became the number-one trader among Persian Gulf states, surpassing even Saudi Arabia, due primarily to a high level of reexports, notably textiles, electronics, and gold. One-quarter of U.A.E. imports were reexported, and Iran was a major customer. Among all Arab states, the U.A.E. became the number one importer and the number two exporter. In addition, it ranked second (behind Qatar) in per capita income. The U.A.E. also led the Arab world in Internet use.

In July 2001 a high-level official U.A.E. delegation led by Minister of State for Foreign Affairs Sheikh Hamdan ibn Zayid, a son of the president, visited Tehran to congratulate Mohammad Khatami on his reelection as president of Iran. The visit was also symbolic politically—it was the first group of senior emissaries to arrive in Iran in nearly a decade. Though the U.A.E.-Iranian dispute over the islands of Abu Musa and the two Tunbs continued, the atmosphere and public rhetoric improved.

(WILLIAM A. RUGH)

UNITED KINGDOM

Area: 244,101 sq km (94,248 sq mi)
Population (2001 est.): 59,953,000
Capital: London
Chief of state: Queen Elizabeth II
Head of government: Prime Minister Tony Blair

Domestic Affairs. In 2001 Tony Blair, the United Kingdom's prime minister since 1997, confirmed his place as the towering figure in British politics both by leading the Labour Party to its second successive landslide election victory (*see* Sidebar) and by winning overwhelming political and public support for his international role in the fight against terrorism following the terrorist attacks in the United States on September 11.

Blair's year had started less auspiciously, with two major shocks. On January 24 he dismissed Peter Mandelson as Northern Ireland secretary. Mandelson had been accused of giving misleading information about his contacts with two controversial Indian businessmen, the Hinduja brothers, over their applications for British passports. For more than a decade, Mandelson had been one of Blair's closest political associates. Following Mandelson's earlier resignation in December 1998, Blair had provoked criticism by restoring his colleague to the cabinet just 10 months later. On March 9 the report of an official inquiry into the affair cleared Mandelson of any impropriety in his dealings with the Hindujas. It was too late for the former minister, however, and Mandelson acknowledged that his future lay outside the ranks of government.

By this time Blair was engulfed in a more enduring domestic crisis. On February 20 the U.K.'s first case of foot-and-mouth disease in 20 years was diagnosed among pigs at an abattoir in Essex, 64 km (40 mi) northeast of London. (*See* AGRICULTURE: *Special Report.*) It turned out that the disease had spread to many parts of the U.K. At its peak in March, over 40 new cases a day were being confirmed. For a while, town dwellers were advised to stay away from the countryside, particularly the normally popular—and heavily infected—tourist destinations of Devon, in the southwest of England, and the Lake District, in the northwest. As a result, much of rural

A pub owner in Oldham, Eng., surveys damage to her establishment that occurred during race riots in the city in late May.

Britain suffered a double loss—the destruction of millions of pigs and sheep in the infected areas and the short-term collapse of tourist income. The rest of Britain, notably London, also suffered a loss of income as overseas tourists, especially from the U.S., decided not to go to the U.K. for the time being.

So intense was the crisis that Blair took the unprecedented step (for peacetime) of obtaining parliamentary approval to postpone for five weeks local elections due to be held on May 3. This was also the widely expected date for the general election, which was postponed until June 7. By late April the number of new cases had declined to fewer than 20 a day, but the disease lingered through the summer. By September the total number of infected farms had passed 2,000, which made it the worst foot-and-mouth outbreak on record. During the last three months of the year, however, no new cases were reported, and the outbreak was officially declared to be over by year's end.

Following Labour's reelection on June 7, Blair made a number of changes to his cabinet. He promoted David Blunkett (*see* BIOGRAPHIES) from education secretary to home secretary, moved Jack Straw from home secretary to foreign secretary, and demoted Robin Cook from foreign secretary to leader of the House of Commons (a position that mainly involved managing day-to-day government business in Parliament). John Prescott and Gordon Brown retained their positions as deputy prime minister and chancellor of the Exchequer, respectively. A record 7 of the 23 members of Blair's new cabinet were women.

The front ranks of the Conservative Party took longer to sort out. At 7:30 AM on June 8, as the scale of his party's election defeat became clear, William Hague announced his intention to resign as party leader. Five candidates stood in the contest to succeed him. Following two early rounds of voting, in July three candidates remained: Kenneth Clarke, the former chancellor, who argued that the Conservatives needed to become more centrist and pro-European; Michael Portillo, the former defense secretary and onetime right-winger, who argued that the party should be less authoritarian and socially more liberal; and Iain Duncan Smith (*see* BIOGRAPHIES), who had no government experience and who retained his right-wing, anti-European Union (EU) views. On July 17, 59 Conservative MPs voted for Clarke, 54 for Duncan Smith, and 53 for Portillo.

Clarke and Duncan Smith went forward to a runoff ballot in which, for the first time, the party's 320,000 local members decided the victor. The result was announced on September 13. On a 79% turnout, Duncan Smith defeated Clarke 61–39%. Clarke and Portillo both declined to serve in Duncan Smith's shadow cabinet, as did a number of other prominent Conservative MPs, fearing that the party would be too right-wing for them. Duncan Smith's first major act was to give Blair full support in his policy toward terrorism. As a result, normal political contest was placed in abeyance, as were all attempts to make an early assessment of Duncan Smith's skills as a partisan opposition leader.

On the night of May 26, the U.K.'s generally good relations between its different racial groups were jolted by street battles between groups of whites and Asians in the northern city of Oldham. In the days that followed, riots took place in Leeds, Burnley, and Bradford. Although the riots subsequently died down, they provided a grim reminder that all was not well, especially in northern inner-city areas that contained significant amounts of poverty, bad housing, and unemployment.

On November 8 Henry McLeish resigned as Scotland's first minister following allegations that he had improperly claimed £36,000 (£1 = about $1.42) in office expenses while he was a member of Parliament at Westminster. On November 22 Jack McConnell, Scotland's education minister, became the country's new first minister, following his election as the new leader of Scotland's Labour Party.

The Economy. In common with much of the world, the British economy experienced a slowdown in 2001, starting in the summer but becoming more severe after September 11. At 2%, however, the growth recorded for the year as a whole compared well with most other industrialized countries. Before September most service sectors prospered, although the tourist-related businesses in parts of the U.K. were badly affected by the foot-and-mouth disease outbreak, which reduced access to the countryside during the spring and the early summer months. Airlines and hotels suffered in the immediate aftermath of the terrorist attacks in the U.S. in September. Many manufacturers, however, found it hard to increase sales, especially exports, at a time when the pound sterling was widely regarded as overvalued against the euro, the EU's single currency, at around £ = €1.60 throughout the year.

By midyear, unemployment had fallen below 5% (according to the definition set by the International Labour Organization), but then it started to rise gradually as the effects of the economic slowdown made themselves felt. Inflation remained steady at 2–2.5%. This allowed the Bank of England to reduce its main "repo" rate in stages from 6% in January to 5% in July. Following the events of September 11, the bank authorized two further quarter-point reductions in quick succession, followed by an additional half-point reduction on November 8, to take the rate to 4%, its lowest since 1963. This helped to sustain consumer confidence as well as reduce the cost for home buyers. In addition, retail sales leading up to Christmas were well above those in 2000.

Speaking to Labour's annual conference on October 2, Blair held out the prospect of a referendum before the next election (to be held by May 2006 at the latest) on whether Great Britain should adopt the euro. He continued to say that the decision would depend on the achievement of five economic conditions, of which the most important was that there be sustained convergence between the economies of the U.K. and the 12 euro-zone countries.

In October Railtrack—a privatized company floated in 1996 to run Britain's railway tracks and stations—collapsed as the costs of improving safety in the wake of serious crashes in 1999 and 2000 spiraled beyond the company's capacity to fund improvements. This was the first failure of a major company established during the wave of privatizations in the 1980s and '90s. Stephen Byers, the transport secretary, announced that a new company would be established as a nonprofit trust to run the tracks and stations.

Foreign Affairs. As soon as the terrorist attacks took place on September 11, Blair committed Great Britain to full support of the United States. The prime minister agreed to deploy British military forces, including bombers and undercover troops. Blair and Straw engaged in intense diplomatic activity, in coordination with U.S. Pres. George W. Bush's administration, in order to maximize the coalition against the al-Qaeda terrorist group in Afghanistan. Between them in the weeks following September 11, Blair and Straw visited Russia, Pakistan, India, Oman, Egypt, Iran, Syria, Saudi Arabia, and Israel. In addition, they helped to secure NATO and EU support for military action against the terrorists. Blair's visit to Damascus in October to meet Syria's president, Bashar al-Assad, was the first in modern times by a British prime minister. Despite some embarrassment at a joint press conference—when Assad and Blair made clear their different views of what constituted "terrorism," especially in the context of the dispute between Israel and the Palestinians—their private

The British Election of 2001

On June 7, 2001, the U.K.'s Labour Party won a second consecutive landslide victory over the Conservatives. Although Labour's majority in Parliament was reduced fractionally, from 179 to 167 in the 659-seat House of Commons, this was still a massive victory by historical standards. It was larger than that achieved by any party in the 60 years prior to Labour's return to power in 1997.

Labour won 413 seats (6 fewer than four years earlier), while the Conservatives claimed 166 (a net increase of just one). The Liberal Democrats took 52 seats, 6 more than in 1997. This gave the House of Commons its highest number of third-party members since 1929. Labour's victory was less emphatic in terms of votes cast. The party's share of the total vote across the U.K. was 40.7% (down 2.5% from 1997), while the Conservatives won 31.7% (up 1%) and the Liberal Democrats tallied 18.3% (up 1.5%). (Smaller parties won 9.3% of the total vote and 28 seats.) Despite its huge majority in terms of seats, Labour's share of the popular vote was lower than that achieved by any other victorious party since 1974.

Labour's main achievement during the campaign was to consolidate its support among the United Kingdom's traditionally Conservative-voting middle classes. Such voters dominate the swing seats that tend to determine the outcome of general elections. Labour's success in managing the country's economy over the previous four years—with falling unemployment, low inflation, and the lowest interest rates for home buyers in 30 years—together with promises of significantly higher spending on health, education, and public transport in the years ahead proved decisive in retaining the support of these voters and hence almost all the seats the party had gained in 1997.

In contrast, the Conservatives were handicapped by past failings and an unpopular leader. Opinion polls found that most voters continued to blame the pre-1997 Conservative administration, rather than the post-1997 Labour government, for Britain's continuing problems, especially the inferior quality of its public services. Moreover, William Hague, who had been elected Conservative leader following the party's defeat in 1997, turned out to be a vote loser. He was a sharp, quick-witted debater in the House of Commons, but most voters watching him on television regarded him as too lightweight to become prime minister.

One feature of this election that shocked people from all parties was the sharp fall in turnout. Just 59% of registered electors cast their votes. This was 12 percentage points lower than in 1997 and by far the lowest general election turnout since the advent of universal adult suffrage in 1928. The decline of ideology and firm, class-based party loyalties, the lack of positive enthusiasm toward Labour, the continuing unpopularity of the Conservatives, and polls showing that Labour was certain to be reelected by a large majority were all cited as contributory reasons for the jump in the number of nonvoters.

(PETER KELLNER)

talks paved the way for fresh diplomatic moves, including those by the United States, to advance the peace process in the Middle East. These were subsequently disrupted, however, by continued suicide bombing raids organized by radical Palestinians and by reprisals by Israeli forces.

Blair received strong support for his antiterrorist strategy from the Conservatives and Liberal Democrats in the House of Commons, but a small minority of MPs from Blair's own Labour Party expressed opposition to military action. A substantially larger block of Labour (and also Liberal Democrat) MPs opposed Blair's willingness (announced by his media spokesman on May 2) to support the development by the U.S. of its proposed National Missile Defense system. The prime minister received widespread support, however, both within and beyond his party, for setting out an ambitious vision for global action beyond the fight against terrorism.

Northern Ireland. On October 23 the Irish Republican Army (IRA) announced that it had decommissioned a portion of its arsenal. Although no details were published, the Independent International Commission on Decommissioning (IICD) confirmed that "we have now witnessed an event—which we regard as significant—in which the IRA has put a quantity of arms completely beyond use. The material in question includes arms, ammunition, and explosives." The action was believed to have involved the injection of concrete into two IRA arms dumps in Ireland. Blair described the IRA's decision as "a very significant milestone." The following day John Reid, the Northern Ireland secretary, announced that some police and army watchtowers in Northern Ireland would be dismantled and that some terrorist escaped prisoners would be granted an amnesty. David Trimble, the leader of the Ulster Unionist Party (UUP), said his party would resume its place on the Northern Ireland Executive.

This rapid sequence of events revived the peace process at a critical time. For much of the year there had been deadlock, with the Unionists threatening to withdraw completely from the executive in protest against the IRA's refusal to start decommissioning its weapons and the IRA saying it would not be forced to act in response to Unionist ultimatums.

Trimble had to tread a narrow line between destroying the peace process and losing unionist support to the rival Democratic Unionist Party (DUP), which blamed him for conceding too much to the nationalists. The U.K. general election in June produced a shift in Northern Ireland, with its own distinct party structure, toward militancy. Among unionist parties the UUP lost 4 of its 10 seats, while the DUP gained 3 seats to end up with 5. Among nationalist parties the Social and Democratic Labour Party (SDLP) retained its three seats but, for the first time, saw its support overtaken by that of Sinn Fein, the political arm of the IRA, which doubled its representation to end up with four seats. Sinn Fein MPs, however, continued their refusal to take their seats in the House of Commons, as to do so would have required them to swear an oath of allegiance to the British crown.

On July 1 Trimble resigned as first minister in protest against the IRA's inaction; twice Reid suspended the Northern Ireland Executive for 24 hours—in August and September—in order to buy time. Under the terms of the 1998 Good Friday Agreement, such suspensions allowed a six-week breathing space without the need for more drastic action. After the September suspension, however, Reid warned that without a resumption of cooperation between unionists and nationalists, the peace process might collapse altogether.

Trimble threatened to provoke this very outcome if decommissioning had not started by October 25. As this deadline approached, the IRA came under mounting pressure to act. Two external events helped to tilt the balance of debate inside the IRA and Sinn Fein. The first was the capture of three IRA members in Colombia, where they were accused of forging links with the Revolutionary Armed Forces of Colombia (FARC) guerrillas who financed many of their operations by dealing in drugs. This embarrassed Sinn Fein, whose tough antidrug policies in Ireland had helped them gain popular support on low-income housing estates. Second, the September 11 terrorist attacks led to increased pressure from the United States on the IRA to give up its weapons. On September 19 the IRA offered to "intensify [its] engagement" with the IICD.

One month later, and just 48 hours before the Ulster Unionist deadline, the IICD reported that decommissioning had in fact taken place. This prompted the Unionists to agree to rejoin, and therefore effectively to revive, the executive and to nominate Trimble to resume his position as first minister. A minority within his own party, together with the whole of the rival DUP, opposed him, but he was supported by most of his party as well as the SDLP, Sinn Fein, and the small cross-community Alliance Party. On November 6 after four days of wrangling and legal maneuvers, the assembly reelected Trimble as first minister.

(PETER KELLNER)

A Protestant father and son stand on a railing in front of a large Loyalist mural in Belfast, N.Ire., on October 24.

AP/Wide World Photos

UNITED STATES

Area: 9,363,364 sq km (3,615,215 sq mi), including 204,446 sq km of inland water but excluding the 155,534 sq km of the Great Lakes that lie within U.S. boundaries
Population (2001 est.): 286,067,000; significant revision based on the 2000 census
Capital: Washington, D.C.
Head of state and government: Presidents Bill Clinton and, from January 20, George W. Bush

Resilience had been a fundamental element of the American character from colonial times, but in 2001 the United States' ability to recover from adversity was severely tested. Its national economy, weary from years as the engine of world growth, finally slipped into recession. An energy crisis threatened further disruption, producing major bankruptcies. Terrorist attacks on September 11 coupled with a subsequent public health scare sent shock waves across the nation; the dispirited American morale slowed economic activity further, and the U.S. was soon plunged into a distant Asian war against an implacable fundamentalist regime.

Within weeks, however, the country had righted its listing self-confidence. Security measures gradually began restoring trust in public institutions. A series of government economic measures, including 11 interest-rate reductions and substantial emergency spending, established a foundation under the rocky economy. The Taliban regime in Afghanistan was rapidly uprooted and dispersed by a devastating show of American military technology. By year's end the United States was on the road to recovery, its position as the world's economic, cultural, and military leader not only restored but burnished in a year of challenges.

Security Crisis. Authorities responded immediately to the September 11 events, bolstering safety measures at public buildings, upgrading screening at airports, freezing assets of groups with suspected terrorist ties, and detaining more than 1,000 noncitizens for questioning. The measures included such extraordinary steps as the granting of authority to air force generals to shoot down hijacked civilian airliners and a provision for wartime military tribunals to try suspected alien terrorists. Some measures prompted criticism from civil liberties groups, but public opinion polls showed that the measures were widely supported.

In a September 20 address to Congress, Pres. George W. Bush announced the creation of an Office of Homeland Security under former Pennsylvania governor Tom Ridge to coordinate the antiterrorism efforts of 40 federal agencies. (*See* BIOGRAPHIES.) Within days the new agency confronted a new threat when several employees of a tabloid newspaper publisher in Florida contracted anthrax, an infectious disease ordinarily confined to farm animals, via suspicious mail. Additional anthrax spores were soon discovered in a variety of places, including the offices of Senate Majority Leader Tom Daschle (*see* BIOGRAPHIES), post offices, and various news organizations. Most of the spores were traced to mail originating near Trenton, N.J., but a connection to the September 11 terrorism was never established. By year's end two forms of anthrax had killed 5 persons and sickened 14.

Congress approved a variety of measures to counter economic and security concerns following the terrorist attacks; $15 billion was appropriated to assist U.S. airline firms, including $5 billion in grants; lawmakers appropriated an immediate $40 billion in additional spending for a variety of causes, including stepped-up military activity and assistance to affected areas, such as New York City; and President Bush received authority to expend half of the funds at his discretion. Congress also authorized the use of force to respond to the attacks, provided for federal takeover of some 28,000 airport security workers, and approved an antiterrorism law that allowed expanded law-enforcement powers over money laundering, electronic and telephone eavesdropping, and detention of suspected terrorists.

By year's end the death toll from the attacks had been revised sharply downward. At one point unofficial estimates had projected up to 10,000 deaths in New York and 500 or more at the Pentagon near Washington. Authorities in December, while cautioning that the precise number of deaths might never be known, put the toll at nearly 2,900 in New York City, with an additional 189 at the Pentagon and 44 in Pennsylvania, where another hijacked plane crashed after passengers attempted to overpower the terrorists.

Domestic Issues. The September 11 events proved to be a critical turning point for President Bush and his administration. Bush was inaugurated in January after having lost the popular vote and enjoying the weakest mandate of any recent U.S. president. (*See* Sidebar.) Congress was nominally in Republican hands but was almost evenly divided. Bush surprised many observers by pushing an aggressively conservative agenda, including a 10-year, $1.6 trillion tax cut, expanded energy exploration, a faith-based social assistance initiative, and withdrawal from several international treaties.

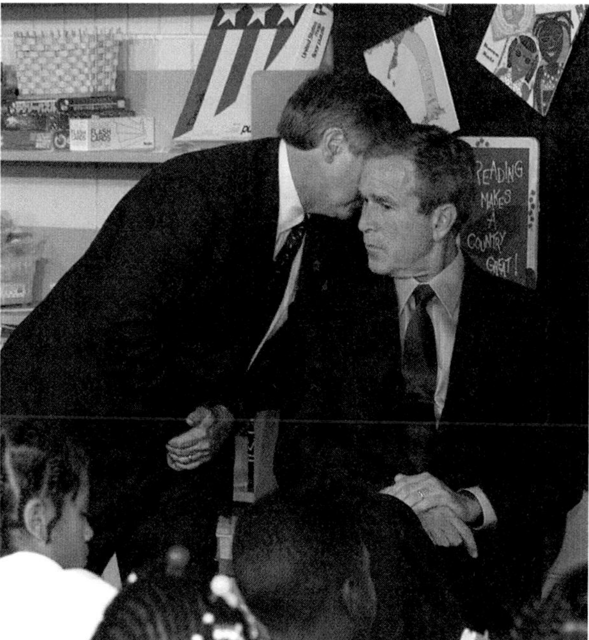

During a visit to an elementary school in Sarasota, Fla., on the morning of September 11, Pres. George W. Bush receives word of the terrorist attacks from his chief of staff, Andy Card.

AP/Wide World Photos

Firefighters and rescue/recovery personnel work at the World Trade Center site.

Mario Tama/Getty Images

Following compromise with congressional Democrats, Bush signed an 11-year, $1,350,000,000,000 tax reduction bill on June 7 that provided instant $300–$600 rebates to most taxpayers, reduced the four major marginal rates, repealed the estate tax, increased the child-care credit, and provided relief for married couples and incentives for savings.

In late May veteran Republican lawmaker Sen. James M. Jeffords of Vermont announced that he would leave the GOP and become an Independent caucusing with Senate Democrats. That turned the Senate, previously divided 50–50 but under Republican organization, over to a 50–49–1 configuration under Democratic control. Jeffords cited disappointment with conservative GOP policies. With Congress now officially divided along partisan lines, Bush's agenda bogged down over the summer, and the president, while still enjoying general popular support, was widely viewed as tentative and ineffective in his public appearances.

Within days of September 11, however, Bush had shed that image. He delivered a thoughtful eulogy to victims at the National Cathedral service in Washington, D.C., and won praise for his presence in an early visit to the World Trade Center site. Bush's September 20 speech to a special joint session of Congress received widespread acclaim for its eloquence and delivery and helped launch Bush's personal approval ratings in public opinion polls to record levels through the remainder of the year.

During the fall, measures responding to the terrorist assault were approved by Congress with only modest opposition, particularly legislation covering military preparedness and disaster relief. In the realm of ongoing domestic policy, however, entrenched partisan arguments stopped passage of numerous bills, including several that had been debated for years. Among legislation failing to pass Congress during 2001 were the president's energy security bill (which included oil exploration in an Alaskan wilderness area), campaign finance reform, fast-track trade-negotiation authority, Bush's faith-based social initiative, an agriculture subsidy bill, a federal patients' bill of rights, and a fiscal stimulus bill that administration partisans said was vital to the national economic recovery.

At year's end Congress did approve a compromise education-reform act cosponsored by Democratic Sen. Edward Kennedy of Massachusetts. The bill required for the first time annual reading and mathematics testing for students in grades three through eight nationwide. It also required school districts to close the gap between poor and middle-class achievement and mandated that consistently underperforming schools allot part of their federal financial assistance to tutoring or providing transportation to other schools. (*See* EDUCATION: *Special Report.*)

Debate over the wisdom and ethics of advanced scientific research grew in intensity during the year. The U.S. House of Representatives approved a bill banning cloning of humans from embryos and prohibiting creation of cloned embryos for research, but the Senate delayed the measure. Under pressure to take a position, President Bush announced in August that he would allow federal funding only for research on the approximately 60 colonies of embryo cells that had been already created, saying he did not believe taxpayer dollars should support further destruction of human embryos. A National Academy of Sciences panel quickly published a report detailing problems with the Bush position, and little was settled on the subject.

Recent FBI figures revealed that the incidence of serious crime had remained virtually unchanged following eight years of significant decline. The figures showed a modest 0.3% reduction in seven index crimes during the first half of 2001. On June 11 Timothy McVeigh (*see* OBITUARIES)—the main perpetrator of the 1995 Oklahoma City, Okla., bombing of the Alfred P. Murrah Federal Building that killed 168 persons—was executed at a U.S. prison in Terre Haute, Ind. It was the first federal execution since 1963. A second federal prisoner, Juan Raul Garza, convicted of three 1993 drug-related murders, was put to death eight days later in the same prison.

Republican businessman Michael Bloomberg (*see* BIOGRAPHIES) prevailed in the highest-profile election of 2001, the race to succeed Rudolph Giuliani as mayor of New York City. Bloomberg spent a record $69 million of personal funds on the campaign. The year's most bizarre political story involved the disappearance from Washington, D.C., of a 24-year-old government intern, Chandra Levy, shortly before she was to return home to Modesto, Calif. Her parents hired lawyers and investigators and turned a glaring media spotlight on their hometown congressman, Democratic Rep. Gary Condit, who eventually admitted to a "close relationship" with the missing woman. Levy remained missing at year's end, and Condit announced that he would launch an uphill bid for reelection.

The Economy. The national economic expansion ended with a whimper during 2001. A panel of the National Bureau of Economic Research (NBER) declared in November that the nation's economic growth had ended the previous March, exactly 10 years after it had started, which made it the longest-running expansion since the organization began keeping records in 1854. Government figures showed that gross domestic product had increased by a modest 1.2% in the first quarter and an anemic 0.3% in the second, followed by a 1.3% retraction in the third quarter. Though recessions had traditionally been declared after two consecutive quarters of negative growth, NBER economists, noting continued economic deterioration, cited other factors in their assessment.

The trauma of September 11 effectively kicked the national economy while it was down. The events further shook consumer confidence, which had been declining, and markedly reduced personal and business travel, entertainment expenditures, and other economic activity. The national jobless rate, which had bottomed at 3.9% in 2000, had started to climb early in the year; it jumped from 4.9% to 5.4% in October, the biggest one month jump in two decades. By December unemployment had soared to 5.8%, the highest level in six years. Another victim of the terrorist-exacerbated recession was the short-lived federal budget surplus: after a record $237 billion in black ink during fiscal 2000, the U.S. ended fiscal 2001 on September 30 with a fast-diminishing $127 billion surplus, with many fiscal 2002 projections anticipating a return to deficit spending.

Even so, the recession's impact was cushioned by several events. Fearing an overexuberant stock market and inflation, the nation's Federal Reserve System had nudged up interest rates six times in 1999–2000. In 2001, however, the Fed sharply reversed field and lowered its key federal funds rate on 11 occasions, from 6.5% to 1.75%, in a desperate attempt to revive the failing national economy. The actions provided a ripple effect that lowered borrowing costs across the board for credit cards, mortgages, and businesses. Additionally, as the recession reduced energy demand, oil prices began dropping worldwide, providing further relief to consumers. The nation's major automobile manufacturers began offering no-interest loans in a successful effort to maintain high demand, and new auto sales continued through the last months of 2001 at record levels. The federal government further contributed with cash tax rebates and at least $60 billion in emergency spending following the terrorist attacks.

By year's end some economists were predicting imminent resumption of national economic expansion. Two major measurements of consumer confidence were rising sharply in December. The Dow Jones Industrial Average, which had dipped as low as 8,235 in the wake of September 11, finished the year over 10,000 and rising. The national inflation rate dropped back to a modest 2.6%, and productivity gains remained strong, which led several economists to predict an end to the recession as the country put memories of the attacks behind it.

The recession helped avoid a widely predicted energy disaster in California and neighbouring states. As the year began, California was suffering under a mishandled deregulation of electricity that led to severe power shortages and the bankruptcy of a major state public utility. Rolling blackouts plagued the state during January, and many analysts predicted further outages and economic disruption during the summer, when air-conditioner use would be high. A combination of state government assistance to the utilities, a cool summer, upgrading of electrical distribution line efficiency, reduced usage due to recession and conservation, and the worldwide energy surplus largely prevented serious incidents.

During the height of the crisis, California Gov. Gray Davis denounced out-of-state energy companies for taking advantage of the state and its consumers, and he specifically named the Houston, Texas-based Enron Corp. Late in 2001 Enron—the seventh largest American corporation, with over $100 billion in revenue in 2000—filed for Chapter 11 bankruptcy protection. The company, listing $49.5 billion in assets, became the largest company in U.S. history to go under. The failure was only tangentially related to its long-running exploitation of deregulated markets for wholesale natural gas and electricity. Analysts discovered that key company officials, while operating largely unregulated marketplaces trading derivative energy contracts, were simultaneous running private off-book partnerships and profiting personally, even while they overstated Enron profits. The company's failure was particularly hard on employees, many of whom had retirement funds tied up in near-worthless company stock.

The world's leading software company, Microsoft Corp., avoided a court-ordered breakup by settling its antitrust case with the Bush administration Justice Department. The company had been found guilty of monopolistic practices in a case brought by the Bill Clinton administration and ordered divided into at least two parts. An appeals court panel in June confirmed that Microsoft had monopoly power but disqualified the original trial judge for injudicious comments outside the courtroom. After Microsoft allowed computer makers to disable some parts of its Windows operating system and replace them with software from other firms, the replacement

(continued on page 516)

Sen. James Jeffords (centre), who in late May switched his party affiliation from Republican to Independent, shown on June 5 with Democratic senators Ted Kennedy (left), Joseph Lieberman (second from right), and Christopher Dodd (right).

AP/Wide World Photos

The U.S. Census of 2000

by Eric Schmitt

AP/Wide World Photos

The 2000 census of the United States revealed a nation that had become ethnically and racially more diverse as cities and suburbs filled with new immigrants. It also showed that the migration from the Frost Belt to the Sun Belt was continuing. About 44% of the nation's 30.5 million foreign-born residents, or 13.3 million people, arrived in the U.S. in the 1990s. By 2000 immigrants constituted 11% of the country's population, the largest share since the 1930s, and nearly one in five Americans did not speak English at home. Overall, the nation's population grew by about 13% to 281.4 million.

The Hispanic population rose 58% in the last decade, which brought it into rough parity, or better, with African Americans as the country's largest minority. U.S. Census Bureau figures showed that the number of Hispanics, who have Spanish-speaking ancestry but may belong to any race, soared to 35.3 million from the 22.4 million in the 1990 census. By contrast, the number of African Americans increased by about 16% to 34.7 million from the 30 million counted in the 1990 census. Demographers had long anticipated that Hispanics would supplant African Americans as the nation's largest minority, but earlier census reports had forecast that this would not happen until 2005.

While Hispanics remained concentrated primarily in the Southwest, California, Florida, and New York, new immigrants from Mexico and Central America moved to states such as North Carolina, Georgia, and Iowa, where the Hispanic population was almost nonexistent a decade ago. Hispanics often became a mainstay in many low-paying, labour-intensive industries. In Atlanta, Ga., and Memphis, Tenn., for instance, they dominated the construction and landscaping trades. In eastern North Carolina they processed hogs. In Arkansas they plucked chickens.

In the 2000 census, for the first time, Americans were allowed to identify themselves as a member of more than one race, choosing from six racial categories; this option was taken by nearly seven million people, about 2% of the overall population. Demographers concluded that the growing waves of immigrants and the increasing numbers of interracial marriages accounted for this result. The new multiracial measurement was especially striking in regard to young people. For example, African Americans aged 17 and younger were nearly four times as likely as those 50 and older to identify themselves as belonging to more than one race.

By permitting people to choose an array of racial identities—white, African American, Asian, American Indian, Alaska native, Pacific islander, native Hawaiian, or "some other race"—the 2000 census presented a matrix of 63 racial categories, compared with 5 a decade ago. The American Indian category offered one of the more interesting glimpses into the census's new racial classification. The number of American Indians and Alaska natives who defined themselves by only that category grew by 26% in the past decade to 2.5 million. When, however, the number of people who said they were part Indian were added, the total ballooned to 4.1 million, a 110% increase since 1990.

The changing face of the U.S. was reflected in cities, suburbs, and rural areas. For the first time, nearly half of the nation's 100 largest cities were home to more African Americans, Hispanics, Asians, and other minorities than to non-Hispanic whites. While the population of the country's fastest-growing cities, such as Las Vegas, Nev., and Phoenix, Ariz., increased in all racial and ethnic categories, the vast majority of U.S. cities —71 of the top 100—lost non-Hispanic white residents. As whites left many urban cores in the 1990s for suburbs and beyond, the nation's largest gained 3.8 million Hispanic residents, a 43% increase from a decade ago. Many cities, including Boston, Los Angeles, and Dallas, Texas, would have lost population in the 1990s were it not for large gains in the number of Hispanics.

The mixture of white flight from urban downtowns and the influx of Hispanics, in particular, underscored the extent to which immigration and higher birthrates among the foreign-born had changed the complexion of cities, fueling a renaissance in some urban centres and forcing civic leaders to confront difficult decisions on how to cope with a new and fast-changing citizenry. Overall, the nation's largest cities grew nearly twice as fast in the 1990s as in the 1980s, with three out of every four urban centres gaining population. In the cities with more than 100,000 people, however, the growth was uneven. Reversing a 50-year

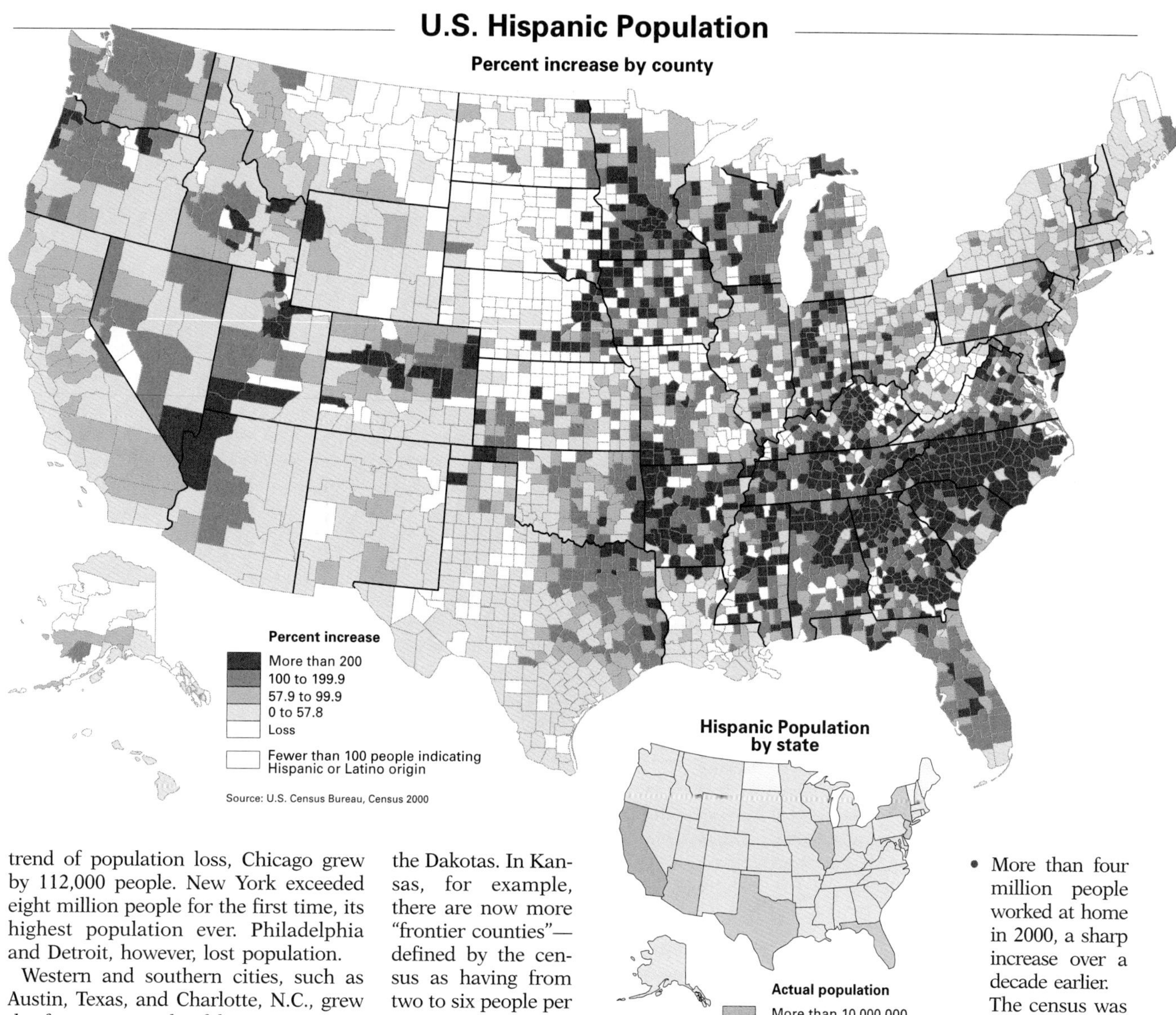

trend of population loss, Chicago grew by 112,000 people. New York exceeded eight million people for the first time, its highest population ever. Philadelphia and Detroit, however, lost population.

Western and southern cities, such as Austin, Texas, and Charlotte, N.C., grew the fastest, a result of booming economies and an influx of immigrants. Urban industrial centres in the Rust Belt, such as Cleveland, Ohio, and Pittsburgh, Pa., and such Middle Atlantic and Northeastern cities as Hartford, Conn., and Baltimore, Md., generally declined as jobs and people migrated elsewhere. A small but growing number of cities with declining populations, such as Pittsburgh and Philadelphia, began to embrace new strategies to attract immigrants to replenish shrinking neighbourhoods, fill labour shortages, and inject greater ethnic diversity into their communities.

Even as most cities were thriving in the 1990s, many rural areas, particularly in the Great Plains, continued to empty out. The Census Bureau found that 676 of the nation's 3,141 counties lost people. Most of the decline took place in wheat, ranching, and oil country in Texas, Oklahoma, Iowa, Nebraska, Kansas, Minnesota, and the Dakotas. In Kansas, for example, there are now more "frontier counties"—defined by the census as having from two to six people per square mile—than there were in 1890.

In a preview of official 2000 census data to be released in 2002 from the questionnaire known as the long form, the Census Bureau disclosed results of a test survey of 700,000 households. Highlights from that survey include the following:

- More than two million grandparents are rearing their grandchildren, the first time the Census Bureau has kept track of that statistic.
- In 2000, 82% of people aged 25 and older had graduated from high school and 25% had at least a bachelor's degree. In 1990 the figures were 75% and 20%, respectively.
- More than 90% of households owned a car, van, or truck in 2000, the highest share ever, and 18% owned three or more vehicles.
- More than four million people worked at home in 2000, a sharp increase over a decade earlier.

The census was not without political controversy. In March the Census Bureau decided against statistically adjusting the 2000 population tally. Several congressional Democrats and Democratic-leaning groups argued that adjusted figures should be used because the 2000 census, while touted as the most accurate in history, still missed millions of people, mainly racial minorities and renters, and double-counted others, mainly whites and homeowners. At stake was what population counts would be used to allocate federal aid and redraw congressional and other legislative districts. About $185 billion a year was distributed on the basis of population counts from the 1990 census.

Eric Schmitt is national immigration and census correspondent for the New York Times.

(continued from page 513)
judge approved a settlement allowing the company to stay intact.

Foreign Policy. Within hours of the September 11 attacks, the Bush administration began preparations for a military assault on the al-Qaeda network in Afghanistan and started assembling international support for the mission. The partners took pains to assure that it was international terrorists and their protectors who were targets, not Islam. In the end some 60 countries offered tangible assistance, including Muslim Pakistan as well as Russia, which provided access to military bases in nearby Tajikistan. The U.S. doubled its military presence in the region to 50,000 during the month the hostilities began.

Demands that the Afghan Taliban regime locate and turn over Osama bin Laden (*see* BIOGRAPHIES) to international forces were met by evasion, then refusal. U.S.-dominated military action started with cruise missile, bomber, and fighter jet attacks throughout Afghanistan on October 7, followed by continued military operations in support of the Northern Alliance Afghan resistance fighters. At the beginning U.S. preparations were met by a hailstorm of criticism and doubts; critics suggested that Americans would be repeating Russian mistakes in Afghanistan or would be bogged down in a Vietnam-style Asian conflict. Instead, the operation was largely completed in 11 weeks as the Taliban was driven from power, replaced by a UN-brokered coalition.

In his September 20 congressional speech, President Bush declared, "From this day forward, any nation that continues to harbor or support terrorism will be regarded by the U.S. as a hostile regime." By year's end neither Bin Laden nor Taliban leader Mullah Mohammad Omar had been located. While continuing to search for Taliban and al-Qaeda leadership in the area, the U.S. turned its attention toward other countries facilitating terrorist activity. The ongoing confrontation with rogue organizations and states, especially those believed to be developing chemical, biological, or nuclear weapons, continued to dominate world affairs.

Cooperation on Afghanistan was a highlight of improved U.S. relations with Russia. In mid-November, Russian Pres. Vladimir Putin visited Washington and Bush's ranch in Crawford, Texas. Talks appeared promising when Putin said he would consider allowing the U.S. to test a missile defense system even though the test would be an apparent violation of the 1972 Anti-Ballistic Missile (ABM) Treaty, provided the two countries could agree on nuclear weapons reductions. Bush announced that the U.S. would slash nuclear warheads from 7,000 to the 1,700–2,200 range over the next decade, and Putin hinted at similar reductions in the Russian 5,800-warhead arsenal. The two were never able to hammer out an agreement on the antimissile test, however, and in December Bush announced that the U.S. would withdraw from the treaty and thereby leave the way open for missile defense testing.

The long-running U.S. effort to broker a lasting peace in the Middle East appeared to collapse during the year. Talks between Israeli and Palestinian leaders sponsored by former president Clinton had fallen apart in late 2000, producing violence that escalated during 2001. After a period of inaction, the Bush administration attempted to revive talks but without success, and after September 11 Israeli advocates successfully likened Palestinian bombing and assaults to the terrorist attacks in the U.S. President Bush pointedly declined to condemn Israeli military responses against the Palestinian population and refused to meet with Palestinian leader Yasir Arafat.

Free-trade advocates scored a major advance at an international meeting in Doha, Qatar, when major countries agreed to begin a new three-year round of trade negotiations. The talks would be aimed at reducing agricultural trade barriers and industrial tariffs. The U.S. made concessions, putting its antidumping law under review in spite of opposition from American steel interests and agreeing that less-developed nations could override drug patents in the interests of public health. Most analysts declared that no new trade agreement could be negotiated, however, unless the U.S. Senate voted fast-track negotiating authority to President Bush. The U.S. normalized trade relations with China during the year after having cleared the way for China's membership in the World Trade Organization.

During 2001 the focus of war concerns shifted to Asia, including Afghanistan. U.S. military efforts aggravated the decades-long conflict between India and Pakistan, and the two countries, both possessing nuclear weapons, were at the brink of war at year's end. Ironically, in an effort to encourage cooperation in the Afghan operation, the U.S. had lifted sanctions imposed on both countries following their 1998 nuclear tests. Problems with North Korea, one of the world's last communist regimes, continued to fester and led to periodic threats of war against the U.S. and its allies, including Japan.

The Bush administration's efforts to build a coalition to support military measures in Afghanistan reversed what critics had labeled U.S. rejection of international solutions to world problems, including its refusal to sign the ABM Treaty and the Comprehensive Test Ban Treaty. Earlier in the year the Bush administration had officially rejected the Kyoto Protocol, suggesting that the anti-global-warming treaty would affect the global economy disproportionately. In late summer the U.S. sent a delegation to the UN World Conference Against Racism in Durban, S.Af., but walked out in protest against proposed conference resolutions calling for reparations to blacks for slavery and for condemnation of Israel for alleged racism against Palestinians. (DAVID C. BECKWITH)

DEVELOPMENTS IN THE STATES

After close to a decade of uninterrupted sunny economic times, states were plunged into multiple new problem areas at the end of 2001. Most states started modest belt-tightening early in the year as the slackening national economy produced slow revenue growth with additional outlays remaining modest. Following the September 11 terrorist attacks, however, matters worsened dramatically, with revenues dropping as travel, commerce, incomes, and other state taxation sources were severely and adversely affected.

States also scrambled to revamp public safety and health security measures in the national emergency, beefing up security in public places and overhauling outdated emergency procedures. At year-end virtually all states were facing budget shortfalls for the year—either higher expenditures or lower revenues, or both—and many began spending cutbacks to balance their budgets. The problems complicated the always-thorny relationship between the federal government and the states over which level of government should have the authority and responsibility for handling aspects of the crisis.

All 50 states held regular legislative sessions during the year, and two dozen staged special sessions later, often to deal with budget and security problems. Democrats made gains in limited state elections, picking up governorships in New Jersey and Virginia previously held by Republicans and improving their status

Election Reform Debate in the U.S.

Amid calls for a radical overhaul of the U.S. electoral system, George W. Bush was inaugurated as president of the United States on Jan. 20, 2001. The 2000 presidential election exposed several deficiencies in the conduct of American elections: the possibility that a candidate could win more popular votes than his opponent and still lose the electoral college tally—Bush defeated Al Gore 271–266 despite winning 500,000 fewer votes nationwide; faulty and outdated election equipment—a General Accounting Office audit found that nearly three-fifths of voting sites had problems in 2000; a lack of uniform rules for election recounts; early and incorrect media projections; confusing ballot design, most notably in Florida, where possibly thousands of people were led to vote mistakenly for a candidate; and low voter turnout. As legislators throughout the U.S. debated election reform, by year's end media analyses of disputed ballots still showed the 2000 race too close to call.

Many proposed election reforms, such as the abolition of the electoral college and the creation of a national holiday for election day, were discarded quickly owing to a lack of support, though in early 2001 momentum in favour of reform suggested that major changes, such as a uniform national poll closing time, would be enacted by year's end. Of the more than 1,500 bills proposed in Congress and in all 50 states, however, few were enacted. Partisan wrangling hampered reform efforts early in the year. Receiving the most support were proposals to eliminate punch-card ballot systems, which had led to high rates of uncounted ballots and which tended to be concentrated in poorer areas, in favour of optical scanning systems. Some studies found that as many as two million votes were uncounted nationwide because of faulty election equipment. Despite the efforts of the bipartisan National Commission on Federal Election Reform, led by former presidents Gerald Ford and Jimmy Carter, by May the election reform movement had stalled in the U.S. Congress and in many states. In December, however, the House of Representatives overwhelmingly approved (362–63) a bill that provided funds to states to modernize election equipment and establish national voting standards, and at year's end many predicted that a compromise between the House and Senate would result in the enactment of election reforms in early 2002.

The most sweeping election reform package was adopted in Florida, the state that had endured a five-week standoff in the presidential election before Bush was declared the winner by a margin of only 537 votes after the Supreme Court halted a recount. On May 9 Florida Gov. Jeb Bush, the brother of the president, approved a uniform statewide ballot design and the elimination of punch cards in favour of optical scanners or other advanced technologies by 2002. The new law also established standardized procedures for the review of ballots during manual recounts—a key point of contention between the Gore and Bush camps. Nevertheless, the U.S. Commission on Civil Rights issued a report a few weeks later that criticized Florida election officials, finding them "grossly derelict" both before and during the November 2000 standoff. The commission's report, which was criticized by Republicans, also found that African Americans were 10 times more likely than white voters to have their votes uncounted and claimed that the reforms enacted in Florida would not entirely eliminate this disparity.

(MICHAEL LEVY)

Members of the Joint Selection Committee to Examine Election Issues study a sample ballot from a voting machine similar to ones used in Florida during the 2000 presidential election.

AP/Wide World Photos

in state legislatures. Entering 2002 the GOP would hold 27 governorships and the Democrats 21, with two independents. Party control of state legislatures was deadlocked, with Republicans and Democrats each controlling 17 states and 15 states under split control. (Nebraska had a nonpartisan unicameral legislature.)

Government Structures, Powers. Stung by criticism of 2000 election procedures, numerous states pursued reform measures early in 2001. (*See* Sidebar.) Florida, Georgia, and Maryland approved sweeping reforms, including complete overhauls of voting equipment statewide. Seven states, including California, either banned or phased out punch-card ballots. Ohio, Nevada, Tennessee, and Virginia clarified what counts as a vote on a punch card; Colorado, Kansas, Virginia, and Washington set up new rules for recounts; and Colorado, Florida, Indiana, Iowa, Kansas, Oregon, and South Dakota either established or upgraded statewide voter-registration databases. A consensus on proper steps was slow in arriving, however, and political considerations in Congress prevented federal assistance or leadership for state election reform. By year's end the momentum for reform had largely dissipated.

A majority of state legislatures enacted new redistricting plans for U.S. Congress and state legislative districts following tabulation of the 2000 U.S. census. (*See* Special Report.) In a key 5–4 decision, the U.S. Supreme Court ruled that states may concentrate African Americans, Hispanics, or other minorities in specific districts as long as they do so for political, not racial, reasons.

Government Relations. The U.S. Supreme Court again bolstered state powers against federal encroachment, ruling 5–4 in separate civil rights cases involving Alabama that states may not be sued for discriminating against employees with disabilities or for policies that have a "discriminatory effect" on racial minorities. In a setback for states, however, the high court ruled 5–4 in a Massachusetts case that tobacco companies have a free-speech right to advertise their products;

the federal government had preempted the issue, leaving states virtually powerless to restrict tobacco promotion, the court said.

The proper division between state and national government responsibilities was at the centre of numerous other controversies during the year. As states scrambled to fund security and health programs made necessary after September 11, they looked to the federal government for assistance, with mixed results. New York state was pledged $20 billion in U.S. aid for extraordinary expenses related to the World Trade Center disaster, but assistance to less-affected states lagged behind their expenses.

In early November, U.S. Attorney General John Ashcroft moved to invalidate Oregon's assisted-suicide law on grounds that the federal Controlled Substances Act barred doctors from prescribing lethal drugs to dying patients. Oregon voters had twice approved a Death with Dignity law, and more than 70 patients had taken advantage of it since 1997. State authorities obtained a temporary court order effectively barring federal intervention.

Security. States moved quickly to address public health and safety concerns arising from September 11 and its aftermath. Some 35 states named security directors or created task forces to help prevent and deal with terrorism, particularly biological threats. Physical security around state capitols, transportation terminals, and public buildings was stepped up.

After it was revealed that the September 11 terrorists had used driver's permits to open bank accounts and rent cars and apartments, several states immediately tightened rules for obtaining driver's licenses. A Florida executive order limited foreigners to a 30-day temporary permit while authorities investigated their identification. New Jersey stopped issuing licenses to immigrants whose visas were to expire within a year.

Finances. As the national economy slowed, legislators began modest belt-tightening measures early in the year. An unprecedented seven consecutive years of multibillion-dollar tax reductions came to an end as states enacted relatively minimal tax and spending changes during 2001 legislative sessions. The cautious outlook changed dramatically after September 11 as anticipated tax revenue plummeted, new security costs escalated, and social spending began to ascend.

Health and Welfare. Problems with managed health care continued to preoccupy state lawmakers, with a focus emerging on improving patient knowledge about plans and service. A majority of states set up information and complaint-resolution systems, often including publishing health maintenance organization (HMO) "report cards," provider profiles, and state-run ombudsman services. North Carolina became the 46th state to adopt a patients' bill of rights.

A San Francisco resident shops in the dark at an auto parts store during a statewide rolling blackout on March 19.

AP/Wide World Photos

As states' fiscal problems mounted, additional states diverted their share of the 25-year, $207 billion tobacco settlement money away from public health and toward other needs. Maryland became the first state with a tobacco buyout, appropriating $5.9 million to wean tobacco farmers over to alternative crops such as grapes or raspberries. The 1996 federal welfare-reform act mandated a cutoff of assistance to recipients after five consecutive years, beginning in October 2001. But state welfare authorities reported that because of strong economic conditions over that period, few recipients were affected by the deadline. Massachusetts joined Maine in providing expanded services to HIV-positive patients on Medicaid, bidding to delay onset of full-blown AIDS. The Wisconsin Supreme Court upheld a novel order prohibiting a deadbeat dad from having any more children while he was on probation. The court's four male judges endorsed the court's ruling, while the three female jurists voted against it.

Law and Justice. After eight consecutive years of declining crime rates, incidence of major violent and property offenses leveled off during 2001. The number of inmates in state prisons nationwide also was flat as California inaugurated a new program to divert nonviolent drug offenders from incarceration to treatment. Nationwide, 66 convicts were executed.

By an 8–0 vote, the U.S. Supreme Court declared that federal law prohibited the use of marijuana as a medical treatment for diseases such as cancer, glaucoma, or AIDS. The ruling did not directly invalidate medical marijuana laws in nine states but allowed authorities to pursue violators even in those states on federal drug charges. Nevada became the first state to approve Internet gambling, another practice forbidden by federal law. State officials planned to overturn the federal law in court.

Energy and Environment. California's 1996 law partially deregulating the electricity industry put the state at the centre of a national crisis in early 2001. California had loosened regulation on power generators while retaining retail price caps, and that led to power shortages and financial trouble for several large utilities. In January state officials decided to buy more than $40 billion worth of electricity on behalf of Pacific Gas & Electric Co., Southern California Edison Corp., and San Diego Gas & Electric Co., all then suffering from high wholesale electricity prices. The state signed multiple-year contracts with energy producers that guaranteed delivery of electricity at set prices and thereby allowed the state to escape the spot market, where prices had soared to as high as $500 per megawatt hour. A combination of the contracts, conservation efforts, a cool summer, and declining energy prices helped the state avoid widely predicted blackouts, and by year's end the contracts were being criticized for overcommitting and overpaying for the electricity.

When California's problems spilled over into neighbouring states, Nevada repealed an electricity deregulation plan it had approved in 1999. Even so, Maryland, New York, Texas, and Virginia moved toward deregulation during the year, which brought to 24 the number of states pursuing a free market in electrical energy. (DAVID C. BECKWITH)

URUGUAY

Area: 176,215 sq km (68,037 sq mi)
Population (2001 est.): 3,303,000
Capital: Montevideo
Head of state and government: President Jorge Batlle Ibáñez

The year 2001 was a difficult one for Uruguay. Pres. Jorge Batlle Ibáñez's first full calendar year in office confronted him with a worsening of Uruguay's economic situation exacerbated by an outbreak of foot-and-mouth disease that seriously disrupted Uruguay's meat exports. The government had hoped that 2001 would bring modest economic growth after two years of recession. Unfortunately, the continued devaluation of the Brazilian currency—the real—and the deepening economic and political crisis in Argentina had adverse effects on both Uruguayan exports and tourism. With these internal and external conditions, unemployment skyrocketed to some 16%, and the gross domestic product rate was –1.1% for the first half of the year. The only good news on the economic front was the continued low inflation rate of 4–5%.

Batlle's approval rating remained relatively high by Uruguayan standards, owing in part to his continued support of a commission he established in 2000 to investigate the disappearance of some 180 Uruguayans during the period of military dictatorship from 1973 to 1985. The ruling Colorado Party's coalition with the Blanco Party remained intact despite strains produced by the stagnant economy. The leftist Broad Front coalition began to voice greater criticism of the administration's economic program and supported increased work stoppages by the labour unions. Nevertheless, Broad Front leader Tabaré Vázquez Rosas adopted a moderate tone on most issues in a clear effort to build on the coalition's more than 40% approval rating in the polls. He clearly had his eye on the next presidential election, which, however, would not take place until October 2004.

Uruguay qualified for the association football (soccer) World Cup finals to be held in 2002 in South Korea and Japan.

(MARTIN WEINSTEIN)

UZBEKISTAN

Area: 447,400 sq km (172,700 sq mi)
Population (2001 est.): 25,155,000
Capital: Tashkent
Chief of state and head of government: President Islam Karimov, assisted by Prime Minister Otkir Sultonov

Through much of 2001, Uzbekistan's position in the world community became more and more difficult. Although there was some understanding for the country's security concerns, it was criticized for its intransigence in the fields of economic reform, human rights, and restrictions on the information media and religious expression. Many international observers pointed out that the repressive policies of the Uzbek leadership were fueling the religious extremism that they feared. An international outcry occurred after the death of human rights activist Shovruk Ruzimuradov in police custody in July.

Relations with neighbouring Tajikistan and Kyrgyzstan worsened as citizens of those countries were injured or killed by Uzbek mines that were placed in border areas to hinder incursions by armed militants. Within Uzbekistan itself, arrests and trials of persons accused of religious extremism continued throughout the year. Leaflets of the banned Islamic group Hizb ut-Tahrir appeared in cities in various parts of the country, and numerous individuals were prosecuted on charges that they were members of the organization. Hizb ut-Tahrir activists insisted that they wanted to create an Islamic state in Central Asia by peaceful means, but the Uzbek authorities considered it a terrorist group.

Already in February, Uzbek officials announced that the continuing drought in the region would probably reduce the amount of cotton that would be produced in 2001, which would in turn affect Uzbekistan's foreign export earnings. In April the International Monetary Fund withdrew from Uzbekistan on the grounds that the Uzbek authorities had failed to implement genuine economic reform as prescribed by the Fund. Two months later the European Bank for Reconstruction and Development warned that it would reduce its level of investment if economic reform was not accelerated. The World Bank considered reducing its credit program for the same reason. While the international lending agencies expressed their dissatisfaction with the rate of reform, foreign investors were quietly withdrawing from Uzbekistan, and by the end of the year many international companies had either closed down or drastically reduced their activities. Many small businesses suffered when the tourism industry effectively collapsed after the beginning of the campaign against the Taliban and al-Qaeda in Afghanistan.

After the terrorist attacks in the United States, Uzbekistan quickly joined the international antiterrorist coalition, permitting U.S. forces the use of an air base near Karshi. According to official statements, the base was to be used for search and rescue operations, but by the end of October a small U.S. military presence had already been well established in Uzbekistan.

(BESS BROWN)

VANUATU

Area: 12,190 sq km (4,707 sq mi)
Population (2001 est.): 195,000
Capital: Vila
Chief of state: President John Bernard Bani
Head of government: Prime Ministers Barak Sopé and, from April 13, Edward Natapei

Vanuatu faced a political crisis in March 2001 when Prime Minister Barak Sopé lost support in Parliament and the speaker, a Sopé supporter, refused to allow consideration of a vote of no confidence. After the acting chief justice of the Supreme Court ruled that the speaker's action was unconstitutional, Sopé's government was defeated and replaced by a coalition of the Vanua'aku Party and the Union of Moderate Parties led by Prime Minister Edward Natapei. In November police attempts to search for documents related to Sopé's controversial business dealings while in office were thwarted by armed villagers.

In late September 2001, Finance Minister Joe Carl met with representatives of the Organisation for Economic Co-operation and Development in Vila, where he expressed his concern over the pressure exerted by the OECD in demanding details of the island's international tax-haven revenue. In June 2000 the OECD had included Vanuatu on a list of nations that sheltered money-laundering activities and maintained unacceptable taxation structures and had threatened sanctions unless action was taken to address the situation. Carl complained that the OECD had not offered an alternative means whereby the country could raise revenue. In October 2001 Vanuatu was accepted for membership (effective in November) in the World Trade Organization. Vanuatu's annual exports totaled about $25 million, mostly coconut products, beef, cocoa, timber, and kava root. Tourism strengthened in the wake of violence and political instability in neighbouring Fiji and the Solomon Islands. In November Natapei rejected suggestions that Vanuatu might offer refugee-processing facilities for asylum seekers (mostly from Afghanistan and Iraq) arriving in Australian waters via Indonesia.

The release of the 1999 census report indicated that the population of Vanuatu at that time was 186,678, an increase of 31% over 1989.

(BARRIE MACDONALD)

AP/Wide World Photos

Pope John Paul II prepares to send a message to Roman Catholics in Oceania on November 22; the message, which included a one-paragraph apology for sexual abuse by Roman Catholic clergy, was the first personally sent by a pope over the Internet.

VATICAN CITY STATE

Area: 44 ha (109 ac)
Population (2001 est.): 900
Chief of state: (sovereign pontiff) Pope John Paul II
Head of administration: Secretary of State Angelo Cardinal Sodano, who heads a pontifical commission of five cardinals

The year 2001 was important in terms of the octogenarian pontiff's desire to strengthen the Vatican's pastoral mission around the globe. Pope John Paul II visited areas of the world that had long viewed the Roman Catholic Church's activities with suspicion, if not open hostility. The pope followed in the footsteps of Saint Paul, traveling to Malta, Greece, and Damascus. He also went to Eastern Europe and Central Asia, making pastoral visits to Ukraine and Kazakhstan. The personal courage involved in undertaking the latter visit was astounding, considering that the trip was completed only days before the U.S. began its bombing in nearby Afghanistan. As with all of his pastoral visits, the aim was to strengthen the Vatican's role as a major player in global affairs. One of the chief areas of resistance in this process was China, and it was remarkable that China manifested an open attitude during the year toward the possibility of reestablishing diplomatic relations with the Vatican after a rupture that had lasted 50 years. A low point in relations between China and the Vatican had been reached in 2000 when the pope canonized 120 Chinese martyrs to communism on the same day as China's national holiday. The pope hoped to strengthen ties with the estimated 10 million Catholics who lived in the world's most populous country. Consistent with the Vatican's mission of bringing peace to the world, the pope expressed horror at the many atrocities committed throughout the globe in 2001, and Vatican officials reiterated the urge for rich nations to devote more attention to the problem of poverty, encouraging steps such as abolishing the debt of poor countries and providing mechanisms to ensure that all nations could derive benefits from the global market.

(GREGORY O. SMITH)

VENEZUELA

Area: 916,445 sq km (353,841 sq mi)
Population (2001 est.): 24,632,000
Capital: Caracas
Head of state and government: President Hugo Chávez Frías

The municipal and parish councilmen that Venezuelans elected on Dec. 3, 2000, assumed office in January 2001. This act completed Pres. Hugo Chávez Frías's demolition of the post-1958 system of the political parties that had governed Venezuela over four decades. Chávez's Fifth Republic Movement and its ally, the Movement to Socialism, as well as other political parties opposed to the previously dominant Democrat Action (AD) party and Social Christians, had captured 72% of all municipal and parish council seats. On October 25, however, the pro-Chávez parties suffered a stinging rebuke when their candidates ran for leadership positions in the Venezuelan Confederation of Workers.

The defeat was so overwhelming (unofficial tallies gave the pro-Chávez slates less than 10% of the total vote) that the National Electoral Council had not released the results as of mid-November. The victorious forces were the same groups that for more than four decades had been part of the AD and the Social Christians. Their victory did not signal the return to favour of these organizations, however. Rather, it indicated that organized labour had emerged as an autonomous political force in Venezuela, one whose support future governments could not take for granted.

Chávez saw his plans to remake Venezuela in the image of his leftist ideology derailed on several other fronts. First, in May he introduced legislation into the National Assembly that would have increased the national government's control over education, private as well as public. Proposals that required the imposition of government overseers with powers to dismiss administrators and teachers evoked intense opposition from the Roman Catholic Church and associations of middle-class parents whose children attended public schools. Chávez and the governing political party backed away from what threatened to become an ugly and possibly violent confrontation. In addition, they declined to press the influential association of taxi drivers when the drivers resisted attempts to regulate them and to integrate them into the ruling political party. Finally, the Chávez government even had difficulty in controlling the capital city of Caracas. The 1999 constitution provided for the election of a "high mayor" to replace the appointed Federal District governor, traditionally the highest local executive authority in Caracas. The first elected high mayor of Caracas was Alfredo Peña, once Chávez's chief of staff. Peña broke with the president, successfully resisted his efforts to control the capital city police forces, and even suggested that it would be necessary to remove the president in a revocatory referendum. On December 10 the business group Fedecámaras and the one-million-strong Confederation of Venezuelan Workers staged a nationwide strike to protest new economic laws—involving the agriculture, fishing, and oil industries—that they believed would "lead the country to economic disaster."

Pres. Hugo Chávez of Venezuela hoists a youngster at the opening ceremony of a school in Caucagua on November 14.

AP/Wide World Photos

Venezuela's central bank reported that the economic recovery that had begun in the second quarter of 2000 slowed in the third quarter of 2001. The communications sector failed to sustain earlier rates of growth, and the financial sector did not recover from the contraction that it experienced in 1999 and 2000. On November 1 the central bank reported that inflation was running at roughly 10% for the year, down slightly from 2000. Private consumption, which had fallen by 15% between May 1999 and May 2000, grew by 5% during the first half of 2001. Total public-sector debt stood at 31% of the country's gross domestic product, up from 29% for 2000.

The Chávez government's handling of foreign policy created two important problems for Venezuela. First, insurgency continued to simmer in neighbouring Colombia, and Chávez's ambiguous position toward the rebel cause raised tensions with Bogotá and Washington. The U.S. government was especially unhappy with Venezuela's unwillingness to allow overflights by military aircraft attempting to track drug-smuggling guerrillas. Second, after U.S. Pres. George W. Bush initiated the bombing of Afghanistan in October, relations between Venezuela and the U.S. deteriorated further when Chávez equated civilian casualties from the bombing with the deaths caused by terrorists on September 11. This position isolated the Chávez government within the Western Hemisphere and hardened opposition by the government's domestic critics. (DAVID J. MYERS)

VIETNAM

Area: 331,041 sq km (127,816 sq mi)
Population (2001 est.): 79,939,000
Capital: Hanoi
Chief of state: President Tran Duc Luong
Head of government: Prime Minister Phan Van Khai

In February 2001 a wave of protests among ethnic minorities swept through the central highlands of Vietnam. The demonstrators were angry over government corruption and encroachment on their ancestral lands by members of the Vietnamese majority. These developments quickly had an impact on political maneuvering prior to the ninth National Congress of the Communist Party of Vietnam. The stewardship of Secretary-General Le Kha Phieu came under challenge by senior retired leaders. Phieu also was implicated in a wiretapping scandal involving the military intelligence service.

Prior to the National Congress, party delegates decided to select Nong Duc Manh as party leader. Manh, a member of the Tay ethnic minority group, was respected for his considerable legislative experience as chairman of the National Assembly.

The National Congress was held on April 19–22. The party set a goal of doubling the country's gross domestic product by 2010 and achieving an annual growth rate of 7.5% for the first five years. Secretary-General Manh quickly stamped his authority on Vietnam's ongoing reform program. He immediately reshuffled key party and military leadership posts. He then ordered the implementation of a directive requiring all party and state officials to publicly declare their assets in an effort to curb corruption.

In June Manh obtained approval from the party's Central Committee for controversial plans to construct a costly hydroelectric scheme at Son La in the north. This project was designed to provide future energy for industry and to control flooding. It would also displace 100,000 persons who would need to be resettled. In August Manh received party endorsement to carry out a thorough reform of the state-owned enterprise sector. In September he personally addressed the problem of ethnic minority grievances by visiting the central highlands. He directed government officials to work closely with local elders, ordered a step-up in the recruitment of ethnic minorities for government service, and offered financial support for the ailing coffee-growing industry.

The National Congress reaffirmed Vietnam's commitment to a policy aimed at diversifying foreign relations. In March Vietnam hosted a visit by Russian Pres. Vladimir Putin. The two countries agreed to form a "strategic partnership" involving long-term economic cooperation and Russian arms sales. In October Russia announced that it would withdraw the last of its military forces from the Cam Ranh Bay naval station. Vietnam received visits by a number of Chinese officials, including Defense Minister Chi Haotian in February, Vice Pres. Hu Jintao in April, and National People's Congress Chairman Li Peng in September. In midyear Vietnam, as chairman of the Standing Committee of the Association of Southeast Asian Nations (ASEAN), hosted the annual meeting of ASEAN foreign ministers, a meeting of the ASEAN Regional Forum, and a meeting of the "ASEAN Plus Three" (China, Japan, and South Korea). In July Vietnam hosted a groundbreaking visit by Kim Yong Nam, president of North Korea's Supreme People's Assembly, and in October the two countries agreed to expand bilateral trade and investment. Vietnam responded to the September 11 terrorist attacks in the U.S. by offering sympathy and condemning terrorism but warned against "overreacting" to the attacks. In the final quarter of the year, Vietnam and the U.S. ratified the Bilateral Trade Agreement, which meant that Vietnamese exports would be subject to much lower tariffs. (CARLYLE A. THAYER)

YEMEN

Area: 555,000 sq km (214,300 sq mi)
Population (2001 est.): 18,078,000
Capital: San'a'
Chief of state: President Maj. Gen. 'Ali 'Abdallah Salih
Head of government: Prime Ministers 'Abd al-Karim al-Iryani and, from March 31, 'Abd al-Qadir al-Ba Jamal

In February 2001, for the first time ever, Yemen held elections for local councils; of the more than 20,000 candidates, 7,000 representatives were chosen. Voters also approved a referendum that would extend the term of the president from five to seven years, a constitutional change that could allow Pres. Maj. Gen. 'Ali 'Abdallah Salih to remain in office until 2013. On April 28 President Salih appointed 111 members to the newly created Consultative Council, which would form the upper house of the parliament.

In March 2001 President Salih reshuffled the cabinet and appointed as prime minister 'Abd al-Qadir al-Ba Jamal, a southerner from the Hadramawt; he had served as foreign minister and minister of oil when Yemen was unified in 1990. Prior to unification Ba Jamal had served in the People's Democratic Republic of Yemen's (South Yemen's) pro-Marxist government as planning and oil minister. Outgoing prime minister 'Abd al-Karim al-Iryani, a veteran politician who had served in many cabinets (before and after unity), became a senior presidential adviser. The new 35-member cabinet, all of whom belonged to the president's party, included Wahiba Fare, Yemen's first woman minister; she became minister of state for human rights.

Yemeni and U.S. authorities continued their intense investigation into the October 2000 terrorist attack on the USS *Cole;* several arrests were made. Following the September 2001 attacks in the U.S., Yemen cooperated with U.S. investigators, arrested dozens of suspects, and froze the bank accounts of two honey stores that were suspected of having links to terrorists. (WILLIAM A. RUGH)

YUGOSLAVIA

Area: 102,173 sq km (39,449 sq mi)
Population (2001 est.): 10,677,000
Capital: Belgrade
Chief of state: President Vojislav Kostunica
Head of government: Prime Ministers Zoran Zizic and, from July 24, Dragisa Pesic

Yugoslavia made significant advances in returning to the international fold in 2001. All international sanctions were lifted; former strongman Slobodan Milosevic was extradited to the International Criminal Tribunal for the Former Yugoslavia (ICTY); the national currency was stabilized; and nearly one-fourth of the country's foreign debt was erased. Domestically, the privatization process was initiated, and an unexpectedly strong voter turnout among Serbs in Kosovo brought some measure of hope to a country ravaged by more than a decade of conflict, isolation, and economic mismanagement.

There was no progress over Yugoslavia's future status as a federation, however. The ruling coalition government was split and perpetually on the verge of collapse; the opposition was marginalized; and political parties continued to exert influence over media much as they had during the 13 years of the Milosevic regime. The government seemed far too occupied with internal rivalries to be able to push through legal, social, and economic reforms that could rid the country of the burdens of recent decades.

Milosevic's arrest on April 1 and his extradition to the ICTY on June 28 revealed the extent of government infighting. The ruling coalition, the Democratic Opposition of Serbia (DOS), led by Serbian Premier Zoran Djindjic, clashed with Yugoslav Pres. Vojislav Kostunica, whose Democratic Party of Serbia was the strongest member of the DOS, over the particulars of a draft extradition law and how Yugoslavia should cooperate with the ICTY. Kostunica demanded a thorough legal review of the draft law, while Djindjic pushed through a document on cooperation with the ICTY and authorized Milosevic's extradition.

The situation in Yugoslavia's constituent republic of Montenegro remained precarious. Pres. Milo Djukanovic's drive for Montenegro's independence from Yugoslavia was imperiled by boycotts from the opposition, pressure from the international community, the worsening economic situation, and fissures within the pro-independence bloc. In April Djukanovic's Democratic Party of Socialists of Montenegro and other parties that favoured independence for the republic barely won the parliamentary election. A broad consensus was lacking even on the rules and conditions for a proposed referendum, and there was considerable wrangling over whether a simple majority or a two-thirds majority would be needed to express the "national will." Clearly, there was no large majority that would vote in favour of Montenegrin independence; opinion surveys in November indicated 52% favoured independence, 33% opposed it, and 15% remained undecided. Observers were predicting that the economic and political situation could tilt undecided voters against independence. The referendum on the issue was tentatively scheduled to take place in April 2002.

Parliamentary elections in the Serbian province of Kosovo (under UN control) went on as planned in November without violence and with the participation of a significant number of ethnic Serbs who heeded Belgrade's call to vote and who ignored demands by their local leaders that they boycott the balloting. The Organization for Security and Cooperation in Europe conducted the elections, and international observers generally agreed that the vote was a step toward stability. Kosovar Albanians generally opted for a more moderate approach to government and independence, while the Serbs expressed hope for a negotiated future in which they might secure real power in a new provincial assembly. The international community rejected a call for independence by moderate ethnic Albanian leader Ibrahim Rugova, whose Democratic League of Kosovo won 47 of 120 seats in the parliament. Two other pro-independence Albanian parties headed by former guerrilla leaders won 34 seats; the only slate of Kosovo Serb candidates, called the Return coalition, took 22 seats.

The hoped-for upturn in the Yugoslav economy was not evident in 2001. According to one study, conducted by an influential nongovernmental group of economists in Serbia called G17 Plus, one out of seven citizens was worse off at the end of 2001 than the previous year. Experts suggested that Yugoslavia would require an influx of about $15 billion over the next five years to stabilize the economy. Unemployment stood at almost 30%, and officials estimated that about 40% of the population lived below the poverty line. The foreign debt rose 20% to $12 billion, and prices on basic commodities jumped 120%.

There were positive indicators, however. According to an International Monetary Fund (IMF) report in September, the Yugoslav tax system had been successfully adjusted to European standards, budgetary discipline had been restored, the central bank had taken control over the flow of currency, and the government no longer printed money to cover the budget deficit or bail out bankrupt state companies. In addition, foreign currency exchange stabilized, foreign currency reserves continued to rise, and for the first time in nearly a decade, citizens were opening savings accounts. A key privatization law, a precondition for foreign capital investment, was also passed by the parliament. These changes led to Yugoslavia's reentry into the IMF, the World Bank, and other Western institutions. A donors' conference in June pledged $1.3 billion in developmental aid for Yugoslavia, and in November the Paris Club of creditors wrote off $3 billion of Yugoslavia's debt to that organization.

(MILAN ANDREJEVICH)

Supporters of the pro-independence Liberal Alliance of Montenegro rally in Podgorica, Yugos., on April 16.

Milos Bicanski/AFP Worldwide

ZAMBIA

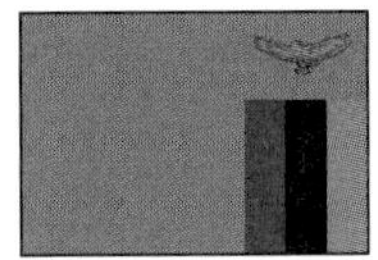

Area: 752,614 sq km (290,586 sq mi)
Population (2001 est.): 9,770,000
Capital: Lusaka
Head of state and government: President Frederick Chiluba

The companies that had taken over the Zambian government's holdings in the copper-mining industry in 2000 started 2001 in a buoyant mood, promising considerable increases in copper output. Encouraged by the apparent success of the government's privatization program, the Dutch oil company Shell resumed operations in Zambia after a 19-year interval.

Early in the year the World Bank released the first $2.5 million installment of its pledge of $30 million for major rehabilitation work on the country's railroad and freight infrastructure, and on April 17 the International Monetary Fund announced that it would make available a loan of $126 million to support Zambia's economic program. Sixteen donor groups representing various countries also made possible a government scheme to give doctors and nurses a substantial pay raise, and in June the European Union made a donation for road improvements.

There were difficulties, however. By the end of 2000, inflation had risen to 28.7%, and to counter this trend the government

Zambian Pres. Frederick Chiluba (left) speaks with South African Pres. Thabo Mbeki before the opening session of the Organization of African Unity summit in Lusaka on July 9.

Alexander Joe/AFP Worldwide

began the year by ordering foreign investors to keep 75% of their earnings in Zambia. In February heavy rains caused floods at the confluence of the Zambezi and Luangwa rivers, threatening more than 30,000 people with famine. Then in October falling copper prices forced the South African Metorex Group to put its Chibuluma opencast mine on a care and maintenance basis less than a year after it had started operations.

Agitation by members of the ruling Movement for Multiparty Democracy (MMD) for a third term in office for Pres. Frederick Chiluba caused a violent reaction in many quarters and even from some members of the MMD itself. A conference of the MMD at the end of April changed the party's rules to allow the president to stand for a further term. Chiluba then dismissed a number of ministers who had opposed the change, including the vice president, Lieut. Gen. Christon Tembo, who formed his own party, the Forum for Democracy and Development. On May 4, however, Chiluba announced that he would not, after all, stand for a third term, and in August Levy Mwanawasa, a lawyer and former vice president, was adopted as the MMD's presidential candidate at the next election.

On November 22, Chiluba formally dissolved the country's National Assembly and called for presidential and general elections to be held on December 27. There were 11 presidential candidates. Even before early results suggested that both the presidential and parliamentary elections would be close, opposition parties accused the government of ballot rigging, and clashes ensued between protesters and riot police. (KENNETH INGHAM)

ZIMBABWE

Area: 390,757 sq km (150,872 sq mi)
Population (2001 est.): 11,365,000
Capital: Harare
Head of state and government: President Robert Mugabe

Throughout 2001 government policy in Zimbabwe was mainly focused upon victory in the elections scheduled for 2002. On January 25 a sharp fall in market interest rates was engineered in spite of urgent warnings from leading bankers. An International Monetary Fund (IMF) team that visited Zimbabwe in March—not impressed by the economic situation—refused to provide any new funds and threatened that if the government did not pay a debt of $73.6 million later in the year, it could be suspended from the IMF. Nevertheless, Finance Minister Simba Makoni, presenting his budget on November 1, said that public spending would double in the next financial year while taxation would be cut. At the same time, he admitted that gross domestic product growth would fall by 7.3% in 2001 and by a further 5.3% in 2002, largely as a result of a 12% cut in agricultural output due to the government's land-reform program.

That program, launched the previous year and involving the forcible occupation of white-owned land by men claiming to be veterans of the 1970s war of independence, was represented by the government as a fulfillment of unfinished business arising from the war. Great Britain, President Mugabe claimed, had failed to carry out the terms of the independence agreement regarding the transfer of land to black ownership and was now conducting a neocolonial campaign on behalf of white farmers. It was a point of view that won the almost unanimous sympathy of African leaders at a summit meeting held in Lusaka in July. It led, however, to clashes with the law courts. Chief Justice Anthony Gubbay was forced to resign in March after the president said that he could not offer protection against people who threatened Gubbay's life. Two other judges resigned in similar circumstances later in the year. Gubbay was replaced by Godfrey Chidyausiku, a friend of the president, and three other black judges were appointed to the bench. Late in the year the Supreme Court ruled that land reform could proceed.

Frequently, journalists of the country's only independent daily newspaper, the *Daily News*, were subjected to harassment for their criticism of government policy. In April two bills were hurried through the parliament, one strengthening the government's control over broadcasting and the other banning donations to political parties by foreign organizations. Members of opposition parties were also harassed and were sometimes subjected to violence by vigilantes. In February Morgan Tsvangirai, leader of the Movement for Democratic Change, was arrested and charged with inciting the violent overthrow of the president. Later in the year his car was attacked by a hostile crowd.

South African Pres. Thabo Mbeki consistently advocated a cooperative approach to Mugabe, and after the outbreak of further violence on white-owned farms in August, he agreed to cooperate with the president of Nigeria in organizing a meeting of Commonwealth foreign ministers aimed at effecting an accommodation between Zimbabwe and Britain over land reform. Although Mugabe accepted the meeting's recommendation that law and order should be restored in Zimbabwe, there was no letup in the activities of vigilantes, and the newly constituted Supreme Court declared the president's method of land reform legal. (KENNETH INGHAM)

Alder, Phillip. Syndicated Bridge Columnist. Associate Editor, *The Bridge World.* Author of *Get Smarter at Bridge.* •SPORTS AND GAMES: *Contract Bridge*

Alexander, Steve. Freelance Technology Writer. •COMPUTERS AND INFORMATION SYSTEMS

Allaby, Michael. Freelance Writer. Author of *Encyclopedia of Weather and Climate* and *Basics of Environmental Science.* •THE ENVIRONMENT: *Environmental Issues; International Activities*

Allan, J.A. Professor of Geography, School of Oriental and African Studies, University of London. Author of *The Water Question in the Middle East* and *Water and Peace in the Middle East.* •WORLD AFFAIRS: *Libya*

Anam, Mahfuz. Editor, *The Daily Star,* Bangladesh. •WORLD AFFAIRS: *Bangladesh*

Andrades, Jorge Adrián. Freelance Journalist. •SPORTS AND GAMES: *Equestrian Sports:* Polo

Andrejevich, Milan. Senior Editor, *Post-Tribune* (Gary, Ind.). Adjunct Professor of Communications and History, Valparaiso University and Indiana University Northwest. Author of *The Sandžak: A Perspective of Serb-Muslim Relations.* •WORLD AFFAIRS: *Bosnia and Herzegovina; Yugoslavia*

Anthony, John Duke. President and CEO, National Council on U.S.-Arab Relations; Consultant to U.S. Departments of Defense and State. •WORLD AFFAIRS: *Oman; Qatar*

Archibald, John J. Retired Feature Writer, St. Louis (Mo.) *Post-Dispatch.* Member of the American Bowling Congress Hall of Fame. •SPORTS AND GAMES: *Bowling:* U.S. Tenpins

Aurora, Vincent. Lecturer in French and Romance Philology, Columbia University, New York City. Author of *Michel Leiris' "Failles": Immobile in mobili.* •LITERATURE: *French:* France

Bahry, Louay. Adjunct Professor of Political Science, University of Tennessee. Author of *The Baghdad Bahn.* •WORLD AFFAIRS: *Bahrain; Iraq*

Balaban, Avraham. Professor and Chairman, Department of African and Asian Languages and Literatures, University of Florida. Author of *Shiv'ah.* •LITERATURE: *Jewish:* Hebrew

Bamia, Aida A. Professor of Arabic Language and Literature, University of Florida. •LITERATURE: *Arabic*

Barrett, David B. Research Professor of Missiometrics, Regent University, Virginia Beach, Va. Author of *World Christian Encyclopedia* and *Schism and Renewal in Africa.* •RELIGION: *Tables (in part)*

Barry, John. Professor of Spanish, Roosevelt University, Chicago. Editor, *Voces en el viento: Nuevas ficciones desde Chicago.* •LITERATURE: *Spanish:* Latin America

Barzel, Ann. Senior Editor, *Dance Magazine.* •PERFORMING ARTS: *Dance:* World

Beattie, Ted A. President, American Zoo and Aquarium Association; President and CEO, John G. Shedd Aquarium, Chicago. •THE ENVIRONMENT: *Zoos*

Beckwith, David C. Vice President, National Cable Television Association. •WORLD AFFAIRS: *United States; United States:* State and Local Affairs

Benedetti, Laura. John L. Loeb Associate Professor of the Humanities, Harvard University. Author of *La sconfitta di Diana. Un percorso per la* Gerusalemme liberata. •LITERATURE: *Italian*

Bernstein, Ellen. Freelance Writer and Editor, specializing in health and medicine, Chicago. •HEALTH AND DISEASE, HEALTH AND DISEASE: Sidebar

Bird, Thomas E. The Jewish Studies Program, Queens College, City University of New York. Coeditor of *Hryhorij Savyc Skovoroda: An Anthology of Critical Articles.* •LITERATURE: *Jewish:* Yiddish

Boggan, Tim. Historian, U.S.A. Table Tennis Association (USATT). Author of *Winning Table Tennis* and *History of U.S. Table Tennis, vol. 1.* •SPORTS AND GAMES: *Table Tennis*

Bonds, John B. Adjunct Professor of History, The Citadel, Charleston, S.C. •SPORTS AND GAMES: *Sailing (Yachting)*

Bradley, Bill. Freelance Journalist; Publisher, *Billiard News.* •BIOGRAPHIES *(in part);* SPORTS AND GAMES: *Billiard Games*

Bradsher, Henry S. Foreign Affairs Analyst. Author of *Afghan Communism and Soviet Intervention.* •BIOGRAPHIES *(in part);* WORLD AFFAIRS: *Philippines*

Brady, Conor. Editor, *The Irish Times,* Dublin. •WORLD AFFAIRS: *Ireland*

Brecher, Kenneth. Professor of Astronomy and Physics; Director, Science and Mathematics Education Center, Boston University. •MATHEMATICS AND PHYSICAL SCIENCES: *Astronomy*

Brockmann, Stephen. Associate Professor of German, Carnegie Mellon University, Pittsburgh, Pa. Author of *Literature and German Reunification.* •LITERATURE: *German*

Brokopp, John G. Specialist and Writer on equestrian racing and casino gambling; Director of Public Relations, National Jockey Club. Author of *Thrifty Gambling* and *The Insider's Guide to Internet Gambling: Your Sourcebook for Safe and Profitable Gambling.* •SPORTS AND GAMES: *Equestrian Sports:* Thoroughbred Racing: *United States*

Brown, Bess. Political Officer, OSCE Centre, Ashgabat, Turkmenistan. Author of *Authoritarianism in the New States of Central Asia.* •WORLD AFFAIRS: *Kazakhstan; Kyrgyzstan; Tajikistan; Turkmenistan; Uzbekistan*

Buchan, David. International Energy Editor, *Financial Times,* London. Author of *The Single Market and Tomorrow's Europe: A Progress Report from the European Commission.* •BIOGRAPHIES *(in part);* WORLD AFFAIRS: *France*

Bungs, Dzintra. Consultant, Stiftung Wissenschaft und Politik, Berlin. Author of *The Baltic States: Problems and Prospects of Membership of the European Union.* •WORLD AFFAIRS: *Latvia*

Burks, Ardath W. Professor Emeritus of Asian Studies, Rutgers University, New Brunswick, N.J. Author of *Japan: A Postindustrial Power.* •BIOGRAPHIES *(in part);* WORLD AFFAIRS: *Japan*

Burns, Erik T. Bureau Chief, Dow Jones Newswires, Lisbon. •WORLD AFFAIRS: *Portugal*

Byrne, Justin. Researcher, Center for Advanced Study in the Social Sciences, Instituto Juan March de Estudios e Investigaciones, Madrid. •WORLD AFFAIRS: *Spain*

Cadoux, Charles. Professor of Public Law, University of Aix-Marseille III, Aix-en-Provence, Fr. •WORLD AFFAIRS: *Dependent States:* Indian Ocean and Southeast Asia

Cafferty, Bernard. Associate Editor, *British Chess Magazine.* Author of *The Soviet Championships.* •SPORTS AND GAMES: *Chess*

Calhoun, David R. Freelance Editor and Author. •BIOGRAPHIES *(in part)*

Calvo, Guillermo A. Chief Economist, Inter-American Development Bank, Washington, D.C.; Director, Center for International Economics, and Professor of Economics, University of Maryland, College Park. •WORLD AFFAIRS: *Special Report:* Dollarization: Is It Worth It?

Campbell, Paul J. Professor of Mathematics and Computer Science, Beloit College, Beloit, Wis. Author of *For All Practical Purposes.* •MATHEMATICS AND PHYSICAL SCIENCES: *Mathematics*

Campbell, Robert. Architect and Architecture Critic. Author of *Cityscapes of Boston: An American City Through Time.* •ARCHITECTURE AND CIVIL ENGINEERING: *Architecture*

Carter, Robert W. Journalist. •SPORTS AND GAMES: *Equestrian Sports:* Show Jumping and Dressage; Steeplechasing; Thoroughbred Racing: *International*

Cenzer, Matthew A. Lecturer in History, Northwestern University, Evanston, Ill. •WORLD AFFAIRS: *Burundi; Comoros; Djibouti; Liberia; Mauritius; Nigeria; Rwanda; Seychelles; Sierra Leone*

Chappell, Duncan. President, Mental Health Review Tribunal, Sydney. Author of *Violence at Work.* •LAW, CRIME, AND LAW ENFORCEMENT: *Crime*

Cheadle, Bruce. Journalist, Canadian Press news agency. •SPORTS AND GAMES: *Curling*

Cheuse, Alan. Writing Faculty, English Department, George Mason University, Fairfax, Va.; Book Commentator, National Public Radio. Author of *The Light Possessed* and *Listening to the Page: Adventures in Reading and Writing.* •LITERATURE: *English:* United States

Cioroslan, Dragomir. National Team Coach, U.S.A. Weightlifting, Inc.; Executive Board Member, International Weightlifting Federation. Author of *Banish Your Belly.* •SPORTS AND GAMES: *Weight Lifting*

Claiborn, Charles D. Professor, Division of Psychology in Education, Arizona State University. •EDUCATION: *Special Report:* Does Testing Deserve a Passing Grade?

Clark, David Draper. Managing Editor, *World Literature Today.* •LITERATURE: *English:* Other Literature in English

Clark, Janet H. Editor, Standard & Poor's, London. •NOBEL PRIZES *(in part)*

Collins, Nigel. Editor in Chief, *The Ring, KO, World Boxing,* and *Boxing 2002.* •SPORTS AND GAMES: *Boxing*

Cosgrave, Bronwyn. Associate Editor, *British Vogue.* Author of *Costume and Fashion: A Complete History.* •BIOGRAPHIES *(in part);* FASHIONS

Coveney, Michael. Theatre Critic, *The Daily Mail.* Author of *The Andrew Lloyd Webber Story* and others. •PERFORMING ARTS: *Theatre:* Great Britain and Ireland

Craine, Anthony G. Writer. •BIOGRAPHIES *(in part)*

Crampton, Richard J. Professor of East European History, University of Oxford, Oxford, Eng. Author of *A Concise History of Bulgaria* and *Eastern Europe in the Twentieth Century—and After.* •WORLD AFFAIRS: *Bulgaria*

Crisp, Brian F. Associate Professor of Political Science, University of Arizona. Author of *Democratic Institutional Design.* •WORLD AFFAIRS: *Colombia*

Curwen, Peter. Professor of Business and Management, Sheffield Hallam University, Sheffield, Eng. Author of *The U.K. Publishing Industry* and others. •MEDIA AND PUBLISHING: *Book Publishing* (international)

Cuttino, John Charles. Lyndon B. Johnson School of Public Affairs, University of Texas at Austin. •WORLD AFFAIRS: *Brazil*

Dailey, Meghan. Art Historian and Critic, New York. •ART, ANTIQUES, AND COLLECTIONS: *Art Exhibitions; Painting and Sculpture;* BIOGRAPHIES *(in part)*

Davis, Stephen P. Associate Editor, Encyclopædia Britannica. •BIOGRAPHIES *(in part)*

Deeb, Marius K. Professor of Middle East Studies, SAIS, Johns Hopkins University, Washington, D.C. Author of *Syria's War on Lebanon and the Peace Process 1974–2001* and others. •BIOGRAPHIES *(in part);* WORLD AFFAIRS: *Egypt; Jordan*

de la Barre, Kenneth. Fellow, Arctic Institute of North America; Research Associate, Yukon College, Northern Research Institute. •WORLD AFFAIRS: *Arctic Regions*

Denselow, Robin. Music Writer, *The Guardian;* Correspondent, BBC Television's *Newsnight.* Author of *When the Music's Over: The Politics of Pop.* •PERFORMING ARTS: *Music:* Popular (international)

Dietz, Henry A. Professor, Department of Government, University of Texas at Austin. Author of *Urban Poverty, Political Participation and the State: Lima 1970–1990.* •WORLD AFFAIRS: *Peru*

Dooling, Dave. Manager, NASA Microgravity Outreach, Infinity Technology, Inc. Coauthor of *Engineering Tomorrow.* •MATHEMATICS AND PHYSICAL SCIENCES: *Space Exploration; Space Exploration:* Sidebar

Dowd, Siobhan. Columnist, *Literary Review* (London); *Glimmer Train* (U.S.). Author of *This Prison Where I Live* and *Roads of the Roma*. •LITERATURE: *English:* United Kingdom

Ehringer, Gavin Forbes. Freelance Writer and Photographer; Correspondent, *People Magazine, Rocky Mountain News,* and *Western Horseman*. Coauthor of *Rodeo in America: Wranglers, Roughstock and Paydirt*. •SPORTS AND GAMES: *Introduction; Rodeo*

El Guindi, Fadwa. Adjunct Professor of Anthropology, University of Southern California. Author of *Veil: Modesty, Privacy and Resistance*. •ANTHROPOLOGY AND ARCHAEOLOGY: *Anthropology:* Cultural

Esteban, Verónica. Journalist and Judicial Interpreter. •LITERATURE: *Spanish:* Spain

Fagan, Brian. Professor of Anthropology, University of California, Santa Barbara. Author of *The Little Ice Age: How Climate Made History, 1300–1850* and *Floods, Famines, and Emperors: El Niño and the Collapse of Civilizations*. •ANTHROPOLOGY AND ARCHAEOLOGY: *Archaeology:* Western Hemisphere

Farr, David M.L. Professor Emeritus of History, Carleton University, Ottawa. •BIOGRAPHIES *(in part);* WORLD AFFAIRS: *Canada*

Fealy, Greg. Research Fellow in Indonesian History, Research School of Pacific and Asian Studies, Australian National University, Canberra. Author of *The Release of Indonesia's Political Prisoners: Domestic Versus Foreign Policy, 1975–1979*. •WORLD AFFAIRS: *Indonesia; Special Report:* Resisting Disintegration in Post-Suharto Indonesia

Fendell, Robert J. Freelance Writer on automobiles and racing. Author of *The Encyclopedia of Auto Racing Greats*. •SPORTS AND GAMES: *Automobile Racing:* Sidebar; *Automobile Racing:* U.S. Auto Racing *(in part)*

Fisher, Sharon. Central European Specialist, PlanEcon, Inc., Washington, D.C. •WORLD AFFAIRS: *Czech Republic; Slovakia*

Flink, Steve. Senior Correspondent, *Tennis Week*. Author of *The Greatest Tennis Matches of the Twentieth Century*. •SPORTS AND GAMES: *Tennis*

Flores, Ramona Monette Sargan. Professor, University of the Philippines, Quezon City. •MEDIA AND PUBLISHING: *Radio* (international); *Television* (international); *Television:* Sidebar

Follett, Christopher. Denmark Correspondent, *The Times;* Local Correspondent for Reuters News Agency, Copenhagen; Editor, *Copenhagen This Week*. Author of *Fodspor paa Cypern*. •WORLD AFFAIRS: *Denmark*

Ford, Brian J. Royal Literary Fellow, Open University, United Kingdom; Fellow, Cardiff University, Wales. Author of *BSE: The Facts*. •AGRICULTURE AND FOOD SUPPLIES: *Special Report:* Trouble on the Hoof: Disease Outbreaks in Europe

Fridovich, Irwin. James B. Duke Professor of Biochemistry, Emeritus, Duke University Medical Center, Durham, N.C. •LIFE SCIENCES: *Molecular Biology (in part)*

Fridovich-Keil, Judith L. Associate Professor, Department of Genetics, Emory University School of Medicine, Atlanta, Ga. •LIFE SCIENCES: *Molecular Biology (in part)*

Fuller, Elizabeth. Editor, *Newsline*, Radio Free Europe/Radio Liberty, Prague. •WORLD AFFAIRS: *Armenia; Azerbaijan; Georgia*

Furmonavičius, Darius. Ph.D. candidate, Department of European Studies, University of Bradford, Eng. •WORLD AFFAIRS: *Lithuania*

Gallagher, Tom. Professor of European Peace Studies, University of Bradford, Eng. Author of *Outcast Europe: The Balkans 1789–1989*. •WORLD AFFAIRS: *Romania*

Ganado, Albert. Lawyer; Chairman, Malta National Archives Advisory Committee; President, Malta Historical Society. Coauthor of *A Study in Depth of 143 Maps Representing the Great Siege of Malta of 1565* and others. •WORLD AFFAIRS: *Malta*

Garcia-Zamor, Jean-Claude. Professor of Public Administration, Florida International University. •WORLD AFFAIRS: *Haiti*

Garrod, Mark. Golf Correspondent, PA Sport, U.K. Honorary Secretary of the Association of Golf Writers. •SPORTS AND GAMES: *Golf*

Gaughan, Thomas. Library Director, Muhlenberg College, Allentown, Pa. •BIOGRAPHIES *(in part);* LIBRARIES AND MUSEUMS: *Libraries; Libraries:* Sidebar

George, Nicholas. Stockholm Correspondent, *Financial Times*. •WORLD AFFAIRS: *Sweden*

Gibbons, J. Whitfield. Professor of Ecology, Savannah River Ecology Laboratory, University of Georgia. Coauthor of *Ecoviews: Snakes, Snails and Environmental Tales*. •LIFE SCIENCES: *Zoology*

Gill, Martin J. Information and Computer Expert, F.A.O. EASTFISH; Editor, *Eurofish*. •AGRICULTURE AND FOOD SUPPLIES: *Fisheries*

Gobbie, Donn. CEO, American Badminton League. •SPORTS AND GAMES: *Badminton*

Goldsmith, Arthur. Freelance Writer. Author of *The Camera and Its Images*. •ART, ANTIQUES, AND COLLECTIONS: *Photography*

Graham, John W. Chair, Canadian Foundation for the Americas; Former Canadian Ambassador. •WORLD AFFAIRS: *Dominican Republic; Suriname*

Greskovic, Robert. Dance Critic, *The Wall Street Journal*. Author of *Ballet, 101*. •PERFORMING ARTS: *Dance:* North America

Griffiths, A.R.G. Associate Professor in History, Flinders University of South Australia. Author of *Contemporary Australia* and *Beautiful Lies*. •WORLD AFFAIRS: *Australia; Nauru; Palau; Papua New Guinea*

Grossman, Sandra A. Deputy Director, The Cuba Program, Inter-American Dialogue, Washington, D.C. •WORLD AFFAIRS: *Cuba*

Guthridge, Guy G. Manager, Antarctic Information Program, U.S. National Science Foundation. •WORLD AFFAIRS: *Antarctica*

Haddad, Mahmoud. Associate Professor of History, Balamand University, Lebanon. •WORLD AFFAIRS: *Lebanon; Saudi Arabia*

Halman, Talat S. Professor and Chairman, Department of Turkish Literature, Bilkent University, Ankara, Turkey. Author of *Doğrusu*. •LITERATURE: *Turkish*

Hammer, William R. Professor and Chair, Department of Geology, Augustana College, Rock Island, Ill. Author of *Gondwana Dinosaurs from the Jurassic of Antarctica*. •LIFE SCIENCES: *Paleontology*

Henry, Alan. Grand Prix Editor, *Autocar* (London). Motor Racing Correspondent, *The Guardian*. Author of *Mercedes in Motorsport* and *50 Years of World Championship Grand Prix Motor Racing*. •SPORTS AND GAMES: *Automobile Racing:* Grand Prix Racing

Hobbs, Greg. Chief Writer, *AFL Record*. Author of *One Hundred and Twenty-Five Years of the Melbourne Demons*. •SPORTS AND GAMES: *Football:* Australian

Hoffman, Dean A. Executive Editor, *Hoof Beats*. Author of *The Hambletonian: America's Trotting Classic*. •SPORTS AND GAMES: *Equestrian Sports:* Harness Racing

Hoke, John. Publisher, *Amateur Wrestling News*. •SPORTS AND GAMES: *Wrestling*

Hollar, Sherman. Assistant Editor, Encyclopædia Britannica. •BIOGRAPHIES *(in part);* DISASTERS; OBITUARIES *(in part)*

Homel, David. Freelance Writer; Lecturer, Concordia University, Montreal. Author of *Get on Top* and others. •LITERATURE: *French:* Canada

Hope, Thomas W. Owner, Hope Reports, Inc.; Former Film Producer. Author of *Large Screen Presentation Systems*. •PERFORMING ARTS: *Motion Pictures:* Nontheatrical Films

IEIS. International Economic Information Services. •ECONOMIC AFFAIRS: *World Economy; Stock Exchanges* (international)

Ingham, Kenneth. Emeritus Professor of History, University of Bristol, Eng. Author of *Politics in Modern Africa: The Uneven Tribal Dimension* and others. •WORLD AFFAIRS: *Angola; Congo, Democratic Republic of the; Kenya; Malawi; Mozambique; Sudan, The; Tanzania; Uganda; Zambia; Zimbabwe*

Ingram, Derek. President Emeritus, Commonwealth Journalists Association; Founding Editor, Gemini News Service. Author of *A Much-Too-Timid Commonwealth* and others. •WORLD AFFAIRS: *Commonwealth of Nations*

Ionescu, Dan. Broadcaster/Editor, Radio Free Europe/Radio Liberty. Contributor to *Transitions*. •WORLD AFFAIRS: *Moldova*

Isaacson, Lanae Hjortsvang. Editor, *Nordic Women Writers*. •LITERATURE: *Danish*

Iyob, Ruth. Associate Professor of Political Science, University of Missouri, St. Louis. •WORLD AFFAIRS: *Eritrea*

Jamail, Milton. Lecturer, Department of Government, University of Texas at Austin. Author of *Full Count: Inside Cuban Baseball*. •SPORTS AND GAMES: *Baseball:* Latin America

Joffé, George. Director, Centre of North African Studies, University of Cambridge. Editor, *Perspectives on Development: The Euro-Mediterranean Partnership*. •WORLD AFFAIRS: *Algeria; Morocco; Tunisia*

Johnson, Steve. Media Critic, *Chicago Tribune*. •MEDIA AND PUBLISHING: *Radio* (U.S.); *Television* (U.S.)

Johnson, Todd M. Director, World Evangelization Research Center. Coauthor of *World Christian Encyclopedia*. •RELIGION: *Tables (in part)*

Joireman, Sandra F. Associate Professor of Politics and International Relations, Wheaton College, Wheaton, Ill. Author of *Property Rights and Political Development in Ethiopia and Eritrea*. •WORLD AFFAIRS: *Ethiopia*

Jones, David G.C. Tutor, Department of Continuing Education, University of Aberystwyth, Aberystwyth, Wales. Author of *Atomic Physics*. •MATHEMATICS AND PHYSICAL SCIENCES: *Physics*

Jones, Mark P. Associate Professor of Political Science, Michigan State University. Author of *Electoral Laws and the Survival of Presidential Democracies*. •WORLD AFFAIRS: *Argentina*

Kaiser, Robert G. Associate Editor, *The Washington Post*. Author of *Why Gorbachev Happened: His Triumphs and His Failure* and others. •SPECIAL REPORT: *9-11*

Kanduza, Ackson M. Associate Professor and Chair, Department of History, University of Swaziland. Author of *Political Economy of Democratisation in Swaziland*. •WORLD AFFAIRS: *Swaziland*

Karimi-Hakkak, Ahmad. Professor of Persian Languages and Literature, University of Washington. Author of *Recasting Persian Poetry: Scenarios of Poetic Modernity in Iran*. •LITERATURE: *Persian*

Kazamaru, Yoshihiko. Literary Critic. •LITERATURE: *Japanese*

Kelleher, John A. Journalist and Editorial Consultant; Former Editor, *Dominion* and *Dominion Sunday Times* (Wellington). •WORLD AFFAIRS: *New Zealand*

Kelling, George H. Lieutenant Colonel, U.S. Army (ret.). Author of *Countdown to Rebellion: British Policy in Cyprus 1939–1955*. •WORLD AFFAIRS: *Cyprus*

Kellner, Peter. Journalist, *The Observer, London Evening Standard*. Author of *The New Mutualism* and others. •BIOGRAPHIES *(in part);* WORLD AFFAIRS: *United Kingdom; United Kingdom:* Sidebar

Kessler, Clive S. Professor of Sociology, University of New South Wales, Sydney. •WORLD AFFAIRS: *Malaysia*

Knox, Paul. International Affairs Reporter, *The Globe and Mail*, Toronto. •WORLD AFFAIRS: *Bolivia; Ecuador*

Kobliner, Beth. Journalist. Author of *Get a Financial Life*. •ECONOMIC AFFAIRS: *Stock Exchanges* (North America)

Kovel, Ralph and Terry. Publishers. Authors of *Kovels on Antiques and Collectibles*. •ART, ANTIQUES, AND COLLECTIONS: *Antiques and Collectibles*

Krause, Stefan. Freelance Political Analyst, Brussels. •WORLD AFFAIRS: *Greece; Macedonia*

Kruger, Linda M. Managing Editor, *Collectors News*. •ART, ANTIQUES, AND COLLECTIONS: Sidebar

Kuiper, Kathleen. Senior Editor, Encyclopædia Britannica. Editor, *Merriam-Webster's Encyclopedia of Literature*. •BIOGRAPHIES *(in part)*; LITERATURE: *Japanese:* Sidebar

Kuptsch, Christiane. Research Officer, International Institute for Labour Studies, International Labour Office. Coeditor of *Social Security at the Dawn of the 21st Century*. •SOCIAL PROTECTION (international)

Lamb, Kevin M. Special Projects Writer, *Dayton* (Ohio) *Daily News*. Author of *Quarterbacks, Nickelbacks & Other Loose Change*. •SPORTS AND GAMES: *Football:* Canadian, U.S.

Langeneckert, Sandra. Senior Copy Editor, Encyclopædia Britannica. •BIOGRAPHIES *(in part)*

Lawler, Nancy Ellen. Professor Emeritus, Oakton Community College, Des Plaines, Ill. Author of *Soldiers of Misfortune* and others. •BIOGRAPHIES *(in part)*; WORLD AFFAIRS: *Benin; Burkina Faso; Cameroon; Central African Republic; Congo, Republic of the; Côte d'Ivoire; Gabon; Guinea; Mali; Mauritania; Niger; Senegal; Togo*

Lawson, Fred H. James Irvine Professor of Government, Mills College, Oakland, Calif. Author of *Why Syria Goes to War*. •WORLD AFFAIRS: *Syria*

Le Comte, Douglas. Meteorologist, Climate Prediction Center, National Oceanic and Atmospheric Administration. •EARTH SCIENCES: *Meteorology and Climate*

Legassick, Martin. Professor of History, University of the Western Cape, Bellville, S.Af. Author of *Skeletons in the Cupboard: South African Museums and the Trade in Human Remains 1907–1917*. •WORLD AFFAIRS: *South Africa*

Levine, Steven I. Mansfield Professor of Asia Pacific Studies, The Mansfield Center, University of Montana, Missoula. •WORLD AFFAIRS: *China; Taiwan*

Levy, Michael I. Editor, Encyclopædia Britannica. •BIOGRAPHIES *(in part)*; WORLD AFFAIRS: *United States:* Sidebar

Lindstrom, Sieg. Managing Editor, *Track & Field News*. •SPORTS AND GAMES: *Track and Field Sports (Athletics)*

Litweiler, John. Jazz Critic. Author of *The Freedom Principle: Jazz After 1958* and *Ornette Coleman: A Harmolodic Life*. •BIOGRAPHIES *(in part)*; OBITUARIES *(in part)*; PERFORMING ARTS: *Music:* Jazz

Logan, Robert G. Sportswriter, *Daily Herald* (Arlington Heights, Ill.). Author of *The Bulls and Chicago: A Stormy Affair* and others. •SPORTS AND GAMES: *Basketball:* United States

Longmore, Andrew. Chief Sports Feature Writer, *The Independent*; Former Assistant Editor, *The Cricketer*. Author of *The Complete Guide to Cycling*. •SPORTS AND GAMES: *Cricket*

Luling, Virginia. Independent Researcher, Survival International. Author of *Somali Sultanate: The Geledi City-State over 150 Years*. •WORLD AFFAIRS: *Somalia; Somalia:* Sidebar

Lundin, Immi. Freelance Journalist and Literary Critic. •LITERATURE: *Swedish*

Macdonald, Barrie. Professor of History, Massey University, Palmerston, N.Z. •WORLD AFFAIRS: *Dependent States:* Pacific; *Fiji; Kiribati; Marshall Islands; Micronesia, Federated States of; Samoa; Solomon Islands; Tonga; Tuvalu; Vanuatu*

McGregor, Alan. Freelance Journalist. •WORLD AFFAIRS: *Switzerland*

McLachlan, Keith S. Professor Emeritus, School of Oriental and African Studies, University of London. Coeditor of *Landlocked States of Africa and Asia*. Author of *Boundaries of Modern Iran*. •WORLD AFFAIRS: *Iran*

McLellan, Joseph. Music Critic Emeritus, *The Washington Post*. •PERFORMING ARTS: *Music:* Classical

Malik, Mohan. Associate Professor, Asia-Pacific Center for Security Studies, Honolulu. •WORLD AFFAIRS: *Myanmar (Burma)*

Manghnani, Murli H. Professor of Geophysics, University of Hawaii at Manoa, Honolulu. •EARTH SCIENCES: *Geophysics*

Mango, Andrew. Foreign Affairs Analyst. Author of *Atatürk: The Biography of the Founder of Modern Turkey* and *Turkey: The Challenge of a New Role*. •WORLD AFFAIRS: *Turkey*

Marples, David R. Professor of History, University of Alberta. Author of *Belarus: A Denationalized Nation* and *Lenin's Revolution: Russia, 1917–1921*. •WORLD AFFAIRS: *Belarus; Ukraine*

Matthíasson, Björn. Economist, Ministry of Finance, Iceland. •WORLD AFFAIRS: *Iceland*

Mazie, David M. Freelance Journalist. •SOCIAL PROTECTION (U.S.)

Michael, Tom. Editor, Encyclopædia Britannica. •BIOGRAPHIES *(in part)*; OBITUARIES *(in part)*; SPORTS AND GAMES: *Basketball:* International

Middlebrook, Kevin J. Director, Center for U.S.-Mexican Studies, University of California, San Diego. Editor of *Conservative Parties, the Right, and Democracy in Latin America*. •WORLD AFFAIRS: *Mexico*

Mora, Frank O. Associate Professor and Chair of International Studies, Rhodes College, Memphis, Tenn. •WORLD AFFAIRS: *Paraguay*

Morgan, Paul. Editor, *Rugby World*. •SPORTS AND GAMES: *Football:* Rugby Football

Morris, Jacqui M. Freelance Editor; Lecturer, University of Sussex, Brighton, Eng.; Former Editor, *Oryx, The International Journal of Conservation*. •THE ENVIRONMENT: *Wildlife Conservation*

Morrison, Graham. Press Officer, British Fencing Association; Correspondent, *Daily Telegraph; Country Life*. •SPORTS AND GAMES: *Fencing*

Murphy, Colin J. Freelance Writer and Editor. •BIOGRAPHIES *(in part)*

Myers, David J. Professor of Political Science, Pennsylvania State University. •WORLD AFFAIRS: *Venezuela*

Newton, Clyde. Editor and Publisher, *Sumo World*. Author of *Dynamic Sumo*. •SPORTS AND GAMES: *Wrestling:* Sumo

Noda, Hiroki. Staff Reporter, *Jiji Press Ltd.*, Japan. •SPORTS AND GAMES: *Baseball:* Japan

O'Brien, Dan. Senior Editor/Economist (Europe), Economist Intelligence Unit. •WORLD AFFAIRS: *Austria*

Ogden, Shepherd. Founder and President, The Cook's Garden. Author of *Straight Ahead Organic* and others. •THE ENVIRONMENT: *Gardening*

O'Leary, Christopher. Senior Editor, *Investment Dealers Digest*. •ECONOMIC AFFAIRS: *Business Overview*

Oppenheim, Lois Hecht. Professor of Political Science and Vice President for Academic Affairs, University of Judaism, Los Angeles. Author of *Politics in Chile: Democracy, Authoritarianism and the Search for Development*. •WORLD AFFAIRS: *Chile*

O'Quinn, Jim. Editor in Chief, *American Theatre*. •PERFORMING ARTS: *Theatre:* U.S. and Canada

Orr, Jay. Editor and Senior Music Writer, Country.com. •BIOGRAPHIES *(in part)*; PERFORMING ARTS: *Music:* Popular (U.S.)

Orwig, Sarah Forbes. Associate Editor, Encyclopædia Britannica. •BIOGRAPHIES *(in part)*

Osborne, Keith L. Editor, *British Rowing Almanack*. Author of *Boat Racing in Britain, 1715–1975* and *One Man Went to Row*. •SPORTS AND GAMES: *Rowing*

Paarlberg, Philip L. Professor of Agricultural Economics, Purdue University, West Lafayette, Ind. •AGRICULTURE AND FOOD SUPPLIES: *Agriculture*

Paradkar, Shalaka. Content Manager, Industrial Credit and Investment Corporation of India. •BIOGRAPHIES *(in part)*; OBITUARIES *(in part)*; WORLD AFFAIRS: *India:* Sidebar

Parker, Ines. Freelance Writer. •WORLD AFFAIRS: *Belize*

Parsons, Neil. Professor of History, University of Botswana. Author of *King Khama, Emperor Joe, and the Great White Queen*. •WORLD AFFAIRS: *Botswana*

Pérez, Orlando J. Associate Professor of Political Science, Central Michigan University. Editor of *Post-Invasion Panama: The Challenges of Democratization in the New World Order*. •WORLD AFFAIRS: *Panama*

Peszek, Luan. Publications Director and Editor, *U.S.A. Gymnastics*. Author of *Gymnastics Almanac*. •SPORTS AND GAMES: *Gymnastics*

Peterson, Mark. Associate Professor of Korean Studies, Brigham Young University. Author of *Korean Adoption and Inheritance* and others. •WORLD AFFAIRS: *Korea, Dem. People's Republic of; Korea, Republic of*

Prasad, H.Y. Sharada. Vice President, Indian Council for Cultural Relations; Former Information Adviser to the Prime Minister of India. •WORLD AFFAIRS: *India*

Primorac, Max. Executive Director, Institute of World Affairs, Zagreb, Croatia. •WORLD AFFAIRS: *Croatia*

Rauch, Robert. Freelance Editor and Writer. •BIOGRAPHIES *(in part)*; NOBEL PRIZES *(in part)*; OBITUARIES *(in part)*

Raun, Toivo U. Professor of Central Eurasian Studies, Indiana University. Author of *Estonia and the Estonians*. •WORLD AFFAIRS: *Estonia*

Rebelo, L.S. Professor Emeritus, Department of Portuguese Studies, King's College, University of London. •LITERATURE: *Portuguese:* Portugal

Reid, Ron. Staff Writer, *Philadelphia Inquirer*. •SPORTS AND GAMES: *Ice Hockey; Ice Skating*

Renwick, David. Freelance Journalist. •WORLD AFFAIRS: *Antigua and Barbuda; Bahamas, The; Barbados; Dependent States:* Caribbean and Bermuda; *Dominica; Grenada; Guyana; Jamaica; Saint Kitts and Nevis; Saint Lucia; Saint Vincent and the Grenadines; Trinidad and Tobago*

Robbins, Paul. International Correspondent, *Ski Trax;* Nordic Correspondent, *Ski Racing*. •SPORTS AND GAMES: *Skiing*

Robinson, David. Film Critic and Historian. Author of *A History of World Cinema* and *Chaplin: His Life and Art*. •PERFORMING ARTS: *Motion Pictures*

Roby, Anne. Freelance Journalist. •WORLD AFFAIRS: *Andorra; Liechtenstein; Luxembourg; Monaco*

Rohwedder, Cecilie. Staff Reporter, *The Wall Street Journal Europe*. •WORLD AFFAIRS: *Germany*

Rollin, Jack. Editor, *Rothmans Football Yearbook*. Author of *World Cup 1930–1990* and others. •SPORTS AND GAMES: *Football:* Association Football (Soccer)

Rose, Leo E. Professor Emeritus of Political Science, University of California, Berkeley. •WORLD AFFAIRS: *Bhutan; Nepal*

Rugh, William A. President and CEO, AMIDEAST; Former U.S. Ambassador to Yemen and the United Arab Emirates. Author of *The Arab Press*. •WORLD AFFAIRS: *United Arab Emirates; Yemen*

Rutherford, Andrew. Professor of Law and Criminal Policy, University of Southampton, Eng. Author of *Transforming Criminal Policy* and others. •LAW, CRIME, AND LAW ENFORCEMENT: *Prisons and Penology*

Sabo, Anne G. Assistant Professor of Norwegian, St. Olaf College, Northfield, Minn. •LITERATURE: *Norwegian*

Sahadevan, Ponmoni. Associate Professor, Jawaharlal Nehru University, New Delhi. Author of *Conflict and Peacemaking in South Asia*. •WORLD AFFAIRS: *Maldives*

Sanders, Alan J.K. Former Lecturer in Mongolian Studies, School of Oriental and African Studies, University of London. Author of *Historical Dictionary of Mongolia;* Coauthor of *Colloquial Mongolian*. •WORLD AFFAIRS: *Mongolia*

Sandvik, Gudmund. Professor Emeritus of Legal History, Faculty of Law, University of Oslo. •WORLD AFFAIRS: *Norway*

Saracino, Peter. Freelance Defense Journalist. •MILITARY AFFAIRS

Sarahete, Yrjö. Secretary Emeritus, Fédération Internationale des Quilleurs. •SPORTS AND GAMES: *Bowling:* World Tenpins

Saunders, Christopher. Professor of Historical Studies, University of Cape Town, S.Af. Coauthor of *Historical Dictionary of South Africa* and *South Africa: A Modern History*. •WORLD AFFAIRS: *Cape Verde; Chad; Equatorial Guinea; Gambia, The; Guinea-Bissau; Lesotho; Madagascar; Namibia; São Tomé and Príncipe*

Schmidt, Fabian. Head of the Bosnian Program, Deutsche Welle. •WORLD AFFAIRS: *Albania*

Schmitt, Eric. National Immigration and Census Correspondent, *The New York Times*. •WORLD AFFAIRS: *United States:* Special Report: The U.S. Census of 2000

Schroeder, Patricia S. President and CEO, Association of American Publishers. Author of *24 Years of House Work...and the Place Is Still a Mess*. •MEDIA AND PUBLISHING: *Book Publishing* (U.S.)

Schulz, Nancy. Freelance Journalist. •MEDIA AND PUBLISHING: *Book Publishing:* Sidebar

Schuster, Angela M.H. Director of Publications, World Monuments Fund; Contributing Editor, *Archaeology;* Editor, *The Explorers Journal*. •ANTHROPOLOGY AND ARCHAEOLOGY: *Archaeology:* Eastern Hemisphere

Sego, Stephen. Freelance Journalist; Former Director, Radio Free Afghanistan. •BIOGRAPHIES *(in part);* WORLD AFFAIRS: *Afghanistan*

Seligson, Mitchell A. Daniel H. Wallace Professor of Political Science, University of Pittsburgh. Editor of *Elections and Democracy in Central America, Revisited*. •WORLD AFFAIRS: *Costa Rica*

Seno, Alexandra A. Correspondent, *Asiaweek*. •WORLD AFFAIRS: *Cambodia*

Serafin, Steven R. Director, Writing Center, Hunter College, City University of New York. Editor of *The Continuum Encyclopedia of American Literature*. •NOBEL PRIZES *(in part)*

Settergren, Amy. Department of History, Northwestern University, Evanston, Ill. •BIOGRAPHIES *(in part);* WORLD AFFAIRS: *Ghana*

Shelley, Andrew. Director, Women's International Squash Players Association; Technical Director, World Squash Federation. Author of *Squash Rules: A Players Guide*. •SPORTS AND GAMES: *Squash*

Shepherd, Melinda C. Associate Editor, Encyclopædia Britannica. •OBITUARIES *(in part);* WORLD AFFAIRS: *Dependent States:* Europe and the Atlantic

Shubinsky, Valery. Correspondent, *Vecherny Peterburg*. •LITERATURE: *Russian*

Siler, Shanda. Editorial Assistant, Encyclopædia Britannica. •BIOGRAPHIES *(in part);* OBITUARIES *(in part)*

Simons, Paul. Freelance Journalist. Author of *The Action Plant*. •LIFE SCIENCES: *Botany*

Simpson, Jane. Freelance Writer. •PERFORMING ARTS: *Dance:* European

Sklar, Morton. Executive Director, World Organization Against Torture USA; Judge, Administrative Tribunal for OAS. Editor, *The Status of Human Rights in the United States* and *Torture in the U.S.* Author of *The Right to Travel* and others. •SOCIAL PROTECTION: *Human Rights*

Smentkowski, Brian. Associate Professor of Political Science, Southeast Missouri State University, Cape Girardeau, Mo. *(The author acknowledges research assistance of Benjamin Lowrance)* •LAW, CRIME, AND LAW ENFORCEMENT: *Court Decisions*

Smith, Gregory O. Academic Development Officer, European School of Economics. •WORLD AFFAIRS: *San Marino; Vatican City State*

Snodgrass, Donald R. Institute Fellow Emeritus, Harvard University. Coauthor of *Economics of Development, 5th ed*. •WORLD AFFAIRS: *Sri Lanka*

Sparks, Karen J. Managing Editor, Encyclopædia Britannica. •BIOGRAPHIES *(in part);* OBITUARIES *(in part);* LIBRARIES AND MUSEUMS: *Museums*

Stern, Irwin. Lecturer in Foreign Languages, North Carolina State University. Editor of *Dictionary of Brazilian Literature*. •LITERATURE: *Portuguese:* Brazil

Stewart, Alan. Freelance Journalist. Author of *How to Make It in IT*. •COMPUTERS AND INFORMATION SYSTEMS: *Microelectronics; Telecommunications*

Summerhill, Edward. Editor, Finnish News Agency; Former Part-Time Staff Member, Reuters. •WORLD AFFAIRS: *Finland*

Sumner, David E. Professor of Journalism and Head of the Magazine Program, Ball State University, Muncie, Ind. •MEDIA AND PUBLISHING: *Magazines*

Susel, Rudolph M. Editor, *American Home*. •WORLD AFFAIRS: *Slovenia*

Susser, Leslie D. Diplomatic Correspondent, *The Jerusalem Report*. Coauthor of *Shalom Friend: The Life and Legacy of Yitzhak Rabin*. •BIOGRAPHIES *(in part);* WORLD AFFAIRS: *Israel*

Swift, Richard N. Professor Emeritus of Politics, New York University. •WORLD AFFAIRS: *Multinational and Regional Organizations; United Nations*

Szilagyi, Zsofia. Freelance Writer. •WORLD AFFAIRS: *Hungary*

Tao, Amy R. Freelance Writer and Editor. •BIOGRAPHIES *(in part)*

Taylor, Jolanda Vanderwal. Associate Professor of Dutch and German, University of Wisconsin, Madison. Author of *A Family Occupation: Children of the War and the Memory of World War II in Dutch Literature of the 1980s*. •LITERATURE: *Netherlandic;* WORLD AFFAIRS: *The Netherlands*

Taylor-Robinson, Michelle M. Associate Professor of Political Science, Texas A&M University. Coauthor of *Negotiating Democracy: Transitions from Authoritarian Rule*. •WORLD AFFAIRS: *Honduras*

Teague, Elizabeth. Research Analyst, Foreign and Commonwealth Office, London. *(The opinions expressed are personal and do not necessarily represent those of the British government.)* •WORLD AFFAIRS: *Russia*

Tétreault, Mary Ann. Una Chapman Cox Distinguished Professor of International Affairs, Trinity University, San Antonio, Texas. Author of *Stories of Democracy: Politics and Society in Contemporary Kuwait* and others. •WORLD AFFAIRS: *Kuwait*

Thayer, Carlyle A. Professor of Politics, Australian Defence Force Academy, Canberra. Author of *The Vietnam People's Army Under Doi Moi*. •WORLD AFFAIRS: *Vietnam*

Thomas, R. Murray. Professor Emeritus of Education, University of California, Santa Barbara. Author of *Recent Theories of Human Development*. •EDUCATION

Thyagarajan, S. Deputy Editor and Hockey Correspondent, *The Hindu*. •SPORTS AND GAMES: *Field Hockey*

Tikkanen, Amy. Freelance Writer and Editor. •BIOGRAPHIES *(in part)*

Todd Middleton, Amy. Assistant Vice President, Sotheby's. •ART, ANTIQUES, AND COLLECTIONS: *Art Auctions and Sales*

Tucker, Emma. Correspondent, *Financial Times*. •WORLD AFFAIRS: *European Union*

Turner, Darrell J. Freelance Writer; Former Religion Writer, *The Journal Gazette* (Fort Wayne, Ind.). •RELIGION

Uddin, Shantha. Director, Research and Reference Center/Permissions, Encyclopædia Britannica. •RELIGION: Sidebar

Uhlick, Lawrence R. Executive Director and General Counsel, Institute of International Bankers. •ECONOMIC AFFAIRS: *Banking*

UNHCR. The Office of the United Nations High Commissioner for Refugees. •SOCIAL PROTECTION: *Refugees and International Migration*

Urbansky, Julie. Media and Public Relations Director, U.S. Bobsled and Skeleton Federation. •SPORTS AND GAMES: *Bobsledding and Luge*

Verdi, Robert. Senior Writer, *New York Times Magazine* group; Contributing Columnist, *Chicago Tribune*. •SPORTS AND GAMES: *Baseball* (U.S. and Canada)

Walker, Thomas W. Professor of Political Science and Director, Latin American Studies Program, Ohio University. Coauthor of *Repression, Resistance, and Democratic Transition in Central America*. •WORLD AFFAIRS: *Nicaragua*

Wallenfeldt, Jeff. Senior Editor, Encyclopædia Britannica. •BIOGRAPHIES *(in part)*

Wang Xiaoming. Professor of Chinese Literature, East China Normal University, Shanghai. Author of *The Cold Face of Reality: A Biography of Lu Xun*. •LITERATURE: *Chinese*

Wanninger, Richard S. Freelance Journalist. •SPORTS AND GAMES: *Volleyball*

Watson, Rory. Freelance Journalist specializing in European Union affairs. Coauthor of *The American Express Guide to Brussels*. •WORLD AFFAIRS: *Belgium*

Weil, Eric. Sports Editor, *Buenos Aires Herald*. •SPORTS AND GAMES: *Football:* Association Football (Soccer): *Latin America*

Weinstein, Martin. Professor of Political Science, William Paterson University of New Jersey, Wayne, N.J. Author of *Uruguay: Democracy at the Crossroads*. •WORLD AFFAIRS: *Uruguay*

White, Martin L. Freelance Writer, Chicago. •OBITUARIES *(in part)*

Whitney, Barbara. Copy Supervisor, Encyclopædia Britannica. •BIOGRAPHIES *(in part);* MEDIA AND PUBLISHING: *Television:* Sidebar; OBITUARIES *(in part)*

Whitten, Phillip. Editor in Chief, *Swimming World*. Author of *The Complete Book of Swimming* and others. •SPORTS AND GAMES: *Swimming*

Wilkinson, Earl J. Executive Director, International Newspaper Marketing Association. Author of *Branding and the Newspaper Consumer*. •MEDIA AND PUBLISHING: *Newspapers*

Wilkinson, John R. Sportswriter, Coventry Newspapers. •SPORTS AND GAMES: *Cycling*

Williams, Victoria C. Assistant Professor of the Humanities, Alvernia College, Reading, Pa.; Independent Consultant on International Affairs. •LAW, CRIME, AND LAW ENFORCEMENT: *International Law*

Wilson, Derek. Correspondent, BBC, Rome. Author of *Rome, Umbria and Tuscany*. •BIOGRAPHIES *(in part);* WORLD AFFAIRS: *Italy*

Wise, Larry. Freelance Writer; Former World Champion Archer and Professional Coach. Author of *Tuning Your Compound Bow* and others. •SPORTS AND GAMES: *Archery*

Woodrow, Robert. Former Assistant Managing Editor, *Asiaweek*. •BIOGRAPHIES *(in part);* WORLD AFFAIRS: *Laos; Thailand*

Woods, Elizabeth. Writer. Author of *If Only Things Were Different (I): A Model for a Sustainable Society, Bird Salad,* and others. •LITERATURE: *English:* Canada

Woods, Michael. Science Editor, *The Toledo Blade*. Author of *Ancient Technology*. •MATHEMATICS AND PHYSICAL SCIENCES: *Chemistry;* NOBEL PRIZES *(in part)*

Woodward, Kenneth L. Religion Editor, *Newsweek*. Author of *The Book of Miracles: The Meaning of the Miracle Stories in Christianity, Judaism, Buddhism, Hinduism, and Islam*. •RELIGION: *Special Report:* Christianity's Newest Converts

Woodward, Ralph Lee, Jr. Neville G. Penrose Professor of Latin American Studies, Texas Christian University. Author of *Central America, a Nation Divided*. •WORLD AFFAIRS: *El Salvador; Guatemala*

Wyllie, Peter J. Emeritus Professor of Geology, California Institute of Technology, Pasadena. Author of *The Dynamic Earth* and *The Way the Earth Works*. •EARTH SCIENCES: *Geology and Geochemistry*

Zegura, Stephen L. Professor of Anthropology, University of Arizona. •ANTHROPOLOGY AND ARCHAEOLOGY: *Anthropology:* Physical

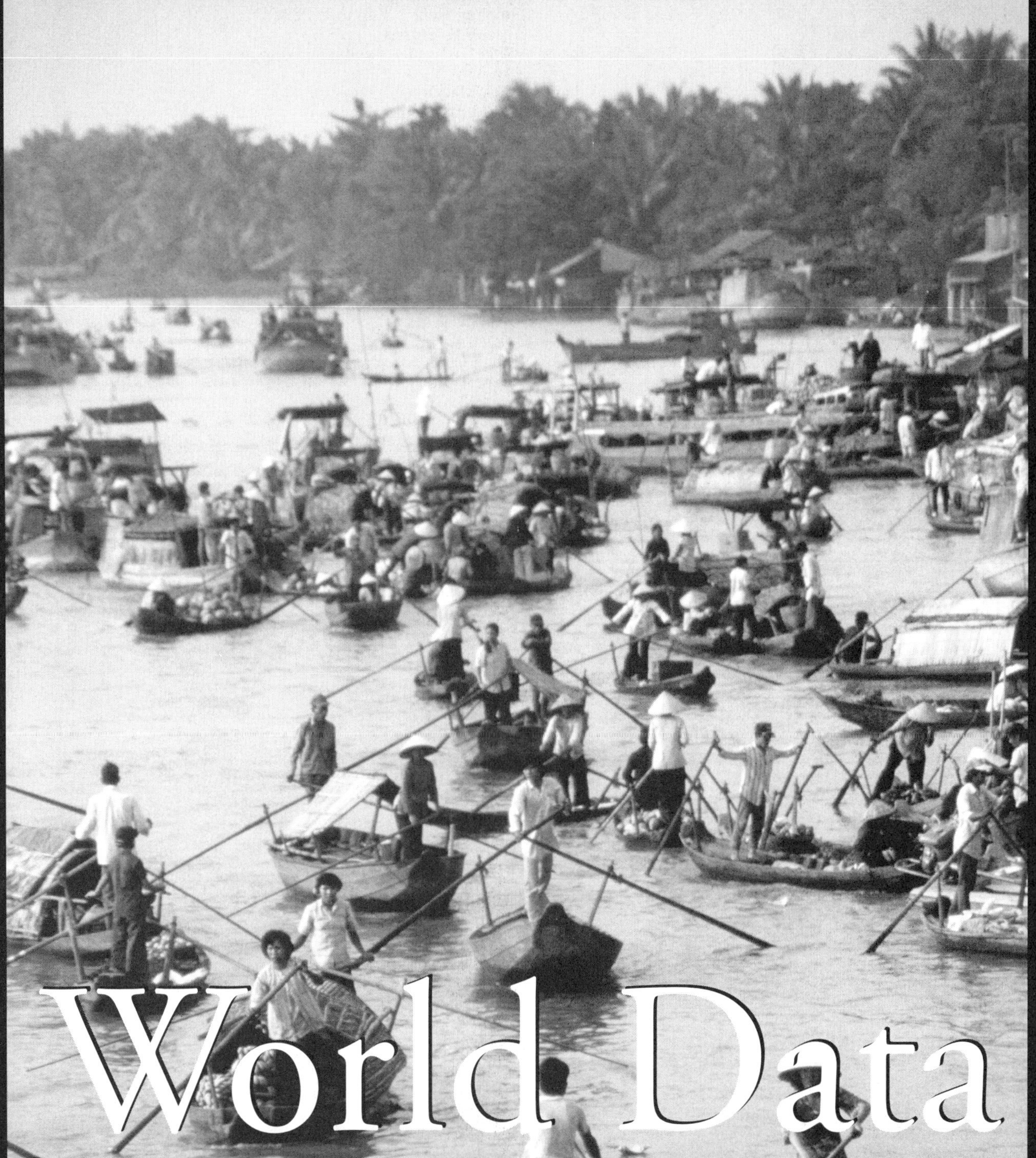

World Data

A female born in East Africa can expect to live 46.5 years—her counterpart in Western Europe will live, on average, 35 years longer.

CONTENTS

INTRODUCTION

Britannica World Data provides a statistical portrait of some 217 countries and dependencies of the world, at a level appropriate to the significance of each. It contains 213 country statements (the "Nations of the World" section), ranging in length from one to seven pages, and permits, in the 20 major thematic tables (the "Comparative National Statistics" [CNS] section), comparisons among these larger countries and 4 other states.

Updated annually, *Britannica World Data* is particularly intended as direct, structured support for many of Britannica's other reference works—encyclopaedias, yearbooks, atlases—at a level of detail that their editorial style or design do not permit.

Like the textual, graphic, or cartographic modes of expression of these other products, statistics possess their own inherent editorial virtues and weaknesses. Two principal goals in the creation of *Britannica World Data* were up-to-dateness and comparability, each possible to maximize separately, but not always possible to combine. If, for example, research on some subject is completed during a particular year (*x*), figures may be available for 100 countries for the preceding year (*x* – 1), for 140 countries for the year before that (*x* – 2), and for 180 countries for the year before that (*x* – 3).

Which year should be the basis of a thematic compilation for 217 countries so as to give the best combination of up-to-dateness and comparability? And, should *x* – 1 be adopted for the thematic table, ought up-to-dateness in the country table (for which year *x* is already available) be sacrificed for agreement with the thematic table? In general, the editors have opted for maximum up-to-dateness in the country statistical boxes and maximum comparability in the thematic tables.

Comparability, however, also resides in the meaning of the numbers compiled, which may differ greatly from country to country. The headnotes to the thematic tables explain many of these methodological problems; the Glossary serves the same purpose for the country statistical pages. Published data do not always provide the researcher or editor with a neat, unambiguous choice between a datum compiled on two different bases (say, railroad track length, or route length), one of which is wanted and the other not. More often a choice must be made among a variety of official, private, and external intergovernmental (UN, FAO, IMF) sources, each reporting its best data but each representing a set of problems: (1) of methodological variance from (or among) international conventions; (2) of analytical completeness (data for a single year may, successively, be projected [based on 10 months' data], preliminary [for 12 months], final, revised or adjusted, etc.); (3) of time frame, or accounting interval (data may represent a full Gregorian calendar year [preferred], a fiscal year, an Islamic or other national or religious year, a multiyear period or average [when a one-year statement would contain unrepresentative results]); (4) of continuity with previous data; and the like. Finally, published data on a particular subject may be complete and final but impossible to summarize in a simple manner. The education system of a single country may include, for example, public and private sectors; local, state, or national systems; varying grades, tracks, or forms within a single system; or opportunities for double-counting or fractional counting of a student, teacher, or institution. When no recent official data exist, or they exist, but may be suspect, the tables may show unofficial estimates, a range (of published opinion), analogous data, or no data at all.

The published basis of the information compiled is the statistical collections of Encyclopædia Britannica, Inc., some of the principal elements of which are enumerated in the Bibliography. Holdings for a given country may include any of the following: the national statistical abstract; the constitution; the most recent censuses of population; periodic or occasional reports on vital statistics, social indicators, agriculture, mining, labour, manufacturing, domestic and foreign trade, finance and banking, transportation, and communications. Further information is received in a variety of formats—telephone, letter, fax, microfilm and microfiche, and most recently, in electronic formats such as computer disks, CD-ROMs, and the Internet. So substantial has the resources of the Internet become that it was decided to add uniform resource locators (URLs) to the great majority of country pages and a number of the CNS tables (summary world sites with data on all countries still being somewhat of a rarity) so as to apprise the reader of the possibility and means to access current information on these subjects year-round.

The recommendations offered are usually to official sites (national statistical offices, general national governments, central banks, embassies, intergovernmental organizations [especially the UN Development Programme], and the like). Though often dissimilar in content, they will usually be updated year-round, expanded as opportunity permits, and lead on to related sites, such as parliamentary offices, information offices, diplomatic and consular sites, news agencies and newspapers, and, beyond, to the myriad academic, commercial, and private sites now accessible from the personal computer. While these URLs were correct and current at the time of writing, they may be subject to change.

The great majority of the social, economic, and financial data contained in this work should not be interpreted in isolation. Interpretive text of long perspective, such as that of the *Encyclopædia Britannica* itself; political, geographic, and topical maps, such as those in the *Britannica Atlas;* and recent analysis of political events and economic trends, such as that contained in the articles of the *Book of the Year,* will all help to supply analytic focus that numbers alone cannot. By the same token, study of those sources will be made more concrete by use of *Britannica World Data* to supply up-to-date geographic, demographic, and economic detail.

GLOSSARY

A number of terms that are used to classify and report data in the "Nations of the World" section require some explanation.

Those italicized terms that are used regularly in the country compilations to introduce specific categories of information (*e.g., birth rate, budget*) appear in this glossary in italic boldface type, followed by a description of the precise kind of information being offered and how it has been edited and presented.

All other terms are printed here in roman boldface type. Many terms have quite specific meanings in statistical reporting, and they are so defined here. Other terms have less specific application as they are used by different countries or organizations. Data in the country compilations based on definitions markedly different from those below will usually be footnoted.

Terms that appear in small capitals in certain definitions are themselves defined at their respective alphabetical locations.

Terms whose definitions are marked by an asterisk (*) refer to data supplied only in the larger two- to four-page country compilations.

access to services, a group of measures indicating a population's level of access to public services, including electrical power, treated public drinking water, sewage removal, and fire protection.*

activity rate, *see* participation/activity rates.

age breakdown, the distribution of a given population by age, usually reported here as percentages of total population in 15-year age brackets. When substantial numbers of persons do not know, or state, their exact age, distributions may not total 100.0%.

area, the total surface area of a country or its administrative subdivisions, including both land and inland (nontidal) water area. Land area is usually calculated from "mean low water" on a "plane table," or flat, basis.

area and population, a tabulation usually including the first-order administrative subdivisions of the country (such as the states of the United States), with capital (headquarters, or administrative seat), area, and population. When these subdivisions are especially numerous or, occasionally, nonexistent, a planning, electoral, census, or other nonadministrative scheme of regional subdivisions has been substituted.

associated state, *see* state.

atheist, in statements of religious affiliation, one who professes active opposition to religion; "nonreligious" refers to those professing only no religion, nonbelief, or doubt.

balance of payments, a financial statement for a country for a given period showing the balance among: (1) transactions in goods, services, and income between that country and the rest of the world, (2) changes in ownership or valuation of that country's monetary gold, SPECIAL DRAWING RIGHTS, and claims on and liabilities to the rest of the world, and (3) unrequited transfers and counterpart entries needed (in an accounting sense) to balance transactions and changes among any of the foregoing types of exchange that are not mutually offsetting. Detail of national law as to what constitutes a transaction, the basis of its valuation, and the size of a transaction visible to fiscal authorities all result in differences in the meaning of a particular national statement.*

balance of trade, the net value of all international goods trade of a country, usually excluding reexports (goods received only for transshipment), and the percentage that this net represents of total trade.

Balance of trade refers only to the "visible" international trade of goods as recorded by customs authorities and is thus a segment of a country's BALANCE OF PAYMENTS, which takes all visible and invisible trade with other countries into account. (Invisible trade refers to imports and exports of money, financial instruments, and services such as transport, tourism, and insurance.) A country has a favourable, or positive (+), balance of trade when the value of exports exceeds that of imports and negative (–) when imports exceed exports.

barrel (bbl), a unit of liquid measure. The barrel conventionally used for reporting crude petroleum and petroleum products is equal to 42 U.S. gallons, or 159 litres. The number of barrels of crude petroleum per metric ton, ranging typically from 6.20 to 8.13, depends upon the specific gravity of the petroleum. The world average is roughly 7.33 barrels per ton.

birth rate, the number of live births annually per 1,000 of midyear population. Birth rates for individual countries may be compared with the estimated world annual average of 22.5 births per 1,000 population in 2000.

budget, the annual receipts and expenditures—of a central government for its activities only;

Abbreviations

Measurements

cu m	cubic metre(s)
kg	kilograms(s)
km	kilometre(s)
kW	kilowatt(s)
kW-hr	kilowatt-hour(s)
metric ton-km	metric ton-kilometre(s)
mi	mile(s)
passenger-km	passenger-kilometre(s)
passenger-mi	passenger-mile(s)
short ton-mi	short ton-mile(s)
sq km	square kilometre(s)
sq m	square metre(s)
sq mi	square mile(s)
troy oz	troy ounce(s)
yr	year(s)

Political Units and International Organizations

CACM	Central American Common Market
Caricom	Caribbean Community and Common Market
CFA	Communauté Financière Africaine
CFP	Comptoirs Françaises du Pacifique
CIS	Commonwealth of Independent States
CUSA	Customs Union of Southern Africa
E.Ger.	East Germany
EC	European Communities
EU	European Union
FAO	United Nations Food and Agriculture Organization
IMF	International Monetary Fund
OECD	Organization for Economic Cooperation and Development
OECS	Organization of Eastern Caribbean States
U.A.E.	United Arab Emirates
U.K.	United Kingdom
UNDP	United Nations Development Programme
U.S.	United States
U.S.S.R.	Union of Soviet Socialist Republics
W.Ger.	West Germany

Months

Jan.	January	Oct.	October
Feb.	February	Nov.	November
Aug.	August	Dec.	December
Sept.	September		

Miscellaneous

AIDS	Acquired Immune Deficiency Syndrome
avg.	average
c.i.f.	cost, insurance, and freight
commun.	communications
CPI	consumer price index
est.	estimate(d)
excl.	excluding
f.o.b.	free on board
GDP	gross domestic product
GNP	gross national product
govt.	government
incl.	including
mo.	month(s)
n.a.	not available (in text)
n.e.s.	not elsewhere specified
no.	number
pl.	plural
pos.	position
pub. admin.	public administration
PVC	Polyvinyl Chloride
SDR	Special Drawing Right
SITC	Standard International Trade Classification
svcs.	services
teacher tr.	teacher training
transp.	transportation
voc.	vocational
$	dollar (of any currency area)
£	pound (of any currency area)
...	not available (in tables)
—	none, less than half the smallest unit shown, or not applicable (in tables)

does not include state, provincial, or local governments or semipublic (parastatal, quasi-nongovernmental) corporations unless otherwise specified. Figures for budgets are limited to ordinary (recurrent) receipts and expenditures, wherever possible, and exclude capital expenditures—*i.e.,* funds for development and other special projects originating as foreign-aid grants or loans.

When both a recurrent and a capital budget exist for a single country, the former is the budget funded entirely from national resources (taxes, duties, excises, etc.) that would recur (be generated by economic activity) every year. It funds the most basic governmental services, those least able to suffer interruption. The capital budget is usually funded by external aid and may change its size considerably from year to year.

capital, usually, the actual seat of government and administration of a state. When more than one capital exists, each is identified by kind; when interim arrangements exist during the creation or movement of a national capital, the de facto situation is described.

Anomalous cases are annotated, such as those in which (1) the de jure designation under the country's laws differs from actual local practice (*e.g.,* Benin's designation of one capital in constitutional law, but another in actual practice), (2) international recognition does not validate a country's claim (as with the proclamation by Israel of a capital on territory not internationally recognized as part of Israel), or (3) both a state and a capital have been proclaimed on territory recognized as part of another state (as with the Turkish Republic of Northern Cyprus).

capital budget, *see* budget.

causes of death, as defined by the World Health Organization (WHO), "the disease or injury which initiated the train of morbid events leading directly to death, or the circumstances of accident or violence which produced the fatal injury." This principle, the "underlying cause of death," is the basis of the medical judgment as to cause; the statistical classification system according to which these causes are grouped and named is the *International List of Causes of Death,* the latest revision of which is the Tenth. Reporting is usually in terms of events per 100,000 population. When data on actual causes of death are unavailable, information on morbidity, or illness rate, usually given as reported cases per 100,000 of infectious diseases (notifiable to WHO as a matter of international agreement), may be substituted.

chief of state/head of government, paramount national governmental officer(s) exercising the highest executive and/or ceremonial roles of a country's government. In general usage, the chief of state is the formal head of a national state. The primary responsibilities of the chief of state may range from the purely ceremonial—convening legislatures and greeting foreign officials—to the exercise of complete national executive authority. The head of government, when this function exists separately, is the officer nominally charged (by the constitution) with the majority of actual executive powers, though they may not in practice be exercised, especially in military or single-party regimes in which effective power may reside entirely outside the executive governmental machinery provided by the constitution. A prime minister, for example, usually the actual head of government, may in practice exercise only Cabinet-level authority.

In communist countries an official identified as the chief of state may be the chairman of the policy-making organ, and the official given as the head of government the chairman of the nominal administrative/executive organ.

c.i.f. (trade valuation): *see* imports.

colony, an area annexed to, or controlled by, an independent state but not an integral part of it; a non-self-governing territory. A colony has a charter and may have a degree of self-government. A crown colony is a colony originally chartered by the British government.

commonwealth (U.K. and U.S.), a self-governing political entity that has regard to the common weal, or good; usually associated with the United Kingdom or United States. Examples include the Commonwealth of Nations (composed of independent states [from 1931 onward]), Puerto Rico since 1952, and the Northern Marianas since 1979.

communications, collectively, the means available for the public transmission of information within a country. Data are tabulated for: daily newspapers and their total circulation; radio and television as total numbers of receivers; telephone data as "main lines," or the number of subscriber lines (not receivers) having access to the public switched network; cellular telephones as number of subscribers; and facsimile machines and personal computers as number of units. For each, a rate per 1,000 persons is given.

constant prices, an adjustment to the members of a financial time series to eliminate the effect of inflation year by year. It consists of referring all data in the series to a single year so that "real" change may be seen.

constitutional monarchy, *see* monarchy.

consumer price index (CPI), also known as the retail price index, or the cost-of-living index, a series of index numbers assigned to the price of a selected "basket," or assortment, of basic consumer goods and services in a country, region, city, or type of household in order to measure changes over time in prices paid by a typical household for those goods and services. Items included in the CPI are ordinarily determined by governmental surveys of typical household expenditures and are assigned weights relative to their proportion of those expenditures. Index values are period averages unless otherwise noted.

coprincipality, *see* monarchy.

current prices, the valuation of a financial aggregate as of the year reported.

daily per capita caloric intake (supply), the calories equivalent to the known average daily supply of foodstuffs for human consumption in a given country divided by the population of the country (and the proportion of that supply provided, respectively, by vegetable and animal sources). The daily per capita caloric intake of a country may be compared with the corresponding recommended minimum daily requirement. The latter is calculated by the Food and Agriculture Organization of the United Nations from the age and sex distributions, average body weights, and environmental temperatures in a given region to determine the calories needed to sustain a person there at normal levels of activity and health. The daily per capita caloric requirement ranges from 2,200 to 2,500.

de facto population, for a given area, the population composed of those actually present at a particular time, including temporary residents and visitors (such as immigrants not yet granted permanent status, "guest" or expatriate workers, refugees, or tourists), but excluding legal residents temporarily absent.

de jure population, for a given area, the population composed only of those legally resident at a particular time, excluding temporary residents and visitors (such as "guest" or expatriate workers, refugees, or tourists), but including legal residents temporarily absent.

deadweight tonnage, the maximum weight of cargo, fuel, fresh water, stores, and persons that may safely by carried by a ship. It is customarily measured in long tons of 2,240 pounds each, equivalent to 1.016 metric tons. Deadweight tonnage is the difference between the tonnage of a fully loaded ship and the fully unloaded tonnage of that ship. *See also* gross ton.

death rate, the number of deaths annually per 1,000 of midyear population. Death rates for individual countries may be compared with the estimated world annual average of 9.0 deaths per 1,000 population in 2000.

density (of population), usually, the DE FACTO POPULATION of a country divided by its total area. Special adjustment is made for large areas of inland water, desert, or other uninhabitable areas—*e.g.,* excluding the ice cap of Greenland.

dependent state, constitutionally or statutorily organized political entity outside of and under the jurisdiction of an independent state (or a federal element of such a state) but not formally annexed to it (*see* Table).

Dependent states[1]

Australia
Christmas Island
Cocos (Keeling) Islands
Norfolk Island

Denmark
Faroe Islands
Greenland

France
French Guiana
French Polynesia
Guadeloupe
Martinique
Mayotte
New Caledonia
Réunion
Saint Pierre and Miquelon
Wallis and Futuna

Netherlands, The
Aruba
Netherlands Antilles

New Zealand
Cook Islands
Niue
Tokelau

United Kingdom
Anguilla
Bermuda
British Virgin Islands
Cayman Islands
Falkland Islands
Gibraltar
Guernsey
Isle of Man
Jersey
Montserrat
Pitcairn Island
Saint Helena and Dependencies
Turks and Caicos Islands

United Nations
East Timor

United States
American Samoa
Guam
Northern Mariana Islands
Puerto Rico
Virgin Islands (of the U.S.)

[1]Excludes territories (1) to which Antarctic Treaty is applicable in whole or in part, (2) without permanent civilian population, (3) without internationally recognized civilian government (Western Sahara, Gaza Strip), or (4) representing unadjudicated unilateral or multilateral territorial claims.

direct taxes, taxes levied directly on firms and individuals, such as taxes on income, profits, and capital gains. The *immediate* incidence, or burden, of direct taxes is on the firms and individuals thus taxed; direct taxes on firms may, however, be passed on to consumers and other economic units in the form of higher prices for goods and services, blurring the distinction between direct and indirect taxation.

distribution of income/wealth, the portion of personal income or wealth accruing to households or individuals constituting each respective decile (tenth) or quintile (fifth) of a country's households or individuals.*

divorce rate, the number of legal, civilly recognized divorces annually per 1,000 population.

doubling time, the number of complete years required for a country to double its population at its current rate of natural increase.

earnings index, a series of index numbers comparing average wages in a collective industrial sample for a country or region with the same industries at a previous period to measure changes over time in those wages. It is most commonly reported for wages paid on a daily, weekly, or monthly basis; annual figures may represent total income or averages of these shorter periods. The scope of the earnings index varies from country to country. The index is often limited to earnings in manufacturing industries. The index for each country applies to all wage earners in a designated group and ordinarily takes into account basic wages (overtime is normally distinguished), bonuses, cost-of-living allowances, and contributions toward social security. Some countries include payments in kind. Contributions toward social security by employers are usually excluded, as are social security benefits received by wage earners.

economically active population, *see* population economically active.

education, tabulation of the principal elements of a country's educational establishment, classified as far as possible according to the country's own system of primary, secondary, and higher levels (the usual age limits for these levels being identified in parentheses), with total number of schools (physical facilities) and of teachers and students (whether full- or part-time). The student-teacher ratio is calculated whenever available data permit.

educational attainment, the distribution of the population age 25 and over with completed educations by the highest level of formal education attained or completed; it must sometimes be reported, however, for age groups still in school or for the economically active only.

emirate, *see* monarchy.

enterprise, a legal entity formed to conduct a business, which it may do from more than one establishment (place of business or service point).

ethnic/linguistic composition, ethnic, racial, or linguistic composition of a national population, reported here according to the most reliable breakdown available, whether published in official sources (such as a census) or in external analysis (when the subject is not addressed in national sources).

exchange rate, the value of one currency compared with another, or with a standardized unit of account such as the SPECIAL DRAWING RIGHT, or as mandated by local statute when one currency is "tied" by a par value to another. Rates given usually refer to free market values when the currency has no, or very limited, restrictions on its convertibility into other currencies.

exports, material goods legally leaving a country (or customs area) and subject to customs regulations. The total value and distribution by percentage of the major items (in preference to groups of goods) exported are given, together with the distribution of trade among major trading partners (usually single countries or trading blocs). Valuation of goods exported is free on board (f.o.b.) unless otherwise specified. The value of goods exported and imported f.o.b. is calculated from the cost of production and excludes the cost of transport.

external debt, public and publicly guaranteed debt with a maturity of more than one year owed to nonnationals of a country and repayable in foreign currency, goods, or services. The debt may be an obligation of a national or subnational governmental body (or an agency of either), of an autonomous public body, or of a private debtor that is guaranteed by a public entity. The debt is usually either outstanding (contracted) or disbursed (drawn).

external territory (Australia), *see* territory.

federal, consisting of first-order political subdivisions that are prior to and independent of the central government in certain functions.

federal republic, *see* republic.

federation, union of coequal, preexisting political entities that retain some degree of autonomy and (usually) right of secession within the union.

fertility rate, *see* total fertility rate.

financial aggregates, tabulation of seven-year time series, providing principal measures of the financial condition of a country, including: (1) the exchange rate of the national crurency against the U.S. dollar, the pound sterling, and the International Monetary Fund's SPECIAL DRAWING RIGHT (SDR), (2) the amount and kind of international reserves (holdings of SDRs, gold, and foreign currencies) and reserve position of the country in the IMF, and (3) principal economic rates and prices (central bank discount rate, government bond yields, and industrial stock [share] prices). For BALANCE OF PAYMENTS, the origin in terms of component balance of trade items and balance of invisibles (net) is given.*

fish catch, the live-weight equivalent of the aquatic animals (including fish, crustaceans, mollusks, etc., but excluding whales, seals, and other aquatic mammals) caught in freshwater or marine areas by national fleets and landed in domestic or foreign harbours for commercial, industrial, or subsistence purposes.

f.o.b. (trade valuation), *see* exports.

food, *see* daily per capita caloric intake.

form of government/political status, the type of administration provided for by a country's constitution—whether or not suspended by extralegal military or civil action, although such de facto administrations are identified—together with the number of members (elected, appointed, and ex officio) for each legislative house, named according to its English rendering. Dependent states (*see* Table) are classified according to the status of their political association with the administering country.

gross domestic product (GDP), the total value of the final goods and services produced by residents and nonresidents within a given country during a given accounting period, usually a year. Unless otherwise noted, the value is given in current prices of the year indicated. The *System of National Accounts* (SNA, published under the joint auspices of the UN, IMF, OECD, EC, and World Bank) provides a framework for international comparability in classifying domestic accounting aggregates and international transactions comprising "net factor income from abroad," the measure that distinguishes GDP and GNP.

gross national product (GNP), the total value of final goods and services produced both from within a given country *and* from external (foreign) transactions in a given accounting period, usually a year. Unless otherwise noted, the value is given in current prices of the year indicated. GNP is equal to GROSS DOMESTIC PRODUCT (*q.v.*) adjusted by net factor income from abroad, which is the income residents receive from abroad for factor services (labour, investment, and interest) less similar payments made to nonresidents who contribute to the domestic economy.

gross ton, volumetric unit of measure (equaling 100 cubic feet [2.83 cu m]) of the permanently enclosed volume of a ship, above and below decks available for cargo, stores, or passenger accommodation. Net, or register, tonnage exempts certain nonrevenue spaces—such as those devoted to machinery, bunkers, crew accommodations, and ballast—from the gross tonnage. *See also* deadweight tonnage.

head of government, *see* chief of state/head of government.

health, a group of measures including number of accredited physicians currently practicing or employed and their ratio to the total population; total hospital beds and their ratio; and INFANT MORTALITY RATE.

household, economically autonomous individual or group of individuals living in a single dwelling unit. A family household is one composed principally of individuals related by blood or marriage.

household income and expenditure, data for average size of a HOUSEHOLD (by number of individuals) and median household income. Sources of income and expenditures for major items of consumption are given as percentages.

In general, household income is the amount of funds, usually measured in monetary units, received by the members (generally those 14 years old and over) of a household in a given time period. The income can be derived from (1) wages or salaries, (2) nonfarm or farm SELF-EMPLOYMENT, (3) transfer payments, such as pensions, public assistance, unemployment benefits, etc., and (4) other income, including interest and dividends, rent, royalties, etc. The income of a household is expressed as a gross amount before deductions for taxes. Data on expenditure refer to consumption of personal or household goods and services; they normally exclude savings, taxes, and insurance; practice with regard to inclusion of credit purchases differs markedly.

immigration, usually, the number and origin of those immigrants admitted to a nation in a legal status that would eventually permit the granting of the right to settle permanently or to acquire citizenship.*

imports, material goods legally entering a country (or customs area) and subject to customs regulations; excludes financial movements. The total value and distribution by percentage of the major items (in preference to groups of goods) imported are given, together with the direction of trade among major trading partners (usually single countries), trading blocs (such as the European Union), or customs areas (such as Belgium-Luxembourg). The value of goods imported is given free on board (f.o.b.) unless otherwise specified; f.o.b. is defined above under EXPORTS.

The principal alternate basis for valuation of goods in international trade is that of cost, insurance, and freight (c.i.f.); its use is restricted to imports, as it comprises the principal charges needed to bring the goods to the customs house in the country of destination. Because it inflates the value of imports relative to exports, more countries have, latterly, been estimating imports on an f.o.b. basis as well.

incorporated territory (U.S.), *see* territory.

independent, of a state, autonomous and controlling both its internal and external affairs. Its date usually refers to the date from which the country was in effective control of these affairs within its present boundaries, rather than the date independence was proclaimed or the date recognized as a de jure act by the former administering power.

indirect taxes, taxes levied on sales or transfers of selected intermediate goods and services, including excises, value-added taxes, and tariffs, that are ordinarily passed on to the ultimate consumers of the goods and services. Figures given for individual countries are limited to indirect taxes levied by their respective central governments unless otherwise specified.

infant mortality rate, the number of children per 1,000 live births who die before their first birthday. Total infant mortality includes neonatal mortality, which is deaths of children within one month of birth.

invisibles (invisible trade), *see* balance of trade.

kingdom, *see* monarchy.

labour force, portion of the POPULATION ECONOMICALLY ACTIVE (PEA) comprising those most fully employed or attached to the labour market (the unemployed are considered to be "attached" in that they usually represent persons previously employed seeking to be reemployed), particularly as viewed from a short-term perspective. It normally includes those who are self-employed, employed by others (whether full-time, part-time, seasonally, or on some other less than full-time, basis), and, as noted above, the unemployed (both those previously employed and those seeking work for the first time). In the "gross domestic product and labour force" table, the majority of the labour data provided refer to population economically active, since PEA represents the longer-term view of working population and, thus, subsumes more of the marginal workers who are often missed by shorter-term surveys.

land use, distribution by classes of vegetational cover or economic use of the land area only (excluding inland water, for example, but not marshland), reported as percentages. The principal categories utilized include: (1) forest, which includes natural and planted tracts, (2) meadows and pastures, which includes land in temporary or permanent use whose principal purpose is the growing of animal fodder, (3) agricultural and under permanent cultivation, which includes temporary and permanent cropland, as well as land left fallow less than five years, but capable of being returned to production without special preparation, and (4) other, which includes built-up, wasteland, watercourses, and the like.

leisure, the principal monetary expenditures, uses, or reported preferences in the use of the individual's free time for recreation, rest, or self-improvement.*

life expectancy, the number of years a person born within a particular population group (age cohort) would be expected to live, based on actuarial calculations.

literacy, the ability to read and write a language with some degree of competence; the precise degree constituting the basis of a particular national statement is usually defined by the national census and is often tested by the census enumerator. Elsewhere, particularly where much adult literacy may be the result of literacy campaigns rather than passage through a formal educational system, definition and testing of literacy may be better standardized.

major cities, usually the five largest cities proper (national capitals are always given, regardless of size); fewer cities may be listed if there are fewer urban localities in the country. For multipage tables, 10 or more may be listed.* Populations for cities will usually refer to the city proper—*i.e.,* the legally bounded corporate entity, or the most compact, contiguous, demographically urban portion of the entity defined by the local authorities. Occasionally figures for METROPOLITAN AREAS are cited when the relevant civil entity at the core of a major agglomeration had an unrepresentatively small population.

manufacturing, mining, and construction enterprises/retail sales and service enterprises, a detailed tabulation of the principal industries in these sectors, showing for each industry the number of enterprises and employees, wages in that industry as a percentage of the general average wage, and the value of that industry's output in terms of value added or turnover.*

marriage rate, the number of legal, civilly recognized marriages annually per 1,000 population.

material well-being, a group of measures indicating the percentage of households or dwellings possessing certain goods or appliances, including automobiles, telephones, television receivers, refrigerators, air conditioners, and washing machines.*

merchant marine, the privately or publicly owned ships registered with the maritime authority of a nation (limited to those in Lloyd's of London statistical reporting of 100 or more GROSS TONS) that are employed in commerce, whether or not owned or operated by nationals of the country.

metropolitan area, a city and the region of dense, predominantly urban, settlement around the city; the population of the whole usually has strong economic and cultural affinities with the central city.

military expenditure, the apparent value of all identifiable military expenditure by the central government on hardware, personnel, pensions, research and development, etc., reported here both as a percentage of the GNP, with a comparison to the world average, and as a per capita value in U.S. dollars.

military personnel, *see* total active duty personnel.

mobility, the rate at which individuals or households change dwellings, usually measured between censuses and including international as well as domestic migration.*

monarchy, a government in which the CHIEF OF STATE holds office, usually hereditarily and for life, but sometimes electively for a term. The state may be a coprincipality, emirate, kingdom, principality, sheikhdom, or sultanate. The powers of the monarch may range from absolute (*i.e.,* the monarch both reigns and rules) through various degrees of limitation of authority to nominal, as in a constitutional monarchy, in which the titular monarch reigns but others, as elected officials, effectively rule.

monetary unit, currency of issue, or that in official use in a given country; name, spelling, and abbreviation in English according to International Monetary Fund recommendations or local practice; name of the lesser, usually decimal, monetary unit constituting the main currency; and valuation in U.S. dollars and U.K. pounds sterling, usually according to free-market or commercial rates.

See also exchange rate.

natural increase, also called natural growth, or the balance of births and deaths, the excess of births over deaths in a population; the rate of natural increase is the difference between the BIRTH RATE and the DEATH RATE of a given population. The estimated world average during 2000 was 13.5 per 1,000 population, or 1.35% annually. Natural increase is added to the balance of migration to calculate the total growth of that population.

net material product, *see* material product.

nonreligious, *see* atheist.

official language(s), that (or those) prescribed by the national constitution for day-to-day conduct and publication of a country's official business or, when no explicit constitutional provision exists, that of the constitution itself, the national gazette (record of legislative activity), or like official documents. Other languages may have local protection, may be permitted in parliamentary debate or legal action (such as a trial), or may be "national languages," for the protection of which special provisions have been made, but these are not deemed official. The United States, for example, does not yet formally identify English as "official," though it uses it for virtually all official purposes.

official name, the local official form(s), short or long, of a country's legal name(s) taken from the country's constitution or from other official documents. The English-language form is usually the protocol form in use by the country, the U.S. Department of State, and the United Nations.

official religion, generally, any religion prescribed or given special status or protection by the constitution or legal system of a country. Identification as such is not confined to constitutional documents utilizing the term explicitly.

organized territory (U.S.), *see* territory.

overseas department (France), *see* department.

overseas territory (France), *see* territory.

parliamentary state, *see* state.

part of a realm, a dependent Dutch political entity with some degree of self-government and having a special status above that of a colony (*e.g.,* the prerogative of rejecting for local application any law enacted by The Netherlands).

participation/activity rates, measures defining differential rates of economic activity within a population. Participation rate refers to the percentage of those employed or economically active who possess a particular characteristic (sex, age, etc.); activity rate refers to the fraction of the total population who *are* economically active.

passenger-miles, or **passenger-kilometres,** aggregate measure of passenger carriage by a specified means of transportation, equal to the number of passengers carried multiplied by the number of miles (or kilometres) each is transported. Figures given for countries are often calculated from ticket sales and ordinarily exclude passengers carried free of charge.

people's republic, *see* republic.

place of birth/national origin, if the former, numbers of native- and foreign-born population of a country by actual place of birth; if the latter, any of several classifications, including those based on origin of passport at original admission to country, on cultural heritage of family name, on self-designated (often multiple) origin of (some) ancestors, and on other systems for assigning national origin.*

political status, *see* form of government/political status.

population, the number of persons present within a country, city, or other civil entity at the date of a census of population, survey, cumulation of a civil register, or other enumeration. Unless otherwise specified, populations given are DE FACTO, referring to those actually present, rather than DE JURE, those legally resident but not necessarily present on the referent date. If a time series, noncensus year, or per capita ratio referring to a country's total population is cited, it will usually refer to midyear of the calendar year indicated.

population economically active, the total number of persons (above a set age for economic labour, usually 10–15 years) in all employment statuses—self-employed, wage- or salary-earning, part-time, seasonal, unemployed, etc. The International Labour Organisation defines the economically active as "all persons of either sex who furnish the supply of labour for the production of economic goods and services." National practices vary as regards the treatment of such groups as armed forces, inmates of institutions, persons seeking their first job, unpaid family workers, seasonal workers and persons engaged in part-time economic activities. In some countries, all or part of these groups may be included among the economically active, while in other countries the same groups may be treated as inactive. In general, however, the data on economically active population do not include students, persons occupied solely in family or household work, retired persons, persons living entirely on their own means, and persons wholly dependent upon others.

See also labour force.

population projection, the expected population in the years 2010 and 2020, embodying the country's own projections wherever possible. Estimates of the future size of a population are usually based on assumed levels of fertility, mortality, and migration. Projections in the tables, unless otherwise specified, are medium (*i.e.,* most likely) variants, whether based on external estimates by the United Nations, World Bank, or U.S. Department of Commerce or on those of the country itself.

price and earnings indexes, tabulation comparing the change in the CONSUMER PRICE INDEX over a period of seven years with the change in the general labour force's EARNINGS INDEX for the same period.

principality, *see* monarchy.

production, the physical quantity or monetary value of the output of an industry, usually tabulated here as the most important items or groups of items (depending on the available detail) of primary (extractive) and secondary (manufactured) production, including construction. When a single consistent measure of value, such as VALUE ADDED, can be obtained, this is given, ranked by value; otherwise, and more usually, quantity of production is given.

public debt, the current outstanding debt of all periods of maturity for which the central government and its organs are obligated. Publicly guaranteed private debt is excluded. For countries that report debt under the World Bank Debtor Reporting System (DRS), figures for outstanding, long-term EXTERNAL DEBT are given.

quality of working life, a group of measures including weekly hours of work (including overtime); rates per 100,000 for job-connected injury, illness, and mortality; coverage of labour force by insurance for injury, permanent disability, and death; workdays lost to labour strikes and stoppages; and commuting patterns (length of journey to work in minutes and usual method of transportation).*

railroads, mode of transportation by self-driven or locomotive-drawn cars over fixed rails. Length-of-track figures include all mainline and spurline running track but exclude switching sidings and yard track. Route length, when given, does not compound multiple running tracks laid on the same trackbed.

recurrent budget, *see* budget.

religious affiliation, distribution of nominal religionists, whether practicing or not, as a percentage of total population. This usually assigns to children the religion of their parents.

republic, a state with elected leaders and a centralized presidential form of government, local subdivisions being subordinate to the national government. A *federal republic* (as distinguished from a unitary republic) is a republic in which power is divided between the central government and the constituent subnational administrative divisions (*e.g.,* states, provinces, or cantons) in whom the central government itself is held to originate, the division of power being defined in a written constitution and jurisdictional disputes usually being settled in a court; sovereignty usually rests with the authority that has the power to amend the constitution. A *unitary republic* (as distinguished from a federal republic) is a republic in which power originates in a central authority and is not derived from constituent subdivisions. A *people's republic,* in the dialectics of Communism, is the first stage of development toward a communist state, the second stage being a *socialist republic.* An *Islamic republic* is structured around social, ethical, legal, and religious precepts central to the Islamic faith.

retail price index, *see* consumer price index.

retail sales and service enterprises, *see* manufacturing, mining, and construction enterprises/retail sales and service enterprises.

roundwood, wood obtained from removals from forests, felled or harvested (with or without bark), in all forms.

rural, *see* urban-rural.

self-employment, work in which income derives from direct employment in one's own business, trade, or profession, as opposed to work in which salary or wages are earned from an employer.

self-governing, of a state, in control of its internal affairs in degrees ranging from control of most internal affairs (though perhaps not of public order or of internal security) to complete control of all internal affairs (*i.e.,* the state is autonomous) but having no control of external affairs or defense. In this work the term self-governing refers to the final stage in the successive stages of increasing self-government that generally precede independence.

service/trade enterprises, *see* manufacturing, mining, and construction enterprises/retail sales and service enterprises.

sex distribution, ratios, calculated as percentages, of male and female population to total population.

sheikhdom, *see* monarchy.

social deviance, a group of measures, usually reported as rates per 100,000 for principal categories of socially deviant behaviour, including specified crimes, alcoholism, drug abuse, and suicide.*

social participation, a group of measures indicative of the degree of social engagement displayed by a particular population, including rates of participation in such activities as elections, voluntary work or memberships, trade unions, and religion.*

social security, public programs designed to protect individuals and families from loss of income owing to unemployment, old age, sickness or disability, or death and to provide other services such as medical care, health and welfare programs, or income maintenance.

socialist republic, *see* republic.

sources of income, *see* household income and expenditure.

Special Drawing Right (SDR), a unit of account utilized by the International Monetary Fund (IMF) to denominate monetary reserves available under a quota system to IMF members to maintain the value of their national currency unit in international transactions.*

state, in international law, a political entity possessing the attributes of: territory, permanent civilian population, government, and the capacity to conduct relations with other states. Though the term is sometimes limited in meaning to fully independent and internationally recognized states, the more general sense of an entity possessing a *preponderance* of these characteristics is intended here. It is, thus, also a first-order civil administrative subdivision, especially of a federated union. An associated state is an autonomous state in free association with another that conducts its external affairs and defense; the association may be terminated in full independence at the instance of the autonomous state in consultation with the administering power. A *parliamentary state* is an independent state of the Commonwealth that is governed by a parliament and that may recognize the British monarch as its titular head.

structure of gross domestic product and labour force, tabulation of the principal elements of the national economy, according to standard industrial categories, together with the corresponding distribution of the labour force (when possible POPULATION ECONOMICALLY ACTIVE) that generates the GROSS DOMESTIC PRODUCT.

sultanate, *see* monarchy.

territory, a noncategorized political dependency; a first-order administrative subdivision; a dependent political entity with some degree of self-government, but with fewer rights and less autonomy than a colony because there is no charter. An *external territory* (Australia) is a territory situated outside the area of the country. An *organized territory* (U.S.) is a territory for which a system of laws and a settled government have been provided by an act of the United States Congress. An *overseas territory* (France) is an overseas subdivision of the French Republic with elected representation in the French Parliament, having individual statutes, laws, and internal organization adapted to local conditions.

ton-miles, or **ton-kilometres,** aggregate measure of freight hauled by a specified means of transportation, equal to tons of freight multiplied by the miles (or kilometres) each ton is transported. Figures are compiled from waybills (nationally) and ordinarily exclude mail, specie, passengers' baggage, the fuel and stores of the conveyance, and goods carried free.

total active duty personnel, full-time active duty military personnel (excluding militias and part-time, informal, or other paramilitary elements), with their distribution by percentages among the major services.

total fertility rate, the sum of the current age-specific birth rates for each of the child-bearing years (usually 15–49). It is the probable number of births, given present fertility data, that would occur during the lifetime of each woman should she live to the end of her child-bearing years.

tourism, service industry comprising activities connected with domestic and international travel for pleasure or recreation; confined here to international travel and reported as expenditures in U.S. dollars by tourists of all nationalities visiting a particular country and, conversely, the estimated expenditures of that country's nationals in all countries of destination.

transfer payments, *see* household income and expenditure.

transport, all mechanical methods of moving persons or goods. Data reported for national establishments include: for railroads, length of track and volume of traffic for passengers and cargo (but excluding mail, etc.); for roads, length of network and numbers of passenger cars and of commercial vehicles (*i.e.,* trucks and buses); for merchant marine, the number of vessels of more than 100 gross tons and their total deadweight tonnage; for air transport, traffic data for passengers and cargo and the number of airports with scheduled flights.

unincorporated territory (U.S.), *see* territory.

unitary republic, *see* republic.

urban-rural, social characteristic of local or national populations, defined by predominant economic activities, "urban" referring to a group of largely nonagricultural pursuits, "rural" to agriculturally oriented employment patterns. The distinction is usually based on the country's own definition of urban, which may depend only upon the size (population) of a place or upon factors like employment, administrative status, density of housing, etc.

value added, also called value added by manufacture, the gross output value of a firm or industry minus the cost of inputs—raw materials, supplies, and payments to other firms—required to produce it. Value added is the portion of the sales value or gross output value that is actually created by the firm or industry. Value added generally includes labour costs, administrative costs, and operating profits.

The Nations of the World

Afghanistan

Official name: Afghanistan[1].
Form of government: interim regime[2].
Head of state and government: interim Premier[2].
Capital: Kabul.
Official languages: Dari (Persian); Pashto.
Official religion: Islam.
Monetary unit: 1 afghani (Af) = 100 puls (puli); valuation (Sept. 28, 2001) 1 U.S.$ = Af 4,750[3]; 1 £ = Af 6,981.

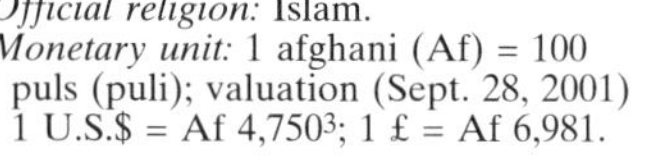

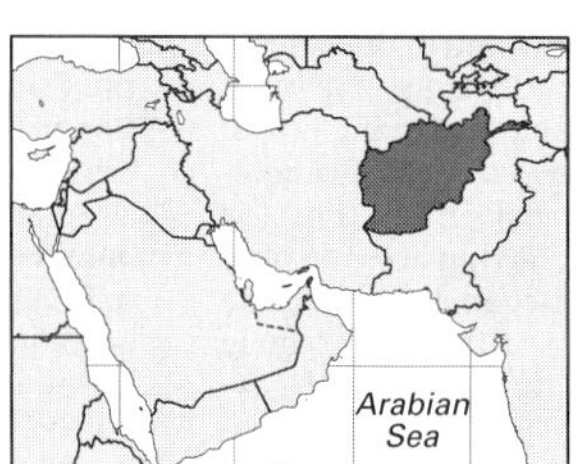

Area and population[4]		area		population
Geographic regions	Principal cities	sq mi	sq km	1993 estimate
Central	Kabul	11,657	30,192	3,481,400
East	Jalālābād	9,802	25,386	1,567,500
East-central	Bāmiān	21,739	56,304	685,600
North	Mazār-e Sharīf	29,520	76,457	2,421,900
North-east	Kondūz	30,233	78,304	2,518,300
South	Gardeyz	19,525	50,569	1,659,600
South-west	Kandahār (Qandahār)	77,000	199,430	2,188,700
West	Herāt	46,187	119,624	1,497,500
TOTAL		251,825[5]	652,225[5]	16,020,500

Demography

Population (2001): 26,813,000[6].
Density (2001): persons per sq mi 106.5, persons per sq km 41.1.
Urban-rural (1999): urban 21.5%; rural 78.5%.
Sex distribution (2000): male 51.31%; female 48.69%.
Age breakdown (2000): under 15, 43.8%; 15–29, 25.4%; 30–44, 16.8%; 45–59, 9.1%; 60–74, 4.2%; 75 and over, 0.7%.
Population projection: (2010) 33,864,000; (2020) 41,735,000.
Doubling time: 29 years.
Ethnolinguistic composition (early 1990[6]): Pashtun 52.4%; Tajik 20.4%; Ḥazāra 8.8%; Uzbek 8.8%; Chahar Aimak 2.8%; Turkmen 1.9%; other 4.9%.
Religious affiliation (2000): Sunnī Muslim 89.2%; Shīʿī Muslim 8.9%; Zoroastrian 1.4%; Hindu 0.4%; other 0.1%.
Major cities (1988): Kabul 2,454,000[7]; Kandahār (Qandahār) 225,500; Herāt 177,300; Mazār-e Sharīf 130,600; Jalālābād 55,000.

Vital statistics

Birth rate per 1,000 population (2000): 41.8 (world avg. 22.5).
Death rate per 1,000 population (2000): 18.0 (world avg. 9.0).
Natural increase rate per 1,000 population (2000): 23.8 (world avg. 13.5).
Total fertility rate (avg. births per childbearing woman; 2000): 5.9.
Life expectancy at birth (2000): male 46.6 years; female 45.1 years.

National economy

Budget (1997–98). Revenue: primarily from narcotics trade. Expenditures: more than 90% of revenue used to finance war effort.
Gross national product (1998): U.S.$6,738,000,000 (U.S.$280 per capita).

Structure of gross domestic product and labour force	1992–93			
	in value Af '000,000[8]	% of total value	labour force	% of labour force
Agriculture	61,400	48.5	4,276,100	67.2
Manufacturing; Mining and public utilities	32,800	25.9	298,900	4.7
Construction	12,400	9.8	81,400	1.3
Transp. and commun.	5,300	4.2	139,900	2.2
Trade	12,400	9.8	420,600	6.6
Pub. admin., services	2,400	1.9	929,300	14.6
Other			214,300	3.4
TOTAL	126,700	100.0[9]	6,360,500	100.0

Public debt (external, outstanding; 1993): U.S.$5,381,000,000.
Production (metric tons except as noted). Agriculture, forestry, fishing (1999): wheat 2,834,000, rice 450,000, grapes 330,000, barley 300,000, corn (maize) 240,000, potatoes 235,000, apricots 37,500, opium poppy 4,600[10]; livestock (number of live animals) 14,300,000 sheep, 2,200,000 goats, 1,500,000 cattle, 1,160,000 asses; roundwood (1998) 8,091,000 cu m; fish catch (1997) 1,250. Mining and quarrying (1997): salt 13,000; copper (metal content) 5,000. Manufacturing (by production value in Af '000,000; 1988–89): food products 4,019; leather and fur products 2,678; textiles 1,760; printing and publishing 1,070; industrial chemicals (including fertilizers) 1,053; footwear 999. Energy production (consumption): electricity (kW-hr; 1996) 593,000,000 (703,000,000); coal (metric tons; 1996) 4,000 (4,000); petroleum products (metric tons; 1996) none (254,000); natural gas (cu m; 1996) 160,169,000 (160,169,000).
Population economically active (1994)[11]: total 5,557,000; activity rate of total population 29.4% (participation rates: female 9.0%; unemployed [1995] *c.* 8%).

Consumer price index (1990 = 100)	1988	1989	1990	1991	1992	1993	1994
Consumer price index	64.3	83.1	100.0	266.0	420.8	563.9	676.7

Tourism: receipts (1997) U.S.$1,000,000; expenditures (1997) U.S.$1,000,000.
Land use (1994): forested 2.9%; meadows and pastures 46.0%; agricultural and under permanent cultivation 12.4%; other 38.7%.

Foreign trade[12]

Balance of trade (current prices)	1993	1994	1995	1996	1997	1998
U.S.$'000,000	+263	−245	−193	−371	−376	−300
% of total	23.6%	54.6%	36.8%	59.8%	55.3%	50.0%

Imports (1997): U.S.$525,000,000 (1995; food 18.8%, machinery and transport equipment 15.2%, unspecified commodities 46.5%). *Major import sources* (1997): Singapore 19.2%; Japan 18.5%; China 6.9%; India 4.8%; Russia 4.0%.
Exports (1997): U.S.$149,000,000 (1995; carpets and rugs 54.3%, dried fruits and nuts 15.6%). *Major export destinations* (1997): Pakistan 20.1%; Belgium-Luxembourg 8.7%; France 7.4%; United States 6.7%; Japan 6.0%.

Transport and communications

Transport. Railroads (1997): length 16 mi (25 km). Roads (1996): total length 21,000 km (paved 13%). Vehicles (1996): passenger cars 31,000; trucks and buses 25,000. Merchant marine: none. Air transport[13]: passenger-km (1995) 276,000,000; metric ton-km cargo 38,000,000; airports (1996) 3.

Communications Medium	date	unit	number	units per 1,000 persons
Daily newspapers	1996	circulation	113,000	5.0
Radio	1997	receivers	2,750,000	116
Television[14]	1997	receivers	270,000	11
Telephones	1999	main lines	29,000	1.2

Education and health

Educational attainment (1980). Population age 25 and over having: no formal schooling 88.5%; some primary education 6.8%; complete primary 0.3%; some secondary 1.2%; postsecondary 3.2%. *Literacy* (1995): Total population age 15 and over literate 31.5%; males 47.2%; females 15.1%.

Education (1995–96)	schools	teachers	students	student/ teacher ratio
Primary	2,146	21,869	1,312,197	60.0
Secondary	...	19,085	512,851	26.9
Higher	...	...	12,800	...

Health: physicians (1997) 2,555[6] (1 per 9,091 persons); hospital beds, n.a.; infant mortality rate (2000) 149.3.
Food (1999): daily per capita caloric intake 1,755 (vegetable products 79%, animal products 21%); 72% of FAO recommended minimum requirement.

Military

Total active duty personnel (1999): no national military from 1992[15].

[1]No official long-form name as of Dec. 20, 2001. [2]From Dec. 22, 2001. [3]Black market rate in April 2000: 1 U.S.$ = Af 64,000; most currency transactions are conducted with the Pakistan rupee or U.S. dollar. [4]A 1993 administrative reorganization created 32 provinces (*wilayah*), for which a detailed breakdown of area and population is unavailable. [5]Detailed breakdown does not account for 6,162 sq mi (15,959 sq km), which is included in the total. [6]Includes Afghan refugees (estimated to number about 2.0 million in Pakistan and about 2.0 million in Iran in August 2001). [7]1999 estimate for urban agglomeration. [8]At prices of 1978–79. [9]Detail does not add to total given because of rounding. [10]Represents 75% of world production; production declined significantly in 2001. [11]Based on settled population only. [12]Exports are f.o.b. and imports are c.i.f. [13]Ariana Afghan Airlines only. [14]Officially outlawed in 1998–2001. [15]UN international peacekeeping force for Kabul (and eventually four other cities) from Dec. 22, 2001; 3,000–5,000 troops expected by mid-January 2002.

Internet resources for further information:
- **Online Center for Afghan Studies http://www.afghan-politics.org**

Albania

Official name: Republika e Shqipërisë (Republic of Albania).
Form of government: unitary multiparty republic with one legislative house (Assembly [140]).
Chief of state: President.
Head of government: Prime Minister.
Capital: Tirana (Tiranë).
Official language: Albanian.
Official religion: none.
Monetary unit: 1 lek = 100 qindars; valuation (Sept. 28, 2001) 1 U.S.$ = 141.35 leks; 1 £ = 207.74 leks.

Area and population

Provinces	Capitals	area sq mi	area sq km	population 2001 census
Berat	Berat	353	915	128,410
Bulqizë	Bulqizë	277	718	42,985
Delvinë	Delvinë	142	367	10,859
Devoll	Bilisht	166	429	34,744
Dibër	Peshkopi	294	761	86,144
Durrës	Durrës	176	455	182,988
Elbasan	Elbasan	498	1,290	224,974
Fier	Fier	328	850	200,154
Gjirokastër	Gjirokastër	439	1,137	55,991
Gramsh	Gramsh	268	695	35,723
Has	Krumë	144	374	19,842
Kavajë	Kavajë	152	393	78,415
Kolonjë	Ersekë	311	805	17,179
Korçë	Korçë	676	1,752	143,499
Krujë	Krujë	144	372	64,357
Kuçovë	Kuçovë	43	112	35,571
Kukës	Kukës	369	956	64,054
Kurbin[1]	Laç	91	235	54,519
Lezhë	Lezhë	185	479	68,218
Librazhd	Librazhd	425	1,102	72,520
Lushnjë	Lushnjë	275	712	144,351
Malësi e Madhe	Koplic	346	897	36,770
Mallakastër	Ballsh	125	325	39,881
Mat	Burrel	397	1,028	61,906
Mirditë	Rrëshen	335	867	37,055
Peqin	Peqin	74	191	32,920
Përmet	Përmet	359	929	25,837
Pogradec	Pogradec	280	725	70,900
Pukë	Pukë	399	1,034	34,454
Sarandë	Sarandë	282	730	35,235
Shkodër	Shkodër	630	1,631	185,794
Skrapar	Çorovoda	299	775	29,874
Tepelenë	Tepelenë	315	817	32,465
Tiranë	Tirana (Tiranë)	461	1,193	523,150
Tropojë	Bajram	403	1,043	28,154
Vlorë	Vlorë	621	1,609	147,267
TOTAL		11,082	28,703	3,087,159

Demography

Population (2001): 3,091,000.
Density (2001): persons per sq mi 278.9, persons per sq km 107.7.
Urban-rural (1999): urban 41.0%; rural 59.0%.
Sex distribution (2000): male 48.90%; female 51.10%.
Age breakdown (2000): under 15, 30.2%; 15–29, 26.6%; 30–44, 19.8%; 45–59, 13.2%; 60–74, 7.9%; 75 and over, 2.3%.
Population projection: (2010) 3,248,000; (2020) 3,497,000.
Doubling time: 54 years.
Ethnic composition (1989): Albanian 98.0%; Greek 1.8%; Macedonian 0.2%.
Religious affiliation (2000): Muslim 38.8%; Roman Catholic 16.7%; nonreligious 16.6%; Albanian Orthodox 10.4%; other Orthodox 5.7%; other 11.8%.
Major cities (1991): Tirana (1999) 279,000; Durrës 86,900; Shkodër 83,700; Elbasan 83,200.

Vital statistics

Birth rate per 1,000 population (2000): 19.5 (world avg. 22.5).
Death rate per 1,000 population (2000): 6.0 (world avg. 9.0).
Natural increase rate per 1,000 population (2000): 13.5 (world avg. 13.5).
Total fertility rate (avg. births per childbearing woman; 2000): 2.4.
Marriage rate per 1,000 population (1990): 8.9.
Divorce rate per 1,000 population (1990): 0.8.
Life expectancy at birth (2000): male 68.8 years; female 74.9 years.

National economy

Budget (2000). Revenue: 120,588,000,000 leks (taxes 86.3%, of which value-added tax 31.6%, import duties and export taxes 18.8%, income tax 11.9%, social security contributions 11.2%, other 12.8%; nontax revenue 13.7%). Expenditures: 169,423,000,000 leks (current expenditure 79.3%, of which social security 22.1%, interest on debt 17.5%, wages 15.2%, government operations 11.4%, other 13.1%; capital expenditure 20.7%).
Public debt (1999): U.S.$849,100,000.
Production (metric tons except as noted). Agriculture, forestry, fishing (2000): cereals 580,000; vegetables and melons 444,000 (mainly beans, peas, onions, tomatoes, cabbage, eggplants, and carrots), watermelons 240,000, potatoes 180,000; livestock (number of live animals) 1,941,000 sheep, 1,120,000 goats, 720,000 cattle, 4,000,000 poultry; roundwood (2000) 409,000 cu m; fish catch (1999) 3,055. Mining and quarrying (1999): chromium ore 79,000; copper ore 34,000. Manufacturing (1999): cement 106,000; bread 67,000; rolled steel 20,000; cheese 7,000; beer 91,000 hectolitres; wine 10,000 hectolitres. Construction (1990): 12,428 units. Energy production (consumption): electricity (kW-hr; 1999) 5,396,000,000 (5,396,000,000); coal (metric tons; 1996) 111,000 (91,000); crude petroleum (barrels; 1999) 2,368,000 (3,257,000[2]); petroleum products (metric tons; 1996) 282,000 (363,000); natural gas (cu m; 1996) 22,911,000 (22,911,000).
Gross national product (1999): U.S.$3,146,000,000 (U.S.$930 per capita).

Structure of gross domestic product and labour force

	1999 in value '000,000 leks	1999 % of total value	1995 labour force	1995 % of labour force
Agriculture	266,270	52.6	778,000	58.7
Manufacturing, mining, public utilities	60,026	11.8	95,000	7.2
Construction	68,387	13.5	21,000	1.6
Transp. and commun.	16,531	3.3	30,000	2.3
Trade			62,000	4.7
Pub. admin., defense	94,991	18.8	...	...
Services			79,000	6.0
Other	—	—	260,000[3]	19.6[3]
TOTAL	506,205	100.0	1,325,000	100.0[4]

Population economically active (2000): total 1,940,000; activity rate of total population 57.0% (participation rates [1998]: ages 15–64, 69.9%; female 49.9%; unemployed 16.8%).

Price index (1995 = 100)

	1994	1995	1996	1997	1998	1999	2000
Consumer price index	92.8	100.0	112.7	150.1	181.1	181.8	187.0

Household income and expenditure. Average household size (1998): 3.9; annual income per rural household (1989) 80,835 leks (U.S.$ value, n.a.); sources of income: wages 53.0%, transfers from relatives abroad 21.5%, social insurance 11.4%; expenditure: n.a.
Tourism (1999): receipts U.S.$211,000,000; expenditures U.S.$12,000,000.

Foreign trade

Balance of trade (current prices)

	1994	1995	1996	1997	1998	1999	2000
U.S.$'000,000	–460	–475	–678	–535	–621	–846	–814
% of total	62.0%	53.7%	58.2%	62.8%	60.2%	60.6%	61.4%

Imports (2000): U.S.$1,070,000,000 (manufactured goods 23.8%; machinery and transport equipment 21.6%; food and beverages 19.8%; mineral fuels 9.0%; chemicals 7.0%; crude materials 1.4%). *Major import sources:* Italy 36.2%; Greece 28.0%; Germany 5.5%; Turkey 5.5%.
Exports (2000): U.S.$256,000,000 (miscellaneous manufactured articles 68.0%; manufactured goods 12.1%; crude materials 8.7%; food and beverages 6.6%). *Major export destinations:* Italy 70.3%; Greece 12.9%; Germany 6.6%.

Transport and communications

Transport. Railroads (1998): length 670 km; passenger-km 116,000,000; metric ton-km cargo 25,000. Roads (1998): total length 18,000 km (paved 30%). Vehicles (1998): passenger cars 90,766; trucks and buses 34,378. Merchant marine (1992): vessels (100 gross tons and over) 24; total deadweight tonnage 80,954. Air transport (1997): passenger-km 3,519,000; short ton-mi 223,000, metric ton-km 325,000; airports (1999) with scheduled flights 1.

Communications

Medium	date	unit	number	units per 1,000 persons
Daily newspapers	1996	circulation	116,000	37
Radio	1997	receivers	810,000	259
Television	1998	receivers	430,000	137
Telephones	1999	main lines	140,392	45
Cellular telephones	1998	subscribers	11,008	3.5
Internet	1999	users	2,500	0.8

Education and health

Educational attainment (1989). Population age 10 and over having: primary education 65.3%; secondary 29.1%; higher 5.6%. *Literacy* (1989): total population age 10 and over literate 91.8%; males 95.5%; females 88.0%.

Education (1996)

	schools	teachers	students	student/ teacher ratio
Primary (age 6–13)	1,782[5]	31,369	558,101	17.8
Secondary (age 14–17)	162[6]	4,147	71,391	17.2
Voc., teacher tr.	259[6]	2,174	18,504	8.5
Higher	10	2,348	34,257	14.6

Health (1995): physicians 4,848 (1 per 657 persons); hospital beds (1994) 10,200 (1 per 333 persons); infant mortality rate per 1,000 live births (2000) 41.3.
Food (1999): daily per capita caloric intake 2,717 (vegetable products 73%, animal products 27%); 113% of FAO recommended minimum requirement.

Military

Total active duty personnel (2000): 47,000 (army 85.1%, navy 5.3%, air force 9.6%). *Military expenditure as percentage of GNP* (1997): 1.4% (world 2.6%); per capita expenditure U.S.$19.

[1]Name changed from Laç to Kurbin in 1999. [2]1996. [3]Includes 171,000 undistributed unemployed. [4]Detail does not add to total given because of rounding. [5]1995. [6]1990.

Internet resources for further information:

- **Bank of Albania http://www.bankofalbania.org**

Algeria

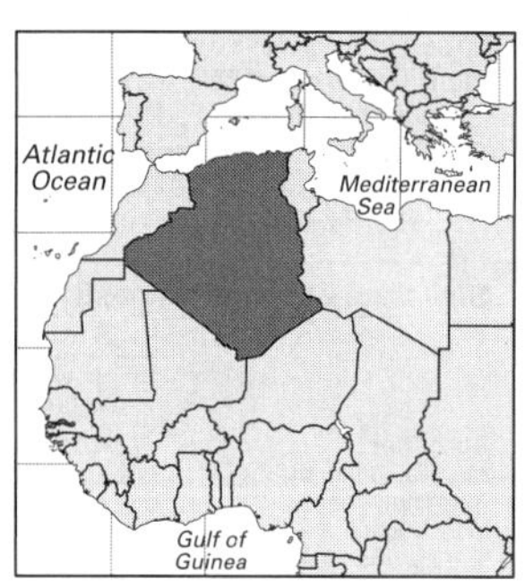

Official name: Al-Jumhūrīyah al-Jazā'irīyah ad-Dīmuqrāṭīyah ash-Sha'bīyah (Arabic) (People's Democratic Republic of Algeria).
Form of government: multiparty republic with two legislative bodies (Council of the Nation [144][1]; National People's Assembly [380]).
Chief of state: President.
Head of government: Prime Minister.
Capital: Algiers.
Official language: Arabic.
Official religion: Islam.
Monetary unit: 1 Algerian dinar (DA) = 100 centimes; valuation (Sept. 28, 2001) 1 U.S.$ = DA 75.35; 1 £ = DA 110.74.

Population (1998 census)

Provinces	population	Provinces	population	Provinces	population
Adrar	313,417	El-Bayadh	172,957	Ouargla	444,683
Aïn Defla	658,897	El-Oued	525,083	Oum el-Bouaghi	529,540
Aïn Temouchent	337,570	Et-Tarf	350,789	Relizane	646,175
Alger	2,423,694	Ghardaïa	311,678	Saïda	313,351
Annaba	559,898	Guelma	444,231	Sétif	1,299,116
Batna	987,475	Illizi	34,189	Sidi bel-Abbès	535,634
Béchar	232,012	Jijel	582,865	Skikda	793,146
Bejaïa	836,301	Khenchela	345,009	Souk Ahras	365,106
Biskra	568,701	Laghouat	326,862	Tamanrasset	138,704
Blida	796,616	Mascara	651,239	Tébessa	565,125
Bordj Bou Arreridj	561,471	Médéa	859,273	Tiaret	770,194
Bouira	637,042	Mila	663,578	Tindouf	27,053
Boumerdes	608,806	Mostaganem	636,884	Tipaza	507,959
Constantine	807,371	M'Sila	835,701	Tissemsilt	274,380
Djelfa	805,298	Naâma	131,846	Tizi Ouzou	1,100,297
Ech-Cheliff	874,917	Oran	1,208,171	Tlemcen	873,039
				TOTAL	29,273,343[2]

Demography

Area: 919,595 sq mi, 2,381,741 sq km.
Population (2001): 30,821,000.
Density (2001): persons per sq mi 33.5, persons per sq km 12.9.
Urban-rural (1998): urban 80.8%; rural 19.2%.
Sex distribution (1998): male 50.56%; female 49.44%.
Age breakdown (1998): under 15, 36.2%; 15–29, 30.6%; 30–44, 17.7%; 45–59, 8.9%; 60–74, 5.1%; 75 and over, 1.5%.
Population projection: (2010) 35,022,000; (2020) 40,365,000.
Doubling time: 49 years.
Ethnic composition (2000): Algerian Arab 59.1%; Berber 26.2%, of which Arabized Berber 3.0%; Bedouin Arab 14.5%; other 0.2%.
Religious affiliation (2000): Muslim 99.7%, of which Sunnī 99.1%, Ibāḍīyah 0.6%; Christian 0.3%.
Major cities (1998): Algiers 1,519,570; Oran 692,516; Constantine 462,187; Annaba 348,554; Batna 242,514; Blida 226,512; Sétif 211,859.

Vital statistics

Birth rate per 1,000 population (2000): 19.8 (world avg. 22.5).
Death rate per 1,000 population (2000): 5.5 (world avg. 9.0).
Natural increase rate per 1,000 population (2000): 14.3 (world avg. 13.5).
Total fertility rate (avg. births per childbearing woman; 2000): 2.8.
Marriage rate per 1,000 population (2000): 5.8.
Life expectancy at birth (2000): male 68.3 years; female 71.0 years.
Notified cases of infectious diseases per 100,000 population (1996): measles 67.8; typhoid fever 15.2; hepatitis 11.3; dysentery 10.1; meningitis 9.4.

National economy

Budget (1997). Revenue: DA 926,600,000,000 (taxes on hydrocarbons 63.9%, value-added taxes 16.0%). Expenditures: DA 845,100,000,000 (current expenditure 69.4%, development expenditure 30.6%).
Land use (1994): forested 1.6%; meadows and pastures 13.3%; agricultural and under permanent cultivation 3.4%; other (mostly desert) 81.7%.
Production (metric tons except as noted). Agriculture, forestry, fishing (1999): wheat 1,503,000, potatoes 1,100,000, tomatoes 790,000, barley 481,000, dates 427,600, onions 400,000, olives 311,200, oranges 307,300, grapes 190,300; livestock (number of live animals) 18,000,000 sheep, 3,200,000 goats; roundwood (1997) 2,735,000 cu m; fish catch (1997) 99,332. Mining and quarrying (1999): iron ore (gross weight) 2,330,000; phosphate rock (gross weight) 1,300,000; mercury 12,000 flasks. Manufacturing (value added in U.S.$'000,000; 1995): iron and steel 634; food products 622; fabricated metal products 518; cement, bricks, and tiles 394; transport equipment 352; electrical machinery 241. Energy production (consumption): electricity (kW-hr; 1996) 20,654,000,000 (20,378,000,000); coal (metric tons; 1996) 22,000 (1,202,000); crude petroleum (barrels; 2000) 307,091,000 ([1996] 165,220,000); petroleum products (metric tons; 1996) 39,628,000 (7,510,000); natural gas (cu m; 2000) 89,300,000,000 (25,981,000,000).
Household income and expenditure. Average household size (1998) 7.1; income per household: n.a.; sources of income (1997): wages and salaries 43.2%, self-employment 39.1%, transfers 17.7%; expenditure (1995): food and beverages 58.5%, transportation and communications 9.5%, clothing and footwear 13.9%, health 4.4%, other 13.7%.
Gross national product (1999): U.S.$46,548,000,000 (U.S.$1,550 per capita).

Structure of gross domestic product and labour force

	1996			
	in value DA '000,000	% of total value	labour force	% of labour force
Agriculture	277,842	12.3	881,000	12.1
Petroleum and natural gas	761,084[3]	33.8[3]		
Other mining	5,216	0.2	676,000	9.3
Manufacturing	165,875[3]	7.4[3]		
Public utilities, construction	268,873	12.0	677,000	9.3
Transp. and commun.	148,886	6.6	750,000	10.3
Trade, restaurants	352,464	15.7	615,000	8.5
Pub. admin., defense	...	...	1,479,000	20.3
Services	58,950	2.6		
Other	212,300	9.4	2,200,000[4]	30.2
TOTAL	2,251,490	100.0	7,278,000	100.0

Population economically active (1994): total 6,814,000; activity rate of population 24.8% (participation rates [1987] ages 15–64, 44.3%; female 9.2%; unemployed [February 2000] 29.8%).

Price and earnings indexes (1995 = 100)

	1994	1995	1996	1997	1998	1999	2000
Consumer price index	77.1	100.0	118.7	128.7	131.7	135.2	133.7[5]
Earnings index[6]	90.9	100.0	110.0	...	...	...	...

Public debt (external, outstanding; 1999): U.S.$25,913,000,000.
Tourism: receipts from visitors (1998) U.S.$24,000,000; expenditures by nationals abroad (1997) U.S.$64,000,000.

Foreign trade[7]

Balance of trade (current prices)

	1994	1995	1996	1997	1998	1999
U.S.$'000,000	−979	−1,425	+4,484	+5,206	+1,122	+2,591
% of total	5.4%	6.8%	19.8%	23.1%	5.4%	11.8%

Imports (1996): U.S.$9,102,000,000 (food 27.5%, machinery and apparatus 15.8%, transport equipment 7.0%). *Major import sources* (1997): France 28.3%; Italy 8.7%; U.S. 8.6%; Spain 7.4%; Brazil 5.3%.
Exports (1996): U.S.$13,586,000,000 (crude and refined petroleum 61.7%, natural gas 31.7%, dates 0.5%). *Major export destinations* (1997): Italy 19.5%; U.S. 17.3%; France 14.2%; Spain 10.2%; The Netherlands 5.6%.

Transport and communications

Transport. Railroads (1997): route length 2,451 mi, 3,945 km; (1996) passenger-km 1,826,000,000; metric ton-km cargo 2,139,000,000. Roads (1995): total length 63,643 mi, 102,424 km (paved 69%). Vehicles (1996): passenger cars 725,000; trucks and buses 780,000. Air transport (1998)[8]: passenger-km 2,901,000,000; metric ton-km cargo 18,285,000; airports (1996) 28.

Communications

Medium	date	unit	number	units per 1,000 persons
Daily newspapers	1996	circulation	1,080,000	38
Radio	1997	receivers	7,100,000	253
Television	1999	receivers	3,300,000	110
Telephones	1999	main lines	1,600,000	53
Cellular telephones	1999	subscribers	72,000	2.4
Personal computers	1999	units	180,000	6.0
Internet	1999	users	20,000	0.7

Education and health

Educational attainment (1998). Percentage of economically active population age 6 and over having: no formal schooling 30.1%; primary education 29.9%; lower secondary 20.7%; upper secondary 13.4%; higher 4.3%; other 1.6%. *Literacy* (1998): total population age 10 and over literate 15,314,109 (68.1%); males literate 8,650,719 (76.3%); females literate 6,663,392 (59.7%).

Education (1996–97)

	schools	teachers	students	student/ teacher ratio
Primary (age 6–11)	15,426	170,956	4,674,947	27.3
Secondary (age 12–17)	3,954[9]	151,948	2,618,242	17.2
Higher[9]	...	19,910	347,410	17.4

Health (1996): physicians 27,650 (1 per 1,015 persons); hospital beds 34,544 (1 per 812 persons); infant mortality rate per 1,000 live births (2000) 51.1.
Food (1999): daily per capita caloric intake 2,965 (vegetable products 90%, animal products 10%); 124% of FAO recommended minimum requirement.

Military

Total active duty personnel (1999): 122,000 (army 86.1%, navy 5.7%, air force 8.2%). *Military expenditure as percentage of GNP* (1997): 3.9% (world 2.6%); per capita expenditure U.S.$61.

[1]Includes 48 nonelected seats appointed by the president. [2]Sum of provincial populations; actual census total equals 29,272,343. [3]Petroleum and natural gas includes (and Manufacturing excludes) refined petroleum and manufacture of hydrocarbons. [4]Estimated number of unemployed. [5]Average of 2nd quarter and 3rd quarter. [6]Public workers only; all data based on January averages of gross income. [7]Imports c.i.f.; exports f.o.b. [8]Air Algérie. [9]1995–96.

Internet resources for further information:
- **Statistiques Algérie**
  http://www.ons.dz/them_sta.htm

American Samoa

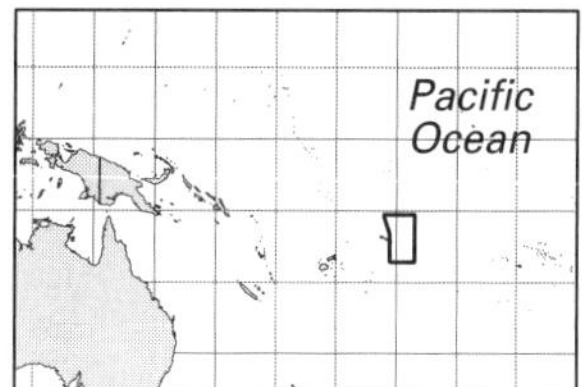

Official name: American Samoa (English); Amerika Samoa (Samoan).
Political status: unincorporated and unorganized territory of the United States with two legislative houses (Senate [18]; House of Representatives [18])[1].
Chief of state: President of the United States.
Head of government: Governor.
Capital: Fagatogo[2] (legislative and judicial) and Utulei (executive).
Official languages: English; Samoan.
Official religion: none.
Monetary unit: 1 dollar (U.S.$) = 100 cents; valuation (Sept. 28, 2001) 1 U.S.$ = £0.68.

Area and population

	area		population
Districts and islands	sq mi	sq km	2000 census
Eastern District	25.9	67.1	23,441
Tutuila Island (part)	25.3	65.5	21,673
Aunu'u Island	0.6	1.6	1,768
Western District	28.8	74.6	32,435
Tutuila Island (part)	28.8	74.6	32,435
Manu'a District (Manu'a Islands)	21.9	56.7	1,378
Ofu Island	2.8	7.2	289
Olosega Island	2.0	5.2	216
Ta'u Island	17.1	44.3	873
Rose Island[3]	0.1	0.3	0
Swains Island[3]	0.6	1.5	37
LAND AREA	77.3	200.2	—
INLAND WATER AREA	7.1	18.4	—
TOTAL AREA	84.4	218.6	57,291

Demography

Population (2001): 58,000.
Density (2000): persons per sq mi 769.3, persons per sq km 297.1.
Urban-rural (1998): urban 51.5%; rural 48.5%.
Sex distribution (2000): male 50.51%; female 49.49%.
Age breakdown (2000): under 15, 38.8%; 15–29, 24.1%; 30–44, 17.8%; 45–59, 11.7%; 60–74, 6.3%; 75 and over, 1.3%.
Population projection: (2010) 70,000; (2020) 86,000.
Doubling time: 32 years.
Ethnic composition (1990): Samoan 88.6%; Tongan 3.7%; Caucasian 1.9%; Asian 1.8%; other 4.0%.
Religious affiliation (1995): 4 major Protestant groups 60.1%; Roman Catholic 19.4%; Mormon 12.5%; other 8.0%.
Major villages (1990): Tafuna 5,174; Nu'uuli 3,893; Pago Pago 3,519 (urban agglomeration [1999] 14,000); Leone 3,013; Fagatogo 2,323[2].

Vital statistics

Birth rate per 1,000 population (2000): 25.8 (world avg. 22.5); legitimate, n.a.; illegitimate, n.a.
Death rate per 1,000 population (2000): 4.3 (world avg. 9.0).
Natural increase rate per 1,000 population (2000): 21.5 (world avg. 13.5).
Total fertility rate (avg. births per childbearing woman; 2000): 3.6.
Marriage rate per 1,000 population (1993): 6.1.
Divorce rate per 1,000 population (1993): 0.5.
Life expectancy at birth (2000): male 70.7 years; female 79.8 years.
Major causes of death per 100,000 population (1998): heart diseases 80.5; malignant neoplasms (cancers) 61.2; cerebrovascular diseases 39.7[4]; chronic obstructive pulmonary diseases 28.2[4]; accidents 21.5[4]; influenza and pneumonia 8.2[4].

National economy

Budget (1992). Revenue: U.S.$146,905,000 (U.S. government grants 73.5%; taxes 16.4%; insurance claims 3.5%; other 6.6%). Expenditures: U.S.$165,-950,000 (general government 45.7%; education and culture 21.0%; health and welfare 16.0%; economic development 5.6%; public works and parks 5.1%; other 6.6%).
Gross national product (at current market prices; 1997): U.S.$253,000,000 (U.S.$4,300 per capita).

Structure of labour force

	1995	
	labour force[5]	% of labour force
Agriculture, forestry, and fishing	307	2.2
Manufacturing and public utilities	4,295	31.2
Mining; Construction	671	4.9
Transportation and communications	848	6.1
Trade	1,685	12.2
Finance	187	1.4
Public administration	2,366	17.2
Services; Other	3,426	24.8
TOTAL	13,785	100.0

Production (metric tons except as noted). Agriculture, forestry, fishing (1999): coconuts 4,700, taros 1,500, fruits (excluding melons) 1,200, bananas 750, vegetables and melons 490; livestock (number of live animals; 1999) 10,700 pigs, 37,000 chickens; forestry, n.a.; fish catch (1998) 910, of which tunas, bonitos, and billfish 865. Mining and quarrying: n.a. Manufacturing (1994): canned tuna shipped to U.S. 211,600,000; other manufactures include garments, handicrafts, soap, and alcoholic beverages. Construction: n.a. Energy production (consumption): electricity (kW-hr; 1996) 130,000,000 (130,000,000); coal, none (n.a.); crude petroleum, none (n.a.); petroleum products (metric tons; 1996) none (92,000); natural gas, none (n.a.).
Public debt: n.a.
Population economically active (1994): total 16,822; activity rate of total population 30.5% (participation rates: ages 16–64, 51.2%; female 39.5%; unemployed 16.7%[6]).

Price index (1990 = 100)

	1990	1991	1992	1993	1994	1995	1996
Consumer price index	100.0	104.0	109.0	109.0	111.0	113.0	118.0

Household income and expenditure. Average household size (1995) 6.3; income per household (1995): U.S.$15,715; sources of income: n.a.; expenditure (1988): food and beverages 44.3%, housing and furnishings 23.4%, transportation and communications 14.9%, clothing and footwear 5.8%, other 11.6%.
Tourism: receipts from visitors (1997) U.S.$10,000,000; expenditures by nationals abroad (1996) U.S.$2,000,000.
Land use (1993): forested 70%; agricultural and under permanent cultivation 15%; other 15%.

Foreign trade[7]

Balance of trade (current prices)

	1986	1987	1988	1989	1990	1991
U.S.$'000,000	–59.6	–58.2	–33.0	–70.3	–54.3	–45.0
% of total	10.5%	9.2%	4.7%	10.3%	8.1%	6.4%

Imports (1994): U.S.$429,000,000 (petroleum and petroleum products 8.8%, food and beverages 5.2%, transport equipment 3.7%, remainder unknown). *Major import sources* (1991): United States 28.7%; Australia 5.6%; New Zealand 4.1%; Japan 3.8%; other South Pacific countries[8] 3.6%; other Asian countries[9] 3.1%.
Exports (1999): U.S.$312,800,000 (1991; tuna in airtight containers 97.4%, pet food 1.4%). *Major export destinations:* United States 100.0%.

Transport and communications

Transport. Railroads: none. Roads (1991): total length 217 mi, 350 km (paved, 43%). Vehicles (1997): passenger cars 5,300; buses 199[10]; motorcycles 27[10]. Merchant marine (1990): vessels (100 gross tons and over) 3; total deadweight tonnage 143. Air transport (1990): incoming flights 4,426; incoming passengers 66,580; incoming cargo 706 metric tons; airports (1994) with scheduled flights 3.

Communications

Medium	date	unit	number	units per 1,000 persons
Daily newspapers	1996	circulation	5,000	85
Radio	1997	receivers	57,000	929
Television	1997	receivers	14,000	221
Telephones	1999	main lines	13,900	248
Cellular telephones	1999	subscribers	2,377	42

Education and health

Educational attainment (1995). Percentage of population age 25 and over having: no formal schooling to some secondary education 32.7%; completed secondary 61.3%; higher 6.0%. *Literacy* (1990): total population age 10 and over literate 33,993 (99.4%); males literate 17,704 (99.4%); females literate 16,589 (99.5%).

Education (1997–98)

	schools	teachers	students	student/ teacher ratio
Primary (age 6–14)	32	524[11]	10,350	15.0[11]
Secondary (age 14–18)	9	266[11]	3,339	14.2[11]
Vocational[11]	...	21	160	7.6
Higher	1	...	1,463[12]	...

Health (1991): physicians 26 (1 per 1,888 persons); hospital beds (1995) 140 (1 per 4.7 persons); infant mortality rate per 1,000 live births (2000) 10.6.
Food: daily per capita caloric intake, n.a.

Military

Military defense is the responsibility of the United States.

[1]The House of Representatives includes an elected representative from Swains Island. [2]The seat of the legislature, as defined by the Constitution of American Samoa, is at Fagatogo, one of a number of villages within an urban agglomeration collectively known as Pago Pago. [3]Not within district administrative structure. Swains Island is administered by a village government and a representative of the governor. [4]1997. [5]Does not include unemployed. [6]1995. [7]Imports c.i.f.; exports f.o.b. [8]South Pacific nations not including Australia and New Zealand. [9]Asian nations not including Japan. [10]1994. [11]1991. [12]American Samoa Community College at Mapusaga, 1990 figures.

Internet resources for further information:
- **U.S. Department of the Interior: Pacific Web http://www.pacificweb.org**
- **Bank of Hawaii: Economics Research Center http://www.boh.com/econ/pacific**

Andorra

Official name: Principat d'Andorra (Principality of Andorra).
Form of government: parliamentary coprincipality with one legislative house (General Council [28]).
Chiefs of state: President of France; Bishop of Urgell, Spain.
Head of government: Head of Government.
Capital: Andorra la Vella.
Official language: Catalan.
Official religion: none[1].
Monetary unit: There is no local currency of issue; the French franc and Spanish peseta are both in circulation. 1 franc (F) = 100 centimes; 1 peseta (Pta) = 100 céntimos. Valuation (Sept. 28, 2001) 1 U.S.$ = F 7.20, 1 £ = F 10.59; 1 U.S.$ = Ptas 182.70, 1 £ = Ptas 268.52.

Area and population

Parishes	Capitals	area sq mi	area sq km	population 2000[2] estimate
Andorra la Vella	Andorra la Vella	49[3]	127[3]	21,189
Canillo	Canillo }	74	191	2,706
Encamp	Encamp }			10,595
La Massana	La Massana	25	65	6,276
Les Escaldes–Engordany	—	[3]	[3]	15,299
Ordino	Ordino	33	85	2,283
Sant Julià de Lòria	Sant Julià de Lòria	[3]	[3]	7,623
TOTAL		181	468	65,971

Demography

Population (2001): 66,900.
Density (2001): persons per sq mi 369.7, persons per sq km 143.0.
Urban-rural (1999): urban 93%; rural 7%.
Sex distribution (2000[2]): male 52.19%; female 47.81%.
Age breakdown (2000[2]): under 15, 15.4%; 15–29, 20.9%; 30–44, 29.3%; 45–59, 18.6%; 60–74, 10.5%; 75 and over, 5.3%.
Population projection: (2010) 73,000; (2020) 80,000.
Doubling time: 74 years.
Ethnic composition (by nationality; 2000[2]): Spanish 41.8%; Andorran 34.5%; Portuguese 10.5%; French 6.6%; British 1.4%; Moroccan 0.7%; German 0.5%; other 4.0%.
Religious affiliation (2000): Roman Catholic 89.1%; other Christian 4.3%; Muslim 0.6%; Hindu 0.5%; nonreligious 5.0%; other 0.5%.
Major urban areas (2000[2]): Andorra la Vella 21,189; Les Escaldes–Engordany 15,299; Encamp 10,595.

Vital statistics

Birth rate per 1,000 population (1999): 12.6[4] (world avg. 22.5).
Death rate per 1,000 population (1999): 3.1[4] (world avg. 9.0).
Natural increase rate per 1,000 population (1999): 9.5[4] (world avg. 13.5).
Total fertility rate (avg. births per childbearing woman; 2000): 1.2.
Marriage rate per 1,000 population (1998): 3.2.
Life expectancy at birth (2000): male 80.6 years; female 86.6 years.
Major causes of death per 100,000 population (1996–98 avg.): cancers (neoplasms) 102.7; diseases of the circulatory system 95.6; diseases of the respiratory system 26.2; accidents and violence 20.0; diseases of the digestive system 17.5.

National economy

Budget (1997). Revenue: Ptas 50,720,000,000 (extraordinary income 45.9%, indirect taxes 41.1%, property income 7.3%). Expenditures: Ptas 50,720,000,000 (extraordinary expenditures 43.0%, current expenditures 30.8%, development expenditures 26.2%).
Public debt (1995): about U.S.$500,000,000.
Production. Agriculture (1997): tobacco 1,047 metric tons; other traditional crops include hay, potatoes, and grapes; livestock (number of live animals; 1997) 2,021 sheep[5], 1,187 cattle, 738 horses. Quarrying: small amounts of marble are quarried. Manufacturing (value of recorded exports in Ptas '000; 1997): electrical machinery and apparatus 1,397,000; motor vehicles and parts 947,000; newspapers and periodicals 743,000; clothing 632,000; toys and games 459,000; other products include furniture, cigarettes, and liqueurs. Construction (approved new building construction; 1998): 181,700 sq m. Energy production (consumption): electricity (kW-hr; 1997) 116,000,000 ([1999] 393,000,000); coal, none (n.a.); crude petroleum, none (n.a.); petroleum products, none (n.a.); natural gas, none (n.a.).
Tourism (1999): 9,422,000 visitors; number of hotels 271.
Population economically active (1997)[6]: total 29,088; activity rate of total population 44.5% (participation rates: ages 15–64, 60.9%; female, n.a.; unemployed [1998] unofficially, none[7]).

Price and earnings indexes (1997 = 100)[8]

	1993	1994	1995	1996	1997	1998	1999
Consumer price index	...	...	...	...	100.0	101.6	104.3
Annual earnings index[9]	85.5	91.2	95.5	98.6	100.0	101.6	103.7

Gross national product (1998): U.S.$1,110,000,000 (U.S.$16,930 per capita)[10].

Structure of labour force[6]

	1997 labour force	1997 % of labour force
Agriculture } Mining }	199	0.7
Manufacturing	1,253	4.3
Construction	4,699	16.2
Public utilities	...	...
Transp. and commun.	...	...
Trade	5,570	19.1
Restaurants, hotels	5,470	18.8
Finance, real estate, insurance	1,276	4.4
Pub. admin., defense	3,636	12.5
Services	5,284	18.2
Other	1,701	5.8
TOTAL	29,088	100.0

Land use (1994): forested 22.0%; meadows and pastures 56.0%; agricultural and under permanent cultivation 2.0%; other 20.0%.
Household expenditure (1997)[11]: food, beverages, and tobacco 25.5%, housing and energy 19.4%, transportation 17.7%, clothing and footwear 9.2%.

Foreign trade

Balance of trade (current prices)

	1994	1995	1996	1997	1998	1999
Ptas '000,000	−117,876	−125,510	−129,577	−150,013	−152,777	−164,572
% of total	89.7%	91.1%	91.7%	91.4%	89.8%	92.5%

Imports (1997): Ptas 157,054,000,000 (food, beverages, and tobacco 30.2%; machinery and apparatus 14.0%; chemicals and chemical products 8.7%; transport equipment 7.7%; textiles and wearing apparel 7.6%; photographic and optical goods and watches and clocks 4.5%). *Major import sources:* Spain 40.2%; France 29.2%; U.K. 5.7%; U.S. 4.9%; Germany 4.6%.
Exports (1997): Ptas 7,041,000,000 (electrical machinery and apparatus 19.8%; motor vehicles and parts 13.4%; newspapers, books, and periodicals 10.6%; clothing 9.0%; toys and games 6.5%). *Major export destinations:* Spain 47.4%; France 41.6%; Belgium 3.4%; The Netherlands 2.6%.

Transport and communications

Transport. Railroads: none; however, both French and Spanish railways stop near the border. Roads (1994): total length 167 mi, 269 km (paved 74%). Vehicles (1996): passenger cars 35,358; trucks and buses 4,238. Airports (1997) with scheduled flights: none.

Communications

Medium	date	unit	number	units per 1,000 persons
Daily newspapers	1996	circulation	4,000	62
Radio	1997	receivers	16,000	247
Television	1998	receivers	30,000	457
Telephones	1999	main lines	33,607	510
Cellular telephones	1999	subscribers	20,600	312
Internet	1999	users	5,000	76

Education and health

Educational attainment (mid-1980s). Percentage of population age 15 and over having: no formal schooling 5.5%; primary education 47.3%; secondary education 21.6%; postsecondary education 24.9%; unknown 0.7%. *Literacy:* resident population is virtually 100% literate.

Education (1996–97)

	schools	teachers	students	student/ teacher ratio
Primary/Lower secondary (age 7–15)	12	...	5,424	...
Upper secondary	6	...	2,655	...
Higher	...	...	932[12]	...

Health (1998): physicians 190 (1 per 345 persons); hospital beds 203 (1 per 323 persons); infant mortality rate per 1,000 live births (1998–2000 avg.) 4.1.
Food: n.a.

Military

Total active duty personnel (1996): none. France and Spain are responsible for Andorra's external security; the police force is assisted in alternate years by either French gendarmerie or Barcelona police.

[1]Roman Catholicism enjoys special recognition in accordance with Andorran tradition. [2]January 1. [3]Andorra la Vella includes Les Escaldes–Engordany and Sant Julià de Lòria. [4]Official government figures. [5]Large herds of sheep and goats from Spain and France feed in Andorra in the summer. [6]Labour force receiving wages only; total population economically active equals 33,203. [7]The restricted size of the indigenous labour force has in the near past necessitated immigration to serve the tourist trade. [8]All indexes are end of year. [9]Official minimum salary. [10]Tourism (including winter-season sports, fairs, festivals, and income earned from low-duty imported manufactured items) and the banking system are the primary sources of GNP. [11]Weights of consumer price index components. [12]1997–98.

Internet resources for further information:
- **Andorra National Information Centre**
  http://www.andorra.ad/cniauk.html
- **Department d'Estudis i d'Estadística**
  http://www.finances.ad/estudis/indexDEE.htm

Angola

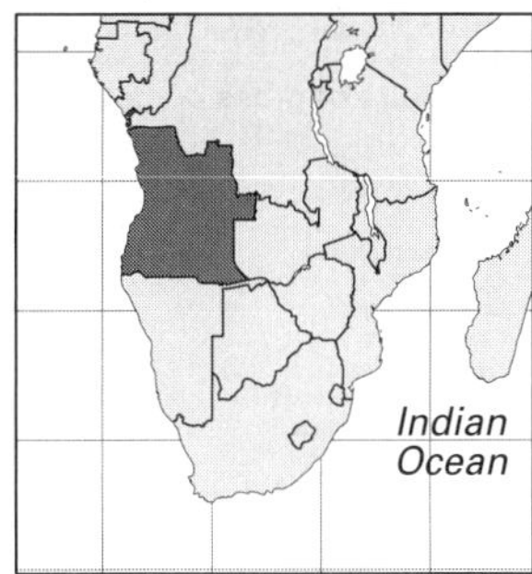

Official name: República de Angola (Republic of Angola).
Form of government: unitary multiparty republic with one legislative house (National Assembly [220])[1].
Head of state and government: President[2].
Capital: Luanda.
Official language: Portuguese.
Official religion: none.
Monetary unit: 1 refloated kwanza[3] = 100 lwei; valuation (Sept. 28, 2001) 1 U.S.$ = refloated kwanza 24.08; 1 £ = refloated kwanza 35.39.

Area and population

Provinces	Capitals	area sq mi	area sq km	population 2001 estimate
Bengo	Caxito	12,112	31,371	...
Benguela	Benguela	12,273	31,788	...
Bié	Kuito	27,148	70,314	...
Cabinda	Cabinda	2,807	7,270	...
Cunene	N'Giva	34,495	89,342	...
Huambo	Huambo	13,233	34,274	...
Huíla	Lubango	28,958	75,002	...
Kuando Kubango	Menongue	76,853	199,049	...
Kuanza Norte	N'Dalatando	9,340	24,190	...
Kuanza Sul	Sumbe	21,490	55,660	...
Luanda	Luanda	934	2,418	...
Lunda Norte	Lucapa	39,685	102,783	...
Lunda Sul	Saurimo	17,625	45,649	...
Malanje	Malanje	37,684	97,602	...
Moxico	Lwena	86,110	223,023	...
Namibe	Namibe	22,447	58,137	...
Uíge	Uíge	22,663	58,698	...
Zaire	M'Banza Kongo	15,494	40,130	...
TOTAL		481,354[4]	1,246,700	10,366,000

Demography

Population (2001): 10,366,000.
Density (2001): persons per sq mi 21.5, persons per sq km 8.3.
Urban-rural (1999): urban 43.2%; rural 56.8%.
Sex distribution (2000): male 50.59%; female 49.41%.
Age breakdown (2000): under 15, 43.2%; 15–29, 26.5%; 30–44, 16.9%; 45–59, 8.7%; 60 and over, 4.7%.
Population projection: (2010) 12,646,000; (2020) 15,750,000.
Doubling time: 33 years.
Ethnic composition (1983): Ovimbundu 37.2%; Mbundu 21.6%; Kongo 13.2%; Luimbe-Nganguela 5.4%; Nyaneka-Humbe 5.4%; Chokwe 4.2%; Luvale (Luena) 3.6%; Luchazi 2.4%; Ambo (Ovambo) 2.4%; Lunda 1.2%; Mbunda 1.2%; other 2.2%.
Religious affiliation (2001): Christian 94.1%, of which Roman Catholic 62.1%, Protestant 15.0%; traditional beliefs 5.0%, other 0.9%.
Major cities (1999): Luanda 2,555,000; Huambo 400,000[5]; Benguela 155,000[6]; Lobito 150,000[6]; Lubango 105,000[7].

Vital statistics

Birth rate per 1,000 population (2000): 46.9 (world avg. 22.5).
Death rate per 1,000 population (2000): 25.0 (world avg. 9.0).
Natural increase rate per 1,000 population (2000): 21.9 (world avg. 13.5).
Total fertility rate (avg. births per childbearing woman; 2000): 6.5.
Life expectancy at birth (2000): male 37.1 years; female 39.6 years.
Major causes of death (percentage of total deaths; 1990): diarrheal diseases 25.8%; malaria 19.4%; cholera 7.3%; acute respiratory infections 6.8%.

National economy

Budget (1999). Revenue: NKz 7,540,000,000[3] (tax revenue 99.4%, of which petroleum corporate taxes 71.1%, tax on goods 20.5%, import duties 3.0%; nontax revenue 0.6%). Expenditures: NKz 8,940,000,000[3]; defense and internal security 41%; administration 16.1%; interest 10.7%; economic services 10.3%; education 4.8%; health 2.8%; other 14.3%).
Public debt (external, outstanding; 1999): U.S.$9,428,000,000.
Tourism: receipts (1999) U.S.$13,000,000; expenditures (1997) U.S.$70,000,000.
Household income and expenditure. Average household size (1998) 5.0; annual income per household: n.a.; sources of income: n.a.; expenditure: n.a.
Production (metric tons except as noted). Agriculture, forestry, fishing (2000): cassava 3,129,734, corn (maize) 428,045, sugarcane 330,000, bananas 290,000, oil palm fruit 250,000, sweet potatoes 182,050, millet 101,736, dry beans 67,509, pineapples 32,000, peanuts (groundnuts) 23,000, coffee 4,260; livestock (number of live animals) 4,042,000 cattle, 2,150,000 goats, 800,000 pigs, 350,000 sheep, 6,400,000 chickens; roundwood (2000) 6,676,000 cu m; fish catch (1999) 177,497. Mining and quarrying (1999): diamonds 1,080,000 carats. Manufacturing (1999): bread 87,500; frozen fish 57,700; wheat flour 57,500; soap 8,565; salt 7,803; leather shoes 25,000 pairs; beer 160,900 hectolitres; fabric 316,000 sq m. Construction (value in NKz '000,000[3]; 1986): residential 608; nonresidential 1,977. Energy production (consumption): electricity (kW-hr; 1998) 1,885,000,000 (1,885,000,000); coal, none (none); crude petroleum (barrels; 1999) 278,900,000 (14,100,000); petroleum products (metric tons; 1999) 1,956,000 (1,124,000); natural gas (cu m; 1996) 179,389,000 (179,389,000).
Gross national product (at current market prices; 1999): U.S.$3,276,000,000 (U.S.$270 per capita).

Structure of gross domestic product and labour force

	1999 in value NKz '000,000,000[8]	% of total value	labour force	% of labour force
Agriculture	1,076	6.9	4,132,000 (Agriculture, Mining)	72.1
Mining	10,968	70.1		
Manufacturing	562	3.6	1,597,000 (Manufacturing through Services)	27.9
Construction	529	3.4		
Finance, Trade, Public utilities, Transp. and commun.	1,370	8.8		
Pub. admin., defense, Services	1,102	7.0		
Other	37[9]	0.2[9]	...	...
TOTAL	15,644	100.0	5,729,000	100.0

Population economically active (1999): total 5,729,000; activity rate of total population 57.7% (participation rates over age 10 [1991] 60.1%; female 38.4%).

Price and earnings indexes (1995 = 100)

	1995	1996	1997	1998	1999	2000
Consumer price index	100.0	4,245.2	13,550.1	25,327.3	43,661	61,311
Monthly earnings index	100.0	...	...	...	...	...

Land use (1995): forested 18.5%; meadows and pastures 43.3%; agricultural and under permanent cultivation 2.8%; other 35.4%.

Foreign trade

Balance of trade (current prices)

	1995	1996	1997	1998	1999
U.S.$'000,000	+1,871	+3,055	+2,529	+1,464	+2,077
% of total	33.6%	42.8%	33.9%	26.0%	24.1%

Imports (1999): U.S.$3,267,000,000 (1991; current consumption goods 50.2%, capital goods 20.2%, intermediate consumption goods 18.9%, transport equipment 6.8%). *Major import sources* (1999): Portugal 18.8%; U.S. 14.6%; South Africa 11.9%; France 8.2%; U.K. 6.2%; Spain 5.9%; Brazil 5.1%.
Exports (1999): U.S.$5,344,000,000 (mineral fuels 87.8%, diamonds 11.8%). *Major export destinations* (1999): U.S. 59.5%; China 8.2%; Taiwan 7.7%; Germany 2.4%; France 2.1%.

Transport and communications

Transport. Railroads (1998): route length 1,834 mi, 2,952 km; passenger-mi 203,000,000[10], passenger-km 326,000,000[10]; short ton-mi cargo 1,178,000,000[10], metric ton km cargo 1,720,000,000[10]. Roads (1998): total length 45,128 mi, 72,626 km (paved 25%). Vehicles (1997): passenger cars 207,000; trucks and buses 25,000. Merchant marine (1998): vessels (100 gross tons and over) 123; total deadweight tonnage 73,907. Air transport (1997): passenger-mi 385,000,000, passenger-km 620,000,000; short ton-mi cargo 60,300,000, metric ton-km cargo 97,000,000; airports (1999) with scheduled flights 17.

Communications

Medium	date	unit	number	units per 1,000 persons
Daily newspapers	1996	circulation	128,000	14
Television	1999	receivers	190,000	19
Telephones	1999	main lines	96,350	9.7
Cellular telephones	1999	subscribers	24,000	2.4
Personal computers	1999	units	12,000	1.2
Internet	1999	users	10,000	1.0

Education and health

Educational attainment: n.a. *Literacy* (1998): percentage of population age 15 and over literate 41.7%; males literate 55.6%; females literate 28.5%.

Education (1991–92)

	schools[11]	teachers	students	student/teacher ratio
Primary (age 7–10)	6,308	31,062	989,443	...
Secondary (age 11–16)	5,276	5,138[12]	196,099	...
Voc., teacher tr.	...	566[12]	22,888	...
Higher	1	787	6,331	8.0

Health (1997): physicians 736 (1 per 12,985 persons); hospital beds (1990) 11,857 (1 per 845 persons); infant mortality rate per 1,000 live births (2000) 195.8.
Food (1999): daily per capita caloric intake 1,873 (vegetable products 92%, animal products 8%); 82% of FAO recommended minimum requirement.

Military

Total active duty personnel (2000): 107,500 (army 93.0%, navy 1.4%, air force 5.6%). *Military expenditure as percentage of GNP* (1997): 20.5% (world 2.6%); per capita expenditure U.S.$147.

[1]Long-term civil war resumed in September 1998 and continued in September 2001. [2]President annulled post of Prime Minister in January 1999. [3]The refloated kwanza (or [second] new kwanza), equal to 1,000 readjusted kwanza, was introduced on Jan. 1, 2000; previously, in July 1995, the readjusted kwanza, equal to 1,000 new kwanza (NKz), was introduced. [4]Detail does not add to total given because of rounding. [5]1995. [6]1983. [7]1984. [8]In refloated kwanza. [9]Import duties. [10]1988. [11]1985–86. [12]1989–90.

Internet resources for further information:
- **Official Home Page of the Republic of Angola http://www.angola.org**
- **Bank of Angola http://www.ebonet.net/bna/bna_blind.htm**

Antigua and Barbuda

Official name: Antigua and Barbuda.
Form of government: constitutional monarchy with two legislative houses (Senate [17]; House of Representatives [17[1]]).
Chief of state: British Monarch represented by Governor-General.
Head of government: Prime Minister.
Capital: Saint John's.
Official language: English.
Official religion: none.
Monetary unit: 1 Eastern Caribbean dollar (EC$) = 100 cents; valuation (Sept. 28, 2001) 1 U.S.$ = EC$2.70; 1 £ = EC$3.97.

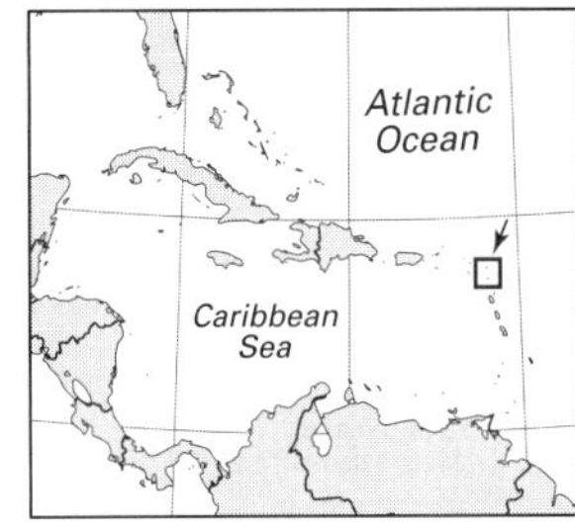

Area and population	area		population
			1991
Parishes[2]	sq mi	sq km	census
Saint George	9.3	24.1	4,473
Saint John's	28.5	73.8	35,635
Saint Mary	22.0	57.0	5,303
Saint Paul	18.5	47.9	6,117
Saint Peter	12.7	32.9	3,622
Saint Phillip	17.0	44.0	2,964
Islands[2]			
Barbuda	62.0	160.6	1,241
Redonda	0.5	1.3	0
TOTAL	170.5	441.6	59,355[3]

Demography

Population (2001): 71,500[4].
Density (2001): persons per sq mi 419.4, persons per sq km 161.9.
Urban-rural (1995): urban 36.5%; rural 63.5%.
Sex distribution (1991): male 48.20%; female 51.80%.
Age breakdown (1991): under 15, 30.4%; 15–29, 27.8%; 30–44, 20.5%; 45–59, 10.2%; 60–74, 7.7%; 75 and over, 3.4%.
Population projection: (2010) 75,000; (2020) 79,000.
Doubling time: 50 years.
Ethnic composition (1994): black 91.3%; mixed 3.7%; white 2.4%; Syrian/Lebanese 0.6%; Indo-Pakistani 0.4%; Amerindian 0.3%; other 1.3%.
Religious affiliation (1991): Protestant 73.7%, of which Anglican 32.1%, Moravian 12.0%, Methodist 9.1%, Seventh-day Adventist 8.8%; Roman Catholic 10.8%; Jehovah's Witness 1.2%; Rastafarian 0.8%[5]; other religion/no religion/not stated 13.5%.
Major cities (1991): Saint John's 22,342[6].

Vital statistics

Birth rate per 1,000 population (2000): 20.2 (world avg. 22.5); (1988) legitimate 23.4%; illegitimate 76.6%.
Death rate per 1,000 population (2000): 6.0 (world avg. 9.0).
Natural increase rate per 1,000 population (2000): 14.2 (world avg. 13.5).
Total fertility rate (avg. births per childbearing woman; 2000): 2.3.
Marriage rate per 1,000 population (1995): 22.1.
Divorce rate per 1,000 population (1988): 0.2.
Life expectancy at birth (2000): male 68.2 years; female 72.8 years.
Major causes of death per 100,000 population (1993–95): diseases of the circulatory system 258.1, of which cerebrovascular disease 103.3, diseases of pulmonary circulation and other forms of heart disease 76.9; malignant neoplasms (cancers) 104.9; endocrine and metabolic disorders 73.7.

National economy

Budget (1998). Revenue: EC$362,300,000 (taxes on international transactions 35.6%, of which import duties 15.8%; consumption taxes 24.9%; nontax revenue 12.5%; corporate income taxes 7.1%). Expenditures: EC$427,300,000 (current expenditures 90.1%; development expenditures 9.9%).
Public debt (external, outstanding; end of 1998): U.S.$406,400,000.
Production (metric tons except as noted). Agriculture, forestry, fishing (1999): tropical fruit (including papayas, guavas, soursops, and oranges) 6,500, mangoes 1,300, eggplants 250, lemons and limes 220, carrots 210, "Antiguan Black" pineapples 150; livestock (number of live animals) 15,700 cattle, 12,200 sheep; roundwood, n.a.; fish catch (1997) 500. Mining and quarrying: crushed stone for local use. Manufacturing (1994): beer and malt 166,000 cases; T-shirts 179,000 units; other manufactures include cement, handicrafts, and furniture, as well as electronic components for export. Construction (1998): gross value of building applications EC$323,000,000. Energy production (consumption): electricity (kW-hr; 1997) 153,700,000 (115,300,000); coal, none (none); crude petroleum, none (none); petroleum products (metric tons; 1996) negligible (105,000); natural gas, none (none).
Population economically active (1991): total 26,753; activity rate of total population 45.1% (participation rates: ages 15–64, 69.7%; female 45.6%; unemployed [end of 1999] *c.* 5%).

Price and earnings indexes (1996 = 100)	1994	1995	1996	1997	1998	1999
Consumer price index	98.2	96.9	100.0	98.9	103.6	...
Annual earnings index[7]	...	...	100.0	100.0	106.0	106.0

Household income and expenditure. Average household size (1991) 3.2; income per household: n.a.; sources of income: n.a.; expenditure: n.a.

Gross national product (1999): U.S.$606,000,000 (U.S.$8,990 per capita).

Structure of gross domestic product and labour force	1998		1991	
	in value EC$'000,000	% of total value	labour force	% of labour force
Agriculture, fishing	56.1	3.4	1,040	3.9
Quarrying	24.3	1.5	64	0.2
Manufacturing	31.7	1.9	1,444	5.4
Construction	166.5	10.0	3,109	11.6
Public utilities	42.6	2.5	435	1.6
Transp. and commun.	289.6	17.4	2,395	9.0
Trade, restaurants, and hotels	323.7	19.4	8,524	31.9
Finance, real estate	235.7	14.1	1,454	5.4
Pub. admin., defense	247.1	14.8	2,572	9.6
Services	104.4	6.3	5,207	19.5
Other	144.5[8]	8.7[8]	509	1.9
TOTAL	1,666.2	100.0	26,753	100.0

Land use (1994): forested 11.0%; meadows and pastures 9.0%; agricultural and under permanent cultivation 18.0%; other 62.0%.
Tourism: receipts from visitors (1999) U.S.$291,000,000; expenditures by nationals abroad (1997) U.S.$26,000,000.

Foreign trade

Balance of trade (current prices)	1994	1995	1996	1997	1998
U.S.$'000,000	–263	–276	–301	–294	–321
% of total	74.8%	72.4%	80.0%	79.5%	81.6%

Imports (1998)[9]: U.S.$357,500,000 (agricultural products 11.0%, other [including petroleum products for reexport] 89%). *Major import sources* (1997): United States 26.3%; United Kingdom 10.0%; Caricom 7.8%.
Exports (1998): U.S.$36,200,000 (reexports [significantly, petroleum products reexported to neighbouring islands] 59.1%, domestic exports 40.9%). *Major export destinations* (1994)[9]: United States 40.0%; others include the United Kingdom, Canada, and Caricom.

Transport and communications

Transport. Railroad[10]. Roads (1996): total length 155 mi, 250 km (paved, n.a.). Vehicles (1995): passenger cars 13,588; trucks and buses 1,342. Merchant marine (1992): vessels (100 gross tons and over) 292; total deadweight tonnage 997,381. Air transport (1995): passenger-mi 157,000,000, passenger-km 252,000,000; (1991) short ton-mi cargo 137,000, metric ton-km cargo 200,000; airports (1996) with scheduled flights 2.

Communications Medium	date	unit	number	units per 1,000 persons
Daily newspapers	1996	circulation	6,000	87
Radio	1997	receivers	36,000	523
Television	1997	receivers	31,000	451
Telephones	1999	main lines	36,500	518
Cellular telephones	1999	subscribers	8,500	121

Education and health

Educational attainment (1991). Percentage of population age 25 and over having: no formal schooling 1.1%; primary education 50.5%; secondary 33.4%; higher (not university) 5.4%; university 6.2%; other/unknown 3.4%. *Literacy* (1995): percentage of total population age 15 and over literate, 90.0%.

Education (1996–97)	schools	teachers	students	student/teacher ratio
Primary (age 5–11)	58	559	12,229	21.9
Secondary (age 12–16)	13	389	4,260	11.0
Higher[11]	1	16	46	2.9

Health (1996): physicians 75 (1 per 915 persons); hospital beds 255 (1 per 269 persons); infant mortality rate per 1,000 live births (2000) 23.0.
Food (1999): daily per capita caloric intake 2,396 (vegetable products 68%, animal products 32%); 102% of FAO recommended minimum requirement.

Military

Total active duty personnel (2000): a 170-member defense force (army 73.5%, navy 26.5%) is part of the Eastern Caribbean regional security system. Military expenditure as percentage of GNP (1998): 0.7%[9] (world average, n.a.).

[1]Directly elected seats only; attorney general and speaker may serve ex officio if they are not elected to House of Representatives. [2]Community councils on Antigua and the local government council on Barbuda are the organs of local government. [3]Unadjusted de jure population excluding institutionalized population; de jure population adjusted for undercount (including institutionalized population) is 63,896. [4]Includes evacuees from Montserrat. [5]Increased to more than 3% of population by 2000. [6]Large settlements include (1991): All Saints 2,230; Liberta 1,473; Codrington 814. [7]Public sector only. [8]Net indirect taxes less imputed bank service charges. [9]Estimated percentages. [10]Mostly nonoperative privately owned tracks. [11]1994–95.

Internet resources for further information:
- **Antigua and Barbuda High Commission (London)** **http://www.antigua-barbuda.com**
- **Ministry of Foreign Affairs** **http://www.foreignaffairs.gov.ag**

Argentina

Official name: República Argentina (Argentina Republic).
Form of government: federal republic with two legislative houses (Senate [72]; Chamber of Deputies [257]).
Head of state and government: President[1].
Capital: Buenos Aires.
Official language: Spanish.
Official religion: Roman Catholicism.
Monetary unit: 1 peso (pl. pesos) (Arg$) = 100 centavos; valuation (Sept. 28, 2001) 1 U.S.$ = Arg$1.00; 1 £ = Arg$1.47.

Area and population

Provinces	Capitals	area sq mi	area sq km	population 2000 estimate
Buenos Aires	La Plata	118,754	307,571	14,214,701
Catamarca	Catamarca	39,615	102,602	318,147
Chaco	Resistencia	38,469	99,633	951,795
Chubut	Rawson	86,752	224,686	448,028
Córdoba	Córdoba	63,831	165,321	3,090,803
Corrientes	Corrientes	34,054	88,199	921,933
Entre Ríos	Paraná	30,418	78,781	1,113,438
Formosa	Formosa	27,825	72,066	504,185
Jujuy	San Salvador de Jujuy	20,548	53,219	604,002
La Pampa	Santa Rosa	55,382	143,440	306,113
La Rioja	La Rioja	34,626	89,680	280,198
Mendoza	Mendoza	57,462	148,827	1,607,618
Misiones	Posadas	11,506	29,801	995,326
Neuquén	Neuquén	36,324	94,078	560,726
Río Negro	Viedma	78,384	203,013	618,486
Salta	Salta	60,034	155,488	1,067,347
San Juan	San Juan	34,614	89,651	578,504
San Luis	San Luis	29,633	76,748	363,345
Santa Cruz	Río Gallegos	94,187	243,943	206,897
Santa Fe	Santa Fe	51,354	133,007	3,098,661
Santiago del Estero	Santiago del Estero	52,645	136,351	725,993
Tierra del Fuego[2]	Ushuaia	8,210	21,263	115,538
Tucumán	San Miguel de Tucumán	8,697	22,524	1,293,349
Other federal entity				
Distrito Federal	Buenos Aires	77	200	3,046,662
TOTAL		1,073,400[3]	2,780,092	37,031,802[3]

Demography

Population (2001): 37,487,000[4].
Density (2001): persons per sq mi 34.9, persons per sq km 13.5.
Urban-rural (2000): urban 89.6%; rural 10.4%.
Sex distribution (2000): male 49.05%; female 50.95%.
Age breakdown (2000): under 15, 27.7%; 15–29, 25.6%; 30–44, 18.8%; 45–59, 14.6%; 60–74, 9.6%; 75 and over, 3.7%.
Population projection: (2010) 41,474,000; (2020) 45,347,000.
Ethnic composition (2000): European extraction 86.4%; mestizo 6.5%; Amerindian 3.4%; Arab 3.3%; other 0.4%.
Religious affiliation (2000): Roman Catholic 79.8%; Protestant 5.4%; Muslim 1.9%; Jewish 1.3%; other 11.6%.
Major cities (1999): Buenos Aires 2,904,192 (12,423,000[5]); Córdoba 1,275,585; Rosario 1,000,000; Mar del Plata 579,483; La Plata 556,308.

Vital statistics

Birth rate per 1,000 population (2000): 18.6 (world avg. 22.5).
Death rate per 1,000 population (2000): 7.6 (world avg. 9.0).
Natural increase rate per 1,000 population (2000): 11.0 (world avg. 13.5).
Total fertility rate (avg. births per childbearing woman; 2000): 2.5.
Life expectancy at birth (2000): male 71.7 years; female 78.6 years.
Major causes of death per 100,000 population (1998): diseases of the circulatory system 265.8; neoplasms (cancers) 146.3; diseases of the respiratory system 91.0; accidents 30.5.

National economy

Budget (1999). Revenue: Arg$56,621,300,000 (current revenue 98.2%, of which tax revenue 90.4%, nontax revenue 7.8%; capital revenue 1.8%). Expenditure: Arg$63,662,000,000 (social security 35.3%; debt service 13.6%; general public services 8.4%; education 5.0%; health 5.0%; economic services 3.9%; defense 3.3%).
Public debt (external, outstanding; 1999): U.S.$84,568,000,000.
Tourism (1999): receipts U.S.$2,812,000,000; expenditures U.S.$4,107,000,000.
Gross national product (1999): U.S.$276,097,000,000 (U.S.$7,550 per capita).

Structure of gross domestic product and labour force

	1999 in value Arg$'000,000	1999 % of total value	1996 labour force	1996 % of labour force
Agriculture	12,329	4.4	190,300[6]	1.5[6]
Mining	4,821	1.7		
Manufacturing	48,471	17.1	1,999,600	15.9
Construction	15,970	5.6	1,217,400	9.7
Public utilities	6,041	2.1	115,700	0.9
Transp. and commun.	22,614	8.0	873,300	6.9
Trade, restaurants	45,806	16.2	2,523,800	20.0
Finance, real estate	56,466	20.0	1,021,800	8.1
Pub. admin., defense	53,609	18.9	1,010,500	8.0
Services			3,573,000	28.4
Other	16,643	6.0	63,500	0.5
TOTAL	282,769[3]	100.0	12,588,900[6]	100.0[3]

Production (metric tons except as noted). Agriculture, forestry, fishing (1999): soybeans 19,500,000, sugarcane 16,700,000, wheat 14,200,000, corn (maize) 13,500,000, sunflower seeds 7,100,000, potatoes 3,450,000, grapes 2,425,000; livestock (number of live animals) 55,000,000 cattle, 14,000,000 sheep; roundwood (1998) 11,428,000 cu m; fish catch 1,012,804. Mining and quarrying (1999): silver 1,149,970 troy oz; gold 655,870 troy oz. Manufacturing (1999): cement 7,187,000; vegetable oil 5,658,000; wheat flour 3,563,000; sugar 1,578,000; paper 1,130,000; wine 12,809,000 hectolitres; beer 12,503,000 hectolitres. Energy production (consumption): electricity (kW-hr; 1996) 69,746,000,000 (73,109,000,000); coal (metric tons; 1996) 311,000 (1,396,000); crude petroleum (barrels; 1996) 275,000,000 (175,000,000); petroleum products (metric tons; 1996) 20,782,000 (19,152,000); natural gas (cu m; 1996) 29,693,000,000 (31,883,000,000).
Population economically active (1995): total 14,345,171; activity rate of total population 41.5% (participation rates: ages 15–64, 64.5%; female 36.9%; unemployed [1996] 17.0%).

Price and earnings indexes (1995 = 100)

	1995	1996	1997	1998	1999	2000
Consumer price index	100.0	100.2	100.7	101.6	100.4	99.5
Monthly earnings index[7]	100.0	100.7	...	...	...	...

Household size and expenditure. Average household size (1991) 3.8; expenditure (1985–86): food 38.2%, transportation 11.6%, housing 9.3%, energy 9.0%, clothing 8.0%, health 7.9%, recreation 7.5%, other 8.5%.

Foreign trade[8]

Balance of trade (current prices)

	1995	1996	1997	1998	1999	2000
U.S.$'000,000	+3,005	+1,621	−2,183	−3,117	−775	−2,537
% of total	7.7%	3.5%	4.0%	5.6%	1.6%	5.1%

Imports (1999): U.S.$25,508,000,000 (machinery and transport equipment 46.5%, chemical products 19.4%, manufactured products 15.0%, food products and live animals 4.4%). *Major import sources:* Brazil 21.9%; U.S. 19.6%[9]; France 5.9%[10]; Germany 5.5%; Italy 5.3%; Japan 4.2%; Spain 3.9%.
Exports (1999): U.S.$23,333,000,000 (food products and live animals 35.1%, petroleum and petroleum products 12.1%, machinery and transport equipment 12.0%, manufactured products 10.8%, vegetable and animal oils 9.9%, crude materials 8.0%, chemical products 7.7%). *Major export destinations:* Brazil 24.4%; U.S. 11.4%; Chile 8.0%; The Netherlands 4.3%; Spain 4.1%; Uruguay 3.5%; Italy 3.0%.

Transport and communications

Transport. Railroads (1999): route length 33,958 km; passenger-km 9,102,000,000; metric ton-km cargo 9,101,852,000. Roads (1996): total length 135,630 mi, 218,276 km (paved 29%). Vehicles (1997): passenger cars 4,901,608; commercial vehicles and buses 1,379,044. Air transport (1999): passenger-km 11,735,034,000; metric ton-km cargo 1,306,500; airports (1997) 39.

Communications

Medium	date	unit	number	units per 1,000 persons
Daily newspapers	1996	circulation	4,320,000	123
Radio	1998	receivers	21,500,000	595
Television	1998	receivers	10,600,000	293
Telephones	1999	main lines	7,223,168	197
Cellular telephones	1999	subscribers	4,434,000	121
Personal computers	1999	units	1,800,000	49
Internet	1999	users	900,000	25

Education and health

Educational attainment (1991). Percentage of population age 25 and over having: no formal schooling 5.7%; less than primary education 22.3%; primary 34.6%; incomplete secondary 12.5%; complete secondary 12.8%; higher 12.0%. *Literacy* (1995): percentage of total population age 15 and over literate 96.2%; males literate 96.2%; females literate 96.2%.

Education (1998–99)

	schools	teachers	students	student/ teacher ratio
Primary (age 6–12)	22,395	313,764[11]	5,262,066	16.1[11]
Secondary (age 13–17)[12]	6,373	233,564[13]	2,539,749	9.6[13]
Higher	1,700	118,695[13]	1,342,565	7.8[13]

Health: physicians (1992) 88,800 (1 per 376 persons); hospital beds (1996) 115,803 (1 per 304 persons); infant mortality rate (2000) 18.3.
Food (1999): daily per capita caloric intake 3,176 (vegetable products 68%, animal products 32%); 135% of FAO recommended minimum requirement.

Military

Total active duty personnel (2000): 71,100 (army 57.8%, navy 24.2%, air force 17.6%). *Military expenditure as percentage of GNP* (1997): 1.2% (world 2.6%); per capita expenditure U.S.$104.

[1]Assisted by a ministerial coordinator who exercises general administration of the country. [2]Area of Tierra del Fuego (province since 1991) excludes claims to British-held islands in the South Atlantic Ocean. [3]Detail does not add to total given because of rounding. [4]Includes about 2 million illegal immigrants from Bolivia and Paraguay. [5]Urban agglomeration. [6]Based on October survey; data for agriculture and mining sectors are incomplete. [7]Manufacturing sector only. [8]Import figures are f.o.b. in balance of trade and c.i.f. in commodities and trading partners. [9]Includes Puerto Rico. [10]Includes Monaco. [11]1996. [12]Secondary includes vocational and teacher training. [13]1994–95.

Internet resources for further information:
- **National Institute of Statistics and Censuses http://www.indec.mecon.ar**

Armenia

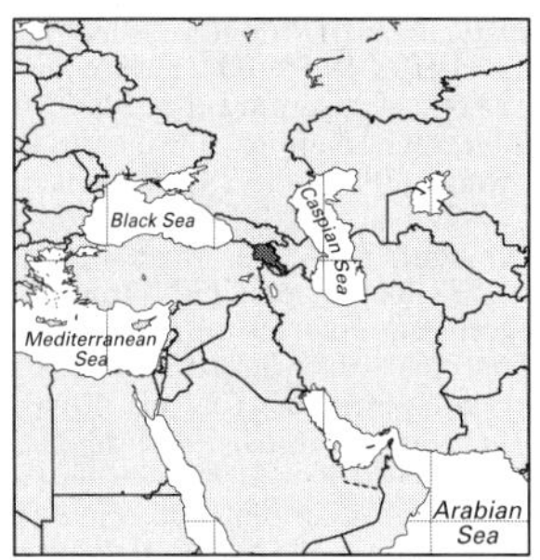

Official name: Hayastani Hanrapetut'yun (Republic of Armenia).
Form of government: unitary multiparty republic with a single legislative body (National Assembly [131]).
Head of state: President.
Head of government: Prime Minister.
Capital: Yerevan.
Official language: Armenian.
Official religion: none[1].
Monetary unit: 1 dram = 100 lumas; valuation (Sept. 28, 2001) official, 1 U.S.$ = 554.14 drams; 1 £ = 814.42 drams.

Area and population

	area		population
Regions	sq mi	sq km	2000 estimate
Aragatsotn	1,064	2,755	167,500
Ararat	812	2,104	310,800
Armavir	479	1,241	322,300
Gegharkunik	1,573	4,073	278,600
Lori	1,464	3,791	394,400
Kotayk	811	2,100	329,400
Shirak	1,034	2,679	362,300
Syunik	1,739	4,505	163,900
Vayots-Dzor	891	2,308	69,200
Tavush	1,043	2,702	156,800
Cities			
Yerevan	81	210	1,248,200
Other	493[2]	1,278[2]	
TOTAL	11,484[3]	29,743[3, 4]	3,803,400

Demography

Population (2001): 3,807,000; *c.* (de facto; 2000) 3,000,000[5].
Density (2001): persons per sq mi 331.5, persons per sq km 128.0.
Urban-rural (1998): urban 69.4%; rural 30.6%.
Sex distribution (2000): male 48.73%; female 51.27%.
Age breakdown (2000): under 15, 24.3%; 15–29, 24.0%; 30–44, 23.6%; 45–59, 13.9%; 60–74, 11.6%; 75 and over, 2.6%.
Population projection: (2010) 3,828,000; (2020) 3,951,000.
Doubling time: n.a.; doubling time exceeds 100 years.
Ethnic composition (1989): Armenian 93.3%; Azerbaijani 2.6%; other 4.1%.
Religious affiliation (1995): Armenian Apostolic 64.5%; other Christian 1.3%; other (mostly nonreligious) 34.2%.
Major cities (2000): Yerevan 1,248,200; Gyumri 163,000[6]; Kirovakan 76,000[6].

Vital statistics

Birth rate per 1,000 population (2000): 11.0 (world avg. 22.5); (1993) legitimate 86.0%; illegitimate 14.0%.
Death rate per 1,000 population (2000): 9.5 (world avg. 9.0).
Natural increase rate per 1,000 population (2000): 1.5 (world avg. 13.5).
Total fertility rate (avg. births per childbearing woman; 2000): 1.5.
Marriage rate per 1,000 population (1999): 3.3.
Divorce rate per 1,000 population (1999): 0.3.
Life expectancy at birth (2000): male 62.0 years; female 71.0 years.
Major causes of death per 100,000 population (1999): circulatory diseases 342.1; cancers 106.0; respiratory diseases 36.2; accidents and violence 33.2.

National economy

Budget (2000). Revenue: 202,005,000,000 drams (tax revenue 96.7%, of which value-added tax 33.4%, excise tax 12.5%, payroll tax 11.6%, enterprise profit tax 10.1%, income tax 7.3%, other taxes 21.8%; grants 3.3%). Expenditures: 267,411,000,000 drams (current expenditures 79.1%, of which pensions and social welfare 24.8%, wages 13.7%, interest 6.5%, health 5.5%, education 3.3%, other 25.3%; capital expenditure and net lending 20.9%).
Public debt (external, outstanding; 1999): U.S.$681,900,000.
Tourism (1998): receipts from visitors U.S.$6,000,000; expenditures by nationals abroad U.S.$45,000,000.
Land use (1994): forest 13.4%; pasture 23.1%; agriculture 20.1%; other 43.4%.
Gross national product (1999): U.S.$1,878,000,000 (U.S.$490 per capita).

Structure of net material product and labour force

	2000			
	in value '000,000 drams	% of total value	labour force	% of labour force
Agriculture	231,908	22.5	555,800	38.7
Manufacturing, mining; Public utilities	226,898	22.0	192,900	13.4
Construction	112,743	10.9	53,000	3.7
Transp. and commun.	71,698	6.9	47,400	3.3
Trade	94,878	9.2	107,900	7.5
Pub. admin., defense	—	—	27,900	2.0
Services	—	—	287,900	20.0
Other	294,330	28.5	164,100[7]	11.4[7]
TOTAL	1,032,455	100.0	1,436,900	100.0

Production (metric tons except as noted). Agriculture, forestry, fishing (2000): potatoes 320,000, wheat 142,000, grapes 110,000, tomatoes 110,000, watermelons 90,000, apples 50,600, barley 48,000; livestock (number of live animals) 540,000 sheep and goats, 478,730 cattle, 70,566 pigs, 4,100,000 poultry; roundwood (1998) 35,700 cu m; fish catch (1998) 1,135. Mining and quarrying (1998): copper 9,200,000; gold (metal content) 400 kg; molybdenum 1,800. Manufacturing (value in '000,000 drams; 1994): machine-building and metalworking equipment 18,436; food products 13,842; chemicals 5,330; metals 5,259; construction materials 3,154; textiles 2,500; leather products 2,335. Construction (1995): 284,000 sq m. Energy production (consumption): electricity (kW-hr; 2000) 5,958,000,000 (5,958,000,000); coal (metric tons; 2000) none (5,000); crude petroleum (barrels; 1996) none (1,026,000); petroleum products (metric tons; 1996) none (358,000); natural gas (cu m; 1996) none (1,050,700).
Population economically active (2000): total 1,436,900; activity rate of total population 37.8% (participation rates [1996] ages 16–60, 75.1%; unemployed [2000] 10.7%).

Price and earnings indexes (1995 = 100)

	1995	1996	1997	1998	1999	2000
Consumer price index	100	119	135	147	147.9	146.7
Earnings index	...	...	...	...	...	...

Household income and expenditure. Average household size (1997) 4.5; income per household (1994) 47,352 drams (U.S.$153); sources of income (1994): wages and salaries 52.3%, agricultural income 7.7%, other 40.0%; expenditure (1994): goods and services 78.0%, taxes and payments to government 22.0%.

Foreign trade

Balance of trade (current prices)

	1994	1995	1996	1997	1998	1999	2000
U.S.$'000,000	–178.3	–403.0	–469.2	–659.8	–640.0	–474.0	–592.0
% of total	29.3%	42.7%	44.7%	58.7%	47.0%	49.0%	49.1%

Imports (2000): U.S.$899,000,000 (minerals and chemicals 29.4%, food 16.6%, jewelry 12.6%, machinery and equipment 2.7%). *Major import sources:* EU countries 33.6%; former Soviet Union (FSU) 18.7%, of which Russia 14.7%; U.S. 11.5%; Iran 9.3%.
Exports (2000): U.S.$307,000,000 (jewelry 39.4%, machinery and equipment 14.3%, mineral products 12.4%, agricultural products 9.8%). *Major export destinations:* Belgium 24.5%; Russia 14.7%; U.S. 12.4%; Iran 9.1%; Georgia 4.9%.

Transport and communications

Transport. Railroads (1999): length 516 mi, 830 km; passenger-mi 28,832,000, passenger-km 46,400,000; ton-mi cargo 201,262,000, metric ton-km cargo 323,900,000. Roads (1997): length 5,238 mi, 8,431 km (paved 100%). Vehicles (1996): passenger cars 1,300; trucks and buses 4,460. Air transport (2000): passenger-mi 355,672,000, passenger-km 572,400,000; short ton-mi cargo 5,931,000, metric ton-km cargo 9,545,000; airports (1999) 1.

Communications

Medium	date	unit	number	units per 1,000 persons
Daily newspapers	1995	circulation	80,000	23
Television	1998	receivers	840,000	221
Telephones	1999	main lines	547,000	144
Cellular telephones	1999	subscribers	8,148	2.1
Personal computers	1999	units	20,000	5.3
Internet	1999	users	30,000	7.9

Education and health

Educational attainment (1989). Percentage of population age 25 and over having: primary education or no formal schooling 7.4%; some secondary 18.6%; completed secondary and some postsecondary 57.7%; higher 13.8%. *Literacy* (1989): total population age 15 and over literate 98.8%; males literate 99.4%; females literate 98.1%.

Education (1996–97)

	schools	teachers	students	student/teacher ratio
Primary (age 6–13)	1,402	13,620	256,475	18.8
Secondary (age 14–17)	...	57,325	365,025	6.4
Voc., teacher tr.[8]	69	...	25,200	...
Higher	14	4,065	35,517	8.7

Health (1994): physicians 13,000 (1 per 288 persons); hospital beds 30,000 (1 per 125 persons); infant mortality rate (2000) 41.5.
Food (1999): daily per capita caloric intake 2,167 (vegetable products 86%, animal products 14%); 85% of FAO recommended minimum requirement.

Military

Total active duty personnel (2000): 41,300 (army 100%). *Military expenditure as percentage of GNP* (1997): 3.5% (world 2.6%); per capita expenditure U.S.$100.

[1]The constitution provides for the right to practice the religion of one's choice. In practice, the law imposes restrictions on religious freedom. The 1991 Law on Religious Organizations establishes the separation of church and state but recognizes the Armenian Apostolic Church (the Armenian Orthodox Church) as having special status. The law requires all nonapostolic religious denominations to register with the Ministry of Justice and prohibits proselytizing. [2]Area of Lake Sevan. [3]In addition, nearly 20% of neighbouring Azerbaijan (including the 4,400-sq km geographic region of Nagorno-Karabakh [Armenian: Artsakh] has been occupied by Armenian forces since 1993. [4]Detail does not add to total given because of rounding. [5]About 1/5 of Armenia's population has left the country since 1993 because of an energy crisis. [6]1989; reduced in population by evacuation following Dec. 7, 1988, earthquake. [7]Includes 153,900 unemployed. [8]1993–94.

Internet resources for further information:
- **The Embassy of the Republic of Armenia http://www.armeniaemb.org**

Aruba

Official name: Aruba.
Political status: nonmetropolitan territory of The Netherlands with one legislative house (States of Aruba [21]).
Chief of state: Dutch Monarch represented by Governor.
Head of government: Prime Minister.
Capital: Oranjestad.
Official language: Dutch.
Official religion: none.
Monetary unit: 1 Aruban florin[1] (Af.) = 100 cents; valuation (Sept. 28, 2001) 1 U.S.$ = Af. 1.79; 1 £ = Af. 2.63.

Area and population	area[2]		population
			1991
Census region	sq mi	sq km	census
Noord/Tanki Leendert	14	37	10,056
Oranjestad East	5	13	11,266
Oranjestad West	4	10	8,779
Paradera	10	25	6,189
San Nicolas North	9	23	8,206
San Nicolas South	4	10	5,304
Santa Cruz	18	47	9,587
Savaneta	11	28	7,273
TOTAL	75	193	66,687[3, 4]

Demography

Population (2001): 97,200.
Density (2000): persons per sq mi 1,296.0, persons per sq km 503.6.
Urban-rural (2000): urban 67.0%; rural 33.0%.
Sex distribution (1999): male 49.41%; female 50.59%.
Age breakdown (1999): under 15, 22.3%; 15–29, 21.0%; 30–44, 27.8%; 45–59, 18.2%; 60–74, 8.1%; 75 and over, 2.6%.
Population projection: (2010) 102,000; (2020) 104,000.
Linguistic composition (1991): Papiamento 76.6%; English 8.9%; Spanish 7.4%; Dutch 5.4%; Portuguese 0.3%; other 1.4%[5].
Religious affiliation (2000): Christian 96.2%, of which Roman Catholic 81.9%, Protestant 7.3%, other Christian (Jehovah's Witness) 1.3%; Spiritist 1.0%; nonreligious 1.4%; other 1.4%.
Major urban areas: Oranjestad (1998) 28,000; San Nicolas (1991) 13,510.

Vital statistics

Birth rate per 1,000 population (2000): 13.1 (world avg. 22.5); (1998) legitimate 57.5%; illegitimate 42.5%.
Death rate per 1,000 population (2000): 6.1 (world avg. 9.0).
Natural increase rate per 1,000 population (2000): 7.0 (world avg. 13.5).
Total fertility rate (avg. births per childbearing woman; 2000): 1.8.
Marriage rate per 1,000 population (1998): 6.1.
Divorce rate per 1,000 population (1998): 3.6.
Life expectancy at birth (2000): male 75.0 years; female 81.9 years.
Major causes of death per 100,000 population (1998): diseases of the circulatory system 184.0, malignant neoplasms (cancers) 118.0, infectious and parasitic diseases/diseases of the respiratory system 61.7.

National economy

Budget (1999). Revenue: Af. 712,900,000 (tax revenue 85.4%, of which taxes on wages and income 32.1%, import duties 13.7%, taxes on profits 11.2%, excise taxes on gasoline 8.4%; nontax revenue 14.4%). Expenditures: Af. 736,900,000.
Production (metric tons except as noted). Agriculture, forestry, fishing: aloes are cultivated for export; small amounts of tomatoes, beans, cucumbers, gherkins, watermelons, and lettuce are grown on hydroponic farms; divi-divi pods, sour orange fruit, sorghum, and peanuts (groundnuts) are nonhydroponic crops of limited value; (livestock; number of live animals) Aruba has very few livestock; roundwood, n.a.; fish catch (1997) 205. Mining and quarrying: excavation of sand for local use. Manufacturing[6]: rum, cigarettes, aloe products, and soaps. Construction (value of residential and nonresidential buildings completed; 1992): Af. 16,900,000. Energy production (consumption): electricity (kW-hr; 1999) 738,000,000 ([2000] 644,000,000); coal, none (none); crude petroleum (barrels; 1996) none (2,287,000); petroleum products (metric tons; 1996) none (238,000); natural gas, none (none).
Gross domestic product (2000): U.S.$1,970,000,000 (U.S.$21,760 per capita).

Structure of gross domestic product and labour force	1994		1997	
	in value Af. '000,000	% of total value	labour force[7]	% of labour force[7]
Agriculture / Mining	12	0.5	198	0.4
			—	—
Manufacturing	130	5.5	2,627	5.9
Construction	156	6.5	3,395	7.6
Public utilities	77	3.2	810	1.8
Transp. and commun.	204	8.6	3,388	7.5
Trade, restaurants	636	26.7	14,240	31.8
Finance, real estate	254	10.7	4,634	10.3
Pub. admin., defense	316	13.3	4,349	9.7
Services	277	11.6	6,404	14.3
Other	319	13.4	4,795[8]	10.7[8]
TOTAL	2,381	100.0	44,840	100.0

Population economically active (1997[7]): total 44,840; activity rate of total population 48.9% (participation rates: ages 15–64, 68.3%; female 43.8%; unemployed 7.4%).

Price and earnings indexes (1995 = 100)	1994	1995	1996	1997	1998	1999	2000
Consumer price index	97.0	100.0	103.0	106.0	108.0	111.0	98.0
Earnings index[9]	92.6	100.0	103.2	106.4	108.9	...	...

Public debt (external, outstanding; December 2000): U.S.$209,800,000.
Household income and expenditure (1999): average household size 3.6; average annual income per household: Af. 39,000 (U.S.$21,800); sources of income: n.a.; expenditure (1994)[10]: transportation and communications 20.7%, food and beverages 18.4%, clothing and footwear 11.3%, household furnishings 10.4%, housing 9.8%.
Tourism: receipts from visitors (2000) U.S.$837,300,000; expenditures by nationals abroad (1999) U.S.$122,000,000.
Land use (1998): forest, negligible; meadows and pastures, negligible, agricultural and under permanent cultivation 11.0%; other (dry savanna and built-up) 89.0%.

Foreign trade

Balance of trade (current prices)	1995	1996	1997	1998	1999	2000
U.S.$'000,000	–425	–308	–391	–354	–594	–32
% of total	13.6%	8.1%	10.2%	13.2%	17.3%	0.6%

Imports (1999): U.S.$2,003,000,000 (petroleum [all forms] and free-zone imports 61.0%, electrical and nonelectrical machinery 8.0%, base and fabricated metals 4.3%). *Major import sources* (1999)[11]: United States 63.3%; The Netherlands 11.1%; Venezuela 3.0%; Netherlands Antilles 2.8%.
Exports (1999): U.S.$1,420,000,000 (petroleum [all forms] and free-zone exports 97.9%). *Major export destinations*[11]: United States 41.4%; Colombia 20.3%; The Netherlands 12.1%; Netherlands Antilles 8.4%.

Transport and communications

Transport. Railroads: none. Roads (1984): total length 236 mi, 380 km (paved 100%). Vehicles (1999): passenger cars 38,834; trucks and buses 990. Air transport (1998)[12]: passenger-mi 318,000,000, passenger-km 511,000,000; short ton-mi cargo, n.a., metric ton-mi cargo, n.a.; airports (1998) with scheduled flights 1.

Communications				units
Medium	date	unit	number	per 1,000 persons
Daily newspapers	1996	circulation	73,000	851
Radio	1997	receivers	50,000	558
Television	1997	receivers	20,000	223
Telephones	1999	main lines	36,557	388
Cellular telephones	2000	subscribers	24,313	251

Education and health

Educational attainment (1991). Percentage of population age 25 and over having: no formal schooling or incomplete primary education 15.0%; completed primary 37.3%; completed lower secondary/vocational 28.1%; completed upper secondary/vocational 4.0%; higher vocational 5.5%; undergraduate 5.3%; graduate 1.7%; other 3.1%. *Literacy* (1990): percentage of total population age 15 and over literate 95.0%.

Education (1998–99)	schools	teachers	students	student/ teacher ratio
Primary (age 6–12)	33	397	8,456	21.3
Secondary (age 12–17) / Voc., teacher tr.	15	470	7,157	15.2
Higher	2	53	394	7.4

Health (1999): physicians (1997) 103 (1 per 870 persons); hospital beds 308 (1 per 306 persons); infant mortality rate per 1,000 live births (2000) 6.5.
Food (1997): n.a.

Military

Total active duty personnel (1999): a 45-member Dutch naval/air force contingent is stationed in Aruba and the Netherlands Antilles.

[1]The Aruban florin (Af.) is pegged to the U.S. dollar at a fixed rate of Af. 1.79 = 1 U.S.$. [2]Areas for census regions are approximate. [3]Includes 27 persons not distributed by census region. [4]Unadjusted census total; adjusted census total equals 67,423. [5]Most Arubans are racially and ethnically mixed; ethnic composition (1998): Amerindian/other 80%; other (primarily Dutch, Spanish and/or black) 20%. [6]Servicing facilities include a free zone, offshore corporate banking facilities, casino/resort complexes, a petroleum transshipment terminal, a cruise ship terminal, and ship repair and bunkering facilities. [7]Based on labour force survey of October 1. [8]Includes 3,339 unemployed. [9]Minimum wage in service and trade industries. [10]Weights of consumer price index components. [11]Excludes petroleum (all forms) and free-zone trade. [12]Air Aruba only.

Internet resources for further information:

- **Aruba Central Bureau of Statistics http://www.arubastatistics.com/toc.htm**
- **Centrale Bank van Aruba http://www.cbaruba.org**

Australia

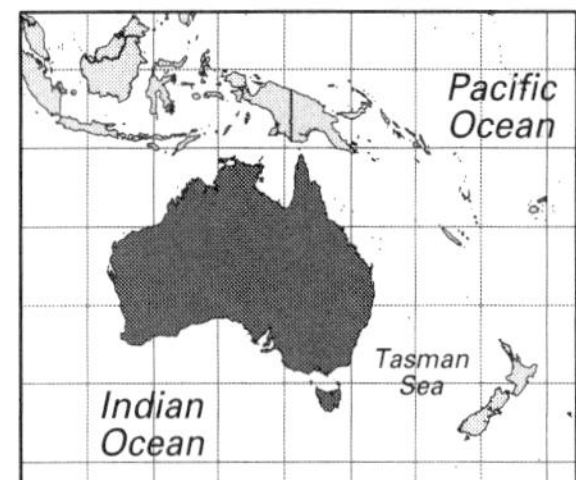

Official name: Commonwealth of Australia.
Form of government: federal parliamentary state (formally a constitutional monarchy) with two legislative houses (Senate [76]; House of Representatives [150]).
Chief of state: British Monarch represented by Governor-General.
Head of government: Prime Minister.
Capital: Canberra.
Official language: English.
Official religion: none.
Monetary unit: 1 Australian dollar ($A) = 100 cents; valuation (Sept. 28, 2001) 1 U.S.$ = $A 2.03; 1 £ = $A 2.98.

Area and population

		area		population
				1999
States	Capitals	sq mi	sq km	estimate
New South Wales	Sydney	309,130	800,640	6,411,680
Queensland	Brisbane	668,210	1,730,650	3,512,360
South Australia	Adelaide	379,720	983,480	1,493,070
Tasmania	Hobart	26,410	68,400	470,260
Victoria	Melbourne	87,810	227,420	4,712,170
Western Australia	Perth	976,790	2,529,880	1,861,020
Territories				
Australian Capital Territory	Canberra	940	2,430	310,170
Northern Territory	Darwin	520,900	1,349,130	192,880
TOTAL		2,969,910	7,692,030	18,966,790[1]

Demography

Population (2001): 19,358,000.
Density (2001): persons per sq mi 6.5, persons per sq km 2.5.
Urban-rural (2000): urban 85.0%; rural 15.0%.
Sex distribution (1999): male 49.77%; female 50.23%.
Age breakdown (1999): under 15, 20.7%; 15–24, 14.2%; 25–44, 30.7%; 45–64, 22.2%; 65 and over, 12.2%.
Population projection: (2010) 20,925,000; (2020) 22,409,000.
Doubling time: over 100 years.
Ethnic composition (1999): white 91.4%; Asian 6.4%; aboriginal 1.5%; other 0.7%.
Religious affiliation (1996): Christian 70.9%, of which Roman Catholic 27.0%, Anglican Church of Australia 22.0%, other Protestant 21.9% (Uniting Church and Methodist 7.5%, Presbyterian 3.8%), Orthodox 2.8%, other Christian 2.4%; Muslim 1.1%; Buddhist 1.1%; Jewish 0.4%; Hindu 0.4%; no religion 16.6%; other 9.5%.
Metropolitan areas (1999): Sydney 4,041,400; Melbourne 3,417,200; Brisbane 1,601,400; Perth 1,364,200; Adelaide 1,092,900; Newcastle 479,300; Gold Coast–Tweed 391,200; Canberra-Queanbeyan 348,600; Wollongong 262,600; Hobart 194,200.
Place of birth (1999): 76.4% native-born; 23.6% foreign-born, of which Europe 10.8% (United Kingdom 6.5%[2], Italy 1.3%, Greece 0.7%, Germany 0.7%, The Netherlands 0.5%, other Europe 1.1%), Asia and Middle East 2.7%, New Zealand 1.9%, Africa, the Americas, and other 8.2%.
Mobility (1995–96). Population age 15 and over living in the same residence as in 1994: 81.6%; different residence between states, regions, and neighbourhoods 18.4%.
Households (1996). Total number of households 7,100,000. Average household size 2.6; couples only 34.1%, couples with dependent children only 40.6%, couples with nondependent children 9.0%, single parent with children 9.9%, other 6.4%.
Immigration (1996): permanent immigrants admitted 96,970, from United Kingdom and Ireland 12.8%, New Zealand 11.8%, China 7.6%, Vietnam 4.8%, Hong Kong 4.6%, India 4.4%, Philippines 3.9%, South Africa 3.2%, Bosnia and Herzegovina 3.2%, Yugoslavia 3.1%, Sri Lanka 2.2%. Refugee arrivals (1998–99): 8,790.

Vital statistics

Birth rate per 1,000 population (2000): 13.0 (world avg. 22.5); (1997) legitimate 72.0%; illegitimate 28.0%.
Death rate per 1,000 population (2000): 7.6 (world avg. 9.0).
Natural increase rate per 1,000 population (2000): 5.4 (world avg. 13.5).
Total fertility rate (avg. births per childbearing woman; 2000): 1.8.
Marriage rate per 1,000 population (1999): 6.0.
Divorce rate per 1,000 population (1999): 2.8.
Life expectancy at birth (2000): male 76.0 years; female 81.0 years.
Major causes of death per 100,000 population (1999): diseases of the circulatory system 210.2; cancers 184.8; respiratory diseases 42.1; accidents, poisoning, and violence 27.9; diabetes 15.5; suicides 13.1.

Social indicators

Educational attainment (1999). Percentage of population age 15 to 64 having: no formal schooling and incomplete secondary education 38.0%; completed secondary 18.3%; postsecondary, technical, or other certificate/diploma 28.3%; university 15.4%.
Quality of working life (1999–2000). Average workweek: 35.7 hours (16.8%[3] overtime). Annual rate per 100,000 workers for: accidental injury and industrial disease, 3,200[4]; death, n.a. Proportion of employed persons insured for damages or income loss resulting from: injury 100%[4]; permanent disability 100%[4]; death 100%[4]. Working days lost to industrial disputes per 1,000 employees (1999): 87. Means of transportation to work (1986): private automobile 69.4%; public transportation 10.1%; motorcycle and bicycle 3.2%; foot 6.6%; other 10.7%. Discouraged job seekers (considered by employers to be too young or too old, having language or training limitations, or no vacancies in line of work; 1999): 1.1% of labour force.

Distribution of household income (1997–98)

percentage of household income by quintile

lowest	second	third	fourth	highest
3.8%	9.0%	15.0%	23.9%	48.3%

Access to services (1976). Proportion of dwellings having access to: electricity 99.5%; bathroom 96.0%; flush toilet 92.2%; kitchen 97.9%; public sewer 73.4%.
Social participation. Eligible voters participating in last national election (1996): 95.8%; voting is compulsory. Population age 16 and over participating in voluntary work: n.a. Trade union membership in total workforce (1996): 31%.
Social deviance (1999). Offense rate per 100,000 population for: murder 1.8; sexual assault 74.2; assault 704.5; auto theft 684.8; burglary and housebreaking 2,191.6; armed robbery 49.8. Incidence per 100,000 in general population of (1996): alcoholism, n.a.; prisoners with drug offenses 539.5; suicide 13.1.
Material well-being (1995). Households possessing: automobile 85%; telephone 95%; refrigerator 99.7%; air conditioner 32.3%[5]; personal computers 54.0%[3]; washing machine 90.0%; central heating 3.9%[5]; swimming pool 10.1%[5].

National economy

Gross national product (1999): U.S.$397,345,000,000 (U.S.$20,950 per capita).

Structure of gross domestic product and labour force

	1997–98[6]		1999–2000	
	in value $A '000,000	% of total value	labour force	% of labour force
Agriculture	16,668	3.0	437,500	4.6
Mining	23,769	4.3	78,200	0.8
Manufacturing	65,878	11.8	1,113,100	11.6
Construction	30,003	5.4	695,400	7.3
Public utilities	14,292	2.6	64,500	0.7
Transp. and commun.	49,129	8.8	576,600	6.0
Trade[7]	110,688	19.9	2,252,300	23.5
Finance, real estate	92,060	16.5	1,316,200	13.7
Pub. admin., defense	23,185	4.2	345,800	3.6
Services	88,849	15.9	2,006,800	21.0
Other	42,402[8]	7.6[8]	691,500[9]	7.2[9]
TOTAL	556,923	100.0	9,577,900	100.0

Budget (1998–99). Revenue: $A 146,444,000,000 (income tax 70.3%, of which individual 52.4%, corporate 14.2%; excise duties and sales tax 22.1%). Expenditures: $A 140,814,000,000 (social security and welfare 37.5%; health 16.6%; economic and public services 11.2%; defense 8.0%; education 6.9%; interest on public debt 5.3%).
Public debt (1999–2000): $A 72,358,000,000.
Tourism (1999): receipts from visitors U.S.$7,525,000,000; expenditures by nationals abroad U.S.$5,792,000,000.

Manufacturing, mining, and construction enterprises (2000)[10]

	no. of estab-lishments	no. of employees	Turnover per person employed ($A '000)	annual turnover ($A '000,000)
Manufacturing[11]				
Food, beverages, and tobacco	3,912[12]	170,600	287.7	49,085
Metal products	9,348[13]	149,200	262.8	39,207
Machinery and equipment	8,988[14]	198,100	221.8	43,935
Chemical, petroleum, and coal products	3,038[12]	96,500	348.2	33,602
Printing and publishing	5,265[14]	103,800	158.0	16,402
Miscellaneous manufacturing	7,134[12]	55,600	121.0	6,727
Wood and paper products	4,218[13]	60,200	198.7	11,963
Nonmetallic mineral products	2,138[12]	35,400	280.5	9,930
Textile, clothing, footwear, and leather	6,720[12]	68,000	142.7	9,705
Mining[15]				
Coal, oil, and gas	254[14]	26,769	813.9	21,788
Metallic minerals	261[14]	24,106	645.3	15,556
Nonmetallic minerals[16]	699	8,799	254.6	2,240
Construction[17]	194,300	484,100	119.6	57,899

Production (gross value in $A '000 except as noted). Agriculture, forestry, fishing (1998–99): livestock slaughtered 7,401,400 (cattle 4,476,600, sheep and lambs 1,045,500, poultry 1,174,300, pigs 689,700); wheat 3,860,000, wool 2,139,100, seed cotton 1,353,000, grapes 1,115,600, sugarcane 1,044,000, barley 885,000, canola 638,000, potatoes 486,000, rice 332,000, apples 325,000, oranges 307,000, sorghum 285,000, bananas 264,000, lupins 244,000, tomatoes 222,000, carrots 162,000, oats 157,000, pears 114,000, sunflower seeds 74,000, peaches 65,000, corn (maize) 60,000, tobacco 40,000, pineapples 39,000; livestock (number of live animals; 1999) 115,456,000 sheep and lamb, 26,578,000 cattle, 2,626,000 pigs, 93,578,000 poultry; roundwood (1999) 22,938,000 cu m; fish catch (1998) 201,216 metric tons. Mining and quarrying (metric tons [tons of contained metal]; 1997–98): iron ore 169,568,000; bauxite 50,418,000; zinc 2,029,000; copper 1,665,000; lead 943,000; uranium oxide 5,797; gold 330,095 kg; diamonds (1998–99) 36,000,000 carats. Manufacturing (value added in U.S.$'000,000 except as noted; 1995): food products 12,239; transport equipment 5,745; printing and publishing 5,252; metal products 4,840; nonferrous metals 4,766; nonelectrical machinery 4,054. Construction (buildings completed, by value in $A '000; 1998–99): new dwellings 17,080,000; alterations and additions to dwellings 3,194,000; nonresidential 14,016,000.

Retail and service enterprises (2000)

	no. of establishments	no. of employees	total wages and salaries ($A '000,000)	annual turnover ($A '000,000)
Retail[18]				
Motor vehicle dealers, gasoline and tire dealers	37,305	220,661	2,572[19]	44,954
Food stores	53,166	406,299	2,461[19]	54,674[11]
Department and general stores	459	87,148	1,175[19]	12,367[11]
Clothing, fabric, and furniture stores	21,688	91,138	965[19]	9,636[11]
Household appliances and hardware stores	14,268	75,355	629	15,332[11]
Recreational goods	...	...	...	6,879[11]
Services				
Real estate agents[11]	7,589	52,079	1,847.5	3,902.7
Pubs, taverns, and bars[15]	4,792	81,724	...	8,253.3
Dental services[15]	5,257	24,108	568.4	1,685.2
Consulting engineering services[12]	5,514	30,736	1,242	3,233.3
Legal services[11]	10,819	73,186	2,181.0	7,034.3
Accounting services[12]	8,389	66,792	...	4,939.1
Computing services[11]	14,731	74,395	4,065.0	10,474.0
Travel agency services[17]	3,266	24,451	647.9	1,979.5
Market research services[11]	272	10,744	203.4	455.8
Private security services[11]	1,714	31,752	756.2	1,394.8

Energy production (consumption): electricity (kW-hr; 1994) 167,151,000,000 (167,151,000,000); coal (metric tons; 1994) 176,078,000 (52,678,000); crude petroleum (barrels; 1994) 159,160,000 (202,490,000); petroleum products (metric tons; 1994) 33,086,000 (33,707,000); natural gas (cu m; 1994) 25,185,000,000 (17,438,000,000).

Population economically active (1999–2000): total 9,577,900; activity rate of total population 50.5% (participation rates: over age 15, 63.4%; female 43.6%; unemployed 6.9%).

Price and earnings indexes (1995 = 100)

	1994	1995	1996	1997	1998	1999	2000
Consumer price index	95.6	100.0	102.6	102.9	103.7	105.3	110.0
Weekly earnings index	95.1	100.0	104.0	108.3	112.7	115.7	121.5

Household income and expenditure (1998–99). Average household size (1996) 2.6; average annual income per household $A 45,708 (U.S.$24,200); sources of income: wages and salaries 39.9%, self-employment 32.1%, transfer payments 10.1%, other 17.9%; expenditure: food and nonbeverages 18.2%, transportation and communications 16.9%, housing 13.9%, recreation 12.7%, household durable goods 6.0%, household services and operation 5.9%, clothing and footwear 4.6%, health 4.6%, alcoholic beverages 2.9%, energy 2.6%, other 11.7%.

Financial aggregates

	1994	1995	1996	1997	1998	1999	2000
Exchange rate, $A 1.00 per:							
U.S. dollar	0.73	0.74	0.78	0.74	0.63	0.65	0.58
£	0.48	0.47	0.50	0.45	0.38	0.40	0.38
SDR	0.53	0.50	0.55	0.48	0.44	0.48	0.43
International reserves (U.S.$)							
Total (excl. gold; '000,000)	11,285	11,896	14,485	16,845	14,641	21,212	18,118
SDRs ('000,000)	73	55	37	19	18	72	94
Reserve pos. in IMF ('000,000)	506	502	482	727	1,256	1,633	1,243
Foreign exchange ('000,000)	10,706	11,340	13,967	16,099	13,366	19,507	16,782
Gold ('000,000 fine troy oz)	7.90	7.90	7.90	2.56	2.56	2.56	2.56
% world reserves	0.9	0.9	0.9	0.3	0.3	0.3	0.3
Interest and prices							
Central bank discount (%)	5.75	5.75	5.75	...	...	...	...
Govt. bond yield (short-term; %)	8.19	8.42	7.53	6.00	5.02	5.55	6.18
Industrial share prices (1995 = 100)	100.7	100.0	112.1	125.2	131.3	145.1	156.6
Balance of payments (U.S.$'000,000)							
Balance of visible trade	−3,277	−4,223	−635	1,849	−5,367	−9,767	...
Imports, f.o.b.	50,648	57,443	61,032	63,044	61,215	65,826	...
Exports, f.o.b.	47,371	53,220	60,397	64,893	55,848	56,059	...
Balance of invisibles	−14,139	−15,431	−15,380	−14,580	−12,878	−13,408	...
Balance of payments, current account	−17,416	−19,654	−16,015	−12,731	−18,245	−23,175	...

Land use (1998): agricultural and under permanent cultivation 7.0%; other 93.0% (of which, meadows and pastures 54.0%).

Foreign trade[20]

Balance of trade (current prices)

	1995	1996	1997	1998	1999	2000
$A '000,000	−5,810	−1,424	−1,423	−7,746	−14,551	−6,376
% of total	3.9%	0.9%	0.8%	4.2%	7.7%	2.8%

Imports (1999–2000): $A 110,083,000,000 (machinery and transport equipment 46.6%, of which road motor vehicles 11.6%, office machines and automatic data-processing equipment 6.9%, telecommunications equipment 6.2%; basic manufactures 12.4%, of which textile yarn and fabrics 2.4%, paper and paperboard products 2.1%; chemicals and related products 11.4%; mineral fuels and lubricants 7.0%; food and live animals 3.6%). *Major import sources:* U.S. 20.9%; Japan 12.8%; China 6.8%; U.K. 5.8%; Germany 5.3%; New Zealand 4.0%; Singapore 4.0%.

Exports (1999–2000): $A 97,255,000,000 (crude materials excluding fuels 18.9%, of which metalliferous ores and metal scrap 11.6%, textile fibres and their waste 4.4%; mineral fuels and lubricants 18.6%, of which coal, coke, and briquettes 8.6%, petroleum, petroleum products, and natural gas 7.3%; food and live animals 17.3%, of which cereals and cereal preparations 5.1%, meat and meat preparations 4.6%, dairy products 2.4%; basic manufactures 12.7%). *Major export destinations:* Japan 19.3%; U.S. 9.8%; South Korea 7.8%; New Zealand 6.9%; China 5.1%; Singapore 5.0%; Taiwan 4.8%.

Trade by commodity group (1999–2000)

SITC Group	imports U.S.$'000,000	imports %	exports U.S.$'000,000	exports %
00 Food and live animals	2,488	3.6	10,570	17.3
01 Beverages and tobacco	445	0.6	988	1.6
02 Crude materials, excluding fuels	1,162	1.7	11,556	18.9
03 Mineral fuels, lubricants, and related materials	4,832	7.0	11,366	18.6
04 Animal and vegetable oils, fat, and waxes	174	0.3	190	0.3
05 Chemicals and related products, n.e.s.	7,863	11.4	2,638	4.3
06 Basic manufactures	8,614	12.4	7,746	12.7
07 Machinery and transport equipment	32,305	46.6	7,302	11.9
08 Miscellaneous manufactured articles	9,759	14.1	2,409	3.9
09 Goods not classified by kind	1,614	2.3	6,421	10.5
TOTAL	69,256	100.0	61,186	100.0

Direction of trade (1999–2000)

	imports U.S.$'000,000	imports %	exports U.S.$'000,000	exports %
Africa	627	0.9	1,363	2.2
Asia	31,198	45.1	37,117	60.7
Japan	8,895	12.8	11,828	19.3
South America	403	0.6	498	0.8
North and Central America	16,018	23.1	7,020	11.5
United States	14,462	20.9	6,025	9.8
Europe	16,512	23.8	8,254	13.5
European Union	15,321	22.1	7,573	12.4
Russia	37	—	119	0.2
Other Europe	1,154	1.7	562	0.9
Oceania	4,220	6.1	5,663	9.2
New Zealand	2,750	4.0	4,235	6.9
Other	278	0.4	1,271	2.1
TOTAL	69,256	100.0	61,186	100.0

Transport and communications

Transport. Railroads (1998–99)[21]: route length 22,233 mi, 35,780 km; passengers carried 595,200,000; short ton-mi cargo 87,262,000,000, metric ton-km cargo 127,400,000,000. Roads (2000): total length 502,356 mi, 808,465 km (paved 40%). Vehicles (1999): passenger cars 9,719,900; trucks and buses 2,214,900. Merchant marine (1999): vessels (150 gross tons and over) 77; total deadweight tonnage 2,505,369. Air transport (1999)[22]: passenger-mi 46,646,591,000, passenger-km 75,070,556,000; short ton-mi cargo 1,156,331,000, metric ton-km cargo 1,688,215,000; airports (1996) with scheduled flights 400.

Communications

Medium	date	unit	number	units per 1,000 persons
Daily newspapers	1996	circulation	5,370,000	296
Radio	1997	receivers	25,500,000	1,391
Television	1999	receivers	13,400,000	706
Telephones	1999	main lines	9,857,000	519
Cellular telephones	1999	subscribers	6,501,000	343
Personal computers	1999	units	8,900,000	469
Internet	1999	users	6,000,000	316

Education and health

Literacy (1996): total population literate, virtually 100%[23].

Education (1996)

	schools	teachers	students	student/teacher ratio
Primary (age 6–12)	7,713	102,267	1,848,169	18.1
Secondary (age 13–17)	1,917	101,706	1,294,846	12.7
Vocational[24]	541	26,345	985,428	37.4
Higher	44[25]	26,920	634,094	23.6

Health: physicians (1999–2000) 55,200 (1 per 345 persons); hospital beds (1998–99) 77,631 (1 per 243 persons); infant mortality rate (2000) 6.0.

Food (1999): daily per capita caloric intake 3,150 (vegetable products 69%, animal products 31%); (1997) 118% of FAO recommended minimum requirement.

Military

Total active duty personnel (2000): 50,600 (army 47.7%, navy 24.7%, air force 27.6%). *Military expenditure as percentage of GNP* (1997): 2.2% (world 2.6%); per capita expenditure U.S.$460.

[1]Total includes 3,180 persons in nondelimited areas. [2]Includes both Northern Ireland and Republic of Ireland. [3]1994. [4]1992–93. [5]1983. [6]At 1996–97 prices. [7]Trade includes hotels and restaurants. [8]Import duties less imputed bank service charges. [9]Mostly unemployed. [10]Excludes operations of single-establishment enterprises employing fewer than four persons. [11]1998–99. [12]1995–96. [13]1994–95. [14]1993–94. [15]1997–98. [16]1990–91. [17]1996–97. [18]1991–92. [19]1985–86. [20]Exports and imports are f.o.b. in the balance of trade table. [21]Government railways only. [22]Includes Qantas and Ansett Australia. [23]A national survey conducted in 1996 put the number of persons who had very poor literacy and numeracy skills at about 17% of the total population (age 15 to 64). [24]Includes special education. [25]1991.

Internet resources for further information:

- **Australian Bureau of Statistics http://www.abs.gov.au**

Austria

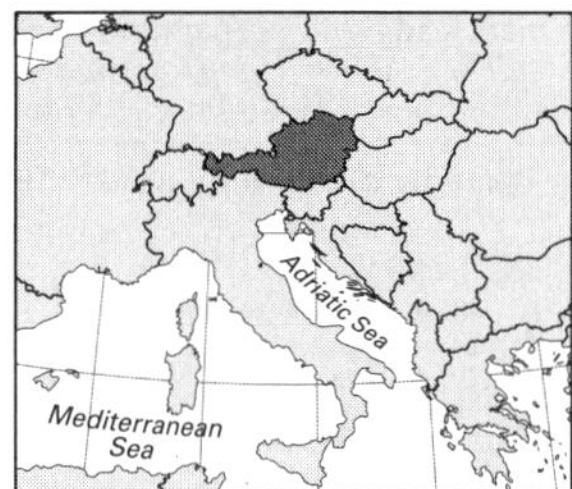

Official name: Republik Österreich (Republic of Austria).
Form of government: federal state with two legislative houses (Federal Council [64]; National Council [183]).
Chief of state: President.
Head of government: Chancellor.
Capital: Vienna.
Official language: German.
Official religion: none.
Monetary unit: 1 Austrian Schilling (S) = 100 Groschen; valuation (Sept. 28, 2001) 1 U.S.$ = S 15.11; 1 £ = S 22.21; 1 € = S 13.7603.

Area and population

		area		population
States	Capitals	sq mi	sq km	2001 census
Burgenland	Eisenstadt	1,531	3,966	278,600
Kärnten	Klagenfurt	3,681	9,533	561,114
Niederösterreich	Sankt Pölten	7,403	19,174	1,549,640
Oberösterreich	Linz	4,626	11,980	1,382,017
Salzburg	Salzburg	2,762	7,154	518,580
Steiermark	Graz	6,327	16,388	1,185,911
Tirol	Innsbruck	4,883	12,647	675,063
Vorarlberg	Bregenz	1,004	2,601	351,565
Wien (Vienna)	—	160	415	1,562,676
TOTAL		32,378[1]	83,858	8,065,166

Demography

Population (2001): 8,069,000.
Density (2001): persons per sq mi 249.2, persons per sq km 96.2.
Urban-rural (1999): urban 64.6%; rural 35.4%
Sex distribution (2000): male 48.61%; female 51.39%.
Age breakdown (2000): under 15, 16.7%; 15–29, 18.8%; 30–44, 25.1%; 45–59, 18.7%; 60–74, 13.5%; 75 and over, 7.2%.
Population projection: (2010) 8,033,000; (2020) 8,078,000.
Doubling time: not applicable; population is stable.
Ethnic composition (national origin; 1998): Austrian 91.2%; citizens of former Yugoslavia 4.0%; Turkish 1.6%; other 3.2%.
Religious affiliation (1995): Roman Catholic 75.1%; nonreligious and atheist 8.6%; Protestant (mostly Lutheran) 5.4%; Muslim 2.1%; Eastern Orthodox 0.7%; Jewish 0.1%; other 1.9%; unknown 6.1%.
Major cities (2000[2]): Vienna 1,608,144; Graz 240,967; Linz 188,022; Salzburg 144,247; Innsbruck 111,752; Klagenfurt 91,141.

Vital statistics

Birth rate per 1,000 population (1999): 9.5 (world avg. 22.5); legitimate 69.5%; illegitimate 30.5%.
Death rate per 1,000 population (1999): 9.4 (world avg. 9.0).
Natural increase rate per 1,000 population (1999): 0.1 (world avg. 13.5).
Total fertility rate (avg. births per childbearing woman; 1999): 1.3.
Marriage rate per 1,000 population (1999): 4.9.
Divorce rate per 1,000 population (1999): 2.3.
Life expectancy at birth (1999): male 75.1 years; female 80.9 years.
Major causes of death per 100,000 population (1998): diseases of the circulatory system 527.9, of which ischemic heart diseases 217.2; malignant neoplasms (cancers) 231.5.

National economy

Budget (1997). Revenue: S 950,820,000,000 (tax revenue 92.0%, of which social security contributions 37.7%, individual income taxes 17.3%, value-added taxes 16.2%). Expenditures: S 1,017,870,000 (social security and welfare 42.0%; health 14.4%; education 9.2%; interest 9.2%; defense 2.0%).
National debt (end of year 1998): U.S.$133,897,000,000.
Production (metric tons except as noted). Agriculture, forestry, fishing (2000): sugar beets 2,600,000, corn (maize) 1,800,000, wheat 1,313,000, barley 855,000, potatoes 496,000, apples 410,000, grapes 364,000, rye 183,000, rapeseed 140,000, triticale 135,000; livestock (number of live animals) 3,790,000 pigs, 2,150,000 cattle, 13,540,000 chickens; roundwood (1999) 14,083,000 cu m; fish catch (1997) 3,486. Mining and quarrying (1999): iron ore 1,747,000; magnesite 748,600; talc 129,600. Manufacturing (value added in S '000,000,000; 1997): nonelectrical machinery and apparatus 46.1; food and beverages 44.1; electrical machinery and apparatus 42.9; fabricated metals 36.9; chemicals and chemical products 28.6; transport equipment 22.0. Energy production (consumption): electricity (kW-hr; 1999) 60,348,000,000 ([1996] 55,787,000,000); hard coal (metric tons; 1999) negligible ([1996] 3,795,000); lignite (metric tons; 1999) 1,137,000 ([1996] 1,659,000); crude petroleum (barrels; 1999) 7,054,000 ([1996] 63,566,000); petroleum products (metric tons; 1996) 8,227,000 (10,503,000); natural gas (cu m; 1999) 1,833,000,000 ([1996] 8,042,000,000).
Tourism (U.S.$'000,000; 1999): receipts U.S.$12,533; expenditures U.S.$9,803.
Population economically active (1999): total 3,909,000; activity rate of total population 48.3% (participation rates: ages 15–64 [1998] 70.7%; female 43.2%; unemployed [October 1999–September 2000] 6.0%).

Price and earnings indexes (1996 = 100)

	1996	1997	1998	1999	2000
Consumer price index	100.0	101.8	103.0	103.8	106.2[3]
Annual earnings index	100.0	100.5	104.0	104.6	...

Gross national product (at current market prices; 1999): U.S.$205,743,000,000 (U.S.$25,430 per capita).

Structure of gross domestic product and labour force

	1998		1999	
	in value S '000,000	% of total value	labour force	% of labour force
Agriculture, forestry	56,750	2.2	233,900	6.0
Mining	8,760	0.3	11,600	0.3
Manufacturing	492,470	18.9	797,100	20.4
Construction	205,580	7.9	360,500	9.2
Public utilities	63,900	2.4	31,700	0.8
Transp. and commun.	184,050	7.0	261,600	6.7
Trade, restaurants	404,940	15.5	848,600	21.7
Finance, real estate	540,220	20.7	396,400	10.1
Pub. admin., defense	164,010	6.3	250,900	6.4
Services	335,520	12.9	698,600	17.9
Other	154,700[4]	5.9[4]	18,100	0.5
TOTAL	2,610,910[1]	100.0	3,909,000	100.0

Household income and expenditure. Average household size (1999) 2.5; sources of income (1995): wages and salaries 54.8%, transfer payments 25.9%; expenditure (1995): transportation and communications 15.4%, housing 15.4%, food and beverages 15.3%, cafe and hotel expenditures 12.6%.
Land use (1994): forested 39.2%; meadows and pastures 24.3%; agricultural and under permanent cultivation 18.3%; other 18.2%.

Foreign trade[5]

Balance of trade (current prices)

	1994	1995	1996	1997	1998	1999
S '000,000,000	–116.4	–88.0	–100.6	–75.3	–67.4	–69.5
% of total	10.2%	7.1%	7.6%	5.0%	4.2%	4.0%

Imports (1999): S 898,800,000,000 (machinery and transport equipment 41.3%, of which road vehicles 12.1%, electrical machinery and apparatus 7.5%; chemicals and related products 10.3%; food products 5.2%; clothing 4.4%). *Major import sources:* Germany 41.9%; Italy 7.6%; United States 5.3%; France 5.0%; Switzerland 3.4%; Hungary 3.3%.
Exports (1999): S 829,300,000,000 (machinery and transport equipment 43.1%, of which road vehicles 10.0%, electrical machinery and apparatus 8.1%; chemical products 9.4%; fabricated metals 4.9%); paper and paper products 4.7%. *Major export destinations:* Germany 34.9%; Italy 8.4%; Switzerland 6.0%; Hungary 4.9%; United States 4.6%; France 4.4%.

Transport and communications

Transport. Railroads[6]: (1999) length 5,643 km; (1998) passenger-km 7,971,000,000; (1998) metric ton-km cargo 15,348,000,000. Roads (1997): total length 200,000 km (paved 100%). Vehicles (1999): passenger cars 4,009,604; trucks and buses 328,591. Air transport[7] (1999): passenger-km 12,460,000,000; metric ton-km cargo 361,348,000; airports (1999) with scheduled flights 6.

Communications

Medium	date	unit	number	units per 1,000 persons
Daily newspapers	1996	circulation	2,382,000	296
Radio	1996	receivers	6,000,000	744
Television	1998	receivers	4,200,000	520
Telephones	1999	main lines	3,863,000	477
Cellular telephones	1999	subscribers	4,206,000	520
Personal computers	1999	units	2,100,000	260
Internet	1999	users	1,840,000	227

Education and health

Educational attainment (1993). Percentage of population age 25 and over having: lower-secondary education 37.5%; vocational education ending at secondary level 44.6%; completed upper secondary 6.1%; higher vocational 5.5%; higher 6.3%. *Literacy:* virtually 100%.

Education (1999–2000)

	schools	teachers	students	student/ teacher ratio
Primary/lower secondary (age 6–13)	4,544	68,147	655,335	9.6
Upper secondary/voc. (age 14–17)	711	41,341	315,590	7.6
Higher[8]	19	16,239	228,936	14.1

Health: physicians (2000) 24,223[9] (1 per 335 persons); hospital beds (1998) 68,918 (1 per 117 persons); infant mortality rate per 1,000 live births (1999) 4.4.
Food (1998): daily per capita caloric intake 3,531 (vegetable products 65%, animal products 35%); 134% of FAO recommended minimum requirement.

Military

Total active duty personnel (2000): 35,500 (army 100%[10]). *Military expenditure as percentage of GNP* (1997): 0.9% (world 2.6%); per capita expenditure U.S.$222.

[1]Detail does not add total given because of rounding. [2]January 1. [3]Average of second and third quarters. [4]Value-added tax less imputed bank service charges and subsidies. [5]Imports c.i.f., exports f.o.b. [6]Federal railways only. [7]Austrian Airlines and Lauda Air. [8]1998–99; universities only. [9]Excludes 5,632 doctors in training. [10]Includes 6,500 troops in air command.

Internet resources for further information:
- **Austrian Central Office of Statistics http://www.statistik.at**
- **Austrian Press and Information Service (Washington, D.C.) http://www.austria.org/index.html**

Azerbaijan

Official name: Azärbayean Respublikası (Azerbaijani Republic).
Form of government: unitary multiparty republic with a single legislative body (National Assembly [124[1]]).
Head of state and government: President assisted by Prime Minister.
Capital: Baku (Azerbaijani: Bakı).
Official language: Azerbaijani.
Official religion: none.
Monetary unit: 1 manat (A.M.) = 100 gopik; valuation (Sept. 28, 2001) free rate, 1 U.S.$ = A.M. 4,694; 1 £ = A.M. 6,898.

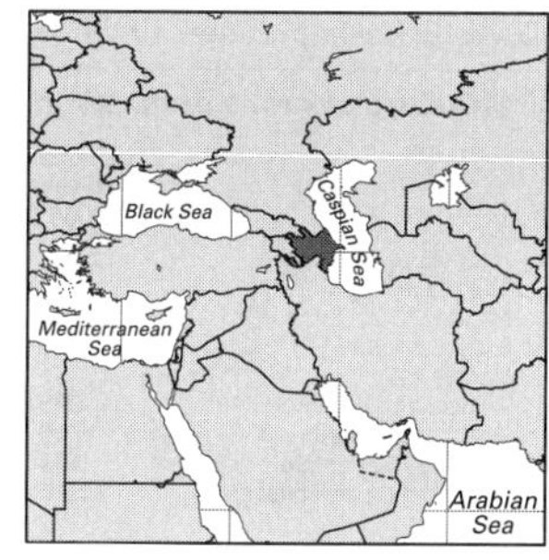

Area and population

Administative/ geographic units	Capitals	area sq mi	area sq km	population 1991 estimate
Autonomous Republic				
Naxçıvan	Naxçıvan	2,100	5,500	305,700
Geographic region				
Nagorno-Karabakh[2]	Xankändi (Stepanakert)	1,700	4,400	193,300
Capital city				
Baku (Bakı)	—	...	...	1,713,300
Others[3]	—	29,600	76,700	4,924,300
TOTAL		33,400	86,600	7,136,600

Demography

Population (2001): 8,105,000.
Density (2001): persons per sq mi 242.7, persons per sq km 93.6.
Urban-rural (1998): urban 56.6%; rural 43.4%.
Sex distribution (1999): male 49.1%; female 50.9%.
Age breakdown (1999): under 15, 32.8%; 15–29, 25.9%; 30–44, 22.3%; 45–59, 10.0%; 60–69, 5.9%; 70 and over, 3.1%.
Population projection: (2010) 8,549,000; (2020) 9,475,000.
Doubling time: 93 years.
Ethnic composition (1995): Azerbaijani 89.0%; Russian 3.0%; Lezgian 2.2%; Armenian 2.0%; other 3.8%.
Religious affiliation (1995): Muslim 93.4% of which Shīʿī 65.4%, Sunnī 28.0%; Russian Orthodox 1.1%; Armenian Apostolic (Orthodox) 1.1%; other 4.4%.
Major cities (1997): Baku 1,727,200; Gäncä (formerly Kirovabad) 291,900; Sumqayıt (Sumgait) 248,500; Mingäçevir (Mingechaur) 97,200.

Vital statistics

Birth rate per 1,000 population (2001): 13.7 (world avg. 22.5); (1994) legitimate 94.8%; illegitimate 5.2%.
Death rate per 1,000 population (2001): 6.2 (world avg. 9.0).
Natural increase rate per 1,000 population (2001): 7.5 (world avg. 13.5).
Total fertility rate (avg. births per childbearing woman; 2001): 1.6.
Marriage rate per 1,000 population (1994): 6.3.
Divorce rate per 1,000 population (1994): 0.8.
Life expectancy at birth (2001): male 68.0 years; female 75.0 years.
Major causes of death per 100,000 population (1994): diseases of the circulatory system 336.3; accidents, poisoning, and violence 99.1; diseases of the respiratory system 98.6; malignant neoplasms (cancers) 67.6; diseases of the digestive system 31.7; infectious and parasitic diseases 29.0; endocrine and metabolic disorders 14.2; diseases of the nervous system 12.1.

National economy

Budget (1998). Revenue: A.M. 2,318,400,000,000 (tax revenue 93.7%, of which value-added tax 30.0%, individual income tax 17.8%, enterprise profits tax 14.1%, tax on international trade 12.6%, property tax 7.4%, excise tax 4.1%, other taxes 7.7%; nontax revenue 6.3%). Expenditures: A.M. 2,642,200,000,000 (social protection 23.3%; education 21.4%; national economy 8.6%; health 5.8%; culture 3.5%; other 37.4%).
Public debt (external, outstanding; 1999): U.S.$493,300,000.
Production (metric tons except as noted). Agriculture, forestry, fishing (1999): cereals 932,111, fruit 482,846, vegetables (except potatoes) 369,000, potatoes 334,000, cotton lint 39,000, tobacco leaves 9,000, tea 856; livestock (number of live animals) 5,502,800 sheep and goats, 1,909,800 cattle, 55,800 horses, 26,100 pigs, 13,300,000 poultry; roundwood (1993) 17,000 cu m; fish catch (1998) 4,678. Mining and quarrying (1996): iron ore 1,000,000; alunite 600,000. Manufacturing (value of production in A.M. '000,000,000; 1998): oil refinery products 2,980; electricity and gas 2,005; food products 1,972; textiles 468; chemicals 320; machine-building and metalworking equipment 249; minerals 137. Construction (1998): completed residential 532,000 sq m. Energy production (consumption): electricity (kW-hr; 1997) 16,800,000,000 (16,800,-000,000); coal (metric tons; 1994) none (8,000); crude petroleum (barrels; 1997) 66,703,000 (76,672,000); petroleum products (metric tons; 1998) 7,800,000 (6,200,000); natural gas (cu m; 1998) 6,000,000,000 (6,000,000,000).
Household income and expenditure. Average household size (1997) 5.2; income per household: n.a.; sources of income (1993): wages and salaries 50.9%, agricultural income 24.0%, social benefits 10.2%; expenditure: food 61.2%, clothing 11.1%, services 3.0%.
Tourism (1999): receipts from visitors U.S.$81,000,000; expenditures by nationals abroad U.S.$139,000,000.
Gross national product (at current market prices; 1999): U.S.$3,705,000,000 (U.S.$460 per capita).

Structure of gross domestic product and labour force

	1998 in value A.M. '000,000[4]	1998 % of total value[4]	1998 labour force	1998 % of labour force
Agriculture	3,472,700	21.8	835,500	22.3
Mining, Manufacturing	3,807,200	23.9	240,200	6.4
Public utilities	286,700	1.8	95,500	2.6
Construction	2,803,600	17.6	155,600	4.2
Transp. and commun.	2,198,300	13.8	168,300	4.5
Trade	971,700	6.1	704,000	18.8
Finance	270,800	1.7	11,000	0.3
Pub. admin., defense	} 2,118,700	} 13.3	68,000	1.8
Services			590,500	15.8
Other			875,200[5]	23.4[5]
TOTAL	15,929,700	100.0	3,743,800	100.0[6]

Population economically active (1998): total 3,743,800, activity rate of total population 47.1% (participation rates: ages 15–59 [male], 15–54 [female] 85.9%; female 82.1%; unemployed 1.3%).

Price and earnings indexes (1995 = 100)

	1995	1996	1997	1998	1999	2000
Consumer price index	100.0	119.9	99.5	99.2	90.7	92.3
Monthly earnings index	...	...	...	...	...	...

Land use (1994): forest 11.0%; pasture 25.4%; agriculture 48.5%; other 15.1%.

Foreign trade[7]

Balance of trade (current prices)

	1994	1995	1996	1997	1998	1999
U.S.$'000,000	–140.4	–122.0	–329.4	–13.0	–471	–106
% of total	9.9%	10.1%	20.7%	0.8%	28.0%	5.4%

Imports (1998): U.S.$1,077,169,100 (machinery and equipment 40.4%, food 16.4%, metals 12.4%, chemical products 7.4%). *Major import sources:* Turkey 20.4%; Russia 18.0%; Ukraine 8.6%; U.K. 6.4%; Germany 4.3%; U.A.E. 4.2%; Iran 4.0%; U.S. 3.7%.
Exports (1998): U.S.$606,150,500,000 (petroleum products 69.1%, textile 9.2%, food 7.7%, machinery and equipment 6.0%, metals 2.2%). *Major export destinations:* Turkey 22.4%; Russia 17.4%; Georgia 12.7%; Italy 7.4%.

Transport and communications

Transport. Railroads (1998): length 2,120 km; passenger-km (1996) 550,000,000; metric ton-km cargo 4,613,000,000. Roads (1998): total length 45,870 km (paved 93.8%). Vehicles (1998): passenger cars 281,100; trucks and buses 104,300. Merchant marine (1998): vessels (100 gross tons and over) 69; total deadweight tonnage, n.a. Air transport (1995): passenger-km 1,650,000,000; metric ton-km cargo 183,000,000; airports (1998) 3.

Communications

Medium	date	unit	number	units per 1,000 persons
Daily newspapers	1995	circulation	210,000	28
Radio	1997	receivers	175,000	23
Television	1998	receivers	1,950,000	253
Telephones	1999	main lines	730,000	95
Cellular telephones	1999	subscribers	180,000	23
Internet	1999	users	8,000	1.0

Education and health

Educational attainment (1995). Percentage of population age 15 and over having: primary education or no formal schooling 12.1%, some secondary 9.1%; completed secondary and some postsecondary 27.5%; higher 7.6%. *Literacy* (1989): percentage of total population 15 and over literate 97.3%; males literate 98.9%; females 95.9%.

Education (1995–96)

	schools	teachers	students	student/ teacher ratio
Primary (age 6–13)	4,462	34,201	697,510	20.4
Secondary (age 14–17)	...	105,656	812,660	7.7
Voc., teacher tr.	78[8]	...	26,585	...
Higher	23[8]	18,184[8]	120,870[8]	6.6

Health (1998): physicians 28,850 (1 per 276 persons); hospital beds 71,100 (1 per 110 persons); infant mortality rate per 1,000 live births (2001) 30.0.
Food (1999): daily per capita caloric intake 2,224 (vegetable product 84%, animal products 16%); (1997) 87% of FAO recommended minimum.

Military

Total active duty personnel (2000): 72,100 (army 85.7%, navy 3.1%, air force 11.2%). *Military expenditure as percentage of GNP* (1997): 1.9% (world 2.6%); per capita expenditure (1997) U.S.$29.

[1]Excludes one vacant seat reserved for Nagorno-Karabakh representative. [2]Controlled by Armenian forces from mid-1993. [3]Includes 59 districts and 10 cities with limited self-government in 1999; some districts and cities have been controlled by Armenian forces from mid-1993. [4]At factor cost. [5]Includes 42,329 unemployed and 832,871 undistributed employed. [6]Detail does not add to total given because of rounding. [7]Imports c.i.f., exports f.o.b. [8]1994–95.

Internet resources for further information:
- **Statistical Committee of Azerbaijan Republic http://www.azeri.com/goscomstat**
- **Azerbaijan Republic http://www.president.az/azerbaijan/azerbaijan.htm**

Bahamas, The

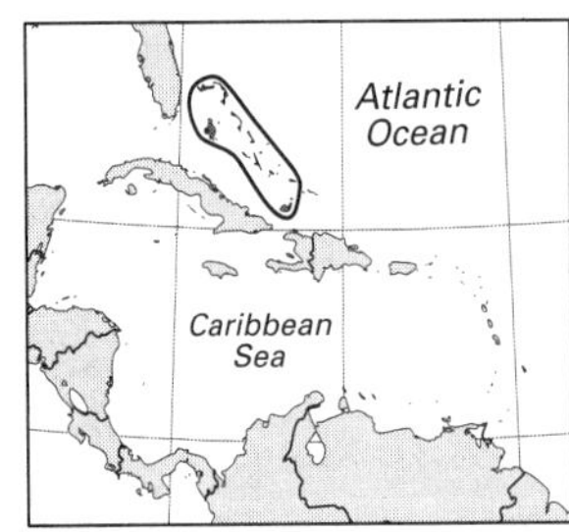

Official name: The Commonwealth of The Bahamas.
Form of government: constitutional monarchy with two legislative houses (Senate [16]; House of Assembly [40]).
Chief of state: British Monarch represented by Governor-General.
Head of government: Prime Minister.
Capital: Nassau.
Official language: English.
Official religion: none.
Monetary unit: 1 Bahamian dollar (B$) = 100 cents; valuation (Sept. 28, 2001) 1 U.S.$ = B$1.00; 1 £ = B$1.47.

Area and population

Islands and Island Groups[2]	area[1] sq mi	area[1] sq km	population 1990 census
Abaco, Great and Little	649	1,681	10,034
Acklins	192	497	405
Andros	2,300	5,957	8,187
Berry Islands	12	31	628
Bimini Islands	9	23	1,639
Cat Island	150	388	1,698
Crooked and Long Cay	93	241	412
Eleuthera	187	484	7,993
Exuma, Great, and Exuma Cays	112	290	3,556
Grand Bahama	530	1,373	40,898
Harbour Island	3	8	1,219
Inagua, Great and Little	599	1,551	985
Long Island	230	596	2,954
Mayaguana	110	285	312
New Providence	80	207	172,196
Ragged Island	14	36	89
Rum Cay	30	78	53
San Salvador	63	163	465
Spanish Wells	10	26	1,372
Other uninhabited cays and rocks	9	23	—
TOTAL	5,382	13,939[3]	255,095

Demography

Population (2001): 298,000.
Density (2001)[4]: persons per sq mi 76.6, persons per sq km 29.6.
Urban-rural (2000): urban 88.3%; rural 11.7%.
Sex distribution (1995): male 48.91%; female 51.09%.
Age breakdown (1995): under 15, 31.4%; 15–29, 27.9%; 30–44, 22.5%; 45–59, 11.4%; 60–74, 5.0%; 75 and over, 1.8%.
Population projection: (2010) 315,000; (2020) 324,000.
Doubling time: 55 years.
Ethnic composition (1996): black 86.0%; white 6.0%; mixed/other 8.0%.
Religious affiliation (1995): non-Anglican Protestant 45.4% of which Baptist 17.5%; Roman Catholic 16.8%; Anglican 10.8%; nonreligious 5.3%; Spiritist 1.5%; other (mostly independent and unaffiliated Christian) 20.2%.
Major cities (1990): Nassau 172,196[5]; Freeport/Lucaya 26,574; Marsh Harbour 3,611; Bailey Town 1,490; Dunmore Town (Harbour Island) 1,219.

Vital statistics

Birth rate per 1,000 population (2000): 19.5 (world avg. 22.5); (1995) legitimate 45.7%; illegitimate 54.3%.
Death rate per 1,000 population (2000): 6.8 (world avg. 9.0).
Natural increase rate per 1,000 population (2000): 12.7 (world avg. 13.5).
Total fertility rate (avg. births per childbearing woman; 2000): 2.3.
Marriage rate per 1,000 population (1996): 9.3.
Life expectancy at birth (2000): male 68.3 years; female 73.9 years.
Major causes of death per 100,000 population (1995): diseases of the circulatory system 160.1; endocrine and metabolic disorders 137.4; malignant neoplasms (cancers) 85.6.[6]

National economy

Budget (1998–99). Revenue: B$730,102,000 (import taxes 45.1%, stamp taxes from imports 11.0%, business and professional licenses 7.4%, departure taxes 6.6%, fines and forfeits 6.1%). Expenditures: B$748,150,000 (education 19.7%, health 15.5%, interest on public debt 13.2%, general administration 12.8%, public order 11.1%, tourism 6.0%, defense 3.7%).
National debt (December 2000): U.S.$1,521,000,000.
Production (value of production in B$'000 except as noted). Agriculture, forestry, fishing (1998): crayfish 54,100, poultry products 28,300, citrus and other fruit 21,300, fish 6,600, ornamental plants and flowers 6,000; roundwood (1998) 117,000 cu m. Mining and quarrying (value of export production; 1996): salt 18,100; aragonite 4,900. Manufacturing (value of export production; 1996): pharmaceuticals and other chemical products (1995) 74,200; rum 5,200. Construction (value of construction completed in B$'000,000; 1998): residential 141; nonresidential 353. Energy production (consumption): electricity (kW-hr; 1996) 1,340,000,000 (1,340,000,000); crude petroleum, none (none); petroleum products (metric tons; 1996) none (555,000).
Tourism: receipts (2000) U.S.$1,814,000,000; expenditures (1999) U.S.$309,000,000.
Household income and expenditure. Average household size (1996) 3.9; income per household (1996) B$27,252 (U.S.$27,252); sources of income: n.a.; expenditure (1995)[7]: housing 32.8%, transportation and communications 14.8% food and beverages 13.8%, household furnishings 8.9%.

Gross national product (1998): U.S.$3,432,000,000 (U.S.$11,890 per capita).

Structure of gross domestic product and labour force

	1995 in value B$'000,000	1995 % of total value	1996 labour force	1996 % of labour force
Agriculture, fishing	100	3.3	6,445	4.4
Manufacturing	80	2.6	5,400	3.7
Mining	26	0.8	1,665	1.1
Public utilities	116	3.8		
Construction	71	2.3	12,045	8.2
Transp. and commun.	295	9.6	11,475	7.8
Trade, restaurants	705	23.0	38,700	26.4
Finance, real estate	599	19.5	11,125	7.6
Pub. admin., defense	210	6.8	42,295	28.8
Services	301	9.8		
Other	568[8]	18.5[8]	17,485[9]	11.9[9]
TOTAL	3,069[3]	100.0	146,635	100.0[3]

Population economically active (1996): total 146,635; activity rate of total population 51.6% (participation rates: [1994] ages 15–64, 77.8%; female 47.5%; unemployed [1998] 9.5%).

Price and earnings indexes (1995 = 100)

	1994	1995	1996	1997	1998	1999	2000
Consumer price index	98.0	100.0	101.4	101.9	103.3	104.6	106.3[10]
Annual earnings index	...	...	...	...	...	...	...

Land use (1994): forest 32.4%; pasture 0.2%; agriculture 1.0%; other 66.4%.

Foreign trade[11]

Balance of trade (current prices)

	1994	1995	1996	1997	1998	1999
B$'000,000	–904	–1,067	–1,187	–1,441	–1,516	–1,421
% of total	73.0%	75.2%	76.9%	79.9%	71.6%	59.4%

Imports (1999): B$1,907,000,000 (machinery and transport equipment 30.8%; food products 13.7%; chemicals and chemical products 11.7%; petroleum for domestic use 8.7%). *Major import sources* (1998)[12]: U.S. 91.5%; EC 1.6%.
Exports (1999): B$486,300,000 (domestic exports 48.3%, of which crayfish 14.9%, rum 6.4%; reexports 44.2%; petroleum exports 7.5%). *Major export destinations* (1998)[12]: U.S. 56.5%; EC 31.4%; Canada 2.1%.

Transport and communications

Transport. Railroads: none. Roads (1995): total length 1,522 mi, 2,450 km (paved 57%). Vehicles (1996)[13]: passenger cars 89,263; trucks and buses 17,228. Merchant marine (1992): vessels (100 gross tons and over) 1,061; total deadweight tonnage 33,081,652. Air transport (1997)[14]: passenger-mi 87,000,000, passenger-km 140,000,000; short ton-mi cargo 312,000, metric ton-km cargo 455,000; airports (1997) with scheduled flights 22.

Communications

Medium	date	unit	number	units per 1,000 persons
Daily newspapers	1996	circulation	28,000	99
Radio	1997	receivers	215,000	744
Television	1997	receivers	67,000	232
Telephones	1999	main lines	111,184	381
Cellular telephones	1999	subscribers	15,911	55

Education and health

Educational attainment (1990). Percentage of population age 25 and over having: no formal schooling 3.5%; incomplete primary education 25.4%; complete primary/incomplete secondary 57.6%; complete secondary/higher 13.5%. *Literacy* (1995): total percentage age 15 and over literate 98.2%.

Education (1996–97)

	schools	teachers	students	student/ teacher ratio
Primary (age 5–10)	113	1,540	34,199	22.2
Secondary (age 11–16)[15]	...	1,352	27,970	20.7
Higher[16]	1	160	3,463	21.6

Health: physicians (1996) 419 (1 per 678 persons); hospital beds (1997) 1,119 (1 per 258 persons); infant mortality rate per 1,000 live births (2000) 17.0.
Food (1999): daily per capita caloric intake 2,500 (vegetable products 71%, animal products 29%); 103% of FAO recommended minimum requirement.

Military

Total active duty personnel (2000): 860 (paramilitary coast guard 100%). *Military expenditure as percentage of GNP* (1997): 0.9% (world 2.6%); per capita expenditure U.S.$100.

[1]Includes areas of lakes and ponds, as well as lagoons and sounds almost entirely surrounded by land; area of land only is about 3,890 sq mi (10,070 sq km). [2]For local administrative purposes, The Bahamas are divided into 25 districts comprising parts of an island, a single island, or a group of islands. [3]Detail does not add to total given because of rounding. [4]Land area only. [5]Population cited is for New Providence Island. [6]All rates include AIDS-related deaths. [7]Weights of retail price index components. [8]Includes net indirect taxes (B$503,000,000) and statistical discrepancy (B$65,000,000). [9]Includes 615 not adequately defined and 16,870 unemployed. [10]Average of 2nd and 3rd quarters. [11]Imports c.i.f.; exports f.o.b. [12]Excludes all petroleum imports/exports. [13]New Providence and Grand Bahama only. [14]Bahamasair; scheduled traffic only. [15]Public sector only. [16]College of The Bahamas only; 1997–98.

Internet resources for further information:
- **The Central Bank of The Bahamas http://www.bahamascentralbank.com**

Bahrain

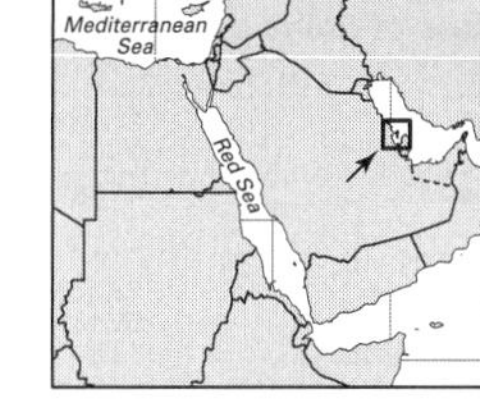

Official name: Dawlat al-Baḥrayn (State of Bahrain).
Form of government: monarchy (emirate)[1, 2].
Chief of state: Emir.
Head of government: Prime Minister.
Capital: Manama.
Official language: Arabic.
Official religion: Islam.
Monetary unit: 1 Bahrain dinar (BD) = 1,000 fils; valuation (Sept. 28, 2001) 1 BD = U.S.$2.63 = £1.82.

Area and population

	area		population
Regions[3]	sq mi	sq km	1991 census
Al-Gharbīyah (Western)	60.3	156.1	22,034
Al-Ḥadd	2.3	6.0	8,610
Jidd (Judd) Ḥafṣ	8.3	21.6	44,769
Al-Manāmah (Manama)	10.0	25.8	136,999
Al-Muḥarraq	6.2	16.0	74,245
Ar-Rifāʿ	112.6	291.6	49,752
Ash-Shamālīyah (Northern)	14.2	36.8	33,763
Ash-Sharqīyah (Eastern)	...	...	3,242[4]
Sitrah	11.1	28.8	36,755
Al-Wusṭā (Central)	13.6	35.2	34,304
Towns with special status			
Ḥammād	5.1	13.1	29,055
Madīnat ʿĪsā	4.8	12.4	34,509
Islands			
Ḥawār and other[5]	19.5	50.6	[3]
TOTAL	268.0	694.2[6]	508,037

Demography

Population (2001): 701,000.
Density (2001): persons per sq mi 2,616.8, persons per sq km 1,010.2.
Urban-rural (1995): urban 90.3%; rural 9.7%.
Sex distribution (1999): male 58.60%; female 41.40%.
Age breakdown (1999): under 15, 30.9%; 15–29, 28.4%; 30–44, 29.1%; 45–59, 8.0%; 60–74, 3.0%; 75 and over, 0.6%.
Population projection: (2010) 803,000; (2020) 899,000.
Doubling time: 41 years.
Ethnic composition (1991): Bahraini Arab 63.6%; Persian, Indian, Pakistani, and other Asians 30.3%; other Arab 3.5%; European 1.2%; other 1.4%.
Religious affiliation (1991): Muslim 81.8%, of which Shīʿī 61.3%, Sunnī 20.5%; Christian 8.5%; other 9.7%.
Major cities (1991): Manama (1992) 140,401; Ar-Rifāʿ 45,956; Al-Muḥarraq 45,337; Madīnat ʿĪsā 34,509.

Vital statistics

Birth rate per 1,000 population (2000): 20.6 (world avg. 22.5); legitimate 100%.
Death rate per 1,000 population (2000): 3.9 (world avg. 9.0).
Natural increase rate per 1,000 population (2000): 16.7 (world avg. 13.5).
Total fertility rate (avg. births per childbearing woman; 2000): 2.8.
Marriage rate per 1,000 population (1999): 5.5.
Divorce rate per 1,000 population (1999): 1.3.
Life expectancy at birth (2000): male 70.6 years; female 75.5 years.
Major causes of death per 100,000 population (1999): diseases of the circulatory system 65.4; malignant neoplasms (cancers) 31.1; metabolic and immunity diseases 19.4; diseases of the respiratory system 17.1; accidents and violence 11.7; diseases of the digestive system 9.3; congenital anomalies 8.6.

National economy

Budget (1999). Revenue: BD 566,000,000 ([1995] entrepreneurial and property income 57.7%, import duties 8.4%, foreign grants 6.7%). Expenditures: BD 726,000,000 ([1995] general administration and public order 33.2%, defense 17.3%, education 13.4%, fuel and energy 9.6%, health 9.3%, transportation and communications 9.0%).
Population economically active (1991): total 226,448; activity rate of total population 44.6% (participation rates: ages 15–64, 66.1%; female 17.5%; unemployed [1997] *c.* 30%).

Price and earnings indexes (1995 = 100)

	1992	1993	1994	1995	1996	1997	1998
Consumer price index	94.1	96.5	97.4	100.0	99.5	102.0	101.6
Earnings index	...	...	...	...	...	...	...

Production (metric tons except as noted). Agriculture, forestry, fishing (1999): fruit (excluding melons) 21,800, dates 16,800, cow's milk 14,000, tomatoes 4,600, hen's eggs 2,968; livestock (number of live animals) 17,100 sheep, 16,000 goats, 13,000 cattle; fish catch (1998) 9,849. Manufacturing (barrels; 1994): gas oil 28,900,000; fuel oil 20,900,000; kerosene 10,400,000; gasoline 7,700,000; jet fuel 7,100,000; naphtha 1,860,000; propane 1,500,000; butane 1,190,000; aluminum (1998) 712,200 metric tons. Construction (permits issued; 1998): residential 6,105; nonresidential 703. Energy production (consumption): electricity (kW-hr; 1998) 5,773,000,000 (5,226,000,000); crude petroleum (barrels; 1998) 13,751,000 ([1996] 82,723,000); petroleum products (metric tons; 1996) 13,100,000 (538,000); natural gas (cu m; 1998) 10,068,000,000 (10,068,000,000).
Gross national product (1998): U.S.$4,909,000,000 (U.S.$7,640 per capita).

Structure of gross domestic product and labour force

	1998		1991	
	value in BD '000,000[7]	% of total value	labour force	% of labour force
Agriculture	21.0	0.9	5,108	2.3
Mining	316.3	13.6	3,638	1.6
Manufacturing	296.1	12.7	26,618	11.8
Construction	94.5	4.1	26,738	11.6
Public utilities	43.8	1.9	2,898	1.3
Transp. and commun.	192.7	8.3	13,789	6.1
Trade	235.0	10.1	29,961	13.2
Finance	825.7	35.5	17,256	7.6
Pub. admin., defense	433.7	18.7	83,944	37.1
Services	116.8	5.0		
Other	–250.2[8]	–10.8[8]	16,498	7.3
TOTAL	2,325.2[6]	100.0	226,448	100.0[6]

Public debt (1999): BD 589,800,000 (U.S.$1,568,632,000).
Household income and expenditure. Average household size (1991) 5.8; income per household: n.a.; sources of income: n.a.; expenditure (1984): food and tobacco 33.3%, housing 21.2%, household durable goods 9.8%, transportation and communications 8.5%, recreation 6.4%, clothing and footwear 5.9%, education 2.7%, health 2.3%, energy and water 2.2%.
Land use (1994): meadows and pastures 5.8%; agricultural and under permanent cultivation 2.9%; built-on and wasteland 91.3%.
Tourism (1999): receipts from visitors U.S.$408,000,000; expenditures by nationals abroad U.S.$159,000,000.

Foreign trade[9]

Balance of trade (current prices)

	1995	1996	1997	1998	1999	2000
BD '000,000	+149.3	+160.5	+134.6	–111.3	+188.0	+412.8
% of total	5.1%	4.8%	4.3%	4.3%	6.1%	10.6%

Imports (1998): BD 1,340,900,000 (machinery and transport equipment 27.6%, crude petroleum products 20.4%, food and live animals 12.8%, chemicals 11.2%). *Major import sources:* Japan 11.5%; United States 10.4%; Australia 9.7%; United Kingdom 7.4%; Saudi Arabia 7.2%; Italy 5.8%; Germany 5.7%.
Exports (1998): BD 1,229,600,000 (petroleum products 51.8%, metal and metal products 29.5%). *Major export destinations:* Saudi Arabia 8.2%; United States 6.0%; Japan 4.4%; India 2.8%; Taiwan 2.6%.

Transport and communications

Transport. Railroads: none. Roads (1998): total length 3,164 km (paved 77%). Vehicles (1997): passenger cars 149,636; trucks and buses 32,213. Merchant marine (1992): vessels (100 gross tons and over) 87; total deadweight tonnage 192,487. Air transport (1999)[10]: passenger-km 2,835,900,000; metric ton-km cargo 118,681,000; airports (1997) with scheduled flights 1.

Communications

Medium	date	unit	number	units per 1,000 persons
Daily newspapers	1996	circulation	67,000	117
Radio	1997	receivers	338,000	580
Television	1999	receivers	270,000	405
Telephones	1999	main lines	165,369	248
Cellular telephones	1999	subscribers	133,468	200
Personal computers	1999	units	93,000	139
Internet	1999	users	30,000	45

Education and health

Educational attainment (1991). Percentage of population age 25 and over having: no formal education 38.4%; primary education 26.2%; secondary 25.1%; higher 10.3%. *Literacy* (1995): percentage of population age 15 and over literate 85.2%; males literate 89.1%; females literate 79.4%.

Education (1997–98)[11]

	schools	teachers	students	student/teacher ratio
Primary (age 6–11)	132	3,761	69,422	18.5
Secondary (age 12–17)	48	2,409	34,654	14.4
Voc., teacher tr.	7	721	7,528	10.4
Higher[12]	4[13]	655[14]	7,676[14]	11.7[14]

Health (1998): physicians 709 (1 per 907 persons); hospital beds 1,832 (1 per 351 persons); infant mortality rate per 1,000 live births (2000) 20.5.

Military

Total active duty personnel (2000): 11,000 (army 77.3%, navy 9.1%, air force 13.6%). *Military expenditure as percentage of GNP* (1997): 10.3% (world 2.6%); per capita expenditure U.S.$883.

[1]Appointed 40-member Consultative Council is an advisory body only. [2]Referendum in February 2001 approved creation of constitutional monarchy and reestablishment of parliament by 2004. [3]Regions have no administrative function; the creation of four actual administrative units was begun in 1997. [4]Ash-Sharqīyah includes population of Ḥawār and other islands. [5]The International Court of Justice awarded the jurisdiction of Ḥawār to Bahrain in early 2001. Jurisdiction of islets nearby to Ḥawār was to be split between Bahrain and Qatar. [6]Detail does not add to total given because of rounding. [7]In purchasers' value at current prices. [8]Less imputed bank service charges. [9]Imports c.i.f. [10]One-fourth apportionment of international flights of Gulf Air (jointly administered by the governments of Bahrain, Oman, Qatar, and the United Arab Emirates). [11]Public education only. [12]Public and private education. [13]1987–88. [14]1993–94.

Internet resources for further information:
- **State of Bahrain**
http://www.bahrain.gov.bh

Bangladesh

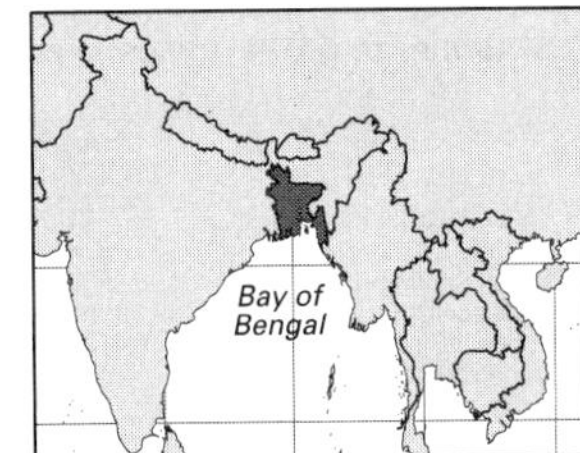

Official name: Gana Prajatantri Bangladesh (People's Republic of Bangladesh).
Form of government: unitary multiparty republic with one legislative house (Parliament [330[1]]).
Chief of state: President.
Head of government: Prime Minister.
Capital: Dhaka.
Official language: Bengali (Bangla).
Official religion: Islam.
Monetary unit: 1 Bangladesh taka (Tk) = 100 paisa; valuation (Sept. 28, 2001) 1 U.S.$ = Tk 56.95; 1 £ = Tk 83.70.

Area and population

Divisions	Administrative centres	area sq mi	area sq km	population 1991 census[2]
Barisal	Barisal	5,134	13,297	7,757,334
Chittagong	Chittagong	7,906	20,476	20,823,477
Dhaka	Dhaka	12,015	31,119	33,939,848
Khulna	Khulna	8,600	22,274	13,243,054
Rajshahi	Rajshahi	13,326	34,513	27,499,727
Sylhet	Sylhet	4,863	12,596	7,149,372
Tribal region				
Chittagong Hill Tracts[3]	Rangamati	5,133	13,295	1,042,373
TOTAL		56,977	147,570	111,455,185

Demography

Population (2001): 131,270,000.
Density (2001): persons per sq mi 2,303.9, persons per sq km 889.5.
Urban-rural (2000): urban 25.0%; rural 75.0%.
Sex distribution (1996): male 51.72%; female 48.28%.
Age breakdown (1996): under 15, 42.0%; 15–29, 26.4%; 30–44, 17.8%; 45–59, 8.9%; 60–74, 3.8%; 75 and over, 1.1%.
Population projection: (2010) 150,392,000; (2020) 169,613,000.
Doubling time: 39 years.
Ethnic composition (1997): Bengali 97.7%; tribal 1.9%, of which Chakma 0.4%, Saontal 0.2%, Marma 0.1%; other 0.4%.
Religious affiliation (2000): Muslim 85.8%; Hindu 12.4%; Christian 0.7%; Buddhist 0.6%; other 0.5%.
Major cities (1991)[4]: Dhaka 6,105,160; Chittagong 2,040,663; Khulna 877,388; Rajshahi 517,136; Mymensingh 185,517[5].

Vital statistics

Birth rate per 1,000 population (2000): 27.0 (world avg. 22.5).
Death rate per 1,000 population (2000): 9.1 (world avg. 9.0).
Natural increase rate per 1,000 population (2000): 17.9 (world avg. 13.5).
Total fertility rate (avg. births per childbearing woman; 2000): 3.0.
Marriage rate per 1,000 population (1996): 10.1.
Divorce rate per 1,000 population (1981): 3.6.
Life expectancy at birth (2000): male 59.0 years; female 60.0 years.
Major causes of death (1990; percentage of recorded deaths): typhoid fever 19.8%; old age 14.8%; tetanus 10.1%; tuberculosis and other respiratory diseases 8.7%; diarrhea 6.4%; suicide, accidents, and poisoning 5.1%; high blood pressure and heart diseases 5.0%.

National economy

Budget (1998–99). Revenue: Tk 210,000,000,000 (value-added tax 37.4%; customs duties 24.0%; income taxes 11.7%; service charges 5.0%; public telephone enterprises 4.3%; interest receipts 2.8%). Expenditures: Tk 157,500,000,000 (goods and services 52.4%; transfer payments 28.4%; interest payments 16.3%).
Production (metric tons except as noted). Agriculture, forestry, fishing (2000): paddy rice 35,821,000, sugarcane 6,951,000, wheat 1,900,000, jute 1,852,000, bananas 562,000, pulses 500,000, oilseeds 415,000, mangoes 187,000, pineapples 146,000, tea 56,000; livestock (number of live animals) 33,800,000 goats, 23,652,000 cattle, 1,121,000 sheep, 828,000 buffalo, 139,300,000 chickens, 13,000,000 ducks; roundwood 33,629,000 cu m; fish catch (1998) 839,141. Mining and quarrying (1997–98): marine salt 350,000; industrial limestone 26,000. Manufacturing (value added in U.S.$'000,000; 1995): textiles 651; industrial chemicals 441; food products 331; wearing apparel 242; tobacco products 347; transport equipment 128; iron and steel 108. Construction: n.a. Energy production (consumption): electricity (kW-hr; 1996) 12,404,000,000 (12,404,000,000); coal (metric tons; 1996) none (negligible); crude petroleum (barrels; 1996) 52,000 (10,423,000); petroleum products (metric tons; 1996) 688,000 (2,049,000); natural gas (cu m; 1996) 8,278,000,000 (8,278,000,000).
Household income. Average household size (1995–96) 5.3; average annual income per household Tk 52,389 (U.S.$1,277); sources of income: self-employment 56.9%, wages and salaries 28.1%, transfer payments 9.1%, other 5.9%; expenditure: food and drink 57.7%, housing and rent 11.1%, clothing and footwear 6.5%, energy 5.6%, other 19.1%.
Population economically active (1995–96): total 56,014,000; activity rate of total population 46.0% (participation rates: over age 10, 64.8%; female 38.1%; unemployed 2.5%[6]).

Price and earnings indexes (1995 = 100)

	1994	1995	1996	1997	1998	1999	2000
Consumer price index	92.1	100.0	104.1	109.5	118.6	125.9	128.8
Earnings index[7]	93.9	100.0	106.0	111.0	123.0	…	…

Public debt (external, outstanding; 1998): U.S.$15,804,000,000.
Gross national product (1998): U.S.$44,244,000,000 (U.S.$350 per capita).

Structure of gross domestic product and labour force

	1997–98		1995–96	
	in value Tk '000,000	% of total value	labour force	% of labour force
Agriculture	443,560	28.6	34,530,000	61.7
Mining	149,156	9.6	23,000	—
Manufacturing			4,085,000	7.3
Construction	92,333	6.0	1,015,000	1.8
Public utilities	32,161	2.1	103,000	0.2
Transp. and commun.	173,110	11.2	2,308,000	4.1
Trade	138,256	8.9	6,060,000	10.8
Finance	30,452	2.0	213,000	0.4
Public admin., defense	92,039	5.9	7,677,000	13.7
Services and other	397,267	25.7		
TOTAL	1,548,334	100.0	56,014,000	100.0

Land use (1998): pasture 4.6%; agriculture 68.6%; forest and other 26.8%.
Tourism (1999): receipts U.S.$50,000,000; expenditures U.S.$212,000,000.

Foreign trade[8]

Balance of trade (current prices)

	1994	1995	1996	1997	1998	1999
Tk '000,000	–59,233	–107,720	–110,988	–99,478	–118,772	–149,493
% of total	21.7%	29.7%	28.7%	23.0%	24.8%	28.0%

Imports (1997–98): Tk 341,850,000,000 (textile yarn, fabrics, and made-up articles 24.6%; machinery and transport equipment 12.5%; petroleum and products 5.8%; iron and steel 5.2%; cereals and cereal preparations 3.9%). *Major import sources:* India 15.0%; Western Europe 13.0%; China 10.0%; Japan 9.0%; South Korea 7.0%; Hong Kong 6.0%; Singapore 5.0%; U.S. 5.0%.
Exports (1997–98): Tk 203,970,000,000 (ready-made garments 61.9%; fish and prawns 7.3%; jute manufactures 6.5%; hides, skins, and leather 4.0%; raw jute 2.4%; tea 1.0%). *Major export destinations:* Western Europe 49.0%; U.S. 32.0%; Hong Kong 3.0%; Japan 2.7%; Canada 2.0%; Pakistan 1.2%.

Transport and communications

Transport. Railroads (1998–99): route length 1,699 mi, 2,734 km; passenger-mi 3,094,000,000, passenger-km 4,980,000,000; short ton-mi cargo 567,000,000, metric ton-km cargo 828,000,000. Roads (1996): total length 126,773 mi, 204,022 km (paved 12%). Vehicles (1998): passenger cars 54,784; trucks and buses 69,394. Merchant marine (1992): vessels (100 gross tons and over) 301; total deadweight tonnage 566,775. Air transport (1999)[9]: passenger-mi 2,153,757,000, passenger-km 3,466,143,000; short ton-mi cargo 94,885,000, metric ton-km cargo 138,530,000; airports with scheduled flights (1997) 8.

Communications

Medium	date	unit	number	units per 1,000 persons
Daily newspapers	1996	circulation	1,117,000	9.0
Radio	1998	receivers	8,000,000	64
Television	1999	receivers	940,000	7.4
Telephones	1999	main lines	432,968	3.4
Cellular telephones	1999	subscribers	149,000	1.2
Personal computers	1999	units	130,000	1.0
Internet	1999	users	50,000	0.4

Education and health

Educational attainment (1991). Percentage of population age 25 and over having: no formal schooling 65.4%; primary education 17.1%; secondary 13.8%; postsecondary 3.7%. *Literacy* (1995): total population age 15 and over literate 38.1%; males literate 49.4%; females literate 26.1%.

Education (1996–97)

	schools	teachers	students	student/ teacher ratio
Primary (age 6–10)	61,638	249,928	17,319,000	69.3
Secondary (age 11–17)	13,087	156,137	5,957,000	38.2
Voc., teacher tr.	165	1,896[10]	41,650	16.1[10]
Higher[11]	3,123	77,644	2,573,439	33.1

Health (1997): physicians 26,608 (1 per 4,627 persons); hospital beds 39,900 (1 per 3,086 persons); infant mortality rate (2000) 73.0.
Food (1999): daily per capita caloric intake 2,201 (vegetable products 97%, animal products 3%); (1997) 95% of FAO recommended minimum requirement.

Military

Total active duty personnel (2000): 137,000 (army 87.6%, navy 7.7%, air force 4.7%). *Military expenditure as percentage of GNP* (1997): 1.4% (world 2.6%); per capita expenditure U.S.$5.

[1]Includes 30 seats reserved for women. [2]Adjusted for underenumeration. [3]Autonomous region for non-Bengali tribal people was created by accord signed in December 1997 and formally established in May 1999. [4]Metropolitan population. [5]Municipal population. [6]Excluding underemployment. [7]Wage earnings in manufacturing. [8]Imports figures are f.o.b. in balance of trade. [9]Bangladesh Biman only. [10]Excludes teachers' training school data. [11]Excludes professional and technical colleges.

Internet resources for further information:

- **Government of the People's Republic of Bangladesh http://www.bangladeshgov.org**

Barbados

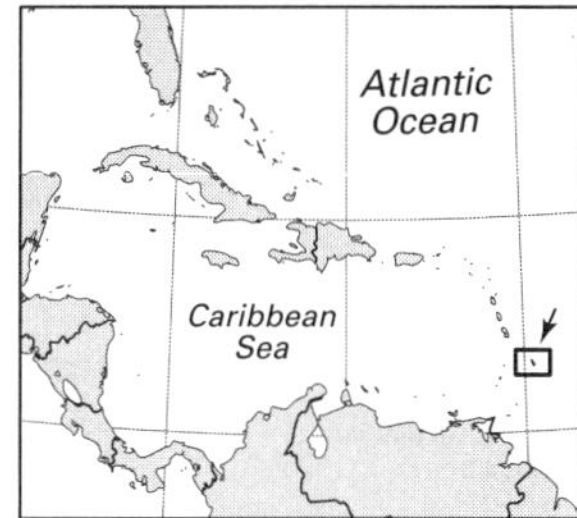

Official name: Barbados.
Form of government: constitutional monarchy with two legislative houses (Senate [21]; House of Assembly [28]).
Chief of state: British Monarch represented by Governor-General.
Head of government: Prime Minister.
Capital: Bridgetown.
Official language: English.
Official religion: none.
Monetary unit: 1 Barbados dollar (BDS$) = 100 cents; valuation (Sept. 28, 2001) 1 U.S.$ = BDS$2.00; 1 £ = BDS$2.94.

Area and population

	area		population
Parishes[1]	sq mi	sq km	1990 census
Christ Church	22	57	47,050
St. Andrew	14	36	6,346
St. George	17	44	17,905
St. James	12	31	21,001
St. John	13	34	10,206
St. Joseph	10	26	7,619
St. Lucy	14	36	9,455
St. Michael[2]	15	39	97,516
St. Peter	13	34	11,263
St. Philip	23	60	20,540
St. Thomas	13	34	11,590
TOTAL	166	430[3]	260,491

Demography

Population (2001): 269,000.
Density (2001): persons per sq mi 1,618, persons per sq km 624.
Urban-rural (1998): urban 48.9%; rural 51.1%.
Sex distribution (2000): male 48.07%; female 51.93%.
Age breakdown (2000): under 15, 22.0%; 15–29, 24.2%; 30–44, 26.1%; 45–59, 15.7%; 60–74, 7.9%; 75 and over, 4.1%.
Population projection: (2010) 275,000; (2020) 283,000.
Doubling time: n.a.; doubling time exceeds 100 years.
Ethnic composition (1990): black 92.5%; white 3.2%; mixed 2.8%; other 1.5%.
Religious affiliation (1995): Protestant 63.0%, of which Anglican 26.3%, Pentecostal 10.6%, Methodist 5.7%; Roman Catholic 4.8%; other Christian 2.0%; nonreligious/other 30.2%.
Major cities (1990): Bridgetown 6,070 (urban agglomeration [1999] 133,000); Speightstown, *c.* 3,500.

Vital statistics

Birth rate per 1,000 population (2000): 13.6 (world avg. 22.5); (1979) legitimate 26.9%; illegitimate 73.1%.
Death rate per 1,000 population (2000): 8.7 (world avg. 9.0).
Natural increase rate per 1,000 population (2000): 4.9 (world avg. 13.5).
Total fertility rate (avg. births per childbearing woman; 2000): 1.6.
Marriage rate per 1,000 population (1995): 13.5.
Divorce rate per 1,000 population (1995): 1.5.
Life expectancy at birth (2000): male 70.4 years; female 75.6 years.
Major causes of death per 100,000 population (1995): diseases of the circulatory system 369.7; malignant neoplasms (cancers) 163.6; endocrine and metabolic disorders 151.3; diseases of the respiratory system 56.3; accidents, poisonings, and violence 36.4; diseases of the digestive system 34.5; infectious and parasitic diseases 27.6; diseases of the nervous system 23.0.

National economy

Budget (1997–98). Revenue: BDS$1,458,274,000[4] (tax revenue 94.7%, of which goods and services taxes 49.5%, personal income and company taxes 29.5%, import duties 8.8%; nontax revenue 5.3%). Expenditures: BDS$1,508,869,000 (current expenditure 83.2%, of which education 18.8%, economic services 11.5%, health 10.9%, social security and welfare 8.3%).
Production (metric tons except as noted). Agriculture, forestry, fishing (1998): raw sugar 48,000, sweet potatoes 5,100, cucumbers 1,400, yams 1,320, cabbage 1,200, pumpkins 1,000, cassava 820, carrots 785, tomatoes 650, onions 480, lettuce 445; livestock (number of live animals) 41,000 sheep, 33,000 pigs, 23,000 cattle, 4,500 goats; roundwood, n.a.; fish catch (1997) 2,764. Manufacturing (value added in BDS$'000; 1995): food, beverages, and tobacco (mostly sugar, molasses, rum, beer, and cigarettes) 108,000; paper products, printing, and publishing 33,400; metal products and assembly-type goods (mostly electronic components) 28,000; textiles and wearing apparel 11,700. Construction (value added in BDS$; 1996): 151,400,000. Energy production (consumption): electricity (kW-hr; 1996) 650,000,000 (571,000,000); coal, none (none); crude petroleum (barrels; 1996) 364,000 (1,552,000); petroleum products (metric tons; 1996) 255,000 (288,000); natural gas (cu m; 1996) 29,112,000 (29,112,000).
Household income and expenditure. Average household size (1990) 3.5; income per household (1988) BDS$13,455 (U.S.$6,690); sources of income: n.a.; expenditure (1994): food 39.4%, housing 16.8%, transportation 10.5%, household operations 8.1%, alcohol and tobacco 6.4%, fuel and light 5.2%, clothing and footwear 5.0%, other 8.6%.
Population economically active (1997): total 135,800; activity rate of total population 51.3% (participation rates: ages 15 and over, 67.5%, female 62.1%, unemployed 14.5%).

Price and earnings indexes (1995 = 100)

	1994	1995	1996	1997	1998	1999	2000
Consumer price index	98.2	100.0	102.4	110.3	108.9	110.6	113.3
Hourly earnings index	...	...	...	...	...	...	...

Gross national product (1999): U.S.$2,294,000,000 (U.S.$8,600 per capita).

Structure of gross domestic product and labour force

	1997			
	in value BDS$'000,000	% of total value	labour force	% of labour force
Agriculture, fishing	174.9	4.0	6,100	4.5
Mining	20.2[5]	0.5[5]	...	...
Manufacturing	225.8	5.2	10,700	7.8
Construction	182.9	4.2	10,200	7.5
Public utilities	127.4[5]	2.9[5]	1,500	1.1
Transp. and commun.	339.6	7.8	4,700	3.4
Trade, restaurants	1,117.6	25.6	28,200	20.7
Finance, real estate	614.3	14.1	8,100	5.9
Pub. admin., defense	611.0	14.0	46,900	34.4
Services	157.8	3.6		
Other	799.1[6]	18.3[6]	20,000[7]	14.7[7]
TOTAL	4,370.6	100.0[3]	136,400	100.0

Public debt (external, outstanding; 1999): U.S.$359,100,000.
Tourism: receipts from visitors (1999) U.S.$677,000,000; expenditures by nationals abroad (1998) U.S.$82,000,000.

Foreign trade[8]

Balance of trade (current prices)

	1995	1996	1997	1998	1999	2000
BDS$'000,000	–1,063	–1,106	–1,425	–1,510	–1,684	–1,767
% of total	52.7%	49.6%	55.7%	59.7%	61.4%	61.9%

Imports (1997): BDS$1,991,001,000 (retained imports 92.7%, of which capital goods 20.4%, food and beverages 15.0%, construction materials 8.2%, chemicals 5.6%, fuels 3.7%; reexported imports 7.3%). *Major import sources* (1997): U.S. 45.4%[9]; Trinidad and Tobago 9.2%; U.K. 8.1%; Canada 3.9%; Jamaica 1.2%.
Exports (1997): BDS$565,887,000 (domestic exports 74.4%, of which sugar 12.7%, chemicals 10.0%, electrical components 9.2%, rum 4.9%, margarine and lard 2.0%, clothing 1.2%; reexports 25.6%). *Major export destinations* (1997): U.K. 17.1%; U.S. 14.7%[9]; Jamaica 6.6%; Trinidad and Tobago 5.5%; St. Lucia 3.7%; Canada 3.5%; Guyana 2.8%.

Transport and communications

Transport. Railroads: none. Roads (1996): total length 1,025 mi, 1,650 km (paved 96%). Vehicles (1995): passenger cars 43,711; trucks and buses 10,583[10]. Merchant marine (1992): vessels (100 gross tons and over) 37; total deadweight tonnage 84,000. Air transport (1995): passenger arrivals 699,000, passenger departures 707,400; cargo unloaded 8,382 metric tons, cargo loaded 4,717 metric tons; airports (1997) with scheduled flights 1.

Communications

Medium	date	unit	number	units per 1,000 persons
Daily newspapers	1996	circulation	53,000	199
Radio	1997	receivers	237,000	888
Television	1999	receivers	78,000	292
Telephones	1999	main lines	115,000	430
Cellular telephones	1999	subscribers	30,000	112
Personal computers	1999	units	21,000	79
Internet	1999	users	6,000	22

Education and health

Educational attainment (1990). Percentage of population age 25 and over having: no formal schooling 0.4%; primary education 23.7%; secondary 60.3%[11]; higher 11.2%; other 4.4%. *Literacy* (1995): total population age 15 and over literate 97.4%; males literate 98.0%; females literate 96.8%.

Education (1995–96)

	schools	teachers	students	student/ teacher ratio
Primary (age 3–11)	79	994	18,513	18.6
Secondary (age 12–16)	21	1,263	21,455	17.0
Vocational[12]	8	79	996	12.6
Higher	4	544[13]	6,622	...

Health (1992): physicians 312 (1 per 842 persons); hospital beds 1,966 (1 per 134 persons); infant mortality rate per 1,000 live births (2000) 12.4.
Food (1999): daily per capita caloric intake 3,203 (vegetable products 74%, animal products 26%); 132% of FAO recommended minimum requirement.

Military

Total active duty personnel (2000): 610 (army 82.0%, navy 18.0%). *Military expenditure as percentage of GNP* (1996): 0.8% (world 2.6%); per capita expenditure U.S.$54.

[1]Parishes and city of Bridgetown have no local administrative function. [2]Includes city of Bridgetown. [3]Detail does not add to total given because of rounding. [4]Current revenue only. [5]Mining excludes natural gas; Public utilities includes natural gas. [6]Net indirect taxes. [7]Unemployed. [8]Import figures are in c.i.f. [9]Includes Puerto Rico. [10]Includes taxis. [11]Includes composite senior. [12]1987–88. [13]1984.

Internet resources for further information:
- **Barbados Statistical Services http://www.bgis.gov.bb/stats**
- **Central Bank of Barbados http://www.centralbank.org.bb**

Belarus

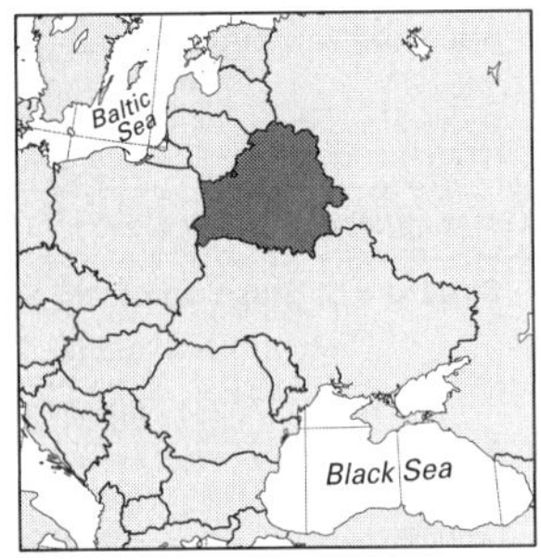

Official name: Respublika Belarus (Republic of Belarus).
Form of government[1]: republic with two legislative bodies (Council of the Republic [64]; House of Representatives [110]).
Head of state and government: President assisted by Prime Minister.
Capital: Minsk.
Official languages: Belarusian; Russian.
Official religion: none.
Monetary unit: rubel[2] (Rbl; plural rubli) valuation (Sept. 28, 2001) free rate, 1 U.S.$ = (new) Rbl 1,482; 1 £ = (new) Rbl 2,178.

Area and population		area		population
				1999
Provinces	Capitals	sq mi	sq km	census
Brest	Brest	12,700	32,800	1,485,100
Homel (Gomel)	Homel	15,600	40,400	1,545,100
Hrodno (Grodno)	Hrodno	9,700	25,000	1,185,200
Mahilyoŭ (Mogilyov)	Mahilyoŭ	11,200	29,100	1,213,500
Minsk (Mensk)	Minsk	15,500	40,200	1,558,600
Vitebsk	Vitebsk	15,500	40,100	1,377,200
City				
Minsk (Mensk)	—	4	4	1,680,500
TOTAL		80,200[5]	207,600[4]	10,045,200

Demography

Population (2001): 9,986,000.
Density (2001): persons per sq mi 124.5, persons per sq km 48.1.
Urban-rural (2000): urban 69.7%; rural 30.3%.
Sex distribution (2000): male 46.94%; female 53.06%.
Age breakdown (2000): under 15, 18.9%; 15–29, 22.2%; 30–44, 23.4%; 45–59, 16.5%; 60–69, 10.4%; 70 and over, 8.6%.
Population projection: (2010) 9,923,000; (2020) 9,904,000.
Doubling time: not applicable; population is declining.
Ethnic composition (1999): Belarusian 81.2%; Russian 11.4%; Polish 3.9%; Ukrainian 2.4%; other 1.1%.
Religious affiliation (1995): Belarusian Orthodox 31.6%; Roman Catholic 17.7%; other (mostly nonreligious) 50.7%.
Major cities (2000): Minsk 1,688,000; Homel 487,000; Mahilyoŭ 358,000.

Vital statistics

Birth rate per 1,000 population (1999): 9.3 (world avg. 22.5); legitimate 82.2%; illegitimate 17.8%.
Death rate per 1,000 population (1999): 14.2 (world avg. 9.0).
Natural increase rate per 1,000 population (1999): –4.9 (world avg. 13.5).
Total fertility rate (avg. births per childbearing woman; 1998): 1.3.
Marriage rate per 1,000 population (1999): 7.3.
Divorce rate per 1,000 population (1999): 4.7.
Life expectancy at birth (1999): male 62.2 years; female 73.9 years.
Major causes of death per 100,000 population (1999): diseases of the circulatory system 750.4; malignant neoplasms (cancers) 198.9; accidents and violence 170.4; diseases of the respiratory system 72.2.

National economy

Budget (1997). Revenue: (old) Rbl 111,736,000,000,000 (value-added tax 30.0%, taxes on profits 14.8%, taxes on income 10.2%, excise taxes 13.1%, taxes on international trade 8.3%, other 23.6%). Expenditures: (old) Rbl 115,875,000,000,000 (education 20.1%, health 15.8%, subsidies 11.1%, capital expenditure 8.6%, Chernobyl expenditures 6.5%, transfers 5.8%, lending minus repayments 1.8%, other 30.3%[5]).
Public debt (external, outstanding; 1999): U.S.$851,000,000.
Household income and expenditure. Average household size (1998) 3.6; income per household (1995) (old) Rbl 2,400,000; sources of income (1997): wages and salaries 55.5%, business activities 20.5%, transfers 15.5%, agricultural income 1.4%; expenditure (1997): retail goods 74.9%, savings 18.6%.
Production (metric tons except as noted). Agriculture, forestry, fishing (1999): potatoes 8,000,000, cereal 3,353,000, other vegetables 1,145,000, sugar beets 1,000,000, fruit 299,350; livestock (number of live animals) 4,515,000 cattle, 3,608,000 pigs, 233,200 horses, 182,000 sheep and goats, 40,000,000 poultry; roundwood (1998) 17,745,000 cu m; fish catch (1998) 457. Mining and quarrying (1997): potash 3,400,000; peat 3,036,000. Manufacturing (value of production in [old] Rbl '000,000; 1994): machine-building equipment 1,086,650; chemical products 659,438; food products 562,438; construction materials 142,555. Construction (1991): 5,395,000 sq m. Energy production (consumption): electricity (kW-hr; 1997) 26,057,000,000 (33,677,000,000); coal (1994) none (1,199,000); crude petroleum (barrels; 1997) 13,355,000 (86,406,000); petroleum products (1997) 9,589,000 (10,473,000); natural gas (cu m; 1997) 242,000,000 (16,402,000,000).
Population economically active (1997): 4,369,900; activity rate of total population 42.7% (participation rate: ages 16–59 [male], 16–54 [female] 81.8%; female 53.6%; unemployed [1998] 2.6%).

Price and earnings indexes (1995 = 100)	1995	1996	1997	1998
Consumer price index	100.0	152.7	204.5	246.1
Monthly earnings index	100.0	160.5	240.1	350.2

Gross national product (1999): U.S.$26,299,000,000 (U.S.$2,620 per capita).

Structure of gross domestic product and labour force	1997			
	in value (old) Rbl '000,000[6]	% of total value[6]	labour force	% of labour force
Agriculture	42,445	14.1	762,500	17.4
Mining / Manufacturing	111,024	36.9	1,204,300	27.6
Public utilities	8,723	2.9	197,600	4.5
Construction	21,535	7.1	311,800	7.1
Transp. and commun.	37,910	12.6	309,100	7.1
Trade	28,196	9.4	461,600	10.6
Finance / Public admin., defense / Services	31,940	10.6	915,400	20.9
Other	19,341	6.4	207,600[7]	4.8[7]
TOTAL	301,114	100.0	4,369,900	100.0

Tourism (1999): receipts U.S.$13,000,000; expenditures U.S.$116,000,000.
Land use (1994)[8]: forested 33.7%; meadows and pastures 14.1%; agricultural and under permanent cultivation 30.5%; other 21.7%.

Foreign trade[9]

Balance of trade (current prices)	1994	1995	1996	1997	1998	1999	2000
U.S.$'000,000	–556	–856	–1,287	–1,388	–1,388	–765	–1,097
% of total	10.0%	8.3%	10.2%	8.7%	8.7%	6.1%	6.9%

Imports (1997): U.S.$8,689,000,000 (industrial products 96.3%, of which petroleum and gas 24.0%, machinery and metalworking 21.7%, chemical and petroleum products 16.8%, iron and steel 10.1%, food and beverages 9.6%, light industry 4.6%, wood and paper products 2.8%; agricultural products 3.7%). *Major import sources:* Russia 53.8%; Ukraine 11.1%; Germany 8.0%; Poland 2.9%; Italy 1.8%; U.S. 1.6%.
Exports (1997): U.S.$7,301,000,000 (industrial products 98.3%, of which machinery and metalworking 32.9%, chemical and petroleum products 20.9%, light industry 9.5%, petroleum and gas 8.2%, iron and steel 8.1%, food and beverages 7.5%, wood and paper products 7.1%, construction materials 2.2%; agricultural products 1.7%). *Major export destinations:* Russia 64.8%; Ukraine 5.8%; Poland 3.4%; Germany 3.0%.

Transport and communications

Transport. Railroads (1998): length 5,488 km; (1997) passenger-km 12,909,-000,000; metric ton-km cargo 30,636,000,000. Roads (1998): total length 53,407 km (paved 98.6%). Vehicles (1998[10]): passenger cars 1,132,843; trucks and buses 8,867. Air transport (1997): passenger-km 910,000,000; metric ton-km cargo 84,000,000; airports 1.

Communications				units
Medium	date	unit	number	per 1,000 persons
Daily newspapers	1997	circulation	1,437,000	140
Radio	1998	receivers	3,021,000	296
Television	1999	receivers	3,300,000	327
Telephones	2000	main lines	2,638,000	263
Cellular telephones	2000	subscribers	22,230	2.2
Internet	2000	users	50,000	5.0

Education and health

Educational attainment (1999). Percentage of population age 15 and over having: no formal schooling 14.8%; primary and secondary education 71.2%; higher 14.0%.

Education (1997–98)	schools	teachers	students	student/teacher ratio
Primary (age 6–13) / Secondary (age 14–17)	4,835	145,300	1,580,000	10.9
Voc., teacher tr.	156	8,800	125,600	14.3
Higher	59	16,300	224,500	13.8

Literacy (1989): total population age 15 and over literate 7,690,000 (97.9%); males literate 3,661,000 (99.4%); females literate 4,029,000 (96.6%).
Health (1995): physicians 46,000 (1 per 224 persons); hospital beds 127,000 (1 per 81 persons); infant mortality rate per 1,000 live births (1999) 11.5.
Food (1999): daily per capita caloric intake 3,171 (vegetable products 72%, animal products 28%); 124% of FAO recommended minimum requirement.

Military

Total active duty personnel (2000): 83,100 (army 52.3%, air force and air defense 27.1%, other 20.6%). *Military expenditure as percentage of GNP* (1997): 1.7% (world 2.6%); per capita expenditure U.S.$81.

[1]Legal status of new constitution approved by referendum on Nov. 27, 1996, and legislative bodies established per this constitution are controversial. Council of the Republic contains 8 unelected seats. [2]Rubel re-denominated Jan. 1, 2000; 1,000 (old) rubli = 1 (new) rubel. [3]Minsk province includes Minsk city. [4]Rounded area figures; exact area figures are 80,153 sq mi (207,595 sq km). [5]Includes expenditure arrears and statistical discrepancy. [6]At factor cost. [7]Includes 126,200 unemployed and 81,400 undistributed employed. [8]25% of Belarusian territory severely affected by radioactive fallout from Chernobyl. [9]Imports in c.i.f. [10]January 1.

Internet resources for further information:
- **Ministry of Statistics and Analysis http://president.gov.by/Minstat/en/main.html**
- **The Native Byelorussian WWW-server for Businessmen http://www.belarus.net**

Belgium

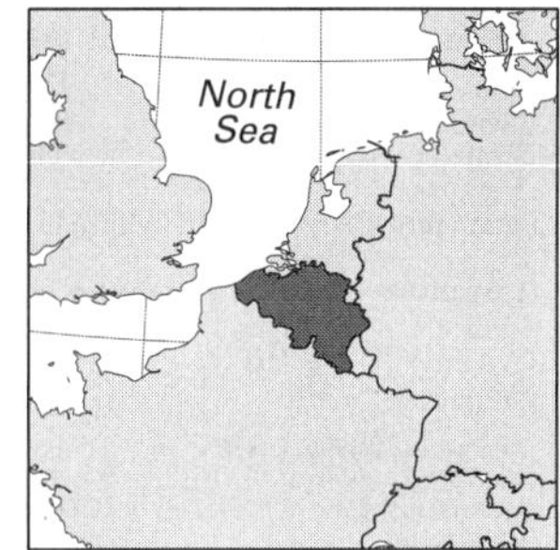

Official name: Koninkrijk België (Dutch); Royaume de Belgique (French) (Kingdom of Belgium).
Form of government: federal constitutional monarchy with a Parliament composed of two legislative chambers (Senate [71[1]]; House of Representatives [150]).
Chief of state: Monarch.
Head of government: Prime Minister.
Capital: Brussels.
Official languages: Dutch; French; German.
Official religion: none.
Monetary unit: 1 Belgian franc (BF) = 100 centimes; valuation (Sept. 28, 2001) 1 U.S.$ = BF 44.30; 1£ = BF 65.10; 1 € = BF 40.3399.

Area and population

Regions[2] / Provinces	Capitals	area sq mi	area sq km	population 2000[3] estimate
Brussels[4]	—	62	161	959,318
Flanders	—	5,221[5]	13,522	5,940,251
Antwerp	Antwerp	1,107	2,867	1,643,972
East Flanders	Ghent	1,151	2,982	1,361,623
Flemish Brabant[6]	Leuven	813	2,106	1,014,704
Limburg	Hasselt	935	2,422	791,178
West Flanders	Brugge	1,214	3,145	1,128,774
Wallonia	—	6,504[5]	16,844	3,339,516
Hainaut	Mons	1,462	3,786	1,279,467
Liège	Liège	1,491	3,862	1,019,442
Luxembourg	Arlon	1,714	4,440	246,820
Namur	Namur	1,415	3,666	443,903
Walloon Brabant[6]	Wavre	421	1,091	349,884
TOTAL		11,787	30,528[5]	10,239,085

Demography

Population (2001): 10,268,000.
Density (2000): persons per sq mi 871.2, persons per sq km 336.4.
Urban-rural (1996)[7]: urban 96.8%; rural 3.2%.
Sex distribution (2000): male 48.89%; female 51.11%.
Age breakdown (2000): under 15, 17.5%; 15–29, 18.8%; 30–44, 22.9%; 45–59, 18.8%; 60–74, 14.8%; 75 and over, 7.2%.
Population projection: (2010) 10,350,000; (2020) 10,323,000.
Nationality (1992): Belgian 91.0%; Italian 2.4%; Moroccan 1.4%; French 0.9%; Turkish 0.8%; Dutch 0.6%; other 2.9%.
Religious affiliation (1995): Roman Catholic 87.9%; Muslim 2.5%; other Christian 2.4%, of which Protestant 1.0%; Jewish 0.3%; other 6.9%.
Major cities (2000[3]): Brussels 959,318[4]; Antwerp 446,525; Ghent 224,180; Charleroi 200,827; Liège 185,639.

Vital statistics

Birth rate per 1,000 population (2000): 10.9 (world avg. 22.5).
Death rate per 1,000 population (2000): 10.1 (world avg. 9.0).
Natural increase rate per 1,000 population (2000): 0.8 (world avg. 13.5).
Total fertility rate (avg. births per childbearing woman; 2000): 1.5.
Marriage rate per 1,000 population (1999): 4.3.
Divorce rate per 1,000 population (1994): 2.2.
Life expectancy at birth (2000): male 74.5 years; female 81.3 years.
Major causes of death per 100,000 population (1992): diseases of the circulatory system 383.3; malignant neoplasms (cancers) 272.6; diseases of the respiratory system 90.6; accidents and violence 40.9.

National economy

Budget (1999). Revenue: €107,764,000,000 (social security contributions 29.6%, taxes on goods and services 26.9%, income tax 26.7%). Expenditures: €109,772,000,000 (transfer payments 49.4%, interest on debt 15.1%, other 35.5%).
Public debt (1999): U.S.$250,459,000,000.
Production (metric tons except as noted). Agriculture, forestry, fishing (2000)[7]: sugar beets 6,200,000, potatoes 3,000,000, wheat 1,634,000, apples 497,075, barley 370,000, tomatoes 300,000; livestock (number of live animals) 7,671,000 pigs, 3,085,000 cattle, 152,000 sheep, 67,000 horses; roundwood (2000)[7] 4,400,000 cu m; fish catch (1999) 29,900. Mining and quarrying (1997): limestone 30,000,000; granite (Belgium bluestone) 2,115,000 cu m; marble 400 cu m. Manufacturing (value added in BF '000,000; 1996): metal products 468,894; food 263,382; chemicals 243,787; printing 69,991; textiles 66,524; furniture 58,115. Construction (1993): residential 33,063,000 cu m; nonresidential 42,864,000 cu m. Energy production (consumption): electricity (kW-hr; 1998) 83,244,000,000 ([1996] 80,241,000,000); coal (metric tons; 1996) negligible (11,556,000); crude petroleum (barrels; 1996) none (231,305,000); petroleum products (metric tons; 1996) 28,400,000 (17,684,000); natural gas (cu m; 1996) 2,514,000 (14,086,000,000).
Household income and expenditure. Avg. household size (1999) 2.5; sources of income (1992): wages 49.6%, transfer payments 20.7%, property income 18.8%, self-employment 10.9%; expenditure (1992): food 18.0%, housing 17.0%, transp. 13.3%, health 11.8%, durable goods 10.7%, clothing 7.7%.
Land use (1994)[7]: forest 21.3%; pasture 21.0%; agriculture 24.2%; other 33.5%.
Population economically active (1999): total 3,905,500; activity rate 38.2% (participation rates: ages 15–64, 58.0%; female 42.7%; unemployed 9.6%).

Price and earnings indexes (1995 = 100)

	1994	1995	1996	1997	1998	1999	2000
Consumer price index	98.6	100.0	102.1	103.7	104.7	105.9	108.6
Earnings index	...	...	...	...	...	...	...

Gross national product (1999): U.S.$252,051,000,000 (U.S.$24,650 per capita).

Structure of gross domestic product and labour force

	1999 in value BF '000,000	% of total value	labour force	% of labour force
Agriculture	124,128	1.4	80,900	2.1
Mining	14,080	0.2	4,400	0.1
Manufacturing	1,644,106	18.7	651,000	16.7
Construction	435,122	5.0	229,800	5.9
Public utilities	233,994	2.7	28,200	0.7
Transp. and commun.	596,727	6.8	265,500	6.8
Trade	1,180,565	13.5	613,700	15.7
Finance	2,473,438	28.2	581,200	14.9
Pub. admin., defense / Services	2,071,216	23.6	1,450,800	37.1
Other	—	—	—	—
TOTAL	8,773,376	100.0[5]	3,905,500[8]	100.0[8]

Tourism (1999): receipts U.S.$7,039,000,000; expenditures U.S.$10,057,000,000.

Foreign trade[7]

Balance of trade (current prices)

	1995	1996	1997	1998	1999	2000
BF '000,000	+415,800	+364,000	+442,700	+562,000	+581,000	+542,822
% of total	4.2%	3.5%	3.8%	4.6%	4.4%	4.2%

Imports (1999): BF 6,237,963,000,000 (machinery and transport equipment 31.9%; basic manufactures 20.8%; chemicals 16.4%; food 7.8%; mineral fuels 5.7%, of which petroleum products 4.3%; diamonds 3.9%). *Major import sources:* Germany 17.4%; The Netherlands 16.7%; France 13.7%; U.K. 8.6%; U.S. 7.5%.
Exports (1999): BF 6,780,785,000,000 (machinery and transport equipment 30.0%; chemicals 20.3%, of which plastics 4.4%; food 8.7%; iron and steel 4.0%; textiles 3.7%; petroleum products 2.5%). *Major export destinations:* Germany 17.9%; France 17.7%; The Netherlands 12.8%; U.K. 10.0%; U.S. 5.2%.

Transport and communications

Transport. Railroads (1999): route length 3,380 km; passenger-km 7,354,000,000; metric ton-km cargo 7,392,000,000. Roads (1997): total length 143,800 km (paved 97%). Vehicles (1998): passenger cars 4,491,734; trucks and buses 453,122. Merchant marine (1992): vessels (100 gross tons and over) 232; total deadweight tonnage 218,506. Air transport (2000)[9]: passenger-km 19,378,689,000; metric ton-km cargo 568,244,000; airports (1999) 2.

Communications

Medium	date	unit	number	units per 1,000 persons
Daily newspapers	1996	circulation	1,625,000	161
Radio	1997	receivers	8,075,000	795
Television	1999	receivers	5,300,000	518
Telephones	1999	main lines	5,100,000	502
Cellular telephones	1999	subscribers	3,193,000	315
Personal computers	1999	units	3,200,000	313
Internet	1999	users	1,400,000	137

Education and health

Educational attainment (1981). Percentage of population age 15 and over having: less than secondary education 44.4%; lower secondary 26.5%; upper secondary 17.0%; vocational 2.9%; teacher's college 0.6%; university 3.5%.
Literacy (1995): virtually 99% literate.

Education (1999–2000)

	schools[10]	teachers	students	student/teacher ratio
Primary (age 6–12)	4,401	82,168[11]	778,000	...
Secondary (age 12–18)	1,727	115,262	779,000	...
Voc., teacher tr.[12]	304	...	155,192[10]	...
Higher	151	38,014[10]	298,000	...

Health: physicians (1998) 40,300 (1 per 253 persons); hospital beds (1994) 77,181 (1 per 131 persons); infant mortality rate (2000) 4.8.
Food (1999)[7]: daily per capita caloric intake 3,625 (vegetable products 68%, animal products 32%); 137% of FAO recommended minimum requirement.

Military

Total active duty personnel (2000): 39,250 (army 68.3%, navy 6.6%, air force 21.9%, medical service 3.6%). *Military expenditure as percentage of GNP* (1997): 1.5% (world 2.6%); per capita expenditure U.S.$362.

[1]Excludes children of the monarch serving ex officio from age 18. [2]Corresponding to three language-based federal community councils: Dutch (Flanders), French (Wallonia), and bilingual (Brussels-Capital) having authority in cultural affairs; a fourth (German) community council (within Wallonia; 1999 population 70,472) lacks expression as an administrative region. [3]January 1. [4]Brussels Capital Region. [5]Detail does not add to total given because of rounding. [6]Former Brabant province divided on Jan. 1, 1995. [7]Includes Luxembourg. [8]Includes 375,000 unemployed. [9]Sabena airlines only. [10]1996–97. [11]Includes preschool teachers. [12]1991–92.

Internet resources for further information:
- **Belgian Federal Government On Line http://belgium.fgov.be**
- **National Bank of Belgium http://www.nbb.be/sg/En/homee2.htm**

Belize

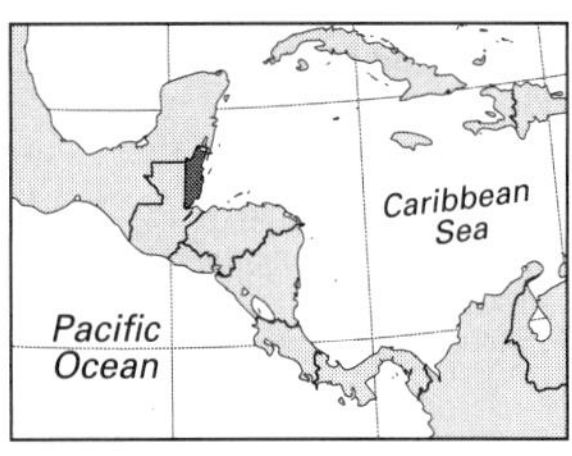

Official name: Belize.
Form of government: constitutional monarchy with two legislative houses (Senate [8[1]]; House of Representatives [29[2]]).
Chief of state: British Monarch represented by Governor-General.
Head of government: Prime Minister.
Capital: Belmopan.
Official language: English.
Official religion: none.
Monetary unit: 1 Belize dollar (BZ$) = 100 cents; valuation (Sept. 28, 2001) 1 U.S.$ = BZ$2.00[3]; 1 £ = BZ$2.94.

Area and population

		area		population
				2000
Districts	**Capitals**	sq mi	sq km	census
Belize	Belize City	1,663	4,307	68,197
Cayo	San Ignacio/Santa Elena	2,006	5,196	52,564
Corozal	Corozal	718	1,860	32,708
Orange Walk	Orange Walk	1,790	4,636	38,890
Stann Creek	Dangriga	986	2,554	24,548
Toledo	Punta Gorda	1,704	4,413	23,297
TOTAL		8,867[4]	22,965[4, 5]	240,204

Demography

Population (2001): 247,000.
Density (2001): persons per sq mi 27.9, persons per sq km 10.8.
Urban-rural (2000): urban 47.7%; rural 52.3%.
Sex distribution (2000): male 50.49%; female 49.51%.
Age breakdown (1998): under 15, 41.2%; 15–29, 26.5%; 30–44, 16.7%; 45–59, 8.8%; 60–74, 5.0%; 75 and over, 1.8%.
Population projection: (2010) 308,000; (2020) 392,000.
Doubling time: 26 years.
Ethnic composition (1991): mestizo (Spanish-Indian) 43.6%; Creole (predominantly black) 29.8%; Mayan Indian 11.0%; Garifuna (black-Carib Indian) 6.7%; white 3.9%; East Indian 3.5%; other or not stated 1.5%.
Religious affiliation (1991): Roman Catholic 57.7%; Protestant 34.3%, of which Anglican 7.0%, Pentecostal 6.3%, Methodist 4.2%, Seventh-day Adventist 4.1%, Mennonite 4.0%; other Christian 1.7%; nonreligious/other 6.3%.
Major cities (2000): Belize City 49,050; Orange Walk 13,483; San Ignacio/Santa Elena 13,260; Dangriga 8,814; Belmopan 8,130.

Vital statistics

Birth rate per 1,000 population (2000): 32.3 (world avg. 22.5); (1997) legitimate 40.3%; illegitimate 59.7%.
Death rate per 1,000 population (2000): 4.8 (world avg. 9.0).
Natural increase rate per 1,000 population (2000): 27.5 (world avg. 13.5).
Total fertility rate (avg. births per childbearing woman; 2000): 4.1.
Marriage rate per 1,000 population (1997): 6.6.
Divorce rate per 1,000 population (1997): 0.2.
Life expectancy at birth (2000): male 68.7 years; female 73.3 years.
Major causes of death per 100,000 population (1995): diseases of the circulatory system 119.8; accidents and violence 57.1; diseases of the respiratory system 47.8; malignant neoplasms 38.1; infectious and parasitic diseases 23.7.

National economy

Budget (1997). Revenue: BZ$324,600,000 (tax revenue 77.4%, of which import duties 25.7%, general sales taxes 23.6%; grants 12.7%; nontax revenue 9.2%). Expenditures: BZ$362,300,000 (education 20.5%; transportation and communication 16.7%; general admin. 11.4%; health 8.2%; defense 5.4%).
Production (metric tons except as noted). Agriculture, forestry, fishing (1998): sugarcane 1,208,000, oranges 170,000, bananas 81,000, grapefruits 41,000, corn (maize) 37,000, rice 17,000, red kidney beans 5,000, coconuts 3,000; livestock (number of live animals; 1999) 58,000 cattle, 23,000 pigs, 1,400,000 chickens; roundwood (1998) 187,600 cu m; fish catch (1998) 2,620, of which shrimp 1,682, conchs 253, lobsters 251, freshwater and marine fish 111. Mining and quarrying (1997): sand and gravel 350,000; limestone 310,000. Manufacturing (1996): sugar (1997) 123,800; molasses (1997) 51,800; flour 13,000; orange concentrate 113,000 hectolitres; beer 34,000 hectolitres; grapefruit concentrate 34,000 hectolitres; cigarettes 80,000,000 units; garments 2,100,000 units. Energy production (consumption): electricity (kW-hr; 1996) 152,000,000 (177,000,000); coal, none (none); crude petroleum, none (none); petroleum products (metric tons; 1996) none (116,000); natural gas, none (none).
Household income and expenditure. Average household size (2000) 4.5; average annual income of employed head of household (1993) BZ$6,450[6] (U.S.$3,225[6]); sources of income, n.a.; expenditure (1990): food, beverages, and tobacco 34.0%, transportation 13.7%, energy and water 9.1%, housing 9.0%, clothing and footwear 8.8%, household furnishings 8.0%.
Tourism (1999): receipts from visitors U.S.$112,000,000; expenditures by nationals abroad U.S.$24,000,000.
Land use (1994): forested 92.1%; meadows and pastures 2.2%; agricultural and under permanent cultivation 3.6%; other 2.1%.
Population economically active (1998[7]): total 85,595; activity rate of total population 36.2% (participation rates: ages 14–64, 64.1%; female 34.5%; unemployed 14.3%).

Price and earnings indexes (1995 = 100)

	1994	1995	1996	1997	1998	1999	2000
Consumer price index	97.2	100.0	106.4	107.5	106.6	105.3	105.9
Monthly earnings index[8]	96.3	100.0	102.5	98.8	…	…	…

Gross national product (1999): U.S.$673,000,000 (U.S.$2,730 per capita).

Structure of gross domestic product and labour force

	1998		1997[7]	
	in value BZ$'000[9]	% of total value[9]	labour force	% of labour force
Agriculture, fishing, forestry	213,600	20.1	21,140	26.1
Mining	6,200	0.6	95	0.1
Manufacturing	139,800	13.1	7,980	9.9
Construction	59,600	5.6	3,835	4.7
Public utilities	35,100	3.3	985	1.2
Transp. and commun.	109,400	10.3	3,655	4.5
Trade, restaurants	199,100	18.7	15,155	18.7
Finance, real estate, insurance	143,000	13.4	2,360	2.9
Pub. admin., defense	133,600	12.6	15,140	18.7
Services	68,100	6.4		
Other	–44,200[10]	–4.2[10]	10,595[11]	13.1[11]
TOTAL	1,063,300	100.0[5]	80,940	100.0[5]

Public debt (external, outstanding; 1999): U.S.$294,600,000.

Foreign trade[12]

Balance of trade (current prices)

	1995	1996	1997	1998	1999	2000
BZ$'000,000	–193.6	–175.7	–219.7	–257.4	–379.3	–480.0
% of total	23.0%	20.8%	23.8%	27.6%	33.9%	39.1%

Imports (1998): BZ$594,100,000 (machinery and transport equipment 25.6%; food and beverages 16.7%; mineral fuels and lubricants 11.1%; chemicals and chemical products 10.7%). *Major import sources:* U.S. 53.6%; Mexico 11.7%; U.K. 4.7%; Caricom 3.6%; other EU 5.3%.
Exports (1998): BZ$336,700,000 (domestic exports 90.9%, of which raw sugar 26.4%, bananas 14.6%, marine products 12.9%, citrus concentrate 12.8%, garments 11.7%; reexports 9.1%). *Major export destinations*[13]: U.S. 42.6%; U.K. 33.3%; Caricom 7.5%; other EU 11.9%.

Transport and communications

Transport. Railroads: none. Roads (1995): total length 1,398 mi, 2,250 km (paved 18%). Vehicles (1997): passenger cars 9,695; trucks and buses 11,698. Merchant marine (1992): vessels (100 gross tons and over) 32; total deadweight tonnage 45,706. Air transport (1998)[14]: passenger arrivals 199,475, passenger departures 193,620; cargo loaded 166 metric tons, cargo unloaded 1,082 metric tons. Airports (1997) with scheduled flights 9.

Communications

Medium	date	unit	number	units per 1,000 persons
Daily newspapers	1996	circulation	0	0
Radio	1997	receivers	133,000	571
Television	1998	receivers	42,000	183
Telephones	1999	main lines	36,632	156
Cellular telephones	1999	subscribers	6,193	26
Personal computers	1999	units	25,000	106
Internet	1999	users	12,000	51

Education and health

Educational attainment (1991). Percentage of population age 25 and over having: no formal schooling 13.0%; primary education 64.3%; secondary 14.9%; higher 6.6%; other 1.2%. *Literacy* (1991): total population age 14 and over literate 75,500 (70.3%).

Education (1997–98)

	schools	teachers	students	student/ teacher ratio
Primary (age 5–12)	247	2,015	53,118	26.4
Secondary (age 13–16)	30	726	11,260	15.5
Higher	12	228	2,753	12.1

Health (1998): physicians 155 (1 per 1,558 persons); hospital beds 554 (1 per 435 persons); infant mortality rate per 1,000 live births (2000) 26.0.
Food (1999): daily per capita caloric intake 2,889 (vegetable products 79%, animal products 21%); 128% of FAO recommended minimum requirement.

Military

Total active duty personnel (2000): 1,050 (army 100%).[15] *Military expenditure as percentage of GNP* (1998): 1.4% (world, n.a.); per capita expenditure U.S.$35.

[1]Excludes president of the Senate, who may be elected by the Senate from outside its appointed membership. [2]Excludes speaker of the House of Representatives, who may be elected by the House from outside its elected membership. [3]The Belize dollar is officially pegged to the U.S. dollar. [4]Includes offshore cays totaling 266 sq mi (689 sq km). [5]Detail does not add to total given because of rounding. [6]Estimated figure for about 33,000 employed heads of household. [7]Based on April survey. [8]In manufacturing, transportation, trade, and finance. [9]At factor cost. [10]Less imputed bank service charges. [11]Includes 335 not adequately defined and 10,260 unemployed. [12]Imports c.i.f.; exports f.o.b. [13]Domestic exports only. [14]Belize international airport only. [15]Foreign forces (2000): British army 180.

Internet resources for further information:
- **Government of Belize http://www.belize.gov.bz**

Benin

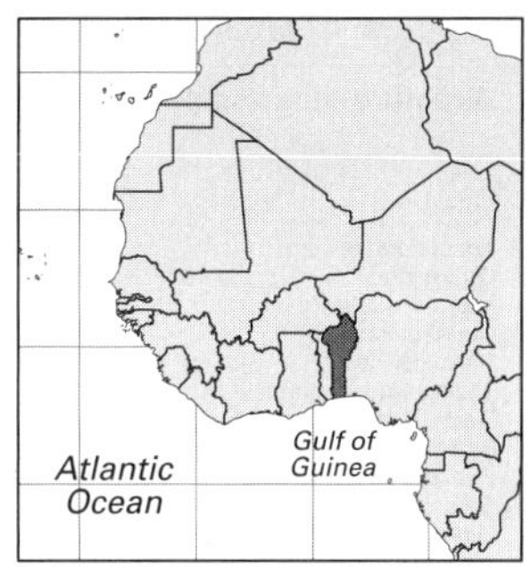

Official name: République du Bénin (Republic of Benin).
Form of government: multiparty republic with one legislative house (National Assembly [83]).
Head of state and government: President, assisted by Prime Minister[1].
Capital[2]: Porto-Novo.
Official language: French.
Official religion: none.
Monetary unit: 1 CFA franc (CFAF) = 100 centimes; valuation (Sept. 28, 2001) 1 U.S.$ = CFAF 720.28; 1 £ = CFAF 1,059.

Area and population		area[3]		population
				1992
Departments[4]	Capitals	sq mi	sq km	census
Alibori	...	10,150	26,310	...[5]
Atacora	Natitingou	7,600	19,700	649,308[6]
Atlantique	...	1,150	2,920	1,066,373[7]
Borgou	Parakou	9,650	25,060	827,925[5]
Collines	...	5,500	14,240	...[8]
Couffo	Aplahoue	1,000	2,620	...[9]
Donga	Djougou	4,550	11,820	...[6]
Littoral	Cotonou	150	350	...[7]
Mono	Lokossa	850	2,200	676,377[9]
Ouémé	Porto-Novo	550	1,450	876,574[10]
Plateau	Ketou	1,200	3,060	...[10]
Zou	Abomey	1,950	5,030	818,998[8]
TOTAL		44,300	114,760	4,915,555

Demography

Population (2001): 6,591,000.
Density (2001): persons per sq mi 148.8, persons per sq km 57.4.
Urban-rural (1999): urban 41.5%; rural 58.5%.
Sex distribution (2000): male 49.21%; female 50.79%.
Age breakdown (2000): under 15, 47.5%; 15–29, 27.7%; 30–44, 13.9%; 45–59, 7.1%; 60–74, 3.1%; 75 and over, 0.7%.
Population projection: (2010) 8,411,000; (2020) 10,588,000.
Doubling time: 30 years.
Ethnic composition (1992): Fon 39.7%; Yoruba (Nago) 12.1%; Adjara 11.1%; Bariba 8.6%; Aizo 8.6%; Somba (Otomary) 6.6%; Fulani 5.6%; other 7.7%.
Religious affiliation (1992): Christian 35.4%, of which Roman Catholic 25.9%, Protestant 9.5%; traditional beliefs, including voodoo 35.0%; Muslim 20.6%; other 9.0%.
Major cities (1994): Cotonou 750,000; Porto-Novo 200,000; Djougou 132,000; Abomey-Calavi 125,565[11]; Parakou 120,000.

Vital statistics

Birth rate per 1,000 population (2000): 44.8 (world avg. 22.5).
Death rate per 1,000 population (2000): 14.5 (world avg. 9.0).
Natural increase rate per 1,000 population (2000): 30.3 (world avg. 13.5).
Total fertility rate (avg. births per childbearing woman; 2000): 6.3.
Life expectancy at birth (2000): male 49.2 years; female 51.2 years.

National economy

Budget (1998). Revenue: CFAF 255,100,000,000 (tax revenue 71.5%; grants 17.3%; nonfiscal receipts 11.2%). Expenditures: CFAF 233,400,000,000 (current expenditures 64.5%, of which debt service 12.7%; development expenditure 34.3%).
Production (metric tons except as noted). Agriculture, forestry, fishing (1999): cassava 2,377,339, yams 1,770,973, corn (maize) 822,739, seed cotton 436,240, sorghum 153,782, tomatoes 149,427, oil palm fruit 135,000, peanuts (groundnuts) 121,263, dry beans 94,342, karité nuts (shea nuts) 15,000; livestock (number of live animals; 1999) 1,345,000 cattle, 1,087,000 goats, 634,000 sheep, 470,000 pigs, 29,000,000 chickens; roundwood (1998) 5,994,000 cu m; fish catch (1997) 43,771. Manufacturing (1998): cement 380,000[12]; cotton fibre 175,000; meat 70,000; wheat flour 12,500; palm oil 11,000. Energy production (consumption): electricity (kW-hr; 1996) 6,000,000 (269,432,000); coal, none (none); crude petroleum (barrels; 1996) 652,000 (negligible); petroleum products (metric tons; 1996) none (149,000); natural gas, none (none).
Public debt (external, outstanding; 1999): U.S.$1,472,000,000.
Gross national product (1999): U.S.$2,320,000,000 (U.S.$380 per capita).

Structure of gross domestic product and labour force	1997		1992	
	in value CFAF '000,000,000	% of total value	labour force[13]	% of labour force[13]
Agriculture	477.3	41.0	1,147,746	55.0
Mining	4.8	0.4	661	0.0
Manufacturing	102.4	8.8	160,406	7.7
Public utilities	10.0	0.9	1,176	0.1
Construction	54.6	4.7	51,655	2.5
Transp. and communications	88.2	7.6	52,837	2.5
Trade	222.6	19.1	432,501	20.7
Finance			3,106	0.1
Pub. admin., defense	86.5	7.4	164,544	7.9
Services	117.5	10.1		
Other	—	—	70,814	3.4
TOTAL	1,163.9	100.0	2,085,446	100.0[14]

Population economically active (1997): total 2,608,000; activity rate of total population 44.2% (participation rates: ages 15–64, 84.3%; female 48.3%; unemployed, n.a.).

Price and earnings indexes (1995 = 100)	1994	1995	1996	1997	1998	1999	2000
Consumer price index	87.4	100.0	104.9	108.6	114.8	115.2	120.0
Hourly earnings index	...	...	...	...	...	...	...

Household income and expenditure. Average household size (1992) 5.9; income per household (1983) U.S.$240; sources of income; self-employement 73.7%, wages and salaries 26.3%; expenditure: n.a.
Land use (1995): agricultural and under permanent cultivation 17.0%; other 83.0% (of which [1994] forested 30.7%, meadows and pastures 4.0%).
Tourism (1998): receipts from visitors U.S.$33,000,000; expenditures by nationals abroad U.S.$7,000,000.

Foreign trade[15]

Balance of trade (current prices)	1995	1996	1997	1998	1999	2000
CFAF '000,000,000	–162.6	0.0	0.0	–153.5	–163.1	–160.8
% of total	27.9%	—	—	23.9%	24.7%	23.1%

Imports (1997): CFAF 300,800,000,000 (cotton yarn and fabric 20.2%; machinery and transport equipment 16.2%; rice 7.4%; iron and steel 4.5%). *Major import sources* (1995): France 27.1%; United Kingdom 9.6%; China 9.3%; Thailand 9.1%; Hong Kong 8.8%; The Netherlands 5.6%; United States 4.8%; Germany 4.3%.
Exports (1997): CFAF 231,100,000,000 (cotton yarn 51.6%, reexport 38.5%, cotton seed 2.8%, crude petroleum 2.2%). *Major export destinations* (1997): Brazil 18.0%; Portugal 11.0%; Morocco 10.0%; India 6.5%; Libya 6.0%; Italy 4.5%; United States 4.5%.

Transport and communications

Transport. Railroads (1997): length 359 mi, 578 km; passenger-mi 75,683,000, passenger-km 121,800,000; short ton-mi cargo 193,495,000, metric ton-km cargo 311,400,000. Roads (1996): total length 4,217 mi, 6,787 km (paved 20.0%). Vehicles (1996): passenger cars 37,772; trucks and buses 8,058. Merchant marine (1992): vessels (100 gross tons and over) 12; total deadweight tonnage 210. Air transport (1998)[16]: passenger-mi 160,477,000, passenger-km 258,263,000; short ton-mi cargo 8,404,000, metric ton-km cargo 13,524,000; airports (1998) with scheduled flights 1.

Communications				units
				per 1,000
Medium	date	unit	number	persons
Daily newspapers	1996	circulation	12,000	2
Radio	1996	receivers	620,000	110
Television	1998	receivers	65,000	10.8
Telephones	1998	main lines	38,354	6.1
Cellular telephones	1998	subscribers	6,286	1.0
Internet	1999	users	10,000	1.6

Education and health

Educational attainment (1992). Percentage of population age 25 and over having: no formal schooling 78.5%; primary education 10.8%; some secondary 8.2%; secondary 1.2%; postsecondary 1.3%. *Literacy* (1995): total percentage of population age 15 and over literate 37.0%; males literate 48.7%; females literate 25.8%.

Education (1996–97)	schools	teachers	students	student/ teacher ratio
Primary	3,072	13,957	779,329	55.8
Secondary	145[17]	5,352	146,135	27.3
Voc., teacher tr.[17]	14	283	4,873	17.2
Higher	16[17]	962	14,085	14.6

Health: physicians (1993) 363 (1 per 14,216 persons); hospital beds (1993) 1,235 (1 per 4,182 persons); infant mortality rate (2000) 90.8.
Food (1999): daily per capita caloric intake 2,489 (vegetable products 96%, animal products 4%); 108% of FAO recommended minimum requirement.

Military

Total active duty personnel (2000): 4,750 (army 94.7%, navy 2.1%, air force 3.2%). *Military expenditure as percentage of GNP* (1997): 1.3% (world 2.6%); per capita expenditure U.S.$5.

[1]Office of Prime Minister vacant from May 1998. [2]Porto-Novo, the official capital established under the constitution, is the seat of the legislature, but the president and most government ministers reside in Cotonou. [3]Estimated figures. [4]Administrative structure announced in 1997. [5]Borgou includes Alibori. [6]Atacora includes Donga. [7]Atlantique includes Littoral. [8]Zou includes Collines. [9]Mono includes Couffo. [10]Ouémé includes Plateau. [11]1992. [12]1996. [13]Age 10 years and over. [14]Detail does not add to total given because of rounding. [15]Import figures are c.i.f. in balance of trade and f.o.b. in commodities and trading partners. [16]Represents 1/11 of the traffic of Air Afrique, which is operated by 11 West African states. [17]1993–94.

Internet resources for further information:
- **Découvrez la République du Bénin http://planben.intnet.bj**

Bermuda

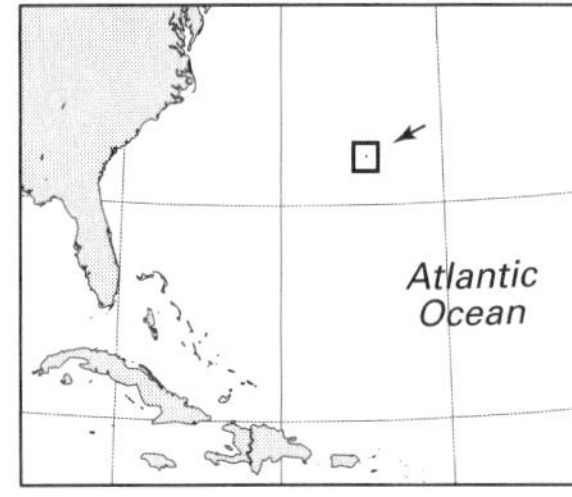

Official name: Bermuda.
Political status: colony (United Kingdom) with two legislative houses (Senate [11]; House of Assembly [40]).
Chief of state: British Monarch, represented by Governor.
Head of government: Premier.
Capital: Hamilton.
Official language: English.
Official religion: none.
Monetary unit: 1 Bermuda dollar (Bd$) = 100 cents; valuation (Sept. 28, 2001) 1 U.S.$ = Bd$1.00[1]; 1 £ = Bd$1.47.

Area and population	area		population
			1991
Municipalities	sq mi	sq km	census
Hamilton	0.3	0.8	1,100
St. George	0.5	1.3	1,648
Parishes			
Devonshire	2.0	5.1	7,371
Hamilton	2.0	5.1	4,680
Paget	2.1	5.3	4,877
Pembroke[2]	1.8	4.6	10,407
St. George's[3, 4]	3.5	8.0	2,975
Sandys	2.1	5.4	6,437
Smith's	1.8	4.7	5,261
Southampton	2.2	5.6	5,804
Warwick	2.0	5.1	7,900
TOTAL	20.5[5, 6]	53.1[5, 6]	58,460[7]

Demography

Population (2001): 63,500.
Density (2001): persons per sq mi 3,098, persons per sq km 1,196.
Urban-rural (2000): urban 100.0%; rural, none.
Sex distribution (1999): male 48.57%; female 51.43%.
Age breakdown (1999): under 15, 19.8%; 15–29, 18.3%; 30–44, 27.5%; 45–59, 19.4%; 60–74, 11.2%; 75 and over, 3.8%.
Population projection: (2010) 67,000; (2020) 69,000.
Ethnic composition (1991): black 57.8%; white 36.2%; other 6.0%.
Religious affiliation (2000): Protestant 67.2%, of which Anglican 37.2%; Roman Catholic 16.0%; unaffiliated Christian 7.0%; nonreligious 4.0%; other 5.8%.
Major cities (1991): St. George 1,648; Hamilton 1,100.

Vital statistics

Birth rate per 1,000 population (1999): 13.2 (world avg. 22.5); legitimate 61.7%; illegitimate 38.3%.
Death rate per 1,000 population (1999): 7.1 (world avg. 9.0).
Natural increase rate per 1,000 population (1999): 6.1 (world avg. 13.5).
Total fertility rate (avg. births per childbearing woman; 2000): 1.8.
Marriage rate per 1,000 population (1999): 17.5.
Divorce rate per 1,000 population (1996): 3.7.
Life expectancy at birth (2000): male 74.9 years; female 78.9 years.
Major causes of death per 100,000 population (1993): diseases of the circulatory system 318.6; malignant neoplasms (cancers) 212.4; infectious and parasitic diseases 61.4; accidents and violence 39.8.

National economy

Budget (1999). Revenue: Bd$562,200,000 (customs duty 31.3%; payroll tax 27.0%; fees, sales, recoveries, and other miscellaneous receipts 15.0%; tax on international companies 6.3%). Expenditures: Bd$545,700,000 (current expenditure 91.4%, of which public debt 2.3%; development expenditure 8.6%).
Public debt (external, outstanding; 1998): n.a.
Production (value in Bd$'000 except as noted). Agriculture, forestry, fishing (1996): vegetables 3,000, milk 2,060, fruits 800, eggs 450, honey 181; livestock (number of live animals; 1999) 900 horses, 600 cattle, 45,000 chickens; roundwood, n.a.; fish catch (metric tons; 1998) 457, of which crustaceans and mollusks 38. Mining and quarrying: crushed stone for local use. Manufacturing: industries include pharmaceuticals, cosmetics, electronics, fish processing, handicrafts, and small boat building[8]. Construction (2000): residential 35,600; nonresidential 111,000. Energy production (consumption): electricity (kW-hr; 1996) 525,000,000 (525,000,000); coal, none (none); crude petroleum, none (none); petroleum products (metric tons; 1996) none (151,000); natural gas, none (none).
Land use (1988): forested 20.0%; meadows and pastures 0.9%; agricultural and under permanent cultivation 3.1%; built-on, wasteland, and other 76.0%.
Tourism: receipts from visitors (1998) U.S.$487,000,000; expenditures by nationals abroad (1997) U.S.$148,000,000.
Population economically active (1991): total 35,222; activity rate of total population 60.2%[7] (participation rates: ages 15–64, 80.9%[7]; female 47.1%[7]; unemployed [1995] 1.5%).

Price and earnings indexes (1995 = 100)	1994	1995	1996	1997	1998	1999	2000
Consumer price index	97.5	100.0	102.5	104.6	106.7	109.3	112.3
Weekly earnings index[9]	97.1	100.0	103.0	...	...	...	...

Gross national product (1997): U.S.$2,128,000,000 (U.S.$34,470 per capita).

Structure of gross domestic product and labour force	1995–96		1997[10]	
	in value U.S.$'000	% of total value	labour force[11]	% of labour force
Agriculture, fishing	...	...	400	1.1
Quarrying	...	...	106	0.3
Manufacturing	...	...	889	2.5
Construction	...	...	2,043	5.8
Public utilities	...	...	522	1.5
Transp. and commun.	...	...	2,220	6.3
Trade, restaurants	...	...	10,914	30.9
Finance, real estate	...	...	5,240	14.8
Pub. admin., defense	...	...	4,608	13.1
Services	...	...	5,687	16.1
Other[12]	...	...	2,667	7.6
TOTAL	2,024,000	100.0	35,296	100.0

Household income and expenditure (1993). Average household size 2.5; average annual income per household Bd$65,676 (U.S.$65,676); sources of income: wages and salaries 65.3%, imputed income from owner occupancy 10.6%, self-employment 9.0%, net rental income 4.8%, pensions 3.3%, interest 3.3%, dividends 2.1%, other 1.7%; expenditure: housing 27.7%, household furnishings 16.6%, food and nonalcoholic beverages 14.6%, health care 7.6%, transportation 7.3%, foreign travel 6.0%, clothing and footwear 4.9%, recreation 4.8%, education 3.8%, energy 3.3%, alcohol and tobacco 2.2%, other 1.2%.

Foreign trade

Balance of trade (current prices)	1993	1994	1995	1996	1997	1998
Bd$'000,000	–495	–514	–496	–514	–554	–564
% of total	86.4%	87.4%	82.1%	82.4%	81.0%	80.3%

Imports (1999): Bd$720,000,000 (machinery 20.4%; food, beverages, and tobacco 18.7%; chemicals and chemical products 9.4%; transport equipment 9.0%; clothing 5.3%). *Major import sources:* United States 74.1%; Canada 6.6%; United Kingdom 4.6%.
Exports (1993): Bd$35,272,000 (reexports 99.99%, of which drugs and medicine 71.12%; Bermuda-originated exports 0.01%). *Major export destinations* (1995): United States 49.8%; United Kingdom 6.2%; nonspecified 44.0%.

Transport and communications

Transport. Railroads: none. Roads (1997): total length 140 mi, 225 km (paved 100%)[13]. Vehicles (1996): passenger cars 21,220; trucks and buses 4,007. Merchant marine (1990): vessels (100 gross tons and over) 105; total deadweight tonnage 7,800,242. Air transport (1996): passenger arrivals 519,772, passenger departures 516,759; cargo unloaded 5,909 metric tons, cargo loaded 727 metric tons; airports (1998) with scheduled flights 1.

Communications				units
Medium	date	unit	number	per 1,000 persons
Daily newspapers	1996	circulation	17,000	277
Radio	1997	receivers	82,000	1,328
Television	1997	receivers	66,000	1,069
Telephones	1999	main lines	54,933	879
Cellular telephones	1998	subscribers	12,572	202

Education and health

Educational attainment (1991). Percentage of total population age 25 and over having: no formal schooling 0.5%; incomplete or complete primary 18.2%; incomplete or complete secondary 62.9%; higher 18.4%. *Literacy* (1997): total population age 15 and over literate, 98%.

Education (1996–97)	schools	teachers	students	student/ teacher ratio
Primary (age 5–11)	26	478	5,883	12.3
Secondary (age 12–16)	...	355	3,726	10.5
Higher	1	...	543	...

Health (1996): physicians 96 (1 per 639 persons); hospital beds 251[14] (1 per 244 persons); infant mortality rate per 1,000 live births (1997–99 avg.) 3.2.
Food (1999): daily per capita caloric intake 2,883 (vegetable products 73%, animal products 27%); 114% of FAO recommended minimum requirement.

Military

Total active duty personnel (1997): 700; part-time defense force assists police and is drawn from Bermudian conscripts.

[1]The Bermuda dollar is at par with the U.S. dollar. [2]Excludes the area and population of the city of Hamilton. [3]Excludes the area and population of the town of St. George. [4]Includes the 2.0 sq mi (5.2 sq km) area of the former U.S. military base closed in 1995. [5]Includes 0.4 sq mi (1.1 sq km) of uninhabited islands. [6]Detail (including areas cited in footnote 5) does not add to total given because of rounding. [7]Excludes 12,624 short-term visitors, 2,889 on-base military personnel, and 864 institutionalized persons. [8]The economy of Bermuda is overwhelmingly based on service industries such as tourism, insurance companies, offshore financial centres, e-commerce companies, and ship repair facilities. [9]Service industry. [10]August. [11]Employed only; excludes family workers. [12]Extra-territorial organizations and bodies. [13]Excludes 138 mi (222 km) of paved private roads. [14]Excludes beds in geriatric, rehabilitation, and hospice units.

Internet resources for further information:

- **Bermuda Online: Economy http://bermuda-online.org/economy.htm**

Bhutan

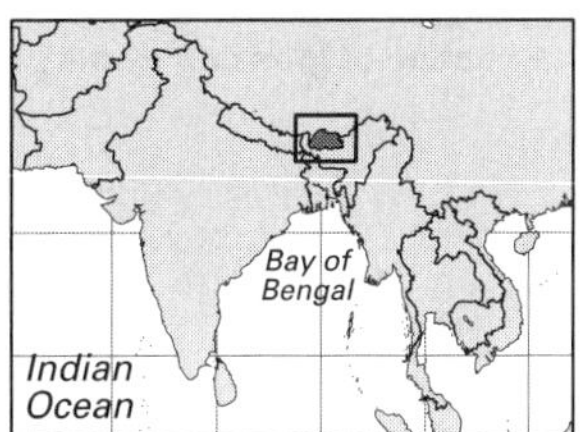

Official name: Druk-Yul (Kingdom of Bhutan).
Form of government: constitutional[1] monarchy with one legislative house (National Assembly [150[2]]).
Chief of state: Monarch[1].
Head of government: Chairman of Council of Ministers[1].
Capital: Thimphu.
Official language: Dzongkha (a Tibetan dialect).
Official religion: Mahāyāna Buddhism.
Monetary unit: 1 ngultrum[3] (Nu) = 100 chetrum; valuation (Sept. 28, 2001) 1 U.S.$ = Nu 47.85; 1 £ = Nu 70.32.

Area and population

		area		population
Districts	**Capitals**	sq mi	sq km	1998 estimate
Bumthang	Jakar	1,150	2,990	...
Chirang	Damphu	310	800	...
Dagana	Dagana	540	1,400	...
Gaylegphug	Gaylegphug	1,020	2,640	...
Ha	Ha	830	2,140	...
Lhuntshi	Lhuntshi	1,120	2,910	...
Mongar	Mongar	710	1,830	...
Paro	Paro	580	1,500	...
Pema Gatsel	Pema Gatsel	150	380	...
Punakha	Punakha	2,330	6,040	...
Samchi	Samchi	830	2,140	...
Samdrup Jongkhar	Samdrup Jongkhar	900	2,340	...
Shemgang	Shemgang	980	2,540	...
Tashigang	Tashigang	1,640	4,260	...
Thimphu	Thimphu	630	1,620	...
Tongsa	Tongsa	570	1,470	...
Wangdi Phodrang	Wangdi Phodrang	1,160	3,000	...
TOTAL		18,150[4, 5]	47,000[4, 5]	633,000[6]

Demography

Population (2001): 692,000[6].
Density (2001): persons per sq mi 38.1, persons per sq km 14.7.
Urban-rural (1999): urban 7.0%; rural 93.0%.
Sex distribution (1988): male 50.97%; female 49.03%.
Age breakdown (1988): under 15, 40.3%; 15–29, 26.4%; 30–44, 16.5%; 45–59, 10.5%; 60–74, 5.2%; 75 and over, 1.1%.
Population projection: (2010) 837,000; (2020) 1,018,000.
Doubling time: 27 years.
Ethnic composition (1993): Bhutiā (Ngalops) 50.0%; Nepalese (Gurung) 35.0%; Sharchops 15.0%.
Religious affiliation (2000): Buddhist 74.0%; Hindu 20.5%; other 5.5%.
Major cities (1997 est.): Thimphu 45,000; Phuntsholing 45,000.

Vital statistics

Birth rate per 1,000 population (2001): 35.2 (world avg. 22.5).
Death rate per 1,000 population (2001): 9.0 (world avg. 9.0).
Natural increase rate per 1,000 population (2001): 26.2 (world avg. 13.5).
Total fertility rate (avg. births per childbearing woman; 2001): 5.2.
Marital status of population 15 years and over (1985): married 71.2%; single 19.7%; widowed 7.5%; divorced 1.6%.
Divorce rate per 1,000 population: n.a.
Life expectancy at birth (1999): male 61.0 years; female 64.0 years.
Major causes of death (percentage distribution; 1989): respiratory tract infections 19.5%; diarrhea/dysentery 15.2%; skin infections 12.2%; parasitic worm infestations 10.0%; malaria 9.4%.

National economy

Budget (1998–99). Revenue: Nu 6,844,000,000 (internal revenue 45.2%, grants from government of India 33.2%, grants from UN and other international agencies 21.6%). Expenditures: Nu 6,999,000,000 (capital expenditures 59.3%, current expenditures 40.7%).
Public debt (external, outstanding; 1999): U.S.$181,800,000.
Production (metric tons except as noted). Agriculture, forestry, fishing (1999): oranges 58,000, rice 50,000, corn (maize) 39,000, potatoes 34,100, sugarcane 12,800, green peppers and chilies 8,500, millet 7,000, apples 5,500, wheat 5,000, barley 4,000, pulses 1,600; livestock (number of live animals) 435,000 cattle, 74,900 pigs, 58,500 sheep, 42,100 goats, 29,900 horses; roundwood (1998) 1,702,000 cu m; fish catch (1997) 330. Mining and quarrying (1997): limestone 270,000; dolomite 250,000; gypsum 50,000. Manufacturing (value in Nu '000,000; 1994): chemical products 419.0; cement 255.1; wood board products 230.6; distillery products 178.3; processed fruits 103.0. Construction (number of buildings completed; 1977–78): residential 10; nonresidential (guest house) 1. Energy production (consumption): electricity (kW-hr; 1996) 1,737,000,000 (261,000,000); coal (metric tons; 1996) 2,000 (23,000); crude petroleum, none (n.a.); petroleum products (metric tons; 1996) none (39,000); natural gas, none (n.a.).
Household income and expenditure. Average household size (1980) 5.4[6]; income per household: n.a.; sources of income: n.a.; expenditure (1979): food 72.3%, clothing 21.2%, energy 3.7%, household durable goods 0.7%, personal effects and other 2.1%.
Tourism (1999): receipts from visitors U.S.$9,000,000; expenditures by nationals abroad, n.a.
Gross national product (at current market prices; 1999): U.S.$399,000,000 (U.S.$510 per capita).

Structure of gross domestic product and labour force

	1997		1984	
	in value Nu '000,000	% of total value	labour force	% of labour force
Agriculture	5,288	38.4	303,000[7]	87.2
Mining	310	2.2	3,000[7]	0.9
Manufacturing	1,742	12.7		
Construction	1,206	8.8		
Trade	1,014	7.4		
Public utilities	1,732	12.6		
Transportation and communications	1,018	7.4		
Finance	495	3.6		
Pub. admin., defense	1,363	9.9	12,000[7]	3.4
Services			30,000[7]	8.5[8]
Other	–417[9]	–3.0[9]	...	...
TOTAL	13,751	100.0	348,000	100.0

Population economically active (1984)[6]: total 348,000; activity rate of total population 53.4% (participation rates: ages 15–64, 94.8%; female 55.0%; unemployed 6.5%).

Price and earnings indexes (1995 = 100)

	1992	1993	1994	1995	1996	1997	1998
Consumer price index	76.8	85.4	91.3	100.0	108.8	115.9	126.5
Earnings index	...	...	...	...	...	...	...

Land use (1994): forested 66.0%; meadows and pastures 5.8%; agricultural and under permanent cultivation 2.8%; other 25.4%.

Foreign trade[10]

Balance of trade (current prices)

	1993	1994	1995	1996	1997	1998
Nu '000,000	–754.9	–793.7	–292.8	–971.4	–703.9	–952.2
% of total	15.9%	16.0%	4.2%	12.0%	7.6%	10.0%

Imports (1997): Nu 4,978,000,000 ([11]petroleum products 4.6%, rice 4.6%, vegetable fats and oils 3.0%, steel products 2.4%, wheat 2.0%, industrial machinery 1.7%). *Major import source* (1997–98): India 70.5%.
Exports (1997): Nu 4,274,100,000 ([11]electricity 21.0%, calcium carbide 15.0%, particle board 8.0%, cement 7.1%). *Major export destination* (1997–98): India 94.5%.

Transport and communications

Transport. Railroads: none. Roads (1996): total length 1,998 mi, 3,285 km (paved 61%). Vehicles (1988): passenger cars 2,590; trucks and buses 1,367. Merchant marine: none. Air transport (1996): passenger-mi 29,000,000, passenger-km 46,000,000; metric ton-km cargo, n.a.; airports (1997) with scheduled flights 1.

Communications

Medium	date	unit	number	units per 1,000 persons
Radio	1997	receivers	37,000	19
Television	1999	receivers	13,000	20
Telephones	1999	main lines	11,800	18
Personal computers	1999	units	3,000	4.6
Internet	1999	users	500	0.8

Education and health

Educational attainment: n.a. *Literacy* (1995 est.): total population age 15 and over literate 42.2%; males literate 56.2%; females literate 28.1%

Education (1994)

	schools	teachers	students	student/teacher ratio
Primary (age 7–11)	235[12]	1,611	60,089	37.3
Secondary (age 12–16)	31[13]	544	7,299	13.4
Voc., teacher tr.	8[13]	95	1,822[13]	12.2[13]
Higher	2[13]	57[13]	2,055	9.1[13]

Health: physicians (1994) 100 (1 per 8,000 persons); hospital beds 970 (1 per 825 persons); infant mortality rate per 1,000 live births (2001) 56.0.
Food (1975–77): daily per capita caloric intake 2,058 (vegetable products 98%, animal products 2%); 89% of FAO recommended minimum requirement.

Military

Total active duty personnel (1993): about 7,000 (army 100%).

[1]There is no formal constitution, but a form of constitutional monarchy is in place; reforms in July 1998 curtailed the powers of the monarchy and increased the powers of the Council of Ministers. [2]Includes 45 nonelective seats occupied by representatives of the King and religious groups. [3]Indian currency is also accepted legal tender; the ngultrum is at par with the Indian rupee. [4]2,700 sq mi (7,000 sq km) are not included in the estimated district area totals. [5]Three districts are not listed: Chhukha, created in 1987 from Samchi, Paro, and Thimphu districts; Gasa, created in 1992 from Punakha; and Tashi Yangtse, created in 1992 from Tashigang. [6]Excludes nearly 100,000 Bhutanese of Nepalese origin declared stateless by the Bhutanese government in late 1990. [7]Derived value. [8]Includes 6.5% with no occupation. [9]Imputed bank service charges. [10]Import figures are c.i.f. in balance of trade, commodities, and trading partners. [11]1996. [12]1993. [13]1990.

Internet resources for further information:
- **The Library of Congress Country Studies: Bhutan http://lcweb2.loc.gov/frd/cs/bttoc.html**

Bolivia

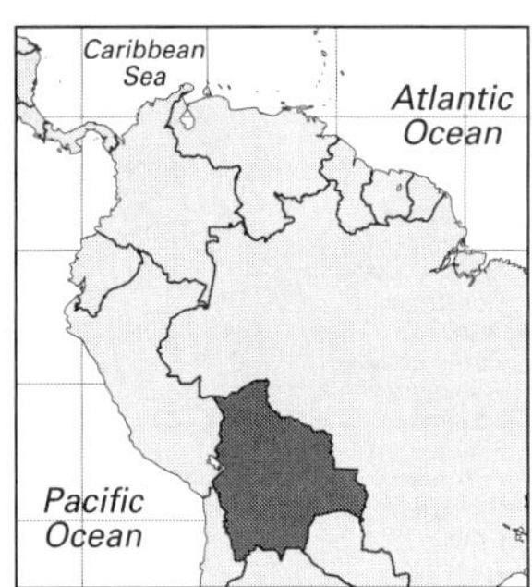

Official name: República de Bolivia (Republic of Bolivia).
Form of government: unitary multiparty republic with two legislative houses (Chamber of Senators [27]; Chamber of Deputies [130]).
Head of state and government: President.
Capitals: La Paz (administrative); Sucre (judicial).
Official languages: Spanish, Aymara, Quechua.
Official religion: Roman Catholicism.
Monetary unit: 1 boliviano (Bs) = 100 centavos; valuation (Sept. 28, 2001) 1 U.S.$ = Bs 6.74; 1 £ = Bs 9.91.

Area and population

Departments	Capitals	area sq mi	area sq km	population 2000[1, 2] estimate
Beni	Trinidad	82,458	213,564	366,047
Chuquisaca	Sucre	19,893	51,524	589,948
Cochabamba	Cochabamba	21,479	55,631	1,524,724
La Paz	La Paz	51,732	133,985	2,406,377
Oruro	Oruro	20,690	53,588	393,991
Pando	Cobija	24,644	63,827	57,316
Potosí	Potosí	45,644	118,218	774,696
Santa Cruz	Santa Cruz	143,098	370,621	1,812,522
Tarija	Tarija	14,526	37,623	403,079
TOTAL		424,164	1,098,581	8,328,700

Demography

Population (2001): 8,516,000.
Density (2001): persons per sq mi 20.1, persons per sq km 7.8.
Urban-rural (2000): urban 63.7%; rural 36.3%.
Sex distribution (2000): male 49.99%; female 50.01%.
Age breakdown (2000): under 15, 39.1%; 15–29, 28.1%; 30–44, 16.6%; 45–59, 9.9%; 60–74, 4.5%; 75 and over, 1.8%.
Population projection: (2010) 10,229,000; (2020) 12,193,000.
Doubling time: 34 years.
Ethnic composition (1996): Indian 55.0%; mestizo 30.0%; white 15.0%.
Religious affiliation (1995): Roman Catholic 88.5%; Protestant 9.0%; other 2.5%.
Major cities (2000)[2]: Santa Cruz 1,016,137; La Paz 1,000,899; Cochabamba 607,129; El Alto 568,919; Oruro 232,311; Sucre 192,238.

Vital statistics

Birth rate per 1,000 population (2000): 31.9 (world avg. 22.5).
Death rate per 1,000 population (2000): 8.6 (world avg. 9.0).
Natural increase rate per 1,000 population (2000): 23.3 (world avg. 13.5).
Total fertility rate (avg. births per childbearing woman; 2000): 3.7.
Marriage rate per 1,000 population: n.a.
Life expectancy at birth (2000): male 61.2 years; female 66.3 years.
Major causes of death (percentage of total registered deaths; 1980–81): infectious and parasitic diseases 23.9%; diseases of the circulatory system 19.5%; diseases of the respiratory system 14.0%; accidents, homicides, and violence 9.8%; diseases of the digestive system 8.6%.

National economy

Budget (1998). Revenue: Bs 11,698,500,000 (tax revenue 78.9%, of which indirect taxes 49.0%, taxes on petroleum and petroleum products 18.8%; nontax revenue 8.9%). Expenditures: Bs 13,681,300,000 (current expenditure 78.8%, of which wages and salaries 31.3%, transfers 21.9%; capital expenditure 21.2%).
Production (metric tons except as noted). Agriculture, forestry, fishing (1999): sugarcane 4,160,000, soybeans 762,000, potatoes 783,000, bananas and plantains 767,000, corn (maize) 613,000, cassava 400,000, rice 189,000, sorghum 148,000, wheat 140,000; livestock (number of live animals) 8,575,000 sheep, 6,556,000 cattle, 2,715,000 pigs, 1,500,000 goats, 631,000 asses, 322,000 horses; roundwood (1998) 1,989,000 cu m; fish catch (1998) 6,055. Mining and quarrying (metric tons of pure metal; 1998): zinc 150,709; lead 13,848; tin 10,542; silver 402; gold 14.4. Manufacturing (value added in U.S.$'000; 1994): petroleum products 375; food products 169; beverages 99; nonmetal mineral products 36; textiles 23; printing and publishing 19; nonferrous metals 18. Construction (1985)[3]: residential dwellings 226. Energy production (consumption): electricity (kW-hr; 1998) 3,771,000,000 (3,252,000,000); coal, none (none); crude petroleum (barrels; 1998) 12,628,000 (10,382,000); petroleum products (metric tons; 1996) 1,325,000 (1,480,000); natural gas (cu m; 1998) 3,106,000,000 (1,511,000,000).
Population economically active (1997): total 3,645,165; activity rate of total population 46.6% (participation rates: ages 15–64, 72.1%; female 43.7%; unemployed 2.1%).

Price and earnings indexes (1995 = 100)

	1995	1996	1997	1998	1999	2000
Consumer price index	100.0	112.4	117.7	126.8	129.5	135.5
Monthly earnings index[4]	100.0	108.8	117.1	146.3	161.0	173.2

Tourism (1999): receipts U.S.$179,000,000; expenditures U.S.$165,000,000.
Gross national product (at current market prices; 1999): U.S.$8,092,000,000 (U.S.$990 per capita).

Structure of gross domestic product and labour force

	1999 in value Bs '000[5]	1999 % of total value[5]	1997 labour force[6]	1997 % of labour force[6]
Agriculture	3,105,038	14.1	1,541,859	42.3
Mining	1,998,841	9.1	63,871	1.7
Manufacturing	3,649,645	16.6	393,451	10.8
Construction	824,155	3.7	187,015	5.1
Public utilities	452,631	2.1	11,029	0.3
Transp. and commun.	2,383,850	10.9	170,531	4.7
Trade	1,866,818	8.5	632,415	17.3
Finance	2,235,150	10.2	78,842	2.2
Pub. admin., defense	1,954,104	8.9	490,728	13.5
Services	1,658,209	7.6		
Other	1,820,911[7]	8.3[7]	75,424[8]	2.1[8]
TOTAL	21,949,352	100.0	3,645,165	100.0

Public debt (external, outstanding; 1999): U.S.$3,864,000,000.
Household income and expenditure. Average household size (1997): 4.4; average annual income per household: n.a.; sources of income: n.a.; expenditure (1988): food 35.5%, transportation and communications 17.7%, housing 14.8%, household durable goods 7.3%, clothing and footwear 5.1%, beverages and tobacco 4.5%, recreation 2.7%, health 2.1%, education 0.3%.
Land use (1994): forested 53.5%; meadows and pastures 24.4%; agricultural and under permanent cultivation 2.2%; other 19.9%.

Foreign trade[9]

Balance of trade (current prices)

	1995	1996	1997	1998	1999
U.S.$'000,000	–162.5	–313.4	–531.6	–721.0	–487.9
% of total	6.9%	12.1%	18.6%	24.6%	18.8%

Imports (1998): U.S.$1,983,000,000 (raw materials 42.2%, of which raw materials for industry 32.8%; capital goods 40.0%, of which transportation equipment 23.1%, capital goods for industry 15.9%; consumer goods 18.2%, of which nondurable consumer goods 9.3%, durable consumer goods 8.9%; other 0.4%). *Major import sources:* U.S. 26.3%; Japan 20.0%; Brazil 10.3%; Argentina 10.0%; Chile 6.0%; Peru 3.7%; France 1.1%.
Exports (1998): U.S.$1,104,900,000 (zinc 14.1%; soybeans 13.6%; gold 10.1%; silver 6.6%; oils 5.8%; natural gas 5.1%; tin 5.1%; timber 4.6%). *Major export destinations:* U.S. 18.4%; U.K. 17.8%; Peru 11.9%; Argentina 10.9%; Chile 2.9%; Brazil 2.4%; Germany 1.9%.

Transport and communications

Transport. Railroads (1997): route length 2,187 mi, 3,519 km; passenger-mi 84,900,000, passenger-km 136,700,000; short ton-mi cargo 358,900,000, metric ton-km cargo 524,200,000. Roads (1996): total length 30,696 mi, 49,400 km (paved 6%[10]). Vehicles (1996): passenger cars 223,829; trucks and buses 138,536. Merchant marine (1992): vessels (100 gross tons and over) 1; total deadweight tonnage 15,765. Air transport (1998)[11]: passenger-mi 1,222,606,000, passenger-km 1,967,597,000; short ton-mi cargo 28,743,000, metric ton-km cargo 41,964,000; airports (1997) with scheduled flights 14.

Communications

Medium	date	unit	number	units per 1,000 persons
Daily newspapers	1996	circulation	420,000	55
Radio	1997	receivers	5,250,000	675
Television	1999	receivers	960,000	118
Telephones	1999	main lines	502,000	62
Cellular telephones	1999	subscribers	420,344	52
Personal computers	1999	units	100,000	12.3
Internet	1999	users	78,000	9.6

Education and health

Educational attainment (1992). Percentage of population age 25 and over having: no formal schooling 23.3%; some primary 20.3%; primary education 21.7%; some secondary 9.0%; secondary 6.5%; some higher 5.0%; higher 4.8%; not specified 9.4%. *Literacy* (1995): total population age 15 and over literate 82.3%; males literate 92.1%; females literate 79.4%.

Education (1997)

	schools	teachers	students	student/ teacher ratio
Primary (age 6–13)	9,758[12]	61,451	1,430,020	23.3
Secondary (age 14–17)	724[12]	15,178	272,584	18.0
Voc., teacher tr.	47[12]			
Higher	10[13]	4,261[13]	160,917	25.7[13]

Health (1996): physicians 4,346 (1 per 1,747 persons); hospital beds (1998) 11,548 (1 per 689 persons); infant mortality rate (2000) 60.4.
Food (1999): daily per capita caloric intake 2,237 (vegetable products 82%, animal products 18%); 94% of FAO recommended minimum requirement.

Military

Total active duty personnel (2000): 32,500 (army 76.9%, navy 13.8%, air force 9.2%). *Military expenditure as percentage of GNP* (1997): 1.9% (world 2.6%); per capita expenditure U.S.$20.

[1]January 1. [2]Projections based on 1992 census. [3]National government sponsored only. [4]December. [5]In 1990 prices. [6]Population 10 years of age and over. [7]Net import duties. [8]Unemployed. [9]Import figures are f.o.b. in balance of trade and c.i.f. for commodities and trading partners. [10]1995. [11]LAB airlines only. [12]1986–87. [13]1991–92.

Internet resources for further information:
- **Instituto Nacional de Estadística http://www.ine.gov.bo**
- **UNDP Bolivia http://guf.pnud.bo/bolbrief.htm**

Bosnia and Herzegovina[1]

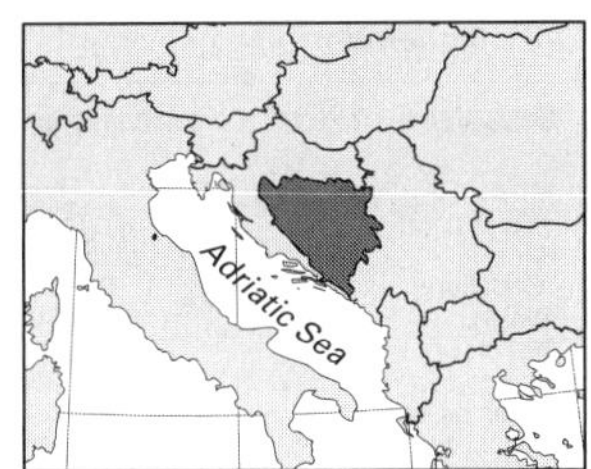

Official name: Bosna i Hercegovina (Bosnia and Herzegovina).
Form of government: federal multiparty republic with bicameral legislature (House of Peoples [15[2]]; House of Representatives [42]).
Chiefs of state: Tripartite presidency.
Head of government: Prime Minister (Chairman of the Council of Ministers).
Capital: Sarajevo.
Official language: Bosnian.
Official religion: none.
Monetary unit: 1 marka[3, 4] (KM) = 100 pfenning; valuation (Sept. 28, 2001) 1 U.S.$ = KM 2.15; 1 £ = KM 3.16.

Area and population

Autonomous regions / Cantons	Principal cities	area sq mi	area sq km	population 1991 estimate[5]
Federation of Bosnia and Herzegovina	Sarajevo	10,068	26,076	2,742,000
Central Bosnia	Travnik	1,240[6]	3,200[6]	305,000
Goražde	Goražde	170[6]	440[6]	78,000
Neretva	Mostar	1,680[6]	4,360[6]	253,000
Posavina	Orašje	90[6]	240[6]	61,000
Sarajevo	Sarajevo	460[6]	1,190[6]	526,000
Tuzla-Podrinje	Tuzla	1,120[6]	2,890[6]	555,000
Una-Sava	Bihać	1,690[6]	4,390[6]	358,000
Western Bosnia	Livno	1,910[6]	4,930[6]	117,000
Western Herzegovina	Ljubuški	450[6]	1,160[6]	60,000
Zenica-Doboj	Zenica	1,270[6]	3,300[6]	429,000
Republika Srpska	Banja Luka	9,673	25,053	1,628,000
TOTAL		19,741	51,129	4,370,000

Demography

Population (2001)[7]: 3,922,000.
Density (2001)[7]: persons per sq mi 198.7, persons per sq km 76.7.
Urban-rural (1999): urban 42.5%; rural 57.5%.
Sex distribution (2000): male 50.66%; female 49.34%.
Age breakdown (2000): under 15, 20.4%; 15–29, 22.3%; 30–44, 26.2%; 45–59, 17.2%; 60–74, 11.9%; 75 and over, 2.0%.
Population projection: (2010) 4,103,000; (2020) 4,182,000.
Ethnic composition (1999): Bosniac 44.0%; Serb 31.0%; Croat 17.0%; other 8.0%.
Religious affiliation (1999): Sunnī Muslim 43.0%; Serbian Orthodox 30.0%; Roman Catholic 18.0%; other (mostly nonreligious) 9.0%.
Major cities (1991): Sarajevo (1997) 360,000; Banja Luka (1997) 160,000; Zenica 96,027; Tuzla 83,770; Mostar 75,865.

Vital statistics

Birth rate per 1,000 population (2000): 12.9 (world avg. 22.5); (1993) legitimate 92.6%; illegitimate 7.4%.
Death rate per 1,000 population (2000): 7.9 (world avg. 9.0).
Natural increase rate per 1,000 population (2000): 5.0 (world avg. 13.5).
Total fertility rate (avg. births per childbearing woman; 2000): 1.7.
Marriage rate per 1,000 population (1991): 6.0.
Divorce rate per 1,000 population (1991): 0.3.
Life expectancy at birth (2000): male 68.8 years; female 74.4 years.
Major causes of death per 100,000 population (1989): circulatory diseases 344.1; malignant neoplasms (cancers) 122.6; accidents, violence, and poisoning 47.1; digestive system diseases 29.2; respiratory diseases 29.0.

National economy

Budget (1998). Revenue: KM 3,148,000,000 (tax revenue 64.6%, of which taxes on goods and services 37.8%, customs duties 12.9%; nontax revenue 35.4%). Expenditures: KM 3,657,000,000 (social funds 24.9%; district, canton, or municipal expenditures 22.7%; disability benefits 10.2%; defense 10.1%).
Public debt (external, outstanding; 1999): U.S.$1,826,000,000.
Gross national product (1999): U.S.$4,706,000,000 (U.S.$1,210 per capita).

Structure of gross domestic product and labour force

	1998 in value U.S.$'000,000	1998 % of total value	1990 labour force[8]	1990 % of labour force[9]
Agriculture	624	16.0	39,053	3.8
Manufacturing, mining	874	22.4	496,190	48.3
Construction	222	5.7	74,861	7.3
Public utilities	82	2.1	22,345	2.2
Transp. and commun.	308	7.9	68,798	6.7
Trade, restaurants	667	17.1	130,914	12.8
Finance, real estate	218	5.6	38,686	3.8
Pub. admin., defense	335	8.6	155,411	15.1
Services / Other	569	14.6		
TOTAL	3,899	100.0	1,026,258	100.0

Production (metric tons except as noted). Agriculture, forestry, fishing (1999): potatoes 380,000, wheat 188,000, corn (maize) 160,000, cabbages 80,000, oats 51,000, plums 25,000, tobacco 4,300; livestock (number of live animals) 350,000 cattle, 285,000 sheep; roundwood (1998) 40,000 cu m; fish catch (1997) 2,550. Mining (1996): iron ore (gross weight) 100,000; bauxite 75,000; kaolin 3,000; barite (concentrate) 2,000. Manufacturing (1996): cement 150,000; crude steel 115,000; pig iron 100,000. Energy production (consumption): electricity (kW-hr; 1996) 2,203,000,000 (2,408,000,000); coal (metric tons; 1996) 1,640,000 (1,640,000); petroleum products (metric tons; 1996) none (516,000); natural gas (cu m; 1996) none (252,000,000).
Population economically active (1991): total 992,000; activity rate of total population 22.7% (participation rates: ages 15–64, 35.6%; female [1990] 37.7%; unemployed [December 2000] *c.* 40%).
Household income and expenditure. Average household size (1991) 3.4; income per household (1990) Din 72,850[10] (U.S.$6,437); sources of income (1990): wages 53.2%, transfers 18.2%, self-employment 12.0%, other 16.6%; expenditure (1988): food 41.3%, clothing 8.3%, fuel and lighting 7.8%, housing 7.8%, transportation 6.0%, beverages and tobacco 5.7%.

Price and earnings indexes (1995 = 100)

	1995	1996	1997	1998	1999	2000
Retail price index[9]	100.0	75.5	83.7	87.9	87.6	88.7
Monthly earnings index	...	...	...	...	...	...

Tourism (1999): receipts from visitors U.S.$21,000,000; expenditures by nationals abroad, n.a.
Land use (1994): forested 53.1%; meadows and pastures 23.5%; agricultural and under permanent cultivation 15.7%; other 7.7%.

Foreign trade[10]

Balance of trade (current prices)

	1995	1996	1997	1998	1999	2000
U.S.$'000,000	–930	+336	–1,758	–1,709	–1,415	–1,661
% of total	75.4%	100.0%	60.4%	51.1%	42.1%	46.2%

Imports (2000): U.S.$2,629,000,000. *Major import sources:* Croatia 20.6%; Italy 15.9%; Slovenia 14.2%; Germany 10.7%; Yugoslavia 5.7%.
Exports (2000): U.S.$968,000,000. *Major export destinations:* Italy 23.4%; Yugoslavia 21.6%; Switzerland 11.9%; Germany 9.2%; Croatia 7.9%.

Transport and communications

Transport. Railroads (1999)[11]: length 1,031 km; passenger-km 31,100,000; metric ton-km cargo 92,800,000. Roads (1996): total length 21,846 km (paved 52%). Vehicles (1996): passenger cars 96,182; trucks and buses 10,919. Air transport (1998)[12]: passenger-km 40,390,000; metric ton-km 430,000. Airports (1997) with scheduled flights 1.

Communications

Medium	date	unit	number	units per 1,000 persons
Daily newspapers	1995	circulation	520,000	155
Radio	1997	receivers	940,000	282
Television	1997	receivers	...	...
Telephones	1999	main lines	368,000	100
Cellular telephones	1999	subscribers	52,607	14.3

Education and health

Educational attainment: n.a. *Literacy:* n.a.

Education (1990–91)

	schools	teachers	students	student/ teacher ratio
Primary (age 7–14)	2,205	23,369	539,875	23.1
Secondary (age 15–18)	238	9,030	172,063	19.1
Higher	44	2,802	37,541	13.4

Health: physicians (1998) 5,000[10] (1 per 700 persons); hospital beds (1996) 15,586 (1 per 208 persons); infant mortality rate (2000) 25.2.
Food (1999): daily per capita caloric intake 2,960 (vegetable products 86%, animal products 14%); 117% of FAO recommended minimum requirement.

Military

Total active duty personnel (2000): n.a.; about 20,000 troops of the NATO-commanded Stabilization Force are stationed in Bosnia and Herzegovina to assure implementation of the Dayton accords. *Military expenditure as percentage of GNP* (1997): 5.9% (world 2.6%); per capita expenditure U.S.$78.

[1]Government structure provided for by Dayton accords and constitutions of 1993 and 1994 is being implemented in stages since formal signing of peace accord on Dec. 14, 1995. [2]All seats are nonelective. [3]An interim currency, the marka (or "convertible mark"; KM), was introduced on June 22, 1998, to replace another interim currency, the Bosnian dinar (BD), at a rate of 1 KM to 100 BD. [4]The KM is pegged to the German Mark (DM) at a rate of 1 KM to 1 DM. [5]Unofficial estimates based on 1991 census. [6]Areas of cantons are approximated figures. [7]Excludes nearly 300,000 refugees in adjacent countries and Western Europe. [8]Excludes 28,000 workers in the private sector. [9]Federation of Bosnia and Herzegovina only. [10]Estimated figures. [11]1991–95 war destroyed much infrastructure; limited service resumed in 1998. [12]Air Bosna only.

Internet resources for further information:
- **Central Bank of Bosnia and Herzegovina http://www.cbbh.gov.ba**
- **Embassy of Bosnia and Herzegovina (Washington, D.C.) http://www.bosnianembassy.org**
- **Office of the High Representative in Bosnia and Herzegovina http://www.ohr.int**

Botswana

Official name: Republic of Botswana.
Form of government: multiparty republic with one legislative body[1] (National Assembly [47[2]]).
Head of state and government: President.
Capital: Gaborone.
Official language: English[3].
Official religion: none.
Monetary unit: 1 pula (P) = 100 thebe; valuation (Sept. 28, 2001) 1 U.S.$ = P 6.00; 1 £ = P 8.81.

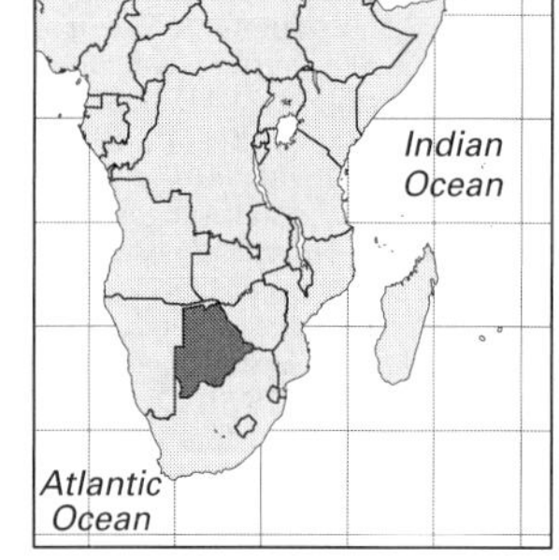

Area and population

Districts	Capitals	area sq mi	area sq km	population 1997 estimate
Barolong	...	773	2,003	19,837
Central	Serowe	57,039	147,730	457,349
Ghanzi	Ghanzi	45,525	117,910	27,099
Kgalagadi	Tsabong	41,290	106,940	34,537
Kgatleng	Mochudi	3,073	7,960	63,712
Kweneng	Molepolole	13,857	35,890	189,672
Ngwaketse	Kanye	10,219	26,467	143,370
North East	Masunga	1,977	5,120	47,312
North West				
Chobe	Kasane	8,031	20,800	16,845
Ngamiland	Maun	33,359	86,400	104,090[4]
Okavango	Orapa	8,776	22,730	[4]
South East	Ramotswa	687	1,780	54,091
Towns[5]				
Francistown	—	31	79	88,195
Gaborone	—	65	169	183,487
Jwaneng	—	39	100	14,866
Lobatse	—	16	42	29,872
Orapa	—	7	17	10,244
Selebi-Pikwe	—	19	50	45,651
Sowa	—	61	159	3,154
TOTAL		224,607[6]	581,730	1,533,383

Demography

Population (2001): 1,586,000.
Density (2001): persons per sq mi 7.1, persons per sq km 2.7.
Urban-rural (1999): urban 29.4%; rural 70.6%.
Sex distribution (2000): male 48.58%; female 51.42%.
Age breakdown (2000): under 15, 40.6%; 15–29, 30.8%; 30–44, 15.0%; 45–59, 7.7%; 60–74, 4.3%; 75 and over, 1.6%.
Population projection: (2010) 1,502,000; (2020) 1,318,000.
Doubling time: n.a.; doubling time exceeds 100 years.
Ethnic composition (2000): Tswana 66.8%; Kalanga 14.8%; Ndebele 1.7%; Herero 1.4%; San (Bushman) 1.3%; Afrikaner 1.3%.
Religious affiliation (2000): traditional beliefs 38.8%; African Christian 30.7%; Protestant 10.9%; Roman Catholic 3.7%.
Major cities (1997): Gaborone 183,487; Francistown 88,195; Selebi-Pikwe 45,651; Molepolole 36,931; Kanye 31,354.

Vital statistics

Birth rate per 1,000 population (2001): 28.8 (world avg. 22.5); (1986) legitimate 28.8%[7]; illegitimate 71.2%[7].
Death rate per 1,000 population (2001): 24.8 (world avg. 9.0).
Natural increase rate per 1,000 population (2001): 4.0 (world avg. 13.5).
Total fertility rate (avg. births per childbearing woman; 2001): 3.7.
Marriage rate per 1,000 population (1987): 1.6.
Life expectancy at birth (2001): male 36.8 years; female 37.5 years.

National economy

Budget (1997–98). Revenue: P 8,468,900,000 (mineral royalties 57.7%, customs and excise taxes 14.0%, property income 13.2%, non-mineral income tax 6.4%). Expenditures: P 7,616,400,000 (education 24.2%, defense 8.4%, health 5.1%, interest 1.3%).
Population economically active (1995): total 439,933; activity rate of total population 29.9% (participation rates: ages 15–64, 59.6%[8]; female 35.5%, unemployed 21.5%).

Price and earnings indexes (1995 = 100)

	1994	1995	1996	1997	1998	1999	2000
Consumer price index	90.5	100.0	110.1	119.6	127.6	136.6	148.5
Monthly earnings index	93.5	100.0	...	...	...	...	...

Public debt (external, outstanding; 1999): U.S.$442,300,000.
Tourism (1999): receipts U.S.$234,000,000; expenditures U.S.$143,000,000.
Production (metric tons except as noted). Agriculture, forestry, fishing (1999): cereals 19,800 (of which sorghum 13,000, corn [maize] 5,000, millet 1,300), pulses 16,000, vegetables and melons 15,000, tubers 12,000, fruits 9,500; livestock (number of live animals) 2,380,000 cattle, 1,835,000 goats, 250,000 sheep, 237,500 mules and asses, 33,000 horses; roundwood (1998) 1,066,000 cu m; fish catch (1998) 2,000. Mining and quarrying (1998): nickel 19,432; copper 15,593; cobalt 352; diamonds 19,773,000 carats. Manufacturing (value added in P '000,000; 1994): food products 164.3; wearing apparel 78.9; paper and paper products 28.0; industrial chemicals 18.7; wood products 17.5. Construction (value added in P '000,000; 1995–96): 877,900. Energy production (consumption): electricity (kW-hr; 1993) 970,000,000 (970,000,000); coal (metric tons; 1992) 901,452 (n.a.); crude petroleum, none (n.a.).

Gross national product (1999): U.S.$5,139,000,000 (U.S.$3,240 per capita).

Structure of gross domestic product and labour force

	1996–97 in value P '000,000	1996–97 % of total value	1995 labour force	1995 % of labour force
Agriculture	617,200	3.4	53,779	12.2
Mining	6,486,800	36.0	15,133	3.4
Manufacturing	853,300	4.7	29,530	6.7
Construction	988,000	5.5	41,025	9.3
Public utilities	314,400	1.7	2,805	0.6
Transp. and commun.	621,700	3.4	7,715	1.8
Trade[9]	3,016,800	16.7	54,156	12.3
Finance	1,885,900	10.5	4,096	0.9
Pub. admin., defense	2,998,000	16.6	102,564	23.3
Services	695,100	3.9	14,948	3.4
Other	–462,100[10]	–2.5[10]	114,182[11]	26.0[11]
TOTAL	18,015,100	100.0[6]	439,933	100.0[6]

Household income and expenditure (1991). Average household size 4.8; average annual income per household (1985–86) P 3,910 (U.S.$2,080); sources of income (1987): wages and salaries 73.3%, self-employment 15.9%, transfers 10.8%; expenditure: food 39.4%, household durable goods 14.0%, rent and services 13.3%, transportation 13.1%, clothing 5.6%, health 2.3%.
Land use (1994): forest 46.8%; pasture 45.2%; agriculture 0.7%; other 7.3%.

Foreign trade[12]

Balance of trade (current prices)

	1994	1995	1996	1997	1998	1999
P '000,000	1,216.3	1,623.6	2,398.9	2,140.7	217.7	2,064.5
% of total	14.0%	15.6%	17.3%	11.5%	1.1%	9.2%

Imports (1997): P 8,255,800,000 (machinery and transport equipment 37.6%, of which transport equipment 20.0%; food, beverages, and tobacco 13.1%; metal and metal products 10.7%; chemical and rubber products 9.1%). *Major import sources:* Customs Union of Southern Africa (CUSA) 72.4%; South Korea 9.5%; Zimbabwe 4.5%; U.K. 2.0%; U.S. 1.1%.
Exports (1997): P 10,390,700,000 (diamonds 73.8%; vehicles and parts 11.4%; copper-nickel matte 4.6%; textiles 2.4%; meat products 2.2%). *Major export destinations*: U.K. 56.2%; CUSA 14.3%; Zimbabwe 3.7%; U.S. 1.0%.

Transport and communications

Transport. Railroads (1996–97): length 705 mi, 1,135 km; passenger-km 96,000,000; metric ton-km cargo 795,000. Roads (1996): total length 11,388 mi, 18,327 km (paved 25%). Vehicles (1996): passenger cars 30,517; trucks and buses 59,710. Merchant marine: none. Air transport (1998)[13]: passenger-km 56,835,000; metric ton-km cargo 211,000; airports (1998) 7.

Communications

Medium	date	unit	number	units per 1,000 persons
Daily newspapers	1996	circulation	40,000	27
Radio	1997	receivers	237,000	154
Television	1999	receivers	33,000	21
Telephones	1999	main lines	123,819	79
Cellular telephones	1999	subscribers	120,000	77
Personal computers	1999	units	50,000	32
Internet	1999	users	12,000	7.7

Education and health

Educational attainment (1993). Percentage of population age 25 and over having: no formal schooling 34.7%; primary education 44.1%; some secondary 19.8%; postsecondary 1.4%. *Literacy* (2000): total population over age 15 literate 934,200 (77.2%); males literate 449,200 (74.4%); females literate 485,000 (79.8%).

Education (1997)

	schools	teachers	students	student/teacher ratio
Primary (age 6–13)	714	11,454	322,268	28.1
Secondary (age 14–18)	274	6,772	116,076	17.1
Voc., teacher tr.	53	2,889	11,482	4.0
Higher	1	507[14]	8,007	10.0[14]

Health (1994): physicians 339 (1 per 4,395 persons); hospital beds (1993) 3,299 (1 per 434 persons); infant mortality rate (2001) 63.2.
Food (1998): daily per capita caloric intake 2,159 (vegetable products 82%, animal products 18%); 93% of FAO recommended minimum requirement.

Military

Total active duty personnel (2000): 9,000 (army 94.4%, navy, none [land locked], air force 5.6%). *Military expenditure as percentage of GNP* (1997): 5.1% (world 2.6%); per capita expenditure U.S.$168.

[1]In addition, the House of Chiefs, a 15-member body consisting of chiefs, subchiefs, and associated members, serves in an advisory capacity to the government. [2]Includes four specially elected members, the speaker elected from outside of the National Assembly, and 2 ex officio members. [3]Tswana is the national language. [4]Ngamiland includes Okavango. [5]Areas are included with respective district totals; population figures are not included with district totals. [6]Detail does not add to total given because of rounding. [7]Registered births only. [8]1991. [9]Includes hotels. [10]Imputed bank service charge. [11]Includes 94,528 unemployed. [12]Import figures are f.o.b. in balance of trade and c.i.f. in commodities and trading partners. [13]Air Botswana only. [14]1994.

Internet resources for further information:
- **Bank of Botswana http://www.bankofbotswana.bw**
- **Republic of Botswana: The Government of Botswana Web Site http://www.gov.bw/home.html**

Brazil

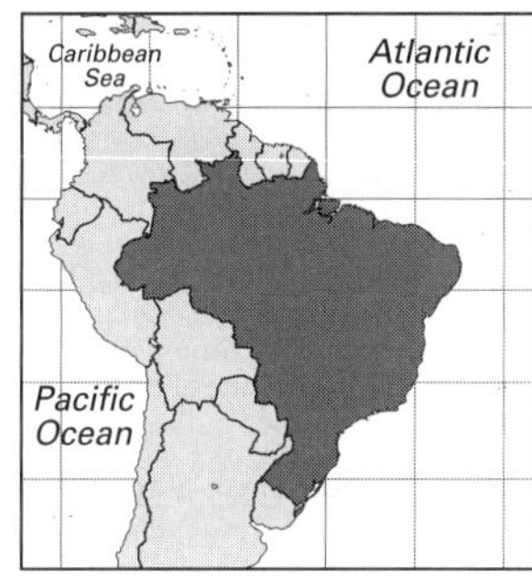

Official name: República Federativa do Brasil (Federative Republic of Brazil).
Form of government: multiparty federal republic with 2 legislative houses (Federal Senate [81]; Chamber of Deputies [513]).
Chief of state and government: President.
Capital: Brasília.
Official language: Portuguese.
Official religion: none.
Monetary unit: 1 real[1] = 100 centavos; valuation (Sept. 28, 2001) 1 U.S.$ = 2.67 reais; 1 £ = 3.92 reais.

Area and population

		area		population
States	**Capitals**	sq mi	sq km	2000 census[2]
Acre	Rio Branco	59,132	153,150	557,337
Alagoas	Maceió	10,785	27,933	2,817,903
Amapá	Macapá	55,388	143,454	475,843
Amazonas	Manaus	609,200	1,577,820	2,840,889
Bahia	Salvador	219,034	567,295	13,066,764
Ceará	Fortaleza	56,505	146,348	7,417,402
Espírito Santo	Vitória	17,836	46,194	3,093,171
Goiás	Goiânia	131,772	341,289	4,994,897
Maranhão	São Luís	128,713	333,366	5,638,381
Mato Grosso	Cuiabá	350,120	906,807	2,498,150
Mato Grosso do Sul	Campo Grande	138,286	358,159	2,075,275
Minas Gerais	Belo Horizonte	227,176	588,384	17,835,488
Pará	Belém	483,850	1,253,165	6,188,685
Paraíba	João Pessoa	21,848	56,585	3,436,718
Paraná	Curitiba	77,108	199,709	9,558,126
Pernambuco	Recife	38,200	98,938	7,910,992
Piauí	Teresina	97,444	252,379	2,840,969
Rio de Janeiro	Rio de Janeiro	16,954	43,910	14,367,225
Rio Grande do Norte	Natal	20,582	53,307	2,770,730
Rio Grande do Sul	Porto Alegre	108,905	282,062	10,178,970
Rondônia	Porto Velho	92,090	238,513	1,377,792
Roraima	Boa Vista	86,918	225,116	324,152
Santa Catarina	Florianópolis	36,851	95,443	5,333,284
São Paulo	São Paulo	96,066	248,809	36,966,527
Sergipe	Aracaju	8,514	22,050	1,779,522
Tocantins	Palmas	107,499	278,421	1,155,251
Federal District				
Distrito Federal	Brasília	2,248	5,822	2,043,169
Disputed areas[3]		1,149	2,977	—
TOTAL		3,300,171[4, 5]	8,547,404[4, 5]	169,543,612

Demography

Population (2001): 172,118,000.
Density (2001): persons per sq mi 52.2, persons per sq km 20.1.
Urban-rural (1997): urban 79.6%; rural 20.4%.
Sex distribution (2000)[6]: male 49.26%; female 50.74%.
Age breakdown (2000)[6]: under 15, 29.0%; 15–29, 28.4%; 30–44, 22.2%; 45–59, 12.5%; 60–74, 6.3%; 75 and over, 1.6%.
Population projection: (2010) 184,306,000; (2020) 194,224,000.
Doubling time: 74 years.
Racial composition (1997)[7]: white 54.4%; mulatto and mestizo 39.9%; black and black/Amerindian 5.2%; Asian 0.4%; Amerindian 0.1%.
Religious affiliation (1995)[8]: Catholic 74.3%[9], of which Roman Catholic 72.3%[9]; Protestant 23.2%, of which Pentecostal 19.1%; other Christian 0.9%; New-Religionist 0.3%; Buddhist 0.3%; Jewish 0.2%; Muslim 0.1%; other 0.7%.
Major cities[10] *and metropolitan areas* (2000)[2]: São Paulo 9,785,640 (17,833,757); Rio de Janeiro 5,850,544 (10,871,960); Salvador 2,439,881 (3,018,326); Belo Horizonte 2,229,697 (4,208,508); Fortaleza 2,138,234 (2,843,304); Brasília 2,043,169 (2,043,169); Curitiba 1,586,898 (2,697,924); Recife 1,421,947 (3,316,451); Manaus 1,394,724 (1,403,796); Porto Alegre 1,320,069 (3,507,624); Belém 1,271,615 (1,807,556); Goiânia 1,083,396 (1,616,370); Guarulhos 1,048,280[11]; Campinas 951,824 (1,717,410).

Other principal cities[10] (2000)[2]

	population		population		population
Aracaju	460,898	Niterói	458,465[13]	São João de Meriti	449,562[13]
Campo Grande	654,832	Nova Iguaçu	915,364[13]	São Jose dos Campos	532,403
Contagem	531,715[12]	Osasco	650,993[11]	São Luis	834,968
Duque de Caxias	767,724[13]	Ribeirão Preto	502,333	Sorocaba	487,907
Jaboatão	567,319[14]	Santo André	648,443[11]	Teresina	676,596
João Pessoa	594,922	São Bernardo do Campo	688,161[11]	Uberlândia	487,887
Maceió	794,894	São Gonçalo	889,828[11]		
Natal	709,422				

Families (1996). Average family size 3.9; 1–2 persons 25.2%, 3 persons 20.3%, 4 persons 22.2%, 5–6 persons 23.3%, 7 or more persons 9.0%.
Domestic migration. Percent of population moving to different *município* between 1991 and 1996: 7.6%.
Number of emigrants/immigrants (1986–96): 2,355,057/169,303. Emigrants' most popular destinations in order of preference are the United States, Japan, and the United Kingdom.

Vital statistics

Birth rate per 1,000 population (2000): 18.8 (world avg. 22.5).
Death rate per 1,000 population (2000): 9.4 (world avg. 9.0).
Natural increase rate per 1,000 population (2000): 9.4 (world avg. 13.5).
Total fertility rate (avg. births per childbearing woman; 2000): 2.1.
Marriage rate per 1,000 population (1995): 4.7.
Divorce rate per 1,000 population (1995): 0.6.
Life expectancy at birth (2000): male 58.5 years; female 67.6 years.
Major causes of death per 100,000 population (1996)[15]: diseases of the circulatory system 225; accidents, murder, and violence 108; malignant neoplasms (cancers) 93; diseases of the respiratory system 80; infectious and parasitic diseases 47; diseases of the digestive system 35; endocrine, metabolic, and nutritional disorders 33; ill-defined conditions 124.

Social indicators

Educational attainment (1996). Percentage of population age 25 and over having: no formal schooling or less than one year of primary education 17.7%; lower primary only 19.1%; upper primary 30.7%; complete primary to some secondary 11.6%; complete secondary to some higher 13.9%; complete higher 6.2%; unknown 0.8%.

Distribution of income (1995)

percentage of national income by decile/quintile

1	2	3	4	5	6	7	8	9	10 (highest)
0.8	1.7	—5.7—		—9.9—		—17.7—		16.3	47.9

Quality of working life. Annual estimated rate per 100,000 insured workers (1990) for: on-the-job injury 2,032; industrial illness 17; death 4. Proportion of labour force participating in national social insurance system (1990): 50.1%. Proportion of formally employed population receiving minimum wage (1993): 25.0%.
Access to services (1997)[7]. Proportion of households having access to: electricity 93.3%, of which urban households having access 99.0%, rural households having access 68.8%; safe public (piped) water supply 73.8%, of which urban households having access 87.4%, rural households having access 14.9%; public (piped) sewage system 40.8%, of which urban household having access 49.4%, rural households having access 3.5%; no sewage disposal 10.0%, of which urban households having no disposal 3.7%, rural households having no disposal 37.2%.
Social participation. Voting is mandatory for national elections; abstention is punishable by a fine. Trade union membership in total workforce (1991): 16,748,155. Practicing Roman Catholic population in total affiliated Roman Catholic population (2000): large cities 10–15%; towns and rural areas 60–70%.
Social deviance. Annual murder rate per 100,000 population (1996): Brazil 23, Rio de Janeiro only 69, São Paulo only 55.
Leisure. Favourite leisure activities include: playing soccer, dancing, rehearsing all year in neighbourhood samba groups for celebrations of Carnival, and competing in water sports, volleyball, and basketball.
Material well-being (1997)[7]. Households possessing: telephone lines 27.9%, of which urban 33.2%, rural 4.9%; television receiver 86.2%, of which urban 92.7%, rural 58.4%; refrigerator 80.3%, of which urban 88.1%, rural 46.6%; washing machine 31.7%, of which urban 36.9%, rural 9.3%.

National economy

Gross national product (at current market prices; 1999): U.S.$730,424,000,000 (U.S.$4,350 per capita).

Structure of gross domestic product and labour force

	1998			
	in value R$ '000,000[1, 16]	% of total value	labour force[7, 17]	% of labour force
Agriculture	75,764	8.4	16,338,100	21.3
Mining	5,759	0.6	861,600	1.1
Public utilities	24,745	2.8		
Manufacturing	182,662	20.3	8,230,600	10.7
Construction	92,321	10.3	4,980,000	6.5
Transportation and communications	50,390	5.6	2,786,600	3.6
Trade	65,236	7.2	9,417,000[18]	12.2[18]
Finance, real estate	196,879	21.9	1,308,700[19]	1.7[19]
Pub. admin., defense	139,291	15.5	26,040,500[20]	33.9[20]
Services	113,287	12.6		
Other	–46,520[21]	–5.2[21]	6,922,600[22]	9.0[22]
TOTAL	899,814	100.0	76,885,700	100.0

Budget. Revenue (1995): R$320,178,000,000 (development receipts 62.6%, of which credits 58.4%; current receipts 37.4%, of which social contributions 19.3% [including social security 9.2%], taxes 13.3%). Expenditures: R$320,178,000,000 (administration and planning 59.5%; social welfare 13.9%; regional development 6.0%; health and sanitation 4.9%; agriculture 3.1%; education 2.7%; defense and public order 2.6%).
Public debt (external, outstanding; 1999): U.S.$95,233,000,000.
Production ('000 metric tons except as noted). Agriculture, forestry, fishing (2000): sugarcane 324,668, soybeans 32,687, corn (maize) 32,038, cassava 22,960, oranges 22,745, rice 11,168, bananas 6,339, tomatoes 3,043, dry beans 3,037, potatoes 2,582, seed cotton 1,915, wheat 1,895, coffee 1,824, coconuts 1,822, papayas 1,700, cashew apples 1,500, pineapples 1,353, apples 1,160, onions 1,078, grapes 978, sorghum 842, mangoes 605, tobacco 594, sweet potatoes 500, lemons and limes 480, oil palm fruit 387, maté 220, cacao beans 210, sisal 195, peanuts (groundnuts) 188, cashews 154, garlic 72, natural rubber 70, Brazil nuts 23; livestock (number of live animals) 167,471,000 cattle, 27,320,000 pigs, 18,300,000 sheep, 6,400,000 horses; roundwood (1999) 197,897,000 cu m, of which fuelwood 90,210,000 cu m, sawlogs and veneer logs 46,779,000 cu m, pulpwood 30,701,000 cu m; fish catch (1997) 820, of which freshwater fishes 267. Mining and quarrying (value of export production in U.S.$'000,000; 1998): iron ore 3,066; ferroniobium 242; silicon 135; bauxite 122; kaolin (clay) 106; ferrosilicon 101; granite (1996) 97; copper 89; manganese 52; nickel 52; gold production for both domestic use and export

1,594,000 troy oz; Brazil is also a world-leading producer of high-quality grade quartz and tantalum. Manufacturing (value added in R$'000,000; 1995): industrial chemicals 21,937; transport equipment 20,434; food products 18,117; fabricated and base metals 13,813; electrical machinery 9,563; nonelectrical machinery 8,122; paper and paper products 5,667; cement, bricks, and tiles 5,125; pharmaceuticals 4,958; textiles 4,907; printing and publishing 4,807.

Land use (1994): forested 57.7%; meadows and pastures 21.9%; agricultural and under permanent cultivation 6.0%; other 14.4%.

Manufacturing enterprises (1995)

	no. of enter-prises	number of labourers[23]	wages of labourers as a % of avg. of all mfg. wages	value added in producer's prices (in R$'000,000)
Industrial chemicals	1,817	218,756	164.3	21,937
Transport equipment	711	262,712	157.7	20,434
Food products	4,241	527,064	60.6	18,117
Fabricated metals, iron and steel, and nonferrous metals	2,050	325,406	114.2	13,813
Electrical machinery	1,081	191,740	126.6	9,563
Nonelectrical machinery	1,694	227,196	124.7	8,122
Paper and paper products	676	103,339	114.1	5,667
Nonmetallic mineral products	1,508	126,925	88.2	5,125
Pharmaceuticals	359	51,953	178.6	4,958
Textiles	1,192	208,857	66.8	4,907
Publishing and printing	782	105,165	132.1	4,807
Clothing and footwear	1,681	299,193	49.8	4,706
Beverages	451	76,452	87.1	4,027
Plastics	724	101,971	81.0	3,111
Paints, soaps, and perfumes	249	31,143	116.7	2,553
Rubber products	407	49,368	111.5	1,767

Population economically active (1998)[7, 17]: total 76,885,700; activity rate of total population 47.4% (participation rates: ages 15–59 [1997] 72.0%; female 40.7%; unemployed [May 1999] officially 8%).

Price and earnings indexes (1995 = 100)

	1994	1995	1996	1997	1998	1999	2000
Consumer price index	60.2	100.0	115.8	123.8	127.7	133.9	143.4
Monthly earnings index[24]	73.9	100.0	118.3	128.5	138.8	146.8	161.8

Tourism (1999): receipts from visitors U.S.$3,994,000,000; expenditures by nationals abroad U.S.$3,059,000,000.

Retail trade enterprises (1996)

	no. of businesses	total no. of employees	annual wage as a % of all trade wages	annual values of sales in R$'000,000[1]
General merchandise stores (including food products)	10,382	437,452	131.2	35,766
Vehicles, new and used	9,348	202,892	229.9	30,926
Gas stations	20,388	210,250	124.7	23,199
Electronics, kitchen equipment, musical instruments	18,245	158,755	143.7	14,855
Metal products, lumber, glass, and construction materials	81,303	386,285	90.1	14,047
Vehicles, parts	55,534	252,731	110.6	10,881
Pharmaceutical and cosmetic products	50,778	240,633	94.2	9,658
Clothing and apparel	128,908	428,150	76.4	9,023
Food, beverages, and tobacco	135,672	378,102	60.7	6,900

Households. Average household size (1997) 3.8.

Family income and expenditure. Average family size (1997) 3.5[7]; annual income per family (1993) Cr$608,364 (U.S.$2,178[7, 25]); sources of income (1987–88)[26]: wages and salaries 62.4%, self-employed 14.7%, transfers 10.9%, other 12.0%; expenditure (1995–96)[27]: housing, energy, and household furnishings 28.8%, food and beverages 23.4%, transportation and communications 13.8%, health care 9.2%, education and recreation 8.4%.

Financial aggregates[28]

	1995	1996	1997	1998	1999	2000
Exchange rate, reais[1] per:						
U.S. dollar	.973	1.039	1.116	1.209	1.789	1.955
£	1.508	1.506	1.846	2.011	2.892	2.917
SDR	1.446	1.495	1.506	1.702	2.455	2.548
International reserves (U.S.$)						
Total (excl. gold; '000,000)	49,708	58,323	50,827	42,580	34,796	32,488
SDRs ('000,000)	1	1	1	2	10	—
Reserve pos. in IMF ('000,000)	—	—	—	—	—	—
Foreign exchange ('000,000)	49,707	58,322	50,826	42,578	34,786	32,488
Gold ('000,000 fine troy oz.)	4.58	3.69	3.03	4.60	3.17	1.89
% world reserves	0.50	0.41	0.34	0.48	0.44	0.20
Interest and prices						
Central bank discount (%)	...	25.34	45.09	39.41	21.37	18.89[29]
Govt. bond yield (%)	...	...	...	...	...	...
Industrial share prices	...	...	...	...	...	...
Balance of payments (U.S.$'000,000)						
Balance of visible trade	–3,157	–5,453	–8,372	–6,603	–1,207	...
Imports, f.o.b.	49,663	53,304	61,358	57,739	49,219	...
Exports, f.o.b.	46,506	47,851	52,986	51,136	48,012	...
Balance of invisibles	–14,979	–17,795	–23,839	–27,226	–23,866	...
Balance of payments current account	–18,136	–23,248	–30,491	–33,829	–25,073	...

Energy production (consumption): electricity (kW-hr; 1998) 288,996,000,000 (287,864,000,000); coal (metric tons; 1999) 4,284,000 ([1996] 17,294,000); crude petroleum (barrels; 1999) 398,228,000 ([1996] 485,343,000); petroleum products (metric tons; 1996) 57,378,000 (66,388,000); natural gas (cu m; 1999) 11,854,000,000 ([1996] 4,936,000,000); carburant alcohol (barrels; 1997) 76,650,000 (76,650,000).

Foreign trade[30]

Balance of trade (current prices)

	1994	1995	1996	1997	1998	1999
U.S.$'000,000	+10,861	–3,157	–5,453	–8,372	–6,603	–1,207
% of total	14.0%	3.3%	5.4%	7.3%	6.1%	1.2%

Imports (1998): U.S.$60,793,000,000 (nonelectrical machinery and apparatus 19.7%; chemicals and chemical products 16.2%; electrical machinery and apparatus 12.8%; motor vehicles 9.5%; mineral fuels 9.3%). *Major import sources:* United States 23.6%; Argentina 13.9%; Germany 9.0%; Japan 5.6%; Italy 5.5%; France 3.4%; United Kingdom 2.6%; Canada 2.4%; Spain 2.1%; China 1.9%.

Exports (1998): U.S.$51,120,000,000 (food products 20.3%, of which coffee 4.6%, sugar [all forms] 4.0%, vegetables and fruit 3.3%; road vehicles 9.4%; nonelectrical machinery and apparatus 8.5%; iron and steel 7.2%; iron ore 6.4%; chemicals and chemical products 6.2%; soybeans 4.3%). *Major export destinations:* United States 19.3%; Argentina 13.2%; Germany 5.9%; The Netherlands 5.4%; Japan 4.3%; Belgium–Luxembourg 4.3%; Italy 3.8%; United Kingdom 2.6%; France 2.5%; Paraguay 2.4%.

Transport and communications

Transport. Railroads (1998)[31]: route length (1997) 18,458 mi, 29,706 km; passenger-mi 8,676,000,000, passenger-km 12,667,000,000; short ton-mi cargo 96,741,000,000, metric ton-km cargo 141,239,000,000. Roads (1997): total length 1,030,652 mi, 1,658,677 km (paved 9%). Vehicles (1998): passenger cars 21,313,351; trucks and buses 3,743,836. Air transport (1999)[32]: passenger-mi 21,765,000,000, passenger-km 35,028,000,000; short ton-mi cargo 891,000,000, metric ton-km cargo 1,301,000,000; airports (1995) with scheduled flights 139.

Communications

Medium	date	unit	number	units per 1,000 persons
Daily newspapers	1996	circulation	6,472,000	41
Radio	1997	receivers	71,000,000	446
Television	1999	receivers	56,000,000	336
Telephones	1999	main lines	24,985,000	150
Cellular telephones	1999	subscribers	15,033,000	90
Personal computers	1999	units	6,100,000	37
Internet	1999	users	3,500,000	21

Education and health

Literacy (2000)[33]: total population age 15 and over literate 103,500,000 (85.3%); males literate 50,300,000 (85.1%); females literate 53,200,000 (85.4%).

Education (1998)

	schools	teachers	students	student/ teacher ratio
Primary (age 7–14)	187,497	1,460,469	35,845,742	24.5
Secondary (age 15–17)	17,602	380,222	6,968,531	18.3
Higher[34]	900	173,705	1,948,200	11.2

Health (1997): physicians 205,828 (1 per 774 persons); hospital beds 496,740 (1 per 321 persons); infant mortality rate per 1,000 live births (2000) 38.0.

Food (1997): daily per capita caloric intake 2,974 (vegetable products 80%, animal products 20%); 124% of FAO recommended minimum requirement.

Military

Total active duty personnel (2000): 287,600 (army 65.7%, navy 16.9%, air force 17.4%). *Military expenditure as percentage of GNP* (1997): 1.8% (world 2.6%); per capita expenditure U.S.$89.

[1]The real (R$) replaced the cruzeiro real (CR$) on July 1, 1994, at a rate of 2,750 cruzeiros reais to 1 real (a rate par to the U.S.$ on that date). Previously, the cruzeiro real replaced the cruzeiro (Cr$) at a rate of 1,000 cruzeiros to 1 cruzeiro real on Aug. 2, 1993; the cruzeiro replaced the new cruzado (NCz$) at a rate of 1 to 1 on March 16, 1990; and the new cruzado replaced the (old) cruzado (Cz$) at a rate of 1,000 (old) to 1 new on Jan. 15, 1989. [2]Preliminary figures. [3]Area in dispute between Ceará and Piauí. [4]Detail does not add to total given because of rounding. [5]Land area excluding inland water is 3,265,076 sq mi (8,456,508 sq km). [6]Estimated figures. [7]Excludes rural population of Acre, Amapá, Amazonas, Pará, Rondônia, and Roraima. [8]Christian data include nominal Christians. [9]Includes syncretic Afro-Catholic cults having Spiritist beliefs and rituals. [10]Populations are for *municípios,* which may include adjacent urban or rural districts. [11]Within São Paulo metropolitan area. [12]Within Belo Horizonte metropolitan area. [13]Within Rio de Janeiro metropolitan area. [14]Within Recife metropolitan area. [15]Projected rates based on about 71% of total deaths. [16]At factor cost. [17]Excludes members of armed forces in barracks. [18]Excludes restaurants and hotels. [19]Includes activities not adequately defined. [20]Includes restaurants and hotels. [21]Less imputed bank service charges. [22]Unemployed. [23]End of year. [24]Minimum wages. [25]Based on end-of-year exchange rate. [26]Based on 10,408,833 families in Brazil's nine largest metropolitan regions. [27]Based on survey of 11 metropolitan areas only. [28]End-of-period figures. [29]September. [30]Imports f.o.b. in balance of trade c.i.f. in commodities and trading partners. [31]Includes suburban services. [32]TAM Regional, TAM Meridional, VARIG, and VASP airlines only. [33]In the late 1990s, functional literacy was 30.5% of total population over age 15. [34]1997.

Internet resources for further information:

- **IBGE: Instituto Brasileiro de Geografia e Estatística**
  http://www.ibge.gov.br/ibge/default.php
- **Central Bank of Brazil: Economic Data**
  http://www.bcb.gov.br/defaulti.htm

Brunei

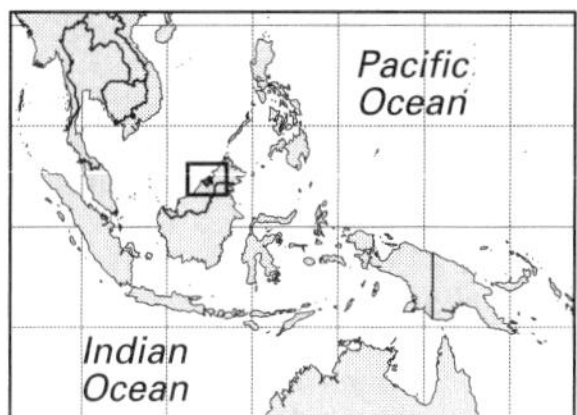

Official name: Negara Brunei Darussalam (State of Brunei, Abode of Peace).
Form of government: monarchy (sultanate)[1].
Head of state and government: Sultan.
Capital: Bandar Seri Begawan.
Official language: Malay[2].
Official religion: Islam.
Monetary unit: 1 Brunei dollar (B$) = 100 cents; valuation (Sept. 28, 2001) 1 U.S.$ = B$1.77; 1 £ = B$2.60.

Area and population

Districts	Capitals	area sq mi	area sq km	population 1998 estimate
Belait	Kuala Belait	1,052	2,724	65,300
Brunei and Muara	Bandar Seri Begawan	220	571	213,800
Temburong	Bangar	504	1,304	9,300
Tutong	Tutong	450	1,166	35,200
TOTAL		2,226	5,765	323,600

Demography

Population (2001): 344,000.
Density (2001): persons per sq mi 154.5, persons per sq km 59.7.
Urban-rural (1999): urban 72.0%; rural 28.0%.
Sex distribution (1998): male 53.06%; female 46.94%.
Age breakdown (1996): under 15, 32.9%; 15–29, 27.5%; 30–44, 25.5%; 45–59, 9.4%; 60 and over, 4.7%.
Population projection: (2010) 408,000; (2020) 475,000.
Doubling time: 36 years.
Ethnic composition (1999): Malay 67.6%; Chinese 14.9%; other indigenous 5.9%; Indian and other 11.6%.
Religious affiliation (2000): Muslim 64.4%; traditional beliefs 11.2%; Buddhist 9.1%; Christian 7.7%; other religions and nonreligious 7.6%.
Major cities (1991): Bandar Seri Begawan (1999) 85,000[3]; Kuala Belait 21,163; Seria 21,082; Tutong 13,049.

Vital statistics

Birth rate per 1,000 population (1999): 22.3 (world avg. 22.5); (1982) legitimate 99.6%; illegitimate 0.4%.
Death rate per 1,000 population (1999): 2.8 (world avg. 9.0).
Natural increase rate per 1,000 population (1999): 19.5 (world avg. 13.5).
Total fertility rate (avg. births per childbearing woman; 1999): 2.7.
Marriage rate per 1,000 population (1995): 6.1.
Divorce rate per 1,000 population (1992): 1.1.
Life expectancy at birth (1999): male 74.0 years; female 76.0 years.
Major causes of death per 100,000 population (1994): cardiovascular disease 51.8; malignant neoplasms (cancers) 41.8; accidents, poisoning, and violence 20.0; pneumonia 12.3; congenital anomalies 7.3.

National economy

Budget (1998). Revenue: B$2,775,000,000 (tax revenue 54.6%, of which corporate income tax 47.3%, import duty 7.2%; nontax revenue 45.4%, of which property income 33.8%, commercial receipts 10.9%). Expenditures: B$4,295,000,000 (current expenditure 65.5%; capital expenditure 34.5%).
Public debt (external, outstanding): none.
Tourism (1995): receipts from visitors U.S.$40,000,000; expenditures by nationals abroad U.S.$1,000,000.
Production (metric tons except as noted). Agriculture, forestry, fishing (1999): vegetables and melons 8,700, fruits (excluding melons) 5,225, cassava 1,500, pineapples 700, rice 290; livestock (number of live animals) 6,000 buffalo, 4,500 pigs, 3,302 goats, 1,924 cattle, 4,929,000 chickens; roundwood (1998) 296,000 cu m; fish catch (1997) 4,677. Mining and quarrying: other than petroleum and natural gas, none except sand and gravel for construction. Manufacturing (1998): gasoline 187,600; distillate fuel oils 147,800; kerosene 76,500. Construction (value in B$'000,000; 1989): residential 26.2; nonresidential 5.1. Energy production (consumption): electricity (kW-hr; 1996) 1,575,000,000 (1,575,000,000); coal, none (none); crude petroleum (barrels; 1996) 60,000,000 (900,000); petroleum products (metric tons; 1996) 851,000 (909,000); natural gas (cu m; 1996) 9,218,000,000 (1,269,000,000).
Population economically active (1991): total 111,955; activity rate of total population 43.0% (participation rates: ages 15–64, 67.6%; female 32.9%; unemployed 4.7%).

Price and earnings indexes (1995 = 100)

	1991	1992	1993	1994	1995	1996	1997
Consumer price index	87.2	88.3	92.2	94.3	100.0	101.8	103.7
Earnings index	…	…	…	…	…	…	…

Household income and expenditure. Average household size (1991) 5.8; income per household: n.a.; sources of income: n.a.; expenditure (1990): food 38.7%, transportation and communications 19.9%, housing 18.6%, clothing 6.4%, other 16.4%.
Gross national product (at current market prices; 1998): U.S.$7,209,000,000 (U.S.$22,278 per capita).

Structure of gross domestic product and labour force

	1998 in value B$'000,000	1998 % of total value	1991 labour force	1991 % of labour force
Agriculture	231	2.8	2,162	1.9
Mining / Manufacturing	2,975	36.7	9,397	8.4
Construction	539	6.7	14,145	12.6
Public utilities	88	1.1	2,223	2.0
Transportation and communications	351	4.3	5,392	4.8
Trade	780	9.6	15,404	13.8
Finance	520	6.4	5,807	5.2
Services	2,847	35.1	52,121	46.6
Other	–220	–2.7	5,304[4]	4.7[4]
TOTAL	8,111	100.0	111,955	100.0

Land use (1994): forested 85.4%; meadows and pastures 1.1%; agricultural and under permanent cultivation 1.3%; other 12.2%.

Foreign trade[5]

Balance of trade (current prices)

	1993	1994	1995	1996	1997	1998
B$'000,000	+577.5	+530.0	+338.0	+153.2	+819.0	+135
% of total	8.6%	8.8%	5.2%	2.1%	11.5%	2.2%

Imports (1997): B$3,154,000,000 (machinery and transport equipment 39.0%, manufactured goods 25.5%, miscellaneous manufactured articles 11.6%, food and live animals 11.1%, chemicals 6.4%, crude materials 3.4%, beverages and tobacco 1.9%). *Major import sources:* ASEAN 45.5%, of which Singapore 25.6%, Malaysia 13.6%; EEC 17.9%; Japan 11.2%; United States 10.0%.
Exports (1997): B$3,973,000,000 (natural gas 46.8%, crude petroleum 41.5%, petroleum products 2.8%). *Major export destinations:* Japan 53.1%; ASEAN 20.9%, of which Thailand 11.2%, Singapore 6.6%; South Korea 18.1%; Taiwan 2.7%.

Transport and communications

Transport. Railroads[6]: length 12 mi, 19 km. Roads (1996): total length 1,064 mi, 1,712 km (paved 75%). Vehicles (1997): passenger cars 91,047; trucks and buses 15,918. Merchant marine (1992): vessels (100 gross tons and over) 51; total deadweight tonnage 349,718. Marine transport (1998): cargo loaded 25,900,000 metric tons, cargo unloaded 1,195,200 metric tons. Air transport (1998): passenger-mi 1,742,000,000, passenger-km 2,803,000,000; short ton-mi cargo 75,020,000, metric ton-km cargo 109,527,000; airports (1996) with scheduled flights 1.

Communications

Medium	date	unit	number	units per 1,000 persons
Daily newspapers	1996	circulation	21,000	69
Radio	1997	receivers	93,000	302
Television	1999	receivers	205,000	637
Telephones	1999	main lines	79,086	246
Cellular telephones	1999	subscribers	66,000	205
Personal computers	1999	units	20,000	62
Internet	1999	users	25,000	78

Education and health

Educational attainment (1991). Percentage of population age 25 and over having: no formal schooling 17.0%; primary education 43.3%; secondary 26.3%; postsecondary and higher 12.9%; not stated 0.5%. *Literacy* (1995): percentage of total population age 15 and over literate 89.1%; males literate 93.2%; females literate 84.6%.

Education (1998)

	schools	teachers	students	student/teacher ratio
Primary (age 5–11)[7]	184	3,858	58,548	15.2
Secondary (age 12–20)	38	2,636	30,956	11.7
Voc., teacher tr.	9	516	2,553	4.9
Higher	4	370	2,080	5.6

Health (1996): physicians 281 (1 per 1,086 persons); hospital beds 961 (1 per 317 persons); infant mortality rate per 1,000 live births (1999) 6.0.
Food (1999): daily per capita caloric intake 2,793 (vegetable products 82%, animal products 18%); (1997) 125% of FAO recommended minimum requirement.

Military

Total active duty personnel (2000): 5,000[8] (army 78.0%, navy 14.0%, air force 8.0%). British troops (a Gurkha batallion; 2000): 1,050. *Military expenditure as percentage of GNP* (1997): 4.6% (world 2.6%); per capita expenditure U.S.$1,190.

[1]A nonelective 21-member body advises the sultan on legislative matters. [2]All official documents that must be published by law in Malay are, however, also required to be issued in an official English version as well. [3]Urban agglomeration. [4]Mostly unemployed. [5]Import data is c.i.f. [6]Privately owned. [7]Includes preprimary. [8]All services form part of the army.

Internet resources for further information:
- **Brunei Darussalam http://www.brunet.bn**
- **The Government of Brunei Darussalam http://www.brunei.gov.bn/index.htm**

Bulgaria

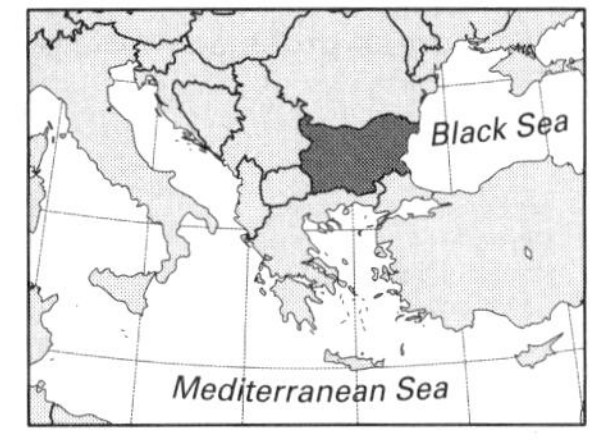

Official name: Republika Bŭlgaria (Republic of Bulgaria).
Form of government: unitary multiparty republic with one legislative body (National Assembly [240]).
Chief of state: President.
Head of government: Prime Minister.
Capital: Sofia.
Official language: Bulgarian.
Official religion: none[1].
Monetary unit: 1 lev (Lw; leva)[2] = 100 stotinki; valuation (Sept. 28, 2001) 1 U.S.$ = 2.14 (new) leva; 1 £ = 3.14 (new) leva.

Area and population

Districts	area sq km	population 2000[3] estimate	Districts	area sq km	population 2000[3] estimate
Blagoevgrad	6,452.3	345,138	Ruse	2,791.3	275,538
Burgas	7,747.9	427,152	Shumen	3,379.8	214,877
Dobrich	4,723.2	225,978	Silistra	2,847.0	152,392
Gabrovo	2,023.0	153,485	Sliven	3,544.1	229,690
Khaskovo	5,539.0	291,770	Smolyan	3,193.9	145,940
Kurdzhali	3,208.8	201,162	Sofiya[4]	7,059.0	262,151
Kyustendil	3,051.5	170,559	Sofiya-Grad[5]	1,344.4	1,211,531
Lovech	4,128.5	176,389	Stara Zagora	5,152.0	385,195
Montana	3,627.6	191,129	Targovishte	2,560.2	144,601
Pazardzhik	4,459.3	315,225	Varna	3,818.9	440,563
Pernik	2,392.8	153,321	Veliko Turnovo	4,662.6	301,284
Pleven	4,338.0	319,356	Vidin	3,033.4	138,794
Plovdiv	5,962.2	729,447	Vratsa	3,937.6	255,589
Razgrad	2,637.6	164,971	Yambol	3,355.5	167,649
			TOTAL	110,971.4	8,190,876

Demography

Population (2001): 7,953,000[6].
Density (2001): persons per sq mi 185.6, persons per sq km 71.7.
Urban-rural (1999): urban 68.0%; rural 32.0%.
Sex distribution (2000): male 48.48%; female 51.52%.
Age breakdown (2000): under 15, 15.6%; 15–29, 21.8%; 30–44, 20.0%; 45–59, 20.5%; 60–74, 16.3%; 75 and over, 5.8%.
Population projection: (2010) 7,229,000; (2020) 6,528,000.
Ethnic composition (1992): Bulgarian 83.2%; Turkish 9.4%; Gypsy 3.6%; other 1.3%.
Religious affiliation (1995): Bulgarian Orthodox 36.5%, Protestant 1.4%, Roman Catholic 0.8%; Sunnī Muslim 13.1%; other/nonreligious 47.8%.
Major cities (2000[3]): Sofia 1,133,183; Plovdiv 344,976; Varna 296,204.

Vital statistics

Birth rate per 1,000 population (1999): 8.8 (world avg. 22.5).
Death rate per 1,000 population (1999): 13.6 (world avg. 9.0).
Natural increase rate per 1,000 population (1999): –4.8 (world avg. 13.5).
Total fertility rate (avg. births per childbearing woman; 1999): 1.2.
Life expectancy at birth (2000): male 67.5 years; female 74.6 years.
Major causes of death per 100,000 population (1999): diseases of the circulatory system 893.1; malignant neoplasms (cancers) 194.8; diseases of the respiratory system 52.5; accidents, poisoning, and violence 56.1.

National economy

Budget (1998). Revenue: 8,913,064,200,000 (old) leva (tax revenue 79.4%, of which social insurance 22.9%, value-added tax 20.6%, income tax 11.5%, profit tax 9.6%, excises 7.6%, customs and duties 5.0%, other 2.2%; nontax revenue 20.0%; other 0.6%). Expenditures: 8,689,188,600,000 (old) leva (social insurance 27.1%; administration 16.3%; wages 12.9%; interest on debt 11.0%; capital expenditure 10.9%; defense 10.8%; education 10.2%).
Public debt (external, outstanding; 1999): U.S.$7,602,000,000.
Gross national product (1999): U.S.$11,572,000,000 (U.S.$1,410 per capita).

Structure of gross domestic product and labour force

	1997 in value '000,000 (old) leva	% of total value	labour force	% of labour force
Agriculture, forestry, and fishing	3,987,312	23.3	800,353	22.3
Manufacturing, mining	3,457,569	20.2	812,941	22.7
Construction	422,179	2.5	139,002	3.9
Transp. and commun.	1,124,858	6.6	228,231	6.4
Trade	1,468,148	8.6	382,505	10.7
Public utilities, housing	603,460	3.5	88,764	2.5
Finance	2,793,211	16.3	49,608	1.4
Pub. admin., defense	555,899	3.3	78,899	2.2
Services	824,866	4.8	488,097	13.6
Other	1,866,231[7]	10.9[7]	513,400[8]	14.3[8]
TOTAL	17,103,433	100.0	3,581,800	100.0

Production (metric tons except as noted). Agriculture, forestry, fishing (1999): wheat 3,000,000, corn (maize) 1,100,000, sunflower seeds 700,000, grapes 636,000, barley 500,000; livestock (number of live animals) 2,774,000 sheep, 1,721,000 pigs, 1,048,000 goats, 671,000 cattle; roundwood (1998) 3,041,000 cu m; fish catch (1998) 10,756. Mining and quarrying (1997): iron ore 895,000; lead 72,975; zinc 72,755; manganese 55,600; silver 23,790 kg. Manufacturing (value of production in '000,000 (old) leva; 1997): food, beverages, and tobacco 2,834,413; chemical and oil processing 1,633,583; machine and metalworking 1,460,220; metallurgy 890,614; electronic and electrical equipment 524,383. Construction (1998): residential 421,241 sq m; nonresidential 162,357. Energy production (consumption): electricity (kW-hr; 1998) 42,803,000,000 (42,803,000,000); coal (metric tons; 1998) 31,248,000 (34,200,000); crude petroleum (barrels; 1998) 232,360 (50,979,000); petroleum products (metric tons; 1996) 5,810,000 (4,361,000); natural gas (cu m; 1996) 44,000,000 (6,197,000,000).
Household income and expenditure. Average household size (1998) 3.0; income per household (1999) 4,179 (new) leva (U.S.$2,276); sources of income (1999): wages and salaries 39.6%, transfer payments 16.8%, self-employment in agriculture 16.7%; expenditure (1999): food 41.8%, housing and energy 11.3%, transportation 5.4%, clothing 5.0%, household durable goods 3.1%, education and culture 3.1%, health 2.7%, other 27.6%.
Population economically active (1997): total 3,581,800; activity rate of total population 51.9% (participation rates: age 16–59 [male], 16–54 [female] 57.3%; female 47.6%; unemployed 13.7%).

Price and earnings indexes (1995 = 100)

	1994	1995	1996	1997	1998	1999	2000
Consumer price index	61.7	100.0	221.6	2,567.0	3,047.2	3,124.8	3,447.1
Monthly earnings index	68.4	100.0	174.4	1,864.4	...	...	...

Tourism (1999): receipts U.S.$932,000,000; expenditures by nationals abroad U.S.$524,000,000.

Foreign trade[9]

Balance of trade (current prices)

	1995	1996	1997	1998	1999	2000
'000,000 (new) leva	–20.3	–32.3	+12.9	–1,195	–2,740	–3,581
% of total	2.8%	1.8%	0.0%	7.3%	15.9%	14.9%

Imports (1997): 8,268,462,200 (new) leva (petroleum and natural gas 28.7%; machine-building and metalworking equipment 13.9%; chemical products 9.9%; electrical and electronic equipment 6.6%; food, beverages, and tobacco 6.3%; textiles and knitwear 4.5%). *Major import sources:* Russia 28.0%; Germany 11.8%; Italy 7.2%; Greece 4.2%; U.S. 3.7%; Ukraine 3.7%.
Exports (1997): 8,281,386,500 (new) leva (chemicals and plastics 22.3%; food, beverages, and tobacco 13.5%; machine-building and metalworking equipment 9.6%; clothing and footwear 7.1%). *Major export destinations:* Italy 11.7%; Germany 9.5%; Turkey 9.0%; Greece 8.2%; Russia 7.9%.

Transport and communications

Transport. Railroads (1998): track length 6,470 km; (1997) passenger-km 5,866,000,000; metric ton-km cargo 7,444,000,000. Roads (1998): length 37,320 km (paved 92%). Vehicles (1998): cars 1,730,506; trucks and buses 251,382. Merchant marine (1998): vessels (100 gross tons and over) 107; deadweight tonnage (1995) 391,000. Air transport (1997): passenger-mi 1,258,742,000, passenger-km 2,025,752,000; short ton-mi cargo 18,872,000, metric ton-km cargo 30,371,000; airports (1997) with scheduled flights 3.

Communications

Medium	date	unit	number	units per 1,000 persons
Daily newspapers	1998	circulation	2,145,000	254
Television	1998	receivers	3,400,000	418
Telephones	1999	main lines	2,933,000	363.4
Cellular telephones	1999	subscribers	350,000	43.4
Personal computers	1999	units	220,000	27.3
Internet	1999	users	235,000	29.1

Education and health

Educational attainment (1992). Percentage of population age 25 and over having: no formal schooling 4.7%; incomplete primary education 12.5%; primary 31.9%; secondary 35.7%; higher 15.0%. *Literacy* (1995): total population age 15 and over literate 98.0%; males 98.8%; females 97.4%.

Education (1997–98)

	schools	teachers	students	student/ teacher ratio
Primary (age 6–14) / Secondary (age 15–17)	3,258	69,850	940,794	13.5
Voc., teacher tr.	545	18,563	196,351	10.6
Higher	86	22,382	266,747	11.9

Health (1998): physicians 28,823 (1 per 285 persons); hospital beds 85,408 (1 per 97 persons); infant mortality rate per 1,000 live births (1999) 14.6.
Food (1999): daily per capita caloric intake 2,847 (vegetable products 76%, animal products 24%); 114% of FAO recommended minimum requirement.

Military

Total active duty personnel (2000): 79,760 (army 53.2%, navy 6.6%, air force 22.9%, other 17.3%). *Military expenditure as percentage of GNP* (1997): 3.0% (world 2.6%); per capita expenditure U.S.$114.

[1]Bulgaria has no official religion; the 1991 constitution, however, refers to Eastern Orthodoxy as the "traditional" religion. [2]The lev was re-denominated as of July 5, 1999; as of this date 1,000 (old) leva = 1 (new) lev. [3]January 1. [4]District nearly encircles Sofiya-Grad district on north, east, and south. [5]Sofiya-Grad includes Sofia city and immediately adjacent urban and rural areas. [6]Adjusted to account for March 2001 preliminary census results totaling 7,973,000. [7]Indirect taxes less bank service charges. [8]Includes 22,000 undistributable employed and 491,400 unemployed. [9]Imports c.i.f.; exports f.o.b.

Internet resources for further information:
- **National Statistical Institute of the Republic of Bulgaria http://www.acad.bg/BulRTD/nsi/index.htm**

Burkina Faso

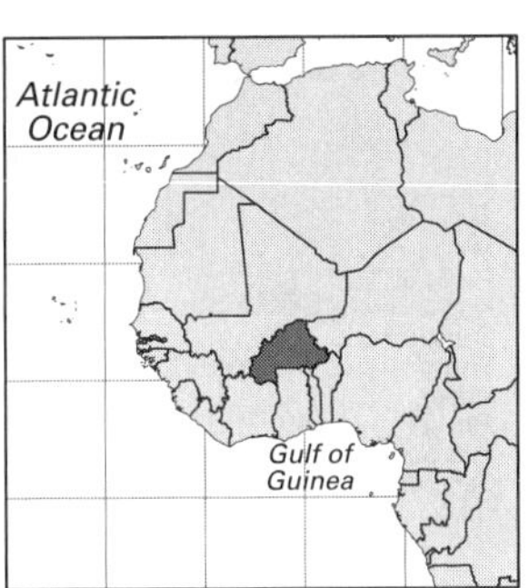

Official name: Burkina Faso (Burkina Faso).
Form of government: multiparty republic with one advisory body (Chamber of Representatives [178[1]]) and one legislative body (National Assembly [111]).
Chief of state: President.
Head of government: Prime Minister.
Capital: Ouagadougou.
Official language: French.
Official religion: none.
Monetary unit: 1 CFA franc (CFAF) = 100 centimes; valuation (Sept. 28, 2001) 1 U.S.$ = CFAF 720.28; 1 £ = CFAF 1,058.

Population[2]

Provinces	Capitals	population estimate[3]	Provinces	Capitals	population estimate[3]
Balé	Boromo	169,543	Mouhoun	Dédougou	237,048
Bam	Kongoussi	212,295	Nahouri	Pô	121,314
Banwa	Solenzo	214,234	Namentenga	Boulsa	251,909
Bazéga	Kombissiri	214,450	Nayala	Toma	136,273
Bougouriba	Diébougou	76,444	Noumbiel	Batié	51,449
Boulgou	Tenkodogo	415,414	Oubritenga	Ziniaré	198,130
Boulkiemde	Koudougou	421,083	Oudalan	Gorom-Gorom	136,583
Comoé	Banfora	240,942	Passoré	Yako	271,216
Ganzourgou	Zorgho	257,707	Poni	Gaoua	196,568
Gnagna	Bogandé	307,386	Sanguié	Réo	249,169
Gourma	Fada N'Gourma	221,956	Sanmatenga	Kaya	460,684
Houet	Bobo-Dioulasso	674,916	Séno	Dori	202,972
Ioba	Dano	159,422	Sissili	Léo	153,560
Kadiogo	Ouagadougou	976,513	Soum	Djibo	253,867
Kénédougou	Orodara	198,936	Sourou	Tougan	189,726
Komondjari	Gayéri	49,389	Tapoa	Diapaga	235,288
Kompienga	Pama	73,949	Tuy	Houndé	160,249
Kossi	Nouna	217,866	Yagha	Sebba	116,985
Koulpélogo	Ouargaye	188,760	Yatenga	Ouahigouya	443,967
Kouritenga	Koupéla	250,699	Ziro	Sapouy	117,774
Kourwéogo	Boussé	117,370	Zondoma	Gourcy	127,580
Léraba	Sindou	93,351	Zoundwéogo	Manga	196,698
Loroum	Titao	111,707	TOTAL		10,373,341

Demography

Area: 105,946 sq mi, 274,400 sq km.
Population (2001): 12,272,000.
Density (2001): persons per sq mi 115.8, persons per sq km 44.7.
Urban-rural (1999): urban 17.0%; rural 83.0%.
Sex distribution (2000): male 48.76%; female 51.24%.
Age breakdown (2000): under 15, 47.6%; 15–29, 27.5%; 30–44, 13.0%; 45–59, 7.3%; 60–74, 3.8%; 75 and over, 0.8%.
Population projection: (2010) 15,424,000; (2020) 19,402,000.
Ethnic composition (1983): Mossi 47.9%; Mande 8.8%; Fulani 8.3%; Lobi 6.9%; Bobo 6.8%; Senufo 5.3%; Grosi 5.1%; Gurma 4.8%; Tuareg 3.3%.
Religious affiliation (2000): Muslim 48.6%; traditional beliefs 34.1%; Christian 16.7%, of which Roman Catholic 9.5%.
Major cities (1993): Ouagadougou 690,000; Bobo-Dioulasso 300,000; Koudougou 105,000; Ouahigouya 38,902[4]; Banfora 35,319[4].

Vital statistics

Birth rate per 1,000 population (2000): 45.3 (world avg. 22.5).
Death rate per 1,000 population (2000): 17.0 (world avg. 9.0).
Natural increase rate per 1,000 population (2000): 28.3 (world avg. 13.5).
Total fertility rate (avg. births per childbearing woman; 2000): 6.4.
Life expectancy at birth (2000): male 46.3 years; female 47.2 years.

National economy

Budget (1999). Revenue: CFAF 238,100,000,000 (tax revenue 93.4%, of which sales tax 43.3%, import duties 25.3%, personal income taxes 22.6%, other 2.2%; nontax revenue 6.6%). Expenditures: CFAF 246,900,000,000 (wages and salaries 27.5%; investment 27.3%; health and education 22.4%; transfers 17.3%; debt service 5.5%).
Public debt (external, outstanding; 1999): U.S.$1,295,000,000.
Household income and expenditure. Average household size (1985) 6.2; average annual income per household CFAF 303,000 (U.S.$640); sources of income: n.a.; expenditure (1985)[5]: food 38.7%, transportation 18.6%, electricity and fuel 13.7%, beverages 9.0%, health 5.2%, housing 5.1%.
Tourism: receipts (1998) U.S.$42,000,000; expenditures (1994) U.S.$23,000,000.
Production (metric tons except as noted). Agriculture, forestry, fishing (1999): sorghum 1,178,400, millet 945,000, corn (maize) 468,900, sugarcane 400,000, peanuts (groundnuts) 281,400, seed cotton 280,000, rice 94,200, pulses 22,000, sweet potatoes 17,300, sesame 12,600, cassava 2,000; livestock (number of live animals) 7,950,000 goats, 6,350,000 sheep, 4,550,000 cattle, 21,000,000 chickens; roundwood (1998) 10,794,000 cu m; fish catch (1998) 8,335. Mining and quarrying (1999): gold 869 kg[6]; silver 120 kg. Manufacturing (1999): sugar 29,905; flour 21,454; edible oils 11,850; soap 9,910; beer 387,000 hectolitres; soft drinks 155,000 hectolitres; printed fabric 1,462,000 sq m; bicycles 24,079 units; mopeds 17,364 units; cigarettes 60,000,000 packets. Construction (value added in CFAF; 1995): 62,400,000,000. Energy production (consumption): electricity (kW-hr; 1998) 267,000,000 (267,000,000); crude petroleum, none (n.a.); petroleum products (metric tons; 1996) none (315,000).
Gross national product (1999): U.S.$2,602,000,000 (U.S.$240 per capita).

Structure of gross domestic product and labour force

	1999 in value CFAF '000,000	1999 % of total value	1991 labour force	1991 % of labour force
Agriculture	469,000	29.5	4,293,784	91.8
Mining } Manufacturing }	325,400	20.5	2,590 / 51,694	0.1 / 1.1
Construction	85,200	5.4	11,016	0.2
Public utilities	13,800	0.9	3,844	0.1
Transp. and commun.	65,000	4.1	15,041	0.3
Trade	189,200	11.9	120,314	2.6
Finance	...	...	2,075	—
Pub. admin., defense } Services }	352,400	22.2	111,556	2.4
Other	88,600[7]	5.6[7]	67,279[8]	1.4[8]
TOTAL	1,588,600	100.0[9]	4,679,193	100.0

Population economically active (1991): total 4,679,193; activity rate 50.9% (participation rates: over age [1988] 10, 78.1%; female 48.7%; unemployed 1.1%).

Price and earnings indexes (1995 = 100)

	1994	1995	1996	1997	1998	1999	2000
Consumer price index	93.1	100.0	106.2	108.6	114.2	112.9	112.5
Earnings index	...	...	...	...	...	...	...

Land use (1994): forest 50.5%; pasture 21.9%; agriculture 13.0%; other 14.6%.

Foreign trade

Balance of trade (current prices)

	1994	1995	1996	1997	1998	1999
CFAF '000,000	−114.4	−163.9	−227.2	−204.6	−231.4	−212.1
% of total	30.0%	34.4%	41.5%	38.0%	49.1%	40.4%

Imports (1999): CFAF 368,700,000,000 (capital equipment 36.8%, petroleum products 16.9%, food products 12.3%, raw materials 9.5%). *Major import sources* (1998): France 29.8%; Côte d'Ivoire 17.4%; Japan 5.4%; United States 3.6%; Italy 3.3%; The Netherlands 3.0%; Germany 2.9%.
Exports (1999): CFAF 156,600,000,000 (raw cotton 53.4%, live animals 10.1%, hides and skins 7.5%, gold 5.9%). *Major export destinations* (1998): France 23.1%; Belgium 10.8%; Côte d'Ivoire 9.8%; Singapore 3.6%; Mali 1.7%.

Transport and communications

Transport. Railroads (1995)[10]: route length 386 mi, 622 km; passenger-km 202,000,000; metric ton-km cargo 45,000,000. Roads (1996): total length 7,519 mi, 12,100 km (paved 16%). Vehicles (1996): passenger cars 38,220; trucks and buses 17,980. Merchant marine: none. Air transport (1993): passenger-km 217,154,000; metric ton-km cargo 34,204,000; airports (1998) 2.

Communications

Medium	date	unit	number	units per 1,000 persons
Daily newspapers	1996	circulation	14,000	1.3
Radio	1997	receivers	370,000	34.0
Television	1998	receivers	120,000	10.6
Telephones	1999	main lines	47,338	4.1
Cellular telephones	1999	subscribers	5,036	0.4
Personal computers	1999	units	12,000	1.0
Internet	1999	users	4,000	0.3

Education and health

Educational attainment (1985). Percentage of population age 10 and over having: no formal schooling 86.1%; some primary 7.3%; general secondary 2.2%; specialized secondary and postsecondary 3.8%; other 0.6%. *Literacy* (1995): percentage of total population age 15 and over literate 23.0%; males literate 31.2%; females literate 13.1%.

Education (1995–96)

	schools	teachers	students	student/ teacher ratio
Primary	3,568	14,037	702,204	50.0
Secondary	252	4,162	137,257	33.0
Vocational	41	731	9,539	13.0
Higher	9	632	9,531	15.1

Health (1991): physicians 341 (1 per 27,158 persons); hospital beds 5,041 (1 per 1,837 persons); infant mortality rate (2000) 108.5.
Food (1999): daily per capita caloric intake 2,376 (vegetable products 95%, animal products 5%); 100% of FAO recommended minimum requirement.

Military

Total active duty personnel (2000): 5,800 (army 96.6%, air force 3.4%). *Military expenditure as percentage of GNP* (1997): 2.8% (world 2.6%); per capita expenditure U.S.$6.

[1]All seats are appointed or indirectly elected. [2]In 1997 the number of first-order administrative subdivisions was increased from 30 to 45. [3]Actual date is unknown. Probable date is 1995–97. [4]1985. [5]Weights of consumer price index components; Ouagadougou only. [6]Officially marketed gold only; does not include substantial illegal production. [7]Includes indirect taxes less imputed bank service charges and subsidies. [8]Includes 49,819 unemployed. [9]Detail does not add to total given because of rounding. [10]Passenger-km and metric ton-km cargo figures are based on traffic between Abidjan, Côte d'Ivoire, and Ouagadougou.

Internet resources for further information:
- **Embassy of Burkina Faso (Washington D.C.) http://www.burkinaembassy-usa.org/indepth.htm**

Burundi

Official name: Republika y'u Burundi (Rundi); République du Burundi (French) (Republic of Burundi).
Form of government: transitional regime[1, 2].
Head of state and government: President assisted by Vice President.
Capital: Bujumbura.
Official languages: Rundi; French.
Official religion: none.
Monetary unit: 1 Burundi franc (FBu) = 100 centimes; valuation (Sept. 28, 2001) 1 U.S.$ = FBu 847.30; 1 £ = FBu 1,245.

Area and population

Provinces	Capitals	area sq mi	area sq km	population 1990 census
Bubanza	Bubanza	420	1,089	222,953
Bujumbura	Bujumbura	509	1,319	608,931
Bururi	Bururi	952	2,465	385,490
Cankuzo	Cankuzo	759	1,965	142,707
Cibitoke	Cibitoke	631	1,636	279,843
Gitega	Gitega	764	1,979	565,174
Karuzi	Karuzi	563	1,457	287,905
Kayanza	Kayanza	476	1,233	443,116
Kirundo	Kirundo	658	1,703	401,103
Makamba	Makamba	757	1,960	223,799
Muramvya	Muramvya	593[3]	1,535[3]	441,653[3]
Muyinga	Muyinga	709	1,836	373,382
Mwaro	Mwaro	[3]	[3]	[3]
Ngozi	Ngozi	569	1,474	482,246
Rutana	Rutana	756	1,959	195,834
Ruyigi	Ruyigi	903	2,339	238,567
TOTAL LAND AREA		10,019	25,949	
INLAND WATER		721	1,867	
TOTAL		10,740	27,816	5,292,793[4]

Demography

Population (2001): 6,224,000.
Density (2001)[5]: persons per sq mi 621.2, persons per sq km 239.9.
Urban-rural (1999): urban 8.6%; rural 91.4%.
Sex distribution (2000): male 49.54%; female 50.46%.
Age breakdown (2000): under 15, 47.1%; 15–29, 26.6%; 30–44, 14.8%; 45–59, 7.2%; 60–74, 3.2%; 75 and over, 1.0%.
Population projection: (2010) 7,669,000; (2020) 9,553,000.
Doubling time: 29 years.
Ethnic composition (1995): Rundi 98.0%, of which Hutu 82.5%, Tutsi 14.5%; Twa Pygmy 1.0%; other 2.0%.
Religious affiliation (1990): Roman Catholic 65.1%; Protestant 13.8%; Muslim 1.6%; nonreligious 18.6%; traditional beliefs 0.3%; other 0.6%.
Major cities (1990): Bujumbura (1994) 300,000; Gitega 101,827; Bururi 15,816; Ngozi 14,511; Cibitoke 8,280.

Vital statistics

Birth rate per 1,000 population (2000): 40.5 (world avg. 22.5).
Death rate per 1,000 population (2000): 16.4 (world avg. 9.0).
Natural increase rate per 1,000 population (2000): 24.1 (world avg. 13.5).
Total fertility rate (avg. births per childbearing woman; 2000): 6.3.
Life expectancy at birth (2000): male 45.2 years; female 47.2 years.
Major causes of death: n.a.; however, major health problems include malaria, influenza, diarrheal diseases, measles, and AIDS.

National economy

Budget (1999). Revenue: FBu 70,400,000,000 (tax revenue 92.9%, of which taxes on goods and services 39.3%, taxes on international trade 23.3%, income tax 13.8%, corporate tax 13.1%, administrative receipts 3.4%; non-tax revenue 7.1%). Expenditures: FBu 99,000,000,000 (wages and salaries 29.1%, goods and services 28.0%, subsidies and transfers 8.5%, public debt 6.1%).
Public debt (external, outstanding; 1999): U.S.$1,050,000,000.
Production (metric tons except as noted). Agriculture, forestry, fishing (1999): bananas 1,511,270, sweet potatoes 734,172, cassavas 617,483, dry beans 227,428, sugarcane 175,000, corn (maize) 128,706, yams and taros 102,861, sorghum 59,992, rice 58,630, coffee 30,000, potatoes 24,393, millet 10,105, peanuts (groundnuts) 9,883, wheat 7,085; livestock (number of live animals) 593,657 goats, 329,000 cattle, 165,000 sheep, 61,000 pigs, 4,400,000 chickens; roundwood (1998) 1,799,000 cu m; fish catch (1998) 32,039. Mining and quarrying (1995): peat 8,000; kaolin clay 5,000; gold 10 kg. Manufacturing (1998): beer 1,036,321 hectolitres; carbonated beverages 60,390 hectolitres; cottonseed oil 133,600 litres; cigarettes 316,820,000 units; blankets 174,407 units; footwear (1994) 74,890 pairs. Construction: n.a. Energy production (consumption): electricity (kW-hr; 1998): 107,081,000 (112,209,000); coal, none (n.a.); crude petroleum, none (n.a.); petroleum products (metric tons; 1998) none (60,667); natural gas, none (n.a.); peat (metric tons; 1995) 8,000 (8,000).
Household income and expenditure. Average household size (1998) 5.0; income per household: n.a.; sources of income: n.a.; expenditure[6]: (1990) food 59.6%, clothing and footwear 11.1%, furniture and household goods 6.0%, energy and water 5.8%, housing 4.4%, other 13.1%.
Land use (1994): forested 12.7%; meadows and pastures 38.6%; agricultural and under permanent cultivation 45.9%; other 2.8%.
Gross national product (at current market prices; 1999): U.S.$823,000,000 (U.S.$120 per capita).

Structure of gross domestic product and labour force

	1999 in value FBu '000,000	1999 % of total value	1990 labour force	1990 % of labour force
Agriculture	183,000	46.3	2,574,443	93.1
Mining	2,900 (Mining and Public utilities)	0.7 (Mining and Public utilities)	1,419	—
Public utilities			1,672	0.1
Manufacturing	26,400	6.7	33,867	1.2
Construction	18,400	4.7	19,737	0.7
Transp. and communications	14,200	3.6	8,504	0.3
Trade	14,800	3.7	25,822	0.9
Finance	...	...	2,005	0.1
Pub. admin., defense	72,500	18.4	85,191 (Pub. admin., defense and Services)	3.1 (Pub. admin., defense and Services)
Services	9,600	2.4		
Other	53,100[7]	13.4[7]	13,270	0.5
TOTAL	394,900	100.0[3]	2,765,945[3]	100.0

Population economically active (1997): total 3,475,000; activity rate of total population 63.1% (participation rates (1991): ages 15–64, 91.4%; female 48.9%; unemployed, n.a.).

Price and earnings indexes (1995 = 100)

	1994	1995	1996	1997	1998	1999	2000
Consumer price index	83.8	100.0	126.4	165.8	186.5	192.8	239.7
Earnings index	...	...	...	...	...	...	...

Tourism (1999): receipts from visitors U.S.$1,000,000; expenditures by nationals abroad U.S.$8,000,000.

Foreign trade

Balance of trade (current prices)

	1994	1995	1996	1997	1998	1999
FBu '000,000	–26,434	–24,018	–26,039	–12,482	–26,700	–21,100
% of total	30.6%	31.1%	53.6%	16.9%	31.8%	24.7%

Imports (1998): FBu 55,300,000,000 (1994; machinery and transport equipment 21.3%, food and food products 17.9%, petroleum products 8.2%, pharmaceutical products 6.4%). *Major import sources* (1997): Belgium-Luxembourg 23.2%; France 21.0%; Zambia 8.2%; The Netherlands 7.5%; Germany 6.4%; Japan 5.2%; United States 1.2%; Kenya 1.2%.
Exports (1998): FBu 28,600,000,000 (coffee 79.7%, tea 17.1%, animal hides and skins 0.2%). *Major export destinations* (1997): United Kingdom 25.2%; Germany 21.4%; Belgium-Luxembourg 10.0%; France 8.1%; United States 0.9%; Rwanda 0.4%.

Transport and communications

Transport. Railroads: none. Roads (1996): total length 8,997 mi, 14,480 km (paved 7%). Vehicles (1996): passenger cars 19,200; trucks and other vehicles 18,240. Air transport (1998)[8]: passenger arrivals 12,113, departures 11,725; cargo loaded 1,490 metric tons, unloaded 9,329 metric tons; airports (1998) 1.

Communications

Medium	date	unit	number	units per 1,000 persons
Daily newspapers	1996	circulation	20,000	3.2
Radio	1997	receivers	440,000	69
Television	1999	receivers	100,000	15.2
Telephones	1999	main lines	18,993	2.9
Cellular telephones	1999	subscribers	800	0.1
Internet	1999	users	2,000	0.3

Education and health

Educational attainment: n.a. *Literacy* (1995): percentage of total population age 15 and over literate 35.3%; males literate 49.7%; females literate 22.5%.

Education (1996)

	schools	teachers	students	student/ teacher ratio
Primary (age 6–11)	1,418[9]	10,400[9]	453,746	...
Secondary (age 12–18)	113[10]	2,562[10]	56,887	...
Vocational and teacher training	...	...	5,712	...
Higher	8[10]	556[9]	4,379	...

Health (1996): physicians 329 (1 per 16,507 persons); hospital beds 3,560 (1 per 1,526 persons); infant mortality rate per 1,000 live births (2000) 71.5.
Food (1999): daily per capita caloric intake 1,628 (vegetable products 97%, animal products 3%); 70% of FAO recommended minimum requirement.

Military

Total active duty personnel (2000): 40,000 (army 100%). *Military expenditure as percentage of GNP* (1997): 6.1% (world 2.6%); per capita expenditure U.S.$11.

[1]Transitional government following military coup of July 1996 was modified into a "new" transitional government between November 2001 and November 2004 per implementation of the Tutsi-Hutu agreement (Arusha Accords) on July 23, 2001. [2]150-member Transitional Parliament and new 50-member Senate expected to be installed in late 2001. [3]Mwaro province was created in 1999 from part of Muramvya province. [4]Detail does not add to total given because of rounding. [5]Based on land area. [6]Weights of consumer price index components. [7]Indirect taxes less subsidies. [8]Figures for Bujumbura airport only. [9]1992–93. [10]1990–91.

Cambodia

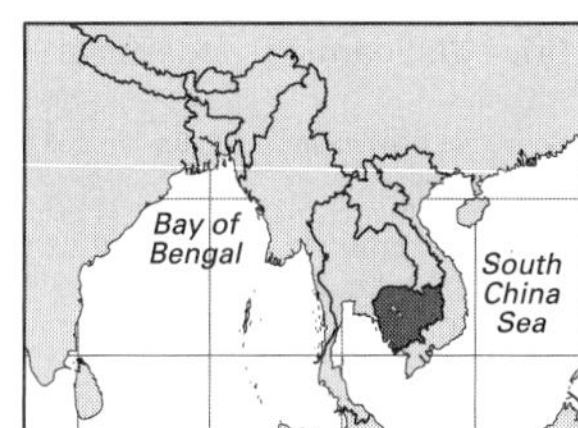

Official name: Preah Reach Ana Pak Kampuchea (Kingdom of Cambodia).
Form of government: constitutional monarchy with two legislative houses (Senate [61[1]]; National Assembly [122]).
Chief of state: King.
Head of government: Prime Minister[2].
Capital: Phnom Penh.
Official language: Khmer.
Official religion: Buddhism.
Monetary unit: 1 riel = 100 sen; valuation (Sept. 28, 2001) 1 U.S.$ = 3,835 riels; 1 £ = 5,636 riels.

Area and population

Provinces	Capitals	area sq mi	area sq km	population 1998 census
Banteay Mean Chey	...	2,579	6,679	577,772
Bat Dambang	Bat Dambang	4,518	11,702	793,129
Kampong Cham	Kampong Cham	3,783	9,799	1,608,914
Kampong Chhnang	Kampong Chhnang	2,132	5,521	417,693
Kampong Spueu	Kampong Spueu	2,709	7,017	598,882
Kampong Thum	Kampong Thum	5,334	13,814	569,060
Kampot	Kampot	1,881	4,873	528,405
Kandal	...	1,378	3,568	1,075,125
Kaoh Kong	Krong Kaoh Kong	4,309	11,160	132,106
Kracheh	Kracheh	4,283	11,094	263,175
Mondol Kiri	Senmonorom	5,517	14,288	32,407
Otdar Mean Cheay	...	2,378	6,158	68,279
Pousat	Pousat	4,900	12,692	360,445
Preah Vihear	Phum Tbeng Mean Cheay	5,324	13,788	119,261
Prey Veaeng	Prey Veaeng	1,885	4,883	946,042
Rotanak Kiri	Lumphat	4,163	10,782	94,243
Siem Reab	Siem Reab	3,976	10,299	696,164
Stueng Traeng	Stueng Traeng	4,283	11,092	81,074
Svay Rieng	Svay Rieng	1,145	2,966	478,252
Takaev	Takaev	1,376	3,563	790,168
Municipalities				
Kaeb	...	130	336	28,660
Pailin	...	310	803	22,906
Phnom Penh	...	112	290	999,804
Preah Sihanouk	...	335	868	155,690
TOTAL LAND AREA		68,740	178,035	
INLAND WATER		1,158	3,000	
TOTAL		69,898	181,035	11,437,656

Demography

Population (2001): 12,720,000.
Density (2001)[3]: persons per sq mi 185.0, persons per sq km 71.4.
Urban-rural (1998): urban 20.9%; rural 79.1%.
Sex distribution (1998): male 48.19%; female 51.81%.
Age breakdown (1998): under 15, 42.8%; 15–29, 26.1%; 30–44, 17.3%; 45–59, 8.6%; 60–74, 4.2%; 75 and over, 1.0%.
Population projection: (2010) 16,345,000; (2020) 20,012,000.
Doubling time: 28 years.
Ethnic composition (1994): Khmer 88.6%; Vietnamese 5.5%; Chinese 3.1%; Cham 2.3%; other (Thai, Lao, and Kola) 0.5%.
Religious affiliation (2000): Buddhist 84.7%; Chinese folk religionist 4.7%; traditional beliefs 4.3%; Muslim 2.3%; Christian 1.1%; other 2.9%.
Major cities (1998): Phnom Penh 999,804; Preah Sihanouk 155,690; Kaeb 28,660; Pailin 22,906.

Vital statistics

Birth rate per 1,000 population (2001): 35.9 (world avg. 22.5).
Death rate per 1,000 population (2001): 10.7 (world avg. 9.0).
Natural increase rate per 1,000 population (2001): 25.2 (world avg. 13.5).
Total fertility rate (avg. births per childbearing woman; 2001): 5.0.
Life expectancy at birth (2001): male 54.0 years; female 59.0 years.
Major causes of death per 100,000 population: n.a.; however, major health problems include tuberculosis, malaria, and pneumonia. Violence, acts of war, and military ordnance (especially unexploded mines) remain hazards.

National economy

Budget (1999). Revenue: 1,224,000,000,000 riels (taxes on international trade 36.0%; indirect taxes 27.1%, of which value-added taxes 13.7%; nontax revenue 28.2%). Expenditures: 1,485,000,000,000 riels (current expenditure 74.4%, of which civil administration 36.1%, defense and security 30.7%; development expenditure 25.6%).
Public debt (external, outstanding; 1999): U.S.$2,136,000,000.
Production (metric tons except as noted). Agriculture, forestry, fishing (1999): rice 3,800,000, bananas 145,000, sugarcane 138,000, roots and tubers 111,000 (of which cassava 67,500, sweet potatoes 25,000), oranges 63,000, corn (maize) 50,000, rubber 40,000, mangoes 33,000, soybeans 27,700, tobacco leaves 10,000; livestock (number of live animals; 1999) 2,821,000 cattle, 2,438,000 pigs, 694,000 buffalo, 16,498,000 chickens and ducks; roundwood (1998) 8,008,000 cu m; fish catch (1997) 114,600. Mining and quarrying (1995): legal mining is confined to fertilizers, salt, and construction materials. Manufacturing (value added in '000,000 riels; 1995): glass and glass products 42,659; cigarettes 1,064.5; wearing apparel 37,567; rubber products 30,114; processed meat, fish, fruits, and vegetables 24,521; sawmilling and planing of wood 18,099; tobacco products 10,163. Construction: n.a. Energy production (consumption): electricity (kW-hr; 1996) 201,000,000 (201,000,000); petroleum products (metric tons; 1996) none (163,000).

Household income and expenditure. Average household size (1998) 5.2.
Gross domestic product (1999): U.S.$3,023,000,000 (U.S.$260 per capita).

Structure of gross domestic product and labour force

	1998 in value '000,000,000 riels	1998 % of total value	1996 labour force	1996 % of labour force
Agriculture	5,443	50.6	3,732,000	72.6
Mining	33	0.3		
Manufacturing	665	6.2		
Construction	794	7.4		
Public utilities	95	0.9		
Transp. and commun.	445	4.1	1,406,000	27.4
Trade	1,530	14.3		
Public admin., defense	344	3.2		
Services, Other	1,401	13.0		
TOTAL	10,750	100.0	5,138,000	100.0

Population economically active (1996): total 4,904,294; activity rate of total population 47.4% (participation rates: ages 15 and over, 78.9%; female 52.7%).

Price and earnings indexes (1995 = 100)

	1994	1995	1996	1997	1998	1999	2000
Consumer price index	99.0	100.0	110.1	113.6	130.4	135.6	134.5
Earnings index	...	...	...	...	...	...	...

Tourism (1999): receipts U.S.$190,000,000; expenditures U.S.$18,000,000.
Land use (1994): forested 69.1%; meadows and pastures 8.5%; agricultural and under permanent cultivation 21.7%; other 0.7%.

Foreign trade[4]

Balance of trade (current prices)

	1994	1995	1996	1997	1998	1999
U.S.$'000,000	–275	–425	–459	–268	–228	–294
% of total	22.9%	21.0%	26.1%	13.3%	10.2%	13.6%

Imports (1998): U.S.$1,334,000,000 (cigarettes 11.2%; petroleum products 10.4%; motorcycles 2.8%; clothing 1.6%). *Major import sources* (1996): Singapore 34.2%; Thailand 23.9%; Vietnam 7.3%.
Exports (1998): U.S.$999,000,000 (reexports 39.6%; garments 39.0%; sawn timber and logs 17.8%, rubber 2.5%). *Major export destinations* (1996): Thailand 13.0%; Singapore 13.0%; India 9.3%.

Transport and communications

Transport. Railroads (1995): length (1999) 403 mi, 649 km; passenger-km 38,443,600; metric ton-km 7,797,600. Roads (1997): total length 22,226 mi, 35,769 km (paved 8%). Vehicles (1997): passenger cars 52,919; trucks and buses 13,574. Merchant marine (1992): vessels (100 gross tons and over) 3; total deadweight tonnage 3,839. Air transport (1977): passenger-mi 26,098,800, passenger-km 42,000,000; short ton-mi cargo 274,000, metric ton-km cargo 400,000; airports (1997) with scheduled flights 8.

Communications

Medium	date	unit	number	units per 1,000 persons
Daily newspapers	1996	circulation	17,000	1.7
Radio	1997	receivers	1,340,000	128
Television	1999	receivers	98,000	9.0
Telephones	1999	main lines	27,704	2.5
Cellular telephones	1999	subscribers	89,117	8.1
Personal computers	1999	units	13,000	1.2
Internet	1999	users	4,000	0.4

Education and health

Educational attainment (1998). Percentage of population age 25 and over having: no formal schooling 2.1%; some primary education 56.6%; primary 24.7%; some secondary 11.8%; secondary and above 4.8%. *Literacy* (1998): percentage of total population age 15 and over literate 67.3%; males literate 79.5%; females literate 57.0%.

Education (1997–98)

	schools	teachers	students	student/ teacher ratio
Primary (age 6–10)	5,026	43,282	2,011,772	46.5
Secondary (age 11–16)	440[5]	16,820	302,951	18.0
Voc., teacher tr.	65[5]	2,315	9,983	4.3
Higher	9[5]	1,001	8,901	8.9

Health: physicians (1994) 1,200 (1 per 7,900 persons); hospital beds (1994) 12,098[6] (1 per 791 persons); infant mortality rate (2001) 76.0.
Food (1999): daily per capita caloric intake 2,000 (vegetable products 93%, animal products 7%); (1997) 90% of FAO recommended minimum requirement.

Military

Total active duty personnel (2000)[7]: 140,000 (army 64.3%, navy 2.1%, air force 1.4%, provincial 32.2%). *Military expenditure as percentage of GNP* (1997): 4.1% (world 2.6%); per capita expenditure U.S.$11.

[1]All seats appointed in 1999; all seats to be elected in future. [2]A single prime minister was head of government from November 1998 per the king's forced moral persuasion. [3]Based on land area. [4]Trade balance statistics indicate imports are f.o.b. [5]1992–93. [6]Public hospitals only. [7]Figures include provincial and exclude paramilitary forces.

Internet resources for further information:
- **Cambodian Information Center http://www.cambodia.org**
- **National Institute of Statistics http://www.nis.gov.kh**

Cameroon

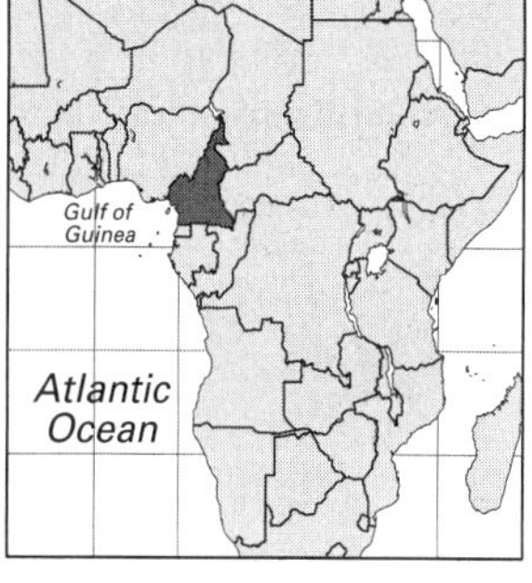

Official name: République du Cameroun (French); Republic of Cameroon (English).
Form of government: unitary multiparty republic with one legislative house (National Assembly [180]).
Chief of state: President.
Head of government: Prime Minister.
Capital: Yaoundé.
Official languages: French; English.
Official religion: none.
Monetary unit: 1 CFA franc (CFAF) = 100 centimes; valuation (Sept. 28, 2001) 1 U.S.$ = CFAF 720.28; 1 £ = CFAF 1,058.

Area and population

Regions	Capitals	area sq mi	area sq km	population 1987 census
Adamoua	Ngaoundéré	24,591	63,691	495,200
Centre	Yaoundé	26,613	68,926	1,651,600
Est	Bertoua	42,089	109,011	517,200
Extrême-Nord	Maroua	13,223	34,246	1,855,700
Littoral	Douala	7,814	20,239	1,354,800
Nord	Garoua	25,319	65,576	832,200
Nord-Ouest	Bamenda	6,877	17,810	1,237,400
Ouest	Bafoussam	5,356	13,872	1,339,800
Sud	Ebolowa	18,189	47,110	373,800
Sud-Ouest	Buea	9,448	24,471	838,000
LAND AREA		179,519	464,952	
INLAND WATER		4,051	10,492	
TOTAL		183,569[1]	475,442[1]	10,495,700

Demography

Population (2001): 15,803,000.
Density (2001)[2]: persons per sq mi 88.0; persons per sq km 34.0.
Urban-rural (1999): urban 48.1%; rural 51.9%.
Sex distribution (2000): male 50.21%; female 49.79%.
Age breakdown (2000): under 15, 42.7%; 15–29, 27.9%; 30–44, 15.6%; 45–59, 8.7%; 60–74, 4.1%; 75 and over, 1.0%.
Population projection: (2010) 19,202,000; (2020) 22,869,000.
Doubling time: 28 years.
Ethnic composition (1983): Fang 19.6%; Bamileke and Bamum 18.5%; Duala, Luanda, and Basa 14.7%; Fulani 9.6%; Tikar 7.4%; Mandara 5.7%; Maka 4.9%; Chamba 2.4%; Mbum 1.3%; Hausa 1.2%; French 0.2%; other 14.5%.
Religious affiliation (2000): Roman Catholic 26.4%; traditional beliefs 23.7%; Muslim 21.2%; Protestant 20.7%.
Major cities (1992): Douala 1,200,000; Yaoundé 800,000; Garoua 160,000; Maroua 140,000; Bafoussam 120,000.

Vital statistics

Birth rate per 1,000 population (2000): 36.6 (world avg. 22.5).
Death rate per 1,000 population (2000): 11.9 (world avg. 9.0).
Natural increase rate per 1,000 population (2000): 24.7 (world avg. 13.5).
Total fertility rate (avg. births per childbearing woman; 2000): 4.9.
Life expectancy at birth (2001): male 54.0 years; female 55.6 years.
Major causes of death per 100,000 population: n.a.; however, major health problems include measles, malaria, tuberculosis of respiratory system, anemias, meningitis, and intestinal obstruction and hernia.

National economy

Budget (1998–99). Revenue: CFAF 838,000,000,000 (taxes on goods and services 40.5%; income tax 20.8%; customs duties 16.5%; oil revenue 15.9%). Expenditures: CFAF 1,023,000,000,000 (current expenditure 80.9%, of which debt services 27.6%, wages and salaries 26.9%, goods and services 16.3%, transfers 9.8%; capital expenditure 19.1%).
Public debt (external, outstanding; 1999): U.S.$7,614,000,000.
Gross national product (1999): U.S.$8,798,000,000 (U.S.$600 per capita).

Structure of gross domestic product and labour force

	1998–99 in value CFAF '000,000,000	1998–99 % of total value	1985 labour force	1985 % of labour force
Agriculture	1,789	33.1	2,900,871	74.0
Mining	243	4.5	1,793	0.1
Manufacturing	703	13.0	174,498	4.5
Construction	157	2.9	66,684	1.7
Public utilities	119	2.2	3,522	0.1
Transp. and commun.			51,688	1.3
Trade			154,014	3.9
Finance	2,395	44.3	8,009	0.2
Services			292,922	7.5
Public admin., defense				
Other	...	...	263,634	6.7
TOTAL	5,406	100.0	3,917,635	100.0

Household income and expenditure. Average household size (1998) 5.7; average annual income per household (1983)[3] U.S.$420; sources of income: n.a.; expenditure (1993)[3]: food 49.1%, housing 18.0%, transportation and communications 13.0%, health 8.6%, clothing 7.6%, recreation 2.4%.
Population economically active (1991): total 4,740,000; activity rate of total population 40.0% (participation rates [1985]: ages 15–69, 66.3%; female 38.5%; unemployed, n.a.).

Price and earnings indexes (1995 = 100)

	1995	1996	1997	1998	1999	2000
Consumer price index	100.0	103.9	108.9	112.4	114.4	115.8
Earnings index	...	...	...	...	...	...

Production (metric tons except as noted). Agriculture, forestry, fishing (1999): cassava 1,500,000, sugarcane 1,350,000, plantains 1,000,000, bananas 990,000, corn (maize) 600,000, sorghum 500,000, vegetables and melons 430,000, sweet potatoes 220,000, seed cotton 190,000, palm oil 150,000, cacao 150,000, yams 130,000, peanuts (groundnuts) 100,000, millet 71,000, rice 65,000, coffee 61,500, natural rubber 54,000, palm kernels 52,000; livestock (number of live animals) 5,900,000 cattle, 3,880,000 sheep, 3,850,000 goats, 1,430,000 pigs; roundwood (1998) 15,172,000 cu m; fish catch (1998) 97,000. Mining and quarrying (1996): pozzolana 100,000; aluminum 82,000; limestone 50,000; tin ore and concentrate 1. Manufacturing (value added in CFAF '000,000; 1994): beverages 49,314; wood and wood products 42,756; rubber and plastic products 38,928; food products 30,030; iron and steel products 29,424; textiles 20,113; refined petroleum products 17,888; industrial chemicals 8,559; pottery, china, and earthenware 6,773; paper products 3,652. Construction (1983): residential 230,400 sq m; nonresidential 51,100 sq m. Energy production (consumption): electricity (kW-hr; 1996) 2,753,000,000 (2,753,000,000); coal (metric tons; 1996) 1,000 (1,000); crude petroleum (barrels; 1996) 42,770,000 (6,856,000); petroleum products (metric tons; 1996) 1,040,000 (1,107,000); natural gas, none (n.a.).
Land use (1994): forested 77.1%; meadows and pastures 4.3%; agricultural and under permanent cultivation 15.1%; other 3.5%.
Tourism (1995): receipts U.S.$36,000,000; expenditures U.S.$105,000,000.

Foreign trade

Balance of trade (current prices)

	1994	1995	1996	1997	1998	1999
CFAF '000,000,000	+223.7	+398.8	+277.5	+290.6	+209.4	+112.4
% of total	15.7%	24.4%	18.1%	15.6%	10.7%	6.0%

Imports (1998–99): CFAF 881,500,000,000 (semifinished goods 15.9%; industrial equipment 13.3%; food and beverages 11.3%; minerals 10.6%; transport equipment 10.3%; unrecorded trade 6.1%). *Major import sources:* France 25.6%; Germany 6.4%; U.S. 5.7%; Japan 5.0%; Belgium-Luxembourg 4.8%; Italy 4.3%; The Netherlands 2.6%; United Kingdom 2.6%.
Exports (1998–99): CFAF 993,900,000,000 (crude petroleum 31.6%; lumber 12.1%; coffee 7.5%; cocoa 7.4%; aluminum 5.0%; cotton 4.7%). *Major export destinations:* Italy 22.4%; France 12.6%; Spain 9.4%; The Netherlands 9.4%; Portugal 3.3%; Germany 1.9%.

Transport and communications

Transport. Railroads (1997): route length 625 mi, 1,006 km; (1995) passenger-mi 197,000,000, passenger-km 317,000,000; short ton-mi cargo 556,000,000, metric ton-km cargo 812,000,000. Roads (1997): total length 30,074 mi, 48,400 km (paved 8%). Vehicles (1997): passenger cars 98,000; trucks and buses 64,350. Merchant marine (1992): vessels (100 gross tons and over) 47; total deadweight tonnage 39,797. Air transport (1996): passenger-mi 347,970,000, passenger-km 560,000,000; short ton-mi cargo 56,540,000, metric ton-km cargo 91,000,000; airports (1998) with scheduled flights 5.

Communications

Medium	date	unit	number	units per 1,000 persons
Daily newspapers	1996	circulation	91,000	6.7
Radio	1997	receivers	2,270,000	163
Television	1998	receivers	480,000	33.5
Telephones	1999	main lines	94,599	6.4
Cellular telephones	1997	subscribers	4,200	0.3
Personal computers	1999	units	40,000	2.7
Internet	1999	users	20,000	1.4

Education and health

Educational attainment (1976). Percentage of population age 15 and over having: no schooling 51.1%; primary education 41.7%; some postprimary 0.2%; secondary 5.7%; some postsecondary 0.3%; higher 0.2%; other 0.8%. *Literacy* (1995): percentage of total population age 15 and over literate 63.4%; males literate 75.0%; females literate 52.1%.

Education (1994–95)

	schools	teachers	students	student/ teacher ratio
Primary (age 6–14)	6,801	40,970	1,896,722	46.3
Secondary (age 15–24)	388[4]	14,917	459,068	30.8
Vocational	220[4]	5,885	91,779	15.6
Higher[5]	5[4]	1,086	33,177	30.5

Health: physicians (1996) 1,031 (1 per 13,510 persons); hospital beds (1988) 29,285 (1 per 371 persons); infant mortality rate (2000) 70.9.
Food (1999): daily per capita caloric intake 2,260 (vegetable products 94%, animal products 6%); 97% of FAO recommended minimum requirement.

Military

Total active duty personnel (2000): 13,100 (army 87.8%, navy 9.9%, air force 2.3%). *Military expenditure as percentage of GNP* (1997): 3.0% (world 2.6%); per capita expenditure U.S.$16.

[1]Detail does not add to total given because of rounding. [2]Based on land area. [3]Weights of consumer price index components. [4]1986–87. [5]1990–91.

Internet resources for further information:
- **Investir en Zone Franc http://www.izf.net/izf/Index.htm**

Canada

Official name: Canada.
Form of government: federal multiparty parliamentary state with two legislative houses (Senate [105]; House of Commons [301]).
Chief of state: Queen of Canada (British Monarch).
Representative of chief of state: Governor-General.
Head of government: Prime Minister.
Capital: Ottawa.
Official languages: English; French.
Official religion: none.
Monetary unit: 1 Canadian dollar (Can$) = 100 cents; valuation (Sept. 28, 2001) 1 U.S.$ = Can$1.58; 1 £ = Can$2.32.

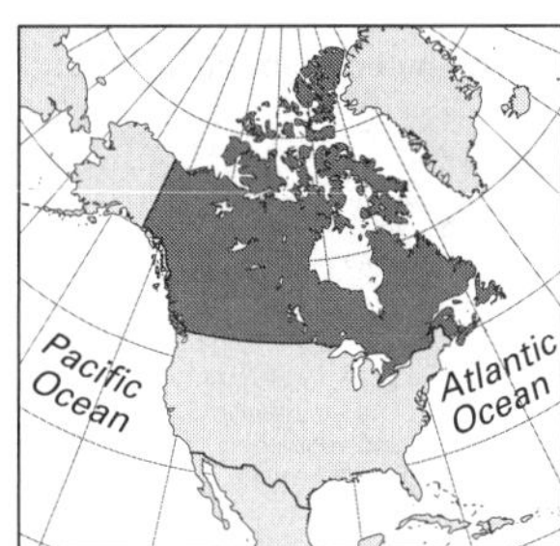

Area and population

		area		population
				2001
Provinces	**Capitals**	sq mi	sq km	estimate
Alberta	Edmonton	255,287	661,190	3,064,200
British Columbia	Victoria	365,948	947,800	4,095,900
Manitoba	Winnipeg	250,947	649,950	1,150,000
New Brunswick	Fredericton	28,355	73,440	757,100
Newfoundland and Labrador	St. John's	156,649	405,720	533,800
Nova Scotia	Halifax	21,425	55,490	942,700
Ontario	Toronto	412,581	1,068,580	11,874,400
Prince Edward Island	Charlottetown	2,185	5,660	138,500
Quebec	Quebec	594,860	1,540,680	7,410,500
Saskatchewan	Regina	251,866	652,330	1,015,800
Territories				
Northwest Territories	Yellowknife	1,322,910[1]	3,426,320[1]	40,900
Nunavut[2]	Iqaluit	[1]	[1]	28,200
Yukon Territory	Whitehorse	186,661	483,450	29,900
TOTAL		3,849,674	9,970,610	31,081,900

Demography

Population (2001): 31,081,900.
Density (2001)[3]: persons per sq mi 8.7, persons per sq km 3.4.
Urban-rural (1996): urban 77.9%; rural 22.1%.
Sex distribution (2001): male 49.51%; female 50.49%.
Age breakdown (2001): under 15, 18.8%; 15–29, 20.3%; 30–44, 24.4%; 45–59, 19.7%; 60–74, 11.1%; 75 and over, 5.7%.
Population projection: (2010) 33,132,000; (2020) 35,187,000.
Doubling time: not applicable; doubling time exceeds 100 years.
Ethnic origin (1996): British 11.5%; French 9.4%; other European 13.1%, of which Southern European 4.8%, Western European 3.9%, Eastern European 3.0%; Asian origin 7.0%; Amerindian and Inuktitut (Eskimo) 1.7%; Latin American origin 1.4%; Arab origin 0.6%; African origin 0.5%; multiple origin and other 54.8%[4].
Religious affiliation (2000): Roman Catholic 41.8%; Protestant 39.7%; Eastern Orthodox 1.9%; Jewish 1.3%; Muslim 1.0%; Hindu 1.0%; Buddhist 0.8%; nonreligious 10.9%; other 1.6%.
Major metropolitan areas (1999): Toronto 4,680,300; Montreal 3,438,500; Vancouver 2,016,600; Ottawa-Hull 1,065,000; Calgary 933,700; Edmonton 929,100; Quebec 688,100; Winnipeg 677,600; Hamilton 665,200; London 418,700.

Other metropolitan areas (1999)

	population		population		population
Chicoutimi-Jonquière	162,300	Regina	199,200	Sherbrooke	153,100
Halifax	352,600	St. Catharines–Niagara	389,600	Sudbury	160,400
Kitchener	415,000	St. John's	127,200	Trois Rivières	141,800
Oshawa	292,900	Saskatoon	231,400	Victoria	316,200
				Windsor	300,000

Place of birth (1996): 83.4% native-born; 16.6% foreign-born, of which U.K. 2.2%, other European 4.2%, Asian countries 5.2%, U.S. 0.8%, other 4.2%.
Mobility (1996). Population living in the same residence as in 1991: 56.7%; different residence, same municipality 23.0%; same province, different municipality 3.3%; different province 13.4%; different country 3.5%.
Households (1999). Total number of households 11,553,000. Average household size 2.5; (1997) 1 person 25.2%, 2 persons 33.0%, 3 persons 16.7%, 4 persons 16.3%, 5 or more persons 8.8%. Family households (1999): 8,139,700 (70.6%), nonfamily 3,413,300 (29.4%, of which 1 person 83.6%).
Immigration (1999–2000): permanent immigrants admitted 252,088; from Asia 62.1%, of which India 11.6%, Philippines 5.6%, Vietnam 0.7%, Hong Kong 0.3%; United States 2.4%; United Kingdom 2.1%; refugee arrivals 22,899.

Vital statistics

Birth rate per 1,000 population (2000): 11.3 (world avg. 22.5); (1997) legitimate 72.3%; illegitimate 27.7%.
Death rate per 1,000 population (2000): 7.4 (world avg. 9.0).
Natural increase rate per 1,000 population (2000): 3.9 (world avg. 13.5).
Total fertility rate (avg. births per childbearing woman; 2000): 1.6.
Marriage rate per 1,000 population (2000): 5.0.
Divorce rate per 1,000 population (2000): 2.2.
Life expectancy at birth (2000): male 76.0 years; female 83.0 years.
Major causes of death per 100,000 population (1997): diseases of the circulatory system 220.8; malignant neoplasms (cancers) 181.5; diseases of the respiratory system 52.7; accidents and violence 39.7 (including suicide 12.0).

Social indicators

Educational attainment (1996). Percentage of population age 15 and over having: no formal schooling or not known 4.2%; at least primary education 12.3%; some secondary 19.6%; completed secondary 19.8%; postsecondary 30.5%; university graduates 13.6%.

Distribution of income (1996)

percentage of household income by quintile

1	2	3	4	5 (highest)
6.1%	11.9%	17.4%	24.0%	40.6%

Quality of working life. Average workweek (1997): 31.3 hours. Annual rate per 100,000 workers for (1997): injury, accident, or industrial illness 1,330; death 2.7. Average days lost to labour stoppages per 1,000 employee-workdays (1997): 0.9. Average duration of journey to work (1996): n.a.; mode of transportation: automobile 80.6%, public transportation 10.1%, other 9.3%. Rate per 1,000 workers of discouraged (unemployed no longer seeking work; 1983): 10.5.
Access to services (1999). Proportion of households having access to: electricity 100.0%; public water supply 99.8%[5]; public sewage collection 99.3%[5].
Social participation. Eligible voters participating in last national election (November 2000): 61.2%. Population over 18 years of age participating in voluntary work (2000): 26.7%. Union membership in total workforce (1999): 32.9%. Practicing religious population in total affiliated population (1996): 92.5%.
Social deviance (2000). Offense rate per 100,000 population for: violent crime 981, of which assault 758.9, sexual assault 78.2, homicide 1.6; property crime 4,067, of which auto theft 521, burglary 954.
Leisure (1998). Favourite leisure activities (hours weekly): television 15.4; social time 13.3; reading 2.8; sports and entertainment 1.4.
Material well-being (1998). Households possessing: automobile 78.8%, of which two or more 34.5%; telephone 98.2%; colour television 98.8%; refrigerator 99.8%; central air conditioner 33.1%; cable television 66.5%; video recorder 88.1%; microwave oven 88.7%; home computers 45.1%.

National economy

Gross national product (1999): U.S.$614,003,000,000 (U.S.$20,140 per capita).

Structure of gross domestic product and labour force

	2000			
	in value Can$'000,000[6]	% of total value	labour force	% of labour force
Agriculture	22,862	2.5	655,700	4.1
Mining	36,125	3.9		
Manufacturing	169,471	18.2	2,344,800	14.7
Construction	48,534	5.2	866,100	5.4
Public utilities	28,234	3.0	116,400	0.7
Transportation	44,658	4.8	779,800	4.9
Trade	105,479	11.3	2,318,100	14.5
Finance	177,925	19.1	867,000	5.4
Pub. admin., defense	51,009	5.6	761,700	4.8
Services[7]	245,259	26.4	6,200,000	38.7
Other	—	—	1,089,600[8]	6.8[8]
TOTAL	929,556[9]	100.0	15,999,200	100.0

Budget (1999–2000). Revenue: Can$172,532,000,000 (individual income taxes 47.8%, value-added tax 20.3%, corporate income tax 13.0%, contributions to social security 10.8%, import duties 1.3%). Expenditures: Can$169,966,000,000 (social services 29.6%, public debt interest 24.5%, defense and social protection 10.8%, education 2.6%, health 1.0%).
National debt (1997): Can$619,710,000,000.
Tourism (1999): receipts U.S.$10,171,000,000; expenditures U.S.$11,345,000,000.

Manufacturing, mining, and construction enterprises (1999)

	no. of establishments[10]	no. of employees	weekly wages as a % of avg. of all mfg. wages	annual value added[10] (Can$'000,000)
Manufacturing				
Food and beverages	3,202	230,100	102.1	20,110
Transport equipment	1,224	246,300	148.4	19,430
Chemicals and related products	1,396	90,000	145.7	12,860
Machinery	4,000	92,100	140.1	9,130
Electrical and electronic products	1,176	129,900	142.3	8,520
Printing, publishing, and related products	4,655	150,300	107.7	8,500
Paper and related products	651	99,300	157.5	7,890
Wood	2,201	142,800	113.0	7,880
Primary metals	417	84,000	157.0	7,790
Metal fabricating	3,287	182,000	123.2	6,290
Rubber and plastic	1,394	104,000	112.8	5,900
Textiles	1,057	53,300	91.0	3,600
Nonmetallic mineral products	1,519	51,500	122.8	3,440
Wearing apparel	1,923	89,400	72.4	3,220
Petroleum and coal products	170	14,800	180.2	2,560
Furniture and fixtures	1,965	61,800	94.6	2,310
Tobacco products industries	17	4,300	211.7	1,220
Mining	13,692	169,700	182.3	29,650
Construction	203,253	524,500	114.5	28,182

Production (metric tons except as noted). Agriculture, forestry, fishing (2001): wheat 20,695,300, barley 11,103,300, rapeseed 7,778,000, corn (maize) 7,550,000, potatoes 4,568,500, oats 2,838,300, soybeans 2,040,100, vegetables 2,135,000 (of which tomatoes 670,000, carrots 278,608, onions 189,334, cabbage 167,450), dry peas 2,175,400, sugar beets 821,000, linseed 703,700, apples 580,000; livestock (number of live animals) 12,860,000 cattle, 12,600,000 pigs, 694,800 sheep, 385,000 horses; roundwood (2000) 148,871,000 cu m; fish catch (1999) 1,135,516. Mining and quarrying (1999): iron ore 33,004,000; zinc 960,099; copper 580,036; nickel 177,029; lead 156,102; uranium 9,892; molybdenum 6,293; silver 1,173 kg; gold 157,790 kg. Manufacturing (value of shipments in Can$'000,000; 1999): transportation equipment 125,034.3; food 52,352.8; electrical machinery 36,760.6; paper products 33,150.3; wood industries 30,600.6; metal products 26,883.9; printing and publishing 16,526.3; machinery 16,890.5; rubber and plastic products 16,885.0; furniture 8,506.4; wearing apparel 6,996.3; textile 3,683.3. Construction (value of building permits in Can$'000,000; 1999): residential 19,956.9; nonresidential 15,813.5.

Retail trade (2000)

	no. of enterprises	no. of employees[11]	weekly wages as a % of all wages	annual sales (Can$'000,000)
Motor vehicle dealers	...	79,800	143.5	73,104
Food stores	...	213,400	84.2	61,090
Service stations	...	63,700	143.5	22,364
Department stores	...	[12]	81.7	[12]
Clothing stores	...	50,200	79.4	15,278
Pharmacies	...	52,400	...	13,499
Furniture and appliance stores	...	62,100	119.2	15,159
Automotive stores	...	31,500	143.5	88,687
General merchandise	...	231,700[12]	81.7	31,297[12]
Sporting goods	...	...	...	332[13]
General stores	...	[12]	81.7	[12]
Hardware stores	...	17,300	81.7	486[13]
Shoe stores	...	18,400	79.4	1,770
Jewelry stores	...	14,000	...	315[13]
Variety stores	...	45,100	92.0	805[13]

Energy production (consumption): electricity (kW-hr; 1999) 541,900,000,000 (545,460,300,000); coal (metric tons; 2000) 69,164,000 (60,761,000); crude petroleum (barrels; 1997) 719,729,000 (608,411,000); petroleum products (metric tons; 1997) 95,026,000 (81,240,000); natural gas (cu m; 1999) 163,384,000,000 ([1998]; 89,163,000,000).

Population economically active (2000): total 15,999,200; activity rate of total population 52.0% (participation rates: ages 15 and over 65.9%; female 45.9%; unemployed [2001] 7.3%).

Price and earnings indexes (1995 = 100)

	1994	1995	1996	1997	1998	1999	2000
Consumer price index	97.9	100.0	100.4	101.3	101.2	102.9	108.1
Hourly earnings index[14]	98.6	100.0	103.2	104.1	106.3	106.4	112.3

Household income and expenditure (1999). Average household size 2.6; average annual income per family (1999) Can$63,818 (U.S.$43,413); sources of income (1995): wages and salaries 57.0%, transfer payments 20.7%, property and entrepreneurial income 13.7%, profits 8.6%; expenditure (1999): housing 27.2%, food, alcohol, and tobacco 19.3%, transportation and communications 18.2%, recreation 7.9%, utilities 6.4%, clothing 6.2%, household durable goods 3.9%, health 3.3%, education 2.0%.

Financial aggregates

	1995	1996	1997	1998	1999	2000
Exchange rate, Can$ per:						
U.S. dollar	1.37	1.37	1.42	1.53	1.44	1.50
£	2.17	2.33	2.34	2.55	2.33	2.24
SDR	2.03	1.97	1.93	2.16	1.98	1.95
International reserves (U.S.$)						
Total (excl. gold; '000,000)	15,049	20,422	17,823	23,308	28,126	31,924
SDRs ('000,000)	1,177	1,168	1,126	1,098	527	574
Reserve pos. in IMF ('000,000)	1,243	1,226	1,575	2,299	3,168	2,509
Foreign exchange ('000,000)	12,629	18,028	15,122	19,991	24,432	28,841
Gold ('000,000 fine troy oz)	3.41	3.09	3.09	2.49	1.81	1.18
% world reserves	0.38	0.34	0.35	0.26	0.18	0.12
Interest and prices						
Central bank discount (%)	5.79	3.25	4.50	5.25	5.00	6.00
Govt. bond yield (%)	8.28	7.50	6.42	5.47	5.69	5.89
Industrial share prices (1995 = 100)	100.0	118.8	145.7	152.4	159.2	216.7
Balance of payments (U.S.$'000,000)						
Balance of visible trade, of which:	22,341	31,091	17,223	12,775	22,756	36,610
Imports, f.o.b.	−167,513	−174,352	−200,516	−204,631	−220,064	−244,538
Exports, f.o.b.	189,854	205,443	217,739	217,406	242,820	281,148
Balance of invisibles	−31,034	−27,713	−27,288	−23,908	−25,029	−23,944
Balance of payments, current account	−8,693	−3,378	−10,065	−11,133	−2,273	+12,666

Land use (1994): forested 53.6%; meadows and pastures 3.0%; agricultural and under permanent cultivation 4.9%; built-on, wasteland, and other 38.5%.

Foreign trade

Balance of trade (current prices)

	1994	1995	1996	1997	1998	1999	2000
Can$'000,000,000	+19.3	+38.7	+42.2	+25.5	+19.8	+35.1	+59.3
% of total	4.5%	7.9%	8.3%	4.5%	3.2%	5.2%	7.5%

Imports (2000): Can$363,281,300,000 (1999; machinery and transport equipment 56.3%, of which motor vehicles 23.2%; chemical products 6.9%; food 5.4%; petroleum and energy products 3.3%; forestry products 0.8%). *Major import sources* (1999): U.S. 67.2%; Japan 4.7%; Mexico 3.0%; China 2.8%; U.K. 2.5%; Germany 2.2%; France 1.7%; Taiwan 1.4%; Italy 1.1%; South Korea 1.1%.

Exports (2000): Can$422,558,700,000 (1999; machinery and transport equipment 50.3%, of which motor vehicles 26.5%; mineral fuels 8.2%, of which crude petroleum 3.1%; food 7.1%; lumber 5.5%; newsprint and paper products 3.5%; wood pulp 1.9%). *Major export destinations* (1999): U.S. 86.8%; Japan 2.5%; U.K. 1.3%; South Korea 0.6%.

Trade by commodities (1998)

	imports		exports	
SITC Group	U.S.$'000,000	%	U.S.$'000,000	%
00 Food and live animals	9,629.6	4.8	12,443.0	5.8
01 Beverages and tobacco	1,065.2	0.5	1,039.0	0.5
02 Crude materials, excluding fuels	5,718.0	2.8	19,337.5	9.0
03 Mineral fuels, lubricants, and related materials	6,847.8	3.5	17,584.3	8.2
04 Animal and vegetable oils, fats, and waxes	...	...	...	...
05 Chemicals and related products, n.e.s.	16,363.1	8.1	11,792.8	5.5
06 Basic manufactures	27,121.9	13.5	34,591.1	16.1
07 Machinery and transport equipment	105,052.9	52.2	88,180.3	41.2
08 Miscellaneous manufactured articles	23,369.9	11.6	13,996.2	6.5
09 Goods not classified by kind	5,568.9	2.8	14,280.2	6.7
TOTAL	201,219.3[15]	100.0[15]	214,187.9[15]	100.0[15]

Direction of trade (1999)

	imports		exports	
	U.S.$'000,000	%	U.S.$'000,000	%
Africa	1,440	0.7	993	0.4
Asia	28,838	13.8	11,587	4.9[15]
China	6,017	2.9	1,673	0.7
Japan	10,104	4.8	5,254	2.2
Taiwan	3,100	1.5	740	0.3
Other	9,617	4.6	3,920	1.6
Americas	153,335	73.2	211,454	89.4
United States	143,498	68.5	208,013	88.0
Mexico	6,263	3.0	1,025	0.4
Other Americas	3,574	1.7	2,416	1.0
Europe	24,904	11.9	11,587	4.9
EU	21,524	10.3	10,427	4.4
Other Europe	3,380	1.6	1,160	0.5
Oceania	1,077	0.5	758	0.3
TOTAL	214,161[15, 16]	100.0[15, 16]	237,337[15]	100.0[15]

Transport and communications

Transport. Railroads (1998): length 65,403 km; passenger-km 1,458,000,000; metric ton-km cargo 299,508,000,000. Roads (1999): total length 901,903 km (paved 35%). Vehicles (1998): passenger cars 13,887,270; trucks and buses 3,694,125. Merchant marine (1993): vessels (100 gross tons and over) 1,049; total deadweight tonnage 1,910,000. Air transport (2000): passenger-km 68,202,000,000; metric ton-km cargo 1,786,600,000; airports (1997) with scheduled flights 269.

Communications

Medium	date	unit	number	units per 1,000 persons
Daily newspapers	1996	circulation	4,718,000	159
Radio	1997	receivers	32,300,000	1,077
Television	1998	receivers	21,450,000	715
Telephones	1999	main lines	19,957,000	655
Cellular telephones	1999	subscribers	6,876,000	256
Personal computers	1999	units	11,000,000	361
Internet	1999	users	11,000,000	361

Education and health

Literacy (1996): total population age 15 and over literate virtually 100%.

Education (1998–99)

	schools[17]	teachers	students	student/teacher ratio
Primary (age 6–14) } Secondary (age 14–18) }	15,566	296,901	5,369,716	18.1
Postsecondary	270	65,429	494,955	7.6
Higher[17]	75	33,702	573,099	17.0

Health: physicians (2000) 60,559 (1 per 508 persons); hospital beds (1997) 161,867 (1 per 185 persons); infant mortality rate (2000) 5.1.

Food (1999): daily per capita caloric intake 3,161 (vegetable products 71%, animal products 29%); 119% of FAO recommended minimum requirement.

Military

Total active duty personnel (2001): 56,800 (army 32.7%, navy 15.8%, air force 23.7%, not identified by service 27.8%). *Military expenditure as percentage of GNP* (1997): 1.3% (world 2.6%); per capita expenditure U.S.$257.

[1]Area for Northwest Territories includes Nunavut. [2]Nunavut came into existence on April 1, 1999. [3]Based on land area of 3,558,096 sq mi (9,215,430 sq km). [4]Includes 35.8% population of mixed origin. [5]1990. [6]At prices of 1997. [7]Services includes communications. [8]Unemployed. [9]GDP at current values in 2000 was Can$1,067,956,000,000. [10]1993. [11]1984. [12]Department and General stores included with General merchandise. [13]1997. [14]Manufacturing only. [15]Detail does not add to total because of discrepancies in estimates. [16]Total for imports includes U.S.$3,299,000,000 (1.7% of total imports; mostly special transactions) not distributable by region. [17]1997–98.

Internet resources for further information:

- **Statistics Canada http://www.statcan.ca**

Cape Verde

Official name: República de Cabo Verde (Republic of Cape Verde).
Form of government: multiparty republic with one legislative house (National Assembly [72]).
Chief of state: President.
Head of government: Prime Minister.
Capital: Praia.
Official language: Portuguese.
Official religion: none.
Monetary unit: 1 escudo (C.V.Esc.)[1] = 100 centavos; valuation (Sept. 28, 2001) 1 U.S.$ = C.V.Esc. 119.75; 1 £ = C.V.Esc. 176.00.

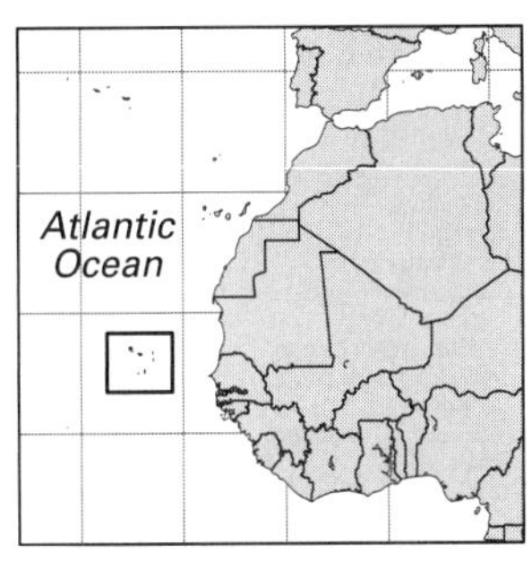

Area and population

Island Groups / Islands/Counties[2] / Counties	Capitals	area sq mi	area sq km	population 2000 census
Leeward Islands		696[3]	1,803	287,323
Brava	Nova Sintra	26	67	6,820
Fogo				
Mosteiros[4]	…	184	476	9,479
São Filipe	São Filipe			27,930
Maio	Porto Inglês	104	269	6,742
Santiago		383	991	236,352
Praia	Praia	153	396	106,052
Santa Catarina	Assomada	94	243	49,970
Santa Cruz	Pedra Badejo	58	149	32,822
São Domingos[4]	…			13,296
São Miguel[4]	…	78	203	16,153
Tarrafal	Tarrafal			18,059
Windward Islands		861[3]	2,230	147,489
Boa Vista	Sal Rei	239	620	4,193
Sal	Santa Maria	83	216	14,792
Santo Antão		300	779	47,124
Paúl	Pombas	21	54	8,325
Porto Novo	Porto Novo	215	558	17,239
Ribeira Grande	Ponta do Sol	64	167	21,560
São Nicolau	Ribeira Brava	150	388	13,536
São Vicente[5]	Mindelo	88	227	67,844
TOTAL		1,557	4,033	434,812

Demography

Population (2001): 446,000.
Density (2001): persons per sq mi 286.2, persons per sq km 110.5.
Urban-rural (1990): urban 29.7%; rural 70.3%.
Sex distribution (2000): male 48.17%; female 51.83%.
Age breakdown (2000): under 15, 43.6%; 15–29, 24.8%; 30–44, 17.1%; 45–59, 5.8%; 60–74, 6.3%; 75 and over, 2.4%.
Population projection: (2010) 474,000; (2020) 492,000.
Doubling time: 32 years.
Ethnic composition (1986): mixed 71.0%; black 28.0%; white 1.0%.
Religious affiliation (2000): Roman Catholic 91.4%; Muslim 2.8%; other 5.8%.
Major cities (2000): Praia 94,757; Mindelo 62,970; São Filipe 7,894.

Vital statistics

Birth rate per 1,000 population (2000): 29.7 (world avg. 22.5); (1989) legitimate 28.9%; illegitimate 71.1%.
Death rate per 1,000 population (2000): 7.4 (world avg. 9.0).
Natural increase rate per 1,000 population (2000): 22.3 (world avg. 13.5).
Total fertility rate (avg. births per childbearing woman; 2000): 4.2.
Marriage rate per 1,000 population (1990): 4.5.
Divorce rate per 1,000 population: n.a.
Life expectancy at birth (2000): male 65.6 years; female 72.3 years.
Major causes of death per 100,000 population (1987): enteritis and other diarrheal diseases 97.4; heart disease 77.9; malignant neoplasms (cancers) 47.9; pneumonia 46.4; accidents, poisoning, and violence 44.0.

National economy

Budget (1998). Revenue: C.V.Esc. 11,656,000,000 (tax revenue 72.1%, of which taxes on international trade 42.1%, income taxes 26.3%, other taxes 3.7%; nontax revenue 27.9%). Expenditures: C.V.Esc. 19,037,000,000 (current expenditure 56.3%, of which wages and salaries 25.7%, transfers 14.0%, public debt 9.9%, goods and services 1.8%; capital expenditure 43.7%).
Public debt (external, outstanding; 1999): U.S.$265,100,000.
Production (metric tons except as noted). Agriculture, forestry, fishing (1999): sugarcane 12,500, corn (maize) 10,000, bananas 6,000, coconuts 5,000, vegetables (including melons) 4,800, fruits (except melons) 4,500, sweet potatoes 3,800, cassava 3,000, potatoes 2,000; livestock (number of live animals) 636,000 pigs, 112,000 goats, 22,000 cattle, 9,000 sheep; roundwood, n.a.; fish catch (1998) 9,999. Mining and quarrying (1992): salt 4,000. Manufacturing (1998): flour 25,916; bread 5,628[6]; paint 628[7]; canned tuna 337[6]; cigarettes 43[7]; beer 4,324,560 litres; soft drinks 922,714[7] litres. Construction (1982): residential C.V.Esc. 365,800,000; nonresidential C.V.Esc. 1,700,000. Energy production (consumption): electricity (kW-hr; 1998) 100,764,000,000 (80,039,000,000); coal, none (none); crude petroleum, none (none); petroleum products (metric tons; 1998) none (98,392); natural gas, none (none).
Tourism: receipts from visitors (1999) U.S.$23,000,000; expenditures by nationals abroad (1998) U.S.$24,000,000.
Land use (1994): forest 0.2%; pasture 6.2%; agriculture 11.2%; other 82.4%.
Gross national product (1999): U.S.$569,000,000 (U.S.$1,330 per capita).

Structure of gross domestic product and labour force

	1998 in value C.V.Esc. '000,000	1998 % of total value	1990 labour force	1990 % of labour force
Agriculture	5,960	12.2	29,876	24.7
Manufacturing	4,992	10.3	5,520	4.6
Public utilities			883	0.7
Mining			410	0.3
Construction	4,304	8.8	22,722	18.9
Transp. and commun.	8,575	17.6	6,138	5.1
Trade	9,240	19.0	12,747	10.6
Finance	5,704	11.7	821	0.7
Pub. admin., defense	6,577	13.5	17,358	14.4
Services	3,315	6.8		
Other	…	…	24,090	20.0
TOTAL	48,667	100.0[3]	120,565	100.0

Population economically active (1997): total 160,000; activity rate of total population 41.2% (participation rates (1990): ages 15–64, 64.3%; female 39.0%; unemployed [1990] 25.8%).

Price and earnings indexes (1995 = 100)

	1993	1994	1995	1996	1997	1998	1999
Consumer price index	89.0	92.0	100.0	106.0	115.0	120.0	126.0
Monthly earnings index	85.8	87.9	100.0	…	…	…	…

Household income and expenditure. Average household size (1990) 5.1; income per household: n.a.; sources of income: n.a.; expenditure (1988): food 51.1%, housing, fuel, and power 13.5%, beverages and tobacco 11.8%, transportation and communications 8.8%, household durable goods 6.9%, other 7.9%.

Foreign trade

Balance of trade (current prices)

	1993	1994	1995	1996	1997	1998
U.S.$'000,000	–170.3	–171.2	–208.4	–176.1	–171.0	–176.2
% of total	81.3%	80.9%	80.6%	74.8%	68.0%	76.2%

Imports (1998): C.V.Esc. 19,999,000,000 (food 39.0%, machinery and apparatus 19.4%, nonmetallic mineral products 9.7%, metal products 8.2%, transport equipment 7.8%). *Major import sources* (1998): Portugal 49.9%; The Netherlands 11.8%; U.S. 3.1%; Spain 2.7%.
Exports (1998): C.V.Esc. 2,702,000,000 (shoes 22.5%; clothing 7.1%; fish and fish preparations 6.7%; reexports 62.1%). *Major export destinations* (1998): Portugal 89.3%; Spain 7.9%.

Transport and communications

Transport. Railroads: none. Roads (1996): total length 680 mi, 1,095 km (paved 78%). Vehicles (1996): passenger cars 3,280; trucks and buses 820. Merchant marine (1992): vessels (100 gross tons and over) 42: total deadweight tonnage 30,921. Air transport (1994)[8]: passenger-mi 106,000,000, passenger-km 171,000,000; short ton-mi cargo 13,156,000, metric ton-km cargo 19,207,000; airports (1997) with scheduled flights 9.

Communications

Medium	date	unit	number	units per 1,000 persons
Radio	1997	receivers	71,000	179.0
Television	1999	receivers	2,000	4.7
Telephones	1999	main lines	46,865	110.4
Cellular telephones	1999	subscribers	8,068	19.0
Personal computers	1998	units	…	…
Internet	1999	users	5,000	11.8

Education and health

Educational attainment (1990). Percentage of population age 25 and over having: no formal schooling 47.9%; primary 40.9%; incomplete secondary 3.9%; complete secondary 1.4%; higher 1.5%; unknown 4.4%. *Literacy* (1995): total population age 15 and over literate 71.6%; males 81.4%; females 63.8%.

Education (1993–94)

	schools	teachers	students	student/ teacher ratio
Primary (age 7–12)	370[9]	2,657	78,173	29.4
Secondary (age 13–17)	16[10]	438	11,808	27.0
Voc., teacher tr.	3[10]	94[11]	2,289	…
Higher	…	…	…	…

Health (1996): physicians 66 (1 per 5,818 persons); hospital beds (1987) 625 (1 per 550 persons); infant mortality rate per 1,000 live births (2000) 54.6.
Food (1999): daily per capita caloric intake 3,166 (vegetable products 84%, animal products 16%); 135% of FAO recommended minimum requirement.

Military

Total active duty personnel (2000): 1,100 (army 90.9%, air force 9.1%). *Military expenditure as percentage of GNP* (1997): 0.9% (world 2.6%); per capita expenditure U.S.$10.

[1]Fixed par value rate, announced March 13, 1998, between the Cape Verde escudo and Portuguese escudo became effective Jan. 1, 1999. [2]Island/county areas are coterminous except Fogo, Santiago, and Santo Antão islands. [3]Detail does not add to total given because of rounding. [4]Created after the 1990 census. [5]Includes Santa Luzia Island, which is uninhabited. [6]1995. [7]1996. [8]TACV airline only. [9]1991. [10]1986–87. [11]Vocational teachers only.

Internet resources for further information:
- **Instituto Nacional de Estatistica de Cabo Verde http://www.ine.cv**
- **Banco de Cabo Verde http://www.bcv.cv**

Central African Republic

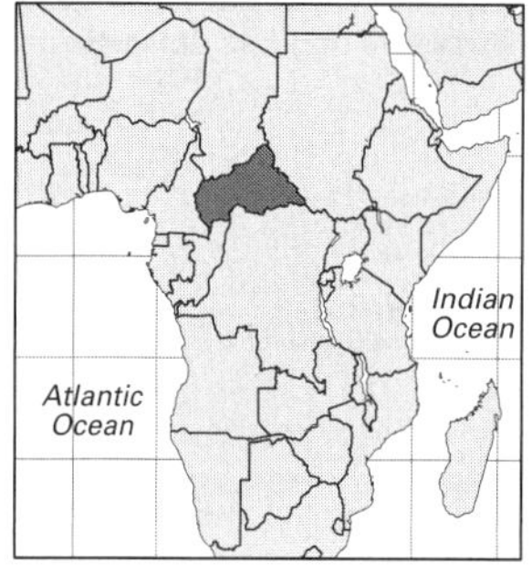

Official name: République Centrafricaine (Central African Republic).
Form of government: multiparty republic with one legislative body (National Assembly [109[1]]).
Chief of state: President.
Head of government: Prime Minister.
Capital: Bangui.
Official languages: French; Sango.
Official religion: none.
Monetary unit: 1 CFA franc (CFAF) = 100 centimes; valuation (Sept. 28, 2001) 1 U.S.$ = CFAF 720.28; 1 £ = CFAF 1,058.

Area and population

Prefectures	Capitals	area sq mi	area sq km	population 1988 census
Bamingui-Bangoran	Ndélé	22,471	58,200	28,643
Basse-Kotto	Mobaye	6,797	17,604	194,750
Haut-Mbomou	Obo	21,440	55,530	27,113
Haute-Kotto	Bria	33,456	86,650	58,838
Kemo	Sibut	6,642	17,204	82,884
Lobaye	Mbaïki	7,427	19,235	169,554
Mambéré-Kadéï	Berbérati	11,661	30,203	230,364
Mbomou	Bangassou	23,610	61,150	119,252
Nana-Gribizi	Kaga-Bandoro	7,721	19,996	95,497
Nana-Mambéré	Bouar	10,270	26,600	191,970
Ombella-M'poko	Boali	12,292	31,835	180,857
Ouaka	Bambari	19,266	49,900	208,332
Ouham	Bossangoa	19,402	50,250	262,950
Ouham-Pendé	Bozoum	12,394	32,100	287,653
Sangha-Mbaéré	Nola	7,495	19,412	65,961
Vakaga	Birao	17,954	46,500	32,118
Autonomous commune				
Bangui	Bangui	26	67	451,690
TOTAL		240,324	622,436	2,688,426

Demography

Population (2001): 3,577,000.
Density (2001): persons per sq mi 14.9, persons per sq km 5.7.
Urban-rural (1999): urban 40.7%; rural 59.3%.
Sex distribution (2001): male 49.43%; female 50.57%.
Age breakdown (2001): under 15, 43.5%; 15–29, 28.0%; 30–44, 14.9%; 45–59, 8.1%; 60–74, 4.2%; 75 and over, 1.3%.
Population projection: (2010) 4,135,000; (2020) 4,672,000.
Doubling time: 37 years.
Ethnolinguistic composition (1988): Baya (Gbaya) 23.7%; Banda 23.4%; Mandjia 14.7%; Ngbaka 7.6%; Sara 6.5%; Mbum 6.3%; Kare 2.4%; French 0.1%; other 15.3%.
Religious affiliation (2000): Christian 67.8%, of which Roman Catholic 18.4%, Protestant 14.4%, African Christian 11.6%, other Christian 23.4%; Muslim 15.6%; traditional beliefs 15.4%; other 1.2%.
Major cities (1994): Bangui 524,000; Berbérati 47,000; Bouar 43,000; Bambari 41,000; Carnot 41,000; Bossangoa 33,000.

Vital statistics

Birth rate per 1,000 population (2000): 37.5 (world avg. 22.5).
Death rate per 1,000 population (2000): 18.4 (world avg. 9.0).
Natural increase rate per 1,000 population (2000): 19.1 (world avg. 13.5).
Total fertility rate (avg. births per childbearing woman; 2000): 5.0.
Life expectancy at birth (2000): male 42.3 years; female 45.8 years.

National economy

Budget (1997). Revenue: CFAF 45,000,000,000 (taxes 94.2%, of which international trade tax 38.0%, indirect domestic tax 36.7%, other 19.5%; nontax receipts 5.8%). Expenditures: CFAF 82,900,000,000 (current expenditure 63.0%, of which wages 32.1%; capital expenditure 37.0%).
Public debt (external, outstanding; 1999): U.S.$830,100,000.
Production (metric tons except as noted). Agriculture, forestry, fishing (1999): cassava 559,000, yams 360,000, bananas 115,000, peanuts (groundnuts) 110,000, taro 100,000, corn (maize) 95,000, sugarcane 90,000, plantains 82,000, seed cotton 36,000, sesame seeds 36,000, pulses 29,000, sorghum 29,000, oranges 22,000, paddy rice 21,000, millet 12,000, coffee 12,000; livestock (number of live animals) 2,992,100 cattle, 2,350,000 goats, 622,000 pigs, 20,600 sheep, 3,900,000 chickens; roundwood (1998) 3,518,000 cu m; fish catch (1998) 13,000. Mining and quarrying (1997): gold 29 kg, diamonds 486,800 carats[2]. Manufacturing (value added in U.S.$'000; 1994): food, beverages, and tobacco 19,000; chemical products 3,000; wood products 2,000; textiles, wearing apparel, and leather products 1,000; transport equipment 1,000. Construction (1992)[3]: residential 10,052 sq m; nonresidential 82,411 sq m. Energy production (consumption): electricity (kW-hr; 1996) 104,000,000 (104,000,000); coal, none (none); crude petroleum, none (none); petroleum products (metric tons; 1996) none (92,000); natural gas, none (none).
Household income and expenditure. Average household size (1998) 5.9; average annual income per household (1988) CFAF 91,985 (U.S.$435); sources of income: n.a.; expenditure (1991)[4]: food 70.5%, clothing 8.5%, other manufactured products 7.6%, energy 7.3%, services (including transportation and communications, recreation, and health) 6.1%.
Gross national product (1999): U.S.$1,035,000,000 (U.S.$290 per capita).

Structure of gross domestic product and labour force

	1997 in value CFAF '000,000	1997 % of total value	1988 labour force	1988 % of labour force
Agriculture	303,700	51.1	1,113,900	80.4
Mining	21,600	3.6	15,400	1.1
Manufacturing	48,000	8.0	22,400	1.6
Construction	26,600	4.5	7,000	0.5
Public utilities	4,800	0.8	1,500	0.1
Transp. and commun.	14,700	2.5	1,500	0.1
Trade	79,900	13.4	118,000	8.5
Services	29,600	5.0	15,600	1.1
Pub. admin., defense	32,000	5.4	91,700	6.6
Other	33,700[5]	5.7[5]	—	—
TOTAL	594,600	100.0	1,387,000	100.0

Population economically active (1988): total 1,186,972; activity rate of total population 48.2% (participation rates: ages 15–64, 78.3%; female 46.8%; unemployed 7.5%).

Price and earnings indexes (1995 = 100)

	1993	1994	1995	1996	1997	1998	1999
Consumer price index[3]	67.4	83.9	100.0	103.7	105.4	103.4	101.9
Earnings index	...	...	100.0	...	...	...	...

Land use (1994): forest 75.0%; meadows 4.8%; agriculture 3.2%; other 17.0%.
Tourism (1997): receipts U.S.$5,000,000; expenditures U.S.$39,000,000.

Foreign trade

Balance of trade (current prices)

	1992	1993	1994	1995	1996	1997
CFAF '000,000,000	–10.1	–4.5	+6.6	–1.6	+2.8	+5.3
% of total	15.2%	6.7%	4.1%	0.9%	1.9%	3.0%

Imports (1997): CFAF 84,400,000,000 (1992; food products 22.2%, transportation equipment 16.6%, chemical products 13.7%, energy products 11.0%). *Major import sources:* France 30.5%; Côte d'Ivoire 18.0%; Cameroon 10.8%; Germany 3.6%; Belgium-Luxembourg 3.6%; United States 2.4%.
Exports (1997): CFAF 89,700,000,000 (diamonds 38.7%, wood 25.4%, cotton 16.1%, coffee 10.3%). *Major export destinations:* Belgium-Luxembourg 36.2%; Côte d'Ivoire 5.2%; Spain 4.4%; France 3.0%; Democratic Republic of the Congo 1.8%; Republic of the Congo 1.1%.

Transport and communications

Transport. Railroads: none. Roads (1996): total length 14,900 mi, 24,000 km (paved 2%). Vehicles (1995): passenger cars 9,500; trucks and buses 7,000. Merchant marine: vessels (100 gross tons and over) none. Air transport (1996)[6]: passenger-mi 139,644,000, passenger-km 224,736,000; short ton-mi cargo 11,247,000, metric ton-km cargo 16,420,000; airports[7] (1998) 1.

Communications

Medium	date	unit	number	units per 1,000 persons
Daily newspapers	1996	circulation	6,000	1.8
Radio	1997	receivers	283,000	83.0
Television	1999	receivers	20,000	5.6
Telephones	1999	main lines	9,860	2.8
Cellular telephones	1999	subscribers	4,162	1.2
Personal computers	1999	units	5,000	1.4
Internet	1999	users	1,000	0.3

Education and health

Educational attainment (1988). Percentage of population age 10 and over having: no formal schooling 59.3%; primary education 29.6%; lower secondary 7.5%; upper secondary 2.3%; higher 1.3%. *Literacy* (1995): total population age 15 and over literate 60.0%; males literate 68.5%; females literate 52.4%.

Education (1991–92)

	schools	teachers	students	student/ teacher ratio
Primary (age 6–11)	930[8]	4,004[8]	277,961	...
Secondary (age 12–18)	46[8]	845[8]	42,263	...
Vocational	[9]	[9]	1,477	...
Higher[10]	1	139	2,923	21.0

Health (1992): physicians 157 (1 per 18,660 persons); hospital beds (1991) 4,258 (1 per 672 persons); infant mortality rate (2000) 106.7.
Food (1999): daily per capita caloric intake 1,978 (vegetable products 91%, animal products 9%); 88% of FAO recommended minimum requirement.

Military

Total active duty personnel (2000): 3,150[11] (army 95.2%; navy, none; air force 4.8%). *Military expenditure as percentage of GNP* (1997): 3.9% (world 2.6%); per capita expenditure U.S.$12.

[1]Number increased as of November–December 1998 elections. [2]An unknown but substantial amount is believed to be smuggled out of the country annually. [3]Bangui only. [4]Weights of consumer price index components. [5]Indirect taxes and customs duties. [6]Represents 1/11 of the traffic of Air Afrique, which is operated by 11 West African states. [7]International air service only. [8]1990–91. [9]Included with secondary. [10]University of Bangui only. [11]Excludes 1,000 gendarmerie, who are part of the armed forces.

Internet resources for further information:
- **Central African Republic http://www.africa.co.uk/country/cenafrep.htm**
- **Investir en Zone Franc http://www.izf.net/izf/Index.htm**

Chad

Official name: Jumhūrīyah Tshad (Arabic); République du Tchad (French) (Republic of Chad).
Form of government: unitary republic with one legislative body (National Assembly [125]).
Chief of state: President.
Head of government: Prime Minister.
Capital: N'Djamena.
Official languages: Arabic; French.
Official religion: none.
Monetary unit: 1 CFA franc (CFAF) = 100 centimes; valuation (Sept. 28, 2001) 1 U.S.$ = CFAF 720.28; 1 £ = CFAF 1,058.

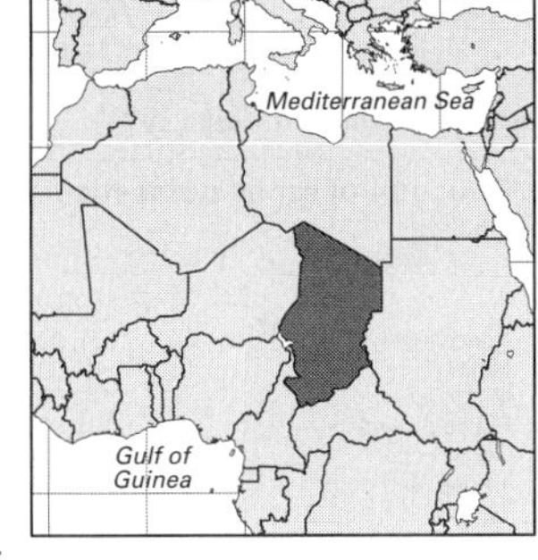

Area and population

Préfectures[1]	Capitals	area sq mi	area sq km	population 1993 census
Batha	Ati	34,285	88,800	288,458
Biltine	Biltine	18,090	46,850	184,807
Borkou-Ennedi-Tibesti	Faya Largeau	231,795	600,350	73,185
Chari-Baguirmi	N'Djamena	32,010	82,910	1,251,906
Guéra	Mongo	22,760	58,950	306,253
Kanem	Mao	44,215	114,520	279,927
Lac	Bol	8,620	22,320	252,932
Logone Occidental	Moundou	3,357	8,695	455,489
Logone Oriental	Doba	10,825	28,035	441,064
Mayo-Kebbi	Bongor	11,625	30,105	825,158
Moyen-Chari	Sarh	17,445	45,180	738,595
Ouaddaï	Abéché	29,436	76,240	543,900
Salamat	Am Timan	24,325	63,000	184,403
Tandjilé	Laï	6,965	18,045	453,854
TOTAL		495,755[2]	1,284,000	6,279,931

Demography

Population (2001): 8,707,000.
Density (2001): persons per sq mi 17.6, persons per sq km 6.8.
Urban-rural (1999): urban 23.4%; rural 76.6%.
Sex distribution (2000): male 48.50%; female 51.50%.
Age breakdown (2000): under 15, 47.7%; 15–29, 26.1%; 30–44, 14.1%; 45–59, 7.6%; 60–74, 3.7%; 75 and over, 0.8%.
Population projection: (2010) 11,616,000; (2020) 15,772,000.
Doubling time: 21 years.
Ethnolinguistic composition (1993): Sara 27.7%; Sudanic Arab 12.3%; Mayo-Kebbi peoples 11.5%; Kanem-Bornu peoples 9.0%; Ouaddaï peoples 8.7%; Hadjeray (Hadjaraï) 6.7%; Tangale (Tandjilé) peoples 6.5%; Gorane peoples 6.3%; Fitri-Batha peoples 4.7%; Fulani (Peul) 2.4%; other 4.2%.
Religious affiliation (1993): Muslim 53.9%; Christian 34.7%, of which Roman Catholic 20.3%, Protestant 14.4%; traditional beliefs 7.4%; other 4.0%.
Major cities (1993): N'Djamena 530,965; Moundou 282,103; Bongor 196,713; Sarh 193,753; Abéché 187,936; Doba 185,461.

Vital statistics

Birth rate per 1,000 population (2000): 48.8 (world avg. 22.5).
Death rate per 1,000 population (2000): 15.7 (world avg. 9.0).
Natural increase rate per 1,000 population (2000): 33.1 (world avg. 13.5).
Total fertility rate (avg. births per childbearing woman; 2000): 6.6.
Life expectancy at birth (2000): male 48.5 years; female 52.6 years.

National economy

Budget (1998). Revenue: CFAF 127,100,000,000 (tax revenue 54.9%, of which taxes on international trade 21.6%, income tax 18.3%, taxes on goods and services 11.3%, other taxes 3.7%; nontax revenue 5.1%; grants 40.0%). Expenditures: CFAF 153,800,000,000 (current expenditure 49.0%, of which government salaries 20.5%, materials and supply 10.7%, defense 6.2%, debt service 5.8%, transfer payments 5.6%, other 0.2%; capital expenditure 51.0%).
Public debt (external, outstanding; 1999): U.S.$1,045,000,000.
Tourism (1994): receipts from visitors U.S.$12,000,000; expenditures by nationals abroad U.S.$26,000,000.
Production (metric tons except as noted). Agriculture, forestry, fishing (1999): sorghum 636,900, peanuts (groundnuts) 471,150, millet 365,600, cassava 275,000, seed cotton 261,272, yams 240,000, corn (maize) 172,100, rice 100,000; livestock (number of live animals) 5,582,092 cattle, 4,968,256 goats, 2,431,555 sheep, 700,000 camels, 4,800,000 chickens; roundwood (1998) 1,919,000 cu m; fish catch (1998) 84,000. Mining and quarrying (1997): aggregate (gravel) 170,000; limited commercial production of natron (10,000) and salt; artisanal gold production. Manufacturing (1998): cotton fibre 61,700[3]; refined sugar 29,000; soap 2,958[3]; woven cotton fabrics 1,100,000 metres; edible oil 160,000 hectolitres; beer 135,000 hectolitres; cigarettes 43,000,000 packs; bicycles 3,444 units[3]. Energy production (consumption): electricity (kW-hr; 1998) 74,878,000 (56,489,000); coal, none (none); crude petroleum, none (none); petroleum products (metric tons; 1998) none (47,057); natural gas, none (none).
Household income and expenditure (1993). Average household size 5.0; average annual income per household CFAF 96,806 (U.S.$458); sources of income (1995–96; urban) informal-sector employment and entrepreneurship[4] 36.7%, transfers 24.8%, wages 23.6%, ownership of real estate 8.6%; expenditure (1983)[5]: food 45.3%, health 11.9%, energy 5.8%, clothing 3.3%.
Population economically active (1997): total 3,433,000; activity rate of total population 47.9% (participation rates: over age 15, 72.3%; female 44.5%; unemployed [1993] 0.6%).

Price and earnings indexes (1995 = 100)

	1994	1995	1996	1997	1998	1999	2000
Consumer price index	91.7	100.0	112.4	118.7	133.1	124.1	128.8
Earnings index	...	...	...	...	...	...	...

Gross national product (1999): U.S.$1,555,000,000 (U.S.$210 per capita).

Structure of gross domestic product and labour force

	1998 in value CFAF '000,000	1998 % of total value	1993 labour force	1993 % of labour force
Agriculture	376,700	38.3	1,903,492	83.0
Manufacturing	117,800	12.0	33,670	1.5
Construction	15,400	1.6	10,885	0.5
Mining	5,400	0.5	756	—
Public utilities			2,026	0.1
Transp. and commun.	239,900	24.4	13,252	0.6
Trade and finance			179,169	7.8
Pub. admin., defense	104,700	10.6	61,875	2.7
Services	92,100	9.4	79,167	3.4
Other	32,200[6]	3.3[6]	9,311	0.4
TOTAL	984,200	100.0[2]	2,293,603	100.0

Land use (1994): forested 25.7%; meadows and pastures 35.7%; agricultural and under permanent cultivation 2.6%; other 36.0%.

Foreign trade[7]

Balance of trade (current prices)

	1994	1995	1996	1997	1998	1999	2000
CFAF '000,000	–16,150	–61,127	–47,838	–56,602	–55,752	–70,385	–76,387
% of total	8.9%	20.1%	16.4%	17.0%	15.3%	22.1%	22.7%

Imports (1998): CFAF 175,000,000,000 (1983; petroleum products 16.8%; cereal products 16.8%; pharmaceutical products and chemicals 11.5%; machinery and transport equipment 8.5%, of which transport equipment 7.3%; electrical equipment 5.7%; textiles 2.9%; raw and refined sugar 2.3%). *Major import sources* (1997[8]): France 41.3%; Nigeria 10.1%; Cameroon 7.2%; India 5.8%; Belgium-Luxembourg 5.1%; Italy 4.3%; Portugal 2.9%.
Exports (1998): CFAF 145,300,000,000 (cotton lint 59.3%; other 40.7%). *Major export destinations* (1997[8]): Portugal 29.9%; Germany 14.2%; Thailand 7.5%; Costa Rica 6.0%; Hong Kong 4.8%; Taiwan 4.8%; France 3.7%.

Transport and communications

Transport. Railroads: none. Roads (1996): total length 33,400 km (paved 1%). Vehicles (1996): passenger cars 10,560; trucks and buses 14,550. Air transport (1996)[9]: passenger km 233,000,000; metric ton-km cargo 37,000,000; airports (1998) with scheduled flights 1.

Communications

Medium	date	unit	number	units per 1,000 persons
Daily newspapers	1997	circulation	2,000	0.2
Radio	1997	receivers	1,310,000	205.9
Television	1999	receivers	10,300	1.4
Telephones	2000	main lines	9,700	1.3
Internet	2000	users	1,000	0.1

Education and health

Educational attainment (1993). Percentage of economically active population age 15 and over having: no formal schooling 81.1%; Qur'ānic education 4.2%; primary education 11.2%; secondary education 2.7%; higher education 0.3%; professional education 0.5%. *Literacy* (1995): percentage of total population age 15 and over literate 48.1%; males literate 62.1%; females literate 34.7%.

Education (1995–96)

	schools	teachers	students	student/teacher ratio
Primary (age 6–12)	2,660	9,395	591,493	63.0
Secondary (age 13–19)	153	2,468	90,100	36.5
Voc., teacher tr.	18	216	2,926	13.5
Higher[10]	8	288	3,446	12.0

Health (1993): physicians 217 (1 per 27,765 persons); hospital beds 3,962 (1 per 1,521 persons); infant mortality rate per 1,000 live births (2000) 96.7.
Food (1999): daily per capita caloric intake 2,206 (vegetable products 93%, animal products 7%); 93% of FAO recommended minimum requirement.

Military

Total active duty personnel (2000): 30,350[11] (army 82.4%; navy, none; air force 1.2%; paramilitary 16.4%). *Military expenditure as percentage of GNP* (1997): 2.7% (world 2.6%); per capita expenditure U.S.$6.

[1]Chad was administratively reorganized into 28 departments in *c.* 2000; details not yet available. [2]Detail does not add to total given because of rounding. [3]1996. [4]Not reported to fiscal authorities. [5]Capital city only. [6]VAT and import taxes. [7]Import figures are c.i.f. in balance of trade and f.o.b. in commodities and trading partners. [8]Based on direction of trade data (analysis of reports of trading partners, rather than country's own customs data). [9]One-eleventh portion of total traffic of Air Afrique, which is operated by 11 West African states. [10]Universities and equivalent institutions only. [11]Excludes 990 French troops.

Internet resources for further information:
- **CIA World Factbook—Chad http://www.odci.gov/cia/publications/factbook/geos/cd.html**
- **Investir en Zone Franc http://www.izf.net/izf/Index.htm**

Chile

Official name: República de Chile (Republic of Chile).
Form of government: multiparty republic with two legislative houses (Senate [49[1]]; Chamber of Deputies [120]).
Head of state and government: President.
Capital: Santiago[2].
Official language: Spanish.
Official religion: none.
Monetary unit: 1 peso (Ch$) = 100 centavos; valuation (Sept. 28, 2001) 1 U.S.$ = Ch$695.35; 1 £ = Ch$1,021.

Area and population[3]

Regions	Capitals	area sq mi	area sq km	population 2000 estimate
Aisén del General Carios Ibáñez del Campo	Coihaique	42,095	109,025	95,000
Antofagasta	Antofagasta	48,820	126,444	468,400
Araucanía	Temuco	12,300	31,858	874,200
Atacama	Copiapó	29,179	75,573	273,600
Bío-Bío	Concepción	14,258	36,929	1,936,300
Coquimbo	La Serena	15,697	40,656	577,900
Libertador General Bernardo O'Higgins	Rancagua	6,319	16,365	788,800
Los Lagos	Puerto Montt	25,868	66,997	1,061,500
Magallanes y la Antártica Chilena	Punta Arenas	50,979	132,034	157,800
Maule	Talca	11,700	30,302	915,200
Santiago, Región Metropolitana de	Santiago	5,926	15,349	6,102,200
Tarapacá	Iquique	22,663	58,698	399,000
Valparaíso	Valparaíso	6,331	16,396	1,561,400
TOTAL		292,135[4]	756,626[4]	15,211,300

Demography

Population (2001): 15,402,000.
Density (2001): persons per sq mi 52.7, persons per sq km 20.4.
Urban-rural (1999): urban 85.4%; rural 14.6%.
Sex distribution (2000): male 49.51%; female 50.49%.
Age breakdown (2000): under 15, 28.5%; 15–29, 24.2%; 30–44, 22.9%; 45–59, 14.3%; 60–74, 7.5%; 75 and over, 2.6%.
Population projection: (2010) 17,010,000; (2020) 18,774,000.
Doubling time: 62 years.
Ethnic composition (1992): European and mestizo 89.7%; Araucanian (Mapuche) 9.6%; Aymara 0.5%; Rapa Nui Polynesian 0.2%.
Religious affiliation (1992): Roman Catholic 76.7%; Protestant 13.2%; atheist and nonreligious 5.8%; other 4.3%.
Major cities (1999): Greater Santiago 4,640,635; Concepción 362,589; Viña del Mar 330,736; Valparaíso 283,489; Talcahuano 269,265; Temuco 253,451.

Vital statistics

Birth rate per 1,000 population (2000): 17.2 (world avg. 22.5).
Death rate per 1,000 population (2000): 5.5 (world avg. 9.0).
Natural increase rate per 1,000 population (2000): 11.7 (world avg. 13.5).
Total fertility rate (avg. births per childbearing woman; 2000): 2.2.
Life expectancy at birth (2000): male 72.4 years; female 79.2 years.
Major causes of death per 100,000 population (1994): diseases of the circulatory system 149.5; malignant neoplasms (cancers) 111.9; accidents and adverse effects 64.3; diseases of the respiratory system 61.2.

National economy

Budget (1999). Revenue: Ch$7,580,300,000,000 (income from taxes 85.3%, nontax revenue 14.7%). Expenditures: Ch$8,392,800,000,000 (social security and welfare 29.1%, transfers 24.3%, wages 19.6%, capital expenditure 16.6%, economic affairs and services 8.3%).
Public debt (external, outstanding; 1999): U.S.$5,655,000,000.
Population economically active (1999): total 5,822,700; activity rate of total population 38.6% (participation rates [1995]: ages 15–64, 58.6%; female 32.4%; unemployed [1999] 9.7%).

Price and earnings indexes (1995 = 100)

	1994	1995	1996	1997	1998	1999	2000
Consumer price index	92	100	107	114	120	124	129
Hourly earnings index	89	100	115	125	135	142	150

Production (metric tons except as noted). Agriculture, forestry, fishing (1999): sugar beets 3,100,000, grapes 1,575,000, tomatoes 1,243,000, wheat 1,196,600, apples 1,165,000, corn (maize) 624,000, potatoes 994,694, onions (dry) 262,000, oats 201,000, barley 81,000, rice 61,000; livestock (number of live animals) 4,134,000 cattle, 4,116,000 sheep, 2,221,000 pigs; roundwood (1998) 31,670,000 cu m; fish catch (1998) 3,265,300. Mining (1998): iron 8,277,000; copper 3,843,000; zinc 26,000; molybdenum 25,000; silver 1,300,000 kg; gold 43,253 kg. Manufacturing (value added in Ch$'000,000; 1997): food products 3,810,200; metal and metal products 2,631,900; petroleum and petroleum products 1,100,200; paper and paper products 964,900; beverages 807,400; nonmetallic mineral products 593,000. Construction (1994): residential 7,049,369 sq m; nonresidential 2,875,935 sq m. Energy production (consumption): electricity (kW-hr; 1999) 38,389,000,000 (31,204,000,000); coal (metric tons; 1996) 1,119,000 (3,558,000); crude petroleum (barrels; 1996) 3,364,000 (61,498,000); petroleum products (metric tons; 1996) 8,608,000 (10,373,000); natural gas (cu m; 1996) 2,056,000,000 (1,983,000,000).
Gross national product (1999): U.S.$69,602,000,000 (U.S.$4,630 per capita).

Structure of gross domestic product and labour force

	1999 in value Ch$'000,000[6]	1999 % of total value	1998[5] labour force	1998[5] % of labour force
Agriculture	586,000	7.3	809,000	13.8
Mining	801,900	10.0		
Manufacturing	1,177,500	14.7	1,015,000	17.3
Public utilities	189,500	2.4		
Construction	374,000	4.7	533,000	9.1
Transp. and commun.	735,800	9.2	456,000	7.8
Trade	1,375,000	17.1	1,075,000	18.4
Finance	1,079,800	13.5	437,000	7.5
Pub. admin., defense; Services	1,707,700	21.2	1,478,000	25.3
Other	–6,500[7]	–0.1[7]	47,000[8]	0.8[8]
TOTAL	8,020,700	100.0	5,852,000[9]	100.0

Household income and expenditure. Average household size (1998) 4.6; average annual income per household (1994) Ch$5,981,706 at November prices (U.S.$12,552); sources of income (1990): wages and salaries 75.1%, transfer payments 12.0%, other 12.9%; expenditure (1989): food 27.9%, clothing 22.5%, housing 15.2%, transportation 6.4%.
Tourism (1999): receipts U.S.$894,000,000; expenditures U.S.$806,000,000.

Foreign trade

Balance of trade (current prices)

	1995	1996	1997	1998	1999	2000
U.S.$'000,000	+1,381	–1,091	–1,557	–2,516	+1,665	+1,482
% of total	4.5%	3.4%	4.5%	7.8%	5.6%	4.3%

Imports (1999): U.S.$15,137,000,000 (intermediate goods 59.5%; capital goods 21.8%; consumer goods 18.7%). *Major import sources:* U.S. 20.8%; Argentina 13.9%; Brazil 6.7%; Japan 4.4%; Germany 4.3%; France 2.9%.
Exports (1999): U.S.$15,616,000,000 (mining products 44.4%, of which copper 37.7%; industrial products 38.5%; foodstuffs 17.1%). *Major export destinations:* U.S. 19.4%; Japan 14.3%; United Kingdom 6.8%; Argentina 4.6%; Brazil 4.3%; Germany 3.5%; Taiwan 3.2%.

Transport and communications

Transport. Railroads (1999): route length 5,410 mi, 8,707 km; passenger-km 605,900,000; metric ton-km cargo 2,329,246,000[10]. Roads (1996): total length 49,590 mi, 79,800 km (paved 14%). Vehicles (1999): passenger cars 1,323,800; trucks and buses 687,500. Air transport (1999): passenger-km 10,650,500,000; metric ton-km cargo 2,107,000,000; airports (1998) with scheduled flights 23.

Communications

Medium	date	unit	number	units per 1,000 persons
Daily newspapers	1996	circulation	1,410,000	98
Radio	1997	receivers	5,180,000	354
Television	1999	receivers	3,600,000	240
Telephones	1999	main lines	3,109,000	207
Cellular telephones	1999	subscribers	2,260,687	150
Personal computers	1999	units	1,000,000	66.6
Internet	1999	users	700,000	46.6

Education and health

Educational attainment (1992). Percentage of population age 25 and over having: no formal schooling 5.7%; primary education 44.2%; secondary 42.2%; higher 7.9%. *Literacy* (1995): total population age 15 and over literate 95.2%; males 95.4%; females 95.0%.

Education (1995)

	schools	teachers	students	student/ teacher ratio
Primary (age 6–13)	8,702	80,155	2,149,501	26.8
Secondary (age 14–17)[11]	2,956[12]	51,042	679,165	13.3
Higher	201[12]	18,084[13]	367,094	...

Health (1999): physicians 17,853 (1 per 841 persons); hospital beds (1998) 41,706 (1 per 355 persons); infant mortality rate (2000) 9.6.
Food (1999): daily per capita caloric intake 2,858 (vegetable products 79%, animal products 21%); 117% of FAO recommended minimum requirement.

Military

Total active duty personnel (2000): 87,000 (army 58.6%, navy 27.6%, air force 12.8%). *Military expenditure as percentage of GNP* (1997): 3.9% (world 2.6%); per capita expenditure U.S.$196.

[1]Includes 11 nonelective seats. [2]Legislative bodies meet in Valparaíso. [3]Excludes the 480,000-sq mi (1,250,000-sq km) section of Antarctica claimed by Chile (and administered as part of Magallanes y la Antártica Chilean region) and "inland" (actually tidal) water areas. The 1992 census population of Chilean-claimed Antarctica was 126. [4]Includes 205 sq mi (530 sq km) of waters, known as Laguna del Desierto, lost in a border dispute with Argentina, resolved on Oct. 21, 1994. [5]Excludes all or some classes or elements of the military. [6]In constant prices of 1986. [7]Less imputed bank service charges. [8]Includes unemployed not previously employed. [9]Detail does not add to total given because of rounding. [10]1994. [11]Includes vocational. [12]1988. [13]Universities only.

Internet resources for further information:

- **Instituto Nacional de Estadísticas http://www.ine.cl**
- **Gobierno de Chile http://www.gobiernodechile.cl**

China

Official name: Chung-hua Jen-min Kung-ho-kuo (People's Republic of China).
Form of government: single-party people's republic with one legislative house (National People's Congress [2,989]).
Chief of state: President.
Head of government: Premier.
Capital: Peking (Beijing).
Official language: Mandarin Chinese.
Official religion: none.
Monetary unit: 1 Renminbi (yuan) (Y) = 10 jiao = 100 fen; valuation (Sept. 28, 2001) 1 U.S.$ = Y 8.28; 1 £ = Y 12.16.

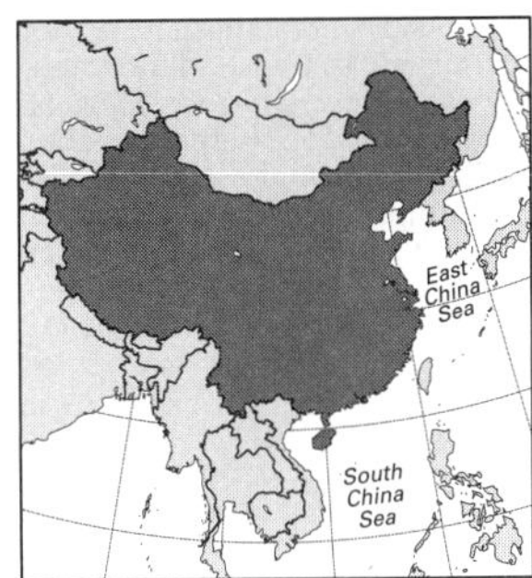

Area and population[1, 2]

Provinces	Capitals	area sq mi	area sq km	population 2000 estimate
Anhwei (Anhui)	Ho-fei (Hefei)	54,000	139,900	59,860,000
Chekiang (Zhejiang)	Hang-chou (Hangzhou)	39,300	101,800	46,770,000
Fukien (Fujian)	Fu-chou (Fuzhou)	47,500	123,100	34,710,000
Hainan (Hainan)	Hai-k'ou (Haikou)	13,200	34,300	7,870,000
Heilungkiang (Heilongjiang)	Harbin	179,000	463,600	36,890,000
Honan (Henan)	Cheng-chou (Zhengzhou)	64,500	167,000	92,560,000
Hopeh (Hebei)	Shih-chia-chuang (Shijiazhuang)	78,200	202,700	67,440,000
Hunan (Hunan)	Ch'ang-sha (Changsha)	81,300	210,500	64,400,000
Hupeh (Hubei)	Wu-han (Wuhan)	72,400	187,500	60,280,000
Kansu (Gansu)	Lan-chou (Lanzhou)	141,500	366,500	25,620,000
Kiangsi (Jiangxi)	Nan-ch'ang (Nanchang)	63,600	164,800	41,400,000
Kiangsu (Jiangsu)	Nanking (Nanjing)	39,600	102,600	74,380,000
Kirin (Jilin)	Ch'ang-ch'un (Changchun)	72,200	187,000	27,280,000
Kwangtung (Guangdong)	Canton (Guangzhou)	76,100	197,100	86,420,000
Kweichow (Guizhou)	Kuei-yang (Guiyang)	67,200	174,000	35,250,000
Liaoning (Liaoning)	Shen-yang (Shenyang)	58,300	151,000	42,380,000
Shansi (Shanxi)	T'ai-yüan (Taiyuan)	60,700	157,100	32,970,000
Shantung (Shandong)	Chi-nan (Jinan)	59,200	153,300	90,790,000
Shensi (Shaanxi)	Sian (Xi'an)	75,600	195,800	36,050,000
Szechwan (Sichuan)	Ch'eng-tu (Chengdu)	210,800	546,000	83,290,000
Tsinghai (Qinghai)	Hsi-ning (Xining)	278,400	721,000	5,180,000
Yunnan (Yunnan)	K'un-ming (Kunming)	168,400	436,200	42,880,000
Autonomous regions				
Inner Mongolia (Nei Monggol)	Hu-ho-hao-t'e (Hohhot)	454,600	1,177,500	23,760,000
Kwangsi Chuang (Guangxi Zhuang)	Nan-ning (Nanning)	85,100	220,400	44,890,000
Ningsia Hui (Ningxia Hui)	Yin-ch'uan (Yinchuan)	25,600	66,400	5,620,000
Sinkiang Uighur (Xinjiang Uygur)	Wu-lu-mu-c'hi (Urumqi)	635,900	1,646,900	19,250,000
Tibet (Xizang)	Lhasa	471,700	1,221,600	2,620,000
Municipalities				
Chungking (Chongqing)	—	8,900	23,000	30,900,000
Peking (Beijing)	—	6,500	16,800	13,820,000
Shanghai (Shanghai)	—	2,400	6,200	16,740,000
Tientsin (Tianjin)	—	4,400	11,300	10,010,000
TOTAL		3,696,100[3]	9,572,900[3]	1,262,280,000[4]

Demography

Population (2001): 1,274,915,000.
Density (2001): persons per sq mi 344.9, persons per sq km 133.2.
Urban-rural (2000): urban 36.1%; rural 63.9%.
Sex distribution (2000): male 51.63%; female 48.37%.
Age breakdown (1998): under 15, 24.3%; 15–29, 24.6%; 30–44, 24.8%; 45–59, 15.2%; 60–74, 8.8%; 75 and over, 2.3%.
Population projection: (2010) 1,357,864,000; (2020) 1,433,111,000.
Doubling time: 88 years.
Ethnic composition (1990): Han (Chinese) 91.96%; Chuang 1.37%; Manchu 0.87%; Hui 0.76%; Miao 0.65%; Uighur 0.64%; Yi 0.58%; Tuchia 0.50%; Mongolian 0.42%; Tibetan 0.41%; Puyi 0.23%; Tung 0.22%; Yao 0.18%; Korean 0.17%; Pai 0.14%; Hani 0.11%; Kazakh 0.10%; Tai 0.09%; Li 0.09%; other 0.51%.
Religious affiliation (2000): nonreligious 42.1%; Chinese folk-religionist 28.5%; Buddhist 8.4%; atheist 8.1%; Christian 7.1%; traditional beliefs 4.3%; Muslim 1.5%.
Major cities (1998): Shanghai 8,937,175; Peking 6,633,929; Tientsin 4,835,327; Wu-han 3,911,824; Shen-yang 3,876,289; Canton 3,306,277; Chungking 3,193,889; Harbin 2,586,978; Nanking 2,388,915; Sian 2,294,790; Ch'eng-tu 2,146,126; Ch'ang-ch'un 2,072,324; Talien (Dalian) 2,000,944; T'ai-yüan 1,768,530; Tsinan 1,713,036; Ch'ing-tao (Qingdao) 1,702,108; Cheng-chou 1,465,069; Tzu-po (Zibo) 1,458,060; Lan-chou 1,429,673; K'un-ming 1,350,640; Hang-chou 1,346,148; Ch'ang-sha (Changsha) 1,334,036; Kuei-yang (Guiyang) 1,320,566.
Households. Average rural household size (1996) 4.4; urban household size (1998) 3.2. Family households (1990): 277,390,000 (99.4%); collective 1,671,000 (0.6%).

Vital statistics

Birth rate per 1,000 population (2001): 14.9 (world avg. 22.5).
Death rate per 1,000 population (2001): 7.0 (world avg. 9.0).
Natural increase rate per 1,000 population (2001): 7.9 (world avg. 13.5).
Total fertility rate (avg. births per childbearing woman; 2001): 1.8.
Marriage rate per 1,000 population (1996): 7.6.
Divorce rate per 1,000 population (1996): 0.9.
Life expectancy at birth (2001): male 69.0 years; female 73.0 years.
Major causes of death per 100,000 population (1998)[5]: diseases of the circulatory system 244.3; malignant neoplasms (cancers) 139.3; diseases of the respiratory system 86.8; accidents, violence, and intoxication 38.7; digestive diseases 18.7.

Social indicators

Educational attainment (1997). Percentage of population age 15 and over having: no schooling and incomplete primary 20.7%; completed primary 37.6%; some secondary and complete secondary 39.2%; college and postsecondary education 2.5%.

Distribution of urban household income (1996)

avg. per capita income by quintile (avg. Y 4,845)

first quintile	second quintile	third quintile	fourth quintile	fifth quintile
Y 2,801	Y 3,780	Y 4,580	Y 5,599	Y 8,039

Quality of working life (1991). Average workweek: 48 hours. Annual rate per 100,000 workers for: injury or accident, n.a.; industrial illness, n.a.; death, n.a. Funds for pensions and social welfare relief (1996): Y 181,780,000,000. Average days lost to labour stoppages per 1,000 workdays: n.a. Average duration of journey to work: n.a. Method of transport: n.a. Rate per 1,000 workers of discouraged (unemployed no longer seeking work): n.a.
Access to services. Proportion of communes having access to electricity (1979) 87.1%. Percentage of urban population with: safe public water supply (1996) 95.0%; public sewage collection, n.a.; public fire protection, n.a.
Social participation. Eligible voters participating in last national election: n.a. Population participating in voluntary work: n.a. Trade union membership in total labour force (1996): 14.7%. Practicing religious population in total affiliated population: n.a.
Social deviance. Annual reported arrest rate per 100,000 population (1986) for: property violation 20.7; infringing personal rights 7.2; disruption of social administration 3.3; endangering public security 1.0[6].
Leisure. Favourite leisure activities: n.a.
Material well-being. Urban families possessing (number per family; 1996): bicycles 1.9; televisions 1.2; washing machines 0.9; refrigerators 0.7; sewing machines 0.6; cameras 0.3. Rural families possessing (number per family; 1998): bicycles 1.4; televisions 1.3; sewing machines 0.7; washing machines 0.2.

National economy

Gross national product (at current market prices; 1998): U.S.$923,560,000,000 (U.S.$750 per capita).

Structure of gross domestic product and labour force

	1998			
	in value Y '000,000,000	% of total value	labour force ('000)	% of labour force
Agriculture	1,429.87	18.0	332,320	47.5
Mining }	3,354.09	42.2	7,210	1.0
Manufacturing }			83,190	11.9
Construction	560.89	7.0	33,270	4.8
Public utilities	...	...	2,830	0.4
Transp. and commun.	502.93	6.3	20,000	2.9
Trade	660.96	8.3	46,450	6.6
Finance	...	...	4,080	0.6
Pub. admin.	...	... }		
Services	1,446.54	18.2 }	170,220[7]	24.3[7]
Other	...	... }		
TOTAL	7,955.28	100.0	699,570	100.0

Budget (1997). Revenue: Y 492,650,000,000 (taxes on goods and services 66.6%; grants 12.3%; income taxes 8.2%; import duties 6.5%; nontax revenue 2.3%). Expenditures: Y 601,720,000,000 (defense 13.6%; general public services 7.5%; agriculture 6.0%; industry 2.9%; public order 2.6%; education 2.0%; utilities 1.8%; other economic affair expenditures 5.9%; nonfunctional expenditures 56.3%).
Public debt (external, outstanding; 1999): U.S.$108,163,000,000.
Tourism: receipts from visitors (1999) U.S.$14,098,000,000; expenditures by nationals abroad (1999) U.S.$10,864,000,000.

Retail and catering enterprises (1996)

	no. of enter-prises	no. of employees	annual wage as a % of all wages	annual gross output value (Y '000,000)
Retail trade	13,963,162	31,892,181	...	...
Food, beverage, and tobacco	5,177,416	10,738,924	...	241,350
Articles for daily use	3,242,769	8,614,944	...	88,470
Textile goods, garments, shoes, and hats	2,018,136	4,030,888	...	125,250
Sundry goods for daily use	799,486	1,670,984	...	...
Hardwares, electrical appliances, and chemicals	583,466	1,828,788	...	...
Medicines and medical appliances	123,534	405,424	...	57,980
Books and newspapers	140,856	365,424	...	23,110
Other	1,877,499	4,236,805	...	...
Catering trade	2,587,730	7,753,108	...	...
Restaurants	1,181,732	4,321,824	...	...
Fast-food eateries	397,561	1,049,829	...	...
Other	1,008,437	2,381,455	...	...

Production (metric tons except as noted). Agriculture, forestry, fishing (2000): grains—rice 190,168,000, corn (maize) 105,231,000, wheat 99,370,000, sorghum 2,784,000, barley 3,940,000, millet 2,091,000; oilseeds—soybeans 15,400,000, peanuts (groundnuts) 15,067,000, rapeseed 11,350,000, sunflower seeds 2,100,000; fruits and nuts—watermelons 38,382,000, apples 22,888,000, pears 8,618,000, cantaloupes 6,418,000, oranges 3,508,000; other—sweet potatoes 121,024,000, sugarcane 70,205,000, potatoes 62,036,000, cabbage 20,209,000, tomatoes 19,309,000, sugar beets 7,700,000, cucumbers 17,176,000, seed cotton 13,050,000, onions 12,176,000, eggplants 11,915,000, garlic 6,466,000, tobacco leaves 2,509,000, tea 721,000; livestock (number of live animals) 437,551,000 pigs, 148,401,000 goats, 131,095,000 sheep, 104,582,000 cattle, 22,599,000 water buffalo, 9,348,000 asses, 8,916,000 horses, 3,625,000,000 chickens, 611,899,000 ducks; roundwood (1999) 291,330,000 cu m; fish catch (1998) 17,229,957. Mining and quarrying (1998): metal concentrates—zinc 1,540,000, copper 1,150,000, lead 733,000, antimony 80,000, tin 79,000, tungsten 24,000; metal ores—iron ore 210,000,000, bauxite 8,500,000, manganese ore 6,100,000, silver 1,400, gold 178; nonmetals—salt 22,420,000, gypsum 7,900,000, soda ash 7,200,000, barite 3,200,000, fluorspar 2,550,000, magnesite 2,200,000, talc 2,200,000, asbestos 250,000. Manufacturing (1998): cement 536,000,000; rolled steel 105,180,000; chemical fertilizer 30,100,000; sulfuric acid 21,710,000; paper and paperboard 21,260,000; sugar 8,260,000; cotton yarn 5,420,000; cotton fabrics 24,100,000,000 m; colour television sets 34,970,000 units; bicycles 23,125,000 units; household washing machines 12,073,000 units; household refrigerators 10,600,000 units; motor vehicles 1,630,000 units. Construction (1996): residential 1,221,880,000 sq m; nonresidential 406,380,000 sq m. Distribution of industrial production (percentage of total value of output by sector; 1978 [1996]): state-operated enterprises 80.6% (28.5%); collectives 19.2% (39.4%); privately operated enterprises 0.2% (32.1%). Retail sales (percentage of total sales by sector; 1978 [1996]): state-operated enterprises 90.5% (27.3%); collectives 7.4% (18.4%); privately operated enterprises 2.1% (54.3%).

Manufacturing and mining enterprises (1996)

	no. of enter-prises	no. of employees[8]	annual wages as a % of avg. of all wages[9]	annual gross output value (Y '000,000)
Manufacturing				
Machinery, transport equipment, and metal manufactures,	23,032	21,560	96.7	880,886
of which,				
Metal products	2,641	1,810,000	...	23,593
Industrial equipment	8,875	7,020,000	...	183,951
Transport equipment	4,303	3,540,000	...	187,581
Electronic goods	1,579	1,630,000	...	70,046
Measuring equipment	1,179	820,000	...	14,738
Textiles	4,031	6,340,000	95.5	161,949
Garments	1,177	1,680,000	...	11,359
Foodstuffs,	18,191	4,710,000	87.5	383,264
of which,				
Food processing	14,520	3,170,000	...	196,393
Beverages	3,367	1,210,000	...	70,368
Tobacco manufactures	304	330,000	...	116,503
Chemicals,	10,707	8,140,000	92.1	537,768
of which,				
Pharmaceuticals	2,044	1,020,000	...	53,749
Plastics	1,667	1,050,000	...	15,167
Secondary forest products (including paper and stationery)	3,664	2,310,000	96.1	51,238
Primary forest products	877	1,140,000	114.3	16,750
Mining				
Nonferrous and ferrous metals	1,163	810,000	107.6	22,711
Crude petroleum	71	1,250,000	...	149,525
Coal	2,011	5,050,000	119.8	105,946

Energy production (consumption): electricity (kW-hr; 1996) 1,081,310,000,000 (1,078,910,000,000); coal (metric tons; 1996) 1,397,000,000 (1,383,170,000); crude petroleum (barrels; 1996) 1,152,000,000 (1,157,000,000); petroleum products (metric tons; 1996) 121,858,000 (130,506,000); natural gas (cu m; 1996) 20,067,000,000 (20,067,000,000).

Financial aggregates[10]

	1994	1995	1996	1997	1998	1999	2000
Exchange rate, Y per:							
U.S. dollar	8.45	8.32	8.30	8.28	8.28	8.28	8.28
£	13.18	12.90	12.95	13.58	13.74	13.41	12.59
SDR	12.33	12.36	11.93	11.17	11.66	11.36	10.78
International reserves (U.S.$)							
Total (excl. gold; '000,000)	52,914	75,377	107,039	142,762	149,188	157,728	168,278
SDRs ('000,000)	539	582	614	602	676	741	798
Reserve pos. in IMF ('000,000)	755	1,216	1,396	2,270	3,553	2,312	1,905
Foreign exchange	51,620	73,579	105,029	139,890	144,959	154,675	165,574
Gold ('000,000 fine troy oz)	12.7	12.7	12.7	12.7	12.7	12.7	12.7
% world reserves	1.4	1.4	1.4	1.4	1.4	1.3	1.3
Interest and prices							
Central bank discount (%)	10.08	10.44	9.00	8.55	4.59	3.24	3.24
Govt. bond yield (%)	...	...	...	...	...	...	...
Industrial share prices	...	...	...	...	...	...	...
Balance of payments (U.S.$'000,000)							
Balance of visible trade,	+7,290	+18,050	+19,535	+46,222	+46,614	+36,207	...
of which:							
Imports, f.o.b.	−95,271	−110,060	−131,542	−136,448	−136,915	−158,509	...
Exports, f.o.b.	102,561	128,110	151,077	182,670	183,529	194,716	...
Balance of invisibles	−382	−16,432	−12,292	−9,259	−15,142	−20,540	...
Balance of payments, current account	+6,908	+1,618	+7,243	+36,963	+31,472	15,667	...

Household income and expenditure (1996). Average household size (2000) 3.4; rural household 4.4, urban household (1998) 3.2. Average annual income per household Y 13,459; rural household Y 12,406, urban household (1998) Y 17,248. Sources of income: rural household—income from household businesses 79.6%, wages 16.1%, other 4.3%; urban household—wages 80.5%, business income 5.9%, other 13.6%. Expenditure: rural household—food 56.3%, housing 13.9%, cultural activities 8.4%, clothing 7.2%, household materials 5.4%, health 3.7%, transportation 3.0%; urban household (1998)—food 44.5%, clothing 11.1%, housing 9.4%, household materials 8.2%, education 6.3%, transportation and communications 5.9%, health 4.7%.

Population economically active (1998): total 699,570,000; activity rate of total population 55.7% (participation rates: over age 15 [1996] 75.9%; female 49.7%[11]; unemployed 3.1%). Urban workforce by sector 1978 (1998): state enterprises 74,500,000 (90,580,000); collectives 20,000,000 (19,630,000); self-employment or privately run enterprises 150,000 (96,570,000).

Price and earnings indexes (1995 = 100)

	1994	1995	1996	1997	1998	1999	2000
Consumer price index	85.6	100.0	108.3	111.3	110.5	109.0	109.3
Annual earnings index[12]	82.2	100.0	112.1	116.1	114.8	...	...

Land use (1999): meadows and pastures 42.9%; agricultural and under permanent cultivation 14.5%; forested and other 42.6%.

Foreign trade[13]

Balance of trade (current prices)

	1994	1995	1996	1997	1998	1999
U.S.$'000,000	+7,290	+18,050	+19,535	+46,222	+46,614	+36,207
% of total	3.7%	7.6%	6.9%	14.5%	14.5%	10.3%

Imports (1998): U.S.$140,166,000,000 (machinery and transport equipment 40.5%; products of textile industries, rubber and metal products 22.2%; chemical and related products 14.4%; inedible raw materials 7.6%; mineral fuel and lubricants 4.8%; food and live animals 2.7%). *Major import sources:* Japan 20.1%; United States 12.1%; Taiwan 11.9%; South Korea 10.7%; Germany 5.0%; Hong Kong 4.8%; Singapore 3.0%; Russia 2.6%; France 2.3%; Australia 1.9%; Malaysia 1.9%.

Exports (1998): U.S.$183,757,000,000 (machinery and transport equipment 27.3%; products of textile industries, rubber and metal products 17.6%; food and live animals 5.8%; chemicals and allied products 5.6%; mineral fuels and lubricants 2.8%; inedible raw materials 1.9%). *Major export destinations:* Hong Kong 21.1%; United States 20.7%; Japan 16.2%; Germany 4.0%; South Korea 3.4%; The Netherlands 2.8%; United Kingdom 2.5%.

Transport and communications

Transport. Railroads (1998): length 35,781 mi, 57,584 km; passenger-mi 229,657,000,000, passenger-km 369,598,000,000; short ton-mi cargo 843,302,-000,000, metric ton-km cargo 1,231,200,000,000. Roads (1998): total length 794,405 mi, 1,278,474 km (paved 93%). Vehicles (1998): passenger cars 6,548,300; trucks and buses 6,278,900. Merchant marine (1992): vessels (100 gross tons and over) 2,390: total deadweight tonnage 20,657,996. Air transport (1998): passenger-mi 49,725,000,000, passenger-km 80,024,000,000; short ton-mi cargo 2,291,000,000, metric ton-km cargo 3,345,000,000; airports (1996) with scheduled flights 113.

Communications

Medium	date	unit	number	units per 1,000 persons
Daily newspapers	1994	circulation	27,790,000	23
Radio	1997	receivers	417,000,000	335
Television	1999	receivers	370,000,000	292
Telephones	1999	main lines	108,716,000	86
Cellular telephones	1999	subscribers	43,296,000	34
Personal computers	1999	units	15,500,000	12
Internet	1999	users	8,900,000	7.0

Education and health

Literacy (1995): total population age 15 and over literate 81.5%; males literate 89.9%; females literate 72.7%.

Education (1998)

	schools	teachers	students	student/ teacher ratio
Primary (age 7–13)	609,626	5,819,000	139,538,000	24.0
Secondary (age 13–17)	77,888	3,697,000	63,010,000	17.0
Secondary specialized	4,109	279,000	4,981,000	17.9
Higher	1,022	407,000	3,409,000	8.4

Health (1998): physicians 1,999,500 (1 per 629 persons); hospital beds 2,913,700 (1 per 431 persons); infant mortality rate per 1,000 live births (2001) 38.0.

Food (1999): daily per capita caloric intake 3,042 (vegetable products 81%, animal products 19%); (1997) 129% of FAO recommended minimum.

Military

Total active duty personnel (2000): 2,470,000 (army 74.1%, navy 8.9%, air force 17.0%). *Military expenditure as percentage of GNP* (1997): 2.2% (world 2.6%); per capita expenditure U.S.$61.

[1]Names of the provinces, autonomous regions, and municipalities are stated in conventional form, followed by Pinyin transliteration; names of capitals are stated in conventional form or Wade-Giles transliteration, followed by Pinyin transliteration. [2]Data for Taiwan, Quemoy and Matsu (parts of Fukien province occupied by Taiwan); Hong Kong (which reverted to China from British administration on July 1, 1997) and Macau (which reverted to China from Portuguese administration on Dec. 20, 1999) are excluded. [3]Includes 4,600 sq mi (11,900 sq km) not shown separately. [4]Sum of provincial and autonomous region populations; national total may differ. [5]Based on urban sample population. [6]Excludes arrests for anti-Communist activities. [7]Includes 5,710,000 persons who are unemployed. [8]In state-owned and collective-owned industries only. [9]1979. [10]Exchange rates and international reserves are period average figures. [11]1987. [12]Average annual wage in industrial establishments in urban areas. [13]Imports and exports f.o.b.

Internet resource for further information:

- **Embassy of The People's Republic of China http://www.china-embassy.org**
- **China Statistical Information Net http://www.stats.gov.cn/english/index.html**

Colombia

Official name: República de Colombia (Republic of Colombia).
Form of government: unitary, multiparty republic with two legislative houses (Senate [102]; House of Representatives [163[1]]).
Head of state and government: President.
Capital: Santafé de Bogotá, D.C.
Official language: Spanish.
Official religion: none.
Monetary unit: 1 peso (Col$) = 100 centavos; valuation (Sept. 28, 2001) 1 U.S.$ = Col$2,193; 1 £ = Col$3,172.

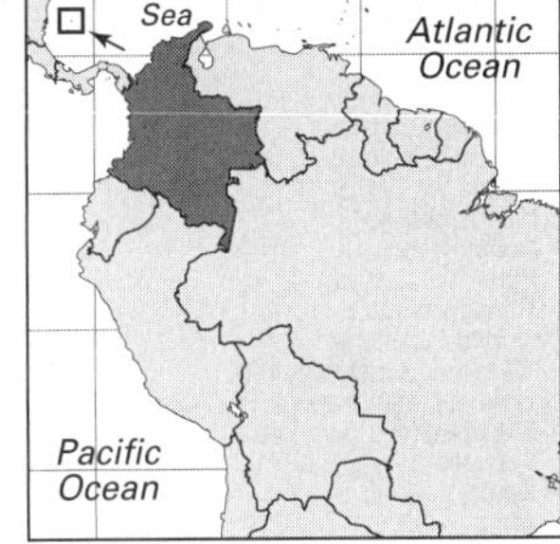

Area and population

Departments	Capitals	area sq mi	area sq km	population 1999 estimate
Antioquia	Medellín	24,445	63,912	5,300,000
Atlántico	Barranquilla	1,308	3,388	2,081,000
Bolívar	Cartagena	10,030	25,978	1,951,000
Boyacá	Tunja	8,953	23,189	1,355,000
Caldas	Manizales	3,046	7,888	1,094,000
Caquetá	Florencia	34,349	88,965	410,000
Cauca	Popayán	11,316	29,308	1,234,000
Cesar	Valledupar	8,844	22,905	944,000
Chocó	Quibdó	17,965	46,530	406,000
Córdoba	Montería	9,660	25,020	1,308,000
Cundinamarca	Santafé de Bogotá, D.C.	8,735	22,623	2,099,000
Huila	Neiva	7,680	19,890	911,000
La Guajira	Riohacha	8,049	20,848	475,000
Magdalena	Santa Marta	8,953	23,188	1,260,000
Meta	Villavicencio	33,064	85,635	686,000
Nariño	Pasto	12,845	33,268	1,603,000
Norte de Santander	Cúcuta	8,362	21,658	1,316,000
Orinoquía-Amazonía[2]	...	186,519	483,083	1,162,000
Quindío	Armenia	712	1,845	552,000
Risaralda	Pereira	1,598	4,140	928,000
San Andrés y Providencia	San Andrés	17	44	71,000
Santander	Bucaramanga	11,790	30,537	1,939,000
Sucre	Sincelejo	4,215	10,917	779,000
Tolima	Ibagué	9,097	23,562	1,293,000
Valle	Cali	8,548	22,140	4,104,000
Capital District				
Santafé de Bogotá, D.C.		613[3]	1,587[3]	6,276,000
TOTAL		440,762[3]	1,141,568[3]	41,537,000

Demography

Population (2001): 43,071,000[4].
Density (2001): persons per sq mi 97.7, persons per sq km 37.7.
Urban-rural (1999): urban 73.5%; rural 26.5%.
Sex distribution (2000): male 49.14%; female 50.86%.
Age breakdown (2000): under 15, 32.2%; 15–29, 26.6%; 30–44, 22.6%; 45–59, 11.6%; 60–74, 5.6%; 75 and over, 1.4%.
Population projection: (2010) 49,665,000; (2020) 56,569,000.
Ethnic composition (2000): mestizo 47.3%; mulatto 23.0%; white 20.0%; black 6.0%; black-Amerindian 1.0%; Amerindian/other 2.7%.
Religious affiliation (1995): Roman Catholic 91.9%; other 8.1%.
Major cities (1999): Santafé de Bogotá, D.C., 6,276,428; Cali 2,110,571; Medellín 1,957,928; Barranquilla 1,226,292; Bucaramanga 520,874.

Vital statistics

Birth rate per 1,000 population (2000): 22.9 (world avg. 22.5).
Death rate per 1,000 population (2000): 5.7 (world avg. 9.0).
Natural increase rate per 1,000 population (2000): 17.2 (world avg. 13.5).
Total fertility rate (avg. births per childbearing woman; 2000): 2.7.
Life expectancy at birth (2000): male 66.4 years; female 74.3 years.
Major causes of death per 100,000 population (1994): accidents, violence, and suicides 114.5, of which homicide with firearms 73.1; malignant neoplasms (cancers) 58.3; ischemic heart disease 50.4; infectious and parasitic diseases 13.7.

National economy

Budget (1998). Revenue: Col$16,706,000,000,000 (tax revenue 70.8%, nontax revenue 25.6%, transfers 3.6%). Expenditures: Col$21,526,000,000,000 (current expenditure 77.0%, of which wages 23.9%, interest 12.2%, goods and services 10.9%; capital expenditure 23.0%).
Public debt (external, outstanding; 1999): U.S.$19,434,000,000.
Land use (1994): forest 22.0%; pasture 18.2%; agriculture 5.7%; other 54.1%.
Tourism (1999): receipts U.S.$938,000,000; expenditures U.S.$1,078,000,000.
Production (metric tons except as noted). Agriculture, forestry, fishing (1999): sugarcane 36,900,000, plantains 2,789,000, potatoes 2,705,413, rice 2,059,374, cassava 1,956,051, bananas 1,570,000, corn 974,583, coffee 648,000; livestock (number of live animals) 25,614,200 cattle, 2,195,600 sheep, 2,764,000 pigs; roundwood (1998) 18,618,000 cu m; fish catch (1998) 167,464. Mining and quarrying (1997): iron ore 631,500; salt 560,300; gold 521,800 troy oz; silver 109,500 troy oz; emeralds 6,305,903 carats[5]. Manufacturing (value added in Col$'000,000; 1996): processed food 9,362,300; beverages 2,485,900; textiles 2,107,300; machinery and electrical apparatus 2,049,000; transport equipment 1,632,700; paper products 1,581,700. Energy production (consumption): electricity (kW-hr; 1996) 44,605,000,000 (44,769,000,000); coal (metric tons; 1996) 30,065,000 (4,919,000); petroleum (barrels; 1996) 237,395,000 (113,211,000); petroleum products (metric tons; 1996) 13,310,000 (10,913,000); natural gas (cu m; 1996) 5,674,035,000 (5,674,035,000).
Gross national product (1999): U.S.$90,007,000,000 (U.S.$2,170 per capita).

Structure of gross domestic product and labour force

	1998 in value Col$'000,000	1998 % of total value	1997 labour force	1997 % of labour force
Agriculture	10,330,739	13.7	3,478,832	22.8
Mining	3,213,148	4.3	110,969	0.7
Manufacturing	10,809,494	14.4	1,996,470	13.1
Construction	3,778,973	5.0	798,739	5.2
Public utilities	[6]	[6]	132,999	0.9
Transp. and commun.	6,007,799	8.0	831,591	5.5
Trade	8,790,382	11.7	3,330,221	21.8
Finance	[6]	[6]	753,572	4.9
Pub. admin., defense	6,783,180	9.0	3,744,301	24.5
Services	[6]	[6]		
Other	25,471,697[6]	33.9[6]	81,777[7]	0.6[7]
TOTAL	75,185,412	100.0	15,259,471	100.0

Population economically active (1998): total 6,550,679[8]; activity rate 47.4% (participation rates: ages 15–69, 67.7%; female 45.1%; unemployed 19.7%).

Price and earnings indexes (1995 = 100)

	1994	1995	1996	1997	1998	1999	2000
Consumer price index	82.7	100.0	120.2	142.5	172.0	191.3	209.4
Earnings index	99.2	100.0	107.4	108.9	109.2	112.3	114.7

Household income and expenditure. Average household size (1998) 5.3; sources of income (1992): wages 45.1%, self-employment 35.4%, transfer payments 14.2%; expenditure (1992): food 34.2%, transportation 18.5%, housing 7.8%, health care 6.4%, household durable goods 5.7%, clothing 4.5%.

Foreign trade[9]

Balance of trade (current prices)

	1995	1996	1997	1998	1999	2000
U.S.$'000,000	–2,865.0	–2,206.7	–2,886.5	–2,874.1	+1,586.3	+2,256.8
% of total	12.5%	9.4%	11.1%	11.7%	7.4%	9.5%

Imports (1998): U.S.$14,634,000,000 (1997; machinery and transport equipment 41.2%, chemicals 21.0%, vegetable products 7.7%, metals 5.1%, food and tobacco 4.4%, paper and paper products 3.4%). *Major import sources* (1997): U.S. 41.5%; Venezuela 10.0%; Germany 5.0%; Japan 4.3%.
Exports (1998): U.S.$11,362,000,000 (1997; petroleum products 23.5%, coffee 19.6%, chemicals 9.4%, coal 7.7%, food and tobacco 5.9%, textiles and apparel 5.5%). *Major export destinations* (1997): U.S. 37.8%; Venezuela 8.9%; Germany 6.3%; Ecuador 4.7%; Peru 4.7%; Japan 3.1%.

Transport and communications

Transport. Railroads (1997): route length 2,000 mi, 3,230 km; passenger mi 9,646,000[10], passenger-km 15,524,000[10]; metric ton-km cargo 736,247,000. Roads (1997): total length 71,800 mi, 115,564 km (paved 12%). Vehicles (1996): cars 762,000; trucks 672,000. Air transport (1997): passenger-km 5,991,000,000; metric ton-km cargo 836,000,000; airports (1998) 43.

Communications

Medium	date	unit	number	units per 1,000 persons
Daily newspapers	1996	circulation	1,800,000[11]	46[11]
Radio	1997	receivers	21,000,000	524
Television	1999	receivers	8,273,000	199
Telephones	1999	main lines	6,665,000	160
Cellular telephones	1999	subscribers	3,134,000	75
Personal computers	1999	units	1,400,000	34
Internet	1999	users	664,000	16.0

Education and health

Educational attainment (1985). Percentage of population age 25 and over having: no schooling 15.3%; primary education 50.1%; secondary 25.4%; higher 6.8%; not stated 2.4%. *Literacy* (1995): population age 15 and over literate 91.3%; males literate 91.2%; females literate 91.4%.

Education (1999)

	schools	teachers	students	student/ teacher ratio
Primary (6–10)	60,183	214,911	5,162,260	24.0
Secondary (11–16)	13,421	200,337	3,594,083	17.9
Higher[12]	266	75,568	673,353	8.9

Health: physicians (1997) 40,355 (1 per 1,102 persons); hospital beds 40,043 (1 per 1,000 persons); infant mortality rate (1999) 25.6.
Food (1999): daily per capita caloric intake 2,567 (vegetable products 83%, animal products 17%); 111% of FAO recommended minimum requirement.

Military

Total active duty personnel (2000): 153,000 (army 85.0%, navy 9.8%, air force 5.2%). *Military expenditure as percentage of GNP* (1997): 3.7% (world 2.6%); per capita expenditure U.S.$91.

[1]Two seats are occupied by representatives from indigenous communities. [2]Geographic designation for eight political entities in eastern Colombia elevated to departmental status in the early 1990s. [3]Detail does not add to total given because of rounding. [4]De jure figure; about 2,000,000 Colombians left the country between 1997 and 2000 because of the violence and high unemployment. [5]1995. [6]Services include public utilities and finance. [7]Activities not adequately described. [8]The data relate to Bogota, Barranquilla, Medellín, Cali, Bucaramanga, Manizales, and Pasto. [9]Import figures are f.o.b. in balance of trade and c.i.f. in commodities and trading partners. [10]1992. [11]Circulation for 26 newspapers only. [12]1996.

Internet resources for further information:
- **National Administration Department of Statistics http://www.dane.gov.co**

Comoros[1]

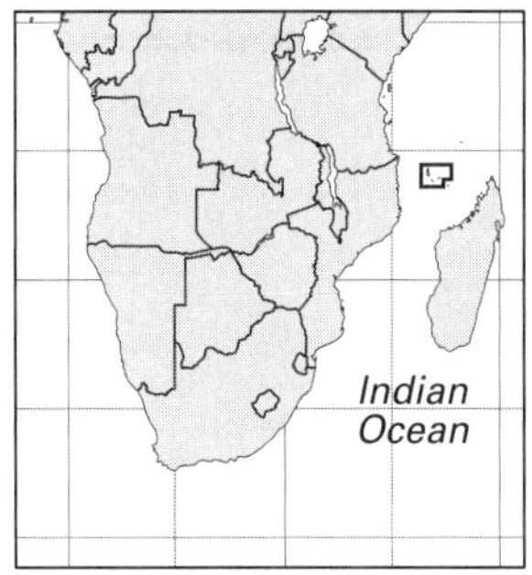

Official name: Jumhurīyat al-Qumur al-Ittihādīyah al-Islāmīyah (Arabic); République Fédérale Islamique des Comores (French) (Federal Islamic Republic of the Comoros)[2].
Form of government: transitional government[3].
Head of state and government: Head of State assisted by Prime Minister.
Capital: Moroni.
Official languages: Comorian; Arabic; French.
Official religion: Islam.
Monetary unit: 1 Comorian franc (CF) = 100 centimes; valuation (Sept. 28, 2001) 1 U.S.$ = CF 550.15; 1 £ = CF 808.55.

Area and population

Islands	Capitals	area sq mi	area sq km	population 2000 estimate
Mwali (Mohéli)	Fomboni	112	290	28,600
Nzwani (Anjouan)[4]	Mutsamudu	164	424	219,500
Ngazidja (Grande-Comore)	Moroni	443	1,148	261,100
TOTAL		719	1,862	509,200[5]

Demography

Population (2001): 566,000[6].
Density (2001): persons per sq mi 787.5, persons per sq km 304.1.
Urban-rural (1995): urban 24.1%; rural 75.9%.
Sex distribution (2000): male 49.62%; female 50.38%.
Age breakdown (2000): under 15, 42.7%; 15–29, 28.6%; 30–44, 15.9%; 45–59, 8.1%; 60–74, 3.9%; 75 and over, 0.8%.
Population projection[6]: (2010) 734,000; (2020) 950,000.
Doubling time: 23 years.
Ethnic composition (1995): nearly all Comorian (a mixture of Bantu, Arab, Malay, and Malagasy peoples).
Religious affiliation (2000): Sunnī Muslim 98.0%; Christian 1.2%; other 0.8%.
Major cities (1995): Moroni 34,168; Mutsamudu (1991) 20,000; Domoni (1990) 8,000; Fomboni (1990) 5,600.

Vital statistics

Birth rate per 1,000 population (2000): 40.0 (world avg. 22.5).
Death rate per 1,000 population (2000): 9.6 (world avg. 9.0).
Natural increase rate per 1,000 population (2000) 30.4 (world avg. 13.5).
Total fertility rate (avg. births per childbearing woman; 2000): 5.4.
Marriage rate per 1,000 population: n.a.[7]
Divorce rate per 1,000 population: n.a.
Life expectancy at birth (2000): male 57.8 years; female 62.2 years.
Major causes of death per 100,000 population: n.a.; however, major diseases include malaria (afflicts 80–90% of the adult population), tuberculosis, leprosy, and kwashiorkor (a nutritional deficiency disease).

National economy

Budget (1998). Revenue: CF 14,066,000,000 (tax revenue 64.0%, grants 29.4%, nontax revenue 6.6%). Expenditures: CF 16,307,000,000 (current expenditures 85.4%, development expenditures 14.6%).
Production (metric tons except as noted). Agriculture, forestry, fishing (1997): coconuts 60,000[8], bananas 60,000[9], cassava 50,700, taro 8,500, corn (maize) 3,800, rice 2,900, cloves 2,000[9], vanilla 180[9], ylang-ylang essence 67[9], other export crops grown in small quantities include coffee, cinnamon, and tuberoses; livestock (number of live animals; 1998) 40,000 goats, 40,000 cattle; roundwood, n.a.; fish catch (1997) 12,500. Mining and quarrying: sand, gravel, and crushed stone from coral mining for local construction. Manufacturing: products of small-scale industries include processed vanilla and ylang-ylang, cement, handicrafts, soaps, soft drinks, woodwork, and clothing. Construction: n.a. Energy production (consumption): electricity (kW-hr; 1999) 34,900,000 (22,000,000); coal, none (none); crude petroleum, none (none); petroleum products (metric tons; 1996) none (22,000); natural gas, none (none).
Population economically active (1991): total 215,000; activity rate of total population 44.4% (participation rates: ages 10 years and over, 57.8%; female 40.0%; unemployed [2000] 20%).

Price and earnings indexes (1995 = 100)

	1994	1995	1996	1997	1998	1999
Consumer price index	93.4	100.0	102.4	104.0	105.9	106.8
Monthly earnings index[10]	88.3	100.0	...	...	...	...

Tourism: receipts from visitors (1999) U.S.$24,700,000; expenditures by nationals abroad (1998) U.S.$3,000,000.
Public debt (external, outstanding; 1999): U.S.$179,900,000.
Household income and expenditure. Average household size (1995) 6.3[11]; average annual income per household (1995) CF 188,985 (U.S.$505)[11]; sources of income: n.a.; expenditure (1993)[12]: food and beverages 67.3%, clothing and footwear 11.6%, tobacco and cigarettes 4.1%, energy 3.8%.
Gross national product (at current market prices; 1999): U.S.$189,000,000 (U.S.$350 per capita).

Structure of gross domestic product and labour force

	2000 in value CF '000,000	2000 % of total value	1980 labour force[13]	1980 % of labour force
Agriculture, fishing	44,082	40.9	53,063	53.3
Mining	...	...	62	0.1
Manufacturing	4,488	4.2	3,946	4.0
Construction	6,733	6.2	3,267	3.3
Public utilities	1,654	1.5	129	0.1
Transportation and communications	5,715	5.3	2,118	2.1
Trade, restaurants, hotels	27,155	25.2	1,873	1.9
Finance, insurance	4,648	4.3	237	0.2
Public admin., defense	15,420	14.3	2,435	2.5
Services	595	0.6	4,646	4.7
Other	–2,689[14]	–2.5[14]	27,687[15]	27.8[15]
TOTAL	107,801	100.0	99,463	100.0

Land use (1994)[8]: forested 17.9%; meadows and pastures 6.7%; agricultural and under permanent cultivation 44.9%; other 30.5%.

Foreign trade[16]

Balance of trade (current prices)

	1994	1995	1996	1997	1998	1999
CF '000,000,000	–17.2	–19.2	–22.2	–23.6	–19.6	–20.7
% of total	64.8%	69.4%	82.0%	81.8%	78.8%	70.9%

Imports (1999): CF 24,929,000,000 (iron and steel 28.5%, rice 18.9%, cement 13.4%, meat and fish 6.1%, petroleum products 5.5%). *Major import sources:* France 32%; South Africa 8%; Réunion 8%; United Arab Emirates 6%; Kenya 6%.
Exports (1999): CF 4,248,000,000 (vanilla 43.2%, cloves 27.7%, ylang-ylang 13.3%). *Major export destinations:* United States 26.8%; France 25.4%; Germany 12.2%; Singapore 8.6%.

Transport and communications

Transport. Railroads: none. Roads (1996): total length 559 mi, 900 km (paved [1995] 76%). Vehicles (1996): passenger cars 9,100; trucks and buses 4,950. Merchant marine (1992): vessels (100 gross tons and over) 6; total deadweight tonnage 3,579. Air transport (1996): passenger-mi 1,900,000, passenger-km 3,000,000; short ton-mi cargo, n.a., metric ton-mi cargo, n.a.; airports (1997) with scheduled flights 2.

Communications

Medium	date	unit	number	units per 1,000 persons
Daily newspapers	1997	circulation	0	0
Radio	1997	receivers	90,000	170
Television	1997	receivers	1,000	1.8
Telephones	1999	main lines	6,521	12

Education and health

Educational attainment (1980). Percentage of population age 25 and over having: no formal schooling 56.7%; Qur'anic school education 8.3%; primary 3.6%; secondary 2.0%; higher 0.2%; not specified 29.2%. *Literacy* (1995)[8]: total population age 15 and over literate 192,000 (57.0%); males literate 108,000 (64.0%); females literate 84,000 (50.0%).

Education (1995–96)

	schools	teachers	students	student/ teacher ratio
Primary (age 7–12)	327	1,508	78,527	52.1
Secondary (age 13–19)	...	591	21,192	35.9
Higher	...	...	348	...

Health (1995): physicians 64[17] (1 per 7,800[17] persons); hospital beds 1,450[17] (1 per 342[17] persons); infant mortality rate per 1,000 live births (2000) 86.3.
Food (1997)[8]: daily per capita caloric intake 1,800 (vegetable products 94%, animal products 6%); 77% of FAO recommended minimum requirement.

Military

Total active duty personnel (1997): 1,500. *Military expenditure as percentage of GNP:* n.a.

[1]Excludes Mayotte, an overseas possession of France, unless otherwise indicated. [2]Long-form name change to the Union of the Comoro Islands is pending from May 1999. [3]Looser federation arrangement is expected in early 2002 per agreement signed in February 2001 by the leaders of the Comorian islands (except Mayotte). [4]Secession from the Comoros from October 1997 ended February 2001. [5]Projection based on 1991 census. [6]100,000 to 150,000 Comorians live abroad in France or Mayotte. [7]In the early 1990s, 20% of adult men had more than one wife. [8]Includes Mayotte. [9]1998. [10]July average for government employees only. [11]Based on sample survey of 2,004 households on all three islands. [12]Weights of consumer price index components for Moroni. [13]The wage labour force was very small in 1995; total of less than 7,000 including government employees, and less than 2,000 excluding them. [14]Less imputed bank service charge. [15]Not adequately defined. [16]Imports c.i.f.; exports f.o.b. [17]Estimated figure.

Internet resources for further information:
- **Indian Ocean Commission**
  http://www.coi-info.org

Congo, Democratic Republic of the

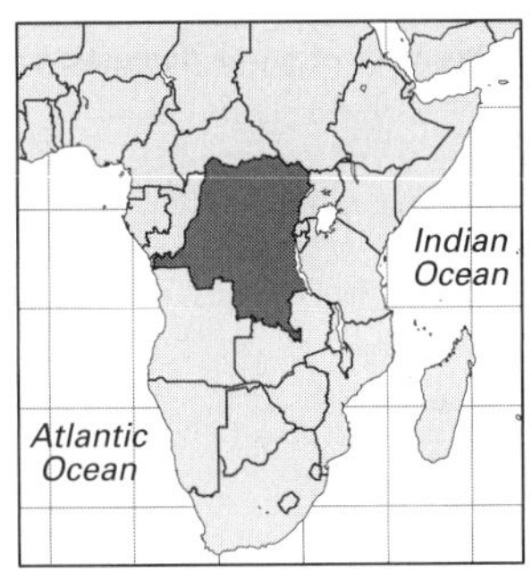

Official name: République Democratique du Congo (Democratic Republic of the Congo).
Form of government: transitional military regime[1] with one legislative body (Assembly[2] [300 nonelected seats]).
Chief of state: President.
Capitals: Kinshasa (executive and judicial[2, 3]); Lubumbashi (legislative[2]).
Official languages: French; English.
Official religion: none.
Monetary unit: Congolese franc (FC)[4]; valuation (Sept. 28, 2001) 1 U.S.$ = FC 4.50; 1 £ = FC 6.61.

Area and population

		area		population
				1998
Provinces	**Capitals**	sq mi	sq km	estimate
Bandundu	Bandundu	114,154	295,658	5,201,000
Bas-Congo	Matadi	20,819	53,920	2,835,000
Equateur	Mbandaka	155,712	403,292	4,820,000
Kasai-Occidental	Kananga	59,746	154,742	3,337,000
Kasai-Oriental	Mbuji-Mayi	65,754	170,302	3,830,000
Katanga	Lubumbashi	191,845	496,877	4,125,000
Maniema	Kindu	51,062	132,250	1,246,787
Nord-Kivu	Goma	22,967	59,483	3,564,434
Orientale	Kisangani	194,302	503,239	5,566,000
Sud-Kivu	Bukavu	25,147	65,130	2,837,779
City				
Kinshasa	—	3,848	9,965	4,787,000
TOTAL		905,354[5]	2,344,858	42,150,000

Demography

Population (2001): 53,625,000[6].
Density (2001): persons per sq mi 59.2, persons per sq km 22.9.
Urban-rural (1999): urban 29.9%; rural 70.1%.
Sex distribution (2000): male 49.40%; female 50.60%.
Age breakdown (2000): under 15, 48.3%; 15–29, 26.9%; 30–44, 13.8%; 45–59, 7.0%; 60–74, 3.3%; 75 and over, 0.7%.
Population projection: (2010) 69,846,000, (2020) 92,377,000.
Doubling time: 23 years.
Ethnic composition (1983): Luba 18.0%; Kongo 16.1%; Mongo 13.5%; Rwanda 10.3%; Azande 6.1%; Bangi and Ngale 5.8%; Rundi 3.8%; Teke 2.7%; Boa 2.3%; Chokwe 1.8%; Lugbara 1.6%; Banda 1.4%; other 16.6%.
Religious affiliation (1995): Roman Catholic 41.0%; Protestant 32.0%; indigenous Christian 13.4%, of which Kimbanguist 13.0%; other Christian 0.8%; Muslim 1.4%; traditional beliefs and other 11.4%.
Major cities (1994): Kinshasa 4,655,313; Lubumbashi 851,381; Mbuji-Mayi 806,475; Kolwezi 417,800; Kisangani 417,517; Kananga 393,030.

Vital statistics

Birth rate per 1,000 population (2000): 46.4 (world avg. 22.5).
Death rate per 1,000 population (2000): 15.4 (world avg. 9.0).
Natural increase rate per 1,000 population (2000): 31.0 (world avg. 13.5).
Total fertility rate (avg. births per childbearing woman; 2000): 6.9.
Life expectancy at birth (2000): male 47.6 years; female 50.8 years.

National economy

Budget (1999). Revenue: FC 2,328,600,000 (tax revenue 76.9%, of which taxes on international trade 18.5%, taxes on goods and services 13.8%, income tax 12.6%; nontax revenue 12.8%). Expenditures: FC 4,113,800,000; wages and salaries 50.5%; defense 14.6%; investment 13.5%; interest on debt 7.2%).
Public debt (external, outstanding; 1999): U.S.$8,188,000,000.
Tourism (1997): receipts U.S.$9,000,000; expenditures U.S.$7,000,000.
Production (metric tons except as noted). Agriculture, forestry, fishing (2000): cassava 15,959,000, plantains 1,800,000, sugarcane 1,669,000, corn (maize) 1,184,000, oil palm fruit 900,000, peanuts (groundnuts) 382,000, sweet potatoes 370,000, rice 337,800, bananas 312,000, yams 255,000, mangoes 216,000, papayas 213,000, pineapples 196,000, oranges 185,000, dry beans 122,000, coffee 36,000, seed cotton 28,000, natural rubber 8,000; livestock (number of live animals) 4,131,321 goats, 1,048,710 pigs, 822,355 cattle, 924,000 sheep, 21,559,000 chickens; roundwood (2000) 50,754,000 cu m; fish catch (1999) 208,862. Mining and quarrying (1999): copper (metal content) 29,600; cobalt (metal content) 1,600; zinc (metal content) 1,300; gold 207 kg; diamonds 20,100,000 carats. Manufacturing (1999): iron and steel 965,000; cement 172,900; sugar 73,400; soap 46,773; tires 41,000 units; printed fabrics 13,615,000 sq m; matches 2,500,000 packs; shoes 848,000 pairs; beer 1,398,000 hectolitres; soft drinks 738,000 hectolitres. Energy production (consumption): electricity (kW-hr; 1999) 5,087,000,000 (5,087,000,000); coal (metric tons; 1996) 95,000 (140,000); crude petroleum (barrels; 1996) 8,403,000 (505,000); petroleum products (metric tons; 1996) 48,000 (459,000); natural gas, none (none).
Household income and expenditure. Average household size (1998) 2.3; average annual income per household (1982) Z 1,200[4] (U.S.$209); sources of income: n.a.; expenditure (1985): food 61.7%, housing and energy 11.5%, clothing and footwear 9.7%, transportation 5.9%, furniture and utensils 4.9%.
Gross national product (2000): U.S.$4,417,000,000 (U.S.$85 per capita).

Structure of gross domestic product and labour force

	1999		1993	
	in value FC '000,000	% of total value	labour force	% of labour force
Agriculture	27,138,200	53.9	9,432,000	65.0
Mining	4,120,300	8.2		
Manufacturing	2,144,000	4.3		
Construction	1,178,300	2.3	2,321,000	16.0
Public utilities	1,089,400	2.2		
Transp. and commun.	1,204,800	2.4		
Trade	8,686,900	17.2		
Pub. admin., defense	2,096,300	4.2	2,757,000	19.0
Finance and services	2,589,400	5.1		
Other	121,900	0.2		
TOTAL	50,369,500	100.0	14,510,000	100.0

Population economically active (1997): total 19,618,000; activity rate 42.0% (participation rates [1987]: over age 10, 57.4%; female 43.5%).

Price and earnings indexes (1995 = 100)

	1993	1994	1995	1996	1997
Consumer price index	0.1	15.6	100.0	758.8	2,090.7
Earnings index	…	…	…	…	…

Land use (1994): forested 76.7%; meadows and pastures 6.6%; agricultural and under permanent cultivation 3.5%; other 13.2%.

Foreign trade

Balance of trade (current prices)

	1996	1997	1998	1999	2000
U.S.$'000,000	+249	+56	−50	−175	−275
% of total	8.2%	2.2%	2.1%	8.6%	15.3%

Imports (1999): U.S.$1,108,000,000 (non-oil 95.0%; oil 5.0%). *Major import sources*[7] (1999): South Africa 22.0%; Belgium 15.8%; Nigeria 10.0%; Zambia 5.3%; France 4.6%; U.S. 3.2%; China 3.2%; Germany 2.7%; The Netherlands 2.5%.
Exports (1999): U.S.$933,000,000 (diamonds 61.3%, crude petroleum 12.4%, coffee 9.8%, cobalt 8.6%, copper 5.1%). *Major export destinations* (1999): Belgium-Luxembourg 63.8%; U.S. 19.0%; Finland 4.1%; Italy 3.0%.

Transport and communications

Transport. Railroads (1996)[8]: length 5,138 km; passenger-km 29,000,000[9]; metric ton-km cargo 176,000,000[9]. Roads (1996): total length 154,027 km (paved 2%). Vehicles (1996): passenger cars 787,000; trucks and buses 60,000. Air transport (1996): passenger-km 279,000,000; metric ton-km cargo 42,000,000; airports (1997) with scheduled flights 22.

Communications

Medium	date	unit	number	units per 1,000 persons
Daily newspapers	1996	circulation	124,000	2.7
Radio	1997	receivers	18,030,000	376.0
Television	1997	receivers	6,478,000	135.0
Telephones	1999	main lines	20,000	0.4
Cellular telephones	1999	subscribers	10,000	0.2
Internet	1998	users	…	…

Education and health

Educational attainment: n.a. *Literacy* (1995): percentage of total population age 15 and over literate 77.3%; males literate 86.6%; females literate 67.7%.

Education (1994–95)

	schools	teachers	students	student/ teacher ratio
Primary (age 6–11)	14,885	121,054	5,417,506	44.8
Secondary (age 12–17)	4,276[10]	59,325[10]	640,298[11]	22.6[10]
Voc., teacher tr.	[10]	[10]	701,148[11]	[10]
Higher	…	3,873[12]	93,266	15.9[12]

Health: physicians (1990) 2,469 (1 per 15,584 persons); hospital beds (1986) 68,508 (1 per 487 persons); infant mortality rate (2000) 101.6.
Food (1999): daily per capita caloric intake 1,637 (vegetable products 97%, animal products 3%); 72% of FAO recommended minimum requirement.

Military

Total active duty personnel (2000): 55,900 (army 99.4%, navy 0.6%; up to 12,000 foreign forces support the government, and about 15,000 foreign forces oppose the government[13]. *Military expenditure as percentage of GNP* (1997): 5.0% (world 2.6%), per capita expenditure U.S.$5.

[1]The civil war begun in August 1998 was halted by cease-fire in September 1999 and resumed in November 1999. [2]From August 2000. [3]Kisangani to become the judicial capital when the civil war ends per July 2000 announcement. [4]The new zaïre (NZ) replaced the (old) zaïre (Z) at a rate of 3,000,000 (old) zaïres to 1 NZ on Oct. 22, 1993; the Congolese franc (FC) replaced the new zaïre (NZ) at a rate of FC 1 to NZ 100,000 on July 1, 1998. Both zaïres ceased to be legal tender on June 30, 1999. [5]Detail does not add to total given because of rounding. [6]Figure includes 1998–2001 war deaths approaching 3 million in the eastern DRC (mostly from starvation, disease, and deprivation) and an unknown figure in western DRC. [7]DOT (Direction of Trade) valuation; the valuation as the sum of all known trading partners, by external analysis, rather than as the reported sum of the country's own trade data. [8]Traffic statistics are for services operated by the Zaire National Railways (SNCZ), which controls more than 90% of the country's total rail facility. [9]1994. [10]Secondary includes Voc., teacher tr. [11]1993–94. [12]1989. [13]UN peacekeeping force numbered 2,400 troops in August 2001.

Internet resource for further information:
- **Zaire—A Country Study http://lcweb2.loc.gov/frd/cs/zrtoc.html**

Congo, Republic of the

Official name: République du Congo (Republic of the Congo).
Form of government: transitional[1] regime with one legislative house (National Transitional Council [75]).
Chief of state and government: President.
Capital: Brazzaville.
Official language: French[2].
Official religion: none.
Monetary unit: 1 CFA franc (CFAF) = 100 centimes; valuation (Sept. 28, 2001) 1 U.S.$ = CFAF 720.28; 1 £ = CFAF 1,059.

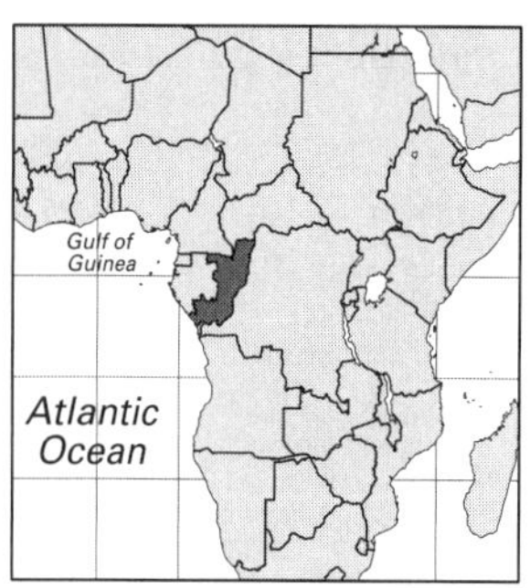

Area and population

Regions	Capitals	area sq mi	area sq km	population 1992 estimate
Bouenza	Madingou	4,733	12,258	177,357
Cuvette Est	Owando	28,900	74,850	151,839
Cuvette Ouest	Ewo			
Kouilou	Pointe-Noire	5,270	13,650	89,296
Lékoumou	Sibiti	8,089	20,950	74,420
Likouala	impfondo	25,500	66,044	70,675
Niari	Loubomo	10,007	25,918	120,077
Plateaux	Djambala	14,826	38,400	119,722
Pool	Kinkala	13,110	33,955	182,671
Sangha	Ouesso	21,542	55,795	35,961
Communes				
Brazzaville	—	39	100	937,579
Loubomo	—	7	18	83,605
Mossendjo	—	2	5	16,405
Nkayi	—	3	8	42,465
Ouesso	—	2	5	16,171
Pointe-Noire	—	17	44	576,206
TOTAL		132,047	342,000	2,694,449

Demography

Population (2001): 2,894,000.
Density (2001): persons per sq mi 21.9, persons per sq km 8.5.
Urban-rural (1999): urban 61.8%; rural 38.2%.
Sex distribution (2000): male 49.17%; female 50.83%.
Age breakdown (2000): under 15, 42.5%; 15–29, 28.7%; 30–44, 16.1%; 45–59, 7.7%; 60–74, 4.1%; 75 and over, 0.9%.
Population projection: (2010) 3,491,000; (2020) 4,209,000.
Doubling time: 30 years.
Ethnic composition (1983): Kongo 51.5%; Teke 17.3%; Mboshi 11.5%; Mbete 4.9%; Punu 3.0%; Sango 2.7%; Maka 1.8%; Pygmy 1.5%; other 5.8%.
Religious affiliation (2000): Roman Catholic 49.3%; Protestant 17.0%; African Christians 12.6%; unaffiliated Christians 11.9%; traditional beliefs 4.8%; other 4.4%.
Major cities (1992): Brazzaville 937,579; Pointe-Noire 576,206; Loubomo 83,605; Nkayi 42,465; Mossendjo 16,405.

Vital statistics

Birth rate per 1,000 population (2000): 38.6 (world avg. 22.5).
Death rate per 1,000 population (2000): 16.4 (world avg. 9.0).
Natural increase rate per 1,000 population (2000): 22.2 (world avg. 13.5).
Total fertility rate (avg. births per childbearing woman; 2000): 5.1.
Life expectancy at birth (2000): male 44.5 years; female 50.5 years.
Major causes of morbidity and mortality in the 1990s included malaria, acute respiratory infections, diarrhea, trauma, helminthiasis, and sexually transmitted diseases.

National economy

Budget (1999). Revenue: CFAF 390,600,000,000 (petroleum revenue 70.6%; nonpetroleum receipts 27.8%; grants 1.6%). Expenditures: CFAF 475,400,000,000 (current expenditure 81.3%, of which debt service 35.4%; salaries 21.2%; transfers and subsidies 5.5%; capital expenditure 18.7%).
Public debt (external, outstanding; 1999): U.S.$3,932,000,000.
Production (metric tons except as noted). Agriculture, forestry, fishing (2000): cassava 790,000, sugarcane 450,000, oil palm fruit 90,000, plantains 78,000, bananas 52,000, sweet potatoes 22,000, peanuts (groundnuts) 25,000, avocados 25,000, yams 13,500, pineapples 13,000, cacao beans 1,800, coffee 1,400, rubber 1,000; livestock (number of live animals) 285,000 goats, 116,000 sheep, 77,000 cattle, 46,000 pigs; roundwood (2000) 3,243,000 cu m; fish catch (1999) 43,886. Mining and quarrying (1998): 10 kg. Manufacturing (1998): residual fuel oil 240,000; cement 110,000; distillate fuel oils 85,000; aviation gas 48,000; gasoline 45,400; kerosene 44,600; refined sugar 42,861; wheat flour 4,002; dried, cured, or salted fish 4,000[3]; cigarettes 380,000,000 cartons; mechanical cultivators 294,404 units[3]; beer 342,000 hectolitres; soft drinks 165,000 hectolitres; cotton textiles 1,800,000 m[4]; veneer sheets 50,000 cu m; footwear 300,000 pairs[5]. Energy production (consumption): electricity (kW-hr; 1998) 408,000,000 (535,000,000); crude petroleum (barrels; 1996) 77,837,000 (11,882,000); petroleum products (metric tons; 1996) 534,000 (507,000); natural gas (cu m; 1996) 3,357,000 (3,357,000).
Household income and expenditure. Average household size (1984) 5.2; income per household: n.a.; sources of income: n.a.; expenditure (1977)[6, 7]: food, beverages, and tobacco 62.0%, housing 10.1%, transportation and recreation 8.6%, clothing and footwear 6.9%, fuel, energy, and water 5.7%, health and medical care 3.8%.
Gross national product (at current market prices; 1999): U.S.$1,571,000,000 (U.S.$550 per capita).

Structure of gross domestic product and labour force

	1999 in value CFAF '000,000[8]	1999 % of total value	1991 labour force	1991 % of labour force
Agriculture, forestry, fishing	119,800	9.0	471,000	59.1
Petroleum	692,300	52.1		
Manufacturing, mining	79,300	6.0	101,000	12.7
Construction	26,200	2.0		
Public utilities	9,300	0.7		
Trade	116,700	8.8		
Transp. and commun.	72,000	5.4	225,000	28.2
Pub. admin., defense	122,200	9.2		
Services	91,100	6.9		
Other	36,400	2.7	—	—
TOTAL	1,328,900[9]	100.0[9]	797,000	100.0

Population economically active (1997): total 1,110,000; activity rate of total population 42.0% (participation rates [1984]: ages 15–64, 54.0%; female [1997] 43.4%; unemployed[10] [1984] 2.3%).

Price and earnings indexes (1995 = 100)

	1993	1994	1995	1996
Consumer price index[7]	55.0	82.4	100	99.8
Earnings index	...	...	...	...

Land use (1994): forested 58.3%; meadows and pastures 29.3%; agricultural and under permanent cultivation 0.5%; other 11.9%.
Tourism (1999): receipts U.S.$12,000,000; expenditures U.S.$60,000,000.

Foreign trade

Balance of trade (current prices)

	1994	1995	1996	1997	1998	1999
CFAF '000,000,000	+192.2	+260.8	+499.5	+547.2	+348.7	+644.1
% of total	22.0%	28.7%	45.4%	41.9%	34.6%	46.0%

Imports (1999): CFAF 378,100,000,000 (machinery and transport equipment 20.8%, basic manufactures 20.1%, food and live animals 20.0%, chemicals and chemical products 14.2%, mineral fuels 12.1%). *Major import sources:* France 23.2%; U.S. 7.8%; Italy 7.8%; Hong Kong 4.9%; Belgium 3.8%; U.K. 3.1%; The Netherlands 2.9%.
Exports (1999): CFAF 1,022,200,000,000 (petroleum and petroleum products 91.9%, wood and wood products 4.3%, other 3.8%). *Major export destinations:* Taiwan 31.5%; U.S. 22.8%; South Korea 15.3%; Germany 6.7%; France 2.6%; Italy 2.3%.

Transport and communications

Transport. Railroads: (1998) length 894 km; passenger-km 242,000,000; metric ton-km cargo 135,000,000. Roads (1997): total length 12,800 km (paved 10%). Vehicles (1997): passenger cars 37,240; trucks and buses 15,500. Air transport (1998)[11]: passenger-km 258,272,000; metric ton-km cargo 13,524,000; airports (1998) with scheduled flights 10.

Communications

Medium	date	unit	number	units per 1,000 persons
Daily newspapers	1995	circulation	20,000	7.8
Radio	1997	receivers	341,000	126
Television	1997	receivers	33,000	12
Telephones	1999	main lines	22,000	7.7
Cellular telephones	1998	subscribers	3,390	1.2
Internet	1998	users	...	...

Education and health

Educational attainment (1984). Percentage of population age 25 and over having: no formal schooling 58.7%; primary education 21.4%; secondary education 16.9%; postsecondary 3.0%. *Literacy* (1995): total population age 15 and over literate 80.7%; males literate 87.5%; females literate 74.4%.

Education (1996–97)

	schools	teachers	students	student/ teacher ratio
Primary (age 6–13)	1,612	6,926	489,546	70.7
Secondary (age 14–18)	238[12]	5,466	190,409	34.8
Voc., teacher tr.	60[12]	1,746	23,606	13.5
Higher[13]	12	1,341	16,602	12.4

Health: physicians (1995) 632 (1 per 4,083 persons); hospital beds (1989) 4,817 (1 per 446 persons); infant mortality rate per 1,000 live births (2000) 101.6.
Food (1999): daily per capita caloric intake 2,212 (vegetable products 94%, animal products 6%); 100% of FAO recommended minimum requirement.

Military

Total active duty personnel (2000): 8,000 (army 75.0%, navy 10.0%, air force 15.0%). *Military expenditure as percentage of GNP* (1997): 4.1% (world 2.6%); per capita expenditure U.S.$28.

[1]From February 1998 through September 2001. [2]"Functional" national languages are Lingala and Monokutuba. [3]1992. [4]1993. [5]1990. [6]European households only; Brazzaville. [7]Cost-of-living components. [8]At current factor cost. [9]Detail does not add to total given because of rounding. [10]Previously employed only. [11]Represents 1/11 of the traffic of Air Afrique, which is operated by 11 African states. [12]1989. [13]1995.

Internet resources for further information:
- **Investir en Zone Franc http://www.izf.net/izf/Index.htm**

Costa Rica

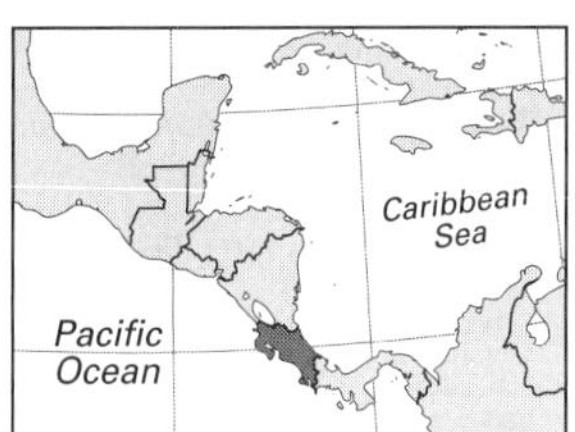

Official name: República de Costa Rica (Republic of Costa Rica).
Form of government: unitary multiparty republic with one legislative house (Legislative Assembly [57]).
Head of state and government: President.
Capital: San José.
Official language: Spanish.
Official religion: Roman Catholicism.
Monetary unit: 1 Costa Rican colón (₡) = 100 céntimos; valuation (Sept. 28, 2001) 1 U.S.$ = ₡333.77; 1 £ = ₡490.54.

Area and population

Provinces	Capitals	area sq mi	area sq km	population 2000 census
Alajuela	Alajuela	3,766	9,753	716,935
Cartago	Cartago	1,207	3,125	432,923
Guanacaste	Liberia	3,915	10,141	264,474
Heredia	Heredia	1,026	2,657	354,926
Limón	Limón	3,548	9,188	340,756
Puntarenas	Puntarenas	4,354	11,277	358,137
San José	San José	1,915	4,959	1,356,442
TOTAL		19,730[1]	51,100	3,824,593

Demography

Population (2001): 3,936,000.
Density (2001): persons per sq mi 199.5, persons per sq km 77.0.
Urban-rural (1999): urban 47.6%; rural 52.4%.
Sex distribution (2000): male 50.04%; female 49.96%.
Age breakdown (2000): under 15, 32.1%; 15–29, 27.1%; 30–44, 21.6%; 45–59, 11.7%; 60–74, 5.6%; 75 and over, 1.9%.
Population projection: (2010) 4,493,000; (2020) 5,052,000.
Doubling time: 40 years.
Ethnic composition (2000): white 77.0%; mestizo 17.0%; black/mulatto 3.0%; East Asian (mostly Chinese) 2.0%; Amerindian 1.0%.
Religious affiliation (1995): Roman Catholic 86.0%; Protestant 9.3%, of which Pentecostal 4.9%; other Christian 2.4%; other 2.3%.
Major cities/metropolitan areas (2000)[2]: San José 344,349[3] (1,082,269); Limón 61,494[4]; Alajuela 53,430[4] (209,098); San Isidro de El General 45,145[4]; Liberia 36,407[4]; Cartago 33,539[5] (303,010); Heredia 30,968[4] (258,815).

Vital statistics

Birth rate per 1,000 population (1999): 21.7 (world avg. 22.5); legitimate 51.0%; illegitimate 49.0%.
Death rate per 1,000 population (1999): 4.2 (world avg. 9.0).
Natural increase rate per 1,000 population (1999): 17.5 (world avg. 13.5).
Total fertility rate (avg. births per childbearing woman; 1999): 2.6.
Marriage rate per 1,000 population (1999): 7.3.
Divorce rate per 1,000 population (1995): 1.4.
Life expectancy at birth (1999): male 74.2 years; female 79.9 years.
Major causes of death per 100,000 population (1999): diseases of the circulatory system 127.6; malignant neoplasms (cancers) 87.2; accidents and violence 50.1; diseases of the respiratory system 44.5.

National economy

Budget (1998). Revenue: ₡459,700,000,000 (general sales tax 38.3%, selective taxes on goods and services 21.6%, income and profit taxes 19.3%, import duties 11.0%). Expenditures: ₡562,300,000,000 (current expenditures 91.3%, development expenditures 8.7%).
Public debt (external, outstanding; 1999): U.S.$3,186,000,000.
Gross national product (1999): U.S.$12,828,000,000 (U.S.$3,570 per capita).

Structure of gross domestic product and labour force

	1998 in value ₡'000,000,000	% of total value	labour force	% of labour force
Agriculture, forestry, fishing	410	15.2	261,584	19.0
Mining	505	18.7	1,595	0.1
Manufacturing			203,501	14.8
Construction	67	2.5	81,176	5.9
Public utilities	82	3.0	13,103	1.0
Transp. and commun.	170	6.3	73,272	5.3
Trade, restaurants	554	20.5	251,735	18.3
Finance, real estate	312	11.6	70,119	5.1
Public administration	367	13.6	333,685	24.2
Services	229	8.5		
Other	—	—	86,770[6]	6.3[6]
TOTAL	2,696	100.0[1]	1,376,540	100.0

Production (metric tons except as noted). Agriculture, forestry, fishing (1999): sugarcane 3,950,000, bananas 2,101,000, oil palm fruit 440,000, pineapples 400,000, oranges 283,200, rice 262,200, coffee 147,000, cassava 119,500, potatoes 91,700, plantains 90,000, other products include other tropical fruits, cut flowers, and ornamental plants grown for export; livestock (number of live animals) 1,617,000 cattle, 290,000 pigs, 17,000,000 chickens; roundwood (1998) 5,311,000 cu m; fish catch (1997) 33,613, of which shrimp 5,717. Mining and quarrying (1997): limestone 1,500,000; gold 17,700 troy oz. Manufacturing (value added in ₡'000,000; 1996): food products 90,498; beverages 43,101; fertilizers and pesticides 18,360; plastic products 12,196; radio, television, and communications equipment 10,955; paper and paper products 10,589; wearing apparel 9,519. Construction (completed; 1997): 1,760,000 sq m. Energy production (consumption): electricity (kW-hr; 1996) 4,853,000,000 (4,997,000,000); coal, none (none); crude petroleum (barrels; 1996) none (4,523,000); petroleum products (metric tons; 1996) 597,000 (1,387,000); natural gas, none (none).
Population economically active (1998): total 1,376,540; activity rate of total population 41.2% (participation rates: ages 12–59, 59.3%; female 32.6%; unemployed [1999] 6.0%).

Price and earnings indexes (1995 = 100)

	1995	1996	1997	1998	1999	2000	2001
Consumer price index	100.0	117.5	133.1	148.6	163.5	181.5	197.3[7]
Monthly earnings index[8]	100.0	115.1	132.7	155.0	...	...	...

Tourism (1999): receipts U.S.$1,002,000,000; expenditures U.S.$428,000,000.
Household income and expenditure. Average household size (1997) 4.1; average annual household income (1997) ₡1,468,597 (U.S.$6,314); sources of income (1987–88): wages and salaries 61.0%, self-employment 22.6%, transfers 9.6%; expenditure (1987–88): food and beverages 39.1%, housing and energy 12.1%, transportation 11.6%, household furnishings 10.9%.
Land use (1994): forested 30.8%; meadows and pastures 45.8%; agricultural and under permanent cultivation 10.4%; other 13.0%.

Foreign trade[9]

Balance of trade (current prices)[10]

	1994	1995	1996	1997	1998
U.S.$'000,000	–1,715	–1,590	–1,617	–2,009	–3,208
% of total	29.0%	23.8%	22.6%	25.3%	34.5%

Imports (1998)[10]: U.S.$6,255,000,000 (raw materials for industry 50.6%, capital goods for industry 14.9%, nondurable consumer goods 11.9%, durable consumer goods 8.6%). *Major import sources*[11]: U.S. 38.8%; Japan 7.6%; Mexico 6.9%; Venezuela 3.8%; Guatemala 3.1%.
Exports (1998): U.S.$3,047,000,000 (bananas 21.8%, coffee 13.3%, processed food and tobacco products 9.3%, fish and shrimp 7.6%, machinery and metal products 6.0%, tropical fruit 5.5%). *Major export destinations*[12]: U.S. 42%; United Kingdom 7%; Germany 7%; The Netherlands 6%; Guatemala 5%.

Transport and communications

Transport. Railroads[13]. Roads (1997): total length 22,119 mi, 35,597 km (paved 17%). Vehicles (1997): passenger cars 294,083; trucks and buses 163,428. Merchant marine (1992): vessels (100 gross tons and over) 24; total deadweight tonnage 8,368. Air transport (1998)[14]: passenger-mi 2,167,000,000, passenger-km 3,487,000,000; short-ton mi cargo 61,904,000, metric ton-km cargo 90,378,000; airports (1996) 14.

Communications

Medium	date	unit	number	units per 1,000 persons
Daily newspapers	1996	circulation	320,000	94
Radio	1997	receivers	980,000	283
Television	1999	receivers	900,000	242
Telephones	1999	main lines	802,597	216
Cellular telephones	1999	subscribers	138,727	37
Personal computers	1999	units	400,000	108
Internet	1999	users	150,000	40

Education and health

Educational attainment (1996). Percentage of population age 5 and over having: no formal schooling 11.7%; incomplete primary education 28.5%; complete primary 25.8%; incomplete secondary 16.0%; complete secondary 9.0%; higher 8.5%; other/unknown 0.5%. *Literacy* (1995): total population age 15 and over literate 2,118,000 (94.8%); males literate 1,054,000 (94.7%); females literate 1,064,000 (95.0%).

Education (1998)

	schools	teachers	students	student/ teacher ratio
Primary (age 7–12)	3,711	19,235	529,637	27.5
Secondary (age 13–17)	353[15]	10,943	202,415	18.5
Higher	40[15]	...	83,106[15]	...

Health (1997): physicians 5,500 (1 per 630 persons); hospital beds 5,953 (1 per 582 persons); infant mortality rate per 1,000 live births (1999) 11.8.
Food (1999): daily per capita caloric intake 2,761 (vegetable products 82%, animal products 18%); 123% of FAO recommended minimum requirement.

Military

Paramilitary expenditure as percentage of GNP (1997): 0.6% (world 2.6%); per capita expenditure U.S.$17. The army was officially abolished in 1948. Paramilitary (police) forces had 8,400 members in 2000.

[1]Detail does not add to total given because of rounding. [2]January 1 estimate. [3]Population of San José canton. [4]District population. [5]Population of two districts. [6]Includes 10,235 not adequately defined and 76,535 unemployed. [7]March. [8]Data for July average of each year. [9]Imports c.i.f.; exports f.o.b. [10]Includes goods imported for reassembly. [11]Excludes goods imported for reassembly. [12]Estimated figures. [13]Rail service was suspended in June 1995 because of a lack of funds and was resumed (in part) from October 1998. [14]Lacsa (Costa Rican Airlines) only. [15]1997.

Internet resources for further information:
- **Central Bank of Costa Rica: Economic Indicators http://websiec.bccr.fi.cr/indicadores/indice.web**
- **Government of Costa Rica http://www.casapres.go.cr**

Côte d'Ivoire

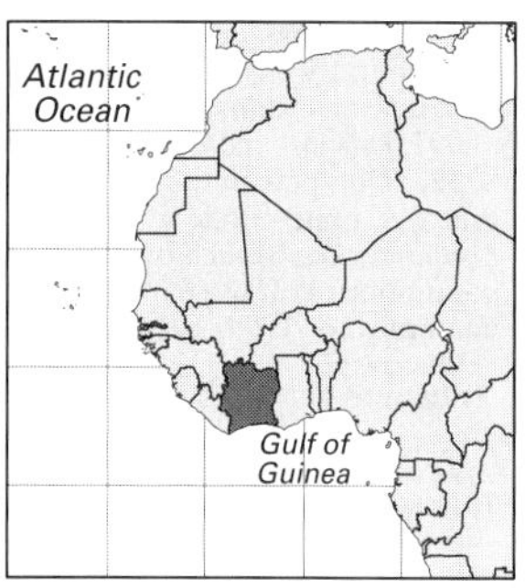

Official name: République de Côte d'Ivoire (Republic of Côte d'Ivoire [Ivory Coast][1]).
Form of government[2]: republic with one legislative house (National Assembly [225[3]]).
Chief of state and government: President assisted by Prime Minister.
Capital: Abidjan (de facto; legislative).
Capital designate: Yamoussoukro (de jure; administrative).
Official language: French.
Official religion: none.
Monetary unit: 1 CFA franc (CFAF) = 100 centimes; valuation (Sept. 28, 2001) 1 U.S.$ = CFAF 720.28; 1 £ = CFAF 1,058.

Area and population

		area		population
Regions	Capitals	sq mi	sq km	2000 estimate
Agnebi	Agboville	3,510	9,080	641,400
Bas-Sassandra	San-Pédro	9,960	25,800	937,700
Denguélé	Odienné	7,950	20,600	246,400
Dix-huit Montagnes	Man	11,870	30,750	1,445,800
Haut-Sassandra	Daloa	7,610	19,700	1,456,600
Lacs	Yamoussoukro	3,450	8,940	531,600
Lagunes	Abidjan	5,480	14,200	3,894,300
Marahoué	Bouaflé	4,210	10,900	783,600
Moyen-Comoé	Abengourou	2,660	6,900	434,200
Nzi-Comoé	Dimbokro	7,550	19,560	809,400
Savanes	Korhogo	15,570	40,323	1,081,000
Sud-Bandama	Divo	4,110	10,650	735,100
Sud-Comoé	Aboisso	2,410	6,250	328,500
Vallée du Bandama	Bouaké	11,020	28,530	1,188,000
Worodougou	Séguéla	11,820	30,620	514,700
Zanzan	Bondoukou	14,670	38,000	746,300
TOTAL		124,504[4]	322,463[4]	15,724,800[4]

Demography

Population (2001): 16,393,000.
Density (2001): persons per sq mi 131.7, persons per sq km 50.8.
Urban-rural (1998): urban 45.3%; rural 54.7%.
Sex distribution (2000): male 50.84%; female 49.16%.
Age breakdown (2000): under 15, 46.5%; 15–29, 27.8%; 30–44, 14.5%; 45–59, 7.6%; 60–74, 3.0%; 75 and over, 0.6%.
Population projection: (2010) 20,003,000; (2020) 23,748,000.
Ethnolinguistic composition (1988)[5]: Akan 41.8%; Voltaic 16.3%; Malinke 15.9%; Kru 14.6%; Southern Mande 10.7%; other 0.7%.
Religious affiliation (1988): Muslim 38.7%; Catholic 20.8%; animist 17.0%; atheist 13.4%; Protestant 5.3%, excluding Harrism (1.4%); other 3.4%.
Major cities (1995): Abidjan (1996) 2,500,000; Bouaké 330,000; Daloa 123,000; Yamoussoukro 110,000.

Vital statistics

Birth rate per 1,000 population (2000): 40.8 (world avg. 22.5).
Death rate per 1,000 population (2000): 16.6 (world avg. 9.0).
Natural increase rate per 1,000 population (2000): 24.2 (world avg. 13.5).
Total fertility rate (avg. births per childbearing woman; 2000): 5.8.
Life expectancy at birth (2000): male 43.7 years; female 46.6 years.

National economy

Budget (1997). Revenue: CFAF 1,372,100,000,000 (tax revenue 81.1%, of which import taxes and duties 22.7%, export taxes 12.6%, taxes on profits 10.7%, income tax 7.1%; nontax revenue 15.7%; grants 3.2%). Expenditures: CFAF 1,191,300,000,000 (wages and salaries 34.3%, capital expenditure 31.3%, debt service 25.5%; other 8.9%).
Production (metric tons except as noted). Agriculture, forestry, fishing (1999): yams 2,923,175, cassava 1,672,599, plantains 1,405,441, paddy rice 1,161,518, sugarcane 1,155,000, cacao beans 1,153,000, corn (maize) 571,018, coffee 365,000, cotton seed 270,000, palm oil 250,200, bananas 241,017, coconuts 193,000, rubber 118,860; livestock (number of live animals) 1,370,000 sheep, 1,330,000 cattle, 1,070,000 goats, 275,000 pigs, 29,000,000 chickens; roundwood (1998) 13,283,000 cu m; fish catch (1997) 67,617. Mining and quarrying (1997): gold 4,000 kg; diamonds 84,300 carats. Manufacturing (value added in CFAF '000,000,000; 1993): meat products 717, chemicals 357, cocoa and chocolate 275, leather products 275, fabricated metal products 191. Energy production (consumption): electricity (kW-hr; 1996) 3,221,000,000 (2,309,000,000); crude petroleum (barrels; 1996) 9,258,000 (31,446,000); petroleum products (metric tons; 1996) 2,192,000 (2,161,000).
Household income and expenditure. Average household size (1998) 8.0; expenditure (1992–93)[6]: food 48.0%, transportation 12.2%, clothing 10.1%, energy and water 8.5%, housing 7.8%, household equipment 3.4%.
Population economically active (1997): total 5,684,000; activity rate of total population 37.7% (participation rates: [1994] over ages 10, 64.3%; female 33.0%).

Price and earnings indexes (1995 = 100)

	1994	1995	1996	1997	1998	1999	2000
Consumer price index	87.5	100.0	102.5	106.6	111.6	112.5	115.2
Minimum earnings index	90.9	100.0	102.7	108.3	...	...	...

Gross national product (1999): U.S.$10,387,000,000 (U.S.$670 per capita).

Structure of gross domestic product and labour force

	1996		1994	
	in value CFAF '000,000,000	% of total value	labour force	% of labour force
Agriculture	1,531.7	28.0	2,886,000	51.1
Manufacturing, mining, and public utilities	954.5	17.4	650,000	11.5
Construction	156.3	2.9		
Transp. and commun.	514.4	9.4	2,112,000	37.4
Trade	929.5	17.0		
Public admin., defense	438.3	8.0		
Services	693.1	12.7		
Other (customs receipts)	255.8	4.7		
TOTAL	5,473.6	100.0[4]	5,648,000	100.0

Public debt (external, outstanding; 1999): U.S.$9,699,000,000.
Tourism (1998): receipts U.S.$108,000,000; expenditures U.S.$237,000,000.

Foreign trade

Balance of trade (current prices)

	1994	1995	1996	1997	1998	1999
CFAF '000,000,000	+700	+681	+777	+777	+810	+830
% of total	28.2%	21.7%	21.6%	19.5%	19.9%	19.2%

Imports (1997): CFAF 1,602,000,000,000 (food and food products 19.4%, machinery and transport equipment 18.6%, crude and refined petroleum 18.5%, plastics 4.6%, iron and steel products 4.4%). *Major import sources* (1995): France 32.0%; Nigeria 19.6%; U.S. 5.9%; Ghana 4.0%; Germany 3.9%; Italy 3.8%.
Exports (1997): CFAF 2,379,000,000,000 (cocoa beans and products 33.5%, petroleum products 16.8%, coffee and coffee products 7.3%, wood and wood products 7.0%, fish products 5.3%, cotton and cotton cloth 3.0%). *Major export destinations:* France 17.3%; The Netherlands 13.2%; United States 7.5%; Italy 5.3%; Mali 4.9%; Germany 4.8%.

Transport and communications

Transport. Railroads (1995): route length 639 km; passenger-km 129,000,000; metric ton-km cargo 58,000,000. Roads (1996): total length 50,400 km (paved 9.7%). Vehicles (1996): passenger cars 293,000; trucks and buses 163,000. Air transport (1996): passenger-km 307,000,000; metric ton-km cargo 44,000,000; airports (1998) 5.

Communications

Medium	date	unit	number	units per 1,000 persons
Daily newspapers	1996	circulation	231,000	17
Radio	1998	receivers	1,600,000	97
Television	1998	receivers	1,000,000	65
Telephones	1999	main lines	219,283	14
Cellular telephones	1999	subscribers	257,134	16.5
Personal computers	1999	units	80,000	5.1
Internet	1999	users	20,000	1.3

Education and health

Educational attainment (1988). Percentage of population age 6 and over having: no formal schooling 60.0%; Koranic school 3.6%; primary education 24.8%; secondary 10.7%; higher 0.9%. *Literacy* (1995): percentage of population age 15 and over literate 40.1%; males 49.9%; females 30.0%.

Education (1995–96)

	schools	teachers	students	student/ teacher ratio
Primary (age 7–12)	7,401	40,529	1,662,285	41.0
Secondary (age 13–19)	147	15,959	489,740	30.7
Vocational[7]	...	1,424	11,037	7.8
Higher[7]	...	1,657	43,147	26.0

Health: physicians (1996) 1,318 (1 per 11,111 persons); hospital beds (1993) 7,928 (1 per 1,698 persons); infant mortality rate (2000) 95.1.
Food (1999): daily per capita caloric intake 2,582 (vegetable products 97%, animal products 3%); 112% of FAO recommended minimum requirement.

Military

Total active duty personnel (2000): 8,400[8] (army 81.0%, navy 10.7%, air force 8.3%). *Military expenditure as percentage of GNP* (1997): 1.1% (world avg. 2.6%); per capita expenditure U.S.$7.

[1]Since 1986, Côte d'Ivoire has requested that the French form of the country's name be used as the official protocol version in all languages. [2]Referendum approving new constitution took place on July 24, 2000. Effective status of the constitution was still in question as of late September 2001. [3]Includes vacant/unoccupied seats. [4]Detail does not add to total given because of rounding. [5]"Ivoirian" nationals only, representing about 60% of the de facto population in 1999. [6]Weights of consumer price index components for a worker's family living in the capital city. [7]1994–95. [8]Excludes 500 French troops.

Internet resources for further information:

- **Côte d'Ivoire—A Country Study http://lcweb2.loc.gov/frd/cs/citoc.html**

Croatia

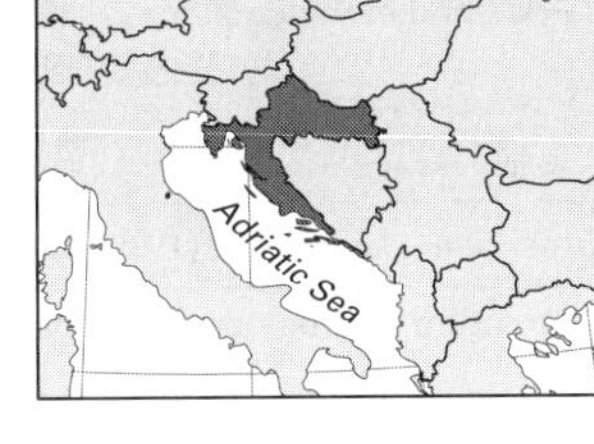

Official name: Republika Hrvatska (Republic of Croatia).
Form of government: multiparty republic with one legislative house (House of Representatives [151[1]])[2].
Head of state: President.
Head of government: Prime Minister.
Capital: Zagreb.
Official language: Croatian (Serbo-Croatian).
Official religion: none.
Monetary unit: 1 kuna (HrK; plural kune)[3] = 100 lipa; valuation (Sept. 28, 2001) 1 U.S.$ = HrK 8.29; 1 £ = HrK 12.18.

Area and population

Counties	area sq km	population 2001 preliminary census[4]	Counties	area sq km	population 2001 preliminary census[4]
Bjelovar-Bilogora	2,638	131,343	Šibenik-Knin	2,994	112,070
Dubrovnik-Neretva	1,782	121,871	Sisak-Moslavina	4,448	183,531
Istria	2,813	205,717	Slavonski Brod-Posavina	2,027	172,993
Karlovac	3,622	140,125	Split-Dalmatia	4,524	456,967
Koprivnica-Križevci	1,734	123,736	Varaždin	1,260	183,730
Krapina-Zagorje	1,230	142,006	Virovitica-Podravina	2,021	92,381
Lika-Senj	5,350	52,221	Vukovar-Srijem	2,448	197,838
Medimurje	730	116,225	Zadar	3,643	158,936
Osijek-Baranja	4,149	326,446	Zagreb	3,078	304,186
Požega-Slavonia	1,821	84,562	**City**		
Primorje-Gorski kotar	3,590	304,410	Zagreb	640	770,058
			TOTAL	56,542	4,381,352

Demography

Population (2001): 4,393,000.
Density (2001): persons per sq mi 201.3, persons per sq km 77.7.
Urban-rural (2000): urban 57.7%; rural 42.3%.
Sex distribution (2000): male 48.58%; female 51.42%.
Age breakdown (2000): under 15, 18.0%; 15–29, 20.1%; 30–44, 21.6%; 45–59, 19.6%; 60–74, 15.4%; 75 and over, 5.3%.
Population projection: (2010) 4,505,000; (2020) 4,560,000.
Ethnic composition (2000): Croat 82.0%; Serb 5.9%; other 12.1%.
Religious affiliation (2000): Christian 95.2%, of which Roman Catholic 88.5%, Eastern Orthodox 5.6%, Protestant 0.6%; Sunnī Muslim 2.3%; nonreligious/atheist 2.5%.
Major cities (1991): Zagreb (2000) 770,058; Split 200,459; Rijeka 167,964; Osijek 129,792; Zadar 76,343.

Vital statistics

Birth rate per 1,000 population (1999): 9.9 (world avg. 22.5); legitimate 91.8%; illegitimate 8.2%.
Death rate per 1,000 population (1999): 11.4 (world avg. 9.0).
Natural increase rate per 1,000 population (1999): –1.5 (world avg. 13.5).
Total fertility rate (avg. births per childbearing woman; 2000): 1.9.
Marriage rate per 1,000 population (1999): 5.2.
Divorce rate per 1,000 population (1999): 0.8.
Life expectancy at birth (2000): male 70.0 years; female 77.5 years.
Major causes of death per 100,000 population (1996): diseases of the circulatory system 547.4; cancers 227.2; accidents, violence, and poisoning 70.7; diseases of the digestive system 52.1; diseases of the respiratory system 41.4.

National economy

Budget (1999). Revenue: HrK 67,907,000,000 (sales tax 34.1%, social security 32.2%, excise taxes 9.5%). Expenditures: HrK 70,358,000,000 (social security and welfare 37.8%, health 14.0%, defense 7.7%, education 7.4%).
Population economically active (1991): total 2,040,000; activity rate 42.6% (participation rates: ages 15–64, 61.1%; female 42.8%; unemployed [March 1998] 17.4%).

Price and earnings indexes (1995 = 100)

	1995	1996	1997	1998	1999	2000	2001
Consumer price index	100.0	104.3	108.6	115.6	119.9	126.4	134.3[5]
Annual earnings index	100.0	111.8	130.7	147.5	168.1	182.9	...

Production (metric tons except as noted). Agriculture, forestry, fishing (1999): corn (maize) 2,135,000, sugar beets 1,114,000, potatoes 729,000, wheat 558,000, grapes 394,000, barley 125,000, soybeans 116,000, sunflower seed 72,400, plums 38,000; livestock (number of live animals) 1,362,000 pigs, 489,000 sheep, 439,000 cattle; roundwood (1998) 3,398,000 cu m; fish catch (1997) 19,885. Mining and quarrying (1998): gypsum 100,000; ferrochromium 15,000. Manufacturing (value added in U.S.$'000,000; 1996): food products 895; transport equipment 425; electrical machinery 362; textiles 285; wearing apparel 260. Construction (value in HrK '000,000; 1997): residential 3,404; nonresidential 9,434. Energy production (consumption): electricity (kW-hr; 1998) 10,356,000,000 ([1996] 12,878,000,000); hard coal (metric tons; 1998) 48,000 ([1996] 117,000); lignite (metric tons; 1996) 2,000 (149,000); crude petroleum (barrels; 1998) 8,532,000 ([1996] 38,248,000); petroleum products (metric tons; 1996) 4,500,000 (3,393,000); natural gas (cu m; 1998) 1,566,000,000 ([1996] 2,584,000,000).
Gross national product (1999): U.S.$20,222,000,000 (U.S.$4,530 per capita).

Structure of gross domestic product and labour force

	1998 in value HrK '000,000[3]	1998 % of total value	1991 labour force	1991 % of labour force
Agriculture	9,840	6.6	265,000	13.0
Mining	616	0.4	613,000	30.0
Manufacturing	32,881	22.2		
Construction	7,807	5.3	98,000	4.8
Public utilities	4,439	3.0	32,700	1.6
Transp. and commun.	10,608	7.2	120,000	5.9
Trade	16,672	11.2	163,000	8.0
Finance, real estate	17,639	11.9	60,400	3.0
Pub. admin., defense	11,878	8.0	315,000	15.4
Services	13,108[6]	8.8[6]	80,700	4.0
Other	22,803[7]	15.4[7]	292,200[8]	14.3[8]
TOTAL	148,291	100.0	2,040,000	100.0

Public debt (external, outstanding; 1999): U.S.$5,433,000,000.
Household income and expenditure. Average household size (1991) 3.1; income per household (1990) Din 165,813[3] (U.S.$14,650); sources (1990): self-employment 40.8%, wages 40.2%, transfers 12.1%, other 6.9%; expenditure (1988): food 34.2%, transportation 9.3%, clothing 8.6%, housing 8.3%, energy 7.6%, drink and tobacco 5.1%, durable goods 4.5%, health care 4.3%.
Tourism (1999): receipts from visitors U.S.$2,493,000,000; expenditures by nationals abroad U.S.$751,000,000.
Land use (1994): forest 37.1%; pasture 19.3%; agriculture 21.6%; other 22.0%.

Foreign trade[9]

Balance of trade (current prices)

	1995	1996	1997	1998	1999	2000
U.S.$'000,000	–2,877	–3,276	–4,933	–3,842	–3,496	–3,455
% of total	23.7%	26.6%	37.2%	29.7%	28.9%	28.0%

Imports (1998): U.S.$8,383,000,000 (machinery and transport equipment 35.2%; chemicals and chemical products 11.7%; food and live animals 8.1%; mineral fuels and lubricants 7.1%). *Major import sources:* Germany 19.2%; Italy 17.9%; Slovenia 8.6%; Austria 7.3%; France 4.8%.
Exports (1998): U.S.$4,541,000,000 (machinery and transport equipment 30.4%; clothing 12.2%; chemical and chemical products 12.7%; food 8.4%; mineral fuels and lubricants 5.8%). *Major export destinations:* Italy 17.7%; Germany 16.9%; Bosnia and Herzegovina 14.4%; Slovenia 9.5%; Austria 5.4%.

Transport and communications

Transport. Railroads (1997): length 2,726 km; passenger-km 981,000,000; metric ton-km cargo 1,876,000,000. Roads (1997): total length 27,840 km (paved 82%). Vehicles (1997): passenger cars 932,278; trucks and buses 114,505. Merchant marine (1994): cargo ships 155. Air transport (1997): passenger-km 546,000,000; metric ton-km cargo 2,997,000; airports (1997) 4.

Communications

Medium	date	unit	number	units per 1,000 persons
Daily newspapers	1996	circulation	515,000	118
Radio	1997	receivers	1,510,000	350
Television	1998	receivers	1,250,000	293
Telephones	1999	main lines	1,634,000	384
Cellular telephones	1999	subscribers	295,000	69
Personal computers	1999	units	300,000	71
Internet	1999	users	200,000	47

Education and health

Educational attainment (1991). Percentage of population age 15 and over having: no schooling or unknown 10.1%; less than full primary education 21.2%; primary 23.4%; secondary 36.0%; postsecondary and higher 9.3%. *Literacy* (1995): population age 15 and over literate 98.3%; males 99.4%; females 97.3%.

Education (1997–98)

	schools	teachers	students	student/ teacher ratio
Primary (age 7–14)	2,127	26,199	423,165	16.2
Secondary (age 15–18)	577	16,942	199,863	11.8
Voc., teacher tr.	2	72	848	11.8
Higher	67	6,181	89,173	14.4

Health (1997): physicians 9,315 (1 per 501 persons); hospital beds 27,472 (1 per 170 persons); infant mortality rate per 1,000 live births (2000) 7.4.
Food (1999): daily per capita caloric intake 2,617 (vegetable products 81%, animal products 19%); 103% of FAO recommended minimum requirement.

Military

Total active duty personnel (2000): 61,000 (army 86.9%, navy 4.9%, air force and air defense 8.2%). *Military expenditure as percentage of GNP* (1997): 6.3% (world 2.6%); per capita expenditure U.S.$345.

[1]Includes six seats representing Croatians abroad. [2]A constitutional amendment in March 2001 abolished the former upper house (House of Counties). [3]On Jan. 1, 1990, the Yugoslav new dinar (Din), equal to 10,000 Yugoslav old dinars (Din), was introduced. On Dec. 23, 1991, the Croatian dinar (HrD) was introduced at parity with the Yugoslav new dinar, which it replaced as Croatia's official currency. On May 30, 1994, the kuna (HrK), equal to 1,000 Croatian dinars, was introduced. [4]De facto population including permanent nonresidents, excluding temporary visitors. [5]May. [6]Includes not adequately defined. [7]Import and turnover taxes less imputed bank service charges. [8]Includes unemployed and private sector. [9]Imports c.i.f.; exports f.o.b.

Internet resources for further information:

- **Croatian Bureau of Statistics http://www.dzs.hr/Eng/Default2.htm**
- **Ministry of Foreign Affairs http://www.mvp.hr**

Cuba

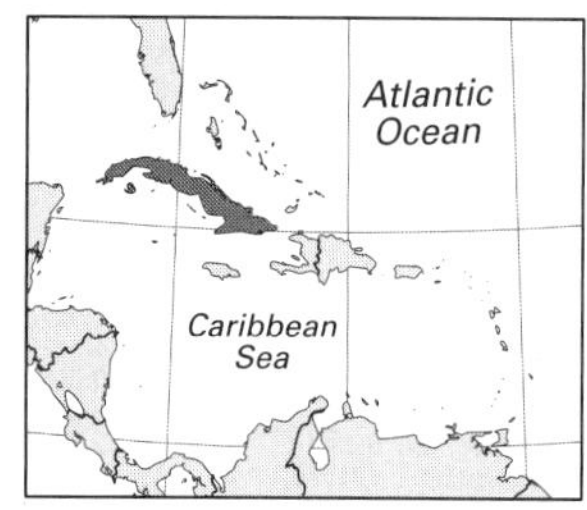

Official name: República de Cuba (Republic of Cuba).
Form of government: unitary socialist republic with one legislative house (National Assembly of the People's Power [601]).
Head of state and government: President.
Capital: Havana.
Official language: Spanish.
Official religion: none.
Monetary unit: 1 Cuban peso (CUP) = 100 centavos; valuation (Sept. 28, 2001) 1 U.S.$ = 21.00 CUP; 1 £ = 30.86 CUP.

Area and population

Provinces	Capitals	area sq mi	area sq km	population 1998[1] estimate
Camagüey	Camagüey	6,174	15,990	780,762
Ciego de Avila	Ciego de Avila	2,668	6,910	403,134
Cienfuegos	Cienfuegos	1,613	4,178	391,666
Ciudad de la Habana[2]	—	281	727	2,198,392
Granma	Bayamo	3,232	8,372	824,897
Guantánamo	Guantánamo	2,388	6,186	508,864
Holguín	Holguín	3,591	9,301	1,020,660
La Habana[3]	Havana	2,213	5,731	693,889
Las Tunas	Las Tunas	2,544	6,589	523,810
Matanzas	Matanzas	4,625	11,978	654,516
Pinar del Río	Pinar del Río	4,218	10,925	729,330
Sancti Spíritus	Sancti Spíritus	2,604	6,744	457,921
Santiago de Cuba	Santiago de Cuba	2,382	6,170	1,023,293
Villa Clara	Santa Clara	3,345	8,662	832,356
Special municipality				
Isla de la Juventud	Nueva Gerona	926	2,398	78,818
TOTAL		42,804	110,861	11,122,308

Demography

Population (2001): 11,190,000.
Density (2001): persons per sq mi 261.4, persons per sq km 100.9.
Urban-rural (1999): urban 75.2%; rural 24.8%.
Sex distribution (2000): male 50.00%; female 50.00%.
Age breakdown (2000): under 15, 21.4%; 15–29, 22.7%; 30–44, 26.2%; 45–59, 16.1%; 60–74, 9.2%; 75 and over, 4.4%.
Population projection: (2010) 11,532,000; (2020) 11,805,000.
Ethnic composition (1994): mixed 51.0%; white 37.0%; black 11.0%; other 1.0%.
Religious affiliation (1995): Roman Catholic 39.5%; Protestant 2.4%; other Christian 0.2%; other (mostly Santería) 57.9%.
Major cities (1993): Havana 2,175,995; Santiago de Cuba 440,084; Camagüey 293,961; Holguín 242,085; Guantánamo 207,796.

Vital statistics

Birth rate per 1,000 population (2000): 12.7 (world avg. 22.5).
Death rate per 1,000 population (2000): 7.3 (world avg. 9.0).
Natural increase rate per 1,000 population (2000): 5.4 (world avg. 13.5).
Total fertility rate (avg. births per childbearing woman; 2000): 1.6.
Marriage rate per 1,000 population (1999): 5.1.
Divorce rate per 1,000 population (1993): 6.0.
Life expectancy at birth (2000): male 73.8 years; female 78.3 years.
Major causes of death per 100,000 population (1998): heart disease 142.6; malignant neoplasms (cancers) 111.0; cerebrovascular disease 52.9; accidents 39.0; influenza and pneumonia 31.3; diseases of the blood vessels 21.9.

National economy

Budget (1999). Revenue: CUP 13,575,000,000. Expenditures: CUP 14,270,000,000 (education and health 26.5%; investment 11.9%; other 61.6%).
Public debt (external, outstanding; 1999): U.S.$11,078,000,000.
Production (metric tons except as noted). Agriculture, forestry, fishing (2000): sugarcane 36,000,000, rice 368,770, oranges and tangerines 447,000, potatoes 344,215, plantains 329,000, grapefruit 232,879, cassava 210,000, tomatoes 181,000, corn (maize) 185,286, bananas 133,280; livestock (number of live animals) 4,700,000 cattle, 2,800,000 pigs, 15,000,000 chickens; roundwood (2000) 1,593,000 cu m; fish catch (1999) 122,425. Mining and quarrying (1998): nickel 67,700; chromite 30,000. Manufacturing (value added in U.S.$'000,000; 1990): tobacco products 2,629; food products 1,033; beverages 358; chemical products 354; transport equipment 225; nonelectrical machinery 176. Construction (gross value of construction in CUP '000,000; 1989): residential 227; nonresidential 872. Energy production (consumption): electricity (kW-hr; 1996) 13,236,000,000 (13,236,000,000); coal (metric tons; 1996) none (163,000); crude petroleum (barrels; 1996) 9,377,000 (9,899,000); petroleum products (metric tons; 1996) 4,767,000 (8,240,000); natural gas (cu m; 1996) 43,002,000 (43,002,000).
Household income and expenditure. Average household size (1999) 3.6; average annual income per household (1982) CUP 3,680 (U.S.$4,330); sources of income (1982): wages and salaries 57.3%, bonuses and other payments 42.7%; personal consumption (1989): food 26.7%, other retail purchases 60.5%, transportation services 5.4%, energy 2.7%, value of self-produced and consumed food 1.5%, household repairs 1.3%, other 1.9%.
Population economically active (1988): total 4,570,236; activity rate of total population 43.7% (participation rates: over age 15, 56.9%; female [1998] 37.0%; unemployed [1998] 6.0%).

Price and earnings indexes (1985 = 100)

	1983	1984	1985	1986	1987	1988	1989
Implicit consumer price deflator index	94.9	98.0	100.0	101.4	102.8	103.1	…
Monthly earnings index[4]	95.9	99.0	100.0	100.1	98.1	99.6	100.0

Gross domestic product (1999): U.S.$18,600,000,000 (U.S.$1,700 per capita).

Structure of gross domestic product and labour force

	1999 in value[5] CUP '000,000	1999 % of total value	1989 labour force[4]	1989 % of labour force
Agriculture	1,122.9	7.2	721,100	20.4
Mining	186.0	1.2	767,500	21.8
Manufacturing	4,594.9	29.3		
Public utilities	430.2	2.7		
Construction	632.0	4.0	344,300	9.8
Transp. and commun.	911.7	5.8	235,900	6.7
Finance, insurance	637.0	4.1	21,700	0.6
Trade	3,370.2	21.5	395,300	11.2
Public administration	—	—	151,700	4.3
Services	3,789.5	24.2	835,700	23.7
Other	—	—	53,400	1.5
TOTAL	15,674.4	100.0	3,526,600	100.0

Tourism: receipts from visitors (1999) U.S.$1,714,000,000; expenditures by nationals abroad (1990) U.S.$48,000,000.
Land use (1994): forested 23.7%; meadows and pastures 27.0%; agricultural and under permanent cultivation 30.7%; other 18.6%.

Foreign trade[6]

Balance of trade (current prices)

	1994	1995	1996	1997	1998	1999
U.S.$'000,000	−797	−1,166	−1,179	−1,200	−1,300	−1,800
% of total	24.4%	28.3%	24.4%	25.2%	25.5%	39.1%

Imports (1999): U.S.$3,200,000,000 (1996; mineral fuels and lubricants 27.9%, food and live animals 19.8%, machinery and transport equipment 16.1%, basic manufactures 14.9%, chemicals 8.7%, inedible crude materials 2.8%). *Major import sources* (1999): Spain 19.5%; France 8.2%; Canada 8.1%; China 7.7%; Italy 7.0%; Russia 3.8%.
Exports (1999): U.S.$1,400,000,000 (1996; sugar 52.8%, minerals and concentrates 23.7%, fish products 6.8%, raw tobacco and tobacco products 5.9%, citrus and other agricultural products 2.1%). *Major export destinations* (1999): Russia 23.3%; Canada 14.5%; The Netherlands 12.9%; Spain 8.0%; China 3.6%.

Transport and communications

Transport. Railroads (1999): length 2,987 mi, 4,807 km; (1997) passenger-km 1,962,200; metric ton-km cargo 1,074,800,000. Roads (1997): total length 37,815 mi, 60,858 km (paved 49%). Vehicles (1998): passenger cars 172,574; trucks and buses 185,495. Air transport (1997): passenger-km 3,543,176,000; metric ton-km cargo 56,239,000; airports with scheduled flights (1999) 14.

Communications

Medium	date	unit	number	units per 1,000 persons
Daily newspapers	1996	circulation	1,300,000	118
Radio	1997	receivers	3,900,000	352
Television	1999	receivers	2,750,000	246
Telephones	1999	main lines	434,000	39
Cellular telephones	1999	subscribers	5,136	0.5
Personal computers	1999	units	110,000	9.9
Internet	1999	users	34,800	3.1

Education and health

Educational attainment (1981). Percentage of population age 25 and over having: no formal schooling or some primary education 39.6%; completed primary 26.6%; secondary 29.6%; higher 4.2%. *Literacy* (1995): total population age 15 and over literate 95.7%; males 96.2%; females 95.3%.

Education (1999–2000)

	schools	teachers	students	student/ teacher ratio
Primary (age 6–11)	9,375	76,300	987,900	12.9
Secondary (age 12–17)	2,018	70,900	857,700	12.1
Voc., teacher tr.	618[7]	27,267[8]	244,253[8]	9.0[8]
Higher	37	23,500	106,500	4.5

Health (1998): physicians 63,554 (1 per 175 persons); hospital beds 80,684 (1 per 123 persons); infant mortality rate per 1,000 live births (2000) 7.5.
Food (1999): daily per capita caloric intake 2,490 (vegetable products 86%, animal products 14%); 108% of FAO recommended minimum requirement.

Military

Total active duty personnel (2000): 58,000 (army 77.6%, navy 5.2%, air force 17.2%). *Military expenditure as percentage of GDP* (1997): 2.3% (world 2.6%); per capita expenditure: U.S.$65.

[1]July 1. [2]Province coextensive with the city of Havana. [3]Province bordering the city of Havana on the east, south, and west. [4]State sector only; excludes military and unemployed. [5]At constant 1981 prices. [6]Imports c.i.f.; exports f.o.b. [7]1989–90. [8]1995–96.

Internet resources for further information:

- **Cuba: the Web Site of the Government of the Republic of Cuba http://www.cubagob.cu**

Cyprus

Island of Cyprus

Area: 3,572 sq mi, 9,251 sq km.
Population (2001): 873,000[1].

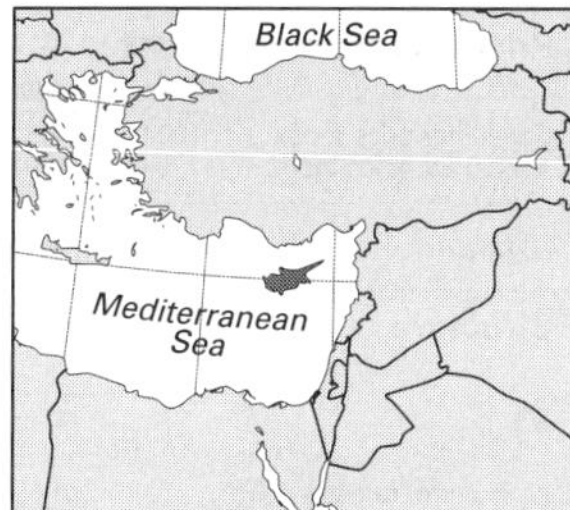

Two de facto states currently exist on the island of Cyprus: the Republic of Cyprus (ROC), predominantly Greek in character, occupying the southern two-thirds of the island, which is the original and still the internationally recognized de jure government of the whole island; and the Turkish Republic of Northern Cyprus (TRNC), proclaimed unilaterally Nov. 15, 1983, on territory originally secured for the Turkish Cypriot population by the July 20, 1974, intervention of Turkey. Only Turkey recognizes the TRNC, and the two ethnic communities have failed to reestablish a single state. Provision of separate data below does not imply recognition of either state's claims but is necessitated by the continuing lack of unified data.

Republic of Cyprus

Official name: Kipriakí Dimokratía (Greek); Kıbrıs Cumhuriyeti (Turkish) (Republic of Cyprus).
Form of government: unitary multiparty republic with a unicameral legislature (House of Representatives [80[2]]).
Head of state and government: President.
Capital: Lefkosia (Nicosia).
Official languages: Greek; Turkish.
Monetary unit: 1 Cyprus pound (£C) = 100 cents; valuation (Sept. 28, 2001) 1 £C = U.S.$1.59 = £1.08.

Demography

Area[3]: 2,276 sq mi, 5,896 sq km.
Population (2001): 675,000[4].
Urban-rural (1999[5]): urban 68.9%; rural 31.1%.
Age breakdown (1999[5]): under 15, 23.8%; 15–29, 21.5%; 30–44, 22.3%; 45–59, 17.2%, 60–74, 10.6%; 75 and over, 4.6%.
Ethnic composition (2000): Greek Cypriot 91.8%; Armenian 3.3% Arab 2.9%, of which Lebanese 2.5%; British 1.4%; other 0.6%.
Religious affiliation (1995): Greek Orthodox 93.4%; Armenian Apostolic 2.9%; Roman Catholic 1.5%; Muslim 1.0%; other 1.2%.
Urban areas (1999[5]): Lefkosia 195,000[6]; Limassol 154,400; Larnaca 68,500.

Vital statistics

Birth rate per 1,000 population (1999): 12.8 (world avg. 22.5).
Death rate per 1,000 population (1999): 7.6 (world avg. 9.0).
Natural increase rate per 1,000 population (1999): 5.2 (world avg. 13.5).
Life expectancy at birth (1998–99): male 75.3 years; female 80.1 years.

National economy

Budget (1998). Revenue: £C 1,473,900,000 (income taxes 19.7%, value-added taxes 15.3%, social security contributions 14.9%). Expenditures: £C 1,731,-500,000 (current expenditures 89.7%, development expenditures 10.3%).
Tourism (1999): receipts U.S.$1,885,000,000; expenditures U.S.$289,000,000.
Household expenditure (1994): food and beverages 23.0%, transportation and communications 14.5%, expenditures in cafes and hotels 14.5%.
Gross national product (at current market prices; 1999): U.S.$9,086,000,000 (U.S.$11,950 per capita).

Structure of gross domestic product and labour force

	1998			
	in value £C '000,000	% of total value	labour force	% of labour force
Agriculture, fishing	204.6	4.4	29,000	9.3
Mining	13.0	0.3	600	0.2
Manufacturing	508.0	10.9	40,200	13.0
Construction	357.0	7.7	24,500	7.9
Public utilities	99.9	2.1	1,600	0.5
Transportation and communications	393.3	8.5	19,600	6.3
Trade	911.2	19.6	77,800	25.0
Finance, insurance	890.2	19.1	24,600	7.9
Pub. admin., defense	635.6	13.7	71,100	22.9
Services	400.9	8.6		
Other	236.4	5.1	21,800[7]	7.0[7]
TOTAL	4,650.1	100.0	310,800	100.0

Production. Agriculture (in '000 metric tons; 1997): grapes 101.0, potatoes 81.5, oranges 50.5, grapefruit 47.0, tomatoes 34.0, lemons 23.0. Manufacturing (value added in £C '000,000; 1996): food 84.7; cement, bricks, and tiles 48.2; wearing apparel 38.0; beverages 37.4; fabricated metal products 34.8. Energy production: electricity (kW-hr; 1998) 2,954,000,000.

Foreign trade[8]

Imports (1998): £C 1,904,700,000 (consumer goods 34.2%; transport equipment 12.9%; capital goods 11.2%; mineral fuels 6.6%). *Major import sources:* U.S. 12.5%; U.K. 11.3%; Italy 9.4%; Germany 8.5%; Greece 8.2%.
Exports (1998): £C 551,134,000 (reexports 55.6%[9]; domestic exports 38.7%, of which clothing 5.3%, chemicals 5.2%; ships' stores 5.7%). *Major export destinations:* U.K. 14.6%; Russia 10.3%, Greece 9.8%; Lebanon 5.5%; United Arab Emirates 4.9%.

Transport and communications

Transport. Roads (1997): total length 10,654 km (paved 58%). Vehicles (1997): cars 234,976; trucks and buses 108,452. Merchant marine (1992): vessels 1,416; deadweight tonnage 36,198,083. Air transport (1998)[10]: passenger-km 2,711,000,000; metric ton-km cargo 38,158,000; airports (1996) 2.

Communications

Medium	date	unit	number	units per 1,000 persons
Daily newspapers[11]	1996	circulation	84,000	111
Radio[11]	1997	receivers	310,000	406
Television	1999	receivers	120,000	180
Telephones	1999	main lines	421,600	634
Cellular telephones	1999	subscribers	151,649	228
Personal computers	1999	units	130,000	195
Internet	1999	users	88,000	132

Education and health

Educational attainment (1997). Percentage of population age 20 and over having: no formal schooling 4%; higher education 17%.

Education (1996–97)

	schools	teachers	students	student/ teacher ratio
Primary (age 6–11)	376	4,159	64,761	15.6
Secondary (age 12–17) / Vocational	125	5,757	61,266	10.6
Higher	35	812	9,982	12.3

Health (1997): physicians 1,725 (1 per 379 persons); hospital beds 3,113 (1 per 210 persons); infant mortality rate per 1,000 live births (2000) 8.1.

Internet resources for further information:
- **Central Bank of Cyprus http://www.centralbank.gov.cy**
- **Rep. of Cyprus Statistical Service http://www.pio.gov.cy/dsr**

Turkish Republic of Northern Cyprus

Official name: Kuzey Kıbrıs Türk Cumhuriyeti (Turkish) (Turkish Republic of Northern Cyprus).
Capital: Lefkoşa (Nicosia).
Official language: Turkish.
Monetary unit: 1 Turkish lira (LT) = 100 kurush; valuation (Sept. 28, 2001) 1 U.S.$ = LT 1,530,500; 1 £ = LT 2,249,377.
Population (2001): 198,000[1] (Lefkoşa 36,834[12]; Gazimağusa 23,295[12]).
Ethnic composition (1996): Turkish Cypriot/Turkish 96.4%; other 3.6%.

Structure of gross domestic product and labour force

	1998		1995	
	in value LT '000,000,000	% of total value	labour force	% of labour force
Agriculture and fishing	18,076	7.9	17,383	22.6
Mining and manufacturing	17,203	7.5	8,348	10.8
Construction	10,132	4.4	9,584	12.4
Public utilities	10,836	4.7		
Transportation and communications	22,713	9.9	6,510	8.5
Trade, restaurants	36,624	16.0	8,367	10.9
Pub. admin.	49,486	21.6	16,589	21.5
Finance, real estate	25,077	10.9	9,673	12.6
Services	20,514	8.9		
Other	18,823[13]	8.2[13]	567[14]	0.7[14]
TOTAL	229,484	100.0	77,021	100.0

Budget (1998). Revenue: U.S.$406,200,000 (aid from Turkey 33.3%, direct taxes 25.2%, indirect taxes 19.8%, loans 7.3%). Expenditures: U.S.$406,200,000 (investments 13.6%, defense 10.4%, other 76.0%).
Imports (1998): U.S.$390,100,000 (transport equipment 18.6%, prepared foodstuffs 12.3%). *Major import sources:* Turkey 59.3%; U.K. 12.8%.
Exports (1998): U.S.$53,400,000 (ready-made garments 40.2%, citrus fruits 24.0%). *Major export destinations:* Turkey 50.7%; U.K. 30.9%.

Education (1998–99)

	schools	teachers	students	student/ teacher ratio
Primary (age 7–11)	91	1,093	16,773	15.3
Secondary (age 12–17)	30	1,256	13,981	11.1
Vocational	10	363	1,890	5.2
Higher	8	884	21,912	24.8

Health (1998): physicians 451 (1 per 416 persons); hospital beds 1,002 (1 per 187 persons); infant mortality rate per 1,000 live births 5.8.

Internet resources for further information:
- **Turkish Republic of Northern Cyprus http://www.cypnet.com/.ncyprus/root.html**

[1]Includes 75,000 "settlers" from Turkey and 31,000 Turkish military in the TRNC; excludes 3,200 British military in the Sovereign Base Areas (SBA) in the ROC and 1,300 UN peacekeeping forces. [2]Twenty-four seats reserved for Turkish Cypriots are not occupied. [3]Area includes 99 sq mi (256 sq km) of British military SBA and *c.* 107 sq mi (*c.* 278 sq km) of the UN Buffer Zone. [4]Excludes British and UN military forces. [5]January 1. [6]ROC only. [7]Includes 10,400 unemployed. [8]Imports c.i.f.; exports f.o.b. [9]Mainly cigarettes, vehicles, and consumer electronics. [10]Cyprus Airways. [11]Island of Cyprus. [12]1996 census. [13]Import duties. [14]Unemployed.

Czech Republic

Official name: Česká Republika.
Form of government: unitary multiparty republic with two legislative houses (Senate [81]; Chamber of Deputies [200]).
Chief of state: President.
Head of government: Prime Minister.
Capital: Prague.
Official language: Czech.
Official religion: none.
Monetary unit: 1 koruna (Kč) = 100 halura; valuation (Sept. 28, 2001) 1 U.S.$ = 37.24 Kč
1 £ = 54.73 Kč

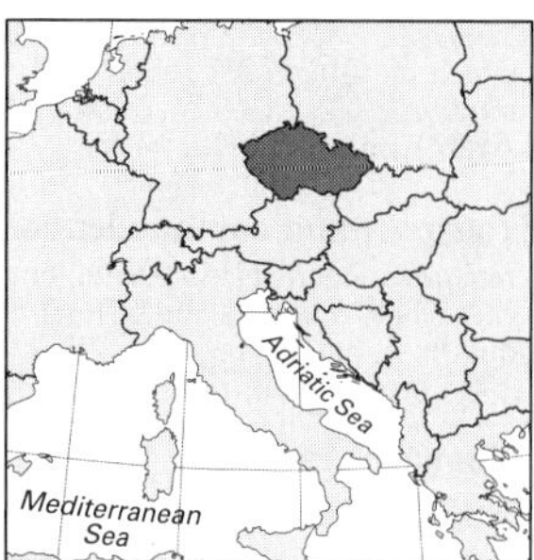

Area and population

Regions[1]	area sq km	population 2000 estimate	Regions[1]	area sq km	population 2000 estimate
Brno	7,067	1,136,664	Pardubice	4,519	508,484
Budejovice	10,056	625,975	Plzeň	7,560	551,613
Hradec Králové	4,757	551,293	Střed	11,014	1,112,627
Jihlava	6,925	521,149	Ústí	5,335	827,014
Karlovy Vary	3,315	304,675	Zlín	3,965	598,061
Liberec	3,163	429,060	**Capital city**[1]		
Olomouc	5,139	641,572	Prague (Praha)	496	1,184,494
Ostrava	5,555	1,280,258	TOTAL	78,866	10,272,939

Demography

Population (2001): 10,269,000.
Density (2001): persons per sq mi 337.2, persons per sq km 130.2.
Urban-rural (1999): urban 74.6%; rural 25.4%.
Sex distribution (2000[2]): male 48.66%; female 51.34%.
Age breakdown (2000[2]): under 15, 16.6%; 15–29, 23.5%; 30–44, 20.2%; 45–59, 21.5%; 60–74, 12.8%; 75 and over, 5.4%.
Population projection: (2010) 10,236,000; (2020) 10,105,000.
Ethnic composition (1991): Czech 81.2%; Moravian 13.2%; Slovak 3.1%; Polish 0.6%; German 0.5%; Silesian 0.4%; Gypsy 0.3%; Hungarian 0.2%; Ukrainian 0.1%; other 0.4%.
Religious affiliation (1991): Catholic 40.9% of which Roman Catholic 39.0%, Hussite Church of the Czech Republic 1.7%; Protestant 2.5%, of which Evangelical Church of Czech Brethren 2.0%; not stated 16.2%; nonreligious/other 40.4%.
Major cities (2000)[2]: Prague 1,186,855; Brno 383,569; Ostrava 321,263; Plzeň 167,534; Olomouc 103,015; Liberec 99,588.

Vital statistics

Birth rate per 1,000 population (1999): 8.7 (world avg. 22.5); legitimate 79.4%; illegitimate 20.6%.
Death rate per 1,000 population (1999): 10.7 (world avg. 9.0).
Natural increase rate per 1,000 population (1999): –2.0 (world avg. 13.5).
Total fertility rate (avg. births per childbearing woman; 1999): 1.1.
Marriage rate per 1,000 population (1999): 5.2.
Divorce rate per 1,000 population (1999): 2.3.
Life expectancy at birth (2000): male 71.1 years; female 78.2 years.
Major causes of death per 100,000 population (1999): diseases of the circulatory system 586.3; malignant neoplasms (cancers) 274.1; accidents, poisoning, and violence 67.3; diseases of the respiratory system 45.3.

National economy

Budget (1998). Revenue: Kč 596,193,000,000 (social security contributions 45.1%, of which from employers 30.8%; value-added tax 20.0%; excise tax 11.4%; corporate tax 8.6%; personal income tax 6.1%). Expenditures: Kč 638,019,000,000 (social security and welfare 36.4%; health 17.9%; education 9.6%; defense 4.8%; police 4.5%).
Public debt (external, outstanding; 1998): U.S.$12,901,000,000.
Production (metric tons except as noted). Agriculture, forestry, fishing (2000): cereals 6,507,000 (of which wheat 4,117,000, barley 1,709,000, corn [maize] 234,000), sugar beets 2,686,000, potatoes 1,417,000, rapeseed 854,000; livestock (number of live animals) 3,688,000 pigs, 1,574,000 cattle, 29,500,000 chickens; roundwood (1999) 14,203,000 cu m; fish catch (1997) 20,881. Mining and quarrying (1998): kaolin 3,720,000; feldspar 360,000. Manufacturing (value added in Kč '000,000,000; 1997): nonelectrical machinery and apparatus 45.8; food products 38.0; fabricated metals 36.3; motor vehicles 30.6; electrical machinery and apparatus 28.8; iron and steel 25.2. Energy production (consumption): electricity (kW-hr; 1999) 64,692,000,000 (61,417,000,000); hard coal (metric tons; 1999) 14,342,000 ([1996] 13,035,000); lignite (metric tons; 1999) 44,790,000 ([1996] 54,181,000); crude petroleum (barrels; 1996) 1,031,000 (55,833,000); petroleum products (metric tons; 1996) 5,845,000 (6,130,000); natural gas (cu m; 1998) 304,000,000 ([1996] 8,990,000,000).
Tourism (1999): receipts from visitors U.S.$3,035,000,000; expenditures by nationals abroad U.S.$1,474,000,000.
Household income and expenditure. Average household size (1998) 2.8; disposable income per household (1998) Kč 289,851 (U.S.$8,979); sources of income (1996): wages and salaries 56.2%, transfer payments 20.3%, rent 6.0%; expenditure (1999): food and beverages 26.6%, transportation and communications 13.8%, recreation 11.3%, energy 9.9%.
Population economically active (1998): total 5,232,500; activity rate of total population 50.9% (participation rates: ages 15–64, 72.5%; female 44.3%; unemployed [July 1999–June 2000] 9.2%).

Price and earnings indexes (1995 = 100)

	1995	1996	1997	1998	1999	2000
Consumer price index	100.0	108.8	118.0	130.7	133.5	138.7
Annual earnings index	100.0	118.4	130.8	143.1	154.9	163.5[3]

Gross national product (1999): U.S.$51,623,000,000 (U.S.$5,020 per capita).

Structure of gross domestic product and labour force

	1999		1997	
	in value Kč '000,000	% of total value	labour force[5]	% of labour force
Agriculture, forestry	62,700	3.4	296,000	5.7
Mining	[4]	[4]	96,000	1.9
Manufacturing	575,100[4]	31.3[4]	1,428,000	27.5
Construction	126,400	6.9	501,000	9.7
Public utilities	[4]	[4]	94,000	1.8
Transportation and communications	163,000	8.9	392,000	7.6
Trade, hotels	242,000	13.2	871,000	16.8
Finance, real estate	265,000	14.4	358,000	6.9
Pub. admin., defense }	243,400	13.3	328,000	6.3
Services }			759,000	14.6
Other	158,700[6]	8.6[6]	61,000	1.2
TOTAL	1,836,300	100.0	5,184,000	100.0

Land use (1994): forested 33.3%; meadows and pastures 11.3%; agricultural and under permanent cultivation 43.0%; other 12.4%.

Foreign trade

Balance of trade (current prices)

	1994	1995	1996	1997	1998	1999
Kč '000,000	–39,535	–99,569	–148,911	–148,221	–71,615	–68,124
% of total	4.1%	8.1%	10.9%	9.3%	3.8%	3.5%

Imports (1998): Kč 985,355,000,000 (machinery and apparatus 31.0%, chemicals and chemical products 11.0%, transport equipment 9.0%, mineral fuels 6.2%). *Major import sources* (1999): Germany 33.9%; Slovakia 6.1%; Austria 5.6%; France 5.3%; Italy 5.3%; Russia 4.8%.
Exports (1998): Kč 913,740,000,000 (machinery and apparatus 32.7%, transport equipment 9.8%, chemicals and chemical products 6.9%, iron and steel 6.2%, fabricated metals 5.5%). *Major export destinations* (1999): Germany 42.1%; Slovakia 8.2%; Austria 6.4%; Poland 5.5%; France 3.9%.

Transport and communications

Transport. Railroads (1999): length 9,444 km; passenger-km 6,957,000,000; metric ton-km cargo 16,713,000,000. Roads (1997): total length 125,905 km (paved, n.a.). Vehicles (1999): passenger cars 3,695,792; trucks and buses 426,684. Merchant marine (1993): vessels (oceangoing) 18; total deadweight tonnage 514,126. Air transport (1999): passenger-km 4,353,602,000; metric ton-km 30,326,000; airports (1997) with scheduled flights 2.

Communications

Medium	date	unit	number	units per 1,000 persons
Daily newspapers	1996	circulation	2,620,000	254
Television	1999	receivers	5,000,000	486
Telephones	1999	main lines	3,694,000	359
Cellular telephones	1999	subscribers	1,944,553	189
Personal computers	1999	units	1,100,000	107
Internet	1999	users	700,000	68

Education and health

Educational attainment (1991). Percentage of adult population having: no schooling through complete primary education 31.7%; secondary 58.6%; higher 8.5%; unknown 1.2%. *Literacy* (1998): 99%.

Education (1999–2000)

	schools	teachers	students	student/ teacher ratio
Primary (age 6–14)	4,088	65,259[7]	1,071,318	16.7[7]
Secondary (age 15–18)	345	10,419[7]	126,797	12.1[7]
Voc., teacher tr.	1,409	...	180,114	...
Higher[8]	23	13,216[7]	183,954	12.5[7]

Health (2000[2]): physicians 39,245 (1 per 262 persons); hospital beds 103,280[9] (1 per 100 persons); infant mortality rate per 1,000 live births (1999) 4.6.
Food (1998): daily per capita caloric intake 3,292 (vegetable products 75%, animal products 25%); 133% of FAO recommended minimum requirement.

Military

Total active duty personnel (2000): 57,500 (army 43.5%, air force 23.2%, ministry of defense 33.3%). *Military expenditure as percentage of GNP* (1997): 1.9% (world 2.6%); per capita expenditure: U.S.$193.

[1]New local government structure as of November 2000 elections. [2]January 1. [3]Average of second and third quarters. [4]Manufacturing includes Mining and Public utilities. [5]Population 15 and over only. [6]Taxes less subsidies and imputed bank charges. [7]1997–98. [8]Universities only. [9]Excludes long-term care facilities; includes 20,687 beds in therapeutic baths.

Internet resources for further information:
- **Czech Statistical Office http://www.czso.cz**

Denmark

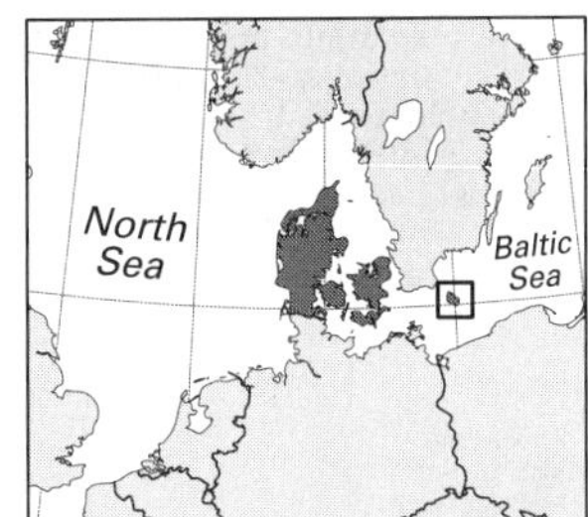

Official name: Kongeriget Danmark (Kingdom of Denmark).
Form of government: parliamentary state and constitutional monarchy with one legislative house (Folketing [179]).
Chief of state: Danish Monarch.
Head of government: Prime Minister.
Capital: Copenhagen.
Official language: Danish.
Official religion: Evangelical Lutheran.
Monetary unit: 1 Danish krone (Dkr; plural kroner) = 100 øre; valuation (Sept. 28, 2001) 1 U.S.$ = Dkr 8.17; 1 £ = Dkr 12.00.

Area and population[1]

Counties	Capitals	area sq mi	area sq km	population 2001 census
Århus	Århus	1,761	4,561	640,637
Bornholm	Rønne	227	588	44,126
Frederiksborg	Hillerød	520	1,347	368,116
Fyn	Odense	1,346	3,486	472,064
København	—	203	526	615,115
Nordjylland	Ålborg	2,383	6,173	494,833
Ribe	Ribe	1,209	3,132	224,446
Ringkøbing	Ringkøbing	1,874	4,854	273,517
Roskilde	Roskilde	344	891	233,212
Sønderjylland	Åbenrå	1,521	3,939	253,249
Storstrøm	Nykøbing Falster	1,312	3,398	259,691
Vejle	Vejle	1,157	2,997	349,186
Vestsjælland	Sorø	1,152	2,984	296,875
Viborg	Viborg	1,592	4,122	233,921
Municipalities				
Copenhagen (København)	—	34	88	499,148
Frederiksberg	—	3	9	91,076
TOTAL		16,639[2]	43,096[2]	5,349,212

Demography

Population (2001): 5,358,000.
Density (2001): persons per sq mi 322.0, persons per sq km 124.3.
Urban-rural (2001): urban 85.1%; rural 14.9%.
Sex distribution (2001): male 49.43%; female 50.57%.
Age breakdown (2001): under 15, 18.6%; 15–29, 18.5%; 30–44, 22.3%; 45–59, 20.8%; 60–74, 12.7%; 75 and over, 7.1%.
Population projection: (2010) 5,525,000; (2020) 5,706,000.
Ethnic composition (2001)[3]: Danish 95.2%; Asian 1.7%, of which Turkish 0.7%; residents of former Yugoslavia 0.7%; African 0.5%; German 0.2%; English 0.2%; other 1.5%.
Religious affiliation (1998): Christian 87.5%, of which Evangelical Lutheran 85.8%; Muslim 2.2%; other/nonreligious 10.3%.
Major urban areas (2001): Greater Copenhagen 1,081,673; Århus 286,688; Odense 144,849; Ålborg 119,996; Frederiksberg 91,076.

Vital statistics

Birth rate per 1,000 population (2000): 12.6 (world avg. 22.5); (1995) legitimate 53.5%; illegitimate 46.5%.
Death rate per 1,000 population (2000): 10.9 (world avg. 9.0).
Natural increase rate per 1,000 population (2000): 1.7 (world avg. 13.5).
Total fertility rate (avg. births per childbearing woman; 2000): 1.7.
Marriage rate per 1,000 population (2000): 7.2.
Divorce rate per 1,000 population (2000): 2.7.
Life expectancy at birth (2001): male 74.3 years; female 79.1 years.
Major causes of death per 100,000 population (1995): malignant neoplasms (cancers) 296.6; ischemic heart disease 242.3; cerebrovascular disease 105.9.

National economy

Budget (1997)[4]. Revenue: Dkr 612,077,000,000 (direct taxes 52.2%, indirect taxes 30.7%). Expenditures: Dkr 626,536,000,000 (social security assistance 31.8%, education 12.2%, welfare services 10.1%, health 8.4%, defense 2.8%).
National debt (end of year; 1996): Dkr 664,128,000,000.
Tourism (1999): receipts U.S.$3,682,000,000; expenditures U.S.$5,084,000,000.
Population economically active (2000): total 2,877,000; activity rate of total population 54.0% (participation rates: ages 16–66 77.5%; female 46.5%; unemployed [May 2000–April 2001 avg.] 5.3%).

Price and earnings indexes (1995 = 100)

	1994	1995	1996	1997	1998	1999	2000
Consumer price index	98.0	100.0	102.1	104.4	106.3	108.9	107.2
Hourly earnings index	96.7	100.0	...	...	...	...	...

Household income and expenditure. Average household size (2001) 2.2; income per household (1988) Dkr 199,354 (U.S.$29,613); expenditure (1993): housing 22.9%, food and beverages 17.9%, transportation and communications 15.5%, recreation 8.3%, household furnishings 6.1%, energy 6.1%.
Production (in Dkr '000,000 except as noted). Agriculture, forestry, fishing (value added; 2000): meat 21,059 (of which pork 17,032, beef 2,654), milk 11,254, cereals 7,458 (of which wheat 3,732, barley 3,214), flowers and plants 2,602, mink furs 2,118; livestock (number of live animals) 11,921,573 pigs, 1,867,937 cattle; roundwood (2000) 3,086,000 cu m; fish catch (1999) 1,447,664 metric tons. Mining and quarrying (1994): sand and gravel 24,829,000 cu m; chalk 3,522,000 cu m. Manufacturing (value added in Dkr '000,000; 1994): food products 38,325, of which meat 11,170; nonelectrical machinery and apparatus 23,331; chemicals and chemical products 18,504; electrical machinery and apparatus 14,428; printing and publishing 9,649; fabricated metals 9,479. Construction (completed; 2000): residential 2,184,000 sq m; nonresidential 4,284,000 sq m. Energy production (consumption): electricity (kW-hr; 1999) 38,604,000,000 ([1996] 39,582,000,000); coal (metric tons; 1996) none (10,948,000); crude petroleum (barrels; 2000) 136,095,000 ([1996] 80,374,000); petroleum products (metric tons; 1996) 10,426,000 (7,730,000); natural gas (cu m; 2000) 8,168,000,000 ([1996] 4,185,000,000).
Gross national product (1999): U.S.$170,685,000,000 (U.S.$32,050 per capita).

Structure of gross domestic product and labour force

	1999 in value Dkr '000,000[5]	1999 % of total value[5]	2000 labour force	2000 % of labour force
Agriculture, fishing	36,258	3.1	107,900	3.7
Mining	11,430	1.0		
Manufacturing	149,842	12.8	464,300	16.1
Construction	43,598	3.7	167,600	5.8
Public utilities	20,022	1.7	16,200	0.6
Transp. and commun.	79,561	6.8	183,400	6.4
Trade, restaurants	156,035	13.3	503,000	17.5
Finance, real estate	163,052	13.9	344,200	12.0
Pub. admin., defense	217,713	18.6	962,200	33.4
Services	112,645	9.6		
Other	180,747[6]	15.4[6]	128,200[7]	4.5[7]
TOTAL	1,170,903	100.0[2]	2,877,000	100.0

Land use (1994): forested 10.5%; meadows and pastures 7.5%; agricultural and under permanent cultivation 55.9%; other 26.1%.

Foreign trade[8]

Balance of trade (current prices)

	1995	1996	1997	1998	1999	2000
Dkr '000,000	+26,171	+32,889	+24,353	+13,776	+30,911	+42,495
% of total	4.9%	6.0%	4.0%	2.2%	4.8%	5.6%

Imports (2000): Dkr 360,790,000,000 (machinery and apparatus 14.2%, chemicals and chemical products 12.3%, food and live animals 8.2%, transport equipment and parts 7.8%, fuels 5.4%). *Major import sources:* Germany 21.0%; Sweden 12.2%; The Netherlands 8.6%; U.K. 7.6%; Norway 5.1%; France 5.1%.
Exports (2000): Dkr 403,285,000,000 (machinery and apparatus 23.5%, food and live animals 18.4%, pharmaceuticals 5.1%, mineral fuels and lubricants 4.8%, furniture 3.8%). *Major export destinations:* Germany 18.9%; Sweden 13.0%; U.K. 9.8%; Norway 5.5%; France 4.9%.

Transport and communications

Transport. Railroads (2001): route length 2,743 km; passenger-km 5,318,000,000; metric ton-km cargo 2,025,000,000. Roads (2001): total length 71,663 km (paved 100%). Vehicles (2001): passenger cars 1,854,060; trucks and buses 335,690. Air transport (1996)[9]: passenger-km 5,376,000,000; metric ton-km cargo 170,768,000; airports (1996) with scheduled flights 13.

Communications

Medium	date	unit	number	units per 1,000 persons
Daily newspapers	1998	circulation	1,613,000	284
Radio	1997	receivers	6,020,000	1,145
Television	1999	receivers	3,300,000	621
Telephones	1999	main lines	3,638,000	684
Cellular telephones	1999	subscribers	2,629,000	495
Personal computers	1999	units	2,200,000	414
Internet	1999	users	1,500,000	282

Education and health

Educational attainment (2000). Percentage of population age 25–69 having: completed lower secondary or not stated 34.6%; completed upper secondary or vocational 42.3%; undergraduate 17.6%; graduate 5.5%. *Literacy:* 100%.

Education (1998–99)

	schools	teachers[10]	students	student/teacher ratio
Primary/lower secondary (age 7–15)	1,836	58,500	651,667	...
Upper secondary (age 16–18)	154	11,000	65,022	...
Vocational	177	12,000	180,784	...
Higher	158	8,000	170,169	...

Health: physicians (1994) 14,497 (1 per 358 persons); hospital beds (1999) 23,352 (1 per 228 persons); infant mortality rate per 1,000 live births (2001) 5.0.
Food (1999): daily per capita caloric intake 3,317 (vegetable products 63%, animal products 37%); 123% of FAO recommended minimum requirement.

Military

Total active duty personnel (2000): 21,810 (army 58.9%, navy 18.6%, air force 22.5%). *Military expenditure as percentage of GNP* (1997): 1.8% (world 2.6%); per capita expenditure U.S.$529.

[1]Excludes the Faroe Islands and Greenland. [2]Detail does not add to total given because of rounding. [3]Based on nationality. [4]Includes both central and local governments. [5]At constant 1995 prices. [6]Taxes on products less imputed bank service charges. [7]Includes 10,500 not adequately defined and 117,700 unemployed. [8]Imports c.i.f., exports f.o.b. [9]Danish share of Scandinavian Airlines System (scheduled air service only) and Maersk Air. [10]1993–94.

Internet resources for further information:
- **Statistics Denmark http://www.dst.dk/dst/yearbook**

Djibouti

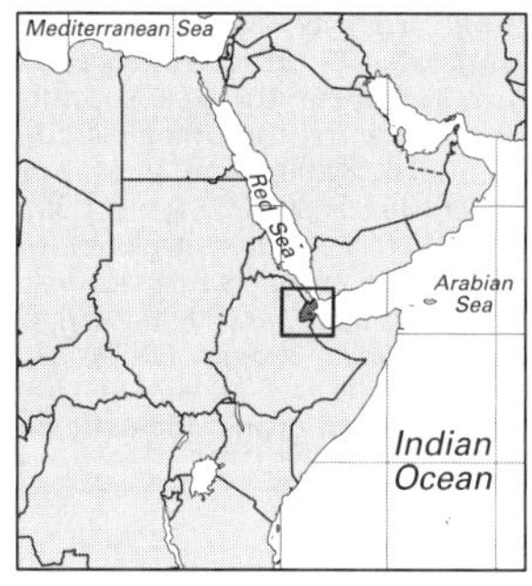

Official name: Jumhūrīyah Jībūtī (Arabic); République de Djibouti (French) (Republic of Djibouti).
Form of government: multiparty republic with one legislative house (National Assembly [65]).
Head of state and government: President.
Capital: Djibouti.
Official languages: Arabic; French.
Official religion: none.
Monetary unit: 1 Djibouti franc (DF) = 100 centimes; valuation (Sept. 28, 2001) 1 U.S.$ = DF 177.72; 1 £ = DF 261.20.

Area and population

		area[1]		population
Districts	Capitals	sq mi	sq km	1982 estimate
ʿAlī Sabīḥ (Ali-Sabieh)	ʿAlī Sabīḥ	925	2,400	15,000
Dikhil	Dikhil	2,775	7,200	30,000
Djibouti	Djibouti	225	600	200,000
Obock	Obock	2,200	5,700	15,000
Tadjoura (Tadjourah)	Tadjoura	2,825	7,300	30,000
TOTAL		8,950	23,200	335,000[2]

Demography

Population (2001): 461,000.
Density (2001): persons per sq mi 51.5, persons per sq km 19.9.
Urban-rural (1999): urban 83.1%; rural 16.9%.
Sex distribution (1999): male 51.66%; female 48.34%.
Age breakdown (1999): under 15, 47.5%; 15–29, 28.9%; 30–44, 13.1%; 45–59, 5.2%; 60–74, 4.7%; 75 and over, 0.6%.
Population projection: (2010) 579,000; (2020) 729,000.
Doubling time: 27 years.
Ethnic composition (2000): Somali 46.0%; Afar 35.4%; Arab 11.0%; mixed African and European 3.0%; French 1.6%; other/unspecified 3.0%.
Religious affiliation (1995): Sunnī Muslim 97.2%; Christian 2.8%, of which Roman Catholic 2.2%, Orthodox 0.5%, Protestant 0.1%.
Major city and towns (1991): Djibouti 383,000[3]; ʿAlī Sabīḥ 8,000; Tadjoura 7,500; Dikhil 6,500.

Vital statistics

Birth rate per 1,000 population (2000): 41.0 (world avg. 22.5).
Death rate per 1,000 population (2000): 14.9 (world avg. 9.0).
Natural increase rate per 1,000 population (2000): 26.1 (world avg. 13.5).
Total fertility rate (avg. births per childbearing woman; 2000): 5.8.
Marriage rate per 1,000 population (1982): 6.7.
Divorce rate per 1,000 population (1982): 1.9.
Life expectancy at birth (2000): male 49.0 years; female 52.7 years.
Major causes of death (percentage of total deaths [infants and children to age 10, district of Djibouti only]; 1984): diarrhea and acute dehydration 16.0%; malnutrition 16.0%; poisoning 11.0%; tuberculosis 6.0%; acute respiratory disease 6.0%; malaria 6.0%; anemia 6.0%; heart disease 2.0%; kidney disease 1.0%; other ailments 19.0%; no diagnosis 11.0%.

National economy

Budget (1998)[4]. Revenue: DF 23,154,000,000 (tax revenue 87.5%, of which domestic consumption taxes 27.1%, wages and salary tax 13.7%, surcharge on khat 8.9%, income and profit tax 6.1%; nontax revenue 12.5%). Expenditures: DF 30,427,000,000 (current expenditures 80.0%, of which general administration 26.7%, defense and mobilization 20.0%, education 8.7%, health 5.4%; capital expenditures 20.0%).
Tourism (1995): receipts from visitors U.S.$4,000,000; expenditures by nationals abroad U.S.$4,000,000.
Production (metric tons except as noted). Agriculture, forestry, fishing (1999): vegetables and melons 22,390, of which tomatoes 1,000, eggplant 45; livestock (number of live animals) 511,000 goats, 463,000 sheep, 269,000 cattle, 66,000 camels, 8,500 asses; roundwood, n.a.; fish catch (1998) 350. Mining and quarrying: mineral production limited to locally used construction materials and evaporated salt. Manufacturing (1999): structural detail, n.a.; main products include furniture, nonalcoholic beverages, meat and hides, light electromechanical goods, and mineral water. Construction (1989): 53,900 sq m. Energy production (consumption): electricity (kW-hr; 1996) 185,000,000 (185,000,000); firewood and charcoal, n.a. (n.a.); coal, none (n.a.); crude petroleum, none (n.a.); petroleum products (metric tons; 1996) none (119,000); natural gas, none (n.a.); geothermal, wind, and solar resources are substantial but largely undeveloped.
Population economically active (1991): total 282,000; activity rate of total population 61.5% (participation rates: over age 10, 70.4%; female 40.8%; unemployed [1987] *c.* 40–50%).

Price and earnings indexes (1990 = 100)

	1990	1991	1992	1993	1994	1995	1996
Consumer price index[5]	100.0	106.8	110.4	115.3	122.8	128.8	134.2
Earnings index	...	...	...	...	...	...	...

Household income and expenditure. Average household size (1985)[6] 7.2; income per household: n.a.; sources of income (1976): wages and salaries 51.6%, self-employment 36.0%, transfer payments 10.5%, other 1.9%; expenditure (expatriate households; 1984): food 50.3%, energy 13.1%, recreation 10.4%, housing 6.4%, clothing 1.7%, personal effects 1.4%, health care 1.0%, household goods 0.3%, other 15.4%.
Public debt (external, outstanding; 1999): U.S.$252,700,000.
Gross national product (1999): U.S.$511,000,000 (U.S.$790 per capita).

Structure of gross domestic product and labour force

	1998		1991	
	in value DF '000,000	% of total value	labour force	% of labour force
Agriculture	2,917	3.2	212,000	75.2
Mining	—	—	31,000	11.0
Manufacturing	4,239	4.6		
Construction	6,971	7.6		
Public utilities	4,850	5.3		
Transp. and commun.	15,824	17.4	39,000	13.8
Trade	14,481	15.9		
Finance	8,772	9.6		
Pub. admin., defense	18,469	20.3		
Services	4,340	4.8		
Other	10,335	11.3	...	...
TOTAL	91,198	100.0	282,000	100.0

Land use (1994): forested 0.9%; meadows and pastures 56.1%; agricultural and under permanent cultivation[7]; built-on, wasteland, and other 43.0%.

Foreign trade

Balance of trade (current prices)

	1993	1994	1995	1996	1997	1998
U.S.$'000,000	–183.9	–180.7	–169.2	–161.1	–161.4	–179.7
% of total	56.4%	61.6%	69.0%	67.0%	65.3%	60.3%

Imports (1998): U.S.$238,800,000 (food, beverages, khat, and tobacco 53.2%; petroleum products 12.4%; machinery and electric appliances 10.9%; base metals and base metal products 4.9%; chemical products 4.6%; transport equipment 4.3%; clothing and footwear 3.7%). *Major import sources:* France 12.5%; Ethiopia 12.0%; Italy 9.2%; U.K. 6.2%; Saudi Arabia 5.7%; Japan 4.2%.
Exports (1998): U.S.$59,100,000,000 (1992; unspecified special transactions 60.0%; live animals [including camels] 21.3%; basic manufactures 5.2%; crude materials 4.5%). *Major export destinations:* Somalia 53.0%; Yemen 22.5%; Ethiopia 5.0%; Saudi Arabia 0.7%.

Transport and communications

Transport. Railroads (1997): length (1989) 66 mi, 106 km; passenger-mi 361,000,000, passenger-km 762,000,000; short ton-mile cargo 144,000,000, metric ton-km cargo 232,000,000. Roads (1996): total length 1,796 mi, 2,890 km (paved 13%). Vehicles (1996): passenger cars 9,200; trucks and buses 2,040. Merchant marine (1992): vessels (100 gross tons and over) 10; total deadweight tonnage 4,090. Air transport (1997): passengers handled 107,369; metric tons of freight handled 7,290; airports (1998) with scheduled flights 1.

Communications

Medium	date	unit	number	units per 1,000 persons
Daily newspapers	1995	circulation	500	0.8
Radio	1997	receivers	52,000	84
Television	1999	receivers	30,000	67
Telephones	1999	main lines	8,831	19.8
Cellular telephones	1999	subscribers	280	0.6
Internet	1999	users	750	1.7

Education and health

Educational attainment: n.a. *Literacy* (1995): percentage of population age 15 and over literate 46.2%; males literate 60.3%; females literate 32.7%.

Education (1996–97)

	schools	teachers	students	student/ teacher ratio
Primary (age 6–11)	81[8]	1,005[8]	33,960	...
Secondary (age 12–18) / Voc., teacher tr.	26[9]	628[8]	11,628	...
Higher	1[9]	13[9]	130[8]	...

Health (1996): physicians 60 (1 per 7,100 persons); hospital beds[10] (1989) 1,383 (1 per 369 persons); infant mortality rate per 1,000 live births (2000) 103.3.
Food (1999): daily per capita caloric intake 2,129 (vegetable products 90%, animal products 10%); 92% of FAO recommended minimum requirement.

Military

Total active duty personnel (2000): 11,400[11] (army 70.2%, navy 1.8%, air force 1.8%, paramilitary 26.2%). *Military expenditure as percentage of GNP* (1997): 4.1% (world 2.6%); per capita expenditure U.S.$47.

[1]Original figures are those given in sq km; sq mi equivalent is rounded to appropriate level of generality. [2]Includes 45,000 persons not distributed by district. [3]1995 estimate. [4]Preliminary. [5]Based on expatriates' expenditures. [6]City of Djibouti only. [7]In 1988–89 only 1,005 acres (407 hectares) of land were cultivated. [8]1995–96. [9]1991. [10]Public health facilities only. [11]Excludes 3,200 French troops.

Dominica

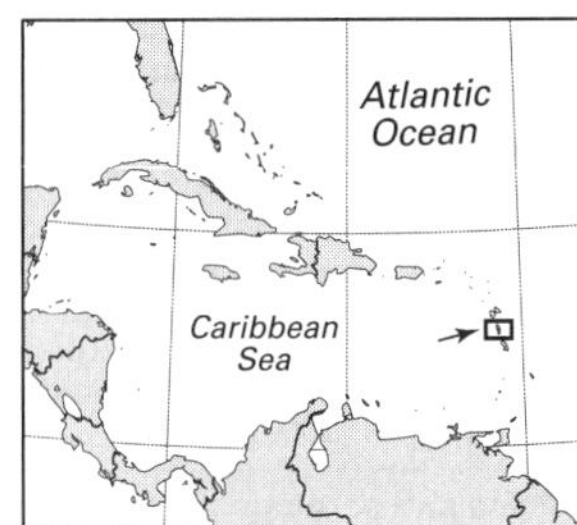

Official name: Commonwealth of Dominica.
Form of government: multiparty republic with one legislative house (House of Assembly [32[1]]).
Chief of state: President.
Head of government: Prime Minister.
Capital: Roseau.
Official language: English.
Official religion: none.
Monetary unit: 1 East Caribbean dollar (EC$) = 100 cents; valuation (Sept. 28, 2001) 1 U.S.$ = EC$2.70; 1 £ = EC$3.97.

Area and population	area		population
			1991
Parishes	sq mi	sq km	census
St. Andrew	69.3	179.6	11,106
St. David	49.0	126.8	6,977
St. George	20.7	53.5	20,365
St. John	22.5	58.5	4,990
St. Joseph	46.4	120.1	6,183
St. Luke	4.3	11.1	1,552
St. Mark	3.8	9.9	1,943
St. Patrick	32.6	84.4	8,929
St. Paul	26.0	67.4	7,495
St. Peter	10.7	27.7	1,643
TOTAL	285.3[2]	739.0[2]	71,183[3]

Demography

Population (2001): 71,700.
Density (2001): persons per sq mi 247.2; persons per sq km 95.6.
Urban-rural (2000): urban 70%; rural 30%.
Sex distribution (2001): male 51%; female 49%.
Age breakdown (2000): under 15, 29.1%; 15–29, 27.2%; 30–44, 23.7%; 45–59, 9.6%; 60–74, 7.0%; 75 and over, 3.4%.
Population projection: (2010) 72,000; (2020) 72,000.
Doubling time: 63 years.
Ethnic composition (1991): black 89.1%; mixed race 7.2%; Amerindian/Carib 2.4%; white 0.4%; other 0.7%; not stated 0.2%.
Religious affiliation (1991): Roman Catholic 70.1%; six largest Protestant groups 17.2%, of which Seventh-day Adventist 4.6%, Pentecostal 4.3%, Methodist 4.2%; other 8.9%; nonreligious 2.9%; unknown 0.9%.
Major towns (1991): Roseau 15,853; Portsmouth 3,621; Marigot 2,919; Atkinson 2,518; Mahaut 2,372.

Vital statistics

Birth rate per 1,000 population (2000): 18.3 (world avg. 22.5); (1991) legitimate 24.1%; illegitimate 75.9%.
Death rate per 1,000 population (2000): 7.3 (world avg. 9.0).
Natural increase rate per 1,000 population (2000): 11.0 (world avg. 13.5).
Total fertility rate (avg. births per childbearing woman; 2000): 2.0.
Marriage rate per 1,000 population (1996): 3.1.
Divorce rate per 1,000 population (1996): 0.7.
Life expectancy at birth (2000): male 70.5 years; female 76.3 years.
Major causes of death per 100,000 population (1994): diseases of the circulatory system 237.8, of which hypertensive disease 93.8, diseases of pulmonary circulation and other forms of heart disease 72.0; malignant neoplasms (cancers) 125.0; endocrine and metabolic disorders 59.8; infectious and parasitic diseases 46.2; diseases of the respiratory system 38.0.

National economy

Budget (1998–99). Revenue: EC$232,700,000 (tax revenue 73.9%, of which consumption taxes on imports 26.9%, income taxes 20.9%; nontax revenue 14.7%; grants 9.2%). Expenditures: EC$260,300,000 (current expenditures 77.1%; development expenditures 22.9%).
Public debt (external, outstanding; 1999): U.S.$89,000,000.
Land use (1994): forested 66.0%; meadows and pastures 3.0%; agricultural and under permanent cultivation 23.0%; other 8.0%.
Tourism: receipts from visitors (1999) U.S.$47,300,000; expenditures by nationals abroad (1998) U.S.$8,000,000.
Gross national product (at current market prices; 1999): U.S.$238,000,000 (U.S.$3,260 per capita).

Structure of gross domestic product and labour force	1998		1991	
	in value EC$'000,000[4]	% of total value[4]	labour force[5]	% of labour force[5]
Agriculture	121.2	20.3	7,344	30.8
Mining	5.3	0.9	65	0.3
Manufacturing	52.5	8.8	1,947	8.2
Construction	46.7	7.8	2,819	11.8
Public utilities	29.9	5.0	304	1.3
Transportation and communications	100.5	16.8	1,202	5.0
Trade, hotels, restaurants	83.2	13.9	3,658	15.4
Finance, real estate	83.9	14.0	810	3.4
Services	120.8	20.2	3,446	14.5
Pub. admin., defense			1,520	6.4
Other	−45.5[6]	−7.6[6]	699	2.9
TOTAL	598.4[7]	100.0[7]	23,814	100.0

Population economically active (1991): total 26,364; activity rate of total population 38.0% (participation rates: ages 15–64, 62.4%; female 34.5%; unemployed [1994] 23%).

Price and earnings indexes (1995 = 100)	1995	1996	1997	1998	1999	2000	2001
Consumer price index	100.0	101.7	104.2	105.2	106.4	107.3	108.5[8]
Earnings index	...	...	...	...	...	...	...

Household income and expenditure. Average household size (1991) 3.6; income per household: n.a.; sources of income: n.a.; expenditure (1984)[9]: food and nonalcoholic beverages 43.1%, housing and utilities 16.1%, transportation 11.6%, clothing and footwear 6.5%, household furnishings 6.0%.
Production (metric tons except as noted). Agriculture, forestry, fishing (1998): bananas 28,640[10], root crops 23,168 (of which dasheens 11,903, yams 7,560, tanias 3,534), plantains 22,236, grapefruit 19,100, coconuts 8,906, oranges 7,230, limes 3,560, mangoes 1,700, pepper 340, bay oil 12; livestock (number of live animals: 1999) 13,400 cattle, 9,700 goats, 7,600 sheep; roundwood, n.a.; fish catch (1997) 855 metric tons. Mining and quarrying: pumice, limestone, and sand and gravel are quarried primarily for local consumption. Manufacturing (value of production in EC$'000; 1998): toilet soap 21,816; laundry soap 16,467; crude coconut oil 1,848; toothpaste 1,662 metric tons; other products include fruit juices, beer, garments, bottled spring water, and cardboard boxes. Energy production (consumption): electricity (kW-hr; 1996) 37,000,000 (37,000,000); coal, none (none); crude petroleum, none (none); petroleum products (metric tons; 1996) none (26,000); natural gas, none (none).

Foreign trade[11]

Balance of trade (current prices)	1995	1996	1997	1998	1999	2000
EC$'000,000	−194.9	−212.4	−193.3	−196.8	−196.2	−253.1
% of total	44.4%	43.4%	40.3%	36.6%	40.0%	46.9%

Imports (1999): EC$343,400,000 (food and beverages 20.8%; machinery 16.4%; transport equipment 9.3%; mineral fuels 6.4%). *Major import sources:* U.S. 30.7%; Caricom 27.0%; U.K. 8.8%; Japan 7.8%; France 5.0%.
Exports (1999): EC$147,400,000 (manufactured exports 61.7%, of which coconut-based laundry and toilet soaps 26.7%; agricultural exports 38.3%, of which bananas 27.1%). *Major export destinations:* Caricom 55.3%; U.K. 27.5%; Guadeloupe 4.9%; U.S. 4.0%.

Transport and communications

Transport. Railroads: none. Roads (1996): total length 485 mi, 780 km (paved 50%). Vehicles (1994): passenger cars 6,581; trucks and buses 2,825. Merchant marine (1992): vessels (100 gross tons and over) 7; total deadweight tonnage 3,153. Air transport: (1991) passenger arrivals 43,312, passenger departures, n.a.; (1997) cargo unloaded 575 metric tons, cargo loaded 363 metric tons; airports (1996) with scheduled flights 2.

Communications				units
Medium	date	unit	number	per 1,000 persons
Radio	1997	receivers	46,000	608
Television	1997	receivers	6,000	79
Telephones	1999	main lines	21,332	296
Cellular telephones	1998	subscribers	650	8.9

Education and health

Educational attainment (1991). Percentage of population age 25 and over having: no formal schooling 4.2%; primary education 78.4%; secondary 11.0%; higher vocational 2.3%; university 2.8%; other/unknown 1.3%. *Literacy* (1994): total population age 15 and over literate, *c.* 44,000 (90.0%).

Education (1997–98)	schools	teachers	students	student/ teacher ratio
Primary	63	587	13,636	23.2
Secondary	15	293	5,455	18.6
Higher[12]	2	34	484	14.2

Health (1998): physicians 38 (1 per 2,007 persons); hospital beds 262 (1 per 291 persons); infant mortality rate per 1,000 live births (2000) 17.1.
Food (1999): daily per capita caloric intake 2,947 (vegetable products 79%, animal products 21%); 122% of FAO recommended minimum requirement.

Military

Total active duty personnel (1999): none[13].

[1]Includes 22 seats that are elective (including speaker if elected from outside of the House of Assembly) and 10 seats that are nonelective (including 9 appointees of the president and the attorney general serving ex officio). [2]Total area of Dominica per more recent survey is 290 sq mi (750 sq km). [3]March 2001 preliminary census total equals 71,727. [4]At current factor cost. [5]Employed persons only. [6]Less imputed banking service charge. [7]Detail does not add to total given because of rounding. [8]April. [9]Weights of consumer price index components. [10]Export production only. [11]Imports c.i.f.; exports f.o.b. [12]1992–93. [13]300-member police force includes a coast guard unit.

Internet resources for further information:
- **Eastern Caribbean Central Bank http://www.eccb-centralbank.org**

Dominican Republic

Official name: República Dominicana (Dominican Republic).
Form of government: multiparty republic with two legislative houses (Senate [30]; Chamber of Deputies [149]).
Head of state and government: President.
Capital: Santo Domingo.
Official language: Spanish.
Official religion: none[1].
Monetary unit: 1 Dominican peso (RD$) = 100 centavos; valuation (Sept. 28, 2001) 1 U.S.$ = RD$16.30; 1 £ = RD$23.96.

Area and population

Provinces	area sq km	population 2000 estimate	Provinces	area sq km	population 2000 estimate
Azua	2,532	243,157	Monte Plata	2,633	174,126
Baoruco	1,283	124,592	Pedernales	2,077	19,698
Barahona	1,739	179,945	Peravia[2]	1,648	223,273
Dajabón	1,021	78,045	Puerto Plata	1,857	302,799
Duarte	1,605	318,151	Salcedo	440	106,450
Elías Piña	1,424	66,267	Samaná	854	82,135
El Seíbo (El Seybo)	1,786	105,447	San Cristóbal	1,265	519,906
Espaillat	838	228,173	San Juan	3,571	265,562
Hato Mayor	1,329	87,595	San Pedro de Macorís	1,255	260,629
Independencia	2,008	41,778	Sánchez Ramírez	1,196	194,282
La Altagracia	3,010	128,627	Santiago	2,836	836,614
La Romana	654	213,628	Santiago Rodríguez	1,112	65,853
La Vega	2,286	390,314	Valverde	823	198,979
María Trinidad Sánchez	1,271	142,030			
Monseñor Nouel	992	174,923	**National district**		
Monte Cristi	1,925	103,711	Santo Domingo	1,401	2,677,055
			TOTAL	48,671[3]	8,553,744

Demography

Population (2001): 8,693,000.
Density (2001): persons per sq mi 462.6, persons per sq km 178.6.
Urban-rural (2000): urban 65.2%; rural 34.8%.
Sex distribution (2000): male 50.80%; female 49.20%.
Age breakdown (2000): under 15, 34.5%; 15–29, 27.3%; 30–44, 20.3%; 45–59, 10.8%; 60–74, 5.7%; 75 and over, 1.4%.
Population projection: (2010) 9,995,000; (2020) 11,489,000.
Doubling time: 34 years.
Ethnic composition (2000): mulatto 69.5%; white 17.0%; local black 9.4%; Haitian black 2.4%; other/unknown 1.7%.
Religious affiliation (1995): Roman Catholic 81.8%; Protestant 6.4%; other Christian 0.6%; other 11.2%.
Major urban centres (1993): Santo Domingo 1,609,966[4]; Santiago 365,463; La Romana 140,204; San Pedro de Macorís 124,735; San Francisco de Macorís 108,485.

Vital statistics

Birth rate per 1,000 population (2000): 25.2 (world avg. 22.5).
Death rate per 1,000 population (2000): 4.7 (world avg. 9.0).
Natural increase rate per 1,000 population (2000): 20.5 (world avg. 13.5).
Total fertility rate (avg. births per childbearing woman; 2000): 3.0.
Marriage rate per 1,000 population (1994): 2.0.
Life expectancy at birth (2000): male 71.1 years; female 75.4 years.
Major causes of death per 100,000 population (1985)[5]: diseases of the circulatory system 165; infectious diseases 85; malignant neoplasms (cancers) 45.

National economy

Budget (1998). Revenue: RD$38,566,000,000 (tax revenue 93.8%, of which taxes on goods and services 47.7%, import duties 27.0%, income taxes 17.9%; nontax revenue 5.3%). Expenditures: RD$41,179,000,000 (current expenditure 72.2%; development expenditure 27.8%).
Public debt (external, outstanding; 1999): U.S.$3,665,000,000.
Gross national product (1999): U.S.$16,130,000,000 (U.S.$1,1920 per capita).

Structure of gross domestic product and labour force

	1998		1997	
	in value RD$'000,000	% of total value	labour force	% of labour force
Agriculture	28,171	11.6	529,000	16.7
Mining	4,722	2.0	8,400	0.3
Manufacturing	40,215	16.6	483,300	15.3
Construction	29,307	12.1	153,600	4.9
Public utilities	5,105	2.1	20,300	0.6
Transp. and commun.	28,061	11.6	202,700	6.4
Trade, restaurants	48,063	19.9	647,600	20.5
Finance, real estate	21,172	8.8	34,000	1.1
Pub. admin., defense	18,839	7.8	125,400	4.0
Services }	18,255	7.5	447,500	14.2
Other }			503,700[6]	16.0[6]
TOTAL	241,910	100.0	3,155,500	100.0

Production (metric tons except as noted). Agriculture, forestry, fishing (1998): sugarcane 5,097,000, rice 475,000, bananas 359,000, plantains 341,000, cacao beans 59,000, coffee 57,000, pulses 56,000; livestock (number of live animals) 2,528,000 cattle, 960,000 pigs, 38,000,000 chickens; roundwood (1997) 982,300 cu m; fish catch (1997) 14,536. Mining (1998): nickel (metal content) 25,200; gold 40,700 troy oz. Manufacturing (1998)[7]: cement 1,872,000; refined sugar 105,000; beer 2,990,000 hectolitres; rum 420,000 hectolitres. Energy production (consumption): electricity (kW-hr; 2000) 9,788,000,000 (5,777,000,000); coal (metric tons; 1996) none (128,000); crude petroleum (barrels; 1996) none (17,035,000); petroleum products (metric tons; 1996) 2,147,000 (3,671,000); natural gas, none (none).
Tourism (1999): receipts U.S.$2,524,000,000; expenditures U.S.$282,000,000.
Population economically active (1993): total 2,556,225; activity rate of total population 35.0% (participation rates: ages 15–64, 54.3%; female 24.9%; unemployed [2000] 13.9%).

Price and earnings indexes (1995 = 100)

	1995	1996	1997	1998	1999	2000	2001
Consumer price index	100.0	105.4	114.1	119.7	127.4	137.2	148.2[8]
Annual earnings index[9]	100.0	100.0	120.0	120.0	...	...	...

Household income and expenditure. Average household size (1993) 3.9; average income: n.a.; sources of income: n.a.; expenditure (1980–85): food and beverages 46.0%, housing 10.0%, household goods 8.0%.
Land use (1994): forested 12.4%; meadows and pastures 43.4%; agricultural and under permanent cultivation 30.6%; other 13.6%.

Foreign trade[10]

Balance of trade (current prices)

	1995	1996	1997	1998	1999	2000
U.S.$'000,000	–2,292	–2,635	–3,175	–4,008	–4,402	–5,450
% of total	56.8%	58.2%	61.0%	69.3%	73.2%	73.8%

Imports (1998): U.S.$4,897,000,000[11] (capital goods 22.1%; consumer durables 13.2%; crude petroleum and petroleum products 11.0%). *Major import sources* (1997)[12]: U.S. 56%; Venezuela 23%; Mexico 9%; Japan 4%.
Exports (1998): U.S.$889,000,000[13] (ships' stores 15.8%; ferronickel 15.0%; cacao and cocoa 13.6%; raw sugar 13.2%; raw coffee 7.2%). *Major export destinations* (1997): U.S. 53.9%; Belgium 11.9%; Puerto Rico 7.0%.

Transport and communications

Transport. Railroads (1997)[14]: route length 1,083 mi, 1,743 km. Roads (1996): total length 7,829 mi, 12,600 km (paved 49%). Vehicles (1996): passenger cars 224,000; trucks and buses 151,550. Air transport (1997)[15]: passenger-mi 9,823,000, passenger-km, 15,808,000; short ton-mi cargo 7,962,000, metric ton-km cargo 11,624,000; airports (1997) 7.

Communications

Medium	date	unit	number	units per 1,000 persons
Daily newspapers	1996	circulation	416,000	53
Radio	1997	receivers	1,440,000	179
Television	1997	receivers	770,000	96
Telephones	1999	main lines	820,926	99
Cellular telephones	1999	subscribers	420,080	51

Education and health

Educational attainment: n.a. *Literacy* (1995): total population age 15 and over literate, *c.* 4,164,000 (82.1%); males literate, *c.* 2,118,000 (82.0%); females literate, *c.* 2,046,000 (82.2%).

Education (1994–95)

	schools	teachers	students	student/ teacher ratio
Primary (age 6–13)	4,001	42,135	1,462,722	34.7
Secondary (age 14–17)	...	10,757	240,441	22.4
Voc. teacher tr.	...	1,297	22,795	17.6
Higher[16]	...	9,041	176,995	19.6

Health: physicians (1997) 17,460 (1 per 460 persons); hospital beds (1996) 11,921 (1 per 662 persons); infant mortality rate per 1,000 live births (2000) 35.9.
Food (1999): daily per capita caloric intake 2,333 (vegetable products 85%, animal products 15%); 103% of FAO recommended minimum.

Military

Total active duty personnel (2000): 24,500 (army 61.2%, navy 16.3%, air force 22.5%). *Military expenditure as percentage of GNP* (1997): 1.1% (world 2.6%); per capita expenditure U.S.$21.

[1]Roman Catholicism is the state religion per concordat with Vatican City. [2]Includes San José de Ocoa province created in January 2001. [3]Mainland total 48,512 sq km and offshore islands total 159 sq km. [4]Urban population of national district. [5]Projected rates based on about 60% of total deaths. [6]Unemployed. [7]Excludes free-zone sector for reexport (mostly ready-made garments) employing (1998) 195,000. [8]July. [9]Minimum wage for medium-sized businesses in private sector. [10]Excludes free zones. [11]Excludes 1998 imports of free zones equaling U.S.$2,701,000,000. [12]Estimated figures. [13]Excludes 1998 reexports of free zones equaling U.S.$4,100,000,000. [14]Most track is privately owned and serves the sugar industry only. [15]Aerochago and Dominair airlines. [16]1996–97.

Internet resources for further information:
- **Banco Central de la República Dominicana http://www.bancentral.gov.do**
- **Oficina Nacional de Estadística http://www.one.gov.do**

Ecuador

Official name: República del Ecuador (Republic of Ecuador).
Form of government: unitary multiparty republic with one legislative house (National Congress [121]).
Head of state and government: President.
Capital: Quito.
Official language: Spanish[1].
Official religion: none.
Monetary unit[2]: 1 dollar (U.S.$); valuation (Sept. 28, 2001) 1 U.S.$ = £ 0.68.

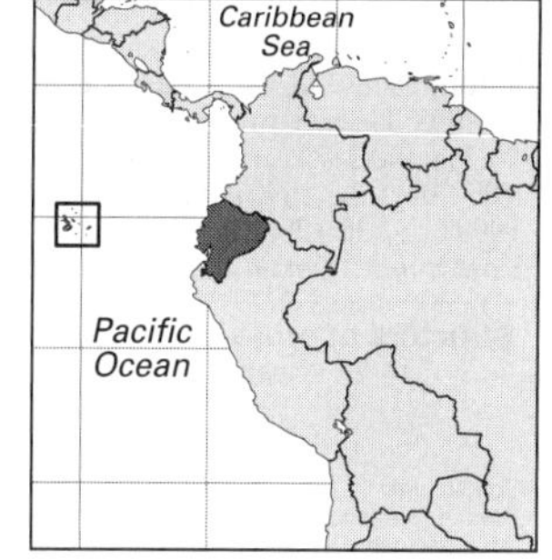

Area and population

Regions / Provinces	Capitals	area sq mi	area sq km	population 2000 estimate
Amazonica				
Morona-Santiago	Macas	13,100	33,930	143,000
Napo[3]	Tena	9,918	25,690	162,000
Pastaza	Puyo	11,496	29,774	62,000
Sucumbíos	Nueva Loja	7,076	18,327	145,000
Zamora-Chinchipe	Zamora	8,923	23,111	103,000
Costa				
El Oro	Machala	2,259	5,850	560,000
Esmeraldas	Esmeraldas	5,884	15,239	434,000
Guayas	Guayaquil	7,916	20,503	3,421,000
Los Ríos	Babahoyo	2,770	7,175	663,000
Manabí	Portoviejo	7,289	18,879	1,268,000
Insular				
Galápagos	Puerto Baquerizo Moreno	3,093	8,010	17,000
Sierra				
Azuay	Cuenca	3,137	8,125	627,000
Bolívar	Guaranda	1,521	3,940	184,000
Cañar	Azogues	1,205	3,122	217,000
Carchi	Tulcán	1,392	3,605	167,000
Chimborazo	Riobamba	2,536	6,569	425,000
Cotopaxi	Latacunga	2,344	6,072	303,000
Imbabura	Ibarra	1,760	4,559	330,000
Loja	Loja	4,257	11,026	429,000
Pichincha	Quito	4,987	12,915	2,466,000
Tungurahua	Ambato	1,288	3,335	447,000
TOTAL		105,037[4, 5]	272,045[5]	12,646,000[6]

Demography

Population (2001): 12,879,000.
Density (2001): persons per sq mi 122.6, persons per sq km 47.3.
Urban-rural (1998): urban 61.0%; rural 39.0%.
Sex distribution (1998): male 50.23%; female 49.77%.
Age breakdown (1997): under 15, 35.4%; 15–29, 29.1%; 30–59, 28.9%; 60 and over, 6.6%.
Population projection: (2010) 14,899,000; (2020) 16,904,000.
Ethnic composition (1989): Amerindian 40.0%; mestizo 40.0%; white 15.0%; black 5.0%.
Religious affiliation (1995): Roman Catholic 93.4%; other 6.6%.
Major cities (2000): Guayaquil 2,118,000; Quito 1,616,000; Cuenca 278,000; Machala 217,000; Portoviejo 181,000; Ambato 174,000.

Vital statistics

Birth rate per 1,000 population (2000): 26.5[7] (world avg. 22.5).
Death rate per 1,000 population (2000): 5.5[7] (world avg. 9.0).
Natural increase rate per 1,000 population (2000): 21.0[7] (world avg. 13.5).
Total fertility rate (avg. births per childbearing woman; 2000): 3.2.
Marriage rate per 1,000 population (1997): 5.6[6].
Life expectancy at birth (2000): male 68.3 years; female 74.0 years.
Major causes of death per 100,000 population (1995): circulatory diseases 55.1; accidents, poisoning, and violence 29.2; pneumonia 27.2; diabetes mellitus 15.4; neoplasms (cancers) 12.7; parasitic diseases 12.2.

National economy

Budget (1996). Revenue: S/. 10,233,300,000,000 (petroleum revenue 45.9%, indirect taxes 30.9%, direct taxes 11.1%). Expenditures: S/. 11,836,700,000,000 (administration 40.8%, debt service 20.7%, subsidies 7.4%).
Public debt (external, outstanding; 1999): U.S.$12,756,000,000.
Production (metric tons except as noted). Agriculture, forestry, fishing (1999): sugarcane 6,800,000, bananas 4,563,000, rice 1,043,000, corn (maize) 688,000; livestock (live animals) 5,534,000 cattle, 2,892,000 pigs, 2,182,000 sheep, 64,736,000 chickens; roundwood (1998) 11,340,000 cu m; fish catch (1997) 688,297. Mining and quarrying (1994): limestone 1,900,000; gold 7,000 kg. Manufacturing (value added in S/. '000,000; 1996): chemical products 2,364,091; food products 1,779,894; nonmetallic mineral products 453,148; textiles 305,369. Construction (in S/.; 1992)[8]: residential 93,166,704,000; nonresidential 58,102,274,000. Energy production (consumption): electricity (kW-hr; 1996) 9,260,000,000 (9,260,000,000); crude petroleum (barrels; 1996) 137,203,000 (58,373,000); petroleum products (metric tons; 1996) 7,130,000 (5,726,000); natural gas (cu m; 1996) 534,000,000 (534,000,000).
Household income and expenditure. Average household size (1990) 4.1; average annual income per household (1995) S/. 9,825,610 (U.S.$3,830); sources of income (1995): self-employment 70.9%, wages 16.0%, transfer payments 6.7%, other 6.4%; expenditure (1995): food and tobacco 37.9%, transportation and communications 15.0%, clothing 9.2%, household furnishings 6.5%.
Population economically active (1997): total 3,373,810; activity rate of total population 44.9% (participation rates: ages 15 and over, 64.2%; female 39.1%.

Price and earnings indexes (1995 = 100)

	1994	1995	1996	1997	1998	1999	2000
Consumer price index	81.4	100.0	124.4	162.5	221.1	336.7	660.2
Monthly earnings index[9]	68.7	100.0	136.4	171.8	217.0	292.7	...

Gross national product (1999): U.S.$16,841,000,000 (U.S.$1,360 per capita).

Structure of gross domestic product and labour force

	1998 in value S/. '000,000[10]	1998 % of total value[10]	1997 labour force	1997 % of labour force
Agriculture	39,342	17.3	520,970	15.4
Mining	30,788	13.5	11,240	0.3
Manufacturing	35,239	15.5	475,280	14.1
Construction	5,837	2.6	185,130	5.5
Public utilities	3,176	1.4	10,230	0.3
Transp. and commun.	14,236	6.2	175,580	5.2
Trade	30,784	13.5	870,900	25.8
Finance	8,083	3.6	138,550	4.1
Pub. admin., defense	15,508	6.8	983,140	29.1
Services	43,166	18.9		
Other	1,519[11]	0.7[11]	2,790[12]	0.1[12]
TOTAL	227,678	100.0	3,373,810	100.0[4]

Tourism (1999): receipts U.S.$343,000,000; expenditures U.S.$271,000,000.

Foreign trade[13]

Balance of trade (current prices)

	1995	1996	1997	1998	1999	2000
U.S.$'000,000	+532.4	+1,510.5	+709.5	−809.8	+1,714.1	+1,674.3
% of total	6.6%	18.3%	7.3%	8.8%	23.8%	20.8%

Imports (1997): U.S.$4,510,600,000 (machines and transport equipment 35.6%; industrial supplies 34.9%; consumer goods 14.1%; food and live animals 7.6%; mineral fuels 7.6%). *Major import sources:* U.S. 30.5%; Colombia 10.6%; Venezuela 6.7%; Japan 5.8%; Germany 4.2%; Spain 3.6%.
Exports (1997): U.S.$5,214,100,000 (food and live animals 56.6%, of which bananas 25.4%, crustaceans 16.8%; crude petroleum 26.9%). *Major export destinations:* U.S. 38.2%; Colombia 6.8%; Italy 5.2%; Chile 4.6%.

Transport and communications

Transport. Railroads (1995): route length 966 km; passenger-km 47,000,000; metric ton-km cargo 2,592,000. Roads (1997): total length 43,197 km (paved 19%). Vehicles (1996): passenger cars 464,902; trucks and buses 52,630. Air transport (1998): passenger-km 923,822,000; metric ton-km cargo 116,378,000.

Communications

Medium	date	unit	number	units per 1,000 persons
Daily newspapers	1996	circulation	820,000	70
Radio	1997	receivers	4,150,000	348
Television	1998	receivers	2,500,000	205
Telephones	1999	main lines	1,129,528	91
Cellular telephones	1999	subscribers	383,185	31
Personal computers	1999	units	250,000	20
Internet	1999	users	35,000	2.8

Education and health

Educational attainment (1990). Percentage of population age 25 and over having: no formal schooling 2.2%; incomplete primary 54.3%; primary 28.0%; postsecondary 15.5%. *Literacy* (1995): total population age 15 and over literate 90.1%; males 92.0%; females 88.2%.

Education (1996–97)

	schools	teachers	students	student/ teacher ratio
Primary (age 4–12)	17,367	74,601	1,888,172	25.3
Secondary (age 12–18) / Vocational	2,207[14]	62,630[15]	813,557[15]	13.0[15]
Higher	21[14]	12,856[16]	206,541[16]	16.1[16]

Health (1997): physicians 20,243 (1 per 590 persons); hospital beds 18,510 (1 per 645 persons); infant mortality rate (2000) 35.1.
Food (1999): daily per capita caloric intake 2,679 (vegetable products 84%, animal products 16%); (1997) 117% of FAO recommended minimum requirement.

Military

Total active duty personnel (2000): 57,500 (army 87.0%, navy 7.8%, air force 5.2%). *Military expenditure as percentage of GNP* (1997): 4.0% (world 2.6%); per capita expenditure U.S.$62.

[1]Quechua and Shuar are also official languages for the indigenous peoples. [2]The United States dollar became the principal national currency from March 2000 and was formally adopted as the national currency on Sept. 9, 2000; the pegged value of the Sucre (S/.), the former national currency, to the U.S. dollar from March 2000 was S/. 25,000 = 1 U.S.$. [3]Includes Orellana province (pop. 70,000) created in 1998. [4]Detail does not add to total given because of rounding. [5]Includes 884 sq mi (2,289 sq km) in nondelimited areas. [6]Total includes 73,000 persons in nondelimited areas. [7]Excluding nomadic Indian tribes. [8]Authorized construction in Cuenca, Guayaquil, and Quito only. [9]General minimum wage. [10]At constant 1975 prices. [11]Minus imputed bank services plus gross import duties. [12]Activities not adequately defined. [13]Import figures are f.o.b. in balance of trade and c.i.f. for commodities and trading partners. [14]1986–87. [15]1992–93. [16]1990–91.

Internet resources for further information:
- **Instituto Nacional de Estadistica y Censos (in Spanish) http://www4.inec.gov.ec**
- **Banco Central del Ecuador http://www.bce.fin.ec**

Egypt

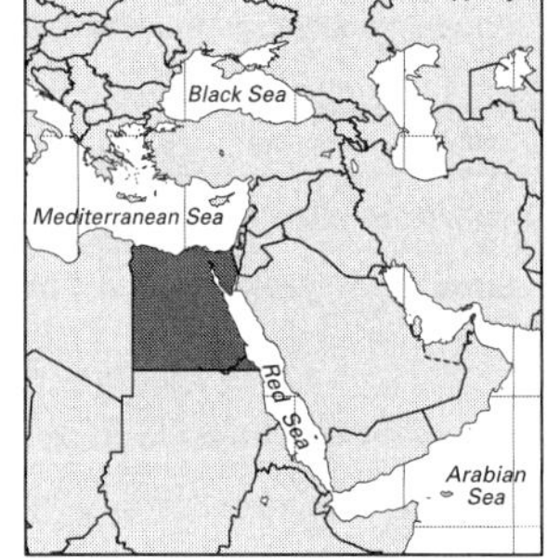

Official name: Jumhūrīyah Miṣr al-ʿArabīyah (Arab Republic of Egypt).
Form of government: republic with one legislative house (People's Assembly [454[1]]).
Chief of state: President.
Head of government: Prime Minister.
Capital: Cairo.
Official language: Arabic.
Official religion: Islam.
Monetary unit: 1 Egyptian pound (£E) = 100 piastres; valuation (Sept. 28, 2001) 1 U.S.$ = £E 4.26; 1 £ = £E 6.26.

Area and population

Regions / Governorates	Capitals	area sq mi	area sq km	population 1996 census
Frontier				
Al-Baḥr al-Aḥmar	Al-Ghurdaqah	78,643	203,685	155,695
Janūb Sīnāʾ	Aṭ-Ṭūr	12,796	33,140	54,495
Maṭrūḥ	Marsā Maṭrūḥ	81,897	212,112	211,866
Shamāl Sīnāʾ	Al-ʿArish	10,646	27,574	252,750
Al-Wādī al-Jadīd	Al-Kharijah	145,369	376,505	141,737
Lower Egypt				
Al-Buḥayrah	Damanhūr	3,911	10,129	3,981,209
Ad-Daqahlīyah	Al-Manṣūrah	1,340	3,471	4,223,655
Dumyāṭ	Dumyāṭ	227	589	914,614
Al-Gharbīyah	Ṭanṭā	750	1,942	3,404,827
Al-Ismāʿīlīyah (Ismailia)	—	557	1,442	715,009
Kafr ash-Shaykh	Kafr ash-Shaykh	1,327	3,437	2,222,920
Al-Minūfīyah	Shibīn al-Kawm	592	1,532	2,758,499
Al-Qalyūbīyah	Banhā	387	1,001	3,302,860
Ash-Sharqīyah	Az-Zaqāzīq	1,614	4,180	4,287,848
Upper Egypt				
Aswān	Aswān	262	679	973,671
Asyūṭ	Asyūṭ	600	1,553	2,802,185
Banī Suwayf	Banī Suwayf	510	1,322	1,860,180
Al-Fayyūm	Al-Fayyūm	705	1,827	1,989,881
Al-Jīzah	Al-Jīzah	32,859	85,105	4,779,865
Al-Minyā	Al-Minyā	873	2,262	3,308,875
Qinā	Qinā	693	1,796	2,441,420
Sawhāj	Sawhāj	597	1,547	3,125,000
Urban				
Būr Saʿīd (Port Said)	—	28	72	469,533
Al-Iskandarīyah (Alexandria)	—	1,034	2,679	3,328,196
Al-Qāhirah (Cairo)	—	83	214	6,789,497
Al-Uqṣur (Luxor)	—	21	55	360,503
As-Suways (Suez)	—	6,888	17,840	417,610
TOTAL		385,210[2]	997,690	59,274,400[3]

Demography

Population (2001): 65,239,000.
Density (2000): persons per sq mi 169.4; persons per sq km 65.4.
Urban-rural (1996): urban 43.0%; rural 57.0%.
Sex distribution (2000): male 50.50%; female 49.50%.
Age breakdown (2000): under 15, 35.1%; 15–29, 28.5%; 30–44, 19.0%; 45–59, 11.3%; 60–74, 5.0%; 75 and over, 1.0%.
Population projection: (2010) 74,878,000; (2020) 84,773,000.
Doubling time: 40 years.
Ethnic composition (2000): Egyptian Arab 84.1%; Sudanese Arab 5.5%; Arabized Berber 2.0%; Bedouin 2.0%; Rom (Gypsy) 1.6%; other 4.8%.
Religious affiliation (1997): Sunnī Muslim 89%; Christian 11%[4].
Major cities ('000; 1996): Cairo 6,789 (10,345[5]); Alexandria 3,328; Al-Jīzah 2,222; Shubrā al-Khaymah 871; Port Said 470; Suez 418.

Vital statistics

Birth rate per 1,000 population (2000): 25.4 (world avg. 22.5).
Death rate per 1,000 population (2000): 7.8 (world avg. 9.0).
Natural increase rate per 1,000 population (2000): 17.6 (world avg. 13.5).
Total fertility rate (avg. births per childbearing woman; 2000): 3.2.
Life expectancy at birth (2000): male 61.3 years; female 65.5 years.

National economy

Budget (1998–99). Revenue: £E 71,295,000,000 (income and profits taxes 21.9%, sales taxes 20.1%, customs duties 14.2%, Suez Canal fees 4.1%, oil revenue 3.1%). Expenditures: £E 75,285,000,000 (current expenditure 79.1%, of which wages and pensions 31.7%, public debt interest 20.8%, defense 11.0%, capital expenditure 20.9%).
Public debt (external, outstanding; 1999): U.S.$25,998,000,000.
Population economically active (1999–2000): total 18,818,000; activity rate 29.7% (participation rates (1995): ages 15–64, 49.8%; female 22.0%; unemployed 7.4%).

Price and earnings indexes (1995 = 100)

	1994	1995	1996	1997	1998	1999	2000
Consumer price index	86.4	100.0	108.3	112.8	114.4	120.4	123.7
Annual earnings index	93.2	100.0	...	...	...	...	...

Production ('000; metric tons except as noted). Agriculture, forestry, fishing (2000): sugarcane 15,668, wheat 6,564, corn (maize) 6,395, rice 5,996, tomatoes 5,900, potatoes 1,784, oranges 1,550, watermelons 1,507; livestock ('000; number of live animals) 4,450 sheep, 3,300 goats, 3,200 buffalo, 3,180 cattle, 88,000 chickens; roundwood (2000) 2,883,000 cu m; fish catch (1999) 606,780. Mining and quarrying (1998–99): iron ore 3,002; gypsum 2,666; salt 2,588; phosphate rock 1,165; kaolin 314. Manufacturing (1999–2000): cement 26,000; nitrate fertilizers 1,550; sugar 1,285; cotton yarn 280; refrigerators 585,000; automobiles 48,167 units. Construction (1992–93): urban residential units 123,098. Energy production (consumption): electricity ('000,000 kW-hr; 1996) 50,258 (50,258); coal ('000 metric tons; 1999) n.a. (1,544[6]); crude petroleum ('000 barrels; 1999) 303,576 (210,243); petroleum products ('000 metric tons; 1999) 28,538 (23,761); natural gas ('000,000 cu m; 1995) 13,568 (13,568).
Gross national product (1999): U.S.$86,544,000,000 (U.S.$1,380 per capita).

Structure of gross domestic product and labour force

	1998–99[7]		1995	
	in value £E '000,000	% of total value	labour force	% of labour force
Agriculture	45,530	17.0	5,215,600	29.4
Mining (petroleum)	67,401	25.1	40,700	0.2
Manufacturing			2,183,500	12.3
Construction	15,580	5.8	967,600	5.5
Public utilities	4,824	1.8	166,800	0.9
Transp. and commun.	24,874[8]	9.3[8]	907,600	5.1
Trade	50,379[9]	18.8[9]	1,587,700	9.0
Finance	16,736	6.2	282,700	1.6
Pub. admin., defense, services	22,164	8.2	3,990,800	22.5
Other	20,910	7.8	2,382,900[10]	13.5[10]
TOTAL	268,398	100.0	17,725,900	100.0

Household income and expenditure. Average household size (1986) 4.9; expenditure (1986–87)[11]: food 55.7%, clothing 10.9%, housing 10.5%.
Tourism (1999): receipts U.S.$3,903,000,000; expenditures U.S.$1,078,000,000.

Foreign trade

Balance of trade (current prices)

	1995	1996	1997	1998	1999	2000
U.S.$'000,000	–7,597	–8,390	–8,632	–10,214	–9,928	–8,321
% of total	46.3%	46.7%	43.9%	53.7%	48.7%	37.4%

Imports (1999): U.S.$15,165,000,000 (machinery and transport equipment 32.7%; foodstuffs 21.2%; iron and steel products 7.7%; wood and paper 6.2%; chemical products 5.1%). *Major import sources* (1999): U.S. 14.3%; Germany 8.6%; Italy 6.5%; France 4.9%.
Exports (1999): U.S.$5,327,000,000 (petroleum and petroleum products 22.9%; cotton yarn, textiles, and clothing 9.7%; basic metals and manufactures 9.4%). *Major export destinations* (1999): U.S. 12.3%; Italy 9.9%; The Netherlands 7.0%; France 3.7%.

Transport and communications

Transport. Railroads (1999): length 4,810 km; passenger-km (1998) 56,667,000,000; metric ton-km cargo (1996) 4,117,000,000. Roads (1998): length 64,000 km (paved 78%). Vehicles (1998): passenger cars 1,154,753; trucks and buses 510,766. Inland water (1999): Suez Canal, number of transits 13,490; metric ton cargo 384,994,000. Air transport (1999): passenger-km 9,074,000,000; metric ton-km cargo 269,520,000; airports (1998) 11.

Communications

Medium	date	unit	number	units per 1,000 persons
Daily newspapers	1996	circulation	2,400,000	38.0
Radio	1997	receivers	20,500,000	330
Television	1999	receivers	11,400,000	183
Telephones	1999	main lines	4,666,000	75
Cellular telephones	1999	subscribers	480,974	77
Personal computers	1999	units	750,000	12
Internet	1999	users	200,000	3.2

Education and health

Literacy (1995): total population age 15 and over literate 51.4%; males 63.6%; females 38.8%.

Education (1998–99)

	schools	teachers	students	student/ teacher ratio
Primary (age 6–11)[12, 13]	15,566	314,528	7,351,118	23.4
Secondary (age 12–17)[12, 13]	8,887	272,687	5,394,019	19.8
Vocational	1,767	145,050	1,852,332	12.8
Higher	356	...	1,316,491[14]	...

Health: physicians (1996) 129,000 (1 per 472 persons); hospital beds (1994) 113,020 (1 per 515 persons); infant mortality rate (2000) 62.3.
Food (1999): daily per capita caloric intake 3,323 (vegetable products 93%, animal products 7%); 120% of FAO recommended minimum requirement.

Military

Total active duty personnel (2000): 448,500 (army 71.3%, navy 4.1%, air force [including air defense] 24.6%). *Military expenditure as percentage of GNP* (1997): 2.8% (world 2.6%); per capita expenditure U.S.$3.4.

[1]Includes 10 nonelective seats. [2]Detail does not add to total given because of rounding. [3]Excludes 2,180,000 Egyptians abroad. [4]According to the 1986 census, the Christian population of Egypt was 5.9% of the total; this figure is considered by some external authorities to understate significantly the Christian population. [5]1999 urban agglomeration. [6]1995. [7]At 1996–97 factor cost. [8]Transportation includes earnings from traffic on the Suez Canal. [9]Trade includes restaurants and hotels. [10]Unemployed and those seeking work for the first time. [11]Weight of consumer price components; urban households only. [12]Data exclude 2,655 primary and secondary schools in the Al-Azhar education system. [13]Includes preparatory. [14]1996–97.

Internet resources for further information:

- **Egypt State Information Service http://www.sis.gov.eg**
- **Ministry of Economy http://www.economy.gov.eg**

El Salvador

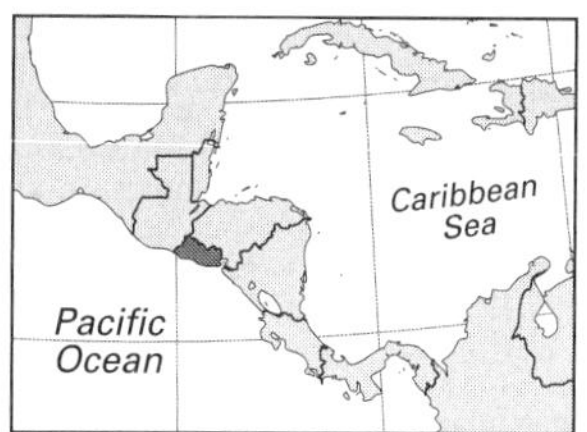

Official name: República de El Salvador (Republic of El Salvador).
Form of government: republic with one legislative house (Legislative Assembly [84]).
Chief of state and government: President.
Capital: San Salvador.
Official language: Spanish.
Official religion: none[1].
Monetary unit[2]: 1 colón (₡) = 100 centavos; valuation (Sept. 28, 2001) 1 U.S.$ = ₡8.75; 1 £ = ₡12.86.

Area and population

Departments	Capitals	area sq mi	area sq km	population 1998 estimate[3]
Ahuachapán	Ahuachapán	479	1,240	307,056
Cabañas	Sensuntepeque	426	1,104	151,079
Chalatenango	Chalatenango	779	2,017	193,866
Cuscatlán	Cojutepeque	292	756	198,643
La Libertad	Nueva San Salvador	638	1,653	642,159
La Paz	Zacatecoluca	473	1,224	283,209
La Unión	La Unión	801	2,074	283,246
Morazán	San Francisco	559	1,447	171,692
San Miguel	San Miguel	802	2,077	463,049
San Salvador	San Salvador	342	886	1,884,700
San Vicente	San Vicente	457	1,184	157,173
Santa Ana	Santa Ana	781	2,023	531,516
Sonsonate	Sonsonate	473	1,225	429,143
Usulután	Usulután	822	2,130	334,795
TOTAL		8,124	21,041[4]	6,031,326

Demography

Population (2001): 6,238,000.
Density (2001): persons per sq mi 767.8, persons per sq km 296.5.
Urban-rural (2000): urban 46.6%; rural 53.4%.
Sex distribution (2000): male 48.65%; female 51.35%.
Age breakdown (2000): under 15, 38.0%; 15–29, 28.7%; 30–44, 16.6%; 45–59, 9.5%; 60–74, 5.3%; 75 and over 1.9%.
Population projection: (2010) 7,293,000; (2020) 8,494,000.
Doubling time: 31 years.
Ethnic composition (2000): mestizo 88.3%; Amerindian 9.1%, of which Pipil 4.0%, white 1.6%; other/unknown 1.0%.
Religious affiliation (1995): Roman Catholic 78.2%; Protestant 17.1%, of which Pentecostal 13.3%; other Christian 1.9%; other 2.8%.
Major urban areas (1992): San Salvador 415,346 (metro area 1,522,126); Soyapango 261,122[5]; Santa Ana 139,389; Mejicanos 131,972[5]; San Miguel 127,696.

Vital statistics

Birth rate per 1,000 population (2000): 29.0 (world avg. 22.5); (1998) legitimate 27.2%; illegitimate 72.8%.
Death rate per 1,000 population (2000): 6.3 (world avg. 9.0).
Natural increase rate per 1,000 population (2000): 22.7 (world avg. 13.5).
Total fertility rate (avg. births per childbearing woman; 2000): 3.4.
Marriage rate per 1,000 population (1998): 4.4.
Divorce rate per 1,000 population (1998): 0.5.
Life expectancy at birth (2000): male 66.1 years; female 73.5 years.
Major causes of death per 100,000 population (1998)[6]: accidents and violence 118; diseases of the circulatory system 89; diseases of the respiratory system 60; malignant neoplasms (cancers) 58; ill-defined conditions 116.

National economy

Budget. Revenue (1997): ₡11,345,000,000 (sales taxes 50.2%, corporate taxes 14.7%, individual income taxes 11.7%, import duties 11.2%). Expenditures: ₡12,027,000,000 (education 19.6%, police 16.3%, general public services 13.6%, transportation and communications 12.4%, health 10.3%, defense 7.1%).
Public debt (external, outstanding; 1999): U.S.$2,649,000,000.
Production (metric tons except as noted). Agriculture, forestry, fishing (1999): sugarcane 5,500,000, corn (maize) 683,500, sorghum 181,500, coffee 143,800, dry beans 71,700, bananas 70,000, rice 60,400, yautia 53,000, tobacco 1,100; livestock (number of live animals) 1,141,000 cattle, 335,000 pigs; roundwood (1998) 5,129,000 cu m; fish catch (1997) 10,987, of which crustaceans 3,920. Mining and quarrying (1997): limestone 3,000,000 metric tons. Manufacturing (value added in ₡'000,000; 1996): food products 1,426; wearing apparel 1,009; soaps, cleansers, and cosmetics 932; refined petroleum 865; beverages 756; textiles 589; nonmetallic mineral products 453. Energy production (consumption): electricity (kW-hr; 1998) 3,868,000,000 (3,906,000,000); coal, none (none); crude petroleum (barrels; 1996) none (5,358,000); petroleum products (metric tons; 1996) 698,000 (1,348,000); natural gas, none (none).
Household income and expenditure. Average household size (1992–93): 4.8; average income per household (1992–93): ₡22,930 (U.S.$2,562); expenditure (1990–91)[7]: food and beverages 37.0%, housing 12.1%, transportation and communications 10.2%, clothing and footwear 6.7%.
Land use (1994): forested 5.0%; meadows and pastures 29.5%; agricultural and under permanent cultivation 35.2%; other 30.3%.
Population economically active (1995): total 2,136,400; activity rate of total population 39.1% (participation rates: ages 15–64, 62.9%; female 37.1%; unemployed [1998] 7.5%).

Price and earnings indexes (1995 = 100)

	1995	1996	1997	1998	1999	2000	2001
Consumer price index	100.0	109.8	114.7	117.6	118.2	120.9	125.7[8]
Monthly earnings index[9]	100.0	108.5	116.7	121.9	...	...	...

Gross national product (at current market prices; 1999): U.S.$11,806,000,000 (U.S.$1,920 per capita).

Structure of gross domestic product and labour force

	1998 in value ₡'000,000	1998 % of total value	1997 labour force	1997 % of labour force
Agriculture	12,532	12.1	547,100	24.3
Mining	417	0.4	1,700	0.1
Manufacturing	22,591	21.8	334,100	14.8
Construction	4,389	4.2	138,700	6.1
Public utilities	1,681	1.6	15,200	0.7
Transp. and commun.	8,304	8.0	96,700	4.3
Trade	19,850	19.1	445,100	19.7
Finance, real estate	12,191	11.7	30,300	1.3
Public admin., defense	7,116	6.9 }	467,100	20.7
Services }	14,795	14.2 }		
Other }			180,000[10]	8.0[10]
TOTAL	103,864[4]	100.0	2,256,000	100.0

Tourism (1999): receipts U.S.$211,000,000; expenditures U.S.$80,000,000.

Foreign trade[11]

Balance of trade (current prices)

	1995	1996	1997	1998	1999	2000
U.S.$'000,000	–1,855.3	–1,646.5	–1,607.6	–1,849.6	–1,965.7	–2,454.2
% of total	48.2%	44.6%	37.5%	42.3%	45.8%	47.8%

Imports (1997): U.S.$2,961,500,000 (chemicals and chemical products 17.0%, food and beverages 13.6%, nonelectrical machinery and equipment 12.8%, mineral fuels 11.4%). *Major import sources:* U.S. 41.4%; Guatemala 10.9%; Mexico 7.9%; Costa Rica 3.9%; Germany 3.2%.
Exports (1997): U.S.$1,353,900,000 (coffee 38.1%, paper and paper products 4.8%, pharmaceuticals 3.9%, raw sugar 3.9%, refined petroleum products 3.3%). *Major export destinations:* Guatemala 19.5%; U.S. 19.2%; Germany 17.5%; Honduras 10.0%; Costa Rica 8.2%.

Transport and communications

Transport. Railroads (1997): route length 562 km[12]; (1996) passenger-km 4,800,000; (1996) metric ton-km cargo 17,300,000. Roads (1997): total length 10,029 km (paved 20%). Vehicles (1997): passenger cars 177,488; trucks and buses 184,859. Air transport: (1996) passenger-km 2,181,000,000; (1995) metric ton-km cargo 16,006,000; airports (1997) with scheduled flights 1.

Communications

Medium	date	unit	number	units per 1,000 persons
Daily newspapers	1996	circulation	278,000	49
Radio	1997	receivers	2,750,000	475
Television	1999	receivers	1,777,000	196
Telephones	1999	main lines	468,068	78
Cellular telephones	1999	subscribers	382,610	64
Personal computers	1999	units	100,000	17
Internet	1999	users	40,000	6.7

Education and health

Educational attainment (1992). Percentage of population over age 25 having: no formal schooling 34.7%; incomplete primary education 37.6%; complete primary[13] 10.8%; secondary 9.4%; higher technical 2.4%; incomplete undergraduate 1.1%; complete undergraduate 2.9%; other/unknown 1.1%.
Literacy (1992): total population age 15 and over literate 2,326,800 (74.1%); males literate 1,141,007 (77.4%); females literate 1,185,793 (71.3%).

Education (1996)

	schools	teachers	students	student/teacher ratio
Primary (age 7–15)	5,025	34,496	1,130,900	32.8
Secondary (age 16–18)	...	9,255	143,588	15.5
Higher	...	5,919	112,266	19.0

Health: physicians (1997) 6,177 (1 per 936 persons); hospital beds (1996) 9,571 (1 per 593 persons); infant mortality rate per 1,000 live births (2000) 29.2.
Food (1997): daily per capita caloric intake 2,562 (vegetable products 88%, animal products 12%); 112% of FAO recommended minimum requirement.

Military

Total active duty personnel (2000): 16,800 (army 89.3%, navy 4.2%, air force 6.5%). *Military expenditure as percentage of GNP* (1997): 0.9% (world 2.6%); per capita expenditure U.S.$17.

[1]Roman Catholicism, although not official, enjoys special recognition in the constitution. [2]The U.S. dollar was legal tender in El Salvador from Jan. 1, 2001 (along with the colón) at a pegged rate of 1 U.S.$ = ₡8.75. [3]Official projection based on 1992 census. [4]Detail does not add to total given because of rounding. [5]Within San Salvador metropolitan area. [6]Projected rates based on about 78% of total deaths. [7]536,628 urban households only. [8]June. [9]Private sector only. [10]Unemployed. [11]Imports c.i.f., exports f.o.b. [12]283 km were operational in 1997. [13]Education completed through ninth grade.

Internet resources for further information:
- **Banco Central de Reserva de El Salvador http://www.bcr.gob.sv**

Equatorial Guinea

Official name: República de Guinea Ecuatorial (Spanish); République du Guinée Équatoriale (French) (Republic of Equatorial Guinea).
Form of government: republic with one legislative house (House of Representatives of the People [80]).
Chief of state: President.
Head of government: Prime Minister.
Capital: Malabo.
Official languages: Spanish; French.
Official religion: none.
Monetary unit: 1 CFA franc (CFAF) = 100 centimes; valuation (Sept. 28, 2001) 1 U.S.$ = CFAF 720.28; 1 £ = CFAF 1,058.

Area and population

Regions / Provinces	Capitals	area sq mi	area sq km	population 1987 estimate
Insular		785[1]	2,034	70,280
Annobón	Palé	7	17	2,360
Bioko Norte	Malabo	300	776	56,600
Bioko Sur	Luba	479	1,241	11,320
Continental		10,045[1]	26,017	259,950
Centro-Sur	Evinayong	3,834	9,931	55,970
Kie-Ntem	Ebebiyin	1,522	3,943	74,050
Litoral[2]	Bata	2,573	6,665	75,640
Wele-Nzas	Mongomo	2,115	5,478	54,290
TOTAL		10,831[1]	28,051	330,230

Demography

Population (2001): 486,000.
Density (2001): persons per sq mi 44.9, persons per sq km 17.3.
Urban-rural (1998): urban 45.7%; rural 54.3%.
Sex distribution (2000): male 48.71%; female 51.29%.
Age breakdown (2000): under 15, 42.7%; 15–29, 26.8%; 30–44, 15.9%; 45–59, 8.6%; 60–74, 4.9%; 75 and over, 1.1%.
Population projection: (2010) 604,000; (2020) 755,000.
Doubling time: 28 years.
Ethnic composition (1995): Fang 82.9%; Bubi 9.6%; other 7.5%.
Religious affiliation (2000): Roman Catholic 80.1%; Muslim 4.0%; African Christian 3.7%; Protestant 3.1%; other 9.1%.
Major cities (1983): Malabo 47,500[3]; Bata 37,000[3]; Ela-Nguema 6,179; Campo Yaunde 5,199; Los Angeles 4,079.

Vital statistics

Birth rate per 1,000 population (2000): 38.1 (world avg. 22.5); legitimate, n.a.; illegitimate, n.a.
Death rate per 1,000 population (2000): 13.4 (world avg. 9.0).
Natural increase rate per 1,000 population (2000): 24.7 (world avg. 13.5).
Total fertility rate (avg. births per childbearing woman; 2000): 4.9.
Marriage rate per 1,000 population: n.a.
Divorce rate per 1,000 population: n.a.
Life expectancy at birth (2000): male 51.5 years; female 55.7 years.
Major causes of death per 100,000 population: n.a.; however, major diseases include malaria (about 24% of total mortality), respiratory infections (12% of mortality), cholera, leprosy, trypanosomiasis (sleeping sickness), and waterborne (especially gastrointestinal) diseases.

National economy

Budget (1996). Revenue: CFAF 24,637,000,000 (domestic revenue 95.1%, of which oil revenue 46.9%, tax revenue 36.8%, nontax revenue 11.4%; foreign grants 4.9%). Expenditures: CFAF 32,955,000,000 (current expenditure 60.6%, of which goods and services 23.8%, salaries 17.3%, interest on debt 15.6%, transfers 3.9%; capital expenditure 9.7%).
Public debt (external, outstanding; 1999): U.S.$207,900,000.
Gross national product (at current market prices; 1999): U.S.$516,000,000 (U.S.$1,170 per capita).

Structure of gross domestic product and labour force

	1998 in value CFAF '000,000	1998 % of total value	1983 labour force	1983 % of labour force
Agriculture, fishing	40,480	15.0	59,390	57.9
Forestry	17,719	6.6		
Crude petroleum	164,969	61.3	1,616	1.6
Manufacturing	1,007	0.4		
Construction	7,752	2.9	1,929	1.9
Public utilities	3,368	1.3	224	0.2
Transportation and communications	2,100	0.8	1,752	1.7
Trade	9,625	3.6	3,059	3.0
Finance, real estate	2,135	0.8	409	0.4
Pub. admin., defense	12,723	4.7	8,377	8.2
Services	4,959	1.8		
Other	2,427[4]	0.9[4]	25,809	25.2
TOTAL	269,266[2]	100.0[2]	102,565	100.0[2]

Production (metric tons except as noted). Agriculture, forestry, fishing (1999): roots and tubers 84,000 (of which cassava 49,000, sweet potatoes 35,000), bananas 15,000, coconuts 8,000, coffee 6,300, palm oil 5,000, cacao beans 5,000, palm kernels 3,000; livestock (number of live animals) 36,000 sheep, 8,100 goats, 5,300 pigs, 4,800 cattle; roundwood (1998) 811,000 cu m; fish catch (1997) 6,090. Mining and quarrying: details, n.a.; however, in addition to quarrying for construction materials, unexploited deposits of iron ore, lead, zinc, manganese, and molybdenum are present. Manufacturing (1998): sawn timber 21,500 cu m; processed timber 3,900 cu m. Construction: n.a. Energy production (consumption): electricity (kW-hr; 1996) 20,000,000 (20,000,000); coal, none (none); crude petroleum (barrels; 1999) 39,487,000 ([1996] 37,000); petroleum products (metric tons; 1996) none (42,000); natural gas, none (none).
Population economically active (1997): total 177,000; activity rate of total population 40.0% (participation rates: ages 15–64, 74.7%; female 35.4%; unemployed [1983] 24.2%).

Price and earnings indexes (1995 = 100)

	1992	1993	1994	1995	1996	1997	1998
Consumer price index	61.3	64.1	89.7	100.0	104.5	107.7	116.2
Earnings index	...	...	...	...	...	...	...

Household income and expenditure. Average household size (1980) 4.5; income per household: n.a.; sources of income (1988): wages and salaries 57.0%, business income 42.0%, other 1.0%; expenditure (1988): food and beverages 62.0%, clothing and footwear 10.0%; medical care 6.0%.
Tourism: tourism is a government priority but remains undeveloped.
Land use (1994): forested 65.2%; meadows and pastures 3.7%; agricultural and under permanent cultivation 8.2%; built-on, wasteland, and other 22.9%.

Foreign trade[5]

Balance of trade (current prices)

	1994	1995	1996	1997	1998
CFAF '000,000,000	–1.0	–5.1	–26.1	+85.0	+15.6
% of total	1.4%	5.6%	11.5%	17.1%	5.5%

Imports (1998): CFAF 256,200,000,000 (petroleum sector 83.1%; other 16.9%). *Major import sources:* United States 35.4%; France 15.0%; Spain 9.9%; Cameroon 9.9%; United Kingdom 6.2%; The Netherlands 5.7%.
Exports (1998): CFAF 271,800,000,000 (petroleum 87.6%; wood 9.2%; cocoa 1.5%). *Major export destinations:* United States 62.0%; Spain 17.3%; China 8.9%; Japan 3.4%; France 3.4%.

Transport and communications

Transport. Railroads: none. Roads (1996): total length 1,740 mi, 2,800 km (paved 13%). Vehicles (1994): passenger cars 6,500; trucks and buses 4,000. Merchant marine (1992): vessels (100 gross tons and over) 3; total deadweight tonnage 6,699. Air transport (1996): passenger-mi 4,000,000, passenger-km 7,000,000; short ton-mi cargo 700,000, metric ton-km cargo 1,000,000; airports (1998) with scheduled flights 1.

Communications

Medium	date	unit	number	units per 1,000 persons
Daily newspapers	1996	circulation	2,000	4.9
Radio	1997	receivers	180,000	428
Television	1997	receivers	4,000	9.8
Telephones	1999	main lines	5,580	12.9
Cellular telephones	1999	units	297	0.7
Internet	1998	users	...	...

Education and health

Educational attainment (1983). Percentage of population age 15 and over having: no schooling 35.4%; some primary education 46.6%; primary 13.0%; secondary 2.3%; postsecondary 1.1%; not specified 1.6%. *Literacy* (1995): percentage of total population age 15 and over literate 77.8%; males literate 89.3%; females literate 67.4%.

Education (1993–94)

	schools	teachers	students	student/ teacher ratio
Primary (age 6–11)	781	1,381	75,751	54.9
Secondary (age 12–17)	...	466	14,511	31.1
Voc., teacher tr.	...	122	2,105	17.3
Higher	...	58	578	10.0

Health: physicians (1996) 106 (1 per 4,065 persons); hospital beds (1990) 992 (1 per 350 persons); infant mortality rate per 1,000 live births (2000) 94.8.
Food: daily per capita caloric intake, n.a.

Military

Total active duty personnel (2000): 1,320 (army 83.3%, navy 9.1%, air force 7.6%). *Military expenditure as percentage of GNP* (1996): 1.5% (world 2.6%); per capita expenditure U.S.$6.

[1]Detail does not add to total given because of rounding. [2]Includes three islets in Corisco Bay. [3]1995. [4]Import duties. [5]Imports c.i.f.; exports f.o.b.

Internet resources for further information:

- **Investir en Zone Franc**
  http://www.izf.net/izf/Index.htm

Eritrea

Official name: State of Eritrea.
Form of government: transitional regime with one interim legislative body (Transitional National Assembly [150][1]).
Head of state and government: President.
Capital: Asmara.
Official language: none.
Official religion: none.
Monetary unit: nakfa[2] = 100 cents; valuation (Sept. 28, 2001) 1 U.S.$ = Nfa 13.50; 1 £ = Nfa 19.84.

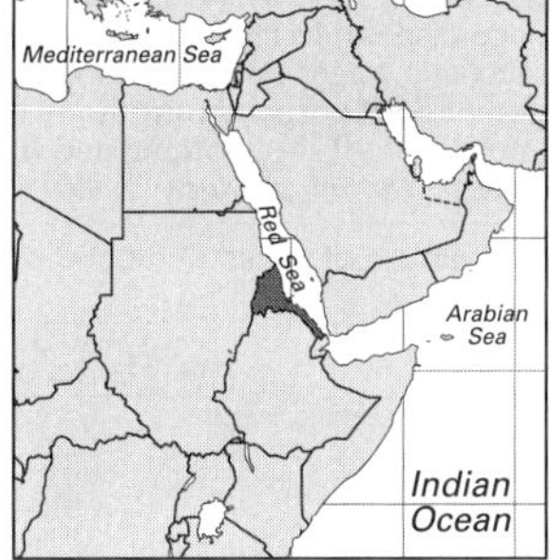

Area and population

		area[3]		population
Regions[4]	Capitals	sq mi	sq km	1997 estimate
Anseba	Keren	8,960	23,200	...
Debub	Mendefera	3,090	8,000	...
Debub-Keih-Bahri	Asseb (Aseb)	10,660	27,600	...
Gash-Barka	Barentu	12,820	33,200	...
Maekel	Asmara (Asmera)	500	1,300	...
Semien-Keih-Bahri	Massawa (Mitsiwa)	10,730	27,800	...
TOTAL		46,770[5]	121,100	3,590,000

Demography

Population (2001): 4,298,000[6].
Density (2001): persons per sq mi 91.9, persons per sq km 35.5.
Urban-rural (1992): urban 16.3%; rural 83.7%.
Sex distribution (2000): male 49.86%; female 50.14%.
Age breakdown (2000): under 15, 42.9%; 15–29, 29.0%; 30–44, 14.1%; 45–59, 8.9%; 60–74, 4.1%; 75 and over, 1.0%.
Population projection[6]: (2010) 5,709,000; (2020) 7,399,000.
Doubling time: 23 years.
Ethnolinguistic composition (2000): Tigrinya (Tigray) 51.8%; Tigré 17.9%; Afar 8.1%; Saho 4.3%; Kunama 4.1%; other 13.8%.
Religious affiliation (2000): Christian 50.5%, of which Eritrean Orthodox 46.1%; Muslim 44.7%; other 4.8%.
Major cities (1992): Asmara 400,000; Asseb 50,000; Keren 40,000; Massawa 40,000; Mendefera 14,833[7].

Vital statistics

Birth rate per 1,000 population (2000): 42.7 (world avg. 22.5).
Death rate per 1,000 population (2000): 12.3 (world avg. 9.0).
Natural increase rate per 1,000 population (2000): 30.4 (world avg. 13.5).
Total fertility rate (avg. births per childbearing woman; 2000): 5.9.
Marriage rate per 1,000 population (1992): 6.8.
Divorce rate per 1,000 population: n.a.
Life expectancy at birth (2000): male 53.4 years; female 58.3 years.
Major causes of death per 100,000 population: n.a.; morbidity (principal causes of illness) arises mainly in malaria and other infectious diseases, parasitic infections, malnutrition, diarrheal diseases, and dysenteries.

National economy

Budget (1997). Revenue: Nfa 1,967,400,000 (taxes 48.8%, of which direct taxes 22.8%, import duties 15.2%, indirect taxes 10.8%; nontax revenue 51.2%). Expenditures: Nfa 2,588,800,000 (current expenditure 55.8%, of which wages and salaries 27.3%, materials 20.1%; capital 44.2%).
Public debt (external, outstanding; 1999): U.S.$253,800,000.
Production (metric tons except as noted). Agriculture, forestry, fishing (1999): cereals 270,000, sorghum 150,000, roots and tubers 125,000, barley 40,000, millet 30,000, pulses 30,000, vegetables and melons 28,000, wheat 15,000, corn (maize) 15,000, sesame seeds 4,200, dry beans 3,000, peanuts (groundnuts) 1,800, chickpeas 1,000; livestock (number of live animals) 1,530,000 sheep, 1,400,000 goats, 1,320,000 cattle, 69,000 camels; fish catch (1996) 3,272, of which artisanal fisheries 818. Mining and quarrying (1995): salt 305,120; marble and granite are quarried, as are sand and aggregate (gravel) for construction; deposits of copper, zinc, mica, gold, iron, manganese, nickel, and lead exist but remain unexploited. Manufacturing (gross value in Nfa '000; 1997): food production 203,700; beverages 159,600; leather products and shoes 69,400; textile products 62,800; chemical products 59,700; metal products 44,300; nonmetallic products 28,500; tobacco and matches 16,600; paper and printing products 11,300. Construction (1997): Nfa 270,794,000. Energy production: energy resources include hydroelectricity, fossil fuels, geothermal power, coal, biogas, solar power, and wind; commercial electricity production for 1997 was 179,192,000 kW-hr.
Tourism (1999): receipts from visitors U.S.$28,000,000.
Household income and expenditure. Average household size (1998) 4.7; average annual income per household: n.a.; sources of income: n.a.; expenditure: n.a.
Persons economically active: n.a.

Price and earnings indexes (December 1992 = 100)

	1991	1992	1993	1994	1995
Consumer price index[8]	91.9	100.0	119.2	127.4	141.3
Earnings index	...	...	...	...	...

Gross national product (at current market prices; 1999): U.S.$779,000,000 (U.S.$200 per capita).

Structure of gross domestic product and labour force

	1999		1992	
	in value Br '000,000	% of total value	labour force	% of labour force
Agriculture	853.6	14.7	647	2.6
Manufacturing	741.2	12.7	11,894	48.3
Mining	4.7	0.1	292	1.2
Public utilities	84.0	1.4	2,284	9.3
Construction	624.9	10.7	298	1.2
Transp. and commun.	542.7	9.3	3,126	12.7
Trade	1,139.4	19.6	597	2.4
Finance	249.5	4.3	382	1.6
Pub. admin., defense	1,014.4	17.4		
Services	66.5	1.1	5,001	20.3
Other	507.6[9]	8.7[9]		
TOTAL	5,828.3[5]	100.0	24,621[5]	100.0[5]

Land use (1994): forested 7.3%; agricultural and under permanent cultivation 5.1%; meadows and pastures 69.0%; other (predominantly barren land) 18.6%.

Foreign trade[10]

Balance of trade (current prices)

	1993	1994	1995	1996	1997	1998	1999
U.S.$'000,000	–239.0	–331.4	–323.2	–418.5	–441.1	–498.9	–480.7
% of total	58.1%	72.0%	66.7%	68.7%	80.4%	89.9%	90.2%

Imports (1998): U.S.$526,800,000 (machinery and transport equipment 38.3%, manufactured goods 23.9%, food products 17.1%, chemical products 5.7%, animal and vegetable oil 2.6%, raw materials 1.6%, petroleum and petroleum products 1.5%). *Major import sources:* Italy 17.4%; United Arab Emirates 16.2%; Germany 5.7%; United Kingdom 4.5%; United States 4.2%; Japan 4.0%; The Netherlands 2.2%; Djibouti 2.1%; Belgium 1.8%; Ethiopia 0.9%.
Exports (1998): U.S.$27,900,000 (raw materials 45.5%, food products 29.6%, manufactured goods 13.2%, machinery and transport equipment 2.4%, chemical products 2.1%). *Major export destinations:* The Sudan 27.2%; Japan 13.2%; United Arab Emirates 7.3%; Ethiopia 26.5%; Italy 5.3%; The Netherlands 2.9%; United States 2.0%; Germany 1.8%.

Transport and communications

Transport. Railroads (1998): a 190-mi (306-km) rail line that formerly connected Massawa and Agordat is currently under reconstruction. A 43-mi (70-km) section of the Asmara–Massawa line was opened. A 24-mi (38-km) section between Amatere and Demas townships was reopened on Jan. 4, 1997. Roads (1996): total length 2,491 mi, 4,010 km (paved 22%). Vehicles (1996): automobiles 5,940, trucks and buses, n.a. Merchant marine: vessels (100 gross tons and over) n.a. Air transport (1993)[11]: passenger arrivals 47,645[12], passenger departures 42,548[12]; short ton cargo handled 25,907[13], metric ton cargo handled 28,557[13]; airports (1997) with scheduled flights 2.

Communications

Medium	date	unit	number	units per 1,000 persons
Radio	1995	receivers	310,000	89.6
Television	1999	receivers	60,000	15.1
Telephones	1999	main lines	27,375	6.9
Internet	1999	users	900	0.2

Education and health

Literacy (1993): total population literate *c.* 20%.

Education (1996–97)

	schools	teachers	students	student/ teacher ratio
Primary (age 7–12)	549	5,476	240,737	44.0
Secondary (age 13–18)	86[14]	1,959	88,054	44.9
Voc., teacher tr.	4[14]	112	1,145	10.2
Higher[15]	1	198	3,096	15.6

Health (1993): physicians 69 (1 per 36,000 persons); hospital beds (1986–87): 2,449 (1 per 1,100 persons); infant mortality rate per 1,000 live births (2000) 76.7.
Food (1999): daily per capita caloric intake 1,646 (vegetable 93.6%, animal products 6.4%); 71% of FAO recommended minimum requirement.

Military

Total active duty personnel (2000): estimated strength of Eritrean armed forces (predominantly former guerrillas) is between 200,000 and 250,000. UN peacekeeping force along Eritrean-Ethiopian border (October 2001): 3,900.

[1]New constitution adopted on May 23, 1997; scheduled election date for permanent legislature is December 2001. [2]The nakfa was introduced in July 1997 as the new national currency. [3]Approximate figures. The published total area is 46,774 sq mi (121,144 sq km); water area is 7,776 sq mi (20,140 sq km). [4]On May 20, 1995, a resolution was approved dividing the country into six administrative regions. [5]Detail does not add to total given because of rounding. [6]Estimate of the U.S. Bureau of the Census, International Data Base. [7]1989. [8]Asmara only; year-end. [9]Including indirect taxes less subsidies. [10]Imports c.i.f. [11]Asmara airport only. [12]January to June only. [13]1987–88. [14]1992–93. [15]1997–98.

Estonia

Official name: Eesti Vabariik (Republic of Estonia).
Form of government: unitary multiparty republic with a single legislative body (Riigikogu[1] [101]).
Chief of state: President.
Head of government: Prime Minister.
Capital: Tallinn.
Official language: Estonian.
Official religion: none.
Monetary unit: 1 kroon (EEK) = 100 sents; valuation (Sept. 28, 2001) 1 U.S.$ = EEK 17.18; 1 £ = EEK 25.26.

Area and population

Counties	Capitals	area sq mi	area sq km	population 2000 census[2]
Harju	Tallinn	1,672	4,332	529,600
Hiiu	Kärdla	395	1,023	10,500
Ida-Viru	Jõhvi	1,299	3,364	181,200
Järva	Paide	1,013	2,623	38,800
Jõgeva	Jõgeva	1,005	2,604	38,500
Lääne	Haapsalu	920	2,383	28,700
Lääne-Viru	Rakvere	1,338	3,465	67,900
Pärnu	Pärnu	1,856	4,806	91,500
Põlva	Põlva	836	2,165	32,700
Rapla	Rapla	1,151	2,980	37,600
Saare	Kuressaare	1,128	2,922	36,000
Tartu	Tartu	1,156	2,993	149,800
Valga	Valga	789	2,044	35,800
Viljandi	Viljandi	1,321	3,422	58,100
Võru	Võru	890	2,305	40,000
TOTAL		16,769[3, 4, 5]	43,431[3, 4, 5]	1,376,700

Demography

Population (2001): 1,363,000.
Density (2001)[3]: persons per sq mi 81.3, persons per sq km 31.4.
Urban-rural (1999): urban 69.1%; rural 30.9%.
Sex distribution (2000[6]): male 46.52%; female 53.48%.
Age breakdown (2000[6]): under 15, 18.0%; 15–29, 21.9%; 30–44, 21.5%; 45–59, 18.3%; 60–74, 15.0%; 75 and over, 5.3%.
Population projection: (2010) 1,312,000; (2020) 1,274,000.
Ethnic composition (2000[6]): Estonian 65.3%; Russian 28.1%; Ukrainian 2.5%; Belarusian 1.5%; Finnish 0.9%; other 1.7%.
Religious affiliation (1995): Christian 38.1%, of which Orthodox 20.4%, Evangelical Lutheran 13.7%; other (mostly nonreligious) 61.9%.
Major cities (2001[6]): Tallinn 399,850; Tartu 101,240; Narva 68,538; Kohtla-Järve 47,484; Pärnu 44,978.

Vital statistics

Birth rate per 1,000 population (2000): 9.6 (world avg. 22.5); legitimate 45.5%; illegitimate 54.5%.
Death rate per 1,000 population (2000): 13.5 (world avg. 9.0).
Natural increase rate per 1,000 population (2000): –3.9 (world avg. 13.5).
Total fertility rate (avg. births per childbearing woman; 1999): 1.2.
Marriage rate per 1,000 population (1998): 3.7.
Divorce rate per 1,000 population (1998): 3.1.
Life expectancy at birth (1999): male 65.4 years; female 76.1 years.
Major causes of death per 100,000 population (1998): diseases of the circulatory system 732.8; malignant neoplasms (cancers) 235.1; accidents, violence and homicide 162.2; diseases of the digestive system 44.4.

National economy

Budget (1998). Revenue: EEK 24,130,000,000 (social security contributions 32.9%, value-added taxes 26.6%, excise taxes 11.6%, personal income taxes 11.4%). Expenditures: EEK 24,103,000,000 (social security and welfare 30.6%, health 16.4%, education 8.6%, police 7.3%, defense 4.0%).
Public debt (external, outstanding; 1999): U.S.$205,500,000.
Production (metric tons except as noted). Agriculture, forestry, fishing (1999): potatoes 340,000, barley 198,000, wheat 135,000, oats 85,000, rye 44,000, rapeseed 30,000; livestock (number of live animals) 326,400 pigs, 307,500 cattle; roundwood (1998) 6,061,000 cu m; (1997) fish catch 123,873. Mining and quarrying (1998): oil shale 10,913,000; peat 333,500. Manufacturing (value of production in EEK '000,000; 1996): meat and meat products 2,888; dairy products 2,260; wood products (excluding furniture) 2,054; beverages 1,566; fish and fish products 1,492; furniture 1,483; textiles 1,471. Energy production (consumption): electricity (kW-hr; 1998) 8,521,000,000 (5,579,000,000); hard coal (metric tons; 1996) none (97,000); lignite (metric tons; 1996) 14,700,000 (16,000,000); crude petroleum, none (n.a.); petroleum products (metric tons; 1996) 344,000 (1,200,000); natural gas (cu m; 1996) none (689,000,000).
Tourism (1999): receipts U.S.$560,000,000; expenditures U.S.$217,000,000.
Population economically active (1997): total 707,800[7]; activity rate of total population 48.4% (participation rates: ages 15–64, 71.3%; female 47.9%; unemployed [July 2000–June 2001] 13.4%).

Price and earnings indexes (1995 = 100)

	1995	1996	1997	1998	1999	2000	2001
Consumer price index	100.0	123.1	136.1	147.2	152.1	158.2	167.9[8]
Annual earnings index	100.0	118.7	123.0	139.7	144.0	...	...

Household income and expenditure (1998). Average household size 2.3; average disposable income per household EEK 53,049 (U.S.$3,769); sources of income: wages and salaries 63.8%, transfers 24.1%, self-employment 6.2%, other 5.9%; expenditure[9]: food and beverages 35.5%, housing 14.6%, transportation 10.7%, clothing and footwear 9.0%.
Gross national product (1999): U.S.$4,906,000,000 (U.S.$3,400 per capita).

Structure of gross domestic product and labour force

	1998 in value EEK '000,000	1998 % of total value	1997 labour force[10, 11]	1997 % of labour force[10, 11]
Agriculture, fishing, forestry	4,079	5.6	60,800	8.5
Mining	763	1.0	7,600	1.1
Manufacturing	10,038	13.7	144,100	20.1
Public utilities	2,517	3.4	17,600	2.5
Construction	3,999	5.5	47,400	6.6
Trade, restaurants	12,818	17.5	105,200	14.7
Transp. and commun.	8,900	12.2	59,400	8.3
Finance, real estate	9,519	13.0	42,600	5.9
Pub. admin., defense	2,853	3.9	34,300	4.8
Services	5,909	8.1	95,800	13.3
Other	11,821[12]	16.1[12]	103,200[13]	14.4[13]
TOTAL	73,213[14]	100.0	717,800[14]	100.0[14]

Land use (1994): forest 44.7%; pasture 7.2%; agriculture 32.2%; other 15.9%.

Foreign trade[15]

Balance of trade (current prices)

	1995	1996	1997	1998	1999	2000
EEK '000,000	–8,046	–13,861	–20,925	–21,812	–17,070	–18,369
% of total	16.0%	21.7%	20.4%	19.3%	16.5%	14.6%

Imports (2000): EEK 72,246,000,000 (electrical and nonelectrical machinery 38.5%, fabricated and base metals 8.1%, textiles and apparel 7.5%). *Major import sources:* Finland 27.4%; Sweden 9.8%; Germany 9.5%; Russia 8.5%; Japan 6.1%.
Exports (2000): EEK 53,877,000,000 (electrical and nonelectrical machinery 37.5%, wood and wood products 13.4%, textiles and clothing 11.3%). *Major export destinations:* Finland 32.3%; Sweden 20.5%; Germany 8.5%; Latvia 7.0%; United Kingdom 4.4%.

Transport and communications

Transport. Railroads (1998): route length 1,018 km; passenger-km 236,000,000; metric ton-km cargo 6,079,000,000. Roads (1998): total length 16,430 km (paved 51%). Vehicles (1998): passenger cars 451,000; trucks and buses 86,900. Air transport (1998)[16]: passenger-km 166,742,000; metric ton-km cargo 901,000; airports (1997) 1.

Communications

Medium	date	unit	number	units per 1,000 persons
Daily newspapers	1996	circulation	255,000	174
Radio	1997	receivers	1,010,000	693
Television	1999	receivers	800,000	568
Telephones	1999	main lines	515,486	366
Cellular telephones	1999	subscribers	387,000	275
Personal computers	1999	units	195,000	138
Internet	1999	users	200,000	142

Education and health

Educational attainment (1989). Percentage of persons age 25 and over having: no formal schooling 2.2%; primary education 39.0%; secondary 45.1%; higher 13.7%.

Education (1995–96)

	schools	teachers	students	student/ teacher ratio
Primary (age 7–12)	727	...	125,718	...
Secondary (age 13–17)	...	9,299	95,342	10.3
Vocational	...	1,793	16,870	9.4
Higher[17]	37	...	40,621	...

Health (1998): physicians 4,471 (1 per 324 persons); hospital beds 10,509 (1 per 138 persons); infant mortality rate per 1,000 live births (2000) 8.4.
Food (1999): daily per capita caloric intake 3,154 (vegetable products 74%, animal products 26%); 123% of FAO recommended minimum requirement.

Military

Total active duty personnel (2000): 4,710 (army 91.7%, navy 5.3%, air force 3.0%). *Military expenditure as a percentage of GNP* (1997): 1.5% (world 2.6%); per capita expenditure U.S.$76.

[1]Official legislation bans translation of parliament's name. [2]March 2000 preliminary de jure figures. [3]Area used by Estonian government to calculate population densities. [4]Total area including the Estonian portion of Lake Peipus (590 sq mi [1,529 sq km]), Lake Võrtsjärv, and Muuga harbour is 17,462 sq mi (45,227 sq km). [5]Total includes 1,596 sq mi (4,133 sq km) of Baltic Sea islands. [6]January. [7]First quarter average. [8]June. [9]For a two-adult household with one child. [10]Ages 15–69 only. [11]Annual average. [12]Includes net taxes (EEK 8,406,000,000) less imputed bank service charges (EEK 1,000,000,000). [13]Includes 33,800 not adequately defined and 69,400 unemployed. [14]Detail does not add to total given because of rounding. [15]Imports c.i.f.; exports f.o.b. [16]Estonian Air. [17]1998–99.

Internet resource for further information:
- **Estonian Ministry of Economic Affairs http://www.mineco.ee/english**
- **Statistical Office of Estonia http://www.stat.ee**

Ethiopia

Official name: Federal Democratic Republic of Ethiopia.
Form of government: federal republic[1] with two legislative houses (Federal Council [108]; Council of People's Representatives [546]).
Chief of state: President.
Head of government: Prime Minister.
Capital: Addis Ababa.
Official language: none[2].
Official religion: none.
Monetary unit: 1 birr (Br) = 100 cents; valuation (Sept. 28, 2001) 1 U.S.$ = Br 8.42; 1 £ = Br 12.37.

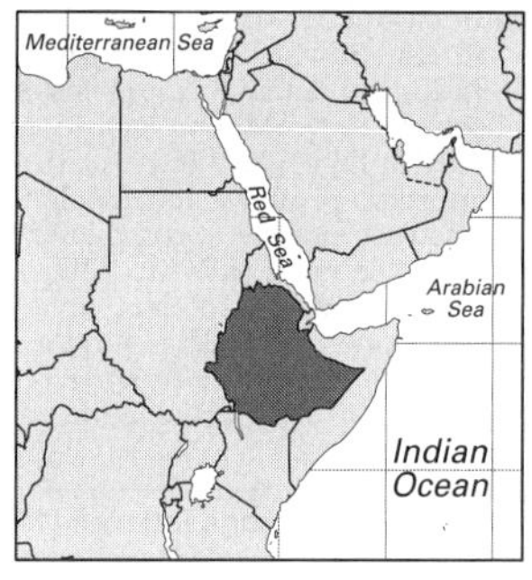

Area and population		area		population
				1994
Regional states	Capitals	sq mi	sq km	census
Afar	Aysaita	...	...	1,106,383
Amhara	Bahir Dar	66,000	170,000	13,834,297
Benishangul/ Gumuz	Asosa	20,000	51,000	460,459
Gambella	Gambella	9,758	25,274	181,862
Harari	Harer (Harar)	131	340	131,139
Oromiya	Addis Ababa	136,560	353,690	18,732,525
Somali	Jijiga	116,000	300,000	3,439,860[3]
Southern Nations, Nationalities and Peoples'	Awasa	44,000	114,000	10,377,028
Tigray	Mekele	31,000	80,000	3,136,267
Cities				
Addis Ababa	...	208	540	2,300,000
Dire Dawa	...	500	1,300	251,864
TOTAL		437,794	1,133,882	...

Demography

Population (2001): 65,892,000.
Density (2001): persons per sq mi 150.5, persons per sq km 58.1.
Urban-rural (1999): urban 17.2%; rural 82.8%.
Sex distribution (2000): male 50.19%; female 49.81%.
Age breakdown (2000): under 15, 47.0%; 15–29, 26.4%; 30–44, 14.2%; 45–59, 7.9%; 60–74, 3.7%; 75 and over, 0.8%.
Population projection: (2010) 82,312,000; (2020) 103,163,000.
Ethnolinguistic composition (1994): Galla (Oromo) 31.8%; Amharic 29.3%; Somali 6.2%; Tigrinya 5.9%; Walaita 4.6%; Gurage 4.2%; Sidamo 3.4%; Afar 1.9%; Hadya-Libide 1.7%; other 11.0%.
Religious affiliation (1994): Ethiopian Orthodox 50.3%; Muslim 32.9%; Protestant 10.1%; traditional beliefs 4.8%; Roman Catholic 0.6%; other 1.3%.
Major cities (1994): Addis Ababa 2,112,737; Dire Dawa 164,851; Harer 131,139; Nazret 127,842; Gonder 112,249.

Vital statistics

Birth rate per 1,000 population (2000): 45.1 (world avg. 22.5).
Death rate per 1,000 population (2000): 17.6 (world avg. 9.0).
Natural increase rate per 1,000 population (2000): 27.5 (world avg. 13.5).
Total fertility rate (avg. births per childbearing woman; 2001): 7.1.
Life expectancy at birth (2000): male 44.4 years; female 45.9 years.
Major causes of death (1987–88)[4, 5]: infectious and parasitic diseases 33.1%; respiratory diseases 15.7%; digestive system diseases 10.7%.

National economy

Budget (1997–98). Revenue: Br 9,686,000,000 (taxes 54.4%, of which import duties 21.0%, income and profit tax 17.1%, sales tax 12.2%, export duties 1.9%; nontax revenue 29.2%; grants 13.1%; privatization receipts 3.3%). Expenditures: Br 7,140,000,000 (general services 45.2%, of which defense 29.3%; social services 24.1%, of which education 15.8%, public health 5.6%; debt payment 12.3%).
Public debt (external, outstanding; 1999): U.S.$5,360,000,000.
Tourism (1999): receipts U.S.$16,000,000; expenditures U.S.$55,000,000.
Gross national product (1999): U.S.$6,524,000,000 (U.S.$100 per capita).

Structure of gross domestic product and labour force[4]	1997–98		1995[6]	
	in value Br '000,000[7]	% of total value	labour force	% of labour force
Agriculture	6,687.0	45.7	21,605,317	88.6
Manufacturing, mining	1,055.8	7.2	401,535	1.6
Construction	412.1	2.8	61,232	0.3
Public utilities	223.1	1.5	17,066	0.1
Transp. and commun.	907.8	6.2	103,154	0.4
Trade	1,263.3	8.7	935,937	3.8
Finance	999.2	6.8	19,451	0.1
Pub. admin., defense	1,848.3	12.7		
Services	1,234.4	8.4	1,252,224	5.1
Other	—	—		
TOTAL	14,631.0	100.0	24,395,916	100.0

Production (metric tons except as noted). Agriculture, forestry, fishing (1999): corn (maize) 2,840,000, sugarcane 2,200,000, sorghum 1,340,000, wheat 1,150,000, barley 970,000, millet 381,486, potatoes 370,000, yams 267,000, coffee 232,020, seed cotton 45,500; livestock (number of live animals) 35,095,230 cattle, 22,000,000 sheep, 16,950,000 goats, 8,580,000 horses, mules, and asses, 1,050,000 camels; roundwood (1998) 50,148,000 cu m; fish catch (1998) 14,000. Mining and quarrying (1995): cement 400,000; limestone 200,000; salt 165,000; gold 4,500 kg; platinum 48 troy oz. Manufacturing (gross value in Br '000; 1997): food 1,351,200; beverages 876,408; textiles 593,341; leather and shoes 483,364; cigarettes 240,371; paper and paper products 126,316; chemicals 29,688. Construction (authorized; 1987–88)[4, 8]: residential 260,251 sq m; nonresidential 63,346 sq m, of which commercial 16,994 sq m. Energy production (consumption)[4]: electricity (kW-hr; 1996) 1,675,000,000 (1,675,000,000); coal, none (n.a.); crude petroleum (barrels; 1996) n.a. (5,549,000); petroleum products (metric tons; 1996) 612,000 (861,000); natural gas, n.a. (n.a.).
Land use (1994): forest 13.3%; pasture 20.0%; agriculture 11.0%; other 55.7%.
Population economically active (1997): total 26,408,000; activity rate of total population 44.8% (participation rates [1995]: ages 15–64, 72.2%; female [1997] 41.0%; unemployed [1994] 62.9%).

Price index (1995 = 100)	1993	1994	1995	1996	1997	1998	1999
Consumer price index	84.5	90.9	100.0	94.6	91.4	98.9	110.0

Household income and expenditure. Average household size (1998) 5.0; income per household (1981–82)[4] Br 1,728 (U.S.$835); sources of income (1981–82): self-employment 79.5%, wages and salaries 0.2%, other 20.3%; expenditure (1988)[4]: food 66.7%, fuel and power 15.9%, clothing and footwear 6.8%, health care 3.1%, education 2.5%, household goods 2.1%.

Foreign trade

Balance of trade (current prices)	1993	1994	1995	1996	1997	1998
U.S.$'000,000	–507.1	–553.7	–713.7	–384.7	–430.5	–473.9
% of total	56.0%	42.7%	45.8%	27.0%	26.8%	29.4%

Imports (1997–98): Br 7,615,100,000 (consumer goods 24.9%, semifinished goods 17.2%, petroleum products 16.2%, transport equipment 13.2%, food and live animals 13.9%, machinery 13.1%, raw materials 2.1%). *Major import sources:* Japan 10.5%; Germany 9.8%; Saudi Arabia 9.7%; Italy 9.5%; U.K. 6.0%; India 5.7%; U.S. 4.7%.
Exports (1997–98): Br 3,966,000,000 (coffee 69.8%, hides 8.4%, pulses 2.5%, petroleum products 0.2%). *Major export destinations:* Germany 24.8%; Japan 12.2%; Saudi Arabia 9.9%; Italy 6.8%; U.S. 6.8%; Belgium 4.4%; France 3.6%.

Transport and communications

Transport. Railroads (1996–97)[9]: length 782 km; passenger-km 157,000,000; metric ton-km cargo 106,000,000. Roads (1996): total length 19,500 km (paved 15%). Vehicles (1997): passenger cars 52,012; trucks and buses 39,936. Air transport (1997)[10]: passenger-km 1,915,000,000; metric ton-km cargo 328,000,000; airports (1997) 31.

Communications				units
Medium	date	unit	number	per 1,000 persons
Daily newspapers	1997	circulation	86,00	1.5
Radio	1997	receivers	11,750,000	202
Television	1999	receivers	350,00	6.1
Telephones	1999	main lines	194,49	3.2
Personal computers	1999	units	45,00	0.7
Internet	1999	users	8,000	0.1

Education and health

Educational attainment: n.a. *Literacy* (1995): total population age 15 and over literate 35.5%; males 45.5%; females 25.3%.

Education (1994–95)	schools	teachers	students	student/ teacher ratio
Primary (age 7–12)	9,276	83,113	2,722,192	32.8
Secondary (age 13–18)	1,209[11]	22,779	747,142	32.8
Voc., teacher tr.	...	826	9,103	11.0
Higher	11[12]	1,937	32,671	16.9

Health: physicians (1988)[4] 1,466 (1 per 30,195 persons); hospital beds (1986–87)[4] 11,745 (1 per 3,873 persons); infant mortality rate (2000) 101.3.
Food (1998): daily per capita caloric intake 1,805 (vegetable products 94%, animal products 6%); 77% of FAO recommended minimum.

Military

Total active duty personnel (2000): 352,500 (army 99.3%, air force 0.7%); UN peacekeeping troops along Ethiopian-Eritrean border (October 2001): 3,900.
Military expenditure as percentage of GNP (1997): 1.9% (world 2.6%); per capita expenditure U.S.$2.

[1]Federal republic formally established on Aug. 22, 1995. [2]Amharic is the "working" language. [3]1997 enumeration. [4]Includes Eritrea. [5]Percentage of illnesses in a sample population of hospital outpatients. [6]For age 10 and up. [7]At 1980–81 factor cost. [8]Addis Ababa only. [9]Includes 62 mi (100 km) of the Chemin de Fer Djibouti-Ethiopiën (CDE) in Djibouti. [10]Ethiopian Airlines only. [11]1985–86. [12]1983–84.

Internet resources for further information:

- **Ethiopian Embassy (Washington, D.C.) http://www.ethiopianembassy.org**

Faroe Islands[1]

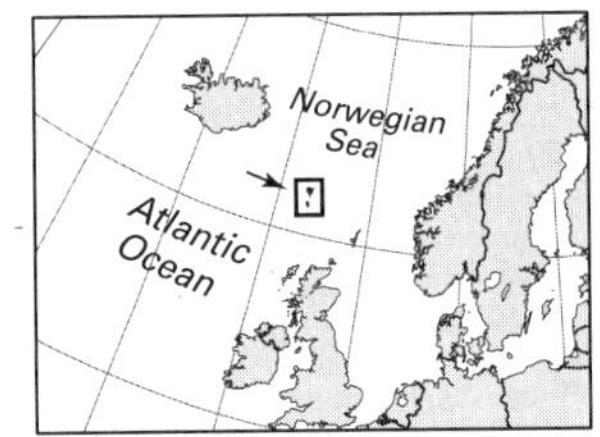

Official name: Føroyar (Faroese); Færøerne (Danish) (Faroe Islands).
Political status: self-governing region of the Danish realm with a single legislative body (Lagting [32]).
Chief of state: Danish Monarch represented by High Commissioner.
Head of home government: Prime Minister
Capital: Tórshavn (Thorshavn).
Official languages: Faroese; Danish.
Official religion: Evangelical Lutheran.
Monetary unit: 1 Danish krone[2] (Dkr) = 100 øre; valuation (Sept. 28, 2001) 1 U.S.$ = Dkr 8.17; 1£ = Dkr 12.00.

Area and population

Districts	Capitals	area sq mi	area sq km	population 2000 estimate
Klaksvík	...	[3]	[3]	5,233
Nordhara Eysturoy (Østerø Nordre)	...	[4]	[4]	1,575
Nordhoy (Norderøernes)	...	93[3]	241[3]	715
Sandoy (Sandø)	...	48	125	1,450
Streymoy (Strømø)	...	151[5]	392[5]	4,177
Sudhuroy (Suderø)	...	65	167	4,973
Sydhra Eysturoy (Østerø Søndre)	...	110[4]	286[4]	8,660
Tórshavn (Thorshavn)	...	[5]	[5]	16,801
Vágar (Vágø)	...	73	188	2,652
TOTAL		540	1,399	46,236

Demography

Population (2001): 46,600.
Density (2001): persons per sq mi 86.3; persons per sq km 33.3.
Urban-rural (2000): urban[6] 36.3%; rural 63.7%.
Sex distribution (2000): male 51.76%; female 48.24%.
Age breakdown (2000): under 15, 23.0%; 15–29, 21.1%; 30–44, 19.5%; 45–59, 18.4%; 60–74, 11.5%; 75 and over, 6.5%.
Population projection: (2010) 52,600; (2020) 60,200.
Ethnic composition (2000): Faroese 97.0%; Danish 2.5%; other Scandinavian 0.4%; other 0.1%.
Religious affiliation (1995): Evangelical Lutheran Church of Denmark 80.8%; Plymouth Brethren 10.1%; Roman Catholic 0.2%; other (mostly nonreligious) 8.9%.
Major towns (2000): Tórshavn 16,673; Klaksvík 4,762; Runavík 2,461; Tvøroyri 1,822.

Vital statistics

Birth rate per 1,000 population (2000): 15.2 (world avg. 22.5); (1998) legitimate 62.0%; illegitimate 38.0%.
Death rate per 1,000 population (2000): 7.8 (world avg. 9.0).
Natural increase rate per 1,000 population (2000): 7.4 (world avg. 13.5).
Total fertility rate (avg. births per childbearing woman; 2000): 2.3.
Marriage rate per 1,000 population (1998): 4.7.
Divorce rate per 1,000 population (1994): 0.8.
Life expectancy at birth (2000): male 75.0 years; female 81.9 years.
Major causes of death per 100,000 population (1992): diseases of the circulatory system 354.5, of which ischemic heart disease 222.1, cerebrovascular disease 81.2; malignant neoplasms (cancers) 192.2; diseases of the respiratory system 59.8, of which pneumonia 36.3, bronchitis, emphysema, and asthma 17.1; suicides 8.5; automobile accidents 4.3.

National economy

Budget (1999). Revenue: Dkr 3,104,530,000 (income taxes 33.8%; customs and excise duties 32.4%; transfers from the Danish government 30.4%). Expenditures: Dkr 3,105,530,000 (health and social welfare 43.3%; education 16.6%; debt service 7.7%; agriculture, fishing, and commerce 7.5%; administration 6.0%).
Gross national product (at current market prices; 2000): U.S.$1,029,000,000 (U.S.$22,460 per capita).

Structure of gross domestic product and labour force

	1999 in value Dkr '000,000	1999 % of total value	1977 labour force	1977 % of labour force
Agriculture	53	0.8	282	1.6
Fishing	1,344	20.5	3,032	17.2
Mining	18	0.3	3,854 (Mining and Manufacturing)	21.9 (Mining and Manufacturing)
Manufacturing	744	11.4		
Construction	321	4.9	1,952	11.1
Public utilities	150	2.3	[7]	[7]
Transp. and commun.	552	8.4	1,944	11.1
Trade, hotels	768	11.7	2,237[7]	12.7[7]
Finance and real estate	1,145	17.5	[7]	[7]
Pub. admin., defense	1,556	23.8	2,927	16.6
Services	234	3.6	796	4.5
Other	–340[8]	–5.2[8]	561[9]	3.2[9]
TOTAL	6,546[10]	100.0	17,585	100.0[10]

Production (metric tons except as noted). Agriculture, forestry, fishing (2000): potatoes 1,500, other vegetables, grass, hay, and silage are produced; livestock (number of live animals) 68,100 sheep, 2,000 cattle; fish catch (1999) 358,013 (of which blue whiting 105,106, mackeral 56,476, saithe 34,423, cod 33,725, capelin 24,275, prawns, shrimps, and other crustaceans 20,916, haddock 19,697). Mining and quarrying: negligible[11]. Manufacturing (value added in Dkr '000,000; 1999): processed fish 393; all other manufacturing 351; important products include handicrafts and woolen textiles and clothing. Construction (1993): completed dwellings 41. Energy production (consumption): electricity (kW-hr; 1999) 201,000,000 ([1997] 181,000,000); coal, none (none); crude petroleum, none (none); petroleum products (metric tons; 1996) none (206,000); natural gas, none (none).
Population economically active (1997): total 26,500; activity rate of total population c. 60% (participation rates: age 14–64, n.a.; female c. 46%; unemployed c. 10%).

Price and earnings indexes (1995 = 100)

	1995	1996	1997	1998	1999	2000
Consumer price index	100.0	102.6	106.0	109.6	114.6	119.6
Hourly wage index	100.0	100.0	101.5	102.5	104.4	109.3

Public debt (to Denmark; end of 1999): U.S.$653,000,000.
Household income and expenditure. Average household size (1977) 3.7; average annual income per household: n.a.; sources of income[12]: self-employment 11.7%, wages and salaries 88.3%; expenditure (1980): food and beverages 40.9%, fuel and energy 18.9%, housing 17.5%, clothing and footwear 11.3%, other 11.4%.
Tourism (1987): receipts from visitors U.S.$10,000,000; expenditures by nationals abroad U.S.$42,600,000.
Land use (1994): forested, none; meadows and pastures, none; agricultural and under permanent cultivation 2.1%; other 97.9%.

Foreign trade

Balance of trade (current prices)

	1995	1996	1997	1998	1999	2000
Dkr '000,000	+260	+270	+198	+331	–24	–404
% of total	6.8%	5.9%	4.0%	6.0%	0.4%	5.1%

Imports (1999): Dkr 3,276,000,000 (goods for household consumption 25.7%; machinery and transport equipment 16.1%; petroleum products 8.1%). *Major import sources:* Denmark 27.8%; Norway 26.1%; Germany 7.2%; United Kingdom 5.9%; Sweden 4.5%.
Exports (1999): Dkr 3,252,154,000 (fish for human consumption 90.3%, of which frozen fish 29.9%, fresh chilled fish 15.3%, dried, salted, and smoked fish 13.8%; ships 4.3%). *Major export destinations:* Denmark 32.1%; United Kingdom 21.2%; France 9.4%; Spain 6.7%; Germany 6.7%; United States 4.6%.

Transport and communications

Transport. Railroads: none. Roads (1998): total length 285 mi, 458 km (paved, n.a.). Vehicles (2000): passenger cars 14,608; trucks and buses 3,455. Merchant marine (1998): vessels (20 gross tons and over) 232; total gross tonnage 77,435. Air transport (1998): airports with scheduled flights 1.

Communications

Medium	date	unit	number	units per 1,000 persons
Daily newspapers	1996	circulation	6,000	136
Radio	1997	receivers	26,000	582
Television	1997	receivers	15,000	333
Telephones	1999	main lines	25,000	556
Cellular telephones	1999	subscribers	11,000	244
Internet	1998	users	5,000	113

Education and health

Education (1997–98)

	schools	teachers	students	student/ teacher ratio
Primary (first 7 grades)	68 (Primary and Secondary)	...	5,037	...
Secondary			2,750	...
Voc., teacher tr.	11	...	2,195[13]	...
Higher[14]	1	18	70[15]	...

Health (1998): physicians 83 (1 per 537 persons); hospital beds 277 (1 per 161 persons); infant mortality rate per 1,000 live births (2000) 6.9.
Food (1979–81): daily per capita caloric intake 3,195 (vegetable products 68%, animal products 32%); 120% of FAO recommended minimum requirement.

Military

Defense responsibility lies with Denmark.

[1]English-language alternative spelling is Faeroe Islands. [2]The local currency, the Faroese króna (Fkr), is equivalent to the Danish krone. Banknotes used are Faroese or Danish; coins are Danish. [3]Nordhoy contains Klaksvík. [4]Sydhra Eysturoy contains Nordhara Eysturoy. [5]Streymoy contains Tórshavn. [6]Tórshavn only. [7]Trade, hotels includes Public utilities and Finance and real estate. [8]Imputed bank service charges. [9]Not adequately defined. [10]Detail does not add to total given because of rounding. [11]The maritime boundary demarcation agreement between the Shetland Islands (U.K.) and the Faroes in May 1999 allowed for the exploration of deep-sea petroleum. [12]Percentages refer to principal sources of income of economically active population. [13]1996–97. [14]University of the Faroe Islands. [15]Full-time students only.

Internet resources for further information:
- **Statistics Faroe Islands http://www.hagstova.Fo/Welcome_uk.html**
- **Governmental Bank: Information Memorandum on the Faroe Islands http://www.landsbank.fo**

Fiji

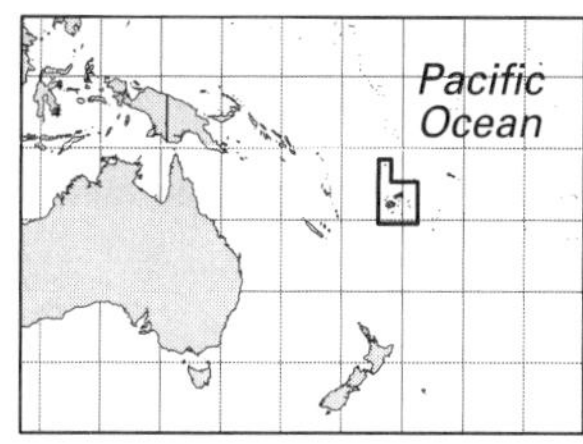

Official name: Republic of the Fiji Islands[1].
Form of government: multiparty republic with two legislative houses (Senate [32[2]]; House of Representatives [71]).
Chief of state: President.
Head of government: Prime Minister.
Capital: Suva.
Official language: [3].
Official religion: none
Monetary unit: 1 Fiji dollar (F$) = 100 cents; valuation (Sept. 28, 2001) 1 U.S.$ = F$2.32; 1 £ = F$3.41.

Area and population		area		population
Divisions				1996
Provinces	Capitals	sq mi	sq km	census
Central	Suva			
Naitasiri	—	643	1,666	126,641
Namosi	—	220	570	5,742
Rewa	—	105	272	101,547
Serua	—	320	830	15,461
Tailevu	—	369	955	48,216
Eastern	Levuka			
Kadavu	—	185	478	9,535
Lau	—	188	487	12,211
Lomaiviti	—	159	411	16,214
Rotuma	—	18	46	2,810
Northern	Labasa			
Bua	—	532	1,379	14,988
Cakaudrove	—	1,087	2,816	44,321
Macuata	—	774	2,004	80,207
Western	Lautoka			
Ba	—	1,017	2,634	212,197
Nadroga-Navosa	—	921	2,385	54,083
Ra	—	518	1,341	30,904
TOTAL	—	7,055[4]	18,272[4]	775,077

Demography

Population (2001): 827,000.
Density (2001): persons per sq mi 117.3, persons per sq km 45.3.
Urban-rural (1996): urban 46.4%; rural 53.6%.
Sex distribution (2000): male 50.25%; female 49.75%.
Age breakdown (2000): under 15, 33.4%; 15–29, 28.3%; 30–44, 20.3%; 45–59, 12.1%; 60–74, 5.2%; 75 and over, 0.7%.
Population projection: (2010) 938,000; (2020) 1,067,000.
Doubling time: 39 years.
Ethnic composition (1996): Fijian 50.8%; Indian 43.7%[5]; other 5.5%.
Religious affiliation (1986): Christian 52.9%; Hindu 38.1%; Muslim 7.8%; Sikh 0.7%; other 0.5%.
Major cities (1996; "urban centres"): Suva 167,421; Lautoka 42,917; Nadi 30,791; Labasa 24,187; Nausori 21,645.

Vital statistics

Birth rate per 1,000 population (2000): 23.5 (world avg. 22.5).
Death rate per 1,000 population (2000): 5.8 (world avg. 9.0).
Natural increase rate per 1,000 population (2000): 17.7 (world avg. 13.5).
Total fertility rate (avg. births per childbearing woman; 2000): 2.9.
Life expectancy at birth (2000): male 65.5 years; female 70.5 years.
Major causes of death per 100,000 population (1987): diseases of the circulatory system 153.4; malignant neoplasms (cancers) 35.5; accidents, poisoning, and violence 32.2; diseases of the respiratory system 31.7.

National economy

Budget (1998). Revenue: F$848,646,000 (income taxes, estate taxes, and gift duties 58.4%; customs duties and port dues 27.0%; fees, royalties, and sales 5.5%). Expenditures: F$1,029,456,000 (departmental expenditure 61.1%; public-debt charges 35.8%; pensions and gratuities 3.1%).
Production (metric tons except as noted). Agriculture, forestry, fishing (1999): sugarcane 4,398,000, coconuts 209,000, cassava 27,000, taro 26,000, paddy rice 18,000, sweet potatoes 7,400, bananas 6,400, yams 3,400, tomatoes 2,800, pineapples 2,500; livestock (number of live animals) 345,000 cattle, 235,000 goats, 112,000 pigs; roundwood (1998) 594,000 cu m; fish catch (1998) 28,212. Mining and quarrying (1995): gold 3,477 kg; silver 1,572 kg. Manufacturing (U.S.$'000,000; 1994): food products 84; wearing apparel 28; wood and wood products 16; beverages 15; chemical products 13. Construction (1995): residential 97,000 sq m; nonresidential 64,000 sq m. Energy production (consumption): electricity (kW-hr; 1996) 545,000,000 (545,000,000); coal (metric tons; 1996) none (22,000); crude petroleum, none (n.a.); petroleum products (metric tons; 1996) none (219,000); natural gas, none (n.a.).
Tourism (1999): receipts from visitors U.S.$275,000,000; expenditures by nationals abroad U.S.$66,000,000.
Land use (1994): forested 64.9%; agricultural and under permanent cultivation 14.2%; meadows and pastures 9.5%; other 11.4%.
Population economically active (1986): total 241,160; activity rate of total population 33.7% (participation rates: ages 15–64, 56.0%; female 21.2%; unemployed [1990] 6.4%).

Price and earnings indexes (1995 = 100)	1994	1995	1996	1997	1998	1999	2000
Consumer price index	97.9	100.0	103.1	106.5	112.6	114.8	116.1
Earnings index	...	...	...	...	...	...	...

Gross national product (1999): U.S.$1,848,000,000 (U.S.$2,310 per capita).

Structure of gross domestic product and labour force	1997		1986	
	in value F$'000[6]	% of total value[6]	labour force	% of labour force
Agriculture	323,600	17.3	106,305	44.1
Mining	62,722	3.4	1,345	0.5
Manufacturing	267,452	14.3	18,106	7.5
Construction	82,306	4.4	11,786	4.9
Public utilities	78,967	4.2	2,154	0.9
Transp. and commun.	245,294	13.1	13,151	5.4
Trade	310,196	16.6	26,010	10.8
Finance	249,115	13.3	6,016	2.5
Pub. admin., defense / Services	364,640	19.5	36,619	15.2
Other	–115,828[7]	–6.17	19,668[8]	8.2[8]
TOTAL	1,868,464	100.0	241,160	100.0

Public debt (external, outstanding; 1999): U.S.$120,700,000.
Household income and expenditure. Average household size (1986) 5.7; income per household (1980) F$2,837 (U.S.$3,546); sources of income (1973): wages and salaries 81.5%, self-employment 9.1%, other 9.4%; expenditure (1991[9]): food, beverages, and tobacco 41.5%, housing and energy 21.4%, transportation and communications 12.9%, household durable goods 6.5%.

Foreign trade

Balance of trade (current prices)	1993	1994	1995	1996	1997	1998
F$'000,000	–521.42	–409.36	–454.45	–225.26	–334.16	–204.8
% of total	30.7%	20.4%	22.9%	10.9%	16.8%	9.2%

Imports (1997): F$1,392,664,000 (durable manufactures 27.6%; machinery and transport equipment 20.6%; food, beverages, and tobacco 14.8%; petroleum products 14.1%; miscellaneous manufactured consumer articles 12.4%; chemicals 7.8%). *Major import sources:* Australia 45.2%; New Zealand 15.4%; Japan 6.9%; United States 5.2%; Singapore 4.2%; China 2.9%; Taiwan 2.4%; Hong Kong 2.2%; Thailand 1.9%; United Kingdom 1.8%.
Exports (1997)[10]: F$714,621,000 (sugar 24.4%; clothing 23.5%; gold 8.7%; fish 5.3%; timber 3.5%; molasses 1.8%; coconut oil 0.8%). *Major export destinations*[11]: Australia 40.5%; United Kingdom 21.4%; Japan 13.4%; United States 10.2%; New Zealand 6.3%; Malaysia 2.4%.

Transport and communications

Transport. Railroads (1995)[12]: length 370 mi, 595 km. Roads (1995): total length 3,200 mi, 5,100 km (paved 20%). Vehicles (1995): passenger cars 49,712; trucks and buses 33,928. Merchant marine (1992). vessels (100 gross tons and over) 64; total deadweight tonnage 60,444. Air transport (1996)[13]: passenger-km 1,194,652,000; metric ton-km cargo 75,367,000; airports(1997) with scheduled flights 13.

Communications Medium	date	unit	number	units per 1,000 persons
Daily newspapers	1996	circulation	40,000	51
Radio	1997	receivers	500,000	636
Television	1999	receivers	88,908	111
Telephones	1999	main lines	81,518	101
Cellular telephones	1999	subscribers	23,380	29
Personal computers	1999	units	40,000	50
Internet	1999	users	7,500	9.3

Education and health

Educational attainment (1986). Percentage of population age 25 and over having: no formal schooling 28.3%; primary only 19.1%; some secondary 44.1%; secondary 4.1%; postsecondary 3.3%; other 1.1%. *Literacy* (1995): total population age 15 and over literate 91.6%; males 93.8%; females 89.3%.

Education (1997)	schools	teachers	students	student/ teacher ratio
Primary (age 5–15)	693[14]	5,011	142,781	28.5
Secondary (age 16–19)	142[14]	3,519	70,098	19.9
Voc., teacher tr.[14]	45	625	7,283	11.6
Higher[15]	5[16]	277	7,908	28.5

Health (1998): physicians 252 (1 per 3,147 persons); hospital beds 1,797 (1 per 441 persons); infant mortality rate per 1,000 live births (2000) 14.5.
Food (1999): daily per capita caloric intake 2,934 (vegetable products 81%, animals products 19%); 129% of FAO recommended minimum requirement.

Military

Total active duty personnel (2000): 3,500 (army 91.4%, navy 8.6%, air force, none). *Military expenditure as percentage of GNP* (1997): 2.4% (world 2.6%); per capita expenditure U.S.$61.

[1]The long-form name in Fijian is Kai Vakarairai ni Fiji. [2]All seats are nonelected. [3]English, Fijian, and Hindustani (Fijian Hindi) have equal status per 1998 constitution. [4]Detail does not add to total given because of rounding. [5]The emigration of Indian population after the coup in 1987 has resulted in the reemergence of a Fijian majority. [6]Constant 1989 prices. [7]Less imputed bank service charges. [8]Not stated and unemployed. [9]Weights of consumer price index components based on 3,000 urban households. [10]Excludes reexports valued at F$138,906,000. [11]Based on exports of local products only. [12]Owned by the Fiji Sugar Corporation. [13]Air Pacific only. [14]1992. [15]1991. [16]1983.

Internet resources for further information:

- **Fiji Islands Statistics Bureau http://www.statsfiji.gov.fj**
- **Fiji Government Online http://www.fiji.gov.fj**

Finland

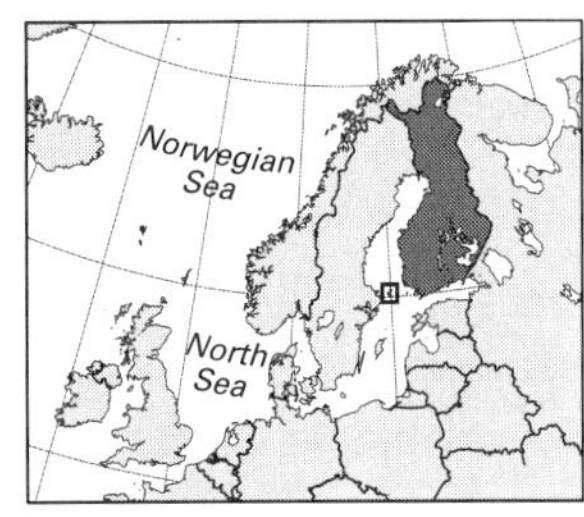

Official names[1]: Suomen Tasavalta (Finnish); Republiken Finland (Swedish) (Republic of Finland).
Form of government: multiparty republic with one legislative house (Parliament [200[2]]).
Chief of state: President.
Head of government: Prime Minister.
Capital: Helsinki.
Official languages: none[1].
Official religion: none.
Monetary unit: 1 markka (Fmk) = 100 penniä, valuation (Sept. 28, 2001) 1 U.S.$ = Fmk 6.53; 1 £ = Fmk 9.60; 1 € = Fmk 5.94573.

Area and population

		area		population
Provinces	**Capitals**	sq mi	sq km	2000 estimate[3]
Eastern Finland	Mikkeli	23,444	60,720	595,113
Lapland	Rovaniemi	38,203	98,946	194,352
Oulu	Oulu	23,773	61,572	453,469
Southern Finland	Hämeenlinna	13,273	34,378	2,068,259
Western Finland	Turku	31,265	80,976	1,834,403
Autonomous Territory				
Åland (Ahvenamaa)	Mariehamn (Maarianhamina)	599	1,552	25,706
TOTAL		130,559[4, 5]	338,145[4, 5]	5,171,302

Demography

Population (2001): 5,185,000.
Density (2000)[6]: persons per sq mi 44.1, persons per sq km 17.0.
Urban-rural (2000): urban 60.4%; rural 39.6%[7].
Sex distribution (2000[3]): male 48.79%; female 51.21%.
Age breakdown (2000[3]): under 15, 18.2%; 15–29, 18.7%; 30–44, 21.8%; 45–59, 21.5%; 60–74, 13.4%; 75 and over, 6.4%.
Population projection: (2010) 5,252,000; (2020) 5,292,000.
Ethnolinguistic composition (by place of birth; 2000[3]): Finland 97.5%; Russia 0.6%; Sweden 0.5%; Africa 0.2%.
Religious affiliation (2000[3]): Evangelical Lutheran 85.2%; Finnish (Greek) Orthodox 1.1%; nonreligious 12.6%; other 1.1%.
Major cities (2000[3]): Helsinki 551,123 (metro area 945,725); Espoo 209,667[8]; Tampere 193,174; Vantaa 176,386[8]; Turku 172,107; Oulu 117,670.

Vital statistics

Birth rate per 1,000 population (1999): 11.2 (world avg. 22.5); legitimate 61.3%; illegitimate 38.7%.
Death rate per 1,000 population (1999): 9.5 (world avg. 9.0).
Natural increase rate per 1,000 population (1999): 1.7 (world avg. 13.5).
Total fertility rate (avg. births per childbearing woman; 1999): 1.7.
Marriage rate per 1,000 population (1999): 4.7.
Divorce rate per 1,000 population (1999): 2.7.
Life expectancy at birth (1999): male 73.7 years; female 81.0 years.
Major causes of death per 100,000 population (1997): ischemic heart diseases 245.4; malignant neoplasms (cancers) 202.7; cerebrovascular diseases 103.2; accidents and violence 83.3; diseases of the respiratory system 77.8.

National economy

Budget (2000). Revenue: Fmk 199,579,000,000 (income and property taxes 33.7%, value-added taxes 27.7%, excise duties 13.8%). Expenditures: Fmk 199,575,000,000 (social security and health 21.8%, education 14.0%, interest on state debt 13.4%, agriculture and forestry 6.6%, defense 4.9%).
National debt (December 1998): U.S.$82,690,000,000.
Tourism (in U.S.$'000,000; 1999): receipts 1,517; expenditures 2,021.
Production (metric tons except as noted). Agriculture, forestry, fishing (1999): silage 6,799,000, barley 1,568,000, sugar beets 1,172,000, oats 990,000, potatoes 791,000, wheat 254,000; livestock (number of live animals; 2000) 1,541,000 pigs, 1,101,000 cattle, (1999) 195,000 reindeer; roundwood (1999) 53,851,000 cu m; fish catch (1997) 196,513. Mining and quarrying (1998): chromite (gross weight) 498,000; gold 5,000 kilograms. Manufacturing (value added in Fmk '000,000; 1998): wood pulp, paper, and paper products 24,304; radio, television, and communications equipment 21,271; nonelectrical machinery 17,398; food and beverages 11,505; fabricated metals 9,485; printing and publishing 9,368; wood and wood products (excluding furniture) 7,498. Energy production (consumption): electricity (kW-hr; 1999) 66,655,000,000 (77,779,000,000); coal (metric tons; 1996) none (7,704,000); crude petroleum (barrels; 1996) none (71,746,000); petroleum products (metric tons; 1996) 11,861,000 (10,355,000); natural gas (cu m; 1996) none (3,582,000,000).
Population economically active (1999): total 2,557,000; activity rate of total population 49.5% (participation rates: ages 15–64, 73.6%; female 47.8%; unemployed [October 1999–September 2000] 10.0%).

Price and earnings indexes (1995 = 100)

	1994	1995	1996	1997	1998	1999	2000
Consumer price index	99.0	100.0	100.6	101.8	103.2	104.4	109.3
Annual earnings index	95.5	100.0	103.9	106.0	...	...	...

Household income and expenditure (1998). Average household size 2.2; disposable income per household Fmk 146,400 (U.S.$27,395); sources of gross income: wages and salaries 55.4%, transfer payments 27.4%, other 17.2%; expenditure: housing and energy 27.3%, transportation and communications 18.9%, food, beverages, and tobacco 16.5%.
Gross national product (1999): U.S.$127,764,000,000 (U.S.$24,730 per capita).

Structure of gross domestic product and labour force

	1999			
	in value Fmk '000,000	% of total value	labour force	% of labour force
Agriculture, fishing	7,891	1.1	121,000	4.7
Forestry	15,202	2.1	23,000	0.9
Mining	1,743	0.2	488,000	19.1
Manufacturing	155,340	21.5		
Public utilities	12,838	1.8	...	...
Construction	35,276	4.9	149,000	5.8
Transp. and commun.	57,720	8.0	168,000	6.6
Trade, restaurants	76,872	10.6	355,000	13.9
Finance, real estate	131,859	18.2	267,000	10.4
Pub. admin., defense	112,477	15.5	116,000	4.5
Services	17,809	2.5	603,000	23.6
Other	98,587[9]	13.6[9]	267,000[10]	10.4[10]
TOTAL	723,614	100.0	2,557,000	100.0[4]

Land use (1994): forested 76.1%; meadows and pastures 0.4%; agricultural and under permanent cultivation 8.5%; other 15.0%.

Foreign trade[11]

Balance of trade (current prices)

	1994	1995	1996	1997	1998	1999
Fmk '000,000	+33,552	+47,466	+44,164	+51,845	+57,750	+56,807
% of total	12.2%	15.6%	13.6%	13.9%	14.3%	13.9%

Imports (1999): Fmk 176,536,000,000 (electrical machinery and apparatus 16.7%; nonelectrical machinery and apparatus 15.4%; mineral fuels 8.5%; automobiles 8.4%). *Major import sources:* Germany 15.3%; Sweden 11.2%; U.S. 7.9%; Russia 7.2%; U.K. 6.6%; Japan 6.2%; France 4.3%.
Exports (1999): Fmk 233,343,000,000 (electrical machinery and apparatus 23.7%; paper and paper products 20.5%; nonelectrical machinery and apparatus 11.8%; wood products and furniture 7.2%). *Major export destinations:* Germany 13.1%; Sweden 9.9%; U.K. 9.1%; U.S. 7.9%; France 5.3%; The Netherlands 4.3%; Russia 4.1%.

Transport and communications

Transport. Railroads: route length (1999) 5,836 km; passenger-km 3,415,000,000; metric ton-km cargo 9,753,000,000. Roads (2000[3, 12]): total length 77,900 km (paved 65%). Vehicles (2000[3]): passenger cars 2,069,055; trucks and buses 300,048. Air transport (1999): passenger-km 12,916,000,000; metric ton-km cargo 315,883,000; airports (1999) 27.

Communications

Medium	date	unit	number	units per 1,000 persons
Daily newspapers	1996	circulation	2,332,000	455
Radio	1997	receivers	7,700,000	1,498
Television	1997	receivers	3,200,000	623
Telephones	1999	main lines	2,850,000	552
Cellular telephones	1999	subscribers	3,364,000	651
Personal computers	1999	units	1,860,000	360
Internet	1999	users	2,143,000	415

Education and health

Educational attainment (end of 1998). Percentage of population age 25 and over having: incomplete upper-secondary education 40.7%; complete upper secondary or vocational 33.6%; higher 25.7%. *Literacy:* virtually 100%.

Education (1999–2000)

	schools	teachers	students	student/ teacher ratio
Primary/Lower Secondary (age 7–15)	4,101	41,631[13]	591,272	...
Upper Secondary (age 16–18)	456	6,693 [13]	130,624	...
Voc. (incl. higher)	398	...	258,845	...
Higher[14]	20	7,252[13]	152,466	...

Health (1999): physicians 15,794[15] (1 per 327 persons); hospital beds (1998) 39,718 (1 per 130 persons); infant mortality rate per 1,000 live births 4.2.
Food (1998): daily per capita caloric intake 3,180 (vegetable products 61%, animal products 39%); 117% of FAO recommended minimum requirement.

Military

Total active duty personnel (2000): 31,700 (army 75.7%, navy 15.8%, air force 8.5%). *Military expenditure as percentage of GNP* (1997): 1.7% (world 2.6%); per capita expenditure U.S.$381.

[1]Finnish and Swedish were official languages until mid-1995 and national languages thereafter. [2]Includes one representative from Åland not taking part in the 1999 general elections. [3]January 1. [4]Detail does not add to total given because of rounding. [5]Total includes land area of 117,580 sq mi (304,530 sq km) and inland water area of 12,979 sq mi (33,615 sq km). [6]Based on land area only. [7]Includes semi-urban (16.5% of total). [8]Within Helsinki metro area. [9]Taxes less subsidies and imputed bank service charges. [10]Includes 261,000 unemployed persons not previously employed and 6,000 not adequately defined. [11]Imports c.i.f., exports f.o.b. [12]Excludes Åland Islands. [13]1998–99. [14]Universities only. [15]Registered professionals of working age.

Internet resources for further information:
- **Embassy of Finland (Washington, D.C.) http://www.finland.org/facts.html**
- **Statistics Finland http://www.stat.fi/index_en.html**

France

Official name: République Française (French Republic).
Form of government: republic with two legislative houses (Parliament; Senate [321], National Assembly [577]).
Chief of state: President.
Head of government: Prime Minister.
Capital: Paris.
Official language: French.
Official religion: none.
Monetary unit: 1 franc (F) = 100 centimes; valuation (Sept. 28, 2001) 1 U.S.$ = F 7.20; 1 £ = F 10.59; 1 € = F 6.55957.

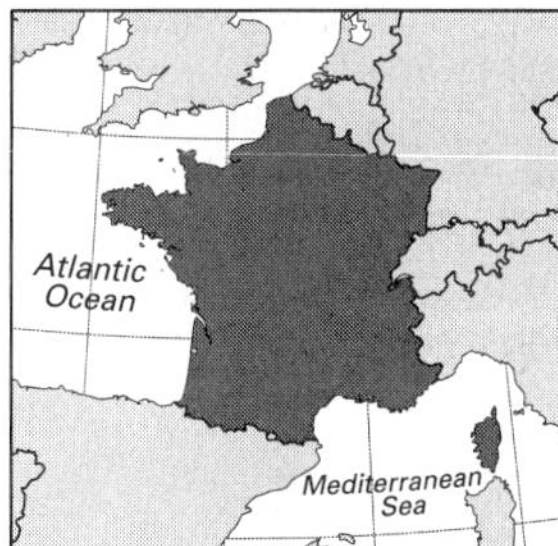

Area and population

Regions / Departments	Capitals	area sq mi	area sq km	population 1999 census
Alsace	Strasbourg			
Bas-Rhin	Strasbourg	1,836	4,755	1,026,120
Haut-Rhin	Colmar	1,361	3,525	708,025
Aquitaine	Bordeaux			
Dordogne	Périgueux	3,498	9,060	388,293
Gironde	Bordeaux	3,861	10,000	1,287,334
Landes	Mont-de-Marsan	3,569	9,243	327,334
Lot-et-Garonne	Agen	2,070	5,361	305,380
Pyrénées-Atlantiques	Pau	2,952	7,645	600,018
Auvergne	Clermont-Ferrand			
Allier	Moulins	2,834	7,340	344,721
Cantal	Aurillac	2,211	5,726	150,778
Haute-Loire	Le Puy	1,922	4,977	209,113
Puy-de-Dôme	Clermont-Ferrand	3,077	7,970	604,266
Basse-Normandie	Caen			
Calvados	Caen	2,142	5,548	648,385
Manche	Saint-Lô	2,293	5,938	481,471
Orne	Alençon	2,356	6,103	292,337
Bourgogne	Dijon			
Côte-d'Or	Dijon	3,383	8,763	506,755
Nièvre	Nevers	2,632	6,817	225,198
Saône-et-Loire	Mâcon	3,311	8,575	544,893
Yonne	Auxerre	2,868	7,427	333,221
Bretagne	Rennes			
Côtes-d'Armor	Saint-Brieuc	2,656	6,878	542,373
Finistère	Quimper	2,600	6,733	852,418
Ille-et-Vilaine	Rennes	2,616	6,775	867,533
Morbihan	Vannes	2,634	6,823	643,873
Centre	Orléans			
Cher	Bourges	2,793	7,235	314,428
Eure-et-Loir	Chartres	2,270	5,880	407,665
Indre	Châteauroux	2,622	6,791	231,139
Indre-et-Loire	Tours	2,366	6,127	554,003
Loir-et-Cher	Blois	2,449	6,343	314,968
Loiret	Orléans	2,616	6,775	618,126
Champagne-Ardenne	Châlons su Marne			
Ardemmes	Charleville-Mézières	2,019	5,229	290,130
Aube	Troyes	2,318	6,004	292,131
Haute-Marne	Chaumont	2,398	6,211	194,873
Marne	Châlons-sur-Marne	3,151	8,162	565,229
Corse[1] (Corsica)	Ajaccio			
Corse-du-Sud	Ajaccio	1,550	4,014	118,593
Haute-Corse	Bastia	1,802	4,666	141,603
Franche-Comté	Besançon			
Doubs	Besançon	2,021	5,234	499,062
Haute-Saône	Vesoul	2,070	5,360	229,732
Jura	Lons-le-Saunier	1,930	4,999	250,857
Territoire de Belfort	Belfort	235	609	137,408
Haute-Normandie	Rouen			
Eure	Évreux	2,332	6,040	541,054
Seine-Maritime	Rouen	2,424	6,278	1,239,138
Île-de-France	Paris			
Essonne	Évry	696	1,804	1,134,238
Hauts-de-Seine	Nanterre	68	176	1,428,881
Paris	Paris	40	105	2,125,246
Seine-et-Marne	Melun	2,284	5,915	1,193,767
Seine-Saint-Denis	Bobigny	91	236	1,382,861
Val-de-Marne	Créteil	95	245	1,227,250
Val-d'Oise	Pontoise	481	1,246	1,105,464
Yvelines	Versailles	882	2,284	1,354,304
Languedoc-Roussillon	Montpellier			
Aude	Carcassonne	2,370	6,139	309,770
Gard	Nîmes	2,260	5,853	623,125
Hérault	Montpellier	2,356	6,101	896,441
Lozère	Mende	1,995	5,167	73,509
Pyrénées-Orientales	Perpignan	1,589	4,116	392,803
Limousin	Limoges			
Corrèze	Tulle	2,261	5,857	232,576
Creuse	Guéret	2,149	5,565	124,470
Haute-Vienne	Limoges	2,131	5,520	353,893
Lorraine	Metz			
Meurthe-et-Moselle	Nancy	2,024	5,241	713,779
Meuse	Bar-le-Duc	2,400	6,216	192,198
Moselle	Metz	2,400	6,216	1,023,447
Vosges	Épinal	2,268	5,874	380,952
Midi-Pyrénées	Toulouse			
Ariège	Foix	1,888	4,890	137,205
Aveyron	Rodez	3,373	8,736	263,808
Gers	Auch	2,416	6,257	172,335
Haute-Garonne	Toulouse	2,436	6,309	1,046,338
Haute-Pyrénées	Tarbes	1,724	4,464	222,368
Lot	Cahors	2,014	5,217	160,197
Tarn	Albi	2,223	5,758	343,402
Tarn-et-Garonne	Montauban	1,435	3,718	206,034
Nord-Pas-de-Calais	Lille			
Nord	Lille	2,217	5,742	2,555,020
Pas-de-Calais	Arras	2,576	6,671	1,441,568
Pays de la Loire	Nantes			
Loire-Atlantique	Nantes	2,631	6,815	1,134,266
Maine-et Loire	Angers	2,767	7,166	732,942
Mayenne	Laval	1,998	5,175	285,338
Sarthe	Le Mans	2,396	6,206	529,851
Vendée	La Roche-sur-Yon	2,595	6,720	539,664
Picardie	Amiens			
Aisne	Laon	2,845	7,369	535,842
Oise	Beauvais	2,263	5,860	766,441
Somme	Amiens	2,382	6,170	555,551
Poitou-Charentes	Poitiers			
Charente	Angoulême	2,300	5,956	339,628
Charente-Maritime	La Rochelle	2,650	6,864	557,024
Deux-Sèvres	Niort	2,316	5,999	344,392
Vienne	Poitiers	2,699	6,990	399,024
Provence-Alpes–Côte d'Azur	Marseille			
Alpes-de-Haute-Provence	Digne	2,674	6,925	139,561
Alpes-Maritimes	Nice	1,660	4,299	1,011,326
Bouches-du-Rhône	Marseille	1,964	5,087	1,835,719
Hautes-Alpes	Gap	2,142	5,549	121,419
Var	Toulon	2,306	5,973	898,441
Vaucluse	Avignon	1,377	3,567	499,685
Rhône-Alpes	Lyon			
Ain	Bourg-en-Bresse	2,225	5,762	515,270
Ardèche	Privas	2,135	5,529	286,023
Drôme	Valence	2,521	6,530	437,778
Haute-Savoie	Annecy	1,694	4,388	631,679
Isère	Grenoble	2,869	7,431	1,094,006
Loire	Saint-Étienne	1,846	4,781	728,524
Rhône	Lyon	1,254	3,249	1,578,869
Savoie	Chambéry	2,327	6,028	373,258
TOTAL		210,026	543,965	60,186,184

Demography

Population (2001): 59,090,000.
Density (2001): persons per sq mi 281.3, persons per sq km 108.6.
Urban-rural (1999): urban 75.5%; rural 24.5%.
Sex distribution (1999): male 48.56%; female 51.44%.
Age breakdown (1999): under 15, 17.9%; 15–29, 20.2%; 30–44, 21.9%; 45–59, 18.7%; 60–74, 13.6%; 75 and over, 7.7%.
Population projection: (2010) 60,596,000; (2020) 61,371,000.
Doubling time: not applicable; doubling time exceeds 100 years.
Ethnic composition (2000): French 65.9%; Italian 1.9%; Portuguese 1.5%; Fleming 1.4%; Basque 1.3%; Jewish 1.2%; German (mostly Alsatian) 1.2%; Catalan 0.5%; other 25.1%.
Religious affiliation (2000): Roman Catholic 82.3%; Muslim 7.1%; atheist 4.4%; Protestant 3.7%; Orthodox 1.1%; Jewish 1.0%; other 0.4%.
Major cities (1999): Paris 2,125,246 (metropolitan area 9,644,507); Marseille 798,430 (1,349,772); Lyon 445,452 (1,348,832); Toulouse 390,350 (761,090); Nice 342,738 (888,784); Nantes 270,251 (544,932); Strasbourg 264,115 (427,245); Montpellier 225,392 (287,981); Bordeaux 215,363 (753,931).
National origin (1990): French 93.6%, of which Martiniquais 0.2%, Guadeloupian 0.2%, Réunionese 0.2%; Portuguese 1.1%; Algerian 1.1%; Moroccan 1.0%; Italian 0.4%; Spanish 0.4%; Turkish 0.3%; other 2.1%.
Mobility (1990). Population living in same residence as in 1982: 51.4%; same region 89.0%; different region 8.8%; different country 2.2%.
Households (1993). Average household size 2.6; 1 person 27.7%, 2 persons 32.0%, 3 persons 17.4%, 4 persons 14.7%, 5 persons or more 8.2%. Family households (1990): 14,118,940 (72.1%); nonfamily 5,471,460 (27.9%, of which 1-person 24.6%).
Immigration (1998): immigrants admitted 100,014 (Algeria 15.3%, Turkey 6.0%, Tunisia 4.9%, Sri Lanka 1.7%, Vietnam 1.0%).

Vital statistics

Birth rate per 1,000 population (1998): 12.7 (world avg. 22.5); (1997) legitimate 59.9%; illegitimate 40.1%.
Death rate per 1,000 population (1998): 9.0 (world avg. 9.0).
Natural increase rate per 1,000 population (1998): 3.7 (world avg. 13.5).
Total fertility rate (avg. births per childbearing woman; 2000): 1.7.
Marriage rate per 1,000 population (1998): 4.6.
Divorce rate per 1,000 population (1998): 2.0.
Life expectancy at birth (2000); male 74.8 years; female 82.9 years.
Major causes of death per 100,000 population (1997): heart disease and other circulatory diseases 291.6; malignant neoplasms (cancers) 252.2; accidents and violence 74.4; respiratory diseases 74.4; digestive tract diseases 44.8.

Social indicators

Educational attainment (1990). Percentage of population age 25 and over having: primary 22.1%; lower secondary 7.8%; higher secondary and vocational 29.4%; postsecondary 11.6%; undeclared attainment 29.1%.

Distribution of income (1984)

percentage of household income by quintile				
1	2	3	4	5 (highest)
7.1%	12.3%	17.1%	23.2%	40.3%

Quality of working life. Average workweek (1994): 38.9 hours. Annual rate per 100,000 workers for: injury or accident 5,322 (deaths 0.8%); accidents in transit to work 708 (deaths 68.3); industrial illness 16.6[2]; death 4.8[2]. Average days lost to labour stoppages per 1,000 workers (1994): 21.0. Average length of journey to work (1990): 8.7 mi (14 km).
Access to services (1992). Proportion of dwellings having: central heating 86.0%; piped water 97.0%; indoor plumbing 95.8%.
Social participation. Eligible voters participating in last (May and June 1997) national election: *c.* 78%. Population over 15 years of age participating in voluntary associations: 28.0%.

Social deviance. Offense rate per 100,000 population (1998) for: murder 1.6, rape 13.4, other assault 583.8; theft (including burglary and housebreaking) 6,107.6. Incidence per 100,000 in general population of: alcoholism, n.a. (deaths related to alcoholism; 1991) 5.0; suicide (1993) 21.1.
Leisure (1987–88). Participation rate for favourite leisure activities: watching television 82%; reading magazines 79%; listening to radio 75%; entertaining relatives 64%; visiting relatives 61%; attending fairs/expositions 56%.
Material well-being (1994). Households possessing: automobile 79.5%; colour television 92.4%; VCR 52.8%; refrigerator 99.0%, washing machine 89.4%.

National economy

Gross national product (1999): U.S.$1,453,211,000,000 (U.S.$24,170 per capita).

Structure of gross domestic product and labour force

	1998[3]			
	in value F '000,000	% of total value	labour force	% of labour force
Agriculture	242,185	3.2	986,600	3.9
Mining	4	4	246,800	1.0
Manufacturing	1,411,010[4]	18.5[4]	3,973,400	15.6
Construction	361,253	4.7	1,371,100	5.4
Public utilities	213,198	2.8	205,100	0.8
Transp. and commun.	326,007[5]	4.3[5]	1,001,600	3.9
Trade[6]	1,726,864[5]	22.7[5]	3,812,400	15.0
Finance	383,133	5.0	683,300	2.7
Pub. admin., defense	1,601,161	21.0	5,767,600	22.6
Services	1,588,888	20.9	4,381,700	17.2
Other	–235,465[7]	–3.1[7]	3,029,600[8]	11.9[8]
TOTAL	7,618,234	100.0	25,459,200	100.0

Budget (1998). Revenue: F 1,331,838,000,000 (value-added taxes 58.3%, personal income tax 22.2%, corporate income tax 16.5%). Expenditure: F 1,585,307,000,000 (education 21.1%, defense 15.0%, health and social services 4.6%, research and development 2.5%).

Manufacturing enterprises (1995)

	no. of enter-prises[9]	no. of employees	annual salaries as a % of avg. of all salaries[9]	annual value added (F '000,000)
Food products	55,197	545,900	87	208,065
Transport equipment	4,293	508,700	108	167,357
Electrical machinery	15,620	433,600	118	156,221
Iron and steel	27,847	403,800	96	131,376
Mechanical equipment	32,134	390,300	104	127,637
Petroleum refineries	180	46,200	174	117,041
Printing, publishing	30,359	231,900	125	83,083
Textiles and wearing apparel	29,701	281,500	78	63,633
Rubber products	5,875	204,200	94	57,758
Chemical products	1,442	102,100	128	51,146
Paper and paper products	1,916	101,500	102	38,585
Metal products	442	43,700	103	28,115
Glass products	1,536	52,400	104	16,638
Footwear	4,236	55,400	75	12,970

Production (metric tons except as noted). Agriculture, forestry, fishing (2000): wheat 37,559,000, sugar beets 31,454,000, corn (maize) 16,469,000, barley 9,927,000, grapes 7,627,000, potatoes 6,652,000, rapeseed 3,569,000, apples 2,157,000, dry peas 1,918,000, sunflower seeds 1,813,000, triticale 1,213,000, tomatoes 898,000, carrots 633,000, green peas 550,000, lettuce 513,000, oats 503,000, peaches 476,000, sorghum 400,000, cauliflower 385,000, string beans 369,000, onions 361,000, cantaloupes 313,000; livestock (number of live animals) 20,527,000 cattle, 14,635,000 pigs, 10,004,000 sheep, 1,190,000 goats; roundwood 50,170,000 cu m; fish catch (1999) 845,649. Mining and quarrying (1998): potash 656,000; iron ore 250,000; bauxite 130,800[10]; uranium 470; gold 122,170 troy oz; silver 32,150 troy oz. Manufacturing (1996): cement 19,896,000[10]; crude steel 17,633,000; pig iron 12,132,000; paper products 8,556,000; rubber products 619,400[10], of which tires 59,268,000 units[10]; aluminum 616,900; automobiles 3,200,000 units[10]. Construction (dwelling units authorized; 1998) 373,600.

Retail trade enterprises (1995[11])

	no. of enter-prises	no. of employees	weekly wages as a % of all wages	annual turnover (F '000,000)
Large food stores	4,373	385,402	...	617,222
Clothing stores	51,873	195,535	...	126,504
Pharmacies	22,301	126,508	...	121,980
Small food stores	64,565	163,474	...	110,928
butcher shops	21,548	59,962	...	36,732
Furniture stores	7,179	53,080	...	54,390
Electrical and electronics stores	10,990	55,560	...	43,995
Department stores	736	35,074	...	27,741
Publishing and paper	15,083	40,375	...	24,591
Gas, coal, and other energy products	6,042	25,375	...	19,204

Energy production (consumption)[12]: electricity (kW-hr; 1997) 515,468,000,000 (450,072,000,000); coal (metric tons; 1997) 7,298,000 (21,527,000); crude petroleum (barrels; 1997) 13,048,000 (651,981,000); petroleum products (metric tons; 1997) 79,634,000 (70,965,000); natural gas (cu m; 1997) 1,437,900,000 (37,102,600,000).
Population economically active (1998[11]): total 25,459,200; activity rate of total population 43.4% (participation rates: ages 15–64, 67.6%[13]; female 45.8%; unemployed 11.9%).

Price and earnings indexes (1995 = 100)

	1994	1995	1996	1997	1998	1999	2000
Consumer price index	98.3	100.0	102.0	103.2	103.9	104.5	106.3
Earnings index	99.2	100.0	101.9	104.7	107.6	110.0	115.0

Household income and expenditure (1995). Average household size 2.6; average annual income per household F 302,560 (U.S.$60,610); sources of income: wages and salaries 70.0%, self-employment 24.4%, social security 5.6%, expenditure (1997): housing 22.5%, food 17.9%, transportation 16.3%, health 10.3%, recreation and education 7.4%, clothing 5.2%.
Tourism (1999): receipts U.S.$31,507,000,000; expenditures U.S.$18,631,000,000.
Public debt (1998): F 5,030,000,000,000 (U.S.$853,000,000,000).

Financial aggregates	1995	1996	1997	1998	1999	2000
Exchange rate, F per:[14]						
U.S. dollar	4.90	5.24	5.99	5.62	1.00	1.07
£	7.60	8.90	9.90	9.35	1.62	1.60
SDR	7.28	7.53	8.08	7.92	1.37	1.40
International reserves (U.S.$)						
Total (excl. gold; '000,000)	26,853	26,796	30,927	44,312	39,701	37,039
SDRs ('000,000)	955	981	971	1,107	347	402
Reserve pos. in IMF ('000,000)	2,756	2,695	2,859	4,452	5,241	4,522
Foreign exchange	23,142	23,120	27,097	38,753	33,933	32,114
Gold ('000,000 fine troy oz)	81.85	81.85	81.89	102.37	97.24	97.25
% world reserves	9.1	9.0	9.2	10.6	10.1	10.2
Interest and prices						
Central bank discount (%)	...	...	...	...	...	...
Govt. bond yield (%)	7.59	6.39	5.63	4.72	4.69	5.45
Industrial share prices (1995 = 100)	100.0	113.2	149.0	200.9	248.6	335.9
Balance of payments (U.S.$'000,000)						
Balance of visible trade	+11,000	+14,940	+26,900	+24,940	+17,990	+1,130
Imports, f.o.b.	267,630	266,910	259,170	278,080	282,060	294,400
Exports, f.o.b.	278,630	281,850	286,070	303,020	300,050	295,530
Balance of invisibles	–160	+5,620	+10,900	+12,760	+17,050	+19,340
Balance of payments, current account	+10,840	+20,560	+37,800	+37,700	+35,040	+20,470

Land use (1994): forest 27.3%; pasture 19.3%; agriculture 35.4%; other 18.0%.

Foreign trade

Balance of trade (current prices)

	1995	1996	1997	1998	1999[15]	2000[15]
F '000,000,000	+62.7	+85.7	+170.4	+160.1	+18.4	+2.8
% of total	2.2%	3.0%	5.3%	4.6%	3.4%	0.9%

Imports (1998): F 1,687,500,000,000 (machinery and transport equipment 39.1%; chemicals 12.2%; agricultural products 7.9%; fuels 5.9%). *Major import sources:* Germany 17.2%; Italy 9.9%, U.K. 8.4%; U.S. 8.2%; Belg.-Lux. 7.7%; Spain 7.1%.
Exports (1998): F 1,773,200,000,000 (machinery and transport equipment 43.8%, of which transport equipment 17.7%; chemical products 12.7%; agricultural products 12.0%; plastics 3.3%). *Major export destinations:* Germany 16.1%; U.K. 10.0%; Italy 9.2%; Spain 8.7%; Belg.-Lux. 7.7%; U.S. 7.4%.

Transport and communications

Transport. Railroads (1999): route length 31,821 km[16]; passenger-km 66,590,000,000; metric ton-km cargo 52,110,000,000. Roads (1999[11]): total length 893,300 km (paved 100%). Vehicles (1998): passenger cars 26,800,000; trucks and buses 5,500,000. Merchant marine (1998): vessels (100 gross tons and over) 808; total deadweight tonnage 4,850,000. Air transport (1999): passenger-km 89,066,600,000; metric ton-km cargo 4,774,900,000; airports (1996) 61.

Communications

Medium	date	unit	number	units per 1,000 persons
Daily newspapers	1996	circulation	12,725,000	218
Radio	1997	receivers	55,300,000	946
Television	1999	receivers	36,500,000	623
Telephones	1999	main lines	34,100,000	582
Cellular telephones	1999	subscribers	21,434,000	366
Personal computers	1999	units	13,000,000	222
Internet	1999	users	5,370,000	91.7

Education and health

Literacy (1980): total population literate 41,112,000 (98.8%); males literate 19,933,000 (98.9%); females literate 21,179,000 (98.7%).

Education (1996–97)

	schools	teachers	students	student/teacher ratio
Primary (age 6–10)	35,019	211,192	4,004,704	19.0
Secondary (age 11–18) / Voc., teacher tr.	11,212[17]	483,493	4,333,690 / 1,646,377	12.4
Higher	1,062[18]	141,410	2,062,495	14.6

Health: physicians (1996) 171,704 (1 per 346 persons); hospital beds (1998) 651,208 (1 per 91 persons); infant mortality rate (2000) 4.5.
Food (1999): daily per capita caloric intake 3,575 (vegetable products 62%, animal products 38%); 141% of FAO recommended minimum requirement.

Military

Total active duty personnel (2000): 294,430 (army 57.5%, navy 16.8%, air force 20.5%, unallocated 5.2%). *Military expenditure as percentage of GNP* (1997): 3.0% (world 2.6%); per capita expenditure U.S.$708.

[1]Expect evolving autonomy from central government between 2001 and 2004. [2]1989. [3]Labor survey is from Jan. 1, 1998. [4]Manufacturing includes mining. [5]Trade includes communications. [6]Includes hotels. [7]Imputed rents and imputed bank service charges. [8]Unemployed. [9]1991. [10]1995. [11]January 1. [12]All energy statistics include Monaco. [13]1994. [14]Beginning in 1999 exchange rates expressed in Euros. [15]In billions of Euros. [16]1997. [17]1995–96. [18]1988–89.

Internet resources for further information:
- **INSEE http://www.insee.fr/fr/home/home_page.asp**
- **City Population http://www.citypopulation.de**

French Guiana

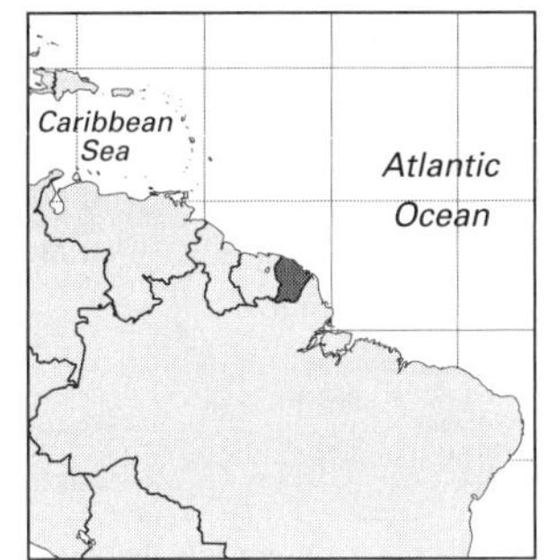

Official name: Département de la Guyane française (Department of French Guiana).
Political status: overseas department of France with two legislative houses (General Council [19]; Regional Council [31]).
Chief of state: President of France.
Heads of government: Prefect (for France); President of the General Council (for French Guiana); President of the Regional Council (for French Guiana).
Capital: Cayenne.
Official language: French.
Official religion: none.
Monetary unit: 1 French franc (F) = 100 centimes; valuation (Sept. 28, 2001) 1 U.S.$ = F 7.20; 1 £ = F 10.59.

Area and population

		area		population
Arrondissements	**Capitals**	sq mi	sq km	1999 census
Cayenne	Cayenne	17,590	45,559	119,660
Saint-Laurent-du-Maroni	Saint-Laurent-du-Maroni	15,809	40,945	37,553
TOTAL		33,399	86,504	157,213

Demography

Population (2001): 168,000.
Density (2001): persons per sq mi 5.0, persons per sq km 1.9.
Urban-rural (2000): urban 78.2%; rural 21.8%.
Sex distribution (1999): male 50.36%; female 49.64%.
Age breakdown (1999): under 15, 34.0%; 15–29, 24.2%; 30–44, 23.3%; 45–59, 12.5%; 60–74, 4.3%; 75 and over, 1.7%.
Population projection: (2010) 204,000; (2020) 233,000.
Doubling time: 40 years.
Ethnic composition (2000): Guianese Mulatto 37.9%; French 8.0%; Haitian 8.0%; Surinamese 6.0%; Antillean 5.0%; Chinese 5.0%; Brazilian 4.9%; East Indian 4.0%; other (other West Indian, Hmong, other South Americans) 21.2%.
Religious affiliation (1995): Roman Catholic 82.1%; other 17.9%.
Major cities (1999)[1]. Cayenne 50,594 (urban agglomeration 84,181); Saint-Laurent-du-Maroni 19,211; Kourou 19,107; Matoury 18,032[2]; Rémire-Montjoly 15,555[2].

Vital statistics

Birth rate per 1,000 population (2000): 22.4 (world avg. 22.5); (1993) legitimate 20.0%; illegitimate 80.0%.
Death rate per 1,000 population (2000): 4.7 (world avg. 9.0).
Natural increase rate per 1,000 population (2000): 17.7 (world avg. 13.2).
Total fertility rate (avg. births per childbearing woman; 2000): 3.2.
Marriage rate per 1,000 population (1993): 5.0.
Divorce rate per 1,000 population (1993): 0.4.
Life expectancy at birth (2000): male 75.0 years; female 81.9 years.
Major causes of death per 100,000 population (1996): diseases of the circulatory system 307.0; malignant neoplasms (cancers) 225.0; violence and suicide 114.0; diseases of the respiratory system 54.0; diseases of the digestive system 52.0%; infectious and parasitic diseases 40.0.

National economy

Budget (1995). Revenue: F 945,000,000 (current receipts 78.2%, of which taxes 50.8%, revenue from French central government 22.5%; development receipts 21.8%). Expenditures: F 945,000,000 (current expenditures 78.2%; capital expenditures 21.8%).
Production (metric tons except as noted). Agriculture, forestry, fishing (2000): rice 31,000, cassava 10,400, sugarcane 5,300, cabbages 4,800, taro 4,100, bananas 3,900, tomatoes 3,100, cucumbers 2,800, plantains 2,600, lemons and limes 1,300; livestock (number of live animals) 10,500 pigs, 9,000 cattle; roundwood (1998) 118,000 cu m; fish catch (1998) 7,709. Mining and quarrying: gold (2000) 90,000 troy oz.[3]; stone, sand, and gravel (1994) 1,034 metric tons. Manufacturing (1998): pork 1,245; chicken meat 461; finished wood products 3,172 cu m[4]; rum 2,728 hectolitres; other products include leather goods, clothing, rosewood essence, yogurt, and beer. Number of satellites launched from the European Space Agency, Kourou (1999): 10[5]. Construction (authorized, 1996): residential 169,400 sq m; nonresidential authorized 85,900 sq m. Energy production (consumption): electricity (kW-hr; 1998) 566,000,000 ([1996] 455,000,000); coal, none (none); crude petroleum, none (none); petroleum products (metric tons; 1996) none (285,000); natural gas, none (none).
Public debt (external, outstanding; 1999): n.a.
Household income and expenditure. Average household size (1999) 3.3; income per household (1980) F 75,762 (U.S.$16,776); sources of income (1989): wages and salaries 64.4%, industrial and commercial profits 15.4%, pensions and rents 18.0%, other 2.2%; expenditure (1994)[6]: food and beverages 28.7%, housing 11.7%, energy 9.0%, clothing and footwear 6.4%, health 2.7%, other 41.5%.
Land use (1994): forested 90.6%; meadows and pastures 0.1%; agricultural and under permanent cultivation 0.2%; other 9.1%.
Gross national product (at current market prices; 1997): U.S.$1,430,000,000 (U.S.$9,410 per capita).

Structure of gross domestic product and labour force

	1992		1990	
	in value F '000,000	% of total value	labour force	% of labour force
Agriculture, forestry, fishing	578	7.2	4,177	8.7
Mining	726	9.1	250	0.5
Manufacturing			2,477	5.1
Construction	868	10.9	4,440	9.2
Public utilities	47	0.6	403	0.8
Finance, real estate	1,185	14.8	408	0.8
Transp. and commun.	921	11.5	1,867	3.8
Trade	961	12.0	3,152	6.5
Pub. admin., defense	1,856	23.3	12,068	25.0
Services	909	11.4	7,352	15.2
Other	–75	–0.9	11,722[7]	24.3[7]
TOTAL	7,976[8]	100.0[8]	48,306	100.0[8]

Population economically active (1998): total 61,100; activity rate of total population 39.0% (participation rates (1990): ages 15–64, 67.3%; female 38.2%; unemployed [1998] 21.4%).

Price and earnings indexes (December 1990 = 100)[9]

	1994	1995	1996	1997	1998	1999	2000
Consumer price index	108.9	110.1	111.2	112.2	112.5	118.2	128.9
Monthly earnings index[10]	109.4	112.3	112.3	114.5	127.8	...	...

Tourism (1999): receipts U.S.$50,000,000; expenditures, n.a.

Foreign trade

Balance of trade (current prices)

	1993	1994	1995[11]	1996[11]	1997	1998
F '000,000	–2,740	–2,919	–2,983	–2,878	–2,913	–2,852
% of total	70.0%	63.8%	68.9%	64.4%	61.4%	70.9%

Imports (1998): F 3,449,000,000 (food products 21.3%; unspecified 78.7%). *Major import sources* (1997): France 51.6%; United States 14.3%; Trinidad and Tobago 6.0%.
Exports (1996): F 856,000,000 (gold 21.5%; shrimp 20.5%; parts for air and space vehicles 14.6%; rice 7.0%). *Major export destinations* (1997): France 61.5%; Switzerland 6.6%; United States 2.2%.

Transport and communications

Transport. Railroads: none. Roads (1996): total length 774 mi, 1,245 km (paved, n.a.). Vehicles (1993): passenger cars 29,100; trucks and buses 10,600. Merchant marine: n.a. Air transport (1998): passenger arrivals 204,078, passenger departures 199,637; cargo unloaded 4,083 metric tons, cargo loaded 2,483 metric tons; airports (1998) with scheduled flights 1.

Communications

Medium	date	unit	number	units per 1,000 persons
Daily newspapers	1996	circulation	2,000	7.0
Radio	1997	receivers	104,000	650
Television	1997	receivers	30,000	172
Telephones	1999	main lines	49,000	282
Cellular telephones	1999	subscribers	18,000	103

Education and health

Educational attainment (1990). Percentage of population age 25 and over having: incomplete primary education or no declaration 61.7%; completed primary 5.3%; some secondary 15.9%; completed secondary 8.2%; some higher 4.9%; completed higher 4.0%. *Literacy* (1982): total population age 16 and over literate 38,964 (82.0%); males literate 21,021 (82.5%); females literate 17,943 (81.3%).

Education (1994–95)

	schools	teachers	students	student/ teacher ratio
Primary (age 6–11)	131	1,267	27,700[12]	19.2
Secondary (age 12–18)	28	968	17,100[12]	14.3
Higher[13]	1	...	239	...

Health: physicians (1998) 223 (1 per 684 persons); hospital beds (1996) 730 (1 per 196 persons); infant mortality rate per 1,000 live births (2000) 14.0.
Food (1992): daily per capita caloric intake 2,900 (vegetable products 70%, animal products 30%); 128% of FAO recommended minimum requirement.

Military

Total active duty personnel (1999): 2,200[14].

[1]Commune population. [2]Within Cayenne urban agglomeration. [3]Officially declared figure; unofficial total is 240,000 troy oz. [4]1996. [5]In 1991 the European Space Agency accounted for 28.7% of GDP, 28.2% of employed labour force, and 70.9% of imports. [6]Weights of consumer price index components. [7]Unemployed. [8]Detail does not add to the total given because of rounding. [9]Indexes based on end-of-year figures. [10]Based on minimum-level wage in public administration. [11]Excludes December. [12]1996–97. [13]Université des Antilles et de la Guyane, Cayenne campus: 1997–98. [14]Includes French Foreign Legion troops assigned to guard the Kourou Space Centre.

Internet resources for further information:
- **Chambre de Commerce et l'Industrie: Guyane** **http://www.guyane.cci.fr**
- **Ministère de l'Outre-mer (Paris)** **http://www.outre-mer.gouv.fr/domtom/guyane/index.htm**

French Polynesia

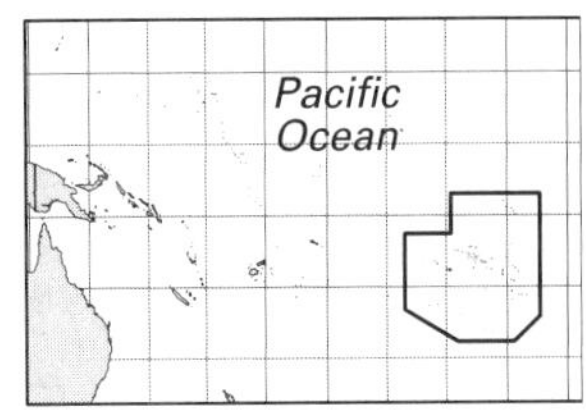

Official name: Territoire de la Polynésie française (French); Polynesia Farani (Tahitian) (Territory of French Polynesia).
Political status: overseas territory (France) with one legislative house (Territorial Assembly [49]).
Chief of state: President of France.
Head of government: High Commissioner (for France); President of the Council of Ministers (for French Polynesia).
Capital: Papeete.
Official languages: French; Tahitian.
Official religion: none.
Monetary unit: 1 Franc de la Comptoirs française du pacifique (CFPF) = 100 centimes; valuation (Sept. 28, 2001) 1 U.S.$ = CFPF 130.21; 1 £ = CFPF 191.37.

Area and population

		area		population
				1996
Circumscriptions	**Capitals**	sq mi	sq km	census
Îles Australes	Mataura	57	148	6,563
Îles Marquises	Talohae	405	1,049	8,064
Îles sous le Vent	Uturoa	156	404	26,838
Îles Tuamotu et Gambler	Papeete	280	726	15,370
Îles du Vent	Papeete	461	1,194	162,686
TOTAL		1,544[1]	4,000[1]	219,521

Demography

Population (2001): 238,000.
Density (2001)[2]: persons per sq mi 175.1, persons per sq km 67.6.
Urban-rural (1999): urban 57.0%; rural 43.0%.
Sex distribution (1996): male 51.92%; female 48.08%.
Age breakdown (1996): under 15, 33.7%; 15–29, 27.3%; 30–44, 21.6%; 45–59, 11.4%; 60–74, 5.0%; 75 and over, 1.0%.
Population projection: (2010) 269,000; (2020) 309,000.
Doubling time: 44 years.
Ethnic composition (1996): Polynesian and part-Polynesian 82.8%; European (mostly French) 11.9%; Asian (mostly Chinese) 4.7%; other 0.6%.
Religious affiliation (1995): Protestant 50.2%, of which Evangelical Church of French Polynesia (Presbyterian) 46.1%; Roman Catholic 39.5%; other Christian 9.9%, of which Mormon 5.9%; other 0.4%.
Major cities (1996)[3]: Faaa 25,888[4]; Papeete 25,553 (urban agglomeration [1999] 121,000); Punaauia 19,524[4]; Pirae 13,974[4]; Mahina 11,640[4].

Vital statistics

Birth rate per 1,000 population (2001): 20.7 (world avg. 22.5); (1996) legitimate 35.4%; illegitimate 64.6%.
Death rate per 1,000 population (2001): 4.8 (world avg. 9.0).
Natural increase rate per 1,000 population (2001): 15.9 (world avg. 13.5).
Total fertility rate (avg. births per childbearing woman; 2001): 2.5.
Marriage rate per 1,000 population (1996): 5.7.
Life expectancy at birth (2001): male 70.0 years; female 75.0 years.
Major causes of death per 100,000 population (1994–95): diseases of the circulatory system 123; malignant neoplasms (cancers) 104; accidents, suicide, and violence 52; respiratory diseases 47; diseases of the digestive system 17.

National economy

Budget (1998). Revenue: CFPF 85,671,000,000 (indirect taxes 60.3%, direct taxes and nontax revenue 39.7%). Expenditures: CFPF 114,143,000,000 (current expenditure 72.5%; capital expenses 27.5%).
Public debt (external, outstanding; 1995): U.S.$863,000,000[5].
Production (metric tons except as noted). Agriculture, forestry, fishing (1999): coconuts 85,000, copra (1998) 11,000, cassava 5,500, potatoes 5,000, pineapples 3,500, sugarcane 2,800, watermelon 1,100, tomatoes 900, cucumbers 700, bananas 650; livestock (number of live animals) 33,000 pigs, 6,500 cattle, 16,000 goats; roundwood, n.a.; fish catch (1998) 11,406; export production of black pearls (1998) 6,050 kg. Mining and quarrying: estimated annual production of phosphates range from 1,000,000 to 1,200,000 tons. Manufacturing (1999): coconut oil 6,386; other manufactures include *monoï* oil (primarily refined coconut and sandalwood oils), beer, printed cloth, and sandals. Construction (buildings completed; 1994): 102,305 sq m. Energy production (consumption): electricity (kW-hr; 1996) 360,000,000 (360,000,000); coal, none (none); crude petroleum, none (none); petroleum products (metric tons; 1996) none (183,000); natural gas, none (none).
Tourism (1998): number of visitors 189,000; receipts from visitors U.S.$354,000,000; number of hotel rooms 3,021; occupancy percentage 59.0%; expenditures by nationals abroad, n.a.
Household income and expenditure (1986). Average household size (1996) 4.3; average annual income per household CFPF 2,153,112 (U.S.$17,831); sources of income (1993): salaries 61.9%, self-employment 21.5%, transfer payments 16.6%; expenditure: food and beverages 32.1%, household furnishings 12.3%, transportation 12.2%, energy 8.1%, recreation and education 6.9%, clothing 6.3%.
Gross domestic product (at current market prices; 1999): U.S.$3,908,000,000 (U.S.$16,930 per capita).

Structure of gross domestic product and labour force

	1993		1996	
	in value CFPF '000,000	% of total value	labour force	% of labour force
Agriculture	12,872	3.9	10,888	12.5
Manufacturing[6]	22,034	6.7	6,424	7.4
Construction	18,735	5.7	4,777	5.5
Public utilities	6,917	2.1	459	0.5
Transp. and commun.	...	...	3,788	4.4
Trade	...	...	9,357	10.7
Finance, real estate	...	...	1,865	2.1
Pub. admin., defense	94,557	28.7	13,475	15.5
Services[7]	174,151	52.9	23,514	27.0
Other	—	—	12,574[8]	14.4[8]
TOTAL	329,266	100.0	87,121	100.0

Population economically active (1996): total 87,121; activity rate of total population 39.7% (participation rates: ages 14 and over, 68.3%; female 38.7%; unemployed 13.2%).

Price and earnings indexes (1990 = 100)[9]

	1993	1994	1995	1996	1997	1998	1999
Consumer price index	103.9	105.6	106.8	108.0	109.1	110.0	111.1
Monthly earnings index	106.6	...	...	...	...	...	...

Land use (1998): forested and other 81.4%; meadows and pastures 5.5%; agricultural and under permanent cultivation 13.1%.

Foreign trade[10]

Balance of trade (current prices)

	1994	1995	1996	1997	1998	1999
CFPF '000,000	–65,539	–73,835	–71,118	–82,819	–99,800	–81,654
% of total	59.5%	67.8%	60.3%	71.5%	75.1%	65.7%

Imports (1997): CFPF 99,300,000,000 (machinery and appliances 16.3%, food products 6.8%, pharmaceutical products 3.1%, metal manufactures 2.6%). *Major import sources* (1996): France 43.9%; United States 13.7%; Australia 7.0%; New Zealand 6.6%; Japan 3.5%; Italy 3.3%; Germany 3.1%.
Exports (1997): CFPF 16,481,000,000 (black cultured pearls 61.6%, coconut oil 1.6%, mother-of-pearl 1.4%, vanilla 0.5%[11]). *Major export destinations* (1996): Japan 40.6%; France 28.7%; United States 8.7%; New Caledonia 2.9%.

Transport and communications

Transport. Railroads: none. Roads (1996): total length 549 mi, 884 km (paved 44%). Motor vehicles (1993): passenger cars 37,000; trucks and buses 15,300. Merchant marine (1992): vessels (100 gross tons and over) 41; total deadweight tonnage 16,547. Air transport (1998): passengers carried 1,219,907; freight handled 9,542 metric tons; airports (1994) with scheduled flights 17.

Communications

Medium	date	unit	number	units per 1,000 persons
Daily newspapers	1996	circulation	24,000	110
Radio	1997	receivers	128,000	574
Television	1999	receivers	43,000	186
Telephones	1999	main lines	52,272	226
Cellular telephones	1999	subscribers	21,929	95
Personal computers	1995	units	20,000	1.2
Internet	1999	users	5,000	22

Education and health

Educational attainment (1996). Percentage of population age 15 and over having: no formal schooling 4.9%; primary education 37.4%; secondary 49.0%; higher 8.7%. *Literacy* (1983): total population age 15 and over literate 98,314 (95.0%); males literate 51,910 (94.9%); females literate 46,404 (95.0%).

Education (1996–97)

	schools	teachers	students	student/ teacher ratio
Primary (age 6–10)	170	2,811	29,415	10.5
Secondary (age 11–17)	32[12]	1,897	28,438	15.0
Vocational[13]	[14]	316	3,730	11.8
Higher[15]	4	70	701	10.0

Health (1996): physicians 384 (1 per 175 persons); hospital beds 981 (1 per 447 persons); infant mortality rate per 1,000 live births (2001) 9.0.
Food (1999): daily per capita caloric intake 2,969 (vegetable products 72%, animal products 28%); (1997) 130% of FAO recommended minimum.

Military

Total active duty personnel (2000): 3,100 French military personnel. *Military expenditure as percentage of GNP:* n.a.

[1]Approximate total area including inland water; total land area is 1,359 sq mi (3,521 sq km). [2]Based on land area. [3]Populations cited are for communes. [4]Part of Papeete urban agglomeration. [5]Includes long-term private debt not guaranteed by the government. [6]Includes mining. [7]Includes finance, real estate, trade, and transportation and communications. [8]Includes not adequately defined and unemployed. [9]All end-of-year. [10]Imports c.i.f.; exports f.o.b. [11]Remaining exports are primarily professional goods including military and aeronautical equipment and parts. [12]1989–90. [13]1991–92. [14]Included with secondary schools. [15]1988–89.

Internet resources for further information:
- **Polynésie française**
http://www.ciral.ulaval.ca./alx/amlxmonde/pacifique/polfr.htm
http://www.outre-mer.gouv.fr/domtom/polynesie/index.htm

Gabon

Official name: République Gabonaise (Gabonese Republic).
Form of government: unitary multiparty republic with a Parliament comprising two legislative houses (Senate [91]; National Assembly [120]).
Chief of state: President.
Head of government: Prime Minister.
Capital: Libreville.
Official language: French.
Official religion: none.
Monetary unit: 1 CFA franc (CFAF) = 100 centimes; valuation (Sept. 28, 2001) 1 U.S.$ = CFAF 720.28; 1 £ = CFAF 1,091.

Area and population

Provinces	Capitals	area sq mi	area sq km	population 1993 census[1]
Estuaire	Libreville	8,008	20,740	463,187
Haut-Ogooué	Franceville	14,111	36,547	104,301
Moyen-Ogooué	Lambaréné	7,156	18,535	42,316
Ngounié	Mouila	14,575	37,750	77,781
Nyanga	Tchibanga	8,218	21,285	39,430
Ogooué-Ivindo	Makokou	17,790	46,075	48,862
Ogooué-Lolo	Koulamoutou	9,799	25,380	43,915
Ogooué-Maritime	Port-Gentil	8,838	22,890	97,913
Woleu-Ntem	Oyem	14,851	38,465	97,271
TOTAL		103,347[2]	267,667	1,014,976

Demography

Population (2001): 1,221,000.
Density (2001): persons per sq mi 11.8, persons per sq km 4.6.
Urban-rural (1998): urban 46.9%; rural 53.1%.
Sex distribution (2001): male 49.77%; female 50.23%.
Age breakdown (1999): under 15, 33.3%; 15–29, 25.7%; 30–44, 15.3%; 45–59, 16.2%; 60–74, 8.0%; 75 and over, 1.4%.
Population projection: (2010) 1,309,000; (2020) 1,386,000.
Doubling time: 68 years.
Ethnic composition (1983): Fang 35.5%; Punu, Sira, and Nzebi 16.9%; Mpongwe 15.1%; Mbete 14.2%; other 18.3%.
Religious affiliation (2000): Christian 90.6%, of which Roman Catholic 56.6%, Protestant 17.7%; Muslim 3.1%; traditional beliefs 1.7%.
Major cities (1993); Libreville 362,386; Port-Gentil 80,841; Franceville 30,246; Oyem 22,669; Moanda 21,921.

Vital statistics

Birth rate per 1,000 population (2001): 27.4 (world avg. 22.5).
Death rate per 1,000 population (2001): 17.2 (world avg. 9.0).
Natural increase rate per 1,000 population (2001): 10.2 (world avg. 13.5).
Total fertility rate (avg. births per childbearing woman; 2001): 3.7.
Life expectancy at birth (2001): male 48.5 years; female 50.8 years.
Major causes of death per 100,000 population: n.a.; however, in the 1990s major causes of morbidity and mortality included malaria, shigellosis (infection with dysentery), tetanus, cardiovascular diseases, trypanosomiasis, and tuberculosis.

National economy

Budget (1997). Revenue: CFAF 914,700,000,000 (oil revenues 62.4%; taxes on international trade 18.8%; customs duties 10.7%; other revenues 8.1%). Expenditures: CFAF 756,100,000,000 (current expenditure 71.5%, of which wages and salaries 25.0%, service on public debt 23.5%; capital expenditure 28.5%).
Public debt (external, outstanding; 1999): U.S.$3,290,000,000.
Tourism (1999): receipts from visitors U.S.$11,000,000; expenditures by nationals abroad U.S.$183,000,000.
Production (metric tons except as noted). Agriculture, forestry, fishing (1999): roots and tubers 436,300 (of which cassava 225,000, yams 150,000, taro 58,500), plantains 280,000, sugarcane 175,000, corn (maize) 31,000, peanuts (groundnuts) 17,000, bananas 11,500, natural rubber 11,000, palm oil 3,000, cacao beans 700; livestock (number of live animals) 212,000 pigs, 195,000 sheep, 90,000 goats, 35,000 cattle, 3,100,000 chickens; roundwood (1998) 5,332,000 cu m; fish catch (1997) 44,772. Mining and quarrying (1997): manganese ore 1,995,500; uranium ore 516,000. Manufacturing (1995): fuel oil 295,000; diesel and gas oil 274,000; cement 130,000; kerosene 88,000; wheat flour 27,000; refined sugar 15,000; beer 816,419 hectolitres; soft drinks 415,613 hectolitres; plywood 52,500,000 cu m; textiles are also significant. Energy production (consumption): electricity (kW-hr) 1,076,000,000 (917,000,000); crude petroleum (barrels; 1997) 135,873,000 ([1996] 6,120,000); petroleum products (metric tons; 1997) 676,300 (549,500); natural gas (cu m; 1996) 826,000,000 (826,000,000).
Household income and expenditure. Average household size (1998) 6.1; income per household: n.a.; sources of income (1983): private sector 73.4%, public sector 26.6%; expenditure (1969)[3]: food and tobacco 54.7%, clothing and footwear 17.5%, housing 13.0%, recreation 6.6%, transportation and communications 6.3%, health care 1.9%.
Population economically active (1997): total 542,000; activity rate of total population 45.5% (participation rates [1985]: ages 15–64, 68.2%; female 44.5%; unemployed [1996] 20%).

Price and earnings indexes (1995 = 100)

	1995	1996	1997	1998
Consumer price index	100.0	100.7	104.7	108.4
Earnings index	100.0	103.6	102.5	101.2

Gross national product (1999): U.S.$3,987,000,000 (U.S.$3,300 per capita).

Structure of gross domestic product and labour force

	1997 in value CFAF '000,000	1997 % of total value	1993 labour force	1993 % of labour force
Agriculture, forestry, fishing	224,500	7.4	156,000[4]	41.6
Mining	1,306,100	43.3		
Manufacturing	167,100	5.5	43,000[4]	11.5
Construction	116,300	3.9		
Public utilities	36,400	1.2		
Transp. and commun.	143,400	4.8		
Trade	245,800	8.2		
Finance	13,000	0.4	115,000[4]	30.7
Services	345,400	11.5		
Pub. admin., defense	267,100	8.9	61,000[4]	16.2
Other	148,600[5]	4.9[5]	...	...
TOTAL	3,013,700	100.0	376,000[2]	100.0

Land use (1994): forested 77.2%; meadows and pastures 18.2%; agricultural and under permanent cultivation 1.8%; other 2.8%.

Foreign trade

Balance of trade (current prices)

	1992	1993	1994	1995	1996	1997
CFAF '000,000	+362,800	+419,400	+882,000	+870,800	+1,095,800	+1,198,200
% of total	43.6%	46.7%	50.6%	49.3%	52.5%	50.9%

Imports (1997): CFAF 578,100,000,000 (machinery and mechanical equipment 26.4%, food and agricultural products 23.1%, consumer products 15.5%, transport equipment 11.5%, metals 6.2%). *Major import sources:* France 39.1%; Belgium 9.7%; U.S. 8.1%; U.K. 4.3%; Japan 4.0%.
Exports (1997): CFAF 1,776,300,000,000 (crude petroleum and petroleum products 77.1%, wood 14.5%, manganese ore and concentrate 5.0%, uranium ore and concentrate 0.7%). *Major export destinations:* U.S. 68.2%; France 8.1%; other EU 4.4%; Japan 3.2%; Africa 1.6%.

Transport and communications

Transport. Railroads (1998): route length 506 mi, 814 km; passenger-km 85,000,000[6]; metric ton-km cargo carried 503,000,000[7]. Roads (1996): total length 4,760 mi, 7,670 km (paved 8.2%). Vehicles (1997): passenger cars 24,750; trucks and buses 16,490. Merchant marine (1992): vessels (100 gross tons and over) 29; total deadweight tonnage 30,186. Air transport (1996): passenger-mi 452,000,000, passenger-km 728,000,000; short ton-mi cargo 62,100,000, metric ton-km cargo 100,000,000; airports (1997) 17.

Communications

Medium	date	unit	number	units per 1,000 persons
Daily newspapers	1997	circulation	33,000	30.0
Radio	1997	receivers	195,000	16.1
Television	1999	receivers	300,000	251
Telephones	1999	main lines	37,978	31.7
Cellular telephones	1999	subscribers	8,891	7.4
Personal computers	1999	units	10,000	8.4
Internet	1999	users	3,000	2.5

Education and health

Educational attainment of economically active population (1993): none, or incomplete primary 37.7%; complete primary 32.1%; complete secondary 16.4%; postsecondary certificate or degree 13.8%. *Literacy* (1995): total population age 15 and over literate 63.2%; males literate 73.7%; females literate 53.3%.

Education (1995–96)

	schools	teachers	students	student/teacher ratio
Primary	1,147	4,944	250,606	50.7
Secondary	88	2,683	72,888	27.2
Voc., teacher tr.	11	411	7,664	18.6
Higher[8, 9]	2	299	3,000	10.0

Health: physicians (1989) 448 (1 per 2,377 persons); hospital beds (1988) 5,329 (1 per 199 persons); infant mortality rate per 1,000 live births (1998) 83.1.
Food (1998): daily per capita caloric intake 2,560 (vegetable products 87%, animal products 13%), 109% of FAO recommended minimum requirement.

Military

Total active duty personnel (2000): 4,700 (army 68.1%, navy 10.6%, air force 21.3%), excluding 700 French troops. *Military expenditure as percentage of GNP* (1997): 2.0% (world 2.6%); per capita expenditure U.S.$76.

[1]De jure; excludes nonnationals numbering 100,000 to 150,000 (mainly West African) prior to their large-scale expulsion in February 1995. [2]Detail does not add to total given because of rounding. [3]Libreville only. [4]Derived values. [5]Import duties. [6]1996. [7]1995. [8]Universities only. [9]1991–92.

Internet resources for further information:
- **Gabon: The Country Fact Book**
  http://www.gabon-net.com/english/facts.html

Gambia, The

Official name: The Republic of the Gambia.
Form of government: multiparty republic[1] with one legislative house (National Assembly [49[2]]).
Head of state and government: President[1].
Capital: Banjul.
Official language: English.
Official religion: none.
Monetary unit: 1 dalasi (D) = 100 butut; valuation (Sept. 28, 2001) 1 U.S.$ = D 16.55; 1 £ = D 24.32.

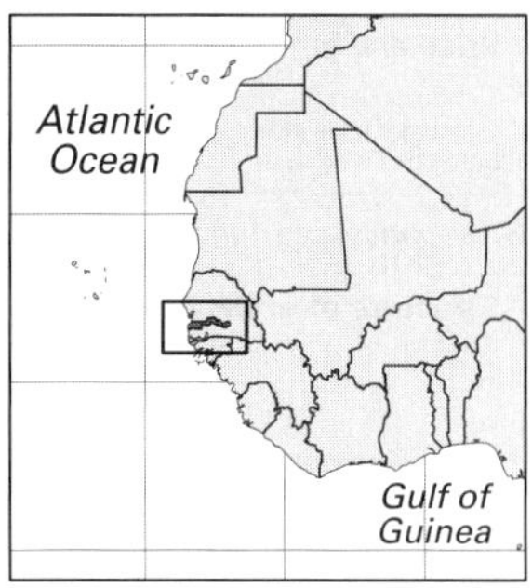

Area and population

		area		population
Divisions	Capitals	sq mi	sq km	1993 census[3]
Kombo St. Mary[4, 5]	Kanifing	29	76	228,214
Lower River	Mansakonko	625	1,618	65,146
Janjanbureh Island	Janjanbureh	1,117	2,894	156,021
North Bank	Kerewan	871	2,256	156,462
Upper River	Basse	799	2,069	155,059
Western	Brikama	681	1,764	234,917
City				
Banjul[5]	—	5	12	42,326
TOTAL		4,127[6]	10,689[6]	1,038,145

Demography

Population (2001): 1,411,000.
Density (2001)[7]: persons per sq mi 424.4, persons per sq km 158.7.
Urban-rural (1999): urban 36.8%; rural 63.2%.
Sex distribution (2000): male 49.97%; female 50.03%.
Age breakdown (2000): under 15, 45.3%; 15–29, 26.1%; 30–44, 15.6%; 45–59, 8.7%; 60–74, 3.5%; 75 and over, 0.8%.
Population projection: (2010) 1,833,000; (2020) 2,365,000.
Doubling time: 24 years.
Ethnic composition (1993): Malinke 34.1%; Fulani 16.2%; Wolof 12.6%; Diola 9.2%; Soninke 7.7%; other 20.2%.
Religious affiliation (1993): Muslim 95.0%; Christian 4.1%; traditional beliefs and other 0.9%.
Major cities/urban areas (1993): Serekunda 151,450[4]; Brikama 42,480; Banjul 42,326 (Greater Banjul 270,540[5]); Bakau 38,062[4]; Farafenni 21,142.

Vital statistics

Birth rate per 1,000 population (2000): 42.3 (world avg. 22.5).
Death rate per 1,000 population (2000): 13.2 (world avg. 9.0).
Natural increase rate per 1,000 population (2000): 29.1 (world avg. 13.5).
Total fertility rate (avg. births per childbearing woman; 2000): 5.8.
Marriage rate per 1,000 population: n.a.
Divorce rate per 1,000 population: n.a.
Life expectancy at birth (2000): male 51.3 years; female 55.2 years.
Major causes of death per 100,000 population: n.a.; however, major infectious diseases include malaria, gastroenteritis and dysentery, pneumonia and bronchitis, measles, schistosomiasis, and whooping cough.

National economy

Budget (1999). Revenue: D 944,500,000 (tax revenue 81.9%, of which import duties and excises 29.0%, income taxes 19.4%, sales tax 6.9%; nontax revenue 11.1%; grants 7.0%). Expenditures: D 1,118,200,000 (wages and salaries 26.9%; interest payments 22.2%; goods and services 16.9%; education and culture 13.1%; health 7.9%; defense 3.6%).
Production (metric tons except as noted). Agriculture, forestry, fishing (1999): peanuts (groundnuts) 123,000, millet 83,000, paddy rice 31,700, corn (maize) 20,400, sorghum 18,000, cassava 6,000, seed cotton 4,740, pulses (mostly beans) 4,000, palm oil 3,000, palm kernels 2,000; livestock (number of live animals) 360,000 cattle, 265,000 goats, 190,000 sheep; roundwood (1998) 661,000 cu m; fish catch (1998) 29,002, of which Atlantic Ocean 26,702, inland water 2,300. Mining and quarrying: sand and gravel are excavated for local use. Manufacturing (value of production in D '000; 1982): processed food, including peanut and palm-kernel oil 62,878; beverage 10,546; textiles 3,253; chemicals and related products 1,031; nonmetals 922; printing and publishing 358; leather 150. Construction: n.a. Energy production (consumption): electricity (kW-hr; 1998) 122,187,000 (122,187,000); coal, none (none); crude petroleum, none (none); petroleum products (metric tons; 1998) none (44,000); natural gas, none (none).
Population economically active (1998): total 575,140; activity rate of total population 47.3% (participation rates: [1983] ages 15–64, 78.2%; female 46.3%; unemployed, n.a.).

Price and earnings indexes (1995 = 100)

	1993	1994	1995	1996	1997	1998	1999
Consumer price index	91.9	93.5	100.0	101.1	103.9	105.1	109.1
Earnings index	...	...	...	...	...	...	...

Tourism (1997): receipts from visitors U.S.$32,000,000; expenditures by nationals abroad U.S.$16,000,000.
Household income and expenditure. Average household size (1998) 9.4; income per household: n.a.; sources of income: n.a.; expenditure (1991)[8]: food and beverages 58.0%, clothing and footwear 17.5%, energy and water 5.4%, housing 5.1%, education, health, transportation and communications, recreation, and other 14.0%.
Public debt (external, outstanding; 1999): U.S.$425,400,000.
Gross national product (at current market prices; 1999): U.S.$415,000,000 (U.S.$330 per capita).

Structure of gross domestic product and labour force

	1999		1983	
	in value D '000,000	% of total value	labour force	% of labour force
Agriculture	1,466.5	29.6	239,940	73.7
Mining	9	9	66	0.0
Manufacturing	234.6	4.7	8,144	2.5
Construction	236.2[9]	4.8[9]	4,373	1.3
Public utilities	82.0	1.7	1,233	0.4
Transp. and commun.	717.6	14.5	8,014	2.5
Trade	735.0	14.8	16,551	5.1
Finance	299.8	6.0	4,577	1.4
Public administration	421.6	8.5	8,295	2.5
Services	204.4	4.1	9,381	2.9
Other	557.9[10]	11.3[10]	25,049[11]	7.7[11]
TOTAL	4,955.6	100.0	325,623	100.0

Land use (1994): forested 10.0%; meadows and pastures 19.0%; agricultural and under permanent cultivation 17.2%; built-on area, wasteland, and other 53.8%.

Foreign trade[12]

Balance of trade (current prices)

	1994	1995	1996	1997	1998	1999
D '000,000	–1,695.0	–1,586.0	–2,318.5	–1,624.0	–2,319.4	–2,106.2
% of total	71.5%	83.6%	84.7%	84.4%	80.2%	96.3%

Imports (1999): D 2,186,820,000 (food 32.9%; basic manufactures 23.9%; machinery and transport equipment 20.7%; mineral fuels and lubricants 7.2%; chemicals and related products 7.3%; vegetable oils 3.0%). *Major import sources:* China 17.2%; Hong Kong 10.6%; U.K. 8.7%; The Netherlands 7.3%; Senegal 5.2%; France 4.7%; Côte d'Ivoire 4.3%; Thailand 1.0%.
Exports (1999): D 80,600,000 (domestic exports 13.3%, of which groundnuts 8.3%, fish products 2.2%; reexports 86.7%). *Major export destinations:* Belgium-Luxembourg 61.0%; Japan 19.4%; U.K. 6.8%; Spain 1.8%.

Transport and communications

Transport. Railroads: none. Roads (1996): total length 1,678 mi, 2,700 km (paved 35%). Vehicles (1996): passenger cars 8,640; trucks and buses 9,000. Merchant marine (1992): vessels (100 gross tons and over) 11; total deadweight tonnage 2,029. Air transport (1994): passenger-mi 31,100,000, passenger-km 50,000,000; cargo 3,107,000 short ton-mi, metric ton-km 5,000,000; airports (1997) with scheduled flights 1.

Communications

Medium	date	unit	number	units per 1,000 persons
Daily newspapers	1996	circulation	2,000	1.7
Radio	1997	receivers	196,000	165
Television	1999	receivers	4,000	3.1
Telephones	1999	main lines	29,216	23.0
Cellular telephones	1999	subscribers	5,307	4.2
Internet	1999	users	3,000	2.4

Education and health

Educational attainment (1973). Percentage of population age 20 and over having: no formal schooling 90.8%; primary education 6.2%; secondary 2.6%; higher 0.4%. *Literacy* (1995): total population age 15 and over literate 38.6%; males literate 52.8%; females literate 24.9%.

Education (1998–99)

	schools	teachers	students	student/ teacher ratio
Primary (age 8–14)	331	4,572	150,403	32.9
Secondary (age 15–21)[13]	85	1,936	46,769	24.2
Postsecondary	4	155[14]	1,082[14]	7.0

Health: physicians (1997) 43 (1 per 28,791 persons); hospital beds (1994) 780 (1 per 1,428 persons); infant mortality rate per 1,000 live births (2000) 79.3.
Food (1999): daily per capita caloric intake 2,598 (vegetable products 95%, animal products 5%); 109% of FAO recommended minimum requirement.

Military

Total active duty personnel (2000): 800 (army 100%). *Military expenditure as percentage of GNP* (1997): 3.7% (world 2.6%); per capita expenditure U.S.$12.

[1]Established by new constitution effective Jan. 16, 1997. Presidential elections of September 1996 did not meet international standards. [2]Includes 4 nonelective seats. [3]Preliminary. [4]Kombo St. Mary includes the urban areas of Serekunda and Bakau. [5]Kombo St. Mary and Banjul city make up Greater Banjul. [6]Includes inland water area of 2,077 sq km (802 sq mi). [7]Based on land area only. [8]Low-income population in Banjul and Kombo St. Mary only; weights of consumer price index components. [9]Construction includes mining. [10]Indirect taxes. [11]Not adequately defined. [12]Imports c.i.f. in balance of trade and f.o.b. in commodities and trading partners. [13]Includes teacher training and vocational. [14]1994.

Internet resources for further information:

- **Official WWW Site of The Republic of The Gambia**
  http://www.Gambia.com

Georgia

Official name: Sak'art'velo (Georgia).
Form of government: unitary multiparty republic with a single legislative body (Parliament [235]).
Head of state and government: President, assisted by Minister of State.
Capital: T'bilisi.
Official language: Georgian.
Official religion: none[1].
Monetary unit: 1 Georgian lari[2] = 100 tetri; valuation (Sept. 28, 2001) 1 U.S.$ = 2.07 lari; 1 £ = 3.04 lari.

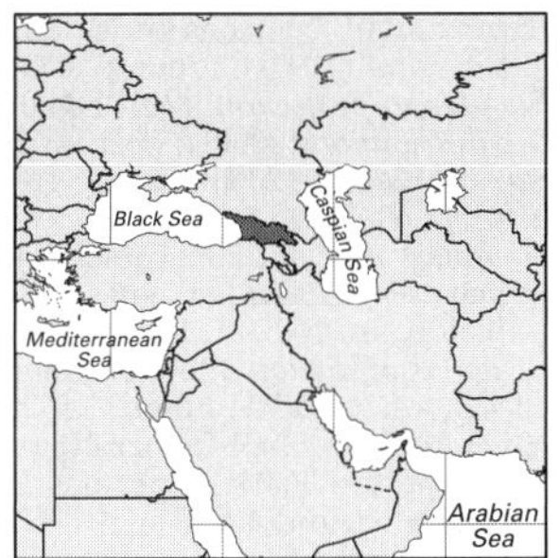

Area and population

Autonomous republics	Capitals	area sq mi	area sq km	population 1993[3] estimate
Abkhazia[4]	Sokhumi (Sukhumi)	3,320	8,600	516,600
Ajaria (Achara)	Bat'umi	1,158	3,000	386,700
Regions				
Guria	Ozurget'i	21,892	56,700	160,800
Imereti	K'ut'aisi			788,900
Kakheti	T'elavi			464,000
Kvemo Kartli	Rust'avi			601,500
Mts'khet'a-Mtianeti	Mts'khet'a			43,800
Ragha-Lechkhumi & Kvemo Svaneti	Ambrolauri			45,400
Samegrelo & Zemo Svaneti	Zugdidi			418,100
Samtskhe-Javakheti	Akhalts'ikhe			198,800
Shida Kartli[5]	Gori			485,900
City				
T'bilisi	...	541	1,400	1,271,800
TOTAL		26,911	69,700	5,405,400[6]

Demography

Population (2001): 4,989,000.
Density (2001): persons per sq mi 185.4, persons per sq km 71.6.
Urban-rural (2000): urban 60.7%; rural 39.3%.
Sex distribution (2000): male 47.55%; female 52.45%.
Age breakdown (2000): under 15, 20.2%; 15–29, 23.8%; 30–44, 22.3%; 45–59, 15.5%; 60–74, 14.4%; 75 and over, 3.8%.
Population projection: (2010) 4,815,000; (2020) 4,785,000.
Ethnic composition (1989): Georgian 70.1%; Armenian 8.1%; Russian 6.3%; Azerbaijani 5.7%; Ossetian 3.0%; Greek 1.9%; Abkhazian 1.8%; other 3.1%.
Religious affiliation (1995): Christian 46.2%, of which Georgian Orthodox 36.7%, Armenian Apostolic 5.6%, Russian Orthodox 2.7%, other Christian 1.2%; Sunni Muslim 11.0%; other (mostly nonreligious) 42.8%.
Major cities (1997): T'bilisi (1998) 1,398,968; K'ut'aisi 240,000; Rust'avi 158,000; Bat'umi 137,100; Zugdidi 105,000[7].

Vital statistics

Birth rate per 1,000 population (2000): 10.9 (world avg. 22.5).
Death rate per 1,000 population (2000): 14.5 (world avg. 9.0).
Natural increase rate per 1,000 population (2000): –3.6 (world avg. 13.5).
Total fertility rate (avg. births per childbearing woman; 2000): 1.4.
Marriage rate per 1,000 population (1996): 3.7.
Life expectancy at birth (2000): male 60.9 years; female 68.2 years.
Major causes of death per 100,000 population (1995): diseases of the circulatory system 569.6; malignant neoplasms (cancers) 63.4; accidents, poisoning, and violence 44.7; diseases of the digestive system 30.3.

National economy

Budget (1998). Revenue: 726,200,000 lari[2] (tax revenue 65.6%, of which value-added tax 34.9%, excise tax 14.9%; extrabudgetary revenue 21.7%; nontax revenue 8.0%; grants 4.7%). Expenditures: 938,800,000 lari[2] (current expenditure 89.5%; development expenditure 5.9%; net lending 4.6%).
Public debt (external, outstanding; 1999): U.S.$1,308,000,000.
Population economically active (1993): total 1,920,000[8]; activity rate of total population 35.7% (participation rates: ages 16–59 [male], 16–54 [female] 58.1%; female [1996] 46.0%; urban unemployed [April–June 2000] 24.7%[9]).

Price and earnings indexes (1995 = 100)

	1995	1996	1997	1998	1999	2000
Consumer price index	100.0	113.5	122.1	135.2	149.9	156.8
Annual earnings index	100.0	213.2	319.2	407.2	496.0	...

Production (metric tons except as noted). Agriculture, forestry, fishing (1999): corn (maize) 486,000, potatoes 433,000, tomatoes 310,000, wheat 243,500, grapes 230,000, apples 110,000, tea 60,000, sunflower seed 43,000; livestock (number of live animals) 1,051,000 cattle, 550,000 sheep; roundwood, n.a.; fish catch (1997) 6,933. Mining and quarrying (1996): manganese ore 97,000. Manufacturing (1995)[10]: steel 88,000; cigarettes 1,900,000,000 units; wine 412,000 hectolitres; beer 67,000 hectolitres. Energy production (consumption): electricity (kW-hr; 1996) 7,195,000,000 (7,315,000,000); coal (metric tons; 1996) 20,000 (230,000); crude petroleum (barrels; 1996) 938,000 (938,000); petroleum products (metric tons; 1996) 22,000 (104,000); natural gas (cu m; 1996) 2,896,000 (917,831,000).
Tourism (in U.S.$'000,000; 1999): receipts 400; expenditures 270.
Gross national product (at current market prices; 1999): U.S.$3,362,000,000 (U.S.$620 per capita).

Structure of net material product and labour force

	1997 in value '000,000 lari[2, 11]	1997 % of total value	1995 labour force[12]	1995 % of labour force
Agriculture	1,917	28.2	516,000	29.6
Mining, Manufacturing, Public utilities	653	9.6	264,000	15.2
Construction	326	4.8	90,000	5.2
Transp. and commun.	673	9.9	52,000	3.0
Trade, restaurants	1,496	22.0	257,000	14.8
Finance, real estate	...	...	10,000	0.6
Pub. admin., defense	...	...	35,000	2.0
Services	...	...	516,000	29.6
Other	25.5	1,733		
TOTAL	6,798	100.0	1,740,000	100.0

Household income and expenditure (1993). Average household size 4.0; income per household: n.a.; sources of income: wages and salaries 34.5%, benefits 21.9%, agricultural income 21.6%, other 22.0%; expenditure: taxes 42.5%, retail goods 32.3%, savings 16.4%, transportation 4.2%.

Foreign trade[13]

Balance of trade (current prices)

	1995	1996	1997	1998	1999	2000
U.S.$'000,000	–337	–519	–657	–475	–382	–370
% of total	31.8%	56.5%	59.4%	64.1%	44.2%	36.0%

Imports (2000): U.S.$700,200,000 (mineral fuels 16.7%; wheat and flour 7.6%; medicines 6.5%; tobacco products 4.2%; unspecified 54.4%). *Major import sources:* Turkey 15.5%; Russia 12.9%; United States 10.1%; Azerbaijan 8.1%; Germany 8.0%.
Exports (2000): U.S.$329,900,000 (scrap metals 11.5%; wine 8.6%; nuts 6.8%; fertilizers 4.7%; precious metallic ores 4.5%). *Major export destinations:* Turkey 22.3%; Russia 20.6%; Germany 9.4%; Azerbaijan 6.4%; Ukraine 5.9%.

Transport and communications

Transport. Railroads (1997): 1,546 km; (1995) passenger-km 371,000,000; (1993) metric ton-km cargo 1,750,000,000. Roads (1996): 20,700 km (paved 93%). Vehicles (1996): passenger cars 427,000; trucks and buses 41,510. Air transport (1997)[14]: passenger-km 127,077,000; metric ton-km cargo 840,000; airports (1997) with scheduled flights 1.

Communications

Medium	date	unit	number	units per 1,000 persons
Daily newspapers	1996	circulation	0	—
Radio	1997	receivers	3,020,000	586
Television	1998	receivers	2,580,000	506
Telephones	1999	main lines	671,511	133
Cellular telephones	2000	subscribers	185,000	37
Internet	1999	users	20,000	4.0

Education and health

Education (1996–97)

	schools	teachers	students	student/ teacher ratio
Primary (age 6–9)	3,201	16,542	293,325	17.7
Secondary (age 10–16)	3,139[15]	55,817	424,465	7.6
Voc., teacher tr.	...	2,146	19,593	9.1
Higher	23	25,549	163,345	6.4

Food (1999): daily per capita caloric intake 2,347 (vegetable products 84%, animal products 16%); 92% of FAO recommended minimum requirement.
Health (1997): physicians 21,846 (1 per 236 persons); hospital beds 24,500 (1 per 210 persons); infant mortality rate per 1,000 live births (2000) 52.9.

Military

Total active duty personnel (2000): 26,900 (army 88.5%, air force 6.9%, navy 3.0%, centrally controlled units/other 1.6%). About 5,000 Russian troops remained in Georgia in mid-2000[16]. *Military expenditure as percentage of GNP* (1997): 1.4% (world 2.6%); per capita expenditure U.S.$31.

[1]Special recognition is given to the Georgian Orthodox Church. [2]The Georgian lari, introduced Sept. 25, 1995, replaced the Georgian coupon, at a rate of 1,000,000 coupons to 1 lari. [3]January 1. [4]Abkhazia has had de facto autonomy from Georgia since 1993. Its final status was unresolved in August 2001. [5]The northern 1,505 sq mi- (3,900 sq km-) area of Shida Kartli is the autonomous region of South Ossetia. In March 1997 the separatist region of South Ossetia was given this status by the Georgian government, but its final status was unresolved in August 2001. [6]Excludes population of 23,200 with unknown distribution by autonomous republic or district. [7]Includes internally displaced persons from Abkhazia. [8]Excludes informal sector. [9]Includes long-term unemployed. [10]Excludes Abkhazia and South Ossetia. [11]Includes official estimates for informal sector. [12]Employed persons in formal sector only. [13]Imports c.i.f.; exports f.o.b. [14]Orbi Georgian Airways. [15]1995–96. [16]Withdrawal of Russian troops from Georgia began in June 2001 with the closure of the first of four Russian military bases.

Internet resources for further information:
- **National Bank of Georgia**
  http://www.nbg.gov.ge
- **Social-Economic Situation in Georgia**
  http://www.parliament.ge/GENERAL/stat/emain.htm

Germany

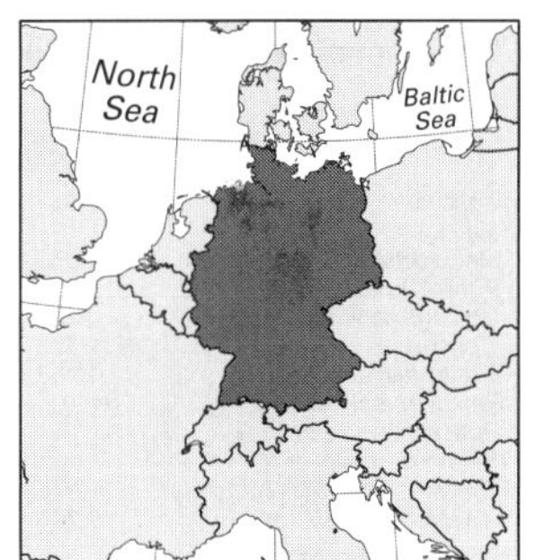

Official name: Bundesrepublik Deutschland (Federal Republic of Germany).
Form of government: federal multiparty republic with two legislative houses (Federal Council [69]; Federal Diet [672]).
Chief of state: President.
Head of government: Chancellor.
Capital: Berlin, some ministries remain in Bonn.
Official language: German.
Official religion: none.
Monetary unit: 1 Deutsche Mark (DM) = 100 Pfennige; valuation (Sept. 28, 2001) 1 U.S.$ = DM 2.15; 1 £ = DM 3.16; 1 € = 1.95583.

Area and population

States / Administrative districts	Capitals	area sq mi	area sq km	population 2000[1] estimate
Baden-Württemberg	Stuttgart	13,804	35,752	10,475,900[2]
Freiburg	Freiburg	3,613	9,357	2,125,400
Karlsruhe	Karlsruhe	2,671	6,919	2,676,300
Stuttgart	Stuttgart	4,076	10,558	3,917,300
Tübingen	Tübingen	3,443	8,918	1,757,000
Bayern	Munich	27,240	70,551[2]	12,155,000
Mittelfranken	Ansbach	2,798	7,246	1,683,300
Niederbayern	Landshut	3,988	10,330	1,170,200
Oberbayern	Munich	6,768	17,530	4,033,600
Oberfranken	Bayreuth	2,792	7,230	1,114,200
Oberpfalz	Regensburg	3,741	9,690	1,074,300
Schwaben	Augsburg	3,859	9,994	1,745,600
Unterfranken	Würzburg	3,294	8,532	1,333,800
Berlin	—	344	891	3,386,700
Brandenburg	Potsdam	11,381	29,476	2,601,200
Bremen	Bremen	156	404	663,100
Hamburg	Hamburg	292	755	1,704,700
Hessen	Wiesbaden	8,152	21,114[2]	6,052,000
Darmstadt	Darmstadt	2,874	7,445	3,719,400
Giessen	Giessen	2,078	5,381	1,063,500
Kassel	Kassel	3,200	8,289	1,269,100
Mecklenburg-Vorpommern	Schwerin	8,946	23,170	1,789,300
Niedersachsen	Hannover	18,383	47,612[2]	7,898,800
Braunschweig	Braunschweig	3,126	8,097	1,669,600
Hannover	Hannover	3,493	9,046	2,152,800
Lüneburg	Lüneburg	5,986	15,505	1,660,700
Weser-Ems	Oldenburg	5,778	14,965	2,415,700
Nordrhein-Westfalen	Düsseldorf	13,158	34,078[2]	17,999,800[2]
Arnsberg	Arnsberg	3,090	8,002	3,814,300
Detmold	Detmold	2,517	6,518	2,048,600
Düsseldorf	Düsseldorf	2,042	5,289	5,264,500
Köln	Köln	2,844	7,365	4,263,700
Münster	Münster	2,665	6,903	2,608,800
Rheinland-Pfalz	Mainz	7,662[2]	19,846[2]	4,030,800[2]
Koblenz	Koblenz	3,117	8,072	1,516,200
Rheinhessen-Pfalz	Mainz	2,646	6,852	2,003,000
Trier	Trier	1,901	4,923	511,500
Saarland	Saarbrücken	992	2,570	1,071,500
Sachsen	Dresden	7,109	18,413	4,459,700
Chemnitz	—	2,354	6,097	1,638,900
Dresden	—	3,062	7,930	1,724,700
Leipzig	—	1,693	4,836	1,096,100
Sachsen-Anhalt	Magdeburg	7,895[2]	20,447[2]	2,648,700
Dessau	Dessau	1,652	4,280	552,400
Halle	Halle/Saale	1,710	4,430	876,100
Magdeburg	Magdeburg	4,532	11,738	1,220,200
Schleswig-Holstein	Kiel	6,089	15,770	2,777,300
Thüringen	Erfurt	6,244	16,171	2,449,100
TOTAL		137,846[2]	357,021[2]	82,163,500[2]

Demography

Population (2001): 82,386,000.
Major cities (1999): Berlin 3,392,900; Hamburg 1,701,800; Munich 1,193,600; Cologne 963,200; Frankfurt am Main 644,700; Essen 600,700; Dortmund 590,300; Stuttgart 581,200; Düsseldorf 568,500; Bremen 542,300; Duisburg 521,300; Hannover 515,200; Leipzig 490,000; Nürnberg 486,400.

Other principal cities (1999)

	population		population		population
Aachen	243,600	Heidelberg	139,400	Oberhausen	222,300
Augsburg	254,500	Heilbronn	119,900	Offenbach am Main	116,400
Bergisch Gladbach	106,300	Herne	176,200	Oldenburg	154,100
Bielefeld	321,600	Hildesheim	104,600	Osnabrück	164,900
Bochum	392,900	Ingolstadt	114,500	Paderborn	136,800
Bonn	304,100	Kaiserslautern	100,300	Pforzheim	117,500
Bottrop	121,500	Karlsruhe	276,700	Potsdam	129,500
Braunschweig	246,800	Kassel	196,700	Recklingshausen	125,200
Bremerhaven	123,800	Kiel	235,500	Regensburg	125,200
Chemnitz	266,000	Koblenz	108,700	Remscheld	119,500
Cottbus	112,200	Krefeld	242,800	Reutlingen	110,200
Darmstadt	137,600	Leverkusen	161,100	Rostock	205,900
Dresden	477,700	Lübeck	213,800	Saarbrücken	184,300
Erfurt	202,100	Ludwigshafen		Salzgitter	113,700
Erlangen	100,600	am Rhein	164,200	Schwerin	104,200
Freiburg		Magdeburg	238,000	Siegen	109,600
im Breisgau	201,000	Mainz	185,600	Solingen	165,400
Fürth	109,700	Mannheim	308,400	Ulm	116,100
Gelsenkirchen	283,300	Moers	106,900	Wiesbaden	268,200
Gera	115,800	Mönchengladbach	264,100	Witten	103,000
Göttingen	125,400	Mülheim		Wolfsburg	122,200
Hagen	206,400	an der Ruhr	174,300	Wuppertal	370,700
Halle an der Saale	258,400	Münster	264,700	Würzburg	126,000
Hamm	181,500	Neuss	149,100	Zwickau	104,900

Density (2001): persons per sq mi 597.7, persons per sq km 230.8.
Urban-rural (1997[1]): urban 82.4%; rural 17.6%.
Population projection: (2010) 84,013,000; (2020) 84,897,000.
Sex distribution (2000[1]): male 48.79%; female 51.21%.
Age breakdown (2000[1]): under 15, 15.7%; 15–29, 17.6%; 30–44, 24.7%; 45–59, 19.1%; 60–74, 15.9%; 75 and over, 7.0%.
Doubling time: not applicable; doubling time exceeds 100 years.
Ethnic composition (by nationality; 2000): German 82.2%; Turkish 3.4%, of which Kurdish 0.7%; Italian 1.0%; Greek 0.7%; Polish 0.4%; other 12.3%.
Religious affiliation: (2000) Lutheran 37.0%, Roman Catholic 34.9%, Muslim 4.4%, atheist 2.2%, other 21.5%.
Households (2000). Number of households 38,124,000; average household size 2.2; 1 person 36.0%, 2 persons 33.4%, 3 persons 14.7%, 4 persons 11.5%, 5 or more persons 4.4%.

Vital statistics

Birth rate per 1,000 population (1999): 9.4 (world avg. 22.5); legitimate 77.8%; illegitimate 22.2%.
Death rate per 1,000 population (1999): 10.3 (world avg. 9.0).
Natural increase rate per 1,000 population (1999): –0.9 (world avg. 13.5).
Total fertility rate (avg. births per childbearing woman; 1999): 1.4.
Marriage rate per 1,000 population (1999): 5.2.
Divorce rate per 1,000 population (1999): 2.3.
Life expectancy at birth (1997–99): male 74.4 years; female 80.6 years.
Major causes of death per 100,000 population (1999): diseases of the circulatory system 494.7; malignant neoplasms (cancers) 256.8, of which bronchial, lung, and tracheal 48.5; diseases of the respiratory system 62.7, of which pneumonia 23.1, chronic bronchitis 4.7; suicide 14.9.

Social indicators

Educational attainment (2000). Percentage of population age 25 and over having: primary and lower secondary 50.6%; intermediate secondary 17.9%; vocational secondary 8.7%; post-secondary and higher (all levels) 22.8%.
Quality of working life. Average workweek (1998): 39.8 hours. Annual rate per 100,000 workers (1993) for: injuries or accidents at work 4,808; deaths, including commuting accidents, 6.7. Proportion of labour force insured for damages of income loss resulting from: injury, virtually 100%; permanent disability, virtually 100%; death, virtually 100%. Average days lost to labour stoppages per 1,000 workers (1996): 4.1.

Distribution of income (1993)[3]

percentage of household income by quintile

1	2	3	4	5 (highest)
6.5	1.8	17.3	27.2	37.2

Access to services. Proportion of dwellings (1996) having: electricity, virtually 100%; piped water supply, virtually 100%; flush sewage disposal (1993) 98.4%; public fire protection, virtually 100%.
Social participation. Eligible voters participating in last (September 1998) national election *c.* 81%. Trade union membership in total workforce (1994): *c.* 27%. Practicing religious population (1994): 5% of Protestants and 25% of Roman Catholics "regularly" attend religious services.
Social deviance (1996). Offense rate per 100,000 population for: murder and manslaughter 3.3; sexual abuse 46.0, of which rape and forcible sexual assault 13.4, child molestation 7.3; assault and battery 116.9; theft 688.9. Incidence per 100,000 in general population (late 1970s) of: alcoholism 2,500–3,000; drug and substance abuse 650; suicide (1996) 14.9.
Material well-being (2000[1]; median income). Households possessing: automobile 75.4%; telephone 96.7%; colour television receiver 95.5%; refrigerator 79.3%; washing machine 97.9%; home freezer 73.8%; personal computer 48.2%; video recorder 83.8%.

Recreational and leisure activities[3]

(Monthly household expenditures, 1997; median income)

Activity	DM	percentage
Vacations	203	24.0
Expenditures for motor vehicles	119	14.0
Sporting and camping equipment and sporting events	121	14.3
Televisions, radios, and their fees	91	10.7
Books, newspapers, and magazines	66	7.8
Gardening and pets	54	6.4
Games and toys	38	4.5
Visits to theatre and cinema	23	2.7
Photographic and moviemaking equipment and film	21	2.5
Tools	8	0.9
Other activities	103	12.2
TOTAL	847	100.0

National economy

Budget (2000). Revenue: DM 1,910,161,000,000 (taxes 84.7%, interest 7.7%). Expenditures: DM 1,873,837,000,000 (pensions and other social security payments 34.4%, purchase of current goods and services 21.9%, personnel costs 18.4%).
Total national debt (1998): DM 718,440,000,000.
Production (value of production in DM except as noted; 1999–2000). Agriculture, forestry, fishing: cereal grains 7,007,000,000, flowers and ornamental plants 3,010,000,000, sugar beets 2,541,000,000, grapes for wine 2,289,000,000, fruits 2,095,000,000, potatoes 2,024,000,000, vegetables 1,960,000,000, tree nurseries 1,870,000,000, oilseed crops 1,601,000,000; livestock (number of live animals; 2000) 27,049,000 pigs, 14,658,000 cattle, 2,100,000 sheep, 110,000,000 chickens; roundwood (2000) 37,634,000 cu m; fish catch (metric tons; 1999) 312,492. Mining and quarrying (metric tons;

1998): potash 37,100,000. Manufacturing (value added at factor cost in DM '000,000; 1996): capital equipment 252,226, of which machinery 90,213, transport equipment 80,418; electrical equipment 57,269; chemicals (including pharmaceuticals) 60,842; food and beverages 39,184; plastics and other synthetic products 27,853; glass and ceramic products 22,730; furniture and other wood products 16,651; paper products 12,948; textiles 8,636; clothing 5,467. Construction (newly completed buildings, sq m; 1996): residential 43,937,000; nonresidential 43,593,000.

Manufacturing, mining, and construction enterprises (1997)

	no. of enter-prises	no. of employees	wages as a % of avg. of all wages	annual gross production value (DM '000,000)[4]
Manufacturing	44,514	6,162,900	100.0	2,077,699
of which				
Road and motor vehicles	1,000	695,800	117.9	303,801
Machinery (nonelectric)	6,461	981,500	106.1	254,366
Chemical	1,709	500,500	121.2	220,367
Food and beverages	4,812	502,100	76.4	219,025
Machinery and appliances (electric)	2,248	446,000	105.2	210,357
Petroleum and natural gas[4]	53	23,000	124.1	123,801
Rubber and plastic products	2,923	343,000	87.5	86,006
Glass and ceramics	3,747	257,400	89.5	70,439
Textiles	1,296	131,600	74.5	31,429
Wood and wood products	2,014	115,700	81.7	30,423
Mining and quarrying[4]	787	169,000	105.3	29,094
Construction[4]	24,848	1,403,000	100.0	249,327

Energy production (consumption): electricity (kW-hr; 1997) 546,412,000,000 (544,063,000,000); hard coal (metric tons; 1997) 51,212,000 (72,236,000); lignite (metric tons; 1997) 177,159,000 (179,403,000); crude petroleum (barrels; 1997) 20,553,000 (745,355,000); petroleum products (metric tons; 1997) 93,230,000 (113,289,000); natural gas (cu m; 1997) 23,925,000,000 (108,390,000,000).
Gross national product (at current market prices; 1999): U.S.$2,103,804,000,000 (U.S.$25,620 per capita).

Structure of gross domestic product and labour force

	1999		2000	
	in value DM '000,000	% of total value	labour force	% of labour force
Agriculture	42,240	1.2	987,000	2.4
Public utilities, mining	82,600	2.4	290,000[5]	0.7
Manufacturing	826,960	23.8	8,694,000[5]	21.6
Construction	189,830	5.4	3,118,000	7.7
Transportation and communications	204,630	5.9	2,008,000	5.0
Trade[6]	420,700	12.2	6,409,000	15.9
Finance, real estate	1,077,270[7]	30.9[7]	1,333,000	3.3
Services	[7]	[7]	10,628,000	26.4
Pub. admin., defense	770,600	22.1	3,136,000	7.8
Other	–137,800[8]	–3.9[8]	3,723,000[9]	9.2[9]
TOTAL	3,480,060	100.0	40,326,000	100.0

Population economically active (2000): total 40,326,000; activity rate of total population 49.0% (participation rates[10]: ages 15–64, 70.7%; female 43.8%; unemployed 9.2%).

Price and earnings indexes (1995 = 100)

	1994	1995	1996	1997	1998	1999	2000
Consumer price index	98.2	100.0	101.5	103.3	104.3	104.9	107.0
Hourly earnings index	...	...	...	...	...	...	...

Household income and expenditure. Average annual income per household (1998) DM 75,144 (U.S.$42,702); sources of take-home income[11]: wages 77.6%, self-employment 12.0%, transfer payments 10.4%; expenditure: rent 24.7%, food and beverages 13.9%, transportation 13.7%, entertainment, education, and leisure 11.8%, household operations, durables, and maintenance 7.0%, clothing and footwear 5.5%.
Tourism (1999): receipts U.S.$16,730,000,000; expenditures U.S.$48,495,000,000.

Financial aggregates[12]

	1994	1995	1996	1997	1998	1999	2000
Exchange rate, DM per[13]:							
U.S. dollar	1.5488	1.4335	1.5548	1.7341	1.7597	0.9386	1.0854
£	2.4207	2.2219	2.6285	2.8399	2.9148	1.5188	1.6456
SDR	2.2610	2.1309	2.2357	2.4180	2.3556	1.3662	1.4002
International reserves (U.S.$)							
Total (excl. gold; '000,000)	77,363	85,005	83,178	77,587	74,024	61,039	56,890
SDRs ('000,000)	1,114	2,001	1,907	1,788	1,868	1,959	1,763
Reserve pos. in IMF ('000,000)	4,030	5,210	5,468	5,946	8,023	6,419	5,460
Foreign exchange	72,219	77,794	75,083	69,853	64,133	52,661	49,667
Gold ('000,000 fine troy oz)	95.18	95.18	95.18	95.18	118.98	111.52	111.52
% world reserves	10.46	10.48	10.52	10.69	12.31	11.56	11.73
Interest and prices							
Central bank discount (%)	4.5	3.0	2.5	2.5	2.5	...	...
Govt. bond yield (%)	6.7	6.5	5.6	5.1	4.4	4.3	5.2
Industrial share prices (1995 = 100)[14]	102.7	100.0	114.1	156.3	200.0	207.3	258.7
Balance of payments (U.S.$'000,000,000)							
Balance of visible trade	51.68	66.12	71.21	71.75	79.04	70.06	57.29
Imports, f.o.b.	378.59	457.10	488.22	439.3	460.95	472.67	491.87
Exports, f.o.b.	430.27	523.22	519.44	511.08	539.99	542.72	549.17
Balance of invisibles	–71.86	–87.67	–84.99	–74.52	–82.48	–88.00	–76.00
Balance of payments, current account	–20.94	–22.56	–13.78	–2.77	–3.44	–17.94	–18.71

Service enterprises (1991)

	no. of enter-prises	no. of employees	weekly wages as a % of all wages	annual turnover (DM '000,000)
Gas	151	37,000	...	42,228
Water	183	40,000	...	3,443
Electrical power	462	296,000	...	147,076
Transport				
air	133	57,390	...	20,270
buses	6,054	192,869	...	12,586
rail	1	416,199	...	14,697
shipping	1,449	9,076	...	...
Communications				
press	2,452	240,075	...	31,096
film[15]	615	3,000	...	836
Postal services	17,616[16]	652,573	...	68,346
Hotels and restaurants	135,141	652,251	...	60,257
Wholesale trade	36,605[16]	1,214,000	...	1,015,984
Retail trade	152,629	2,241,000	...	605,755

Land use (1994): forest 30.6%; pasture 15.1%; agriculture 19.9%; other 34.4%.

Foreign trade

Balance of trade (current prices)

	1995	1996	1997	1998	1999[17]	2000[17]
DM '000,000,000	+103.40	+117.35	+137.35	+148.66	+76.90	+55.88
% of total	7.4%	8.0%	8.4%	8.4%	8.2%	4.9%

Imports (2000): DM 1,064,308,800,000 (machinery and transport equipment 37.0%, of which road transport equipment 8.3%, electrical machinery other than office equipment 7.9%; chemicals and chemical products 8.9%, of which organic chemical products 2.5%, unfabricated plastics 1.4%; mineral fuels 8.7%, of which crude petroleum and petroleum products 6.5%, natural gas 1.8%; food and beverages 6.1%, of which fruits and vegetables 1.8%, meat and meat products 0.7%, coffee, tea, and cocoa 0.6%; iron and steel 2.2%; furniture 1.3%). *Major import sources:* France 9.6%; The Netherlands 8.8%; U.S. 8.5%; U.K. 7.0%; Italy 6.6%; Japan 4.9%; Belgium 4.8%.
Exports (2000): DM 1,167,343,300,000 (machinery and transport equipment 51.2%, of which road transport equipment 17.4%, electrical machinery other than office equipment 8.4%; chemicals and chemical products 12.7%, of which organic chemical products 2.4%, unfabricated plastics 2.2%). *Major export destinations:* France 11.4%; U.S. 10.2%; U.K. 8.3%; Italy 7.6%; The Netherlands 6.4%; Austria 5.3%; Belgium 5.1%; Spain 4.5%; Switzerland 4.3%; Poland 2.4%; Japan 2.2%; Sweden 2.2%.

Transport and communications

Transport. Railroads (1999): length 51,209 mi[10], 82,413 km[10]; passengers carried 1,943,000,000; passenger-mi 45,725,000,000, passenger-km 73,587,000,000; short ton-mi cargo 48,874,000,000, metric ton-km cargo 71,356,000,000. Roads (1999): total length 143,372 mi, 230,735 km (paved 99%). Vehicles (2000[1]): passenger cars 42,423,300; trucks and buses 2,576,000. Merchant marine (1998): vessels (100 gross tons and over) 1,158; total deadweight tonnage 8,083,600. Air transport (1999): passengers carried 41,118,000; passenger-mi 55,219,396,000, passenger-km 88,867,173,000; short ton-mi cargo 4,519,788,000, metric ton-km cargo 6,598,776,000; airports (1997) 35.

Communications

Medium	date	unit	number	units per 1,000 persons
Daily newspapers	1996	circulation	25,500,000	311
Radio	1997	receivers	77,800,000	948
Television	1999	receivers	47,600,000	580
Telephones	1999	main lines	48,500,000	590
Cellular telephones	1999	subscribers	23,470,000	286
Personal computers	1999	units	24,400,000	297
Internet	1999	users	14,400,000	175

Education and health

Health (2000): physicians 294,676 (1 per 279 persons); dentists 63,156 (1 per 1,302 persons); hospital beds (1999) 565,268 (1 per 145 persons); infant mortality rate per 1,000 live births (1999) 4.5.

Education (1999–2000)

	schools	teachers	students	student/ teacher ratio
Primary (age 6–10)	17,503	192,659	3,488,300	17.9
Secondary (age 10–19)	19,897	421,002	5,827,714	13.8
Voc., teacher tr.	9,580	112,577	2,656,450	23.5
Higher[18]	335	152,401	1,838,456	12.1

Food (1999): daily per capita caloric intake 3,411 (vegetable products 69%, animal products 31%); 128% of FAO recommended minimum requirement.

Military

Total active duty personnel (2000): 321,000 (army 68.9%, navy 8.3%, air force 22.8%). *Military expenditure as percentage of GNP* (1997): 1.6% (world 2.6%); per capita expenditure U.S.$401.

[1]January 1. [2]Detail does not add to total given because of rounding. [3]Former West Germany only. [4]1996. [5]Manufacturing includes mining. [6]Include hotels. [7]Finance, real estate includes Services. [8]Less imputed bank service charges. [9]Unemployed. [10]1998. [11]1997. [12]End-of-period figures unless footnoted otherwise. [13]Beginning in 1999 exchange rates expressed in euros (€). [14]Period averages. [15]1984. [16]1990. [17]In billions of Euros. [18]1995–96.

Internet resources for further information:
- **Federal Statistical Office of Germany**
http://www.statistik-bund.de/e_home.htm

Ghana

Official name: Republic of Ghana.
Form of government: unitary multiparty republic with one legislative house (House of Parliament [200]).
Head of state and government: President.
Capital: Accra.
Official language: English.
Official religion: none.
Monetary unit: 1 cedi (₵) = 100 pesewas; valuation (Sept. 28, 2001) 1 U.S.$ = ₵7,200; 1 £ = ₵10,582.

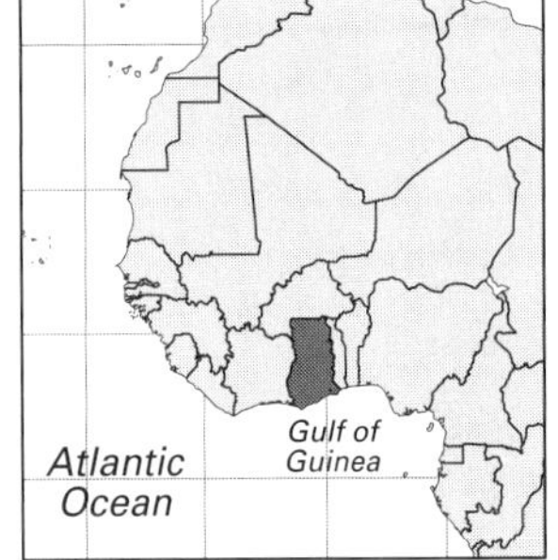

Area and population

Regions[2]	Capitals	area sq mi	area sq km	population 1991[1] estimate
Ashanti	Kumasi	9,417	24,389	2,485,766
Brong-Ahafo	Sunyani	15,273	39,557	1,432,971
Central	Cape Coast	3,794	9,826	1,359,861
Eastern	Koforidua	7,461	19,323	2,003,235
Greater Accra	Accra	1,253	3,245	1,696,170
Northern	Tamale	27,175	70,384	1,389,105
Upper East	Bolgatanga	3,414	8,842	921,196
Upper West	Wa	7,134	18,476	526,398
Volta	Ho	7,942	20,570	1,432,971
Western	Sekondi-Takoradi	9,236	23,921	1,374,483
TOTAL		92,098[3]	238,533	14,622,156

Demography

Population (2001): 19,894,000.
Density (2001): persons per sq mi 216.0, persons per sq km 83.4.
Urban-rural (1999): urban 37.8%; rural 62.2%.
Sex distribution (1999): male 49.77%; female 50.23%.
Age breakdown (2000): under 15, 41.9%; 15–29, 27.7%; 30–44, 17.4%; 45–59, 7.8%; 60–74, 4.2%; 75 and over, 1.0%.
Population projection: (2010) 22,650,000; (2020) 25,223,000.
Doubling time: 37 years.
Ethnolinguistic composition (1983): Akan 52.4%; Mossi 15.8%; Ewe 11.9%; Ga-Adangme 7.8%; Gurma 3.3%; Yoruba 1.3%; other 7.5%.
Religious affiliation (2000): Christian 55.4%, of which Protestant 16.6%, African Christian 14.4%, Roman Catholic 9.5%; traditional beliefs 24.4%; Muslim 19.7%; other 0.5%.
Major cities (2001[1]): Accra 1,551,200; Kumasi 610,600; Tamale 259,200; Tema 225,900; Obuasi 118,000.

Vital statistics

Birth rate per 1,000 population (2001): 29.0 (world avg. 22.5); legitimate, n.a.; illegitimate, n.a.
Death rate per 1,000 population (2001): 10.3 (world avg. 9.0).
Natural increase rate per 1,000 population (2001): 18.7 (world avg. 13.5).
Total fertility rate (avg. births per childbearing woman; 2001): 3.8.
Life expectancy at birth (2001): male 55.9 years; females 58.7 years.
Major causes of death per 100,000 population: n.a.; however, principal infectious diseases as a percentage of outpatients (1989): malaria 43.8%, respiratory infections (including tuberculosis) 8.0%, diarrheal diseases 6.7%, intestinal worms 3.1%.

National economy

Budget (1996). Revenue: ₵1,997,600,000,000 (excise and value-added taxes 36.7%, of which petroleum tax 14.5%; import-export duties 27.3%; income taxes 21.7%; nontax revenue 14.4%). Expenditures (1995): ₵1,697,893,000,000 (1994; education 22.3%; debt service 20.1%; health 6.9%; transportation and communications 5.3%; social security and welfare 3.6%; defense 2.9%).
Public debt (external, outstanding; 1999): U.S.$5,647,000,000.
Production (metric tons except as noted). Agriculture, forestry, fishing (2000): roots and tubers 12,893,000 (of which cassava 7,845,000, yams 3,249,000, taro 1,707,000), cereals 1,686,000 (of which corn [maize] 1,014,000, sorghum 302,000, rice 210,000, millet 160,000), bananas and plantains 2,061,000, cacao 409,000, coconuts 310,000, oranges 270,000, tomatoes 216,000, peanuts (groundnuts) 212,000, sugarcane 147,000, palm kernels 34,000, lemons and limes 30,000, pulses 20,000; livestock (number of live animals) 2,739,000 goats, 2,516,000 sheep, 1,273,000 cattle, 352,000 pigs, 17,467,000 chickens; roundwood (1998) 21,905,000 cu m; fish catch (1998) 442,692. Mining and quarrying (1998): manganese ore 384,173; bauxite 341,121; gold 113,054 kg; diamonds 805,742 carats. Manufacturing (value added in ₵; 1993): tobacco 71,474,700,000; footwear 60,350,600,000; chemical products 40,347,600,000; beverages 36,167,000,000; metal products 35,121,700,000; petroleum products 32,143,500,000; textiles 18,278,600,000; machinery and transport equipment 9,525,700,000. Construction (value added in ₵; 1994) 171,129,000,000. Energy production (consumption): electricity (kW-hr; 1996) 6,631,000,000 (6,405,000,000); coal (metric tons; 1998) none (3,000); crude petroleum (barrels; 1998) none (7,315,000); petroleum products (metric tons; 1998) 926,000 (1,077,000); natural gas, none (n.a.).
Tourism (1999): receipts U.S.$304,000,000; expenditures U.S.$36,000,000.
Household income and expenditure. Average household size (1984) 4.9; average annual income per household (1978) ₵9,600 (U.S.$[4]); sources of income: n.a.; expenditure (1978): food 57.4%, clothing 14.3%, housing 11.5%, transportation and communications 3.3%, health care 1.3%.
Gross national product (1999): U.S.$7,451,000,000 (U.S.$400 per capita).

Structure of gross domestic product and labour force

	1996 in value ₵'000,000	1996 % of total value	1984 labour force	1984 % of labour force
Agriculture	4,895,000	46.0	3,310,967	59.4
Mining	190,000	1.8	26,828	0.5
Manufacturing	964,000	9.1	588,418	10.5
Construction	376,000	3.5	64,686	1.2
Public utilities	215,000	2.0	15,437	0.3
Transp. and commun.	431,000	4.0	122,806	2.2
Trade[5]	2,176,000	20.5	792,147	14.2
Finance	404,000	3.8	27,475	0.5
Pub. admin., defense } Services }	957,000	9.0	97,548	1.7
			376,168	6.7
Other	26,000[6]	0.2[6]	157,624[7]	2.8[7]
TOTAL	10,633,000[3]	100.0[3]	5,580,104	100.0

Population economically active (1984): total 5,580,104; activity rate of total population 45.4% (participation rates: over age 15, 82.5%; female 51.2%; unemployed 2.8%).

Price and earnings indexes (1995 = 100)

	1994	1995	1996	1997	1998	1999	2000
Consumer price index	62.7	100.0	146.6	187.4	214.8	241.5	302.3
Monthly earnings index	...	...	...	...	...	...	...

Land use (1994): forest 42.2%; pasture 36.9%; agriculture 19.0%; other 1.9%.

Foreign trade

Balance of trade (current prices)

	1994	1995	1996	1997	1998	1999
U.S.$'000,000	–353.1	–256.6	–366.0	–638.3	–805.5	–1,111.5
% of total	12.6%	4.6%	10.4%	17.6%	16.2%	20.8%

Imports (1998): U.S.$2,896,900,000 (petroleum [all forms] 7.4%; unspecified 92.6%). *Major import sources* (1999): Nigeria 14.9%; U.K. 9.5%; Côte d'Ivoire 9.0%; U.S. 8.1%; France 7.7%.
Exports (1998): U.S.$2,091,400,000 (gold 32.9%; cacao 25.9%; wood products 8.2%; cocoa products 3.8%). *Major export destinations* (1999): Togo 12.6%; U.K. 11.6%; U.S. 9.4%; Italy 8.9%; The Netherlands 7.5%.

Transport and communications

Transport. Railroads (1993): route length 592 mi, 953 km; passenger-mi 731,400,000, passenger-km 1,177,000,000; short ton-mi cargo 93,906,000, metric ton-km cargo 137,100,000. Roads (1996): total length 24,000 mi, 38,700 km (paved 40%). Vehicles (1996): passenger cars 90,000; trucks and buses 45,000. Merchant marine (1992): vessels (100 gross tons and over) 155; total deadweight tonnage 130,977. Air transport (1996)[8]: passenger-mi 407,073,000, passenger-km 655,122,000; short ton-mi cargo 20,239,000, metric ton-km cargo 29,549,000; airports (1996) with scheduled flights 1.

Communications

Medium	date	unit	number	units per 1,000 persons
Daily newspapers	1996	circulation	250,000	14
Radio	1997	receivers	4,400,000	236
Television	1999	receivers	2,266,000	118
Telephones	1999	main lines	158,555	8.3
Cellular telephones	1999	subscribers	70,026	3.7
Personal computers	1999	units	50,000	2.6
Internet	1999	users	20,000	1.0

Education and health

Educational attainment (1984). Percentage of population age 25 and over having: no formal schooling 60.4%; primary education 7.1%; middle school 25.4%; secondary 3.5%; vocational and other postsecondary 2.9%; higher 0.6%. *Literacy* (2000): total population age 15 and over literate 8,070,000 (70.2%); males literate 4,520,000 (79.8%); females literate 3,550,000 (61.2%).

Education (1991–92)

	schools	teachers	students	student/ teacher ratio
Primary (6–12)	11,056	66,068	1,796,490	27.2
Secondary (13–20)	5,540	43,367	816,578	18.8
Voc., teacher tr.[9]	957	422	13,232	31.4
Higher[9]	16	700	9,274	13.2

Health: physicians (1994) 735 (1 per 22,970 persons); hospital beds (1994) 26,455 (1 per 638 persons); infant mortality rate per 1,000 live births (2001) 56.5.
Food (1998): daily per capita caloric intake 2,568 (vegetable products 97%, animal products 3%): 112% of FAO recommended minimum.

Military

Total active duty personnel (2000): 7,000 (army 71.4%, navy 14.3%, air force 14.3%). *Military expenditure as percentage of GNP* (1997): 0.7% (world 2.8%); per capita expenditure U.S.$3.

[1]January 1. [2]Government administration has been decentralized to the local level of 103 district assemblies, 4 municipal assemblies, and 3 metropolitan assemblies. [3]Detail does not add to total given because of rounding. [4]Unofficial 1978 exchange rate (7.5 to 9.9 times the official rate) does not permit meaningful conversion into other currencies. [5]Trade includes hotels. [6]Import duties and statistical adjustments less imputed bank service charges. [7]Unemployed only. [8]Ghana Airways only. [9]1989–90.

Internet resources for further information:
- **Ghana Home Page http://www.ghanaweb.com/GhanaHomePage**
- **Bank of Ghana http://www.bog.gov.gh**

Greece

Official name: Elliniki Dhimokratía (Hellenic Republic).
Form of government: unitary multiparty republic with one legislative house (Greek Chamber of Deputies [300]).
Chief of state: President.
Head of government: Prime Minister.
Capital: Athens.
Official language: Greek.
Official religion: Eastern Orthodox.
Monetary unit: 1 drachma (Dr) = 100 lepta; valuation (Sept. 28, 2001) 1 U.S.$ = Dr 374.16; 1 £ = Dr 549.91; 1 € = Dr 340.750.

Area and population

Regions[1]	Principal cities	area sq mi	area sq km	population 2001 census
Insular				
Aegean, Northern	Mitilíni	1,481	3,836	200,066
Aegean, Southern	Ermoúpolis	2,041	5,286	298,745
Crete	Iráklion	3,218	8,336	601,159
Ionian Islands	Kérkira	891	2,307	214,274
Mainland				
Attica	Athens	1,470	3,808	3,764,348
Epirus	Ioánnina	3,553	9,203	352,420
Greece, Central	Lamía	6,004	15,549	608,655
Greece, Western[2]	Pátrai	4,382	11,350	742,419
Macedonia, Central[3]	Thessaloníki	7,393	19,147	1,862,833
Macedonia, Eastern and Thrace	Komotiní	5,466	14,157	604,254
Macedonia, Western	Kozáni	3,649	9,451	302,750
Peloponnese	Trípolis	5,981	15,490	632,955
Thessaly	Lárisa	5,420	14,037	754,893
TOTAL		50,949	131,957	10,939,771

Demography

Population (2001): 10,975,000.
Density (2001): persons per sq mi 215.4, persons per sq km 83.2.
Urban-rural (2000): urban 60.1%; rural 39.9%.
Sex distribution (1998): male 49.29%; female 50.71%.
Age breakdown (1998): under 15, 15.6%; 15–29, 22.1%; 30–44, 21.5%; 45–59, 18.1%; 60–74, 16.3%; 75 and over, 6.5%.
Population projection: (2010) 11,114,000; (2020) 10,988,000.
Ethnic composition (1995)[4]: Greek 98.5%; Turkish 0.9%; other 0.6%.
Religious affiliation (1995): Christian 95.2%, of which Eastern Orthodox 94.0%, Roman Catholic 0.5%; Muslim 1.3%; other 3.5%.
Major cities (1991): Athens 772,072 (urban agglomeration [1999]; 3,112,000); Thessaloníki 383,967; Piraeus (Piraiévs) 182,671[5]; Pátrai 152,570; Peristérion 137,288[5]; Iráklion 116,178.

Vital statistics

Birth rate per 1,000 population (2000): 11.7 (world avg. 22.5); (1998) legitimate 96.2%; illegitimate 3.8%.
Death rate per 1,000 population (2000): 10.5 (world avg. 9.0).
Natural increase rate per 1,000 population (2000): 1.2 (world avg. 13.5).
Total fertility rate (avg. births per childbearing woman; 2000): 1.3.
Marriage rate per 1,000 population (1998): 5.3.
Divorce rate per 1,000 population (1997): 0.8.
Life expectancy at birth (2000): male 75.9 years; female 81.2 years.
Major causes of death per 100,000 population (1998): diseases of the circulatory system 490.6; malignant neoplasms (cancers) 208.5; ill-defined conditions 81.6; diseases of the respiratory system 63.7.

National economy

Budget (1999). Revenue: Dr 12,409,000,000,000 (indirect taxes 47.2%, direct taxes 32.6%, nontax revenue 20.2%). Expenditures: Dr 17,737,000,000,000 (debt service 36.8%, health and social insurance 12.4%, education and culture 7.9%, agriculture 7.1%, defense 5.9%).
Public debt (1997): U.S.$18,331,000,000.
Tourism (1999): receipts U.S.$8,783,000,000; expenditures U.S.$3,989,000,000.
Production (metric tons except as noted). Agriculture, forestry, fishing (2000): sugar beets 2,906,000, olives 2,000,000, tomatoes 1,960,000, corn (maize) 1,850,000, wheat 1,770,000, seed cotton 1,250,000, grapes 1,200,000, oranges 950,000, peaches and nectarines 900,000, potatoes 890,000, apples 326,000, barley 255,000, lemons and limes 155,000, tobacco 129,900; livestock (number of live animals) 9,041,000 sheep, 5,293,000 goats, 906,000 pigs, 590,000 cattle; roundwood (1999) 2,215,260 cu m; fish catch (1997) 214,228. Mining and quarrying: bauxite (1999) 1,813,000; nickel (1998) 18,000[6]. Manufacturing (value added in Dr '000,000,000; 1999): food 573; paints, soaps, varnishes, drugs, and medicines 371; electrical machinery 287; textiles 259; cement, bricks, and tiles 227; beverages 214. Energy production (consumption): electricity (kW-hr; 1999) 44,724,000,000 ([1997] 36,528,000,000); hard coal (metric tons; 1996) none (1,484,000); lignite (metric tons; 1999) 61,464,000 ([1996] 61,410,000); crude petroleum (barrels; 1996) 3,144,000 (128,379,000); petroleum products (metric tons; 1996) 18,572,000 (15,174,000); natural gas (cu m; 1996) 53,868,000 (57,430,000).
Household income and expenditure. Average household size (1993–94) 2.9; income per household Dr 3,900,000 (U.S.$15,660); sources of income (1995): wages and salaries 36.6%, transfer payments 19.0%, other 44.4%; expenditure: food and beverages 32.7%, transportation and communications 13.5%, housing 11.5%, cafe/hotel expenditures 7.6%, household furnishings 7.4%.
Gross national product (1999): U.S.$127,648,000,000 (U.S.$12,110 per capita).

Structure of gross domestic product and labour force

	1999 in value Dr '000,000,000	1999 % of total value	1998 labour force	1998 % of labour force
Agriculture	2,645	6.9	704,200	15.8
Mining	187	0.5	18,300	0.4
Manufacturing	4,023	10.5	577,900	13.0
Construction	2,865	7.5	282,300	6.4
Public utilities	802	2.1	35,300	0.8
Transp. and commun.	2,206	5.8	244,800	5.5
Trade, restaurants	7,427	19.5	917,000	20.6
Finance, real estate	7,316	19.2	290,600	6.5
Pub. admin., defense	2,355	6.2	896,800	20.2
Services	4,659	12.2		
Other	3,662[7]	9.6[7]	478,500[8]	10.8[8]
TOTAL	38,147	100.0	4,445,700	100.0

Population economically active (1998): total 4,445,700; activity rate of total population 42.3% (participation rates: ages 15 and over, 50.1%; female 39.4%; unemployed 10.8%).

Price and earnings indexes (1995 = 100)

	1995	1996	1997	1998	1999	2000	2001
Consumer price index	100.0	108.2	114.7	119.6	122.8	126.6	130.2[9]
Hourly earnings index	100.0	108.6	118.3	123.9	...	...	...

Land use (1994): forest 20.3%; pasture 40.7%; agriculture 27.2%; other 11.8%.

Foreign trade[10]

Balance of trade (current prices)

	1994	1995	1996	1997	1998	1999
Dr '000,000,000	–2,931.0	–3,471.0	–4,311.8	–5,235.2	–5,730.5	–4,773.6
% of total	39.2%	40.6%	48.6%	52.6%	47.2%	44.3%

Imports (1998): Dr 8,933,500,000,000 (machinery and transport equipment 34.7%; chemicals and chemical products 12.3%; food products 10.9%; mineral fuels 7.3%). *Major import sources:* Italy 15.9%; Germany 14.9%; France 8.6%; U.K. 6.4%; The Netherlands 6.2%; U.S. 4.6%.
Exports (1998): Dr 3,203,000,000,000 (food 18.4%, of which fruits and nuts 7.7%; clothing and apparel 16.8%; petroleum 6.4%; aluminum 4.2%; tobacco products 4.1%). *Major export destinations:* Germany 18.3%; Italy 11.9%; U.K. 7.0%; U.S. 4.7%; France 4.6%; Bulgaria 4.1%.

Transport and communications

Transport. Railroads (1997): route length 2,503 km; passenger-km 1,783,000,000; metric ton-km cargo 330,000,000. Roads (1996): total length 117,000 km (paved 92%). Vehicles (1998): passenger cars 2,675,676; trucks and buses 1,013,677. Merchant marine (1998): vessels (100 gross tons and over) 1,903; total deadweight tonnage, n.a. Air transport (1999)[11]: passenger-km 8,305,451,000; metric ton-km cargo 103,243,000; airports (1997) 36.

Communications

Medium	date	unit	number	units per 1,000 persons
Daily newspapers	1996	circulation	1,600,000	150
Radio	1997	receivers	5,020,000	470
Television	1999	receivers	5,100,000	471
Telephones	1999	main lines	5,611,000	518
Cellular telephones	1999	subscribers	3,904,000	360
Personal computers	1999	units	640,000	59
Internet	1999	users	750,000	69

Education and health

Educational attainment (1991). Percentage of population age 25 and over having: no formal schooling (illiterate) 6.8%; some primary education 10.6%; completed primary 39.7%; lower secondary 10.8%; higher secondary 20.6%; some postsecondary 4.9%; completed higher 6.6%. *Literacy* (2000): total population age 15 and over literate 9,080,000 (97.2%); males literate 4,570,000 (98.6%); females literate 4,510,000 (96.0%).

Education (1998–99)

	schools	teachers	students	student/ teacher ratio
Primary (age 6–12)	6,549	45,876	646,559	14.1
Secondary (age 12–18)	2,921	48,754	598,237	12.3
Voc., teacher tr.	637	11,270	139,422	12.4
Higher[12]	...	13,793	185,146	13.4

Health (1997): physicians 43,030 (1 per 248 persons); hospital beds 52,474 (1 per 204 persons); infant mortality rate per 1,000 live births (1999) 6.7.
Food (1999): daily per capita caloric intake 3,689 (vegetable products 78%, animal products 22%); 148% of FAO recommended minimum requirement.

Military

Total active duty personnel (2000): 159,200 (army 69.1%, navy 11.9%, air force 19.0%). *Military expenditure as percentage of GNP* (1997): 4.6% (world 2.6%); per capita expenditure U.S.$527.

[1]Created for planning and economic development; local administration is based on 52 departments and one autonomous self-governing monastic region (Mount Athos). [2]Corresponds to the northwestern part of the Peloponnese. [3]Includes Mount Athos (Ávion Óros). [4]Greek government states there are no ethnic divisions in Greece; data exclude resident aliens. [5]Within Athens urban agglomeration. [6]Metal content of ore. [7]Taxes less imputed bank service charges and subsidies. [8]Unemployed. [9]March. [10]Imports c.i.f.; exports f.o.b. [11]Olympic Airways. [12]Includes higher technical education.

Internet resources for further information:
- **National Statistical Service of Greece http://www.statistics.gr/**

Greenland

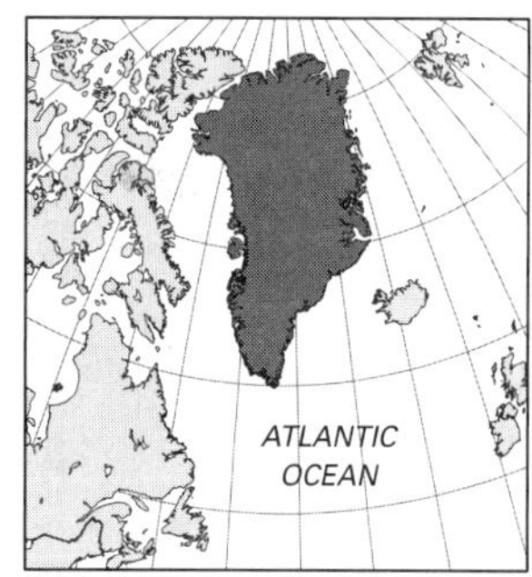

Official name: Kalaallit Nunaat (Greenlandic); Grønland (Danish) (Greenland).
Political status: integral part of the Danish realm with one legislative house (Parliament [31]).
Chief of state: Danish Monarch.
Heads of government: High Commissioner (for Denmark); Prime Minister (for Greenland).
Capital: Nuuk (Godthåb).
Official languages: Greenlandic; Danish.
Official religion: Evangelical Lutheran (Lutheran Church of Greenland).
Monetary unit: 1 Danish krone (Dkr) = 100 øre; valuation (Sept. 28, 2001) 1 U.S.$ = Dkr 8.17; 1 £ = Dkr 12.00.

Area and population

Counties / Communes	area		population
	sq mi	sq km	2000[1] estimate
Avanersuaq (Nordgrønland)	41,200	106,700	
Qaanaaq (Thule)	...	...	864
Kitaa (Vestgrønland)	46,000	119,100	
Aasiaat (Egedesminde)	...	...	3,446
Ilulissat (Jakobshavn)	...	...	4,663
Ivittuut (Ivigtut)	...	...	164
Kangaatsiaq (Kangâtsiaq)	...	...	1,495
Maniitsoq (Sukkertoppen)	...	...	3,725
Nanortalik	...	...	2,555
Narsaq (Narssaq)	...	...	2,082
Nuuk (Godthåb)	...	...	13,838
Paamiut (Frederikshåb)	...	...	2,085
Qaqortoq (Julianehåb)	...	...	3,416
Qasigiannguit (Christianshåb)	...	...	1,516
Qeqertarsuaq (Godhavn)	...	...	1,050
Sisimiut (Holsteinsborg)	...	...	5,371
Upernavik	...	...	2,902
Uummannaq (Umanaq)	...	...	2,761
Tunu (Østgrønland)	44,700	115,900	
Illoqqortoormiit (Scoresbysund)	...	...	551
Ammassalik	...	...	2,911
TOTAL (ICE-FREE)	131,900	341,700	
PERMANENT ICE[3]	708,100	1,833,900	
TOTAL	840,000	2,175,600	56,124[2]

Demography

Population (2001): 56,300.
Density[3] (2001): persons per sq mi 0.43, persons per sq km 0.16.
Urban-rural (2001[1]): urban (town) 84.3%; rural (settlement) 15.7%.
Sex distribution (2000[1]): male 53.43%; female 46.57%.
Age breakdown (2000[1]): under 15, 27.1%; 15–29, 19.2%; 30–44, 29.3%; 45–59, 16.4%; 60–69, 5.3%; 70 and over, 2.7%.
Population projection: (2010) 56,900; (2020) 57,600.
Doubling time: 76 years.
Ethnic composition (2000): Greenland Eskimo 79.1%; Danish 13.6%; other 7.3%.
Religious affiliation (2000): Protestant 69.2%, of which Evangelical Lutheran 64.2%, Pentecostal 2.8%; other Christian 27.4%; other/nonreligious 3.4%.
Major towns (2001[1]): Nuuk (Godthåb) 13,650; Sisimiut (Holsteinsborg) 5,165; Ilulissat (Jakobshavn) 4,165; Aasiaat (Egedesminde) 3,239; Qaqortoq (Julianehåb) 3,111.

Vital statistics

Birth rate per 1,000 population (2000): 16.8 (world avg. 22.5); (1993) legitimate 29.2%; illegitimate 70.8%.
Death rate per 1,000 population (2000): 7.6 (world avg. 9.0).
Natural increase rate per 1,000 population (2000): 9.2 (world avg. 13.5).
Total fertility rate (avg. births per childbearing woman; 2000): 2.5.
Marriage rate per 1,000 population (1993): 7.1.
Divorce rate per 1,000 population (1993): 2.7.
Life expectancy at birth (2000): male 64.5 years; female 71.7 years.
Major causes of death per 100,000 population (1995): diseases of the circulatory system 214.4, of which cerebrovascular disease 68.8, ischemic heart disease 64.9; malignant neoplasms (cancers) 198.7; suicides 90.5; accidents 80.6.

National economy

Budget (1998). Revenue: Dkr 4,304,000,000 (block grant from Danish government 59.8%; taxes and royalties for Greenland treasury 13.5%; import duties 11.3%; EEC fishery license fees 6.4%; other 6.6%). Expenditures (1997): Dkr 5,987,442,000 (current expenditure 93.3%, of which wages and salaries 35.9%, social welfare 22.3%, culture and education 15.3%, health 10.7%, defense 5.5%; capital [development] expenditure 6.7%).
Public debt (external, outstanding; 1995): U.S.$243,000,000.
Tourism (1997): number of overnight visitors 181,043.
Production (metric tons except as noted). Fishing, animal products: fish catch (1998) 372,974 (by local boats 128,630, of which shrimp 73,581, halibut 29,965, cod 11,776; by foreign boats 123,748); livestock (number of live animals; 1999) 22,000 sheep, 4,800 reindeer; animal products (value of external sales in Dkr '000; 1998) sealskins 31,044, polar bear skins 579. Mining[4]: none. Manufacturing: principally handicrafts and fish processing. Construction: residential (1992[1]) 18,624 sq m; nonresidential (1985) 12,300 sq m. Energy production (consumption): electricity (kW-hr; 1998) 205,700,000 (158,300,000); coal, none (none); crude petroleum, none (n.a.); petroleum products (metric tons; 1991) none (214,000); natural gas, none (none).
Gross national product (1997): U.S.$1,142,000,000 (U.S.$20,381 per capita).

Structure of gross domestic product and labour force

	1998		2000	
	in value Dkr '000,000	% of total value	labour force	% of labour force
Fishing, hunting, and sheep farming	...	...	...	...
Mining	...	...	...	...
Manufacturing	...	...	...	...
Construction	...	...	...	...
Transp. and commun.	...	...	...	...
Trade, restaurants	...	...	...	...
Public utilities	...	...	...	...
Public administration	...	...	...	...
Private services	...	...	...	...
Other	...	...	...	...
TOTAL	7,719	100.0	31,518[1]	100.0

Population economically active (2000[1]): total 31,518; activity rate of total population 56.2% (participation rates: ages 15–60, 86.6%; female [1987] 43.4%; unemployed [1999] 10.0%).

Price and earnings indexes (January 1995 = 100)[5]

	1995	1996	1997	1998	1999
Consumer price index	100.0	100.7	101.6	102.1	103.0
Monthly earnings index	100.0	102.4	103.5	103.0	102.9

Household income and expenditure. Average household size (1998): 2.6; income per person (1997): Dkr 144,700 (U.S.$17,700); sources of income: n.a.; expenditure (1994): food, beverages, and tobacco 41.6%, housing and energy 22.4%, transportation and communications 10.2%, recreation 6.4%.
Land use (1994): forested 0.03%; meadows and pastures 0.69%; agricultural and under permanent cultivation, none; other (principally ice cap) 99.28%.

Foreign trade

Balance of trade (current prices)

	1995	1996	1997	1998	1999
DKr '000,000	–625	–784	–857	–947	–859
% of total	7.3%	16.8%	19.5%	21.8%	18.2%

Imports (1999): Dkr 2,789,000,000 (1998; machinery and transport equipment 26.1%; manufactured goods 14.9%; food and live animals 12.1%; miscellaneous manufactured articles 11.4%; petroleum and petroleum products 9.3%; beverages and tobacco 4.0%). *Major import sources* (1998): Denmark 65.2%; Norway 12.0%; U.S. 3.0%; Japan 2.9%; Germany 2.3%; Sweden 1.8%.
Exports (1999): Dkr 1,930,000,000 (1998; fish and fish products 91.7%, of which shrimp 69.0%). *Major export destinations* (1998): Denmark 84.3%; U.K. 3.5%; Japan 3.4%; U.S. 2.1%; Norway 1.6%.

Transport and communications

Transport. Railroads: none. Roads (1998): total length 93 mi, 150 km (paved 60%). Vehicles (1998): passenger cars 2,242; trucks and buses 1,474. Merchant marine (1992): vessels (100 gross tons and over) 82; total deadweight tonnage, 54,169. Air transport (1998)[6]: passenger-mi 103,769,000, passenger-km 167,000,000; short ton-mi cargo 232,000[7] metric ton-km cargo 339,000; airports (1998) with scheduled flights 18.

Communications

Medium	date	unit	number	units per 1,000 persons
Daily newspapers	1996	circulation	1,000	18
Radio	1997	receivers	27,000	482
Television	1997	receivers	22,000	393
Telephones	1999	main lines	26,000	464
Cellular telephones	1999	subscribers	14,000	250

Education and health

Educational attainment. n.a. *Literacy* (1999): total population age 15 and over literate: virtually 100%.

Education (1998–99)

	schools	teachers	students	student/ teacher ratio
Primary (age 6–15)	88	975	9,341	9.6
Secondary (age 15–19)	3	...	1,746	5.9
Voc., teacher tr.[8]	8	110	650	
Higher[9]	2	35	200	5.7

Health (1998): physicians 84 (1 per 668 persons); hospital beds (1993) 465 (1 per 125 persons); infant mortality rate per 1,000 live births (2000) 18.3.

Military

Total active duty personnel. Denmark is responsible for Greenland's defense. Greenlanders are not liable for military service.

[1]January 1. [2]Includes 729 people not distributed by county. [3]Area of permanent ice not distributable by county; population density calculated with reference to ice-free area only. [4]Greenland's only mine closed in 1990. [5]All figures denote January. [6]Greenlandair only. [7]1985. [8]1986–87.

Internet resources for further information:
- **Greenland Home Rule http://www.gh.gl**
- **Statistics Greenland http://www.statgreen.gl**
- **Danmarks Statistik http://www.dst.dk/dst/665**

Grenada

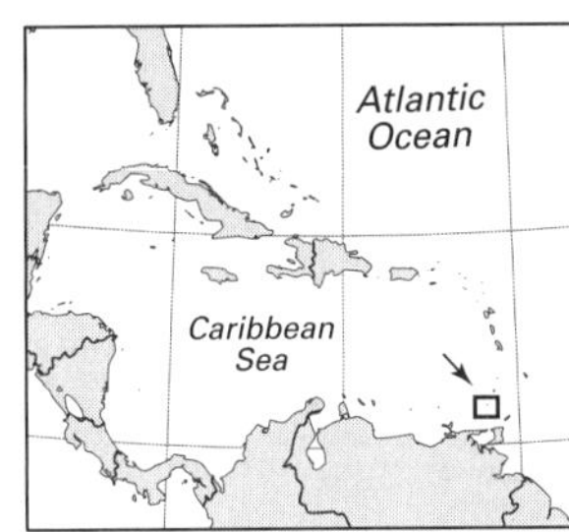

Official name: Grenada.
Form of government: constitutional monarchy with two legislative houses (Senate [13]; House of Representatives [15[1]]).
Chief of state: British Monarch represented by Governor-General.
Head of government: Prime Minister.
Capital: St. George's.
Official language: English.
Official religion: none.
Monetary unit: 1 East Caribbean dollar (EC$) = 100 cents; valuation (Sept. 28, 2001) 1 U.S.$ = EC$2.70; 1 £ = EC$3.97.

Area and population

Local Councils	Principal towns	area sq mi	area sq km	population 1991 census
Carriacou	Hillsborough	10	26	5,726
Petite Martinique	...	3	8	
St. Andrew	Grenville	38	99	24,135
St. David	...	17	44	11,011
St. George	...	25[2]	65[2]	27,373
St. John	Gouyave	14	35	8,752
St. Mark	Victoria	10	25	3,861
St. Patrick	Sauteurs	16	42	10,118
Town				
St. George's	—	[2]	[2]	4,621
TOTAL		133	344	95,597

Demography

Population (2001): 102,000.
Density (2001): persons per sq mi 766.9, persons per sq km 296.5.
Urban-rural (2000)[3]: urban 38.3%; rural 61.7%.
Sex distribution (2000): male 51.70%; female 48.30%.
Age breakdown (2000): under 15, 38.1%; 15–29, 33.3%; 30–44, 17.7%; 45–59, 4.9%; 60–74, 4.7%; 75 and over, 1.3%.
Population projection: (2010) 109,000; (2020) 116,000.
Doubling time: 47 years.
Ethnic composition (2000): black 51.7%; mixed 40.0%; Indo-Pakistani 4.0%; white 0.9%; other 3.4%.
Religious affiliation (1995): Roman Catholic 57.8%; Protestant 37.6%, of which Anglican 14.4%, Pentecostal 8.3%, Seventh-day Adventist 7.0%; other 4.6%, of which Rastafarian *c.* 3.0%.
Major localities (1991): St. George's 4,621 (urban agglomeration [1999] 35,000); Gouyave 3,100; Grenville 2,300; Victoria 2,100.

Vital statistics

Birth rate per 1,000 population (2000): 23.2 (world avg. 22.5); (1987) legitimate 18.1%; illegitimate 81.9%.
Death rate per 1,000 population (2000): 8.0 (world avg. 9.0).
Natural increase rate per 1,000 population (2000): 15.2 (world avg. 13.5).
Total fertility rate (avg. births per childbearing woman; 2000): 2.6.
Marriage rate per 1,000 population (1991): 4.3.
Divorce rate per 1,000 population (1991): 0.8.
Life expectancy at birth (2000): male 62.7 years; female 66.3 years.
Major causes of death per 100,000 population (1987): diseases of the circulatory system 264.3; malignant neoplasms (cancers) 82.8; endocrine and metabolic diseases 57.3; diseases of the respiratory system 45.6; diseases of the digestive system 38.2; ill-defined conditions 209.1.

National economy

Budget (1998). Revenue: EC$229,000,000 (current revenue 90.0%, of which tax on international trade 52.3%, general sales taxes 17.8%, income taxes 9.6%; grants from abroad 10.0%). Expenditures: EC$281,700,000 (current expenditure 73.7%, of which wages 37.2%, transfers 16.1%, debt 11.6%; capital expenditure 26.3%).
Public debt (external, outstanding; 1999): U.S.$122,000,000.
Tourism (1999): receipts from visitors U.S.$63,000,000; expenditures by nationals abroad U.S.$5,000,000.
Gross national product (at current market prices; 1999): U.S.$334,000,000 (U.S.$3,440 per capita).

Structure of gross domestic product and labour force

	1997 in value EC$'000,000[4]	1997 % of total value[4]	1991 labour force[5]	1991 % of labour force[5]
Agriculture	53.8	9.5	4,223	17.1
Quarrying	3.1	0.5	126	0.5
Manufacturing	39.9	7.0	1,881	7.6
Construction	41.7	7.3	3,168	12.9
Public utilities	28.7	5.1	350	1.4
Transportation and communications	139.1	24.5	1,614	6.5
Trade, restaurants	113.6	20.0	5,149	20.9
Finance, real estate	77.4	13.6	866	3.5
Pub. admin., defense	93.6	16.5	1,738	7.1
Services	15.7	2.8	3,372	13.7
Other	–38.7[6]	–6.8[6]	2,163	8.8
TOTAL	567.9	100.0	24,650	100.0

Production (metric tons except as noted). Agriculture, forestry, fishing (1999): coconuts 6,800, sugarcane 6,600, bananas 4,400, roots and tubers 3,000, nutmeg 2,500, grapefruit 2,000, mangoes 1,800, avocados 1,700, cacao 1,100, oranges 900, other crops include cotton, limes, cinnamon, cloves, and pimiento; livestock (number of live animals) 13,000 sheep, 7,000 goats, 5,300 pigs; roundwood, n.a.; fish catch (1998) 1,713. Mining and quarrying: excavation of gravel for local use. Manufacturing (value of production in EC$'000; 1997): wheat flour 13,390; soft drinks 9,798; beer 7,072; animal feed 5,852; rum 5,497; toilet paper 4,237; malt 4,192; stout 3,835; cigarettes 1,053. Construction: n.a. Energy production (consumption): electricity (kW-hr; 1996) 95,000,000 (95,000,000); coal, none (none); crude petroleum, none (none); petroleum products (metric tons; 1996) none (55,000); natural gas, none (none).
Household income and expenditure. Average household size (1991) 3.7; income per household (1988) EC$7,097 (U.S.$2,629); sources of income: n.a.; expenditure (1987): food, beverages, and tobacco 40.7%, household furnishings and operations 13.7%, housing 11.9%, transportation 9.1%, personal effects and medical care 8.6%.
Population economically active (1988): total 38,920; activity rate of total population 39.9% (participation rate: ages 15–65, 72.7%; female 48.6%; unemployed [1997] 17.0%).

Price and earnings indexes (1995 = 100)

	1993	1994	1995	1996	1997	1998	1999
Consumer price index	94.6	98.2	100.0	102.0	103.0	104.7	105.0
Annual earnings index[7]	89.7	95.1	100.0	....	...	...	...

Land use (1994): forested 9.0%; meadows and pastures 3.0%; agricultural and under permanent cultivation 35.0%; other 53.0%.

Foreign trade[8]

Balance of trade (current prices)

	1993	1994	1995	1996	1997
U.S.$'000,000	–122.5	–94.8	–106.3	–126.4	–140.7
% of total	74.0%	65.8%	63.0%	75.0%	73.1%

Imports (1997): U.S.$166,600,000 (machinery and transport equipment 25.8%; food 21.6%; basic manufactures 18.6%; chemicals and chemical products 7.4%). *Major import sources:* Trinidad and Tobago 40.4%; United States 24.6%; United Kingdom 7.1%; Barbados 3.8%; Japan 3.8%; St. Vincent and the Grenadines 1.6%.
Exports (1997): U.S.$25,900,000 (domestic exports 91.5%, of which nutmeg 26.3%, fish 14.3%, cocoa beans 7.3%, clothing 4.6%; reexports 8.5%). *Major export destinations:* Germany 46.9%; United States 12.2%; St. Lucia 6.1%; Trinidad and Tobago 6.1%.

Transport and communications

Transport. Railroads: none. Roads (1996): total length 646 mi, 1,040 km (paved 61%). Vehicles (1991)[9]: passenger cars 4,739; trucks and buses 3,068. Merchant marine (1992): vessels (100 gross tons and over) 3; total deadweight tonnage 484. Air transport (1997)[10]: passengers 322,000; cargo 2,300 metric tons; airports (1998) with scheduled flights 2.

Communications

Medium	date	unit	number	units per 1,000 persons
Radio	1997	receivers	57,000	615
Television	1997	receivers	33,000	353
Telephones	1999	main lines	27,484	298
Cellular telephones	1999	subscribers	1,410	15

Education and health

Educational attainment (1991). Percentage of population age 25 and over having: no formal schooling 1.8%; primary education 74.9%; secondary 15.5%; higher 4.7%, of which university 2.8%; other/unknown 3.1%. *Literacy* (1995): total population age 15 and over literate 50,000 (85.0%).

Education (1996–97)

	schools	teachers	students	student/ teacher ratio
Primary (age 5–11)[11]	58	879	23,449	26.7
Secondary (age 12–16)[11]	19[12]	381[12]	7,367	19.3
Vocational	...	...	...	...
Higher[12, 13]	1	66	651	9.9

Health (1997): physicians 80 (1 per 1,236 persons); hospital beds 340 (1 per 290 persons); infant mortality rate per 1,000 live births (2000) 14.6.
Food (1999): daily per capita caloric intake 2,685 (vegetable products 80%, animal products 20%); 111% of FAO recommended minimum requirement.

Military

Total active duty personnel (1997)[14]: *Military expenditure as percentage of GNP:* n.a.; per capita expenditure, n.a.

[1]Excludes the speaker, who may be elected from outside its elected membership. [2]St. George local council includes St. George's town. [3]Urban defined as St. George's town and St. George local council. [4]At factor cost. [5]Employed persons only. [6]Less imputed bank service charges. [7]Private sector only. [8]Imports c.i.f.; exports f.o.b. [9]Registered vehicles only. [10]Point Salines airport. [11]Excludes private schools. [12]1994–95. [13]Excludes Grenada Teachers' College. [14]The 730-member police force includes an 80-member paramilitary unit and a 30-member coast guard unit.

Internet resources for further information:
- **Eastern Caribbean Central Bank**
  http://www.eccb-centralbank.org

Guadeloupe

Official name: Département de la Guadeloupe (Department of Guadeloupe).
Political status: overseas department (France[1]) with two legislative houses (General Council [42]; Regional Council [43]).
Chief of state: President of France.
Heads of government: Commissioner of the Republic (for France); President of the General Council (for Guadeloupe); President of the Regional Council (for Guadeloupe).
Capital: Basse-Terre.
Official language: French.
Official religion: none.
Monetary unit: 1 French franc (F) = 100 centimes; valuation (Sept. 28, 2001) 1 U.S.$ = F 7.20; 1 £ = F 10.59.

Area and population

		area		population
Arrondissements	Capitals	sq mi	sq km	1999 census
Basse-Terre[2]	Basse-Terre	330	855	175,691
Pointe-à-Pitre[3]	Pointe-à-Pitre	299	775	210,875
Saint-Martin-Saint-Barthélemy[4]	Marigot	28	74	35,930
TOTAL		687[5, 6]	1,780[5, 6]	422,496

Demography

Population (2001): 432,000.
Density (2001): persons per sq mi 628.8, persons per sq km 242.7.
Urban-rural (1999)[7]: urban 99.6%; rural 0.4%.
Sex distribution (1999): male 48.11%; female 51.89%.
Age breakdown (1999): under 15, 23.6%; 15–29, 22.4%; 30–44, 24.3%; 45–59, 15.7%; 60–74, 9.3%; 75 and over, 4.7%.
Population projection: (2010) 470,000; (2020) 502,000.
Doubling time: 62 years.
Ethnic composition (2000): Creole (mulatto) 76.7%; black 10.0%; Guadeloupe mestizo (French-East Asian) 10.0%; white 2.0%; other 1.3%.
Religious affiliation (1995): Roman Catholic 81.1%; Jehovah's Witness 4.8%; Protestant 4.7%; other 9.4%.
Major communes (1999): Les Abymes 63,054; Saint-Martin 29,078; Le Gosier 25,360; Baie-Mahault 23,389; Pointe-à-Pitre 20,948; Le Moule 20,827.

Vital statistics

Birth rate per 1,000 population (2000): 17.2 (world avg. 22.5); (1997) legitimate 37.0%; illegitimate 63.0%.
Death rate per 1,000 population (2000): 6.0 (world avg. 9.0).
Natural increase rate per 1,000 population (2000): 11.2 (world avg. 13.5).
Total fertility rate (avg. births per childbearing woman; 2000): 1.9.
Marriage rate per 1,000 population (1997): 4.7.
Divorce rate per 1,000 population (1997): 1.3.
Life expectancy at birth (2000): male 73.8 years; female 80.3 years.
Major causes of death per 100,000 population (1996): diseases of the circulatory system 183.7; malignant neoplasms (cancers) 134.8; accidents, violence, and poisoning 68.1; diseases of the respiratory system 32.1; diseases of the digestive system 31.4; endocrine and metabolic diseases 26.2; infectious and parasitic diseases 23.8.

National economy

Budget (1998). Revenue: F 4,227,000,000 (tax revenues 69.0%, of which direct taxes 42.5%, value-added taxes 25.1%; advances, loans, and transfers 26.8%). Expenditures: F 7,874,000,000 (current expenditures 70.6%, capital [development] expenditures 10.6%; advances and loans 18.8%).
Public debt (external, outstanding; 1990[8]): U.S.$58,000,000.
Tourism (1999): receipts from visitors U.S.$375,000,000; expenditures, n.a.
Production (metric tons except as noted). Agriculture, forestry, fishing (1999): sugarcane 499,980, bananas 141,140, yams 9,030, pineapples 6,900, plantains 5,870, sweet potatoes 3,410, melons 3,240, tomatoes 3,080, lettuce 3,030, cucumbers and gherkins 2,620; livestock (number of live animals) 80,410 cattle, 63,000 goats, 15,000 pigs; roundwood (1998) 15,000 cu m; fish catch (1998) 9,084. Mining and quarrying (1993): pumice 210,000. Manufacturing (1996): cement 282,571; raw sugar 48,896; rum 66,483 hectolitres; other products include clothing, wooden furniture and posts, and metalware. Construction (buildings authorized; 1992): residential 358,474 sq m; nonresidential 160,084 sq m. Energy production (consumption): electricity (kW-hr; 1996) 1,098,000,000 (987,600,000); coal, none (none); crude petroleum, none (none); petroleum products (metric tons; 1996) none (456,000); natural gas, none (none).
Population economically active (1998): total 182,200; activity rate of total population 41.8% (participation rates: ages [1995] 15–64, 73.2%; female 46.8%; unemployed 30.7%).

Price and earnings indexes (1995 = 100)[9]

	1990	1991	1992	1993	1994	1995	1996[10]
Consumer price index	87.5	89.2	91.4	93.3	96.9	100.0	99.3
Monthly earnings index[11]	92.0	93.8	96.3	96.6	98.0	100.0	100.8

Gross national product (1995): U.S.$3,877,000,000 (U.S.$9,145 per capita).

Structure of gross domestic product and labour force

	1995		1998	
	in value F '000,000	% of total value	labour force	% of labour force
Agriculture	1,080.7	4.1	8,200	4.5
Mining, manufacturing	1,744.9	6.6	7,900	4.3
Construction	1,880.1	7.2	13,000	7.1
Public utilities	...	...	...	...
Transp. and commun.	2,156.2	8.2	4,200	2.3
Trade[12]	6,121.6	23.4	20,700	11.4
Finance, real estate	1,043.2	4.0	3,500	1.9
Pub. admin., defense	9,926.7	37.9	43,400	23.8
Services	3,210.2	12.2	24,400	13.4
Other	−957.4[13]	−3.6[13]	56,900[14]	31.2[14]
TOTAL	26,206.2	100.0	182,200	100.0[6]

Household income and expenditure. Average household size (1990) 3.4; income per household (1988) F 105,400 (U.S.$17,700); sources of income (1988): wages and salaries 78.9%, self-employment 12.7%, transfer payments 8.4%; expenditure (1994–95): housing 26.2%, food and beverages 21.4%, transportation and communications 14.1%, household durables 6.0%, culture and leisure 4.2%.
Land use (1994): forest 39.1%; pasture 14.2%; agriculture 16.0%; other 30.7%.

Foreign trade

Balance of trade (current prices)

	1993	1994	1995	1996	1997	1998
F '000,000	−7,309	−7,693	−8,655	−9,635	−9,274	−9,996
% of total	83.2%	82.0%	84.3%	83.6%	86.3%	88.2%

Imports (1998): F 10,663,000,000 (consumer goods 23.7%, food and agriculture products 21.1%, machinery and equipment 19.7%, transport vehicles and parts 12.3%). *Major import sources:* France 63.4%; Germany 4.4%; Italy 3.5%; Martinique 3.4%; U.S. 2.9%; Japan 1.9%.
Exports (1998): F 667,000,000 (1995; bananas 25.4%, sugar 11.4%, rum 4.4%, melons 2.9%). *Major export destinations:* France 68.5%; Martinique 9.4%; Italy 4.8%; Belgium-Luxembourg 3.3%; French Guiana 3.0%.

Transport and communications

Transport. Railroads: none. Roads (1998): total length 1,988 mi, 3,415 km (paved [1986] 80%). Vehicles (1993); passenger cars 101,600; trucks and buses 37,500. Merchant marine (1992): vessels (100 gross tons and over) 20; deadweight tonnage 4,430. Air transport (1998): passenger arrivals and departures 1,807,100; cargo handled 16,496 metric tons, cargo unloaded 5,493 metric tons; airports (1997) with scheduled flights 7.

Communications

Medium	date	unit	number	units per 1,000 persons
Daily newspapers	1995	circulation	35,000	81
Radio	1997	receivers	113,000	258
Television	1999	receivers	118,000	262
Telephones	1999	main lines	201,000	447
Cellular telephones	1999	subscribers	88,000	196
Personal computers	1998	units	...	...
Internet	1998	users	...	...

Education and health

Educational attainment (1990). Percentage of population age 25 and over having: incomplete primary, or no declaration 59.8%; primary education 14.5%; secondary 19.0%; higher 6.7%. *Literacy* (1982): total population age 15 and over literate 225,400 (90.1%); males literate 108,700 (89.7%); females literate 116,700 (90.5%).

Education (1998–99)

	schools	teachers	students	student/teacher ratio
Primary (age 6–10)	348	2,936	40,042	13.6
Secondary (age 11–17) Vocational	85	3,392	51,491	15.2
Higher[15]	1	...	10,919	...

Health (1998): physicians 760 (1 per 550 persons); hospital beds 2,796 (1 per 149 persons); infant mortality rate per 1,000 live births (2000) 9.8.
Food (1995): daily per capita caloric intake 2,732 (vegetable products 75%, animal products 25%); 129% of FAO recommended minimum requirement.

Military

Total active duty personnel (1994): 535 French troops.

[1]Guadeloupe elects 4 deputies and 2 senators to French parliament. [2]Comprises Basse-Terre 327 sq mi (848 sq km), pop. 172,693, and Îles des Saintes 5 sq mi (13 sq km), pop. 2,998. [3]Comprises Grande-Terre 228 sq mi (590 sq km), pop. 196,767; Marie-Galante 61 sq mi (158 sq km), pop. 12,488; La Désirade 8 sq mi (20 sq km), pop. 1,620; and the uninhabited Îles de la Petite-Terre. [4]Comprises the French part of Saint-Martin 20 sq mi (54 sq km), pop. 29,079; Saint-Barthélemy 8 sq mi (21 sq km), pop. 6,852; and the small, uninhabited island of Tintamarre. [5]Total area includes 29 sq mi (75 sq km) not allocated by arrondissement. [6]Detail does not add to total given because of rounding. [7]Urban defined as locality with 2,000 or more inhabitants. [8]Includes external long-term private debt not guaranteed by the government. [9]Base and indexes are end of year unless footnoted. [10]March. [11]Based on minimum-level wage of public employees. [12]Includes hotels. [13]Less imputed bank service charges. [14]Includes 55,900 unemployed. [15]University of Antilles-French Guiana, Guadeloupe campus.

Internet resources for further information:

- **Ministère de l'Outre-mer (Paris) http://www.outre-mer.gouv.fr/domtom/guadeloupe**

Guam

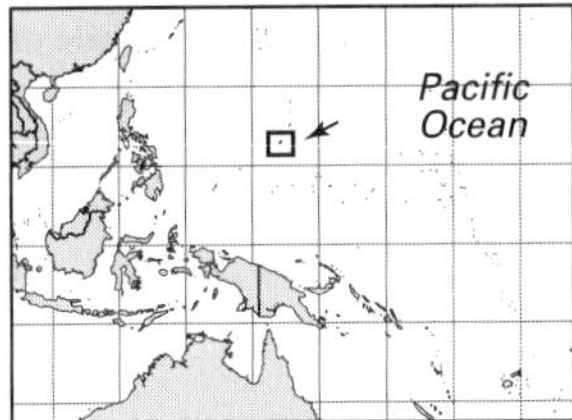

Official name: Teritorion Guam (Chamorro); Territory of Guam (English).
Political status: self-governing, organized, unincorporated territory of the United States with one legislative house (Guam Legislature [15]).
Chief of state: President of the United States.
Head of government: Governor.
Capital: Agana (Hagåtña).
Official languages: Chamorro; English.
Official religion: none.
Monetary unit: 1 United States dollar (U.S.$) = 100 cents; valuation (Sept. 28, 2001) 1 U.S.$ = £0.68.

Area and population

	area		population[1]
			2000
Election Districts	sq mi	sq km	census
Agana	1	3	1,100
Agana Heights	1	3	3,940
Agat	11	29	5,656
Asan	6	16	2,090
Barrigada	9	23	8,652
Chalan Pago-Ordot	6	16	5,923
Dededo	30	78	42,980
Inarajan	19	49	3,052
Mangilao	10	26	13,313
Merizo	6	16	2,163
Mongmong-Toto-Maite	2	5	5,845
Piti	7	18	1,666
Santa Rita	16	42	7,500
Sinajana	1	3	2,853
Talofofo	17	44	3,215
Tamuning	6	16	18,012
Umatac	6	16	887
Yigo	35	91	19,474
Yona	20	52	6,484
TOTAL	209[2]	541[2, 3]	154,805

Demography

Population (2001): 158,000.
Density (2001)[2]: persons per sq mi 728.1, persons per sq km 281.6.
Urban-rural (1999): urban 39.0%; rural 61.0%.
Sex distribution (1990): male 53.99%; female 46.01%.
Age breakdown (1990): under 15, 29.8%; 15–29, 29.9%; 30–44, 22.4%; 45–59, 11.2%; 60–74, 5.2%; 75 and over, 1.5%.
Population projection: (2010) 184,000; (2020) 211,000.
Doubling time: 32 years.
Ethnic composition (1990): Pacific Islander 42.4%, of which Chamorro 37.5%; Asian 29.5%, of which Filipino 22.6%, Korean 3.0%; white 14.4%; mixed 9.7%; black 2.4%; other 1.6%.
Religious affiliation (1995): Roman Catholic 74.7%; Protestant 12.8%; other Christian 2.4%; other 10.1%.
Major populated places (1990): Tamuning 9,534; Apra Harbor 7,956; Mangilao 5,608; Andersen Air Force Base 5,531; Agana (Hagåtña) 1,139.

Vital statistics

Birth rate per 1,000 population (2001): 27.0 (world avg. 22.5); (1997) legitimate 50.1%; illegitimate 49.9%.
Death rate per 1,000 population (2001): 4.8 (world avg. 9.0).
Natural increase rate per 1,000 population (2001): 22.2 (world avg. 13.5).
Total fertility rate (avg. births per childbearing woman; 2001): 4.0.
Marriage rate per 1,000 population (1997): 9.5.
Divorce rate per 1,000 population (1995): 4.3.
Life expectancy at birth (2001): male 72.0 years; female 77.0 years.
Major causes of death per 100,000 population (1996): heart diseases 134.5; malignant neoplasms (cancers) 73.8; accidents, poisonings, and violence 35.2; diabetes mellitus 28.3; pneumonia 9.7; liver diseases 9.7.

National economy

Budget (1997–98). Revenue: U.S.$738,100,000 (local taxes 68.7%, federal contributions 25.5%, interest 2.2%, licenses, fees, and permits 1.7%). Expenditures: U.S.$501,900,000 (current expenditures 80.2%, debt service 10.6%, capital expenditures 8.6%).
Public debt (external, outstanding): n.a.
Tourism (1999): receipts from visitors U.S.$1,908,000,000.
Land use (1998): forested 14.6%; meadows and pastures 14.5%; agricultural and under permanent cultivation 21.8%; other 49.1%.
Production. Agriculture, forestry, fishing (value of production in U.S.$'000; 1996): eggplant 625, long beans 592, bananas 418, cucumbers 348, watermelons 232, papayas 101; livestock (number of live animals) 205,000 poultry, 4,000 pigs, 610 goats; fish catch (metric tons; 1998) 253, value of aquaculture production (1996) U.S.$1,442,000. Mining and quarrying: sand and gravel. Manufacturing (value of sales in U.S.$'000; 1997): printing and publishing 40,307; food processing 24,333; stone, clay, and glass products 16,914; fabricated metal products 4,367. Construction (gross value of building and construction permits in U.S.$; 1998): residential 125,207,000; nonresidential 196,681,000. Energy production (consumption): electricity (kW-hr; 1996) 825,000,000 (825,000,000); petroleum products (metric tons; 1996) none (1,329,000).
Gross domestic product (1998): U.S.$3,302,700,000 (U.S.$20,660 per capita).

Structure of gross domestic product and labour force

	1995		1999	
	in value U.S.$'000,000	% of total value	labour force[4]	% of labour force
Agriculture	5	5	300	0.5
Manufacturing	5	5	1,880	3.0
Construction	379.0	12.5	6,490	10.2
Trade	622.9	20.6	13,690	21.6
Transp. and commun.	5	5	5,230	8.3
Finance	5	5	2,720	4.3
Pub. admin. (local)	513.3	16.9	} 19,760	} 31.2
Pub. admin., defense (federal)	452.7	14.9		
Services	486.9	16.1	13,280	21.0
Other	575.4[5]	19.0[5]	—	—
TOTAL	3,030.2	100.0	63,350	100.0[3]

Population economically active (1997): total 71,400; activity rate of total population 45.7% (participation rates: over age 16 [1994] 69.3%[6]; female [1994] 43.3%[6]; unemployed [June 1999] 15.2%).

Price and earnings indexes (1996 = 100)

	1996	1997	1998	1999
Consumer price index	100.0	101.6	101.2	100.9
Hourly earnings index	...	...	...	...

Household income and expenditure. Average household size (1998) 3.9[7]; average annual income per household (1998) U.S.$47,374[7]; sources of income: n.a.; expenditure (1978): housing 28.6%, food 24.1%, transportation 18.0%, clothing 10.6%, entertainment 5.1%, medical care 4.7%.

Foreign trade

Balance of trade (current prices)

	1991	1992	1993	1994	1995	1996
U.S.$'000,000	–358	–384	–355	–528	–584	–600
% of total	74.3%	74.4%	70.3%	86.3%	88.0%	88.2%

Imports (1998–99[8]): U.S.$205,800,000 (food products 34.2%; leather products including footwear 15.8%; motor vehicles and parts 14.3%; construction materials 6.4%; clothing 5.0%). *Major import sources:* n.a.
Exports (1999): U.S.$75,700,000 (food products 54.7%, of which fish 53.8%; petroleum and natural gas products 20.0%; tobacco products 6.7%). *Major export destinations:* Japan 53.9%; Federated States of Micronesia 18.6%; Palau 6.3%; Hong Kong 2.0%.

Transport and communications

Transport. Railroads: none. Roads (1999): total length 550 mi, 885 km (paved 76%). Vehicles (1995): passenger cars 79,800; trucks and buses 34,700. Merchant marine (1992): vessels (100 gross tons and over) 5, total deadweight tonnage 50; surface cargo loaded, unloaded, or transshipped (1998) 2,053,000 metric tons. Air transport (1998): passenger arrivals 1,375,000; passenger departures 1,378,000; cargo loaded and unloaded (1997) 35,295 metric tons; airports (1999) with scheduled flights 1.

Communications

Medium	date	unit	number	units per 1,000 persons
Daily newspapers	1996	circulation	28,000	178
Radio	1997	receivers	221,000	1,400
Television	1997	receivers	106,000	668
Telephones	1999	main lines	77,609	472
Cellular telephones	1999	subscribers	20,000	122

Education and health

Educational attainment (1995). Percentage of population age 25 and over having: no formal schooling to some secondary education 26.9%; completed secondary 55.4%; completed higher 17.7%. *Literacy* (1990): total population age 15 and over literate 99.0%; males literate 99.0%; females literate 99.0%.

Education (1996)

	schools	teachers	students	student/ teacher ratio
Primary (age 5–10)	24	1,091	18,896	17.3
Secondary (age 11–18) } Vocational }	6	943	18,068	19.2
Higher	5	...	3,383	...

Health (1999): physicians 130[9] (1 per 1,169 persons); hospital beds 192[10] (1 per 792 persons); infant mortality rate per 1,000 live births (2001) 10.0.

Military

Total active duty U.S. personnel (2000): 3,740 (army, 1.0%; navy 49.5%; air force 49.5%).

[1]Includes active-duty military personnel, U.S. Department of Defense employees, their dependents, and Guamanian nationals. [2]Total area per most recent survey including area designated as inland water equals 217 sq mi (561 sq km). [3]Detail does not add to total given because of rounding. [4]Employed persons only. [5]Other includes Agriculture, Manufacturing, Transportation and communications, and Finance. [6]Excludes nonimmigrant aliens and civilians living on military reservations. [7]Excludes U.S. military and dependents. [8]Fiscal year November 1998–October 1999. [9]Members of Guam Medical Society only. [10]Guam Memorial Hospital only.

Internet resources for further information:
- **The Official Guam U.S.A. Website http://ns.gov.gu**
- **Government of Guam: Economic Overview http://www.admin.gov.gu/commerce/economy.htm**

Guatemala

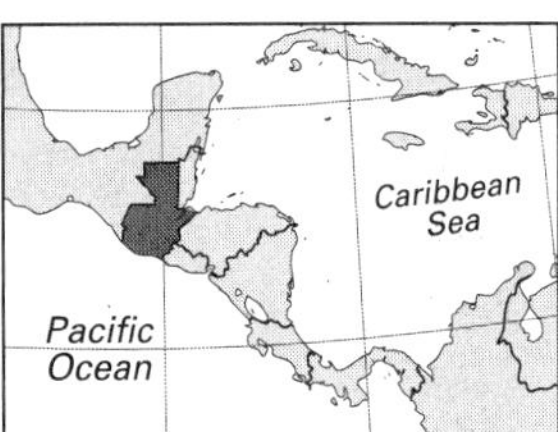

Official name: República de Guatemala (Republic of Guatemala).
Form of government: republic with one legislative house (Congress of the Republic [113]).
Head of state and government: President.
Capital: Guatemala City.
Official language: Spanish.
Official religion: none
Monetary unit: 1 quetzal (Q) = 100 centavos; valuation (Sept. 28, 2001) 1 U.S.$ = Q 7.94; 1 £ = Q 11.66.

Area and population

Departments	Capitals	area sq mi	area sq km	population 2000 estimate[1]
Alta Verapaz	Cobán	3,354	8,686	814,300
Baja Verapaz	Salamá	1,206	3,124	203,430
Chimaltenango	Chimaltenango	764	1,979	427,602
Chiquimula	Chiquimula	917	2,376	313,150
El Progreso	Guastatoya (Progreso)	742	1,922	143,197
Escuintla	Escuintla	1,693	4,384	483,768
Guatemala	Guatemala City	821	2,126	2,578,526
Huehuetenango	Huehuetenango	2,857	7,400	879,987
Izabal	Puerto Barrios	3,490	9,038	333,956
Jalapa	Jalapa	797	2,063	270,055
Jutiapa	Jutiapa	1,243	3,219	385,909
Petén	Flores	13,843	35,854	333,389
Quetzaltenango	Quetzaltenango	753	1,951	678,251
Quiché	Santa Cruz del Quiché	3,235	8,378	588,831
Retalhuleu	Retalhuleu	717	1,856	241,921
Sacatepéquez	Antigua Guatemala	180	465	259,265
San Marcos	San Marcos	1,464	3,791	844,486
Santa Rosa	Cuilapa	1,141	2,955	319,814
Sololá	Sololá	410	1,061	307,791
Suchitepéquez	Mazatenango	969	2,510	403,609
Totonicapán	Totonicapán	410	1,061	361,303
Zacapa	Zacapa	1,039	2,690	212,794
TOTAL		42,042[2]	108,889	11,385,334

Demography

Population (2001): 11,687,000.
Density (2001): persons per sq mi 278.0, persons per sq km 107.3.
Urban-rural (2000): urban 39.4%; rural 60.6%.
Sex distribution (1998): male 50.44%; female 49.56%.
Age breakdown (1998): under 15, 44.2%; 15–29, 28.0%; 30–44, 14.6%; 45–59, 7.9%; 60–74, 4.3%; 75 and over, 1.0%.
Population projection: (2010) 14,631,000; (2020) 18,123,000.
Doubling time: 25 years.
Ethnic composition (1994): Amerindian 42.8%; non-Amerindian 57.2%.
Religious affiliation (1995): Roman Catholic 75.9%, of which Catholic/traditional syncretist 25.0%; Protestant 21.8%; other Christian 1.3%; other 1.0%.
Major cities (1995)[3]: Guatemala City 1,167,495; Mixco 436,668; Villa Nueva 165,567; Chinautla 61,335; Amatitlan 40,229.

Vital statistics

Birth rate per 1,000 population (2000): 35.1 (world avg. 22.5).
Death rate per 1,000 population (2000): 6.9 (world avg. 9.0).
Natural increase rate per 1,000 population (2000): 28.2 (world avg. 13.5).
Total fertility rate (avg. births per childbearing woman; 2000): 4.7.
Marriage rate per 1,000 population (1995): 4.6.
Divorce rate per 1,000 population (1995): 0.05.
Life expectancy at birth (2000): male 63.5 years; female 69.0 years.
Major causes of death per 100,000 population (1988): infectious and parasitic diseases 121.6; diseases of the respiratory system 110.8; perinatal causes 58.7; malnutrition 50.2; dehydration 18.5.

National economy

Budget (1998). Revenue: Q 11,997,000,000 (tax revenue 90.3%, nontax revenue 8.9%). Expenditures: Q 14,828,000,000 (current expenditures 61.7%, of which disbursements for wages and salaries 25.3%, transfer payments 18.0%; capital expenditures 38.3%).
Public debt (external, outstanding; 1999): U.S.$3,129,000,000.
Tourism (1999): receipts U.S.$570,000,000; expenditures U.S.$183,000,000.
Production (metric tons except as noted). Agriculture, forestry, fishing (1999): sugarcane 15,459,000, corn (maize) 1,109,000 bananas 733,000, oil palm fruit 340,000, coffee 200,000, tomatoes 149,000; livestock (number of live animals) 2,300,000 cattle, 825,000 pigs, 24,000,000 chickens; roundwood (1998) 12,995,000 cu m; fish catch (1998) 10,847. Mining and quarrying (1997): gypsum 30,000; iron ore 3,300; antimony ore 880. Manufacturing (value added in Q '000,000; 1998[4]): food and beverage products 298; clothing and textiles 119; machinery and metal products 55. Construction (value of buildings authorized in Q '000,000; 1991)[5]: residential 170.2; nonresidential 127.5. Energy production (consumption): electricity (kW-hr; 1996) 3,500,000,000 (3,500,000,000); crude petroleum (barrels; 1996) 5,256,000 (5,198,000); petroleum products (metric tons; 1996) 687,000 (1,990,000).
Household income and expenditure. Average household size (1994) 5.2; income per household (1989) Q 4,306 (U.S.$1,529); sources of income: n.a.; expenditure (1981): food 64.4%, housing and energy 16.0%, transportation and communications 7.0%, household furnishings 5.0%, clothing 3.1%.
Gross national product (1999): U.S.$18,625,000,000 (U.S.$1,680 per capita).

Structure of gross domestic product and labour force

	1998 in value Q '000,000[4]	1998 % of total value	1995 labour force	1995 % of labour force
Agriculture	1,103	23.4	1,798,227	58.1
Mining	30	0.6	3,095	0.1
Manufacturing	640	13.6	420,928	13.6
Construction	113	2.4	126,898	4.1
Public utilities	162	3.4	9,285	0.3
Transp. and commun.	426	9.0	77,377	2.5
Trade	1,162	24.6	225,940	7.3
Finance, real estate	461	9.8		
Pub. admin., defense	356	7.5	371,407	12.0
Services	269	5.7		
Other	—	—	61,901[6]	2.0[6]
TOTAL	4,722	100.0	3,095,058	100.0

Population economically active (1996): total 3,183,173; activity rate of total population 29.1% (participation rates [1994] ages 15–64, 51.0%; female 19.5%; unemployed [1995] 1.4%[7]).

Price and earnings indexes (1995 = 100)

	1994	1995	1996	1997	1998	1999	2000
Consumer price index	92.2	100.0	111.1	121.3	129.8	136.1	144.2
Annual earnings index[8]	82.4	100.0	121.8	136.7	151.0	...	...

Land use (1998): forested and nonarable land 58.4%; meadows and pastures 24.0%; agricultural and under permanent cultivation 17.6%.

Foreign trade[9]

Balance of trade (current prices)

	1995	1996	1997	1998	1999	2000
U.S.$'000,000	–692.0	–849.7	–1,198.7	–1,582.9	–1,613.0	–1,727.7
% of total	13.8%	17.3%	20.4%	23.5%	25.2%	24.3%

Imports (1998): U.S.$4,650,900,000 (intermediate goods 34.9%, consumer goods 29.5%, capital goods 26.3%, lubricants and fuels 6.1%, construction materials 3.2%). *Major import sources:* United States 41.5%; Mexico 10.4%; Japan 4.5%; Venezuela 3.3%; Germany 2.8%.
Exports (1998): U.S.$2,846,700,000 (coffee 20.4%, sugar 11.0%, bananas 6.2%, petroleum 2.0%). *Major export destinations:* United States 32.2%; Germany 4.3%; Mexico 4.1%; Japan 2.2%.

Transport and communications

Transport. Railroads (1996): route length 884 km; passenger-km (1995) 16,580,000; metric ton-km cargo 85,615,000. Roads (1996): total length 13,100 km (paved 28%). Vehicles (1996): passenger cars 102,000; trucks and buses 97,000. Air transport (1995)[10]: passenger-km 500,000,000; metric ton-km cargo 70,000,000; airports (1996) 2.

Communications

Medium	date	unit	number	units per 1,000 persons
Daily newspapers	1996	circulation	338,000	33
Radio	1997	receivers	835,000	79
Television	1998	receivers	660,000	61
Telephones	1999	main lines	610,701	55
Cellular telephones	1999	subscribers	337,800	30
Personal computers	1999	units	110,000	9.9
Internet	1999	users	65,000	5.9

Education and health

Educational attainment (1994). Percentage of population age 25 and over having: no formal schooling 45.2%; incomplete primary education 20.8%; complete primary 18.0%; some secondary 4.8%; secondary 7.2%; higher 4.0%. *Literacy* (1995): total population age 15 and over literate 55.6%; males literate 62.5%; females literate 48.6%.

Education (1996)

	schools	teachers	students	student/teacher ratio
Primary (age 7–12)	12,409	43,403	1,510,811	34.8
Secondary (age 13–18)	1,274[11]	22,624	375,528	16.6
Voc., teacher tr.	626[11]			
Higher	5[12]	4,346[12]	80,228[13]	16.0[12]

Health (1988): physicians (1997) 9,812 (1 per 1,072 persons); hospital beds (1995) 10,974 (1 per 909 persons); infant mortality rate (2000) 47.0.
Food (1999): daily per capita caloric intake 2,331 (vegetable products 92%, animal products 8%); (1997) 106% of FAO recommended minimum.

Military

Total active duty personnel (2000): 31,400 (army 93.0%, navy 4.8%, air force 2.2%). *Military expenditure as percentage of GNP* (1996): 1.4% (world 2.6%); per capita expenditure U.S.$23.

[1]Adjusted for underenumeration in 1994 census. [2]Detail does not add to total given because of rounding. [3]Municipal population. [4]At prices of 1958. [5]Private construction in Guatemala City metropolitan area only. [6]Persons in activities not adequately defined. [7]Registered unemployed; majority of economically active population is estimated to be underemployed. [8]Based on employees entitled to social security. [9]Import figures are f.o.b. in balance of trade and c.i.f. for commodities and trading partners. [10]Aviateca Airlines only. [11]1991. [12]1989. [13]1995.

Internet resources for further information:
- **Banco de Guatemala (Spanish only) http://www.banguat.gob.gt**
- **Instituto Nacional de Estadistica http://www.ine.gob.gt**

Guernsey[1]

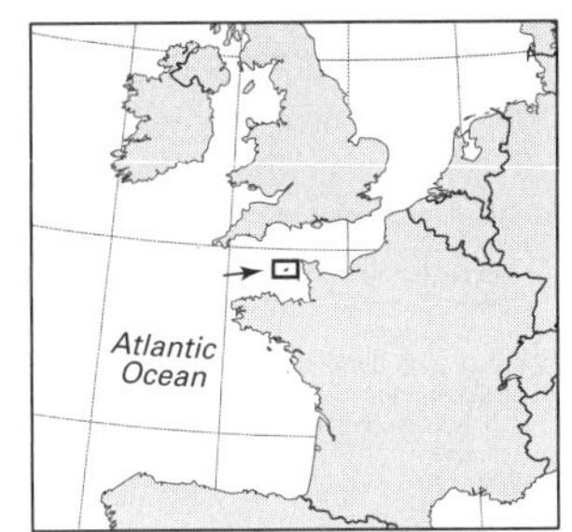

Official name: Bailiwick of Guernsey.
Political status: crown dependency (United Kingdom) with one legislative house (States of Deliberation [57[2, 3, 4]]).
Chief of state: British Monarch represented by Lieutenant Governor.
Head of government: [5].
Capital: St. Peter Port.
Official language: English.
Official religion: n.a.
Monetary unit: 1 Guernsey pound[6] = 100 pence; valuation (Sept. 28, 2001) 1 Guernsey pound = U.S.$1.47.

Area and population	area		population
			1996
	sq mi	sq km	census
Parishes of Guernsey	24.3	63.0	58,581
Castel	3.9	10.1	8,922
Forest	1.6	4.1	1,423
St. Andrew	1.7	4.5	2,342
St. Martin	2.8	7.3	6,082
St. Peter Port	2.6	6.6	16,194
St. Peter	2.4	6.2	2,151
St. Sampson	2.3	6.0	8,540
St. Saviour	2.4	6.3	2,469
Torteval	1.2	3.1	954
Vale	3.4	8.8	9,504
Dependencies of Guernsey	5.9	15.1	2,797
Alderney	3.1	7.9	2,147[7]
Brechou	0.1	0.3	0
Herm	0.5	1.3	97
Jethou	0.1	0.2	3
Lihou	0.1	0.2	0
Little Sark	0.4	1.0	} 550
Sark (Great Sark)	1.6	4.2	
TOTAL	30.2	78.1	61,378

Demography

Population (2001): 64,300.
Density (2001): persons per sq mi 2,129.1, persons per sq km 823.3.
Sex distribution (1996): male 48.13%; female 51.87%.
Age breakdown (1996): under 15, 17.6%; 15–29, 20.6%; 30–44, 22.3%; 45–59, 19.0%; 60–74, 13.2%; 75 and over, 7.3%.
Population projection: (2010) 66,000; (2020) 67,000.
Doubling time: n.a.; doubling time exceeds 100 years.
Population by place of birth (1996): Guernsey 65.5%, United Kingdom 27.2%, Portugal 1.9%, Jersey 0.7%, Ireland 0.7%, Alderney 0.3%, Sark 0.1%, other 3.6%.
Religious affiliation (*c.* 1990): Anglican 65.2%; other 34.8%.
Major cities (1996)[8]: St. Peter Port 16,194; Vale 9,504; Castel 8,922; St. Sampson 8,540; St. Martin 6,082.

Vital statistics

Birth rate per 1,000 population (2000): 10.5 (world avg. 22.5).
Death rate per 1,000 population (2000): 9.3 (world avg. 9.0).
Natural increase rate per 1,000 population (2000): 1.2 (world avg. 13.5).
Total fertility rate (avg. births per childbearing woman; 2000): 1.3.
Marriage rate per 1,000 population (1995): 6.0.
Divorce rate per 1,000 population (1993): 2.5.
Life expectancy at birth (2000): male 76.7 years; female 82.8 years.
Major causes of death per 100,000 population (1993): diseases of the circulatory system 423.5; malignant neoplasms (cancers) 288.0; diseases of the respiratory system 133.8; endocrine and metabolic disorders 25.4; accidents, poisoning, and violence 22.0; diseases of the digestive system 11.8.

National economy

Budget (1999). Revenue: £306,991,000 (income tax 79.7%; custom duties and excise taxes 5.7%; document duties 2.7%; corporation taxes 2.1%; automobile taxes 1.9%). Expenditures: £244,418,000 (welfare 31.1%; health 26.2%; education 15.9%; administrative services 6.7%; law and order 4.9%; community services 4.1%).
Public debt: n.a.
Gross national product (at current market prices; 2000): U.S.$1,883,550,000 (U.S.$30,840 per capita).

Structure of gross domestic product and labour force	1999		1996	
	in value £'000	% of total value	labour force	% of labour force
Horticulture, fishing	25,596	2.2	1,893	6.2
Mining	—		—	—
Manufacturing	38,812	3.4	2,084	6.8
Construction	59,623	5.2	2,676	8.7
Public utilities	[9]	[9]	447	1.5
Transp. and commun.	[10]	[10]	1,260	4.1
Finance, real estate[11]	706,483[9]	61.7[9]	5,928	19.3
Pub. admin., defense }	302,010[10]	26.4[10]	1,908	6.2
Services }			14,252	46.4
Other	12,998	1.1	245	0.8
TOTAL	1,145,522	100.0	30,693	100.0

Production (metric tons except as noted). Agriculture, forestry, fishing (1999): tomatoes 2,449[12], flowers 1,153,857 boxes, of which roses 287,915 boxes, freesia 184,467 boxes, carnations 161,273 boxes; livestock (number of live animals) 3,262 cattle; roundwood n.a.; fish catch (1997)[13]: 4,368, of which crustaceans 2,934 (sea spiders and crabs 2,713), molluscs 743 (abalones, winkles, and conch 438), marine fish 691. Mining and quarrying: n.a. Manufacturing: milk 98,830 hectolitres. Construction: n.a. Energy production (consumption): electricity (kW-hr; 1999–2000), n.a. (273,013,000).
Household income and expenditure (1999). Average household size (1996) 2.6; expenditure: housing 21.6%, food 12.7%, household goods and services 11.2%, recreation services 9.2%, transportation 8.5%, clothing and footwear 5.6%, personal goods 4.9%, energy 4.1%.
Population economically active (1999): total 31,153; activity rate of total population 48.8% (participation rates: ages 15–64, n.a.; female n.a.; unemployed n.a.).

Retail price and earnings indexes (1994 = 100)	1995	1996	1997	1998	1999	2000	2001
Consumer price index[14]	103.0	105.5	108.8	113.2	115.7	120.1	124.0
Earnings index	...	...	...	...	...	...	...

Tourism (1996): receipts U.S.$275,000,000.

Foreign trade

Imports (1997): principal imports, n.a. *Major import sources* (1997): mostly United Kingdom.
Exports (1999): £525,718,000 (mostly flowers and tomatoes). *Major export destinations* (1999): mostly United Kingdom.

Transport and communications

Transport. Railroads: n.a. Vehicles (2000): passenger cars 37,598; trucks and buses 7,338. Air transport: (2000) passenger arrivals 884,284; (1996) freight loaded and unloaded 7,616 metric tons; airports (1999) with scheduled flights 2[15].

Communications				units per 1,000
Medium	date	unit	number	persons
Daily newspapers	1998	circulation	15,784	260
Telephones	1999	main lines	50,739	834
Cellular telephones	1999	subscribers	15,320	251

Education and health

Educational attainment: n.a. *Literacy* (1993): percentage of total population age 15 and over literate 100.0%; males literate 100.0%; females literate 100.0%.

Education (1999)	schools	teachers	students	student/ teacher ratio
Primary (age 5–10)	22[16]	253	4,977	19.9
Secondary (age 11–16)	8[16]	295	3,900	13.2
Higher	1	...	211[17]	...

Health (1999): physicians 93 (1 per 654 persons); hospital beds, n.a.; infant mortality rate per 1,000 live births (2000) 5.1.
Food (1999)[18]: daily per capita caloric intake 3,318 (vegetable products 68%, animal products 32%); 132% of FAO recommended minimum requirement.

Military

Total active duty personnel[19]: n.a.

[1]Data excludes Alderney and Sark unless otherwise noted. [2]Elected only; excludes those serving ex-officio. [3]Headed by the Bailiff. [4]Alderney and Sark have their own parliaments. The States of Alderney has an elected president and 12 people's deputies. The Chief Please of Sark consists of 40 *tenants* or landowners and 12 people's deputies. [5]The government of Guernsey is conducted by committees appointed by the States of Deliberation. [6]Equivalent in value to pound sterling (£). [7]Based on 1996 estimate. [8]Parishes. [9]Utilities and trade included in Finance, real estate. [10]Transportation is included in Public administration, defense and Services. [11]Mostly from 79 banks (located offshore) and 581 insurance companies (352 offshore and 217 domestic). [12]1998. [13]Includes Jersey. [14]March. [15]Includes one airport on Alderney. [16]1992. [17]Full students. [18]Data for the United Kingdom. [19]The United Kingdom is responsible for defense.

Internet resources for further information:
- **The States of Guernsey http://www.gov.gg**

Guinea

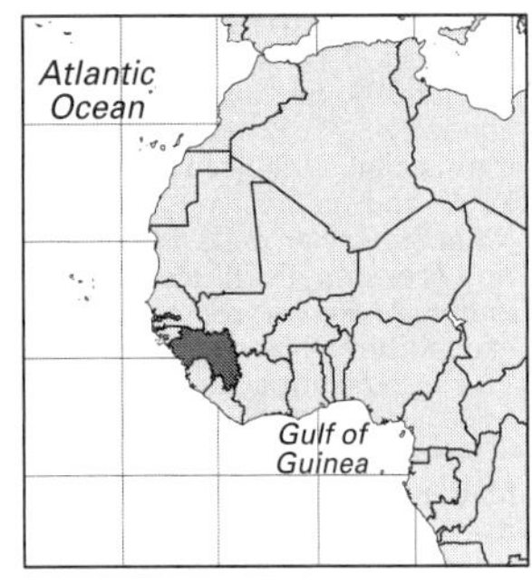

Official name: République de Guinée (Republic of Guinea).
Form of government: unitary multiparty republic with one legislative house (National Assembly [114 seats]).
Head of state and government: President assisted by extraconstitutional Prime Minister.
Capital: Conakry.
Official language: French.
Official religion: none.
Monetary unit: 1 Guinean franc (GF) = 100 cauris; valuation (Sept. 28, 2001) 1 U.S.$ = GF 1,960; 1 £ = GF 2,881.

Area and population

Regions[1]	Capitals	area sq mi	area sq km	population 1983 census
Beyla	Beyla	6,738	17,452	161,347
Boffa	Boffa	1,932	5,003	141,719
Boké	Boké	3,881	10,053	225,207
Conakry	Conakry	119	308	705,280
Coyah (Dubréka)	Coyah	2,153	5,576	134,190
Dabola	Dabola	2,317	6,000	97,986
Dalaba	Dalaba	1,313	3,400	132,802
Dinguiraye	Dinguiraye	4,247	11,000	133,502
Faranah	Faranah	4,788	12,400	142,923
Forécariah	Forécariah	1,647	4,265	116,464
Fria	Fria	840	2,175	70,413
Gaoual	Gaoual	4,440	11,500	135,657
Guéckédou	Guéckédou	1,605	4,157	204,757
Kankan	Kankan	7,104	18,400	229,861
Kérouané	Kérouané	3,070	7,950	106,872
Kindia	Kindia	3,409	8,828	216,052
Kissidougou	Kissidougou	3,425	8,872	183,236
Koubia	Koubia	571	1,480	98,053
Koundara	Koundara	2,124	5,500	94,216
Kouroussa	Kouroussa	4,647	12,035	136,926
Labé	Labé	973	2,520	253,214
Lélouma	Lélouma	830	2,150	138,467
Lola	Lola	1,629	4,219	106,654
Macenta	Macenta	3,363	8,710	193,109
Mali	Mali	3,398	8,800	210,889
Mamou	Mamou	2,378	6,160	190,525
Mandiana	Mandiana	5,000	12,950	136,317
Nzérékoré	Nzérékoré	1,460	3,781	216,355
Pita	Pita	1,544	4,000	227,912
Siguiri	Siguiri	7,626	19,750	209,164
Télimélé	Télimélé	3,119	8,080	243,256
Tougué	Tougué	2,394	6,200	113,272
Yomou	Yomou	843	2,183	74,417
TOTAL		94,926[2]	245,857	5,781,014

Demography

Population (2001): 7,614,000.
Density (2001): persons per sq mi 80.2, persons per sq km 31.0.
Urban-rural (1998): urban 31.3%; rural 68.7%.
Sex distribution (1998): male 50.28%; female 49.72%.
Age breakdown (1999): under 15, 43.6%; 15–29, 26.9%; 30–44, 16.0%; 45–59, 9.0%; 60–74, 3.9%; 75 and over, 0.6%.
Population projection: (2010) 9,281,000; (2020) 11,440,000.
Doubling time: 31 years.
Ethnic composition (1996): Fulani 38.6%; Malinke 23.2%; Susu 11.0%; Kissi 6.0%; Kpelle 4.6%; other 16.6%.
Religious affiliation (1996): Muslim 85.0%; Christian 10.0%; other 5.0%.
Major cities (2001): Conakry 1,565,200; Kankan 88,800; Labe 64,500; Kindia 56,000; Nzérékoré 55,000; Kissidougou 40,400.

Vital statistics

Birth rate per 1,000 population (2001): 39.8 (world avg. 22.5).
Death rate per 1,000 population (2001): 17.5 (world avg. 9.0).
Natural increase rate per 1,000 population (2001): 22.3 (world avg. 13.5).
Total fertility rate (avg. births per childbearing woman; 2001): 5.4.
Life expectancy at birth (2001): male 43.5 years; female 48.4 years.

National economy

Budget (1998). Revenue: GF 624,500,000,000 (current revenues 79.5%, of which indirect taxes 34.8%, mining sector 20.2%, tax on trade 11.5%, direct taxes 7.7%, nontax revenue 5.3%; foreign aid 20.5%). Expenditures: GF 655,600,000,000 (wages and salaries 27.6%, goods and services 13.6%, interest 9.8%, transfers 8.1%; capital spending 38.2%).
Production (metric tons except as noted). Agriculture, forestry, fishing (1999): roots and tubers 1,064,888 (of which cassava 811,869, sweet potatoes 134,940, yams 88,635), fruits 996,078 (of which plantains 429,000, bananas 150,000, pineapples 71,858), paddy rice 750,000, vegetables and melons 420,000, sugarcane 220,000, peanuts (groundnuts) 173,682, corn (maize) 88,690; livestock (number of live animals) 2,368,000 cattle, 864,000 goats, 687,000 sheep, 54,000 pigs, 8,900,000 chickens; roundwood (1998) 8,650,000 cu m; fish catch (1997) 102,589. Mining and quarrying (1996): bauxite 15,888,600; alumina 564,237; gold 7,863 kg[3]. Manufacturing (value of production in GF '000; 1985): corrugated and sheet iron 571,081; plastics 462,242; tobacco products 375,154; cement 326,138; printed matter 216,511. Energy production (consumption): electricity (kW-hr; 1996) 541,000,000 (541,000,000); petroleum products (metric tons; 1996) none (356,000).
Gross national product (1999): U.S.$3,556,000,000 (U.S.$490 per capita).

Structure of gross domestic product and labour force

	1998 in value GF '000,000,000[4]	1998 % of total value	1983 labour force	1983 % of labour force
Agriculture, forestry, fishing	824.8	20.6	1,423,615	78.2
Mining	630.3	15.7	12,241	0.7
Manufacturing	153.9	3.8	11,215	0.6
Construction	350.6	8.7	9,115	0.5
Public utilities	20.8	0.5	3,205	0.2
Transp. and commun.	243.6	6.1	29,496	1.6
Trade, finance	1,116.8	27.8	40,865	2.0
Pub. admin., defense Services	166.1	4.1	137,600	7.5
Other	505.8[5]	12.6[5]	155,679	8.5
TOTAL	4,012.7	100.0[2]	1,823,031	100.0

Public debt (external, outstanding; 1999): U.S.$3,057,000,000.
Population economically active (1997): total 3,321,000; activity rate of total population 44.8% (participation rates [1983]: ages 15–64, 63.5%; female 47.3%; unemployed, n.a.).

Price and earnings indexes (1995 = 100)

	1994	1995	1996	1997	1998
Consumer price index	94.7	100.0	102.9	104.9	110.3
Annual salary index	...	...	...	...	...

Household income and expenditure. Average household size (1997): 4.1; average annual income per capita (1984) GS 7,660 (U.S.$305); expenditure (1985): food 61.5%, health 11.2%, clothing 7.9%, housing 7.3%.
Tourism (1999): receipts U.S.$7,000,000; expenditures U.S.$31,000,000.
Land use (1994): forest 27.3%; pasture 43.5%; agriculture 3.3%; other 25.9%.

Foreign trade

Balance of trade (current prices)

	1993	1994	1995	1996	1997	1998
U.S.$'000,000	−21.6	−169.7	−39.0	+111.2	+117.6	+137.4
% of total	1.9%	14.1%	3.2%	9.6%	10.3%	10.7%

Imports (1997): U.S.$571,800,000 (capital goods 52.4%, consumer products 18.0%, food 17.1%, petroleum 12.5%). *Major import sources:* France 24.8%; U.S. 9.8%; Belgium 7.9%; Côte d'Ivoire 6.6%; China 5.6%.
Exports (1998): U.S.$709,200,000 (bauxite 45.7%, gold 17.7%, alumina 14.1%, diamonds 7.2%, fish 5.4%, coffee 3.3%). *Major export destinations:* U.S. 16.4%; Hong Kong 14.7%; Belgium 13.7%; Spain 12.4%; Ireland 12.2%.

Transport and communications

Transport. Railroads (1998): route length 662 km; (latest) passenger-km 41,500,000; metric ton-km cargo 7,300,000. Roads (1997): total length 30,500 km (paved 16.5%). Vehicles (1996): passenger cars 14,100; trucks and buses 21,000. Air transport (1995): passenger-km 52,000,000; metric ton-km cargo 5,000,000; airports (1998) 1.

Communications

Medium	date	unit	number	units per 1,000 persons
Daily newspapers	1988	circulation	13,000	2.0
Radio	1998	receivers	325,000	43
Television	1999	receivers	343,000	44
Telephones	1999	main lines	46,246	6.0
Cellular telephones	1999	subscribers	25,182	3.2
Personal computers	1998	units	26,720	3.5
Internet	1999	users	5,000	0.6

Education and health

Educational attainment of those age 6 and over having attended school (1983): primary 55.2%; secondary 32.7%; vocational 3.4%; higher 8.7%. *Literacy* (1995): percentage of total population age 15 and over literate 35.9%; males 49.9%; females 21.9%.

Education (1997–98)

	schools	teachers	students	student/ teacher ratio
Primary (age 7–12)	3,723	13,883	674,732	48.6
Secondary (age 13–18)	239	4,958	143,245	28.9
Voc., teacher tr.[6]	55	1,268	8,569	6.8
Higher[7, 8]	2	947	8,151	8.6

Health: physicians (1991) 920 (1 per 6,840 persons); hospital beds (1988) 3,382 (1 per 1,652 persons); infant mortality rate (2001) 120.0.
Food (1999): daily per capita caloric intake 2,133 (vegetable products 97%, animal products 3%); 92% of FAO recommended minimum requirement.

Military

Total active duty personnel (2000): 9,700 (army 87.6%, navy 4.1%, air force 8.2%). *Military expenditure as percentage of GNP* (1997): 1.5% (world 2.6%); per capita expenditure U.S.$7.

[1]Regions represent second-level administration; Guinea is divided into 7 provinces and 1 city (Conakry) at the first level of administration. [2]Detail does not add to total given because of rounding. [3]1995 reported figure to government of artisanal production; excludes artisanal production smuggled out of country. [4]1994 prices. [5]Includes services and indirect taxes. [6]1995–96. [7]1996–97. [8]Universities only.

Internet resources for further information:
- **Welcome to Guinea http://www.guinee.net**

Guinea-Bissau

Official name: Répubica da Guiné-Bissau (Republic of Guinea-Bissau).
Form of government: transitional regime with one legislative house (National People's Assembly [102]).
Chief of state: President.
Head of government: Prime Minister.
Capital: Bissau.
Official language: Portuguese.
Official religion: none.
Monetary unit: 1 CFA franc[1] (CFAF) = 100 centimes; valuation (Sept. 28, 2001) 1 U.S.$ = CFAF 720.28; 1 £ = CFAF 1,059.

Area and population

		area		population
Regions	Chief towns	sq mi	sq km	1991 census
Bafatá	Bafatá	2,309	5,981	143,377
Biombo	Quinhámel	324	840	60,420
Bolama	Bolama	1,013	2,624	26,691
Cacheu	Cacheu	1,998	5,175	146,980
Gabú	Gabú	3,533	9,150	134,971
Oio	Bissorã	2,086	5,403	156,084
Quinara	Fulacunda	1,212	3,138	44,793
Tombali	Catió	1,443	3,736	72,441
Autonomous Sector				
Bissau	—	30	78	197,610
TOTAL		13,948[2]	36,125[2]	983,367

Demography

Population (2001): 1,316,000.
Density (2001)[3]: persons per sq mi 121.2, persons per sq km 46.8.
Urban-rural (1996): urban 22.0%; rural 78.0%.
Sex distribution (1997): male 48.52%; female 51.48%.
Age breakdown (1997): under 15, 42.7%; 15–29, 28.1%; 30–44, 15.4%; 45–59, 9.2%; 60–74, 3.8%; 75 and over, 0.8%.
Population projection: (2010) 1,614,000; (2020) 1,998,000.
Doubling time: 29 years.
Ethnic composition (1995): Balante 30%; Fulani 20%; Mandyako 14%; Malinke 13%; Pepel 7%; nonindigenous Cape Verdean mulatto 2%; other 14%.
Religious affiliation (2000): traditional beliefs 45.2%; Muslim 39.9%; Christian 13.2%, of which Roman Catholic 9.9%; other 1.7%.
Major cities (1997): Bissau 200,000 (urban agglomeration [1999] 274,000); Bafatá 15,000; Cacheu 14,000; Gabú 10,000.

Vital statistics

Birth rate per 1,000 population (2000): 39.6 (world avg. 22.5).
Death rate per 1,000 population (2000): 15.6 (world avg. 9.0).
Natural increase rate per 1,000 population (2000): 24.0 (world avg. 13.5).
Total fertility rate (avg. births per childbearing woman; 2000): 5.3.
Marriage rate per 1,000 population (1981): 0.1.
Divorce rate per 1,000 population: n.a.
Life expectancy at birth (2000): male 46.8 years; female 51.4 years.
Major causes of death per 100,000 population: n.a.; however, major diseases include tuberculosis of the respiratory system, whooping cough, typhoid fever, cholera, bacillary dysentery and amebiasis, malaria, pneumonia, and meningococcal infections; malnutrition is widespread.

National economy

Budget (1998). Revenue: CFAF 10,500,000,000 (foreign grants 37.1%; taxes on international trade 21.6%, of which import duties 12.9%; nontax revenues 19.8%, of which fishing licenses 7.3%; taxes on goods and services 10.7%; income taxes 8.2%). Expenditures: CFAF 30,200,000,000 (current expenditures 75.2%, of which scheduled external interest payments 27.0%; capital expenditures 24.8%).
Production (metric tons except as noted). Agriculture, forestry, fishing (1999): rice 130,000, oil palm fruit 80,000, roots and tubers 77,500, coconuts 44,000, cashew nuts 38,000, plantains 36,000, millet 30,000, peanuts (groundnuts) 18,000; livestock (number of live animals) 520,000 cattle, 340,000 pigs, 315,000 goats, 280,000 sheep; roundwood (1998) 589,000 cu m; fish catch (1997) 7,250, of which marine fish 5,664, crustaceans and molluscs 1,336. Mining and quarrying: extraction of construction materials only. Manufacturing (1997): processed wood 21,400; fresh pork 9,720; wood products 7,000; dried and smoked fish 6,600; fresh beef 3,850; soap 3,000; vegetable oils 41,000 hectolitres; distilled liquor 13,000 hectolitres. Energy production (consumption): electricity (kW-hr; 1999) 27,500,000 (10,200,000); coal, none (none); crude petroleum, none (none); petroleum products (metric tons; 1996) none (75,000); natural gas, none (none).
Population economically active (1992): total 471,000; activity rate of total population 46.9% (participation rates [1991]: over age 10, 67.1%; female 40.5%; unemployed, n.a.).

Price and earnings indexes (1995 = 100)

	1995	1996	1997	1998	1999	2000	2001
Consumer price index	100.0	150.7	224.7	239.4	237.7	258.2	275.7[4]
Monthly earnings index	...	...	...	...	...	...	...

Public debt (external, outstanding; 1999): U.S.$831,700,000.
Gross national product (at current market prices; 1999): U.S.$194,000,000 (U.S.$160 per capita).

Structure of gross domestic product and labour force

	1998		1994	
	in value CFAF '000,000	% of total value	labour force	% of labour force
Agriculture	74,831	61.7	365,000	77.2
Mining, Manufacturing, Public utilities	11,134	9.2	21,000	4.5
Construction	4,071	3.4		
Transportation and communications	2,333	1.9	87,000	18.3
Trade	23,624	19.5		
Finance, services	897	0.7		
Pub. admin., defense	3,067	2.5		
Other	1,357[5]	1.1[5]		
TOTAL	121,313[6]	100.0	473,000	100.0

Tourism: n.a.
Land use (1994): forested 38.1%; meadows and pastures 38.4%; agricultural and under permanent cultivation 12.1%; other 11.4%.
Household income and expenditure. Average household size (1996) 6.9; income per household: n.a; sources of income: n.a.; expenditure: n.a.

Foreign trade[7]

Balance of trade (current prices)

	1994	1995	1996	1997	1998	1999
CFAF '000,000	–15,950	–24,680	–24,210	–23,500	–21,400	–28,000
% of total	32.5%	50.1%	52.3%	29.3%	40.4%	31.6%

Imports (1997): CFAF 51,800,000,000 (foodstuffs 35.1%, of which rice 25.1%; transport equipment 14.1%; fuel and lubricants 10.7%; construction materials 9.6%). *Major import sources* (1999): Portugal 24.0%; Senegal 18.2%; China 12.9%; Japan 8.1%; The Netherlands 6.7%.
Exports (1997): CFAF 28,300,000,000 (cashews 94.0%; sawn wood 1.6%; shrimp 0.8%; logs 0.8%). *Major export destinations* (1999): India 85.2%; Spain 1.7%; other/unspecified 13.1%.

Transport and communications

Transport. Railroads: none. Roads (1996): total length 2,734 mi, 4,400 km (paved 10%). Vehicles (1996): passenger cars 7,120; trucks and buses 5,640. Merchant marine (1992): vessels (100 gross tons and over) 19; total deadweight tonnage 1,846. Air transport (1996): passenger-mi 6,200,000, passenger-km 10,000,000; short ton-mi cargo, n.a., metric ton-km cargo, n.a., airports (1997) with scheduled flights 2.

Communications

Medium	date	unit	number	units per 1,000 persons
Daily newspapers	1996	circulation	6,000	5.1
Radio	1997	receivers	49,000	41
Television	1997	receivers	0	0
Telephones	1998	main lines	8,079	6.6
Internet	1999	users	1,500	1.2

Education and health

Educational attainment (1979). Percentage of population age 7 and over having: no formal schooling or knowledge of reading and writing 90.4%; primary education 7.9%; secondary 1.0%; technical 0.5%; higher 0.2%. *Literacy* (1995): total population age 15 and over literate 54.9%; males literate 68.0%; females literate 42.5%.

Education (1994–95)

	schools	teachers	students	student/ teacher ratio
Primary (age 7–13)	...	...	100,369	...
Secondary (age 13–18)	...	...	7,000[8]	...

Health: physicians (1991) 184 (1 per 5,556 persons); hospital beds (1993) 1,300 (1 per 834 persons); infant mortality rate per 1,000 live births (2000) 112.3.
Food (1999): daily per capita caloric intake 2,245 (vegetable products 93%, animal products 7%); 97% of FAO recommended minimum requirement.

Military

Total active duty personnel (2000): 7,250[9] (army 93.8%, navy 4.8%, air force 1.4%). *Military expenditure as percentage of GNP* (1997): 3.2% (world 2.6%); per capita expenditure U.S.$7.

[1]The CFA franc replaced the Guinea-Bissau peso in May 1997. [2]Includes water area of about 3,089 sq mi (8,000 sq km). [3]Based on land area of 10,859 sq mi (28,125 sq km). [4]June. [5]Indirect taxes. [6]Detail does not add to total given because of rounding. [7]Imports c.i.f.; exports f.o.b. [8]1993–94. [9]Excludes 2,000 paramilitary (gendarmes).

Internet resources for further information:
- **Afristat http://www.afristat.org**
- **Investir en Zone Franc http://www.izf.net/izf/Index.htm**

Guyana

Official name: Co-operative Republic of Guyana.
Form of government: unitary multiparty republic with one legislative house (National Assembly [65[1]]).
Head of state and government: President.
Capital: Georgetown.
Official language: English.
Official religion: none.
Monetary unit: 1 Guyana dollar (G$) = 100 cents; valuation (Sept. 28, 2001) 1 U.S.$ = G$180.00; 1 £ = G$264.55.

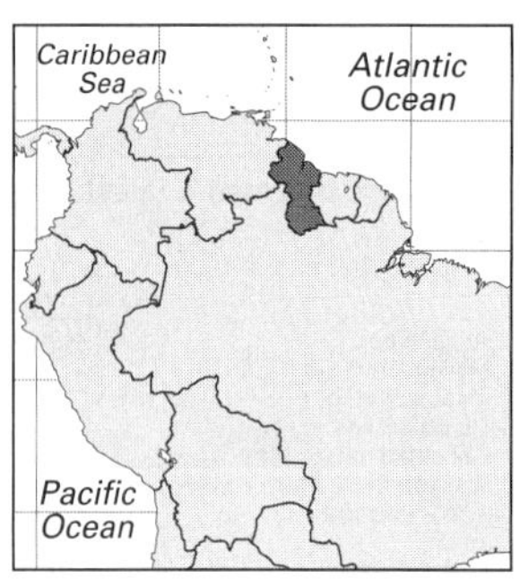

Area and population

Administrative Regions		Capitals	area sq mi	area sq km	population 1986 estimate
Region 1	(Barima–Waini)	Mabaruma	7,853	20,339	18,516
Region 2	(Pomeroon–Supenaam)	Anna Regina	2,392	6,195	41,966
Region 3	(Essequibo Islands–West Demerara)	Vreed en Hoop	1,450	3,755	102,760
Region 4	(Demerara–Mahaica)	Paradise	862	2,233	310,758
Region 5	(Mahaica–Berbice)	Fort Wellington	1,610	4,170	55,556
Region 6	(East Berbice–Corentyne)	New Amsterdam	13,998	36,255	148,967
Region 7	(Cuyuni–Mazaruni)	Bartica	18,229	47,213	17,941
Region 8	(Potaro–Siparuni)	Mahdia	7,742	20,052	5,672
Region 9	(Upper Takutu–Upper Essequibo)	Lethem	22,313	57,790	15,338
Region 10	(Upper Demerara–Berbice)	Linden	6,595	17,081	38,598
TOTAL			83,044[2]	215,083[2]	756,072

Demography

Population (2001): 776,000.
Density (2000)[3]: persons per sq mi 10.2, persons per sq km 3.9.
Urban-rural (1998): urban 37.1%; rural 62.9%.
Sex distribution (1995): male 49.46%; female 50.54%.
Age breakdown (1995): under 15, 32.2%; 15–29, 30.1%; 30–44, 22.2%; 45–59, 9.5%; 60–74, 4.8%; 75 and over, 1.2%.
Population projection: (2010) 807,000; (2020) 834,000.
Doubling time: 74 years.
Ethnic composition (1992–93): East Indian 49.4%; black (African Negro and Bush Negro) 35.6%; mixed 7.1%; Amerindian 6.8%; Portuguese 0.7%; Chinese 0.4%.
Religious affiliation (1995): Christian 40.9%, of which Protestant 27.5% (including Anglican 8.6%), Roman Catholic 11.5%, Ethiopian Orthodox 1.1%; Hindu 34.0%; Muslim 9.0%; other 16.1%.
Major cities (1997): Georgetown 230,000; Linden 35,000; New Amsterdam 25,000; Corriverton 24,000.

Vital statistics

Birth rate per 1,000 population (2000): 17.9 (world avg. 22.5).
Death rate per 1,000 population (2000): 8.4 (world avg. 9.0).
Natural increase rate per 1,000 population (2000): 9.5 (world avg. 13.5).
Total fertility rate (avg. births per childbearing woman; 2000): 2.1.
Life expectancy at birth (2000): male 61.1 years; female 67.2 years.
Major causes of death per 100,000 population (1994)[4]: diseases of the circulatory system 274.3, of which cerebrovascular disease 99.2, ischemic heart diseases 75.2, diseases of pulmonary circulation and other forms of heart disease 57.9; accidents and violence 76.1; endocrine and metabolic disorders 58.9; diseases of the respiratory system 50.1.

National economy

Budget (1999): Revenue: G$36,544,000,000 (tax revenue 91.6%, of which consumption taxes 32.0%, income taxes on companies 22.2%, personal income taxes 15.5%, import duties 11.4%; nontax revenue 8.2%). Expenditures: G$41,983,000,000 (current expenditure 71.2%, of which debt charges 13.8%; development expenditure 28.8%).
Production (metric tons except as noted). Agriculture, forestry, fishing (1999): rice 365,469, raw sugar 321,438, coconuts 56,449, cassava (manioc) 25,957, plantains 14,000, bananas 11,177, pineapples 7,000; livestock (number of live animals) 220,000 cattle, 130,000 sheep, 11,600,000 chickens; roundwood 442,000 cu m; fish catch (1997) 57,409, of which shrimps and prawns 19,060. Mining and quarrying (1999): bauxite 2,359,272; gold 414,905 troy oz; diamonds (1998) 34,385 carats. Manufacturing (1999): flour 35,290; rum 137,800 hectolitres; beer and stout 129,200 hectolitres; soft drinks 3,975,000 cases; pharmaceuticals 7,600,000 tablets; garments 2,900,000 units. Construction: n.a. Energy production (consumption): electricity (kW-hr; 2000) 477,900,000 ([1996] 255,000,000); coal, none (none); crude petroleum, none (none); petroleum products (metric tons; 1996) none (311,000); natural gas, none (none).
Population economically active (1992–93); total 278,000; activity rate of total population 38.8% (participation rates: ages 15–64, 61.8%; female 34.1%; unemployed [1998] *c.* 12%).

Price and earnings indexes (1995 = 100)

	1994	1995	1996	1997	1998	1999	2000
Consumer price index[5]	89.8	100.0	107.1	110.9	116.0	124.7	132.4
Earnings index	...	...	...	...	...	...	...

Gross national product (at current market prices; 1999): U.S.$651,000,000 (U.S.$760 per capita).

Structure of gross domestic product and labour force

	1999 in value G$'000,000	1999 % of total value	1980 labour force	1980 % of labour force
Sugar	16,142[6]	13.4[6]	50,316	20.4
Other agriculture	17,543[7]	14.5[7]		
Fishing, forestry	8,851	7.3		
Mining	13,923	11.5	9,669	3.9
Manufacturing	3,681[8, 9]	3.1[8, 9]	28,980	11.8
Construction	4,771	4.0	7,024	2.8
Public utilities	[9]	[9]	2,850	1.2
Transp. and commun.	7,138	5.9	9,412	3.8
Trade	4,268	3.5	15,231	6.2
Finance, real estate	7,235	6.0	2,944	1.2
Pub. admin., defense	16,976	14.1	29,948	12.1
Services	1,570	1.3	29,295	11.9
Other	18,570[10]	15.4[10]	61,002[11]	24.7[11]
TOTAL	120,668	100.0	246,671	100.0

Public debt (external, outstanding; 1999): U.S.$1,238,000,000.
Household income and expenditure. Average household size (1997) 4.5.
Tourism: receipts from visitors (1998) U.S.$52,000,000; expenditures by nationals abroad (1997) U.S.$22,000,000.
Land use (1994): forested 83.8%; meadows and pastures 6.3%; agricultural and under permanent cultivation 2.5%; other 7.4%.

Foreign trade[12]

Balance of trade (current prices)

	1994	1995	1996	1997	1998	1999
U.S.$'000,000	–42.9	–40.8	–20.2	–34.2	–54.2	–25.2
% of total	4.4%	4.0%	1.7%	2.8%	4.7%	2.3%

Imports (1999): U.S.$550,200,000 (consumer goods 35.2%; capital goods 29.6%; fuels and lubricants 13.1%). *Major import sources* (1998)[13]: U.S. 28%; Trinidad and Tobago 21%; Netherlands Antilles 14%; U.K. 7%; Japan 3%.
Exports (1999): U.S.$525,000,000 (domestic exports 96.1%, of which sugar 25.9%, gold 20.7%; bauxite 14.7%, rice 13.5%, timber 7.1%; reexports 3.9%). *Major export destinations* (1998)[13]: U.S. 24%; Canada 23%; U.K. 19%; Netherlands Antilles 10%.

Transport and communications

Transport. Railroads: [14]. Roads (1996): total length 4,952 mi, 7,970 km (paved 7%). Vehicles (1995): passenger cars 24,000; trucks and buses 9,000. Air transport (1996)[15]: passenger-mi 154,000,000, passenger-km 248,000,000; short ton-mi cargo 2,300,000, metric ton-km cargo 3,300,000; airports (1996) with scheduled flights 1[16].

Communications

Medium	date	unit	number	units per 1,000 persons
Daily newspapers	1996	circulation	42,000	54
Radio	1997	receivers	420,000	539
Television	1999	receivers	60,000	77
Telephones	1999	main lines	64,034	82
Cellular telephones	1999	subscribers	2,815	3.6
Personal computers	1999	units	21,000	27
Internet	1999	users	3,000	3.8

Education and health

Educational attainment (1980). Percentage of population age 25 and over having: no formal schooling 8.1%; primary education 72.8%; secondary 17.3%; higher 1.8%. *Literacy* (1995): total population age 15 and over literate, *c.* 511,000 (98.1%); males literate, *c.* 254,000 (98.6%); females literate, *c.* 257,000 (97.5%).

Education (1996–97)

	schools	teachers	students	student/ teacher ratio
Primary (age 6–11)	420	3,461	102,000	29.5
Secondary (age 12–17)	...	2,150[17]	62,043	29.5[17]
Higher	...	612[17]	8,965	12.5[17]

Health: physicians (1997) 153 (1 per 5,090 persons); hospital beds (1996) 3,242 (1 per 240 persons); infant mortality rate per 1,000 live births (2000) 39.1.
Food (1999): daily per capita caloric intake 2,569 (vegetable products 84%, animal products 16%); 113% of FAO recommended minimum requirement.

Military

Total active duty personnel (2000): 1,600 (army 87.5%, navy 6.3%, air force 6.2%) *Military expenditure as percentage of GNP* (1997): 1.1% (world 2.6%); per capita expenditure U.S.$10.

[1]Includes 12 indirectly elected seats. [2]Includes inland water area equaling *c.* 7,000 sq mi (*c.* 18,000 sq km). [3]Based on land area only. [4]Projected rates based on about 78% of total deaths. [5]Weights of consumer price index components for Georgetown only. [6]Includes sugar manufacturing. [7]Includes rice manufacturing. [8]Excludes sugar and rice manufacturing. [9]Manufacturing includes Public utilities. [10]Indirect taxes less subsidies. [11]Represents "not stated." [12]Imports c.i.f.; exports f.o.b. [13]Estimated figures. [14]No public railways. [15]Scheduled traffic only. [16]International only; domestic air service is provided on a charter basis. [17]1995–96.

Internet resources for further information:

- **Guyana News and Information http://www.guyana.org**

Haiti

Official name: Repiblik Dayti (Haitian Creole); République d'Haïti (French) (Republic of Haiti).
Form of government: multiparty republic with two legislative houses (Senate [27[1]]; Chamber of Deputies [82]).
Chief of state: President.
Head of government: Prime Minister.
Capital: Port-au-Prince.
Official languages: Haitian Creole; French.
Official religion: none[2].
Monetary unit: 1 gourde (G) = 100 centimes; valuation (Sept. 28, 2001) 1 U.S.$ = G 25.00; 1 £ = G 36.74.

Area and population

		area		population
				1997
Departements	Capitals	sq mi	sq km	estimate
Artibonite	Gonaïves	1,924	4,984	1,052,834
Centre	Hinche	1,419	3,675	508,199
Grand'Anse	Jérémie	1,278	3,310	660,420
Nord	Cap-Haïtien	813	2,106	785,687
Nord-Est	Fort-Liberté	697	1,805	255,601
Nord-Ouest	Port-de-Paix	840	2,176	439,984
Ouest	Port-au-Prince	1,864	4,827	2,651,115
Sud	Les Cayes	1,079	2,794	671,112
Sud-Est	Jacmel	781	2,023	466,810
TOTAL		10,695	27,700	7,491,762[3]

Demography

Population (2001): 6,965,000[4].
Density (2001): persons per sq mi 651.2, persons per sq km 251.4.
Urban-rural (1999): urban 35.1%; rural 64.9%.
Sex distribution (2000): male 49.26%; female 50.74%.
Age breakdown (2000): under 15, 41.1%; 15–29, 28.7%; 30–44, 15.2%; 45–59, 8.6%; 60–74, 5.0%; 75 and over, 1.4%.
Population projection[4]: (2010) 7,950,000; (2020) 9,072,000.
Doubling time: 41 years.
Ethnic composition (2000): black 94.2%; mulatto 5.4%; other/unspecified 0.4%.
Religious affiliation (1995): Roman Catholic 68.5%[5]; Protestant 24.1%, of which Baptist 5.9%, Pentecostal 5.3%, Seventh-day Adventist 4.6%; other 7.4%.
Major cities (1997): Port-au-Prince 917,112 (metropolitan area 1,556,588); Carrefour 306,074[6]; Delmas 257,247[6]; Cap-Haïtien 107,026; Pétion-Ville 76,155[6].

Vital statistics

Birth rate per 1,000 population (2000): 32.0 (world avg. 22.5).
Death rate per 1,000 population (2000): 15.1 (world avg. 9.0).
Natural increase rate per 1,000 population (2000): 16.9 (world avg. 13.5).
Total fertility rate (avg. births per childbearing woman; 2000): 4.5.
Life expectancy at birth (2000): male 47.5 years; female 51.1 years.
Major causes of death per 100,000 population (1982)[7]: infectious and parasitic diseases 46.0; diseases of the circulatory system 11.9; diseases associated with malnutrition 8.5; ill-defined conditions 115.2.

National economy

Budget (1998)[8]. Revenue: G 5,371,000,000 (general sales tax 26.4%; customs duties 20.1%; excises 15.9%; taxes on income and profits 11.7%). Expenditures: G 6,036,000,000 (current expenditure 80.0%, of which interest on public debt 7.2%; development expenditure 20.0%).
Production (metric tons except as noted). Agriculture, forestry, fishing (1999): sugarcane 1,000,100, cassava (manioc) 325,000, plantains 290,000, bananas 290,000, mangoes 225,000, corn (maize) 215,000, yams 195,000, sweet potatoes 172,000, rice 102,000, sorghum 96,000, avocados 45,000, coffee 28,000, sisal 5,700, cacao 4,500; livestock (number of live animals) 1,618,000 goats, 1,300,000 cattle, 800,000 pigs, 490,000 horses; roundwood (1998) 6,397,000 cu m; fish catch (1997) 5,630. Mining and quarrying: small amounts of limestone, calcareous clay, salt, and marble. Manufacturing (1995–96): cigarettes 837,900,000 units; malt liquor 13,800,000 bottles; beer 4,200,000 bottles; articles assembled for reexport (gross export value in U.S.$'000,000; 1997–98) 211.2, of which garments 199.3, travel goods and handbags 2.8, sports equipment and toys 2.3; cement and essential oils (mostly amyris, neroli, and vetiver) are also manufactured. Energy production (consumption): electricity (kW-hr; 1996) 633,000,000 (633,000,000); coal (metric tons) none (none); crude petroleum, none (none); petroleum products (metric tons; 1996) none (341,000); natural gas, none (none).
Land use (1994): forested 5.1%; meadows and pastures 18.0%; agricultural and under permanent cultivation 33.0%; other 43.9%.
Population economically active (1996): total 3,209,000; activity rate of total population 49.3% (participation rates: ages 15–64 [1990] 64.8%; female 43.0%; unemployed unofficially about 60%).

Price and earnings indexes (1995 = 100)

	1995	1996	1997	1998	1999	2000	2001
Consumer price index	100.0	120.6	145.4	160.8	174.8	198.7	225.6[9]
Daily earnings index[10]	100.0	100.0	100.0	100.0	100.0	…	…

Household income and expenditure. Average household size (1982) 4.4; average annual income of urban wage earners (1984): G 1,545 (U.S.$309); expenditure (1996)[11]: food, beverages, and tobacco 49.4%, housing and energy 9.1%, transportation 8.7%, clothing and footwear 8.5%.
Public debt (external, outstanding; 1999): U.S.$1,049,000,000.
Gross national product (1999): U.S.$3,584,000,000 (U.S.$460 per capita).

Structure of gross domestic product and labour force

	1997–98[12]		1990	
	in value G '000,000[13]	% of total value	labour force	% of labour force
Agriculture, forestry	1,403	30.2	1,535,444	57.3
Mining	10	0.2	24,012	0.9
Manufacturing	330	7.1	151,387	5.6
Construction	562	12.1	28,001	1.0
Public utilities	42	0.9	2,577	0.1
Transp. and commun.	98	2.1	20,691	0.8
Trade, restaurants	622	13.4	352,970	13.2
Finance, real estate	366	7.9	5,057	0.2
Services	216	4.6	155,347	5.8
Pub. admin., defense	829	17.8		
Other	174[14]	3.7[14]	403,654[15]	15.1[15]
TOTAL	4,652	100.0	2,679,140	100.0

Tourism (1998): receipts from visitors U.S.$57,000,000; expenditures by nationals abroad U.S.$37,000,000.

Foreign trade[12, 16, 17]

Balance of trade (current prices)

	1994–95	1995–96	1996–97	1997–98	1998–99	1999–2000
U.S.$'000,000	–344.1	–540.2	–511.1	–527.2	–769.5	–897.3
% of total	55.6%	64.6%	56.7%	48.1%	67.9%	71.8%

Imports (1997–98): U.S.$811,500,000 ([18]food and live animals 27%, machinery and transport equipment 16%, petroleum and derivatives 9%, animal and vegetable oils 7%). *Major import sources* (1998)[18]: United States 60%; Japan 4%; Dominican Republic 4%; France 3%; Colombia 3%.
Exports (1997–98): U.S.$284,300,000 ([18]reexports [mostly clothing] 74%, handicrafts [includes wood carvings, paintings, and woven sisal products] 7%, coffee 7%). *Major export destinations* (1998)[18]: United States 88%; Belgium 3%, France 3%.

Transport and communications

Transport. Railroad (1998) none. Roads (1996): total length 2,585 mi, 4,160 km (paved 24%). Vehicles (1996): passenger cars 32,000; trucks and buses 21,000. Air transport (1994)[19]: passenger arrivals 167,882, passenger departures 177,072; cargo unloaded 11,967 metric tons, cargo loaded 10,087 metric tons; airports (1997) with scheduled flights 2.

Communications

Medium	date	unit	number	units per 1,000 persons
Daily newspapers	1996	circulation	20,000	3.1
Radio	1997	receivers	415,000	63
Television	1997	receivers	38,000	5.8
Telephones	1999	main lines	70,000	10
Cellular telephones	1999	subscribers	25,000	3.7

Education and health

Educational attainment (1986–87). Percentage of population age 25 and over having: no formal schooling 59.5%; primary education 30.5%; secondary 8.6%; vocational and teacher training 0.7%; higher 0.7%. *Literacy* (1995): total population age 15 and over literate 1,930,000 (45.0%); males literate 992,000 (48.0%); females literate 938,000 (42.2%).

Education (1994–95)

	schools	teachers	students	student/ teacher ratio
Primary (age 6–12)	10,071	30,205	1,110,398	36.8
Secondary (age 13–18) Voc., teacher tr.	1,038	…	195,418	…
Higher[20, 21]	2	817	12,204	14.9

Health: physicians (1993–94) 641[22] (1 per 9,846 persons); hospital beds (1996) 5,241 (1 per 1,242 persons); infant mortality rate (2000) 97.1.
Food (1999): daily per capita caloric intake 1,977 (vegetable products 94%, animal products 6%); 87% of FAO recommended minimum requirement.

Military

Total active duty personnel:[23].

[1]Statutory membership; some seats occupied from May 2000 through July 2001 did not meet statutory guidelines. [2]Roman Catholicism has special recognition. [3]Official population projection based on 1982 census. [4]De facto estimate(s). [5]About 80% of all Roman Catholics also practice voodoo. [6]Within Port-au-Prince metropolitan area. [7]Public health facilities only. [8]Excludes G 3,700,000,000 in foreign grants. [9]May. [10]Standard minimum wage rate. [11]Weights of consumer price index components. [12]For fiscal year ending September 30. [13]At prices of 1975–76. [14]Indirect taxes including import duties. [15]Includes 63,975 not adequately defined and 339,679 officially unemployed. [16]Includes reexports. [17]Import figures c.i.f., export figures f.o.b. [18]Estimated percentages. [19]Port-au-Prince Airport only. [20]Port-au-Prince universities only. [21]1997–98. [22]Public health services only. [23]The Haitian army was disbanded in 1995. A UN force supervised the creation of a 5,300-member (2000) national police force between 1995 and 1997.

Internet resources for further information:
- **Embassy of Haiti (Washington, D.C.) (mostly French language) http://www.haiti.org**

Honduras

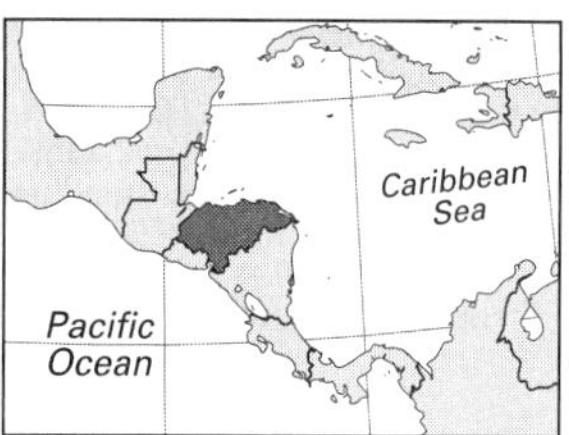

Official name: República de Honduras (Republic of Honduras).
Form of government: multiparty republic with one legislative house (National Assembly [128]).
Head of state and government: President.
Capital: Tegucigalpa[1].
Official language: Spanish.
Official religion: none.
Monetary unit: 1 Honduran lempira (L) = 100 centavos; valuation (Sept. 28, 2001) 1 U.S.$ = L 15.61; 1 £ = L 22.94.

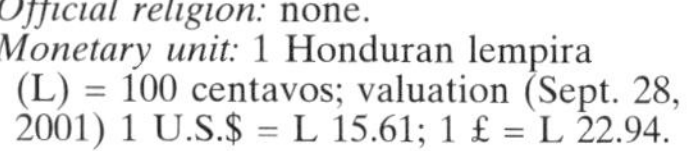

Area and population

Departments	Administrative centres	area sq mi	area sq km	population 1991 estimate
Atlántida	La Ceiba	1,641	4,251	255,000
Choluteca	Choluteca	1,626	4,211	309,000
Colón	Trujillo	3,427	8,875	164,000
Comayagua	Comayagua	2,006	5,196	257,000
Copán	Santa Rosa de Copán	1,237	3,203	226,000
Cortés	San Pedro Sula	1,527	3,954	706,000
El Paraíso	Yuscarán	2,787	7,218	277,000
Francisco Morazán	Tegucigalpa	3,068	7,946	878,000
Gracias a Dios	Puerto Lempira	6,421	16,630	37,000
Intibucá	La Esperanza	1,186	3,072	130,000
Islas de la Bahía	Roatán	100	261	24,000
La Paz	La Paz	900	2,331	112,000
Lempira	Gracias	1,656	4,290	180,000
Ocotepeque	Nueva Ocotepeque	649	1,680	77,000
Olancho	Juticalpa	9,402	24,351	309,000
Santa Bárbara	Santa Bárbara	1,975	5,115	291,000
Valle	Nacaome	604	1,565	121,000
Yoro	Yoro	3,065	7,939	355,000
TOTAL		43,277[2]	112,088[2]	4,708,000

Demography

Population (2001): 6,626,000.
Density (2001)[3]: persons per sq mi 152.6, persons per sq km 58.9.
Urban-rural (1999): urban 43.7%; rural 56.3%.
Sex distribution (1999): male 48.94%; female 51.06%.
Age breakdown (1998): under 15, 42.6%; 15–29, 28.4%; 30–44, 16.2%; 45–59, 7.8%; 60–74, 3.9%; 75 and over, 1.1%.
Population projection: (2010) 7,979,000; (2020) 9,166,000.
Doubling time: 26 years.
Ethnic composition (2000): mestizo 86.6%; Amerindian 5.5%; black (including Black Carib) 4.3%; white 2.3%; other 1.3%.
Religious affiliation (1995): Roman Catholic 86.7%; Protestant 10.4%, of which Pentecostal 5.7%; other 2.9%.
Major cities (1999): Tegucigalpa 988,400[4]; San Pedro Sula 452,100; El Progreso 104,100; La Ceiba 103,400; Choluteca 92,400.

Vital statistics

Birth rate per 1,000 population (2000): 32.7 (world avg. 22.5).
Death rate per 1,000 population (2000): 5.3 (world avg. 9.0).
Natural increase rate per 1,000 population (2000): 27.4 (world avg. 13.5).
Total fertility rate (avg. births per childbearing woman; 2000): 4.3.
Marriage rate per 1,000 population (1983): 4.9.
Divorce rate per 1,000 population (1983): 0.4.
Life expectancy at birth (2000): male 67.9 years; female 72.1 years.
Major causes of death per 100,000 population (1983): diseases of the circulatory system 48.4; infectious and parasitic diseases 46.6; accidents and violence 42.2; diseases of the respiratory system 26.3.

National economy

Budget (1998). Revenue: L 13,197,000,000 (current revenue 99.8%, of which indirect taxes 65.1%, direct taxes 25.6%, nontax revenue 6.9%, transfers 2.2%). Expenditures: L 11,367,000,000 (current expenditure 72.6%; capital expenditure 27.4%).
Production (metric tons except as noted). Agriculture, forestry, fishing (1999): sugarcane 4,286,000, bananas 861,000, oil palm fruit 522,000, corn (maize) 478,000, plantains 250,000, coffee 164,000, oranges 79,000, cantaloupes 78,000, sorghum 71,000, pineapples 70,000; livestock (number of live animals) 2,061,000 cattle, 700,000 pigs, 18,000,0000 chickens; roundwood (1998) 7,176,000 cu m; fish catch (1998) 14,881. Mining and quarrying (1997): gypsum 28,000; salt 25,000; zinc 25,500; lead 3,400; gold 150 kilograms. Manufacturing (value added in L '000,000; 1996): food products 1,937.3; wearing apparel 1,266.4; beverages 699.6; nonmetallic mineral products 503.6; wood products 325.7; consumer chemicals 319.7. Construction (value of private construction in L '000,000; 1999)[5]: residential 813.8; nonresidential 890.7. Energy production (consumption): electricity (kW-hr; 1996) 2,815,000,000 (2,819,000,000); coal, none (none); crude petroleum (barrels; 1992) none (3,064,000); petroleum products (metric tons; 1996) none (1,157,000).
Household income and expenditure. Average household size (1988) 5.4; income per household: n.a.; sources of income (1985): wages and salaries 58.8%, transfer payments 1.8%, other 39.4%; expenditure (1986): food 44.4%, utilities and housing 22.4%, clothing and footwear 9.0%, household furnishings 8.3%, health care 7.0%, transportation 3.0%, other 5.9%.
Land use (1998): forested and other 67.9%; meadows and pastures 13.8%; agricultural and under permanent cultivation 18.3%.
Gross national product (1999): U.S.$4,829,000,000 (U.S.$760 per capita).

Structure of gross domestic product and labour force

	1999 in value L '000,000[6]	% of total value	labour force	% of labour force
Agriculture	10,635	16.2	834,900	39.2
Mining	1,325	2.0	4,200	0.2
Manufacturing	12,916	19.6	249,000	11.7
Construction	3,516	5.4	158,300	7.4
Public utilities	3,208	4.9	20,100	0.9
Transp. and commun.	3,423	5.2	58,600	2.7
Trade	8,365	12.7	240,400	11.3
Finance, real estate	10,950	16.7	48,400	2.3
Public admin., defense	4,153	6.3	517,400	24.3
Services	7,261	11.0		
TOTAL	65,752	100.0	2,131,300	100.0

Public debt (external, outstanding; 1999): U.S.$4,231,000,000.
Population economically active (1999): total 2,131,300; activity rate of total population 33.4% (participation rates: over age 15 [1998] 61.2%; female [1998] 34.6%; unemployed [1998] 4.3%).

Price and earnings indexes (1995 = 100)

	1994	1995	1996	1997	1998	1999	2000
Consumer price index	77.2	100.0	123.8	148.8	169.2	188.9	209.8
Daily earnings index[7]	84.4	100.0	119.3	158.0	184.9	...	...

Tourism (1999): receipts U.S.$195,000,000; expenditures U.S.$94,000,000.

Foreign trade[8]

Balance of trade (current prices)

	1994	1995	1996	1997	1998	1999
U.S.$'000,000	−382	−273	−341	−505	−683	−1,254
% of total	15.8%	9.5%	10.7%	14.1%	17.1%	32.5%

Imports (1999): U.S.$2,727,800,000 (machinery and electrical equipment 20.8%, industrial chemicals 13.0%, transport equipment 12.1%, food products 10.3%, mineral fuels and lubricants 9.4%). *Major import sources:* United States 47.1%; Guatemala 7.4%; Mexico 4.8%; Japan 4.7%; Costa Rica 2.5%.
Exports (1999): U.S.$1,303,900,000 (coffee 20.5%, shrimp and lobsters 15.5%, melons 3.7%, lead and zinc 3.4%). *Major export destinations:* United States 35.4%; Germany 7.5%; El Salvador 6.4%; Guatemala 5.8%; Nicaragua 4.8%.

Transport and communications

Transport. Railroads (1989): length (1999) 614 mi, 988 km; passenger-km 7,700,000; metric ton-km cargo 30,200,000. Roads (1999): total length 9,073 mi, 14,602 km (paved 18%). Vehicles (1995): passenger cars 81,439; trucks and buses 170,006. Merchant marine (1992): vessels (100 gross tons and over) 966; total deadweight tonnage 1,437,321. Air transport (1995): passenger-mi 212,000,000, passenger-km 341,000,000; short ton-mi cargo 23,000,000, metric ton-km cargo 33,000,000; airports (1996) with scheduled flights 8.

Communications

Medium	date	unit	number	units per 1,000 persons
Daily newspapers	1996	circulation	320,000	55
Radio	1997	receivers	2,450,000	410
Television	1999	receivers	600,000	95
Telephones	1999	main lines	279,197	44
Cellular telephones	1999	subscribers	78,588	12
Personal computers	1999	units	60,000	9.5
Internet	1999	users	20,000	3.2

Education and health

Educational attainment (1988). Percentage of population age 10 and over having: no formal schooling 33.4%; primary education 50.1%; secondary education 13.4%; higher 3.1%. *Literacy* (1995): total population age 15 and over literate 72.7%; males literate 72.6%; females literate 72.7%.

Education (1999)

	schools	teachers	students	student/ teacher ratio
Primary (age 7–13)	8,768	33,431	1,099,714	32.9
Secondary (age 14–19) Voc., teacher tr.	661[9]	14,539	187,561	12.9
Higher	8[9]	3,600	52,139	14.5

Health: physicians (1993) 3,803 (1 per 1,358 persons); hospital beds (1999) 5,720 (1 per 1,098 persons); infant mortality rate (2000) 31.3.
Food (1999): daily per capita caloric intake 2,396 (vegetable products 84%, animal products 16%); (1997) 106% of FAO recommended minimum.

Military

Total active duty personnel (2000): 8,300 (army 66.3%, navy 12.0%, air force 21.7%). *Military expenditure as percentage of GNP* (1995): 1.3% (world 2.7%); per capita expenditure U.S.$9.

[1]Tegucigalpa and adjacent city of Comayagüela jointly form the capital according to the constitution. [2]The 1993 area is 43,433 sq mi (112,492 sq km); breakdown by department is not available. [3]Based on the revised area. [4]Population cited is for Central District (Tegucigalpa and Comayagüela). [5]Tegucigalpa, San Pedro Sula, and 10 other urban centres. [6]At factor cost. [7]Official minimum wages in all sectors. [8]Import figures are f.o.b. in balance of trade and c.i.f. for commodities and trading partners. [9]1995.

Internet resources for further information:

- **Banco Central de Honduras http://www.bch.hn/frames.htm**
- **Instituto Nacional de Estadística http://www.ine.online.hn**

Hong Kong

Official name: Xianggang Tebie Xingzhengqu (Chinese); Hong Kong Special Administrative Region (English).
Political status: special administrative region[1] (People's Republic of China) with one legislative house (Legislative Council [60[2]]).
Head of state and government: Chief Executive.
Capital: None[3].
Official languages: Chinese; English.
Official religion: none.
Monetary unit: 1 Hong Kong dollar (HK$) = 100 cents; valuation (Sept. 28, 2001) 1 U.S.$ = HK$7.80; 1 £ = HK$11.46.

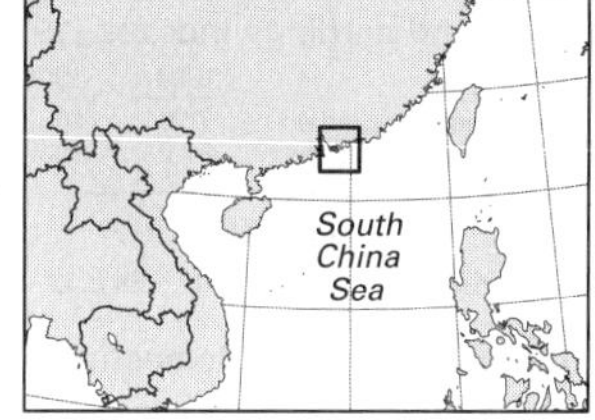

Area and population

Area	area sq mi	area sq km	population 2001 census[4]
Hong Kong Island	30.9	80.1	1,337,800
Kowloon and New Kowloon	18.0	46.5	2,025,800
New Territories	372.7	965.3	3,345,600
Marine	—	—	5,900
TOTAL	421.6	1,091.9	6,715,100

Demography

Population (2001): 6,732,000.
Density (2001): persons per sq mi 15,968.0, persons per sq km 6,165.5.
Urban-rural (2000): urban 100.0%.
Sex distribution (2001): male 48.97%; female 51.03%.
Age breakdown (2001): under 15, 16.5%; 15–29, 21.6%; 30–44, 28.9%; 45–59, 18.0%; 60–74, 10.6%; 75 and over, 4.4%.
Population projection: (2010) 7,312,000; (2020) 8,015,000.
Doubling time: not applicable; doubling time exceeds 100 years.
Linguistic composition (1991)[5]: Chinese 96.8%, of which Cantonese 88.7%; English 2.2%; other 1.0%.
Religious affiliation (1994): Buddhist and Taoist 73.8%; Christian 8.4%, of which Protestant 4.3%, Roman Catholic 4.1%; New Religionist 3.2%; Muslim 0.8%; Hindu 0.2%; nonreligious/atheist 13.5%; other 0.1%.

Vital statistics

Birth rate per 1,000 population (2000): 8.1 (world avg. 22.5); (1985) legitimate 94.5%; illegitimate 5.5%.
Death rate per 1,000 population (2000): 5.1 (world avg. 9.0).
Natural increase rate per 1,000 population (2000): 3.0 (world avg. 13.5).
Total fertility rate (avg. births per childbearing woman; 2000): 1.3.
Marriage rate per 1,000 population (2000): 4.6.
Life expectancy at birth (2000): male 77.0 years; female 82.2 years.
Major causes of death per 100,000 population (1999): malignant neoplasms (cancers) 162.5; diseases of the circulatory system 134.4; diseases of the respiratory system 92.9; accidents and poisoning 29.0; diseases of the digestive system 20.8; diseases of the genitourinary system 21.0.

National economy

Budget (1999–2000). Revenue: HK$229,322,000,000 (earning and profit taxes 28.5%; capital revenue 25.0%; indirect taxes 17.8%, of which entertainment and stamp duties 9.8%, duties 3.2%). Expenditures: HK$278,416,000,000 (education 18.8%; housing 16.9%; health 11.6%; social welfare 10.2%; law and order 9.8%; transportation and public works 8.7%; culture and recreation 3.5%).
Gross domestic product (1999): U.S.$158,737,000,000 (U.S.$23,620 per capita).

Structure of gross domestic product and labour force

	1999 in value HK$'000,000	1999 % of total value	1998 labour force	1998 % of labour force
Agriculture	1,171	0.1		
Mining	307	—	391,900	11.7
Manufacturing	65,767	5.5		
Construction	66,111	5.5	319,500	9.5
Public utilities	34,358	2.8	[6]	[6]
Transp. and commun.	110,314	9.2	363,300	10.8
Trade	289,873	24.1	973,900	29.0
Finance, insurance, and real estate	266,069	22.1	419,000	12.5
Pub. admin., defense, and services	247,399	20.5	705,300	21.0
Other	122,582[7]	10.2[7]	185,800[6, 8]	5.5[6, 8]
TOTAL	1,203,951	100.0	3,358,700	100.0

Tourism (1999): receipts from visitors U.S.$7,210,000,000.
Production (metric tons except as noted). Agriculture, forestry, fishing (1999): vegetables 48,000, fruits and nuts 3,770, field crops 540, milk 241, eggs 3,530,000 units; livestock (number of live animals) 415,000 pigs[9], 36 cattle; roundwood (1996) 206,000 cu m; fish catch 127,880. Manufacturing (value added in HK$; 1997): publishing and printed materials 13,398,000,000; textiles 9,316,000,000; wearing apparel 9,089,000,000; electrical and electronic products 7,551,000,000; machinery and equipment 6,123,000,000; office equipment 3,997,000,000; basic metals and fabricated metal products 3,889,000,000. Construction (1998)[10]: residential 1,564,000 sq m; nonresidential 1,652,000 sq m. Energy production (consumption): electricity (kW-hr; 1995) 27,916,000,000 (33,979,000,000); coal (metric tons; 1995) none (9,109,000); petroleum products (metric tons; 1995) none (3,387,000).
Population economically active (2000): total 3,382,700; activity rate of total population 49.3% (participation rates: over age 15, 60.7%; female 49.1%; unemployed 5.0%).

Price and earnings indexes (1995 = 100)

	1994	1995	1996	1997	1998	1999	2000
Consumer price index	97.3	100.0	106.3	112.5	115.7	111.1	107.1
Daily earnings index[11]	89.5	100.0	104.5	...	...	...	...

Household income and expenditure. Average household size (2000) 3.3; monthly income per household (1996) HK$17,500 (U.S.$2,300); sources of income: n.a.; expenditure (1994–95): food 29.5%, housing 28.8%, transportation and vehicles 7.8%, clothing and footwear 6.7%, durable goods 5.5%.
Land use (1995): forested 20.1%; agricultural and under permanent cultivation 5.8%; fishponds 1.5%; built-on, scrublands, and other 72.6%.

Foreign trade[12]

Balance of trade (current prices)

	1995	1996	1997	1998	1999	2000
HK$'000,000	−146,994	−137,664	−159,141	−81,443	−43,718	−85,273
% of total	5.2%	4.7%	5.8%	2.9%	1.6%	2.6%

Imports (2000): HK$1,657,962,000,000 (machinery and transport equipment 42.7%, manufactured goods 17.0%, chemicals and other related products 6.3%, food and beverages 4.1%, mineral fuels and lubricants 2.1%). *Major import sources:* China 43.1%; Japan 12.0%; Taiwan 7.5%; U.S. 6.8%; South Korea 4.9%; Singapore 4.5%.
Exports (2000): HK$180,967,000,000[13] (clothing accessories and apparel 42.8%, electrical machinery 15.8%, textile fabrics 5.1%, office and automatic data-processing machines 3.2%, jewelry 3.2%, printed materials 2.5%, telecommunications equipment 2.3%, watches and clocks 1.7%, articles of artificial resins and plastics 0.8%). *Major export destinations:* U.S. 30.1%; China 29.9%; U.K. 5.9%; Germany 5.1%; Taiwan 3.3%; Japan 2.8%.

Transport and communications

Transport. Railroads (1995): route length 21 mi, 34 km; passenger-mi 2,231,000,000, passenger-km 3,591,000,000; short ton-mi cargo 68,000,000[14], metric ton-km cargo 99,000,000[14]. Roads (2000): total length 1,183 mi, 1,904 km (paved 100%). Vehicles (2000): passenger cars 332,000; trucks and buses 133,000. Air transport (2000): passenger arrivals 11,566,000, passenger departures 11,458,000; airports (1997) with scheduled flights 1.

Communications

Medium	date	unit	number	units per 1,000 persons
Daily newspapers	1996	circulation	5,000,000	792
Radio	1998	receivers	3,700,000	553
Television	1998	receivers	1,749,000	262
Telephones	2000	main lines	3,946,000	575
Cellular telephones	1999	subscribers	4,275,000	647
Personal computers	1999	units	2,000,000	303
Internet	1999	users	2,430,000	368

Education and health

Educational attainment (1996). Percentage of population age 15 and over having: no formal schooling 9.5%; primary education 22.6%; secondary 46.6%; matriculation 6.1%; nondegree higher 4.8%; higher degree 10.4%.
Literacy (1995): total population age 15 and over literate 92.2%; males literate 96.0%; females literate 88.2%.

Education (2000–2001)

	schools	teachers[15]	students	student/ teacher ratio[15]
Primary (age 6–11)	816	22,344	493,979	22.0
Secondary (age 12–18)	525	24,453	456,693	18.5
Vocational	1[16]	1,058	22,279	21.0
Higher	28	5,892	59,479	10.1

Health (2000): physicians 10,130[17] (1 per 658 persons); hospital beds 35,100 (1 per 190 persons); infant mortality rate per 1,000 live births (2000) 2.9.
Food (1999): daily per capita caloric intake 3,231 (vegetable products 63%, animal products 37%); 141% of FAO recommended minimum requirement.

Military

Total active duty personnel [18].

[1]On July 1, 1997, Hong Kong reverted to China as a special administrative region in which the existing socioeconomic system would remain unchanged for a period of 50 years. [2]24 seats are directly elected by ordinary voters; the remaining 36 seats are elected/appointed by special interest groups and a committee. [3]Victoria, for some time, had been regarded as the capital because it had been the seat of the British administration of the Crown Colony. [4]Preliminary. [5]Excludes about 59,000 Vietnamese refugees, about 1% of the population. [6]Other includes Public utilities. [7]Indirect taxes less subsidies. [8]Includes 157,600 unemployed. [9]Excludes local pigs not slaughtered in abattoirs. [10]Usable floor area only. [11]September. [12]Imports are c.i.f., exports f.o.b. [13]Excludes reexports valued at HK$1,391,722,000,000. [14]1994. [15]1999–2000. [16]The Hong Kong Institute of Vocational Education was formed in 1999. It is composed of the two former technical colleges and the seven former technical institutes. [17]Registered personnel; all may not be present and working in the country. [18]British forces completed their final withdrawal on June 30, 1997. On July 1, 1997, the recently passed Garrison Law took effect, allowing for an unarmed garrison to be established in Hong Kong and used only at the governor's request.

Internet resources for further information:
- **Census and Statistics Department http://www.info.gov.hk/censtatd**

Hungary

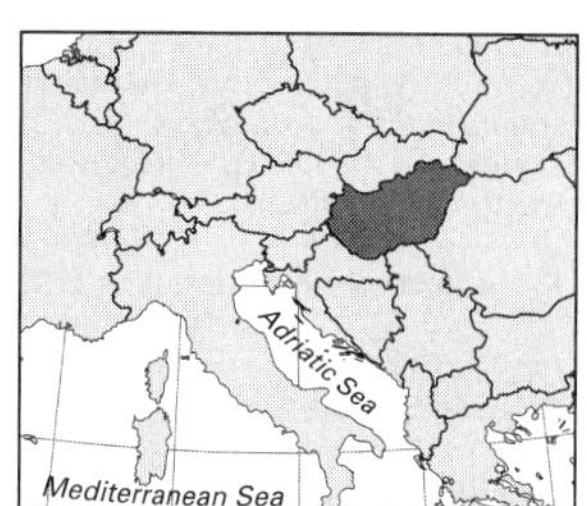

Official name: Magyar Köztársaság (Republic of Hungary).
Form of government: unitary multiparty republic with one legislative house (National Assembly [386[1]]).
Chief of state: President.
Head of government: Prime Minister.
Capital: Budapest.
Official language: Hungarian.
Official religion: none.
Monetary unit: 1 forint (Ft) = 100 filler; valuation (Sept. 28, 2001) 1 U.S.$ = Ft 281.88; 1 £ = Ft 414.28.

Area and population

		area		population
Counties	Capitals	sq mi	sq km	2000[2] estimate
Bács-Kiskun	Kecskemét	3,251	8,420	532,000
Baranya	Pécs	1,710	4,430	401,000
Békés	Békéscsaba	2,174	5,631	392,000
Borsod-Abaúj-Zemplén	Miskolc	2,798	7,247	730,000
Csongrád	Szeged	1,646	4,263	418,000
Fejér	Székesfehérvár	1,688	4,373	426,000
Győr-Moson-Sopron	Győr	1,568	4,062	424,000
Hajdú-Bihar	Debrecen	2,398	6,211	542,000
Heves	Eger	1,404	3,637	323,000
Jász-Nagykun-Szolnok	Szolnok	2,165	5,607	412,000
Komárom-Esztergom	Tatabánya	869	2,251	310,000
Nógrád	Salgótarján	982	2,544	217,000
Pest	Budapest[3]	2,468	6,393	1,033,000
Somogy	Kaposvár	2,331	6,036	330,000
Szabolcs-Szatmár-Bereg	Nyíregyháza	2,292	5,937	570,000
Tolna	Szekszárd	1,430	3,703	244,000
Vas	Szombathely	1,288	3,336	266,000
Veszprém	Veszprém	1,791	4,639	373,000
Zala	Zalaegerszeg	1,461	3,784	293,000
Capital City				
Budapest[3]		203	525	1,812,000
TOTAL		35,919[4]	93,030[4]	10,043,000[4, 5]

Demography

Population (2001): 10,190,000.
Density (2001): persons per sq mi 283.7, persons per sq km 109.5.
Urban-rural (1999): urban 63.3%; rural 36.7%.
Sex distribution (2000): male 47.71%; female 52.29%.
Age breakdown (2000): under 15, 17.1%; 15–29, 22.6%; 30–44, 20.2%; 45–59, 20.5%; 60–74, 14.0%; 75 and over, 5.6%.
Population projection: (2010) 9,911,000; (2020) 9,562,000.
Ethnic composition (1998): Hungarian 92%; Rom (Gypsy) 4%; German 2%; Slovak 1%; other 1%.
Religious affiliation (1995): Roman Catholic 63.1%; Protestant 25.5% (of which Reformed 19.8%, Lutheran 4.5%); Jewish 0.8%; other 10.6%.
Major cities (2000[2]): Budapest 1,811,552; Debrecen 203,648; Miskolc 172,357; Szeged 158,158; Pécs 157,332; Győr 127,119.

Vital statistics

Birth rate per 1,000 population (1999): 9.4 (world avg. 22.5); legitimate 72.0%; illegitimate 28.0%.
Death rate per 1,000 population (1999): 14.2 (world avg. 9.0).
Natural increase rate per 1,000 population (1999): –4.8 (world avg. 13.5).
Total fertility rate (avg. births per childbearing woman; 1999): 1.3.
Marriage rate per 1,000 population (1999): 4.5.
Life expectancy at birth (1999): male 66.3 years; female 75.1 years.
Major causes of death per 100,000 population (1999): diseases of the circulatory system 728.4; malignant neoplasms (cancers) 340.3.

National economy

Budget (1999). Revenue: Ft 4,955,000,000,000 (social security contributions 29.6%, value-added taxes 19.0%, personal income taxes 15.5%, excise taxes 9.4%). Expenditures: Ft 5,396,000,000,000 (current expenditures 93.9%, development expenditures 6.1%).
Production (metric tons except as noted). Agriculture, forestry, fishing (2000): corn (maize) 5,000,000, wheat 3,709,000, sugar beets 2,300,000, barley 905,000, apples 520,000, grapes 500,000, sunflower seeds 485,000; livestock (number of live animals) 5,335,000 pigs, 857,000 cattle; roundwood (1999) 4,287,500 cu m; fish catch (1997) 21,916. Mining and quarrying (1999): bauxite 935,000. Manufacturing (value added in Ft '000,000; 1998): refined petroleum products 296,000; food and beverages 278,800; electrical machinery and apparatus 218,000; transportation equipment 168,800; paints, soaps, and pharmaceuticals 100,800. Energy production (consumption): electricity (kW-hr; 1999) 37,154,000,000 (33,348,000,000); hard coal (metric tons; 1999) 732,000 (1,110,000); lignite (metric tons; 1999) 13,704,000 (14,341,000); crude petroleum (barrels; 1999) 8,349,000 (51,633,000); petroleum products (metric tons; 1996) 6,333,000 (6,168,000); natural gas (cu m; 1999) 3,625,000,000 (12,365,000,000).
Land use (1994): forested 19.1%; meadows and pastures 12.4%; agricultural and under permanent cultivation 53.9%; other 14.6%.
Public debt (external, outstanding; 1998): U.S.$15,941,000,000.
Population economically active (1999): total 4,096,200; activity rate of total population 40.7% (participation rates: ages 15–64, 59.9%; female 44.5%; unemployed 7.0%).

Price and earnings indexes (1995 = 100)

	1994	1995	1996	1997	1998	1999	2000
Consumer price index	77.9	100.0	123.6	146.2	167.1	183.8	201.9
Annual earnings index	87.2	100.0	120.4	147.2	174.2	202.2	...

Tourism (U.S.$'000,000; 1999): receipts 3,394; expenditures 1,191.
Gross national product (1999): U.S.$46,751,000,000 (U.S.$4,640 per capita).

Structure of gross domestic product and labour force

	1999			
	in value Ft '000,000	% of total value	labour force	% of labour force
Agriculture, forestry	490,200	4.3	270,400	6.6
Mining	28,800	0.3	24,400	0.6
Manufacturing	2,374,300	20.8	928,900	22.7
Construction	457,800	4.0	253,000	6.2
Public utilities	392,700	3.4	89,800	2.2
Transp. and commun.	1,019,600	8.9	308,300	7.5
Trade, restaurants	1,338,100	11.7	650,700	15.9
Finance, real estate	1,928,800	16.9	264,800	6.5
Public administration, defense	723,400	6.3	301,900	7.4
Services	1,241,000	10.9	719,200	17.6
Other	1,441,900[6]	12.6[6]	284,700[7]	7.0[7]
TOTAL	11,436,500[4]	100.0[4]	4,096,200[4]	100.0[4]

Household income and expenditure. Average household size (1998) 2.5; income per household[8] (1998) Ft 1,828,441 (U.S.$8,528); sources of income (1998): wages 49.9%, transfers 17.9%, self-employment 17.2%, other 15.0%; expenditure (1999): food and beverages 33.6%; transportation and communications 14.9%; energy 14.6%; housing 8.0%.

Foreign trade

Balance of trade (current prices)

	1994	1995	1996	1997	1998	1999
Ft '000,000,000	–389.6	–318.3	–490.0	–378.4	–567.3	–707.1
% of total	14.7%	9.2%	10.3%	5.1%	5.4%	5.6%

Imports (1999): Ft 6,645,600,000,000 (nonelectrical machinery 16.3%, electrical machinery 12.4%, road vehicles 8.6%, computers and office machines 6.7%, telecommunications equipment 6.1%). *Major import sources:* Germany 29.2%; Austria 8.9%; Italy 7.7%; Russia 5.9%; France 4.7%.
Exports (1999): Ft 5,938,500,000,000 (nonelectrical machinery 16.8%, office machines and computers 13.4%, electrical machinery 11.0%, road vehicles 9.0%, telecommunications equipment 7.9%). *Major export destinations:* Germany 38.4%; Austria 9.6%; Italy 5.9%; The Netherlands 5.2%; U.S. 5.2%.

Transport and communications

Transport. Railroads (1999): route length 7,768 km[9]; passenger-km 9,514,000,000; metric ton-km cargo 7,733,000,000. Roads (1997): total length 188,203 km (paved 43%). Vehicles (1999): passenger cars 2,255,526; trucks and buses 321,634. Air transport (1999): passenger-km 3,513,000,000; metric ton-km cargo 55,500,000; airports (1997) with scheduled flights 1.

Communications

Medium	date	unit	number	units per 1,000 persons
Daily newspapers	1996	circulation	1,895,000	186
Radio	1997	receivers	7,000,000	689
Television	1998	receivers	4,500,000	445
Telephones	1999	main lines	3,609,000	358
Cellular telephones	1999	subscribers	1,620,000	161
Personal computers	1998	units	600,000	59
Internet	1999	users	453,000	45

Education and health

Educational attainment (1990). Population age 25 and over having: no formal schooling 1.3%; primary education 57.9%; secondary 30.7%; higher 10.1%.

Education (1999–2000)

	schools	teachers	students	student/ teacher ratio
Primary (age 6–13)	3,696	82,829	960,601	11.6
Secondary (age 14–17)	1,054	32,317	386,579	12.0
Vocational	356	5,002	117,038	23.4
Higher	89	21,138	278,997	13.2

Health (1999): physicians 32,240[10] (1 per 312 persons); hospital beds 83,992 (1 per 120 persons); infant mortality rate per 1,000 live births 8.4.
Food (1998): daily per capita caloric intake 3,408 (vegetable products 69%, animal products 31%); 130% of FAO recommended minimum requirement.

Military

Total active duty personnel (2000): 43,790 (army 53.7%, air force 26.3%, headquarters staff 20.0%). *Military expenditure as percentage of GNP* (1997): 1.9% (world 2.6%); per capita expenditures U.S.$129.

[1]Excludes 13 seats set aside for ethnic minorities. [2]January 1. [3]Budapest acts as the capital of Pest county even though it is administratively not part of Pest county. [4]Detail does not add to total given because of rounding. [5]February 2001 preliminary census total equals 10,197,119. [6]Represents net taxes on commodities less imputed bank service charge. [7]Unemployed. [8]Adjusted disposable income including government transfers. [9]1998. [10]In active service.

Internet resources for further information:
- **Embassy of the Republic of Hungary http://www.hungaryemb.org**
- **Hungarian Central Statistical Office http://www.ksh.hu/eng/index.html**

Iceland

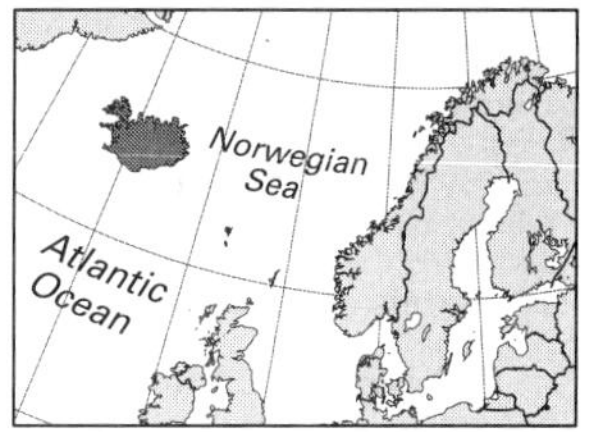

Official name: Lýdhveldidh Ísland (Republic of Iceland).
Form of government: unitary multiparty republic with one legislative house (Althing [63]).
Chief of state: President.
Head of government: Prime Minister.
Capital: Reykjavík.
Official language: Icelandic.
Official religion: Evangelical Lutheran.
Monetary unit: 1 króna (ISK) = 100 aurar; valuation (Sept. 28, 2001) 1 U.S.$ = ISK 101.25; 1 £ = ISK 148.81.

Area and population

		area		population
Constituencies[2]	Principal centres	sq mi	sq km	2000[1] estimate
Austurland	Egilsstadhir	8,491	21,991	11,930
Nordhurland eystra	Akureyri	8,636	22,368	26,471
Nordhurland vestra	Saudhárkrókur	5,055	13,093	9,424
Reykjanes	…	765[3]	1,982[3]	80,146
Reykjavík	Reykjavík	[3]	[3]	111,345
Sudhurland	Selfoss	9,735	25,214	21,123
Vestfirdhir	Ísafjördhur	3,657	9,470	8,144
Vesturland	Borgarnes	3,360	8,701	14,266
TOTAL		39,699	102,819	282,849

Demography

Population (2001): 284,000.
Density (2001)[4]: persons per sq mi 30.9, persons per sq km 11.9.
Urban-rural (1999): urban 93.5%; rural 6.5%.
Sex distribution (2000): male 50.07%; female 49.93%.
Age breakdown (2000): under 15, 23.2%; 15–29, 22.7%; 30–44, 22.2%; 45–59, 16.9%; 60–74, 9.9%; 75 and over, 5.1%.
Population projection: (2010) 314,000; (2020) 351,000.
Doubling time: 87 years.
Ethnic composition (1999)[5]: Icelandic 94.7%; Danish 0.8%; Swedish 0.6%; persons born in the United States 0.5%; Poland 0.5%; German 0.3%; other 2.6%.
Religious affiliation (2000): Protestant 92.3%, of which Evangelical Lutheran 87.8%, other Lutheran 3.9%; Roman Catholic 1.5%; other and not specified 6.2%.
Major cities (2000): Reykjavík 111,345 (urban area 174,991); Kópavogur 23,518[6]; Hafnarfjördhur 19,640[6]; Akureyri 15,385; Gardhabær 8,050[6].

Vital statistics

Birth rate per 1,000 population (1999): 14.8 (world avg. 22.5); (1999) legitimate 37.4%; illegitimate 62.6%.
Death rate per 1,000 population (1999): 6.9 (world avg. 9.0).
Natural increase rate per 1,000 population (1999): 7.9 (world avg. 13.5).
Total fertility rate (avg. births per childbearing woman; 1999): 2.0.
Marriage rate per 1,000 population (1999): 5.6.
Divorce rate per 1,000 population (1999): 1.7.
Life expectancy at birth (1998–99): male 77.5 years; female 81.4 years.
Major causes of death per 100,000 population (1995): diseases of the circulatory system 308.2, of which ischemic heart diseases 164.9, cerebrovascular disease 81.9; malignant neoplasms (cancers) 176.2; diseases of the respiratory system 95.3.

National economy

Budget (1997). Revenue: ISK 193,567,000,000 (indirect taxes 49.1%, of which value-added taxes 26.0%; direct taxes 44.4%; nontax revenue 6.5%). Expenditures: ISK 197,804,000,000 (health and welfare 39.6%; education 14.3%; general administration 8.7%; communications 7.5%; cultural affairs 6.2%; agriculture 4.0%).
Public debt (2000): U.S.$2,242,600,000.
Production (metric tons except as noted). Agriculture, forestry, fishing (1999): potatoes 9,000, silage 1,612,500 cu m, hay 722,800 cu m; livestock (number of live animals) 490,500 sheep, 77,300 horses, 74,500 cattle; fish catch (value in ISK '000,000; 1999) cod 21,548, shrimp 7,583, redfish 4,922, haddock 4,348, herring 2,883, Greenland halibut 1,882. Mining and quarrying (1998): diatomite 27,100. Manufacturing (value added in ISK '000,000; 1993): preserved and processed fish 17,534; printing and publishing 5,020; fabricated metal products 3,996; meat 2,569; wood furniture 2,275. Construction (completed; 1997): residential 581,000 cu m; nonresidential 1,299,000 cu m. Energy production (consumption): electricity (kW-hr; 1998) 5,131,000,000 ([1996] 5,131,000,000); coal (metric tons; 1996) none (66,000); crude petroleum, none (none); petroleum products (metric tons; 1996) none (623,000).
Land use (1994): forested 1.2%; meadows and pastures 22.7%; agricultural and under permanent cultivation 0.1%; other 76.0%.
Population economically active (1998): total 152,100; activity rate of total population 55.5% (participation rates: ages 16–74, 79.5%; female 46.8%; unemployed 2.7%).

Price and earnings indexes (1995 = 100)

	1994	1995	1996	1997	1998	1999	2000
Consumer price index	98.4	100.0	102.3	104.1	105.9	109.3	114.9
Hourly earnings index	96.8	100.0	…	…	…	…	…

Tourism (1999): receipts U.S.$227,000,000; expenditures U.S.$430,000,000.
Gross national product (1999): U.S.$8,197,000,000 (U.S.$29,540 per capita).

Structure of gross domestic product and labour force

	1996		1998	
	in value ISK '000,000[7]	% of total value[7]	labour force	% of labour force
Agriculture	8,883	1.8	6,500	4.3
Fishing	38,285	7.9	6,200	4.1
Fish processing	17,718	3.6	7,400	4.9
Manufacturing	47,928	9.9	17,400	11.4
Construction	25,976	5.3	10,900	7.2
Public utilities	16,431	3.4	1,500	1.0
Transp. and commun.	33,265	6.8	10,800	7.1
Trade, restaurants	53,310	10.9	25,000	16.5
Finance, real estate	78,215	16.1	14,200	9.4
Public administration	53,188	11.0	7,000	4.6
Health, education, other services	21,917	4.5	40,900	27.0
Other	91,338[8]	18.8[8]	3,788[9]	2.5[9]
TOTAL	486,454	100.0	151,688[10]	100.0

Household income and expenditure. Average household size (1990)[11] 3.6; annual income per household (1995)[11] ISK 1,976,066 (U.S.$30,546); sources of income (1995): wages and salaries 74.1%, pension 10.5%, self-employment 2.7%, other 12.7%; expenditure (1995): food and beverages 24.0%, transportation and communications 20.8%, recreation and education 13.9%, household furnishings and equipment 8.3%, clothing and footwear 8.0%, energy 4.3%, health 4.0%.

Foreign trade[12]

Balance of trade (current prices)

	1995	1996	1997	1998	1999	2000
ISK '000,000	+2,993	–10,304	–12,014	–39,516	–36,189	–55,331
% of total	1.3%	3.9%	4.4%	12.6%	11.1%	15.7%

Imports (1999): ISK 182,321,500,000 (nonelectrical machinery and apparatus 11.2%; road vehicles 11.0%; food products 8.9%; chemicals 8.0%; electrical machinery and apparatus 6.3%; crude petroleum and petroleum products 5.2%). *Major import sources:* Germany 11.8%; U.S. 10.9%; Norway 10.4%; U.K. 9.2%; Denmark 8.1%; Sweden 6.2%; Japan 5.5%.
Exports (1999): ISK 144,928,100,000 (marine products 61.2%, of which frozen fish 36.3%, salted fish 15.0%; lobster and shrimp 8.3%; aluminum 15.6%; transportation equipment 4.5%). *Major export destinations:* U.K. 19.6%; U.S. 14.7%; Germany 13.1%; The Netherlands 6.0%; France 5.2%; Spain 5.2%.

Transport and communications

Transport. Railroads: none. Roads (1996): total length 7,691 mi, 12,378 km (paved 25%). Vehicles (1999): passenger cars 151,409; trucks and buses 19,428. Merchant marine (1992): vessels (100 gross tons and over) 394; total deadweight tonnage 114,851. Air transport (1999)[13]: passenger-mi 2,272,749,000, passenger-km 3,657,642,000; short ton-mi cargo 50,966,000, metric ton-km cargo 74,409,000; airports (1996) with scheduled flights 24.

Communications

Medium	date	unit	number	units per 1,000 persons
Daily newspapers	1996	circulation	145,000	535
Radio	1997	receivers	260,000	950
Television	1999	receivers	145,000	523
Telephones	1999	main lines	188,800	681
Cellular telephones	1999	subscribers	172,614	623
Personal computers	1999	units	100,000	361
Internet	1999	users	150,000	541

Education and health

Educational attainment: n.a. *Literacy:* virtually 100%.

Education (1998–99)

	schools[14]	teachers	students	student/ teacher ratio
Primary/lower secondary (age 7–15)	205	3,518	42,421	12.1
Upper Secondary (age 16–19)	35	1,483	18,097	12.2
Higher	14	508[14]	8,158	15.7[14]

Health: physicians (1997) 884 (1 per 307 persons); hospital beds (1993) 2,798[15] (1 per 95 persons); infant mortality rate (1999) 2.4.
Food (1999): daily per capita caloric intake 3,313 (vegetable products 59%, animal products 41%); 125% of FAO recommended minimum requirement.

Military

Total active duty personnel (2000): 120 coast guard personnel; NATO-sponsored U.S.-manned Iceland Defense Force: 1,640. *Military expenditure as percentage of GNP* (1997): none (world average 2.6%).

[1]December 1. [2]Constituencies are electoral districts. Actual local administration is based on towns or rural districts. [3]Reykjanes includes Reykjavík. [4]Population density calculated with reference to 9,191 sq mi (23,805 sq km) area free of glaciers, lava fields, and lakes. [5]By country of birth. [6]Within Reykjavík urban area. [7]Breakdown by sector is estimated. [8]Indirect taxes, statistical discrepancy, and production of private nonprofit institution less imputed bank service charges and subsidies. [9]Unemployed. [10]Detail does not add to total given because of rounding. [11]Based on sample survey. [12]Imports c.i.f.; exports f.o.b. [13]Icelandair only. [14]1996–97. [15]Excludes nursing wards in old-age homes.

Internet resources for further information:
- **Statistics Iceland http://www.statice.is**
- **The Icelandic Government (some Icelandic only) http://brunnur.stjr.is/interpro/stjr/stjr.nsf/pages/english-index**
- **Central Bank of Iceland http://www.sedlabanki.is/interpro/sedlabanki/sedlabanki.nsf/pages/english-front**

India

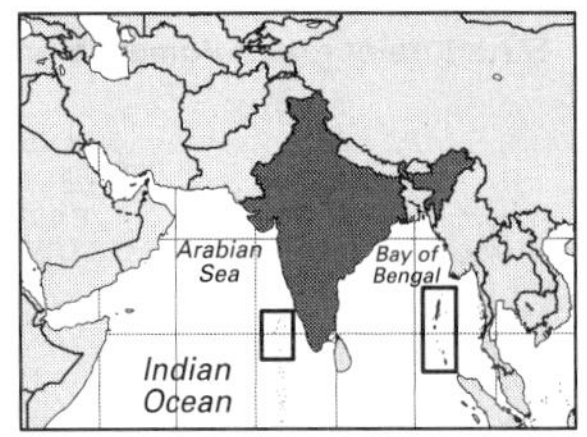

Official name: Bharat (Hindi); Republic of India (English).
Form of government: multiparty federal republic with two legislative houses (Council of States [245[1]], House of the People [545[2]]).
Chief of state: President.
Head of government: Prime Minister.
Capital: New Delhi.
Official languages: Hindi; English.
Official religion: none.
Monetary unit: 1 Indian rupee (Re, plural Rs) = 100 paise; valuation (Sept. 28, 2001) 1 U.S.$ = Rs 47.85; 1 £ = Rs 70.32.

Area and population

		area		population
States	**Capitals**	sq mi	sq km	2001 preliminary census
Andhra Pradesh	Hyderabad	106,204	275,068	75,727,541
Arunachal Pradesh	Itanagar	32,333	83,743	1,091,117
Assam	Dispur	30,285	78,438	26,638,407
Bihar	Patna	38,301	99,200	82,878,796
Chhattisgarh[3]	Raipur	52,199	135,194	20,795,956
Goa	Panaji	1,429	3,702	1,343,998
Gujarat	Gandhinagar	75,685	196,024	50,596,992
Haryana	Chandigarh	17,070	44,212	21,082,989
Himachal Pradesh	Shimla	21,495	55,673	6,077,248
Jammu and Kashmir[4]	Srinagar	39,146	101,387	10,069,917
Jharkhand[3]	Ranchi	28,833	74,677	26,909,428
Karnataka	Bangalore	74,051	191,791	52,733,958
Kerala	Trivandrum	15,005	38,863	31,838,619
Madhya Pradesh	Bhopal	119,016	308,252	60,385,118
Maharashtra	Mumbai (Bombay)	118,800	307,690	96,752,247
Manipur	Imphal	8,621	22,327	2,388,634
Meghalaya	Shillong	8,660	22,429	2,306,069
Mizoram	Aizawl	8,139	21,081	891,058
Nagaland	Kohima	6,401	16,579	1,988,636
Orissa	Bhubaneshwar	60,119	155,707	36,706,920
Punjab	Chandigarh	19,445	50,362	24,289,296
Rajasthan	Jaipur	132,139	342,239	56,473,122
Sikkim	Gangtok	2,740	7,096	540,493
Tamil Nadu	Chennai (Madras)	50,216	130,058	62,110,839
Tripura	Agartala	4,049	10,486	3,191,168
Uttaranchal[3]	Dehra Dun	19,739	51,125	8,479,562
Uttar Pradesh	Lucknow	93,933	243,286	166,052,859
West Bengal	Kolkata (Calcutta)	34,267	88,752	80,221,171
Union Territories				
Andaman and Nicobar Islands	Port Blair	3,185	8,249	356,265
Chandigarh	Chandigarh	44	114	900,914
Dadra and Nagar Haveli	Silvassa	190	491	220,451
Daman and Diu	Daman	43	112	158,059
Lakshadweep	Kavaratti	12	32	60,595
Pondicherry	Pondicherry	190	492	973,829
National Capital Territory				
Delhi	Delhi	573	1,483	13,782,976
TOTAL		1,222,559[4, 5]	3,166,414[4]	1,027,015,247

Demography

Population (2001): 1,029,991,000.
Density (2000)[4]: persons per sq mi 842.5, persons per sq km 325.3.
Urban-rural (2000): urban 28.4%; rural 71.6%.
Sex distribution (2001): male 51.73%; female 48.27%.
Age breakdown (2000): under 15, 33.6%; 15–29, 27.7%; 30–44, 19.8%; 45–59, 11.9%; 60–74, 5.6%; 75 and over, 1.4%.
Population projection: (2010) 1,168,000,000; (2020) 1,312,000,000.
Doubling time: 44 years.
Major cities (1991; *urban agglomerations,* 1995): Greater Mumbai (Greater Bombay) 9,925,891 (15,093,000); Delhi 7,206,704 (9,882,000); Kolkata (Calcutta) 4,399,819 (11,673,000); Chennai (Madras) 3,841,396 (5,906,000); Bangalore 3,302,296 (4,749,000); Hyderabad 3,145,939 (5,343,000); Ahmadabad 2,954,526 (3,688,000); Kanpur 1,879,420 (2,356,000); Nagpur 1,624,752 (1,847,000); Lucknow 1,619,115 (2,029,000); Pune 1,566,651 (2,940,000); New Delhi[6] 301,297.

Other principal cities (1991)

	population		population		population
Agra	891,790	Hubli-Dharwad	648,298	Rajkot	612,458
Prayagraj (Allahabad)	806,486	Indore	1,091,674	Ranchi	599,306
Amritsar	708,835	Jabalpur	764,586	Sholapur (Solapur)	604,215
Aurangabad	573,272	Jaipur	1,458,183	Srinagar	850,000[10]
Bareilly	590,661	Jodhpur	666,279	Surat	1,505,872
Bhopal	1,062,771	Kalyan[8]	1,014,557	Thane (Thana)[8]	803,389
Chandigarh	510,565	Kota	537,371	Trivandrum	699,872
Cochin (Kochi)	582,588	Ludhiana	1,042,740	Vadodara (Baroda)	1,061,598
Coimbatore	816,321	Madurai	940,989	Varanasi (Benares)	932,399
Faridabad	617,717	Meerut	753,778	Vijayawada	701,827
Guwahati	584,342	Mysore	606,755	Vishakhapatnam	752,037
Gwalior	690,765	Nashik (Nasik)	656,925		
Howrah (Haora)[7]	950,435	Patna	917,243		
		Pimpri-Chinchwad[9]	517,083		

Linguistic composition (1991)[11]: Hindi 27.58% (including associated languages and dialects, 39.85%); Bengali 8.22%; Telugu 7.80%; Marathi 7.38%; Tamil 6.26%; Urdu 5.13%; Gujarati 4.81%; Kannada 3.87%; Malayalam 3.59%; Oriya 3.32%; Punjabi 2.76%; Assamese 1.55%; Bhili/Bhilodi 0.66%; Santhali 0.62%; Kashmiri 0.47%[12]; Gondi 0.25%; Sindhi 0.25%; Nepali 0.25%; Konkani 0.21%; Tulu 0.18%; Kurukh 0.17%; Manipuri 0.15%; Bodo 0.14%; Khandeshi 0.12%; other 3.26%. Hindi (66.00%) and English (19.00%) are also spoken as lingua francas (second languages).
Religious affiliation (2000): Hindu 73.72%; Muslim 11.96%, of which Sunnī 8.97%, Shīʿī 2.99%; Christian 6.08%, of which Independent 2.99%, Protestant 1.47%, Roman Catholic 1.35%, Orthodox 0.27%; traditional beliefs 3.39%; Sikh 2.16%; Buddhist 0.71%; Jain 0.40%; Bahāʾī 0.12%; Zoroastrian (Parsi) 0.02%; other 1.44%.
Households (1991)[13]. Total households 151,032,898. Average household size 5.6; 1–2 persons 12.1%, 3–5 persons 44.4%, 6–8 persons 30.5%, 9 or more persons 13.0%. Average number of rooms per household 2.2; 1 room 40.5%, 2 rooms 30.6%, 3 rooms 13.8%, 4 rooms 7.1%, 5 rooms 3.2%, 6 or more rooms 3.9%, unspecified number of rooms 0.9%. Average number of persons per room 2.6.

Vital statistics

Birth rate per 1,000 population (2000): 24.8 (world avg. 22.5).
Death rate per 1,000 population (2000): 8.9 (world avg. 9.0).
Natural increase rate per 1,000 population (2000): 15.9 (world avg. 13.5).
Total fertility rate (avg. births per childbearing woman; 2000): 3.1.
Marital status of male (female) population age 6 and over (1992–93): single 48.3% (37.1%); married 47.5% (55.2%); widowed 3.6% (7.2%); divorced or separated 0.6% (0.5%).
Life expectancy at birth (2000): male 61.9 years; female 63.1 years.
Major causes of death per 100,000 population (1987)[14]: diseases of the circulatory system 227; infectious and parasitic diseases 215; diseases of the respiratory system 108; certain conditions originating in the perinatal period 108; accidents, homicide, and other violence 102; diseases of the digestive system 48; diseases of the nervous system 43; malignant neoplasms (cancers) 41; endocrine, metabolic, and nutritional disorders 30; diseases of the blood and blood-forming organs 25; ill-defined conditions 129.

Social indicators

Educational attainment (1991)[13, 15]. Percentage of population age 25 and over having: no formal schooling 57.5%; incomplete primary education 28.0%; complete primary or some secondary 7.2%; complete secondary or higher 7.3%.

Distribution of expenditure (1994)

percentage of household expenditure by decile/quintile

1	2	3	4	5	6	7	8	9	10 (highest)
4.1	5.1	—13.0—		—16.8—		—21.7—		14.3	25.0

Quality of working life. Average workweek (1989): 42 hours[16]. Rate of fatal (nonfatal) injuries per 100,000 industrial workers (1989) 17 (3,625)[16]. Agricultural workers in servitude to creditors (early 1990s) 10–20%.
Access to services (1991). Percentage of total (urban, rural) households having access to: electricity for lighting purposes 42.4% (75.8%, 30.5%); attached toilet or nearby latrine 23.7% (63.9%, 9.5%). Source of drinking water: piped water 32.3%, well 32.2%, hand pump or tube well 30.0%, river or canal 2.0%, public tank 1.3%, other 2.2%.
Social participation. Eligible voters participating in September/October 1999 national election: 59.6%. Trade union membership (1998): *c.* 16,000,000 (primarily in the public sector).
Social deviance (1990)[17]. Offense rate per 100,000 population for: murder 4.1; dacoity (gang robbery) 1.3; theft and housebreaking 56.6; riots 12.0. Rate of suicide per 100,000 population (1991): 9.0.
Material well-being (1994). Households possessing: black and white television receivers 18.8%, colour television receivers 6.3%, videocassette recorders 1.3%, refrigerators 6.9%, washing machines 2.3%.

National economy

Gross national product (1999): U.S.$441,834,000,000 (U.S.$440 per capita).

Structure of gross domestic product and labour force

	1999–2000[18]		1993–94	
	in value Rs '000,000,000[19]	% of total value	labour force	% of labour force
Agriculture, forestry	4,940	27.9	240,700,000	64.7
Mining	332	1.9	2,600,000	0.7
Manufacturing	2,793	15.8	39,100,000	10.5
Construction	1,039	5.9	11,900,000	3.2
Public utilities	440	2.5	1,500,000	0.4
Transp. and commun. } Trade, restaurants }	3,600	20.3	10,400,000	2.8
			27,500,000	7.4
Finance, real estate	2,075	11.7 }	38,300,000	10.3
Pub. admin., defense } Services }	2,504	14.1 }		
TOTAL	17,723	100.0[5]	372,000,000	100.0

Budget (1999–2000). Revenue: Rs 3,288,000,000,000 (tax revenue 48.6%, of which excise taxes 19.4%, customs duties 15.3%, corporation taxes 9.4%; nontax revenue 36.5%, of which economic services 20.7%, interest receipts 10.0%; other sources of revenue 14.9%). Expenditures: Rs 3,288,000,000,000 (interest payments and debt servicing 26.8%; transportation 11.0%; defense 10.5%; grants in aid to state governments 9.4%; communications 7.2%; agriculture 5.0%; social services 4.7%).
Public debt (external, outstanding; 1999): U.S.$82,380,000,000.
Production (in '000 metric tons except as noted). Agriculture, forestry, fishing (2000): sugarcane 315,100; cereals 239,814 (of which rice 134,150, wheat 74,251, corn [maize] 11,500, sorghum 9,500, millet 9,000); fruits 49,199 (of which mangoes 15,642, bananas 13,900, oranges 3,000, apples 1,580, pineapples 1,440, lemons and limes 1,000); oilseeds 31,015[20] (of which rapeseed 6,120, peanuts [groundnuts] 6,100, soybeans 5,400, sunflower seeds 1,200,

castor beans 810, sesame 620); pulses 14,237[20] (of which chickpeas 5,754[20], dry beans 3,600[20], pigeon peas 2,450[20]), coconuts 11,100, seed cotton 6,172, eggplants 6,100, jute 1,500, tea 749, tobacco 702, natural rubber 620, garlic 517, cashews 450, betel 315, coffee 282, ginger 235, pepper 58; livestock (number of live animals; 2000) 218,800,000 cattle, 123,000,000 goats, 93,772,000 water buffalo, 57,900,000 sheep, 16,500,000 pigs, 1,030,000 camels; roundwood (1999) 302,794,000 cu m, of which fuelwood 278,755,000 cu m, industrial roundwood 24,038,000; fish catch (metric tons; 1997) 5,378,000, of which marine fish 2,478,000, freshwater fish 2,435,000, crustaceans 465,000. Mining and quarrying (1998): limestone 108,920; iron ore 44,200[21, 22]; bauxite 6,658[22]; manganese 610[21]; chromium 1,311; zinc 197[21]; copper 43[21, 22]; gold 76,615 troy oz[21]; gem diamonds 20,000 carats. Manufacturing (value added in Rs '000,000,000; 1999): iron and steel 188.1; industrial chemicals 167.7; paints, soaps, varnishes, drugs, and medicines 164.2; transport equipment 159.7; food products 139.0; textiles 136.8; electrical machinery 118.6; nonelectrical machinery 116.3; refined petroleum 79.2; cements, bricks, and tiles 67.2; fabricated metal products 39.5; nonferrous base metals 37.5.

Manufacturing enterprises (1995–96)[23]

	no. of factories	no. of persons engaged	avg. wages as a % of avg. of all wages	annual value added (Rs '000,000)[24]
Chemicals and chemical products,	9,206	758,500	140.3	237,093
of which fertilizers/pesticides	753	104,500	217.4	59,521
drugs and medicine	2,542	204,600	129.3	40,050
synthetic fibres	395	97,100	183.8	68,420
paints, soaps, and cosmetics	1,958	104,300	129.0	23,459
Transport equipment,	6,120	838,600	142.7	120,207
of which motor vehicles	3,758	392,400	162.4	77,240
motorcycles and bicycles	1,243	124,900	123.6	21,957
Textiles	16,228	1,579,400	80.2	99,855
Iron and steel	3,519	507,700	152.9	97,274
Nonelectrical machinery/apparatus	9,075	548,400	137.2	92,762
Food products,	22,878	1,285,900	60.4	92,163
of which refined sugar	1,285	341,000	92.0	28,125
Electrical machinery/apparatus,	5,472	443,700	149.4	84,320
of which industrial machinery	2,048	165,600	190.8	35,717
Refined petroleum	161	31,100	349.3	52,778
Bricks, cement, plaster products	10,067	394,500	70.3	49,413
Nonferrous basic metals	3,301	228,700	124.3	42,252
Fabricated metal products	7,984	277,700	98.6	32,565
Paper and paper products	2,742	175,200	99.5	26,380
Wearing apparel	3,463	263,700	55.0	23,485

Energy production (consumption): electricity (kW-hr; 1999) 473,214,000,000 ([1996] 433,914,000,000); coal (metric tons; 1999) 292,356,000 ([1996] 319,233,000); crude petroleum (barrels; 1999) 247,426,000 ([1996] 492,646,000); petroleum products (metric tons; 1996) 47,648,000 (67,219,000); natural gas (cu m; 1999) 20,006,000,000 ([1996] 27,113,000,000).

Financial aggregates[25]

	1995	1996	1997	1998	1999	2000	2001
Exchange rate, Rs per:							
U.S. dollar	35.18	35.93	39.28	42.48	43.49	46.75	46.64[26]
£	54.53	61.01	64.96	70.67	70.30	69.76	66.49[26]
SDR	52.30	51.67	53.00	59.81	59.69	60.91	58.80[26]
International reserves (U.S.$)							
Total (excl. gold; '000,000)	17,922	20,170	24,688	27,341	32,667	37,902	40,172[26]
SDRs ('000,000)	139	122	77	83	4	2	2[26]
Reserve pos. in IMF ('000,000)	316	306	287	300	671	637	616[26]
Foreign exchange ('000,000)	17,467	19,742	24,324	26,958	31,992	37,264	39,554[26]
Gold ('000,000 fine troy oz)	12.780	12.781	12.740	11.487	11.502	11.502	11.502[26]
% world reserves	1.4	1.4	1.4	1.2	1.2	1.2	1.2[26]
Interest and prices							
Central bank discount (%)	12.0	12.0	9.0	9.0	8.0	8.0	...
Advance (prime) rate (%)	15.5	16.0	13.8	13.5	12.5	12.3	...
Industrial share prices (1995 = 100)[27]	100.0	91.3	84.5	76.8	...	...	...
Balance of payments (U.S.$'000,000)							
Balance of visible trade	–6,718	–10,052	–10,028	–10,752	–8,028	...	...
Imports, f.o.b.	37,957	43,789	45,730	44,828	45,556	...	...
Exports, f.o.b.	31,239	33,737	35,702	34,076	37,528	...	...
Balance of invisibles	+1,155	+4,096	+7,063	+3,849	+5,244	...	...
Balance of payments, current account	–5,563	–5,956	–2,965	–6,903	–2,784	...	...

Land use (1994): forested 23.0%; meadows and pastures 3.8%; agricultural and under permanent cultivation 57.1%; other 16.1%.

Population economically active (1993–94): total 372,000,000; activity rate of total population *c.* 41% (participation rates: n.a.; female 32.5%; unemployed[28]).

Price and earnings indexes (1995 = 100)

	1994	1995	1996	1997	1998	1999	2000
Consumer price index	90.7	100.0	109.0	116.8	132.2	138.4	144.0
Earnings index	...	...	...	...	...	...	...

Household income and expenditure. Average household size (1991)[13] 5.6; sources of income (1984–85): salaries and wages 42.2%, self-employed 39.7%, interest 8.6%, profits and dividends 6.0%, rent 3.5%; expenditure (1995–96): food and beverages 49.2%, transportation and communications 12.3%, clothing and footwear 11.4%, housing 5.2%, household furnishings 5.0%.

Service enterprises (net value added in Rs '000,000,000; 1995–96): wholesale and retail trade 1,315; finance and insurance 861; transport and storage 632; community, social, and personal services 594; construction 566; real estate and business services 286; electricity, gas, and steam 240.

Tourism (1999): receipts from visitors U.S.$3,036,000,000; expenditures by nationals abroad U.S.$2,010,000,000.

Foreign trade[29, 30]

Balance of trade (current prices)

	1994–95	1995–96	1996–97	1997–98	1998–99	1999–2000
Rs '000,000	–72,970	–163,250	–200,030	–252,680	–385,080	–399,140
% of total	4.2%	7.1%	7.8%	9.5%	12.6%	11.0%

Imports (1999–2000): Rs 2,006,570,000,000 (crude petroleum and refined petroleum 22.3%; precious and semiprecious stones 11.6%; chemicals 6.0%; nonelectrical machinery 5.8%; electronic goods 5.6%). *Major import sources:* Belgium 7.7%; U.S. 7.5%; U.K. 5.8%; Switzerland 5.5%; Japan 5.1%; Saudi Arabia 4.8%; United Arab Emirates 4.5%; Malaysia 4.3%; Germany 3.9%.

Exports (1999–2000): Rs 1,607,430,000,000 (cut and polished diamonds and jewelry 20.0%; cotton ready-made garments 9.2%; cotton yarn, fabrics, and thread 7.9%; leather and leather manufactures 4.2%; drugs and pharmaceuticals 4.2%; fabricated metals 3.2%). *Major export destinations:* U.S. 22.2%; Hong Kong 6.7%; U.K. 5.6%; United Arab Emirates 5.6%; Germany 4.6%; Japan 4.5%; Belgium 3.6%; Italy 3.0%; Russia 2.5%.

Transport and communications

Transport. Railroads (1998–99): route length 39,028 mi, 62,809 km; (1999–2000) passenger-mi 261,254,000,000, passenger-km 420,449,000,000; (1999–2000) short ton-mi cargo 209,259,000,000, metric ton-km cargo 305,513,000,000. Roads (1996): total length 2,062,727 mi, 3,319,644 km (paved 46%). Vehicles (1996): passenger cars 4,189,000; trucks and buses 2,234,000. Air transport (1999[31]): passenger-mi 11,456,000,000, passenger-km 18,436,000,000; short ton-mi cargo 329,421,000, metric ton-km cargo 480,946,000; airports (1996) with scheduled flights 66.

Communications

Medium	date	unit	number	units per 1,000 persons
Daily newspapers	1993	circulation	18,800,000	21
Radio	1997	receivers	116,000,000	120
Television	1999	receivers	75,000,000	75
Telephones	1999	main lines	26,511,000	27
Cellular telephones	1999	subscribers	1,884,000	1.9
Personal computers	1999	units	3,300,000	3.3
Internet	1999	users	2,800,000	2.8

Education and health

Literacy (2001): total population age 7 and over literate 566,715,000 (65.4%); males literate 339,969,000 (75.8%); females literate 226,746,000 (54.2%).

Education (1997–98)

	schools	teachers	students	student/teacher ratio
Primary (age 6–10)	610,763	1,871,542	108,781,792	50.1
Secondary (age 11–17)	261,736	2,081,223	57,433,776	27.6
Higher	26,491	651,766	6,944,069	10.7

Health: physicians (1992) 410,875 (1 per 2,173 persons); hospital beds (1993) 659,000 (1 per 1,364 persons); infant mortality rate (2000) 64.9.

Food (1999): daily per capita caloric intake 2,417 (vegetable products 92%, animal products 8%); 109% of FAO recommended minimum requirement.

Military

Total active duty personnel (2000): 1,303,000 (army 84.4%, navy 4.1%, air force 11.5%); personnel in paramilitary forces 1,069,000. *Military expenditure as percentage of GNP* (1997): 2.8% (world 2.6%); per capita expenditure U.S.$11.

[1]Council of States can have a maximum of 250 members; a maximum of 12 of these members may be nominated by the president. [2]Includes 2 nonelective seats. [3]Created November 2000. [4]Excludes 46,660 sq mi (120,849 sq km) of territory claimed by India as part of Jammu and Kashmir but occupied by Pakistan or China; inland water constitutes 9.6% of total area of India (including all of Indian-claimed Jammu and Kashmir). [5]Detail does not add to total given because of rounding. [6]Within Delhi urban agglomeration. [7]Within Calcutta urban agglomeration. [8]Within Greater Mumbai urban agglomeration. [9]Within Pune urban agglomeration. [10]1990 estimate. [11]Mother tongue unless otherwise noted. [12]1981. [13]Excludes Jammu and Kashmir. [14]Projected rates based on about 3.5% of total deaths (317,392 registered deaths out of an estimated total of nearly 9,000,000 deaths). [15]No formal schooling (1991): males 43.3%, females 72.8%; complete secondary or higher education (1991): males 10.6%, females 3.7%. [16]Data apply to the workers employed in the "organized sector" only (28.2 million in 1997–98, of which 19.4 million are employed in the public sector and 8.8 million are employed in the private sector); few legal protections exist for the more than 350 million workers in the "unorganized sector." [17]Crimes reported to National Crime Records Bureau by police authorities of state governments. [18]April 1–March 31. [19]At factor cost. [20]1998. [21]Approximate metal content of ore. [22]1999. [23]Establishments using power with at least 10 workers on any workday and all establishments employing 20 or more workers. [24]In factor values. [25]End-of-period unless otherwise noted. [26]March. [27]Period average. [28]Average number of registered unemployed in February 2000 was 40,395,000. [29]Imports c.i.f.; exports f.o.b. [30]Fiscal year beginning April 1. [31]Air India and Indian Airlines.

Internet resources for further information:

- **India Image: Directory of Government Web Sites http://www.nic.in**
- **Census of India http://www.censusindia.net**
- **Press Information Bureau (Government of India) http://pib.nic.in**

Indonesia

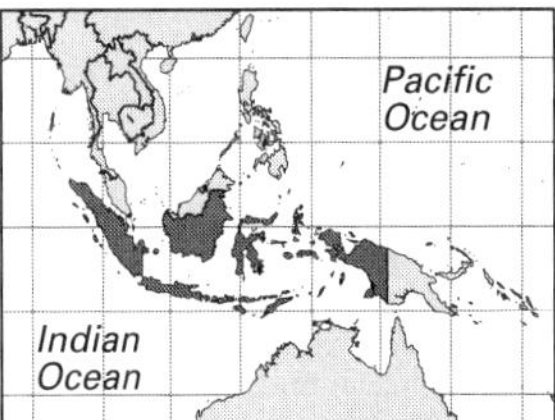

Official name: Republik Indonesia (Republic of Indonesia).
Form of government: unitary multiparty republic with two legislative houses (People's Consultative Assembly [700[1]]; House of People's Representatives [500[2]]).
Head of state and government: President.
Capital: Jakarta.
Official language: Indonesian (Bahasa Indonesia).
Official religion: monotheism.
Monetary unit: 1 Indonesian rupiah (Rp) = 100 sen; valuation (Sept. 28, 2001) 1 U.S.$ = Rp 9,707; 1 £ = Rp 14,267.

Area and population

Island(s) Provinces	area sq km	population 1999 estimate
Bali and the Lesser Sunda Islands[3]	73,135	10,824,100
Bali	5,633	3,052,700
East Nusa Tenggara	47,349	3,850,100
West Nusa Tenggara	20,153	3,921,300
Celebes (Sulawesi)[4]	191,800	14,768,400
Central Sulawesi	63,689	2,129,000
Gorontalo[5]	12,151	2,804,400
North Sulawesi	15,337	
Southeast Sulawesi	38,140	1,744,900
South Sulawesi	62,483	8,090,100
Java[4]	127,499	121,193,000
Banten[6]	8,232	[7]
Central Java	32,549	31,043,700
East Java	47,923	35,160,100
Jakarta[8]	664	9,604,900
West Java	34,945	42,332,200[7]
Yogyakarta[9]	3,186	3,052,100
Kalimantan[4, 10]	547,891	11,396,100
Central Kalimantan	153,564	1,771,000
East Kalimantan	210,985	2,579,400
South Kalimantan	36,535	3,102,500
West Kalimantan	146,807	3,943,200
Maluku (Moluccas)	77,871	2,223,000
Maluku	...	...
North Maluku	...	...
Papua (Irian Jaya)[4, 11]	421,981	2,165,300
Sumatra[4]	482,393	43,947,100
Aceh[9]	55,390	4,144,500
Bangka-Belitung[5]	[12]	[12]
Bengkulu	19,789	1,557,000
Jambi	53,436	2,589,800
Lampung	35,385	7,080,800
North Sumatra	71,680	11,955,400
Riau	94,561	4,290,600
South Sumatra	109,254[12]	7,734,200[12]
West Sumatra	42,898	4,594,800
TOTAL	1,922,570[3]	206,517,000[3]

Demography

Population (2001): 212,195,000.
Density (2001)[3]: persons per sq mi 285.9, persons per sq km 110.4.
Urban-rural (2001): urban 42.0%; rural 58.0%.
Sex distribution (1995): male 49.77%; female 50.23%.
Age breakdown (1995): under 15, 35.6%; 15–29, 27.5%; 30–44, 19.6%; 45–59, 10.8%; 60–74, 5.4%; 75 and over, 1.1%.
Population projection: (2010) 237,973,000; (2020) 261,802,000.
Ethnolinguistic composition (1990): Javanese 39.4%; Sundanese 15.8%; Indonesian (Malay) 12.1%; Madurese 4.3%; Minang 2.4%; other 26.0%.
Religious affiliation (1990): Muslim 87.2%; Christian 9.6%, of which Roman Catholic 3.6%; Hindu 1.8%; Buddhist 1.0%; other 0.4%.
Major cities (1995): Jakarta (1996) 9,341,000; Surabaya (1996) 2,743,000; Bandung (1996) 2,429,000; Medan 1,909,700; Palembang 1,283,100; Tangerang 1,144,500; Semarang 1,097,800; Ujung Pandang 1,029,900; Malang 716,400; Bandar Lampung 598,900.

Vital statistics

Birth rate per 1,000 population (2001): 20.8 (world avg. 22.5).
Death rate per 1,000 population (2001): 7.2 (world avg. 9.0).
Natural increase rate per 1,000 population (2001): 13.6 (world avg. 13.5).
Total fertility rate (avg. births per childbearing woman; 2001): 2.4.
Marriage rate per 1,000 population (1997–98): 8.1[13].
Life expectancy at birth (2001): male 65.0 years; female 69.0 years.
Major causes of death (percent distribution, 1986): infectious and parasitic diseases 43.5%; diseases of the respiratory system 21.9%; cardiovascular diseases 9.7%; diseases of the nervous system 6.0%.

National economy

Budget (1999–2000). Revenue: RP 188,428,500,000,000 (income tax 31.7%, oil and gas revenues 31.0%, value-added tax 17.6%, nontax revenue 9.1%, excise taxes 5.5%). Expenditures: RP 204,900,300,000,000 (development 23.9%, subsidies 22.9%, salaries 15.7%, debt repayment 10.1%, transfers 8.5%).
Production (metric tons except as noted). Agriculture, forestry, fishing (2000): rice 51,000,000, palm fruit oil 34,000,000, sugarcane 21,400,000, cassava 16,347,000, corn (maize) 9,169,000, natural rubber 1,488,000; livestock (number of live animals) 14,121,000 goats, 12,102,000 cattle, 7,502,000 sheep, 2,859,000 buffalo; roundwood (1999) 190,601,000 cu m; fish catch (1998) 3,699,000. Mining and quarrying (1998): copper concentrate 2,640,000; nickel ore 1,642,000; bauxite 513,000; gold 118,246 kg. Manufacturing (value added in RP '000,000,000; 1997)[14]: transport equipment 10,038.6; textiles 9,629.7; food products 9,028.1; electrical machinery 6,654.7; wood products, except furniture 6,092.8; industrial chemicals 5,019.3; paper and paper products 4,121.2. Energy production (consumption): electricity (kW-hr; 1996) 73,794,000,000 (73,794,000,000); coal (metric tons; 1999) 70,704,000 ([1996] 15,796,000); crude petroleum (barrels; 1999) 500,642,000 ([1996] 311,201,000); petroleum products (metric tons; 1996) 43,307,000 (40,759,000); natural gas (cu m; 1998) 84,348,000,000 ([1996] 38,885,000,000).
Gross national product (1999): U.S.$125,043,000,000 (U.S.$600 per capita).

Structure of gross domestic product and labour force

	1999 in value Rp '000,000,000	% of total value	labour force[15]	% of labour force[15]
Agriculture	218,044	19.5	38,378,000	43.2
Mining	112,638	10.1	726,000	0.8
Manufacturing	284,804	25.4	11,516,000	13.0
Construction	73,418	6.5	3,415,000	3.9
Public utilities	13,369	1.2	188,000	0.2
Transp. and commun.	66,077	5.9	4,206,000	4.7
Trade	183,627	16.4	17,529,000	19.7
Finance, real estate	55,098	4.9	634,000	0.7
Pub. admin., defense	56,745	5.1	12,225,000	13.8
Services	55,622	5.0		
Other	...	...	...	...
TOTAL	1,119,442	100.0	88,817,000	100.0

Public debt (external, outstanding; 1999): U.S.$72,554,000,000.
Population economically active (1999): total 94,800,000; activity rate 46.0% (participation rates: over age 15, 70.7%; unemployed 6.3%).

Price and earnings indexes (1995 = 100)

	1994	1995	1996	1997	1998	1999	2000
Consumer price index	91.4	100.0	108.0	115.2	181.7	218.9	227.0
Earnings index[16]	83.9	100.0	105.4	116.1	133.9	155.4	...

Household income and expenditure. Average household size (1998) 4.1.
Tourism (1999): receipts U.S.$4,710,000,000; expenditures U.S.$2,353,000,000.

Foreign trade[17]

Balance of trade (current prices)

	1993	1994	1995	1996	1997	1998	1999
U.S.$'000,000	+8,872	+11,496	+8,883	+5,285	+9,456	+18,428	+20,643
% of total	13.4%	16.8%	10.8%	5.6%	9.3%	22.4%	25.2%

Imports (1998): U.S.$27,336,900,000 (machinery and transport equipment 36.3%, basic manufactures 16.6%, chemicals 15.1%, mineral fuels 9.8%, food and live animals 9.6%). *Major import sources:* Japan 15.7%; U.S. 12.9%; Singapore 9.3%; Germany 8.7%; Australia 6.4%; South Korea 5.6%.
Exports (1998): U.S.$48,847,600,000 (crude petroleum 8.3%, natural gas 7.8%, garments 5.4%, plywood 4.3%, processed rubber 2.3%). *Major export destinations:* Japan 18.7%; U.S. 14.4%; Singapore 10.6%; Australia 3.1%.

Transport and communications

Transport. Railroads (1999): route length 6,458 km; passenger-km 18,585,000,000; metric ton-km cargo 5,035,000,000. Roads (1997): length 341,467 km (paved 56%). Vehicles (1998): passenger cars 2,734,769; trucks and buses 2,189,876. Air transport (1999): passenger-km 12,389,000,000; metric ton-km cargo 340,932,000; airports (1996) 81.

Communications

Medium	date	unit	number	units per 1,000 persons
Daily newspapers	1996	circulation	4,665,000	23
Radio	1998	receivers	26,000,000	128
Television	1999	receivers	30,000,000	143
Telephones	1999	main lines	6,080,200	29
Cellular telephones	1999	subscribers	2,221,000	11
Personal computers	1999	units	1,900,000	9.1
Internet	1999	users	900,000	4.3

Education and health

Educational attainment (1990). Percentage of population age 25 and over having: no schooling 34.6%; less than complete primary 28.2%; primary 23.3%; secondary 12.5%; higher 1.4%. *Literacy* (1995 est.): total population age 15 and over literate 83.8%; males literate 89.6%; females literate 78.0%.

Education (1997–98)

	schools	teachers	students	student/ teacher ratio
Primary (age 7–12)	151,064	1,158,616	25,689,693	22.1
Secondary (age 13–18)	29,398	654,505	10,821,139	16.5
Voc., teacher tr.	4,006	127,270	1,862,060	14.6
Higher	1,391	181,545	2,051,001	11.3

Health: physicians (1996) 31,435 (1 per 6,259 persons); hospital beds (1997) 121,996 (1 per 1,638 persons); infant mortality rate (2001) 42.0.
Food (1999): daily per capita caloric intake 2,931 (vegetable products 95%, animal products 5%); (1997) 136% of FAO recommended minimum.

Military

Total active duty personnel (2000): 297,000 (army 77.4%, navy 13.5%, air force 9.1%). *Military expenditure as percentage of GNP* (1997): 2.3% (world 2.6%); per capita expenditure U.S.$24.

[1]Includes the 500 members of the House of People's Representatives plus 200 other appointees. [2]Includes 38 nonelective seats reserved for the military. [3]Excludes area and population of East Timor; the UN assumed formal control of East Timor on Oct. 26, 1999. [4]Includes area and population of nearby islands. [5]Formally established February 2001. [6]Formally established November 2000. [7]West Java includes Banten. [8]Formally a metropolitan district. [9]Formally a special autonomous district. [10]Kalimantan is the name of the Indonesian part of the island of Borneo. [11]Locally West Papua; increased autonomy from October 2001. [12]South Sumatra includes Bangka-Belitung. [13]Muslim population only. [14]Medium and large establishments only. [15]Employed people only. [16]Based on minimum monthly wages. [17]Imports and exports are f.o.b. in balance of trade.

Internet resources for further information:

- **Central Bureau of Statistics http://www.bps.go.id**

Iran

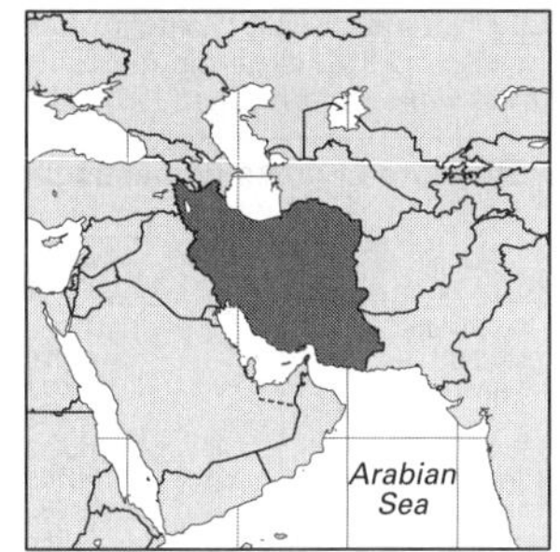

Official name: Jomhūrī-ye Eslāmī-ye Īrān (Islamic Republic of Iran).
Form of government: unitary Islamic republic with one legislative house (Islamic Consultative Assembly [290]).
Supreme political/religious authority: Leader[1].
Head of state and government: President.
Capital: Tehrān.
Official language: Farsī (Persian).
Official religion: Islam.
Monetary unit: 1 rial (Rls); valuation (Sept. 28, 2001) 1 U.S.$ = Rls 1,750[2]; 1 £ = Rls 2,572[2].

Area and population

Provinces	area sq km	1996 census population	Provinces	area sq km	1996 census population
Ardabīl	17,881	1,168,000	Khūzestān	63,213	3,747,000
Āzārbāyjān-e Gharbī	37,463	2,496,000	Kohgīlūyeh va Būyer Aḩmad	15,563	544,000
Āzārbāyjān-e Sharqī	45,481	3,326,000	Kordestān	28,817	1,346,000
Būshehr	23,168	744,000	Lorestān	28,392	1,584,000
Chahār Maḩāll va Bakhtīārī	16,201	761,000	Markazī	29,406	1,229,000
Eşfahān	107,027	3,923,000	Māzandarān	23,833	2,602,000
Fārs	121,825	3,817,000	Qazvīn	15,502	968,000
Gīlān	13,952	2,242,000	Qom	11,237	853,000
Golestān	20,893	1,426,000	Semnān	96,816	501,000
Hamadān	19,547	1,678,000	Sīstān va Balūchestān	178,431	1,723,000
Hormozgān	71,193	1,062,000	Tehrān	19,196	10,344,000
Īlām	20,150	488,000	Yazd	73,467	751,000
Kermān	181,814	2,004,000	Zanjān	21,841	901,000
Kermānshāh	24,641	1,779,000	TOTAL	1,629,918[3]	60,055,000
Khorāsān	302,966	6,048,000			

Demography

Population (2001): 63,442,000[4, 5].
Density (2001): persons per sq mi 100.8, persons per sq km 38.9.
Urban-rural (2000): urban 63.8%; rural 36.2%.
Sex distribution (2000): male 50.73%; female 49.27%.
Age breakdown (2000): under 15, 34.4%; 15–29, 32.0%; 30–44, 17.9%; 45–59, 9.2%; 60–74, 5.1%; 75 and over, 1.4%.
Population projection: (2010) 70,494,000; (2020) 80,482,000.
Doubling time: 54 years.
Ethnic composition (1995): Persian 51%; Azerbaijani 24%; Gīlaki/Mazāndarānī 8%; Kurd 7%; Arab 3%; Lurī 2%; Balochi 2%; other 3%.
Religious affiliation (2000): Muslim 95.6% (Shīʿī 90.1%, Sunnī 5.5%); Zoroastrian 2.8%; Christian 0.5%; other 1.1%.
Major cities (1996): Tehrān 6,758,845; Mashhad 1,887,405; Eşfahān 1,266,072; Tabriz 1,191,043; Shīrāz 1,053,025; Karaj 940,968; Ahvāz 804,980.

Vital statistics

Birth rate per 1,000 population (2000): 18.3 (world avg. 22.5).
Death rate per 1,000 population (2000): 5.5 (world avg. 9.0).
Natural increase rate per 1,000 population (2000): 12.8 (world avg. 13.5).
Total fertility rate (avg. births per childbearing woman; 2000): 2.2.
Life expectancy at birth (2000): male 68.3 years; female 71.5 years.
Major causes of death per 100,000 population (1990)[6]: diseases of the circulatory system 304; accidents and violence 108; malignant neoplasms (cancers) 61; diseases of the respiratory system 48; infectious diseases 34.

National economy

Budget (2000–01). Revenue: Rls 150,212,000,000,000 (petroleum and natural gas revenue 55.2%; taxes 22.6%, of which corporate 8.9%; import duties 4.6%; other 17.6%). Expenditures: Rls 136,761,000,000,000 (current expenditure 65.1%; development expenditure 22.0%; other 12.9%).
Public debt (external, outstanding; 2000): U.S.$6,184,000,000.
Tourism (1999): receipts U.S.$662,000,000; expenditures U.S.$918,000,000.
Gross national product (1999): U.S.$113,729,000,000 (U.S.$1,810 per capita).

Structure of gross domestic product and labour force

	1999–2000 in value Rls '000,000,000[7]	1999–2000 % of total value[7]	1996 labour force	1996 % of labour force
Agriculture, forestry	86,997	20.9	3,357,263	21.0
Petroleum, natural gas	35,044	8.4	} 119,884	} 0.7
Other mining	2,740	0.7		
Manufacturing	70,655	17.0	2,551,962	15.9
Construction	14,083	3.4	1,650,481	10.3
Public utilities	7,421	1.8	150,631	0.9
Transp. and commun.	34,387	8.3	972,792	6.1
Trade, restaurants	76,802	18.4	1,927,067	12.0
Finance, real estate	44,759	10.7	301,962	1.9
Pub. admin., defense	35,652	8.5	1,618,100	10.1
Services	8,628	2.1	1,664,402	10.4
Other	–951[8]	–0.2[8]	1,712,028[9]	10.7[9]
TOTAL	416,698	100.0	16,026,572	100.0

Production (metric tons except as noted). Agriculture, forestry, fishing (1998): wheat 8,673,000, sugar beets 5,587,000, potatoes 3,433,000, tomatoes 3,400,000, rice 2,348,000, barley 1,999,000, grapes 2,350,000, apples 2,200,000, oranges 1,850,000, onions 1,667,000, corn (maize) 1,155,000, lemons 1,000,000, dates 930,000, seed cotton 441,000, pistachios 291,000; livestock (number of live animals) 55,000,000 sheep, 8,100,000 cattle; roundwood (2000) 1,151,000 cu m; fish catch (1999) 419,000. Mining and quarrying (1998): copper ore 14,500,000; iron ore 12,300,000; gypsum 9,750,000; lead-zinc ore 1,520,000; chromite 860,000. Manufacturing (value added in U.S.$'000,000; 1995): iron and steel 1,393; food products 1,170; textiles 989; transport equipment 763; electrical machinery 716; bricks, tiles, and cement 703. Energy production (consumption): electricity (kW-hr; 2000–01) 120,611,000,000 (120,611,000,000); coal (metric tons; 1997) 1,750,000 (1,320,000); crude petroleum (barrels; 1999–2000) 1,255,000,000 (496,000,000); petroleum products (metric tons; 1997) 50,135,000 (53,936,000); natural gas (cu m; 1999–2000) 80,000,000,000 (58,700,000,000).
Population economically active (2000–01): total 18,700,000; activity rate 29.3% (participation rates: over age 15 [1996] 44.0%; female [1996] 12.7%; unemployed 13.9%).

Price and earnings indexes (1997–98 = 100)

	1995–96	1996–97	1997–98	1998–99	1999–2000	2000–01
Consumer price index	68.4	88.4	100.0	118.1	141.8	159.7
Daily earnings index[10]	59.4	79.5	100.0	113.3	128.5	142.3

Household income and expenditure. Average household size (1999): 5.0; income per urban household (1988) Rls 1,339,970 (U.S.$19,536); sources of urban income (1988): wages 37.4%, self-employment 30.5%, other 32.1%; expenditure (1990–91): food, beverages, and tobacco 42.6%[11], housing and energy 24.9%, clothing 11.8%, household furnishings 6.4%.
Land use (1994): forest 7.0%; pasture 26.9%; agriculture 11.1%; other 55.0%.

Foreign trade

Balance of trade (current prices)

	1994–95	1995–96	1996–97	1997–98	1998–99	1999–2000
U.S.$'000,000	+7,633	+5,586	+7,910	+4,258	–1,168	+6,215
% of total	24.4%	17.9%	21.5%	13.1%	4.3%	18.7%

Imports (1998–99): U.S.$14,286,000,000 (nonelectrical machinery 24.4%, electrical machinery 10.6%, iron and steel 9.0%, transportation equipment 9.3%, grains and derivatives 6.1%). *Major import sources:* Germany 11.6%; Italy 8.3%; Japan 7.0%; Belgium 6.3%; U.A.E. 5.3%; Argentina 4.4%.
Exports (1998–99): U.S.$13,118,000,000 (petroleum and natural gas 75.7%, fruit 4.5%, carpets 4.3%, iron and steel 1.1%). *Major export destinations:* U.K. 16.8%; Japan 15.7%; Italy 8.6%; U.A.E. 6.7%; South Korea 5.0%; Greece 5.0%; Turkey 3.8%.

Transport and communications

Transport. Railroads (1999): route length 3,915 mi, 6,300 km; passenger-km 6,103,000,000[12]; metric ton-km cargo 14,400,000,000[12]. Roads (1997): length 102,976 mi, 165,724 km (paved 50%). Vehicles (1996): passenger cars 1,793,000; trucks and buses 692,000. Air transport (2000)[13]: passenger-km 6,228,670,000; metric ton-km cargo 72,150,000; airports (1996) with scheduled flights 19.

Communications

Medium	date	unit	number	units per 1,000 persons
Daily newspapers	1996	circulation	1,651,000	28
Radio	1997	receivers	17,000,000	280
Television	1999	receivers	10,500,000	157
Telephones	1999	main lines	8,371,000	125
Cellular telephones	1999	subscribers	490,478	7.3
Personal computers	1999	units	3,500,000	52
Internet	1999	users	100,000	1.5

Education and health

Educational attainment (1986). Percentage of population age 25 and over having: no formal schooling 12.8%; secondary education 38.0%; higher 7.8%.
Literacy (1997): total population age 15 and over literate 73.4%; males literate 79.7%; females literate 65.9%.

Education (1997–98)

	schools	teachers	students	student/ teacher ratio
Primary (age 7–11)	63,101[14]	298,755[14]	8,938,000	30.9[14]
Secondary (age 12–18)[15]	...	280,309	8,776,792	31.3
Higher	...	40,477[14, 16]	1,284,658	...

Health (1998–99): physicians 60,000 (1 per 1,033 persons); hospital beds 98,669 (1 per 628 persons); infant mortality rate (2000) 30.0.
Food (1999): daily per capita caloric intake 2,898 (vegetable products 91%, animal products 9%); 120% of FAO recommended minimum requirement.

Military

Total active duty personnel (2000): 513,000 (revolutionary guard corps 24.4%, army 63.4%, navy 3.5%, air force 8.7%). *Military expenditure as percentage of GNP* (1997): 3.0% (world 2.6%); per capita expenditure U.S.$78.

[1]Not required to be a supreme theological authority. [2]Official floating rate. [3]Detail does not add to total given because of rounding. [4]De jure estimate. [5]Excludes roughly 2,000,000 Afghan refugees and less than 400,000 Iraqi refugees in mid-2001. [6]Projected rates based on about 20% of total deaths. [7]At factor cost. [8]Less imputed bank service charge. [9]Includes 1,455,000 unemployed. [10]Construction sector only. [11]Includes café and hotel expenditures. [12]1997. [13]Iran Air. [14]1996–97. [15]Includes vocational and teacher training. [16]Excludes private universities.

Internet resources for further information:

- **Embassy of the Islamic Republic of Iran (London) http://www.iran-embassy.org.uk**
- **Statistical Centre of Iran http://www.sci.or.ir**

Iraq

Official name: Al-Jumhūrīyah al-ʿIrāqīyah (Republic of Iraq).
Form of government: unitary multiparty[1] republic with one legislative house (National Assembly [220[2]]).
Head of state and government: President.
Capital: Baghdad.
Official language: Arabic[3].
Official religion: Islam.
Monetary unit: 1 Iraqi dinar (ID) = 20 dirhams = 1,000 fils; valuation (Sept. 28, 2001) 1 ID = U.S.$3.22 = £2.17.

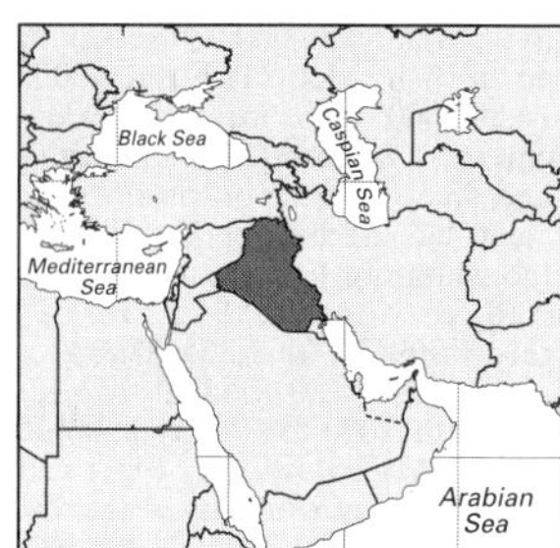

Area and population		area[4]		population
				1991
Governorates	Capitals	sq mi	sq km	estimate
Al-Anbār	Ar-Ramādī	53,208	137,808	865,500
Bābil	Al-Ḥillah	2,163	5,603	1,221,100
Baghdād	Baghdad	1,572	4,071	3,910,900
Al-Baṣrah[4]	Basra	7,363	19,070	1,168,800
Dhī Qār	An-Nāṣirīyah	4,981	12,900	1,030,900
Diyālā	Baʿqūbah	6,828	17,685	1,037,600
Karbalāʾ	Karbalāʾ	1,944	5,034	567,600
Maysān	Al-ʿAmārah	6,205	16,072	524,200
Al-Muthannā	As-Samāwah	19,977	51,740	350,000
An-Najaf	An-Najaf	11,129	28,824	666,400
Nīnawā	Mosul	14,410	37,323	1,618,700
Al-Qādisiyah	Ad-Dīwānīyah	3,148	8,153	595,600
Ṣalāḥ ad-Dīn	Tikrīt	9,407	24,363	772,200
At-Taʾmīm	Karkūk (Kirkūk)	3,737	9,679	605,900
Wāsiṭ	Al-kūt	6,623	17,153	605,700
Kurdish Autonomous Region[5]				
Dahūk	Dahūk	2,530	6,553	309,300
Irbīl	Irbīl	5,820	15,074	928,400
As-Sulaymānīyah	As-Sulaymānīyah	6,573	17,023	1,124,200
LAND AREA		167,618	434,128	
OTHER[6]		357	924	
TOTAL		167,975	435,052	17,903,000

Demography

Population (2001): 23,332,000.
Density (2001): persons per sq mi 138.9, persons per sq km 53.6.
Urban-rural (1999): urban 76.4%; rural 23.6%.
Sex distribution (2001): male 50.57%; female 49.43%.
Age breakdown (2000): under 15, 42.1%; 15–29, 30.4%; 30–44, 15.6%; 45–59, 7.4%; 60–74, 3.5%; 75 and over, 1.0%.
Population projection: (2010) 29,672,000; (2020) 36,908,000.
Doubling time: 25 years.
Ethnic composition (2000): Arab 64.7%; Kurd 23.0%; Azerbaijani 5.6%; Turkmen 1.2%; Persian 1.1%; other 4.4%.
Religious affiliation (2000): Shīʿī Muslim 62.0%; Sunnī Muslim 34.0%; Christian (primarily Chaldean rite and Syrian rite Roman Catholic and Nestorian) 3.2%; other (primarily Yazīdī syncretist) 0.8%.
Major cities (1987): Baghdad (1999; urban agglomeration) 4,689,000; Mosul 664,221; Irbīl 485,968; Karkūk (Kirkūk) 418,624; Al-Baṣrah 406,296.

Vital statistics

Birth rate per 1,000 population (2001): 34.6 (world avg. 22.5).
Death rate per 1,000 population (2001): 6.2 (world avg. 9.0).
Natural increase rate per 1,000 population (2001): 28.4 (world avg. 13.5).
Total fertility rate (avg. births per childbearing woman; 2001): 4.8.
Marriage rate per 1,000 population (1992): 7.8.
Life expectancy at birth (2001): male 65.9 years; female 68.0 years.
Major causes of death. Prior to the Gulf War (1990) the leading causes (in descending order) were: circulatory diseases, injury and poisoning, cancer, and congenital anomalies; since 1990, additional mortality has been attributed to deprivation of medical care and malnutrition consequent upon the imposition of UN sanctions, especially among children and other vulnerable populations.

National economy

Budget (1992). Revenue: ID 13,935,000,000. Expenditures: ID 13,935,000,000. Details of more recent budgets are not available.
Production (metric tons except as noted). Agriculture, forestry, fishing (2000): dates 540,000, wheat 384,000, watermelons 380,000, tomatoes 300,000, oranges 270,000, grapes 270,000, barley 226,000, cantaloupes 195,000, potatoes 150,000, rice 130,000, cucumbers 125,000; livestock (number of live animals) 6,100,000 sheep, 1,150,000 cattle; roundwood (2000) 177,000 cu m; fish catch (1999) 26,789. Mining and quarrying (1995): sulfur 475,000; phosphate rock 440,000. Manufacturing (value added in U.S.$'000,000; 1994): refined petroleum 127; bricks, tiles, and cement 100; industrial chemicals 79; food products 59; metal products 28. Construction (authorized; 1991): residential 4,558,000 sq m; nonresidential 410,000 sq m. Energy production (consumption): electricity (kW-hr; 1997) 29,950,000,000 (29,950,000,000); coal, none (none); crude petroleum (barrels; 1997) 419,584,000 (214,678,000); petroleum products (metric tons; 1997) 23,730,000 (21,531,000); natural gas (cu m; 1997) 3,620,000,000 (3,620,000,000).
Household income and expenditure (1988). Average household size 8.9; sources of income: self-employment 33.9%, wages and salaries 23.9%, transfers 23.0%, rent 18.6%; expenditure: food and beverages 50.2%, housing and energy 19.9%, clothing and footwear 10.6%.
Gross domestic product (1999): U.S.$19,000,000,000 (U.S.$850 per capita).

Structure of gross domestic product and labour force	1995		1988	
	in value ID '000,000[7]	% of total value	labour force	% of labour force
Agriculture	1,255,760	47.2	477,264	11.6
Mining	−2,090	−0.1	60,701	1.5
Manufacturing	19,077	0.7	337,293	8.2
Construction	11,913	0.4	460,788	11.2
Public utilities	1,498	0.1	41,200	1.0
Transp. and commun.	514,105	19.3	266,233	6.4
Trade	712,987	26.8	281,877	6.8
Finance, real estate	79,686	3.0	41,532	1.0
Pub. admin., defense	59,050	2.2		
Services	37,110	1.5	2,160,406	52.3
Other	−30,399[8]	−1.1[8]		
TOTAL	2,658,697	100.0	4,127,294	100.0

Public debt (external, outstanding; 1999): U.S.$23,000,000,000.
Population economically active (1988): total 4,127,294; activity rate of total population 24.7% (participation rates: ages 15–64, 45.3%; female 12.0%).

Price index (1995 = 100)	1990	1991	1992	1993	1994	1995	1996
Consumer price index	0.2	0.6	1.7[9]	5.2[9]	20[9]	100[9]	550[9]

Tourism (1995): receipts U.S.$13,000,000; expenditures, n.a.
Land use (1994): forest 0.4%; pasture 9.1%; agriculture 13.1%; other 77.4%.

Foreign trade[10, 11]

Balance of trade (current prices)[9]	1990	1991	1992	1993	1994	1995
U.S.$'000,000	+5,587	−1,633	−2,199	−1,956	−1,518	−2,081
% of total	36.6%	66.3%	73.3%	68.8%	66.5%	71.3%

Imports (1995): U.S.$2,500,000,000[9] (agricultural products 42.7%, of which cereals 9.9%; unspecified 57.3%). *Major import sources* (1996)[12]: Turkey 36.5%; Jordan 26.3%; Malaysia 3.7%; Australia 3.0%.
Exports (1995): U.S.$419,000,000[9] (mostly crude petroleum and petroleum products). *Major export destinations* (1996): Jordan 91.5%; Turkey 5.8%.

Transport and communications

Transport. Railroads (1997): route length 2,032 km; passenger-km 1,169,000,000; metric ton-km cargo 956,000,000. Roads (1999): total length 45,550 km (paved 84%). Vehicles (1996): passenger cars 772,986; trucks and buses 323,906. Air transport: [13].

Communications				units per 1,000
Medium	date	unit	number	persons
Daily newspapers	1996	circulation	407,000	20
Radio	1997	receivers	4,850,000	229
Television	1997	receivers	1,750,000	78
Telephones	1999	main lines	675,000	30

Education and health

Educational attainment (1987). Percentage of population age 10 and over having: no formal schooling 52.8%; primary education 21.5%; secondary 11.6%; higher 4.1%; unknown 10.0%. *Literacy* (1995): total population age 15 and over literate 58.0%; males 70.7%; females 45.0%.

Education (1995–96)	schools	teachers	students	student/ teacher ratio
Primary (age 6–11)	8,145	145,455	2,903,923	20.0
Secondary (age 12–17)	2,635[14]	52,393	1,037,482	19.8
Voc., teacher tr.	310[14]	9,903	122,939	12.4
Higher[14]	12	11,847	201,984	17.0

Health (1993): physicians 8,787 (1 per 2,181 persons); hospital beds 27,202 (1 per 704 persons); infant mortality rate per 1,000 live births (2001) 60.0.
Food (1999): daily per capita caloric intake 2,446 (vegetable products 96%, animal products 4%); 101% of FAO recommended minimum requirement.

Military

Total active duty personnel (2000): 429,000 (army 91.3%, navy 0.5%, air force 8.2%). *Military expenditure as percentage of GDP* (1997): 4.9% (world 2.6%); per capita expenditure U.S.$59.

[1]Multipartyism is officially authorized, but political power is in fact concentrated in a single-party apparatus. [2]Elective seats as of March 2000 elections; 30 additional seats allotted to the Kurdish Autonomous Region were filled by presidential appointment. [3]Kurdish is official in the Kurdish Autonomous Region only. [4]Includes territory ceded to Kuwait as of Jan. 15, 1993. [5]De facto self-government from 1992 through September 2001. [6]Territorial water at the mouth of the Shaṭṭ al-ʿArab. [7]At factor cost. [8]Imputed bank service charge. [9]Estimated figure(s). [10]Imports c.i.f.; exports f.o.b. [11]UN-imposed trade sanctions in place from August 1990 through September 2001. [12]Based on estimated imports equaling U.S.$1,513,000,000. [13]Scheduled domestic and limited international air service resumed in 2000 and 2001, respectively. [14]1994–95.

Internet resources for further information:
- **Permanent Mission of Iraq to the United Nations (official site) http://www.undp.org/missions/iraq**
- **Iraq Foundation (unofficial) http://www.iraqfoundation.org**

Ireland

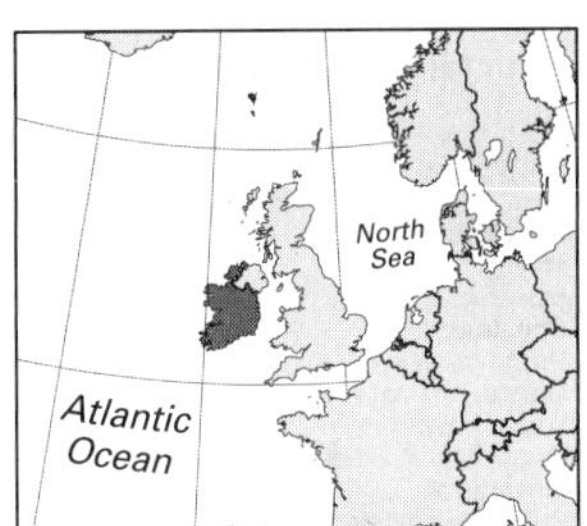

Official name: Éire (Irish); Ireland[1] (English).
Form of government: unitary multiparty republic with two legislative houses (Senate [60[2]]; House of Representatives [166]).
Chief of state: President.
Head of government: Prime Minister.
Capital: Dublin.
Official languages: Irish; English.
Official religion: none.
Monetary unit: 1 Irish pound (£Ir) = 100 new pence; valuation (Sept. 28, 2001) 1 £Ir = U.S.$1.16 = £0.78; 1 £Ir = € 1.269738.

Area and population

Provinces Counties/County Boroughs (C.B.)	area sq km	population 1996 census
Connacht	17,122	433,231
Galway	5,940	131,613
Galway C.B.		57,241
Leitrim	1,525	25,057
Mayo	5,398	111,524
Roscommon	2,463	51,975
Sligo	1,796	55,821
Leinster	19,633	1,924,702
Carlow	896	41,616
Dublin C.B.	[3]	481,854
Dun Laoghaire	[3]	189,999
Fingal	[3]	167,683
Kildare	1,694	134,992
Kilkenny	2,062	75,336
Laoighis	1,719	52,945
Longford	1,044	30,166
Louth	823	92,166
Meath	2,336	109,732
Offaly	1,998	59,117
South Dublin	[3]	218,728
Westmeath	1,763	63,314
Wexford	2,351	104,371

Provinces Counties/County Boroughs (C.B.)	area sq km	population 1996 census
Wicklow	2,025	102,683
Munster	24,127	1,033,903
Clare	3,188	94,006
Cork	7,460	293,323
Cork C.B.		127,187
Kerry	4,701	126,130
Limerick	2,686	113,003
Limerick C.B.		52,039
Tipperary North Riding	1,996	58,021
Tipperary South Riding	2,258	75,514
Waterford	1,838	52,140
Waterford C.B.		42,540
Ulster (part of)	8,012	234,251
Cavan	1,891	52,944
Donegal	4,830	129,994
Monaghan	1,291	51,313
TOTAL LAND AREA	68,895[4]	
INLAND WATER	1,390	
TOTAL	70,285[5]	3,626,087

Demography

Population (2001): 3,823,000.
Density (2001): persons per sq mi 140.9, persons per sq km 54.4.
Urban-rural (1996): urban 58.0%; rural 42.0%.
Sex distribution (2000): male 49.59%; female 50.41%.
Age breakdown (2000): under 15, 21.9%; 15–29, 24.9%; 30–44, 21.1%; 45–59, 16.9%; 60–74, 10.3%; 75 and over, 4.9%.
Population projection: (2010) 4,161,000; (2020) 4,372,000.
Ethnic composition (2000): Irish 95.0%; British 1.7%, of which English 1.4%; Ulster Irish 1.0%; U.S. white 0.8%; other 1.5%.
Religious affiliation (1991): Roman Catholic 91.6%; Church of Ireland (Anglican) 2.5%; Presbyterian 0.4%; other 5.5%.
Major cities (1996)[6]: Dublin 481,854 (urban agglomeration [1999] 977,000); Cork 127,187; Galway 57,241; Limerick 52,039; Waterford 42,540.

Vital statistics

Birth rate per 1,000 population (2000): 14.5 (world avg. 22.5).
Death rate per 1,000 population (2000): 8.1 (world avg. 9.0).
Natural increase rate per 1,000 population (2000): 6.4 (world avg. 13.5).
Marriage rate per 1,000 population (1999): 4.9.
Total fertility rate (avg. births per childbearing woman; 2000): 1.9.
Life expectancy at birth (2000): male 74.1 years; female 79.7 years.
Major causes of death per 100,000 population (1998): heart and circulatory diseases 364.4, of which ischemic heart diseases 199.3; malignant neoplasms (cancers) 206.9; respiratory disease 131.8, of which pneumonia 62.0.

National economy

Budget (2000). Revenue: £Ir 21,741,000,000 (income taxes 33.0%, value-added tax 27.0%, excise taxes 15.4%). Expenditures: £Ir 19,297,000,000 (social welfare 27.9%, health 20.9%, education 14.9%, debt service 10.5%).
Public debt (1996): U.S.$47,876,000,000.
Gross national product (1999): U.S.$80,559,000,000 (U.S.$21,470 per capita).

Structure of gross domestic product and labour force

	2000			
	in value £Ir '000,000[7]	% of total value[7]	labour force	% of labour force
Agriculture	2,872	4.0	130,900	7.5
Mining, Manufacturing, Public utilities, Construction	30,781	42.8		
Mining, Manufacturing			309,900	17.7
Public utilities				
Construction			166,300	9.5
Transp. and commun.	11,803	16.4	100,800	5.8
Trade			362,800	20.8
Pub. admin., defense	2,460	3.4	77,800	4.5
Services	24,612	34.2	310,100	17.8
Finance			212,100	12.2
Other	–626[8]	–0.9[8]	74,900[9]	4.3[9]
TOTAL	71,912[4]	100.0[4]	1,745,600	100.0[4]

Tourism (1999): receipts U.S.$3,392,000,000; expenditures U.S.$2,620,000,000.
Production (metric tons except as noted). Agriculture, forestry, fishing (2000): sugar beets 1,564,000, barley 1,129,000, wheat 706,000, potatoes 381,000, oats 128,000, milk (1995) 51,900,000 hectolitres; livestock (number of live animals) 8,393,000 sheep, 6,607,500 cattle, 1,763,000 pigs; roundwood (2000) 2,673,000 cu m; fish catch (1999) 329,777. Mining and quarrying (1999): gypsum 480,000; zinc ore 199,300[10]; lead ore 44,100[10]. Manufacturing (value added in £Ir '000,000; 1995): office equipment and computers 2,163; basic chemicals 2,112; reproduction of recorded media 1,531; pharmaceuticals 884; alcoholic beverages 735. Construction (1998): residential 6,098,000 sq m; nonresidential 4,122,000 sq m. Energy production (consumption): electricity (kW-hr; 1997) 19,856,000,000 (19,856,000,000); coal (metric tons; 1997) none (3,070,000); crude petroleum (barrels; 1997) none (20,800,000); petroleum products (metric tons; 1997) 2,795,000 (5,616,000); natural gas (cu m; 1997) 1,012,000,000 (3,242,000,000).
Population economically active (2000): total 1,745,600; activity rate 46.1% (participation rates: ages 15–64, *c.* 68%; female 40.3%; unemployed 4.3%).

Price and earnings indexes (1995 = 100)

	1994	1995	1996	1997	1998	1999	2000
Consumer price index	97.5	100.0	101.7	103.2	105.7	107.4	110.7
Weekly earnings index	97.8	100.0	102.5	105.4	110.2	...	...

Household income and expenditure. Average household size (1997) 3.1; income per household (1994–95): £Ir 16,224 (U.S.$25,100); expenditure (1996)[11]: food and beverages 35.4%, transportation 13.9%, rent/household goods 11.6%.

Foreign trade[12]

Balance of trade (current prices)

	1993	1994	1995	1996	1997	1998	1999
£Ir '000,000	+4,945	+5,470	+7,206	+7,978	+9,454	+13,939	+17,855
% of total	14.2%	13.7%	14.9%	15.1%	15.4%	18.2%	20.5%

Imports (1999): £Ir 34,682,100,000 (machinery and transport equipment 51.5%, chemicals 11.2%, manufactured goods 11.0%, food 5.8%, petroleum and petroleum products 2.8%). *Major import sources:* U.K. 33.1%; U.S. 16.7%; Germany 6.2%; Japan 5.8%; France 4.1%.
Exports (1999): £Ir 52,537,200,000 (machinery and transport equipment 38.8%, chemical products 31.6%, manufactured goods 11.1%, food 8.2%). *Major export destinations:* U.K. 22.0%; U.S. 15.4%; Germany 11.9%; France 8.4%; The Netherlands 6.0%.

Transport and communications

Transport. Railroads (1999): route length 1,945 km; passenger-km 1,295,000,000; metric ton-km cargo 570,000,000. Roads (1999): length 92,500 km (paved 94%). Vehicles (2000): passenger cars 1,269,245; trucks and buses 188,814. Air transport (1998)[13]: passenger-km 6,466,383,000; metric ton-km cargo 129,648,000; airports (1996) 9.

Communications

Medium	date	unit	number	units per 1,000 persons
Daily newspapers	1996	circulation	543,000	150
Radio	1998	receivers	2,150,000	580
Television	1999	receivers	2,144,000	578
Telephones	1999	main lines	1,770,000	477
Cellular telephones	1999	subscribers	1,655,000	446
Personal computers	1999	units	1,500,000	404
Internet	1999	users	679,000	183

Education and health

Educational attainment (1991). Percentage of population age 15 and over having: primary education or no schooling 33.7%; secondary 42.7%; some postsecondary 12.6%; university or like institution 11.0%.

Education (1998–99)

	schools	teachers	students	student/teacher ratio
Primary (age 6–11)[14]	3,303	21,500	452,533	21.0
Secondary (age 12–18)	432	12,180	211,369	17.4
Voc., teacher tr.	330	8,640	151,136	17.5
Higher	24	5,644	107,213	19.0

Health: physicians (1998) 8,114 (1 per 457 persons); hospital beds (1995) 11,953[15] (1 per 301 persons); infant mortality rate (2000) 5.6.
Food (1999): daily per capita caloric intake 3,649 (vegetable products 67%, animal products 33%); 145% of FAO recommended minimum requirement.

Military

Total active duty personnel (2000): 11,460 (army 81.2%, navy 9.6%, air force 9.2%). *Military expenditure as percentage of GNP* (1997): 1.2% (world 2.6%); per capita expenditure U.S.$203.

[1]As provided by the constitution; the 1948 Republic of Ireland Act provides precedent for this longer formulation of the official name but, per official sources, "has not changed the usage *Ireland* as the name of the state in the English language." [2]Includes 11 nonelective seats. [3]Dublin C.B. includes Dun Laoghaire, Fingal, and South Dublin. [4]Detail does not add to total given because of rounding. [5]Area per more recent survey is 70,273 sq km. [6]Populations for Ireland's five administrative county boroughs. [7]At factor cost. [8]Statistical discrepancy. [9]Unemployed. [10]Metal content of ores. [11]November. [12]Imports c.i.f.; exports f.o.b. [13]Aer Lingus only. [14]National schools only. [15]Acute-care public hospitals only.

Internet resources for further information:

- **Central Statistics Office (Ireland) http://www.cso.ie**
- **Central Bank of Ireland http://www.centralbank.ie**

Isle of Man

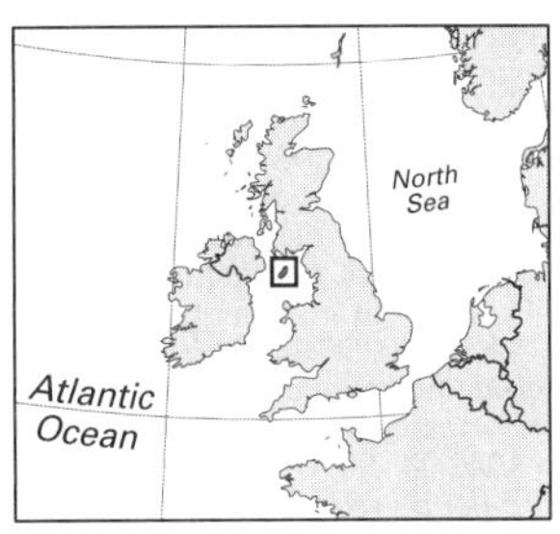

Official name: Isle of Man[1].
Political status: crown dependency (United Kingdom) with two legislative bodies[2] (Legislative Council [11[3]]; House of Keys [24]).
Chief of state: British Monarch represented by Lieutenant-Governor.
Head of government: Chief Minister assisted by the Council of Ministers.
Capital: Douglas.
Official language: English.
Official religion: none.
Monetary unit: 1 Manx pound (£M)[4] = 100 new pence; valuation (Sept. 28, 2001) 1 £M = U.S.$1.47.

Area and population

	area sq km	population 1996 census		area sq km	population 1996 census
Towns			**Parishes** (cont.)		
Castletown	0.4	2,958	Ballaugh	24.6	812
Douglas	6.7	23,487	Braddan	45.1	2,527
Peel	1.3	3,819	Bride	23.5	405
Ramsey	1.2	6,874	German	46.1	1,038
			Jurby	19.1	624
Villages			Lezayre	65.3	1,047
Laxey	5	1,433	Lonan	38.1[5]	1,292
Onchan	26.4	8,656	Malew	51.7	2,140
Port Erin	2.6	3,218	Marown	26.6	1,564
Port St. Mary	1.4	1,874	Maughold	36.2	858
			Michael	35.5	1,261
Parishes			Patrick	42.9	1,198
Andreas	31.9	1,144	Rushen	26.2	1,441
Arbory	18.1	1,622	Santon	17.2	422
			TOTAL	588.1	71,714

Demography

Population (2001): 73,500.
Density (2001): persons per sq mi 323.6, persons per sq km 125.0.
Urban-rural (1999): urban 76.3%; rural 23.7%.
Sex distribution (1996): male 48.52%; female 51.48%.
Age breakdown (1996): under 15, 17.6%; 15–29, 19.0%; 30–44, 20.6%; 45–59, 19.5%; 60–74, 14.4%; 75 and over, 8.9%.
Population projection: (2010) 77,000; (2020) 80,000.
Population by place of birth (1996): Isle of Man 49.9%; United Kingdom 44.1%, of which England 37.5%, Scotland 3.3%, Northern Ireland 2.1%; Ireland 2.4%.
Religious affiliation (2000): Christian 63.7%, of which Anglican 40.5%, Methodist 9.9%, Roman Catholic 8.2%; other (mostly nonreligious) 36.3%.
Major towns (1996): Douglas 23,487; Onchan 8,656; Ramsey 6,874; Peel 3,819; Port Erin 3,218.

Vital statistics

Birth rate per 1,000 population (1999): 12.3 (world avg. 22.5); legitimate 68.1%; illegitimate 31.9%.
Death rate per 1,000 population (1999): 13.5 (world avg. 9.0).
Natural increase rate per 1,000 population (1999): –1.2 (world avg. 13.5).
Total fertility rate (avg. births per childbearing woman; 1999): 1.6.
Marriage rate per 1,000 population (1999): 5.5.
Divorce rate per 1,000 population (1996): 4.0.
Life expectancy at birth (1999): male 73.9 years; female 80.8 years.
Major causes of death per 100,000 population (1998): diseases of the circulatory system 504.3, of which ischemic heart diseases 247.3, cerebrovascular disease 96.7; neoplasms (cancers) 298.4; diseases of the respiratory system 225.2.

National economy

Budget (1997–98). Revenue: £265,716,000 (customs duties and excise taxes 51.7%; income taxes 43.7%, of which resident 34.6%, nonresident 9.1%; interest on investments 4.2%). Expenditures: £240,140,000 (health and social security 42.2%; education 19.2%; transportation 6.4%; home affairs 6.3%; tourism and recreation 5.4%).
Public debt: n.a.
Production. Agriculture, forestry, fishing (1998): main crops include hay, oats, barley, wheat, and orchard crops; livestock (number of live animals) 173,900 sheep, 34,000 cattle, 6,600 pigs; roundwood n.a.; fish catch (value of catch in £ sterling; 1997): scallops 1,666,000; whitefish 244,000; herring 138,000. Mining and quarrying: sand and gravel. Manufacturing (value added in U.S.$; 1996–97): electrical and nonelectrical machinery/apparatus, textiles, other 103,700,000; food and beverages 18,600,000. Energy production (consumption): electricity (kW-hr; 1997–98) n.a. (275,400,000); crude petroleum, none (n.a.); petroleum products, n.a. (n.a.); natural gas, none (n.a.).
Household income and expenditure. Average household size (1996) 2.4; income per household (1981–82)[6, 7]: £7,479 (U.S.$13,721); sources of income (1981–82)[6, 7]: wages and salaries 64.1%, transfer payments 16.9%, interest and dividends 11.2%, self-employment 6.6%; expenditure (1981–82)[6, 7]: food and beverages 31.0%, transportation 14.9%, energy 11.0%, housing 7.9%, clothing and footwear 7.0%.
Gross national product (at current market prices; 1997–98): U.S.$1,282,000,000 (U.S.$17,730 per capita).

Structure of gross domestic product and labour force

	1997–98		1996	
	in value £ '000[8]	% of total value[8]	labour force	% of labour force
Agriculture, fishing	10,726	1.5	938	2.7
Mining Manufacturing	80,981	11.2	3,562	10.2
Construction	44,587	6.2	3,372	9.7
Public utilities	15,062	2.1	462	1.3
Transp. and commun.	63,198	8.8	2,688	7.7
Trade, hotels	69,109	9.6	4,457	12.8
Finance, real estate, insurance	320,414[9]	44.5[9]	5,941	17.1
Pub. admin., defense	40,850	5.7	2,147	6.2
Services	167,826[9]	23.3[9]	10,005	28.7
Other	–93,071	–12.9	1,239[10]	3.6[10]
TOTAL	719,682	100.0	34,811	100.0

Population economically active (1996): total 34,811; activity rate of total population 48.5% (participation rates: ages 16 and over 59.8%; female 44.0%; unemployed 3.5%).

Price and earnings indexes (1995 = 100)

	1993	1994	1995	1996	1997	1998
Retail price index	94.6	97.2	100.0	102.9	105.2	108.3
Weekly earnings index[11]	92.7	95.0	100.0	102.9	110.0	115.0

Tourism: receipts from visitors (1997–98) U.S.$68,000,000; expenditures by nationals abroad, n.a.
Land use: n.a.

Foreign trade

Imports (1998): n.a. *Major import sources* (1998): mostly the United Kingdom.
Exports (1998): traditional exports include scallops, herring, beef, lambs, and tweeds. *Major export destinations* (1998): mostly the United Kingdom.

Transport and communications

Transport. Railroads (1998): route length 32 mi, 52 km[12]. Roads (1998): total length, more than 500 mi, more than 805 km (paved, n.a.). Vehicles (1998): passenger cars 40,168; trucks and buses, n.a. Merchant marine (1999): vessels (100 gross tons and over) 219; total deadweight tonnage, n.a. Air transport (1998)[13]: passenger-mi 526,161,000, passenger-km 846,775,000; short ton-mi cargo 115,000, metric ton-km cargo 168,000; airports (1999) with scheduled flights 1.

Communications

Medium	date	unit	number	units per 1,000 persons
Daily newspapers	1997	circulation	—[14]	—
Television	1997	receivers	27,000	375
Telephones	1996	main lines	46,000	641

Education and health

Educational attainment: n.a. *Literacy:* n.a.

Education (1998–99)

	schools	teachers	students	student/ teacher ratio
Primary (age 5–10)	33	...	6,210	...
Secondary (age 11–16)	5	...	4,732	...
Higher[15]	1	...	1,128[16]	...

Health (1998): physicians 117 (1 per 619 persons); hospital beds 505 (1 per 143 persons); infant mortality rate per 1,000 live births (1997–99 avg.) 3.7.
Food (1998)[17]: daily per capita caloric intake 3,257 (vegetable products 68%, animal products 32%); 129% of FAO recommended minimum requirement.

Military

Total active duty personnel: [18].

[1]Ellan Vannin in Manx Gaelic. [2]Collective name is Tynwald. [3]Includes 3 nonelected seats. [4]Equivalent in value to pound sterling (£). [5]Lonan includes Laxey. [6]Fiscal year ending March 31st. [7]Based on survey of 259 households; "high income" and "pensioner" households are excluded. [8]At factor cost. [9]Most GDP in 1999 was derived from 66 banks (most of which are "offshore"), 77 investment businesses, and 193 insurance companies. [10]Includes 5 not adequately defined and 1,234 unemployed. [11]June only. [12]Length of three tourist (novel) railways operating in summer. [13]Manx Airlines. [14]Isle of Man has 2 weekly newspapers and 1 biweekly newspaper. [15]1997–98. [16]Includes enrollees at Isle of Man College and students abroad. [17]Data for United Kingdom. [18]The United Kingdom is responsible for defense.

Internet resources for further information:
- **Isle of Man Government**
http://www.gov.im

Israel

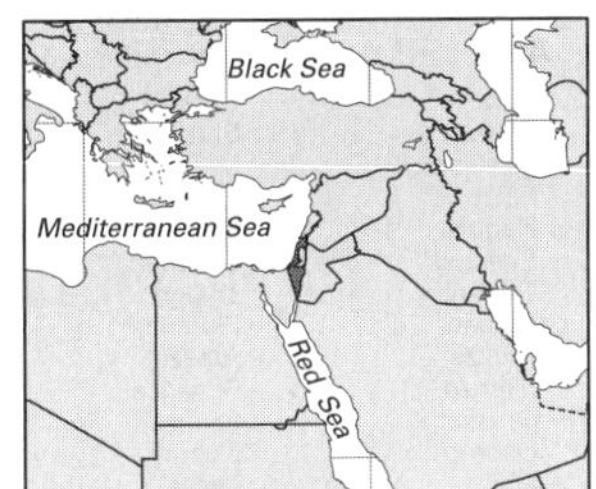

Official name: Medinat Yisra'el (Hebrew); Isrā'īl (Arabic) (State of Israel).
Form of government: multiparty republic with one legislative house (Knesset [120]).
Chief of state: President.
Head of government: Prime Minister.
Capital: Jerusalem is the proclaimed capital of Israel and the actual seat of government, but recognition of its status as capital by the international community has largely been withheld pending final settlement of territorial and other issues through peace talks between Israel and the Arab parties concerned.
Official languages: Hebrew; Arabic.
Official religion: none.
Monetary unit: 1 New (Israeli) sheqel (NIS) = 100 agorot; valuation (Sept. 28, 2001) 1 U.S.$ = NIS 4.36; 1 £ = NIS 6.40.

Area and population

Districts	Capitals	area[1] sq mi	area[1] sq km	population 2001[2] estimate
Central (Ha Merkaz)	Ramla	493	1,276	1,457,500
Haifa (Hefa)	Haifa	333	863	818,500
Jerusalem (Yerushalayim)	Jerusalem	225	582	758,300
Northern (Ha Zafon)	Tiberias	1,275	3,302	1,083,300
Southern (Ha Darom)	Beersheba	5,494	14,231	899,400
Tel Aviv	Tel Aviv–Yafo	66	171	1,153,800
TOTAL		7,886	20,425	6,170,800[3]

Demography

Population (2001): 6,258,000.
Density (2001)[3]: persons per sq mi 793.6, persons per sq km 306.4.
Urban-rural (2000): urban 90.6%; rural 9.4%.
Sex distribution (2000): male 49.33%; female 50.67%.
Age breakdown (2000): under 15, 28.6%; 15–29, 25.1%; 30–44, 18.7%; 45–59, 14.5%; 60–74, 8.8%; 75 and over, 4.3%.
Population projection: (2010) 7,003,000, (2020) 7,710,000.
Ethnic composition (2000): Jewish 78.1%; Arab and other 21.9%.
Religious affiliation (2000): Jewish 78.1%; Muslim (mostly Sunnī) 15.1%; Christian 2.1%; Druze 1.6%; other 3.1%.
Major cities (2001[2]): Jerusalem 657,500; Tel Aviv–Yafo 354,400; Haifa 270,500; Rishon LeZiyyon 202,200; Petah Tiqwa 167,500; Holon 165,700.

Vital statistics

Birth rate per 1,000 population (2000): 21.7 (world avg. 22.5); (1994)[4] legitimate 98.2%; illegitimate 1.8%.
Death rate per 1,000 population (2000): 6.0 (world avg. 9.0).
Natural increase rate per 1,000 population (2000): 15.7 (world avg. 13.5).
Total fertility rate (avg. births per childbearing woman; 2000): 3.0.
Marriage rate per 1,000 population (1999): 6.6.
Divorce rate per 1,000 population (1999): 1.7.
Life expectancy at birth (2000): male 76.6 years; female 80.4 years.
Major causes of death per 100,000 population (1997): diseases of the circulatory system 210; malignant neoplasms (cancers) 140; diabetes mellitus 42; accidents and violence 20; diseases of the respiratory system 19.

National economy

Budget (2000). Revenue: NIS 178,037,000,000 (tax revenue 74.6%, of which income tax and property tax 34.7%, value-added tax 26.0%, sales tax and fuel tax 4.7%; nontax revenue 18.5%; grants 6.9%). Expenditures: NIS 188,927,000,000 (defense 20.7%; education 14.8%; interest on loans 13.9%; labour and welfare 12.1%; health 8.5%).
Public debt (external, outstanding; 1999): U.S.$27,323,000,000.
Gross national product (1999): U.S.$99,574,000,000 (U.S.$16,310 per capita).

Structure of net domestic product and labour force

	1999 in value NIS '000,000[5]	1999 % of total value[5]	2000 labour force	2000 % of labour force
Agriculture	4,419	2.3	47,900	2.0
Manufacturing, mining	35,501	18.6	396,600	16.3
Construction	16,401	8.6	116,400	4.8
Public utilities	3,299	1.7	19,300	0.8
Transp. and commun.	13,122	6.9	144,900	6.0
Trade	21,526	11.2	295,600	12.1
Finance	51,754[6]	27.1[6]	433,700[6]	17.8[6]
Public and community services	48,297[7]	25.3[7]	712,100[7]	29.2[7]
Services	8,403[8]	4.4[8]	34,700[8]	1.4[8]
Other	–11,690[9]	–6.1[9]	233,800[10]	9.6[10]
TOTAL	191,032	100.0	2,435,000	100.0

Production (metric tons except as noted). Agriculture, forestry, fishing (2000): tomatoes 550,200, grapefruit 370,000, potatoes 348,600, oranges 300,000, seed cotton 112,000, corn (maize) 82,160, apples 81,500; livestock (number of live animals) 388,000 cattle, 350,000 sheep; roundwood (2000) 113,000 cu m; fish catch (1999) 24,661. Mining and quarrying (1999): phosphate rock 4,100,000, potash 1,750,000. Manufacturing (1996): cement 6,723,000; polyethylene 144,147[11]; sulfuric acid 130,000[11]; paper 114,403; cardboard 113,278; chlorine 34,630; wine 12,733,000 litres[11]. Construction (2000): residential 7,101,000 sq m; nonresidential 2,354,000 sq m. Energy production (consumption): electricity (kW-hr; 2000) 42,916,000 (39,317,000); coal (metric tons; 1996) none (7,808,000); crude petroleum (barrels; 1996) 29,000 (77,000,000); petroleum products (metric tons; 1996) 9,963,000 (9,579,000); natural gas (cu m; 1996) 13,143,000 (13,143,000).
Population economically active (2000)[12]: total 2,435,000; activity rate 39.9% (participation rates: over ages 15, 54.3%; female 45.6%; unemployed 8.8%).

Price and earnings indexes (1995 = 100)

	1994	1995	1996	1997	1998	1999	2000
Consumer price index	90.9	100.0	111.3	121.3	127.9	134.5	135.6
Daily earnings index	87.1	100.0	113.9	130.8	143.9	155.4	160.1

Household income and expenditure (1999). Average household size 3.6; monthly income per household[12] (1995) NIS 6,125 (U.S.$2,034); sources of income (1993)[13]: salaries and wages 63.4%, allowances and assistance 18.9%, self-employment 14.6%; expenditure (1998): housing 23.7%, food, beverages, and tobacco 21.1%, household durable goods 8.2%.
Tourism (1999): receipts U.S.$2,974,000,000; expenditures U.S.$2,566,000,000.

Foreign trade

Balance of trade (current prices)

	1995	1996	1997	1998	1999	2000
U.S.$'000,000	–9,527	–9,824	–7,064	–4,736	–6,073	–4,346
% of total	20.3%	19.6%	13.8%	9.3%	10.8%	6.5%

Imports (2000): U.S.$35,749,500,000 (investment goods 21.3%; diamonds 17.0%; consumer goods 12.3%; fuel and lubricants 6.0%). *Major import sources:* U.S. 20.7%; Belgium 11.1%; Germany 8.1%; U.K. 7.6%; Italy 5.3%.
Exports (2000): U.S.$31,403,700,000 (machinery and transport equipment 39.7%; diamonds 23.7%; chemicals 13.4%; apparel 4.9%; food, beverages, and tobacco 3.1%). *Major export destinations:* U.S. 35.5%; U.K. 5.5%; Belgium 5.4%; Germany 4.5%; Hong Kong 3.4%; Japan 3.3%.

Transport and communications

Transport. Railroads (1999): route length 610 km; passenger-km 529,000,000; metric ton-km cargo 1,128,000,000. Roads (1999): total length 15,464 km (paved 100%). Vehicles (2000): passenger cars 1,316,765; trucks and buses 319,581. Air transport (2000)[14]: passenger-km 14,125,067,000; metric ton-km cargo 1,288,345,000; airports (1999) with scheduled flights 7.

Communications

Medium	date	unit	number	units per 1,000 persons
Daily newspapers	1997	circulation	1,650,000	288
Radio	1997	receivers	3,070,000	524
Television	1999	receivers	1,690,000	288
Telephones	1999	main lines	2,877,000	471
Cellular telephones	1999	subscribers	2,880,000	472
Personal computers	1999	units	1,500,000	221
Internet	1999	users	800,000	131

Education and health

Educational attainment (2000). Percentage of population age 15 and over having: no formal schooling 3.3%; primary 1.9%; secondary 57.4%; postsecondary, vocational, and higher 37.4%. *Literacy* (2000): total population age 15 and over literate 96.7%.

Education (2000–01)

	schools	teachers	students	student/ teacher ratio
Primary (age 6–13)	2,137	58,785	559,541	9.5
Secondary (age 14–17)[15]	707	76,915	473,092	6.2
Vocational, teacher tr.	113	...	118,605	...
Higher	7	10,171	219,763	21.6

Health (2000): physicians 21,500 (1 per 284 persons); hospital beds 38,577 (1 per 158 persons); infant mortality rate (2000) 5.1.
Food (1999): daily per capita caloric intake 3,542 (vegetable products 81%, animal products 19%); 138% of FAO recommended minimum.

Military

Total active duty personnel (2000): 172,500 (army 75.4%, navy 3.8%, air force 20.8%). *Military expenditure as percentage of GNP* (1997): 9.7% (world 2.6%); per capita expenditure U.S.$1,698.

[1]Excluding West Bank (2,278 sq mi [5,900 sq km]), Gaza Strip (140 sq mi [363 sq km]), Golan Heights (454 sq mi [1,176 sq km]), East Jerusalem (27 sq mi [70 sq km]), Sea of Galilee (63 sq mi [164 sq km]), and the Dead Sea (120 sq mi [310 sq km]). [2]January 1. [3]Includes 2001 population of Golan Heights (34,800) and East Jerusalem and excludes 2001 Jewish population of the West Bank and Gaza Strip (198,500). [4]Jewish population only. [5]At factor cost; 1999 GDP equals NIS 417,446,000,000. [6]Finance includes other business activities. [7]Public and community services includes education, health, and social services. [8]Services includes private households with domestic personnel. [9]Less imputed bank service charges. [10]Includes 213,800 unemployed. [11]1993. [12]Civilian labour force. [13]Urban population only. [14]El Al only. [15]Includes intermediate schools.

Internet resources for further information:
- **Central Bureau of Statistics (Israel) http://www.cbs.gov.il**

Italy

Official name: Repubblica Italiana (Italian Republic).
Form of government: republic with two legislative houses (Senate [321[1]]; Chamber of Deputies [630]).
Chief of state: President.
Head of government: Prime Minister.
Capital: Rome.
Official language: Italian.
Official religion: none.
Monetary unit: 1 lira (Lit, plural lire) = 100 centesimi; valuation (Sept. 28, 2001) 1 U.S.$ = Lit 2,126; 1 £ = Lit 3,125; 1 € = Lit 1,936.27.

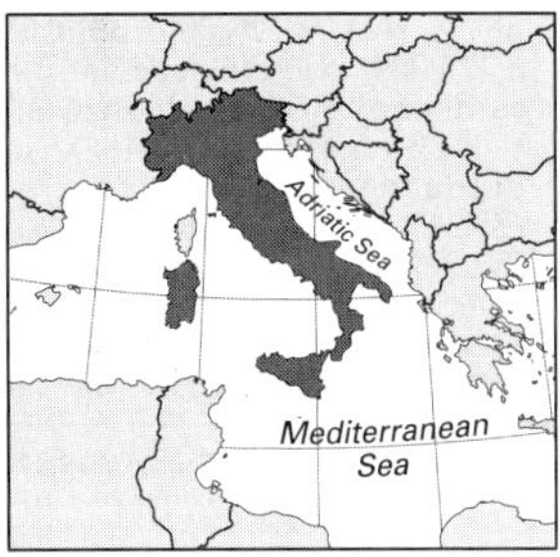

Area and population

Regions Provinces[2]	Capitals	area sq mi	 sq km	population 2000 estimate[3]
Abruzzo	L'Aquila	4,168	10,794	1,279,016
Chieti	Chieti	999	2,587	390,133
L'Aquila	L'Aquila	1,944	5,034	303,839
Pescara	Pescara	473	1,225	294,168
Teramo	Teramo	752	1,948	290,876
Basilicata	Potenza	3,858	9,992	606,183
Matera	Matera	1,331	3,447	206,193
Potenza	Potenza	2,527	6,545	399,990
Calabria	Catanzaro	5,823	15,080	2,050,478
Catanzaro	Catanzaro	924	2,392	381,737
Cosenza	Cosenza	2,568	6,650	745,406
Crotone	Crotone	662	1,716	174,158
Reggio di Calabria	Reggio di Calabria	1,229	3,183	572,546
Vibo Valentia	Vibo Valentia	440	1,139	176,631
Campania	Naples	5,249	13,595	5,780,958
Avellino	Avellino	1,078	2,792	440,482
Benevento	Benevento	800	2,071	293,458
Caserta	Caserta	1,019	2,639	855,693
Napoli	Naples	452	1,171	3,099,366
Salerno	Salerno	1,900	4,922	1,091,959
Emilia-Romagna	Bologna	8,542	22,123	3,981,146
Bologna	Bologna	1,429	3,702	917,110
Ferrara	Ferrara	1,016	2,632	348,705
Forlì-Cesena	Forlì	969	2,510	354,426
Modena	Modena	1,039	2,690	625,766
Parma	Parma	1,332	3,449	397,092
Piacenza	Piacenza	1,000	2,589	266,085
Ravenna	Ravenna	718	1,859	350,646
Reggio nell'Emilia	Reggio nell'Emilia	885	2,292	449,285
Rimini	Rimini	154	400	272,031
Friuli-Venezia Giulia	Trieste	3,029	7,845	1,185,172
Gorizia	Gorizia	180	467	138,305
Pordenone	Pordenone	878	2,273	280,326
Trieste	Trieste	82	212	247,723
Udine	Udine	1,889	4,893	518,818
Lazio	Rome	6,642	17,203	5,264,077
Frosinone	Frosinone	1,251	3,239	494,019
Latina	Latina	869	2,251	510,109
Rieti	Rieti	1,061	2,749	150,587
Roma	Rome	2,066	5,352	3,817,133
Viterbo	Viterbo	1,395	3,612	292,229
Liguria	Genoa	2,092	5,418	1,625,870
Genova	Genoa	709	1,836	907,583
Imperia	Imperia	446	1,155	216,386
La Spezia	La Spezia	341	882	222,140
Savona	Savona	596	1,545	279,761
Lombardia	Milan	9,211	23,857	9,065,440
Bergamo	Bergamo	1,051	2,722	965,133
Brescia	Brescia	1,846	4,782	1,098,481
Como	Como	497	1,288	539,472
Cremona	Cremona	684	1,771	334,317
Lecco	Lecco	315	816	309,484
Lodi	Lodi	302	783	195,720
Mantova	Mantova	903	2,339	374,008
Milano	Milan	765	1,980	3,757,609
Pavia	Pavia	1,145	2,965	497,575
Sondrio	Sondrio	1,240	3,212	177,367
Varese	Varese	463	1,199	816,274
Marche	Ancona	3,743	9,693	1,460,989
Ancona	Ancona	749	1,940	444,056
Ascoli Piceno	Ascoli Piceno	806	2,087	369,791
Macerata	Macerata	1,071	2,774	302,648
Pesaro e Urbino	Pesaro	1,117	2,892	344,494
Molise	Campobasso	1,713	4,438	327,987
Campobasso	Campobasso	1,123	2,909	236,418
Isernia	Isernia	590	1,529	91,569
Piemonte	Turin	9,807[4]	25,399	4,287,465
Alessandria	Alessandria	1,375	3,560	430,983
Asti	Asti	583	1,511	210,347
Biella	Biella	352	913	189,506
Cuneo	Cuneo	2,665	6,903	557,430
Novara	Novara	530	1,373	343,556
Torino	Turin	2,637	6,830	2,214,282
Verbano-Cusio-Ossola	Verbania	858	2,221	160,751
Vercelli	Vercelli	806	2,088	180,610
Puglia	Bari	7,470	19,348	4,085,239
Bari	Bari	1,980	5,129	1,576,050
Brindisi	Brindisi	710	1,838	411,563
Foggia	Foggia	2,774	7,185	693,900
Lecce	Lecce	1,065	2,759	815,855
Taranto	Taranto	941	2,437	587,871
Sardegna	Cagliari	9,301	24,090	1,651,888
Cagliari	Cagliari	2,662	6,895	766,066
Nuoro	Nuoro	2,720	7,044	269,422
Oristano	Oristano	1,016	2,631	157,215
Sassari	Sassari	2,903	7,520	459,185
Sicilia (Sicily)	Palermo	9,926	25,709	5,087,794
Agrigento	Agrigento	1,175	3,042	469,288
Caltanissetta	Caltanissetta	822	2,128	282,256
Catania	Catania	1,371	3,552	1,100,208
Enna	Enna	989	2,562	181,749
Messina	Messina	1,254	3,248	676,895
Palermo	Palermo	1,927	4,992	1,238,061
Ragusa	Ragusa	623	1,614	301,854
Siracusa	Siracusa	814	2,109	403,478
Trapani	Trapani	951	2,462	434,005
Toscana	Florence	8,877	22,992[5]	3,536,392
Arezzo	Arezzo	1,248	3,232	321,725
Firenze	Florence	1,365	3,536	953,973
Grosseto	Grosseto	1,739	4,504	215,445
Livorno	Livorno	468	1,213	334,223
Lucca	Lucca	684	1,773	375,103
Massa-Carrara	Massa-Carrara	447	1,157	199,534
Pisa	Pisa	945	2,448	386,298
Pistoia	Pistoia	373	965	269,265
Prato	Prato	133	344	228,027
Siena	Siena	1,475	3,821	252,799
Trentino-Alto Adige	Bolzano	5,258	13,618	936,256
Bolzano-Bozen	Bolzano	2,857	7,400	462,542
Trento	Trento	2,401	6,218	473,714
Umbria	Perugia	3,265	8,456	835,488
Perugia	Perugia	2,446	6,334	612,629
Terni	Terni	819	2,122	222,859
Valle d'Aosta	Aosta	1,259	3,262	120,343
Veneto	Venice	7,090	18,364	4,511,714
Belluno	Belluno	1,420	3,678	211,048
Padova	Padova	827	2,142	849,592
Rovigo	Rovigo	691	1,789	243,520
Treviso	Treviso	956	2,477	784,055
Venezia	Venice	950	2,460	814,581
Verona	Verona	1,195	3,096	821,563
Vicenza	Vicenza	1,051	2,722	787,355
TOTAL		116,324[5]	301,277[5]	57,679,895

Demography

Population (2001): 57,892,000.
Density (2001): persons per sq mi 497.8, persons per sq km 192.2.
Urban-rural (2000): urban 67.0%; rural 33.0%.
Sex distribution (2000): male 48.55%; female 51.45%.
Age breakdown (2000): under 15, 14.4%; 15–29, 19.5%; 30–44, 23.1%; 45–59, 19.1%; 60–74, 16.1%; 75 and over, 7.8%.
Population projection: (2010) 57,409,000; (2020) 55,540,000.
Doubling time: not applicable; population stable.
Ethnolinguistic composition (2000): Italian 96.0%; North African Arab 0.9%; Italo-Albanian 0.8%; Albanian 0.5%; German 0.4%; Austrian 0.4%; other 1.0%.
Religious affiliation (1996): Roman Catholic 81.7%; nonreligious 13.6%; Muslim 1.2%; other 3.5%.
Major cities (2000[3, 6]): Rome 2,643,581; Milan 1,300,977; Naples 1,002,619; Turin 903,703; Palermo 683,794; Genoa 636,104; Bologna 381,161; Florence 376,682; Catania 337,862; Bari 331,848; Venice 277,305.
National origin (1991): Italian 99.3%; foreign-born 0.7%, of which European 0.3%, African 0.2%, Asian 0.1%, other 0.1%.
Mobility (1991). Population living in the same commune as in 1986: 93.3%; another commune, same province 3.4%; different province 2.5%; abroad 0.8%.
Households. Average household size (1991) 2.7; composition of households: 1 person 19.5%, 2 persons 21.9%, 3 persons 25.2%, 4 persons 21.4%, 5 or more persons 12.0%. Family households (1991): 15,538,335 (73.8%); non-family 5,527,105 (26.2%), of which one-person 19.5%.
Immigration (1997): immigrants 162,857, from Europe 41.1%, of which EU countries 14.2%; Africa 25.5%; Asia 19.0%; Western Hemisphere 14.0%.

Vital statistics

Birth rate per 1,000 population (2000): 9.1 (world avg. 22.5); (1998) legitimate 91.0%; illegitimate 8.0%.
Death rate per 1,000 population (2000): 10.1 (world avg. 9.0).
Natural increase rate per 1,000 population (2000): –1.0 (world avg. 13.5).
Total fertility rate (avg. births per childbearing woman; 2000): 1.2.
Marriage rate per 1,000 population (1998): 4.8.
Divorce rate per 1,000 population (1994): 0.5.
Life expectancy at birth (2001): male 75.9 years; female 82.5 years.
Major causes of death per 100,000 population (1996): diseases of the circulatory system 418.3; malignant neoplasms 272.8; diseases of the respiratory system 56.2; accidents and violence 48.8; diseases of the digestive system 45.6.

Social indicators

Educational attainment (1995). Percentage of labour force age 15 and over having: basic literacy or primary education 40.4%; secondary 30.5%; post-secondary technical training 5.1%; some college 19.2%; college degree 4.3%.
Quality of working life. Average workweek (1995): 37.0 hours. Annual rate per 100,000 workers (1996) for: injury or accident 3,208; death 7.5. Percentage of labour force insured for damages or income loss (1992) resulting from: injury 100%; permanent disability 100%; death 100%. Number of working days lost to labour stoppages per 1,000 workers (1996): 97. Average duration of journey to work: n.a. Rate per 1,000 workers of discouraged (unemployed no longer seeking work; 1990): 1.1.
Material well-being. Rate per 1,000 of population possessing (1995): telephone 434; automobile 550; television 436.
Social participation. Eligible voters participating in last national election (May 13, 2001): 81.2%. Trade union membership in total workforce (1990): *c.* 28%.
Social deviance (1999). Offense rate per 100,000 population for: murder 1.4; rape 68.3; assault 210.4[7]; theft, including burglary and housebreaking 2,567; suicide 6.3[8].
Access to services (1999). Nearly 100% of dwellings have access to electricity, a safe water supply, and toilet facilities.

Leisure (1998). Favourite leisure activities (as percentage of household spending on culture): cinema 21.8%; sporting events 14.6%; theatre 13.8%.

National economy

Gross national product (1999): U.S.$1,162,910,000,000 (U.S.$20,170 per capita).

Structure of gross domestic product and labour force

	1999			
	in value (Lit '000,000,000)	% of total value	labour force	% of labour force
Agriculture	58,865	2.8	1,371,000	5.9
Mining	[9]	[9]	[9]	[9]
Manufacturing	558,617[9]	26.3[9]	5,252,000[9]	22.7[9]
Construction	94,722	4.4	1,508,000	6.5
Public utilities	[9]	[9]	[9]	[9]
Transp. and commun.	146,610	6.9	1,413,000	6.1
Trade	332,374	15.6	4,729,000	20.4
Finance	159,090	7.5	8,862,000	38.3
Pub. admin., defense	270,080	12.7		
Services	269,140	12.6		
Other	238,667[10]	11.2[10]	[11]	[11]
TOTAL	2,128,165	100.0	23,135,000	100.0[4]

Budget (1999). Revenue: Lit 620,534,000,000,000 (income taxes 46.9%, of which individual 37.5%, corporate 9.4%; value-added and excise taxes 30.6%). Expenditures: Lit 668,251,000,000,000 (1995; debt service 27.5%; social security 18.4%; education 9.1%; transportation 4.7%; defense 2.8%).
Public debt (1999): U.S.$766,000,000,000.
Tourism (1999): receipts U.S.$28,359,000,000; expenditures U.S.$16,913,000,000.

Manufacturing, mining, and construction enterprises (1995)

	no. of enterprises	no. of employees[12]	hourly wages as a % of avg. of all wages	annual value added (Lit '000,000,000)
Manufacturing				
Metal products	5,780	360,979	...	36,249
Machinery (nonelectrical)	4,503	379,027	...	35,221
Industrial chemicals	1,206	180,836	...	27,505
Electrical machinery	2,962	303,439	...	26,306
Food products	2,549	224,025	...	22,878
Transport equipment	1,122	275,077	...	22,642
Printing, publishing[13]	2,086	148,757	...	16,150
Pottery, ceramics, and glass	2,128	149,586	...	14,361
Textiles[14]	3,514	215,387	...	14,335
Rubber and plastic products	1,836	123,119	...	12,711
Wearing apparel	2,436	114,059	...	7,279
Paper and paper products[13]	...	...	...	...
Petroleum and gas	108	22,566	...	4,221
Mining and quarrying	340	20,013	...	5,991
Construction	6,228	1,564,100	...	94,887

Production (metric tons except as noted). Agriculture, forestry, fishing (2001): sugar beets 12,000,000, corn (maize) 11,300,000, grapes 9,770,000, tomatoes 6,990,000, wheat 6,500,000, olives 2,780,000, oranges 2,270,000, apples 2,160,000, potatoes 2,100,000, peaches and nectarines 1,730,000, rice 1,300,000, barley 1,250,000, soybeans 1,100,000; livestock (number of live animals) 10,970,000 sheep, 8,400,000 pigs, 7,180,000 cattle, 100,000,000 chickens; roundwood (2000) 9,329,000 cu m; fish catch (1999) 540,523. Mining and quarrying (1998): rock salt 3,413,522; feldspar 2,503,541; barite 31,792; lead 10,102; zinc 5,242. Manufacturing (1998): cement 33,714,914[7]; crude steel 25,782,300; pig iron 10,792,700; glass 3,981,104[7]; textiles 2,340,600[15]; sulfuric acid 2,013,400; wine 56,896,000 hectolitres; beer 10,616,173 hectolitres[7]; olive oil (2000) 493,000; 6,995,818 washing machines[7]; 5,908,224 refrigerators[7]; 2,723,541 motorized road vehicles, of which 1,378,517 automobiles, 1,062,570 motorcycles, 282,454 trucks and buses; 2,779,827 colour televisions[7]. Construction (1998): residential 56,268,471 cu m; commercial 67,443,808 cu m.

Service enterprises (1997)

	no. of enterprises[16]	no. of employees	hourly wage as a % of all wages	annual value added (Lit '000,000,000)
Public utilities	327	257,000[7]	...	102,495[7]
Transportation / Communications	3,230	1,413,000	...	146,610
Finance	...	424,000[15]	...	159,090
Wholesale and retail trade	8,115	4,729,000	...	332,374
Pub. admin., services	...	4,251,900[15]	...	270,080

Energy production (consumption): electricity (kW-hr; 1996) 241,413,000,000 (278,802,000,000); coal (metric tons; 1996) none (16,335,000); crude petroleum (barrels; 1996) 39,802,000 (588,438,000); petroleum products (metric tons; 1996) 80,002,000 (86,550,000); natural gas (cu m; 1996) 19,993,000,000 (56,284,000,000).
Population economically active (1999): total 23,135,000; activity rate of total population 40.1% (participation rates: ages 15–64, 57.7%[8] female 38.2%; unemployed 11.4%).

Price and earnings indexes (1995 = 100)

	1995	1996	1997	1998	1999	2000
Consumer price index	100.0	104.0	106.1	108.2	110.0	112.8
Earnings index	100.0	103.2	106.9	109.9	112.4	114.7

Household income and expenditure (1995). Average household size 2.7; average annual income per household (1984) Lit 19,692,000 (U.S.$11,208); sources of income (1996): salaries and wages 38.8%, property income and self-employment 38.5%, transfer payments 22.0%; expenditure (1997): food and beverages 18.1%, housing 18.0%, transportation and communications 13.3%, recreation and education 8.4%.

Financial aggregates

	1995	1996	1997	1998	1999	2000
Exchange rate, Lit per:						
U.S. dollar	1,628.9	1,530.6	1,759.2	1,653.1	1,927.8	2,080.9
£	2,571.2	2,690.8	2,909.4	2,749.9	3,116.1	3,105.1
SDR	2,355.7	2,200.9	2,373.6	2,327.6	2,645.9	2,711.2
International reserves (U.S.$)						
Total (excl. gold; '000,000)	34,905	45,948	55,739	29,888	...	25,566
SDRs ('000,000)	53	29	67	111	168	238
Reserve pos. in IMF ('000,000)	1,963	1,855	2,241	4,330	3,546	2,906
Foreign exchange ('000,000)	32,942	44,064	54,431	25,447	18,623	22,423
Gold ('000,000 fine troy oz)	66.67	66.67	66.67	83.36	78.83	78.83
% world reserves	7.3	7.3	7.5	8.6	8.2	8.3
Interest and prices						
Central bank discount (%)	9.00	7.50	5.50	3.00	...	...
Govt. bond yield (%)	11.98	8.93	6.47	4.55	4.04	5.29
Industrial share prices (1990 = 100)	95.4	96.0	137.7	220.5	245.5	319.0
Balance of payments (U.S.$'000,000)						
Balance of visible trade	44,082	60,822	39,877	35,361	23,437	10,717
Imports, f.o.b.	−187,254	−190,021	−200,527	−206,941	−212,420	−228,019
Exports, f.o.b.	231,336	250,843	240,404	242,572	235,856	238,736
Balance of invisibles	−18,378	−20,823	−7,474	−15,363	−15,326	−16,477
Balance of payments, current account	25,704	−39,999	32,403	19,998	8,111	−5,760

Land use (1994): forest 23.0%; pasture 15.4%; agriculture 37.9%; other 23.7%.

Foreign trade[17]

Balance of trade (current prices)

	1995	1996	1997	1998	1999	2000
Lit '000,000,000	+45,514	+67,599	+51,541	+47,398	+24,853	+3,358
% of total	6.3%	9.5%	6.7%	5.9%	3.1%	0.3%

Imports (1999): Lit 394,271,000,000,000 (machinery and transport equipment 38.4%, of which transport equipment 15.1%; chemicals 13.6%; metal 9.8%; food 7.5%; textiles 5.2%; plastics 2.3%). *Major import sources:* Germany 19.0%; France 12.6%; The Netherlands 6.3%; U.K. 6.1%; U.S. 4.9%; Belgium-Luxembourg 4.6%; Spain 4.3%.
Exports (1999): Lit 419,124,000,000,000 (machinery and transport equipment 41.7%, of which transport equipment 11.5%, electrical machinery 9.8%; textiles and wearing apparel 10.7%; chemicals 8.9%; plastics 3.7%). *Major export destinations:* Germany 16.5%; France 13.0%; U.S. 9.5%; U.K. 7.1%; Spain 6.3%.

Transport and communications

Transport. Railroads (1998): length 19,527 km[15]; passenger-km 41,392,000,000; metric ton-km cargo 22,386,000,000. Roads (1997): total length 308,139 km (paved 100%). Vehicles (1998): passenger cars 31,370,000; trucks and buses 5,127,000. Merchant marine (1995): vessels (100 gross tons and over) 1,355; total deadweight tonnage 6,905,313. Air transport (1996): passenger-km 29,471,000,000; metric ton-km cargo 1,219,000,000; airports (1997) 34.

Communications

Medium	date	unit	number	units per 1,000 persons
Daily newspapers	1997	circulation	5,970,000	104
Radio	1997	receivers	50,500,000	880
Television	1998	receivers	28,000,000	488
Telephones	1999	main lines	26,506,000	460
Cellular telephones	1999	subscribers	30,296,000	526
Personal computers	1999	units	11,000,000	191
Internet	1999	users	3,300,000	57

Education and health

Literacy (1995): total population age 15 and over literate 48,100,000 (98.1%); males literate 23,800,000 (98.6%); females literate 24,300,000 (97.6%).

Education (1998–99)

	schools	teachers	students	student/teacher ratio
Primary (age 6–10)	19,073	281,909	2,859,379	10.1
Secondary (age 11–18)	8,695	208,620	1,775,009	8.5
Voc., teacher tr.	6,883	295,482	2,543,750	8.6
Higher[18, 19]	48	58,874	1,601,873	27.2

Health (1997): physicians (1993) 207,319 (1 per 193 persons); hospital beds 334,613 (1 per 172 persons); infant mortality rate (2001) 5.8.
Food (1999): daily per capita caloric intake 3,629 (vegetable products 74%, animal products 26%); 144% of FAO recommended minimum requirement.

Military

Total active duty personnel (2000): 250,600 (army 61.0%, navy 15.2%, air force 23.8%). *Military expenditure as percentage of GNP* (1997): 2.0% (world 2.6%); per capita expenditure U.S.$395.

[1]Includes 6 nonelective seats in May 2001 (4 presidential appointees and 2 former presidents serving ex officio). [2]Six provinces were created in 1992. [3]Resident population only. [4]Detail does not add to total given because of rounding. [5]The total area for Italy, per 1998 survey, is 301,337 sq km (116,347 sq mi). [6]January 1. [7]1995. [8]1996. [9]Manufacturing includes Mining and Public utilities. [10]Other includes indirect import charges and building rental less imputed bank service charges. [11]The 2,637,000 unemployed are not calculated separately. [12]Total number of persons engaged. [13]Printing, publishing includes Paper and paper products. [14]1993. [15]1997. [16]Enterprises with 20 or more persons engaged. [17]Imports c.i.f.; exports f.o.b. [18]Universities only. [19]1994–95.

Internet resources for further information:

- **National Statistical Institute http://www.istat.it/homeing.html**

Jamaica

Official name: Jamaica.
Form of government: constitutional monarchy with two legislative houses (Senate [21]; House of Representatives [60]).
Chief of state: British Monarch represented by Governor-General.
Head of government: Prime Minister.
Capital: Kingston.
Official language: English.
Monetary unit: 1 Jamaica dollar (J$) = 100 cents; valuation (Sept. 28, 2001) 1 U.S.$ = J$45.55; 1 £ = J$66.94.

Area and population

Parishes	Capitals	area sq mi	area sq km	population 2000[1] estimate
Clarendon	May Pen	462	1,196	228,300
Hanover	Lucea	174	450	67,500
Kingston	2	8	22	3
Manchester	Mandeville	321	830	188,800
Portland	Port Antonio	314	814	79,400
Saint Andrew	2	166	431	716,000
Saint Ann	Saint Ann's Bay	468	1,213	164,900
Saint Catherine	Spanish Town	460	1,192	413,200
Saint Elizabeth	Black River	468	1,212	148,600
Saint James	Montego Bay	230	595	180,800
Saint Mary	Port Maria	236	611	112,800
Saint Thomas	Morant Bay	287	743	92,400
Trelawny	Falmouth	338	875	72,500
Westmoreland	Savanna-la-Mar	312	807	140,600
TOTAL		4,244	10,991	2,605,800

Demography

Population (2001): 2,624,000.
Density (2001): persons per sq mi 618.2, persons per sq km 238.7.
Urban-rural (1998): urban 55.1%; rural 44.9%.
Sex distribution (1998): male 49.85%; female 50.15%.
Age breakdown (1998): under 15, 31.5%; 15–29, 27.5%; 30–44, 20.9%; 45–59, 10.4%; 60–74, 6.6%; 75 and over, 3.1%.
Population projection: (2010) 2,800,000; (2020) 3,070,000.
Doubling time: 47 years.
Ethnic composition (2000): local black 77.0%; local mulatto 14.6%; Haitian 2.0%; East Indian 1.7%; black-East Indian 1.6%; other 3.1%.
Religious affiliation (1995): Protestant 39.0%, of which Pentecostal 10.5%, Seventh-day Adventist 6.1%, Baptist 5.3%; Roman Catholic 10.4%; Anglican 3.7%; other (including nonreligious) 46.9%[4].
Major cities (1991): Kingston 103,771[5] (metropolitan area 587,798); Spanish Town 92,383; Portmore 90,138; Montego Bay 83,446; May Pen 46,785.

Vital statistics

Birth rate per 1,000 population (2000): 20.0 (world avg. 22.5).
Death rate per 1,000 population (2000): 5.1 (world avg. 9.0).
Natural increase rate per 1,000 population (2000): 14.9 (world avg. 13.5).
Total fertility rate (avg. births per childbearing woman; 1997): 2.8.
Marriage rate per 1,000 population (1996): 7.4.
Life expectancy at birth (2000): male 73.3 years; female 77.3 years.
Major causes of death per 100,000 population (1991): diseases of the circulatory system 189.4; malignant neoplasms (cancers) 84.1; endocrine and metabolic disorders 51.3; diseases of the respiratory system 30.1.

National economy

Budget (1998–99). Revenue J$74,096,000,000 (tax revenue 90.4%, of which income taxes 34.9%, consumption taxes 28.3%, custom duties 9.6%; nontax revenue 9.6%). Expenditures: J$93,267,000,000 (current expenditure 91.5%, of which debt interest 37.4%).
Public debt (external, outstanding; 1999): U.S.$2,905,000,000.
Production (metric tons except as noted). Agriculture, forestry, fishing (1999): sugarcane 2,400,000, yams 198,400, vegetables and melons 183,701, citrus fruits 154,000, bananas 130,000, coconuts 115,000, pumpkins, squash, and gourds 42,000, plantains 33,500, sweet potatoes 27,000, cabbages 23,000, carrots 22,000, tomatoes 18,000; livestock (number of live animals) 440,000 goats, 400,000 cattle, 180,000 pigs; roundwood (1998) 342,700 cu m; fish catch (1998) 6,720. Mining and quarrying (1998): bauxite 4,034,600; alumina 3,440,000; gypsum 154,500. Manufacturing (valued added in constant 1991–95 prices, J$'000,000; 1995): machinery and equipment 593.6; food processing 580.3; petroleum products 351.3; rubber and plastic products 324.1; textiles and clothing 257.0; tobacco and tobacco products 255.2; metal and nonmetallic products 223.6. Construction (1995): residential units completed 7,067[6]; factory space completed 6,989 sq m[7]. Energy production (consumption): electricity (kW-hr; 1996) 6,038,000,000 (6,038,000,000); coal, none (none); crude petroleum (barrels; 1996) none (7,828,000); petroleum products (metric tons; 1996) 1,055,000 (3,135,000); natural gas, none (none).
Population economically active (October 1999): total 1,115,600; activity rate of total population 43.1% (participation rates: ages 14 and over 64.1%; female 44.7%; unemployed 16.0%).

Price and earnings indexes (1995 = 100)

	1994	1995	1996	1997	1998	1999	2000
Consumer price index	83.4	100.0	126.4	138.6	150.6	159.5	172.6
Earnings index	...	...	...	...	...	...	...

Gross national product (1999): U.S.$6,311,000,000 (U.S.$2,430 per capita).

Structure of gross domestic product and labour force

	2000 in value J$'000,000	% of total value	labour force	% of labour force
Agriculture	20,765.5	6.9	195,700	17.7
Mining	13,826.6	4.6	4,600	0.4
Manufacturing	42,903.8	14.4	69,600	6.3
Construction	30,924.9	10.3	81,500	7.4
Public utilities	12,877.3	4.3	6,300	0.6
Transp. and commun.	31,704.3	10.6	59,400	5.4
Trade	78,184.6	26.2	206,300	18.7
Pub. admin., defense	36,326.7	12.2	254,800	23.0
Finance, real estate	42,756.9	14.3	53,100	4.8
Services	8,910.0	3.0	2,300	0.2
Other	–20,497.9[8]	–6.8[8]	171,800[9]	15.5[9]
TOTAL	298,682.7	100.0	1,105,400	100.0

Household income and expenditure. Average household size (1991) 4.2; average annual income per household (1988) J$8,356 (U.S.$1,525); sources of income (1989): wages and salaries 66.1%, self-employment 19.3%, transfers 14.6%; expenditure (1988)[10]: food and beverages 55.6%, housing 7.9%, fuel and other household supplies 7.4%, health care 7.0%, transportation 6.4%.
Tourism: receipts (2000) U.S.$1,332,600,000; expenditures (1999) U.S.$227,-000,000.

Foreign trade

Balance of trade (current prices)

	1994	1995	1996	1997	1998	1999	2000
U.S.$'000,000	–551.2	–829.3	–994.2	–1,120.8	–1,101.9	–1,654.8	–1,906.8
% of total	28.7%	18.7%	23.5%	24.8%	25.7%	40.1%	42.4%

Imports (1999): U.S.$2,892,761,000 (raw materials 50.5%, of which fuels 10.8%; consumer goods 33.2%, of which food 9.4%; capital goods 16.3%, of which machinery and apparatus 7.6%). *Major import sources* (1997): U.S. 48.1%; Trinidad and Tobago 7.8%; Japan 6.9%; France 5.0%; U.K. 3.7%; Canada 3.0%; Mexico 2.6%.
Exports (1999): U.S.$1,237,982,000 (crude materials 55.7%; food 19.1%; beverages and tobacco 4.8%; chemicals 3.6%; machinery and transport equipment 2.2%; manufactured goods 0.7%). *Major export destinations:* U.S. 33.4%; Canada 14.1%; U.K. 13.4%; The Netherlands 10.2%; Norway 5.8%; Japan 2.3%.

Transport and communications

Transport. Railroads (1991): route length 129 mi; 208 km; passenger-mi 12,127,000[7], passenger-km 19,516,000[7]; short ton-mi cargo 1,700,000, metric ton-km cargo 2,482,000. Roads (1996): total length 11,800 mi, 19,000 km (paved 71%). Vehicles (1999–00): passenger cars 160,948; trucks and buses 55,596. Air transport (1999)[11]: passenger-mi 1,037,565,000, passenger-km 1,669,803,000; short ton-mi cargo 20,186,000, metric ton-km cargo 29,471,000; airports (1997) with scheduled flights 4.

Communications

Medium	date	unit	number	units per 1,000 persons
Daily newspapers	1996	circulation	158,000	63
Radio	1997	receivers	1,215,000	483
Television	1998	receivers	480,000	187
Telephones	1999	main lines	509,646	197
Cellular telephones	1999	subscribers	144,388	56
Personal computers	1999	units	110,000	43
Internet	1999	users	60,000	23

Education and health

Educational attainment (1982). Percentage of population age 25 and over having: no formal schooling 3.2%; some primary education 79.8%; some secondary 15.0%; complete secondary and higher 2.0%. *Literacy* (2000): total population age 15 and over literate 88%; males 83%; females 91%.

Education (1999–2000)

	schools	teachers	students	student/ teacher ratio
Primary (age 6–11)[12]	788[13]	9,908	325,298	32.8
Secondary (age 12–16)	134	8,903	167,098	18.8
Voc., teacher tr.	17	1,091	17,388	15.9
Higher	15[14]	1,047[15]	24,200[16]	17.9[15]

Health (2000)[17]: physicians 435 (1 per 5,988 persons); hospital beds 3,511 (1 per 742 persons); infant mortality rate 14.6.
Food (1999): daily per capita caloric intake 2,708 (vegetable products 83%, animal products 17%); 121% of FAO recommended minimum requirement.

Military

Total active duty personnel (2000): 2,830 (army 88.3%; coast guard 6.7%; air force 5.0%). *Military expenditure as percentage of GNP* (1997): 0.9% (world 2.6%); per capita expenditure U.S.$20.

[1]Year end. [2]The parishes of Kingston and Saint Andrew are jointly administered from the Half Way Tree section of Saint Andrew. [3]Kingston included with Saint Andrew. [4]Includes *c.* 0.7% Rastafarian. [5]City of Kingston is coextensive with Kingston parish. [6]51% public sector. [7]1990. [8]Less imputed service charges. [9]Unemployed. [10]Weights of consumer price index components. [11]Air Jamaica only. [12]Includes lower-secondary students at all-age schools. [13]1991–92. [14]1988–89. [15]1987–88. [16]1994–95. [17]Public health only.

Internet resources for further information:

- **Statistics Institute of Jamaica http://www.statinja.com**

Japan

Official name: Nihon (Japan).
Form of government: constitutional monarchy with a national Diet consisting of two legislative houses (House of Councillors [247]; House of Representatives [480]).
Chief of state: Emperor.
Head of government: Prime Minister.
Capital: Tokyo.
Official language: Japanese.
Official religion: none.
Monetary unit: 1 yen (¥) = 100 sen; valuation (Sept. 28, 2001) 1 U.S.$ = ¥119.13; 1 £ = ¥175.08.

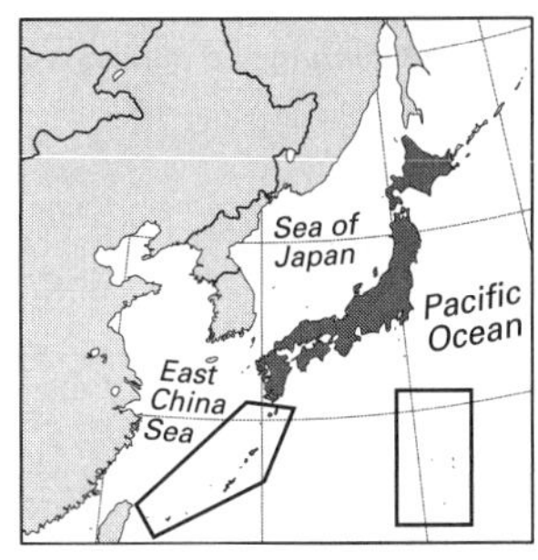

Area and population

Regions / Prefectures	Capitals	area sq mi	area sq km	population 2000[1] estimate
Chūbu				
Aichi	Nagoya	1,984	5,139	7,043,000
Fukui	Fukui	1,619	4,192	829,000
Gifu	Gifu	4,091	10,596	2,108,000
Ishikawa	Kanazawa	1,621	4,198	1,181,000
Nagano	Nagano	5,245	13,585	2,214,000
Niigata	Niigata	4,857	12,579	2,476,000
Shizuoka	Shizuoka	3,001	7,773	3,767,000
Toyama	Toyama	1,642	4,252	1,121,000
Yamanashi	Kōfu	1,723	4,463	888,000
Chūgoku				
Hiroshima	Hiroshima	3,269	8,467	2,879,000
Okayama	Okayama	2,738	7,092	1,951,000
Shimane	Matsue	2,559[2]	6,629[2]	761,000
Tottori	Tottori	1,349[2]	3,494[2]	613,000
Yamaguchi	Yamaguchi	2,358	6,107	1,528,000
Hokkaidō				
Hokkaidō (Territory)	Sapporo	32,247	83,520	5,683,000
Kantō				
Chiba	Chiba	1,989	5,151	5,926,000
Gumma	Maebashi	2,454	6,356	2,025,000
Ibaraki	Mito	2,353	6,094	2,985,000
Kanagawa	Yokohama	928	2,403	8,490,000
Saitama	Urawa	1,467	3,799	6,938,000
Tochigi	Utsunomiya	2,476	6,414	2,005,000
Kinki				
Hyōgo	Kōbe	3,236	8,381	5,551,000
Mie	Tsu	2,231	5,778	1,857,000
Nara	Nara	1,425	3,692	1,443,000
Shiga	Ōtsu	1,551	4,016	1,343,000
Wakayama	Wakayama	1,024	4,725	1,070,000
Kyūshū				
Fukuoka	Fukuoka	1,916	4,963	5,016,000
Kagoshima	Kagoshima	3,539	9,167	1,786,000
Kumamoto	Kumamoto	2,860	7,408	1,859,000
Miyazaki	Miyazaki	2,986	7,735	1,170,000
Nagasaki	Nagasaki	1,588	4,113	1,517,000
Ōita	Ōita	2,447	6,338	1,221,000
Saga	Saga	942	2,440	877,000
Ryukyu				
Okinawa	Naha	871	2,255	1,318,000
Shikoku				
Ehime	Matsuyama	2,190	5,672	1,493,000
Kagawa	Takamatsu	727	1,883	1,023,000
Kōchi	Kōchi	2,744	7,107	814,000
Tokushima	Tokushima	1,601	4,146	824,000
Tohoku				
Akita	Akita	4,484[3]	11,613[3]	1,189,000
Aomori	Aomori	3,714[3]	9,619[3]	1,476,000
Fukushima	Fukushima	5,322	13,784	2,127,000
Iwate	Morioka	5,898	15,277	1,416,000
Miyagi	Sendai	2,815	7,292	2,365,000
Yamagata	Yamagata	3,601	9,327	1,244,000
Metropolis				
Tōkyō[4]	Tokyo	836	2,166	12,059,000
Urban prefectures				
Kyōto[5]	Kyōto	1,781	4,613	2,644,000
Ōsaka[5]	Ōsaka	722	1,869	8,805,000
TOTAL		145,883[6, 7]	377,835[6, 7]	126,919,000[7]

Demography

Population (2001): 127,100,000.
Density (2001): persons per sq mi 871.2, persons per sq km 336.4.
Urban-rural (1999): urban 78.6%; rural 21.4%.
Sex distribution (1999[8]): male 48.9%; female 51.1%.
Age breakdown (1999[8]): under 15, 14.8%; 15–29, 20.9%; 30–44, 19.3%; 45–59, 22.2%; 60–74, 16.0%; 75 and over, 6.8%.
Population projection: (2010) 127,626,000; (2020) 124,248,000.
Doubling time: not applicable; doubling time exceeds 100 years.
Composition by nationality (1997[9]): Japanese 99.1%; Korean 0.5%; Chinese 0.2%; other 0.2%.
Place of birth (1995): 99.3% native-born; 0.7% foreign-born (mainly Korean).
Immigration (1998[9]): permanent immigrants/registered aliens admitted 1,482,707, from North and South Korea 43.5%, Taiwan, Hong Kong, and China 17.0%, Brazil 15.7%, Philippines 6.3%, United States 2.9%, Peru 2.7%, Thailand 1.4%, United Kingdom 1.0%, Indonesia 0.8%, Vietnam 0.8%, Canada 0.6%, Iran 0.5%, India 0.5%, other 6.3%.
Major cities (2000): Tokyo 8,130,000; Yokohama 3,427,000; Ōsaka 2,599,000; Nagoya 2,171,000; Sapporo 1,822,000; Kōbe 1,494,000; Kyōto 1,468,000; Fukuoka 1,341,000; Kawasaki 1,250,000; Hiroshima 1,126,000; Kita-Kyūshū 1,011,000; Sendai 1,008,000.

Other principal cities (1995)

	population		population		population
Akashi	287,613	Kagoshima	546,294	Ōita	426,981
Akita	312,035	Kakogawa	260,588	Okayama	616,056
Amagasaki	488,574	Kanazawa	453,977	Okazaki	322,615
Aomori	294,165	Kashiwa	317,752	Omiya	433,768
Asahikawa	360,569	Kasugai	277,579	Ōtsu	276,331
Chiba	856,882	Kawagoe	323,345	Sagamihara	570,594
Fujisawa	368,636	Kawaguchi	448,801	Sakai	802,965
Fukui	255,601	Kōchi	322,077	Shimonoseki	259,791
Fukushima	285,745	Koriyama	324,831	Shizuoka	474,089
Fukuyama	374,510	Koshigaya	298,285	Suita	342,794
Funabashi	540,814	Kumamoto	650,322	Takamatsu	330,997
Gifu	407,145	Kurashiki	422,824	Takatsuki	362,259
Hachinohe	242,654	Machida	360,418	Tokorozawa	320,448
Hachiōji	503,320	Maebashi	284,780	Tokushima	268,712
Hakodate	298,868	Matsudo	461,489	Toyama	325,303
Hamamatsu	561,568	Matsuyama	460,870	Toyohashi	352,913
Higashi-Ōsaka	517,228	Miyazaki	300,054	Toyonaka	398,912
Himeji	470,986	Morioka	286,478	Toyota	341,038
Hirakata	400,130	Nagano	358,512	Urawa	453,300
Hiratsuka	253,818	Nagasaki	438,724	Utsunomiya	435,446
Ibaraki	258,237	Naha	301,928	Wakayama	393,951
Ichihara	277,080	Nara	359,234	Yamagata	254,485
Ichikawa	440,527	Neyagawa	258,440	Yao	276,658
Ichinomiya	267,359	Niigata	494,785	Yokkaichi	285,777
Iwaki	360,497	Nishinomiya	390,388	Yokosuka	432,202

Religious affiliation (1995): Shintō and related religions 93.1%[10]; Buddhism 69.6%; Christian 1.2%; other 8.1%.
Households (1995). Total households 43,899,923; average household size 2.8; composition of households 1 person 25.6%, 2 persons 23.0%, 3 persons 18.5%, 4 persons 18.8%, 5 persons 8.0%, 6 or more persons 6.1%. Family households 32,533,000 (74.1%); nonfamily 11,366,900 (25.9%), of which 1 person 11,239,400 (25.6%).

Type of household (1998)

Total number of occupied dwelling units: 43,922,000

	number of dwellings	percentage of total
by kind of dwelling		
exclusively for living	41,744,000	95.0
mixed use	124,000	0.3
combined with nondwelling	2,054,000	4.7
detached house	23,469,000	56.2
apartment building	16,420,000	39.3
tenement (substandard or overcrowded building)	1,735,000	4.2
other	120,000	0.3
by legal tenure of householder		
owned	26,468,000	60.3
rented	16,730,000	38.1
other	724,000	1.6
by kind of amenities		
flush toilet	36,461	83.0
bathroom	41,919	95.4
by year of construction		
prior to 1945	1,647,000	3.8
1945–70	8,077,000	18.9
1971–80	11,492,000	26.8
1981–90	11,973,000	28.0
1991–98 (Sept.)	9,650,000	22.5

Mobility (October 1990). Population living in same residence as in October 1985, 74.7%; different residence, same town 9.5%; same prefecture 7.9%; different prefecture 7.6%; different country 0.3%.

Vital statistics

Birth rate per 1,000 population (1999): 9.3 (world avg. 22.5); (1985) legitimate 99.0%; illegitimate 1.0%.
Death rate per 1,000 population (1999): 7.8 (world avg. 9.0).
Natural increase rate per 1,000 population (1999): 1.5 (world avg. 13.5).
Total fertility rate (avg. births per childbearing woman; 1999): 1.4.
Marriage rate per 1,000 population (1998): 6.3; (1996) average age at first marriage men 28.5 years, women 26.4 years.
Divorce rate per 1,000 population (1998): 0.7.
Life expectancy at birth (2000): male 77.5 years; female 84.0 years.
Major causes of death per 100,000 population (1998): malignant neoplasms (cancers) 226.7; circulatory diseases 224.3, of which cerebrovascular disease 110.0; pneumonia and bronchitis 71.9; accidents and adverse effects 56.5, of which suicide 25.4; nephritis, nephrotic syndrome, and nephrosis 13.3; cirrhosis of the liver 12.9; diabetes mellitus 10.0.

Social indicators

Educational attainment (1990). Percentage of population age 25 years and over having: primary education 34.3%; secondary 44.5%; postsecondary 21.2%.

Distribution of income (1999)

percentage of average household income by quintile

1	2	3	4	5 (highest)
11.1	15.6	19.0	22.7	31.6

Quality of working life. Average hours worked per month (1998): 153.5. Annual rate of industrial deaths per 100,000 workers (1998): 1.7. Proportion of labour force insured for damages or income loss resulting from injury, permanent disability, and death (1991): 50.1%. Average man-days lost to labour stoppages per 1,000,000 workdays (1998): 6.8. Average duration of journey to work (1996): 19.0 minutes (1983; 26.7% private automobile. 67.4% public transportation, 5.5% taxi, 0.4% other). Rate per 1,000 workers of discouraged (unemployed no longer seeking work: 1997): 89.4.

Access to services (1989). Proportion of households having access to: gas supply 64.6%; safe public water supply 94.0%; public sewage collection 89.4%.

Social participation. Eligible voters participating in last national election (October 1996): 59.6%. Population 15 years and over participating in social-service activities on a voluntary basis (1991): 26.3%. Trade union membership in total workforce (1996): 18.7%.

Social deviance (1998). Offense rate per 100,000 population for: homicide 1.1; rape 1.5; robbery 2.7; larceny and theft 1,415. Incidence in general population of: alcoholism, n.a.; drug and substance abuse, n.a. Rate of suicide per 100,000 population: 25.4.

Leisure/use of personal time

Discretionary daily activities (1996)
(Population age 10 years and over)

	weekly average hrs./min.
Total discretionary daily time	6:12
of which	
Hobbies and amusements	0:36
Sports	0:13
Learning (except schoolwork)	0:12
Social activities	0:04
Associations	0:27
Radio, television, newspapers, and magazines	2:59
Rest and relaxation	1:15
Other activities	0:20

Major leisure activities (1996)
(Population age 15 years and over)

	percentage of participation		
	male	female	total
Sports	81.7	70.5	76.1
Light gymnastics	25.9	30.6	28.3
Swimming	24.6	20.9	22.8
Bowling	33.7	24.6	29.2
Learning (except schoolwork)	30.7	30.6	30.6
Travel (1991)			
Domestic	72.7	68.3	70.4
Foreign	10.4	7.6	9.0

Material well-being (1994). Households possessing: automobile 79.7%; telephone, virtually 100%; colour television receiver 99.3%; refrigerator 98.9%; air conditioner 72.3%; washing machine 99.4%; vacuum cleaner 98.7%; videocassette recorder 82.8%; camera 86.8%; microwave oven 84.3%; compact disc player 53.8%.

National economy

Gross national product (at current market prices; 1999): U.S.$4,045,545,000,000 (U.S.$32,035 per capita).

Structure of gross domestic product and labour force

1998	in value ¥'000,000,000	% of total value	labour force	% of labour force
Agriculture, fishing	8,619	1.7	3,430,000	5.0
Mining	995	0.2	60,000	0.1
Manufacturing	117,216	23.5	13,820,000	20.3
Construction	46,122	9.3	6,620,000	9.7
Public utilities	15,049	3.0	370,000	0.5
Transportation and communications	32,623	6.5	4,050,000	6.0
Trade	58,582	11.8	14,830,000	21.8
Finance	94,819	19.0	5,930,000	8.7
Pub. admin., defense	41,528	8.3	} 15,660,000	23.1
Services	91,023	18.3		
Other	–8,077[11]	–1.6[11]	3,150,000[12]	4.7[12]
TOTAL	498,499	100.0	67,930,000[7]	100.0[7]

Budget (2000–01). Revenue: ¥52,377,000,000,000 (income tax 35.7%; corporation tax 19.0%; value-added tax 18.8%; liquor and tobacco tax 6.4%; fuel taxes 4.0%; stamp and customs duties 2.9%). Expenditures: ¥70,057,000,000,000 (debt service 31.4%; social security 23.9%; public works 14.2%; national defense 7.0%).

Public debt (1998): U.S.$2,412,200,000,000 (¥278,847,900,000,000).

Population economically active (1998): total 67,930,000; activity rate of total population 53.7% (participation rates: age 15 and over, 63.7%[13]; female 40.7%; unemployed 4.1%).

Price and earnings indexes (1995 = 100)

	1994	1995	1996	1997	1998	1999	2000
Consumer price index	100.1	100.0	100.1	101.8	102.5	102.2	101.5
Monthly earnings index	97.9	100.0	101.9	103.4	103.1	103.6	104.6

Household income and expenditure (1999). Average household size 2.8; average annual income per household ¥6,896,100 (U.S.$49,163); sources of income (1994): wages and salaries 59.0%, transfer payments 20.5%, self-employment 12.8%, other 7.3%; expenditure (1999): food 23.7%, transportation and communications 10.6%, recreation 10.3%, fuel, light, and water charges 6.7%, housing 6.5%, clothing and footwear 5.4%, education 4.2%, furniture and household utensils 3.6%, medical care 3.5%.

Tourism (1999): receipts from visitors U.S.$3,428,000,000; expenditures by nationals abroad U.S.$32,808,000,000.

Land use (1994): forested 66.4%; meadows and pastures 1.8%; agricultural and under permanent cultivation 11.7%; other 20.1%.

Manufacturing and mining enterprises (1998)

	no. of establish-ments	avg. no. of persons engaged	annual wages as a % of avg. of all mfg. wages	annual value added (¥'000,000,000)
Electrical machinery	29,738	1,666,000	104.3	18,429
Transport equipment	14,245	893,000	126.3	13,116
Nonelectrical machinery	42,398	1,085,000	115.9	12,325
Food, beverages, and tobacco	48,595	1,276,000	69.2	12,515
Chemical products	5,426	383,000	134.4	11,329
Fabricated metal products	46,248	772,000	97.5	7,511
Printing and publishing	27,411	543,000	118.2	6,979
Ceramic, stone, and clay	18,792	396,000	100.9	4,486
Iron and steel	5,653	261,000	136.5	4,389
Plastic products	19,649	438,000	88.8	4,159
Paper and paper products	10,368	260,000	99.4	3,045
Apparel products	29,201	492,000	50.3	2,085
Nonferrous metal products	3,786	149,000	118.3	1,871
Precision instruments	5,993	192,000	98.6	1,859
Textiles	13,482	219,000	80.0	1,522
Rubber products	4,616	139,000	101.0	1,507
Furniture and fixtures	14,003	185,000	85.5	1,320
Lumber and wood products	14,517	182,000	71.2	1,256
Petroleum and coal products	1,199	32,000	161.7	899
Leather products	4,279	52,000	66.2	311
Mining and quarrying	590	11,137	109.3	85

Energy production (consumption): electricity (kW-hr; 1996) 1,012,145,000,000 (1,012,145,000,000); coal (metric tons; 1996) 6,480,000 (132,582,000); crude petroleum (barrels; 1996) 3,796,000 (1,616,793,000); petroleum products (metric tons; 1996) 185,422,000, of which (by volume) diesel 34.3%, heavy fuel oil 22.0%, gasoline 20.7%, kerosene and jet fuel 12.4% (197,099,000); natural gas (cu m; 1996) 2,298,200,000 (65,530,400,000). Composition of energy supply by source (1998): crude oil and petroleum products 50.9%, coal 17.0%, natural gas 12.8%, nuclear power 14.2%, hydroelectric power 4.1%, other 1.0%. Domestic energy demand by end use (1998): mining and manufacturing 46.3%, residential and commercial 26.3%, transportation 25.2%, other 2.2%.

Financial aggregates

	1994	1995	1996	1997	1998	1999	2000
Exchange rate[14], ¥ per:							
U.S. dollar	99.74	102.30	116.00	129.95	115.60	102.20	114.90
£	157.59	158.56	196.97	214.11	192.30	165.20	171.45
SDR	145.61	152.86	166.80	175.34	162.77	140.27	149.70
International reserves (U.S.$)							
Total (excl. gold; '000,000)	125,860	183,250	216,648	219,648	215,471	286,916	354,902
SDRs ('000,000)	2,083	2,707	2,648	2,638	2,663	2,656	2,437
Reserve pos. in IMF ('000,000)	8,100	8,100	6,671	9,144	9,593	6,552	5,253
Foreign exchange ('000,000)	115,146	172,443	207,335	207,866	203,215	277,708	347,212
Gold ('000,000 fine troy oz)	24.23	24.23	24.23	24.23	24.23	24.23	24.55
% world reserves	2.6	2.7	2.7	2.7	2.5	2.6	2.6
Interest and prices							
Central bank discount (%)[14]	1.75	0.50	0.50	0.50	0.50	0.50	0.50
Govt. bond yield (%)	3.71	2.27	2.23	1.69	1.10	1.77	1.75
Industrial share prices (1995 = 100)	115.8	100.0	116.3	101.1	85.4	100.4	112.0
Balance of payments (U.S.$'000,000,000)							
Balance of visible trade	144.19	131.79	83.56	101.60	122.39	123.32	116.72
Imports, f.o.b.	241.51	296.93	316.72	307.64	251.66	280.37	342.80
Exports, f.o.b.	385.70	428.72	400.28	409.24	374.04	403.69	459.51
Balance of invisibles	–13.93	–20.8	–17.68	–7.25	–1.69	–16.45	0.16
Balance of payments, current account	130.26	111.04	65.88	94.35	120.70	106.87	116.88

Retail and wholesale trade and services (1997)

	no. of establish-ments	avg. no. of em-ployees	annual sales (¥'000,000,000)
Retail trade	1,419,696	7,351,000	147,743
Food and beverages	526,460	2,795,000	42,825
Grocery	60,630	711,000	16,647
Liquors	83,770	248,000	5,493
General merchandise	5,078	505,000	21,022
Department stores	2,364	489,000	20,627
Motor vehicles and bicycles	87,837	558,000	19,598
Apparel and accessories	209,420	726,000	13,356
Furniture and home furnishings	134,868	541,000	12,583
Gasoline service stations	71,599	413,000	11,837
Books and stationery	68,289	667,000	5,218
Wholesale trade	391,574	4,165,000	479,813
Machinery and equipment	89,576	1,074,000	117,627
General machinery except electrical	36,685	366,000	30,827
Motor vehicles and parts	17,659	216,000	31,757
General merchandise	1,309	58,000	71,761
Farm, livestock, and fishery products	39,952	411,000	51,416
Food and beverages	87,437	519,000	46,432
Minerals and metals	18,191	211,000	44,279
Building materials	46,526	379,000	31,978
Textiles, apparel, and accessories	35,480	398,000	25,955
Chemicals	15,998	158,000	19,950
Drugs and toilet goods	17,514	255,000	20,033

Production (metric tons except as noted). Agriculture, forestry, fishing (2000): rice 11,863,000, sugar beets 3,800,000, potatoes 2,900,000, cabbages 2,600,000, sugarcane 1,512,000, sweet potatoes 1,073,000, onions 1,049,000, tomatoes 804,000, apples 800,000, cucumbers 767,000, wheat 689,000, carrots 677,000, watermelons 581,000, lettuce 540,000, eggplant 477,000, pears 424,000, spinach 330,000, cantaloupes 300,000, persimmons 279,000, pumpkins 254,000, taro 248,000, grapes 238,000, soybeans 235,000, barley 214,000, strawberries 205,000, yams 200,000, peaches 175,000, peppers 171,000, plums 119,000, cauliflower 116,000; livestock (number of live animals) 9,879,000 pigs, 4,658,000 cattle, 296,000,000 chickens; roundwood (1999) 19,031,000 cu m; fish catch (1998) 5,315,000, of which mackerel 1,122,000, sardines 739,000, squid 385,000, Alaska pollack 316,000, crabs 44,000. Mining and quarrying (1999): limestone 180,193,000; silica stone 18,312,000; dolomite 3,648,000; pyrophyllite 694,000; zinc 64,263; lead 6,074; copper 1,038; silver 94,004 kg; gold 9,405 kg. Manufacturing (1999): crude steel 94,192,000; steel products 86,335,000[15]; cement 80,120,000; pig iron 74,520,000; sulfuric acid 6,493,000; plastic products 6,035,000[15]; fertilizers 4,156,000[15]; spun yarn 507,475[15]; newsprint 3,192,300; synthetic fabrics 2,087,000 sq m[15]; cotton fabrics 814,000,000 sq m[15]; finished products (in number of units) 552,269,000 watches and clocks, 30,350,000[16] air conditioners, 12,051,000[15] videocassette recorders, 10,326,000 cameras, 9,684,000[15] video cameras, 9,639,000[15] computers, 8,100,000 passenger cars, 3,444,000 colour television receivers, 6,056,000[15] facsimile machines, 5,975,000[13] bicycles, 4,851,000[15] electric refrigerators, 4,468,000[15] automatic washing machines, 2,959,000[15] microwave ovens, 2,252,000 motorcycles, 1,903,000[16] photocopy machines. Construction (value in ¥'000,000; 1996): residential 44,240,000; nonresidential 28,800,000.

Foreign trade

Balance of trade (current prices)

	1995	1996	1997	1998	1999	2000
¥'000,000,000	+9,998	+6,737	+9,982	+13,991	+12,279	+10,734
% of total	13.7%	8.1%	10.9%	16.0%	14.8%	11.6%

Imports (1998): ¥36,654,000,000,000 (machinery and transport equipment 27.6%, food products 13.0%, petroleum and petroleum products 9.5%, chemicals and chemical products 7.4%, textiles 5.2%). *Major import sources:* United States 23.9%; China 13.2%; Australia 4.6%; South Korea 4.3%; Indonesia 3.9%; Germany 3.8%; Taiwan 3.6%; Malaysia 3.1%; Thailand 3.0%; United Arab Emirates 2.9%.

Exports (1998): ¥50,645,000,000,000 (electrical machinery 23.2%, motor vehicles 12.9%, chemicals 7.0%, scientific and optical equipment 4.2%, iron and steel products 3.8%, textiles and allied products 2.0%). *Major export destinations:* United States 30.5%; Taiwan 6.6%; Hong Kong 6.5%; China 5.2%; Germany 4.9%; South Korea 4.0%; Singapore 3.8%; United Kingdom 3.8%; The Netherlands 2.8%; Thailand 2.1%.

Trade by commodity group (1998)

	imports		exports	
SITC group	U.S.$'000,000	%	U.S.$'000,000	%
00 Food and live animals; 01 Beverages and tobacco	41,252	14.7	1,621	0.4
02 Crude materials, excluding fuels	23,185[17]	8.3[17]	2,876[17]	0.7[17]
03 Mineral fuels, lubricants, and related materials	43,336	15.4	1,485	0.4
04 Animal and vegetable oils, fats, and waxes	[17]	[17]	[17]	[17]
05 Chemicals and related products, n.e.s.	20,345	7.2	26,374	6.8
06 Basic manufactures	28,441	10.1	42,450	10.9
07 Machinery and transport equipment	74,716	26.6	267,884	69.0
08 Miscellaneous manufactured articles	43,328	15.4	32,558	8.4
09 Goods not classified by kind	5,316	1.9	12,467	3.2
TOTAL	280,634[18]	100.0[18]	388,136[18]	100.0[18]

Direction of trade (1999)

	imports		exports	
	U.S.$'000,000	%	U.S.$'000,000	%
Africa	3,930	1.3	4,311	1.0
Asia	154,654	49.8	167,690	40.0
South America	6,907	2.2	4,830	1.2
North America and Central America	77,865	25.0	150,301	35.8
United States	67,529	21.7	130,195	31.0
other North and Central Am.	10,336	3.3	20,106	4.8
Europe	53,750	17.3	80,432	19.2
EU	42,820	13.8	74,542	17.8
Russia	3,767	1.2	483	0.1
other Europe	7,163	2.3	5,407	1.3
Oceania	15,416	5.0	10,233	2.4
TOTAL	310,733[18]	100.0[18]	419,207[18]	100.0[18]

Transport and communications

Transport. Railroads (1998): length 16,937[16] mi, 27,258[16] km; rolling stock—locomotives 1,787[19], passenger cars 25,973[19], freight cars 12,688[19]; passengers carried 22,013,000,000; passenger-mi 241,674,000,000, passenger-km 388,938,000,000; short ton-mi cargo 15,699,000,000, metric ton-km cargo 22,920,000,000. Roads (1998): total length 718,300 mi, 1,156,000 km (paved 73%). Vehicles (1998): passenger cars 51,222,000; trucks 18,425,000; buses 236,000. Merchant marine (1999): vessels (100 gross tons and over) 6,140; total deadweight tonnage 16,198,000. Air transport (1998): passengers carried 102,749,000; passenger-mi 97,744,600,000, passenger-km 157,305,000,000; short ton-mi cargo 4,920,000,000, metric ton-km cargo 7,183,000,000; airports (1996) with scheduled flights 73.

Distribution of traffic (1998)

	cargo carried[16] ('000,000 tons)	% of national[16] total	passengers carried ('000,000)	% of national total
Road	6,177	90.8	52,819	70.5
Rail (intercity)	74	1.1	22,014	29.4
Urban transport (1997)	—	—	13,149	…
road	—	—	10,385	…
rail (subways)	—	—	2,764	…
Inland water	547	8.0	148[16]	0.2[16]
Air	1	0.0	87	0.1
TOTAL	6,799	100.0[7]	74,918[20]	100.0[20]

Communications

Medium	date	unit	number	units per 1,000 persons
Daily newspapers	1998	circulation	72,410,000	572
Radio	1997	receivers	120,500,000	955
Television	1997	receivers	86,500,000	686
Telephones	1999	main lines	70,530,000	558
Cellular telephones	1999	subscribers	56,846,000	449
Personal computers	1999	units	36,300,000	287
Internet	1999	users	27,060,000	214

Radio and television broadcasting (1994): total radio stations 1,340, of which commercial 481; total television stations 14,625, of which commercial 7,736. Commercial broadcasting hours (by percentage of programs; 1994): reports—radio 13.0%, television 21.0%; education—radio 3.4%, television 12.0%; culture—radio 14.9%, television 24.7%; entertainment—radio 67.6%, television 40.0%. Advertisements (daily average; 1994): radio 148, television 295.

Other communications media (1996)

	titles
Print	
Books (new)	60,462
of which	
Social sciences	12,607
Fiction	11,680
Arts	8,358
Engineering	5,479
Natural sciences	4,533
History	3,824
Philosophy	2,794
Magazines/journals	4,178
Weekly	112
Monthly	2,848
Cinema	
Feature films	610
Domestic	289
Foreign	321

	traffic ('000)
Electronic	
Telegram	40,368
Domestic	40,198
International	170
Fax service	1,015[21]
Post	
Mail	25,385,000
Domestic	24,971,000
International	414,000
Parcels	392,300
Domestic	386,000
International	6,300

Education and health

Literacy: total population age 15 and over literate, virtually 100%.

Education (1999)

	schools	teachers	students	student/ teacher ratio
Primary (age 6–11)	24,188	411,439	7,500,317	18.2
Secondary (age 12–17)	16,701	533,436	8,455,588	15.8
Higher	1,269	170,218	3,135,392	18.4

Health (1998): physicians 248,611 (1 per 508 persons); dentists 88,061 (1 per 1,436 persons); nurses 985,821 (1 per 128 persons); pharmacists 205,953 (1 per 614 persons); midwives 24,202 (1 per 5,223 persons); hospital beds 1,656,415 (1 per 76 persons), of which general 76.1%, mental 21.7%, tuberculosis 1.6%, other 0.6%; infant mortality rate per 1,000 live births (1999) 3.4.

Food (1999): daily per capita caloric intake 2,782 (vegetable products 79%, animal products 21%); 119% of FAO recommended minimum.

Military

Total active duty personnel (2000): 236,700[22] (army 62.7%, navy 18.0%, air force 18.7%). *Military expenditure as percentage of GNP* (1997): 1.0% (world 2.6%); per capita expenditure U.S.$325.

[1]October 1. [2]Excludes Lake Naka (38 sq mi [98 sq km]), which is part of both Shimane and Tottori prefectures. [3]Excludes Lake Towada (23 sq mi [60 sq km]), which is part of both Akita and Aomori prefectures. [4]Part of Kantō geographic region, [5]Part of Kinki geographic region. [6]1987 survey (includes Lake Naka and Lake Towada); total area per 1996 survey equals 145,884 sq mi (377,837 sq km). [7]Detail does not add to total given because of rounding. [8]August 1. [9]January 1. [10]Many Japanese practice both Shintōism and Buddhism. [11]Import duties and statistical discrepancy less imputed bank service charge. [12]Includes 2,790,000 unemployed. [13]1997. [14]End of period. [15]1998. [16]1996. [17]Crude materials includes Animal and vegetable oils, fats, and waxes. [18]Detail does not add to total given because of statistical discrepancies in the data. [19]1995. [20]Totals do not include Urban transport or Inland water. [21]Number of subscribers. [22]Includes 1,400 personnel not allocated to specific branch.

Internet resources for further information:

- **Bank of Japan http://www.boj.or.jp/en/index.htm**
- **Economic Planning Agency of Japan http://www.epa.go.jp/e-e/menu.html**
- **Statistics Bureau and Statistics Center (Japan) http://www.stat.go.jp/english/1.htm**

Jersey

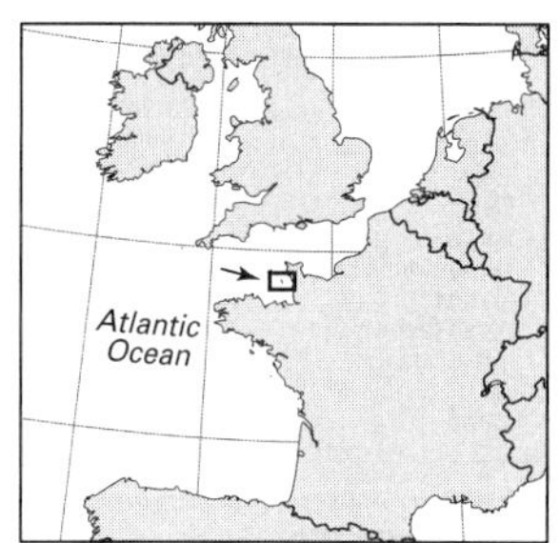

Official name: Bailiwick of Jersey.
Political status: crown dependency (United Kingdom) with one legislative house (States of Jersey [57][1]).
Chief of state: British Monarch represented by Lieutenant Governor.
Head of government: [2].
Capital: Saint Helier.
Official language: English[3].
Official religion: none.
Monetary unit: 1 Jersey pound (£J) = 100 pence; valuation (Sept. 28, 2001) 1 Jersey pound = U.S.$1.47; at par with the British pound.

Area and population	area		population
			1996
Parishes	sq mi	sq km	census
Grouville	3.0	7.8	4,658
St. Brelade	4.9	12.8	9,560
St. Clement	1.6	4.2	7,986
St. Helier	3.3	8.6	27,523
St. John	3.4	8.7	2,520
St. Lawrence	3.7	9.5	4,773
St. Martin	3.8	9.9	3,423
St. Mary	2.5	6.5	1,475
St. Ouen	5.8	15.0	3,685
St. Peter	4.5	11.6	4,228
St. Saviour	3.6	9.3	12,680
Trinity	4.7	12.3	2,639
TOTAL	44.9	116.2	85,150

Demography

Population (2001): 89,400.
Density (2001): persons per sq mi 1,991.1, persons per sq km 769.4.
Sex distribution (2000): male 49.07%; female 50.93%.
Age breakdown (2000): under 15, 17.7%; 15–29, 15.8%; 30–44, 27.2%; 45–59, 19.7%; 60–74, 12.9%; 75 and over, 6.7%.
Population projection: (2010) 91,900; (2020) 93,100.
Population by place of birth (1996): Jersey 52.7%; United Kingdom, Guernsey, or Isle of Man 34.5%; Portugal 5.4%; Ireland 2.6%; France 1.1%; other European Union 1.1%; other 2.6%.
Religious affiliation (2000)[4]: Christian 86.0%, of which Anglican 44.1%, Roman Catholic 14.6%, other Protestant 6.9%, unaffiliated Christian 20.1%; nonreligious/atheist 13.4%; other 0.6%.
Major cities (1996)[5]: St. Helier 27,523; St. Saviour 12,680; St. Brelade 9,560.

Vital statistics

Birth rate per 1,000 population (2000): 11.6 (world avg. 22.5).
Death rate per 1,000 population (2000): 9.3 (world avg. 9.0).
Natural increase rate per 1,000 population (2000): 2.3 (world avg. 13.5).
Total fertility rate (avg. births per childbearing woman; 2000): 1.6.
Marriage rate per 1,000 population: n.a.
Divorce rate per 1,000 population: n.a.
Life expectancy at birth (2000): male 76.1 years; female 81.1 years.
Major causes of death per 100,000 population: n.a.

National economy

Budget (2000). Revenue: £388,389,000 (corporate income tax 43.0%, individual income tax 26.9%, self-employment tax 11.6%, spirits and tobacco tax 6.0%, international business 5.4%, tax on fuel 3.0%). Expenditures: £300,030,000 (current expenditure 79.2%, of which health 27.8%, education 21.3%, social security 20.5%; capital expenditure 20.8%).
Production. Agriculture, forestry, fishing: fruits and vegetables, mostly potatoes and greenhouse tomatoes; greenhouse flowers are important export crops; livestock (number of live animals; 1999) 7,315 cattle, of which about 4,500 dairy cattle; roundwood, none; fish catch (metric tons; 1997)[4]: 4,368, of which crustaceans 2,934 (including sea spiders and crabs 2,713); mollusks 743 (including abalones, winkles, and conch 438); marine fish 691. Mining and quarrying: n.a. Manufacturing: light industry, mainly electrical goods, textiles and clothing; dairy products (including 179 hectolitres of milk in 1999). Construction: n.a. Energy production (consumption): electricity (kW-hr; 1995) 266,000,000 (467,000,000); crude petroleum, none (n.a.); petroleum products, n.a. (n.a.); natural gas, none (n.a.).
Gross national product (at current market prices; 1995): U.S.$2,670,000,000 (U.S.$30,940 per capita).

Structure of gross domestic product and labour force	1996			
	in value[6] £J'000,000	% of total value	labour force	% of labour force
Agriculture, fishing	74	5.0	2,162	4.6
Mining	...	...	193	0.4
Manufacturing	30	2.0	1,727	3.7
Construction	...	...	4,187	8.9
Public utilities	...	...	619	1.3
Transp. and commun.	...	...	2,602	5.5
Trade, hotels, restaurants	354[7]	24.0[7]	10,961	23.3
Finance, real estate[8]	811	55.0	11,604	24.7
Pub. admin., defense	...	...	2,140	4.6
Services	...	...	9,248	19.7
Other	206[9]	14.0[9]	1,549[10]	3.3[10]
TOTAL	1,475	100.0	46,992	100.0

Household income and expenditure. Average household size (1996) 2.4; income per household: n.a.; sources of income: n.a.; expenditure (1998–99)[11]: housing 20.1%, recreation 16.5%, transportation 12.8%, household furnishings 11.6%, food 11.5%, alcoholic beverages 6.0%, clothing and footwear 5.5%.
Population economically active (1996): total 46,992; activity rate of total population 55.2% (participation rates: ages 15–64, n.a.; female 44.6%; unemployed 3.3%).

Price index (1995 = 100)[12]	1995	1996	1997	1998	1999	2000
Consumer price index	100.0	103.6	107.2	111.7	115.6	120.2

Public debt: none.
Tourism (1996): receipts U.S.$429,000,000; expenditures by nationals abroad, n.a.; number of visitors for at least one night 670,000.
Land use (1997): land under cultivation 56.8%, other 43.2%.

Foreign trade

Imports: [13]. *Major import sources* (1999): mostly the United Kingdom.
Exports: [13]; agricultural exports (1996): £45,400,000 (potatoes 61.2%, greenhouse tomatoes 17.2%, zucchini 6.4%, greenhouse carnations and narcissus 6.0%). *Major export destinations:* mostly the United Kingdom.

Transport and communications

Transport. Railroads: none. Roads (1995): total length 346 mi, 557 km (paved 100%). Vehicles (1995): passenger cars 58,491; trucks and buses 9,109. Air transport (1999)[14]: passenger-mi 553,291,000, passenger-km 890,438,000; short ton-mi cargo 632,000, metric ton-km cargo 923,000; airports (1999) with scheduled flights 1.

Communications				units
Medium	date	unit	number	per 1,000 persons
Daily newspapers	1997	circulation	25,542	299
Telephones	1998	main lines	68,721	781
Cellular telephones	1998	subscribers	18,255	208
Internet	1999	users	1,000	12

Education and health

Educational attainment: n.a. *Literacy* (1996): total population age 15 and over literate 71,033 (100.0%).

Education (1996)	schools	teachers	students	student/ teacher ratio
Primary (age 5–10)	32	313[15]	6,906	...
Secondary (age 11–16)	14	373[15]	4,924	...
Voc., teacher tr.	...	...	...	...
Higher	1	...	1,298	...

Health (1995): physicians 95 (1 per 895 persons); hospital beds 651 (1 per 130 persons); infant mortality rate per 1,000 live births (2000) 5.7.
Food (1998): daily per capita caloric intake, n.a.

Military

Total active duty personnel (2000): none; defense is the responsibility of the United Kingdom.

[1]53 elected members include 12 senators popularly elected for six-year terms, 12 constables popularly elected triennially, and 29 deputies also popularly elected triennially; 4 nonelected members include the bailiff, the dean of Jersey, the attorney general, and the solicitor general. [2]Executive committees appointed by the States of Jersey (alternately called States Assembly). [3]Until the 1960s French was an official language of Jersey and is still used by the court and legal professions; Jerriais, a Norman-French dialect, is spoken by a small number of residents. [4]Includes Guernsey. [5]Population of parishes. [6]Calculation based on percentage distribution. [7]Represents tourism-related businesses. [8]Jersey is an international finance centre with 79 banks in 1998 and over 33,000 registered companies; of more than U.S.$160,000,000,000 deposited in the island, 62 percent is in foreign (not £J or £) currency. [9]Represents investment income from abroad received by residents. [10]Unemployed seeking work. [11]Weights of retail price index components. [12]June. [13]Customs ceased recording imports and exports as of 1980. [14]Jersey European Airways. [15]1990.

Internet resources for further information:

- **An Introduction to Jersey**
  http://www.adwebjersey.co.uk/states.html
- **This is Jersey**
  http://www.thisisjersey.com

Jordan

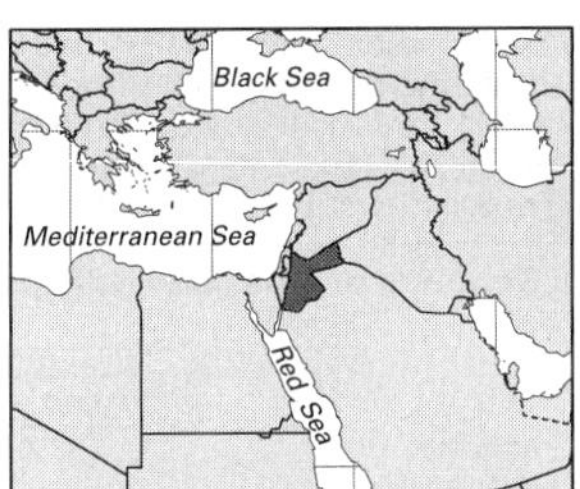

Official name: Al-Mamlakah al-Urdunnīyah al-Hāshimīyah (Al-Urdun) (Hashemite Kingdom of Jordan).
Form of government: constitutional monarchy with two legislative houses (Senate [40[1]]; House of Representatives [80]).
Head of state and government: King assisted by Prime Minister.
Capital: Amman.
Official language: Arabic.
Official religion: Islam.
Monetary unit: 1 Jordan dinar (JD) = 1,000 fils; valuation (Sept. 28, 2001) JD 1.00 = U.S.$1.41 = £0.96.

Area and population

		area		population
Governorates	Capitals	sq mi	sq km	1999 estimate[2]
ʻAjlūn	ʻAjlun	159	412	105,500
ʻAmman	Amman	3,178	8,231	1,809,800
Al-ʻAqabah	Al-ʻAqabah	2,542	6,583	95,400
Al-Balqāʼ	Aṣ-Ṣalt	415	1,076	312,200
Irbid	Irbid	626	1,621	848,300
Jarash	Jarash	155	402	139,800
Al-Karak	Al-Karak	1,242	3,217	191,400
Maʻān	Maʻān	12,804	33,163	92,700
Mādabā	Mādabā	775	2,008	121,300
Al-Mafraq	Al-Mafraq	10,207	26,435	219,000
Aṭ-Ṭafīlah	Aṭ-Ṭafīlah	816	2,114	72,500
Az-Zarqāʼ	Az-Zarqāʼ	1,575	4,080	747,900
TOTAL		34,495[3]	89,342	4,755,800

Demography

Population (2001): 5,132,000.
Density (2001): persons per sq mi 148.8, persons per sq km 57.4.
Urban-rural (2000): urban 74.2%; rural 25.8%.
Sex distribution (2001): male 52.35%; female 47.65%.
Age breakdown (2000): under 15, 37.9%; 15–29, 30.9%; 30–44, 18.3%; 45–59, 7.8%; 60–74, 4.2%; 75 and over, 0.9%.
Population projection: (2010) 6,486,000; (2020) 7,920,000.
Doubling time: 30 years.
Ethnic composition (2000): Arab 97.8%, of which Jordanian 32.4%, Palestinian 32.2%, Iraqi 14.0%, Bedouin 12.8%; Armenian 1.7%; Circassian 1.2%.
Religious affiliation (2000): Shiʼi Muslim 59.5%; Sunnī Muslim 36.5%; Christian 3.2%.
Major cities (1994): Amman 969,598; Az-Zarqāʼ 350,849; Irbid 208,329; Ar-Ruṣayfah 137,247; Wādi Essier 89,104; Al-ʻAqabah 62,773.

Vital statistics

Birth rate per 1,000 population (2000): 26.2 (world avg. 22.5).
Death rate per 1,000 population (2000): 2.6 (world avg. 9.0).
Natural increase rate per 1,000 population (2000): 23.6 (world avg. 13.5).
Total fertility rate (avg. births per childbearing woman; 2000): 3.4.
Life expectancy at birth (2000): male 74.9 years; female 79.9 years.
Major causes of death per 100,000 population: n.a.

National economy

Budget (1998 est.). Revenue: JD 1,688,000,000 (taxes 50.8%, of which sales tax 20.7%, custom duties 17.1%, income and profits taxes 8.3%; nontax 37.1%, of which licenses and fees 11.4%; external aid 12.0%). Expenditures: JD 2,047,000,000 (current 81.9%, of which defense 24.1%, interest expense 11.7%, wages and salaries 17.2%; capital construction 18.1%).
Public debt (external, outstanding; 1999): U.S.$7,546,000,000.
Production (metric tons except as noted). Agriculture, forestry, fishing (1999): tomatoes 305,100, watermelons 97,400, potatoes 92,600, cucumbers 73,900, bananas 72,500, olives 55,000, lemons and limes 41,600, apples 34,200, pumpkins and squash 31,400, cabbages 28,400; livestock (number of live animals) 2,000,000 sheep, 795,000 goats, 65,000 cattle, 18,000 camels; roundwood (1998) 3,000 cu m; fish catch (1998) 470. Mining and quarrying (1998): phosphate ore 5,925,000; potash 1,527,000. Manufacturing (value added in JD '000; 1997): chemicals 130,276; nonmetallic mineral products, pottery, and china 114,897; tobacco 96,380; food products 80,994; refined petroleum 60,028; plastic products 25,627. Construction (permits issued; 1998): residential 3,427,600 sq m; nonresidential 669,600. Energy production (consumption): electricity (kW-hr; 1996) 6,058,000,000 (6,058,000,000); crude petroleum (barrels; 1996) 14,400 (23,790,000); petroleum products (metric tons; 1996) 3,102,000 (3,932,000).
Land use (1994): forest 0.8%; pasture 8.9%; agriculture 4.6%; other 85.7%.
Tourism (1999): receipts U.S.$795,000,000; expenditures U.S.$355,000,000.
Population economically active (1993): total 859,300; activity rate of total population 22.2% (participation rates: over age 15, 43.6%; female 14.0%; unemployed [1996] 13.0%).

Price and earnings indexes (1995 = 100)

	1994	1995	1996	1997	1998	1999	2000
Consumer price index	97.7	100.0	106.5	109.7	113.1	113.8	114.6
Daily earnings index	...	...	...	...	...	...	...

Gross national product (1999): U.S.$7,717,000,000 (U.S.$1,630 per capita).

Structure of gross domestic product and labour force

	1997		1993	
	in value JD '000,000	% of total value	labour force	% of labour force
Agriculture	151.1	3.1	54,995	6.4
Mining	202.4	4.1	91,086	10.6
Manufacturing	840.1	17.0		
Construction	224.2	4.5	60,151	7.0
Public utilities	117.8	2.4	6,015	0.7
Transp. and commun.	672.9	13.6	57,573	6.7
Trade[4]	546.0	11.0	129,754	15.1
Finance	804.3	16.3	24,920	2.9
Pub. admin., defense	890.9	18.0	434,806	50.6
Services[5]	216.5	4.4		
Other	279.6[6]	5.6[6]		
TOTAL	4,945.8	100.0	859,300	100.0

Household income and expenditure. Average household size (1995) 6.1; income per household (1995) JD 4,010 (U.S.$5,725); sources of income (1995): wages and salaries 51.4%, rent and property income 23.8%, transfer payments 13.7%, self-employment 11.1%; expenditure (1992): food and beverages 40.6%, housing and energy 26.9%, transportation 11.2%, clothing and footwear 8.2%, education 3.5%, health care 2.2%.

Foreign trade

Balance of trade (current prices)

	1995	1996	1997	1998	1999	2000
JD '000,000	–1,349.3	–1,851.0	–1,609.0	–1,436.5	–1,336.4	–1,872.8
% of total	35.2%	41.8%	38.2%	36.0%	34.0%	41.0%

Imports (1998): JD 2,719,900,000 (machinery and transport equipment 28.5%; food and live animals 19.6%; chemicals and chemical products 12.7%; mineral fuels 9.4%; iron and steel 4.0%). *Major import sources:* Germany 9.8%; United States 9.5%; Iraq 8.8%; Japan 5.8%; United Kingdom 5.1%; Italy 4.9%.
Exports (1998): JD 1,275,600,000 (domestic goods 81.9%, of which chemicals and chemical products 25.3%, phosphate fertilizers 11.0%, potash 8.7%, fruits, vegetables, and nuts 8.3%, machinery and transport equipment 3.5%; reexports 18.1%). *Major export destinations*[7]: India 11.2%; Iraq 10.3%; Saudi Arabia 9.9%; Lebanon 2.9%; Kuwait 2.6%.

Transport and communications

Transport. Railroads (1995): route length 677 km; passenger traffic was negligible; metric ton-km cargo 1,336,000,000[8]. Roads (1998): total length 7,133 km (paved 100%). Vehicles (1996): passenger cars 213,874; trucks and buses 79,153. Merchant marine (1995): vessels (1,000 gross tons and over) 1; total deadweight tonnage 15,794. Air transport (1998)[9]: passenger-km 4,064,737,000; metric ton-km cargo 219,219,000; airports (1997) 2.

Communications

Medium	date	unit	number	units per 1,000 persons
Daily newspapers	1996	circulation	250,000	57
Radio	1997	receivers	1,660,000	395
Television	1999	receivers	540,000	83
Telephones	1999	main lines	565,000	85
Cellular telephones	1999	subscribers	118,000	18
Personal computers	1999	units	90,000	14
Internet	1999	users	120,000	19

Education and health

Educational attainment (2000). Percentage of population age 25 and over having: no formal schooling 16.7%; primary education 49.2%; secondary 16.7%; postsecondary and vocational 9.5%; higher 8.2%. *Literacy* (2000): percentage of population age 15 and over literate 88.8%; males literate 94.9%; females literate 84.4%.

Education (1995–96)

	schools	teachers	students	student/ teacher ratio
Primary (age 6–14)	2,531	51,721	1,074,877	20.8
Secondary (age 15–17)	741[10]	8,615	143,014	16.6
Voc., teacher tr.	54[10]	2,306	33,109	14.4
Higher	55[11]	4,821[12]	99,020[12]	20.5

Health (1998): physicians 7,480 (1 per 625 persons); hospital beds 8,565 (1 per 546 persons); infant mortality rate per 1,000 live births (2000) 21.1.
Food (1999): daily per capita caloric intake 2,834 (vegetable products 89%, animal products 11%); 115% of FAO recommended minimum requirement.

Military

Total active duty personnel (2000): 103,800 (army 86.6%, navy 0.5%, air force 12.9%). *Military expenditure as percentage of GDP* (1997): 9.0% (world 2.6%); per capita expenditure U.S.$145.

[1]Appointed by king. [2]January 1. [3]Detail does not add to total given because of rounding. [4]Includes hotels. [5]Includes domestic help employed in households. [6]Imputed bank service charges. [7]Domestic exports only. [8]For Aqaba Railway Corporation only. [9]Royal Jordanian airlines only. [10]1993–94. [11]1988–89. [12]Includes community colleges.

Internet resources for further information:
- **Dept. of Statistics http://www.dos.gov.jo**
- **Jordan National Information System http://www.nic.gov.jo**

Kazakhstan

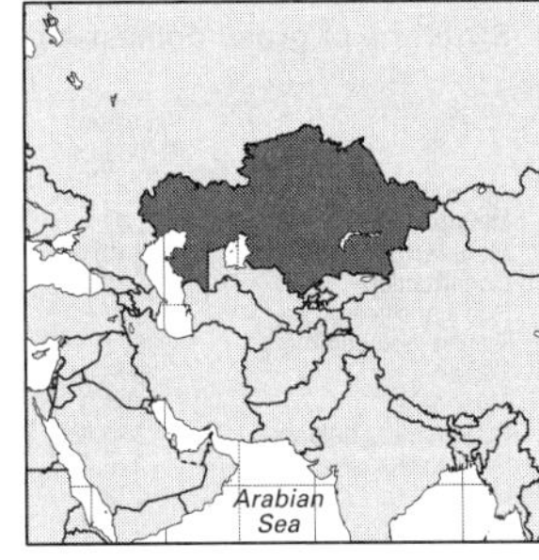

Official name: Qazaqstan Respūblīkasy (Republic of Kazakhstan).
Form of government: unitary republic with a Parliament consisting of two chambers (Senate [39[1]] and Assembly [77]).
Head of state and government: President assisted by Prime Minister.
Capital: Astana[2].
Official language: Kazakh[3].
Official religion: none.
Monetary unit: 1 tenge (T) = 100 tiyn; valuation (Sept. 28, 2001) free rate, 1 U.S.$ = 147.84 tenge; 1 £ = 217.27 tenge.

Area and population

Provinces	Capitals	area sq mi	area sq km	population 1999 census
Almaty (Alma-Ata)	Almaty (Alma-Ata)	86,500[4]	224,200[4]	1,559,522
Aqmola	Astana[2]	35,500[5, 6]	92,000[5, 6]	835,661
Aqtöbe	Aqtöbe	116,050	300,600	682,793
Atyraū	Atyraū	45,800	118,600	439,900
Batys Qazaqstan	Oral	58,400	151,300	617,624
Mangghystaū	Aqtaū	63,950	165,600	316,847
Ongtüstik Qazaqstan	Shymkent	45,300	117,300	1,976,689
Pavlodar	Pavlodar	48,200	124,800	806,034
Qaraghandy	Qaraghandy	165,250	428,000	1,411,401
Qostanay	Qostanay	44,000[5]	113,000[5]	1,019,560
Qyzylorda	Qyzylorda	87,250[7]	226,000[7]	596,344[7]
Shyghys Qazaqstan	Shyghys Qazaqstan	109,400	283,300	1,530,792
Soltüstik Qazaqstan	Petropavl	47,500	123,200	725,932
Zhambyl	Zhambyl (Aullye-Ata)	55,700	144,300	983,935
Cities				
Almaty (Alma-Ata)	—	4	4	1,130,068
Astana	—	6	6	319,318
Bayqongyr (Leninsk)[7]	—	...	...	...
TOTAL		1,052,100[8]	2,724,900	14,952,420

Demography

Population (2001): 14,868,000.
Density (2001): persons per sq mi 14.1, persons per sq km 5.5.
Urban-rural (1997): urban 57.0%; rural 43.0%.
Sex distribution (1997): male 48.61%; female 51.39%.
Age breakdown (1997): under 15, 29.3%; 15–29, 25.4%; 30–44, 22.2%; 45–59, 12.9%; 60 and over, 10.2%.
Population projection: (2010) 15,352,000; (2020) 16,477,000.
Ethnic composition (1995)[9]: Kazakh 46.0%; Russian 34.7%; Ukrainian 4.9%; German 3.1%; Uzbek 2.3%; Tatar 1.9%; other 7.1%.
Religious affiliation (1995): Muslim (mostly Sunnī) 47.0%; Russian Orthodox 8.2%; Protestant 2.1%; other (mostly nonreligious) 42.7%.
Major cities (1999): Almaty (Alma-Ata) 1,129,400; Qaraghandy (Karaganda) 436,900; Shymkent (Chimkent) 360,100; Taraz 330,100.

Vital statistics

Birth rate per 1,000 population (2001): 16.5 (world avg. 22.5); (1994) legitimate 86.6%; illegitimate 13.4%.
Death rate per 1,000 population (2001): 10.1 (world avg. 9.0).
Natural increase rate per 1,000 population (2001): 6.4 (world avg. 13.5).
Total fertility rate (avg. births per childbearing woman; 2001): 2.0.
Marriage rate per 1,000 population (1996): 6.4.
Divorce rate per 1,000 population (1996): 2.5.
Life expectancy at birth (2001): male 59.0 years; female 71.0 years.
Major causes of death per 100,000 population (1996): diseases of the circulatory system 436.2; malignant neoplasms (cancers) 133.0; accidents, poisoning, and violence 101.1; diseases of the respiratory system 71.0.

National economy

Budget (1998). Revenue: 262,916,000,000 tenge (taxes on goods and services 32.6%, social security contributions 23.4%, income, profits, and capital gains taxes 8.5%, taxes on international trade 3.7%, payroll taxes 3.2%). Expenditures: 318,252,000,000 tenge (social security and welfare 38.1%, general public services 7.9%, health 7.7%, public order 7.3%, defense 5.1%).
Public debt (external, outstanding; 1999): U.S.$2,995,000,000.
Population economically active (1995): total 6,976,000; activity rate of total population 41.8% (participation rates: ages 16–59 [male], 16–54 [female] 80.1%; female [1994] 48.0%; unemployed 2.3%).

Price and earnings indexes (1995 = 100)

	1994	1995	1996	1997	1998	1999	2000
Consumer price index	36.2	100.0	139.3	163.4	175.0	189.6	214.6
Monthly earnings index	36.1	100.0	142.9	178.5	202.3	229.5	288.5

Production (metric tons except as noted). Agriculture, forestry, fishing (1999): wheat 11,242,000, barley 2,265,000, potatoes 1,695,000, oats 194,000, sugar beets 294,000; livestock (number of live animals) 9,556,000 sheep and goats, 3,958,000 cattle, 986,000 horses, 892,000 pigs; roundwood (1998) 315,000 cu m; fish catch (1997) 41,367. Mining and quarrying (1998): titanium 12,000,000; magnesium 9,000,000; iron ore 8,693,000; nickel 6,000,000; bauxite 3,400,000; chromite 1,600,000. Manufacturing (value of production in '000,000 tenge; 1996): food products 107,397; nonferrous metallurgy 89,052; ferrous metallurgy 81,026; machinery 52,168; chemical products 28,974; construction materials 23,239. Construction (1994): residential 2,300,000 sq m. Energy production (consumption): electricity (kW-hr; 1996) 58,657,000,000 (65,502,000,000); coal (metric tons; 1996) 76,597,000 (55,852,000); crude petroleum (barrels; 1996) 150,000,000 (63,000,000); petroleum products (metric tons; 1996) 10,894,000 (10,627,000); natural gas (cu m; 1996) 7,107,000,000 (10,609,000,000).
Gross national product (1999): U.S.$18,732,000,000 (U.S.$1,250 per capita).

Structure of gross domestic product and labour force

	1998 in value '000,000 tenge	1998 % of total value	1995 labour force	1995 % of labour force
Agriculture	147,385	8.4	1,442,000	20.7
Manufacturing, mining, public utilities	383,614	21.9	1,372,000	19.7
Construction	77,652	4.4	364,000	5.2
Transp. and commun.	192,944	11.0	507,000	7.3
Trade	303,133	17.4	1,035,000	14.8
Finance	} 642,992	} 36.8	334,000	4.8
Pub. admin., defense			} 1,664,000	} 23.9
Services				
Other	...	...	258,000[10]	3.7[10]
TOTAL	1,747,720	100.0[8]	6,976,000	100.0[8]

Household income and expenditure. Average household size (1989) 4.0; income per household: n.a.; sources of income (1994): salaries and wages 67.7%, social benefits 16.9%, agricultural income 5.8%, other 9.6%; expenditure (1994): retail goods 60.6%, taxes 16.8%, services 11.7%, other 10.9%.

Foreign trade[11]

Balance of trade (current prices)

	1994	1995	1996	1997	1998	1999
U.S.$'000,000	–920	+114.1	–335.0	–276.4	–750.1	+686.0
% of total	12.3%	1.1%	2.6%	2.0%	6.0%	5.7%

Imports (1998): U.S.$6,574,700,000 (electrical equipment and mechanical tools 18.3%, vehicles 5.9%, nonfood consumer goods 5.4%, foodstuffs 3.7%, petroleum products 2.8%). *Major import sources:* Russia 39.4%; Germany 8.6%; U.S. 6.3%; U.K. 5.0%; Uzbekistan 2.3%.
Exports (1998): U.S.$5,773,800,000 (oil and gas condensate 28.6%, rolled ferrous metal 8.9%, refined copper 8.8%, coal 5.6%, grain 5.1%). *Major export destinations:* Russia 28.9%; U.K. 9.0%; China 7.2%; Switzerland 6.1%.

Transport and communications

Transport. Railroads: (1999) route length 13,500 km; (1998) passenger-km 13,000,000,000; metric ton-km cargo 107,500,000,000. Roads (1997): total length 125,796 km (paved 83%). Vehicles (1997): passenger cars 973,323; trucks and buses 361,920. Air transport (1995): passenger-km 2,429,000,000; metric ton-km cargo 237,000,000; airports (1997) with scheduled flights 20.

Communications

Medium	date	unit	number	units per 1,000 persons
Radio	1997	receivers	6,470,000	395
Television	1998	receivers	3,890,000	238
Telephones	1999	main lines	1,760,000	108
Cellular telephones	1999	subscribers	49,500	3.0
Personal computers	...	units	...	...
Internet	1999	users	70,000	4.3

Education and health

Educational attainment (1989). Population age 25 and over having: primary education or no formal schooling 16.2%; some secondary 19.8%; completed secondary and some postsecondary 54.1%; higher 9.9%. *Literacy* (1989): population age 15 and over literate 97.5%; males 99.1%; females 96.1%.

Education (1996–97)

	schools	teachers	students	student/ teacher ratio
Primary (age 7–13)	8,611[12]	262,000[12]	1,342,035	11.7[12]
Secondary (age 14–17)	...	...	1,743,623	...
Voc., teacher tr.	3,504[13]	...	177,679	...
Higher	69[13]	...	260,043[12]	...

Health (1997): physicians 55,800 (1 per 287 persons); hospital beds 136,000 (1 per 115 persons); infant mortality rate per 1,000 live births (2001) 43.0.

Military

Total active duty personnel (2000): 64,000 (army 70.3%, air force 29.7%). *Military expenditure as percentage of GNP* (1997): 1.3% (world avg. 2.6%); per capita expenditure U.S.$41.

[1]Includes 7 nonelective seats. [2]City of Akmola (Kazakh: Aqmola; new capital replacing Almaty) was renamed Astana on May 6, 1998. [3]Russian commands equal status with Kazakh at state-owned organizations and bodies of local government per a law effective July 16, 1997. [4]Area of Almaty city included with Almaty province. [5]Excludes parts of the former Torghay province incorporated into Aqmola and Qostanay provinces in 1997. The total area of Torghay province was 43,150 sq mi (111,800 sq km). [6]Area of Astana city is included with Aqmola province. [7]Bayqongyr city included with Qyzylorda province. [8]Detail does not add to total given because of rounding. [9]Kazakh and Russian percents for 1998 equaled 52 and 31, respectively. [10]Includes 139,600 undistributed unemployed and 118,400 undistributed employed. [11]Imports and exports are f.o.b. in balance of trade. [12]1995–96. [13]1994–95.

Internet resources for further information:
- **National Bank of Kazakhstan**
  http://www.nationalbank.kz/eng
- **Agency on Statistics of Kazakhstan**
  http://www.kazstat.asdc.kz/indexe.htm

Kenya

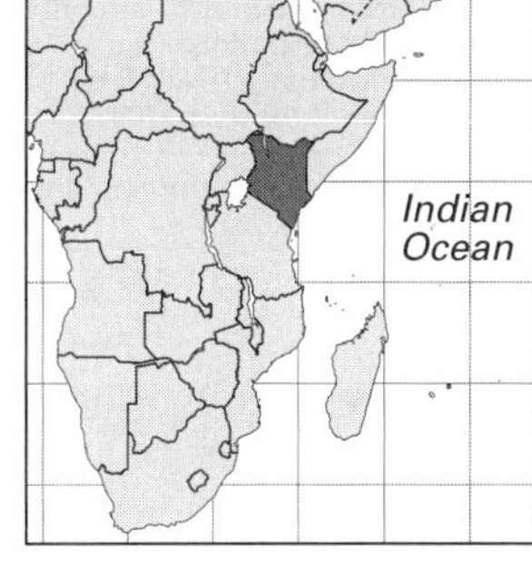

Official name: Jamhuri ya Kenya (Swahili); Republic of Kenya (English).
Form of government: unitary multiparty republic with one legislative house (National Assembly [224[1]]).
Head of state and government: President.
Capital: Nairobi.
Official languages: Swahili; English.
Official religion: none.
Monetary unit: 1 Kenya shilling[2] (K Sh) = 100 cents; valuation (Sept. 28, 2001) 1 U.S.$ = K Sh 79.11; 1 £ = K Sh 116.26.

Area and population

Provinces	Provincial headquarters	area sq mi	area sq km	population 1999 census[3]
Central	Nyeri	5,087	13,176	3,724,159
Coast	Mombasa	32,279	83,603	2,487,264
Eastern	Embu	61,734	159,891	4,631,779
North Eastern	Garissa	48,997	126,902	962,143
Nyanza	Kisumu	6,240	16,162	4,392,196
Rift Valley	Nakuru	67,131	173,868	6,987,036
Western	Kakamega	3,228	8,360	3,358,776
Special area				
Nairobi	—	264	684	2,143,254
TOTAL		224,961[4]	582,646	28,686,607

Demography

Population (2001)[5]: 30,766,000.
Density (2001): persons per sq mi 136.8, persons per sq km 52.8.
Urban-rural (1999): urban 32.2%; rural 67.8%.
Sex distribution (1999): male 49.52%; female 50.48%.
Age breakdown (1999): under 15, 43.6%; 15–29, 31.2%; 30–44, 14.1%; 45–59, 7.0%; 60–74, 3.3%; 75 and over, 0.8%.
Population projection[5]: (2010) 33,068,000; (2020) 34,001,000.
Doubling time: 39 years.
Ethnic composition (1989): Kikuyu 17.7%; Luhya 12.4%; Luo 10.6%; Kalenjin 9.8%; Kamba 9.8%; other 39.7%.
Religious affiliation (2000): Christian 79.3%, of which Roman Catholic 22.0%, African Christian 20.8%, Protestant 20.1%; Muslim 7.3%; other 13.4%
Major cities (1999): Nairobi 2,143,254[6]; Mombasa 465,000[6]; Nakuru 231,262; Kisumu 185,100[6]; Meru 126,427; Eldoret 104,900[6].

Vital statistics

Birth rate per 1,000 population (2000): 29.4 (world avg. 22.5).
Death rate per 1,000 population (2000): 14.1 (world avg. 9.0).
Natural increase rate per 1,000 population (2000): 15.3 (world avg. 13.5).
Total fertility rate (avg. births per childbearing woman; 2000): 3.7.
Life expectancy at birth (2000): male 47.0 years; female 49.0 years.
Major causes of death per 100,000 population: n.a.; however, major infectious diseases include AIDS, malaria, gastroenteritis, venereal diseases, diarrhea and dysentery, trachoma, amebiasis, and schistosomiasis.

National economy

Budget (1996–97). Revenue: K Sh 155,032,000,000 (tax revenue 83.4%, nontax revenue 12.9%, grants 3.7%). Expenditures: K Sh 168,403,000,000 (1995–96; recurrent expenditure 80.7%, of which interest on debt 24.3%, administration 21.9%, education 19.3%, defense 5.9%, health 5.8%; development expenditure 19.3%).
Production (metric tons except as noted). Agriculture, forestry, fishing (1999): sugarcane 5,200,000, corn (maize) 2,100,000, cassava 920,000, sweet potatoes 720,000, plantains 380,000, potatoes 350,000, pineapples 290,000, pulses 240,000, tea 220,000, bananas 220,000, wheat 135,000, sorghum 130,000, coffee 66,000, coconuts 65,000, barley 50,000, millet 50,000, tomatoes 31,000, sisal 26,000, seed cotton 15,000, tobacco 10,000, cotton seeds 8,000, cashew nuts 8,000, sunflower seeds 5,500; livestock (number of live animals) 13,392,000 cattle, 7,600,000 goats, 5,800,000 sheep; roundwood (1998) 29,337,000 cu m; fish catch (1998) 172,592, of which freshwater fish 95.0%. Mining and quarrying (1995): soda ash 218,450; fluorite 80,230; salt 71,400. Manufacturing (value added in K£'000[2]; 1994): food products 639,000; machinery and transport equipment 233,000; beverages and tobacco 190,000; chemical products 168,000; metal products 125,000; paper and paper products 87,000; plastic products 65,000; clothing and footwear 55,000. Construction (1990): residential 411,000 sq m; nonresidential 182,000 sq m. Energy production (consumption): electricity (kW-hr; 1996) 3,745,000,000 (3,920,000,000); coal (metric tons; 1996) none (100,000); crude petroleum (barrels; 1996) none (13,487,000); petroleum products (metric tons; 1996) 1,722,000 (2,016,000).
Public debt (external, outstanding; 1999): U.S.$5,385,000,000.
Household income and expenditure. Average household size (1998): 3.4; average annual income per household: n.a.; sources of income: n.a.; expenditure (1980): food 46.5%, housing 10.0%, furniture and utensils 9.4%, transportation 8.4%, clothing and footwear 7.7%, energy 2.6%, health 2.2%.
Tourism (1999): receipts from visitors U.S.$304,000,000; expenditures by nationals abroad U.S.$115,000,000.
Population economically active (1997): total 14,592,000; activity rate of total population 50.0% (participation rates [1985]: ages 15–64, 76.2%; female [1997] 46.1%; unemployed, n.a.).

Price and earnings indexes (1995 = 100)

	1994	1995	1996	1997	1998	1999	2000
Consumer price index	99.2	100.0	108.8	121.9	129.0	132.4	140.1
Earnings index	...	...	...	...	...	...	...

Gross national product (1999): U.S.$10,696,000,000 (U.S.$360 per capita).

Structure of gross domestic product and labour force

	1996 in value K Sh '000,000	1996 % of total value	1995 labour force[7]	1995 % of labour force[7]
Agriculture	130,471	30.0	294,000	18.9
Mining	741	0.2	5,000	0.3
Manufacturing	45,645	10.5	205,000	13.1
Construction	20,012	4.6	76,000	4.9
Public utilities	5,515	1.3	23,000	1.5
Transp. and commun.	34,277	7.9	79,000	5.1
Trade	82,895	19.0	135,000	8.7
Finance	79,055	18.1	78,000	5.0
Pub. admin., defense / Services	36,869	8.5	663,000	42.6
Other	—	—	—	—
TOTAL	435,480	100.0[4]	1,558,000	100.0

Land use (1994): forest 29.5%; pasture 37.4%; agriculture 8.0%; other 25.1%.

Foreign trade[8]

Balance of trade (current prices)

	1995	1996	1997	1998	1999	2000
K Sh '000,000	–57,884	–50,260	–70,714	–71,780	–76,246	–104,430
% of total	22.9%	17.5%	22.8%	22.8%	23.8%	28.3%

Imports (1997): U.S.$3,294,000,000 (machinery and transport equipment 28.9%, manufactured goods 22.0%, mineral fuels 15.6%, chemical products 14.5%, food and beverages 12.4%). *Major import sources:* Middle East 15.8%; U.K. 10.7%; U.S. 7.9%; Japan 7.4%; India 7.5%; South Africa 7.4%; Germany 6.0%; Italy 5.2%; United States 3.6%; Saudi Arabia 2.0%.
Exports (1997): U.S.$2,105,000,000 (tea 20.5%, coffee [not roasted] 14.3%, petroleum products 7.8%, horticulture 7.3%, fruits and vegetables 3.1%, cement 2.1%, soda ash 1.1%, hides and skins 0.6%). *Major export destinations:* Uganda 15.1%; Tanzania 12.9%; U.K. 11.4%; Germany 6.8%; The Netherlands 4.8%; U.S. 3.0%.

Transport and communications

Transport. Railroads (1996): route length 1,885 mi, 3,034 km; passenger-mi 239,000,000; passenger-km 385,000,000; short ton-mi cargo 813,000,000, metric ton-km cargo 1,309,000,000. Roads (1996): total length 39,600 mi, 63,800 km (paved 14%). Vehicles (1996): passenger cars 278,000; trucks and buses 81,200. Merchant marine (1992): vessels (100 gross tons and over) 29; total deadweight tonnage 11,649. Air transport (1996): passenger-mi 1,062,000,000, passenger-km 1,709,000,000; short ton-mi cargo 126,100,000, metric ton-km cargo 203,000,000; airports (1997) with scheduled flights 11.

Communications

Medium	date	unit	number	units per 1,000 persons
Daily newspapers	1996	circulation	263,000[9]	9.4[9]
Radio	1997	receivers	3,070,000	107
Television	1999	receivers	660,000	23.0
Telephones	1999	main lines	304,626	10.6
Cellular telephones	1999	subscribers	23,757	0.8
Personal computers	1999	units	125,000	4.4
Internet	1999	users	35,000	1.2

Education and health

Educational attainment (1979). Percentage of population age 25 and over having: no formal schooling 58.6%; primary education 32.2%; some secondary 7.9%; complete secondary and higher 1.3%. *Literacy* (1995): total population over age 15 literate 77.3%; males literate 85.6%; females literate 69.1%.

Education (1993)

	schools	teachers	students	student/teacher ratio
Primary (age 5–11)	15,906	181,975	5,544,998	30.5
Secondary (age 12–17)	2,878	41,484	632,388	15.2
Voc., teacher tr.	62	...	29,593[10]	...
Higher	14	4,392[10, 11]	88,180[10]	8.1[10, 11]

Health (1994): physicians 4,558 (1 per 5,999 persons); hospital beds 37,271 (1 per 734 persons); infant mortality rate per 1,000 live births (2000): 68.7.
Food (1999): daily per capita caloric intake 1,887 (vegetable products 88%, animal products 12%); 81% of FAO recommended minimum requirement.

Military

Total active duty personnel (2000): 22,200 (army 82.0%, navy 4.5%, air force 13.5%). *Military expenditure as percentage of GNP* (1997): 7.2% (world 2.6%); per capita expenditure U.S.$7.

[1]Includes 14 nonelective seats. [2]Kenya pound (K£) as a unit of account equals 20 K Sh. [3]Preliminary. [4]Detail does not add to total given because of rounding. [5]Not based on August 1999 census results. [6]1989 census. [7]Employed persons only. [8]Import figures are c.i.f. [9]Circulation for four newspapers only. [10]1993. [11]Universities only.

Internet resources for further information:
- **Central Bank of Kenya http://www.africaonline.co.ke/cbk**
- **Ministry of Finance and Planning http://www.treasury.go.ke**

Kiribati

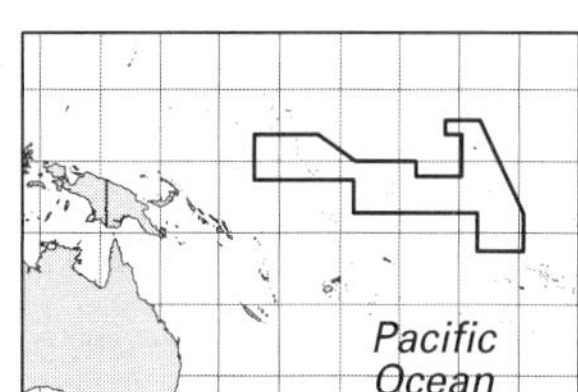

Official name: Republic of Kiribati.
Form of government: unitary republic with a unicameral legislature (House of Assembly [42[1]]).
Head of state and government: President.
Capital: Bairiki, on Tarawa Atoll.
Official language: English.
Official religion: none.
Monetary unit: 1 Australian Dollar ($A) = 100 cents; valuation (Sept. 28, 2001) 1 U.S.$ = $A 2.03; 1 £ = $A 2.98.

Area and population

		area[2]		population
Island Groups				1995
Islands	Capitals	sq mi	sq km	census
Gilberts Group	Bairiki Islet	110	286[3]	71,757
Abaiang	Tuarabu	7	18	6,020
Abemama	Kariatebike	11	27	3,442
Aranuka	Takaeang	5	12	1,015
Arorae	Roreti	3	9	1,248
Banaba	Anteeren	2	6	339
Beru	Taubukinberu	7	18	2,784
Butaritari	Butaritari	5	13	3,909
Kuria	Tabontebike	6	16	971
Maiana	Tebangetua	6	17	2,184
Makin	Makin	3	8	1,830
Marakei	Rawannawi	5	14	2,724
Nikunau	Rungata	7	19	2,009
Nonouti	Teuabu	8	20	3,042
Onotoa	Buariki	6	16	1,918
Tabiteuea North	Utiroa	10	26	3,383
Tabiteuea South	Buariki	5	12	1,404
Tamana	Bakaka	2	5	1,181
Tarawa North	Abaokoro	6	15	4,004
Tarawa South	Bairiki	6	16	28,350
Line Group	Kiritimati	192	496	5,818
Northern		167	432	5,818
Kiritimati (Christmas)	London	150	388	3,225
Tabuaeran (Fanning)	Paelau	13	34	1,615
Teraina (Washington)	Washington	4	10	978
Southern (Caroline [Millennium], Flint, Malden, Starbuck, Vostok)		25	64	—
Phoenix Group (Birnie, Enderbury, Kanton [Canton], McKean, Manra [Sydney], Nikumaroro [Gardner], Orona [Hull], Rawaki [Phoenix])	Kanton	11	29	83
TOTAL		313	811	77,658

Demography

Population (2001): 94,000.
Density (2001)[4]: persons per sq mi 335.7, persons per sq km 129.5.
Urban-rural (1998): urban 37.0%; rural 63.0%.
Sex distribution (1995): male 49.55%; female 50.45%.
Age breakdown (1995): under 15, 41.2%; 15–29, 25.8%; 30–44, 18.3%; 45–59, 9.3%; 60–74, 4.4%; 75 and over, 1.0%.
Population projection: (2010) 115,000; (2020) 143,000.
Doubling time: 28 years.
Ethnic composition (1995): I-Kiribati 97.7%; mixed (part I-Kiribati and other) 1.5%; Tuvaluan 0.3%; European 0.2%; other 0.3%.
Religious affiliation (1995): Roman Catholic 54.3%; Kiribati Protestant (Congregational) 37.9%; Bahā'ī 2.6%; other Protestant 2.5%; other Christian (Mormon) 1.7%; other/nonreligious 1.0%.
Major cities (1999): Tarawa (urban area) 32,000.

Vital statistics

Birth rate per 1,000 population (2000): 33.1 (world avg. 22.5); legitimate, n.a.; illegitimate, n.a.
Death rate per 1,000 population (2000): 8.4 (world avg. 9.0).
Natural increase rate per 1,000 population (2000): 24.7 (world avg. 13.5).
Total fertility rate (avg. births per childbearing woman; 1999): 4.4.
Marriage rate per 1,000 population (1988): 5.2.
Life expectancy at birth (1999): male 56.5 years; female 62.4 years.
Major causes of death per 100,000 population (1993): senility without mention of psychosis 61.2; stroke 39.1; diarrhea 37.8; hepatitis 32.5; diabetes mellitus 28.6; malnutrition 23.4; meningitis 18.2.

National economy

Budget (1997). Revenue: $A 79,100,000 (nontax revenue 46.6%, tax revenue 20.4%, grants 33.0%). Expenditures: $A 79,100,000 (current expenditure 66.3%, of which wages 25.4%; capital expenditure 33.7%).
Public debt (external, outstanding; 1993): U.S.$18,000,000.
Tourism (1999): receipts from visitors U.S.$2,000,000; expenditures by nationals abroad U.S.$2,000,000.
Production (metric tons except as noted). Agriculture, forestry, fishing (1999): coconuts 85,000, roots and tubers 6,500 (of which taro 1,600), vegetables and melons 5,000, bananas 4,700, tropical fruit 1,150; livestock (number of live animals) 9,500 pigs, 300,000 chickens; fish catch (1997) 23,000. Mining and quarrying: none. Manufacturing (1996): processed copra 9,321; other important products are processed fish, baked goods, clothing, and handicrafts. Energy production (consumption): electricity (kW-hr; 1996) 7,000,000 (7,000,000); coal, none (n.a.); crude petroleum, none (n.a.); petroleum products (metric tons; 1996) none (7,000).
Gross national product (1999): U.S.$81,000,000 (U.S.$910 per capita).

Structure of gross domestic product and labour force

	1996		1990	
	in value[5] $A '000	% of total[5] value	labour force	% of labour force
Agriculture, fishing	4,832	12.4	23,137[6]	71.0[6]
Mining	—	—	—	—
Manufacturing	344	0.9	622	1.9
Construction	1,024	2.6	339	1.0
Public utilities	947	2.4	301	0.9
Transp. and commun.	4,822	12.4	921	2.8
Trade	7,238	18.5	1,341	4.1
Finance	2,215	5.7	441	1.4
Pub. admin., defense	12,780	32.8	2,123	6.5
Services	1,346	3.4	2.286	7.0
Other	3,470[7]	8.9[7]	1,099[8]	3.4[8]
TOTAL	39,018	100.0	32,610	100.0

Population economically active (1995): total 38,407; activity rate of total population 49.5% (participation rates: over age 15, 84.0%; female 47.8%; unemployed 0.2%).

Price and earnings indexes (1990 = 100)

	1991	1992	1993	1994	1995	1996	1997
Consumer price index	103.7	109.2	115.6	123.0	127.4	126.7	126.6
Earnings index	...	...	...	...	...	...	...

Household income and expenditure. Average household size (1995) 6.5; income per household: n.a.; sources of income (1978): wages 69.7%, self-employment 21.4%, transfer payments 6.0%, other 2.9%; expenditure (1982): food 50.0%, tobacco and alcohol 14.0%, clothing 8.0%, transportation 8.0%, housing, energy, and household operation 7.5%.
Land use (1994): forest 2.7%; agricultural and under permanent cultivation 50.7%; other 46.6%.

Foreign trade

Balance of trade[9] (current prices)

	1992	1993	1994	1995	1996	1997
$A '000	–44,882	–36,443	–29,303	–38,826	–40,382	–44,104
% of total	88.8%	80.7%	68.1%	69.0%	73.1%	72.3%

Imports (1996): $A 47,829,000 (food and live animals 33.4%; machinery and transport equipment 18.1%; basic manufactures 14.6%; mineral fuels 10.3%; beverages and tobacco 6.7%; chemicals 6.6%; crude materials 2.1%). *Major import sources:* Australia 46.1%; Fiji 18.7%; Japan 8.6%; New Zealand 8.4%; China 5.9%; United States 3.3%.
Exports (1996): $A 7,447,000 (domestic exports 91.7%, of which copra 62.8%, pet fish 11.6%, fish and fish preparations 4.0%, seaweed 3.6%; reexports 8.3%). *Major export destinations* (1994): Japan 32.9%; United States 17.1%; Hong Kong 12.9%; Bangladesh 8.6%; Germany 8.6%; Malaysia 7.1%.

Transport and communications

Transport. Roads (1996): total length 416 mi, 670 km (paved 5%). Vehicles (1988): passenger cars 222; trucks and buses 115. Merchant marine (1992): vessels (100 gross tons and over) 7; total deadweight tonnage 2,685. Air transport (1996): passenger-mi 4,350,000, passenger-km 7,000,000; short ton-mi cargo 621,000, metric ton-km cargo 1,000,000; airports 9.

Communications

Medium	date	unit	number	units per 1,000 persons
Radio	1997	receivers	17,000	212
Television	1997	receivers	1,000	15
Telephones	1999	main lines	3,502	43
Cellular telephones	1999	subscribers	200	2.4
Internet	1998	users	...	...

Education and health

Educational attainment (1995). Percentage of population age 25 and over having: no schooling 7.8%; primary education 68.5%; secondary or higher 23.7%.
Literacy (1995): population age 15 and over literate 90%.

Education (1997)

	schools	teachers	students	student/ teacher ratio
Primary (age 6–13)	86	727	17,594	24.2
Secondary (age 14–18)	9[10]	215	4,403	20.5
Voc., teacher tr.	[11]	23	333	14.5
Higher[11]	—	—	—	—

Health: physicians (1998) 26 (1 per 3,378 persons); hospital beds (1990) 283 (1 per 253 persons); infant mortality rate per 1,000 live births (1999) 56.8.
Food (1999): daily per capita caloric intake 2,982 (vegetable products 89%, animal products 11%); (1997) 131% of FAO recommended minimum.

[1]Includes two nonelective members. [2]Includes uninhabited islands. [3]Detail does not add to total given because of rounding. [4]Based on inhabited island areas (280 sq mi, [726 sq km]) only. [5]1991 constant prices. [6]Includes 20,568 persons engaged in "village work" (subsistence agriculture or fishing). [7]Indirect taxes less subsidies and imputed bank service charge. [8]Includes 900 unemployed. [9]Exports do not include reexports. [10]Includes vocational. [11]54 students overseas in 1993.

Internet resources for further information:

- **The Secretariat of the Pacific Community http://www.spc.org.nc**

Korea, North

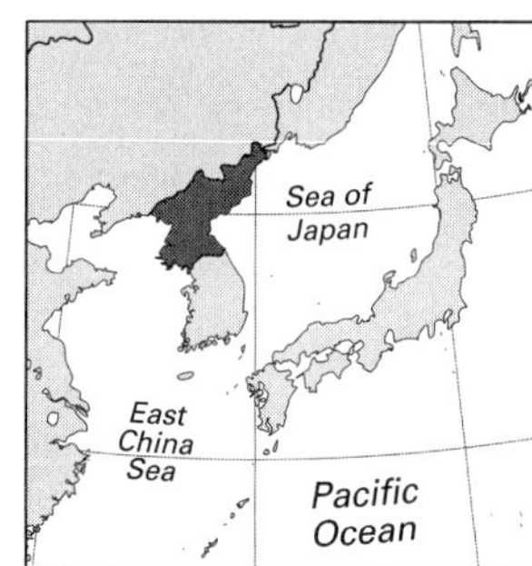

Official name: Chosŏn Minjujuŭi In'min Konghwaguk (Democratic People's Republic of Korea).
Form of government: unitary single-party republic with one legislative house (Supreme People's Assembly [687]).
Chief of state: Chairman of the National Defense Commission[1].
Head of state and government: Premier.
Capital: P'yŏngyang.
Official language: Korean.
Official religion: none.
Monetary unit: 1 won = 100 chŏn; valuation (Sept. 28, 2001) 1 U.S.$ = 2.20 won; 1 £ = 3.23 won.

Area and population

Provinces	Capitals	area sq mi	area sq km	population[2] 1987 estimate
Chagang-do	Kanggye	6,551	16,968	1,156,000
Kangwŏn-do	Wŏnsan	4,306	11,152	1,227,000
North Hamgyŏng (Hamgyŏng-pukto)	Ch'ŏngjin	6,784	17,570	2,003,000
North Hwanghae (Hwanghae-pukto)	Sariwŏn	3,091	8,007	1,409,000
North Pyŏngan (P'yŏngan-pukto)	Sinŭiju	4,707[3]	12,191[3]	2,380,000
South Hamgyŏng (Hamgyŏng-namdo)	Hamhŭng	7,324	18,970	2,547,000
South Hwanghae (Hwanghae-namdo)	Haeju	3,090	8,002	1,914,000
South Pyŏngan (P'yŏngan-namdo)	P'yŏngsan	4,470	11,577	2,653,000
Yanggang-do	Hyesan	5,528	14,317	628,000
Special cities				
Kaesŏng	—	485	1,255	331,000
Namp'o	—	291	753	715,000
P'yŏngyang	—	772	2,000	2,355,000
Special district				
Hyangsan-chigu	—	3	3	28,000
TOTAL		47,399	122,762	19,346,000

Demography

Population (2001): 21,968,000.
Density (2001): persons per sq mi 463.5, persons per sq km 178.9.
Urban-rural (1998): urban 62.2%; rural 37.8%.
Sex distribution (2000): male 48.48%; female 51.52%.
Age breakdown (2000): under 15, 25.6%; 15–29, 24.5%; 30–44, 24.7%; 45–59, 14.4%; 60–74, 9.0%; 75 and over, 1.8%.
Population projection: (2010) 23,753,000; (2020) 25,143,000.
Ethnic composition (1999): Korean 99.8%; Chinese 0.2%.
Religious affiliation (1980): atheist or nonreligious 68.3%; traditional beliefs 15.6%; Ch'ŏndogyo 13.9%; Buddhist 1.7%; Christian 0.5%.
Major cities (1993): P'yŏngyang 2,500,000[4,5]; Namp'o 731,448; Hamhŭng 709,000; Ch'ŏngjin 582,480; Kaesŏng 334,433; Sinŭiju 326,011.

Vital statistics

Birth rate per 1,000 population (2000): 20.4 (world avg. 22.5).
Death rate per 1,000 population (2000): 6.9 (world avg. 9.0).
Natural increase rate per 1,000 population (2000): 13.5 (world avg. 13.5).
Total fertility rate (avg. births per childbearing woman; 2000): 2.3.
Marriage rate per 1,000 population (1987): 9.3.
Divorce rate per 1,000 population (1987): 0.2.
Life expectancy at birth (2000): male 67.8 years; female 73.9 years.
Major causes of death per 100,000 population (1986); diseases of the circulatory system 224.9; malignant neoplasms (cancers) 69.0; diseases of the digestive system 51.6; diseases of the respiratory system 46.7; injuries and poisoning 38.2; infectious and parasitic diseases 19.4.

National economy

Budget (1999). Revenue: 19,801,000,000 won (turnover tax and profits from state enterprises). Expenditures: 20,018,200,000 won (1994; national economy 67.8%, social and cultural affairs 19.0%, defense 11.6%).
Population economically active (1997)[6]: total 11,898,000; activity rate of total population 55.8% (participation rates [1988–93]: ages 15–64, 49.5%; female 46.0%; unemployed, n.a.).
Production (metric tons except as noted). Agriculture, forestry, fishing (2000): rice 1,690,000, potatoes 1,402,000, corn (maize) 1,041,000, cabbages 630,000, apples 650,000, sweet potatoes 468,000, soybeans 350,000, wheat 157,500, pears 130,000, watermelons 104,000, peaches and nectarines 100,000, barley 88,500, cucumbers and gherkins 64,000, tomatoes 62,000, tobacco leaves 62,000, millet 45,000, oats 11,000; livestock (number of live animals) 2,970,000 pigs, 2,100,000 goats, 600,000 cattle, 190,000 sheep, 10,371,000 chickens; roundwood (2000) 4,900,000 cu m; fish catch (1999): 278,500. Mining and quarrying (1997): iron ore (metal content) 4,700,000; magnesite (metal content) 1,600,000; phosphate rock 520,000; sulfur 250,000; tungsten 900,000; zinc 210,000; lead (metal content) 40,000; fluorspar 39,000; graphite 40,000; copper 16,000; silver 50; gold 5,000 kg. Manufacturing (1996): cement 17,000,000; crude steel 8,100,000; pig iron 6,600,000; coke 3,450,000; steel semimanufactures 2,700,000[7]; chemical fertilizers 2,500,000[7]; meat 259,200[7]; gasoline 8,600,000 barrels; textile fabrics 350,000,000 sq m[7]. Construction: n.a. Energy production (consumption): electricity (kW-hr; 1999) 28,600,000 (28,600,000); coal (metric tons; 1999) 85,500,000 (87,600,000); crude petroleum (barrels; 1999) none (26,000,000); petroleum products (metric tons; 1996) 2,785,000 (4,258,000).
Household income and expenditure. Average household size (1987) 4.8; average annual income per household (1980) 3,677 won (U.S.$4,275); sources of income: n.a.; expenditure (1984)[8]: food 46.5%, clothing 29.9%, furniture 3.8%, energy 3.3%, housing 0.6%.
Public debt (external, outstanding; 1996): U.S.$12,000,000,000.
Gross national product (1999): U.S.$9,912,000,000 (U.S.$457 per capita).

Structure of gross domestic product and labour force

	1999 in value U.S.$'000,000	1999 % of total value	1997 labour force	1997 % of labour force
Agriculture	...	...	3,853,000	32.4
Mining and manufacturing	...	...		
Construction	...	...		
Public utilities	...	...		
Transp. and commun.	...	...		
Trade	...	...	8,045,000	67.6
Finance	...	...		
Pub. admin., defense	...	...		
Services	...	...		
Other	...	...		
TOTAL	22,600	100.0	11,898,000	100.0

Land use (1994): forested 61.2%; meadows and pastures 0.4%; agricultural and under permanent cultivation 16.6%; other 21.8%.

Foreign trade[9]

Balance of trade (current prices)

	1994	1995	1996	1997	1998	1999
U.S.$'000,000	–429.5	–880.0	–1,050	–390	–320	–450
% of total	20.4%	42.7%	36.3%	18.1%	22.2%	30.4%

Imports (1999): U.S.$965,000,000 (crude petroleum, coal and coke, industrial machinery and transport equipment [including trucks], industrial chemicals, textile yarn and fabrics, and grain are among the major imports). *Major import sources* (1995): China 30.0%; Japan 15.8%; Austria 9.3%; Ukraine 5.9%.
Exports (1999): U.S.$515,000,000 (minerals [including lead, magnesite, zinc], metallurgical products [iron and steel, nonferrous metals], cement, agricultural products [including fish, grain, fruit and vegetables, tobacco], and manufactured goods [textile fabrics, clothing] are among the major exports). *Major export destinations* (1995): Japan 31.4%; Austria 17.3%; India 6.9%.

Transport and communications

Transport. Railroads (1999): length 8,533 km. Roads (1997): total length 14,526 mi, 23,377 km (paved 8%). Vehicles (1990): passenger cars 248,000. Merchant marine (1992): vessels (100 gross tons and over) 100; total deadweight tonnage 951,222. Air transport (1997): passenger-mi 177,712,000, passenger-km 286,000,000; short ton-mi cargo 18,600,000; metric ton-km cargo 30,000,000; airports (1999) with scheduled flights 1.

Communications

Medium	date	unit	number	units per 1,000 persons
Daily newspapers	1996	circulation	4,500,000	199
Radio	1997	receivers	3,360,000	146
Television	1997	receivers	1,200,000	52
Telephones	1999	main lines	1,100,000	46

Education and health

Educational attainment (1987–88). Percentage of population age 16 and over having attended or graduated from postsecondary-level school: 13.7%.
Literacy (1997): 95%.

Education (1988)

	schools	teachers	students	student/ teacher ratio
Primary (age 6–9)	4,810[10]	59,000	1,543,000	26.2
Secondary (age 10–15)[10]	4,840	111,000	2,468,000	22.2
Voc., teacher tr.	473[11]	...	220,000[10]	...
Higher	46	23,000	325,000	14.1

Health (1993): physicians 61,200 (1 per 370 persons); hospital beds (1989) 290,590 (1 per 74 persons); infant mortality rate (2000) 24.3.
Food (1999): daily per capita caloric intake 2,100 (vegetable products 94%, animal products 6%); 90% of FAO recommended minimum requirement.

Military

Total active duty personnel (1999): 1,082,000 (army 87.8%, navy 4.2%, air force 8.0%). *Military expenditure as percentage of GNP* (1997): 27.5% (world 2.6%); per capita expenditure U.S.$282.

[1]Position in effect from Sept. 5, 1998. It is defined as an enhanced military post with revised constitutional powers. [2]Civilian population only; UN cites a 1993 census total of 21,123,376, but details are not available. [3]North P'yŏngan includes special district of Hyangsan-chigu. [4]1996 estimate. [5]Urban agglomeration for 1999 equals 3,136,000. [6]The Democratic People's Republic of Korea categorizes economically active as including students in higher education, retirees, and heads of households, as well as those in the civilian labour force. [7]1994. [8]Workers and clerical workers only. [9]Imports are f.o.b. [10]1987. [11]1986.

Internet resources for further information:

- **Korean News http://www.kcna.co.jp**
- **United States Department of Energy http://www.eia.doe.gov/emeu/cabs/nkorea.html**

Korea, South

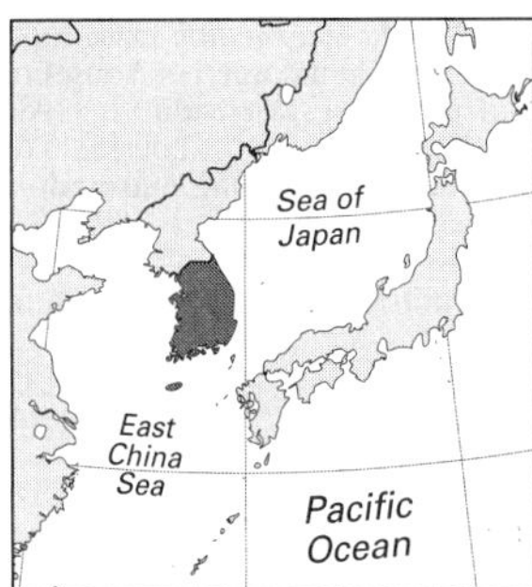

Official name: Taehan Min'guk (Republic of Korea).
Form of government: unitary multiparty republic with one legislative house (National Assembly [273]).
Head of state and government: President, assisted by Prime Minister.
Capital: Seoul.
Official language: Korean.
Official religion: none.
Monetary unit: 1 won (W) = 100 chon; valuation (Sept. 28, 2001) 1 U.S.$ = W 1,310; 1 £ = W 1,925.

Area and population

		area		population
Provinces	**Capitals**	sq mi	sq km	2000 census[1]
Cheju	Cheju	713	1,846	513,000
Kangwŏn	Ch'unch'ŏn'	6,399	16,572	1,487,000
Kyŏnggi	Suwŏn	3,913	10,135	8,979,000
North Chŏlla	Chŏnju	3,108	8,050	1,890,000
North Ch'ungch'ŏng	Ch'ŏngju	2,870	7,432	1,466,000
North Kyŏngsang	Taegu	7,345	19,024	2,726,000
South Chŏlla	Kwangju	4,628	11,987	1,996,000
South Ch'ungch'ŏng	Taejŏn	3,315	8,586	1,846,000
South Kyŏngsang	Masan	4,060	10,515	2,978,000
Metropolitan cities				
Inch'ŏn	Inch'ŏn	373	965	2,476,000
Kwangju	Kwangju	193	501	1,352,000
Pusan	Pusan	293	760	3,664,000
Sŏul (Seoul)	Seoul	234	606	9,891,000
Taegu	Taegu	342	886	2,480,000
Taejŏn	Taejŏn	208	540	1,367,000
Ulsan	Ulsan	408	1,056	1,014,000
TOTAL		38,402	99,461	46,125,000

Demography

Population (2001): 47,676,000.
Density (2001): persons per sq mi 1,241.5, persons per sq km 479.3.
Urban-rural (2001): urban 82.0%; rural 18.0%.
Sex distribution (2001): male 50.42%; female 49.58%.
Age breakdown (1998): under 15, 22.0%; 15–29, 26.8%; 30–44, 26.2%; 45–59, 14.8%; 60–74, 8.1%; 75 and over, 2.1%.
Population projection: (2010) 50,886,000; (2020) 52,759,000.
Doubling time: 83 years.
Ethnic composition (1990): Korean 99.9%; other 0.1%.
Religious affiliation (1995): religious 50.7%, of which Buddhist 23.2%, Protestant 19.7%, Roman Catholic 6.6%, Confucian 0.5%, Wonbulgyo 0.2%, Ch'ŏndogyo 0.1%, other 0.4%; nonreligious 49.3%.
Major cities (2000)[1]: Seoul 9,891,000; Pusan 3,664,000; Taegu 2,480,000; Inch'ŏn 2,476,000; Taejŏn 1,367,000.

Vital statistics

Birth rate per 1,000 population (1999): 15.3 (world avg. 22.5).
Death rate per 1,000 population (1999): 5.8 (world avg. 9.0).
Natural increase rate per 1,000 population (1999): 9.5 (world avg. 13.5).
Total fertility rate (avg. births per childbearing woman; 1999): 1.7.
Marriage rate per 1,000 population (1997): 6.8.
Divorce rate per 1,000 population (1997): 1.6.
Life expectancy at birth (1999): male 70.5 years; female 78.4 years.
Major causes of death per 100,000 population (1997): diseases of the circulatory system 121.5; malignant neoplasms (cancers) 115.4; accidents, poisoning, and violence 70.6; diseases of the digestive system 34.4.

National economy

Budget (1998). Revenue: W 96,673,000,000,000 (taxes on income and profits 28.9%, taxes on goods and services 28.1%, nontax revenue 18.1%, social security contributions 10.9%, education tax 5.4%). Expenditures: W 115,689,000,000,000 (economic services 24.6%, education 15.4%, defense 11.8%, social security and welfare 10.6%, general public services 9.4%, housing and community amenities 6.3%).
Public debt (external, outstanding; 1999): U.S.$57,231,000,000.
Production (metric tons except as noted). Agriculture, forestry, fishing (2000): rice 7,067,000, cabbages 2,755,000, dry onions 936,000, tangerines 601,000, apples 491,000; livestock (number of live animals) 7,864,000 pigs, 2,486,000 cattle, 97,000,000 chickens; roundwood 1,722,000 cu m; fish catch (1998) 2,026,934. Mining and quarrying (1998): copper ore 226,000; iron ore 133,000; zinc concentrate 10,488. Manufacturing (2000): cement 51,424,000; finished steel 48,865,000; synthetic resin 8,657,000; computer peripherals U.S.$12,060,000,000; mobile phones U.S.$12,019,000,000; colour television receivers U.S.$1,773,000,000; motor vehicles 3,115,000 units. Construction (permits authorized; 2000): residential 41,283,000 sq m; nonresidential 39,775,000 sq m. Energy production (consumption): electricity (kW-hr; 1999) 239,328,000,000 ([1996] 227,554,000,000); coal (metric tons; 1999) 4,140,000 ([1996] 50,277,000); crude petroleum (barrels; 1996) none (721,829,000); petroleum products (metric tons; 1996) 83,721,000 (74,869,000); natural gas (cu m; 1996) none (12,814,000,000).
Household income and expenditure (2000)[2]. Average household size (1998) 3.6; income per household W 54,025,000 (U.S.$47,769); sources of income: wages 53.0%, other 47.0%; expenditure: food and beverages 27.5%, transportation and communications 16.4%, education and recreation 16.2%, clothing and footwear 5.7%, utilities 5.1%, health care 4.1%, household durable goods 3.7%, housing 3.3%, other 18.0%.
Gross national product (1999): U.S.$397,910,000,000 (U.S.$8,490 per capita).

Structure of gross domestic product and labour force

	2000			
	in value W '000,000,000[3]	% of total value	labour force	% of labour force
Agriculture	24,859.8	6.0	2,288,000	10.4
Mining	1,439.4	0.3	18,000	0.1
Manufacturing	163,014.5	39.6	4,244,000	19.3
Construction	36,881.8	9.0	1,583,000	7.2
Public utilities	12,265.2	3.0	12,928,000	58.9
Transp. and commun.	41,276.1	10.0		
Trade	58,469.5	14.2		
Finance	83,860.0	20.4		
Pub. admin., defense	29,171.7	7.1		
Services	30,396.9	7.4		
Other	–69,946.4[4]	–17.0[4]	889,000[5]	4.1[5]
TOTAL	411,688.5	100.0	21,950,000	100.0

Population economically active (2000): total 21,950,000; activity rate 46.4% (participation rates: ages 15 and over, 60.7%; female [1998] 38.8%; unemployed 4.1%).

Price and earnings indexes (1995 = 100)

	1994	1995	1996	1997	1998	1999	2000
Consumer price index	95.7	100.0	104.9	109.6	117.8	118.8	121.5
Monthly earnings index	91.0	100.0	112.2	118.0	114.3	131.3	142.4

Tourism (1999): receipts U.S.$6,802,000,000; expenditures U.S.$3,975,000,000.

Foreign trade[6]

Balance of trade (current prices)

	1995	1996	1997	1998	1999	2000
U.S.$'000,000	–10,061	–20,624	–8,452	+39,031	+23,934	+11,787
% of total	3.9%	7.4%	3.0%	17.3%	9.1%	3.5%

Imports (2000): U.S.$160,481,000,000 (electric and electronic products 27.0%, crude petroleum 15.7%, machinery and transport equipment 13.2%, manufactured consumer goods 10.0%, chemicals 7.4%, iron and steel products 3.7%). *Major import sources:* Japan 19.8%; U.S. 18.2%; China 8.0%; Saudi Arabia 6.0%; Australia 3.7%; Malaysia 3.0%.
Exports (2000): U.S.$172,267,500,000 (electric and electronic products 36.0%, machinery and transport equipment 18.2%, chemicals 7.0%, crude materials and fuels 6.7%). *Major export destinations:* U.S. 21.8%; Japan 11.9%; China 10.7%; Hong Kong 6.2%; Taiwan 4.7%; Singapore 3.3%; U.K. 3.1%.

Transport and communications

Transport. Railroads (1998): length (2000) 6,706 km; passenger-km 30,072,000,000; metric ton-km cargo 12,708,000,000. Roads (2000): total length 88,775 km (paved 76%). Vehicles (2000): passenger cars 8,084,000; trucks and buses 3,938,000. Air transport (1998): passenger-km 47,712,000,000; metric ton-km cargo 7,280,640,000; airports (1996) with scheduled flights 14.

Communications

Medium	date	unit	number	units per 1,000 persons
Daily newspapers	1995	circulation	17,700,000	394
Radio	1997	receivers	47,500,000	1,033
Television	1999	receivers	16,896,000	361
Telephones	2000	main lines	21,931,000	464
Cellular telephones	2000	subscribers	26,816,000	567
Personal computers	1999	units	8,519,000	182
Internet	2000	users	19,040,000	403

Education and health

Educational attainment (1995). Percentage of population age 25 and over having: no formal schooling 8.5%; primary education or less 17.7%; some secondary and secondary 53.1%; postsecondary 20.6%. *Literacy* (1995): total population age 15 and over literate 98.0%; males 99.3%; females 96.7%.

Education (1999)

	schools	teachers	students	student/ teacher ratio
Primary (age 6–13)	14,334	163,741	4,469,703	27.3
Secondary (age 14–19)	4,684	198,548	4,148,096	20.9
Vocational, teacher training	172	12,089	880,870	72.9
Higher[7]	158	41,226	1,587,667	38.5

Health (1999): physicians 69,724 (1 per 672 persons); hospital beds (1997) 220,427 (1 per 209 persons); infant mortality rate per 1,000 live births 10.0.
Food (1999): daily per capita caloric intake 3,073 (vegetable products 86%, animal products 14%); (1997) 131% of FAO recommended minimum.

Military

Total active duty personnel (2000): 683,000 (army 82.0%, navy 8.8%, air force 9.2%); U.S. military forces (2001): 36,000. *Military expenditure as percentage of GNP* (1997): 3.4% (world 2.6%); per capita expenditure U.S.$326.

[1]Preliminary. [2]Excludes farm households. [3]At 1995 constant prices. [4]Import duties less imputed bank service charges. [5]Unemployed. [6]Imports c.i.f.; exports f.o.b. [7]Excludes graduate schools.

Internet resources for further information:
- **National Statistical Office http://www.nso.go.kr/eng**

Kuwait

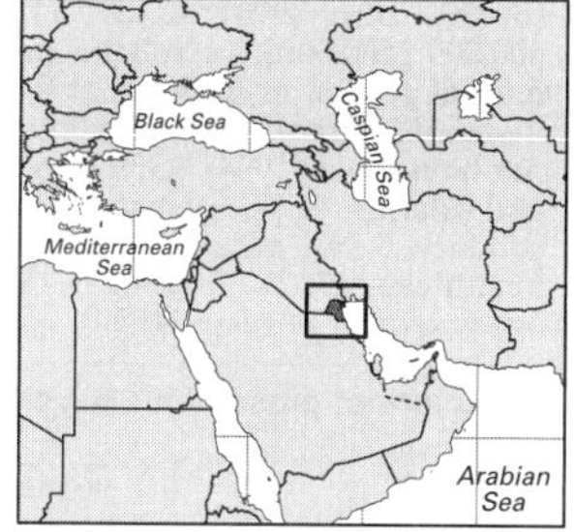

Official name: Dawlat al-Kuwayt (State of Kuwait).
Form of government: constitutional monarchy with one legislative body (National Assembly [65[1]]).
Head of state and government: Emir[2].
Capital: Kuwait City.
Official language: Arabic.
Official religion: Islam.
Monetary unit: 1 Kuwaiti dinar (KD) = 1,000 fils; valuation[3] (Sept. 28, 2001) 1 KD = U.S.$3.33 = £2.22.

Area and population		area		population
				1998
Governorates	**Capitals**	sq mi	sq km	estimate
Al-Aḥmadī	Al-Aḥmadī	1,984	5,138	313,424
Al-Farwānīyah	Al-Farwānīyah	[4]	[4]	498,584
Al-Jahrā'	Al-Jahrā'	4,372	11,324	252,157
Capital	Kuwait City	38	98	305,694
Ḥawallī	Ḥawallī	138[4]	358[4]	496,245
Islands[5]	—	347	900	...
TOTAL		6,880[6]	17,818	1,866,104

Demography

Population (2001): 2,275,000.
Density (2001): persons per sq mi 330.7, persons per sq km 127.7.
Urban-rural (1995): urban 97.0%; rural 3.0%.
Sex distribution (2000): male 60.04%; female 39.96%.
Age breakdown (2000): under 15, 29.4%; 15–29, 28.2%; 30–44, 25.8%; 45–59, 12.6%; 60–74, 3.5%; 75 and over, 0.5%.
Population projection: (2010) 2,865,000; (2020) 3,495,000.
Doubling time: 37 years.
Ethnic composition (2000): Arab 74%, of which Kuwaiti 30%, Palestinian 17%, Jordanian 10%, Bedouin 9%; Kurd 10%; Indo-Pakistani 8%; Persian 4%; other 4%.
Religious affiliation (1995): Muslim 85%, of which Sunnī 45%, Shīʿī 30%; other Muslim 10%; other (mostly Christian and Hindu) 15.0%.
Major cities (1995): As-Sālimīyah 130,215; Qalīb ash-Shuyūkh 102,178; Ḥawallī 82,238; Kuwait City 28,859 (urban agglomeration [1999] 1,165,000).

Vital statistics

Birth rate per 1,000 population (2000): 22.0 (world avg. 22.5).
Death rate per 1,000 population (2000): 2.4 (world avg. 9.0).
Natural increase rate per 1,000 population (2000): 19.6 (world avg. 13.5).
Total fertility rate (avg. births per childbearing woman; 2000): 3.3.
Marriage rate per 1,000 population (1999): 7.0.
Divorce rate per 1,000 population (1999): 3.9.
Life expectancy at birth (2000): male 75.3 years; female 76.9 years.
Major causes of death per 100,000 population (1998): circulatory diseases 84.2; accidents and violence 31.7; cancers 22.9; congenital anomalies 12.4; endocrine and metabolic diseases 11.5; respiratory diseases 10.7.

National economy

Budget[7] (2001–02). Revenue: KD 2,224,000,000 (oil revenue 79.2%). Expenditures: KD 4,295,000,000 (transfers 21.2%, defense 20.9%, education 9.1%, economic development 8.0%, health 6.3%).
Tourism (2000): receipts from visitors U.S.$243,000,000; expenditures by nationals abroad U.S.$2,510,000,000.
Gross national product (1998): U.S.$42,387,000,000 (U.S.$20,910 per capita).

Structure of gross domestic product and labour force	1999			
	in value KD '000,000[8]	% of total value	labour force	% of labour force
Agriculture	35.7	0.4	22,619	1.8
Mining (oil sector)	3,354.4	37.1	7,581	0.6
Manufacturing	1,100.6	12.2	77,879	6.4
Construction	229.4	2.5	118,301	9.7
Public utilities	–42.8	–0.5	7,907	0.6
Transp. and commun.	505.9	5.6	41,584	3.4
Trade[9]	646.6	7.2	196,079	16.0
Finance and business services	1,278.6	14.2	45,821	3.7
Pub. admin., defense Services	2,277.8	25.2	614,876	50.1
Other	–353.4[10]	–3.9[10]	93,487[11]	7.6[11]
TOTAL	9,032.8	100.0	1,226,134	100.0[6]

Production (metric tons except as noted). Agriculture, forestry, fishing (2000): cucumber and gherkins 33,004, tomatoes 31,788, eggplants 12,002, onions 3,377, garlic 539; livestock (number of live animals) 450,000 sheep, 150,000 goats, 20,400 cattle, 8,900 camels; fish catch (1999) 6,535. Mining and quarrying (1997): sulfur 600,000; lime 40,000. Manufacturing (value added in KD '000,000; 1997): refined petroleum products 3,632; industrial chemicals 962; fabricated metal products 68; food products 55; clothing and apparel 37. Construction (floor area of new construction; 1998): residential 2,983,000 sq m; nonresidential 220,000 sq m. Energy production (consumption): electricity (kW-hr; 1998) 29,988,000,000 ([1996] 25,925,000,000); crude petroleum (barrels; 1999) 795,000,000 ([1998] 314,515,000); petroleum products (metric tons; 1996) 36,572,000 (6,478,000); natural gas (cu m; 1998) 11,081,000,000 (11,081,000,000).

Population economically active (1999): total 1,226,134; activity rate of total population 53.9% (participation rates [1995]: ages 15–59, 70.7%; female 26.1%; unemployed 0.7%).

Price and earnings indexes (1995 = 100)	1993	1994	1995	1996	1997	1998	1999
Consumer price index	95.0	97.4	100.0	103.6	104.2	104.4	104.5
Earnings index	...	...	...	...	...	...	...

Household income and expenditure. Average household size (1995) 3.9; annual income per household (1973)[12] KD 4,246 (U.S.$12,907); sources of income (1986): wages and salaries 53.8%, self-employment 20.8%, other 25.4; expenditure (1992): food, beverages, and tobacco 37.0%, housing and energy 18.7%, transportation 15.3%, household appliances and services 11.1%, clothing and footwear 10.0%, education and health 2.5%.
Land use (1994): forest 0.1%; pasture 7.7%; agriculture 0.3%; other 91.9%.

Foreign trade[13]

Balance of trade (current prices)	1994	1995	1996	1997	1998	1999
KD '000,000	+1,289	+1,530	+2,168	+1,783	+259	+1,378
% of total	24.5%	24.8%	30.2%	26.3%	4.7%	22.9%

Imports (1999): KD 2,318,305,000 (machinery and transport equipment 39.7%, manufactured goods 16.3%, food and live animals 14.9%, miscellaneous manufactured articles 14.5%, chemical products 8.7%, inedible crude materials except fuel 1.9%). *Major import sources:* Japan 12.8%; U.S. 12.3%; Germany 7.7%; Saudi Arabia 6.2%; U.K. 5.8%; Italy 5.8%; France 3.7%; India 3.7%.
Exports (1999)[14]: KD 3,696,000,000 (crude petroleum and petroleum products 96.5%, chemicals 2.9%). *Major export destinations:* Saudi Arabia 11.5%; U.A.E. 9.3%; India 8.6%; Singapore 7.3%; China 4.4%; Belgium-Luxembourg 4.4%; Pakistan 4.1%.

Transport and communications

Transport. Railroads: none. Roads (1997): total length 2,765 mi, 4,450 km (paved 81%). Vehicles (1998): passenger cars 747,042; trucks and buses 140,480. Merchant marine (1998): vessels (100 gross tons and over) 202; total deadweight tonnage (1992) 3,188,526. Air transport (2000): passenger-mi 3,813,469,000, passenger-km 6,137,195,000; short ton-mi cargo 151,120,000, metric ton-km cargo 243,204,000; airports (1999) with scheduled flights 1.

Communications				units per 1,000
Medium	date	unit	number	persons
Daily newspapers	1990	circulation	005,000	077
Radio	1997	receivers	1,175,000	678
Television	1999	receivers	910,000	520
Telephones	1999	main lines	456,000	240
Cellular telephones	1999	subscribers	30,000	158
Personal computers	1999	units	230,000	120
Internet	1999	users	100,000	54

Education and health

Educational attainment (1988). Percentage of population age 25 and over having: no formal schooling 44.8%; primary education 8.6%; some secondary 15.1%; complete secondary 15.1%; higher 16.4%. *Literacy* (1995): total population age 15 and over literate 79.3%; males literate 82.3%; females literate 76.0%.

Education (1998–99)	schools	teachers	students	student/ teacher ratio
Primary (age 6–9)	179[15]	10,389	139,690	13.4
Secondary (age 10–17)	117[15]	19,702	228,810	11.6
Voc., teacher tr.	39	1,030	4,457	4.3
Higher[16]	1	942	15,726	16.7

Health (1998): physicians 3,447 (1 per 541 persons); hospital beds 4,389[17] (1 per 425 persons); infant mortality rate per 1,000 live births (2000) 11.5.
Food (1999): daily per capita caloric intake 3,167 (vegetable products 76%, animal products 24%); 131% of FAO recommended minimum requirement.

Military

Total active duty personnel (2000): 15,300 (army [including central staff] 71.9%, navy 11.8%, air force 16.3%). *Military expenditure as percentage of GNP* (1997): 7.5% (world 2.6%); per capita expenditure U.S.$1,525.

[1]Fifty elected seats in National Assembly may include Cabinet ministers; Cabinet ministers not elected to National Assembly serve ex officio. [2]Assisted by prime minister. [3]Composite rate; pegged rate to a basket of currencies. [4]Ḥawallī includes Al-Farwānīyah. [5]Bubian Island 333 sq mi (863 sq km) and Warba Island 14 sq mi (37 sq km). [6]Detail does not add to total given because of rounding. [7]Approved budget. [8]In purchasers' prices. [9]Trade includes restaurants and hotels. [10]Includes import duties and imputed bank service charges. [11]Not stated. [12]Kuwaiti households only. [13]Imports and exports are f.o.b. in the balance of trade table. [14]Total exports and reexports include oil and non-oil, but breakdown by destination is derived from non-oil exports. [15]Government schools only. [16]University only. [17]Public hospitals only.

Internet resources for further information:

- **Central Bank of Kuwait http://www.cbk.gov.kw**
- **Ministry of Planning http://www.mop.gov.kw/indexe.htm**

Kyrgyzstan

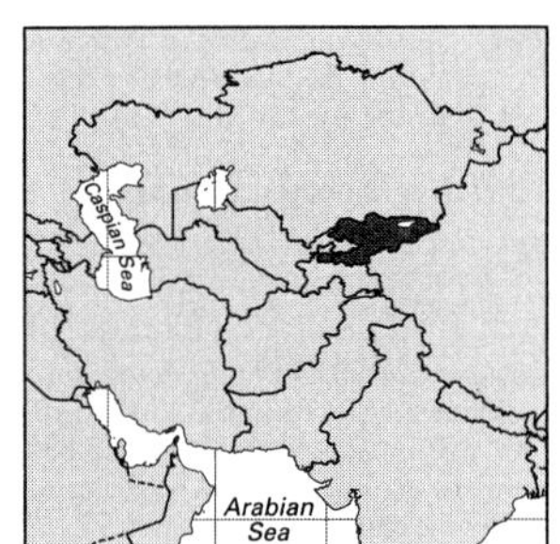

Official name: Respublika Kirgizstan (Kyrgyz); Kyrgyz Respublikasy (Russian) (Kyrgyz Republic).
Form of government: unitary multiparty republic with two legislative houses (Assembly of People's Representatives [45]; Legislative Assembly [60]).
Head of state and government: President assisted by Prime Minister.
Capital: Bishkek.
Official languages: Kyrgyz; Russian.
Official religion: none.
Monetary unit: 1 som (K.S.) = 100 tyiyn; valuation (Sept. 28, 2001) 1 U.S.$ = K.S. 47.70; 1 £ = K.S. 70.10.

Area and population

Provinces	Capitals	area sq mi	area sq km	population 1999 census
Batken	Batken	6,600	17,000	382,426
Chüy (Chu)	Kara-Balta	7,800	20,200	770,811
Jalal-Abad (Dzhalal-Abad)	Jalal-Abad (Dzhalal-Abad)	13,000	33,700	869,259
Naryn	Naryn	17,500	45,200	249,115
Osh	Osh	11,300	29,200	1,175,998
Talas	Talas	4,400	11,400	199,872
Ysyk-Köl (Issyk-Kul)	Ysyk-Köl (Issyk-Kul)	16,600	43,100	413,149
City				
Bishkek (Frunze)	—	40	100	762,308
TOTAL		77,200[1]	199,900	4,822,938

Demography

Population (2001): 4,934,000.
Density (2001): persons per sq mi 64.4, persons per sq km 24.9.
Urban-rural (1999): urban 40.0%; rural 60.0%.
Sex distribution (1997): male 49.37%; female 50.63%.
Age breakdown (1997): under 15, 37.3%; 15–29, 26.3%; 30–44, 19.5%; 45–59, 8.8%; 60–74, 6.5%; 75 and over, 1.6%.
Population projection: (2010) 5,423,000; (2020) 6,023,000.
Doubling time: 53 years.
Ethnic composition (1999): Kyrgyz 64.9%; Uzbek 13.8%; Russian 12.5%; Hui 1.1%; Ukrainian 1.0%; Uighur 1.0%; other 5.7%.
Religious affiliation (1997): Muslim (mostly Sunnī) 75.0%; Christian 6.7%, of which Russian Orthodox 5.6%; other (mostly nonreligious) 18.3%.
Major cities (1999 est.): Bishkek (Frunze) 619,000; Osh 220,500; Jalal-Abad 74,200[2]; Tokmok 71,200[2]; Kara-Köl 64,300[2].

Vital statistics

Birth rate per 1,000 population (2001): 20.6 (world avg. 22.5); (1994) legitimate 83.2%; illegitimate 16.8%.
Death rate per 1,000 population (2001): 7.3 (world avg. 9.0).
Natural increase rate per 1,000 population (2001): 13.3 (world avg. 13.5).
Total fertility rate (avg. births per childbearing woman; 2001): 2.5.
Marriage rate per 1,000 population (1995): 6.0.
Divorce rate per 1,000 population (1995): 1.3.
Life expectancy at birth (2001): male 64.0 years; female 72.0 years.
Major causes of death per 100,000 population (1996): diseases of the circulatory system 278.5; diseases of the respiratory system 75.0; malignant neoplasms (cancers) 25.7; accidents, poisoning, and violence 21.4; infectious and parasitic diseases 12.6; diseases of the digestive system 9.8.

National economy

Budget (1998). Revenue: K.S. 6,090,700,000 (tax revenue 79.9%, of which taxes on goods and services 54.2%, taxes on income and profits 14.6%, taxes on international trade 6.2%; nontax revenue 18.7%). Expenditures: K.S. 7,531,600,000 (education 22.3%; social security 13.0%; general public services 13.5%; health 12.8%; economic development 11.2%; defense 6.5%).
Public debt (external, outstanding; 1999): U.S.$1,130,400,000.
Land use (1994): forest 3.7%; pasture 45.4%; agriculture 7.2%; other 43.7%.
Population economically active (1995): total 1,692,000; activity rate of total population 37.2% (1993; participation rates: ages 16–59 [male], 16–54 [female] 81.1%; female 49.0%; (1996) unemployed 4.3%).

Price and earnings indexes (1995 = 100)

	1994	1995	1996	1997	1998	1999	2000
Consumer price index	...	100.0	131.9	162.9	179.9	244.5	290.2
Monthly earnings index	63.4	100.0	133.3	184.7	228.3	...	...

Production (metric tons except as noted). Agriculture, forestry, fishing (1999): grain 1,630,000, potatoes 957,000, vegetables (other than potatoes) and melons 485,000, fruit (excluding melons) 109,000, seed cotton 87,000; livestock (number of live animals) 3,570,000 sheep and goats, 825,000 cattle, 320,000 horses, 80,000 pigs; roundwood (1998) 42,400 cu m; fish catch (1997) 300. Mining and quarrying (1998): antimony 1,297; mercury 630; uranium 450; gold 21 kg. Manufacturing (value of production in '000,000 som; 1994): textiles 1,112; processed foods 729; ferrous and nonferrous metals 678; machinery and metalwork 650; construction materials 258; footwear and leather goods 89. Construction (1992): residential 1,232,000 sq m. Energy production (consumption): electricity (kW-hr; 1996) 13,480,000,000 (11,400,000,000); coal (metric tons; 1996) 410,000 (1,018,000); crude petroleum (barrels; 1996) 600,000 (500,000); petroleum products (metric tons; 1996) 3,000 (566,000); natural gas (cu m; 1996) 26,000,000 (1,053,000,000).
Household income and expenditure. Average household size (1999) 4.3; income per household (1994) 4,359 som (U.S.$325); sources of income (1990): wages and salaries 49.7%, pensions and stipends 11.1%, income from agricultural products 3.5%, other 35.7%; expenditure (1990): food and clothing 48.0%, health care 13.1%, housing 5.9%, cultural affairs 5.2%, appliances 4.4%.
Gross national product (1999): U.S.$1,465,000,000 (U.S.$300 per capita).

Structure of gross domestic product and labour force

	1998 in value K.S. '000,000	1998 % of total value	1997 labour force	1997 % of labour force
Agriculture	12,324.2	36.0	815,600	48.3
Mining, Manufacturing	5,559.2	16.3	171,600	10.2
Public utilities	812.8	2.4	...	...
Construction	1,537.3	4.5	57,000	3.4
Transp. and commun.	1,535.0	4.5	79,200	4.7
Trade	4,501.8	13.2	172,400	10.2
Finance	410.1	1.2	14,300	0.8
Public admin., defense	1,035.5	3.0	60,300	3.6
Services	3,492.5	10.2	269,700	16.0
Other	2,973.0	8.7	49,200	2.9
TOTAL	34,181.4	100.0	1,689,300	100.0[1]

Tourism (1998): receipts from visitors, U.S.$8,000,000; expenditures by nationals abroad, U.S.$3,000,000.

Foreign trade[3]

Balance of trade (current prices)

	1994	1995	1996	1997	1998	1999
U.S.$'000,000	–86.1	–122.1	–251.7	–15.3	–220.8	–84.3
% of total	11.2%	13.0%	19.2%	1.2%	17.1%	8.4%

Imports (1997): U.S.$709,300,000 (oil and gas 24.8%, machine-building equipment 21.7%, chemical products 13.5%, food products 11.7%, light industrial products 6.8%). *Major import sources:* Russian Federation 26.9%; Uzbekistan 18.1%; Kazakhstan 9.8%; Turkey 6.2%; United States 5.6%.
Exports (1997): U.S.$603,800,000 (metals 36.3%, electricity 13.8%, food products 13.2%, machinery 10.2%, light industrial products 10.0%, construction materials 4.4%). *Major export destinations:* Switzerland 26.9%; Uzbekistan 16.8%; Russian Federation 16.4%; Kazakhstan 14.4%; China 5.2%.

Transport and communications

Transport. Railroads (1999): length 424 km; (1995) passenger-km 30,000,000; metric ton-km cargo 403,000,000. Roads (1996): total length 18,500 km (paved 91%). Vehicles (1996): passenger cars 146,000; trucks and buses, n.a. Air transport (1996): passenger-km 4,408,000,000; metric ton-km cargo 65,199,000; airports (1997) with scheduled flights 2.

Communications

Medium	date	unit	number	units per 1,000 persons
Daily newspapers	1996	circulation	67,000	15
Radio	1997	receivers	520,000	113
Television	1998	receivers	220,000	47
Telephones	1999	main lines	356,000	76
Cellular phones	1999	subscribers	2,574	0.6
Personal computers	...	units	...	...
Internet	1999	users	10,000	2.1

Education and health

Educational attainment (1989). Percentage of population age 19 and over having: primary education 4.7%; some secondary 20.9%; completed secondary 44.4%; some postsecondary 19.3%; higher 10.7%. *Literacy* (1989): total population age 15 and over literate 4,130,562 (97.0%); males literate 2,048,536 (98.6%); females literate 2,082,026 (95.5%).

Education (1995–96)

	schools	teachers	students	student/ teacher ratio
Primary (age 6–13)	1,885	24,086	473,077	19.7
Secondary (age 14–17)	1,474[4]	38,915	498,849	12.8
Voc., teacher tr.	53[4]	3,371	32,005	9.5
Higher	23[4]	3,691	49,744	13.5

Health (1997): physicians 15,100 (1 per 307 persons); hospital beds 40,700 (1 per 114 persons); infant mortality rate per 1,000 live births (2001) 39.0.
Food (1999): daily per capita caloric intake 2,833 (vegetable products 81%, animal products 19%); (1997) 111% of FAO recommended minimum.

Military

Total active duty personnel (2000): 9,000 (army 73.3%, air force 26.7%). *Military expenditure as percentage of GNP* (1997): 1.6% (world 2.6%); per capita expenditure U.S.$35.

[1]Detail does not add to total given because of rounding. [2]1991. [3]Imports and exports in balance of trade are f.o.b. [4]1993–94.

Internet resources for further information:
- **National Statistical Committee of the Kyrgyz Republic http://nsc.bishkek.su/Eng/Home/Start.html**
- **Embassy of the Kyrgyz Republic http://www.kyrgyzstan.org**

Laos

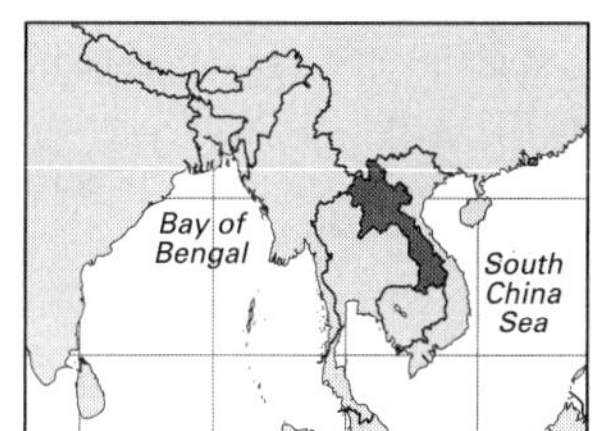

Official name: Sathalanalat Paxathipatai Paxaxôn Lao (Lao People's Democratic Republic).
Form of government: unitary single-party people's republic with one legislative house (National Assembly[1] [99]).
Chief of state: President.
Head of government: Prime Minister.
Capital: Vientiane (Viangchan).
Official language: Lao.
Official religion: none.
Monetary unit: 1 kip (KN) = 100 at; valuation (Sept. 28, 2001) managed floating rate, 1 U.S.$ = KN 7,600; 1 £ = KN 11,170.

Area and population

Provinces	Capitals	area sq mi	area sq km	population 1995 estimate
Attapu	Attapu	3,985	10,320	87,700
Bokèo	Houayxay	2,392	6,196	114,900
Bolikhamxai	Pakxan	5,739	14,863	164,900
Champasak	Pakxé	5,952	15,415	503,300
Houaphan	Xam Nua	6,371	16,500	247,300
Khammouan	Thakhek	6,299	16,315	275,400
Louangnamtha	Louangnamtha	3,600	9,325	115,200
Louangphrabang	Louangphrabang	6,515	16,875	367,200
Oudomxay	Xay	5,934	15,370	211,300
Phôngsali	Phôngsali	6,282	16,270	153,400
Salavan	Salavan	4,128	10,691	258,300
Savannakhét	Savannakhét	8,407	21,774	674,900
Special Region	...	2,743	7,105	54,200
Viangchan	Muang Phôn-Hông	6,149	15,927	286,800
Xaignabouli	Xaignabouli	6,328	16,389	293,300
Xékong	Thong	2,959	7,665	64,200
Xiangkhoang	Phônsavan	6,131	15,880	201,200
Municipalities				
Viangchan	Vientiane (Viangchan)	1,514	3,920	531,800
TOTAL		91,429[2]	236,800	4,605,300

Demography

Population (2001): 5,636,000.
Density (2001): persons per sq mi 61.6, persons per sq km 23.8.
Urban-rural (1999): urban 23.0%; rural 77.0%.
Sex distribution (1996): male 49.42%; female 50.58%.
Age breakdown (1996): under 15, 44.2%; 15–29, 25.4%; 30–44, 16.0%; 45–59, 8.7%; 60–74, 4.5%; 75 and over, 1.2%.
Population projection: (2010) 6,993,000; (2020) 8,637,000.
Doubling time: 30 years.
Ethnic composition (2000): Lao-Lum (Lao) 53.0%; Lao-Theung (Mon-Khmer) 23.0%; Lao-Tai (Tai) 13.0%; Lao-Soung (Miao [Hmong] and Man [Yao]) 10.0%; other (ethnic Chinese or Vietnamese) 1.0%.
Religious affiliation (2000): Buddhist 48.8%; traditional beliefs 41.7%; nonreligious 4.3%; Christian 2.1%; other 3.1%.
Major cities (1995): Vientiane (Viangchan) 528,100; Louangphrabang 55,300; Savannakhét 47,500; Salavan 42,500; Pakxé 32,500.

Vital statistics

Birth rate per 1,000 population (2001): 36.5 (world avg. 22.5).
Death rate per 1,000 population (2001): 13.1 (world avg. 9.0).
Natural increase rate per 1,000 population (2001): 23.4 (world avg. 13.5).
Total fertility rate (avg. births per childbearing woman; 2001): 5.0.
Marriage rate per 1,000 population: n.a.
Divorce rate per 1,000 population: n.a.
Life expectancy at birth (2001): male 53.0 years; female 55.0 years.
Major causes of death per 100,000 population (incomplete, 1990): malaria 7.6; pneumonia 3.0; meningitis 1.5; diarrhea 1.2; tuberculosis 0.8.

National economy

Budget (1998–99). Revenue: KN 1,312,100,000,000 (taxes 52.3%, foreign grants 37.0%, nontax revenue 10.7%). Expenditures: KN 1,685,100,000,000 (current expenditure 31.8%, capital expenditure 68.2%).
Public debt (external, outstanding; 1999): U.S.$2,471,000,000.
Tourism (1999): receipts from visitors U.S.$97,000,000; expenditures by nationals abroad U.S.$12,000,000.
Population economically active (1989): total 1,888,000; activity rate of total population 49.0% (participation rates [1985]: ages 15–64, 84.2%; female 45.3%; unemployed [1994] 2.6%).

Price and earnings indexes (1995 = 100)

	1994	1995	1996	1997	1998	1999	2000
Consumer price index	83.6	100.0	113.0	144.1	275.2	628.7	786.4
Earnings index	...	...	....	...	...	...	...

Production (metric tons except as noted). Agriculture, forestry, fishing (1999): rice 2,103,000, sugarcane 174,000, corn (maize) 96,000, sweet potatoes 81,000, cassava 70,000, pineapples 34,000, melons 33,000, potatoes 33,000, oranges 28,000, seed cotton 26,000, bananas 22,000, coffee 18,000; livestock (number of live animals) 1,937,000 pigs, 1,497,000 cattle, 1,286,000 water buffalo, 200,000 goats, 28,000 horses, 13,882,000 chickens; roundwood (1998) 4,591,000 cu m; fish catch (1997) 40,000. Mining and quarrying (1997): gypsum 145,000; rock salt 18,000; tin (metal content) 618. Manufacturing (1998): plastic products 3,225; tobacco 1,000; detergent 912; nails 624; clothing 23,000,000 pieces; cigarettes 55,000,000 packs; beer 332,000 hectolitres; soft drinks 125,000 hectolitres. Construction: n.a. Energy production (consumption): electricity (kW-hr; 1996) 1,294,000,000 (517,000,000); coal (metric tons; 1996) 1,000 (1,000); crude petroleum, n.a. (n.a.); petroleum products (metric tons; 1996) none (107,000); natural gas, n.a. (n.a.).
Gross national product (1999): U.S.$1,476,000,000 (U.S.$290 per capita).

Structure of gross domestic product and labour force

	1998 in value KN '000,000[3]	1998 % of total value	1989 labour force	1989 % of labour force
Agriculture	517,100	52.1	1,359,000	72.0
Manufacturing	164,500	16.6		
Mining	4,100	0.4		
Construction	26,700	2.7		
Public utilities	20,500	2.1		
Transp. and commun.	56,800	5.7		
Trade	119,900	12.1	58,533	8.1
Finance	29,800	3.0		
Pub. admin., defense; Services	43,100	4.3		
Other	10,400	1.0		
TOTAL	992,900	100.0	1,888,000	100.0

Household income and expenditure. Average household size (1995) 6.1%; average annual income per household KN 3,710 (U.S.$371); sources of income: n.a.; expenditure: n.a.
Land use (1994): forested 54.4%; meadows and pastures 3.5%; agricultural and under permanent cultivation 3.9%; other 38.2%.

Foreign trade[4]

Balance of trade (current prices)

	1994	1995	1996	1997	1998	1999
U.S.$'000,000	–263.7	–239.3	–366.8	–347.0	–183.3	–214.0
% of total	30.5%	25.6%	36.2%	32.6%	19.9%	25.6%

Imports (1998): U.S.$552,800,000 (consumption goods 42.3%; investment goods 41.0%, of which construction and electrical equipment 14.7%, motor vehicles 7.1%; materials for garment assembly 12.1%). *Major import sources* (1997): Thailand 52.0%; Vietnam 3.9%; Japan 1.6%; Hong Kong 1.5%; China 0.8%.
Exports (1998): U.S.$369,500,000 (wood products 34.3%; garments 20.8%; electricity 18.0%; coffee 14.3%). *Major export destinations* (1997): Vietnam 42.7%; Thailand 22.1%; France 6.3%; Belgium 5.6%; Germany 5.1%.

Transport and communications

Transport. Railroads: none. Roads (1996): total length 13,870 mi, 22,321 km (paved [1995] 14%). Vehicles (1996): passenger cars 16,320; trucks and buses 4,200. Merchant marine (1992): vessels (100 gross tons and over) 1; total deadweight tonnage 1,469. Air transport (1995): passenger-mi 29,000,000, passenger-km 48,000,000; short ton-mi cargo 3,000,000, metric ton-km cargo 5,000,000; airports (1996) with scheduled flights 11.

Communications

Medium	date	unit	number	units per 1,000 persons
Daily newspapers	1996	circulation	18,000	3.7
Radio	1997	receivers	730,000	145
Television	1999	receivers	51,000	9.6
Telephones	1999	main lines	34,493	6.5
Cellular telephones	1999	subscribers	9,048	1.7
Personal computers	1999	units	12,000	2.3
Internet	1999	users	2,000	0.4

Education and health

Educational attainment (1985). Percentage of population age 6 and over having: no schooling 49.3%; primary 41.2%; secondary 9.1%; higher 0.4%. *Literacy* (1995): total population age 15 and over literate 56.6%; males literate 69.4%; females literate 44.4%.

Education (1996–97)

	schools	teachers	students	student/ teacher ratio
Primary (age 6–10)	7,896	25,831	786,335	30.4
Secondary (age 11–16)	750[5]	10,717	180,160	16.8
Voc., teacher tr.	139[6]	1,600[7]	9,400[7]	5.9[7]
Higher	9[5]	1,369	12,732	9.3

Health: physicians (1995) 3,100 (1 per 1,563 persons); hospital beds (1990) 10,364 (1 per 402 persons); infant mortality rate (2001) 91.0.
Food (1999): daily per capita caloric intake 2,152 (vegetable products 93%, animal products 7%); (1997) 97% of FAO recommended minimum requirement.

Military

Total active duty personnel (2000): 29,100 (army 85.9%, navy 2.1%, air force 12.0%). *Military expenditure as percentage of GNP* (1997): 3.4% (world 2.6%); per capita expenditure U.S.$12.

[1]Formerly known as the Supreme People's Assembly. [2]Detail does not add to total given because of rounding. [3]At constant 1990 prices. [4]Import figures are c.i.f. in balance of trade and commodities. [5]1989–90. [6]1988–89. [7]1995–96.

Internet resources for further information:
- **Discovering Laos http://www.laoembassy.com/discover/index.htm**

Latvia

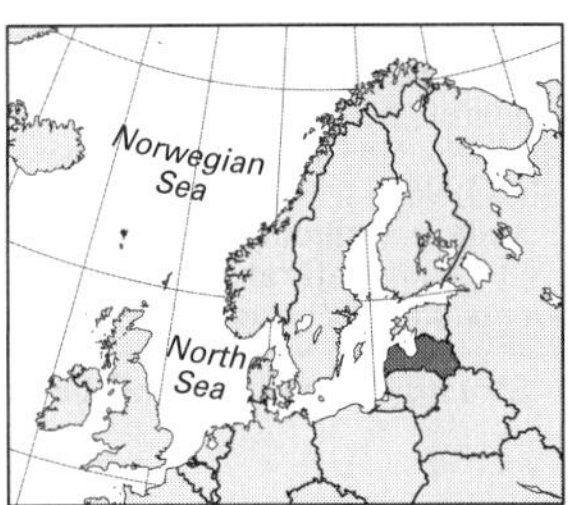

Official name: Latvijas Republika (Republic of Latvia).
Form of government: unitary multiparty republic with a single legislative body (Parliament, or Saeima [100]).
Chief of state: President.
Head of government: Prime Minister.
Capital: Riga.
Official language: Latvian.
Official religion: none.
Monetary unit: 1 lats (Ls; plural lati) = 100 santimi; valuation (Sept. 28, 2001) 1 U.S.$ = 0.62 lats; 1 £ = 0.91 lats.

Area and population

Cities	area sq km	population 2000 census[1]	Districts	area sq km	population 2000 census[1]
Daugavpils	72	114,829	Jelgava	1,604	37,110
Jelgava	60	63,269	Krāslava	2,285	36,825
Jūrmala	100	55,671	Kuldīga	2,502	38,198
Liepāja	60	89,439	Liepāja	3,594	46,851
Rēzekne	17	39,462	Limbaži	2,602	40,160
Riga	307	764,328	Ludza	2,569	35,112
Ventspils	46	43,891	Madona	3,346	46,412
			Ogre	1,840	62,908
Districts			Preiļi	2,041	41,722
Aizkraukle	2,565	41,881	Rēzekne	2,655	42,930
Alūksne	2,243	26,418	Rīga (Riga)	3,059	143,764
Balvi	2,386	30,651	Saldus	2,182	39,000
Bauska	1,882	53,178	Talsi	2,751	49,842
Cēsis	3,067	60,614	Tukums	2,447	53,889
Daugavpils	2,525	42,743	Valka	2,437	34,324
Dobele	1,633	40,275	Valmiera	2,365	60,345
Gulbene	1,877	28,226	Ventspils	2,472	14,610
Jēkabpils	2,998	56,462	TOTAL	64,589	2,375,339

Demography

Population (2001): 2,358,000.
Density (2001): persons per sq mi 94.5, persons per sq km 36.5.
Urban-rural (2000[2]): urban 68.9%; rural 31.1%.
Sex distribution (2000[1]): male 46.03%; female 53.97%.
Age breakdown (2000[2]): under 15, 17.8%; 15–29, 21.2%; 30–44, 22.1%; 45–59, 18.2%; 60–74, 15.4%; 75 and over, 5.3%.
Population projection: (2010) 2,219,000; (2020) 2,119,000.
Ethnic composition (2000): Latvian 57.6%; Russian 29.6%; Belarusian 4.1%; Ukrainian 2.7%; Polish 2.5%; Lithuanian 1.4%; other 2.1%.
Religious affiliation (1995): Christian 39.6%, of which Protestant 16.7% (of which Lutheran 14.6%), Roman Catholic 14.9%, Orthodox 8.0%; Jewish 0.6%; other (mostly nonreligious) 59.8%.
Major cities (2000[2]): Riga (2001) 755,600; Daugavpils 114,829; Liepāja 89,439; Jelgava 63,269; Jūrmala 55,671.

Vital statistics

Birth rate per 1,000 population (1999): 8.0 (world avg. 22.5); (1998) legitimate 62.9%; illegitimate 37.1%.
Death rate per 1,000 population (1999): 13.5 (world avg. 9.0).
Natural increase rate per 1,000 population (1999): –5.5 (world avg. 13.5).
Total fertility rate (avg. births per childbearing woman; 1999): 1.2.
Marriage rate per 1,000 population (1999): 3.9.
Divorce rate per 1,000 population (1999): 2.5.
Life expectancy at birth (1999): male 64.9 years; female 76.2 years.
Major causes of death per 100,000 population (1998): diseases of the circulatory system 775.6; malignant neoplasms (cancers) 231.8; accidents, poisoning, and violence 161.8; diseases of the digestive system 42.2.

National economy

Budget (1998). Revenue: Ls 1,577,400,000 (social security contributions 27.1%, value-added taxes 20.1%, personal income taxes 13.9%, excises 10.7%, nontax revenue 10.1%). Expenditures: Ls 1,572,300,000 (social security and welfare 34.4%, education 15.7%, health 9.4%, police 5.8%, defense 2.4%).
Production (metric tons except as noted). Agriculture, forestry, fishing (1999): grasses for forage and silage 13,800,000, hay 1,355,000, potatoes 795,500, sugar beets 451,500, wheat 351,900, barley 232,600, rye 88,700; livestock (number of live animals) 403,400 pigs, 375,700 cattle; roundwood (1998) 10,030,000 cu m; fish catch (1997) 106,027. Mining and quarrying (1998): peat 171,700; gypsum 119,100. Manufacturing (value added in Ls '000,000; 1996): alcoholic beverages 58.7; fish processing 32.8; dairy products 26.9; bakery products 26.4; sawn wood 23.3; wearing apparel 20.5; veneer/plywood 20.5. Energy production (consumption): electricity (kW-hr; 1998) 5,797,000,000 (5,133,000,000); coal (1996) none (293,000); crude petroleum, none (none); petroleum products (1996) none (2,079,000); natural gas (cu m; 1996) none (938,000,000).
Household income and expenditure. Average household size (1996) 2.7; annual disposable income per household (1996) Ls 1,659 (U.S.$3,011); sources of income (1998): wages and salaries 55.8%, pensions and transfers 25.7%, self-employment 9.5%; expenditure (1998): food, beverages, and tobacco 46.4%, housing and energy 16.6%, transportation and communications 9.8%, clothing and footwear 6.9%.
Public debt (external, outstanding; 1999): U.S.$864,800,000.
Gross national product (1999): U.S.$5,913,000,000 (U.S.$2,420 per capita).

Structure of gross domestic product and labour force

	1998			
	in value Ls '000,000	% of total value	labour force[3]	% of labour force[3]
Agriculture, forestry	155.0	4.1	184,000	15.2
Mining and quarrying	5.0	0.1	2,000	0.2
Manufacturing	662.9	17.6	171,000	14.1
Construction	169.2	4.5	63,000	5.2
Public utilities	127.4	3.4	19,000	1.6
Transp. and commun.	464.5	12.3	90,000	7.4
Trade	606.1	16.1	191,000	15.7
Finance, real estate	298.4	7.9	62,000	5.1
Pub. admin., defense	329.5	8.7	64,000	5.3
Services	461.4	12.2	197,000	16.2
Other	494.1[4]	13.1[4]	169,500[5]	14.0[5]
TOTAL	3,773.5	100.0	1,212,500	100.0

Population economically active (1997): total 1,186,100; activity rate of total population 48.2% (participation rates: ages 15–64, 70.2%; female 48.1%; unemployed [1998] 7.6%).
Tourism (in U.S.$'000,000; 1999): receipts 118; expenditures 268.

Price and earnings indexes (1995 = 100)

	1995	1996	1997	1998	1999	2000	2001
Consumer price index	100.0	117.6	127.5	133.5	136.6	140.3	145.0[6]
Annual earnings index	100.0	114.9	139.7	148.8	154.7	159.6	...

Land use (1994): forested 44.4%; meadows and pastures 12.4; agricultural and under permanent cultivation 27.0%; other 16.2%.

Foreign trade[7]

Balance of trade (current prices)

	1995	1996	1997	1998	1999	2000
Ls '000,000	–272	–483	–610	–812	–716	–803
% of total	16.5%	23.3%	23.9%	27.5%	26.2%	26.2%

Imports (1998): Ls 1,881,000,000 (machinery and equipment 20.5%, chemicals and chemical products 11.1%, mineral fuels 10.5%, transport vehicles 10.4%, base and fabricated metals 8.4%). *Major import sources:* Germany 16.8%; Russia 11.8%; Finland 9.5%; Sweden 7.2%; Estonia 6.6%.
Exports (1998): Ls 1,069,000,000 (wood and paper products 33.5%, textiles and clothing 16.1%, food and beverages 9.8%, base and fabricated metals 9.8%). *Major export destinations:* Germany 15.6%; U.K. 13.5%; Russia 12.1%; Sweden 10.3%; Lithuania 7.4%.

Transport and communications

Transport. Railroads (1998): length 2,413 km; passenger-km (1998) 1,059,000,000; metric-km cargo (1998) 12,995,000,000. Roads (1997): total length 55,942 km (paved 38%). Vehicles (1997): passenger cars 431,816; trucks and buses 95,329. Air transport (1998): passenger-km 298,000,000; metric ton-km cargo 9,000,000; airports with scheduled flights (1996) 1.

Communications

Medium	date	unit	number	units per 1,000 persons
Daily newspapers	1996	circulation	616,000	247
Radio	1997	receivers	1,760,000	713
Television	1999	receivers	1,808,000	755
Telephones	1999	main lines	731,527	306
Cellular telephones	1999	subscribers	274,344	115
Personal computers	1999	units	200,000	84
Internet	1999	users	105,000	44

Education and health

Educational attainment (2000). Percentage of population age 15 and over having: incomplete primary education 2.4%; complete primary 6.1%; lower secondary 26.5%; upper secondary 51.1%; higher 13.9%. *Literacy* (1995): percentage of total population age 15 and over literate 99.6%.

Education (1996–97)

	schools	teachers	students	student/ teacher ratio
Primary	1,074	10,883[8]	146,653	13.5[8]
Secondary	...	24,112	196,148	8.1
Vocational	...	5,740	43,170	7.5
Higher	28	4,486	56,187	12.5

Health (1998): physicians 6,900 (1 per 355 persons); hospital beds 23,165 (1 per 106 persons); infant mortality rate per 1,000 live births (1999) 11.4.
Food (1999): daily per capita caloric intake 2,904 (vegetable products 75%, animal products 25%); 113% of FAO recommended minimum requirement.

Military

Total active duty personnel (2000): 5,050[9] (army 47.5%, navy 16.6%, air force 4.2%, national guard 31.7%). *Military expenditure as percentage of GNP* (1997): 0.9% (world 2.6%); per capita expenditure U.S.$39.

[1]Preliminary figures. [2]January 1. [3]Annual average official estimate. [4]Indirect taxes less subsidies. [5]Represents nonworking job seekers, of which 91,800 (7.6%) are registered unemployed. [6]June. [7]Imports c.i.f.; exports f.o.b. [8]Full-time teachers only. [9]Excludes 3,500 border guards classified as paramilitary.

Internet resources for further information:
- **Bank of Latvia http://www.bank.lv**
- **Central Statistical Bureau of Latvia http://www.csb.lv**

Lebanon

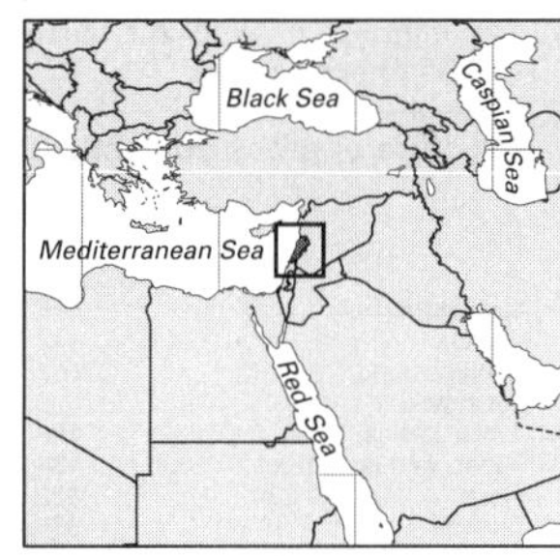

Official name: Al-Jumhūrīyah al-Lubnānīyah (Lebanese Republic).
Form of government: unitary multiparty republic with one legislative house (National Assembly [128])[1].
Chief of state: President.
Head of government: Prime Minister.
Capital: Beirut.
Official language: Arabic.
Official religion: none.
Monetary unit: 1 Lebanese pound (£L) = 100 piastres; valuation (Sept. 28, 2001) 1 U.S.$ = £L 1,512; 1 £ = £L 2,222.

Area and population

		area		population
Governorates	Capitals	sq mi	sq km	1996 estimate
Bayrūt	Beirut (Bayrūt)	7	18	407,403
Al-Biqāʿ	Zaḥlah	1,653	4,280	399,890
Jabal Lubnān	Bʿabdā	753	1,950	1,145,458
Al-Janūb	Sidon (Ṣaydā)	772[2]	2,001[2]	283,056
An-Nabaṭīyah	An-Nabaṭīyah	[2]	[2]	205,412
Ash-Shamāl	Tripoli (Ṭarābulus)	765	1,981	670,609
TOTAL		4,016[3]	10,400[3]	3,111,828

Demography

Population (2001): 3,628,000.
Density (2001): persons per sq mi 903.3, persons per sq km 348.8.
Urban-rural (1999): urban 89.4%; rural 10.6%.
Sex distribution (2000): male 48.44%; female 51.56%.
Age breakdown (2000): under 15, 27.9%; 15–29, 33.5%; 30–44, 19.0%; 45–59, 10.1%; 60–74, 7.2%; 75 and over, 2.3%.
Population projection: (2010) 4,056,000; (2020) 4,417,000.
Doubling time: 50 years.
Ethnic composition (1996): Arab *c.* 93%, of which Lebanese *c.* 84%, Palestinian *c.* 9%; Armenian *c.* 6%; Kurd and other *c.* 1%.
Religious affiliation (1995): Muslim 55.3%, of which Shīʿī 34.0%, Sunnī 21.3%; Christian 37.6%, of which Catholic 25.1% (Maronite 19.0%, Greek Catholic or Melchite 4.6%), Orthodox 11.7% (Greek Orthodox 6.0%, Armenian Apostolic 5.2%), Protestant 0.5%; Druze 7.1%.
Major cities (1994)[4]: Beirut 1,100,000; Tripoli 240,000; Sidon (Ṣaydā) 150,000; Jūniyah 100,000; Zaḥlah 100,000; Tyre 80,000.

Vital statistics

Birth rate per 1,000 population (2000): 20.3 (world avg. 22.5).
Death rate per 1,000 population (2000): 6.4 (world avg. 9.0).
Natural increase rate per 1,000 population (2000): 13.9 (world avg. 13.5).
Total fertility rate (avg. births per childbearing woman; 2000): 2.1.
Life expectancy at birth (1999): male 68.9 years; female 73.7 years.
Major causes of death: n.a.

National economy

Budget (2000). Revenue: £L 4,091,435,000,000 (1998; tax revenue 74.6%, of which customs revenues 44.1%, income tax 9.0%, taxes on goods and services 8.4%, property tax 8.4%, miscellaneous taxes and fees 2.1%; nontax revenue 25.4%). Expenditures: £L 8,190,034,000,000 (current expenditures 81.1%, of which debt service 40.0%, public services 13.3%, defense 9.7%, education 8.3%, social security 6.4%, health 2.6%; capital expenditures 18.9%).
Production (metric tons except as noted). Agriculture, forestry, fishing (2000): tomatoes 335,000, sugar beets 330,000, potatoes 270,000, grapes 250,000, cucumbers and gherkins 190,000, oranges 160,000, apples 120,000, lemons and limes 109,000, olives 105,000, onions 85,000; livestock (number of live animals) 445,000 goats, 380,000 sheep, 77,000 cattle, 63,500 pigs, 32,000,000 chickens; roundwood (2000) 412,150 cu m; fish catch (1999) 3,860. Mining and quarrying (1996): lime 16,000; salt 4,000; gypsum 2,000. Manufacturing (1999): cement 2,715,000; flour 411,300; olive oil 6,000. Construction (1999): 6,700,000 sq m[5]. Energy production (consumption): electricity (kW-hr; 2000) 9,236,000,000 (1998; 9,010,000,000); coal, n.a. (none); crude petroleum (barrels; 1998) none (1,358,000); petroleum products (metric tons; 1998) none (3,204,000).
Gross national product (1999): U.S.$15,796,000,000 (U.S.$3,700 per capita).

Structure of gross domestic product and labour force

	1995			
	in value U.S.$'000,000	% of total value	labour force	% of labour force
Agriculture	380	4.0	143,900	14.0
Mining	—	—		
Manufacturing	1,235	13.0	277,600	27.0
Construction	950	10.0		
Public utilities / Transp. and commun.	2,375[6]	25.0[6]		
Trade	2,660	28.0	606,500	59.0
Finance / Real estate and business services / Services	1,900	20.0		
Pub. admin., defense	[6]	[6]		
TOTAL	9,500	100.0	1,028,000	100.0

Population economically active (1995): total 1,028,000; activity rate of total population 25.4% (participation rates: over age 15 [1988] 44%; female *c.* 30%; unemployed n.a.).

Price and earnings indexes (1995 = 100)

	1993	1994	1995	1996	1997
Consumer price index	87.1	94.3	100.0	88.7	90.5
Wages index[7]	58.1	88.0	100.0	...	...

Public debt (external, outstanding; 1999): U.S.$5,568,000,000.
Household income and expenditure. Average household size (1998) 4.4; average annual income per household (1994) £L 2,400,000 (U.S.$1,430); sources of income (1974): wages 27.9%, transfers 3.0%, other 69.1%; expenditure (1966)[8]: food 42.8%, housing 16.8%, clothing 8.6%, health care 7.2%.
Tourism (1999): receipts from visitors U.S.$673,000,000.
Land use (1994): forested 7.8%; meadows and pastures 1.0%; agricultural and under permanent cultivation 29.9%; wasteland and other areas 61.3%.

Foreign trade[9]

Balance of trade (current prices)

	1995	1996	1997	1998	1999	2000
U.S.$'000,000	–5,770	–6,643	–6,880	–6,408	–5,530	–5,514
% of total	74.5%	76.4%	84.1%	82.9%	80.3%	79.4%

Imports (2000): £L 6,228,000,000 (1995; machinery and transport equipment 27.0%, metals and metal products 9.8%, mineral products 8.8%, processed food 7.8%, chemicals 6.7%). *Major import sources* (1999): Italy 10.9%; France 9.6%; Germany 8.9%; U.S. 8.1%; Switzerland 7.1%.
Exports (2000): £L 714,000,000 (1995; pharmaceuticals and detergents 15.2%, food and beverages 15.1%, machinery and transport equipment 10.2%, paper products 8.9%, aluminum products 6.1%, metals and metal products 4.3%, gold products 2.6%). *Major export destinations*[10] (1999): Saudi Arabia 10.5%; U.A.E. 8.0%; France 7.7%; U.S. 6.2%; Syria 4.8%; Jordan 4.0%.

Transport and communications

Transport. Railroads (1999)[11]: length 222 km. Roads (1996): total length 6,350 km (paved 95%). Vehicles (1997): passenger cars 1,299,398; trucks and buses 85,242. Merchant marine (1992): vessels (100 gross tons and over) 163; total deadweight tonnage 438,165. Air transport (1997)[12]: passenger-km 2,116,000,000; metric ton-km cargo 319,000,000; airports (1999) 1.

Communications

Medium	date	unit	number	units per 1,000 persons
Daily newspapers	1996	circulation	435,000	141
Radio	1997	receivers	2,850,000	907
Television	1998	receivers	1,120,000	351
Telephones	1999	main lines	650,000	201
Cellular telephones	1999	subscribers	627,000	194
Personal computers	1999	units	150,000	42
Internet	1999	users	200,000	56

Education and health

Educational attainment: n.a. *Literacy* (1995): total population age 15 and over literate 1,829,000 (92.4%); males literate 94.7%; females literate 90.3%.

Education (1996–97)

	schools	teachers	students	student/ teacher ratio
Primary (age 5–9)	2,160	22,810[13]	382,309	...
Secondary (age 10–16)	1,405[13]	21,344[13]	292,002	...
Voc., teacher tr.	275[14]	7,745	55,848	7.2
Higher	20	10,444[15]	81,588[15]	7.8[15]

Health (1997): physicians 7,203 (1 per 476 persons); hospital beds (1995) 11,596 (1 per 319 persons); infant mortality rate per 1,000 live births (2000) 29.3.
Food (1999): daily per capita caloric intake 3,256 (vegetable products 86%, animal products 14%); 131% of FAO recommended minimum.

Military

Total active duty personnel (2000): Lebanese national armed forces 63,570 (army 95.4%, navy 1.9%, air force 2.7%). External regular military forces include: UN peacekeeping force in Lebanon (August 2001) 4,486; Syrian army 22,000. *Military expenditure as percentage of GDP* (1997): 3.0% (world 2.6%); per capita expenditure: U.S.$135.

[1]The current legislature was elected between August and September 2000; one-half of its membership is Christian and one-half Muslim/Druze. [2]Al-Janūb includes An-Nabaṭīyah. [3]Includes water area of 66 sq mi (170 sq km) not distributed by governorate. [4]Urban agglomerations. [5]Permits authorized. [6]Public utilities and transportation and communications includes public administration and defense. [7]Based on minimum wage, in real terms. [8]Weights based on consumer price index components. For capital city only. [9]Imports are c.i.f. [10]Domestic exports only; reexports not included. [11]Apart from a 14-mi (23-km) section delivering oil from the Zahrani refinery to a thermal power station serving Beirut, no passenger or general cargo track is currently in use. [12]MEA-Airliban international flights only [13]1981–82. [14]1994–95. [15]1995–96.

Internet resources for further information:
- **Central Administration for Statistics** **http://www.cas.gov.lb**
- **U.S. Embassy of Lebanon** **http://www.lebanonembassy.org**
- **Bank of Lebanon** **http://www.bdl.gov.lb**

Lesotho

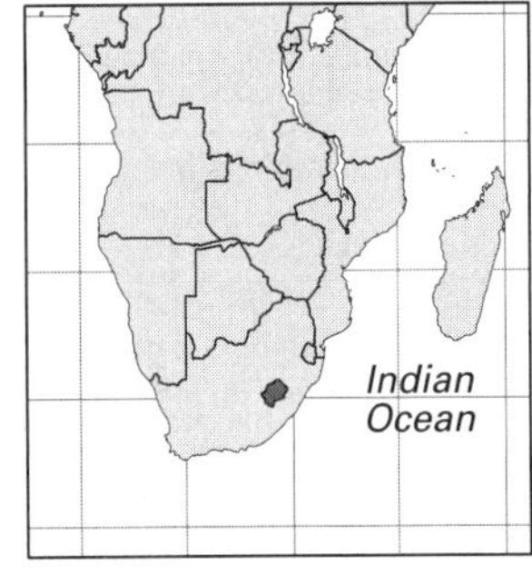

Official name: Lesotho (Sotho); Kingdom of Lesotho (English).
Form of government[1]: transitional regime with 2 legislative houses (Senate [33]; National Assembly [80]).
Chief of state: King.
Head of government: Prime Minister.
Capital: Maseru.
Official languages: Sotho; English.
Official religion: Christianity.
Monetary unit: 1 loti (plural maloti [M]) = 100 lisente; valuation (Sept. 28, 2001) 1 U.S.$ = M 9.01; 1 £ = M 13.24.

Area and population

Districts	Capitals	area sq mi	area sq km	population 1995 estimate[2]
Berea	Teyateyaneng	858	2,222	206,200
Butha-Buthe	Butha-Buthe	682	1,767	135,400
Leribe	Hlotse	1,092	2,828	349,500
Mafeteng	Mafeteng	818	2,119	259,000
Maseru	Maseru	1,652	4,279	400,200
Mohale's Hoek	Mohale's Hoek	1,363	3,530	231,300
Mokhotlong	Mokhotlong	1,573	4,075	100,300
Qacha's Nek	Qacha's Nek	907	2,349	86,800
Quthing	Quthing	1,126	2,916	151,900
Thaba-Tseka	Thaba-Tseka	1,649	4,270	136,200
TOTAL		11,720	30,355	2,056,800

Demography

Population (2001): 2,177,000[3].
Density (2001)[3]: persons per sq mi 185.8, persons per sq km 71.7.
Urban-rural (1996): urban 16.9%; rural 83.1%.
Sex distribution (1996): male 49.20%; female 50.80%.
Age breakdown (1996): under 15, 43.1%; 15–29, 27.6%; 30–44, 15.0%; 45–59, 8.6%; 60–74, 4.8%; 75 and over, 0.9%.
Population projection[3]: (2010) 2,339,000; (2020) 2,382,000.
Doubling time: 41 years.
Ethnic composition (2000): Sotho 80.3%; Zulu 14.4%; other 5.3%.
Religious affiliation (2000): Christian 91.0%, of which Roman Catholic 37.5%, Protestant (mostly Presbyterian) 13.0%, African Christian 11.8%; other (mostly traditional beliefs) 9.0%.
Major urban centres (1996): Maseru 137,837; Teyateyaneng 48,869; Maputsoe 27,951; Hlotse 23,122; Mafeteng 20,804.

Vital statistics

Birth rate per 1,000 population (2000): 31.7 (world avg. 22.5).
Death rate per 1,000 population (2000): 14.6 (world avg. 9.0).
Natural increase rate per 1,000 population (2000): 17.1 (world avg. 13.5).
Total fertility rate (avg. births per childbearing woman; 2000): 4.2.
Life expectancy at birth (2000): male 49.8 years; female 51.8 years.
Major causes of death per 100,000 population: n.a.; however, major diseases include typhoid fever and infectious and parasitic diseases.

National economy

Budget (1999–2000). Revenue: M 2,580,700,000 (customs receipts 45.8%, grants and nontax revenue 28.8%, income tax 13.5%, sales tax 10.2%). Expenditures: M 2,913,500,000 (personal emoluments 41.9%, capital expenditure 32.4%, subsidies and transfers 13.0%, interest payments 12.7%).
Production (metric tons except as noted). Agriculture, forestry, fishing (1999): corn (maize) 125,000, roots and tubers 85,000, sorghum 33,000, vegetables 19,000, wheat 15,000, fruit 14,000, dry beans 9,300, dry peas 3,000; livestock (number of live animals) 720,000 sheep, 560,000 goats, 510,000 cattle, 152,000 asses, 98,000 horses, 63,000 pigs, 1,700,000 chickens; roundwood (1998) 1,594,000 cu m; fish catch (1998) 30. Mining and quarrying (1998): diamonds 2,398 carats. Manufacturing (value added in U.S.$'000,000; 1995): food products 58; beverages 38; textiles 14; chemical products 9; metal products 4; wearing apparel 4. Construction (permits issued in M '000,000; 1999): residential 3.76; nonresidential 65.10. Energy production (consumption): electricity (kW-hr; 1988) 1,000,000 (n.a.); coal, none (n.a); petroleum, none (n.a.); natural gas, none (n.a.).
Public debt (external, outstanding; 1999): U.S.$661,800,000.
Tourism (1999): receipts from visitors U.S.$19,000,000; expenditures by nationals abroad U.S.$12,000,000.
Population economically active (1993): total 617,871; activity rate of total population 45.1% (participation rates: ages 15–64 [1986] 79.8%; female 23.7%; unemployed [1992] 35.0%).

Price and earnings indexes (1995 = 100)

	1994	1995	1996	1997	1998	1999	2000
Consumer price index	91.5	100.0	109.3	...	...	135.2	143.5
Annual earnings index[4]	86.6	100.0	114.2	126.1	146.9	164.6	179.3

Household income and expenditure. Average household size (1996) 5.0; average annual income per household (1986–87) M 2,832 (U.S.$1,297); sources of income (1986–87): transfer payments 44.7%, self-employment 27.8%, wages and salaries 22.4%, other 5.1%; expenditure (1989): food 48.0%, clothing 16.4%, household durable goods 11.9%, housing and energy 10.1%, transportation 4.7%.

Gross national product (at current market prices; 1999): U.S.$1,158,000,000 (U.S.$550 per capita).

Structure of gross domestic product and labour force

	1998 in value M '000,000[5]	1998 % of total value[5]	1986 labour force	1986 % of labour force
Agriculture	645.7	16.9	474,171	66.2
Mining	2.6	0.1	6,446	0.9
Manufacturing	508.5	13.3	19,339	2.7
Construction	573.9	15.1	31,516	4.4
Public utilities	168.5	4.4	1,433	0.2
Transp. and commun.	131.0	3.4	5,014	0.7
Trade	352.9	9.3	22,204	3.1
Finance	330.4	8.7	3,581	0.5
Pub. admin., defense	661.8	17.4	17,907	2.5
Services	41.5	1.1	126,780	17.7
Other	390.9[6]	10.3[6]	7,879	1.1
TOTAL	3,807.7	100.0	716,270[7]	100.0[7]

Land use (1998): meadows and pastures 65.9%; agricultural and under permanent cultivation 10.7%; other 23.4%.

Foreign trade[8]

Balance of trade (current prices)

	1994	1995	1996	1997	1998	1999
U.S.$'000,000	–666.7	–825.2	–811.8	–828.3	–672.5	–606.7
% of total	69.9%	72.1%	68.5%	67.9%	63.5%	63.7%

Imports (1998): M 5,199,800,000 (1990; manufactured goods [excluding chemicals, machinery, and transport equipment] 42.5%; food and live animals 19.1%; machinery and transport equipment 15.3%; petroleum products 8.6%). *Major import sources:* Customs Union of Southern Africa 88.7%; Asia 7.2%; Europe 2.3%, of which European Economic Community 2.0%; the Americas 1.3%.
Exports (1998): M 1,109,600,000 (manufactured goods 71.6%; machinery and transport equipment 15.1%; food and live animals 4.0%; beverages and tobacco 3.5%; crude materials 1.8%). *Major export destinations:* Customs Union of Southern Africa 65.5%; the Americas 33.6%; Europe 0.5%.

Transport and communications

Transport. Railroads (1999): length 1.6 mi, 2.6 km. Roads (1996): total length 3,079 mi, 4,955 km (paved 18%). Vehicles (1996): passenger cars 12,610; trucks and buses 25,000. Merchant marine: vessels (100 gross tons and over) none. Air transport (1996): passenger-mi 3,900,000, passenger-km 6,200,000; short ton-mi cargo 395,000, metric ton-km cargo 577,000; airports (1997).

Communications

Medium	date	unit	number	units per 1,000 persons
Daily newspapers	1996	circulation	15,000	7.6
Radio	1997	receivers	104,000	52
Television	1999	receivers	33,000	16
Telephones	1998	main lines	21,000	10
Cellular telephones	1998	subscribers	9,831	4.8
Personal computers	...	units	...	...
Internet	1999	users	1,000	0.5

Education and health

Educational attainment (1986–87). Percentage of population age 10 and over having: no formal education 22.9%; primary 52.8%; secondary 23.2%; higher 0.6%. *Literacy* (1995): total population age 15 and over literate 849,700 (71.3%); males literate 468,000 (81.1%); females literate 381,700 (62.3%).

Education (1996–97)

	schools	teachers	students	student/ teacher ratio
Primary (age 6–12)	1,249	7,898	374,628	47.4
Secondary (age 13–17)	187[9]	2,817	67,454	23.9
Vocational	9[9]	61	678	11.1
Higher	1[9]	574	4,614	8.0

Health: physicians (1995) 105 (1 per 18,527 persons); hospital beds (1992) 2,400 (1 per 765 persons); infant mortality rate per 1,000 live births (2000) 83.0.
Food (1999): daily per capita caloric intake 2,300 (vegetable products 95%, animal products 5%); (1997) 101% of FAO recommended minimum requirement.

Military

Total active duty personnel (2000): 2,000[10]. *Military expenditure as percentage of GNP* (1997): 2.5% (world 2.6%); per capita expenditure U.S.$16.

[1]Traditionally a hereditary monarchy; the Interim Political Authority, which was mandated in December 1998 to make Lesotho more democratic, has implemented a new electoral system for elections in early 2002. [2]De jure population. [3]Excludes absentee miners working in South Africa. [4]Based on average annual wages, including overtime, of mine workers. [5]At 1995 prices. [6]Indirect taxes less imputed bank service charges. [7]Approximately 117,600 persons (*c.* 40% of Lesotho's adult male labour force) were employed as mine workers in South Africa in 1993; by May 2000 this figure had declined to 54,000. [8]Import figures are f.o.b. in balance of trade and c.i.f. in commodities and trading partners. [9]1993–94. [10]Royal Lesotho Defence Force.

Internet resources for further information:

- **Central Bank of Lesotho http://www.centralbank.org.ls**

Liberia

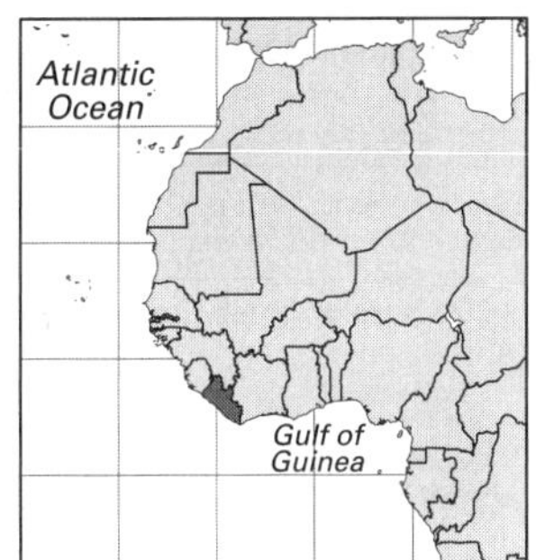

Official name: Republic of Liberia.
Form of government: multiparty republic with two legislative houses (Senate [26]; House of Representatives [64]).
Head of state and government: President.
Capital: Monrovia.
Official language: English.
Official religion: none.
Monetary unit: 1 Liberian dollar (L$) = 100 cents; valuation (Sept. 28, 2001) 1 U.S.$ = L$1.00[1]; 1 £ = L$1.47.

Area and population

Counties	Capitals	area sq mi	area sq km	population 1986 estimate
Bomi	Tubmanburg	755	1,955	67,300
Bong	Gbarnga	3,127	8,099	268,100
Gbarpolu	Bopulu	2,982	7,723	[2]
Grand Bassa	Buchanan	3,382	8,759	166,900
Grand Cape Mount	Robertsport	2,250	5,827	83,900
Grand Gedeh	Zwedru	6,575[3]	17,029[3]	109,000[3]
Grand Kru	Barclayville	[4]	[4]	[4]
Lofa	Voinjama	4,493	11,367	261,000[2]
Margibi	Kakata	1,260	3,263	104,000
Maryland	Harper	2,066[4]	5,351[4]	137,700[4]
Montserrado	Bensonville	1,058	2,740	582,400
Nimba	Sanniquellie	4,650	12,043	325,700
River Gee	Fish Town	[3]	[3]	[3]
Rivercess	Rivercess City	1,693	4,385	39,900
Sinoe	Greenville	3,959	10,254	65,400
TOTAL		38,250[5]	99,067[5, 6]	2,221,300[7]

Demography

Population (2001): 3,226,000.
Density (2001)[5]: persons per sq mi 85.5, persons per sq km 33.3.
Urban-rural (1999): urban 44.2%; rural 55.8%.
Sex distribution (2000): male 49.37%; female 50.63%.
Age breakdown (2000): under 15, 43.0%; 15–29, 26.9%; 30–44, 15.2%; 45–59, 9.5%; 60–74, 4.2%; 75 and over, 1.2%.
Population projection: (2010) 4,073,000; (2020) 5,294,000.
Doubling time: 23 years.
Ethnic composition (1984): Kpelle 19.4%; Bassa 13.9%; Grebo 9.0%; Gio 7.8%; Kru 7.3%; Mano 7.1%; other 35.5%.
Religious affiliation (1995): traditional beliefs 63.0%; Christian 21.0%, of which Protestant 13.5%, African Christian 5.1%, Roman Catholic 2.4%; Muslim 16.0%.
Major cities (1999): Monrovia 479,000; Harbel 60,000[8]; Gbarnga 30,000[9]; Buchanan 25,000[8]; Yekepa 16,000[8].

Vital statistics

Birth rate per 1,000 population (2000): 47.2 (world avg. 22.5).
Death rate per 1,000 population (2000): 16.6 (world avg. 9.0).
Natural increase rate per 1,000 population (2000): 30.6 (world avg. 13.5).
Total fertility rate (avg. births per childbearing woman; 2000): 6.4.
Marriage rate per 1,000 population: n.a.
Divorce rate per 1,000 population: n.a.
Life expectancy at birth (2000): male 49.6 years; female 52.5 years.
Major causes of death per 100,000 population: n.a.; however, major health problems include complications during pregnancy, malaria, pneumonia, anemia, malnutrition, measles, and AIDS. Violence and acts of war were major causes of both morbidity and mortality from 1990 onward.

National economy

Budget (1999). Revenue: U.S.$65,500,000,000 (tax revenue 92.2%, of which import duties and consular fees 29.9%, maritime revenue 23.2%, income and profit taxes 22.4%, sales tax 15.9%, property taxes 0.5%). Expenditures: U.S.$67,500,000,000 (current expenditure 85.2%, of which goods and services 49.3%, wages 21.6%, subsidies and transfers 8.8%, interest on debt 5.2%; development expenditure 8.3%; other 6.5%).
Tourism: n.a.
Population economically active (1997): total 1,183,000; activity rate 51.4% (participation rates: ages 10–64 [1994] 64.0%; female 39.5%; unemployed [1996] 95%).

Price and earnings indexes (1990 = 100)

	1989	1990	1991	1992	1993	1994	1995
Consumer price index	79.8	100.0	110.0	121.0	133.1	146.4	161.0
Earnings index	...	...	...	...	...	...	...

Production (metric tons except as noted). Agriculture, forestry, fishing (1999): cassava 313,000, sugarcane 250,000, rice 210,000, oil palm fruit 152,000, bananas 90,000, plantains 35,000, natural rubber 35,000, yams 20,000, coffee 3,000, cacao beans 500; livestock (number of live animals) 220,000 goats, 210,000 sheep, 120,000 pigs, 36,000 cattle, 3,500,000 chickens; roundwood (1998) 3,021,000 cu m; fish catch (1998) 10,830. Mining and quarrying (1998): diamonds 7,719 carats[10]; gold 72 kg[10]. Manufacturing (1996): palm oil 45,000; cement 8,300[11]; cigarettes 22,000,000 units[12]; soft drinks 171,000 hectolitres[13]; beer 158,000 hectolitres[13]. Construction: n.a. Energy production (consumption): electricity (kW-hr; 1996) 488,000,000 (488,000,000); coal, none (none); crude petroleum, none (none); petroleum products (metric tons; 1994) none (106,000); natural gas, none (none).
Public debt (external, outstanding; 1999): U.S.$1,062,000,000.
Household income and expenditure. Average household size (1983) 4.3; income per household: n.a.; sources of income: n.a.; expenditure: n.a.
Gross national product (1996): U.S.$1,174,000,000 (U.S.$490 per capita).

Structure of gross domestic product and labour force

	1999 in value U.S.$'000,000	1999 % of total value	1994 labour force	1994 % of labour force
Agriculture	337.7	75.3	676,000	68.1
Mining	9.8	2.2	77,000	7.7
Manufacturing	21.4	4.8		
Construction	6.9	1.5		
Public utilities	2.3	0.5		
Transp. and commun.	21.6	4.8		
Trade	17.0	3.8		
Finance	13.3	3.0		
Pub. admin., defense	11.2	2.5		
Services	10.3	2.3	240,000	24.2
Other	–3.2[14]	–0.7[14]		
TOTAL	448.3	100.0	993,000	100.0

Land use (1994): forested 47.8%; meadows and pastures 20.8%; agricultural and under permanent cultivation 3.8%; other 27.6%.

Foreign trade

Balance of trade (current prices)

	1994	1995	1996	1997	1998	1999
U.S.$'000,000	–5,393	–4,829	–2,718	–217.9	–118.5	–111.8
% of total	81.7%	71.7%	54.5%	81.1%	58.1%	50.1%

Imports (1999): U.S.$167,500,000 (food and live animals 31.9%, machinery and transport equipment 21.7%, petroleum and petroleum products 10.4%, basic manufactures 10.2%, chemicals 7.9%, beverages and tobacco 4.2%). *Major import sources* (1998): South Korea 26.8%; Italy 21.7%; Japan 16.9%; France 13.4%; Croatia 5.7%; Singapore 4.8%.
Exports (1999): U.S.$55,700,000 (rubber 56.9%, logs and timber 39.1%, cocoa 2.0%, coffee 1.8%). *Major export destinations* (1999): United States 54.3%; France 24.3%; Singapore 5.2%; Belgium 4.4%; Italy 3.3%; Malaysia 2.4%.

Transport and communications

Transport. Railroads (1998): route length 304 mi, 490 km; short ton-mi cargo 534,000,000, metric ton-km cargo 860,000,000. Roads (1996): total length 6,600 mi, 10,600 km (paved 6%). Vehicles (1996): passenger cars 9,400; trucks and buses 25,000. Merchant marine (1992): vessels (100 gross tons and over) 1,672; total deadweight tonnage 97,373,965. Air transport (1992): passenger-mi 4,300,000, passenger-km 7,000,000; short ton-mi cargo 68,000, metric ton-km cargo 100,000; airports (1998) with scheduled flights 1.

Communications

Medium	date	unit	number	units per 1,000 persons
Daily newspapers	1996	circulation	35,000	16
Radio	1997	receivers	790,000	329
Television	1997	receivers	70,000	29
Telephones	1999	main lines	6,600	2.2

Education and health

Educational attainment, n.a. *Literacy* (1995): total population age 15 and over literate 705,000 (38.3%); males literate 523,000 (53.9%); females literate 182,000 (22.4%).

Education (1980)

	schools	teachers	students	student/ teacher ratio
Primary (age 6–12)	1,651	9,099	167,000[11]	...
Secondary (age 13–18)	419	1,129	51,666	45.8
Voc., teacher tr.	6	63	2,322	36.9
Higher	3	...	5,716[11]	...

Health: physicians (1992) 257 (1 per 8,333 persons); hospital beds, n.a.; infant mortality rate (2000) 134.6.
Food (1999): daily per capita caloric intake 2,089 (vegetable products 97%, animal products 3%); 90% of FAO recommended minimum requirement.

Military

Total active duty personnel: About 11,000–15,000 in all armed forces as of 2000. West African (ECOMOG) peacekeepers withdrew in January 1999 and the civil war resumed in remote locales as of April 1999. The fighting continued as of November 2001. *Military expenditure as percentage of GNP:* n.a.

[1]Par value rate to U.S.$ ineffective from January 1998; the independent free market exchange rate was roughly L$60 = U.S.$1 in August 2001. [2]Population for Gbarpolu (created late 2000) included with Lofa. [3]Figures for River Gee (created mid-2000) included with Grand Gedeh. [4]Figures for Grand Kru included with Maryland. [5]Total area per more recent survey is 37,743 sq mi (97,754 sq km). [6]Detail does not add to total given because of rounding. [7]Includes 10,000 persons not allocated by county. [8]1985. [9]1986. [10]Export figure. [11]1993. [12]1992. [13]1988. [14]Import duties less imputed bank service charges.

Internet resources for further information:
- **Liberian Daily News Bulletin (link) http://www.africanews.org/west/liberia**

Libya

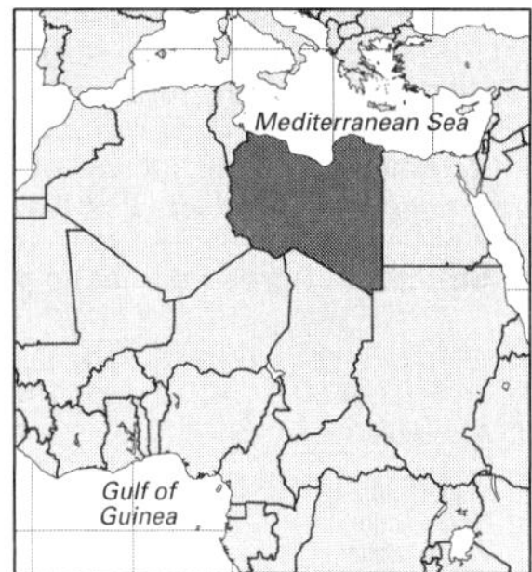

Official name: Al-Jamāhīrīyah al-ʿArabīyah al-Lībīyah ash-Shaʿbīyah al-Ishtirākīyah al-Uẓmá (Socialist People's Libyan Arab Jamahiriya).
Form of government: socialist state with one policy-making body (General People's Congress [760]).
Chief of state: Muammar al-Qaddafi (de facto)[1]; Secretary of General People's Congress (de jure).
Head of government: Secretary of the General People's Committee (prime minister).
Capital: Tripoli[2].
Official language: Arabic.
Official religion: Islam.
Monetary unit: 1 Libyan dinar (LD) = 1,000 dirhams; valuation (Sept. 28, 2001) 1 U.S.$ = LD 0.64; 1 £ = LD 0.95.

Area and population

Administrative regions[3]	Capitals	area sq mi	area sq km	population 1988 estimate
Banghāzī	Banghāzī	5,800	15,000	512,200
Al-Jabal al-Akhḍar	Al-Bayḍā'	14,300	37,000	308,300
Al-Jabal al-Gharbī	Gharyān	33,600	87,000	204,300
Khalīj Surt	Surt	145,200	376,000	382,100
Al-Kufrah	Al-Kufrah	186,900	484,000	23,800
Margib	Al-Khums	11,200	29,000	408,900
Marzūq	Marzūq	135,100	350,000	45,200
Nikāt al-Khums	Zuwārah	39,000	101,000	196,000
Sabhā	Sabhā	31,700	82,000	121,700
Ṭarābulus	Tripoli (Ṭarābulus)	1,200	3,000	1,083,100
Ṭubruq	Ṭubruq	32,400	84,000	110,900
Wādī al-Ha'iṭ	Awbārī	40,500	105,000	49,600
Az-Zāwiyah	Az-Zāwiyah	1,500	4,000	326,500
TOTAL		678,400	1,757,000	3,772,600

Demography

Population (2001): 5,241,000.
Density (2001): persons per sq mi 7.7, persons per sq km 3.0.
Urban-rural (2000): urban 87.6%; rural 12.4%.
Sex distribution (2000): male 51.44%; female 48.56%.
Age breakdown (2000): under 15, 35.9%; 15–29, 32.1%; 30–44, 18.4%; 45–59, 7.9%; 60–74, 4.5%; 75 and over, 1.2%.
Population projection: (2010) 6,447,000; (2020) 7,740,000.
Doubling time: 29 years.
Ethnic composition (1995): Libyan Arab 78%; Berber 1%; other 21% (mostly Egyptians, Sudanese, and Chadians).
Religious affiliation (1995): Sunnī Muslim 97.0%; other 3.0%.
Major cities (1995): Tripoli 1,140,000; Banghāzī 650,000; Miṣrātah 280,000; Surt 150,000; Az-Zāwiyah (1988) 89,338.

Vital statistics

Birth rate per 1,000 population (2000): 27.7 (world avg. 22.5).
Death rate per 1,000 population (2000): 3.5 (world avg. 9.0).
Natural increase rate per 1,000 population (2000): 24.2 (world avg. 13.5).
Total fertility rate (avg. births per childbearing woman; 2000): 3.7.
Marriage rate per 1,000 population (1991): 5.1[4].
Divorce rate per 1,000 population (1988): 0.6[4].
Life expectancy at birth (2000): male 73.3 years; female 77.7 years.
Major causes of death per 100,000 population: n.a.; however, the main causes of hospital mortality in 1987 were injuries and poisoning 15.5%, diseases of the circulatory system 11.6%, conditions originating in the perinatal period 11.4%, diseases of the respiratory system 7.0%, neoplasms (cancers) 4.4%.

National economy

Budget (1998). Revenue: LD 5,311,000,000 (oil revenues 68.4%, other 31.6%). Expenditures: LD 5,311,000,000 (1990–91: current expenditures 55.7%, of which municipalities 39.4%, education and scientific research 4.3%, health 2.7%; capital expenditures 44.3%, of which agriculture and land reclamation 13.6%, industry 5.3%).
Production (metric tons except as noted). Agriculture, forestry, fishing (1998): tomatoes 250,000, potatoes 230,000, olives 200,000, onions 190,000, watermelons 180,000, barley 135,000, wheat 30,000; livestock (number of live animals; 1998) 3,700,000 sheep, 1,300,000 goats, 155,000 cattle, 103,000 camels, 24,000,000 chickens; roundwood (1998) 651,000 cu m; fish catch (1998) 33,594. Mining and quarrying (1997): lime 280,000; gypsum 180,000; salt 32,000. Manufacturing (value of production in '000,000 LD; 1996): base metals 212, electrical equipment 208, petrochemicals 175, food products 79, cement and other building materials 68. Energy production (consumption): electricity (kW-hr; 1996) 18,300,000,000 (18,300,000,000); coal (metric tons; 1996) none (5,000); crude petroleum (barrels; 1999) 481,380,000 ([1996] 112,725,000); petroleum products (metric tons; 1996) 14,070,000 (7,863,000); natural gas (cu m; 1996) 6,392,000,000 (5,192,000,000).
Land use (1994): forested 0.5%; meadows and pastures 7.6%; agricultural and under permanent cultivation 1.2%; desert and built-up areas 90.7%.
Population economically active (1996): total 1,224,000; activity rate of total population 26.1% (participation rates [1993]: ages 10 and over, 35.2%; female 9.8%; unemployed [1999] 30.0%).

Price index (1995 = 100)

	1989	1990	1991	1992	1993	1994	1995
Consumer price index	33.9	38.4	42.9	49.3	59.2	76.9	100.0

Public debt (2000): n.a.[5]
Gross domestic product (1998): U.S.$32,662,500,000 (U.S.$6,700 per capita).

Structure of gross domestic product and labour force

	1996 in value LD '000,000	% of total value	labour force	% of labour force
Agriculture	782.5	6.6	219,500	17.0
Mining and quarrying	3,036.5	25.8	31,000	2.5
Manufacturing	1,107.0	9.4	128,500	10.5
Construction	797.0	6.8	171,000	14.0
Public utilities	240.5	2.0	35,500	2.9
Transp. and commun.	1,025.5	8.7	104,000	8.5
Trade	1,345.5	11.4	73,000	6.0
Finance, insurance	739.5	6.3	22,000	1.8
Pub. admin., defense	2,247.5	19.1	439,500	35.9
Services	461.0	3.9		
TOTAL	11,782.5	100.0	1,224,000	100.0

Household income and expenditure. Average household size (1980) 5.1; income per household: n.a.; sources of income: n.a.; expenditure (1977): food 37.2%, housing and energy 32.2%, transportation 9.4%, education and recreation 8.5%, clothing 6.9%, health care 3.3%.
Tourism (1999): receipts U.S.$28,000,000; expenditures U.S.$150,000,000.

Foreign trade[6]

Balance of trade (current prices)[7]

	1994	1995	1996	1997	1998	1999
U.S.$'000,000	+1,026	+2,781	+2,519	+2,716	+471	+2,974
% of total	6.5%	18.2%	15.1%	15.9%	3.9%	25.7%

Imports (1997)[8]: U.S.$5,593,000,000 (machinery 25.9%; food products 20.0%; road vehicles 10.1%; chemical products 7.5%). *Major import sources:* Italy 15.8%; Germany 12.8%; Japan 8.1%; U.K. 7.8%; France 6.2%.
Exports (1997): U.S.$9,029,000,000 (crude petroleum 76.4%; refined petroleum 16.5%; iron and steel 1.5%). *Major export destinations:* Italy 36.2%; Germany 15.0%; Spain 9.1%; Turkey 5.6%; Austria 5.2%.

Transport and communications

Transport. Railroads: none. Roads (1996): total length 81,600 km (paved 57%). Vehicles (1996): passenger cars 809,514; trucks and buses 357,528. Merchant marine (1992): vessels (100 gross tons and over) 150; total deadweight tonnage 1,223,589. Air transport (1997): passenger-km 377,000,000; metric ton-km cargo, n.a.; airports with scheduled flights: n.a.

Communications

Medium	date	unit	number	units per 1,000 persons
Daily newspapers	1996	circulation	71,000	14
Radio	1997	receivers	1,350,000	259
Television	1999	receivers	730,000	133
Telephones	1999	main lines	550,000	101
Cellular telephones	1999	subscribers	20,000	3.6

Education and health

Educational attainment (1984). Percentage of population age 25 and over having: no formal schooling (illiterate) 59.7%; incomplete primary education 15.4%; complete primary 8.5%; some secondary 5.2%; secondary 8.5%; higher 2.7%. *Literacy* (1995): percentage of total population age 15 and over literate 76.2%; males literate 87.9%; females literate 63.0%.

Education (1995–96)

	schools	teachers	students	student/ teacher ratio
Primary (age 6–12)	2,733[9]	122,020	1,333,679	10.9
Secondary (age 13–18)	...	17,668	189,202[10]	...
Voc., teacher tr.	480	...	147,689[11]	...
Higher	13	...	126,348	...

Health: physicians (1997) 6,092 (1 per 781 persons); hospital beds (1998) 18,100[12] (1 per 312 persons); infant mortality rate (2000) 30.1.
Food (1999): daily per capita caloric intake 3,277 (vegetable products 88%, animal products 12%); 138% of FAO recommended minimum requirement.

Military

Total active duty personnel (2000): 76,000 (army 59.2%, navy 10.5%, air force 30.3%). *Military expenditure as percentage of GNP* (1995): 6.1% (world 2.7%); per capita expenditure U.S.$389.

[1]No formal titled office exists. [2]Policy-making body (General People's Congress) may meet in Surt or Tripoli. [3]Libya is divided into 26 administrative regions as of 1998; area and population breakdown is not available. [4]Registered events; incomplete to some degree. [5]Libya had no foreign debt in 2000. [6]Imports f.o.b. in balance of trade and c.i.f. in commodities and trading partners. [7]Per IMF *International Financial Statistics* (November 2000). [8]Per UN *International Trade Statistics Yearbook* (1998). [9]1994–95. [10]1992–93. [11]1993–94. [12]Includes beds in clinics.

Internet resources for further information:
- **CIA World Factbook—Libya**
  http://www.odci.gov/cia/publications/factbook/geos/ly.html

Liechtenstein

Official name: Fürstentum Liechtenstein (Principality of Liechtenstein).
Form of government: constitutional monarchy with one legislative house (Diet [25]).
Chief of state: Prince.
Head of government: Prime Minister.
Capital: Vaduz.
Official language: German.
Official religion: none.
Monetary unit: 1 Swiss franc (Sw F) = 100 centimes; valuation (Sept. 28, 2001) 1 U.S.$ = Sw F 1.62; 1 £ = Sw F 2.38.

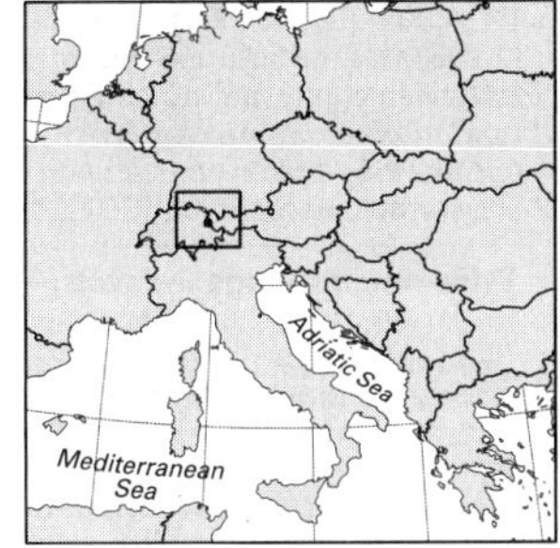

Area and population

Regions / Communes	area sq mi	area sq km	population 2000 estimate
Oberland	48.3	125.2	21,906[1]
Balzers	7.6	19.6	4,230
Planken	2.0	5.3	367
Schaan	10.3	26.8	5,365
Triesen	10.2	26.4	4,349
Triesenberg	11.5	29.8	2,531
Vaduz	6.7	17.3	4,974
Unterland	13.4[2]	34.8	10,857
Eschen	4.0	10.3	3,718
Gamprin	2.4	6.1	1,176
Mauren	2.9	7.5	3,264
Ruggell	2.9	7.4	1,707
Schellenberg	1.4	3.5	992
TOTAL	61.8[1]	160.0	32,673

Demography

Population (2001): 33,000.
Density (2000): persons per sq mi 534.1, persons per sq km 206.3.
Urban-rural: n.a.
Sex distribution (2000): male 48.70%; female 51.30%.
Age breakdown (2000): under 15, 18.7%; 15–29, 22.3%; 30–44, 25.4%; 45–59, 19.4%; 60–74, 9.7%; 75 and over, 4.5%.
Population projection: (2010) 37,000; (2020) 41,000.
Doubling time: n.a.; doubling time exceeds 100 years.
Ethnic composition (2000): Liechtensteiner 65.5%; Swiss 11.9%; Austrian 6.2%; German 3.4%; Italian 2.8%; other 10.2%.
Religious affiliation (1998): Roman Catholic 80.0%; Protestant 7.5%; Muslim 3.3%; Eastern Orthodox 0.7%; atheist 0.6%; other 7.9%.
Major cities (1999): Schaan 5,262; Vaduz 5,106.

Vital statistics

Birth rate per 1,000 population (2000): 11.8 (world avg. 22.5); (1997) legitimate 86.0%; illegitimate 14.0%.
Death rate per 1,000 population (2000): 6.7 (world avg. 9.0).
Natural increase rate per 1,000 population (2000): 5.1 (world avg. 13.5).
Total fertility rate (avg. births per childbearing woman; 2000): 1.5.
Marriage rate per 1,000 population (1998): 13.2.
Divorce rate per 1,000 population (1994): 1.4.
Life expectancy at birth (2000): male 75.2 years; female 82.5 years.
Major causes of death per 100,000 population (1998): diseases of the circulatory system 284.2; malignant neoplasms (cancers) 128.0; old age 49.9; diseases of the respiratory system 31.2; accidents, poisonings, and acts of violence 28.1; diseases of the digestive tract 24.9.

National economy

Budget (1999). Revenue: Sw F 690,200,000 (taxes and duties 78.2%, investment income 11.3%, charges and fees 8.5%, real estate capital-gains taxes and death and estate taxes 2.0%). Expenditures: Sw F 537,200,000 (financial affairs 35.8%, social welfare 17.0%, education 15.1%, transportation 9.1%, general administration 9.4%, public safety 4.9%, health 4.7%).
Public debt: none.
Tourism (1999): 124,173 tourist overnight stays; receipts from visitors, n.a.; expenditures by nationals abroad, n.a.
Population economically active (2000): total 16,368; activity rate of total population 50.1% (participation rates: ages 15–64, 71.2%; female 40.3%; unemployed 1.8%).

Price and earnings indexes (1995 = 100)

	1993	1994	1995	1996	1997	1998	1999
Consumer price index	97.4	98.2	100.0	100.8	101.3	101.4	102.2
Earnings index	...	...	...	...	...	...	...

Household income and expenditure. Average household size (1990) 2.7; income per household: n.a.; sources of earned income (1987): wages and salaries 92.9%, self-employment 7.1%; expenditure (1990)[2]: rent 20.9%, food 17.7%, transportation 11.0%, education and self-improvement 9.7%, clothing 7.0%, health 4.7%.
Production (metric tons except as noted). Agriculture, forestry, fishing (1987): silo corn (maize) 27,880, potatoes 1,040, wheat 460, barley 416, grapes (2000) 150; livestock (number of live animals; 2000) 6,000 cattle, 3,000 pigs, 2,900 sheep; commercial timber (1998) 19,527 cu m; fish catch, n.a. Mining and quarrying: n.a. Manufacturing (1997): processed milk 13,304; milk for whipped cream 262; yogurt 82; cheese 3; wine (1993) 635.2 hectolitres; small-scale precision manufacturing includes optical lenses, electron microscopes, electronic equipment, and high-vacuum pumps; metal manufacturing, construction machinery, and ceramics are also important. Construction (1997): residential 344,515 cu m; nonresidential 282,145 cu m. Energy production (consumption): electricity (kW-hr; 1997) 75,842,000 (295,031,000[3]); coal (metric tons; 1996) none (24); petroleum products (metric tons; 1995) none (49,291); natural gas (cu m; 1994) none (19,350,000).
Gross domestic product (1996): U.S.$714,000,000 (U.S.$23,000 per capita).

Structure of gross domestic product and labour force

	1996 in value U.S.$	1996 % of total value	2000 labour force	2000 % of labour force
Agriculture	...	...	277	1.7
Manufacturing	...	...	4,393	26.8
Construction	...	...	1,448	8.8
Public utilities	...	...	163	1.0
Transportation and communications	...	...	561	3.4
Trade, public accommodation	...	...	2,287	14.0
Finance, insurance, real estate	...	...	1,282	7.8
Pub. admin., defense	...	...	1,253	7.7
Services	...	...	4,405	26.9
Other	...	...	299[4]	1.8[4]
TOTAL	714,000,000	100.0	16,368[5]	100.0[1]

Land use (latest): forested 34.8%; meadows and pastures 15.7%; agricultural and under permanent cultivation 24.3%; other 25.2%.

Foreign trade

Balance of trade (current prices)

	1992	1993	1994	1995	1996	1997
Sw F '000,000	+947.1	+1,024.2	+1,043.3	+1,078.0	+1,165.3	+1,515.0
% of total	30.6%	33.8%	33.1%	33.5%	34.0%	39.1%

Imports (1997): Sw F 1,179,318,000 (machinery and transport equipment 35.2%; other finished goods 23.6%; metal products 12.5%; limestone, cement, and other building materials 12.4%; unrefined and semifabricated metal 5.7%; chemical products 5.2%). *Major import sources:* n.a.
Exports (1997): Sw F 2,694,357,000 (machinery and transport equipment 49.2%; metal products 15.1%; other finished goods 12.7%; limestone, cement, and other building materials 9.8%; chemical products 7.7%; food and beverages 4.2%). *Major export destinations* (1998): European Economic Community countries 49.5%; Switzerland 12.7%; other 37.8%.

Transport and communications

Transport. Railroads (1998): length 11.5 mi, 18.5 km; passenger and cargo traffic, n.a. Roads (1999): total length 201 mi, 323 km. Vehicles (1999): passenger cars 21,150; trucks and buses (1998) 2,684. Merchant marine: none. Air transport: none.

Communications

Medium	date	unit	number	units per 1,000 persons
Daily newspapers	1996	circulation	19,000	602
Radio	1997	receivers	21,000	658
Television	1997	receivers	12,000	364
Telephones	1999	main lines	19,763	597

Education and health

Educational attainment (1990). Percentage of population not of preschool age or in compulsory education having: no formal schooling 0.3%; primary and lower secondary education 39.3%; higher secondary and vocational 47.6%; some postsecondary 7.4%; university 4.2%; other and unknown 1.1%.
Literacy: virtually 100%.

Education (1998–99)

	schools	teachers	students	student/ teacher ratio
Primary (age 7–12)	14	151	2,048	13.6
Secondary (age 13–19)	9	162	1,859	11.5
Vocational[6]	2	309	2,307	7.5

Health: physicians (1997) 41 (1 per 764 persons); hospital beds 108 (1 per 288 persons); infant mortality rate per 1,000 live births (2000) 5.7.
Food (1999)[7]: daily per capita caloric intake 3,600 (vegetable products 65%, animal products 35%); 134% of FAO recommended minimum requirement.

Military

Total active duty personnel: none. *Military expenditure as percentage of GNP:* none.

[1]Detail does not add to total given because of rounding. [2]Household expenditures are taken from a 1986 Swiss sample survey; a similarity of consumption patterns is assumed. [3]2000. [4]Unemployed. [5]Excludes 10,643 foreign employees. [6]1997–98. [7]Figures are derived from statistics for Switzerland and Austria.

Lithuania

Official name: Lietuvos Respublika (Republic of Lithuania).
Form of government: unitary multiparty republic with a single legislative body, the Seimas (141).
Head of state: President.
Head of government: Prime Minister.
Capital: Vilnius.
Official language: Lithuanian.
Official religion: none.
Monetary unit: 1 litas (LTL) = 100 centai; valuation (Sept. 28, 2001) 1 U.S.$ = LTL 4.00[1]; 1 £ = LTL 5.88.

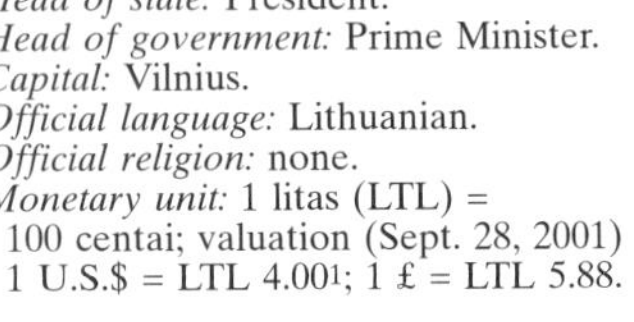

Area and population

Provinces	Capitals	area sq mi	area sq km	population 2001 estimate[2]
Alytus	Alytus	2,095	5,425	202,000
Kaunas	Kaunas	3,154	8,170	749,000
Klaipėda	Klaipėda	2,219	5,746	402,800
Marijampolė	Marijampolė	1,723	4,463	198,000
Panevėžys	Panevėžys	3,043	7,881	320,100
Šiauliai	Šiauliai	3,379	8,751	394,300
Tauragė	Tauragė	1,496	3,874	142,400
Telšiai	Telšiai	1,598	4,139	188,700
Utena	Utena	2,780	7,201	199,400
Vilnius	Vilnius	3,726	9,650	895,900
TOTAL		25,212[3]	65,300	3,692,600[4]

Demography

Population (2001): 3,691,000[5].
Density (2001): persons per sq mi 146.4, persons per sq km 56.5.
Urban-rural (2001)[2]: urban 68.1%; rural 31.9%.
Sex distribution (2001)[2]: male 47.14%; female 52.86%.
Age breakdown (2001)[2]: under 15, 19.1%; 15–29, 22.0%; 30–44, 23.0%; 45–59, 17.0%; 60–74, 13.8%; 75 and over, 5.1%.
Population projection: (2010) 3,658,000; (2020) 3,623,000.
Ethnic composition (1997): Lithuanian 81.6%; Russian 8.2%; Polish 6.9%; Belarusian 1.5%; Ukrainian 1.0%; other 0.8%.
Religious affiliation (1995): Roman Catholic 72.2%; Orthodox 3.3%; Protestant 1.3%; other (mostly nonreligious) 23.2%.
Major cities (2001)[2]: Vilnius 576,400; Kaunas 409,800; Klaipėda 201,800; Šiauliai 146,200; Panevėžys 133,600; Alytus 77,600.

Vital statistics

Birth rate per 1,000 population (2000): 9.2 (world avg. 22.5); (1998) legitimate 82.0%; illegitimate 18.0%.
Death rate per 1,000 population (2000): 10.5 (world avg. 9.0).
Natural increase rate per 1,000 population (2000): –1.3 (world avg. 13.5).
Total fertility rate (avg. births per childbearing woman; 2000): 1.3.
Marriage rate per 1,000 population (2000): 4.6.
Divorce rate per 1,000 population (2000): 2.9.
Life expectancy at birth (2000): male 67.6 years; female 77.9 years.
Major causes of death per 100,000 population (1997): diseases of the circulatory system 613.9; malignant neoplasms (cancers) 199.7; accidents, injury, homicide 146.9.

National economy

Budget (1998). Revenue: LTL 9,378,000,000 (value-added tax 38.5%, individual income tax 25.8%, excise taxes 14.3%, nontax revenue 7.5%). Expenditures: LTL 9,916,000,000 (education 27.7%, police 12.3%, social security and welfare 10.0%, health 6.6%, defense 4.5%).
Gross national product (1999): U.S.$9,751,000,000 (U.S.$2,640 per capita).

Structure of gross national product and labour force

	1998 in value LTL '000,000	% of total value	labour force[6]	% of labour force
Agriculture, forestry	3,881	9.1	356,000	20.1
Mining	9,051	21.2	3,100	0.2
Manufacturing			286,900	16.2
Construction	3,043	7.1	118,200	6.7
Public utilities	...	...	40,600	2.3
Transp. and commun.	3,666	8.6	96,900	5.5
Trade	6,796	15.9	265,400	15.0
Finance, real estate	4,181	9.8	58,600	3.3
Pub. admin., defense	2,568	6.0	69,100	3.9
Services	5,148	12.0	361,300	20.4
Other	4,433[7]	10.4[7]	113,700[8]	6.4[8]
TOTAL	42,768[3]	100.0[3]	1,769,800	100.0

Production (metric tons except as noted). Agriculture, forestry, fishing (1999): hay 2,621,000, potatoes 1,699,000, sugar beets 890,000, wheat 837,300, barley 835,000, cabbages 200,000, apples 100,000, oats 75,000, rapeseed 71,900; livestock (number of live animals) 1,168,000 pigs, 928,000 cattle; roundwood (1998) 4,879,000 cu m; fish catch (1997) 19,837. Mining and quarrying (1998): limestone 250,000; peat 195,300. Manufacturing (value of production in LTL '000,000; 1997): food and beverages 5,785; refined petroleum products 3,488; wearing apparel 1,378; textiles 1,312; chemicals and chemical products 1,222; wood and wood products (excluding furniture) 902. Energy production (consumption): electricity (kW-hr; 2000) 11,388,000,000 ([1996] 11,630,000,000); coal (metric tons; 1996) none (338,000); crude petroleum (barrels; 1996) 1,136,000 (27,583,000); petroleum products (metric tons; 1996) 3,974,000 (2,993,000); natural gas (cu m; 1996) none (2,327,000,000).
Public debt (external outstanding; 1999): U.S.$1,891,500,000.
Population economically active (1997)[9]: total 1,819,800; activity rate of total population 49.1% (participation rates: ages 14–64, 71.1%; female 47.3%; registered unemployed [2000] 11.5%).

Price and earnings indexes (1995 = 100)

	1995	1996	1997	1998	1999	2000	2001[10]
Consumer price index	100.0	124.6	135.7	142.5	143.6	145.1	147.0
Annual earnings index	100.0	135.1	166.7	187.7	198.6	203.4	...

Household income and expenditure. Average household size (1997) 2.9; average annual household disposable income (1997): LTL 12,914 (U.S.$3,228); sources of income (1998): wages and salaries 52.7%, transfers 21.3%, self-employment 14.8%, other 11.2%; expenditure (1998): food, beverages, and expenditures in cafes/hotels 54.6%, housing and energy 12.4%, transportation and communications 8.6%, clothing and footwear 8.0%.
Land use (1994): forested 30.4%; meadows and pastures 7.6%; agricultural and under permanent cultivation 53.9%; other 8.1%.
Tourism (1999): receipts from visitors U.S.$550,000,000; expenditures by nationals abroad U.S.$341,000,000.

Foreign trade[11]

Balance of trade (current prices)

	1995	1996	1997	1998	1999	2000
LTL '000,000	–3,774	–4,815	–7,136	–8,332	–7,323	–6,588
% of total	14.8%	12.7%	18.8%	21.9%	23.4%	17.8%

Imports (1998): LTL 23,174,000,000 (machinery/apparatus 18.4%, mineral fuels 14.3%, motor vehicles 11.4%, chemicals and chemical products 9.2%, textiles and clothing 8.8%). *Major import sources:* Russia 21.1%; Germany 18.2%; Poland 5.5%; Italy 4.4%; Denmark 3.8%.
Exports (1998): LTL 14,842,000,000 (mineral fuels 18.6%, textiles and clothing 18.6%, food products 12.3%, machinery/apparatus 10.8%, chemicals and chemical products 9.6%). *Major export destinations:* Russia 16.5%; Germany 13.1%; Latvia 11.1%; Belarus 8.9%; Ukraine 7.8%.

Transport and communications

Transport. Railroads (1998): route length 1,241 mi, 1,997 km; passenger-mi 444,000,000, passenger-km 715,000,000; short ton-mi cargo 5,661,000,000, metric ton-km cargo 8,265,000,000. Roads (1998): total length 44,350 mi, 71,375 km (paved 91%). Vehicles (1998): passenger cars 980,910; trucks and buses 105,022. Air transport (1998)[12]: passenger-mi 190,503,000, passenger-km 306,585,000; short ton-mi cargo 1,781,000, metric ton-km cargo 2,600,000; airports with scheduled flights (1996) 3.

Communications

Medium	date	unit	number	units per 1,000 persons
Daily newspapers	1996	circulation	344,000	93
Radio	1997	receivers	1,900,000	513
Television	1999	receivers	1,555,000	420
Telephones	1999	main lines	1,153,000	312
Cellular telephones	1999	subscribers	332,000	90
Personal computers	1999	units	220,000	59
Internet	1999	users	103,000	28

Education and health

Educational attainment (1989). Percentage of population age 25 and over having: no schooling 9.1%; incomplete and complete primary education 21.3%; incomplete and complete secondary 57.0%; postsecondary 12.6%. *Literacy* (1995): total population age 15 and over literate 99.2%.

Education (1996–97)

	schools	teachers	students	student/ teacher ratio
Primary (7–10)[13]	...	14,095	225,071	16.0
Secondary (11–18)[13]	...	32,172	325,480	10.1
Voc., teacher tr.[14]	104	5,078	56,400	11.1
Higher	...	13,136	83,645	6.4

Health (1998): physicians 14,622 (1 per 253 persons); hospital beds 35,612 (1 per 104 persons); infant mortality rate per 1,000 live births (2000) 8.5.
Food (1999): daily per capita caloric intake 2,959 (vegetable products 77%, animal products 23%); 116% of FAO recommended minimum requirement.

Military

Total active duty personnel (2000): 12,700[15] (army 73.5%, navy 4.4%, air force 6.3%, volunteer national defense force 15.8%). *Military expenditure as percentage of GNP* (1997): 0.8% (world 2.6%); per capita expenditure U.S.$34.

[1]Pegged value to U.S.$ since April 1994. [2]January 1. [3]Detail does not add to total given because of rounding. [4]Unadjusted preliminary April 2001 census figure equals 3,496,000. [5]Excludes April 2001 census results. [6]Annual average. [7]Taxes less imputed bank service charges and subsidies. [8]Unemployed. [9]As of September. [10]May. [11]Imports c.i.f.; exports f.o.b. [12]Lithuanian and Lietuva airlines. [13]Excludes special education. [14]1998–99. [15]Excludes 3,900 paramilitary in border police or coast guard.

Internet resources for further information:

- **Lithuanian Department of Statistics http://www.std.lt**
- **Bank of Lithuania http://www.lbank.lt/eng/default.htm**

Luxembourg

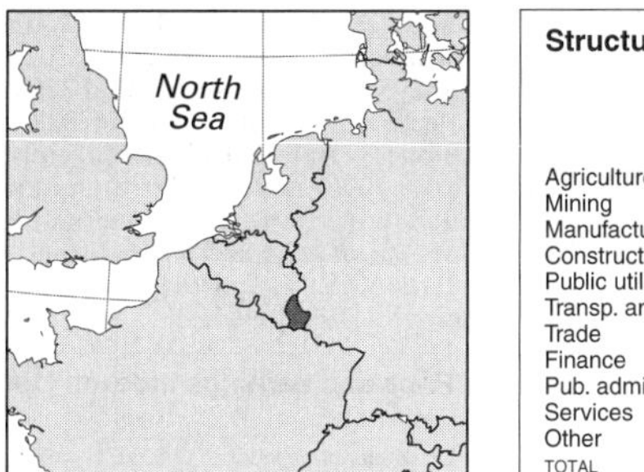

Official name: Groussherzogtum Lëtzebuerg (Luxemburgian); Grand-Duché de Luxembourg (French); Grossherzogtum Luxemburg (German) (Grand Duchy of Luxembourg).
Form of government: constitutional monarchy with two legislative houses (Council of State [21][1]; Chamber of Deputies [60]).
Chief of state: Grand Duke.
Head of government: Prime Minister.
Capital: Luxembourg.
Official language: none; Luxemburgian (national); French (used for most official purposes); German (lingua franca).
Official religion: none.
Monetary unit: 1 Luxembourg franc (Lux F) = 100 centimes; valuation (Sept. 28, 2001) 1 U.S.$ = Lux F 44.30; 1 £ = Lux F 65.10; 1 € = Lux F 40.3399.

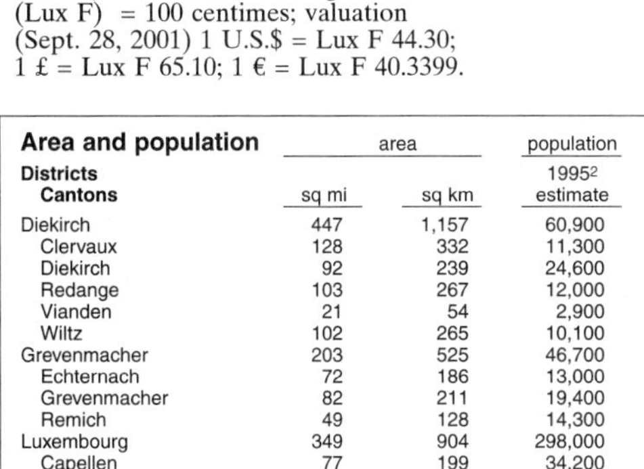

Area and population	area		population
Districts / **Cantons**	sq mi	sq km	1995[2] estimate
Diekirch	447	1,157	60,900
Clervaux	128	332	11,300
Diekirch	92	239	24,600
Redange	103	267	12,000
Vianden	21	54	2,900
Wiltz	102	265	10,100
Grevenmacher	203	525	46,700
Echternach	72	186	13,000
Grevenmacher	82	211	19,400
Remich	49	128	14,300
Luxembourg	349	904	298,000
Capellen	77	199	34,200
Esch	94	243	122,700
Luxembourg (Ville et Campagne)	92	238	120,500
Mersch	86	224	20,600
TOTAL	999	2,586	406,600[3]

Demography

Population (2001): 444,000.
Density (2001): persons per sq mi 444.7, persons per sq km 171.8.
Urban-rural (1999): urban 91.1%; rural 8.9%.
Sex distribution (2000): male 49.16%; female 50.84%.
Age breakdown (2000): under 15, 18.9%; 15–29, 18.3%; 30–44, 25.3%; 45–59, 18.7%; 60–74, 13.1%; 75 and over, 5.7%.
Population projection: (2010) 493,000; (2020) 542,000.
Ethnic composition (nationality; 1999[2]): Luxemburger 64.4%; Portuguese 13.0%; Italian 4.7%; French 4.1%; Belgian 3.2%; German 2.4%; English 1.1%; other 7.1%.
Religious affiliation (1996): Roman Catholic 95.1%; other 4.9%.
Major cities (2000[2])[4]: Luxembourg 80,700; Esch-sur-Alzette 25,200; Differdange 17,300; Dudelange 17,100; Petange 13,700.

Vital statistics

Birth rate per 1,000 population (2000): 12.5 (world avg. 22.5); (1998) legitimate 82.5%; illegitimate 17.5%.
Death rate per 1,000 population (2000): 8.9 (world avg. 9.0).
Natural increase rate per 1,000 population (2000): 3.6 (world avg. 13.5).
Total fertility rate (avg. births per childbearing woman; 2000): 1.7.
Marriage rate per 1,000 population (1999): 4.8.
Divorce rate per 1,000 population (1999): 2.4.
Life expectancy at birth (2000): male 73.8 years; female 80.6 years.
Major causes of death per 100,000 population (1997): circulatory diseases 371.7, of which ischemic heart disease and myocardial infarction 118.8, cerebrovascular disease 104.5; malignant neoplasms (cancers) 281.4.

National economy

Budget (1998). Revenue: Lux F 170,310,600,000 (income and excise taxes 58.2%, customs taxes 13.4%). Expenditures: Lux F 170,413,400,000 (social security 21.3%, education 11.7%, transportation 8.2%, administration 6.5%, defense 2.7%, debt service 0.9%).
Public debt (1997): U.S.$668,420,000.
Production (metric tons except as noted). Agriculture, forestry, fishing (1999): barley 63,200, wheat 60,100, potatoes 21,100, oats 11,700, sugar beets 7,500, apples 2,150; livestock (number of live animals) 207,862 cattle, 85,830 pigs; roundwood (1997) 315,500 cu m. Mining and quarrying (1999): gypsum and anhydrite 400,000. Manufacturing (1999): rolled steel 4,239,000; crude steel 2,600,000; cement 600,000; wine (1994) 179,998 hectolitres. Construction (1997): residential 440,840 sq m; nonresidential 93,100 sq m. Energy production (consumption): electricity (kW-hr; 1998) 382,000,000 (5,856,000,000); coal (metric tons; 1997) none (194,000); crude petroleum, none (none); petroleum products (metric tons; 1997) none (1,615,000); natural gas (cu m; 1997) none (730,700,000).
Land use (1992): forested 34.2%; meadows and pastures 25.6%; agricultural and under permanent cultivation 23.2%; other 17.0%.
Gross national product (1999): U.S.$18,545,000,000 (U.S.$42,930 per capita).

Structure of gross domestic product and labour force	1999		1998	
	in value Lux F '000,000[5]	% of total value	labour force	% of labour force
Agriculture	5,500	1.0	5,500	2.3
Mining	900	0.2	32,600	13.7
Manufacturing	95,100	16.5		
Construction	39,400	6.8	25,700	10.8
Public utilities	8,400	1.4	2,100	0.9
Transp. and commun.	6	6	17,500	7.4
Trade	134,400	23.2	47,600	20.1
Finance	256,200	44.3	20,700	8.7
Pub. admin., defense	6	6	37,900	16.0
Services	114,200[6]	19.7[6]	47,600	20.1
Other	−76,000[7]	−13.1[7]	...	...
TOTAL	578,100	100.0	237,200	100.0

Population economically active (1999): total 248,300; activity rate of total population 57.9% (participation rates: ages 15–64 [1997] 51.4%; female [1997] 38.2%; unemployed 2.9%).

Price and earnings indexes (1995 = 100)	1995	1996	1997	1998	1999	2000	2001
Consumer price index	100.0	101.4	102.8	103.8	104.8	108.1	110.4[8]
Hourly earnings index	...	...	...	...	...	...	...

Household income and expenditure. Average household size (1991) 2.6; income per household (1992) Lux F 1,438,000 (U.S.$44,700); sources of income (1992): wages and salaries 67.1%, transfer payments 28.1%, self-employment 4.8%; expenditure (1994): food, beverages, and tobacco 19.7%, housing 17.3%, transportation and communications 16.2%, household goods and furniture 9.9%, clothing and footwear 8.2%, health 7.9%.
Tourism (1997): receipts from visitors U.S.$297,000,000.

Foreign trade[9]

Balance of trade (current prices)	1995	1996	1997	1998	1999	2000
Lux F '000,000	−62,400	−71,100	−82,800	−82,200	−109,400	−105,700
% of total	12.0%	13.9%	14.4%	8.0%	15.4%	13.4%

Imports (1999): Lux F 409,000,000,000 (machinery and transport equipment 20.2%; transport equipment 18.4%; fabricated metals 10.9%; chemicals and chemical products 9.5%; food products 6.6%). *Major import sources:* Belgium 34.9%; Germany 25.5%; France 11.9%; U.S. 9.1%; The Netherlands 3.7%.
Exports (1999): Lux F 299,600,000,000 (fabricated metals 28.3%; machinery and equipment 20.5%; chemicals and chemical products 6.3%; food products 4.0%). *Major export destinations:* Germany 25.4%; France 21.1%; Belgium 13.0%; U.K. 8.1%; Italy 5.3%; The Netherlands 5.0%.

Transport and communications

Transport. Railroads (1999): route length 170 mi, 274 km; passenger-mi 192,600,000, passenger-km 310,000,000; short ton-mi cargo 410,000,000, metric ton-km cargo 660,000,000. Roads (1999): total length 3,209 mi, 5,166 km (paved 100%). Vehicles (2000[2]): passenger cars 263,683; trucks and buses 20,228. Merchant marine (1992): vessels (100 gross tons and over) 54; total deadweight tonnage 2,603,611. Air transport (1999): passengers carried 1,599,000; cargo 448,393 metric tons; airports (1999) with scheduled flights 1.

Communications Medium	date	unit	number	units per 1,000 persons
Daily newspapers	1996	circulation	135,000	325
Radio	1997	receivers	285,000	677
Television	1998	receivers	165,000	389
Telephones	1999	main lines	310,893	724
Cellular telephones	1999	subscribers	209,000	487
Personal computers	1999	units	170,000	396
Internet	1999	users	75,000	175

Education and health

Educational attainment: n.a. *Literacy* (1995): virtually 100% literate.

Education (1998–99)	schools	teachers	students	student/ teacher ratio
Primary (age 6–11)[10]	...	1,922	29,533	15.4
Secondary (age 12–18)	...	1,691	9,471	5.6
Voc., teacher tr.	...	2,743	20,763	7.6
Higher	5	...	2,716	...

Health (1996[2]): physicians 908 (1 per 454 persons); hospital beds (1995[2]) 4,443 (1 per 92 persons); infant mortality rate per 1,000 live births (2000) 4.8.
Food (1995): daily per capita caloric intake 3,530 (vegetable products 68%, animal products 32%); 134% of FAO recommended minimum.

Military

Total active duty personnel (2000): 899 (army 100.0%). *Military expenditure as percentage of GNP* (1997): 0.8% (world 2.6%); per capita expenditure U.S.$318.

[1]Has limited legislative authority. [2]January 1. [3]Detail does not add to total given because of rounding. [4]Commune population. [5]In constant 1995 prices. [6]Transportation and communications and Public administration are included with Services. [7]Imputed bank service charges. [8]July. [9]Imports c.i.f.; exports f.o.b. [10]Public schools only.

Internet resources for further information:
- **STATEC: Luxembourg in Figures http://statec.gouvernement.lu**

Macau[1]

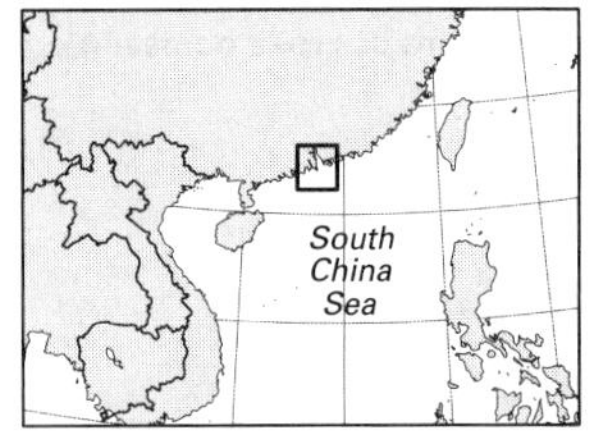

Official name: Aomen Tebie Xingzhengqu (Chinese); Regiño Administrativa Especial de Macau (Portuguese) (Macau Special Administrative Region).
Political status: special administrative region (China) with one legislative house (Legislative Council [27[2]]).
Head of state and government: Chief Executive.
Capital: Macau.
Official languages: Chinese; Portuguese.
Official religion: none.
Monetary unit: 1 pataca (MOP) = 100 avos; valuation (Sept. 28, 2001) 1 U.S.$ = MOP 8.03; 1 £ = MOP 11.81.

Area and population

	area		population
			1991
Geographical areas	sq mi	sq km	census
Islands	5.3	13.8	10,148
Coloane	2.9	7.6	3,111
Taipa	2.4	6.2	7,037
Macau	3.0	7.8	326,460
Marine	—	—	2,856
TOTAL	8.3[3]	21.6[3]	339,464

Demography

Population (2001): 445,000.
Density (2001)[3]: persons per sq mi 48,901, persons per sq km 18,856.
Urban-rural (1999): urban, virtually 100%[4].
Sex distribution (1998): male 47.55%; female 52.45%.
Age breakdown (1998): under 15, 24.0%; 15–29, 23.0%; 30–44, 29.4%; 45–59, 13.8%; 60–74, 6.7%; 75 and over, 3.1%.
Population projection: (2010) 518,000; (2020) 604,000.
Doubling time: over 100 years.
Nationality (1991): Chinese 68.2%; Portuguese 27.9%; English 1.8%; other 2.1%.
Religious affiliation (1998): nonreligious 60.8%; Buddhist 16.7%; other 22.5%.
Major city (2000 est.): Macau 437,900.

Vital statistics

Birth rate per 1,000 population (2001): 9.4 (world avg. 22.5); legitimate, n.a.; illegitimate, n.a.
Death rate per 1,000 population (2001): 4.5 (world avg. 9.0).
Natural increase rate per 1,000 population (2001): 4.9 (world avg. 13.5).
Total fertility rate (avg. births per childbearing woman; 2001): 1.1.
Marriage rate per 1,000 population (1998): 3.4.
Divorce rate per 1,000 population (1998): 0.6.
Life expectancy at birth (2001): male 77.0 years; female 81.0 years.
Major causes of death per 100,000 population (1998): diseases of the circulatory system 117.1; malignant neoplasms (cancers) 77.8; diseases of the respiratory system 39.3; accidents, poisoning, and violence 23.9; diseases of the genitourinary system 11.4; diseases of the digestive system 11.1; infectious and parasitic diseases 10.0; endocrine and metabolic disorders 3.9; obstetric and perinatal disorders 3.3.

National economy

Budget (1998). Revenue: 14,831,099,000 patacas (recurrent receipts 69.1%, autonomous agency receipts 21.4%, capital receipts 2.2%). Expenditures: 14,831,099,000 patacas (recurrent payments 61.1%, autonomous agency expenditures 21.4%, capital payments 17.5%).
Tourism (1999): receipts from visitors U.S.$2,466,000,000; expenditures by nationals abroad U.S.$131,000,000.
Land use (1992): built-on area, wasteland, and other 100.0%.
Gross domestic product (at current market prices; 1999): U.S.$6,161,000,000 (U.S.$14,200 per capita).

Structure of labour force

	1998	
	labour force	% of labour force
Agriculture	300	0.1
Mining	100	—
Manufacturing	41,500	19.7
Construction	11,800	5.6
Public utilities	1,400	0.7
Transportation and communications	13,700	6.5
Trade	54,600	25.9
Finance	13,600	6.5
Public administration / Services	64,000	30.4
Other	9,700	4.6
TOTAL	210,700	100.0

Production (metric tons except as noted). Agriculture, forestry, fishing (1999): eggs 650; livestock (number of live animals) 500,000 chickens; fish catch (1997) 1,500. Quarrying (value added in '000,000 patacas; 1997): 13. Manufacturing (value added in '000,000 patacas; 1997): wearing apparel 2,161; textiles 607; electrical appliances 131; printing and publishing 97; nonmetallic mineral products 92; food products 83; footwear 53. Construction (1998): residential 742,955 sq m; nonresidential 226,237 sq m. Energy production (consumption): electricity (kW-hr; 1996) 1,620,000,000 (1,794,000,000); coal (metric tons) none (none); crude petroleum (barrels) none (none); petroleum products (metric tons; 1996) none (459,000); natural gas, none (none).
Public debt (long-term, external; 1995): U.S.$506,000,000.
Population economically active (1998): total 210,700; activity rate of total population 48.9% (participation rates: age 15–64, 70.2%; female 44.8%; unemployed [1999] 6.6%).

Price and earnings indexes (1995 = 100)

	1995	1996	1997	1998	1999	2000
Consumer price index[5]	100.0	99.4	102.8	103.0	99.7	98.1
Earnings index	...	...	...	...	...	...

Household income and expenditure. Average household size (1991) 3.5; income per household: n.a.; sources of income: n.a.; expenditure (1987–88): food 38.3%, housing 19.7%, education, health, and other services 12.1%, transportation 7.4%, clothing and footwear 6.8%, energy 4.0%, household durable goods 3.7%, other goods 8.0%.

Foreign trade[6]

Balance of trade (current prices)

	1995	1996	1997	1998	1999	2000
'000,000 patacas	–354	–32	+526	+1,487	+1,280	+2,283
% of total	1.1%	0.1%	1.6%	4.6%	3.8%	5.9%

Imports (1998): 15,596,446,000 patacas (raw materials 54.1%, capital goods 14.2%, foodstuffs 9.3%, fuels and lubricants 6.3%). *Major import sources:* China 32.7%; Hong Kong 23.7%; European Economic Community 10.5%; Taiwan 9.9%; Japan 7.8%; United States 4.7%.
Exports (1998): 17,083,616,000 patacas (garments 76.4%, textiles 4.5%, machinery and mechanical appliances 3.5%, textile yarn and thread 3.1%, footwear 2.2%). *Major export destinations:* United States 47.7%; European Economic Community 30.5%; Hong Kong 7.6%; China 6.8%; Taiwan 1.5%; Japan 0.7%.

Transport and communications

Transport. Railroads: none. Roads (1996): total length 31 mi, 50 km (paved 100%). Vehicles (1998): passenger cars 45,184; trucks and buses 6,578. Merchant marine (1990): vessels 6; total gross tonnage 3,512. Air transport: none.

Communications

Medium	date	unit	number	units per 1,000 persons
Daily newspapers	1996	circulation	200,000	455
Radio	1997	receivers	160,000	356
Television	1999	receivers	125,492	287
Telephones	1999	main lines	178,445	408
Cellular telephones	1999	subscribers	88,561	203
Personal computers	1999	units	60,000	137
Internet	1999	users	40,000	92

Education and health

Educational attainment (1991). Population age 25 and over having: no formal schooling 13.1%; incomplete primary education 16.0%; completed primary 19.9%; some secondary 45.1%; post-secondary 5.9%. *Literacy* (1995): percentage of population age 15 and over literate 91.7%; males literate 95.6%; females literate 88.2%.

Education (1997–98)

	schools	teachers	students	student/ teacher ratio
Primary (age 6–11)	81	1,744	47,235	27.1
Secondary (age 12–18)	47	1,577	28,280	17.9
Teacher tr.	2	47	699	14.9
Higher	7	818	7,682	9.4

Health (1998): physicians 369 (1 per 1,167 persons); hospital beds 1,086 (1 per 396 persons); infant mortality rate per 1,000 live births (2001) 8.0.
Food (1998): daily per capita caloric intake 2,471 (vegetable products 76%, animal products 24%); 108% of FAO recommended minimum requirement.

Military

Total active duty personnel: The People's Liberation Army is responsible for Macau's defense and security.

[1]Macau reverted to Chinese sovereignty on Dec. 20, 1999. [2]Includes 10 directly elected seats, 7 seats appointed by the chief executive, and 10 seats appointed by special-interest groups. [3]Landfill in late 1990s increased total area to 9.1 sq mi (23.6 sq km). [4]About 1% of Macau's population live on sampans and other vessels. [5]Excluding rent; base year is July 1995–June 1996. [6]Import figures are c.i.f.

Internet resources for further information:
- **Government of Macau Special Administrative Region, P.R.C.**
  http://www.macau.gov.mo
- **Macau Census and Statistics Service**
  http://www.dsec.gov.mo

Macedonia

Official name[1]: Republika Makedonija (Republic of Macedonia).
Form of government: unitary multiparty republic with a unicameral legislative (Assembly [120]).
Head of state: President.
Head of government: Prime Minister.
Capital: Skopje.
Official language: Macedonian[2].
Official religion: none.
Monetary unit: denar; valuation (Sept. 28, 2001) 1 U.S.$ = 66.21 denar; 1 £ = 97.30 denar.

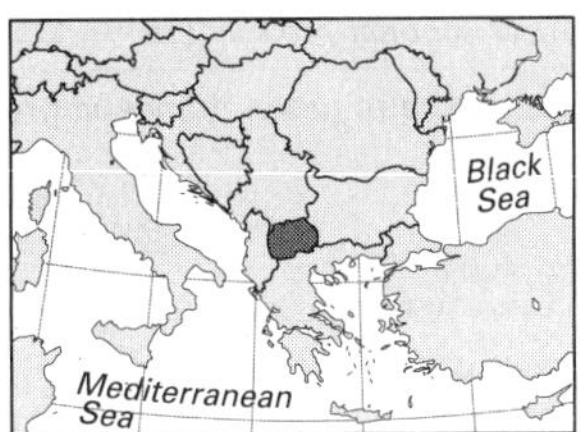

Area and population

Administrative districts[3]	area sq km	population 1994 census	Administrative districts[3]	area sq km	population 1994 census
Berovo	806	19,737	Negotino	734	23,094
Bitola	1,798	106,012	Ohrid	1,069	60,841
Brod	924	10,912	Prilep	1,675	93,248
Debar	274	26,449	Probištip	326	16,373
Delčevo	589	25,052	Radoviš	735	30,378
Demir Hisar	443	10,321	Resen	739	17,467
Gevgelija	757	34,767	Skopje	1,818	541,280
Gostivar	1,341	108,189	Štip	815	50,531
Kavadarci	1,132	41,801	Struga	507	62,305
Kičevo	854	53,044	Strumica	952	89,759
Kočani	570	48,105	Sveti Nikole	649	21,391
Kratovo	376	10,855	Tetovo	1,080	174,748
Kriva Palanka	720	25,112	Titov Veles	1,536	65,523
Kruševo	239	11,981	Valandovo	331	12,049
Kumanovo	1,212	126,543	Vinica	432	19,010
			TOTAL	25,713[4]	1,936,877

Demography

Population (2001): 2,046,000.
Density (2001): persons per sq mi 206.0, persons per sq km 79.6.
Urban-rural (2000): urban 62.0%; rural 38.0%.
Sex distribution (2000): male 50.06%; female 49.94%.
Age breakdown (2000): under 15, 23.4%; 15–29, 24.3%; 30–44, 21.6%; 45–59, 16.5%; 60–64, 11.1%; 65 and over, 3.0%.
Population projection: (2010) 2,115,000; (2020) 2,171,000.
Ethnic composition (2000): Macedonian 53.9%; Albanian 18.0%; Turkish 7.7%; Roma (Gypsy) 5.3%; Aromanian 3.0%, Serbian 2.1%; Croat 2.0%; other 6.0%.
Religious affiliation (1995): Serbian (Macedonian) Orthodox 54.2%; Sunnī Muslim 30.0%; other 15.8%.
Major cities (1994): Skopje 440,577; Bitola 75,386; Prilep 67,371; Kumanovo 66,237; Tetovo 50,376.

Vital statistics

Birth rate per 1,000 population (2000): 13.7 (world avg. 22.5); (1998) legitimate 90.5%; illegitimate 9.5%.
Death rate per 1,000 population (2000): 7.7 (world avg. 9.0).
Natural increase rate per 1,000 population (2000): 6.0 (world avg. 13.5).
Total fertility rate (avg. births per childbearing woman; 2000): 1.8.
Marriage rate per 1,000 population (1998): 7.0.
Life expectancy at birth (2000): male 71.6 years; female 76.2 years.
Major causes of death per 100,000 population (1997): diseases of the circulatory system 462.8; malignant neoplasms 138.3; diseases of the respiratory system 39.5; accidents, violence, and poisoning 32.4; diseases of the digestive system 15.9.

National economy

Budget (1996). Revenue: 64,184,000,000 denar (social security contributions 38.1%, income and profits tax 17.1%, excise taxes 16.3%, sales tax 11.3%, import duties 10.4%). Expenditure: 63,970,000,000 denar (1995; pensions 24.1%, wages and salaries 22.7%, health 13.3%).
Production (metric tons except as noted). Agriculture, forestry, fishing (1999): wheat 378,000, grapes 244,000, corn (maize) 200,000, potatoes 180,000; livestock (number of live animals) 1,550,000 sheep, 290,000 cattle, 60,000 pigs, 3,340,000 chickens; roundwood (1998) 720,000 cu m; fish catch (1997) 1,388 (all freshwater). Mining and quarrying (1998[5]): lead 17,000; copper 8,000; zinc 3,500; iron 1,000; refined silver 20,000 kg. Manufacturing (1998): cement 461,195; steel sheets 276,464; detergents 21,990; wool yarn 3,252; refrigerators 4,007 units; freezers 3,488 units; leather footwear 1,382,000 pairs; cotton fabric 13,700,000 sq m; cigarettes 7,009,000 units. Construction (value in '000,000 denars; 1998) residential 331; nonresidential 834. Energy production (consumption): electricity (kW-hr; 1996) 6,489,000,000 (6,489,000,000); coal (metric tons; 1996) 7,195,000 (7,330,000); crude petroleum (barrels; 1996) none (6,047,000); petroleum products (metric tons; 1996) 770,000 (1,383,000); natural gas (cu m; 1993) none (269,100,000).
Population economically active (1998): total 823,800; activity rate 41.1% (participation rates: ages 15–64, 61.2%; female 38.5%; unemployed 34.5%).

Price and earnings indexes (1995 = 100)

	1994	1995	1996	1997	1998	1999
Consumer price index	85.9	100.0	102.7	103.8	104.4	103.0
Earnings index[6]	90.6	100.0	102.8	...	...	...

Gross national product (1999): U.S.$3,348,000,000 (U.S.$1,660 per capita).

Structure of gross domestic product and labour force

	1997 in value '000,000 denar	1997 % of total value	1998 labour force	1998 % of labour force
Agriculture	20,764	11.2	94,800	11.5
Mining and manufacturing	38,351	20.7	173,800	21.1
Construction	10,131	5.5	...	...
Public utilities	4,904	2.6	...	...
Transp. and commun.	11,301	6.1	...	...
Trade	20,104	10.9	55,400	6.7
Finance	10,157	5.5	...	...
Pub. admin., defense	32,271	17.4	72,700	8.8
Services	7,268	3.9	35,600	4.3
Other	29,730[7]	16.1[7]	391,500[8]	47.5[8]
TOTAL	184,982[9]	100.0[9]	823,800	100.0[9]

External debt (1999): U.S.$1,135,000,000.
Household income and expenditure (1994). Average household size 3.8; income per household Din 49,635 (U.S.$1,223); sources of income: wages and salaries 59.9%, transfer payments 17.0%, transfers from abroad 13.4%, other 9.7%; expenditure: food 42.2%, fuel and lighting 7.5%, clothing and footwear 7.4%, transportation and communications 7.2%, drink and tobacco 7.0%, health care 4.7%, education and entertainment 3.2%.
Tourism (1998): receipts from visitors U.S.$15,000,000; expenditures by nationals abroad U.S.$30,000,000.
Land use (1994): forested 38.9%; meadows and pastures 24.7%; agricultural and under permanent cultivation 25.7%; other 10.7%.

Foreign trade

Balance of trade (current prices)

	1994	1995	1996	1997	1998	1999
U.S.$'000,000	–397.8	–514.9	–316.5	–387.6	–604.0	–603.8
% of total	15.5%	17.6%	11.0%	13.9%	18.7%	20.2%

Imports (1998): U.S.$1,310,697,000 (machinery and transport equipment 19.1%, manufactured products 14.5%, food products 13.4%, chemical products 10.6%, petroleum products 8.5%). *Major import sources:* Germany 13.3%; Yugoslavia 12.8%; Slovenia 7.8%; Ukraine 6.2%; Italy 5.7%; U.S. 5.3%.
Exports (1998): U.S.$1,914,663,000 (manufactured products 34.2%, machinery and transport equipment 7.5%, food products 5.0%, chemical products 5.0%, raw materials 4.3%). *Major export destinations:* Germany 21.4%; Yugoslavia 18.3%; United States 13.3%; Italy 7.0%; Greece 6.4%.

Transport and communications

Transport. Railroads (1998): length 575 mi, 925 km; passenger-mi 93,200,000, passenger-km 150,000,000; short ton-mi cargo 279,000,000, metric ton-km cargo 408,000,000. Roads (1998): length 7,154 mi, 11,513 km (paved 63%). Vehicles (1998): passenger cars 288,678; trucks and buses 24,745. Merchant marine: n.a. Air transport (1998): passenger-mi 553,460,000, passenger-km 890,710,000; short ton-mile cargo transported 239,200,000, metric tons cargo transported 163,840,000; airports (1997) with scheduled flights 2.

Communications

Medium	date	unit	number	units per 1,000 persons
Daily newspapers	1996	circulation	41,000	20
Radio	1997	receivers	410,000	204
Television	1999	receivers	500,000	248
Telephones	1999	main lines	471,000	234
Cellular telephones	1998	subscribers	48,000	24
Personal computers	1999	units	2,000	1.1
Internet	1999	users	30,000	15

Education and health

Educational attainment (1981). Percentage of population age 15 and over having: less than full primary education 45.3%; primary 28.1%; secondary 21.2%; postsecondary and higher 5.1%; unknown 0.3%. *Literacy* (1981): total population age 10 and over literate 1,365,000 (89.1%); males literate 729,000 (94.2%); females literate 636,000 (83.8%).

Education (1997–98)

	schools	teachers	students	student/ teacher ratio
Primary (age 7–14)	1,043	13,376	256,275	19.2
Secondary (age 15–18)	93	5,226	84,059	16.1
Higher[10]	30	1,385	36,141	26.1

Health (1998): physicians 4,508 (1 per 445 persons); hospital beds 10,333 (1 per 194 persons); infant mortality rate per 1,000 live births (2000) 13.4.

Military

Total active duty personnel (2000): 16,000 (army 95.6%, air force 4.4%). *Military expenditure as percentage of GNP* (1997): 2.5% (world 2.6%); per capita expenditure U.S.$42.

[1]Member of the United Nations under the name The Former Yugoslav Republic of Macedonia. [2]Final approval of Albanian as second official language at the local level only was pending in October 2001. [3]Local government reorganized September 1996 from 34 administrative districts into 123 municipalities. [4]Total includes 280 sq km of inland water not distributed by district. [5]Contained metal. [6]Based on nominal net wages per worker. [7]Includes import duties, customs imputed rents, and statistical discrepancy. [8]Includes 284,064 unemployed. [9]Detail does not add to total given because of rounding. [10]1998–99.

Internet resources for further information:

- **Secretariat of Information http://www.sinf.gov.mk**
- **National Bank of the Republic of Macedonia http://www.nbrm.gov.mk**

Madagascar

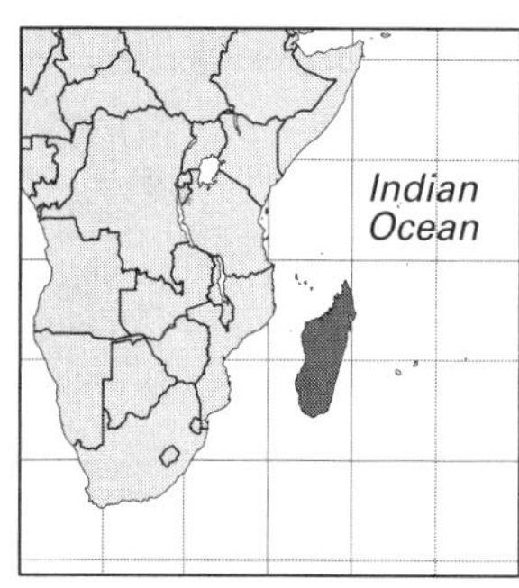

Official name: Repoblikan'i Madagasikara (Malagasy); République de Madagascar (French) (Republic of Madagascar).
Form of government: federal[1] multiparty republic with two legislative houses (Senate [90]; National Assembly [150]).
Heads of state and government: President assisted by Prime Minister.
Capital: Antananarivo.
Official languages: [2].
Official religion: none.
Monetary unit: 1 Malagasy franc (FMG) = 100 centimes; valuation (Sept. 28, 2001) 1 U.S.$ = FMG 6,177; 1 £ = FMG 9,078.

Area and population

Autonomous provinces[1]	Capitals	area sq mi	area sq km	population 1993 census
Antananarivo	Antananarivo	22,503	58,283	3,483,236
Antsirañana	Antsirañana	16,620	43,046	942,410
Fianarantsoa	Fianarantsoa	39,526	102,373	2,671,150
Mahajanga	Mahajanga	57,924	150,023	1,330,612
Toamasina	Toamasina	27,765	71,911	1,935,330
Toliary	Toliary	62,319	161,405	1,729,419
TOTAL		226,658	587,041	12,092,157

Demography

Population (2001): 15,983,000.
Density (2001): persons per sq mi 70.5, persons per sq km 27.2.
Urban-rural (1999): urban 29.0%; rural 71.0%.
Sex distribution (2000): male 49.70%; female 50.30%.
Age breakdown (2000): under 15, 45.0%; 15–29, 26.5%; 30–44, 15.8%; 45–59, 7.9%; 60–74, 3.8%; 75 and over, 1.0%.
Population projection: (2010) 20,993,000; (2020) 28,405,000.
Doubling time: 25 years.
Ethnic composition (1983): Malagasy 98.9%, of which Merina 26.6%, Betsimisaraka 14.9%, Betsileo 11.7%, Tsimihety 7.4%, Sakalava 6.4%; Comorian 0.3%; Indian and Pakistani 0.2%; French 0.2%; other 0.4%.
Religious affiliation (2000): Christian 49.5%, of which Protestant 22.7%, Roman Catholic 20.3%; traditional beliefs 48.0; Muslim 1.9%; other 0.6%.
Major cities (1993): Antananarivo 1,103,304; Toamasina 137,782; Antsirabe 126,062; Fianarantsoa 109,248; Mahajanga 106,780.

Vital statistics

Birth rate per 1,000 population (2000): 42.9 (world avg. 22.5).
Death rate per 1,000 population (2000): 12.7 (world avg. 9.0).
Natural increase rate per 1,000 population (2000): 30.2 (world avg. 13.5).
Total fertility rate (avg. births per childbearing woman; 2000): 5.8.
Life expectancy at birth (2000): male 52.7 years; female 57.3 years.
Major causes of death per 100,000 population: n.a.; however, major causes of death in the 1990s included maternal and perinatal diseases, malaria, infectious and parasitic diseases, malnutrition, diarrhea, and respiratory diseases.

National economy

Budget (1999). Revenue: FMG 2,667,000,000,000 (taxes 96.7%, of which duties on trade 55.5%, value-added tax 15.0%, income tax 14.9%; nontax receipts 3.3%). Expenditures: FMG 3,791,000,000,000 (current expenditure 57.4%, of which debt service 13.0%, general administration 10.8%, education 10.3%, defense 7.5%, health 4.0%, agriculture 1.5%; capital expenditure 42.6%).
Public debt (external, outstanding; 1999): U.S.$4,023,000,000.
Production (metric tons except as noted). Agriculture, forestry, fishing (2000): paddy rice 2,300,000, cassava 2,228,000, sugarcane 2,200,000, sweet potatoes 476,000, potatoes 293,000, bananas 265,000, mangoes 206,000, corn (maize) 155,000, taro 155,000, oranges 85,000, coconuts 85,000, dry beans 84,000, coffee 65,000, pineapples 52,000, peanuts (groundnuts) 35,000, seed cotton 32,000; livestock (number of live animals) 10,364,000 cattle, 900,000 pigs, 1,370,000 goats, 800,000 sheep, 20,000,000 chickens; roundwood (2000) 10,359,000 cu m; fish catch (1999) 141,057. Mining and quarrying (1998): chromite ore 119,000; marine salt 30,000; graphite 14,300; mica 431; gold 200 kg[3]; in addition, a wide variety of semiprecious stones and gemstones are produced. Manufacturing (1998): refined sugar 79,775 metric tons, cement 44,327 metric tons, soap 14,513, cigarettes 3,303 metric tons, beer 207,400 hectolitres, fuel oil 217,800 cu m, gas oil 110,800 cu m, kerosene 75,200 cu m, gasoline 92,700 cu m, shoes 511,000 pairs. Construction (1986)[4]: residential 19,700 sq m; nonresidential 5,700 sq m. Energy production (consumption): electricity (kW-hr; 1998) 642,000,000 (642,000,000); coal (metric tons; 1996) none (14,000); crude petroleum (barrels; 1996) none (1,530,000); petroleum products (metric tons; 1996) 191,000 (358,000); natural gas, none (n.a.).
Population economically active (1993): total 5,914,000; activity rate of total population 48.9% (participation rates [1995]: over age 10, 59.4%; female 38.4%; unemployed, n.a.).

Price and earnings indexes (1995 = 100)

	1993	1994	1995	1996	1997	1998	1999
Consumer price index	48.3	67.1	100.0	119.8	125.1	132.9	146.1
Annual earnings index[5]	55.2	71.4	100.0	...	...	...	...

Gross national product (1999): U.S.$3,712,000,000 (U.S.$250 per capita).

Structure of gross domestic product and labour force

	1999 in value FMG '000,000[6]	1999 % of total value[6]	1993 labour force	1993 % of labour force
Agriculture	6,366.1	30.0	5,100,000	86.2
Manufacturing / Mining	2,916.7	13.8	86,000	1.5
Public utilities / Construction	355.0	1.7	46,000	0.8
Transp. and commun.	4,034.7	19.0	42,000	0.7
Trade	2,624.2	12.4	149,000 (Trade and Finance)	2.5 (Trade and Finance)
Finance	7	7		
Services	3,948.5[7]	18.6[7]	243,000	4.1
Pub. admin., defense	1,266.0	6.0	208,000	3.5
Other	–308[8]	–1.5[8]	40,000	0.7
TOTAL	21,202.6	100.0	5,914,000	100.0

Household income and expenditure. Average household size (1993) 4.6[9]; average annual income per household: n.a.; sources of income (1975)[9]: wages and salaries 58.8%, self-employment 14.1%, other 27.1%; expenditure (1983)[4, 10]: food 60.4%, fuel and light 9.1%, clothing and footwear 8.6%, household goods and utensils 2.4%.
Land use (1994): forest 39.9%; pasture 41.3%; agriculture 5.3%; other 13.5%.
Tourism (1999): receipts from visitors U.S.$100,000,000; expenditures by nationals abroad U.S.$111,000,000.

Foreign trade

Balance of trade

	1993	1994	1995	1996	1997	1998
FMG '000,000,000	–396.7	–161.9	–764.5	–840.4	–1,253.1	–1,480.3
% of total	28.4%	6.1%	19.6%	25.7%	35.5%	36.1%

Imports (1998): FMG 2,748,989,000,000 (chemical products 14.9%; food 14.1%; minerals 11.2%, of which crude petroleum 7.1%; machinery and equipment 9.3%). *Major import sources* (1999): France 24.1%; Iran 7.1%; Japan 6.2%; South Africa 6.0%; U.S. 4.0%.
Exports (1998): FMG 1,273,787,000,000 (coffee 17.2%; cotton fabrics 14.1%; minerals 11.3%; shrimp 6.0%; cloves and clove oil 3.9%; vanilla 3.0%). *Major export destinations* (1998): France 39.4%; Mauritius 6.8%; U.S. 5.5%; Germany 4.5%; Italy 3.7%.

Transport and communications

Transport. Railroads: route length (1998) 680 mi, 1,095 km; passenger-mi 21,748,000, passenger-km 35,000,000; short ton-mi cargo 44,117,000, metric ton-km cargo 71,000,000. Roads (1996): total length 30,967 mi, 49,837 km (paved 17%). Vehicles (1996): passenger cars 62,000; trucks and buses 16,460. Air transport (1998): passenger-mi 519,000,000, passenger-km 836,000,000; short ton-mi cargo 20,230,000, metric ton-km cargo 29,533,000; airports (1994) with scheduled flights 44.

Communications

Medium	date	unit	number	units per 1,000 persons
Daily newspapers	1996	circulation	66,000	4.6
Radio	1997	receivers	3,050,000	209
Television	1998	receivers	340,000	22.0
Telephones	1999	main lines	50,226	3.2
Cellular telephones	1998	subscribers	12,784	0.9
Personal computers	1998	users	25,000	1.7
Internet	1999	users	8,000	0.5

Education and health

Educational attainment: n.a. *Literacy* (1995): percentage of total population age 15 and over literate 45.7%; males literate 59.8%; females literate 32.0%.

Education (1995–96)

	schools	teachers	students	student/ teacher ratio
Primary (age 6–13)	13,325	44,145	1,638,187	37.1
Secondary (age 14–18)	1,142[11]	16,795	302,036	18.0
Voc., teacher tr.	61[12]	1,150	8,479	7.3
Higher	5[9]	921	18,458	20.0

Health: physicians (1996) 1,470 (1 per 9,351 persons); hospital beds (1989) 10,900 (1 per 1,029 persons); infant mortality rate (2000) 87.0.
Food (1999): daily per capita caloric intake 1,994 (vegetable products 90%, animal products 10%); 88% of FAO recommended minimum requirement.

Military

Total active duty personnel (1999): 21,000 (army 95.2%, navy 2.4%, air force 2.4%). *Military expenditure as percentage of GNP* (1997): 1.5% (world 2.6%); per capita expenditure U.S.$4.

[1]Each of the six autonomous provinces is adopting its own statutory laws per article 2 of the 1998 constitution. [2]The 1998 constitution identifies Malagasy as the "national" language, although neither Malagasy nor French, the languages of the two official texts of the constitution, is itself "official." [3]1994. [4]Antananarivo only. [5]Average salary, all public employees, including military. [6]At factor cost. [7]Included with Services. [8]Less imputed bank charges. [9]Malagasy households only. [10]Weights of consumer price index components; excludes housing. [11]1988–89. [12]1987–88.

Internet resources for further information:
- **Mission of Madagascar to the United Nations (Geneva; French, summary only in English) http://www3.itu.ch/MISSIONS/Madagascar**

Malawi

Official name: Republic of Malawi.
Form of government: multiparty republic with one legislative house (National Assembly [192]).
Head of state and government: President.
Capital: [1].
Official language: none.
Official religion: none.
Monetary unit: 1 Malawi kwacha (MK) = 100 tambala; valuation (Sept. 28, 2001) 1 U.S.$ = MK 61.48; 1 £ = MK 90.36.

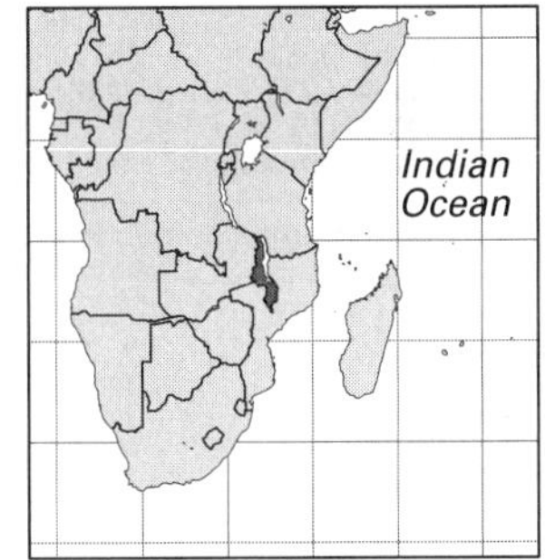

Area and population		area		population
Regions / Districts	Capitals	sq mi	sq km	1998 census
Central	Lilongwe	13,742	35,592	4,066,340
Dedza	Dedza	1,399	3,624	486,682
Dowa	Dowa	1,174	3,041	411,387
Kasungu	Kasungu	3,042	7,878	480,659
Lilongwe	Lilongwe	2,378	6,159	1,346,360
Mchinji	Mchinji	1,296	3,356	324,941
Nkhotakota	Nkhotakota	1,644	4,259	229,460
Ntcheu	Ntcheu	1,322	3,424	370,757
Ntchisi	Ntchisi	639	1,655	167,880
Salima	Salima	848	2,196	248,214
Northern	Mzuzu	10,398	26,931	1,233,560
Chitipa	Chitipa	1,656	4,288	126,799
Karonga	Karonga	1,295	3,355	194,572
Likoma	Likoma	7	18	8,074
Mzimba	Mzimba	4,027	10,430	610,994
Nkhata Bay	Nkhata Bay	1,572	4,071	164,761
Rumphi	Rumphi	1,841	4,769	128,360
Southern	Blantyre	12,260	31,753	4,633,968
Balaka	Balaka	847	2,193	253,098
Blantyre	Blantyre	777	2,012	809,397
Chikwawa	Chikwawa	1,836	4,755	356,682
Chiradzulu	Chiradzulu	296	767	236,050
Machinga	Machinga	1,456	3,771	369,614
Mangochi	Mangochi	2,422	6,273	610,239
Mulanje	Mulanje	794	2,056	428,322
Mwanza	Mwanza	886	2,295	138,015
Nsanje	Nsanje	750	1,942	194,924
Phalombe	Phalombe	538	1,394	231,990
Thyolo	Thyolo	662	1,715	458,976
Zomba	Zomba	996	2,580	546,661
TOTAL LAND AREA		36,400	94,276	
INLAND WATER		9,347	24,208	
TOTAL		45,747	118,484	9,933,868

Demography

Population (2001): 10,491,000.
Density (2001)[2]: persons per sq mi 288.2, persons per sq km 111.3.
Urban-rural (1998): urban 10.7%; rural 89.3%.
Sex distribution (1998): male 48.89%; female 51.11%.
Age breakdown (1987): under 15, 46.0%; 15–29, 25.4%; 30–44, 14.5%; 45–59, 8.1%; 60 and over, 6.0%.
Population projection: (2010) 11,621,000; (2020) 12,318,000.
Ethnic composition (2000): Chewa 34.7%; Maravi 12.2%; Ngoni 9.0%; Yao 7.9%; Tumbuka 7.9%; Lomwe 7.7%; Ngonde 3.5%; other 17.1%.
Religious affiliation (1995): Christian 50.3%, of which Protestant 20.5%, Roman Catholic 18.0%; Muslim 20.0%; traditional beliefs 10.0%; other 19.7%.
Major cities (1998): Blantyre 478,155; Lilongwe 435,964; Mzuzu 87,030.

Vital statistics

Birth rate per 1,000 population (2000): 38.5 (world avg. 22.5).
Death rate per 1,000 population (2000): 22.4 (world avg. 9.0).
Natural increase rate per 1,000 population (2000): 16.1 (world avg. 13.5).
Total fertility rate (avg. births per childbearing woman; 2000): 6.3.
Life expectancy at birth (2000): male 37.2 years; female 38.0 years.
Major causes of death per 100,000 population (1986)[3]: infectious and parasitic diseases 711, of which malaria 270, diarrheal diseases 148, measles 128; malnutrition 267; diseases of the respiratory system 265.

National economy

Budget (1997–98). Revenue: MK 8,366,200,000 (tax revenue 96.7%, of which income tax 40.3%, sales tax 35.1%; nontax revenue 3.3%). Expenditures: MK 12,785,600,000 (administration 17.3%, education 16.5%, health 7.0%).
Public debt (external, outstanding; 1999): U.S.$2,596,000,000.
Production (metric tons except as noted). Agriculture (1999): corn (maize) 2,480,000, sugarcane 1,900,000, potatoes 385,000, plantains 205,000, cassava 200,000, tobacco 113,000, peanuts (groundnuts) 100,000, bananas 95,000; livestock (number of live animals) 1,260,000 goats, 750,000 cattle, 230,000 pigs, 110,000 sheep; roundwood (1998) 9,692,000 cu m; fish catch (1998) 41,111. Mining and quarrying (1998): limestone 171,900; gemstone 934 kg. Manufacturing (value added in MK '000; 1986): chemicals 30,805; textiles 19,630; food products 11,988; beverages 11,988; tobacco 9,480. Construction (value in MK; 1994): 41,700,000[4]. Energy production (consumption): electricity (kW-hr; 1996) 874,000,000 (874,000,000); coal (metric tons; 1996) none (17,000); petroleum products (metric tons; 1996) none (199,000).
Land use (1994): forested 39.3%; meadows and pastures 19.6%; agricultural and under permanent cultivation 18.1%; other 23.0%.
Population economically active (1987): total 3,457,753; activity rate 43.3% (participation rates: age 15–64, 84.6%; female 51.5%; unemployed 5.4%).

Price and earnings indexes (1995 = 100)	1994	1995	1996	1997	1998	1999	2000
Consumer price index	54.5	100.0	137.6	150.2	194.9	282.4	365.6
Earnings index	...	...	...	...	...	...	...

Gross national product (1999): U.S.$1,961,000,000 (U.S.$180 per capita).

Structure of gross domestic product and labour force	1998		1987	
	in value MK '000,000[5]	% of total value[5]	labour force	% of labour force
Agriculture	4,582.8	36.3	2,967,933	85.8
Mining	111.9	0.9	7,164	0.2
Manufacturing	1,659.1	13.1	97,776	2.8
Construction	228.3	1.8	46,875	1.4
Public utilities	170.5	1.3	8,833	0.2
Transp. and commun.	531.0	4.2	24,863	0.7
Trade	3,117.1	24.7	94,445	2.7
Finance	1,088.5	8.6	5,590	0.3
Public administration	1,220.9	9.6	147,039	4.3
Services	262.0	2.1		
Other	–332.5[6]	–2.6[6]	57,235	1.6
TOTAL	12,639.6	100.0	3,457,753	100.0

Household income and expenditure. Average household size (1998) 4.3; income per household n.a.; sources of income: n.a.; expenditure (1990)[7]: food 55.5%, clothing and footwear 11.7%, housing 9.6%, household goods 8.4%.
Tourism: receipts (1999) U.S.$20,000,000; expenditures (1994) U.S.$15,000,000.

Foreign trade[8]

Balance of trade (current prices)	1994	1995	1996	1997	1998	1999
MK '000,000	+247.3	+1,840	+1,632	+1,118	+5,734	+970
% of total	4.6%	17.4%	12.5%	6.8%	21.0%	2.6%

Imports (1995): MK 7,254,949,000 (1990; transport equipment 9.2%, petroleum products 8.3%, clothing 3.8%, pharmaceutical products 2.2%). *Major import sources:* South Africa 44.4%; Germany 4.5%; U.K. 4.3%; United States 3.7%.
Exports (1995): MK 6,192,563,000 (tobacco 63.2%, tea 6.7%, sugar 6.5%, cotton 0.9%). *Major export destinations:* South Africa 16.2%; Germany 14.7%; Japan 11.1%; U.S. 10.9%; Mozambique 7.6%.

Transport and communications

Transport. Railroads (1995–96): route length 495 mi, 797 km; passenger-km 18,048,000; metric ton-km cargo 43,431,000. Roads (1997): total length 10,222 mi, 16,451 km (paved 19%). Vehicles (1996): passenger cars 27,000; trucks and buses 29,700. Air transport (1995)[9]: passenger-km 110,000,000, metric ton-km cargo 14,000,000; airports (1997) 5.

Communications				units
Medium	date	unit	number	per 1,000 persons
Daily newspapers	1996	circulation	22,000[10]	2.3[10]
Radio	1997	receivers	2,600,000	258
Television	1999	receivers	27,000	2.5
Telephones	1999	main lines	41,362	4.1
Cellular telephones	1999	subscribers	22,500	2.2
Personal computers	1999	units	10,000	1.0
Internet	1999	users	2,000	0.2

Education and health

Educational attainment (1987). Percentage of population age 25 and over having: no formal education 55.0%; primary education 39.8%; secondary and higher 5.2%. *Literacy* (1995): total population age 15 and over literate 56.4%; males literate 71.9%; females literate 41.8%.

Education (1995–96)	schools	teachers	students	student/ teacher ratio
Primary (age 6–13)	3,706	49,138	2,887,107	58.8
Secondary (age 14–18)	94[11]	2,948	139,386	47.3
Teacher tr., voc.	13[11]	224	2,525	11.3
Higher	6[12]	531	5,561	10.5

Health: physicians (1989) 186 (1 per 47,634 persons); hospital beds (1987) 12,617 (1 per 627 persons); infant mortality rate (1999) 123.4.
Food (1999): daily per capita caloric intake 2,164 (vegetable products 98%, animal products 2%); 91% of FAO recommended minimum requirement.

Military

Total active duty personnel (2000): 5,000 (army 100%; navy, none; air force, none). *Military expenditure as percentage of GNP* (1997): 1.0% (world 2.6%); per capita expenditure U.S.$3.

[1]A capital is not designated in the 1994 constitution. Current government operations are divided between Lilongwe (ministerial, financial, and legislative) and Blantyre (executive and judicial). [2]Based on land area. [3]Estimates based on reported inpatient deaths in hospitals, constituting an estimated 8% of total deaths. [4]Cities of Blantyre, Lilongwe, and Mzuzu only. [5]At constant prices of 1994. [6]Less imputed bank service charges. [7]Weights of consumer price index components, cities of Blantyre and Lilongwe only. [8]Import figures are f.o.b. in balance of trade and c.i.f. in commodities and trading partners. Reexports included in balance of trade, excluded from commodities and trading partners. [9]Air Malawi only. [10]Circulation for one newspaper only. [11]1989–90. [12]Universities only.

Internet resources for further information:
- **National Statistical Office of Malawi http://www.nso.malawi.net**

Malaysia

Official name: Malaysia.
Form of government: federal constitutional monarchy with two legislative houses (Senate [70[1]]; House of Representatives [193]).
Chief of state: Yang di-Pertuan Agong (Paramount Ruler).
Head of government: Prime Minister.
Capital: Kuala Lumpur[2].
Official language: Malay.
Official religion: Islam.
Monetary unit: 1 ringgit, or Malaysian dollar (RM) = 100 cents; valuation[3] (Sept. 28, 2001) 1 U.S.$ = RM 3.80; 1 £ = RM 5.58.

Area and population		area		population
Regions				2000
States	Capitals	sq mi	sq km	census[4]
East Malaysia				
Sabah	Kota Kinabalu	28,460	73,711	2,449,389
Sarawak	Kuching	48,050	124,449	2,012,616
West Malaysia				
Johor	Johor Baharu	7,330	18,985	2,565,701
Kedah	Alor Setar	3,639	9,425	1,572,107
Kelantan	Kota Baharu	5,765	14,931	1,289,199
Melaka	Melaka	637	1,651	602,867
Negeri Sembilan	Seremban	2,565	6,643	830,080
Pahang	Kuantan	13,886	35,965	1,231,176
Perak	Ipoh	8,110	21,005	2,030,382
Perlis	Kangar	307	795	198,335
Pulau Pinang	George Town	399	1,033	1,225,501
Selangor	Shah Alam	3,054	7,910	3,947,527[5]
Terengganu	Kuala Terengganu	5,002	12,955	879,691
Federal Territories				
Kuala Lumpur	—	94	243	1,297,526
Labuan	—	38	98	70,517
Putrajaya	—	18	46	5
TOTAL		127,354	329,845	22,202,614

Demography

Population (2001): 22,602,000.
Density (2001): persons per sq mi 177.5, persons per sq km 68.5.
Urban-rural (2001): urban 58.0%; rural 42.0%.
Sex distribution (2000[4]): male 50.45%; female 49.55%.
Age breakdown (1999): under 15, 33.5%; 15–29, 28.2%; 30–44, 21.0%; 45–59, 11.3%; 60–74, 4.9%, 75 and over, 1.1%.
Population projection: (2010) 26,625,000; (2020) 31,306,000.
Doubling time: 37 years.
Ethnic composition (1999): Malay and other indigenous 57.9%; Chinese 24.7%; Indian 7.0%; other nonindigenous 3.2%; noncitizen 7.2%.
Religious affiliation (2000): Muslim 47.6%; Chinese folk religionist 24.1%; Christian 8.3%; Hindu 7.3%; Buddhist 6.6%; other 6.1%.
Major cities (1991): Kuala Lumpur 1,145,342; Ipoh 382,853; Johor Baharu 328,436; Melaka 296,897; Petaling Jaya 254,350.

Vital statistics

Birth rate per 1,000 population (2001): 23.5 (world avg. 22.5).
Death rate per 1,000 population (2001): 4.4 (world avg. 9.0).
Natural increase rate per 1,000 population (2001): 19.1 (world avg. 13.5).
Total fertility rate (avg. births per childbearing woman; 1999): 3.1.
Life expectancy at birth (2001): male 70.3 years; female 75.2 years.
Major causes of death per 100,000 population (1997): diseases of the circulatory system 59.7; accidents and violence 34.8; malignant neoplasms 22.3; infectious and parasitic diseases 18.6; respiratory diseases 10.2.

National economy

Budget (1999). Revenue: RM 59,157,000,000 (income tax 42.5%, taxes on goods and services 24.6%, nontax revenue 19.0%, taxes on international trade 9.1%). Expenditures: RM 71,429,000,000 (education 21.5%, defense and internal security 12.9%, general administration 12.7%, interest payments 11.1%, health 6.2%, transport and communications 6.1%, social security 5.7%, agriculture 3.2%).
Tourism (1999): receipts from visitors U.S.$3,540,000,000; expenditures by nationals abroad (1997) U.S.$1,973,000,000.
Population economically active (1999): total 9,010,000; activity rate 39.7% (participation rates: ages 15–64, 60.6%; female [1997] 34.0%; unemployed 3.0%).
Production (metric tons except as noted). Agriculture, forestry, fishing (2000):

Price index (1995 = 100)	1994	1995	1996	1997	1998	1999	2000
Consumer price index	95.0	100.0	103.5	106.2	111.8	114.9	116.7

palm fruit oil 56,600,000, rice 2,037,000, sugarcane 1,600,000, rubber 768,900, bananas 545,000, pineapples 134,000; livestock (number of live animals) 1,829,000 pigs, 723,000 cattle, 120,000,000 chickens; roundwood 29,461,000 cu m; fish catch (1998) 1,153,719. Mining and quarrying (1998): iron ore 316,808; bauxite 134,077; copper concentrates 53,001; tin concentrates 5,756. Manufacturing (1999): cement 10,104,000; iron and steel bars and rods 2,261,000; refined sugar 1,226,000; plywood 3,701,000 cu m; radio receivers 32,957,000 units; automotive tires 24,984,000 units. Construction (completed; 1986)[6]: residential 8,809,100 sq m; nonresidential 959,900 sq m. Energy production (consumption): electricity (kW-hr; 1996) 53,000,000,000 (52,986,000,000); coal (metric tons; 1996) 83,000 (2,416,000); crude petroleum (barrels; 1996) 258,000,000 (132,000,000); petroleum products (metric tons; 1996) 11,406,000 (17,007,000); natural gas (cu m; 1996) 35,268,000,000 (18,885,000,000).
Gross national product (1999): U.S.$76,944,000,000 (U.S.$3,390 per capita).

Structure of gross domestic product and labour force	1999			
	in value RM '000,000[7]	% of total value	labour force	% of labour force
Agriculture	17,998	9.3	1,389,000	15.4
Mining	13,973	7.3	42,000	0.5
Manufacturing	57,760	30.0	2,379,000	26.4
Construction	6,922	3.6	804,000	8.9
Public utilities	6,631	3.5	72,000	0.8
Transp. and commun.	15,592	8.1	442,000	4.9
Trade	29,154	15.1	1,449,000	16.1
Finance	23,753	12.3	420,000	4.7
Pub. admin., defense	14,195	7.4	875,000	9.7
Services	15,251	7.9	1,138,000	12.6
Other	–8,720[8]	–4.5[8]		
TOTAL	192,509	100.0	9,010,000	100.0

Public debt (external, outstanding; 1999): U.S.$18,929,000,000.
Household income and expenditure. Average household size (2000) 4.5; annual income per household (1997) RM 31,280 (U.S.$11,120); sources of income: n.a.; expenditure (1983): food 28.7%, transportation 20.9%, recreation and education 11.0%, housing 10.2%, household durable goods 7.7%.

Foreign trade[9]

Balance of trade (current prices)	1994	1995	1996	1997	1998	1999
U.S.$'000,000	+1,577	–104	+3,848	+3,509	+17,505	+22,648
% of total	1.4%	0.1%	2.6%	2.3%	13.9%	15.6%

Imports (1998): RM 228,309,000,000 (machinery and transport equipment 63.0%, basic manufactures 11.1%, chemicals 7.1%, food 4.6%, mineral fuels 3.1%). *Major import sources:* Japan 20.8%; U.S. 17.4%; Singapore 14.0%; Taiwan 5.3%; South Korea 5.2%; Thailand 3.8%.
Exports (1998): RM 286,756,000,000 (machinery and transport equipment 59.2%, basic manufactures 8.3%, animal and vegetable oils 7.5%, mineral fuels 6.2%, chemicals 3.5%, inedible crude materials 3.3%). *Major export destinations:* U.S. 21.9%; Singapore 16.5%; Japan 11.6%; The Netherlands 5.1%; Taiwan 4.5%; Hong Kong 4.2%; United Kingdom 3.8%.

Transport and communications

Transport. Railroads (1999): route length 2,227 km; passenger-km 1,332,000,000[10]; metric ton-km cargo 912,000,000[10]. Roads (1998): total length 66,437 km (paved 76%). Vehicles (1998): passenger cars 3,517,484; trucks and buses 644,792. Air transport (1999): passenger-km 33,708,000,000; metric ton-km cargo 1,424,556,000; airports (1997) 39.

Communications				units
Medium	date	unit	number	per 1,000 persons
Daily newspapers	1996	circulation	3,345,000	163
Radio	1997	receivers	9,100,000	434
Television	1999	receivers	3,800,000	174
Telephones	1999	main lines	4,431,000	203
Cellular telephones	1999	subscribers	2,990,000	137
Personal computers	1999	units	1,500,000	69
Internet	1999	users	1,500,000	69

Education and health

Educational attainment (1996). Percentage of population age 25 and over having: no formal schooling 16.7%; primary education 33.7%; secondary 42.8%; higher 6.8%. *Literacy* (1995): total population age 15 and over literate 83.5%; males literate 89.1%; females literate 78.1%.

Education (1998)	schools	teachers	students	student/ teacher ratio
Primary (age 7–12)	7,124	154,829	2,872,000	18.5
Secondary (age 13–19)	1,486	97,083	1,866,000	19.2
Voc., teacher tr.	78	5,056	24,000	4.7
Higher	51	15,684[11]	230,000[11]	14.7[11]

Health (1998): physicians 15,016 (1 per 1,402 persons); hospital beds 42,398 (1 per 497 persons); infant mortality rate per 1,000 live births (2001) 7.9.
Food (1999): daily per capita caloric intake 2,946 (vegetable products 81%, animal products 19%); (1997) 132% of FAO recommended minimum.

Military

Total active duty personnel (2000): 96,000 (army 83.4%, navy 8.3%, air force 8.3%). *Military expenditure as percentage of GDP* (1997): 2.2% (world 2.6%); per capita expenditure U.S.$102.

[1]Includes 40 appointees of the Paramount Ruler; the remaining 30 are indirectly elected at different times. [2]The transfer to the new federal administrative centre at Putrajaya will occur between 1999 and 2005. [3]Pegged to the U.S. dollar at RM 3.80 = 1 U.S.$ on Oct. 6, 2000. [4]Preliminary. [5]Includes population data for Putrajaya. [6]Results of the Central Bank Survey of four major towns: Kuala Lumpur, Shah Alam, Kelang, and Seberang Prai. [7]At constant prices of 1987. [8]Net bank service charges. [9]Import figures are f.o.b. in balance of trade. [10]Peninsular Malaysia and Singapore. [11]1996.

Internet resources for further information:
- **Department of Statistics http://www.statistics.gov.my**
- **Malaysian Information Services (English) http://penerangan.gov.my**

Maldives

Official name: Divehi Jumhuriyya (Republic of Maldives).
Form of government: republic with one legislative house (Majlis[1] [42[2, 3]]).
Head of state and government: President.
Capital: Male.
Official language: Divehi.
Official religion: Islam.
Monetary unit: 1 Maldivian rufiyaa (Rf) = 100 laari; valuation (Sept. 28, 2001) 1 U.S.$ = Rf 11.77; 1 £ = Rf 17.30.

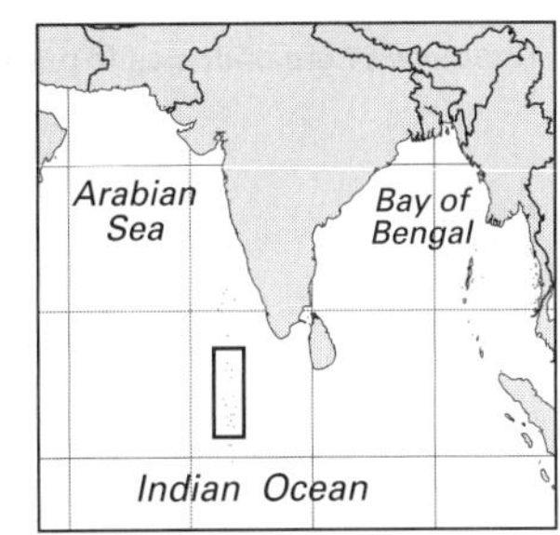

Area and population[4]

Administrative atolls	Capitals	area sq mi	area sq km	population 2000 census
North Thiladhunmathi (Haa-Alifu)	Dhidhdhoo	...	...	14,161
South Thiladhunmathi (Haa-Dhaalu)	Nolhivaranfaru	...	...	16,956
North Miladhunmadulu (Shaviyani)	Farukolhu-funadhoo	...	...	11,406
South Miladhunmadulu (Noonu)	Manadhoo	...	...	10,429
North Maalhosmadulu (Raa)	Ugoofaaru	...	...	14,486
South Maalhosmadulu (Baa)	Eydhafushi	...	...	9,612
Faadhippolhu (Lhaviyani)	Naifaru	...	...	9,385
Male (Kaafu)	Thulusdhoo	...	...	13,474
Ari Atoll Uthuru Gofi (Alifu)	Rasdhoo	...	...	5,518
Ari Atoll Dhekunu Gofi (Alifu)	Mahibadhoo	...	...	7,803
Felidhu Atoll (Vaavu)	Felidhoo	...	...	1,753
Mulakatholhu (Meemu)	Muli	...	...	5,084
North Nilandhe Atoll (Faafu)	Magoodhoo	...	...	3,827
South Nilandhe Atoll (Dhaalu)	Kudahuvadhoo	...	...	5,067
Kolhumadulu (Thaa)	Veymandoo	...	...	9,305
Hadhdhunmathi (Laamu)	Hithadhoo	...	...	11,588
North Huvadhu Atoll (Gaafu-Alifu)	Viligili	...	...	8,249
South Huvadhu Atoll (Gaafu-Dhaalu)	Thinadhoo	...	...	11,886
Foammulah (Gnyaviyani)	Foahmulah	...	...	7,528
Addu Atoll (Seenu)	Hithadhoo	...	...	18,515
Capital island				
Male (Maale)		...	...	74,069
TOTAL		115	298	270,101

Demography

Population (2001): 275,000.
Density (2001): persons per sq mi 2,391, persons per sq km 922.8.
Urban-rural (1999): urban 28.0%; rural 72.0%.
Sex distribution (2000): male 50.80%; female 49.20%.
Age breakdown (2000): under 15, 40.7%; 15–29, 28.5%; 30–44, 17.1%; 45–59, 7.7%; 60–74, 5.1%; 75 and over, 0.9%.
Population projection: (2010) 326,000; (2020) 394,000.
Doubling time: 23 years.
Ethnic composition: the majority is principally of Sinhalese and Dravidian extraction; Arab, African, and Negrito influences are also present.
Religious affiliation: virtually 100% Sunnī Muslim.
Major city (2000): Male 74,069.

Vital statistics

Birth rate per 1,000 population (2001): 36.3 (world avg. 22.5).
Death rate per 1,000 population (2001): 6.3 (world avg. 9.0).
Natural increase rate per 1,000 population (2001): 30.0 (world avg. 13.5).
Total fertility rate (avg. births per childbearing woman; 2001): 5.5.
Marriage rate per 1,000 population (1996): 9.6.
Divorce rate per 1,000 population (1996): 2.8.
Life expectancy at birth (2001): male 68.0 years; female 66.0 years.
Major causes of death per 100,000 population (1988): rheumatic fever 106.0; ischemic heart diseases 65.0; bronchitis, emphysema, and asthma 61.0; tetanus 23.5; tuberculosis 13.0; accidents and suicide 10.0.

National economy

Budget (1998). Revenue: Rf 1,941,400,000 (taxation 45.9%, nontax revenue 45.8%, foreign aid 8.2%). Expenditures: Rf 2,216,300,000 (general public services 40.7%, education 19.0%, housing 10.5%, health 10.0%, transportation and communications 9.5%).
Public debt (external, outstanding; 1999): U.S.$192,500,000.
Production (metric tons except as noted). Agriculture, forestry, fishing (1999): vegetables and melons 25,300, coconuts 13,000, fruits (excluding melons) 8,850, roots and tubers (including cassava, sweet potatoes, and yams) 7,010; fish catch (1997) 107,676. Mining and quarrying: coral for construction materials. Manufacturing: details, n.a.; however, major industries include boat building and repairing, coir yarn and mat weaving, coconut and fish processing, lacquerwork, garment manufacturing, and handicrafts. Energy production (consumption): electricity (kW-hr; 1996) 63,000,000 (63,000,000); petroleum products (metric tons; 1996) none (97,000).
Tourism (1999): receipts from visitors U.S.$334,000,000; expenditures by nationals abroad U.S.$45,000,000.
Population economically active (1995): total 67,476; activity rate of total population 27.6% (participation rates: ages 15–64, 62.6%; female 27.1%; unemployed [1995] 0.9%).

Price index (1995 = 100)

	1994	1995	1996	1997	1998	1999	2000
Consumer price index	94.8	100.0	106.3	114.3	112.7	116.0	114.7

Household income and expenditure (1990). Average household size 7.2; annual income per household Rf 2,616 (U.S.$274), sources of income: n.a.; expenditure (1981)[5]: food and beverages 61.8%, housing equipment 17.0%, clothing 8.0%, recreation and education 5.9%, transportation 2.6%, health 2.5%, rent 1.6%.
Gross national product (1999): U.S.$322,000,000 (U.S.$1,200 per capita).

Structure of gross domestic product and labour force

	1997 in value Rf '000[6]	1997 % of total value	1990 labour force	1990 % of labour force
Agriculture[7]	262,200	17.0	14,117	25.0
Mining	24,200	1.6	496	0.9
Manufacturing } Public utilities }	90,400	5.9	8,441	15.0
			445	0.8
Construction	171,500	11.1	3,151	5.6
Transp. and commun.	110,700	7.2	5,321	9.4
Trade	302,800	19.7	8,884	15.7
Finance	454,500	29.6	1,058	1.9
Public administration, defense } Services }	121,200	7.9	11,848	21.0
Other	...	...	2,674	4.7
TOTAL	1,537,500	100.0	56,435	100.0

Land use (1994): forested 3.3%; meadows and pastures 3.3%; agricultural and under permanent cultivation 10.0%; built-on, wasteland, and other 83.4%.

Foreign trade[8]

Balance of trade (current prices)

	1995	1996	1997	1998	1999	2000
U.S.$'000,000	–186.1	–206.3	–233.8	–235.3	–290.4	–266.1
% of total	65.3%	63.5%	61.5%	60.7%	69.5%	63.7%

Imports (1996): Rf 3,551,289,000 (machinery and transport equipment 27.9%, basic manufactures 23.7%, food and live animals 21.4%, petroleum products 9.1%). *Major import sources:* Singapore 32.0%; India 12.0%; Malaysia 8.5%; Sri Lanka 7.6%; United Kingdom 3.6%; Japan 3.5%.
Exports (1996): Rf 699,190,000 (canned fish 28.0%, yellowfin tuna 20.5%, apparel and clothing 17.4%, dried skipjack tuna 11.0%). *Major export destinations:* United Kingdom 21.7%; Sri Lanka 18.3%; United States 10.2%; Germany 10.8%; Japan 10.6%; Thailand 9.5%.

Transport and communications

Transport. Railroads: none. Roads: total length, n.a. Vehicles (1997): passenger cars 1,716; trucks and buses 586. Merchant marine (1992): vessels (100 gross tons and over) 44; total deadweight tonnage 78,994. Air transport (1995): passengers carried 159,000; passenger-km 71,000,000; airports (1997) with scheduled flights 5.

Communications

Medium	date	unit	number	units per 1,000 persons
Daily newspapers	1996	circulation	5,000	19
Radio	1997	receivers	34,000	129
Television	1999	receivers	10,650	38
Telephones	1999	main lines	22,179	80
Cellular telephones	1999	subscribers	2,926	11
Personal computers	1999	units	5,000	18
Internet	1999	users	3,000	11

Education and health

Educational attainment (1990). Percentage of population age 15 and over having: no standard passed 25.6%; primary standard 37.2%; middle standard 25.9%; secondary standard 6.3%; preuniversity 3.4%; higher 0.4%; not stated 1.2%. *Literacy* (1995): total population age 15 and over literate 93.2%; males literate 93.0%; females literate 93.3%.

Education (1998)

	schools	teachers	students	student/ teacher ratio
Primary (age 6–11)	228	1,992	48,895	24.5
Secondary (age 11–18)	9[9]	291[9]	15,933[10]	12.3[9]
Voc., teacher tr.	10[9]	52[9]	452[10]	8.9[9]
Higher	—	—	—	—

Health (1996): physicians 99 (1 per 1,995 persons); hospital beds 318 (1 per 806 persons); infant mortality rate per 1,000 live births (2001) 40.
Food (1999): daily per capita caloric intake 2,298 (vegetable products 81%, animal products 19%); (1997) 104% of FAO recommended minimum requirement.

Military

Total active duty personnel: Maldives maintains a single security force numbering about 700–1,000; it performs both army and police functions.

[1]Also known or translated as People's Majlis, Citizens' Council, or Citizens' Assembly. [2]Excludes nonelective seats. [3]The new constitution went into effect Jan. 1, 1998. [4]Maldives is divided into 20 administrative districts corresponding to atoll groups; arrangement shown here is from north to south. Total area excludes 34,634 sq mi (89,702 sq km) of tidal waters. [5]Weights of consumer price index components. [6]At 1985 prices. [7]Primarily fishing. [8]Import figures are f.o.b. in balance of trade and c.i.f. for commodities and trading partners. [9]1986. [10]1992.

Mali

Official name: République du Mali (Republic of Mali).
Form of government: multiparty republic with one legislative house (National Assembly [147])[1].
Chief of state: President.
Head of government: Prime Minister.
Capital: Bamako.
Official language: French.
Official religion: none.
Monetary unit: 1 CFA franc (CFAF) = 100 centimes; valuation (Sept. 28, 2001) 1 U.S.$ = CFAF 720.28; 1 £ = CFAF 1,059.

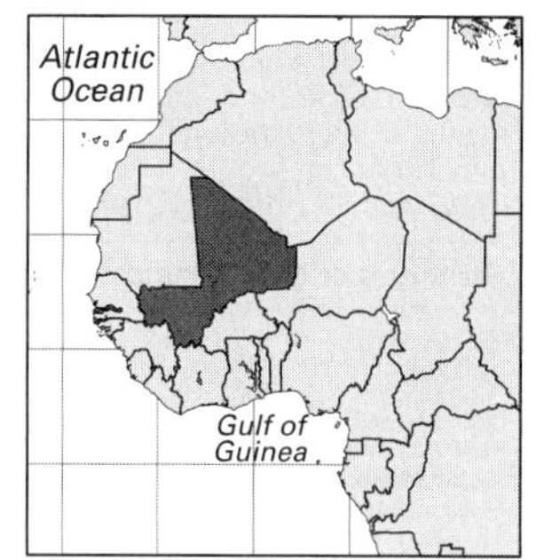

Area and population

Regions	Capitals	area sq mi	area sq km	population 1995 estimate
Gao	Gao	65,858	170,572	408,000[2]
Kayes	Kayes	46,233	119,743	1,245,000
Kidal	Kidal	58,467	151,430	[2]
Koulikoro	Koulikoro	37,007	95,848	1,462,000
Mopti	Mopti	30,509	79,017	1,423,000
Ségou	Ségou	25,028	64,821	1,579,000
Sikasso	Sikasso	27,135	70,280	1,521,000
Tombouctou	Timbuktu (Tombouctou)	191,743	496,611	462,000
District				
Bamako	Bamako	97	252	913,000
TOTAL		482,077	1,248,574	9,013,000

Demography

Population (2001): 11,009,000.
Density (2001): persons per sq mi 22.8, persons per sq km 8.8.
Urban-rural (1998): urban 28.7%; rural 71.3%.
Sex distribution (2001): male 48.9%; female 51.1%.
Age breakdown (2001): under 15, 47.2%; 15–29, 26.8%; 30–44, 13.3%; 45–59, 7.9%; 60–74, 4.0%; 75 and over, 0.8%.
Population projection: (2010) 14,349,000; (2020) 18,984,000.
Doubling time: 24 years.
Ethnic composition (2000): Bambara 30.6%; Senufo 10.5%; Fula Macina (Niafunke) 9.6%; Soninke 7.4%; Tuareg 7.0%; Maninka 6.6%; Songhai 6.3%; Dogon 4.3%; Bobo 3.5%; other 14.2%.
Religious affiliation (2000): Muslim 82%; traditional beliefs 16%; Christian 2%.
Major cities (1996): Bamako 809,552; Ségou 106,799; Mopti 86,355; Sikasso 90,174; Gao 62,667.

Vital statistics

Birth rate per 1,000 population (2001): 48.8 (world avg. 22.5).
Death rate per 1,000 population (2001): 18.7 (world avg. 9.0).
Natural increase rate per 1,000 population (2001): 30.1 (world avg. 13.5).
Total fertility rate (avg. births per childbearing woman; 2001): 6.8.
Life expectancy at birth (2001): male 45.8 years; female 48.2 years.
Major causes of death per 100,000 population: n.a.; morbidity ([notified cases of illness] by cause as a percentage of all reported infectious disease; 1985): malaria 62.1%; measles 10.3%; amebiasis 10.3%; syphilis and gonococcal infections 6.0%; influenza 4.9%.

National economy

Budget (1999). Revenue: CFAF 356,000,000,000 (tax revenue 66.1%, grants 23.4%, nontax revenue 10.5%). Expenditures: CFAF 417,400,000,000 (current expenditure 46.3%, of which wages and salaries 15.6%, education 10.3%, defense 8.3%, interest on public debt 3.6%, health 2.8%; capital expenditure 53.7%).
Public debt (external, outstanding; 1999): U.S.$2,798,000,000.
Tourism (1999): receipts from visitors U.S.$50,000,000; expenditures by nationals abroad U.S.$29,000,000.
Population economically active (1997): total 5,042,000; activity rate of total population 51.5% (participation rates [1987] ages 15–64, 67.4%; female 46.3%; unemployed 0.8%).

Price and earnings indexes (1995 = 100)

	1994	1995	1996	1997	1998	1999	2000
Consumer price index	88.2	100.0	106.8	106.4	110.7	109.4	108.6
Hourly earnings index	...	...	...	100.0	...	...	...

Production (metric tons except as noted). Agriculture, forestry, fishing (2001): millet 802,500, rice 745,100, sorghum 591,700, seed cotton 480,000, corn (maize) 322,700, sugarcane 300,000, peanuts (groundnuts) 140,000, sweet potatoes 15,000; livestock (number of live animals) 14,550,000 goats and sheep, 6,200,000 cattle, 652,000 asses, 292,000 camels, 136,000 horses, 65,000 pigs; roundwood (2000) 6,596,900 cu m; fish catch (1999) 98,776. Mining and quarrying (1999): limestone 20,000[3]; phosphate 3,000[3]; iron oxide 708[3]; gypsum 500[3]; gold 23,689 kg; silver 250 kg. Manufacturing (1999): sugar 27,000; cement 20,000; soap 10,097[4]; soft drinks 68,609 hectolitres[4]; beer 41,690 hectolitres[4]; shoes 111,000 pairs[4]; cigarettes 114,928 cartons[4]. Construction: n.a. Energy production (consumption): electricity (kW-hr; 1997) 391,000,000 (391,000,000); coal, none (n.a.); crude petroleum, none (n.a.); petroleum products (metric tons; 1997) none (154,000); natural gas, none (n.a.).
Gross national product (at current market prices; 1999): U.S.$2,577,000,000 (U.S.$240 per capita).

Structure of gross domestic product and labour force

	1999 in value CFAF '000,000	1999 % of total value	1987 labour force	1987 % of labour force
Agriculture	393,100	43.8	2,802,722	82.2
Mining	51,400	5.8	1,524	—
Manufacturing	71,500	8.0	186,243	5.5
Construction	42,400	4.7	13,065	0.4
Public utilities			3,157	0.1
Transp. and commun.	48,100	5.4	6,174	0.2
Trade	133,700	14.9	158,892	4.7
Finance			320	—
Pub. admin., defense	53,700	6.0	158,704	4.6
Services	51,400	5.7	...	...
Other	51,400[5]	5.7[5]	78,470	2.3
TOTAL	896,700	100.0	3,409,271	100.0

Household income and expenditure. Average household size (1997) 5.0; average annual income per household: n.a.; sources of income: n.a.; expenditure (1986–87)[6]: food 54.6%, clothing 14.2%, transportation and communications 11.9%, housing and energy 8.7%, household durable goods 4.2%.
Land use (1994): forested 5.7%; meadows and pastures 24.6%; forest 9.7%; agricultural and under permanent cultivation 2.1%; other 63.6%.

Foreign trade[7]

Balance of trade (current prices)

	1994	1995	1996	1997	1998	1999
CFAF '000,000,000	−162.5	−154.4	−173.3	−110.5	−117.5	−142.0
% of total	30.3%	25.9%	28.2%	14.4%	15.1%	16.9%

Imports (1999): CFAF 490,600,000,000 (machinery, appliances, and transport equipment 31.1%; petroleum products 14.3%; food products 13.9%; construction products 10.5%; chemicals 10.2%). *Major import sources:* African countries 49.9%, of which Côte d'Ivoire 18.9%; France 18.7%; China 4.4%; Germany 2.7%; Belgium-Luxembourg 2.4%.
Exports (1999): CFAF 348,600,000,000 (raw cotton and cotton products 43.9%; gold 40.8%; live animals 9.4%). *Major export destinations:* Western Europe, U.S., and other non-Asian industrial countries 52.7%; Asian countries 33.9%; African countries 8.4%.

Transport and communications

Transport. Railroads (1995): route length 398 mi, 641 km; passenger-mi 577,600,000, passenger-km 929,600,000; short ton-mi cargo 337,280,000, metric ton-km cargo 542,800,000. Roads (1996): total length 9,383 mi, 15,100 km (paved 12%). Vehicles (1996): passenger cars 26,190; trucks and buses 18,240. Merchant marine: vessels (100 gross tons and over) none. Air transport (1997)[8]: passenger-mi 150,400,000, passenger-km 242,000,000; short ton-mi cargo 23,600,000, metric ton-km cargo 38,000,000; airports (1999) with scheduled flights 9.

Communications

Medium	date	unit	number	units per 1,000 persons
Daily newspapers	1997	circulation	45,000	4.6
Radio	1997	receivers	1,600,000	163
Television	1999	receivers	130,000	12
Telephones	1999	main lines	26,758	2.5
Cellular phones	1999	subscribers	4,473	0.4
Personal computers	1999	units	11,000	1.1
Internet	1999	users	1,000	0.1

Education and health

Educational attainment (1987). Percentage of population age 6 and over having: no formal schooling 86.0%; primary education 12.5%; secondary 1.2%; postsecondary and higher 0.3%. *Literacy* (1995): Percentage of total population age 15 and over literate 1,760,000 (31.0%); males literate 1,084,000 (39.4%); females literate 676,000 (23.1%).

Education (1997–98)

	schools	teachers	students	student/ teacher ratio
Primary (age 6–14)	2,511	10,853	862,875	79.5
Secondary (age 15–17)	307[9]	4,549[10]	166,372	...
Vocational	...	21,737	7,200	3.0
Higher	7	796[11]	13,847	17.4

Health: physicians (1993) 483 (1 per 18,376 persons); hospital beds (1987) 3,430 (1 per 2,253 persons); infant mortality rate per 1,000 live births (2001) 121.4.
Food (1999): daily per capita caloric intake 2,314 (vegetable products 91%, animal products 9%); 90% of FAO recommended minimum requirement.

Military

Total active duty personnel (1999): 7,350 (army 93.9%, navy 0.7%, air force 5.4%). *Military expenditure as percentage of GNP* (1997): 1.7% (world 2.6%); per capita expenditure U.S.$4.

[1]Multiparty legislative elections held in March 1997 were annulled by the constitutional court; new elections were held in July and August. [2]Kidal region was created in May 1991 from the northern half of Gao region as a concession to Tuareg separatists. Separate data not available. [3]1997. [4]1995. [5]Import taxes. [6]Weights of consumer price index components. [7]Imports are in c.i.f. [8]Represents 1/11 of the traffic of Air Afrique, which is operated by 11 West African states. [9]1991–92. [10]1995–96. [11]1996–97.

Internet resources for further information:
- **Embassy of Mali (Washington, D.C.) http://www.maliembassy-usa.org**
- **Investir en Zone Franc http://www.izf.net/izf/Index.htm**

Malta

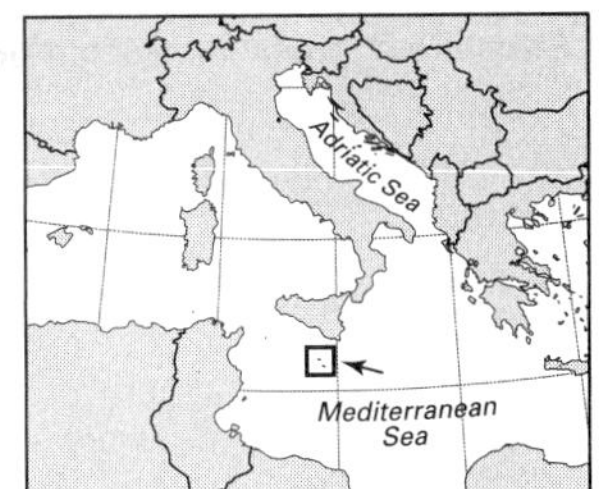

Official name: Repubblikka ta' Malta (Maltese); Republic of Malta (English).
Form of government: unitary multiparty republic with one legislative house (House of Representatives [65]).
Chief of state: President.
Head of government: Prime Minister.
Capital: Valletta.
Official languages: Maltese; English.
Official religion: Roman Catholicism.
Monetary unit: 1 Maltese lira (Lm) = 100 cents = 1,000 mils; valuation[1] (Sept. 28, 2001) 1 U.S.$ = Lm 0.44; 1 £ = Lm 0.65.

Area and population

Census regions[3]	area sq mi	area sq km	population 1999[2] census
Gozo and Comino	27	70	29,180
Inner Harbour	6	15	87,413
Northern	30	78	45,043
Outer Harbour	12	32	113,119
South Eastern	20	53	51,484
Western	27	69	52,279
TOTAL	122	316[4]	378,518

Demography

Population (2001): 381,000.
Density (2001): persons per sq mi 3,123, persons per sq km 1,206.
Urban-rural (2000): urban 90.5%; rural 9.5%.
Sex distribution (2000): male 49.49%; female 50.51%.
Age breakdown (2000): under 15, 20.3%; 15–29, 21.6%; 30–44, 20.8%; 45–59, 20.4%; 60–74, 12.0%; 75 and over, 4.9%.
Population projection: (2010) 404,000; (2020) 427,000.
Ethnic composition (by nationality; 2000): Maltese 93.8%; British 2.1%; Arab 2.0%; other 2.1%.
Religious affiliation (1996): Roman Catholic 93.4%; other 6.6%.
Major cities (1999[2]): Birkirkara 21,350; Qormi 17,881; Sliema 12,308; Hamrun 11,014; Valletta 7,100.

Vital statistics

Birth rate per 1,000 population (2000): 12.7 (world avg. 22.5); (1998) legitimate 91.8%; illegitimate 8.2%.
Death rate per 1,000 population (2000): 7.7 (world avg. 9.0).
Natural increase rate per 1,000 population (2000): 5.0 (world avg. 13.5).
Total fertility rate (avg. births per childbearing woman; 2000): 1.9.
Marriage rate per 1,000 population (1998): 6.3.
Divorce rate per 1,000 population: n.a.
Life expectancy at birth (2000): male 75.5 years; female 80.6 years.
Major causes of death per 100,000 population (1998): diseases of the circulatory system 353.1; malignant neoplasms 191.2; diseases of the respiratory system 79.7; endocrine and metabolic diseases of the blood 33.1; accidents, poisoning, and violence 26.5; diseases of the digestive system 23.6.

National economy

Budget (1999). Revenue: Lm 637,852,000 (direct taxes 42.7%; indirect taxes 32.6%; nontax revenue 23.1%; foreign grants 1.5%). Expenditures: Lm 690,965,000 (recurrent expenditures 84.6%, of which social security 27.2%[5], education 10.4%[5], health 10.0%[5], debt service 4.9%[5], defense 4.2%[5]; capital expenditure 15.4%).
Public debt (1998): U.S.$2,224,400,000.
Production (metric tons except where noted). Agriculture, forestry, fishing (1999): vegetables 58,850 (of which tomatoes 32,800, cabbage 3,500, melons 2,600, garlic 2,000, onions 1,200), potatoes 32,000, grapes 10,000, barley 2,000; livestock (number of live animals; 1999) 69,000 pigs, 21,000 cattle, 16,000 sheep, 9,050 goats; fish catch 979,432. Quarrying (value of production in Lm; 1996): 6,898,000. Manufacturing (value of sales in Lm; 1994–95): machinery and transport equipment 402,993,000; food 103,733,000; textiles and wearing apparel 80,813,000; paper and printing 40,610,000; chemicals 35,151,000. Construction (buildings completed; 1996): residential 3,360[6]; nonresidential 1,859. Energy production (consumption): electricity (kW-hr; 1996) 1,514,000,000 (1,514,000,000); coal (metric tons; 1996) none (310,000); crude petroleum, none (n.a.); petroleum products (metric tons; 1996) none (342,000).
Population economically active (1998): total 144,824; activity rate of total population 38.4% (participation rates: ages 15–64 [1985] 45.9%; female 27.6%; unemployed 5.1%).

Price and earnings indexes (1995 = 100)

	1994	1995	1996	1997	1998	1999	2000
Consumer price index	96.2	100.0	102.5	105.7	108.2	110.5	113.1
Average weekly earnings	96.8	100.0	104.3	...	...	...	...

Household income and expenditure. Average household size (1985) 3.3; average annual income per household (1982) Lm 4,736 (U.S.$11,399); sources of income (1993): wages and salaries 63.8%, professional and unincorporated enterprises 19.3%, rents, dividends, and interest 16.9%; expenditure (1993): food and beverages 27.9%, transportation and communications 15.7%, household furnishings and operations 9.5%, recreation, entertainment, and education 7.2%, clothing and footwear 6.9%, housing 5.5%, health 3.3%, tobacco 2.6%.

Tourism (1999): receipts from visitors U.S.$675,000,000; expenditures by nationals abroad U.S.$201,000,000.
Gross domestic product (1999): U.S.$3,492,000,000 (U.S.$9,210 per capita).

Structure of gross domestic product and labour force

	1998 in value Lm '000	% of total value	labour force	% of labour force
Agriculture	32,605	2.7	2,522	1.7
Manufacturing	271,334	22.7	33,924	23.4
Mining	36,073	3.0		
Construction			5,440	3.8
Public utilities	7	7	2,004	1.4
Transp. and commun.	75,819	6.3	10,199	7.0
Trade	136,096	11.4	24,256[8]	16.7[8]
Finance	96,941	8.1	5,370	3.7
Pub. admin., defense	279,887[7]	23.4[7]	32,151	22.2
Services	134,308	11.2	16,630	11.5
Other	134,869	11.3	12,328[9]	8.5[9]
TOTAL	1,197,932	100.0[4]	144,824	100.0[4]

Land use (1994): agricultural and under permanent cultivation 40.6%; other (infertile clay soil with underlying limestone) 59.4%.

Foreign trade[10]

Balance of trade (current prices)

	1993	1994	1995	1996	1997	1998	1999
Lm '000,000	–312.6	–326.4	–362.8	–383.7	–352.5	–335.1	–348.6
% of total	23.2%	21.6%	21.2%	23.5%	21.8%	19.2%	18.0%

Imports (1998): Lm 1,034,994,000 (machinery and transport equipment 50.3%, manufactured and semimanufactured goods 24.8%, food 9.3%, chemicals 7.7%, mineral fuels 3.8%). *Major import sources:* Italy 19.3%; France 17.8%; U.K. 12.4%; Germany 10.5%; U.S. 8.9%.
Exports (1998): Lm 703,442,000 (machinery and transport equipment 64.6%, manufactured 27.7%, food and live animals 2.0%). *Major export destinations:* France 20.5%; U.S. 18.0%; Singapore 14.3%; Germany 12.8%; U.K. 7.8%; Italy 4.7%.

Transport and communications

Transport. Railroads: none. Roads (1997): total length 1,219 mi, 1,961 km (paved 94%). Vehicles (1998): passenger cars 185,247; trucks and buses 49,520. Merchant marine (1992): vessels (100 gross tons and over) 889; total deadweight tonnage 17,073,207. Air transport (1998): passenger-mi 1,172,982,000, passenger-km 1,887,736,000; short ton-mi cargo 7,689,800; metric ton-km cargo 11,227,000; airports (1999) with scheduled flights 1.

Communications

Medium	date	unit	number	units per 1,000 persons
Daily newspapers	1996	circulation	54,000	145
Radio	1997	receivers	255,000	680
Television	1999	receivers	212,000	549
Telephones	1999	main lines	198,000	513
Cellular telephones	1999	subscribers	38,000	98
Personal computers	1998	units	100,000	260
Internet	1999	users	30,000	77

Education and health

Educational attainment (1967). Percentage of economically active population having: no formal schooling 10.8%; primary education 60.4%; lower secondary 3.4%; upper secondary 17.6%; technical secondary 3.9%; post-secondary and higher 3.9%. *Literacy* (2000): total population age 15 and over literate 279,000 (92.1%); males literate 138,000 (91.4%); females literate 141,000 (92.8%).

Education (1995–96)

	schools	teachers	students	student/ teacher ratio
Primary (age 5–10)	111	1,990	35,479	17.8
Secondary (age 11–17)	59	2,679	29,907	20.9
Voc., teacher tr.	22	541	4,539	8.4
Higher[11]	1	470	5,805	12.3

Health (1996): physicians 925 (1 per 403 persons); hospital beds 2,140 (1 per 174 persons); infant mortality rate per 1,000 live births (2000) 5.9.
Food (1999): daily per capita caloric intake 3,482 (vegetable products 72%, animal products 28%); 139% of FAO recommended minimum requirement.

Military

Total active duty personnel (2000): 2,140 (army 100%). *Military expenditure as percentage of GNP* (1997): 0.9% (world 2.6%); per capita expenditure U.S.$81.

[1]The Maltese lira is tied to the currencies of several principal trading partners. [2]January 1. [3]Actual local administration in 2001 was based on 68 local councils. [4]Detail does not add to total given because of rounding. [5]1997. [6]Dwellings completed. [7]Pub. admin., defense includes Public utilities. [8]Includes hotels and catering. [9]Includes 7,437 unemployed. [10]Import figures are f.o.b. in balance of trade and c.i.f. for commodities and trading partners. [11]1994–95.

Internet resources for further information:
- **Central Office of Statistics http://www.magnet.mt/info/general.html**

Marshall Islands

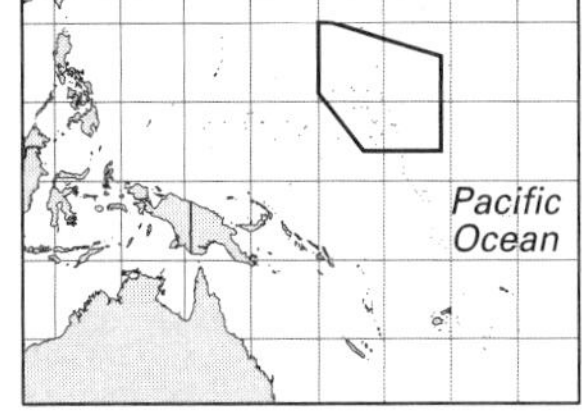

Official name: Majōl (Marshallese); Republic of the Marshall Islands (English).
Form of government: unitary republic with two legislative houses (Council of Iroij [12][1]; Nitijela [33]).
Head of state and government: President.
Capital: Majuro.
Official languages: Marshallese (Kajin-Majōl); English.
Official religion: none.
Monetary unit: 1 U.S. dollar (U.S.$) = 100 cents; valuation (Sept. 28, 2001) 1 U.S.$ = £0.68.

Area and population

Atolls/Islands	area sq mi	area sq km	population 1999 census[2]
Ailinglaplap	5.67	14.68	1,959
Ailuk	2.07	5.36	...
Arno	5.00	12.95	2,069
Aur	2.17	5.62	...
Bikini	2.32	6.01	...
Ebon	2.22	5.75	902
Enewetak	2.26	5.85	...
Jabat	0.22	0.57	...
Jaluit	4.38	11.34	1,609
Kili	0.36	0.93	...
Kwajalein	6.33	16.39	10,902
Lae	0.56	1.45	...
Lib	0.36	0.93	...
Likiep	3.96	10.26	...
Majuro	3.75	9.71	23,676
Maloelap	3.75	9.71	...
Mejit	0.72	1.86	...
Mili	6.15	15.93	1,032
Namorik	1.07	2.77	...
Namu	2.42	6.27	903
Rongelap	3.07	7.95	...
Ujae	0.72	1.86	...
Ujelang	0.67	1.74	...
Utrik	0.94	2.43	...
Wotho	1.67	4.32	...
Wotje	3.16	8.18	866
Other atolls	4.10	10.62	...
TOTAL	70.07	181.48[3]	50,840

Demography

Population (2001): 52,300.
Density (2001): persons per sq mi 746.4, persons per sq km 288.2.
Urban-rural (1999): urban 71.0%; rural 29.0%.
Sex distribution (2000): male 42.45%; female 57.55%.
Age breakdown (1997): under 15, 50.2%; 15–29, 26.0%; 30–44, 13.9%; 45–59, 6.5%; 60–74, 2.6%; 75 and over, 0.8%.
Population projection: (2010) 59,600; (2020) 68,800.
Doubling time: 19 years.
Ethnic composition (nationality; 2000): Marshallese 88.5%; U.S. white 6.5%; other Pacific islanders and East Asians 5.0%.
Religious affiliation (1995): Protestant 62.8%; Roman Catholic 7.1%; Mormon 3.1%; Jehovah's Witness 1.0%; other (mostly nonreligious) 26.0%.
Major cities: Majuro (1999) 23,676; Ebeye (1988) 8,324.

Vital statistics

Birth rate per 1,000 population (2000): 41.8 (world avg. 22.5).
Death rate per 1,000 population (2000): 4.9 (world avg. 9.0).
Natural increase rate per 1,000 population (2000): 36.9 (world avg. 13.5).
Total fertility rate (avg. births per childbearing woman; 2000): 6.6.
Life expectancy at birth (2000): male 63.7 years; female 67.4 years.
Major causes of death per 100,000 population (1990–93)[4]: infectious and parasitic diseases 169.9; circulatory diseases 155.1; respiratory diseases 105.1; malignant neoplasms (cancers) 68.4; digestive diseases 63.3; accidents, injuries, and violence 36.7.

National economy

Budget (1997–98). Revenue: U.S.$61,400,000 (U.S. government grants 59.7%, income tax 12.7%, import tax 10.7%, value-added and excise taxes 4.4%, fishing rights 2.9%, fees and charges 2.1%). Expenditures: U.S.$50,900,000 (wages and salaries 33.4%, goods and services 32.4%, capital expenditures 14.3%, interest payments 10.8%, subsidies 7.1%).
Production (metric tons except as noted). Agriculture, forestry, fishing (1997): coconuts 140,000, copra 18,000, cassava 12,000, sweet potatoes 3,000, bananas 2,000; livestock (number of live animals) 32,000 pigs, 14,000 cattle; roundwood, n.a.; fish catch (1998) 400. Mining and quarrying: high-grade phosphate mining on Ailinglaplap Atoll, quarrying of sand and aggregate for local construction only. Manufacturing (1995): copra 7,728; coconut oil and processed (chilled or frozen) fish are important products; the manufacture of handicrafts and personal items (clothing, mats, boats, etc.) by individuals is also significant. Construction (1994): value added U.S.$9,300,000. Energy production (consumption): electricity (kW-hr; 1994) 57,891,000 (57,891,000); coal, none (n.a.); gasoline, oil, and lubricants (barrels; 1988)[5] n.a. (84,588).
Public debt (external, outstanding; 1996–97): U.S.$124,900,000.
Gross national product (at current market prices; 1999): U.S.$99,000,000 (U.S.$1,950 per capita).

Structure of gross domestic product and labour force

	1996–97 in value U.S.$'000	1996–97 % of total value	1988 labour force	1988 % of labour force
Agriculture	14,400	14.8	2,150	18.7
Mining	300	0.3	2	—
Manufacturing	2,200	2.3	945	8.2
Public utilities	2,400	2.5	82	0.7
Construction	6,600	6.8	1,076	9.4
Transp. and commun.	6,400	6.6	537	4.7
Trade, restaurants, hotels	17,300	17.8	1,394	12.1
Finance, insurance, real estate	14,700	15.2	833	7.3
Public administration	12,100	12.5	3,035	26.4
Services	17,200	17.7		
Other	3,400[6]	3.5[6]	1,434[7]	12.5[7]
TOTAL	97,000	100.0	11,488	100.0

Land use (1989)[8]: forested 22.5%; meadows and pastures 13.5%; agricultural and under permanent cultivation 33.1%; other 30.9%.
Household income and expenditure. Average household size (1988) 8.7; income per household (1979) U.S.$3,366; sources of income: n.a.; expenditure (1982): food 57.7%, housing 15.6%, clothing 12.0%, personal effects and other 14.7%.
Population economically active (1988): total 11,488; activity rate of total population 26.5% (participation rates: over age 14, 54.1%; female 30.1%; unemployed 12.5%).

Price and earnings indexes (1995 = 100)

	1993	1994	1995	1996	1997
Consumer price index	87.4	92.4	100.0	109.6	114.9
Earnings index	...	...	...	...	...

Tourism (1999): receipts from visitors U.S.$4,000,000; expenditures by nationals abroad, n.a.

Foreign trade[9]

Balance of trade (current prices)

	1992	1993	1994	1995	1996	1997
U.S.$'000,000	–52.6	–53.4	–48.2	–52.0	–53.6	–48.3
% of total	74.1%	77.7%	52.1%	53.0%	58.6%	65.6%

Imports (1997): U.S.$60,995,000 (mineral fuels and lubricants 23.4%, food, beverages, and tobacco 22.8%, machinery and transport equipment 9.5%, manufactured goods 7.4%, chemical products 6.6%). *Major import sources:* U.S. 47.2%; Guam 4.8%; Australia 4.0%; Singapore 3.4%; Japan 3.3%.
Exports (1997): U.S.$12,665,000 (chilled fish 78.2%, frozen fish 10.7%, crude coconut oil 9.6%). *Major export destinations:* U.S. *c.* 80.0%; other *c.* 20.0%.

Transport and communications

Transport. Vehicles (1995): passenger cars 1,374; trucks and buses 262. Merchant marine (1992): vessels (100 gross tons and over) 35; total deadweight tonnage 4,182,356. Air transport (1996): passenger-km 28,000,000; metric ton-km cargo 5,000; airports (1997) with scheduled flights 25.

Communications

Medium	date	unit	number	units per 1,000 persons
Telephones	1998	main lines	3,744	62
Cellular telephones	1998	subscribers	345	5.8

Education and health

Educational attainment (1988). Percentage of population age 25 and over having: no grade completed 5.1%; elementary education 43.2%; secondary 39.7%; higher 11.4%; not stated 0.6%. *Literacy* (latest): total population age 15 and over literate 19,377 (91.2%); males literate 9,993 (92.4%); females literate 9,384 (90.0%).

Education (1994–95)

	schools	teachers	students	student/teacher ratio
Primary (age 6–14)	103	669	13,355	20.0
Secondary (age 15–18)	12	144	2,400	16.7
Voc., teacher tr.	...	...	...	...
Higher	...	...	...	...

Health (1997): physicians 34 (1 per 1,785 persons); hospital beds 129 (1 per 470 persons); infant mortality rate per 1,000 live births (2000) 41.0.

Military

Under the 1984 Compact of Free Association, the United States provides for the defense of the Republic of the Marshall Islands.

[1]Council of Iroij is an advisory body only. [2]Partial breakdown of final census results. [3]Detail does not add to total given because of rounding. [4]Registered deaths only. [5]Import only. [6]Import duties less imputed bank service charges. [7]Includes 1,432 unemployed. [8]Data are for the former Trust Territory of the Pacific Islands. [9]Imports c.i.f. in balance of trade table.

Internet resources for further information:
- **RMI Online, Internet Guide to the Republic of the Marshall Islands http://www.rmiembassyus.org**

Martinique

Official name: Département de la Martinique (Department of Martinique).
Political status: overseas department (France) with two legislative houses (General Council [45]; Regional Council [41]).
Chief of state: President of France.
Heads of government: Prefect (for France); President of the General Council (for Martinique); President of the Regional Council (for Martinique).
Capital: Fort-de-France.
Official language: French.
Official religion: none.
Monetary unit: 1 French franc (F) = 100 centimes; valuation (Sept. 28, 2001) 1 U.S.$ = F 7.20; 1 £ = F 10.59.

Area and population

		area		population
				1999
Arrondissements	Capitals	sq mi	sq km	census
Fort-de-France	Fort-de-France	66	171	166,139
Le Marin	Le Marin	158	409	106,818
La Trinité	La Trinité	131	338	85,006
Saint-Pierre	Saint-Pierre	81	210	23,464
TOTAL		436	1,128	381,427

Demography

Population (2001): 388,000.
Density (2001): persons per sq mi 889.9, persons per sq km 344.0.
Urban-rural (1999): urban 94.6%; rural 5.4%.
Sex distribution (1999): male 47.44%; female 52.56%.
Age breakdown (1999): under 15, 22.0%; 15–29, 21.0%; 30–44, 24.4%; 45–59, 16.0%; 60–74, 11.1%; 75 and over, 5.5%.
Population projection: (2010) 415,000; (2020) 436,000.
Doubling time: 72 years.
Ethnic composition (2000): mixed race (black/white/Asian) 93.4%; French (metropolitan and Martinique white) 3.0%; East Indian 1.9%; other 1.7%.
Religious affiliation (1995): Roman Catholic 86.5%; Protestant 8.0% (mostly Seventh-day Adventist); Jehovah's Witness 1.6%, other 3.9%, including Hindu, syncretist, and nonreligious.
Major communes (1999): Fort-de-France 94,049; Le Lamentin 35,460; Le Robert 21,201; Schoelcher 20,845; Sainte-Marie 20,058.

Vital statistics

Birth rate per 1,000 population (2000): 16.1 (world avg. 22.5); (1992) legitimate 34.1%; illegitimate 65.9%.
Death rate per 1,000 population (2000): 6.4 (world avg. 9.0).
Natural increase rate per 1,000 population (2000): 9.7 (world avg. 13.5).
Total fertility rate (avg. births per childbearing woman; 2000): 1.8.
Marriage rate per 1,000 population (1997): 4.1.
Divorce rate per 1,000 population (1996): 1.1.
Life expectancy at birth (2000): male 79.0 years; female 77.5 years.
Major causes of death per 100,000 population (1996): diseases of the circulatory system 206.8; malignant neoplasms (cancers) 150.3; accidents, poisoning, and violence 47.2; diseases of the respiratory system 36.3; endocrine and metabolic disorders 27.8; diseases of the digestive system 27.2.

National economy

Budget (1994). Revenue: F 1,816,000,000 (general receipts from French central government and local administrative bodies 45.0%; tax receipts 34.0%, of which indirect taxes 19.5%, direct taxes 14.5%). Expenditures: F 1,816,000,000 (health and social assistance 42.0%; wages and salaries 16.7%; other administrative services 7.2%; debt amortization 5.0%).
Public debt (1994): U.S.$186,700,000.
Production (metric tons except as noted). Agriculture, forestry, fishing (1999): bananas 321,454, sugarcane 188,827, pineapples 20,200, plantains 13,000, roots and tubers 11,750, lettuce 7,800, yams 4,700, tomatoes 4,300, cucumbers and gherkins 3,200, melons 2,900, coconuts 1,137, sweet potatoes 970; livestock (number of live animals) 42,000 sheep, 33,000 pigs, 30,000 cattle, 21,800 goats; roundwood (1998) 12,000 cu m; fish catch (1998) 5,500. Mining and quarrying (1996): pumice 130,000; sand and gravel for local construction. Manufacturing (1998): cement 225,000; processed pineapples 20,210; sugar 6,543; rum 68,716 hectolitres; other products include clothing, fabricated metals, and yawls and sails. Construction (buildings authorized; 1994): residential permits 6,893; nonresidential 113,279 sq m. Energy production (consumption): electricity (kW-hr; 1996) 906,000,000 (906,000,000); coal, none (none); crude petroleum (barrels; 1996) none (5,827,000); petroleum products (metric tons; 1996) 738,000 (566,000); natural gas, none (none).
Household income and expenditure. Average household size (1997) 3.0; income per household (1989) F 147,150 (U.S.$24,525); sources of income (1989): wages and salaries 80%, other 20%; expenditure (1993): food and beverages 32.1%, transportation and communications 20.7%, housing and energy 10.6%, household durable goods 9.4%, clothing and footwear 8.0%, education and recreation 5.4%, health care 5.2%, other 8.6%.
Tourism (1999): receipts from visitors U.S.$404,000,000; expenditures by nationals abroad, n.a.; number of visitors 904,000.

Gross national product (1998): U.S.$4,888,000,000 (U.S.$12,875 per capita).

Structure of gross domestic product and labour force

	1992		1990	
	in value F '000,000	% of total value	labour force	% of labour force
Agriculture, fishing	1,106.3	5.0	8,445	5.1
Mining, manufacturing	1,770.6	8.0	9,706	5.9
Construction	1,145.3	5.2	9,298	5.6
Public utilities	483.6	2.2		
Transp. and commun.	1,427.6	6.5	6,673	4.0
Trade, restaurants, hotels	4,022.1	18.2	13,965	8.5
Finance, real estate, insurance	2,590.1	11.7	26,489	16.1
Pub. admin., defense	5,416.0	24.5	35,541	21.6
Services	3,906.9	17.7		
Other	224.9[1]	1.0[1]	54,760[2]	33.2[2]
TOTAL	22,093.4	100.0	164,877	100.0

Population economically active (1998): total 165,900; activity rate of total population 41.6% (participation rates: ages 15–64, 71.2%; [1997] female 32.6%; unemployed [1998] 28.2%).

Price and earnings indexes (1995 = 100)

	1994	1995	1996	1997	1998	1999	2000
Consumer price index[3]	98.4	100.0	101.9	102.8	103.0	103.7	105.7
Monthly earnings index[4]	98.0	100.0	100.9	104.9	106.3	106.3	106.8

Land use (1994): forested 45.3%; meadows and pastures 13.2%; agricultural and under permanent cultivation 17.0%; other 24.5%.

Foreign trade[5]

Balance of trade (current prices)

	1995	1996	1997	1998	1999	2000
F '000,000	–8,604	–8,987	–8,676	–8,305	–9,640	–9,436
% of total	78.2%	80.5%	78.6%	71.0%	75.5%	71.0%

Imports (1998): F 9,997,000,000 (1996; consumer goods 23.9%, goods for intermediate consumption [inputs to the manufacturing process changed or destroyed in the final product] 15.9%, automobiles 15.0%, professional equipment 15.2%, energy products 8.3%). *Major import sources* (1996): France 62.3%; Italy 4.1%; Venezuela 3.8%; Germany 3.3%; United States 3.0%; U.K. 2.0%; Guadeloupe 0.9%.
Exports (1998): F 1,692,000,000 (1996; bananas 36.9%, refined petroleum 19.9%, rum 11.3%, yachts and boats 7.1%). *Major export destinations* (1996): France 51.7%; Guadeloupe 21.0%; U.K. 7.2%; French Guiana 3.8%.

Transport and communications

Transport. Railroads: none. Roads (1994): total length 1,299 mi, 2,091 km (paved [1988] 75%). Vehicles (1993): passenger cars 108,300; trucks and buses 32,200. Merchant marine (1992): vessels (100 gross tons and over) 6; total deadweight tonnage 1,121. Air transport (1997): passenger arrivals and departures 1,552,000; cargo handled 14,400 metric tons; airports (1998) with scheduled flights 1.

Communications

Medium	date	unit	number	units per 1,000 persons
Daily newspapers	1996	circulation	32,000	83
Radio	1997	receivers	82,000	213
Television	1999	receivers	66,000	168
Telephones	1999	main lines	172,192	443
Cellular telephones	1999	subscribers	102,000	206
Personal computers	1999	units	36,000	93

Education and health

Educational attainment (1990). Percentage of population age 25 and over having: incomplete primary, or no declaration 54.3%; primary education 18.0%; secondary 20.0%; higher 7.7%. *Literacy* (1982): total population age 15 and over literate 206,807 (92.5%); males literate 97,538 (91.8%); females literate 109,269 (93.2%).

Education (1997)

	schools	teachers	students	student/ teacher ratio
Primary (age 6–11)	273	2,603	55,569	21.3
Secondary (age 12–18)[6]	76	2,888	36,605	12.7
Vocational[6]	...	896	11,101	12.4
Higher	1	99[7]	3,079	45.3[7]

Health (1998): physicians 780 (1 per 487 persons); hospital beds 2,907 (1 per 131 persons); infant mortality rate per 1,000 live births (2000) 8.0.
Food (1998): daily per capita caloric intake 2,865 (vegetable products 75%, animal products 25%); 118% of FAO recommended minimum requirement.

Military

Total active duty personnel (2000): 3,800 French troops.

[1]Import duties, value-added tax less imputed bank service charge. [2]Unemployed. [3]Figures are end-of-year. [4]Based on minimum-level wage of public employees. [5]Imports c.i.f.; exports f.o.b. [6]1995–96. [7]1993–94.

Internet resources for further information:
- **France Overseas**
  http://www.outre-mer.gouv.frdomtom/martinique/index.htm
- **Chambre de Commerce et d'Industrie de la Martinique**
  http://www.martinique.cci.fr

Mauritania

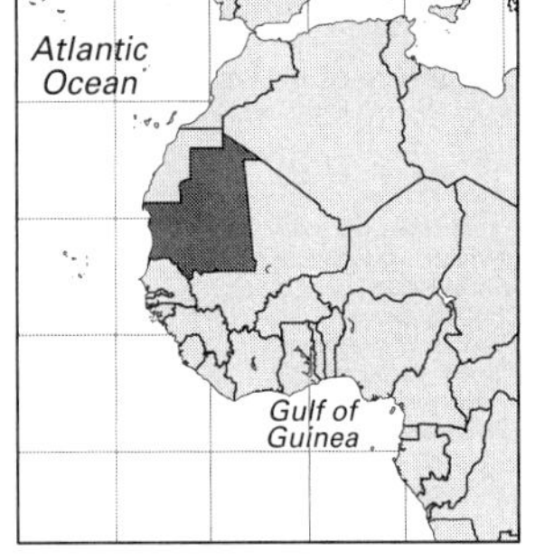

Official name: Al-Jumhūrīyah al-Islāmīyah al-Mūrītānīyah (Arabic) (Islamic Republic of Mauritania).
Form of government: unitary multiparty republic with two legislative houses (Senate [56]; National Assembly [81]).
Head of state and government: President assisted by the Prime Minister.
Capital: Nouakchott.
Official language: Arabic[1].
Official religion: Islam.
Monetary unit: 1 ouguiya (UM) = 5 khoums; valuation (Sept. 28, 2001) 1 U.S.$ = UM 256.12; 1 £ = UM 376.42.

Area and population

Regions	Capitals	area sq mi	area sq km	population 2000 census[2]
El-'Açâba	Kiffa	14,100	36,600	249,596
Adrar	Atar	83,100	215,300	60,847
Brakna	Aleg	13,000	33,800	240,167
Dakhlet Nouadhibou	Nouadhibou	8,600	22,300	75,976
Gorgol	Kaédi	5,300	13,600	248,980
Guidimaka	Sélibaby	4,000	10,300	186,697
Hodh ech-Chargui	Néma	70,600	182,700	275,288
Hodh el-Gharbi	'Ayoûn el-'Atroûs	20,600	53,400	219,167
Inchiri	Akjoujt	18,100	46,800	11,322
Tagant	Tidjikdja	36,800	95,200	61,984
Tiris Zemmour	Zouérate	97,600	252,900	53,586
Trarza	Rosso	26,200	67,800	252,664
Capital District				
Nouakchott	Nouakchott	400	1,000	611,883
TOTAL		398,000[3]	1,030,700	2,548,157

Demography

Population (2001): 2,591,000.
Density (2001): persons per sq mi 6.5, persons per sq km 2.5.
Urban-rural (1999): urban 56.5%; rural 43.5%.
Sex distribution (2000): male 48.68%; female 51.32%.
Age breakdown (2000): under 15, 46.2%; 15–29, 26.6%; 30–44, 15.6%; 45–59, 7.8%; 60–74, 3.3%; 75 and over, 0.5%.
Population projection: (2010) 3,243,000; (2020) 4,161,000.
Doubling time: 24 years.
Ethnic composition (1993)[4]: Moor 70% (of which about 40% "black" Moor [Ḥarāṭīn, or African Sudanic] and about 30% "white" Moor [Bidan, or Arab-Berber]); other black African 30% (mostly Wolof, Tukulor, Soninke, and Fulani).
Religious affiliation (2000): Sunnī Muslim 99.1%; traditional beliefs 0.5%; Christian 0.3%; other 0.1%.
Major cities (2000): Nouakchott 611,883; Nouadhibou 74,414; Kiffa (1999) 50,800; Kaédi (1992) 35,241; Rosso (1992) 30,000.

Vital statistics

Birth rate per 1,000 population (2000): 43.4 (world avg. 22.5).
Death rate per 1,000 population (2000): 14.0 (world avg. 9.0).
Natural increase rate per 1,000 population (2000): 29.4 (world avg. 13.5).
Total fertility rate (avg. births per childbearing woman; 2000): 6.3.
Life expectancy at birth (2000): male 48.7 years; female 52.9 years.

National economy

Budget (1997). Revenue: UM 44,800,000,000 (tax revenue 58.3%, of which taxes on goods and services 26.5%, import taxes 12.1%, income taxes 9.6%; nontax revenue 39.9%, of which fishing royalties and penalties 32.3%). Expenditures: UM 32,110,000,000 (wages and salaries 24.9%; interest on public debt 15.3%; defense 11.4%).
Land use (1994): forested 4.3%; meadows and pastures 38.3%; agricultural and under permanent cultivation 0.2%; desert 57.2%.
Production (metric tons except as noted). Agriculture, forestry, fishing (1999): rice 101,900, sorghum 74,800, dates 22,000, cow peas 22,000, pulses 12,000, millet 10,400; livestock (number of live animals) 6,200,000 sheep, 4,133,000 goats, 1,395,000 cattle, 1,185,000 camels; roundwood (1998) 15,000 cu m; fish catch (metric tons; 1997) 82,000, of which octopuses 23,500[5]. Mining and quarrying (gross weight; 1998): iron ore 11,411,000; gypsum 100,000. Manufacturing (1996): cow's milk 91,000[6]; goat's milk 77,000[6]; meat 58,200, of which fresh mutton and lamb 24,600, fresh beef and veal 10,200; hides and skins 4,600; cement, tiles, and bricks 5.9[7]; fabricated metal products 5.4[7]; paper and paper products 2.1[7]. Energy production (consumption): electricity (kW-hr; 1999) 226,700,000 ([1996] 153,000,000); coal (metric tons; 1996) none (6,000); crude petroleum (barrels; 1996) none (6,927,000); petroleum products (metric tons; 1996) 840,000 (927,000); natural gas, none (none).
Population economically active (1994): total 687,000; activity rate of total population 31.3% (participation rates: over age 10 [1991] 45.5%; female 22.9%).

Price and earnings indexes (1995 = 100)

	1995	1996	1997	1998	1999	2000	2001[8]
Consumer price index[9]	100.0	104.7	109.5	118.3	123.1	127.1	133.0
Hourly earnings index[10]	100.0	100.0	100.0	100.0	100.0	...	...

Household income and expenditure. Average household size (1996): 5.3; expenditure (1990): food and beverages 73.1%, clothing and footwear 8.1%, energy and water 7.7%, transportation and communications 2.0%.
Gross national product (1999): U.S.$1,001,000,000 (U.S.$390 per capita).

Structure of gross domestic product and labour force

	1997 in value UM '000,000	1997 % of total value	1988 labour force	1988 % of labour force
Agriculture, livestock	37,117	22.2	225,238	38.5
Mining	16,075	9.6	6,322	1.1
Manufacturing	16,447	9.9	5,630	1.0
Public utilities }	14,344	8.6	1,326	0.2
Construction }			12,291	2.1
Transp. and commun.	12,627	7.6	8,378	1.4
Trade and finance	25,511	15.3	73,451	12.5
Services	11,270	6.8 }	86,807	14.8
Pub. admin., defense	16,852	10.1 }		
Other	16,688[11]	10.0[11]	166,366[12]	28.4[12]
TOTAL	166,930[3]	100.0[3]	585,809	100.0

Public debt (external, outstanding; 1999): U.S.$2,138,000,000.
Tourism (1999): receipts U.S.$28,000,000; expenditures U.S.$55,000,000.

Foreign trade

Balance of trade (current prices)

	1993	1994	1995	1996	1997	1998
U.S.$'000,000	+2.6	+47.4	+183.8	+133.9	+1.6	+40.0
% of total	0.3%	6.3%	23.9%	16.2%	0.2%	5.9%

Imports (1997): U.S.$403,400,000 (imports for National Industrial and Mining Company 20.2%; petroleum products 13.6%; investment including food aid 10.0%; equipment and machinery 6.5%). *Major import sources:* France 25.5%; Spain 7.5%, Germany 6.7%, Belgium-Luxembourg 6.4%, Thailand 5.1%.
Exports (1997): U.S.$405,000,000 (iron ore 52.4%; fish 47.6%, of which cephalopods 28.3%). *Major export destinations:* Japan 23.3%; Italy 16.7%; France 13.9%; Spain 8.3%; Belgium-Luxembourg 7.1%.

Transport and communications

Transport. Railroads (1998): route length 437 mi, 704 km; passenger-km, negligible; (1997) metric ton-km cargo 2,340,000,000. Roads (1996): total length 4,760 mi, 7,660 km (paved 11%). Vehicles (1996): passenger cars 18,810; trucks and buses 10,450. Air transport (1998)[13]: passenger-km 258,263,000; metric ton-km cargo 13,524,000; airports (1997) with scheduled flights 9.

Communications

Medium	date	unit	number	units per 1,000 persons
Daily newspapers	1996	circulation	1,000	0.4
Radio	1997	receivers	360,000	147
Television	1999	receivers	247,000	100
Telephones	1999	main lines	16,525	6.7
Personal computers	1999	units	70,000	28
Internet	1999	users	12,500	5.1

Education and health

Educational attainment (1988). Percentage of population age 25 and over having: no formal schooling 60.8%; primary and incomplete secondary 34.1%; secondary 3.8%; higher 1.3%. *Literacy* (1995): percentage of total population age 15 and over literate 37.7%; males literate 49.6%; females literate 26.3%.

Education (1995–96)

	schools	teachers	students	student/ teacher ratio
Primary (age 6–11)[14]	2,392	6,225	312,671	50.2
Secondary (age 12–17)	...	1,865	49,221	26.4
Voc., teacher tr.[15]	...	202	2,544	12.6
Higher	...	270	8,496	31.5

Health: physicians (1994) *c.* 200 (1 per 11,085 persons); hospital beds (1988) 1,556 (1 per 1,217 persons); infant mortality rate per 1,000 live births (2000) 78.1.
Food (1999): daily per capita caloric intake 2,702 (vegetable products 85%, animal products 15%); 117% of FAO recommended minimum requirement.

Military

Total active duty personnel (2000): 15,650 (army 95.8%, navy 3.2%, air force 1.0%). *Military expenditure as percentage of GNP* (1997): 2.3% (world 2.6%); per capita expenditure U.S.$10.

[1]The 1991 constitution names Arabic as the official language and the following as national languages: Arabic, Fulani, Soninke, and Wolof. [2]Preliminary figures. [3]Detail does not add to total given because of rounding. [4]Estimated figures. [5]Fish catch (1996) including foreign fishing vessels equals 564,200 metric tons. [6]1994. [7]1993 value added of production in U.S.$'000,000. [8]May. [9]Nouakchott only. [10]Minimum wage. [11]Indirect taxes. [12]Mostly unemployed. [13]Data represent 1/11 of the total scheduled traffic of Air Afrique. [14]1996–97. [15]Excludes health-related programs.

Internet resources for further information:
- **Office National de la Statistique**
  http://www.ons.mr

Mauritius

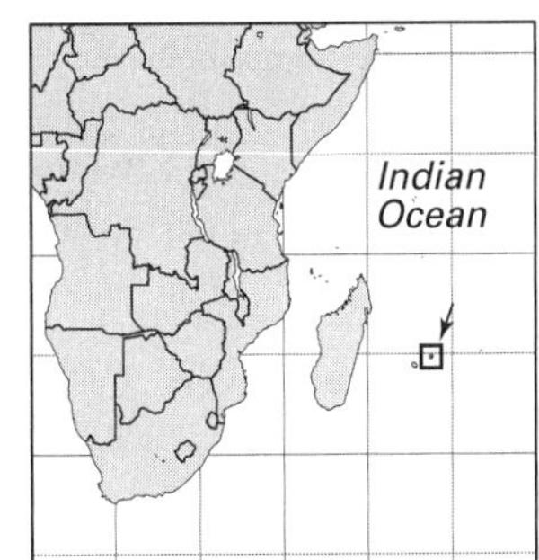

Official name: Republic of Mauritius.
Form of government: republic with one legislative house (National Assembly [70[1]]).
Chief of state: President.
Head of government: Prime Minister.
Capital: Port Louis.
Official language: English.
Official religion: none.
Monetary unit: 1 Mauritian rupee (Mau Re; plural Mau Rs) = 100 cents; valuation (Sept. 28, 2001) 1 U.S.$ = Mau Rs 29.72; 1 £ = Mau Rs 43.68.

Area and population

Islands Districts/Dependencies	Administrative Centres	area sq mi	area sq km	population 2000[2] estimate
Mauritius		720	1,865	1,145,196
Black River	Tamarin	100	259	54,557
Flacq	Centre de Flacq	115	298	125,074
Grand Port	Mahébourg	100	260	107,680
Moka	Moka	89	231	75,159
Pamplemousses	Pamplemousses	69	179	118,221
Plaines Wilhems	Rose Hill	78	203	360,804
Port Louis	Port Louis	17	43	138,531
Rivière du Rempart	Poudre d'Or	57	148	99,012
Savanne	Souillac	95	245	66,158
Mauritian dependencies				
Agalega[3] / Cargados Carajos Shoals (Saint Brandon)[3]	...	27	71	170
Rodrigues[4]	...	40	104	35,546
TOTAL		788[5]	2,040[5]	1,180,912

Demography

Population (2001): 1,195,000.
Density (2001): persons per sq mi 1,516.5, persons per sq km 585.8.
Urban-rural (2000): urban 41.3%; rural 58.7%.
Sex distribution (2000): male 49.47%; female 50.53%.
Age breakdown (2000): under 15, 25.7%; 15–29, 25.6%; 30–44, 24.7%; 45–59, 15.1%; 60–74, 6.8%; 75 and over, 2.1%.
Population projection: (2010) 1,281,000; (2020) 1,364,000.
Doubling time: 70 years.
Ethnic composition (2000): Indo-Pakistani 67.0%; Creole (mixed Caucasian, Indo-Pakistani, and African) 27.4%; Chinese 3.0%; other 2.6%.
Religious affiliation (1990): Hindu 50.6%; Roman Catholic 27.2%; Muslim 16.3%; Protestant 5.2%; Buddhist 0.3%; other 0.4%.
Major urban areas (2000[2]): Port Louis 148,506; Beau Bassin-Rose Hill 102,377; Vacoas-Phoenix 100,490; Curepipe 80,973; Quatre Bornes 78,096.

Vital statistics

Birth rate per 1,000 population (2000): 16.7[6] (world avg. 22.5).
Death rate per 1,000 population (2000): 6.8[6] (world avg. 9.0).
Natural increase rate per 1,000 population (2000): 9.9[6] (world avg. 13.5).
Total fertility rate (avg. births per childbearing woman; 2000): 2.0[6].
Marriage rate per 1,000 population (1998): 9.4[6].
Divorce rate per 1,000 population (1997): 0.8[6].
Life expectancy at birth (2000): male 67.0 years; female 75.0 years.
Major causes of death per 100,000 population (1998): diseases of the circulatory system 331.0; malignant neoplasms (cancers) 65.0; diseases of the respiratory system 63.0; homicide, suicide, and accidents 44.0.

National economy

Budget (1997–98). Revenue: Mau Rs 18,501,000,000 (tax revenue 84.8%, of which import duties 33.3%, taxes on goods and services 32.5%, income tax 13.0%; nontax revenue 14.0%; grants 1.2%). Expenditures: Mau Rs 21,872,000,000 (social security 19.4%, government services 18.8%, education 16.0%, interest on debt 16.0%, economic services 11.4%, health 8.1%).
Tourism (1999): receipts from visitors U.S.$545,000,000; expenditures by nationals abroad U.S.$187,000,000.
Public debt (external, outstanding; 1999): U.S.$1,155,000,000.
Gross national product (1999): U.S.$4,157,000,000 (U.S.$3,540 per capita).

Structure of gross domestic product and labour force

1998	in value Mau Rs '000,000	% of total value	labour force[7, 8]	% of labour force[7, 8]
Agriculture	7,150	7.5	30,400	10.4
Mining	135	0.1	200	0.1
Manufacturing	20,650	21.6	111,200	38.0
Construction	4,940	5.2	8,900	3.0
Public utilities	1,900	2.0	3,200	1.1
Transp. and commun.	9,315	9.7	15,100	5.1
Trade	14,795	15.4	27,800	9.5
Finance	13,585	14.2	13,700	4.7
Pub. admin., defense	8,900	9.3	61,800	21.1
Services	4,860	5.1	17,900	6.1
Other	9,520[9]	9.9[9]	2,600	0.9
TOTAL	95,750	100.0	292,800[8]	100.0[8]

Production (metric tons except as noted). Agriculture, forestry, fishing (1999): sugarcane 3,500,000, vegetables 23,000, potatoes 15,000, roots and tubers 11,750, tomatoes 11,000, bananas 9,400, onions 6,750, cabbages 6,300, pineapples 1,500, peanuts (groundnuts) 600; livestock (number of live animals) 93,000 goats, 27,000 cattle, 20,000 pigs, 7,200 sheep; roundwood (1998) 14,760 cu m; fish catch (1998) 13,734. Manufacturing (value added in Mau Rs '000; 1994): apparel 5,065,000; beverages and tobacco 1,995,800; food products 1,580,400; metal and metal products 882,900; textile yarn and fabrics 676,400; chemical products 505,600. Construction (1998): residential 1,204,000 sq m; nonresidential 276,000 sq m. Energy production (consumption): electricity (kW-hr; 1998) 1,364,800 (1,364,800); coal (metric tons; 1998) none (86,300); petroleum products (metric tons; 1998) none (576,000).
Population economically active (1998): total 507,000; activity rate of total population 43.8% (participation rates: ages 12 and over, 55.6%; female 37.1%; unemployed 5.7%).

Price and earnings indexes (1995 = 100)

	1994	1995	1996	1997	1998	1999	2000
Consumer price index	94.3	100.0	106.6	113.8	121.6	130.0	135.4
Earnings index	...	100.0	...	...	...	...	...

Household income and expenditure. Average household size (2000) 4.2; annual income per household (1996–97) Mau Rs 122,148 (U.S.$6,263); sources of income (1990): salaries and wages 48.4%, entrepreneurial income 41.2%, transfer payments 10.4%; expenditure (1996–97): food, beverages, and tobacco 45.2%, transportation and communications 14.2%, housing and household furnishings 13.2%, clothing and footwear 7.9%, recreation and education 6.0%, energy 4.4%, health 3.8%.
Land use (1994): forested 21.7%; meadows and pastures 3.4%; agricultural and under permanent cultivation 52.2%; other 22.7%.

Foreign trade

Balance of trade (current prices)

	1994	1995	1996	1997	1998	1999
Mau Rs '000,000	–10,451	–7,607	–9,501	–6,381	–10,177	–17,019
% of total	17.8%	12.4%	13.1%	7.5%	11.4%	17.8%

Imports (1998): Mau Rs 49,811,000,000 (manufactured goods classified chiefly by material 34.6%, machinery and transport equipment 22.8%, food 13.8%, chemicals 7.8%, mineral fuels and lubricants 6.3%, inedible crude materials excluding fuels 3.9%, animal and vegetable oils and fats 1.3%). *Major import sources:* France 11.1%; South Africa 10.5%; India 9.3%; Taiwan 5.2%; United Kingdom 5.2%; Japan 5.1%; Hong Kong 5.0%; Germany 4.1%.
Exports (1998): Mau Rs 39,634,000,000 (clothing 55.9%, sugar 21.3%, yarn 3.7%, chemicals 0.5%, other 18.6%). *Major export destinations:* United Kingdom 32.3%; France 17.1%; United States 16.3%; Germany 5.3%; Italy 3.5%.

Transport and communications

Transport. Railroads: none. Roads (1998): total length 1,184 mi, 1,905 km (paved 93%). Vehicles (1998): passenger cars 46,300; trucks and buses 12,100. Air transport (1998)[10]: passenger-km 3,858,695; metric ton-km cargo 819,432,000; airports (1998) with scheduled flights 1.

Communications

Medium	date	unit	number	units per 1,000 persons
Daily newspapers	1996	circulation	85,000	76
Radio	1997	receivers	420,000	371
Television	1999	receivers	265,000	230
Telephones	1999	main lines	257,000	223
Cellular telephones	1999	subscribers	102,000	89
Personal computers	1999	units	110,000	96
Internet	1999	users	55,000	48

Education and health

Educational attainment (1990). Percentage of population age 25 and over having: no formal education 18.3%; incomplete primary 42.6%; primary 6.1%; incomplete secondary 18.0%; secondary 13.1%; higher 1.9%. *Literacy* (1995): percentage of total population age 15 and over literate 82.9%; males literate 87.1%; females literate 78.8%.

Education (1998)

	schools	teachers	students	student/ teacher ratio
Primary (age 5–12)	285	5,065	130,505	25.7
Secondary (age 12–20)	133	4,820	94,364	19.6
Voc., teacher tr.	13	1,170[11]	5,496	...
Higher	3	461	6,429	13.9

Health (1998): physicians 1,033 (1 per 1,123 persons); hospital beds 3,826 (1 per 303 persons); infant mortality rate per 1,000 live births (2000) 17.7[6].
Food (1999): daily per capita caloric intake 2,972 (vegetable products 86%, animal products 14%); 131% of FAO recommended minimum requirement.

Military

Total active duty personnel: none; however, a special 1,500-person paramilitary force ensures internal security. *Military expenditure as percentage of GNP* (1997): 0.3% (world 2.6%); per capita expenditure U.S.$10.

[1]Includes 8 "bonus" seats allocated to minor parties. [2]January 1. [3]Administered directly from Port Louis. [4]Administered by resident commissioner assisted by local council. [5]Detail does not add to total given because of rounding. [6]Excludes Agalega and Cargados Carajos Shoals. [7]Employed persons in large establishments only. [8]Total labour force equals 507,000 and includes 223,000 employees of small businesses or self-employed and 29,000 unemployed. [9]Indirect taxes less imputed bank service charges. [10]Air Mauritius only. [11]1997.

Internet resources for further information:
- **Central Statistical Office http://ncb.intnet.mu/cso.htm**

Mayotte

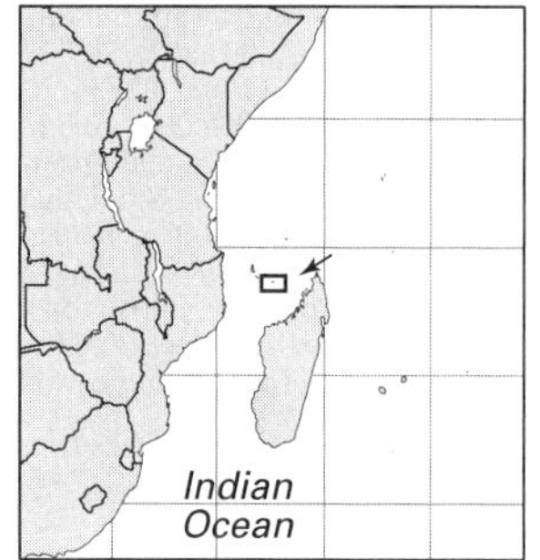

Official name: Collectivité Départementale de Mayotte (Departmental Collectivity of Mayotte)[1].
Political status: overseas dependency of France[2] with one legislative house (General Council [19]).
Chief of state: President of France.
Head of government: Prefect (for France); President of the General Council (for Mayotte).
Capitals: Dzaoudzi (French administrative); Mamoudzou (local administrative)[3].
Official language: French.
Official religion: none.
Monetary unit: 1 French (metropolitan) franc (F) = 100 centimes; valuation (Sept. 28, 2001) 1 U.S.$ = F 7.20; 1 £ = F 10.59.

Area and population

Islands / Communes	Capitals	area sq mi	area sq km	population 1997 census
Grande Terre				
Acoua	Acoua	4.9	12.6	4,446
Bandraboua	Bandraboua	12.5	32.4	6,406
Bandrele	Bandrele	14.1	36.5	4,958
Boueni	Boueni	5.4	14.1	4,673
Chiconi	Chiconi	3.2	8.3	6,042
Chirongui	Chirongui	10.9	28.3	5,144
Dembeni	Dembeni	15.0	38.8	5,554
Kani-Keli	Kani-Keli	7.9	20.5	4,155
Koungou	Koungou	11.0	28.4	10,165
Mamoudzou	Mamoudzou	16.2	41.9	32,733
M'tsangamouji	M'tsangamouji	8.4	21.8	5,098
M'tzamboro	M'tzamboro	5.3	13.7	6,335
Ouangani	Ouangani	7.3	19.0	4,838
Sada	Sada	4.3	11.2	7,434
Tsingoni	Tsingoni	13.4	34.8	5,507
Petite Terre				
Dzaoudzi-Labattoir	Dzaoudzi	2.6	6.7	10,792
Pamandzi	Pamandzi	1.7	4.3	7,040
TOTAL		144.1	373.2[4]	131,320

Demography

Population (2001): 159,000.
Density (2001): persons per sq mi 1,103.4, persons per sq km 426.0.
Urban-rural (1985): urban 59.7%; rural 40.3%.
Sex distribution (2000): male 52.45%; female 47.55%.
Age breakdown (2000): under 15, 46.6%; 15–29, 25.2%; 30–44, 18.1%; 45–59, 7.2%; 60–74, 2.4%; 75 and over, 0.5%.
Population projection: (2010) 225,000; (2020) 304,000.
Doubling time: 20 years.
Place of birth (1997): Mayotte 73.6%[5]; nearby islands of the Comoros 19.9%[5]; metropolitan France 2.8%; other 3.7%.
Ethnic composition (2000): Comorian (Mauri, Mahorais) 92.3%; Swahili 3.2%; white (French) 1.8%; Makua 1.0%; other 1.7%.
Religious affiliation (2000): Sunnī Muslim 96.5%; Christian, principally Roman Catholic, 2.2%; other 1.3%.
Major towns (1997[6]): Mamoudzou 32,733; Dzaoudzi 10,792; Koungou 10,165.

Vital statistics

Birth rate per 1,000 population (2000): 45.3 (world avg. 22.5).
Death rate per 1,000 population (2000): 9.1 (world avg. 9.0).
Natural increase rate per 1,000 population (2000): 36.2 (world avg. 13.5).
Total fertility rate (avg. births per childbearing woman; 2000): 6.3.
Marriage rate per 1,000 population: n.a.; *marital status of adult population* (1997): monogamous marriage 48.5%, polygamous marriage 6.9%, other 44.6%.
Divorce rate per 1,000 population: 16.2.
Life expectancy at birth (2000): male 59.9; female 69.2.
Morbidity (number of reported cases of infectious diseases; 1985): malaria 73; syphilis 63; gonorrhea 61; tuberculosis 14; typhoid 14; leprosy 12.

National economy

Budget (1993). Revenue: F 551,700,000 (current revenue 68.8%, of which subsidies 40.0%, indirect taxes 16.8%, direct taxes 4.9%; development revenue 31.2%, of which loans 11.6%, subsidies 7.9%). Expenditures: F 551,700,000 (current expenditure 68.8%, development expenditure 31.2%).
Production (metric tons except as noted). Agriculture, forestry, fishing (1997): bananas 30,200, cassava 10,000, cinnamon 27,533 kg, ylang-ylang 14,300 kg, vanilla 4,417 kg; livestock (number of live animals; 1997) 25,000 goats, 17,000 cattle, 2,000 sheep; roundwood, n.a.; fish catch (1998) 1,570. Mining and quarrying: negligible. Manufacturing: mostly processing of agricultural products and materials used in housing construction (including siding and roofing materials, joinery, and latticework). Construction (public works authorized in F '000; 1999): residential 128,991; nonresidential 119,294. Energy production (consumption): electricity (kW-hr; 1999) 68,387,000 (68,387,000); coal, none (none); crude petroleum, none (none); petroleum products, none (n.a.); natural gas, none (none).
Gross national product (1998): U.S.$486,409,000 (U.S.$3,704 per capita).

Structure of gross domestic product and labour force

	1997 in value U.S.$'000	% of total value	labour force	% of labour force
Agriculture, forestry, and fishing	...	...	4,824	11.2
Mining	...	...	80	0.2
Manufacturing	...	...	1,083	2.5
Construction	...	...	3,840	9.0
Public utilities	...	...	399	0.9
Transp. and commun.	...	...	1,563	3.6
Trade	...	...	3,057	7.1
Finance, insurance, real estate	...	...	647	1.5
Pub. admin., defense	...	...	4,526	10.6
Services	...	...	5,074	11.8
Other	...	...	17,803[7]	41.5[7]
TOTAL	154,900	100.0	42,896	100.0[4]

Public debt: n.a.
Household income and expenditure. Average household size (1997) 4.6; expenditure (1991)[8]: food 42.2%, clothing and footwear 31.5%, household furnishings 8.8%, energy and water 6.8%, transportation 5.1%.
Population economically active (1997): total 42,896; activity rate of total population 32.7% (participation rates: ages 15–64, 58.6%; female 43.4%; unemployed 41.5%).

Price and earnings indexes (1995 = 100)

	1995	1996	1997	1998	1999
Consumer price index	100.0	105.3	108.9	111.1	112.2
Monthly earnings index[9]	100.0	106.3	109.5	112.2	113.4

Land use (1987): meadows 35.0%; agricultural 29.0%; other 36.0%.
Tourism (number of visitors; 1997): 9,500.

Foreign trade

Balance of trade (current prices)

	1996	1997	1998	1999
F '000,000	–520.8	–620.4	–660.0	–615.7
% of total	92.9%	96.0%	95.7%	96.0%

Imports (1999): F 628,266,000 (1997; food products 23.8%; machinery 20.4%; transport equipment 10.4%; metals and metal products 10.3%; chemical products 7.7%). *Major import sources* (1997): France 66.0%; South Africa 14.0%; Asia 11.0%.
Exports (1999): F 12,540,000 (1997; domestic exports 37.2%, of which ylang-ylang 27.9%, vanilla 3.5%; reexports 62.8%). *Major export destinations* (1997): France 80.0%; Comoros 15.0%.

Transport and communications

Transport. Railroads: none. Roads (1997): total length 145 mi, 233 km (paved 77%). Vehicles (1997): 6,553. Merchant marine: n.a. Air transport (1997): passenger arrivals and departures 75,077; cargo unloaded and loaded 1,119 metric tons; airports (1998) with scheduled flights 1.

Communications

Medium	date	unit	number	units per 1,000 persons
Daily newspapers[10]	1998	circulation	...	...
Radio	1996	receivers	50,000	427
Television	1999	receivers	3,500	30
Telephones	1998	main lines	12,200	95

Education and health

Educational attainment (1991). Percentage of population age 25 and over having: no formal education 72.8%; primary 14.2%; lower secondary 7.5%; higher secondary 3.2%; higher 2.3%. *Literacy* (1997): total population age 15 and over literate 63,053 (86.1%).

Education (1992–93)

	schools	teachers	students	student/ teacher ratio
Primary (age 6–11)	88[11]	555	25,805[12]	38.9
Secondary (age 12–18)	8[12]	246	6,190[12]	16.2
Voc., teacher tr.	2[11]	17[11]	839	23.1[11]
Higher	—	—	—	—

Health: physicians (1997) 57 (1 per 2,304 persons); hospital beds 186 (1 per 706 persons); infant mortality rate per 1,000 live births (2000) 71.3.

Military

Total active duty personnel (2000): 4,200 French troops are assigned to Mayotte and Réunion.

[1]The extraconstitutional status of departmental collectivity (between an overseas department and an overseas territory) was approved by the residents of Mayotte in mid-2000. [2]Final status of Mayotte has not yet been determined; it is claimed by Comoros as an integral part of that country. [3]Representatives of the French government in Mayotte continue to occupy offices in the original capital of Dzaoudzi. Local administrative (General Council) offices are in Mamoudzou. [4]Detail does not add to total given because of rounding. [5]Nearly all ethnic Comorian (a mixture of Bantu, Arab, and Malagasy peoples). [6]Population of communes. [7]Unemployed. [8]Weights of consumer price index components. [9]Based on minimum-level wage of public employees. [10]One weekly newspaper has a total circulation of 15,000. [11]1989–90. [12]1997.

Internet resources for further information:

- **France Overseas http://www.outre-mer.gouv.fr/domtom/mayotte/index.htm**

Mexico

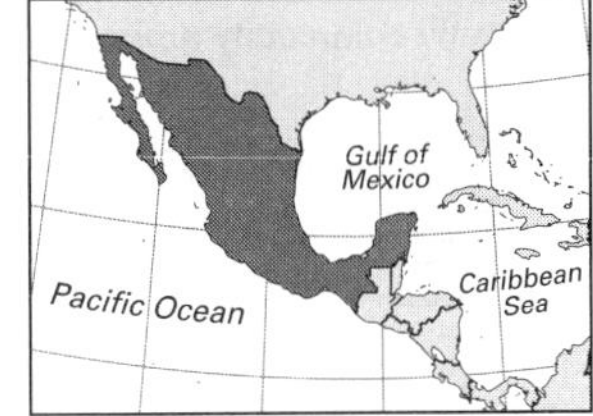

Official name: Estados Unidos Mexicanos (United Mexican States).
Form of government: federal republic with two legislative houses (Senate [128]; Chamber of Deputies [500]).
Head of state and government: President.
Capital: Mexico City.
Official language: Spanish.
Official religion: none.
Monetary unit: 1 Mexican peso[1] (Mex$) = 100 centavos; valuation (Sept. 28, 2001) 1 U.S.$ = Mex$9.51; 1 £ = Mex$13.98.

Area and population

		area		population
States	**Capitals**	sq mi	sq km	2000 census[2]
Aguascalientes	Aguascalientes	2,112	5,471	943,506
Baja California	Mexicali	26,997	69,921	2,487,700
Baja California Sur	La Paz	28,369	73,475	423,516
Campeche	Campeche	19,619	50,812	689,656
Chiapas	Tuxtla Gutiérrez	28,653	74,211	3,920,515
Chihuahua	Chihuahua	94,571	244,938	3,047,867
Coahuila	Saltillo	57,908	149,982	2,295,808
Colima	Colima	2,004	5,191	540,679
Durango	Durango	47,560	123,181	1,445,922
Guanajuato	Guanajuato	11,773	30,491	4,656,761
Guerrero	Chilpancingo	24,819	64,281	3,075,083
Hidalgo	Pachuca	8,036	20,813	2,231,392
Jalisco	Guadalajara	31,211	80,836	6,321,278
México	Toluca	8,245	21,355	13,083,359
Michoacán	Morelia	23,138	59,928	3,979,177
Morelos	Cuernavaca	1,911	4,950	1,552,878
Nayarit	Tepic	10,417	26,979	919,739
Nuevo León	Monterrey	25,067	64,924	3,826,240
Oaxaca	Oaxaca	36,275	93,952	3,432,180
Puebla	Puebla	13,090	33,902	5,070,346
Querétaro	Querétaro	4,420	11,449	1,402,010
Quintana Roo	Chetumal	19,387	50,212	873,804
San Luis Potosi	San Luis Potosi	24,351	63,068	2,296,363
Sinaloa	Culiacán	22,521	58,328	2,534,835
Sonora	Hermosillo	70,291	182,052	2,213,370
Tabasco	Villahermosa	9,756	25,267	1,889,367
Tamaulipas	Ciudad Victoria	30,650	79,384	2,747,114
Tlaxcala	Tlaxcala	1,551	4,016	961,912
Veracruz	Xalapa (Jalapa)	27,683	71,699	6,901,111
Yucatán	Mérida	14,827	38,402	1,655,707
Zacatecas	Zacatecas	28,283	73,252	1,351,207
Federal District				
Distrito Federal	—	571	1,479	8,591,309
CONTINENTAL AREA		756,066[3]	1,958,201[3]	
LAND		736,949	1,908,690	
WATER		19,116	49,511	
INSULAR AREA[4]		1,979	5,127	
TOTAL		758,449[5]	1,964,375[5]	97,361,711

Demography

Population (2001): 99,969,000.
Density (2001): persons per sq mi 132.2, persons per sq km 51.1.
Urban-rural (1990): urban 71.3%; rural 28.7%.
Sex distribution (2000): male 49.28%; female 50.72%.
Age breakdown (2000): under 15, 33.8%; 15–29, 29.8%; 30–44, 19.1%; 45–59, 10.7%; 60–74, 5.2%; 75 and over, 1.4%.
Population projection: (2010) 112,640,000; (2020) 125,610,000.
Doubling time: 39 years.
Ethnic composition (1990): mestizo 60.0%; Amerindian 30.0%; Caucasian 9.0%; other 1.0%.
Religious affiliation (1995): Roman Catholic 90.4%; Protestant (including Evangelical) 3.8%; other 5.8%.
Major cities (2000): Mexico City 8,591,309; Guadalajara 1,647,000; Puebla 1,270,989; Ciudad Netzahualcóyotl 1,224,500; Juárez 1,190,000; Tijuana 1,150,000; Monterrey 1,108,400; León 1,019,510; Mérida 660,848; Chihuahua 650,000.
Place of birth (1990): 93.1% native-born; 6.9% foreign-born and unknown.
Mobility (1990). Population 5 years and older living in the same state as in 1985: 94.3%; different state 4.9%; unspecified 0.8%.
Households. Total households (2000) 21,948,000; distribution by size (1995): 1 person 5.7%, 2 persons 10.9%, 3 persons 15.8%, 4 persons 20.1%, 5 persons 17.7%, 6 persons 11.6%, 7 or more persons 18.2%. Family households (1990): 17,064,507 (98.4%); nonfamily 1,039,738 (1.3%); unspecified 256,554 (0.3%).
Emigration (1998): legal immigrants into the United States 131,600.

Vital statistics

Birth rate per 1,000 population (2000): 23.2 (world avg. 22.5); (1983) legitimate 72.5%; illegitimate 27.5%.
Death rate per 1,000 population (2000): 5.0 (world avg. 9.0).
Natural increase rate per 1,000 population (2000): 18.2 (world avg. 13.5).
Total fertility rate (avg. births per childbearing woman; 2000): 2.7.
Marriage rate per 1,000 population (1997): 7.5.
Divorce rate per 1,000 population (1995): 0.4.
Life expectancy at birth (2000): male 68.5 years; female 74.7 years.
Major causes of death per 100,000 population (1998): diseases of the circulatory system 104.1; malignant neoplasms (cancers) 57.6; diseases of the digestive system 43.5; diseases of the respiratory system 43.3; conditions originating in the perinatal period 20.7.

Social indicators

Access to services (1995). Proportion of dwellings having: electricity 93.2%; piped water supply 85.6%; drained sewage 74.7%.
Educational attainment (1995). Population age 15 and over having: no primary education 13.4%; some primary 22.8%; completed primary 19.3%; incomplete secondary 19.9%; complete secondary 16.3%; higher 8.3%.

Distribution of income (1994)

percentage of household income by quintile				
1	2	3	4	5 (highest)
4.8	8.6	12.8	19.5	54.3

Quality of working life. Average workweek (1997): 44.8 hours[6]. Annual rate (1992) per 100,000 insured workers for: temporary disability 6,426; indemnification for permanent injury 239; death 18. Labour stoppages (1997): 39, involving 9,375 workers. Average duration of journey to work: n.a. Method of transport: n.a. Rate per 1,000 workers of discouraged (unemployed no longer seeking work): n.a.
Social participation. Eligible voters participating in last national election (2000): 64%. Population participating in voluntary work: n.a. Trade union membership in total workforce: n.a. Practicing religious population in total affiliated population: national average of weekly attendance (1993) 11%; (1970) weekly attendance 10% of urban dwellers, 25% of rural dwellers; yearly attendance 55% of urban dwellers, 73% of rural dwellers.
Social deviance (1991). Criminal cases tried by local authorities per 100,000 population for: murder 60.3; rape 22.4; other assault 301.0; theft 703.8. Incidence per 100,000 in general population of: alcoholism, n.a.; drug and substance abuse, n.a.[7]; suicide (1994) 2.47.
Material well-being (1985). Households possessing: radio 96%; television 73%; washing machine 33%; automobile 29%; telephone 27%; refrigerator 23%.

National economy

Gross national product (1999): U.S.$428,877,000,000 (U.S.$4,440 per capita).

Structure of gross domestic product and labour force

	1999			
	in value Mex$'000,000[1, 8]	% of total value	labour force	% of labour force
Agriculture	209,719	5.0	8,209,000	20.7
Mining	51,734	1.2	133,000	0.3
Manufacturing	889,662	21.0	7,345,000	18.5
Construction	201,013	4.8	2,158,000	5.4
Public utilities	48,805	1.1	193,000	0.5
Transp. and commun.	479,260	11.4	1,739,000	4.4
Trade	873,010	20.7	8,390,000	21.1
Finance	570,746	13.5	1,458,000	3.7
Pub. admin., defense } Services }	945,704	22.4	9,278,000	23.3
Other	–47,394[9]	–1.1[9]	848,000[10]	2.1[10]
TOTAL	4,222,259	100.0	39,751,000	100.0

Budget (2000). Revenue: Mex$866,231,000,000[1] (1997; income tax 30.9%, VAT 20.9%, social security contributions 12.3%, excise tax 9.9%, import duties 3.9%). Expenditures: Mex$936,738,000,000[1] (1997; education 22.1%, social security and welfare 18.0%, interest on public debt 13.7%).
Public debt (external, outstanding; 1999); U.S.$87,531,000,000.
Tourism (1999): receipts from visitors U.S.$7,223,000,000; expenditures by nationals abroad U.S.$4,541,000,000.

Manufacturing, mining, and construction enterprises (1993)

	no. of enter-prises	no. of employees ('000)	yearly wages as a % of avg. of all wages[11]	value added (Mex$'000,000[1, 11])
Manufacturing	266,033	3,174.4	97.5	20,950,900
Metal products	46,667[12]	955.6[12]	114.2[12]	6,605,300[12]
Chemicals	7,321	371.2	152.3	4,228,000
Food, beverages, and tobacco	91,894	679.3	86.4	3,378,700
Textiles and apparel	44,071	530.6	80.0	2,414,800
Iron and steel	401	57.4	128.2	1,332,400
Nonmetallic mineral products	24,397	181.8	98.6	1,177,700
Paper and printing	15,022	193.2	100.0	1,127,900
Wood and wood products	31,549	162.6	62.8	497,000
Nonelectrical machinery and transport equipment	[12]	[12]	...[12]	[12]
Electrical machinery	[12]	[12]	...[12]	[12]
Other manufactures	4,711	42.7	...	189,200
Mining	2,845	95.6	161.0	1,643,800
Construction	5,308[11]	342.4[11]	62.1	1,414,800

Production (metric tons except as noted). Agriculture, forestry, fishing (2000): sugarcane 49,274,780, corn (maize) 17,988,060, sorghum 5,981,835, oranges 4,059,769, wheat 3,404,576, tomatoes 2,176,557, bananas 1,978,032, peppers 1,826,140, mangoes 1,499,382, lemons and limes 1,639,196, coconuts 1,213,000, watermelons 1,069,000, avocados 933,337, dry beans 914,379, pineapples 881,000, papayas 748,000, barley 732,706, grapes 446,470, rice 410,210, carrots 372,869, coffee (green) 353,999, cauliflower 205,000; livestock (number of live animals) 30,540,000 cattle, 14,900,000 pigs, 9,600,000 goats, 8,000,000 ducks, 6,250,000 horses, 5,950,000 sheep, 3,000,000 turkeys, 3,280,000 mules, 3,250,000 asses, 476,000,000 chickens; roundwood (2000) 24,122,000 cu m; fish catch (1999) 1,250,592. Mining and quarrying (1999): salt 8,900,000, iron 6,855,219, gypsum 4,100,000, silica 1,700,000, phosphate 950,649, sulfur 855,482, dolomite 415,284, fluorite 557,106, zinc 339,758, copper 340,148, barite 157,952, manganese 169,107, lead 131,402, silver 2,456,000 kg, gold 23,476 kg. Manufacturing (gross value of production in Mex$'000[1]; 1998): machinery and equipment 423,579,725; food, beverages, and tobacco products 279,104,375; chemical products 212,479,904; metal products 108,951,844; mineral products 55,612,499; paper and paper products 56,522,215; textiles 54,458,821. Construction (gross value of new construction, in Mex$'000,000[1]; 1985): residential 154,835; nonresidential 168,096.

Trade and service enterprises (1998)

	no. of establish-ments	no. of employees	yearly wage as a % of avg. of all wages[13]	annual income (Mex$'000,000[1])[14]
Trade	1,497,828	3,790,764	...	565,728,373
Wholesale	110,180	864,569	...	249,597,035
Retail	1,387,648	2,926,195	...	316,131,338
Boutiques (excluding food products)	536,900	1,192,597	...	108,507,889
Food and tobacco speciality stores	768,799	1,234,656	...	65,305,180
Automobile, tire, and auto parts dealers	41,236	164,493	...	47,888,576
Supermarkets and grocery stores	24,697	254,497	...	48,769,283
Gasoline stations	4,345	53,610	...	32,517,091
Other	11,671	26,342	...	13,143,319
Services[14]	711,843	2,766,750	85.2	200,001,682
Professional services	130,475	652,148	77.9	53,533,318
Food and beverage services	677	11,258	...	1,012,369
Transp. and travel agencies	9,967	62,767	133.4	11,858,406
Lodging	9,913	151,445	...	8,960,922
Automotive repair	112,293	252,950	...	7,263,560
Educational services (private)	20,622	247,086	134.3	10,815,238
Medical and social assistance	79,748	203,348	206.4	7,497,794
Amusement services (cinemas and theatres)	4,855	65,608	148.9	9,845,129
Recreation[14]	20,973	65,936	...	3,065,672
Other repair[14]	72,129	104,478	...	2,625,370
Commercial and professional[14] organizations	1,946	11,946	77.9	264,770
Other[14]	248,245	937,780	49.9	83,259,134

Energy production (consumption): electricity (kW-hr; 1997) 170,751,000,000 (172,212,000,000); coal (metric tons; 1997) 10,337,000 (11,538,000); crude petroleum (barrels; 1997) 1,099,400,000 (470,400,000); petroleum products (metric tons; 1997) 72,362,000 (83,281,000); natural gas (cu m; 1997) 29,708,000,000 (30,314,000,000).

Population economically active (1999): total 39,751,000; activity rate of total population 41.2% (participation rates: ages 15–64, 63.4%; female 33.5%; unemployed [2000] 4.0%).

Price and earnings indexes (1995 = 100)

	1994	1995	1996	1997	1998	1999	2000
Consumer price Index	74.1	100.0	134.4	162.1	187.9	219.1	239.9
Monthly earnings index	90.9	100.0	...	156.6	...	...	...

Household income and expenditure. Average household size (1999) 4.4; income per household (1989) Mex$3,461 (U.S.$1,384); sources of income (1992): wages and salaries 61.5%, property and entrepreneurship 29.1%, transfer payments 7.8%, other 1.6%; expenditure (1992): food, beverages, and tobacco 36.9%, housing (includes household furnishings) 25.2%, transportation and communications 10.1%, clothing and footwear 8.5%, recreation and entertainment 5.5%, health and medical services 3.5%.

Financial aggregates[1, 15]

	1994	1995	1996	1997	1998	1999	2000
Exchange rate, Mex$ per:							
U.S. dollar	3.375	6.419	7.599	7.919	9.136	9.560	9.456
£	5.164	10.132	11.867	12.969	15.133	15.470	14.336
SDR	7.774	11.361	11.289	10.906	13.890	13.059	12.472
International reserves (U.S.$)							
Total (excl. gold; '000,000)	6,278	16,847	19,433	28,797	31,799	31,782	35,509
SDRs ('000,000)	177	1,597	257	661	337	790	366
Reserve pos. in IMF ('000,000)	—	—	—	—	—	—	—
Foreign exchange	6,101	15,250	19,176	28,136	31,461	30,992	35,142
Gold ('000,000 fine troy oz)	0.43	0.51	0.26	0.19	0.22	0.16	0.25
% world reserves	0.05	0.06	0.03	0.02	0.03	0.02	0.02
Interest and prices							
Treasury bill rate	14.10	48.44	31.39	19.80	24.76	21.41	15.24
Balance of payments (U.S.$'000,000)							
Balance of visible trade, of which:	−18,464	+7,089	+6,531	+623	−7,743	−5,581	−8,003
Imports, f.o.b.	−79,347	−72,454	−89,469	−109,808	−125,243	−141,973	−174,458
Exports, f.o.b.	60,882	79,543	96,000	110,431	117,500	136,392	166,455
Balance of invisibles	−11,198	−8,665	−8,454	−8,077	−8,044	−8,473	−10,134
Balance of payments, current account	−29,662	−1,576	−2,328	−7,454	−15,724	−14,324	−18,137

Land use (1994): forest 25.5%; pasture 39.0%; agriculture 13.0%; other 22.5%.

Foreign trade

Balance of trade (current prices)

	1995	1996	1997	1998	1999	2000
U.S.$'000,000	−18,464	+6,531	+623	−7,742	−5,361	−8,003
% of total	13.2%	3.5%	0.3%	3.2%	1.9%	2.3%

Imports (2000): U.S.$174,458,000,000 (intermediate goods 76.6%; capital goods 13.8%; consumer goods 9.6%). *Major import sources:* U.S. 73.1%; Japan 3.7%; Germany 3.6%; Canada 2.3%; Italy 1.2%; China 1.1%.

Exports (2000): U.S.$166,455,000,000 (machinery and transport equipment 33.3%; electrical equipment 10.7%; crude petroleum 8.9%; agricultural goods 3.3%). *Major export destinations:* U.S. 88.7%; Europe 3.9%; Canada 2.0%; Japan 0.6%.

Trade by commodity group (1998)

	imports		exports	
SITC group	U.S.$'000,000	%	U.S.$'000,000	%
00 Food and live animals	5,285	4.2	6,135	5.2
01 Beverages and tobacco	...	...	1,035	0.9
02 Crude materials, excluding fuels	4,263	3.4	1,696	1.4
03 Mineral fuels, lubricants, and related materials	2,747	2.2	6,980	5.9
04 Animal and vegetable oils, fats, and waxes	590	0.5	—	—
05 Chemicals and related products, n.e.s.	10,718	8.6	4,231	3.6
06 Basic manufactures	21,537	17.2	11,976	10.2
07 Machinery and transport equipment	59,850	47.8	68,011	58.0
08 Miscellaneous manufactured articles	15,773	12.6	16,976	14.5
09 Goods not classified by kind	4,210	3.4	285	0.3
TOTAL[16]	125,193[17]	100.0[17]	117,325	100.0

Direction of trade (1999)

	imports		exports	
	U.S.$'000,000	%	U.S.$'000,000	%
Western Hemisphere	112,011	78.8	127,982	93.6
United States	105,267	74.1	120,393	88.1
Latin America and the Caribbean	3,795	2.7	5,198	3.8
Canada	2,949	2.0	2,391	1.7
Europe	15,208	10.7	5,889	4.3
EU	14,006	9.9	5,197	3.8
EFTA	776	0.5	455	0.3
Russia	—	—	—	—
Other Europe	426	0.3	237	0.2
Asia	13,354	9.4	2,353	1.7
Japan	5,083	3.6	776	0.6
Other Asia	8,271	5.8	1,577	1.1
Africa	398	0.3	159	0.1
Other	1,093	0.8	320	0.2
TOTAL	142,064	100.0	136,703	100.0[17]

Transport and communications

Transport. Railroads (1998): route length 16,543 mi, 26,623 km; passenger-mi 677,000,000, passenger-km 1,089,000,000; short ton-mi cargo 19,726,000,000, metric ton-km cargo 31,747,000,000. Roads (1999): total length 226,874 mi, 365,119 km (paved 29%). Vehicles (1999): passenger cars 9,842,006; trucks and buses 4,749,789. Air transport (1997): passenger-mi 14,707,000,000, passenger-km 23,668,000,000; short ton-mi cargo 1,426,000,000, metric ton-km cargo 2,295,000; airports (1997) 83.

Communications

Medium	date	unit	number	units per 1,000 persons
Daily newspapers	1996	circulation	9,030,000	97
Radio	1997	receivers	31,000,000	329
Television	1999	receivers	26,000,000	267
Telephones	1999	main lines	10,927,000	112
Cellular telephones	1999	subscribers	7,732,000	79
Personal computers	1999	units	4,300,000	44
Internet	1999	users	1,822,000	19

Education and health

Literacy (1995): total population age 15 and over literate 89.6%; males literate 91.8%; females literate 87.4%.

Education (2000–01)

	schools	teachers	students	student/ teacher ratio
Primary (age 6–12)	99,176	546,717	14,808,300	27.1
Secondary (age 12–18)	44,441	552,735	9,330,900	16.9
Voc., teacher tr.[18]	6,610	63,674	883,000	13.9
Higher	4,081	214,126	2,073,600	9.7

Health: physicians (1994) 146,021 (1 per 613 persons); hospital beds 107,288 (1 per 864 persons); infant mortality rate per 1,000 live births (2000) 26.2.

Food (1999): daily per capita caloric intake 3,168 (vegetable products 82%, animal products 18%); 136% of FAO recommended minimum requirement.

Military

Total active duty personnel (2000): 192,770 (army 74.7%, navy 19.2%, air force 6.1%). *Military expenditure as percentage of GNP* (1997): 1.1% (world 2.6%); per capita expenditure U.S.$44.

[1]The Mexican new peso, equivalent to 1,000 old Mexican pesos, was introduced on Jan. 1, 1993. On Jan. 1, 1996, the name of the currency was changed to Mexican peso. [2]Preliminary. [3]Continental area per more recent survey equals 756,470 sq mi (1,959,248 sq km). [4]Uninhabited (nearly all Pacific) islands directly administered by federal government. [5]Total area based on most recent survey figure for continental area. [6]Manufacturing only. [7]Through 1982, cannabis remained the most abused drug. [8]At factor cost. [9]Imputed bank service charge. [10]Includes 682,000 unemployed persons. [11]1988. [12]Metal products include Nonelectrical machinery and transport equipment and Electrical machinery. [13]1984. [14]1993. [15]Exchange rates and treasury bill rates are expressed in period averages; international reserves are expressed in end-of-period rates. [16]Totals include adjustments of unspecified nature. [17]Detail does not add to total given because of rounding. [18]1996–97.

Internet resources for further information:

- **National Institute of Statistics, Geography, and Informatics http://www.inegi.gob.mx/difusion/ingles/portadai.html**

Micronesia

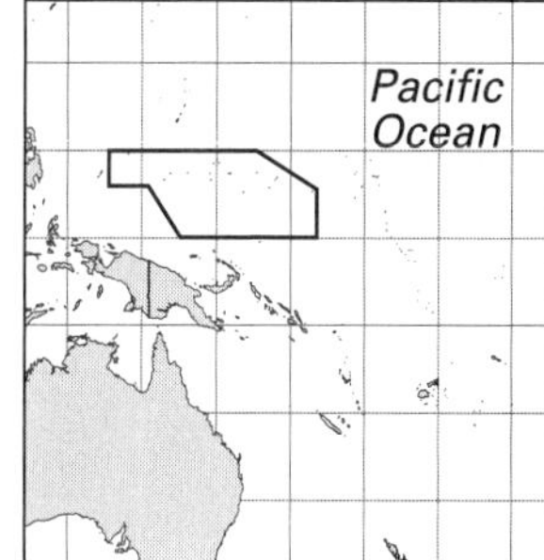

Official name: Federated States of Micronesia.
Form of government: federal nonparty republic in free association with the United States with one legislative house (Congress [14])[1].
Head of state and government: President.
Capital: Palikir, on Pohnpei.
Official language: none.
Official religion: none.
Monetary unit: 1 U.S. dollar (U.S.$) = 100 cents; valuation (Sept. 28, 2001) 1 £ = U.S.$1.47.

Area and population

	area		population
States			1999
Major Islands	sq mi	sq km	estimate
Chuuk (Truk)	49.1	127.2	59,367
Weno (Moen) Islands	7.0	18.1	...
Kosrae	42.3	109.6	7,833
Kosrae Island	42.3	109.6	7,833
Pohnpei	133.3	345.2	37,013
Pohnpei Island	129.0	334.1	...
Yap	45.9	118.9	12,055
Yap Island	38.7	100.2	...
TOTAL	270.8[2]	701.4[2]	116,268

Demography

Population (2001): 118,000.
Density (2001): persons per sq mi 435.7, persons per sq km 168.2.
Urban-rural (2000): urban 28.5%; rural 71.5%.
Sex distribution (2000): male 51.26%; female 48.74%.
Age breakdown (1999): under 15, 40.6%; 15–29, 28.4%; 30–44, 16.5%; 45–59, 9.1%; 60 and over, 5.4%.
Population projection: (2010) 125,000; (2020) 126,000.
Doubling time: 33 years.
Ethnic composition (2000): Chuukese 28.0%; Pohnpeian 24.9%; Yapese 10.6%; Mortlockese 5.6%; Kosraean 5.2%; white (U.S.) 4.5%; Ulithian 3.3%; Carolinian 2.8%; other 15.1%.
Religious affiliation (2000): Christianity is the predominant religious tradition; Roman Catholic 53.9%, Protestant 34.0%; the Kosraeans, Pohnpeians, and Chuukese are mostly Protestant and the Yapese mostly Roman Catholic.
Major cities (1994): Weno (Moen) 16,121; Tol 4,816; Kolonia 6,660.

Vital statistics

Birth rate per 1,000 population (2000): 27.1 (world avg. 22.5); legitimate, n.a.; illegitimate, n.a.
Death rate per 1,000 population (2000): 6.0 (world avg. 9.0).
Natural increase rate per 1,000 population (2000): 21.1 (world avg. 13.5).
Total fertility rate (avg. births per childbearing woman; 2000): 3.8.
Marriage rate per 1,000 population: n.a.
Divorce rate per 1,000 population: n.a.
Life expectancy at birth (2000): male 66.7 years; female 70.6 years.
Major causes of death per 100,000 population (1997)[3]: diseases of the cerebrovascular system 90.3; endocrine and metabolic diseases 64.4; homicide, suicide, and accidents 55.4; diseases of the respiratory system 42.0; malignant neoplasms (cancers) 34.0; infectious and parasitic diseases 26.8 (with especially high morbidity rates for tuberculosis and leprosy).

National economy

Budget (1997–98). Revenue: U.S.$152,300,000 (external grants 60.0%; tax revenue 15.1%; fishing rights fees 13.4%). Expenditures: U.S.$154,700,000 (current expenditures 79.6%, of which government services 71.4%, transfer payments 4.7%, debt services 3.4%; capital expenditure 20.4%).
Public debt (external, outstanding; 1999): U.S.$98,200,000.
Population economically active (1994): total 27,573; activity rate of total population 26.3% (participation rates: ages 15–64, 43.6%; female 33.8%; unemployed 15.3%).

Price and earnings indexes (1995 = 100)

	1994	1995	1996	1997	1998	1999
Price index	96.2	100.0	103.1	105.2	106.8	109.6
Annual wage index	103.2	100.0	97.5	94.2	...	...

Production (metric tons except as noted). Agriculture, forestry, fishing: n.a.; however, Micronesia's major crops include coconuts (which provide annually more than 4,000 tons of copra), breadfruit, cassava, sweet potatoes, peppers, and a variety of tropical fruits (including bananas); livestock comprises mostly pigs and poultry; fish catch (1998) 15,393, of which skipjack tuna 15,000, yellowfin tuna 5,000. Mining and quarrying: quarrying of sand and aggregate for local construction only. Manufacturing: n.a.; however, copra and coconut oil, traditionally important products, are being displaced by garment production; the manufacture of handicrafts and personal items (clothing, mats, boats, etc.) by individuals is also important. Construction: n.a. Energy production (consumption): electricity (kW-hr; 1997) 100,333,000 (100,333,000); coal, none (n.a.); crude petroleum, none (n.a.); petroleum products (metric tons; 1992) none (77,000); natural gas, none (n.a.).

Household income and expenditure. Average household size (1994) 6.8; annual income per household (1994) U.S.$8,645; sources of income (1994): wages and salaries 51.8%, operating surplus 23.0%, social security 2.1%; expenditure (1985): food and beverages 73.5%.
Land use (1984)[4]: forested 22.5%; meadows and pastures 13.5%; agricultural and under permanent cultivation 33.5%; other 30.5%.
Gross national product (1999): U.S.$229,880,000 (U.S.$1,980 per capita).

Structure of gross domestic product and labour force

	1996		1994	
	in value U.S.$'000,000	% of total value	labour force	% of labour force
Agriculture and fishing[5]	34.7	19.1	7,375	26.7
Mining	0.7	0.4	42	0.2
Manufacturing	2.6	1.4	656	2.4
Construction	1.9	1.0	1,171	4.2
Public utilities	2.0	1.1	279	1.0
Transp. and commun.	8.5	4.7	727	2.6
Finance	4.2	2.3	632	2.3
Services	3.1	1.7	2,125	7.7
Trade[6]	43.6	24.0	2,258	8.2
Public administration	80.4	44.3	8,092	29.3
Other	...	...	4,216[7]	15.2[7]
TOTAL	181.6[2]	100.0	27,573	100.0[2]

Tourism (1998): expenditures U.S.$4,383,000; number of visitors 16,283.

Foreign trade

Balance of trade (current prices)

	1992	1993	1994	1995	1996
U.S.$'000,000	–109.1	–93.7	–75.5	–59.1	–52.0
% of total	66.0%	41.4%	43.5%	48.0%	44.1%

Imports (1998): U.S.$82,486,915 (1997; food, beverages, and tobacco 41.9%; manufactured goods 32.0%; machinery and transport equipment 28.4%; petroleum products 11.2%; chemicals 4.4%). *Major import sources* (1997): United States (including Guam) 72.5%; Japan 13.5%; Australia 6.6%.
Exports (1998): U.S.$8,037,207 (1997; marine products 89.2%; agricultural products 4.4%, of which bananas 3.2%, copra 1.2%). *Major export destinations* (1992): Japan 80.0%; United States 9.3%; Guam 8.3%; South Pacific Region 2.4%.

Transport and communications

Transport. Railroads: none. Roads (1990): total length 140 mi, 226 km (paved 17%). Vehicles (1998): passenger cars 2,044; trucks and buses 354. Merchant marine (1997[8]): vessels (100 gross tons and over) 19; deadweight tonnage 9,200. Air transport: n.a.; airports (1997) with scheduled flights 4.

Communications

Medium	date	unit	number	units per 1,000 persons
Radio	1996	receivers	70,000	667
Television	1999	receivers	2,400	21
Telephones	1999	main lines	9,100	78
Internet	1999	users	2,000	17

Education and health

Educational attainment (1998). Percentage of population age 25 and over having: no formal schooling 4.4%; primary education 46.0%; some secondary 18.3%; secondary 12.9%; some college 14.7%; bachelor's degree 2.9%; higher 0.8%. *Literacy* (1994): total population age 10 and over literate 69,779 (93.9%); males literate 35,688 (94.7%); females literate 34,091 (93.0%).

Education (1997–98)

	schools	teachers	students	student/ teacher ratio
Elementary (age 6–12)	171	1,486	25,915	18.6
Secondary (age 13–18)	24	418	6,809	16.2
College	1	71	1,884	26.5

Health (1998): physicians 68 (1 per 1,677 persons); hospital beds (1997) 260 (1 per 447 persons); infant mortality rate per 1,000 live births (2000) 33.5.
Food: daily per capita caloric intake, n.a.

Military

External security is provided by the United States.

[1]On Nov. 3, 1986, the United States unilaterally terminated the UN trusteeship it held over the Federated States of Micronesia (FSM), thus formally initiating their free-association political status. On Dec. 22, 1990, the United Nations Security Council joined the Trusteeship Council, which had endorsed the termination of the trusteeship in May 1986. [2]Detail does not add to total given because of rounding. [3]Based on registered deaths only. [4]Includes all areas formerly constituting the U.S. Trust Territory of the Pacific Islands. [5]Includes subsistence farming and fishing. [6]Includes hotels. [7]Unemployed. [8]January 1.

Internet resources for further information:

- **General Information on The FSM http://www.boh.com/econ/pacific**

Moldova

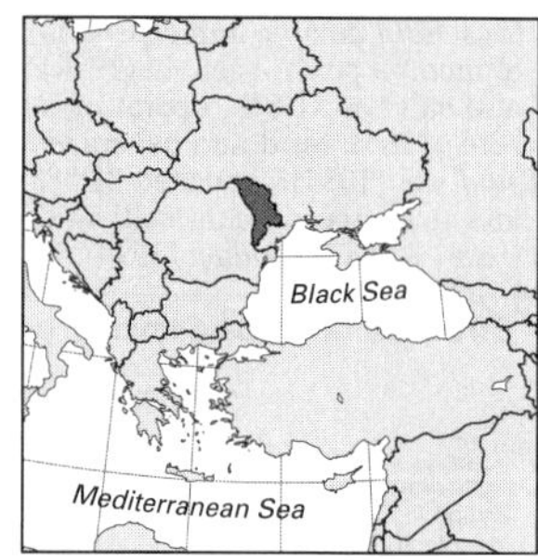

Official name: Republica Moldova (Republic of Moldova).
Form of government: unitary parliamentary republic[1] with a single legislative body (Parliament [101]).
Head of state: President.
Head of government: Prime Minister.
Capital: Chişinău.
Official language: Romanian[2].
Official religion: none.
Monetary unit: 1 Moldovan leu (plural lei) = 100 bani; valuation (Sept. 28, 2001) free rate, 1 U.S.$ = 12.87 Moldovan lei; 1 £ = 18.91 Moldovan lei.

Area and population[3]

Counties	Capitals	area[4] sq mi	area[4] sq km	population 2000 estimate
Bălţi	Bălţi	1,500	4,000	...
Cahul	Cahul	900	2,300	...
Chişinău	Chişinău	1,200	3,000	...
Edinet	Edinet	1,300	3,300	...
Lăpuşna	...	1,300	3,400	...
Orhei	Orhei	1,300	3,500	...
Soroca	Soroca	1,100	2,900	...
Tighina	Tighina	1,000	2,600	...
Ungheni	Ungheni	900	2,200	...
City				
Chişinău	—	200	500	...
Autonomous Region				
Găgăuzia	Comrat	900	2,500	...
Disputed Territory[5]				
Transdniester (Dubăsari)	...	1,400	3,500	...
TOTAL		13,000	33,700	4,298,000[6]

Demography

Population (2001): 4,431,000[6].
Density (2001): persons per sq mi 323.5, persons per sq km 124.9.
Urban-rural (1999): urban 54.4%; rural 45.6%.
Sex distribution (2000): male 47.66%; female 52.34%.
Age breakdown (2000): under 15, 23.2%; 15–29, 24.9%; 30–44, 21.4%; 45–59, 16.3%; 60–74, 11.0%; 75 and over, 3.2%.
Population projection: (2010) 4,535,000; (2020) 4,736,000.
Doubling time: not applicable; doubling time exceeds 100 years.
Ethnic composition (2000): Moldovan 48.2%; Ukrainian 13.8%; Russian 12.9%; Bulgarian 8.2%; Roma (Gypsy) 6.2%; Gagauz 4.2%; other 6.5%.
Religious affiliation (1995): Orthodox 46.0%, of which Romanian Orthodox 35.0%, Russian Orthodox 9.5%; Muslim 5.5%; Catholic 1.8%, of which Roman Catholic 0.6%; Protestant 1.7%; Jewish 0.9%; other (mostly nonreligious) 44.1%.
Major cities (1999): Chişinău 655,000; Tiraspol 200,700; Bălţi 156,600.

Vital statistics

Birth rate per 1,000 population (2000): 12.9 (world avg. 22.5); (1995) legitimate 87.7%; illegitimate 12.3%.
Death rate per 1,000 population (2000): 12.6 (world avg. 9.0).
Natural increase rate per 1,000 population (2000): 0.3 (world avg. 13.5).
Total fertility rate (avg. births per childbearing woman; 2000): 1.6.
Marriage rate per 1,000 population(1994): 7.8.
Life expectancy at birth (2000): male 59.9 years; female 69.2 years.
Major causes of death per 100,000 population (1994): circulatory diseases 500.7; cancers 136.1; accidents and violence 113.3; digestive system diseases 110.4.

National economy

Budget (1997). Revenue: 3,473,000,000 lei (value-added tax 23.8%, excise taxes 12.4%, personal income tax 7.4%, profits tax 6.2%, duties and customs taxes 3.3%). Expenditures: 2,354,000,000,000 lei (current expenditures 94.5%, of which education 20.4%, health care 12.5%, interest payments 9.1%; capital expenditure 5.5%).
Public debt (external, outstanding; 1999): U.S.$722,000,000.
Land use (1994): forest 10.6%; pasture 10.9%; agriculture 75.9%; other 2.6%.
Production (metric tons except as noted). Agriculture, forestry, fishing (2000): sugar beets 1,800,000, corn (maize) 900,000, wheat 770,000, grapes 350,000, potatoes 342,000, apples 215,000; livestock (number of live animals) 974,000 sheep, 705,000 pigs, 416,000 cattle; roundwood (1998) 406,000 cu m; fish catch (1998) 491. Mining and quarrying (1995): sand and gravel 376,000; gypsum 13,600. Manufacturing ('000,000 lei; 1995): food 1,446,824; machinery 383,153; construction materials 164,198; textiles 57,283. Construction (1994): 127,200,000 lei. Energy production (consumption): electricity (kW-hr; 1997): 5,274,000,000 (7,226,000,000); coal (metric tons; 1997) none (322,000); crude petroleum (barrels; 1997) none (none); petroleum products (metric tons; 1997) none (862,000); natural gas (cu m; 1997) none (3,729,000,000).
Population economically active (1994): total (1995) 1,693,000; activity rate of total population 44.8% (participation rates: ages 16–59 [male], 16–54 [female] 85.2%; female 53.0%; unemployed 1.4%).

Price and earnings indexes (1995 = 100)

	1994	1995	1996	1997	1998	1999	2000
Consumer price index	89.2	100.0	120.9	130.6	139.2	203.2	266.8
Earnings index	78.7	100.0	...	...	...	...	...

Gross national product (at current market prices; 1999): U.S.$1,481,000,000 (U.S.$410 per capita).

Structure of gross domestic product and labour force

	1997 in value '000,000 lei	1997 % of total value	1994 labour force	1994 % of labour force
Agriculture	2,248	26.0	767,000	45.1
Manufacturing, mining	1,992	23.0	232,000	13.7
Public utilities	163	1.9	39,000	2.2
Construction	349	4.0	91,000	5.4
Transp. and commun.	293	3.4	73,000	4.3
Trade[7]	652	7.5	107,000	6.3
Finance	341	3.9	20,000	1.2
Pub. admin., defense	1,043	12.0	32,000	1.9
Services	440	5.1	305,000	18.0
Other	1,134[8]	13.1[8]	33,000	1.9
TOTAL	8,655	100.0[9]	1,699,000	100.0

Household income and expenditure. Average household size (1989) 3.4; income per household: n.a.; sources of income (1994): wages and salaries 41.2%, social benefits 15.3%, agricultural income 10.4%, other 33.1%; expenditure (1995): food and drink 49.1%, clothing 9.7%, health 4.1%.

Foreign trade

Balance of trade (current prices)

	1993	1994	1995	1996	1997	1998
U.S.$'000,000	–180	–54	–32	–274	–348	–388
% of total	16.6%	4.2%	2.1%	14.5%	16.4%	23.2%

Imports (1996): 4,967,200,000 lei (mineral products 36.8%, machinery 14.5%, agricultural goods 10.8%, chemical products 6.6%, textiles 5.1%). *Major import sources:* Ukraine 27.5%; Russia 27.3%; Romania 6.7%.
Exports (1996): 3,691,200,000 lei (food and agricultural goods 72.8%, textile products 6.2%, machinery 5.3%, metals and metal products 1.7%). *Major export destinations:* Russia 53.6%; Romania 9.4%; Ukraine 5.9%.

Transport and communications

Transport. Railroads (1997): length 2,710 km; passenger-km 949,300,000; metric ton-km cargo 3,133,600,000[10]. Roads (1995): total length 12,259 km (paved 87.2%). Vehicles (1996): passenger cars 166,757; trucks and buses 67,638. Air transport (1994): passenger-km 225,000; metric ton-km cargo 1,000,000; airports (1997) 1.

Communications

Medium	date	unit	number	units per 1,000 persons
Daily newspapers	1996	circulation	261,000	59
Radio	1997	receivers	3,220,000	736
Television	1998	receivers	1,300,000	297
Telephones	1998	main lines	657,000	150
Cellular telephones	1999	subscribers	18,000	4.1
Personal computers	1999	units	35,000	8.0
Internet	1999	users	25,000	5.7

Education and health

Educational attainment (1989). Percentage of population age 15 and over having: no formal schooling or some primary education 24.5%; some secondary 20.4%; secondary 46.4%; higher 8.7%. *Literacy* (2000): total population age 15 and over literate 98.9%; males 99.6%; females 98.3%.

Education (1996–97)

	schools	teachers	students	student/teacher ratio
Primary (age 7–13)	1,700[11]	14,097	320,725	22.8
Secondary (age 14–17)		28,615[12]	419,256	...
Voc., teacher tr.	64[11]	...	26,105	...
Higher	20[11]	8,814	93,759	10.6

Health (1995): physicians 17,200 (1 per 250 persons); hospital beds 53,000 (1 per 82 persons); infant mortality rate per 1,000 live births (2000) 43.3.
Food (1999): daily per capita caloric intake 2,728 (vegetable products 85%, animal products 15%); 106% of FAO recommended minimum requirement.

Military

Total active duty personnel (2000): 9,500 (army 89.5%, air force 10.5%). *Military expenditure as percentage of GNP* (1997): 1.0% (world 2.6%); per capita expenditure U.S.$14.

[1]Moldova is officially a parliamentary republic from Oct. 27, 2000. [2]Officially designated Moldovan per constitution. [3]Local government structure reorganized in 1999. [4]Area figures are estimated and rounded. [5]Breakaway area from 1991. [6]Includes 600,000 Moldovans working abroad (particularly in Western Europe). [7]Includes hotels. [8]Import and production taxes less subsidies. [9]Detail does not add to total given because of rounding. [10]1995. [11]1995–96. [12]Secondary includes Voc., teacher tr.

Internet resources for further information:
- **Moldova.Net http://www.moldova.net**

Monaco

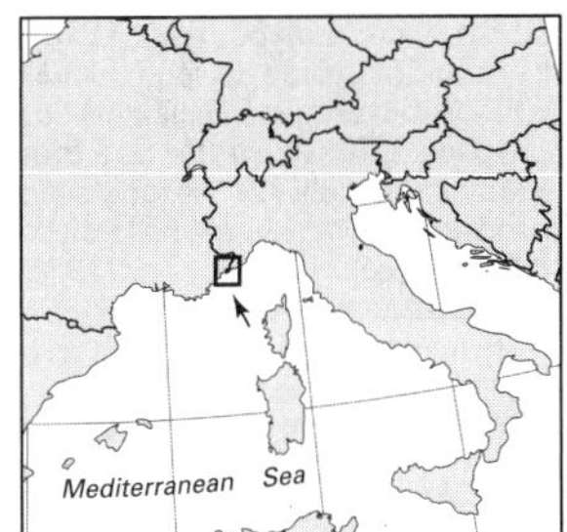

Official name: Principauté de Monaco (Principality of Monaco).
Form of government: constitutional monarchy with one legislative body (National Council [18]).
Chief of state: Prince.
Head of government[1]: Minister of State assisted by the Council of Government.
Capital: [2].
Official language: French.
Official religion: Roman Catholicism.
Monetary unit: 1 French franc (F) = 100 centimes; valuation (Sept. 28, 2001) 1 U.S.$ = F 7.20; 1 £ = F 10.59[3].

Area and population

		area		population
Quarters[2]	Capitals	sq mi	sq km	1990 census
Fontvieille	—	0.13	0.33	1,961
La Condamine	—	0.23	0.61	12,158
Monaco-Ville	—	0.07	0.19	1,151
Monte-Carlo	—	0.32	0.82	14,702
TOTAL		0.75	1.95	29,972

Demography

Population (2001): 31,800.
Density (2001): persons per sq mi 42,400, persons per sq km 16,307.
Urban-rural (2000): urban 100%; rural 0%.
Sex distribution (2000): male 47.58%; female 52.42%.
Age breakdown (2000): under 15, 15.1%; 15–29, 14.0%; 30–44, 21.2%; 45–59, 21.3%; 60–74, 17.2%; 75 and over, 11.2%.
Population projection: (2000) 33,000; (2010) 34,000.
Doubling time: not applicable.
Ethnic composition (2000): French 45.8%; Ligurian (Genoan) 17.2%; Moneguasque 16.9%; British 4.5%; Jewish 1.7%; other 13.9%.
Religious affiliation (2000): Christian 93.2%, of which Roman Catholic 89.3%, Jewish 1.7%; nonreligious and other 5.1%.

Vital statistics

Birth rate per 1,000 population (2000): 9.9 (world avg. 22.5).
Death rate per 1,000 population (2000): 13.1 (world avg. 9.0).
Natural increase rate per 1,000 population (2000): –3.2 (world avg. 13.5).
Total fertility rate (avg. births per childbearing woman; 2000): 1.8.
Marriage rate per 1,000 population (1997): 6.0.
Divorce rate per 1,000 population (1997): 2.5.
Life expectancy at birth (2000): male 74.9 years; female 83.0 years.
Major causes of death per 100,000 population: n.a.; however, principal causes are those of a developed country with an older population.

National economy

Budget (1997). Revenue: F 3,225,658,000 (value-added taxes 50.0%).[4] Expenditures: F 3,139,854,000.
Public debt: n.a.
Production. Agriculture, forestry, fishing: some horticulture and greenhouse cultivation; no agriculture as such. Mining and quarrying: none. Manufacturing: in the 1990s, principal manufactures included chemicals, cosmetics, perfumery, and pharmaceuticals; light electronics and precision instruments; paper and card manufactures; fabricated plastics; and clothing. Construction: n.a. Energy production (consumption): electricity (kW-hr; 1997) 403,000,000 (imported from France); coal, none (n.a.); crude petroleum, none (n.a.); natural gas, none (n.a.).
Gross domestic product (1994): U.S.$765,000,000[5] (U.S.$24,460 per capita).

Distribution of value of sales and labour force

	1992		1990	
	in value F '000,000	% of total value	labour force[6]	% of labour force[6]
Agriculture	...	...	41	0.3
Manufacturing	3,650	11.3	3,754	29.8
Construction, Public utilities	7	7	122	1.0
Hotels, restaurants	1,140	3.5	1,445	11.5
Transportation and communications	...	...	3,491	27.8
Finance, real estate	3,780[7]	11.6[7]		
Services	23,870	73.6		
Pub. admin., defense	...	...	2,828	22.5
Other	—	—	893[8]	7.1[8]
TOTAL	32,440	100.0	12,574	100.0

Population economically active (1990): total 12,574 (42.0%); female participation in labour force 5,002 (39.8%); ages 17–64, 63.6%; unemployed (1996) 3.0%.

Price and earnings indexes (1995 = 100)

	1994	1995	1996	1997	1998	1999	2000
Consumer price index[9]	98.3	100.0	102.0	103.2	103.9	104.5	106.3
Earnings index	99.2	100.0	101.9	104.7	107.6	110.0	115.0

Household income and expenditure. Average household size (1998) 2.2; average annual income per household: n.a.; sources of income: n.a.; expenditure: n.a.
Tourism (1999): 2,219 hotel rooms; 278,000 overnight stays.
Land use (2000): forested 0%; meadows and pastures 0%; agricultural and under permanent cultivation 0%; built-up and other 100%.

Foreign trade

Monaco participates in a customs union (since 1963) with France; separate figures are not available.

Transport and communications

Transport. Railroads (1997): length 1.1 mi, 1.7 km; passengers 2,171,100; cargo 3,357 tons. Roads (1997): total length 31 mi, 50 km (paved 100%). Vehicles (1997): passenger cars 21,120; trucks and buses 2,770. Merchant marine (1997): vessels (100 gross tons and over) 9; total deadweight tonnage (1989) 4,959. Air transport (1999): traffic, not applicable; airports with scheduled flights: none[10].

Communications

Medium	date	unit	number	units per 1,000 persons
Daily newspapers	1999	circulation	10,000	300
Radio	1997	receivers	34,000	1,030
Television	1997	receivers	25,000	758
Telephones	1999	main lines	33,000	990
Cellular telephones	1999	subscribers	12,000	360

Education and health

Education (1996–97)

	schools	teachers	students	student/teacher ratio
Primary (age 6–10)	8	127	1,917	15.1
Secondary (age 11–17)	6	192	2,416	12.6
Vocational	4	89	532	6.0
Higher	1	...	112	...

Literacy: virtually 100%.
Health (1997): physicians 188 (1 per 170 persons); hospital beds 555 (1 per 58 persons); infant mortality rate per 1,000 live births (2000) 5.9.
Food: daily per capita caloric intake, n.a.; assuming consumption patterns similar to France (1999) 3,575 (vegetable products 62%, animal products 38%), 142% of FAO recommended minimum requirement.

Military

Defense responsibility lies with France according to the terms of the Versailles Treaty of 1919.

[1]Under the authority of the prince. [2]The principality is a single administrative unit, and no separate area within it is distinguished as capital. [3]Monégasque coins of equal value to French coins also circulate. [4]The main sources of revenue in 1997 were financial activities (about 50%) and tourism (about 25%); receipts from gambling had declined to about 4%. [5]UN estimate. [6]Officially economically active per 1990 census; the employed labour force in 1998 (including many foreign workers) was 32,697. [7]Finance, real estate includes Construction and Public utilities. [8]Includes not adequately defined. [9]The index is for France, which is united with Monaco in a customs and monetary union. [10]Fixed-wing service is provided at Nice, France; helicopter service is available at Fontvieille; passengers carried (1997) 131,038.

Internet resources for further information:
- **Welcome to Monaco (official guide) http://www.monaco.mc/monaco/index.html**

Mongolia

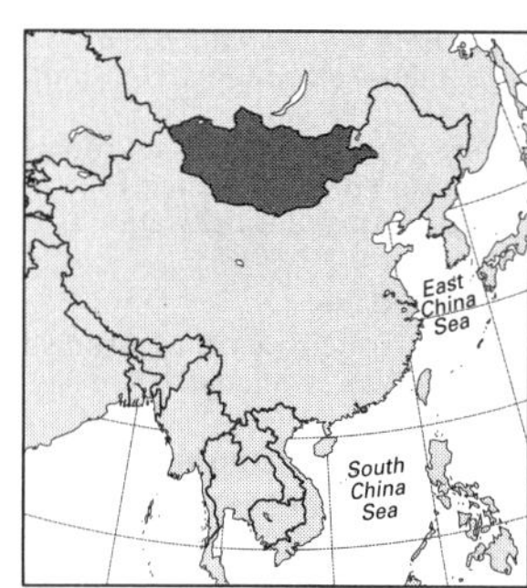

Official name: Mongol Uls (Mongolia).
Form of government: unitary multiparty republic with one legislative house (State Great Hural [76]).
Chief of state: President.
Head of government: Prime Minister.
Capital: Ulaanbaatar (Ulan Bator).
Official language: Khalkha Mongolian.
Official religion: none.
Monetary unit: 1 tugrik (Tug) = 100 möngö; valuation (Sept. 28, 2001) 1 U.S.$ = Tug 1,100; 1 £ = Tug 1,617.

Area and population

		area		population
Provinces	**Capitals**	sq mi	sq km	2000 census[1]
Arhangay	Tsetserleg	21,400	55,300	97,092
Bayan-Ölgiy	Ölgiy	17,600	45,700	91,068
Bayanhongor	Bayanhongor	44,800	116,000	84,779
Bulgan	Bulgan	18,800	48,700	61,776
Darhan-Uul	Darhan	1,270	3,280	83,271
Dornod	Choybalsan	47,700	123,600	75,373
Dornogovĭ	Saynshand	42,300	109,500	50,575
Dundgovĭ	Manalgovi	28,800	74,700	51,517
Dzavhan	Uliastay	31,900	82,500	89,999
Govĭ-Altay	Altay	54,600	141,400	63,673
Govĭ-Sümber	Choyr	2,140	5,540	12,230
Hentiy	Öndörhaan	31,000	80,300	70,946
Hovd	Hovd	29,400	76,100	86,831
Hövsgöl	Mörön	38,800	100,600	119,063
Ömnögovĭ	Dalandzadgad	63,900	165,400	46,858
Orhon	Erdenet	320	840	71,525
Övörhangay	Arvayheer	24,300	62,900	111,421
Selenge	Sühbaatar	15,900	41,200	99,950
Sühbaatar	Baruun-Urt	31,800	82,300	56,166
Töv	Dzüünmod	28,600	74,000	99,268
Uvs	Ulaangom	26,900	69,600	90,037
Autonomous municipality				
Ulaanbaatar	—	1,800	4,700	760,080
TOTAL	...	603,930[2]	1,564,160	2,373,498

Demography

Population (2001): 2,435,000.
Density (2001): persons per sq mi 4.0, persons per sq km 1.6.
Urban-rural (2000): urban 56.6%; rural 43.4%.
Sex distribution (2000): male 49.63%; female 50.37%.
Age breakdown (1999): under 15, 34.6%; 15–29, 30.6%; 30–44, 20.8%; 45–59, 8.3%; 60–69, 3.3%; 70 and over, 2.4%.
Population projection: (2010) 2,787,000; (2020) 3,174,000.
Doubling time: 47 years.
Ethnic composition (1989): Khalkha Mongol 78.8%; Kazakh 5.9%; Dörbed Mongol 2.7%; Bayad 1.9%; Buryat Mongol 1.7%; Dariganga Mongol 1.4%; other 7.6%.
Religious affiliation (1995): Tantric Buddhist (Lamaism) 96.0%; Muslim 4.0%.
Major cities (1999): Ulaanbaatar (Ulan Bator) 691,000; Darhan 72,600; Erdenet 65,700; Choybalsan 38,500; Ölgiy 23,700.

Vital statistics

Birth rate per 1,000 population (2001): 22.4 (world avg. 22.5).
Death rate per 1,000 population (2001): 7.5 (world avg. 9.0).
Natural increase rate per 1,000 population (2001): 14.9 (world avg. 13.5).
Total fertility rate (avg. births per childbearing woman; 2001): 2.4.
Marriage rate per 1,000 population (1999): 9.7.
Divorce rate per 1,000 population (1999): 0.7.
Life expectancy at birth (2001): male 61.0 years; female 65.0 years.
Major causes of death per 100,000 population: n.a.; however, in the early 1990s, major causes of mortality included diseases of the cardiovascular system, diseases of the respiratory system, and diseases of the cerebrovascular system.

National economy

Budget (1999). Revenue: Tug 243,504,400,000 (taxes 67.9%, of which sales tax 27.0%, social security contributions 15.3%, special taxes 10.2%, income taxes 8.5%, custom duties 3.7%; nontax revenue 19.4%). Expenditures: Tug 334,455,400,000 (transfers to provincial governments 11.2%; capital investment 8.8%; wages 7.5%; defense 5.8%; general social services 5.6%).
Public debt (external; 1999): U.S.$816,300,000.
Tourism (1999): receipts U.S.$36,000,000; expenditures U.S.$41,000,000.
Population economically active (1998): total 840,877; activity rate of total population 36.7% (participation rates: ages 15 and over 59.2%; female 48.0%; unemployed 5.7%).

Price and earnings indexes (1995 = 100)

	1993	1994	1995	1996	1997	1998	1999
Consumer price index	34.0	63.8	100.0	149.3	203.9	223.0	239.9
Monthly earnings index	...	59.7	100.0	146.4	185.4	234.4	...

Production (metric tons except as noted). Agriculture, forestry, fishing (1999): wheat 171,520, potatoes 63,765, vegetables and melons 46,524; livestock (number of live animals) 14,694,000 sheep, 11,062,000 goats, 3,726,000 cattle, 3,059,000 horses, 356,500 camels, 21,000 pigs; roundwood (1998) 631,000 cu m; fish catch (1997) 181. Mining and quarrying (1998): fluorspar 612,000; copper 358,400; molybdenum 4,240; gold 9,531 kg. Manufacturing (value added by manufacturing in Tug '000,000; 1996): food products 10,261.3; textiles 6,522.8; beverages 3,316.6; clothing and apparel 2,782.6; nonmetallic mineral products 1,708.8; leather and footwear 1,374.1; wood products 847.0; printing 834.2; chemicals 724.9. Construction (1994): residential 120,400 sq m. Energy production (consumption): electricity (kW-hr; 1996) 2,580,000,000 (2,975,-000,000); coal (metric tons; 1996) 5,111,000 (4,928,000); petroleum products (metric tons; 1996) none (544,000).
Gross national product (1999): U.S.$927,000,000 (U.S.$390 per capita).

Structure of gross domestic product and labour force

	1998			
	in value Tug '000,000[3]	% of total value	labour force	% of labour force
Agriculture	74,200	37.2	394,100	45.9
Manufacturing and mining	64,700	32.5	97,900	11.4
Construction	3,500	1.8	27,500	3.2
Transp. and commun.	8,800	4.4	33,400	3.9
Trade	29,600	14.8	...	...
Services[4]	18,600	9.3	239,700	27.9
Other	...	...	66,700[5]	7.8[5]
TOTAL	199,400	100.0	859,300	100.0[2]

Household income and expenditure (1999): Average household size (2000) 4.4; monthly income per household Tug 67,426 (U.S.$66); sources of income: wages and salaries 36.4%, transfer payments 11.7%, self-employment 41.2%[6], other 10.7%; expenditure: food 41.1%, housing 11.4%, clothing 9.7%, education 7.5%, transportation and communications 7.1%, healthcare 3.6%.
Land use (1998): forest and other 24.4%; pasture 74.8%; agriculture 0.8%.

Foreign trade[7]

Balance of trade (current prices)

	1994	1995	1996	1997	1998	1999
U.S.$'000,000	+97.7	+58.0	–26.6	–16.8	–158.1	–246.9
% of total	15.9%	6.5%	3.0%	1.8%	18.6%	13.9%

Imports (1998): U.S.$582,400,000 (capital equipment 33.5%, energy 15.7%, food 13.9%, consumer goods 12.6%, raw materials and spare parts 10.8%). *Major import sources:* Russia 29.9%; Japan 11.8%; China 11.6%; South Korea 7.5%; United States 7.2%; France 5.3%; Germany 5.1%.
Exports (1998): U.S.$462,300,000 (mineral products 59.0%, textile and cashmere products 13.5%, wool, hides, and leather goods 5.5%). *Major export destinations:* China 29.3%; Switzerland 20.4%; Russia 11.8%; South Korea 9.6%; United States 8.5%.

Transport and communications

Transport. Railroads (1999): length 1,815 km; passenger-km 559,800,000; metric ton-km cargo 1,942,000. Roads (1996): total length 50,000 km (paved 3%). Vehicles (1999): passenger cars 39,921; trucks and buses 31,061. Air transport (1996): passenger-km 525,000,000; metric ton-km cargo 48,000,000; airports (1997) with scheduled flights 1.

Communications

Medium	date	unit	number	units per 1,000 persons
Daily newspapers	1996	circulation	68,000	27
Radio	1997	receivers	360,000	142
Television	1998	receivers	152,000	58
Telephones	1999	main lines	103,400	39
Cellular telephones	1999	subscribers	34,562	13
Personal computers	1999	units	24,000	9.2
Internet	1999	users	6,000	2.3

Education and health

Educational attainment (1989). Percentage of population age 10 and over having: primary education 33.7%; some secondary 31.9%; complete secondary 16.9%; vocational secondary 9.4%; some higher and complete higher 8.1%.
Literacy (2000): percentage of total population age 7 and over literate 97.8%; males literate 98.0%; females literate 97.5%.

Education (1996–97)

	schools	teachers	students	student/ teacher ratio
Primary (age 6–12)	308	7,587	234,193	30.9
Secondary (age 13–16)	337	12,503	184,100	14.7
Vocational (age 16–18)	38	668	11,308	16.9
Higher	86	4,491	44,088	9.8

Health (1999): physicians 6,162 (1 per 384 persons) hospital beds 17,877 (1 per 132 persons); infant mortality rate per 1,000 live births (2001) 61.0.
Food (1999): daily per capita caloric intake 1,963 (vegetable products 55%, animal products 45%); (1997) 81% of FAO recommended minimum.

Military

Total active duty personnel (2000): 9,100 (army 82.4%, air force 17.6%). *Military expenditure as percentage of GNP* (1997): 1.9% (world 2.6%); per capita expenditure U.S.$8.

[1]January 5 de jure figure; rounded de facto figure equals 2,381,500. [2]Detail does not add to total given because of rounding. [3]At constant prices of 1993. [4]Services includes finance, public administration, and defense. [5]Includes unemployed and foreign workers. [6]Includes income from agricultural cooperatives. [7]Imports c.i.f. in balance of trade table.

Internet resources for further information:
- **Mongolia Online http://www.mol.mn**
- **Cyber Mongolia http://www.mongol.net**

Morocco

Official name: Al-Mamlakah al-Maghribīyah (Kingdom of Morocco).
Form of government: constitutional monarchy with two legislative houses (House of Councillors [270[1]]; House of Representatives [325]).
Chief of state and head of government: King assisted by Prime Minister.
Capital: Rabat.
Official language: Arabic.
Official religion: Islam.
Monetary unit: 1 Moroccan dirham (DH) = 100 Moroccan francs; valuation (Sept. 28, 2001) 1 U.S.$ = DH 11.32; 1 £ = DH 16.64.

Population (1994 census)[2]

Regions	Administrative centres	Population
Chaouia-Ouardigha	Settat	1,554,241
Doukkala-Abda	Safi	1,793,458
Fès-Boulemane	Fès	1,322,473
Gharb-Chrarda-Béni Hsen	Kénitra	1,625,082
Grand Casablanca	Casablanca	3,094,203
Guelmim-Es Semara	Guelmim	386,075
Laâyoune-Bojador-Sakia El-Hamra	Laâyoune	175,669
Marrakech-Tensift-El Haouz	Marrakech	2,724,204
Meknès-Tafilalt	Meknès	1,903,790
Oriental	Oujda	1,768,691
Oued Eddahab-Lagouira[3]	Dakhla	36,751
Rabat-Salé-Zemmour-Zaër	Rabat	1,985,602
Sous-Massa-Draâ	Agadir	2,622,947
Tadla-Azilal	Béni Mellal	1,324,662
Tangier-Tetouan	Tangier	2,036,032
Taza-Al Hoceïma-Taounate	Al-Hoceïma	1,719,837
	TOTAL	26,073,717

Demography

Area[2]: 274,461 sq mi, 710,850 sq km.
Population (2001)[2]: 29,237,000.
Density (2001)[2]: persons per sq mi 106.5, persons per sq km 41.1.
Urban-rural (1999): urban 52.7%; rural 47.3%.
Sex distribution (1999): male 49.89%; female 50.11%.
Age breakdown (1999): under 15, 35.7%; 15–29, 28.9%; 30–44, 18.9%; 45–59, 9.2%; 60–74, 5.3%; 75 and over, 2.0%.
Population projection[2]: (2010) 33,678,000; (2020) 38,415,000.
Doubling time: 38 years.
Ethnolinguistic composition (1995): Arab 65%; Berber 33%; other 2%.
Religious affiliation (2000): Muslim (mostly Sunnī) 98.3%; Christian 0.6%; other 1.1%.
Major urban areas (1994): Casablanca 2,940,623; Rabat-Salé 1,385,872; Fès 774,574; Marrakech 745,541; Oujda 678,778; Agadir 550,200.

Vital statistics

Birth rate per 1,000 population (2001): 24.2 (world avg. 22.5).
Death rate per 1,000 population (2001): 5.9 (world avg. 9.0).
Natural increase rate per 1,000 population (2001): 18.3 (world avg. 13.5).
Total fertility rate (avg. birth per childbearing woman; 2001): 3.0.
Life expectancy at birth (2001): male 67.2 years; female 71.7 years.
Major causes of death (1989)[4]: childhood diseases 22.9%; circulatory diseases 15.4%; accidents 7.3%; infectious and parasitic diseases 6.3%; cancers 5.6%.

National economy

Budget. Revenue (1997): DH 79,747,000,000 (taxes on income and profits 25.2%; value-added tax 22.7%; excise taxes 17.9%; international trade 15.0%; stamp tax 4.4%). Expenditures (1997): DH 86,058,000,000 (current expenditure 78.7%, of which wages 39.7%, debt payment 20.1%; capital expenditure 21.3%).
Public debt (external, outstanding; 1999): U.S.$17,284,000,000.
Tourism (1999): receipts U.S.$1,880,000,000; expenditures U.S.$440,000,000.
Production (metric tons except as noted). Agriculture, forestry, fishing (1999): sugar beets 3,223,400, wheat 2,153,540, barley 1,473,980, sugarcane 1,372,900, potatoes 1,140,780, oranges 873,500, tomatoes 857,410; livestock (number of live animals) 16,576,400 sheep, 5,114,400 goats, 2,559,800 cattle, 979,800 asses, 150,000 horses, 100,000 chickens, 36,000 camels; roundwood (1998) 1,746,000 cu m; fish catch (1997) 625,000. Mining and quarrying (1996): phosphate rock 20,792,000; barite 283,000; zinc 152,000; lead 108,000; copper 38,000; silver 199. Manufacturing (value added in DH '000,000; 1996): food 39,280; chemical products 13,508; textiles 12,392. Construction (authorized, urban areas; 1994): residential 7,069,557 sq m; nonresidential 998,424 sq m. Energy production (consumption): electricity (kW-hr; 1996) 12,178,000,000 (13,228,000,000); coal (metric tons; 1996) 504,000 (2,649,000); crude petroleum (barrels; 1996) 30,400 (45,600,000); petroleum products (metric tons; 1996) 5,112,000 (5,888,000); natural gas (cu m; 1996) 20,399,000 (20,399,000).
Population economically active (1998): total 5,137,539; activity rate 34.4% (participation rates: over age 15, 48.1%; female 23.8%; unemployed 19.0%).

Price index (1995 = 100)

	1994	1995	1996	1997	1998	1999	2000
Consumer price index	94.2	100.0	103.0	103.9	106.9	107.6	109.7
Earnings index	...	...	...	...	...	...	...

Gross national product (1999): U.S.$33,715,000,000 (U.S.$1,190 per capita).

Structure of gross domestic product and labour force

	1996		1993	
	in value DH '000,000	% of total value	labour force	% of labour force
Agriculture	65,478	20.4	2,906,000	34.0
Mining	5,539	1.7	2,650,000	31.0
Manufacturing	54,384	16.9		
Construction	13,515	4.2		
Public utilities	24,568	7.7		
Transp. and commun.	18,152	5.7	2,991,000	35.0
Trade	35,755	11.1		
Finance	...	...		
Pub. admin., defense	39,350	12.3		
Services	39,724	12.4		
Other	24,454	7.6		
TOTAL	320,919	100.0	8,547,000	100.0

Household income and expenditure. Average household size (1998) 5.7; expenditure (1994)[5]: food 45.2%, housing 12.5%, transportation 7.6%.

Foreign trade

Balance of trade (current prices)

	1995	1996	1997	1998	1999	2000
DH '000,000	–19,981	–17,830	–16,398	–21,306	–23,294	–25,174
% of total	14.5%	12.9%	10.9%	13.3%	13.9%	14.8%

Imports (1999): DH 95,577,000,000 (1996; capital goods 23.5%; food, beverages, and tobacco 17.1%; energy products 17.0%; consumer goods 14.6%). *Major import sources* (1996): France 20.8%; Spain 8.8%; U.S. 7.4%; Germany 6.1%.
Exports (1999): DH 72,283,000,000 (1996; food 31.6%; consumer goods 23.0%; minerals 11.0%). *Major export destinations* (1996): France 28.3%; Spain 9.9%; Japan 6.9%; India 6.3%; Italy 6.3%.

Transport and communications

Transport. Railroads (1996): route length 1,768 km; passenger-km 1,776,000,000; metric ton-km cargo 4,757,000,000. Roads (1996): total length 57,810 km (paved 52%). Vehicles (1996): passenger cars 1,018,146; trucks and buses 278,075. Air transport (1996): passenger-km 4,489,000,000[6]; metric ton-km cargo 380,000,000; airports (1998) 11.

Communications

Medium	date	unit	number	units per 1,000 persons
Daily newspapers	1996	circulation	704,000	27
Radio	1997	receivers	6,640,000	247
Television	1997	receivers	3,100,000	115
Telephones	1999	main lines	1,515,000	55
Cellular telephones	1999	subscribers	116,645	4.2
Personal computers	1999	units	200,000	7.1
Internet	1999	users	40,000	1.4

Education and health

Educational attainment (1982). Percentage of population age 25 and over having: no formal education 47.8%; some primary education 47.8%; some secondary 3.8%; higher 0.6%. *Literacy* (1995): total population over age 15 literate 43.7%; males literate 56.6%; females literate 31.0%.

Education (1996–97)

	schools	teachers	students	student/ teacher ratio
Primary (age 7–12)	5,806	114,406	3,160,907	27.6
Secondary (age 13–17)	451[7]	84,202	1,345,589	16.0
Vocational[8]	562[9]	...	96,460	...
Higher	13[10]	13,155	31,743	11.0

Health (1994): physicians 8,838 (1 per 2,923 persons); hospital beds 26,407 (1 per 978 persons); infant mortality rate (2001) 48.1.
Food (1999): daily per capita caloric intake 3,010 (vegetable products 94%, animal products 6%); 124% of FAO recommended minimum requirement.

Military

Total active duty personnel (2000): 198,500 (army 88.2%, navy 5.0%, air force 6.8%). *Military expenditure as percentage of GDP* (1997): 4.3% (world 2.6%); per capita expenditure U.S.$49.

[1]All seats indirectly elected; 162 by regional councils; 108 by industry, agriculture, and trade unions. [2]Includes Western Sahara, annexure of Morocco whose unresolved political status (from 1991) is to be eventually decided by a UN-sponsored referendum; Western Sahara area: 97,344 sq mi, 252,120 sq km, Western Sahara population (2001 est.) 251,000. [3]Includes Aousserd province created in late 1990s. [4]Registered deaths of urban population only. [5]Weights of consumer price index components. [6]Royal Air Maroc only. [7]1994–95. [8]Excludes teacher training. [9]1991–92. [10]Universities only.

Internet resources for further information:

- **Moroccan Ministry of Communication http://www.mincom.gov.ma**
- **Moroccan Ministry of Economic Forecasting http://www.mpep.gov.ma**

Mozambique

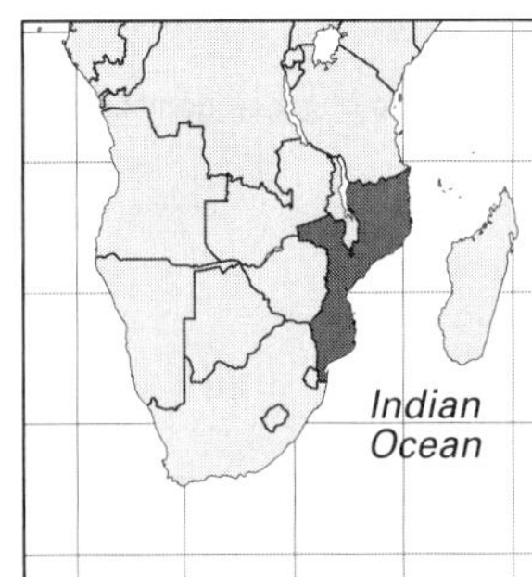

Official name: República de Moçambique (Republic of Mozambique).
Form of government: multiparty republic with a single legislative house (Assembly of the Republic [250]).
Head of state and government: President assisted by the Prime Minister.
Capital: Maputo.
Official language: Portuguese.
Official religion: none.
Monetary unit: 1 metical (Mt; plural meticais) = 100 centavos; valuation (Sept. 28, 2001) 1 U.S.$ = Mt 21,870; 1 £ = Mt 32,142.

Area and population

		area		population
Provinces	Capitals	sq mi	sq km	2000 estimate
Cabo Delgado	Pemba	31,902	82,625	1,465,537
Gaza	Xai-Xai	29,231	75,709	1,203,294
Inhambane	Inhambane	26,492	68,615	1,256,139
Manica	Chimoio	23,807	61,661	1,137,448
Maputo	Maputo	9,944	25,756	933,951
Nampula	Nampula	31,508	81,606	3,265,854
Niassa	Lichinga	49,828	129,055	870,544
Sofala	Beira	26,262	68,018	1,453,928
Tete	Tete	38,890	100,724	1,319,904
Zambézia	Quelimane	40,544	105,008	3,316,703
City				
Maputo	—	232	602	1,018,938
TOTAL LAND AREA		308,642[1]	799,379	
INLAND WATER		5,019	13,000	
TOTAL		313,661	812,379	17,242,240

Demography

Population (2001): 19,371,000[2].
Density (2001)[3]: persons per sq mi 61.9, persons per sq km 23.9.
Urban-rural (2000): urban 40.2%; rural 59.8%.
Sex distribution (2000): male 49.30%; female 50.70%.
Age breakdown (2000): under 15, 42.9%; 15–29, 29.1%, 30–44, 15.1%; 45–59, 8.5%; 60–74, 3.7%; 75 and over, 0.7%.
Population projection: (2010) 20,504,000[2]; (2020) 20,626,000[2].
Doubling time: 48 years.
Ethnic composition: Makuana 15.3%; Makua 14.5%; Tsonga 8.6%; Sena 8.0%; Lomwe 7.1%; Tswa 5.7%; Chwabo 5.5%; other 35.3%.
Linguistic composition (1997): Makua 26.3%; Tsonga 11.4%; Lomwe 7.6%; Sena 7.0%; Portuguese 6.5%; Chuaba 6.3%; other Bantu languages 33.0%; other 1.9%.
Religious affiliation (2000): traditional beliefs 50.4%; Christian 38.4%, of which Roman Catholic 15.8%, Protestant 8.9%; Muslim 10.5%.
Major cities (1997): Maputo 989,386; Matola 440,927; Beira 412,588; Nampula 314,965.

Vital statistics

Birth rate per 1,000 population (2000): 38.0 (world avg. 22.5).
Death rate per 1,000 population (2000): 23.3 (world avg. 9.0).
Natural increase rate per 1,000 population (2000): 14.7 (world avg. 13.5).
Total fertility rate (avg. births per childbearing woman; 2000): 4.9.
Marriage rate per 1,000 population (1974): 0.7.
Divorce rate per 1,000 population (1973): 0.01.
Life expectancy at birth (2000): male 38.3 years; female 36.7 years.

National economy

Budget (1997). Revenue: Mt 4,522,000,000 (1995; sales tax 47.8%, customs taxes 24.0%, individual income tax 16.6%). Expenditures: Mt 8,196,000,000 (current expenditure 52.2%, of which goods and services 23.6%, administrative salaries 22.3%, defense and security 19.4%; capital expenditure 47.8%).
Public debt (external, outstanding; 1999): U.S.$4,625,000,000.
Production (metric tons except as noted). Agriculture, forestry, fishing (2000): cassava 4,643,000, corn (maize) 1,109,000, sugarcane 440,000, coconuts 300,000, sorghum 252,000, rice 158,000, peanuts (groundnuts) 100,000, bananas 59,000; livestock (number of live animals) 1,320,000 cattle, 392,000 goats, 180,000 pigs, 125,000 sheep, 28,000,000 chickens; roundwood (1998) 17,977,000 cu m; fish catch (1998) 36,775. Mining and quarrying (1994): marine salt 40,000; bauxite 9,620; copper 133[4, 5]; garnet 3,000 kg; gemstones 6,865 carats. Manufacturing (value in Mt '000,000; 1995): food processing 696,611; beverages and tobacco 395,871; textiles 207,378; nonmetallic mineral products 140,193; wood and cork products 134,951; chemical products 116,335; rubber products 87,827; clothing 82,123; machinery and transport equipment 72,507. Construction (value in Mt; 1994) 157,700,000. Energy production (consumption): electricity (kW-hr; 1996) 568,000,000 (1,168,000,000); coal, none (none); crude petroleum, none (none[6]); petroleum products (metric tons; 1994) none[6] (251,000); natural gas, none (none).
Household income and expenditure. Average family size (1992–93) 6.7[7]; income per household: n.a.; source of income (1992–93)[7]: wages and salaries 51.6%, self-employment 12.5%, barter 11.5%, private farming 7.7%; expenditure (1992–93)[7]: food, beverages, and tobacco 74.6%; housing and energy 11.7%; transportation and communications 4.7%; clothing and footwear 3.7%; education and recreation 1.4%; health 0.8%.

Population economically active (1980): total 5,671,290; activity rate 48.6% (participation rates: over age 15, 87.3%; female 52.4%; unemployed 1.7%).

Price and earnings indexes (1995 = 100)

	1993	1994	1995	1996	1997	1998	1999
Consumer price index	39.7	64.8	100.0	146.9	156.3	157.1	160.3
Monthly earning index[8]	42.3	70.2	100.0	143.6	...	...	...

Gross national product (1999): U.S.$3,804,000,000 (U.S.$220 per capita).

Structure of gross domestic product and labour force

	1995		1980	
	in value Mt '000,000	% of total value	labour force	% of labour force
Agriculture	5,018,000	25.5	4,754,831	83.8
Mining	3,395,000[9]	17.2[9]	73,425	1.3
Manufacturing			273,369	4.8
Construction	2,405,000	12.2	42,121	0.7
Public utilities	[10]	[10]	[10]	[10]
Transp. and commun.	2,454,000	12.5	77,025	1.4
Finance	...	...	...	...
Trade	2,049,000	10.4	112,244	2.0
Pub. admin., defense	1,657,000	8.4	243,449[10]	4.3[10]
Services	2,191,000[10]	11.1[10]		
Other	514,000	2.6	94,826[11]	1.7[11]
TOTAL	19,685,000[1, 12]	100.0[1]	5,671,290	100.0

Land use (1994): forested 22.1%; meadows and pastures 56.1%; agricultural and under permanent cultivation 4.0%; other 17.8%.

Foreign trade[13]

Balance of trade (current prices)

	1994	1995	1996	1997	1998	1999
Mt '000,000,000	–2,300	–4,954	–6,224	–6,090	–6,793	–11,430
% of total	54.0%	61.2%	55.4%	53.8%	55.0%	62.5%

Imports (1996): U.S.$782,640,000 (machinery and transport equipment 32.3%, food and beverages 18.3%, basic manufactures 17.4%, petroleum products 9.6%). *Major import sources:* South Africa 34.5%; European Union 27.1%; Portugal 6.3%; U.S. 4.2%; Japan 4.0%; Zimbabwe 3.9%.
Exports (1996): U.S.$226,090,000 (food and beverages 66.4%, of which shell fish 38.1%; machinery and transport equipment 11.5%, cotton 5.7%, sugar and honey 5.7%). *Major export destinations:* European Union 34.7%; South Africa 19.4%; India 11.8%; U.S. 11.4%; Japan 7.6%.

Transport and communications

Transport. Railroads (1995): route length 1,940 mi, 3,123 km; passenger-mi 194,000,000, passenger-km 312,000,000; short ton-mi cargo 612,000,000, metric ton-km cargo 893,000,000. Roads (1996): total length 18,890 mi, 30,400 km (paved 18.8%). Vehicles (1995): passengers cars 84,000; trucks and buses 26,800. Air transport (1996): passenger-mi 161,511,000, passenger-km 259,927,000; short ton-mi cargo 3,709,000, metric ton-km cargo 5,415,000; airports (1997) with scheduled flights 7.

Communications

Medium	date	unit	number	units per 1,000 persons
Daily newspapers	1996	circulation	49,000	2.7
Radio	1997	receivers	730,000	40
Television	1999	receivers	95,000	5.0
Telephones	1999	main lines	78,000	4.0
Cellular telephones	1999	subscribers	12,000	0.6
Personal computers	1998	units	40,000	2.1
Internet	1999	users	15,000	0.8

Education and health

Literacy (2000): percentage of total population age 15 and over literate 43.8%; males literate 59.9%; females literate 28.4%.

Education (1995)

	schools	teachers	students	student/ teacher ratio
Primary (age 5–19)	4,167	24,575	1,415,428	57.6
Secondary (age 10–16)[14]	239[15]	4,376	165,868	37.9
Voc., teacher tr.	31[15]	1,239	19,313	15.6
Higher	3[15]	715	6,639	9.2

Health: physicians (1996) 120[16] (1 per 124,697 persons); hospital beds (1997) 12,630 (1 per 1,210 persons); infant mortality rate (2000) 139.9.
Food (1999): daily per capita caloric intake 1,939 (vegetable products 97%, animal products 3%); 83% of FAO recommended minimum requirement.

Military

Total active duty personnel (2000): 5,100–6,100[17]. *Military expenditure as percentage of GNP* (1997): 2.8% (world 2.6%); per capita expenditure U.S.$4.

[1]Detail does not add to total given because of rounding. [2]Estimate from U.S. Census Bureau International Data Base. [3]Based on land area. [4]1990. [5]Metal content only. [6]Internal disorder and a lack of foreign exchange have brought importation of crude petroleum and the production of refined petroleum products practically to a halt. [7]City of Maputo only. [8]Agricultural workers only. [9]Manufacturing includes fishing. [10]Services includes Public utilities. [11]Unemployed. [12]Reported as gross output. [13]Import figures are c.i.f. [14]Includes the two stages of secondary education and the upper-level primary stage. [15]1994. [16]Government personnel only. [17]Estimate; approximately 80% are in the army.

Internet resources for further information:
- **Instituto Nacional de Estatística http://www.ine.gov.mz**

Myanmar (Burma)

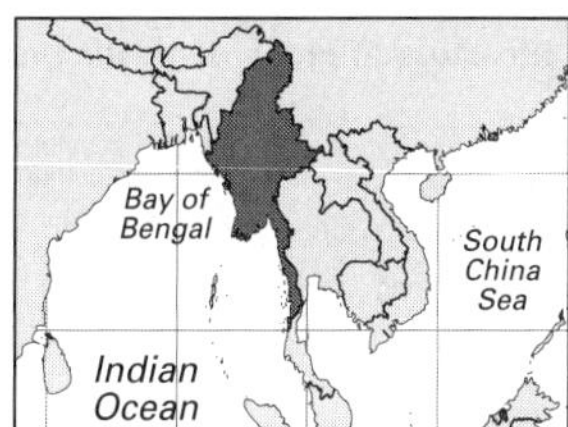

Official name: Pyidaungzu Myanma Naingngandaw (Union of Myanmar).
Form of government: military regime.
Head of state and government: Chairman of the State Peace and Development Council.
Capital: Yangôn (Rangoon).
Official language: Burmese.
Official religion: none.
Monetary unit: 1 Myanmar kyat (K) = 100 pyas; valuation[1] (Sept. 28, 2001) 1 U.S.$ = K 6.61; 1 £ = K 9.71.

Area and population

Divisions	Capitals	area sq mi	area sq km	population 1994 estimate
Irrawaddy (Ayeyarwady)	Bassein (Pathein)	13,567	35,138	6,107,000
Magwe (Magway)	Magwe (Magway)	17,305	44,820	4,067,000
Mandalay	Mandalay	14,295	37,024	5,823,000
Pegu (Bago)	Pegu (Bago)	15,214	39,404	4,607,000
Sagaing	Sagaing	36,535	94,625	4,889,000
Tenasserim (Tanintharyi)	Tavoy (Dawei)	16,735	43,343	1,187,000
Yangôn	Yangôn (Rangoon)	3,927	10,171	5,037,000
States				
Chin	Hakha	13,907	36,019	438,000
Kachin	Myitkyinā	34,379	89,041	1,135,000
Karen	Pa-an (Hpa-an)	11,731	30,383	1,323,000
Kayah	Loi-kaw	4,530	11,733	228,000
Mon	Moulmein (Mawlamyine)	4,748	12,297	2,183,000
Rakhine (Arakan)	Sittwe (Akyab)	14,200	36,778	2,482,000
Shan	Taunggyi	60,155	155,801	4,416,000
TOTAL		261,228	676,577	43,922,000

Demography

Population (2001): 41,995,000.
Density (2001): persons per sq mi 160.8, persons per sq km 62.1.
Urban-rural (1999): urban 27.0%; rural 73.0%.
Sex distribution (1997): male 49.65%; female 50.35%.
Age breakdown (1997): under 15, 33.3%; 15–29, 27.7%, 30–44, 19.8%; 45–59, 11.5%; 60 and over, 7.7%.
Population projection: (2010) 43,674,000; (2020) 44,775,000.
Doubling time: 56 years.
Ethnic composition (2000): Burman 55.9%; Karen 9.5%; Shan 6.5%; Han Chinese 2.5%; Mon 2.3%; Yangbye 2.2%; Kachin 1.5%; other 19.6%.
Religious affiliation (1983): Buddhist 89.4%; Christian 4.9%; Muslim 3.8%; traditional beliefs 1.2%; other 0.7%.
Major cities (1993 est.): Yangôn (Rangoon) 3,361,700; Mandalay 885,300; Moulmein (Mawlamyine) 307,600; Pegu (Bago) 190,900; Bassein (Pathein) 183,900.

Vital statistics

Birth rate per 1,000 population (2001): 24.2 (world avg. 22.5).
Death rate per 1,000 population (2001): 11.7 (world avg. 9.0).
Natural increase rate per 1,000 population (2001): 12.5 (world avg. 13.5).
Total fertility rate (avg. births per childbearing woman; 2001): 3.0.
Marriage rate per 1,000 population: n.a.
Divorce rate per 1,000 population: n.a.
Life expectancy at birth (2001): male 60.0 years; female 59.0 years.
Major causes of death per 100,000 population (1994): infectious and parasitic diseases 27.7; circulatory diseases 17.4; respiratory diseases 15.1; malignant neoplasms (cancers) 7.6; malnutrition 3.2.

National economy

Budget (1998–99). Revenue: K 80,400,000,000 (nontax revenue 55.6%; revenue from taxes 43.7%, of which taxes on goods and services 17.4%, taxes on income 15.3%; foreign grants 0.7%). Expenditures: K 72,100,000,000 (defense 34.0%; agriculture and forestry 13.3%; interest payments 12.5%; education 11.1%; public works and housing 8.7%; general services 6.8%).
Public debt (external, outstanding; 1999): U.S.$5,333,000,000.
Tourism: receipts from visitors (1999) U.S.$35,000,000; expenditures by nationals abroad U.S.$18,000,000.
Production (metric tons except as noted). Agriculture, forestry, fishing (1999): rice 17,075,000, sugarcane 5,429,000, pulses 1,895,000, peanuts (groundnuts) 562,000, plantains 423,000, corn (maize) 303,000, sesame seeds 210,000, seed cotton 158,000, opium poppy (2000) 1,085; livestock (number of live animals) 10,740,000 cattle, 6,100,000 ducks, 3,715,000 pigs, 2,391,000 buffalo; roundwood (1998) 22,430,000 cu m; fish catch (1997) 917,666. Mining and quarrying (1997–98): gypsum 40,642; copper concentrates 14,634; refined lead 1,585; tin concentrates 154; refined silver 9,381 kilograms. Manufacturing (1996): cement 513,000; fresh meat 116,000; fertilizers 66,000; refined sugar 43,000; cheese 29,000; butter 10,100; plywood 24,000 cu m; cigarettes 1,727,000,000 units; clay bricks 60,900,000 units. Construction (units; 1987–88)[2]: residential 1,193; nonresidential 1,483. Energy production (consumption): electricity (kW-hr; 1996) 4,256,000,000 (4,256,000,000); coal (metric tons; 1996) 72,000 (78,000); crude petroleum (barrels; 1996) 2,800,000 (5,300,000); petroleum products (metric tons; 1996) 679,000 (1,227,000); natural gas (cu m; 1996) 1,576,000,000 (1,576,000,000).
Household income and expenditure. Average household size (1994) 5.6; average annual income per household: n.a.; sources of income: n.a.; expenditure (1994)[3]: food and beverages 67.1%, fuel and lighting 6.6%, transportation 4.0%, charitable contributions 3.1%, medical care 3.1%.
Gross national product (1996): U.S.$119,334,000,000 (U.S.$2,610 per capita).

Structure of gross domestic product and labour force

	1997–98 in value K '000,000	% of total value	labour force[4]	% of labour force[4]
Agriculture	659,596	59.5	12,093,000	65.9
Mining	5,547	0.5	121,000	0.7
Manufacturing	78,801	7.1	1,666,000	9.1
Construction	26,494	2.4	400,000	2.2
Public utilities	1,558	0.1	26,000	0.1
Transp. and commun.	43,727	3.9	495,000	2.7
Trade	257,613	23.2	1,781,000	9.7
Finance	3,014	0.3	1,485,000	8.1
Public admin., services	13,293	1.2		
Other	19,911	1.8	270,000	1.5
TOTAL	1,109,554	100.0	18,337,000	100.0

Population economically active (1997–98): total 19,743,000; activity rate of total population 42.5% (participation rates: ages 15–64 [1983] 64.2%; female [1987–88] 35.3%; unemployed 6.2%).

Price and earnings indexes (1995 = 100)

	1994	1995	1996	1997	1998	1999	2000
Consumer price index	79.9	100.0	116.3	150.8	228.5	270.5	270.2
Monthly earnings index	...	...	...	...	...	...	...

Land use (1994): forested 49.3%; meadows and pastures 0.5%; agricultural and under permanent cultivation 15.3%; other 34.9%.

Foreign trade[5]

Balance of trade (current prices)

	1995	1996	1997	1998	1999	2000
K '000,000	–2,738.4	–3,612.5	–7,320.1	–10,183.5	–7,390.4	–6,252.2
% of total	22.1%	29.0%	40.3%	43.0%	34.3%	25.4%

Imports (1997–98): K 12,735,900,000 (machinery and transport equipment 28.6%, intermediate raw materials 19.9%, basic manufactures 15.8%, capital construction materials 12.3%, consumer durable goods 4.3%). *Major import sources:* Singapore 31.1%; Japan 15.3%; Thailand 9.8%; China 9.4%; Malaysia 7.0%; South Korea 5.5%; Indonesia 4.8%.
Exports (1997–98): K 5,415,800,000 (pulses and beans 22.3%, teak 11.1%, fish and fish products 4.6%, hardwood 2.5%, rubber 2.1%). *Major export destinations:* India 22.6%; Singapore 13.2%; Thailand 11.9%; China 10.6%; Hong Kong 5.8%; Japan 3.8%; United States 3.5%.

Transport and communications

Transport. Railroads (1998): route length (1999–2000) 3,955 km; passenger-km 3,948,000,000; metric ton-km cargo 984,000,000. Roads (1996): total length 28,200 km (paved 12%). Vehicles (1996): passenger cars 27,000; trucks and buses 42,000. Air transport (1995–96): passenger-km 438,000,000; metric ton-km cargo 3,212,000; airports (1996) 19.

Communications

Medium	date	unit	number	units per 1,000 persons
Daily newspapers	1996	circulation	449,000	10
Radio	1997	receivers	4,200,000	96
Television	1999	receivers	323,000	7.2
Telephones	1999	main lines	249,083	5.5
Cellular telephones	1999	subscribers	11,389	0.3
Personal computers	1999	units	50,000	1.1
Internet	1999	users	500	0.01

Education and health

Educational attainment (1983). Percentage of population age 25 and over having: no formal schooling 55.8%; primary education 39.4%; secondary 4.6%; religious 0.1%; postsecondary 0.1%. *Literacy* (1995): total population age 15 and over literate 83.1%; males literate 88.7%; females literate 77.7%.

Education (1997–98)

	schools	teachers	students	student/ teacher ratio
Primary (age 5–9)	35,877	167,134	5,145,400	30.8
Secondary (age 10–15)	2,091	56,955	1,545,600	27.1
Voc., teacher tr.[6]	103	2,462	25,374	10.3
Higher	923	17,089	385,300	22.5

Health (1995–96): physicians 12,950 (1 per 3,114 persons); hospital beds 28,732 (1 per 1,404 persons); infant mortality rate per 1,000 live births (2001) 89.0.
Food (1999): daily per capita caloric intake 2,803 (vegetable products 96%, animal products 4%); (1997) 130% of FAO recommended minimum requirement.

Military

Total active duty personnel (2000): 429,000 (army 95.6%, navy 2.3%, air force 2.1%). *Military expenditure as percentage of GNP* (1996): 7.6% (world 2.6%); per capita expenditure U.S.$87.

[1]Pegged rate to the Special Drawing Right of the International Monetary Fund. [2]Construction Corporation activity only. [3]Yangôn only. [4]Employed only. [5]Import figures are c.i.f. in balance of trade and in commodities and trading partners. [6]1994–95.

Internet resources for further information:
- **Myanmar Home Page http://www.myanmar.com/e-index.html**

Namibia

Official name: Republic of Namibia.
Form of government: republic with two legislative houses (National Council[1] [26]; National Assembly [72[2]]).
Head of state and government: President.
Capital: Windhoek.
Official language: English.
Official religion: none.
Monetary unit: 1 Namibian dollar (N$) = 100 cents; valuation (Sept. 28, 2001) 1 U.S.$ = N$9.01; 1 £ = N$13.24.

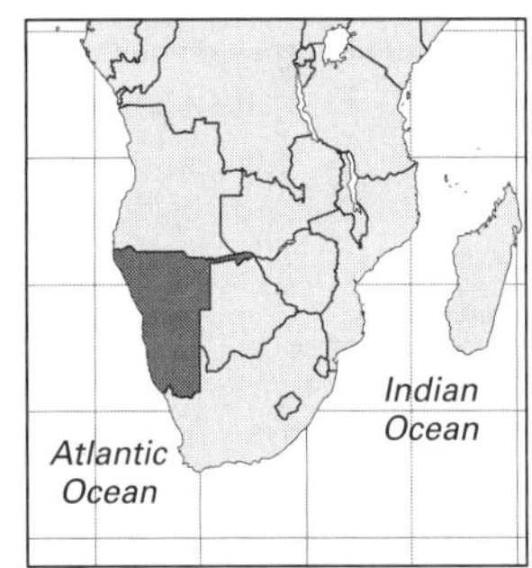

Area and population[3]

		area		population
Regions	Chief towns	sq mi	sq km	1997 estimate
Erongo[3]	Omaruru	24,602	63,719	98,500
Hardap	Mariental	42,428	109,888	80,000
Karas	Keetmanshoop	62,288	161,324	73,000
Khomas	Windhoek	14,210	36,804	174,000
Kunene	Opuwo	55,697	144,254	58,500
Liambezi (Caprivi)	Katima Mulilo	7,541	19,532	92,000
Ohangwena	Oshikango	4,086	10,582	178,000
Okavango	Rundu	16,763	43,417	136,000
Omaheke	Gobabis	32,715	84,731	55,600
Omusati	Ongandjera	5,265	13,637	158,000
Oshana	Oshakati	2,042	5,290	159,000
Oshikoto	Tsumeb	10,273	26,607	176,000
Otjozondjupa	Grootfontein	40,667	105,327	85,000
TOTAL		318,580[4]	825,118[4]	1,523,600

Demography

Population (2001): 1,798,000.
Density (2001): persons per sq mi 5.6, persons per sq km 2.2.
Urban-rural (1999): urban 39.8%; rural 60.2%.
Sex distribution (1999): male 49.85%; female 50.15%.
Age breakdown (1999): under 15, 43.2%; 15–29, 28.6%, 30–44, 15.1%; 45–59, 7.7%; 60–74, 4.0%; 75 and over, 1.4%.
Population projection: (2010) 1,908,000; (2020) 1,956,000.
Doubling time: 51 years.
Ethnic composition (1991): Ovambo 50.7%; Nama 12.5%; Kavango 9.7%; Herero 8.0%; San (Bushman) 1.9%; Tswana 0.4%; other 16.8%.
Religious affiliation (2000): Protestant (mostly Lutheran) 47.5%; Roman Catholic 17.7%; African Christian 10.8%; traditional beliefs 6.0%; other 18.0%.
Major cities (1991 census): Windhoek 147,056; Walvis Bay 22,999; Oshakati 21,603; Rehoboth 21,439; Rundu 19,366; Swakopmund 15,500[5].

Vital statistics

Birth rate per 1,000 population (2001): 34.7 (world avg. 22.5).
Death rate per 1,000 population (2001): 20.9 (world avg. 9.0).
Natural increase rate per 1,000 population (2001): 13.8 (world avg. 13.5).
Total fertility rate (avg. births per childbearing woman; 2001): 4.8.
Life expectancy at birth (2001): male 42.5 years; female 38.7 years.
Major causes of death per 100,000 population: n.a.; however, in the early 1990s, tuberculosis had become a serious problem (especially in the southern regions); AIDS cases, while few, were increasing exponentially.

National economy

Budget (1999–2000). Revenue: N$7,128,400,000 (customs taxes 31.4%, general sales tax 28.2%, individual income taxes 17.9%, nontax revenues 8.9%, mining taxes 3.1%). Expenditures: N$8,009,400,000 (1996–97; education 23.2%, health and welfare 10.3%, transportation 6.1%, defense 5.8%, social security 5.4%).
Tourism (1998): receipts from visitors U.S.$288,000,000; expenditures by nationals abroad U.S.$88,000,000.
Public debt (1997): U.S.$697,000,000.
Production (metric tons except as noted). Agriculture, forestry, fishing (1999): roots and tubers 260,000, cereals 71,100,000 (of which millet 46,300, corn [maize] 18,300, sorghum 3,300, wheat 3,000), fruits 10,000, vegetables and melons 10,000, pulses 8,000; livestock (number of live animals) 2,100,000 sheep, 2,000,000 cattle, 1,700,000 goats; fish catch (1998) 352,188. Mining and quarrying (1998): diamonds 1,440,000 carats (mostly gem quality); zinc 78,617; copper 8,014; uranium 3,257; silver 740,000 troy oz; gold 60,500 troy oz. Manufacturing: n.a.; products include cut gems (primarily diamonds), fur products (karakul), processed foods (fish, meats, and dairy products), textiles, carved wood products, refined metals (copper and lead). Construction (value of buildings completed in N$'000,000; 1994): residential 347.7; nonresidential 160.4. Energy production (consumption): electricity (kW-hr; 1992) 1,714,000,000 (1,714,000,000); coal, none (n.a.); crude petroleum, none (n.a.).
Population economically active: total (1991) 493,580; activity rate of total population, 34.9% (participation rates: ages 15–64, 61.3%; female 43.5%; unemployed 20.1%).

Price and earnings indexes (1995 = 100)

	1994	1995	1996	1997	1998	1999
Consumer price index	90.9	100.0	108.0	117.5	124.8	135.5
Earnings index	...	...	...	...	...	...

Gross national product (1999): U.S.$3,211,000,000 (U.S.$1,890 per capita).

Structure of gross domestic product and labour force

	1998		1991	
	in value N$'000,000	% of total value	labour force[6]	% of labour force
Agriculture	1,804	10.7	189,929	38.5
Mining	1,876	11.2	14,686	3.0
Manufacturing	2,414	14.3	22,884	4.6
Construction	323	1.9	18,638	3.8
Public utilities	353	2.1	2,974	0.6
Transp. and commun.	613	3.6	9,322	1.9
Trade[7]	1,476	8.8	37,820	7.7
Finance	1,480	8.8	8,547	1.7
Services	507	3.0		
Public administration and defense	3,999	23.8	89,541	18.1
Other	1,981[8]	11.8[8]	99,239[9]	20.1[9]
TOTAL	16,826	100.0	493,580	100.0

Household income and expenditure. Average household size (1991) 5.2; average annual income per household (1980) R 3,223 (U.S.$4,143); sources of income (1992): wages and salaries 69.0%, income from property 25.6%, transfer payments 5.4%; expenditure: n.a.
Land use (1994): forested 15.2%; meadows and pastures 46.2%; agricultural and under permanent cultivation 0.8%; other 37.8%.

Foreign trade

Balance of trade (current prices)

	1991	1992	1993	1994	1995	1996
U.S.$'000,000	+102	+79	+122	+165	−98	−25
% of total	4.3%	3.0%	5.0%	6.6%	3.5%	0.9%

Imports (1994): N$4,467,700,000 (machinery and transport equipment 27.1%, of which transport equipment 16.2%; food and live animals 22.3%; minerals and fuels 11.4%; chemical products 8.1%). *Major import sources* (1993): South Africa 87.0%[10]; Germany 3.0%; France 2.0%; Japan 2.0%.
Exports (1994): N$4,692,000,000 (minerals 50.1%, of which diamonds 31.4%; food and live animals 47.0%, of which fish and fish products 28.6%, cattle and meat products 12.6%; karakul pelts 0.2%). *Major export destinations* (1993): U.K. 34.0%; South Africa 27.0%; Japan 10.0%; Spain 6.0%.

Transport and communications

Transport. Railroads: length (1995) 1,480 mi, 2,382 km; passenger-km 34,700,000; metric ton-km 1,077,000,000. Roads (1996): total length 25,130 mi, 65,220 km (paved 7.7%). Vehicles (1996): passenger cars 74,875; trucks and buses 66,500[11]. Merchant marine (1992): vessels (100 gross tons and over) 30; total deadweight tonnage 5,874. Air transport (1996)[12]: passenger-km 756,000,000; metric ton-km cargo 23,000,000; airports (1997) with scheduled flights 11.

Communications

Medium	date	unit	number	units per 1,000 persons
Daily newspapers	1996	circulation	30,000	19
Radio	1997	receivers	232,000	143
Television	1999	receivers	65,000	38
Telephones	1999	main lines	108,000	64
Cellular telephones	1999	subscribers	30,000	18
Personal computers	1999	units	50,000	29
Internet	1999	users	6,000	3.5

Education and health

Educational attainment (1991). Percentage of population age 25 and over having: no formal schooling 35.1%; primary education 31.9%; secondary 28.5%; higher 4.5%. *Literacy* (2000): total population age 15 and over literate 830,200 (82.1%); males literate 416,000 (82.9%); females literate 414,200 (81.2%).

Education (1994)

	schools	teachers	students	student/teacher ratio
Primary (age 6–12)	933	10,912[13]	366,666	32.0[13]
Secondary (age 13–19)	114	2,534[14]	101,838	29.3[14]
Voc., teacher tr.	17	140[15]	1,503	11.9[15]
Higher	7	213[16]	6,523	11.8[16]

Health: physicians (1992) 324 (1 per 4,594 persons); hospital beds (1989) 6,997 (1 per 216 persons); infant mortality rate per 1,000 live births (2001) 71.7.
Food (1999): daily per capita caloric intake 2,096 (vegetable products 89%, animal products 11%); 92% of FAO recommended minimum requirement.

Military

Total active duty personnel (2000): 9,000 (army 98.9%, navy 1.1%[17]). *Military expenditure as percentage of GNP* (1997): 2.7% (world 2.6%); per capita expenditure U.S.$57.

[1]Mostly an advisory body. [2]72 elected and up to 6 appointed members. [3]Includes the 434 sq mi (1,124 sq km) former district of Walvis Bay (1992 population estimate, 23,000) that was jointly administered with South Africa from November 1992 to March 1994. [4]Detail does not add to total given because of rounding. [5]1990 estimate. [6]Includes more than 140,000 nonwage (informal) workers. [7]Includes hotels. [8]Includes import duties and excise taxes. [9]Unemployed. [10]Includes goods from other countries shipped via South Africa. [11]1995. [12]Namib Air only. [13]1992. [14]1990. [15]1989. [16]1991. [17]Coast Guard for fishery protection.

Internet resources for further information:
- **Namibia Fact Sheet http://www.emulateme.com/namibia.htm**
- **Bank of Namibia http://www.bon.com.na**

Nauru

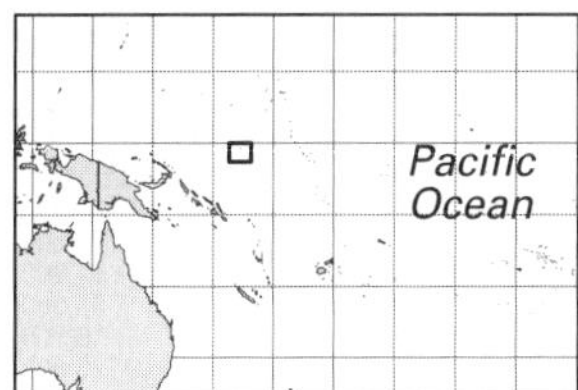

Official name: Naoero (Republic of Nauru).
Form of government: republic with one legislative house (Parliament [18]).
Head of state and government: President.
Capital: [1].
Official language: none.
Official religion: none.
Monetary unit: 1 Australian dollar ($A) = 100 cents; valuation (Sept. 28, 2001) 1 U.S.$ = $A 2.03; 1 £ = $A 2.98.

Area and population

	area		population
			1992
Districts	sq mi	sq km	census[2]
Aiwo	0.4	1.1	1,072
Anabar	0.6	1.5	320
Anetan	0.4	1.0	427
Anibare	1.2	3.1	165
Baitsi	0.5	1.2	450
Boe	0.2	0.5	750
Buada	1.0	2.6	661
Denigomodu	0.3	0.9	2,548
Ewa	0.5	1.2	355
Ijuw	0.4	1.1	206
Meneng	1.2	3.1	1,269
Nibok	0.6	1.6	577
Uaboe	0.3	0.8	447
Yaren	0.6	1.5	672
TOTAL	8.2	21.2	9,919

Demography

Population (2001): 12,100.
Density (2001): persons per sq mi 1,476, persons per sq km 570.8.
Urban-rural (1999): urban 100%; rural 0%.
Sex distribution (1999): male 50.50%; female 49.50%.
Age breakdown (1999): under 15, 41.6%; 15–29, 25.5%; 30–44, 19.7%; 45–59, 10.0%; 60–74, 2.9%; 75 and over 0.3%.
Population projection: (2010) 14,300; (2020) 16,700.
Doubling time: 33 years.
Ethnic composition (1992): Nauruan 68.9%; other Pacific Islander 23.7%, of which Kiribati 12.8%, Tuvaluan 8.7%; Asian 5.9%, of which Filipino 2.5%, Chinese 2.3%; other 1.5%.
Religious affiliation (1995): Protestant 53.5%, of which Congregational 35.3%, Pentecostal 4.8%; Roman Catholic 27.5%; other 19.0%.
Major cities: none; population of Yaren district (1996) 700.

Vital statistics

Birth rate per 1,000 population (2000): 22.9 (world avg. 22.5); legitimate, n.a.; illegitimate, n.a.
Death rate per 1,000 population (2000): 5.1 (world avg. 9.0).
Natural increase rate per 1,000 population (2000): 17.8 (world avg. 13.5).
Total fertility rate (avg. births per childbearing woman; 1999): 3.8.
Marriage rate per 1,000 population (1995): 5.3.
Divorce rate per 1,000 population: n.a.
Life expectancy at birth (1999): male 57.0 years; female 64.1 years.
Major causes of death per 100,000 population: n.a.[3]

National economy

Budget (1999). Revenue: $A 38,700,000[4]. Expenditures: $A 37,200,000.
Public debt (external, outstanding; beginning of 1996): *c.* U.S.$150,000,000.
Tourism: receipts from visitors (1999) virtually none; expenditures by nationals abroad, n.a.
Gross national product (at current market prices; 1997): U.S.$128,000,000 (U.S.$11,538 per capita).

Distribution of gross domestic product and labour force

	1995		1997	
	in value U.S.$'000,000	% of total value	labour force[5, 6, 7]	% of labour force
Agriculture	...	...	...	...
Mining (phosphate)	...	...	528	24.7
Manufacturing	...	...	...	...
Construction	...	...	...	...
Public utilities	...	...	...	...
Transportation and communications	...	...	...	...
Hotels	...	...	137	6.4
Finance[8]	...	...	33	1.6
Services	...	...	...	...
Pub. admin.	...	...	1,238	58.0
Other	...	...	198	9.3
TOTAL	368	100.0	2,134	100.0

Production (metric tons except as noted). Agriculture, forestry, fishing (1999): coconuts 1,600, vegetables 450, tropical fruit (including mangoes) 275; almonds, figs, and pandanus are also cultivated, but most foodstuffs and beverages (including water) are imported; livestock (number of live animals) 3,000 pigs; roundwood, none; fish catch 500. Mining and quarrying (1998): phosphate rock (gross weight) 500,000. Manufacturing: none; virtually all consumer manufactures are imported. Construction: n.a. Energy production (consumption): electricity (kW-hr; 1996) 32,000,000 (32,000,000); coal, none (n.a.); crude petroleum, none (n.a.); petroleum products (metric tons; 1996) none (45,000); natural gas, none (n.a.).
Population economically active (1992): 2,453[6, 9]; activity rate of total population 35.9% (participation rates: over age 15, n.a.; female, n.a.; unemployed, 18.2%).
Price and earnings indexes: [10].
Household income and expenditure. Average household size (1992) 10.0[6]; income per household: n.a.; sources of income: n.a.; expenditure: n.a.
Land use (1995): forested, nil; meadows and pastures, nil; agricultural and under permanent cultivation *c.* 10%[11]; other *c.* 90%[12].

Foreign trade

Balance of trade (current prices)

	1990	1991	1992	1993	1994	1995
U.S.$'000,000	+50	+12	+15	+21	+20	+20
% of total	61.0%	22.2%	27.8%	34.4%	33.3%	33.3%

Imports (1995): U.S.$20,000,000 (agricultural products 20.5%, of which food 14.5%; remainder 79.5%). *Major import sources:* Australia more than 50%; United Kingdom *c.* 10%; New Zealand *c.* 10%.
Exports (1995): U.S.$40,000,000 (phosphate, virtually 100%). *Major export destinations:* New Zealand *c.* 50%; Australia *c.* 25%.

Transport and communications

Transport. Railroads (1997): length 3 mi, 5 km; passenger traffic, n.a.; metric ton-km cargo, n.a. Roads (1996): total length 19 mi, 30 km (paved 79%). Vehicles (1989): passenger cars, trucks, and buses 1,448. Merchant marine (1992): vessels 2, total deadweight tonnage 5,791. Air transport (1996): passenger-mi 151,000,000, passenger-km 243,000,000; short ton-mi cargo 15,000,000, metric ton-km cargo 24,000,000; airports (1999) with scheduled flights 1.

Communications

Medium	date	unit	number	units per 1,000 persons
Daily newspapers	—	circulation	—	—
Radio	1997	receivers	7,000	609
Television	1997	receivers	500	48
Telephones	1998	main lines	1,700	149
Cellular telephones	1998	subscribers	850	75
Personal computers	1998	units	...	...
Internet	1998	users	...	...

Education and health

Educational attainment (1992).[6] Percentage of population age 5 and over having primary education or less 77.4%; secondary education 12.9%; higher 4.1%; not stated 5.6%. *Literacy* (1995): total population age 15 and over literate 99%.

Education (1997)[6]

	schools	teachers	students	student/ teacher ratio
Primary (age 6–13) } Secondary (age 14–17) }	3	64	1,379	21.5
Vocational	3	53	1,113	21.0
Higher	—	—	—	—

Health: physicians (1995) 17 (1 per 637 persons); hospital beds (1990) 207 (1 per 46 persons); infant mortality rate per 1,000 live births (1999) 11.1.
Food (1998)[13]: daily per capita caloric intake 3,011 (vegetable products 70%, animal products 30%); (1997) 132% of FAO recommended minimum requirement.

Military

Total active duty personnel (2001): Nauru does not have any military establishment. The defense is assured by Australia, but no formal agreement exists.

[1]Government offices are located in Yaren district. [2]Preliminary. [3]Morbidity is often associated with dietary and social problems (particularly obesity and alcoholism). In 1989, 32% of adult Nauruans were diagnosed with diabetes mellitus. [4]Largely from phosphate exports. [5]Employed only. [6]Nauruan only. [7]Most non-Nauruans are phosphate industry contract workers. [8]400 offshore banks were registered in Nauru in mid-2001. [9]Excludes activity not stated. [10]Minimum wage remained constant between November 1992 and the end of 1997. [11]Cultivatable coastal strip. [12]Phosphate-extracted interior wasteland. [13]Data for Oceania.

Nepal

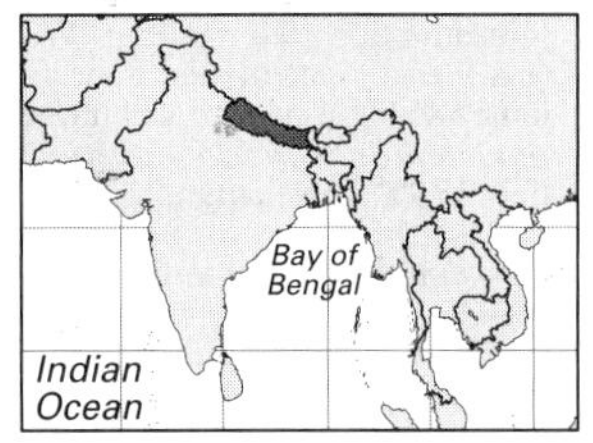

Official name: Nepal Adhirajya (Kingdom of Nepal).
Form of government: constitutional monarchy with a bicameral parliament consisting of two legislative houses (National Council [60[1]]; House of Representatives [205]).
Chief of state: King.
Head of government: Prime Minister.
Capital: Kathmandu.
Official language: Nepali.
Official religion: Hinduism.
Monetary unit: 1 Nepalese rupee (NRs) = 100 paisa (pice); valuation (Sept. 28, 2001) 1 U.S.$ = NRs 76.11; 1 £ = NRs 111.86.

Area and population

Development regions / Zones	Capitals	area sq mi	area sq km	population 1991 census
Eastern	Dhankuta	10,987	28,456	4,446,749
Koshi	Dharan	3,733	9,669	1,728,247
Mechi	Ilam	3,165	8,196	1,118,210
Sagarmatha	Rajbiraj	4,089	10,591	1,600,292
Central	Kathmandu	10,583	27,410	6,183,955
Bagmati	Bhaktapur	3,640	9,428	2,250,805
Janakpur	Sindhulimadi	3,733	9,669	2,061,816
Narayani	Hetauda	3,210	8,313	1,871,334
Western	Pokhara	11,351	29,398	3,770,678
Dhawalagiri	Bagluri	3,146	8,148	490,877
Gandaki	Chame	4,740	12,275	1,266,128
Lumbini	Butawal	3,465	8,975	2,013,673
Mid-western	Surkhet	16,362	42,378	2,410,414
Bheri	Nepalganj	4,071	10,545	1,103,043
Karnali	Manma	8,244	21,351	260,529
Rapti	Tulsipur	4,047	10,482	1,046,842
Far-western	Dipayal	7,544	19,539	1,679,301
Mahakali	Dadeldhura	2,698	6,989	664,952
Seti	Silgadhi	4,846	12,550	1,014,349
TOTAL		56,827	147,181	18,491,097

Demography

Population (2001): 25,284,000.
Density (2001): persons per sq mi 444.9, persons per sq km 171.8.
Urban-rural (1999): urban 11.0%; rural 89.0%.
Sex distribution (1997): male 50.20%; female 49.80%.
Age breakdown (1996): under 15, 43.1%; 15–29, 26.0%; 30–44, 16.0%; 45–59, 9.4%; 60–74, 4.6%; 75 and over, 0.9%.
Population projection: (2010) 30,758,000; (2020) 36,925,000.
Doubling time: 29 years.
Ethnic composition (1991): Nepalese 53.2%; Bihari (including Maithili and Bhojpuri) 18.4%; Tharu 4.8%; Tamang 4.7%; Newar 3.4%; Magar 2.2%; Abadhi 1.7%; other 11.6%.
Religious affiliation (2000): Hindu 75.9%; traditional beliefs 9.3%; Buddhist 8.1%; Muslim 3.8%; Christian 2.4%; other 0.5%.
Major cities (2000 est.): Kathmandu 701,499; Pokhara 168,806; Biratnagar 168,544; Lalitpur 157,495; Birganj 103,880.

Vital statistics

Birth rate per 1,000 population (2001): 34.7 (world avg. 22.5).
Death rate per 1,000 population (2001): 10.3 (world avg. 9.0).
Natural increase rate per 1,000 population (2001): 24.4 (world avg. 13.5).
Total fertility rate (avg. births per childbearing woman; 2001): 4.6.
Life expectancy at birth (2001): male 59.0 years; female 59.0 years.
Major causes of death per 100,000 population: n.a.; however, the leading causes of mortality are infectious and parasitic diseases, diseases of the respiratory system, and diseases of the nervous system.

National economy

Budget (1999). Revenue: NRs 40,698,000,000 (taxes on goods and services 29.2%, taxes on international trade 23.9%, foreign grants 14.5%, income taxes 14.2%, state property revenues 8.4%, administrative fees 5.5%). Expenditures: NRs 58,391,000,000 (education 13.6%, transport and communications 11.4%, fuel and energy 9.0%, health 6.5%, agriculture 5.5%, housing 4.7%, defense 4.5%, public order 4.3%, general public services 3.7%).
Public debt (external, outstanding; 1999): U.S.$2,910,000,000.
Land use (1994): forested 42.0%; meadows and pastures 14.6%; agricultural and under permanent cultivation 17.2%; other 26.2%.
Tourism (1999): receipts from visitors U.S.$168,000,000; expenditures by nationals abroad U.S.$71,000,000.
Production (metric tons except as noted). Agriculture, forestry, fishing (1999): rice 3,710,000, sugarcane 1,972,000, corn (maize) 1,346,000, potatoes 1,091,000, wheat 1,086,000, millet 291,000, pulses 213,000; livestock (number of live animals) 7,030,698 cattle, 6,204,616 goats, 3,470,600 buffalo, 855,159 sheep, 825,132 pigs; roundwood (1998) 21,474,000 cu m; fish catch (1997) 23,206. Mining and quarrying (1997): limestone 369,000; salt 7,000; talc 6,800. Manufacturing (value added in U.S.$'000,000; 1995): textiles 78; food products 74; wearing apparel 54; tobacco products 41; nonmetal mineral products 35. Construction: n.a. Energy production (consumption): electricity (kW-hr; 1996) 1,218,000,000 (1,243,000,000); coal (metric tons; 1996) none (50,000); petroleum products (metric tons; 1996) none (427,000).
Gross national product (1999): U.S.$5,173,000,000 (U.S.$220 per capita).

Structure of gross domestic product and labour force

	1998–99 in value NRs '000,000[2]	1998–99 % of total value[2]	1991 labour force	1991 % of labour force
Agriculture	129,600	37.6	5,961,788	81.2
Mining	1,800	0.5	2,367	—
Manufacturing	31,800	9.2	150,051	2.0
Construction	33,500	9.7	35,658	0.5
Public utilities	5,300	1.5	11,734	0.2
Transp. and commun.	26,800	7.8	50,808	0.7
Trade	38,700	11.2	256,012	3.5
Finance	35,100	10.2	20,847	0.3
Services	29,900	8.7	752,019	10.3
Other	12,400[3]	3.6[3]	98,302	1.3
TOTAL	344,900	100.0	7,339,586	100.0

Population economically active (1991): total 7,339,586; activity rate of total population 39.7% (participation rates: ages 10 years and over, 57.0%; female 45.5%; unemployed [1996] 4.9%).

Price and earnings indexes (1995 = 100)

	1994	1995	1996	1997	1998	1999	2000
Consumer price index	92.9	100.0	109.2	113.6	125.0	135.1	137.1
Monthly earnings index[4]	...	100.0	100.0	100.0	124.1	124.1	...

Household income and expenditure (1984–85). Average household size (1991) 5.6; income per household NRs 14,796 (U.S.$853); sources of income: self-employment 63.4%, wages and salaries 25.1%, rent 7.5%, other 4.0%; expenditure: food and beverages 61.2%, housing 17.3%, clothing 11.7%, health care 3.7%, education and recreation 2.9%, transp. and commun. 1.2%, other 2.0%.

Foreign trade[5]

Balance of trade (current prices)

	1994	1995	1996	1997	1998	1999
U.S.$'000,000	−790.2	−960.9	−1,106.0	−1,278.1	−757.1	−880.7
% of total	51.7%	57.9%	58.7%	60.7%	44.0%	38.3%

Imports (1996–97): NRs 96,006,000,000 (basic manufactured goods 47.6%; machinery and transport equipment 14.7%; chemicals 8.8%; mineral fuels and lubricants 7.5%; food and live animals, chiefly for food 6.6%; crude materials except fuels 5.5%). *Major import sources:* India 23.3%; Hong Kong 14.3%; Singapore 13.0%; Japan 11.2%; China 6.4%; New Zealand 5.1%.
Exports (1996–97): NRs 22,481,000,000 (basic manufactures 48.7%; miscellaneous manufactures 29.2%; food and live animals, chiefly for food 12.6%; chemicals and drugs 5.9%; crude materials except fuels 2.6%). *Major export destinations:* U.S. 34.4%; India 9.5%; Bangladesh 1.4%; China 0.9%.

Transport and communications

Transport. Railroads (1995–96): route length (1999) 59 km; passengers carried 1,379,000; freight handled 5,320 metric tons. Roads (1997): total length 7,700 km (paved 42%). Vehicles (1997–98): passenger cars 47,541; trucks and buses 29,371. Air transport (1995): passenger-km 856,000,000; metric ton-km cargo 93,000,000; airports (1996) with scheduled flights 24.

Communications

Medium	date	unit	number	units per 1,000 persons
Daily newspapers	1996	circulation	250,000	11
Radio	1997	receivers	840,000	38
Television	1999	receivers	150,000	6.7
Telephones	1999	main lines	253,035	11
Cellular telephones	1999	subscribers	5,500	0.2
Personal computers	1999	units	60,000	2.7
Internet	1999	users	35,000	1.6

Education and health

Educational attainment (1981). Percentage of population age 25 and over having: no formal schooling 41.2%; primary education 29.4%; secondary 22.7%; higher 6.8%. *Literacy* (1995): total population age 15 and over literate 27.5%; males literate 40.9%; females literate 14.0%.

Education (1996)

	schools	teachers	students	student/teacher ratio
Primary (age 6–10)	22,218	89,378	3,447,607	38.6
Secondary (age 11–15) / Vocational	7,582[6]	36,127	1,121,335	31.0
Higher	3[7]	4,925[8]	105,694	22.4[8]

Health (1996): physicians 872 (1 per 25,745 persons); hospital beds 3,604 (1 per 6,229 persons); infant mortality rate per 1,000 live births (2001) 74.
Food (1999): daily per capita caloric intake 2,264 (vegetable products 93%, animal products 7%); (1997) 103% of FAO recommended minimum.

Military

Total active duty personnel (2000): 46,000 (army 99.5%, air force 0.5%). *Military expenditure as percentage of GNP* (1997): 0.8% (world 2.6%); per capita expenditure U.S.$2.

[1]Includes 10 members nominated by the king. [2]Estimate. [3]Includes indirect taxes. [4]Minimum monthly wage rates for unskilled industrial workers; 1994–95 = 100. [5]Import figures are f.o.b. in balance of trade and c.i.f. for commodities and trading partners. [6]1995. [7]1993. [8]1991.

Internet resources for further information:
- **Nepal Home Page http://www.info-nepal.com**
- **Central Bank of Nepal http://www.nrb.org.np**

Netherlands, The

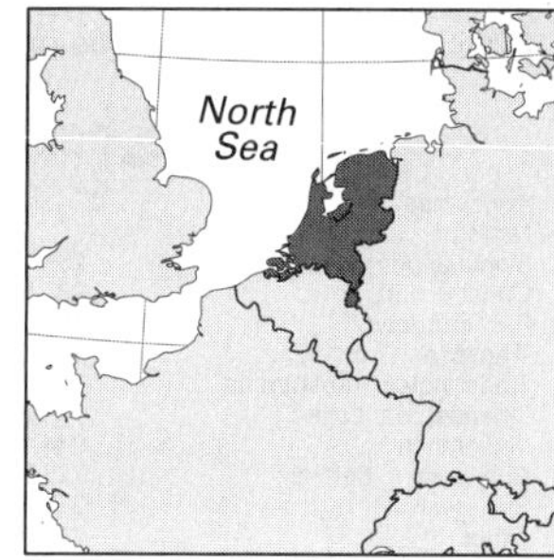

Official name: Koninkrijk der Nederlanden (Kingdom of The Netherlands).
Form of government: constitutional monarchy with a parliament (States General) comprising two legislative houses (First Chamber [75]; Second Chamber [150]).
Chief of state: Monarch.
Head of government: Prime Minister.
Seat of government: The Hague.
Capital: Amsterdam.
Official language: Dutch.
Official religion: none.
Monetary unit: 1 Netherlands guilder (f.) = 100 cents; valuation (Sept. 28, 2001) 1 U.S.$ = f. 2.42; 1 £ = f. 3.56; 1 € = f. 2.20371.

Area and population

		area		population
Provinces	Capitals	sq mi	sq km	2000[1] estimate
Drenthe	Assen	1,035	2,680	469,800
Flevoland	Lelystad	931	2,412	317,200
Friesland	Leeuwarden	2,217	5,741	624,500
Gelderland	Arnhem	1,986	5,143	1,919,200
Groningen	Groningen	1,146	2,967	562,600
Limburg	Maastricht	853	2,209	1,141,200
Noord-Brabant	's-Hertogenbosch	1,962	5,082	2,356,000
Noord-Holland	Haarlem	1,567	4,059	2,518,400
Overijssel	Zwolle	1,320	3,420	1,077,600
Utrecht	Utrecht	554	1,434	1,107,800
Zeeland	Middelburg	1,132	2,932	371,900
Zuid-Holland	The Hague	1,331	3,446	3,397,700
TOTAL		16,033[2, 3]	41,526[2, 3]	15,864,000[2]

Demography

Population (2001): 15,968,000.
Density (2000)[4]: persons per sq mi 1,221.0, persons per sq km 471.4.
Urban-rural (1999): urban 89.3%; rural 10.7%.
Sex distribution (2000[1]): male 49.46%; female 50.54%.
Age breakdown (2000[1]): under 15, 18.6%; 15–29, 19.3%; 30–44, 24.2%; 45–59, 19.8%; 60–74, 12.1%; 75 and over, 6.0%.
Population projection: (2010) 16,638,000; (2020) 17,089,000.
Ethnic composition (by place of origin [including 2nd generation]; 2000[1]): Netherlander 82.5%; Indonesian 2.6%; Turkish 1.9%; Surinamese 1.9%; Moroccan 1.7%; Netherlands Antillean/Aruban 0.7%; other 8.7%[5].
Religious affiliation (1999[1]): Roman Catholic 31.0%; Reformed (NHK) 14.0%; other Reformed 7.0%; Muslim 4.5%; Hindu 0.5%; nonreligious 41.0%; other 2.0%.
Major urban agglomerations (2000[1]): Amsterdam 1,002,868; Rotterdam 989,956; The Hague 610,245; Utrecht 366,186; Eindhoven 302,274.

Vital statistics

Birth rate per 1,000 population (1999): 12.7 (world avg. 22.5); legitimate 77.3%; illegitimate 22.7%.
Death rate per 1,000 population (1999): 8.9 (world avg. 9.0).
Natural increase rate per 1,000 population (1999): 3.8 (world avg. 13.5).
Total fertility rate (avg. births per childbearing woman; 2000): 1.6.
Marriage rate per 1,000 population (2000): 5.3.
Life expectancy at birth (2000): male 75.3 years; female 80.6 years.
Major causes of death per 100,000 population (1999): diseases of the circulatory system 313.3; malignant neoplasms (cancers) 247.2; diseases of the respiratory system 90.8; accidents and violence 32.8.

National economy

Budget (1997). Revenue: f. 324,360,000,000 (social security taxes 41.1%; income and corporate taxes 24.8%; value-added and excise taxes 22.7%; property taxes 3.0%). Expenditures: f. 337,620,000,000 (social security and welfare 37.4%; health 14.8%; education 10.0%; interest payments 9.1%; defense 3.9%; transportation 3.5%).
Public debt (1999): U.S.$251,763,000,000.
Production (metric tons except as noted). Agriculture, forestry, fishing (2000): potatoes 8,200,000, sugar beets 5,504,000, wheat 1,183,000, onions 766,000, tomatoes 600,000, apples 575,000, barley 319,000, flowering bulbs and tubers 55,600 acres (22,500 hectares), of which tulips 24,000 acres (9,700 hectares), cut flowers/plants under glass 14,625 acres (5,917 hectares); livestock (number of live animals; 2000) 13,140,000 pigs, 4,200,000 cattle, 1,401,000 sheep; roundwood (1999) 1,044,000 cu m; fish catch (1997) 550,009. Manufacturing (value added in f. '000,000; 1998): food, beverages and tobacco 24,323; chemicals and chemical products 15,009; printing and publishing 11,267; electric/electronic machinery 10,385. Energy production (consumption): electricity (kW-hr; 1999) 86,616,000,000 (93,505,000,000); coal (metric tons; 1996) negligible (14,996,000); crude petroleum (barrels; 1999) 10,973,000 ([1996] 424,957,000); petroleum products (metric tons; 1996) 65,755,000 (33,662,000); natural gas (cu m; 1999) 70,777,000,000 ([1996] 54,789,000).
Household income and expenditure. Average household size (2000) 2.3; spendable income per household (1997) f. 53,597 (U.S.$27,468); sources of income (1995): wages 48.2%, transfers 29.0%, property income 11.8%; expenditure (1995): housing 15.2%; food and beverages 13.5%; transportation and communications 13.1%; health care 13.1%; recreation 9.9%.

Gross national product (1999): U.S.$397,384,000,000 (U.S.$25,140 per capita).

Structure of gross domestic product and labour force

	1999		1998	
	in value f. '000,000	% of total value	labour force	% of labour force
Agriculture	20,554	2.5	236,000	3.1
Mining	14,503	1.8	11,000	0.1
Manufacturing	125,570	15.2	1,104,000	14.3
Construction	43,091	5.2	451,000	5.8
Public utilities	13,046	1.6	47,000	0.6
Transp. and commun.	55,723	6.8	442,000	5.7
Trade	112,907	13.7	1,487,000	19.2
Finance, real estate	199,652	24.2	1,097,000	14.2
Pub. admin., defense	87,044	10.6	525,000	6.8
Services	84,717	10.3	1,811,000	23.4
Other	67,176[6]	8.1[6]	524,000[7]	6.8[7]
TOTAL	823,983	100.0	7,735,000	100.0

Population economically active (1998): total 7,735,000; activity rate of total population 49.3% (participation rates: ages 15–64, 72.9%; female 42.5%; unemployed [October 1999–September 2000] 2.7%).

Price and earnings indexes (1995 = 100)

	1995	1996	1997	1998	1999	2000	2001[8]
Consumer price index	100.0	102.0	104.2	106.3	108.6	111.4	114.5
Hourly earnings index	100.0	101.7	104.8	108.1	111.3	115.4	117.5

Tourism (1999): receipts U.S.$7,092,000,000; expenditures U.S.$11,366,000,000.
Land use (1994): forested 10.3%; meadows and pastures 31.0%; agricultural and under permanent cultivation 28.0%; other 30.7%.

Foreign trade[9]

Balance of trade (current prices)

	1995	1996	1997	1998	1999	2000
f. '000,000	+31,155	+28,361	+32,732	+26,926	+21,773	+30,243
% of total	5.2%	4.4%	4.5%	3.5%	2.7%	3.1%

Imports (1999): f. 393,845,000,000 (machinery 31.5%, chemicals and chemical products 11.0%, food 8.7%, road vehicles 8.0%). *Major import sources:* Germany 19.3%; Belgium-Luxembourg 10.0%; U.K. 9.7%; U.S. 9.5%; France 6.5%.
Exports (1999): f. 415,618,000,000 (machinery 27.8%, chemicals and chemical products 15.3%, food 13.4%, mineral fuels 5.9%). *Major export destinations:* Germany 26.1%; Belgium-Luxembourg 12.2%; France 10.8%; U.K. 10.8%; Italy 6.0%.

Transport and communications

Transport. Railroads (1999): length 2,808 km; passenger-km 14,330,000,000; metric ton-km cargo 3,521,000,000. Roads (1996): total length 124,530 km (paved 91%). Vehicles (2000): passenger cars 6,343,000; trucks and buses 826,000. Air transport (1999)[10]: passenger-km 58,112,000,000; metric ton-km cargo 3,910,532,000; airports (1996) 6.

Communications

Medium	date	unit	number	units per 1,000 persons
Daily newspapers	1996	circulation	4,753,000	306
Radio	1998	receivers	12,000,000	764
Television	1999	receivers	9,500,000	601
Telephones	1999	main lines	9,610,000	608
Cellular telephones	1999	subscribers	6,900,000	436
Personal computers	1999	units	5,700,000	361
Internet	1999	users	3,000,000	190

Education and health

Educational attainment (1999). Percentage of population ages 15–64 having: primary education 13.4%; lower secondary 10.4%; upper secondary/vocational 53.9%; tertiary vocational 15.5%; university 6.8%.

Education (1999–2000)[11]

	schools	teachers	students	student/ teacher ratio
Primary (age 6–12)	7,224	...	1,543,000	...
Secondary (age 12–18)	635	...	861,000	...
Vocational[12]	65	...	250,000	...
Higher[13]	13	...	150,000	...

Health (1999): physicians 27,090 (1 per 582 persons); hospital beds 81,328 (1 per 194 persons); infant mortality rate per 1,000 live births 5.2.
Food (1999): daily per capita caloric intake 3,243 (vegetable products 64%, animal products 36%); 121% of FAO recommended minimum requirement.

Military

Total active duty personnel (2000): 51,940 (army 44.5%, navy 23.8%, air force 21.8%, paramilitary 10.0%). *Military expenditure as percentage of GNP* (1997): 1.9% (world 2.6%); per capita expenditure U.S.$438.

[1]January 1. [2]Detail does not add to total given because of rounding. [3]Includes inland water area totaling 2,955 sq mi (7,653 sq km). [4]Based on land area only (13,078 sq mi [33,873 sq km]). [5]Includes Netherlander-EU country 4.6%. [6]Imputed value added tax less subsidies and bank service charges. [7]Includes 337,000 registered unemployed. [8]February. [9]Imports c.i.f.; exports f.o.b. [10]KLM only. [11]Public schools only. [12]Colleges only. [13]Universities only.

Internet resources for further information:
- **Statistics Netherlands http://www.cbs.nl/en**

Netherlands Antilles

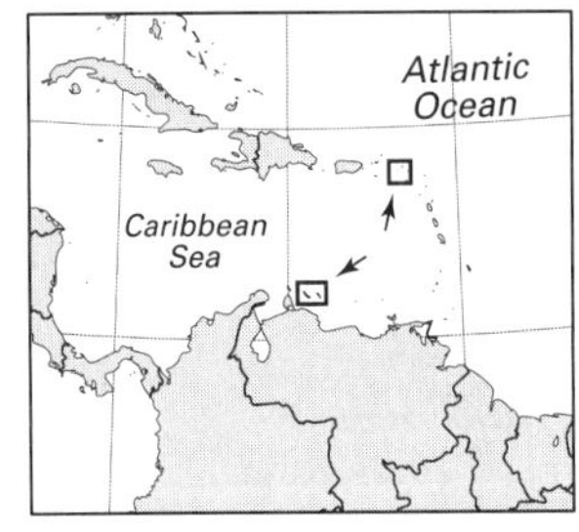

Official name: Nederlandse Antillen (Netherlands Antilles).
Political status: nonmetropolitan territory of The Netherlands with one legislative house (States of the Netherlands Antilles [22])[1].
Chief of state: Dutch Monarch represented by Governor.
Head of government: Prime Minister.
Capital: Willemstad.
Official language: Dutch.
Official religion: none.
Monetary unit: 1 Netherlands Antillean guilder (NA f.) = 100 cents; valuation (Sept. 28, 2001) 1 U.S.$ = NA f. 1.79; 1 £ = NA f. 2.63.

Area and population

Island councils	Capitals	area sq mi	area sq km	population 2000[2] estimate
Leeward Islands				
Bonaire	Kralendijk	111	288	13,724
Curaçao	Willemstad	171	444	143,387
Windward Islands				
Saba	The Bottom	5	13	1,704
Sint Eustatius, or Statia	Oranjestad	8	21	2,249
Sint Maarten (Dutch part only)	Philipsburg	13	34	41,718
TOTAL		308	800	202,782

Demography

Population (2001): 205,000.
Density (2001): persons per sq mi 665.6, persons per sq km 256.2.
Urban-rural (2000): urban 70.0%; rural 30.0%.
Sex distribution (2000)[2]: male 47.99%; female 52.01%.
Age breakdown (2000): under 15, 25.5%; 15–29, 18.2%; 30–44, 26.0%; 45–59, 18.9%; 60–74, 8.6%; 75 and over, 2.8%.
Population projection: (2010) 221,000; (2020) 235,000.
Doubling time: 96 years.
Ethnic composition (2000): local black-other (Antillean Creole) 81.1%; Dutch 5.3%; Surinamese 2.9%; other (significantly West Indian black) 10.7%.
Religious affiliation (1992): Roman Catholic 73.9%; Protestant 10.4%, of which Methodist 3.0%, Seventh-day Adventist 2.2%; Jehovah's Witness 1.5%; Jewish 0.3%; Muslim 0.2%; nonreligious 6.3%; other 8.9%.
Major cities: Willemstad (urban area; 1999) 123,000; Kralendijk (2001) 7,900; Philipsburg (2001) 6,300.

Vital statistics

Birth rate per 1,000 population (1999): 13.7 (world avg. 22.5); (1988)[3] legitimate 51.6%; illegitimate 48.4%.
Death rate per 1,000 population (1999): 6.5 (world avg. 9.0).
Natural increase rate per 1,000 population (1999): 7.2 (world avg. 13.5).
Total fertility rate (avg. births per childbearing woman; 2000): 2.1.
Marriage rate per 1,000 population (1999): 4.7.
Divorce rate per 1,000 population (1999): 2.6.
Life expectancy at birth (2000): male 72.6 years; female 77.0 years.
Major causes of death per 100,000 population (1993): infectious and parasitic diseases/diseases of the respiratory system 209.0; diseases of the circulatory system 180.2; malignant neoplasms (cancers) 117.7.

National economy

Budget (1999). Revenue: NA f. 498,300,000 (tax revenue 83.2%, of which import duties 28.0%, sales tax 20.4%, excise on gasoline 18.8%; nontax revenue 15.3%). Expenditures: NA f. 626,200,000 (current expenditures 91.9%; development expenditures 8.1%).
Production (metric tons except as noted). Agriculture, forestry, fishing: [4]; livestock (number of live animals; 1999) 13,000 goats, 7,300 sheep, 2,600 asses, 135,000 chickens; roundwood, n.a.; fish catch (1997) 1,105. Mining and quarrying (1997): salt 432,225, sulfur by-product 27,600. Manufacturing (1996): residual fuel oil 5,013,000; gas-diesel oils 2,218,000; other manufactures include electronic parts, cigarettes, textiles, rum, and Curaçao liqueur. Energy production (consumption): electricity (kW-hr; 1996) 1,482,000,000 (1,482,000,000); coal, none (none); crude petroleum (barrels; 1996) none (93,334,000); petroleum products (metric tons; 1996) 9,952,000 (851,000); natural gas, none (none).
Land use (1998): forested, negligible; meadows and pastures, negligible; agricultural and under permanent cultivation 10.0%; other (dry savanna) 90.0%.
Tourism (2000): receipts from visitors U.S.$765,000,000; expenditures by nationals abroad U.S.$339,000,000.
Household income and expenditure. Average household size (1999) 3.2; income per household: n.a.; sources of income: n.a.; expenditure (1996)[5, 6]: housing 26.5%, transportation and communications 19.9%, food 14.7%, household furnishings 8.8%, recreation and education 8.2%, clothing and footwear 7.5%.
Gross national product (at current market prices; 1997): U.S.$2,609,000,000 (U.S.$12,490 per capita).

Structure of gross domestic product and labour force

	1995 in value NA f. '000,000	1995 % of total value	1992 labour force	1992 % of labour force
Agriculture / Mining	31.8	0.7	788	0.9
Manufacturing	281.8	6.6	6,935	7.9
Construction	282.5	6.6	6,474	7.4
Public utilities	165.2	3.9	1,241	1.4
Transp. and commun.[7]	557.0	13.1	4,984	5.7
Trade, hotels, restaurants	1,065.0	25.1	20,832	23.7
Finance, real estate, insurance	944.1	22.2	8,190	9.3
Pub. admin., defense	771.9	18.2	24,674	28.1
Services[8]	370.3	8.7		
Other	–219.1[9]	–5.2[9]	13,638[10]	15.5[10]
TOTAL	4,250.5	100.0[11]	87,756	100.0[11]

Population economically active (1992): total 87,756; activity rate of total population 46.3% (participation rates: ages 15–64, 68.6%; female 45.1%; unemployed [1998] 16.7%).

Price index (1996 = 100)

	1995	1996	1997	1998	1999	2000	2001[12]
Consumer price index	96.5	100.0	103.3	104.4	104.8	110.9	112.5
Monthly earnings index[13]	...	100.0	100.0	100.0	...	...	...

Public debt (external, outstanding; 1999): U.S.$294,600,000.

Foreign trade

Balance of trade (current prices)

	1995	1996	1997	1998	1999	2000[14]
NA. f '000,000	–1,939	–2,003	–1,998	–1,815	–1,905	–1,851
% of total	71.3%	70.8%	67.6%	62.6%	60.4%	42.6%

Imports (1999): NA f. 2,375,000,000 (nonpetroleum domestic imports 71.3%, crude petroleum and petroleum products 14.8%, imports of Curaçao free zone 13.9%). *Major import sources* (1998)[15]: Venezuela 37%; United States 22%; Mexico 7%; The Netherlands 5%; Italy 5%.
Exports (1999): NA f. 470,000,000 (reexports of Curaçao free zone 59.1%, nonpetroleum domestic exports 37.5%, petroleum products 3.4%). *Major export destinations* (1998)[15]: United States 23%; Guatemala 10%; The Bahamas 6%; Guyana 6%; Chile 4%.

Transport and communications

Transport. Railroads: none. Roads (1992): total length 367 mi, 590 km (paved, 51%). Vehicles (1996): passenger cars 75,105; trucks and buses 17,753. Air transport (1998)[16]: passenger arrivals and departures 959,000; freight loaded and unloaded 11,100 metric tons; airports (1995) with scheduled flights 6.

Communications

Medium	date	unit	number	units per 1,000 persons
Daily newspapers	1996	circulation	70,000	341
Radio	1997	receivers	217,000	1,039
Television	1997	receivers	69,000	330
Telephones	1999	main lines	79,000	386
Cellular telephones	1998	subscribers	16,000	77

Education and health

Educational attainment (1992). Percentage of employed population having: no formal schooling or some primary education 21.5%; completed primary 50.8%; completed vocational or secondary 24.3%; completed higher 3.4%.
Literacy (1995): total population age 15 and over literate 194,900 (96.6%); males literate 93,300 (96.6%); females literate 101,600 (96.6%).

Education (1997–98)

	schools	teachers	students	student/ teacher ratio
Primary (age 6–12)	85[17]	1,111	24,061	21.7
Secondary (age 12–17)	21	...	8,372	...
Voc., teacher tr.	33	...	8,254	...
Higher	1	97	686	7.1

Health (1997): physicians 339 (1 per 616 persons); hospital beds 1,466 (1 per 142 persons); infant mortality rate per 1,000 live births (2000) 11.7.
Food (1999): daily per capita caloric intake 2,591 (vegetable products 67%, animal products 33%); 107% of FAO recommended minimum requirement.

Military

Total active duty personnel (1999): a 45-member Dutch naval/air force contingent is stationed in the Netherlands Antilles and Aruba.

[1]The Netherlands Antilles included Aruba before Jan. 1, 1986. [2]January 1. [3]Excludes Sint Eustatius. [4]Mostly tomatoes, beans, cucumbers, gherkins, melons, and lettuce grown on hydroponic farms; aloes grown for export, divi-divi pods, and sour orange fruit are nonhydroponic crops. [5]Curaçao only. [6]Weights of consumer price index components. [7]Includes ship repair and transshipment and storage of cargo. [8]Includes extraterritorial organizations and bodies. [9]Less imputed bank service charges. [10]Includes 13,434 unemployed. [11]Detail does not add to total given because of rounding. [12]March. [13]Minimum wages only. [14]Method of calculation is different from 1995–99. [15]Estimated figures. [16]Curaçao airport only. [17]1996–97.

Internet resources for further information:
- **Central Bank of the Netherlands Antilles http://www.centralbank.an**

New Caledonia

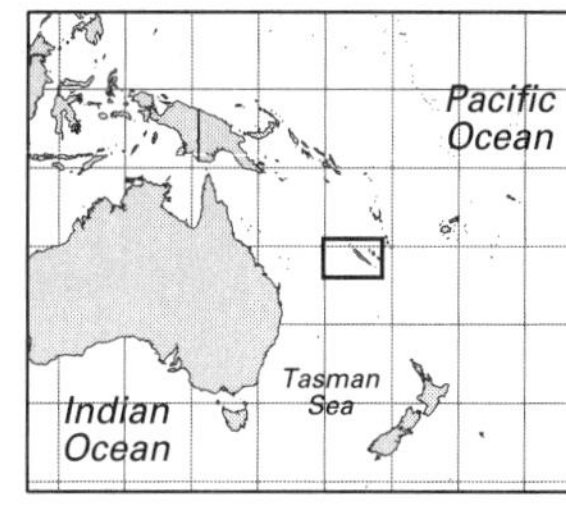

Official name: Nouvelle-Calédonie (New Caledonia)[1].
Political status: overseas country[1] (France) with one legislative house (Congress[2] [54]).
Chief of state: President of France represented by High Commissioner.
Head of government: President.
Capital: Nouméa.
Official language: none[3].
Official religion: none.
Monetary unit: 1 franc of the Comptoirs français du Pacifique (CFPF) = 100 centimes; valuation (Sept. 28, 2001) 1 U.S.$ = CFPF 130.21; 1 £ = CFPF 191.37.

Area and population

Provinces Island(s)	Capitals	area sq mi	area sq km	population 1996 census
Loyauté (Loyalty)	Wé	765	1,981	20,877
Maré		248	642	6,896
Lifou		466	1,207	10,007
Ouvéa		51	132	3,974
Nord (Northern)	Koné	3,305	8,561	41,413
Belep		27	70	923
New Caledonia (part)		3,278	8,491	40,490
Sud (Southern)	Nouméa	3,102	8,033	134,546
New Caledonia (part)		3,043	7,881	132,875
Pins		59	152	1,671
TOTAL		7,172	18,575	196,836

Demography

Population (2001): 216,000.
Density (2001): persons per sq mi 30.1, persons per sq km 11.6.
Urban-rural (1999): urban 75.7%; rural 24.3%.
Sex distribution (1996): male 51.23%; female 48.77%.
Age breakdown (1996): under 15, 30.7%; 15–29, 27.2%; 30–44, 21.3%; 45–59, 13.3%; 60–74, 5.9%; 75 and over, 1.6%.
Population projection: (2010) 249,000; (2020) 286,000.
Doubling time: 47 years.
Ethnic composition (1996): Melanesian 45.3%, of which local (Kanak) 44.1%, Vanuatuan 1.2%; European 34.1%; Wallisian or Futunan 9.0%; Indonesian 2.6%; Tahitian 2.6%, Vietnamese 1.4%; other 5.0%.
Religious affiliation (1995): Roman Catholic 61.3%; Protestant 14.5%, of which Presbyterian 12.3%; Muslim 2.7%; other Christian 2.3%; other 19.2%.
Major cities (1996): Nouméa 76,293 (urban agglomeration 118,823); Mont-Dore 20,780[4]; Dumbéa 13,888[4].

Vital statistics

Birth rate per 1,000 population (2001): 20.1 (world avg. 22.5); (1996) legitimate 36.4%; illegitimate 63.6%.
Death rate per 1,000 population (2001): 4.9 (world avg. 9.0).
Natural increase rate per 1,000 population (2001): 15.2 (world avg. 13.5).
Total fertility rate (avg. births per childbearing woman; 2001): 2.5.
Marriage rate per 1,000 population (1999): 4.5.
Divorce rate per 1,000 population (1996): 0.8.
Life expectancy at birth (2001): male 72.0 years; female 77.0 years.
Major causes of death per 100,000 population (1996): diseases of the circulatory system 124.2; malignant neoplasms (cancers) 110.6; accidents, poisonings, and violence 63.9; diseases of the respiratory system 60.3.

National economy

Budget (1999). Revenue: CFPF 77,477,000,000 (indirect taxes 49.7%, direct taxes 30.9%, French government subsidies 8.6%, tobacco excises 6.3%). Expenditures: CFPF 74,218,000,000 (current expenditure 93.4%, development expenditure 6.6%).
Production (metric tons except as noted). Agriculture, forestry, fishing (1999): roots and tubers 21,100, of which yams 11,000, sweet potatoes 3,000; coconuts 16,000; vegetables 3,785; fruit 3,021; cereals 1,870, of which maize (corn) 1,650; livestock (number of live animals) 120,000 cattle, 38,000 pigs, 390,000 chickens; roundwood (1998) 4,800 cu m; fish catch (1997) 3,421, of which shrimp 1,107, sea urchins and echinoderms 505. Mining and quarrying (metric tons; 1999): nickel ore 6,562,000, of which nickel content (1997) 110,000; cobalt (1997) 800. Manufacturing (metric tons; 1999): cement 92,714; ferronickel (metal content) 45,289; nickel matte (metal content) 11,353; other manufactures include beer, copra cake, and soap. Energy production (consumption): electricity (kW-hr; 1996) 1,476,000,000 (1,476,000,000); coal (metric tons; 1996) none (168,000); crude petroleum, none (none); petroleum products (metric tons; 1996) none (409,000); natural gas, none (none).
Tourism: receipts from visitors (1998) U.S.$110,000,000; expenditures by nationals abroad, n.a.
Population economically active (1996): total 80,589; activity rate of total population 40.9% (participation rates: over age 14, 57.3%; female 39.7%; unemployed 18.6%).

Price and earnings indexes (1995 = 100)[5]

	1994	1995	1996	1997	1998	1999	2000
Consumer price index	98.4	100.0	101.7	103.7	104.0	104.1	106.5
Earnings index[6]	98.4	100.0	101.2	103.1	104.4	105.0	106.1

Public debt (external, outstanding; 1995): U.S.$1,033,000,000[7].
Gross national product (1999): U.S.$3,169,000,000 (U.S.$15,160 per capita).

Structure of gross domestic product and labour force

	1997 in value CFPF '000,000	1997 % of total value	1996 labour force	1996 % of labour force
Agriculture	6,439	1.9	4,663	5.8
Mining	13,307	3.8	4,408[8]	5.5[8]
Manufacturing	38,766	11.1	3,072[9]	3.8[9]
Construction	17,447	5.0	6,890	8.5
Public utilities	5,370	1.5	697	0.8
Transp. and commun.	23,415	6.7	2,968	3.7
Trade	80,054	22.9	8,375	10.4
Finance }	76,543	21.9	5,550	6.9
Services }			17,218	21.4
Pub. admin., defense	87,919	25.2	10,536	13.1
Other	—	—	16,212[10]	20.1[10]
TOTAL	349,260	100.0	80,589	100.0

Household income and expenditure (1991). Average household size (1996) 3.8; average annual income per household CFPF 3,361,233 (U.S.$32,879)[11]; sources of income: wages and salaries 68.2%, transfer payments 13.7%, other 18.1%; expenditure: food and beverages 25.9%, housing 20.4%, transportation and communications 16.1%, recreation 4.8%.
Land use (1994): forested 38.7%; meadows and pastures 11.8%; agricultural and under permanent cultivation 0.7%; other 48.8%.

Foreign trade[12]

Balance of trade (current prices)

	1995	1996	1997	1998	1999	2000
CFPF '000,000	–35,714	–41,616	–40,949	–58,910	–68,125	–44,235
% of total	25.9%	28.8%	26.2%	42.0%	43.2%	22.7%

Imports (1999): CFPF 112,888,000,000 (machinery and apparatus 20.0%, food 16.2%, transportation equipment 15.6%, mineral fuels 9.4%, chemicals and chemical products 7.8%). *Major import sources* (1998): France 52.2%; Australia 13.9%; New Zealand 5.3%; Singapore 4.2%; Japan 3.4%.
Exports (1999): CFPF 44,763,000,000 (ferronickel 54.8%, nickel ore 18.8%, nickel matte 13.9%, shrimp 4.2%). *Major export destinations:* Japan 32.2%; France 22.1%; Taiwan 8.4%; South Korea 7.6%; Australia 7.1%.

Transport and communications

Transport. Railroads: none. Roads (1996): total length 3,582 mi, 5,764 km (paved [1993] 52%). Vehicles: passenger cars (1996) 56,700; trucks and buses (1993) 21,200. Air transport (1999)[13]: passenger arrivals 171,887, passenger departures 170,815; (1998) freight unloaded 3,530 metric tons, freight loaded 1,371 metric tons; airports (1999) with scheduled flights 11.

Communications

Medium	date	unit	number	units per 1,000 persons
Daily newspapers	1996	circulation	24,000	121
Radio	1997	receivers	107,000	533
Television	1999	receivers	101,000	480
Telephones	1999	main lines	50,652	241
Cellular telephones	1999	subscribers	25,450	121
Internet	1999	users	5,000	24

Education and health

Educational attainment (1996). Percentage of population age 14 and over having: no formal schooling 5.7%; primary education 28.9%; lower secondary 30.2%; upper secondary 24.6%; higher 10.5%. *Literacy:* n.a.

Education (1996)

	schools	teachers	students	student/ teacher ratio
Primary (age 6–10)	279	1,622	22,942	14.1
Secondary (age 11–17) }	46	2,021	20,360	13.0
Vocational }	14		5,916	
Higher	4	79	1,749	22.1

Health (1996): physicians 362 (1 per 549 persons); hospital beds 898 (1 per 221 persons); infant mortality rate per 1,000 live births (2001) 7.0.
Food (1999): daily per capita caloric intake 2,772 (vegetable products 73%, animal products 27%); (1997) 122% of FAO recommended minimum requirement.

Military

Total active duty personnel (2000): 3,100 French troops. *Military expenditure as percentage of GNP:* n.a.

[1]The Nouméa Accord granting New Caledonia limited autonomy (with likely independence by 2013) was formally signed on May 5, 1998, approved by referendum in New Caledonia in November 1998, and passed by both houses of the French Parliament by February 1999. [2]Operates in association with 3 provincial assemblies. [3]Kanak languages and French have special recognition per Nouméa Accord. [4]Within Nouméa urban agglomeration. [5]All figures are end-of-year. [6]Based on minimum hourly wage. [7]Includes long-term private debt not guaranteed by the government. [8]Includes metallurgy. [9]Excludes metallurgy. [10]Includes 1,194 military conscripts and 15,018 unemployed. [11]Includes both monetary (92%) and nonmonetary income (8%). [12]Imports c.i.f.; exports f.o.b. [13]La Tontouta international airport only.

Internet resources for further information:
- **Overseas Departments and Territories of France http://www.outre-mer.gouv.fr/domtom/nouvcal/index.htm**
- **New Caledonia Economic Development Agency http://www.adecal.nc**

New Zealand

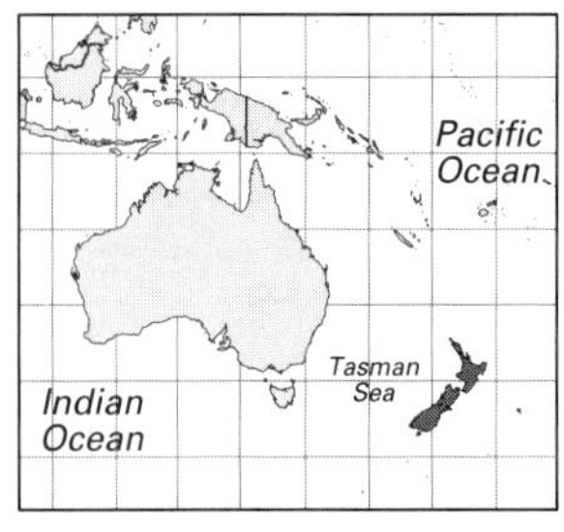

Official name: New Zealand (English); Aotearoa (Māori).
Form of government: constitutional monarchy with one legislative house (House of Representatives [120[1]]).
Chief of state: British Monarch, represented by Governor-General.
Head of government: Prime Minister.
Capital: Wellington.
Official languages: English; Māori.
Official religion: none.
Monetary unit: 1 New Zealand dollar ($NZ) = 100 cents; valuation (Sept. 28, 2001) 1 U.S.$ = $NZ 2.46; 1 £ = $NZ 3.61.

Area and population

Islands / Regional Councils	area sq mi	area sq km	population 2001 preliminary census
North Island	44,702	115,777	2,849,724
Auckland	...	...	1,165,278
Bay of Plenty	...	...	243,078
Gisborne[2]	...	...	44,355
Hawkes Bay	...	...	145,959
Manawatu-Wanganui	...	...	220,650
Northland	...	...	143,661
Taranaki	...	...	101,787
Waikato	...	...	360,495
Wellington	...	...	424,461
South Island	58,384	151,215	942,213
Canterbury	...	...	491,565
Marlborough[2]	...	...	42,240
Nelson[2]	...	...	43,293
Otago	...	...	192,936
Southland	...	...	93,633
Tasman[2]	...	...	44,394
West Coast	...	...	34,152
Offshore islands	1,368	3,542	720
TOTAL	104,454	270,534	3,792,657

Demography

Population (2001): 3,861,000[3].
Density (2001): persons per sq mi 37.0, persons per sq km 14.3.
Urban-rural (2001): urban 86.0%; rural 14.0%.
Sex distribution (2000): male 49.26%; female 50.74%.
Age breakdown (1998): under 15, 22.7%; 15–29, 21.6%; 30–44, 23.3%; 45–59, 17.0%; 60–74, 10.3%; 75 and over, 5.1%.
Population projection: (2010) 4,109,000; (2020) 4,351,000.
Ethnic composition (2000): Anglo-New Zealander 69.4%; Māori 10.0%; British 9.1%; other Polynesian 3.7%; Anglo-Australian 1.7%; Chinese 1.4%; other 4.7%.
Religious affiliation (1996): Christian 60.8%, of which Protestant 39.4% (including Anglican 17.5%), Roman Catholic 13.1%; nonreligious 24.7%; other religions/not specified 14.5%.
Major cities (1999 est.): Auckland 381,800 (urban agglomeration 1,078,000); Christchurch 324,200; Manukau 281,800[4]; North Shore 187,700[4]; Waitakere 170,600[4]; Wellington 166,700.

Vital statistics

Birth rate per 1,000 population (2001): 14.7 (world avg. 22.5); (1996) legitimate 58.0%; illegitimate 42.0%.
Death rate per 1,000 population (2001): 6.9 (world avg. 9.0).
Natural increase rate per 1,000 population (2001): 7.8 (world avg. 13.5).
Total fertility rate (avg. births per childbearing woman; 2001): 2.0.
Life expectancy at birth (2000): male 75.7 years; female 80.8 years.
Major causes of death per 100,000 population (1996): diseases of the circulatory system 317.2; malignant neoplasms (cancers) 200.8; diseases of the respiratory system 86.5; accidents, suicide, homicide, and other violence 47.0.

National economy

Budget (2000–2001). Revenue: $NZ 37,156,000,000 (income taxes 59.4%, taxes on goods and services 34.4%, nontax revenue 6.2%). Expenditures: $NZ 37,019,000,000 (social welfare 37.0%, health 19.0%, education 17.6%).
Production (metric tons except as noted). Agriculture, forestry, fishing (2000): apples 482,000, wheat 360,000, barley 281,000, corn (maize) 174,000; livestock (number of live animals) 45,800,000 sheep, 9,457,000 cattle, 344,000 pigs; roundwood (1999) 17,953,000 cu m; fish catch (1998) 635,711. Mining and quarrying (1998): iron ore and sand concentrate 2,000,000; aluminum metal 315,600; silver 31,500 kg; gold 11,250 kg. Manufacturing (1996–97): wood pulp 1,405,300; chemical fertilizers 1,365,000; yarn 21,302; beer 343,457,000 litres; footwear 2,840,000 pairs[5]; carpets 9,980,000 sq m. Energy production (consumption): electricity (kW-hr; 1996) 35,932,000,000 (35,932,000,000); coal (metric tons; 1996) 3,611,000 (2,438,000); crude petroleum (barrels; 1996) 16,000,000 (35,000,000); petroleum products (metric tons; 1996) 4,481,000 (4,778,000); natural gas (cu m; 1996) 4,781,000,000 (4,780,000,000).
Household income and expenditure. Average household size (1996) 2.8; annual income per household[6] (1996–97) $NZ 59,444 (U.S.$40,143); sources of income (1998): wages and salaries 65.8%, transfer payments 15.2%, self-employment 9.8%, other 9.2%; expenditure (1996–97): housing 20.2%, transportation 18.2%, food 16.4%, household goods 13.7%, clothing 3.8%.
Tourism (1999): receipts U.S.$2,083,000,000; expenditures U.S.$1,493,000,000.
Gross national product (1999): U.S.$53,299,000,000 (U.S.$13,990 per capita).

Structure of gross domestic product and labour force

	1998 in value $NZ '000,000[7]	1998 % of total value	1999 labour force	1999 % of labour force
Agriculture	6,516	7.3	165,500	8.8
Mining	1,159	1.3	3,600	0.2
Manufacturing	15,486	17.4	278,400	14.8
Construction	3,096	3.5	109,500	5.8
Public utilities	2,276	2.6	8,900	0.5
Transp. and commun.	9,928	11.2	110,400	5.9
Trade	12,933	14.5	371,500	19.8
Finance	19,471	21.9	220,100	11.7
Pub. admin., defense / Services	17,423	19.6	478,600	25.5
Other	613	0.7	131,700[8]	7.0[8]
TOTAL	88,901	100.0	1,878,200	100.0

Population economically active (2000): total 1,923,700; activity rate 50.1% (participation rates: over age 15, 66.2%; female 45.3%; unemployed 5.7%).

Price and earnings indexes (1995 = 100)

	1994	1995	1996	1997	1998	1999	2000
Consumer price index	96.4	100.0	102.3	103.5	104.8	104.7	107.4
Hourly earnings index[9]	97.4	100.0	103.7	107.2	...	...	...

Land use (1999): pasture 49.6%; agriculture 12.2%; forest and other 38.2%.

Foreign trade[10]

Balance of trade (current prices)

	1995	1996	1997	1998	1999	2000
$NZ '000,000	+1,068.9	+1,162.0	+902.0	+812.0	–1,896	+338
% of total	2.6%	2.8%	2.2%	1.8%	3.9%	0.6%

Imports (1999): $NZ 24,248,000,000 (machinery 24.6%; transport equipment 17.2%; mineral fuels 5.7%; textiles and textile products 4.7%; plastics 4.1%). *Major import sources:* Australia 22.1%; U.S. 17.7%; Japan 12.6%; China 5.1%; Germany 4.5%; U.K. 4.4%.
Exports (1998–99): $NZ 22,600,000,000 (food 47.2%; wood and wood products 10.6%; machinery 7.7%; metals and metal products 7.2%; wool 3.8%). *Major export destinations:* Australia 21.4%; U.S. 13.3%; Japan 12.7%; U.K. 6.2%; South Korea 3.9%; Germany 2.8%; China 2.7%.

Transport and communications

Transport. Railroads (1999): route length 3,912 km; passengers carried (1998) 11,751,000; metric ton-km cargo 3,960,000,000. Roads (1999): total length 92,075 km (paved 62%). Vehicles (1998–99): passenger cars 1,831,118; trucks and buses (1998) 368,723. Merchant marine (1992): vessels (100 gross tons and over) 139; total deadweight tonnage 279,805. Air transport[11] (1999): passenger-km 19,879,000,000; metric ton-km cargo 851,744,000; airports (1997) 36.

Communications

Medium	date	unit	number	units per 1,000 persons
Daily newspapers	1999	circulation	850,000	223
Radio	1997	receivers	3,750,000	997
Television	1999	receivers	1,975,000	518
Telephones	1999	main lines	1,889,000	496
Cellular telephones	1999	subscribers	1,395,000	366
Personal computers	1999	units	1,250,000	328
Internet	1999	users	700,000	184

Education and health

Educational attainment (1991). Percentage of population age 25 and over having: primary and some secondary education 54.9%; secondary 31.1%; higher 6.9%; not specified 6.1%[6]. *Literacy:* virtually 100.0%.

Education (1999)

	schools	teachers	students	student/ teacher ratio
Primary (age 5–12)[12]	2,366	25,832	478,065	18.5
Secondary (age 13–17)	335	15,401	226,164	14.7
Voc., teacher tr.	29	5,428	111,855	20.6
Higher[13]	7	5,008	105,996	21.2

Health: physicians (1999) 13,360 (1 per 285 persons); hospital beds (2000) 31,425 (1 per 122 persons); infant mortality rate per 1,000 live births (2001) 5.9.
Food (1999): daily per capita caloric intake 3,152 (vegetable products 68%, animal products 32%); 119% of FAO recommended minimum requirement.

Military

Total active duty personnel (2000): 9,230 (army 48.2%, air force 30.3%, navy 21.5%. *Military expenditure as percentage of GNP* (1997): 1.3% (world 2.6%); per capita expenditure U.S.$204.

[1]Includes six elected seats allocated to Māoris. [2]Reorganized as a unitary authority that is administered by a district council with regional powers. [3]Excludes March 2001 preliminary census results. [4]Within Auckland urban agglomeration. [5]1994–95. [6]Disposable income. [7]Constant 1992 prices. [8]Mostly unemployed. [9]In manufacturing. [10]Import figures are f.o.b. in balance of trade and c.i.f. in commodities and trading partners. [11]Air New Zealand only. [12]Includes composite schools that provide both primary and secondary education. [13]Universities only.

Internet resources for further information:
- **Statistics New Zealand/Te Tari Tatau http://www.stats.govt.nz/statsweb.nsf**
- **The Press On-Line New Zealand News http://www.press.co.nz**

Nicaragua

Official name: República de Nicaragua (Republic of Nicaragua).
Form of government: unitary multiparty republic with one legislative house (National Assembly [93[1]]).
Head of state and government: President.
Capital: Managua.
Official language: Spanish.
Official religion: none.
Monetary unit: 1 córdoba oro (C$)[2] = 100 centavos; valuation (Sept. 28, 2001) 1 U.S.$ = C$13.64; 1 £ = C$20.05.

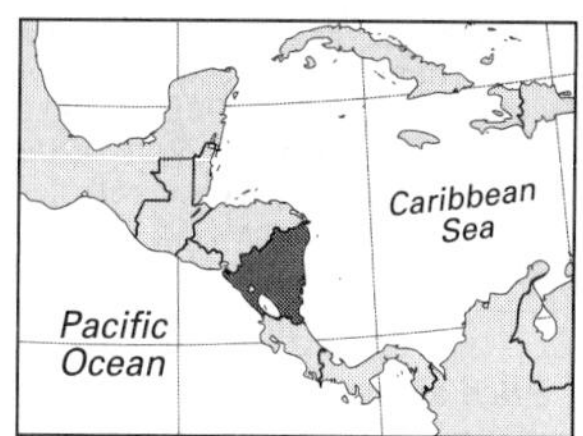

Area and population

Departments	Capitals	area[3] sq mi	area[3] sq km	population 1998 estimate
Boaco	Boaco	1,613	4,177	150,744
Carazo	Jinotepe	417	1,081	160,705
Chinandega	Chinandega	1,862	4,822	383,658
Chontales	Juigalpa	2,502	6,481	159,603
Estelí	Estelí	861	2,230	188,462
Granada	Granada	402	1,040	170,129
Jinotega	Jinotega	3,714	9,620	294,333
León	León	2,107	5,457	359,588
Madriz	Somoto	659	1,708	115,935
Managua	Managua	1,338	3,465	1,196,422
Masaya	Masaya	236	611	270,954
Matagalpa	Matagalpa	2,627	6,804	417,465[4]
Nueva Segovia	Ocotal	1,194	3,093	163,400
Río San Juan	San Carlos	2,912	7,541	81,408
Rivas	Rivas	835	2,162	151,294
Autonomous regions				
North Atlantic	Puerto Cabezas	12,549	32,501	216,737[4]
South Atlantic	Bluefields	10,636	27,546	303,037
TOTAL LAND AREA		46,464	120,340[5]	
INLAND WATER		3,874	10,034	
TOTAL		50,337[5]	130,373[5]	4,803,102[6]

Demography

Population (2001): 4,918,000[7].
Density (2001)[8]: persons per sq mi 104.9, persons per sq km 40.5.
Urban-rural (1998): urban 56.4%; rural 43.6%.
Sex distribution (2000): male 49.96%; female 50.04%.
Age breakdown (2000): under 15, 39.7%; 15–29, 30.6%; 30–44, 17.0%; 45–59, 8.2%; 60–74, 3.7%; 75 and over, 0.8%.
Population projection: (2010) 5,839,000; (2020) 6,808,000.
Doubling time: 30 years.
Ethnic composition (1997): mestizo (Spanish/Indian) 69.0%; white 17.0%; black 9.0%; Amerindian 5.0%.
Religious affiliation (1995): Roman Catholic 72.9%; Protestant 16.7%, of which Evangelical 15.1%, Moravian 1.5%; nonreligious 8.5%; other 1.9%.
Major cities (1995): Managua 864,201; León 123,865; Chinandega 97,387; Masaya 88,971; Granada 71,783; Estelí 71,550.

Vital statistics

Birth rate per 1,000 population (2000): 28.3 (world avg. 22.5).
Death rate per 1,000 population (2000): 4.9 (world avg. 9.0).
Natural increase rate per 1,000 population (2000): 23.4 (world avg. 13.5).
Total fertility rate (avg. births per childbearing woman; 2000): 3.3.
Life expectancy at birth (2000): male 66.8 years; female 70.8 years.
Major causes of death per 100,000 population (1994)[9]: diseases of the circulatory system 126; accidents, injuries, and violence 77; infectious and parasitic diseases 55; conditions originating in the perinatal period 53; diseases of the respiratory system 51.

National economy

Budget (1998). Revenue: C$6,581,000,000 (tax revenue 85.7%, of which import duties 23.0%, excise taxes on petroleum products 16.7%, general sales taxes 14.2%, income taxes 12.3%; grants 10.3%). Expenditures: C$7,037,000,000 (current expenditure 67.2%; development expenditure 31.6%).
Public debt (external, outstanding; 1999): U.S.$5,799,000,000.
Production (metric tons except as noted). Agriculture, forestry, fishing (1999): sugarcane 3,748,000, corn (maize) 302,000, rice 137,000, dry beans 94,000, sorghum 83,000, oranges 71,000, bananas 69,000, coffee 65,000, manioc (cassava) 51,000, soybeans 31,500; livestock (number of live animals) 1,693,000 cattle, 400,000 pigs; roundwood (1998) 4,198,000 cu m; fish catch (1997) 16,130, of which shrimp 6,437. Mining and quarrying (1997): gold 109,000 troy oz. Manufacturing (value added in C$'000,000; 1998[10]): food 1,816; beverages 1,245; cement, bricks, tiles 381; refined petroleum 209; tobacco products 202. Energy production (consumption): electricity (kW-hr; 1998) 2,084,000,000 (1,392,000,000); coal, none (none); crude petroleum (barrels; 1996) none (4,479,000); petroleum products (metric tons; 1996) 593,000 (882,000); natural gas, none (none).
Tourism (1999): receipts from visitors U.S.$107,000,000; expenditures by nationals abroad U.S.$74,000,000.
Land use (1994): forested 26.3%; meadows and pastures 45.3%; agricultural and under permanent cultivation 10.5%; other 17.9%.
Population economically active (1995): total 1,447,847; activity rate of total population 33.2% (participation rates: 15–64, 59.5%; female 29.5%; unemployed [2000] 9.8%).

Price and earnings indexes (1995 = 100)

	1994	1995	1996	1997	1998	1999	2000
Consumer price index	90	100	112	122	145	155	170
Monthly earnings index	98	100	106	119	...	...	...

Gross national product (1999): U.S.$2,012,000,000 (U.S.$410 per capita).

Structure of gross domestic product and labour force

	1997 in value C$'000,000	1997 % of total value	1995 labour force	1995 % of labour force
Agriculture, forestry	6,439	33.8	484,153	33.4
Mining	174	0.9	4,117	0.3
Manufacturing	2,980	15.6	107,919	7.5
Construction	746	3.9	45,362	3.1
Public utilities	230	1.2	6,022	0.4
Transp. and commun.	652	3.4	40,119	2.8
Trade, restaurants	4,587	24.1	205,982	14.2
Finance, real estate	999	5.2	7,143	0.5
Pub. admin., defense	1,218	6.4	233,322	16.1
Services	1,044	5.5		
Other	—	—	313,708[11]	21.7[11]
TOTAL	19,069	100.0	1,447,847	100.0

Household income and expenditure. Average household size (1995) 5.8.

Foreign trade[12]

Balance of trade (current prices)

	1995	1996	1997	1998	1999	2000
U.S.$'000,000	–440.3	–577.1	–793.9	–823.7	–1,153.5	–962.2
% of total	32.5%	38.2%	40.8%	41.8%	51.4%	43.3%

Imports (1999): U.S.$1,845,700,000 (capital goods 32.2%, nondurable consumer goods 23.9%, mineral fuels 8.7%). *Major import sources:* U.S. 34.5%; Costa Rica 11.4%; Guatemala 7.3%; Panama 6.9%.
Exports (1999): U.S.$543,800,000 (coffee 24.9%, manufactured products 19.9%, crustaceans 15.4%, beef 7.7%, raw sugar 5.6%, gold 5.6%). *Major export destinations:* U.S. 37.7%; El Salvador 12.5%; Germany 9.8%; Honduras 6.5%; Costa Rica 5.1%.

Transport and communications

Transport. Railroads:[13]. Roads (1996): total length 18,000 km (paved 10%). Vehicles (1996): passenger cars 73,000; trucks and buses 61,650. Air transport (1995)[14]: passenger-km 78,985,000; metric ton-km cargo 8,985,000; airports (1997) with scheduled flights 10.

Communications

Medium	date	unit	number	units per 1,000 persons
Daily newspapers	1996	circulation	135,000	30
Radio	1997	receivers	1,240,000	265
Television	1999	receivers	340,000	72
Telephones	1999	main lines	150,258	32
Cellular telephones	1999	subscribers	44,249	9.4
Personal computers	1999	units	40,000	8.5
Internet	1999	users	20,000	4.2

Education and health

Educational attainment (1995). Percentage of population age 25 and over having: no formal schooling 30.6%, no formal schooling (literate) 3.9%, primary education 39.2%, secondary 17.0%, technical 3.1%, incomplete undergraduate 2.2%; complete undergraduate 4.0%. *Literacy* (1995): total population age 15 and over literate 1,769,000 (74.0%); males literate 853,000 (74.4%); females literate 916,000 (73.6%).

Education (1997)

	schools	teachers	students	student/ teacher ratio
Primary (age 7–12)	7,224[15]	21,020[16]	783,002[15]	36.3[16]
Secondary (age 13–18)	451[17]	5,990[18]	220,670[18]	36.8[18]
Higher	10[17]	3,840	48,758	12.7

Health: physicians (1997) 3,725 (1 per 1,255 persons); hospital beds (1996) 6,666 (1 per 674 persons); infant mortality rate (2000) 34.8.
Food (1999): daily per capita caloric intake 2,314 (vegetable products 93%, animal products 7%); 103% of FAO recommended minimum requirement.

Military

Total active duty personnel (2000): 16,000 (army 87.5%, navy 5.0%, air force 7.5%). *Military expenditure as percentage of GNP* (1997): 1.5% (world 2.6%); per capita expenditure U.S.$6.

[1]Includes 3 unsuccessful 2001 presidential candidates meeting special conditions. [2]The córdoba oro (gold cordoba), introduced in August 1990, circulated simultaneously with the new córdoba until April 30, 1991, when the new córdoba ceased to be legal tender; on April 30, 1 córdoba oro equaled 5,000,000 new córdobas. [3]Lakes and lagoons are excluded from the areas of departments and autonomous regions. [4]1997 estimate. [5]Detail does not add to total given because of rounding. [6]De jure projection based on 1995 census. [7]De facto estimate. [8]Based on land area. [9]Projected rates based on about 55% of total deaths. [10]At prices of 1980. [11]Includes 68,925 not adequately defined and 244,783 unemployed. [12]Imports f.o.b. in balance of trade and c.i.f. in commodities and trading partners. [13]Railroad service ended in January 1994. [14]Nica only. [15]1998. [16]1996. [17]1994. [18]1995.

Internet resources for further information:
- **Banco Central de Nicaragua http://www.bcn.gob.ni**

Niger

Official name: République du Niger (Republic of Niger).
Form of government: multiparty republic with one legislative house (National Assembly [83]).
Head of state and government: President, assisted by Prime Minister.
Capital: Niamey.
Official language: French.
Official religion: none.
Monetary unit: 1 CFA franc (CFAF) = 100 centimes; valuation (Sept. 28, 2001) 1 U.S.$ = CFAF 720.28; 1 £ = CFAF 1,059.

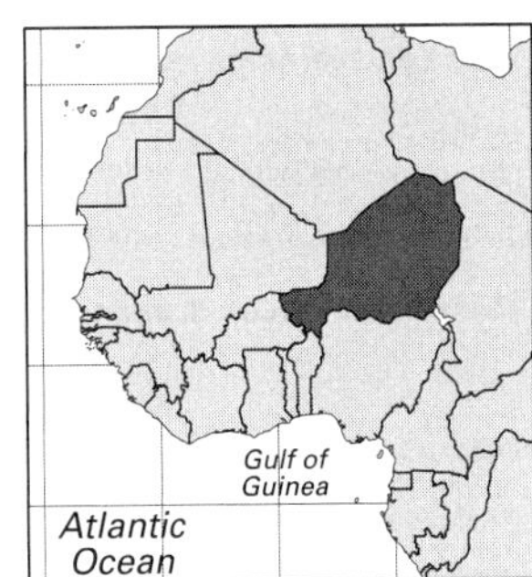

Area and population		area[1]		population
				1990
Departments	Capitals	sq mi	sq km	estimate
Agadez	Agadez	244,869	634,209	189,000
Diffa	Diffa	54,138	140,216	227,000
Dosso	Dosso	11,970	31,002	982,000
Maradi	Maradi	14,896	38,581	1,415,000
Tahoua	Tahoua	41,188	106,677	1,373,000
Tillabéri	Tillabéri	34,604	89,623	1,818,000[2]
Zinder	Zinder	56,151	145,430	1,467,000
City				
Niamey	Niamey	259	670	[2]
TOTAL		458,075	1,186,408	7,471,000

Demography

Population (2001): 10,355,000.
Density (2000)[1]: persons per sq mi 21.2, persons per sq km 8.2.
Urban-rural (1999): urban 20.1%; rural 79.9%.
Sex distribution (2000): male 49.91%; female 50.09%.
Age breakdown (2000): under 15, 48.0%; 15–29, 26.3%; 30–44, 14.1%; 45–59, 7.8%; 60–74, 3.2%; 75 and over, 0.6%.
Population projection: (2010) 13,140,000; (2020) 16,800,000.
Doubling time: 25 years.
Ethnic composition (1988): Hausa 53.0%; Zerma- (Djerma-) Songhai 21.2%; Tuareg 10.4%; Fulani (Peul) 9.8%; Kanuri-Nanga 4.4%; Teda 0.4%; Arab 0.3%; Gurma 0.3%; other 0.2%.
Religious affiliation (2000): Sunnī Muslim 90.7%; traditional beliefs 8.7%; Christian 0.5%; other 0.1%.
Major cities (1988): Niamey 391,876 (urban agglomeration [1999] 731,000); Zinder 119,827; Maradi 110,005; Tahoua 49,948; Agadez 32,272.

Vital statistics

Birth rate per 1,000 population (2000): 51.4 (world avg. 22.5).
Death rate per 1,000 population (2000): 23.2 (world avg. 9.0).
Natural increase rate per 1,000 population (2000): 28.2 (world avg. 13.5).
Total fertility rate (avg. births per childbearing woman; 2000): 7.2.
Marriage rate per 1,000 population: n.a.
Divorce rate per 1,000 population: n.a.
Life expectancy at birth (2000): male 41.4 years; female 41.1 years.
Major causes of death: n.a.; however, among selected major causes of infectious disease registered at medical facilities were malaria, measles, diarrhea, meningitis, pneumonia, diphtheria, tetanus, viral hepatitis, and poliomyelitis; malnutrition and shortages of trained medical personnel are widespread.

National economy

Budget (1998). Revenue: CFAF 164,400,000,000 (taxes 59.3%, external aid and gifts 34.1%, nontax revenue 6.6%). Expenditures: CFAF 188,000,000,000 (current expenditures 69.2%, development expenditures 30.8%).
Public debt (external, outstanding; 1999): U.S.$1,424,000,000.
Tourism (1999): receipts from visitors U.S.$24,000,000; expenditures by nationals abroad (1997) U.S.$26,000,000.
Gross national product (1999): U.S.$1,974,000,000 (U.S.$190 per capita).

Structure of gross domestic product and labour force	1998		1988	
	in value CFAF '000,000	% of total value	labour force[3]	% of labour force
Agriculture	488,900	40.5	1,764,049	76.2
Mining	49,100	4.1	5,295	0.2
Manufacturing	78,100	6.5	65,793	2.8
Construction	24,700	2.0	13,742	0.6
Public utilities	23,400	1.9	1,778	0.1
Transp. and commun.	64,700	5.4	14,764	0.6
Trade and finance	201,200	16.6	210,354	9.1
Pub. admin., defense	96,600	8.0	59,271	2.6
Services	140,800	11.7	63,991	2.8
Other	40,600[4]	3.4[4]	116,657	5.0
TOTAL	1,208,100	100.0[5]	2,315,694	100.0

Production (metric tons except as noted). Agriculture, forestry, fishing (1999): millet 2,253,000, cowpeas 641,000, sorghum 481,000, cassava (manioc) 230,000, onions 180,000, peanuts (groundnuts) 108,100, rice 73,000, tomatoes 65,000, tobacco leaf 930; livestock (number of live animals) 6,469,000 goats, 4,312,000 sheep, 2,174,000 cattle, 530,000 asses, 404,000 camels, 94,000 horses; roundwood (1998) 6,460,000 cu m; fish catch (1997) 6,341. Mining and quarrying: salt (1997) 3,000; uranium (1999) 2,916. Manufacturing (value added in CFAF '000,000; 1997): traditional-sector handicrafts 56,200; food 1,320; soaps and other chemical products 1,249; construction materials 836. Construction (value added in CFAF; 1994): 16,100,000,000. Energy production (consumption): electricity (kW-hr; 1999) 170,200,000 (379,200,000); coal (metric tons; 1996) 173,000 (173,000); crude petroleum, none (none); petroleum products (metric tons; 1996) none (205,000); natural gas, none (none).
Population economically active (1988)[3]: total 2,315,694; activity rate of total population 31.9% (participation rates: ages 15–64, 55.2%; female 20.4%).

Price and earnings indexes (1995 = 100)	1995	1996	1997	1998	1999	2000	2001[6]
Consumer price index	100.0	105.3	108.4	113.3	110.7	113.9	120.5
Annual earnings index	...	...	...	...	...	...	...

Household income and expenditure. Average household size (1998) 6.3; income per household: n.a.; expenditure (1987): food and beverages 43.1%, housing 22.8%, clothing 10.0%.
Land use (1994): forested 2.0%; meadows and pastures 8.2%; agricultural and under permanent cultivation 2.9%; other (largely desert) 86.9%.

Foreign trade

Balance of trade (current prices)	1994	1995	1996	1997	1998	1999
CFAF '000,000	–20,700	–5,500	–2,300	–16,400	–21,100	–17,800
% of total	7.6%	1.9%	0.6%	4.9%	5.7%	4.8%

Imports (1998): CFAF 196,700,000,000 (consumer goods 74.0%, of which food products 24.1%, petroleum products 7.0%; intermediate and capital goods 26.0%). *Major import sources*[7]: France 17%; Côte d'Ivoire 9%; Belgium 5%; Germany 4%; unspecified countries/special categories 37%.
Exports (1998): CFAF 175,600,000,000 (uranium 43.6%; livestock [mostly live cattle, sheep, and goats] 13.8%; cowpeas 7.1%). *Major export destinations*[7]: France 52%; South Korea 34%; United Kingdom 4%.

Transport and communications

Transport. Railroads: none. Roads (1996): total length 6,276 mi, 10,100 km (paved 8%). Vehicles (1996): passenger cars 38,220, trucks and buses 15,200. Air transport (1998)[8]: passenger-mi 160,477,000, passenger-km 258,263,000; short ton-mi cargo 9,263,000, metric ton-km cargo 13,524,000; airports (1996) with scheduled flights 6.

Communications				units per 1,000
Medium	date	unit	number	persons
Daily newspapers	1996	circulation	2,000	0.2
Radio	1997	receivers	680,000	73
Television	1999	receivers	285,000	29
Telephones	1998	main lines	18,114	1.9
Cellular telephones	1998	subscribers	1,349	0.1
Personal computers	1999	units	4,000	0.4
Internet	1999	users	3,000	0.3

Education and health

Educational attainment (1988). Percentage of population age 25 and over having: no formal schooling 85.0%; Koranic education 11.2%; primary education 2.5%; secondary 1.1%; higher 0.2%. *Literacy* (1995): total population age 15 and over literate 641,000 (13.6%); males literate 482,000 (20.9%); females literate 159,000 (6.6%).

Education (1997–98)	schools	teachers	students	student/ teacher ratio
Primary (age 7–12)	3,175	11,545	482,065	41.8
Secondary (age 13–19)[9]	...	3,579	97,675	27.3
Voc., teacher tr.[9]	...	215	2,145	10.0
Higher[10]	2	355	5,569	15.7

Health: physicians (1993) 237 (1 per 35,141 persons); hospital beds (1987) *c.* 3,500 (1 per 2,000 persons); infant mortality rate per 1,000 live births (2000) 124.9.
Food (1999): daily per capita caloric intake 2,064 (vegetable products 95%, animal products 5%); 88% of FAO recommended minimum requirement.

Military

Total active duty personnel (2000): 5,300 (army 98.1%, air force 1.9%). *Military expenditure as percentage of GNP* (1997): 1.1% (world 2.6%); per capita expenditure U.S.$2.

[1]The departmental areas and total shown are obsolete. The total area, according to more recent official estimates, is 489,000 sq mi (1,267,000 sq km); but subtotals distributing this total among the departments remain unpublished. [2]Tillabéri includes Niamey. [3]Excluding nomadic population. [4]Import taxes and duties. [5]Detail does not add to total given because of rounding. [6]June. [7]Estimated figures. [8]Represents 1/11 of the traffic of Air Afrique, which is operated by 11 West African states. [9]1996–97. [10]Université de Niamey and École Nationale d'Administration du Niger only.

Internet resources for further information:
- **The United Nations in Niger**
  http://www.un.ne/home_un_fr/index_un_fr.htm
- **Investir en zone franc**
  http://www.izf.net/izf/Index.htm

Nigeria

Official name: Federal Republic of Nigeria.
Form of government: federal republic with two legislative bodies (Senate [109]; House of Representatives [360])[1].
Head of state and government: President.
Capital: Abuja (Federal Capital Territory)[2, 3].
Official language: English.
Official religion: none.
Monetary unit: 1 Nigerian naira (₦) = 100 kobo; valuation (Sept. 28, 2001) 1 U.S.$ = ₦112.66; 1 £ = ₦165.58.

Area and population

States[4]	area sq km	population 1995 estimate	States[4]	area sq km	population 1995 estimate
Abia	6,320	2,569,362[5]	Kebbi	36,800	2,305,768
Adamawa	36,917	2,374,892	Kogi	29,833	2,346,936
Akwa Ibom	7,081	2,638,413	Kwara	36,825	1,751,464
Anambra	4,844	3,094,783	Lagos	3,345	6,357,253
Bauchi	45,837	4,801,569[6]	Niger	76,363	2,775,526
Bayelsa	10,773	[7]	Nassarawa	27,117	[9]
Benue	34,059	3,108,754	Ogun	16,762	2,614,747
Borno	70,898	2,903,238	Ondo	14,606	4,343,230[8]
Cross River	20,156	2,085,926	Osun	9,251	2,463,185
Delta	17,698	2,873,711	Oyo	28,454	3,900,803
Ebonyi	5,670	[5]	Plateau	30,913	3,671,498[9]
Edo	17,802	2,414,919	Rivers	11,077	4,454,337[7]
Ekiti	6,353	[8]	Sokoto	25,973	4,911,118[10]
Enugu	7,161	3,534,633[5]	Taraba	54,473	1,655,443
Gombe	18,768	[6]	Yobe	45,502	1,578,172
Imo	5,530	2,779,028	Zamfara	39,762	[10]
Jigawa	23,154	3,164,134			
Kaduna	46,053	4,438,007	**Federal Capital Territory**		
Kano	20,131	6,297,165			
Katsina	24,192	4,336,363	Abuja	7,315	423,391
			TOTAL	923,768	98,967,768

Demography

Population (2001): 126,636,000.
Density (2001): persons per sq mi 355.1, persons per sq km 137.1.
Urban-rural (1996): urban 40.1%; rural 59.9%.
Sex distribution (2000): male 50.59%; female 49.41%.
Age breakdown (2000): under 15, 43.8%; 15–29, 27.7%; 30–44, 15.3%; 45–59, 8.7%; 60–74, 3.8%; 75 and over, 0.7%.
Population projection: (2010) 155,588,000; (2020) 187,437,000.
Doubling time: 26 years.
Ethnic composition (1983): Hausa 21.3%; Yoruba 21.3%; Igbo (Ibo) 18.0%; Fulani 11.2%; Ibibio 5.6%; Kanuri 4.2%; Edo 3.4%; Tiv 2.2%; Ijo (Ijaw) 1.8%; Bura 1.7%; Nupe 1.2%; other 8.1%.
Religious affiliation (1995): Muslim 43.0%; Christian 35.3%, of which Protestant 20.0%, Roman Catholic 8.2%; African indigenous 19.0%; other 2.7%.
Major cities (1991): Lagos 5,197,247 (urban agglomeration [1999] 12,763,000); Kano 2,166,554; Ibadan 1,835,300; Kaduna 993,642; Benin City 762,719; Port Harcourt 703,421.

Vital statistics

Birth rate per 1,000 population (2000): 40.2 (world avg. 22.5).
Death rate per 1,000 population (2000): 13.7 (world avg. 9.0).
Natural increase rate per 1,000 population (2000): 26.5 (world avg. 13.5).
Total fertility rate (avg. births per childbearing woman; 2000): 5.7.
Life expectancy at birth (2000): male 51.6 years; female 51.6 years.

National economy

Budget (2000). Revenue: ₦1,927,087,000,000 (tax revenue 33.1%, of which petroleum profit tax 17.3%; import duties, excise taxes, and fees 6.0%; nontax revenue 66.9%, of which oil export proceeds 49.1%). Expenditures: ₦1,834,305,000,000 (1999; recurrent expenditure 75.6%, of which debt service 18.8%, education 5.2%, defense 4.6%, health 2.0%, construction 0.9%, transportation and communications 0.6%; capital expenditure 24.4%).
Public debt (external, outstanding; 1999): U.S.$22,423,000,000.
Production (metric tons except as noted). Agriculture, forestry, fishing (2000): cassava 33,854,000, yams 26,201,000, sorghum 7,711,000, millet 6,105,000, corn (maize) 5,598,000, taro 3,866,000, rice 3,298,000, peanuts (groundnuts) 2,901,000, sweet potatoes 2,468,000, cow peas 2,150,000, plantains 1,902,000, tomatoes 879,000; livestock (number of live animals) 24,300,000 goats, 20,500,000 sheep, 19,830,000 cattle, 4,855,000 pigs; roundwood (2000) 100,637,000 cu m; fish catch (1999) 477,365. Mining and quarrying (1998): limestone 3,660,000; marble 22,460; lead and zinc 682[11]. Manufacturing (value added in ₦'000,000; 1995): food and beverages 25,415; textiles 16,193; chemical products 11,181; machinery and transport equipment 5,639; paper products 2,828. Construction: n.a. Energy production (consumption): electricity (kW-hr; 1997) 14,830,000,000 (14,830,000,000); coal (metric tons; 1997) 50,000 (50,000); crude petroleum (barrels; 2000) 733,139,000 ([1997] 41,257,000); petroleum products (metric tons; 1997) 5,550,000 (6,175,000); natural gas (cu m; 1997) 5,500,000,000 (5,500,000,000).
Tourism (1999): receipts (1998) U.S.$142,000,000; expenditures U.S.$620,000,000.
Household income and expenditure. Avg. household size (1995) 4.7; annual income per household (1992–93) ₦15,000 (U.S.$760): sources of income (1979): self-employment 49.4%, wages 30.2%, interest 5.4%, rent 4.7%, transfer payments 4.3%; expenditures (1979): food 53.0%, fuel and light 11.4%, clothing 6.0%, transportation 4.7%, household goods 3.8%, other 21.1%.
Gross national product (1999): U.S.$31,600,000,000 (U.S.$260 per capita).

Structure of gross domestic product and labour force

	2000		1986	
	in value ₦'000,000	% of total value	labour force	% of labour force
Agriculture	1,191,989	28.5	13,259,000	43.1
Mining[12]	1,657,876	39.7	6,800	0.1
Manufacturing	166,247	4.0	1,263,700	4.1
Construction	31,017	0.7	545,600	1.8
Public utilities	2,212	0.1	130,400	0.4
Transp. and commun.	108,080	2.6	1,111,900	3.6
Trade[13]	533,442	12.8	7,417,400	24.1
Finance	216,270	5.1	120,100	0.4
Pub. admin., defense	226,306	5.4	4,902,100	15.9
Services	53,688	1.3		
Other[14]	–8,948	–0.2	2,008,500[15]	6.5[15]
TOTAL	4,178,179	100.0	30,765,500	100.0

Population economically active (1993–94): total 29,000,000; activity rate 31.0% (participation rates: ages 15–59, 64.4%; female 44.0%).

Price and earnings indexes (1995 = 100)

	1994	1995	1996	1997	1998	1999	2000
Consumer price index	57.9	100.0	129.3	139.9	154.3	164.6	176.0
Earnings index	...	...	...	...	...	...	...

Land use (1994): forest 15.7%; pasture 43.9%; agriculture 35.9%; other 4.5%.

Foreign trade

Balance of trade (current prices)

	1995	1996	1997	1998	1999	2000
₦'000,000	+108,681	+746,996	+395,946	+18,341	+128,904	+820,593
% of total	32.7%	39.9%	19.0%	4.3%	6.2%	24.6%

Imports (1995): ₦111,728,000,000 (machinery and transport equipment 42.0%; manufactured goods [mostly iron and steel products, textiles, and paper products] 24.0%; chemicals 17.0%; food 8.4%). *Major import sources* (1999): U.K. 11.0%; Germany 9.9%; U.S. 9.5%; France 8.4%; China 5.8%; Italy 4.9%.
Exports (1995): ₦220,408,900,000 (crude petroleum 94.8%; cocoa beans 0.7%; rubber 0.3%; other exports include cocoa products, textiles, and cashew nuts). *Major export destinations* (1999): U.S. 36.2%; India 8.6%; Spain 7.5%; France 5.9%.

Transport and communications

Transport. Railroads (1999): length 3,505 km; passenger-km 161,000,000[16]; metric ton-km cargo 108,000,000[16]. Roads (1996): total length 62,598 km (paved 19%). Vehicles (1996): passenger cars 773,000; trucks and buses 68,300[16]. Merchant marine (1992): vessels (100 gross tons and over) 271; total deadweight tonnage 733,329. Air transport[17] (2000): passenger-km 111,566,000; metric ton-km cargo 2,068,000; airports (1996) 12.

Communications

Medium	date	unit	number	units per 1,000 persons
Daily newspapers	1996	circulation	2,500,000	24
Radio	1996	receivers	20,500,000	197
Television	1998	receivers	7,200,000	66
Telephones	1999	main lines	410,000	3.6
Cellular telephones	1998	subscribers	20,000	0.2
Personal computers	1999	units	700,000	6.4
Internet	1999	users	100,000	0.9

Education and health

Literacy (2000): total population age 15 and over literate 40,700,000 (64.1%); males literate 22,600,000 (62.3%); females literate 18,100,000 (56.2%).

Education (1994–95)

	schools	teachers	students	student/ teacher ratio
Primary (age 6–12)	38,649	435,210	16,191,000	37.2
Secondary (age 12–17)	6,074	152,596	4,451,000	29.2
Voc., teacher tr.	376[18]	15,738[19]	391,583[19]	24.9[19]
Higher	31	12,103	228,000	18.8

Health (1995): physicians 27,230 (1 per 3,707 persons); hospital beds 68,350 (1 per 1,477 persons); infant mortality rate (2000) 74.2.
Food (1999): daily per capita caloric intake 2,833 (vegetable products 97%, animal products 3%); 120% of FAO recommended minimum requirement.

Military

Total active duty personnel (2000): 76,500 (army 81.0%, navy 6.6%, air force 12.4%). *Military expenditure as percentage of GNP* (1997): 1.4% (world 2.6%); per capita expenditure U.S.$17.

[1]Civilian government elected in May 1999. [2]Statutory transfer of capital from Lagos to Abuja took place in December 1991. [3]Judiciary and some ministries remain in Lagos, the former capital. [4]In October 1996 six new states were created: Bayelsa, Ebonyi, Ekiti, Gombe, Nassarawa, and Zamfara. [5]Ebonyi is included partly in Abia and partly in Enugu. [6]Bauchi includes Gombe. [7]Rivers includes Bayelsa. [8]Ondo includes Ekiti. [9]Plateau includes Nassarawa. [10]Sokoto includes Zamfara. [11]Metal content. [12]Includes ₦1,653,212,000,000 (39.5%) from petroleum and natural gas. [13]Includes hotels. [14]Less subsidies. [15]Includes 1,263,000 unemployed. [16]1995. [17]Nigeria Airways only. [18]1987–88. [19]1988–89.

Northern Mariana Islands

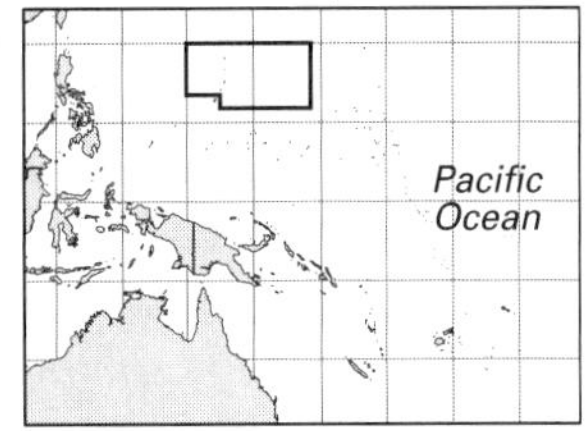

Official name: Commonwealth of the Northern Mariana Islands.
Political status: self-governing commonwealth in association with the United States, having two legislative houses (Senate [9]; House of Representatives [18]).
Chief of state: President of the United States[1].
Head of government: Governor.
Capital: Capital Hill, Saipan.
Official languages[2]: Chamorro, Carolinian, and English.
Official religion: none.
Monetary unit: 1 dollar (U.S.$) = 100 cents; valuation (Sept. 28, 2001) 1 U.S.$ = £0.68.

Area and population

Municipal councils	Seats	area sq mi	area sq km	population 2000[3] census
Northern Islands[4]	...	55.3	143.2	6
Rota (island)	Songsong	32.8	85.0	3,283
Saipan (island)	Chalan Kanoa	46.5	120.4	62,392
Tinian[5]	San Jose	41.9	108.5	3,540
TOTAL		176.5[6]	457.1[6]	69,221[7]

Demography

Population (2001): 73,400.
Density (2001): persons per sq mi 415.9, persons per sq km 160.6.
Urban-rural (1999): urban 55.0%; rural 45.0%.
Sex distribution (1995): male 49.75%; female 50.25%.
Age breakdown (1995): under 15, 24.3%; 15–29, 31.7%; 30–44, 31.6%; 45–59, 9.7%; 60–74, 2.2%; 75 and over, 0.5%.
Population projection: (2010) 97,000; (2020) 121,000.
Doubling time: 38 years.
Ethnic composition (1995)[8]: Filipino 33.1%; Chamorro 24.1%; Chinese 11.5%; Carolinian 10.1%; other Asian 7.6%; Micronesian 7.1%; white 3.0%; other 3.5%.
Religious affiliation (1995)[9]: Roman Catholic 59.6%; Protestant 18.7%; other Christian 1.4%; other 20.3%.
Major villages (1995)[10]: Garapan 6,634; San Antonio 6,256; Chalan Kanoa 6,229; Capital Hill 2,698; San Jose (on Tinian) 1,896; Songsong (on Rota) 1,339.

Vital statistics

Birth rate per 1,000 population (2000): 20.7 (world avg. 22.5); legitimate, 32.4%; illegitimate, 67.6%.
Death rate per 1,000 population (2000): 2.2 (world avg. 9.0).
Natural increase rate per 1,000 population (2000): 18.5 (world avg. 13.5).
Total fertility rate (avg. births per childbearing woman; 1999)[11]: 1.8.
Marriage rate per 1,000 population (1989): 28.5.
Divorce rate per 1,000 population (1986): 2.9.
Life expectancy at birth (1999)[11]: male 72.0 years; female 78.4 years.
Major causes of death per 100,000 population (1994–96 avg.): diseases of the circulatory system 53.3, of which cerebrovascular disease 25.8, ischemic heart diseases 21.8; malignant neoplasms (cancers) 33.3; accidents 29.8; diabetes mellitus 10.9.

National economy

Budget (1994–95). Revenue: U.S.$217,100,000 (local revenue 87.7%, grants from U.S. Office of Insular Affairs for capital improvements 12.3%). Expenditures: U.S.$190,400,000 (general government 46.1%, education 19.6%, health and social welfare 18.4%, public safety 6.6%).
Tourism (1998): receipts from visitors, U.S.$394,000,000; expenditures by nationals abroad, n.a.
Land use (1990): forested, n.a.; meadows and pastures 3.7%; agricultural and under permanent cultivation 4.0%; other 92.3%.
Gross national product (1999): U.S.$664,600,000 (U.S.$9,600 per capita).

Structure of labour force

	1995 labour force	1995 % of labour force
Agriculture, forestry, and fishing	419	1.2
Mining and quarrying	...	...
Manufacturing	7,770	22.8
Public utilities	...	...
Construction	3,627	10.7
Transp. and commun.	2,540	7.5
Trade	5,980	17.6
Finance, insurance, and real estate	723	2.1
Pub. admin., defense	2,552	7.5
Services	10,429	30.6
Other	...	...
TOTAL	34,040	100.0

Production (metric tons except as noted). Agriculture, forestry, fishing (1989): melons 165, cucumbers 83, bananas 46, betelnuts 38, Chinese cabbage 33, coconuts 30, eggplant 23; livestock (number of live animals) 4,513 cattle, 1,260 pigs, 482 goats, 9,580 chickens; roundwood, n.a.; fish catch (1998) 235. Mining and quarrying: negligible amount of quarrying for building material. Manufacturing (value of sales in U.S.$'000,000; 1997): garments 700; stone, glass, or ceramic products 21; food products 6. Construction (new permits in U.S.$'000,000; 1998): 63.3. Energy production (consumption): electricity (kW-hr) n.a.[12]; coal, none (none); crude petroleum, none (none); petroleum products, none (none); natural gas, none (none).
Population economically active (1995): total 37,393; activity rate of total population 63.5% (participation rates: ages 16 and over, 85.3%; female 48.1%; unemployed 7.1%).

Price index (1990 = 100)

	1992	1993	1994	1995	1996	1997
Consumer price index	116.9	122.0	125.4	127.7	131.5	132.9

Public debt (external, outstanding; 1995): U.S.$27,000,000.
Household income and expenditure. Average household size (1995) 4.0; average income per household (1995) U.S.$30,296; sources of income: n.a.; expenditure: n.a.

Foreign trade

Balance of trade (current prices)

	1986	1987	1988	1989	1990	1991
U.S.$'000,000	–33[13]	–93[13]	–208[13]	–162	–138	–129
% of total	57.4%[13]	79.1%[13]	89.4%[13]	34.7%	25.3%	19.7%

Imports (1991): U.S.$392,250,000 (machinery and transport equipment 22.2%, petroleum and petroleum products 20.9%, special transactions not elsewhere specified 14.8%, food 13.9%, manufactured goods 11.7%, manufactured articles 8.8%, beverages and tobacco 5.4%). *Major import sources:* United States 18.2%, Japan 16.6%, other Asian countries 10.3%, Australia 3.4%, unspecified countries 51.5%.
Exports (1999): U.S.$1,049,000,000 (clothing and accessories 99.9%). *Major export destinations:* nearly all to the United States.

Transport and communications

Transport. Railroads: none. Roads (1998): total length *c.* 225 mi, *c.* 360 km (paved, nearly 100%). Vehicles (1993): passenger cars 12,000; trucks and buses 6,300. Merchant marine (1992): vessels (100 gross tons and over) 2; total deadweight tonnage 856. Air transport (1993[14]): aircraft landings 21,555; boarding passengers 590,857; airports (1999) with scheduled flights 2[15].

Communications

Medium	date	unit	number	units per 1,000 persons
Radio	1999	receivers	10,500	152
Television	1999	receivers	4,100	59
Telephones	1999	main lines	24,945	480
Cellular telephones	1999	subscribers	2,905	56
Personal computers	...	units	...	...
Internet	...	users	...	...

Education and health

Educational attainment (1995). Percentage of population age 25 and over having: no formal schooling 0.7%; primary education, 5.5%; some secondary 13.5%; completed secondary 38.8%; some postsecondary 23.3%; completed undergraduate 18.2%. *Literacy* (1990): total population age 10 and over literate 35,490 (98.8%); males literate 18,790 (99.0%); females literate 16,700 (98.6%).

Education (1996–97)

	schools	teachers	students	student/ teacher ratio
Primary (age 6–11)	16[16]	597	6,952	18.4
Secondary (age 12–17)	9[16]		4,003	
Vocational	—	—	—	—
Higher[17]	1	...	845	...

Health: physicians (1986): 23 (1 per 1,326 persons); hospital beds (1998): 74 (1 per 899 persons); infant mortality rate per 1,000 live births (1999): 5.9[11].
Food: n.a.

Military

The United States is responsible for military defense; headquarters of the U.S. Pacific Command are in Hawaii.

[1]Residents elect a nonvoting representative to U.S. Congress. [2]In 1990, 90.5 percent of residents five years old and over spoke English, although 95.2 percent of residents spoke a language other than English at home, of which Chamorro 29.9 percent and Carolinian 4.8 percent. [3]Preliminary results. [4]Comprises the islands of Agrihan, Pagan, and Alamagan, as well as nine other uninhabited islands: Farallon de Pajaros (Uracas), Maug (East, West, and North islands), Asuncion, Guguan, Serigan, Anatahan, and Farallon de Medinilla. [5]Comprises Tinian island and Aguijan island. [6]Area measured at high tide; at low tide, total dry land area is 184.0 square miles (476.6 square km). [7]The 1995 census totaling 58,846 included 27,478 U.S. citizens and 31,368 aliens working primarily in the garment industry. [8]Includes aliens. [9]Unofficial estimate. [10]All villages are unincorporated census designated places. [11]U.S. Census Bureau estimate. [12]The installed electrical capacity in 1992 was 114,020 kilowatts. [13]Estimate. [14]Saipan International Airport only. [15]International flights are regularly scheduled at Saipan and at Rota; Tinian has nonscheduled domestic service. Additional domestic airports mainly handle charter flights. [16]1993–94. [17]Northern Marianas College; 1995–96.

Internet resources for further information:
- **Bank of Hawaii: Economics Research Center**
  http://www.boh.com/econ/pacific
- **CNMI: Central Statistics Division**
  http://www.commerce.gov.mp/csdhome.htm

Norway

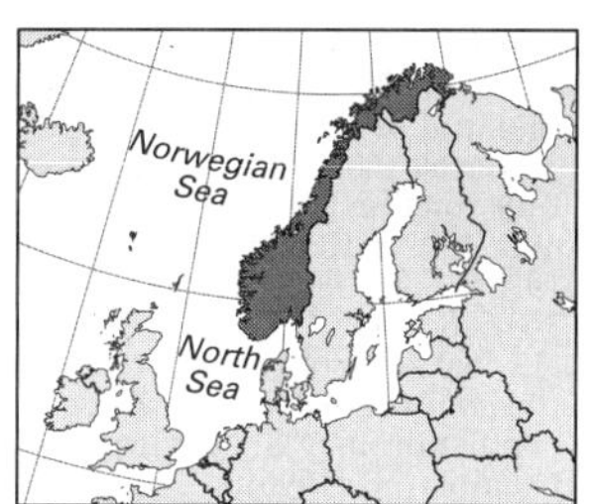

Official name: Kongeriket Norge (Kingdom of Norway).
Form of government: constitutional monarchy with one legislative house (Parliament [165]).
Chief of state: King.
Head of government: Prime Minister.
Capital: Oslo.
Official language: Norwegian.
Official religion: Evangelical Lutheran.
Monetary unit: 1 Norwegian krone (NKr) = 100 øre; valuation (Sept. 28, 2001) 1 U.S.$ = NKr 8.87; 1 £ = NKr 13.04.

Area and population

Counties	Capitals	area[1] sq mi	area[1] sq km	population 2000[2] estimate
Akershus	—	1,898	4,917	467,052
Aust-Agder	Arendal	3,557	9,212	102,178
Buskerud	Drammen	5,763	14,927	236,811
Finnmark	Vadsø	18,779	48,637	74,059
Hedmark	Hamar	10,575	27,388	187,103
Hordaland	Bergen	6,036	15,634	435,219
Møre og Romsdal	Molde	5,832	15,104	243,158
Nordland	Bodø	14,798	38,327	239,109
Nord-Trøndelag	Steinkjer	8,647	22,396	127,108
Oppland	Lillehammer	9,726	25,191	182,701
Oslo	Oslo	175	454	507,467
Østfold	Moss	1,615	4,183	248,217
Rogaland	Stavanger	3,529	9,141	373,210
Sogn og Fjordane	Leikanger	7,189	18,620	107,589
Sør-Trøndelag	Trondheim	7,271	18,838	262,852
Telemark	Skien	5,913	15,315	165,038
Troms	Tromsø	10,032	25,984	151,160
Vest-Agder	Kristiansand	2,811	7,281	155,691
Vestfold	Tønsberg	856	2,216	212,775
TOTAL		125,004[3]	323,758[3]	4,478,497[4]

Demography

Population (2001): 4,516,000.
Density (2001): persons per sq mi 36.1, persons per sq km 13.9.
Urban-rural (1990): urban 75.0%; rural 25.0%.
Sex distribution (2000[2]): male 49.51%; female 50.49%.
Age breakdown (2000[2]): under 15, 20.0%; 15–29, 19.6%; 30–44, 22.3%; 45–59, 18.8%; 60–74, 11.5%; 75 and over, 7.8%.
Population projection: (2010) 4,702,000; (2020) 4,904,000.
Ethnic composition (by country of citizenship; 2000[2]): Norway 96.0%; Sweden 0.6%; Denmark 0.4%; Bosnia and Herzegovina 0.3%; United Kingdom 0.3%; Yugoslavia 0.2%; United States 0.2%; Pakistan 0.2%; Germany 0.1%; Iraq 0.1%; Somalia 0.1%; Iran 0.1%; other 1.4%.
Major cities (2000)[5]: Oslo 507,467; Bergen 229,496; Trondheim 148,859.

Vital statistics

Birth rate per 1,000 population (2000): 13.2 (world avg. 22.5); (1999) legitimate 49.1%; illegitimate 50.9%.
Death rate per 1,000 population (2000): 9.8 (world avg. 9.0).
Natural increase rate per 1,000 population (2000): 3.4 (world avg. 13.5).
Total fertility rate (avg. births per childbearing woman; 1999): 1.9.
Marriage rate per 1,000 population (1998): 5.3.
Divorce rate per 1,000 population (1998): 2.1.
Life expectancy at birth (1999): male 75.6 years; female 81.1 years.
Major causes of death per 100,000 population (1996): malignant neoplasms (cancers) 250.2; ischemic heart disease 205.2; cerebrovascular disease 119.1.

National economy

Budget (1999). Revenue: NKr 609,315,000,000 (value-added taxes 30.7%, tax on income 28.6%, social security taxes 20.2%). Expenditures: NKr 551,803,000,000 (social security and welfare 37.8%, health 15.9%, education 13.6%, debt service 4.6%).
Land use (1994): forested 27.2%; meadows and pastures 0.4%; agricultural and under permanent cultivation 2.9%; built-up and other 69.5%.
Production (metric tons except as noted). Agriculture, forestry, fishing (2000): barley 649,400, potatoes 446,000, oats 372,400, wheat 293,000; livestock (number of live animals) 2,400,000 sheep, 1,042,000 cattle, 690,000 pigs; roundwood (1999) 8,424,000 cu m; fish catch (1999) 2,598,733, of which herring 807,635, cod 256,621[6], saithe 197,857, capelin 86,767. Mining and quarrying (1998)[7]: iron ore 621,000, ilmenite-titanium 589,500, copper 11,400, zinc 1,800. Manufacturing (value added in NKr '000,000; 1997): machinery and transport equipment 27,779; food products 25,646; paper and paper products 18,139; chemical products 10,421; wood products 4,616. Construction (1999): residential 2,919,000 sq m; nonresidential 3,768,000 sq m. Energy production (consumption): electricity (kW-hr; 1996) 104,756,000,000 (103,732,000,000); coal (metric tons; 1996) 230,000 (934,000); crude petroleum (barrels; 1996) 1,193,000,000 (109,000,000); petroleum products (metric tons; 1996) 14,626,000 (8,311,000); natural gas (cu m; 1996) 42,714,000,000 (3,713,000,000).
Household income and expenditure. Average household size (1996–98) 2.2; consumption expenditure per household (1998) NKr 357,458 (U.S.$47,376); expenditure (1996–98): transportation 24.1%, housing 16.6%, food 12.9%, recreation and education 11.3%, household furniture and equipment 8.7%, clothing and footwear 6.1%.
Gross national product (1999): U.S.$149,280,000,000 (U.S.$33,470 per capita).

Structure of gross domestic product and labour force

	1999 in value NKr '000,000	% of total value	labour force	% of labour force
Agriculture	23,163	2.0	102,000	4.4
Mining	2,097	0.2	[8]	[8]
Crude petroleum and natural gas	169,558	14.2	27,000	1.2
Manufacturing	124,769	10.5	305,000[8]	13.1[8]
Construction	48,205	4.0	146,000	6.2
Public utilities	22,856	1.9	18,000	0.8
Transp. and commun.	103,522	8.7	170,000	7.3
Trade	122,097[9]	10.2[9]	411,000	17.6
Finance	191,405	16.0	252,000	10.8
Pub. admin., defense	193,545	16.2 }	825,000	35.4
Services	63,324	5.3 }		
Other	128,286	10.8	76,000[10]	3.2[10]
TOTAL	1,192,826[3]	100.0	2,333,000[3]	100.0

Population economically active (1999): total 2,333,000; activity rate of total population 52.4% (participation rates: ages 16–64 [1996] 79.1%; female 46.0%; unemployed 4.9%).

Price and earnings indexes (1995 = 100)

	1994	1995	1996	1997	1998	1999	2000
Consumer price index	97.6	100.0	101.3	103.9	106.2	108.7	112.0
Hourly earnings index	96.6	100.0	104.2	108.4[11]	...	...	...

Public debt (1997): U.S.$33,763,000,000.
Tourism (1999): receipts from visitors U.S.$2,229,000,000.

Foreign trade[12]

Balance of trade (current prices)

	1994	1995	1996	1997	1998	1999
NKr '000,000	+51,736	+57,256	+90,410	+90,189	+25,998	+84,886
% of total	11.9%	12.1%	16.4%	15.1%	4.5%	13.8%

Imports (1999): NKr 266,676,500,000 (machinery and transport equipment 51.1%, of which road vehicles 8.6%, ships 3.6%; metals and metal products 8.2%, of which iron and steel 2.8%; food products 5.7%, of which fruits and vegetables 1.4%; petroleum products 2.3%). *Major import sources:* Sweden 15.1%; Germany 12.8%; U.K. 9.2%; Denmark 6.8%.
Exports (1999): NKr 355,171,500,000 (petroleum products 41.6%; machinery and transport equipment 14.3%; metals and metal products 10.3%; food products 8.7%, of which fish 8.0%). *Major export destinations:* U.K. 18.2%; The Netherlands 10.5%; Germany 10.0%; Sweden 9.4%.

Transport and communications

Transport. Railroads (1998): route length 4,006 km; passenger-km 2,589,000,000; metric ton-km cargo 2,142,000,000. Roads (2000): total length 90,880 km (paved 74%[13]). Vehicles (1999): passenger cars 1,813,642; trucks and buses 447,583. Merchant marine (1995): vessels (100 gross tons and over) 1,597; total deadweight tonnage 20,834,000. Air transport (1999): passenger-km 10,371,135,000; metric ton-km cargo 1,199,090,000; airports (1996) 50.

Communications

Medium	date	unit	number	units per 1,000 persons
Daily newspapers	1999	circulation	2,294,000	514
Radio	1996	receivers	4,000,000	913
Television	1999	receivers	2,900,000	650
Telephones	1999	main lines	3,176,000	711
Cellular telephones	1999	subscribers	2,744,793	615
Personal computers	1999	units	2,000,000	448
Internet	1999	users	2,000,000	448

Education and health

Educational attainment (1998). Percentage of population age 16 and over having: primary and lower secondary education 30.0%; higher secondary 45.9%; higher 20.8%; unknown 3.3%. *Literacy* (1998): virtually 100% literate.

Education (1998–99)

	schools	teachers	students	student/ teacher ratio
Primary (age 7–12)	3,277	44,972	569,044	12.7
Secondary (age 13–18) and vocational	703	21,068	197,765	9.4
Higher	82	11,590	184,063	15.9

Health: physicians (1996) 15,368 (1 per 285 persons); hospital beds (1998) 21,287 (1 per 208 persons); infant mortality rate (1999) 3.9.
Food (1999): daily per capita caloric intake 3,425 (vegetable products 67%, animal products 33%); 128% of FAO recommended minimum requirement.

Military

Total active duty personnel (2000): 25,800 (army 57.0%, navy 23.6%, air force 19.4%). *Military expenditure as percentage of GNP* (1997): 2.1% (world avg. 2.6%); per capita expenditure U.S.$739.

[1]Excludes Svalbard and Jan Mayen (24,360 sq mi [63,080 sq km]). [2]January 1. [3]Detail does not add to total given because of rounding. [4]Includes the Norwegian population of Svalbard and Jan Mayen, registered as residents in municipalities on the mainland. [5]Population of municipalities. [6]Norwegian catches on quotas bought from other countries are included. [7]Metal content of ore. [8]Manufacturing includes mining. [9]Includes hotels. [10]Unemployed. [11]2nd quarter. [12]Imports c.i.f. in balance of trade. [13]1998.

Internet resources for further information:
- **Statistics Norway http://www.ssb.no/www-open/english**

Oman

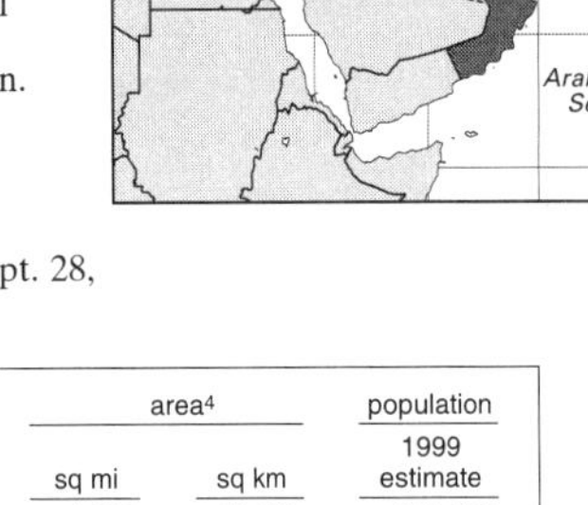

Official name: Salṭanat ʿUmān (Sultanate of Oman).
Form of government: monarchy with two advisory bodies (Council of State [41[1]]; Consultative Council [83[2]]).
Head of state and government: Sultan.
Capital: Muscat[3].
Official language: Arabic.
Official religion: Islam.
Monetary unit: 1 rial Omani (RO) = 1,000 baizas; valuation (Sept. 28, 2001) 1 RO = U.S.$2.56 = £1.75.

Area and population		area[4]		population
Regions	Capitals	sq mi	sq km	1999 estimate
Al-Bāṭinah	Ar-Rustāq; Ṣuḥār	4,850	12,500	648,602
Ad-Dākhilīyah	Nizwā; Samā'il	12,300	31,900	264,700
Ash-Sharqīyah	Ibrā; Ṣūr	14,200	36,800	297,929
Al-Wusṭa	Haymā'	30,750	79,700	19,768
Aẓ-Ẓāhirah	Al-Buraymī; ʿIbrī	17,000	44,000	208,439
Governorates				
Masqaṭ	Muscat (Masqaṭ)	1,350	3,500	635,279
Musandam	Khaṣab	700	1,800	32,965
Ẓufār (Dhofar)	Salālah	38,350	99,300	217,756
TOTAL		119,500	309,500	2,325,438

Demography

Population (2001): 2,497,000.
Density (2001): persons per sq mi 20.9, persons per sq km 8.1.
Urban-rural (1999): urban 82.7%; rural 17.3%.
Sex distribution (2000): male 56.8%; female 43.2%.
Age breakdown (1998): under 15, 36.8%; 15–29, 29.7%; 30–44, 22.1%; 45–59, 7.9%; 60 and over, 3.5%.
Population projection: (2010) 3,359,000; (2020) 4,461,000.
Doubling time: 21 years.
Ethnic composition (1993): Omani Arab 73.5%; Indian 13.3%; Bangladeshi 4.3%; Pakistani (mostly Balochī) 3.1%; Egyptian 1.6%; other 4.2%.
Religious affiliation (1993): Muslim 87.7%, of which Ibāḍiyah Muslim *c.* 75% (principal minorities are Sunnī Muslim and Shīʿī Muslim); Hindu 7.4%; Christian 3.9%; Buddhist 0.5%; other 0.5%.
Major cities (1993): As-Sīb 155,000[5]; Salālah 116,000; Bawshar 107,500[5]; Ṣuḥār 84,300; ʿIbrī 76,000; Muscat 40,900 (urban agglomeration [1999] 887,000).

Vital statistics

Birth rate per 1,000 population (2000): 38.1 (world avg. 22.5).
Death rate per 1,000 population (2000): 4.2 (world avg. 9.0).
Natural increase rate per 1,000 population (2000): 33.9 (world avg. 13.5).
Total fertility rate (avg. births per childbearing woman; 2000): 6.1.
Life expectancy at birth (1999): male 69.7 years; female 74.0 years.
Major causes of death per 100,000 population: n.a.; however, the main causes of hospital deaths in 1995 were diseases of the circulatory system 34.1%, infectious diseases 11.1%, malignant neoplasms (cancers) 9.4%, perinatal problems 7.2%, diseases of the respiratory system 6.3%.

National economy

Budget (2000). Revenue: RO 2,284,300,000 (oil revenue 75.3%; other 24.7%). Expenditures: RO 2,608,200,000 (current expenditure 78.8%, of which civil ministries 41.0%, defense 30.6%, interest paid on loans 4.1%; capital development projects and subsidies 21.2%).
Public debt (external, outstanding; 1999): U.S.$1,768,000,000.
Gross national product (1998): U.S.$13,135,000,000 (U.S.$5,950 per capita).

Structure of gross national product and labour force	2000			
	in value RO '000,000	% of total value	labour force	% of labour force
Agriculture[6]	162.3	2.1	58,595	9.8
Mining	3,749.5	49.3	4,739	0.8
Manufacturing	397.8	5.2	68,304	11.4
Construction	116.3	1.5	116,711	19.5
Public utilities	78.0	1.0	1,188	0.2
Transp. and commun.	461.9	6.1	3,905	0.7
Trade	865.5[7]	11.4[7]	158,509	26.6
Finance	591.1[8]	7.8[8]	6,097	1.0
Pub. admin., defense	699.8	9.2	102,942	17.2
Services	650.5[9]	8.6[9]	76,651	12.8
Other	−169.8[10]	−2.2[10]	—	—
TOTAL	7,602.9	100.0	597,641[11]	100.0[12]

Tourism (1997): receipts U.S.$108,000,000; expenditures U.S.$47,000,000.
Household income and expenditure. Average household size (1999) 6.9; income per household: n.a.; sources of income: n.a.; expenditure (1990): housing and utilities 27.8%, food, beverage, and tobacco 26.4%, transportation 19.8%, clothing and shoes 7.8%, household goods and furniture 6.1%, education, health services, entertainment, and other 12.1%.
Production (metric tons except as noted). Agriculture, forestry, fishing (2000): vegetables and melons 165,000 (of which watermelons 32,000), dates 135,000, bananas 28,000, mangoes 12,000, onions 9,400, potatoes 5,700, papayas 2,900, tobacco leaf 2,450, wheat 1,400; livestock (number of live animals) 729,000 goats, 180,000 sheep, 149,000 cattle, 98,000 camels, 3,400,000 chickens; fish catch (1999) 108,819. Mining and quarrying (2000): copper 26,000; chromite 15,000; silver 4,692 kg; gold 551 kg. Manufacturing (value of production in RO '000,000; 1993): textiles and apparel 78,200; food and beverages 72,930; chemical products 40,950; wood products 5,950; metal products 4,200; paper products 360; other major products include refined petroleum products. Construction (1998): number of residential permits 5,372; nonresidential permits 448; mixed 263. Energy production (consumption): electricity (kW-hr; 1999) 8,600,000,000 (8,600,000,000); crude petroleum (barrels; 2000) 349,500,000 (22,700,000); petroleum products (metric tons; 1996) 3,770,000 (1,656,000); natural gas (cu m; 1999) 5,578,400,000 (5,125,300,000).
Population economically active (1993)[13]: total 704,798; activity rate of total population 34.9% (participation rates: over age 15, 60.9%; female 9.7%; unemployed [1996] *c.* 20%).

Price and earnings indexes (1995 = 100)	1995	1996	1997	1998	1999	2000
Consumer price index	100.0	100.3	100.0	99.5	100.6	101.3
Earnings index	...	...	...	...	...	...

Land use (1994): meadows and pastures 4.7%; agricultural and under permanent cultivation 0.3%; other (mostly desert and developed area) 95.0%.

Foreign trade[14]

Balance of trade (current prices)	1995	1996	1997	1998	1999	2000
RO '000,000	+700	+1,064	+1,001	−66.6	+977.9	+2,414.3
% of total	17.6%	23.2%	20.6%	1.5%	21.4%	38.4%

Imports (2000): RO 1,937,700,000 (machinery and transport equipment 43.1%; basic manufactured goods 16.0%; food and live animals 12.2%; beverages and tobacco 8.7%; miscellaneous manufactured articles 6.6%). *Major import sources:* United Arab Emirates 29.5%; Japan 18.1%; United Kingdom 5.8%; United States 5.4%; Germany 3.7%; South Korea 3.4%; India 3.3%; Saudi Arabia 2.7%.
Exports (2000): RO 4,352,000,000 (domestic exports 88.5%, of which petroleum 82.8%, manufactured goods 2.4% [of which copper and copper products 0.5%], food and live animals 1.9%, mineral fuels 0.7%; reexports 11.5%, of which machinery and transport equipment 7.8%). *Major export destinations*[15]: United Arab Emirates 40.1%; Saudi Arabia 8.4%; Iran 7.8%; Yemen 7.8%; United States 5.5%; United Kingdom 3.8%; Tanzania 2.9%.

Transport and communications

Transport. Railroads: none. Roads (1999): total length 20,518 mi, 33,020 km (paved 24%). Vehicles (1999): passenger cars 229,029; trucks and buses 110,717. Merchant marine (1998): vessels (100 gross tons and over) 20; total deadweight tonnage 15,000. Air transport (2000)[16]: passenger-mi 601,400,000, passenger-km 968,000,000; short ton-mi cargo 11,250,000, metric ton-km cargo 18,106,000; airports (1999) with scheduled flights 6.

Communications				units
Medium	date	unit	number	per 1,000 persons
Daily newspapers	1996	circulation	63,000	28
Radio	1997	receivers	1,400,000	607
Television	1999	receivers	1,415,000	608
Telephones	1999	main lines	220,373	90
Cellular telephones	1999	subscribers	120,941	49
Personal computers	1999	units	65,000	28
Internet	1999	users	50,000	22

Education and health

Educational attainment (1993). Percentage of population age 15 and over having: no formal schooling (illiterate) 41.2%; no formal schooling (literate) 14.9%; primary 18.9%; secondary 21.1%; higher technical 2.0%; higher undergraduate 1.5%; higher graduate 0.1%; other 0.3%. *Literacy* (1995): percentage of total population age 15 and over literate 64.0%; males literate 74.6%; females literate 50.7%.

Education (1998–99)	schools	teachers	students	student/ teacher ratio
Primary (age 6–14)	294	11,447	301,281	26.3
Secondary (age 15–17)[17]	674	12,646	227,026	18.0
Voc., teacher tr.	10	954	9,936	10.4
Higher[18]	1	695	6,605	9.5

Health (1998): physicians 3,061 (1 per 747 persons); hospital beds 5,075 (1 per 444 persons); infant mortality rate per 1,000 live births (2000) 23.3.

Military

Total active duty personnel (2000): 39,800 (army 62.8%, navy 10.6%, air force 10.3%, royal household 16.3%). *Military expenditure as percentage of GDP* (1997): 26.1% (world 2.6%); per capita expenditure U.S.$795.

[1]All seats are nonelected. [2]Filled by 114,000 appointed voters. [3]Most ministries have moved to suburbs. [4]Approximate; no comprehensive survey of surface area has ever been carried out in Oman. [5]Within Muscat urban agglomeration. [6]Agriculture includes fishing. [7]Trade includes restaurants and hotels. [8]Finance includes business services and real estate. [9]Services include education and health. [10]Includes import taxes less bank service charges. [11]Employed only; includes 494,699 expatriate workers in private sector and 102,942 government employees, of which 74.0% are Omani. [12]Detail does not add to total given because of rounding. [13]Non-Omani workers constituted 61.3% of the labour force in 1993. [14]Imports c.i.f.; exports f.o.b. [15]Non-oil exports only; includes reexports. [16]Oman Air only. [17]Includes preparatory. [18]University only.

Internet resources for further information:
- **Ministry of Information http://www.omanet.com**

Pakistan

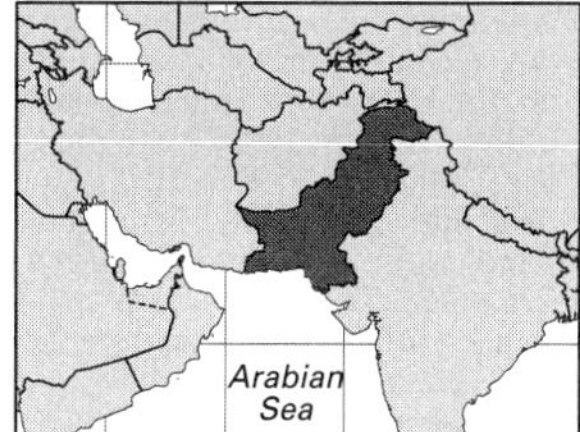

Official name: Islam-i Jamhuriya-e Pakistan (Islamic Republic of Pakistan).
Form of government: interim military regime.
Chief of state and government: President[1].
Capital: Islamabad.
Official language: Urdu.
Official religion: Islam.
Monetary unit: 1 Pakistan rupee (PRs) = 100 paisa, valuation (Sept. 28, 2001) 1 U.S.$ = PRs 64.10; 1 £ = PRs 94.21.

Area and population

Provinces	Capitals	area[2] sq mi	area[2] sq km	population 1998 census[3]
Balochistan	Quetta	134,051	347,190	6,511,000
North-West Frontier	Peshawar	28,773	74,521	17,555,000
Punjab	Lahore	79,284	205,344	72,585,000
Sindh	Karachi	54,407	140,914	29,991,000
Federally Administered Tribal Areas	...	10,509	27,220	3,138,000
Federal Capital Area				
Islamabad	...	350	906	799,000
TOTAL		307,374	796,095	130,579,000

Demography

Population (2001)[3]: 144,617,000.
Density (2001): persons per sq mi 470.5, persons per sq km 181.7.
Urban-rural (2001)[3, 4]: urban 38.0%; rural 62.0%.
Sex distribution (1999)[3, 4]: male 51.89%; female 48.11%.
Age breakdown (1998)[3, 4]: under 15, 43.2%; 15–29, 26.9%; 30–44, 15.6%; 45–59, 8.8%; 60–74, 4.3%; 75 and over, 1.2%.
Population projection[3]: (2010) 171,373,000; (2020) 199,745,000.
Doubling time: 26 years.
Ethnic composition (2000): Punjabi 52.6%; Pashtun 13.2%; Sindhi 11.7%; Urdu-speaking muhajirs 7.5%; Balochi 4.3%; other 10.7%.
Religious affiliation (2000): Muslim 96.1%[5]; Christian 2.5%; Hindu 1.2%; others (including Ahmadiyah) 0.2%.
Major cities (1998): Karachi 9,269,000; Lahore 5,063,000; Faisalabad 1,977,000; Rawalpindi 1,406,000; Multan 1,182,000; Islamabad 525,000.

Vital statistics

Birth rate per 1,000 population (2001): 36.8 (world avg. 22.5).
Death rate per 1,000 population (2001): 10.0 (world avg. 9.0).
Natural increase rate per 1,000 population (2001): 26.8 (world avg. 13.5).
Total fertility rate (avg. births per childbearing woman; 2001): 5.2.
Life expectancy at birth (2001): male 61.0 years; female 60.0 years.
Major cause of death (percentage of total deaths; 1987): malaria 18.2%; childhood diseases 12.1%; diseases of digestive system 9.8%; diseases of respiratory system 9.2%; infection of intestinal tract 7.7%.

National economy

Budget (1999–2000). Revenue: PRs 505,921,000,000 (nontax receipts 23.5%, sales tax 23.1%, income taxes 21.3%, customs duties 12.2%, excise taxes 11.0%). Expenditures: PRs 573,788,000,000 (public-debt service 42.7%, defense 26.2%, development 11.8%, general administration 8.3%, grants and subsidies 5.9%).
Production (metric tons except as noted). Agriculture, forestry, fishing (2000): sugarcane 46,333,000, wheat 21,079,000, rice 7,000,000, seed cotton 5,735,000, potatoes 1,868,000, corn (maize) 1,351,000, chickpeas 565,000, rapeseed 260,000; livestock (number of live animals) 47,400,000 goats, 24,100,000 sheep, 22,700,000 buffalo, 22,000,000 cattle, 148,000,000 chickens; roundwood (1999) 33,075,000 cu m; fish catch (1998) 596,980. Mining and quarrying (1998–99): limestone 9,467,000; rock salt 1,190,000; gypsum 242,000; silica sand 158,000; chromite 18,000. Manufacturing (1998–99): cement 9,635,000; refined sugar 3,568,000; chemical fertilizers 3,543,000, of which urea 3,522,000; cotton yarn 1,540,000; vegetable ghee 842,000; industrial chemicals 387,000; jute textiles 85,500; cotton textiles 385,000,000 sq m; cigarettes 51,578,000,000 units; motor-vehicle tires 845,000 units; bicycles 504,000 units; sewing machines 29,700 units. Energy production (consumption): electricity (kW-hr; 1997–98) 59,088,000,000 ([1996] 56,946,000,000); coal (metric tons; 1997–98) 3,144,000 ([1996] 4,718,000); crude petroleum (barrels; 1997–98) 20,520,000 ([1996] 49,609,000); petroleum products (metric tons; 1996) 5,890,000 (15,842,000); natural gas (cu m; 1997–98) 19,809,000,000 ([1996] 17,894,000).
Household income and expenditure (1988). Average household size 6.3; income per household PRs 25,572 (U.S.$1,420); sources of income: self-employment 56.0%, wages and salaries 22.0%, other 22.0%; expenditure: food 47.0%, housing 12.0%, clothing and footwear 8.0%, other 33.0%.
Population economically active (1999): total 38,590,000; activity rate of total population 28.7% (participation rates: ages 15–64, 43.1%; female [1996–97] 14.4%; unemployed 6.1%).

Price index (1995 = 100)

	1994	1995	1996	1997	1998	1999	2000
Consumer price index	89.0	100.0	110.4	122.9	130.6	136.0	141.9

Gross national product (1999): U.S.$62,915,000,000 (U.S.$470 per capita).

Structure of gross domestic product and labour force

	1999–2000 in value PRs '000,000	1999–2000 % of total value	1999 labour force	1999 % of labour force
Agriculture	762,527	24.0	15,980,000	41.4
Mining	16,851	0.5	4,060,000	10.5
Manufacturing	448,531	14.1		
Construction	96,645	3.1	2,460,000	6.4
Public utilities	119,751	3.8	360,000	0.9
Transp. and commun.	305,919	9.6	2,070,000	5.4
Trade	442,475	14.0	5,290,000	13.7
Finance	230,404	7.3		
Pub. admin., defense	235,543	7.4	5,290,000	13.7
Services	264,279	8.3		
Other	250,760	7.9	3,080,000[6]	8.0[6]
TOTAL	3,173,685	100.0	38,590,000	100.0

Public debt (external, outstanding; 1999): U.S.$28,514,000,000.
Tourism (1999): receipts U.S.$76,000,000; expenditures U.S.$180,000,000.
Land use (1999): pasture 6.5%; agriculture 28.4%; forest and other 65.1%.

Foreign trade[7]

Balance of trade (current prices)

	1995–96	1996–97	1997–98	1998–99	1999–2000
U.S.$'000,000	–3,704	–3,145	–1,868	–2,086	–1,435
% of total	18.2%	16.3%	10.0%	12.2%	8.1%

Imports (1999–2000): U.S.$10,361,000,000 (1998–99; petroleum products 14.7%, fixed vegetable oil and fats 8.9%, specialized machinery 6.9%, organic chemicals 5.6%, wheat 4.1%, general industrial machinery 3.7%, road vehicles and parts 3.4%, iron and steel manufactures 3.2%). *Major import sources* (1998–99): Japan 8.3%; U.S. 7.7%; Saudi Arabia 6.8%; United Arab Emirates 6.7%; Malaysia 6.7%; Kuwait 5.9%; U.K. 4.4%; China 4.2%; Germany 4.2%.
Exports (1999–2000): U.S.$8,569,000,000 (textile fabrics 18.1%, ready-made apparel and made-up articles 14.2%, cotton yarn 12.5%, rice 6.3%, leather goods 6.0%). *Major export destinations* (1998–99): U.S. 21.8%; Hong Kong 7.1%; Germany 6.6%; U.K. 6.6%; United Arab Emirates 5.4%; Japan 3.5%; France 3.2%; The Netherlands 3.1%; Italy 2.7%.

Transport and communications

Transport. Railroads (1998–99): route length 8,774 km; passenger-km 19,164,000,000; metric ton-km cargo 4,020,000,000. Roads (1997–98): total length 149,679 mi, 240,885 km (paved 55%). Vehicles (1998): passenger cars 1,167,635; trucks and buses 251,407. Merchant marine (1992): vessels (100 gross tons and over) 73; total deadweight tonnage 513,823. Air transport (1999): passenger-km 10,466,000,000; metric ton-km cargo 329,832,000; airports (1997) 35.

Communications

Medium	date	unit	number	units per 1,000 persons
Daily newspapers	1995	circulation	2,800,000	21
Radio	1997	receivers	13,500,000	102
Television	1999	receivers	16,000,000	119
Telephones	1999	main lines	2,986,000	22
Cellular telephones	1999	subscribers	278,830	2.1
Personal computers	1999	units	580,000	4.3
Internet	1999	users	80,000	0.6

Education and health

Educational attainment (1990). Percentage of population age 25 and over having: no formal schooling 73.8%; some primary education 9.7%; secondary 14.0%; postsecondary 2.5%. *Literacy* (1995): total population age 15 and over literate 37.8%; males literate 50.0%; females literate 24.4%.

Education (1998–99)

	schools	teachers	students	student/ teacher ratio
Primary (age 5–9)	163,746	374,500	17,298,000	46.2
Secondary (age 10–14)	27,526	262,800	5,664,000	21.6
Voc., teacher tr.	498	7,045	85,000	12.1
Higher	1,026	39,704	989,288	24.9

Health (1998): physicians 82,682 (1 per 1,638 persons); hospital beds 90,659 (1 per 1,494 persons); infant mortality rate per 1,000 live births (2001) 89.0.
Food (1999): daily per capita caloric intake 2,462 (vegetable products 83%, animal products 17%); 107% of FAO recommended minimum.

Military

Total active duty personnel (2000): 587,000 (army 89.9%, navy 3.6%, air force 6.5%). *Military expenditure as percentage of GNP* (1997): 5.7% (world 2.6%); per capita expenditure U.S.$26.

[1]Military leader (from October 1999) who was sworn in as president in June 2001 and was given three years to restore democracy by the Pakistani Supreme Court in May 2000. [2]Excludes 32,494 sq mi (84,159 sq km) area of Pakistani-administered Jammu and Kashmir (comprising both Azad Kashmir [AK] and the Northern Areas [NA]). [3]Excludes Afghan refugees (2001; *c.* 2,000,000) and the population of AK and NA (2001; *c.* 4,200,000). [4]Excludes Federally Administered Tribal Areas. [5]Mostly Sunni, with Shīʿī comprising about 17% of total population. [6]Mostly unemployed. [7]Import figures are f.o.b.

Internet resources for further information:
- **Government of Pakistan: http://www.pak.gov.pk**
- **Statistics Division: http://www.statpak.gov.pk**

Palau

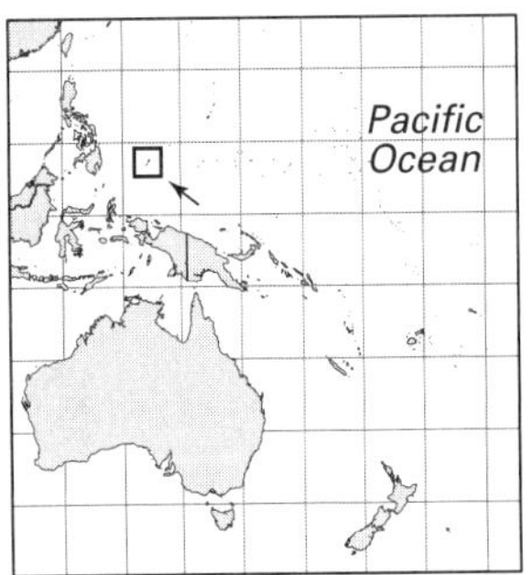

Official name: Belu'u er a Belau (Palauan); Republic of Palau (English).
Form of government: unitary republic with a national congress composed of two legislative houses (Senate [14]; House of Delegates [16]).
Head of state and government: President.
Capital: Koror[1].
Official languages[2]: Palauan; English.
Official religion: none.
Monetary unit: 1 U.S. dollar (U.S.$) = 100 cents; valuation (Sept. 28, 2001) 1 U.S.$ = £0.68.

Area and population

	area		population
			1995
States	sq mi	sq km	census
Aimeliik	20	52	419
Airai	17	44	1,481
Angaur	3	8	193
Hatobohel	1	3	51
Kayangel	1	3	124
Koror	7	18	12,299
Melekeok	11	28	261
Ngaraard	14	36	421
Ngarchelong	4	10	253
Ngardmau	18	47	162
Ngatpang	18	47	221
Ngchesar	16	41	228
Ngeremlengui	25	65	281
Ngiwal	10	26	176
Peleliu	5	13	575
Sonsorol	1	3	80
Other			
Rock Islands	18	47	—
TOTAL	188[3]	488[3]	17,225[4]

Demography

Population (2001): 19,700.
Density (2001): persons per sq mi 104.8, persons per sq km 40.4.
Urban-rural (1990): urban 59.6%; rural 40.4%.
Sex distribution (2000): male 54.63%; female 45.37%.
Age breakdown (2000): under 15, 23.9%; 15–29, 24.2%; 30–44, 29.9%; 45–59, 14.2%; 60–74, 5.5%; 75 and over 2.3%.
Population projection: (2010) 22,200; (2020) 24,200.
Doubling time: 50 years.
Ethnic composition (1997): Palauan 74.5%; Filipino 16.0%; Chinese 3.2%; other Micronesian and other 6.3%.
Religious affiliation (1995): Roman Catholic 38.4%; Protestant 24.7%; Modekne 26.5%; other 10.4%.
Major city (2000): Koror 13,303.

Vital statistics

Birth rate per 1,000 population (2000): 21.1 (world avg. 22.5).
Death rate per 1,000 population (2000): 7.2 (world avg. 9.0).
Natural increase rate per 1,000 population (2000): 13.9 (world avg. 13.5).
Total fertility rate (avg. births per childbearing woman; 1999): 2.5.
Marriage rate per 1,000 population: n.a.
Divorce rate per 1,000 population: n.a.
Life expectancy at birth (1999): male 65.2 years; female 71.5 years.
Major causes of death per 100,000 population (1993): diseases of the circulatory system 192.9; malignant and benign neoplasms (cancers) 136.9; accidents, poisoning, and violence 112.0; diseases of the respiratory system 43.6; infectious and parasitic diseases 43.6.

National economy

Budget (1999). Revenue: U.S.$59,102,000 (grants from the U.S. 40.5%, tax revenue 39.0%, nontax revenue 20.5%). Expenditures: U.S.$69,900,000 (current expenditure 86.0%, of which wages and salaries 38.9%; capital expenditure 14.0%).
Gross national product (at current market prices; 1997)[5]: U.S.$159,800,000 (U.S.$8,806 per capita).

Structure of gross domestic product and labour force

	1998		1995	
	in value U.S.$'000	% of total value	labour force	% of labour force
Agriculture, fisheries	6,135	4.8	724	8.7
Mining	145	0.1		
Manufacturing	1,016	0.8	1,165[6]	14.0[6]
Public utilities	–427	–0.3	[7]	[7]
Construction	10,006	7.7	[6]	[6]
Transportation and communications	20,649	16.0	435[7]	5.2[7]
Trade	34,671	26.8	1,448	17.3
Finance	15,802	12.2	122	1.5
Public administration, defense	28,879	22.3	2,292	27.5
Services	9,214	7.1	1,573	18.8
Other	3,161[8]	2.4[8]	584[9]	7.0[9]
TOTAL	129,251	100.0[3]	8,368	100.0

Production (metric tons except as noted). Agriculture, forestry, fishing (value of sales in U.S.$; 1993): eggs 262,701, fruit and vegetables 126,325, betel nuts 60,376, root crops (taro, cassava, sweet potatoes) 43,718; livestock (number of live animals; 1984) 1,343 pigs, 82 cows, 52 goats, 9,500 poultry; roundwood, n.a.; fish catch (1997) 1,500 (major species are parrot fish, snapper, unicorn fish, and rabbitfish). Mining and quarrying: n.a. Manufacturing: includes handicrafts and small items. Construction: n.a. Energy production (consumption): electricity (kW-hr; 1996) 208,000,000 (208,000,000); coal, none (n.a.); crude petroleum, none (n.a.); petroleum products, none (80,000); natural gas, none (n.a.).
Public debt (external, outstanding; 1998): U.S.$1,433,000.
Tourism (1999): receipts from visitors U.S.$68,200,000.
Population economically active (1995): total 8,368; activity rate of total population 48.6% (participation rates: over age 15, 69.0%; female 39.6%; unemployed 7.0%.
Land use: n.a.
Household income and expenditure. Average household size (2000) 5.7; income per household (1989) U.S.$8,882; sources of income (1989): wages 63.7%, social security 12.0%, self-employment 7.4%, retirement 5.5%, interest, dividend, or net rental 4.3%, remittance 4.1%, public assistance 1.0%, other 2.0%; expenditure (1997): food 42.2%, beverages and tobacco 14.8%, entertainment 13.1%, transportation 6.4%, clothing 5.7%, household goods 2.7%, other 15.1%.

Foreign trade

Balance of trade (current prices)

	1992–93	1993–94	1994–95	1995–96	1996–97	1997–98
U.S.$'000	–24,470	–31,659	–46,569	–58,517	–61,079	–52,127
% of total	40.8%	55.7%	62.7%	67.8%	72.1%	70.1%

Imports (1997–98): U.S.$63,222,000 (1997; machinery and transport equipment 27.8%; food, beverages, and tobacco 27.1%; manufactured articles 27.1%; mineral fuels 13.2%; chemicals and related products 4.5%). *Major import sources* (1997): United States 44.1%; Guam 19.3%; Japan 14.8%; Singapore 14.3%; Taiwan 5.4%; China 2.6%; Hong Kong 1.9%.
Exports (1997–98): U.S.$11,095,000 (mostly high-grade tuna; also garments and handicrafts). *Major export destinations:* mostly Japan.

Transport and communications

Transport. Railroads: none. Roads (1993): total length 40 mi, 64 km (paved 59%). Vehicles (1994): passenger cars and trucks 4,271. Merchant marine (1991): vessels (100 gross tons and over) 4; total deadweight tonnage, n.a. Air transport (1993): passenger arrivals 50,366, passenger departures 49,376; airports (1997) with scheduled flights 1.

Communications

Medium	date	unit	number	units per 1,000 persons
Radio	1997	receivers	12,000	663.0
Television	1997	receivers	11,000	606.0
Telephones	1994	main lines	2,615	160.0

Education and health

Educational attainment (1997). Percentage of population age 25 and over having: no formal schooling 0.1%; some primary education 4.4%; completed primary 5.7%; some secondary 16.3%; completed secondary 41.0%; some post-secondary 13.0%; higher 19.5%. *Literacy* (1997): total population age 15 and over literate 99.9%.

Education (1997)

	schools[10]	teachers[10]	students	student/ teacher ratio
Primary (age 6–13)	26	289	1,450	...
Secondary (age 14–18)	6	[11]	490	...
Higher[12]	1	...	130	...

Health (1990): physicians[13] 10 (1 per 1,518 persons); hospital beds 70 (1 per 200 persons); infant mortality rate per 1,000 live births (1999) 17.7.
Food: daily per capita caloric intake, n.a.

Military

The United States is responsible for the external security of Palau, as specified in the Compact of Free Association of Oct. 1, 1994.

[1]A site on Babelthuap is to be the eventual permanent capital. [2]Sonsorolese-Tobian is also, according to official sources, considered an official language. [3]Detail does not add to total given because of rounding. [4]2000 census total equals 19,129. [5]Gross national product comprises U.S. government spending only. [6]Manufacturing includes Construction. [7]Transportation and communications includes Public utilities. [8]Includes import duties and imputed bank service charge. [9]Unemployed. [10]1987. [11]Included with primary. [12]Palau Community College. [13]Government-employed health personnel only.

Internet resources for further information:
- **Republic of Palau Economic Report (Bank of Hawaii)**
  http://www.boh.com/econ/index.asp
- **Department of the Interior: Office of Insular Affairs**
  http://www.pacificweb.org

Panama

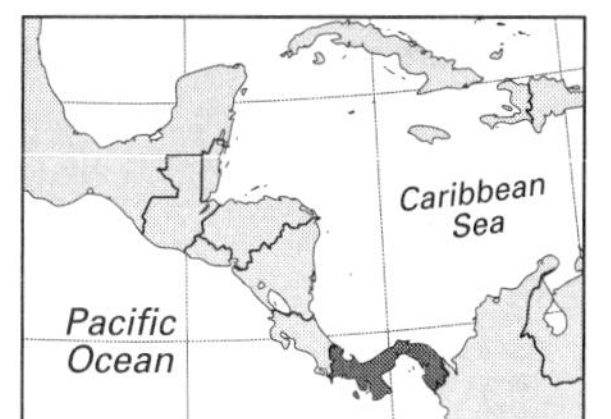

Official name: República de Panamá (Republic of Panama).
Form of government: multiparty republic with one legislative house (Legislative Assembly [71]).
Head of state and government: President assisted by Vice Presidents.
Capital: Panama City.
Official language: Spanish.
Official religion: none.
Monetary unit: 1 balboa (B) = 100 cents; valuation (Sept. 28, 2001) 1 U.S.$ = B 1.00; 1 £ = B 1.47.

Area and population

Provinces	Capitals	area sq mi	area sq km	population 2000 census
Bocas del Toro	Bocas del Toro	1,788	4,631	89,269
Chiriquí	David	2,498	6,471	368,790
Coclé	Penonomé	1,902	4,927	202,461
Colón	Colón	1,888	4,890	204,208
Darién[1]	La Palma	4,282	11,091	40,284[2]
Herrera	Chitré	904	2,341	102,465
Los Santos	Las Tablas	1,469	3,805	83,495
Panamá	Panama City	3,719	9,633	1,385,052
Veraguas	Santiago	4,119	10,668	209,076
Indigenous districts				
Emberá	...	1,698	4,398	8,246
Ngöbe Buglé	...	2,576	6,673	110,080
Kuna de Madungandí	...	895	2,319	3,305
Kuna de Wargandí[1]	...	299	775	[2]
Kuna Yala (San Blas)	El Porvenir	910	2,357	32,446
TOTAL		28,950[3]	74,979	2,839,177

Demography

Population (2001): 2,903,000.
Density (2001): persons per sq mi 100.3, persons per sq km 38.7.
Urban-rural (1999): urban 56.0%; rural 44.0%.
Sex distribution (2000): male 50.46%; female 49.54%.
Age breakdown (1999): under 15, 31.7%; 15–29, 27.4%; 30–44, 20.9%; 45–59, 12.0%; 60–74, 5.9%; 75 and over, 2.1%.
Population projection: (2010) 3,150,000; (2020) 3,443,000.
Doubling time: 49 years.
Ethnic composition (1992): mestizo 64.0%; black and mulatto 14.0%; white 10.0%; Amerindian 8.0%; Asian 4.0%.
Religious affiliation (1995): Roman Catholic 80.2%; Protestant 15.0%, of which Pentecostal 8.4%; other Christian 1.6%; other 3.2%.
Major cities (2000): Panama City 415,964 (urban agglomeration [1999] 1,141,000); San Miguelito 293,745[4]; David 77,734[5]; Arraiján 63,753[5]; La Chorrera 55,871; Colón 42,133.

Vital statistics

Birth rate per 1,000 population (2000): 19.5 (world avg. 22.5).
Death rate per 1,000 population (2000): 5.0 (world avg. 9.0).
Natural increase rate per 1,000 population (2000): 14.5 (world avg. 13.5).
Total fertility rate (avg. births per childbearing woman; 2000): 2.3.
Marriage rate per 1,000 population (1997): 4.1[6].
Divorce rate per 1,000 population (1997): 0.7[6].
Life expectancy at birth (2000): male 72.7 years; female 78.3 years.
Major causes of death per 100,000 population (1997): diseases of the circulatory system 122.1; malignant neoplasms (cancers) 64.4; accidents 37.1; diseases of the respiratory system 25.4; infectious and parasitic diseases 21.2.

National economy

Budget (1997). Revenue: B 2,266,300,000 (tax revenue 70.3%, of which income taxes 20.2%, social security contributions 19.1%; nontax revenue 26.8%, of which entrepreneurial and property income 15.4%). Expenditures: B 2,341,300,000 (social security and welfare 20.5%; health 18.7%; education 18.3%; economic affairs 8.0%; defense 5.0%).
Public debt (external, outstanding; 1999): U.S.$5,678,000,000.
Production (metric tons except as noted). Agriculture, forestry, fishing (1999): sugarcane 2,050,000, bananas 650,000, rice 232,000, plantains 115,000, corn (maize) 89,800, yams 36,900, oranges 27,000, coffee 10,400, tobacco 2,200; livestock (number of live animals; 1999) 1,400,000 cattle, 252,000 pigs, 165,000 horses; roundwood (1998) 1,098,300 cu m; fish catch (value of production in B '000,000; 1998): fish 63, shrimps 40. Mining and quarrying (1997): limestone 326,000; gold 38,600 troy oz. Manufacturing (value of production in B '000,000; 1998): food products 1,203, of which meat 341, dairy products 144; refined petroleum 299; beverages 176; cement, bricks, and tiles 154. Energy production (consumption): electricity (kW-hr; 1998) 4,183,000,000 (3,416,000,000); coal (metric tons; 1996) none (56,000); crude petroleum (barrels; 1996) none (12,615,000); petroleum products (metric tons; 1996) 1,171,000 (1,497,000); natural gas (cu m; 1996) none (60,736,000).
Tourism (1999): receipts from visitors U.S.$538,000,000; expenditures by nationals abroad U.S.$184,000,000.
Household income and expenditure. Average household size (2000) 4.2; average annual income per household (1990) B 5,450 (U.S.$5,450); expenditure (1983–84)[7]: food and beverages 34.9%, transportation and communications 15.1%, housing and energy 12.6%, education and recreation 11.7%.
Population economically active (1998)[6]: total 1,083,580; activity rate of total population 42.2%[8] (participation rates: ages 15–69 [1997] 64.3%, female [1997] 35.6%, unemployed 13.6%).

Price and earnings indexes (1995 = 100)

	1995	1996	1997	1998	1999	2000	2001[9]
Consumer price index	100.0	101.3	102.5	103.2	104.5	106.0	106.5
Monthly earnings index	...	...	...	...	...	...	...

Gross national product (1999): U.S.$8,657,000,000 (U.S.$3,080 per capita).

Structure of gross domestic product and labour force

	1998 in value B '000,000[10]	% of total value	labour force[6]	% of labour force
Agriculture, fishing	545.1	7.9	171,560	15.8
Mining	17.0	0.2	934	0.1
Manufacturing	673.4	9.7	106,076	9.8
Construction	279.4	4.0	80,680	7.4
Public utilities	293.8	4.2	9,827	0.9
Transp. and commun.	901.1	13.0	69,176	6.4
Trade, restaurants	1,410.3	20.3	244,108	22.5
Finance, real estate	1,746.8	25.2	66,264	6.1
Pub. admin.	711.3	10.3	72,696	6.7
Services	397.0	5.7	224,118	20.7
Other	−42.3[11]	−0.6[11]	38,141	3.5
TOTAL	6,932.9	100.0[4]	1,083,580	100.0[3]

Land use (1994): forested 43.8%; meadows and pastures 19.8%; agricultural and under permanent cultivation 8.9%; other 27.5%.

Foreign trade[12, 13]

Balance of trade (current prices)

	1995	1996	1997	1998	1999	2000
B '000,000	−1,958	−2,215	−2,358	−2,693	−2,695	−2,519
% of total	62.9%	66.2%	64.5%	65.6%	62.1%	49.1%

Imports (1998): B 3,398,000,000 (machinery and apparatus 22.9%, transport equipment 15.1%, mineral fuels 10.3%, chemicals and chemical products 9.6%). *Major import sources:* U.S. 39.7%; Colón Free Zone 12.8%; Japan 9.0%; Mexico 4.8%; Ecuador 3.2%.
Exports (1998): B 705,000,000 (bananas 19.7%, shrimps 19.4%, fish 7.9%, sugar 3.6%, clothing 3.6%). *Major export destinations:* U.S. 40.0%; Sweden 7.2%; Costa Rica 6.6%; Spain 5.4%; Belgium 4.3%.

Transport and communications

Transport. Railroads (1997): route length 220 mi, 354 km. Roads (1997): total length 7,022 mi, 11,301 km (paved 33%). Vehicles: passenger cars (1996) 203,760; trucks and buses 74,637. Panama Canal traffic (1997–98): oceangoing transits 13,158; cargo 189,865,000 metric tons. Air transport (1998)[14]: passenger-km 1,373,000,000; metric ton-km cargo 21,778,000; airports (1996) 10.

Communications

Medium	date	unit	number	units per 1,000 persons
Daily newspapers	1996	circulation	166,000	63
Radio	1997	receivers	815,000	306
Television	1998	receivers	530,000	195
Telephones	1999	main lines	462,476	166
Cellular telephones	1999	subscribers	242,000	87
Personal computers	1999	units	90,000	32
Internet	1999	users	45,000	16

Education and health

Educational attainment (1990). Percentage of population age 25 and over having: no formal schooling 11.6%; primary 41.6%; secondary 28.7%; undergraduate 12.4%; graduate 0.7%; other/unknown 5.0%. *Literacy* (1995): total population age 15 and over literate 1,590,000 (90.8%).

Education (1997)

	schools	teachers	students	student/teacher ratio
Primary (age 6–11)	2,866	15,058	377,898	25.1
Secondary (age 12–17) Voc., teacher tr.	417	12,450	223,155	17.9
Higher	14	6,409	95,341	14.9

Health (1998): physicians 3,518 (1 per 772 persons); hospital beds 7,287 (1 per 373 persons); infant mortality rate per 1,000 live births (2000) 20.8.
Food (1999): daily per capita caloric intake 2,496 (vegetable products 78%, animal products 22%); 108% of FAO recommended minimum requirement.

Military

Total active duty personnel (2000): none; Panama has an 11,000-member national police force. *Military expenditure as percentage of GNP* (1997): 1.4% (world avg. 2.6%); per capita expenditure U.S.$43.

[1]Kuna de Wargandí indigenous district (*comarca*) was created in 2000 from part of Darién province. [2]Darién includes Kuna de Wargandí. [3]Detail does not add to total given because of rounding. [4]District adjacent to Panama City within Panama City urban agglomeration. [5]Population of *cabecera*. [6]Excludes indigenous population. [7]Panama City only. [8]Estimated figure. [9]May. [10]At prices of 1982. [11]Imputed finance service charges less import duties. [12]Imports c.i.f.; exports f.o.b. [13]Excludes Colón Free Zone (1998 imports f.o.b. B 5,319,000,000; 1998 reexports f.o.b. B 5,969,000,000, of which machinery and apparatus 28.4%, textiles and clothing 21.3%). [14]COPA only.

Internet resources for further information:
- **Dirección de Estadistica y Censo**
  http://www.contraloria.gob.pa/direcciones/estycenso/index.htm

Papua New Guinea

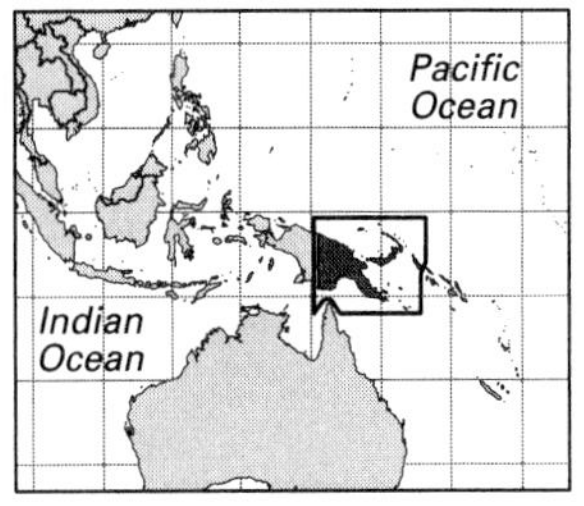

Official name: Independent State of Papua New Guinea.
Form of government: constitutional monarchy with one legislative house (National Parliament [109]).
Chief of state: British Monarch represented by Governor-General.
Head of government: Prime Minister.
Capital: Port Moresby.
Official language: English[1].
Official religion: none.
Monetary unit: 1 Papua New Guinea kina (K) = 100 toea; valuation (Sept. 28, 2001) 1 U.S.$ = K 3.55; 1 £ = K 5.21.

Area and population

		area		population
Provinces	**Administrative centres**	sq mi	sq km	1999 estimate
Central	Port Moresby (Central)	11,400	29,500	167,582
East New Britain	Rabaul	6,000	15,500	251,032
East Sepik	Wewak	16,550	42,800	288,080
Eastern Highlands	Goroka	4,300	11,200	324,259
Enga	Wabag	4,950	12,800	324,118
Gulf	Kerema	13,300	34,500	73,232
Madang	Madang	11,200	29,000	298,896
Manus	Lorengau	800	2,100	40,583
Milne Bay	Alotau (Samarai)	5,400	14,000	193,367
Morobe	Lae	13,300	34,500	456,700
National Capital District	Port Moresby	100	240	298,145
New Ireland	Kavieng	3,700	9,600	111,906
Oro (Northern)	Popondetta	8,800	22,800	117,798
Sandaun (West Sepik)	Vanimo	14,000	36,300	167,959
Simbu (Chimbu)	Kundiawa	2,350	6,100	189,069
Southern Highlands	Mendi	9,200	23,800	413,006
West New Britain	Kimbe	8,100	21,000	184,275
Western	Daru	38,350	99,300	150,682
Western Highlands	Mount Hagen	3,300	8,500	417,507
Autonomous region				
Bougainville[2]	Arawa (Buka)	3,600	9,300	181,321
TOTAL		178,704[3]	462,840	4,649,517[4]

Demography

Population (2001): 5,287,000.
Density (2001): persons per sq mi 29.6, persons per sq km 11.4.
Urban-rural (2000): urban 15.0%; rural 85.0%.
Sex distribution (2000): male 51.30%; female 48.70%.
Age breakdown (2000): under 15, 38.8%; 15–29, 28.7%; 30–44, 17.1%; 45–59, 9.7%; 60–74, 4.7%; 75 and over, 1.0%.
Population projection: (2010) 6,461,000; (2020) 7,748,000.
Ethnic composition (1983): New Guinea Papuan 84.0%; New Guinea Melanesian 15.0%; other 1.0%.
Religious affiliation (1990): non-Anglican Protestant 64.3%, of which Evangelical Lutheran 23.2%, Uniting Church 12.7%, Seventh-day Adventist 8.1%, Pentecostal 7.1%; Roman Catholic 28.3%; Anglican 3.9%; other (mostly animists) 3.5%.
Major cities (1997): Port Moresby 271,813; Lae 113,118; Madang 32,117; Wewak 25,143; Goroka 17,269.

Vital statistics

Birth rate per 1,000 population (2000): 32.7 (world avg. 22.5).
Death rate per 1,000 population (2000): 8.0 (world avg. 9.0).
Natural increase rate per 1,000 population (2000): 24.7 (world avg. 13.5).
Total fertility rate (avg. births per childbearing woman; 2000): 4.4.
Life expectancy at birth (2000): male 61.1 years; female 65.3 years.
Major causes of death per 100,000 population (1993): acute respiratory infections 34.6; pneumonia 27.8; meningitis 7.6; conditions originating from perinatal period 6.2; malaria 3.8.

National economy

Budget (2000). Revenue: K 2,866,700,000 (tax revenue 72.5%, of which income tax 19.5%, corporate tax 18.3%, VAT 11.8%; foreign grants 18.9%, nontax revenue 8.6%). Expenditures: K 3,081,800,000 (current expenditure 70.8%, of which transfer to provincial governments 16.8%, interest payments 12.4%; development expenditure 29.2%).
Public debt (external, outstanding; 1999): U.S.$1,517,000,000.
Production (metric tons except as noted). Agriculture, forestry, fishing (2000): coconuts 826,000, bananas 700,000, sweet potatoes 480,000, sugarcane 430,000, palm oil 299,000, yams 220,000, taro 170,000, cassava 120,000, coffee 83,040, palm kernels 61,000, cacao 39,000, pineapples 11,500, tea 9,000, natural rubber 7,200; livestock (number of live animals) 1,500,000 pigs, 87,000 cattle, 3,600,000 chickens; roundwood (2000) 8,597,000 cu m; fish catch (1999) 53,763. Mining and quarrying (1999): copper 143,900; silver 54,100 kg; gold 63,000 kg. Manufacturing (1998): palm oil 241,485; copra 124,349; coffee 80,700; cocoa 26,852; tea 7,923; rubber 5,645. Construction (value in K; 1998): total 193,500,000. Energy production (consumption): electricity (kW-hr; 1997) 1,161,900,000 (1,790,000,000[5]); coal (metric tons; 1996) none (1,000); crude petroleum (barrels; 1996) 546,000 (7,500); natural gas (cu m; 1996) 83,300,000 (83,300,000); petroleum products (metric tons; 1996) 50,000 (727,000).
Land use (1997): forested 92.3%; agricultural and under permanent cultivation 1.5%; meadows and pastures 0.2%; other 6.0%.
Gross national product (1999): U.S.$3,834,000,000 (U.S.$810 per capita).

Structure of gross domestic product and labour force

	2000		1980	
	in value K '000,000	% of total value	labour force[6]	% of labour force[6]
Agriculture	2,210	25.1	564,500	77.0
Mining	2,313	26.2	4,300	0.6
Manufacturing	806	9.1	14,000	1.9
Construction	628	7.2	21,600	2.9
Public utilities	119	1.3	2,800	0.4
Transp. and commun.	473	5.4	17,400	2.4
Trade	762	8.6	25,100	3.4
Finance	104	1.2	4,500	0.6
Pub. admin., defense Services	937	10.6	77,100	10.5
Other	468[7]	5.3[7]	1,500	0.2
TOTAL	8,820	100.0	732,800	100.0[3]

Population economically active (1990)[6]: total 1,715,330; activity rate 36.9% (participation rates: over age 10, 35.2%[8]; female 41.5%; unemployed 7.7%).

Price and earnings indexes (1995 = 100)

	1994	1995	1996	1997	1998	1999	2000
Consumer price index	85.3	100.0	111.6	116.0	131.8	151.5	175.1
Weekly earnings index	100.0	100.0	...	...	...	...	...

Tourism (1999): receipts U.S.$76,000,000; expenditures U.S.$53,000,000.

Foreign trade

Balance of trade (current prices)

	1995	1996	1997	1998	1999	2000
K '000,000	+1,780.0	+1,318.0	+928.4	+1,356.1	+2,173.1	+1,937.0
% of total	35.5%	24.8%	17.9%	24.2%	28.5%	26.0%

Imports (2000): K 2,758,100,000 (1990; machinery and transport equipment 38.7%; basic manufactures 20.4%; food and live animals 17.9%; chemicals 7.5%; mineral fuels, lubricants, and related materials 2.7%). *Major import sources* (1999): Australia 53.5%; Singapore 12.9%; Japan 5.6%; New Zealand 4.1%; U.S. 3.6%; China 2.6%.
Exports (2000): K 4,695,000,000 (gold 35.3%; crude oil 19.8%; copper 14.7%; coffee 7.0%; palm oil 5.2%; cocoa beans 2.8%). *Major export destinations* (1999): Australia 38.1%; Japan 16.9%; Germany 9.6%; U.S. 6.6%; South Korea 5.8%; China 4.0%; U.K. 2.7%.

Transport and communications

Transport. Railroads: none. Roads (1986): total length 19,736 km (paved 6%). Vehicles (1994): passenger cars 13,000; trucks and buses 32,000. Air transport (1997): passenger-km 735,000,000; metric ton-km cargo 86,000,000; airports (1999) with scheduled flights 42.

Communications

Medium	date	unit	number	units per 1,000 persons
Daily newspapers	1996	circulation	65,000	15
Radio	1997	receivers	410,000	91
Television	1999	receivers	60,000	13
Telephones	1999	main lines	59,773	13
Cellular telephones	1999	units	7,059	1.5
Internet	1999	users	2,000	0.7

Education and health

Educational attainment (1990). Percentage of population age 25 and over having: no formal schooling 82.6%; some primary education 8.2%; completed primary 5.0%; some secondary 4.2%. *Literacy* (1995 est.): total population age 15 and over literate 72.2%; males literate 81.0%; females literate 62.7%.

Education (1997)

	schools	teachers	students	student/ teacher ratio
Primary (age 7–12)	3,518	13,457[9]	587,788	...
Secondary (age 13–16)	159	2,415[10]	74,873	...
Voc., teacher tr.	128	878[10]	15,422	...
Higher	3	957[9]	9,220	...

Health: physicians (1998) 342 (1 per 13,708 persons); hospital beds (1989) 15,335 (1 per 234 persons); infant mortality rate (2000) 59.9.
Food (1999): daily per capita caloric intake 2,186 (vegetable products 89%, animal products 11%); 96% of FAO recommended minimum.

Military

Total active duty personnel (1999): 4,400 (army 86.4%, navy 9.1%, air force 4.5%). *Military expenditure as percentage of GNP* (1997): 1.3% (world 2.6%); per capita expenditure U.S.$14.

[1]The national languages are English, Tok Pisin (English Creole), and Motu. [2]Formal peace agreement signed on Aug. 30, 2001, ended nine years of civil war and promised Bougainville autonomy. [3]Detail does not add to total given because of rounding. [4]Preliminary 2000 census total equals 5,130,000. [5]1996. [6]Citizens of Papua New Guinea over age 10 involved in "money-raising activities" only. [7]Import duties. [8]1980. [9]1995. [10]1992.

Internet resources for further information:
- **Prime Minister's Office of Papua New Guinea http://www.pm.gov.pg/pmsoffice/PMsoffice.nsf**
- **Bank of Hawaii Economic Report http://www.boh.com/econ/pacific**

Paraguay

Official name: República del Paraguay (Spanish); Tetä Paraguáype (Guaraní)(Republic of Paraguay).
Form of government: multiparty republic with two legislative houses (Senate [46[1]]; Chamber of Deputies [80]).
Head of state and government: President.
Capital: Asunción.
Official languages: Spanish; Guaraní.
Official religion: none[2].
Monetary unit: 1 Paraguayan Guaraní (₲) = 100 céntimos; valuation (Sept. 28, 2001) 1 U.S.$ = ₲4,453; 1 £ = ₲6,544.

Area and population

Regions / Departments	Capitals	area sq mi	area sq km	population 1999 estimate
Occidental		95,338	246,925	132,906
Alto Paraguay	Fuerte Olimpo	31,795	82,349	14,389
Boquerón	Filadelfia	35,393	91,669	37,363
Presidente Hayes	Pozo Colorado	28,150	72,907	81,154
Oriental		61,710	159,827	5,222,937
Alto Paraná	Ciudad del Este	5,751	14,895	666,660
Amambay	Pedro Juan Caballero	4,994	12,933	133,573
Asunción[3]	—	45	117	557,776
Caaguazú	Coronel Oviedo	4,430	11,474	455,404
Caazapá	Caazapá	3,666	9,496	143,157
Canindiyú	Salto del Guairá	5,663	14,667	141,504
Central	Asunción	952	2,465	1,278,824
Concepción	Concepción	6,970	18,051	189,813
Cordillera	Caacupé	1,910	4,948	215,638
Guairá	Villarrica	1,485	3,846	174,695
Itapúa	Encarnación	6,380	16,525	478,753
Misiones	San Juan Bautista	3,690	9,556	99,823
Ñeembucú	Pilar	4,690	12,147	87,873
Paraguarí	Paraguarí	3,361	8,705	247,426
San Pedro	San Pedro	7,723	20,002	352,018
TOTAL		157,048	406,752	5,355,843

Demography

Population (2001): 5,636,000.
Density (2001): persons per sq mi 35.9, persons per sq km 13.9.
Urban-rural (1999): urban 54.0%; rural 46.0%.
Sex distribution (1999): male 50.42%; female 49.58%.
Age breakdown (1999): under 15, 39.3%; 15–29, 26.2%; 30–44, 17.9%; 45–59, 9.9%; 60–74, 5.1%; 75 and over, 1.6%.
Population projection: (2010) 6,980,000; (2020) 8,570,000.
Ethnic composition (2000): mixed (white/Amerindian) 85.6%; white 9.3%, of which German 4.4%, Latin American 3.4%; Amerindian 1.8%; black 1.0%; other 2.3%.
Religious affiliation (1995): Roman Catholic 88.5%; Protestant 5.0%; other 6.5%.
Major cities (1992): Asunción 500,938 (urban agglomeration [1999] 1,224,000); Ciudad del Este 133,881; San Lorenzo 133,395[4]; Lambaré 99,572[4]; Fernando de la Mora 95,072[4].

Vital statistics

Birth rate per 1,000 population (2000): 31.3 (world avg. 22.5).
Death rate per 1,000 population (2000): 4.8 (world avg. 9.0).
Natural increase rate per 1,000 population (2000): 26.5 (world avg. 13.5).
Total fertility rate (avg. births per childbearing woman; 2000): 4.2.
Marriage rate per 1,000 population (1999): 3.6[5].
Life expectancy at birth (2000): male 71.2 years; female 76.3 years.
Major causes of death per 100,000 population (1998)[6]: diseases of the circulatory system 129; malignant neoplasms (cancers) 63; accidents 54; diseases of the respiratory system 40; infectious and parasitic diseases 29.

National economy

Budget (1999): Revenue: ₲4,011,200,000,000 (tax revenue 69.4%, of which taxes on goods and services 39.0%, income tax 13.4%, customs duties 10.3%, social security 6.7%; nontax revenue including grants 30.6%). Expenditures: ₲4,605,800,000,000 (current expenditure 75.6%; capital expenditure 24.4%).
Public debt (external, outstanding; 1999): U.S.$1,672,000,000.
Population economically active (1996): total 1,747,488; activity rate 35.3% (participation rates [1992]: ages 12 and over, 51.0%; female 23.8%; unemployed [1998] 7.2%).

Price index (1995 = 100)

	1994	1995	1996	1997	1998	1999	2000
Consumer price index	88.2	100.0	109.8	117.5	131.0	139.9	152.4

Production (metric tons except as noted). Agriculture, forestry, fishing (1999): cassava 3,500,000, soybeans 3,303,500, sugarcane 2,872,270, corn (maize) 817,000, oranges 230,632, seed cotton 202,283, lint cotton 120,000, sweet potatoes 79,365, bananas 69,968; livestock (number of live animals) 9,863,000 cattle, 2,500,000 pigs, 15,000,000 chickens; roundwood (1998) 8,097,000 cu m; fish catch (1998) 26,000. Mining and quarrying (1997): limestone 600,000; kaolin 66,700; gypsum 4,500. Manufacturing (value added in constant prices of 1982, ₲'000,000; 1998): food products 59,100; wood products and furniture 23,500; handicrafts 10,300; printing and publishing 9,200; leather and hides 7,000; textiles 6,600; nonmetal products 6,600; petroleum products 3,800. Energy production (consumption): electricity (kW-hr; 1996) 48,200,000,000 (7,938,000,000); crude petroleum (barrels; 1996) none (1,143,000); petroleum products (metric tons; 1996) 157,000 (1,084,000).
Gross national product (1999): U.S.$8,374,000,000 (U.S.$1,560 per capita).

Structure of gross domestic product and labour force

	1998 in value ₲'000,000,000	1998 % of total value	1996 labour force	1996 % of labour force
Agriculture	7,037.2	28.3	559,042	32.0
Mining	119.6	0.5	2,568	0.1
Manufacturing	3,385.3	13.6	181,983	10.4
Construction	1,291.7	5.2	142,678	8.2
Public utilities	1,498.9	6.0	13,150	0.8
Transp. and commun.	1,216.0	4.9	55,972	3.2
Trade, Finance	5,772.8	23.2	224,210	12.8
Pub. admin., defense	1,454.3	5.9	330,697 (with Services)	18.9
Services, Other	3,077.9	12.4	237,188[7]	13.6[7]
TOTAL	24,853.7	100.0	1,747,488	100.0

Household income and expenditure. Average household size (1999) 4.6; sources of income (1989): wages and salaries 33.9%, transfer payments 2.5%.
Tourism (1999): receipts U.S.$81,000,000; expenditures U.S.$109,000,000.

Foreign trade[8]

Balance of trade (current prices)

	1994	1995	1996	1997	1998	1999
U.S.$'000,000	–1,323.6	–1,887.6	–1,807.0	–1,868.5	–1,866.4	–1,456.7
% of total	44.8%	50.5%	46.4%	46.2%	45.9%	41.8%

Imports (1998): U.S.$2,470,800,000 (machinery and transport equipment 30.6%, of which transport equipment 8.1%; food, beverages, and tobacco 23.7%; fuels and lubricants 7.6%; chemicals and pharmaceuticals 5.4%). *Major import sources:* Brazil 32.2%; U.S. 20.2%; Argentina 15.6%; Hong Kong 6.9%; Japan 2.7%.
Exports (1998): U.S.$1,014,100,000 (soybean flour 43.4%; cotton fibres 9.1%; timber 6.9%; vegetable oil 7.5%, of which soybean oil 6.0%; processed meats 6.7%; hides and skins 3.8%). *Major export destinations:* Brazil 28.1%; Argentina 25.7%; The Netherlands 15.3%; Japan 4.8%; Chile 4.7%; U.S. 2.7%; Italy 2.0%.

Transport and communications

Transport. Railroads (1998): route length 441 km; passenger-km 3,000,000; metric ton-km cargo 5,500,000. Roads (1997): total length 29,500 km (paved 10%). Vehicles (1996): passenger cars 71,000; trucks 50,000. Air transport (1997): passenger-km 215,000,000; metric ton-km cargo 19,000,000; airports (1998) 5.

Communications

Medium	date	unit	number	units per 1,000 persons
Daily newspapers	1996	circulation	213,000	43
Radio	1997	receivers	925,000	182
Television	1999	receivers	1,100,000	205
Telephones	1999	main lines	297,000	55
Cellular telephones	1999	subscribers	435,610	81
Personal computers	1999	units	60,000	11
Internet	1999	users	20,000	3.7

Education and health

Educational attainment (1999). Percentage of population age 15 and over having: no formal schooling 5.5%; primary education 52.8%; secondary 34.0%; higher 7.6%; not stated 0.1%. *Literacy* (1999): percentage of total population age 15 and over literate 92.3%; males literate 94.1%; female literate 90.6%.

Education (1998)

	schools	teachers	students	student/ teacher ratio
Primary (age 7–12)	6,143	59,423	933,289	15.7
Secondary (age 13–18)[9]	1,846	17,668[10]	332,703	16.6[10]
Higher[10]	2	742[11]	42,302	…

Health (1995): physicians 3,730 (1 per 1,294 persons); hospital beds 6,759 (1 per 714 persons); infant mortality rate per 1,000 live births (2000) 30.8.
Food (1999): daily per capita caloric intake 2,588 (vegetable products 76%, animal products 24%); 112% of FAO recommended minimum requirement.

Military

Total active duty personnel (2000): 20,200 (army 73.8%, navy 17.8%, air force 8.4%). *Military expenditure as percentage of GNP* (1997): 1.3% (world 2.6%), per capita expenditure U.S.$25.

[1]Includes one nonelective seat. Former president Juan Carlos Wasmosy became senator-for-life in August 1998. [2]Roman Catholicism, although not official, enjoys special recognition in the 1992 constitution. [3]Asunción is the capital city, not a department. [4]Within Asunción urban agglomeration. [5]Civil Registry records only. [6]Reporting areas only (constituting about 67 percent of the total population). [7]Includes 171,312 unemployed. [8]Imports are f.o.b. [9]Includes vocational and teacher training. [10]1996. [11]1993–94.

Internet resources for further information:

- **Banco Central del Paraguay**
  http://www.bcp.gov.py
- **Dirección General Estadística, Encuestas y Censos**
  http://www.dgeec.gov.py/index.htm

Peru

Official name: República del Perú (Spanish) (Republic of Peru).
Form of government: unitary multiparty republic with one legislative house (Congress [120]).
Head of state and government: President, assisted by Prime Minister.
Capital: Lima.
Official languages: Spanish; Quechua; Aymara.
Official religion: Roman Catholicism.
Monetary unit: 1 nuevo sol (S/.) = 100 céntimos; valuation (Sept. 28, 2001) 1 U.S.$ = S/. 3.48; 1 £ = S/. 5.12.

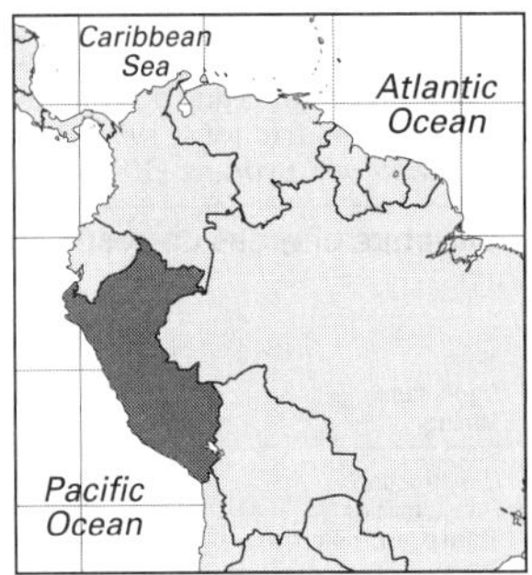

Area and population

Regions[1]	Capitals	area sq mi	area sq km	population 2000 estimate
Andres Avelino Cáceres	...	40,707	105,430	2,215,087
Arequipa	...	24,458	63,345	1,072,958
Chavín	...	15,686	40,627	1,067,282
Grau	...	15,661	40,562	1,739,611
Inca	...	66,696	172,741	1,667,892
José Carlos Mariátegui	...	40,081	103,809	1,623,960
La Libertad	...	9,873	25,570	1,465,970
Loreto	...	142,414	368,852	880,471
Los Libertadores-Wari	...	34,340	88,939	1,600,132
Nor Oriental del Marañón	...	33,486	86,728	2,911,053
San Martín	...	19,789	51,253	743,668
Ucayali	...	39,541	102,411	424,410
Department				
Lima	...	13,437	34,802	7,475,495
Constitutional Province				
Callao	Callao	57	147	773,701
TOTAL		496,225[2]	1,285,216	25,661,690

Demography

Population (2001): 26,090,000.
Density (2001): persons per sq mi 52.6, persons per sq km 20.3.
Urban-rural (2000): urban 72.3%; rural 27.7%.
Sex distribution (2000): male 49.59%; female 50.41%.
Age breakdown (2000): under 15, 33.4%; 15–29, 29.1%; 30–44, 19.3%; 45–59, 10.9%; 60–74, 5.7%; 75 and over, 1.6%.
Population projection: (2010) 29,885,000; (2020) 33,757,000.
Doubling time: 38 years.
Ethnic composition (2000): Quechua 47.0%; mestizo 31.9%; white 12.0%; Aymara 5.4%; Japanese 0.5%; other 3.2%.
Religious affiliation (1995): Roman Catholic 88.8%; Protestant 6.7%; other Christian 1.5%; other 3.0%.
Major cities (1998 est.): metropolitan Lima 7,060,600; Arequipa 710,103; Trujillo 603,657; Chiclayo 469,200; Iquitos 334,013.

Vital statistics

Birth rate per 1,000 population (2000): 24.5 (world avg. 22.5); (1977) legitimate 57.8%; illegitimate 42.2%.
Death rate per 1,000 population (2000): 5.8 (world avg. 9.0).
Natural increase rate per 1,000 population (2000): 18.7 (world avg. 13.5).
Total fertility rate (avg. births per childbearing woman; 2000): 3.0.
Life expectancy at birth (2000): male 67.6 years; female 72.5 years.
Major causes of death per 100,000 population (1989): diseases of the circulatory system 115.3; respiratory diseases 100.2; infectious diseases 84.5; malignant neoplasms 72.9; accidents, poisoning, and violence 53.6.

National economy

Budget (1998). Revenue: S/. 25,980,000,000 (taxes on goods and services 54.3%, income taxes 22.6%, import duties 9.5%, nontax revenue 7.0%, payroll tax 4.9%). Expenditures: S/. 27,389,000,000 (current expenditure 69.5%, capital expenditure 19.4%, interest payments 11.1%).
Public debt (external, outstanding; 1999): U.S.$20,709,000,000.
Tourism (1999): receipts U.S.$890,000,000; expenditures U.S.$443,000,000.
Production (metric tons except as noted). Agriculture, forestry, fishing (1999): sugarcane 6,900,000, potatoes 3,050,000, rice 1,947,000, plantains 1,344,000, corn (maize) 1,058,000, cassava 862,000; livestock (number of live animals) 13,700,000 sheep, 4,898,000 cattle, 2,784,000 pigs, 2,068,000 goats, 79,917,000 chickens; roundwood (1998) 9,157,000 cu m; fish catch (1998) 4,338,437. Mining and quarrying (1998): iron ore 3,224,000; zinc 725,000; copper 356,000; lead 228,000; silver 1,832. Manufacturing (value in S/. '000,000[3]; 1996): processed foods 275.1; base metal products 188.6; textiles and leather products 129.5; industrial chemicals 112.3; wood products 80.0. Construction (value in S/. '000,000[3]; 1996): residential 32.1; nonresidential 26.8. Energy production (consumption): electricity (kW-hr; 1996) 20,038,000,000 (20,038,000,000); coal (metric tons; 1996) 58,000 (302,000); crude petroleum (barrels; 1996) 44,000,000 (52,000,000); petroleum products (metric tons; 1996) 6,956,000 (6,078,000); natural gas (cu m; 1996) 208,000,000 (208,000,000).
Household income and expenditure. Average household size (1993) 5.1; income per household (1988) U.S.$2,173; sources of income (1991): business income 67.1%, wages 23.3%, transfers 7.6%, other 2.0%; expenditure (1990): food 29.4%, recreation and education 13.2%, household durables 10.1%, clothing and footwear 8.5%, transportation 7.5%, health 7.0%.
Gross national product (at current market prices; 1999): U.S.$53,705,000,000 (U.S.$2,130 per capita).

Structure of gross domestic product and labour force

	1998 in value S/. [3]	1998 % of total value	1992 labour force	1992 % of labour force
Agriculture	643,100	13.2	2,658,000	33.0
Mining	533,400	10.9	198,000	2.4
Manufacturing	1,029,300	21.1	840,000	10.4
Construction	473,400	9.7	300,000	3.7
Public utilities	...	...	25,000	0.3
Transp. and commun.	...	...	355,000	4.4
Trade	...	...	1,297,000	16.1
Finance	...	...	192,000	2.4
Services	2,195,700[4]	45.1[4]	2,199,000[5]	27.3[5]
TOTAL	4,874,900	100.0	8,064,000	100.0

Population economically active (1998): total 7,407,280; activity rate of total population 45.7% (participation rates: over age 15, 66.9%; female 43.8%; unemployed 7.7%).

Price and earnings indexes (1995 = 100)

	1994	1995	1996	1997	1998	1999	2000
Consumer price index	90.0	100.0	111.5	121.1	129.9	134.4	139.4
Monthly earnings index[6]	98.5	100.0	106.8	114.8	120.5	122.1	...

Land use (1998): forest and other 75.7%; pasture 21.1%; agricultural 3.2%.

Foreign trade[7]

Balance of trade (current prices)

	1995	1996	1997	1998	1999	2000
U.S.$'000,000	–2,111.6	–1,996.5	–1,738.3	–2,477.2	–612.2	–303.0
% of total	15.9%	14.5%	11.3%	17.8%	4.8%	2.1%

Imports (1998): U.S.$8,200,000,000 (raw and intermediate materials 41.3%, machinery 24.9%, consumer goods 23.0%, transport equipment 6.7%). *Major import sources:* U.S. 32.5%; Colombia 7.4%; Germany 5.6%; Venezuela 4.3%.
Exports (1998): U.S.$5,722,900,000 (gold 16.2%, copper and copper products 13.6%, zinc products 7.8%, fish meal fodder 6.8%, coffee 5.0%, petroleum and derivatives 3.9%, lead products 3.7%, silver 2.3%, tin 2.1%). *Major export destinations:* U.S. 32.3%; Japan 8.7%; United Kingdom 4.8%; Switzerland 4.2%; Spain 4.1%; Venezuela 3.9%; South Korea 3.4%.

Transport and communications

Transport. Railroads (1996): route length 1,992 km; passenger-km 171,091,000; metric ton-km cargo 850,329,000. Roads (1996): total length 73,766 km (paved 12%). Vehicles (1996): passenger cars 557,042; trucks and buses 359,374. Air transport (1996): passenger-km 2,634,000,000; metric ton-km cargo 251,000,000; airports (1996) 27.

Communications

Medium	date	unit	number	units per 1,000 persons
Daily newspapers	1996	circulation	2,000,000	84
Radio	1997	receivers	6,650,000	273
Television	1999	receivers	3,700,000	147
Telephones	1999	main lines	1,688,600	67
Cellular telephones	1999	subscribers	1,013,314	40
Personal computers	1999	units	900,000	36
Internet	1999	users	400,000	16

Education and health

Educational attainment (1993). Percentage of population age 15 and over having: no formal schooling 12.3%; less than primary education 0.3%; primary 31.5%; secondary 35.5%; higher 20.4%. *Literacy* (1995): total population age 15 and over literate 88.0%; males 93.5%; females 82.7%.

Education (1997)

	schools	teachers	students	student/teacher ratio
Primary (age 6–11)	33,017	153,951	4,163,180	27.0
Secondary (age 12–16)	8,452[8]	106,614	1,969,501	18.5
Voc., teacher tr.[8]	2,531	12,392	256,763	20.7
Higher	994[8]	45,443	657,586	14.5

Health: physicians (1996) 24,708 (1 per 969 persons); hospital beds (1994) 42,979 (1 per 538 persons); infant mortality rate per 1,000 live births (2000) 40.6.
Food (1999): daily per capita caloric intake 2,621 (vegetable products 87%, animal products 13%); (1997) 112% of FAO recommended minimum requirement.

Military

Total active duty personnel (2000): 115,000 (army 65.2%, navy 21.7%, air force 13.1%). *Military expenditure as percentage of GNP* (1997): 2.1% (world 2.6%); per capita expenditure U.S.$55.

[1]The nominal regional administrative structure introduced in 1987 coexisted in 2000 with an older departmental structure because of a lack of funding. [2]Detail does not add to total given because of rounding. [3]At 1979 prices. [4]Includes public utilities, transportation and communications, trade, finance, and public administration. [5]Includes public administration and other. [6]Estimate for Lima metropolitan area only; private sector nominal wages. [7]Imports and exports in balance of trade is f.o.b. [8]1996.

Internet resources for further information:
- **Instituto Nacional de Estadística e Informática (Spanish) http://www.inei.gob.pe**

Philippines

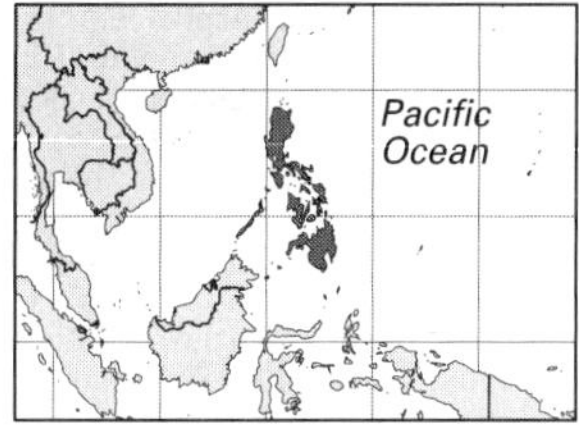

Official name: Republika ng Pilipinas (Pilipino); Republic of the Philippines (English).
Form of government: unitary republic with two legislative houses (Senate [24]; House of Representatives [260[1]]).
Chief of state and head of government: President.
Capital: Quezon City/Manila[2].
Official languages: Pilipino; English.
Official religion: none.
Monetary unit: 1 Philippine peso (₱) = 100 centavos; valuation (Sept. 28, 2001) 1 U.S.$ = ₱ 51.35; 1 £ = ₱ 75.47.

Area and population	area		population
			2000
Regions	sq mi	sq km	census
Bicol	6,808	17,633	4,674,855
Cagayan Valley	10,362	26,838	2,813,159
Caraga	7,277	18,847	2,095,367
Central Luzon	7,039	18,231	8,030,945
Central Mindanao	5,549	14,373	2,598,210
Central Visayas	5,773	14,951	5,701,064
Eastern Visayas	8,275	21,432	3,610,355
Ilocos	4,958	12,840	4,200,478
National Capital	246	636	9,932,560
Nothern Mindanao	5,418	14,033	2,747,585
Southern Mindanao	10,479	27,141	5,189,335
Southern Tagalog	18,117	46,924	11,793,655
Western Mindanao	6,194	16,042	3,091,208
Western Visayas	7,808	20,223	6,208,733
Autonomous Regions			
Cordillera	7,063	18,294	1,365,220
Muslim Mindanao	4,493	11,638	2,412,159
TOTAL	115,860[3]	300,076	76,498,735[4]

Demography

Population (2001): 78,609,000.
Density (2001): persons per sq mi 678.5, persons per sq km 262.0.
Urban-rural (2001): urban 59.0%; rural 41.0%.
Sex distribution (2000): male 50.37%; female 49.63%.
Age breakdown (2000): under 15, 36.2%; 15–29, 28.1%; 30–44, 19.0%; 45–59, 10.7%; 60–74, 4.8%; 75 and over, 1.2%.
Population projection: (2010) 92,896,000; (2020) 108,320,000.
Doubling time: 32 years.
Ethnolinguistic composition (by mother tongue of households; 1995): Pilipino (Tagalog) 29.3%; Cebuano 23.3%; Ilocano 9.3%; Hiligaynon Ilongo 9.1%; Bicol 5.7%; Waray 3.8%; Pampango 3.0%; Pangasinan 1.8%; other 14.7%.
Religious affiliation (1996): Roman Catholic 82.9%; Protestant 5.4%; Muslim 4.6%; Aglipayan (Philippine Independent Church) 2.6%; other 4.5%.
Major cities (2000): Quezon City 2,173,831; Manila 1,581,082; Caloocan 1,177,604; Davao 1,147,116; Cebu 718,821; Zamboanga 601,794.

Vital statistics

Birth rate per 1,000 population (2001): 26.7 (world avg. 22.5); (1982) legitimate 93.9%; illegitimate 6.1%.
Death rate per 1,000 population (2001): 5.3 (world avg. 9.0).
Natural increase rate per 1,000 population (2001): 21.4 (world avg. 13.5).
Total fertility rate (avg. births per childbearing woman; 2001); 3.3.
Life expectancy at birth (2001): male 68.0 years; female 72.0 years.
Major causes of death per 100,000 population (1995): heart disease 73.2; vascular diseases 56.2; pneumonia 49.0; malignant neoplasms (cancers) 41.5; tuberculosis 39.4; accidents 23.0.

National economy

Budget (1998). Revenue: ₱ 462,515,000,000 (income taxes 39.8%, taxes on goods and services 27.8%, international duties 16.5%, nontax revenues 9.9%). Expenditures: ₱ 528,263,000,000 (debt service 20.4%, education 20.1%, transportation and communications 8.5%, public order and safety 7.3%, general administration 6.8%, defense 5.6%).
Production (metric tons except as noted). Agriculture, forestry, fishing (2000): sugarcane 33,732,000, rice 12,415,000, coconuts 5,761,000, corn (maize) 4,486,000, bananas 4,156,000, pineapples 1,524,000; livestock (number of live animals) 10,398,000 pigs, 6,780,000 goats, 3,018,000 buffalo, 142,000,000 chickens; roundwood (1999) 43,399,000 cu m; fish catch (1998) 1,827,971. Mining and quarrying (1999): nickel ore 436,970; copper concentrate 98,857; chrome concentrate 17,562; gold 29,109 kg; silver 16,387 kg. Manufacturing (gross value added in ₱ '000,000; 1998)[5]: food products 246,300; electrical machinery 53,000; chemicals 49,100; petroleum and coal products 41,900. Construction (private, authorized; 1999): residential ₱ 26,647,111,000; nonresidential ₱ 36,181,015,000. Energy production (consumption): electricity (kW-hr; 1996) 34,775,000,000 (34,775,000,000); coal (metric tons; 1996) 1,109,000 (2,589,000); crude petroleum (barrels; 1996) 3,000,000 (117,000,000); petroleum products (metric tons; 1996) 12,260,000 (13,590,000).
Household income and expenditure (2000). Average household size 5.0; income per family ₱ 144,506 (U.S.$3,150); sources of income (1997): wages 45.6%, entrepreneurial income 26.2%, rent 10.3%, transfers 6.8%, other 11.1%; expenditure: food, beverage, and tobacco 45.0%, housing 15.1%, transportation 6.8%, fuel and power 6.2%, education 4.2%, personal care 3.6%.
Gross national product (1999): U.S.$77,967,000,000 (U.S.$1,050 per capita).

Structure of gross domestic product and labour force	1998		2000	
	in value ₱ '000,000	% of total value	labour force	% of labour force
Agriculture	449,888	16.9	11,415,000	35.8
Mining	20,093	0.8	110,000	0.3
Manufacturing	582,894	21.9	2,700,000	8.5
Construction	160,185	6.0	1,485,000	4.7
Public utilities	77,973	2.9	121,000	0.4
Transp. and commun.	139,662	5.2	1,991,000	6.2
Trade	361,159	13.5	4,590,000	14.4
Finances	319,584	12.0	729,000	2.3
Services	555,670	20.8	5,751,000	18.1
Others	—	—	2,956,000[6]	9.3[6]
TOTAL	2,667,108	100.0	31,848,000	100.0

Public debt (external, outstanding; 1999): U.S.$33,568,000,000.
Population economically active (2000): total 31,848,000; activity rate 41.5% (participation rates: ages 15–64, 65.0%; female [1995] 37.4%; unemployed 9.3%).

Price and earnings indexes (1995 = 100)	1994	1995	1996	1997	1998	1999	2000
Consumer price index	92.6	100.0	109.0	115.4	126.6	135.1	141.0
Daily earnings index[7]	100.0	100.0	113.8	127.6	127.6	...	...

Tourism (1999): receipts U.S.$2,534,000,000; expenditures U.S.$1,308,000,000.

Foreign trade[8]

Balance of trade (current prices)	1995	1996	1997	1998	1999	2000
₱ '000,000	−229,214	−299,998	−316,285	−69,991	+231,075	+385,576
% of total	20.3%	21.9%	17.5%	3.0%	8.8%	12.2%

Imports (1999): U.S.$30,723,340,000 (chemicals 8.1%, mineral fuels and lubricants 7.9%, power generating and specialized machinery 7.8%, telecommunications equipment and electrical machinery 7.6%, base metals 4.3%). *Major import sources:* United States 20.7%; Japan 19.9%; South Korea 8.9%; Singapore 5.7%; Taiwan 5.3%; Hong Kong 4.0%.
Exports (1999): U.S.$35,036,560,000 (electronics 56.2%, garments 6.5%, ignition wiring sets 1.5%, woodcraft and furniture 1.4%, coconut oil 1.0%, bananas 0.7%). *Major export destinations:* United States 29.6%; Japan 13.3%; Taiwan 8.5%; The Netherlands 8.2%; Singapore 7.0%; Hong Kong 5.6%.

Transport and communications

Transport. Railroads (2000): route length 897 km; passenger-km 12,000,000; metric ton-km cargo 660,000,000. Roads (1998): total length 199,950 km (paved 39%). Vehicles (1998): passenger cars 745,144; trucks and buses 263,037. Air transport (1999)[9]: passenger-km 10,292,338,000; metric ton-km cargo 240,918,000; airports (1996) with scheduled flights 21.

Communications				units per 1,000
Medium	date	unit	number	persons
Daily newspapers	1996	circulation	5,700,000	82
Radio	1997	receivers	11,500,000	161
Television	1999	receivers	8,200,000	110
Telephones	1999	main lines	2,892,000	39
Cellular telephones	1999	subscribers	2,850,000	38
Personal computers	1999	units	1,260,000	17
Internet	1999	users	500,000	6.7

Education and health

Education attainment (1995). Percentage of population age 15 and over having: no schooling 3.7%; elementary education 35.8%; secondary 38.4%; postsecondary 21.9%; not stated 0.2%. *Literacy* (1995): total population age 15 and over literate 94.6%; males literate 95.0%; females literate 94.3%.

Education (1996–97)	schools	teachers	students	student/ teacher ratio
Primary (age 7–12)	37,645	341,183	11,902,501	34.9
Secondary (age 13–16) / Voc., teacher tr.	6,369	154,705	4,888,246	31.6
Higher	1,316	66,876[10]	2,017,972[10]	30.2[10]

Health: physicians (1993) 78,445 (1 per 849 persons); hospital beds (1998) 81,200 (1 per 903 persons); infant mortality rate per 1,000 live births (2001) 31.0.
Food (1999): daily per capita caloric intake 2,357 (vegetable products 85%, animal products 15%); (1997) 104% of FAO recommended minimum.

Military

Total active duty personnel (2000): 106,000 (army 62.3%, navy 22.6%, air force 15.1%). *Military expenditure as percentage of GNP* (1997): 1.5% (world 2.6%); per capita expenditure U.S.$17.

[1]Includes 38 vacant seats. [2]And other Manila suburbs of the National Capital Region. [3]Detail does not add to total given because of rounding. [4]Includes foreign-service employees stationed abroad. [5]Manufacturing firms with 10 or more workers. [6]Mostly unemployed. [7]Minimum wages in nonagricultural activities in the National Capital Region. [8]Import figures are f.o.b. in balance of trade and c.i.f. for commodities and trading partners. [9]Philippines Airlines only. [10]1995–96.

Internet resources for further information:
- **National Statistics Office http://www.census.gov.ph**
- **Government Website http://www.neda.gov.ph**

Poland

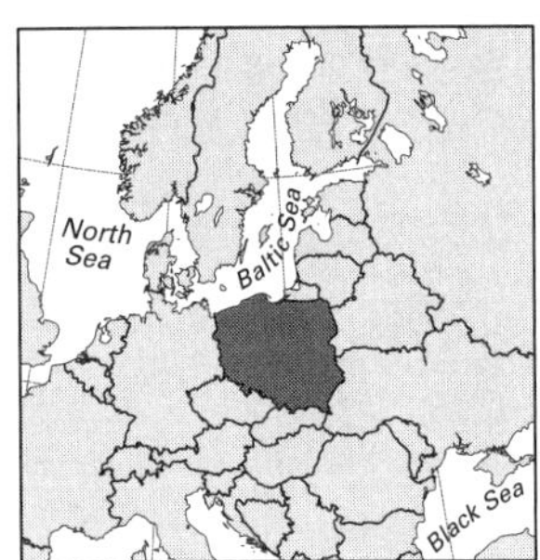

Official name: Rzeczpospolita Polska (Republic of Poland).
Form of government: unitary multiparty republic with two legislative houses (Senate [100]; Diet [460]).
Chief of state: President.
Head of government: Prime Minister.
Capital: Warsaw.
Official language: Polish.
Official religion: none[1].
Monetary unit: 1 zloty (Zł)[2] = 100 groszy; valuation (Sept. 28, 2001) 1 U.S.$ = Zł 4.23; 1 £ = Zł 6.21.

Area and population

		area		population
Provinces[3]	Capitals	sq mi	sq km	2000[4] estimate
Dolnośląskie	Wrocław	7,702	19,948	2,977,611
Kujawsko-pomorskie	Bydgoszcz/Toruń	6,938	17,970	2,100,771
Lubelskie	Lublin	9,697	25,114	2,234,937
Lubuskie	Gorzów Wielkopolski/ Zielona Góra	5,399	13,984	1,023,483
Łódzkie	Łódź	7,034	18,219	2,652,999
Małopolskie	Kraków	5,847	15,144	3,222,525
Mazowieckie	Warsaw (Warszawa)	13,744	35,598	5,069,977
Opolskie	Opole	3,634	9,412	1,088,272
Podkarpackie	Rzeszów	6,921	17,926	2,126,001
Podlaskie	Białystok	7,792	20,180	1,222,709
Pomorskie	Gdańsk	7,063	18,293	2,192,268
Śląskie	Katowice	4,747	12,294	4,865,512
Świętokrzyskie	Kielce	4,507	11,672	1,322,747
Warmińsko-Mazurskie	Olsztyn	9,345	24,203	1,465,577
Wielkopolskie	Poznań	11,516	29,826	3,355,332
Zachodniopomorskie	Szczecin	8,843	22,902	1,732,838
TOTAL		120,728[5]	312,685	38,653,559

Demography

Population (2001): 38,647,000.
Density (2001): persons per sq mi 320.1, persons per sq km 123.6.
Urban-rural (2000): urban 61.8; rural 38.2%.
Sex distribution (1998): male 48.61%; female 51.39%.
Age breakdown (1998): under 15, 20.6%; 15–29, 23.3%; 30–44, 22.2%; 45–59, 17.5%; 60–74, 12.2%; 75 and over, 4.2%.
Population projection: (2010) 38,764,000; (2020) 39,003,000.
Ethnolinguistic composition (1997): Polish 94.2%; Ukrainian 3.9%; German 1.3%; Belarusian 0.6%.
Religious affiliation (1995): Roman Catholic 90.7%; Ukrainian Catholic 1.4%; Polish Orthodox 1.4%; Protestant 0.5%; Jehovah's Witness 0.5%; other (mostly nonreligious) 5.5%.
Major cities (2000[4]): Warsaw 1,615,369; Łódź 800,110; Kraków 738,150; Wrocław 636,785; Poznań 576,899; Gdańsk (1999) 458,988.

Vital statistics

Birth rate per 1,000 population (1999): 9.9 (world avg. 22.5).
Death rate per 1,000 population (1999): 9.9 (world avg. 9.0).
Natural increase rate per 1,000 population (1999): 0.0 (world avg. 13.5).
Total fertility rate (avg. births per childbearing woman; 2000): 1.4.
Marriage rate per 1,000 population (1999): 5.7.
Divorce rate per 1,000 population (1999): 1.1.
Life expectancy at birth (2000): male 69.0 years; female 77.6 years.
Major causes of death per 100,000 population (1998): diseases of the circulatory system 450.9; malignant neoplasms (cancers) 168.6; accidents, poisoning, and violence 73.2; diseases of the respiratory system 36.5.

National economy

Budget (1998). Revenue: Zł 126,560,000,000 (income tax 39.1%, value-added tax 33.9%, excise tax 16.6%). Expenditures: Zł 139,752,000,000 (social security 18.0%, health 15.0%, education 8.1%, welfare 6.6%, defense 6.0%).
Public debt (external, outstanding; 1999): U.S.$34,528,000,000.
Gross national product (1999): U.S.$157,429,000,000 (U.S.$4,070 per capita).

Structure of gross domestic product and labour force

	1998			
	in value Zł '000,000	% of total value	labour force	% of labour force
Agriculture	23,157	4.2	2,946,000	17.2
Mining	13,789	2.5	381,000	2.2
Manufacturing	103,932	18.9	3,205,000	18.7
Public utilities	15,760	2.9	265,000	1.5
Construction	40,811	7.4	1,071,000	6.2
Transp. and commun.	30,946	5.6	958,000	5.6
Trade, restaurants	102,912	18.7	2,336,000	13.6
Finance, real estate	70,129	12.8	818,000	4.8
Pub. admin., defense	25,711	4.7	779,000	4.5
Services	55,099	10.0	2,595,000	15.1
Other	67,222[6]	12.2[6]	1,808,000[7]	10.5[7]
TOTAL	549,467[5]	100.0[5]	17,162,000	100.0[5]

Production (metric tons except at noted). Agriculture, forestry, fishing (1999): (gross value of production in Zł '000,000) potatoes 4,066, wheat 3,747, fruit 3,578, vegetables 3,484, rye 1,420, sugar beets 1,254; livestock (number of live animals) 18,538,000 pigs, 6,555,000 cattle; roundwood (1999) 24,300,000 cu m; fish catch (1997) 390,586. Mining and quarrying (1998): sulfur 1,672,000; copper ore (metal content) 432,243; silver (recoverable metal content) 1,108. Manufacturing (value added in Zł '000,000; 1999): food products 13,764; beverages 13,582; transport equipment 10,596; nonelectrical machinery 7,542; electrical machinery 7,506. Energy production (consumption): electricity ('000,000 kW-hr; 2000) 141,629 ([1996] 136,666); hard coal ('000 metric tons; 2000) 103,173 ([1996] 109,355); lignite ('000 metric tons; 2000) 59,366 ([1996] 63,864); crude petroleum (barrels; 1996) 2,400,000 (107,000,000); petroleum products (metric tons; 1996) 13,691,000 (16,305,000); natural gas (cu m; 2000) 4,970,000,000 ([1996] 14,160,000,000).
Population economically active (1998): total 17,162,000; activity rate of total population 44.4% (participation rates: 15–64, 66.1%; female 45.7%; unemployed [March 2000–February 2001] 14.3%).

Price and earnings indexes (1995 = 100)

	1995	1996	1997	1998	1999	2000	2001[8]
Consumer price index	100.0	119.8	137.9	154.1	165.3	182.1	191.4
Annual earnings index	100.0	126.3	151.6	174.2	189.9	209.6	218.2

Household income and expenditure. Average household size (1997) 2.9; average annual income (1995) Zł 8,431 (U.S.$2,990); sources of income (1996): wages 43.9%, transfers 25.2%, self-employment 21.9%; expenditure (1996): food, beverages, and tobacco 36.3%, housing and energy 19.1%, transportation and communications 11.3%.
Tourism (1999): receipts U.S.$6,100,000,000; expenditures U.S.$3,600,000,000.
Land use (1994): forest 28.8%; meadow 13.3%; agricultural and under permanent cultivation 47.0%; other 10.9%.

Foreign trade[9]

Balance of trade (current prices)

	1995	1996	1997	1998	1999	2000
Zł '000,000	–14,987	–34,412	–54,418	–67,443	–73,656	–75,163
% of total	11.9%	20.7%	24.4%	26.2%	25.3%	21.4%

Imports (1999): Zł 182,362,000,000 (machinery and transport equipment 38.2%, chemicals and chemical products 14.3%, mineral fuels and lubricants 7.2%, food 5.5%). *Major import sources:* Germany 25.2%; Italy 9.4%; France 6.8%; Russia 5.9%; U.K. 4.6%.
Exports (1999): Zł 108,706,000,000 (machinery and transport equipment 30.3%, food 8.5%, chemicals and chemical products 6.2%, mineral fuels and lubricants 5.0%). *Major export destinations:* Germany 36.1%; Italy 6.5%; The Netherlands 5.3%; France 4.8%; U.K. 4.0%.

Transport and communications

Transport. Railroads (2000[4]): length 22,981 km; (1999) passenger-km 26,198,000,000; (1999) metric ton-km cargo 55,471,000,000. Roads (1997): total length 377,048 km (paved 66%). Vehicles (2000[4]): passenger cars 9,283,000; trucks and buses 1,762,000. Air transport (1999[10]): passenger-km 4,632,000,000; metric ton-km cargo 80,304,000; airports (1997) 8.

Communications

Medium	date	unit	number	units per 1,000 persons
Daily newspapers	1996	circulation	4,351,000	113
Radio	1997	receivers	20,200,000	523
Television	1999	receivers	15,000,000	388
Telephones	2000[4]	main lines	10,076,000	261
Cellular telephones	2000[4]	subscribers	3,956,000	102
Personal computers	1999	units	2,400,000	62
Internet	1999	users	2,100,000	54

Education and health

Educational attainment (1995). Percentage of population age 15 and over having: no formal schooling/incomplete primary education 6.3%; primary 33.7%; secondary/vocational 53.2%; higher 6.8%. *Literacy* (2000): 99.8%.

Education (1999–2000)

	schools	teachers	students	student/ teacher ratio
Primary (age 7–12)	17,743	274,600	3,958,000	14.4
Secondary (age 13–18)	8,277	71,500	1,479,400	20.7
Voc., teacher tr.	8,066	89,900	1,552,300	17.3
Higher	287	78,100	1,431,900	18.3

Health (1999): physicians 90,086[4] (1 per 429 persons); hospital beds (2000[4]) 239,341 (1 per 161 persons); infant mortality rate per 1,000 live births 8.9.
Food (1999): daily per capita caloric intake 3,368 (vegetable products 73%, animal products 27%); 129% of FAO recommended minimum.

Military

Total active duty personnel (2000): 217,290 (army 61.1%, navy 7.7%, air force 21.3%, paramilitary 9.9%). *Military expenditure as percentage of GNP* (1997): 2.3% (world 2.6%); per capita expenditure U.S.$145.

[1]Roman Catholicism has special recognition per 1997 concordat with Vatican City. [2]On Jan. 1, 1995, the złoty was redenominated at a rate of 10,000 old złoty to 1 new złoty. [3]New administrative organization effective from Jan. 1, 1999. [4]January 1. [5]Detail does not add to total given because of rounding. [6]Taxes less subsidies. [7]Unemployed. [8]April. [9]Imports c.i.f.; exports f.o.b. [10]LOT only.

Internet resources for further information:
- **Polish Official Statistics**
  http://www.stat.gov.pl/english/index.htm

Portugal

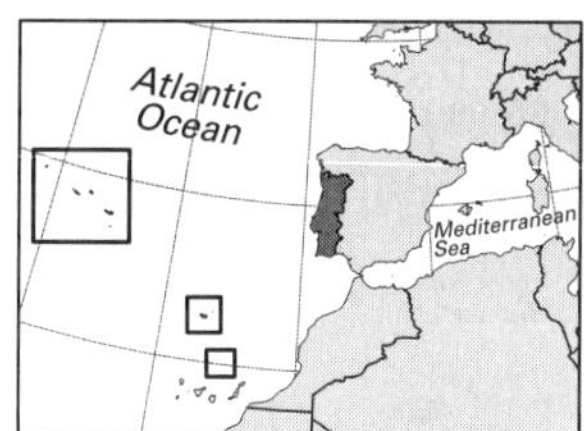

Official name: República Portuguesa (Portuguese Republic).
Form of government: republic with one legislative house (Assembly of the Republic [230]).
Chief of state: President.
Head of government: Prime Minister.
Capital: Lisbon.
Official language: Portuguese.
Official religion: none.
Monetary unit: 1 escudo (Esc) = 100 centavos; valuation (Sept. 28, 2001) 1 U.S.$ = Esc 220.14; 1 £ = Esc 323.54; 1 € = Esc 200.482.

Area and population

Continental Portugal		area		population
		sq mi	sq km	2001[1] census
Regions	**Principal cities**	34,284	88,796	9,833,408
Alentejo	Évora	10,398	26,931	534,365
Algarve	Faro	1,926	4,988	391,819
Centre (Centro)	Coimbra	9,138	23,668	1,779,672
Lisbon and Tagus Valley (Lisboa e Vale do Tejo)	Lisbon	4,607	11,931	3,447,173
North (Norte)	Porto	8,215	21,278	3,680,379
Insular Portugal				
Autonomous Regions		1,209	3,130	484,676
Azores (Açores)	Ponta Delgado	901[2]	2,333[2]	242,073
Madeira	Funchal	308[3]	797[3]	242,603
TOTAL		35,662[4]	92,365[4]	10,318,084[5]

Demography

Population (2001): 10,328,000[5].
Density (2001): persons per sq mi 289.6, persons per sq km 111.8.
Urban-rural (1996): urban 36.0%; rural 64.0%.
Sex distribution (2001): male 48.34%; female 51.66%.
Age breakdown (2000): under 15, 17.1%; 15–29, 23.0%; 30–44, 21.5%; 45–59, 17.8%; 60–74, 14.5%; 75 and over, 6.1%.
Population projection: (2010) 10,448,000; (2020) 10,364,000.
Ethnic composition (2000): Portuguese 91.9%; mixed race 1.6%[6]; Brazilian 1.4%; Marrano 1.2%; other European 1.2%; Han Chinese 0.9%; other 1.8%.
Religious affiliation (1995): Christian 94.8%, of which Roman Catholic 92.2%, Protestant 1.5%, other Christian (Jehovah's Witness 0.7%, Mormon 0.4%) 1.1%; Muslim 0.1%; other and nonreligious 5.1%.
Major cities (2001): Lisbon 556,797 (urban agglomeration 3,447,173); Porto 262,928; Amadora 174,788; Braga 105,000; Coimbra 103,000; Funchal 102,521.

Vital statistics

Birth rate per 1,000 population (2000): 11.5 (world avg. 22.5).
Death rate per 1,000 population (2000): 10.2 (world avg. 9.0).
Natural increase rate per 1,000 population (2000): 1.3 (world avg. 13.5).
Total fertility rate (avg. births per childbearing woman; 2000): 1.5.
Life expectancy at birth (2000): male 72.2 years; females 79.5 years.
Major causes of death per 100,000 population (1998): circulatory diseases 426.5; malignant neoplasms (cancers) 213.9; respiratory diseases 94.9.

National economy

Budget (1997). Revenue: Esc 7,041,700,000,000 (social security contributions 22.5%, general sales tax 19.3%, individual income tax 14.9%, excise tax 11.6%, grants 9.2%, nontax revenue 9.1%). Expenditures: Esc 7,242,200,000,000 (current expenditure 87.3%, development expenditure 12.7%).
Public debt (1996): U.S.$40,504,000,000.
Production (metric tons except as noted). Agriculture, forestry, fishing (2000): potatoes 1,250,000, tomatoes 1,000,000, corn (maize) 905,000, grapes 900,000, sugar beets 475,000, wheat 352,519, olives 260,000, oranges 253,816, apples 180,000, pears 169,931, rice 149,000, cabbages 140,000, carrots 100,000, cork (1998) 163,000; livestock (number of live animals) 5,850,000 sheep, 2,330,000 pigs, 1,245,000 cattle; roundwood (2000) 8,978,000 cu m; fish catch (1999) 215,230. Mining and quarrying (1999): marble 900,000; copper (mine output, copper content) 99,500. Manufacturing (value added in Esc '000,000; 1995): petroleum refining 424,700; machinery and transport equipment 412,300; food and beverages 312,800; wearing apparel and footwear 303,000; textiles 262,100; printing and publishing 133,700; tobacco 130,000. Energy production (consumption): electricity (kW-hr; 1998) 33,144,000,000 ([1997] 37,086,000,000); coal (metric tons; 1997) negligible (5,758,000); crude petroleum (barrels; 1997) none (90,452,000); petroleum products (metric tons; 1997) 11,333,000 (11,100,000); natural gas (cu m; 1997) none (103,328,000).
Tourism (1999): receipts U.S.$5,131,000,000; expenditures U.S.$2,266,000,000.
Land use (1994): forest 35.9%; pasture 10.9%; agriculture 31.5%; other 21.7%.
Population economically active (1999): total 5,046,800; activity rate of total population 50.5% (participation rates: ages 15–64 (1997), 68.5%; female 45.4%; unemployed 4.4%).

Price and earnings indexes (1995 = 100)

	1994	1995	1996	1997	1998	1999	2000
Consumer price index	96.0	100.0	103.1	105.3	108.3	110.8	112.6
Annual earnings index	...	...	...	...	...	...	...

Gross national product (at current market prices; 1999): U.S.$110,175,000,000 (U.S.$11,030 per capita).

Structure of gross domestic product and labour force

	1993		1998	
	in value Esc '000,000	% of total value	labour force	% of labour force
Agriculture	489,476	3.7	639,500	12.8
Mining	113,243	0.8	16,000	0.3
Manufacturing	3,417,963	25.8	1,130,100	22.6
Construction	699,267	5.3	516,700	10.3
Public utilities	551,164	4.2	31,900	0.6
Trade[7]	2,474,801	18.6	899,600	18.0
Finance	1,246,248	9.4	263,000	5.3
Transp. and commun.	825,319	6.2	177,600	3.6
Services	2,477,083	18.7	301,000	6.0
Pub. admin., defense	976,901	7.4	776,400	15.5
Other	...	...	248,100[8]	5.0[8]
TOTAL	13,271,465	100.0[9]	4,999,900[9]	100.0

Household income and expenditure. Average household size (1999) 3.1; income per household: n.a.; sources of income (1994–95): wages and salaries 45.8%, property and entrepreneurial income 32.4%, transfer payments 21.5%; expenditure (1994–95): food 23.9%, housing 20.6%, transportation and communications 18.9%, clothing and footwear 6.3%, health 4.6%, other 25.7%.

Foreign trade[10]

Balance of trade (current prices)

	1995	1996	1997	1998	1999	2000
Esc '000,000,000	–1,527	–1,631	–1,945	–2,454	–2,903	–3,245
% of total	17.9%	17.7%	18.8%	21.6%	23.9%	24.3%

Imports (1999): Esc 7,519,000,000,000 (machinery and transport equipment 37.8%, of which road vehicles and parts 14.5%; basic manufactures 20.1%, of which textiles 5.8%; food products 10.4%; chemicals and chemical products 9.4%; mineral fuels 5.6%). *Major import sources* (1999): Spain 25.3%; Germany 14.7%; France 11.4%; Italy 7.7%; U.K. 7.7%; The Netherlands 4.8%.
Exports (1999): Esc 4,616,000,000,000 (1998; machinery and transport equipment 32.9%, of which transport equipment 15.3%; textiles and wearing apparel 25.5%; footwear 6.6%; chemicals and chemical products 4.7%; food 4.0%; cork and wood products 3.8%). *Major export destinations* (1999): Germany 19.8%; Spain 18.1%; France 13.9%; U.K. 12.0%; U.S. 5.0%; Belgium 4.7%.

Transport and communications

Transport. Railroads (1998): route length 3,259 km; passenger-km 4,602,185; metric ton-km cargo 2,339,895,000. Roads (1996): total length 68,732 km (paved 88%). Vehicles (1998): passenger cars 3,200,000; trucks and buses 1,097,000. Merchant marine (1992): vessels (100 gross tons and over) 332; total deadweight tonnage 1,129,382. Air transport (1998): passenger-km 10,104,000,000; metric ton-km cargo 232,000,000; airports (1998) 16.

Communications

Medium	date	unit	number	units per 1,000 persons
Daily newspapers	1996	circulation	744,000	74
Radio	1997	receivers	3,020,000	298
Television	1999	receivers	5,600,000	547
Telephones	1999	main lines	4,230,000	413
Cellular telephones	1999	subscribers	4,671,000	456
Personal computers	1999	units	930,000	91
Internet	1999	users	700,000	68

Education and health

Educational attainment (1991). Percentage of population age 25 and over having: no formal schooling 16.1%; some primary education 61.5%; some secondary 10.6%; postsecondary 3.5%. *Literacy* (2000): total population age 15 and over literate 92.2%; males 94.8%; females 90.0%.

Education (1996–97)

	schools	teachers	students	student/ teacher ratio
Primary (age 5–11)	11,179	68,194	1,094,313	16.0
Secondary (age 12–19)	663	108,420	714,422	6.6
Vocational	205	5,298	80,130	15.1
Higher	282	16,192	350,850	21.7

Health (1998): physicians 31,087 (1 per 321 persons); hospital beds 39,870 (1 per 250 persons); infant mortality rate per 1,000 live births (2000) 6.1.
Food (1999): daily per capita caloric intake 3,768 (vegetable products 72%, animal products 28%); 154% of FAO recommended minimum requirement.

Military

Total active duty personnel (1999): 44,650 (army 57.4%, navy 26.0%, air force 16.6%). *Military expenditure as percentage of GNP* (1997): 2.4% (world 2.6%); per capita expenditure U.S.$240.

[1]Preliminary de jure figures. [2]Includes the uninhabited Ilhéus in the Azores. [3]Includes the uninhabited Desertas and Selvagens islands associated with Madeira. [4]Includes the 169 sq mi (439 sq km) of water areas comprising the Tagus and Sado estuaries and the Aveiro lagoon. [5]Includes March 2001 preliminary census results totaling 10,318,084. [6]Refugees and descendants of refugees from Angola, Cape Verde, or Mozambique. [7]Includes hotels. [8]Unemployed. [9]Detail does not add to total given because of rounding. [10]Imports c.i.f.; exports f.o.b.

Internet resources for further information:

- **Instituto Nacional de Estatística http://www.ine.pt**
- **Banco de Portugal http://www.bportugal.pt**

Puerto Rico

Official name: Estado Libre Asociado de Puerto Rico; Commonwealth of Puerto Rico.
Political status: self-governing commonwealth in association with the United States, having two legislative houses (Senate [27[1]]; House of Representatives [51[1]]).
Chief of state: President of the United States.
Head of government: Governor.
Capital: San Juan.
Official languages: Spanish; English.
Monetary unit: 1 U.S. dollar (U.S.$) = 100 cents; valuation (Sept. 28, 2001) 1 £ = U.S.$1.47.

Population (2000 census)

Municipio	population	Municipio	population	Municipio	population
Adjuntas	19,143	Fajardo	40,712	Naguabo	23,753
Aguada	42,042	Florida	12,367	Naranjito	29,709
Aguadilla	64,685	Guánica	21,888	Orocovis	23,844
Agunas Buenas	29,032	Guayama	44,301	Patillas	20,152
Aibonito	26,493	Guayanilla	23,072	Peñuelas	26,719
Añasco	28,348	Guaynabo	100,053	Ponce	186,475
Arecibo	100,131	Gurabo	36,743	Quebradillas	25,450
Arroyo	19,117	Hatillo	38,925	Rincón	14,767
Barceloneta	22,322	Hormigueros	16,614	Río Grande	52,362
Barranquitas	28,909	Humacao	59,035	Sabana Grande	25,935
Bayamón	224,044	Isabela	44,444	Salinas	31,113
Cabo Rojo	46,911	Jayuya	17,318	San Germán	37,105
Caguas	140,502	Juana Díaz	50,531	San Juan	434,374
Camuy	35,244	Juncos	36,452	San Lorenzo	40,997
Canóvanas	43,335	Lajas	26,261	San Sebastián	44,204
Carolina	186,076	Lares	34,415	Santa Isabel	21,665
Cataño	30,071	Las Marías	11,061	Toa Alta	63,929
Cayey	47,370	Las Piedras	34,485	Toa Baja	94,085
Ceiba	18,004	Loíza	32,537	Trujillo Alto	75,728
Ciales	19,811	Luquillo	19,817	Utuado	35,336
Cidra	42,753	Manatí	45,409	Vega Alta	37,910
Coamo	37,597	Maricao	6,449	Vega Baja	61,929
Comerío	20,002	Maunabo	12,741	Vieques	9,106
Corozal	36,867	Mayagüez	98,434	Villalba	27,913
Culebra	1,868	Moca	39,697	Yabucoa	39,246
Dorado	34,017	Morovis	29,965	Yauco	46,384
				TOTAL	3,808,610

Demography

Area: 3,515 sq mi, 9,104 sq km.
Population (2001): 3,829,000.
Density (2001): persons per sq mi 1,089.4, persons per sq km 420.6.
Urban-rural (1990): urban 74.9%; rural 25.1%.
Sex distribution (2000): male 48.14%; female 51.86%.
Age breakdown (2000): under 15, 23.8%; 15–34, 30.1%; 35–54, 25.7%; 55–64, 9.2%; 65 and over, 11.2%.
Population projection: (2010) 3,981,000; (2020) 4,085,000.
Doubling time: 90 years.
Linguistic composition (1990): Spanish 51.3%; Spanish-English 46.9%; English 0.5%; other 1.3%.
Religious affiliation (1995): Roman Catholic 64.8%; Protestant 28.7%; other 6.5%.
Major urban agglomerations (1998): San Juan 2,004,054; Ponce 366,273; Caguas 315,921; Mayagüez 258,283; Arecibo 176,814.

Vital statistics

Birth rate per 1,000 population (2000): 15.5 (world avg. 22.5).
Death rate per 1,000 population (2000): 7.7 (world avg. 9.0).
Natural increase rate per 1,000 population (2000): 7.8 (world avg. 13.5).
Total fertility rate (avg. births per childbearing woman; 2000): 1.9.
Marriage rate per 1,000 population (1996): 8.7.
Life expectancy at birth (2000): male 71.1 years; female 80.3 years.
Major causes of death per 100,000 population (1993): heart disease 142.6; cancers 95.4; diabetes 55.1; cerebrovascular disease 38.0; pneumonia and influenza 29.2.

National economy

Budget. Revenue (1997–98): U.S.$8,784,000,000 (tax revenue 68.3%, of which income taxes 45.5%, excise taxes 15.5%, intergovernment transfers 31.7%). Expenditures (1997–98): U.S.$6,263,000,000 (welfare 25.6%; education 20.3%; debt service 9.0%; public safety and protection 8.7%; health 3.5%).
Public debt (outstanding; 1999): U.S.$22,678,200,000.
Tourism (1999): receipts U.S.$2,138,000,000; expenditures U.S.$815,000,000.
Production (in metric tons except as noted). Agriculture, forestry, fishing (1999): sugarcane 307,358, plantains 76,140, bananas 38,215, pineapples 19,204, mangoes 17,245, oranges 16,057, pumpkins, squash, and gourds 16,329, coffee 11,567; livestock (number of live animals) 388,307 cattle, 174,748 pigs; roundwood, n.a.; fish catch (1997) 2,744 metric tons. Mining (value of production in U.S.$'000; 1993): stone 50. Manufacturing (value added in U.S.$'000,000; 1997): chemicals, pharmaceuticals, and allied products 21,393; food 3,532; machinery and metal products 2,940; petroleum products 849; clothing 679. Energy production (consumption): electricity (kW-hr; 1996) 19,029,000,000 (19,029,000,000); coal (metric tons; 1996) none (170,000); crude petroleum (barrels; 1996) none (43,980,000); petroleum products (metric tons; 1996) 5,877,000 (6,743,000); natural gas, none (none).

Gross national product (1997): U.S.$25,380,000,000 (U.S.$7,010 per capita).

Structure of gross domestic product and labour force

	1997–98		1997	
	in value U.S.$'000,000	% of total value	labour force	% of labour force
Agriculture	402.2	0.7	31,000	2.4
Manufacturing	23,015.6	42.8	162,000	12.5
Mining }	1,323.3	2.5	1,000	0.1
Construction }			64,000	4.9
Public utilities }	4,068.9	7.6	15,000	1.1
Transp. and commun. }			44,000	3.4
Trade	6,989.7	13.0	228,000	17.6
Finance, real estate	6,898.4	12.8	37,000	2.9
Pub. admin., defense	5,246.0	9.7	261,000	20.1
Services	5,758.0	10.7	285,000	22.0
Other	123.3[2]	0.2[2]	170,000[3]	13.1[3]
TOTAL	53,825.4	100.0	1,298,000	100.0[4]

Population economically active (1997): total 1,298,000; activity rate 34.1% (participation rates: ages 16 and over, 48.0%; female 39.5%; unemployed 13.1%).

Price and earnings indexes (1995 = 100)

	1993	1994	1995	1996	1997	1998	1999
Consumer price index	93.5	96.2	100.0	105.1	110.8	117.0	123.2
Hourly earnings index[5]	...	...	...	...	...	...	...

Household income and expenditure (1999). Average family size (2000) 3.0; income per family U.S.$32,892; sources of income: wages and salaries 60.6%, transfers 31.3%, rent 6.5%, self-employment 6.1%; expenditure: food and beverages 18.8%, health care 17.8%, transportation 12.8%, housing 12.1%, household furnishings 11.6%, clothing 7.9%, recreation 7.7%.

Foreign trade

Balance of trade (current prices)

	1994	1995	1996	1997	1998	1999
U.S.$'000,000	+5,098	+4,995	+3,884	+2,559	+6,107	+9,602
% of total	13.3%	11.7%	9.2%	5.6%	10.1%	16.0%

Imports (1997–98): U.S.$27,308,700,000 (chemicals [all forms] 26.8%, electrical machinery 11.8%, food 10.2%, transport equipment 9.6%, petroleum and petroleum products 7.2%, nonelectrical machinery 6.8%, professional and scientific instruments 4.2%, clothing and textiles 4.2%). *Major import sources* (1995–96): U.S. 62.5%; Japan 6.4%; Dominican Republic 4.0%; U.K. 2.9%.
Exports (1997–98): U.S.$33,416,400,000 (chemicals and chemical products 43.6%, nonelectrical machinery 13.2%, food 12.1%, electrical machinery 7.7%). *Major export destinations:* U.S. 88.5%; other 11.5%.

Transport and communications

Transport. Railroads (1988)[6]: length 59 mi, 96 km. Roads (1996): total length 8,948 mi, 14,400 km (paved 100%). Vehicles (1996): passenger cars 878,000; trucks and buses 190,000. Merchant marine: n.a. Air transport (1998): passenger arrivals and departures 9,285,000; cargo loaded and unloaded 275,500 metric tons[7]; airports (1998) with scheduled flights 7.

Communications

Medium	date	unit	number	units per 1,000 persons
Daily newspapers	1996	circulation	475,000	128
Radio	1997	receivers	2,700,000	724
Television	1998	receivers	1,250,000	333
Telephones	1999	main lines	1,295,000	342
Cellular telephones	1999	subscribers	814,000	215
Internet	1999	users	200,000	53

Education and health

Educational attainment (1990). Percentage of population age 25 and over having: primary education 26.8%; some secondary 23.5%; complete secondary 21.0%; higher 28.7%. *Literacy* (1995): total population age 15 and over literate 92.8%; males literate 92.7%; females literate 92.8%.

Education (1985–86)

	schools	teachers	students	student/ teacher ratio
Primary (age 5–12)	1,542	18,359	427,582	23.3
Secondary (age 13–18)	395	13,612	334,661	24.6
Voc., teacher tr.	52	...	149,191	...
Higher	45	9,045	156,818	17.3

Health: physicians (1992) 6,269 (1 per 575 persons); hospital beds (1993–94) 9,598 (1 per 381 persons); infant mortality rate (2000) 9.7.

Military

Total active duty personnel (2001): 2,840 U.S. personnel.

[1]Number of members per constitution. Excludes additional seats allotted to either the Senate or House of Representatives to meet 1/3 total representation requirements for minority parties per constitution. [2]Statistical discrepancy. [3]Unemployed. [4]Detail does not add to total given because of rounding. [5]Manufacturing sector only. [6]Privately owned railway for sugarcane transport only. [7]Handled by the Luis Muñoz Marín International Airport only.

Qatar

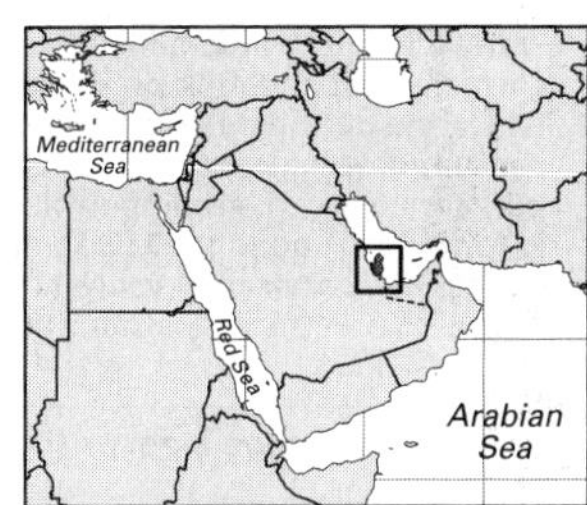

Official name: Dawlat Qaṭar (State of Qatar).
Form of government: monarchy (emirate)[1]; Islamic law is the basis of legislation in the state.
Heads of state and government: Emir assisted by Prime Minister.
Capital: Doha.
Official language: Arabic.
Official religion: Islam.
Monetary unit: 1 riyal (QR) = 100 dirhams; valuation (Sept. 28, 2001) 1 U.S.$ = QR 3.64; 1 £ = QR 5.35.

Area and population

Municipalities	Capitals	area sq mi	area sq km	population 1997 census
Ad-Dawḥah (Doha)	—	51	132	264,009
Al-Ghuwayrīyah	Al-Ghuwayrīyah	240	622	1,716
Jarayān al-Bāṭinah	Jarayān al-Bāṭinah	1,434	3,715	4,742
Al-Jumaylīyah	Al-Jumaylīyah	991[2]	2,565[2]	9,836
Al-Khawr	Al-Khawr	385	996	17,793
Ar-Rayyān	Ar-Rayyān	343	889	169,774
Ash-Shamāl	Madīnat ash-Shamāl	348	901	4,059
Umm Ṣalāl	Umm Ṣalāl Muḥammad	190	493	18,392
Al-Wakrah	Al-Wakrah	430	1,114	31,702
TOTAL		4,412[3]	11,427[3]	522,023

Demography

Population (2001): 596,000.
Density (2001): persons per sq mi 135.1; persons per sq km 52.2.
Urban-rural (1999): urban 92.3%; rural 7.7%.
Sex distribution (2000): male 65.9%; female 34.1%.
Age breakdown (2000): under 15, 26.3%; 15–29, 22.6%; 30–44, 27.1%; 45–59, 19.4%; 60–74, 4.1%; 75 and over, 0.5%.
Population projection: (2010) 756,000; (2020) 870,000.
Doubling time: 53 years.
Ethnic composition (2000): Arab 52.5%, of which Palestinian 13.4%, Qatari 13.3%, Lebanese 10.4%, Syrian 9.4%; Persian 16.5%; Indo-Pakistani 15.2%; black African 9.5%; other 6.3%.
Religious affiliation (2000): Muslim (mostly Sunnī) 82.7%; Christian 10.4%; Hindu 2.5%; other 4.4%.
Major cities (1997): Ad Dawhah (Doha) 264,009 (urban agglomeration [1999] 391,000); Ar-Rayyān 161,453; Al-Wakrah 20,205; Umm Ṣalāl 15,935.

Vital statistics

Birth rate per 1,000 population (2000): 16.1 (world avg. 22.5).
Death rate per 1,000 population (2000): 4.2 (world avg. 9.0).
Natural increase rate per 1,000 population (2000): 11.9 (world avg. 13.5).
Total fertility rate (avg. births per childbearing woman; 2000): 3.3.
Marriage rate per 1,000 population (1994): 2.8.
Divorce rate per 1,000 population (1994): 1.0.
Life expectancy at birth (2000): male 69.9 years; female 74.9 years.
Major causes of death per 100,000 population (1992): diseases of the circulatory system 56.9; injuries and poisoning 36.0; neoplasms (including benign neoplasms) 21.4; certain conditions originating in the perinatal period 11.1; diseases of the respiratory system 7.5; endocrine, metabolic, and nutritional diseases and immunity disorders 7.3; diseases of the digestive system 3.4; signs, symptoms, and ill-defined conditions 10.9.

National economy

Budget (1999–2000). Revenue: QR 14,098,000,000 (crude oil about 90%). Expenditures: QR 14,353,000,000 (current expenditure 91.7%, of which wages and salaries 37.5%; capital expenditure 8.3%).
Production (metric tons except as noted). Agriculture, forestry, fishing (2000): dates 16,500, tomatoes 11,000, pumpkin and squash 8,500, barley 4,650, dry onions 4,000, melons 3,450, watermelons 1,400; livestock (number of live animals; 2000) 215,000 sheep, 179,000 goats, 50,000 camels, 14,200 cattle; fish catch (1999) 4,207. Mining and quarrying (1996): limestone 900,000; sulfur 61,000; gypsum, sand and gravel, and clay are also produced. Manufacturing (value added in QR '000,000; 1994): refined petroleum 919; chemical products 887; iron and steel 319; pottery, china, and earthenware 219; textiles and apparel 193; food, beverages, and tobacco 99; metal products 89; wood products and furniture 79. Construction (1992): residential 12,420 units; nonresidential 1,416 units. Energy production (consumption): electricity (kW-hr; 1996) 6,340,000,000 (6,340,000,000); coal, none (n.a.); crude petroleum (barrels; 1999) 224,910,000 ([1996] 22,425,000); petroleum products (metric tons; 1996) 5,430,000 (745,000); natural gas (cu m; 1996) 13,700,000,000 (13,700,000,000).
Tourism (1994): receipts and expenditures, n.a.; total number of tourists staying in hotels 241,000.
Population economically active (1997): total 280,122; activity rate of total population 53.7% (participation rates: ages 15–64, 59.7%; female 21.0%; unemployed, n.a.).

Price and earnings indexes (1995 = 100)

	1994	1995	1996	1997	1998	1999
Consumer price index	97.1	100.0	107.4	110.4	113.3	115.7
Earnings index	...	...	...	...	...	...

Gross national product (1998): U.S.$6,473,000,000 (U.S.$11,600 per capita).

Structure of gross domestic product and labour force

	2000 in value QR '000,000	2000 % of total value	1988 labour force	1988 % of labour force
Agriculture	290	0.7	4,544	1.6
Oil sector	27,200	51.6	7,657	2.6
Manufacturing	3,745	7.1	10,627	3.6
Construction	2,180	4.1	64,213	21.9
Public utilities	635	1.2	3,672	1.3
Transportation	2,080	3.9	11,877	4.1
Trade	3,350	6.4	34,246	11.7
Finance	4,710	8.9	6,172	2.1
Pub. admin., defense; Services; Other	8,490	16.1	149,560	51.1
TOTAL	52,680	100.0	292,568	100.0

Household income and expenditure. Average household size (1998) 7.0; income per household: n.a.; sources of income (1988): wages and salaries 80.8%, rents and royalties 10.6%, self-employment 5.6%, other 3.0%; expenditure (1993): food 28.7%, transportation 19.3%, housing 12.4%, clothing 10.6%, education 7.6%, health 1.2%.
Land use (1994): meadows and pastures 4.5%; agricultural and under permanent cultivation 0.7%; built-up, desert, and other 94.7%.

Foreign trade

Balance of trade (current prices)[4]

	1995	1996	1997	1998	1999	2000
QR '000,000	+1,940	+4,546	+3,143	+7,134	+18,062	+23,198
% of total	8.1%	19.5%	12.6%	24.2%	52.4%	40.5%

Imports (1999): QR 9,098,400,000 (machinery and transport equipment 34.6%, manufactured goods 19.0%, food and live animals 13.2%, chemicals and chemical products 8.2%, raw materials 3.1%). *Major import sources* (1999): United Kingdom 11.5%; United States 11.4%; Japan 10.3%; UAE 8.0%; Saudi Arabia 7.1%; Germany 6.1%; France 4.9%; Italy 4.9%.
Exports (1999): QR 26,258,000,000 (1994; mineral fuels and lubricants 81.2%, chemicals and chemical products 10.4%, manufactured goods 5.9%). *Major export destinations* (1999): Japan 51.0%; South Korea 12.9%; Singapore 9.1%; U.S. 4.3%; Thailand 3.4%; United Arab Emirates 2.3%; India 1.1%.

Transport and communications

Transport. Railroads: none. Roads (1996): total length 764 mi, 1,230 km (paved 90%). Vehicles (1996): passenger cars 126,000; trucks and buses 64,000. Merchant marine (1998): vessels (100 gross tons and over) 64; total deadweight tonnage 744,181. Air transport (1999)[5]: passenger-mi 1,775,583,000, passenger-km 2,857,529,000; short ton-mi cargo 34,700,000, metric ton-km cargo 104,947,000; airports (1999) with scheduled flights 1.

Communications

Medium	date	unit	number	units per 1,000 persons
Daily newspapers	1995	circulation	90,000	161
Radio	1997	receivers	250,000	432
Television	1998	receivers	490,000	846
Telephones	1999	main lines	154,904	263
Cellular telephones	1999	subscribers	84,365	143.0
Personal computers	1999	units	80,000	135.8
Internet	1999	users	24,000	40.7

Education and health

Educational attainment (1986). Percentage of population age 25 and over having: no formal education 53.3%, of which illiterate 24.3%; primary 9.8%; preparatory (lower secondary) 10.1%; secondary 13.3%; postsecondary 13.3%; other 0.2%. *Literacy* (1995): total population age 15 and over literate 460,000 (79.4%); males literate 298,000 (79.2%); females literate 122,000 (79.9%).

Education (1995–96)[6]

	schools	teachers	students	student/teacher ratio
Primary (age 6–11)	174	5,864	53,631	9.1
Secondary (age 12–17)	123	3,738	37,924	10.1
Vocational[7]	3	120	670	5.6
Higher[8]	1	643	8,475	13.2

Health: physicians (1996) 703 (1 per 793 persons); hospital beds (1995) 892 (1 per 555 persons); infant mortality rate per 1,000 live births (2000) 22.1.

Military

Total active duty personnel (2000): 12,330 (army 68.9%, navy 14.0%, air force 17.1%). *Military expenditure as percentage of GNP* (1996): 10.5% (world 2.6%); per capita expenditure U.S.$1,540.

[1]Provisional constitution of 1970 provided limited constitutional forms but has not been fully implemented. [2]Includes the area of the unpopulated and formerly disputed (with Bahrain) Hawar Islands. The International Court of Justice awarded Hawar to Bahrain in early 2001. Qatar was awarded jurisdiction over some nearby islets. [3]Includes approximately 4 sq mi (10 sq km) of area not distributed by municipalities. [4]Imports f.o.b. in balance of trade and c.i.f. in commodities and trading partners. [5]Qatar Airways. [6]Public schools only; available detail for private schools (1991–92) included 17,728 primary students, 1,695 secondary students, and 1,465 teachers. [7]1994–95. [8]1996–97.

Internet resources for further information:
- **Qatar Ministry of Foreign Affairs http://www.mofa.gov.qa**

Réunion

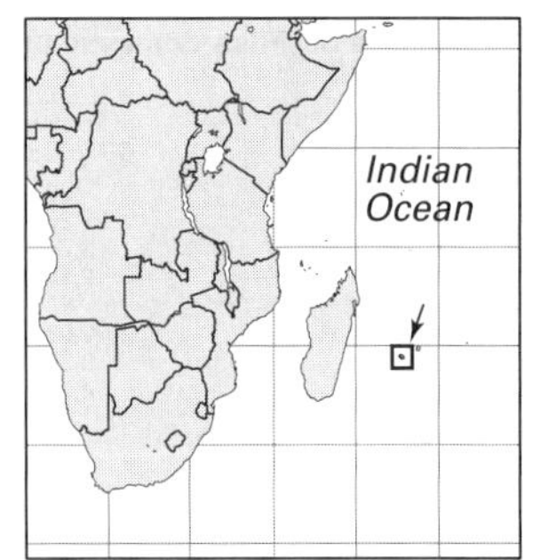

Official name: Département de la Réunion (Department of Réunion).
Political status: overseas department (France) with two legislative houses (General Council [47]; Regional Council [45]).
Chief of state: President of France.
Heads of government: Prefect (for France); President of General Council (for Réunion); President of Regional Council (for Réunion).
Capital: Saint-Denis.
Official language: French.
Official religion: none.
Monetary unit: 1 French franc (F) = 100 centimes; valuation (Sept. 28, 2001) 1 U.S.$ = F 7.20; 1 £ = F 10.59.

Area and population

		area		population
Arrondissements	**Capitals**	sq mi	sq km	1999 census
Saint-Benoît	Saint-Benoît	285	737	101,804
Saint-Denis	Saint-Denis	163	421	236,599
Saint-Paul	Saint-Paul	180	467	138,551
Saint-Pierre	Saint-Pierre	341	883	229,346
TOTAL		968[1, 2]	2,507[1, 2]	706,300

Demography

Population (2001): 733,000.
Density (2001): persons per sq mi 757.2, persons per sq km 292.4.
Urban-rural (1999): urban 71.6%; rural 28.4%[3].
Sex distribution (1999): male 49.15%; female 50.85%.
Age breakdown (1999): under 15, 27.0%; 15–29, 24.8%; 30–44, 24.4%; 45–59, 13.8%; 60–74, 7.2%; 75 and over, 2.8%.
Population projection: (2010) 829,000; (2020) 932,000.
Doubling time: 50 years.
Ethnic composition (2000): mixed race (black-white-South Asian) 42.6%; local white 25.6%; South Asian 23.0%, of which Tamil 20.0%; Chinese 3.4%; East African 3.4%; Malagasy 1.4%; other 0.6%.
Religious affiliation (1995): Roman Catholic 89.4%; Pentecostal 2.7%; other Christian 1.8%; other (mostly Muslim) 6.1%.
Major cities (1999): Saint-Denis 131,557[4] (agglomeration 158,139); Saint-Paul 87,712[4]; Saint-Pierre 68,915[4] (agglomeration 129,238); Le Tampon 60,323[4, 5]; Saint-Louis 43,519[4].

Vital statistics

Birth rate per 1,000 population (1998): 19.3 (world avg. 22.5); (1997) legitimate 41.5%; illegitimate 58.5%.
Death rate per 1,000 population (1998): 5.4 (world avg. 9.0).
Natural increase rate per 1,000 population (1998): 13.9 (world avg. 13.5).
Total fertility rate (avg. births per childbearing woman; 1997): 2.2.
Marriage rate per 1,000 population (1998): 4.8.
Divorce rate per 1,000 population (1997): 1.3.
Life expectancy at birth (1998): male 70.2 years; female 78.5 years.
Major causes of death per 100,000 population (1996): diseases of the circulatory system 170.7; malignant neoplasms (cancers) 98.0; accidents, suicide, and violence 53.0; diseases of the respiratory system 48.5.

National economy

Budget (1998). Revenue: F 4,624,000,000 (receipts from the French central government and local administrative bodies 52.7%, tax receipts 20.2%, loans 8.9%). Expenditures: F 4,300,000,000 (current expenditures 68.7%, development expenditures 31.3%).
Public debt (external, outstanding): n.a.
Tourism (1999): receipts U.S.$270,000,000; expenditures, n.a.
Gross national product (at current market prices; 1998): U.S.$5,070,000,000 (U.S.$7,270 per capita).

Structure of gross domestic product and labour force

	1995		1994	
	in value F '000,000	% of total value	labour force	% of labour force
Agriculture, fishing	1,392	3.6	12,015	5.0
Manufacturing, mining	3,101	8.0	9,854	4.1
Construction }	1,761	4.5	16,711	7.0
Public utilities }			...	...
Transp. and commun.	1,753	4.5	5,495	2.3
Trade, restaurants	6,140	15.8	22,587	9.4
Finance, real estate, business services	9,823	25.4	11,148	4.7
Pub. admin., defense }	16,524	42.7	23,678	9.9
Services }			50,986	21.3
Other	–1,760[6]	–4.5[6]	86,905[7]	36.3[7]
TOTAL	38,734	100.0	239,379	100.0

Production (metric tons except as noted). Agriculture, forestry, fishing (1999): sugarcane 1,800,000, corn (maize) 17,000, cabbages 14,000, pineapples 13,000, tomatoes 11,500, bananas 10,000, pimento 430, ginger 95, vanilla 30, tobacco 20, geranium essence (1998) 6.3; livestock (number of live animals) 89,000 pigs, 38,000 goats, 27,000 cattle; roundwood (1998) 36,100 cu m; fish catch (1998) 6,453. Mining and quarrying: gravel and sand for local use. Manufacturing (value added in F '000,000; 1997): food and beverages 1,019, of which meat and milk products 268; construction materials (mostly cement) 394; fabricated metals 258; printing and publishing 192. Energy production (consumption): electricity (kW-hr; 1998) 1,431,000,000 ([1996] 1,132,000,000); coal, none (none); crude petroleum, none (none); petroleum products (metric tons; 1996) none (509,000); natural gas, none (none).
Population economically active (1998): total 288,760; activity rate of total population 41.2% (participation rates: ages 15–64, 57.5%; female 44.3%; unemployed 41.1%).

Price and earnings indexes (December 1997 = 100)[8]

	1994	1995	1996	1997	1998	1999	2000
Consumer price index	94.8	96.7	98.6	100.0	101.0	102.1	104.4
Monthly earnings index[9]	96.5	98.9	98.9	100.0	101.4	102.8	...

Household income and expenditure. Average household size (1999) 3.3; average annual income per household (1997) F 136,800 (U.S.$23,438); sources of income (1997): wages and salaries and self-employment 41.8%, transfer payments 41.3%, other 16.9%; expenditure (1994–95): food and beverages 22.0%, transportation and communications 19.0%, housing and energy 10.0%, household furnishings 8.0%, recreation 6.0%.
Land use (1994): forested 35.2%; meadows and pastures 4.8%; agricultural and under permanent cultivation 19.6%; other 40.4%.

Foreign trade

Balance of trade (current prices)

	1994	1995	1996	1997	1998	1999
F '000,000	–12,116	–12,458	–13,180	–13,011	–14,095	–12,937
% of total	86.4%	85.7%	86.0%	83.9%	85.3%	85.3%

Imports (1998): F 15,310,000,000 (food and agricultural products 17.1%, transport equipment 14.7%, machinery and apparatus 13.4%, clothing and footwear 6.8%). *Major import sources:* France 66.0%; EC 14.0%.
Exports (1998): F 1,215,000,000 (sugar 58.9%, machinery, apparatus, and transport equipment 17.5%, rum 2.5%, lobster 1.7%). *Major export destinations:* France 70.0%; EC 9.0%; Madagascar 4.5%; Mauritius 2.3%.

Transport and communications

Transport. Railroads:[10]. Roads (1994): total length 1,711 mi, 2,754 km (paved [1991] 79%). Vehicles (1999[11]): passenger cars 190,300; trucks and buses 44,300. Air transport (1998): passenger arrivals 677,487, passenger departures 674,651; cargo unloaded 15,060 metric tons, cargo loaded 7,270 metric tons; airports (1999) with scheduled flights 2.

Communications

Medium	date	unit	number	units per 1,000 persons
Daily newspapers	1996	circulation	83,000	123
Radio	1997	receivers	173,000	252
Television	1997	receivers	127,000	185
Telephones	1999	main lines	268,496	378
Cellular telephones	1998	subscribers	50,300	72

Education and health

Educational attainment (1986–87). Percentage of population age 25 and over having: no formal schooling 18.8%; primary education 44.3%; lower secondary 21.6%; upper secondary 11.0%; higher 4.3%. *Literacy* (1996): total population age 16–66 literate 373,487 (91.3%); males literate 179,154 (89.9%); females literate 194,333 (92.7%).

Education (1997–98)

	schools	teachers	students	student/ teacher ratio
Primary (age 6–10)	351	...	76,364	...
Secondary (age 11–17)	111	...	96,811	...
Higher[12]	1	286	9,103	31.8

Health (1999[11]): physicians 1,346 (1 per 525 persons); hospital beds (1998[11]) 2,734 (1 per 254 persons); infant mortality rate per 1,000 live births (1997) 6.4.
Food (1999): daily per capita caloric intake, n.a.

Military

Total active duty personnel (2000): 4,200 French troops[13].

[1]Detail does not add to total given because of rounding. [2]Indian Ocean islets administered by France from Réunion are excluded from total. Areas of these islets, which have no permanent population, are: Îles Glorieuses 1.9 sq mi (5.0 sq km), Île Juan de Nova 1.7 sq mi (4.4 sq km), Île Tromelin 0.4 sq mi (1.0 sq km), Bassas da India 0.1 sq mi (0.2 sq km), Île Europa 7.8 sq mi (20.2 sq km). [3]Includes semi-urban. [4]Population of commune. [5]Within Saint-Pierre agglomeration. [6]Less imputed bank service charges. [7]Includes 2,621 not adequately defined and 84,284 unemployed. [8]Indexes refer to December. [9]Minimum salary in public administration. [10]No public railways; railways in use are for sugar industry. [11]January 1. [12]University only. [13]Includes troops stationed on Mayotte.

Internet resources for further information:
- **INSEE: Réunion**
  http://www.insee.fr/fr/insee_regions/reunion/home/home_page.asp
- **Ministère de l'Outre-mer (Paris)**
  http://www.outre-mer.gouv.fr/domtom/reunion/index.htm

Romania

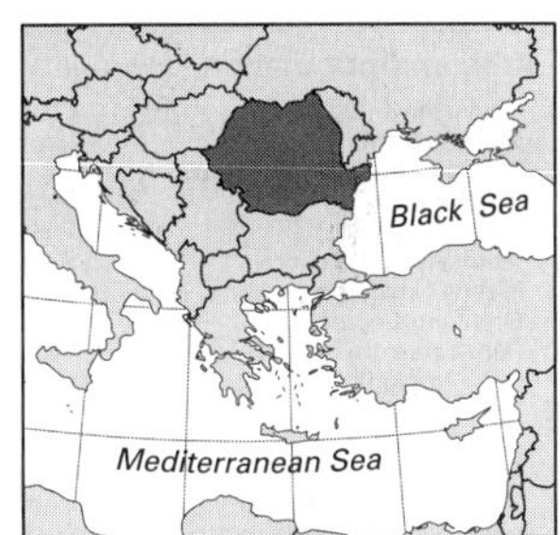

Official name: România (Romania).
Form of government: unitary republic with two legislative houses (Senate [143]; Assembly of Deputies [346[1]]).
Chief of state: President.
Head of government: Prime Minister.
Capital: Bucharest.
Official language: Romanian.
Official religion: none.
Monetary unit: 1 Romanian leu (plural lei) = 100 bani; valuation (Sept. 28, 2001) 1 U.S.$ = 30,485 lei; 1 £ = 44,804 lei.

Area and population

Counties	Capitals	area sq mi	area sq km	population 1997 estimate
Alba	Alba Iulia	2,406	6,231	402,097
Arad	Arad	2,954	7,652	476,988
Argeş	Piteşti	2,626	6,801	676,005
Bacău	Bacău	2,551	6,606	746,131
Bihor	Oradea	2,909	7,535	625,596
Bistriţa-Năsăud	Bistriţa	2,048	5,305	326,539
Botoşani	Botoşani	1,917	4,965	460,115
Brăila	Brăila	1,824	4,724	388,891
Braşov	Braşov	2,066	5,351	636,434
Buzău	Buzău	2,344	6,072	508,492
Călăraşi	Călăraşi	1,959	5,074	332,884
Caraş-Severin	Reşiţa	3,283	8,503	360,773
Cluj	Cluj-Napoca	2,568	6,650	724,355
Constanţa	Constanţa	2,724	7,055	746,686
Covasna	Sfântu Gheorghe	1,431	3,705	231,491
Dâmboviţa	Târgovişte	1,558	4,036	553,986
Dolj	Craiova	2,862	7,413	749,311
Galaţi	Galaţi	1,709	4,425	641,647
Giurgiu	Giurgiu	1,356	3,511	298,795
Gorj	Târgu Jiu	2,178	5,641	397,714
Harghita	Miercurea-Ciuc	2,552	6,610	343,330
Hunedoara	Deva	2,709	7,016	543,109
Ialomiţa	Slobozia	1,718	4,449	304,740
Iaşi	Iaşi	2,112	5,469	823,735
Maramureş	Baia Mare	2,400	6,215	533,672
Mehedinţi	Drobeta-Turnu Severin	1,892	4,900	325,344
Mureş	Târgu Mureş	2,585	6,696	602,626
Neamţ	Piatra Neamţ	2,274	5,890	583,141
Olt	Slatina	2,126	5,507	513,961
Prahova	Ploieşti	1,812	4,694	864,159
Sălaj	Zalău	1,486	3,850	259,304
Satu Mare	Satu Mare	1,701	4,405	392,054
Sibiu	Sibiu	2,093	5,422	444,701
Suceava	Suceava	3,303	8,555	711,568
Teleorman	Alexandria	2,224	5,760	466,010
Timiş	Timişoara	3,356	8,692	692,870
Tulcea	Tulcea	3,255	8,430	265,778
Vâlcea	Râmnicu Vâlcea	2,203	5,705	433,356
Vaslui	Vaslui	2,045	5,297	460,840
Vrancea	Focşani	1,878	4,863	391,762
Municipality				
Bucharest	Bucharest	703	1,820	2,304,934
TOTAL		91,699[2]	237,500	22,545,924

Demography

Population (2001): 22,413,000.
Density (2000): persons per sq mi 244.4, persons per sq km 94.4.
Urban-rural (2000): urban 56.2%; rural 43.8%.
Sex distribution (2000): male 48.84%; female 51.16%.
Age breakdown (2000): under 15, 18.4%; 15–29, 24.1%; 30–44, 21.0%; 45–59, 17.7%; 60–74, 14.3%; 75 and over, 4.5%.
Population projection: (2010) 21,978,000; (2020) 21,313,000.
Ethnic composition (1992): Romanian 90.7%; Hungarian 7.2%; other 2.1%.
Religious affiliation (1992): Romanian Orthodox 86.8%; Protestant 5.5%; Roman Catholic 5.1%; Greek Orthodox 1.0%; Muslim 0.2%; other 1.4%.
Major cities (1997): Bucharest 2,027,512; Iaşi 348,399; Constanţa 344,876; Timişoara 334,098; Cluj-Napoca 332,792; Galaţi 331,360.

Vital statistics

Birth rate per 1,000 population (2000): 10.8 (world avg. 22.5).
Death rate per 1,000 population (2000): 12.3 (world avg. 9.0).
Natural increase rate per 1,000 population (2000): –1.7 (world avg. 13.5).
Total fertility rate (avg. births per childbearing woman; 2000): 1.4.
Marriage rate per 1,000 population (1995): 6.8.
Life expectancy at birth (2000): male 66.1 years; female 74.0 years.
Major causes of death per 100,000 population (1998): circulatory disease 738.6; cancers 173.4; diseases of the digestive system 71.6; respiratory disease 71.0.

National economy

Budget ('000,000,000,000 lei; 1996). Revenue: 76.7 (social security 23.0%, personal income tax 18.2%, value-added tax 15.2%). Expenditures: 85.6 (social security 28.2%, debt service 10.0%, education 9.6%, health 7.5%).
Tourism (1999): receipts U.S.$254,000,000; expenditures U.S.$395,000,000.
Production (metric tons). Agriculture (2000): wheat 4,320,000, corn (maize) 4,200,000, potatoes 3,650,000, sugar beets 1,500,000, grapes 1,250,000; livestock (number of live animals) 7,972,000 sheep, 5,951,000 pigs, 3,154,000 cattle; roundwood (1998) 11,515,000 cu m; fish catch (1998) 9,020. Mining (1995): iron 184,000; bauxite 174,000; zinc 35,000; copper 24,000. Manufacturing (value-added in '000,000,000,000 lei; 1996): food products 5.8; beverages 3.0; iron and steel 1.6; glass products 1.5; textiles 1.4; motor vehicles 1.3; electrical machinery 0.9. Construction (1995): 9,300 dwelling units. Energy production (consumption): electricity (kW-hr; 1996) 61,350,000,000 (62,157,000,000); coal (metric tons; 1996) 41,869,000 (45,477,000); crude petroleum (barrels; 1996) 70,558,000 (100,440,000); petroleum products (metric tons; 1996) 10,956,000 (10,933,000); natural gas (cu m; 1996) 14,460,000,000 (20,401,000,000).
Public debt (external, outstanding; 1999): U.S.$5,985,000,000.
Gross national product (1999): U.S.$33,034,000,000 (U.S.$2,250 per capita).

Structure of gross domestic product and labour force

	1998 in value '000,000,000 lei	% of total value	labour force	% of labour force
Agriculture	20,662.0	19.1	4,342,200	37.5
Industry[3]	37,054.4	34.2	2,750,600	23.8
Construction	7,468.8	6.9	433,500	3.7
Transp. and commun.	9,374.3	8.6	529,400	4.6
Trade	10,907.5	10.1	1,068,000	9.2
Finance			81,800	0.7
Pub. admin.	18,011.1	16.6	1,639,500	14.2
Services				
Other	4,912.8	4.5	732,400[4]	6.3[4]
TOTAL	108,390.5[2]	100.0	11,577,300[2]	100.0

Population economically active (1998): total 11,577,300; activity rate 51.4% (participation rates: ages 15–64, 67.2%[5]; female 42.8%; unemployed 6.3%).

Price and earnings indexes (1995 = 100)

	1994	1995	1996	1997	1998	1999	2000
Consumer price index	75.6	100.0	138.8	353.7	562.7	820.4	1,195.1
Annual earnings index	64.9	100.0	149.0	295.0	502.9	719.6	1,006.0

Household income and expenditure. Average household size (1992) 3.1; income per household (1989) 73,500 lei (U.S.$4,940); sources of income (1982): wages 62.6%; expenditure (1989): food 51.1%; housing 16.4%.

Foreign trade

Balance of trade (current prices)

	1995	1996	1997	1998	1999	2000
U.S.$'000,000	–1,576.7	–2,470.5	–1,980.3	–403.3	–1,087.4	–1,683.1
% of total	9.1%	13.2%	10.5%	9.4%	6.0%	7.5%

Imports (1996): 10,368,000,000,000 lei (mineral fuels 25.4%, machinery and transport equipment 24.1%, textiles 12.0%, chemicals 8.4%). *Major import sources:* Germany 16.5%; Italy 15.6%; Russia 13.1%; France 4.8%.
Exports (1996): 10,272,827,000,000 lei (textiles 20.8%, mineral products 9.2%, chemicals 9.0%, machinery 8.0%, footwear 6.1%). *Major export destinations:* Germany 18.2%, Italy 16.6%; France 5.6%; U.K. 2.9%; U.S. 2.2%.

Transport and communications

Transport. Railroads (1997): length 11,365 km[6]; passenger-km 15,794,000,000; metric ton-km cargo 24,789,000,000. Roads (1996): length 153,358 km (paved 51%). Vehicles (1997): cars 2,605,565; trucks and buses 427,579. Merchant marine (1992): vessels (100 gross tons and over) 439; total deadweight tonnage 4,845,539. Air transport (1998): passenger-km 1,712,300,000; metric ton-km cargo 12,110,000; airports (1997) 8.

Communications

Medium	date	unit	number	units per 1,000 persons
Daily newspapers	1996	circulation	6,800,000	297
Radio	1997	receivers	7,200,000	319
Television	1999	receivers	7,000,000	312
Telephones	1999	main lines	3,740,000	167
Cellular telephones	1999	subscribers	1,356,000	61
Personal computers	1998	units	230,000	10
Internet	1999	users	600,000	28

Education and health

Educational attainment (1992). Percentage of population age 25 and over having: no schooling 5.4%; some primary education 24.4%; some secondary 63.2%; postsecondary 6.9%. *Literacy* (2000): total population age 15 and over literate 98.2%; males 99.1%; females 97.3%.

Education (1996–97)

	schools	teachers	students	student/teacher ratio
Primary (age 6–9)	13,978	175,426	2,546,231	14.5
Secondary (age 10–17)	1,295	64,485	792,788	12.3
Voc., teacher tr.	1,692	10,942	351,900	32.2
Higher	102	23,447	354,488	15.1

Health: physicians (1994) 47,990 (1 per 474 persons); hospital beds (1992) 174,900 (1 per 130 persons); infant mortality rate (2000) 19.8.
Food (1999): daily per capita caloric intake 3,254 (vegetable products 77%, animal products 23%); 132% of FAO recommended minimum requirement.

Military

Total active duty personnel (2000): 207,000 (army 51.2%, navy 10.0%, air force 21.0%, other 17.8%). *Military expenditure as percentage of GNP* (1997): 2.4% (world 2.6%); per capita expenditure U.S.$102.

[1]Includes 19 nonelective seats. [2]Detail does not add to total given because of rounding. [3]Mining, manufacturing, and public utilities. [4]Unemployed. [5]1992. [6]1994.

Internet resources for further information:
- **Embassy of Romania (Washington, D.C.) http://www.roembus.org**

Russia

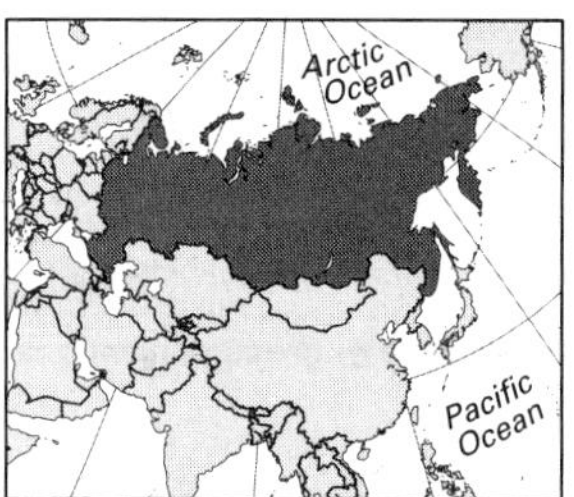

Official name: Rossiyskaya Federatsiya (Russian Federation).
Form of government: federal multiparty republic with a bicameral legislative body (Federal Assembly comprising a Federation Council [178] and a State Duma [450]).
Head of state: President.
Head of government: Prime Minister.
Capital: Moscow.
Official language: Russian.
Official religion: none.
Monetary unit: 1 ruble (Rub) = 100 kopecks; valuation (Sept. 28, 2001) market rate, 1 U.S.$ = Rub 29.47; 1 £ = Rub 43.31.

Area and population

		area		population
Federal Districts[2]	**Capitals**	sq mi	sq km	2000[1] estimate
Central	Moscow	252,000	652,800	37,142,000
Belgorod (region)	Belgorod	10,500	27,100	1,497,000
Bryansk (region)	Bryansk	13,500	34,900	1,443,000
Ivanovo (region)	Ivanovo	9,200	23,900	1,222,000
Kaluga (region)	Kaluga	11,500	29,900	1,081,000
Kostroma (region)	Kostroma	23,200	60,100	786,000
Kursk (region)	Kursk	11,500	29,800	1,316,000
Lipetsk (region)	Lipetsk	9,300	24,100	1,240,000
Moscow (city)		[3]	[3]	8,631,000
Moskva (Moscow; region)	Moskva	18,200[3]	47,000[3]	6,511,000
Oryol (region)	Oryol	9,500	24,700	899,000
Ryazan (region)	Ryazan	15,300	39,600	1,284,000
Smolensk (region)	Smolensk	19,200	49,800	1,133,000
Tambov (region)	Tambov	13,200	34,300	1,269,000
Tula (region)	Tula	9,900	25,700	1,746,000
Tver (region)	Tver	32,500	84,100	1,602,000
Vladimir (region)	Vladimir	11,200	29,000	1,609,000
Voronezh (region)	Voronezh	20,200	52,400	2,459,000
Yaroslavl (region)	Yaroslavl	14,100	36,400	1,414,000
Far Eastern	Khabarovsk	2,400,000	6,215,900	7,159,000
Amur (region)	Blagoveshchensk	140,400	363,700	1,006,000
Chukot (autonomous district)	Anadyr	284,800	737,700	72,000
Kamchatka (region)	Petropaulovsk-Kamchatsky	66,000	170,800	354,000
Khabarovsk (territory)	Khabarovsk	304,500	788,600	1,518,000
Koryak (autonomous district)	Palana	116,400	301,500	29,000
Magadan (region)	Magadan	178,100	461,400	233,000
Primorye (territory)	Vladivostok	64,100	165,900	2,173,000
Sakha (republic)	Yakutsk	1,198,200	3,103,200	977,000
Sakhalin (region)	Yuzhno-Sakhalinsk	33,600	87,100	598,000
Yevreyskaya (autonomous region)	Birobidzhan	13,900	36,000	199,000
North Caucasus	Rostov-na-Donu	227,300	589,200	21,695,000
Adygeya (republic)	Maikop	2,900	7,600	449,000
Astrakhan (region)	Astrakhan	17,000	44,100	1,024,000
Chechnia (republic)	Grozny	[4]	[4]	574,000
Dagestan (republic)	Makhachkala	19,400	50,300	2,149,000
Ingushetiya (republic)	Nazran	7,400[4]	19,300[4]	488,000
Kabardino-Balkariya (republic)	Nalchik	4,800	12,500	792,000
Kalmykiya (republic)	Elista	29,400	76,100	316,000
Karachayevo-Cherkesiya (republic)	Cherkessk	5,400	14,100	435,000
Krasnodar (territory)	Krasnodar	29,300	76,000	5,067,000
Rostov (region)	Rostov-na-donu	38,900	100,800	4,358,000
Severnaya Osetiya–Alania (republic)	Vladikavkaz	3,100	8,000	674,000
Stavropol (territory)	Stavropol	25,700	66,500	2,691,000
Volgograd (region)	Volgograd	44,000	113,900	2,678,000
Northwest	St. Petersburg	648,000	1,677,900	14,515,000
Archangelsk (region)	Archangelsk	158,700	411,000	1,414,000
Kaliningrad (region)	Kaliningrad	5,800	15,100	949,000
Kareliya (republic)	Petrozavodsk	66,600	172,400	766,000
Komi (republic)	Kudymkar	160,600	415,900	1,135,000
Leningrad (region)	St. Petersburg	33,200[5]	85,900[5]	1,674,000
Murmansk (region)	Murmansk	55,900	144,900	983,000
Nenets (autonomous district)	Naryan-Mar	68,100	176,400	46,000
Novgorod (region)	Novgorod	21,400	55,300	729,000
Pskov (region)	Pskov	21,400	55,300	801,000
St. Petersburg (city)		[5]	[5]	4,694,000
Vologda (region)	Vologda	56,300	145,700	1,324,000
Siberia	Novosibirsk	1,974,800	5,114,800	20,792,000
Agin Buryat (autonomous district)	Aginskoye	7,300	19,000	79,000
Altay (republic)	Gorno-Altaisk	35,700	92,600	205,000
Altay (territory)	Barnaul	65,300	169,100	2,653,000
Buryatiya (republic)	Ulan-Ude	135,600	351,300	1,035,000
Chita (region)	Chita	159,300	412,500	1,180,000
Evenk (autonomous district)	Tyra	296,400	767,600	18,000
Irkutsk (region)	Irkutsk	287,900	745,500	2,604,000
Kemerovo (region)	Kemerovo	36,900	95,500	2,987,000
Khakasiya (republic)	Abakan	23,900	61,900	581,000
Krasnoyarsk (territory)	Krasnoyarsk	274,100	710,000	2,978,000
Novosibirsk (region)	Novosibirsk	68,800	178,200	2,744,000
Omsk (region)	Omsk	53,900	139,700	2,163,000
Taymyr (autonomous district)	Dudinka	332,900	862,100	43,000
Tomsk (region)	Tomsk	122,400	316,900	1,067,000
Tuva (republic)	Kyzyl-Orda	65,800	170,500	311,000
Ust-Ordyn Buryat		8,600	22,400	144,000
Urals	Yekaterinburg	690,600	1,788,900	12,597,000
Chelyabinsk (region)	Chelyabinsk	33,900	87,900	3,672,000
Khanty-Mansi (autonomous district)	Khanty-Mansiysk	202,000	523,100	1,363,000
Kurgan (region)	Kurgan	27,400	71,000	1,097,000
Sverdlovsk (region)	Sverdlovsk	75,200	194,800	4,612,000
Tyumen (region)	Tyumen	62,400	161,800	1,358,000
Yamalo-Nenets (autonomous district)	Salekhard	289,700	750,300	495,000
Volga	Nizhny Novgorod	400,100	1,035,900	32,025,000
Bashkortostan (republic)	Ufa	55,400	143,600	4,117,000

Area and population (continued)

Chuvashiya (republic)	Cheboksary	7,100	18,300	1,357,000
Kirov (region)	Kirov	46,600	120,800	1,589,000
Komi-Permyak (autonomous district)	Syktyvkar	12,700	32,900	152,000
Mari-El (republic)	Toshkar-Ola	9,000	23,200	759,000
Mordoviya (republic)	Saransk	10,100	26,200	929,000
Nizhny Novgorod (region)	Nizhny Novgorod	28,900	74,800	3,658,000
Orenburg (region)	Orenburg	47,900	124,000	2,224,000
Penza (region)	Penza	16,700	43,200	1,531,000
Perm (region)	Perm	49,300	127,700	2,814,000
Samara (region)	Samara	20,700	53,600	3,297,000
Saratov (region)	Saratov	38,700	100,200	2,712,000
Tatarstan (republic)	Kazan	26,300	68,000	3,779,000
Udmurtia (republic)	Izhevsk	16,300	42,100	1,639,000
Ulyanovsk (Simbirsk; region)	Simbirsk	14,400	37,300	1,468,000
TOTAL		6,592,800	17,075,400	145,925,000

Demography

Population (2001): 144,417,000.
Density (2001): persons per sq mi 21.9, persons per sq km 8.5.
Urban-rural (2000): urban 73.0%; rural 27.0%.
Sex distribution (2000): male 46.78%; female 53.22%.
Age breakdown (2000): under 15, 18.3%; 15–29, 22.5%; 30–44, 23.3%; 45–59, 17.5%; 60–74, 14.4%; 75 and over, 4.0%.
Population projection: (2010) 141,297,000; (2020) 137,971,000.
Ethnic composition (1997): Russian 86.6%; Tatar 3.2%; Ukrainian 1.3%; Chuvash 0.9%; Bashkir 0.7%; Chechen 0.6%; Mordovian 0.5%; Belorussian 0.3%; other 5.9%.
Religious affiliation (1997): Russian Orthodox 16.3%; Muslim 7.0%; Protestant 0.9%; Jewish 0.4%; other (mostly nonreligious) 75.4%.
Major cities (2000[1]): Moscow 8,369,200; St. Petersburg 4,694,000; Novosibirsk 1,398,800; Nizhny Novgorod 1,357,000; Yekaterinburg 1,266,300; Samara 1,156,100; Omsk 1,148,900; Kazan 1,101,000; Ufa 1,091,200; Chelyabinsk 1,083,000; Rostov-na-Donu 1,012,700; Perm 1,009,700.

Other principal cities (2000[1])

	population		population		population
Astrakhan	486,100	Lipetsk	521,100	Tolyatti	722,900
Barnaul	580,100	Naberezhnye Chelny	514,700	Tomsk	482,100
Irkutsk	593,700	Novokuznetsk	561,600	Tula	506,100
Izhevsk	652,800	Orenburg	523,600	Tyumen	503,400
Kemerovo	492,700	Penza	532,200	Vladivostok	606,200
Khabarovsk	609,400	Ryazan	529,900	Volgograd	993,400
Krasnodar	639,000	Saratov	874,000	Voronezh	907,700
Krasnoyarsk	875,500	Simbirsk (Ulyanovsk)	667,400	Yaroslavl	616,700

Mobility (1989). Population living in the same residence as in 1988: 78.8%; different residence, same oblast 11.5%; different republic 9.7%.
Households (1999). Total family households 52,116,000; average household size 2.8; distribution by size (1995): 1 person 19.2%; 2 persons 26.2%; 3 persons 22.6%; 4 persons 20.5%; 5 persons or more 11.5%. Population in family households (1989): 128,787,000 (87.0%), nonfamily population 19,254,000 (13.0%).

Vital statistics

Birth rate per 1,000 population (2000): 8.3 (world avg. 22.5); legitimate 70.5%; illegitimate 29.5%.
Death rate per 1,000 population (2000): 14.7 (world avg. 9.0).
Natural increase rate per 1,000 population (2000): –6.4 (world avg. 13.5).
Total fertility rate (avg. births per childbearing woman; 2000): 1.3.
Marriage rate per 1,000 population (1999): 6.3.
Divorce rate per 1,000 population (1999): 3.7.
Life expectancy at birth (1999): male 59.9 years; female 72.4 years.
Major causes of death per 100,000 population (1999): circulatory diseases 815.7; accidents, poisoning, and violence 206.1, of which suicide 39.5; murder 26.2; malignant neoplasms (cancers) 205.0; respiratory diseases 64.9; digestive diseases 41.9; infectious and parasitic diseases 24.5.

Social indicators

Educational attainment (1998). Percentage of population age 16 and over having: primary or no formal education 11.2%; some secondary 25.3%; secondary and some postsecondary 40.9%; higher and postgraduate 22.6%.
Quality of working life (1999). Average workweek: 40 hours. Annual rate per 100,000 workers of: injury or accident 520; industrial illness 17.6; death 14.4. Proportion of labour force insured for damages or income loss resulting from: injury 100%; permanent disability 100%; death 100%. Average days lost to labour stoppages per 1,000 workdays (1992): 1.1.
Access to services (1990). Proportion of dwellings having access to: electricity, virtually 100%; safe public water supply 94%; public sewage collection 92%; central heating 92%; bathroom 87%; gas 72%; hot water 79%.
Social participation. Eligible voters participating in last national election (2000): 64.2%. Trade union membership in total workforce (1989): 100%. Practicing religious population in total affiliated population (1991): 32%.
Social deviance. Offense rate per 100,000 population (1999) for: murder 21.3; rape 5.6; serious injury 32.6; larceny-theft 952.5. Incidence per 100,000 population (1992) of: alcoholism 1,727.5; substance abuse 25.1; suicide 26.5.
Material well-being (1999). Durable goods possessed per 100 family households: automobile 37; radio receiver 100; television receiver 112; refrigerator or freezer 93; washing machine 80; camera 35; motorcycle 22; bicycle 51.

National economy

Budget (1999)[6]. Revenue: Rub 615,500,000,000 (tax revenue 82.8%, of which value-added tax 35.9%, profit tax 13.2%, individual income tax 10.9%, excise tax 5.9%; nontax revenue 17.2%). Expenditures: Rub 666,900,000,000 (interest on foreign debt 24.4%; defense 17.4%; social and cultural 12.8%; law enforcement 8.3%; administrative 2.2%).

Public debt (external, outstanding: 1999): U.S.$120,375,000,000.
Gross national product (1999): U.S.$328,995,000,000 (U.S.$2,250 per capita.)

Structure of gross domestic product and labour force

	1999		2000	
	in value Rub '000,000	% of total value	labour force	% of labour force
Agriculture	286,158.0	6.3	8,740,000	12.0
Mining / Manufacturing	1,341,271.3	29.5	14,297,000	19.6
Public utilities	179,516.9	3.9	3,361,000	4.6
Construction	244,830.6	5.4	5,080,000	7.0
Transp. and commun.	423,384.4	9.3	4,919,000	6.7
Trade	910,447.8	20.0	9,320,000	12.8
Finance	377,358.6	8.3	744,000	1.0
Services	354,088.0	7.8	14,643,000	20.1
Pub. admin., defense	201,658.0	4.5	2,858,000	3.9
Other	227,775.7[7]	5.0[7]	8,938,000[8]	12.3[8]
TOTAL	4,546,489.4	100.0	72,900,000	100.0

Production (metric tons except as noted). Agriculture, forestry, fishing (2000): wheat 36,000,000, potatoes 32,597,000, vegetables (other than potatoes) 15,600,000, sugar beets 14,040,800, barley 13,266,000, oats 5,500,000, rye 5,300,000, sunflower seeds 4,300,000, corn (maize) 1,800,000, millet 1,100,000, peas 700,000, buckwheat 650,000, rice 440,000; livestock (number of live animals) 27,500,000 cattle, 18,300,000 pigs; 14,000,000 sheep; roundwood (2000) 158,100,000 cu m; fish catch (1999) 4,209,772. Mining and quarrying (1997): nickel 260,000,000; chrome ore 151,000,000; iron ore 70,800,000; tin 7,500,000; molybdenum 8,500,000; antimony 6,000,000; gold 3,955,000 troy oz. Manufacturing (1999): crude steel 51,500,000; pig iron 41,000,000; rolled steel 40,900,000; cement 28,529,000; mineral fertilizers 11,496,000; sulfuric acid 7,100,000; cellulose 4,225,000; synthetic resins and plastics 2,206,000; cardboard 1,324,000; caustic soda 1,036,000; detergents 386,000; synthetic fibres 136,000; cotton fabrics 1,258,000,000 sq m; silk fabrics 146,000,000 sq m; linen fabrics 90,400,000 sq m; wool fabrics 47,800,000 sq m; cigarettes 283,000,000,000 units; watches 6,300,000 units; television receivers 281,000 units; refrigerators 1,173,000 units; passenger cars 954,000 units; washing machines 999,000 units; vacuum cleaners 746,000 units; tape recorders 700,000 units; bicycles 426,000 units; cameras 181,200 units; motorcycles 26,900 units; sewing machines 22,800 units; leather footwear 29,900,000 pairs; vodka and liquors 13,400,000 hectolitres; champagne 7,300,000 hectolitres; grape wine 1,830,000 hectolitres; beer 446,000 hectolitres; brandy 140,000 hectolitres. Construction (1999): residential 32,000,000 sq m; nonresidential (1995) 26,400,000 sq m.

Manufacturing, mining, and construction enterprises (1995)

	no. of enter-prises	no. of employees	monthly wages as a % of avg. of all wages[9]	value added (Rub '000,000,000)
Manufacturing				
Machinery and metal products	48,905	4,842,000	98.2	27,234
Fuel and energy	1,758	1,554,000	133.3	44,211
Metallurgy	2,158	1,248,000	124.3	26,437
Chemicals	23,027	2,432,000	94.1	17,934
Light industry	23,007	1,368,000	80.0	2,931
Food	14,713	1,514,000	100.1	12,886
Other industries	19,073	2,085,000	...	4,685
Building materials	8,359	994,000	108.2	3,761

Energy production (consumption): electricity (kW-hr; 1999) 846,200,000,000 (832,100,000,000); hard coal (metric tons; 1999) 166,000,000 (1996; 161,020,000); lignite (metric tons; 1999) 83,500,000 ([1996] 86,091,000); crude petroleum (barrels; 1999) 2,115,740,000 ([1996] 1,315,000,000); petroleum products (metric tons; 1996) 157,884,000 (105,168,000); natural gas (cu m; 1999) 564,000,000,000 ([1996] 323,175,000,000); peat (metric tons; 1995) 4,401,000 (3,683,000); oil shale (metric tons; 1994) 2,000,000 (1993; 3,300,000).
Population economically active (2000): total 72,900,000; activity rate of total population 49.9% (participation rates: ages over 15, 78.0%; female 47.6%; unemployed 12.3%).

Price and earnings indexes (1995 = 100)

	1995	1996	1997	1998	1999
Consumer price index	100.0	121.8	111.0	184.4	136.5
Monthly earnings index	100.0	100.4	105.9	83.6	86.4

Household income and expenditure. Average household size (1999): 2.8; income per household: Rub 37,800 (U.S.$1,480); sources of income (1999): wages 64.2%[10], pensions and stipends 13.3%, income from entrepreneurial activities 14.3%, property income 7.3%, other 0.9%; expenditure (1999): food 52.0%, clothing 13.5%, furniture and household appliances 7.3%, housing 4.7%, transportation 2.4%.
Land use (1994): forest 44.9%; pasture 5.2%; agriculture 7.7%; other 42.2%.
Tourism (1999): receipts U.S.$7,510,000,000; expenditures U.S.$7,434,000,000.

Foreign trade[11]

Balance of trade (current prices; non-CIS)

	1995	1996	1997	1998	1999	2000
U.S.$'000,000	+12,233	+13,720	+9,212	+11,071	+34,900	+55,711
% of total	8.2%	8.4%	5.5%	8.0%	30.3%	36.2%

Imports (1999): U.S.$40,200,000,000 (1998; machinery and transport equipment 23.9%, food 17.5%, chemicals 10.3%, ferrous and nonferrous metals 4.6%, wood and wood products 2.6%, fuels and lubricants 2.5%, textiles and clothing 2.2%). *Major import sources* (1999): Germany 13.9%; Belarus 10.6%; Ukraine 8.3%; U.S. 7.9%; Kazakhstan 4.5%; Italy 3.8%; France 3.8%; Finland 3.1%; Poland 2.0%.

Exports (1999): U.S.$75,100,000,000 (fuels and lubricants 43.8%, of which oil and oil products 26.5%; ferrous and nonferrous metals 20.5%; machinery and transport equipment 10.6%; chemicals 8.3%, precious metals 6.4%, forestry products 5.3%). *Major export destinations:* U.S. 8.9%; Germany 8.5%; Ukraine 6.6%; Belarus 5.2%; Italy 5.1%; China 4.9%; The Netherlands 4.8%; Switzerland 4.8%; U.K. 3.9%; Poland 3.9%; Finland 3.3%; Kazakhstan 1.7%.

Trade by commodity group (1996)

	imports		exports	
SITC group	U.S.$'000,000	%	U.S.$'000,000	%
00 Food and live animals	11,028	24.3	1,654	1.9
02 Raw materials, excl. fuels	5,614	12.4	20,843	24.7
03 Mineral fuels, lubricants	1,703	3.6	38,365	45.5
05 Chemicals	6,140	13.5	6,899	8.2
65 Textile yarn, fabrics	894	2.0	555	0.7
07 Machinery and transport equipment	11,859	26.1	7,477	8.8
08 Misc. manufactured articles	8,200	18.1	8,594	10.2
TOTAL	45,438	100.0	84,387	100.0

Direction of trade (1997)

	imports		exports	
	U.S.$'000,000	%	U.S.$'000,000	%
Africa	488	0.9	753	0.9
Asia	5,211	10.0	11,845	14.1
Japan	985	1.9	2,935	3.5
South America	941	1.8	291	0.3
North and Central America	4,942	9.5	6,334	7.5
United States	4,061	7.8	4,951	5.9
Europe	40,218	77.2	64,861	77.1
EU	19,578	37.6	27,998	33.3
EFTA	938	1.8	3,937	4.7
other Europe	19,702	37.8	32,926	39.1
Oceania	326	0.6	32	0.1
TOTAL	52,129[12]	100.0	84,154[12]	100.0

Transport and communications

Transport. Railroads (1999): length 151,000 km; passenger-km 141,700,000,000; metric ton-km cargo 1,205,000,000. Roads (1999): total length 570,719 km (paved 79%). Vehicles (1999): passenger cars 19,717,800; trucks and buses 5,021,000. Air transport (1999): passenger-km 53,400,000,000; metric ton-km cargo 2,300,000,000; airports (1998) 75.

Distribution of traffic (1999)

	cargo carried ('000,000 tons)	% of national total	passengers carried ('000,000)	% of national total
Intercity transport			24,266	53.5
Road	556	22.9	22,883	50.4
Rail	947	39.0	1,338	3.0
Sea and river	122	5.0	23	0.1
Air	0.7	...	22	
Pipeline	802	33.0	—	—
Urban transport			21,077	46.5
Road	—	—	21,077	46.5
Rail	—	—		
TOTAL	2,427.7	100.0[12]	45,343	100.0

Communications

Medium	date	unit	number	units per 1,000 persons
Daily newspapers	1996	circulation	15,517,000	105
Radio	1997	receivers	61,500,000	417
Television	1999	receivers	62,000,000	425
Telephones	1999	main lines	30,949,000	212
Cellular telephones	1999	subscribers	1,370,600	9.4
Personal computers	1999	units	5,500,000	37.7
Internet	1999	users	2,700,000	18.5

Education and health

Health (2000): physicians 682,500 (1 per 214 persons); hospital beds 1,672,400 (1 per 87 persons); infant mortality rate per 1,000 live births (1999) 16.9.

Education (1999–2000)

	schools	teachers	students	student/ teacher ratio
Primary (age 6–13) / Secondary (age 14–17)	67,550	1,787,000	21,316,000	11.9
Voc., teacher tr.	3,911	...	1,694,000	...
Higher	939	255,900	4,073,000	15.9

Food (1999): daily per capita caloric intake 2,879 (vegetable products 77%; animal products 23%); 112% of FAO recommended minimum.

Military

Total active duty personnel (2000): 1,004,100 (army 34.6%, navy 17.1%, air force 18.4%, other 29.9%[13]). *Military expenditure as percentage of GNP* (1997): 5.8% (world 2.6%); per capita expenditure U.S.$283.

[1]January 1. [2]Federal districts were formally established in May 2000. [3]Moskva (Moscow; region) includes Moscow (city). [4]Ingushetiya includes Chechnia. [5]Leningrad region includes St. Petersburg city. [6]Federal budget only. [7]Taxes on products less subsidies and bank service charges. [8]Unemployed. [9]1990. [10]Includes hidden salaries. [11]Imports c.i.f. [12]Detail does not add to total given because of rounding. [13]Represents 300,000 military personnel not included elsewhere (including Ministry of Defense staff and centrally controlled units for electronic warfare).

Internet resources for further information:

- **Russian Statistical Agency http://www.gks.ru/eng/default.asp**
- **Permanent Mission of the Russian Federation to the United Nations http://www.un.int/russia**

Rwanda

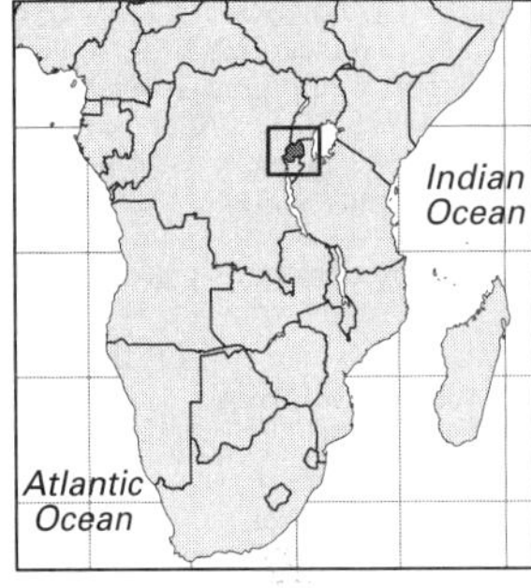

Official name: Repubulika y'u Rwanda (Rwanda); République Rwandaise (French); Republic of Rwanda (English).
Form of government: transitional regime[1] with one legislative body (Transitional National Assembly [74]).
Head of state and government: President assisted by Prime Minister.
Capital: Kigali.
Official languages: Rwanda; French; English.
Official religion: none.
Monetary unit: 1 Rwanda franc (RF); valuation (Sept. 28, 2001) 1 U.S.$ = RF 438.00; 1 £ = RF 643.73.

Area and population

Prefectures	Capitals	area sq mi	area sq km	population 1991 census
Butare	Butare	709	1,837	766,839
Byumba[2]	Byumba	1,838	4,761	783,350
Cyangugu	Cyangugu	712	1,845	515,129
Gikongoro	Gikongoro	794	2,057	464,585
Gisenyi	Gisenyi	791	2,050	734,697
Gitarama	Gitarama	845	2,189	851,516
Kibungo[2]	Kibungo	1,562	4,046	655,368
Kibuye	Kibuye	658	1,705	470,747
Kigali	Kigali (city)	1,159	3,002	918,869
Kigali (city)	—	45	116	237,782
Ruhengeri	Ruhengeri	642	1,663	766,112
Umutara[2]	Nyagatare	...	...	...
TOTAL LAND AREA		9,757[3]	25,271	
TOTAL		10,169	26,338	7,164,994

Demography

Population (2001): 7,313,000.
Density (2001)[4]: persons per sq mi 749.5, persons per sq km 289.4.
Urban-rural (1999): urban 6.0%; rural 94.0%.
Sex distribution (2001): male 49.60%; female 50.40%.
Age breakdown (2001): under 15, 43.0%; 15–29, 30.4%; 30–44, 15.0%; 45–59, 7.3%; 60–74, 3.5%; 75 and over, 0.8%.
Population projection: (2010) 7,876,000; (2020) 8,027,000.
Doubling time: 47 years.
Ethnic composition (1996): Hutu 80.0%; Tutsi 19.0%; Twa 1.0%.
Religious affiliation (1996): Roman Catholic 65.0%; Protestant 9.0%; Muslim 1.0%; indigenous beliefs and other 25.0%.
Major cities (1991): Kigali 237,782; Ruhengeri 29,578[5]; Butare 28,645[5]; Gisenyi 21,918[5].

Vital statistics

Birth rate per 1,000 population (2000): 34.8 (world avg. 22.5).
Death rate per 1,000 population (2000): 21.0 (world avg. 9.0).
Natural increase rate per 1,000 population (2000): 13.8 (world avg. 13.5).
Total fertility rate (avg. births per childbearing woman; 2000): 5.1.
Marriage rate per 1,000 population (1984)[6]: 2.5.
Life expectancy at birth (2000): male 38.6 years; female 40.1 years.
Major causes of death per 100,000 population: n.a.; however, principal causes in 1999 were malaria, bronchopneumonia, diarrhea, AIDS, pulmonary diseases, cerebrospinal meningitis, kwashiorkor, and road accidents.

National economy

Budget (1998). Revenue: RF 99,000,000,000 (grants 33.3%, taxes on goods and services 28.9%, import and export duties 16.0%, income tax 3.4%). Expenditures: RF 117,400,000,000 (capital expenditures 35.9%, wages 24.6%, goods and services 21.7%, transfers 7.9%, debt payment 4.9%).
Production (metric tons except as noted). Agriculture, forestry, fishing (1999): plantains 2,897,433, sweet potatoes 862,562, cassava 316,934, potatoes 175,889, sorghum 107,566, corn [maize] 54,912, coffee 18,800; livestock (number of live animals) 725,541 cattle, 634,046 goats, 290,000 sheep, 159,625 pigs; roundwood (1998) 3,000,000 cu m; fish catch (1998) 6,641. Mining and quarrying (1997): cassiterite (tin ore) 330; wolframite (tungsten ore) 188; gold 17 kg. Manufacturing (1997): cement 58,929; lye soap 6,966; beer 650,000 hectolitres; nonalcoholic beverages 363,000 hectolitres; textiles 5,298,000 metres. Energy production (consumption): electricity (kW-hr; 1998) 153,630,000 (186,080,000); petroleum products (metric tons; 1998) none (95,500); natural gas (cu m; 1996) 179,389 (179,389).
Population economically active (1991): total 3,649,000; activity rate of total population 50.2% (participation rates: ages 14–74 [1989] 46.3%; female 53.5%; unemployed, n.a.).

Price and earnings indexes (1995 = 100)

	1994	1995	1996	1997	1998	1999	2000
Consumer price index	...	100.0	107.4	120.3	127.8	124.7	129.6
Earnings index	100.0	100.0	120.0	...	...	...	...

Public debt (external, outstanding; 1999): U.S.$1,162,000,000.
Tourism: receipts (1993) U.S.$2,000,000; expenditures (1992) U.S.$17,000,000.
Land use (1994): forested 10.1%; meadows and pastures 28.4%; agricultural and under permanent cultivation 47.4%; other 14.1%.
Gross national product (1999): U.S.$2,041,000,000 (U.S.$250 per capita).

Structure of gross domestic product and labour force

	1998 in value RF '000,000	1998 % of total value	1989 labour force	1989 % of labour force
Agriculture	278,600	44.1	2,832,557	90.1
Mining	400	0.1	4,691	0.2
Manufacturing	79,700	12.6	45,089	1.4
Construction	41,500	6.6	38,237	1.2
Public utilities	3,000	0.5	2,562	0.1
Transp. and commun.	26,100	4.1	7,333	0.2
Trade	66,900	10.6	80,026	2.6
Pub. admin., defense	41,700	6.6	123,147	3.9
Services	94,200	14.9		
Other	—	—	9,414	0.3
TOTAL	632,100	100.0[3]	3,143,056	100.0

Household income and expenditure. Average household size (1991) 4.7; average annual income per household (1983) RF 122,870 (U.S.$1,300); sources of income (1977): self-employment 71.0%, salaries and wages 16.5%, transfers 9.5%; expenditure (1982): food 44.2%, housing 13.2%, clothing and footwear 11.4%, transportation 10.3%, household equipment 8.4%.

Foreign trade

Balance of trade (current prices)

	1994	1995	1996	1997	1998	1999
U.S.$'000,000	−335.2	−143.7	−151.3	−184.5	−193.3	−163.3
% of total	83.9%	58.8%	55.0%	52.5%	60.8%	57.2%

Imports (1999): U.S.$224,500,000 (food 16.7%, energy products 16.6%, capital goods 15.8%, intermediate goods 13.1%). *Major import sources* (1998): Kenya 25.8%; U.S. 8.4%; Belgium 5.9%; France 5.2%; Germany 3.8%; The Netherlands 3.1%; Italy 2.8%; U.K. 1.7%; Democratic Republic of the Congo 1.7%.
Exports (1999): U.S.$61,200,000 (coffee 43.3%, tea 28.6%, cassiterite and tin 1.8%). *Major export destinations* (1998): Belgium 47.6%; Germany 25.4%; U.S. 6.3%; Italy 6.3%.

Transport and communications

Transport. Railroads: none. Roads (1996): total length 9,528 mi, 14,900 km (paved 9%). Vehicles (1995): passenger cars 13,000; trucks 17,100. Air transport: (1994) passenger-mi 1,243,000, passenger-km 2,000,000; (1991) metric ton cargo loaded 2,674, metric ton cargo unloaded 4,794; airports (1998) with scheduled flights 2.

Communications

Medium	date	unit	number	units per 1,000 persons
Daily newspapers	1995	circulation	500	0.1
Radio	1997	receivers	601,000	101
Telephones	1999	main lines	12,651	1.8
Cellular telephones	1999	subscribers	11,000	1.5
Internet	1999	users	...	...

Education and health

Educational attainment (1978). Percentage of population age 25 and over having: no formal schooling 76.9%; some primary education 16.8%; complete primary education 4.0%; some secondary and complete secondary education 2.0%; some postsecondary vocational and higher education 0.3%. *Literacy* (1995): percentage of total population age 15 and over literate 67.0%; males literate 73.7%; females literate 60.6%.

Education (1991–92)

	schools	teachers	students	student/ teacher ratio
Primary (age 7–15)	1,710	18,937	1,104,902	58.3
Secondary (age 16–19)[7]	...	3,413	94,586	27.7
Higher[8]	3[9]	646	3,389	5.2

Health: physicians (1992) 150 (1 per 50,000 persons); hospital beds (1990) 12,152 (1 per 588 persons); infant mortality rate (2000) 120.1.
Food (1999): daily per capita caloric intake 2,011 (vegetable products 97%, animal products 3%); 87% of FAO recommended minimum requirement.

Military

Total active duty personnel (2000): 49,000–64,000 (army 100%). *Military expenditure as percentage of GNP* (1997): 4.4% (world 2.6%); per capita expenditure U.S.$10.

[1]Five-year transitional period from November 1994 was extended to July 2003 in June 1999. [2]Umutara prefecture created in 1996 from parts of Byumba and Kibungo prefectures. [3]Detail does not add to total given because of rounding. [4]Based on land area only. [5]De jure population only. [6]Excludes marriages not registered in court. [7]Includes vocational and teacher training. [8]1989–90. [9]1985.

Internet resources for further information:
- **Republic of Rwanda (official website) http://www.rwanda1.com/government/rwandalaunch.html**

Saint Kitts and Nevis

Official name: Federation of Saint Kitts and Nevis[1].
Form of government: constitutional monarchy with one legislative house (National Assembly [15[2]]).
Chief of state: British Monarch represented by Governor-General.
Head of government: Prime Minister.
Capital: Basseterre.
Official language: English.
Official religion: none.
Monetary unit: 1 Eastern Caribbean dollar (EC$) = 100 cents; valuation (Sept. 28, 2001) 1 U.S.$ = EC$2.70; 1 £ = EC$3.97.

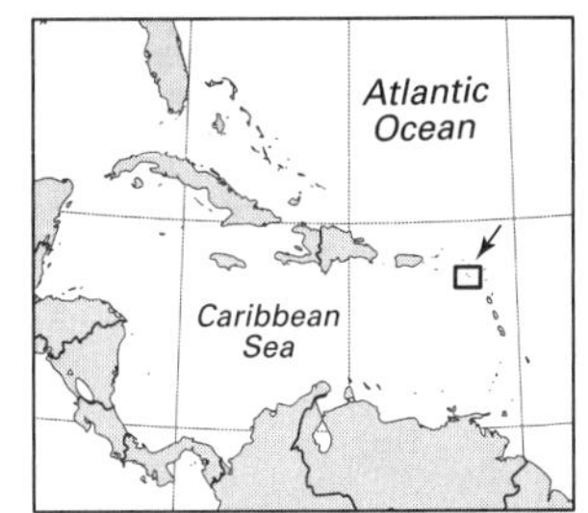

Area and population

Islands	Capitals	area sq mi	area sq km	population 1995 estimate
Nevis[3]	Charlestown	36.0	93.2	8,010
St. Kitts	Basseterre	68.0	176.2	35,340
TOTAL		104.0	269.4	43,350

Demography

Population (2001): 38,800.
Density (2001): persons per sq mi 373.1, persons per sq km 144.0.
Urban-rural (2000): urban 34.2%; rural 65.8%.
Sex distribution (2000): male 49.46%; female 50.54%.
Age breakdown (2000): under 15, 30.3%; 15–29, 24.9%; 30–44, 22.2%; 45–59, 11.2%; 60–74, 7.1%; 75 and over, 4.3%.
Population projection: (2010) 40,300; (2020) 44,500.
Doubling time: 72 years.
Ethnic composition (2000): black 90.4%; mulatto 5.0%; Indo-Pakistani 3.0%; white 1.0%; other/unspecified 0.6%.
Religious affiliation (1995): Protestant 84.6%, of which Anglican 25.2%, Methodist 25.2%, Pentecostal 8.4%, Moravian 7.6%; Roman Catholic 6.7%; Hindu 1.5%; other 7.2%.
Major towns (1994): Basseterre 12,605; Charlestown 1,411.

Vital statistics

Birth rate per 1,000 population (2000): 19.1 (world avg. 22.5); (1983) legitimate 19.2%; illegitimate 80.8%.
Death rate per 1,000 population (2000): 9.4 (world avg. 9.0).
Natural increase rate per 1,000 population (2000): 9.7 (world avg. 13.5).
Total fertility rate (avg. births per childbearing woman; 2000): 2.4.
Marriage rate per 1,000 population: n.a.
Divorce rate per 1,000 population: n.a.
Life expectancy at birth (2000): male 67.9 years; female 73.7 years.
Major causes of death per 100,000 population (1985): diseases of the circulatory system 443.2, of which cerebrovascular disease 220.5, diseases of pulmonary circulation and other heart disease 122.7; malignant neoplasms (cancers) 95.5.

National economy

Budget (1999). Revenue: EC$252,400,000 (tax revenue 72.8% of which taxes on income and profits 19.6%, consumption taxes 16.3%, import duties 15.4%, taxes on domestic goods and services 14.9%; nontax revenue 26.1%). Expenditures: EC$298,300,000 (current expenditure 88.4%; development expenditure 11.6%).
Production (metric tons except as noted). Agriculture, forestry, fishing (1999): sugarcane 196,784, tropical fruit 1,300, coconuts 1,000, roots and tubers 700, potatoes 211, pulses 210, cabbages 175, sweet potatoes 170, tomatoes 120, onions 75; sea island cotton is grown on Nevis; livestock (number of live animals) 14,500 goats, 8,000 sheep, 3,600 cattle, 3,000 pigs; roundwood, n.a.; fish catch (1997) 161. Mining and quarrying: excavation of sand for local use. Manufacturing (2001): raw sugar 20,193; carbonated beverages 45,000 hectolitres[4]; beer 20,000 hectolitres[4]; other manufactures include electronic components, garments, footwear, and batik. Construction (value added; 1994): EC$57,000,000. Energy production (consumption): electricity (kW-hr; 1996) 82,000,000 (82,000,000); coal, none (none); crude petroleum, none (none); petroleum products (metric tons; 1996) none (33,000); natural gas, none (none).
Gross national product (1999): U.S.$259,000,000 (U.S.$6,330 per capita).

Structure of gross domestic product and labour force

	1999 in value EC$'000,000	1999 % of total value	1994 labour force[5]	1994 % of labour force[5]
Sugarcane	7.7	0.9	1,525[6]	9.2[6]
Other agriculture, forestry, fisheries	17.2	2.1	914	5.5
Mining	2.3	0.3	29	0.2
Manufacturing	70.5	8.7	1,290[7]	7.8[7]
Construction	89.4	11.0	1,745	10.5
Public utilities	12.9	1.6	416	2.5
Transp. and commun.	96.4	11.9	534	3.2
Trade, restaurants	162.8	20.1	3,367	20.3
Finance, real estate	112.8	13.9	3,708[8]	22.3[8]
Pub. admin., defense	129.5	16.0	2,738	16.5
Services	29.5	3.6	[8]	[8]
Other	80.7[9]	9.9[9]	342	2.1
TOTAL	811.8[10]	100.0[10]	16,608	100.0[10]

Household income and expenditure. Average household size (1980) 3.7; average annual income per wage earner (1994) EC$9,940 (U.S.$3,681); sources of income: n.a.; expenditure (1978)[11]: food, beverages, and tobacco 55.6%, household furnishings 9.4%, housing 7.6%, clothing and footwear 7.5%, fuel and light 6.6%, transportation 4.3%, other 9.0%.
Public debt (external, outstanding; 1999): U.S.$131,700,000.
Population economically active (1980): total 17,125; activity rate of total population 39.5% (participation rates: ages 15–64, 69.5%; female 41.0%; unemployed [1997] 4.5%).

Price and earnings indexes (1995 = 100)

	1995	1996	1997	1998	1999	2000
Consumer price index	100.0	102.1	111.2	115.0	119.5	115.3[12]
Earnings index	...	...	...	...	...	...

Land use (1994): forested 17%; meadows and pastures 3%; agricultural and under permanent cultivation 39%; other 41%.
Tourism: receipts from visitors (1999) U.S.$67,000,000; expenditures by nationals abroad (1998) U.S.$6,000,000.

Foreign trade

Balance of trade (current prices)

	1994	1995	1996	1997	1998	1999
EC$'000,000	−211	−217	−263	−291	−239	−260
% of total	53.3%	52.4%	43.3%	57.0%	47.5%	50.2%

Imports (1997): EC$401,100,000 (machinery and transport equipment 30.3%, basic and miscellaneous manufactures 20.6%, food 16.1%, chemicals and chemical products 8.2%). *Major import sources:* United States 45.5%; Caricom countries 13.4%, of which Trinidad and Tobago 9.8%; United Kingdom 9.7%.
Exports (1997): EC$109,900,000 (food 56.0%, machinery and transport equipment [mostly electronic goods] 31.7%). *Major export destinations* (1997): United States 55.0%; United Kingdom 32.6%; Caricom countries 2.9%.

Transport and communications

Transport. Railroads (1995)[13]: length 22 mi, 36 km. Roads (1996): total length 199 mi, 320 km (paved 43%). Vehicles (1995): passenger cars 5,200; trucks and buses 2,300. Merchant marine (1992): vessels (100 gross tons and over) 1; total deadweight tonnage 550. Air transport: passenger arrivals (1992) 123,195[14]; passenger departures, n.a.; cargo handled, n.a.; airports (1998) with scheduled flights 2.

Communications

Medium	date	unit	number	units per 1,000 persons
Radio	1997	receivers	28,000	701
Television	1997	receivers	10,000	264
Telephones	1999	main lines	20,059	515
Cellular telephones	1999	units	700	18

Education and health

Educational attainment (1980). Percentage of population age 25 and over having: no formal schooling 1.1%; primary education 29.6%; secondary 67.2%; higher 2.1%. *Literacy* (1990): total population age 15 and over literate 25,500 (90.0%); males literate 13,100 (90.0%); females literate 12,400 (90.0%).

Education (1997–98)

	schools	teachers	students	student/ teacher ratio
Primary (age 5–12)	23	320	5,928	18.5
Secondary (age 13–17)	9	341	4,548	13.3
Higher[15]	1	51	394	7.7

Health (1998): physicians 50 (1 per 815 persons); hospital beds 244 (1 per 167 persons); infant mortality rate per 1,000 live births (2000): 16.7.
Food (1998): daily per capita caloric intake 2,766 (vegetable products 75%, animal products 25%); 114% of FAO recommended minimum requirement.

Military

Total active duty personnel: in July 1997 the National Assembly approved a bill creating a 50-member army. *Military expenditure as percentage of GNP* (1998): 3.5%[16] (world, n.a.); per capita expenditure U.S.$226[16].

[1]Both Saint Christopher and Nevis and the Federation of Saint Christopher and Nevis are officially acceptable, variant, short- and long-form names of the country. [2]Includes 4 nonelective seats. [3]Nevis has full internal self-government. The Nevis legislature is subordinate to the National Assembly only with regard to external affairs and defense. [4]1995. [5]Employed persons only. [6]Includes sugar manufacturing. [7]Excludes sugar manufacturing. [8]Finance, real estate includes Services. [9]Net of indirect taxes less imputed service charge. [10]Detail does not add to total given because of rounding. [11]Weights of consumer price index components. [12]Average of first quarter. [13]Light railway serving the sugar industry on Saint Kitts. [14]Saint Kitts airport only. [15]1992–93. [16]May include expenditure for police.

Internet resources for further information:

- **Official web site of the Government of St. Kitts & Nevis http://www.stkittsnevis.net**

Saint Lucia

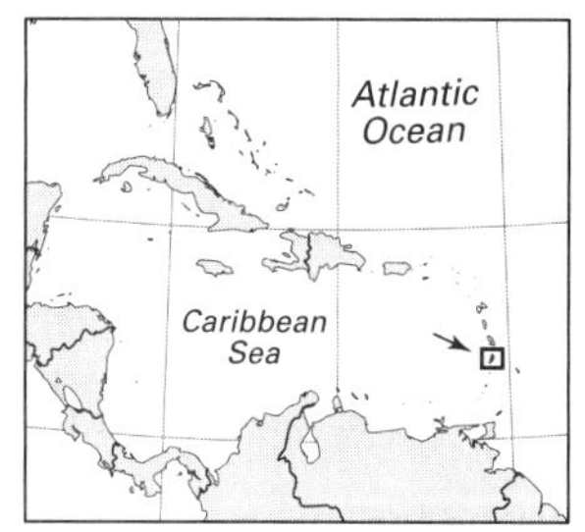

Official name: Saint Lucia.
Form of government: constitutional monarchy with a Parliament consisting of two legislative chambers (Senate [11]; House of Assembly [17[1]]).
Chief of state: British Monarch represented by Governor-General.
Head of government: Prime Minister.
Capital: Castries.
Official language: English.
Official religion: none.
Monetary unit: 1 Eastern Caribbean dollar (EC$) = 100 cents; valuation (Sept. 28, 2001) 1 U.S.$ = EC$2.70; 1 £ = EC$3.97.

Area and population

		area		population
Districts	Capitals	sq mi	sq km	1999 estimate
Anse-la-Raye	Anse-la-Raye	18	47	6,203
Canaries	Canaries			1,923
Castries	Castries	31	79	61,823
Choiseul	Choiseul	12	31	7,255
Dennery	Dennery	27	70	12,778
Gros Islet	Gros Islet	39	101	13,994
Laborie	Laborie	15	38	8,727
Micoud	Micoud	30	78	17,423
Soufrière	Soufrière	19	51	8,953
Vieux Fort	Vieux Fort	17	44	14,624
TOTAL		238[2]	617[2]	153,703

Demography

Population (2001): 158,000.
Density (2001): persons per sq mi 663.9, persons per sq km 256.1.
Urban-rural (1998): urban 37.3%; rural 62.7%.
Sex distribution (1997): male 48.34%; female 51.66%.
Age breakdown (1999): under 15, 33.5%; 15–29, 30.9%; 30–44, 20.4%; 45–59, 8.0%; 60–74, 4.9%; 75 and over, 2.3%.
Population projection: (2010) 177,000; (2020) 199,000.
Doubling time: 42 years.
Ethnic composition (2000): black 50%; mulatto 44%; East Indian 3%; white 1%; other 2%.
Religious affiliation (1995): Roman Catholic 79.2%; Protestant 19.4%, of which Pentecostal 5.4%, Seventh-day Adventist 5.2%; other 1.4%.
Major city (1997): Castries city proper 2,249 (urban area 16,187).

Vital statistics

Birth rate per 1,000 population (2000): 22.2 (world avg. 22.5); legitimate (1998) 14.2%; illegitimate 85.8%.
Death rate per 1,000 population (2000): 5.4 (world avg. 9.0).
Natural increase rate per 1,000 population (2000): 16.8 (world avg. 13.5).
Total fertility rate (avg. births per childbearing woman; 2000): 2.4.
Marriage rate per 1,000 population (1997): 3.1.
Divorce rate per 1,000 population (1997): 0.2.
Life expectancy at birth (2000): male 68.7 years; female 76.1 years.
Major causes of death per 100,000 population (1996): diseases of the circulatory system 282.9; malignant neoplasms (cancers) 74.1; diseases of the respiratory system 41.5; infectious and parasitic diseases 37.4; endocrine and metabolic disorders 19.0; ill-defined conditions 63.2.

National economy

Budget (1998–99). Revenue: EC$469,900,000 (current revenue 86.9%, of which consumption duties on imported goods 24.4%; taxes on income and profits 21.9%; import duties 14.7%; nontax revenue 9.2%; grants 3.9%). Expenditures: EC$496,600,000 (current expenditures 69.4%; development expenditures and net lending 30.6%).
Public debt (external, outstanding; 1999): U.S.$125,600,000.
Tourism: receipts from visitors (1999) U.S.$311,000,000; expenditures by nationals abroad (1997) U.S.$29,000,000.
Production (metric tons except as noted). Agriculture, forestry, fishing (1999): bananas 80,000, mangoes 27,000, coconuts 12,000, yams 3,800, tropical fruit 2,750, grapefruit 1,393, plantains 1,296, cassava 980, vegetables 950, oranges 705; livestock (number of live animals; 1999) 14,750 pigs, 12,500 sheep, 12,450 cattle, 9,800 goats; roundwood, n.a.; fish catch (1998) 1,462. Mining and quarrying: excavation of sand for local construction and pumice. Manufacturing (value of production in EC$'000; 1998): alcoholic beverages and tobacco 31,120; paper products and cardboard boxes 28,747; electrical and electronic components 16,245; food 9,535; garments 6,563; textiles 3,999; refined coconut oil 2,330; copra 1,330. Construction (buildings approved; 1994): residential 61,400 sq m; nonresidential 41,350 sq m. Energy production (consumption): electricity (kW-hr; 1998) 235,881,000 (213,000,000); coal, none (none); crude petroleum, none (none); petroleum products (metric tons; 1998) none (25,000); natural gas, none (none).
Household income and expenditure. Average household size (1991) 4.0; income per household: n.a.; sources of income: n.a.; expenditure (1982)[3]: food 46.8%, housing 13.5%, clothing and footwear 6.5%, transportation and communications 6.3%, household furnishings 5.8%, other 21.1%.
Population economically active (1998): total 73,660; activity rate of total population 49.2% (participation rates: ages 15–64, 79.1%; female 44.4%; unemployed 22.2%).

Price and earnings indexes (1995 = 100)

	1993	1994	1995	1996	1997	1998	1999
Consumer price index	92.0	94.5	100.0	101.8	102.0	104.2	109.7
Earnings index	...	...	...	...	...	...	...

Gross national product (at current market prices; 1999): U.S.$590,000,000 (U.S.$3,820 per capita).

Structure of gross domestic product and labour force

	1998			
	in value EC$'000,000[4]	% of total value[4]	labour force[5]	% of labour force
Agriculture	114	8.1	17,310	23.5
Mining	7	0.5	221	0.3
Manufacturing	83	5.9	6,850	9.3
Construction	103	7.3	5,893	8.0
Public utilities	73	5.2	1,105	1.5
Transportation and communications	253	18.0	4,788	6.5
Trade, restaurants	374	26.6	19,225	26.1
Finance, real estate	305	21.7	3,168	4.3
Pub. admin., defense	206	14.7	9,797	13.3
Services	51	3.6	1,252	1.7
Other	–165[6]	–11.7[6]	4,051	5.5
TOTAL	1,404	100.0[7]	73,660	100.0

Land use (1994): forested 13%; meadows and pastures 5%; agricultural and under permanent cultivation 30%; other 52%.

Foreign trade

Balance of trade (current prices)

	1994	1995	1996	1997	1998
U.S.$'000,000	–165.7	–155.2	–177.6	–209.1	–201.1
% of total	45.3%	40.5%	47.3%	56.2%	56.2%

Imports (1998): U.S.$279,600,000 (food 21.7%; machinery and transportation equipment 21.1%; manufactured goods 19.0%; chemicals and chemical products 8.6%; crude petroleum and petroleum products 8.5%). *Major import sources:* United States 40.0%; Caricom countries 21.2%, of which Trinidad and Tobago 11.5%; United Kingdom 9.2%; Japan 4.4%; Canada 2.8%.
Exports (1998): U.S.$78,500,000 (bananas 50.5%; clothing 7.5%; primarily paper and paperboard 5.9%; beer 5.0%). *Major export destinations:* United Kingdom 60.0%; United States 21.0%; Caricom countries 16.3%.

Transport and communications

Transport. Railroads: none. Roads (1997): total length 750 mi, 1,210 km (paved 5%). Vehicles (1997): passenger cars 14,783; trucks and buses 1,020. Merchant marine (1992): vessels (100 gross tons and over) 7; total deadweight tonnage 2,070. Air transport (1999)[8]: passenger arrivals and departures 912,000; cargo unloaded and loaded 4,600 metric tons; airports (1998) with scheduled flights 2.

Communications

Medium	date	unit	number	units per 1,000 persons
Radio	1997	receivers	100,000	668
Television	1997	receivers	40,000	267
Telephones	1999	main lines	44,465	289
Cellular telephones	1998	subscribers	1,900	12.5

Education and health

Educational attainment (1980). Percentage of population age 25 and over having: no formal schooling 17.5%; primary education 74.4%; secondary 6.8%; higher 1.3%. *Literacy* (1995): about 82%.

Education (1997–98)

	schools	teachers	students	student/teacher ratio
Primary (age 5–11)	84	1,160	30,536	26.3
Secondary (age 12–16)	17	620	11,405	18.4
Vocational[9]	1	34	806	23.7
Higher[9]	1	389	870	2.4

Health (1997): physicians 81 (1 per 1,847 persons); hospital beds 527 (1 per 284 persons); infant mortality rate per 1,000 live births (2000) 15.6.
Food (1999): daily per capita caloric intake 2,812 (vegetable products 77%, animal products 23%); 116% of FAO recommended minimum requirement.

Military

Total active duty personnel (1997): [10].

[1]Represents elected seats only. Attorney general and speaker serve ex officio. [2]Total includes the uninhabited 30 sq mi (78 sq km) Central Forest Reserve. [3]Castries area only. [4]At factor cost in current prices. [5]Based on the percentage given. [6]Less imputed bank service charges. [7]Detail does not add to total given because of rounding. [8]Combined data for both Castries and Vieux Fort airports. [9]1992–93. [10]The 300-member police force includes a specially trained paramilitary unit and a coast guard unit.

Internet resources for further information:
- **Saint Lucian Government Statistics Department http://www.stats.gov.lc**

Saint Vincent and the Grenadines

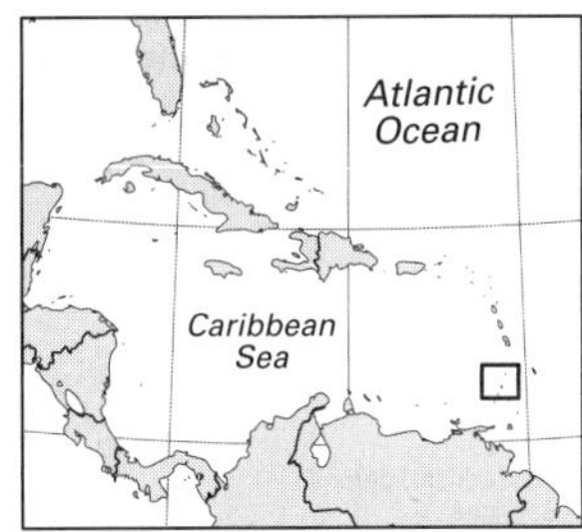

Official name: Saint Vincent and the Grenadines.
Form of government: constitutional monarchy with one legislative house (House of Assembly [21[1]]).
Chief of state: British Monarch represented by Governor-General.
Head of government: Prime Minister.
Capital: Kingstown.
Official language: English.
Official religion: none.
Monetary unit: 1 Eastern Caribbean dollar (EC$) = 100 cents; valuation (Sept. 28, 2001) 1 U.S.$ = EC$2.70; 1 £ = EC$3.97.

Area and population

Census Divisions[2]	area sq mi	area sq km	population 1999[3] estimate
Island of Saint Vincent			
Barrouallie	14.2	36.8	5,437
Bridgetown	7.2	18.6	7,874
Calliaqua	11.8	30.6	21,219
Chateaubelair	30.9	80.0	6,319
Colonarie	13.4	34.7	8,252
Georgetown	22.2	57.5	7,638
Kingstown (city)	1.9	4.9	16,175
Kingstown (suburbs)	6.4	16.6	11,258
Layou	11.1	28.7	6,268
Marriaqua	9.4	24.3	9,274
Sandy Bay	5.3	13.7	2,921
Saint Vincent Grenadines			
Nothern Grenadines	9.0	23.3	5,761
Southern Grenadines	7.5	19.4	2,984
TOTAL	150.3	389.3[4]	111,380

Demography

Population (2001): 113,000.
Density (2001): persons per sq mi 751.8, persons per sq km 290.3.
Urban-rural (2000): urban 54.4%; rural 45.6%.
Sex distribution (1999): male 50.50%; female 49.50%.
Age breakdown (1999): under 15, 31.3%; 15–29, 31.2%; 30–44, 19.6%; 45–59, 9.4%; 60–74, 5.9%; 75 and over, 2.6%.
Population projection: (2010) 117,000; (2020) 122,000.
Doubling time: 58 years.
Ethnic composition (1999): black 65.5%; mulatto 23.5%; Indo-Pakistani 5.5%; white 3.5%; black-Amerindian 2.0%.
Religious affiliation (1995): Protestant 57.6%; unaffiliated Christian 20.6%; Roman Catholic 10.7%; Hindu 3.3%; Muslim 1.5%; other/nonreligious 6.3%.
Major city (1999[3]): Kingstown 16,175.

Vital statistics

Birth rate per 1,000 population (2000): 18.3 (world avg. 22.5).
Death rate per 1,000 population (2000): 6.2 (world avg. 9.0).
Natural increase rate per 1,000 population (2000): 12.1 (world avg. 13.5).
Total fertility rate (avg. births per childbearing woman; 2000): 2.1.
Marriage rate per 1,000 population (1997): 4.6.
Divorce rate per 1,000 population (1997): 0.8.
Life expectancy at birth (2000): male 70.6 years; female 74.1 years.
Major causes of death per 100,000 population (1997): diseases of the circulatory system 228.4, of which ischemic heart disease 94.4, cerebrovascular diseases 70.1; malignant neoplasms (cancers) 90.0; endocrine and metabolic disorders 56.6; diseases of the respiratory system 42.2; infectious and parasitic diseases 36.8.

National economy

Budget (1998). Revenue: EC$285,200,000 (current revenue 73.8%, of which income tax 25.1%, consumption duties on imports 23.3%, taxes on goods and services 9.3%, import duties 7.9%; grants 14.5%; nontax revenue 9.5%; capital revenue 2.2%). Expenditures: EC$303,100,000 (current expenditure 65.9%; development expenditure 34.1%).
Public debt (external, outstanding; 1999): U.S.$159,800,000.
Production (metric tons except as noted). Agriculture, forestry, fishing (1999): bananas 43,000, coconuts 23,600, roots and tubers 9,000, eddoes and dasheens[5] 4,247[6], corn (maize) 2,000, sweet potatoes 1,500, mangoes 1,400, yams 1,200, oranges 960, lemons and limes 870, ginger 892[6], arrowroot starch 177[6], nutmegs 105[6], soursops, guavas, and papayas are also important; livestock (number of live animals) 13,000 sheep, 9,400 pigs, 6,200 cattle; roundwood, n.a.; fish catch (1998) 835. Mining and quarrying: sand and gravel for local use. Manufacturing (export value of manufactures in U.S.$'000,000; 1995): packaged flour 8.7; packaged rice 6.4; other goods (mostly garments, sporting goods, and electronic goods) 8.1. Construction (gross floor area planned; 1997): 530,500 sq m. Energy production (consumption): electricity (kW-hr; 1998) 82,773,000 (82,773,000); coal, none (none); crude petroleum, none (none); petroleum products (metric tons; 1996) none (41,000); natural gas, none (none).
Tourism: receipts from visitors (1999) U.S.$77,000,000; expenditures by nationals abroad (1998) U.S.$8,000,000.
Gross national product (1999): U.S.$301,000,000 (U.S.$2,640 per capita).

Structure of gross domestic product and labour force

	1998 in value EC$'000,000	1998 % of total value	1991 labour force	1991 % of labour force
Agriculture, forestry, fishing	78.3	9.2	8,377	20.1
Mining	2.3	0.3	98	0.2
Manufacturing	49.5	5.8	2,822	6.8
Construction	101.9	11.9	3,535	8.5
Public utilities	40.6	4.7	586	1.4
Transp. and commun.	148.4	17.4	2,279	5.5
Trade, restaurants	128.6	15.1	6,544	15.7
Finance, real estate	71.6	8.4	1,418	3.4
Pub. admin., defense	129.6	15.2	7,696	18.5
Services	12.9	1.5		
Other	90.5[7]	10.6[7]	8,327[8]	20.0[8]
TOTAL	854.2	100.0[4]	41,682	100.0[3]

Population economically active (1991): total 41,682; activity rate of total population 39.1% (participation rates: ages 15–64, 67.5%; female 35.9%; unemployed [1996] more than 30%).

Price and earnings indexes (1995 = 100)

	1995	1996	1997	1998	1999	2000	2001[9]
Consumer price index	100.0	104.4	104.9	107.1	108.2	108.4	109.1
Daily earnings index	...	...	...	...	...	...	...

Household income and expenditure. Average household size (1991) 3.9; income per household (1988) EC$4,579 (U.S.$1,696); sources of income: n.a.; expenditure (1975–76); food and beverages 59.8%, clothing 7.7%, household furnishings 6.6%, housing 6.3%, energy 6.2%, other 13.4%.
Land use (1994): forested 36%; meadows and pastures 5%; agricultural and under permanent cultivation 28%; other 31%.

Foreign trade[10]

Balance of trade (current prices)

	1995	1996	1997	1998	1999	2000
U.S.$'000,000	–93.3	–85.5	–135.6	–143.0	–142.4	–115.6
% of total	52.3%	48.0%	59.4%	59.0%	61.0%	54.9%

Imports (1998): U.S.$169,100,000 (basic manufactures 33.7%; food products 23.1%; machinery and transport equipment 22.2%; chemical products 9.7%; fuels 5.6%). *Major import sources:* U.S. 39.4%; Caricom countries 24.5%, of which Trinidad and Tobago 16.8%; U.K. 12.5%; other 6.8%.
Exports (1998): U.S.$49,600,000 (domestic exports 94.1%, of which bananas 41.5%, packaged flour 13.9%, packaged rice 12.9%, eddoes and dasheens[5] 3.8%; reexports 5.9%). *Major export destinations:* Caricom countries 49.1%, of which Trinidad and Tobago 11.0%, St. Lucia 10.4%; U.K. 42.2%; U.S. 5.2%; other 3.5%.

Transport and communications

Transport. Railroads: none. Roads (1996): total length 646 mi, 1,040 km (paved 31%). Vehicles (1997): passenger cars 6,089; trucks and buses 3,670. Merchant marine (1997): vessels (100 gross tons and over) 946; total deadweight tonnage 1,253,000. Air transport (1997): passenger arrivals 125,400; passenger departures 130,166; airports (1998) with scheduled flights 5.

Communications

Medium	date	unit	number	units per 1,000 persons
Radio	1995	receivers	65,000	591
Television	1995	receivers	17,700	161
Telephones	1999	main lines	23,631	212
Cellular telephones	1999	subscribers	1,420	13
Internet	1998	users	...	...

Education and health

Educational attainment (1980). Percentage of population age 25 and over having: no formal schooling 2.4%; primary education 88.0%; secondary 8.2%; higher 1.4%. *Literacy* (1991): total population age 15 and over literate 64,000 (96.0%).

Education (1997–98)

	schools	teachers	students	student/ teacher ratio
Primary (age 5–11)	60	1,007	21,347	21.2
Secondary (age 12–18)	21	379	7,775	20.5
Voc., teacher tr.[11]	3	49[12]	415	...

Health (1998): physicians 59 (1 per 1,883 persons); hospital beds 209 (1 per 531 persons); infant mortality rate per 1,000 live births (1999) 17.7.
Food (1999): daily per capita caloric intake 2,540 (vegetable products 83%, animal products 17%); 105% of FAO recommended minimum requirement.

Military

Total active duty personnel (1992): 634-member police force includes a coast guard and paramilitary unit.

[1]Includes 6 nonelective seats; excludes speaker who may be elected from within or from outside of the House of Assembly membership. [2]For statistical purposes and the election of legislative representatives only. [3]January 1. [4]Detail does not add to total given because of rounding. [5]Varieties of taro roots. [6]1997. [7]Net of indirect taxes less imputed bank service charges. [8]Unemployed. [9]Average of second quarter. [10]Exports c.i.f. in balance of trade and f.o.b. in commodities and trading partners. [11]1996–97. [12]1993–94.

Internet resources for further information:
- **Eastern Caribbean Central Bank http://www.eccb-centralbank.org**

Samoa[1]

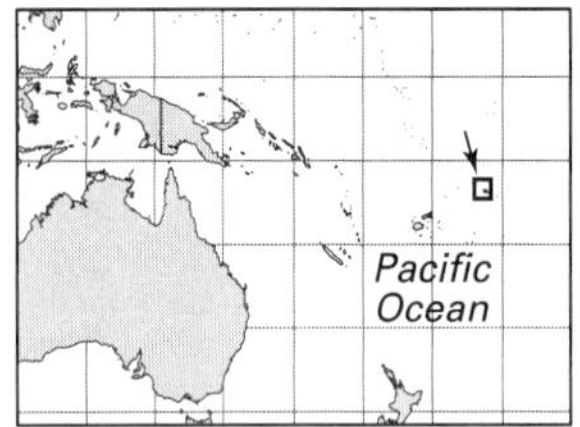

Official name: Malo Sa'oloto Tuto'atasi o Samoa (Samoan); Independent State of Samoa (English).
Form of government: constitutional monarchy[2] with one legislative house (Legislative Assembly [49]).
Chief of state: Head of State.
Head of government: Prime Minister.
Capital: Apia.
Official languages: Samoan; English.
Official religion: none.
Monetary unit: 1 tala (SA$[3], plural tala) = 100 sene; valuation (Sept. 28, 2001) 1 U.S.$ = SA$3.44; 1 £ = SA$5.06.

Area and population

Islands / Political Districts	area sq mi	area sq km	population 1991 census
Savaii	659	1,707	45,050
Fa'aseleleaga			...
Gaga'emauga			...
Gaga'ifomauga			...
Palauli			...
Satupa'itea			...
Vaisigano			...
Upolu	432	1,119	116,248
A'ana			...
Aiga-i-le-Tai			...
Atua			...
Tuamasaga			...
Vaa-o-Fonoti			...
TOTAL	1,093[4]	2,831[4]	161,298

Demography

Population (2001): 179,000.
Density (2001): persons per sq mi 163.8, persons per sq km 63.2.
Urban-rural (1999): urban 21.0%; rural 79.0%.
Sex distribution (1991): male 52.45%; female 47.55%.
Age breakdown (1991): under 15, 40.6%; 15–29, 29.9%; 30–44, 14.6%; 45–59, 8.8%; 60–74, 5.0%; 75 and over, 1.1%.
Population projection: (2010) 176,000; (2020) 178,000.
Doubling time: 31 years.
Ethnic composition (1997): Samoan (Polynesian) 92.6%; Euronesian (European and Polynesian) 7.0%; European 0.4%.
Religious affiliation (1995): Mormon 25.8%; Congregational 24.6%; Roman Catholic 21.3%; Methodist 12.2%; Pentecostal 8.0%; Seventh-day Adventist 3.9%; other Christian 1.7%; other 2.5%.
Major city (1999): Apia 38,000.

Vital statistics

Birth rate per 1,000 population (2001): 28.2 (world avg. 22.5); (1978) legitimate 43.5%; illegitimate 56.5%.
Death rate per 1,000 population (2001): 5.7 (world avg. 9.0).
Natural increase rate per 1,000 population (2001): 22.5 (world avg. 13.5).
Total fertility rate (avg. births per childbearing woman; 2001): 4.3.
Marriage rate per 1,000 population (1992)[5]: 5.0.
Divorce rate per 1,000 population (1989)[5]: 0.2.
Life expectancy at birth (2001): male 67.0 years; female 73.0 years.
Major causes of death (percent distribution; 1992)[5]: congestive heart failure 14.0%; malignant neoplasms (cancers) 11.0%; cerebrovascular diseases 8.0%; injury and poisoning 8.0%; pneumonia 6.0%; septicemia 6.0%; diabetes mellitus 4.0%; intestinal infectious diseases 2.0%.

National economy

Budget (1998–99). Revenue: SA$276,900,000 (tax revenue 56.1%; grants 30.7%; nontax revenue 13.2%). Expenditures: SA$279,400,000 (current expenditure 61.9%; development expenditure 32.3%; net lending 5.8%).
Public debt (external, outstanding; 1999): U.S.$156,500,000.
Production (metric tons except as noted). Agriculture, forestry, fishing (1999): coconuts 130,000, taro 36,900, bananas 10,000, papayas 10,000, pineapples 5,700, mangoes 4,900, avocados 1,700, cacao beans 400; livestock (number of live animals) 178,800 pigs, 26,000 cattle, 350,000 chickens; roundwood (1998) 131,000 cu m; fish catch (1997) 4,590. Mining and quarrying: n.a. Manufacturing (in WS$'000; 1990): beer 8,708; cigarettes 6,551; coconut cream 5,576; sawn wood 3,662; coconut oil 3,442; corned meat 2,905; soap 1,487; paints 1,457. Construction (permits issued in WS$; 1995): residential 7,749,000; commercial, industrial, and other 30,867,000. Energy production (consumption): electricity (kW-hr; 1996) 65,000,000 (65,000,000); coal, none (n.a.); crude petroleum, none (n.a.); petroleum products (metric tons; 1996) none (43,000).
Household income and expenditure. Average household size (1981) 5.1; income per household (1972) WS$1,518 (U.S.$2,200); sources of income (1972): wages 49.4%, self-employment 22.8%, remittances, gifts, and other assistance 18.0%, land rent 8.7%, other 1.1%; expenditure (1987)[6]: food 58.8%, transportation 9.0%, housing and furnishings 5.1%, fuel and lighting 5.0%, clothing 4.2%, other goods and services 1.9%, other 16.0%.
Tourism (1999): receipts from visitors U.S.$42,000,000; expenditures by nationals abroad U.S.$4,000,000.
Gross national product (1999): U.S.$181,000,000 (U.S.$1,070 per capita).

Structure of gross domestic product and labour force

	1997 in value WS$'000	1997 % of total value	1986 labour force	1986 % of labour force
Agriculture	102,700	17.2	29,023	63.6
Mining	...	... }	1,587 }	3.5 }
Manufacturing	112,400	18.9 }		
Construction	32,000	5.4	62	0.1
Public utilities	14,800	2.5	855	1.9
Transp. and commun.	65,800	11.0	1,491	3.3
Trade	101,900	17.1	1,710	3.7
Finance	43,300	7.3	842	1.8
Pub. admin., defense	54,600	9.2 }	9,436 }	20.7 }
Services	67,600	11.4 }		
Other	...	...	629	1.4
TOTAL	595,100	100.0	45,635	100.0

Population economically active (1994): total 47,207; activity rate of total population 28.7% (participation rates: ages 15–64 [1981] 48.6%; female [1991] 32.0%).

Price and earnings indexes (1995 = 100)

	1994	1995	1996	1997	1998	1999	2000
Consumer price index	103.0	100.0	105.4	112.6	115.1	115.4	116.5
Earnings index	...	...	...	...	...	...	...

Land use (1994): forested 47.3%; meadows and pastures 0.4%; agricultural and under permanent cultivation 43.1%; other 9.2%.

Foreign trade[7]

Balance of trade (current prices)

	1995	1996	1997	1998	1999	2000
WS$'000	–213,494	–222,258	–208,846	–242,409	–285,070	–301,774
% of total	83.0%	81.7%	73.0%	73.7%	69.8%	76.3%

Imports (1997): WS$247,377,000 ([1996]; food 33.9%, industrial supplies 26.4%, machinery 16.9%, petroleum products 11.8%, consumer goods 11.0%). *Major import sources:* New Zealand 37.9%; Australia 20.7%; United States 15.6%; Fiji 15.0%; Japan 4.5%; Hong Kong 0.9%; Singapore 0.5%.
Exports (1997): WS$38,531,000 (fresh fish 33.0%, copra 21.1%, coconut oil 18.1%, coconut cream 12.8%, beer 4.3%, kava 4.0%, copra meal 1.5%). *Major export destinations:* New Zealand 48.1%; American Samoa 15.3%; Australia 9.2%; United States 3.3%; Germany 2.9%.

Transport and communications

Transport. Railroads: none. Roads (1996): total length 491 mi, 790 km (paved 42%). Vehicles (1995): passenger cars 1,068; trucks and buses 1,169. Merchant marine (1997): vessels (100 gross tons and over) 7; total deadweight tonnage 6,501. Air transport (1996): passenger-km 265,000,000; metric ton-km cargo 26,000,000; airports (1997) with scheduled flights 3.

Communications

Medium	date	unit	number	units per 1,000 persons
Radio	1997	receivers	178,000	1,035
Television	1998	receivers	9,000	52
Telephones	1998	main lines	8,480	49
Cellular telephones	1999	subscribers	3,000	17
Personal computers	1999	units	1,000	5.6
Internet	1999	users	500	2.8

Education and health

Educational attainment (1981). Percentage of population age 25 and over having: some primary education 16.5%; complete primary 24.5%; some secondary 52.1%; complete secondary 3.1%; higher 2.0%; unknown 1.8%.
Literacy (1981): virtually 100%.

Education (1996)

	schools	teachers	students	student/ teacher ratio
Primary (age 5–11)	155[8]	1,479	35,378	23.9
Secondary (age 12–18)	38[9]	665	12,672	19.1
Voc., teacher tr.	4[10]	37[11]	228[11]	6.2[11]
Higher[10]	6	25	271	10.8

Health: physicians (1996) 62 (1 per 2,919 persons); hospital beds (1991) 863 (1 per 255 persons); infant mortality rate per 1,000 live births (2001) 27.0.
Food (1992): daily per capita caloric intake 2,828 (vegetable products 74%, animal products 26%); 124% of FAO recommended minimum requirement.

Military

No military forces are maintained; New Zealand is responsible for defense.

[1]In July 1997 the short-form name of the country was officially changed from Western Samoa to Samoa. [2]According to the constitution, the current Head of State, paramount chief HH Malietoa Tanumafili II, will hold office for life. Upon his death, the monarchy will functionally cease, and future Heads of State will be elected by the Legislative Assembly. [3]Symbol of the monetary unit changed from WS$ to SA$ as of July 1997. [4]Total includes 2 sq mi (5 sq km) of uninhabited islands. [5]Registered only. [6]Consumer price index components. [7]Import figures are c.i.f. in balance of trade and in commodities and trading partners. [8]1995. [9]1982. [10]1983. [11]1986–87.

Internet resources for further information:
- **Central Bank of Samoa http://www.cbs.gov.ws**

San Marino

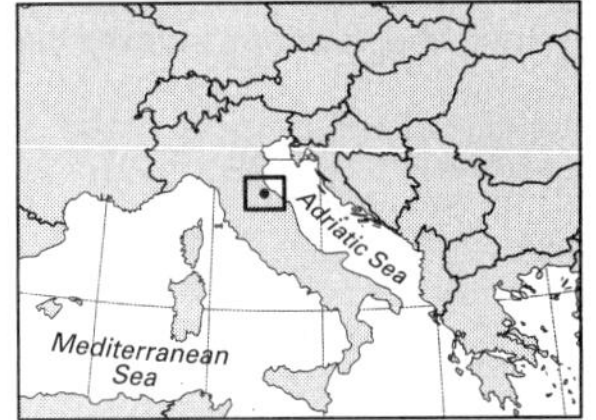

Official name: Serenissima Repubblica di San Marino (Most Serene Republic of San Marino).
Form of government: unitary multiparty republic with one legislative house (Great and General Council [60]).
Head of state and government: Captains-Regent (2).
Capital: San Marino.
Official language: Italian.
Official religion: none.
Monetary unit: 1 Italian lira (Lit; plural lire) = 100 centesimi; valuation (Sept. 28, 2001) 1 U.S.$ = Lit 2,126; 1 £ = Lit 3,125; 1 € = Lit 1,936.27.

Area and population

		area		population
Castles	Capitals	sq mi	sq km	1997[1] estimate
Acquaviva	Acquaviva	1.88	4.86	1,264
Borgo Maggiore	Borgo	3.48	9.01	5,358
Chiesanuova	Chiesanuova	2.11	5.46	866
Città	San Marino	2.74	7.09	4,350
Domagnano	Domagnano	2.56	6.62	2,207
Faetano	Faetano	2.99	7.75	870
Fiorentino	Fiorentino	2.53	6.56	1,798
Montegiardino	Montegiardino	1.28	3.31	717
Serravalle/Dogano	Serravalle	4.07	10.53	8,085
TOTAL		23.63[2]	61.19	25,515

Demography

Population (2001): 27,200.
Density (2001): persons per sq mi 1,152.4, persons per sq km 445.0.
Urban-rural (1999): urban 96.2%; rural 3.8%.
Sex distribution (2000): male 48.34%; female 51.66%.
Age breakdown (2000): under 15, 15.7%; 15–29, 18.8%; 30–44, 25.5%; 45–59, 18.8%; 60–74, 14.0%; 75 and over, 7.2%.
Population projection: (2010) 31,200; (2020) 36,200.
Doubling time: not applicable; natural population growth is negligible.
Ethnic composition (1997[1]): Sammarinesi 83.1%; Italian 12.0%; other 4.8%.
Religious affiliation (2000): Roman Catholic 88.7%; Pentecostal 1.8%; other 9.5%.
Major cities (1997[1]): Serravalle/Dogano 4,802; Borgo Maggiore 2,394; San Marino 2,294; Murata 1,549; Domagnano 1,048.

Vital statistics

Birth rate per 1,000 population (2000): 10.9 (world avg. 22.5); (1985) legitimate 95.2%; illegitimate 4.8%.
Death rate per 1,000 population (2000): 7.6 (world avg. 9.0).
Natural increase rate per 1,000 population (2000): 3.3 (world avg. 13.5).
Total fertility rate (avg. births per childbearing woman; 2000): 1.3.
Marriage rate per 1,000 population (1992–96): 8.1.
Divorce rate per 1,000 population (1991–95): 1.0.
Life expectancy at birth (2000): male 77.6 years; female 85.0 years.
Major causes of death per 100,000 population (1994–98): disease of the circulatory system 338.3; malignant neoplasms (cancers) 224.5; accidents, violence, and suicide 60.9; diseases of the respiratory system 9.5.

National economy

Budget (1997). Revenue: Lit 411,000,000,000 (taxes on goods and services 37.2%; taxes on income and profits 31.6%; social security 19.7%). Expenditures: Lit 448,000,000,000 (current expenditures 90.4%, of which social security and subsidies 48.2%, wages and salaries 31.2%; capital expenditures 6.9%; other 2.7%).
Public debt: n.a.
Tourism: number of tourist arrivals (1999) 3,148,000; receipts from visitors (1994) U.S.$252,500,000; expenditures by nationals abroad, n.a.
Population economically active (1999): total 19,347; activity rate of total population 73.2% (participation rates: ages 15–64, 88.4%; female 41.2%; unemployed 4.4%).

Price and earnings indexes (1990 = 100)

	1991	1992	1993	1994	1995	1996	1997
Consumer price index	82.2	86.6	90.7	95.2	100.0	104.9	107.0
Annual earnings index	...	81.8	87.9	93.9	100.0	110.9	118.4

Household income and expenditure. Total number of households (1997[1]) 10,093; average household size 2.5; income per household: n.a.; sources of income: n.a.; expenditure (1991)[3]: food, beverages, and tobacco 22.1%, housing, fuel, and electrical energy 20.9%, transportation and communications 17.6%, clothing and footwear 8.0%, furniture, appliances, and goods and services for the home 7.2%, education 7.1%, health and sanitary services 2.6%, other goods and services 14.5%.
Production (metric tons except as noted). Agriculture, forestry, fishing[4]: wheat *c.* 4,400, grapes *c.* 700, barley *c.* 500; livestock (number of live animals; 1998) 831 cattle, 748 pigs. Manufacturing (1998): processed meats 324,073 kg, of which beef 226,570 kg, pork 87,764 kg, veal 7,803 kg; cheese 61,563 kg; butter 12,658 kg; milk 1,167,620 litres; yogurt 5,131 litres; other major products include electrical appliances, musical instruments, printing ink, paint, cosmetics, furniture, floor tiles, gold and silver jewelry, clothing, and postage stamps. Construction (new units completed; 1998): residential 69; nonresidential 165. Energy production (consumption): all electrical power is imported via electrical grid from Italy (consumption, n.a.); coal, none (n.a.); crude petroleum, none (n.a.); petroleum products, none (n.a.); natural gas, none (n.a.).
Gross national product (at current market prices; 1998): U.S.$344,000,000 (U.S.$13,200 per capita).

Structure of labour force (1999)

	labour force	% of labour force
Agriculture	254	1.3
Manufacturing	5,962	30.8
Construction and public utilities	1,608	8.3
Transportation and communications	396	2.1
Trade	3,508	18.1
Finance and insurance	533	2.8
Services	2,021	10.4
Public administration and defense	4,211	21.8
Other	854[5]	4.4[5]
TOTAL	19,347	100.0

Land use (1985): agricultural and under permanent cultivation 74%; meadows and pastures 22%; forested, built-on, wasteland, and other 4%.

Foreign trade

Balance of trade (current prices)

	1992	1993	1994	1995	1996
U.S.$'000,000	–50.3	–48.8	–41.2	–3.3	+22.6
% of total	1.4%	1.4%	1.3%	0.1%	0.7%

Imports (1996): U.S.$1,719,300,000 (manufactured goods of all kinds, oil, and gold). *Major import source:* Italy.
Exports (1996): U.S.$1,741,900,000 (manufactured goods, traditionally wine, wheat, woolen goods, furniture, wood, ceramics, building stone, dairy products, meat, and postage stamps). *Major export destination:* Italy.

Transport and communications

Transport. Railroads: none (nearest rail terminal is at Rimini, Italy, 17 mi [27 km] northeast). Roads (1999): total length 156 mi, 252 km. Vehicles (1999): passenger cars 26,320; trucks and buses 2,763. Merchant marine: vessels (100 gross tons and over) none. Air transport: airports with scheduled flights, none; there is, however, a heliport that provides passenger and cargo service between San Marino and Rimini, Italy, during the summer months.

Communications

Medium	date	unit	number	units per 1,000 persons
Daily newspapers	1996	circulation	2,000	72
Radio	1998	receivers	16,000	610
Television	1998	receivers	9,055	358
Telephones	1999	main lines	19,970	769
Cellular telephones	1999	subscribers	10,000	369

Education and health

Educational attainment (1997[1]). Percentage of population age 14 and over having: basic literacy[6] or primary education 35.6%; secondary 30.7%; some postsecondary 27.9%; higher degree 5.8%. *Literacy* (1997[1]): total population age 15 and over literate 21,885 (99.1%); males literate 10,546 (99.4%); females literate 11,339 (98.8%).

Education (1997–98)

	schools	teachers	students	student/teacher ratio
Primary (age 6–10)	14	196	1,227	6.3
Secondary (age 11–18)	4	151	1,083	7.2
Voc., teacher tr.	...	49	380	7.8
Higher	1	...	...	...

Health (1999): physicians 84 (1 per 315 persons); hospital beds 143 (1 per 185 persons); infant mortality rate per 1,000 live births (2000) 6.3.
Food (1999)[7]: daily per capita caloric intake 3,269 (vegetable products 82%, animal products 18%); 130% of FAO recommended minimum requirement.

Military

Total active duty personnel (2000): none[8]. *Military expenditure as percentage of national budget* (1992): 1.0% (world 3.6%); per capita expenditure (1987) U.S.$155.

[1]January 1. [2]Detail does not add to total given because of rounding. [3]Weighting coefficients for component expenditures are those of the 1991 official Italian consumer price index for the North-Central region of Italy. [4]Early 1980s. [5]Unemployed. [6]Includes 0.9 percent illiterate population. [7]Figures are for Italy. [8]Defense is provided by a public security force of about 50; all fit males ages 16–55 constitute a militia.

Internet resources for further information:
• San Marino http://www.emulateme.com/sanmarino.htm

São Tomé and Príncipe

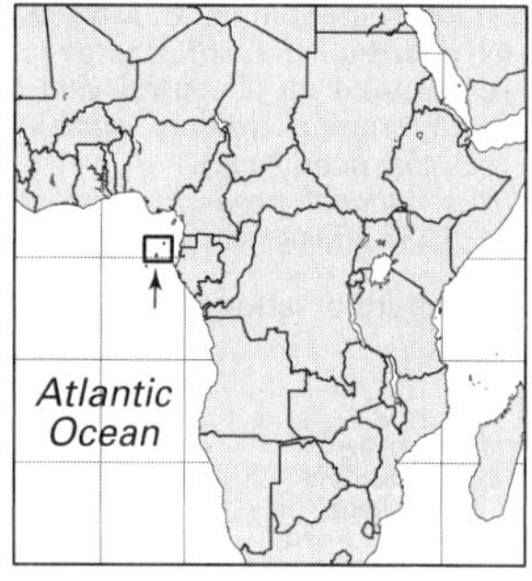

Official name: República democrática de São Tomé e Príncipe (Democratic Republic of São Tomé and Príncipe).
Form of government: Multiparty republic with one legislative house (National Assembly [55]).
Chief of state: President.
Head of government: Prime Minister.
Capital: São Tomé.
Official language: Portuguese.
Official religion: none.
Monetary unit: 1 dobra (Db) = 100 cêntimos; valuation (Sept. 28, 2001) 1 U.S.$ = Db 8,937; 1 £ = Db 13,135.

Area and population

Islands / Districts	Capitals	area sq mi	area sq km	population 1991 census[1]
São Tomé		332	859	114,507
Aqua Grande	São Tomé	7	17	43,420
Cantagalo	Santana	46	119	11,421
Caué	São João Angolares	103	267	5,541
Lemba	Neves	88	229	9,448
Lobata	Guadalupe	41	105	13,101
Mé-Zóchi	Trindade	47	122	31,576
Autonomous Island		55	142	5,639
Príncipe	Santo António	55	142	5,639
TOTAL		386	1,001	120,146

Demography

Population (2001): 147,000.
Density (2001): persons per sq mi 379.9, persons per sq km 146.5.
Urban-rural (1999): urban 46.0%; rural 54.0%.
Sex distribution (2000): male 49.26%, female 50.74%.
Age breakdown (2000): under 15, 47.7%; 15–29, 27.4%; 30–44, 12.6%; 45–59, 6.3%; 60–74, 4.7%; 75 and over, 1.3%.
Population projection: (2010) 177,000; (2020) 218,000.
Doubling time: 20 years.
Ethnic composition (2000): black-white admixture 79.5%; Fang 10.0%; angolares (descendants of former Angolan slaves) 7.6%; Portuguese 1.9%; other 1.0%.
Religious affiliation (1995): Roman Catholic, about 89.5%; remainder mostly Protestant, predominantly Seventh-day Adventist and an indigenous Evangelical Church.
Major cities (1991): São Tomé 43,420; Trindade 11,388[2]; Santana 6,190[2]; Neves 5,919[2]; Santo Amaro 5,878[2].

Vital statistics

Birth rate per 1,000 population (2000): 43.0 (world avg. 22.5).
Death rate per 1,000 population (2000): 7.8 (world avg. 9.0).
Natural increase rate per 1,000 population (2000): 35.2 (world avg. 13.5).
Total fertility rate (avg. births per childbearing woman; 2000): 6.1.
Marriage rate per 1,000 population: n.a.
Divorce rate per 1,000 population: n.a.
Life expectancy at birth (2000): male 63.8 years; females 66.7 years.
Major causes of death per 100,000 population (1987): malaria 160.6; direct obstetric causes 76.7; pneumonia 74.0; influenza 61.5; anemias 47.3; hypertensive disease 32.1.

National economy

Budget (1997). Revenue: Db 55,528,000,000 (grants 43.7%; taxes 38.2%, of which import taxes 8.5%, sales taxes 7.5%, export taxes 3.4%; nontax revenue 18.1%). Expenditures: Db 140,174,000,000 (capital 60.3%; recurrent expenditure 39.7%, of which debt service 15.9%, personnel costs 8.4%, transfers 6.3%, goods and services 5.0%, defense 1.2%).
Public debt (external, outstanding; 1999): U.S.$233,200,000.
Tourism (1997): receipts from visitors U.S.$2,000,000; expenditures by nationals abroad U.S.$1,000,000.
Production (metric tons except as noted). Agriculture, forestry, fishing (1999): coconuts 28,000, taro 23,060, bananas 18,000, vegetables 6,100, cassava 4,840, cacao 4,197, fruits (other than melon) 2,100, corn (maize) 1,487, yams 1,200, coffee 58; livestock (number of live animals) 4,750 goats, 4,000 cattle, 2,550 sheep, 2,100 pigs; roundwood (1998) 9,000 cu m; fish catch (1998) 3,305, principally marine fish and shellfish. Mining and quarrying: some quarrying to support local construction industry. Manufacturing (value in Db; 1995): beer 880,000; clothing 679,000; lumber 369,000; bakery products 350,000; palm oil 228,000; soap 133,000; ceramics 87,000. Construction (1972): buildings authorized 44 (5,561 sq m, of which residential 3,698, mixed residential-commercial 1,361, commercial 502). Energy production (consumption): electricity (kW-hr; 1996) 15,000,000 (15,000,000); coal, none (n.a.); crude petroleum, none (n.a.); petroleum products (metric tons; 1996) none (25,000); natural gas, none (n.a.).
Household income and expenditure. Average household size (1981): 4.0; income per household: n.a.; sources of income: n.a.; expenditure (1995)[3]: food 71.9%, housing and energy 10.2%, transportation and communications 6.4%, clothing and other items 5.3%, household durable goods 2.8%, education and health 1.7%.
Population economically active (1994): total 51,789; activity rate of total population 40.8% (participation rates [1981] ages 15–64, 61.1%; female [1991] 32.4%; unemployed [1994] 29.0%).

Price and earnings indexes (1995 = 100)

	1993	1994	1995	1996	1997
Consumer price index	57.5	72.9	100.0	137.6	231.4
Earnings index	...	...	...	...	...

Gross national product (1999): U.S.$40,000,000 (U.S.$270 per capita).

Structure of gross domestic product and labour force

	1997 in value Db '000,000	1997 % of total value	1994 labour force	1994 % of labour force
Agriculture	46,682	23.3	14,022	27.1
Mining	...	...	...	...
Manufacturing, Public utilities	7,875	4.0	2,327	4.5
Construction	29,469	14.7	3,365	6.5
Transp. and commun.	37,508	18.8	2,829	5.5
Trade			5,184	10.0
Finance	15,134	7.6	194	0.3
Pub. admin., defense	44,669	22.3	4,023	7.8
Services	18,664	9.3	...	...
Other	...	...	19,845[4]	38.3[4]
TOTAL	200,001	100.0	51,789	100.0

Land use (1994): meadows and pastures 1.3%; agricultural and under permanent cultivation 54.0%; forest, built-on, wasteland, and other 44.7%.

Foreign trade

Balance of trade (current prices)

	1993	1994	1995	1996	1997	1998
U.S.$'000,000	−20.4	−18.5	−18.3	−14.9	−13.9	−12.1
% of total	66.2%	61.3%	64.2%	60.3%	56.7%	56.3%

Imports (1997): U.S.$19,200,000 (capital goods 29.2%, food and other agricultural products 19.8%, petroleum products 19.8%). *Major import sources:* Portugal 26.3%; France 17.9%; Angola 6.7%; Belgium 5.8%; Japan 3.3%; Germany 1.6%; Gabon 0.8%; Italy 0.4%.
Exports (1997): U.S.$5,300,000 (cocoa 86.8%). *Major export destinations:* The Netherlands 50.9%; Germany 5.7%; Portugal 5.7%.

Transport and communications

Transport. Railroads: none. Roads (1996): total length 199 mi, 320 km (paved 68%). Vehicles (1996): passenger cars 4,040; trucks and buses 1,540. Merchant marine (1992): vessels (100 gross tons and over) 4; total deadweight tonnage 2,277. Air transport (1997): passenger-mi 6,000,000, passenger-km 9,000,000; short ton-mi cargo 700,000, short ton-km cargo 1,000,000; airports (1998) 2.

Communications

Medium	date	unit	number	units per 1,000 persons
Radio	1997	receivers	38,000	272
Television	1997	receivers	23,000	163
Telephones	1999	main lines	4,526	32

Education and health

Educational attainment (1981). Percentage of population age 25 and over having: no formal schooling 56.6%; incomplete primary education 18.0%; primary 19.2%; incomplete secondary 4.6%; complete secondary 1.3%; post-secondary 0.3%. *Literacy* (1981): total population age 15 and over literate 28,114 (54.2%); males literate 17,689 (70.2%); females literate 10,425 (39.1%).

Education (1997)

	schools	teachers	students	student/ teacher ratio
Primary (age 6–13)	69	638	21,760	34.1
Secondary (age 14–18)[5]	10	415	12,280	29.6
Voc., teacher tr.	...	...	...	...
Higher	...	...	...	...

Health: physicians (1996) 61 (1 per 2,147 persons); hospital beds (1983) 640 (1 per 158 persons); infant mortality rate per 1,000 live births (2000) 50.4.
Food (1999): daily per capita caloric intake 2,269 (vegetable products 95%, animal products 5%); 97% of FAO recommended minimum requirement.

Military

Total active duty personnel: a police force of about 900 men from 1992. *Military expenditure as percentage of GNP* (1997): 0.9% (world 2.6%); per capita expenditure U.S.$2.

[1]Preliminary. [2]1981. [3]Weights based on CPI components. [4]Includes 15,000 unemployed. [5]Includes vocational.

Internet resources for further information:
- **São Tomé e Príncipe Homepage (unofficial) http://www.stome.com**

Saudi Arabia

Official name: Al-Mamlakah al-ʿArabīyah as-Saʿūdīyah (Kingdom of Saudi Arabia).
Form of government: monarchy[1].
Head of state and government: King.
Capital: Riyadh.
Official language: Arabic.
Official religion: Islam.
Monetary unit: 1 Saudi riyal (SRls) = 100 halalah; valuation (Sept. 28, 2001) 1 U.S.$ = SRls 3.75; 1 £ = SRls 5.51.

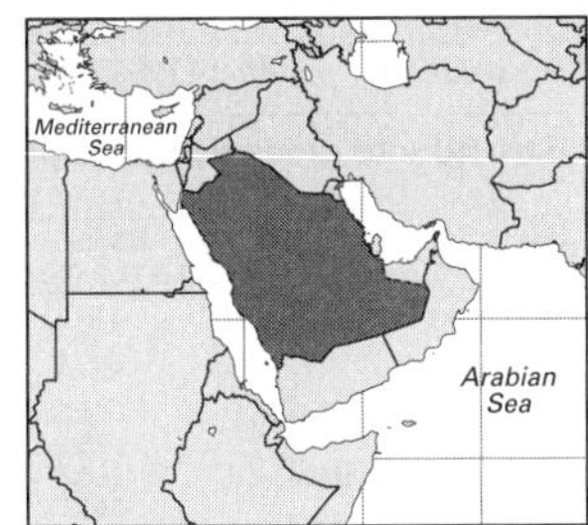

Area and population

Geographic Regions / Administrative Regions[3]	Capitals	area[2] sq mi	area[2] sq km	population 1992 census
Al-Gharbīyah (Western)		—	—	5,884,774
Al-Bāḥah	Al-Bāḥah	6,000	15,000	332,157
Al-Madīnah al-Munawwarah	Medina (Al-Madīnah)	67,000	173,000	1,084,947
Makkah al-Mukarramah	Mecca (Makkah)	63,000	164,000	4,467,670
Al-Janūbīyah (Southern)		—	—	2,507,123
ʿAsīr	Abha	31,000	81,000	1,340,168
Jīzān	Jīzān	7,000	17,000	865,961
Najrān	Najrān	46,000	119,000	300,994
Ash-Shamālīyah (Northern)		—	—	983,422
Al-Ḥudūd ash-Shamālīyah (Northern Borders)	ʿArʿar	46,000	120,000	229,060
Al-Jawf[3] / Al-Qurrayāt[3]	Sakākah / Al-Qurrayāt	54,000	139,000	268,228
Tabūk	Tabūk	42,000	108,000	486,134
Ash-Sharqīyah (Eastern)		—	—	2,575,820
Ash-Sharqīyah (Eastern)	Ad-Dammām	274,000	710,000	2,575,820
Al-Wūsṭā (Central)		—	—	4,997,249
Ḥāʾil	Ḥāʾil	48,000	125,000	411,284
Al-Qaṣīm	Buraydah	25,000	65,000	750,979
Ar-Riyāḍ	Riyadh (Ar-Riyāḍ)	159,000	412,000	3,834,986
TOTAL		868,000	2,248,000	16,948,388

Demography

Population (2001): 22,757,000.
Density (2001)[2]: persons per sq mi 26.2, persons per sq km 10.1.
Urban-rural (2000): urban 83.0%; rural 17.0%.
Sex distribution (2000): male 55.33%; female 44.67%.
Age breakdown (2000): under 15, 42.6%; 15–29, 22.8%; 30–44, 17.9%; 45–59, 12.1%; 60–74, 3.9%; 75 and over, 0.7%.
Population projection: (2010) 30,546,000; (2020) 41,880,000.
Doubling time: 22 years.
Ethnic composition (2000): Arab 88.1%, of which Saudi Arab 74.2%, Bedouin 3.9%, Gulf Arab 3.0%; Indo-Pakistani 5.5%; African black 1.5%; Filipino 1.0%; other 3.9%.
Religious affiliation (1992): Sunnī Muslim 93.3%; Shīʿī Muslim 3.3%; Christian 3.0%; other 0.4%.
Major cities (1992): Riyadh (Ar-Riyāḍ) 2,776,096; Jiddah 2,046,251; Mecca (Makkah) 965,697; Medina 608,295; Aṭ-Ṭāʾif 416,121.

Vital statistics

Birth rate per 1,000 population (2000): 37.5 (world avg. 22.5).
Death rate per 1,000 population (2000): 6.0 (world avg. 9.0).
Natural increase rate per 1,000 population (2000): 31.5 (world avg. 13.5).
Total fertility rate (avg. births per childbearing woman; 2000): 6.3.
Life expectancy at birth (2000): male 66.1 years; female 69.5 years.
Major causes of death per 100,000 population: n.a.

National economy

Budget (2000). Revenue: SRls 157,000,000,000 (oil revenues 75.1%). Expenditures: SRls 185,000,000,000 (defense and security 40.5%, human resource development 26.6%, public administration, municipal transfers, and subsidies 16.5%, health and social development 8.9%).
Public debt: n.a.
Production (metric tons except as noted). Agriculture, forestry, fishing (2000): wheat 2,046,000, alfalfa 1,400,000, dates 712,000, potatoes 394,000, watermelons 285,000, tomatoes 277,000, grapes 259,000, sorghum 204,000, barley 192,000, cantaloupes 140,500, dry onions 95,000; livestock (number of live animals) 7,576,000 sheep, 4,305,000 goats, 400,000 camels, 297,000 cattle; fish catch (1999) 51,949. Mining and quarrying (1999): gypsum 330,000; silver 20,000 kg; gold 9,000 kg. Manufacturing (value added in U.S.$'000,000; 1995): industrial chemicals 3,014; cement, glass, and other nonmetal mineral products 943; refined petroleum 830; iron and steel 561; metal products 589; food, beverages, and tobacco 493; plastic products 221. Energy production (consumption): electricity (kW-hr; 1996) 104,118,000,000 (104,118,000,000); coal, none (none); crude petroleum (barrels; 2000) 2,939,000,000 ([1996] 635,000,000); petroleum products (metric tons; 1996) 97,311,000 (45,396,000); natural gas (cu m; 1999) 46,200,000,000 ([1996] 41,339,000,000).
Population economically active (1994): total 5,614,000; activity rate of total population 32.2% (participation rates [1988] ages 15–64, 59.1%, female 3.5%; unemployed [1997] *c.* 25%).

Price and earnings indexes (1995 = 100)

	1994	1995	1996	1997	1998	1999	2000
Consumer price index	95.4	100.0	101.2	101.3	100.7	99.3	98.5
Earnings index	...	...	...	...	...	...	...

Gross national product (1999): U.S.$139,365,000,000 (U.S.$6,900 per capita).

Structure of gross domestic product and labour force

	1999 in value[4] SRls '000,000	1999 % of total value	1990 labour force	1990 % of labour force
Agriculture	34,443	6.6	569,200	9.9
Mining	180,551 (Mining and Oil sector)	34.6 (Mining and Oil sector)	3,500	0.1
Oil sector			46,800	0.8
Manufacturing	34,465	6.6	374,900	6.5
Construction	48,462	9.3	944,100	16.4
Public utilities	924	0.2	126,900	2.2
Transp. and commun.	34,191	6.6	262,300	4.5
Trade	37,557	7.2	898,300	15.6
Finance	30,699[5]	5.9[5]	99,000	1.7
Pub. admin., defense	103,094	19.7	624,800	10.8
Services	15,034	2.9	1,822,000 (Services and Other)	31.6 (Services and Other)
Other	2,569[6]	0.5[6]		
TOTAL	521,989	100.0[7]	5,771,800	100.0[7]

Household income and expenditure. Average household size (1992) 6.1; income per household: n.a.; sources of income: n.a.; expenditure (1994)[8]: food and tobacco 38.5%, transportation and communications 16.4%, housing 15.2%, clothing 8.8%, household furnishings 9.7%, education and entertainment 2.3%, other 9.1%.
Tourism (in U.S.$'000,000): receipts (1997) 1,420; expenditures, n.a.
Land use (1994): forested 0.8%; meadows and pastures 55.8%; agricultural and under permanent cultivation 1.8%; built-on, waste, and other 41.6%.

Foreign trade[9]

Balance of trade (current prices)

	1994	1995	1996	1997	1998	1999
SRls '000,000,000	+72.2	+82.2	+123.5	+119.8	+33.0	+85.1
% of total	29.2%	28.1%	37.3%	35.8%	12.8%	28.9%

Imports (1999): SRls 104,980,000,000 (machinery and appliances 24.0%, transport equipment 14.5%, chemicals and chemical products 9.0%, base metals and articles 8.4%, vegetables 7.3%, textiles and clothing 6.2%). *Major import sources:* U.S. 18.9%; Japan 9.2%; U.K. 8.1%; Germany 7.3%; Italy 4.2%.
Exports (1999): SRls 190,100,000,000[10] (crude petroleum 72.8%; refined petroleum 15.8%; chemical products 4.8%; plastic products 1.9%). *Major export destinations*[11]: U.S. 16.3%; Japan 14.9%; S. Korea 9.6%; Singapore 6.0%; The Netherlands 4.2%.

Transport and communications

Transport. Railroads (1997–98): route length 1,390 km; passenger-km 222,000,000 metric ton-km cargo 856,000,000. Roads (1996): total length 162,000 km (paved 42.7%). Vehicles (1996): passenger cars 1,744,000; trucks and buses 1,192,000. Merchant marine (1998): vessels (100 gross tons and over) 279; total deadweight tonnage 1,278,000. Air transport (1997): passenger-km 18,949,000,000; metric ton-km cargo 2,650,000,000; airports (1998) with scheduled flights 28.

Communications

Medium	date	unit	number	units per 1,000 persons
Daily newspapers	1996	circulation	1,105,000	59
Radio	1997	receivers	6,250,000	313
Television	1999	receivers	5,500,000	256
Telephones	1999	main lines	2,706,000	129
Cellular telephones	1999	subscribers	837,000	40
Personal computers	1999	units	1,200,000	56
Internet	1999	users	300,000	14

Education and health

Educational attainment (1986). Percentage of population age 25 and over having: no formal schooling 31.8%; primary, secondary, or higher education 68.2%. *Literacy* (1995): percentage of population age 15 and over literate 62.8%; males literate 71.5%; females literate 50.2%.

Education (1998–99)

	schools	teachers	students	student/ teacher ratio
Primary (age 6–12)	12,234	189,008	2,259,849	12.0
Secondary (age 13–18)	9,018	139,946	1,739,934	12.4
Voc., teacher tr.[13]	...	6,878	56,972	8.3
Higher[13]	72	9,427	165,545	17.6

Health (1995): physicians 30,306 (1 per 590 persons); hospital beds 41,916 (1 per 427 persons); infant mortality rate per 1,000 live births (2000) 52.9.
Food (1999): daily per capita caloric intake 2,953 (vegetable products 85%, animal products 15%); 138% of FAO recommended minimum requirement.

Military

Total active duty personnel (2000): 126,500 (army 59.3%, navy 12.3%, air force 28.4%); U.S. military (2001) 5,200. *Military expenditure as percentage of GDP* (1997): 14.5% (world 2.6%); per capita expenditure U.S.$1,050.

[1]Assisted by the Consultative Council consisting of 90 appointed members. [2]Estimated; not adjusted to reflect June 2000 Saudi Arabia boundary agreement with Yemen. [3]Al-Jawf and Al-Qurrayāt merged in 1993. [4]In producers' values at current prices. [5]Finance includes real estate and business services. [6]Other equals import duties less imputed bank services charge. [7]Detail does not add to total given because of rounding. [8]Urban middle-income households only. [9]Imports c.i.f., exports f.o.b. [10]Includes reexports. [11]1998. [12]Domestic and international operation of Saudi Arabian Airlines. [13]1997–98.

Internet resources for further information:
- **Ministry of Information http://www.saudinf.com**

Senegal

Official name: République du Sénégal (Republic of Senegal).
Form of government: multiparty republic with one legislative house (National Assembly [120])[1].
Head of state and government: President assisted by Prime Minister.
Capital: Dakar.
Official language: French.
Official religion: none.
Monetary unit: 1 CFA franc (CFAF) = 100 centimes; valuation (Sept. 28, 2001) 1 U.S.$ = CFAF 720.28; 1 £ = CFAF 1,059.

Area and population

Regions	Capitals	area sq mi	area sq km	population 1994 estimate
Dakar	Dakar	212	550	1,869,000
Diourbel	Diourbel	1,683	4,359	750,000
Fatick	Fatick	3,064	7,935	569,000
Kaolack	Kaolack	6,181	16,010	948,000
Kolda	Kolda	8,112	21,011	689,000
Louga	Louga	11,270	29,188	525,000
Saint-Louis	Saint-Louis	17,034	44,117	749,000
Tambacounda	Tambacounda	23,012	59,602	449,000
Thiès	Thiès	2,549	6,601	1,115,000
Ziguinchor	Ziguinchor	2,834	7,339	467,000
TOTAL		75,951	196,712	8,127,000[2]

Demography

Population (2001): 10,285,000.
Density (2000): persons per sq mi 135.4, persons per sq km 52.3.
Urban-rural (2000): urban 47.4%; rural 52.6%.
Sex distribution (2000): male 48.98%; female 50.02%.
Age breakdown (2000): under 15, 44.6%; 15–29, 27.5%; 30–44, 15.6%; 45–59, 7.7%; 60–74, 3.7%; 75 and over, 0.9%.
Population projection: (2010) 13,221,000; (2020) 16,855,000.
Doubling time: 24 years.
Ethnic composition (1988): Wolof 48.1%; Serer 12.6%; Peul (Fulani) and Tukulor 21.7%; Diola 5.0%; Malinke (Mandingo) 3.7%; other 8.9%.
Religious affiliation (1988): Sunnī Muslim 92.0%; traditional beliefs and other 6.0%; Christian (predominantly Roman Catholic) 2.0%.
Major cities (1994): Dakar 785,071 (urban agglomeration 1,869,323[3]); Thiès 216,381; Kaolack 193,115; Ziguinchor 161,680; Rufisque 138,837[4]; Saint-Louis 132,444.

Vital statistics

Birth rate per 1,000 population (2000): 37.9 (world avg. 22.5).
Death rate per 1,000 population (2000): 8.6 (world avg. 9.0).
Natural increase rate per 1,000 population (2000): 29.3 (world avg. 13.5).
Total fertility rate (avg. births per childbearing woman; 2000): 5.2.
Marriage rate per 1,000 population: n.a.[5]
Divorce rate per 1,000 population: n.a.
Life expectancy at birth (2000): male 60.6 years; female 63.8 years.
Major causes of death (percentage of officially confirmed deaths from infectious diseases only; 1988): malaria 44.8%; tetanus 17.8%; meningitis 15.3%; tuberculosis of respiratory system 10.4%.

National economy

Budget (1997). Revenue: CFAF 432,200,000,000 (value-added taxes 30.3%, individual income tax 12.4%, taxes on petroleum products 9.1%, corporate income tax 6.7%). Expenditures: CFAF 432,200,000,000 (current expenditures 73.5%, of which education 19.0%, defense 9.3%, health 3.7%; development expenditure 26.5%).
Production (metric tons except as noted). Agriculture, forestry, fishing (2000): sugarcane 887,000, peanuts (groundnuts) 828,000, millet 506,000, watermelons 260,000, paddy rice 240,000, sorghum 147,000, mangoes 75,000, corn (maize) 66,000, oil palm fruit 64,000, onions 61,000, cassava 42,000; livestock (number of live animals) 4,300,000 sheep, 3,595,000 goats, 2,960,000 cattle, 510,000 horses; roundwood (1998) 4,934,000 cu m; fish catch (1998) 425,766. Mining and quarrying (1996): phosphate 1,376,000; salt 87,600[6]. Manufacturing (1996): tobacco 1,425,000; phosphates 1,384,000; cement 811,000; peanut oil 91,200; vegetable oil 84,200; sugar 68,400; soap 46,300. Construction (authorized; 1993)[4]: residential 357,000 sq m; nonresidential 235,000 sq m. Energy production (consumption): electricity (kW-hr; 1998) 1,160,000,000 (1,160,000,000); coal, none (none); crude petroleum (barrels; 1998) none (6,392,000); petroleum products (metric tons; 1998) 852,000 (895,000); natural gas, none (none).
Population economically active (1991): total 2,739,476; activity rate of total population 36.1% (participation rates [1988]: ages 15–60, 53.1%; female 25.6%; unemployed [1992] 24.4%).

Price and earnings indexes (1995 = 100)

	1994	1995	1996	1997	1998	1999	2000
Consumer price index[7]	92.7	100.0	102.8	104.4	105.6	106.5	107.2
Hourly earnings index	...	...	...	...	...	...	...

Household income and expenditure. Average household size (1991) 8.7; average annual income per household: n.a.; sources of income: n.a.; expenditure (early 1980s): food 49%, clothing and footwear 11%, housing 7%, education 6%.

Public debt (external, outstanding; 1999): U.S.$3,111,000,000.
Gross national product (1999): U.S.$4,685,000,000 (U.S.$500 per capita).

Structure of gross domestic product and labour force

	1997		1991	
	in value CFAF '000,000,000	% of total value	labour force	% of labour force
Agriculture	476.9	18.3	1,789,467	65.3
Mining	406.5	15.6	1,998	0.1
Manufacturing			161,124	5.9
Public utilities	51.3	2.0	...	...
Construction	126.5	4.8	60,935	2.2
Transp. and commun.	286.7	11.0	58,081	2.1
Trade[8]	649.5	24.9	378,241	13.8
Finance	...	...	4,623	0.2
Services	416.4	16.0	...	...
Pub. admin., defense	193.2	7.4	268,721	9.8
Other	—	—	16,286	0.6
TOTAL	2,607.0	100.0	2,739,476	100.0

Tourism (1999): receipts U.S.$166,000,000; expenditures (1997) U.S.$53,000,000.
Land use (1994): forested 39.5%; meadows and pastures 29.6%; agricultural and under permanent cultivation 12.2%; other 18.7%.

Foreign trade[9]

Balance of trade (current prices)

	1994	1995	1996	1997	1998	1999	2000
CFAF '000,000,000	–215.7	–219.8	–143.9	–154.7	–258.9	–273.2	–261.6
% of total	21.4%	20.3%	12.5%	12.5%	18.5%	17.8%	15.6%

Imports (1998): CFAF 793,000,000,000 (1995; agricultural products 34.5%, of which rice 7.1%, fixed vegetable oils 5.2%; capital goods 15.0%[10]; refined petroleum 11.0%[10]). *Major import sources:* France 35.8%; United States 5.9%; Germany 5.2%; Spain 4.6%; Nigeria 4.4%.
Exports (1998): CFAF 575,700,000,000 (1995[10]; fish and crustaceans 28.0%; chemical products 12.0%; peanut [groundnut] oil 11.0%; phosphates 3.0%). *Major export destinations:* France 9.8%; Mali 8.5%; Mauritania 3.9%; Cameroon 1.6%.

Transport and communications

Transport. Railroads: (1995) route length 761 mi, 1,225 km; (1993) passenger-mi 128,000,000, passenger-km 206,000,000; short ton-mi cargo 476,000,000, metric ton-km cargo 695,000,000. Roads (1996): total length 9,060 mi, 14,700 km (paved 29%). Vehicles (1996): passenger cars 85,488, trucks and buses 36,962. Merchant marine (1992): vessels (100 gross tons and over) 183; total deadweight tonnage 27,473. Air transport (1996)[11]: passenger-mi 139,644,000, passenger-km 224,736,000; short ton-mi cargo 11,247,000, metric ton-km cargo 16,420,000; airports (1996) with scheduled flights 7.

Communications

Medium	date	unit	number	units per 1,000 persons
Daily newspapers	1996	circulation	45,000	5.3
Radio	1997	receivers	1,240,000	141
Television	1998	receivers	370,000	41
Telephones	1999	main lines	166,000	18
Cellular telephones	1999	subscribers	88,000	9.5
Personal computers	1999	units	140,000	15
Internet	1999	users	30,000	3.2

Education and health

Educational attainment (1988). Percentage of population age 6–34 having: no formal schooling 62.6%; primary education 25.7%; secondary 8.4%; higher 0.8%; other 2.5%. *Literacy* (1995): percentage of total population age 15 and over literate 1,960,000 (37.3%); males literate 1,220,000 (47.2%); females literate 740,000 (27.6%).

Education (1996–97)

	schools	teachers	students	student/ teacher ratio
Primary (age 6–12)	3,530	16,567	954,758	57.6
Secondary (age 13–18)	359[12]	6,219	206,934	33.3
Vocational	19[12]	182[12]	4,624	40.1[12]
Higher[12, 13]	2	784	16,733	21.3

Health (1992): physicians 520 (1 per 14,825 persons); hospital beds 7,408 (1 per 1,041 persons); infant mortality rate per 1,000 live births (2000): 58.1.
Food (1999): daily per capita caloric intake 2,307 (vegetable products 91%, animal products 9%); 97% of FAO recommended minimum requirement.

Military

Total active duty personnel (2000): 9,400[14] (army 85.1%, navy 6.4%, air force 8.5%). *Military expenditure as percentage of GNP* (1997): 1.6% (world 2.6%); per capita expenditure U.S.$7.

[1]Former Senate abolished by promulgation of January 2001 constitutional referendum. [2]Detail does not add to total given because of rounding. [3]Urbanized area of Pikine (1994 population estimate 855,287) is within Dakar urban agglomeration. [4]Within Dakar urban agglomeration. [5]In 1996 about half of all women lived in polygamous unions. [6]1994. [7]Capital region only. [8]Includes hotels. [9]Imports f.o.b.; exports c.i.f. [10]Estimated figure(s). [11]Represents 1/11 of total international scheduled traffic of Air Afrique (government-supported airline of 11 West African countries). [12]1992–93. [13]Universities only; 1994–95. [14]Excludes 1,170 French troops.

Internet resources for further information:
- **République du Sénégal (French language only)**
http://www.primature.sn

Seychelles

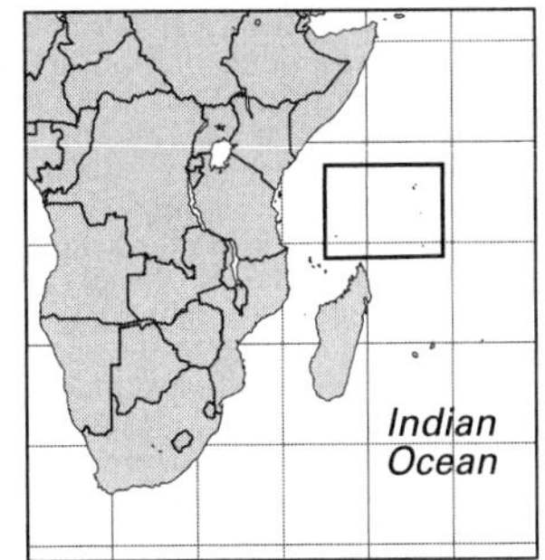

Official name: Repiblik Sesel (Creole); Republic of Seychelles (English); République des Seychelles (French).
Form of government: multiparty republic with one legislative house (National Assembly [34]).
Head of state and government: President.
Capital: Victoria.
Official languages: none[1].
Official religion: none.
Monetary unit: 1 Seychelles rupee (SR) = 100 cents; valuation (Sept. 28, 2001) 1 U.S.$ = SR 5.49; 1 £ = SR 8.06.

Area and population

Island Groups	Capital	area sq mi	area sq km	population 1997 census
Central (Granitic) group				
La Digue and satellites	—	6	15	1,998
Mahé and satellites	Victoria	59	153	67,338
Praslin and satellites	—	15	40	6,091
Silhouette	—	8	20	449
Other islands	—	2	4	0
Outer (Coralline) islands	—	86	223	0
TOTAL		176	455	75,876

Demography

Population (2001): 80,600.
Density (2001): persons per sq mi 457.8, persons per sq km 177.1.
Urban-rural (1999): urban 63.0%; rural 37.0%.
Sex distribution (2000): male 48.30%; female 51.70%.
Age breakdown (2000): under 15, 28.8%; 15–29, 29.6%; 30–44, 24.6%; 45–59, 8.6%; 60–74, 5.8%; 75 and over, 2.6%.
Population projection: (2010) 93,000; (2020) 109,000.
Doubling time: 65 years.
Ethnic composition (2000): Seychellois Creole (mixture of Asian, African, and European) 93.2%; British 3.0%; French 1.8%; Chinese 0.5%; Indian 0.3%; other unspecified 1.2%.
Religious affiliation (1996): Roman Catholic 86.6%; other Christian (mostly Anglican) 9.3%; Hindu 1.3%; other 2.8%.
Major city (1999): Victoria 28,000.

Vital statistics

Birth rate per 1,000 population (2000): 18.0 (world avg. 22.5); (1998) legitimate 24.7%; illegitimate 75.3%.
Death rate per 1,000 population (2000): 6.7 (world avg. 9.0).
Natural increase rate per 1,000 population (2000): 11.3 (world avg. 13.5).
Total fertility rate (avg. births per childbearing woman; 2000): 1.9.
Marriage rate per 1,000 population (1998): 4.5.
Divorce rate per 1,000 population (1998): 1.0.
Life expectancy at birth (2000): male 64.9 years; female 76.1 years.
Major causes of death per 100,000 population (1998): diseases of the circulatory system 238.4, of which cerebrovascular disease 74.0; malignant neoplasms (cancers) 105.3; accidents 57.0; diseases of the respiratory system 52.0; diseases of the digestive system 51.9; infectious and parasitic diseases 36.8.

National economy

Budget (1999). Revenue: SR 1,399,600,000 (1997; customs taxes and duties 42.3%, transfers from Social Security Fund 17.4%, administrative fees 11.2%, income tax 10.5%, business taxes 6.1%, fees and fines 1.3%, grants 0.2%). Expenditures: SR 1,754,000,000 (1997; wages and salaries 27.4%, capital expenditure 17.5%, transfers 17.2%, debt service 16.5%, defense 3.3%).
Tourism (1999): receipts from visitors U.S.$112,000,000; expenditures by nationals abroad U.S.$21,000,000.
Land use (1994): forested 11.1%; agricultural and under permanent cultivation 15.6%; built-on, wasteland, and other 73.3%.
Gross national product (1999): U.S.$520,000,000 (U.S.$6,500 per capita).

Structure of gross domestic product and labour force

	1997 in value SR '000,000	% of total value	labour force[2]	% of labour force
Agriculture	109.8	4.1	1,759	6.2
Mining, manufacturing	355.7	13.1	3,553[3]	12.6[3]
Construction	218.5	8.1	2,521	8.9
Public utilities	57.6	2.1	[3]	[3]
Trade	248.0	9.2	2,360	8.3
Transportation and communications	823.8	30.4	3,121	11.0
Finance	286.0	10.6	1,518	5.4
Pub. admin., defense	371.0	13.7	2,595	9.2
Services	65.1	2.4	9,871	34.9
Other	171.9[4]	6.3[4]	999	3.5
TOTAL	2,707.4	100.0	28,297	100.0

Production (metric tons except as noted). Agriculture, forestry, fishing (1999): coconuts 3,200, bananas 1,950, cinnamon 650, tea 260; livestock (number of live animals) 18,200 pigs, 5,150 goats, 1,400 cattle, 540,000 chickens; fish catch (1999) 4,418, of which (1998) jack 30.2%, snapper 18.3%, capitaine 8.3%, mackerel 4.8%. Mining and quarrying (1998): guano 5,000. Manufacturing (1999): canned tuna 33,234; soft drinks 105,610 hectolitres; beer and stout 67,680 hectolitres; fruit juices 22,530 hectolitres; cigarettes 60,300,000 units. Energy production (consumption): electricity (kW-hr; 1999) 172,400,000 (172,400,000); coal, none (n.a.); crude petroleum, none (n.a.); petroleum products (metric tons; 1996) none (55,000); natural gas, none (n.a.).
Population economically active (1999): total 30,786; activity rate of total population 38.3% (participation rates: ages 15–64 [1989] 74.3%; female [1989] 42.5%; unemployed 11.5%).

Price and earnings indexes (1995 = 100)

	1994	1995	1996	1997	1998	1999	2000
Consumer price index	100.3	100.0	98.9	99.5	102.1	108.6	115.4
Monthly earnings index	96.0	100.0	...	...	...	...	...

Public debt (external, outstanding; 1999): U.S.$132,200,000.
Household income and expenditure. Average household size (1997) 4.2; average annual income per household (1978) SR 18,480 (U.S.$2,658); sources of income: wages and salaries 77.2%, self-employment 3.8%, transfer payments 3.2%; expenditure (1991–92): food and beverages 47.6%, housing 15.1%, clothing and footwear 8.6%, transportation 8.0%, energy and water 7.4%, recreation 6.7%, household and personal goods 6.6%.

Foreign trade

Balance of trade (current prices)

	1994	1995	1996	1997	1998	1999
SR '000,000	–786.7	–855.7	–1,188.7	–1,131.4	–1,140.1	–1,544.3
% of total	60.6%	62.8%	46.1%	49.4%	49.6%	50.0%

Imports (1999): SR 2,316,200,000 (manufactured goods 30.8%, machinery and transport equipment 29.5%, food, beverages, and tobacco 22.2%, mineral fuels [including petroleum], lubricants, and related materials 9.9%, chemicals 6.0%). *Major import sources* (1997): South Africa 14.5%; United Kingdom 11.8%; Bahrain 11.2%; Singapore 11.2%; France 9.6%; Italy 4.7%; Japan 3.1%; India 2.6%; The Netherlands 2.5%.
Exports (1999): SR 771,900,000[5] (canned tuna 70.2%, petroleum products 21.9%[6], other fish, including dried shark fins 1.9%, frozen prawns 1.0%, cinnamon bark 0.3%). *Major export destinations* (1997)[7]: France 29.2%; Germany 27.3%; Italy 24.0%; Japan 7.0%; South Africa 4.0%; United Kingdom 3.7%.

Transport and communications

Transport. Railroads: none. Roads (1999): total length 263 mi, 424 km (paved 87%). Vehicles (1997): passenger cars 7,120; trucks and buses 1,980. Merchant marine (1992): vessels (100 gross tons and over) 9; total deadweight tonnage 3,337. Air transport (1999): passenger arrivals 155,000, passenger departures 156,000; metric ton cargo unloaded 4,526, metric ton cargo loaded 1,960; airports (1998) with scheduled flights 2.

Communications

Medium	date	unit	number	units per 1,000 persons
Daily newspapers	1996	circulation	3,000	46
Radio	1997	receivers	42,000	560
Television	1998	receivers	12,000	149
Telephones	1999	main lines	16,635	207
Cellular telephones	1999	subscribers	16,316	203
Internet	1998	users	2,000	25

Education and health

Educational attainment (1994). Percentage of population age 12 and over having: primary education 37.0%; some secondary 16.8%; complete secondary 19.0%; vocational 15.2%; postsecondary 3.0%; not stated 9.0%. *Literacy* (1994): total population age 12 and over literate 49,136 (87.5%); males literate 24,086 (86.3%); females literate 25,050 (88.6%).

Education (2000)

	schools	teachers	students	student/ teacher ratio
Primary (age 6–15)	25	708	10,026	14.2
Secondary (age 16–18)	13	535	7,742	14.5
Voc., teacher tr.	1[8]	134	1,818	13.6

Health (1999): physicians 104 (1 per 773 persons); hospital beds 445 (1 per 181 persons); infant mortality rate per 1,000 live births (2000) 17.7.
Food (1999): daily per capita caloric intake 2,422 (vegetable products 82%, animal products 18%); 104% of FAO recommended minimum requirement.

Military

Total active duty personnel (2000): 450[9]. *Military expenditure as percentage of GNP* (1997): 3.8% (world 2.6%); per capita expenditure U.S.$194.

[1]Creole, English, and French are all national languages per 1993 constitution. [2]Excludes unemployed, self-employed, and domestic workers. [3]Mining, manufacturing includes Public utilities. [4]Import duties less bank service charges. [5]Includes SR 194,200,000 of reexports. [6]Items reexported. [7]Domestic exports only. [8]1994. [9]All services form part of the army.

Internet resources for further information:
- **Seychelles in Figures http://www.seychelles.net/hendrick**

Sierra Leone

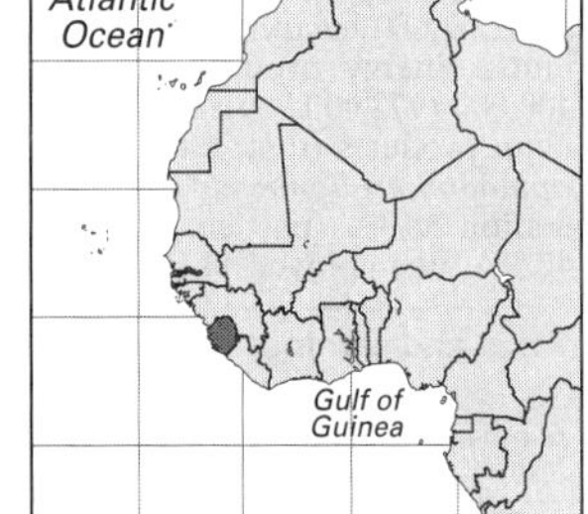

Official name: Republic of Sierra Leone.
Form of government: republic with one legislative body (Parliament [80[1]])[2].
Head of state and government: President.
Capital: Freetown.
Official language: English.
Official religion: none.
Monetary unit: 1 leone (Le) = 100 cents; valuation (Sept. 28, 2001) 1 U.S.$ = Le 1,967; 1 £ = Le 2,891.

Area and population		area		population
Provinces				1985
Districts	**Capitals**	sq mi	sq km	census[3]
Eastern Province	Kenema	6,005	15,553	960,551
Kailahun	Kailahun	1,490	3,859	233,839
Kenema	Kenema	2,337	6,053	337,055
Kono	Sefadu	2,178	5,641	389,657
Northern Province	Makeni	13,875	35,936	1,259,641
Bombali	Makeni	3,083	7,985	317,729
Kambia	Kambia	1,200	3,108	186,231
Koinaduga	Kabala	4,680	12,121	183,286
Port Loko	Port Loko	2,208	5,719	329,344
Tonkolili	Magburaka	2,704	7,003	243,051
Southern Province	Bo	7,604	19,694	741,377
Bo	Bo	2,015	5,219	268,671
Bonthe (incl. Sherbro)	Bonthe	1,339	3,468	105,007
Moyamba	Moyamba	2,665	6,902	250,514
Pujehun	Pujehun	1,585	4,105	117,185
Western Area[4]	Freetown	215	557	554,243
TOTAL		27,699	71,740	3,515,812

Demography

Population (2001): 5,427,000[5].
Density (2001): persons per sq mi 195.9, persons per sq km 75.6.
Urban-rural (2000): urban 36.6%; rural 63.4%.
Sex distribution (2000): male 48.44%; female 51.56%.
Age breakdown (2000): under 15, 44.7%; 15–29, 26.1%; 30–44, 14.9%; 45–59, 9.2%; 60–74, 4.3%; 75 and over, 0.8%.
Population projection: (2010) 6,930,000; (2020) 8,820,000.
Doubling time: 27 years.
Ethnic composition (2000): Mende 26.0%; Temne 24.6%; Limba 7.1%; Kuranko 5.5%; Kono 4.2%; Fulani 3.8%; Bullom-Sherbro 3.5%; other 25.3%.
Religious affiliation (2000): Sunnī Muslim 45.9%; traditional beliefs 40.4%; Christian 11.4%; other 2.3%.
Major cities (1985): Freetown 469,776; Koidu-New Sembehun 80,000; Bo 26,000; Kenema 13,000; Makeni 12,000.

Vital statistics

Birth rate per 1,000 population (2000): 45.6 (world avg. 22.5).
Death rate per 1,000 population (2000): 19.6 (world avg. 9.0).
Natural increase rate per 1,000 population (2000): 26.0 (world avg. 13.5).
Total fertility rate (avg. births per childbearing woman; 2000): 6.1.
Life expectancy at birth (2000): male 42.4 years; female 48.2 years.
Major causes of death per 100,000 population: n.a.; however, the major diseases are malaria, tuberculosis, leprosy, measles, tetanus, and diarrhea.

National economy

Budget (1996–97). Revenue: Le 85,708,000,000 (customs duties 47.4%; excise taxes 25.4%; corporate income tax 9.5%; personal income tax 7.3%). Expenditures: Le 143,293,000,000 (recurrent expenditures 75.6%, of which transfers 24.4%, wages and salaries 19.8%, goods and services 18.9%, debt service 12.5%; capital expenditures 24.4%).
Gross national product (1999): U.S.$653,000,000 (U.S.$130 per capita).
Production (metric tons except as noted). Agriculture, forestry, fishing (1999):

Structure of gross domestic product and labour force	1994–95		1997	
	in value Le '000,000	% of total value	labour force	% of labour force
Agriculture	275,327.5	38.8	1,052,000	63.8
Mining	119,229.2	16.8		
Manufacturing	61,475.3	8.6	297,000	18.0
Construction	15,788.2	2.2		
Public utilities	2,816.8	0.4		
Transp. and commun.	61,267.5	8.6		
Trade[6]	98,270.1	13.8		
Finance	14,732.2	2.1	300,000	18.2
Pub. admin., defense	19,844.9	2.8		
Services	12,308.9	1.7		
Other	29,329.7[7]	4.2[7]		
TOTAL	710,389.3[8]	100.0	1,649,000	100.0

rice 247,235, cassava 239,597, oil palm fruit 163,000, pulses 40,000, peanuts (groundnuts) 29,010, plantains 26,000, tomatoes 25,000, sugarcane 21,000, sweet potatoes 20,000, coffee 17,350, sorghum 17,200, cacao beans 10,920, mangoes 6,500, millet 4,725; livestock (number of live animals) 400,000 cattle, 350,000 sheep, 190,000 goats, 52,000 pigs; roundwood (1998) 3,315,000 cu m; fish catch (1998) 52,700. Mining and quarrying (1997)[9]: bauxite (1994) 735,000; rutile and ilmenite (titanium ores) (1994) 184,000; diamonds 104,000 carats; gold 322 troy oz. Manufacturing (value added in Le '000,000; 1993): food 36,117; chemicals 10,560; earthenware 1,844; printing and publishing 1,171; metal products 1,073; furniture 647. Construction (value added in Le; 1994–95): 15,788,200,000. Energy production (consumption): electricity (kW-hr; 1996) 241,000,000 (241,000,000); crude petroleum (barrels; 1996) none (1,657,000); petroleum products (metric tons; 1996) 173,000 (128,000).
Household income and expenditure. Average household size (1998) 6.3; average annual income per household (1984): U.S.$320; sources of income (1984): self-employment 61.6%, wages and salaries 27.9%, other 10.5%; expenditure (1989): food 66.2%, clothing 9.9%, housing 5.8%, transportation 4.4%, household goods 4.0%, recreation and education 3.8%, health 3.5%.
Public debt (external, outstanding; 1999): U.S.$938,000,000.
Population economically active (1996): total 1,610,000; activity rate of total population 34.8% (participation rates [1991]: ages 10–64, 53.3%; female 32.4%; unemployed [registered; 1992] 10.6%).

Price index (1995 = 100)	1994	1995	1996	1997	1998	1999	2000
Consumer price index	79.4	100.0	123.1	141.5	191.8	257.2	255.1

Tourism (1999): receipts U.S.$8,000,000; expenditures U.S.$4,000,000.
Land use (1994): forest 28.5%; pasture 30.7%; agriculture 7.5%; other 33.3%.

Foreign trade[10]

Balance of trade (current prices)	1995	1996	1997	1998	1999	2000
Le '000,000	−84,480	−150,622	−64,598	−137,744	−142,509	−287,868
% of total	70.1%	63.6%	67.7%	86.8%	86.3%	84.3%

Imports (1999): Le 153,856,000,000 (1995–96; food and live animals 51.6%; fuels 11.6%; chemicals 10.2%; machinery and transport equipment 8.9%; beverages and tobacco 2.7%; crude minerals 2.5%). *Major import sources* (1998): U.K. 20.0%; U.S. 13.0%; Belgium 7.5%; Italy 6.5%; Nigeria 5.5%.
Exports (1999): Le 11,347,000,000 (1995–96; mineral exports 56.4%, of which diamonds 50.6%, rutile [titanium ore] 5.7%; cocoa 5.0%; coffee 3.7%; reexports 4.8%). *Major export destinations* (1999): Belgium 40.8%; United States 7.5%; Spain 6.1%; U.K. 4.1%.

Transport and communications

Transport. Railroads (1995): length 52 mi, 84 km. Roads (1996): total length 7,270 mi, 11,700 km (paved 11%). Vehicles (1996): passenger cars 17,640; trucks and buses 10,890. Air transport (1996): passenger-mi 15,000,000, passenger-km 24,000,000; short ton-mi cargo 1,400,000, metric ton-km cargo 2,000,000; airports (1998) with scheduled flights 1.

Communications				units
				per 1,000
Medium	date	unit	number	persons
Daily newspapers	1996	circulation	20,000	4.7
Radio	1997	receivers	1,121,000	253
Television	1998	receivers	60,000	13
Telephones	1998	main lines	17,000	3.8
Personal computers	1999	units	100	—
Internet	1999	users	2,000	0.4

Education and health

Educational attainment (1985). Percentage of population age 5 and over having: no formal schooling 64.1%; primary education 18.7%; secondary 9.7%; higher 1.5%. *Literacy* (1995): total population age 15 and over literate 791,000 (31.4%); males literate 555,000 (45.4%); females 236,000 (18.2%).

Education (1992–93)	schools	teachers	students	student/ teacher ratio
Primary (age 5–11)	1,643	10,595	267,425	25.2
Secondary (age 12–18)	167	4,313	70,900	16.4
Voc., teacher tr.	44	709	7,756	10.9
Higher[11]	2	257	2,571	10.0

Health: physicians (1996) 339 (1 per 13,696 persons); hospital beds (1988) 4,025 (1 per 980 persons); infant mortality rate per 1,000 live births (2000) 148.7.
Food (1999): daily per capita caloric intake 2,017 (vegetable products 96%, animal products 4%); 88% of FAO recommended minimum requirement.

Military

Total active duty personnel (2000): 3,000 (army *c.* 93%, navy *c.* 7%, air force, none)[12]. *Military expenditure as percentage of GNP* (1997): 5.9% (world 2.6%); per capita expenditure U.S.$10.

[1]Includes 12 paramount chiefs elected to represent each of the provincial districts. [2]Attempts by UN forces to implement the peace agreement signed July 1999 ending nine years of civil war were only partially successful as of October 2001. [3]Preliminary figures exclude adjustment for underenumeration; adjusted total is 3,760,000. [4]Not officially a province; the administration of the Western Area is split among Greater Freetown (the city and its suburbs) and other administrative bodies. [5]Includes about 200,000 (mid-2001) Sierra Leonean refugees in neighbouring countries (mostly Guinea). [6]Includes hotels. [7]Import duties less imputed bank service charges. [8]Detail does not add to total given because of rounding. [9]All mining and quarrying production was suspended or greatly reduced after 1994 because of the civil war. [10]Import c.i.f.; exports f.o.b. [11]1990–91. [12]UN troops authorized from October 1999 numbered 13,500 in June 2001.

Internet resources for further information:
- **Sierra Leone Web http://www.Sierra-Leone.org**
- **Sierra Leone on the Web http://www.sierra-leone.gov.sl**

Singapore

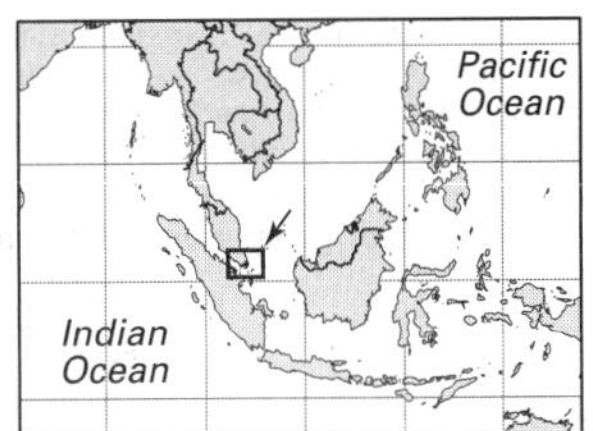

Official name: Hsin-chia-p'o Kung-ho-kuo (Mandarin Chinese); Republik Singapura (Malay); Singapore Kudiyarasu (Tamil); Republic of Singapore (English).
Form of government: unitary multiparty republic with one legislative house (Parliament [93[1]]).
Chief of state: President.
Head of state government: Prime Minister.
Capital: Singapore.
Official languages: Chinese; Malay; Tamil; English.
Official religion: none.
Monetary unit: 1 Singapore dollar (S$) = 100 cents; valuation (Sept. 28, 2001) 1 U.S.$ = S$1.77; 1 £ = S$2.60.

Population (1990 census)

Census division[2]	population	Census division[2]	population	Census division[2]	population
Alexandra	27,245	Henderson	18,445	Nee Soon East	58,651
Aljunied	51,669	Hong Kah Central	48,379	Nee Soon South	49,771
Ang Mo Kio	35,814	Hong Kah North	33,265	Pasir Panjang	35,824
Ayer Rajah	44,977	Hong Kah South	37,900	Paya Lebar	41,903
Bedok	22,032	Hougang	36,774	Potong Pasir	32,992
Boon Lay	39,249	Jalan Besar	28,298	Punggol	68,270
Boon Teck	22,652	Jalan Kayu	34,907	Queenstown	19,676
Braddell Heights	47,738	Joo Chiat	35,777	Radin Mas	35,730
Brickworks	10,593	Jurong	74,696	Sembawang	28,039
Bukit Batok	44,918	Kaki Bukit	32,782	Serangoon Gardens	44,702
Bukit Gombak	46,149	Kallang	34,178	Siglap	36,022
Bukit Merah	18,666	Kampong Chai Chee	33,928	Tampines East	41,474
Bukit Panjang	95,827	Kampong Glam	29,481	Tampines North	73,634
Bukit Timah	47,056	Kampong Kembangan	33,510	Tampines West	38,833
Buona Vista	23,873	Kampong Ubi	40,682	Tanah Merah	32,314
Cairnhill	48,445	Kebun Baru	36,878	Tanglin	43,544
Changi	50,003	Kim Keat	28,538	Tanjong Paper	29,217
Changkat	41,995	Kim Seng	23,683	Teck Ghee	26,622
Cheng San	27,821	Kolam Ayer	22,420	Telok Blangah	29,157
Chong Boon	32,174	Kreta Ayer	29,631	Thomson	71,345
Chong Pang	38,613	Kuo Chuan	26,968	Tiong Bahru	27,468
Chua Chu Kang	43,465	Leng Kee	28,886	Toa Payoh	22,811
Clementi	37,635	Macpherson	23,764	Ulu Pandan	42,923
Eunos	52,976	Marine Parade	31,003	West Coast	46,052
Fengshan	27,285	Moulmein	33,872	Whampoa	18,285
Geylang Serai	36,800	Mountbatten	23,891	Yio Chu Kang	28,589
Geylang West	31,560	Nee Soon Central	47,032	Yuhua	32,733
				TOTAL	3,016,379[3]

Demography

Area: 263.6 sq mi, 682.7 sq km.
Population (2001): 3,322,000[4].
Density (2001): persons per sq mi 12,602, persons per sq km 4,866.
Urban-rural: urban 100.0%.
Sex distribution (2000): male 49.96%; female 50.04%.
Age breakdown (2000): under 15, 21.5%; 15–34, 30.1%; 35–54, 33.9%; 55–74, 12.1%; 75 and over, 2.4%.
Population projection: (2010) 3,827,000; (2020) 4,570,000.
Ethnic composition (2000): Chinese 76.8%; Malay 13.9%; Indian 7.9%.
Religious affiliation (2000)[5]: Buddhist 42.5%; Muslim 14.9%; Christian 14.6%; Taoist 8.5%; Hindu 4.0%; traditional beliefs 0.6%; nonreligious 14.9%.

Vital statistics

Birth rate per 1,000 population (2000): 13.6 (world avg. 22.5).
Death rate per 1,000 population (2000): 4.5 (world avg. 9.0).
Natural increase rate per 1,000 population (2000): 9.1 (world avg. 13.5).
Total fertility rate (avg. births per childbearing woman; 2000): 1.6.
Marriage rate per 1,000 population (1999): 6.7.
Life expectancy at birth (2000): male 76.0 years; female 80.0 years.
Major causes of death per 100,000 population (1999): diseases of the circulatory system 172.6; malignant neoplasms (cancers) 128.3; diseases of the respiratory system 54.6; accidents and violence 17.8.

National economy

Budget (2000). Revenue: S$33,526,600,000 (income tax 40.0%, nontax revenue 24.6%, goods and services tax 6.7%, motor vehicle taxes 6.5%, customs and excise duties 5.3%). Expenditures: S$18,896,900,000 (security 47.0%, education 20.6%, communications 12.8%, health 5.2%, trade and industry 2.1%).
Production (metric tons except as noted). Agriculture, forestry, fishing (2000): vegetables and fruits 4,811; livestock (number of live animals) 2,000,000 chickens; fish catch (1999) 6,489. Mining and quarrying (value of output in S$; 1994): granite 75,800,000. Manufacturing (value added in S$'000,000; 1996): electronic products 16,982.1; chemical products 3,326.5; machinery and equipment 2,623.3; transport equipment 2,216.1; fabricated metal products 2,121.1; petroleum products 2,038.3. Construction (starts; 2000): residential 1,472,000 sq m; nonresidential 1,272,000 sq m. Energy production (consumption): electricity (kW-hr; 1996) 23,458,000,000 (23,458,000,000); crude petroleum (barrels; 1996) none (432,000,000); petroleum products (metric tons; 1996) 51,025,000 (20,777,000).
Tourism (1999): receipts U.S.$5,974,000,000; expenditures U.S.$2,749,000,000.
Population economically active (2000): total 2,192,300; activity rate of total population 67.2% (participation rates: ages 15 and over, 85.6%; female 55.5%; unemployed 3.5%).

Price and earnings indexes (1995 = 100)

	1994	1995	1996	1997	1998	1999	2000
Consumer price index	98.3	100.0	101.4	103.4	103.1	103.2	104.6
Monthly earnings index	94.0	100.0	105.8	111.8	114.9	118.0	128.4

Gross national product (1999): U.S.$95,429,000,000 (U.S.$29,660 per capita).

Structure of gross domestic product and labour force

	2000			
	in value S$'000,000[6]	% of total value[6]	labour force[7]	% of labour force[7]
Agriculture Quarrying	190.8	0.1	12,600	0.6
Manufacturing	36,974.4	26.5	434,900	20.8
Construction	9,555.2	6.8	274,000	13.1
Public utilities	2,333.9	1.7	...	...
Transp. and commun.	19,557.0	14.0	196,500	9.4
Trade	27,272.2	19.5	401,300	19.2
Finance	35,666.1	25.5	322,500	15.4
Services	14,990.5	10.7	452,500	21.6
Other	–6,700.6[8]	–4.8[8]	500	—
TOTAL	139,839.5	100.0	2,094,800	100.0[9]

Household income and expenditure. Average household size (2000) 3.7; income per household (2000) S$59,316 (U.S.$34,406); sources of income: n.a.; expenditure (1998): food 23.7%, transportation and communications 22.8%, housing costs and furnishings 21.6%, education 6.9%, clothing and footwear 4.1%, health 3.3%, other 17.6%.

Foreign trade[10]

Balance of trade (current prices)

	1995	1996	1997	1998	1999	2000
S$'000,000	–8,802	–8,912	–10,993	+8,896	+6,147	+5,651
% of total	2.6%	2.5%	2.4%	2.5%	1.6%	1.2%

Imports (2000): S$232,175,000,000 (office machines 12.4%, crude petroleum 6.5%, petroleum products 5.6%, telecommunications apparatus 4.7%, electric power machinery 4.7%, scientific instruments 3.7%, industrial machinery 2.1%). *Major import sources* (1999): U.S. 17.0%; Japan 16.6%; Malaysia 15.6%; China 5.1%; Thailand 4.7%; Taiwan 4.0%; South Korea 3.8%.
Exports (2000): S$237,826,000,000 (office machines 22.6%, petroleum products 7.2%, telecommunications apparatus 5.5%, electrical generators 3.4%, optical instruments 2.6%, industrial machinery 1.4%, clothing 1.3%). *Major export destinations* (1999): U.S. 19.2%; Malaysia 16.6%; Hong Kong 7.7%; Japan 7.4%; Taiwan 4.9%; Thailand 4.4%; United Kingdom 3.7%.

Transport and communications

Transport. Railroads (2000): length 117 km. Roads (1997): total length 3,017 km (paved 97%). Vehicles (2000): passenger cars 413,545; trucks and buses 147,325. Air transport (1999): passenger-km 64,528,800,000; metric ton-km cargo 5,481,708,000; airports (2000) 1.

Communications

Medium	date	unit	number	units per 1,000 persons[11]
Daily newspapers	2000	circulation	1,197,301	367
Radio	1997	receivers	2,550,000	821
Television	1999	receivers	1,200,000	373
Telephones	2000	main lines	1,936,000	593
Cellular telephones	2000	subscribers	2,442,000	748
Personal computers	1999	units	1,700,000	528
Internet	2000	users	1,940,000	595

Education and health

Educational attainment (2000)[11]. Percentage of population age 15 and over having: no schooling 19.6%; primary education 23.1%; secondary 39.5%; postsecondary 17.8%. *Literacy* (1995)[11]: total population age 15 and over literate 90.8%; males literate 95.6%; females literate 86.1%.

Education (2000)

	schools	teachers	students	student/ teacher ratio
Primary (age 6–11)	201	12,287	305,992	24.5
Secondary (age 12–18)	180	11,340	201,107	17.7
Voc., teacher tr.	10	1,257	15,974	12.7
Higher	8	7,318	111,538	15.2

Health (2000): physicians 5,577 (1 per 585[11] persons); hospital beds 11,798 (1 per 277[11] persons); infant mortality rate per 1,000 live births 2.5.
Food (1988–90): daily per capita caloric intake 3,121 (vegetable products 76%, animal products 24%); 136% of FAO recommended minimum requirement.

Military

Total active duty personnel (2000): 60,500 (army 82.7%, navy 7.4%, air force 9.9%). *Military expenditure as percentage of GNP* (1997): 5.7% (world 2.6%); per capita expenditure U.S.$1,665.

[1]Includes 10 nonelective seats. [2]The census divisions have no administrative function. [3]Preliminary de facto census figure; 2000 preliminary de facto census total equals 4,017,733. [4]De jure population including citizens (3,010,000) and permanent residents; total estimated population in 2001 including nonresidents equals 4,130,000. [5]De jure population aged 15 years and over. [6]At prices of 1990. [7]Employed only. [8]Imputed bank service charges. [9]Detail does not add to total given because of rounding. [10]Imports c.i.f., exports f.o.b. [11]De jure population.

Internet resources for further information:

- **Statistics Singapore http://www.singstat.gov.sg**

Slovakia

Official name: Slovenská Republika (Slovak Republic).
Form of government: unitary multiparty republic with one legislative house (National Council [150]).
Chief of state: President.
Head of government: Prime Minister.
Capital: Bratislava.
Official language: Slovak.
Official religion: none.
Monetary unit: 1 Slovak koruna (Sk) = 100 halura; valuation (Sept. 28, 2001) 1 U.S.$ = Sk 47.93; 1 £ = Sk 70.45.

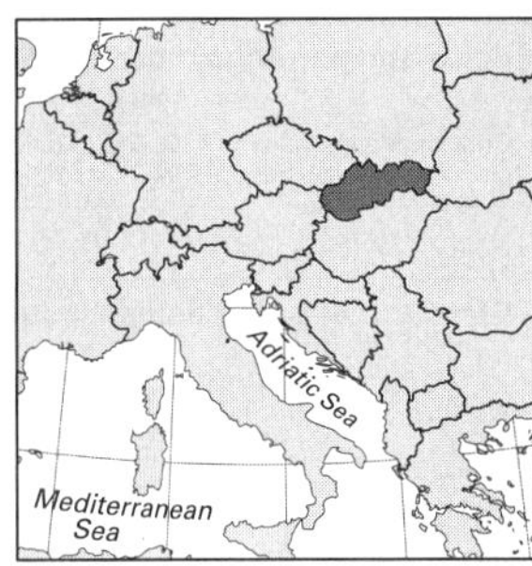

Area and population

Regions[1]	Capitals	area sq mi	area sq km	population 2001 census
Banská Bystrica	Banská Bystrica	3,651	9,455	662,121
Bratislava	Bratislava	793	2,053	599,015
Košice	Košice	2,607	6,753	766,012
Nitra	Nitra	2,449	6,343	713,422
Prešov	Prešov	3,472	8,993	789,968
Trenčín	Trenčín	1,738	4,501	605,582
Trnava	Trnava	1,602	4,148	551,003
Žilina	Žilina	2,621	6,788	692,332
TOTAL		18,933	49,035[3]	5,379,455[3]

Demography

Population (2001): 5,410,000[4].
Density (2001): persons per sq mi 285.7, persons per sq km 110.3.
Urban-rural (1998): urban 60.2%; rural 39.8%.
Sex distribution (2001[5]): male 48.61%; female 51.39%.
Age breakdown (2000[5]): under 15, 19.8%; 15–29, 24.9%; 30–44, 21.8%; 45–59, 18.1%; 60–74, 11.0%; 75 and over, 4.4%.
Population projection: (2010) 5,480,000; (2020) 5,559,000.
Doubling time: not applicable; population growth is negligible.
Ethnic composition (2000[5]): Slovak 85.6%; Hungarian 10.5%; Rom (Gypsy) 1.7%; Czech 1.1%; Ruthenian and Ukrainian 0.6%; other 0.5%.
Religious affiliation (1991): Roman Catholic 60.4%; nonreligious and atheist 9.8%; Protestant 8.0%, of which Slovak Evangelical 6.2%, Reformed Christian 1.6%; Greek Catholic 3.4%; Eastern Orthodox 0.7%; other 17.7%.
Major cities (2000[5]): Bratislava 448,292; Košice 241,874; Prešov 93,977; Nitra 87,591; Žilina 86,818; Banská Bystrica 84,272.

Vital statistics

Birth rate per 1,000 population (2000): 10.2 (world avg. 22.5); (1999) legitimate 83.1%; illegitimate 16.9%.
Death rate per 1,000 population (2000): 9.8 (world avg. 9.0).
Natural increase rate per 1,000 population (2000): 0.4 (world avg. 13.5).
Total fertility rate (avg. births per childbearing woman; 2000): 1.3.
Marriage rate per 1,000 population (1999): 5.1.
Divorce rate per 1,000 population (1999): 1.8.
Life expectancy at birth (2000): male 69.7 years; female 78.0 years.
Major causes of death per 100,000 population (1997): diseases of the circulatory system 529; malignant neoplasms (cancers) 209; diseases of the respiratory system 70; diseases of the digestive system 41.

National economy

Budget (1998). Revenue: Sk 304,100,000,000 (tax revenue 87.5%, of which social security contribution 33.0%, value-added tax 18.2%, income tax 14.0%; nontax revenue 12.5%). Expenditures: Sk 340,200,000,000 (current expenditure 86.1%, of which social welfare 31.6%, wages 16.6%, health 13.1%, debt service 5.1%; investment 13.9%).
Public debt (external, outstanding; 1999): U.S.$4,457,000,000.
Production (metric tons except as noted). Agriculture, forestry, fishing (1999): sugar beets 1,405,000, wheat 1,187,000, corn [maize] 779,000, barley 724,000, potatoes 384,000, rapeseed 237,000, sunflower seeds 125,000; livestock (number of live animals) 1,592,599 pigs, 704,792 cattle, 326,199 sheep; roundwood (1998) 5,532,000 cu m; fish catch (1998) 2,531. Mining and quarrying (1998): iron ore 899,000; gold 10,900 troy oz. Manufacturing (1998): crude steel 3,700,000; pig iron 3,100,000; cement 3,000,000; plastic and resins 405,270[6]; flour 328,000[6]; nitrogenous fertilizers 226,102[6]; aluminum ingot 108,000; beer 5,577,000 hectolitres[6]. Construction (1997): residential 281,298 dwellings. Energy production (consumption): electricity (kW-hr; 1998) 25,465,000,000 (21,020,000,000); coal (metric tons; 1996) 3,829,000 (7,142,000); crude petroleum (barrels; 1997) 462,800 (38,497,000); petroleum products (metric tons; 1996) 3,930,000 (2,134,000); natural gas (cu m; 1997) 284,000,000 (5,743,400,000).
Population economically active (1999): total 2,662,000; activity rate of total population 47.6% (participation rates [1997]: ages 15–64, 76.8%; female 67.3%; unemployed [1999] 17.1%).

Price and earnings indexes (1995 = 100)

	1995	1996	1997	1998	1999	2000	2001[7]
Consumer price index	100.0	105.8	112.3	119.8	132.5	148.4	159.8
Annual earnings index	100.0	114.6	127.2	136.1	148.3	162.0	177.6

Household income and expenditure. Average household size (1997) 3.2; income per household (1997) Sk 74,052 (U.S.$2,194); sources of income (1999): wages and salaries 62.4%, transfer payments 25.6%; expenditure (1999): food, beverages, and tobacco 31.0%, housing and energy 14.6%, transportation and communications 10.4%, clothing and footwear 8.6%.
Gross national product (1999): U.S.$20,318,000,000 (U.S.$3,770 per capita).

Structure of gross domestic product and labour force

	1999 in value Sk '000,000	1999 % of total value	1998 labour force	1998 % of labour force
Agriculture	33,200	4.3	183,253	8.9
Mining and manufacturing	185,600	23.8	553,877	26.9
Construction	31,300	4.0	154,427	7.5
Public utilities	30,000	3.8	55,594	2.7
Transp. and commun.	68,200	8.8	152,368	7.4
Trade	168,600	21.6	350,034	17.0
Finance	[8]	[8]	172,958	8.4
Pub. admin., defense	94,300	12.1	436,513	21.2
Services	128,000[8]	16.4[8]		
Other	40,000[9]	5.1[9]		
TOTAL	779,300[2]	100.0[2]	2,059,024[10]	100.0[10]

Land use (1994): forested 40.6%; meadows and pastures 17.0%; agricultural and under permanent cultivation 32.9%; other 9.5%.

Foreign trade

Balance of trade (current prices)

	1995	1996	1997	1998	1999	2000
U.S.$'000,000	–228	–2,293	–2,081	–2,353	–1,093	–897
% of total	1.3%	11.5%	9.7%	9.9%	5.1%	3.6%

Imports (1999): U.S.$11,321,000,000 (machinery and transport equipment 37.7%; semimanufactured products 18.3%; mineral fuels 12.9%; chemicals and chemical products 11.3%). *Major import sources* (2000): Germany 25.0%; Czech Republic 18.7%; Russia 17.0%; Italy 6.2%; Austria 3.9%.
Exports (1999): U.S.$10,229,000,000 (machinery and transport equipment 39.5%; manufactured goods 27.3%; chemicals and chemical products 7.9%; mineral fuels 4.8%). *Major export destinations* (2000): Germany 26.7%; Czech Republic 20.0%; Italy 9.1%; Austria 8.3%; Poland 5.8%; Hungary 4.8%.

Transport and communications

Transport. Railroads (1997): length 3,673 km; passenger-km 3,057,000,000; metric ton-km cargo 12,373,000,000. Roads (1997): total length 17,627 km (paved, n.a.). Vehicles (1997): passenger cars 1,135,914; trucks and buses 100,254. Merchant marine: n.a. Air transport (1997): passenger-km 231,396,000; metric ton-km cargo 729,000; airports (1998) with scheduled flights 2.

Communications

Medium	date	unit	number	units per 1,000 persons
Daily newspapers	1996	circulation	989,000	184
Television	1999	receivers	2,250,000	417
Telephones	1999	main lines	1,655,000	307
Cellular telephones	1999	subscribers	918,039	170
Personal computers	1999	units	590,000	109
Internet	1999	users	600,000	111

Education and health

Educational attainment (1991). Percentage of adult population having: incomplete primary education 0.7%; primary and incomplete secondary 37.9%; complete secondary 50.9%; higher 9.5%; unknown 1.0%. *Literacy* (1997): total population age 15 and over literate 4,253,972 (100%).

Education (1997–98)

	schools	teachers	students	student/ teacher ratio
Primary (age 6–14)	2,482	39,535	645,941	16.3
Secondary (age 15–18)	198	5,849	80,116	13.7
Voc., teacher tr.	365	10,104	116,681	11.5
Higher	18	8,544	83,942	9.8

Health (1997): physicians 17,940 (1 per 300 persons); hospital beds 61,288 (1 per 88 persons); infant mortality rate per 1,000 live births (2000) 8.3.
Food (1998): daily per capita caloric intake 2,953 (vegetable products 72%, animal products 28%); 121% of FAO recommended minimum requirement.

Military

Total active duty personnel (2000): 38,600 (army 61.7%, air force 29.8%, headquarters staff 8.5%). *Military expenditure as percentage of GNP* (1997): 2.1% (world 2.6%); per capita expenditure U.S.$167.

[1]Based on administrative reorganization effective from July 1996. [2]Detail does not add to total given because of rounding. [3]De jure figure; 2001 de facto census total equals 5,193,376. [4]De jure estimate not adjusted for May 2001 de jure census results. [5]January 1. [6]1997. [7]May. [8]Services include finance. [9]Bank service charges and indirect taxes. [10]Excluding 407,000 unemployed and women on regular and additional maternity leave and including employees with a second job.

Internet resources for further information:
- **Statistical Office of the Slovak Republic http://www.statistics.sk**
- **National Bank of Slovakia http://www.nbs.sk**

Slovenia

Official name: Republika Slovenija (Republic of Slovenia).
Form of government: unitary multiparty republic with two legislative houses (National Council [40]; National Assembly [90]).
Head of state: President.
Head of government: Prime Minister.
Capital: Ljubljana.
Official language[1]: Slovene.
Official religion: none.
Monetary unit: 1 Slovene tolar (SIT; plural tolarji) = 100 stotin; valuation (Sept. 28, 2001) 1 U.S.$ = 241.71 tolarji; 1 £ = 355.23 tolarji.

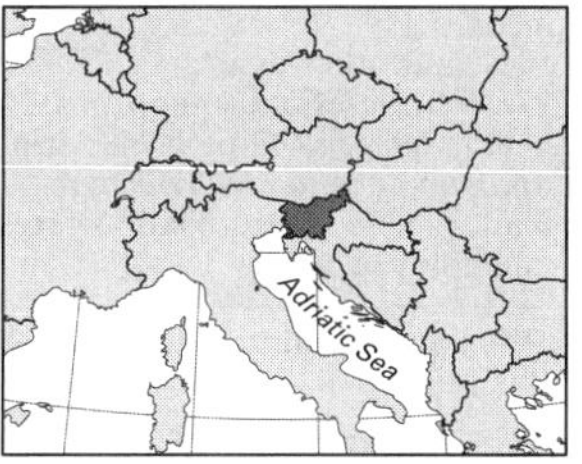

Area and population

Statistical regions[2]	Principal cities	area sq mi	area sq km	population 1998 estimate
Dolenjska	Novo mesto	653	1,690	105,926
Gorenjska	Kranj	825	2,137	195,580
Goriška	Nova Gorica	898	2,325	119,967
Koroška	Ravne na Koroškem	401	1,041	73,961
Notranjsko-kraška	Postojna	562	1,456	50,163
Obalno Kraško	Koper	403	1,044	102,565
Osrednjeslovenska	Ljubljana	1,367	3,540	517,022
Podravska	Maribor	838	2,170	319,617
Pomurska	Murska Sobota	516	1,337	125,441
Savinjska	Celje	920	2,384	255,541
Spodnjeposavska	Krško	342	885	70,187
Zasavska	Trbovlje	102	264	46,633
TOTAL		7,827	20,273	1,982,603

Demography

Population (2001): 1,991,000.
Density (2001): persons per sq mi 254.4, persons per sq km 98.2.
Urban-rural (1999): urban 50.3%; rural 49.7%.
Sex distribution (2000): male 48.84%; female 51.16%.
Age breakdown (2000): under 15, 16.1%; 15–29, 21.9%; 30–44, 23.4%; 45–59, 19.6%; 60–74, 14.0%; 75 and over, 5.0%.
Population projection: (2010) 2,006,000; (2020) 1,985,000.
Ethnic composition (1991): Slovene 87.8%; Croat 2.8%; Serb 2.4%; Bosnian Muslim 1.4%; Hungarian 0.4%; other 5.2%.
Religious affiliation (1995): Christian 86.2%, of which Roman Catholic 82.7%, Orthodox 2.0%, Protestant 1.3%; Muslim 1.0%; other 12.8%.
Major cities (2000[3]): Ljubljana 270,986; Maribor 115,532; Kranj 51,923; Celje 49,572; Koper 47,905.

Vital statistics

Birth rate per 1,000 population (1999): 8.8 (world avg. 22.5); legitimate 64.4%; illegitimate 35.6%.
Death rate per 1,000 population (1999): 9.5 (world avg. 9.0).
Natural increase rate per 1,000 population (1999): –0.7 (world avg. 13.5).
Total fertility rate (avg. births per childbearing woman; 1999): 1.2.
Marriage rate per 1,000 population (1999): 3.9.
Divorce rate per 1,000 population (1999): 1.1.
Life expectancy at birth (2000): male 71.0 years; female 79.0 years.
Major causes of death per 100,000 population (1999): diseases of the circulatory system 390.8; malignant neoplasms (cancers) 247.3; diseases of the respiratory system 79.6; accidents and violence 74.8.

National economy

Budget (2000). Revenue: SIT 1,725,791,000,000 (taxes on goods and services 34.9%, social security contributions 32.0%, personal income tax 15.0%, non-tax revenue 7.3%). Expenditures: SIT 1,781,311,000,000 (current expenditures 90.4%, development expenditures 9.6%).
Public debt (external, outstanding; 2000): U.S.$2,665,000,000.
Production (metric tons except as noted). Agriculture, forestry, fishing (2000): silage 1,900,000, sugar beets 467,000, corn (maize) 308,000, potatoes 194,000, wheat 150,000, grapes 98,000, apples 81,000; livestock (number of live animals) 552,000 pigs, 471,000 cattle; roundwood (1999) 2,133,000 cu m; fish catch (1997) 3,262. Mining and quarrying (1998): ferrosilicon 10,000; kaolin 10,000. Manufacturing (value added in SIT '000,000; 1997): base and fabricated metals 89,189; food, beverages, and tobacco products 81,998; chemicals and chemical products 81,408; electrical machinery 81,068; paper and paper products and printing and publishing 60,075. Energy production (consumption): electricity (kW-hr; 1999) 12,456,000,000 (10,432,000,000); coal (metric tons; 1998) 5,200,000 ([1997] 5,456,000); crude petroleum (barrels; 1999) 6,000 ([1996] 3,335,000); petroleum products (metric tons; 1996) 389,000 ([1998] 2,328,000); natural gas (cu m; 1999) 5,700,000 (996,000,000).
Land use (1994): forest 53.2%; pasture 24.8%; agricultural 11.6%; other 10.4%.
Household income and expenditure (1999). Average household size 2.8[4]; income per household SIT 2,557,500 (U.S.$14,070); sources of income: wages 58.8%, transfers 29.7%, self-employment 7.0%, other 4.5%; expenditure: transportation and communications 18.9%, food and beverages 18.6%, housing 11.3%, recreation 8.2%, clothing and footwear 8.1%.
Gross national product (at current market prices; 1999): U.S.$19,862,000,000 (U.S.$10,000 per capita).

Structure of gross domestic product and labour force

	1999 in value SIT '000,000	% of total value	labour force[5]	% of labour force[5]
Agriculture, forestry	115,484	3.2	96,000	10.0
Mining	36,503	1.0	6,000	0.6
Manufacturing	866,778	23.8	278,000	28.9
Construction	193,157	5.3	45,000	4.7
Public utilities	96,060	2.6	8,000	0.8
Transp. and commun.	256,337	7.0	54,000	5.6
Trade, restaurants	457,620	12.6	143,000	14.9
Finance, real estate	517,280	14.2	70,000	7.3
Pub. admin., defense	180,101	5.0	49,000	5.1
Services	459,667	12.6	141,000	14.7
Other	458,450[6]	12.6[6]	71,000[7]	7.4[7]
TOTAL	3,637,437	100.0[8]	963,000[8]	100.0

Population economically active (1998): total 967,000; activity rate 49.6% (participation rates: ages 15–64, 69.1%; female 46.3%; unemployed[9] [2000] 12.2%).

Price and earnings indexes (1995 = 100)

	1995	1996	1997	1998	1999	2000	2001
Consumer price index	100.0	109.8	119.0	128.4	136.3	148.4	156.3[10]
Annual earnings index	100.0	114.8	128.0	140.3	153.5	169.4	...

Tourism (2000): receipts U.S.$957,000,000; expenditures U.S.$517,000,000.

Foreign trade[11]

Balance of trade (current prices)

	1995	1996	1997	1998	1999	2000
U.S.$'000,000	–1,176	–1,111	–985	–1,062	–1,537	–1,384
% of total	6.6%	6.3%	5.6%	5.5%	8.3%	7.3%

Imports (2000): U.S.$10,115,000,000 (machinery and transport equipment 34.2%, other manufactured goods 21.9%, chemicals and chemical products 12.4%, mineral fuels 9.1%, food products 5.1%). *Major import sources:* Germany 19.0%; Italy 17.4%; France 10.3%; Austria 8.2%; Croatia 4.4%.
Exports (2000): U.S.$8,731,000,000 (machinery and transport equipment 36.0%, other manufactured goods 27.3%, chemicals and chemical products 11.2%, food products 2.3%). *Major export destinations:* Germany 27.2%; Italy 13.6%; Croatia 7.9%; Austria 7.5%; France 7.1%.

Transport and communications

Transport. Railroads (1999): length 746 mi, 1,201 km; passenger-km 625,-000,000; metric ton-km cargo 2,784,000,000. Roads (1999): total length 12,507 mi, 20,128 km (paved 81%). Vehicles (1999): passenger cars 829,674; trucks and buses 67,111. Air transport (1999): passenger-mi 517,000,000, passenger-km 832,000,000; short ton-mi cargo 2,849,000, metric ton-km cargo 4,160,000; airports (1999) with scheduled flights 3.

Communications

Medium	date	unit	number	units per 1,000 persons
Daily newspapers	1996	circulation	397,000	199
Radio	1997	receivers	630,000	317
Television	1998	receivers	710,000	358
Telephones	1999	main lines	786,229	399
Cellular telephones	1999	subscribers	613,780	309
Personal computers	1999	units	500,000	252
Internet	1999	users	250,000	126

Education and health

Educational attainment (1991). Percentage of population age 25 and over having: no formal schooling 0.7%; incomplete and complete primary education 45.1%; incomplete and complete secondary 42.4%; higher 10.4%; unknown 1.4%. *Literacy* (2000): 99.7%.

Education (1998–99)

	schools	teachers	students	student/ teacher ratio
Primary (age 7–14)	444	15,140	189,564	12.5
Secondary (age 15–18)	201	8,816	116,672[12]	...
Higher	...	4,482	74,642	16.7

Health (1999): physicians 4,486 (1 per 440 persons); hospital beds 10,959 (1 per 180 persons); infant mortality rate per 1,000 live births 4.5.

Military

Total active duty personnel (2000): 9,000 (army 100%). *Military expenditure as percentage of GNP* (1997): 5.2% (world 2.6%); per capita expenditure U.S.$614.

[1]Hungarian and Italian are official in autochthonous Hungarian and Italian communities. [2]Actual first-order administration is based on 192 municipalities. [3]Populations of municipalities, which may include nearby small towns and rural areas. [4]January. [5]Second quarter. [6]Corrections less imputed bank service charges. [7]Unemployed. [8]Detail does not add to total given because of rounding. [9]Registered. [10]February. [11]Imports c.i.f.; exports f.o.b. [12]1997–98.

Internet resources for further information:
- **Statistical Office of the Republic of Slovenia http://www.sigov.si/zrs/eng/index.html**
- **Bank of Slovenia http://www.bsi.si**

Solomon Islands

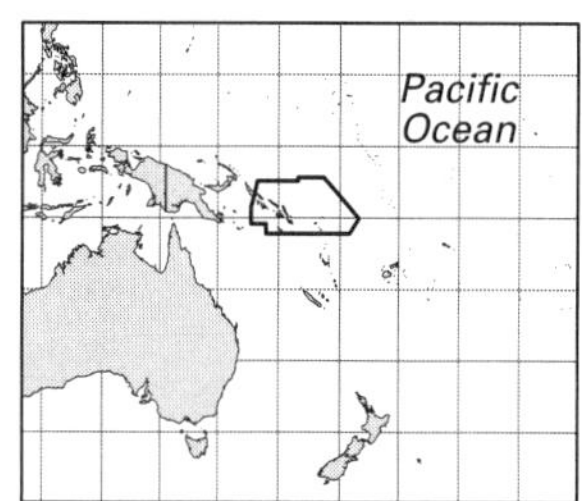

Official name: Solomon Islands.
Form of government: constitutional monarchy with one legislative house (National Parliament [50]).
Chief of state: British Monarch represented by Governor-General.
Head of government: Prime Minister.
Capital: Honiara.
Official language: English.
Official religion: none.
Monetary unit: 1 Solomon Islands dollar (SI$) = 100 cents; valuation (Sept. 28, 2001) 1 U.S.$ = SI$5.43; 1 £ = SI$7.97.

Area and population

Provinces	Capitals	area sq mi	area sq km	population 1997 estimate
Central Islands	Tulagi	237	615	30,071[1]
Choiseul	Taro	1,481	3,837	[2]
Guadalcanal	Honiara	2,060	5,336	61,243
Isabel	Buala	1,597	4,136	22,653
Makira	Kira Kira	1,231	3,188	29,110
Malaita	Auki	1,631	4,225	105,882
Rennell and Bellona	Tigoa	259	671	[1]
Temotu	Santa Cruz	334	865	21,159
Western	Gizo	2,114	5,475	95,193[2]
Capital Territory				
Honiara	—	8	22	45,610
TOTAL		10,954[3]	28,370	410,921

Demography

Population (2001): 480,000.
Density (2001): persons per sq mi 43.9, persons per sq km 16.9.
Urban-rural (1999): urban 19.0%; rural 81.0%.
Sex distribution (1996): male 51.65%; female 48.35%.
Age breakdown (1996): under 15, 43.7%; 15–29, 28.7%; 30–44, 15.2%; 45–59, 8.1%; 60–74, 3.6%; 75 and over, 0.7%.
Population projection: (2010) 610,000; (2020) 748,000.
Doubling time: 21 years.
Ethnic composition (1986): Melanesian 94.2%; Polynesian 3.7%; other Pacific Islander 1.4%; European 0.4%; Asian 0.2%; other 0.1%.
Religious affiliation (1995): Christian 85.6%, of which Protestant 67.1% (including Church of Melanesia [Anglican] 31.0%), Roman Catholic 17.4%; traditional beliefs 3.1%; other 11.3%.
Major cities (1986)[4]: Honiara 43,643[5] (urban agglomeration [1999] 68,000); Gizo 3,727; Auki 3,262; Kira Kira 2,585; Buala 1,913.

Vital statistics

Birth rate per 1,000 population (2001): 38.3 (world avg. 22.5).
Death rate per 1,000 population (2001): 4.8 (world avg. 9.0).
Natural increase rate per 1,000 population (2001): 33.5 (world avg. 13.5).
Total fertility rate (avg. births per childbearing woman; 2001): 5.4.
Marriage rate per 1,000 population: n.a.
Divorce rate per 1,000 population: n.a.
Life expectancy at birth (2001): male 68.0 years; female 70.0 years.
Major causes of death per 100,000 population (1990): respiratory diseases 22.4; diarrheal diseases 13.6; malaria 10.0.

National economy

Budget (1998). Revenue: SI$557,800,000 (foreign grants 33.0%, taxes on foreign trade 25.8%, income taxes 19.5%, taxes on goods and services 13.1%, nontax revenue 8.6%). Expenditures: SI$558,700,000 (capital expenditure 35.9%, administrative 28.6%, wages and salaries 27.2%, interest payments 8.3%).
Tourism: receipts from visitors (1999) U.S.$6,000,000; expenditures by nationals abroad U.S.$7,000,000.
Land use (1994): forested 87.5%; meadows and pastures 1.4%; agricultural and under permanent cultivation 2.0%; other 9.1%.
Gross national product (at current market prices; 1999): U.S.$320,000,000 (U.S.$750 per capita).

Structure of gross domestic product and labour force

	1996 in value SI$ '000[6]	1996 % of total value	1993 labour force[7]	1993 % of labour force
Agriculture	107,400	32.9	8,106	27.4
Mining	200	0.1	2,844	9.6
Manufacturing	11,300	3.5		
Construction	19,600	6.0	977	3.3
Public utilities	5,100	1.6	245	0.8
Transportation and communications	18,500	5.7	1,723	5.8
Trade	28,900	8.8	3,390	11.5
Finance	13,500	4.1	1,144	3.9
Pub. admin., defense	68,100	20.8	4,303	14.6
Services			6,845	23.1
Other	54,300	16.6	...	...
TOTAL	326,900	100.0[3]	29,577	100.0

Household income and expenditure. Average household size (1996) 5.8; average annual income per household[8] (1983) SI$1,010 (U.S.$1,160); sources of income (1983): wages and salaries 74.1%, self-employment, remittances, gifts, and other assistance 25.9%; expenditure (1992)[9]: food 46.8%, housing 11.0%, household operations 10.9%, transportation 9.9%, recreation and health 7.9%, clothing 5.7%, drinks and tobacco 5.0%.
Population economically active (1993): total 29,577[7]; activity rate of total population 8.3% (participation rates: ages 15–60 [1986] 98.6%; female 22.6%; unemployed n.a.).

Price and earnings indexes (1995 = 100)

	1993	1994	1995	1996	1997	1998	1999
Consumer price index	80.5	91.2	100.0	111.8	120.8	135.7	146.9
Annual earnings index[7]	142.8	...	...	...	...	...	...

Production (metric tons except as noted). Agriculture, forestry, fishing (1999): coconuts 240,000, palm oil fruit 140,000, sweet potatoes 73,000, taro 32,000, yams 24,500, vegetables and melons 6,850, cacao beans 3,454; livestock (number of live animals) 58,000 pigs, 10,000 cattle, 185,000 chickens; roundwood (1998) 872,000 cu m; fish catch (1997) 53,442. Mining and quarrying (1998): gold 33,300 troy oz. Manufacturing (1997): palm oil 30,100, copra 23,500, coconut oil 3,900, cocoa 2,200, (1996) sawnwood 12,000 cu m. Construction (gross value in SI$ in Honiara; 1994): residential 9,508,000; nonresidential 11,151,000. Energy production (consumption): electricity (kW-hr; 1996) 32,000,000 (32,000,000); coal none (n.a.); petroleum products (metric tons; 1996) none (52,000); natural gas, none (n.a.).
Public debt (external, outstanding; 1999): U.S.$120,400,000.

Foreign trade[10]

Balance of trade (current prices)

	1993	1994	1995	1996	1997	1998
U.S.$'000,000	–7.81	–0.06	+13.77	+10.96	–28.08	–18.07
% of total	2.9%	0.0%	4.3%	3.5%	8.2%	6.0%

Imports (1996): SI$536,870,000 (machinery and transport equipment 30.3%, basic manufactured goods 22.2%, food and live animals 15.1%, mineral fuels and lubricants 11.3%). *Major import sources:* Australia 44.1%; Japan 12.5%; Singapore 7.0%; United States 2.1%; Thailand 1.8%; United Kingdom 1.6%.
Exports (1996): SI$656,300,000 (timber products 60.6%, fish products 18.3%, palm oil products 10.9%, copra 4.1%, cacao beans 2.2%). *Major export destinations:* Japan 40.1%; South Korea 19.4%; United Kingdom 18.4%; Thailand 3.8%; Australia 2.3%; Singapore 2.2%.

Transport and communications

Transport. Railroads: none. Roads (1996): total length 1,360 km (paved 2.5%). Vehicles (1993): passenger cars 2,052; trucks and buses 2,574. Merchant marine (1992): vessels (100 gross tons and over) 33; total deadweight tonnage 4,985. Air transport (1999): passenger-km 47,278,000; metric ton-km cargo 1,250,000; airports (1997) with scheduled flights 21.

Communications

Medium	date	unit	number	units per 1,000 persons
Radio	1997	receivers	57,000	141
Television	1998	receivers	6,000	14
Telephones	1999	main lines	8,132	19
Cellular telephones	1999	subscribers	1,093	2.5
Personal computers	1999	units	18	0.04
Internet	1999	users	2,000	4.7

Education and health

Educational attainment (1986)[11]. Percentage of population age 25 and over having: no schooling 44.4%; primary education 46.2%; secondary 6.8%; higher 2.6%. *Literacy* (1976): total population age 15 and over literate 55,500 (54.1%); males 33,600 (62.4%); females 21,900 (44.9%).

Education (1994)

	schools	teachers	students	student/ teacher ratio
Primary (age 7–12)	520	2,510	73,120	29.1
Secondary (age 13–18)	23	618	7,981	12.9
Voc., teacher tr.[12]	1	...	...	...
Higher[12]	1	...	...	...

Health (1997): physicians 31 (1 per 13,258 persons); hospital beds 210 (1 per 1,957 persons); infant mortality rate per 1,000 live births (2001) 22.0.
Food (1999): daily per capita caloric intake 2,222 (vegetable products 92%, animal products 8%); (1997) 97% of FAO recommended minimum requirement.

Military

Total active duty personnel: no military forces are maintained, but a police force of 475 provides internal security.

[1]Central Islands includes Rennell and Bellona. [2]Western includes Choiseul. [3]Detail does not add to total given because of rounding. [4]Ward populations. [5]1996. [6]At 1985 factor cost. [7]Persons employed in the monetary sector only; 1990 = 100. [8]Public-service earnings. [9]Retail price index components. [10]Import figures are f.o.b. [11]Indigenous population only. [12]Vocational and teacher training are carried out at the College of Higher Education.

Internet resources for further information:
- **Solomon Islands Home Page http://www.solomons.com**

Somalia[1]

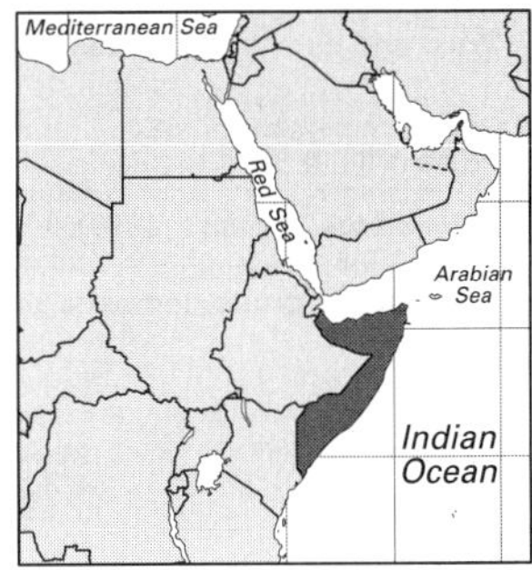

Official name: Soomaaliya (Somali)(Somalia).
Form of government: transitional regime[2] with one legislative body (Transitional National Assembly [245[3]]).
Head of state and government: President assisted by Prime Minister.
Capital: Mogadishu.
Official languages: Somali; Arabic.
Official religion: Islam.
Monetary unit: 1 Somali shilling (So.Sh.) = 100 cents; valuation (Sept. 28, 2001) 1 U.S.$ = So.Sh. 2,620[4]; 1 £ = So.Sh. 3,851.

Area and population

		area		population
				1980
Regions[5]	Capitals	sq mi	sq km	estimate
Bakool	Xuddur	10,000	27,000	148,700
Banaadir	Mogadishu (Muqdisho)	400	1,000	520,100
Bari[6]	Boosaaso	27,000	70,000	222,300
Bay	Baydhabo	15,000	39,000	451,000
Galguduud	Dhuusamarreeb	17,000	43,000	255,900
Gedo	Garbahaarrey	12,000	32,000	235,000
Hiiraan	Beledweyne	13,000	34,000	219,300
Jubbada Dhexe	Bu'aale	9,000	23,000	147,800
Jubbada Hoose	Kismaayo	24,000	61,000	272,400
Mudug[6]	Gaalkacyo	27,000	70,000	311,200
Nugaal[6]	Garoowe	19,000	50,000	112,200
Sanaag[7]	Ceerigaabo	21,000	54,000	216,500
Shabeellaha Dhexe	Jawhar	8,000	22,000	352,000
Shabeellaha Hoose	Marka	10,000	25,000	570,700
Togdheer[7]	Burao	16,000	41,000	383,900
Woqooyi Galbeed[7]	Hargeysa	17,000	45,000	655,000
TOTAL		246,000[8]	637,000	5,074,000

Demography

Population (2001): 7,489,000.
Density (2001): persons per sq mi 30.4, persons per sq km 11.8.
Urban-rural (1999): urban 27.1%; rural 72.9%.
Sex distribution (2000): male 50.18%; female 49.82%.
Age breakdown (2000): under 15, 44.4%; 15–29, 26.8%; 30–44, 17.9%; 45–59, 6.6%; 60–74, 3.5%; 75 and over, 0.8%.
Population projection: (2010) 9,922,000; (2020) 13,023,000.
Doubling time: 24 years.
Ethnic composition (1983): Somali 98.3%[9]; Arab 1.2%; Bantu 0.4%; other 0.1%.
Religious affiliation (1995): Sunnī Muslim 99.9%; other 0.1%.
Major cities (1990): Mogadishu 1,162,000[10]; Hargeysa 90,000; Kismaayo 90,000; Berbera 70,000; Marka 62,000.

Vital statistics

Birth rate per 1,000 population (2000): 47.7 (world avg. 22.5).
Death rate per 1,000 population (2000): 18.7 (world avg. 9.0).
Natural increase rate per 1,000 population (2000): 29.0 (world avg. 13.5).
Total fertility rate (avg. births per childbearing woman; 2000): 7.2.
Life expectancy at birth (2000): male 44.7 years; female 47.9 years.

National economy

Budget (1991). Revenue: So.Sh. 151,453,000,000 (domestic revenue sources, principally indirect taxes and import duties 60.4%; external grants and transfers 39.6%). Expenditures: So.Sh. 141,141,000,000 (general services 46.9%; economic and social services 31.2%; debt service 7.0%).
Public debt (external, outstanding; 1999): U.S.$1,859,000,000.
Production (metric tons except as noted). Agriculture, forestry, fishing (1999): fruits (excluding melons) 210,000, sugarcane 210,000, corn (maize) 150,000, cassava 65,000, bananas 55,000, sorghum 55,000, sesame seed 22,000, beans 14,000, dates 10,000, seed cotton 4,550, other forest products include khat, frankincense, and myrrh; livestock (number of live animals) 13,000,000 sheep, 12,000,000 goats, 6,000,000 camels, 5,000,000 cattle; roundwood (1998) 7,955,000 cu m; fish catch (1998) 16,000. Mining and quarrying (1992): salt 2,000 metric tons. Manufacturing (value added in So.Sh. '000,000; 1988): food 794; cigarettes and matches 562; hides and skins 420; paper and printing 328; plastics 320; chemicals 202; beverages 144. Construction (value added in So.Sh.; 1991): 51,100,000,000. Energy production (consumption): electricity (kW-hr; 1998) 265,000,000 (246,000,000); coal, none (n.a.); crude petroleum (barrels; 1991) n.a. (806,000); petroleum products (metric tons; 1991) none (59,000); natural gas, none (n.a.).
Household income and expenditure. Average household size (1980) 4.9; income per household: n.a.; sources of income: n.a.; expenditure (1983)[11]: food and tobacco 62.3%, housing 15.3%, clothing 5.6%, energy 4.3%, other 12.5%.
Population economically active (1991): total 3,215,000; activity rate of total population 40.9% (participation rates [1987] over age 10, 63.1%; female 48.7%; unemployed n.a.).

Price and earnings indexes (1990 = 100)

	1989	1990	1991	1992	1993	1994	1995
Consumer price index[12]	100.0	240.0	372.2	507.4	630.7	749.8	872.1
Earnings index	...	...	...	...	...	...	...

Gross national product (1996): U.S.$706,000,000 (U.S.$110 per capita).

Structure of gross domestic product and labour force

	1991			
	in value So.Sh. '000,000	% of total value	labour force	% of labour force
Agriculture	867,500	64.5	2,275,000	70.8
Mining	2,700	0.2		
Manufacturing	59,200	4.4	336,000	10.4
Construction	51,100	3.8		
Public utilities	9,400	0.7		
Transp. and commun.	80,700	6.0		
Trade	125,000	9.3		
Finance	45,700	3.4	604,000	18.8
Pub. admin., defense	80,700	6.0		
Services	30,900	2.3		
Other	–8,100	–0.6		
TOTAL	1,344,900[8]	100.0	3,215,000	100.0

Tourism: n.a.
Land use (1994): forest 25.5%; pasture 68.6%; agriculture 1.6%; other 4.3%.

Foreign trade[13]

Balance of trade (current prices)

	1993	1994	1995	1996	1997	1998
U.S.$'000,000	–146	–133	–48	–95	–112	–140
% of total	38.4%	32.8%	14.2%	21.0%	25.8%	27.2%

Imports (1998): U.S.$327,000,000 (1995; agricultural products 38.0%, of which raw sugar 16.1%, rice 7.8%, wheat 5.0%; unspecified 62.0%). *Major import sources* (1997): Djibouti 20%; Kenya 11%; Belarus 11%; India 10%; Saudi Arabia 9%; Brazil 9%.
Exports (1998): U.S.$187,000,000 (1995; agricultural products 51.4%, of which live sheep and goats 40.0%, bananas 6.9%, live camels and cattle 4.3%; other 48.6%). *Major export destinations* (1997): Saudi Arabia 57%; United Arab Emirates 15%; Italy 12%; Yemen 8%.

Transport and communications

Transport. Railroads: none. Roads (1996): total length 13,700 mi, 22,100 km (paved 12%). Vehicles (1996): passenger cars 1,020; trucks and buses 6,440. Merchant marine (1992): vessels (100 gross tons and over) 28; total deadweight tonnage 18,496. Air transport (1991): passenger-mi 81,000,000, passenger-km 131,000,000; short ton-mi cargo 3,000,000, metric ton-km cargo 5,000,000; airports (1998) with scheduled flights 1.

Communications

Medium	date	unit	number	units per 1,000 persons
Daily newspapers	1996	circulation	10,000	1.2
Radio	1997	receivers	470,000	53
Television	1997	receivers	135,000	15
Telephones	1999	main lines	15,000	2.1

Education and health

Educational attainment: n.a. *Literacy* (1995): percentage of total population age 15 and over literate 24%; males literate 36%; females literate 14%.

Education (1989–90)

	schools	teachers	students	student/ teacher ratio
Primary (age 6–14)	1,125	8,208	377,000	20.9
Secondary (age 15–18)	82	2,109	44,000	20.3
Voc., teacher tr.	21	498	10,400	9.7
Higher	1	549	4,640	...

Health: physicians (1997) 265 (1 per 25,034 persons); hospital beds (1985) 5,536 (1 per 1,130 persons); infant mortality rate (2000) 125.8.
Food (1999): daily per capita caloric intake 1,555 (vegetable products 60%, animal products 40%); 67% of FAO recommended minimum requirement.

Military

Total active duty personnel: clan warfare between 1991 and mid-2001. *Military expenditure as percentage of GNP* (1990): 0.9% (world 4.3%); per capita expenditure U.S.$1.

[1]Proclamation of the "Republic of Somaliland" in May 1991 on territory corresponding to the former British Somaliland (which unified with the former Italian Trust Territory of Somalia to form Somalia in 1960) had not received international recognition as of November 2001. This entity represented about a quarter of Somalia's territory. [2]From August 2000. [3]Includes 44 seats allotted to each of 4 major clans, 24 seats allotted to minor clans and tribes, 25 seats allotted to women, and 20 nominees of president. [4]In April 2001 about 17,000 So.Sh. equaled 1 U.S.$ on the black market. [5]Local governments operate in only a few areas in mid-2001. [6]Part of "autonomous region" of Puntland (within Somalia) from 1998. [7]Part of "Republic of Somaliland" from 1991. [8]Detail does not add to total given because of rounding. [9]The Somali are divided into six major clans, of which four are predominantly pastoral (representing *c.* 70% of the population) and two are predominantly agricultural (representing *c.* 20% of the population); the remainder are urban dwellers with less clan identification. [10]1999. [11]Mogadishu only. [12]Reported inflation rate. [13]Imports c.i.f.; exports f.o.b.

Internet resources for further information:
- **Somalia Web Page**
  http://www.abyssiniacybergateway.net/somalia

South Africa

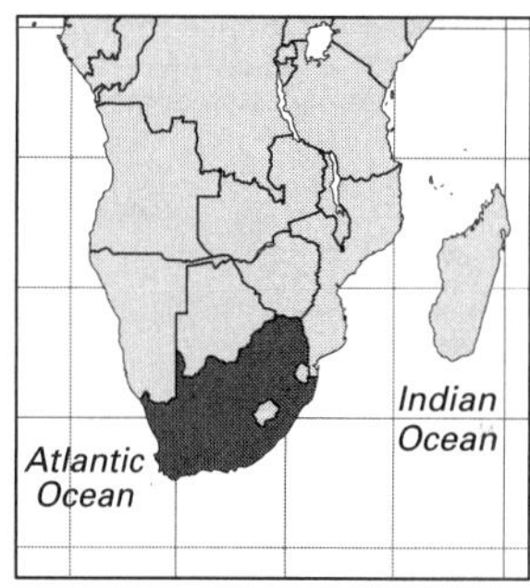

Official name: Republic of South Africa (English).
Form of government: multiparty republic with two legislative houses (National Council of Provinces [90]; National Assembly [400]).
Head of state and government: President.
Capitals (de facto): Pretoria/Tshwane[1] (executive); Bloemfontein/Mangaung[1] (judicial); Cape Town (legislative).
Official languages: [2].
Official religion: none.
Monetary unit: 1 rand (R) = 100 cents; valuation (Sept. 28, 2001) 1 U.S.$ = R 9.01; 1 £ = R 13.24.

Area and population

		area		population
Provinces	Capitals	sq mi	sq km	1999 estimate
Eastern Cape	Bisho	65,475	169,580	6,658,670
Free State	Bloemfontein	49,993	129,480	2,714,654
Gauteng	Johannesburg	6,568	17,010	7,807,273
KwaZulu–Natal	Pietermaritzburg	35,560	92,100	8,924,643
Mpumalanga	Nelspruit	30,691	79,490	3,003,327
Northern Cape	Kimberley	139,703	361,830	875,222
Northern Province	Pietersburg	47,842	123,910	5,337,267
North West	Mafikeng/Mmabatho	44,911	116,320	3,562,280
Western Cape	Cape Town	49,950	129,370	4,170,970
TOTAL		470,693	1,219,090	43,054,306

Demography

Population (2001): 43,586,000.
Density (2001): persons per sq mi 92.6, persons per sq km 35.8.
Urban-rural (1996): urban 53.7%; rural 46.3%.
Sex distribution (1996): male 47.98%; female 52.02%.
Age breakdown (1996): under 15, 33.9%; 15–29, 28.6%; 30–44, 19.4%; 45–59, 9.9%; 60–74, 5.3%; 75 and over, 1.7%; unknown, 1.2%.
Population projection[3]: (2010) 41,108,000; (2020) 36,744,000.
Ethnic composition (1999): black 77.2%, of which Zulu *c.* 22.0%, Xhosa *c.* 18.0%, Pedi *c.* 9.0%, Sotho *c.* 7.0%, Tswana *c.* 7.0%, Tsonga *c.* 3.5%, Swazi *c.* 3.0%; white 10.5%; Coloured 8.8%; Asian 2.5%; other 1.0%.
Religious affiliation (2000): Christian 83.1%, of which black independent churches 39.1%, Protestant 31.8%, Roman Catholic 7.1%; traditional beliefs 8.4%; Hindu 2.4%; Muslim 2.4%; nonreligious 2.4%; Bahā'ī 0.6%; Jewish 0.4%; other 0.3%.
Major cities (1996)[3]: Cape Town 2,415,408; Durban 2,117,650[4]; Johannesburg 1,480,530[4, 5]; Pretoria 1,104,479[1]; Soweto 1,098,094; Port Elizabeth 749,921[4].

Vital statistics

Birth rate per 1,000 population (2000): 21.6 (world avg. 22.5).
Death rate per 1,000 population (2000): 14.7 (world avg. 9.0).
Natural increase rate per 1,000 population (2000): 6.9 (world avg. 13.5).
Marriage rate per 1,000 population (1996): 3.6.
Total fertility rate (avg. births per childbearing woman; 2000): 2.5.
Life expectancy at birth (2000): male 51.4 years; female 54.1 years.
Major causes of death per 100,000 population (1993–94): accidents and violence 221.9; diseases of the circulatory system 102.3; infectious and parasitic diseases 51.8; ill-defined conditions 424.0.

National economy

Budget (1999–2000). Revenue: R 196,302,000,000 (personal income taxes 43.9%, value-added taxes 23.7%, company income taxes 11.1%). Expenditures: R 223,564,000,000 (education 21.4%, interest on public debt 19.9%, health 13.4%, police and prisons 9.7%, defense 4.8%).
Public debt (external, outstanding; 1999): U.S.$10,627,000,000.
Production (in R '000,000 except as noted). Agriculture, forestry, fishing (in value of production; 1998): poultry 7,987, corn (maize) 4,374, beef 3,201, temperate fruits 2,968, sugarcane 2,650, milk 2,298, vegetables 2,155, citrus fruits 1,849, potatoes 1,467, grapes 1,413, wheat 1,410, sheep and goat meat 952; roundwood (2000) 30,616,000 cu m; fish catch (1999) 592,144 metric tons. Mining and quarrying (in value of sales; 1998): gold 24,155; rough diamonds (1995) 16,431; coal 17,878; platinum-group metals (1997) 8,511; iron ore 2,492; copper 1,612; nickel (1997) 1,004. Manufacturing (in U.S.$'000,000 value added; 1995): food products 3,028; iron and steel 2,700; transport equipment 2,334; metal products 1,825; nonelectrical machinery 1,819; beverages 1,660; refined petroleum 1,457. Energy production (consumption): electricity (kW-hr; 1999) 203,532,000,000 ([1998] 187,517,000,000); coal (metric tons; 1999) 223,357,000 ([1997] 149,076,000[6]); crude petroleum (barrels; 1999) 5,493,000 ([1997] 159,061,000[6]); petroleum products (metric tons; 1997) 19,193,000[6] (17,252,000[6]); natural gas (cu m; 1999): 1,616,500,000[6] (1,616,500,000[6]).
Tourism (1999): receipts U.S.$2,526,000,000; expenditures U.S.$1,806,000,000.
Household income and expenditure. Average household size (1996) 4.5; average annual disposable income per household (1996)[7] R 47,600 (U.S.$11,070); expenditure (1998): food, beverages, and tobacco 31.3%; transportation 14.3%; housing 9.3%; household furnishings and operation 8.9%.
Population economically active (1999): total 12,553,000; activity rate of total population 29.3% (participation rates [1995]: over age 15, *c.* 53%; female 43.6%; unemployed [1999] 25.2%).

Price and earnings indexes (1995 = 100)

	1994	1995	1996	1997	1998	1999	2000
Consumer price index	92.0	100.0	107.4	116.5	124.6	130.5	138.1
Monthly earnings index	...	...	...	...	...	...	...

Gross national product (1999): U.S.$133,569,000,000 (U.S.$3,170 per capita).

Structure of gross domestic product and labour force

	1999			
	in value R '000,000	% of total value	labour force	% of labour force
Agriculture	26,634	3.7	935,000	7.4
Mining	47,139	6.5	435,000	3.5
Manufacturing	132,640	18.2	1,385,000	11.0
Construction	20,918	2.9	548,000	4.4
Public utilities	23,785	3.3	113,000	0.9
Transp. and commun.	73,146	10.0	552,000	4.4
Trade	95,211	13.1	1,787,000	14.2
Finance, real estate	140,632	19.3	855,000	6.8
Pub. admin., defense	123,782	17.0	2,620,000	20.9
Services	22,108	3.0		
Other	22,060	3.0	3,323,000[8]	26.5[8]
TOTAL	728,055	100.0	12,553,000	100.0

Land use (1994): forest 6.7%; pasture 66.7%; agriculture 10.8%; other 15.8%.

Foreign trade

Balance of trade (current prices)

	1995	1996	1997	1998	1999	2000
R '000,000	+2,783	+11,547	+13,202	+2,192	+16,091	+22,094
% of total	1.4%	4.6%	4.8%	0.8%	5.2%	5.6%

Imports (1995): R 98,614,000,000 (machinery and apparatus 31.9%, chemicals and chemical products 12.5%, motor vehicles 11.6%). *Major import sources* (1999): Germany 14.5%; U.S. 13.3%; U.K. 9.4%; Japan 7.5%; France 4.3%.
Exports (1995): R 101,397,000,000 (gold 19.9%, base metals and metal products 15.4%, gem diamonds 9.8%, food 7.4%). *Major export destinations* (1999): U.K. 8.3%; U.S. 8.2%; Germany 7.0%; Japan 5.2%; Italy 4.2%; unspecified 21.8%.

Transport and communications

Transport. Railroads: route length (1998) 20,319 km[9]; passenger-km (1997–98) 1,775,000,000[9]; metric ton-km cargo (1997–98) 103,866,000,000. Roads (1999): length 331,265 km (paved 41%). Vehicles (1996): passenger cars 3,966,252; trucks and buses 1,904,871. Air transport (2000)[10]: passenger-km 19,320,000,000; metric ton-km cargo 677,048,000; airport (1996) 24.

Communications

Medium	date	unit	number	units per 1,000 persons
Daily newspapers	1996	circulation	1,288,000	31
Radio	1997	receivers	13,750,000	324
Television	1999	receivers	5,450,000	124
Telephones	1999	main lines	5,493,000	125
Cellular telephones	1999	subscribers	5,269,000	120
Personal computers	1999	units	2,400,000	55
Internet	1999	users	1,820,000	42

Education and health

Educational attainment (1994). Percentage of population age 25 and over having: no formal schooling 14.5%; primary/incomplete secondary 61.6%; secondary/incomplete higher 20.4%; complete higher 3.1%; other/unknown 0.4%. *Literacy* (1995): total population age 15 and over literate: 81.8%.

Education (1999)

	schools	teachers	students	student/ teacher ratio
Primary (age 6–12)	14,897	159,432	5,578,978	35.0
Secondary (age 13–17)[11]	8,493	152,305	5,008,932	32.9
Higher	241	27,099[12]	669,115	...

Health: physicians (1998) 29,020 (1 per 1,476 persons); hospital beds 99,313[13] (1 per 431 persons); infant mortality rate per 1,000 live births (2000) 58.9.
Food (1999): daily per capita caloric intake 2,805 (vegetable products 87%, animal products 13%); 114% of FAO recommended minimum.

Military

Total active duty personnel (2000): 63,389 (army 67.0%, navy 8.2%, air force 15.2%, intraservice medical service 9.6%). *Military expenditure as percentage of GNP* (1997): 1.8% (world 2.6%); per capita expenditure U.S.$55.

[1]Renamed within larger municipality in December 2000. [2]Afrikaans; English; Ndebele; Pedi (North Sotho); Sotho (South Sotho); Swazi; Tsonga; Tswana (West Sotho); Venda; Xhosa; Zulu. [3]Census population of urban areas (not necessarily metropolitan areas). [4]Name change pending late 2001. [5]The 1991 population of the Witwatersrand (including East Rand [1,379,000], Far East Rand [701,000], and West Rand [870,000] urban areas) was 4,866,000. [6]Includes Botswana, Lesotho, Namibia, and Swaziland. [7]Estimated figures. [8]Includes 160,000 not adequately defined and 3,163,000 unemployed. [9]Excludes suburban lines. [10]SAA only. [11]Includes combined and intermediate. [12]1996. [13]Public hospitals.

Internet resources for further information:
- **South African Reserve Bank http://www.resbank.co.za**
- **Statistics South Africa http://www.statssa.gov.za**

Spain

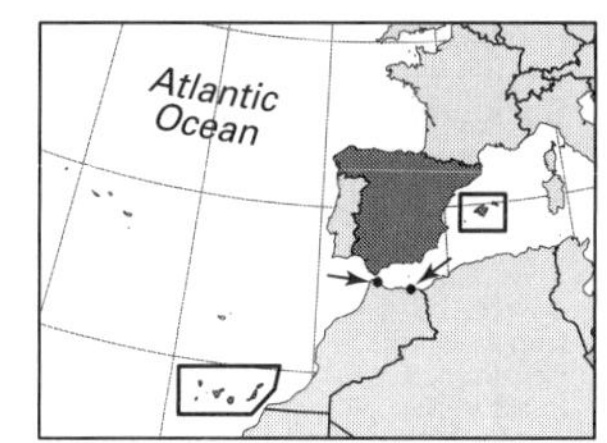

Official name: Reino de España (Kingdom of Spain).
Form of government: constitutional monarchy with two legislative houses (Senate [259[1]]; Congress of Deputies [350]).
Chief of state: King.
Head of government: Prime Minister.
Capital: Madrid.
Official languages: Castilian Spanish[2].
Official religion: none.
Monetary unit: 1 peseta (Pta) = 100 céntimos; valuation (Sept. 28, 2001) 1 U.S.$ = Ptas 182.70; 1 £ = Ptas 268.52; 1 € = Ptas 166.386[3].

Area and population

Autonomous communities	Capitals	area sq mi	area sq km	population 2000[4] estimate
Andalucía	Seville	33,822	87,599	7,340,052
Aragón	Zaragoza	18,425	47,720	1,189,909
Asturias	Oviedo	4,094	10,604	1,076,567
Baleares (Balearic Islands)	Palma de Mallorca	1,927	4,992	845,630
Canarias (Canary Islands)	Santa Cruz de Tenerife	2,875	7,447	1,716,276
Cantabria	Santander	2,504	5,321	531,159
Castilla-La Mancha	Toledo	30,680	79,461	1,734,261
Castilla y León	Valladolid	36,380	94,224	2,479,118
Cataluña	Barcelona	12,399	32,113	6,261,999
Ceuta	—	8	20	75,241
Extremadura	Mérida	16,075	41,634	1,069,420
Galicia	Santiago de Compostela	11,419	29,575	2,731,900
La Rioja	Logroño	1,948	5,045	264,178
Madrid	Madrid	3,100	8,028	5,205,408
Melilla	—	5	12	66,263
Murcia	Murcia	4,368	11,314	1,149,328
Navarra	Pamplona	4,012	10,391	543,757
País Vasco (Basque Country)	Vitoria (Gasteiz)	2,793	7,234	2,098,596
Valencia	Valencia	8,979	23,255	4,120,729
TOTAL		195,364[5, 6]	505,990[6]	40,499,791

Demography

Population (2001): 40,144,000.
Density (2001): persons per sq mi 205.5, persons per sq km 79.3.
Urban-rural (1990): urban 78.4%; rural 21.6%.
Sex distribution (2001)[7]: male 48.86%; female 51.14%.
Age breakdown (2001)[7]: under 15, 14.9%; 15–29, 22.2%; 30–44, 23.4%; 45–59, 17.8%; 60–74, 14.3%; 75 and over, 7.4%.
Population projection: (2010) 40,289,000; (2020) 39,362,000.
Ethnolinguistic composition (1991): Spanish 74.4%; Catalan 16.9%; other 8.7%.
Religious affiliation (2000): Roman Catholic 92.0%; Muslim 0.5%; Protestant 0.3%; other 7.2%.
Major cities (2000)[4, 8]: Madrid 2,882,860; Barcelona 1,496,266; Valencia 739,014; Seville 700,716; Zaragoza 604,631.

Vital statistics

Birth rate per 1,000 population (2000): 9.8 (world avg. 22.5).
Death rate per 1,000 population (2000): 9.1 (world avg. 9.0).
Natural increase rate per 1,000 population (2000): 0.7 (world avg. 13.5).
Total fertility rate (avg. births per childbearing woman; 1999): 1.2.
Life expectancy at birth (1999): male 74.4 years; female 81.6 years.
Major causes of death per 100,000 population (1998): circulatory diseases 337.1; malignant neoplasms (cancers) 231.4; respiratory diseases 95.7.

National economy

Budget (2000). Revenue: Ptas 18,736,200,000,000 (indirect taxes 45.7%, of which value-added tax on products 30.2%; direct taxes 42.7%; other taxes on production 11.6%). Expenditures: Ptas 19,762,900,000,000 (health 21.6%; public debt 14.2%; pensions 5.0%; defense 4.9%; public works 4.8%).
Tourism (1999): receipts U.S.$32,497,000,000; expenditures U.S.$5,523,000,000.
Gross national product (1999): U.S.$583,082,000,000 (U.S.$14,800 per capita).

Structure of gross domestic product and labour force

	2000 in value Ptas '000,000	% of total value	labour force	% of labour force
Agriculture	3,309,160	3.3	1,196,900	7.1
Mining	15,789,795	15.6	64,000	0.4
Manufacturing			2,927,900	17.4
Public utilities	3,955,530	3.9	97,600	0.6
Construction	8,056,403	8.0	1,776,800	10.5
Transp. and commun.	...	...	911,900	5.4
Trade and hotels	59,995,170	59.5	3,618,800	21.5
Finance			1,527,300	9.1
Services			3,802,800	22.6
Pub. admin., defense				
Other	9,766,668[9]	9.7[9]	920,300[10]	5.4[10]
TOTAL	100,872,726	100.0	16,844,200[5]	100.0

Production (metric tons except as noted). Agriculture, forestry, fishing (2000): barley 11,283,100, sugar beets 8,343,800, wheat 7,333,100, grapes 5,646,400, olives 4,182,900, corn (maize) 3,866,700, tomatoes 3,597,000, potatoes 3,138,000, oranges 2,706,000; livestock (number of live animals) 23,700,000 sheep, 23,682,000 pigs, 6,203,000 cattle, 2,873,000 goats; roundwood (1999) 15,113,000 cu m; fish catch (1997) 1,341,000. Mining and quarrying (metal content in metric tons; 1998): zinc 128,000; iron ore 52,000[11]; lead 19,000. Manufacturing (value added in U.S.$'000; 1994): machinery and transport equipment 20,322,000; food products 11,072,000; chemical products 8,618,000; publishing products 6,082,000; wood products 3,208,000. Construction (2000): dwellings 594,820. Energy production (consumption): electricity (kW-hr; 1995) 166,380,000,000 (170,866,000,000); coal (metric tons; 1995) 28,403,000 (42,640,000); crude petroleum (barrels; 1995) 6,000,000 (415,000,000); petroleum products (metric tons; 1995) 47,064,000 (42,327,000); natural gas (cu m; 1995) 178,000,000 (8,879,000,000).
Public debt (2000): Ptas 51,372,300,000,000 (U.S.$335,122,000,000).
Population economically active (2000): total 16,844,200; activity rate of total population 41.6% (participation rates: ages [1995] 16–64, 60.7%, female 38.3%; unemployed 22.9%).

Price and earnings indexes (1995 = 100)

	1994	1995	1996	1997	1998	1999	2000
Consumer price index	95.5	100.0	103.6	105.6	107.5	110.0	113.8
Monthly earnings index	95.4	100.0	105.3	109.6	...	115.5	...

Household income and expenditure. Average household size (1991) 3.4; income per household (2000) Ptas 3,205,693 (U.S.$18,470); expenditure (1995): housing 26.0%, food 24.0%, transportation 12.8%, clothing and footwear 7.4%, household goods and services 6.1%.

Foreign trade[12]

Balance of trade (current prices)

	1995	1996	1997	1998	1999	2000
Ptas '000,000,000	−2,767.1	−2,504.5	−2,699.1	−3,547.1	−5,231.4	−7,161.1
% of total	10.8%	8.8%	8.1%	9.8%	13.1%	14.9%

Imports (2000): Ptas 27,643,097,000,000 (machinery 12.5%; energy products 12.0%; transportation equipment 10.9%; agricultural products 8.1%). *Major import sources:* France 17.1%; Germany 14.9%; Italy 14.3%; U.K. 7.0%.
Exports (2000): Ptas 20,482,039,900,000 (transport equipment 19.5%; agricultural products 12.9%; machinery 7.9%). *Major export destinations:* France 19.4%; Germany 12.4%; Portugal 9.4%; Italy 8.8%; U.K. 8.3%.

Transport and communications

Transport. Railroads (2000)[13]: route length 13,832 km; passenger-km 18,547,000,000; metric ton-km cargo 11,620,000,000. Roads (1997): length 346,548 km (paved 99%). Vehicles (1999): cars 16,847,000; trucks and buses 3,659,000. Air transport (1999): passenger-km 60,696,083,000; metric ton-km cargo 6,406,562,000; airports (1997) with scheduled flights 25.

Communications

Medium	date	unit	number	units per 1,000 persons
Daily newspapers	1996	circulation	3,931,000	99
Radio	1998	receivers	12,000,000	332
Television	1998	receivers	22,000,000	553
Telephones	1999	main lines	16,480,000	412
Cellular telephones	1999	subscribers	12,300,000	307
Personal computers	1999	units	4,800,000	120
Internet	1999	users	4,652,000	116

Education and health

Educational attainment (1997). Percentage of economically active population age 16 and over having: no formal schooling 6.4%[14]; primary 26.6%; secondary 58.9%; higher 8.1%.

Education (1997–98)

	schools	teachers	students	student/ teacher ratio
Primary (age 6–11)	16,540[15]	170,184	2,633,678	15.5
Secondary (age 12–18)[16]	25,775[17]	278,075	3,706,935	13.3
Higher	1,415[17]	101,626	1,746,170	17.2

Health (1995): physicians 162,650 (1 per 241 persons); hospital beds (1999) 164,097 (1 per 244 persons); infant mortality rate (2000) 5.0.
Food (1999): daily per capita caloric intake 3,353 (vegetable products 72%, animal products 28%); 136% of FAO recommended minimum requirement.

Military

Total active duty personnel (2000): 166,050 (army 60.2%, navy 22.3%, air force 17.5%). *Military expenditure as percentage of GNP* (1997): 1.5% (world 2.6%); per capita expenditure U.S.$196.

[1]At the March 2000 elections, 208 seats were directly elected and 51 indirectly elected by the parliaments of the autonomous communities. [2]The constitution states that "Castilian is the Spanish official language of the State," but that "all other Spanish languages will also be official in the corresponding Autonomous Communities." [3]Euro banknotes and coins are to be introduced on Jan. 1, 2002 (at the latest). All national currencies are to be phased out by Feb. 28, 2002. [4]De jure population for January 1. [5]Detail does not add to total given because of rounding. [6]Includes other enclaves (*plazas de soberanía*). [7]Estimate based on 1991 census. [8]For municipios, which may contain rural population. [9]Import taxes and value-added tax on products. [10]Includes 507,000 unemployed persons not previously employed. [11]The decrease in iron ore production is due to the lack of mining at Minas de Alquife (Granada). [12]Imports in c.i.f., exports f.o.b. [13]Spanish National Railways (RENFE) only. [14]Includes illiterate. [15]1993–94. [16]Includes vocational. [17]1992–93.

Internet resources for further information:
- **"Sí Spain" (Embassy of Spain, Ottawa, Canada) http://www.sispain.org**
- **National Institute of Statistics http://www.ine.es**

Sri Lanka

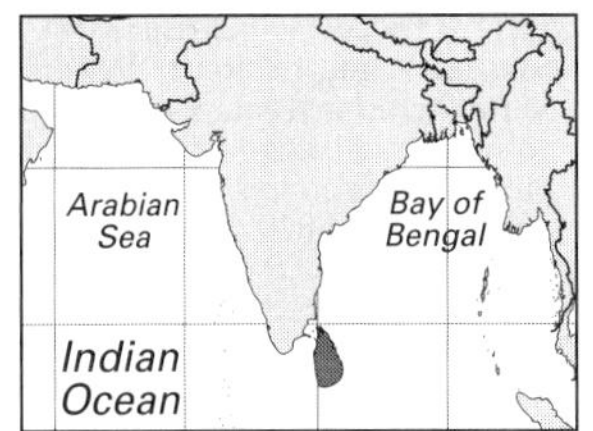

Official name: Śri Lanka Prajatantrika Samajavadi Janarajaya (Sinhala); Ilangai Jananayaka Socialisa Kudiarasu (Tamil) (Democratic Socialist Republic of Sri Lanka).
Form of government: unitary multiparty republic with one legislative house (Parliament [225]).
Head of state and government: President assisted by Prime Minister.
Capitals: Colombo (executive); Sri Jayewardenepura Kotte (Colombo suburb; legislative and judicial).
Official languages: Sinhala; Tamil.
Official religion: none.
Monetary unit: 1 Sri Lanka rupee (SL Rs) = 100 cents; valuation (Sept. 28, 2001) 1 U.S.$ = SL Rs 90.17; 1 £ = SL Rs 132.52.

Area and population

Districts	Capitals	area sq mi	area sq km	population 1994 estimate
Amparai	Amparai	1,705	4,415	512,000
Anuradhapura	Anuradhapura	2,772	7,179	750,000
Badulla	Badulla	1,104	2,861	735,000
Batticaloa	Batticaloa	1,102	2,854	443,000
Colombo	Colombo	270	699	2,062,000
Galle	Galle	638	1,652	983,000
Gampaha	Gampaha	536	1,387	1,568,000
Hambantota	Hambantota	1,007	2,609	537,000
Jaffna	Jaffna	396	1,025	896,000
Kalutara	Kalutara	617	1,598	969,000
Kandy	Kandy	749	1,940	1,286,000
Kegalle	Kegalle	654	1,693	763,000
Kilinochchi	Kilinochchi	494	1,279	110,000
Kurunegala	Kurunegala	1,859	4,816	1,481,000
Mannar	Mannar	771	1,996	140,000
Matale	Matale	770	1,993	434,000
Matara	Matara	495	1,283	810,000
Monaragala	Monaragala	2,177	5,639	367,000
Mullaitivu	Mullaitivu	1,010	2,617	98,000
Nuwara Eliya	Nuwara Eliya	672	1,741	541,000
Polonnaruwa	Polonnaruwa	1,271	3,293	336,000
Puttalam	Puttalam	1,186	3,072	626,000
Ratnapura	Ratnapura	1,264	3,275	972,000
Trincomalee	Trincomalee	1,053	2,727	327,000
Vavuniya	Vavuniya	759	1,967	119,000
TOTAL		25,332	65,610	17,865,000

Demography

Population (2001): 19,399,000.
Density (2001): persons per sq mi 765.8, persons per sq km 295.7.
Urban-rural (2000): urban 24.0%; rural 76.0%.
Sex distribution (1998): male 50.97%; female 49.03%.
Age breakdown (1996): under 15, 28.0%; 15–29, 26.9%; 30–44, 22.5%; 45–59, 13.6%; 60–74, 7.0%; 75 and over, 2.0%.
Population projection: (2010) 20,832,000; (2020) 22,120,000.
Ethnic composition (2000): Sinhalese 72.4%; Tamil 17.8%; Sri Lankan Moor 7.4%; other 2.4%.
Religious affiliation (2000): Buddhist 68.4%; Hindu 11.3%; Christian 9.4%; Muslim 9.0%; other 1.9%.
Major cities (1997): Colombo 800,982; Dehiwala–Mount Lavinia 220,780; Moratuwa 213,000; Kandy 150,532; Jaffna 145,600.

Vital statistics

Birth rate per 1,000 population (2000): 17.5 (world avg. 22.5); (1986) legitimate 96.3%; illegitimate 3.7%.
Death rate per 1,000 population (2000): 5.8 (world avg. 9.0).
Total fertility rate (avg. births per childbearing woman; 2000): 2.1.
Marriage rate per 1,000 population (1997): 8.9.
Life expectancy at birth (2000): male 71.0 years; female 76.0 years.
Major causes of death per 100,000 population (1989): diseases of the circulatory system 47.8; violence and poisoning 38.6; malignant neoplasms 26.7.

National economy

Budget (2000). Revenue: SL Rs 233,974,000,000 (sales and turnover tax 22.8%, excise taxes 19.9%, nontax revenue 13.8%, income taxes 12.5%, import duties 11.5%). Expenditures: SL Rs 329,012,000,000 (interest payments 21.1%, defense 11.7%, transport and communications 11.7%, social welfare 10.5%, education 9.5%, administration 8.5%).
Public debt (external, outstanding; 1999): U.S.$7,649,000,000.
Production (metric tons except as noted). Agriculture, forestry, fishing (2000): rice 2,767,000, coconuts 1,950,000, sugarcane 1,114,000, plantains 600,000; livestock (number of live animals) 1,616,700 cattle, 727,700 buffalo, 514,400 goats; roundwood (1999) 10,344,000 cu m; fish catch (1998) 266,100. Mining and quarrying (1998); limestone 950,000; titanium concentrate 23,000; graphite 5,000; gemstones U.S.$63,000,000. Manufacturing (value added, in U.S.$'000,000; 1995): food, beverages, and tobacco 601; textiles and apparel 391; petrochemicals 116. Construction (units completed; 1993): residential 1,128; nonresidential 96. Energy production (consumption): electricity (kW-hr; 1997) 5,148,000,000 ([1996] 4,366,000,000); coal (metric tons, 1996) none (negligible); crude petroleum (barrels; 1996) none (15,063,000); petroleum products (metric tons; 1996) 1,908,000 (2,188,000).

Gross national product (1998): U.S.$15,176,000,000 (U.S.$810 per capita).

Structure of gross domestic product and labour force

	2000 in value SL Rs '000,000[1]	% of total value[1]	labour force[2]	% of labour force[2]
Agriculture	222,100	19.8	2,290,000	33.4
Mining	21,700	1.9	77,800	1.1
Manufacturing	188,200	16.7	1,013,200	14.8
Construction	80,800	7.2	320,600	4.7
Public utilities			25,000	0.4
Transp. and commun.			278,100	4.1
Trade			767,700	11.2
Finance	612,300	54.4	122,600	1.8
Pub. admin., defense			1,153,700	16.8
Services				
Other			804,600[3]	11.7[3]
TOTAL	1,125,100	100.0	6,853,300	100.0

Population economically active: total (1997) 6,213,086; activity rate 40.2% (participation rates: ages 15 and over, 55.2%; female 32.4%; unemployed [2000] 8.0%[2]).

Price and earnings indexes (1995 = 100)

	1993	1994	1995	1996	1997	1998	1999
Consumer price index	85.6	92.9	100.0	115.9	127.0	138.9	145.4
Average wage index[4]	96.7	98.9	100.0	109.3	117.0	132.1	134.3

Household income and expenditure (1992). Average household size (1994) 4.6[2]; income per household SL Rs 116,100 (U.S.$2,600); sources of income: wages 48.5%, property income and self-employment 41.8%, transfers 9.7%; expenditure: food 58.6%, transportation 16.0%, clothing 8.4%.
Tourism (1999): receipts U.S.$275,000,000; expenditures U.S.$219,000,000.

Foreign trade

Balance of trade (current prices)

	1994	1995	1996	1997	1998	1999
SL Rs '000,000	–77,022	–77,084	–74,275	–41,449	–63,164	–91,443
% of total	19.5%	16.5%	14.1%	7.0%	9.4%	12.4%

Imports (1999): U.S.$5,981,000,000 (textile products 22.1%, machinery and equipment 11.3%, transport equipment 8.7%, petroleum 8.4%, processed foods 6.7%). *Major import sources:* Japan 10.4%; India 9.5%; Singapore 8.4%; U.K. 4.7%; U.S. 4.0%.
Exports (1999): U.S.$4,600,000,000 (clothing and accessories 52.7%, tea 13.5%, gems 4.7%, coconuts 1.8%). *Major export destinations:* U.S. 39.6%; U.K. 13.3%; Germany 4.8%; Japan 3.5%; The Netherlands 2.4%.

Transport and communications

Transport. Railroads (1998): route length 1,447 km; passenger-km 3,264,000,000; metric ton-km cargo 132,000,000. Roads (1996): total length 99,200 km (paved 40%). Vehicles (1996): passenger cars 107,000; trucks and buses 150,160. Air transport (1999): passenger-km 5,156,000,000; metric ton-km cargo 669,700,000; airports (1996) 1.

Communications

Medium	date	unit	number	units per 1,000 persons
Daily newspapers	1996	circulation	530,000	29
Radio	1997	receivers	3,850,000	211
Television	1999	receivers	1,900,000	102
Telephones	1999	main lines	679,207	36
Cellular telephones	1999	subscribers	227,941	12
Personal computers	1999	units	105,000	5.6
Internet	1999	users	65,000	3.5

Education and health

Educational attainment (1981). Percentage of population age 25 and over having: no schooling 15.5%; less than complete primary education 12.1%; complete primary 52.3%; postprimary 14.7%; secondary 3.0%; higher 1.1%; unspecified 1.3%. *Literacy* (1995): percentage of population age 15 and over literate 90.2%; males literate 93.4%; females literate 87.2%.

Education (1995)

	schools	teachers	students	student/ teacher ratio
Primary (age 5–10)	9,657	70,537	1,962,498	27.8
Secondary (age 11–17)	5,771[5]	103,572	2,314,054	22.3
Voc., teacher tr.[6]	23	437	8,908	20.4
Higher	8[6]	2,636	63,660	24.2

Health (1999): physicians 6,938 (1 per 2,740 persons); hospital beds (1997) 52,298 (1 per 355 persons); infant mortality rate (2000) 17.0.
Food (1999): daily per capita caloric intake 2,411 (vegetable products 94%, animal products 6%); (1997) 109% of FAO recommended minimum.

Military

Total active duty personnel (2000): 112,500 (army 82.2%, navy 8.9%, air force 8.9%). *Military expenditure as percentage of GNP* (1997): 5.1% (world 2.6%); per capita expenditure U.S.$41.

[1]Provisional. [2]Excludes the Northern and Eastern provinces where Tamils are in the majority. [3]Mainly unemployed. [4]Agricultural minimum rates. [5]1992. [6]1991.

Internet resources for further information:
- **Central Bank of Sri Lanka http://www.centralbanklanka.org**
- **Statistics http://www.lk/statistics.html**

Sudan, The

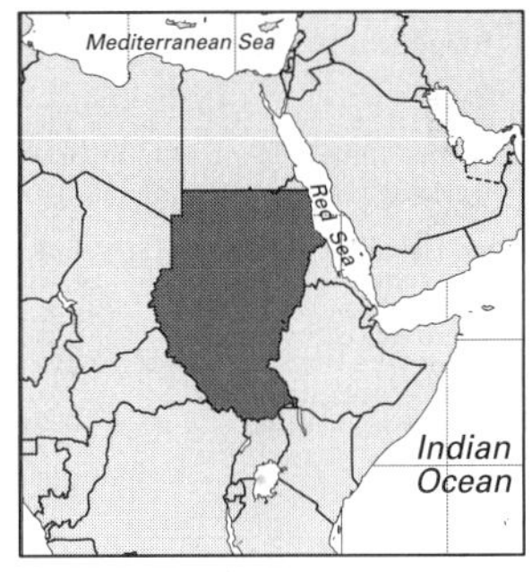

Official name: Jumhūrīyat as-Sūdān (Republic of the Sudan).
Form of government: federal republic[1] with one legislative body (National Assembly [360[2]]).
Head of state and government: President.
Capitals: Khartoum (executive); Omdurman (legislative).
Official language: Arabic[3].
Official religion: [4].
Monetary unit: 1 Sudanese dinar (Sd)[5]; valuation (Sept. 28, 2001) 1 U.S.$ = Sd 258.70; 1 £ = Sd 380.21.

Area and population

States[6]	area sq km	population 2000 estimate	States[6]	area sq km	population 2000 estimate
Bahr el-Ghazal[7]	...	2,256,942	Red Sea	...	709,637
Blue Nile	...	633,129	River Nile	...	895,893
Equatoria	...	1,234,486	Sinnar	...	1,132,758
Gedaref	...	1,414,531	Southern Darfur	...	2,708,007
Gezira	...	3,310,928	Southern Kordofan	...	1,066,117
Kassalā	...	1,433,730	Upper Nile	...	1,342,943
Khartoum	...	4,740,290	Western Darfur	...	1,531,682
Northern	...	578,376	Western Kordofan	...	1,078,330
Northern Darfur	...	1,409,894	White Nile	...	1,431,701
Northern Kordofan	...	1,439,930	TOTAL	2,503,890[8]	30,349,304[9, 10]

Demography

Population (2001): 36,080,000.
Density (2001): persons per sq mi 37.3, persons per sq km 14.4.
Urban-rural (1999): urban 35.2%; rural 64.8%.
Sex distribution (2000): male 50.66%; female 49.34%.
Age breakdown (2000): under 15, 45.0%; 15–29, 27.5%; 30–44, 15.4%; 45–59, 8.4%; 60–74, 3.2%; 75 and over, 0.5%.
Population projection: (2000) 45,485,000; (2010) 56,162,000.
Doubling time: 25 years.
Ethnic composition (1983): Sudanese Arab 49.1%; Dinka 11.5%; Nuba 8.1%; Beja 6.4%, Nuer 4.9%; Azande 2.7%; Bari 2.5%; Fur 2.1%; other 12.7%.
Religious affiliation (2000): Sunnī Muslim 70.3%; Christian 16.7%, of which Roman Catholic *c.* 8%, Anglican *c.* 6%; traditional beliefs 11.9%; other 1.1%.
Major cities (1993): Omdurman 1,267,077; Khartoum 924,505; Khartoum North 879,105; Port Sudan 305,385; Kassalā 234,270; Nyala 228,778.

Vital statistics

Birth rate per 1,000 population (2000): 38.6 (world avg. 22.5).
Death rate per 1,000 population (2000): 10.3 (world avg. 9.0).
Natural increase rate per 1,000 population (2000): 28.3 (world avg. 13.5).
Total fertility rate (avg. births per childbearing woman; 2000): 5.5.
Life expectancy at birth (2000): male 55.5 years; female 57.7 years.
Major causes of death per 100,000 population: n.a.

National economy

Budget (1999–2000). Revenue: Sd 206,700,000,000[5] (import duties 26.0%, non-tax revenue 25.8%, excise duties 11.9%, taxes on business profits 11.1%). Expenditures: Sd 227,200,000,000[5] (current expenditure 85.8%, development expenditure 14.2%).
Public debt (external, outstanding; 1999): U.S.$8,852,000,000.
Tourism (1999): receipts U.S.$2,000,000; expenditures U.S.$35,000,000.
Production (metric tons except as noted). Agriculture, forestry, fishing (1999): sugarcane 5,950,000, sorghum 3,045,000, peanuts (groundnuts) 980,000, millet 499,000, sesame seeds 220,000, seed cotton 205,000, dates 175,500, tea 170,000, wheat 168,000, gum arabic (1998–99) 28,000; livestock (number of live animals) 42,500,000 sheep, 37,500,000 goats, 35,000,000 cattle, 3,150,000 camels; roundwood (1998) 9,486,000 cu m; fish catch (1997) 48,072. Mining and quarrying (1998): salt 45,000; gold 161,000 troy oz. Manufacturing (1999): raw sugar 622,000; flour 532,000; cement 267,000; vegetable oils 100,000; cattle hides and horsehides (1996) 34,700; shoes 48,000,000 pairs. Construction: n.a. Energy production (consumption): electricity (kW-hr; 1999) 2,243,000,000 (1,317,000,000); coal, none (none); crude petroleum (barrels; 1999–2000[11]) 60,700,000 ([1996] 7,616,000); petroleum products (metric tons; 1996) 878,000 (1,039,000); natural gas, none (none).
Gross national product (1999): U.S.$9,435,000,000 (U.S.$330 per capita).

Structure of gross domestic product and labour force

	1999 in value Sd '000,000,000[12]	1999 % of total value	1983 labour force[13]	1983 % of labour force[13]
Agriculture	1,040	42.6	4,028,705	63.5
Mining	21	0.9	6,534	0.1
Manufacturing	217	8.9	266,693	4.2
Construction	157	6.4	139,282	2.2
Public utilities	19	0.8	43,728	0.7
Transportation and communications	142	5.8	215,474	3.4
Trade, hotels	492	20.1	314,676	5.0
Finance, Services, Pub. admin., defense	354	14.5	550,409	8.7
Other	—	—	777,480[14]	12.2[14]
TOTAL	2,442	100.0	6,342,981	100.0

Population economically active (1993): total 8,866,000; activity rate of total population 32.3% (participation rates: ages 15–64 [1983] 57.4%; female 22.3%; unemployed *c.* 30.0%).

Price and earnings indexes (1995 = 100)

	1994	1995	1996	1997	1998	1999	2000
Consumer price index	59.4	100.0	232.8	341.5	399.9	463.8	488.1[15]
Earnings index	...	...	...	...	...	...	...

Household income and expenditure. Average household size: n.a.; income per household: n.a.[16]; expenditure (1983): food and beverages 63.6%, housing 11.5%, household goods 5.5%, clothing and footwear 5.3%.
Land use (1994): forested 18.1%; meadows and pastures 46.3%; agricultural and under permanent cultivation 5.5%; desert and other 30.1%.

Foreign trade[17]

Balance of trade (current prices)

	1994	1995	1996	1997	1998	1999
U.S.$'000,000	–676	–663	–927	–985	–1,329	–632
% of total	41.0%	37.4%	42.8%	45.2%	52.7%	28.8%

Imports (1999): U.S.$1,412,000,000 (machinery and equipment 25.4%; foodstuffs 19.5%, of which wheat and wheat flour 8.7%; petroleum products 13.0%; transport equipment 9.3%). *Major import sources:* Saudi Arabia 11.8%; France 8.6%; Italy 6.3%; U.A.E. 5.5%; Germany 5.4%; U.K. 5.1%.
Exports (1999): U.S.$780,000,000 (crude petroleum 35.4%; sesame seeds 16.3%; sheep and lambs 13.0%; gold 7.1%; cotton 5.8%). *Major export destinations:* Saudi Arabia 18.1%; Japan 15.7%; U.K. 9.2%; South Korea 7.9%; Italy 7.1%.

Transport and communications

Transport. Railroads: route length (1998) 4,595 km; (1995–96) passenger-km 161,000,000; (1995–96) metric ton-km cargo 1,965,000,000. Roads (1996): total length 11,900 km (paved 36%). Vehicles (1996): passenger cars 285,000; trucks and buses 53,000. Air transport (1998)[18]: passenger-km 530,671,000; metric ton-km cargo 20,293,000; airports (1997) with scheduled flights 3.

Communications

Medium	date	unit	number	units per 1,000 persons
Daily newspapers	1996	circulation	737,000	24
Radio	1997	receivers	7,550,000	235
Television	1999	receivers	5,000,000	147
Telephones	1999	main lines	251,420	7.4
Cellular telephones	1999	subscribers	13,000	0.4
Personal computers	1999	units	85,000	2.5
Internet	1999	users	5,000	0.1

Education and health

Educational attainment (1983). Percentage of population age 25 and over having: no formal schooling 76.7%; complete secondary 2.0%; higher 0.8%.
Literacy (1995): total population age 15 and over literate 8,720,000 (50.8%); males 5,460,000 (63.5%); females 3,260,000 (38.3%).

Education (1996–97)

	schools	teachers	students	student/ teacher ratio
Primary (age 7–12)	11,158	102,987	3,000,048	29.1
Secondary (age 13–18)	...	15,504	405,583	26.2
Vocational	...	761	26,421	34.7
Higher[19]	6	1,417	52,260	36.9

Health: physicians (1994) 2,736 (1 per 10,900 persons); hospital beds (1990) 19,449 (1 per 1,369 persons); infant mortality rate (2000) 70.2.
Food (1998): daily per capita caloric intake 2,444 (vegetable products 80%, animal products 20%); 104% of FAO recommended minimum.

Military

Total active duty personnel (2000): 104,500 (army 95.7%, navy 1.4%, air force 2.9%). *Military expenditure as percentage of GNP* (1997): 4.6% (world 2.6%); per capita expenditure U.S.$13.

[1]A state of emergency introduced Dec. 12, 1999, was extended through November 2001; elections to National Assembly were held in December 2000. [2]Includes 90 indirectly elected or appointed seats. [3]English has been designated the "principal" language in southern Sudan. [4]Islamic law and custom are sources of national law per 1998 constitution. [5]The Sudanese dinar (Sd), introduced May 1992 at a value equal to 10 Sudanese pounds (LSd), officially replaced the Sudanese pound on March 1, 1999. [6]Local administrative reorganization into 26 new states was announced in February 1994 and confirmed in June 1998. Names listed below are English-language variants; six southern states are excluded. [7]Includes Western Bahr el-Ghazal and Northern Bahr el-Ghazal. [8]Including *c.* 130,000 sq km of inland water area. [9]Summary total; actual total per official source is 31,081,000. [10]Population estimates are unavailable for six states in southern Sudan experiencing civil war since 1983. [11]Production from August 1999 through July 2000. [12]At factor cost. [13]Excludes nomads, the homeless, and institutionalized persons. [14]Includes 592,759 unemployed not previously employed. [15]April. [16]Average annual income of paid worker (1992) U.S.$216. [17]Imports c.i.f.; exports f.o.b. [18]Sudan Airways only. [19]Universities only.

Internet resources for further information:

- **Ministry of Foreign Affairs**
  http://www.sudmer.com

Suriname

Official name: Republiek Suriname (Republic of Suriname).
Form of government: multiparty republic with one legislative house (National Assembly [51]).
Head of state and government: President.
Capital: Paramaribo.
Official language: Dutch.
Official religion: none.
Monetary unit: 1 Suriname guilder (Sf) = 100 cents; valuation (Sept. 28, 2001) 1 U.S.$ = Sf 2,178; 1 £ = Sf 3,202.

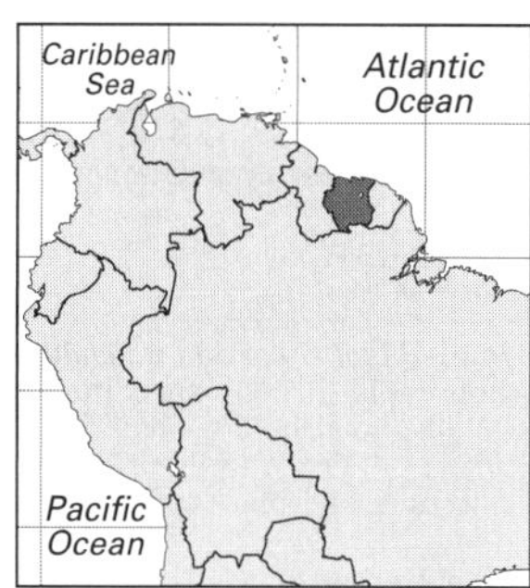

Area and population

Districts	Capitals	area sq mi	area sq km	population 1996 estimate
Brokopondo	Brokopondo	2,843	7,364	7,200
Commewijne	Nieuw Amsterdam	908	2,353	20,900
Coronie	Totness	1,507	3,902	2,900
Marowijne	Albina	1,786	4,627	12,600
Nickerie	Nieuw Nickerie	2,067	5,353	33,600
Para	Onverwacht	2,082	5,393	14,400
Saramacca	Groningen	1,404	3,636	13,000
Sipaliwini	[1]	50,412	130,566	23,500
Wanica	Lelydorp	171	443	72,400
Town district				
Paramaribo	Paramaribo	71	183	222,800
TOTAL		63,251[2]	163,820[2]	423,400[3]

Demography

Population (2001): 434,000.
Density (2001): persons per sq mi 6.9, persons per sq km 2.6.
Urban-rural (1998): urban 51.0%; rural 49.0%.
Sex distribution (2000): male 50.77%; female 49.23%.
Age breakdown (2000): under 15, 32.1%; 15–29, 27.2%; 30–44, 22.7%; 45–59, 9.9%; 60–74, 6.4%; 75 and over, 1.7%.
Population projection: (2010) 450,000; (2020) 457,000.
Doubling time: 45 years.
Ethnic composition (1999): Indo-Pakistani 37.0%; Suriname Creole 31.0%; Javanese 15.0%; Bush Negro 10.0%; Amerindian 2.5%; Chinese 2.0%; white 1.0%; other 1.5%.
Religious affiliation (1995): Hindu 27.4%; Roman Catholic 21.0%; Muslim 19.6%; Protestant (mostly Moravian) 16.4%; other 15.6%.
Major cities (1996/1997): Paramaribo 222,800 (urban agglomeration 289,000); Lelydorp 15,600; Nieuw Nickerie 11,100; Mungo (Moengo) 6,800; Meerzorg 6,600.

Vital statistics

Birth rate per 1,000 population (2000): 21.1 (world avg. 22.5).
Death rate per 1,000 population (2000): 5.7 (world avg. 9.0).
Natural increase rate per 1,000 population (2000): 15.4 (world avg. 13.5).
Total fertility rate (avg. births per childbearing woman; 2000): 2.5.
Marriage rate per 1,000 population (1991): 4.9.
Divorce rate per 1,000 population (1991): 2.5.
Life expectancy at birth (2000): male 68.7 years; female 74.1 years.
Major causes of death per 100,000 population (1992): noncommunicable diseases 769.0; external and other causes 608.1; communicable and perinatal diseases 232.8; ill-defined diseases 279.0.

National economy

Budget (1996). Revenue: Sf 90,874,600,000 (direct taxes 42.2%; indirect taxes 32.2%; bauxite levy 25.0%; other 0.6%). Expenditures: Sf 96,957,700,000 (current expenditures 99.6%, of which wages and salaries 28.5%, transfers 13.7%, debt service 1.7%; capital expenditures 0.4%).
Production (metric tons except as noted). Agriculture, forestry, fishing (1999): rice 180,400, sugarcane 90,000, bananas 55,000, plantains 13,000, oranges 12,000, coconuts 9,400, cassava 4,000, cucumbers 3,220, watermelons 2,700, tomatoes 1,625, cabbage 990, grapefruit 940; livestock (number of live animals) 102,000 cattle, 25,000 pigs, 10,600 sheep, 10,000 goats, 2,200,000 chickens; roundwood (1998) 183,000 cu m; fish catch (1997) 13,000. Mining and quarrying (1997): bauxite 3,877,000; gold 6,993 troy oz. Manufacturing (value of production at factor cost in Sf; 1993): food products 992,000,000; beverages 558,000,000; tobacco 369,000,000; chemical products 291,000,000; pottery and earthenware 258,000,000; wood products 180,000,000. Construction (value of building authorized; 1985): residential Sf 46,500,000; nonresidential Sf 8,100,000. Energy production (consumption): electricity (kW-hr; 1996) 1,621,000,000 (1,621,000,000); hard coal (metric tons) none (n.a.); crude petroleum (barrels; 1996) 1,519,000 (1,227,000); petroleum products (metric tons; 1996) none (478,000); natural gas, none (none).
Household income and expenditure. Average household size (1998) 4.8; income per household: n.a.; sources of income (1975): wages and salaries 74.6%, transfer payments 3.2%, other 22.2%; expenditure (1968–69): food and beverages 40.0%, household furnishings 12.3%, clothing and footwear 11.0%, transportation and communications 9.5%, recreation and education 8.4%, energy 6.9%, housing 4.4%, other 7.5%.
Land use (1994): forested 96.2%; meadows and pastures 0.1%; agricultural and under permanent cultivation 0.4%; other 3.3%.
Gross national product (at current market prices; 1998): U.S.$684,000,000 (U.S.$1,660 per capita).

Structure of gross domestic product and labour force

	1996 in value Sf '000,000[4]	1996 % of total value[4]	1994 labour force	1994 % of labour force
Agriculture, forestry	104.4	7.0	19,940[5]	20.3[5]
Mining	190.8	12.9	3,181	3.2
Manufacturing	148.9	10.1	4,432	4.5
Construction	47.3	3.2	1,656	1.7
Public utilities	126.7	8.6	1,288	1.3
Transp. and commun.	139.3	9.4	2,112	2.1
Trade[6]	123.9	8.4	4,383	4.5
Finance, real estate	551.3	37.2	1,954	2.0
Pub. admin., defense	289.0	19.5	38,552	39.2
Services	7.4	0.5	2,010	2.0
Other	–248.0[7]	–16.7[7]	18,732[8]	19.1[8]
TOTAL	1,481.0	100.0[3]	98,240	100.0[3]

Public debt (external, outstanding; 1996): U.S.$216,500,000.
Population economically active (1994): total 98,240; activity rate of total population 24.3% (participation rates[9, 10]: ages 15–64, 56.0%; female 37.5%; unemployed [1996] 10.7%).

Price and earnings indexes (1995 = 100)

	1993	1994	1995	1996	1997	1998	1999
Consumer price index	6.4	29.8	100.0	99.3	106.4	126.6	251.8
Earnings index	...	...	...	...	...	...	...

Tourism (1999): receipts from visitors U.S.$53,000,000; expenditures by nationals abroad U.S.$11,000,000[11].

Foreign trade

Balance of trade (current prices)

	1991	1992	1993	1994	1995	1996
U.S.$'000,000	–117.9	–110.8	–77.2	–99.3	+38.3	+18.8
% of total	11.3%	10.2%	8.0%	20.4%	4.6%	2.2%

Imports (1995): Sf 258,916,700,000 (raw materials 36.4%, investment goods 25.2%, fuels and lubricants 11.1%, food and live animals 9.7%, cars and motorcycles 3.8%). *Major import sources:* U.S. 42.1%; The Netherlands 19.8%; Trinidad and Tobago 7.4%; Netherlands Antilles 2.6%; Japan 2.1%.
Exports (1995): Sf 211,020,600,000 (1994; alumina 63.6%, shrimp and fish 9.7%, rice 9.6%, aluminum 9.3%, petroleum 3.0%, bananas 2.9%). *Major export destinations:* The Netherlands 27.9%; Norway 24.9%; U.S. 22.3%; Japan 6.1%; Brazil 5.2%.

Transport and communications

Transport. Railroads (1997)[12]: length 187 mi, 301 km; passengers, not applicable; cargo, n.a. Roads (1996): total length 2,815 mi, 4,530 km (paved 26%). Vehicles (1996): passenger cars 46,408; trucks and buses 19,255. Merchant marine (1992): vessels (100 gross tons and over) 24; total deadweight tonnage 15,721. Air transport (1996): passenger-mi 548,885,000, passenger-km 883,347,000; short ton-mi cargo 65,865,000, metric ton-km cargo 106,000,000; airports (1998) with scheduled flights 1.

Communications

Medium	date	unit	number	units per 1,000 persons
Daily newspapers	1996	circulation	50,000	122
Radio	1997	receivers	300,000	728
Television	1999	receivers	98,000	236
Telephones	1999	main lines	67,308	163
Cellular telephones	1999	subscribers	18,000	43
Internet	1999	users	7,236	17.5

Education and health

Educational attainment: n.a. *Literacy* (1995): total population age 15 and over literate 271,000 (93.0%); males literate 137,000 (95.1%); females literate 134,000 (91.0%).

Education (1995–96)

	schools	teachers	students	student/ teacher ratio
Primary (age 6–11)	304	3,611	75,585	20.9
Secondary (age 12–18)	104	2,286	31,918	13.9
Teacher training	1	...	1,462	...
Higher	1	155	1,335	8.6

Health: physicians (1998) 166 (1 per 2,518 persons); hospital beds (1998) 1,449 (1 per 288 persons); infant mortality rate per 1,000 live births (2000) 25.1.
Food (1999): daily per capita caloric intake 2,604 (vegetable products 85%, animal products 15%); 116% of FAO recommended minimum requirement.

Military

Total active duty personnel (2000): 2,040[13] (army 78.4%, navy 11.8%, air force 9.8%). *Military expenditure as percentage of GNP* (1997): 1.2% (world 2.6%); per capita expenditure U.S.$43.

[1]No capital; administered from Paramaribo. [2]Area excludes 6,809 sq mi (17,635 sq km) of territory disputed with Guyana. [3]Detail does not add to total given because of rounding. [4]At factor cost; 1980 prices. [5]Derived value. [6]Includes hotels. [7]Indirect taxes less subsidies and imputed bank service charges. [8]Includes 11,300 unemployed. [9]Districts of Wanica and Paramaribo only. [10]1992. [11]1998. [12]There are no public railways operating in Suriname. [13]All services are part of the army.

Internet resources for further information:
- **Suriname Home Page http://www.sesrtcic.org/dir-sur/surhome.htm**

Swaziland

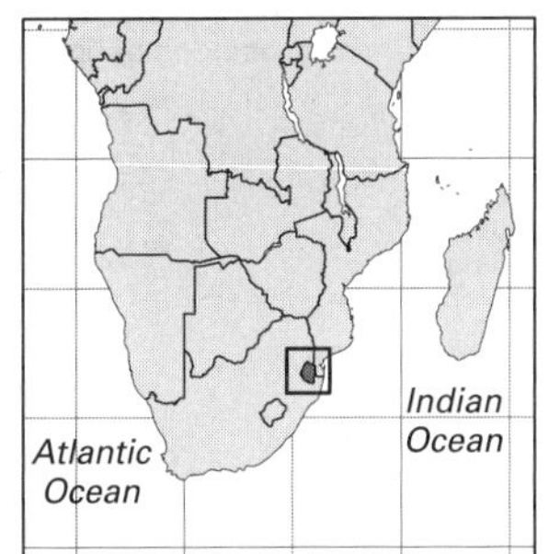

Official name: Umbuso weSwatini (Swazi); Kingdom of Swaziland (English).
Form of government[1]: monarchy with two legislative houses (Senate [30[2]]; House of Assembly [65[3]]).
Head of state and government: King, assisted by Prime Minister.
Capitals: Mbabane (administrative and judicial); Lozitha and Ludzidzini (royal); Lobamba (legislative).
Official languages: Swazi; English.
Official religion: none.
Monetary unit: 1 lilangeni[4] (plural emalangeni [E]) = 100 cents; valuation (Sept. 28, 2001) 1 U.S.$ = E 9.01; 1 £ = E 13.24.

Area and population

Districts	Capitals	area sq mi	area sq km	population 1997 census
Hhohho	Mbabane	1,378	3,569	269,826
Lubombo	Siteki	2,296	5,947	201,696
Manzini	Manzini	1,571	4,068	292,100
Shiselweni	Nhlangano	1,459	3,780	217,100
TOTAL		6,704	17,364	980,722[5]

Demography

Population (2001): 1,104,000.
Density (2001): persons per sq mi 164.7; persons per sq km 63.6.
Urban-rural (1997): urban 22.6%; rural 77.4%.
Sex distribution (1997): male 48.28%; female 51.72%.
Age breakdown (1997): under 15, 42.5%; 15–29, 29.2%; 30–44, 15.5%; 45–59, 7.8%; 60–74, 3.3%; 75 and over, 1.2%; unknown 0.5%.
Population projection: (2010) 1,216,000; (2020) 1,296,000.
Doubling time: 32 years.
Ethnic composition (2000): Swazi 82.3%; Zulu 9.6%; Tsonga 2.3%; Afrikaner 1.4%; mixed (black-white) 1.0%; other 3.4%.
Religious affiliation (1995): Christian 66.7%, of which African indigenous 44.7%, Protestant 14.8%, Roman Catholic 5.3%; other (mostly traditional beliefs) 33.3%.
Major cities (1986): Mbabane 38,290; Manzini 18,084 (urban agglomeration 46,058); Big Bend 9,676; Simunye/Ngomane 9,060; Mhlume 6,509.

Vital statistics

Birth rate per 1,000 population (2000): 40.6 (world avg. 22.5).
Death rate per 1,000 population (2000): 20.4 (world avg. 9.0).
Natural increase rate per 1,000 population (2000): 20.2 (world avg. 13.5).
Total fertility rate (avg. births per childbearing woman; 2000): 5.9.
Life expectancy at birth (2000): male 39.5 years; female 41.4 years.
Major causes of death (1992)[6]: accidents and injuries 15.8%; infectious intestinal diseases 13.3%; tuberculosis 10.3%; malnutrition 6.2%; respiratory diseases 5.3%; circulatory diseases 5.0%; digestive diseases 4.6%.

National economy

Budget (1999–2000). Revenue: E 2,436,400,000 (receipts from Customs Union of Southern Africa 50.1%; tax on income and profits 25.8%; sales tax 12.0%; foreign-aid grants 3.5%; property income 2.1%; fees, services, and fines 1.1%). Expenditures: E 2,630,700,000 (recurrent expenditure 78.2%, of which general administration 28.0%, education 17.3%, economic services 11.2%, justice and police 8.0%, health 6.5%, defense 4.8%).
Gross national product (1999): U.S.$1,379,000,000 (U.S.$1,350 per capita).

Structure of gross domestic product and labour force

	1999		1986	
	in value E '000	% of total value	labour force	% of labour force
Agriculture	904,900	11.7	30,197	18.8
Mining	51,400	0.7	5,245	3.3
Manufacturing	2,148,700	27.7	14,742	9.2
Construction	278,800	3.6	7,661	4.8
Public utilities	117,700	1.5	1,315	0.8
Transp. and commun.	290,600	3.7	7,526	4.7
Trade	530,500	6.8	12,348	7.7
Finance	333,300	4.3	1,931	1.2
Pub. admin., defense	1,158,100	15.0	32,309	20.1
Services	82,100	1.1		
Other	1,849,700[7]	23.9[7]	47,081[8]	29.4[8]
TOTAL	7,746,000[9]	100.0	160,355	100.0

Population economically active (1986): total 160,355; activity rate of total population 23.5% (participation rates: ages 15 and over, 44.1%; female 34.2%; unemployed 27.0%).

Price and earnings indexes (1995 = 100)

	1994	1995	1996	1997	1998	1999	2000
Consumer price index	89.1	100.0	106.4	114.0	123.3	130.8	146.7
Weekly earnings index[10]	...	100.0	100.0	95.7	95.7	98.3	...

Public debt (external, outstanding; 1999): U.S.$205,500,000.
Production (metric tons except as noted). Agriculture, forestry, fishing (1999): sugarcane 3,700,000, corn (maize) 113,000, oranges 31,200, grapefruit and pomelo 25,400, seed cotton 16,200, roots and tubers 8,300 (of which potatoes 6,000, sweet potatoes 2,300), pineapples 8,000, dry beans 5,000, peanuts (groundnuts) 4,600; livestock (number of live animals) 652,000 cattle, 438,000 goats, 31,000 pigs, 26,000 sheep, 980,000 chickens; roundwood (1998) 1,494,000 cu m; fish catch (1998) 60. Mining and quarrying (1999): asbestos 22,912; diamonds 64,000 carats[11]. Manufacturing (value added in U.S.$'000; 1994): food and beverages 244,000, of which beverage processing 153,000; paper and paper products 35,000; textiles 19,000; printing and publishing products 18,000; clothing 7,000; metal and metal products 7,000. Construction (value in E; 1996)[12]: residential 34,100,000; nonresidential 17,500,000. Energy production (consumption): electricity (kW-hr; 1991) 387,000,000 (815,000,000); coal (metric tons; 1999) 426,299 (1989; 28,454); crude petroleum, n.a. (n.a.).
Household income and expenditure. Average household size (1986) 5.7; annual income per household (1985) E 332 (U.S.$151); sources of income (1985): wages and salaries 44.4%, self-employment 22.2%, transfers 12.2%, other 21.2%; expenditure (1985): food and beverages 33.5%, rent and fuel 13.4%, household durable goods 12.8%, transportation and communications 8.8%, clothing and footwear 6.0%, recreation 3.3%.
Tourism (1999): receipts U.S.$35,000,000; expenditures U.S.$45,000,000.

Foreign trade

Balance of trade (current prices)

	1995	1996	1997	1998	1999
U.S.$'000,000	–197	–204	–127	–100	–130
% of total	10.2%	10.7%	6.2%	4.9%	6.6%

Imports (1998): U.S.$1,068,000,000 (machinery and transport equipment 26.2%; manufactured items 17.0%; foodstuffs 15.8%; chemicals 13.9%; minerals, fuels, and lubricants 11.8%). *Major import sources* (1997–98): South Africa 82.9%; U.K. 1.7%; U.S. 0.9%; Zimbabwe 0.2%; Spain 0.2%.
Exports (1998): U.S.$921,000,000 (sugar 11.0%; wood and wood products 8.1%; refrigerators 7.5%; cotton yarn 2.3%; paper and paper products 2.0%; canned fruits 1.4%; citrus fruits 1.3%; asbestos 1.0%). *Major export destinations* (1997): South Africa 74.0%; Italy 8.7%; Mozambique 5.2%; U.S. 2.4%; U.K. 2.1%; Zimbabwe 1.7%.

Transport and communications

Transport. Railroads (1995)[13]: length 187 mi, 301 km; passenger-mi 752,000,000[14], passenger-km 1,210,000,000[14]; short ton-mi cargo 1,993,000,000[15], metric ton-km cargo 2,910,000,000[15]. Roads (1996): total length 2,367 mi, 3,810 km (paved 29%). Vehicles (1997): passenger cars 31,882; trucks and buses 32,772. Air transport (1995)[16]: passenger-mi 30,710,000, passenger-km 49,423,000; short ton-mi cargo 87,000, metric ton-km cargo 127,000; airports (1997) with scheduled flights 1.

Communications

Medium	date	unit	number	units per 1,000 persons
Daily newspapers	1996	circulation	24,000	24.3
Radio	1997	receivers	155,000	153
Television	1999	receivers	110,000	104
Telephones	1999	main lines	30,569	28.8
Cellular telephones	1999	subscribers	14,000	13.2
Personal computers	1998	units	278	0.3
Internet	1999	users	5,000	4.7

Education and health

Educational attainment (1986). Percentage of population age 25 and over having: no formal schooling 42.1%; some primary education 23.9%; complete primary 10.5%; some secondary 19.2%; complete secondary and higher 4.3%.
Literacy (1995): total population age 15 and over literate 76.7%; males literate 78.0%; females literate 75.6%.

Education (1997)

	schools	teachers	students	student/teacher ratio
Primary (age 6–13)	529	6,094	205,829	33.8
Secondary (age 14–18)	175	3,067	58,197	19.0
Voc., teacher tr.[17]	5	228	2,958	13.0
Higher	1	190[17]	2,132	9.1[17]

Health: physicians (1996) 148 (1 per 6,663 persons); hospital beds (1984) 1,608 (1 per 396 persons); infant mortality rate per 1,000 live births (2000) 109.0.
Food (1999): daily per capita caloric intake 2,698 (vegetable products 87%, animal products 13%); 116% of FAO recommended minimum requirement.

Military

Total active duty personnel: n.a. *Military expenditure as percentage of GNP* (1997): 2.7% (world 2.6%); per capita expenditure U.S.$34.

[1]The Constitutional Review Committee appointed in August 1996 presented a draft constitution to the King in August 2001; promulgation of a new constitution expected by August 2003. [2]Includes 20 nonelective seats. [3]Includes 10 nonelective seats. [4]The lilangeni is at par with the South African rand. [5]Includes residents abroad. [6]Percentage of deaths of known cause at government, mission, and private hospitals. [7]Includes indirect taxes less imputed bank service charges and subsidies. [8]Includes 43,925 unemployed. [9]Detail does not add to total given because of rounding. [10]Manufacturing sector only. [11]1994. [12]Urban areas under the jurisdiction of the Manzini and Mbabane town councils only. [13]Swaziland's only passenger train service was terminated in May 2000. [14]1988. [15]1991. [16]Royal Swazi National Airways only; international flights only. [17]1993–94.

Internet resources for further information:
- **Central Bank of Swaziland http://www.centralbank.sz**
- **Swaziland on the Internet http://www.realnet.co.sz**

Sweden

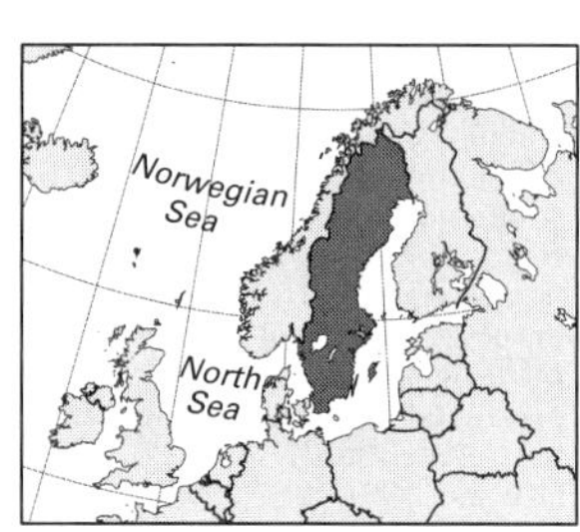

Official name: Konungariket Sverige (Kingdom of Sweden).
Form of government: constitutional monarchy and parliamentary state with one legislative house (Parliament [349]).
Chief of state: King.
Head of government: Prime Minister.
Capital: Stockholm.
Official language: Swedish.
Official religion: none[1].
Monetary unit: 1 Swedish krona (SKr) = 100 ore; valuation (Sept. 28, 2001) 1 U.S.$ = SKr 10.67; 1 £ = SKr 15.68.

Area and population

Counties	Capitals	area sq mi	area sq km	population 2001[2] estimate
Blekinge	Karlskrona	1,136	2,941	150,392
Dalarna	Falun	10,885	28,193	278,259
Gävleborg	Gävle	7,024	18,192	279,262
Gotland	Visby	1,212	3,140	57,313
Halland	Halmstad	2,106	5,454	275,004
Jämtland	Östersund	19,090	49,443	129,566
Jönköping	Jönköping	4,044	10,475	327,829
Kalmar	Kalmar	4,313	11,171	235,391
Kronoberg	Växjö	3,266	8,458	176,639
Norrbotten	Luleå	38,190	98,911	256,238
Örebro	Örebro	3,288	8,517	273,615
Östergötland	Linköping	4,078	10,562	411,345
Skåne	Malmo	4,258	11,027	1,129,424
Södermanland	Nyköping	2,341	6,062	256,033
Stockholm	Stockholm	2,506	6,490	1,823,210
Uppsala	Uppsala	2,698	6,989	294,196
Värmland	Karlstad	6,790	17,586	275,003
Västerbotten	Umeå	21,390	55,401	255,640
Västernorrland	Härnösand	8,370	21,678	246,903
Västmanland	Västerås	2,433	6,302	256,889
Västra Götaland	Göteborg	9,244	23,942	1,494,641
TOTAL LAND AREA		158,662	410,934	
INLAND WATER		15,070	39,030	
TOTAL		173,732	449,964	8,882,792

Demography

Population (2001): 8,888,000.
Density (2001)[3]: persons per sq mi 51.2, persons per sq km 19.8.
Urban-rural (1999): urban 83.3%; rural 16.7%.
Sex distribution (2000): male 49.42%; female 50.58%.
Age breakdown (2000[2]): under 15, 18.5%; 15–29, 18.3%; 30–44, 20.8%; 45–59, 20.3%; 60–74, 13.3%; 75 and over, 8.8%.
Population projection: (2010) 9,055,000; (2020) 9,307,000.
Ethnic composition (1997[2]): Swedish 89.3%; Finnish 2.3%; Yugoslavian 0.8%; Iranian 0.6%; Bosnian 0.5%; other 6.5%.
Religious affiliation (1999): Church of Sweden 86.5% (nominally; about 30% nonpracticing); Muslim 2.3%; Roman Catholic 1.8%; Pentecostal 1.1%; other 8.3%.
Major cities (2000): Stockholm 743,703; Göteborg 462,470; Malmö 257,574; Uppsala 188,478; Linköping 132,500.

Vital statistics

Birth rate per 1,000 population (2000): 9.9 (world avg. 22.5); (1999) legitimate 48.2%; illegitimate 51.8%.
Death rate per 1,000 population (2000): 10.6 (world avg. 9.0).
Natural increase rate per 1,000 population (2000): –0.7 (world avg. 13.5).
Total fertility rate (avg. births per childbearing woman; 2000): 1.5.
Marriage rate per 1,000 population (1999): 3.6.
Divorce rate per 1,000 population (1999): 2.4.
Life expectancy at birth (2000): male 77.1 years; female 82.5 years.
Major causes of death per 100,000 population (1997): heart disease 508.8; malignant neoplasms (cancers) 240.0; cerebrovascular disease 116.2.

National economy

Budget (1999). Revenue: SKr 725,104,000,000 (value-added and excise taxes 34.8%, social security 32.1%, income and capital gains taxes 18.8%, property taxes 5.4%). Expenditures: SKr 643,147,000,000 (health and social affairs 25.5%, debt service 14.0%, defense 6.9%, education 4.5%).
Public debt (2000): U.S.$61,046,000,000.
Production (metric tons except as noted). Agriculture, forestry, fishing (2001): sugar beets 2,752,600, wheat 2,390,000, barley 1,600,000, potatoes 991,000, oats 990,000; livestock (number of live animals) 1,891,456 pigs, 1,713,000 cattle, 451,594 sheep; roundwood (2000) 55,250,000 cu m; fish catch (1999) 357,317. Mining and quarrying (1998): iron ore 20,930,000; zinc 297,000; copper 270,000. Manufacturing (value added, in SKr '000,000; 1999): transport equipment 76,274; machinery, except electrical 76,133; paper products 46,363; electrical machinery 40,603; food 21,474; wood products 15,825; iron and steel 14,671. Construction (dwellings completed; 1999): 11,712. Energy production (consumption): electricity (kW-hr; 1999) 154,663,000,000 (158,882,000,000); coal (metric tons; 1997) none (3,113,000); crude petroleum (barrels; 1997) none (146,382,000); petroleum products (metric tons; 1997) 18,840,000 (12,757,000); natural gas (cu m; 1997) none (856,941,000).
Tourism (1999): receipts U.S.$3,894,000,000; expenditures U.S.$7,557,000,000.
Land use (1994): forest 68.0%; pasture 1.4%; agriculture 6.8%; other 23.8%.
Gross national product (1998): U.S.$236,940,000 (U.S.$26,750 per capita).

Structure of gross domestic product and labour force

	1999 in value SKr '000,000	% of total value	labour force	% of labour force
Agriculture	39,072	2.3	104,000	2.4
Mining	5,262	0.3		
Manufacturing	409,630	24.5	797,000	18.5
Public utilities	46,896	2.8		
Construction	71,310	4.3	225,000	5.2
Transp. and commun.	134,251	8.0	787,000	18.3
Trade	222,173	13.3		
Finance	414,456	24.8	504,000	11.7
Pub. admin., defense	329,909	19.7	208,000	4.8
Services	70,468	4.2	1,442,000	33.5
Other	–69,514[4]	–4.2[4]	241,000[5]	5.6[5]
TOTAL	1,673,913	100.0[6]	4,308,000	100.0

Population economically active (1999): total 4,308,000; activity rate of total population 48.6% (participation rates: ages 16–64, 77.2%; female 47.7%; unemployed 5.6%).

Price and earnings indexes (1995 = 100)

	1994	1995	1996	1997	1998	1999	2000
Consumer price index	98.0	100.0	100.0	101.0	101.0	101.1	102.0
Hourly earnings index	97.9	100.0	101.9	103.4	103.1	...	...

Household income and expenditure. Average household size (1999) 2.2; median income per household (1994) SKr 396,100 (U.S.$51,330); sources of income (1992): wages and salaries 58.9%, transfer payments 25.8%, self-employment 15.3%; expenditure (1995): housing and energy 29.6%, food 20.9%, transportation 16.1%, education and recreation 9.2%.

Foreign trade

Balance of trade (current prices)

	1995	1996	1997	1998	1999	2000
SKr '000,000	82,735	120,000	131,600	129,700	135,100	134,903
% of total	8.1%	11.8%	11.6%	10.7%	10.7%	10.6%

Imports (1999): SKr 565,950,000,000 (machinery and transport equipment 42.4%; manufactured goods 13.6%; chemicals 10.3%; food 5.7%). *Major import sources* (1998): Germany 19.0%; U.K. 10.2%; Norway 7.6%; Denmark 6.5%; U.S. 6.2%.
Exports (1999): SKr 700,853,000,000 (machinery and transport equipment 50.8%, of which electrical machinery 21.1%, road vehicles 12.6%; paper products 8.1%; chemicals 9.6%; iron and steel products 4.6%). *Major export destinations* (1998): Germany 11.2%; U.K. 9.1%; Norway 8.8%; U.S. 8.8%.

Transport and communications

Transport. Railroads (2000[2]): length 6,811 mi, 10,961 km; (1999) passenger-km 7,638,000,000; metric ton-km cargo 19,088,000,000. Roads (2000[2]): total length 130,500 mi, 210,000 km (paved 74%). Vehicles (2000[2]): passenger cars 3,890,159; trucks and buses 352,897. Merchant marine (2000[2]): vessels (100 gross tons and over) 412; total deadweight tonnage 2,861,000. Air transport (2000[7]): passenger-km 11,261,000; metric ton-km cargo 286,404,000; airports (1996) 48.

Communications

Medium	date	unit	number	units per 1,000 persons
Daily newspapers	1996	circulation	3,933,000	446
Radio	1997	receivers	8,250,000	932
Television	1999	receivers	4,900,000	553
Telephones	1999	main lines	5,889,000	665
Cellular telephones	1999	subscribers	5,165,000	583
Personal computers	1999	units	4,000,000	451
Internet	1999	users	3,666,000	414

Education and health

Educational attainment (2000[2]). Percentage of population age 16–64 having: primary education 32.0%; lower secondary education 28.0%; higher secondary 16.0%; some postsecondary 24.0%. *Literacy* (2000): virtually 100%.

Education (1999–2000)

	schools	teachers	students	student/ teacher ratio
Primary (age 7–12)	5,048	100,827	1,034,881	10.3
Secondary (age 13–18)		30,295	312,936	10.3
Higher	64	29,487[8]	372,108	...

Health (1999): physicians 24,200 (1 per 366 persons); hospital beds 32,755 (1 per 271 persons); infant mortality rate per 1,000 live births (2000) 3.5.
Food (1999): daily per capita caloric intake 3,141 (vegetable 67%, animal 33%) 117% of FAO recommended minimum requirement.

Military

Total active duty personnel (2000): 53,100 (army 66.1%, navy 17.3%, air force 16.6%). *Military expenditure as percentage of GNP* (1997): 2.5% (world 2.6%); per capita expenditure U.S.$626.

[1]As of January 1, 2000, the Church of Sweden (Lutheran Church) ceased being the official religion. [2]January 1. [3]Density based on land area only. [4]Includes statistical discrepancies less imputed bank service charges. [5]Unemployed. [6]Detail does not add to total given because of rounding. [7]One-third of SAS. [8]1994–95.

Internet resources for further information:
- **Statistics Sweden http://www.scb.se/eng/index.asp**

Switzerland

Official name: Confédération Suisse (French); Schweizerische Eidgenossenschaft (German); Confederazione Svizzera (Italian) (Swiss Confederation)[1].
Form of government: federal state with two legislative houses (Council of States [46]; National Council [200]).
Head of state and government: President of the Federal Council.
Capitals: Bern (administrative); Lausanne (judicial).
Official languages: French; German; Italian; Romansh (locally).
Official religion: none.
Monetary unit: 1 Swiss Franc (Sw F) = 100 centimes; valuation (Sept. 28, 2001) 1 U.S.$ = Sw F 1.62; 1 £ = Sw F 2.38.

Area and population

		area		population
Cantons	Capitals	sq mi	sq km	2000[2] estimate
Aargau	Aarau	542	1,404	540,600
Appenzell Ausser-Rhoden[3]	Herisau	94	243	53,700
Appenzell Inner-Rhoden[3]	Appenzell	66	172	14,900
Basel-Landschaft[3]	Liestal	200	518	258,600
Basel-Stadt[3]	Basel	14	37	188,500
Bern	Bern	2,301	5,959	943,400
Fribourg	Fribourg	645	1,671	234,300
Genève	Geneva	109	282	403,100
Glarus	Glarus	264	685	38,700
Graubünden	Chur	2,743	7,105	186,000
Jura	Delémont	324	838	68,800
Luzern	Luzern	576	1,493	345,400
Neuchâtel	Neuchâtel	310	803	165,600
Nidwalden[3]	Stans	107	276	37,700
Obwalden[3]	Sarnen	190	491	32,200
Sankt Gallen	Sankt Gallen	782	2,026	447,600
Schaffhausen	Schaffhausen	115	298	73,600
Schwyz	Schwyz	351	908	128,200
Solothurn	Solothurn	305	791	243,900
Thurgau	Frauenfeld	383	991	227,300
Ticino	Bellinzona	1,086	2,812	308,500
Uri	Altdorf	416	1,077	35,500
Valais	Sion	2,017	5,224	275,600
Vaud	Lausanne	1,240	3,212	616,300
Zug	Zug	92	239	07,800
Zürich	Zürich	668	1,729	1,198,600
TOTAL		15,940	41,284	7,164,400[4]

Demography

Population (2001): 7,222,000.
Density (2001): persons per sq mi 453.1, persons per sq km 174.9.
Urban-rural (1999): urban 67.5%; rural 32.5%.
Sex distribution (2000[2]): male 48.86%; female 51.14%.
Age breakdown (2000[2]): under 15, 17.4%; 15–29, 18.3%; 30–44, 24.4%; 45–59, 19.8%; 60–74, 13.0%; 75 and over, 7.1%.
Population projection: (2010) 7,323,000; (2020) 7,333,000.
National composition (2000[2])[4]: Swiss 80.4%; former Yugoslav 4.7%; Italian 4.6%; Portuguese 1.9%; German 1.4%; Spanish 1.2%; other 5.8%.
Religious affiliation (1990): Roman Catholic 46.2%; Protestant 40.0%; Muslim 2.2%; Orthodox Christian 1.0%; Jewish 0.3%; other 10.3%.
Major urban agglomerations (2000[2]): Zürich 943,400; Geneva 457,500; Basel 401,600; Bern 319,100; Lausanne 288,100; Luzern 181,400.

Vital statistics

Birth rate per 1,000 population (1999): 11.0 (world avg. 22.5); legitimate 90.0%; illegitimate 10.0%.
Death rate per 1,000 population (1999): 8.7 (world avg. 9.0).
Natural increase rate per 1,000 population (1999): 2.3 (world avg. 13.5).
Total fertility rate (avg. births per childbearing woman; 1999): 1.5.
Marriage rate per 1,000 population (1999): 5.7.
Life expectancy at birth (1998–99): male 76.7 years; female 82.6 years.
Major causes of death per 100,000 population (1996): diseases of the circulatory system 364.2; malignant neoplasms (cancers) 213.6; diseases of the respiratory system 53.3; accidents, suicide, violence 51.9.

National economy

Budget (1997)[5]. Revenue: Sw F 99,349,000,000 (social security contributions 46.7%, taxes on goods and services 20.2%, income taxes 11.6%). Expenditures: Sw F 103,528,000,000 (social security and welfare 50.5%, health 19.7%, economic affairs 10.4%, defense 5.2%, education 2.3%).
National debt (end of year; 2000): Sw F 108,108,000,000.
Tourism (1999): receipts from visitors U.S.$7,739,000,000; expenditures by nationals abroad U.S.$6,842,000,000.
Production (metric tons except as noted). Agriculture, forestry, fishing (2000): cow's milk 3,910,000, sugar beets 1,410,000, potatoes 584,000, wheat 548,200, apples 380,000, barley 273,000, grapes 164,500; livestock (number of live animals) 1,600,000 cattle, 1,450,000 pigs; roundwood (1999) 5,000,000 cu m; fish catch (1998) 1,709. Mining (1998): salt 300,000.[6] Manufacturing (value added in Sw F '000,000; 1997): machinery and transport equipment 22,530; chemicals and chemical products 19,414; iron and steel 7,972; food products 7,720. Energy production (consumption): electricity (kW-hr; 1999) 66,696,000,000 ([1996] 56,117,000,000); coal (metric tons; 1996) none (183,000); crude petroleum (barrels; 1996) none (38,534,000); petroleum products (metric tons; 1996) 5,103,000 (11,738,000); natural gas (cu m; 1996) negligible (2,902,000,-000).
Gross national product (1999): U.S.$273,856,000,000 (U.S.$38,380 per capita).

Structure of gross domestic product and labour force

	1994		1999	
	in value Sw F '000,000	% of total value	labour force[7]	% of labour force[7]
Agriculture	9,230	2.6	187,000	4.8
Manufacturing	80,997	23.0	683,000	17.6
Mining	...	...	5,000	0.1
Public utilities	7,741	2.2	25,000	0.7
Construction	24,749	7.0	289,000	7.5
Transp. and commun.	22,173	6.3	253,000	6.5
Trade, restaurants	61,092	17.3	887,000	22.9
Finance, insurance[8]	84,744	24.0	580,000	15.0
Pub. admin., defense	45,647	12.9	150,000	3.9
Services	27,769	7.9	814,000	21.0
Other	–11,218[9]	–3.2[9]	—	—
TOTAL	352,924	100.0	3,873,000[10]	100.0

Population economically active (1999): total 3,984,000; activity rate of total population 55.6% (participation rates: ages 15 and over, 67.8%; female 44.4%; unemployed [April 2000–March 2001] 1.9%).

Price and earnings indexes (1995 = 100)

	1995	1996	1997	1998	1999	2000	2001
Consumer price index	100.0	100.8	101.3	101.4	102.2	103.8	105.3[11]
Annual earnings index	100.0	101.2	101.7	102.4	102.7	...	...

Household income and expenditure (1998). Average household size 2.4; average gross income per household Sw F 100,272 (U.S.$69,162); sources of income (1996): wages 58.5%, transfers 25.6%; expenditure (1998): housing 26.2%, food 13.2%, recreation 11.4%.
Land use (1994): forested 31.6%; meadows and pastures 29.0%; agricultural and under permanent cultivation 11.0%; other 28.4%.

Foreign trade[12]

Balance of trade (current prices)

	1995	1996	1997	1998	1999	2000
Sw F '000,000	+1,753	+1,925	+330	+2,247	+1,030	–2,066
% of total	0.9%	1.0%	0.1%	1.0%	0.5%	0.8%

Imports (2000): Sw F 128,615,000,000 (machinery 24.6%, chemical products 17.1%, vehicles 11.6%, food products 7.7%). *Major import sources:* Germany 31.2%; France 10.8%; Italy 10.0%; U.S. 6.8%; The Netherlands 6.1%.
Exports (2000): Sw F 126,549,000,000 (machinery 29.3%, chemical products 28.4%, precision instruments, watches, jewelry 16.2%, fabricated metals 8.6%). *Major export destinations:* Germany 22.2%; U.S. 11.6%; France 9.0%; Italy 7.6%; U.K. 5.4%.

Transport and communications

Transport. Railroads: length (1997) 3,129 mi, 5,035 km; passenger-km 14,104,000,000; metric ton-km cargo 8,688,000,000. Roads (1998): total length 44,248 mi, 71,211 km. Vehicles (1999): passenger cars 3,467,275; trucks and buses 313,646. Air transport (1999)[13]: passenger-km 31,767,000,000; metric ton-km cargo 1,776,000,000; airports (1996) with scheduled flights 5.

Communications

Medium	date	unit	number	units per 1,000 persons
Daily newspapers	1996	circulation	2,383,000	337
Radio	1997	receivers	7,100,000	1,002
Television	1999	receivers	3,700,000	518
Telephones	1999	main lines	4,992,000	699
Cellular telephones	1999	subscribers	2,935,000	411
Personal computers	1999	units	3,300,000	462
Internet	1999	users	1,427,000	200

Education and health

Educational attainment (1997). Percentage of resident Swiss and resident alien population age 25–64 having: lower secondary education or less 20%; vocational 50%; upper secondary 7%; higher technical 13%; university 10%.
Health (1998): physicians 22,950[14] (1 per 310 persons); hospital beds 45,989 (1 per 155 persons); infant mortality rate per 1,000 live births (1999) 3.4.
Food (1999): daily per capita caloric intake 3,258 (vegetable products 67%, animal products 33%); 121% of FAO recommended minimum.

Military

Total active duty personnel (2000): 3,470[15]. *Military expenditure as percentage of GNP* (1997): 1.4% (world 2.6%); per capita expenditure U.S.$545.

[1]Short-form name in Romansh is Svizzra. [2]January 1. [3]Demicanton; functions as a full canton. [4]Includes 1,406,600 resident aliens; excludes 107,010 refugees. [5]Consolidated central government. [6]Cut and polished diamond exports (1998): U.S.$1,340,000,000. [7]Excludes unemployed. [8]Includes consulting services. [9]Import duties less imputed bank charges. [10]Labour force includes 956,000 foreign workers. [11]May. [12]Imports c.i.f.; exports f.o.b. [13]Swissair only. [14]Estimated figure. [15]Excludes 361,200 reservists.

Internet resources for further information:
- **Embassy of Switzerland (Washington, D.C.) http://www.swissemb.org**
- **Swiss Federal Statistical Office http://www.statistik.admin.ch/eindex.htm**

Syria

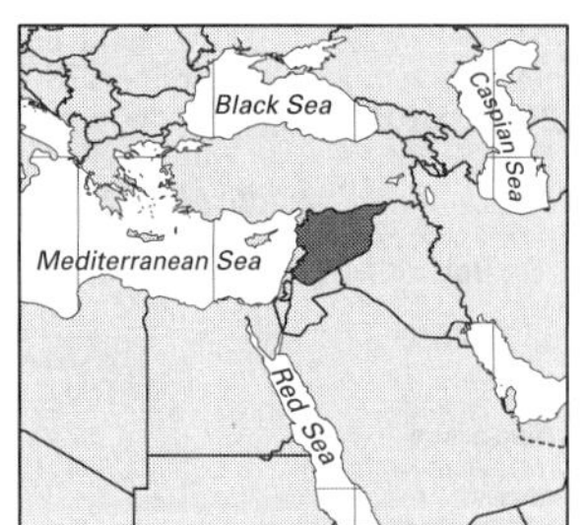

Official name: Al-Jumhūrīyah al-ʿArabīyah as-Sūrīyah (Syrian Arab Republic).
Form of government: unitary multiparty[1] republic with one legislative house (People's Council [250]).
Head of state and government: President.
Capital: Damascus.
Official language: Arabic.
Official religion: none[2].
Monetary unit: 1 Syrian pound (LS) = 100 piastres; valuation[3] (Sept. 28, 2001) 1 U.S.$ = LS 51.85; 1 £ = LS 76.20.

Area and population

		area		population
Governorates	**Capitals**	sq mi	sq km	1995 estimate
Darʿā	Darʿā	1,440	3,730	623,000
Dayr az-Zawr	Dayr az-Zawr	12,765	33,060	722,000
Dimashq	Damascus	6,962	18,032	1,730,000
Ḥalab	Aleppo	7,143	18,500	3,035,000
Ḥamāh	Ḥamāh	3,430	8,883	1,120,000
Al-Ḥasakah	Al-Ḥasakah	9,009	23,334	1,050,000
Ḥimṣ	Homs	16,302	42,223	1,247,000
Idlib	Idlib	2,354	6,097	922,000
Al-Lādhiqīyah	Latakia	887	2,297	766,000
Al-Qunayṭirah	Al-Qunayṭirah	719[4]	1,861[4]	50,000
Ar-Raqqah	Ar-Raqqah	7,574	19,616	566,000
As-Suwaydāʾ	As-Suwaydāʾ	2,143	5,550	270,000
Ṭarṭūs	Ṭarṭūs	730	1,892	596,000
Municipality				
Damascus	—	41	105	1,489,000
TOTAL		71,498[4]	185,180[4]	14,186,000

Demography

Population (2001): 16,729,000.
Density (2001): persons per sq mi 234.0, persons per sq km 90.3.
Urban-rural (1999): urban 54.0%; rural 46.0%.
Sex distribution (2000): male 51.23%; female 48.77%.
Age breakdown (2000): under 15, 40.1%; 15–29, 30.6%; 30–44, 16.6%; 45–59, 7.4%; 60–74, 3.8%; 75 and over, 1.5%.
Population projection: (2010) 20,606,000; (2020) 24,676,000.
Doubling time: 27 years.
Ethnic composition (2000): Syrian Arab 74.9%; Bedouin Arab 7.4%; Kurd 7.3%; Palestinian Arab 3.9%; Armenian 2.7%; other 3.8%.
Religious affiliation (1992): Muslim 86.0%, of which Sunnī 74.0%, ʿAlawite (Shīʿī) 12.0%; Christian 5.5%; Druze 3.0%; other 5.5%.
Major cities (1994): Aleppo 1,591,400; Damascus 1,549,932; Homs 644,204; Latakia 306,535; Ḥamāh 229,000.

Vital statistics

Birth rate per 1,000 population (2000): 31.1 (world avg. 22.5).
Death rate per 1,000 population (2000): 5.3 (world avg. 9.0).
Natural increase rate per 1,000 population (2000): 25.8 (world avg. 13.5).
Total fertility rate (avg. births per childbearing woman; 2000): 4.1.
Marriage rate per 1,000 population (1995)[5]: 8.4.
Life expectancy at birth (2000): male 67.4 years; female 69.6 years.
Major causes of death per 100,000 population (1989): n.a.; however, the leading causes of mortality among the total population were diseases of the circulatory system 39.6%, injuries and poisoning 9.1%, diseases of the nervous system 7.4%, diseases of the respiratory system 7.4%.

National economy

Budget (1999). Revenue: LS 255,300,000,000 (current revenues 85.4%, capital [development] revenues 14.6%). Expenditures: LS 255,300,000,000 (current expenditures 56.4%, capital [development] expenditures 43.6%).
Public debt (external, outstanding; 1999): U.S.$16,142,000,000.
Gross national product (1999): U.S.$15,172,000,000 (U.S.$970 per capita).

Structure of gross domestic product and labour force

	1999			
	in value LS '000,000[6]	% of total value	labour force	% of labour force
Agriculture	196,743	24.0	1,163,672	25.7
Mining	221,416[7]	27.0[7]	10,868	0.2
Manufacturing			520,734	11.5
Construction	27,433	3.3	582,382	12.9
Public utilities	[7]	[7]	3,386	0.1
Transp. and commun.	104,053	12.7	224,527	5.0
Trade	152,866	18.6	647,195	14.3
Finance	35,095	4.3	33,474	0.7
Pub. admin.	64,859	7.9	909,242	20.1
Services	18,862	2.3		
Other	...	...	431,778[8]	9.5[8]
TOTAL	821,327	100.0[9]	4,527,258	100.0

Production (metric tons except as noted). Agriculture, forestry, fishing (2000): wheat 3,104,969, sugar beets 1,300,000, seed cotton 930,000, grapes 451,000, olives 750,000, tomatoes 610,000, potatoes 450,000, oranges 400,000, apples 320,000, eggplants 128,000; livestock (number of live animals) 15,000,000 sheep, 1,200,000 goats, 905,000 cattle; roundwood (2000) 50,400 cu m; fish catch (1999) 14,024. Mining and quarrying (1999): phosphate rock 2,127,000; gypsum 232,000; salt 104,000; marble blocks 16,000,000 cu m. Manufacturing (1998): cement 5,016,000; refined sugar 89,000; cottonseed cake 226,000; olive oil 145,000; soap 89,000; vegetable oil 65,000; glass and pottery products 57,000; television receivers 150,500 units; refrigerators 136,900 units. Construction (1993): residential 628,000 sq m; nonresidential 209,000 sq m. Energy production (consumption): electricity (kW-hr; 1999) 21,568,000,000 (21,568,000,000); crude petroleum (barrels; 1996) 189,426,000 (84,083,000); petroleum products (metric tons; 1996) 11,580,000 (10,287,000); natural gas (cu m; 1996) 2,614,000,000 (2,614,000,000).
Population economically active (1999): total 4,527,258; activity rate of total population 28.8% (participation rates: ages 10 and over, 32.9%; female 11.3%; unemployed 9.5%).

Price and earnings indexes (1995 = 100)

	1993	1994	1995	1996	1997	1998	1999
Consumer price index	80.3	92.6	100.0	108.2	110.8	110.2	107.3
Earnings index	...	...	...	...	...	...	...

Average household size (1999): 5.0; income per household: n.a.; sources of income: n.a.; expenditure (1987)[10]: food 58.8%, rent, fuel, and light 16.0%, clothing 7.5%, household goods 5.8%, transportation 2.4%, education and recreation 2.1%.
Tourism (1998): receipts U.S.$1,360,000,000; expenditures U.S.$630,000,000.
Land use (1994): steppe and pasture 45.2%; agricultural and under permanent cultivation 30.1%; forested 2.6%; other 22.1%.

Foreign trade[11]

Balance of trade (current prices)

	1994	1995	1996	1997	1998	1999
LS '000,000	–21,550	–12,860	–15,500	–1,250	–11,280	–4,130
% of total	21.3%	13.8%	14.7%	1.4%	14.8%	5.0%

Imports (1999): LS 43,010,000,000 (basic metals and manufactures 16.9%, food and beverages 13.8%, machinery and transport equipment 13.0%, textiles 9.9%, chemicals and chemical products 8.9%, resins 5.8%). *Major import sources:* Germany 7.0%; France 5.7%; Italy 5.6%; Turkey 4.7%; United States 4.6%; Japan 4.1%; China 3.3%; Belgium 2.9%.
Exports (1999): LS 38,880,000,000 (crude petroleum and petroleum products 62.9%, fresh vegetables and fruits 12.4%, textiles and fabrics 7.2%, raw cotton 4.5%, live animals and meat 1.3%). *Major export destinations:* Italy 26.6%; France 20.6%; Turkey 9.2%; Saudi Arabia 8.3%; Spain 6.9%; Lebanon 4.0%.

Transport and communications

Transport. Railroads (1998): route length 2,425 km; passenger-km 181,575,000; metric ton-km cargo (1997) 1,364,000,000. Roads (1998): total length 41,451 km (paved 23%). Vehicles (1998): passenger cars 138,900; trucks and buses 282,664. Air transport (2000): passenger-km 1,421,537,000; metric ton-km cargo 20,813,000; airports (1999) with scheduled flights 5.

Communications

Medium	date	unit	number	units per 1,000 persons
Daily newspapers	1996	circulation	287,000	20
Radio	1997	receivers	4,150,000	278
Television	1999	receivers	1,070,000	66.4
Telephones	1999	main lines	1,600,000	99.3
Cellular telephones	1999	units	4,000	0.4
Personal computers	1999	units	230,000	22.7
Internet	1999	users	20,000	2.0

Education and health

Educational attainment (1984). Percentage of population age 10 and over having: no schooling 20.1%; knowledge of reading and writing 26.3%; primary education 29.3%; secondary 18.4%; certificate 3.3%; higher 2.7%. *Literacy* (1995): percentage of population age 15 and over literate 74.4%; males literate 88.3%; females literate 60.4%.

Education (1996–97)

	schools	teachers	students	student/ teacher ratio
Primary (age 6–11)	10,783	114,689	2,690,205	23.5
Secondary (age 12–18)	2,526[12]	52,182	865,042	16.6
Voc., teacher tr.	292[12]	12,479	92,622	7.4
Higher[13]	4[12]	4,773	215,734	45.2

Health (1998): physicians 22,293 (1 per 694 persons); hospital beds (1995) 17,623 (1 per 832 persons); infant mortality rate (2000) 34.8.
Food (1999): daily per capita caloric intake 3,272 (vegetable products 88%, animal products 12%); 132% of FAO recommended minimum requirement.

Military

Total active duty personnel (2000): 316,000 (army 68.0%, navy 1.9%, air force 30.1%). *Military expenditure as percentage of GNP* (1997): 5.6% (world 2.6%); per capita expenditure U.S.$211.

[1]Parties ideologically compatible with the Baʿth Party. [2]Islam is required to be the religion of the head of state and is the basis of the legal system. [3]Exchange rate most commonly used for commerce; Syria had five different exchange rates in February 2000. [4]Includes territory in the Golan Heights recognized internationally as part of Syria. [5]Syrian Arabs only. [6]In purchasers' values. [7]Manufacturing and Mining includes Public utilities. [8]Unemployed. [9]Detail does not add to total given because of rounding. [10]Weights of consumer price index components for Damascus only. [11]Import figures are c.i.f. [12]1994–95. [13]University-level institutions only.

Taiwan

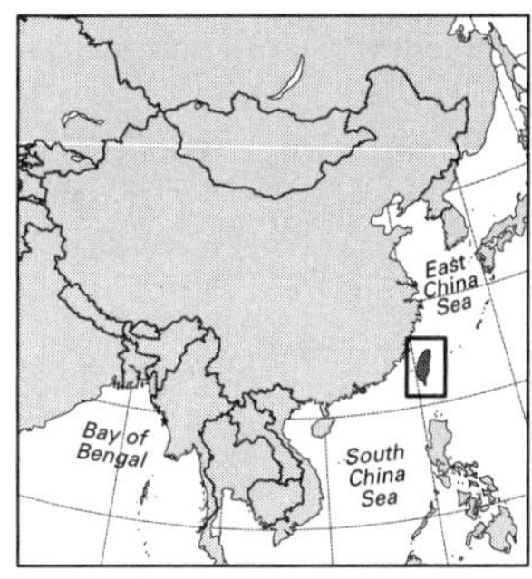

Official name: Chung-hua Min-kuo (Republic of China).
Form of government: multiparty republic with a Legislature (Legislative Yuan [225])[1].
Chief of state: President.
Head of government: Premier.
Capital: Taipei.
Official language: Mandarin Chinese.
Official religion: none.
Monetary unit: 1 New Taiwan dollar (NT$) = 100 cents; valuation (Sept. 28, 2001) 1 U.S.$ = NT$34.51; 1 £ = NT$50.72.

Area and population

	area	population		area	population
Taiwan area		2001			2001
Counties	sq km	estimate	**Municipalities**	sq km	estimate
Chang-hua	1,074	1,311,675	Chia-i	60	266,858
Chia-i	1,902	562,813	Chi-lung	133	389,732
Hsin-chu	1,428	442,766	Hsin-chu	104	371,017
Hua-lien	4,629	352,778	Kao-hsiung	154	1,493,854
I-lan	2,137	466,051	T'ai-chung	163	977,131
Kao-hsiung	2,793	1,234,896	T'ai-nan	176	738,494
Miao-li	1,820	559,526	Taipei	272	2,641,036
Nan-t'ou	4,106	540,987	**non-Taiwan area**		
P'eng-hu	127	90,719	**Counties**		
P'ing-tung	2,776	906,505	Kinmen (Quemoy)		
T'ai-chung	2,051	1,497,607	Lienchiang (Matsu)	179	63,876
T'ai-nan	2,016	1,106,821			
T'ai-pei	2,052	3,589,787			
T'ai-tung	3,515	244,275	TOTAL	36,179[2]	22,339,536
T'ao-yüan	1,221	1,748,057			
Yün-lin	1,291	742,275			

Demography

Population (2001)[3]: 22,340,000.
Density (2001)[2, 3]: persons per sq mi 1,598.9, persons per sq km 617.3.
Urban-rural (1991)[4]: urban 74.7%; rural 25.3%.
Sex distribution (2001)[3]: male 51.10%; female 48.90%.
Age breakdown (2000): under 15, 21.1%; 15–29, 25.4%; 30–44, 25.4%; 45–59, 16.0%; 60–74, 9.0%; 75 and over, 3.1%.
Population projection: (2010) 24,168,000; (2020) 26,332,000.
Ethnic composition (1997). Han Chinese, Chinese mainland minorities, and others 98.2%; indigenous tribal peoples 1.8%, of which Ami 0.6%.
Religious affiliation (1997)[5, 6]: Buddhism 22.4%; Taoism 20.7%; I-kuan Tao 4.3%; Protestant 1.6%; Roman Catholic 1.4%; other Christian 0.3%; Muslim 0.2%; Bahā'ī 0.1%; other 49.0%.
Major cities (2000): Taipei 2,646,753; Kao-hsiung 1,482,899; T'ai-chung 954,177; T'ai-nan 732,241; Chung-ho (1998) 388,174; Chi-lung 386,430.

Vital statistics

Birth rate per 1,000 population (2000): 13.8 (world avg. 22.5).
Death rate per 1,000 population (2000): 5.7 (world avg. 9.0).
Natural increase rate per 1,000 population (2000): 8.1 (world avg. 13.5).
Total fertility rate (avg. births per childbearing woman; 2000): 1.8.
Life expectancy at birth (2000): male 73.6 years; female 79.3 years.
Major causes of death per 100,000 population (2000)[4]: malignant neoplasms 142.3; cerebrovascular diseases 60.1; heart disease 47.6; accidents and suicide 47.4; diabetes 42.6; liver diseases 23.3; kidney diseases 17.5; pneumonia 14.9.

National economy

Budget (1999[7]). Revenue: NT$2,218,135,000,000 (income taxes 19.5%, of which business tax 8.8%, land tax 6.7%, commodity tax 6.6%, customs duties 4.6%). Expenditures: NT$2,217,846,000,000 (administration and defense 25.5%, education 15.3%).
Population economically active (1990): total 10,236,324; activity rate 50.5% (participation rates: ages 15–64, 72.5%; female 38.5%; unemployed [2000] 3.0%).

Price and earnings indexes (1995 = 100)

	1994	1995	1996	1997	1998	1999	2000
Consumer price index	96.4	100.0	103.1	104.0	105.7	105.9	107.2
Monthly earnings index[8]	94.8	100.0	104.2	108.9	112.0	115.8	...

Production (metric tons except as noted). Agriculture, forestry, fishing (2000): sugarcane 2,894,000, rice 1,559,000, citrus fruits 440,382, pineapples 357,535, bananas 198,454, sweet potatoes 198,000; livestock (number of live animals) 7,494,954 pigs, 202,491 goats, 161,700 cattle; timber 21,134 cu m; fish catch 1,356,275. Mining and quarrying (1990): silver 3,926 kg. Manufacturing (2000): cement 17,572,303; steel ingots 17,302,396; paperboard 3,233,864; fertilizers 1,706,861; polyester filament 1,639,139; polyvinyl chloride plastics 1,386,933; telephones 4,722,353 units; televisions 1,153,217 units. Construction (2000): total residential and nonresidential 56,121,000 sq m. Energy production (consumption): electricity (kW-hr; 2000) 175,165,000,000 ([1996] 111,140,000,000); coal (metric tons; 1996) 147,500 (29,983,000); crude petroleum (barrels; 1996) 335,000 (226,387,000); natural gas (cu m; 1996) 870,000,000 (4,500,000,000).
Tourism (1999): receipts from visitors U.S.$3,571,000,000; expenditures by nationals abroad U.S.$5,635,000,000.

Gross national product (2000): U.S.$314,421,000,000 (U.S.$14,216 per capita).

Structure of gross domestic product and labour force[4]

	2000			
	in value NT$'000,000	% of total value	labour force[9]	% of labour force[9]
Agriculture	199,430	2.1	740,000	7.6
Mining	40,782	0.4	11,000	0.1
Manufacturing	2,549,927	26.3	2,655,000	27.1
Construction	336,703	3.5	832,000	8.5
Public utilities	207,271	2.1	36,000	0.4
Transp. and commun.	652,924	6.7	481,000	4.9
Trade	1,856,026	19.2	2,163,000	22.1
Finance	2,248,185	23.2	725,000	7.4
Pub. admin., defense	987,409	10.2	1,849,000	18.9
Services	912,265	9.4		
Other	–303,983[10]	–3.1[10]	293,000[11]	3.0[11]
TOTAL	9,686,939	100.0	9,785,000	100.0

Household income and expenditure (1999). Average household size (2000) 3.3; income per household NT$1,181,082 (U.S.$37,153); expenditure: food, beverage, and tobacco 25.1%, rent, fuel, and power 24.9%, education and recreation 13.0%, transportation 11.1%, health care 11.0%, clothing 4.1%, furniture 2.9%.

Foreign trade[12]

Balance of trade (current prices)

	1995	1996	1997	1998	1999	2000
U.S.$'000,000	+8,109	+13,572	+7,656	+5,917	+10,901	+8,310
% of total	3.8%	6.2%	3.2%	2.7%	4.7%	2.8%

Imports (2000): U.S.$140,010,600,000 (electronic machinery 19.5%, nonelectrical machinery 12.2%, minerals 10.1%, chemicals 9.3%, metals and metal products 7.9%, transportation equipment 3.4%). *Major import sources:* Japan 27.5%; U.S. 17.9%; South Korea 6.4%; Germany 4.0%; Malaysia 3.8%; Singapore 3.6%.
Exports (2000): U.S.$148,320,600,000 (machinery and electric 55.7%, textile products 10.3%, plastic articles 6.1%, transportation equipment 3.9%). *Major export destinations:* U.S. 23.5%; Hong Kong 21.1%; Japan 11.2%; Singapore 3.7%; Germany 3.3%.

Transport and communications

Transport. Railroads (2000): track length 3,879 km; passenger-km 12,606,000,000; metric ton-km cargo 1,179,000,000. Roads (2000): total length 20,375 km (paved 89%[13]). Vehicles (2000): passenger cars 4,716,000; trucks and buses 833,000. Air transport (1998): passenger-km 39,218,000,000; metric ton-km cargo 4,129,300,000; airports (1996) 13.

Communications

Medium	date	unit	number	units per 1,000 persons
Radio	1996	receivers	8,620,000	402
Television	1999	receivers	9,200,000	418
Telephones	2000	main lines	12,642,000	570
Cellular telephones	2000	subscribers	17,874,000	806
Personal computers	1999	units	4,353,000	198
Internet	2000	users	4,650,000	210

Education and health

Educational attainment (1999). Percentage of population age 25 and over having: no formal schooling 7.0%; less than complete primary education 6.3%; primary 21.3%; incomplete secondary 25.7%; secondary 21.8%; some college 10.4%; higher 7.5%. *Literacy* (1999): population age 15 and over literate 16,414,896 (94.6%); males 8,641,549 (97.6%); females 7,773,347 (91.4%).

Education (1999–2000)

	schools	teachers	students	student/ teacher ratio
Primary (age 6–12)	2,583	98,745	1,927,179	19.5
Secondary (age 13–18)	972	78,506	1,288,827	16.4
Vocational	199	20,203	467,207	23.1
Higher	141	41,949	994,283	23.7

Health (1999): physicians 28,216 (1 per 780 persons); hospital beds 122,937 (1 per 179 persons); infant mortality rate per 1,000 live births (2000) 7.1.

Military

Total active duty personnel (2000): 370,000 (army 64.9%, navy 16.8%, air force 18.4%). *Military expenditure as percentage of GNP* (1997): 4.6% (world 2.6%); per capita expenditure U.S.$606.

[1]The National Assembly became a nonstanding body with limited specialized authority per April 2000 amendment; the Legislature is the formal lawmaking body. [2]Total area per more recent survey is 36,188 sq km. [3]Includes Quemoy and Matsu groups. [4]For Taiwan area only, excluding Quemoy and Matsu groups. [5]Formal subscribers to religious beliefs. [6]Almost all Taiwanese adults engage in religious practices stemming from one or a combination of traditional folk religions. [7]General government. [8]In manufacturing. [9]Civilian employed persons only. [10]Import duties less imputed bank service charge. [11]Unemployed. [12]Imports c.i.f. [13]1996.

Internet resources for further information:

- **The Republic of China Yearbook 2001 http://www.gio.gov.tw/taiwan-website/5-gp/yearbook/index.htm**
- **Directorate-General of Budget, Accounting and Statistics (Taiwan) http://www.dgbasey.gov.tw/english/dgbas_e0.htm**
- **National Statistics of Taiwan, the Republic of China http://www.stat.gov.tw**

Tajikistan

Official name: Jumhurii Tojikistan (Republic of Tajikistan).
Form of government: parliamentary republic with two legislative houses (National Assembly [33[1]]; Assembly of Representatives [63]).
Chief of state: President.
Head of government: Prime Minister.
Capital: Dushanbe.
Official language: Tajik (Tojik).
Official religion: none.
Monetary unit: 1 somoni = 100 dinars[2]; valuation (Sept. 28, 2001) 1 U.S.$ = 2.56 somoni; 1 £ = 3.76 somoni.

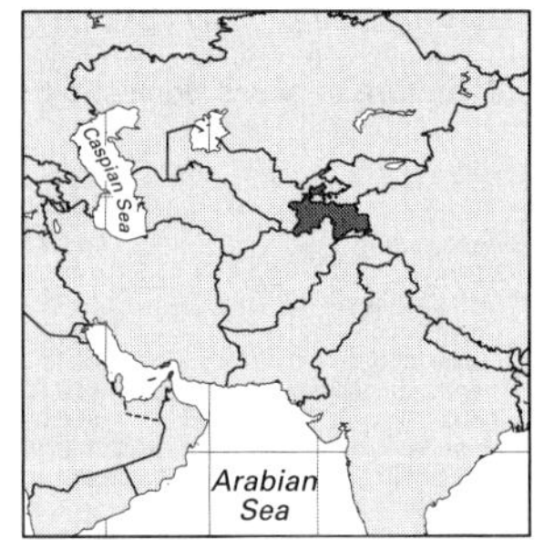

Area and population		area		population
				1999
Oblasts	**Capitals**	sq mi	sq km	census
Leninobod	Khujand	10,100	26,100	1,870,000
Khatlon (Qŭrghonteppa)	Qŭrghonteppa	9,500	24,600	2,151,000
Autonomous oblast				
Kŭhistoni Badakhshon (Gorno-Badakhshan)	Khorugh	24,600	63,700	206,000
City				
Dushanbe	—	100	300	562,000
Other[3]	—	11,000	28,400	1,338,000
TOTAL		55,300	143,100	6,127,000

Demography

Population (2001): 6,252,000.
Density (2001): persons per sq mi 113.1, persons per sq km 43.7.
Urban-rural (1999): urban 33.0%; rural 67.0%.
Sex distribution (2000): male 49.81%; female 50.19%.
Age breakdown (2000): under 15, 39.4%; 15–29, 27.7%; 30–44, 18.4%; 45–59, 7.6%; 60–74, 5.4%; 75 and over, 1.5%.
Population projection: (2010) 7,233,000; (2020) 8,506,000.
Doubling time: 39 years.
Ethnic composition (2000): Tajik 64.9%; Uzbek 25.9%; Russian 3.5%; Tatar 1.4%; Kyrgyz 1.3%; other 3.0%.
Religious affiliation (1995): Sunnī Muslim 80.0%; Shīʿī Muslim 5.0%; Russian Orthodox 1.5%; Jewish 0.1%; other (mostly nonreligious) 13.4%.
Major cities (1998 est.): Dushanbe 513,000; Khujand 163,000.

Vital statistics

Birth rate per 1,000 population (2001): 24.7 (world avg. 22.5); (1994) legitimate 90.8%; illegitimate 9.2%.
Death rate per 1,000 population (2001): 6.4 (world avg. 9.0).
Natural increase rate per 1,000 population (2001): 18.3 (world avg. 13.5).
Total fertility rate (avg. births per childbearing woman; 2001): 4.4.
Marriage rate per 1,000 population (1994): 6.8.
Divorce rate per 1,000 population (1994): 0.8.
Life expectancy at birth (2001): male 65.0 years; female 71.0 years.
Major causes of death per 100,000 population (1993): diseases of the circulatory system 225.5; violence, poisoning, and accidents 184.0; diseases of the respiratory system 160.6; infectious and parasitic diseases 129.9; malignant neoplasms (cancers) 42.3; diseases of the digestive system 20.9.

National economy

Budget (1998). Revenue: 115,144,000,000 Tajik rubles (tax revenue 96.6%, of which taxes on aluminum and cotton 35.6%, income and profit taxes 18.4%, value-added tax 17.2%, customs duties 10.7%; nontax revenue 3.4%). Expenditures: 153,797,000,000 Tajik rubles (national economy 26.2%, education 14.4%, defense 8.8%, law enforcement 8.3%, health 7.6%, state bodies and administration 5.7%).
Production (metric tons except as noted). Agriculture, forestry, fishing (1999): vegetables and melons 526,300, grain 521,000, milk 302,000, potatoes 136,000; livestock (number of live animals) 2,247,000 sheep and goats, 911,500 cattle, 2,000 pigs, 600,000 poultry; roundwood, n.a.; fish catch (1997) 285. Mining and quarrying (1998): aluminum 195,630; lead 3,500[4]; gold 3.2. Manufacturing (value of production in '000,000 Tajik rubles; 1996): ferrous and nonferrous metals 80,333; textiles 35,023; grain mill products 23,526; bakery products 16,908; basic chemicals 7,586; jewelry 3,552; processed fruits and vegetables 2,339. Energy production (consumption): electricity (kW-hr; 1996) 15,000,000,000 (15,320,000,000); coal (metric tons; 1996) 20,000 (120,000); crude petroleum (barrels; 1996) 146,600 (146,600); petroleum products (metric tons; 1996) n.a. (1,116,000); natural gas (cu m; 1996) 54,000,000 (1,276,000).
Public debt (external, outstanding; 1999): U.S.$594,900,000.
Tourism: receipts from visitors, n.a.; expenditures by nationals abroad, n.a.
Land use (1994): forest 3.8%; pasture 24.8%; agriculture 6.0%; other 65.4%.
Population economically active (1998): total 1,855,000; activity rate of total population 30.4% (participation rates: ages 16–59 [male], 16–54 [female] 60.3%; female [1996] 46.5%; unemployed 3.0%).

Price and earnings indexes (1995 = 100)							
	1994	1995	1996	1997	1998	1999	2000
Consumer price index	18.4	100.0	298.0	511.0	524.8	682.8	1,096.6
Monthly earnings index	47.7	100.0	383.7	680.6	1,175.1	1,487.7	2,048.6

Gross national product (1999): U.S.$1,749,000,000 (U.S.$280 per capita).

Structure of gross domestic product and labour force				
	1998			
	in value '000,000 Tajik rubles	% of total value	labour force	% of labour force
Agriculture	202,897	19.8	1,167,000	62.9
Mining / Manufacturing	185,144	18.1	149,000	8.0
Public utilities	...	...	...	...
Construction	18,751	1.8	52,000	2.8
Transp. and commun.	9,932	1.0	52,000	2.8
Trade	166,881	16.3	63,000	3.4
Finance	...	...	...	...
Public administration, defense	...	...	20,000	1.1
Services	225,036	21.9	281,000	15.1
Other	216,570[5]	21.1	71,000[6]	3.8[6]
TOTAL	1,025,211	100.0	1,855,000	100.0[7]

Household income and expenditure. Average household size (1989) 6.1; (1995) income per household: 18,744 Tajik rubles (U.S.$114); sources of income (1995): wages and salaries 34.5%, self-employment 34.0%, borrowing 2.4%, pension 2.0%, other 27.1%; expenditure: food 81.5%, clothing 10.2%, transport 2.5%, fuel 2.1%, other 3.7%.

Foreign trade[8]

Balance of trade (current prices)						
	1995	1996	1997	1998	1999	2000
U.S.$'000,000	–59	–16	–63	–145	–27	–47
% of total	3.6%	1.0%	4.1%	11.0%	2.0%	2.9%

Imports (1998): U.S.$731,000,000 (electricity 16.0%, petroleum products and natural gas 15.6%, alumina 15.0%, grain and flour 5.6%). *Major import sources* (1996): Uzbekistan 29.8%; Switzerland 14.9%; United Kingdom 11.7%; Russia 11.1%; Kazakhstan 7.8%; Turkmenistan 3.9%; Ukraine 2.9%.
Exports (1998): U.S.$586,000,000 (aluminum 39.9%, cotton fibre 19.1%, electricity 17.6%). *Major export destinations* (1996): The Netherlands 28.3%; Uzbekistan 24.8%; Switzerland 10.8%; Russia 10.2%; Kazakhstan 3.2%.

Transport and communications

Transport. Railroads (1995): length 294.5 mi, 474.0 km; passenger-mi 77,000,000, passenger-km 124,000,000; short ton-mi cargo 1,449,000,000, metric ton-km cargo 2,115,000,000. Roads (1996): total length 8,500 mi, 13,700 km (paved 83%). Vehicles (1996): passenger cars 680,000; trucks and buses, 8,190. Merchant marine: vessels (100 gross tons and over) n.a.; total deadweight tonnage, n.a. Air transport (1995): passenger-mi 1,386,000,000, passenger-km 2,231,000,000; short ton-mi cargo 140,000,000, metric ton-km cargo 205,000,000; airports (1997) with scheduled flights 1.

Communications				units
Medium	date	unit	number	per 1,000 persons
Daily newspapers	1996	circulation	120,000	21
Radio	1997	receivers	850,000	143
Television	1999	receivers	2,000,000	328
Telephones	1999	main lines	212,500	35
Cellular phones	1999	subscribers	625	0.1
Personal computers	...	units	...	...
Internet	1999	users	2,000	0.3

Education and health

Educational attainment (1989). Percentage of population age 25 and over having: primary education or no formal schooling 16.3%; some secondary 21.1%; completed secondary and some postsecondary 55.1%; higher 7.5%. *Literacy* (1995): percentage of total population age 15 and over literate 98.7%; males literate 99.3%; females literate 98.1%.

Education (1996–97)	schools	teachers	students	student/ teacher ratio
Primary (age 6–13)	3,432	27,172	638,674	23.5
Secondary (age 14–17)[9]	...	112,532	688,150	6.1
Voc., teacher tr.	...	...	29,482[10]	...
Higher	...	...	76,613	...

Health (1996): physicians 12,456 (1 per 475 persons); hospital beds 43,400 (1 per 136 persons); infant mortality rate per 1,000 live births (2001) 54.0.
Food (1999): daily per capita caloric intake 1,927 (vegetable products 93%, animal products 7%); (1997) 75% of FAO recommended minimum requirement.

Military

Total active duty personnel (2000): 6,000 (army 100%); more than 8,200 Russian troops remained in Tajikistan in late 2000. *Military expenditure as percentage of GNP* (1997): 1.7% (world 2.6%); per capita expenditure U.S.$19.

[1]Eight members are appointed by the President. [2]The somoni (equal to 1,000 Tajik rubles) was introduced on Oct. 30, 2000. [3]No oblast-level administration. [4]1996. [5]Includes 111,441,000,000 rubles in undistributed GDP and 105,129,000,000 rubles in indirect taxes. [6]Mostly unemployed. [7]Detail does not add to total given because of rounding. [8]Import total in balance of trade is c.i.f. [9]Excludes special education. [10]1994–95.

Internet resources for further information:
- **Interactive Central Asia Resource Project http://www.icarp.org**
- **Interstate Statistical Committee of the Commonwealth of Independent States http://www.cisstat.com/eng/macro0.htm**

Tanzania

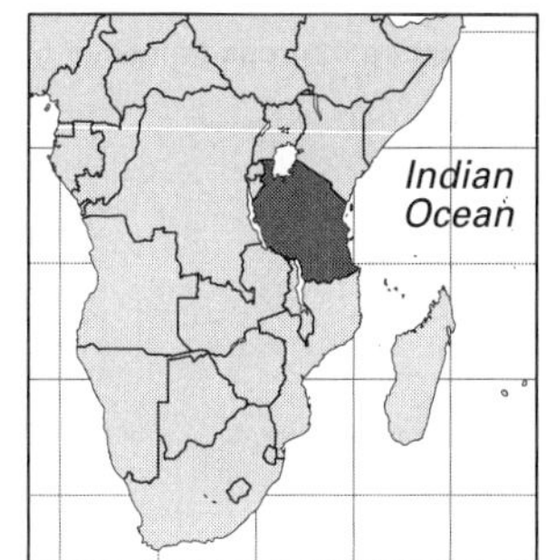

Official name: Jamhuri ya Muungano wa Tanzania (Swahili); United Republic of Tanzania (English).
Form of government: unitary multiparty republic with one legislative house (National Assembly [275[1]]).
Head of state and government: President.
Seat of government: Dar es Salaam (Capital designate, Dodoma)[2].
Official languages: Swahili; English.
Official religion: none.
Monetary unit: 1 Tanzania shilling (T Sh) = 100 cents; valuation (Sept. 28, 2001) 1 U.S.$ = T Sh 892.75; 1 £ = T Sh 1,313.

Area and population

Administrative Regions	area sq km	population 1995 estimate	Administrative Regions	area sq km	population 1995 estimate
Mainland Tanzania (Tanganyika)			Rukwa	68,635	843,424
Arusha	82,306	1,640,399	Ruvuma	63,498	950,649
Dar es Salaam	1,393	1,651,534	Shinyanga	50,781	2,151,539
Dodoma	41,311	1,502,344	Singida	49,341	960,947
Iringa	56,864	1,467,144	Tabora	76,151	1,257,650
Kagera	28,388	1,652,991	Tanga	26,808	1,590,381
Kigoma	37,037	1,043,491	**Autonomous Territory**		
Kilimanjaro	13,309	1,345,523	Zanzibar and Pemba[3]		
Lindi	66,046	784,658	Pemba	906	322,466
Mara	19,566	1,178,340	Zanzibar	1,554	456,934
Mbeya	60,350	1,791,522	TOTAL LAND AREA	883,749	
Morogoro	70,799	1,525,577	INLAND WATER	59,050	
Mtwara	16,707	1,079,495	TOTAL	942,799[4]	28,251,511
Mwanza	19,592	2,280,206			
Pwani (Coast)	32,407	774,297			

Demography

Population (2001): 36,232,000.
Density (2001)[5]: persons per sq mi 99.3, persons per sq km 38.3.
Urban-rural (1999): urban 31.7%; rural 68.3%.
Sex distribution (2000): male 49.69%; female 50.31%.
Age breakdown (2000): under 15, 44.9%; 15–29, 28.8%; 30–44, 14.1%; 45–59, 7.7%; 60–74, 3.6%; 75 and over, 0.9%.
Population projection: (2010) 44,957,000; (2020) 54,774,000.
Doubling time: 25 years.
Ethnolinguistic composition (1987): Nyamwezi and Sukuma 21.1%; Swahili 8.8%; Hehet and Bena 6.9%; Haya 5.9%; Makonde 5.9%; Nyakyusa 5.4%; Chagga 4.9%; other 41.1%.
Religious affiliation (1997): Christian *c.* 44%; Muslim *c.* 37%; animist *c.* 19%.

Vital statistics

Birth rate per 1,000 population (2000): 40.2 (world avg. 22.5).
Death rate per 1,000 population (2000): 12.9 (world avg. 9.0).
Natural increase rate per 1,000 population (2000): 27.3 (world avg. 13.5).
Total fertility rate (avg. births per childbearing woman; 2000): 5.5.
Life expectancy at birth (2000): male 51.3 years; female 53.2 years.
Major causes of death per 100,000 population: n.a.; however, the major diseases include malaria, bilharziasis, tuberculosis, and sleeping sickness.

National economy

Budget (1998–99). Revenue: T Sh 689,470,000,000 (import duties 31.7%, sales and excise tax 23.7%, income tax 23.6%). Expenditures: T Sh 898,800,000,000 (wages 24.5%, interest payments on debt 12.9%).
Public debt (external, outstanding; 1999): U.S.$6,595,000,000.
Tourism (1998): receipts from visitors U.S.$570,000,000; expenditures by nationals abroad U.S.$493,000,000.
Gross national product (1999)[6]: U.S.$8,515,000,000 (U.S.$260 per capita).

Structure of gross domestic product and labour force

	1999		1991	
	in value T Sh '000,000	% of total value	labour force	% of labour force
Agriculture	2,611,946	40.1	10,540,000	80.3
Mining	88,516	1.4		
Manufacturing	432,843	6.6	614,000	4.7
Construction	303,092	4.6		
Public utilities	92,647	1.4		
Transp. and commun.	288,699	4.4		
Trade	734,298	11.3		
Finance	830,380	12.7	1,969,000	15.0
Pub. admin., defense	471,424	7.2		
Services	156,184	2.4		
Other	514,321[7]	7.9[7]	...	...
TOTAL	6,524,350	100.0	13,123,000	100.0

Production (metric tons except as noted). Agriculture (1999): cassava 7,181,500, corn (maize) 2,457,745, sugarcane 1,354,999, bananas 751,601, plantains 752,000, rice 676,000, sorghum 561,030, sweet potatoes 500,000, coconuts 400,000, millet 194,372; livestock (number of live animals) 14,350,000 cattle, 9,900,000 goats, 4,150,000 sheep, 28,000,000 chickens; roundwood (1998) 39,022,000 cu m; fish catch (1998) 348,000. Mining and quarrying (1994): gemstones (including emeralds, sapphires, and rubies) 33,000 kg; gold 3,370 kg; diamonds 15,700 carats. Manufacturing (1999): cement 833,000; petroleum products 287,000; sugar 153,000; iron sheets 23,000; rolled steel 9,500; beer 1,239,000 hectolitres; cigarettes 3,400,000,000 units; textiles 49,800,000 sq m. Energy production (consumption): electricity (kW-hr; 1996) 1,737,000,000 (1,737,000,000); coal (metric tons; 1995) 5,000 (5,000); crude petroleum (barrels; 1996) none (4,317,000); petroleum products (metric tons; 1996) 583,000 (656,000).
Population economically active (1994): total 13,852,000; activity rate 48.0% (participation rates [1991]: over age 10, 87.8%; female 40.0%).

Price index (1995 = 100)

	1994	1995	1996	1997	1998	1999	2000
Consumer price index	77.9	100.0	121.0	140.4	158.4	170.9	181.0

Household income and expenditure. Average household size (1998) 5.4; income per household: n.a.; sources of income: n.a.; expenditure (1994): food 64.2%, clothing 9.9%, housing 8.3%, energy 7.6%, transportation 4.1%.
Land use (1995): forested 37.0%; meadows and pastures 39.6%; agricultural and under permanent cultivation 4.2%; other 19.2%.

Foreign trade

Balance of trade (current prices)

	1994	1995	1996	1997	1998	1999
T Sh '000,000	–385,977	–433,525	–363,605	–379,905	–517,779	–809,445
% of total	42.1%	35.7%	29.2%	30.2%	36.6%	49.6%

Imports (1999): U.S.$1,630,600,000 (consumer goods 33.9%, machinery 20.9%, transport equipment 18.2%, food 10.8%). *Major import sources:* Japan 10.9%; U.K. 7.8%; U.S. 6.0%; Kenya 5.8%; India 5.6%.
Exports (1999): U.S.$541,000,000 (cashew nuts 18.3%, coffee 14.2%, minerals 13.2%, tobacco 8.0%, cotton 5.2%, tea 4.5%). *Major export destinations:* India 19.5%; U.K. 17.0%; Japan 8.0%; The Netherlands 5.7%; Singapore 4.5%; Germany 4.0%; Kenya 3.8%; U.S. 3.3%.

Transport and communications

Transport. Railroads (1997): length 3,569 km; passenger-journeys 694,000,000[8]; metric ton-km cargo 1,354,000,000[8]. Roads (1996): length 88,200 km (paved 4.2%). Vehicles (1996): passenger cars 23,760; trucks and buses 115,700. Merchant marine (1992): vessels (100 gross tons and over) 43; deadweight tonnage 48,465. Air transport (1995)[9]: passenger-km 184,383,000; metric ton-km 2,904,000; airports (1998) with scheduled flights 11.

Communications

Medium	date	unit	number	units per 1,000 persons
Daily newspapers	1996	circulation	120,000	3.9
Radio	1997	receivers	8,800,000	280
Television	1999	receivers	690,000	20
Telephones	1999	main lines	149,611	4.4
Cellular telephones	1999	subscribers	50,950	1.5
Personal computers	1999	units	80,000	2.3
Internet	1999	users	25,000	0.7

Education and health

Educational attainment (1978). Percentage of population age 10 and over having: no schooling 48.6%; some primary education 40.7%; completed primary 8.7%; secondary and higher 1.9%. *Literacy* (1995): percentage of population age 15 and over literate 67.8%; males 79.4%; females 56.8%.

Education (1996)[10]

	schools	teachers	students	student/ teacher ratio
Primary (age 7–13)	10,927	108,874	3,942,888	36.2
Secondary (age 14–19)	491[11]	11,659	199,093	17.1
Teacher training	40[11]	1,062	12,571	11.8
Higher	...	1,650	12,776	7.7

Health (1993): physicians 1,365 (1 per 20,511 persons); hospital beds 26,820 (1 per 1,000 persons); infant mortality rate (2000) 81.0.
Food (1999): daily per capita caloric intake 1,940 (vegetable products 94%, animal products 6%); 84% of FAO recommended minimum requirement.

Military

Total active duty personnel (2000): 34,000 (army 88.2%, navy 2.9%, air force 8.9%). *Military expenditure as percentage of GNP* (1997): 1.3% (world 2.6%); per capita expenditure U.S.$3.

[1]Includes 5 indirectly elected seats from Zanzibar and Pemba and 37 indirectly elected seats for women and the attorney general serving ex officio. [2]The movement of the capital from Dar es Salaam to Dodoma began in the early 1980s and was scheduled to be completed by 1992; as of 1999 only the prime minister's office and legislature were located in Dodoma. [3]Has local internal government structure; Zanzibar has 3 administrative regions, Pemba has 2. [4]A recent survey indicates a total area of 364,901 sq mi (945,090 sq km). [5]Based on the total area of 364,901 sq mi (945,090 sq km). [6]Mainland Tanzania only. [7]Includes bank service charge. [8]Tanzanian Railways only; 1995. [9]Air Tanzania only. [10]Excludes Zanzibar and Pemba. [11]1994.

Internet resources for further information:

- **National Bureau of Statistics http://www.tanzania.go.tz/statistics.html#top**
- **Bank of Tanzania http://www.bot-tz.org**

Thailand

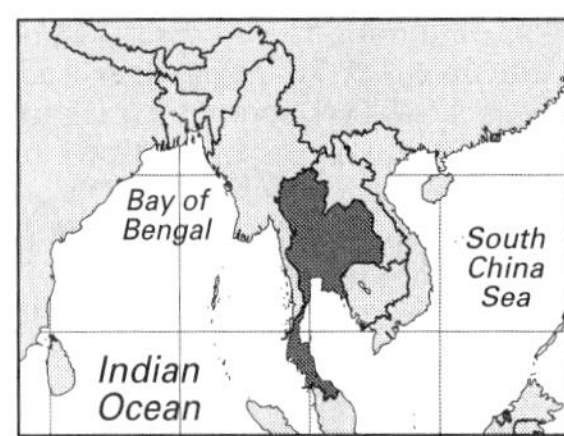

Official name: Muang Thai, or Prathet Thai (Kingdom of Thailand).
Form of government: constitutional monarchy with two legislative houses (Senate [200]; House of Representatives [500]).
Chief of state: King.
Head of government: Prime Minister.
Capital: Bangkok.
Official language: Thai.
Official religion: Buddhism.
Monetary unit: 1 Thai baht (B) = 100 stangs; valuation (Sept. 28, 2001) 1 U.S.$ = B 44.48; 1 £ = B 65.37.

Area and population	area		population
			2000
Regions[1]	sq mi	sq km	census[2]
Bangkok Metropolis	604	1,565	6,320,174
Central	39,512	102,335	14,101,530
Northeastern	65,196	168,855	20,759,899
Northern	65,500	169,645	11,367,826
Southern	27,303	70,715	8,057,518
TOTAL	198,115	513,115	60,606,947

Demography

Population (2001): 61,251,000.
Density (2001): persons per sq mi 315.1, persons per sq km 121.7.
Urban-rural (2001): urban 22.0%; rural 78.0%.
Sex distribution (2000): male 49.24%; female 50.76%.
Age breakdown (1999): under 15, 26.0%; 15–29, 27.7%; 30–44, 23.3%; 45–59, 14.1%; 60–74, 7.2%; 75 and over, 1.7%.
Population projection: (2010) 65,788,000; (2020) 68,980,000.
Doubling time: 70 years.
Ethnic composition (2000): Tai peoples 81.4%, of which Thai (Siamese) 34.9%, Lao 26.5%; Han Chinese 10.6%; Malay 3.7%; Khmer 1.9%; other 2.4%.
Religious affiliation (1996): Buddhist 92.6%; Muslim 5.3%; Christian 1.3%; other 0.8%.
Major cities (1996)[3]: Bangkok 5,584,963; Nonthaburi 271,084; Nakhon Ratchasima 180,000; Chiang Mai 170,217; Udon Thani 159,595.

Vital statistics

Birth rate per 1,000 population (2001): 16.1 (world avg. 22.5).
Death rate per 1,000 population (2001): 6.0 (world avg. 9.0).
Natural increase rate per 1,000 population (2001): 10.1 (world avg. 13.5).
Total fertility rate (avg. births per childbearing woman; 2001): 1.8.
Marriage rate per 1,000 population (1998): 5.4.
Divorce rate per 1,000 population (1998): 1.1.
Life expectancy at birth (2001): male 71.0 years; female 76.0 years.
Major causes of death per 100,000 population (1997): diseases of the heart 71.9; accidents, homicide, and poisonings 62.2; malignant neoplasms (cancers) 43.7; hypertension and cerebrovascular disease 13.4; diseases of the liver and the pancreas 10.5; pneumonia and other lung diseases 10.4.

National economy

Budget (1998). Revenue: B 753,569,000,000 (taxes on goods and services 48.6%; income taxes 28.5%; taxes on international trade 9.0%). Expenditures: B 854,264,000,000 (education 23.1%; transportation and communications 15.9%; defense 10.3%; health 9.2%; agriculture 7.5%; public order and safety 6.1%; housing 4.8%).
Production (metric tons except as noted). Agriculture, forestry, fishing (2000): sugarcane 51,210,472, rice 23,402,900, cassava 18,508,568, corn (maize) 4,571,450, pineapples 2,280,959, natural rubber 2,235,680, bananas 1,720,000, soybeans 346,127, tobacco 74,200; livestock (number of live animals) 7,682,000 pigs, 6,100,000 cattle, 2,100,000 buffalo, 172,000,000 chickens; roundwood (1999) 36,631,000 cu m; fish catch (1998) 2,900,320. Mining and quarrying (1998): limestone 37,251,000; gypsum 4,334,000; kaolin clay 266,000; zinc ore 195,122; lead ore 15,346; fluorite 3,743; tin concentrates 2,028. Manufacturing (1996): cement 38,739,000; refined sugar 6,323,000; crude steel 2,143,000; paper products 608,000; unwrought tin 10,981; beer 6,323,000 hectolitres. Construction (1990): residential 16,343,000 sq m; nonresidential 13,449,000 sq m. Energy production (consumption): electricity (kW-hr; 1996) 91,467,000,000 (92,183,000,000); coal (metric tons; 1996) 21,477,000 (24,826,000); crude petroleum (barrels; 1996) 8,900,000 (221,000,000); petroleum products (metric tons; 1996) 33,390,000 (35,863,000); natural gas (cu m; 1996) 13,274,000,000 (13,274,000,000).
Tourism (1999): receipts from visitors U.S.$6,695,000,000; expenditures by nationals abroad U.S.$1,843,000,000.
Land use (1998): meadows and pastures 1.6%; agricultural and under permanent cultivation 39.8%; forested and other 58.6%.
Population economically active (2000)[4]: total 33,973,000; activity rate of total population 54.4% (participation rates: over age 13, 69.7%; female 45.0%; unemployed 2.4%).

Price and earnings indexes (1995 = 100)							
	1994	1995	1996	1997	1998	1999	2000
Consumer price index	94.5	100.0	105.8	111.8	120.8	121.1	123.0
Monthly earnings index	87.3	100.0	108.5	117.0	…	…	…

Gross national product (1999): U.S.$121,051,000,000 (U.S.$2,010 per capita).

Structure of gross domestic product and labour force	1998		2000	
	in value B '000,000	% of total value	labour force[4]	% of labour force[4]
Agriculture	683,400	14.2	16,095,500	47.4
Mining	85,600	1.8	38,900	0.1
Manufacturing	1,362,600	28.3	4,784,800	14.1
Construction	228,100	4.7	1,280,000	3.8
Public utilities	132,000	2.7	172,500	0.5
Transp. and commun.	385,900	8.0	951,200	2.8
Trade	677,900	14.1	4,801,500	14.1
Finance Pub. admin., defense Services	1,262,000	26.2	4,864,800	14.3
Other	…	…	983,800[5]	2.9[5]
TOTAL	4,817,500	100.0	33,973,000	100.0

Public debt (external, outstanding; 1998): U.S.$28,113,000,000.
Household income and expenditure (1998). Average household size (2000) 3.9; average annual income per household B 149,904 (U.S.$3,624); sources of income: wages and salaries 40.1%, self-employment 29.8%, transfer payments 7.9%, other 22.2%; expenditure: food, tobacco, and beverages 37.7%, housing 21.4%, transportation and communications 13.3%, medical and personal care 5.1%, clothing 3.5%, education 2.3%.

Foreign trade[6]

Balance of trade (current prices)						
	1995	1996	1997	1998	1999	2000
U.S.$'000,000	−7,968	−9,488	+1,572	+16,238	+14,013	+11,757
% of total	6.7%	8.0%	1.4%	18.2%	14.1%	9.5%

Imports (1998): B 1,778,564,000,000 (electrical machinery 26.2%, power generating equipment 14.6%, mineral fuels and lubricants 8.0%, iron and steel products 8.0%, plastics 4.2%, organic chemicals 3.3%, aircraft and parts 2.7%). *Major import sources:* Japan 23.6%; U.S. 14.0%; Singapore 5.6%; Taiwan 5.2%; Malaysia 5.1%; Germany 4.3%; China 4.2%; South Korea 3.5%.
Exports (1998): B 2,242,579,000,000 (electrical machinery 18.9%, power generating equipment 18.6%, garments 6.1%, rubber products 4.1%, live fish 4.0%, meat and fish preparations 3.9%, cereals 3.9%). *Major export destinations:* U.S. 22.3%; Japan 13.7%; Singapore 8.6%; Hong Kong 5.1%; The Netherlands 4.0%; U.K. 3.9%; Malaysia 3.3%; China 3.2%.

Transport and communications

Transport. Railroads (1998[7]): route length 4,623 km; passenger-km 10,680,000,000; metric ton-km cargo 2,832,000,000. Roads (1996): total length 64,600 km (paved 98%). Vehicles (1999): passenger cars 1,661,000; trucks and buses 2,855,000. Air transport (1999): passenger-km 38,345,195,000; metric ton-km cargo 1,670,717,000; airports (1996) 25.

Communications				units
Medium	date	unit	number	per 1,000 persons
Daily newspapers	1996	circulation	3,800,000	64
Radio	1997	receivers	13,959,000	234
Television	1999	receivers	17,600,000	289
Telephones	1999	main lines	5,216,000	86
Cellular telephones	1999	subscribers	2,339,000	38
Personal computers	1999	units	1,382,000	23
Internet	1999	users	800,000	13

Education and health

Educational attainment (1990). Percentage of population age 25 and over having: no formal schooling 11.8%; primary education 71.3%; secondary 9.5%; postsecondary 6.6%; unknown 0.8%. *Literacy* (1995): total population age 15 and over literate 93.8%; males literate 96.0%; females literate 91.6%.

Education (1997–98)	schools	teachers	students	student/ teacher ratio
Primary (age 7–12)	34,001[8]	445,542[9]	5,927,902	19.3[9]
Secondary (age 13–18)	2,318[9]	107,025[9]	3,358,470	19.8[9]
Voc., teacher tr.	679[9]	40,116[9]	738,861	19.8[9]
Higher	102[9]	38,423[8]	1,522,142	31.8[8]

Health (1997): physicians 16,569 (1 per 3,553 persons); hospital beds 132,405 (1 per 445 persons); infant mortality rate (2001) 18.0.
Food (1999): daily per capita caloric intake 2,411 (vegetable products 88%, animal products 12%); (1997) 109% of FAO recommended minimum requirement.

Military

Total active duty personnel (2000): 301,000 (army 63.1%, navy 22.6%, air force 14.3%). *Military expenditure as percentage of GNP* (1997): 2.3% (world 2.6%); per capita expenditure U.S.$57.

[1]Actual local administration is based on 76 provinces. [2]Preliminary. [3]Based on registration records. [4]August; economically active persons 13 years and over. [5]Mostly unemployed. [6]Import figures are f.o.b. in balance of trade and c.i.f. for commodities and trading partners. [7]Traffic data refer to fiscal year ending September 30. [8]1995–96. [9]1993.

Internet resources for further information:
- **National Statistical Office Thailand**
  http://www.nso.go.th
- **Bank of Thailand**
  http://www.bot.or.th/bothomepage/index/index_e.asp

Togo

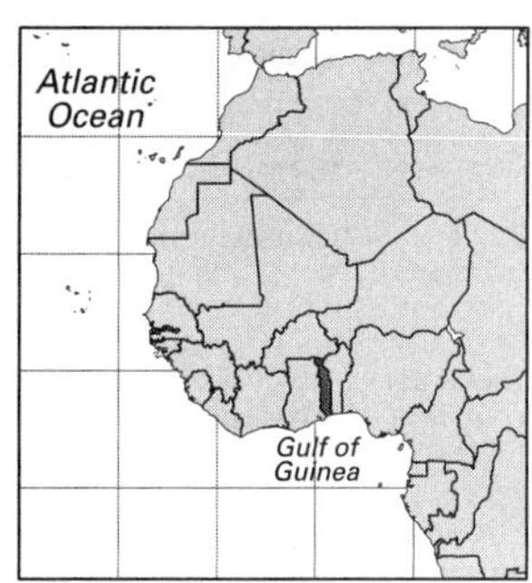

Official name: République Togolaise (Togolese Republic).
Form of government: multiparty republic[1] with one legislative body (National Assembly [81]).
Chief of state: President[1].
Head of government: Prime Minister.
Capital: Lomé.
Official language: French.
Official religion: none.
Monetary unit: 1 CFA franc (CFAF) = 100 centimes; valuation (Sept. 28, 2001) 1 U.S.$ = CFAF 720.28; 1 £ = CFAF 1,059.

Area and population

Regions / Prefectures	Capitals	area sq mi	area sq km	population 1989 estimate
Centrale	Sokodé			339,000
Sotouboua	Sotouboua	2,892	7,491	162,500
Tchamba	Tchamba	1,214	3,143	54,500
Tchaoudjo	Sokodé	984	2,549	122,000
De la Kara	Kara			531,500
Assoli	Bafilo	362	938	41,000
Bassar	Bassar	2,444	6,330	152,000
Binah	Pagouda	180	465	61,000
Doufelgou	Niamtougou	432	1,120	75,000
Kéran	Kandé	419	1,085	49,500
Kozah	Kara	653	1,692	153,000
Des Plateaux	Atakpamé			810,500
Amou	Amlamé	773	2,003	98,500
Haho	Notsé	1,406	3,641	139,000
Kloto	Kpalimé	1,072	2,777	233,500
Ogou	Atakpamé	2,349	6,083	204,000
Wawa	Badou	954	2,471	135,500
Des Savanes	Dapaong			410,500
Oti	Sansanné-Mango	1,453	3,762	98,500
Tône	Dapaong	1,869	4,840	312,000
Maritime	Lomé			1,300,000[2]
Golfe	Lomé	133	345	560,000
Lacs	Aného	275	713	172,500
Vo	Vogan	290	750	125,000
Yoto	Tabligbo	483	1,250	187,000
Zio	Tsévié	1,288	3,337	255,000
TOTAL		21,925	56,785	3,391,500

Demography

Population (2001): 5,153,000.
Density (2001): persons per sq mi 235.0, persons per sq km 90.7.
Urban-rural (1998): urban 32.2%; rural 67.8%.
Sex distribution (2000): male 49.20%; female 50.80%.
Age breakdown (2000): under 15, 46.1%; 15–29, 27.8%; 30–44, 14.7%; 45–59, 7.5%; 60–74, 3.2%; 75 and over, 0.7%.
Population projection: (2010) 6,245,000; (2020) 7,197,000.
Ethnic composition (2000): Ewe 22.2%; Kabre 13.4%; Wachi 10.0%; Mina 5.6%; Kotokoli 5.6%; Bimoba 5.2%; Losso 4.0%; Gurma 3.4%; Lamba 3.2%; Adja 3.0%; other 24.4%.
Religious affiliation (1993): traditional beliefs 50%; Christian 35%, of which Roman Catholic 23%; Muslim 15%.
Major cities (1997): Lomé 375,000 (urban agglomeration [1999] 790,000); Sokodé 51,000; Kara 35,000; Kpalimé 30,000; Atakpamé 30,000.

Vital statistics

Birth rate per 1,000 population (2000): 38.0 (world avg. 22.5).
Death rate per 1,000 population (2000): 11.2 (world avg. 9.0).
Natural increase rate per 1,000 population (2000): 26.8 (world avg. 13.5).
Total fertility rate (avg. births per childbearing woman; 2000): 5.5.
Life expectancy at birth (2000): male 52.8 years; female 56.7 years.

National economy

Budget (1998). Revenue: CFAF 142,400,000,000 (tax revenue 81.0%, of which taxes on international trade 40.3%, public enterprise taxes 10.0%, sales tax 9.6%; grants 10.4%; nontax revenue 8.6%). Expenditures: CFAF 187,500,000,000 (current expenditure 70.9%, of which wages 31.4%, materials and supplies 20.2%; transfers 14.0%; other 5.4%; debt service 9.6%).
Production (metric tons except as noted). Agriculture, forestry, fishing (1997): yams 696,147, cassava 579,381, corn (maize) 350,484, vegetables 150,000, sorghum 136,558, oil palm fruit 115,000, rice 86,663, millet 40,693, peanuts (groundnuts) 27,157, bananas 16,100, coffee 14,000, coconuts 14,000, pulses 6,000; livestock (number of live animals) 1,110,000 goats, 850,000 pigs, 740,000 sheep, 222,800 cattle, 7,500,000 chickens; roundwood (1998) 1,182,000 cu m; fish catch (1997) 14,290. Mining and quarrying (1996): phosphate rock 2,700,000; limestone is quarried for cement manufacture. Manufacturing (value added in CFAF '000,000; 1998): food products, beverages, and tobacco manufactures 41,400; metallic goods 12,000; nonmetallic manufactures 8,500; textiles, clothing, and leather 4,900; wood products 4,700; paper, printing, and publishing 4,600; chemicals 3,600. Construction (value added in CFAF; 1995): 19,958,000,000. Energy production (consumption): electricity (kW-hr; 1997) 34,700,000 (282,200,000); petroleum products (metric tons; 1998) none (231,000).
Household income and expenditure. Average household size (1998) 6.0; average annual income per household (1980) CFAF 102,000 (U.S.$452); sources of income: n.a.; expenditure (1987): food and beverages 45.9%, household durable goods 13.9%, clothing 11.4%, housing 5.9%, services 20.5%.

Gross national product (1999): U.S.$6,794,000,000 (U.S.$320 per capita).

Structure of gross domestic product and labour force

	1998 in value CFAF '000,000,000	1998 % of total value	1994 labour force	1994 % of labour force
Agriculture	375.1	42.1	1,041,000	67.7
Mining	52.0	5.8	177,000	11.5
Manufacturing	81.3	9.1		
Construction	27.2	3.1		
Public utilities	27.5	3.1		
Transp. and commun.	47.3	5.3	318,000	20.7
Trade and finance	151.1	17.0		
Pub. admin., defense	62.1	7.0		
Services	67.0	7.5		
TOTAL	890.6	100.0	1,538,000[3]	100.0[3]

Public debt (external, outstanding; 1999): U.S.$1,263,000,000.
Population economically active (1994): total 1,538,000; activity rate of total population 33.8% (participation rates over age 10, 50.7%; female 35.6%; unemployed 16–18%).

Price and earnings indexes (1995 = 100)

	1994	1995	1996	1997	1998	1999	2000
Consumer price index	85.9	100.0	104.7	113.3	114.4	114.3	116.5
Hourly earnings index	...	...	...	...	...	...	...

Tourism (1999): receipts U.S.$6,000,000; expenditures U.S.$2,000,000.

Foreign trade[4]

Balance of trade (current prices)

	1994	1995	1996	1997	1998
CFAF '000,000	+7,800	+2,500	−21,300	−17,700	−18,600
% of total	3.2%	0.7%	5.2%	3.4%	3.7%

Imports (1998): CFAF 263,400,000,000 (consumer goods 55.8%; capital equipment 18.8%; intermediate goods 18.0%; petroleum products 7.4%). *Major import sources* (1998): Ghana 21%; France 12.7%; China 12.0%; Nigeria 2.1%; Japan 1.8%.
Exports (1998): CFAF 244,800,000,000 (domestic exports 80.4%, of which cotton 24.5%, phosphates 22.0%, coffee 9.1%, cocoa 4.3%; reexports 19.6%). *Major export destinations* (1998): Canada 12.1%; Bolivia 9.5%; Nigeria 7.4%; France 3.8%; Ghana 3.1%.

Transport and communications

Transport. Railroads (1996): route length 395 km; (1996) passenger-km 16,500,000; metric ton-km cargo 49,000,000. Roads (1996): total length 7,520 km (paved 32%). Vehicles (1996): passenger cars 79,200; trucks and buses 34,240. Merchant marine (1992): vessels (100 gross tons and over) 8; total deadweight tonnage 20,633. Air transport (1996)[5]: passenger-km 224,736,000; metric ton-km cargo 16,420,000; airports (1998) 2.

Communications

Medium	date	unit	number	units per 1,000 persons
Daily newspapers	1996	circulation	15,000	3.6
Radio	1998	receivers	720,000	167
Television	1999	receivers	100,000	21
Telephones	1999	main lines	38,166	7.8
Cellular telephones	1999	subscribers	17,000	3.5
Personal computers	1999	units	80,000	16
Internet	1999	users	15,000	3.1

Education and health

Educational attainment (1981). Percentage of population age 25 and over having: no formal schooling 76.5%; primary education 13.5%; secondary 8.7%; higher 1.3%. *Literacy* (1995): total population age 15 and over literate 51.7%; males 67.0%; females 37.0%.

Education (1996–97)

	schools	teachers	students	student/ teacher ratio
Primary (age 6–11)	3,283[6]	18,535	859,574	46.4
Secondary (age 12–18)	314[7]	4,736[6]	169,178	...
Vocational	18[8]	653	9,076	13.9
Higher[9]	1	443	11,639	26.3

Health: physicians (1995) 320 (1 per 13,158 persons); hospital beds (1990) 5,307 (1 per 694 persons); infant mortality rate (2000) 71.6.
Food (1999): daily per capita caloric intake 2,527 (vegetable products 96%, animal products 4%); 110% of FAO recommended minimum requirement.

Military

Total active duty personnel (2000): 6,950 (army 93.5%, navy 2.9%, air force 3.6%). *Military expenditure as percentage of GNP* (1997): 2.0% (world 2.6%); per capita expenditure U.S.$6.

[1]Personal military-supported rule from 1967 continues under constitution approved by referendum in September 1992. [2]1981. [3]Detail does not add to total given because of rounding. [4]Import figures are f.o.b.; 1995–98 data are estimates. [5]Represents 1/11 of the traffic of Air Afrique, which is operated by 11 West African states. [6]1995–96. [7]1990. [8]1987. [9]University only.

Internet resources for further information:
- **President of the Republic http://www.republicoftogo.com/english/index.htm**
- **Investir en Zone Franc http://www.izf.net/izf/index.htm**

Tonga

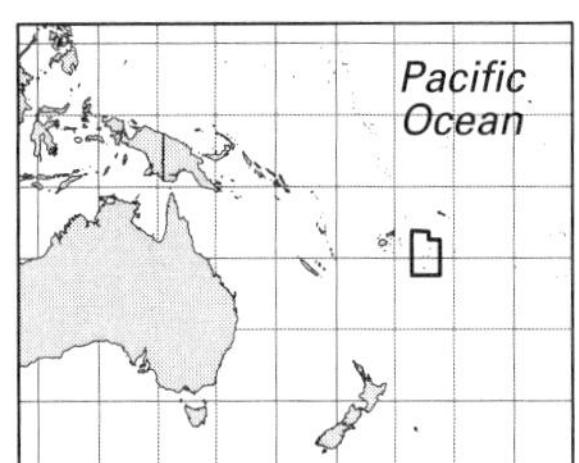

Official name: Pule'anga Fakatu'i 'o Tonga (Tongan); Kingdom of Tonga (English).
Form of government: constitutional monarchy with one legislative house (Legislative Assembly [30[1]]).
Head of state and government: King assisted by Privy Council.
Capital: Nuku'alofa.
Official languages: Tongan; English.
Official religion: none.
Monetary unit: 1 pa'anga[2] (T$) = 100 seniti; valuation (Sept. 28, 2001) 1 U.S.$ = T$2.03; 1 £ = T$2.98.

Area and population

Divisions	Capitals	area sq mi	area sq km	population 1996 census
'Eua[3]	'Ohonua	33.7	87.4	4,934
Ha'apai[4]	Pangai	42.5	110.0	8,138
Niuas[5]	Hihifo	27.7	71.7	2,018
Tongatapu[3]	Nuku'alofa	100.6	260.5	66,979
Vava'u[4]	Neiafu	46.0	119.2	15,715
TOTAL LAND AREA		278.1[6]	720.3[6]	
INLAND WATER		11.4	29.6	
TOTAL		289.5	749.9	97,784

Demography

Population (2001): 101,000.
Density (2001)[7]: persons per sq mi 363.2, persons per sq km 140.2.
Urban-rural (1999): urban 45.0%; rural 55.0%.
Sex distribution (1996): male 50.74%; female 49.26%.
Age breakdown (1996): under 15, 39.1%; 15–29, 28.0%; 30–44, 15.1%; 45–59, 10.0%; 60–74, 6.0%; 75 and over, 1.8%.
Population projection: (2010) 104,000; (2020) 108,000.
Doubling time: 33 years.
Ethnic composition (1996): Tongan and part Tongan 98.2%; other 1.8%.
Religious affiliation (1998): Free Wesleyan 41.2%; Roman Catholic 15.8%; Mormon 13.6%; other (mostly other Protestant) 29.4%.
Major cities (1986): Nuku'alofa (1996) 22,400[8]; Neiafu 3,879; Haveluloto 3,070.

Vital statistics

Birth rate per 1,000 population (2000): 27.2 (world avg. 22.5).
Death rate per 1,000 population (2000): 6.1 (world avg. 9.0).
Natural increase rate per 1,000 population (2000): 21.1 (world avg. 13.5).
Total fertility rate (avg. births per childbearing woman; 1999): 3.6.
Marriage rate per 1,000 population (1992): 8.2.
Divorce rate per 1,000 population (1992): 1.1.
Life expectancy at birth (1999): male 67.7 years; female 72.2 years.
Major causes of death per 100,000 population (1993)[9]: circulatory diseases 58.1; nervous system diseases 51.0; senility 27.6; diabetes mellitus 17.3.

National economy

Budget (1997–98). Revenue: T$63,000,000 (foreign-trade taxes 47.9%, government services revenue 20.0%, direct taxes 13.8%, indirect taxes 11.6%, interest and rent 3.5%). Expenditures[10]: T$63,000,000 (education 18.4%, general administration 13.8%, health 13.2%, law and order 12.5%, public works and communications 9.2%, agriculture 6.2%).
Production (metric tons except as noted). Agriculture, forestry, fishing (1999): yams 31,000, cassava 28,000, taro 27,200, coconuts 24,500, fruits 12,500, vegetables 7,308, sweet potatoes 5,137; livestock (number of live animals) 80,853 pigs, 13,939 goats, 11,400 horses, 9,318 cattle, 266,000 chickens; roundwood (1998) 4,600 cu m; fish catch (1997) 2,739. Mining and quarrying (1982): coral 150,000; sand 25,000. Manufacturing (output in T$'000,000; 1996): food products and beverages 8,203; paper products 1,055; chemical products 964; metal products 889; textile and wearing apparel 742; nonmetallic products 715. Construction (value in T$; 1984): residential 9,552,300; nonresidential 11,377,100. Energy production (consumption): electricity (kW-hr; 1996) 34,000,000 (34,000,000); petroleum (barrels) none (none); petroleum products (metric tons; 1996) n.a. (38,000).
Gross national product (1999): U.S.$172,000,000 (U.S.$1,730 per capita).

Structure of gross domestic product and labour force

	1997–98 in value T$'000,000	1997–98 % of total value	1990 labour force	1990 % of labour force
Agriculture	74.9	32.1	11,682	36.5
Mining	0.7	0.3	4,665	14.6
Manufacturing	7.6	3.3		
Construction	10.5	4.5	1,257	3.9
Public utilities	3.7	1.6	408	1.3
Transp. and commun.	17.1	7.3	1,821	5.7
Trade	25.6	11.0	2,597	8.1
Finance	24.3	10.4	1,188	3.7
Pub. admin., defense	30.9	13.2	7,052	22.0
Services	11.4	4.9		
Other	26.5	11.4	1,343	4.2
TOTAL	233.2	100.0	32,013	100.0

Population economically active (1996–97): total 33,908; activity rate 34.7% (participation rates: ages 15 and over 57.0%; female 36.0%; unemployed 13.3%).

Price and earnings indexes (1995 = 100)

	1994	1995	1996	1997	1998	1999	2000
Consumer price index	98.6	100.0	103.0	105.2	108.6	113.9	120.6
Quarterly earnings index	...	...	...	...	...	...	...

Public debt (external, outstanding; 1999): U.S.$63,500,000.
Household income and expenditure. Average household size (1996) 6.0; income per household: n.a.; sources of income: n.a.; expenditure (1991–92)[11]: food 43.2%, transportation 15.5%, household 14.2%, housing 6.4%, tobacco and beverages 5.4%, clothing and footwear 4.2%.
Tourism (1999): receipts U.S.$9,000,000; expenditures (1997) U.S.$3,000,000.
Land use (1994): forest 11.1%; pasture 5.6%; agriculture 66.7%; other 16.6%.

Foreign trade[12]

Balance of trade (current prices)

	1994	1995	1996	1997	1998	1999
T$'000,000	–72.8	–79.6	–75.5	–79.3	–90.8	–96.4
% of total	66.5%	68.3%	69.9%	75.6%	79.6%	70.7%

Imports (1998–99): T$104,900,000 (food and live animals 31.8%, basic manufactures 17.4%, machinery and transport equipment 17.0%, mineral fuels 11.8%, chemicals 7.8%). *Major import sources:* New Zealand 35.0%; Australia 28.6%; U.S. 13.1%; Fiji 8.6%; Japan 4.9%.
Exports (1998–99): T$12,000,000 (squash 35.8%, fish 24.2%, vanilla beans 6.7%, root crops 2.5%). *Major export destinations:* Japan 40.8%; U.S. 17.5%; New Zealand 14.2%; Fiji 5.8%; Australia 3.3%.

Transport and communications

Transport. Railroads: none. Roads (1996): total length 680 km (paved 27%). Vehicles (1996): passenger cars 1,140, commercial vehicles 780. Merchant marine (1992): vessels (100 gross tons and over) 15; total deadweight tonnage 13,740. Air transport (1996): passenger-km 11,000,000; metric ton-km cargo 1,000,000; airports (1996) with scheduled flights 6.

Communications

Medium	date	unit	number	units per 1,000 persons
Daily newspapers	1996	circulation	7,000	72
Radio	1997	receivers	61,000	619
Television	1997	receivers	2,000	21
Telephones	1999	main lines	9,100	93
Cellular telephones	1999	subscribers	140	1.4

Education and health

Educational attainment (1996). Percentage of population age 25 and over having: primary education 26%; lower secondary 58%; upper secondary 8%; higher 6%; not stated 2%. *Literacy:* n.a.

Education (1994)

	schools	teachers	students	student/ teacher ratio
Primary (age 6–11)	115	701	16,540	23.6
Secondary (age 12–18)	38	809	15,702	19.4
Voc., teacher tr.	9	67	824	12.3
Higher[13]	1	19	226	11.9

Health: physicians (1997) 43 (1 per 2,279 persons); hospital beds (1992) 307 (1 per 320 persons); infant mortality rate per 1,000 live births (1999) 37.9.
Food (1992): daily per capita caloric intake 2,946 (vegetable products 82%, animal products 18%); 129% of FAO recommended minimum requirement.

Military

Total active duty personnel (1996): 125-member naval force; an air force was created in 1996. *Military expenditure as percentage of GNP* (1989): 4.9% (world 4.9%); per capita expenditure U.S.$21.

[1]Includes 12 nonelective seats and 9 nobles elected by the 33 hereditary nobles of Tonga. [2]The pa'anga was pegged at par to the Australian dollar through Feb. 8, 1991, but beginning Feb. 11, 1991, it was linked to a weighted basket of foreign currencies. [3]'Eua and Tongatapu together comprise Tongatapu island group. [4]Also the name of an island group. [5]Also known as Niuatoputapu island group. [6]Total includes 27.6 sq mi (71.5 sq km) of uninhabited islands. [7]Based on land area. [8]Population of urban agglomeration (1999) is 37,000. [9]Reported inpatient deaths at all hospitals. [10]Excludes amortization of public debt and sinking funds. [11]Current weight of consumer price index components. [12]Import data used is c.i.f. [13]1992.

Internet resources for further information:
- **Tonga on the Net http://www.tongatapu.net.to**

Trinidad and Tobago

Official name: Republic of Trinidad and Tobago.
Form of government: multiparty republic with two legislative houses (Senate [31]; House of Representatives [36[1]]).
Chief of state: President.
Head of government: Prime Minister.
Capital: Port of Spain.
Official language: English.
Official religion: none.
Monetary unit: 1 Trinidad and Tobago dollar (TT$) = 100 cents; valuation (Sept. 28, 2001) 1 U.S.$ = TT$6.05; 1 £ = TT$8.89.

Area and population

	area[2] sq km	population 1990 census
Trinidad		
Counties		
Couva/Tabaquite/Talparo	701	
Diego Martin	122	
Mayaro/Rio Claro	907	
Penal/Debe	259	
Princes Town	551	996,815
Sangre Grande	881	
San Juan/Laventille	200	
Siparia	570	
Tunapuna/Piarco	526	

	area[2] sq km	population 1990 census
Cities		
Port of Spain	10	50,878
San Fernando	8	30,092
Boroughs		
Arima	10	29,695
Chaguanas	60	56,601
Point Fortin	23	20,025
Tobago (Unitary State)		
Counties		
Eastern Tobago	231	50,282
Western Tobago	69	
TOTAL	5,128	1,234,388

Demography

Population (2001): 1,298,000.
Density (2001): persons per sq mi 655.6, persons per sq km 253.1.
Urban-rural (1999): urban 73.6%; rural 26.4%.
Sex distribution (1998): male 49.81%; female 50.19%.
Age breakdown (1995): under 15, 30.3%; 15–29, 26.6%; 30–44, 22.0%; 45–59, 12.3%; 60–74, 6.5%; 75 and over, 2.3%.
Population projection: (2010) 1,353,000; (2020) 1,418,000.
Ethnic composition (2000): black 39.2%; East Indian 38.6%; mixed 16.3%; Chinese 1.6%; white 1.0%; other/not stated 3.3%.
Religious affiliation (1990): six largest Protestant bodies 29.7%; Roman Catholic 29.4%; Hindu 23.7%; Muslim 5.9%; other 11.3%.
Major cities (1990): Chaguanas 56,601; Port of Spain 43,396[3]; San Fernando 30,115[4]; Arima 29,483[4]; Point Fortin 20,025; Scarborough 4,000.

Vital statistics

Birth rate per 1,000 population (1997): 14.5 (world avg. 22.5).
Death rate per 1,000 population (1997): 7.2 (world avg. 9.0).
Natural increase rate per 1,000 population (1997): 7.3 (world avg. 13.5).
Total fertility rate (avg. births per childbearing woman; 2000): 1.8.
Marriage rate per 1,000 population (1996): 5.6.
Divorce rate per 1,000 population (1996): 1.2.
Life expectancy at birth (2000): male 65.4 years; female 70.6 years.
Major causes of death per 100,000 population (1994): diseases of the circulatory system 286.4; malignant neoplasms (cancers) 94.3; endocrine and metabolic disorders 90.0; accidents, violence, and homicide 52.8.

National economy

Budget (1999). Revenue: TT$9,789,000,000 (company taxes 21.2%, of which petroleum sector 9.2%; individual income taxes 20.3%; value-added taxes 17.0%; nontax revenues 8.3%). Expenditures: TT$11,076,000,000 (current expenditures 95.6%; development expenditures 4.4%).
Production (metric tons except as noted). Agriculture, forestry, fishing (1999): sugarcane 1,200,000, coconuts 22,000, oranges 15,000, rice 7,037, pigeon peas 3,180, cocoa 1,270, coffee 367; livestock (number of live animals) 59,000 goats, 8,500,000 chickens; roundwood (1998) 60,000 cu m; fish catch (1997) 15,012. Mining and quarrying (1999): natural asphalt 12,600. Manufacturing (1999): anhydrous ammonia and urea (nitrogenous fertilizers) 3,946,800; methanol 2,149,800; steel billets 723,900; cement 688,400; steel wire rods 638,200; refined sugar 43,600; beer and stout 418,800 hectolitres[3]; rum 78,000 hectolitres[3]. Energy production (consumption): electricity (kW-hr; 1997) 4,848,000,000 ([1996] 4,541,000,000); coal, none (none); crude petroleum (barrels; 1999) 35,903,000 ([1996] 39,840,000); petroleum products (metric tons; 1996) 5,454,000 (1,448,000); natural gas (cu m; 1999) 9,296,000,000 ([1996] 7,509,000,000).
Household income and expenditure. Average household size (1998) 3.8; average income per household (1988) TT$21,760 (U.S.$5,661); expenditure (1993): food, beverages, and tobacco 25.5%, housing 21.6%, transportation 15.2%, household furnishings 14.3%, clothing and footwear 10.4%.
Tourism (1998): receipts from visitors U.S.$201,000,000; expenditures by nationals abroad U.S.$67,000,000.
Land use (1994): forested 45.8%; meadows and pastures 2.1%; agricultural and under permanent cultivation 23.8%; other 28.3%.
Gross national product (at current market prices; 1999): U.S.$6,142,000,000 (U.S.$4,750 per capita).

Structure of gross domestic product and labour force

	1999		1998	
	in value TT$'000,000	% of total value	labour force	% of labour force
Agriculture	891	2.2	41,300	7.4
Petroleum, natural gas, quarrying	8,834[5]	21.5[5]	21,700[6]	3.9[6]
Manufacturing	3,333[6]	8.1[6]	59,800[5]	10.7[5]
Construction	4,232	10.3	83,500	14.9
Public utilities	849	2.1	6,900	1.2
Transp. and commun.	3,827	9.3	38,100	6.8
Trade	6,944	16.9	98,600	17.6
Finance, real estate	5,706	13.9	43,100	7.7
Pub. admin., defense	3,918	9.5	165,400	29.6
Services	2,605	6.3		
Other	−957	−0.2[7]	400	0.1
TOTAL	41,044[8]	100.0[8]	558,700[8]	100.0[8]

Population economically active (1998): total 558,700; activity rate of total population 43.6% (participation rates: [1995] ages 15–64, 65.4%; female 38.3%; unemployed [1999] 13.1%).

Price and earnings indexes (1995 = 100)

	1995	1996	1997	1998	1999	2000	2001
Consumer price index	100.0	103.4	107.2	113.2	117.1	121.2	126.0
Weekly earnings index[9]	100.0	102.5	109.5	114.9	...	...	...

Public debt (external, outstanding; 1999): U.S.$1,485,000,000.

Foreign trade[10]

Balance of trade (current prices)

	1994	1995	1996	1997	1998	1999
TT$'000,000	+4,354	+3,938	+1,488	−2,818	−4,666	+398
% of total	24.5%	16.2%	5.5%	8.1%	14.1%	1.1%

Imports (1998): TT$18,887,000,000 (machinery and apparatus 30.8%, fuels 12.2%, food 7.3%, transport equipment 6.2%). *Major import sources* (1999): United States 39.8%; Venezuela 11.9%; Japan 5.1%; Canada 4.9%; United Kingdom 4.7%.
Exports (1998): TT$14,221,000,000 (refined petroleum 29.6%, crude petroleum 10.6%, anhydrous ammonia 10.6%, iron and steel 8.8%, reexports 7.1%, methanol 6.3%). *Major export destinations* (1999): United States 39.3%; Caricom 26.1%, of which Jamaica 8.7%, Barbados 5.3%; EC 5.7%.

Transport and communications

Transport. Railroads: none. Roads (1995): total length 8,320 km (paved 51%). Vehicles (1996): passenger cars 122,000; trucks and buses 24,000. Air transport (2000)[11]: passenger-km 2,869,000,000; metric ton-km cargo 55,021,000; airports (1996) with scheduled flights 2.

Communications

Medium	date	unit	number	units per 1,000 persons
Daily newspapers	1996	circulation	156,000	123
Radio	1997	receivers	680,000	535
Television	1999	receivers	435,000	338
Telephones	1999	main lines	279,000	217
Cellular telephones	1999	subscribers	38,659	30
Personal computers	1999	units	70,000	54
Internet	1999	users	30,000	23

Education and health

Educational attainment (1990). Percentage of population age 25 and over having: no formal schooling 4.5%; primary education 56.4%; secondary 32.1%; higher 3.4%; other/not stated 3.6%. *Literacy* (1995): total population age 15 and over literate 886,000 (97.9%).

Education (1996–97)

	schools	teachers	students	student/teacher ratio
Primary (age 5–11)	476	7,311	181,030	24.8
Secondary (age 12–16)	...	5,070	104,349	20.6
Higher[12]	1	510	6,641	13.0

Health: physicians (1997) 1,074 (1 per 1,183 persons); hospital beds (1996) 6,622 (1 per 191 persons); infant mortality rate (1997) 17.1.
Food (1998): daily per capita caloric intake 2,711 (vegetable products 85%, animal products 15%); 112% of FAO recommended minimum requirement.

Military

Total active duty personnel (2000): 2,700 (army 74.1%, coast guard 25.9%). *Military expenditure as percentage of GNP* (1997): 1.5% (world 2.6%); per capita expenditure U.S.$65.

[1]Excludes speaker, who may be elected from outside the House of Representatives. [2]Area figures for counties are estimated. [3]1996. [4]1991. [5]Includes refined petroleum and petrochemicals. [6]Excludes refined petroleum and petrochemicals. [7]Net of value-added taxes less imputed bank service charges. [8]Detail does not add to total given because of rounding. [9]Manufacturing only. [10]Imports c.i.f.; exports f.o.b. [11]BWIA only. [12]1998–99; University of the West Indies, St. Augustine campus only.

Internet resources for further information:
- **Central Bank of Trinidad and Tobago http://www.central-bank.org.tt**

Tunisia

Official name: Al-Jumhūrīyah at-Tūnisīyah (Republic of Tunisia).
Form of government: multiparty republic with one legislative house (Chamber of Deputies [182]).
Chief of state: President.
Head of government: Prime Minister.
Capital: Tunis.
Official language: Arabic.
Official religion: Islam.
Monetary unit: 1 dinar (D) = 1,000 millimes; valuation (Sept. 28, 2001) 1 U.S.$ = D 1.43; 1 £ = D 2.10.

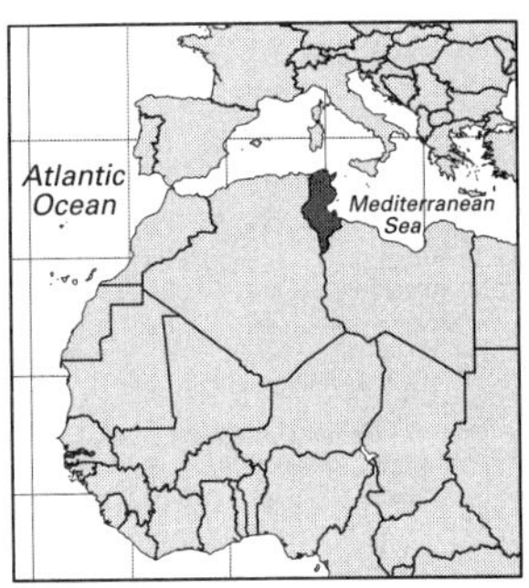

Area and population

		area		population
Governorates	Capitals	sq mi	sq km	2000 estimate
Al-Ariānah	Al-Ariānah	602[1]	1,558[1]	363,500
Bājah	Bājah	1,374	3,558	317,500
Banzart	Bizerte (Banzart)	1,423	3,685	518,400
Bin ʿArūs	Bin ʿArūs	294	761	445,300
Jundūbah	Jundūbah	1,198	3,102	424,900
Al-Kāf	Al-Kāf	1,917	4,965	280,600
Madanīn	Madanīn	3,316	8,588	421,500
Al-Mahdīyah	Al-Mahdīyah	1,145	2,966	366,200
Manūbah	Manūbah	[1]	[1]	313,800
Al-Munastīr	Al-Munastīr	393	1,019	413,000
Nābul	Nābul	1,076	2,788	632,200
Qābis	Qābis	2,770	7,175	332,300
Qafṣah	Qafṣah	3,471	8,990	327,800
Al-Qaṣrayn	Al-Qaṣrayn	3,114	8,066	416,300
Al-Qayrawān	Al-Qayrawān	2,591	6,712	563,300
Qibilī	Qibilī	8,527	22,084	141,400
Ṣafāqis	Safāqis	2,913	7,545	808,000
Sīdī Bū Zayd	Sīdī Bū Zayd	2,700	6,994	398,900
Siliānah	Siliānah	1,788	4,631	255,500
Sūsah	Sūsah	1,012	2,621	492,000
Tatāuīn	Tatāuīn	15,015	38,889	147,300
Tawzar	Tawzar	1,822	4,719	96,300
Tūnis	Tunis (Tūnis)	134	346	930,700
Zaghwān	Zaghwān	1,069	2,768	154,100
TOTAL		63,378[2]	164,150[2]	9,560,800

Demography

Population (2001): 9,828,000.
Density (2001): persons per sq mi 155.1, persons per sq km 59.9.
Urban-rural (2000): urban 62.6%; rural 37.4%.
Sex distribution (2000): male 50.40%; female 49.60%.
Age breakdown (2000): under 15, 29.7%; 15–29, 30.4%; 30–44, 21.2%; 45–59, 10.6%; 60–74, 6.8%; 75 and over, 1.3%.
Population projection: (2010) 11,124,000; (2020) 12,507,000.
Doubling time: 50 years.
Ethnic composition (2000): Tunisian Arab 67.2%; Bedouin Arab 26.6%; Algerian Arab 2.4%; Berber 1.4%; other 2.4%.
Religious affiliation (2000): Sunnī Muslim 98.9%; Christian 0.5%; other 0.6%.
Major cities (commune; 1994): Tunis 674,100; Ṣafāqis 230,900; Al-Ariānah 152,700; Ettadhamen 149,200; Sūsah 125,000.

Vital statistics

Birth rate per 1,000 population (2000): 17.1 (world avg. 22.5).
Death rate per 1,000 population (2000): 5.6 (world avg. 9.0).
Natural increase rate per 1,000 population (2000): 11.5 (world avg. 13.5).
Total fertility rate (avg. births per childbearing woman; 2000): 2.1.
Marriage rate per 1,000 population (1995): 6.0.
Life expectancy at birth (2000): male 70.1 years; female 74.2 years.
Major causes of death (1992)[3]: complications of pregnancy and childbirth 31.6%, circulatory diseases 22.4%, accidents and poisoning 14.9%, respiratory diseases 7.2%.

National economy

Budget (2000). Revenue: D 7,625,000,000 (tax revenue 91.1%, of which goods and services 39.1%, income tax 20.0%, social security 17.8%, import duties 9.8%; nontax revenue 8.9%). Expenditures: D 8,454,000,000 (current expenditure 77.2%, of which interest on public debt 10.3%; development expenditure 22.8%).
Public debt (external, outstanding; 1999): U.S.$9,487,000,000.
Production (metric tons except as noted). Agriculture, forestry, fishing (2000): wheat 1,144,000, olives 1,000,000, tomatoes 905,000, barley 416,000, potatoes 295,000, oranges 116,000, apples 108,000, dates 104,000; livestock (number of live animals) 6,600,000 sheep, 1,400,000 goats, 790,000 cattle; roundwood (2000) 2,841,800 cu m; fish catch (2000) 90,100. Mining and quarrying (2000): phosphate rock 8,301,200; iron ore (1998) 140,000; zinc 28,200. Manufacturing (2000): cement 5,398,900; phosphoric acid 845,000; flour 745,500; semolina 620,500; lime 432,000; crude steel 183,300; sugar 92,000. Energy production (consumption): electricity (kW-hr; 2000) 9,221,900,000 (8,150,400,000); coal (metric tons; 1996) 2,000 (2,000); crude petroleum (barrels; 1999) 30,956,000 (1996; 7,097,000); petroleum products (metric tons; 1996) 1,844,000 (3,106,000); natural gas (cu m; 2000) 1,862,500,000 ([1997] 2,107,300,000).
Household income and expenditure. Average household size (1999) 4.9; income per household: n.a.; sources of income: n.a.; expenditure (1995): food and beverages 37.7%, housing and energy 22.2%, health and personal care 9.6%, transportation 8.9%, recreation 8.7%, other 12.9%.
Gross national product (1999): U.S.$19,757,000,000 (U.S.$2,090 per capita).

Structure of gross domestic product and labour force

	2000		1994	
	in value D '000,000	% of total value	labour force	% of labour force
Agriculture	3,248.3	12.2	501,000	21.6
Mining	234.5	0.9	36,800	1.6
Public utilities	1,287.6	4.8		
Manufacturing	4,889.0	18.3	455,700	19.6
Construction	1,252.4	4.7	305,800	13.2
Transp. and commun.	2,069.9	7.8	[4]	[4]
Trade	5,646.9	21.2	315,600	13.6
Finance	3,590.9	13.5		
Pub. admin., defense			667,100[4]	28.7[4]
Services				
Other	4,461.7[5]	16.7[5]	38,600	1.7
TOTAL	26,683.2[6]	100.0[6]	2,320,600	100.0

Population economically active (1997): total 3,502,000; activity rate of total population 37.9% (participation rates [1989]: ages 15–64, 42.2%; female [1997] 30.9%; unemployed [2000] 15.9%).

Price and earnings indexes (1995 = 100)

	1994	1995	1996	1997	1998	1999	2000
Consumer price index	94.1	100.0	103.7	107.5	110.9	113.9	115.8
Hourly earnings index	...	...	...	...	...	...	...

Land use (1994): forested 4.3%; meadows and pastures 20.0%; agricultural and under permanent cultivation 31.9%; other 43.8%.
Tourism (1999): receipts U.S.$1,560,000,000; expenditures U.S.$235,000,000.

Foreign trade[7]

Balance of trade (current prices)

	1995	1996	1997	1998	1999	2000
D '000,000	–2,291	–2,126	–2,608	–2,944	–3,103	–3,723
% of total	18.1%	16.5%	17.5%	18.4%	18.2%	18.9%

Imports (2000): D 11,728,000,000 (textiles, clothing, and leather 22.9%, nonelectrical equipment 20.3%, electrical equipment 10.2%, transport equipment 10.2%). *Major import sources:* France 26.3%; Italy 19.1%; Germany 10.0%; U.S. 4.6%; Libya 3.7%.
Exports (2000): D 8,005,000,000 (textiles, clothing, and leather products 46.6%, mineral fuels and lubricants 12.1%, electrical equipment 10.1%, phosphates and phosphate derivatives 9.0%). *Major export destinations:* France 26.8%; Italy 23.0%; Germany 12.5%; Belgium 5.1%; Libya 3.6%.

Transport and communications

Transport. Railroads (2000): route length 2,169 km; passenger-km 1,196,000,000; metric ton-km cargo 2,365,000,000. Roads (1997): total length 23,100 km (paved 79%). Vehicles (1996): passenger cars 269,000; trucks and buses 312,000. Air transport (2000)[8]: passenger-km 2,694,167,000; metric ton-km cargo 20,821,000; airports (1998) 5.

Communications

Medium	date	unit	number	units per 1,000 persons
Daily newspapers	1996	circulation	280,000	31
Radio	1997	receivers	2,060,000	224
Television	1999	receivers	1,800,000	190
Telephones	1999	main lines	850,381	90
Cellular telephones	1999	subscribers	55,258	5.8
Personal computers	1999	units	145,000	15
Internet	1999	users	30,000	3.2

Education and health

Educational attainment (1989). Percentage of population age 25 and over having: no formal schooling 54.9%; primary 26.9%; secondary 14.3%; higher 3.4%; unspecified 0.5%. *Literacy* (2000): total population age 10 and over literate 74.4%; males literate 83.5%; females literate 65.3%.

Education (1999–2000)

	schools	teachers	students	student/teacher ratio
Primary (age 6–11)	4,497	60,912	1,413,795	23.2
Secondary (age 12–18)	1,301	52,432	965,607	18.4
Teacher tr.[9]	...	237	3,839	16.2
Higher	95	6,641[10]	180,044	18.3[10]

Health (2000): physicians 7,444 (1 per 1,284 persons); hospital beds (1999) 16,256 (1 per 581 persons); infant mortality rate (2000) 25.8.
Food (1999): daily per capita caloric intake 3,388 (vegetable products 91%, animal products 9%); 142% of FAO recommended minimum requirement.

Military

Total active duty personnel (2000): 35,000 (army 77.1%, navy 12.9%, air force 10.0%). *Military expenditure as percentage of GNP* (1997): 2.0% (world 2.6%); per capita expenditure U.S.$39.

[1]Al-Ariānah includes Manūbah. [2]Total includes 3,714 sq mi (9,620 sq km) of territory that is not distributed by governorate. [3]12,000 reported deaths from urban areas only, including complete figures for Tunis. [4]Services includes transportation and communications. [5]Indirect taxes less subsidies. [6]Detail does not add to total given because of rounding. [7]Imports c.i.f. [8]Tunis Air only. [9]1987–88. [10]1996–97.

Internet resources for further information:
- **Tunisia Online http://www.tunisiaonline.com**
- **National Statistics Institute (French only) http://www.ins.nat.tn**

Turkey

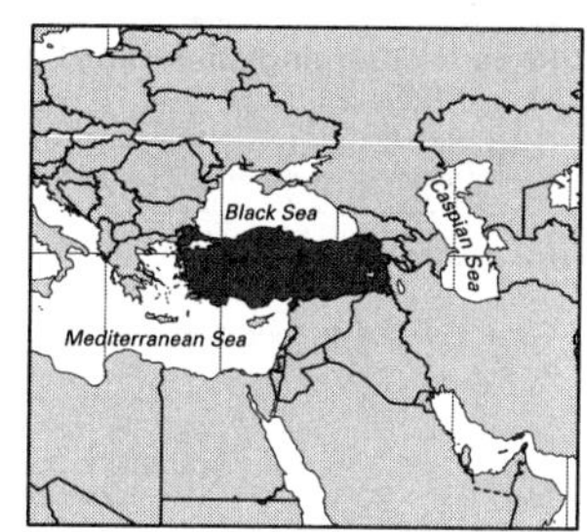

Official name: Türkiye Cumhuriyeti (Republic of Turkey).
Form of government: multiparty republic with one legislative house (Turkish Grand National Assembly [550]).
Chief of state: President.
Head of government: Prime Minister.
Capital: Ankara.
Official language: Turkish.
Official religion: none.
Monetary unit: 1 Turkish lira (LT) = 100 kurush; valuation (Sept. 28, 2001) 1 U.S.$ = LT 1,530,500; 1 £ = LT 2,249,400.

Area and population	area		population
Geographic regions[1]	sq mi	sq km	1997 estimate
Akdeniz kıyısı (Mediterranean Coast)	22,933	59,395	6,266,958
Batı Anadolu (West Anatolia)	29,742	77,031	4,074,955
Doğu Anadolu (East Anatolia)	68,074	180,180	7,351,461
Güneydoğu Anadolu (Southeast Anatolia)	15,347	35,880	3,205,251
İç Anadolu (Central Anatolia)	91,254	236,347	14,049,774
Karadeniz kıyısı (Black Sea Coast)	31,388	81,295	6,816,009
Marmara ve Ege kıyıları (Marmara and Aegean coasts)	33,035	85,560	13,677,750[2]
Trakya (Thrace)	9,175	23,764	7,168,094[2]
TOTAL	300,948	779,452	62,610,252

Demography

Population (2001): 66,229,000.
Density (2001): persons per sq mi 220.1, persons per sq km 85.0.
Urban-rural (1997): urban 64.7%; rural 35.3%.
Sex distribution (2000): male 50.57%; female 49.43%.
Age breakdown (2000): under 15, 29.1%; 15–29, 28.8%; 30–44, 21.5%; 45–59, 11.8%; 60–74, 6.8%; 75 and over, 2.0%.
Population projection: (2010) 74,119,000; (2020) 80,544,000.
Doubling time: 54 years.
Ethnic composition (2000)[3]: Turk 65.1%; Kurd 18.9%; Crimean Tatar 7.2%; Arab 1.8%; Azerbaijani 1.0%; Yoruk 1.0%; other 5.0%.
Religious affiliation (2000): Muslim 97.2%, of which Sunnī *c.* 67%, Shīʿī *c.* 30% (including nonorthodox Alevi *c.* 26%); Christian (mostly Eastern Orthodox) 0.6%; other 2.2%.
Major cities (1997): Istanbul 8,260,438; Ankara 2,984,099; İzmir 2,081,556; Adana 1,041,509; Bursa 1,066,559; Gaziantep 712,800; Konya 623,333.

Vital statistics

Birth rate per 1,000 population (2000): 18.7 (world avg. 22.5).
Death rate per 1,000 population (2000): 6.0 (world avg. 9.0).
Natural increase rate per 1,000 population (2000): 12.7 (world avg. 13.5).
Total fertility rate (avg. births per childbearing woman; 2000): 2.2.
Marriage rate per 1,000 population (1997): 7.8.
Divorce rate per 1,000 population (1997): 0.5.
Life expectancy at birth (2000): male 68.6 years; female 73.4 years.
Major causes of death per 100,000 population (1995)[4]: diseases of the circulatory system 322; malignant neoplasms (cancers) 71; accidents and violence 32; infectious and parasitic diseases 20; ill-defined conditions 129.

National economy

Budget (2000). Revenue: LT 33,756,347,000,000,000 (tax revenue 78.5%, nontax revenue 10.3%, special funds 9.7%, other 1.5%). Expenditures: LT 46,602,627,000,000,000 (interest payments 38.3%, personnel 24.7%, investments 5.5%).
Public debt (external, outstanding; 1999): U.S.$50,095,000,000.
Production (in '000 metric tons except as noted). Agriculture, forestry, fishing (2000): wheat 21,000, sugar beets 18,000, barley 8,000, tomatoes 6,800, potatoes 5,350, grapes 3,550, apples 2,300, seed cotton 2,200, corn (maize) 2,800, olives 1,700, cottonseed 1,500, oranges 1,035, sunflower seeds 825, lentils 590, hazelnuts 470, peaches 430, tobacco 189, raisins 250[5], tea 120[5], garlic 106[5], attar of roses 800 kg[6]; livestock (number of live animals) 29,435,000 sheep, 11,031,000 cattle, 615,000[7] angora goats; roundwood (2000) 17,767,000 cu m; fish catch (1999) 638,097. Construction (2000): residential 43,607,000 sq m; nonresidential 14,999,000 sq m. Mining (1999): boron minerals 2,600; chromite 770; copper ore (metal content) 45. Manufacturing (1995)[8]: refined petroleum 4,583; food products 3,944; textiles 3,907; transport equipment 3,048; iron and steel 2,453; paints, soaps, and pharmaceuticals 2,301. Energy production (consumption): electricity (kW-hr; 1999) 115,424,000,000 ([1997] 80,862,000,000); hard coal (metric tons; 1999) 2,738,000 ([1996] 8,145,000); lignite (metric tons; 1999) 64,896,000 ([1996] 54,961,000); crude petroleum (barrels; 1999) 21,013,000 ([1996] 193,791,000); petroleum products (metric tons; 1996) 22,906,000 (26,183,000); natural gas (cu m; 1997) 250,800,000 ([1996] 8,541,800,000).
Tourism (1999): receipts from visitors U.S.$5,203,000,000; expenditures by nationals abroad U.S.$1,471,000,000.
Household income and expenditure (1994). Average household size (1999) 4.6; income per household LT 165,089,000 (U.S.$5,576); expenditure: food, tobacco, and café expenditures 38.5%, housing 22.8%, clothing 9.0%.
Population economically active (1997)[9]: total 22,359,000; activity rate of total population 35.8% (participation rates: ages 15–64, 53.1%; female 26.8%; unemployed [2000] 6.6%).

Price and earnings indexes (1995 = 100)	1994	1995	1996	1997	1998	1999	2000
Consumer price index	53.2	100.0	180.3	335.0	618.5	1,019.7	1,245.8
Annual earnings index[10]	52.5	100.0	190.4	376.8	650.3	...	...

Gross national product (1999): U.S.$186,490,000,000 (U.S.$2,900 per capita).

Structure of gross domestic product and labour force	2000		1998	
	in value LT '000,000,000,000	% of total value	labour force[9]	% of labour force[9]
Agriculture	12,749	14.5	8,918,000	39.6
Mining }	20,347	23.2	154,000	0.7
Manufacturing }			3,267,000	14.5
Construction	4,617	5.3	1,277,000	5.7
Public utilities	2,251	2.6	115,000	0.5
Transp. and commun.	12,419	14.1	957,000	4.3
Trade	17,567	20.0	2,860,000	12.7
Finance, real estate	8,090	9.2	511,000	2.3
Pub. admin., defense	9,000	10.3 }	3,026,000	13.4
Services	3,365	3.8 }		
Other	–2,645[11]	–3.0[11]	1,428,000[12]	6.3[12]
TOTAL	87,760	100.0	22,513,000	100.0

Land use (1994): forested 26.2%; meadows and pastures 16.1%; agricultural and under permanent cultivation 36.1%; other 21.6%.

Foreign trade[13]

Balance of trade (current prices)	1995	1996	1997	1998	1999	2000
U.S.$'000,000	–14,073	–20,403	–22,298	–18,947	–14,104	–26,659
% of total	24.5%	30.5%	29.8%	26.0%	21.0%	32.8%

Imports (2000): U.S.$53,983,000,000 (mineral fuels 17.6%; nonelectrical machinery 14.3%; electrical machinery 11.2%; transport equipment 10.1%; iron and steel 5.1%; chemicals 3.7%). *Major import sources:* Germany 13.2%; Italy 8.0%; U.S. 7.2%; France 6.5%; U.K. 5.0%.
Exports (2000): U.S.$27,324,000,000 (textiles and clothing 22.6%; electrical and electronic machinery 7.1%; vehicles 5.7%; iron and steel 5.7%). *Major export destinations:* Germany 18.8%; U.S. 11.2%; Russia and Eastern Europe 10.8%; U.K. 7.4%; Italy 6.3%; France 6.0%.

Transport and communications

Transport. Railroads (2000): length 5,388 mi, 8,671 km; passenger-km 6,122,000,000; metric ton-km cargo 10,032,000,000. Roads (2000): total length 238,379 mi, 383,636 km (paved [1997] 25%). Vehicles (2000): passenger cars 4,283,080; trucks and buses 1,488,016. Air transport (2000)[14]: passenger-km 16,492,416; metric ton-km cargo 379,630,000; airports (1996) 26.

Communications				units
Medium	date	unit	number	per 1,000 persons
Daily newspapers	1996	circulation	6,845,000	111
Radio	1997	receivers	11,300,000	181
Television	1999	receivers	21,500,000	331
Telephones	1999	main lines	18,054,000	278
Cellular telephones	1999	subscribers	8,122,000	125
Personal computers	1999	units	2,200,000	34
Internet	1999	users	1,500,000	23

Education and health

Educational attainment (1993). Percentage of population age 25 and over having: no formal schooling 30.5%; incomplete primary education 6.6%; complete primary 40.4%; incomplete secondary 3.1%; complete secondary or higher 19.1%; unknown 0.3%. *Literacy* (1995): total population age 15 and over literate 33,605,000 (82.3%); males literate 19,191,000 (91.7%); females literate 14,414,000 (72.4%).

Education (1996–97)	schools	teachers	students	student/ teacher ratio
Primary (age 6–10)	47,313	217,131	6,389,060	29.4
Secondary (age 11–16)	11,144	139,497	3,427,715	24.6
Voc., teacher tr.	4,046	72,537	1,333,177	18.4
Higher	817[15]	50,313	1,434,033	28.5

Health: physicians (1997) 73,659[16] (1 per 853 persons); hospital beds (1997) 144,984 (1 per 431 persons); infant mortality rate (2000) 48.9.
Food (1999): daily per capita caloric intake 3,469 (vegetable products 89%, animal products 11%); 138% of FAO recommended minimum requirement.

Military

Total active duty personnel (2000): 609,700 (army 81.2%, navy 9.0%, air force 9.8%). *Military expenditure as percentage of GNP* (1997): 4.0% (world 2.6%); per capita expenditure U.S.$124.

[1]Administratively divided into 81 provinces as of 1999. [2]Estimated figures. [3]Per unofficial source. [4]Projected rates based on about 42% of total deaths. [5]1998. [6]1993. [7]1997. [8]Value added in U.S.$'000,000. [9]Civilian population only. [10]Istanbul wage earners only. [11]Import duties less imputed bank charges. [12]Unemployed. [13]Imports c.i.f.; exports f.o.b. [14]Turkish Airlines only. [15]1995–96. [16]Includes assistant doctors.

Internet resources for further information:
- **Ministry of Foreign Affairs http://www.mfa.gov.tr**
- **Republic of Turkey http://www.turkey.org**
- **State Institute of Statistics http://www.die.gov.tr**

Turkmenistan

Official name: Türkmenistan (Turkmenistan).
Form of government: unitary republic with one legislative body (Majlis [Parliament; 50]).
Head of state and government: President assisted by the People's Council[1].
Capital: Ashgabat (formerly Ashkhabad).
Official language: Turkmen.
Official religion: none.
Monetary unit: manat; valuation (Sept. 28, 2001) 1 U.S.$ = 5,200 manat; 1 £ = 7,642 manat.

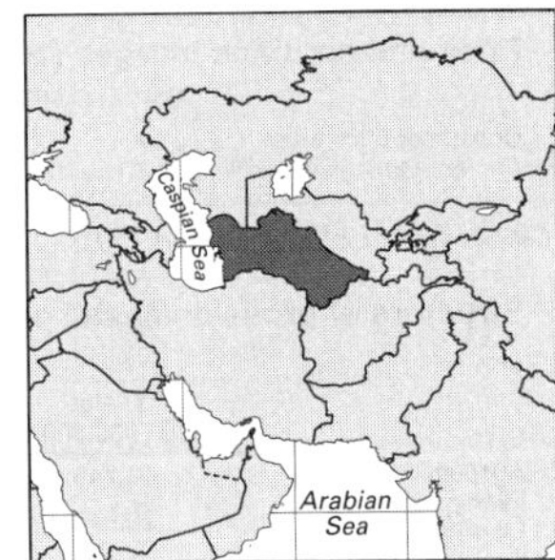

Area and population

		area		population
Provinces	**Capitals**	sq mi	sq km	1999 estimate
Ahal	Ashgabat	37,500[2]	97,100[2]	722,800
Balkan	Nebitdag	53,500	138,600	424,700
Dashhowuz	Dashhowuz	28,100	72,700	1,059,800
Lebap	Turkmenabad (Chärjew)	36,000	93,200	1,034,700
Mary	Mary	33,400	86,400	1,146,800
City				
Ashgabat	—	[2]	[2]	604,700
TOTAL		188,500[3]	488,100[3]	4,993,500

Demography

Population (2001): 5,462,000.
Density (2001): persons per sq mi 29.0, persons per sq km 11.2.
Urban-rural (1999): urban 45.0%; rural 55.0%.
Sex distribution (1996): male 49.59%; female 50.41%.
Age breakdown (1995): under 15, 40.4%; 15–29, 27.6%; 30–44, 18.7%; 45–59, 7.5%; 60–74, 4.7%; 75 and over, 1.1%.
Population projection: (2010) 6,444,000; (2020) 7,726,000.
Doubling time: 34 years.
Ethnic composition (1997): Turkmen 77.0%; Uzbek 9.2%; Russian 6.7%; Kazakh 2.0%; Tatar 0.8%; other 4.3%.
Religious affiliation (1995): Muslim (mostly Sunnī) 87.0%; Russian Orthodox 2.4%; other (mostly nonreligious) 10.6%.
Major cities (1999 est.): Ashgabat 605,000; Turkmenabad (Chärjew) 203,000; Dashhowuz 165,000; Mary 123,000; Nebitdag 119,000.

Vital statistics

Birth rate per 1,000 population (2000): 28.9 (world avg. 22.5); (1998) legitimate 96.2%; illegitimate 3.8%.
Death rate per 1,000 population (2000): 9.0 (world avg. 9.0).
Natural increase rate per 1,000 population (2000): 19.9 (world avg. 13.5).
Total fertility rate (avg. births per childbearing woman; 2000): 1.8.
Marriage rate per 1,000 population (1994): 8.7.
Divorce rate per 1,000 population (1994): 1.5.
Life expectancy at birth (2000): male 57.3 years; female 64.7 years.
Major causes of death per 100,000 population (1994): diseases of the circulatory system 337.1; diseases of the respiratory system 150.3; infectious and parasitic diseases 75.7; accidents, poisoning, and violence 60.1; malignant neoplasms (cancers) 56.8; diseases of the digestive system 31.1.

National economy

Budget (1999). Revenue: 3,693,100,000,000 manat (value-added tax 25.6%, pension and social security fund 22.5%, repayments of scheduled gas 13.0%, excise tax 10.2%, personal income tax 6.1%). Expenditures: 3,894,300,000,000 manat (education 26.9%, pension and social security 15.6%, defense and security 14.9%, health 14.1%, agriculture 5.7%).
Public debt (external, outstanding; 1999): U.S.$1,678,000,000.
Production (metric tons except as noted). Agriculture, forestry, fishing (1999): cereals 1,567,200, seed cotton 1,300,000, vegetables and melons 336,400, fruit excluding melons 193,600; livestock (number of live animals) 6,025,000 sheep and goats, 880,000 cattle, 48,000 pigs, 4,250,000 poultry; roundwood (1990) 4,000,000 cu m; fish catch (1997) 8,828. Mining and quarrying (1996): gypsum 169,577, sodium sulphate 30,820, sulfur 8,112. Manufacturing (value of production in '000,000 manat; 1994): ferrous and nonferrous metals 278; machinery and metalworks 223; food products 129; chemical products 90; construction materials 52; wood products 31. Construction (1994): 1,700,000 sq m. Energy production (consumption): electricity (kW-hr; 1996) 10,100,000,000 (7,300,000,000); coal (metric tons; 1996) none (100,000); crude petroleum (barrels; 1996) 28,000,000 (29,000,000); petroleum products (metric tons; 1996) 2,223,000 (2,266,000); natural gas (cu m; 1996) 33,991,000,000 (10,803,000,000).
Household income and expenditure. Average household size (1998) 5.0; income per household: n.a.); sources of income (1996): wages and salaries 70.6%, pensions and grants 20.9%, self-employment (mainly agricultural income) 2.3%, nonwage income of workers 1.1%; expenditure (1996): goods 26.8%, services 13.5%, taxes and other payments 9.4%.
Land use (1994): forested 8.2%; meadows and pastures 61.6%; agricultural and under permanent cultivation 3.0%; other 27.2%.
Population economically active (1996): total 1,680,000; activity rate of total population 36.8% (participation rates [1995]: ages 16–59 [male] 16–54 [female] 81.0%; female 41.0%; unemployed 3.0%[4]).

Price and earnings indexes (1994 = 100)[5]

	1994	1995	1996	1997	1998
Consumer price index	100	1,362	7,431	27,502	32,122
Monthly earnings index	100	739	6,334	11,282	16,163

Gross national product (1999): U.S.$3,205,000,000 (U.S.$670 per capita).

Structure of gross domestic product and labour force

	1998		1996	
	in value '000,000 manat	% of total value	labour force	% of labour force
Agriculture	3,256,000	24.6	746,000	44.4
Mining, Manufacturing, Public utilities	3,862,000	29.2	165,000	9.8
Construction	1,582,000	11.9	155,000	9.2
Transp. and commun.	1,372,000	10.4	83,000	4.9
Trade	687,000	5.2	106,700	6.4
Finance	...	...	8,000	0.5
Public administration, defense	...	...	25,000	1.5
Services	1,678,000	12.7	347,000	20.7
Other	804,000	6.1	44,000	2.6
TOTAL	13,241,000	100.0[3]	1,680,000[3]	100.0

Tourism: receipts from visitors (1998) U.S.$192,000,000; expenditures (1997) U.S.$125,000,000.

Foreign trade[6]

Balance of trade (current prices)

	1994	1995	1996	1997	1998
U.S.$'000,000	+485	+536	+329	−231	−523
% of total	12.5%	15.4%	10.8%	13.0%	30.0%

Imports (1998): U.S.$1,137,100,000 (machinery and equipment 39.1%, food products 8.0%, chemicals 5.1%, medicines 1.8%). *Major import sources:* Ukraine 16.1%; Turkey 13.1%; Russia 11.6%; Germany 6.9%; U.S. 6.4%; Uzbekistan 5.2%; Armenia 3.0%.
Exports (1998): U.S.$614,100,000 (natural gas and oil products 54.6%, cotton 22.0%, electricity 5.2%). *Major export destinations:* Iran 24.1%; Turkey 18.3%; Azerbaijan 6.9%; U.K. 4.9%; Russia 4.7%; Tajikistan 4.5%.

Transport and communications

Transport. Railroads (1996): length 1,317 mi, 2,120 km; passenger-km 2,104,000,000, metric ton-km cargo 6,779,000,000. Roads (1996): total length 13,700 km (paved 83%). Vehicles (1995): passenger cars 220,000; trucks and buses, 58,200. Air transport (1996): passenger-km 1,562,000,000; metric ton-km cargo 143,000,000; airports (1997) with scheduled flights 1.

Communications

Medium	date	unit	number	units per 1,000 persons
Radio	1997	receivers	1,225,000	289
Television	1998	receivers	865,000	201
Telephones	1999	main lines	359,000	82
Cellular phones	1999	subscribers	4,000	0.9
Internet	1999	users	2000	0.5

Education and health

Educational attainment (1989). Percentage of population age 25 and over having: primary education or no formal schooling 13.6%; some secondary 21.3%; completed secondary and some postsecondary 56.8%; higher 8.3%. *Literacy* (1989): total population age 15 and over literate 3,453,000 (97.7%); males literate 1,714,000 (98.8%); females literate 1,739,000 (96.6%).

Education (1994–95)

	schools	teachers	students	student/ teacher ratio
Primary (age 6–13), Secondary (age 14–17)	1,900	72,900	940,600	12.9
Voc., teacher tr.	78	...	26,000	...
Higher	15	...	29,435[7]	...

Health (1995): physicians 13,500 (1 per 330 persons); hospital beds 46,000 (1 per 97 persons); (2000) infant mortality rate per 1,000 live births 73.3.
Food (1999): daily per capita caloric intake 2,746 (vegetable products 82%, animal products 18%); (1997) 107% of FAO recommended minimum.

Military

Total active duty personnel (2000): 17,500 (army 82.9%; air force 17.1%). *Military expenditure as percentage of GNP* (1997): 4.6% (world 2.6%); per capita expenditure U.S.$71.

[1]The People's Council is the ultimate representative organ of governmental supervision and is composed of the president, membership of the Majlis, elected members, and a variety of ex officio members of national, provincial, and local government. [2]Ahal includes Ashgabat. [3]Detail does not add to total given because of rounding. [4]Every Turkmen citizen is guaranteed employment, so that unemployment does not officially exist. However, the 1995 Household Survey indicates an unemployment rate of about 3 percent of the labour force (defined as those actively seeking employment but not employed as a proportion of the labour force). [5]December. [6]Import data in balance of trade is c.i.f. [7]1995–96.

Internet resources for further information:
- **United Nations in Turkmenistan http://www.untuk.org**
- **Interstate Statistical Committee of the Commonwealth of Independent States http://www.cisstat.com/eng/macro0.htm**

Tuvalu

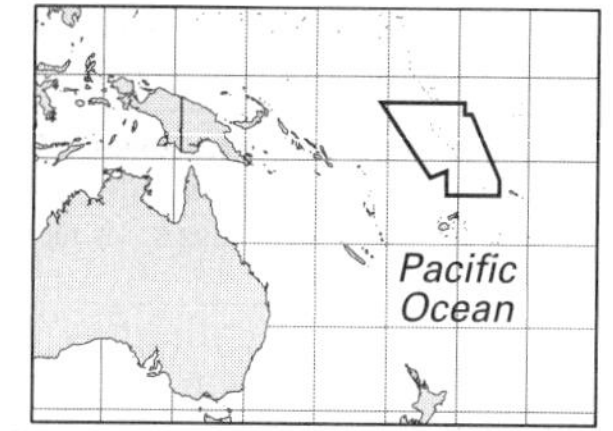

Official name: Tuvalu.
Form of government: constitutional monarchy with one legislative house (Parliament [12]).
Chief of state: British Monarch, represented by Governor-General.
Head of government: Prime Minister.
Capital: government offices are at Vaiaku, Fongafale islet, of Funafuti atoll.
Official language: none.
Official religion: none.
Monetary units[1]: 1 Tuvalu dollar = 1 Australian dollar ($T = $A) = 100 Tuvalu and Australian cents; valuation (Sept. 28, 2001) 1 U.S.$ = $A 2.03; 1 £ = $A 2.98.

Area and population

	area		population
Islands[2]	sq mi	sq km	2000 estimate
Funafuti	1.08	2.79	4,590
Nanumaga	1.07	2.78	770
Nanumea	1.49	3.87	1,010
Niulakita	0.16	0.42	3
Niutao	0.98	2.53	1,120[3]
Nui	1.09	2.83	690
Nukufetau	1.15	2.99	800
Nukulaelae	0.70	1.82	360
Vaitupu	2.16	5.60	1,410
TOTAL	9.90[4, 5]	25.63	10,750

Demography

Population (2001): 11,000.
Density (2001): persons per sq mi 1,110, persons per sq km 429.
Urban-rural (1999): urban 51.0%; rural 49.0%.
Sex distribution (1997): male 48.59%; female 51.41%.
Age breakdown (1997): under 15, 35.7%; 15–29, 23.2%; 30–44, 23.4%; 45–59, 10.5%; 60–74, 6.1%; 75 and over, 1.1%.
Population projection: (2010) 12,600; (2020) 14,800.
Doubling time: 52 years.
Ethnic composition (2000): Tuvaluan (Polynesian) 96.3%; mixed (Pacific Islander/European/Asian) 1.0%; Micronesian 1.0%; European 0.5%; other 1.2%.
Religious affiliation (1995): Church of Tuvalu (Congregational) 85.4%; Seventh-day Adventist 3.6%; Roman Catholic 1.4%; Jehovah's Witness 1.1%; Bahā'i 1.0%; other 7.5%.
Major locality (1995): Fongafale, on Funafuti atoll, 4,000.

Vital statistics

Birth rate per 1,000 population (2000): 21.4 (world avg. 22.5); (1989) legitimate 82.2%; illegitimate 17.8%.
Death rate per 1,000 population (2000): 7.8 (world avg. 9.0).
Natural increase rate per 1,000 population (2000): 13.6 (world avg. 13.5).
Total fertility rate (avg. births per childbearing woman; 1998): 3.1.
Marriage rate per 1,000 population: n.a.
Divorce rate per 1,000 population: n.a.
Life expectancy at birth (1998): male 62.7 years; female 65.1 years.
Major causes of death per 100,000 population (1985): diseases of the digestive system 170.0; diseases of the circulatory system 150.0; diseases of the respiratory system 120.0; diseases of the nervous system 120.0; malignant neoplasms (cancers) 70.0; infectious and parasitic diseases 40.0; endocrine and metabolic disorders 20.0; ill-defined conditions 430.0.

National economy

Budget (1996). Revenue: $A 7,905,000 (nontax revenues 67.2%; taxes 32.8%). Expenditures: $A 8,203,000 (1987; capital [development] expenditures 68.9%, of which marine transport 20.7%, education 13.0%, fisheries 5.6%, health 3.1%; current expenditures 31.1%).
Public debt (external; 1993): U.S.$6,000,000.
Gross national product (at current market prices; 1998): U.S.$14,700,000 (U.S.$1,400 per capita).

Structure of gross domestic product and labour force

	1995		1991	
	in value[6] $A	% of total value	labour force	% of labour force
Agriculture, fishing, forestry	3,152,000	22.2	4,020	68.0
Mining	317,000	2.2	—	—
Manufacturing[7]	452,000	3.2	60	1.0
Construction	1,963,000	13.9	240	4.0
Public utilities	345,000	2.4	—	—
Transp. and commun.	599,000	4.2	60	1.0
Trade, hotels, and restaurants	2,043,000	14.4	240	4.0
Finance	1,390,000	9.8	—	—
Pub. admin., defense / Services	3,922,000	27.7	1,290	22.0
TOTAL	14,183,000	100.0	5,910	100.0

Production (metric tons except as noted). Agriculture[8], forestry, fishing (1999): coconuts 1,800, bananas 180, hens' eggs 12, other agricultural products include breadfruit, pulaka (taro), pandanus fruit, sweet potatoes, and pawpaws; livestock (number of live animals) 27,000 chickens, 12,600 pigs, 7,000 ducks; forestry, n.a.; fish catch (1998) 400. Mining and quarrying[9]: n.a. Manufacturing (1988): copra 90; handicrafts and baked goods are also important. Construction: n.a.; however, the main areas of construction activity are roadworks, coastal protection, government facilities, and water-related infrastructure projects. Energy production (consumption): electricity (kW-hr; 1992) 1,300,000 (1,300,000); coal, none (none); crude petroleum, none (n.a.); petroleum products, none (n.a.); natural gas, none (none).
Tourism (1998): receipts from visitors U.S.$200,000; expenditures by nationals abroad, n.a.
Population economically active (1991): total 5,910; activity rate of total population 65.3% (participation rates: ages 15–64, 85.5%; female [1979] 51.3%; unemployed [1979] 4.0%).

Price and earnings indexes (1990 = 100)

	1992	1993	1994	1995	1996	1997	1998
Consumer price index	100.1	102.3	103.7	109.0	109.8	111.5	112.4
Earnings index	...	...	...	...	...	...	...

Household income and expenditure. Average household size (1979) 6.4; average annual income per household $A 2,575 (U.S.$2,044); sources of income (1987): agriculture and other 45.0%, cash economy only 38.0%, overseas remittances 17.0%; expenditure (1992)[10]: food 45.5%, housing and household operations 11.5%, transportation 10.5%, alcohol and tobacco 10.5%, clothing 7.5%, other 14.5%.
Land use (1987): agricultural and under permanent cultivation 73.6%[11]; scrub 16.1%; other 10.3%.

Foreign trade[12]

Balance of trade (current prices)

	1993	1994	1995	1996	1997	1998
$A '000	–9,344	–10,513	–6,373	–5,638	–7,771	–11,341
% of total	91.8%	93.0%	94.4%	88.6%	91.2%	98.8%

Imports (1998): $A 11,408,000 (1989; food 29.3%, manufactured goods 28.2%, petroleum and petroleum products 12.8%, machinery and transport equipment 12.2%, chemicals 7.1%, beverages and tobacco 3.9%). *Major import sources* (1995): Fiji 65.8%; Australia 17.1%; New Zealand 3.9%; United Kingdom 3.3%; United States 2.0%; Germany 1.3%; The Netherlands 1.3%.
Exports (1998): $A 67,000 (1989; clothing and footwear 29.5%, copra 21.5%, fruits and vegetables 8.0%). *Major export destinations* (1995): South Africa 63.6%; Colombia 9.1%; Belgium-Luxembourg 9.1%.

Transport and communications

Transport. Railroads: none. Roads (1996): total length 8 km (paved, none). Vehicles[13]: n.a. Merchant marine (1992): vessels (100 gross tons and over) 6; total deadweight tonnage 16,005. Air transport (1977): passenger arrivals (Funafuti) 1,443; cargo, n.a.; airports (1997) with scheduled flights 1.

Communications

Medium	date	unit	number	units per 1,000 persons
Radio	1997	receivers	4,000	384
Television	1996	receivers	100	13
Telephones	1999	main lines	630	55

Education and health

Educational attainment (1991). Percentage of population age 25 and over having: no formal schooling 0.8%; primary education 71.4%; secondary 16.2%; higher 7.0%. *Literacy* (1990): total population literate in Tuvaluan 8,593 (95.0%); literacy in English estimated at 45.0%.

Education (1991)

	schools	teachers[14]	students	student/ teacher ratio
Primary (age 5–11)	11	72	1,906[15]	...
Secondary (age 12–18)	1	21	314	...
Vocational	1	10	58	...
Higher	—	—	—	—

Health (1999): physicians 8 (1 per 1,375 persons); hospital beds (1990) 30 (1 per 302 persons); infant mortality rate per 1,000 live births (1998): 26.2.

Military

Total active duty personnel: none; Tuvalu relies on Australian-trained volunteers from Fiji and Papua New Guinea.

[1]The value of the Tuvalu dollar is pegged to the value of the Australian dollar, which is also legal currency in Tuvalu. [2]Local government councils have been established on all islands except Niulakita. [3]Niutao includes Niulakita. [4]Another survey puts the area at 9.4 sq mi (24.4 sq km). [5]Detail does not add to total given because of rounding. [6]At 1988 factor cost. [7]Including cottage industry. [8]Because of poor soil quality, only limited subsistence agriculture is possible on the islands. [9]Research into the mineral potential of Tuvalu's maritime exclusive economic zone (289,500 sq mi [750,000 sq km] of the Pacific Ocean) is currently being conducted by the South Pacific Geo-Science Commission. [10]Weights of consumer price index components. [11]Capable of supporting coconut palms, pandanus, and breadfruit. [12]Imports are c.i.f. [13]There are several cars, tractors, trailers, and light trucks on Funafuti; a few motorcycles are in use on most islands. [14]1990. [15]1994.

Uganda

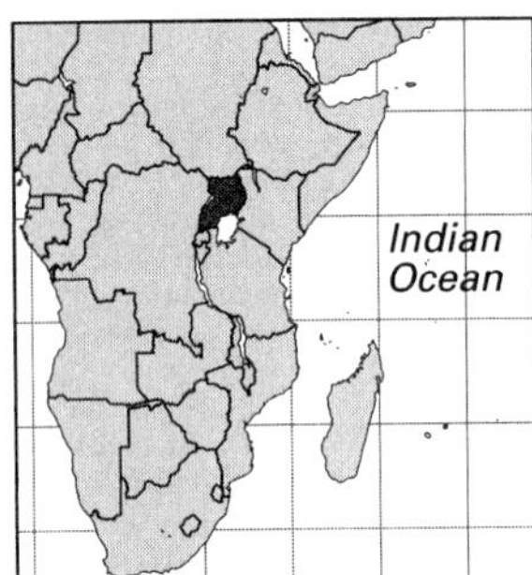

Official name: Republic of Uganda.
Form of government: nonparty republic with one legislative house (Parliament [305[1]])[2].
Head of state and government: President.
Capital: Kampala.
Official language: English.
Official religion: none.
Monetary unit: 1 Uganda shilling (U Sh) = 100 cents; valuation (Sept. 28, 2001) 1 U.S.$ = U Sh 1,757; 1 £ = U Sh 2,582.

Area and population

		area		population
Geographic regions[3]	Principal cities	sq mi	sq km	1999 estimate
Central	Kampala	23,749	61,510	6,046,000
Eastern	Jinja	15,426	39,953	5,469,500
Northern	Gulu	32,687	84,658	4,106,500
Western	Mbarara	21,204	54,917	5,997,700
TOTAL		93,065[4, 5]	241,038[4]	21,619,700

Demography

Population (2001): 23,986,000.
Density (2001)[6]: persons per sq mi 315.3, persons per sq km 121.7.
Urban-rural (1999–2000): urban 13.0%; rural 87.0%.
Sex distribution (2000): male 49.55%; female 50.45%.
Age breakdown (2000): under 15, 51.1%; 15–29, 26.2%; 30–44, 13.6%; 45–59, 5.7%; 60–74, 2.9%; 75 and over, 0.5%.
Population projection: (2010) 31,395,000; (2020) 42,005,000.
Doubling time: 22 years.
Ethnolinguistic composition (1991): Ganda 18.1%; Nkole 10.7%; Kiga 8.4%; Soga 8.2%; Lango 5.9%; Lugbara 4.7%; Gisu 4.5%; Acholi 4.4%.
Religious affiliation (1995): Christian 66%, of which Roman Catholic 33%, Protestant 33% (of which mostly Anglican); traditional beliefs 18%; Muslim 16%.
Major cities (1991): Kampala 1,154,000[7]; Jinja 61,000; Mbale 53,600; Masaka 49,100; Gulu 42,800; Entebbe 41,600.

Vital statistics

Birth rate per 1,000 population (2000): 48.0 (world avg. 22.5).
Death rate per 1,000 population (2000): 22.4 (world avg. 9.0).
Natural increase rate per 1,000 population (2000): 25.6 (world avg. 13.5).
Total fertility rate (avg. births per childbearing woman; 2000): 7.0.
Life expectancy at birth (2000): male 42.2 years; female 43.7 years.

National economy

Budget (1997–98). Revenue: U Sh 1,193,100,000,000 (taxes 62.7%, of which customs duties 25.5%, sales taxes 20.2%, income taxes 10.5%; grants 33.3%). Expenditures: U Sh 1,239,900,000,000 (current expenditures 58.7%, of which wages and salaries 20.6%, education 16.6%, security 11.0%, health 4.3%; capital expenditures 41.3%).
Public debt (external, outstanding; 1999): U.S.$3,564,000,000.
Production (metric tons except as noted). Agriculture, forestry, fishing (1999): plantains 9,400,000, cassava 3,400,000, sweet potatoes 2,520,000, sugarcane 1,600,000, corn (maize) 780,000, millet 638,000, sorghum 454,000, potatoes 449,000, coffee 198,000, peanuts (groundnuts) 183,000, rice 96,000; livestock (number of live animals) 5,700,000 cattle, 3,650,000 goats, 1,970,000 sheep, 960,000 pigs, 23,000,000 chickens; roundwood (1998) 15,649,000 cu m; fish catch (1998) 220,626. Mining and quarrying (1997): gold 3,000 kg. Manufacturing (1998): cement 278,800; sugar 93,000; soap 36,100; metal products 22,400; meat 3,706; footwear 995,000 pairs; beer 552,000 hectolitres. Energy production (consumption): electricity (kW-hr; 1998) 1,282,800,000 (872,000,000); coal (metric tons) none (none); crude petroleum (barrels) none (none); petroleum products (metric tons; 1996) none (319,000); natural gas (cu m) none (none).
Tourism (1999): receipts from visitors U.S.$149,000,000; expenditures by nationals abroad U.S.$141,000,000.
Land use (1994): forest 31.5%; pasture 9.1%; agriculture 34.0%; other 25.4%.
Gross national product (1999): U.S.$6,794,000,000 (U.S.$330 per capita).

Structure of gross domestic product and labour force

	1998–99		1991	
	in value U Sh '000,000	% of total value	labour force	% of labour force
Agriculture	3,489,000	40.3	6,724,000	80.4
Mining	49,000	0.6	478,000	5.7
Manufacturing	690,000	8.0		
Construction	565,000	6.5		
Public utilities	108,000	1.2		
Transp. and commun.	335,000	3.9	1,163,000	13.9
Trade	1,091,000	12.6		
Finance, Pub. admin., defense	1,279,000	14.8		
Services	281,000	3.2		
Other	778,000	9.0	...	...
TOTAL	8,665,000	100.0[5]	8,365,000	100.0

Population economically active (1991): total 8,365,000; activity rate of total population 49.6% (participation rates: ages 15–64, 78.9%[8]; female 35.2%).

Price and earnings indexes (1995 = 100)

	1994	1995	1996	1997	1998	1999	2000
Consumer price index	92.0	100.0	107.0	115.0	115.0	122.0	125.0
Earnings index	...	...	...	...	...	...	...

Household income and expenditure (1999–2000)[8]. Average household size 5.2; income per household: U Sh 141,000 (U.S.$91[9]); sources of income: wages and self-employment 78.0%; transfers 13.0%; rent 9.0%; expenditure: food and beverages 51.0%; rent, energy, and services 17.0%; education 7.0%; household durable goods 6.0%; transportation 5.0%; health 4.0%.

Foreign trade[10]

Balance of trade (current prices)

	1995	1996	1997	1998	1999	2000
U Sh '000,000,000	–578.2	–633.8	–831.1	–952.7	–1,207.0	–1,727.0
% of total	39.3%	34.1%	41.1%	50.1%	44.6%	53.2%

Imports (1997–98): U.S.$1,411,100,000 (1996; machinery and transport equipment 33.8%, basic manufactures 22.0%, chemicals 15.9%, food and live animals 7.3%). *Major import sources* (1996): Kenya 21.5%; U.K. 14.2%; Japan 9.1%; United Arab Emirates 6.1%; Germany 4.2%; U.S. 3.1%.
Exports (1997–98): U.S.$458,400,000 (unroasted coffee 58.7%, tea 7.6%, fish 6.1%, cotton 2.5%). *Major export destinations* (1996): U.K. 20.8%; Belgium-Luxembourg 12.3%; Spain 9.1%; U.S. 8.1%; France 6.4%; Germany 4.3%.

Transport and communications

Transport. Railroads (1998): route length 1,241 km; passenger-km (1996) 27,000,000; metric ton-km cargo (1996) 236,000,000. Roads (1996): total length 26,800 km (paved 7.7%). Vehicles (1996): passenger cars 35,361; trucks and buses 48,430. Merchant marine (1992): vessels (100 gross tons and over) 2; total deadweight tonnage 8,600[11]. Air transport (1997): passenger-km 52,117,000; metric ton-km cargo 5,000,000; airports (1998) 1.

Communications

Medium	date	unit	number	units per 1,000 persons
Daily newspapers	1997	circulation	40,000	2.1
Radio	1997	receivers	2,600,000	130
Television	1998	receivers	580,000	28.0
Telephones	1999	main lines	57,239	2.5
Cellular telephones	1999	subscribers	56,358	2.4
Personal computers	1999	units	55,000	2.4
Internet	1999	users	25,000	1.1

Education and health

Educational attainment (1991). Percentage of population age 25 and over having: no formal schooling or less than one full year 46.9%; primary education 42.1%; secondary 10.5%; higher 0.5%. *Literacy* (1999–2000): population age 10 and over literate 65.0%; males literate 74.0%; females literate 57.0%.

Education (1995)

	schools	teachers	students	student/ teacher ratio
Primary (age 5–11)[12]	8,531	76,134	2,636,409	34.6
Secondary (age 12–15)[12]	...	14,447	255,158	17.7
Voc., teacher tr.[12]	...	1,788	36,063	20.2
Higher	...	2,006	29,343	14.6

Health (1993): physicians 840 (1 per 22,399 persons); hospital beds (1989) 20,136 (1 per 817 persons); infant mortality rate (2000) 93.3.
Food (2000): daily per capita caloric intake 2,238 (vegetable products 94%, animal products 6%); 96% of FAO recommended minimum requirement.

Military

Total active duty personnel (2000): 50,000–60,000[13]. *Military expenditure as percentage of GNP* (1997): 4.2% (world 2.6%); per capita U.S.$12.

[1]Includes 10 ex officio members (ministers who are not elected to Parliament). [2]New constitution promulgated on Oct. 8, 1995. [3]The 39 administrative districts in Uganda as of 1994 were increased to 45 administrative districts in 1997. Eight additional administrative districts were announced in November 2000 and 3 more in July 2001, for a total of 56 administrative districts. [4]Includes water area of 16,984 sq mi (43,989) sq km; Uganda's portion of Lake Victoria comprises 11,954 sq mi (30,960 sq km). [5]Detail does not add to total given because of rounding. [6]Based on land area only. [7]1998. [8]Based on nationally representative household survey. [9]The household income for urban areas is U Sh 302,900 (U.S.$195). [10]Imports c.i.f.; exports f.o.b. [11]1988. [12]Public sector only. [13]Breakdown by branch of service is unavailable.

Internet resources for further information:
- **Uganda Bureau of Statistics http://www.ubos.org**

Ukraine

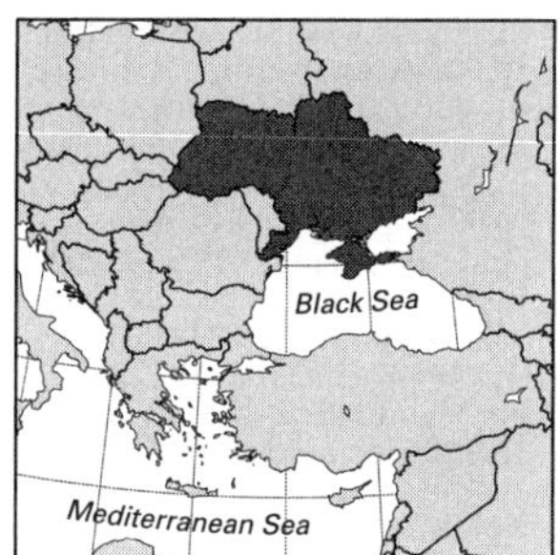

Official name: Ukrayina (Ukraine).
Form of government: unitary multiparty republic with a single legislative body (Supreme Council [450]).
Head of state: President.
Head of government: Prime Minister.
Capital: Kiev (Kyyiv).
Official language: Ukrainian.
Official religion: none.
Monetary unit: hryvnya (pl. hryvnyas)[1]; (Sept. 28, 2001) free rate, 1 U.S.$ = 5.33 hryvnyas; 1 £ = 7.83 hryvnyas.

Area and population

Autonomous republic	area sq km	population 1998 estimate
Crimea (Krym)	26,100	2,157,700
Cities		
Kiev	800	2,629,300
Sevastopol	900	397,300
Provinces		
Cherkasy	20,900	1,478,700
Chernihiv	31,900	1,318,500
Chernivtsi	8,100	938,500
Dnipropetrovsk	31,900	3,775,400
Donetsk	26,500	5,064,400
Ivano-Frankivsk	13,900	1,463,600
Kharkiv	31,400	3,024,400
Kherson	28,500	1,246,800
Khmelnytsky	20,600	1,485,700
Kirovohrad	24,600	1,197,800

Provinces	area sq km	population 1998 estimate
Kyyiv (Kiev)	28,100	1,864,000
Luhansk	26,700	2,706,400
Lviv	21,800	2,739,600
Mykolayiv	24,600	1,322,500
Odessa	33,300	2,547,800
Poltava	28,800	1,708,300
Rivne	20,100	1,192,200
Sumy	23,800	1,369,800
Ternopil	13,800	1,168,400
Vinnytsya	26,500	1,847,100
Volyn	20,200	1,067,900
Zakarpatska	12,800	1,288,200
Zaporizhzhya	27,200	2,042,500
Zhytomyr	29,900	1,457,100
TOTAL	603,700	50,499,900

Demography

Population (2001): 48,767,000.
Density (2001): persons per sq mi 209.2, persons per sq km 80.8.
Urban-rural (1999): urban 67.9%; rural 32.1%.
Sex distribution (1999): male 46.30%; female 53.70%.
Age breakdown (1999): under 15, 18.4%; 15–29, 21.7%; 30–44, 21.8%; 45–59, 17.7%; 60–74, 15.6%; 75 and over, 4.8%.
Population projection: (2010) 46,193,000; (2020) 44,362,000.
Ethnic composition (2000): Ukrainian 70.4%; Russian 20.0%; Polish 2.3%; Rom (Gypsy) 1.3%; Ruthenian 1.1%; other/unspecified 4.9%.
Religious affiliation (1995): Ukrainian Orthodox (Russian patriarchy) 19.5%; Ukrainian Orthodox (Kiev patriarchy) 9.7%; Ukrainian Catholic (Uniate) 7.0%; Protestant 3.6%; other Orthodox 1.6%; Roman Catholic 1.2%; Jewish 0.9%; other (mostly nonreligious) 56.5%.
Major cities (1998): Kiev 2,629,300; Kharkiv 1,521,400; Dnipropetrovsk 1,122,400; Donetsk 1,065,400; Odessa 1,027,400; Zaporizhzhya 863,100.

Vital statistics

Birth rate per 1,000 population (2000): 7.9[2] (world avg. 22.5); (1993) legitimate 87.0%; illegitimate 13.0%.
Death rate per 1,000 population (2000): 13.9[2] (world avg. 9.0).
Natural increase rate per 1,000 population (2000): –6.0[2] (world avg. 13.5).
Total fertility rate (avg. births per childbearing woman; 2000): 1.3.
Life expectancy at birth (2000): male 60.6 years; female 72.0 years.
Major causes of death per 100,000 population (1995): circulatory diseases 874.0; neoplasms (cancers) 199.0; accidents 160.0; respiratory diseases 89.0.

National economy

Budget (1998). Revenue: 36,892,000,000 hryvnyas (tax revenue 95.5%, of which taxes on goods and services 31.5%, payroll tax 29.3%, income tax 26.3%, property tax 3.0%, excise tax 2.6%, other 2.8%; nontax revenue 4.5%). Expenditures: 39,714,000,000 hryvnyas (social security 36.3%; national economy 15.1%; education 11.3%; health 9.1%; defense 3.4%).
Public debt (external; 1999): U.S.$10,027,000,000.
Production (metric tons except as noted). Agriculture, forestry, fishing (1999): potatoes 15,405,100, sugar beets 13,890,000, wheat 13,476,200, barley 6,382,100, corn (maize) 1,732,500, rye 908,000, oats 759,300; livestock (number of live animals) 11,722,000 cattle, 10,083,000 pigs, 2,026,000 sheep and goats; roundwood (1998) 10,052,000 cu m; fish catch (1998) 462,308. Mining and quarrying (1998): iron ore 50,700,000; manganese 2,226,000; uranium 500,000. Manufacturing (value of production in '000,000 hryvnyas; 1997): iron and steel 12,832; food products 12,221; nonelectrical machinery 3,447; fabricated metal products 2,951; industrial chemicals 2,705. Energy production (consumption): electricity (kW-hr; 1999) 172,104,000,000 (146,700,000,000); hard coal (metric tons; 1999) 81,648,000 ([1996] 79,500,000); lignite (metric tons; 1999) 1,188,000 ([1996] 4,300,000); crude petroleum (barrels; 1999) 27,795,000 ([2000] 126,290,000); petroleum products (1996) 11,759,000 (16,168,000); natural gas (cu m; 1999) 15,740,000,000 (78,013,000,000).
Population economically active (1997): total 22,598,000; activity rate of total population 44.6% (participation rates: ages 16–59 [male] 15–64 [female] 79.7%; female [1994] 51.0%; unemployed [1999–2000] 4.3%[3]).

Price and earnings indexes (1997 = 100)

	1997	1998	1999	2000[4]
Consumer price index	100.0	110.6	135.7	167.1
Monthly earnings index	100.0	105.6	...	...

Gross national product (1999): U.S.$41,991,000,000 (U.S.$840 per capita).

Structure of gross domestic product and labour force

	1998		1997	
	in value '000,000 hryvnyas	% of total value	labour force	% of labour force
Agriculture	12,000	11.4	4,903,000	21.7
Mining; Manufacturing; Public utilities	26,000	24.8	4,822,000	21.3
Construction	5,000	4.8	1,194,000	5.3
Transp. and commun.	14,000	13.3	1,308,000	5.8
Trade	8,000	7.6	1,522,000	6.7
Finance; Pub. admin., defense; Services	26,000	24.8	3,440,000	15.2
Other	14,000[5]	13.3[5]	5,409,000[6]	23.9[6]
TOTAL	105,000	100.0	22,598,000	100.0[7]

Tourism (1997): receipts U.S.$270,000,000; expenditures U.S.$305,000,000.
Household income and expenditure (1996). Average household size (1998) 3.0; income per household (1996) 4,968 hryvnyas[1] (U.S.$2,715); sources of income (1995): wages and salaries 66.4%, sales of agricultural products 9.3%, subsidies 6.9%, pensions 6.5%, remuneration from abroad 5.3%; expenditures (1995): food and beverages 43.1%, consumer goods 27.5%, services 7.2%, housing 6.7%, taxes 6.2%.

Foreign trade

Balance of trade (current prices)

	1994	1995	1996	1997	1998	1999
U.S.$'000,000	–2,575	–2,702	–4,296	–4,205	–2,584	–482
% of total	8.5%	8.7%	12.1%	12.0%	8.6%	1.9%

Imports (1999): U.S.$12,945,000,000 (fuel and energy products 39.9%; machinery 17.4%; chemicals and chemical products 11.3%; food and raw materials 7.0%). *Major import sources:* Russia 47.9%; Germany 7.3%; Turkmenistan 3.7%; U.S. 3.1%; Belarus 2.6%.
Exports (1999): U.S.$12,463,000,000 (ferrous and nonferrous metals 39.1%; food and raw materials 11.4%; machinery 11.1%; chemicals and chemical products 11.1%). *Major export destinations:* Russia 19.2%; China 5.9%; Turkey 5.4%; Germany 4.5%; Italy 3.7%; U.S. 3.5%.

Transport and communications

Transport. Railroads (1998): length 22,564 km; passenger-km 54,500,000,000; metric ton-km cargo (1997) 160,419,000,000. Roads (1997): total length 172,378 km (paved 95%). Vehicles (1997): passenger cars 4,885,691. Air transport (1998): passenger-km 1,972,134,000; metric ton-km cargo 27,395,000[8]; airports (1998) with scheduled flights 12.

Communications

Medium	date	unit	number	units per 1,000 persons
Daily newspapers	1996	circulation	2,780,000	54
Radio	1997	receivers	45,050,000	889
Television	1998	receivers	21,000,000	418
Telephones	1999	main lines	10,074,000	202
Cellular telephones	1999	subscribers	216,567	4.4
Personal computers	1999	units	800,000	16
Internet	1999	users	200,000	4.0

Education and health

Educational attainment (1989). Percentage of population age 15 and over having: some primary education 6.8%; completed primary 13.8%; some secondary 18.4%; completed secondary 31.1%; some postsecondary 19.5%; higher 10.4%. *Literacy* (1989): percentage of total population age 15 and over literate 98.4%; males literate 99.5%; females literate 97.4%.

Education (1995–96)

	schools	teachers	students	student/ teacher ratio
Primary (age 6–13); Secondary (age 14–17)	21,900	576,000[9]	7,007,000	...
Voc., teacher tr.	782	...	618,000	...
Higher	255	...	922,800	...

Health (1998): physicians 150,382 (1 per 334 persons); hospital beds 508,030 (1 per 99 persons); infant mortality rate per 1,000 live births (2000) 21.7.
Food (1999): daily per capita caloric intake 2,809 (vegetable products 78%, animal products 22%); 110% of FAO recommended minimum requirement.

Military

Total active duty personnel (2000): 303,800 (army 49.8%, air force 31.6%, navy 4.3%, headquarters 14.3%). *Military expenditure as percentage of GNP* (1997) 3.7% (world 2.6%); per capita expenditure U.S.$85.

[1]On Sept. 2, 1996, the karbovanets, a transitional currency, was replaced by the hryvnya at a 100,000-to-1 ratio. [2]Average of April to September only. [3]Official figure; August 1999–July 2000 average. [4]April. [5]Less imputed bank service charges, net indirect taxes, and taxes on production. [6]Includes 2,646,000 self-employed and 2,763,000 unemployed. [7]Detail does not add to total given because of rounding. [8]10 Ukrainian airlines only. [9]1994–95.

Internet resources for further information:
- **National Bank of Ukraine**
  http://www.bank.gov.ua/ENGL/DEFAULT.htm

United Arab Emirates

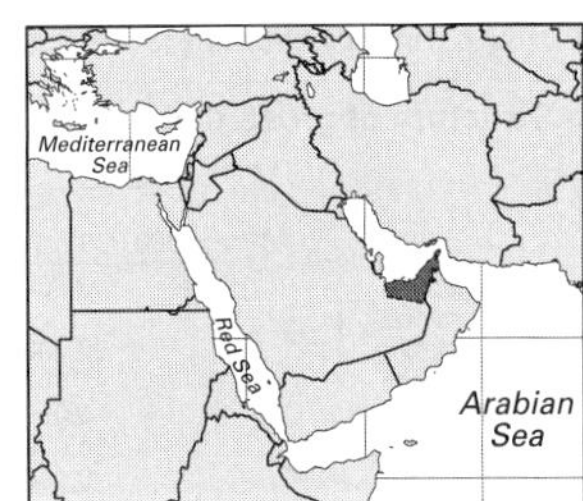

Official name: Al-Imārāt al-ʿArabīyah al-Muttaḥidah (United Arab Emirates).
Form of government: federation of seven emirates with one appointive advisory body (Federal National Council [40[1]]).
Chief of state: President.
Head of government: Prime Minister.
Capital: Abu Dhabi.
Official language: Arabic.
Official religion: Islam.
Monetary unit: 1 U.A.E. dirham (Dh) = 100 fils; valuation (Sept. 28, 2001) 1 U.S.$ = Dh 3.67; 1 £ = Dh 5.40.

Area and population		area		population
				2001
Emirates	Capitals	sq mi	sq km	estimate
Abū Ẓaby (Abu Dhabi)	Abu Dhabi	28,210[2]	73,060[2]	1,186,000
ʿAjmān (Ajman)	ʿAjmān	100	260	174,000
Dubayy (Dubai)	Dubai	1,510	3,900	913,000
Al-Fujayrah (Fujairah)	Al-Fujayrah	500	1,300	98,000
Ra's al-Khaymah (Ras al-Khaimah)	Ra's al-Khaymah	660	1,700	171,000
Ash-Shāriqah (Sharjah)	Sharjah	1,000	2,600	520,000
Umm al-Qaywayn (Umm al-Qaiwain)	Umm al-Qaywayn	300	780	46,000
TOTAL		32,280	83,600	3,108,000

Demography

Population (2001): 3,108,000.
Density (2001): persons per sq mi 96.3, persons per sq km 37.2.
Urban-rural (1998): urban 85.1%; rural 14.9%.
Sex distribution (2001): male 67.54%; female 32.46%.
Age breakdown (2001): under 15, 26.2%; 15–29, 29.2%; 30–44, 33.4%; 45–59, 9.6%; 60–74, 1.4%; 75 and over, 0.2%.
Population projection: (2010) 3,751,000; (2020) 4,257,000.
Doubling time: 50 years.
Ethnic composition (2000): Arab 48.1%, of which UAE Arab 12.2%, UAE Bedouin 9.4%, Egyptian Arab 6.2%, Omani Arab 4.1%, Saudi Arab 4.0%; South Asian 35.7%, of which Pashtun 7.1%, Balochi 7.1%, Malayali 7.1%; Persian 5.0%; Filipino 3.4%; white 2.4%; other 5.4%.
Religious affiliation (1995): Muslim 96.0% (Sunnī 80.0%, Shīʿī 16.0%); other (mostly Christian and Hindu) 4.0%.
Major cities (1995): Dubai 669,181; Abu Dhabi 398,695; Sharjah 320,095; Al-ʿAyn 225,970; ʿAjmān 114,395; Ra's al-Khaymah 77,550.

Vital statistics

Birth rate per 1,000 population (2000): 18.0 (world avg. 22.5).
Death rate per 1,000 population (2000): 3.7 (world avg. 9.0).
Natural increase rate per 1,000 population (2000): 14.3 (world avg. 13.5).
Total fertility rate (avg. births per childbearing woman; 2000): 3.3.
Marriage rate per 1,000 population (1999): 3.5.
Divorce rate per 1,000 population (1999): 0.9.
Life expectancy at birth (1999): male 71.6 years; female 76.6 years.
Major causes of death per 100,000 population (1998): cardiovascular diseases 44.1; accidents and poisoning 31.1; malignant neoplasms (cancers) 15.3; congenital anomalies 9.4.

National economy

Budget (1999). Revenue: Dh 52,003,000,000 (oil revenue 54.2%, non-oil revenue 45.8%). Expenditures: Dh 77,089,000,000 (current expenditures 66.2%, capital [development] expenditure 33.8%).
Gross national product (1999): U.S.$52,098,000,000 (U.S.$17,965 per capita).

Structure of gross domestic product and labour force	2000			
	in value Dh '000,000[3]	% of total value[3]	labour force	% of labour force
Agriculture	7,017	2.9	142,213	7.8
Crude petroleum production / Mining and quarrying	82,655	34.2	41,148	2.3
Manufacturing	28,846	11.9	194,765	10.7
Construction	17,247	7.1	344,179	18.9
Public utilities	4,627	1.9	17,759	1.0
Transp. and commun.	16,153	6.7	127,214	7.0
Trade	27,294	11.3	310,430	17.1
Finance, real estate	32,981	13.6	68,127	3.7
Pub. admin., defense	24,637	10.2	237,391	13.0
Services	5,441	2.2	295,774	16.2
Other	–5,010[4]	–2.0[4]	41,000[5]	2.3[5]
TOTAL	241,888	100.0	1,820,000	100.0

Public debt: n.a.
Tourism (1999): total number of tourist arrivals 3,392,000.
Production (metric tons except as noted). Agriculture, forestry, fishing (2000): tomatoes 780,000, dates 318,000, cantaloupes and watermelons 64,000, cabbages 58,132, pumpkins and squash 31,252, eggplants 28,068, lemons and limes 18,137, cucumbers and gherkins 14,836, mangoes 10,300; livestock (number of live animals) 1,200,000 goats, 467,281 sheep, 200,000 camels, 110,000 cattle, 14,650,000 chickens; fish catch (1999) 117,607. Mining and quarrying (1998): sulfur 268,000; gypsum 110,000; chromite 54,000; lime 50,000. Manufacturing (value of production in Dh '000,000; 1993): chemical products 13,086; fabricated metal products 2,234; food, beverages, and tobacco 2,122; nonmetallic mineral products 2,025; basic metal manufactures 1,992; textiles, clothing, and leather products 1,135. Energy production (consumption): electricity (kW-hr; 1997) 20,571,000,000 (20,571,000,000); crude petroleum (barrels; 2000) 769,000,000 ([1997] 86,000,000); petroleum products (metric tons; 1997) 18,995,000 (7,190,000); natural gas (cu m; 1997) 35,859,000,000 (28,839,000,000).
Population economically active (2001): total 1,947,000; activity rate of total population 59.2% (participation rates [1995]: over age 15, 55.4%; female 13.2%; unemployment [2000] 2.3%).

Price and earnings indexes (1995 = 100)	1991	1992	1993	1994	1995	1996	1997
Consumer price index[6]	81.5	86.9	91.3	95.8	100.0	103.2	106.7
Annual earnings index	...	...	104.1	101.1	100.0	103.0	102.7

Household income and expenditure. Average household size (1999) 6.1; income per household: n.a.; sources of income: n.a.; expenditure (1991): rent, fuel, and light 23.9%, food 22.7%, transportation and communications 14.1%, durable household goods 11.6%, education, recreation, and entertainment 8.6%.
Land use (1994): forested, virtually none; meadows and pastures 2.4%; agricultural and under permanent cultivation 0.5%; built-on, wasteland, and other 97.1%.

Foreign trade

Balance of trade (current prices)	1995	1996	1997	1998	1999	2000
Dh '000,000,000	+22.6	+29.5	+30.4	+5.7	+16.2	+41.8
% of total	11.0%	12.7%	12.2%	2.6%	6.7%	15.1%

Imports (1997): Dh 109,100,000,000 (machinery and transport equipment 38.4%, basic manufactures 24.8%, food and live animals 9.7%, chemicals 6.1%, crude minerals 1.6%, mineral fuels 1.4%). *Major import sources:* Japan 10.2%; United States 9.4%; United Kingdom 8.7%; China 8.0%; Germany 6.9%; India 5.8%; Italy 5.2%; South Korea 5.1%.
Exports (1997): Dh 139,500,000,000 (crude petroleum 37.6%, natural gas 7.1%, refined petroleum products 4.8%). *Major export destinations:* Japan 36.2%; India 6.6%; Singapore 6.4%; South Korea 6.1%; Iran 3.7%; Oman 3.7%.

Transport and communications

Transport. Railroads: none. Roads (1999): total length 2,355 mi, 3,791 km (paved 100%). Vehicles (1996): passenger cars 201,000; trucks and buses 56,950. Merchant marine (1992): vessels (100 gross tons and over) 276; total deadweight tonnage 1,491,728. Air transport (2000)[7]: passenger-mi 12,149,300,000, passenger-km 19,552,500,000; short ton-mi cargo 887,000,000, metric ton-km cargo 1,427,500,000; airports (1999) with scheduled flights 6.

Communications Medium	date	unit	number	units per 1,000 persons
Daily newspapers	1996	circulation	384,000	170
Radio	1997	receivers	820,000	355
Television	1999	receivers	740,000	252
Telephones	1999	main lines	975,178	332
Cellular telephones	1999	subscribers	832,267	283
Personal computers	1999	units	300,000	102
Internet	1999	users	400,000	136

Education and health

Educational attainment (1995). Percentage of population age 10 and over having: no formal schooling 47.6%; primary education 27.8%; secondary 16.0%, higher 8.6%. *Literacy* (1995): total population age 15 and over literate 79.2%; males literate 78.9%; females literate 79.8%.

Education (1998–99)	schools	teachers	students	student/ teacher ratio
Primary (age 6–11) / Secondary (age 12–18)	512[8]	16,148[9]	270,486	16.1[9]
		12,388[10]	198,439	12.0[10]
Vocational	...	249[9]	3,113	7.7[9]
Higher	4[9]	510[11]	17,950[9]	19.2[11]

Health (1999): physicians 6,059 (1 per 485 persons); hospital beds 7,448 (1 per 394 persons); infant mortality rate per 1,000 live births (1999) 8.8.
Food (1999): daily per capita caloric intake 3,182 (vegetable products 75%, animal products 25%); 132% of FAO recommended minimum requirement.

Military

Total active duty personnel (2000): 65,000 (army 90.7%, navy 3.1%, air force 6.2%). *Military expenditure as percentage of GDP* (1997): 6.9% (world 2.6%); per capita expenditure U.S.$1,004.

[1]All appointed seats. [2]Approximate, based on reported total and on reported partial areas for smaller emirates. [3]At factor cost. [4]Imputed bank service charges. [5]Unemployed. [6]Abu Dhabi only. [7]Emirates Air and one-fourth apportionment of Gulf Air. [8]1991–92. [9]1996–97. [10]1994–95. [11]1992–93.

Internet resources for further information:
• **U.A.E. Home Page http://www.emirates.org**

United Kingdom

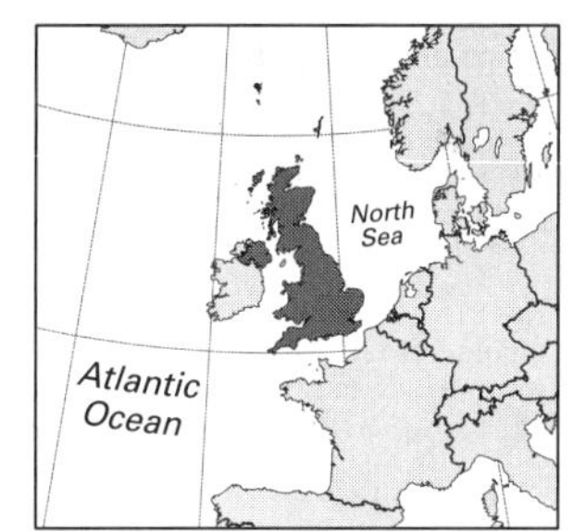

Official name: United Kingdom of Great Britain and Northern Ireland.
Form of government: constitutional monarchy with two legislative houses (House of Lords [695]; House of Commons [659]).
Chief of state: Sovereign.
Head of government: Prime Minister.
Capital: London.
Official language: English.
Official religion: Churches of England and Scotland "established" (protected by the state, but not "official") in their respective countries; no established church in Northern Ireland or Wales.
Monetary unit: 1 pound sterling (£) = 100 new pence; valuation (Sept. 28, 2001) 1 £ = U.S.$1.47; 1 U.S.$ = £0.68.

Population (1999 estimate)

Countries[1]	population		population		population
England	49,752,900[2]	Peterborough	156,500	Scotland	5,119,200[2]
Counties		Plymouth	253,200	**Unitary Districts**	
Bedfordshire	378,800	Poole	140,800	Aberdeen City	212,600
Buckinghamshire	482,500	Portsmouth	188,700	Aberdeenshire	227,500
Cambridgeshire	568,400	Reading	147,300	Angus	109,900
Cheshire	670,600	Redcar and		Argyll and Bute	89,700
Cornwall	494,700	Cleveland	137,000	City of Edinburgh	451,700
Cumbria	491,800	Rutland	37,000	Clackmannanshire	48,500
Derbyshire	737,600	Slough	111,100	Dumfries and	
Devon	697,700	South		Galloway	146,800
Dorset	389,200	Gloucestershire	244,500	Dundee City	144,500
Durham	506,300	Southampton	215,200	East Ayrshire	121,000
East Sussex	496,200	Southend	176,700	East Dumbarton-	
Essex	1,306,200	Stockton-on-		shire	110,700
Gloucestershire	562,000	Tees	182,400	East Lothian	90,400
Hampshire	1,248,700	Stoke-on-Trent	250,800	East Renfrewshire	89,300
Hertfordshire	1,043,000	Swindon	181,200	Eileane Siar[5]	27,500
Isle of Wight[3]	128,300	Telford and		Falkirk	144,400
Kent	1,344,000	Wrenkin	149,900	Fife	349,200
Lancashire	1,137,100	Thurrock	134,800	Glasgow City	611,500
Leicestershire	606,800	Torbay	124,200	Highland	208,600
Lincolnshire	628,600	Warrington	190,700	Inverclyde	85,200
Norfolk	796,500	West Berkshire	144,600	Midlothian	81,700
North Yorkshire	569,800	Windsor and		Moray	85,200
Northamptonshire	621,200	Maidenhead	141,300	North Ayrshire	139,400
Northumberland	310,100	Wokingham	144,800	North Lanarkshire	327,900
Nottinghamshire	748,400	York	177,800	Orkney Islands	19,700
Oxfordshire	626,200	**Metropolitan**		Perth and Kinross	134,000
Shropshire	282,500	**Counties/Greater**		Renfrewshire	177,200
Somerset	493,100	**London**		Scottish Borders	106,400
Staffordshire	809,800	Greater London[4]	7,285,100	Shetland Islands	22,800
Suffolk	674,600	Greater		South Ayrshire	114,300
Surrey	1,078,100	Manchester	2,577,000	South Lanarkshire	307,600
Warwickshire	507,900	Merseyside	1,403,600	Stirling	84,700
West Sussex	760,700	South Yorkshire	1,302,400	West Dumbarton-	
Wiltshire	429,100	Tyne and Wear	1,108,400	shire	95,000
Worcestershire	539,800	West Midlands	2,626,500	West Lothian	154,700
Unitary Councils		West Yorkshire	2,115,400		
Bath and				Northern Ireland	1,691,800[2]
NE Somerset	168,600	Wales	2,937,000	**Districts**	
Blackburn with		**Unitary Districts**		Antrim	50,800
Darwen	138,400	Blaenau Gwent	71,800	Ards	71,400
Blackpool	150,000	Bridgend	131,600	Armagh	54,000
Bournemouth	162,500	Caerphilly	170,100	Ballymena	59,200
Bracknell Forest	111,500	Cardiff	324,400	Ballymoney	25,900
Brighton and		Carmarthenshire	168,900	Banbridge	39,800
Hove	258,100	Ceredigion	71,700	Belfast	284,300
Bristol	405,300	Conway	112,100	Carrickfergus	37,800
Darlington	100,500	Denbighshire	91,000	Castlereagh	66,800
Derby	236,500	Flintshire	147,400	Coleraine	55,700
East Riding of		Gwynedd	116,400	Cookstown	31,700
Yorkshire	315,700	Isle of Anglesey	65,300	Craigavon	79,700
Halton	121,100	Merthyr Tydfil	56,200	Derry	106,600
Hartlepool	92,000	Monmouthshire	86,700	Down	63,800
Herefordshire	168,300	Neath and		Dungannon	48,200
Kingston upon		Port Talbot	138,300	Fermanagh	57,400
Hull	257,900	Newport	138,300	Larne	30,900
Leicester	291,000	Pembrokeshire	113,700	Limvady	31,900
Luton	183,300	Powys	126,300	Lisburn	111,300
Medway	243,200	Rhondda, Cynon,		Magherafelt	39,000
Middlesborough	144,300	Taff	240,500	Moyle	15,400
Milton Keynes	206,800	Swansea	229,700	Newry and Mourne	87,700
NE Lincolnshire	156,000	Torfaen	89,800	Newtownabbey	81,300
North Lincolnshire	152,000	The Vale of		North Down	75,700
North Somerset	189,800	Glamorgan	121,300	Omagh	47,800
Nottingham City	284,300	Wrexham	125,500	Strabane	37,600
				TOTAL	59,500,900

Demography

Population (2001): 59,953,000.
Area: 94,248 sq mi; 244,101 sq km, of which England 50,351 sq mi, 130,410 sq km; Wales 8,015 sq mi, 20,758 sq km; Scotland 30,421 sq mi, 78,789 sq km; Northern Ireland (figures represent remainder) 5,461 sq mi, 14,144 sq km.
Density (2001): persons per sq mi 636.1, persons per sq km 245.6.
Urban-rural (1999): urban 88.2%; rural 10.8%.
Age breakdown (1999): under 15, 20.4%; 15–29, 18.0%; 30–44, 22.8%; 45–59, 18.4%; 60–74, 13.1%; 75 and over, 7.3%.
Population projection: (2010) 60,913,000; (2020) 61,742,000.
Ethnic composition (1998): white 93.2%; black 1.8%; Asian Indian 1.7%; Pakistani 1.2%; Bangladeshi 0.5%; Chinese 0.2%; other and not stated 1.4%.
Sex distribution (1999): male 49.24%; female 50.76%.
Religious affiliation (2000): Christian 66.4%, of which Protestant 53.3% (Anglican 45.0%), Roman Catholic 9.6%, Orthodox 0.9%; Muslim 2.0%; Hindu 0.7%; Sikh 0.5%; Jewish 0.4%; other/nonreligious 30.0%.
Major cities (1999): Greater London 7,285,000; Birmingham 1,013,200; Leeds 726,800; Glasgow 668,100; Sheffield 530,600; Bradford 483,700; Liverpool 458,000; Edinburgh 451,700; Manchester 431,100; Bristol 405,200; Kirklees 392,200; Wirral 326,600.
Mobility (1991)[6]. Population living in the same residence as 1990: 90.1%; different residence, same country (of Great Britain) 8.1%; different residence, different country of Great Britain 1.2%; from outside Great Britain 0.6%.
Households (1994)[6]. Average household size 2.4; 1 person 27%, 2 persons 34%, 3 persons 16%, 4 persons 15%, 5 persons 6%, 6 or more persons 2%. Family household: 16,900,000 (72.0%), nonfamily 6,600,000 (28.0%, of which 1-person 12.0%).
Immigration (1998): permanent residents 332,000, from Australia 7.5%, United States 5.7%, New Zealand 4.2%, South Africa 3.6%, Bangladesh, India, and Sri Lanka 3.0%, Canada 1.5%, Pakistan 1.2%, other 73.3%, of which EU 8.7%.

Vital statistics

Birth rate per 1,000 population (1999): 11.8 (world avg. 22.5); legitimate 61.2%; illegitimate 38.8%.
Death rate per 1,000 population (1999): 10.6 (world avg. 9.0).
Natural increase rate per 1,000 population (1999): 1.2 (world avg. 13.5).
Total fertility rate (avg. births per childbearing woman; 1999): 1.7.
Marriage rate per 1,000 population (1999): 5.1.
Divorce rate per 1,000 population (1999): 2.7.
Life expectancy at birth (1997–99): male 74.9 years; female 79.8 years.
Major causes of death per 100,000 population (1999): diseases of the circulatory system 420.7, of which ischemic heart disease 221.9, cerebrovascular disease 108.4; malignant neoplasms (cancers) 260.2; diseases of the respiratory system 184.5, of which pneumonia 110.8; diseases of the digestive system 42.0; diseases of the endocrine system 14.4, of which diabetes mellitus 11.3; diseases of the genitourinary system 14.2; suicide 7.5.

Social indicators

Educational attainment (1981). Percentage of population age 25 and over having: primary or secondary education only 89.7%; some postsecondary 4.8%; bachelor's or equivalent degree 4.9%; higher university degree 0.6%.

Distribution of disposable income (1998–99)

percentage of household income by quintile				
1	2	3	4	5 (highest)
7.8	11.0	10.0	22.1	12.5

Quality of working life (1999). Average workweek (hours): male 41.4, female 37.5. Annual rate per 100,000 workers for (1996): injury or accident 553.6; death 1.0. Proportion of labour force (employed persons) insured for damages or income loss resulting from: injury 100%; permanent disability 100%; death 100%. Average days lost to labour stoppages per 1,000 employee workdays 1999: 0.04. Principal means of transport to work (1991; London only): public transportation 81%, private automobile 15%, motor or pedal cycle 2%, other 2%.
Access to services (1991)[6]. Proportion of households having access to: bath or shower 98.7%; toilet 99.8%; central heating 81.1%.
Social participation. Eligible voters participating in last national election (May 1997): 71.4%. Population age 16 and over participating in voluntary work (1987)[6]: 22%. Trade union membership in total workforce (1998) 26.7%.
Social deviance (1998–99). Offense rate per 100,000 population for: theft and handling stolen goods 3,574.2; burglary 1,599.8; violence against the person 387.9; fraud and forgery 291.9; robbery 111.3; sexual offense 58.6.
Leisure (1994). Favourite leisure activities (hours weekly): watching television 17.1; listening to radio 10.3; reading 8.8, of which books 3.8, newspapers 3.3; gardening 2.1.
Material well-being (1999). Households possessing: automobile 71.0%, telephone 95.0%, television receiver 98.3% (colour 95%)[7], refrigerator 98.5%, central heating 90.0%, washing machine 91.0%, video recorder 86.0%.

National economy

Budget (1999). Revenue: £328,168,000,000 (income tax 39.3%, customs and excise taxes 32.4%, social security contributions 17.2%). Expenditures: £336,930,000,000 (1996–97; social security 24.9%, health 11.0%, debt interest 7.2%, defense 7.2%).
Total national debt (March 31, 2000): £421,635,700,000 (U.S.$672,551,100,000).
Gross national product (at current market prices; 1999): U.S.$1,403,843,000,000 (U.S.$23,590 per capita).

Structure of gross domestic product and labour force

	1999		2000	
	in value £'000,000	% of total value	labour force	% of labour force
Agriculture	10,695	1.2	342,000	1.2
Mining[8]	20,495	2.3	272,000	0.9
Manufacturing	167,530	18.8	3,958,000	13.5
Construction	46,340	5.2	1,188,000	4.0
Public utilities	20,490	2.3	135,000	0.5
Transp. and commun.	78,420	8.8	1,415,000	4.8
Trade[9]	132,770	14.9	4,095,000	13.9
Finance	249,510	28.0	988,000	3.4
Pub. admin., defense	150,595	16.9	5,979,000	20.3
Services	47,230	5.3	5,942,000	20.2
Other	–32,970[10]	–3.7[10]	5,098,000[11]	17.3[11]
TOTAL	891.106[2]	100.0	29,412,000	100.0

Land use (1994): forested 10.4%; meadows and pastures 45.9%; agricultural and under permanent cultivation 24.8%; other 18.9%.
Tourism (1999): receipts from visitors U.S.$20,223,000,000; expenditures by nationals abroad U.S.$35,631,000,000.
Production (metric tons except as noted). Agriculture, forestry, fishing (2001): wheat 12,060,000, sugar beets 10,000,000, barley 6,690,000, potatoes 6,647,000, rapeseed 1,129,000, oats 680,000, carrots 674,000, green peas 436,000; livestock (number of live animals) 42,000,000 sheep, 11,000,000 cattle, 6,500,000 pigs; roundwood (1999) 7,451,000 cu m; fish catch (1999) 992,552. Mining and quarrying (1999): limestone 91,485,000; lead 1,000. Manufacturing (value added in £'000,000; 1998): electrical and optical equipment 19,478; food and beverages 19,337; iron and ferro-alloys 17,375; paper, printing, and publishing 17,717; transport equipment 16,968; chemicals and chemical products 14,582; machinery and equipment 13,295; textiles and leather products 6,704. Construction (value in £; 1995)[6]: residential 7,135,000,000; nonresidential 13,877,000,000.

Financial aggregates

	1994	1995	1996	1997	1998	1999	2000
Exchange rate							
U.S. dollar per £	1.53	1.58	1.56	1.64	1.66	1.62	1.52
SDRs per £	1.07	1.04	1.18	1.22	1.18	1.18	1.14
International reserves (U.S.$)							
Total (excl. gold; '000,000,000)	41.01	42.02	39.90	32.32	32.21	35.87	43.89
SDRs ('000,000,000)	0.49	0.41	0.34	0.47	0.47	0.51	0.33
Reserve pos. in IMF ('000,000)	1.99	2.42	2.43	2.97	4.38	5.28	4.28
Foreign exchange	38.53	39.18	37.12	28.88	27.36	30.08	39.28
Gold ('000,000 fine troy oz)	18.44	18.43	18.43	18.42	23.00	20.55	15.67
% world reserves	2.0	2.0	2.0	2.1	2.4	2.1	1.6
Interest and prices							
Central bank discount (%)	...	...	...	...	...	...	...
Govt. bond yield (%) long term	8.05	8.26	8.10	7.09	5.45	4.70	4.68
Industrial share prices (1995 = 100)	77.9	89.4	96.1	100.0	113.3	...	...
Balance of payments (U.S.$'000,000,000)							
Balance of visible trade,	−16,127	−18,266	−18,870	−19,490	−35,020	−42,340	−43,580
Imports, f.o.b.	222,263	259,154	278,400	−300,800	−305,800	−311,280	−326,760
Exports, f.o.b.	206,136	240,888	259,530	281,310	271,780	268,940	283,180
Balance of invisibles	13,736	7,697	19,110	30,320	34,870	26,360	19,120
Balance of payments, current account	−2,391	−10,569	240	10,830	−150	−15,980	−24,460

Manufacturing, mining, and construction enterprises (1997)

	no. of establishments	no. of employees	annual wages as a % of avg. of all wages	annual value added (£'000,000)
Manufacturing				
Food, beverages, and tobacco	15,106	880,000	92.5	33,718
Paper and paper products; printing and publishing	62,641	879,000	113.8	31,386
Chemical products	8,242	532,000	127.0	28,814
Metal manufacturing	61,867	939,000	94.7	26,381
Machinery and equipment	28,199	759,000	107.9	25,727
Electrical and data-processing equipment	10,466	397,000	101.2	13,279
Transport equipment	2,723	249,000	116.4	9,698
Rubber and plastics	8,049	312,000	90.7	9,115
Textiles	11,615	335,000	76.2	7,465
Wood and wood products	15,851	157,000	74.2	3,696
Furniture	7,529	132,000	86.7	3,452
Clothing and footwear	8,640	185,000	56.7	3,333
Mining[12]				
Extraction of coal, mineral oil, and natural gas	358	80,000[13]	...	10,261
Extraction of minerals other than fuels	921	30,200	...	1,090
Construction[12]	199,363	1,016,000[13]	...	19,274

Retail trade enterprises (1992)

	no. of enterprises	no. of employees	weekly wage as a % of all wages	annual turnover (£'000,000)[14]
Food and grocery, of which	60,119	854,000	...	51,462
large grocery	71	579,000	...	40,837
other grocery	18,557	95,000	...	4,086
meats	12,149	58,000	...	2,523
Household goods, of which	45,532	299,000	...	20,881
electrical and musical goods	10,887	87,000	...	7,270
furniture	11,927	60,000	...	4,575
Drink, confectionery, and tobacco, of which	46,671	254,000	...	13,810
tobacco and confectionery	41,502	215,000	...	10,880
Clothing and footwear, of which	24,923	264,000	...	12,428
women's, girls', and infants' wear	13,624	102,000	...	4,771
footwear	3,098	67,000	...	2,589
men's and boys' wear	3,751	37,000	...	2,063
Pharmaceuticals	7,560	87,000	...	5,231

Energy production (consumption): electricity (kW-hr; 1997) 344,955,000,000 (361,529,000,000); coal (metric tons; 1997) 45,895,000 (63,128,000); crude petroleum (barrels; 1997) 892,985,000 (648,791,000); petroleum products (metric tons; 1997) 89,779,000 (72,673,000); natural gas (cu m; 1997) 104,174,000,000 (102,506,000,000).
Population economically active (2000): total 29,412,000, activity rate of total population 49.2% (participation rates: ages 16–64, 74.3%; female 44.5%; unemployed 5.5%).

Price and earnings indexes (1995 = 100)

	1994	1995	1996	1997	1998	1999	2000
Consumer price index	96.7	100.0	102.4	105.7	109.3	111.0	114.2
Monthly earnings index	96.7	100.0	103.5	108.0	113.5	119.0	124.4

Household income and expenditure (1998–99). Average household size 2.4; average annual disposable income per household £19,230 (U.S.$31,990); sources of income: wages and salaries 65.7%, social security benefits 12.1%, income from self-employment 9.6%, dividends and interest 4.5%; expenditure: food and beverages 20.8%, transport and vehicles 17.2%, housing 15.8%, household goods 8.5%, clothing 5.8%, energy 3.1%.

Foreign trade

Balance of trade (current prices)

	1995	1996	1997	1998	1999	2000
£'000,000	−14,702	−16,549	−15,540	−25,466	−29,765	−34,856
% of total	4.6%	4.7%	4.3%	7.2%	8.2%	8.6%

Imports (1999): £194,434,000,000 (machinery and transport equipment 46.0%, of which electrical equipment 21.2%, road vehicles 12.5%; chemicals 9.7%, of which plastics 2.0%, organic chemicals 1.5%; clothing and footwear 4.9%; food 4.7%; petroleum and petroleum products 2.5%; textiles 2.3%; paper and paperboard 2.2%). *Major import sources:* Germany 13.8%; U.S. 12.7%; France 9.3%; The Netherlands 7.0%; Belgium-Luxembourg 4.9%; Japan 4.8%; Italy 4.8%; Ireland 4.4%; Spain 3.1%; Switzerland 2.8%.
Exports (1999): £165,667,000,000 (machinery and transport equipment 47.5%, of which electrical equipment 21.6%, road vehicles 9.1%; chemicals 13.9%, of which organic chemicals 3.3%; petroleum and petroleum products 5.5%; professional and scientific 4.1%; food 2.0%; iron and steel products 1.6%). *Major export destinations:* U.S. 14.7%; Germany 12.3%; France 10.1%; The Netherlands 8.2%; Ireland 6.5%; Belgium-Luxembourg 5.5%; Italy 4.7%; Spain 4.5%; Sweden 2.4%; Japan 2.0%; Switzerland 1.7%.

Transport and communications

Transport. Railroads (1999–2000)[6]: length 23,518 mi[15], 37,849 km[15]; passenger-mi 23,800,000,000, passenger-km 38,300,000,000; ton-mi cargo 12,800,000,000, metric ton-km cargo 18,400,000,000. Roads (1999)[6]: total length 231,097 mi, 371,914 km (paved 100%). Vehicles (1999): passenger cars 23,393,000, trucks and buses 2,368,000. Merchant marine (1992): vessels (over 100 gross tons) 1,631; total deadweight tonnage 4,355,063. Air transport (1999): passenger-mi 99,628,300,000, passenger-km 160,336,400,000; short ton-mi cargo 3,422,000,000, metric ton-km cargo 4,924,900,000; airports (1997) 57.

Communications

Medium	date	unit	number	units per 1,000 persons
Daily newspapers	1996	circulation	19,332,000	332
Radio	1997	receivers	84,500,000	1,443
Television	1999	receivers	38,800,000	652
Telephones	1999	main lines	33,750,000	567
Cellular telephones	1999	subscribers	27,185,000	457
Personal computers	1999	units	18,000,000	303
Internet	1999	users	12,500,000	210

Education and health

Literacy (1990): total population literate, virtually 100%[16].

Education (1998–99)[17]

	schools	teachers	students	student/teacher ratio
Primary (age 5–10)	31,956	226,696	5,028,684	22.2
Secondary (age 11–19)		230,635	3,694,311	16.0
Voc., teacher tr.	...	...	586,000[18]	...
Higher[19, 20]	70	c. 48,000	c. 810,000	c. 17.0

Health (1993)[6]: physicians 92,474 (1 per 629 persons); hospital beds 283,814 (1 per 205 persons); infant mortality rate (1999) 5.8.
Food (1999): daily per capita caloric intake 3,318 (vegetable products 68%, animal products 32%); 132% of FAO recommended minimum requirement.

Military

Total active duty personnel (2001): 211,430 (army 53.9%, navy 20.6%, air force 25.5%). *Military expenditure as percentage of GNP* (1997): 2.7% (world 2.6%); per capita expenditure U.S.$600.

[1]The reorganization of first-order administrative units was completed in 1999; England's former 46 counties (including 7 metropolitan counties) reorganized into 35 counties, 45 unitary districts, 6 metropolitan counties, and Greater London; Wales's former 8 counties reorganized into 22 unitary districts; Scotland's former 9 regions and 3 island councils organized into 32 unitary districts; Northern Ireland remained. [2]Detail does not add to total given because of rounding. [3]Only unitary district with county status. [4]Has administrative authority from July 2000. [5]Formerly Western Isles. [6]Great Britain only. [7]1992. [8]Includes petroleum extraction. [9]Includes hotels. [10]Plus rent; less imputed bank service charges. [11]Includes 1,619,000 unemployed and 3,139,000 self-employed not distributed by sector and 207,000 military personnel. [12]1993. [13]1992. [14]Includes value-added taxes. [15]1990. [16]A survey in 1986–87, however, put the number of functional illiterates at 9–12% of the adult population. [17]Public sector only. [18]1992–93. [19]1994–95. [20]Universities only.

Internet resources for further information:
- **Office for National Statistics http://www.statistics.gov.uk**

United States

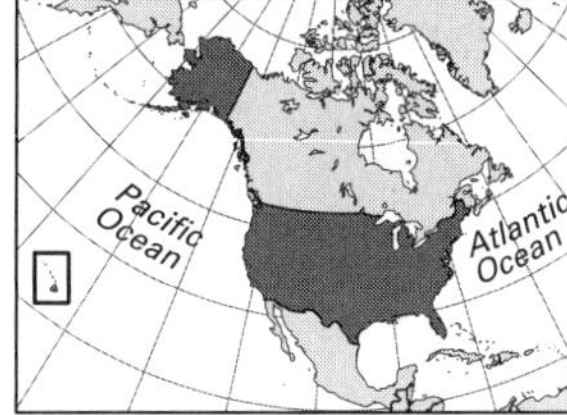

Official name: United States of America.
Form of government: federal republic with two legislative houses (Senate [100]; House of Representatives [435[1]]).
Head of state and government: President.
Capital: Washington, D.C.
Official language: none.
Official religion: none.
Monetary unit: 1 dollar (U.S.$) = 100 cents; valuation (Sept. 28, 2001) 1 U.S.$ = £0.68; 1 £ = U.S.$1.47.

Area and population

States	Capitals	area sq mi	area sq km	population 2000 census (prelim.)
Alabama	Montgomery	51,718	133,950	4,447,100
Alaska	Juneau	587,875	1,522,595	626,932
Arizona	Phoenix	114,006	295,275	5,130,632
Arkansas	Little Rock	53,182	137,741	2,673,400
California	Sacramento	158,647	410,895	33,871,648
Colorado	Denver	104,100	269,619	4,301,261
Connecticut	Hartford	5,006	12,966	3,405,565
Delaware	Dover	2,026	5,247	783,600
Florida	Tallahassee	58,680	151,981	15,982,378
Georgia	Atlanta	58,930	152,629	8,186,453
Hawaii	Honolulu	6,459	16,729	1,211,537
Idaho	Boise	83,574	216,456	1,293,953
Illinois	Springfield	57,918	150,008	12,419,293
Indiana	Indianapolis	36,420	94,328	6,080,485
Iowa	Des Moines	56,276	145,755	2,926,324
Kansas	Topeka	82,282	213,110	2,688,418
Kentucky	Frankfort	40,411	104,664	4,041,769
Louisiana	Baton Rouge	47,719	123,592	4,468,976
Maine	Augusta	33,128	85,801	1,274,923
Maryland	Annapolis	10,455	27,078	5,296,486
Massachusetts	Boston	8,262	21,399	6,349,097
Michigan	Lansing	96,705	250,466	9,938,444
Minnesota	St. Paul	86,943	225,182	4,919,479
Mississippi	Jackson	47,695	123,530	2,844,658
Missouri	Jefferson City	69,709	180,546	5,595,211
Montana	Helena	147,046	380,849	902,195
Nebraska	Lincoln	77,359	200,360	1,711,263
Nevada	Carson City	110,567	286,368	1,998,257
New Hampshire	Concord	9,283	24,043	1,235,786
New Jersey	Trenton	7,790	20,176	8,414,350
New Mexico	Santa Fe	121,598	314,939	1,819,046
New York	Albany	53,013	137,304	18,976,457
North Carolina	Raleigh	52,672	136,420	8,049,313
North Dakota	Bismarck	70,704	183,123	642,200
Ohio	Columbus	44,828	116,104	11,353,140
Oklahoma	Oklahoma City	69,903	181,049	3,450,654
Oregon	Salem	97,052	251,364	3,421,399
Pennsylvania	Harrisburg	45,759	118,516	12,281,054
Rhode Island	Providence	1,213	3,142	1,048,319
South Carolina	Columbia	31,117	80,593	4,012,012
South Dakota	Pierre	77,121	199,743	754,844
Tennessee	Nashville	42,145	109,155	5,689,283
Texas	Austin	266,873	691,201	20,851,820
Utah	Salt Lake City	84,904	219,901	2,233,169
Vermont	Montpelier	9,615	24,903	608,827
Virginia	Richmond	40,598	105,149	7,078,515
Washington	Olympia	68,126	176,446	5,894,121
West Virginia	Charleston	24,232	62,761	1,808,344
Wisconsin	Madison	65,500	169,645	5,363,675
Wyoming	Cheyenne	97,819	253,351	493,782
District				
District of Columbia	—	68	176	572,059
TOTAL		3,675,031[2]	9,518,323[2]	281,421,906

Demography

Population (2001): 286,067,000[3].
Density (2001)[3]: persons per sq mi 77.8, persons per sq km 30.5.
Urban-rural (2000): urban 77.2%; rural 22.8%.
Sex distribution (2000): male 49.06%; female 50.94%.
Age breakdown (2000): under 15, 21.4%; 15–29, 20.8%; 30–44, 23.3%; 45–59, 18.2%; 60–74, 10.4%; 75 and over, 5.9%.
Population projection: (2010) 308,761,000; (2020) 334,548,000.
Doubling time: not applicable; doubling time exceeds 100 years.
Population by race and Hispanic[4] origin (1999): non-Hispanic white 71.9%; non-Hispanic black 12.1%; Hispanic 11.6%; Asian and Pacific Islander 3.7%; American Indian and Eskimo 0.7%.
Religious affiliation (1995): Christian 85.3%, of which Protestant 57.9%, Roman Catholic 21.0%, other Christian 6.4%; Jewish 2.1%; Muslim 1.9%; nonreligious 8.7%; other 2.0%.
Mobility (1999). Population living in the same residence as in 1998: 84.0%; different residence, same county 9.0%; different county, same state 3.0%; different state 3.0%; moved from abroad 1.0%.
Households (1999). Total households 103,874,000 (married-couple families 54,770,000 [52.7%]). Average household size (1998) 2.6; 1 person 25.6%, 2 persons 32.2%, 3 persons 16.9%, 4 persons 15.0%, 5 or more persons 10.2%. Family households: 71,535,000 (68.9%); nonfamily 32,339,000 (31.1%), of which 1-person 82.2%.
Immigration (1998[5]): permanent immigrants admitted 660,477, from Mexico 19.9%, China 5.6%, India 5.5%, Philippines 5.2%, Dominican Republic 3.1%, Cuba 2.9%, Vietnam 2.7%, Ukraine 2.6%, Jamaica 2.3%, El Salvador 2.2%, South Korea 2.2%, Pakistan 2.0%, Russia 1.7%. Refugee arrivals (1998[5]): 54,645.

Components of population change (1990–99)

States	Net change in population	Annual percentage change	Births	Deaths	Net migration
Alabama	329,473	0.8	568,961	387,158	147,670
Alaska	69,457	1.3	98,976	22,291	–7,228
Arizona	1,112,993	2.9	670,677	317,200	759,516
Arkansas	200,749	0.9	330,123	244,180	114,806
California	3,333,694	1.2	5,227,258	2,039,044	145,480
Colorado	761,660	2.3	513,908	225,699	473,451
Connecticut	–5,085	–0.1	423,922	268,782	–160,225
Delaware	87,370	1.3	97,768	58,165	47,767
Florida	2,173,173	1.7	1,781,648	1,370,234	1,761,759
Georgia	1,310,091	2.0	1,053,424	525,580	782,247
Hawaii	77,268	0.7	173,388	67,676	–28,444
Idaho	244,966	2.4	166,298	77,951	156,619
Illinois	697,768	0.6	1,735,493	971,944	–65,781
Indiana	398,745	0.8	779,368	482,740	102,117
Iowa	92,582	0.4	349,191	256,794	185
Kansas	176,464	0.7	348,226	215,686	43,924
Kentucky	273,933	0.8	494,758	340,897	120,072
Louisiana	150,209	0.4	629,286	362,228	–116,849
Maine	25,112	0.2	137,791	107,664	–5,015
Maryland	390,881	0.9	687,293	375,178	78,766
Massachusetts	158,744	0.3	778,803	506,880	–113,179
Michigan	568,488	0.6	1,287,572	763,166	44,082
Minnesota	399,843	0.9	603,264	338,093	134,672
Mississippi	193,144	0.8	389,349	246,225	50,020
Missouri	351,437	0.7	697,038	492,127	146,526
Montana	83,714	1.1	103,358	69,332	49,688
Nebraska	87,611	0.6	217,510	139,754	9,855
Nevada	607,578	4.5	227,622	110,437	490,393
New Hampshire	91,882	0.9	142,027	83,680	33,535
New Jersey	395,662	0.5	1,079,022	667,367	–15,993
New Mexico	224,775	1.5	254,934	111,862	81,703
New York	205,823	0.1	2,539,280	1,519,562	–813,895
North Carolina	1,018,341	1.6	967,386	586,354	637,309
North Dakota	–5,134	–0.1	78,833	54,150	–29,817
Ohio	409,539	0.4	1,454,713	957,171	–88,003
Oklahoma	212,468	0.7	437,373	298,499	73,594
Oregon	473,817	1.7	399,411	255,204	329,610
Pennsylvania	111,174	0.1	1,438,566	1,163,384	–164,008
Rhode Island	–12,645	–0.1	125,103	89,187	–48,561
South Carolina	399,426	1.2	498,067	301,259	202,618
South Dakota	37,129	0.6	98,048	62,765	1,846
Tennessee	606,332	1.3	687,916	463,719	382,135
Texas	3,057,806	1.8	3,025,567	1,254,005	1,286,244
Utah	406,986	2.3	369,419	98,393	135,960
Vermont	30,982	0.6	67,101	44,797	8,678
Virginia	683,715	1.1	872,681	477,233	288,267
Washington	889,692	1.8	729,025	372,964	533,631
West Virginia	13,451	0.1	198,388	184,750	–187
Wisconsin	358,492	0.8	637,733	412,353	133,112
Wyoming	26,013	0.6	60,099	32,704	–1,382
District					
District of Columbia	–87,900	–1.7	87,167	59,836	–115,231
TOTAL/RATE	23,899,888	1.0	36,820,132	20,934,303	8,014,059

Major cities (1999): New York 7,428,162; Los Angeles 3,633,591; Chicago 2,799,050; Houston 1,845,967; Philadelphia 1,417,601; San Diego 1,238,974; Phoenix 1,211,466; San Antonio 1,147,213; Dallas 1,076,214; Detroit 965,084.

Other principal cities (1999)

	population		population		population
Akron	211,822	Honolulu	395,327	Pittsburgh	336,882
Albuquerque	420,578	Indianapolis	738,907	Portland (Ore.)	503,637
Anaheim	300,650	Jacksonville	695,877	Raleigh	261,205
Anchorage	257,808	Jersey City	230,458	Riverside	265,721
Arlington (Tex.)	311,962	Kansas City (Mo.)	437,764	Rochester	214,470
Atlanta	401,726	Las Vegas	418,658	Sacramento	406,899
Austin	587,873	Lexington (Ky.)	243,785	St. Louis	333,960
Bakersfield	222,352	Lincoln	215,928	St. Paul	256,213
Baltimore	632,681	Long Beach	435,027	St. Petersburg	234,647
Baton Rouge	210,667	Louisville	253,128	San Francisco	746,777
Birmingham	249,459	Madison	210,674	San Jose	867,675
Boston	555,249	Memphis	606,109	Santa Ana	309,290
Buffalo	295,619	Mesa (Ariz.)	368,811	Seattle	537,150
Charlotte	520,829	Miami	369,253	Stockton	245,020
Cincinnati	330,914	Milwaukee	572,424	Tampa	290,973
Cleveland	501,662	Minneapolis	353,395	Toledo	307,946
Colorado Springs	350,199	Nashville	506,385	Tucson	466,591
Columbus	671,247	New Orleans	460,913	Tulsa	381,579
Corpus Christi	281,774	Newark	263,087	Virginia Beach	433,461
Denver	499,775	Norfolk	225,875	Washington, D.C.	519,000
El Paso	612,770	Oakland	365,210	Wichita	335,562
Fort Worth	502,369	Oklahoma City	475,322		
Fresno	404,141	Omaha	386,742		

Place of birth (1999): native-born 245,295,000 (90.3%); foreign-born 26,448,000 (9.7%), of which Mexico 7,197,000, Philippines 1,455,000, China and Hong Kong 985,000, Cuba 943,000, Vietnam 966,000, India 839,000, El Salvador 761,000, South Korea 611,000.

Vital statistics

Birth rate per 1,000 population (1999): 14.3 (world avg. 22.5); (1998) legitimate 67.2%; illegitimate 32.8%.
Death rate per 1,000 population (1999): 8.7 (world avg. 9.0).
Natural increase rate per 1,000 population (1999): 5.6 (world avg. 13.5).
Total fertility rate (avg. births per childbearing woman; 1999): 2.0.
Marriage rate per 1,000 population (1998): 8.3; median age at first marriage (1991): men 26.3 years, women 24.1 years.
Divorce rate per 1,000 population (1998): 3.1.
Life expectancy at birth (1998): white male 74.8 years, black and other male 68.9[6] years; white female 79.9 years, black and other female 76.1[6] years.

Vital statistics (1998)

States	Live births	Birth rate per 1,000 population	Death rate per 1,000 population	Infant mortality rate per 1,000 live births[7]	Abortion rate per 1,000 live births[8]	Life expectancy[9]
Alabama	62,074	14.3	10.1	9.5	248.8	73.6
Alaska	9,926	16.2	4.2	7.5	196.1	. . .
Arizona	78,243	16.8	8.2	7.1	248.3	76.1
Arkansas	36,865	14.5	10.8	8.7	170.5	74.3
California	521,661	16.0	6.9	5.9	434.8	75.9
Colorado	59,577	15.0	6.7	7.0	294.7	77.0
Connecticut	43,820	13.4	9.1	7.2	383.7	76.9
Delaware	10,578	14.2	8.9	7.8	582.5	74.8
Florida	195,637	13.1	10.6	7.1	466.3	75.8
Georgia	122,368	16.0	7.9	8.6	329.5	73.6
Hawaii	17,583	14.7	6.8	6.6	430.1	78.2
Idaho	19,391	15.8	7.5	6.8	111.1	76.9
Illinois	182,588	15.2	8.7	8.4	366.0	74.9
Indiana	85,122	14.4	8.9	8.2	169.1	75.4
Iowa	37,282	13.0	9.9	6.2	163.0	77.3
Kansas	38,422	14.6	9.3	7.4	268.8	76.8
Kentucky	54,329	13.8	9.6	7.3	152.7	74.4
Louisiana	66,888	15.3	9.2	9.5	228.7	73.0
Maine	13,733	11.0	9.8	5.1	215.8	73.1
Maryland	71,972	14.0	8.2	8.8	428.2	76.4
Massachusetts	81,411	13.2	9.0	5.2	502.5	74.8
Michigan	133,666	13.6	8.7	8.2	364.0	75.0
Minnesota	65,202	13.8	7.9	5.9	237.0	77.8
Mississippi	42,939	15.6	10.1	10.6	72.6	73.0
Missouri	75,358	13.9	10.1	7.6	150.7	75.3
Montana	10,579	12.3	9.0	6.9	270.3	76.2
Nebraska	23,534	14.2	9.1	7.4	172.4	76.9
Nevada	28,699	16.4	8.3	6.5	640.0	74.2
New Hampshire	14,429	12.2	8.1	4.3	204.1	76.7
New Jersey	114,550	14.1	8.8	6.3	531.4	75.4
New Mexico	27,318	15.7	7.7	6.1	185.9	75.7
New York	258,207	14.2	8.6	6.7	648.5	74.7
North Carolina	111,688	14.8	9.0	9.2	344.5	74.5
North Dakota	7,932	12.4	9.3	6.2	117.6	77.6
Ohio	152,794	13.6	9.5	7.8	266.1	75.3
Oklahoma	49,461	14.8	10.2	7.5	196.9	75.1
Oregon	45,273	13.8	9.0	5.8	373.8	76.4
Pennsylvania	145,899	12.2	10.6	7.6	270.1	75.4
Rhode Island	12,599	12.7	9.7	7.0	468.8	76.5
South Carolina	53,877	14.0	9.1	9.6	216.1	73.5
South Dakota	10,288	13.9	9.3	7.7	95.2	76.9
Tennessee	77,396	14.3	10.0	8.6	245.9	74.3
Texas	342,283	17.3	7.2	6.4	275.7	75.1
Utah	45,165	21.5	5.6	5.8	101.0	77.7
Vermont	6,582	11.1	8.4	6.1	294.1	76.5
Virginia	94,351	13.9	8.0	7.8	334.8	75.2
Washington	79,663	14.0	7.5	5.6	323.8	76.8
West Virginia	20,747	11.5	11.5	9.6	141.5	74.3
Wisconsin	67,450	12.9	8.8	6.5	192.6	76.9
Wyoming	6,252	13.0	8.0	5.8	. . .	76.2
District						
District of Columbia	7,686	14.7	11.4	13.2	2,333.3	68.0
TOTAL/RATE	3,941,553	14.6	8.7	7.2	349.8	75.8

Major causes of death per 100,000 population (1998[10]): cardiovascular diseases 347.7, of which ischemic heart disease 170.3, cerebrovascular diseases 58.5, atherosclerosis 5.7; malignant neoplasms (cancers) 199.4; diseases of the respiratory system 74.9, of which pneumonia 32.6; accidents and adverse effects 34.5, of which motor-vehicle accidents 15.5; diabetes mellitus 23.9; AIDS 17.2; suicide 10.8; chronic liver disease and cirrhosis 10.8.

Death rates by major causes (1997)

States	Total rate of death per 100,000 population	Circulatory diseases	Cancer	Pulmonary diseases	Suicide and homicide	Other
Alabama	1,001.5	381.0	221.7	66.8	23.9	308.1
Alaska	422.6	113.1	102.1	21.7	30.0	155.7
Arizona	813.7	277.9	185.5	54.5	26.1	269.7
Arkansas	1,103.7	433.0	240.3	97.5	25.9	307.0
California	696.0	264.6	161.1	51.8	19.4	199.1
Colorado	658.3	210.5	145.1	43.9	20.4	238.4
Connecticut	899.6	356.0	218.3	58.2	11.8	255.3
Delaware	889.9	319.7	228.1	47.4	16.3	278.4
Florida	1,054.3	408.2	260.0	68.4	22.0	295.7
Georgia	792.8	293.0	174.0	57.0	20.8	248.0
Hawaii	665.1	260.4	155.6	59.8	15.6	173.7
Idaho	741.7	266.8	160.9	58.7	20.9	234.4
Illinois	865.1	335.0	205.8	60.7	17.4	246.2
Indiana	906.0	349.4	210.3	65.3	19.8	261.2
Iowa	970.9	395.1	222.0	75.7	14.6	263.5
Kansas	915.3	346.6	201.1	66.2	18.4	283.0
Kentucky	972.3	382.8	229.5	64.0	19.1	276.9
Louisiana	919.3	330.8	214.9	58.1	28.2	287.3
Maine	965.6	356.3	239.9	63.5	12.8	293.1
Maryland	820.4	286.9	198.8	51.2	21.1	262.4
Massachusetts	893.9	325.5	223.7	55.7	10.3	278.7
Michigan	852.3	337.7	200.6	58.9	18.4	236.7
Minnesota	787.8	269.1	187.3	64.0	12.9	254.5
Mississippi	1,007.3	423.3	214.2	68.0	26.6	275.2
Missouri	1,005.6	410.3	221.4	68.6	21.1	284.2
Montana	884.0	301.8	203.5	61.9	25.0	291.8
Nebraska	922.3	364.5	195.4	66.5	14.5	281.4
Nevada	797.9	280.0	189.6	47.6	35.0	245.7
New Hampshire	806.5	297.7	205.8	58.8	13.8	230.4
New Jersey	895.8	341.8	225.5	51.3	11.8	265.4
New Mexico	731.5	233.7	159.9	44.4	26.8	266.7
New York	874.7	380.1	206.0	44.2	13.9	230.5
North Carolina	889.2	330.4	204.3	70.4	21.4	262.7
North Dakota	919.5	360.3	206.3	75.2	12.5	265.2
Ohio	941.7	368.3	220.7	61.5	14.5	276.7
Oklahoma	1,023.3	411.9	218.1	72.1	23.7	297.5
Oregon	887.0	311.0	208.7	79.2	20.6	267.5
Pennsylvania	1,064.3	420.1	251.1	69.6	18.2	305.3

Death rates by major causes (1997) (continued)

States	Total rate of death per 100,000 population	Circulatory diseases	Cancer	Pulmonary diseases	Suicide and homicide	Other
Rhode Island	994.5	400.0	249.7	69.3	10.1	265.4
South Carolina	896.0	338.9	203.2	75.7	21.0	257.2
South Dakota	930.3	366.0	209.8	77.4	20.2	256.9
Tennessee	981.1	385.2	220.9	74.9	24.0	276.1
Texas	734.5	276.6	165.6	52.2	18.6	221.5
Utah	562.3	188.5	103.6	42.5	17.7	210.0
Vermont	857.9	314.6	208.8	58.9	12.4	263.2
Virginia	799.7	292.1	192.0	60.0	18.9	236.7
Washington	739.0	258.1	178.9	60.0	17.7	224.3
West Virginia	1,150.0	449.4	262.0	68.1	19.7	350.8
Wisconsin	868.4	336.1	204.6	71.2	15.2	241.3
Wyoming	780.6	265.4	175.9	48.6	24.2	266.5
District						
District of Columbia	1,158.7	369.0	254.8	63.5	54.8	416.6
U.S. RATE	864.7	331.3	201.6	59.7	18.8	253.3

Morbidity rates of infectious diseases per 100,000 population (1998): chlamydia 223.4; gonorrhea 131.7; chicken pox 30.5; AIDS 17.2; syphilis 14.0; salmonellosis 16.2; shigellosis 8.7; hepatitis A (infectious) 8.6; tuberculosis 6.8; lyme disease 6.2; hepatitis B (serum) 3.8; pertussis 2.7.

Leading cause of death by age group (1997)

	Number of deaths			Total death rate (per 100,000 population)	Percentage of all deaths
	Total	Male	Female		
All ages[11]	2,314,245	1,154,039	1,160,206	864.7	100.0
1 to 4 years	5,501	3,121	2,380	35.8	0.24
Accidents	2,005	1,192	813	13.1	0.09
Malignant neoplasms	438	240	198	2.9	0.02
Homicide	375	209	166	2.4	0.02
Circulatory diseases	212	119	93	1.4	0.01
HIV infection	147[6]	74[6]	77[6]	0.9[6]	0.01
5 to 14 years	8,061	4,763	3,298	20.8	0.35
Accidents	3,371	2,110	1,261	8.7	0.14
Malignant neoplasms	1,030	560	470	2.7	0.04
Homicide	457	295	162	1.2	0.02
Circulatory diseases	313	180	133	0.8	0.01
Suicide	307	233	74	0.8	0.01
15 to 24 years	31,544	23,312	8,232	86.2	1.36
Accidents	13,367	9,791	3,567	36.5	0.58
Homicide	6,146	5,302	844	16.8	0.26
Suicide	4,186	3,559	627	11.4	0.18
Malignant neoplasms	1,645	981	664	4.5	0.07
Circulatory diseases	1,098	674	424	3.0	0.04
25 to 44 years	134,946	89,848	45,098	161.4	5.83
Accidents	27,129	20,412	6,717	32.4	1.17
Malignant neoplasms	21,706	9,841	11,865	26.0	0.94
HIV infection	11,066	8,569	2,497	13.2	0.49
Circulatory diseases	19,978	13,468	6,510	23.9	0.86
Suicide	12,402	9,907	2,495	14.8	0.54
45 to 64 years	376,875	229,463	147,412	679.7	16.28
Malignant neoplasms	131,743	69,819	61,924	237.6	5.69
Circulatory diseases	129,553	86,304	43,249	233.7	5.60
Accidents	17,251	12,411	5,110	31.6	0.74
Diabetes mellitus	12,705	6,655	6,050	22.9	0.55
Liver disease and cirrhosis	10,875	7,852	3,023	19.8	0.47
65 and over	1,728,872	787,427	941,445	5,073.6	74.70
Circulatory diseases	841,690	372,792	468,898	2,470.1	36.36
Malignant neoplasms	382,913	199,617	183,296	1,123.7	16.54
Pneumonia and influenza	77,561	34,011	43,550	227.6	3.35
Diabetes mellitus	47,289	19,966	27,323	138.8	2.04
Accidents	31,386	15,526	15,860	92.1	1.36

Incidence of chronic health conditions per 1,000 population (1996): chronic sinusitis 125.0; arthritis 126.8; deformities or orthopedic impairments 111.2; hypertension 106.8; hay fever 89.4; hearing impairment 83.1; heart conditions 77.9; asthma 55.0; chronic bronchitis 53.4; migraine 43.5.

Social indicators

Educational attainment (1996). Percentage of population age 25 and over having: some primary 9.3%; incomplete secondary 16.5%; secondary 35.1%; some postsecondary 25.5%; 4-year higher degree or more 13.6%. Number of earned degrees (1995): bachelor's degree 1,192,000; master's degree 405,000; doctor's degree 43,000; first-professional degrees (in fields such as medicine, theology, and law) 77,000.

Distribution of income (1998)

percentage of disposable family income by quintile

1	2	3	4	5 (highest)
4.2	9.9	15.7	23.0	47.3

Quality of working life (1999). Average workweek: 39.5 hours. Annual rate per 100,000 workers for (1995): injury or accident 2,720; death 4.0. Proportion of labour force insured for damages or income loss resulting from: injury, permanent disability, and death (1988) 56.6%. Average days per 1,000 workdays lost to labour stoppages (1996): 1.6. Average duration of journey to work (1990): 22.4 minutes (private automobile 94.7%, of which drive alone 80.0%, carpool 14.7%; take public transportation 5.3%). Rate per 1,000 employed workers of discouraged workers (unemployed no longer seeking work; 1992): 6.9.

Access to services (1995). Proportion of occupied dwellings having access to: electricity, virtually 100.0%; safe public water supply 99.4% (12.6% from wells); public sewage collection 77.0%; septic tanks 22.8%.
Social participation. Eligible voters participating in last presidential election (2000): 51.2%. Population age 18 and over participating in voluntary work (1999): 66.0%. Trade-union membership in total workforce (1996): 14.5%. Practicing religious population in total affiliated population (church attendance; 1987) once a week 47%; once in six months 67%; once a year 74%.
Social deviance (1998). Offense rate per 100,000 population for: murder 6.3; rape 34.4; robbery 165.2; aggravated assault 360.5; motor-vehicle theft 459.0; burglary and housebreaking 862.0; larceny-theft 2,728.1; drug-abuse violation 434.2 (1995); drunkenness 200.2 (1995). Drug and substance users (population age 26 and over; 1994): alcohol 41.2%; tobacco (cigarettes) 33.5%; marijuana 16.0%; cocaine 0.4%; analgesics 1.3%; tranquilizers 0.2%; stimulants 0.4%; hallucinogens 1.2%; heroin, n.a. Rate per 100,000 population of suicide (1997): 11.5.

Crime rates per 100,000 population in metropolitan areas[12] (1999)

	violent crime				
	total	murder	rape	robbery	assault
Atlanta	2,794	35.6	79.9	1,014	1,665
Baltimore[7]	2,420	43.4	66.7	1,199	1,111
Boston	1,308	5.6	60.7	444	797
Chicago	...	22.9	...	731	1,172
Dallas	1,434	17.7	61.6	591	764
Detroit	2,277	43.0	81.8	811	1,342
Houston	1,166	13.1	40.5	452	660
Los Angeles	1,290	11.7	35.4	397	845
Miami	2,129	17.1	30.6	833	1,248
Minneapolis	1,399	13.3	128	593	665
New York	1,063	9.0	22.9	486	545
Pittsburgh	904	14.5	41.0	469	379
St. Louis	2,279	38.9	43.1	836	1,361
San Francisco	878	8.6	25.8	465	378
Washington, D.C.	1,628	46.4	47.8	644	889

	property crime			
	total	burglary	larceny	auto theft
Atlanta	11,015	2,134	7,058	1,824
Baltimore[7]	8,363	1,772	5,363	1,227
Boston	5,009	615	3,176	1,218
Chicago	6,198	1,083	3,988	1,126
Dallas	8,317	1,824	4,834	1,659
Detroit	8,246	1,894	3,579	2,774
Houston	5,973	1,340	3,579	1,053
Los Angeles	3,320	592	2,049	679
Miami	8,717	1,985	5,182	1,550
Minneapolis	7,299	1,574	4,631	1,094
New York	2,969	545	1,890	534
Pittsburgh	5,404	925	3,531	949
St. Louis	12,007	2,352	7,665	1,990
San Francisco	4,920	740	3,382	800
Washington, D.C.	6,434	976	4,176	1,282

Leisure (1997). Favourite leisure activities (percentage of total population age 18 and over that undertook activity at least once in the previous year): movie 66.0%, amusement park 57.0%, sports event 41.0%, exercise program 76.0%, home improvement 66.0%; charity work 43.0%, playing sports 45.0%.
Material well-being (1995). Occupied dwellings with householder possessing: automobile 84.9%[13]; telephone 93.9%; radio receiver 99.0%; television receiver 98.3%; air conditioner 68.4%[14]; washing machine 77.1%[14]; videocassette recorder 81.0%; cable television 63.4%.
Recreational expenditures (1998): U.S.$494,700,000,000 (television and radio receivers, computers, and video equipment 18.7%; sports supplies 11.7%; golfing, bowling, and other participatory activities 11.4%; nondurable toys and sports equipment 9.5%; magazines and newspapers 6.4%; books and maps 5.6%; spectator amusements 4.8%, of which theatre and opera 1.9%, movies 1.4%, spectator sports 1.5%; flowers, seeds, and potted plants 3.3%).

National economy

Budget (2000). Revenue: U.S.$2,046,800,000,000 (individual income tax 49.3%, social-insurance taxes and contributions 33.8%, corporation income tax 11.5%, excise taxes 3.4%, customs duties 1.0%, other 1.0%). Expenditures: U.S.$1,741,000,000,000 (social security and medicare 32.4%, defense 17.4%, interest on debt 15.1%, other 35.1%).
Total national debt (2000): U.S.$5,686,338,000,000.

Manufacturing, mining, and construction enterprises (1998)

	no. of enter-prises	no. of employees	hourly wages as a % of all wages[15]	value added (U.S.$'000,000)
Manufacturing				
Chemical and related products	12,371	820,200	131.0	158,700
Food and related products	20,878	1,561,400	90.1	122,000
Electric and electronic machinery	17,104	1,582,300	100.9	168,300
Machinery, except electrical	56,383	1,978,200	113.2	153,300
Transportation equipment	12,387	1,561,700	137.23	164,700
Printing and publishing	62,355	1,534,300	104.0	96,300
Fabricated metal products	37,985	1,549,500	100.4	104,700
Instruments and related products	11,727	907,100[16]	106.0	59,000
Paper and related products	6,496	626,300[16]	118.0	54,900
Rubber and plastic products	14,515	1,018,000	92.2	54,900
Primary metals	6,275	692,200	119.9	54,800
Stone, clay, and glass products	16,393	505,400	102.9	42,100
Lumber and wood	36,735	757,300	85.4	43,900
Apparel and related products	23,411	829,300	66.3	25,400
Textile-mill products	6,155	561,900	79.8	25,600
Petroleum and coal products	2,147	106,100	162.1	30,100
Furniture and fixtures	12,095	523,900	84.6	25,200
Tobacco products	105	38,000[16]	127.4	17,900
Leather and leather products	1,839	101,100[16]	72.6	4,400
Miscellaneous manufacturing industries	18,043	394,000	85.1	26,600
Mining				
Oil and gas extraction	17,219	272,764	124.1	79,700[17]
Coal mining	1,820	86,824	142.7	17,283[17]
Nonmetallic, except fuels	5,516	97,761	112.0	9,619[17]
Metal mining	696	48,533	126.2	7,180[17]
Construction				
Special trade contractors	415,423	3,446,000	130.4	122,422[17]
Heavy construction contractors	39,542	852,000	121.5	49,066[17]
General contractors and operative builders	184,512	1,269,000	124.3	63,743[17]

Gross national product (2000): U.S.$9,860,800,000,000 (U.S.$35,040 per capita).

Structure of gross domestic product and labour force

	1999			
	in value U.S.$'000,000,000	% of total value	labour force[18]	% of labour force[18]
Agriculture	125.4	1.3	3,281,000	2.4
Mining	111.8	1.2	565,000	0.4
Manufacturing	1,500.8	16.1	20,070,000	14.4
Construction	416.4	4.5	8,987,000	6.4
Public utilities	216.0	2.3	9,554,000	6.8
Transp. and commun.	563.6	6.1		
Trade[19]	1,499.7	16.1	27,572,000	19.8
Finance	1,792.1	19.3	8,815,000	6.3
Public administration, defense	1,158.4	12.4	5,958,000	4.3
Services	1,986.9	21.4	48,687,000	34.9
Other	–71.9	–0.8	5,880,000[20]	4.2
TOTAL	9,299.2	100.0[21]	139,368,000[21]	100.0[21]

Gross domestic product and national income

(in U.S.$'000,000,000)

	1996	1997	1998	1999	2000
Gross domestic product	7,576.1	8,110.9	8,511.0	9,299.2	9,963.1
By type of expenditure					
Personal consumption expenditures	5,151.4	5,493.7	5,807.9	6,268.7	6,757.3
Durable goods	632.1	673.0	724.7	761.3	820.3
Nondurable goods	1,545.1	1,600.6	1,662.4	1,845.5	2,010.0
Services	2,974.3	3,220.1	3,420.8	3,661.9	3,927.0
Gross private domestic investment	1,117.0	1,256.0	1,367.1	1,650.1	1,832.7
Fixed investment	1,101.5	1,188.6	1,307.8	1,606.8	1,778.2
Changes in business inventories	15.4	67.4	59.3	43.3	54.5
Net exports of goods and services	–98.7	–90.4	151.0	261.0	–370.7
Exports	855.2	965.4	959.0	990.2	1,097.3
Imports	953.9	1,058.8	1,110.2	1,224.2	1,468.0
Government purchases of goods and services	1,406.4	1,454.6	1,487.1	1,634.4	1,743.7
Federal	523.1	520.2	520.6	568.6	595.2
State and local	886.8	934.4	966.5	1,003.8	1,148.6
By major type of product					
Goods output	2,799.8	2,978.5	3,104.0	3,510.2	3,793.4
Durable goods	1,232.3	1,343.8	1,416.2	1,687.3	1,843.9
Nondurable goods	1,567.5	1,634.8	1,687.8	1,831.9	1,949.5
Services	4,105.2	4,414.1	4,641.0	4,934.6	5,254.0
Structures	671.1	718.3	765.9	854.3	915.6
National income (incl. capital consumption adjustment)	6,164.2	6,646.5	6,994.7	7,469.7	8,002.0
By type of income					
Compensation of employees	4,448.5	4,687.2	4,981.0	5,299.8	5,638.2
Proprietors' income	527.7	551.2	577.2	663.5	710.4
Rental income of persons	150.2	158.2	162.6	143.4	140.0
Corporate profits	670.2	817.9	824.6	856.0	946.2
Net interest	403.3	432.0	449.3	507.1	567.2
By industry division (excl. capital consumption adjustment)					
Agriculture, forestry, fishing	114.1	106.0	104.2	109.2	...
Mining and construction	325.9	357.6	381.1	433.1	...
Manufacturing	1,069.1	1,150.0	1,168.7	1,193.3	...
Durable	628.6	659.4	684.2	704.6	...
Nondurable	440.5	491.6	484.4	488.7	...
Transportation	196.5	208.0	216.2	236.9	...
Communications	148.5	139.3	149.3	161.9	...
Public utilities	126.5	133.6	135.3	135.9	...
Wholesale and retail trade	857.8	927.4	989.2	1,077.0	...
Finance, insurance, real estate	1,037.0	1,192.0	1,273.5	1,366.9	...
Services	1,441.1	1,513.6	1,624.9	1,782.9	...
Government and government enterprise	843.1	877.5	906.3	953.2	...
Other	–8.9	–8.0	–20.4	–11.0	...

Business activity (1997): number of businesses 23,645,000 (sole proprietorships 72.6%, active corporations 19.9%, active partnerships 7.5%), of which services 10,114,000, wholesaling and retailing 4,455,000; business receipts U.S.$18,057,000,000,000 (active corporations 88.0%, sole proprietorships 4.8%, active partnerships 7.2%), of which wholesaling and retailing U.S.$5,136,000,000,000, services U.S.$2,130,000,000,000; net profit U.S.$1,270,000,000,000 (active corporations 72.0%, sole proprietorships 14.7%, partnerships 13.3%), of which services U.S.$203,000,000,000, wholesaling and retailing U.S.$10,000,000,000. New business starts and business failures (1995): total number of new business starts 168,158; total failures 71,194, of which commercial service 21,850, retail trade 12,952; failure rate per 10,000 concerns 90.0; current liabilities of failed concerns U.S.$37,507,000,000; average liability U.S.$526,830. Business expenditures for new plant and equipment (1995): total U.S.$594,465,000,000, of which trade, services, and communications U.S.$244,829,000,000, manufacturing businesses U.S.$172,308,000,000 (durable goods 53.0%, nondurable goods 47.0%), public utilities U.S.$42,816,000,000, transportation U.S.$37,021,000,000, mining and construction U.S.$35,985,000.

Components of gross domestic product (1997)

States	Gross state product (U.S.$'000,000,000)	Personal income (U.S.$'000,000,000)	Disposable personal income (U.S.$'000,000,000)	Per capita disposable personal income (U.S.$)
Alabama	103.1	89.3	78.8	18,728
Alaska	24.5	15.2	12.9	23,733
Arizona	121.2	100.2	86.1	19,880
Arkansas	58.5	49.4	43.7	17,972
California	1,033.0	846.8	718.0	22,859
Colorado	126.1	105.1	88.7	24,008
Connecticut	134.6	117.2	96.4	29,312
Delaware	31.6	20.9	17.7	23,285
Florida	380.6	364.0	313.8	22,386
Georgia	229.5	178.9	153.5	21,204
Hawaii	38.0	30.5	26.4	23,064
Idaho	29.1	24.6	21.3	18,385
Illinois	393.5	332.0	280.3	24,384
Indiana	161.7	136.1	111.6	20,568
Iowa	80.5	66.0	57.2	20,859
Kansas	71.7	62.4	53.5	21,118
Kentucky	100.1	80.4	69.7	18,472
Louisiana	124.4	89.1	78.9	18,768
Maine	30.2	27.2	23.7	19,542
Maryland	153.8	146.1	122.4	24,409
Massachusetts	221.0	191.0	157.4	26,378
Michigan	272.6	244.1	206.6	22,086
Minnesota	149.4	123.0	101.5	23,306
Mississippi	58.3	49.4	44.7	16,914
Missouri	152.1	127.8	110.3	21,200
Montana	19.2	17.3	15.1	17,728
Nebraska	48.8	39.1	33.8	21,649
Nevada	57.4	44.5	37.6	24,564
New Hampshire	38.1	32.5	28.2	24,175
New Jersey	294.1	260.7	219.9	27,656
New Mexico	45.2	33.3	29.3	17,910
New York	651.7	548.9	456.6	25,637
North Carolina	218.9	172.1	148.3	20,934
North Dakota	15.8	12.9	11.4	18,572
Ohio	320.5	270.4	230.8	21,467
Oklahoma	76.6	67.4	59.0	18,454
Oregon	98.4	77.6	65.2	21,282
Pennsylvania	339.9	308.3	264.5	22,625
Rhode Island	27.8	25.3	21.9	23,378
South Carolina	93.3	77.7	67.8	18,737
South Dakota	20.2	15.5	14.0	20,173
Tennessee	147.0	121.9	107.8	20,875
Texas	601.6	459.6	406.7	21,172
Utah	55.4	41.7	35.6	18,305
Vermont	15.2	13.5	11.7	20,333
Virginia	211.3	175.9	149.1	23,059
Washington	172.3	148.5	128.6	23,598
West Virginia	38.2	34.0	30.2	17,187
Wisconsin	147.3	125.1	105.2	21,258
Wyoming	17.6	10.8	9.3	20,375
District				
District of Columbia	52.4	18.9	15.8	29,535
TOTAL/AVERAGE	8,103.2	6,770.6	5,782.7	22,312

Retail and wholesale trade and services (1997)

	no. of establish-ments	no. of employees	hourly wage as a % of all wages[15]	annual sales or receipts (U.S.$'000,000)
Retail trade	1,588,700	22,003,000	68.7	2,546,300
Automotive dealers	200,900[22]	2,312,000[22]	93.5[22]	631,600[22]
Food stores	176,600	3,162,000	68.8	428,800
General merchandise group stores	35,300	2,445,000	74.7	322,500
Eating and drinking places	478,600	7,597,000	50.0[23]	245,300
Gasoline service stations	[22]	[22]	[22]	[22]
Building materials, hardware, garden supply, and mobile home dealers	69,500	857,000	74.2	144,700
Furniture, home furnishings, equipment stores	116,400	867,000	92.2	141,800
Apparel and accessory stores	125,100	1,085,000	67.8	112,600
Drugstores and proprietary stores	47,600	724,000	79.8	90,700[6]
Liquor stores	29,100	129,000	...	22,800[6]
Wholesale trade	521,100	6,509,000	110.1	4,235,400
Durable goods	337,300	3,887,000	114.9	2,299,500
Professional and commercial equipment	49,700	760,000	136.6	387,500
Motor vehicles, automotive equipment	48,100	555,000	101.8	561,800
Machinery, equipment, and supplies	77,600	780,000	115.9	330,500
Electrical goods	44,300	548,000	117.5	381,000
Metals and minerals, except petroleum	12,600	174,000	109.1	150,500
Lumber and other construction materials	22,400	258,000	101.8	118,800
Hardware, plumbing, heating equipment and supplies	26,900	280,000	106.4	109,000
Furniture and home furnishings	18,600	192,000	100.8	82,700
Miscellaneous durable goods	37,100	341,000	89.6	177,600
Nondurable goods	183,900	2,622,000	97.3	1,935,900
Groceries and related products	41,900	858,000	101.5	590,000
Petroleum and petroleum products	12,700	152,000	93.8	272,500
Farm-products raw materials	10,300	98,000	79.2	166,800
Drugs, drug proprietaries, and druggists' sundries	8,100	190,000	142.6	203,100
Paper and paper products	19,700	297,000	104.9	134,200
Apparel and accessories	21,300	215,000	97.6	125,900
Beer, wine, and distilled alcoholic beverages	4,900	152,000	115.0	69,700
Chemicals and allied products	15,900	166,000	119.7	128,900
Miscellaneous nondurable goods	49,000	495,000	84.0	244,000

Retail and wholesale trade and services (1997) (continued)

	no. of establish-ments	no. of employees	hourly wage as a % of all wages[15]	annual sales or receipts (U.S.$'000,000)
Services	2,077,700	25,278,000	101.6	1,843,800
Health	466,400	5,520,000	107.1	398,500
Business, except computer services	294,000	7,179,000	100.9	304,400
Computer and data-processing services	103,300	1,421,000	168.4	224,100
Legal services	165,800	956,000	145.3	122,600
Automotive repair, services, garages	191,900	1,094,000	86.7	99,600
Management and public relations	108,100	941,000	139.6	101,300
Hotels and motels	55,900	1,686,000	70.1	97,900
Amusement and recreation	46,000	571,000	76.4	67,900
Engineering services	82,200	934,000	139.5	108,600
Personal services	204,500	1,303,000	72.2	53,100
Motion pictures	46,000	571,000	111.4	67,900

Daily consumption of water (1995)

(in gallons)

States	Total consumption ('000,000,000)	Per capita	Irrigation	Public consumption	Industrial processes	Thermo-electric
Alabama	6,967	1,670	139	875	753	5,200
Alaska	318	350	1	90	197	30
Arizona	6,775	1,620	5,670	846	197	62
Arkansas	8,326	3,540	5,940	419	187	1,780
California	45,072	1,130	28,900	5,740	802	9,630
Colorado	13,738	3,590	12,700	732	191	115
Connecticut	4,427	389	28	448	11	3,940
Delaware	1,483	1,050	48	101	64	1,270
Florida	18,079	509	3,470	2,360	649	11,600
Georgia	5,718	799	722	1,250	676	3,070
Hawaii	1,860	853	652	218	20	970
Idaho	13,330	13,000	13,000	254	76	...
Illinois	19,757	1,680	180	1,950	527	17,100
Indiana	9,000	1,570	116	784	2,410	5,690
Iowa	2,888	1,070	39	418	301	2,130
Kansas	5,101	2,040	3,380	384	77	1,260
Kentucky	4,358	1,150	12	521	375	3,450
Louisiana	9,506	2,270	769	677	2,580	5,480
Maine	314	178	27	135	16	136
Maryland	7,655	289	57	907	331	6,360
Massachusetts	5,499	189	82	759	88	4,570
Michigan	11,997	1,260	227	1,490	1,910	8,370
Minnesota	3,258	736	157	573	438	2,090
Mississippi	2,786	1,140	1,740	377	294	375
Missouri	6,937	1,320	567	757	63	5,550
Montana	8,813	10,200	8,550	161	80	22
Nebraska	10,403	6,440	7,550	328	175	2,350
Nevada	2,241	1,480	1,640	479	95	27
New Hampshire	1,296	388	6	130	50	1,110
New Jersey	6,091	269	125	1,120	486	4,360
New Mexico	3,451	2,080	2,990	337	69	55
New York	16,591	567	30	3,140	321	13,100
North Carolina	8,983	1,070	239	939	385	7,420
North Dakota	1,038	1,750	117	85	17	819
Ohio	10,427	944	27	1,560	650	8,190
Oklahoma	1,870	543	864	597	285	124
Oregon	7,130	2,520	6,170	572	379	9
Pennsylvania	9,606	802	16	1,730	1,930	5,930
Rhode Island	406	138	2	121	7	275
South Carolina	6,180	1,690	53	614	703	4,810
South Dakota	403	631	269	97	32	5
Tennessee	10,023	1,920	24	831	868	8,300
Texas	29,290	1,300	9,450	3,420	2,920	13,500
Utah	4,337	2,200	3,530	506	253	48
Vermont	534	967	4	66	12	452
Virginia	8,183	826	30	911	622	6,620
Washington	8,798	1,620	6,470	1,300	652	376
West Virginia	4,557	2,530	...	217	1,330	3,010
Wisconsin	7,134	1,420	169	692	453	5,820
Wyoming	7,028	14,700	6,590	100	118	220
District						
District of Columbia	10	18	...	...	1	10
TOTAL/AVERAGE	389,972	1,280	133,538	43,118	26,126	187,190

Production. Agriculture, forestry, fishing (value of production/catch in U.S.$'000,000 except as noted; 2000): corn (maize) 18,621, soybeans 13,073, wheat 5,970, cotton lint 4,781, grapes 3,063, potatoes 2,539, tobacco 2,056, oranges 1,752, apples 1,554, head lettuce 1,259, tomatoes 1,160, rice 1,073, strawberries 1,013, almonds 852, peanuts (groundnuts) 844, sorghum 822, onions 732, cottonseed 677, barley 632, bell peppers 614, broccoli 597, peaches 495, sweet corn 474, carrots 436, dry beans 423, grapefruit 423, cantaloupes 359, cabbage 332, lemons 318, avocados 318, sweet cherries 286, cauliflower 259, pears 255, sunflower seeds 241, watermelons 236, pecans 234; livestock (number of live animals; 2000) 98,048,000 cattle, 59,337,000 pigs, 7,215,000 sheep, 5,320,000 horses, 1,720,000,000 chickens; roundwood (1998) 420,458,000 cu m; fish and shellfish catch (1998) 3,128, of which fish 1,447 (including salmon 257, Alaska pollack 190), shellfish 1,682 (including shrimp 516, crabs 473). Mining (metal content in metric tons except as noted; 1996): iron 39,342,000; copper 1,910,000; zinc 620,000; lead 430,000; molybdenum 57,000; vanadium 2,700; mercury 550; silver 1,800,000 kg; gold 325,000 kg; helium 101,000,000 cu m. Quarrying (metric tons; 1996): crushed stone 1,300,000,000; sand and gravel 992,000,000; cement 75,000,000; clay 44,000,000; phosphate rock 43,000,000; common salt 40,000,000; gypsum 17,000,000; lime 18,900,000. Manufacturing (1996): motor vehicles 329,155; industrial machinery 135,393; electronic components 127,996; computers and office equipment 103,270; meat products 102,103; aircraft 83,394; commercial printing 67,842; medical instruments 47,406; cigarettes 28,987; household furniture 25,426; photographic equipment 22,297; household appliances 22,157; missiles and space vehicles 17,928; ships and boats 15,634; toys and sporting goods 14,748; audio and video equipment 11,266. Construction (completed; 1996): private U.S.$427,776,000,000, of which residential U.S.$246,899,000,000, nonresidential U.S.$140,692,000,000; public U.S.$141,-132,000,000.

Energy production (consumption): electricity (kW-hr; 1994) 3,268,250,000,000 (3,312,888,000,000); coal (metric tons; 1994) 937,580,000 (843,873,000); crude petroleum (barrels; 1994) 2,464,000,000 (5,024,000,000); petroleum products (metric tons; 1994) 704,201,000 (737,681,000); natural gas (cu m; 1994) 530,014,000,000 (592,209,000,000). Domestic production of energy by source (1994): coal 31.2%, natural gas 27.6%, crude petroleum 19.9%, other[24] 21.3%.

Energy consumption by sector

('000,000,000,000 Btu)

States	Total	Residential	Commercial	Industrial	Trans-portation	Per capita ('000,000 Btu)
Alabama	1,975.1	353.2	182.6	991.3	448.0	457.3
Alaska	696.8	49.5	66.7	419.2	161.4	1,143.6
Arizona	1,114.9	251.6	238.2	226.8	398.3	244.7
Arkansas	1,012.9	195.3	119.4	430.2	268.0	401.5
California	7,697.1	1,340.4	1,193.5	2,289.7	2,873.5	238.5
Colorado	1,133.5	255.0	240.2	302.4	335.9	291.2
Connecticut	824.5	254.7	189.9	164.4	215.5	252.2
Delaware	273.2	57.3	42.8	106.0	67.1	373.4
Florida	3,579.4	1,002.7	761.1	582.0	1,233.6	244.3
Georgia	2,634.5	561.8	391.9	835.7	845.1	351.9
Hawaii	241.9	21.5	23.8	76.3	120.3	203.9
Idaho	491.1	91.1	82.9	202.0	115.1	405.8
Illinois	3,897.4	986.5	722.4	1,356.5	832.0	327.6
Indiana	2,663.7	503.5	301.9	1,242.7	615.6	454.2
Iowa	1,090.7	240.5	156.3	417.5	276.4	382.4
Kansas	1,060.0	210.9	183.3	389.3	276.5	408.5
Kentucky	1,776.8	327.7	199.6	848.0	401.5	454.6
Louisiana	3,994.9	326.6	222.0	2,617.3	829.0	918.0
Maine	538.4	102.1	57.8	271.9	106.6	433.5
Maryland	1,349.2	387.6	322.3	277.7	361.6	264.8
Massachusetts	1,533.5	426.4	371.3	312.9	422.9	250.7
Michigan	3,249.2	795.9	577.8	1,099.5	776.0	332.4
Minnesota	1,688.9	377.8	227.5	635.6	448.0	360.4
Mississippi	1,098.4	205.3	117.5	432.4	343.2	402.3
Missouri	1,744.8	459.4	337.1	374.8	573.5	323.0
Montana	395.1	70.4	55.6	167.6	101.5	449.6
Nebraska	604.4	140.5	123.2	160.1	180.6	364.8
Nevada	575.3	108.9	88.8	198.1	179.5	343.2
New Hampshire	302.2	83.9	55.6	78.9	83.8	257.7
New Jersey	2,574.8	565.3	520.4	655.0	834.1	319.8
New Mexico	595.2	87.5	101.8	217.5	188.4	344.1
New York	4,129.6	1,104.7	1,118.9	949.8	956.2	227.7
North Carolina	2,416.5	583.1	414.1	773.3	646.0	325.4
North Dakota	351.9	61.7	46.5	168.2	75.5	549.1
Ohio	4,115.7	930.8	649.2	1,640.5	895.2	367.9
Oklahoma	1,405.6	273.1	196.2	550.3	386.0	423.8
Oregon	1,108.1	234.9	180.0	386.3	306.9	341.8
Pennsylvania	3,927.3	935.8	607.8	1,477.9	905.0	326.7
Rhode Island	235.9	72.1	52.2	52.4	59.2	238.9
South Carolina	1,426.8	291.5	191.0	614.1	330.2	379.4
South Dakota	244.8	61.8	41.1	61.5	80.4	331.6
Tennessee	2,067.8	475.3	139.4	905.1	548.0	385.2
Texas	11,278.2	1,310.2	1,080.4	6,542.3	2,345.3	580.2
Utah	674.4	120.0	106.5	254.2	193.7	327.5
Vermont	162.5	46.1	27.3	36.7	52.4	275.7
Virginia	2,115.3	518.7	451.9	532.5	612.2	314.1
Washington	1,835.3	435.5	321.2	757.8	320.8	380.6
West Virginia	803.4	150.9	97.2	391.1	164.2	442.5
Wisconsin	1,791.6	403.6	278.9	708.8	400.3	346.0
Wyoming	423.1	41.0	44.5	235.3	102.3	882.1
District						
Dist. of Columbia	177.4	38.3	110.0	3.2	25.9	335.4
TOTAL/AVERAGE	93,398.5	18,930.0	14,429.2	35,420.3	24,619.0	349.0

Energy consumption by source (1997): petroleum and petroleum products 38.6%, natural gas 24.1%, coal 22.3%, other[24] 15.0%; by end use: industrial 38.0%, residential and commercial 35.5%, transportation 26.5%.

Energy consumption by source

('000,000,000,000 Btu)

States	Petroleum	Natural gas	Coal	Hydroelectric power	Nuclear electric power
Alabama	562.5	336.3	887.5	114.6	315.6
Alaska	224.0	443.6	11.2	13.1	...
Arizona	427.4	121.7	343.2	98.0	306.4
Arkansas	309.7	277.7	260.2	28.9	141.9
California	3,341.9	1,865.1	53.9	487.6	362.2
Colorado	412.2	314.7	340.3	17.6	...
Connecticut	412.5	131.5	24.4	15.7	66.1
Delaware	139.0	55.9	50.8	0.0	...
Florida	1,629.6	510.7	694.5	2.2	270.6
Georgia	1,017.1	392.2	725.6	51.6	317.9
Hawaii	221.4	2.8	3.6	1.1	...
Idaho	159.4	69.0	7.3	138.9	...
Illinois	1,272.8	1,140.6	906.9	1.1	741.2
Indiana	859.2	579.8	1,372.1	4.6	...
Iowa	371.3	274.3	380.5	9.7	41.7
Kansas	379.7	362.0	338.6	0.1	87.2
Kentucky	599.1	248.0	951.8	36.2	...
Louisiana	1,612.2	1,737.7	205.6	10.0	167.5
Maine	253.2	5.8	5.9	76.3	53.8
Maryland	518.2	198.1	292.2	25.4	128.5
Massachusetts	690.7	367.5	113.1	16.8	56.6
Michigan	998.4	1,026.7	789.3	26.2	285.0
Minnesota	638.6	375.1	345.5	92.9	128.5
Mississippi	424.0	277.4	128.1	0.0	98.0
Missouri	721.1	297.5	629.7	12.8	94.4
Montana	175.3	63.2	135.7	143.0	...
Nebraska	235.6	133.8	179.0	16.6	100.5
Nevada	216.1	127.6	169.5	22.4	...
New Hampshire	156.6	19.4	36.2	29.2	104.6
New Jersey	1,228.0	624.6	62.4	0.0	117.1
New Mexico	209.4	228.2	279.2	2.2	...
New York	1,569.3	1,159.9	294.3	343.3	374.2

Energy consumption by source (continued)

('000,000,000,000 Btu)

States	Petroleum	Natural gas	Coal	Hydroelectric power	Nuclear electric power
North Carolina	885.1	220.8	687.0	66.2	358.2
North Dakota	119.8	51.5	404.1	40.8	...
Ohio	1,236.6	972.0	1,448.8	4.1	147.9
Oklahoma	469.6	580.2	349.9	21.5	...
Oregon	363.9	175.3	20.3	491.3	...
Pennsylvania	1,329.3	752.7	1,432.3	23.2	729.5
Rhode Island	97.3	87.7	0.1	9.4	...
South Carolina	445.1	154.1	352.5	23.6	462.9
South Dakota	116.7	37.4	33.2	82.5	...
Tennessee	690.9	289.3	648.6	111.6	243.5
Texas	5,166.4	4,123.0	1,475.4	9.9	379.9
Utah	251.6	167.8	355.0	10.8	...
Vermont	85.2	7.4	...	41.0	40.4
Virginia	792.9	248.4	378.8	6.2	279.2
Washington	842.1	247.5	90.9	1,045.5	59.4
West Virginia	257.6	164.5	898.3	14.8	...
Wisconsin	550.0	408.0	452.8	29.3	107.5
Wyoming	145.5	107.6	473.0	12.7	...
District					
District of Columbia	35.4	34.2	0.6	0.0	...
TOTAL	35,886.2	22,598.1	20,519.6	3,881.3	7,167.6

Household income[25] level by selected characteristics (1998)

Characteristics	Number of households ('000)	Number ('000) Under $15,000	$15,000–$34,999	$35,000–$74,999	$75,000 and over	Median income ($)
Total/Average	103,874	18,798	28,285	35,272	20,860	38,885
Age of householder						
15 to 24 years	5,770	1,743	2,269	1,483	274	23,564
25 to 34 years	18,819	2,699	5,453	7,694	2,973	40,069
35 to 44 years	23,968	2,626	5,376	9,916	6,051	48,451
45 to 54 years	20,158	2,078	3,950	7,744	6,387	54,148
55 to 64 years	13,571	2,370	3,271	4,580	3,350	43,167
65 years and over	21,589	7,311	7,964	4,247	1,824	21,729
Size of household						
One person	26,606	10,388	9,199	5,703	1,314	20,154
Two persons	34,262	4,233	10,106	12,807	7,115	41,512
Three persons	17,386	1,916	3,955	6,970	4,544	46,069
Four persons	15,030	1,180	2,808	6,259	4,784	55,886
Five persons	6,962	681	1,351	2,841	2,089	53,706
Six persons	2,367	267	555	856	690	49,080
Seven or more persons	1,261	132	309	495	324	46,646
Educational attainment of householder Total[26]	98,104	17,055	26,016	34,448	20,585	40,296
Less than 9th grade	7,047	3,314	2,455	1,070	208	16,154
Some high school	9,407	3,405	3,360	2,179	463	20,724
High school graduate	30,613	5,881	9,671	11,263	3,797	34,373
Some college, no degree	17,833	2,334	4,936	7,182	3,381	41,658
Associate degree	7,468	779	1,690	3,251	1,748	48,604
Bachelor's degree	16,781	936	2,867	6,535	6,442	62,188
Master's degree	5,961	265	769	2,911	2,784	71,086
Professional degree	1,623	93	145	414	971	95,309
Doctorate degree	1,373	48	122	413	789	84,100

Household income and expenditure. Average household size (1997) 2.6; average (median) annual income per household U.S.$37,005, of which average white household U.S.$35,766, average Hispanic[4] household U.S.$22,860, average black household U.S.$22,393; sources of income: wages and salaries 55.8%, transfer payments 16.5%, self-employment 7.9%, other 19.8%; expenditure: transportation 18.6%, housing 18.4%, food 14.0%, fuel and utilities 6.8%, household furnishings 5.9%, recreation 5.5%, health 5.4%, wearing apparel 5.3%, education 1.5%, other 18.6%.

Financial aggregates

	1994	1995	1996	1997	1998	1999	2000
Exchange rate, U.S.$ per:							
£[27]	1.53	1.58	1.56	1.65	1.66	1.62	1.49
SDR[27]	1.43	1.52	1.45	1.38	1.36	1.37	1.32
International reserves (U.S.$)[28]							
Total (excl. gold; '000,000,000)	63.28	74.78	64.04	58.91	70.71	60.50	56.60
SDRs ('000,000,000)	10.04	11.04	10.31	10.03	10.60	10.35	10.54
Reserve pos. in IMF ('000,000,000)	12.03	14.65	15.43	18.07	24.11	17.97	14.82
Foreign exchange ('000,000,000)	41.22	49.10	38.29	30.81	36.00	32.18	31.24
Gold ('000,000 fine troy oz)	261.73	261.70	261.66	261.61	261.78	261.67	261.61
% world reserves	28.70	29.00	28.86	29.52	27.09	27.13	27.52
Interest and prices							
Central bank discount (%)[28]	4.75	5.25	5.00	5.00	4.50	5.00	6.00
Govt. bond yield (%)[27]	6.26	6.26	6.44	6.35	5.26	5.49	6.22
Industrial share prices[27] (1995 = 100)	84.1	100.0	123.5	159.3	198.7	251.3	272.8
Balance of payments (U.S.$'000,000,000)							
Balance of visible trade	−164.33	−158.78	−189.25	−181.87	−231.10	−343.26	−449.57
Imports, f.o.b.	−668.87	−743.52	−803.23	−870.57	−913.60	−1,029.92	−1,224.43
Exports, f.o.b.	504.54	584.71	613.98	688.70	682.50	686.66	774.86
Balance of invisibles	162.83	10.55	40.52	52.58	87.25	5.86	4.88
Balance of payments, current account	−1.50	−148.23	−148.73	−129.29	−143.85	−337.4	−444.69

Average employee earnings

	average hourly earnings in U.S.$		average weekly earnings in U.S.$	
	Feb. 1999	Feb. 2000	Feb. 1999	Feb. 2000
Manufacturing				
Durable goods	13.66	14.19	564.16	588.89
Lumber and wood products	11.26	11.61	453.78	469.04
Furniture and fixtures	11.06	11.50	440.17	457.70
Stone, clay, and glass products	13.64	13.99	576.96	593.18
Primary metal industries	15.41	16.29	673.42	723.28
Fabricated metal products	13.29	13.65	555.52	576.03
Machinery, except electrical	14.72	15.39	619.71	652.54
Electrical and electronic equipment	13.25	13.71	544.58	567.59
Transportation equipment	17.50	18.65	768.25	818.74
Instruments and related products	13.94	14.41	578.51	595.13
Miscellaneous manufacturing	11.17	11.56	442.33	455.46
Nondurable goods	12.97	13.38	525.29	543.23
Food and kindred products	11.91	12.25	489.50	501.03
Tobacco manufactures	17.80	17.32	662.16	680.68
Textile mill products	10.60	10.84	426.12	447.69
Apparel and other textile products	8.65	9.01	322.65	338.78
Paper and allied products	15.70	16.03	675.10	689.29
Printing and publishing	13.67	14.13	515.36	536.53
Chemicals and allied products	17.20	17.80	734.44	756.50
Petroleum and coal products	21.43	22.03	927.92	962.71
Rubber and miscellaneous plastics products	12.16	12.53	503.42	518.74
Leather and leather products	9.56	9.87	355.63	370.13
Nonmanufacturing				
Metal mining	18.16	18.63	793.59	815.99
Coal mining	19.11	19.40	865.68	873.00
Oil and gas extraction	16.98	16.68	696.18	738.47
Nonmetallic minerals, except fuels	14.81	15.22	662.00	672.02
Construction	16.66	17.37	633.08	672.09
Transportation and public utilities	15.56	16.06	606.84	613.49
Wholesale trade	14.38	14.96	550.75	571.47
Retail trade	8.98	9.34	256.83	266.19
Finance, insurance, and real estate	14.55	14.91	528.17	536.76
Hotels, motels, and tourist courts	9.20	9.53	280.60	289.71
Health services	14.06	14.55	462.57	480.15
Legal services	18.74	19.75	652.15	693.23
Miscellaneous services	18.38	18.67	637.79	681.46

Median household income[25]

(in constant 1999 U.S.$)

States	1995	1996	1997	1998	1999
Alabama	28,413	32,175	33,153	37,067	36,213
Alaska	52,422	56,042	49,818	51,812	51,509
Arizona	33,739	33,593	33,984	37,909	37,119
Arkansas	28,219	28,800	27,156	28,276	29,762
California	40,457	41,211	41,203	41,838	43,744
Colorado	44,499	43,482	44,876	47,628	48,346
Connecticut	43,993	44,723	45,657	47,535	50,798
Delaware	38,182	41,739	44,669	42,374	46,839
Florida	32,517	32,535	33,688	35,680	35,876
Georgia	37,276	34,505	38,056	39,519	39,433
Hawaii	46,844	44,354	42,490	41,729	44,373
Idaho	35,721	36,855	34,674	37,490	35,906
Illinois	41,618	41,999	42,852	44,132	46,392
Indiana	36,496	37,320	40,367	40,608	40,929
Iowa	38,829	35,262	35,067	37,837	41,238
Kansas	33,168	34,600	37,857	37,522	37,476
Kentucky	32,588	34,417	34,723	37,053	33,901
Louisiana	30,553	32,133	34,524	32,436	32,695
Maine	37,013	36,841	34,018	36,427	38,932
Maryland	44,865	46,713	48,459	51,121	52,310
Massachusetts	42,168	41,936	43,620	43,280	44,192
Michigan	39,820	41,650	40,214	42,745	46,238
Minnesota	41,467	43,525	44,182	48,984	47,240
Mississippi	29,011	28,326	29,582	29,763	32,540
Missouri	38,070	36,383	37,942	41,089	41,466
Montana	30,343	30,457	30,322	32,274	31,244
Nebraska	35,997	36,117	36,011	37,217	38,787
Nevada	39,446	40,923	40,331	40,634	41,680
New Hampshire	42,821	41,843	42,556	45,951	46,167
New Jersey	48,017	50,403	49,846	50,926	49,930
New Mexico	28,413	26,637	31,229	32,240	32,475
New York	36,105	37,599	37,159	38,220	40,058
North Carolina	34,959	37,802	37,202	36,630	37,340
North Dakota	31,799	33,416	32,864	30,973	32,877
Ohio	38,197	36,176	37,507	39,785	39,617
Oklahoma	28,763	29,133	32,543	34,472	32,919
Oregon	39,763	37,686	38,663	39,930	40,713
Pennsylvania	37,741	37,057	38,943	39,877	37,995
Rhode Island	38,654	39,273	36,119	41,585	42,936
South Carolina	31,780	36,808	35,564	34,002	36,563
South Dakota	32,334	31,351	30,823	33,510	35,982
Tennessee	31,719	32,694	31,800	34,844	36,536
Texas	35,024	35,117	36,408	36,573	38,978
Utah	39,879	39,328	44,401	45,277	46,094
Vermont	36,976	34,358	36,385	40,242	41,630
Virginia	39,597	41,635	44,590	44,312	45,750
Washington	38,882	38,943	46,256	48,468	45,639
West Virginia	27,198	26,808	28,533	27,294	29,433
Wisconsin	44,771	42,474	41,100	42,240	45,825
Wyoming	34,467	32,867	34,693	36,029	37,395
District					
District of Columbia	33,613	33,942	33,071	34,171	38,686
U.S. AVERAGE	37,251	37,686	38,411	39,744	40,816

Average annual expenditure of "consumer units" (households, plus individuals sharing households or budgets; 1997–98): total U.S.$35,535, of which housing U.S.$11,713, transportation U.S.$6,616, food U.S.$4,810, pensions and social security U.S.$2,982, health care U.S.$1,903, clothing U.S.$1,674, other U.S.$5,837.

Selected household characteristics (1996). Total number of households 99,627,000, of which (by race) white 84.8%, black 11.6%, other 3.6%; in central cities 31.4%[17], in suburbs 46.3%[17], outside metropolitan areas 22.3%[17]; (by tenure[17]) owned 64,045,000 (64.7%), rented 34,946,000 (35.3%); family households 69,594,000, of which married couple 76.9%, female head with own children[29] under age 18, 11.0%, female head without own children[29] under 18, 7.0%; nonfamily households 30,033,000, of which female living alone 48.6%, male living alone 34.2%, other 17.2%.

Population economically active (1999): total 139,368,000[18]; activity rate of total population 51.1% (participation rates: ages 15–64, 80.0%; female 46.5%; unemployed 4.2%).

Price and earnings indexes (1995 = 100)

	1994	1995	1996	1997	1998	1999	2000
Consumer price index	97.3	100.0	102.9	105.3	107.0	109.3	113.0
Hourly earnings index[30]	97.5	100.0	103.3	106.4	109.1	112.4	116.2

Tourism (1998): receipts from visitors U.S.$91,246,000,000; expenditures by nationals abroad U.S.$75,902,000,000; number of foreign visitors 46,395,000 (13,422,000 from Canada, 9,276,000 from Mexico, 10,675,000 from Europe); number of nationals traveling abroad 56,287,000 (18,338,000 to Mexico, 14,880,000 to Canada).

Land use (1994): forested 32.3%; meadows and pastures 26.1%; agricultural and under permanent cultivation 20.5%; other 21.0%.

Foreign trade

Balance of trade (current prices)

	1995	1996	1997	1998	1999	2000
U.S.$'000,000,000	–158.8	–189.2	–181.9	–231.1	–343.3	–435.23
% of total	12.0%	13.4%	–11.7%	14.5%	20.0%	21.8%

Imports (1999): U.S.$1,025,032,000,000 (machinery and transport equipment 41.6%, of which motor vehicles and parts 14.3%; wearing apparel 6.9%; chemicals and chemical products 6.1%; petroleum and petroleum products 6.3%; food and live animals 3.4%). *Major import sources:* Canada 19.3%; Japan 12.8%; Mexico 10.7%; China 8.0%; Germany 5.4%; United Kingdom 3.8%; Taiwan 3.4%; South Korea 3.0%; France 2.5%; Italy 2.2%; Malaysia 2.1%; Singapore 1.8%; Thailand 1.4%; Philippines 1.2%; Brazil 1.1%.

Exports (1999): U.S.$695,009,000,000 (machinery and transport equipment 47.1%, of which motor vehicles and parts 7.7%; chemicals and related products 8.1%; scientific and precision equipment 4.5%; food and live animals 5.3%). *Major export destinations:* Canada 23.9%; Mexico 12.2%; Japan 8.3%; United Kingdom 5.4%; Germany 3.8%; South Korea 3.3%; Taiwan 2.8%; The Netherlands 2.8%; France 2.7%; Singapore 2.3%; Brazil 1.9%; China 1.9%.

Trade by commodity group (1998)

	imports		exports	
SITC Group	U.S.$'000,000	%	U.S.$'000,000	%
00 Food and live animals	35,807[31]	3.8[31]	38,295	5.6
01 Beverages and tobacco	8,200	0.9	7,833	1.2
02 Crude materials, excluding fuels	22,758	2.4	26,236	3.8
03 Mineral fuels, lubricants, and related materials	62,224	6.6	10,414	1.5
04 Animal and vegetable oils, fat, and waxes	[31]	[31]	2,667	0.4
05 Chemicals and related products, n.e.s.	55,481	5.9	67,245	9.9
06 Basic manufactures	118,510	12.5	62,926	9.2
07 Machinery and transport equipment	431,318	45.7	357,786	52.6
08 Miscellaneous manufactured articles	168,880	17.9	77,739	11.4
09 Goods not classified by kind	39,581	4.2	29,294	4.3
TOTAL	944,350[32]	100.0[32]	680,435	100.0[32]

Direction of trade (1999)

	imports		exports	
	U.S.$'000,000	%	U.S.$'000,000	%
Africa	17,969	1.7	9,911	1.4
South Africa	3,327	0.3	2,809	0.4
Other Africa	14,642	1.4	7,102	1.0
Americas	369,601	35.2	304,596	44.1
Canada	198,829	19.0	162,956	23.6
Caribbean countries and Central America	20,285	1.9	19,949	2.9
Mexico	109,499	10.4	86,383	12.5
South America	40,988	3.9	35,308	5.1
Asia	423,146	40.4	190,325	27.6
China	98,678	9.4	25,715	3.7
Japan	134,009	12.8	57,733	8.4
Other Asia	190,459	18.2	106,877	15.5
Europe	229,766	21.9	171,925	24.9
EU	199,581	19.0	151,865	22.0
Russia	6,094	0.6	2,186	0.3
Other Europe	24,091	2.3	17,874	2.6
Oceania	7,951	0.8	13,555	2.0[21]
Australia	5,828	0.6	11,344	1.6
Other Oceania	2,123	0.2	2,211	0.3
TOTAL	1,048,435[32]	100.0	690,689[32]	100.0

Transport and communications

Transport. Railroads (1997): length[17] 137,900 mi, 222,000 km; passenger-mi 14,000,000,000, passenger-km 22,500,000,000; short ton-mi cargo 1,421,000,000,000, metric ton-km cargo 2,075,000,000. Roads (1998): total length 3,906,292 mi, 6,286,396 km (paved 91.0%). Vehicles (1998): passenger cars 131,839,000; trucks and buses 79,778,000. Merchant marine (1996): vessels (1,000 gross tons and over) 509; total deadweight tonnage 18,585,000. Air transport (1998): passenger-mi 619,500,000,000, passenger-km 997,000,000,000; short ton-mi cargo 18,116,000,000, metric ton-km cargo 26,449,000,000; localities (1996) with scheduled flights 834[33]. Certified route passenger/cargo air carriers (1992) 77; operating revenue (U.S.$'000,000; 1991) 74,942, of which domestic 56,119, international 18,823; operating expenses 76,669, of which domestic 56,596, international 20,073.

Intercity passenger and freight traffic by mode of transportation (1997)

	cargo traffic ('000,000,000 ton-mi)	% of nat'l total	passenger traffic ('000,000,000 passenger-mi)	% of nat'l total
Rail	1,421	39.2	14	0.6
Road	1,051	29.0	1,998	80.7
Inland water	508	14.1	—	—
Air	14	0.4	466	18.8
Petroleum pipeline	628	17.3	—	—
TOTAL	3,622	100.0	2,476[21]	100.0[21]

Communications

Medium	date	unit	number	units per 1,000 persons
Daily newspapers	1996	circulation	57,100,000	215
Radio	1997	receivers	575,000,000	2,116
Television	1999	receivers	233,000,000	843
Telephones	1999	main lines	183,521,000	664
Cellular telephones	1999	subscribers	86,047,000	307
Personal computers	1999	units	141,000,000	510
Internet	1998	users	81,000,000	290

Other communications media (1999)

	titles		titles
Print		General interest	181
Books (new)	119,357	History	151
of which		Home economics	90
Agriculture	1,037	Industrial arts	106
Art	4,795	Journalism and commun.	90
Biography	4,051	Labour and industrial relations	70
Business	3,789	Law	273
Education	3,408	Library and information sciences	118
Fiction	12,372	Literature and language	158
General works	1,456	Mathematics and science	238
History	7,486	Medicine	182
Home economics	2,564	Philosophy and religion	130
Juvenile	9,438	Physical education and recreation	151
Language	2,565	Political science	136
Law	3,078	Psychology	138
Literature	3,646	Sociology and anthropology	149
Medicine	6,153	Zoology	94
Music	1,593	**Cinema**	
Philosophy, psychology	5,861	Feature films	461
Poetry, drama	2,455		traffic
Religion	6,044	**Cellular telephones**	
Science	7,862	Number of subscribers	86,047,000
Sociology, economics	14,579		(pieces of mail)
Sports, recreation	3,252	**Post**	
Technology	8,896	Mail	201,576,000,000
Travel	2,977	Domestic	200,613,000,000
Periodicals[7]	3,731	International	963,000,000
of which			
Agriculture	153		
Business and economics	262		
Chemistry and physics	170		
Children's periodicals	78		
Education	203		
Engineering	265		
Fine and applied arts	145		

Education and health

Literacy: studies in the late 1980s indicated that adult "functional" literacy may not exceed 85%.

Education (1995–96)

	schools	teachers	students	student/teacher ratio
Primary (age 5–13)[34]	85,393[35]	1,784,000	33,410,000	18.7
Secondary and vocational (age 14–17)		1,187,000	17,390,000	14.6
Higher, including teacher-training colleges	5,758[36]	833,000	14,210,000	17.1

Food (1999): daily per capita caloric intake 3,754 (vegetable products 72%, animal products 28%); 142% of FAO recommended minimum requirement. Per capita consumption of major food groups (kilograms annually; 1995): milk 255.7; fresh fruits 123.2; cereal products 114.5; fresh vegetables 110.4; red meat 74.8; sweeteners 69.3; potatoes 58.7; poultry products 43.8; fats and oils 30.8; fish and shellfish 21.8.

Health (1995): doctors of medicine 720,300[37] (1 per 365 persons), of which office-based practice 427,300 (including specialties in internal medicine 17.0%, general and family practice 14.0%, pediatrics 7.9%, obstetrics and gynecology 6.8%, general surgery 5.6%, psychiatry 5.4%, anesthesiology 5.6%, orthopedics 4.0%, ophthalmology 4.3%); doctors of osteopathy 35,700; nurses 2,116,000 (1 per 124 persons); dentists 190,000 (1 per 1,385 persons); hospital beds 1,081,000 (1 per 243 persons), of which nonfederal 92.9% (community hospitals 80.8%, psychiatric 10.2%, long-term general and special 1.8%), federal 7.1%; infant mortality rate per 1,000 live births (1997) 7.1.

Physicians and nurses (1997)[38]

States	Physicians Total	Physicians Rate per 100,000 population	Nurses Total	Nurses Rate per 100,000 population
Alabama	8,399	194	33,200	768
Alaska	975	160	6,700	1,099
Arizona	9,094	200	34,600	760
Arkansas	4,622	185	18,500	733
California	78,502	244	178,500	555
Colorado	9,099	234	31,300	796
Connecticut	11,236	344	33,000	1,010
Delaware	1,688	230	8,000	1,088
Florida	34,100	232	123,700	843
Georgia	15,292	204	54,700	730
Hawaii	3,001	252	9,100	763
Idaho	1,817	150	7,200	596
Illinois	30,373	253	107,200	894
Indiana	11,238	192	47,600	812
Iowa	4,885	171	29,900	1,048
Kansas	5,246	202	22,300	857
Kentucky	8,018	205	31,500	806
Louisiana	10,364	239	33,600	772
Maine	2,663	214	13,300	1,071
Maryland	18,469	362	43,400	852
Massachusetts	24,597	402	72,900	1,192
Michigan	21,329	218	81,100	829
Minnesota	11,590	247	48,200	1,028
Mississippi	4,273	156	20,600	754
Missouri	12,175	225	52,300	967
Montana	1,655	188	7,300	831
Nebraska	3,530	213	15,100	911
Nevada	2,837	169	10,400	620
New Hampshire	2,694	230	11,100	947
New Jersey	23,101	287	66,500	825
New Mexico	3,595	209	12,000	696
New York	68,107	375	169,500	934
North Carolina	16,688	225	65,500	881
North Dakota	1,401	219	7,200	1,123
Ohio	25,688	230	103,000	920
Oklahoma	5,514	166	19,900	599
Oregon	7,152	221	27,500	848
Pennsylvania	33,849	282	129,800	1,081
Rhode Island	3,199	324	11,400	1,155
South Carolina	7,609	201	29,200	771
South Dakota	1,309	177	7,500	1,017
Tennessee	12,983	242	47,300	881
Texas	37,987	196	127,100	656
Utah	4,060	197	13,300	644
Vermont	1,698	288	5,200	883
Virginia	15,708	233	55,600	825
Washington	12,859	229	44,000	784
West Virginia	0,006	210	15,400	848
Wisconsin	11,630	224	46,400	892
Wyoming	801	167	4,400	917
District				
District of Columbia	3,722	702	8,600	1,623
TOTAL/AVERAGE	656,197	245	2,203,000	823

Military

Total active duty personnel (2000): 1,365,800 (army 34.6%, navy 27.1%, air force 25.9%, marines 12.4%). *Military expenditure as percentage of GNP* (1997): 3.3% (world 2.6%); per capita expenditure U.S.$1,024. *Military aid* (1993): total $4,143,000,000 (Middle East 76.2%, of which Israel 43.4%, Egypt 31.4%; Europe 20.8%, of which Turkey 10.9%; Latin America 1.8%).

[1]Excludes 5 delegates having only committee voting rights. [2]Total area per most recent official survey equals 3,675,267 sq mi (9,518,898 sq km), of which land area equals 3,536,278 sq mi (9,158,918 sq km), inland water area equals 78,937 sq mi (204,446 sq km), and Great Lakes water area equals 60,052 sq mi (155,534 sq km). [3]Includes military personnel residing overseas. [4]Persons of Hispanic origin may be of any race. [5]Fiscal year ending Sept. 30, 1996. [6]1996. [7]1997. [8]1995. [9]1989–91. [10]Data for 12-month period ending February 28. [11]Includes deaths with age not known. [12]Estimated crimes include unreported crimes. [13]1988. [14]1993. [15]2000. [16]1992. [17]1994. [18]Excludes military personnel overseas. [19]Includes hotels. [20]Unemployed. [21]Detail does not add to total given because of rounding. [22]Automotive dealers includes Gasoline service stations. [23]Excludes tips. [24]Includes hydroelectric, nuclear, and geothermal power. [25]Gross income from all sources, including transfer payments to individuals. [26]Householder 25 years old or older. [27]Period average. [28]End-of-year. [29]"Own children" includes adopted children and stepchildren. [30]Manufacturing sector only. [31]Animal and vegetable oils included in Food and live animals. [32]Detail does not add to total given because of statistical discrepancies in the data. [33]Includes 292 localities in Alaska. [34]Primary includes kindergarten. [35]1993–94. [36]1992–93. [37]646,000 professionally active. [38]Nonfederal physicians and nurses only.

Internet resources for further information:

- **U.S. Census Bureau http://www.census.gov**
- **Statistical Abstract of the United States http://www.census.gov/prod/www/statistical-abstract-us.html**

Uruguay

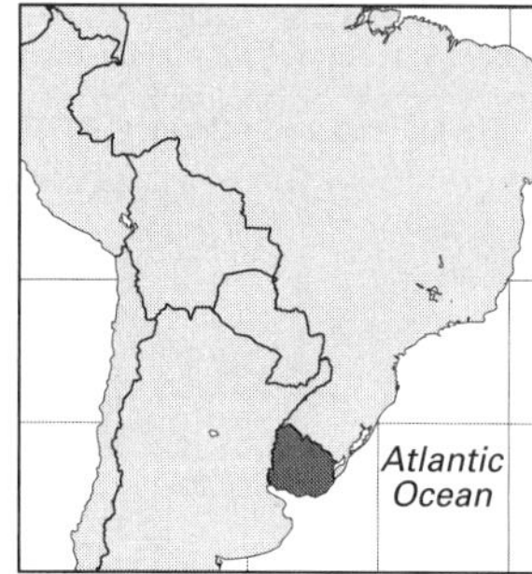

Official name: República Oriental del Uruguay (Oriental Republic of Uruguay).
Form of government: republic with two legislative houses (Senate [31][1]; Chamber of Representatives [99]).
Head of state and government: President.
Capital: Montevideo.
Official language: Spanish.
Official religion: none.
Monetary unit: 1 peso uruguayo[2] ($U) = 100 centesimos; valuation (Sept. 28, 2001) 1 U.S.$ = $U 13.69; 1 £ = $U 20.12.

Area and population

Departments	Capitals	area sq mi	area sq km	population 1996 census
Artigas	Artigas	4,065	11,928	75,786
Canelones	Canelones	1,751	4,536	410,524
Cerro Largo	Melo	5,270	13,648	81,218
Colonia	Colonia del Sacramento	2,358	6,106	117,380
Durazno	Durazno	4,495	11,643	56,986
Flores	Trinidad	1,986	5,144	25,348
Florida	Florida	4,022	10,417	68,257
Lavalleja	Minas	3,867	10,016	60,618
Maldonado	Maldonado	1,851	4,793	113,884
Montevideo	Montevideo	205	530	1,378,705
Paysandú	Paysandú	5,375	13,922	107,706
Río Negro	Fray Bentos	3,584	9,282	48,730
Rivera	Rivera	3,618	9,370	97,959
Rocha	Rocha	4,074	10,551	71,492
Salto	Salto	5,468	14,163	115,244
San José	San José de Mayo	1,927	4,992	91,874
Soriano	Mercedes	3,478	9,008	83,741
Tacuarembó	Tacuarembó	5,961	15,438	84,078
Treinta y Tres	Treinta y Tres	3,679	9,529	49,846
TOTAL LAND AREA		67,574	175,016	
INLAND WATER		463	1,199	
TOTAL		68,037	176,215	3,139,376

Demography

Population (2001): 3,303,000.
Density (2001): persons per sq mi 48.6, persons per sq km 18.7.
Urban-rural (1996): urban 88.7%; rural 11.3%.
Sex distribution (2000): male 48.51%; female 51.49%.
Age breakdown (2000): under 15, 24.8%; 15–29, 23.4%; 30–44, 19.4%; 45–59, 15.3%; 60–74, 11.9%; 75 and over, 5.2%.
Population projection: (2010) 3,540,000; (2020) 3,794,000.
Ethnic composition (1990): white (mostly Spanish, Italian, or mixed Spanish-Italian) 86.0%; mestizo 8.0%; mulatto or black 6.0%.
Religious affiliation (1997): Roman Catholic 78.5%[3]; Protestant 4.5%; other Christian 3.5%; Jewish 0.9%; other 12.6%.
Major cities (1996): Montevideo 1,378,707; Salto 93,113; Paysandú 74,568; Las Piedras 66,584; Rivera 62,859.

Vital statistics

Birth rate per 1,000 population (2000): 17.4 (world avg. 22.5).
Death rate per 1,000 population (2000): 9.1 (world avg. 9.0).
Total fertility rate (avg. births per childbearing woman; 2000): 2.4.
Marriage rate per 1,000 population (1996): 5.6.
Divorce rate per 1,000 population (1996): 2.1.
Life expectancy at birth (2000): male 71.9 years; female 78.8 years.
Major causes of death per 100,000 population (1990): diseases of the circulatory system 378.4; malignant neoplasms 222.8; respiratory diseases 76.3.

National economy

Budget (1998). Revenue: $U 70,664,000,000 (taxes on goods and services 39.4%, social security contributions 28.6%, income taxes 12.6%, nontax revenue 7.1%, receipts from foreign trade 3.7%). Expenditures: $U 72,673,000,000 (social security and welfare 61.4%, general public services 7.4%, education 7.0%, health 5.8%, interest payments 4.7%).
Public debt (external, outstanding; 1999): U.S.$5,108,000,000.
Production (metric tons except as noted). Agriculture, forestry, fishing (1999): rice 1,328,000, wheat 377,000, corn (maize) 243,000, oranges 186,000, sugarcane 185,000, sunflower seed 161,000; livestock (number of live animals) 15,500,000 sheep, 10,700,000 cattle; roundwood (1998) 6,163,000 cu m; fish catch (1998) 140,609. Mining and quarrying (1997): hydraulic cement 770,000; gypsum 183,000. Manufacturing (value added in U.S.$'000,000; 1995): food products 1,012; beverages 426; chemical products 402; textiles 281; tobacco products 211. Construction (approvals; 1994): residential 301,666 sq m; nonresidential 177,752 sq m. Energy production (consumption): electricity (kW-hr; 1996) 6,666,000,000 (6,538,000,000); crude petroleum, none (13,942,000); petroleum products (metric tons; 1996) 1,821,000 (1,626,000).
Land use (1998): forested and other 15.2%; meadows and pastures 77.3%; agricultural and under permanent cultivation 7.5%.
Household income and expenditure. Avg. household size (1985) 3.3; avg. annual income per household (1985) NUr$266,261[2] (U.S.$2,625); sources of income[4]: wages 53.5%, self-employment 17.0%, transfer payments and other 29.5%; expenditure (1982–83)[5]: food 39.9%, housing 17.6%, transportation and communications 10.4%, health care 9.3%, clothing 7.0%.
Gross national product (1999): U.S.$20,604,000,000 (U.S.$6,220 per capita).

Structure of gross domestic product and labour force

	1998 in value $U '000	1998 % of total value	1993 labour force	1993 % of labour force
Agriculture	18,511,900	8.5	47,700	3.8
Mining	569,800	0.3	2,100	0.2
Manufacturing	38,748,000	17.8	254,300	20.2
Construction	10,621,000	4.9	86,400	6.9
Public utilities	9,990,500	4.6	16,900	1.3
Transp. and commun.	15,871,100	7.3	67,900	5.4
Trade	25,725,000	11.8	231,300	18.3
Finance	58,364,300	26.7	68,400	5.4
Pub. admin., defense	22,148,900	10.1	455,800	36.1
Services	25,876,000	11.8		
Other	–8,282,000[6]	–3.8[6]	30,200[7]	2.4[7]
TOTAL	218,144,500	100.0	1,261,000	100.0

Population economically active (1998): total 1,239,400[8]; activity rate 47.0% (participation rates: ages 14 and over, 60.4%; female 44.0%).

Price and earnings indexes (1995 = 100)

	1994	1995	1996	1997	1998	1999	2000
Consumer price index	70.3	100.0	128.3	153.8	170.4	180.0	188.6
Monthly earnings index[8]	72.4	100.0	115.1	138.2	155.9	167.3	...

Tourism (1999): receipts U.S.$653,000,000; expenditures U.S.$280,000,000.

Foreign trade[9]

Balance of trade (current prices)

	1995	1996	1997	1998	1999	2000
U.S.$'000,000	–563.0	–686.9	–704.4	–772.1	–896.6	–936.8
% of total	11.6%	12.3%	11.2%	12.0%	16.4%	16.4%

Imports (1999): U.S.$3,356,770,000 (machinery and appliances 22.2%; chemical products 14.6%; mineral products 11.6%; transport equipment 9.1%; processed foods 7.1%; synthetic plastics, resins, and rubber 7.0%; metal products 4.8%). *Major import sources* (1998): Argentina 22.0%; Brazil 20.8%; United States 12.1%; France 4.7%; Italy 4.6%; Spain 3.7%.
Exports (1999): U.S.$2,236,848,000 (live animals and live-animal products 30.1%; vegetable products 15.8%; textiles and textile products 11.8%; hides and skins 9.8%; processed foods 5.4%). *Major export destinations* (1998): Brazil 33.8%; Argentina 18.5%; United States 5.7%; Germany 4.0%.

Transport and communications

Transport. Railroads (1996): route length 2,073 km; metric ton-km cargo 180,000,000. Roads (1997): length 8,683 km[10] (paved 30%). Vehicles (1997): passenger cars 516,889; trucks and buses 50,264. Air transport (1996): passenger-km 640,000,000; metric ton-km cargo 62,000,000; airports (1997) 1.

Communications

Medium	date	unit	number	units per 1,000 persons
Daily newspapers	1996	circulation	950,000	293
Radio	1997	receivers	1,970,000	603
Television	1999	receivers	1,760,000	531
Telephones	1999	main lines	896,849	271
Cellular telephones	1999	subscribers	316,131	95
Personal computers	1999	units	330,000	100
Internet	1999	users	330,000	100

Education and health

Educational attainment (1996). Percentage of population age 25 and over having: no formal schooling 3.4%; primary education 53.6%; secondary 31.7%; higher 10.1%; unknown 1.2%. *Literacy* (1995 est.): population age 15 and over literate 97.3%; males 96.9%; females 97.7%.

Education (1997)

	schools	teachers	students	student/teacher ratio
Primary (age 6–11)	2,410	16,721	348,195	20.8
Secondary (age 12–17)	413	19,104	192,399	10.1
Vocational	101	...	58,246	...
Higher	2	9,907[11]	79,691[11]	8.0[11]

Health (1999): physicians 12,357 (1 per 263 persons); hospital beds 6,651 (1 per 488 persons); infant mortality rate (2000) 15.1.
Food (1999): daily per capita caloric intake 2,862 (vegetable products 61%, animal products 39%); (1997) 107% of FAO recommended minimum.

Military

Total active duty personnel (2000): 23,700 (army 64.1%, navy 23.2%, air force 12.7%). *Military expenditure as percentage of GNP* (1997): 1.4% (world 2.6%); per capita expenditure U.S.$88.

[1]Includes the vice president, who serves as ex officio presiding officer. [2]The peso uruguayo (Uruguayan peso [$U]) replaced the new Uruguayan peso (NUr$) on March 1, 1993. [3]About 30–40% of Roman Catholics are estimated to be nonreligious. [4]Salaried employees only. [5]Weights of consumer price index components in Montevideo. [6]Includes indirect taxes less imputed bank service charges. [7]Includes unemployed not previously employed. [8]From urban areas only. [9]Import figures are f.o.b. in balance of trade. [10]Excludes streets under local control. [11]1996.

Internet resources for further information:

- **Instituto Nacional de Estadística—Uruguay http://www.ine.gub.uy/principal.htm**
- **Uruguay: Datos Estadísticos http://www.rau.edu.uy/uruguay/generalidades/Uy.estad.htm**

Uzbekistan

Official name: Ŭzbekiston Respublikasi (Republic of Uzbekistan).
Form of government: multiparty republic with a single legislative body (Supreme Assembly [250]).
Heads of state and government: President assisted by Prime Minister.
Capital: Tashkent (Toshkent).
Official language: Uzbek.
Official religion: none.
Monetary unit: sum (plural sumy); valuation (Sept. 28, 2001) 1 U.S.$ = 425.99 sumy; 1 £ = 626.08 sumy.

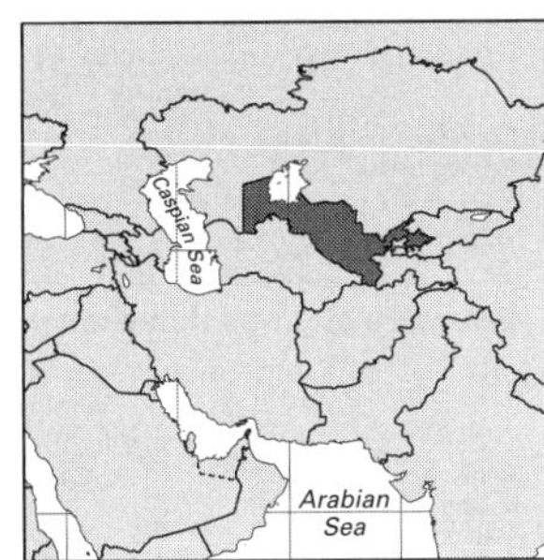

Area and population

Autonomous Republic	Administrative centres	area sq mi	area sq km	population 1993 estimate
Qoraqalpoghiston	Nuqus	63,700	164,900	1,343,000
Provinces				
Andijon	Andijon	1,600	4,200	1,899,000
Bukhoro	Bukhara (Bukhoro)	15,200	39,400	1,262,000
Farghona	Fergana (Farghona)	2,700	7,100	2,338,000
Jizzakh	Jizzakh	7,900	20,500	831,000
Khorazm	Urganch	2,400	6,300	1,135,000
Namangan	Namangan	3,100	7,900	1,652,000
Nawoiy	Nawoiy	42,800	110,800	715,000
Qashqadaryo	Qarshi	11,000	28,400	1,812,000
Samarqand	Samarkand (Samarqand)	6,300	16,400	2,322,000
Sirdaryo	Guliston	2,000	5,100	600,000
Surkhondaryo	Termiz	8,000	20,800	1,437,000
Tashkent (Toshkent)	Tashkent (Toshkent)	6,000[1]	15,600[1]	2,236,000
City				
Tashkent (Toshkent)	—	[1]	[1]	2,121,000
TOTAL		172,700	447,400	21,703,000

Demography

Population (2001): 25,155,000.
Density (2001): persons per sq mi 145.7, persons per sq km 56.2.
Urban-rural (1999): urban 37.1%; rural 62.9%.
Sex distribution (1999): male 49.55%; female 50.45%.
Age breakdown (1999): under 15, 37.9%; 15–29, 27.7%; 30–44, 19.4%; 45–59, 8.1%; 60–74, 5.5%; 75 and over, 1.4%.
Population projection: (2010) 29,280,000; (2020) 34,465,000.
Doubling time: 44 years.
Ethnic composition (1998): Uzbek 75.8%; Russian 6.0%; Tajik 4.8%; Kazakh 4.1%; Tatar 1.6%; other 7.7%.
Religious affiliation (2000): Muslim (mostly Sunnī) 76.2%; nonreligious 18.1%; Russian Orthodox 0.8%; Jewish 0.2%; other 4.7%.
Major cities (1998 est.): Tashkent 2,124,000; Samarkand 388,000; Namangan 291,000; Andijon 288,000; Bukhara 220,000.

Vital statistics

Birth rate per 1,000 population (2001): 21.7 (world avg. 22.5); (1994) legitimate 96.5%; illegitimate 3.5%.
Death rate per 1,000 population (2001): 5.9 (world avg. 9.0).
Natural increase rate per 1,000 population (2001): 15.8 (world avg. 13.5).
Total fertility rate (avg. births per childbearing woman; 2001): 3.1.
Marriage rate per 1,000 population (1994): 7.9.
Divorce rate per 1,000 population (1994): 1.1.
Life expectancy at birth (2001): male 66.0 years; female 72.0 years.
Major causes of death per 100,000 population (1993): diseases of the circulatory system 303.6; diseases of the respiratory system 115.0; accidents, poisoning, and violence 50.0; cancers 48.7; infectious and parasitic diseases 38.4; diseases of the digestive system 31.8; diseases of the nervous system 10.3; endocrine and metabolic disorders 10.3.

National economy

Budget (1998). Revenue: 440,140,000,000 sumy (taxes on income and profits 31.5%, value-added tax 30.2%, excise taxes 18.9%, property and land taxes 12.5%, other 6.9%). Expenditures: 488,297,000,000 sumy (social and cultural affairs 34.2%, investments 19.4%, national economy 11.2%, transfers 9.2%, administration 2.3%, interest on debt 2.0%, other 21.7%).
Household income and expenditure (1995). Average household size (1998) 5.5; income per household 35,165 sumy (U.S.$1,040); sources of income: wages and salaries 63.0%, subsidies, grants, and nonwage income 34.9%, other 2.1%; expenditure: food and beverages 71%, clothing and footwear 14%, recreation 6%, household durables 4%, housing 3%.
Public debt (external, outstanding; 1999): U.S.$3,421,000,000.
Production (metric tons except as noted). Agriculture, forestry, fishing (1999): seed cotton 3,680,000, vegetables 2,800,000, fruit (except grapes) and berries 1,350,000, grapes 650,000, potatoes 649,600, rice 541,000, barley 109,000; livestock (number of live animals) 8,000,000 sheep, 5,225,200 cattle, 697,900 goats, 208,000 pigs, 13,935,000 chickens; roundwood (1990) 15,000 cu m; fish catch (1998) 2,798. Mining and quarrying (1998): copper 89,930; zinc 38,000; uranium 2,000; gold 85. Manufacturing (metric tons except as noted; 1998): cement 3,358,000; cotton fibre 1,138,000; mineral fertilizer 897,000; steel 360,000; ferrous metal products 322,000; television sets 192,468 units; passenger cars 54,456; video recorders 50,096 units; refrigerators 16,000 units; tractors 3,000 units. Construction (1992): residential 7,000,000,000 sq m. Energy production (consumption): electricity (kW-hr; 1998) 46,056,000,000 (46,100,000,000); coal (metric tons; 1998) 2,952,000 (2,792,000); crude petroleum (barrels; 1998) 59,400,000 (57,870,000); petroleum products (metric tons; 1998) 8,104,000 (6,934,000); natural gas (cu m; 1998) 51,245,000,000 (44,246,000,000).
Gross national product (1999): U.S.$17,613,000,000 (U.S.$720 per capita).

Structure of gross domestic product and labour force

1999	in value '000,000 sumy	% of total value	labour force[2]	% of labour force[2]
Agriculture	521,627	26.9	3,091,000	35.0
Manufacturing and mining	283,425	14.6	1,126,000	12.8
Construction	149,803	7.7	578,000	6.5
Transp. and commun.	120,125	6.2	379,000	4.3
Trade	169,344	8.7	716,000	8.1
Finance / Pub. admin., defense / Services	399,882	20.6	2,003,000	22.7
Other	297,903[3]	15.3[3]	938,000[4]	10.6[4]
TOTAL	1,942,109	100.0	8,831,000[5]	100.0

Population economically active (1999): total 8,831,000; activity rate of total population 36.4% (participation rates: ages 16–59 [male], 16–54 [female] 70.4%; female [1994] 43.0%; unemployed 0.6%[6]).

Price and earnings indexes (1995 = 100)

	1994	1995	1996	1997	1998
Consumer price index	44.4	100	...	...	...
Monthly earnings index	28.5	100	202.4	345.5	506.0

Tourism (1997): receipts U.S.$19,000,000.
Land use (1994): forested 2.9%; meadows and pastures 46.5%; agricultural and under permanent cultivation 10.1%; other 40.5%.

Foreign trade

Balance of trade (current prices)

	1993	1994	1995	1996	1997	1998
U.S.$'000,000	−378	+214	+237	−706	−72	+171
% of total	6.2%	3.8%	3.5%	9.1%	1.0%	3.0%

Imports (1998): U.S.$2,717,000,000 (machinery and metalworking products 49.6%, food products 20.9%, other 29.5%). *Major import sources:* Western Europe 30.6%; Russia 20.5%; Asia 14.2%; Kazakhstan 5.2%; Ukraine 3.2%.
Exports (1998): U.S.$2,888,000,000 (cotton fibre 41.5%, energy 22.7%, gold 6.0%, other 29.8%). *Major export destinations:* Western Europe 33.7%; Russia 22.6%; Asia 11.6%; Ukraine 5.4%; Kazakhstan 5.4%; Tajikistan 2.9%; Turkmenistan 2.5%.

Transport and communications

Transport. Railroads (1997): length 3,655 km; (1995) passenger-km 2,500,000,000; (1995) metric ton-km cargo 16,907,000,000. Roads (1997): total length 84,400 km (paved 87%). Vehicles (1994): passenger cars 865,300; buses 14,500. Air transport (1996): passenger-km 3,460,000,000; metric ton-km cargo 321,000,000; airports (1998) with scheduled flights 9.

Communications

Medium	date	unit	number	units per 1,000 persons
Daily newspapers	1996	circulation	75,000	3.3
Television	1999	receivers	6,700,000	276
Telephones	1999	main lines	1,599,000	66
Cellular telephones	1999	subscribers	40,389	1.7
Internet	1999	users	7,500	0.3

Education and health

Educational attainment (1989). Percentage of population age 25 and over having: primary education or no formal schooling 13.3%; some secondary 19.8%; completed secondary and some postsecondary 57.7%; higher 9.2%. *Literacy* (1997): percentage of total population age 15 and over literate 99.0%.

Education (1995–96)

	schools	teachers	students	student/ teacher ratio
Primary (age 6–13) / Secondary (age 14–17)	9,300	413,000	5,090,000	12.3
Voc., teacher tr.[7]	248	22,164[8]	240,100	...
Higher[8]	55	...	272,300	...

Health (1995): physicians 76,000 (1 per 302 persons); hospital beds 192,000 (1 per 120 persons); infant mortality rate per 1,000 live births (2001) 38.0.
Food (1999): daily per capita caloric intake 2,870 (vegetable products 85%, animal products 15%); (1997) 112% of FAO recommended minimum requirement.

Military

Total active duty personnel (2000): 78,100 (army 64.0%, air force 11.7%, other 24.3%). *Military expenditure as percentage of GNP* (1996): 2.5% (world 2.6%); per capita expenditure U.S.$62.

[1]Tashkent province includes Tashkent City. [2]August. [3]Includes value-added taxes: excise taxes plus net import taxes minus subsidies. [4]Includes 882,600 persons on forced leave and 55,400 unemployed. [5]Detail does not add to total given because of rounding. [6]Official unemployment rate. [7]1998. [8]1992–93.

Internet resources for further information:
- **Welcome to Uzbekistan http://www.gov.uz**
- **UNDP in Uzbekistan http://www.undp.uz**

Vanuatu

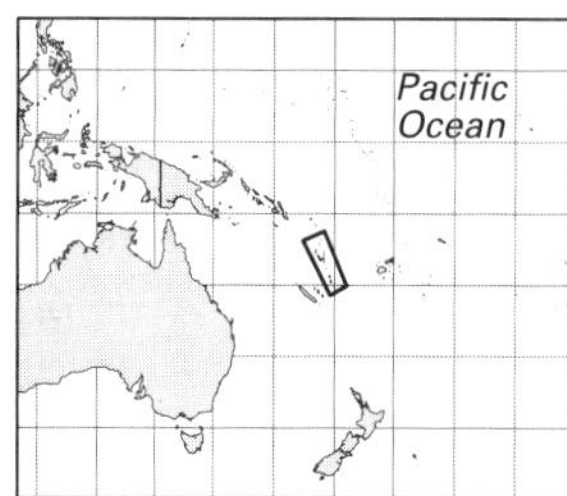

Official name: Ripablik blong Vanuatu (Bislama); République de Vanuatu (French); Republic of Vanuatu (English).
Form of government: republic with a single legislative house (Parliament [52]).
Chief of state: President.
Head of government: Prime Minister.
Capital: Vila.
Official languages: Bislama; French; English.
Official religion: none.
Monetary unit: vatu (VT); valuation (Sept. 28, 2001) 1 U.S.$ = VT 148.40; 1 £ = VT 218.10.

Area and population

		area		population
				1999
Provinces	Capitals	sq mi	sq km	census
Malampa	Lakatoro	1,073	2,779	33,773
Penama	Longana	463	1,198	28,914
Sanma	Luganville	1,640	4,248	37,141
Shefa	Vila	562	1,455	55,900
Tafea	Isangel	628	1,627	29,412
Torba	Sola	341	882	8,079
TOTAL		4,707	12,190[1]	193,219[2]

Demography

Population (2001): 195,000.
Density (2001): persons per sq mi 41.4, persons per sq km 16.0.
Urban-rural (1999): urban 21.5%; rural 78.5%.
Sex distribution (1999): male 51.46%; female 48.54%.
Age breakdown (1999): under 15, 37.8%; 15–29, 29.4%; 30–44, 18.2%; 45–59, 9.7%; 60–74, 4.0%; 75 and over, 0.9%.
Population projection: (2010) 221,000; (2020) 250,000.
Doubling time: 26 years.
Ethnic composition (1989): Ni-Vanuatu 97.9%; European 1.0%; other Pacific Islanders 0.4%; other 0.7%.
Religious affiliation (1989): Christian 89.7%, of which Presbyterian 35.8%, Roman Catholic 14.5%, Anglican 14.0%, Seventh-day Adventist 8.2%; Custom (traditional beliefs) 4.6%; unknown 4.0%; nonreligious 1.7%.
Major towns (1999): Vila (Port-Vila) 30,139; Luganville 11,360.

Vital statistics

Birth rate per 1,000 population (2001): 32.1 (world avg. 22.5).
Death rate per 1,000 population (2001): 5.6 (world avg. 9.0).
Natural increase rate per 1,000 population (2001): 26.5 (world avg. 13.5).
Total fertility rate (avg. births per childbearing woman; 2001): 4.4.
Marriage rate per 1,000 population (1985): *c.* 7.4.
Divorce rate per 1,000 population (1985): less than 0.7.
Life expectancy at birth (2001): male 67.0 years; female 70.0 years.
Major causes of death per 100,000 population (1994)[3]: diseases of the circulatory system 39.0; diseases of the respiratory system 30.4; malignant neoplasms (cancers) 29.2; infectious and parasitic diseases 25.0; diseases of the digestive system 9.7.

National economy

Budget (1998). Revenue: VT 8,536,000,000 (taxes on international trade 33.0%; taxes on goods and services 32.0%; foreign grants 20.9%; nontax revenue 10.2%). Expenditures: VT 12,611,000,000 (current expenditure 58.0%, of which general public services 17.2%, education 13.2%, public order and safety 8.4%, health 6.6%, economic affairs and services 5.8%; capital expenditure 42.0%).
Public debt (external, outstanding; 1999): U.S.$63,400,000.
Household income and expenditure (1985)[4]. Average household size (1989) 5.1; income per household U.S.$11,299; sources of income: wages and salaries 59.0%, self-employment 33.7%; expenditure (1990)[4, 5]: food and nonalcoholic beverages 30.5%, housing 20.7%, transportation 13.2%, health and recreation 12.3%, tobacco and alcohol 10.4%.
Production (metric tons except as noted). Agriculture, forestry, fishing (1999): coconuts 339,000, roots and tubers 65,000, bananas 12,500, vegetables and melons 9,800, peanuts (groundnuts) 1,750, cacao beans 1,500, corn (maize) 700; livestock (number of live animals) 151,000 cattle, 62,000 pigs, 12,000 goats, 320,000 chickens; roundwood (1998) 63,200 cu m; fish catch (1997) 2,589. Mining and quarrying: small quantities of coral-reef limestone, crushed stone, sand, and gravel. Manufacturing (value added in VT '000,000; 1995): food, beverages, and tobacco 645; wood products 423; fabricated metal products 377; paper products 125; chemical, rubber, plastic, and nonmetallic products 84; textiles, clothing, and leather 54. Construction (approvals in Vila and Luganville; 1992): residential 20,386 sq m; nonresidential 19,876 sq m. Energy production (consumption): electricity (kW-hr; 1996) 30,000,000 (30,000,000); coal, none (none); crude petroleum, none (none); petroleum products (metric tons; 1996) none (20,000); natural gas, none (none).
Land use (1994): forested 75.0%; meadows and pastures 2.0%; agricultural 11.8%; other 11.2%.
Population economically active (1989): total 66,957; activity rate of total population 47.0% (participation rates: ages 15–64, 85.0%; female 46.3%; unemployed 0.5%).

Price and earnings indexes (1995 = 100)

	1993	1994	1995	1996	1997	1998	1999
Consumer price index	95.6	97.8	100.0	100.9	103.8	107.2	109.3
Earnings index	...	...	...	...	...	...	...

Gross national product (1999): U.S.$227,000,000 (U.S.$1,180 per capita).

Structure of gross domestic product and labour force

	1997		1989	
	in value VT '000,000	% of total value	labour force	% of labour force
Agriculture	7,193	24.7	49,811	74.4
Mining	...	...	1	—
Manufacturing	1,442	5.0	891	1.3
Construction	1,613	5.5	1,302	1.9
Public utilities	500	1.7	109	0.2
Transportation and communications	2,138	7.3	1,031	1.5
Trade	9,551	32.7	2,713	4.1
Finance	2,042	7.0	646	1.0
Pub. admin., defense	3,362	11.5	7,892	11.8
Services	1,883	6.5		
Other	−548[6]	−1.9[6]	2,561	3.8
TOTAL	29,176	100.0	66,957	100.0

Tourism (1999): receipts from visitors U.S.$56,000,000; expenditures by nationals abroad U.S.$9,000,000.

Foreign trade[7]

Balance of trade (current prices)

	1994	1995	1996	1997	1998	1999
VT '000,000	−7,493	−7,486	−7,520	−6,801	−6,934	−6,187
% of total	56.3%	54.1%	52.7%	45.4%	44.5%	39.9%

Imports (1997): VT 10,888,000,000 (machinery and transport equipment 25.7%, food and live animals 19.7%, basic manufactures 15.2%, mineral fuels 10.6%, chemical products 6.2%, beverages and tobacco 3.6%). *Major import sources:* Australia 42.1%; France 13.5%; New Zealand 12.2%; Japan 7.3%; Fiji 6.0%.
Exports (1997): VT 4,087,000,000 (copra 49.0%, timber 12.3%, beef 10.2%, cacao beans 5.9%). *Major export destinations*[8]: European Union 45.9%; Bangladesh 12.6%; Japan 10.4%; New Caledonia 4.5%; Australia 2.3%.

Transport and communications

Transport. Railroads: none. Roads (1996): total length 665 mi, 1,070 km (paved 24%). Vehicles (1996): passenger cars 4,000; trucks and buses 2,600. Merchant marine (1992): vessels (100 gross tons and over) 280; total deadweight tonnage 3,259,594. Air transport (1999): passenger-mi 110,800,000, passenger-km 178,316,000; short ton-mi cargo 1,318,000, metric ton-km 1,924,000; airports (1996) with scheduled flights 29.

Communications

Medium	date	unit	number	units per 1,000 persons
Radio	1997	receivers	62,000	350
Television	1997	receivers	2,000	14
Telephones	1999	main lines	5,500	30
Cellular telephones	1999	subscribers	300	1.6
Personal computers	...	units	...	...
Internet	...	users	...	...

Education and health

Educational attainment (1989). Percentage of population age 6 and over having: no formal schooling or less than one year 22.3%; some primary education 52.6%; lower-level secondary 18.3%; upper-level secondary and higher 4.8%; not stated 2.0%. *Literacy* (1979): total population age 15 and over literate 32,120 (52.9%); males 18,550 (57.3%); females 13,570 (47.8%).

Education (1992)

	schools	teachers	students	student/ teacher ratio
Primary (age 6–11)[9]	272	852	26,267	30.8
Secondary (age 11–18)	27	220	4,269	19.4
Voc., teacher tr.	...	50[10]	444	...
Higher	1[11]	13[12]	124[13]	...

Health (1997): physicians 21 (1 per 8,524 persons); hospital beds 573 (1 per 312 persons); infant mortality rate per 1,000 live births (2001) 30.0.
Food (1999): daily per capita caloric intake 2,766 (vegetable products 86%, animal products 14%); (1997) 121% of FAO recommended minimum.

Military

Total active duty personnel: Vanuatu has a paramilitary force of about 300.

[1]Detail does not add to total given because of rounding. [2]De facto figure; de jure figure equals 186,678. [3]Deaths reported to the Ministry of Health only. [4]Vila and Luganville only. [5]Weights of consumer price index components. [6]Imputed bank service charges. [7]Imports c.i.f.; exports f.o.b. [8]Destination of domestic exports only. [9]Excludes independent private schools. [10]1981. [11]1989. [12]1983. [13]1991.

Internet resources for further information:

- **Vanuatu Online**
  http://www.vanuatu.net.vu/VanuatuOnlineDirectory.html
- **New Zealand Ministry of Foreign Affairs: Vanuatu**
  http://www.mft.govt.nz/foreign/regions/5thpacific/country/vanuatupaper.html

Venezuela

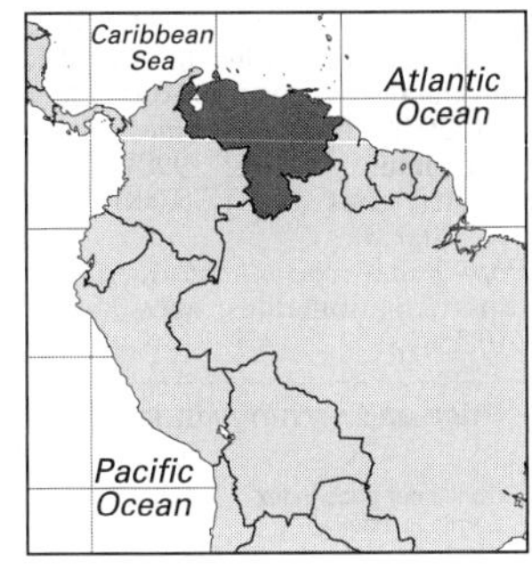

Official name[1]: República Bolivariana de Venezuela (Bolivarian Republic of Venezuela).
Form of government[1]: federal multiparty republic with a unicameral legislature (National Assembly [165]).
Head of state and government: President.
Capital: Caracas.
Official language: Spanish.
Official religion: none.
Monetary unit: 1 bolívar (B, plural Bs) = 100 céntimos; valuation (Sept. 28, 2001) 1 U.S.$ = Bs 742.90; 1 £ = Bs 1,091.

Area and population

States	Capitals	area sq mi	area sq km	population 1997 estimate
Amazonas	Puerto Ayacucho	69,554	180,145	96,976
Anzoátegui	Barcelona	16,700	43,300	1,077,435
Apure	San Fernando de Apure	29,500	76,500	415,051
Aragua	Maracay	2,708	7,014	1,399,987
Barinas	Barinas	13,600	35,200	545,013
Bolívar	Ciudad Bolívar	91,900	238,000	1,207,527
Carabobo	Valencia	1,795	4,650	1,935,461
Cojedes	San Carlos	5,700	14,800	241,365
Delta Amacuro	Tucupita	15,500	40,200	123,491
Falcón	Coro	9,600	24,800	719,458
Guárico	San Juan de Los Morros	25,091	64,986	605,878
Lara	Barquisimeto	7,600	19,800	1,491,940
Mérida	Mérida	4,400	11,300	706,870
Miranda	Los Teques	3,070	7,950	2,424,862
Monagas	Maturín	11,200	28,900	573,967
Nueva Esparta	La Asunción	440	1,150	349,139
Portuguesa	Guanare	5,900	15,200	764,284
Sucre	Cumaná	4,600	11,800	799,935
Táchira	San Cristóbal	4,300	11,100	981,607
Trujillo	Trujillo	2,900	7,400	573,537
Vargas	La Guaira	578	1,497	[2]
Yaracuy	San Felipe	2,700	7,100	487,441
Zulia	Maracaibo	24,400	63,100	2,974,233
Other federal entities				
Dependencias Federales[3]	—	50	120	...
Distrito Federal	Caracas	167	433	2,281,695[2]
TOTAL		353,841[4]	916,445	22,777,152

Demography

Population (2001): 24,632,000.
Density (2001): persons per sq mi 69.6, persons per sq km 26.9.
Urban-rural (1997): urban 86.1%; rural 13.9%.
Sex distribution (1997): male 50.35%; female 49.65%.
Age breakdown (1997): under 15, 35.4%; 15–29, 27.6%; 30–44, 19.9%; 45–59, 10.8%; 60–74, 5.0%; 75 and over, 1.3%.
Population projection: (2010) 28,716,000; (2020) 32,911,000.
Ethnic composition (1993): mestizo 67%; white 21%; black 10%; Indian 2%.
Religious affiliation (2000): Roman Catholic 89.5%; Protestant 2.0%; other Christian 1.4%; Spiritist 1.1%; nonreligious/atheist 2.2%; other 3.8%.
Major cities (2000 est.): Caracas 1,975,787; Maracaibo 1,764,038; Valencia 1,338,833; Barquisimeto 875,790; Ciudad Guayana 704,168.

Vital statistics

Birth rate per 1,000 population (2000): 21.1 (world avg. 22.5); (1974) legitimate 47.0%; illegitimate 53.0%.
Death rate per 1,000 population (2000): 4.9 (world avg. 9.0).
Total fertility rate (avg. births per childbearing woman; 2000): 2.5.
Marriage rate per 1,000 population (1997): 3.8.
Divorce rate per 1,000 population (1997): 0.9.
Life expectancy at birth (2000): male 70.1 years; female 76.3 years.
Major causes of death per 100,000 population (1996): heart diseases 102.9; cancers 59.0; accidents 35.8; cardiovascular diseases 33.0.

National economy

Budget (1998). Revenue: Bs 9,017,475,000,000 (tax revenues 73.6%; nontax revenues 26.4%, of which oil revenues 24.9%). Expenditures: Bs 10,460,235,000,000 (subsidies 43.7%, goods and services 23.9%; capital expenditure 18.9%; debt service 11.8%).
Public debt (external, outstanding; 1999): U.S.$25,216,000,000.
Tourism (1999): receipts U.S.$656,000,000; expenditures U.S.$1,646,000,000.
Production (metric tons except as noted). Agriculture, forestry, fishing (1999): sugarcane 6,850,000, corn (maize) 1,024,000, bananas 1,000,394, rice 670,000, plantains 578,000, cassava 588,000, sorghum 402,000, potatoes 352,000; livestock (number of live animals) 15,992,400 cattle, 4,500,000 pigs, 4,000,000 goats, 110,000,000 chickens; roundwood (1998) 2,038,000 cu m; fish catch (1998) 506,177. Mining and quarrying (1998): iron ore 19,305,000; bauxite 4,633,000; gold 14,046 kg; diamonds (1997) 401,068 carats. Manufacturing (value added in 1984 Bs '000,000; 1997): ferrous and nonferrous metals 16,355; food products 13,277; chemicals 10,004; beverages 9,480; clothing, textiles, leather, and shoes 8,311; metal products 6,413. Energy production (consumption): electricity (kW-hr; 1996) 74,968,000,000 (74,817,000,000); coal (metric tons; 1996) 3,486,000 (328,000); crude petroleum (barrels; 1996) 1,005,526,000 (370,722,000); petroleum products (metric tons; 1996) 54,847,000 (23,096,000); natural gas (cu m; 1996) 39,411,000,000 (39,411,000,000).
Gross national product (1999): U.S.$87,313,000,000 (U.S.$3,680 per capita).

Structure of gross domestic product and labour force

	1998 in value Bs '000,000	1998 % of total value	1997 labour force	1997 % of labour force
Agriculture	2,394,000	5.0	792,482	8.3
Petroleum and natural gas } Mining	5,846,000	12.1	93,846	1.0
Manufacturing	7,728,000	16.0	1,211,413	12.7
Construction	3,190,000	6.6	745,094	7.8
Public utilities	942,000	2.0	71,399	0.8
Transp. and commun.	4,773,000	9.9	551,947	5.8
Trade	8,490,000	17.6	2,061,940	21.7
Finance	7,577,000	15.7	460,837	4.8
Pub. admin., defense	2,857,000	5.9 }	2,482,055	26.1
Services	4,398,000	9.1 }		
Other	...	...	1,036,112[5]	10.9[5]
TOTAL	48,195,000	100.0[4]	9,507,125	100.0[4]

Population economically active (1997): total 9,507,125; activity rate 41.7% (participation rates: over age 15, 64.6%; female 35.9%; unemployed 10.6%).

Price index (1995 = 100)

	1994	1995	1996	1997	1998	1999	2000
Consumer price index	62.5	100.0	199.9	299.9	407.2	503.2	584.7

Household income and expenditure. Average household size (1990) 5.1; average annual income per household (1981) Bs 42,492 (U.S.$9,899); expenditure (1995): food 40.6%, housing 13.8%, transportation and communications 8.6%, clothing 5.3%, health 3.1%, education and recreation 2.9%.
Land use (1998): forest and other 75.3%; pasture 20.7%; agriculture 4.0%.

Foreign trade[6]

Balance of trade (current prices)

	1995	1996	1997	1998	1999	2000
Bs '000,000	+1,407.7	+5,996.8	+3,858.3	+1,642.2	+4,388.5	+11,694.7
% of total	27.2%	44.3%	23.1%	9.6%	21.7%	37.1%

Imports (1998)[7]: U.S.$7,794,000,000 (processed industrial supplies 28.0%, machinery 22.1%, transport equipment 22.1%, manufactured consumer goods 17.8%, construction materials 5.4%). *Major import sources:* U.S. 46.0%; Andean Pact countries 7.0%; Japan 5.0%; Germany 4.1%; Italy 3.9%.
Exports (1998): U.S.$17,534,000,000 (crude petroleum and petroleum products 69.8%, basic and precious metals 6.6%). *Major export destinations:* U.S. 48.5%; Andean Pact countries 11.1%; Canada 2.1%; United Kingdom 2.0%.

Transport and communications

Transport. Railroads (1996): length (1994) 627 km; passenger-km 149,905; metric ton-km cargo 54,474,000. Roads (1997): total length 95,664 km (paved 36%). Vehicles (1997): passenger cars 1,505,000; trucks and buses 542,000. Merchant marine (1992): vessels (over 100 gross tons) 271; total deadweight tonnage 1,355,419. Air transport (1996): passenger-km 5,800,000,000; metric ton-km cargo 639,000,000; airports (1997) with scheduled flights 20.

Communications

Medium	date	unit	number	units per 1,000 persons
Daily newspapers	1996	circulation	4,600,000	206
Radio	1997	receivers	10,750,000	472
Television	1998	receivers	4,300,000	185
Telephones	1999	main lines	2,586,000	109
Cellular telephones	1999	subscribers	3,400,000	143
Personal computers	1999	units	1,000,000	42
Internet	1999	users	525,000	22

Education and health

Educational attainment (1993). Percentage of population age 25 and over having: no formal schooling 8.0%; primary education or less 43.7%; some secondary and secondary 38.3%; postsecondary 10.0%. *Literacy* (1995 est.): total population age 15 and over literate 91.1%; males 91.8%; females 90.3%.

Education (1996–97)

	schools	teachers	students	student/ teacher ratio
Primary (age 7–12)	14,601	202,195	4,262,221	21.1
Secondary (age 13–17)[8]	2,177	39,601	377,984	9.5
Higher	99[9]	43,833[9]	717,192	12.6[10]

Health (1997): physicians 28,341 (1 per 804 persons); hospital beds 38,924 (1 per 585 persons); infant mortality rate (2000) 26.2.
Food (1999): daily per capita caloric intake 2,229 (vegetable products 84%, animal products 16%); (1997) 90% of FAO recommended minimum.

Military

Total active duty personnel (2000): 79,000 (army 72.1%, navy 19.0%, air force 8.9%). *Military expenditure as percentage of GNP* (1997): 2.2% (world 2.6%); per capita expenditure U.S.$82.

[1]Based on the new constitution, which was approved by referendum on Dec. 15, 1999. [2]Distrito Federal includes Vargas. [3]A new federal entity (the Caribbean Federal Territory) was under consideration in late 2001. [4]Detail does not add to total given because of rounding. [5]Mostly unemployed. [6]Imports and exports are f.o.b. in balance of trade. [7]Data is for first six months of 1998. [8]Includes vocational and teacher training. [9]1990–91. [10]1991–92.

Internet resources for further information:

- **Central Office of Statistics and Informatics http://www.ocei.gov.ve**
- **Embassy of the Republic of Venezuela http://www.embassy.org/embassies/ve.html**

Vietnam

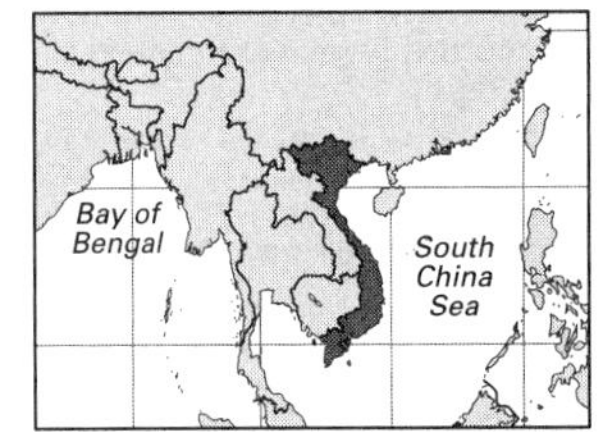

Official name: Cong Hoa Xa Hoi Chu Nghia Viet Nam (Socialist Republic of Vietnam).
Form of government: socialist republic with one legislative house (National Assembly [450]).
Head of state: President.
Head of government: Prime Minister.
Capital: Hanoi.
Official language: Vietnamese.
Official religion: none.
Monetary unit: 1 dong (D) = 10 hao = 100 xu; valuation (Sept. 28, 2001) 1 U.S.$ = D 15,003; 1 £ = D 22,050.

Area and population

		area		population
Economic Regions[1]	**Principal cities**	sq mi	sq km	1993 estimate
Central Highlands	Da Lat	21,455	55,569	2,903,500
North Central Coast	Hue	19,763	51,187	9,516,900
Northeastern South Region	Ho Chi Minh City	9,066	23,481	8,692,900
North Mountains and Midlands	Thai Nguyen	39,749	102,949	12,109,300
Mekong River Delta	Long Xuyen	15,280	39,575	15,531,600
Red River Delta	Hanoi	4,810	12,457	13,808,800
South Central Coast	Da Nang	17,692	45,823	7,374,700
TOTAL		127,816[2]	331,041	70,982,500[3]

Demography

Population (2001): 79,939,000.
Density (2001): persons per sq mi 625.4, persons per sq km 241.5.
Urban-rural (1999): urban 23.5%; rural 76.5%.
Sex distribution (1999): male 49.15%; female 50.85%.
Age breakdown (2001): under 15, 32.1%; 15–29, 29.4%; 30–44, 21.1%; 45–59, 9.7%; 60–74, 5.8%; 75 and over, 1.9%.
Population projection: (2010) 90,192,000; (2020) 100,985,000.
Doubling time: 46 years.
Ethnic composition (1989): Vietnamese 86.8%; Tho (Tay) 1.9%; Tai 1.6%; Chinese (Hoa) 1.4%; Khmer 1.4%; Muong 1.4%; Nung 1.1%; other 4.4%.
Religious affiliation (1995): Buddhist 66.7%; Christian 8.7%, of which Roman Catholic 7.7%, Protestant 1.0%; Cao Dai (a New-Religionist group) 3.5%; Hoa Hao (a New-Religionist group) 2.1%; other 19.0%.
Major cities (1992): Ho Chi Minh City 4,549,000[4]; Hanoi 2,154,900[5]; Haiphong 783,133; Da Nang 382,674; Buon Ma Thuot 282,095; Nha Trang 221,331; Hue 219,149; Can Tho 215,587.

Vital statistics

Birth rate per 1,000 population (2000): 21.6 (world avg. 22.5).
Death rate per 1,000 population (2000): 6.3 (world avg. 9.0).
Natural increase rate per 1,000 population (2000): 15.3 (world avg. 13.5).
Total fertility rate (avg. births per childbearing woman; 2000): 2.5.
Life expectancy at birth (2000): male 66.8 years; female 71.9 years.

National economy

Budget (1998). Revenue: D 73,000,000,000,000 (tax revenue 80.8%, of which taxes on trade 20.4%, corporate income taxes 17.9%, turnover taxes 16.2%; nontax revenues 16.3%; grants 2.9%). Expenditures: D 80,200,000,000,000 (current expenditures 67.6%, of which social services 30.4%; capital expenditures 25.6%; other 6.8%).
Public debt (external, outstanding; 1999): U.S.$20,529,000,000.
Gross national product (1999): U.S.$28,733,000,000 (U.S.$370 per capita).

Structure of gross domestic product and labour force

	1998		1997	
	in value D '000,000,000[6]	% of total value	labour force	% of labour force
Agriculture, forestry, fishing	57,422	23.5	25,400,000	68.5
Public utilities	5,099	2.1	200,000	0.5
Mining	15,063	6.2	200,000	0.5
Manufacturing	42,613	17.4	3,300,000	8.9
Construction	20,434	8.3	1,000,000	2.7
Transp. and commun.	9,548	3.9	900,000	2.4
Trade and restaurants	49,210	20.1	3,200,000	8.6
Finance, insurance	16,287	6.7	700,000	1.9
Pub. admin., defense, services, other	29,065	11.9	2,200,000	5.9
TOTAL	244,741	100.0[2]	37,000,000[2]	100.0[2]

Tourism (1997): receipts from visitors U.S.$88,000,000; expenditures by nationals abroad, n.a.
Production (metric tons except as noted). Agriculture, forestry, fishing (2000): rice 32,554,000, sugarcane 15,145,000, cassava 2,036,000, corn (maize) 1,929,000, sweet potatoes 1,658,000, bananas 1,269,000, coconuts 940,000, coffee 802,000, oranges 427,000, groundnuts (peanuts) 353,000, natural rubber 291,000, pineapples 291,000, pimento 75,000, tea 69,700; livestock (number of live animals) 54,500,000 ducks, 20,194,000 pigs, 4,137,000 cattle, 2,897,000 buffalo; roundwood (1999) 36,730,000 cu m, of which fuelwood 32,174,000 cu m, industrial roundwood 4,556,000 cu m; fish catch (1997) 1,546,000, of which marine fish 668,000. Mining and quarrying (1998): phosphate rock (gross weight) 860,000; tin (metal content) 5,000. Manufacturing (gross value of production in D '000,000,000; 1998[6]): food and beverages 36.5; cement, bricks, pottery, and glass 13.7; textiles 8.4; chemicals and chemical products 8.1; footwear and leather tanning 7.1; electric and electronic products 6.2. Energy production (consumption): electricity (kW-hr; 1998) 21,847,000,000 ([1996] 16,320,000,000); coal (metric tons; 1998) 10,800,000 ([1996] 5,551,000); crude petroleum (barrels; 1998) 83,000,000 ([1996] 283,300); petroleum products (metric tons; 1996) 38,000 (5,483,000); natural gas (cu m; 1996): 7,700,000 (7,700,000).
Population economically active (1989): total 30,521,019; activity rate 47.4% (participation rates: ages 15–64, 79.9%; female 51.7%; unemployed [1997] 10.3%).

Price and earnings indexes (1995 = 100)

	1995	1996	1997	1998	1999	2000	2001
Consumer price index	100.0	105.7	109.1	117.0	121.8	119.7	118.9[7]
Earnings index	...	...	...	...	...	...	...

Household income and expenditure. Average household size (1989) 4.8; income per household (1990)[8] D 577,008 (U.S.$93); sources of income: n.a.; expenditure (1990): food 62.4%, clothing 5.0%, household goods 4.6%, education 2.9%, housing 2.5%.
Land use (1994): forested 29.6%; meadows and pastures 1.0%; agricultural and under permanent cultivation 21.5%; other 47.9%.

Foreign trade[9]

Balance of trade (current prices)

	1994	1995	1996	1997	1998	1999[10]
U.S.$'000,000	–1,772	–3,183	–4,307	–2,447	–2,162	–83
% of total	17.9%	23.4%	22.7%	11.8%	10.3%	0.4%

Imports (1998): U.S.$11,527,000,000 (machinery equipment [including aircraft] 17.8%; petroleum products 7.2%; textiles, clothing, and leather 7.1%; iron and steel 4.5%; unspecified 50.1%). *Major import sources:* Singapore 13.4%; South Korea 12.1%; Japan 11.8%; Taiwan 10.8%; China 9.1%.
Exports (1998): U.S.$9,365,000,000 (garments 14.4%; crude petroleum 13.2%; rice 10.9%; footwear 10.7%; fish, crustaceans, and mollusks 8.7%; coffee 6.3%). *Major export destinations:* Japan 18.0%; Germany 9.2%; U.S. 6.2%; France 5.8%; Australia 5.4%.

Transport and communications

Transport. Railroads (1999): route length 1,952 mi, 3,142 km; passenger-mi 1,694,000,000, passenger-km 2,727,000,000; short ton-mile cargo 958,000,000, metric ton-km cargo 1,398,000,000. Roads (1996): total length 58,000 mi, 93,300 km (paved 25%). Vehicles (1994): passenger cars, trucks, and buses 200,000. Air transport (1999)[11]: passenger-mi 2,380,000,000, passenger-km 3,831,000,000; short ton-mile cargo 67,436,000, metric ton-km cargo 98,455,000; airports (1997) with scheduled flights 12.

Communications

Medium	date	unit	number	units per 1,000 persons
Daily newspapers	1996	circulation	300,000	4.1
Radio	1997	receivers	8,200,000	109
Television	1999	receivers	14,500,000	187
Telephones	2000	main lines	2,800,000	36
Cellular telephones	1999	subscribers	328,671	4.2
Personal computers	1999	units	700,000	9.0
Internet	1999	users	100,000	1.3

Education and health

Educational attainment (1989). Percentage of population age 25 and over having: no formal education (illiterate) 16.6%; incomplete and complete primary 69.8%; incomplete and complete secondary 10.6%; higher 2.6%; unknown 0.4%. *Literacy* (2000): percentage of population age 15 and over literate 93.3%; males 95.7%; females 91.0%.

Education (1997–98)

	schools	teachers	students	student/ teacher ratio
Primary (age 7–12)	...	324,431	10,431,337	32.2
Secondary (age 13–18)	...	226,491	6,642,350	29.3
Vocational[12]	...	9,336	172,400	18.5
Higher	109[13]	23,522[12]	509,300[12]	21.7[12]

Health (1999): physicians 37,100 (1 per 2,092 persons); hospital beds (1997) 197,900 (1 per 380 persons); infant mortality rate per 1,000 live births (2000) 31.1.
Food (1999): daily per capita caloric intake 2,564 (vegetable products 89%, animal products 11%); 119% of FAO recommended minimum requirement.

Military

Total active duty personnel (2000): 484,000 (army 85.1%, navy 8.7%, air force 6.2%). *Military expenditure as percentage of GNP* (1997): 2.8% (world 2.6%); per capita expenditure U.S.$45.

[1]Seven economic regions are divided into 57 provinces and 4 municipalities as of the administrative reorganization of 1997. [2]Detail does not add to total given because of rounding. [3]Total includes 1,044,800 persons not distributed in geographic and region estimates. [4]1999. [5]1993. [6]Estimated figures at prices of 1994. [7]April. [8]Wage workers and government officials only. [9]Imports c.i.f.; exports f.o.b. [10]Estimated figures. [11]Vietnam Airlines only. [12]1996–97. [13]1995–96.

Internet resources for further information:

- **Ministry of Foreign Affairs**
  http://www.mofa.gov.vn

Virgin Islands (U.S.)

Official name: Virgin Islands of the United States.
Political status: organized unincorporated territory of the United States with one legislative house (Senate [15]).
Chief of state: President of the United States.
Head of government: Governor.
Capital: Charlotte Amalie.
Official language: English.
Official religion: none.
Monetary unit: 1 U.S. dollar (U.S.$) = 100 cents; valuation (Sept. 28, 2001) 1 £ = U.S.$1.47.

Area and population

		area		population
Islands[1]	**Principal Towns**	sq mi	sq km	2000 census
St. Croix	Christiansted	84	218	53,234
St. John	—	20	52	4,197
St. Thomas	Charlotte Amalie	32	83	51,181
TOTAL		136	353	108,612[2]

Demography

Population (2001): 122,000[3].
Density (2001): persons per sq mi 898.6, persons per sq km 346.2.
Urban-rural (1998): urban 45.7%; rural 54.3%.
Sex distribution (2000): male 46.91%; female 53.09%.
Age breakdown (2000): under 15, 27.8%; 15–29, 22.4%; 30–44, 17.9%; 45–59, 19.1%; 60–74, 9.7%; 75 and over, 3.1%.
Population projection[3]: (2010) 133,000; (2020) 144,000.
Doubling time: 65 years.
Ethnic composition (1995): black 76.7%, of which Hispanic 6.7%; white 10.4%, of which Hispanic 1.5%; other 12.9%, of which Hispanic 9.1%.
Religious affiliation (1993): Baptist 42.0%; Roman Catholic 34.0%; Episcopalian 17.0%; other 7.0%.
Major towns (2000): Charlotte Amalie 11,004; Christiansted 2,637; Frederiksted 732.

Vital statistics

Birth rate per 1,000 population (2000): 16.0 (world avg. 22.5); (1998) legitimate 30.2%[4]; illegitimate 69.8%.
Death rate per 1,000 population (2000): 5.4 (world avg. 9.0).
Natural increase rate per 1,000 population (2000): 10.6 (world avg. 13.5).
Total fertility rate (avg. births per childbearing woman; 2000): 2.3.
Marriage rate per 1,000 population (1993): 35.1.
Divorce rate per 1,000 population (1993): 4.5.
Life expectancy at birth (2000): male 74.2 years; female 82.5 years.
Major causes of death per 100,000 population (1997): diseases of the heart 111.3; malignant neoplasms (cancers) 103.9; cerebrovascular diseases 44.5; diabetes mellitus 32.3; accidents 31.4; homicide 27.1.

National economy

Budget. Revenue (1998): U.S.$459,485,000 (personal income tax 45.7%, gross receipts tax 18.5%, property tax 9.9%, corporate income tax 5.4%, excise tax 3.7%). Expenditures (1998): U.S.$398,394,000 (education 30.4%, health 17.8%, executive branch 7.8%, public safety 7.6%, public works 6.3%, College of the Virgin Islands 5.7%).
Production. Agriculture, forestry, fishing (value of sales in U.S.$'000; 1998): milk 1,263, livestock and livestock products 655 (of which cattle and calves 439, hogs and pigs 46), ornamental plants and other nursery products 364, vegetables 329 (notably tomatoes and cucumbers), fruits and nuts 185 (notably mangoes, bananas, and avocados), poultry 21; livestock (number of live animals) 3,636 cattle, 3,074 sheep, 2,944 goats, 1,436 hogs and pigs, 3,538 chickens; roundwood, n.a.; fish catch (1998) 910 metric tons. Mining and quarrying: sand and crushed stone for local use. Manufacturing (U.S.$'000[5]; 1997): food and food products 31,949; stone, clay, and glass products 21,897; print and publishing 21,127; transportation equipment 4,920; fabricated metal products 3,352. Construction: n.a. Energy production (consumption): electricity (kW-hr; 1996) 1,075,000,000 (1,075,000,000); coal (metric tons; 1996) none (250,000); crude petroleum (barrels; 1996) none (119,528,000); petroleum products (metric tons; 1996) 15,096,000 (2,284,000); natural gas, none (none).
Tourism (1999): receipts from visitors U.S.$940,000,000; number of hotel rooms (1997) 4,406; occupancy percentage 61.3%[6]; expenditures by nationals abroad, n.a.
Household income and expenditure. Average household size (1990) 3.1; average annual income per household (1989) U.S.$29,953; sources of income (1984): wages and salaries 65.7%, transfer payments 13.0%, interest, dividends, and rent 12.7%, self-employment 2.6%; expenditure n.a.
Population economically active (1995)[7]: total 47,810; activity rate of total population 46.6%[8] (participation rates: ages 16–64, 72.5%[8]; female 47.8%[8]; unemployed 5.3%).

Price and earnings indexes (1995 = 100)

	1994	1995	1996	1997	1998	1999	2000
Consumer price index[9]	97.3	100.0	102.9	105.3	107.0	109.3	113.0
Annual earnings index	...	...	...	...	...	...	...

Gross national product (at current market prices; 1997): U.S.$2,666,000,000 (U.S.$18,287 per capita).

Structure of gross domestic product and labour force

	1989		1995	
	in value U.S.$'000,000	% of total value	labour force[10]	% of labour force
Agriculture, fishing	...	...	3,110	6.5
Mining	...	...	[11]	[11]
Manufacturing	...	...	2,370[12]	5.0[12]
Construction	...	...	1,140[11]	2.4[11]
Public utilities	...	...	[12]	[12]
Transp. and commun.	...	...	2,560	5.4
Trade, hotels, restaurants	...	...	9,740	20.4
Finance, insurance, real estate	...	...	1,830	3.8
Pub. admin., defense	...	...	13,770	28.8
Services	...	...	10,490	21.9
Other	...	...	2,800[13]	5.8[13]
TOTAL	1,344[14]	100.0	47,810	100.0

Public debt (1999): U.S.$1,200,000,000.
Land use (1994): forested 5.9%; meadows and pastures 26.5%; agricultural and under permanent cultivation 20.6%; other 47.0%.

Foreign trade

Balance of trade (current prices)

	1982	1983	1984	1985	1986	1987
U.S.$'000,000	–300.2	–1,019.5	–786.4	–383.5	–523.8	–1,175
% of total	2.9%	12.2%	9.0%	5.4%	11.0%	21.1%

Imports (1995): U.S.$3,200,300,000[15]. *Major import sources:* United States 32.6%; other countries 67.4%.
Exports (1995): U.S.$3,026,300,000[16]. *Major export destinations:* United States 92.7%; other countries 7.3%.

Transport and communications

Transport. Railroads: none. Roads (1996): total length 532 mi, 856 km (paved, n.a.). Vehicles (1993): passenger cars 51,000; trucks and buses 13,300. Merchant marine (1992): vessels (100 gross tons and over) 1. Shipping (1988): cruise ship arrivals 1,228; passenger arrivals 1,062,010. Air transport (1989)[17]: passenger arrivals and departures 1,897,000; cargo loaded and unloaded 4,600 metric tons; airports (1999) with scheduled flights 2.

Communications

Medium	date	unit	number	units per 1,000 persons
Daily newspapers	1996	circulation	4[illegible],000	3[illegible]1
Radio	1996	receivers	107,000	927
Television	1996	receivers	67,000	580
Telephones	1999	main lines	67,229	562
Cellular telephones	1998	subscribers	25,000	211

Education and health

Educational attainment (1997). Percentage of population age 25 and over having: incomplete primary education 4.4%; completed lower secondary 18.5%; incomplete upper secondary 27.3%; completed upper secondary 24.0%; incomplete undergraduate 14.0%; completed undergraduate 11.8%. *Literacy:* n.a.

Education (1997–98)[18]

	schools	teachers	students	student/ teacher ratio
Primary (age 5–12)	62[19]	777	11,926	15.3
Secondary (age 12–18)	...	782	9,982	12.8
Higher	1	266[19]	3,103	11.0[19]

Health (1989): physicians 130 (1 per 780 persons); hospital beds 252 (1 per 402 persons); infant mortality rate per 1,000 live births (2000) 9.6.
Food: daily per capita caloric intake, n.a.

Military

Total active duty personnel: no domestic military force is maintained; the United States is responsible for defense and external security.

[1]May be administered by officials assigned by the governor. [2]De jure figure. [3]De facto estimate not adjusted for 2000 census. [4]Percentage of legitimate births may be an underestimation due to the common practice of consensual marriage. [5]Figures are for value of sales. [6]1993. [7]Excludes armed forces. [8]1990. [9]U.S. mainland. [10]Employed labour force as of September 30; excludes armed forces. [11]Construction includes mining. [12]Manufacturing includes public utilities. [13]Includes 2,740 unemployed. [14]Tourism accounts for more than 70% of gross domestic product. [15]Breakdown of 1992 imports from U.S. only, totaling U.S.$1,768,000,000: crude petroleum 60.7%, food and beverages 4.5%, iron and steel (all forms) 4.5%, fuel oils 3.2%. [16]Breakdown of 1999 exports to U.S. only, totaling U.S.$2,971,899,000: petroleum products 90.4%, chemicals and chemical products 2.4%, antibiotics 0.4%, alcoholic beverages 0.3%. [17]St. Croix and St. Thomas airports. [18]Public schools only. [19]1992–93.

Internet resources for further information:
- **U.S. Department of the Interior: Pacific Web http://www.pacificweb.org**
- **U.S. Census Bureau: Economic Census of Outlying Areas http://www.census.gov/csd/oat**

Yemen

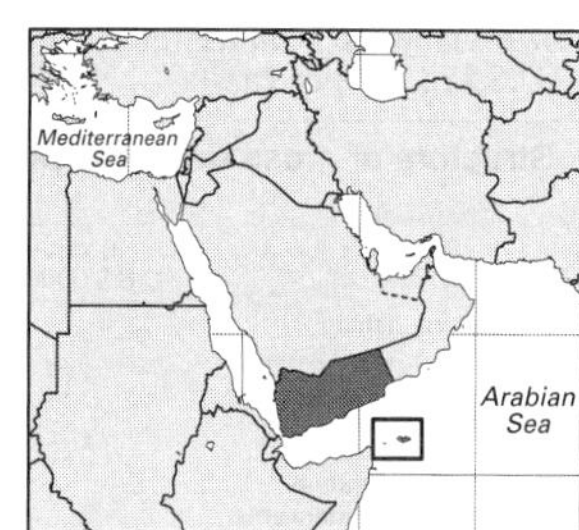

Official name: Al-Jumhūrīyah al-Yamanīyah (Republic of Yemen).
Form of government: multiparty republic with two legislative houses (Consultative Council [111[1]]; House of Representatives [301]).
Head of state: President.
Head of government: Prime Minister.
Capital: Ṣanʿāʾ.
Official language: Arabic.
Official religion: Islam.
Monetary unit: 1 Yemeni Rial (YRls) = 100 fils; valuation (Sept. 28, 2001): 1 U.S.$ = YRls 169.33; 1 £ = YRls 248.86.

Area and population

Governorates	Capitals	area sq mi	area sq km	population 1994 census
Northern Yemen				
Al-Bayḍāʾ	Al-Bayḍāʾ	4,310	11,170	509,265
Dhamār	Dhamār	3,430	8,870	1,050,346
Ḥajjah	Ḥajjah	3,700	9,590	1,262,590
Al-Ḥudaydah	Al-Ḥudaydah	5,240	13,580	1,749,944
Ibb	Ibb	2,480	6,430	1,959,313
Al-Jawf	Al-Jawf	...	...	157,096
Al-Maḥwīt	Al-Maḥwīt	830	2,160	403,465
Maʾrib	Maʾrib	15,400	39,890	167,388
Ṣaʿdah	Ṣaʿdah	4,950	12,810	486,059
Ṣanʿāʾ	Ṣanʿāʾ	7,840	20,310	1,910,286
Taʿizz	Taʿizz	4,020	10,420	2,205,947
Southern Yemen				
Abyān	Zinjibār	8,297	21,489	414,543
ʿAdan	Aden	2,695	6,980	562,162
Ḥaḍramawt	Al-Mukallā	59,991	155,376	870,025
Laḥij	Laḥij	4,928	12,766	634,652
Al-Mahrah	Al-Ghayḍah	25,618	66,350	112,512
Shabwah	ʿAtāq	28,536	73,908	377,080
TOTAL		182,278[2, 3]	472,099[2]	14,832,673

Demography

Population (2001): 18,078,000.
Density (2000)[4]: persons per sq mi 84.4, persons per sq km 32.6.
Urban-rural (1998): urban 36.1%; rural 63.9%.
Sex distribution (2000): male 50.98%; female 49.02%.
Age breakdown (2000): under 15, 47.5%; 15–29, 27.8%; 30–44, 13.2%; 45–59, 7.1%; 60–74, 3.3%; 75 and over, 1.1%.
Population projection: (2010) 24,637,000; (2020) 34,195,000.
Doubling time: 21 years.
Ethnic composition (2000): Arab 92.8%; Somali 3.7%; black 1.1%; Indo-Pakistani 1.0%; other 1.4%.
Religious affiliation (1995): Muslim 99.9%, of which Sunnī *c.* 60%, Shīʿī *c.* 40%; other 0.1%.
Major cities (1994): Ṣanʿāʾ 954,400; Aden 398,300; Taʿizz 317,600; Al-Ḥudaydah 298,500; Al-Mukallā 122,400.

Vital statistics

Birth rate per 1,000 population (2000): 43.4 (world avg. 22.5).
Death rate per 1,000 population (2000): 9.9 (world avg. 9.0).
Natural increase rate per 1,000 population (2000): 33.5 (world avg. 13.5).
Total fertility rate (avg. births per childbearing woman; 2000): 7.1.
Life expectancy at birth (2000): male 58.1 years; female 61.6 years.
Major causes of death per 100,000 population: n.a.; however, infant, child, and maternal mortality were very high in the late 1990s.

National economy

Budget (2000). Revenue: YRls 388,950,000,000 (1999; tax revenue 90.1%, of which oil revenue 64.1%, taxes on income and profits 9.4%, custom duties 7.8%; nontax revenue 9.9%). Expenditures: YRls 422,250,000,000 (1999; wages and salaries 23.0%; defense 18.1%; economic development 17.5%; interest on debt 13.8%; subsidies 7.7%).
Population economically active (1999): total 4,118,000; activity rate of total population 24.3% (participation rates [1994]: age 15 and over, 45.8%; female 18.2%; unemployed [1995] 30%).

Price index (1995 = 100)

	1993	1994	1995	1996	1997	1998	1999
Consumer price index	44.0	64.0	100.0	130.0	137.0	148.0	167.9

Production (metric tons except as noted). Agriculture, forestry, fishing (2000): sorghum 401,212, tomatoes 244,720, potatoes 213,445, grapes 162,315, oranges 175,095, wheat 137,166, bananas 94,114, onions 70,838, millet 67,234, papayas 64,195; livestock (number of live animals) 4,760,389 sheep, 4,214,170 goats, 1,282,975 cattle, 500,000 asses, 185,000 camels, 28,000,000 chickens; roundwood (1998) 324,000 cu m; fish catch (1999) 123,252. Mining and quarrying (1999): gypsum 103,000; salt 149,000. Manufacturing (value of production in YRls '000,000; 1996): food, beverages, and tobacco 43,927; chemicals and chemical products 42,369; nonmetallic mineral products 8,571; paper products 8,562; basic metal industries 3,040; clothing, textiles, and leather 1,693; wood products 392. Construction: n.a. Energy production (consumption): electricity (kW-hr; 1999) 2,633,000,000 (2,633,000,000); coal, none (n.a.); crude petroleum (barrels; 2000) 160,600,000 ([1996] 40,559,000); petroleum products (metric tons; 1996) 3,494,000 (3,304,000); natural gas (cu m; 2000) none (none).
Gross national product (1999): U.S.$6,386,000,000 (U.S.$360 per capita).

Structure of gross domestic product and labour force

	1999 in value Y Rls '000,000[5]	% of total value[5]	labour force	% of labour force
Agriculture	186,054	17.5	1,996,000	48.5
Mining	296,447	27.9	13,000	0.3
Manufacturing	83,829	7.9	206,000	5.0
Public utilities	8,401	0.8	382,000	9.3
Construction	41,867	3.9	21,000	0.5
Transp. and commun.	127,814	12.0	210,000	5.1
Trade	106,790	10.0	440,000	10.7
Finance, real estate	62,429	5.9	49,000	1.2
Pub. admin., defense	121,982	11.5	389,000	9.4
Services	19,009	1.8	412,000	10.0
Other	8,935[6]	0.8[6]	...	...
TOTAL	1,063,557	100.0	4,118,000	100.0

Household income and expenditure. Average household size (1998) 7.1; income per household YRls 29,035 (U.S.$217).
Tourism (2000): receipts U.S.$64,000,000; expenditures U.S.$83,000,000.
Public debt (external, outstanding; 1999): U.S.$3,729,000,000.
Land use (1994): forest 3.8%; pasture 30.4%; agriculture 2.9%; other 62.9%.

Foreign trade[7]

Balance of trade

	1994	1995	1996	1997	1998	1999
U.S.$'000,000	–1,154.5	+242.8	+634.6	+490.2	–700.5	+900.0
% of total	31.2%	7.3%	13.5%	10.9%	18.9%	22.7%

Imports (1999): U.S.$1,535,900,000 (food and live animals 36.2%, of which cereals and related products 17.1%; machinery 15.3%; chemicals and chemical products 8.5%; mineral fuels 7.4%). *Major import sources:* U.A.E. 11.7%; Saudi Arabia 10.2%; U.S. 5.5%; Australia 4.8%; U.K. 4.7%; Kuwait 4.6%.
Exports (1999): U.S.$2,435,800,000 (crude petroleum 87.5%; petroleum products 8.0%; coffee 0.5%; fish 0.5%). *Major export destinations:* China 28.8%; Thailand 25.5%; South Korea 14.5%; Singapore 8.6%.

Transport and communications

Transport. Railroads: none. Roads (1996): total length 64,725 km (paved 8.1%). Vehicles (1996): passenger cars 240,567; trucks and buses 291,149. Air transport (2000): passenger-km 1,574,000,000; metric ton-km cargo 32,000,000; airports (1998) with scheduled flights 12.

Communications

Medium	date	unit	number	units per 1,000 persons
Daily newspapers	1996	circulation	230,000	15
Radio	1997	receivers	1,050,000	64
Television	1999	receivers	5,000,000	286
Telephones	1999	main lines	291,359	16.7
Cellular telephones	1999	subscribers	27,677	1.6
Internet	1999	users	10,000	0.6

Education and health

Educational attainment (1998). Percentage of population age 10 and over having: no formal schooling 49.5%; reading and writing ability 32.2%; primary education 11.0%; secondary education 4.6%; higher 2.7%. *Literacy* (1998): percentage of total population age 10 and over literate 50.5%; males literate 71.8%; females literate 29.1%.

Education (1996–97)

	schools	teachers	students	student/ teacher ratio
Primary (age 7–12)	11,013[8]	90,478	2,699,788	29.8
Secondary (age 13–18)[9]	1,224[10]	11,130[10]	354,288	...
Voc., teacher tr.[9, 10]	125	369	15,074	40.9
Higher	2	1,991	65,675	...

Health (1998): physicians 3,883 (1 per 4,211 persons); hospital beds 9,143 (1 per 1,788 persons); infant mortality rate per 1,000 live births (2000) 70.3.
Food (1999): daily per capita caloric intake 2,002 (vegetable products 94%, animal products 6%); 83% of FAO recommended minimum requirement.

Military

Total active duty personnel (2000): 66,300 (army 92.0%, navy 2.7%, air force 5.3%). *Military expenditure as percentage of GNP* (1997): 8.1% (world 2.6%); per capita expenditure U.S.$26.

[1]All seats are nonelected. [2]An agreement to resolve the long-undemarcated northeastern boundary with Saudi Arabia (which increased Yemen's total area to roughly 214,300 sq mi [555,000 sq km]) was signed in June 2000. [3]Detail does not add to total given because of rounding. [4]Based on the higher total area estimate of 214,300 sq mi (555,000 sq km). [5]In purchasers' value at current prices. [6]Includes import duties of 31.0 million Yemeni Rials less imputed bank service charges. [7]Imports are c.i.f. [8]1993–94. [9]Public schools only, which comprise the vast majority of schools in Yemen. [10]1994–95.

Internet resources for further information:
- **The Yemen Times http://www.yementimes.com**
- **Yemen Info Homepage http://www.yemeninfo.gov.ye**

Yugoslavia

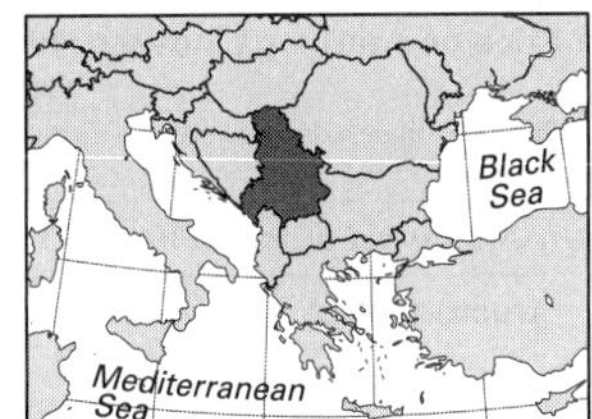

Official name: Savezna Republika Jugoslavija (Federal Republic of Yugoslavia).
Form of government: federal multiparty republic with two legislative houses (Chamber of Republics [40]; Chamber of Citizens [138]).
Chief of state: Federal President.
Head of government: Prime Minister.
Capital: Belgrade.
Official language: Serbian (Serbo-Croatian).
Official religion[1]: none.
Monetary unit: 1 Yugoslav new dinar (second) = 100 paras; valuation (Sept. 28, 2001) 1 U.S.$ = 67.30 Yugoslav new dinars; 1 £ = 98.91 Yugoslav new dinars[2].

Area and population

		area		population
Republics	**Capitals**	sq mi	sq km	1997 estimate
Montenegro (Crna Gora)	Podgorica	5,333	13,812	631,164
Serbia (Srbija)	Belgrade	21,609	55,968	5,762,954
Autonomous province[3]				
Vojvodina	Novi Sad	8,304	21,506	1,954,432
Geographical region				
Kosovo (Kosova)[4, 5]	Priština	4,203	10,887	2,227,742
TOTAL		39,449	102,173	10,576,292

Demography

Population (2001): 10,677,000.
Density (2001): persons per sq mi 270.7, persons per sq km 104.5.
Urban-rural (1999): urban 52.0%; rural 48.0%.
Sex distribution (1999): male 49.53%; female 50.47%.
Age breakdown (1991): under 15, 22.8%; 15–29, 21.6%; 30–44, 21.7%; 45–59, 17.1%; 60–74, 12.2%; 75 and over, 3.5%; unknown, 1.1%.
Population projection: (2010) 10,667,000; (2020) 10,561,000.
Ethnic composition (1991): Serb 62.6%; Albanian 16.5%; Montenegrin 5.0%; multi-ethnic 3.4%; Hungarian 3.3%; Sandzak and Bosniak Muslim 3.2%; Romany (Gypsy) 1.4%; Croat 1.1%; other 3.5%.
Religious affiliation (1995): Serbian Orthodox 62.6%; Muslim 19.0%; Roman Catholic 5.8%; other, mostly nonreligious 12.6%.
Major cities (1999): Belgrade 1,168,454; Novi Sad 179,626; Niš 175,391; Kragujevac 147,305; Podgorica 117,875.

Vital statistics

Birth rate per 1,000 population (1997): 12.4 (world avg. 22.5).
Death rate per 1,000 population (1997): 10.6 (world avg. 9.0).
Natural increase rate per 1,000 population (1997): 1.8 (world avg. 13.5).
Total fertility rate (avg. births per childbearing woman; 1997): 1.7.
Marriage rate per 1,000 population (1997): 5.3.
Life expectancy at birth (1995): male 69.9 years; female 74.7 years.
Major causes of death per 100,000 population (1997): diseases of the circulatory system 585.0; malignant neoplasms (cancers) 169.0; accidents, violence, and poisoning 45.0; diseases of the respiratory system 39.0.

National economy

Budget (1998). Revenue: 44,200,696,000 Yugoslav new dinars (turnover tax 30.3%, social security tax 22.1%, income tax 20.6%). Expenditure: 44,200,-696,000 Yugoslav new dinars (government 20.8%, health 20.0%, education 12.2%, other 47.0%).
Public debt (external, outstanding; 1999): U.S.$7,416,000,000.
Production (metric tons except as noted). Agriculture, forestry, fishing (2000): corn (maize) 2,944,302, wheat 1,927,273, sugar beets 1,070,033, potatoes 690,446, grapes 362,628, plums 362,121, cabbages 285,317, watermelons 244,407; livestock (number of live animals) 4,087,000 pigs, 1,917,000 sheep, 1,452,000 cattle, 21,118,000 poultry; roundwood 1,140,000 cu m; fish catch 9,940. Mining and quarrying (1998): copper ore 19,939,000; lead-zinc ore 1,249,000; magnesite 81,000; aluminum and ingots 61,000; salt 19,305; asbestos ore 19,000; refined silver 34,000 kg. Manufacturing (1998): wheat flour 830,000; crude steel 949,000; pig iron 826,000; sulfuric acid 211,000; nitric acid 185,000; electrolytic copper 94,000; refined lead 24,000; welded pipes 43,000; rolled copper 27,055; medicines 22,871. Construction (residential units constructed; 1998): 14,768. Energy production (consumption): electricity (kW-hr; 1999) 34,456,000,000 (34,456,000,000); coal (metric tons; 1999) 40,619,000 (40,619,000); crude petroleum (barrels; 1999) 5,229,000 (5,229,000); petroleum products (metric tons; 1998) 763,000 (1,383,000[6]); natural gas (cu m; 1998) 731,000,000 (2,935,400,000[6]).
Land use (1994): forested 17.3%; meadows and pastures 20.7%; agricultural and under permanent cultivation 40.0%; other 22.0%.
Population economically active (1998): total 4,508,900; activity rate 42.6% (1998; participation rates: over age 15, 58.3%; female [1995] 43.7%; [1999] unemployed 19.8%).

Price and earnings indexes (1997 = 100)

	1997	1998	1999	2000
Consumer price index	100.0	129.9	188.2	348.0
Annual earnings index	...	...	...	...

Household income and expenditure. Average household size (1999) 3.2; income per household (1998) 34,582 Yugoslav new dinars (U.S.$3,400); sources of income (1998): wages and salaries 50.3%, pensions 14.8%, self-employment 9.2%, other 25.7%; expenditure (1998): food 52.8%, fuel and light 10.4%, beverages and tobacco 7.3%, clothing and footwear 6.7%, health 5.0%, transportation and communications 4.9%, education 2.1%, housing 1.1%, other 9.1%.
Gross domestic product (1999): U.S.$18,491,000,000 (U.S.$1,742 per capita).

Structure of gross material product and labour force

	1997		1998	
	in value '000,000 Yugoslav new dinars	% of total value	labour force	% of labour force
Agriculture	19,679.5	21.8	102,700	2.3
Mining; Manufacturing	30,790.3	34.1	835,800	18.5
Construction	5,809.4	6.4	126,900	2.8
Public utilities	239.8	0.3	55,000	1.2
Transp. and commun.	9,671.4	10.7	142,800	3.2
Trade	15,085.4	16.7	293,800	6.5
Finance	...	...	...	...
Pub. admin., defense; Services	9,098.8	10.1	615,900	13.7
Other	—	—	2,336,000[7]	51.8[7]
TOTAL	90,374.6	100.0[8]	4,508,900	100.0

Tourism (2000): receipts from visitors U.S.$17,000,000; expenditures, n.a.

Foreign trade

Balance of trade (current prices)

	1995	1996	1997	1998	1999
Din '000,000	−2,193	−10,442	−12,225	−18,470	−19,829
% of total	29.5%	34.2%	28.5%	26.0%	37.8%

Imports (1998): Din 44,805,000,000 (manufactured goods 20.8%, machinery and transport equipment 18.4%, chemicals 16.9%, mineral fuels and lubricants 15.0%, food and live animals 8.2%). *Major import sources:* Germany 12.5%; Italy 10.9%; Russia 10.7%; Macedonia 5.2%.
Exports (1998): Din 26,335,000,000 (manufactured goods 38.5%, machinery and transport equipment 14.2%, chemicals 13.4%, food 8.3%). *Major export destinations:* Italy 11.6%; Macedonia 10.8%; Germany 8.9%; Russia 8.6%; Switzerland 5.3%; Greece 4.0%; U.K. 3.6%; Hungary 2.9%.

Transport and communications

Transport. Railroads (1999): length 4,069 km; passenger-km 1,614,000,000; metric ton-km cargo 2,570,000,000. Roads (1998): total length 50,497 km (paved 60%). Vehicles (1994): passenger cars 1,400,000; trucks and buses 132,000. Merchant marine (1998): cargo vessels 22. Air transport (1998): passenger-mi 551,155,000, passenger-km 887,000,000; short ton-mi cargo 3,730,000,000, metric ton-km cargo 6,003,000,000; airports (1999) 5.

Communications

Medium	date	unit	number	units per 1,000 persons
Daily newspapers	1995	circulation	1,363,000	256
Radio	1997	receivers	1,384,000	131
Television	1999	receivers	2,900,000	272
Telephones	1999	main lines	2,281,000	214
Cellular telephones	1999	subscribers	605,697	57
Personal computers	1999	units	220,000	40
Internet	1999	users	80,000	7.5

Education and health

Educational attainment (1991). Percentage of population age 15 and over having: less than full primary education 33.5%; primary 25.0%; secondary 32.2%; postsecondary and higher 9.3%. *Literacy* (1991): total population age 10 and over literate 93.0%; males literate 97.2%; females literate 88.9%.

Education (1998–99)

	schools	teachers	students	student/ teacher ratio
Primary (age 7–14)	4,431	52,294	864,199	16.5
Secondary (age 15–18)	561	27,766	367,587	13.2
Higher	83	10,998	147,981	13.5

Health (1997): physicians 22,498 (1 per 471 persons); hospital beds 58,576 (1 per 181 persons); infant mortality rate per 1,000 live births 14.3.
Food (1999): daily per capita caloric intake 2,963 (vegetable products 66%, animal products 34%); 111% of FAO recommended minimum.

Military

Total active duty personnel (2000)[9]: 97,700 (army 75.7%, air force 17.1%, navy 7.2%). *Military expenditure as percentage of government expenditure* (1991): 3.9% (world 4.0%); per capita expenditure U.S.$167.

[1]Government gives "preferential treatment" to the Serbian Orthodox Church according to the U.S. Department of State, *Country Reports on Human Rights Practices for 1996.* [2]Montenegro adopted the Deutsche Mark as its legal tender in mid-November 2000. [3]Vojvodina is administratively part of the Republic of Serbia. [4]Region under interim UN administration from mid-1999. [5]Kosovo adopted the Deutsche Mark as its official currency in September 1999. [6]1996. [7]Includes 1,069,600 unemployed. [8]Detail does not add to total given because of rounding. [9]39,100 troops from over 30 NATO and non-NATO countries were deployed in Kosovo by September 2001.

Internet resources for further information:
- **Federal Statistical Office of Yugoslavia http://www.szs.sv.gov.yu/homee.htm**
- **Federal Republic of Yugoslavia Official Web Site http://www.gov.yu**

Zambia

Official name: Republic of Zambia.
Form of government: multiparty republic with one legislative house (National Assembly [156[1]]).
Head of state and government: President.
Capital: Lusaka.
Official language: English.
Official religion: none[2].
Monetary unit: 1 Zambian kwacha (K) = 100 ngwee; valuation (Sept. 28, 2001) 1 U.S.$ = K 3,800; 1 £ = K 5,585.

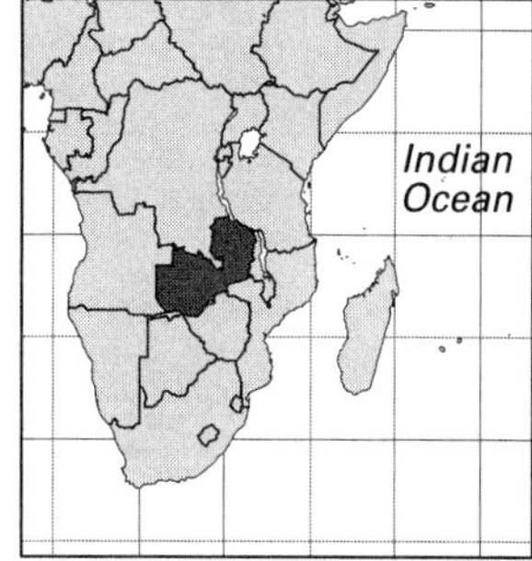

Area and population

Provinces	Capitals	area sq mi	area sq km	population 1990 census
Central	Kabwe	36,446	94,395	725,611
Copperbelt	Ndola	12,096	31,328	1,579,542
Eastern	Chipata	26,682	69,106	973,818
Luapula	Mansa	19,524	50,567	526,705
Lusaka	Lusaka	8,454	21,896	1,207,980
North-Western	Solwezi	48,582	125,827	383,146
Northern	Kasama	57,076	147,826	867,795
Southern	Livingstone	32,928	85,283	946,353
Western	Mongu	48,798	126,386	607,497
TOTAL		290,586	752,614	7,818,447

Demography

Population (2001): 9,770,000.
Density (2001): persons per sq mi 33.6, persons per sq km 13.0.
Urban-rural (1998): urban 43.9%; rural 56.1%.
Sex distribution (2000): male 49.73%; female 50.27%.
Age breakdown (2000): under 15, 47.6%; 15–29, 30.6%; 30–44, 12.4%; 45–59, 5.5%; 60–74, 3.1%; 75 and over, 0.8%.
Population projection: (2010) 11,482,000; (2020) 13,365,000.
Doubling time: 35 years.
Ethnolinguistic composition (1990): Bemba peoples 39.7%; Maravi (Nyanja) peoples 20.1%; Tonga peoples 14.8%; North-Western peoples 8.8%; Barotze peoples 7.5%; Tumbuka peoples 3.7%; Mambwe peoples 3.4%; other 2.0%.
Religious affiliation (1995): Christian 47.8%, of which Protestant 22.9%, Roman Catholic 16.9%, African Christian 5.6%; traditional beliefs 27.0%; Muslim 1.0%; other 24.2%.
Major cities (1990): Lusaka 982,362 (urban agglomeration, 1,577,000[3]); Ndola 370,000; Kitwe 290,000; Chingola 167,954; Kabwe 159,000; Mufulira 152,944.

Vital statistics

Birth rate per 1,000 population (2000): 41.9 (world avg. 22.5); legitimate, n.a.; however, marriage is both early and universal, suggesting that legitimate births are a relatively high proportion of all births.
Death rate per 1,000 population (2000): 22.1 (world avg. 9.0).
Natural increase rate per 1,000 population (2000): 19.8 (world avg. 13.5).
Total fertility rate (avg. births per childbearing woman; 2000): 5.6.
Life expectancy at birth (2000): male 37.1 years; female 37.4 years.
Major causes of death per 100,000 population: n.a.

National economy

Budget (1998). Revenue: K 1,529,054,000,000 (tax revenue 71.5%, of which income tax 24.9%, excise taxes 13.8%, value-added tax 13.1%, company income tax 5.9%; grants 26.0%; nontax revenue 2.5%). Expenditures: K 1,943,165,000,000 (current expenditures 65.0%, of which debt service 21.7%, education 7.7%, transfers 7.7%, health 5.7%, defense 1.4%; capital expenditures 35.0%).
Public debt (external, outstanding; 1999): U.S.$4,498,000,000.
Production (metric tons except as noted). Agriculture, forestry, fishing (2000): sugarcane 1,600,000, corn (maize) 1,260,000, cassava 1,020,000, fruits and vegetables 380,000 (of which onions 27,000, tomatoes 25,000, oranges 3,500), millet 71,000, seed cotton 62,000, wheat 60,000, sweet potatoes 56,000, peanuts (groundnuts) 55,000, soybeans 30,000, sorghum 26,000, potatoes 11,000, sunflower seeds 7,500, tobacco 3,100; livestock (number of live animals) 2,373,000 cattle, 1,249,000 goats, 330,000 pigs, 140,000 sheep, 29,000,000 chickens; roundwood (2000) 8,053,000 cu m; fish catch (1999) 71,507. Mining and quarrying (1999): copper (metal content) 260,000; cobalt (metal content) 4,700; silver 8,000 kg; gold 740 kg[4]. Manufacturing (value added in K '000,000; 1994): food products 39,765.1; beverages 36,596.5; chemicals and pharmaceuticals 32,141.5; textiles 15,358.5; tobacco 14,060.2; iron and steel, nonferrous metals, and fabricated metal products 13,874.6. Construction (value added in K; 1995): 45,663,000,000. Energy production (consumption): electricity (kW-hr; 1996) 7,795,000,000 (6,315,000,000); coal (metric tons; 1996) 350,000 (345,000); crude petroleum (barrels; 1996) none (4,178,000); petroleum products (metric tons; 1996) 515,000 (453,000); natural gas, none (n.a.).
Household income and expenditure. Average household size (1997) 5.0; average annual income per household (1981) K 1,041 (U.S.$908); sources of income (1981): wages and salaries 94.0%, other 6.0%; expenditure (1977): food 37.7%, housing 11.0%, clothing 8.3%, transportation 4.3%, education 2.1%, health 1.0%.
Tourism (1999): receipts U.S.$85,000,000; expenditures, n.a.
Population economically active (1996): total 3,454,000; activity rate of total population 38.2% (participation rates [1991]: over age 10, 52.6%; female 29.6%; unemployed 17.4%[5]).

Price and earnings indexes (1995 = 100)

	1991	1992	1993	1994	1995	1996	1997
Consumer price index	6.2	16.8	48.5	74.5	100.0	146.3	182.6
Earnings index	...	...	...	...	...	...	...

Gross national product (1999): U.S.$3,222,000,000 (U.S.$330 per capita).

Structure of gross domestic product and labour force

	1998 in value K '000,000	1998 % of total value	1990 labour force	1990 % of labour force
Agriculture	1,080,000	17.3	1,872,000	68.9
Mining	378,000	6.1	56,800	2.1
Manufacturing	713,000	11.4	50,900	1.9
Construction	316,000	5.1	29,100	1.1
Public utilities	241,000	3.9	8,900	0.3
Transp. and commun.	362,000	5.8	25,600	0.9
Trade	1,201,000	19.2	30,700	1.1
Finance	1,014,000	16.2	24,200	0.9
Pub. admin., defense; Services	560,000	9.0	111,600	4.1
Other	376,000[6]	6.0[6]	506,100	18.6
TOTAL	6,241,000	100.0	2,716,000[7]	100.0[7]

Land use (1994): forest 43.0%; pasture 40.4%; agriculture 7.1%; other 9.5%.

Foreign trade

Balance of trade (current prices)

	1994	1995	1996	1997	1998
U.S.$'000,000	+63	–8	–62	–27	–148
% of total	3.0%	0.3%	3.0%	1.1%	7.8%

Imports (1998): U.S.$1,022,000,000 (1995; machinery 24.5%; transport equipment 13.4%; chemicals and chemical products 13.3%; crude petroleum 11.3%; cereals and related products 6.5%). *Major import sources* (1999): South Africa 50.3%; Zimbabwe 9.3%; United Kingdom 5.9%; Saudi Arabia 5.7%.
Exports (1998): U.S.$873,600,000 (copper 49.3%; cobalt 17.7%; nonmetal exports 33.0%). *Major export destinations* (1999): Japan 11.3%; United Kingdom 8.5%; India 6.6%; Thailand 5.7%; Saudi Arabia 4.8%; U.S. 4.5%; Germany 4.1%.

Transport and communications

Transport. Railroads (1997)[8]: length 787 mi, 1,266 km; passenger-mi 166,000,000, passenger-km 267,000,000; short ton-mi cargo 316,000,000, metric ton-km cargo 462,000,000. Roads (1997): total length 24,170 mi, 38,898 km (paved 18%). Vehicles (1995): passenger cars 157,000; trucks and buses 81,000. Merchant marine: vessels (100 gross tons and over) none. Air transport (1996)[9]: passenger arrivals and departures 284,000; metric ton cargo unloaded and loaded 8,800; airports (1998) with scheduled flights 4.

Communications

Medium	date	unit	number	units per 1,000 persons
Daily newspapers	1996	circulation	114,000	14
Radio	1997	receivers	1,030,000	120
Television	1999	receivers	1,300,000	156
Telephones	1999	main lines	83,064	9.3
Cellular telephones	1999	subscribers	28,190	3.1
Internet	1999	users	15,000	1.5

Education and health

Educational attainment (1993)[10]. Percentage of population age 14 and over having: no formal schooling 18.6%; some primary education 54.8%; some secondary 25.1%; higher 1.5%. *Literacy* (1995): population age 15 and over literate 3,890,000 (78.2%); males literate 2,060,000 (85.6%); females literate 1,830,000 (71.3%).

Education (1996)

	schools	teachers	students	student/ teacher ratio
Primary (age 7–13)	3,907	38,528[11]	1,670,000	...
Secondary (age 14–18)	246	5,786[12]	255,000	...
Voc., teacher tr.	26[13]	846[13]	7,982[14]	...
Higher	2	640	4,470	7.0

Health: physicians (1993) 786 (1 per 10,917 persons); hospital beds (1989) 22,461 (1 per 349 persons); infant mortality rate per 1,000 live births (2000) 92.4.
Food (1999): daily per capita caloric intake 1,934 (vegetable products 95%, animal products 5%); 84% of FAO recommended minimum requirement.

Military

Total active duty personnel (2000): 21,600 (army 92.6%; navy, none; air force 7.4%). *Military expenditure as percentage of GNP* (1997): 1.1% (world 2.6%); per capita expenditure U.S.$4.

[1]Includes 5 nonelective seats. [2]In 1996 Zambia was declared a Christian nation per the preamble of a constitutional amendment. [3]1999 estimate. [4]In 1997 legal and illegal exports of emeralds were estimated to equal U.S.$20,000,000 (about 20% of world total). [5]1987. [6]Less imputed bank service charge. [7]Detail does not add to total given because of rounding. [8]Excludes Tanzania-Zambia Railway Authority (TAZARA) data. [9]Lusaka airport only. [10]Based on a sample survey of 35,502 persons. [11]1995. [12]1988. [13]1989. [14]1990.

Internet resources for further information:
- **Zambian National WWW Server (Zamnet) http://www.zamnet.zm**

Zimbabwe

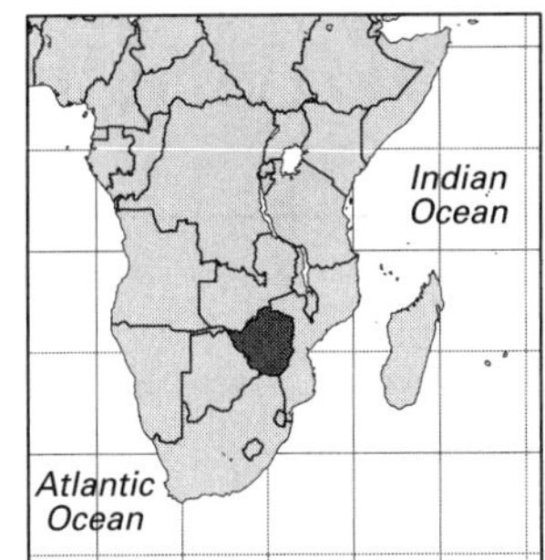

Official name: Republic of Zimbabwe.
Form of government: multiparty republic with one legislative house (House of Assembly [150[1]]).
Head of state and government: President.
Capital: Harare.
Official language: English.
Official religion: none.
Monetary unit: 1 Zimbabwe dollar (Z$) = 100 cents; valuation (Sept. 28, 2001) 1 U.S.$ = Z$55.45; 1 £ = Z$81.49.

Area and population

Provinces	Capitals	area sq mi	area sq km	population 1992 census
Bulawayo[2]	—	185	479	620,936
Harare[2]	—	337	872	1,478,810
Manicaland	Mutare	14,077	36,459	1,537,676
Mashonaland Central	Bindura	10,945	28,347	857,318
Mashonaland East	Marondera	12,444	32,230	1,033,336
Mashonaland West	Chinhoyi	22,178	57,441	1,116,928
Masvingo	Masvingo	21,840	56,566	1,221,845
Matabeleland North	Lupane	28,967	75,025	640,957
Matabeleland South	Gwanda	20,916	54,172	591,747
Midlands	Gweru	18,983	49,166	1,302,214
TOTAL		150,872	390,757	10,401,767

Demography

Population (2001): 11,365,000.
Density (2001): persons per sq mi 75.3, persons per sq km 29.1.
Urban-rural (1998): urban 33.9%; rural 66.1%.
Sex distribution (2001): male 50.52%; female 49.48%.
Age breakdown (2000): under 15, 39.6%; 15–29, 33.1%; 30–44, 14.8%; 45–59, 7.2%; 60–74, 4.1%; 75 and over, 1.2%.
Population projection: (2010) 11,057,000; (2020) 9,997,000.
Doubling time: not applicable; doubling time exceeds 100 years.
Ethnic composition (2000): Shona 67.1%; Ndebele 13.0%; Chewa 4.9%; British 3.5%; other 11.5%.
Religious affiliation (1995): Christian 45.4%, of which Protestant (including Anglican) 23.5%, African indigenous 13.5%, Roman Catholic 7.0%; animist 40.5%; other 14.1%.
Major cities (1992): Harare 1,184,169; Bulawayo 620,936; Chitungwiza 274,035; Mutare 131,808; Gweru 124,735.

Vital statistics

Birth rate per 1,000 population (2000): 25.0 (world avg. 22.5).
Death rate per 1,000 population (2000): 22.4 (world avg. 9.0).
Natural increase rate per 1,000 population (2000): 2.6 (world avg. 13.5).
Total fertility rate (avg. births per childbearing woman; 2000): 3.3.
Life expectancy at birth (2000): male 39.2 years; female 36.3 years.
Major causes of death per 100,000 population (1990): infectious and parasitic diseases 64.7; accidents and poisoning 44.4; diseases of the circulatory system 40.9; diseases of the respiratory system 39.5; malignant neoplasms (cancers) 28.4; diseases of the digestive system 12.1; diseases of the nervous system 9.4; endocrine and metabolic disorders 4.9.

National economy

Budget (1997–98). Revenue: Z$57,596,000,000 (tax revenue 93.0%, of which income tax 48.0%, sales tax 20.4%, customs duties 17.3%, excise tax 4.2%; nontax revenue 7.0%). Expenditures: Z$70,332,000,000 (recurrent expenditures 92.1%, of which goods and services 48.5%, interest payments 25.0%, transfer payments 18.4%).
Population economically active (1992): total 3,600,000; activity rate of total population 34.6% (participation rates: over age 15, 63.4%; female 39.8%; unemployed 7.2%[3]).

Price and earnings indexes (1995 = 100)

	1993	1994	1995	1996	1997	1998	1999
Consumer price index	66.7	81.6	100.0	121.4	144.2	190.1	301.3
Earnings index	…	…	…	…	…	…	…

Production (metric tons except as noted). Agriculture, forestry, fishing (1999): sugarcane 4,657,000, corn (maize) 1,520,000, wheat 320,000, seed cotton 268,000, tobacco 193,000, cassava 170,000, vegetables (including melons) 122,000, peanuts (groundnuts) 113,000, soybeans 107,000, sorghum 85,000, bananas 82,000, oranges 72,000, millet 53,000; livestock (number of live animals) 5,500,000 cattle, 2,770,000 goats, 525,000 sheep, 272,000 pigs, 15,000,000 chickens; roundwood (1998) 8,378,000 cu m; fish catch (1998) 16,386 metric tons. Mining and quarrying (value of production in Z$; 1997): gold 3,076,800,000; nickel 944,500,000; asbestos 927,900,000; coal 817,100,000; chrome 263,500,000; copper 162,300,000. Manufacturing (value in Z$; 1994): foodstuffs 6,746,300,000; metals and metal products 5,662,700,000; chemicals and petroleum products 3,314,800,000; beverages and tobacco 3,208,400,000; textiles 2,607,700,000; clothing and footwear 1,732,200,000; paper, printing, and publishing 1,553,700,000; transport equipment 1,454,400,000; wood and furniture 1,136,500,000; nonmetallic mineral products 1,076,600,000; other manufactured goods 323,300,000. Construction (Z$; 1996): residential 1,045,301,000; commercial 182,000,000; industrial 76,021,000. Energy production (consumption): electricity (kW-hr; 1996) 7,819,000,000 (10,991,000,000); coal (metric tons; 1996) 5,247,000 (5,242,000); crude petroleum, none (none); petroleum products (metric tons; 1996) none (1,375,000).
Public debt (external, outstanding; 1999): U.S.$3,211,000,000.
Household income and expenditure. Average household size (1992) 4.8; income per household Z$1,689 (U.S.$2,628); sources of income: n.a.; expenditure (1990[4]): food, beverages, and tobacco 39.1%, housing 18.7%, clothing and footwear 9.8%, transportation 8.4%, education 7.6%, household durable goods 7.2%, health 2.8%, recreation 2.0%, other 4.4%.
Gross national product (1999): U.S.$6,302,000,000 (U.S.$530 per capita).

Structure of gross domestic product and labour force

	1996 in value Z$'000,000[5]	1996 % of total value[5]	1995 labour force[6]	1995 % of labour force[6]
Agriculture	15,283	20.0	334,000	26.9
Mining	3,846	5.0	59,000	4.7
Manufacturing	14,668	19.2	185,900	15.0
Construction	1,943	2.5	71,800	5.8
Public utilities	2,409	3.2	9,500	0.8
Transp. and commun.	4,200	5.5	50,900	4.1
Trade	15,630	20.5	100,600	8.2
Finance	7,896	10.4	21,100	1.7
Pub. admin., defense	3,324	4.4	406,800	32.8
Services	5,472	7.2		
Other	1,572[7]	2.1[7]	…	…
TOTAL	76,243	100.0	1,239,600	100.0

Tourism: receipts (1999) U.S.$202,000,000; expenditures (1998) U.S.$131,-000,000.

Foreign trade

Balance of trade (current prices)

	1994	1995	1996	1997	1998	1999
U.S.$'000,000	+169	+89	+249	+230	+79	+276
% of total	4.5%	2.0%	5.2%	4.5%	2.0%	8.3%

Imports (1998): U.S.$1,968,000,000 (1996; machinery and transport equipment 38.7%, of which transport equipment 9.1%; manufactured goods 16.7%, of which textiles 2.6%, paper and paperboard 1.8%; fuels 10.4%, of which petroleum 9.7%). *Major import sources* (1996): South Africa 38.3%; U.K. 7.9%; Japan 5.1%; U.S. 5.0%; Germany 4.9%; France 3.1%; Italy 2.5%; The Netherlands 1.8%.
Exports (1998)[8]: U.S.$2,047,000,000 (1996; domestic exports 86.8%, of which tobacco 30.5%, gold sales 12.3%, ferroalloys 6.7%, nickel metal 3.2%, cotton 2.7%, asbestos 2.6%, cut flowers 1.4%, corn [maize] 1.2%). *Major export destinations* (1996): U.K. 10.1%; South Africa 9.6%; Germany 7.9%; U.S. 6.7%; Japan 5.1%; Zambia 4.3%; Italy 4.3%; Botswana 4.0%; The Netherlands 3.8%.

Transport and communications

Transport. Railroads (1998): route length 2,759 km; passenger-km 408,223,000; metric ton-km cargo 4,603,000. Roads (1996): total length 18,338 km (paved 47%). Vehicles (1996): passenger cars 323,000; trucks and buses 32,000. Air transport (1999)[9]: passenger-km 874,998,000; metric ton-km cargo 35,062,000; airports (1997) with scheduled flights 7.

Communications

Medium	date	unit	number	units per 1,000 persons
Daily newspapers	1996	circulation	209,000	19
Radio	1997	receivers	1,140,000	102
Television	1999	receivers	2,074,000	183
Telephones	1999	main lines	238,956	21
Personal computers	1999	units	150,000	13
Internet	1999	users	20,000	1.8

Education and health

Educational attainment (1992). Percentage of population age 25 and over having: no formal schooling 22.3%; primary 54.3%; secondary 13.1%; higher 3.4%. *Literacy* (1995): percentage of total population age 15 and over literate 85.1%; males literate 90.4%; females literate 79.9%.

Education (1998)

	schools	teachers	students	student/teacher ratio
Primary (age 7–13)	4,706	64,538	2,507,098	38.8
Secondary (age 14–19)	1,530	30,482	847,296	27.8
Voc., teacher tr.[10]	25	1,479	27,431	18.5
Higher[11]	28[10]	3,581	46,492	13.0

Health: physicians (1996) 1,603 (1 per 6,904 persons); hospital beds (1996) 22,975 (1 per 501 persons); infant mortality rate (2000) 62.3.
Food (1999): daily per capita caloric intake 2,076 (vegetable products 95%, animal products 5%); 87% of FAO recommended minimum requirement.

Military

Total active duty personnel (2000): 40,000 (army 87.5%, air force 12.5%). *Military expenditure as percentage of GNP* (1997): 3.8% (world 2.6%); per capita expenditure U.S.$29.

[1]Includes 30 nonelective seats. [2]City with provincial status. [3]Does not take into consideration seasonal unemployment of communal workers; 1986–87. [4]Based on consumer price index. [5]At factor cost. [6]Wage-earning workers only. [7]Less imputed bank service charges. [8]Excludes gold sales and reexports. [9]Air Zimbabwe only. [10]1992. [11]Includes postsecondary vocational and teacher training at the higher level.

Internet resources for further information:
- **Reserve Bank of Zimbabwe http://www.rbz.co.zw**

Comparative National Statistics

World and regional summaries

region/bloc	area and population, 2001						gross national product, 1999						labour force, 1990		
	area		population			population projection, 2020	total ('000,000 U.S.$)	% agricul-ture	% industry	% ser-vices	growth rate, 1990–99	GNP per capita (U.S.$)	total ('000)	% male	% female
	square miles	square kilometres	total	per sq mi	per sq km										
World	52,433,570	135,802,510	6,130,169,000	116.9	45.1	7,477,335,000	29,278,809	4	30	65	2.5	5,120	2,353,806	63.8	36.2
Africa	11,717,370	30,348,110	816,524,000	69.7	26.9	1,163,522,000	539,367	18	34	48	2.5	700	242,784	65.6	34.4
Central Africa	2,552,970	6,612,160	96,826,000	37.9	14.6	158,008,000	26,211	34	33	33	1.3	290	26,428	64.7	35.3
East Africa	2,473,670	6,406,670	252,375,000	102.0	39.4	361,044,000	67,422	31	18	51	2.9	280	85,082	58.8	41.2
North Africa	3,287,800	8,515,320	176,446,000	53.7	20.7	239,962,000	228,722	15	38	46	3.3	1,390	40,016	84.6	15.4
Southern Africa	1,032,300	2,673,660	50,251,000	48.7	18.8	43,696,000	144,456	4	33	63	1.3	3,040	14,532	64.3	35.7
West Africa	2,370,630	6,140,300	240,626,000	101.5	39.2	360,812,000	72,556	36	40	24	3.0	320	76,726	63.8	36.2
Americas	16,247,180	42,080,010	841,294,000	51.8	20.0	1,015,255,000	11,470,019	3	27	70	3.0	13,970	293,723	66.5	33.5
Anglo-America[3]	8,301,330	21,500,350	317,195,000	38.2	14.8	369,868,000	9,496,848	2	26	72	3.0	30,750	135,438	58.7	41.3
Canada	3,849,670	9,970,610	31,002,000	8.1	3.1	35,187,000	614,003	2	31	67	2.8	20,140	13,360	60.2	39.8
United States	3,615,220	9,363,360	286,067,000	79.1	30.6	334,548,000	8,879,500	2	26	72	3.0	31,910	122,005	58.6	41.4
Latin America	7,945,850	20,579,660	524,099,000	66.0	25.5	645,387,000	1,973,172	8	29	63	3.4	3,850	158,285	73.1	26.9
Caribbean	90,710	234,920	37,061,000	408.6	157.8	43,730,000	100,928	6	35	59	2.8	2,720	13,813	66.9	33.1
Central America	201,480	521,840	35,555,000	181.4	70.1	51,478,000	59,430	16	22	62	4.4	1,690	9,520	78.5	21.5
Mexico	758,450	1,964,380	99,969,000	131.8	50.9	125,610,000	428,877	5	27	68	2.8	4,440	30,487	72.9	27.1
South America	6,895,210	17,858,520	350,514,000	50.8	19.6	424,569,000	1,383,937	9	30	62	3.6	4,030	104,465	73.6	26.4
Andean Group	2,112,160	5,470,480	130,590,000	61.8	23.9	171,108,000	325,560	9	29	62	3.8	2,580	34,715	75.6	24.4
Brazil	3,300,170	8,547,400	172,118,000	52.2	20.1	194,224,000	730,424	9	29	62	3.0	4,350	55,026	72.6	27.4
Other South America	1,482,880	3,840,640	47,806,000	32.2	12.4	59,237,000	327,953	7	32	61	4.8	6,650	14,724	72.4	27.6
Asia	12,312,740	31,889,660	3,714,141,000	301.7	116.5	4,539,614,000	7,109,229	8	37	55	3.7	2,120	1,464,452	64.5	35.5
Eastern Asia	4,546,090	11,774,380	1,503,611,000	330.7	127.7	1,673,386,000	5,887,883	5	39	56	3.1	3,970	775,590	57.4	42.6
China	3,696,100	9,572,900	1,274,915,000	344.9	133.2	1,433,111,000	979,894	17	50	33	10.8	780	669,693	56.7	43.3
Japan	145,880	377,840	127,100,000	871.2	336.4	124,248,000	4,054,545	2	37	61	1.4	32,030	62,202	62.1	37.9
South Korea	38,400	99,460	47,676,000	1,241.5	479.3	52,759,000	397,910	5	44	51	5.7	8,490	18,664	66.2	33.8
Other Eastern Asia	665,710	1,724,180	53,920,000	81.0	31.3	63,268,000	455,534	3	33	64	5.5	8,670	25,031	58.8	41.2
South Asia	1,939,160	5,022,390	1,378,341,000	710.8	274.4	1,783,298,000	572,958	28	25	47	5.5	440	411,136	77.4	22.6
India	1,222,560	3,166,410	1,029,991,000	842.5	325.3	1,311,747,000	441,834	29	25	47	5.9	440	322,944	74.8	25.2
Pakistan	307,370	796,100	144,617,000	470.5	181.7	199,745,000	62,915	26	25	49	3.5	470	33,698	87.5	12.5
Other South Asia	409,230	1,059,880	203,733,000	497.8	192.2	271,806,000	68,209	25	28	48	4.9	380	54,494	86.2	13.8
Southeast Asia	1,742,140	4,512,020	519,510,000	298.2	115.1	651,001,000	592,688	18	36	46	5.3	1,160	189,297	63.0	37.0
Southwest Asia	4,085,340	10,580,770	312,679,000	76.5	29.6	431,929,000	830,134	11	37	52	2.8	2,740	88,429	69.4	30.6
Central Asia	1,545,790	4,003,400	56,671,000	36.7	14.2	73,197,000	42,764	21	29	50	–4.3	770	20,728	54.8	45.2
Gulf Cooperation Council	1,031,340	2,671,040	31,934,000	31.0	12.0	55,862,000	307,707	4	50	46	2.2	9,300	6,511	91.7	8.3
Iran	629,310	1,629,920	63,442,000	100.8	38.9	80,482,000	113,729	20	36	44	3.4	1,810	15,253	82.0	18.0
Other Southwest Asia	878,900	2,276,410	160,632,000	182.8	70.6	222,388,000	365,934	14	26	60	4.0	2,410	45,936	68.7	31.3
Europe	8,868,680	22,969,900	726,833,000	82.0	31.6	720,645,000	9,684,865	3	30	67	1.3	13,350	340,666	57.1	42.9
Eastern Europe	7,437,100	19,262,130	335,196,000	45.1	17.4	322,138,000	805,089	8	35	57	–3.2	2,380	171,080	50.6	49.4
Russia	6,592,800	17,075,400	144,417,000	21.9	8.5	137,971,000	328,995	7	35	59	–6.0	2,250	72,286	47.6	52.4
Ukraine	233,100	603,700	48,767,000	209.2	80.8	44,362,000	41,991	14	35	52	–10.8	840	25,401	48.0	52.0
Other Eastern Europe	611,200	1,583,030	142,012,000	232.4	89.7	139,805,000	434,103	8	35	57	1.3	2,940	73,393	54.4	45.6
Western Europe	1,431,580	3,707,770	391,637,000	273.6	105.6	398,507,000	8,879,776	2	29	68	1.8	22,990	169,586	63.6	36.4
European Union (EU)	1,249,710	3,236,710	378,771,000	303.1	117.0	384,973,000	8,434,344	2	29	68	1.8	22,580	163,771	63.6	36.4
France	210,030	543,960	59,090,000	281.3	108.6	61,371,000	1,453,211	2	26	72	1.5	24,170	25,404	60.1	39.9
Germany	137,850	357,020	82,386,000	597.7	230.8	84,897,000	2,103,804	1	30	69	1.4	26,620	38,981	60.7	39.3
Italy	116,350	301,340	57,892,000	497.6	192.1	55,540,000	1,162,910	3	31	67	1.4	20,170	23,339	68.1	31.9
Spain	195,360	505,990	40,144,000	205.5	79.3	39,362,000	583,082	4	32	64	2.3	14,800	14,456	75.5	24.5
United Kingdom	94,250	244,100	59,953,000	636.1	245.6	61,742,000	1,403,843	2	31	67	2.5	23,500	27,766	61.4	38.6
Other EU	495,870	1,284,300	79,306,000	159.9	61.8	82,061,000	1,727,494	4	29	67	2.4	22,250	33,825	63.4	36.6
Non-EU	181,870	471,060	12,866,000	70.7	27.3	13,534,000	445,432	3	29	68	1.7	35,080	5,815	61.9	38.1
Oceania	3,287,600	8,514,830	31,377,000	9.5	3.7	38,299,000	469,240	4	26	71	3.9	15,510	12,181	63.0	37.0
Australia	2,969,910	7,692,030	19,358,000	6.5	2.5	22,409,000	397,345	3	26	71	4.1	20,950	7,963	61.9	38.1
Pacific Ocean Islands	317,690	822,800	12,019,000	37.8	14.6	15,890,000	71,895	8	23	69	2.9	6,370	4,218	65.0	35.0

[1]Refers only to the outstanding long-term external public and publicly guaranteed debt of the 137 countries that report under the World Bank's Debtor Reporting System (DRS). [2]World total includes

Africa

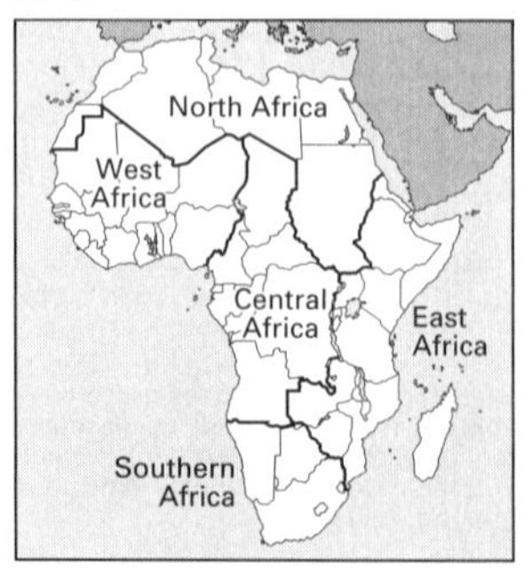

Americas

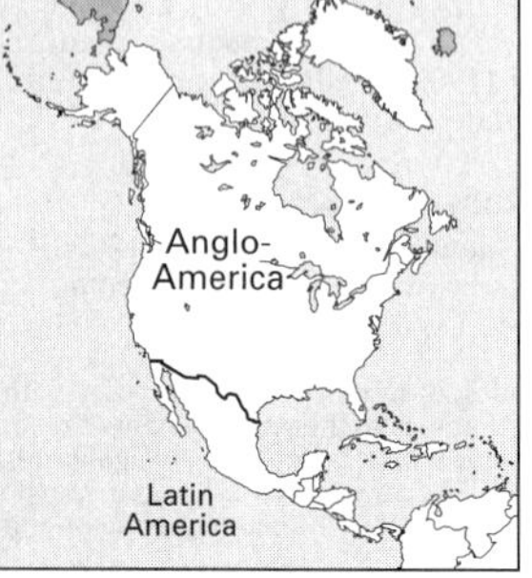

Asia

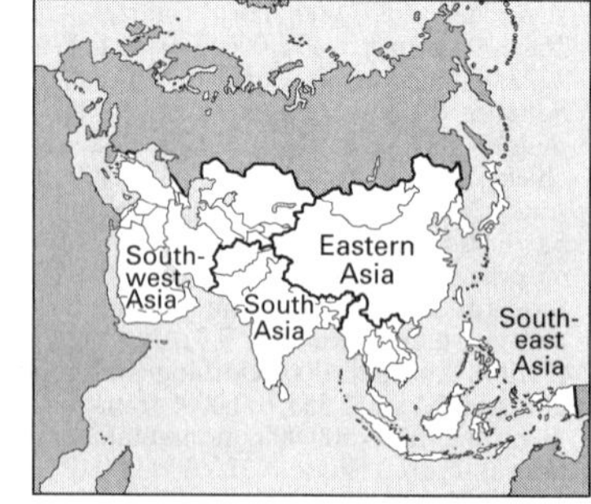

economic indicators							social indicators								region/bloc
pop. per 1,000 ha of arable land, 1998	electricity consump-tion (kW-hr per capita), 1996	trade ('000,000 U.S.$), 1998			debt ('000,000 U.S.$), 1999[1]		life expec-tancy (years), 2000		health			food (% FAO recom-mended minimum), 1998	literacy (%) (latest)		
		imports (c.i.f.)	exports (f.o.b.)	balance	total	% of GNP	male	female	pop. per doctor (latest)	infant mor-tality per 1,000 births, 2000	pop. having safe water (%); (1989–98)		male	female	
4,270	2,345	5,670,613	5,474,996[2]	–195,617[2]	1,464,107	24.0	64.7	68.9	730	53.6	76	118	83.7	71.0	World
4,300	507	140,047	126,853	–13,194	236,331	48.0	51.1	53.2	2,560	86.9	57	104	65.9	45.5	Africa
4,100	126	7,828	6,994	–834	34,588	134.3	46.9	50.4	12,890	107.8	44	83	77.7	56.4	Central Africa
5,590	142	18,172	16,013	–2,159	45,902	77.9	45.0	46.5	13,620	95.4	44	84	65.4	44.1	East Africa
4,100	693	56,196	52,715	–3,481	87,534	44.0	63.2	66.8	890	57.7	82	125	64.8	40.1	North Africa
2,990	3,888	29,439	25,891	–3,548	10,458	7.7	49.6	50.8	1,610	63.0	70	116	81.6	80.0	Southern Africa
3,940	128	28,412	25,240	–3,172	57,849	79.6	50.3	51.5	6,260	86.6	52	113	58.4	37.5	West Africa
2,240	6,200	1,528,175	1,425,746	–102,429	398,042	20.6	68.6	75.2	520	25.4	83	128	91.3	89.9	Americas
1,350	13,421	1,165,588	1,104,705	–60,883	—	—	74.4	80.2	370	6.7	91	140	96.1	95.7	Anglo-America[3]
660	17,455	219,150	198,530	–20,620	—	—	76.0	83.0	540	5.1	100	119	96.6	96.6	Canada
1,530	12,980	944,644	904,575	–40,069	—	—	74.2	79.9	360	6.8	90	142	95.7	95.3	United States
3,720	1,737	362,587	321,041	–41,546	398,042	20.6	65.2	72.2	690	32.6	78	119	87.8	85.6	Latin America
6,390	1,610	28,950	25,256	–3,694	10,091	26.6	67.6	72.4	380	43.5	77	102	83.8	83.0	Caribbean
4,930	629	23,202	34,805	+11,603	24,967	41.2	66.9	72.2	950	35.8	76	105	73.6	68.1	Central America
3,800	1,754	137,709	104,240	–33,469	87,531	18.6	68.5	74.7	810	26.2	85	135	91.8	87.4	Mexico
3,450	1,861	172,726	156,740	–15,986	275,453	20.2	63.8	71.5	710	33.0	76	117	88.4	87.0	South America
8,900	1,575	68,680	60,121	–8,559	87,634	26.6	67.9	74.3	830	31.3	79	106	92.6	88.7	Andean Group
3,040	2,026	63,314	59,053	–4,261	95,233	13.0	58.5	67.6	770	38.0	76	122	83.3	83.2	Brazil
1,580	2,009	40,732	37,556	–3,166	92,586	30.4	71.4	78.1	410	20.7	71	129	96.0	95.7	Other South America
7,200	1,140	1,378,224	1,283,051	–95,173	595,398	20.9	65.8	69.0	970	50.9	75	117	81.2	63.7	Asia
10,930	1,775	807,833	749,452	–58,381	166,210	12.1	70.3	74.6	610	26.5	71	125	91.4	77.0	Eastern Asia
10,010	891	140,385	154,843	+14,458	108,163	11.1	69.6	73.3	620	28.9	67	126	89.9	72.7	China
27,880	8,074	281,243	254,114	–27,129	—	—	77.5	84.1	530	3.9	97	123	100.0	100.0	Japan
27,180	5,022	93,282	81,259	–12,023	57,231	14.2	70.8	78.5	740	7.9	93	131	99.3	96.7	South Korea
13,400	4,270	292,923	259,236	–33,687	816	94.7	71.2	76.9	500	18.4	96	107	95.9	91.4	Other Eastern Asia
6,520	402	68,420	61,099	–7,321	139,322	24.4	61.3	62.4	2,100	70.3	80	108	62.4	35.5	South Asia
6,080	459	43,458	38,604	–4,854	82,380	18.5	61.9	63.1	1,920	64.9	81	112	65.5	37.7	India
6,920	407	9,308	8,873	–435	28,514	48.5	60.3	61.9	1,840	82.5	79	106	50.0	24.4	Pakistan
9,710	104	15,654	13,622	–2,032	28,428	41.3	59.1	59.1	5,080	84.6	78	89	53.5	30.9	Other South Asia
8,050	613	283,858	269,222	–14,636	186,531	37.6	64.5	69.5	3,120	40.3	70	120	91.8	83.3	Southeast Asia
3,010	2,105	218,113	203,278	–14,835	103,335	25.5	65.8	70.3	610	52.3	79	116	86.7	72.4	Southwest Asia
1,430	2,675	11,237	10,253	–984	9,819	25.1	59.2	67.7	330	77.1	85	98	98.8	96.1	Central Asia
7,610	6,472	94,584	85,454	–9,130	1,768	12.8	67.7	71.1	620	46.2	95	122	73.8	55.8	Gulf Cooperation Council
3,640	1,180	13,107	11,983	–1,124	6,184	5.6	68.3	71.1	1,200	30.0	95	117	78.4	65.8	Iran
3,810	1,545	99,185	95,588	–3,597	85,563	35.5	66.6	70.9	690	51.8	65	122	87.8	68.1	Other Southwest Asia
2,480	5,603	2,539,663	2,499,599	–40,064	232,295	28.0	70.0	77.9	300	10.8	99	125	99.0	97.5	Europe
1,570	4,419	247,515	240,899	–6,616	232,295	28.0	64.1	73.9	290	18.1	95	116	99.1	96.6	Eastern Europe
1,170	5,588	42,476	52,731	+10,255	120,375	32.1	62.0	72.7	240	20.3	. . .	111	99.5	96.8	Russia
1,530	3,482	14,676	14,204	–472	10,027	26.7	60.4	71.9	330	21.7	97	112	99.5	97.4	Ukraine
2,470	3,550	190,363	173,964	–16,399	101,893	24.4	67.5	75.9	370	15.1	94	122	98.7	96.1	Other Eastern Europe
5,040	6,660	2,292,148	2,258,700	–33,448	—	—	75.0	81.5	300	5.1	100	134	98.9	98.2	Western Europe
4,960	6,433	2,168,432	2,121,340	–47,092	—	—	74.9	81.5	290	5.1	100	134	98.8	98.1	European Union (EU)
3,180	7,518	285,520	307,195	+21,675	—	—	74.9	82.9	330	4.5	100	141	98.9	98.7	France
6,910	6,582	463,263	474,552	+11,289	—	—	74.3	80.8	290	4.8	100	128	100.0	100.0	Germany
6,960	4,870	215,911	209,376	–6,535	—	—	75.9	82.4	180	5.9	100	143	97.8	96.4	Italy
2,790	4,384	130,073	132,526	+2,453	—	—	75.3	82.5	240	5.0	99	136	98.1	95.1	Spain
9,450	6,232	309,790	319,251	+9,461	—	—	75.0	80.5	720	5.6	100	129	100.0	100.0	United Kingdom
4,720	7,815	763,875	678,440	–85,435	—	—	74.8	80.9	320	4.9	100	132	97.9	97.2	Other EU
9,170	13,533	123,716	137,360	+13,644	—	—	76.3	82.3	480	4.4	100	123	99.9	99.9	Non-EU
540	7,735	84,504	75,492	–9,012	2,042	33.7	73.2	78.8	480	24.0	86	117	96.3	94.0	Oceania
350	9,820	66,843	59,534	–7,309	—	—	76.9	82.7	400	5.0	95	120	99.5	99.5	Australia
5,530	4,009	17,661	15,958	–1,703	2,042	33.7	67.0	72.2	770	40.3	68	111	89.8	82.7	Pacific Ocean Islands

U.S.$64,255,000,000 undistributable by region. [3]Anglo-America includes Canada, the United States, Greenland, Bermuda, and St. Pierre and Miquelon.

Europe

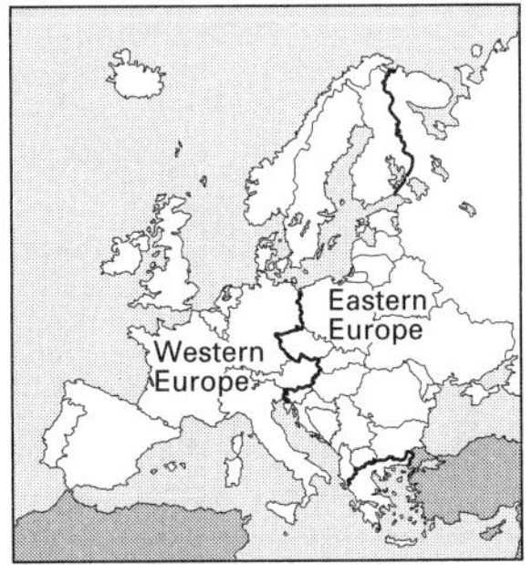

Eastern Europe

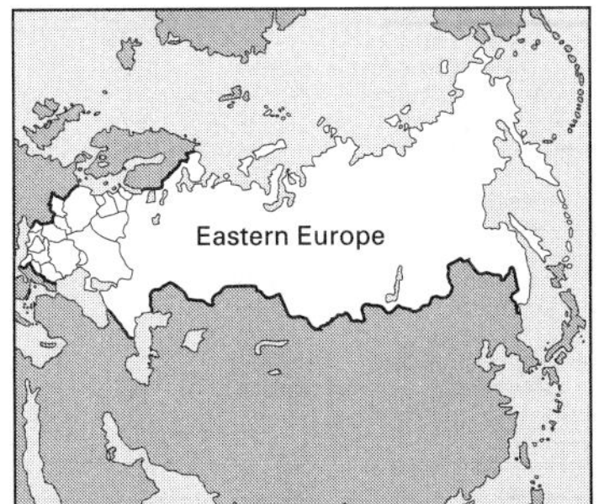

Oceania

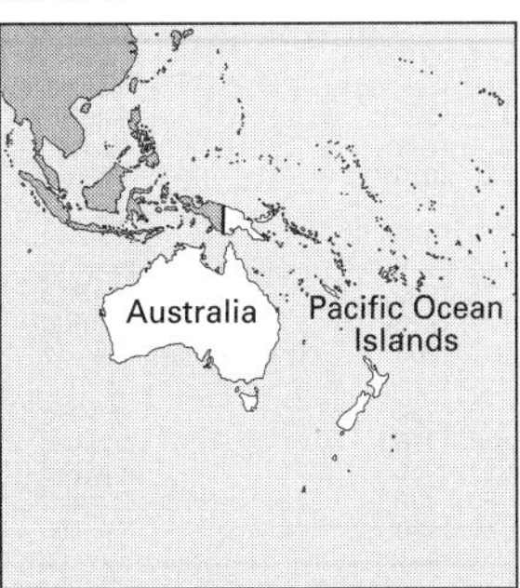

Government and international organizations

This table summarizes principal facts about the governments of the countries of the world, their branches and organs, the topmost layers of local government constituting each country's chief administrative subdivisions, and the participation of their central governments in the principal intergovernmental organizations of the world.

In this table "date of independence" may refer to a variety of circumstances. In the case of the newest countries, those that attained full independence after World War II, the date given is usually just what is implied by the heading—the date when the country, within its present borders, attained full sovereignty over both its internal and external affairs. In the case of longer established countries, the choice of a single date may be somewhat more complicated, and grounds for the use of several different dates often exist. The reader should refer to appropriate Britannica articles on national histories and relevant historical acts. In cases of territorial annexation or dissolution, the date given here refers either to the final act of union of a state composed of smaller entities or to the final act of separation from a larger whole (*e.g.*, the separation of Bangladesh from Pakistan in 1971).

The date of the current, or last, constitution is in some ways a less complicated question, but governments sometimes do not, upon taking power, either adhere to existing constitutional forms or trouble to terminate the previous document and legitimize themselves by the installation of new constitutional forms. Often, however, the desire to legitimize extraconstitutional political activity by associating it with existing forms of long precedent leads to partial or incomplete modification, suspension, or abrogation of a constitution, so that the actual day-to-day conduct of government may be largely unrelated to the provisions of a constitution still theoretically in force. When a date in this column is given in italics, it refers to a document that has been suspended, abolished by extraconstitutional action, or modified extensively.

The characterizations adopted under "type of government" represent a compromise between the forms provided for by the national constitution and the more pragmatic language that a political scientist might adopt to describe these same systems. For an explanation of the application of these terms in the Britannica World Data, *see* the Glossary at page 533.

The positions denoted by the terms "chief of state" and "head of government" are usually those identified with those functions by the constitution. The duties of the chief of state may range from largely ceremonial responsibilities, with little or no authority over the day-to-day conduct of government, to complete executive authority as the effective head of government. In certain countries, an official of a political party or a revolutionary figure outside the constitutional structure may exercise the powers of both positions.

Membership in the legislative house(s) of each country as given here includes all elected or appointed members, as well as ex officio members (those who by virtue of some other office or title are members of the body), whether voting or nonvoting. The legislature of a country with a unicameral system is shown as the upper house in this table.

The number of administrative subdivisions for each country is listed down to the second level. A single country may, depending on its size, complexity, and historical antecedents, have as many as five levels of administrative subordination or it may have none at all. Each level of subordination may have several kinds of subdivisions.

Government and international organizations

country	date of independence[a]	date of current or last constitution[b]	type of government	executive branch[c]		legislative branch[d]		admin. subdivisions		seaward claims	
				chief of state	head of government	upper house (members)	lower house (members)	first-order (number)	second-order (number)	territorial (nautical miles)	fishing/economic (nautical miles)
Afghanistan	Aug. 19, 1919	—	[1]	[1]		...	...	...	...	—	—
Albania	Nov. 28, 1912	Nov. 28, 1998	republic	president	prime minister	140	—	12	36	12	[2]
Algeria	July 5, 1962	Dec. 7, 1996[3]	republic	president	prime minister	144	380	48	553	12	[4]
American Samoa	—	July 1, 1967	territory (U.S.)	U.S. president	governor	18	18	4	14	12	200
Andorra	Dec. 6, 1288	May 4, 1993	parl. coprincipality	[6]	head of govt.	28	—	7	...	—	—
Angola	Nov. 11, 1975	Aug. 27, 1992	republic	president[7]		220[8]	—	18	163	20	200
Antigua and Barbuda	Nov. 1, 1981	Nov. 1, 1981	constitutional monarchy	British monarch	prime minister	17[9]	17	30	—	12[10]	200[10]
Argentina	July 9, 1816	Aug. 24, 1994[11]	federal republic	president[12]		72	257	24	503	12	200
Armenia	Sept. 23, 1991	July 5, 1995	republic	president	prime minister	131	—	11	...	—	—
Aruba	—	Jan. 1, 1986	overseas territory (Neth.)	Dutch monarch	[13]	21	—	...	...	12	200
Australia	Jan. 1, 1901	July 9, 1900	federal parl. state[15]	British monarch	prime minister	76	150	8	*c.* 900	12	200
Austria	Oct. 30, 1918	Oct. 1, 1920[16]	federal state	president	chancellor	64	183	9	99	—	—
Azerbaijan	Aug. 30, 1991	Nov. 12, 1995[17]	republic	president[18]		124[19]	—	2	71	...	...
Bahamas, The	July 10, 1973	July 10, 1973	constitutional monarchy	British monarch	prime minister	16	40	—	25	12	200
Bahrain	Aug. 15, 1971	June 1973[20]	monarchy (emirate)	emir	prime minister	40[21]	...	...	—	12	[22]
Bangladesh	March 26, 1971	Dec. 16, 1972	republic	president	prime minister	330	—	7	64	12	200
Barbados	Nov. 30, 1966	Nov. 30, 1966	constitutional monarchy	British monarch	prime minister	21	28	—	—	12	200
Belarus	Aug. 25, 1991	Nov. 27, 1996[23]	republic	president[18]		64[23]	110[23]	7	118	—	—
Belgium	Oct. 4, 1830	Feb. 17, 1994	fed. const. monarchy	monarch	prime minister	71[24]	150	[25]	589	12	[22]
Belize	Sept. 21, 1981	Sept. 21, 1981	constitutional monarchy	British monarch	prime minister	8	29	[26]	...	12[27]	200
Benin	Aug. 1, 1960	Dec. 2, 1990	republic	president		83	—	12	77	200	200
Bermuda	—	June 8, 1968	dependent territory (U.K.)	British monarch	[28]	11	40	11	—	12	200
Bhutan	March 24, 1910	—	[29]	monarch	chairman CM	150	—	20	196	—	—
Bolivia	Aug. 6, 1825	Feb. 2, 1967	republic	president		27	130	9	112	—	—
Bosnia and Herzegovina	March 3, 1992	Dec. 14, 1995[30]	federal republic	[31]	chairman CM	15	42	2	10[32]	...	...
Botswana	Sept. 30, 1966	Sept. 30, 1966	republic	president		15[21]	47	19	...	—	—
Brazil	Sept. 7, 1822	Oct. 5, 1988[16]	federal republic	president		81	513	27	5,656	12	200
Brunei	Jan. 1, 1984	*Sept. 29, 1959*	monarchy (sultanate)	sultan		21[21]	—	4	...	12	200
Bulgaria	Oct. 5, 1908	July 12, 1991	republic	president	prime minister	240	—	28	259	12	200
Burkina Faso	Aug. 5, 1960	June 11, 1991	republic	president	prime minister	178[21]	111	45	382	—	—
Burundi	July 1, 1962	July 23, 2001[33]	republic[34]	president[35]		[36]	[36]	15	116	—	—
Cambodia	Nov. 9, 1953	March 4, 1999[37]	constitutional monarchy	king	prime minister	61	122	24	183	12	200
Cameroon	Jan. 1, 1960	Jan. 18, 1996	republic	president	prime minister	180	—	10	56	50	[2]
Canada	July 1, 1867	April 17, 1982	federal parl. state[15]	Canadian GG[38]	prime minister	105	301	13	...	12	200
Cape Verde	July 5, 1975	Sept. 25, 1992	republic	president	prime minister	72	—	17	...	12[10]	200[10]
Central African Republic	Aug. 13, 1960	Jan. 14, 1995	republic	president	prime minister	109	—	17	69	—	—
Chad	Aug. 11, 1960	April 14, 1996	republic	president	prime minister	125	—	28	107	—	—
Chile	Sept. 18, 1810	March 11, 1981	republic	president		48	120	13	51	12	200
China	1523 BC	Dec. 4, 1982	people's republic	president	premier SC	2,989	—	31	332	12	[2]
Colombia	July 20, 1810	July 5, 1991	republic	president		102	163	33	1,011	12	200
Comoros	July 6, 1975	Feb. 17, 2001[39]	republic[34]	head of state[18]		—	—	...	...	12[10]	200[10]
Congo, Dem. Rep. of the	June 30, 1960	*April 9, 1994*	republic[34]	president		300	—	11	...	12	200
Congo, Rep. of the	Aug. 15, 1960	Nov. 3, 1997[41]	republic[34]	president		75	...	16	47	200	[2]
Costa Rica	Sept. 15, 1821	Nov. 9, 1949	republic	president		57	—	7	81	12	200
Côte d'Ivoire	Aug. 7, 1960	July 23, 2000[42]	republic	president[18]		225	—	16	58	12	200
Croatia	June 25, 1991	Dec. 22, 1990	republic	president	prime minister	151	—	21	123	12	...
Cuba	May 20, 1902	Feb. 24, 1976	socialist republic	president		601	—	15	169	12	200
Cyprus[43]	Aug. 16, 1960	Aug. 16, 1960	republic	president		56[44]	—	...	647	12	[2]
Czech Republic	Jan. 1, 1993	Jan. 1, 1993	republic	president	prime minister	81	200	14	76	—	—
Denmark	*c.* 800	June 5, 1953	constitutional monarchy	monarch	prime minister	179	—	16	275	3	200
Djibouti	June 27, 1977	Sept. 15, 1992	republic	president		65	—	5	...	12	200
Dominica	Nov. 3, 1978	Nov. 3, 1978	republic	president	prime minister	32	—	37	—	12	200
Dominican Republic	Feb. 27, 1844	Nov. 28, 1966	republic	president		30	149	31	160	6	200
East Timor	—	Oct. 26, 1999[45]	UN transitional admin.	UN administrator[46]		88	—	13	...	...	...
Ecuador	May 24, 1822	Aug. 10, 1998	republic	president		121	—	22	214	200	200

Finally, in the second half of the table are listed the memberships each country maintains in the principal international intergovernmental organizations of the world. This part of the table may also be utilized to provide a complete membership list for each of these organizations as of Dec. 1, 2001.

Notes for the column headings

a. The date may also be either that of the organization of the present form of government or the inception of the present administrative structure (federation, confederation, union, etc.).
b. Constitutions whose dates are in italic type had been wholly or substantially suspended or abolished as of late 2001.
c. For abbreviations used in this column see the list on the facing page.
d. When a legislative body has been adjourned or otherwise suspended, figures in parentheses indicate the number of members in the legislative body as provided for in constitution or law.
e. States contributing funds to or receiving aid from UNICEF in 1997.
f. 15 nations with judicial representation in ICJ in 2001.
g. Palestine (Liberation Organization) also a member.
h. OAU dissolved Sept. 17, 2001. Replaced by the African Union (AU) on Sept. 18, 2001.

International organizations, conventions

ACP	African, Caribbean, and Pacific (Lomé IV) convention
ADB	Asian Development Bank
APEC	Asia-Pacific Economic Cooperation Council
CARICOM	Caribbean Community and Common Market
EU	The European Union
ECOWAS	Economic Community of West African States
FAO	Food and Agriculture Org.
FZ	The Franc Zone
GCC	Gulf Cooperation Council
I-ADB	Inter-American Development Bank
IAEA	International Atomic Energy Agency
IBRD	International Bank for Reconstruction and Development
ICAO	International Civil Aviation Org.
ICJ	International Court of Justice
IDA	International Development Association
IDB	Islamic Development Bank
IFC	International Finance Corporation
ILO	International Labour Org.
IMF	International Monetary Fund
IMO	International Maritime Org.
ITU	International Telecommunication Union
LAS	League of Arab States
OAS	Organization of American States
OAU/AU	Organization of African Unity/African Union
OPEC	Organization of Petroleum Exporting Countries
SPC	South Pacific Commission
UNCTAD	United Nations Conference on Trade and Development
UNESCO	United Nations Educational Scientific and Cultural Org.
UNICEF	United Nations Children's Fund
UNIDO	United Nations Industrial Development Org.
UPU	Universal Postal Union
WHO	World Health Org.
WIPO	World Intellectual Property Org.
WMO	World Meteorological Org.
WTO	World Trade Org.

Abbreviations used in the executive-branch column

CM	Council of Ministers
EC	Executive Council
FC	Federal Council
GG	Governor-General
GPC	General People's Committee
NDC	National Defense Commission
PC	People's Council
PNA	Palestine National Authority
SC	State Council
SPDC	State Peace and Development Council

membership in international organizations																																					country
United Nations (date of admission)	UN organs★ and affiliated intergovernmental organizations																				Commonwealth of Nations	regional multipurpose						economic									
	UNCTAD★	UNICEF★e	ICJ★f	FAO	IAEA	IBRD	ICAO	IDA	IFC	ILO	IMF	IMO	ITU	UNESCO	UNIDO	UPU	WHO	WIPO	WMO	WTO		EU	GCC	LASg	OAS	OAU/AUh	SPC	ACP	ADB	APEC	CARICOM	ECOWAS	FZ	I-ADB	IDBg	OPEC	
1946	●	●		●	●	●	●	●	●	●	●		●	●	●	●	●		●										●						●		Afghanistan
1955	●	●		●	●	●	●	●	●	●	●	●	●	●	●	●	●	●	●	●															●		Albania
1962	●	●		●	●	●	●	●	●	●	●	●	●	●	●	●	●	●	●	5				●		●									●	●	Algeria
—																●											●										American Samoa
1993	●						●						●	●			●	●	●	5																	Andorra
1976	●	●		●	●	●	●	●	●	●	●	●	●	●	●	●	●	●	●	●						●		●									Angola
1981	●	●		●		●	●		●	●	●	●	●	●		●	●	●	●	●	●				●			●			●						Antigua and Barbuda
1945	●	●		●	●	●	●	●	●	●	●	●	●	●	●	●	●	●	●	●					●									●			Argentina
1992	●	●		●	●	●	●	●	●	●	●		●	●	●	●	●	●	●	5																	Armenia
—														14		●			●																		Aruba
1945	●	●		●	●	●	●	●	●	●	●	●	●	●		●	●	●	●	●	●						●		●	●							Australia
1955	●	●		●	●	●	●	●	●	●	●	●	●	●	●	●	●	●	●	●		●							●					●			Austria
1992	●	●		●	●	●	●	●	●	●	●	●	●	●	●	●	●	●	●	5									●						●		Azerbaijan
1973	●	●		●		●	●		●	●	●	●	●	●	●	●	●	●	●	5	●				●			●			●			●			Bahamas, The
1971	●	●		●		●	●		●	●	●	●	●	●	●	●	●	●	●	●			●	●											●		Bahrain
1974	●	●		●	●	●	●	●	●	●	●	●	●	●	●	●	●	●	●	●	●								●						●		Bangladesh
1966	●	●		●		●	●	●	●	●	●	●	●	●	●	●	●	●	●	●	●				●			●			●			●			Barbados
1945	●	●			●	●	●		●	●	●		●	●	●	●	●	●	●	5																	Belarus
1945	●	●		●	●	●	●	●	●	●	●	●	●	●	●	●	●	●	●	●		●							●					●			Belgium
1981	●	●		●		●	●	●	●	●	●	●	●	●	●	●	●	●	●	●	●				●			●			●			●			Belize
1960	●	●		●	●	●	●	●	●	●	●	●	●	●	●	●	●	●	●	●						●		●				●	●		●		Benin
—																●			●																		Bermuda
1971	●	●		●		●	●	●			●		●	●	●	●	●	●		5									●								Bhutan
1945	●	●		●	●	●	●	●	●	●	●	●	●	●	●	●	●	●	●	●					●									●			Bolivia
1992	●	●		●	●	●	●	●	●	●	●	●	●	●	●	●	●	●	●	5																	Bosnia and Herzegovina
1966	●	●		●		●	●	●	●	●	●		●	●	●	●	●	●	●	●	●					●		●									Botswana
1945	●	●	●	●	●	●	●	●	●	●	●	●	●	●	●	●	●	●	●	●					●									●			Brazil
1984	●					●	●				●	●	●			●	●	●	●	●	●									●					●		Brunei
1955	●	●		●	●	●	●		●	●	●	●	●	●	●	●	●	●	●	●																	Bulgaria
1960	●	●		●	●	●	●	●	●	●	●		●	●	●	●	●	●	●	●						●		●				●	●		●		Burkina Faso
1962	●	●		●		●	●	●	●	●	●		●	●	●	●	●	●	●	●						●		●									Burundi
1955	●	●		●	●	●	●	●	●	●	●	●	●	●	●	●	●	●	●	5									●								Cambodia
1960	●	●		●	●	●	●	●	●	●	●	●	●	●	●	●	●	●	●	●	●					●		●					●		●		Cameroon
1945	●	●		●	●	●	●	●	●	●	●	●	●	●		●	●	●	●	●	●				●				●	●				●			Canada
1975	●	●		●		●	●	●	●	●	●	●	●	●	●	●	●	●	●	5						●		●				●					Cape Verde
1960	●	●		●	●	●	●	●	●	●	●		●	●	●	●	●	●	●	●						●		●					●				Central African Republic
1960	●	●		●		●	●	●	●	●	●		●	●	●	●	●	●	●	●						●		●					●		●		Chad
1945	●	●		●	●	●	●	●	●	●	●	●	●	●	●	●	●	●	●	●					●					●				●			Chile
1945	●	●	●	●	●	●	●	●	●	●	●	●	●	●	●	●	●	●	●	●								●	●	●							China
1945	●	●		●	●	●	●	●	●	●	●	●	●	●	●	●	●	●	●	●					●									●			Colombia
1975	●	●		●		●	●	●	●	●	●	●	●	●	●	●	●		●					●		●		●					●		●		Comoros
1960	●	●		●	●	●	●	●	●	●	40	●	●	●	●	●	●	●	●	●						●		●									Congo, Dem. Rep. of the
1960	●	●		●		●	●	●	●	●	●	●	●	●	●	●	●	●	●	●						●		●					●				Congo, Rep. of the
1945	●	●		●	●	●	●	●	●	●	●	●	●	●	●	●	●	●	●	●					●									●			Costa Rica
1960	●	●		●	●	●	●	●	●	●	●	●	●	●	●	●	●	●	●	●						●		●				●	●				Côte d'Ivoire
1992	●	●		●	●	●	●	●	●	●	●	●	●	●	●	●	●	●	●	●														●			Croatia
1945	●	●		●	●		●			●		●	●	●	●	●	●	●	●	●					40												Cuba
1960	●	●		●	●	●	●	●	●	●	●	●	●	●	●	●	●	●	●	●	●																Cyprus[43]
1993	●	●		●	●	●	●	●	●	●	●	●	●	●	●	●	●	●	●	●																	Czech Republic
1945	●	●		●	●	●	●	●	●	●	●	●	●	●	●	●	●	●	●	●		●							●					●			Denmark
1977	●	●				●	●	●	●	●	●	●	●	●	●	●	●		●	●				●		●		●							●		Djibouti
1978	●	●		●		●		●	●	●	●	●	●	●	●	●	●	●	●	●	●				●			●			●						Dominica
1945	●	●		●	●	●	●	●	●	●	●	●	●	●	●	●	●	●	●	●					●			●						●			Dominican Republic
—																																					East Timor
1945	●	●		●	●	●	●	●	●	●	●	●	●	●	●	●	●	●	●	●					●									●			Ecuador

Government and international organizations (continued)

country	date of independence[a]	date of current or last constitution[b]	type of government	executive branch[c]: chief of state	executive branch[c]: head of government	legislative branch[d]: upper house (members)	legislative branch[d]: lower house (members)	admin. subdivisions: first-order (number)	admin. subdivisions: second-order (number)	seaward claims: territorial (nautical miles)	seaward claims: fishing/economic (nautical miles)
Egypt	Feb. 28, 1922	Sept. 11, 1971	republic	president	prime minister	454	—	27	186	12[47]	200[47]
El Salvador	Jan. 30, 1841	Dec. 20, 1983	republic	—president—		84	—	14	262	200	200
Equatorial Guinea	Oct. 12, 1968	Nov. 16, 1991[42]	republic	president	prime minister	80	—	7	18	12	200
Eritrea	May 24, 1993	May 23, 1997[48]	republic[34]	—president—		150	—	6	...	...	...
Estonia	Feb. 24, 1918	July 3, 1992	republic	president	prime minister	101	—	15	46	12	...
Ethiopia	c. 1000 BC	Aug. 22, 1995[49]	federal republic	president	prime minister	108	546	11	57	—	—
Faroe Islands	—	April 1, 1948	part of Danish realm	Danish monarch	[50]	32	—	9	48	3	200
Fiji	Oct. 10, 1970	July 27, 1998	republic	president	prime minister	32	71	4	15	12[10]	200[10]
Finland	Dec. 6, 1917	March 1, 2000	republic	president	prime minister	200	—	6	20	12[51]	12
France	August 843	Oct. 4, 1958[16]	republic	president	prime minister	321	577	22	96	12	200
French Guiana	—	Feb. 28, 1983	overseas dept. (Fr.)	French president	[52]	19	31	2	22	12	200
French Polynesia	—	Sept. 6, 1984	overseas territory (Fr.)	French president	[53]	49	—	5	48	12	200
Gabon	Aug. 17, 1960	March 26, 1991	republic	president	prime minister	91	120	9	37	12	200
Gambia, The	Feb. 18, 1965	Jan. 16, 1997	republic	—president—		49	—	7	45	12	200
Gaza Strip	—	May 4, 1994[54]	interim authority	—chairman PNA—		89	—	5	...	...	...
Georgia	April 9, 1991	Oct. 17, 1995	republic	—president[55]—		235	—	12	74	...	...
Germany	May 5, 1955	May 23, 1949	federal republic	president	chancellor	69	672	16	32	12[47]	200
Ghana	March 6, 1957	Jan. 7, 1993	republic	—president—		200	—	10	110	12	200
Greece	Feb. 3, 1830	April 6, 2001[56]	republic	president	prime minister	300	—	53	448	6/10	[2]
Greenland	—	May 1, 1979	part of Danish realm	Danish monarch	[50]	31	—	19	...	3	200
Grenada	Feb. 7, 1974	Feb. 7, 1974	constitutional monarchy	British monarch	prime minister	13	15	9	...	12	200
Guadeloupe	—	Feb. 28, 1983	overseas dept. (Fr.)	French president	[52]	42	43	3	34	12	200
Guam	—	Aug. 1, 1950	territory (U.S.)	U.S. president	governor	15	—	...	—	12	...
Guatemala	Sept. 15, 1821	Jan. 14, 1986	republic	—president—		113	—	22	313	12	200
Guernsey	—	Jan. 1, 1949[16]	crown dependency (U.K.)	British monarch[57]	[58]	59	—	2	10	...	...
Guinea	Oct. 2, 1958	Dec. 23, 1990[41]	republic	—president[59]—		114	—	8	34	12	200
Guinea-Bissau	Sept. 10, 1974	May 11, 1991	republic[34]	president	prime minister	102	—	9	37	12	200
Guyana	May 26, 1966	Oct. 6, 1980	cooperative republic	—president—		65	—	10	71	12	200
Haiti	Jan. 1, 1804	March 29, 1987	republic	president	prime minister	27	82	9	41	12	200
Honduras	Nov. 5, 1838	Jan. 20, 1982	republic	—president—		128	—	18	297	12	200
Hong Kong	—	July 1, 1997	[60]	—chief executive EC—		60	—	18	...	12	[2]
Hungary	Nov. 16, 1918	Oct. 18, 1989[41]	republic	president	prime minister	386[61]	—	20	195	—	—
Iceland	June 17, 1944	June 17, 1944	republic	president	prime minister	63	—	124	—	12	200
India	Aug. 15, 1947	Jan. 26, 1950	federal republic	president	prime minister	245	545	35	465	12	200
Indonesia	Aug. 17, 1945	Aug. 17, 1945	republic	—president—		700	500	30	...	12[10]	200[10]
Iran	Oct. 7, 1906	Dec. 2–3, 1979	Islamic republic	—president[62]—		290	—	28	282	12	50[63]
Iraq	Oct. 3, 1932	Sept. 22, 1968[64]	republic	—president—		250	—	18	96	12	[2]
Ireland	Dec. 6, 1921	Dec. 29, 1937	republic	president	prime minister	60	166	34	86	12	200
Isle of Man	—	1961[16]	crown dependency (U.K.)	British monarch[57]	chief minister	11	24	24	—	12[65]	...
Israel	May 14, 1948	June 1950[16]	republic	president	prime minister	120	—	6	15	12	[2]
Italy	March 17, 1861	Jan. 1, 1948	republic	president	prime minister	321	630	20	102	12	[2]
Jamaica	Aug. 6, 1962	Aug. 6, 1962	constitutional monarchy	British monarch	prime minister	21	60	13	—	12	200
Japan	c. 660 BC	May 3, 1947	constitutional monarchy	emperor	prime minister	247	480	47	3,233	12[66]	200
Jersey	—	Jan. 1, 1949[16]	crown dependency (U.K.)	British monarch[57]	[67]	57	—	12	—	3	...
Jordan	May 25, 1946	Jan. 8, 1952	constitutional monarchy	—king[18]—		40	80	12	18	3	[2]
Kazakhstan	Dec. 16, 1991	Sept. 6, 1995	republic	—president[18]—		39	77	17	...	—	—
Kenya	Dec. 12, 1963	Dec. 12, 1963	republic	—president—		224	—	8	...	12	200
Kiribati	July 12, 1979	July 12, 1979	republic	—president—		42	—	3	6	12[10]	200[10]
Korea, North	Sept. 9, 1948	Sept. 5, 1998[68]	socialist republic	chairman NDC	premier	687	—	13	172	12	200
Korea, South	Aug. 15, 1948	Feb. 25, 1988	republic	—president[18]—		273	—	16	195	12[69]	12
Kuwait	June 19, 1961	Nov. 16, 1962	const. mon. (emirate)	—emir[18]—		50[70]	—	5	—	12	[2]
Kyrgyzstan	Aug. 31, 1991	May 5, 1993	republic	—president[18]—		45	60	7	39	—	—
Laos	Oct. 23, 1953	Aug. 15, 1991	republic	president	prime minister	99	—	18	133	—	—
Latvia	Nov. 18, 1918	Nov. 7, 1922	republic	president	prime minister	100	—	33	70	12	...
Lebanon	Nov. 26, 1941	Sept. 21, 1990	republic	president	prime minister	128	—	6	c. 700	12	[2]
Lesotho	Oct. 4, 1966	April 2, 1993	[34, 71]	king	prime minister	33[21]	80	10	...	—	—
Liberia	July 26, 1847	Aug. 20, 1995[72]	republic	—president—		26	64	15	...	200	[2]
Libya	Dec. 24, 1951	March 2, 1977	socialist state[73]	leader[74]	sec. GPC	760	—	26	...	12[75]	[2]
Liechtenstein	July 12, 1806	Oct. 5, 1921	constitutional monarchy	prince	head of govt.	25	—	11	—	—	—
Lithuania	Feb. 16, 1918	Nov. 6, 1992	republic	president	prime minister	141	—	10	61	12	...
Luxembourg	May 10, 1867	Oct. 17, 1868	constitutional monarchy	grand duke	prime minister	21[21]	60	3	12	—	—
Macau	—	Dec. 20, 1999	[60]	—chief executive EC—		27	—	...	...	6	12
Macedonia	Nov. 17, 1991	Nov. 17, 1991	republic	president	prime minister	120	—	123	...	—	—
Madagascar	June 26, 1960	April 8, 1998	federal republic	—president[18]—		90	150	6	113	12	200
Malawi	July 6, 1964	May 18, 1994	republic	—president—		192	—	3	27	—	—
Malaysia	Aug. 31, 1957	Aug. 31, 1957	fed. const. monarchy	paramount ruler	prime minister	70	193	16	132	12	200
Maldives	July 26, 1965	Jan. 1, 1998	republic	—president—		42[70]	—	21	201	12[10]	[47]
Mali	Sept. 22, 1960	Feb. 25, 1992	republic	president	prime minister	147	—	9	701	—	—
Malta	Sept. 21, 1964	Dec. 13, 1974	republic	president	prime minister	65	—	1	68	12	25
Marshall Islands	Dec. 22, 1990	May 1, 1979	republic	—president—		12[21]	33	...	—	12[10]	200
Martinique	—	Feb. 28, 1983	overseas dept. (Fr.)	French president	[52]	45	41	4	34	12	200
Mauritania	Nov. 28, 1960	July 21, 1991	republic	—president[18]—		56	81	13	53	12	200
Mauritius	March 12, 1968	March 12, 1992	republic	president	prime minister	70	—	11	130	12	200
Mayotte	—	Dec. 24, 1976	dept. collectivity (Fr.)	French president	[76]	19	—	17	—	12	200
Mexico	Sept. 16, 1810	Feb. 5, 1917	federal republic	—president—		128	500	32	2,443	12	200
Micronesia	Dec. 22, 1990	Jan. 1, 1981	federal republic	—president—		14	—	4	74	12	200
Moldova	Aug. 27, 1991	Aug. 27, 1994	parliamentary republic	president	prime minister	101	—	12	...	—	—
Monaco	Feb. 2, 1861	Dec. 17, 1962	constitutional monarchy	prince	min. of state[77]	18	—	1	—	12	[2]
Mongolia	March 13, 1921	Feb. 12, 1992	republic	president	prime minister	76	—	22	342	—	—
Morocco	March 2, 1956	Oct. 7, 1996	constitutional monarchy	—king[18]—		270	325	17[78]	71[78]	12	200
Mozambique	June 25, 1975	Nov. 30, 1990	republic	—president—		250	—	11	112	12	200
Myanmar (Burma)	Jan. 4, 1948	*Jan. 4, 1974*	republic	—chairman SPDC—		(492)	—	14	58	12	200
Namibia	March 21, 1990	March 21, 1990	republic	—president—		26	72[70]	13	—	12	200
Nauru	Jan. 31, 1968	Jan. 31, 1968	republic	—president—		18	—	1	—	12	200
Nepal	Nov. 13, 1769	Nov. 9, 1990	constitutional monarchy	king	prime minister	60	205	14	75	—	—

United Nations (date of admission)	membership in international organizations: UN organs★ and affiliated intergovernmental organizations																				Commonwealth of Nations	regional multipurpose						economic									country
	UNCTAD★	UNICEF★[e]	ICJ★[f]	FAO	IAEA	IBRD	ICAO	IDA	IFC	ILO	IMF	IMO	ITU	UNESCO	UNIDO	UPU	WHO	WIPO	WMO	WTO		EU	GCC	LAS[g]	OAS	OAU/AU[h]	SPC	ACP	ADB	APEC	CARICOM	ECOWAS	FZ	I-ADB	IDB[g]	OPEC	
1945	●	●	●	●	●	●	●	●	●	●	●	●	●	●	●	●	●	●	●	●				●		●									●		Egypt
1945	●	●		●	●	●	●	●	●	●	●	●	●	●	●	●	●	●	●	●					●									●			El Salvador
1968	●	●		●		●	●	●	●	●	●	●	●	●	●	●	●	●								●		●					●				Equatorial Guinea
1993	●	●		●		●	●	●	●	●	●	●	●	●	●	●	●	●	●							●		●									Eritrea
1991	●	●		●	●	●	●		●	●	●	●	●	●	●	●	●	●	●	●																	Estonia
1945	●	●		●	●	●	●	●	●	●	●	●	●	●	●	●	●		●	5						●		●									Ethiopia
—																●																					Faroe Islands
1970	●	●		●		●	●	●	●	●	●	●	●	●	●	●	●	●	●	●	●						●	●	●								Fiji
1955	●	●		●	●	●	●	●	●	●	●	●	●	●	●	●	●	●	●	●		●							●					●			Finland
1945	●	●	●	●	●	●	●	●	●	●	●	●	●	●	●	●	●	●	●	●		●					●		●				●	●			France
—																●																	●				French Guiana
—																●			●								●						●				French Polynesia
1960	●	●		●	●	●	●	●	●	●	●	●	●	●	●	●	●	●	●	●						●		●					●		●		Gabon
1965	●	●		●		●	●	●	●	●	●	●	●	●	●	●	●	●	●	●	●					●		●				●			●		Gambia, The
—		●														●																					Gaza Strip
1992	●	●		●	●	●	●	●	●	●	●	●	●	●	●	●	●		●	●																	Georgia
1973	●	●	●	●	●	●	●	●	●	●	●	●	●	●	●	●	●	●	●	●		●							●					●			Germany
1957	●	●		●	●	●	●	●	●	●	●	●	●	●	●	●	●	●	●	●	●					●		●				●					Ghana
1945	●	●		●	●	●	●	●	●	●	●	●	●	●	●	●	●	●	●	●		●															Greece
—																●																					Greenland
1974	●	●		●		●	●	●	●	●	●	●	●	●	●	●	●	●		●	●				●			●			●						Grenada
—																●																	●				Guadeloupe
—																●											●										Guam
1945	●	●		●	●	●	●	●	●	●	●	●	●	●	●	●	●	●	●	●					●									●			Guatemala
—																●																					Guernsey
1958	●	●		●		●	●	●	●	●	●	●	●	●	●	●	●	●	●	●						●		●				●			●		Guinea
1974	●	●		●		●	●	●	●	●	●	●	●	●	●	●	●	●	●	●						●		●				●	●		●		Guinea-Bissau
1966	●	●		●		●	●	●	●	●	●	●	●	●	●	●	●	●	●	●	●				●			●			●			●			Guyana
1945	●	●		●	●	●	●	●	●	●	●	●	●	●	●	●	●	●	●	●					●			●			●			●			Haiti
1945	●	●		●	●	●	●	●	●	●	●	●	●	●	●	●	●	●	●	●					●									●			Honduras
—		●										14				●			●	●									●	●							Hong Kong
1955	●	●	●	●	●	●	●	●	●	●	●	●	●	●	●	●	●	●	●	●																	Hungary
1946	●	●		●	●	●	●	●	●	●	●	●	●	●		●	●	●	●	●																	Iceland
1945	●	●		●	●	●	●	●	●	●	●	●	●	●	●	●	●	●	●	●	●								●								India
1950	●	●		●	●	●	●	●	●	●	●	●	●	●	●	●	●	●	●	●									●	●					●	●	Indonesia
1945	●	●		●	●	●	●	●	●	●	●	●	●	●	●	●	●		●																●	●	Iran
1945	●	●		●	●	●	●	●	●	●	●	●	●	●	●	●	●	●	●					●											●	●	Iraq
1955	●	●		●	●	●	●	●	●	●	●	●	●	●	●	●	●	●	●	●		●															Ireland
—																●																					Isle of Man
1949	●	●		●	●	●	●	●	●	●	●	●	●	●	●	●	●	●	●	●														●			Israel
1955	●	●		●	●	●	●	●	●	●	●	●	●	●	●	●	●	●	●	●		●							●					●			Italy
1962	●	●		●	●	●	●		●	●	●	●	●	●	●	●	●	●	●	●	●				●			●			●			●			Jamaica
1956	●	●	●	●	●	●	●	●	●	●	●	●	●	●	●	●	●	●	●	●									●	●				●			Japan
—																●																					Jersey
1955	●	●	●	●	●	●	●	●	●	●	●	●	●	●	●	●	●	●	●	●				●											●		Jordan
1992	●	●		●	●	●	●	●	●	●	●	●	●	●	●	●	●	●	●	5									●						●		Kazakhstan
1963	●	●		●	●	●	●	●	●	●	●	●	●	●	●	●	●	●	●	●	●					●		●									Kenya
1999	●	●		●		●	●	●	●	●	●		●	●		●	●				●						●	●	●								Kiribati
1991	●	●		●			●					●	●	●	●	●	●	●	●																		Korea, North
1991	●	●		●	●	●	●	●	●	●	●	●	●	●	●	●	●	●	●	●									●	●							Korea, South
1963	●	●		●	●	●	●	●	●	●	●	●	●	●	●	●	●	●	●	●			●	●											●	●	Kuwait
1992	●	●		●		●	●	●	●	●	●		●	●	●	●	●	●	●	●									●						●		Kyrgyzstan
1955	●	●		●		●	●	●	●	●	●		●	●	●	●	●	●	●	5									●								Laos
1991	●	●		●	●	●	●	●	●	●	●	●	●	●		●	●	●	●	●																	Latvia
1945	●	●		●	●	●	●	●	●	●	●	●	●	●	●	●	●	●	●	5				●											●		Lebanon
1966	●	●		●		●	●	●	●	●	●		●	●	●	●	●	●	●	●	●					●		●									Lesotho
1945	●	●		●	●	●	●	●	●	●	●	●	●	●	●	●	●	●	●							●		●				●					Liberia
1955	●	●		●	●	●	●	●	●	●	●	●	●	●	●	●	●	●	●					●		●									●	●	Libya
1990	●				●								●			●	●	●		●																	Liechtenstein
1991	●	●		●	●	●	●		●	●	●	●	●	●	●	●	●	●	●	●																	Lithuania
1945	●	●		●	●	●	●	●	●	●	●	●	●	●	●	●	●	●	●	●		●															Luxembourg
—				●								14		14		●			●	●																	Macau
1993	●	●		●	●	●	●	●	●	●	●	●	●	●	●	●	●	●	●	5																	Macedonia
1960	●	●	●	●	●	●	●	●	●	●	●	●	●	●	●	●	●	●	●	●						●		●									Madagascar
1964	●	●		●		●	●	●	●	●	●	●	●	●	●	●	●	●	●	●	●					●		●									Malawi
1957	●	●		●	●	●	●	●	●	●	●	●	●	●	●	●	●	●	●	●	●								●	●					●		Malaysia
1965	●	●		●		●	●	●	●		●	●	●	●	●	●	●		●	●	●								●						●		Maldives
1960	●	●		●	●	●	●	●	●	●	●		●	●	●	●	●	●	●	●						●		●				●	●		●		Mali
1964	●	●		●	●	●	●			●	●	●	●	●	●	●	●	●	●	●	●																Malta
1991	●	●		●	●	●	●	●	●		●	●	●	●		●	●										●	●	●								Marshall Islands
—																●																	●				Martinique
1961	●	●		●		●	●	●	●	●	●	●	●	●	●	●	●	●	●	●				●		●		●							●		Mauritania
1968	●	●		●	●	●	●	●	●	●	●	●	●	●	●	●	●	●	●	●	●					●		●									Mauritius
—																●																	●				Mayotte
1945	●	●		●	●	●	●	●	●	●	●	●	●	●	●	●	●	●	●	●					●					●				●			Mexico
1991	●	●				●	●	●	●		●		●	●		●	●		●								●	●	●								Micronesia
1992	●	●		●	●	●	●	●	●	●	●		●	●	●	●	●	●	●	●																	Moldova
1993	●	●			●		●					●	●	●		●	●	●																			Monaco
1961	●	●		●	●	●	●	●	●	●	●	●	●	●	●	●	●	●	●	●									●								Mongolia
1956	●	●		●	●	●	●	●	●	●	●	●	●	●	●	●	●	●	●	●				●											●		Morocco
1975	●	●		●		●	●	●	●	●	●	●	●	●	●	●	●	●	●	●	●					●		●							●		Mozambique
1948	●	●		●	●	●	●	●	●	●	●	●	●	●	●	●	●	●	●	●									●								Myanmar (Burma)
1990	●	●		●	●	●	●	5	●	●	●	●	●	●	●	●	●	●	●	●	●					●		●									Namibia
1999				●			●						●	●		●	●				●						●	●	●								Nauru
1955	●	●		●		●	●	●	●	●	●	●	●	●	●	●	●	●	●	5									●								Nepal

Government and international organizations (continued)

country	date of independence[a]	date of current or last constitution[b]	type of government	executive branch[c]		legislative branch[d]		admin. subdivisions		seaward claims	
				chief of state	head of government	upper house (members)	lower house (members)	first-order (number)	second-order (number)	territorial (nautical miles)	fishing/economic (nautical miles)
Netherlands, The	March 30, 1814	Feb. 17, 1983	constitutional monarchy	monarch	prime minister	75	150	12	536	12	200
Netherlands Antilles	—	Dec. 29, 1954	overseas territory (Neth.)	Dutch monarch	[13]	22	—	5	—	12	200
New Caledonia	—	February 1999	overseas country (Fr.)	French president[79]	president	54	—	3	33	12	200
New Zealand	Sept. 26, 1907	June 30, 1852[16]	constitutional monarchy	British monarch	prime minister	120	—	16	74	12	200
Nicaragua	April 30, 1838	Jan. 9, 1987	republic	president		93	—	17	151	200	200
Niger	Aug. 3, 1960	Aug. 9, 1999[41]	republic	president[18]		83	—	8	35	—	—
Nigeria	Oct. 1, 1960	May 5, 1999	federal republic	president		109	360	37	990	30	200
Northern Mariana Is.	—	Jan. 9, 1978	commonwealth (U.S.)	U.S. president	governor	9	18	4	—	12	200
Norway	June 7, 1905	May 17, 1814	constitutional monarchy	king	prime minister	165	—	19	435	4	200
Oman	Dec. 20, 1951	Nov. 6, 1996[80]	monarchy (sultanate)	sultan		[81]	—	8	60	12	200
Pakistan	Aug. 14, 1947	*Aug. 14, 1973*	republic	president		(87)	(217)	16[82]	106	12	200
Palau	Oct. 1, 1994	Jan. 1, 1981	republic	president		14	16	16	—	3	200
Panama	Nov. 3, 1903	May 20, 1983[37]	republic	president[83]		71	—	14	74	200	[2]
Papua New Guinea	Sept. 16, 1975	Sept. 16, 1975	constitutional monarchy	British monarch	prime minister	109	—	20	267	12[10]	200[10]
Paraguay	May 14, 1811	June 22, 1992	republic	president		46	80	18	217	—	—
Peru	July 28, 1821	Dec. 29, 1993	republic	president[18]		120	—	14/28[84]	194	200	200
Philippines	July 4, 1946	Feb. 11, 1987	republic	president		24	260[85]	16	80	...	200[10]
Poland	Nov. 10, 1918	Oct. 17, 1997	republic	president	prime minister	100	460	16	373	12	[86]
Portugal	c. 1140	April 25, 1976	republic	president	prime minister	230	—	7	308	12	200
Puerto Rico	—	July 25, 1952	commonwealth (U.S.)	U.S. president	governor	27[87]	51[87]	78	...	12	200
Qatar	Sept. 3, 1971	July 1970[64]	monarchy	emir[18]		35[21]	—	9	—	12	[88]
Réunion	—	Feb. 28, 1983	overseas dept. (Fr.)	French president	[52]	47	45	4	24	12	200
Romania	May 21, 1877	Dec. 13, 1991	republic	president	prime minister	143	346	41	2.687	12[47]	200[47]
Russia	Dec. 8, 1991	Dec. 24, 1993	federal republic	president	prime minister	178	450	7	89	12	...
Rwanda	July 1, 1962	May 5, 1995[89]	republic[34]	president[18]		74	—	12	154	—	—
St. Kitts and Nevis	Sept. 19, 1983	Sept. 19, 1983	constitutional monarchy	British monarch	prime minister	15	—	1	—	12	200
St. Lucia	Feb. 22, 1979	Feb. 22, 1979	constitutional monarchy	British monarch	prime minister	11	17[9]	10	—	12	200
St. Vincent	Oct. 27, 1979	Oct. 27, 1979	constitutional monarchy	British monarch	prime minister	21	—	...	—	12	200
Samoa	Jan. 1, 1962	Oct. 28, 1960	[90]	head of state	prime minister	49	—	11	—	12	200
San Marino	855	Oct. 8, 1600	republic	captains-regent (2)		60	—	9	—	—	—
São Tomé and Príncipe	July 12, 1975	Sept. 10, 1990	republic	president	prime minister	55	—	1	6	12[10]	200[10]
Saudi Arabia	Sept. 23, 1932	[91]	monarchy	king		90[21]	—	13	103	12	[2]
Senegal	Aug. 20, 1960	Jan. 7, 2001[42]	republic	president[18]		120	—	10	30	12[47]	200[47]
Seychelles	June 29, 1976	June 21, 1993	republic	president		34	—	...	...	12	200
Sierra Leone	April 27, 1961	Oct. 1, 1991	republic	president		80	—	4	12	200	[2]
Singapore	Aug. 9, 1965	June 3, 1959[16]	republic	president	prime minister	93	—	—	—	3	12
Slovakia	Jan. 1, 1993	2001[92]	republic	president	prime minister	150	—	8	79	—	—
Slovenia	June 25, 1991	Dec. 23, 1991	republic	president	prime minister	40	90	192	—	...	...
Solomon Islands	July 7, 1978	July 7, 1978	constitutional monarchy	British monarch	prime minister	50	—	10	...	12[10]	200[10]
Somalia	July 1, 1960	July–August 2000[93]	republic[34]	president[18]		245	—	3	...	200	200
South Africa	May 31, 1910	June 30, 1997	republic	president		90	400	9	360	12	200
Spain	1492	Dec. 29, 1978	constitutional monarchy	king	prime minister	259	350	19	50	12	200[94]
Sri Lanka	Feb. 4, 1948	Sept. 7, 1978	republic	president		225	—	...	...	12	200
Sudan, The	Jan. 1, 1956	June 30, 1998	federal republic	president		360	—	26	66	12	[2]
Suriname	Nov. 25, 1975	Nov. 25, 1987	republic	president		51	—	10	...	12	200
Swaziland	Sept. 6, 1968	*Sept. 6, 1968*	monarchy	king[18]		30[21]	65[21]	4	55	—	—
Sweden	before 836	Jan. 1, 1975	constitutional monarchy	king	prime minister	349	—	21	289	12	[22]
Switzerland	Sept. 22, 1499	Jan. 1, 2000	federal state	president FC		46	200	26	187	—	—
Syria	April 17, 1946	March 14, 1973	republic	president		250	—	14	47	35	[2]
Taiwan	Oct. 25, 1945	Dec. 25, 1947[16]	republic	president	premier	225	—	2	25	24	200
Tajikistan	Sept. 9, 1991	Nov. 6, 1994	republic	president	prime minister	33	63	5	...	—	—
Tanzania	Dec. 9, 1961	April 25, 1977	republic	president		275	—	1	25	12	200
Thailand	1350	Oct. 11, 1997	constitutional monarchy	king	prime minister	200	500	76	795	12	200
Togo	April 27, 1960	Sept. 27, 1992[42]	republic	president	prime minister	81	—	5	21	30	200
Tonga	June 4, 1970	Nov. 4, 1875	constitutional monarchy[95]	monarch		30	—	...	...	12	200
Trinidad and Tobago	Aug. 31, 1962	July 27, 1976	republic	president	prime minister	31	36	16	...	12[10]	200[10]
Tunisia	March 20, 1956	June 1, 1959	republic	president	prime minister	182	—	24	257	12	[2]
Turkey	Oct. 29, 1923	Nov. 7, 1982	republic	president	prime minister	550	—	81	849	12[96]	[22]
Turkmenistan	Oct. 27, 1991	May 18, 1992	republic	president PC		50	—	6	...	—	—
Tuvalu	Oct. 1, 1978	Oct. 1, 1986	constitutional monarchy	British monarch	prime minister	12	—	8	—	12[10]	200[10]
Uganda	Oct. 9, 1962	Oct. 8, 1995	republic	president[18]		305	—	56	...	—	—
Ukraine	Aug. 24, 1991	June 28, 1996	republic	president	prime minister	450	—	27	485	12	200
United Arab Emirates	Dec. 2, 1971	Dec. 2, 1971	federation of emirates	president	prime minister	40[21]	—	7	—	12	200
United Kingdom	Dec. 6, 1921	[97]	constitutional monarchy	monarch	prime minister	695	659	...	...	12[65]	200
United States	July 4, 1776	March 4, 1789	federal republic	president		100	435	51	3,043	12	200
Uruguay	Aug. 25, 1828	Feb. 15, 1967	republic	president		31	99	19	...	200	200
Uzbekistan	Aug. 31, 1991	Dec. 8, 1992	republic	president[18]		250	—	14	162	...	...
Vanuatu	July 30, 1980	July 30, 1980	republic	president	prime minister	52	—	6	...	12[10]	200[10]
Venezuela	July 5, 1811	Dec. 20, 1999	federal republic	president		165	—	25	332	12	200
Vietnam	Sept. 2, 1945	April 15, 1992	socialist republic	president	prime minister	450	—	61	479	12	200
Virgin Islands (U.S.)	—	July 22, 1954	territory (U.S.)	U.S. president	governor	15	—	...	...	12	200
West Bank	—	May 4, 1994[54]	interim authority	chairman PNA		89	—	11	...	—	—
Western Sahara	—	—	annexure of Morocco	—	—	—	—	...	...	12	200
Yemen	December 1918	Sept. 29, 1994[99]	republic	president	prime minister	111	301	19	...	12	200
Yugoslavia	Dec. 1, 1918	April 27, 1992	federal republic	federal president	prime minister	40	138	3	25[100]	...	...
Zambia	Oct. 24, 1964	May 28, 1996[3]	republic	president		156	—	9	57	—	—
Zimbabwe	April 18, 1980	April 18, 1980	republic	president		150	—	10	80	—	—

[1]Six-month interim government headed by prime minister announced Dec. 5, 2001. [2]Territorial sea claim. [3]Date president signed new constitution. [4]Varies between 32 and 52 nautical miles. [5]Observer. [6]President of France and Bishop of Urgell, Spain. [7]President annulled post of prime minister in January 1999. [8]Includes 70 UNITA members expelled September 1998. [9]Excludes possible ex officio members. [10]Measured from claimed archipelagic baselines. [11]Promulgation date of significant amendments to July 9, 1853, constitution. [12]Assisted by the ministerial coordinator. [13]Executive responsibilities divided between (for The Netherlands) the governor and (locally) the prime minister. [14]Associate member. [15]Formally a constitutional monarchy. [16]Evolving body of constitutional law. [17]Date of referendum adopting new constitution. [18]Assisted by the prime minister. [19]Excludes one vacant seat reserved for Nagorno-Karabakh representative. [20]The National Action Charter eventually transforming Bahrain into a constitutional monarchy was approved in February 2001. [21]Body with limited or no legislative authority. [22]Defined by the equidistant line. [23]Legal status is controversial. [24]Excludes children of the monarch serving ex officio from age 18. [25]10 provincial councils; 5 region/community councils. [26]6 districts; 8 town boards. [27]3 nautical miles from the mouth of the Sarstoon River (southern boundary with Guatemala) to Ranguana Caye. [28]Executive responsibilities divided between (for the U.K.) the governor and (locally) the premier. [29]Resembles a constitutional monarchy without a formal constitution. [30]Date of international treaty confirming the existence of a single state. [31]Tripartite presidency. [32]Excludes Republika Srpska. [33]Implementation date of Arusha Accords. [34]Transitional government. [35]Assisted by the vice president. [36]New transitional legislative bodies to be installed by the end of 2001. [37]Date significant amendments adopted. [38]Governor-general can exercise all the powers of the reigning monarch of the Commonwealth. [39]Unity agreement date reinstating the Comoros (excepting Mayotte) as a single federated entity. [40]Suspended membership. [41]Transitional constitution. [42]Date of referendum approving new constitution. [43]Republic of Cyprus only. [44]Occupied seats only. [45]Date UN assumed formal transitional administration. [46]Assisted locally by chief minister. [47]Zone defined by geographic coordinates. [48]Date new constitution approved by constituent assembly. [49]Date new republic was formally established. [50]Executive responsibilities divided between (for Denmark) the high commissioner and (locally) the prime minister. [51]3 nautical miles in the Gulf of Finland. [52]Executive responsibilities

membership in international organizations																																					country
United Nations (date of admission)	UN organs★ and affiliated intergovernmental organizations																				Commonwealth of Nations	regional multipurpose						economic										
	UNCTAD★	UNICEF★e	ICJ★f	FAO	IAEA	IBRD	ICAO	IDA	IFC	ILO	IMF	IMO	ITU	UNESCO	UNIDO	UPU	WHO	WIPO	WMO	WTO		EU	GCC	LASg	OAS	OAU/AUh	SPC	ACP	ADB	APEC	CARICOM	ECOWAS	FZ	I-ADB	IDBg	OPEC	
1945	●	●	●	●	●	●	●	●	●	●	●	●	●	●	●	●	●	●	●	●		●							●					●			Netherlands, The
—														14		●			●	●																	Netherlands Antilles
—																●			●								●						●				New Caledonia
1945	●	●		●	●	●	●	●	●	●	●	●	●	●	●	●	●	●	●	●	●						●		●	●							New Zealand
1945	●	●		●	●	●	●	●	●	●	●	●	●	●	●	●	●	●	●	●					●									●			Nicaragua
1960	●	●		●	●	●	●	●	●	●	●		●	●	●	●	●	●	●	●						●		●				●	●		●		Niger
1960	●	●		●	●	●	●	●	●	●	●	●	●	●	●	●	●	●	●	●	●					●		●				●				●	Nigeria
—																●											●										Northern Mariana Is.
1945	●	●		●	●	●	●	●	●	●	●	●	●	●	●	●	●	●	●	●									●					●			Norway
1971	●	●		●		●	●	●	●	●	●	●	●	●	●	●	●	●	●	●			●	●											●		Oman
1947	●	●		●	●	●	●	●	●	●	●	●	●	●	●	●	●	●	●	●	40								●						●		Pakistan
1994		●		●		●	●	●			●			●		●	●										●	●									Palau
1945	●	●		●	●	●	●	●	●	●	●	●	●	●	●	●	●	●	●	●					●									●			Panama
1975	●	●		●		●	●	●	●	●	●	●	●	●	●	●	●	●	●	●	●						●	●	●	●							Papua New Guinea
1945	●	●		●	●	●	●	●	●	●	●	●	●	●	●	●	●	●	●	●					●									●			Paraguay
1945	●	●		●	●	●	●	●	●	●	●	●	●	●	●	●	●	●	●	●					●					●				●			Peru
1945	●	●		●	●	●	●	●	●	●	●	●	●	●	●	●	●	●	●	●									●	●							Philippines
1945	●	●		●	●	●	●	●	●	●	●	●	●	●	●	●	●	●	●	●																	Poland
1955	●	●		●	●	●	●	●	●	●	●	●	●	●	●	●	●	●	●	●		●												●			Portugal
—				14												●	14																				Puerto Rico
1971	●	●		●	●	●	●			●	●	●	●	●	●	●	●	●	●	●			●	●											●	●	Qatar
—																●																	●				Réunion
1955	●	●		●	●	●	●		●	●	●	●	●	●	●	●	●	●	●	●																	Romania
1991	●	●	●		●	●	●	●	●	●	●	●	●	●	●	●	●	●	●	5										●							Russia
1962	●	●		●		●	●	●	●	●	●		●	●	●	●	●	●	●	●						●		●									Rwanda
1983	●	●		●		●		●	●	●	●	●		●	●	●	●	●		●	●				●			●			●						St. Kitts and Nevis
1979	●	●		●		●	●	●	●	●	●	●	●	●	●	●	●	●	●	●	●				●			●			●						St. Lucia
1980	●	●		●		●	●	●		●	●	●	●	●	●	●	●	●		●	●				●			●			●						St. Vincent
1976	●	●		●		●	●	●	●		●	●	●	●		●	●		●	5	●						●	●	●								Samoa
1992	●	●		●		●	●			●	●		●	●		●	●	●	●																		San Marino
1975	●	●		●		●	●	●		●	●	●	●	●	●	●	●	●	●	5						●		●									São Tomé and Príncipe
1945	●	●		●	●	●	●	●	●	●	●	●	●	●	●	●	●	●	●	5			●	●											●	●	Saudi Arabia
1960	●	●		●	●	●	●	●	●	●	●	●	●	●	●	●	●	●	●	●						●		●				●	●		●		Senegal
1976	●	●		●		●	●		●	●	●	●	●	●	●	●	●	●	●	5	●					●		●									Seychelles
1961	●	●	●	●	●	●	●	●	●	●	●	●	●	●	●	●	●	●	●	●	●					●		●				●			●		Sierra Leone
1965	●	●			●	●	●		●	●	●	●	●			●	●	●	●	●	●								●	●							Singapore
1993	●	●		●	●	●	●	●	●	●	●	●	●	●	●	●	●	●	●	●																	Slovakia
1992	●	●		●	●	●	●	●	●	●	●	●	●	●	●	●	●	●	●	●														●			Slovenia
1978	●	●		●		●	●	●	●	●	●	●	●	●		●	●		●	●	●						●	●	●								Solomon Islands
1960	●	●		●		●	●	●	●	●	●	●	●	●	●	●	●	●	●					●		●		●							●		Somalia
1945	●	●		●	●	●	●	●	●	●	●	●	●	●	●	●	●	●	●	●	●					●		●									South Africa
1955	●	●		●	●	●	●	●	●	●	●	●	●	●	●	●	●	●	●	●		●							●					●			Spain
1955	●	●		●	●	●	●	●	●	●	●	●	●	●	●	●	●	●	●	●	●								●								Sri Lanka
1956	●	●		●	●	●	●	●	●	●	●	●	●	●	●	●	●	●	●	5				●		●		●							●		Sudan, The
1975	●	●		●		●	●			●	●	●	●	●	●	●	●	●	●	●					●			●			●			●	●		Suriname
1968	●	●		●		●	●	●	●	●	●		●	●	●	●	●	●	●	●	●					●		●									Swaziland
1946	●	●		●	●	●	●	●	●	●	●	●	●	●	●	●	●	●	●	●		●							●					●			Sweden
—	●	●		●	●	●	●	●	●	●	●	●	●	●	●	●	●	●	●	●									●					●			Switzerland
1945	●	●		●	●	●	●	●	●	●	●	●	●	●	●	●	●		●					●											●		Syria
—																				●									●	●							Taiwan
1992	●	●		●	●	●	●	●	●	●	●	●	●	●	●	●	●	●	●	5									●						●		Tajikistan
1961	●	●		●	●	●	●	●	●	●	●	●	●	●	●	●	●	●	●	●	●					●		●									Tanzania
1946	●	●		●	●	●	●	●	●	●	●	●	●	●	●	●	●	●	●	●									●	●							Thailand
1960	●	●		●		●	●	●	●	●	●	●	●	●	●	●	●	●	●	●						●		●				●	●				Togo
1999	●	●		●		●	●	●	●		●	●	●	●	●	●	●	●		5	●						●	●	●								Tonga
1962	●	●		●		●	●	●	●	●	●	●	●	●	●	●	●	●	●	●	●				●			●			●			●			Trinidad and Tobago
1956	●	●		●	●	●	●	●	●	●	●	●	●	●	●	●	●	●	●	●				●		●									●		Tunisia
1945	●	●		●	●	●	●	●	●	●	●	●	●	●	●	●	●	●	●	●									●						●		Turkey
1992	●	●		●		●	●	5	●	●	●	●	●	●	●	●	●	●	●																●		Turkmenistan
2000	●	●											●	●	●	●	●				●						●	●	●								Tuvalu
1962	●	●		●	●	●	●	●	●	●	●		●	●	●	●	●	●	●	●	●					●		●							●		Uganda
1945	●	●			●	●	●	5	●	●	●	●	●	●	●	●	●	●	●	5																	Ukraine
1971	●	●		●	●	●	●	●	●	●	●	●	●	●	●	●	●	●	●	●			●	●											●	●	United Arab Emirates
1945	●	●	●	●	●	●	●	●	●	●	●	●	●	●	●	●	●	●	●	●	●	●					●		●					●			United Kingdom
1945	●	●	●	●	●	●	●	●	●	●	●	●	5		●	●	●	●	●	●					●		●		●	●				●			United States
1945	●	●		●	●	●	●		●	●	●	●	●	●	●	●	●	●	●	●					●									●			Uruguay
1992	●	●		●	●	●	●	●	●	●	●		●	●	●	●	●	●	●	5									●								Uzbekistan
1981	●	●		●		●	●	●			●	●	●	●	●	●	●		●	●	●						●	●	●								Vanuatu
1945	●	●	●	●	●	●	●		●	●	●	●	●	●	●	●	●	●	●	●					●									●		●	Venezuela
1977	●	●		●	●	●	●	●	●	●	●	●	●	●	●	●	●	●	●	5									●	●							Vietnam
—																●															●						Virgin Islands (U.S.)
—		●																																			West Bank
—																										98											Western Sahara
1947	●	●		●	●	●	●	●	●	●	●	●	●	●	●	●	●	●	●	5				●											●		Yemen
1945	●	●		●	●	●	●	5	5	●	●	●	●	●	●	●	●	●	●																		Yugoslavia
1964	●	●		●	●	●	●	●	●	●	●		●	●	●	●	●	●	●	●	●					●		●									Zambia
1980	●	●		●	●	●	●	●	●	●	●		●	●	●	●	●	●	●	●	●					●		●									Zimbabwe

divided among (for France) the prefect and (locally) the president of the General Council and the president of the Regional Council. [53]Executive responsibilities divided between (for France) the high commissioner and (locally) the president of the territorial government. [54]Date of agreement providing for Palestinian self-rule. [55]Assisted by the minister of state. [56]Date parliament approved constitutional amendments for 78 articles. [57]Represented by the lieutenant governor. [58]Executive committees appointed by the States of Deliberation. [59]Assisted by extraconstitutional prime minister. [60]Special administrative region (China). [61]Excludes 13 seats set aside for ethnic minorities. [62]Shares coexecutive authority with spiritual leader. [63]Sea of Oman only; median line boundaries in Persian Gulf. [64]Provisional constitution. [65]Median line between the Isle of Man and the United Kingdom. [66]3 nautical miles in 5 straits. [67]Executive committees appointed by the States Assembly. [68]Essentially 1992 constitution with new preamble. [69]3 nautical miles in Korea Strait. [70]Elected seats only. [71]Traditionally a hereditary monarchy. [72]Date of peace accord. [73]Formally a *jamahiriya,* translated as "the masses of people"; in fact, a military dictatorship. [74]De facto chief of state. [75]Based on Gulf of Sidra closing line (32° 30′ N), in part. [76]Executive responsibilities divided between (for France) the prefect and (locally) the president of the General Council. [77]Under prince's authority. [78]Includes Western Sahara annexure. [79]Represented by High Commissioner. [80]Basic law promulgated by sultan. [81]Has 2 consultative bodies with advisory authority only. [82]Includes federally administered tribal areas, excludes Jammu and Kashmir. [83]Assisted by vice presidents. [84]Two concomitant administrative systems. [85]Includes vacant seats. [86]Defined by international treaties. [87]Excludes additional seats for both houses of the legislature to meet 1/3 total representation requirements for minority parties per constitution. [88]Limits of continental shelf or median boundaries. [89]Date constitution adopted by transitional legislature. [90]Mixed political system approximating a constitutional monarchy. [91]Royal decrees from March 1, 1992, created first written rules of governance. [92]Many significant constitutional amendments became effective in 2001. [93]Transitional National Charter. [94]Atlantic Ocean only. [95]In practice resembles a system of monarchical absolutism. [96]Black Sea and Mediterranean Sea; 6 nautical miles in Aegean Sea. [97]Based on evolving body of statutes and common law. [98]Membership held by the Sahrawi Arab Democratic Republic. [99]Effective date of significant amendments. [100]Serbia only excluding Kosovo.

Area and population

This table provides the area and population for each of the countries of the world and for all but the smallest political dependencies having a permanent civilian population. The data represent the latest published and unpublished data for both the surveyed area of the countries and their populations, the latter both as of a single year (2001) to provide the best comparability and as of the most recent census to provide the fullest comparison of certain demographic measures that are not always available between successive national censuses. The 2001 midyear estimates represent a combination of national, United Nations (UN) or other international organizations, and *Encyclopædia Britannica* estimates so as to give the best fit to available published series, to take account of unpublished information received via Internet, facsimile, or correspondence, and to incorporate the results of very recent censuses for which published analyses are not yet available.

One principal point to bear in mind when studying these statistics is that all of them, whatever degree of precision may be implied by the exactness of the numbers, are estimates—all of varying, and some of suspect, accuracy—even when they *contain* a very full enumeration. The United States—which has a long tradition both of census taking and of the use of the most sophisticated analytical tools in processing the data—is unable to determine within 1.2% (the estimated 2000 undercount) its total population nationally. And that is an *average* underenumeration. In states and larger cities, where enumeration of particular populations, including illegal, is more difficult, the accuracy of the enumerated count may be off as much as 3.1% at a state level (in New Mexico, for instance) and by a greater percent for a single city. The high accuracy attained by census operations in China may approach 0.25% of rigorously maintained civil population registers. Other national census operations not so based, however, are inherently less accurate. For example, Ethiopia's first-ever census in 1984 resulted in figures that were 30% or more above prevailing estimates; Nigeria's 1991 census corrected decades of miscounts and was well below prevailing estimates. An undercount of 2–8% is more typical, but even census operations offering results of 30% or more above or below prevailing estimates can still represent well-founded benchmarks from which future planning may proceed. The editors have tried to take account of the range of variation and accuracy in published data, but it is difficult to establish a value for many sources of inaccuracy unless some country or agency has made a conscientious effort to establish both the relative accuracy (precision) of its estimate and the absolute magnitude of the quantity it is trying to measure—for example, the number of people in Cambodia who died at the hands of the Khmer Rouge. If a figure of 2,000,000 is adopted, what is its accuracy: ± 1%, 10%, 50%? Are the original data documentary or evidentiary, complete or incomplete, analytically biased or unbiased, in good agreement with other published data?

Many similar problems exist and in endless variations: What is the extent of eastern European immigration to western Europe in search of jobs? How many refugees from Afghanistan, Sierra Leone, or Burundi are there in surrounding countries? How many undocumented aliens are there in the United Kingdom, Japan, or the United States? How many Tamils have left Sri Lanka as a result of civil unrest in their homeland? How many Amerindians exist (remain, preserving their original language and a mode of life unassimilated by the larger national culture) in the countries of South America?

Still, much information is accurate, well founded, and updated regularly. The sources of these data are censuses; national population registers (cumu-

Area and population

country	area			population (latest estimate)					population (latest census)				
	square miles	square kilo-metres	rank	total midyear 2001	rank	density		% annual growth rate 1996–2001	census year	total	male (%)	female (%)	urban (%)
						per sq mi	per sq km						
Afghanistan	251,825	652,225	41	26,813,000	38	106.5	41.1	3.6	1979	13,051,358[1]	51.4	48.6	15.1
Albania	11,082	28,703	142	3,091,000	132	278.9	107.7	–0.5	1989	3,182,417	51.5	48.5	35.7
Algeria	919,595	2,381,741	11	30,821,000	35	33.5	12.9	1.5	1998	29,272,343	50.6	49.4	80.8
American Samoa	77	199	206	58,500	207	759.3	293.8	2.0	2000	57,291	51.4[2]	48.6[2]	33.4[2]
Andorra	181	468	194	66,900	204	369.7	143.0	0.8	2000[3]	65,971	52.2	47.8	93.0[4]
Angola	481,354	1,246,700	24	10,366,000	72	21.5	8.3	1.9	1970	5,673,046	52.1	47.9	14.2
Antigua and Barbuda	171	442	196	71,500	203	419.1	161.8	0.8	1991	63,896	48.2	51.8	36.2
Argentina	1,073,400	2,780,092	8	37,487,000	31	34.9	13.5	1.3	1991	32,615,528	48.9	51.1	88.4
Armenia	11,484	29,743	141	3,807,000	123	331.5	128.0	0.2	1989	3,287,677	49.3	50.7	67.8
Aruba	75	193	207	97,200	196	1,296.3	503.8	2.5	1991	66,687	49.2	50.8	...
Australia	2,969,910	7,692,030	6	19,358,000	53	6.5	2.5	1.1	1996	17,892,423	49.5	50.5	89.3
Austria	32,378	83,858	115	8,069,000	87	249.2	96.2	0.0	1991	7,795,786	48.2	51.8	64.5
Azerbaijan	33,400	86,600	113	8,105,000	86	242.7	93.6	0.9	1999	7,953,000	48.8	51.2	56.9[4]
Bahamas, The	5,382	13,939	159	298,000	175	55.3	21.4	1.1	1990	255,095	49.0	51.0	64.3
Bahrain	268	694	187	701,000	160	2,616.8	1,010.2	3.2	1991	508,037	57.9	42.1	88.4
Bangladesh	56,977	147,570	93	131,270,000	8	2,303.9	889.5	1.6	1991	111,455,185	51.4	48.6	20.2
Barbados	166	430	197	269,000	178	1,617.7	624.5	0.3	1990[6]	257,083	47.7	52.3	37.9[7]
Belarus	80,153	207,595	85	9,986,000	79	124.6	48.1	–0.5	1999	10,045,237[6]	47.0[6]	53.0[6]	69.3[6]
Belgium	11,787	30,528	139	10,268,000	77	871.2	336.4	0.2	1991	9,978,681	48.9	51.1	96.6[8]
Belize	8,867	22,965	150	247,000	180	27.8	10.8	2.5	2000	240,204	50.5	49.5	47.7
Benin	44,300	114,760	101	6,591,000	96	148.8	57.4	3.1	1992	4,915,555	48.6	51.4	35.7
Bermuda	21	54	213	63,500	206	3,024.0	1,176.0	0.7	1991[6]	58,460	48.5	51.5	100.0
Bhutan	18,150	47,000	131	692,000	161	38.2	14.7	2.9	...	...	51.6[10]	48.4[10]	7.0[10]
Bolivia	424,164	1,098,581	28	8,516,000	85	20.1	7.8	2.3	1992	6,420,792	49.4	50.6	57.5
Bosnia and Herzegovina	19,741	51,129	127	3,922,000	119	198.7	76.7	3.8	1991	4,377,033	49.9	50.1	39.6
Botswana	224,607	581,730	47	1,586,000	146	7.1	2.7	1.2	1991	1,326,796	47.8	52.2	23.9
Brazil	3,300,171	8,547,404	5	172,118,000	5	52.2	20.1	1.6	1991	146,825,475	49.4	50.6	75.6
Brunei	2,226	5,765	168	344,000	174	154.4	59.6	2.4	1991	260,482	52.8	47.2	66.6
Bulgaria	42,846	110,971	103	7,953,000	88	185.6	71.7	–0.7	2001	7,977,646	48.7	51.3	67.2[11]
Burkina Faso	105,946	274,400	73	12,272,000	64	115.8	44.7	2.8	1996	10,312,609	48.2	51.8	15.0[10]
Burundi	10,740	27,816	145	6,224,000	100	579.5	223.8	2.8	1990[6]	5,292,793	48.6	51.4	6.3
Cambodia	69,898	181,035	89	12,720,000	63	182.0	70.3	2.7	1998	11,437,656	48.2	51.8	20.9
Cameroon	183,569	475,442	53	15,803,000	59	86.1	33.2	2.6	1987	10,516,232	49.0	51.0	38.3
Canada	3,849,674	9,970,610	2	31,002,000	34	8.1	3.1	0.9	1996	28,846,761	49.1	50.9	77.9
Cape Verde	1,557	4,033	170	446,000	167	286.2	110.5	2.4	2000	434,812	48.4	51.6	53.3
Central African Republic	240,324	622,436	43	3,577,000	127	14.9	5.7	1.9	1988	2,688,426	49.1	50.9	36.5
Chad	495,755	1,284,000	21	8,707,000	83	17.6	6.8	3.4	1993	6,279,931	47.9	52.1	21.4
Chile	292,135	756,626	38	15,402,000	60	52.7	20.4	1.3	1992	13,348,401	49.1	50.9	83.5
China	3,696,100	9,572,900	3	1,274,915,000	1	344.9	133.2	1.1	2000	1,265,830,000	51.6	48.4	36.1
Colombia	440,762	1,141,568	26	43,071,000	27	97.7	37.7	1.9	1993	33,109,840	49.2	50.8	70.3[7]
Comoros	719	1,862	176	566,000	163	787.5	304.1	2.2	1991	446,817	49.5	50.5	28.5
Congo, Dem. Rep. of the	905,354	2,344,858	12	53,625,000	23	59.2	22.9	2.8	1984	29,671,407	49.2	50.8	29.1[12]
Congo, Rep. of the	132,047	342,000	63	2,894,000	134	21.9	8.5	2.3	1984[6]	1,909,248	48.7	51.3	52.0
Costa Rica	19,730	51,100	128	3,936,000	118	199.5	77.0	2.9	2000	3,824,593	50.0	50.0	51.9[10]
Côte d'Ivoire	124,504	322,463	68	16,393,000	56	131.7	50.8	2.3	1988	10,815,694	51.1	48.9	39.0
Croatia	21,831	56,542	126	4,393,000	116	201.2	77.7	0.1	1991	4,784,265	48.5	51.5	54.3
Cuba	42,804	110,861	104	11,190,000	67	261.4	100.9	0.3	1993	10,904,466	50.3	49.7	74.4
Cyprus[13]	3,572	9,251	165	873,000	156	244.4	94.4	1.0	1992[6, 14]	615,013	49.8	50.2	67.7
Czech Republic	30,450	78,866	117	10,269,000	76	337.3	130.2	–0.1	1991	10,302,215	48.5	51.5	75.2
Denmark	16,639	43,096	133	5,358,000	106	322.0	124.3	0.4	1999[3]	5,313,577	49.4	50.6	85.0
Djibouti	8,950	23,200	149	461,000	166	51.5	19.9	1.6	1983	273,974	51.9	48.1	82.8[12]
Dominica	290	750	184	71,700	202	247.2	95.6	–0.4	1991	71,183	49.8	50.2	...
Dominican Republic	18,792	48,671	130	8,693,000	84	462.6	178.6	1.9	1993	7,293,390	48.7	51.3	56.1
East Timor	5,641	14,609	158	897,000	155	159.1	61.4	1.6	1990	747,750	51.7	48.3	7.8
Ecuador	105,037	272,045	74	12,879,000	62	122.6	47.3	1.9	1990	9,648,189	49.7	50.3	55.4

lated periodically); registration of migration, births, deaths, and so on; sample surveys to establish demographic conditions; and the like.

The statistics provided for area and population by country are ranked, and the population densities based on those values are also provided. The population densities, for purposes of comparison within this table, are calculated on the bases of the 2000 midyear population estimate as shown and of total area of the country. Elsewhere in individual country presentations the reader may find densities calculated on more specific population figures and more specialized area bases: land area for Finland (because of its many lakes) or ice-free area for Greenland (most of which is ice cap). The data in this section conclude with the estimated average annual growth rate for the country (including both natural growth and net migration) during the five-year period, 1996–2001.

In the section containing census data, information supplied includes the census total (usually de facto, the population actually present, rather than de jure, the population legally resident, who might be anywhere); the male-female breakdown; the proportion that is urban (usually according to the country's own definition); and finally an analysis of the age structure of the population by 15-year age groups. This last analysis may be particularly useful in distinguishing the type of population being recorded—young, fast-growing nations show a high proportion of people under 30 (many countries in sub-Saharan Africa and the Middle East have about 40% of their population under 15 years), while other nations (for example Sweden, which suffered no age-group losses in World War II) exhibit quite uniform proportions.

Finally, a section is provided giving the population of each country at 10-year intervals from 1950 to 2020. The data for years past represent the best available analysis of the published data by the country itself, by the demographers of the UN, demographers of the U.S. Bureau of the Census, International Data Base, or by the editors of Britannica. The projections for 2010 and 2020 similarly represent the best fit of available data through 2000 with projected population structure and growth rates during the next two decades. The evidence of the last 30 years with respect to similar estimates published about 1970, however, shows how cloudy is the glass through which these numbers are read. In 1970 no respectable Western analyst would have imagined proposing that mainland China could achieve the degree of birth control that it apparently has since then (as evidenced by the results of 1982 and 1990 censuses); on the other hand, even the Chinese admit that their methods have been somewhat Draconian and that they have already seen some backlash in terms of higher birth rates among those who have so far postponed larger families. How much is "some" by 2010? Compound that problem with all the social, economic, political, and biological factors that can affect 217 countries' populations, and the difficulty facing the prospective compiler of such projections may be appreciated.

Specific data about the vital rates affecting the data in this table may be found in great detail in both the country statistical boxes in "The Nations of the World" section and in the *Vital statistics, marriage, family* table, beginning at page 802.

Percentages in this table for male and female population will always total 100.0, but percentages by age group may not, for reasons such as nonresponse on census forms, "don't know" responses (which are common in countries with poor birth registration systems), and the like.

age distribution (%)						population (by decade, '000s)								country
0–14	15–29	30–44	45–59	60–74	75 and over	1950	1960	1970	1980	1990	2000	2010 projection	2020 projection	
44.5	26.9	15.8	8.6	3.6	0.6	8,150	9,829	12,431	14,985	14,750	25,889	33,864	41,735	Afghanistan
33.0	28.9	18.5	11.7	5.9	1.9	1,227	1,623	2,157	2,671	3,258	3,100	3,248	3,497	Albania
36.2	30.6	17.7	8.9	5.1	1.5	8,956	10,800	14,330	18,666	24,698	30,386	35,022	40,365	Algeria
38.1[2]	29.0[2]	18.1[2]	9.4[2]	4.3[2]	1.1[2]	19	20	27	32	47	57	70	86	American Samoa
15.4	20.0	20.3	18.6	10.5	5.3	6	8	19	33	53	66	73	80	Andorra
41.7	23.2	17.0	7.4	3.8	1.0	4,118	4,797	5,606	6,741	8,056	10,145	12,646	15,750	Angola
30.4	27.8	20.5	10.2	7.7	3.4	45	55	66	69	64	71	75	79	Antigua and Barbuda
30.6	23.3	19.3	13.9	9.6	3.3	17,150	20,616	23,962	28,094	32,527	37,032	41,474	45,347	Argentina
30.3	25.7	20.8	13.6	6.4	3.2	1,354	1,867	2,520	3,067	3,545	3,805	3,828	3,951	Armenia
24.4	22.0	27.0	16.1	7.2	3.0	51	57	61	60	64	97	102	104	Aruba
21.5[5]	22.3[5]	23.1[5]	17.1[5]	11.0[5]	5.0[5]	8,219	10,315	12,552	14,741	17,065	19,157	20,925	22,409	Australia
17.4	23.7	21.6	17.2	13.4	6.7	6,935	7,048	7,447	7,549	7,718	8,078	8,033	8,078	Austria
31.8	25.6	24.1	9.5	7.6	1.4	2,896	3,895	5,172	6,165	7,166	8,048	8,549	9,475	Azerbaijan
32.2	30.8	19.7	10.6	5.0	1.8	79	110	170	210	257	295	315	324	Bahamas, The
31.7	28.4	28.2	8.0	3.1	0.6	110	149	210	334	503	691	803	899	Bahrain
41.5	25.2	16.2	8.1	4.3	1.1	45,646	54,622	67,403	88,077	109,897	129,194	150,392	169,613	Bangladesh
24.1	27.1	22.1	11.4	9.9	5.4	209	232	235	249	261	268	275	283	Barbados
19.5	21.8	23.4	16.4	—18.9—		7,745	8,190	9,040	9,650	10,190	10,004	9,923	9,904	Belarus
18.2	21.8	22.5	16.9	14.1	6.6	8,639	9,153	9,690	9,859	9,967	10,251	10,350	10,323	Belgium
43.9[9]	27.9[9]	14.9[9]	7.2[9]	4.4[9]	1.6[9]	68	90	120	146	189	241	308	392	Belize
48.6	24.2	14.5	6.6	4.1	1.9	1,673	2,055	2,620	3,444	4,656	6,396	8,411	10,588	Benin
19.5	24.0	26.8	16.4	—13.3—		37	43	53	55	59	63	67	69	Bermuda
40.2[10]	26.0[10]	17.4[10]	10.1[10]	5.2[10]	1.1[10]	...	...	...	...	519	678	837	1,019	Bhutan
41.2	26.2	16.8	8.9	—6.5—		2,714	3,351	4,212	5,355	6,573	8,329	10,229	12,193	Bolivia
23.5[8]	26.3[8]	22.6[8]	16.9[8]	8.9[8]	2.7[8]	2,662	3,240	3,703	4,092	4,424	3,836	4,103	4,182	Bosnia and Herzegovina
42.8	27.3	14.3	7.3	4.1	2.2	430	497	584	903	1,304	1,576	1,502	1,318	Botswana
34.7	28.1	19.3	10.6	5.7	1.6	53,444	72,594	95,847	118,617	143,581	169,358	184,306	194,224	Brazil
34.5	29.3	24.2	7.9	—4.1—		45	83	128	185	258	336	408	475	Brunei
20.5[11]	19.2[11]	—39.8[11]—		—20.5[11]—		7,251	7,867	8,490	8,862	8,718	8,012	7,229	6,528	Bulgaria
47.9[5]	26.8[5]	12.9[5]	7.6[5]	3.9[5]	0.9[5]	4,376	4,866	5,626	6,939	9,037	11,946	15,424	19,402	Burkina Faso
46.4	25.3	15.4	7.0	4.0	1.7	2,363	2,812	3,513	4,138	5,285	6,055	7,669	9,553	Burundi
42.8	26.1	17.2	8.5	4.3	1.1	4,163	5,364	6,996	6,499	8,965	12,371	16,345	20,012	Cambodia
46.4	24.5	14.6	8.7	4.1	1.6	4,888	5,609	6,727	8,747	11,761	15,422	19,202	22,869	Cameroon
19.9	20.9	25.7	17.2	11.1	5.2	13,737	17,909	21,324	24,561	27,634	30,750	33,132	35,187	Canada
43.6[10]	24.8[10]	17.1[10]	5.8[10]	6.3[10]	2.4[10]	146	197	269	296	342	435	474	492	Cape Verde
43.2	27.5	15.0	9.2	4.1	0.8	1,260	1,467	1,827	2,244	2,803	3,513	4,135	4,672	Central African Republic
48.1	24.6	14.7	7.2	4.2	1.3	2,608	3,042	3,728	4,535	6,018	8,425	11,616	15,772	Chad
29.4	27.3	21.2	12.2	7.2	2.5	6,082	7,608	9,496	11,147	13,100	15,211	17,010	18,774	Chile
27.7[2]	31.0[2]	20.7[2]	12.1[2]	6.9[2]	1.7[2]	556,613	667,070	818,316	981,242	1,133,683	1,261,379	1,357,864	1,433,111	China
34.5	28.5	20.1	10.0	5.3	1.6	12,568	16,857	22,561	28,447	34,970	42,231	49,665	56,569	Colombia
47.6[8]	27.0[8]	13.1[8]	7.7[8]	3.5[8]	1.0[8]	148	183	236	334	429	549	734	950	Comoros
47.3[12]	25.9[12]	14.1[12]	8.1[12]	3.8[12]	0.8[12]	13,569	16,462	21,395	28,129	37,991	51,965	69,846	92,377	Congo, Dem. Rep. of the
44.7	27.2	13.3	9.1	4.6	0.7	768	931	1,183	1,620	2,218	2,831	3,491	4,209	Congo, Rep. of the
32.1[10]	27.1[10]	21.6[10]	11.7[10]	5.6[10]	1.9[10]	862	1,236	1,731	2,246	2,874	3,826	4,493	5,052	Costa Rica
46.8	27.3	15.0	7.5	2.8	0.6	2,860	3,565	5,427	8,261	11,919	15,981	20,003	23,748	Côte d'Ivoire
19.4	20.7	22.7	18.3	12.9	4.5	3,837	4,036	4,205	4,383	4,508	4,282	4,505	4,560	Croatia
22.3	29.4	21.3	14.8	8.4	3.9	5,850	7,028	8,572	9,780	10,603	11,148	11,532	11,805	Cuba
25.4	22.0	22.3	15.4	10.2	4.7	494	573	615	631	757	865	956	1,056	Cyprus[13]
21.0	21.8	22.6	16.8	12.7	5.1	8,925	9,539	9,830	10,292	10,298	10,273	10,236	10,105	Czech Republic
18.2	19.2	22.4	20.5	12.6	7.1	4,271	4,581	4,929	5,123	5,141	5,339	5,525	5,706	Denmark
39.4	32.9	16.9	7.4	2.8	0.6	60	78	158	279	370	451	579	729	Djibouti
33.3	28.3	16.3	9.7	—11.8—		51	60	70	75	72	72	72	72	Dominica
36.5[15]	29.5[15]	18.4[15]	9.6[15]	4.8[15]	1.2[15]	2,353	3,231	4,423	5,697	7,098	8,554	9,995	11,489	Dominican Republic
...	...	...	...	...	...	433	501	605	581	740	885	1,015	1,139	East Timor
38.8	28.5	17.3	9.0	4.7	1.7	3,307	4,421	5,958	8,123	10,264	12,646	14,899	16,904	Ecuador

Area and population (continued)

country	area			population (latest estimate)					population (latest census)				
	square miles	square kilo-metres	rank	total midyear 2001	rank	density		% annual growth rate 1996–2001	census year	total	male (%)	female (%)	urban (%)
						per sq mi	per sq km						
Egypt	385,210	997,690	30	65,239,000	17	169.4	65.4	2.1	1996	59,312,914	51.2	48.8	42.6
El Salvador	8,124	21,041	151	6,238,000	99	767.8	296.5	1.9	1992	5,118,599	48.6	51.4	50.4
Equatorial Guinea	10,831	28,051	144	486,000	164	44.9	17.3	2.5	1983	300,060	48.8	51.2	28.2
Eritrea	46,774	121,144	99	4,298,000	117	91.9	35.5	3.7	1984	2,703,998	49.9	50.1	15.1
Estonia	17,462	45,227	132	1,363,000	148	78.1	30.1	–1.5	2000	1,376,700[6]	46.1	53.9	74.3[10]
Ethiopia	437,794	1,133,882	27	65,892,000	16	150.5	58.1	2.8	1994	53,477,265	50.3	49.7	14.4[12]
Faroe Islands	540	1,399	178	46,600	210	86.2	33.3	1.3	1999[3]	45,409	51.8	48.2	...
Fiji	7,055	18,272	155	827,000	157	117.3	45.3	1.3	1996	775,077	50.8	49.2	46.4
Finland	130,559	338,145	64	5,185,000	109	39.7	15.3	0.2	1990	4,998,478	48.5	51.5	79.7
France	210,026	543,965	49	58,835,000	21	280.1	108.2	0.3	1999	58,518,748	48.6	51.4	75.5
French Guiana	33,399	86,504	114	168,000	186	5.0	1.9	3.3	1999	157,274	50.4	49.6	77.8[4]
French Polynesia	1,544	4,000	171	238,000	181	153.8	59.4	1.6	1996	219,521	51.9	48.1	40.1[4]
Gabon	103,347	267,667	76	1,221,000	151	11.8	4.6	1.1	1993	1,011,710	49.3	50.7	73.2
Gambia, The	4,127	10,689	163	1,411,000	147	341.9	132.0	3.4	1993	1,038,145	50.1	49.9	36.7
Gaza Strip	140	363	200	1,203,000	152	8,589.9	3,312.9	4.4	1995[3, 17]	1,054,000	50.9	49.1	...
Georgia	26,911	69,700	121	4,989,000	112	185.4	71.6	–0.9	1989	5,443,359	47.2	52.8	55.7
Germany	137,847	357,021	62	82,386,000	12	597.7	230.8	0.1	1998[3]	82,037,000	48.8	51.2	87.5[10]
Ghana	92,098	238,533	81	19,894,000	50	216.0	83.4	2.0	1984	12,296,081	49.3	50.7	32.0
Greece	50,949	131,957	96	10,975,000	69	215.4	83.2	0.7	1991	10,264,156	49.3	50.7	58.9
Greenland	836,330	2,166,086	14	56,300	208	0.1	0.0	0.1	2000[3]	56,124	53.4	46.6	81.5
Grenada	133	344	202	102,000	194	769.1	297.4	0.7	1991	95,597	48.8	51.2	33.5
Guadeloupe	658	1,705	177	432,000	171	656.3	253.3	1.0	1999	422,496	48.1	51.9	99.7[4]
Guam	217	561	191	158,000	189	726.9	281.2	1.5	1990	133,152	53.3	46.7	38.2
Guatemala	42,042	108,889	105	11,687,000	65	278.0	107.3	2.7	1994	8,331,874	49.3	50.7	35.0
Guernsey	30	78	211	64,300	205	2,144.7	824.9	0.4	1996[18]	58,681	48.1	51.9	...
Guinea	94,926	245,857	78	7,614,000	89	80.2	31.0	0.8	1996	7,165,750	48.8	51.2	26.0
Guinea-Bissau	13,948	36,125	137	1,316,000	149	94.3	36.4	2.4	1991	983,367	48.4	51.6	20.3[8]
Guyana	83,044	215,083	84	776,000	158	9.3	3.6	–0.1	1991	701,704	49.2	50.8	35.4[12]
Haiti	10,695	27,700	146	6,965,000	93	651.2	251.4	1.4	1982	5,053,792	48.5	51.5	20.6
Honduras	43,433	112,492	102	6,626,000	95	152.6	58.9	3.1	1988	4,376,839	49.6	50.4	39.4
Hong Kong	422	1,092	180	6,732,000	94	15,968.0	6,165.5	0.9	2001	6,715,000	49.0	51.0	100.0
Hungary	35,919	93,030	110	10,190,000	76	283.7	109.5	–0.2	1990	10,375,323	48.1	51.9	61.8
Iceland	39,699	102,819	106	284,000	176	7.2	2.8	1.1	1999[3]	278,717	50.1	49.9	93.5
India	1,222,559	3,166,414	7	1,029,991,000	2	842.5	325.3	1.7	2001	1,027,015,247	51.7	48.3	27.8
Indonesia	742,308	1,922,570	16	212,195,000	4	285.9	110.4	1.5	1990	178,631,196	49.9	50.1	30.9
Iran	629,315	1,629,918	18	63,442,000	18	100.8	38.9	1.2	1996	60,055,488	50.8	49.2	61.3
Iraq	167,975	435,052	58	23,332,000	44	138.9	53.6	3.0	1997	22,017,983	49.7	50.3	74.5[12]
Ireland	27,133	70,273	120	3,823,000	122	140.9	54.4	1.1	1996	3,626,087	49.6	50.4	57.0
Isle of Man	227	588	190	73,500	200	323.6	125.0	0.5	1996[6]	71,714	48.5	51.5	74.7
Israel[21, 22]	7,886	20,425	152	6,258,000	97	793.6	306.4	2.5	1995[6, 23]	5,548,523	49.3	50.7	92.9[12]
Italy	116,347	301,337	71	57,892,000	22	497.6	192.1	0.2	1991	57,103,833	48.6	51.4	67.1[24]
Jamaica	4,244	10,991	162	2,624,000	135	618.2	238.7	0.8	1991	2,374,193	49.0	51.0	50.4
Japan	145,884	377,837	61	127,100,000	9	871.2	336.4	0.2	1995	125,570,246	49.0	51.0	78.1
Jersey	45	116	210	89,400	198	1,985.8	770.4	0.6	1996	85,150	48.6	51.4	...
Jordan[25]	34,495	89,342	112	5,133,000	111	148.8	57.4	3.3	1994	4,139,458	52.2	47.8	78.3
Kazakhstan	1,052,090	2,724,900	9	14,868,000	61	14.1	5.5	–0.9	1999	15,049,100	48.5[26]	51.5[26]	57.2[26]
Kenya	224,961	582,646	46	30,766,000	36	136.8	52.8	1.9	1999	28,686,607	49.5	50.5	32.2[4]
Kiribati	313	811	182	94,100	197	300.8	116.1	2.4	1995	77,658	49.5	50.5	36.5
Korea, North	47,399	122,762	98	21,968,000	49	463.5	178.9	0.4	1993	21,213,378	48.7	51.3	58.9
Korea, South	38,402	99,461	108	47,676,000	25	1,241.5	479.3	0.9	1995[6]	44,608,726	50.2	49.8	81.0[12]
Kuwait	6,880	17,818	156	2,275,000	140	330.7	127.7	3.7	1995	1,575,983	58.0	42.0	97.0[12]
Kyrgyzstan	77,200	199,900	86	4,934,000	113	63.9	24.7	1.3	1999	4,822,938	49.4	50.6	34.8
Laos	91,429	236,800	83	5,636,000	101	61.6	23.8	2.5	1995	4,581,258	49.5	50.5	20.7[12]
Latvia	24,938	64,589	124	2,358,000	139	94.5	36.5	–0.9	2000	2,375,339	46.0	54.0	69.2
Lebanon	4,016	10,400	164	3,628,000	125	903.3	348.8	1.4	1970	2,126,325	50.8	49.2	60.1
Lesotho	11,720	30,355	140	2,177,000	142	185.8	71.7	1.8	1996[6]	1,960,069	49.2	50.8	16.9
Liberia	37,743	97,754	109	3,226,000	131	85.5	33.0	9.7	1984	2,101,628	50.6	49.4	38.8
Libya	678,400	1,757,000	17	5,241,000	108	7.7	3.0	2.3	1995[6]	4,404,986	50.8	49.2	85.3[12]
Liechtenstein	62	160	209	33,000	212	534.1	206.3	1.2	1999[3]	32,426	48.7	51.3	22.2[4]
Lithuania	25,212	65,300	123	3,691,000	124	146.4	56.5	–0.1	1989	3,689,779	47.4	52.6	68.0
Luxembourg	999	2,586	173	444,000	169	444.7	171.8	1.3	1991	384,634	49.0	51.0	85.9[8]
Macau	9.1	23.6	215	445,000	168	48,381.4	18,702.1	1.4	1991	339,464	48.5	51.5	97.0
Macedonia	9,928	25,713	148	2,046,000	143	206.1	79.6	0.5	1994	1,945,932	50.4	49.6	58.7
Madagascar	226,658	587,041	45	15,983,000	57	70.5	27.2	3.1	1993[6]	12,092,157	49.5	50.5	26.4[12]
Malawi	45,747	118,484	100	10,491,000	71	229.3	88.5	2.0	1998	9,933,868	49.0	51.0	14.0
Malaysia	127,354	329,845	66	22,602,000	46	177.5	68.5	2.5	2000	22,202,614	50.4	49.6	50.6[9]
Maldives	115	298	204	275,000	177	2,394.8	924.2	1.9	2000	269,010	51.2	48.8	25.5[29]
Mali	482,077	1,248,574	23	11,009,000	68	22.8	8.8	3.1	1987	7,696,348	48.9	51.1	22.0
Malta	122	316	203	384,000	173	3,152.9	1,214.0	0.6	1995	378,132	49.4	50.6	90.3[4]
Marshall Islands	70	181	208	52,300	209	747.5	289.1	1.5	1999	50,865	51.2	48.8	64.5[30]
Martinique	436	1,128	179	388,000	172	889.0	343.6	0.7	1999	381,427	47.4	52.6	94.6[4]
Mauritania	398,000	1,030,700	29	2,591,000	136	6.5	2.5	2.5	2000	2,548,157	48.7	51.3	57.7[10]
Mauritius	788	2,040	175	1,195,000	153	1,517.0	586.0	1.1	1990	1,056,827	49.9	50.1	39.3
Mayotte	145	375	199	159,000	187	1,097.1	424.2	5.2	1997	131,320	50.7	49.3	...
Mexico	758,449	1,964,375	15	99,969,000	11	131.8	50.9	1.9	2000	97,361,711	48.6	51.4	71.3
Micronesia	271	701	186	118,000	192	435.0	167.9	1.5	1994	105,506	51.1	48.9	28.0[12]
Moldova	13,000	33,700	138	3,611,000	126	277.7	107.1	–1.5	1989	4,337,592	47.5	52.5	46.9
Monaco	0.75	1.95	217	31,800	213	42,456.0	16,329.2	0.5	1990	29,972	47.5	52.5	100.0
Mongolia	603,909	1,564,116	19	2,435,000	138	4.0	1.6	1.4	2000	2,382,500	49.6	50.4	58.6
Morocco[32]	177,117	458,730	55	28,986,000	37	163.7	63.2	1.7	1994	25,821,571[33]	49.7[33]	50.3[33]	51.7[33]
Mozambique	313,661	812,379	35	19,371,000	52	61.8	23.8	1.7	1997	16,099,246	47.9	52.1	28.6
Myanmar (Burma)	261,228	676,577	40	41,995,000	28	160.8	62.1	0.7	1983	35,307,913	49.6	50.4	24.0
Namibia	318,580	825,118	34	1,798,000	145	5.6	2.2	1.8	1991	1,401,711	48.6	51.4	32.8
Nauru	8.2	21.2	216	12,100	216	1,474.1	570.2	2.1	1992	9,919	51.2	48.8	100.0
Nepal	56,827	147,181	94	25,284,000	40	444.9	171.8	2.4	1991	18,491,097	49.9	50.1	9.6

age distribution (%)						population (by decade, '000s)								country
0–14	15–29	30–44	45–59	60–74	75 and over	1950	1960	1970	1980	1990	2000	2010 projection	2020 projection	
37.7	27.6	18.6	10.4	5.0	0.7	20,461	26,085	33,329	40,546	51,959	63,905	74,878	84,773	Egypt
38.7	28.7	16.0	9.2	5.4	1.9	1,940	2,582	3,604	4,566	5,100	6,123	7,293	8,494	El Salvador
41.7	25.1	15.7	11.2	5.3	1.0	211	244	270	256	368	474	604	755	Equatorial Guinea
46.1	23.0	15.9	8.9	4.4	1.6	1,403	1,612	2,153	2,555	2,945	4,136	5,709	7,399	Eritrea
17.7[10]	22.1[10]	21.4[10]	18.4[10]	15.0[10]	5.4[10]	1,101	1,216	1,365	1,473	1,571	1,369	1,312	1,274	Estonia
46.1[16]	26.0[16]	15.1[16]	8.3[16]	3.8[16]	0.7[16]	20,175	24,252	29,673	36,413	48,335	64,117	82,312	103,163	Ethiopia
23.8	19.4	21.0	18.2	11.3	1.8	31	35	39	44	48	46	53	60	Faroe Islands
35.4	27.4	20.7	11.4	4.2	0.9	289	394	520	634	738	816	938	1,067	Fiji
19.3	20.5	24.6	17.1	12.9	5.7	4,009	4,430	4,606	4,800	4,986	5,176	5,252	5,292	Finland
17.9	20.2	21.9	18.7	13.6	7.7	41,736	45,684	50,770	53,880	56,697	58,874	60,596	61,371	France
34.0	24.2	23.3	12.5	4.3	1.7	27	33	49	68	116	165	204	233	French Guiana
33.7	27.3	21.6	11.4	5.0	1.0	62	84	109	151	197	233	269	309	French Polynesia
33.8[15]	23.7[15]	17.0[15]	17.4[15]	6.9[15]	1.2[15]	416	446	514	806	1,069	1,208	1,309	1,386	Gabon
43.8	27.7	15.1	6.8	3.5	1.4	305	391	502	676	962	1,367	1,833	2,365	Gambia, The
50.3	25.8	13.1	6.2	3.7	0.9	...	...	370	456	630	1,147	1,872	2,623	Gaza Strip
24.8	24.1	19.2	17.5	10.8	3.6	3,516	4,147	4,694	5,048	5,457	5,020	4,815	4,785	Georgia
15.8	17.9	24.6	19.3	15.5	6.9	68,373	72,673	77,772	78,289	79,433	82,207	84,013	84,897	Germany
45.0	26.4	14.6	8.1	4.1	1.8	5,297	6,958	8,789	10,998	15,360	19,534	22,650	25,223	Ghana
19.3	22.2	20.3	18.3	14.1	5.9	7,566	8,327	8,793	9,643	10,161	10,904	11,114	10,988	Greece
27.1	19.2	29.3	16.4	—8.0—		23	33	41	50	56	56	57	58	Greenland
42.5[8]	30.4[8]	12.9[8]	6.6[8]	5.5[8]	2.1[8]	76	90	95	89	95	102	109	116	Grenada
23.6	22.4	24.3	15.7	9.3	4.7	206	265	320	327	388	428	470	502	Guadeloupe
30.0	30.0	22.6	10.8	5.5	1.1	60	67	86	107	134	155	184	211	Guam
44.0	26.1	15.8	8.3	—5.8—		2,969	3,963	5,243	6,820	8,749	11,385	14,631	18,123	Guatemala
17.6	20.6	22.3	19.0	13.2	7.3	44	45	51	53	63	64	66	67	Guernsey
44.1[5]	26.5[5]	15.9[5]	9.0[5]	3.9[5]	0.6[5]	2,586	3,019	3,587	4,320	5,936	7,466	9,281	11,440	Guinea
43.9[8]	26.5[8]	16.1[8]	8.8[8]	3.7[8]	1.0[8]	573	617	620	789	996	1,286	1,614	1,998	Guinea-Bissau
35.4[8]	31.5[8]	17.8[8]	9.0[8]	4.8[8]	1.5[8]	428	560	714	759	759	772	807	834	Guyana
39.2	26.9	15.6	10.0	5.4	2.9	3,097	3,723	4,605	5,056	6,028	6,868	7,950	9,072	Haiti
46.8	25.8	14.4	7.9	3.8	1.4	1,390	1,873	2,553	3,316	4,681	6,490	7,979	9,166	Honduras
16.5	21.6	29.0	18.0	10.6	4.3	1,974	3,074	3,942	5,063	5,705	6,665	7,312	8,015	Hong Kong
21.3	19.4	22.5	17.9	13.4	5.6	9,338	9,984	10,337	10,693	10,365	10,206	9,912	9,562	Hungary
23.3	22.7	22.4	16.5	10.0	5.1	143	176	204	228	255	281	314	351	Iceland
33.1[19]	27.8[19]	19.9[19]	12.1[19]	5.6[19]	1.5[19]	369,880	445,857	555,042	690,462	850,558	1,014,004	1,168,205	1,311,747	India
36.6	28.3	18.1	10.6	5.2	1.1	75,449	92,701	119,467	146,449	178,302	209,342	237,973	261,802	Indonesia
44.3	26.6	15.1	8.2	4.8	0.8	16,913	21,554	28,359	38,783	54,134	62,704	70,494	80,482	Iran
43.8[20]	30.2[20]	14.5[20]	6.9[20]	3.6[20]	1.0[20]	5,163	6,822	9,413	13,233	18,135	22,676	29,672	36,908	Iraq
26.7	24.1	20.2	13.8	10.6	4.6	2,969	2,834	2,954	3,421	3,506	3,787	4,161	4,372	Ireland
17.0	10.0	20.6	19.5	14.4	8.9	55	49	52	64	69	73	77	80	Isle of Man
29.2	25.0	19.6	13.1	9.1	4.0	...	2,114	2,958	3,862	4,613	6,110	7,000	7,710	Israel[21, 22]
15.9	23.7	20.9	18.4	14.4	6.7	47,104	50,200	53,822	56,434	56,749	57,762	57,498	55,540	Italy
34.4	30.6	16.6	9.0	—9.4—		1,403	1,629	1,891	2,133	2,369	2,605	2,800	3,070	Jamaica
15.9	21.5	19.7	22.0	15.0	5.9	83,200	93,419	103,720	116,807	123,478	126,870	127,626	124,248	Japan
15.5[9]	24.9[9]	23.5[9]	17.0[9]	11.9[9]	6.8[9]	57	63	71	76	84	89	92	93	Jersey
41.3	31.8	14.6	8.1	3.4	0.8	1,095	1,384	1,795	2,183	3,306	4,970	6,486	7,920	Jordan[25]
31.9[26]	26.3[26]	19.4[26]	13.2[26]	6.9[26]	2.3[26]	6,693	9,982	13,106	14,994	16,708	14,870	15,352	16,477	Kazakhstan
47.8[26]	27.6[26]	13.1[26]	6.6[26]	3.4[26]	1.5[26]	6,121	8,157	11,272	16,685	23,767	30,340	33,068	34,001	Kenya
41.2	25.8	18.3	9.3	4.4	1.0	33	41	49	58	71	92	115	143	Kiribati
29.5[15]	31.9[15]	21.3[15]	11.0[15]	5.0[15]	1.2[15]	9,471	10,392	13,912	17,114	20,019	21,688	23,753	25,143	Korea, North
23.0	27.6	25.7	14.5	7.4	1.9	21,147	25,142	32,976	38,124	42,869	47,275	50,886	52,759	Korea, South
25.4[27]	26.4[27]	34.4[27]	11.1[27]	—2.7[27]—		145	292	748	1,358	2,141	2,190	2,865	3,495	Kuwait
37.5[26]	27.0[26]	16.3[26]	10.9[26]	6.2[26]	2.1[26]	1,740	2,173	2,965	3,631	4,395	4,884	5,423	6,023	Kyrgyzstan
45.4[12]	26.5[12]	14.9[12]	8.1[12]	4.2[12]	1.0[12]	1,886	2,309	2,845	3,293	4,210	5,497	6,993	8,637	Laos
21.4[26]	21.7[26]	20.3[26]	19.2[26]	12.0[26]	5.3[26]	1,949	2,129	2,374	2,544	2,627	2,369	2,219	2,119	Latvia
42.6	23.8	16.7	9.1	—7.7—		1,364	1,786	2,383	3,086	3,147	3,578	4,056	4,417	Lebanon
43.1	27.6	15.0	8.6	4.8	0.9	726	859	1,067	1,344	1,732	2,143	2,339	2,382	Lesotho
43.2	28.2	14.7	7.7	4.4	1.8	824	1,055	1,397	1,892	2,190	3,164	4,073	5,294	Liberia
45.4[12]	26.4[12]	14.7[12]	9.1[12]	3.7[12]	0.6[12]	961	1,338	1,999	3,065	4,140	5,115	6,447	7,740	Libya
18.7	20.6	25.8	20.5	9.7	4.7	14	16	21	26	29	33	37	41	Liechtenstein
22.6	23.8	20.0	17.9	10.9	4.8	2,567	2,779	3,148	3,439	3,722	3,696	3,659	3,623	Lithuania
17.3	21.5	23.8	17.5	12.8	7.1	296	314	339	364	382	439	493	542	Luxembourg
24.1	27.2	29.4	9.6	7.3	2.3	188	169	221	243	332	438	518	604	Macau
24.8	24.1	22.3	15.8	10.6	2.4	1,225	1,366	1,574	1,792	1,893	2,041	2,115	2,171	Macedonia
45.1[15]	26.8[15]	15.1[15]	7.7[15]	4.3[15]	1.0[15]	4,620	5,482	6,766	8,677	11,522	15,506	20,993	28,405	Madagascar
45.7[28]	29.2[28]	13.2[28]	7.5[28]	3.7[28]	0.7[28]	2,817	3,450	4,489	6,129	8,442	10,286	11,621	12,318	Malawi
36.7[9]	27.6[9]	20.0[9]	9.9[9]	4.6[9]	1.2[9]	6,187	7,908	10,466	13,764	17,857	22,195	26,625	31,306	Malaysia
46.4[29]	26.2[29]	14.3[29]	7.7[29]	4.3[29]	0.9[29]	82	106	128	155	215	270	326	394	Maldives
46.1	23.9	15.0	8.9	4.9	1.2	3,688	4,486	5,525	6,731	8,228	10,686	14,349	18,984	Mali
21.9	20.9	22.5	18.8	11.6	4.3	308	329	326	324	354	381	404	427	Malta
51.0[30]	24.5[30]	14.6[30]	5.5[30]	3.6[30]	0.8[30]	11	15	22	31	45	52	60	69	Marshall Islands
22.0	21.0	24.4	16.0	11.1	5.5	222	252	287	326	360	385	415	436	Martinique
46.2[10]	26.6[10]	15.6[10]	7.8[10]	3.3[10]	0.5[10]	960	1,057	1,227	1,550	1,969	2,527	3,243	4,161	Mauritania
29.7	28.9	22.3	10.9	6.6	1.6	479	662	829	966	1,059	1,186	1,281	1,364	Mauritius
43.5	29.9	15.6	6.6	2.7	1.7	17	25	35	52	89	151	225	304	Mayotte
38.3	29.4	16.6	8.9	4.5	1.7	27,737	36,945	50,596	67,570	81,700	98,152	112,840	125,610	Mexico
46.4[31]	26.8[31]	12.6[31]	8.5[31]	4.5[31]	1.1[31]	30	40	57	73	98	117	125	126	Micronesia
27.9	22.9	21.0	15.6	9.7	2.9	2,341	3,004	3,595	4,002	4,245	3,664	3,695	3,859	Moldova
12.3	16.7	21.2	20.4	17.9	10.8	18	21	24	27	30	32	33	34	Monaco
41.9[26]	29.2[26]	14.6[26]	8.5[26]	—5.8[26]—		747	931	1,248	1,663	2,086	2,399	2,787	3,174	Mongolia
37.0[16]	29.6[16]	17.3[16]	9.2[16]	5.4[16]	1.5[16]	8,953	11,640	15,126	19,332	24,117	28,496	33,378	38,058	Morocco[32]
43.5[20]	28.6[20]	15.1[20]	8.5[20]	3.6[20]	0.7[20]	6,250	7,472	9,304	12,103	14,276	19,105	20,504	20,626	Mozambique
38.6	28.7	15.5	10.9	5.2	1.1	19,488	22,836	27,386	33,281	38,519	41,735	43,674	44,775	Myanmar (Burma)
41.7	28.8	14.7	7.8	—6.9—		464	591	765	975	1,409	1,771	1,908	1,956	Namibia
41.8	25.0	20.7	8.2	—2.8—		3	4	7	8	10	12	14	17	Nauru
42.3	25.7	16.7	9.7	4.7	0.9	8,989	10,305	11,919	15,016	19,325	24,702	30,758	36,925	Nepal

Area and population (continued)

country	area			population (latest estimate)					population (latest census)				
	square miles	square kilometres	rank	total midyear 2001	rank	density per sq mi	density per sq km	% annual growth rate 1996–2001	census year	total	male (%)	female (%)	urban (%)
Netherlands, The	16,033	41,526	134	15,968,000	58	996.0	384.5	0.6	2000	15,864,000	49.5	50.5	89.4[10]
Netherlands Antilles	308	800	183	205,000	183	666.7	256.7	0.0	1992	189,474	47.9	52.1	...
New Caledonia	7,172	18,575	154	216,000	182	30.1	11.6	1.7	1996	196,836	51.2	48.8	60.4
New Zealand	104,454	270,534	75	3,861,000	120	37.0	14.3	0.8	1996	3,681,546	49.1	50.9	85.0
Nicaragua	50,337	130,373	97	4,918,000	114	97.7	37.7	2.3	1995	4,357,099	49.3	50.7	54.4
Niger	489,000	1,267,000	22	10,355,000	73	21.2	8.2	2.8	1988	7,228,552	49.5	50.5	15.3
Nigeria	356,669	923,768	32	126,636,000	10	355.1	137.1	2.8	1991	88,514,501	50.3	49.7	35.0[7]
Northern Mariana Islands	184	477	193	73,400	201	398.9	153.9	4.8	1995	58,846	49.8	50.2	28.0[2]
Norway	125,004	323,758	67	4,516,000	115	36.1	13.9	0.6	1990	4,247,546	49.4	50.6	72.0
Oman	119,500	309,500	70	2,497,000	137	20.9	8.1	2.4	1993	2,018,074	58.4	41.6	71.7
Pakistan[34]	307,374	796,095	36	144,617,000	6	470.5	181.7	2.2	1998	130,579,571	52.0	48.0	33.3
Palau	188	488	192	19,700	215	104.7	40.3	2.3	2000	19,129	54.6	45.4	71.4[29]
Panama	28,950	74,979	118	2,903,000	133	100.3	38.7	2.0	2000	2,839,177	50.5	49.5	56.3
Papua New Guinea	178,704	462,840	54	5,287,000	107	29.6	11.4	3.2	2000	5,130,000	51.9	48.1	15.2[2]
Paraguay	157,048	406,752	59	5,636,000	102	35.9	13.9	2.6	1992	4,123,550	50.2	49.8	50.5
Peru	496,225	1,285,216	20	26,090,000	39	52.6	20.3	1.7	1993	22,639,443	49.7	50.3	70.1
Philippines	115,860	300,076	72	78,609,000	14	678.5	262.0	2.4	1995	68,613,706	50.4	49.6	54.0[12]
Poland	120,728	312,685	69	38,648,000	30	320.1	123.6	0.0	1988	37,878,641	48.7	51.3	61.2
Portugal	35,662	92,365	111	10,328,000	74	289.6	111.8	0.5	2001	10,318,084[6]	48.3[6]	51.7[6]	48.2[9]
Puerto Rico	3,515	9,104	166	3,829,000	121	1,089.4	420.6	0.7	2000	3,808,610	48.1	51.9	71.2[2]
Qatar	4,412	11,427	161	596,000	162	135.1	52.2	3.1	1997	522,023	65.6	34.4	91.4[12]
Réunion	968	2,507	174	733,000	159	757.2	292.4	1.7	1999	706,180	49.1	50.9	70.3[4]
Romania	91,699	237,500	82	22,413,000	47	244.4	94.4	–0.2	1992	22,760,449	49.1	50.9	54.4
Russia	6,592,800	17,075,400	1	144,417,000	7	21.9	8.5	–0.4	1989	147,400,537	46.9	53.1	73.6
Rwanda	10,169	26,338	147	7,313,000	91	719.1	277.7	4.2	1991	7,164,994	48.7	51.3	5.4
St. Kitts and Nevis	104	269	205	38,800	211	373.1	144.0	–0.4	1991	40,618	49.1	50.9	48.9[7]
St. Lucia	238	617	189	158,000	188	663.9	256.1	1.4	1991	133,308	48.5	51.5	44.1[7]
St. Vincent and the Grenadines	150	389	198	113,000	193	751.8	290.3	0.3	1991	106,499	49.9	50.1	24.6
Samoa	1,093	2,831	172	179,000	185	163.8	63.2	–0.2	1991	161,298	52.5	47.5	21.2
San Marino	24	61	212	27,200	214	1,152.4	445.0	1.5	1997	25,872[3]	49.3	50.7	96.0[12]
São Tomé and Príncipe	386	1,001	181	147,000	190	379.9	146.5	2.2	1991	117,504	49.4	50.6	44.1[24]
Saudi Arabia	868,000	2,248,000	13	22,757,000	45	26.2	10.1	3.4	1992	16,948,388	55.9	44.1	77.3[7]
Senegal	75,951	196,712	87	10,285,000	75	135.4	52.3	3.0	1988	6,928,405	48.7	51.3	38.6
Seychelles	176	455	195	80,600	199	457.8	177.1	1.4	1997	75,876	49.5	50.5	54.8[12]
Sierra Leone	27,699	71,740	119	5,427,000	104	195.9	75.6	3.2	1985	3,517,530	49.6	50.4	31.8
Singapore	264	683	188	3,322,000	129	12,602.4	4,866.0	1.8	2000[6]	3,263,209	50.0	50.0	100.0
Slovakia	18,933	49,035	129	5,410,000	105	285.8	110.3	0.1	1991	5,268,935	48.9	51.1	56.8
Slovenia	7,827	20,273	153	1,991,000	144	254.4	98.2	0.0	1991	1,974,839	48.5	51.5	48.9
Solomon Islands	10,954	28,370	143	480,000	165	43.9	16.9	3.2	1986	285,176	51.9	48.1	15.7
Somalia	246,000	637,000	42	7,489,000	90	30.4	11.8	3.0	1975	4,089,203	50.1	49.9	25.4
South Africa	470,693	1,219,090	25	43,586,000	26	92.6	35.8	0.7	1996	40,583,573	48.1	51.9	53.7
Spain	195,364	505,990	51	40,144,000	29	205.5	79.3	0.2	1991	38,999,181	49.1	50.9	75.3
Sri Lanka	25,332	65,610	122	19,399,000	51	765.8	295.7	1.2	1981	14,848,364	50.8	49.2	21.5
Sudan, The	966,757	2,503,890	10	36,080,000	33	37.3	14.4	2.9	1993	24,940,683	50.2	49.8	31.3[12]
Suriname	63,251	163,820	92	434,000	170	6.9	2.6	0.7	1980	354,860	49.5	50.5	49.1[12]
Swaziland	6,704	17,364	157	1,104,000	154	164.7	63.6	2.3	1997	929,718	47.3	52.7	23.1
Sweden	173,732	449,964	56	8,888,000	82	51.2	19.8	0.1	1999[3]	8,861,426	49.4	50.6	83.3[4]
Switzerland	15,940	41,284	135	7,222,000	92	453.1	174.9	0.4	1990[36]	6,873,687	49.3	50.7	68.9
Syria	71,498	185,180	88	16,729,000	55	234.0	90.3	2.6	1994	13,812,284	50.7	49.3	52.2[12]
Taiwan	13,972	36,188	136	22,340,000	48	1,598.9	617.3	0.9	1990[6]	20,393,628	52.1	47.9	74.5
Tajikistan	55,300	143,100	95	6,252,000	98	113.1	43.7	1.6	1989	5,108,576	49.7	50.3	32.6
Tanzania	364,901	945,090	31	36,232,000	32	99.3	38.3	2.6	1988	23,174,336	48.9	51.1	18.5
Thailand	198,115	513,115	50	61,251,000	19	309.2	119.4	1.0	2000	60,606,947	49.2	50.8	31.1
Togo	21,925	56,785	125	5,153,000	110	235.0	90.7	3.1	1981	2,719,567	48.7	51.3	15.2
Tonga	290	750	185	101,000	195	347.3	134.1	0.7	1996[6]	97,784	50.7	49.3	32.1
Trinidad and Tobago	1,980	5,128	169	1,298,000	150	655.4	253.1	0.5	1990	1,234,388	50.1	49.9	64.8
Tunisia	63,378	164,150	91	9,828,000	80	155.1	59.9	1.6	1994	8,785,711	50.6	49.4	61.0
Turkey	300,948	779,452	37	66,229,000	15	220.1	85.0	1.5	1997	62,865,574	50.7[2]	49.3[2]	65.0
Turkmenistan	188,500	488,100	52	5,462,000	103	29.0	11.2	3.5	1995	4,483,251	49.6	50.4	46.0
Tuvalu	9.9	25.6	214	11,000	217	1,110.2	428.8	1.5	1991	9,043	48.4	51.6	42.5
Uganda	93,065	241,038	80	23,986,000	43	257.7	99.5	2.8	1991	16,671,705	49.1	50.9	11.3
Ukraine	233,100	603,700	44	48,767,000	24	209.2	80.8	–0.9	1989	51,706,746	46.3	53.7	66.9
United Arab Emirates	32,280	83,600	116	3,108,000	131	96.3	37.2	4.6	1995	2,411,041	66.6	33.4	77.3
United Kingdom	94,248	244,101	79	59,953,000	20	636.1	245.6	0.4	1991[6]	56,467,000	48.4	51.6	89.1[7]
United States	3,615,215[37]	9,363,364[37]	4	286,067,000	3	79.1	30.6	1.2	2000	281,421,906	49.1	50.9	75.2[2]
Uruguay	68,037	176,215	90	3,303,000	129	48.6	18.7	0.9	1996	3,151,662	48.4	51.6	89.3
Uzbekistan	172,700	447,400	57	25,155,000	41	145.7	56.2	1.6	1989	19,905,158	49.3	50.7	40.7
Vanuatu	4,707	12,190	160	195,000	184	41.3	16.0	2.6	1999	193,219	51.5	48.5	21.5
Venezuela	353,841	916,445	33	24,632,000	42	69.6	26.9	2.0	1990	19,405,429	49.7	50.3	84.0
Vietnam	127,816	331,041	65	79,939,000	13	625.4	241.5	1.5	1999	76,324,753	49.2	50.8	23.5
Virgin Islands (U.S.)	136	352	201	122,000	191	898.6	347.2	1.2	1990	101,809	48.3	51.7	37.2
West Bank[38]	2,270	5,900	167	2,268,000	141	999.3	384.5	5.8	1995[3, 17]	1,707,000	51.2	48.8	...
Western Sahara	97,344	252,120	77	251,000	179	2.6	1.0	2.4	1994	252,146	...	...	90.7
Yemen	214,300	555,000	48	18,078,000	54	84.4	32.6	3.4	1994	14,587,807	51.2	48.8	23.5
Yugoslavia	39,449	102,173	107	10,662,000	70	270.7	104.5	–0.2	1991	10,394,026	49.6	50.4	53.2[7]
Zambia	290,586	752,614	39	9,770,000	81	33.6	13.0	2.0	1990	7,818,447	49.2	50.8	42.0
Zimbabwe	150,872	390,757	60	11,365,000	66	75.3	29.1	0.5	1992	10,412,548	48.8	51.2	30.6

[1]Settled population only. [2]1990 census. [3]Civil register; not a census. [4]1999 estimate. [5]1996 estimate. [6]Data are for de jure population. [7]1990 estimate. [8]1991 estimate. [9]1991 census. [10]2000 estimate. [11]1992 census. [12]1995 estimate. [13]Data are for the island of Cyprus (excepting census information). [14]Republic of Cyprus only. [15]1993 estimate. [16]1994 estimate. [17]Projections from 1995 demographic survey. [18]Data exclude Alderney (population 2,297) and Sark (population 604). [19]2001 estimate. [20]1997 estimate. [21]Area figures exclude the West Bank, East Jerusalem, Gaza Strip, and Golan Heights. [22]Population figures include Golan Heights and East Jerusalem and exclude Israelis in the West Bank and Gaza Strip. [23]Includes East

age distribution (%)						population (by decade, '000s)								country
0–14	15–29	30–44	45–59	60–74	75 and over	1950	1960	1970	1980	1990	2000	2010 projection	2020 projection	
18.6	19.3	24.2	19.8	12.1	6.0	10,027	11,417	12,958	14,150	14,952	15,896	16,638	17,089	Netherlands, The
26.0	23.9	25.5	14.3	7.3	3.0	112	136	163	174	188	204	221	235	Netherlands Antilles
30.7	27.2	21.3	13.3	5.9	1.6	59	79	110	140	171	213	249	280	New Caledonia
23.0	22.3	23.0	16.2	10.6	4.9	1,909	2,377	2,820	3,144	3,417	3,833	4,109	4,351	New Zealand
45.1	27.5	15.0	7.2	3.7	1.4	1,098	1,493	2,053	2,804	3,643	4,813	5,839	6,808	Nicaragua
48.7	24.8	14.6	6.8	3.6	1.5	2,482	3,168	4,182	5,629	7,627	10,076	13,140	16,800	Niger
45.5[8]	26.0[8]	15.3[8]	8.8[8]	3.8[8]	0.6[8]	31,797	39,914	51,099	69,593	92,483	123,338	155,588	187,437	Nigeria
24.6	31.9	31.6	9.6	1.8	0.5	6	9	10	17	44	70	97	121	Northern Mariana Islands
18.8	22.9	22.1	15.1	13.9	7.2	3,265	3,581	3,877	4,086	4,241	4,491	4,702	4,904	Norway
41.0	25.5	21.9	7.8	2.9	0.9	489	499	779	1,060	1,625	2,416	3,359	4,461	Oman
43.2	26.9	15.6	8.8	4.3	1.2	39,448	50,387	65,706	85,219	113,975	141,554	171,373	199,745	Pakistan[34]
23.9	24.2	29.9	14.2	5.5	2.3	7	9	12	13	15	19	22	24	Palau
32.0	26.8	20.6	12.0	6.1	2.5	893	1,148	1,531	1,950	2,335	2,847	3,150	3,443	Panama
41.9[2]	28.5[2]	16.6[2]	8.7[2]	— 3.2[2] —		1,412	1,747	2,288	2,991	3,758	5,125	6,461	7,748	Papua New Guinea
40.1	27.6	18.7	8.3	4.2	1.1	1,351	1,774	2,351	3,136	4,219	5,496	6,980	8,570	Paraguay
37.0	28.6	17.7	9.8	— 7.0 —		7,632	9,931	13,193	17,324	21,569	25,662	29,885	33,757	Peru
38.3	28.4	18.3	9.5	4.3	1.2	20,988	27,561	36,850	48,286	60,937	76,797	92,896	108,320	Philippines
25.4	21.2	23.3	15.5	10.4	4.2	24,824	29,561	32,526	35,578	38,057	38,661	38,764	39,003	Poland
20.0[9]	23.7[9]	20.2[9]	17.1[9]	13.7[9]	5.3[9]	8,405	8,826	9,040	9,766	9,896	10,281	10,448	10,364	Portugal
23.8	23.2	20.6	17.1	10.5	4.8	2,218	2,360	2,721	3,210	3,529	3,816	3,981	4,085	Puerto Rico
29.7[20]	30.7[20]	31.0[20]	7.0[20]	1.4[20]	0.2[20]	47	59	151	229	423	580	756	870	Qatar
27.0	24.8	24.4	13.8	7.2	2.8	244	338	447	507	601	722	829	932	Réunion
22.4	22.9	20.8	17.1	— 16.8 —		16,311	18,403	20,253	22,201	23,207	22,443	21,978	21,313	Romania
23.1	22.0	21.9	17.6	11.2	4.2	101,937	119,632	130,425	139,045	148,082	145,230	141,297	137,971	Russia
45.6	28.6	12.4	8.4	3.9	0.9	2,439	3,032	3,769	5,139	6,962	7,229	7,876	8,027	Rwanda
36.9[8]	31.8[8]	14.5[8]	6.0[8]	6.9[8]	3.8[8]	49	51	46	44	41	39	40	44	St. Kitts and Nevis
36.8	29.4	16.3	8.7	6.3	2.5	79	86	101	122	134	156	177	199	St. Lucia
37.2	29.5	16.1	8.3	6.4	2.5	67	80	86	99	105	112	117	122	St. Vincent and the Grenadines
40.5	30.0	14.6	8.7	— 6.0 —		82	111	143	155	170	179	176	178	Samoa
14.6	20.5	25.9	18.5	13.8	6.7	13	15	19	21	23	27	31	36	San Marino
46.9	26.2	12.2	8.0	— 6.7 —		60	64	74	94	117	144	177	218	São Tomé and Príncipe
41.8	26.8	20.4	7.0	3.0	1.0	3,860	4,718	6,109	9,949	15,847	22,024	30,546	41,880	Saudi Arabia
47.5	26.1	13.6	7.8	— 5.0 —		2,654	3,270	4,318	5,640	7,360	9,987	13,221	16,855	Senegal
28.8	27.4	22.6	10.6	7.5	3.1	34	42	54	63	70	79	93	109	Seychelles
43.9[35]	25.6[35]	15.7[35]	9.6[35]	4.5[35]	0.7[35]	2,087	2,396	2,789	3,327	4,227	5,233	6,930	8,820	Sierra Leone
21.5	21.2	28.4	18.2	8.2	2.5	1,022	1,639	2,075	2,282	2,705	3,263	3,827	4,570	Singapore
25.0	22.7	22.8	14.6	10.7	4.2	3,463	3,994	4,528	4,984	5,298	5,403	5,480	5,559	Slovakia
20.0	22.4	23.7	17.4	11.9	4.6	1,467	1,580	1,727	1,901	1,998	1,989	2,006	1,985	Slovenia
47.3	25.7	13.9	8.1	— 4.9 —		107	126	163	232	335	466	610	748	Solomon Islands
45.6	24.9	15.5	7.4	— 5.4 —		2,438	2,956	3,007	5,701	6,675	7,253	9,922	13,023	Somalia
33.9	28.6	19.4	9.8	5.3	1.8	13,596	17,417	22,739	29,252	38,176	43,421	41,108	36,744	South Africa
19.4	24.9	20.0	16.5	13.6	5.6	27,868	30,303	33,779	37,636	38,798	40,128	40,289	39,362	Spain
35.3	29.6	17.9	10.6	5.2	1.4	7,678	9,889	12,514	14,747	16,993	19,246	20,832	22,120	Sri Lanka
43.0	27.0	16.4	9.3	3.7	0.6	8,051	10,589	13,788	19,064	26,627	35,080	45,485	56,162	Sudan, The
39.3	29.5	13.8	10.0	4.5	2.8	208	285	373	355	395	431	450	457	Suriname
44.3	28.6	14.4	7.7	3.4	1.6	277	352	455	606	852	1,083	1,216	1,296	Swaziland
18.5	18.3	20.7	20.3	13.3	8.9	7,041	7,498	8,081	8,310	8,559	8,872	9,005	9,307	Sweden
16.8	22.8	23.2	18.0	12.5	6.7	4,715	5,429	6,270	6,362	6,712	7,185	7,323	7,333	Switzerland
44.7	28.2	14.8	7.3	— 5.0 —		3,495	4,533	6,258	8,774	12,436	16,306	20,606	24,676	Syria
27.1	27.8	23.1	12.3	7.9	1.8	7,619	10,668	14,583	17,705	20,279	22,185	24,168	26,332	Taiwan
42.9	28.1	13.8	9.0	4.6	1.6	1,532	2,083	2,942	3,968	5,213	6,151	7,233	8,506	Tajikistan
45.8	26.7	13.5	7.8	4.5	1.7	7,935	10,260	13,842	18,939	26,244	35,306	44,957	54,774	Tanzania
28.8[2]	30.4[2]	21.2[2]	12.3[2]	5.7[2]	1.6[2]	20,010	26,392	35,037	46,538	54,692	60,766	65,788	68,980	Thailand
49.8	24.8	13.1	6.8	3.3	2.0	1,172	1,456	1,964	2,596	3,691	5,019	6,245	7,197	Togo
39.1	28.0	15.1	10.0	6.0	1.8	50	65	80	92	96	100	104	108	Tonga
33.5	27.2	19.9	10.7	6.4	2.3	668	828	941	1,082	1,227	1,292	1,353	1,418	Trinidad and Tobago
34.8	28.5	18.8	9.6	6.4	1.9	3,517	4,149	5,099	6,443	8,154	9,686	11,124	12,507	Tunisia
35.0[2]	28.6[2]	18.4[2]	10.9[2]	5.6[2]	1.6[2]	21,122	28,217	35,758	44,439	56,098	65,293	74,119	80,544	Turkey
40.5[26]	28.8[26]	15.5[26]	9.1[26]	4.7[26]	1.4[26]	1,211	1,594	2,189	2,860	3,668	5,278	6,444	7,726	Turkmenistan
34.6	24.0	20.7	11.3	— 9.2 —		5	5	6	8	9	11	13	15	Tuvalu
47.3	27.7	13.1	6.9	3.7	1.3	5,522	7,262	9,728	12,298	17,186	23,318	31,395	42,005	Uganda
21.5	21.0	20.6	18.5	10.7	7.7	36,906	42,783	47,317	50,034	51,892	49,235	46,193	44,362	Ukraine
26.3	29.2	33.2	9.6	1.4	0.3	70	90	223	1,042	1,844	3,022	3,751	4,257	United Arab Emirates
19.1	21.9	21.2	16.7	14.1	7.0	50,290	52,372	55,632	56,330	57,561	59,727	60,913	61,742	United Kingdom
21.4	20.8	23.3	18.2	10.4	5.9	152,271	180,671	204,879	227,726	249,806	282,564	308,761	334,548	United States
25.1	22.9	19.6	15.1	12.2	5.1	2,194	2,531	2,824	2,914	3,041	3,278	3,540	3,794	Uruguay
40.8	28.4	15.0	9.3	4.7	1.8	6,314	8,559	11,973	15,977	20,515	24,756	29,280	34,465	Uzbekistan
45.5[26]	26.6[26]	15.2[26]	8.4[26]	3.7[26]	0.6[26]	52	66	85	117	147	190	221	250	Vanuatu
38.3	28.1	18.6	9.3	4.5	1.2	5,094	7,579	10,721	15,091	19,502	24,170	28,716	32,911	Venezuela
39.0[26]	28.7[26]	16.0[26]	9.1[26]	5.6[26]	1.6[26]	25,348	31,656	42,577	53,661	66,338	78,774	90,192	100,985	Vietnam
28.9	23.7	22.0	16.0	7.3	2.2	27	32	63	100	104	121	133	144	Virgin Islands (U.S.)
44.6	28.4	14.0	7.4	4.4	1.2	...	...	608	733	1,011	2,184	3,227	4,128	West Bank[38]
...	...	...	...	...	...	14	32	76	126	191	245	301	357	Western Sahara
47.6[16]	28.7[16]	11.9[16]	7.4[16]	3.6[16]	0.7[16]	4,461	5,483	6,628	8,527	12,023	17,479	24,637	34,195	Yemen
22.8	21.6	21.7	17.1	12.2	3.5	7,106	7,932	8,681	9,515	9,766	10,662	10,667	10,561	Yugoslavia
47.3	28.2	12.9	7.3	3.5	0.7	2,553	3,254	4,252	5,700	7,851	9,582	11,482	13,365	Zambia
45.1	28.3	14.0	7.2	3.9	1.2	2,853	4,011	5,515	7,170	10,103	11,343	11,057	9,997	Zimbabwe

Jerusalem and Israelis in the West Bank, Gaza Strip, and Golan Heights. [24]1992 estimate. [25]Excludes the West Bank. [26]1989 census. [27]1998 official country estimate including nonresidents. [28]1998 estimate. [29]1995 census. [30]1988 census. [31]1980 census. [32]Excludes Western Sahara, an annexure of Morocco. [33]Includes Western Sahara. [34]Excludes Afghan refugees (2001; *c.* 2 million) and the area (32,494 sq mi [84,159 sq km]) and population (2001; *c.* 4.2 million) of Pakistani-occupied Jammu and Kashmir. [35]1985 estimate. [36]Includes resident aliens; excludes seasonal workers. [37]Includes inland water area of 78,937 sq mi (204,446 sq km); excludes Great Lakes water area of 60,052 sq mi (155,534 sq km). [38]Excludes East Jerusalem.

Major cities and national capitals

The following table lists the principal cities or municipalities (those exceeding 100,000 in population [75,000 for Anglo-America, Australia, and the United Kingdom]) of the countries of the world, together with figures for each national capital (indicated by a ★), regardless of size.

Most of the populations given refer to a so-called city proper, that is, a legally defined, incorporated, or chartered area defined by administrative boundaries and by national or state law. Some data, however, refer to the municipality, or commune, similar to the medieval city-state in that the city is governed together with its immediately adjoining, economically dependent areas, whether urban or rural in nature. Some countries define no other demographic or legal entities within such communes or municipalities, but many identify a centre, seat, head (*cabecera*), or locality that corresponds to the most densely populated, compact, contiguous core of the municipality. Because the amount of work involved in carefully defining these "centres" may be considerable, the necessary resources usually exist only at the time of a national census (generally 5 or 10 years apart). Between censuses, therefore, it may be possible only to track the growth of the municipality as a whole. Thus, in order to provide the most up-to-date data for cities in this table, figures referring to municipalities or communes may be given (identified by the abbreviation "MU"), even though the country itself may define a smaller, more closely knit city proper. Specific identification of municipalities is provided in this table *only* when the country also publishes data for a more narrowly defined city proper; it is *not* provided when the sole published figure is the municipality, whether or not this is the proper local administrative term for the entity.

Populations for urban agglomerations as defined by the United Nations are occasionally inset beneath the populations of cities proper. Specifically that is when the urban agglomeration populations are at least three times the size of cities proper.

For certain countries, more than one form of the name of the city is given, usually to permit recognition of recent place-name changes or of *forms* of the place-name likely to be encountered in press stories if the title of the city's entry in the *Encyclopædia Britannica* is spelled according to a different romanization or spelling policy.

Chinese names for China are usually given in their Pinyin spelling, the official Chinese system encountered in official documents and maps. For Taiwan, the Wade-Giles spelling of place-names is used.

Sources for this data were often national censuses and statistical abstracts of the countries concerned, supplemented by Internet sources.

Internet sources for further information

- City Population: http://www.citypopulation.de/cities.html
- The World Gazetteer: http://www.gazetteer.de/st/stata.htm

Major cities and national capitals

country city	population
Afghanistan (early 1990s est.)	
Herāt	186,800
★ Kābul	700,000[1]
agglomeration	2,454,000[2]
Kandahār (Qandahār)	237,500
Mazār-e Sharīf	127,800
Albania (1999 est.)	
★ Tiranë	279,000
Algeria (1998)	
★ Algiers	1,519,570
Annaba	348,554
Batna	242,514
Béchar	131,010
Bejaïa	147,076
Biskra (Beskra)	170,956
Blida (el-Boulaida)	226,512
Bordj Bou Arreridj	128,535
Constantine (Qacentina)	462,187
Djelfa	154,265
Ech-Cheliff (el-Asnam)	179,768
El-Eulma	105,130
El-Wad	104,801
Ghardaïa	110,724
Ghilizane	104,285
Guelma	108,734
Jijel	106,003
Khenchela	106,082
Médéa	123,535
Mostaganem	124,399
Oran (Wahran)	692,516
Saïda	110,865
Sétif (Stif)	211,859
Sidi bel Abbès	180,260
Skikda	152,335
Souq Ahras	115,882
Tébessa (Tbessa)	153,246
Tihert	145,332
Tlemcen (Tilimsen)	155,162
Touggourt	113,625
Wargla (Ouargla)	129,402
American Samoa (1990)	
★ Fagatogo (legislative and judicial)	2,323[3]
★ Utulei (executive)	930[3]
Andorra (1999 est.)	
★ Andorra la Vella	21,513
Angola (1999 est.)	
Huambo	400,000[4]
★ Luanda	2,555,000
Antigua and Barbuda (1991)	
★ Saint John's	22,342
Argentina (1999 est.)	
Almirante Brown	550,000
Avellaneda	342,193
Bahía Blanca	281,161
Belén de Escobar	192,992
Berazategui	296,759
★ Buenos Aires	2,904,192
agglomeration	12,423,000
Caseros	341,398
Catamarca	140,000
Comodoro Rivadavia	144,074
Concordia	131,716
Córdoba	1,275,585
Corrientes	325,628
Esteban Echeverría	234,188
Florencio Valera	331,358
Formosa	197,057
General San Martín	409,879
General Sarmiento	209,450
Godoy Cruz	205,955
Hurlingham	165,986
Ituzaingo	154,437
José Carlos Paz	219,624
La Matanza (San Justo)	1,241,264
La Plata	556,308
La Rioja	138,074
Lanús	470,000
Las Heras	183,511
Lomas de Zamora	609,621
Mar del Plata	579,483
Mendoza	119,681
Mercedes	100,876
Merlo	430,213
Moreno	398,023
Morón	340,645
Neuquén	327,374
Paraná	256,602
Pilar	166,587
Posadas	250,000
Quilmes	550,069
Resistencia	280,000
Río Cuarto	150,000
Rosario	1,000,000
Salta	457,223
San Carlos de Bariloche	105,093
San Fernando	146,896
San Isidro	296,935
San Juan	120,000
San Luis	146,855
San Miguel	246,503
San Miguel de Tucumán	519,252
San Nicolás de los Arroyos	132,909
San Rafael	111,066
San Salvador de Jujuy	226,961
Santa Fe	400,000
Santiago del Estero	202,876
Tigre	299,376
Trelew	101,425
Vicente López	279,464
Villa Krause	100,000
Villa Nueva	224,116
Armenia (1995 est.)	
Gyumri (Kumayri; Leninakan)	120,000[5]
★ Yerevan	1,248,700
Aruba (1998 est.)	
★ Oranjestad	28,000
Australia (1998 est.)	
Adelaide UC[6]	978,100[7]
Adelaide	12,922
Charles Sturt	103,012
Marion	77,547
Onkaparinga	146,367
Port Adelaide Enfield	101,225
Salisbury	112,344
Tea Tree Gully	96,972
Brisbane UC[6]	1,291,117[7]
Brisbane	848,741
Ipswich	132,232
Logan	165,924
Canberra-Queanbeyan UC[6]	322,723[7]
★ Canberra	306,000
Melbourne UC[6]	2,865,329[7]
Banyule	119,486
Bayside	88,449
Boroondara	157,208
Brimbank	158,032
Casey	160,845
Dandenong	132,091
Darebin	129,005
Frankston	111,081
Glen Eira	122,535
Hobsons Bay	80,825
Hume	126,350
Kingston	132,895
Knox	141,016
Manningham	112,503
Maroondah	97,321
Melbourne	44,619
Monash	161,996
Moonee Valley	111,898
Moreland	137,258
Port Philip	78,680
Stonnington	90,546
Whitehorse	145,611
Whittlesea	111,040
Wyndham	80,931
Perth UC[6]	1,096,829[7]
Gosnells	79,372
Melville	95,854
Perth	5,957
Stirling	175,569
Wanneroo	154,641
Sydney UC[6]	3,276,207[7]
Bankstown	167,839
Blacktown	248,525
Blue Mountains	75,855
Campbelltown	149,489
Canterbury	140,435
Fairfield	190,920
Gosford	155,144
Holroyd	86,280
Liverpool	137,066
Parramatta	144,366
Penrith	171,420
Randwick	125,359
Rockdale	90,372
Ryde	97,598
South Sydney	83,752
Sydney	24,883
Other cities	
Ballarat	80,330
Bendigo	86,451
Cairns	118,834
Geelong	186,307
Gold Coast	380,270
Lake Macquarie	180,826
Newcastle	139,171
Shoalhaven	81,253
Toowoomba	86,968
Townsville	87,235
Wollongong	185,397
Austria (2001)	
Graz	226,424
Innsbruck	113,826
Linz	186,298
Salzburg	144,816
★ Vienna	1,562,676
Azerbaijan (1997 est.)	
★ Baku (Baky)	1,727,200
Gäncä (Gyandzha)	291,900
Sumqayit (Sumgait)	248,500
Bahamas, The (1999 est.)	
★ Nassau	214,000[8]
Bahrain (1999 est.)	
★ Al-Manāmah	162,000
Bangladesh (1991)	
Barisal	170,232
Bogra	120,170
Brahmanbaria	109,032
Chittagong	1,392,860
Comilla	135,313
★ Dhaka (Dacca)	3,612,850
agglomeration	11,726,000[2]
Dinajpur	127,815
Jamalpur	103,556
Jessore	139,710
Khulna	663,340
Mymensingh	188,713
Naogaon	101,266
Narayanganj	276,549
Nawabganj (Nowabgonj)	130,577
Pabna	103,277
Rajshahi	294,056
Rangpur	191,398
Sylhet	117,396
Tangail	106,004
Tongi	168,702
Barbados (1990)	
★ Bridgetown	6,070
agglomeration	133,000[2]
Belarus (1998 est.)	
Baranovichi (Baranavichy)	173,000
Bobruysk (Babrujsk)	227,000
Borisov (Barysau)	153,000
Brest (Bierascie)	297,000
Gomel (Homiel)	513,000
Grodno (Horadnia)	306,000
Lida	100,000
★ Minsk	1,717,000
Mogilyov (Mahilou)	369,000
Mozyr (Mazyr)	109,000
Orsha (Vorsha)	138,000
Pinsk	132,000
Soligorsk	102,000
Vitebsk (Viciebsk)	364,000
Belgium (2000 est.)	
Antwerp	446,525
Brugge (Bruges)	116,246
★ Brussels	133,859
agglomeration	1,121,000[2]
Charleroi	200,827
Ghent	224,180
Liège (Luik)	185,639
Namur	105,419
Schaerbeek	105,692
Belize (2000)	
★ Belmopan	8,130
Benin (1992)	
★ Cotonou (official)	533,212
Djougou	132,192
Parakou	106,708
★ Porto-Novo (de facto)	177,660
Bermuda (1995 est.)	
★ Hamilton	1,100
Bhutan (1999 est.)	
★ Thimphu	28,000
Bolivia (2000 est.)	
Cochabamba	607,129
El Alto	568,919
★ La Paz (administrative)	1,000,899
Oruro	232,311
Potosí	147,351
Quillacollo	132,579
Santa Cruz	1,016,137
★ Sucre (judicial)	192,238
Tarija	135,679
Bosnia and Herzegovina (1997 est.)	
Banja Luka	160,000
★ Sarajevo	360,000
Botswana (1997 est.)	
★ Gaborone	183,487
Brazil (2000)[9]	
Águas Lindas de Goiás	105,216
Alagoinhas	112,339
Alvorada	182,864
Americana	181,650
Ananindeua	391,994
Anápolis	279,752
Angra dos Reis	114,237

country city	population
Aparecida de Goiânia	334,994
Apucarana	100,241
Aracaju	460,898
Araçatuba	164,440
Araguaina	105,701
Arapiraca	152,281
Araraquara	173,086
Barbacena	103,522
Barra Mansa	164,963
Barreiras	115,331
Barueri	208,028
Bauru	310,208
Belém	1,271,615
Belford Roxo	433,120
Belo Horizonte	2,229,697
Betim	295,480
Blumenau	241,987
Boa Vista	196,942
Botucatu	103,793
Bragança Paulista	110,982
★ Brasília	1,954,442
Cabo (de Santo Agostinho)	134,356
Cabo Frio	106,326
Cachoeirinha	107,472
Cachoeiro de Itapemirim	154,771
Camaçari	153,829
Camaragibe	128,627
Campina Grande	336,218
Campinas	951,824
Campo Grande	654,832
Campos	363,489
Canoas	305,711
Carapicuíba	343,668
Cariacica	312,542
Caruaru	217,084
Cascavel	228,340
Castanhal	121,174
Catanduva	104,195
Caucaia	225,854
Caxias	103,276
Caxias do Sul	333,201
Chapecó	134,210
Colombo	174,971
Contagem	531,715
Cotia	148,082
Criciúma	152,903
Cubatão	107,260
Cuiabá	475,632
Curitiba	1,586,898
Diadema	356,389
Divinópolis	177,729
Dourados	149,679
Duque de Caxias	767,724
Embu	206,781
Feira de Santana	431,458
Ferraz	140,777
Florianópolis	321,778
Fortaleza	2,138,234
Foz do Iguaçu	256,349
Franca	281,869
Francisco Morato	133,085
Franco de Rocha	100,241
Garanhuns	103,283
Goiânia	1,083,396
Governador Valadares	235,881
Gravataí	211,969
Guarapuava	141,575
Guarujá	265,076
Guarulhos	1,048,280
Hortolândia	151,669
Ibirité	132,131
Ilhéus	161,898
Imperatriz	218,555
Indaiatuba	144,528
Ipatinga	210,777
Itaboraí	176,767
Itabuna	190,888
Itajaí	141,932
Itapecerica da Serra	127,783
Itapetininga	111,774
Itapevi	162,421
Itaquaquecetuba	272,416
Itu	123,881
Jaboatão	567,319
Jacareí	183,444
Jaú	106,954
Jequié	130,207
João Pessoa	594,922
Joinville	414,350
Juàzeiro	132,796
Juàzeiro do Norte	201,950
Juiz de Fora	443,359
Jundiaí	299,669
Lages	152,320
Lauro de Freitas	108,111
Limeira	237,959
Londrina	433,264
Luziânia	129,905
Macaé	125,118
Macapá	270,077
Maceió	794,894
Magé	193,784
Manaus	1,394,724
Marabá	134,258
Maracanaú	174,037
Marília	189,533
Maringá	283,792
Mauá	363,112
Mogi Guaçu	116,117
Moji das Cruzes	301,551
Montes Claros	288,534
Mossoró	197,067
Natal	709,422
Nilópolis	153,572
Niterói	458,465
Nossa Senhora de Socorro	130,255
Nova Friburgo	151,820
Nova Iguaçu	915,364
Novo Hamburgo	231,833
Olinda	361,300
Osasco	650,993
Palmas	133,471
Paranaguá	122,179
Parnaíba	124,942
Parnamirim	107,927
Passo Fundo	163,748
Patos de Minas	111,159
Paulista	262,072
Pelotas	300,952
Petrolina	166,113
Petrópolis	270,489
Pindamonhangaba	118,793
Pinhais	100,601
Piracicaba	316,518
Poços de Caldas	130,594
Ponta Grossa	266,552
Porto Alegre	1,320,069
Porto Velho	273,496
Praia Grande	191,811
Presidente Prudente	185,150
Queimados	121,681
Recife	1,421,947
Ribeirão das Neves	245,143
Ribeirão Pires	104,336
Ribeirão Prêto	502,333
Rio Branco	226,054
Rio Claro	163,341
Rio de Janeiro	5,850,544
Rio Grande	179,422
Rio Verde	106,109
Rondonópolis	141,660
Sabará	111,897
Salvador	2,439,881
Santa Bárbara d'Oeste	167,574
Santa Luzia	184,026
Santa Maria	230,464
Santa Rita	100,259
Santarém	186,518
Santo André	648,443
Santos	415,543
São Bernardo do Campo	688,161
São Caetano do Sul	140,144
São Carlos	183,369
São Gonçalo	889,828
São João de Meriti	449,562
São José	167,268
São José do Rio Prêto	336,998
São José dos Campos	532,403
São José dos Pinhais	183,259
São Leopoldo	192,756
São Luís	834,968
São Paulo	9,785,640
São Vicente	302,541
Sapucaia do Sul	121,739
Serra	320,965
Sete Lagoas	180,211
Sobral	134,371
Sorocaba	487,907
Sumaré	193,266
Susano (Suzano)	221,192
Taboão da Serra	197,460
Taubaté	229,810
Teófilo Otoni	102,500
Teresina	676,596
Teresopolis	114,688
Timon	111,967
Uberaba	243,406
Uberlândia	487,887
Uruguaiana	118,181
Varginha	103,499
Várzea Grande	210,849
Viamão	210,873
Vila Velha	343,567
Vitória	291,889
Vitória da Conquista	225,430
Volta Redonda	242,773
Brunei (1991)	
★ Bandar Seri Begawan	21,484
agglomeration	85,000[2]
Bulgaria (1999 est.)	
Burgas	195,255
Dobrich	100,399
Pleven	121,952
Plovdiv	342,584
Ruse	166,467
Sliven	105,530
★ Sofia	1,122,302
Stara Zagora	147,939
Varna	299,801
Burkina Faso (1993 est.)	
Bobo Dioulasso	300,000
Koudougou	105,000
★ Ouagadougou	690,000
Burundi (1994 est.)	
★ Bujumbura	300,000
Gitega	101,827[10]
Cambodia (1999 est.)	
★ Phnom Penh	938,000
Cameroon (1992 est.)	
Bafoussam	120,000
Bamenda	110,000[5]
Douala	1,200,000
Garoua	160,000
Maroua	140,000
Nkongsamba	112,000[5]
★ Yaoundé	800,000
Canada (1996)	
Abbotsford	105,403
Barrie	79,191
Brampton	268,251
Brantford	84,764
Burlington	136,976
Burnaby	179,209
Calgary	768,082
Cambridge	101,429
Cape Breton	114,733
Coquitlam	101,820
Delta	95,411
East York	107,822
Edmonton	616,306
Etobicoke	328,718
Gatineau	100,702
Gloucester	104,022
Guelph	95,821
Halifax	113,910
Hamilton	322,352
Kamloops	76,394
Kelowna	89,442
Kitchener	178,420
Laval	330,343
London	325,646
Longueuil	127,977
Markham	173,383
Mississauga	544,382
Montreal	1,016,376
Montréal-Nord	81,581
Nepean	115,100
Niagara Falls	76,917
North York	589,653
Oakville	128,405
Oshawa	134,364
★ Ottawa	323,340
Pickering	78,989
Prince George	75,150
Quebec	167,264
Regina	180,400
Richmond	148,867
Richmond Hill	101,725
Saanich	101,388
Saint Catharines	130,926
Saint-Hubert	77,042
Saint John's	101,936
Saskatoon	193,647
Sault Sainte Marie	80,054
Scarborough	558,960
Sherbrooke	76,786
Sudbury	92,059
Surrey	304,477
Thunder Bay	113,662
Toronto	653,734
Vancouver	514,008
Vaughan	132,549
Waterloo	77,949
Windsor	197,694
Winnipeg	618,477
York	146,534
Cape Verde (2000)	
★ Praia	94,757
Central African Republic (1995 est.)	
★ Bangui	553,000
Chad (1993; MU)	
Abéché	187,936
Bongor	196,713
Doba	185,461
Moundou	282,103
★ N'Djamena	530,965
Sarh	193,753
Chile (1999 est.)	
Antofagasta	243,038
Arica	178,547
Calama	121,326
Chillán	162,969
Concepción	362,589
Copiapó	114,615
Coquimbo	126,886
Iquique	159,815
La Serena	123,166
Los Angeles	109,606
Osorno	126,645
Puente Alto	363,012
Puerto Montt	128,945
Punta Arenas	120,148
Quilpué	114,617
Rancagua	202,067
San Bernardo	223,055
★ Santiago (administrative)	202,010[11]
agglomeration	4,640,635
Talca	174,858
Talcahuano	269,265
Temuco	253,451
Valdívia	122,166
★ Valparaíso (legislative)	283,489
Viña del Mar	330,736
China (1999 est.)[12]	
Acheng	234,057
Aksu	220,415
Altay	106,665
Anda	180,795
Ankang	173,450
Anlu	112,529
Anning	128,275
Anqing	356,920
Anqiu	193,258
Anshan	1,285,849
Anshun	217,215
Anyang	527,982
Baicheng	269,732
Baise	119,150
Baishan	253,631
Baiyin	258,885
Baoding	570,167
Baoji	447,105
Baoshan	100,797
Baotou	1,092,819
Bazhong	137,627
Bei'an	217,980
Beihai	196,256
★ Beijing (Peking)	6,633,929
Beiliu	140,015
Beining	101,273
Beipiao	202,807
Bengbu	506,239
Benxi	827,203
Bijie	101,171
Binzhou	230,174
Botou	103,337
Bozhou	253,544
Cangzhou	304,010
Cenxi	113,589
Changchun	2,072,324
Changde	384,433
Changge	117,166
Changji	192,000
Changning	134,592
Changsha	1,334,036
Changshu	264,472
Changyi	133,754
Changzhi	387,002
Changzhou	772,700
Chaohu	280,409
Chaoyang (*Fujian*)	389,558
Chaoyang (*Liaoning*)	295,302
Chaozhou	257,521
Chengde	298,895
Chengdu	2,146,126
Chenghai	166,621
Chenzhou	274,338
Chibi	158,125
Chifeng	453,946
Chongqing (Chungking)	3,193,889
Chuxiong	115,887
Chuzhou	187,985
Cixi	132,588
Conghua	128,328
Da'an	153,718
Dachuan	200,785
Dafeng	153,147
Dali	175,847
Dalian	2,000,944
Dandong	578,723
Dangyang	114,885
Danjiangkou	152,396
Danyang	211,875
Danzhou	212,572
Daqing	811,154
Dashiqiao	186,201
Datong	928,293
Daye	128,561
Dehui	149,275
Dengzhou	119,036
Dexing	104,945
Deyang	246,221
Dezhou	310,538
Dingzhou	131,992
Donggang	104,971
Dongguan	378,354
Dongsheng	113,436
Dongtai	231,444
Dongying	479,941
Dujiangyan	154,867
Dunhua	257,190
Duyun	150,950
Emeishan	124,471
Enping	164,929
Enshi	125,937
Ezhou	301,248
Fangchenggang	119,444
Fanyu	345,275
Feicheng	301,981
Fengcheng (*Guangdong*)	173,112
Fengcheng (*Jiangxi*)	221,652
Fengnan	121,767
Foshan	411,107
Fu'an	100,793
Fujin	123,280
Fuqing	139,426
Fushun	1,271,113
Fuxin	682,966
Fuyang (*Anhui*)	319,816
Fuzhou	1,057,372
Gaizhou	175,467
Ganzhou	271,952
Gao'an	130,520
Gaomi	224,162
Gaoming	121,732
Gaoyao	142,335
Gaoyou	135,728
Gaozhou	204,028
Gejiu	218,921
Genhe	173,188
Gongyi	118,985
Gongzhuling	352,978
Guanghan	121,228
Guangshui	137,189
Guangyuan	257,411
Guangzhou (Canton)	3,306,277
Guichi	103,860
Guigang	290,829
Guilin	458,333
Guiping	151,341
Guixi	102,536
Guiyang	1,320,566
Gujiao	104,560
Haicheng	259,725
Haikou	438,262
Hailar	209,294
Hailin	242,389
Hailun	154,148
Haimen	355,232
Haining	122,973
Hami	205,310
Hancheng	108,702
Hanchuan	171,827
Handan	1,005,834
Hangzhou	1,346,148
Hanzhong	215,284
Harbin	2,586,978
Hebi	276,808
Hechi	108,942
Hechuan	202,218
Hefei	1,000,655
Hegang	591,254
Heihe	112,961
Helong	135,328
Hengshui	212,516
Hengyang	584,346
Heshan	117,049

Major cities and national capitals (continued)

country city	population
Heyuan	164,986
Heze	307,445
Hezhou	113,031
Hohhot	754,749
Honghu	201,421
Hongjiang	130,713
Hongta	110,048
Houma	103,578
Huadian	197,759
Huadu	195,921
Huai'an	155,657
Huaibei	574,904
Huaihua	225,414
Huainan	823,395
Huaiyin	320,841
Huanggang	241,268
Huangshan	130,623
Huangshi	569,394
Huazhou	183,394
Huichun	134,379
Huiyang	192,713
Huizhou	287,178
Hulin	152,353
Huludao	447,986
Huzhou	296,962
Jiamusi	579,093
Ji'an (*Jiangxi*)	178,957
Jiangdu	182,208
Jiangjin	222,571
Jiangmen	333,154
Jiangyan	149,706
Jiangyin	339,420
Jiangyou	221,960
Jianyang (*Sichuan*)	161,496
Jiaohe	170,881
Jiaonan	186,424
Jiaozhou	188,192
Jiaozuo	536,021
Jiaxing	261,465
Jiayuguan	114,510
Jieyang	204,134
Jilin	1,165,418
Jimo	149,083
Jinan	1,713,036
Jinchang	141,578
Jincheng	200,659
Jingdezhen	315,036
Jingjiang	136,204
Jingmen	388,780
Jingzhou	596,860
Jinhua	199,649
Jining (*Inner Mongolia*)	206,514
Jining (*Shandong*)	427,256
Jinjiang	126,102
Jinzhou	658,589
Jishou	114,650
Jiujiang	361,645
Jiutai	198,316
Jixi	752,840
Jiyuan	241,406
Jurong	108,555
Kaifeng	569,300
Kaili	149,939
Kaiping	188,795
Kaiyuan (*Liaoning*)	132,481
Kaiyuan (*Yunnan*)	104,329
Karamay	225,251
Kashgar (Kashi)	205,056
Korla	200,374
Kuitun	144,048
Kunming	1,350,640
Kunshan	177,003
Laiwu	382,785
Laixi	118,709
Laiyang	166,824
Laizhou	206,786
Langfang	241,984
Langzhong	112,118
Lanxi	103,792
Lanzhou	1,429,673
Laohekou	162,343
Lechang	177,572
Leiyang	163,278
Leizhou	226,310
Lengshuijiang	176,182
Leping	129,376
Leqing	103,118
Leshan	410,423
Lhasa	121,568
Lianjiang	246,638
Lianyuan	133,059
Lianyungang	447,918
Liaocheng	275,271
Liaoyang	570,483
Liaoyuan	391,841
Liling	135,453
Linchuan	232,592
Linfen	257,684
Lingbao	114,053
Lingyuan	141,481
Linhai	127,378
Linhe	186,234
Linjiang	114,072
Linqing	143,203
Linyi	569,419
Linzhou	110,526
Liu'an	282,880
Liupanshui	502,327
Liuyang	133,723
Liuzhou	775,823
Liyang	292,482
Longhai	101,884
Longjing	144,940
Longkou	221,823
Longyan	237,385
Loudi	222,375
Lufeng	260,804
Luoding	338,722
Luohe	306,565
Luoyang	1,002,178
Luzhou	371,843
Ma'anshan	393,174
Macheng	175,322
Manzhouli	143,711
Maoming	302,022
Meihekou	255,514
Meizhou	230,419
Mianyang	396,055
Mingguang	112,715
Mishan	153,717
Mudanjiang	641,347
Muling	134,632
Nan'an	108,684
Nanchang	1,264,739
Nanchong	390,603
Nanhai	381,322
Nanjing (Nanking)	2,388,915
Nankang	102,222
Nanning	984,061
Nanping	230,931
Nantong	468,215
Nanyang	477,128
Nehe	128,191
Neijiang	320,777
Ning'an	143,722
Ningbo	704,819
Ningguo	108,767
Panjin	471,729
Panshi	165,101
Panzhihua	488,911
Penglai	114,440
Pengzhou	122,074
Pingdingshan	619,694
Pingdu	198,558
Pingliang	124,447
Pingxiang	392,286
Pizhou	159,194
Pulandian	166,331
Puning	312,498
Putian	145,051
Puyang	289,232
Qianjiang	313,500
Qidong	231,611
Qilin	210,230
Qingdao	1,702,108
Qingyuan	193,284
Qingzhou	193,996
Qinhuangdao	485,143
Qinzhou	172,379
Qiongshan	144,979
Qiqihar (Tsitsihar)	1,115,766
Qitaihe	289,111
Qixia	115,089
Quanzhou	281,906
Qufu	157,201
Quzhou	151,122
Renqiu	158,242
Rizhao	322,190
Rongcheng	203,263
Rugao	276,028
Rui'an	164,563
Rushan	116,166
Ruzhou	102,691
Sanhe	108,252
Sanmenxia	189,084
Sanming	199,201
Sanshui	145,279
Sanya	161,869
Shanghai	8,937,175
Shangqiu	317,948
Shangrao	168,263
Shangyu	116,279
Shangzhi	228,273
Shantou	831,949
Shanwei	171,380
Shaoguan	431,053
Shaoxing	233,954
Shaoyang	311,261
Shenyang	3,876,289
Shenzhen	899,111
Shihezi	330,535
Shijiazhuang	1,338,796
Shishou	140,634
Shiyan	377,232
Shizuishan	313,842
Shouguang	202,067
Shuangcheng	172,936
Shuangliao	135,663
Shuangyashan	431,170
Shulan	208,723
Shunde	339,392
Shuozhou	134,645
Sihui	125,065
Siping	382,652
Songyuan	303,821
Songzi	148,183
Suihua	262,117
Suining	229,229
Suizhou	333,766
Suqian	115,368
Suzhou (*Anhui*)	325,724
Suzhou (*Jiangsu*)	845,687
Tai'an	518,117
Taicang	119,862
Taishan	355,017
Taixing	185,270
Taiyuan	1,768,530
Taizhou (*Jiangsu*)	219,968
Taizhou (*Zhejiang*)	239,271
Tangshan	1,210,842
Taonan	156,464
Tengzhou	452,009
Tianchang	167,508
Tianjin (Tientsin)	4,835,327
Tianmen	367,036
Tianshui	301,570
Tiefa	165,956
Tieli	272,841
Tieling	313,991
Tongchuan	304,809
Tonghua	362,577
Tongliao	305,885
Tongling	292,721
Tongxiang	109,976
Tongzhou	365,003
Tumen	102,191
Ulanhot	182,128
Ürümqi	1,258,457
Wafangdian	305,249
Weifang	621,125
Weihai	287,872
Weinan	210,079
Wendeng	183,952
Wenling	134,074
Wenzhou	512,523
Wuchang	227,856
Wuchuan	184,812
Wudalianchi	157,547
Wuhai	316,718
Wuhan	3,911,824
Wuhu	495,765
Wujiang	176,514
Wujin	141,495
Wuwei	181,328
Wuxi	940,858
Wuxian	176,694
Wuxue	142,136
Wuzhou	253,159
Xiamen (Amoy)	593,401
Xi'an (Sian)	2,294,790
Xiangcheng	103,692
Xiangfan	597,604
Xiangtan	518,783
Xiangxiang	103,871
Xianning	249,234
Xiantao	412,434
Xianyang	460,976
Xiaogan	224,026
Xiaoshan	220,815
Xiaoyi	117,133
Xichang	174,781
Xingcheng	120,431
Xinghua	199,023
Xingning	206,712
Xingping	108,491
Xingtai	387,081
Xinhui	269,528
Xining	604,812
Xinmin	123,655
Xintai	381,637
Xinxiang	583,408
Xinyang	366,304
Xinyi (*Guangdong*)	170,368
Xinyi (*Jiangsu*)	127,496
Xinyu	250,666
Xinzheng	136,980
Xinzhou	143,840
Xishan	171,316
Xuanwei	120,046
Xuanzhou	136,914
Xuchang	275,743
Xuzhou	1,044,729
Ya'an	119,320
Yakeshi	391,627
Yan'an	133,226
Yancheng	332,125
Yangchun	206,440
Yangjiang	295,672
Yangquan	447,229
Yangzhou	395,048
Yanji	329,112
Yantai	818,646
Yanzhou	199,491
Yibin	288,039
Yichang	481,277
Yicheng	116,586
Yichun (*Heilongjiang*)	802,931
Yichun (*Jiangxi*)	198,799
Yima	116,760
Yinchuan	469,180
Yingcheng	120,499
Yingde	205,782
Yingkou	498,300
Yingtan	110,671
Yining	230,429
Yixing	258,808
Yiyang	297,000
Yizheng	166,358
Yong'an	130,688
Yongcheng	118,659
Yongchuan	186,482
Yongzhou	276,669
Yuanjiang	140,406
Yuanping	101,689
Yuci	243,948
Yueyang	448,249
Yuhang	152,429
Yulin (*Guangxi*)	190,418
Yulin (*Shaanxi*)	106,391
Yumen	116,194
Yuncheng	172,620
Yunfu	168,371
Yushu	171,692
Yuyao	136,464
Yuzhou	133,619
Zalantun	143,273
Zaoyang	211,295
Zaozhuang	741,421
Zengcheng	197,023
Zhangjiagang	168,546
Zhangjiajie	115,896
Zhangjiakou	660,504
Zhangqiu	207,212
Zhangshu	112,600
Zhangye	114,592
Zhangzhou	231,333
Zhanjiang	588,583
Zhaodong	227,218
Zhaoqing	311,571
Zhaotong	104,382
Zhaoyuan	172,646
Zhengzhou	1,465,069
Zhenjiang	469,977
Zhijiang	126,808
Zhongshan	390,060
Zhongxiang	224,442
Zhoukou	189,377
Zhoushan	196,368
Zhuanghe	161,223
Zhucheng	145,952
Zhuhai	371,116
Zhuji	116,116
Zhumadian	204,020
Zhuozhou	109,390
Zhuzhou	528,958
Zibo	1,458,060
Zigong	464,497
Zixing	123,747
Ziyang	145,665
Zoucheng	302,856
Zunyi	464,945
Colombia (1999 est.)	
Armenia	281,422
Barrancabermeja	178,020
Barranquilla	1,223,260
Bello	333,470
Bucaramanga	515,555
Buenaventura	224,336
Buga	110,699
Cali	2,077,386
Cartagena	805,757
Cartago	125,884
Cúcuta	606,932
Dos Quebradas	159,363
Envigado	135,848
Florencia	108,574
Floridablanca	221,913
Girardot	110,963
Ibagué	393,664
Itagüí	228,985
Maicao	108,053
Manizales	337,580
Medellín	1,861,265
Montería	248,245
Neiva	300,052
Palmira	226,509
Pasto	332,396
Pereira	381,725
Popayán	200,719
Santa Marta	359,147
★ Santafé de Bogotá, D.C.	6,260,862
Sincelejo	220,704
Soacha	272,058
Sogamoso	107,728
Soledad	295,058
Tuluá	152,488
Tunja	109,740
Valledupar	263,247
Villavicencio	273,140
Comoros (1995 est.)	
★ Moroni	34,168
Congo, Dem. Rep. of the (1994 est.)	
Boma	135,284
Bukavu	201,569
Butembo	109,406
Goma	109,094
Kalemi	101,309
Kananga	393,030
Kikwit	182,142
★ Kinshasa	4,655,313
Kisangani	417,517
Kolwezi	417,810
Likasi	299,118
Lubumbashi	851,381
Matadi	172,730
Mbanadaka	169,841
Mbuji-Mayi	806,475
Mwene-Ditu	137,459
Tshikapa	180,860
Uvira	115,590
Congo, Rep. of the (1992 est.)	
★ Brazzaville	937,579
Pointe-Noire	576,206
Costa Rica (2000 est.)	
★ San José	344,349[13]
Côte d'Ivoire (1995 est.)	
★ Abidjan (de facto; legislative)	3,199,000[2]
Bouaké	330,000
Daloa	123,000
Korhogo	109,445[14]
★ Yamoussoukro (de jure; administrative)	110,000
Croatia (2001)	
Rijeka	147,709
Split	173,692
★ Zagreb	682,598[15]
Cuba (1994 est.)	
Bayamo	137,663
Camagüey	293,961
Ciego de Avila	104,060[5]
Cienfuegos	132,038
Guantánamo	207,796
★ Havana	2,198,392[16]
Holguín	242,085
Las Tunas	126,930
Manzanillo	109,471[5]
Matanzas	123,843
Pinar del Río	128,570
Santa Clara	205,400
Santiago de Cuba	440,084
Cyprus (1998 est.)	
Limassol	152,900
★ Lefkosia (Nicosia)	194,100[17]
Czech Republic (2000 est.)	
Brno	383,569
Olomouc	103,015
Ostrava	321,263
Plzeň	167,534
★ Prague	1,186,855
Denmark (2000 est.; MU)	
Ålborg	161,161
Århus	284,846
★ Copenhagen	495,699
Odense	183,912

country city	population
Djibouti (1995 est.)	
★ Djibouti	383,000
Dominica (1991)	
★ Roseau	15,853
Dominican Republic (1993)	
La Romana	140,204
San Francisco de Macorís	108,485
San Pedro de Macorís	124,735
Santiago	365,463
★ Santo Domingo	1,609,966[18]
East Timor (1999 est.)	
★ Dili	65,000
Ecuador (1997 est.)	
Ambato	160,302
Cuenca	255,028
Duran	135,675
Eloy Alfaro	120,364[4]
Esmeraldas	117,722
Guayaquil	1,973,880
Ibarra	119,243
Loja	117,365
Machala	197,350
Manta	156,981
Milagro	119,371
Portoviejo	167,956
Quevedo	120,640
★ Quito	1,487,513
Riobamba	117,270
Santo Domingo	183,219
Egypt (1996)	
Alexandria	3,328,196
Al-ʿArīsh	100,447
Aswān	219,017
Asyūṭ	343,498
Banhā	145,792
Banī Suwayf	172,032
Bilbays	113,608
Būr Saʿīd (Port Said)	469,533
★ Cairo	6,789,479
Damanhūr	212,203
Al-Fayyūm	260,964
Al-Ismāʿīlīyah	254,477
Al-Jīzah (Giza)	2,221,868
Kafr ad-Dawwar	231,978
Kafr ash-Shaykh	124,819
Al-Maḥallah al-Kubrā	395,402
Mallawī	119,283
Al-Manṣūrah	369,621
Al-Minyā	201,360
Mīt Ghamr	101,801
Qinā	171,275
Sawhāj	170,125
Shibīn al-Kawm	159,909
Shubrā al-Khaymah	870,716
As-Suways (Suez)	417,610
Ṭanṭā	371,010
Al-Uqṣur (Luxor)	360,503
Az-Zaqāzīq	267,351
El Salvador (1992)	
Mejicanos	131,972[19]
San Miguel	127,696
★ San Salvador	415,346
Santa Ana	139,389
Soyapango	261,122[19]
Equatorial Guinea (1995 est.)	
★ Malabo	47,500
Eritrea (1995 est.)	
★ Asmara	431,000
Estonia (2000 est.)	
★ Tallinn	404,000
Tartu	101,000
Ethiopia (1994)	
★ Addis Ababa	2,112,737
Dire Dawa	164,851
Gonder	112,249
Harer (Harar)	131,139
Jima	106,842
Nazret	127,842
Faroe Islands (2000 est.)	
★ Tórshavn	16,474
Fiji (1996)	
★ Suva	77,366
Finland (2000 est.)	
Espoo	209,667
★ Helsinki	551,123
Oulu	117,670
Tampere	193,174
Turku	172,107
Vantaa	176,386
France (1999)	
Aix-en-Provence	134,222
Amiens	135,501
Angers	151,279
Besançon	117,304
Bordeaux	215,118
Boulogne-Billancourt	106,367
Brest	149,634
Caen	113,987
Clermont-Ferrand	137,140
Dijon	149,867
Grenoble	153,317
Le Havre	190,651
Le Mans	146,105
Lille	182,228
Limoges	133,960
Lyon	445,257
Marseille	797,486
Metz	123,776
Montpellier	225,392
Mulhouse	110,359
Nancy	103,605
Nantes	268,695
Nice	342,738
Nîmes	133,424
Orléans	112,833
★ Paris	2,123,261
agglomeration	9,608,000[2]
Perpignan	105,115
Reims	187,206
Rennes	206,229
Rouen	106,035
Saint-Étienne	179,755
Strasbourg	263,940
Toulon	159,389
Toulouse	390,413
Tours	132,820
Villeurbanne	124,215
French Guiana (1999)	
★ Cayenne	50,594
French Polynesia (1996)	
★ Papeete	25,353
agglomeration	121,000[2]
Gabon (1993)	
★ Libreville	362,386
Gambia, The (1993)	
★ Banjul	42,407
agglomeration	270,540
Gaza Strip (1999 est.)	
★ Gaza (Ghazzah; acting administrative centre)	388,031
Jabālyah	113,901[20]
Khān Yūnus	123,175[20]
Georgia (1997 est.)	
Bat'umi (Batumi)	137,100
K'ut'aisi (Kutaisi)	240,000
Rust'avi (Rustavi)	158,000
★ T'bilisi (Tbilisi)	1,398,968[16]
Zugdidi	105,000[21]
Germany (1999 est.)	
Aachen	243,600
Augsburg	254,500
Bergisch Gladbach	105,963[16]
★ Berlin	3,392,900
Bielefeld	321,600
Bochum	392,900
Bonn	304,100
Bottrop	121,500
Braunschweig	246,800
Bremen	542,300
Bremerhaven	123,800
Chemnitz	266,000
Cologne (Köln)	963,200
Cottbus	112,200
Darmstadt	137,600
Dortmund	590,300
Dresden	477,700
Duisburg	521,300
Düsseldorf	568,500
Erfurt	202,100
Erlangen	100,600
Essen	600,700
Frankfurt am Main	644,700
Freiburg im Breisgau	201,000
Fürth	109,700
Gelsenkirchen	283,300
Gera	115,800
Göttingen	127,366[16]
Hagen	206,400
Halle	258,500
Hamburg	1,701,800
Hamm	181,500
Hannover	515,200
Heidelberg	139,400
Heilbronn	119,900
Herne	176,200
Hildesheim	105,405[16]
Ingolstadt	114,500
Kaiserslautern	100,300
Karlsruhe	276,700
Kassel	196,700
Kiel	235,500
Koblenz	108,700
Krefeld	242,800
Leipzig	490,000
Leverkusen	161,100
Lübeck	213,800
Ludwigshafen	164,200
Magdeburg	238,000
Mainz	185,600
Mannheim	308,400
Moers	106,704[16]
Mönchengladbach	264,100
Mülheim an der Ruhr	174,300
Munich (München)	1,193,600
Münster	264,700
Neuss	149,206[16]
Nürnberg	486,400
Oberhausen	222,300
Offenbach am Main	116,400
Oldenburg	154,100
Osnabrück	164,900
Paderborn	131,851[16]
Pforzheim	117,500
Potsdam	129,500
Recklinghausen	126,241[16]
Regensburg	125,200
Remscheid	119,500
Reutlingen	109,000[16]
Rostock	205,900
Saarbrücken	186,402[16]
Salzgitter	113,700
Schwerin	104,200
Siegen	110,847[16]
Solingen	165,400
Stuttgart	581,200
Ulm	116,000
Wiesbaden	268,200
Witten	103,872[16]
Wolfsburg	122,200
Wuppertal	370,700
Würzburg	126,000
Zwickau	104,900
Ghana (1998 est.)	
★ Accra	1,446,000
Kumasi	578,000
Tamale	229,000
Tema	300,000
Greece (1991)	
★ Athens	772,072
Iráklion	116,178
Kallithéa	114,233
Larissa	112,777
Pátrai (Patras)	153,344
Peristérion	137,288
Piraiévs (Piraeus)	182,671
Thessaloníki	383,967
Greenland (2000 est.)	
★ Nuuk (Godthåb)	13,838
Grenada (1991)	
★ Saint George's	4,621
agglomeration	35,000[2]
Guadeloupe (1999)	
★ Basse-Terre	12,549
Guam (1995 est.)	
★ Hagåtña (Agana)	2,000
Guatemala (1994)	
★ Guatemala City	823,301
agglomeration	3,119,000[2]
Mixco	209,791[22]
Villa Nueva	101,295[22]
Guernsey (1996)	
★ St. Peter Port	16,194
Guinea (1999 est.)	
★ Conakry	1,764,000
Guinea-Bissau (1999 est.)	
★ Bissau	274,000
Guyana (1999 est.)	
★ Georgetown	275,000
Haiti (1997 est.)	
Cap-Haïtien	107,026
Carrefour	306,074
Delmas	257,247
★ Port-au-Prince	917,112
Honduras (1999 est.)	
El Progreso	104,100
La Ceiba	103,400
San Pedro Sula	452,100
★ Tegucigalpa	988,400[23]
Hong Kong (2001 est.)	
★ Hong Kong	6,732,100[24]
Hungary (2000 est.)	
★ Budapest	1,811,552
Debrecen	203,648
Győr	127,119
Kecskemét	105,606
Miskolc	172,357
Nyíregyháza	112,419
Pécs	157,332
Szeged	158,158
Székesfehérvár	105,119
Iceland (1999 est.)	
★ Reykjavík	109,184
India (1991)	
Abohar	107,163
Adoni	136,182
Agartala	157,358
Agra	891,790
Ahmadabad	2,876,710
Ahmadnagar	181,339
Aizawl	155,240
Ajmer	402,700
Akola	328,034
Alandur	125,244
Alappuzha (Alleppey)	174,666
Alibag	328,640
Aligarh	480,520
Allahabad (Prayagraj)	792,858
Alwar	205,086
Ambala	119,338
Ambattur	215,424
Amravati	421,576
Amritsar	708,835
Amroha	137,061
Anand	110,266
Anantapur	174,924
Ara (Arrah)	157,082
Asansol	262,188
Avadi	183,215
Baharampur	115,144
Bahraich	135,400
Bally	184,474
Balurghat	119,796
Bangalore	2,660,088
Bankura	114,876
Baranagar (Barahanagar)	224,821
Barasat	102,660
Barddhaman (Burdwan)	245,079
Bareilly	587,211
Barrackpore	133,265
Basirhat	101,409
Bathinda (Bhatinda)	159,042
Beawar	105,363
Belgaum	326,399
Bellary	245,391
Bhagalpur	253,225
Bharatpur	148,519
Bharuch (Broach)	133,102
Bhatpara	304,952
Bhavnagar	402,338
Bhilainagar	395,360
Bhilwara	183,965
Bhimavaram	121,314
Bhind	109,755
Bhiwandi	379,070
Bhiwani	121,629
Bhopal	1,062,771
Bhubaneshwar	411,542
Bhuj	102,176
Bhusawal	145,143
Bid (Bhir)	112,434
Bidar	108,016
Bidhan Nagar	100,048
Bihar Sharif	201,323
Bijapur	186,939
Bikaner	416,289
Bilaspur	179,833
Bokaro (Bokaro Steel City)	333,683
Brahmapur	210,418
Budaun	116,695
Bulandshahr	127,201
Burhanpur	172,710
Burnpur	174,933
Champdani	101,067
Chandannagar	120,378
Chandigarh	504,094
Chandrapur	226,105
Chennai (Madras)	3,841,396
Chhapra	136,877
Chittoor	133,462
Coimbatore	816,321
Cuddalore	144,561
Cuddapah	121,463
Cuttack	403,418
Dabgram	147,217
Darbhanga	218,391
Davanagere	266,082
Dehra Dun	270,159
Delhi	7,206,704
Dewas	164,364
Dhanbad	151,789
Dhule (Dhulia)	278,317
Dibrugarh	120,127
Dindigul	182,447
Durg	150,645
Durgapur	425,836
Eluru	212,866
Erode	159,232
Etawah	124,072
Faizabad	124,437
Faridabad	617,717
Farrukhabad-cum-Fatehgarh	194,567
Fatehpur	117,675
Fīrozabad	215,128
Gadag-Betigeri	134,051
Gandhidham	104,585
Gandhinagar	123,359
Ganganagar	161,482
Gaya	219,675
Ghaziabad	454,156
Gondia	109,470
Gorakhpur	505,566
Gudivada	101,656
Gulbarga	304,099
Guna	100,490
Guntakal	107,592
Guntur	471,051
Gurgaon	121,486
Guwahati (Gauhati)	584,342
Gwalior	690,765
Habra	100,223
Haldia	100,347
Haldwani-cum-Kathgodam	104,195
Halisahar	114,028
Haora (Howrah)	950,435
Hapur	146,262
Haridwar (Hardwar)	147,305
Hathras	113,285
Hindupur	104,651
Hisar (Hissar)	172,677
Hoshiarpur	122,705
Hubli-Dharwad	648,298
Hugli-Chunchura	151,806
Hyderabad	3,145,939
Ichalkaranji	214,950
Imphal	198,535
Indore	1,091,674
Ingraj Bazar (English Bazar)	139,204
Jabalpur	741,927
Jaipur	1,458,183
Jalandhar (Jullundur)	509,510
Jalgaon	242,193
Jalna	174,985
Jammu	225,000[5, 25]
Jamnagar	341,637
Jamshedpur	478,950
Jaunpur	136,062
Jhansi	300,850
Jodhpur	666,279
Junagadh	130,484
Kakinada	279,980
Kalyan	1,014,557
Kamarhati	266,889
Kanchipuram	144,955
Kanchrapara	100,194
Kanpur	1,874,409

Major cities and national capitals (continued)

country city	population
Karimnagar	148,583
Karnal	173,751
Katihar	135,436
Khammam	127,992
Khandwa	143,133
Kharagpur	177,989
Kochi (Cochin)	564,589
Kolhapur	406,370
Kolkata (Calcutta)	4,399,819
Kollam (Quilon)	139,852
Korba	124,501
Kota	537,371
Kozhikode (Calicut)	419,831
Krishnanagar	121,110
Kukatpalle	186,963
Kulti-Barakar	108,518
Kumbakonam	139,483
Kurnool	236,800
Lalbahadur Nagar	155,514
Latur	197,408
Lucknow	1,619,115
Ludhiana	1,042,740
Machilipatnam (Masulipatam)	159,110
Madurai	940,989
Mahbubnagar	116,833
Malegaon	342,595
Malkajgiri	127,178
Mandya	120,265
Mangalore	273,304
Mango	108,100
Mathura	226,691
Maunath Bhanjan	136,697
Medinipur (Midnapore)	125,498
Meerut	753,778
Mira-Bhayandar	175,605
Miraj	121,593
Mizapur-cum-Vindhyachal	169,336
Modinagar	101,660
Moga	108,304
Moradabad	429,214
Morena	147,124
Mumbai (Bombay)	9,925,891
Munger (Monghyr)	150,112
Murwara (Katni)	163,431
Muzaffarnagar	240,609
Muzaffarpur	241,107
Mysore	480,692
Nadiad	167,051
Nagercoil	190,084
Nagpur	1,624,752
Naihati	132,701
Nanded (Nander)	275,083
Nandyal	119,813
Nashik (Nasik)	656,925
Navadwip	125,037
Navsari	126,089
Nellore	316,606
New Bombay	307,724
★ New Delhi	301,297
Neyveli	118,080
Nizamabad	241,034
Noida	146,514
North Barrackpore	100,606
North Dum Dum	149,965
Ongole	100,836
Palghat (Palakkad)	123,289
Pali	136,842
Pallavaram	111,866
Panihati	275,990
Panipat	191,212
Parbhani	190,255
Pathankot	123,930
Patiala	238,368
Patna	917,243
Pilibhit	106,605
Pimpri-Chinchwad	517,083
Pondicherry	203,065
Porbandar	116,671
Proddatur	133,914
Pune	1,566,651
Puri	125,199
Purnia (Purnea)	114,912
Qutubullapur	106,591
Rae Bareli	129,904
Raichur	157,551
Raiganj	151,045
Raipur	438,639
Raj Nandgaon	125,371
Rajahmundry	324,851
Rajapalaiyam	114,202
Rajkot	559,407
Ramagundam	214,384
Rampur	243,742
Ranchi	599,306
Ratlam	183,375
Raurkela Civil Township	140,408
Raurkela Steel Township	215,509
Rewa	128,981
Rishra	102,815
Rohtak	216,096
Sagar	195,346
Saharanpur	374,945
Salem	366,712
Sambalpur	131,138
Sambhal	150,869
Sangli	193,197
Satna	156,630
Shahjahanpur	237,713
Shambajinagar (Aurangābād)	573,272
Shantipur	109,956
Shiliguri (Siliguri)	216,950
Shillong	131,719
Shimoga	179,258
Shivpuri	108,277
Sholapur (Solapur)	604,215
Shrirampur	137,028
Sikandarabad (Secundarabad) Cantonment	171,148
Sikar	148,272
Silchar	115,483
Sirsa	112,841
Sitapur	121,842
Sonipat (Sonepat)	143,922
South Dum Dum	232,811
Srinagar	700,000[5, 25]
Surat	1,498,817
Surendranagar	106,110
Tambaram	107,187
Tenali	143,726
Thalassery (Tellicherry)	103,579
Thane (Thana)	803,389
Thanjavur	202,013
Thiruvananthapuram (Trivandrum)	524,006
Tiruchchirappalli	387,223
Tirunelueli	135,825
Tirupati	174,369
Tirupper (Tiruppur)	235,661
Tiruvannamalai	109,196
Tiruvottiyur	168,642
Titagarh	114,085
Tonk	100,079
Tumkur	138,903
Tuticorin	199,854
Udaipur	308,571
Ujjain	362,266
Ulhasnagar	369,077
Uluberia	155,172
Unnao	107,425
Uttarpara-Kotrung	101,268
Vadodara (Baroda)	1,031,346
Valparai	106,523
Varanasi (Benares)	929,270
Vellore	175,061
Vijayawada	701,827
Vishakhapatnam	752,037
Vizianagaram	160,359
Warangal	447,657
Wardha	102,985
Yamunanagar	144,346
Yavatmal (Yeotmal)	108,578
Indonesia (1995 est.)[26]	
Ambon	249,312
Balikpapan	338,752
Banda Aceh	143,360[10]
Bandar Lampung	457,927[10]
Bandung	2,356,120
Banjarmasin	482,931
Bekasi	644,284[10]
Bengkulu	146,395[10]
Binjai	127,184[10]
Blitar	112,986[10]
Bogor	285,114
Cianjur	114,335[10]
Cibinong	101,317[10]
Cilacap	206,928[10]
Cilegon-Merak	116,981[10]
Cimahi	344,607[10]
Ciomas	187,379[10]
Ciparay	111,467[10]
Ciputat	270,815[10]
Cirebon	254,406
Citeurup	105,079[10]
Denpasar	345,150[10]
Depok (*West Java*)	106,825[10]
Depok (*Yogyakarta*)	661,495[10]
★ Jakarta	9,112,652
Jambi	385,201
Jember	218,529[10]
Karawang (Krawang)	145,041[10]
Kediri	253,760
Klaten	103,327[10]
Kupang	129,259[10]
Lhokseumawe	109,569[10]
Madiun	171,532
Magelang	123,800
Malang	716,862
Manado	332,288
Mataram	275,089[10]
Medan	1,843,919
Padang	534,474
Palembang	1,222,764
Palu	142,767[10]
Pangkalpinang	108,377[10]
Pasuruan	133,685[9]
Pekalongan	301,504
Pekanbaru	438,638
Pemalang	103,540[10]
Pematang Siantar	203,056
Percut	129,036[10]
Pondokgede	263,152[10]
Pontianak	409,632
Probolinggo	120,770
Purwokerto	202,452[10]
Salatiga	103,000
Samarinda	399,175
Semarang	1,104,405
Serang	122,429[10]
Sukabumi	125,766
Surabaya	2,663,820
Surakarta	516,594
Taman	106,975[10]
Tangerang	887,952[10]
Tanjung Balai	101,644[10]
Tanjung Karang	680,332
Tasikmalaya	179,766[10]
Tebingtinggi	129,300
Tegal	289,744
Ujung Pandang	1,060,257
Waru	124,282[10]
Yogyakarta	418,944
Iran (1996)	
Ābādān	206,073
Ahvāz	804,980
Āmol	159,092
Andīmeshk	106,923
Arāk	380,755
Ardabīl	340,386
Bābol	158,346
Bandar 'Abbās	273,578
Bandar-e Būshehr (Būshehr)	143,641
Bīrjand	127,608
Bojnūrd	134,835
Borūjerd	217,804
Būkān	120,020
Dezfūl	202,639
Emāmshahr (Shāhrūd)	104,765
Eṣfahān (Isfahan)	1,266,072
Gonbad-e Kavus	111,253
Gorgān	188,710
Hamadān	401,281
Īlām	126,346
Islāmshahr (Eslāmshahr)	265,450
Karaj	940,968[27]
Kāshān	201,372
Kermān	384,991
Kermānshāh (Bākhtarān)	692,986
Khomeynīshahr	165,888
Khorramābād	272,815
Khorramshahr	105,636
Khvoy (Khoy)	148,944
Mahābād	107,799
Malāyer	144,373
Marāgheh	132,318
Marv Dasht	103,579
Mashhad (Meshed)	1,887,405
Masjed-e Soleymān	116,882
Najafābād	178,498
Neyshābūr	158,847
Orūmīyeh	435,200
Qā'emshahr	143,286
Qarchak	142,690
Qazvīn	291,117
Qods	138,278
Qom	777,677
Rasht	417,748
Sabzevār	170,738
Sanandaj	277,808
Saqqez	115,394
Sārī	195,882
Sāveh	111,245
Shahr-e Kord	100,477
Shīrāz	1,053,025
Sīrjān	135,024
Tabrīz	1,191,043
★ Tehrān	6,758,845
Varāmīn	107,233
Yazd	326,776
Zābol	100,888
Zāhedān	419,518
Zanjān	286,295
Iraq (1987)	
Al-'Amārah	208,797
★ Baghdad	4,689,000[2, 28]
Ba'qūbah	114,516[29]
Al-Baṣrah	406,296
Al-Ḥillah	268,834
Dīwanīyah	196,519
Irbīl	485,968
Karbalā'	296,705
Karkūk	418,624
Al-Kūt	183,183
Mosul	664,221
An-Najaf	309,010
An-Nāṣirīyah	265,937
Ar-Ramādī	192,556
As-Sulaymānīyah	364,096
Ireland (1996)	
Cork	127,092[30]
★ Dublin	480,996[30]
Isle of Man (1996)	
★ Douglas	23,487
Israel (1999 est.)	
Ashdod	155,800
Bat Yam	137,000
Beersheba (Be'er Sheva')	163,700
Bene Beraq	133,900
Haifa (Ḥefa)	265,700
Ḥolon	163,100
★ Jerusalem (Yerushalayim, Al-Quds)	633,700
Netanya	154,900
Petaḥ Tiqwa	159,400
Ramat Gan	126,900
Rishon LeẔiyyon	188,200
Tel Aviv–Yafo	348,100
Italy (2000 est.)[31]	
Bari	331,848
Bergamo	117,837
Bologna	381,161
Brescia	191,317
Cagliari	165,926
Catania	337,862
Ferrara	132,127
Florence (Firenze)	376,682
Foggia	154,891
Forlì	107,475
Genoa (Genova)	636,104
Latina	114,099
Livorno	161,673
Messina	259,156
Milan (Milano)	1,300,977
Modena	176,022
Monza	119,516
Naples (Napoli)	1,002,619
Novara	102,037
Padua (Padova)	211,391
Palermo	683,794
Parma	168,717
Perugia	156,673
Pescara	115,698
Prato	172,473
Ravenna	138,418
Reggio di Calabria	179,617
Reggio nell'Emilia	143,664
Rimini	131,062
★ Rome (Roma)	2,643,581
Salerno	142,055
Sassari	120,803
Siracusa (Syracuse)	126,282
Taranto	208,214
Terni	107,770
Trento	104,906
Trieste	216,459
Turin (Torino)	903,703
Venice (Venezia)	277,305
Verona	255,268
Vicenza	109,738
Jamaica (1991)	
★ Kingston	103,771
agglomeration	655,000[2]
Japan (1995)	
Abiko	124,257
Ageo	206,090
Aizuwakamatsu	119,640
Akashi	287,606
Akishima	107,292
Akita	311,948
Amagasaki	488,586
Anjō	149,464
Aomori	294,167
Asahikawa	360,568
Asaka	110,789
Ashikaga	165,828
Atsugi	208,627
Beppu	128,255
Chiba	856,878
Chigasaki	212,874
Chōfu	198,574
Daitō	128,838
Ebetsu	115,495
Ebina	113,430
Fuchu	216,211
Fuji	229,187
Fujieda	124,822
Fujinomiya	119,536
Fujisawa	368,651
Fukaya	100,285
Fukui	255,604
Fukuoka	1,284,795
Fukushima	285,754
Fukuyama	374,517
Funabashi	540,817
Gifu	407,134
Habikino	117,735
Hachinohe	242,654
Hachiōji	503,363
Hadano	164,722
Hakodate	298,881
Hamamatsu	561,606
Handa	106,452
Higashi-Hiroshima	113,939
Higashi-Kurume	111,097
Higashi-Murayama	135,112
Higashi-Ōsaka	517,232
Hikone	103,508
Himeji	470,986
Hino	166,537
Hirakata	400,144
Hiratsuka	253,822
Hirosaki	177,972
Hiroshima	1,108,888
Hitachi	199,244
Hitachinaka	146,750
Hōfu	118,803
Hoya	100,260
Ibaraki	258,233
Ichihara	277,061
Ichikawa	440,555
Ichinomiya	267,362
Iida	106,772
Ikeda	104,293
Ikoma	106,726
Imabari	120,214
Iruma	144,402
Ise	102,632
Isesaki	120,236
Ishinomaki	121,208
Itami	188,431
Iwaki	360,598
Iwakuni	107,386
Iwatsuki	109,546
Izumi	157,300
Joetsu	132,205
Kadoma	140,506
Kagamigahara	131,955
Kagoshima	546,282
Kakogawa	260,567
Kamakura	170,329
Kanazawa	453,975
Kariya	125,305
Kashihara	121,988
Kashiwa	317,750
Kasugai	277,589
Kasukabe	200,121
Kawachi-Nagano	117,082
Kawagoe	323,353
Kawaguchi	448,854
Kawanishi	144,539
Kawasaki	1,202,820
Kiryū	120,377
Kisarazu	123,499
Kishiwada	194,818
Kita-Kyūshū	1,019,598
Kitami	110,452
Kobe	1,423,792
Kochi	321,999
Kodaira	172,946
Kofu	201,124
Koganei	109,279
Kokubunji	105,786
Komaki	137,165
Komatsu	107,965
Koriyama	326,833
Koshigaya	298,253

country city	population
Kumagaya	156,429
Kumamoto	650,341
Kurashiki	422,836
Kure	209,485
Kurume	234,433
Kusatsu	101,828
Kushiro	199,323
Kuwana	103,044
Kyōto	1,463,822
Machida	360,525
Maebashi	284,788
Matsubara	134,457
Matsudo	461,503
Matsue	147,416
Matsumoto	205,523
Matsuyama	460,968
Matsuzaka	122,449
Minō	127,542
Misato	133,600
Mishima	107,890
Mitaka	165,721
Mito	246,347
Miyakonojō	132,714
Miyazaki	300,068
Moriguchi	157,306
Morioka	286,478
Muroran	109,766
Musashino	135,051
Nagano	358,516
Nagaoka	190,470
Nagareyama	146,245
Nagasaki	438,635
Nagoya	2,152,184
Naha	301,890
Nara	359,218
Narashino	152,887
Neyagawa	258,443
Niigata	494,769
Niihama	127,917
Niiza	144,726
Nishinomiya	390,389
Nobeoka	126,629
Noda	119,790
Numazu	212,241
Obihiro	171,715
Odawara	200,103
Ōgaki	110,760
Ōita	426,979
Okayama	615,757
Okazaki	322,621
Okinawa	115,336
Ōme	137,234
Ōmiya	433,755
Ōmuta	145,085
Ōsaka	2,602,421
Ōta	143,057
Ōtaru	157,022
Ōtsu	276,332
Oyama	150,115
Saga	171,231
Sagamihara	570,597
Sakai	802,993
Sakata	101,230
Sakura	162,624
Sapporo	1,757,025
Sasebo	244,909
Sayama	162,240
Sendai	971,297
Seto	129,393
Shimizu	240,174
Shimonoseki	259,795
Shizuoka	474,092
Sōka	217,930
Suita	342,760
Suzuka	179,800
Tachikawa	157,884
Tajimi	101,270
Takamatsu	331,004
Takaoka	173,607
Takarazuka	202,544
Takasaki	238,133
Takatsuki	362,270
Tama	148,113
Tokorozawa	320,406
Tokushima	268,706
Tokuyama	108,671
★ Tokyo	7,967,614
Tomakomai	169,328
Tondabayashi	121,690
Tottori	146,330
Toyama	325,375
Toyohashi	352,982
Toyokawa	114,380
Toyonaka	398,908
Toyota	341,079
Tsu	163,156
Tsuchiura	132,243
Tsukuba	156,012
Tsuruoka	100,538
Ube	175,116
Ueda	123,284
Uji	184,830
Urawa	453,300
Urayasu	123,654
Utsunomiya	435,357
Wakayama	393,885
Yachiyo	154,509
Yaizu	115,931
Yamagata	254,488
Yamaguchi	135,579
Yamato	203,933
Yao	276,664
Yatsushiro	107,709
Yokkaichi	285,779
Yokohama	3,307,136
Yokosuka	432,193
Yonago	134,762
Zama	118,159
Jersey (1996)	
★ St. Helier	27,523
Jordan (1994)	
★ Amman	969,598
Irbid	208,329
Ar-Ruṣayfah	137,247
Az-Zarqā'	350,849
Kazakhstan (1999)	
Almaty (Alma-Ata)	1,129,400
Aqtaū (Aktau; Shevchenko)	143,400
Aqtöbe (Aktyubinsk)	253,100
★ Astana (Aqmola; Tselinograd)	313,000
Atyraū (Guryev)	142,500
Ekibastuz	127,200
Kökshetaū (Kokchetav)	123,400
Oral (Uralsk)	195,500
Öskemen (Ust-Kamenogorsk)	311,000
Pavlodar	300,500
Petropavl (Petropavlovsk)	203,500
Qaraghandy (Karaganda)	436,900
Qostanay (Kustanay)	221,400
Qyzylord (Kzyl-Orda)	157,400
Rūdny	109,500
Semey (Semipalatinsk)	269,600
Shymkent (Shimkent; Chimkent)	360,100
Taraz (Auliye-Ata; (Dzhambul)	330,100
Temirtaū	170,500
Kenya (1999)	
Eldoret	111,882[32]
Kisumu	192,733[32]
Machakos	143,274
Meru	126,427
Mombasa	461,753[32]
★ Nairobi	2,143,254
Nakuru	231,262
Nyeri	101,238
Kiribati (1990)	
★ Bairiki	2,226
agglomeration	32,000[2]
Korea, North (1987 est.)	
Anju	186,000
Ch'ŏngjin	582,480[1]
Haeju	195,000
Hamhŭng-Hungnam	709,000[1]
Hŭich'ŏn	163,000
Kaesŏng	334,433[1]
Kanggye	211,000
Kimch'aek (Songjin)	179,000
Kusŏng	177,000
Namp'o	731,448[1]
★ P'yŏngyang	3,136,000[2, 28]
Sinp'o	158,000
Sinŭiju	326,011[1]
Sunch'ŏn	356,000
Tanch'ŏn	284,000
Tŏkch'ŏn	217,000
Wŏnsan	274,000
Korea, South (1995)	
Andong	188,443
Ansan	510,314
Anyang	591,106
Asan	154,663
Ch'angwŏn	481,694
Chech'ŏn	137,070
Cheju (Jeju)	258,511
Chinhae	125,997
Chinju	329,886
Ch'ŏnan	330,259
Ch'ŏngju	531,376
Chŏng-ŭp	139,011
Chŏnju	563,153
Ch'unch'ŏn	234,528
Ch'ungju	205,206
Hanam	115,812
Iksan (Iri)	322,685
Inch'ŏn (Incheon)	2,308,188
Kangnŭng	220,403
Kimch'ŏn	147,027
Kimhae	256,370
Kimje	115,427
Kŏje	147,562
Kongju	131,229
Koyang	518,282
Kumi	311,431
Kunp'o	235,233
Kunsan	266,569
Kuri	142,173
Kwangju	1,257,636
Kwangmyŏng	350,914
Kwangyang	122,052
Kyŏngju	273,968
Kyŏngsan	173,746
Masan	441,242
Miryang	121,501
Mokp'o	247,452
Naju	107,831
Namwon	103,544
Namyangju	229,060
P'ohang	508,899
Poryŏng	122,604
Puch'ŏn	779,412
Pusan (Busan)	3,814,325
P'yŏngt'aek	312,927
Sach'ŏn	113,494
Sangju	124,116
★ Seoul (Sŏul)	10,231,217
Shihŭng	133,443
Sŏngnam	869,094
Sŏsan	134,746
Sunch'ŏn	249,263
Suwŏn	755,550
Taegu	2,449,420
Taejŏn	1,272,121
Tongyŏng	131,717
Ŭijŏngbu	276,111
Ŭiwang	108,788
Ulsan	967,429
Wŏnju	237,460
Yŏngch'ŏn	113,511
Yŏngju	131,097
Yŏsu	183,596
Kuwait (1995)	
As-Sālimīyah	130,215
★ Kuwait (Al-Kuwayt)	28,859
agglomeration	1,165,000[2]
Qalīb ash-Shuyūkh	102,178
Kyrgyzstan (1999 est.)	
★ Bishkek (Frunze)	619,000[28]
Osh	220,500[33]
Laos (1999 est.)	
★ Vientiane (Viangchan)	534,000
Latvia (2000 est.)	
Daugavpils	114,510
★ Rīga	788,283
Lebanon (1998 est.)	
Baalbek (Ba'labakk)	150,000
★ Beirut (Bayrūt)	1,500,000
Jūniyah	100,000
Tripoli (Ṭarābulus)	160,000
Lesotho (1996 est.)	
★ Maseru	160,100
agglomeration	373,000[2]
Liberia (1999 est.)	
★ Monrovia	479,000[28]
Libya (1995 est.)	
Banghāzī	650,000
Miṣrātah	280,000
Surt (Sirte)	150,000
★ Tripoli (Ṭarābulus)	1,140,000
Liechtenstein (2000 est.)	
★ Vaduz	5,043
Lithuania (2000 est.)	
Kaunas	412,614
Klaipėda	202,484
Panevėžys	133,696
Šiauliai	146,570
★ Vilnius	577,969
Luxembourg (1999 est.)	
★ Luxembourg	79,800
Macau (2000 est.)	
★ Macau	440,000
Macedonia (1994)	
★ Skopje (Skopije)	444,299
Madagascar (1993)	
★ Antananarivo	1,103,304
Antsirabe	126,062
Fianarantsoa	109,248
Mahajanga	106,780
Toamasina	137,782
Malawi (1998 est.)	
★ Blantyre (executive; judicial)	478,155
★ Lilongwe (ministerial; financial; legislative)	435,964
Malaysia (1991)	
Alor Setar	125,026
George Town (Pinang)	219,376
Ipoh	382,633
Johor Baharu	328,646
Kelang (Port Kelang)	243,698
Kota Baharu	219,713
★ Kuala Lumpur	1,145,075
Kuala Terengganu	228,659
Kuantan	198,356
Kuching	147,729
Petaling Jaya	254,849
Sandakan	126,092
Selayang Baru	124,606
Seremban	182,584
Shah Alam	101,773
Sibu	126,384
Sungai Petani	115,719
Taiping	183,165
Maldives (1995)	
★ Male	62,973
Mali (1996 est.)	
★ Bamako	809,552
Ségou	106,799
Malta (1999 est.)	
★ Valletta	7,100
agglomeration	102,000
Marshall Is. (1999)	
★ Majuro	23,676
Martinique (1999)	
★ Fort-de-France	94,049
Mauritania (1999 est.)	
★ Nouakchott	881,000
Mauritius (1999 est.)	
★ Port Louis	147,648
Beau Bassin/Rose Hill	101,273
Mayotte (1997; MU)	
★ Dzaoudzi (French administrative)	10,796
★ Mamoudzou (local administrative)	32,774
Mexico (2000 est.)	
Acapulco	619,253[34]
Aguascalientes	594,056[34]
Atizapán de Zaragoza (Ciudad López Mateos)	467,000
Boca del Río	124,000
Campeche	195,000
Cancún	400,000
Celaya	270,000
Chalco	123,000
Chetumal	118,000
Chihuahua	650,000
Chilpancingo	140,000
Chimalhuacán	488,000
Ciudad Acuña (Acuña)	108,000
Ciudad Apodaca (Apodaca)	273,000
Ciudad del Carmen	115,000
Ciudad Madero	182,012[34]
Ciudad Obregón	250,000
Ciudad Santa Catarina (Santa Catarina)	226,500
Ciudad Valles	105,000
Ciudad Victoria (Victoria)	248,000
Coacalco	250,000
Coatzacoalcos	229,000
Colima	119,186[34]
Córdoba	138,000
Cuautitlán Izcalli	435,000
Cuautla Morelos	137,000
Cuernavaca	330,000
Culiacán	536,942[34]
Durango	430,000
Ecatepec (de Morelos)	1,619,000
Ensenada	222,687[34]
General Escobedo	230,000
Gómez Palacio	210,000
Guadalajara	1,647,000
Guadalupe	668,500
Hermosillo	544,889[34]
Heroica Nogales (Nogales)	157,000
Huixquilucan	110,000
Iguala	105,000
Irapuato	320,000
Ixtapaluca	240,000
Jiutepec	140,000
Juárez (Ciudad Juárez)	1,190,000
La Paz	162,795[34]
León	1,019,510[34]
Los Mochis	200,000
Los Reyes la Paz	213,040[34]
Matamoros	370,000
Mazatlán	325,000
Mérida	660,848[34]
Metepec	160,000
Mexicali	550,000
★ Mexico City	8,591,309[34]
Minatitlán	150,000
Monclova	192,000
Monterrey	1,108,400
Morelia	549,404[34]
Naucalpan	840,000
Nezahualcóyotl	1,224,500
Nicolás Romero	218,000
Nuevo Laredo	309,000
Oaxaca	252,586[34]
Orizaba	118,400
Pachuca	231,089[34]
Piedras Negras	125,000
Poza Rica de Hidalgo	151,500
Puebla	1,270,989[34]
Puerta Vallarta	150,000
Querétaro	535,468[34]
Reynosa	398,000
Salamanca	140,000
Saltillo	560,000
San Cristóbal de las Casas	112,000
San Luis Potosí	628,134[34]
San Luis Río Colorado	125,000
San Nicolás de los Garzas	495,540[34]
San Pablo de las Salinas	150,000
San Pedro Garza García	126,000
Soledad de Graciano Sanchez	170,000
Tampico	294,789[34]
Tapachula	180,000
Tehuacán	204,358[34]
Tepic	265,681[34]
Texcoco (de Mora)	105,000
Tijuana	1,150,000
Tlalnepantla	715,000
Tlaquepaque	460,000
Toluca	435,000
Tonala	310,000
Torreón	505,000
Tultilan (Buenavista)	192,000
Tuxtla Gutiérrez	425,000
Uruapan	227,000
Valle de Chalco (Xico)	323,000
Veracruz	410,000
Villahermosa	330,605[34]
Xalapa (Jalapa Enríquez)	375,000
Zacatecas	113,780[34]
Zamora de Hidalgo	121,000
Zapopan	912,000
Micronesia	
★ Palikir	—
Moldova (1999 est.)	
Bălţi (Beltsy)	156,600
★ Chişinău (Kishinyov)	655,000
Tighina (Bendery)	128,000[33]
Tiraspol	200,700
Monaco (2000 est.)	
★ Monaco	31,700
Mongolia (2000 est.)	
★ Ulaanbaatar (Ulan Bator)	691,000

Major cities and national capitals (continued)

country city	population
Morocco (1994)	
Agadir	155,240
Beni-Mellal	140,212
Casablanca	2,940,623
El-Jadida	119,083
Fès	541,162
Kenitra	292,627
Khouribga	152,090
Ksar el-Kebir	107,065
Marrakech	621,914
Meknès	459,958
Mohammedia	170,083
Nador	112,450
Oujda	365,582
★ Rabat	623,457
Safi	262,276
Salé	504,420
Tanger	521,735
Temera	126,303
Tétouan	277,516
Mozambique (1997)	
Beira	412,588
Chimoio	177,608
★ Maputo (Lourenço Marques)	989,386
Matola	440,927
Mocuba	124,650
Nacala	164,309
Nampula	314,965
Quelimane	153,187
Tete	104,832
Xai-Xai	103,251
Myanmar (Burma) (1993 est.)	
Bassein (Pathein)	183,900
Henzada	104,700
Lashio	107,600
Mandalay	885,300
Meiktila	129,700
Mergui	122,700
Monywa	138,600
Moulmein (Mawlamyine)	307,600
Myingyan	103,600
Pegu (Bago)	190,900
Pyay (Prome, Pye)	105,700
Sittwe (Akyab)	137,600
Taunggyi	131,500
★ Yangôn (Rangoon)	3,361,700
Namibia (1997 est.)	
★ Windhoek	169,000
Nauru (1992)	
★ Yaren	672
Nepal (2000 est.; MU)	
Biratnagar	168,544
Birganj	103,880
★ Kathmandu	701,499
Lalitpur (Patan)	157,475
Pokhara	168,806
Netherlands, The (1999 est.)	
Almere	136,157
Amersfoort	123,367
★ Amsterdam (capital)	727,053
Apeldoorn	152,860
Arnhem	137,222
Breda	159,042
Dordrecht	119,462
Ede	101,542
Eindhoven	199,877
Emmen	105,497
Enschede	148,814
Groningen	171,193
Haarlem	148,262
Haarlemmermeer	109,377
Leiden	117,389
Maastricht	121,479
Nijmegen	151,864
Rotterdam	592,665
's-Hertogenbosch	128,009
★ The Hague (seat of government)	440,743
Tilburg	190,559
Utrecht	232,718
Zaanstad	135,126
Zoetermeer	108,899
Zwolle	104,431
Netherlands Antilles (1999 est.)	
★ Willemstad	123,000
New Caledonia (1996)	
★ Nouméa	76,293
New Zealand (1999 est.)	
Auckland	381,800
Christchurch	324,200
Dunedin	119,600
Hamilton	117,100
Manukau	281,800
North Shore	187,700
Waitakere	170,600
★ Wellington	166,700
Nicaragua (1995)	
León	123,865
★ Managua	864,201
Niger (1994 est.)	
★ Niamey	420,000
Zinder	100,000
Nigeria (1991)	
Aba	500,183
Abeokuta	352,735
★ Abuja	107,069
Ado-Ekiti	156,122
Akure	239,124
Awka	104,682
Bauchi	206,537
Benin City	762,719
Bida	111,245
Calabar	310,839
Damaturu	141,897
Ede	142,363
Effon-Alaiye	158,977
Enugu	407,756
Gboko	101,281
Gombe	163,604
Gusau	132,393
Ibadan	1,835,300
Ife	186,856
Ijebu-Ode	124,313
Ikare	103,843
Ikire	111,435
Ikorodu	184,674
Ikot Ekpene	119,402
Ilawe-Ekiti	104,049
Ilesha	139,445
Ilorin	532,089
Ise	108,136
Iseyin	170,936
Iwo	125,645
Jimeta	141,724
Jos	510,300
Kaduna	993,642
Kano	2,166,554
Katsina	259,315
★ Lagos	5,195,247
agglomeration	12,763,000[2]
Maiduguri	618,278
Makurdi	151,515
Minna	189,191
Mubi	128,900
Nnewi	121,065
Ogbomosho	433,030
Okene	312,775
Okpogho	105,127
Ondo	146,051
Onitsha	350,280
Oshogbo	250,951
Owerri	119,711
Owo	157,181
Oyo	369,894
Port Harcourt	703,421
Sagamu	127,513
Sango Otta	103,332
Sapele	109,576
Sokoto	329,639
Suleja	105,075
Ugep	134,773
Umuahia	147,167
Warri	363,382
Zaria	612,257
Northern Mariana Is. (1995 est.)	
★ Capital Hill[35]	2,698
Norway (2000 est.; MU)	
Bærum	101,494
Bergen	229,496
★ Oslo	507,467
Stavanger	108,818
Trondheim	148,859
Oman (1993)	
As-Sīb	155,000
Bawshar	107,500
★ Muscat	40,900
agglomeration	887,000[2]
Salālah	116,000
Pakistan (1998)	
Abbottabad	105,999[36]
Bahawalnagar	109,642
Bahawalpur	403,408[36]
Burewala	149,857
Chiniot	169,282
Chishtian Mandi	101,659
Daska	101,500
Dera Ghazi Khan	188,149
Faisalabad (Lyallpur)	1,977,246
Gojra	114,967
Gujranwala	1,124,799
Gujrat	250,121
Hafizabad	130,216
Hyderabad	1,151,274[36]
★ Islamabad	524,500
Jacobabad	137,773
Jaranwala	103,308
Jhang Sadar	292,214
Jhelum	145,847
Kamoke	150,984
Karachi	9,269,265[36]
Kasur	241,649
Khairpur	102,188
Khanewal	132,962
Khanpur	117,764
Kohat	125,271[36]
Lahore	5,063,499[36]
Larkana	270,366
Mardan	244,511[36]
Mingaora	174,469
Mirpur Khas	184,465
Multan	1,182,441[36]
Muridike	108,578
Muzaffargarh	121,641
Nawabshah	183,110
Okara	200,901
Pakpattan	107,791
Peshawar	988,055[36]
Quetta	560,307
Rahimyar Khan	228,479
Rawalpindi	1,406,214[36]
Sadiqabad	141,509
Sahiwal	207,388
Sargodha	455,360[36]
Shekhupura	271,875
Shikarpur	133,259
Sialkot	417,597[36]
Sukkur	329,176
Tando Adam	103,363
Wah	198,431[36]
Palau (2000)	
★ Koror	13,303
Panama (2000)	
★ Panama City	415,964
San Miguelito	293,745[37]
Papua New Guinea (1999 est.)	
Lae	113,118[38]
★ Port Moresby (National Capital District)	298,145
Paraguay (1992)	
★ Asunción	500,938
Ciudad del Este	133,881
San Lorenzo	133,395
Peru (1998 est.)	
Arequipa	710,103
Ayacucho	118,960
Cajamarca	108,009
Chiclayo	469,200
Chimbote	298,800
Chincha Alta	130,000
Cusco	278,590
Huancayo	305,039
Huánuco	129,688
Ica	194,820
Iquitos	334,013
Juliaca	180,000
Lima agglomeration	7,060,600
Ate	324,799[33]
Callao	407,904[33]
Carabayllo	115,000[33]
Chorrillos	238,739[33]
Comas	434,690[33]
El Agustino	159,707[33]
Independencia	191,151[33]
La Victoria	213,239[33]
★ Lima	316,322[33]
Los Olivos	281,115[33]
Lurigancho	110,347[33]
Puente Piedra	131,000[33]
Rímac	190,836[33]
San Borja	109,233[33]
San Juan de Lurigancho	652,681[33]
San Juan de Miraflores	329,023[33]
San Martín de Porras	411,000[33]
San Miguel	126,825[33]
Santa Anita	131,519[33]
Santiago de Surco	224,866[33]
Ventanilla	105,824[33]
Villa el Salvador	296,000[33]
Villa María del Triunfo	301,505[33]
Piura	308,155
Pucallpa	220,866
Puno	101,578
Sullana	170,000
Tacna	215,683
Trujillo	603,657
Philippines (2000)	
Angeles	263,971
Antipolo	200,000[39]
Bacolod	429,076
Bacoor	305,699
Baguio	252,386
Baliuag	119,675
Biñan	201,186
Binangonan	187,691
Butuan	120,000[39]
Cagayan de Oro	345,000[39]
Cainta	242,511
Calamba	160,000[39]
Cebu	718,821
Cotabato	163,849
Dagupan	130,328
Dasmariñas	250,000[39]
Davao	700,000[39]
Dumaguete	102,265
General Mariano Alvarez	112,446
General Santos	250,000[39]
Iloilo	365,820
Kalookan (Caloocan)	1,177,604
Lapu-Lapu	217,019
Las Piñas	472,780
Lucena	196,075
Makati	444,867
Malabon	338,855
Malolos	175,291
Mandaluyong	278,474
Mandaue	259,728
★ Manila	1,581,082
Metro Manila	9,932,560
Marawi	131,090
Marikina	391,170
Meycauayan	163,037
Muntinglupa	379,310
Naga	137,810
Navotas	230,403
Olongapo	194,260
Parañaque	449,811
Pasay	354,908
Pasig	505,058
★ Quezon City	2,173,831
San Fernando	221,857
San Juan del Monte	117,680
San Pablo	105,000[39]
San Pedro	231,403
Santa Rosa	185,633
Tacloban	178,639
Tagig	467,375
Taytay	198,183
Valenzuela	485,433
Zamboanga	135,000[39]
Poland (1999 est.)	
Białystok	283,937
Bielsko-Biała	180,307
Bydgoszcz	386,855
Bytom	205,560
Chorzów	121,708
Częstochowa	257,812
Dąbrowa Górnicza	131,037
Elbląg	129,782
Gdańsk	458,988
Gdynia	253,521
Gliwice	212,164
Gorzów Wielkopolski	126,019
Grudziadz	102,434
Jastrzębie-Zdrój	102,294
Kalisz	106,641
Katowice	345,934
Kielce	212,383
Koszalin	112,375
Kraków	740,666
Legnica	109,335
Łódź	806,728
Lublin	356,251
Olsztyn	170,904
Opole	129,553
Płock	131,011
Poznań	578,235
Radom	232,262
Ruda Śląska	159,665
Rybnik	144,582
Rzeszów	162,049
Słupsk	102,370
Sosnowiec	244,102
Szczecin	416,988
Tarnów	121,494
Toruń	206,158
Tychy	133,178
Wałbrzych	136,923
★ Warsaw (Warszawa)	1,618,468
Włocławek	123,373
Wrocław	637,877
Zabrze	200,177
Zielona Góra	118,182
Portugal (2001)	
Amadora	174,788
Braga	105,000
Coimbra	103,000
Funchal	102,521
★ Lisbon	556,797
agglomeration	3,754,000[2]
Porto	262,928
Puerto Rico (2000)	
Bayamón	203,499[40]
Carolina	168,164[40]
Ponce	155,038[40]
★ San Juan	421,958[40]
agglomeration	1,366,000[2]
Qatar (1997)	
★ Doha	264,009
Ar-Rayyān	161,453
Réunion (1999)	
★ Saint-Denis	131,557
Romania (1997 est.)	
Arad	184,619
Bacău	209,689
Baia Mare	149,496
Botoşani	129,285
Brăila	234,648
Braşov	317,772
★ Bucharest	2,027,512
Buzău	149,080
Cluj-Napoca	332,792
Constanţa	344,876
Craiova	312,891
Drobeta-Turnu Severin	117,882
Galaţi	331,360
Iaşi	348,399
Oradea	223,288
Piatra Neamţ	125,121
Piteşti	187,181
Ploieşti	253,414
Râmnicu Vâlcea	119,340
Satu Mare	129,886
Sibiu	168,949
Suceava	118,162
Timişoara	334,098
Târgu Mureş	165,534
Russia (1999 est.)	
Abakan	169,000
Achinsk	122,400
Almetyevsk	141,000
Angarsk	266,600
Arkhangelsk	366,200
Armavir	166,600
Arzamas	111,300
Astrakhan	488,000
Balakovo	206,300
Balashikha	134,200
Barnaul	586,200
Belgorod	339,100
Berezniki	182,200
Biysk	225,700
Blagoveshchensk	220,900
Bratsk	252,500
Bryansk	461,100
Cheboksary	458,000
Chelyabinsk	1,086,300
Cherepovets	324,500
Cherkessk	122,200
Chita	314,300
Dimitrovgrad	137,200
Dzerzhinsk	278,900
Elektrostal	147,600
Elista	101,700
Engels	189,100
Glazov	106,000
Grozny (Dzhokhar)	186,000
Irkutsk	596,400
Ivanovo	463,400

country city	population
Izhevsk	655,300
Kaliningrad	427,200
Kaliningrad (*Moscow oblast*)	134,000[38]
Kaluga	342,400
Kamensk-Uralsky	192,000
Kamyshin	126,000
Kansk	107,500
Kazan	1,100,800
Kemerovo	496,300
Khabarovsk	614,000
Khimki	133,500
Kineshma	100,000
Kirov	466,100
Kiselyovsk	111,100
Kislovodsk	120,800
Kolomna	151,500
Kolpino	141,200
Komsomolsk-na-Amure	295,100
Kostroma	289,300
Kovrov	161,200
Krasnodar	643,400
Krasnoyarsk	877,800
Kurgan	367,200
Kursk	445,400
Leninsk-Kuznetsky	115,600
Lipetsk	521,600
Lyubertsy	165,100
Magadan	121,800
Magnitogorsk	428,100
Makhachkala	334,900
Maykop	167,000
Mezhdurechensk	104,500
Miass	166,900
Michurinsk	121,800
★ Moscow	8,389,700
Murmansk	382,700
Murom	143,200
Mytishchi	155,700
Naberezhnye Chelny (Brezhnev)	518,300
Nakhodka	159,800
Nalchik	234,700
Nevinnomyssk	132,700
Nikolo-Beryozovka (Neftekamsk)	116,500
Nizhnekamsk	222,000
Nizhnevartovsk	235,600
Nizhny Novgorod (Gorky)	1,364,900
Nizhny Tagil	395,800
Noginsk	117,800
Norilsk	146,500
Novgorod	231,700
Novocheboksarsk	123,600
Novocherkassk	186,500
Novokuybyshevsk	116,400
Novokuznetsk	562,800
Novomoskovsk	139,600
Novorossiysk	204,300
Novoshakhtinsk	103,100
Novosibirsk	1,402,400
Novotroitsk	109,700
Obninsk	108,500
Odintsovo	127,600
Oktyabrsky	111,700
Omsk	1,157,600
Orekhovo-Zuyevo	125,500
Orenburg	526,800
Orsk	274,400
Oryol	346,500
Penza	533,300
Perm	1,017,100
Pervouralsk	136,400
Petropavlovsk-Kamchatsky	196,700
Petrozavodsk	282,500
Podolsk	195,900
Prokopyevsk	240,500
Pskov	202,900
Pyatigorsk	133,100
Rostov-na-Donu	1,017,300
Rubtsovsk	163,900
Ryazan	531,300
Rybinsk (Andropov)	241,800
Saint Petersburg (Leningrad)	4,169,400
Salavat	156,400
Samara (Kuybyshev)	1,168,000
Saransk	316,600
Sarapul	106,800
Saratov	881,000
Sergiev Posad (Zagorsk)	111,800
Serov	100,400
Serpukhov	134,600
Severodvinsk	231,800
Seversk	118,600[39]
Shakhty	224,400
Shchyolkovo	104,900[39]
Simbirsk (Ulyanovsk)	671,700
Smolensk	355,700
Sochi	359,300
Solikamsk	106,400
Stary Oskol	211,800
Stavropol	345,100
Sterlitamak	263,600
Surgut	276,100
Syktyvkar	230,900
Syzran	188,100
Taganrog	287,600
Tambov	315,100
Tobolsk	100,000[39]
Tolyatti	720,300
Tomsk	481,400
Tula	513,100
Tver (Kalinin)	457,100
Tyumen	503,800
Ufa	1,088,900
Ulan-Ude	371,400
Usolye-Sibirskoye	104,100
Ussuriysk	158,400
Ust-Ilimsk	105,500
Velikiye Luki	117,100
Vladikavkaz (Ordzhonikidze)	310,600
Vladimir	339,200
Vladivostok	613,100
Volgodonsk	179,200
Volgograd	1,000,000
Vologda	304,300
Volzhsky	289,500
Voronezh	908,000
Votkinsk	102,000
Yakutsk	195,500
Yaroslavl	620,600
Yekaterinburg (Sverdlovsk)	1,272,900
Yelets	120,300
Yoshkar-Ola	249,800
Yuzhno-Sakhalinsk	179,900
Zelenodolysk	100,600
Zelenograd	206,800
Zheleznodorozhny	100,400
Zlatoust	198,400
Rwanda (1996 est.)	
★ Kigali	356,000
St. Kitts and Nevis (1994 est.)	
★ Basseterre	12,605
St. Lucia (1997 est.)	
★ Castries	16,187
agglomeration	57,000[2]
St. Vincent and the Grenadines (1999 est.)	
★ Kingstown	16,175
Samoa (1999 est.)	
★ Apia	38,000
San Marino (1997 est.)	
★ San Marino	2,294
São Tomé and Príncipe (1991)	
★ São Tomé	43,420
Saudi Arabia (1992)	
Abhā	112,316
ʿArʿar	108,055
Buraydah	248,636
Ad-Dammām	482,321
Ḥafar al-Bāṭin	137,793
Ḥāʾil	176,757
Al-Hufūf	225,847
Jiddah	2,046,251
Al-Jubayl	140,828
Khamīs Mushayṭ	217,870
Al-Kharj	152,071
Al-Khubar	141,683
Mecca (Makkah)	965,697
Medina (Al-Madīnah)	608,295
Al-Mubarraz	219,123
★ Riyadh (Ar-Riyāḍ)	2,776,096
Tabūk	292,555
Aṭ-Ṭāʾif	416,121
Ath-Thuqbah	125,650
Yanbuʿ al-Baḥr	119,819
Senegal (1998 est.)	
★ Dakar	1,999,000[2, 28]
Kaolack	200,000
Mbour	109,317[33]
Rufisque	185,142[33]
Saint-Louis	180,000[33]
Thiès	320,000
Ziguinchor	180,555[33]
Seychelles (1997)	
★ Victoria	24,701[28]
Sierra Leone (1999 est.)	
★ Freetown	822,000[28]
Singapore (2000 est.)[41]	
★ Singapore	3,278,000
Slovakia (2000 est.)	
★ Bratislava	448,292
Košice	241,874
Slovenia (2000 est.)	
★ Ljubljana	270,986
Solomon Islands (2000 est.)	
★ Honiara	50,100
Somalia (1999 est.)	
★ Mogadishu	1,162,000[28]
South Africa (1996)[28]	
Alberton	147,948
Benoni	365,467
★ Bloemfontein[42] (de facto judicial)	333,769
Boksburg	260,905
Botshabelo	177,971
Brakpan	171,359
★ Cape Town (de facto legislative)	2,415,408
Carletonville	164,367
Durban	2,117,650
East London	212,323
Johannesburg	1,480,530
Kimberley	170,432
Klerksdorp	137,318
Krugersdorp	203,168
Mdantsane	182,998
Midrand	126,400
Newcastle	219,682
Paarl	140,376
Pietermaritzburg	378,126
Port Elizabeth	749,921
Potchefstroom	101,682
★ Pretoria[43] (de facto executive)	1,104,479
Rustenburg	104,537
Somerset West	112,489
Soweto	1,098,094
Springs	160,795
Tembisa	282,272
Uitenhage	192,120
Vanderbijlpark	253,335
Vereeniging	346,780
Verwoerdburg	114,575
Welkom	203,296
Westonaria	113,932
Witbank	167,183
Spain (1998 est.)	
Albacete	145,454
Alcalá de Henares	163,831
Alcorcón	143,970
Algeciras	101,972
Alicante (Alacant)	272,432
Almería	168,025
Badajoz	134,710
Badalona	209,606
Barakaldo	98,649
Barcelona	1,505,581
Bilbao	358,467
Burgos	161,984
Cádiz	143,129
Cartagena	175,628
Castellón de la Plana (Castelló de la Plana)	137,741
Córdoba	309,961
Coruña, A (Coruña, La)	243,134
Donostia–San Sebastián	178,229
Elche (Elx)	191,713
Fuenlabrada	167,458
Getafe	143,629
Gijón	265,491
Granada	241,471
Hospitalet de Llobregat	248,521
Huelva	139,991
Jaén	107,184
Jerez de la Frontera	181,602
Laguna, La	127,945
Leganés	173,163
León	139,809
Lleida (Lérida)	112,207
Logroño	125,617
★ Madrid	2,881,506
Málaga	528,079
Mataró	103,265
Móstoles	195,311
Murcia	349,040
Ourense (Orense)	107,965
Oviedo	199,549
Palma (de Mallorca)	319,181
Palmas de Gran Canaria, Las	352,641
Pamplona (Iruña)	171,150
Sabadell	184,859
Salamanca	158,457
Santa Coloma de Gramanet	120,958
Santa Cruz de Tenerife	211,930
Santander	184,165
Sevilla (Seville)	701,927
Tarragona	112,795
Terrassa (Tarrasa)	165,654
Valencia (València)	739,412
Valladolid	319,946
Vigo	283,110
Vitoria–Gasteiz	216,527
Zaragoza (Saragossa)	603,367
Sri Lanka (1997 est.; MU)	
★ Colombo (administrative)	800,982
Dehiwala-Mount Lavinia	220,780
Galle	123,616
Jaffna	145,600
Kandy	150,532
Moratuwa	213,000
Negombo	136,850
★ Sri Jayawardenepura Kotte (legislative and judicial)	118,000[44, 45]
Sudan, The (1993)	
Al-Fāshir	141,884
Juba	114,980
Kassalā	234,270
★ Khartoum (executive)	924,505
Khartoum North	879,105
Kūsti	173,599
Nyala	228,778
★ Omdurman (legislative)	1,267,077
Port Sudan	305,385
Al-Qaḍārif	189,384
Al-Ubayyiḍ	228,096
Wad Madanī	218,714
Suriname (1999 est.)	
★ Paramaribo	233,000[28]
Swaziland (1998 est.)	
★ Lobamba (legislative)	...
★ Lozitha (royal)	...
★ Ludzidzini (royal)	...
★ Mbabane (administrative)	60,000
Sweden (2000 est.; MU)	
Göteborg	462,470
Helsingborg	116,870
Jönköping	116,344
Linköping	132,500
Malmö	257,574
Norrköping	122,212
Örebro	123,503
★ Stockholm	743,703
Umeå	103,970
Uppsala	188,478
Västerås	125,433
Switzerland (1999 est.)	
Basel (Bâle)	168,735
★ Bern (Berne)	123,254
Geneva (Genève)	172,809
Lausanne	114,161
Zürich	336,821
Syria (1994)	
Aleppo (Ḥalab)	1,582,930
★ Damascus (Dimashq)	1,394,322
Darʿā	180,093[44]
Dayr az-Zawr	140,459
Dūmā	131,158[44]
Ḥamāh	264,348
Al-Ḥasakah	106,000[46]
Homs (Ḥims)	540,133
Jaramānah	138,469[44]
Latakia (al-Ladhiqiyah)	311,784
Al-Qāmishlī	144,286
Ar-Raqqah	165,195
Ṭarṭūs	136,812[44]
Taiwan (2000 est.)	
Chang-hua	227,715
Chi-lung (Keelung)	385,201
Chia-i	265,109
Chung-ho	392,176
Chung-li	318,649
Feng-shan	318,562
Féng-yüan	161,032
Hsi-chih	154,976
Hsin-chu	361,958
Hsin-chuang	365,048
Hsin-tien	263,603
Hua-lien	108,407
Kao-hsiung	1,475,505
Lu-chou	160,516
Nan-t'ou	104,723
Pa-te	161,700
Pan-ch-'iao (T'ai-pei-hsien)	523,850
P'ing-chen	188,344
P'ing-tung	214,727
San-chu'ung	380,084
Shu-lin	151,260
T'ai-chung	940,589
T'ai-nan	728,060
T'ai-p'ing	165,524
T'ai-tung	111,039
★ Taipei (T'ai-pei)	2,641,312
Ta-li	171,940
T'ao-yuan	316,438
T'u-ch'eng	224,897
Yung-ho	227,700
Yung-k'ang	193,005
Tajikistan (1998 est.)	
★ Dushanbe	513,000
Khujand (Khudzhand; Leninabad)	163,000[1]
Tanzania (1988)	
Arusha	102,544
★ Dar es Salaam	1,747,000[4]
★ Dodoma (legislative)	189,000[4]
Mbeya	130,798
Morogoro	117,760
Mwanza	172,287
Tanga	137,364
Zanzibar	157,634
Thailand (1999 est.)	
★ Bangkok (Krung Thep)	6,320,174[34]
Chiang Mai	171,594
Hat Yai	156,812
Khon Kaen	126,500[39]
Nakhon Ratchasima	181,400[39]
Nakhon Si Thammarat	105,176
Nonthaburi	292,100[39]
Pak Kret	140,725[38]
Surat Thani	112,504
Ubon Ratchathani	116,300[39]
Udon Thani	156,038
Togo (1999 est.)	
★ Lomé	790,000[28]
Tonga (1999 est.)	
★ Nuku'alofa	37,000
Trinidad and Tobago (1996 est.)	
★ Port-of-Spain	43,396
Tunisia (1994)	
Aryānah	152,700
Ettadhamen	149,200
Kairouan	102,600
Ṣafāqis (Sfax)	230,900
Sūsah	125,000
★ Tunis	674,100
Turkey (1997)	
Adana	1,041,509
Adıyaman	212,475
Afyon	113,510
Aksaray	101,187
Alanya	117,311
★ Ankara	2,984,099
Antakya (Hatay)	139,046
Antalya	512,086
Aydın	133,757
Balıkesir	189,987
Batman	212,726
Bismil	101,409

Major cities and national capitals (continued)

county city	population
Bursa	1,066,559
Çorlu	123,266
Çorum	147,112
Denizli	233,651
Diyarbakır	511,640
Edirne	115,083
Elazığ	250,534
Erzincan	102,304
Erzurum	298,735
Eskişehir	454,536
Gaziantep	712,800
Gebze	235,211
Hatay	139,046
İçel (Mersin)	501,398
İskenderun	161,728
Isparta	134,271
Istanbul	8,260,438
İzmir	2,081,556
Kahramanmaraş (Maras)	303,594
Karabük	103,806
Karaman	104,154
Kayseri	498,233
Kırıkkale	203,496
Kızıltepe	112,015
Kocaeli (İzmit)	198,200
Konya	623,333
Kütahya	162,319
Malatya	400,248
Manisa	201,340
Ordu	117,699
Osmaniye	160,854
Sakarya (Adapazarı)	183,265
Samsun	338,387
Siirt	107,067
Sivas	232,352
Sultanbeyli	144,932
Tarsus	190,184
Tekirdağ	100,557
Trabzon	182,552
Urfa (Şanlıurfa)	410,762
Uşak	124,356
Van	226,965
Viranşehir	106,363
Zonguldak	106,176
Turkmenistan (1999 est.)	
★ Ashkhabad (Ashgabat)	605,000
Chärjew (Chardzhev; Chardzhou)	203,000
Dashhowuz (Dashkhovuz; Tashauz)	165,000
Mary	123,000
Nebitdag	119,000
Tuvalu (1999 est.)	
★ Funafuti	6,000
Uganda (1999 est.)	
★ Kampala	1,154,000[28]
Ukraine (1998 est.)	
Alchevsk	120,900
Berdyansk	132,300
Bila Tserkva (Belaya Tserkov)	215,200
Cherkasy (Cherkassy)	310,600
Chernihiv (Chernigov)	310,800
Chernivtsi (Chernovtsy)	259,000
Dniprodzerzhynsk (Dneprodzerzhinsk)	275,000
Dnipropetrovsk (Dnepropetrovsk)	1,122,400
Donetsk	1,065,400
Horlivka (Gorlovka)	309,300
Ivano-Frankivsk (Ivano-Frankovsk)	237,400
Kam'yanets-Podilskyy (Kamenets-Podolsky)	108,000
Kerch	167,400
Kharkiv (Kharkov)	1,521,400
Kherson	358,700
Khmelnytskyy (Khmelnitsky)	260,100
★ Kiev (Kyyiv)	2,620,900
Kirovohrad	270,200
Kostyantynivka (Konstantinovka)	100,100
Kramatorsk	190,800
Krasnyy Luch	104,500
Kremenchuk (Kremenchug)	240,700
Kryvyy Rih (Krivoy Rog)	715,400
Luhansk (Voroshilovgrad)	475,300
Lutsk	217,900
Lviv (Lvov)	793,700
Lysychansk (Lisichansk)	119,000
Makiyivka (Makeyevka)	394,800
Mariupol (Zhdanov)	504,400
Melitopol	171,000
Mykolayiv (Nikolayev)	517,900
Nikopol	152,000
Odesa (Odessa)	1,027,400
Oleksandriya (Aleksandriya)	101,000
Pavlohrad	130,000
Poltava	317,300
Rivne (Rovno)	244,900
Sevastopol	356,000
Simferopol	341,000
Slov'yansk (Slavyansk)	129,600
Stakhanov	104,500
Sumy	299,800
Syeverodonetsk	129,200
Ternopil (Ternopol)	235,100
Uzhhorod	125,500
Vinnytsya (Vinnitsa)	389,100
Yenakiyeve (Yenakiyevo)	108,700
Yevpatoriya	113,500
Zaporizhzhya (Zaporozhye)	863,100
Zhytomyr (Zhitomir)	297,700
United Arab Emirates (1995)	
★ Abu Dhabi (Abū Ẓaby)	398,695
'Ajmān	114,395
Al-'Ayn	225,970
Dubai (Dubayy)	669,181
Sharjah (Ash-Shāriqah)	320,095
United Kingdom (1999 est.)	
England[47]	
Barnsley	220,937
Birmingham	961,041
Blackburn with Darwen	136,612
Blackpool	151,200
Bolton	258,584
Bournemouth	160,700
Bracknell Forest	110,000
Bradford	457,344
Brighton and Hove	245,000
Bristol	399,600
Bury	176,760
Calderdale	191,585
Cambridge	91,933
Canterbury	123,947
Carlisle	100,562
Chester	115,971
Coventry	294,387
Darlington	101,000
Derby	235,238
Doncaster	288,854
Dudley	304,615
Durham	80,669
Exeter	98,125
Gateshead	199,588
Gloucester	101,608
Halton	123,038
Kingston upon Hull	266,900
Kirklees	373,127
Knowsley	152,091
Lancaster	123,856
Leeds	680,722
Leicester	270,493
Lincoln	81,987
Liverpool	452,450
★ London (Greater London)	7,187,300[16, 48]
Luton	181,500
Manchester	404,861
Milton Keynes	204,415
Newcastle upon Tyne	259,541
North Tyneside	192,286
Norwich	120,895
Nottingham	284,000
Oldham	216,531
Oxford	134,800
Peterborough	159,900
Plymouth	255,800
Poole	139,200
Portsmouth	190,400
Reading	142,851
Rochdale	202,164
Rotherham	251,637
St. Albans	128,700
St. Helens	178,764
Salford	220,463
Sandwell	290,091
Sefton	289,542
Sheffield	501,202
Slough	108,000
Solihull	199,859
South Tyneside	154,697
Southampton	214,859
Southend	172,300
Stockport	284,395
Stockton-on-Tees	179,000
Stoke-on-Trent	254,300
Sunderland	289,040
Swindon	177,118
Tameside	216,431
Thurrock	132,283
Torbay	119,674
Trafford	212,731
Wakefield	310,915
Walsall	259,488
Warrington	187,000
Wigan	306,521
Winchester	96,386
Windsor and Maidenhead	132,465
Wirral	330,795
Wolverhampton	242,190
Worcester	89,481
York	175,925
Northern Ireland[49]	
Belfast	297,200
Craigavon	79,100
Derry (Londonderry)	104,700
Lisburn	106,600
Newtonabbey	79,600
Scotland[50]	
Aberdeen	213,070
Dundee	146,690
Edinburgh	450,180
Glasgow	619,680
Wales[51]	
Cardiff	315,040
Conwy	110,600
Neath Port Talbot	139,459
Newport	136,800
Rhondda, Cynon, Taff	240,117
Swansea	230,200
Torfaen	90,527
Wrexham	125,200
United States (2000)	
Abilene (*Texas*)	115,930
Akron (*Ohio*)	217,074
Albany (*Ga.*)	76,939
Albany (*N.Y.*)	95,658
Albuquerque (*N.M.*)	448,607
Alexandria (*Va.*)	128,283
Alhambra (*Calif.*)	85,804
Allentown (*Pa.*)	106,632
Amarillo (*Texas*)	173,627
Anaheim (*Calif.*)	328,014
Anchorage (*Alaska*)	260,283
Ann Arbor (*Mich.*)	114,024
Antioch (*Calif.*)	90,532
Arden-Arcade (*Calif.*)[52]	96,025
Arlington (*Texas*)	332,969
Arlington (*Va.*)[52]	189,453
Arlington Heights (*Ill.*)	76,031
Arvada (*Colo.*)	102,153
Athens (*Ga.*)	100,266
Atlanta (*Ga.*)	416,474
Augusta (*Ga.*)	195,182
Aurora (*Colo.*)	276,393
Aurora (*Ill.*)	142,990
Austin (*Texas*)	656,562
Bakersfield (*Calif.*)	247,057
Baldwin Park (*Calif.*)	75,837
Baltimore (*Md.*)	651,154
Baton Rouge (*La.*)	227,818
Beaumont (*Texas*)	113,866
Beaverton (*Ore.*)	76,129
Bellevue (*Wash.*)	109,569
Berkeley (*Calif.*)	102,743
Billings (*Mont.*)	89,847
Birmingham (*Ala.*)	242,820
Bloomington (*Minn.*)	85,172
Boise (*Idaho*)	185,787
Boston (*Mass.*)	589,141
Boulder (*Colo.*)	94,673
Brandon (*Fla.*)[52]	77,895
Brick Township (*N.J.*)[52]	76,119
Bridgeport (*Conn.*)	139,529
Brockton (*Mass.*)	94,304
Brownsville (*Texas*)	139,722
Buena Park (*Calif.*)	78,282
Buffalo (*N.Y.*)	292,648
Burbank (*Calif.*)	100,316
Cambridge (*Mass.*)	101,355
Camden (*N.J.*)	79,904
Canton (*Mich.*)[52]	76,366
Canton (*Ohio*)	80,806
Cape Coral (*Fla.*)	102,286
Carlsbad (*Calif.*)	78,247
Carrollton (*Texas*)	109,576
Carson (*Calif.*)	89,730
Cary (*N.C.*)	94,536
Cedar Rapids (*Iowa*)	120,758
Chandler (*Ariz.*)	176,581
Charleston (*S.C.*)	96,650
Charlotte (*N.C.*)	540,828
Chattanooga (*Tenn.*)	155,554
Cheektowaga (*N.Y.*)[52]	79,988
Chesapeake (*Va.*)	199,184
Chicago (*Ill.*)	2,896,016
Chula Vista (*Calif.*)	173,556
Cicero (*Ill.*)	85,616
Cincinnati (*Ohio*)	331,285
Citrus Heights (*Calif.*)	85,071
Clarksville (*Tenn.*)	103,455
Clearwater (*Fla.*)	108,787
Cleveland (*Ohio*)	478,403
Clifton (*N.J.*)	78,672
Clinton Township (*Mich.*)[52]	95,648
Colorado Springs (*Colo.*)	360,890
Columbia (*Md.*)[52]	88,254
Columbia (*Mo.*)	84,531
Columbia (*S.C.*)	116,278
Columbus (*Ga.*)	185,781
Columbus (*Ohio*)	711,470
Compton (*Calif.*)	93,493
Concord (*Calif.*)	121,780
Coral Springs (*Fla.*)	117,549
Corona (*Calif.*)	124,966
Corpus Christi (*Texas*)	277,454
Costa Mesa (*Calif.*)	108,724
Cranston (*R.I.*)	79,269
Dallas (*Texas*)	1,188,580
Daly City (*Calif.*)	103,621
Davenport (*Iowa*)	98,359
Davie (*Fla.*)	75,720
Dayton (*Ohio*)	166,179
Dearborn (*Mich.*)	97,775
Decatur (*Ill.*)	81,860
Denton (*Texas*)	80,537
Denver (*Colo.*)	554,636
Des Moines (*Iowa*)	198,682
Detroit (*Mich.*)	951,270
Dover Township (*N.J.*)[52]	86,327
Downey (*Calif.*)	107,323
Duluth (*Minn.*)	86,918
Durham (*N.C.*)	187,035
East Los Angeles (*Calif.*)[52]	124,283
Edison (*N.J.*)[52]	97,687
El Cajon (*Calif.*)	94,869
El Monte (*Calif.*)	115,965
El Paso (*Texas*)	563,662
Elgin (*Ill.*)	94,487
Elizabeth (*N.J.*)	120,568
Erie (*Pa.*)	103,717
Escondido (*Calif.*)	133,559
Eugene (*Ore.*)	137,893
Evansville (*Ind.*)	121,582
Everett (*Wash.*)	91,488
Fairfield (*Calif.*)	96,178
Fall River (*Mass.*)	91,938
Fargo (*N.D.*)	90,599
Farmington Hills (*Mich.*)	82,111
Fayetteville (*N.C.*)	121,015
Federal Way (*Wash.*)	83,259
Flint (*Mich.*)	124,943
Fontana (*Calif.*)	128,929
Fort Collins (*Colo.*)	118,652
Fort Lauderdale (*Fla.*)	152,397
Fort Smith (*Ark.*)	80,268
Fort Wayne (*Ind.*)	205,727
Fort Worth (*Texas*)	534,694
Fremont (*Calif.*)	203,413
Fresno (*Calif.*)	427,652
Fullerton (*Calif.*)	126,003
Gainesville (*Fla.*)	95,447
Garden Grove (*Calif.*)	165,196
Garland (*Texas*)	215,768
Gary (*Ind.*)	102,746
Gilbert (*Ariz.*)	109,697
Glendale (*Ariz.*)	218,812
Glendale (*Calif.*)	194,973
Grand Prairie (*Texas*)	127,427
Grand Rapids (*Mich.*)	197,800
Greeley (*Colo.*)	76,930
Green Bay (*Wis.*)	102,313
Greensboro (*N.C.*)	223,891
Gresham (*Ore.*)	90,205
Hammond (*Ind.*)	83,048
Hampton (*Va.*)	146,437
Hartford (*Conn.*)	121,578
Hawthorne (*Calif.*)	84,112
Hayward (*Calif.*)	140,030
Henderson (*Nev.*)	175,381
Hialeah (*Fla.*)	226,419
High Point (*N.C.*)	85,839
Hollywood (*Fla.*)	139,357
Honolulu (*Hawaii*)[52]	371,657
Houston (*Texas*)	1,953,631
Huntington Beach (*Calif.*)	189,594
Huntsville (*Ala.*)	158,216
Independence (*Mo.*)	113,288
Indianapolis (*Ind.*)	791,926
Inglewood (*Calif.*)	112,580
Irvine (*Calif.*)	143,072
Irving (*Texas*)	191,615
Jackson (*Miss.*)	184,256
Jacksonville (*Fla.*)	735,617
Jersey City (*N.J.*)	240,055
Joliet (*Ill.*)	106,221
Kalamazoo (*Mich.*)	77,145
Kansas City (*Kan.*)	146,866
Kansas City (*Mo.*)	441,545
Kendall (*Fla.*)[52]	75,226
Kenosha (*Wis.*)	90,352
Killeen (*Texas*)	86,911
Knoxville (*Tenn.*)	173,890
Lafayette (*La.*)	110,257
Lakeland (*Fla.*)	78,452
Lakewood (*Calif.*)	79,345
Lakewood (*Colo.*)	144,126
Lancaster (*Calif.*)	118,718
Lansing (*Mich.*)	119,128
Laredo (*Texas*)	176,576
Las Vegas (*Nev.*)	478,434
Lawrence (*Kan.*)	80,098
Lawton (*Okla.*)	92,757
Lewisville (*Texas*)	77,737
Lexington (*Ky.*)	260,512
Lincoln (*Neb.*)	225,581
Little Rock (*Ark.*)	183,133
Livonia (*Mich.*)	100,545
Long Beach (*Calif.*)	461,522
Los Angeles (*Calif.*)	3,694,820
Louisville (*Ky.*)	256,231
Lowell (*Mass.*)	105,167
Lubbock (*Texas*)	199,564
Lynn (*Mass.*)	89,050
McAllen (*Texas*)	106,414
Macon (*Ga.*)	97,255
Madison (*Wis.*)	208,054
Manchester (*N.H.*)	107,006
Memphis (*Tenn.*)	650,100
Mesa (*Ariz.*)	396,375
Mesquite (*Texas*)	124,523
Metairie (*La.*)[52]	146,136
Miami (*Fla.*)	362,470
Miami Beach (*Fla.*)	87,933
Midland (*Texas*)	94,996
Milwaukee (*Wis.*)	596,974
Minneapolis (*Minn.*)	382,618
Mission Viejo (*Calif.*)	93,102
Mobile (*Ala.*)	198,915
Modesto (*Calif.*)	188,856
Montgomery (*Ala.*)	201,568
Moreno Valley (*Calif.*)	142,381
Naperville (*Ill.*)	128,358
Nashua (*N.H.*)	86,605
Nashville (*Tenn.*)	545,524
New Bedford (*Mass.*)	93,768
New Haven (*Conn.*)	123,626
New Orleans (*La.*)	484,674
New York City (*N.Y.*)	8,008,278
Newark (*N.J.*)	273,546
Newport News (*Va.*)	180,150
Newton (*Mass.*)	83,829
Norfolk (*Va.*)	234,403

[1]1993 estimate. [2]1999 estimate. [3]Eight villages, including Fagatogo, Utulei, and Pago Pago, are collectively known as Pago Pago (1999 agglomeration pop. 14,000). [4]1995 estimate. [5]1991 estimate. [6]Urban Centre ("urban agglomeration") as defined by 1996 census. [7]1996 census. [8]Estimated population of New Providence and adjacent islands. [9]Preliminary census populations for urban areas of *municipios*. [10]1990 census. [11]1992 census. [12]Excludes agricultural population within city limits. [13]San Jose canton. [14]1988 census. [15]As of 1998 administrative reorganization. [16]1998 estimate. [17]Excludes Lefkoşa (Turkish Nicosia), whose population per 1996 census was 36,834. [18]Population of the urban area of the National District. [19]Within San Salvador metropolitan area. [20]1997 census. [21]Includes internally displaced persons from Abkhazia. [22]Within Guatemala City metropolitan area. [23]Population includes Comayagüela. [24]Urban population; Hong Kong is 100% urban. [25]Census not taken because of civil unrest. [26]Urban population (may or may not be city proper; not urban agglomeration). [27]Population of Greater Karaj. [28]Urban agglomeration(s). [29]1985 estimate. [30]County borough population. [31]Commune population. [32]1989 census. [33]1996 estimate. [34]2000 census. [35]Census designated place on the island of Saipan. [36]Includes

county / city	population
Norman (*Okla.*)	95,694
North Charleston (*S.C.*)	79,641
North Las Vegas (*Nev.*)	115,488
Norwalk (*Calif.*)	103,298
Norwalk (*Conn.*)	82,951
Oakland (*Calif.*)	399,484
Oceanside (*Calif.*)	161,029
Odessa (*Texas*)	90,943
Ogden (*Utah*)	77,226
Oklahoma City (*Okla.*)	506,132
Olathe (*Kan.*)	92,962
Omaha (*Neb.*)	390,007
Ontario (*Calif.*)	158,007
Orange (*Calif.*)	128,821
Orem (*Utah*)	84,324
Orlando (*Fla.*)	185,951
Overland Park (*Kan.*)	149,080
Oxnard (*Calif.*)	170,358
Palm Bay (*Fla.*)	79,413
Palmdale (*Calif.*)	116,670
Paradise (*Nev.*)[52]	186,070
Parma (*Ohio*)	85,655
Pasadena (*Calif.*)	133,936
Pasadena (*Texas*)	141,674
Paterson (*N.J.*)	149,222
Pembroke Pines (*Fla.*)	137,427
Peoria (*Ariz.*)	108,364
Peoria (*Ill.*)	112,936
Philadelphia (*Pa.*)	1,517,550
Phoenix (*Ariz.*)	1,321,045
Pittsburgh (*Pa.*)	334,563
Plano (*Texas*)	222,030
Plantation (*Fla.*)	82,934
Pomona (*Calif.*)	149,473
Pompano Beach (*Fla.*)	78,191
Port St. Lucie (*Fla.*)	88,769
Portland (*Ore.*)	529,121
Portsmouth (*Va.*)	100,565
Providence (*R.I.*)	173,618
Provo (*Utah*)	105,166
Pueblo (*Colo.*)	102,121
Quincy (*Mass.*)	88,025
Racine (*Wis.*)	81,855
Raleigh (*N.C.*)	276,093
Rancho Cucamonga (*Calif.*)	127,743
Reading (*Pa.*)	81,207
Redding (*Calif.*)	80,865
Redwood City (*Calif.*)	75,402
Reno (*Nev.*)	180,480
Rialto (*Calif.*)	91,873
Richardson (*Texas*)	91,802
Richmond (*Calif.*)	99,216
Richmond (*Va.*)	197,790
Riverside (*Calif.*)	255,166
Roanoke (*Va.*)	94,911
Rochester (*Minn.*)	85,806
Rochester (*N.Y.*)	219,773
Rockford (*Ill.*)	150,115
Roseville (*Calif.*)	79,921
Roswell (*Ga.*)	79,334
Sacramento (*Calif.*)	407,018
St. Louis (*Mo.*)	348,189
St. Paul (*Minn.*)	287,151
St. Petersburg (*Fla.*)	248,232
Salem (*Ore.*)	136,924
Salinas (*Calif.*)	151,060
Salt Lake City (*Utah*)	181,743
San Angelo (*Texas*)	88,439
San Antonio (*Texas*)	1,144,646
San Bernardino (*Calif.*)	185,401
San Buenaventura (Ventura) (*Calif.*)	100,916
San Diego (*Calif.*)	1,223,400
San Francisco (*Calif.*)	776,733
San Jose (*Calif.*)	894,943
San Leandro (*Calif.*)	79,452
San Mateo (*Calif.*)	92,482
Sandy (*Utah*)	88,418
Sandy Springs (*Ga.*)[52]	85,781
Santa Ana (*Calif.*)	337,977
Santa Barbara (*Calif.*)	92,325
Santa Clara (*Calif.*)	102,361
Santa Clarita (*Calif.*)	151,088
Santa Maria (*Calif.*)	77,423
Santa Monica (*Calif.*)	84,084
Santa Rosa (*Calif.*)	147,595
Savannah (*Ga.*)	131,510
Schaumburg (*Ill.*)	75,386
Scottsdale (*Ariz.*)	202,705
Scranton (*Pa.*)	76,415
Seattle (*Wash.*)	563,374
Shreveport (*La.*)	200,145
Silver Spring (*Md.*)[52]	76,540
Simi Valley (*Calif.*)	111,351
Sioux City (*Iowa*)	85,013
Sioux Falls (*S.D.*)	123,975
Somerville (*Mass.*)	77,478
South Bend (*Ind.*)	107,789
South Gate (*Calif.*)	96,375
Southfield (*Mich.*)	78,296
Spokane (*Wash.*)	195,629
Spring Valley (*Nev.*)[52]	117,390
Springfield (*Ill.*)	111,454
Springfield (*Mass.*)	152,082
Springfield (*Mo.*)	151,580
Stamford (*Conn.*)	117,083
Sterling Heights (*Mich.*)	124,471
Stockton (*Calif.*)	243,771
Sunnyvale (*Calif.*)	131,760
Sunrise (*Fla.*)	85,779
Sunrise Manor (*Nev.*)[52]	156,120
Syracuse (*N.Y.*)	147,306
Tacoma (*Wash.*)	193,556
Tallahassee (*Fla.*)	150,624
Tampa (*Fla.*)	303,447
Tempe (*Ariz.*)	158,625
Thornton (*Colo.*)	82,384
Thousand Oaks (*Calif.*)	117,005
Toledo (*Ohio*)	313,619
Topeka (*Kan.*)	122,377
Torrance (*Calif.*)	137,946
Trenton (*N.J.*)	85,403
Troy (*Mich.*)	80,959
Tucson (*Ariz.*)	486,699
Tulsa (*Okla.*)	393,049
Tuscaloosa (*Ala.*)	77,906
Tyler (*Texas*)	83,650
Vacaville (*Calif.*)	88,625
Vallejo (*Calif.*)	116,760
Virginia Beach (*Va.*)	425,257
Visalia (*Calif.*)	91,565
Vista (*Calif.*)	89,857
Waco (*Texas*)	113,726
Warren (*Mich.*)	138,247
Warwick (*R.I.*)	85,808
★ Washington, D.C.	572,059
Waukegan (*Ill.*)	87,901
Waterbury (*Conn.*)	107,271
West Covina (*Calif.*)	105,080
West Palm Beach (*Fla.*)	82,103
West Valley City (*Utah*)	108,896
Westland (*Mich.*)	86,602
Westminster (*Calif.*)	88,207
Westminster (*Colo.*)	100,940
Whittier (*Calif.*)	83,680
Wichita (*Kan.*)	344,284
Wichita Falls (*Texas*)	104,197
Wilmington (*N.C.*)	75,838
Winston-Salem (*N.C.*)	185,776
Worcester (*Mass.*)	172,648
Yonkers (*N.Y.*)	196,086
Youngstown (*Ohio*)	82,026
Yuma (*Ariz.*)	77,515
Uruguay (1996)	
★ Montevideo	1,378,707
Uzbekistan (1998 est.)	
Andijon (Andizhan)	288,000
Angren	132,000[1]
Bukhoro (Bukhara)	220,000
Chirchiq (Chirchik)	156,000[1]
Farghona (Fergana)	203,000
Jizzakh (Dzhizak)	116,000[1]
Marghilon (Margilan)	129,000[1]
Namangan	291,000
Nawoiy (Navoi)	115,000[1]
Nukus	185,000[1]
Olmaliq (Almalyk)	116,000[1]
Qarshi (Karshi)	177,000[1]
Qŭqon (Kokand)	184,000[1]
Samarqand (Samarkand)	388,000
★ Tashkent (Toshkent)	2,124,000
Urganch (Urgench)	135,000[1]
Vanuatu (1999 est.)	
★ Vila	30,139
Venezuela (2000 est.)[53]	
Acarigua	166,720
Barcelona	311,475
Barinas	228,598
Barquisimeto	875,790
Baruta	213,373
Cabimas	214,000
Calabozo	102,000
★ Caracas	1,975,787
Carúpano	121,892
Catia la Mar	118,466
Ciudad Bolívar	312,691
Ciudad Guayana (San Felix de Guayana)	704,168
Ciudad Ojeda	103,835
Coro	158,763
Cúa	101,868
Cumaná	269,428
El Límon	119,602
El Tigre	119,609
Guacara	137,816
Guanare	112,000
Guarenas	170,204
Guatire	115,264
Los Teques	183,142
Maracaibo	1,764,038
Maracay	459,007
Mariara	101,115
Maturín	283,318
Mérida	230,101
Ocumare del Tuy	101,707
Petare	520,982
Puerto Cabello	169,959
Puerto La Cruz	205,635
Punto Fijo	109,362
San Cristóbal	307,184
Santa Teresa	126,930
Turmero	226,084
Valencia	1,338,833
Valera	116,036
Vietnam (1992 est.)	
Bien Hoa	273,879[32]
Cam Pha	109,086
Cam Ranh	114,041[32]
Can Tho	215,587
Da Lat	106,409
Da Nang	382,674
Haiphong	783,133
★ Hanoi	1,073,760
Ho Chi Minh City (Saigon)	3,015,743
Hong Gai	127,484
Hue	219,149
Long Xuyen	132,681
My Tho	108,404
Nam Dinh	171,699
Nha Trang	221,331
Phan Thiet	114,236[32]
Qui Nhon	163,385
Rach Gia	141,132
Thai Nguyen	127,643
Vinh	112,455
Vung Tau	145,145
Virgin Islands (U.S.) (1990)	
★ Charlotte Amalie	12,331
West Bank (1997)	
Hebron (Al-Khalīl)	119,401
Nābulus	100,231
★ Rām Allāh (Ramallah) (acting administrative centre)	18,017
Western Sahara (1998 est.)	
Laayoune (El Aaiún)	164,000[54]
Yemen (1994)	
Aden	398,300
Al-Ḥudaydah	298,500
Ibb	103,300
Al-Mukallā	122,400
★ Ṣan'ā'	954,400
Ta'izz	317,600
Yugoslavia (2000 est.)[55]	
★ Belgrade (Beograd)	1,194,878
Kragujevac	154,489
Níš	182,583
Novi Sad	182,778
Podgorica (Titograd)	130,875
Priština	186,611
Prizren	115,711
Zambia (1990)	
Chingola	167,954
Kabwe	166,519
Kitwe	338,207
Luanshya	146,275
★ Lusaka	1,577,000[2, 28]
Mufulira	152,944
Ndola	376,311
Zimbabwe (1998 est.)	
Bulawayo	790,000
Chitungwiza	600,000
Gweru	170,000
★ Harare	1,686,000[2, 28]
Kwekwe	100,000
Mutare	165,000

cantonment(s). [37]Urban district adjacent to Panama City. [38]1997 estimate. [39]2000 estimate. [40]Urban population. [41]Urban population; Singapore is 100% urban. [42]Bloemfontein was absorbed into the larger municipality of Manguang in December 2000. [43]Pretoria was absorbed into the larger municipality of Tshwane in December 2000. [44]1994 estimate. [45]Population refers to Kotte only. [46]1992 estimate. [47]All cities and borough councils of England after the local government reorganization of 1995–98. [48]32 borough councils, not listed separately, constitute London (Greater London). [49]Cities and borough councils of Northern Ireland with more than 75,000 population. [50]Cities of Scotland after the local government reorganization of 1994–96. Borough councils do not exist in Scotland. [51]Cities and boroughs in Wales with more than 75,000 population after the local government reorganization of 1994–96. [52]Unincorporated place. [53]Projections based on 1990 census. [54]Urban population of Laayoune and northern Western Sahara. [55]Unofficial estimate.

Language

This table presents estimated data on the principal language communities of the countries of the world. The countries, and the principal languages (occasionally, language families) represented in each, are listed alphabetically. A bullet (●) indicates those languages that are official in each country. The sum of the estimates equals the 2000 population of the country given in the "Area and population" table.

The estimates represent, so far as national data collection systems permit, the distribution of mother tongues (a mother tongue being the language spoken first and, usually, most fluently by an individual). Many countries do not collect any official data whatever on language use, and published estimates not based on census or survey data usually span a substantial range of uncertainty. The editors have adopted the best-founded distribution in the published literature (indicating uncertainty by the degree of rounding shown) but have also adjusted or interpolated using data not part of the base estimate(s). Such adjustments have not been made to account for large-scale refugee movements, as these are of a temporary nature.

A variety of approaches have been used to approximate mother-tongue distribution when census data were unavailabe. Some countries collect data on ethnic or "national" groups only; for such countries ethnic distribution often had to be assumed to conform roughly to the distribution of language communities. This approach, however, should be viewed with caution, because a minority population is not always free to educate its children in its own language and because better economic opportunities often draw minority group members into the majority-language community. For some countries, a given individual may be visible in national statistics only as a passport-holder of a foreign country, however long he may remain resident. Such persons, often guest workers, have sometimes had to be assumed to be speakers of the principal language of their home country. For other countries, the language mosaic may be so complex, the language communities so minute in size, scholarly study so inadequate, or the census base so obsolete that it was possible only to assign percentages to entire groups, or families, of related languages, despite their mutual unintelligibility (Papuan and Melanesian languages in Papua New Guinea, for instance). For some countries in the Americas, so few speakers of any single indigenous language remain that it was necessary to combine these groups as *Amerindian* so as to give a fair impression of their aggregate size within their respective countries.

No systematic attempt has been made to account for populations that may legitimately be described as bilingual, unless the country itself collects data on that basis, as does Bolivia or the Comoros, for example. Where a nonindigenous official or excolonial language constitutes a lingua franca of the country, however, speakers of the language as a second tongue are shown in italics, even though very few may speak it as a mother tongue. No comprehensive effort has been made to distinguish between dialect communities *usually* classified as belonging to the same language, though such distinctions were possible for some countries—*e.g.*, between French and Occitan (the dialect of southern France) or among the various dialects of Chinese.

In giving the names of Bantu languages, grammatical particles specific to a language's autonym (name for itself) have been omitted (the form *Rwanda* is used here, for example, rather than *kinyaRwanda* and *Tswana* instead of *seTswana*). Parenthetical alternatives are given for a number of languages that differ markedly from the name of the people speaking them (such as Kurukh, spoken by the Oraon tribes of India) or that may be combined with other groups sometimes distinguishable in national data but appearing here under the name of the largest member—*e.g.*, "Tamil (and other Indian languages)" combining data on South Asian Indian populations in Singapore. The term *creole* as used here refers to distinguishable dialectal communities related to a national, official, or former colonial language (such as the French creole that survives in Mauritius from the end of French rule in 1810).

Internet resources for further information:

- *Ethnologue* (13th ed.; Summer Institute of Linguistics) http://www.sil.org/ethnologue
- Joshua Project 2000—People's List (Christian interfaith missionary database identifying some 2,000 ethnolinguistic groups) http://www.ad2000.org/peoples/index.htm
- U.S. Census Bureau: http://www.census.gov/ftp/pub/ipc/www/idbconf.html (especially tables 57 and 59)
- Living Languages of the Americas (Summer Institute of Linguistics) http://www.sil.org/lla

Language

Major languages by country	Number of speakers
Afghanistan[1]	
Indo-Aryan languages	
Pashai	160,000
Iranian languages	
Balochi	240,000
● Dari (Persian)	
Chahar Aimak	730,000
Hazara	2,280,000
Tajik	5,280,000
Nuristani group	200,000
Pamir group	160,000
● Pashto	13,560,000
Turkic languages	
Turkmen	500,000
Uzbek	2,280,000
Other	490,000
Albania[1]	
● Albanian	3,419,000
Greek	65,000
Macedonian	5,000
Other	1,000
Algeria	
● Arabic	26,280,000
Berber	4,280,000
English	...
French	*6,000,000*
American Samoa	
● English	2,000
English (lingua franca)	*64,000*
● Samoan	59,000
Tongan	2,000
Other	2,000
Andorra[2]	
● Catalan (Andorran)	22,000
French	5,000
Portuguese	7,000
Spanish	29,000
Other	4,000
Angola[1]	
Ambo (Ovambo)	240,000
Chokwe	430,000
Herero	70,000
Kongo	1,340,000
Luchazi	240,000
Luimbe-Nkangala	550,000
Lunda	120,000
Luvale (Luena)	360,000
Mbunda	120,000
Mbundu	2,190,000
Nyaneka-Nkhumbi	550,000
Ovimbundu (Umbundu)	3,770,000
● Portuguese	*3,600,000*
Other	160,000
Antigua and Barbuda	
● English	*71,000*
English/English Creole	67,000
Other	4,000
Argentina	
Amerindian languages	110,000
Italian	650,000
● Spanish	35,860,000
Other	410,000
Armenia	
● Armenian	3,560,000
Azerbaijani (Azeri)	100,000
Other	160,000
Aruba	
● Dutch	5,000
English	9,000
Papiamento	74,000
Spanish	7,000
Other	1,000
Australia	
Aboriginal languages	51,000
Arabic	187,000
Cantonese	219,000
Dutch	46,000
● English	15,561,000
English (lingua franca)	*18,500,000*
French	44,000
German	111,000
Greek	299,000
Hungarian	30,000
Indonesian Malay	30,000
Italian	423,000
Macedonian	79,000
Maltese	51,000
Mandarin	101,000
Pilipino (Filipino)	78,000
Polish	70,000
Portuguese	27,000
Russian	35,000
Serbo-Croatian	118,000
Spanish	100,000
Turkish	49,000
Vietnamese	154,000
Other/not stated	1,303,000
Austria	
Czech	19,000
● German	7,444,000
Hungarian	34,000
Polish	19,000
Romanian	17,000
Serbo-Croatian	176,000
Slovene	30,000
Turkish	123,000
Other	230,000
Azerbaijan	
Armenian	160,000
● Azerbaijani (Azeri)	7,170,000
Lezgi (Lezgian)	180,000
Russian	240,000
Other	310,000
Bahamas, The	
● English	...
English/English Creole	260,000
French (Haitian) Creole	30,000
Bahrain[2]	
● Arabic	470,000
English	...
Other	220,000
Bangladesh[1]	
● Bengali	126,260,000
Chakma	480,000
English	*3,400,000*
Garo	120,000
Khasi	100,000
Marma (Magh)	250,000
Mro	40,000
Santhali	90,000
Tripuri	90,000
Other	1,770,000
Barbados	
Bajan (English Creole)	254,000
● English	...
Other	13,000
Belarus	
● Belarusian	6,560,000
Polish	50,000
● Russian	3,190,000
Ukrainian	130,000
Other	60,000
Belgium[2, 3]	
Arabic	160,000
● Dutch (Flemish; Netherlandic)	6,080,000
● French (Walloon)	3,350,000
● German	100,000
Italian	250,000
Spanish	50,000
Turkish	90,000
Other	180,000
Belize	
● English	128,000
English Creole (lingua franca)	*190,000*
Garifuna (Black Carib)	17,000
German	4,000
Mayan languages	24,000
Spanish	80,000
Spanish (lingua franca)	*140,000*
Benin[1]	
Adja	710,000
Aizo (Ouidah)	550,000
Bariba	550,000
Dendi	140,000
Djougou	190,000
Fon	2,540,000
● French	*600,000*
Fula (Fulani)	360,000
Somba (Ditamari)	420,000
Yoruba (Nago)	780,000
Other	150,000
Bermuda	
● English	63,000
Portuguese	*6,000*
Bhutan[1]	
Assamese	100,000
● Dzongkha (Bhutia)	330,000
Nepali (Hindi)	230,000
Bolivia	
● Aymara	270,000
Guaraní	10,000
● Quechua	680,000
● Spanish	3,480,000
Spanish-Amerindian (multilingual), of which	3,830,000
Spanish-Aymara	*1,650,000*
Spanish-Guaraní	*30,000*
Spanish-Quechua	*2,160,000*
Other	70,000
Bosnia and Herzegovina[1]	
● Bosnian	1,690,000
● Croatian	650,000
● Serbian	1,190,000
Other	310,000
Botswana[1]	
● English (lingua franca)	*630,000*
Khoekhoe (Hottentot)	39,000
Ndebele	20,000
San (Bushman)	55,000
Shona	196,000
Tswana	1,189,000
Tswana (lingua franca)	*1,260,000*
Other	77,000
Brazil[1]	
Amerindian languages	170,000
German	910,000
Italian	700,000
Japanese	630,000
● Portuguese	162,160,000
Other	1,540,000
Brunei	
Chinese	31,000
English	10,000
● Malay	153,000
Malay-Chinese	3,000
Malay-English	97,000
English-Chinese	7,000
Malay-Chinese-English	13,000
Other	18,000
Bulgaria[1]	
● Bulgarian	6,800,000
Macedonian	200,000
Romany	300,000
Turkish	770,000
Other	100,000
Burkina Faso[4]	
Dogon	40,000
French	40,000
● French (lingua franca)	*4,900,000*
Fula (Fulani)	1,150,000
Gur (Voltaic) languages	
Bwamu	260,000
Gouin (Cerma)	70,000
Grusi (Gurunsi) group	
Ko	20,000
Lyele	290,000
Nuni	140,000
Sissala	10,000
Lobi	230,000
Mossi (Moore) group	
Dagara	370,000
Gurma	680,000
Kusaal	20,000
Mossi (Moore)	6,000,000
Senufo group	
Minianka	—
Senufo	170,000
Kru languages	
Seme (Siamou)	20,000
Mande languages	
Bobo	270,000
Busansi (Bisa)	430,000
Dyula (Jula)	310,000
Marka	200,000
Samo	280,000
Tamashek (Tuareg)	110,000
Other	850,000
Burundi[1]	
● French	*560,000*
● Rundi	5,930,000
Hutu	5,000,000
Tutsi	880,000
Twa	60,000
Other[5]	120,000

Major languages by country	Number of speakers
Cambodia[1]	
Cham	290,000
Chinese	380,000
● Khmer	10,960,000
Vietnamese	680,000
Other[6]	60,000
Cameroon[1]	
Chadic languages	
Buwal	300,000
Hausa	190,000
Kotoko	170,000
Mandara (Wandala)	870,000
Masana (Masa)	610,000
● English	*7,700,000*
● French	*4,600,000*
Niger-Congo languages	
Adamawa-Ubangi languages	
Chamba	370,000
Gbaya (Baya)	190,000
Mbum	200,000
Atlantic languages	
Fula (Fulani)	1,480,000
Benue-Congo languages	
Bamileke (Medumba)-Widikum (Mogha-mo)-Bamum (Mum)	2,860,000
Basa (Bassa)	170,000
Duala	1,680,000
Fang (Pangwe)-Beti-Bulu	3,030,000
Ibibio (Efik)	20,000
Igbo	80,000
Jukun	100,000
Lundu	420,000
Maka	760,000
Tikar	1,140,000
Tiv	400,000
Wute	50,000
Saharan languages	
Kanuri	50,000
Semitic languages	
Arabic	150,000
Other	120,000
Canada	
● English	18,218,000
● French	7,158,000
English-French	116,000
English-other	269,000
French-other	39,000
English-French-other	10,000
Arabic	160,000
Chinese	772,000
Cree	83,000
Dutch	144,000
Eskimo (Inuktitut) languages	29,000
German	486,000
Greek	131,000
Italian	523,000
Pilipino (Filipino)	144,000
Polish	230,000
Portuguese	228,000
Punjābī	218,000
Spanish	230,000
Ukrainian	175,000
Vietnamese	115,000
Other	1,293,000
Cape Verde	
Crioulo (Portuguese Creole)	401,000
● Portuguese	...
Central African Republic	
Banda	820,000
● French	*900,000*
Gbaya (Baya)	830,000
Mandjia	520,000
Mbum	220,000
Ngbaka	270,000
Nzakara	60,000
● Sango (lingua franca)	*3,100,000*
Sara	230,000
Zande (Azande)	70,000
Other	500,000
Chad[1]	
● Arabic	1,040,000
Bagirmi	130,000
Fitri-Batha	390,000
● French	*2,530,000*
Fula (Fulani)	210,000
Gorane	530,000
Hadjarai	560,000
Kanem-Bornu	760,000
Lac-Iro	50,000
Mayo-Kebbi	970,000
Ouaddai	740,000
Sara	2,330,000
Tandjile	550,000
Other	180,000
Chile[1]	
Araucanian (Mapuche)	1,460,000
Aymara	80,000
Rapa Nui	35,000
● Spanish	13,640,000
China[1]	
Achang	30,000
Bulang (Blang)	90,000
Ch'iang (Qiang)	220,000
Chinese (Han)	1,159,850,000
Cantonese (Yüeh [Yue])	*50,000,000*
Hakka	*28,000,000*
Hsiang (Xiang)	*39,000,000*
Kan (Gan)	*22,000,000*
● Mandarin	*899,000,000*
Min	*39,000,000*
Wu	*83,000,000*
Ching-p'o (Jingpo)	130,000
Chuang (Zhuang)	17,230,000
Daghur (Daur)	130,000
Evenk (Ewenki)	30,000
Gelo	490,000
Hani (Woni)	1,400,000
Hui	9,570,000
Kazak	1,240,000
Korean	2,140,000
Kyrgyz	160,000
Lahu	460,000
Li	1,240,000
Lisu	640,000
Manchu	10,930,000
Maonan	80,000
Miao	8,230,000
Mongol	5,350,000
Mulam	180,000
Na-hsi (Naxi)	310,000
Nu	30,000
Pai (Bai)	1,770,000
Pumi	30,000
Puyi (Chung-chia)	2,830,000
Salar	100,000
She	700,000
Shui	380,000
Sibo (Xibe)	190,000
Tai (Dai)	1,140,000
Tajik	40,000
Tibetan	5,110,000
Tu (Monguor)	210,000
T'u-chia (Tujia)	6,350,000
Tung (Dong)	2,800,000
Tung-hsiang (Dongxiang)	420,000
Uighur	8,030,000
Wa (Va)	390,000
Yao	2,370,000
Yi	7,310,000
Other	990,000
Colombia[1]	
Amerindian languages	360,000
Arawakan	40,000
Cariban	30,000
Chibchan	180,000
Other	110,000
English Creole	50,000
● Spanish	41,880,000
Comoros	
● Arabic	...
● Comorian	434,000
Comorian-French	75,000
Comorian-Malagasy	32,000
Comorian-Arabic	10,000
Comorian-Swahili	3,000
Comorian-French-other	23,000
● French	*120,000*
Other	3,000
Congo, Dem. Rep. of the[1]	
Boa	1,220,000
Chokwe	950,000
● English	...
● French	*4,000,000*
Kongo	8,340,000
Kongo (lingua franca)	*16,000,000*
Lingala (lingua franca)	*36,000,000*
Luba	9,340,000
Lugbara	840,000
Mongo	7,000,000
Ngala and Bangi	3,000,000
Rundi	2,000,000
Rwanda	5,340,000
Swahili (lingua franca)	*25,000,000*
Teke	1,420,000
Zande (Azande)	3,170,000
Other	9,340,000
Congo, Rep. of the[1]	
Bobangi	30,000
● French	*1,500,000*
Kongo	1,460,000
Kota	30,000
Lingala (lingua franca)	...
Maka	50,000
Mbete	140,000
Mboshi	330,000
Monokutuba (lingua franca)	*1,700,000*
Punu	90,000
Sango	80,000
Teke	490,000
Other	150,000
Costa Rica	
Chibchan languages	11,000
Bribrí	7,000
Cabécar	4,000
Chinese	7,000
English Creole	73,000
● Spanish	3,553,000
Côte d'Ivoire[1]	
Akan (including Baule and Anyi)	4,800,000
● French	*8,000,000*
Gur ([Voltaic] including Senufo and Lobi)	1,870,000
Kru (including Bete)	1,680,000
Malinke (including Dyula and Bambara)	1,830,000
Southern Mande (including Dan and Guro)	1,230,000
Other (non-Ivoirian population)	4,570,000
Croatia	
● Serbo-Croatian (Croatian)	4,110,000
Other	170,000
Cuba	
● Spanish	11,148,000
Cyprus (island)[1]	
● Greek	640,000
● Turkish	190,000
Other	30,000
Czech Republic[1]	
Bulgarian	3,000
● Czech	8,338,000
German	48,000
Greek	3,000
Hungarian	20,000
Moravian	1,322,000
Polish	60,000
Romanian	1,000
Romany	33,000
Russian	5,000
Ruthenian	2,000
Silesian	44,000
Slovak	311,000
Ukrainian	8,000
Other	70,000
Denmark[2]	
Arabic	39,000
● Danish	5,050,000
English	20,000
German	26,000
South Slavic languages	39,000
Turkish	47,000
Other	119,000
Djibouti[1]	
Afar	160,000
● Arabic	50,000
● French	*70,000*
Somali	200,000
Gadaboursi	...
Issa	...
Issaq	...
Other	40,000
Dominica	
● English	...
English Creole	76,000
French Creole	*69,000*
Dominican Republic	
French (Haitian) Creole	170,000
● Spanish	8,270,000
East Timor	
Portuguese	70,000
Tetum (Tetun)	530,000
Other	270,000
Ecuador	
Quechuan (and other Amerindian languages)	890,000
● Spanish	11,760,000
Egypt[1]	
● Arabic	65,080,000
Other	790,000
El Salvador	
● Spanish	6,123,000
Equatorial Guinea[1]	
Bubi	50,000
Fang	390,000
● French	...
Krio (English Creole)	...
● Spanish	...
Other	40,000
Eritrea	
Cushitic languages	
Afar	180,000
Bilin	130,000
Hadareb (Beja)	160,000
Saho	120,000
Nilotic languages	
Kunama	110,000
Nara	90,000
Semitic languages	
Arabic (Rashaida)	10,000
Tigré	1,310,000
Tigrinya	2,030,000
Estonia[1]	
Belarusian	21,000
● Estonian	936,000
Finnish	13,000
Russian	403,000
Ukrainian	36,000
Other	26,000
Ethiopia[1]	
Afar	1,210,000
Agew (Awngi)	610,000
Amharic	18,750,000
Berta	150,000
Gedeo	550,000
Gumuz	130,000
Gurage	2,720,000
Hadya–Libida	1,090,000
Kaffa	720,000
Kambata	800,000
Kimant	200,000
Oromo (Oromifa)	20,380,000
Sidamo	2,170,000
Somali	3,990,000
Tigrinya	3,780,000
Walaita	3,900,000
Other	5,730,000
Faroe Islands	
● Danish	...
● Faroese	46,000
Fiji[1]	
● English	*170,000*
Fijian	416,000
Hindi	358,000
Other	45,000
Finland	
Finnish	4,789,000
Russian	26,000
Sami (Lapp)	2,000
Swedish	293,000
Other	68,000
France	
Arabic[7]	1,490,000
English[7]	80,000
● French[7, 8, 9]	55,100,000
Basque	*100,000*
Breton	*800,000*
Catalan (Rousillonais)	*260,000*
Corsican	*80,000*
Dutch (Flemish)	*90,000*
German (Alsatian)	*1,000,000*
Occitan	*700,000*
Italian[7]	260,000
Polish[7]	50,000
Portuguese[7]	680,000
Spanish[7]	220,000
Turkish[7]	210,000
Other[7]	750,000
French Guiana	
Amerindian languages	3,000
● French	...
French/French Creoles	155,000
Other	7,000
French Polynesia[10]	
Chinese	13,000
● French	188,000
Polynesian languages	213,000
● Tahitian	...
Other	46,000
Gabon[1]	
Fang	430,000
● French	*1,000,000*
Kota	40,000
Mbete	170,000
Mpongwe (Myene)	180,000
Punu, Sira, Nzebi	200,000
Teke	20,000
Other	160,000
Gambia, The[1]	
● English	...
Gambians	
Aku (Krio)	8,000
Atlantic languages	
Diola (Jola)	126,000
Fula (Fulani)	221,000
Manjak	22,000
Serer	33,000
Wolof	172,000
Mande languages	
Bambara	10,000
Malinke	466,000
Soninke	105,000
Other	17,000
non-Gambians	188,000
Gaza Strip	
Arabic	1,141,000
Hebrew	6,000
Georgia	
Abkhaz	90,000
Armenian	350,000
Azerbaijani (Azeri)	280,000
● Georgian (Kartuli)	3,590,000
Ossetian	120,000
Russian	450,000
Other	160,000
Germany[2]	
● German	75,060,000
Greek	360,000
Italian	610,000
Polish	280,000
South Slavic languages	1,190,000
Turkish	2,110,000
Kurdish	*400,000*
Other	2,590,000
Ghana[1]	
Akan	10,240,000
● English	*1,370,000*
Ewe	2,320,000
Ga-Adangme	1,520,000
Gurma	650,000
Hausa (lingua franca)	*11,700,000*
Mole-Dagbani (Moore)	3,090,000
Yoruba	260,000
Other	1,450,000
Greece	
● Greek	10,400,000
Turkish	100,000
Other	60,000
Greenland[2]	
● Danish	7,000
● Greenlandic	49,000
Grenada	
● English	...
English/English Creole	102,000
Guadeloupe	
● French	...
French/French Creole	407,000
Other	21,000
Guam	
● Chamorro	45,000
Chinese	2,000
Chuukese (Trukese)	2,000
● English	58,000
English (lingua franca)	*153,000*
Japanese	4,000
Korean	5,000
Palauan	2,000
Philippine languages	31,000
Other	6,000
Guatemala	
Garífuna (Black Carib)	30,000
Mayan languages	3,990,000
Cakchiquel	1,020,000
Kekchí	550,000
Mam	310,000
Quiché	1,150,000
● Spanish	7,370,000
Guernsey	
● English	64,000
Norman French	...
Guinea[1]	
Atlantic languages	
Basari-Konyagi	90,000
Fula (Fulani)	2,880,000
Kissi	450,000
Other	230,000
● French	*700,000*
Mande languages	
Kpelle	350,000
Loma	170,000
Malinke	1,730,000
Susu	820,000
Yalunka	220,000
Other	520,000
Other	10,000
Guinea-Bissau[1]	
Balante	390,000
Crioulo (Portuguese Creole)	*570,000*
Ejamat	30,000
French	*130,000*
Fula (Fulani)	280,000
Malinke	170,000
Mandyako	140,000
Mankanya	50,000
Pepel	130,000
● Portuguese	*140,000*
Other	100,000
Guyana	
Amerindian languages	
Arawakan	11,000
Cariban	17,000
● English	...
English/English Creoles	764,000

Language (continued)

Major languages by country	Number of speakers
Haiti	
● French	*1,400,000*
● Haitian (French) Creole	6,868,000
Honduras	
English Creole	12,000
Garifuna (Black Carib)	82,000
Miskito	11,000
● Spanish	6,307,000
Other	78,000
Hong Kong	
Chinese	
● Cantonese	6,014,000
Cantonese (lingua franca)	*6,500,000*
Chiu Chau	95,000
Fukien (Min)	129,000
Hakka	113,000
Putonghua (Mandarin)	75,000
Putonghua (lingua franca)	*1,230,000*
Sze Yap	27,000
● English	150,000
English (lingua franca)	*2,140,000*
Japanese	14,000
Pilipino (Filipino)	7,000
Other	163,000
Hungary	
German	40,000
● Hungarian	9,870,000
Romanian	10,000
Romany	50,000
Serbo-Croatian	20,000
Slovak	10,000
Other	20,000
Iceland[2]	
● Icelandic	268,000
Other	12,000
India	
Afro-Asiatic languages	
Arabic	30,000
Austroasiatic languages	
Ho	1,140,000
Kharia	270,000
Khasi	1,090,000
Korku	560,000
Munda	500,000
Mundari	1,030,000
Santhali	6,250,000
Savara (Sora)	330,000
Other Austroasiatic	190,000
Dravidian languages	
Gondi	2,550,000
Kannada	39,240,000
Khond	260,000
Koya	320,000
Kui	770,000
Kurukh (Oraon)	1,710,000
Malayalam	36,400,000
Tamil	63,510,000
Telugu	79,100,000
Tulu	1,860,000
Other Dravidian	660,000
English	210,000
● English (lingua franca)	*193,000,000*
Indo-Iranian (Indo-Aryan) languages	
Assamese	15,670,000
Bengali	83,390,000
Bhili (Bhilodi)	6,680,000
Barel	*560,000*
Bhilali	*560,000*
Gujarati	48,730,000
Halabi	640,000
● Hindi	404,100,000
Awadhi	*580,000*
Baghelkhandi	*1,660,000*
Bagri	*710,000*
Banjari	*1,060,000*
Bhojpuri	*27,680,000*
Bundelkhandi	*1,990,000*
Chhattisgarhi	*12,690,000*
Dhundhari	*1,160,000*
Garhwali	*2,240,000*
Harauti	*1,480,000*
Haryanvi	*430,000*
Hindi	*279,690,000*
Kangri	*590,000*
Khortha (Khotta)	*1,260,000*
Kumauni	*2,060,000*
Lamani (Banjari)	*2,460,000*
Magahi (Magadhi)	*12,660,000*
Maithili	*9,310,000*
Malvi	*3,560,000*
Mandeali	*530,000*
Marwari	*5,600,000*
Mewari	*2,530,000*
Nagpuri	*930,000*
Nimadi	*1,700,000*
Pahari	*2,610,000*
Rajasthani	*15,970,000*
Sadani (Sadri)	*1,880,000*
Surgujia	*1,250,000*
Surjapuri	*440,000*
Other Hindi dialects	*7,390,000*
Hindi (lingua franca)	*669,000,000*
Kashmiri	4,720,000
Khandeshi	1,170,000
Konkani	2,110,000
Lahnda	30,000
Marathi	74,860,000
Nepali (Gorkhali)	2,490,000
Oriya	33,620,000
Punjabi	28,010,000
Sanskrit	60,000
Sindhi	2,540,000
Kachchhi	*680,000*
Urdu	52,010,000
Sino-Tibetan languages	
Adi	190,000
Angami	120,000
Ao	210,000
Bodo/Boro	1,460,000
Dimasa	110,000
Garo	810,000
Karbi/Makir	440,000
Konyak	170,000
Lotha	100,000
Lushai (Mizo)	650,000
Manipuri (Meithei)	1,520,000
Miri/Mishing	470,000
Nissi/Dafla	210,000
Rabha	170,000
Sema	200,000
Tangkhul	120,000
Thado	130,000
Tripuri	830,000
Kokbarak	*620,000*
Other Sino-Tibetan languages	1,810,000
Other	5,290,000
Indonesia	
Balinese	3,480,000
Banjarese	3,660,000
Batak	4,650,000
Buginese	4,610,000
● Indonesian (Malay)	25,350,000
Javanese	82,540,000
Madurese	9,060,000
Minangkabau	4,940,000
Sundanese	33,010,000
Other	38,040,000
Iran[1]	
Armenian	300,000
Iranian languages	
Bakhtyari (Luri)	1,050,000
Balochi	1,430,000
● Farsi (Persian)	28,610,000
Farsi (lingua franca)	*51,900,000*
Gilaki	3,310,000
Kurdish	5,720,000
Luri	2,710,000
Mazandarani	2,260,000
Other	1,360,000
Semitic languages	
Arabic	1,350,000
Other	150,000
Turkic languages	
Afshari	710,000
Azerbaijani (Azeri)	10,540,000
Qashqa'i	800,000
Shahsavani	380,000
Turkish (mostly Pishagchi, Bayat, and Qajar)	450,000
Turkmen	980,000
Other	130,000
Other	460,000
Iraq[1]	
● Arabic	17,490,000
Assyrian	190,000
Azerbaijani (Azeri)	390,000
Kurdish	4,300,000
Persian	190,000
Other	130,000
Ireland	
● English	3,720,000
● Irish[11]	60,000
Irish	*1,230,000*
Isle of Man	
● English	73,000
Israel[12]	
● Arabic	1,100,000
● Hebrew	3,850,000
Russian	550,000
Other	610,000
Italy[1]	
Albanian	120,000
Catalan	30,000
French	310,000
German	310,000
Greek	40,000
● Italian	54,290,000
Rhaetian	740,000
Friulian	720,000
Ladin	20,000
Romany	110,000
Sardinian	1,530,000
Slovene	120,000
Other	130,000
Jamaica	
● English	...
English/English Creoles	2,460,000
Hindī and other Indian languages	50,000
Other	100,000
Japan[2]	
Ainu	15,000
Chinese	240,000
English	80,000
● Japanese	125,800,000
Korean	660,000
Philippine languages	90,000
Other	50,000
Jersey	
● English	89,000
French	...
Norman French	*6,000*
Jordan[1]	
● Arabic	4,880,000
Armenian	50,000
Kabardian (Circassian)	50,000
Kazakhstan[1]	
Azerbaijani (Azeri)	90,000
Belarusian	150,000
German	460,000
● Kazakh	6,860,000
Korean	90,000
Russian	5,180,000
Tatar	290,000
Ughur	170,000
Ukrainian	740,000
Uzbek	340,000
Other	550,000
Kenya[1]	
Bantu languages	
Bajun (Rajun)	70,000
Basuba	120,000
Embu	360,000
Gusii (Kisii)	1,870,000
Kamba	3,420,000
Kikuyu	6,340,000
Kuria	180,000
Luhya	4,200,000
Mbere	120,000
Meru	1,660,000
Nyika (Mijikenda)	1,450,000
Pokomo	80,000
Swahili	10,000
● Swahili (lingua franca)	*20,000,000*
Taita	300,000
Cushitic languages	
Oromo languages	
Boran	140,000
Gabbra	60,000
Gurreh	160,000
Orma	60,000
Somali languages	
Degodia	190,000
Ogaden	50,000
Somali	310,000
● English (lingua franca)	*2,700,000*
Nilotic languages	
Kalenjin	3,270,000
Luo	3,870,000
Masai	480,000
Sambur	150,000
Teso	260,000
Turkana	410,000
Semitic languages	
Arabic	80,000
Other	680,000
Kiribati[1]	
● English	*23,000*
Kiribati (Gilbertese)	91,000
Tuvaluan (Ellice)	500
Other	600
Korea, North[1]	
Chinese	30,000
● Korean	21,650,000
Korea, South[1]	
Chinese	50,000
● Korean	47,220,000
Kuwait	
● Arabic	1,550,000
Other	440,000
Kyrgyzstan[1]	
Azerbaijani (Azeri)	20,000
German	30,000
Kazakh	50,000
● Kyrgyz	2,920,000
● Russian	790,000
Tajik	40,000
Tatar	60,000
Ukrainian	80,000
Uzbek	690,000
Other	210,000
Laos[1]	
● Lao-Lum (Lao)	2,910,000
Lao-Soung (Miao [Hmong] and Man [Yao])	550,000
Lao-Tai (Tai)	710,000
Lao-Theung (Mon-Khmer)	1,260,000
Other[13]	50,000
Latvia[1]	
Belarusian	90,000
● Latvian	1,340,000
Lithuanian	30,000
Polish	50,000
Russian	780,000
Ukrainian	70,000
Other	40,000
Lebanon[1]	
● Arabic	3,330,000
Armenian	210,000
French	*860,000*
Other	40,000
Lesotho[1]	
● English	*510,000*
● Sotho	1,820,000
Zulu	320,000
Liberia[1]	
Atlantic (Mel) languages	
Gola	130,000
Kissi	130,000
● English	*630,000*
Krio (English Creole)	*2,800,000*
Kru languages	
Bassa	440,000
Belle	20,000
De (Dewoin, Dey)	10,000
Grebo	280,000
Krahn	120,000
Kru (Krumen)	230,000
Mande (Northern) languages	
Gbandi	90,000
Kpelle	610,000
Loma	180,000
Malinke (Mandingo)	160,000
Mende	20,000
Vai	110,000
Mande (Southern) languages	
Gio (Dan)	250,000
Mano	220,000
Other	160,000
Libya	
● Arabic	4,910,000
Berber	50,000
Other[14]	150,000
Liechtenstein[2]	
● German	28,000
Italian	1,000
Other	3,000
Lithuania[1]	
Belarusian	50,000
● Lithuanian	3,020,000
Polish	260,000
Russian	300,000
Ukrainian	40,000
Other	30,000
Luxembourg[2]	
Belgian	15,000
Dutch	4,000
English	5,000
French	19,000
German	11,000
Italian	20,000
Luxemburgian	278,000
Portuguese	257,000
Other	30,000
Macau	
Chinese	
● Cantonese (Yüeh [Yue])	380,000
Mandarin	5,000
Other Chinese languages	40,000
English	2,000
● Portuguese	10,000
Other	5,000
Macedonia[1]	
Albanian	467,000
● Macedonian	1,358,000
Romany	46,000
Serbo-Croatian	41,000
Turkish	81,000
Vlach	9,000
Other	39,000
Madagascar[1]	
French	*2,300,000*
Malagasy	15,340,000
Other	160,000
Malawi[1]	
Chewa (Maravi)	6,060,000
● English	*540,000*
Lomwe	1,910,000
Ngoni	690,000
Yao	1,370,000
Other	350,000
Malaysia	
Bajau	150,000
Chinese	1,350,000
Chinese-others	760,000
Dusun	240,000
English	120,000
English-others	260,000
English (lingua franca)	*7,100,000*
Iban	550,000
Iban-others	90,000
● Malay	10,030,000
Malay-others	3,560,000
Tamil	900,000
Tamil-others	10,000
Other	5,240,000
Maldives	
● Divehi (Maldivian)	285,000
Mali[1]	
Afro-Asiatic languages	
Berber languages	
Tamashek (Tuareg)	780,000
Semitic languages	
Arabic (Mauri)	170,000
● French	*1,100,000*
Niger-Congo languages	
Atlantic languages	
Fula (Fulani) and Tukulor	1,490,000
Dogon	430,000
Gur (Voltaic) languages	
Bwa (Bobo)	260,000
Mossi (Moore)	40,000
Senufo and Minianka	1,280,000
Mande languages	
Bambara	3,410,000
Bambara (lingua franca)	*8,500,000*
Bobo Fing	10,000
Dyula (Jula)	310,000
Malinke, Khasonke, and Wasulunka	710,000
Samo (Duun)	70,000
Soninke	940,000
Nilo-Saharan languages	
Songhai	770,000
Other	30,000
Malta[1]	
● English	13,000
English (lingua franca)	*95,000*
● Maltese	364,000
Other	5,000
Marshall Islands[2]	
● English	*51,600*
● Marshallese	50,000
Other	1,600
Martinique	
● French	...
French/French Creole	372,000
Other	13,000
Mauritania[1]	
● Arabic	...
French	*270,000*
Fula (Fulani)	30,000
Hassānīyah Arabic	2,170,000
Soninke	70,000
Tukulor	140,000
Wolof	180,000
Zenaga	30,000
Other	40,000
Mauritius	
Bhojpuri	226,000
Bhojpuri-other	25,000
Chinese	4,000
● English	2,000
French	41,000
French Creole	732,000
French Creole-other	105,000
Hindi	15,000
Marathi	8,000
Tamil	9,000
Telugu	7,000
Urdu	8,000
Other	3,000
Mayotte[15]	
● Arabic	...
Mahorais (local dialect of Comorian Swahili)	137,000
Other Comorian Swahili dialects	60,000
Malagasy	53,000
● French	66,000
Other	10,000
Mexico	
Amerindian languages	7,800,000
Amuzgo	40,000
Aztec (Nahuatl)	1,770,000
Chatino	40,000
Chinantec	160,000
Chocho	20,000

Major languages by country	Number of speakers
Chol	190,000
Chontal	50,000
Cora	20,000
Cuicatec	20,000
Huastec	180,000
Huave	20,000
Huichol	30,000
Kanjobal	20,000
Mame	20,000
Mayo	60,000
Mazahua	200,000
Mazatec	240,000
Mixe	140,000
Mixtec	570,000
Otomí	420,000
Popoluca	50,000
Purépecha (Tarasco)	140,000
Tarahumara	80,000
Tepehua	10,000
Tepehuan	30,000
Tlapanec	100,000
Tojolabal	50,000
Totonac	310,000
Trique	20,000
Tzeltal	390,000
Tzotzil	350,000
Yaqui	20,000
Yucatec (Mayan)	1,050,000
Zapotec	580,000
Zoque	70,000
Other	350,000
● Spanish	91,080,000
Spanish-Amerindian languages	*6,350,000*
Micronesia	
Chuukese (Trukese)	49,000
English	1,000
Kosraean	9,000
Mortlockese	9,000
Palauan	500
Pohnpeian	28,000
Woleaian	4,000
Yapese	7,000
Other	11,000
Moldova	
Bulgarian	70,000
Gagauz	140,000
● Romanian (Moldovan)	2,660,000
Russian	990,000
Ukrainian	370,000
Other	60,000
Monaco[2]	
English	2,000
● French	13,000
Italian	5,000
Monegasque	5,000
Other	6,000
Mongolia[1]	
Bayad	46,000
Buryat	41,000
Darhat	17,000
Dariganga	34,000
Dörbet	65,000
Dzakhchin	26,000
Kazakh	142,000
● Khalkha (Mongolian)	1,890,000
Khalkha (lingua franca)	*2,150,000*
Ould	10,000
Torgut	12,000
Tuvan (Uryankhai)	24,000
Other	94,000
Morocco	
● Arabic	18,730,000
Berber	9,510,000
French	*11,500,000*
Other	580,000
Mozambique	
Bantu languages	
Chuabo	1,200,000
Lomwe	1,450,000
Makua	5,020,000
Sena	1,340,000
Tsonga (Changana)	2,180,000
Other Bantu languages	6,300,000
● Portuguese	1,240,000
Portuguese (lingua franca)	*7,570,000*
Other	360,000
Myanmar (Burma)[1]	
● Burmese	28,780,000
Burmese (lingua franca)	*33,400,000*
Chin	910,000
Kachin (Ching-p'o)	570,000
Karen	2,600,000
Kayah	170,000
Mon	1,010,000
Rakhine (Arakanese)	1,880,000
Shan	3,530,000
Other	2,290,000
Namibia	
Afrikaans	168,000
Caprivi	83,000
● English	14,000
English (lingua franca)	*340,000*
German	16,000
Herero	142,000
Kavango (Okavango)	172,000
Nama	221,000
Ovambo (Ambo [Kwanyama])	897,000
San (Bushman)	34,000
Tswana	8,000
Other	17,000
Nauru	
Chinese	1,000
English	900
English (lingua franca)	*10,700*
Kiribati (Gilbertese)	2,100
Nauruan	6,800
Tuvaluan (Ellice)	1,000
Nepal	
Austroasiatic (Munda) languages	
Santhali	40,000
English	*7,300,000*
Indo-Aryan languages	
Bengali	40,000
Bhojpuri	1,840,000
Dhanwar	30,000
Hindi	230,000
Hindi (Awadhi dialect)	500,000
Maithili	2,930,000
● Nepali (Eastern Pahari)	12,430,000
Rajbansi	110,000
Tharu	1,330,000
Urdu	270,000
Tibeto-Burman languages	
Bhutia (Sherpa)	160,000
Chepang	30,000
Gurung	300,000
Limbu	340,000
Magar	570,000
Newari	920,000
Rai and Kiranti	590,000
Tamang	1,210,000
Thakali	10,000
Thami	20,000
Other	790,000
Netherlands, The[2]	
Arabic	130,000
● Dutch	15,228,000
Dutch and Frisian	*600,000*
Turkish	103,000
Other	435,000
Netherlands Antilles	
● Dutch	...
English	18,000
Papiamento	190,000
Other	13,000
New Caledonia[1]	
● French	72,000
Indonesian	5,000
Melanesian languages	95,000
Polynesian languages	25,000
Vietnamese	3,000
Other	11,000
New Zealand	
● English	3,338,000
English-Māori	149,000
● Māori	14,000
Other	334,000
Nicaragua	
English Creole	27,000
Misumalpan languages	
Miskito	79,000
Sumo	8,000
● Spanish	4,697,000
Other	2,000
Niger[1]	
Atlantic languages	
Fula (Fulani)	980,000
Berber languages	
Tamashek (Tuareg)	1,050,000
Chadic languages	
Hausa	5,340,000
Hausa (lingua franca)	*7,100,000*
● French	*1,500,000*
Gur (Voltaic) languages	
Gurma	30,000
Saharan languages	
Kanuri	450,000
Teda (Tubu)	40,000
Semitic languages	
Arabic	30,000
Songhai and Zerma	2,140,000
Other	20,000
Nigeria[1]	
Arabic	300,000
Bura	1,900,000
Edo	4,200,000
● English/English Creole (lingua franca)	*56,000,000*
Fula (Fulani)	13,900,000
Hausa	26,300,000
Hausa (lingua franca)	*62,000,000*
Ibibio	6,900,000
Igbo (Ibo)	22,200,000
Ijo (Ijaw)	2,200,000
Kanuri	5,100,000
Nupe	1,500,000
Tiv	2,800,000
Yoruba	26,300,000
Other	9,600,000
Northern Mariana Islands	
● Carolinian	3,400
● Chamorro	21,500
Chinese	5,100
Chuukese (Trukese)	1,700
● English	3,400
English (lingua franca)	*65,100*
Japanese	1,400
Korean	4,700
Palauan	2,500
Philippine languages	24,500
Other	3,600
Norway[2]	
Danish	18,000
English	24,000
● Norwegian	4,332,000
Swedish	13,000
Other	100,000
Oman	
● Arabic (Omani)	1,850,000
Other	560,000
Pakistan	
Balochi	4,260,000
Brahui	1,730,000
English (lingua franca)	*16,000,000*
Pashto	18,600,000
Punjabi	
Punjabi	68,190,000
Hindko	3,440,000
Sindhi	
Saraiki	13,910,000
Sindhi	10,000,000
● Urdu	10,760,000
Other	4,030,000
Palau	
Chinese	300
● English	600
English (lingua franca)	*18,700*
● Palauan	15,500
Philippine languages	1,800
Other	700
Panama	
Amerindian languages	
Bokotá	5,000
Chibchan	
Guaymí (Ngöbe Buglé)	150,000
Kuna	57,000
Teribe	3,000
Chocó	
Emberá	18,000
Wounaan	3,000
Arabic	16,000
Chinese	8,000
English	...
English Creoles	395,000
● Spanish	2,168,000
Papua New Guinea[1]	
● English	*140,000*
Melanesian languages	990,000
Motu	*160,000*
Papuan languages	3,840,000
Tok Pisin (English Creole)	*3,200,000*
Other	100,000
Paraguay	
German	50,000
● Guaraní	2,210,000
Guaraní-Spanish	2,670,000
Portuguese	170,000
● Spanish	360,000
Other	40,000
Peru	
Amerindian languages	
● Aymara	590,000
● Quechua	4,220,000
Other	180,000
● Spanish	20,470,000
Other	200,000
Philippines	
Aklanon	560,000
Bantoanon	70,000
Bicol	4,340,000
Bilaan	40,000
Bontoc	60,000
Butuanon	80,000
Cebuano	17,760,000
Chavacano	470,000
Chinese	70,000
Davaweno (Mansaka)	520,000
● English (lingua franca)	*39,700,000*
Hiligaynon	6,950,000
Ibaloi (Nabaloi)	130,000
Ibanag	280,000
Ifugao	210,000
Ilocano	7,110,000
Ilongot	110,000
Kalinga	130,000
Kankanai	290,000
Kinaray-a (Hamtikanon)	480,000
Maguindanao	1,110,000
Manobo	510,000
Maranao	970,000
Masbateño	530,000
Palawano	80,000
Pampango	2,280,000
Pangasinan	1,380,000
● Pilipino (Filipino; Tagalog)	22,350,000
Romblon	240,000
Samal	480,000
Sambal	200,000
Subanon	310,000
Surigaonon	560,000
Tau Sug	880,000
Tboli	100,000
Tinggian	70,000
Tiruray	70,000
Waray-Waray	2,910,000
Yakan	150,000
Other	1,500,000
Poland	
Belarusian	190,000
German	500,000
● Polish	37,730,000
Ukrainian	230,000
Portugal[2]	
● Portuguese	9,910,000
Other	100,000
Puerto Rico	
● English	20,000
● Spanish	2,010,000
Spanish-English	1,840,000
Other	50,000
Qatar[2]	
● Arabic	240,000
Other[16]	360,000
Réunion	
Chinese	20,000
Comorian	20,000
● French	*220,000*
French Creole	660,000
Malagasy	10,000
Tamil	*140,000*
Other	10,000
Romania	
Bulgarian	9,000
Czech	5,000
German	97,000
Hungarian	1,612,000
Polish	3,000
● Romanian	20,343,000
Romany (Tigani)	164,000
Russian	31,000
Serbo-Croatian	33,000
Slovak	18,000
Tatar	22,000
Turkish	27,000
Ukrainian	63,000
Other	5,000
Russia	
Adyghian	120,000
Armenian	360,000
Avar	530,000
Azerbaijani (Azeri)	280,000
Bashkir	970,000
Belarusian	430,000
Buryat	360,000
Chechen	880,000
Chuvash	1,370,000
Dargin	340,000
Georgian (Kartuli)	90,000
German	350,000
Ingush	210,000
Kabardian	370,000
Kalmyk	150,000
Karachay	150,000
Kazakh	560,000
Komi-Permyak	100,000
Komi-Zyryan	240,000
Kumyk	270,000
Lak	100,000
Lezgi (Lezgian)	240,000
Mari	520,000
Mordvin	730,000
Ossetian	370,000
Romanian	110,000
Romany	130,000
● Russian	126,420,000
Tabasaran	90,000
Tatar	4,690,000
Tuvan	200,000
Udmurt	500,000
Ukrainian	1,860,000
Uzbek	100,000
Yakut	360,000
Other	1,440,000
Rwanda	
● English	...
● French	*500,000*
● Rwanda	7,299,000
St. Kitts and Nevis	
● English	...
English/English Creole	39,000
St. Lucia	
● English	31,000
English/French Creole	126,000
St. Vincent and the Grenadines	
● English	...
English/English Creole	112,000
Other	1,000
Samoa	
● English	1,000
● Samoan	85,000
Samoan-English	93,000
San Marino[1]	
● Italian (Romagnolo)	26,800
São Tomé and Príncipe	
Crioulo (Portuguese Creole)	124,000
English	...
French	1,000
● Portuguese	...
Other	18,000
Saudi Arabia[1]	
● Arabic	20,920,000
Other	1,100,000
Senegal	
● French	*3,500,000*
Senegalese	
Bambara	90,000
Diola	490,000
Fula (Fulani)-Tukulor	2,170,000
Malinke (Mandingo)	370,000
Serer	1,250,000
Soninke	130,000
Wolof	4,800,000
Wolof (lingua franca)	*8,000,000*
Other	440,000
non-Senegalese	220,000
Seychelles	
English	3,000
English (lingua franca)	*29,000*
French	1,000
French (lingua franca)	*78,000*
Seselwa (French Creole)	75,000
Other	3,000
Sierra Leone[1]	
Atlantic languages	
Bullom-Sherbro	200,000
Fula (Fulani)	200,000
Kissi	120,000
Limba	440,000
Temne	1,660,000
● English	*500,000*
Krio (English Creole [lingua franca])	*4,400,000*
Mande languages	
Kono-Vai	270,000
Kuranko	180,000
Mende	1,810,000
Susu	80,000
Yalunka	180,000
Other	90,000
Singapore[1]	
Chinese	2,517,000
● English	*1,226,000*
● Malay	456,000
● Mandarin Chinese	*1,421,000*
● Tamil (and other Indian languages)	259,000
Other	43,000
Slovakia[1]	
Czech, Moravian, and Silesian	59,000
German	5,000
Hungarian	569,000
Polish	3,000
Romany	90,000
Ruthenian, Ukrainian, and Russian	35,000
● Slovak	4,626,000
Other	15,000
Slovenia	
Hungarian	9,000
Serbo-Croatian	155,000
● Slovene	1,725,000
Other	74,000

Language (continued)

Major languages by country	Number of speakers
Solomon Islands[1]	
● English	*9,000*
Melanesian languages	399,000
Papuan languages	40,000
Polynesian languages	17,000
Solomon Island Pidgin (English Creole)	*163,000*
Other	10,000
Somalia[1]	
● Arabic	...
English	...
● Somali	7,130,000
Other	120,000
South Africa	
● Afrikaans	6,220,000
● English	3,700,000
Nguni	
● Ndebele	630,000
● Swazi	1,080,000
● Xhosa	7,700,000
● Zulu	9,840,000
Sotho	
● North Sotho (Pedi)	3,950,000
● South Sotho	3,320,000
● Tswana (Western Sotho)	3,530,000
● Tsonga	1,880,000
● Venda	940,000
Other	620,000
Spain	
Basque (Euskera)	630,000
● Castilian Spanish	29,860,000
Catalan (Català)	6,770,000
Galician (Gallego)	2,560,000
Other	300,000
Sri Lanka	
English	10,000
English-Sinhala	1,060,000
English-Sinhala-Tamil	690,000
English-Tamil	220,000
● Sinhala	11,610,000
Sinhala-Tamil	1,800,000
● Tamil	3,780,000
Other	60,000
Sudan, The[1]	
● Arabic	17,320,000
Arabic (lingua franca)	*21,000,000*
Bari	860,000
Beja	2,240,000
Dinka	4,050,000
Fur	720,000
Lotuko	520,000
Nubian languages	2,840,000
Nuer	1,720,000
Shilluk	600,000
Zande (Azande)	950,000
Other	3,260,000
Suriname	
● Dutch	*110,000*
English/English Creole	*410,000*
Sranantonga	170,000
Sranantonga-other	170,000
Other (mostly Hindī, Javanese, and Saramacca)	90,000
Swaziland[1]	
● English	*50,000*
● Swazi	970,000
Zulu	20,000
Other	80,000
Sweden[2]	
Arabic	68,000
Danish	41,000
English	32,000
Finnish	209,000
German	45,000
Iranian languages	49,000
Norwegian	46,000
Polish	39,000
South Slavic languages	116,000
Spanish	56,000
● Swedish	7,937,000
Turkish	29,000
Other	197,000
Switzerland	
● French	1,380,000
● German	4,570,000
● Italian	550,000
Romansch	40,000
Other	640,000
Syria[1]	
● Arabic	14,680,000
Kurdish	1,470,000
Other	160,000
Taiwan	
Austronesian languages	
Ami	138,000
Atayal	89,000
Bunun	42,000
Paiwan	68,000
Puyuma	10,000
Rukai	11,000
Saisiyat	6,000
Tsou	7,000
Yami	4,000
Chinese languages	
Hakka	2,440,000
● Mandarin	4,460,000
Min (South Fukien)	14,800,000
Other	120,000
Tajikistan	
Russian	610,000
● Tajik (Tojik)	3,920,000
Uzbek	1,460,000
Other	310,000
Tanzania[1]	
Chaga (Chagga), Pare	1,730,000
● English	*3,800,000*
Gogo	1,390,000
Ha	1,210,000
Haya	2,080,000
Hehet	2,430,000
Iramba	1,010,000
Luguru	1,730,000
Luo	290,000
Makonde	2,080,000
Masai	350,000
Ngoni	470,000
Nyakusa	1,910,000
Nyamwesi (Sukuma)	7,450,000
Shambala	1,510,000
● Swahili	3,120,000
Swahili (lingua franca)	*32,000,000*
Tatoga	260,000
Yao	860,000
Other	5,430,000
Thailand[1]	
Chinese	7,570,000
Karen	220,000
Malay	2,270,000
Mon-Khmer languages	
Khmer	790,000
Kuy	670,000
Other	220,000
Tai languages	
Lao	16,790,000
● Thai (Siamese)	32,820,000
Other	430,000
Other	640,000
Togo[1]	
Atlantic (Mel) languages	
Fula (Fulani)	68,000
Benue-Congo languages	
Ana (Ana-Ife)	126,000
Nago	13,000
Yoruba	10,000
Chadic languages	
Hausa	14,000
● French	*2,500,000*
Gur (Voltaic) languages	
Basari	88,000
Chakossi (Akan)	59,000
Chamba	49,000
Dye (Gangam)	47,000
Gurma	170,000
Kabre	692,000
Konkomba	71,000
Kotokoli (Tem)	289,000
Moba	270,000
Mossi (Moore)	13,000
Namba (Lamba)	153,000
Naudemba (Losso)	206,000
Tamberma	28,000
Yanga	15,000
Kwa languages	
Adja (Aja)	157,000
Adele	10,000
Ahlo	9,000
Akposo	134,000
Ane (Basila)	284,000
Anlo	4,000
Anyaga	10,000
Ewe	1,164,000
Fon	50,000
Hwe	6,000
Kebu	58,000
Kpessi	4,000
Peda-Hula (Pla)	20,000
Watyi (Ouatchi)	517,000
Other	212,000
Tonga	
● English	*30,000*
● Tongan	98,000
Other	2,000
Trinidad and Tobago	
● English	...
English Creole[17]	37,000
Hindi	45,000
Trinidad English	1,208,000
● Other	3,000
Tunisia	
● Arabic	6,710,000
Arabic-French	2,520,000
Arabic-French-English	300,000
Arabic-other	10,000
Other-no Arabic	30,000
Other	30,000
Turkey[1]	
Arabic	900,000
Kurdish[18]	6,960,000
● Turkish	57,510,000
Other	300,000
Turkmenistan[1]	
Armenian	37,000
Azerbaijani (Azeri)	40,000
Balochi	40,000
Kazakh	96,000
Russian	329,000
Tatar	40,000
● Turkmen	3,745,000
Ukrainian	25,000
Uzbek	448,000
Other	85,000
Tuvalu	
English	...
Kiribati (Gilbertese)	800
Tuvaluan (Ellice)	10,000
Uganda[1]	
Bantu languages	
Amba	90,000
Ganda (Luganda)	4,220,000
Gisu (Masaba)	1,050,000
Gwere	380,000
Kiga (Chiga)	1,950,000
Konjo	510,000
Nkole (Nyankole and Hororo)	2,500,000
Nyole	320,000
Nyoro	690,000
Ruli	100,000
Rundi	140,000
Rwanda	750,000
Samia	310,000
Soga	1,920,000
Swahili (lingua franca)	*8,200,000*
Toro	680,000
Central Sudanic languages	
Lugbara	1,100,000
Madi	180,000
Ndo	230,000
● English	*2,500,000*
Nilotic languages	
Acholi	1,030,000
Alur	550,000
Kakwa	120,000
Karamojong	490,000
Kumam	160,000
Lango	1,370,000
Padhola	350,000
Sebei (Kupsabiny)	150,000
Teso	1,400,000
Other (mostly Gujarati and Hindi)	580,000
Ukraine	
Belarusian	150,000
Bulgarian	160,000
Hungarian	150,000
Polish	30,000
Romanian	330,000
Russian	16,310,000
● Ukrainian	32,110,000
Other	430,000
United Arab Emirates[2]	
● Arabic	1,270,000
Other[16]	1,750,000
United Kingdom	
● English	58,090,000
Scots-Gaelic	80,000
Welsh	570,000
Other	970,000
United States	
Amharic	40,000
Arabic	420,000
Armenian	180,000
Bengali	50,000
Cajun	40,000
Chinese (including Formosan)	1,550,000
Czech	110,000
Danish	40,000
Dutch	170,000
English	237,320,000
English (lingua franca)	*267,000,000*
Finnish	60,000
French	2,030,000
French Creole (mostly Haitian)	220,000
German	1,850,000
Greek	460,000
Gujarati	120,000
Hebrew	170,000
Hindi (including Urdu)	400,000
Hungarian	180,000
Ilocano	50,000
Italian	1,560,000
Japanese	510,000
Korean	750,000
Kru (Gullah)	80,000
Lithuanian	70,000
Malayalam	40,000
Miao (Hmong)	100,000
Mon-Khmer (mostly Cambodian)	150,000
Navajo	180,000
Norwegian	100,000
Pennsylvania Dutch	100,000
Persian	240,000
Polish	860,000
Portuguese	510,000
Punjābī	60,000
Romanian	80,000
Russian	290,000
Samoan	40,000
Serbo-Croatian	140,000
Slovak	100,000
Spanish	20,720,000
Swedish	90,000
Syriac	40,000
Tagalog	1,010,000
Tai (including Laotian)	250,000
Turkish	50,000
Ukrainian	120,000
Vietnamese	610,000
Yiddish	250,000
Other	810,000
Uruguay	
● Spanish	3,140,000
Other	140,000
Uzbekistan[1]	
Kazakh	1,010,000
Russian	1,490,000
Tajik	1,190,000
Tatar	400,000
● Uzbek	18,770,000
Other	1,910,000
Vanuatu[19]	
● Bislama (English Creole)	120,000
● English	60,000
● French	30,000
Other	2,000
Venezuela	
Amerindian languages	
Goajiro	160,000
Warrau (Warao)	20,000
Other	150,000
● Spanish	23,310,000
Other	520,000
Vietnam[1]	
Bahnar	170,000
Cham	120,000
Chinese (Hoa)	1,100,000
French	*380,000*
Hre	120,000
Jarai	300,000
Khmer	1,090,000
Koho	110,000
Man (Mien, or Yao)	580,000
Miao (Meo, or Hmong)	690,000
Mnong	80,000
Muong	1,120,000
Nung	870,000
Rade (Rhadé)	240,000
Roglai	90,000
San Chay (Cao Lan)	140,000
San Diu	120,000
Sedang	120,000
Stieng	60,000
Tai	1,280,000
Tho (Tay)	1,460,000
● Vietnamese	68,400,000
Other	160,000
Virgin Islands (U.S.)	
● English	98,000
French	3,000
Spanish	16,000
Other	3,000
West Bank[20]	
Arabic	2,010,000
Hebrew	170,000
Western Sahara	
Arabic	245,000
Yemen[1]	
● Arabic	17,400,000
Other	70,000
Yugoslavia[1]	
Albanian	1,760,000
Hungarian	350,000
Macedonian	50,000
Romanian	40,000
Romany	150,000
● Serbo-Croatian (Serbian)	8,020,000
Serbo-Croatian (lingua franca)	*10,100,000*
Slovak	70,000
Vlach	20,000
Other	200,000
Zambia[21]	
Bemba group	
Bemba	2,850,000
Bemba (lingua franca)	*5,000,000*
Bisa	110,000
Lala	230,000
Lamba	210,000
Other	400,000
● English	110,000
English (lingua franca)	*1,800,000*
Lozi (Barotse) group	
Lozi (Barotse)	610,000
Other	110,000
Mambwe group	
Lungu	70,000
Mambwe	110,000
Mwanga (Winawanga)	130,000
Other	10,000
North-Western group	
Kaonde	220,000
Lunda	190,000
Luvale (Luena)	170,000
Other	260,000
Nyanja (Maravi) group	
Chewa	550,000
Ngoni	160,000
Nsenga	410,000
Nyanja (Maravi)	750,000
Nyanja (lingua franca)	*2,500,000*
Other	60,000
Tonga (Ila-Tonga) group	
Ila	90,000
Lenje	150,000
Tonga	1,050,000
Other	120,000
Tumbuka group	
Senga	70,000
Tumbuka	280,000
Other	10,000
Other	90,000
Zimbabwe	
● English	250,000
English (lingua franca)	*5,300,000*
Ndebele (Nguni)	1,840,000
Nyanja	260,000
Shona	8,180,000
Other	810,000

[1]Figures given represent ethnolinguistic groups. [2]Data refer to nationality (usually resident aliens holding foreign passports). [3]Data are partly based on place of residence. [4]Majority of population speak Moore (language of the Mossi); Dyula is language of commerce. [5]Swahili also spoken. [6]English and French also spoken. [7]Based on "nationality" at 1982 census. [8]Includes naturalized citizens. [9]French is the universal language throughout France; traditional dialects and minority languages are retained regionally in the approximate numbers shown, however. [10]Data reflect multilingualism; 2000 population estimate is 233,000. [11]Refers to Irish speakers in Gaeltacht areas. [12]Includes the population of the Golan Heights and East Jerusalem; excludes the Israeli population in the West Bank and Gaza Strip. [13]English and French also spoken. [14]English and Italian also spoken. [15]Data reflect ability to speak the language, not mother tongue; 2000 population estimate is 156,000. [16]Mostly Pakistanis, Indians, and Iranians. [17]Spoken on Tobago only. [18]Other estimates of the Kurdish population range from 6 percent to 20–25 percent. [19]Data reflect multilingualism; 2000 population is 190,000. [20]Excludes East Jerusalem. [21]Groups are officially defined geographic divisions; elements comprising them are named by language.

Religion

The following table presents statistics on religious affiliation for each of the countries of the world. An assessment was made for each country of the available data on distribution of religious communities within the total population; the best available figures, whether originating as census data, membership figures of the churches concerned, or estimates by external analysts in the absence of reliable local data, were applied as percentages to the estimated 2001 midyear population of the country to obtain the data shown below.

Several concepts govern the nature of the available data, each useful separately but none the basis of any standard of international practice in the collection of such data. The word "affiliation" was used above to describe the nature of the relationship joining the religious bodies named and the populations shown. This term implies some sort of formal, usually documentary, connection between the religion and the individual (a baptismal certificate, a child being assigned the religion of its parents on a census form, maintenance of one's name on the tax rolls of a state religion, etc.) but says nothing about the nature of the individual's personal religious practice, in that the individual may have lapsed, never been confirmed as an adult, joined another religion, or may have joined an organization that is formally atheist.

The user of these statistics should be careful to note that not only does the nature of the affiliation (with an organized religion) differ greatly from country to country, but the social context of religious practice does also. A country in which a single religion has long been predominant will often show more than 90% of its population to be *affiliated*, while in actual fact, no more than 10% may actually *practice* that religion on a regular basis. Such a situation often leads to undercounting of minority religions (where someone [head of household, communicant, child] is counted at all), blurring of distinctions seen to be significant elsewhere (a Hindu country may not distinguish Protestant [or even Christian] denominations; a Christian country may not distinguish among its Muslim or Buddhist citizens), or double-counting in countries where an individual may conscientiously practice more than one "religion" at a time.

Until 1989 communist countries had for long consciously attempted to ignore, suppress, or render invisible religious practice within their borders. Countries with large numbers of adherents of traditional, often animist, religions and belief systems usually have little or no formal methodology for defining the nature of local religious practice. On the other hand, countries with strong missionary traditions, or good census organizations, or few religious sensitivities may have very good, detailed, and meaningful data.

The most comprehensive works available are DAVID B. BARRETT (ed.), *World Christian Encyclopedia* (2001); and PETER BRIERLEY, *World Churches Handbook* (1997).

Religion

Religious affiliation	2001 population
Afghanistan	
Sunnī Muslim	23,090,000
Shī'ī Muslim	2,310,000
other	490,000
Albania	
Muslim	1,200,000
Roman Catholic	520,000
Albanian Orthodox	320,000
other	1,050,000
Algeria	
Sunnī Muslim	30,550,000
Ibāḍīyah Muslim	180,000
other	90,000
American Samoa	
Congregational	23,800
Roman Catholic	11,300
other	23,400
Andorra	
Roman Catholic	60,000
other	7,000
Angola	
Roman Catholic	6,440,000
Protestant	1,550,000
African Christian	710,000
other	1,660,000
Antigua and Barbuda	
Protestant	30,000
Anglican	23,000
Roman Catholic	8,000
other	10,000
Argentina	
Roman Catholic	29,920,000
Protestant	2,040,000
Muslim	730,000
Jewish	500,000
nonreligious	880,000
other	3,430,000
Armenia	
Armenian Apostolic (Orthodox)	2,454,000
other	1,353,000
Aruba	
Roman Catholic	80,000
other	18,000
Australia	
Roman Catholic	5,230,000
Anglican	4,260,000
Uniting Church	1,460,000
Presbyterian	740,000
other Protestant	1,400,000
Orthodox	540,000
nonreligious	3,220,000
other	2,510,000
Austria	
Roman Catholic	6,060,000
Protestant (mostly Lutheran)	430,000
atheist and nonreligious	690,000
other	890,000
Azerbaijan	
Shī'ī Muslim	5,299,000
Sunnī Muslim	2,271,000
other	535,000
Bahamas, The	
Protestant	135,000
Roman Catholic	50,000
Anglican	32,000
other	77,000
Bahrain	
Shī'ī Muslim	420,000
Sunnī Muslim	140,000
other	140,000
Bangladesh	
Muslim	112,660,000
Hindu	16,260,000
other	2,360,000
Barbados	
Anglican	89,000
Protestant	80,000
Roman Catholic	12,000
other	88,000
Belarus	
Belarusian Orthodox	3,151,000
Roman Catholic	1,772,000
other	5,062,000
Belgium	
Roman Catholic	8,310,000
nonreligious	600,000
other	1,360,000
Belize	
Roman Catholic	143,000
Protestant	67,000
Anglican	17,000
other	20,000
Benin	
Voodoo (traditional beliefs)	3,390,000
Roman Catholic	1,370,000
Muslim	1,320,000
other	500,000
Bermuda	
Anglican	23,700
Methodist	10,400
Roman Catholic	8,800
other	20,900
Bhutan	
Lamaistic Buddhist	510,000
Hindu	140,000
other	40,000
Bolivia	
Roman Catholic	7,540,000
Protestant	770,000
other	210,000
Bosnia and Herzegovina	
Sunnī Muslim	1,690,000
Serbian Orthodox	1,180,000
Roman Catholic	710,000
other	350,000
Botswana	
African Christian	490,000
Protestant	170,000
Roman Catholic	60,000
other (mostly traditional beliefs)	870,000
Brazil	
Roman Catholic (including syncretic Afro-Catholic cults having Spiritist beliefs and rituals)	124,470,000
Evangelical Protestant	39,850,000
other	7,800,000
Brunei	
Muslim	222,000
other	121,000
Bulgaria	
Bulgarian Orthodox	5,690,000
Muslim (mostly Sunnī)	940,000
other	1,320,000
Burkina Faso	
Muslim	5,960,000
traditional beliefs	4,180,000
Christian	2,040,000
other	80,000
Burundi	
Roman Catholic	4,050,000
nonreligious	1,160,000
other (mostly Protestant)	1,020,000
Cambodia	
Buddhist	10,780,000
Chinese folk-religionist	600,000
traditional beliefs	550,000
Muslim	290,000
other	500,000
Cameroon	
Roman Catholic	4,180,000
traditional beliefs	3,750,000
Muslim	3,350,000
Protestant	3,270,000
other	1,250,000
Canada	
Roman Catholic	14,010,000
Protestant	8,620,000
Anglican	2,490,000
Eastern Orthodox	440,000
Jewish	360,000
Muslim	290,000
Buddhist	190,000
Hindu	180,000
Sikh	170,000
nonreligious	3,880,000
other	380,000
Cape Verde	
Roman Catholic	370,000
other	35,000
Central African Republic	
Roman Catholic	660,000
Muslim	560,000
traditional beliefs	550,000
Protestant	520,000
other	1,290,000
Chad	
Muslim	4,690,000
Roman Catholic	1,770,000
Protestant	1,250,000
traditional beliefs	640,000
other	350,000
Chile	
Roman Catholic	11,810,000
Evangelical Protestant	1,910,000
other	1,690,000
China	
nonreligious	661,390,000
Chinese folk-religionist	256,260,000
atheist	152,990,000
Buddhist	108,110,000
Christian	76,540,000
Muslim	18,360,000
traditional beliefs	1,280,000
Colombia	
Roman Catholic	39,590,000
other	3,480,000
Comoros	
Sunnī Muslim	555,000
other	11,000
Congo, Dem. Rep. of the	
Roman Catholic	21,990,000
Protestant	16,950,000
African Christian	7,170,000
traditional beliefs	5,740,000
Muslim	750,000
other	1,040,000
Congo, Rep. of the	
Roman Catholic	1,430,000
Protestant	490,000
African Christian	360,000
other	610,000
Costa Rica	
Roman Catholic	3,380,000
Protestant	360,000
other	190,000
Côte d'Ivoire	
Muslim	6,340,000
Roman Catholic	3,400,000
traditional beliefs	2,790,000
nonreligious	2,220,000
Protestant	870,000
other	770,000
Croatia	
Roman Catholic	3,890,000
Serbian Orthodox	250,000
Sunnī Muslim	100,000
Protestant	30,000
other	130,000
Cuba	
Roman Catholic	4,420,000
Protestant	270,000
other (mostly Santeria)	6,500,000
Cyprus	
Greek Orthodox	630,000
Muslim (mostly Sunnī)	200,000
other (mostly Christian)	40,000
Czech Republic	
Roman Catholic	4,010,000
Evangelical Church of Czech Brethren	200,000
Czechoslovak Hussite	180,000
Silesian Evangelical	30,000
Eastern Orthodox	20,000
atheist and nonreligious	4,100,000
other	1,730,000
Denmark	
Evangelical Lutheran	4,600,000
Muslim	120,000
other	640,000
Djibouti	
Sunnī Muslim	434,000
other	27,000
Dominica	
Roman Catholic	50,000
Protestant	12,000
other	10,000
Dominican Republic	
Roman Catholic	7,110,000
Protestant	560,000
other	1,020,000
East Timor	
Roman Catholic	780,000
Protestant	50,000
Muslim	30,000
other	40,000
Ecuador	
Roman Catholic	11,910,000
Protestant	440,000
other	530,000
Egypt	
Sunnī Muslim	58,060,000
Coptic Orthodox[1]	6,520,000
other	660,000
El Salvador	
Roman Catholic	4,880,000
Protestant	1,070,000
other	290,000
Equatorial Guinea	
Roman Catholic	390,000
other	110,000
Eritrea	
Eritrean Orthodox	1,980,000
Muslim	1,920,000
other	400,000

Religion (continued)

Religious affiliation	2001 population
Estonia	
Estonian Orthodox	277,000
Evangelical Lutheran	187,000
other	899,000
Ethiopia	
Ethiopian Orthodox	33,110,000
other Christian	7,090,000
Muslim (mostly Sunnī)	21,710,000
traditional beliefs	3,180,000
other	820,000
Faroe Islands	
Evangelical Lutheran	38,000
other	9,000
Fiji	
Christian (mostly Methodist and Roman Catholic)	437,000
Hindu	316,000
Muslim	65,000
other	9,000
Finland	
Evangelical Lutheran	4,420,000
other	770,000
France	
Roman Catholic	38,690,000
nonreligious	9,230,000
Muslim	4,180,000
atheist	2,380,000
Protestant	720,000
Jewish	590,000
other	3,290,000
French Guiana	
Roman Catholic	91,000
other	77,000
French Polynesia	
Protestant	119,000
Roman Catholic	94,000
other	25,000
Gabon	
Roman Catholic	690,000
Protestant	220,000
African Christian	170,000
other	160,000
Gambia, The	
Muslim (mostly Sunnī)	1,340,000
other	70,000
Gaza Strip	
Muslim (mostly Sunnī)	1,190,000
other	20,000
Georgia	
Georgian Orthodox	1,828,000
Sunnī Muslim	549,000
Armenian Apostolic (Orthodox)	279,000
Russian Orthodox	133,000
other (mostly nonreligious)	2,200,000
Germany	
Protestant (mostly Evangelical Lutheran)	29,330,000
Roman Catholic	27,590,000
Muslim	3,660,000
atheist	1,800,000
other (mostly nonreligious)	20,020,000
Ghana	
traditional beliefs	4,860,000
Muslim	3,910,000
Protestant	3,310,000
African Christian	2,870,000
Roman Catholic	1,890,000
other	3,050,000
Greece	
Greek Orthodox	10,010,000
Muslim	360,000
other	500,000
Greenland	
Evangelical Lutheran	36,500
other	19,800
Grenada	
Roman Catholic	54,000
Anglican	14,000
other	34,000
Guadeloupe	
Roman Catholic	350,000
other	82,000
Guam	
Roman Catholic	118,000
Protestant	19,000
other	21,000
Guatemala	
Roman Catholic	8,880,000
Evangelical Protestant	2,540,000
other	270,000
Guernsey	
Anglican	42,000
other	22,000
Guinea	
Muslim	6,470,000
Christian	760,000
other	380,000
Guinea-Bissau	
traditional beliefs	590,000
Muslim	530,000
Christian	170,000
other	20,000
Guyana	
Hindu	264,000
Protestant	145,000
Roman Catholic	89,000
Muslim	70,000
Anglican	67,000
other	142,000
Haiti	
Roman Catholic	4,770,000
Protestant	1,590,000
other	610,000
Honduras	
Roman Catholic	5,740,000
Evangelical Protestant	690,000
other	200,000
Hong Kong	
Buddhist and Taoist	4,970,000
Protestant	290,000
Roman Catholic	280,000
other	1,200,000
Hungary	
Roman Catholic	6,120,000
Protestant	2,470,000
nonreligious	750,000
other	850,000
Iceland	
Evangelical Lutheran	260,000
other	20,000
India	
Hindu	759,350,000
Sunnī Muslim	92,380,000
traditional beliefs	34,930,000
Shīʿī Muslim	30,790,000
independent	30,750,000
Sikh	22,290,000
Protestant	15,130,000
Roman Catholic	13,940,000
Buddhist	7,290,000
Jain	4,160,000
atheist	1,670,000
Bahāʾī	1,190,000
Zoroastrian (Parsi)	210,000
nonreligious	12,910,000
other	3,000,000
Indonesia	
Muslim	185,060,000
Protestant	12,820,000
Roman Catholic	7,600,000
Hindu	3,880,000
Buddhist	2,190,000
other	660,000
Iran	
Shīʿī Muslim	57,180,000
Sunnī Muslim	3,460,000
Zoroastrian	1,780,000
Bahāʾī	430,000
Christian	340,000
other	250,000
Iraq	
Shīʿī Muslim	13,890,000
Sunnī Muslim	8,510,000
Christian	750,000
other	180,000
Ireland	
Roman Catholic	3,500,000
other	320,000
Isle of Man	
Anglican	30,000
Methodist	7,000
Roman Catholic	6,000
other	31,000
Israel	
Jewish[2]	4,960,000
Muslim (mostly Sunnī)	930,000
other	360,000
Italy	
Roman Catholic	46,260,000
nonreligious and atheist	9,600,000
Muslim	680,000
other	1,350,000
Jamaica	
Protestant	1,020,000
Roman Catholic	270,000
Anglican	100,000
other	1,230,000
Japan	
Shintoist[3]	118,270,000
Buddhist[3]	88,490,000
Christian	1,470,000
other	10,250,000
Jersey	
Anglican	55,000
Roman Catholic	21,000
other	14,000
Jordan	
Sunnī Muslim	4,800,000
Christian	210,000
other	120,000
Kazakhstan	
Muslim (mostly Sunnī)	6,988,000
Russian Orthodox	1,216,000
Protestant	318,000
other (mostly nonreligious)	6,345,000
Kenya	
Roman Catholic	6,780,000
African Christian	6,400,000
Protestant	6,170,000
traditional beliefs	3,540,000
Anglican	2,900,000
Muslim	2,240,000
Orthodox	720,000
other	2,030,000
Kiribati	
Roman Catholic	50,000
Congregational	36,000
other	9,000
Korea, North	
atheist and nonreligious	15,000,000
traditional beliefs	3,430,000
Ch'ŏndogyo	3,050,000
other	480,000
Korea, South	
nonreligious	23,490,000
Buddhist	11,040,000
Protestant	9,370,000
Roman Catholic	3,160,000
Confucian	230,000
Wonbulgyo	90,000
other	290,000
Kuwait	
Sunnī Muslim	1,020,000
Shīʿī Muslim	680,000
other Muslim	230,000
other (mostly Christian and Hindu)	340,000
Kyrgyzstan	
Muslim (mostly Sunnī)	3,701,000
Russian Orthodox	276,000
other (mostly nonreligious)	958,000
Laos	
Buddhist	2,750,000
traditional beliefs	2,350,000
other	540,000
Latvia	
Roman Catholic	350,000
Evangelical Lutheran	345,000
Russian Orthodox	181,000
other (mostly nonreligious)	1,482,000
Lebanon	
Shīʿī Muslim	1,230,000
Sunnī Muslim	770,000
Maronite Catholic	690,000
Druze	260,000
Greek Orthodox	220,000
Armenian Apostolic (Orthodox)	190,000
Greek Catholic (Melchite)	170,000
other	110,000
Lesotho	
Roman Catholic	820,000
Protestant	280,000
African Christian	260,000
traditional beliefs	170,000
Anglican	100,000
other	550,000
Liberia	
traditional beliefs	1,390,000
Christian	1,270,000
Muslim	520,000
other	60,000
Libya	
Sunnī Muslim	5,040,000
other	200,000
Liechtenstein	
Roman Catholic	26,000
other	7,000
Lithuania	
Roman Catholic	2,660,000
Russian Orthodox	90,000
other (mostly nonreligious)	940,000
Luxembourg	
Roman Catholic	400,000
other	40,000
Macau	
nonreligious	271,000
Buddhist	75,000
other	100,000
Macedonia	
Serbian (Macedonian) Orthodox	1,210,000
Sunnī Muslim	580,000
other	260,000
Madagascar	
traditional beliefs	7,670,000
Roman Catholic	3,250,000
Protestant	3,630,000
other	1,420,000
Malawi	
Roman Catholic	2,600,000
Protestant	2,070,000
African Christian	1,770,000
Muslim	1,560,000
traditional beliefs	820,000
other	1,730,000
Malaysia	
Muslim	10,770,000
Chinese folk-religionist	5,450,000
Christian	1,880,000
Hindu	1,660,000
Buddhist	1,500,000
other	1,350,000
Maldives	
Sunnī Muslim	273,000
other	2,000
Mali	
Muslim	9,010,000
traditional beliefs	1,760,000
Christian	220,000
other	10,000
Malta	
Roman Catholic	363,000
other	21,000
Marshall Islands	
Protestant	32,800
Roman Catholic	3,700
other	15,700
Martinique	
Roman Catholic	336,000
other	52,000
Mauritania	
Sunnī Muslim	2,720,000
other	20,000
Mauritius	
Hindu	610,000
Roman Catholic	330,000
Muslim	190,000
other	70,000
Mayotte	
Sunnī Muslim	153,000
Christian	5,000
Mexico	
Roman Catholic	90,370,000
Protestant	3,820,000
other Christian	1,820,000
other (mostly nonreligious)	3,970,000
Micronesia	
Roman Catholic	63,600
Protestant	40,100
other	14,200
Moldova	
Romanian Orthodox	1,263,000
Russian (Moldovan) Orthodox	342,000
other (mostly nonreligious)	2,007,000
Monaco	
Roman Catholic	28,000
other	4,000
Mongolia	
Tantric Buddhist (Lamaist)	2,340,000
Muslim	100,000
Morocco	
Muslim (mostly Sunnī)	28,730,000
other	500,000
Mozambique	
traditional beliefs	9,750,000
Roman Catholic	3,060,000
Muslim	2,040,000
Protestant	1,720,000
African Christian	1,400,000
other	1,400,000
Myanmar (Burma)	
Buddhist	37,560,000
Christian	2,060,000
Muslim	1,610,000
traditional beliefs	480,000
Hindu	210,000
other	70,000
Namibia	
Protestant (mostly Lutheran)	850,000
Roman Catholic	320,000
African Christian	200,000
other	430,000
Nauru	
Protestant	6,100
Roman Catholic	3,300
other	2,700
Nepal	
Hindu	19,180,000
traditional beliefs	2,350,000
Buddhist	2,050,000
Muslim	970,000
Christian	600,000
other	140,000
Netherlands, The	
Roman Catholic	4,950,000
Dutch Reformed Church (NHK)	2,240,000
Reformed Churches	1,120,000
Muslim	720,000
nonreligious	6,550,000
other	400,000
Netherlands Antilles	
Roman Catholic	152,000
other	54,000
New Caledonia	
Roman Catholic	132,000
Protestant	31,300
other	52,200

Religious affiliation	2001 population
New Zealand	
Anglican	674,000
Roman Catholic	505,000
Presbyterian	489,000
Methodist	130,000
Baptist	57,000
Mormon	44,000
Ratana	39,000
nonreligious	954,000
other	969,000
Nicaragua	
Roman Catholic	3,590,000
Protestant	810,000
other (mostly nonreligious)	520,000
Niger	
Sunnī Muslim	9,390,000
traditional beliefs	900,000
other	70,000
Nigeria	
Muslim	55,600,000
traditional beliefs	12,500,000
Christian	58,100,000
other	500,000
Northern Mariana Islands	
Roman Catholic	53,600
other	19,700
Norway	
Evangelical Lutheran (Church of Norway)	3,990,000
other	530,000
Oman	
Ibāḍīyāh Muslim	1,840,000
Sunnī Muslim	350,000
Hindu	190,000
Christian	100,000
other	20,000
Pakistan	
Sunnī Muslim	113,950,000
Shīʿī Muslim	25,010,000
Christian	3,560,000
Hindu	1,730,000
other	370,000
Palau	
Roman Catholic	7,600
Modekne	5,200
Protestant	4,900
other	2,100
Panama	
Roman Catholic	2,330,000
Protestant	420,000
other	150,000
Papua New Guinea	
Protestant	3,180,000
Roman Catholic	1,500,000
Anglican	210,000
other	420,000
Paraguay	
Roman Catholic	4,990,000
Protestant	280,000
other	370,000
Peru	
Roman Catholic	23,170,000
Protestant	1,730,000
other (mostly nonreligious)	1,190,000
Philippines	
Roman Catholic	63,530,000
Protestant	4,160,000
Muslim	3,500,000
Aglipayan	2,010,000
Church of Christ (Iglesia ni Cristo)	1,790,000
other	1,620,000
Poland	
Roman Catholic	35,050,000
Polish Orthodox	550,000
other (mostly nonreligious)	3,050,000
Portugal	
Roman Catholic	9,520,000
other	810,000
Puerto Rico	
Roman Catholic	2,480,000
Protestant	1,080,000
other	270,000
Qatar	
Muslim (mostly Sunnī)	490,000
Christian	60,000
other	40,000
Réunion	
Roman Catholic	599,000
Hindu	33,000
other	102,000
Romania	
Romanian Orthodox	19,460,000
Roman Catholic	1,140,000
other	1,810,000
Russia	
Russian Orthodox	23,580,000
Muslim	10,980,000
Protestant	1,320,000
Jewish	590,000
other (mostly nonreligious)	107,960,000
Rwanda	
Roman Catholic	3,730,000
Protestant	1,530,000
traditional beliefs	660,000
Muslim	580,000
Anglican	570,000
other	260,000
St. Kitts and Nevis	
Anglican	10,000
Methodist	10,000
other	15,000
Pentecostal	7,000
other	12,000
St. Lucia	
Roman Catholic	125,000
Protestant	20,000
other	13,000
St. Vincent and the Grenadines	
Anglican	20,000
Pentecostal	17,000
Methodist	12,000
Roman Catholic	12,000
other	52,000
Samoa	
Mormon	46,200
Congregational	44,000
Roman Catholic	38,100
Methodist	21,800
other	29,100
San Marino	
Roman Catholic	24,000
other	3,000
São Tomé and Príncipe	
Roman Catholic	111,000
African Christian	16,000
other	20,000
Saudi Arabia	
Sunnī Muslim	20,490,000
Shīʿī Muslim	840,000
Christian	840,000
Hindu	250,000
other	330,000
Senegal	
Sunnī Muslim	9,010,000
traditional beliefs	640,000
Roman Catholic	480,000
other	160,000
Seychelles	
Roman Catholic	69,800
other	10,800
Sierra Leone	
Sunnī Muslim	2,490,000
traditional beliefs	2,190,000
Christian	620,000
other	130,000
Singapore	
Buddhist and Taoist	1,695,000
Muslim	495,000
Christian	485,000
Hindu	133,000
nonreligious	493,000
other	21,000
Slovakia	
Roman Catholic	3,270,000
Slovak Evangelical	340,000
other (mostly nonreligious)	1,800,000
Slovenia	
Roman Catholic	1,650,000
other	340,000
Solomon Islands	
Protestant	173,000
Anglican	149,000
Roman Catholic	83,000
other	75,000
Somalia	
Sunnī Muslim	7,364,000
other	125,000
South Africa	
Christian	36,220,000
independents	17,040,000
Protestant	13,860,000
Roman Catholic	3,090,000
traditional beliefs	3,660,000
Hindu	1,050,000
Muslim	1,050,000
Bahā'ī	260,000
Jewish	170,000
nonreligious	1,050,000
other	130,000
Spain	
Roman Catholic	36,920,000
Muslim	200,000
other (mostly nonreligious)	3,010,000
Sri Lanka	
Buddhist	13,270,000
Hindu	2,190,000
Muslim	1,750,000
Roman Catholic	1,300,000
other	900,000
Sudan, The	
Sunnī Muslim	25,360,000
Christian	6,020,000
traditional beliefs	4,300,000
other	390,000
Suriname	
Hindu	119,000
Roman Catholic	91,000
Muslim	85,000
Protestant	71,000
other	68,000
Swaziland	
African Christian	480,000
Protestant	160,000
traditional beliefs	120,000
other	340,000
Sweden	
Church of Sweden (Lutheran)	7,690,000
other	1,200,000
Switzerland	
Roman Catholic	3,330,000
Protestant	2,890,000
other	1,000,000
Syria	
Sunnī Muslim	12,380,000
Shīʿī Muslim	2,010,000
Christian	920,000
Druze	500,000
other	920,000
Taiwan	
nonreligious	10,670,000
Buddhist	5,100,000
Taoist	4,040,000
I Kuan Tao	990,000
Protestant	440,000
Roman Catholic	320,000
Tien Te Chiao	210,000
Tien Ti Chiao	190,000
Confucianism (Li)	150,000
Hsuan Yuan Chiao	140,000
Muslim	50,000
Shinto (Tenrikyo)	20,000
Bahā'ī	20,000
Tajikistan	
Sunnī Muslim	4,920,000
Shīʿī Muslim	310,000
Russian Orthodox	90,000
atheist	120,000
other (mostly nonreligious)	820,000
Tanzania	
Christian	18,260,000
Muslim	11,520,000
traditional beliefs	5,830,000
other	620,000
Thailand	
Buddhist	57,920,000
Muslim	2,850,000
Christian	440,000
other	40,000
Togo	
traditional beliefs	1,940,000
Roman Catholic	1,250,000
Sunnī Muslim	970,000
Protestant	530,000
other	450,000
Tonga	
Free Wesleyan	44,000
Roman Catholic	16,000
other	41,000
Trinidad and Tobago	
Roman Catholic	380,000
Hindu	308,000
Protestant	244,000
Anglican	142,000
Muslim	76,000
other	149,000
Tunisia	
Sunnī Muslim	9,720,000
other	104,000
Turkey	
Muslim (mostly Sunnī)	64,360,000
nonreligious	1,340,000
other	530,000
Turkmenistan	
Muslim (mostly Sunnī)	4,752,000
Russian Orthodox	129,000
other (mostly nonreligious)	581,000
Tuvalu	
Congregational	9,400
other	1,600
Uganda	
Roman Catholic	10,050,000
Anglican	9,450,000
Muslim (mostly Sunnī)	1,250,000
traditional beliefs	1,050,000
other	2,190,000
Ukraine	
Ukrainian Orthodox (Russian patriarchy)	9,491,000
Ukrainian Orthodox (Kiev patriarchy)	4,746,000
Ukrainian Autocephalous Orthodox	332,000
Ukrainian Catholic (Uniate)	3,417,000
Protestant	1,736,000
Roman Catholic	576,000
Jewish	423,000
other (mostly nonreligious)	28,044,000
United Arab Emirates	
Sunnī Muslim	2,490,000
Shīʿī Muslim	500,000
other	120,000
United Kingdom	
Christian	49,510,000
Anglican	26,140,000
Roman Catholic	5,590,000
Protestant	5,020,000
Eastern Orthodox	370,000
other Christian	12,390,000
Muslim	1,220,000
Hindu	440,000
Jewish	310,000
Sikh	240,000
other (mostly nonreligious and atheist)	8,240,000
United States	
Christian (professing)	242,011,000
Christian (affiliated)	196,929,000
independent	80,639,000
Protestant	66,287,000
Roman Catholic	59,542,000
Eastern Orthodox	5,915,000
Anglican	2,464,000
other Christian	10,348,000
multi-affiliated Christians	−28,266,000
Christian (unaffiliated)	45,082,000
non-Christian	44,056,000
nonreligious	25,745,000
Jewish	5,771,000
Muslim	4,242,000
Buddhist	2,515,000
atheist	1,181,000
Hindu	1,059,000
New-Religionist	832,000
Bahā'ī	773,000
Ethnic religionist	447,000
Sikh	240,000
Chinese folk-religionist	80,000
other	1,171,000
Uruguay	
Roman Catholic	2,590,000
Protestant	150,000
Mormon	50,000
Jewish	30,000
other	480,000
Uzbekistan	
Muslim (mostly Sunnī)	19,156,000
Russian Orthodox	195,000
other (mostly nonreligious)	5,804,000
Vanuatu	
Presbyterian	70,000
Roman Catholic	28,000
Anglican	27,000
other	69,000
Venezuela	
Roman Catholic	22,050,000
other	2,590,000
Vietnam	
Buddhist	53,290,000
Roman Catholic	6,180,000
New-Religionist	
Cao Dai	2,810,000
Hoa Hao	1,690,000
other	16,500,000
Virgin Islands (U.S.)	
Protestant	56,000
Roman Catholic	41,000
other	24,000
West Bank	
Muslim (mostly Sunnī)	1,860,000
Jewish[4]	230,000
Christian and other	180,000
Western Sahara	
Sunnī Muslim	250,000
other	1,000
Yemen	
Muslim (mostly Sunnī)	18,050,000
other	20,000
Yugoslavia	
Serbian Orthodox	6,680,000
Sunnī Muslim	2,030,000
Roman Catholic	620,000
other (mostly nonreligious)	1,350,000
Zambia	
traditional beliefs	2,640,000
Protestant	2,240,000
Roman Catholic	1,650,000
other	3,240,000
Zimbabwe	
African Christian	4,580,000
traditional beliefs	3,430,000
Protestant	1,400,000
Roman Catholic	1,090,000
other	870,000

[1]Official 1986 census figure is 5.9 percent. [2]Includes the Golan Heights and East Jerusalem; excludes the West Bank and Gaza Strip. [3]Many Japanese practice both Shintoism and Buddhism. [4]Excludes East Jerusalem.

Vital statistics, marriage, family

This table provides some of the basic measures of the factors that influence the size, direction, and rates of population change within a country. The accuracy of these data depends on the effectiveness of each respective national system for registering vital and civil events (birth, death, marriage, etc.) and on the sophistication of the analysis that can be brought to bear upon the data so compiled.

Data on birth rates, for example, depend not only on the completeness of registration of births in a particular country but also on the conditions under which those data are collected: Do all births take place in a hospital? Are the births reported comparably in all parts of the country? Are the records of the births tabulated at a central location in a timely way with an effort to eliminate inconsistent reporting of birth events, perinatal mortality, etc.? Similar difficulties attach to death rates but with the added need to identify "cause of death." Even in a developed country such identifications are often left to nonmedical personnel, and in a developing country with, say, only one physician for every 10,000 population, there will be too few physicians to perform autopsies to assess accurately the cause of death after the fact and also too few to provide ongoing care at a level where records would permit inference about cause of death based on prior condition or diagnosis.

Calculating natural increase, which at its most basic is simply the difference between the birth and death rates, may be affected by the differing degrees of completeness of birth and death registration for a given country. The total fertility rate may be understood as the average number of children that would be borne per woman if all childbearing women lived to the end of their childbearing years and bore children at each age at the average rate for that age. Calculating a meaningful fertility rate requires analysis of changing age structure of the female population over time, changing mortality rates among mothers and their infants, and changing medical practice at births, each improvement of natural survivorship or medical support leading to greater numbers of live-born children and greater numbers of children who survive their first year (the basis for measurement of infant mortality, another basic indicator of demographic conditions and trends within a population).

As indicated above, data for causes of death are not only particularly difficult to obtain, since many countries are not well equipped to collect the data, but also difficult to assess, as their accuracy may be suspect and their meaning may be subject to varying interpretation. Take the case of a citizen of a less developed country who dies of what is clearly a lung infection: Was the death complicated by chronic malnutrition, itself complicated by a parasitic infestation, these last two together so weakening the subject that he died of an infection that he might have survived had his general health been better? Similarly, in a developed country: Someone may die from what is identified in an autopsy as a cerebrovascular accident, but if that accident occurred in a vascular system that was weakened by diabetes, what was the actual cause of death? Statistics on causes of death seek to identify the "underlying" cause (that which sets the final train of events leading to death in motion) but often must settle for the most proximate cause or symptom. Even this kind of analysis may be misleading for those charged with interpreting the data with a view to ordering health-care priorities for a particular country. The eight groups of causes of death utilized here include most, but not all, of the detailed causes classified by the World Health Organization and would not, thus, aggregate to the country's crude death rate for the same year. Among the lesser causes excluded by the present classification are: benign neoplasms; nutritional disorders; anemias; mental disorders; kidney and genito-urinary

Vital statistics, marriage, family

country	vital rates						causes of death (rate per 100,000 population)								
	year	birth rate per 1,000 population	death rate per 1,000 population	infant mortality rate per 1,000 live births	rate of natural increase per 1,000 population	total fertility rate	year	infectious and parasitic diseases	malignant neoplasms (cancers)	endocrine and metabolic disorders	diseases of the nervous system	diseases of the circulatory system	diseases of the respiratory system	diseases of the digestive system	accidents, poisoning, and violence
Afghanistan	2000	41.8	18.0	149.3	23.8	5.9	...	...	...	...	...	...	...	...	...
Albania	2000	19.5	6.0	41.3	13.5	2.4	1993	10.8	53.8	5.1	24.1	187.0	84.5	16.5	41.7
Algeria	2000	19.8	5.5	51.1	14.3	2.8	...	...	...	...	...	...	...	...	...
American Samoa	2000	25.8	4.3	10.6	21.5	3.6	1990	16.4[4]	46.8	16.4[5]	...	131.1[6]	65.6[7]	...	58.5
Andorra	1999	12.6[8]	3.1[8]	4.1[9]	9.5[8]	1.2[10]	...	...	...	...	...	...	...	...	...
Angola	2000	46.9	25.0	195.8	21.9	6.5	...	...	...	...	...	...	...	...	...
Antigua and Barbuda	2000	20.2	6.0	23.0	14.2	2.3	1995	10.4	96.2	57.7	13.3	242.6	42.9	19.2	37.0
Argentina	2000	18.6	7.6	18.3	11.0	2.5	1996	28.1	145.7	19.1[5]	9.7	297.3	64.8	32.5	52.2
Armenia	2000	11.0	9.5	41.5	1.5	1.5	1997	9.2	96.5	32.6	4.4	336.6	38.9	23.9	37.9
Aruba	2000	13.1	6.1	6.5	7.0	1.8	1998	26.1	118.0	29.3[5]	4.3	184.0	35.9	14.1	52.2
Australia	2000	13.0	7.6	6.0	5.4	1.8	1995	6.0	190.0	23.0	17.0	296.0	52.0	21.0	41.0
Austria	1999	9.5	9.4	4.4	0.1	1.3	1997	2.5	233.5	19.9	0.5[14]	532.6	29.9	28.4	54.9
Azerbaijan	2001	13.7	6.2	83.4[10]	7.5	1.6	1995	29.7	61.9	11.8	11.3	335.3	84.9	34.3	45.9
Bahamas, The	2000	19.5	6.8	17.0	12.7	2.3	1995	13.3	85.6	36.3	0.7	160.1	26.6	14.4	40.0
Bahrain	2000	20.6	3.9	20.5	16.7	2.8	1998	5.4	37.8	22.7	4.6	85.9	22.7	13.3	14.5
Bangladesh	2000	27.0	9.1	73.0	17.9	3.0	...	...	...	...	...	...	...	...	...
Barbados	2000	13.6	8.7	12.4	4.9	1.6	1995	27.3	162.5	149.2	22.7	365.5	55.7	34.1	36.0
Belarus	1999	9.3	14.2	11.5	–4.9	1.3[19]	1997	8.8	191.9	8.7[20]	11.5	673.9	68.7	27.5	154.5
Belgium	2000	10.9	10.1	4.8	0.8	1.5	1994	13.4	275.0	21.7	29.2	383.4	92.5	42.6	68.5
Belize	2000	32.3	4.8	26.0	27.5	4.1	1995	23.5	37.7	22.1	6.9	118.9	47.5	16.1	67.3
Benin	2000	44.8	14.5	90.8	30.3	6.3	...	...	...	...	...	...	...	...	...
Bermuda	1999	13.2	7.1	3.2[21]	6.1	1.8	1990	...	181.5	...	...	344.4	25.2	...	38.6
Bhutan	2001	35.2	9.0	56.0	26.2	5.2	...	...	...	...	...	...	...	...	...
Bolivia	2000	31.9	23.3	62.0[23]	23.3	3.7	...	...	...	...	...	...	...	...	...
Bosnia and Herzegovina	2000	12.9	7.9	25.2	5.0	1.7	1989	9.9	122.6[24]	12.6	11.9	344.1	29.0	29.2	47.1
Botswana	2001	28.8	24.8	63.2	4.0	3.7	...	...	...	...	...	...	...	...	...
Brazil	2000	18.8	9.4	38.0	9.4	2.1	1996	33.5	65.9	23.3[20]	9[13]	159.1	56.4	25.9	75.9
Brunei	1999	22.3	2.8	6.0	19.5	2.7	...	...	...	...	...	...	...	...	...
Bulgaria	1999	8.8	13.6	14.6	–4.8	1.2	1998	9.4	192.9	25.4	9.7	954.4	67.6	38.8	60.7
Burkina Faso	2000	45.3	17.0	108.5	28.3	6.4	...	...	...	...	...	...	...	...	...
Burundi	2000	40.5	16.4	71.5	24.1	6.3	...	...	...	...	...	...	...	...	...
Cambodia	2001	35.9	10.7	76.0	25.2	5.0	...	...	...	...	...	...	...	...	...
Cameroon	2000	36.6	11.9	70.9	24.7	4.9	...	...	...	...	...	...	...	...	...
Canada	2000	11.3	7.4	5.1	3.9	1.6	1997	8.3	195.6	23.7	21.9	264.8	66.8	25.4	43.5
Cape Verde	2000	29.7	7.4	54.6	22.3	4.2	...	...	...	...	...	...	...	...	...
Central African Republic	2000	37.5	18.4	106.7	19.1	5.0	...	...	...	...	...	...	...	...	...
Chad	2000	48.8	15.7	96.7	33.1	5.7	...	...	...	...	...	...	...	...	...
Chile	2000	17.2	5.5	9.6	11.7	2.2	1994	14.2	111.9	16.5	8.6	149.5	61.2	37.2	63.6
China	2001	14.9	7.0	38.0	7.9	1.8	1994[26]	15.2	117.7	17.2[20]	4.4	206.4	125.3	25.3	56.6
Colombia	2000	22.9	5.7	24.7	17.2	2.7	1994	13.7	58.3	15.2	4.6	125.3	34.3	15.7	119.5
Comoros	2000	40.0	9.6	86.3	30.4	5.4	...	...	...	...	...	...	...	...	...
Congo, Dem. Rep. of the	2000	46.4	15.4	101.6	31.0	6.9	...	...	...	...	...	...	...	...	...
Congo, Rep. of the	2000	38.6	16.4	101.6	22.2	5.1	...	...	...	...	...	...	...	...	...
Costa Rica	1999	21.7	4.2	11.8	17.5	2.6	1994	9.7	80.0	12.6	8.5	126.6	40.6	24.6	49.7
Côte d'Ivoire	2000	40.8	16.6	95.1	24.2	5.8	...	...	...	...	...	...	...	...	...
Croatia	1999	9.9	11.4	7.4	–1.5	1.9[10]	1996	8.8	227.2	25.4[20]	8.0	547.4	41.4	52.1	70.7
Cuba	2000	12.7	7.3	7.5	5.4	1.6	1995	12.8	133	25.9	11.1	305.5	64.1	24.9	84.6
Cyprus	1999	12.8	7.6	8.1[10]	5.2	2.0	...	...	...	...	...	...	...	...	...
Czech Republic	1999	8.7	10.7	4.6	–2.0	1.1	1998	2.6	272.1	15.0	11.6	586.7	39.9	40.4	68.1
Denmark	2000	12.6	10.9	5.0	1.7	1.7	1996	10.1	289.2	16.5	15.3	428.4	108.1	46.1	64.1

diseases not classifiable under the main groups; maternal deaths (for which data *are* provided, however, in the "Health services" table); diseases of the skin and musculoskeletal systems; congenital and perinatal conditions; and general senility and other ill-defined (ill-diagnosed) conditions, a kind of "other" category.

Expectation of life is probably the most accurate single measure of the quality of life in a given society. It summarizes in a single number all of the natural and social stresses that operate upon individuals in that society. The number may range from as few as 40 years of life in the least developed countries to as much as 80 years for women in the most developed nations. The lost potential in the years separating those two numbers is prodigious, regardless of how the loss arises—wars and civil violence, poor public health services, or poor individual health practice in matters of nutrition, exercise, stress management, and so on.

Data on marriages and marriage rates probably are less meaningful in terms of international comparisons than some of the measures mentioned above because the number, timing, and kinds of social relationships that substitute for marriage depend on many kinds of social variables—income, degree of social control, heterogeneity of the society (race, class, language communities), or level of development of civil administration (if one must travel for a day or more to obtain a legal civil ceremony, one may forgo it). Nevertheless, the data for a single country say specific things about local practice in terms of the age at which a man or woman typically marries, and the overall rate will at least define the number of legal civil marriages, though it cannot say anything about other, less formal arrangements (here the figure for the legitimacy rate for children in the next section may identify some of the societies in which economics or social constraints may operate to limit the number of marriages that are actually confirmed on civil registers). The available data usually include both first marriages and remarriages after annulment, divorce, widowhood, or the like.

The data for families provide information about the average size of a family unit (individuals related by blood or civil register) and the average number of children under a specified age (set here at 15 to provide a consistent measure of social minority internationally, though legal minority depends on the laws of each country). When well-defined family data are not collected as part of a country's national census or vital statistics surveys, data for households have been substituted on the assumption that most households worldwide represent families in some conventional sense. But increasing numbers of households worldwide are composed of unrelated individuals (unmarried heterosexual couples, aged [or younger] groups sharing limited [often fixed] incomes for reasons of economy, or homosexual couples). Such arrangements do not yet represent great numbers overall. Increasing numbers of census programs, however, even in developing countries, are making more adequate provision for distinguishing these nontraditional, often nonfamily households.

Internet resources for further information:

- World Health Organization (World) http://www.who.ch
- Pan American Health Organization (the Americas) http://www.paho.org
- National Center for Health Statistics (U.S.) http://www.cdc.gov/nchs
- U.S. Census Bureau: International Data Base (World) http://www.census.gov/ipc/www/idbprint.html

expectation of life at birth (latest year)		nuptiality, family, and family planning															country
		marriages			age at marriage (latest)						families (F), households (H) (latest)						
		year	total number	rate per 1,000 population	groom (percent)			bride (percent)			families (households)		children		induced abortions		
male	female				19 and under	20–29	30 and over	19 and under	20–29	30 and over	total ('000)	size	number under age 15	percent legitimate	number	ratio per 100 live births	
46.6	45.1	…	…	…	…	…	…	…	…	…	H 2,110	H 6.2	H 2.8[1]	…	…	…	Afghanistan
00.0	71.0	1997	25,260	6.8	1.5[2]	80.4[2]	18.1[2]	24.0[2]	71.4[2]	4.6[2]	F 675	F 3.9	F 1.6	…	…	…	Albania
68.3	71.0	1996	156,870	5.6	0.7[3]	67.1[3]	32.2[3]	29.8[3]	61.4[3]	0.0[3]	H 1,102	H 7.1	H 3.0	…	…	…	Algeria
70.7	79.8	1993	325	6.1	…	…	…	…	…	…	H 7	H 7.0	H 2.7	72.0	…	…	American Samoa
80.6	86.6	1998	208	3.2	…	…	…	…	…	…	…	…	…	…	…	…	Andorra
37.1	39.6	…	…	…	…	…	…	…	…	…	…	H 5.0	…	…	…	…	Angola
68.2	72.8	1998	1,418	22.1	1.0[11]	37.4[12]	61.6	3.7[11]	52.4[12]	43.9	H 18	H 3.2	H 1.2	23.4	…	…	Antigua and Barbuda
71.7	78.6	1996	148,721	4.2	5.6	71.5	22.9	26.0	58.6	15.4	H 10,097	H 3.2	H 1.0	67.5	…	…	Argentina
62.0	71.0	1995	14,200	4.2	5.0[13]	73.8[13]	21.2[13]	39.3[13]	49.9[13]	10.8[13]	H 559	H 4.5	H 1.8	86.0	30,571	59.8	Armenia
75.0	81.9	1998	564	6.1	…	…	…	…	…	…	H 19	H 3.6	…	57.5	…	…	Aruba
76.0	81.0	1996	109,386	6.0	0.7	54.5	44.8	3.6	63.6	32.8	H 6,636	H 2.6	H 0.6	75.0	…	…	Australia
75.1	80.9	1998	39,143	4.8	1.1[15]	49.9[15]	49.0[15]	4.2[15]	62.0[15]	33.8[15]	H 3,058	H 2.6	H 0.5	69.5	…	…	Austria
68.0	75.0	1994	47,147	6.3	1.2[16]	80.4[16]	18.4[16]	24.8[16]	63.9[16]	11.3[16]	H 1,381	H 5.2	H 1.7	94.8	42,134	23.2	Azerbaijan
68.3	73.9	1996	2,628	9.3	…	14.0	86.0	—	26.1	73.9	H 74	H 3.9	…	45.7	…	…	Bahamas, The
70.6	75.5	1998	3,677	5.7	2.6[17]	65.4[17]	32.0[17]	28.0[17]	54.6[17]	17.4[17]	H 67	H 6.5	H 2.2	100.0	…	…	Bahrain
59.0	60.0	1997	1,181,000	9.7	…	…	…	…	…	…	H 19,980	H 5.6	…	…	…	…	Bangladesh
70.4	75.6	1995	3,564	13.5	0.1[18]	40.2[18]	59.7[18]	1.4[18]	53.6[18]	44.9[18]	H 67	H 3.5	H 1.5	26.9	723	19.6	Barbados
62.2	73.9	1997	69,735	6.8	5.4[15]	69.8[15]	24.8[15]	27.1[15]	53.1[15]	19.8[15]	H 2,796	H 3.6	H 0.8	82.2	174,098	181.7	Belarus
74.5	81.3	1996	50,601	5.0	0.6[17]	59.5[17]	39.9[17]	4.0[17]	66.3[17]	29.7[17]	F 3,613	F 2.7	F 0.5	88.7	…	…	Belgium
68.7	73.3	1997	1,543	6.6	6.3[17]	58.4[17]	35.3[17]	23.4[17]	51.0[17]	25.6[17]	H 42	H 5.3	H 2.2	40.3	990	15.1	Belize
49.2	51.2	…	…	…	…	…	…	…	…	…	…	H 5.9	…	…	…	…	Benin
74.9	78.9	1994	944	15.4	0.2[22]	37.4[22]	62.4[22]	1.5[22]	49.4[22]	49.1[22]	H 24	H 2.5	H 0.5	61.7	92	11.0	Bermuda
61.0	64.0	…	…	…	…	…	…	…	…	…	…	H 5.4	…	…	…	…	Bhutan
66.3	61.2	…	…	…	…	…	…	…	…	…	H 1,655	H 3.8	H 1.6	80.9	…	…	Bolivia
68.8	74.4	1991	27,923	6.0	2.3	74.2	23.5	28.6	58.9	12.5	H 1,203	H 3.4	H 1.1	92.6	…	…	Bosnia and Herzegovina
36.8	37.5	1986	1,638	1.5	—	33.0	67.0	5.0	69.2	25.8	H 125	H 5.7	H 2.0	28.8	17	0.1	Botswana
58.5	67.6	1995	…	4.7	7.0[13]	68.7[13]	24.3[13]	31.2[13]	54.3[13]	14.5[13]	F 39,768	F 3.9	1.2	…	…	…	Brazil
74.0	76.0	1995	1,793	6.1	10.6[25]	50.1[25]	39.3[25]	11.4[25]	54.7[25]	33.9[25]	H 45	H 5.8	H 2.0	99.6	…	…	Brunei
67.5	74.6	1996	…	4.3	3.4[17]	73.1[17]	23.5[17]	26.9[17]	60.4[17]	12.7[17]	H 2,795	H 3.0	…	74.3	97,023	134.8	Bulgaria
46.3	47.2	…	…	…	…	…	…	…	…	…	…	H 6.2	…	…	…	…	Burkina Faso
45.2	47.2	…	…	…	…	…	…	…	…	…	…	H 5.0	…	…	…	…	Burundi
54.0	59.0	…	…	…	…	…	…	…	…	…	…	H 5.6	…	…	…	…	Cambodia
54.0	55.6	…	…	…	…	…	…	…	…	…	…	H 5.7	…	…	…	…	Cameroon
76.0	83.0	1995	160,256	5.4	0.9	49.3	49.8	3.6	57.9	38.5	H 11,580	H 2.5	H 0.6	83.8	70,549	18.7	Canada
65.6	72.3	1994	1,200	3.2	…	…	…	…	…	…	F 59	F 5.1	…	28.9	…	…	Cape Verde
42.3	45.8	…	…	…	…	…	…	…	…	…	…	H 5.9	…	…	…	…	Central African Republic
48.5	52.6	…	…	…	…	…	…	…	…	…	…	H 5.0	…	…	…	…	Chad
72.4	79.2	1996	83,547	5.8	4.7	67.5	27.8	18.6	62.2	19.2	H 3,537	H 3.8	…	61.9	67	—	Chile
69.0	73.0	1994	9,290,027	7.8	…	…	…	…	…	…	H 278.6[27]	H 4.1	H 1.1	…	10,500,000	47.7	China
66.4	74.3	…	…	…	…	…	…	…	…	…	F 4,772	F 5.3	F 2.5	75.2	…	…	Colombia
57.8	62.2	…	…	…	…	…	…	…	…	…	…	H 5.6	…	…	…	…	Comoros
47.6	50.8	…	…	…	…	…	…	…	…	…	…	H 2.3	…	…	…	…	Congo, Dem. Rep. of the
44.5	50.5	…	…	…	…	…	…	…	…	…	H 326	H 4.7	H 2.0	…	…	…	Congo, Rep. of the
74.2	79.9	1997	22,422	6.5	7.1[17]	60.9[17]	32.0[17]	26.3[17]	52.0[17]	94.7[17]	H 772	H 4.1	…	50.3	…	…	Costa Rica
43.7	46.6	…	…	…	…	…	…	…	…	…	…	H 8.0	…	…	…	…	Côte d'Ivoire
70.0	77.5	1997	24,517	5.3	1.2[15]	65.2[15]	33.6[15]	13.9[15]	66.8[15]	19.3[15]	H 1,544	H 3.1	H 0.6	92.7	12,339	22.9	Croatia
73.8	78.5	1997	60,220	5.4	5.2[17]	51.8[17]	43.0[17]	18.0[17]	49.4[17]	32.6[17]	F 2,860	F 3.7	H 1.6	…	83,963	57.1	Cuba
75.3	80.1	1996	5,761	7.8	0.8	54.6	44.6	8.1	64.2	27.7	H 160	H 3.5	H 1.1	99.6	…	…	Cyprus
71.1	78.2	1997	57,086	5.6	3.7[15]	66.5[15]	29.8[15]	15.0[15]	65.8[15]	19.2[15]	H 3,557	H 2.9	…	79.4	48,086	53.2	Czech Republic
74.3	79.1	1997	34,108	6.5	0.4[17]	36.2[17]	63.4[17]	1.4[17]	47.9[17]	50.7[17]	H 2,027	H 2.2	…	53.5	17,720	53.2	Denmark

Vital statistics, marriage, family (continued)

country	vital rates						causes of death (rate per 100,000 population)								
	year	birth rate per 1,000 population	death rate per 1,000 population	infant mortality rate per 1,000 live births	rate of natural increase per 1,000 population	total fertility rate	year	infectious and parasitic diseases	malignant neoplasms (cancers)	endocrine and metabolic disorders	diseases of the nervous system	diseases of the circulatory system	diseases of the respiratory system	diseases of the digestive system	accidents, poisoning, and violence
Djibouti	2000	41.0	14.9	103.3	26.1	5.8	…	…	…	…	…	…	…	…	…
Dominica	2000	18.3	7.3	17.1	11.0	2.0	1994	23.1	125.0	59.8	9.5	237.8	38.0	21.7	28.5
Dominican Republic	2000	25.2	4.7	35.9	20.5	3.0	1985[28]	85	45	15[5]	7[14]	165	41	25	*56*
East Timor[29]	…	…	…	…	…	…	…	…	…	…	…	…	…	…	…
Ecuador	2000[1]	26.5	5.5	35.1	21.0	3.2	1995	29.7	50.8	17.5	7.2	80.8	46.0	23.1	65.1
Egypt	2000	25.4	7.8	62.3	17.6	3.2	1992	49.0	22.4	17.3	9.5	313.5	83.4	33.5	28.8
El Salvador	2000	29.0	6.3	29.2	22.7	3.4	1994[30]	42	52	9[5]	2[14]	124	36	14	135
Equatorial Guinea	2000	38.1	13.4	94.8	24.7	4.9	…	…	…	…	…	…	…	…	…
Eritrea	2000	42.7	12.3	76.7	30.4	5.9	…	…	…	…	…	…	…	…	…
Estonia	2000	9.6	13.5	8.4	−3.9	1.2	1995	13.7	221.1	8.2	13.0	771.9	42.5	36.0	198.8
Ethiopia	2000	45.1	17.6	101.3	27.5	7.1	…	…	…	…	…	…	…	…	…
Faroe Islands	2000	13.6	8.7	6.9	22.3	2.3	1992	4.3	191.3	14.9[5]	—	352.8	59.5	14.9	57.4
Fiji	2000	23.5	5.8	14.5	17.7	2.9	…	…	…	…	…	…	…	…	…
Finland	1999	11.2	9.5	4.2	1.7	1.7	1995	7.7	196.6	12.5	20.1	459.7	73.6	38.0	85.8
France	2000	12.3	9.1	4.8	3.2	1.7	1994	12.8	207.7	27.8	20.7	288.2	63.9	43.9	76.1
French Guiana	2000	22.4	4.8	14.0	17.6	3.2	1989	61.7	58.1	16.3	10.9	114.3	20.9	13.6	98.0
French Polynesia	2001	20.7	4.8	9.0	15.9	2.5	1994–95	14.0	104.0	14.0	10.0	123.0	47.0	17.0	52.0
Gabon	2001	27.4	17.2	94.9	10.2	3.7	…	…	…	…	…	…	…	…	…
Gambia, The	2000	42.3	13.2	79.3	29.1	5.8	…	…	…	…	…	…	…	…	…
Gaza Strip	2000	43.1	4.3	26.0	38.8	6.6	…	…	…	…	…	…	…	…	…
Georgia	2000	10.9	14.5	52.9	−3.6	1.4	1990	12.7	100.8	14.6	4.3	548.4	43.3	8.5	56.1
Germany	2000	9.4	10.5	4.8	−1.1	1.4	1995	7.4	260.7	34.5	18.0	525.7	66.0	51.2	48.2
Ghana	2001	29.0	10.3	56.5	18.7	3.8	…	…	…	…	…	…	…	…	…
Greece	2000	11.7	10.5	6.7[23]	1.2	1.3	1998	6.7	213.4	8.3	9.4	492.4	54.9	22.1	42.8
Greenland	2000	16.9	7.6	18.3	9.3	2.4	1995	29.5	198.7	3.9	1.8	214.4	9.6	5.7	206.5
Grenada	2000	23.2	8.0	14.6	15.2	3.2	1987	9.6	82.8	57.3	7.4	264.3	45.6	38.2	…
Guadeloupe	2000	17.3	6.0	9.8	11.3	1.9	1996	23.8	134.8	26.2	…	183.7	32.1	31.4	68.1
Guam	2001	27.0	4.8	10.0	22.2	4.0	1994	1.4	60.0	26.5[5]	6.8	141.8	27.9	1.4	64.1
Guatemala	2000	35.1	6.9	47.0	28.2	4.7	…	…	…	…	…	…	…	…	…
Guernsey	2000	10.5	9.3	5.1	1.2	1.3	1996	5.3	282.3	15.9	15.9	441.1	150.0	49.4	24.7
Guinea	2001	39.8	17.5	120.0	22.3	5.4	…	…	…	…	…	…	…	…	…
Guinea-Bissau	2000	39.6	15.6	112.3	24.0	5.3	…	…	…	…	…	…	…	…	…
Guyana	2000	17.9	8.4	39.1	9.5	2.1	1994	38.9	33.5	45.7	10.6	212.8	44.5	27.6	59.0
Haiti	2000	32.0	15.1	97.1	16.9	4.5	…	…	…	…	…	…	…	…	…
Honduras	2000	32.7	5.3	31.3	27.4	4.3	…	…	…	…	…	…	…	…	…
Hong Kong	2000	8.1	5.1	2.9	3.0	1.3	1998	14.4	160.5	7.4	3.9	126.7	99.6	21.0	21.2
Hungary	1999	9.4	14.2	8.4	−4.8	1.3	1995	7.9	322.0	20.1	11.5	721.4	63.0	115.6	111.5
Iceland	1999	14.8	6.9	2.4	7.9	2.0	1995	6.7	176.4	3.7	19.5	308.6	82.0	3.0	56.6
India	2000	24.8	8.9	64.9	15.9	3.1	…	…	…	…	…	…	…	…	…
Indonesia[29]	2001	20.8	7.2	42.0	13.6	2.4	…	…	…	…	…	…	…	…	…
Iran	2000	18.3	5.5	30.0	12.8	2.2	1990[34]	*34*	*61*	*12*[20]	*26*	*304*	*48*	*24*	*108*
Iraq	2000	35.0	6.4	62.5	28.6	4.9	…	…	…	…	…	…	…	…	…
Ireland	2000	14.5	8.1	5.6	6.4	1.9	1997	4.8	205.6	10.8[5]	0.2[14]	369.9	153.4	9.4	38.4
Isle of Man	1999	12.3	13.5	3.7[35]	−1.2	1.6	1998	2.8	298.4	11.1	31.8	504.3	225.2	38.7	52.5
Israel	2000	21.7	6.0	5.1	15.7	3.0	1995	10.4	148.9	23.4	11.5	278.4	26.5	23.1	35.8
Italy	2000	9.1	10.0	5.9	−0.9	1.2	1995	13.3	258.2	34.7	20.3	424.3	59.1	47.0	49.0
Jamaica	2000	20.0	5.1	14.6	14.9	2.8[36]	1991	8.1	84.1	51.3	7.5	189.5	30.2	14.1	8.4
Japan	1999	9.3	7.8	3.4	1.5	1.4	1997	14.6	220.4	12.4	7.0	237.7	98.0	30.0	52.4
Jersey	2000	11.7	9.3	5.7	2.4	1.6	…	…	…	…	…	…	…	…	…
Jordan	2000	26.2	2.6	21.1	23.6	3.4	…	…	…	…	…	…	…	…	…
Kazakhstan	2001	16.5	10.1	43.0	6.4	2.0	1996	45.7	133.0	10.9	1.4	436.2	71.0	32.9	101.1
Kenya	2000	29.4	14.1	68.7	15.3	3.7	…	…	…	…	…	…	…	…	…
Kiribati	2000	33.1	8.4	56.8[23]	24.7	4.4[23]	…	…	…	…	…	…	…	…	…
Korea, North	2000	20.4	6.9	24.3	13.5	2.3	…	…	…	…	…	…	…	…	…
Korea, South	1999	15.3	5.8	10.0	9.5	1.7	1997	10.8	115.4	20.2	5.1	121.5	24.4	34.4	70.6
Kuwait	2000	22.0	2.4	11.5	19.6	3.3	1997	5.4	22.7	10.6	3.1	84.6	11.0	4.7	34.8
Kyrgyzstan	2001	20.6	7.3	39.0	13.3	2.5	1996	12.6	25.7	8.3	1.5	278.5	75.0	9.8	21.4
Laos	2001	36.5	13.1	91.0	23.4	5.0	…	…	…	…	…	…	…	…	…
Latvia	1999	8.0	13.5	11.4	−5.5	1.2	1998	19.5	231.8	12.2[20]	12.7	775.6	34.6	42.2	161.8
Lebanon	2000	20.3	6.4	29.3	13.9	2.1	…	…	…	…	…	…	…	…	…
Lesotho	2000	31.7	14.6	83.0	17.1	4.2	…	…	…	…	…	…	…	…	…
Liberia	2000	47.2	16.6	134.6	30.6	6.4	…	…	…	…	…	…	…	…	…
Libya	2000	27.7	3.5	30.1	24.2	3.7	…	…	…	…	…	…	…	…	…
Liechtenstein	2000	11.8	6.7	5.7	5.1	1.5	1997	23.0[13]	199.7	…	6.6[13]	613.9	29.0	22.6	146.9
Lithuania	2000	9.2	10.5	8.5	−1.3	1.4	1995	16.4	203.2	8.0	10.3	654.2	40.5	32.1	176.0
Luxembourg	2000	12.5	8.9	4.8	3.6	1.7	1995	4.6	248.5	21.7	14.9	375.1	61.5	40.2	59.0
Macau	2001	9.4	4.5	8.0	4.9	1.1	1998	10.0	77.8	3.9	1.7	117.1	39.3	11.1	23.9
Macedonia	2000	13.7	7.7	13.4	6.0	1.8	1997	17.6	138.3	24.1[5]	28.0	462.8	39.5	15.9	32.4
Madagascar	2000	42.9	12.7	87.0	30.2	5.8	…	…	…	…	…	…	…	…	…
Malawi	2000	38.5	22.4	122.3	16.1	6.3	…	…	…	…	…	…	…	…	…
Malaysia	2001	23.5	4.4	7.9	19.1	3.1[23]	1997	15.2	19.8	3.8	1.1	37.2	8.7	2.1	13.2
Maldives	2001	36.3	6.3	40.0	30.0	5.5	…	…	…	…	…	…	…	—	…
Mali	2000	49.2	19.1	123.3	30.1	6.9	…	…	…	…	…	…	…	…	…
Malta	2000	12.8	7.7	5.9	5.1	1.9	1997	5.1	281.9	25.1	12.8	354.1	70.9	26.1	28.5
Marshall Islands	2000	41.8	4.9	41.0	36.9	6.6	1993[37]	169.9	68.4	…	—	155.1	105.1	63.3	36.7
Martinique	2000	16.1	6.4	8.0	9.7	1.8	1996	21.9	150.1	27.7	…	206.6	36.3	27.2	47.2
Mauritania	2000	43.4	14.0	78.1	29.4	6.3	…	…	…	…	…	…	…	…	…
Mauritius	2000	16.7	6.8	17.7	9.9	2.0	1996	12.1	56.8	24.9	0.8	291.2	34.9	21.7	46.2
Mayotte	2000	45.3	9.1	71.3	36.2	6.3	…	…	…	…	…	…	…	…	…
Mexico	2000	23.2	5.1	26.2	18.1	2.7	1995	22.0	52.9	46.9	6.7	106.8	47.1	42.1	62.4
Micronesia	2000	27.1	6.0	33.5	21.1	3.8	…	…	…	…	…	…	…	…	…
Moldova	2000	12.9	12.6	43.3	0.3	1.6	1995	14.6	133.3	10.7	11.8	559.4	76.3	114.7	113.7
Monaco	2000	9.9	13.1	5.9	−3.2	1.8	…	…	…	…	…	…	…	…	…
Mongolia	2001	22.4	7.5	61.0	14.9	2.4	1994[38]	33	118	3	14	200	110	55	64
Morocco	2001	24.2	5.9	48.1	18.3	3.0	1992	10.2	14.0	12.2	4.9	35.5	9.5	7.9	19.2

expectation of life at birth (latest year)		nuptiality, family, and family planning															country
		marriages			age at marriage (latest)						families (F), households (H) (latest)						
		year	total number	rate per 1,000 popu-lation	groom (percent)			bride (percent)			families (households)		children		induced abortions		
male	female				19 and under	20–29	30 and over	19 and under	20–29	30 and over	total ('000)	size	number under age 15	percent legiti-mate	number	ratio per 100 live births	
49.0	52.7	...	...	...	...	...	...	...	...	...	...	H 5.6	...	96.8	...	...	Djibouti
70.5	76.3	1996	230	3.1	—	37.0	63.0	2.7	56.2	41.1	H 19	H 3.6	H 2.2	24.1	...	...	Dominica
71.1	75.4	1994	14,883	2.0	...	...	...	...	...	...	H 1,804	H 3.9	...	32.8	562	0.5	Dominican Republic
...	...	...	...	...	...	...	...	...	...	...	... ...	... ...	... ...	...	...	...	East Timor[29]
68.3	74.0	1996	72,094	6.2	12.6	61.7	25.7	32.6	51.4	16.0	...	H 4.1	...	67.9	...	...	Ecuador
61.3	65.5	1994	451,817	3.2	3.4	58.7	37.9	11.2	77.1	11.7	H 9,733	H 4.9	H 2.1	100.0	...	...	Egypt
66.1	73.5	1994	27,761	5.1	6.6[25]	54.8[25]	38.6[25]	21.5[25]	51.4[25]	27.1[25]	H 1,092	H 4.8	...	29.4	...	...	El Salvador
51.5	55.7	...	...	...	...	...	...	...	...	...	...	H 4.5	...	...	...	...	Equatorial Guinea
53.4	58.3	1992	68	...	...	...	...	...	...	...	...	[31, 32]	...	...	...	...	Eritrea
65.4	76.1	1998	5,430	3.7	3.2[15]	56.4[15]	40.4[15]	13.9[15]	53.9[15]	32.2[15]	H 427	H 3.1	H 0.8	47.8	16,887	127.1	Estonia
44.4	45.9	...	...	...	...	...	...	...	...	...	...	H 4.5[31, 32]	...	...	...	...	Ethiopia
75.0	81.9	1990	203	4.3	...	...	...	...	...	...	F 14	F 3.0	F 0.9	57.5	26	3.3	Faroe Islands
65.5	70.5	1995	7,903	9.9	...	...	...	...	...	...	F 97	F 6.0	F 2.5	82.7	...	...	Fiji
73.7	81.0	1998	24,023	4.7	1.0[15]	47.1[15]	51.9[15]	3.5[15]	55.9[15]	40.6[15]	H 2,270	H 2.2	...	61.3	10,437	17.2	Finland
74.9	82.9	1997	283,984	4.8	0.2[17]	51.9[17]	47.9[17]	1.4[17]	63.2[17]	35.4[17]	H 20,899	H 2.6	H 1.0	63.9	157,886	22.2	France
72.8	79.6	1992	716	5.3	...	...	...	...	...	...	H 33	H 3.4	H 1.2	20.3	388	16.8	French Guiana
70.0	75.0	1996	1,200	5.7	...	...	...	...	...	...	H 40	H 4.3	H 1.7	40.5	...	...	French Polynesia
48.5	50.8	...	...	...	...	...	...	...	...	...	H 136	H 4.0	...	...	...	...	Gabon
50.9	54.7	...	...	...	...	...	...	...	...	...	...	H 8.3	...	...	...	...	Gambia, The
69.6	72.1	...	...	...	...	...	...	...	...	...	...	...	...	...	...	...	Gaza Strip
60.9	68.2	1996	19,253	3.7	9.1	59.4	31.5	32.7	51.2	16.1	H 1,244	H 4.1	H 1.1	82.3	43,549	77.3	Georgia
74.3	80.8	1997	422,319	5.1	0.7[15]	44.6[15]	54.7[15]	3.7[15]	56.3[15]	40.0[15]	H 37,457	H 2.2	H 0.3	82.0	97,937	12.8	Germany
55.9	58.7	...	...	...	...	...	...	...	...	...	H 2,355	H 4.9	H 2.2	...	...	...	Ghana
75.9	81.2	1998	55,489	5.3	0.9[17]	53.6[17]	45.5[17]	9.6[17]	68.9[17]	21.5[17]	H 2,990	H 3.3	H 0.7	96.7	12,289	12.1	Greece
64.5	71.7	1996	208	3.7	1.1[2]	44.6[2]	54.3[2]	2.7[2]	59.6[2]	37.7[2]	F 31	F 1.8	F 0.5	29.2	962	80.7	Greenland
62.7	66.3	1991	...	4.3	...	...	...	...	...	...	H 24	H 3.7	H 2.2	18.1	...	...	Grenada
73.8	80.3	1997	1,936	4.7	0.5[2]	51.4[2]	48.0[2]	7.2[2]	61.4[2]	31.4[2]	H 112	H 3.4	H 0.9	37.0	561	8.7	Guadeloupe
72.0	77.0	1995	1,507	10.1	3.0[25]	55.5[25]	41.5[25]	9.2[25]	59.3[25]	31.5[25]	H 31	H 4.0	H 1.3	50.1	...	...	Guam
63.5	69.0	1997	51,526	4.9	18.3	56.1	25.6	41.1	40.8	18.1	H 1,806	H 5.2	...	34.8	...	...	Guatemala
76.7	82.8	1996	340	5.8	...	...	...	...	...	...	H 21	H 2.6	H 0.5	73.2	...	...	Guernsey
43.5	48.4	...	...	...	...	...	...	...	...	...	H 1,064	H 4.1	...	...	...	...	Guinea
46.8	51.4	...	...	...	...	...	...	...	...	...	H 124	H 6.9	H 2.8	11.3	...	...	Guinea-Bissau
61.1	67.2	...	...	...	...	...	...	...	...	...	H 150	H 5.1	H 2.1	...	...	...	Guyana
47.5	51.1	...	...	...	...	...	...	...	...	...	H 1,147	H 4.4	H 1.8	...	...	...	Haiti
67.9	72.1	...	...	...	...	...	...	...	...	...	H 463	H 5.7	H 2.8	...	...	...	Honduras
77.0	82.2	1999	31,300	4.6	0.9[15]	42.7[15]	56.4[15]	3.0[15]	63.5[15]	33.5[15]	H 1,840	H 3.3	...	94.5	17,600	25.2	Hong Kong
66.3	75.1	1999	45,600	4.5	3.7[15]	69.1[15]	27.2[15]	17.5[15]	64.8[15]	17.7[15]	F 3,058	F 2.9	F 0.8	72.0	76,600	72.8	Hungary
77.5	81.4	1998	1,238	5.6	0.1[15]	40.7[15]	59.2[15]	1.2[15]	55.6[15]	43.2[15]	H 85	H 2.0	H 1.3	37.4	858	19.8	Iceland
61.9	63.1	...	...	...	...	...	...	...	...	...	H 151,033	H 5.6	H 2.4	...	581,215	...	India
65.0	69.0	1992–93[33]	1,423,774	7.6	...	...	...	...	...	...	H 39,695	H 4.5	H 1.8	...	...	...	Indonesia[29]
68.3	71.5	1996	479,263	7.8	...	...	...	...	...	...	H 9,759	H 4.8	H 2.2	...	...	...	Iran
65.5	67.6	1992	144,055	7.8	...	...	...	...	...	...	H 1,873	H 8.9	H 4.1	...	...	...	Iraq
74.1	79.7	1999	18,526	4.9	0.7[13]	62.2[13]	37.1[13]	1.6[13]	74.7[13]	23.7[13]	H 541	H 3.3	H 1.3	65.5	...	...	Ireland
73.9	80.8	1998	435	6.0	0.2	39.5	60.3	1.6	45.1	53.3	H 29,377	H 2.4	...	68.1	...	...	Isle of Man
76.6	80.5	1997	32,510	5.6	3.5[13]	74.0[13]	22.5[13]	21.2[13]	68.3[13]	10.5[13]	H 1,355	H 3.7	H 1.1	98.5	16,903	14.7	Israel
75.9	82.4	1997	275,381	4.8	0.6[17]	56.2[17]	43.2[17]	4.8[17]	71.5[17]	23.7[17]	F 19,766	F 2.6	F 0.5	90.2	134,137	25.5	Italy
73.3	77.3	1996	18,708	7.4	...	...	...	...	...	...	H 554	H 4.2	H 1.4	14.9	...	...	Jamaica
77.5	84.0	1996	795,000	6.3	1.2	61.6	37.2	2.6	77.0	20.4	H 43,447	H 2.8	...	99.0	338,867	28.1	Japan
76.1	81.1	1994	542	6.4	...	...	...	...	...	...	H 29	H 2.6	H 0.4	88.1	296	28.0	Jersey
74.9	79.9	1996	102,558	6.4	4.4[17]	70.0[17]	25.6[17]	37.3[17]	54.7[17]	8.0[17]	H 11,891	H 6.1	H 3.4	...	...	...	Jordan
59.0	71.0	1996	102,558	6.4	6.0	71.5	22.5	27.9	56.5	15.6	H 3,824	H 4.0	H 1.4	86.6	193,462	76.4	Kazakhstan
47.0	49.0	...	...	...	...	...	...	...	...	...	H 1,938	H 3.4	H 2.7	...	...	...	Kenya
56.5	62.4	...	...	...	...	...	...	...	...	...	H 11	H 6.6	H 2.5	...	...	...	Kiribati
67.8	73.9	...	...	...	...	...	...	...	...	...	H 4,054	H 4.8	H 1.7	...	...	...	Korea, North
70.5	78.4	1995	320,395	7.1	0.3	67.7	32.0	1.7	86.1	12.2	H 12,961	H 3.7	H 1.0	99.5	...	...	Korea, South
75.3	76.9	1997	9,612	5.3	6.1[25]	72.2[25]	21.7[25]	35.9[25]	53.3[25]	10.8[25]	H 246	H 3.9	H 1.6	100.0	...	...	Kuwait
64.0	72.0	1995	26,866	6.0	5.4	79.0	15.6	38.1	52.0	9.9	H 856	H 4.2	H 1.9	83.2	27,111	23.1	Kyrgyzstan
53.0	55.0	...	...	...	...	...	...	...	...	...	...	H 6.0	...	...	...	...	Laos
64.9	76.2	1998	9,641	3.9	—	61.7	38.3	—	69.0	31.0	H 732	H 2.7	H 0.8	62.9	24,227	122.5	Latvia
68.9	73.7	...	...	...	...	...	...	...	...	...	H 405	H 5.3	H 2.2	...	...	...	Lebanon
49.8	51.8	...	...	...	...	...	...	...	...	...	H 330	H 4.8	H 2.0	...	...	...	Lesotho
49.6	52.5	...	...	...	...	...	...	...	...	...	H 474	H 5.0	...	...	...	...	Liberia
73.3	77.7	...	...	...	...	...	...	...	...	...	F 383	F 5.4	F 2.9	...	...	...	Libya
75.2	82.5	1998	423	13.2	—	54.5	44.5	0.0	66.3	29.2	H 8	H 3.0	H 0.7	86.0	...	...	Liechtenstein
67.6	77.9	1997	18,769	5.0	7.1[15]	68.5[15]	24.4[15]	23.0[15]	57.8[15]	19.2[15]	H 1,000	H 2.9	H 0.8	82.0	27,829	71.0	Lithuania
73.8	80.6	1997	2,007	4.8	0.9[15]	49.1[15]	50.0[15]	4.0[15]	61.6[15]	34.4[15]	H 145	H 2.6	H 0.5	82.5	...	...	Luxembourg
77.0	81.0	1998	1,451	3.4	0.6[15]	38.6[15]	60.8[15]	2.8[15]	58.0[15]	39.2[15]	H 99	H 3.5	H 0.9	99.3	...	...	Macau
71.6	76.2	1998	13,993	7.0	5.0	75.1	19.9	26.5	63.8	9.7	H 468	H 3.8	H 1.3	90.5	18,754	57.9	Macedonia
52.7	57.3	...	...	...	...	...	...	...	...	...	H 1,709	H 4.7	H 2.0	...	...	...	Madagascar
37.2	38.0	...	...	...	...	...	...	...	...	...	...	H 4.3	...	...	...	...	Malawi
70.3	75.2	...	...	...	...	...	...	...	...	...	H 3,580	H 4.9	...	...	...	...	Malaysia
68.0	66.0	1995	4,998	19.7	13.7[18]	58.2[18]	29.1[18]	...	...	...	...	H 7.2	...	...	...	...	Maldives
45.5	47.8	...	...	...	...	...	...	...	...	...	H 1,364	H 5.0	...	...	...	...	Mali
75.5	80.6	1998	2,376	6.3	2.0[15]	74.0[15]	24.0[15]	9.5[15]	76.0[15]	14.5[15]	H 76	H 3.3	H 1.2	91.8	...	...	Malta
63.7	67.4	...	...	...	...	...	...	...	...	...	H 5	H 8.7	...	...	...	...	Marshall Islands
75.5	80.6	1993	1,555	4.2	0.1[25]	46.8[25]	53.1[25]	3.3[25]	61.5[25]	35.2[25]	H 107	H 3.3	H 0.8	34.1	1,753	30.6	Martinique
48.7	52.9	...	...	...	...	...	...	...	...	...	H 246	H 5.0	... ...	...	...	...	Mauritania
67.0	75.0	1997	10,887	9.5	1.8[15]	56.2[15]	42.0[15]	25.8[15]	54.0[15]	20.2[15]	F 155	F 5.3	F 2.0	72.8	...	...	Mauritius
57.4	61.6	...	...	...	...	...	...	...	...	...	H 19	H 4.9	H 2.3	89.2	...	...	Mayotte
68.5	74.7	1996	670,523	6.9	14.0	65.1	20.9	32.5	54.7	12.8	H 17,152	H 5.1	H 2.0	72.5	28,734	1.0	Mexico
66.7	70.6	...	...	...	...	...	...	...	...	...	H 11	H 6.8	...	...	...	...	Micronesia
59.9	69.2	1996	26,089	6.0	8.2[17]	70.0[17]	21.8[17]	38.2[17]	45.0[17]	16.8[17]	H 1,144	H 3.4	H 1.1	89.6	44,252	78.4	Moldova
74.9	83.0	...	...	...	...	...	...	...	...	...	H 14	H 2.2	H 0.3	96.8	...	...	Monaco
61.0	65.0	1996	14,200	6.0	...	...	...	...	...	...	F 428	F 4.8	...	...	...	...	Mongolia
67.2	71.7	...	...	...	...	...	...	...	...	...	H 2,819	H 5.8	H 2.5	...	...	...	Morocco

Vital statistics, marriage, family (continued)

country	vital rates						causes of death (rate per 100,000 population)								
	year	birth rate per 1,000 population	death rate per 1,000 population	infant mortality rate per 1,000 live births	rate of natural increase per 1,000 population	total fertility rate	year	infectious and parasitic diseases	malignant neoplasms (cancers)	endocrine and metabolic disorders	diseases of the nervous system	diseases of the circulatory system	diseases of the respiratory system	diseases of the digestive system	accidents, poisoning, and violence
Mozambique	2000	38.0	23.3	139.9	14.5	4.9	...	...	...	...	...	...	...	...	...
Myanmar (Burma)	2000	24.2	11.7	89.0	12.5	3.0	...	...	...	...	...	...	...	...	...
Namibia	2001	34.7	20.9	71.7	13.8	4.8	...	...	...	...	...	...	...	...	...
Nauru	2000	22.9	5.1	11.1[23]	17.8	3.8[23]	...	...	...	...	...	...	...	...	...
Nepal	2001	34.7	10.3	74.0	24.4	4.6	...	...	...	...	...	...	...	...	...
Netherlands, The	1999	12.7	8.9	5.2	3.8	1.6[10]	1995	7.6	236.1	28.1	13.3	335.1	81.8	32.6	33.5
Netherlands Antilles	1999	13.7	6.5	11.7[10]	7.2	2.1[10]	1995[39]	16.7	149.0	61.7	9.9	71.6	40.8	21.4	47.6
New Caledonia	2001	20.1	4.9	7.0	15.2	2.5	1996	17.6	110.6	8.1[16]	14.6	124.2	60.3	19.6	63.7
New Zealand	2001	14.7	6.9	5.9	7.8	2.0	1996	5.6	200.7	22.1	12.3	317.2	86.4	20.9	46.7
Nicaragua	2000	28.3	4.9	34.8	23.4	3.3	1994[38]	*68*	*62*	*25*	*12*	*156*	*64*	*29*	*120*
Niger	2000	51.5	23.2	124.9	28.3	7.2	...	...	...	...	...	...	...	...	...
Nigeria	2000	40.2	13.7	74.2	26.5	5.7	...	...	...	...	...	...	...	...	...
Northern Mariana Islands	2000	20.7	2.2	5.9[23]	18.5	1.8[23]	1994–96	[40]	33.3	10.9[5]	—	53.3	12.6[40]	—	47.0
Norway	2000	13.2	9.8	3.9	3.4	1.9[23]	1994	8.3	238.3	16.4	16.4	450.1	102.2	29.8	51.8
Oman	2000	38.1	4.2	23.3	33.9	6.1	...	...	...	...	...	...	...	...	...
Pakistan	2001	36.8	10.0	89.0	26.8	5.2	...	...	...	...	...	...	...	...	...
Palau	2000	21.1	7.2	17.7[23]	13.9	2.5[23]	1993	43.6	136.9	...	...	192.9	43.6	...	112.0
Panama	2000	19.5	5.0	20.8	14.5	2.3	1997	21.2	64.4	18.2[5]	1.3[14]	122.1	25.4	9.6	37.1
Papua New Guinea	2000	32.7	8.0	59.9	24.7	4.4	...	...	...	...	...	...	...	...	...
Paraguay	2000	31.3	4.8	30.8	26.5	4.2	1994[41]	*29*	*53*	*18*	*6*	*162*	*31*	*18*	*48*
Peru	2000	24.5	5.8	40.6	18.7	3.0	...	...	...	...	...	...	...	...	...
Philippines	2001	26.7	5.3	31.0	21.4	3.3	1996	66.7	42.9	11.0[5]	7.1	136.3	76.9	22.4	43.4
Poland	1999	9.9	9.9	8.9	0.0	1.4[10]	1995	6.4	202.3	14.0	8.1	504.5	34.3	33.0	74.5
Portugal	2000	11.5	10.2	6.1	1.3	1.5	1995	10.2	201.7	43.9	10.0	438.9	80.2	45.7	59.8
Puerto Rico	2000	15.5	7.7	9.7	7.8	1.9	1993	59.4	122.2	66.7	19.2	242.3	80.5	43.9	34.1
Qatar	2000	16.1	4.2	22.1	11.9	3.3	1992	3.4	21.4[24]	7.3[22]	2.6	59.9	7.5	3.4	36.0
Réunion	2000	21.8	5.6	8.7	16.2	1.3	1993	14.9	99.7	22.5	16.0	170.1	41.5	59.5[42]	65.3
Romania	2000	10.8	12.3	19.8	–1.5	1.4	1995	14.1	164.1	10.4	8.8	736.1	75.8	68.2	78.7
Russia	2000	8.3	14.7	16.9	–6.4	1.3	1998	19.0	203.0	11.0[13]	10.9[13]	749.0	57.0	38.0	185.0
Rwanda	2000	35.8	21.0	120.1	14.8	5.1	...	...	...	...	...	...	...	...	...
St. Kitts and Nevis	2000	19.1	9.4	16.7	9.7	2.4	1995	57.8	108.0	55.3	20.1	482.4	65.3	50.3	45.2
St. Lucia	2000	22.2	5.4	16.8	16.8	2.4	1995	20.7	98.6	79.3	13.8	226.9	29.7	21.4	50.3
St. Vincent and the Grenadines	2000	18.3	6.2	17.7[23]	12.1	2.1	1997	36.8	90.0	56.6	14.4	228.4	42.2	28.8	—
Samoa	2001	28.2	5.7	27.0	22.5	4.3	1992[37]	3.1	11.2	9.9	3.1	24.2	9.9	6.8	2.5
San Marino	2000	10.9	7.7	6.3	3.2	1.3	1991–95	...	229.4	2.4[5]	...	324.8	10.7	...	45.2
São Tomé and Príncipe	2000	43.0	7.8	50.4	35.2	6.1	...	...	...	...	...	...	...	...	...
Saudi Arabia	2000	37.5	6.0	52.9	31.5	6.3	...	...	...	...	...	...	...	...	...
Senegal	2000	37.9	8.6	58.1	29.3	5.2	...	...	...	...	...	...	...	...	...
Seychelles	2000	18.0	6.7	17.7	11.3	1.9	1994	43.3	128.6	16.2	16.2	288.4	98.8	39.3	43.3
Sierra Leone	2000	45.6	19.6	148.7	26.0	6.1	...	...	...	...	...	...	...	...	...
Singapore	2000	13.6	4.5	2.5	9.1	1.6	1995	12.4	130.5	10.9	3.0	186.1	97.5	13.7	37.3
Slovakia	2000	10.2	9.8	8.3	0.4	1.3	1997	4.0	209.0	12.0	5.0	529.0	70.0	41.0	69.0
Slovenia	1999	8.8	9.5	4.5	–0.7	1.2	1997	4.4	243.9	36.4	9.0	381.1	81.0	55.2	88.6
Solomon Islands	2001	38.3	4.8	22.0	33.5	5.4	...	...	...	...	...	...	...	...	...
Somalia	2000	47.7	18.7	125.8	29.0	7.2	...	...	...	...	...	...	...	...	...
South Africa	2000	21.6	14.7	58.9	6.9	2.5	1995	71.3	55.8	20.5	10.2	98.5	51.9	15.1	112.0
Spain	2000	9.8	9.1	5.0	0.7	1.2[23]	1995	5.9	219.8	23.1	0.4	333.6	28.0	20.4	41.3
Sri Lanka	2000	17.5	5.8	17.0	11.7	2.1	...	...	...	...	...	...	...	...	...
Sudan, The	2000	38.6	10.3	70.2	28.3	5.5	...	...	...	...	...	...	...	...	...
Suriname	2000	21.1	5.7	25.1	15.4	2.5	1992[43]	*40*	*68*	*40*	*11*	*193*	*37*	*32*	*71*
Swaziland	2000	40.6	20.4	109.0	20.2	5.9	...	...	...	...	...	...	...	...	...
Sweden	2000	10.0	10.6	3.5	–0.6	1.5	1995	8.6	234.6	23.2	14.3	525.5	85.8	33.8	48.9
Switzerland	1999	11.0	8.7	3.4	2.3	1.5	1994	16.3	238.7	23.3[20]	18.1	381.5	64.2	27.1	69.3
Syria	2000	31.1	5.3	34.8	25.8	4.1	...	...	...	...	...	...	...	...	...
Taiwan	2000	13.8	5.7	7.1	8.1	1.8	1992	...	101.5	23.7[5]	...	140.1[18]	24.3[44]	18.2[44]	63.7[44]
Tajikistan	2001	24.7	6.4	54.0	18.3	4.4	1993	128.3	40.7	8.8[2, 20]	7.9[2]	222.8	158.7	20.7	181.3
Tanzania	2000	40.2	12.9	81.0	27.3	5.5	...	...	...	...	...	...	...	...	...
Thailand	2001	16.1	6.0	18.0	10.1	1.8	1994	27.6	49.0	7.5	11.0	89.8	91.4	18.4	73.8
Togo	2000	38.0	11.2	71.6	26.8	5.5	...	...	...	...	...	...	...	...	...
Tonga	2000	27.2	6.1	37.9[23]	21.1	3.6[23]	1992	16.3	54.9	15.2	6.1	158.5	31.5	18.3	4.1
Trinidad and Tobago	1997	14.5	7.2	17.1	7.3	1.8[10]	1994	11.6	94.4	119.3	14.7	286.5	49.0	28.6	52.8
Tunisia	2000	17.1	5.6	25.8	11.5	2.1	...	...	...	...	...	...	...	...	...
Turkey	2000	18.7	6.0	48.9	12.7	2.2	1993[44]	24	80	9[5]	2[13]	369	19	10	33
Turkmenistan	2000	28.9	9.0	73.3	19.9	1.8	1994	75.7	55.4	11.2	7.6	337.2	150.3	7.6	60.1
Tuvalu	2000	21.4	7.8	26.2[19]	13.6	3.1[19]	...	...	...	...	...	...	...	...	...
Uganda	2000	48.0	18.4	93.3	29.6	7.0	...	...	...	...	...	...	...	...	...
Ukraine	2000	7.9[45]	13.9[45]	21.7	–6.0[45]	1.3	1996	17.7	192.5	8.3[20]	1.2	784.5	75.3	4.9	157.2
United Arab Emirates	2000	18.0	3.7	8.8[23]	14.3	3.3	...	...	...	...	...	...	...	...	...
United Kingdom	2000	11.7	10.4	5.6	1.3	1.7	1997	6.8	261.2	13.8	18.5	442.1	165.8	39.5	32.7
United States	1999	14.3	8.7	6.9	5.6	2.0	1997	19.6[46]	201.6	30.3	21.0	354.4	85.2	29.5	55.9
Uruguay	2000	17.4	9.1	15.1	8.3	2.4	1990	16.0	222.8	25.5	16.2	378.4	76.3	39.1	61.7
Uzbekistan	2001	21.7	5.9	38.0	15.8	3.1	1993	38.0	48.2	9.4[25]	8.9[25]	300.3	113.8	31.4	49.5
Vanuatu	2001	32.1	5.6	30.0	26.5	4.4	1994[37]	25.0	29.2	9.1	5.5	39.0	30.4	9.7	9.1
Venezuela	2000	21.1	4.9	26.2	16.2	2.5	1994	33.0	60.5	24.1	7.4	144.7	31.9	19.3	74.1
Vietnam	2000	21.6	6.3	31.1	15.3	2.5	...	...	...	...	...	...	...	...	...
Virgin Islands (U.S.)	2000	16.0	5.4	9.6	10.6	2.3	...	...	...	...	...	...	...	...	...
West Bank	2000	36.7	4.5	22.3	32.2	5.0	...	...	...	...	...	...	...	...	...
Western Sahara	2000	45.1	16.1	133.6	29.0	6.6	...	...	...	...	...	...	...	...	...
Yemen	2000	43.4	9.9	70.3	33.5	7.1	...	...	...	...	...	...	...	...	...
Yugoslavia	1997	12.4	10.6	14.3	1.8	1.7	1995	9.0	167.7[24]	23.8	10.1	573.7	40.9	28.3	42.2
Zambia	2000	41.9	22.1	92.4	19.8	5.6	...	...	...	...	...	...	...	...	...
Zimbabwe	2000	25.0	22.4	62.3	2.6	3.3	1990	64.7	28.4	4.9	9.4	40.8	39.5	12.1	44.9

[1]Excludes nomadic tribes. [2]1991. [3]1986. [4]Septicemia only. [5]Diabetes mellitus only. [6]Cerebrovascular disease and heart disease only. [7]Chronic obstructive pulmonary diseases, pneumonia, and influenza only. [8]Official government figures. [9]1998–2000 average. [10]2000. [11]Under 21 years of age. [12]21–29 years of age. [13]1994. [14]Meningitis only. [15]1996. [16]1989. [17]1995. [18]1993. [19]1998. [20]Includes nutritional disorders. [21]1996–98 average. [22]1990. [23]1999. [24]Includes benign neoplasms (cancers). [25]1992. [26]Results based on a sample population of about 100,000. [27]Millions of households. [28]Projected rates based on about 60 percent of the total deaths. [29]Indonesia includes East Timor. [30]Projected rates based on about 75 percent of the total deaths.

expectation of life at birth (latest year)		nuptiality, family, and family planning															country
		marriages			age at marriage (latest)						families (F), households (H) (latest)						
					groom (percent)			bride (percent)			families (households)		children		induced abortions		
male	female	year	total number	rate per 1,000 population	19 and under	20–29	30 and over	19 and under	20–29	30 and over	total ('000)	size	number under age 15	percent legitimate	number	ratio per 100 live births	
38.3	36.7	...	...	...	...	...	...	...	...	...	F 1,860	F 4.4	F 2.0	73.1	...	...	Mozambique
59.0	63.0	...	...	...	...	...	...	...	...	...	...	H 5.6	...	...	...	...	Myanmar (Burma)
42.5	38.7	...	...	...	...	...	...	...	...	...	...	H 5.2	...	...	...	...	Namibia
57.0	64.1	1995	57	5.3	...	...	...	...	...	...	H 1	H 8.0	H 2.6	...	...	...	Nauru
59.0	59.0	...	...	...	...	...	...	...	...	...	H 3,345	H 5.6	H 2.3	...	...	...	Nepal
75.2	80.7	1998	87,000	5.5	0.5[15]	47.4[15]	52.1[15]	3.2[15]	60.9[15]	35.9[15]	H 6,185	H 2.3	H 0.4	77.3	22,441	11.8	Netherlands, The
72.6	77.0	1998	1,276	6.1	...	...	...	...	...	...	H 41	H 3.7	H 2.1	51.6	...	...	Netherlands Antilles
72.0	77.0	1999	934	4.5	0.1[12]	46.5[12]	53.4[12]	5.0[12]	61.2[12]	33.8[12]	H 51	H 3.8	...	36.4	...	...	New Caledonia
75.7	80.8	1996	21,506	6.0	0.8[12]	50.6[12]	48.6[12]	3.2[12]	60.8[12]	36.0[12]	H 1,178	H 2.8	H 0.7	58.0	11,460	19.3	New Zealand
66.8	70.8	1991	13,122	3.3	...	...	...	...	...	...	H 752	H 5.8	...	...	...	...	Nicaragua
41.4	41.1	...	...	...	...	...	...	...	...	...	H 1,130	H 6.3	...	...	...	...	Niger
51.6	51.6	...	...	...	...	...	...	...	...	...	H 21,283	H 4.7	...	...	...	...	Nigeria
72.0	78.4	...	...	...	...	...	...	...	...	...	H 7	H 4.6	H 1.5	51.2	...	...	Northern Mariana Islands
75.6	81.1	1996	23,172	5.3	0.4	43.5	56.1	2.1	59.1	38.8	H 1,864	H 2.3	...	51.0	13,672	22.6	Norway
69.7	74.0	...	...	...	...	...	...	...	...	...	...	H 8.0	...	...	...	...	Oman
61.0	60.0	...	...	...	...	...	...	...	...	...	...	H 6.3	...	...	...	...	Pakistan
65.2	71.5	...	...	...	...	...	...	...	...	...	...	H 4.9	...	...	...	...	Palau
72.7	78.3	1995	8,841	3.4	2.4	52.3	45.3	10.4	57.2	32.4	H 524	H 4.4	H 1.5	25.5	...	...	Panama
61.1	65.3	...	...	...	...	...	...	...	...	...	H 674	H 4.6	...	...	...	...	Papua New Guinea
71.2	76.3	1994	23,649	5.0	4.2[25]	64.8[25]	31.0[25]	30.4[25]	50.2[25]	19.4[25]	H 868	H 4.7	1.9	68.7	...	...	Paraguay
67.6	72.5	1993	90,000	4.1	...	...	...	...	...	...	H 3,099	H 5.1	...	57.8	...	...	Peru
68.0	72.0	1993	474,407	7.1	4.9	66.3	28.8	18.0	63.8	18.2	F 9,566	F 5.7	F 2.4	93.9	2,315	...	Philippines
69.0	77.6	1996	203,641	5.3	2.8	77.2	20.0	16.6	70.5	12.9	F 9,435	F 3.6	F 0.9	95.0	491	0.1	Poland
72.2	79.5	1997	63,542	6.5	3.1[15]	70.0[15]	26.9[15]	13.9[15]	68.1[15]	18.0[15]	H 3,150	H 3.1	H 0.8	85.5	...	...	Portugal
71.1	80.3	1996	32,572	8.7	8.5	53.8	37.7	19.4	49.3	31.4	H 1,005	H 3.6	H 1.0	59.6	...	...	Puerto Rico
69.9	74.9	1996	1,641	2.9	4.9	67.5	27.6	29.6	59.7	10.7	H 61	H 6.4	...	...	...	...	Qatar
69.3	76.2	1996	3,313	4.9	1.2[22]	65.2[22]	33.6[22]	12.5[22]	66.8[22]	20.7[22]	H 185	H 3.5	...	44.1	4,302	31.7	Réunion
66.1	74.0	1997	147,105	6.5	2.6[15]	76.0[15]	21.4[15]	25.4[15]	62.1[15]	12.5[15]	H 7,115	H 3.1	...	...	456,221	197.2	Romania
59.9	72.4	1995	1,074,900	7.3	6.5	64.5	29.0	28.5	47.7	23.8	H 40,426	H 3.2	H 0.8	70.5	2,766,362	202.8	Russia
38.6	40.1	...	...	...	...	...	...	...	...	...	H 1,509	H 4.7	2.3	94.9	...	...	Rwanda
67.9	73.7	...	...	...	...	...	...	...	...	...	H 12	H 3.7	H 1.4	19.2	...	...	St. Kitts and Nevis
68.7	76.1	1997	467	3.1	0.8[16]	34.4[16]	64.8[16]	3.5[16]	45.1[16]	51.4[16]	H 33	H 4.0	H 2.0	14.2	...	...	St. Lucia
70.6	74.1	1997	508	4.6	1.0[25]	37.0[25]	62.0[25]	4.8[25]	46.3[25]	48.9[25]	H 27	H 3.9	H 2.0	...	...	...	St. Vincent and the Grenadines
67.0	73.0	1997	...	4.6	0.5[18]	51.0[18]	48.5[18]	8.0[18]	65.0[18]	27.0[18]	F 20	F 7.8	F 3.8	43.5	...	...	Samoa
77.6	85.0	1996	191	7.5	0.6[16]	75.1[16]	24.3[16]	5.3[16]	85.3[16]	9.5[16]	H 9	H 2.6	H 0.4	95.2	...	...	San Marino
63.8	66.7	...	...	...	...	...	...	...	...	...	...	H 4.0	...	...	...	...	São Tomé and Príncipe
66.1	69.5	...	...	...	...	...	...	...	...	...	H 1,513	H 6.1	...	...	...	...	Saudi Arabia
60.6	63.8	...	...	...	...	...	...	...	...	...	...	H 8.7	...	...	...	...	Senegal
64.9	76.1	1996	875	11.4	2.0[13]	45.8[13]	42.2[13]	11.2[13]	51.5[13]	29.6[13]	H 13	H 4.8	H 1.9	27.2	387	22.8	Seychelles
42.4	48.2	...	...	...	...	...	...	...	...	...	...	H 6.6	...	...	...	...	Sierra Leone
76.0	80.0	1997	25,667	6.9	0.5	57.3	42.2	3.1	74.5	22.4	H 662	H 4.2	H 1.3	...	14,362	29.6	Singapore
69.7	78.0	1996	27,484	5.1	6.0[17]	76.2[17]	17.8[17]	27.4[17]	62.4[17]	10.2[17]	...	H 3.2	...	83.1	35,879	58.4	Slovakia
71.0	79.0	1996	7,555	3.8	0.5	63.2	36.3	5.8	72.7	21.5	H 637	H 3.1	...	64.4	10,218	54.4	Slovenia
68.0	70.0	...	...	...	...	...	...	...	...	...	...	H 5.8	...	...	...	...	Solomon Islands
44.7	47.9	...	...	...	...	...	...	...	...	...	...	H 4.9	...	...	...	...	Somalia
50.4	51.8	1995	148,148	3.6	0.3	39.7	60.0	2.8	54.9	42.3	H 8,688	H 4.6	...	75.9	...	...	South Africa
74.4	81.6	1996	194,635	5.0	1.2[17]	62.5[17]	36.3[17]	5.0[17]	72.8[17]	22.2[17]	F 10,665	F 3.5	...	89.5	47,832	13.1	Spain
71.0	76.0	1996	170,444	9.3	1.3	64.3	34.4	16.7	67.1	16.2	H 3,282	H 4.6	...	96.3	...	...	Sri Lanka
55.5	57.7	...	...	...	...	...	...	...	...	...	H 3,471	H 5.3	...	...	...	...	Sudan, The
68.7	74.1	1995	2,249	5.5	...	...	...	...	...	...	...	H 4.8	...	...	...	...	Suriname
39.5	41.4	...	...	...	...	...	...	...	...	...	H 122	H 5.7	...	...	1,145	...	Swaziland
77.0	82.4	1996	33,484	3.4	0.3	40.5	59.2	1.5	54.0	44.5	H 3,670	H 2.1	H 0.5	46.1	32,117	33.7	Sweden
76.7	82.6	1997	37,575	5.3	0.4[15]	43.6[15]	56.0[15]	2.8[15]	58.8[15]	38.4[15]	H 3,250	H 2.0	0.4	91.2	...	...	Switzerland
67.4	69.6	1994	115,994	8.4	...	...	...	...	...	...	F 1,151	H 6.2	F 2.4	...	...	...	Syria
73.6	79.3	1998	145,678	6.7	1.5[22]	62.3[22]	36.2[22]	6.0[22]	77.7[22]	16.3[22]	H 5,964	H 3.6	H 1.0	97.2	...	...	Taiwan
65.0	71.0	1994	38,820	6.8	10.7	80.6	8.7	49.6	45.7	4.7	H 799	H 6.1	H 2.7	93.0	35,709	22.0	Tajikistan
51.3	53.2	...	...	...	...	...	...	...	...	...	H 3,435	H 5.2	H 2.3	...	...	...	Tanzania
71.0	76.0	1995	470,751	7.9	...	...	...	...	...	...	H 15,551	H 3.8	...	...	...	...	Thailand
52.8	56.7	...	...	...	...	...	...	...	...	...	H 479	H 6.0	...	...	...	...	Togo
67.7	72.2	1994	748	7.7	16.3	63.0	20.7	5.1	65.0	29.9	F 15	F 6.3	F 2.7	80.6	...	...	Tonga
65.4	70.6	1996	7,118	5.6	4.3	54.9	40.8	20.0	52.8	27.2	H 301	H 3.8	H 1.3	...	9	—	Trinidad and Tobago
72.1	75.4	1997	57,100	6.2	...	60.5[25]	39.5[25]	24.7[25]	62.7[25]	20.2[25]	H 1,703	H 5.1	H 1.9	99.8	23,300	10.9	Tunisia
68.6	73.4	1996	486,734	7.8	5.9[17]	74.5[17]	19.6[17]	31.4[17]	58.5[17]	10.1[17]	...	H 4.5	...	...	...	...	Turkey
57.3	64.7	1993	42,106	10.7	3.0[16]	87.4[16]	9.6[16]	16.1[16]	77.1[16]	6.8[16]	H 598	H 5.6	H 2.4	96.5	39,068	31.3	Turkmenistan
62.7	65.1	...	...	...	...	...	...	...	...	...	H 1	H 6.4	H 2.2	82.2	...	...	Tuvalu
42.2	43.7	...	...	...	...	...	...	...	...	...	H 2,766	H 4.8	...	...	...	...	Uganda
60.6	72.0	1997	345,000	6.5	7.5	68.4	24.1	35.2	45.9	18.9	H 14,507	H 3.2	H 0.8	89.2	957,022	159.5	Ukraine
71.6	76.6	1995	...	2.7	...	...	...	...	...	...	H 247	H 5.3	...	...	...	...	United Arab Emirates
75.0	80.5	1995	282,900	5.5	0.8	49.1	50.1	3.6	57.4	39.0	H 29,533	H 2.4	H 1.7	63.2	167,297	22.8	United Kingdom
74.1	79.7	1996	2,324,000	8.8	4.3[22]	51.8[22]	43.9[22]	10.9[22]	55.8[22]	35.3[22]	H 96,391	H 2.6	F 1.0	67.2	1,359,145	32.0	United States
71.9	78.8	1996	17,596	5.5	6.9[25]	57.2[25]	35.9[25]	23.5[25]	51.4[25]	25.1[25]	H 863	H 3.3	H 0.9	73.8	...	...	Uruguay
66.0	72.0	1994	176,300	7.8	11.2	80.7	8.1	49.3	45.3	5.4	H 3,415	H 5.5	H 2.4	95.8	120,434	18.3	Uzbekistan
67.0	70.0	...	...	...	...	...	...	...	...	...	H 28	H 5.1	H 2.2	...	113	2.4	Vanuatu
70.1	76.3	1996	81,951	3.7	9.5	58.7	31.8	27.9	51.7	20.4	H 2,707	H 5.3	H 2.2	47.0	...	...	Venezuela
66.8	71.9	...	...	...	...	...	...	...	...	...	H 12,958[47]	H 4.8[47]	H 1.9[47]	...	...	...	Vietnam
74.2	82.5	1993	3,646	35.1	0.4	33.6	66.0	1.9	45.9	52.2	H 32	H 3.1	H 1.0	30.2	...	...	Virgin Islands (U.S.)
70.4	73.9	...	...	...	...	...	...	...	...	...	...	...	...	...	...	...	West Bank
48.7	51.3	...	...	...	...	...	...	...	...	...	...	...	...	...	...	...	Western Sahara
58.1	61.6	...	...	...	...	...	...	...	...	...	H 1,848	H 5.6	...	...	...	...	Yemen
69.9	74.7	1997	56,004	5.3	2.3[17]	64.5[17]	33.2[17]	18.7[17]	63.5[17]	17.8[17]	H 2,870	H 3.6	H 0.9	...	91,474	65.1	Yugoslavia
37.1	37.4	...	...	...	...	...	...	...	...	...	H 1,370	H 4.4	H 2.1	...	...	...	Zambia
39.2	36.4	...	...	...	...	...	...	...	...	...	H 2,166	H 4.8	1.1	95.8	...	...	Zimbabwe

[31]Ethiopia includes Eritrea. [32]Based on a sample registration scheme. [33]Muslims only. [34]Projected rates based on about 20 percent of the total deaths. [35]1997–99 average. [36]1997. [37]Registered deaths only. [38]Projected rates based on about 45 percent of the total deaths. [39]Includes Aruba. [40]Diseases of the respiratory system included in infectious and parasitic diseases. [41]Reporting areas only (constituting about 75 percent of the total population). [42]Includes all deaths associated with alcoholism. [43]Projected rates based on about 70 percent of the total deaths. [44]Projected rates based on about 35 percent of the total deaths. [45]Average of April to September only. [46]Of which AIDS, 6.2. [47]Private households only.

National product and accounts

This table furnishes, for most of the countries of the world, breakdowns of (1) gross national product (GNP)—its global and per capita values, and purchasing power parity (PPP), (2) growth rates (1990–99) and principal industrial and accounting components of gross domestic product (GDP), and (3) principal elements of each country's balance of payments, including international goods trade, invisibles, external public debt outstanding, and tourism payments.

Measures of national output. The two most commonly used measures of national output are GDP and GNP. Each of these measures represents an aggregate value of goods and services produced by a specific country. The GDP, the more basic of these, is a measure of the total value of goods and services produced entirely within a given country. The GNP, the more comprehensive value, is composed of both domestic production (GDP) and the net income from current (short-term) transactions with other countries. When the income received from other countries is greater than payments to them, a country's GNP is greater than its GDP. In theory, if all national accounts could be equilibrated, the global summation of GDP would equal GNP.

In the first section of the table, data are provided for the nominal and real GNP. ("Nominal" refers to value in current prices for the year indicated and is distinguished from a "real" valuation, which is one adjusted to eliminate the effect of recent inflation [most often] or, occasionally, of deflation between two given dates.) Both the total and per capita values of this product are denominated in U.S. dollars for ease of comparison, as is a new value for GNP per capita adjusted for purchasing power parity. The latter is a concept that provides a better approximation of the ability of equivalent values of two (or more) national currencies to purchase comparable quantities of goods and services in their respective domestic markets and may differ substantially from two otherwise equal GNP per capita values based solely on currency exchange rates. Beside these are given figures for average annual growth of total and per capita real GNP. GNP per capita provides a rough measure of annual national income per person, but values should be compared cautiously, as they are subject to a number of distortions, notably of exchange rate, but also of purchasing power parity and in the existence of elements of national production that do not enter the monetary economy in such a way as to be visible to fiscal authorities (*e.g.*, food, clothing, or housing produced and consumed within families or communal groups or services exchanged). For reasons of comparability, the majority of the data in this section are taken from the World Bank's *The World Bank Atlas* (annual).

The internal structure of the national product. GDP/GNP values allow comparison of the relative size of national economies, but further information is provided when these aggregates are analyzed according to their industrial sectors of origin, component kinds of expenditure, and cost components.

The distribution of GDP for ten industrial sectors, usually compiled from national sources, is aggregated into three major industrial groups:

1. The primary sector, composed of agriculture (including forestry and fishing) and mineral production (including fossil fuels).

National product and accounts

country	gross national product (GNP), 1999			gross domestic product (GDP), 1990–99			origin of gross domestic product (GDP) by economic sector, 1998 (%)										
	nominal ('000,000 U.S.$)	per capita		average annual growth rates, 1990–99			primary		secondary			tertiary					other
		nominal (U.S.$)	purchasing power parity (PPP; U.S.$)	real GDP (%)	population (%)	real GDP per capita (%)	agriculture	mining	manufacturing	construction	public utilities	transp., communications	trade	financial svcs.	other svcs.	government	
Afghanistan	5,666[1]	250[1]	...	...	...	...	...	...	...	...	...	...	...	...	...	...	...
Albania	3,146	930	3,240	3.4	0.6	2.8	54	[2]	12[2]	13	[2]	3	—18—				—
Algeria	46,548	1,550	4,840	1.7	2.2	–0.5	11	23	10	11	—	—24—				13	8
American Samoa	253[1]	4,300[1]	...	...	...	...	...	...	...	...	...	...	...	...	...	...	...
Andorra	850[3]	13,100[3]	...	...	...	...	...	...	...	...	...	...	...	...	...	...	...
Angola	3,276	270	1,100	–0.5	2.3	–2.8	13	45	6	6	—	—18—		—11—			1
Antigua and Barbuda	606	8,990	9,870	3.8	1.1	2.7	3	1	2	10	3	17	19	14	6	15	10
Argentina	296,097	7,550	11,940	4.9	1.3	3.6	5[3]	2[3]	20[3]	6[3]	2[3]	6[3]	14[3]	18[3]	—24[3]—		3[3]
Armenia	1,878	490	2,360	–3.1	0.8	–3.9	31	[2]	22[2]	9	[2]	5	9	—25—			–1
Aruba	1,728[4, 5]	18,700[4, 5]	...	...	...	...	...	...	...	...	...	...	...	...	...	...	...
Australia	397,345	20,950	23,850	4.1	1.2	2.9	3	4	13	6	2	8	10	16	33	4	1
Austria	205,743	25,430	24,600	1.9	0.5	1.4	3	1	24	7	3	8	19	18	6	10	1
Azerbaijan	3,705	460	2,450	–9.5	1.2	–10.7	20[3]	[2]	25[2, 3]	14[3]	[2]	10[3]	—31[3]—				—
Bahamas, The	3,288[3]	11,830[3]	...	...	...	...	1[6]	15[6]	17[6]	6[6]	2[6]	11[6]	11[6]	19[6]	5[6]	19[6]	–6[6]
Bahrain	4,909[4]	7,640[4]	...	...	...	...	1[7]	17[7]	22[7]	6[7]	2[7]	9[7]	11[7]	18[7]	5[7]	19[7]	–10[7]
Bangladesh	41,071	370	1,530	4.7	1.6	3.1	23	1	18	7	1	10	15	11	11	2	1
Barbados	2,294	8,600	14,010	1.8	0.3	1.5	6	1	10	8	4	8	35	—17—		12	–1
Belarus	26,299	2,620	6,880	–3.1	–0.2	–2.9	13	[8]	36[8]	7	4	12	12	—16—			—
Belgium	252,051	24,650	25,710	1.7	0.3	1.4	1[3]	—	21[3]	5[3]	2[3]	8[3]	12[3]	14[3]	7[3]	24[3]	6[3]
Belize	673	2,730	4,750	3.2	2.5	0.7	18	1	13	5	2	12	15	8	6	6	14
Benin	2,320	380	920	5.0	3.2	1.8	38[3]	[8]	9[3, 8]	4[3]	1[3]	7[3]	18[3]	9[3]	—7[3]—		7[3]
Bermuda	2,128[3]	34,950[3]	...	...	...	...	...	...	...	...	...	...	...	...	...	...	...
Bhutan	399	510	1,260	6.1	2.7	3.4	38	2	12	11	11	8	7	5	—9—		–3
Bolivia	8,092	990	2,300	4.2	2.4	1.8	15	11	18	5	1	12	9	13	6	10	—
Bosnia and Herzegovina	4,706	1,210	...	...	...	...	12	...	24	6	3	9	19	4	14	8	—
Botswana	5,139	3,240	6,540	3.8	2.0	1.8	3	36	5	6	2	4	18	8	4	14	—
Brazil	730,424	4,350	6,840	3.0	1.5	1.5	7[3]	1[3]	19[3]	9[3]	3[3]	5[3]	7[3]	20[3]	11[3]	13[3]	5[3]
Brunei	7,209[4]	22,280[4]	...	...	...	...	3	[8]	37[8]	7	1	4	10	9	—33—		–4
Bulgaria	11,572	1,410	5,070	–2.8	–0.7	–2.1	19	1	17	3	4	7	7	2	—29—		11
Burkina Faso	2,602	240	960	4.2	2.8	1.4	30	[8]	20[8]	5	1	4	12	—22—			6
Burundi	823	120	570	–3.9	1.1	–5.0	46	1[9]	9	5	[9]	4	4	—2—		18	11
Cambodia	3,023	260	1,350	5.2	3.3	1.9	51	—	6	7	1	4	15	5	7	3	1
Cameroon	8,798	600	1,490	1.3	2.8	–1.5	41	5	10	4	1	—35—					4
Canada	614,003	20,140	25,440	2.8	1.1	1.7	2	4	18	6	3	8	12	16	24	6	1
Cape Verde	569	1,330	4,450	4.6	1.4	3.2	12	—	10	9	—	18	19	12	7	14	–1
Central African Republic	1,035	290	1,150	2.0	2.3	–0.3	49	4	8	4	1	2	12	—6—		6	8
Chad	1,555	210	840	2.5	3.4	–0.9	37	1	12	2	1	—24—		—9—		11	3
Chile	69,602	4,630	8,410	7.1	1.5	5.6	7	9	15	5	2	9	18	17	6	2	10
China	979,894	780	3,550	10.8	1.3	9.5	18	[2]	42[2]	7	[2]	6	8	—18—			1
Colombia	90,007	2,170	5,580	3.3	1.9	1.4	14	4	14	5	...	8	12	—34—		9	—
Comoros	189	350	1,430	–0.1	3.0	–3.1	40	...	4	6	1	5	25	3	1	13	2
Congo, Dem. Rep. of the	5,433[4]	110[4]	...	...	...	...	58[7]	4[7]	6[7]	2[7]	2[7]	3[7]	17[7]	—6[7]—		1[7]	1[7]
Congo, Rep. of the	1,571	550	540	–0.8	2.5	–3.3	11[7]	33[7]	8[7]	2[7]	1[7]	12[7]	9[7]	—8[7]—		13[7]	3[7]
Costa Rica	12,828	3,570	7,880	5.0	2.0	3.0	15	[8]	19[8]	2	3	6	21	12	8	14	—
Côte d'Ivoire	10,387	670	1,540	3.6	3.0	0.6	28	[2]	20[2]	5	[2]	8	15	—12—		8	4
Croatia	20,222	4,530	7,260	0.4	–0.6	1.0	7	[8]	24[8]	6	3	8	12	13	—14—		13
Cuba	18,600[5]	1,700[5]	...	...	...	...	7[3]	2[3]	37[3]	5[3]	2[3]	4[3]	21[3]	2[3]	—19[3]—		2[3]
Cyprus[10]	9,086	11,950	19,080	4.2	1.4	2.8	4	—	11	8	2	9	20	19	10	14	3
Czech Republic	51,623	5,020	12,840	0.9	–0.0	0.9	4	[2]	32[2]	7	[2]	9	12	17	—13—		6
Denmark	170,685	32,050	25,600	2.4	0.4	2.0	4[3]	1[3]	20[3]	6[3]	2[3]	10[3]	13[3]	19[3]	6[3]	22[3]	–3[3]
Djibouti	511	790	...	–3.0	2.1	–5.1	3	—	5	8	5	17	16	10	5	20	11
Dominica	238	3,260	5,040	2.4	0.6	1.8	20	1	9	8	5	17	14	14	1	19	–8
Dominican Republic	16,130	1,920	5,210	5.7	1.8	3.9	12	2	17	12	2	12	20	9	8	8	–2
East Timor	113[4, 5]	130[4, 5]	...	...	...	...	...	...	...	...	...	...	...	...	...	...	...
Ecuador	16,841	1,360	2,820	2.1	2.1	0.0	17[3]	15[3]	15[3]	2[3]	1[3]	9[3]	15[3]	12[3]	6[3]	7[3]	1[3]

2. The secondary sector, composed of manufacturing, construction, and public utilities.
3. The tertiary sector, which includes transportation and communications, trade (wholesale and retail), restaurants and hotels, financial services (including banking, real estate, insurance, and business services), other services (community, social, and personal), and government services.

The category "other" contains adjustments such as import duties and bank service charges that are not distributed by sector.

There are three major domestic components of GDP expenditure: private consumption (analyzed in greater detail in the "Household budgets and consumption" table), government spending, and gross domestic investment. The fourth, nondomestic, component of GDP expenditure is net foreign trade; values are given for both exports (a positive value) and imports (a negative value, representing obligations to other countries). The sum of these five percentages, excluding statistical discrepancies and rounding, should be 100% of the GDP.

Balance of payments (external account transactions). The external account records the sum (net) of all economic transactions of a current nature between one country and the rest of the world. The account shows a country's net of overseas receipts and obligations, including not only the trade of goods and merchandise but also such invisible items as services, interest and dividends, short- and long-term investments, tourism, transfers to or from overseas residents, etc. Each transaction gives rise either to a foreign claim for payment, recorded as a deficit (*e.g.*, from imports, capital outflows), or a foreign obligation to pay, recorded as a surplus (*e.g.*, from exports, capital inflows) or a domestic claim on another country. Any international transaction automatically creates a deficit in the balance of payments of one country and a surplus in that of another. Values are given in U.S. dollars for comparability.

External public debt. Because the majority of the world's countries are in the less developed bloc, and because their principal financial concern is often external debt and its service, data are given for outstanding external public and publicly guaranteed long-term debt rather than for total public debt, which is the major concern in the developed countries. For comparability, the data are given in U.S. dollars. The data presented in the table come from the World Bank's *Global Development Finance* (formerly *World Debt Tables*).

Tourist trade. Net income or expenditure from tourism (in U.S. dollars for comparability) is often a significant element in a country's balance of payments. Receipts from foreign nationals reflect payments for goods and services from foreign currency resources by tourists in the given country. Expenditures by nationals abroad are also payments for goods and services, but in this case made by the residents of the given country as tourists abroad. The majority of the data in this section are compiled by the World Tourism Organization.

gross domestic product (GDP) by type of expenditure, 1998 (%)					external public debt outstanding (long-term, disbursed only), 1999						balance of payments, 1999 (current external transactions; '000,000 U.S.$)			tourist trade, 1997 ('000,000 U.S.$)		country
consumption		gross domestic investment	foreign trade		total ('000,000 U.S.$)	creditors (%)		debt service			net transfers		current balance of payments	receipts from foreign nationals	expenditures by nationals abroad	
private	government		exports	imports		official	private	total ('000,000 U.S.$)	repayment (%) principal	repayment (%) interest	goods, merchandise	invisibles				
…	…	…	…	…	…	…	…	…	…	…	…	…	…	1	1	Afghanistan
…	…	…	…	…	849.1	70.7	29.3	27.1	28.4	71.6	–663.0	507.6	–155.4	27	5	Albania
51	17	27	28	–23	25,913	71.3	28.7	4,885	64.7	35.3	3,360	–3,340	20	20	64	Algeria
…	…	…	…	…	…	…	…	…	…	…	…	…	…	10	…	American Samoa
…	…	…	…	…	…	…	…	…	…	…	…	…	…	…	…	Andorra
…	…	…	…	…	9,248	39.6	60.4	1,099	89.6	10.4	1,463.5[4]	–3,323.1[4]	–1,857.6[4]	9	73	Angola
58	22	32	73	–84	…	…	…	…	…	…	–321.0[4]	202.7[4]	88.6[4]	260	26	Antigua and Barbuda
— 71 —		20	10	–13	84,568	24.8	75.2	12,170	48.1	51.9	–770	–11,676	–12,446	5,069	2,680	Argentina
103	11	19	19	–53	681.9	100.0	—	39.8	64.6	35.4	–474.0	167.0	–307.1	7	41	Armenia
73	13	11	— 2 —		…	…	…	…	…	…	–591.7	258.5	–333.2	666	130	Aruba
59	18	24	20	–22	…	…	…	…	…	…	–9,730	–13,340	–23,070	9,026	6,129	Australia
55	20	26	44	–45	…	…	…	…	…	…	–3,649	–2,098	–5,747	12,393	10,992	Austria
78[3]	12[3]	38[3]	28[3]	–55[3]	493.3	91.1	8.9	49.8	81.5	18.5	–408.2	–191.5	–599.7	159	72	Azerbaijan
66[7]	15[7]	23[7]	54[7]	–58[7]	…	…	…	…	…	…	–1,428.2	756.3	–671.9	1,416	250	Bahamas, The
51	21	18	78	–68	…	…	…	…	…	…	672.1	–1,012.5	–340.4	260	129	Bahrain
78	14	13	19	–23	16,962	99.4	0.6	675	72.3	27.7	–1,962.1	1,670.6	–291.5	59	170	Bangladesh
59	21	20	58	–57	359.1	75.4	24.6	84.2	64.4	35.6	–691.7	565.9	–125.8	717	74	Barbados
58	20	27	60	–65	851	52.8	47.2	141	64.5	35.5	–570.0	376.3	–193.7	25	114	Belarus
54	21	21	76	–72	…	…	…	…	…	…	6,642	6,732	13,374	5,275	8,275	Belgium
65	17	27	52	–61	294.6	73.6	26.4	40.2	59.6	40.4	–128.8	51.4	–77.4	87	30	Belize
81	9	18	27	–35	1,472	99.8	0.2	56	64.3	35.7	–158.3[4]	6.8[4]	–151.5[4]	31	7	Benin
…	…	…	…	…	…	…	…	…	…	…	…	…	…	474	148	Bermuda
36[1]	29[1]	44[1]	34[1]	–44[1]	181.8	100.0	—	6.9	71.0	29.0	–24.8[4]	–21.7[4]	–46.5[4]	6	…	Bhutan
75	14	23	20	–32	3,864	99.4	0.6	257	57.0	43.0	–488.0	–67.8	–555.8	170	172	Bolivia
— 100 —		38	35	–73	1,826	92.6	7.4	388	64.3	35.7	–2,072.0	1,284.6	–787.4	15	…	Bosnia and Herzegovina
28	29	28	56	–41	442.3	95.2	4.8	82.5	74.7	25.3	674.5	–157.7	516.8	184	140	Botswana
64	18	21	7	–10	95,233	33.8	66.2	24,374	72.1	27.9	–1,261	–24,139	–25,400	2,595	6,583	Brazil
…	…	…	…	…	…	…	…	…	…	…	175[4]	1,910[4]	2,085[4]	39	…	Brunei
72	15	14	44	–45	7,602	32.8	67.2	632	49.5	50.5	–1,081.0	396.3	–684.7	368	222	Bulgaria
81	10	24	15	–30	1,295	99.7	0.3	53	69.8	30.2	–184.5	–38.6	–223.1	39	32	Burkina Faso
96	12	3	8	–19	1,050	99.9	0.1	20	70.0	30.0	–42.3	15.3	–27.0	1	10	Burundi
96[1]	7[1]	16[1]	28[1]	–46[1]	2,136	100.0	—	28	51.8	48.2	–209.5	143.5	–66.0	143	12	Cambodia
71	9	18	26	–27	7,614	95.2	4.8	346	47.8	52.2	112.4	–343.7	–231.3	39	107	Cameroon
59	20	20	41	–40	…	…	…	…	…	…	22,756	–25,029	–2,273	8,770	11,304	Canada
68	23	40	25	–57	265.1	95.7	4.3	21.6	84.7	15.3	–185.6[4]	127.6[4]	–58.0[4]	15	17	Cape Verde
84	12	14	16	–25	830.1	96.1	3.9	11.9	60.9	39.1	–8.3[4]	–79.1[4]	–87.4[4]	5	39	Central African Republic
90	10	15	18	–33	1,045	98.5	1.5	27	61.1	38.9	–50.3[4]	–155.8[4]	–206.1[4]	9	24	Chad
67	11	26	25	–29	5,655	37.1	62.9	780	60.1	39.9	1,664	–1,744	–80	1,021	946	Chile
46	12	38	— 4 —		108,163	46.6	53.4	15,668	68.2	31.8	36,207	–20,540	15,667	12,074	10,166	China
68	19	20	15	–22	19,434	39.6	60.4	4,775	65.5	34.5	1,776	–1,837	–61	955	958	Colombia
91[1]	15[1]	19[1]	20[1]	–45[1]	179.9	100.0	—	7.1	87.3	12.7	–35.6[4]	40.8[4]	5.2[4]	26	8	Comoros
81[7]	5[7]	9[7]	28[7]	–23[7]	8,188	93.8	6.2	—	—	—	830[1]	–1,375[1]	–515[1]	2	7	Congo, Dem. Rep. of the
46	16	26	67	–55	3,932	80.1	19.9	—	—	—	644.1	–885.7	–241.6	3	36	Congo, Rep. of the
56	16	28	50	–50	3,186	64.0	36.0	475	70.3	29.7	659.6	–1,309.1	–649.5	719	358	Costa Rica
64	11	19	44	–37	9,699	74.8	28.2	992	53.8	46.2	1,832.3[4]	–2,144.9[4]	–312.6[4]	88	282	Côte d'Ivoire
59[1]	29[1]	22[1]	42[1]	–52[1]	5,433	26.3	73.7	667	47.1	52.9	–3,298.7	1,776.5	–1,522.2	2,529	521	Croatia
71[1]	24[1]	7[1]	16[1]	–18[1]	…	…	…	…	…	…	…	…	…	1,338	…	Cuba
64	19	25	44	–52	…	…	…	…	…	…	–2,309.2	2,075.5	–233.7	1,639	278	Cyprus[10]
52	19	30	60	–61	13,440	8.6	91.4	2,470	62.5	37.5	–1,902	870	–1,032	3,647	2,380	Czech Republic
51	26	21	35	–33	…	…	…	…	…	…	6,689	–3,725	2,964	3,156	4,128	Denmark
79	24	15	45	–64	252.7	100.0	—	3.0	68.3	31.7	–179.7[4]	165.3[4]	–14.4[4]	4	5	Djibouti
58[3]	21[3]	34[3]	51[3]	–63[3]	89.0	100.0	—	9.3	75.3	23.7	–58.4	29.0	–29.4	37	7	Dominica
75	8	26	47	–56	3,665	80.5	19.5	331	52.3	47.7	–2,904.4	2,475.2	–429.2	2,107	242	Dominican Republic
…	…	…	…	…	…	…	…	…	…	…	…	…	…	…	…	East Timor
70	12	25	25	–32	12,756	42.7	57.3	1,382	45.2	54.8	1,655	–700	955	290	227	Ecuador

National product and accounts (continued)

country	gross national product (GNP), 1999			gross domestic product (GDP), 1990–99			origin of gross domestic product (GDP) by economic sector, 1998 (%)										
	nominal ('000,000 U.S.$)	per capita		average annual growth rates, 1990–99			primary		secondary			tertiary					other
		nominal (U.S.$)	purchasing power parity (PPP; U.S.$)	real GDP (%)	popu-lation (%)	real GDP per capita (%)	agri-culture	mining	manu-factur-ing	con-struc-tion	public util-ities	transp., commu-nications	trade	finan-cial svcs.	other svcs.	govern-ment	
Egypt	86,544	1,380	3,460	4.6	2.2	2.4	16[3]	[8]	27[3, 8]	5[3]	2[3]	11[3]	19[3]	6[3]	— 7[3] —		7[3]
El Salvador	11,806	1,920	4,260	4.6	1.8	2.8	12	—	22	4	2	8	19	12	7	14	—
Equatorial Guinea	516	1,170	3,910	18.9	2.6	16.3	22	61	—	3	1	1	4	1	2	5	—
Eritrea	779	200	1,040	5.6	3.4	2.2	15	—	13	11	1	9	20	4	1	17	9
Estonia	4,906	3,400	8,190	–1.2	–0.9	–0.3	6	1	14	5	3	12	18	13	14	4	10
Ethiopia	6,524	100	620	5.3	2.9	2.4	46	[8]	7[8]	3	2	6	9	7	8	13	–1
Faroe Islands	976[4]	24,620[4]	…	…	…	…	…	…	…	…	…	…	…	…	…	…	…
Fiji	1,848	2,310	4,780	2.2	1.0	1.2	16	3	15	5	5	14	16	14	— 20 —		–8
Finland	127,764	27,730	22,600	2.4	0.4	2.0	4	—	22	4	2	8	11	11	9	16	13
France	1,453,211	24,170	23,020	1.5	0.4	1.1	3[3]	1[3]	22[3]	5[3]	3[3]	6[3]	14[3, 11]	5[3]	18[3, 11]	19[3]	6[3]
French Guiana	1,543[7]	10,580[7]	…	…	…	…	…	…	…	…	…	…	…	…	…	…	…
French Polynesia	3,908	16,930	22,200	1.6	1.7	–0.1	…	…	…	…	…	…	…	…	…	…	…
Gabon	3,987	3,300	5,280	1.8	1.2	0.6	7[3]	43[3]	6[3]	4[3]	1[3]	5[3]	8[3]	— 11[3] —		9[3]	6[3]
Gambia, The	415	330	1,550	3.0	3.6	–0.6	24	—	5	5	2	14	17	7	5	9	12
Gaza Strip	1,368[4, 5]	1,320[4, 5]	…	…	…	…	13	—	10	8	2	5	15	23	8	16	—
Georgia	3,362	620	2,540	…	…	…	32	[2]	13[2]	4	[2]	11	11	11	— 13 —		5
Germany	2,103,804	26,620	23,510	1.4	0.4	1.0	1	[2]	25[2]	5	[2]	— 17 —		30	— 21 —		1
Ghana	7,451	400	1,850	4.1	2.5	1.6	36	5	9	9	3	4	7	4	3	10	10
Greece	127,648	12,110	15,800	2.5	0.7	1.8	14[3]	1[3]	14[3]	6[3]	2[3]	7[3]	14[3]	3[3]	11[3]	19[3]	9[3]
Greenland	1,142[3]	20,380[3]	…	…	…	…	…	…	…	…	…	…	…	…	…	…	…
Grenada	334	3,440	6,300	2.9	0.7	2.2	9[3]	1[3]	7[3]	7[3]	5[3]	24[3]	20[3]	14[3]	3[3]	16[3]	–6[3]
Guadeloupe	3,706[5, 7]	9,200[5, 7]	…	…	…	…	…	…	…	…	…	…	…	…	…	…	…
Guam	3,301[4, 5]	20,660[4, 5]	…	…	…	…	…	…	…	…	…	…	…	…	…	…	…
Guatemala	18,625	1,680	3,630	4.2	2.7	1.5	23	1	14	2	3	9	25	10	6	8	–1
Guernsey[12]	1,902	29,810	…	…	…	…	…	…	…	…	…	…	…	…	…	…	…
Guinea	3,556	490	1,870	3.9	2.4	1.5	21	16	4	9	1	6	— 28 —		9	4	2
Guinea-Bissau	194	160	630	0.7	2.6	–1.9	62	[2]	9[2]	3	[2]	2	19	— 1 —		3	1
Guyana	651	760	3,330	5.6	0.4	5.2	29	14	9[13]	5	[13]	6	4	6	1	11	15
Haiti	3,584	460	1,470	–2.1	1.3	–3.4	30	—	7	12	1	2	13	8	5	18	4
Honduras	4,829	760	2,270	3.6	3.3	0.3	19	2	19	5	5	5	12	17	11	6	–1
Hong Kong	165,122	24,570	22,570	3.7	1.8	1.9	—	—	6	6	3	9	23	24	— 19 —		10
Hungary	46,751	4,640	11,050	1.1	–0.3	1.4	6[3]	[8]	20[3, 8]	4[3]	3[3]	9[3]	10[3]	16[3]	13[3]	6[3]	13[3]
Iceland	8,197	29,540	27,210	2.7	0.9	1.8	9[3]	—	13[3]	6[3]	3[3]	6[3]	10[3]	15[3]	5[3]	14[3]	18[3]
India	441,834	440	2,230	5.9	1.8	4.1	25	2	15	4	2	7	14	10	6	5	10
Indonesia	125,043	600	2,660	4.6	1.6	3.0	19	13	26	5	1	5	15	8	3	4	1
Iran	113,729	1,810	5,520	3.4	1.5	1.9	20	12	16	4	2	8	17	10	2	10	–1
Iraq	11,500[1, 5]	600[1, 5]	…	…	…	…	…	…	…	…	…	…	…	…	…	…	…
Ireland	80,559	21,470	22,460	6.8	0.7	6.1	8[1]	[14]	38[1, 14]	[14]	[14]	— 18[1] —		— 31[1] —		5[1]	—
Isle of Man	1,319[4, 5]	18,270[4, 5]	…	…	…	…	2[3]	—	12[3]	7[3]	3[3]	10[3]	12[3]	59[3]	4[3]	6[3]	–15[3]
Israel	99,574	16,310	18,070	5.2	2.9	2.3	2[3]	[2]	19[2, 3]	9	[2]	6[3]	12[3]	30[3]	— 28[3] —		–6[3]
Italy	1,162,910	20,170	22,000	1.4	0.2	1.2	3[1]	4[1]	16[1]	5[1]	6[1]	6[1]	19[1]	5[1]	13[1]	22[1]	1[1]
Jamaica	6,311	2,430	3,390	0.4	1.0	–0.6	7	5	14	10	2	11	23	12	3	12	1
Japan	4,054,545	32,030	25,170	1.4	0.3	1.1	2[3]	—	24[3]	10[3]	3[3]	7[3]	12[3]	19[3]	20[3]	8[3]	–5[3]
Jersey	2,670[1, 5]	30,940[1, 5]	…	…	…	…	…	…	…	…	…	…	…	…	…	…	…
Jordan	7,717	1,630	3,880	5.4	4.3	1.1	3	3	12	4	2	14	11	16	5	18	12
Kazakhstan	18,732	1,250	4,790	–6.1	–1.2	–4.9	8	[2]	22[2]	4	[2]	11	17		— 37 —		1
Kenya	10,696	360	1,010	2.3	2.6	–0.3	30[1]	—	10[1]	5[1]	1[1]	8[1]	19[1]	18[1]	— 8[1] —		—
Kiribati	81	910	…	3.6	2.6	1.0	12[1]	—	1[1]	3[1]	2[1]	12[1]	19[1]	6[1]	3[1]	33[1]	9[1]
Korea, North	17,700[3]	740[3]	…	…	…	…	…	…	…	…	…	…	…	…	…	…	…
Korea, South	397,910	8,490	15,530	5.7	1.0	4.7	5	—	31	10	2	7	11	20	8	8	–2
Kuwait	35,152[3]	22,110[3]	…	…	…	…	—	31	12	3	—	6	10	14	— 26 —		–2
Kyrgyzstan	1,465	300	2,420	–5.4	1.0	–6.4	41	[2]	17[2]	3	[2]	2	12	— 14 —		3	8
Laos	1,476	290	1,430	6.5	2.7	3.8	52	—	17	3	2	6	12	3	1	3	1
Latvia	5,913	2,430	6,220	–4.7	–1.0	–3.7	8[1]	[8]	19[1, 8]	4[1]	5[1]			— 51[1] —			13[1]
Lebanon	15,796	3,700	…	7.0	1.3	5.7	…	…	…	…	…	…	…	…	…	…	…
Lesotho	1,158	550	2,350	4.3	2.2	2.1	12[1]	—	14[1]	18[1]	3[1]	3[1]	10[1]	8[1]	1[1]	18[1]	13[1]
Liberia	1,174[1]	490[1]	…	…	…	…	78	2	5	2	—	5	3	3	2	2	–2
Libya	32,663[4, 5]	6,700[4, 5]	…	…	…	…	…	…	…	…	…	…	…	…	…	…	—
Liechtenstein	714[1, 5]	23,000[1, 5]	…	…	…	…	…	…	…	…	…	…	…	…	…	…	…
Lithuania	9,751	2,640	6,490	–4.0	–0.1	–3.9	9	[8]	17[8]	8	4	9	16	9	11	6	11
Luxembourg	18,545	42,930	41,230	5.2	1.4	3.8	1	—	17	7	1	— 24 —		45	— 19 —		–14
Macau	6,161	14,200	16,940	3.7	3.0	0.7	…	…	…	…	…	…	…	…	…	…	…
Macedonia	3,348	1,660	4,590	–0.7	0.8	–1.5	10	[8]	22[8]	6	3	6	13	6	— 19 —		15
Madagascar	3,712	250	790	1.8	3.0	–1.2	33	[8]		— 12[8] —			— 42 —			5	8
Malawi	1,961	180	570	2.0	1.1	0.9	36	1	13	2	1	4	25	9	2	10	–3
Malaysia	76,944	3,390	7,640	7.4	2.7	4.7	9	8	28	4	3	8	16	13	— 16 —		–5
Maldives	322	1,200	…	6.3	2.4	3.9	16	2	7[13]	11	[13]	7	20	— 29 —		8	—
Mali	2,577	240	740	3.7	2.6	1.1	44	6	9	5	—	5	— 16 —		7	4	4
Malta	3,492	9,210	…	5.0	0.8	4.2	2	[15]	19	3[15]	7	6	10	17	9	14	13
Marshall Islands	99	1,950	…	…	…	…	15[3]	—	2[3]	7[3]	2[3]	7[3]	18[3]	15[3]	— 30[3] —		4[3]
Martinique	4,271[3, 5]	11,320[3, 5]	…	…	…	…	…	…	…	…	…	…	…	…	…	…	…
Mauritania	1,001	390	1,550	4.3	3.0	1.3	22[3]	10[3]	10[3]	— 9[3] —		8[3]	15[3]	— 7[3] —		10[3]	9[3]
Mauritius	4,157	3,540	8,950	5.1	1.2	3.9	7	—	21	5	2	10	15	14	5	9	12
Mayotte	486[4]	3,700[4]	…	…	…	…	…	…	…	…	…	…	…	…	…	…	…
Mexico	428,877	4,440	8,070	2.8	1.8	1.0	5	1	21	5	1	11	20	14	— 23 —		–1
Micronesia	212	1,830	…	–0.2	1.6	–1.8	19[1]	—	1[1]	1[1]	1[1]	5[1]	24[1]	3[1]	3[1]	42[1]	1[1]
Moldova	1,481	410	2,100	–11.0	–0.2	–10.8	21	[8]	17[8]	4	2	4	7	6	— 12 —		27
Monaco	793[1, 5]	25,000[1, 5]	…	…	…	…	…	…	…	…	…	…	…	…	…	…	…
Mongolia	927	390	1,610	0.8	1.4	–0.6	33	[8]	24[8]	3	—	7	19		— 14 —		—
Morocco	33,715	1,190	3,320	2.1	1.7	0.4	15[3]	2[3]	18[3]	5[3]	9[3]	6[3]	19[3]		— 13[3] —		13[3]
Mozambique	3,804	220	810	6.9	3.1	3.8	32	—	8	8	1	11	23	—	12	3	2
Myanmar (Burma)	55,700[3, 5]	1,190[3, 5]	…	…	…	…	53	—	6	2	—	5	30	2	— 2 —		—
Namibia	3,211	4,890	5,580	3.2	2.4	0.8	9[3]	12[3]	12[3]	3[3]	3[3]	4[3]	9[3]	8[3]	3[3]	23[3]	14[3]
Nauru	128[4]	11,540[4]	…	…	…	…	…	…	…	…	…	…	…	…	…	…	…
Nepal	5,173	220	1,280	4.8	2.5	2.3	38	1	9	10	2	8	11	10	— 9 —		2

gross domestic product (GDP) by type of expenditure, 1998 (%): consumption: private	consumption: govern-ment	gross domestic invest-ment	foreign trade: exports	foreign trade: imports	external public debt outstanding (long-term, disbursed only), 1999: total ('000,000 U.S.$)	creditors (%): offi-cial	creditors (%): private	debt service: total ('000,000 U.S.$)	repayment (%): princi-pal	repayment (%): inter-est	balance of payments, 1999 (current external transactions; '000,000 U.S.$): net transfers: goods, merchan-dise	net transfers: invisibles	current balance of payments	tourist trade, 1997 ('000,000 U.S.$): receipts from foreign nationals	expendi-tures by nationals abroad	country
74	10	22	17	−23	25,998	97.9	2.1	1,478	56.8	43.2	−9,928	8,293	−1,635	3,727	1,347	Egypt
86	10	17	23	−36	2,649	91.8	8.2	254	54.3	45.7	−1,358.9	1,117.0	−241	75	75	El Salvador
…	…	…	102	−173	207.9	93.7	6.3	1.7	58.8	41.2	26.5[4]	−400.1[4]	−373.6[4]	2	8	Equatorial Guinea
…	…	…	…	…	253.8	100.0	—	3.9	16.7	83.3	−498.9[4]	323.5[4]	−175.4[4]	75	…	Eritrea
59	22	29	78	−88	205.5	81.8	18.2	61.2	80.5	19.5	−877.5	582.9	−294.6	465	118	Estonia
79	14	18	16	−26	5,360	97.6	2.4	147	62.6	37.4	−797.1	480.9	−316.2	36	40	Ethiopia
…	…	…	…	…	…	…	…	…	…	…	51.6[4]	102.4[4]	154.0[4]	…	…	Faroe Islands
72	18	12	67	−69	120.7	100.0	—	29.2	75.3	24.7	−115.6	128.3	12.7	297	53	Fiji
39	21	19	50	−30	…	…	…	…	…	…	11,655	−4,067	7,588	1,963	2,270	Finland
54	24	19	26	−23	…	…	…	…	…	…	19,390	17,190	36,580	28,009	16,576	France
…	…	…	…	…	…	…	…	…	…	…	…	…	…	…	…	French Guiana
…	…	…	…	…	…	…	…	…	…	…	…	…	…	359	…	French Polynesia
40[3]	11[3]	26[3]	64[3]	−42[3]	3,290	96.1	3.9	487	52.6	47.4	202.5[3]	34.6[3]	237.1[3]	7	178	Gabon
76	17	18	51	−62	425.4	100.0	—	16.6	67.2	32.8	−69.0[4]	52.7[4]	−16.3[4]	32	16	Gambia, The
…	…	…	…	…	…	…	…	…	…	…	…	…	…	…	…	Gaza Strip
…	…	…	…	…	1,308	99.8	0.2	80	48.1	51.9	−533.9	335.5	−198.4	416	228	Georgia
57	19	22	29	−27	…	…	…	…	…	…	72,000	−91,310	−19,310	16,509	46,200	Germany
77	10	25	34	−47	5,647	91.2	8.8	391	68.3	31.7	−1,111.5	345.5	−766.0	266	22	Ghana
71	15	21	18	−25	…	…	…	…	…	…	−17,947	12,845	−5,102	3,771	1,325	Greece
…	…	…	…	…	…	…	…	…	…	…	…	…	…	…	…	Greenland
61	18	44	53	−76	122.2	93.9	6.1	6.4	73.4	26.6	−133.4[4]	43.9[4]	−89.5[4]	61	5	Grenada
…	…	…	…	…	…	…	…	…	…	…	…	…	…	499	…	Guadeloupe
…	…	…	…	…	…	…	…	…	…	…	…	…	…	…	…	Guam
87	6	16	19	−27	3,129	80.0	20.0	313	58.5	41.5	1,445.1	−2,471.0	−1,025.9	325	119	Guatemala
…	…	…	…	…	…	…	…	…	…	…	…	…	…	…	…	Guernsey[12]
77	7	17	22	−23	3,057	99.1	0.9	114	61.4	38.6	94.5	−246.1	−151.6	5	23	Guinea
100	9	11	15	−35	837.1	99.9	0.1	8.6	44.2	55.8	−14.4	−12.6	−27.0	…	…	Guinea-Bissau
43[3]	20[3]	43[3]	78[3]	−84[3]	1,238	96.6	3.4	74	52.7	47.3	−25	−50	−75	39	22	Guyana
—103—		13	13	−29	1,049	100.0	—	43	65.1	34.9	−469.7	410.1	−59.6	97	37	Haiti
67	10	30	44	−51	4,231	96.7	3.3	296	59.3	40.7	−709.1	172.3	−536.8	146	62	Honduras
61	9	30	127	−127	…	…	…	…	…	…	−3,159	14,635	11,476	9,242	…	Hong Kong
62	11	29	51	−53	16,064	14.0	86.0	3,282	69.5	30.5	−2,189	83	−2,106	2,582	1,153	Hungary
62	21	22	35	−39	…	…	…	…	…	…	−308	−292	−600	173	324	Iceland
66	13	23	12	−13	82,380	71.1	28.9	8,221	62.7	37.3	−8,029	5,245	−2,784	3,152	1,342	India
53	4	35	40	−33	72,554	75.5	24.5	9,192	59.5	40.5	20,644	−14,859	5,785	5,437	2,436	Indonesia
65	13	22	8	−8	6,184	59.4	40.6	2,971	86.6	13.4	6,215	−1,488	4,727	327	253	Iran
…	…	…	…	…	…	…	…	…	…	…	…	…	…	13	…	Iraq
51	13	24	84	−72	…	…	…	…	…	…	24,178	−23,583	595	3,189	2,223	Ireland
…	…	…	…	…	…	…	…	…	…	…	…	…	…	…	…	Isle of Man
61	30	20	32	−43	…	…	…	…	…	…	−4,408	2,527	−1,881	2,741	3,570	Israel
60	18	20	24	−22	…	…	…	…	…	…	20,383	−14,079	6,304	29,714	16,631	Italy
67	18	29	43	−56	2,905	77.5	22.5	648	52.3	47.7	−1,137.7	882.0	−255.7	1,131	181	Jamaica
61	10	26	11	−9	…	…	…	…	…	…	123,320	−16,450	106,870	4,326	33,041	Japan
…	…	…	…	…	…	…	…	…	…	…	…	…	…	…	…	Jersey
70	27	25	49	−70	7,546	83.2	16.8	559	52.6	47.4	−1,460.1	1,865.0	404.9	774	398	Jordan
75	11	18	32	−37	2,995	77.0	23.0	629	71.7	28.3	343.7	−514.7	−171.0	289	445	Kazakhstan
74	16	17	25	−32	5,385	90.2	9.8	533	78.9	21.1	−829.2	840.2	11.0	377	194	Kenya
…	…	…	…	…	…	…	…	…	…	…	−31.6[1]	29.3[1]	−2.3[1]	2	4	Kiribati
…	…	…	…	…	…	…	…	…	…	…	…	…	…	…	…	Korea, North
55	11	21	48	−35	57,231	27.1	72.9	23,000	81.4	18.6	28,371	−3,894	24,477	5,116	6,262	Korea, South
56	31	14	45	−47	…	…	…	…	…	…	5,571	−509	5,062	188	2,558	Kuwait
88	18	16	36	−58	1,130.4	97.2	2.8	16.5	8.2	91.8	−84.4	−168.9	−253.3	7	4	Kyrgyzstan
…	…	…	…	…	2,471	100.0	—	29	69.0	31.0	−189.5	68.4	−121.1	73	21	Laos
64	26	23	48	−61	864.8	70.2	29.8	41.4	50.7	49.3	−1,027	380	−647	192	326	Latvia
…	…	…	…	…	5,568	16.4	83.6	653	45.6	54.4	…	…	…	1,000	…	Lebanon
116	20	46	27	−109	661.8	91.6	8.4	44.6	55.8	44.2	−606.7	385.9	−220.8	20	8	Lesotho
…	…	…	…	…	1,062	80.7	19.3	—	—	—	−118.5[4]	76.6[4]	−41.9[4]	…	…	Liberia
55[3]	27[3]	12[3]	29[3]	−23[3]	…	…	…	…	…	…	2,974	−838	2,136	6	215	Libya
…	…	…	…	…	…	…	…	…	…	…	…	…	…	…	…	Liechtenstein
63	25	24	47	−59	1,891.5	34.2	65.8	166.7	54.3	45.7	−1,404.6	210.6	−1,194.0	399	290	Lithuania
46	17	21	116	−99	…	…	…	…	…	…	−2,449	3,761	1,312	297	…	Luxembourg
40	11	18	76	−46	…	…	…	…	…	…	…	…	…	2,947	153	Macau
74	18	23	43	−58	1,135	75.4	24.6	377	85.0	15.0	−420.3	108.6	−311.7	14	27	Macedonia
89	7	12	21	−30	4,023	99.1	0.9	147	46.9	53.1	−154[4]	−147[4]	−301[4]	73	48	Madagascar
85	14	14	30	−42	2,596	99.3	0.7	44	62.5	37.5	−93.0[1]	−0.3[1]	−92.7[1]	7	17	Malawi
42	10	27	114	−93	18,929	24.2	75.8	2,278	52.3	47.7	22,648	−10,042	12,606	2,703	2,478	Malaysia
…	…	…	…	…	192.5	84.9	15.1	16.7	73.7	26.3	−262.6	192.6	−70.0	286	38	Maldives
70	14	24	24	−33	2,798	100.0	—	85	75.3	24.7	9.7[3]	−187.7[3]	−178.0[3]	26	42	Mali
62	20	23	88	−94	…	…	…	…	…	…	−571.4	449.0	−112.4	664	191	Malta
…	…	…	…		…	…	…	…	…	…	−35.8[3]	52.2[3]	16.4[3]	3	…	Marshall Islands
…	…	…	…	…	…	…	…	…	…	…	…	…	…	400	…	Martinique
69[3]	20[3]	17[3]	42[3]	−49[3]	2,138	99.1	0.9	88	68.2	31.8	40.0[4]	37.2[4]	77.2[4]	11	24	Mauritania
63	12	25	67	−67	1,155	45.8	54.2	161	62.4	37.6	−547.2	494.9	52.4	475	177	Mauritius
…	…	…	…	…	…	…	…	…	…	…	…	…	…	…	…	Mayotte
68	9	24	31	−33	87,531	24.9	75.1	16,015	61.4	38.6	−5,581	−8,585	−14,166	7,594	3,892	Mexico
…	…	…	…	…	…	…	…	…	…	…	−52.0[3]	115.8[3]	63.8[3]	…	…	Micronesia
71	24	30	—−25—		722	82.5	17.5	98	55.1	44.9	−128.0	83.3	−44.7	4	…	Moldova
…	…	…	…	…	…	…	…	…	…	…	…	…	…	…	…	Monaco
65[3]	16[3]	23[3]	1[3]	−5[3]	816.3	97.4	2.6	20.9	57.2	42.8	−56.4	−55.8	−112.2	22	21	Mongolia
65	18	22	22	−26	17,284	75.9	24.1	2,985	64.6	35.4	−2,448	2,277	−171	1,443	315	Morocco
88	9	23	12	−32	4,625	99.7	0.3	68	47.8	52.2	−491.0[4]	61.7[4]	−429.3[4]	…	…	Mozambique
—89—		12	0	−1	5,333	90.1	9.9	88	72.7	27.3	−1,035.2	669.5	−365.7	34	25	Myanmar (Burma)
55[3]	31[3]	20[3]	53[3]	−58[3]	…	…	…	…	…	…	−172.6[4]	334.4[4]	161.8[4]	336	99	Namibia
…	…	…	…	…	…	…	…	…	…	…	…	…	…	…	…	Nauru
81	9	21	24	−35	2,910	99.3	0.7	99	69.7	30.3	−880.7	891.3	10.6	119	103	Nepal

National product and accounts (continued)

country	gross national product (GNP), 1999			gross domestic product (GDP), 1990–99			origin of gross domestic product (GDP) by economic sector, 1998 (%)										
	nominal ('000,000 U.S.$)	per capita		average annual growth rates, 1990–99			primary		secondary			tertiary					other
		nominal (U.S.$)	purchasing power parity (PPP; U.S.$)	real GDP (%)	popu-lation (%)	real GDP per capita (%)	agri-culture	mining	manu-factur-ing	con-struc-tion	public util-ities	transp., commu-nications	trade	finan-cial svcs.	other svcs.	govern-ment	
Netherlands, The	397,384	25,140	24,410	2.7	0.6	2.1	3	2	17	5	2	7	15	26	11	12	—
Netherlands Antilles	2,400[3, 5]	11,500[3, 5]	...	...	...	...	1[7]	—	7[7]	7[7]	4[7]	13[7]	25[7]	17[7]	9[7]	18[7]	–1[7]
New Caledonia	3,169	15,160	21,130	1.4	2.2	–0.8	2[3]	4[3]	11[3]	5[3]	2[3]	7[3]	23[3]	—20[3]—		25[3]	–1[3]
New Zealand	53,299	13,990	17,630	3.0	1.2	1.8	7	1	17	3	3	11	15	22	—22—		1
Nicaragua	2,012	410	2,060	3.3	2.9	0.4	28	2	21	5	3	5	18	7	4	8	–1
Niger	1,974	190	740	1.8	2.8	–1.0	37[3]	4[3]	7[3]	2[3]	2[3]	6[3]	17[3]	—21[3]—			4[3]
Nigeria	31,600	260	770	2.4	2.9	–0.5	37	26	5	1	—	3	16	5	1	1	5
Northern Mariana Is.	665	9,600	...	...	...	...	...	...	...	...	...	...	...	...	...	...	...
Norway	149,280	33,470	28,140	3.8	0.6	3.2	2	11	12	4	2	9	10	17	5	16	12
Oman	13,135[4]	5,950[4]	...	...	...	...	2[1]	43[1]	4[1]	2[1]	1[1]	6[1]	13[1]	8[1]	8[1]	12[1]	1[1]
Pakistan	62,915	470	1,860	3.5	2.5	1.0	24	—	15	3	4	9	15	8	7	7	8
Palau	129[4, 5]	7,140[4, 5]	...	...	...	...	5	—	1	8	—	16	27	12	7	22	2
Panama	8,657	3,080	5,450	4.3	1.9	2.4	8	—	10	4	4	13	21	25	6	10	–1
Papua New Guinea	3,834	810	2,260	4.9	2.6	2.3	24	26	9	6	1	5	9	1	—13—		6
Paraguay	8,374	1,560	4,380	2.5	2.7	–0.2	28	—	14	5	6	5	23	3	10	6	—
Peru	53,705	2,130	4,480	5.0	1.8	3.2	6[3]	2[3]	19[3]	11[3]	1[3]	4[3]	16[3]	14[3]	13[3]	7[3]	7[3]
Philippines	77,967	1,050	3,990	3.2	2.3	0.9	17	1	22	6	3	5	14	12	11	10	–1
Poland	157,429	4,070	8,390	4.6	0.2	4.4	5	3	22	8	3	6	21	15	3	13	1
Portugal	110,175	11,030	15,860	2.4	0.1	2.3	...	...	...	...	...	...	...	...	...	...	...
Puerto Rico	25,380[3]	7,010[3]	...	...	...	...	1[1]	[15]	41[1]	2[1, 15]	[16]	8[1, 16]	14[1]	13[1]	11[1]	11[1]	–1[1]
Qatar	6,473[4]	11,600[4]	...	...	...	...	1[3]	38[3]	7[3]	7[3]	1[3]	4[3]	8[3]	10[3]	—24[3]—		...
Réunion	5,680[3]	8,260[3]	...	...	...	...	...	...	...	...	...	...	...	...	...	...	...
Romania	33,034	1,470	5,970	–0.9	–0.4	–0.5	19[1]	[2]	34[1, 2]	7[1]	[2]	9[1]	10[1]	—17[1]—			4[1]
Russia	328,995	2,250	6,990	–6.0	–0.1	–5.9	7	[2]	33[2]	8	[2]	—23—		14	9	6	—
Rwanda	2,041	250	880	–2.7	0.3	–3.0	44	—	13	7	—	4	11	—15—		7	–1
St. Kitts	259	6,330	10,400	4.2	–0.7	4.9	6[1]	—	11[1]	12[1]	2[1]	16[1]	23[1]	16[1]	4[1]	18[1]	–8[1]
St. Lucia	590	3,820	5,200	2.4	1.5	0.9	7	—	5	6	4	15	23	15	3	13	9
St. Vincent	301	2,640	4,990	3.3	0.7	2.6	9	—	6	12	5	17	15	8	2	15	11
Samoa	181	1,070	4,070	2.0	0.6	1.4	17[3]	...	19[3]	5[3]	2[3]	11[3]	17[3]	11[3]	7[3]	9[3]	2[3]
San Marino	883[3, 5]	34,330[3, 5]	...	...	...	...	...	...	...	...	...	...	...	...	...	...	...
São Tomé and Príncipe	40	270	...	1.1	2.0	–0.9	23[3]	—	4[3]	15[3]	—	—19[3]—		8[3]	9[3]	22[3]	—
Saudi Arabia	139,365	6,900	11,050	2.2	3.3	–1.1	6[1]	36[1]	9[1]	9[1]	—	6[1]	7[1]	5[1]	3[1]	17[1]	2[1]
Senegal	4,685	500	1,400	3.7	3.1	0.6	18	[5]	13[5]	5	2	12	—21—		20	9	—
Seychelles	520	6,500	...	2.9	1.6	1.3	3	...	14	9	3	15	24	10	2	13	7
Sierra Leone	653	130	440	–4.9	2.1	–7.0	39[7]	17[7]	9[7]	2[7]	—	9[7]	14[7]	2[7]	2[7]	3[7]	4[7]
Singapore	95,429	24,150	22,310	6.6	1.9	4.7	—	—	24	9	2	14	19	28	—11—		–7
Slovakia	20,318	3,770	10,430	1.8	0.2	1.6	4	1	23	5	3	8	—22—		—29—		5
Slovenia	19,862	10,000	16,050	2.4	–0.1	2.5	4[3]	1[3]	25[3]	5[3]	3[3]	7[3]	13[3]	14[3]	12[3]	5[3]	11[3]
Solomon Islands	320	750	2,050	3.7	3.4	0.3	48[1]	—	3[1]	7[1]	2[1]	6[1]	9[1]	4[1]	—21[1]—		—
Somalia	706[1]	110[1]	...	...	...	...	...	...	...	...	...	...	...	...	...	...	...
South Africa	133,569	3,170	8,710	1.2	1.4	–0.2	4	7	19	3	3	10	13	18	—23—		—
Spain	583,082	14,800	17,850	2.3	0.3	2.0	4[1]	[2]	24[1, 2]	8[1]	[2]	—59[1]—					5[1]
Sri Lanka	15,578	820	3,230	5.3	1.3	4.0	19	2	15	7	1	10	19	9	—13—		5
Sudan, The	9,435	330	...	...	...	...	41	—	9	6	1	6	20	—14—			3
Suriname	684[4]	1,660[4]	...	...	...	...	12[1]	11[1]	13[1]	3[1]	9[1]	15[1]	12[1]	14[1]	—13[1]—		–2[1]
Swaziland	1,379	1,350	4,380	2.3	2.5	–0.2	12	1	27	4	2	4	7	4	1	15	23
Sweden	236,940	26,750	22,510	1.6	0.4	1.2	2[1]	—	20[1]	5[1]	3[1]	6[1]	11[1]	23[1]	4[1]	19[1]	7[1]
Switzerland	273,856	38,380	28,760	0.6	0.7	–0.1	...	...	...	...	...	...	...	...	...	...	...
Syria	15,172	970	3,450	5.5	2.8	2.7	28[1]	7[1]	4[1]	4[1]	1[1]	11[1]	26[1]	5[1]	2[1]	10[1]	—
Taiwan	297,953[4]	13,900[4]	...	...	...	...	3	—	27	4	2	7	17	23	10	10	–3
Tajikistan	1,749	280	...	...	...	...	20	[2]	28[2]	2	[2]	—18—		—22—			10
Tanzania	8,515	260	500	3.0	3.1	–0.1	43[3]	1[3]	6[3]	4[3]	2[3]	5[3]	12[3]	12[3]	2[3]	7[3]	6[3]
Thailand	121,051	2,010	5,950	4.9	1.1	3.8	14	2	28	5	3	8	14	—26—			—
Togo	1,398	310	1,380	2.7	3.2	–0.5	42	6	9	3	3	5	17	—8—		7	—
Tonga	172	1,732	...	1.1	0.4	0.7	32	—	3	5	2	7	11	10	—18—		12
Trinidad and Tobago	6,142	4,750	7,690	2.5	0.5	2.0	2	21	8	10	—	—18—		12	17	9	3
Tunisia	19,757	2,090	5,700	4.5	1.6	2.9	12	1	18	5	5	8	—24—			14	13
Turkey	186,490	2,900	6,440	3.7	1.5	2.2	17	1	19	6	2	14	20	—13—		9	–1
Turkmenistan	3,205	670	3,340	–6.6	3.0	–9.6	25	[2]	30[2]	12	[2]	10	5	—13—			5
Tuvalu	7[1]	650[1]	...	...	...	...	22[7]	2[7]	3[7]	14[7]	2[7]	4[7]	14[7]	10[7]	—28[7]—		—
Uganda	6,794	320	1,160	7.1	3.1	4.0	41[1]	—	7[1]	7[1]	1[1]	4[1]	12[1]	7[1]	5[1]	4[1]	12[1]
Ukraine	41,991	840	3,360	–10.8	–0.5	–10.3	11	[2]	25[2]	5	[2]	13	8	—25—			13
United Arab Emirates	48,673[4]	17,870[4]	...	...	...	...	2[1]	35[1]	9[1]	9[1]	1[1]	6[1]	13[1]	13[1]	2[1]	11[1]	–1[1]
United Kingdom	1,403,843	23,500	22,220	2.5	0.4	2.1	1	2	18	5	2	7	13	23	4	15	10
United States	8,879,500	31,910	31,910	3.0	1.0	2.0	2[3]	1[3]	17[3]	4[3]	3[3]	6[3]	17[3]	19[3]	20[3]	13[3]	—
Uruguay	20,604	6,220	8,750	3.7	0.7	3.0	11	—	20	4	4	10	14	21	—15—		1
Uzbekistan	17,613	720	2,230	–1.2	1.9	–3.1	26	[2]	15[2]	8	[2]	6	8	—21—			16
Vanuatu	227	1,180	2,880	2.3	3.1	–0.8	23	—	5	5	2	7	34	7	—17—		—
Venezuela	87,313	3,680	5,420	1.7	2.2	–0.5	5	12	16	7	2	10	18	16	9	6	–1
Vietnam	28,733	370	1,860	8.0	1.8	6.2	26	[8]	—33[8]—			4	19	7	—12—		–1
Virgin Islands (U.S.)	2,666[3]	18,290[3]	...	...	...	...	...	...	...	...	...	...	...	...	...	...	...
West Bank	2,758[4, 5]	1,680[4, 5]	...	...	...	...	7	[2]	17[2]	11	[2]	[17]	14	11	19[17]	10	13
Western Sahara	60[5, 18]	300[5, 18]	...	...	...	...	...	...	...	...	...	...	...	...	...	...	...
Yemen	6,080	360	730	3.5	3.9	–0.4	24	17	10	4	2	7	14	6	2	14	—
Yugoslavia	13,742[4]	1,290[4]	...	...	...	...	20	[8]	36[8]	6	3	12	19	—5—			–1
Zambia	3,222	330	720	–0.4	2.0	–2.4	17	6	11	5	4	6	19	16	—9—		7
Zimbabwe	6,302	530	2,690	1.9	1.3	0.6	14[7]	5[7]	18[7]	2[7]	3[7]	5[7]	18[7]	9[7]	11[7]	4[7]	11[7]

gross domestic product (GDP) by type of expenditure, 1998 (%)					external public debt outstanding (long-term, disbursed only), 1999						balance of payments, 1999 (current external transactions; '000,000 U.S.$)			tourist trade, 1997 ('000,000 U.S.$)		country
consumption		gross domestic invest-ment	foreign trade		total ('000,000 U.S.$)	creditors (%)		debt service			net transfers		current balance of payments	receipts from foreign nationals	expendi-tures by nationals abroad	
private	govern-ment		exports	imports		offi-cial	private	total ('000,000 U.S.$)	repayment (%) principal	repayment (%) interest	goods, merchan-dise	invisibles				
59	14	20	55	–49	…	…	…	…	…	…	17,940	–704	17,236	6,219	10,232	Netherlands, The
67[7]	28[7]	19[7]	72[7]	–85[7]	…	…	…	…	…	…	–1,064[4]	1,008[4]	–56[4]	576	243	Netherlands Antilles
…	…	…	…	…	…	…	…	…	…	…	…	…	…	110	…	New Caledonia
65	15	19	31	–30	…	…	…	…	…	…	–435	–3,161	3,596	2,093	1,451	New Zealand
94	14	34	36	–78	5,799	93.3	6.7	137	43.1	56.9	–1,133.2	481.0	–652.2	74	65	Nicaragua
82[3]	16[3]	12[3]	19[3]	–29[3]	1,424	100.0	—	19	52.6	47.7	–17.6[5]	–134.1[5]	–151.7[5]	18	24	Niger
64	14	29	32	–38	22,423	74.3	25.7	835	67.2	32.8	4,288	–3,782	506	118	1,816	Nigeria
…	…	…	…	…	…	…	…	…	…	…	…	…	…	672	…	Northern Mariana Is.
50	22	28	37	–37	…	…	…	…	…	…	10,119	–4,105	6,014	2,226	4,496	Norway
55	24	23	37	–39	1,768	37.4	62.6	711	82.3	17.7	2,918	–3,110	–192	108	47	Oman
72	12	17	16	–17	28,514	92.5	7.5	1,597	63.1	36.9	–1,874[4]	—[4]	–1,874[4]	117	364	Pakistan
…	…	…	…	…	…	…	…	…	…	…	…	…	…	22[7]	…	Palau
58	16	33	90	–97	5,678	23.6	76.4	619	45.7	54.3	–1,415.0	39.0	–1,376.0	374	164	Panama
55[7]	16[7]	18[7]	49[7]	–37[7]	1,517	95.6	4.4	160	66.9	33.1	856.0	–761.3	94.7	72	81	Papua New Guinea
86	8	23	28	–45	1,672	96.7	3.3	183	62.3	37.7	–334.4	270.8	–63.6	753	195	Paraguay
72	9	24	12	–17	20,709	79.7	20.3	1,957	41.3	58.7	–616	–1,206	–1,822	805	485	Peru
73	13	20	51	–58	33,568	63.8	36.2	5,097	68.1	31.9	4,958	2,952	7,910	2,831	1,936	Philippines
63	16	27	25	–32	33,151	75.6	24.4	2,162	39.1	60.9	–15,072	2,585	–12,487	8,679	6,900	Poland
66	20	26	28	–40	…	…	…	…	…	…	–13,766	4,137	–9,629	4,277	2,164	Portugal
…	…	…	…	…	…	…	…	…	…	…	…	…	…	2,046	869	Puerto Rico
…	…	…	…	…	…	…	…	…	…	…	…	…	…	…	…	Qatar
…	…	…	…	…	…	…	…	…	…	…	…	…	…	249	…	Réunion
76	15	18	26	–34	5,985	64.4	35.6	2,754	85.7	14.3	–1,092	–205	–1,297	526	783	Romania
58	19	15	31	–23	120,375	59.1	40.9	4,470	42.9	57.1	36,130	–11,482	24,648	6,900	10,113	Russia
94	9	16	6	–24	1,162	99.9	0.1	20	60.0	40.0	–140.6	138.1	–2.5	…	…	Rwanda
76[1]	18[1]	24[1]	44[1]	–63[1]	131.7	73.4	26.6	16.9	54.4	45.6	…	…	…	72	6	St. Kitts
69	15	19	65	–68	125.6	88.5	11.5	16.4	63.4	36.8	–201.2[4]	160.2[4]	–41.0[4]	282	29	St. Lucia
74	19	32	47	–72	159.8	63.2	36.8	12.6	49.2	50.8	–119.4[4]	75.1[4]	–44.3[4]	70	7	St. Vincent
…	…	…	…	…	156.5	100.0	—	4.8	70.8	29.2	–97.5	78.7	18.8	41	5	Samoa
66[1]	12[1]	17[1]	234[1]	–229[1]	…	…	…	…	…	…	22.6[1]	–11.9[1]	10.7[1]	…	…	San Marino
…	…	…	…	…	232.2	100.0	—	3.9	64.1	35.9	–12.1[4]	3.6[4]	–8.5[4]	2	1	São Tomé and Príncipe
41	32	21	36	–31	…	…	…	…	…	…	25,039	–24,627	412	1,420	…	Saudi Arabia
76	10	20	32	–38	3,111	99.7	0.3	179	68.2	31.8	–284.3[4]	174.6[4]	–109.7[4]	160	77	Senegal
51	27	37	65	–81	132.2	81.6	18.4	23.4	76.3	23.7	–232.4	118.4	–114.0	122	30	Seychelles
81	11	4	14	–10	938	99.4	0.6	7	57.1	42.9	–126.7[7]	0.2[7]	–126.5[7]	57	2	Sierra Leone
39	10	33	—— 18 ——		…	…	…	…	…	…	11,303	9,951	21,254	6,843	3,224	Singapore
50	22	39	64	–75	4,457	29.6	70.4	[illegible]	67.0	32.1	–1,109	–46	–1,155	546	439	Slovakia
56	21	25	57	–58	…	…	…	…	…	…	–1,245.2	462.8	–782.4	1,188	544	Slovenia
…	…	…	…	…	120.4	97.2	2.8	5.5	72.7	27.3	54.5	–33.1	21.5	7	9	Solomon Islands
…	…	…	…	…	1,859	98.2	1.8	—	—	—	…	…	…	…	…	Somalia
63	20	16	26	–25	9,148	—	100.0	3,162	78.5	21.5	4,150	–4,683	–533	2,297	1,947	South Africa
62	16	22	29	–28	…	…	…	…	…	…	–30,339	16,623	–13,716	26,651	4,467	Spain
71	10	25	36	–42	8,182	92.6	7.4	401	64.1	35.9	–707.4	214.4	–493.0	212	180	Sri Lanka
91	4	18	6	–19	8,852	84.8	15.2	12	45.8	54.2	–475.9	11.1	–464.8	4	34	Sudan, The
…	…	…	…	…	…	…	…	…	…	…	–27.2[4]	–127.7[4]	–154.9[4]	17	4	Suriname
63	25	34	76	–99	205.5	100.0	—	29.0	64.3	35.7	–110.8	128.0	17.2	40	37	Swaziland
50	27	17	44	–38	…	…	…	…	…	…	15,714	–9,732	5,982	3,572	6,579	Sweden
60	15	21	40	–36	…	…	…	…	…	…	723	28,476	29,199	7,902	6,904	Switzerland
69	11	20	30	–31	16,142	93.3	6.7	206	61.7	38.3	216	–15	201	1,035	545	Syria
61	14	22	49	–47	…	…	…	…	…	…	10,531[4]	–6,803[4]	3,728[4]	3,402	6,500	Taiwan
…	…	…	…	…	594.9	90.7	9.3	22.6	88.7	11.3	–38[3]	–36[3]	–74[3]	…	…	Tajikistan
85	8	15	19	–28	6,595	96.7	3.3	150	59.3	40.7	–876.0	69.1	–806.9	392	407	Tanzania
50	10	24	56	–40	31,011	71.3	28.7	4,255	60.0	40.0	14,013	1,585	12,428	7,048	1,888	Thailand
81	11	14	34	–40	1,263	100.0	—	26	65.4	34.6	–98.0	–29.1	–127.1	13	19	Togo
…	…	…	…	…	63.5	98.0	2.0	4.3	81.4	18.6	–67.1[4]	47.8[4]	–19.3[4]	14	3	Tonga
62	16	26	48	–54	1,485	46.3	53.7	401	74.1	25.9	–740.8[4]	97.3[4]	–643.5[4]	108	75	Trinidad and Tobago
60	16	28	42	–46	9,487	67.5	32.5	1,359	63.8	36.2	–2,141	1,698	–443	1,423	160	Tunisia
67	12	24	24	–27	50,095	25.8	74.2	8,559	64.0	36.0	–10,443	9,083	–1,360	8,088	1,716	Turkey
…	…	…	…	…	1,678	23.7	76.3	449	86.2	13.8	–523.0[4]	–411.5[4]	–934.5[4]	74	125	Turkmenistan
…	…	…	…	…	…	…	…	…	…	…	…	…	…	0.3	…	Tuvalu
83[3]	10[3]	15[3]	12[3]	–21[3]	3,564	98.0	2.0	126	65.1	34.9	–596.4	45.6	–550.8	135	137	Uganda
59	23	21	40	–43	10,027	61.5	38.5	1,277	62.4	37.6	244	1,414	1,658	270	305	Ukraine
45[1]	16[1]	26[1]	77[1]	–65[1]	…	…	…	…	…	…	8,254[3]	–1,553[3]	6,701[3]	535	…	United Arab Emirates
65	18	18	27	–28	…	…	…	…	…	…	–42,350	26,370	–15,980	20,039	27,710	United Kingdom
67	15	20	11	–13	…	…	…	…	…	…	–343,260	11,780	–331,480	73,268	51,220	United States
71	14	16	22	–22	5,108	42.1	57.9	917	61.6	38.4	–868.4	263.4	–605.0	759	264	Uruguay
…	…	…	…	…	3,421	54.8	45.2	461	65.7	34.3	171[4]	–210[4]	–39[4]	19	…	Uzbekistan
49[5]	27[5]	34[5]	47[5]	–57[5]	63.4	100.0	—	1.6	53.1	46.9	–51.5	48.4	–3.1	51	5	Vanuatu
73	8	20	20	–20	25,216	18.9	81.1	4,148	54.6	45.4	7,606	–3,917	3,689	1,086	2,381	Venezuela
71	7	29	42	–49	20,529	82.2	17.8	1,347	75.8	24.2	–981[4]	–86[4]	–1,067[4]	88	…	Vietnam
…	…	…	…	…	…	…	…	…	…	…	…	…	…	601	…	Virgin Islands (U.S.)
…	…	…	…	…	…	…	…	…	…	…	…	…	…	…	…	West Bank
…	…	…	…	…	…	…	…	…	…	…	…	…	…	…	…	Western Sahara
61[3]	16[3]	28[3]	43[3]	–48[3]	3,729	95.3	4.7	100	46.0	54.0	357.9	219.2	577.1	69	81	Yemen
…	…	…	…	…	7,416	44.4	55.6	—	—	—	…	…	…	41	…	Yugoslavia
79	16	14	29	–38	4,498	99.3	0.7	416	69.5	30.5	–148[4]	–121[4]	–269[4]	75	59	Zambia
70[3]	17[3]	20[3]	38[3]	–46[3]	3,211	88.7	11.3	480	71.6	28.4	79[4]	–423[4]	–344[4]	230	118	Zimbabwe

[1]1996. [2]Manufacturing includes mining and public utilities. [3]1997. [4]1998. [5]Gross domestic product (GDP). [6]1994. [7]1995. [8]Manufacturing includes mining. [9]Mining includes public utilities. [10]Republic of Cyprus only. [11]Services includes hotels. [12]Excludes Alderney and Sark. [13]Manufacturing includes public utilities. [14]Manufacturing includes mining, construction, and public utilities. [15]Construction includes mining. [16]Transportation, communications includes public utilities. [17]Services includes transportation, communications. [18]1991.

Employment and labour

This table provides international comparisons of the world's national labour forces—giving their size; composition by demographic component and employment status; and structure by industry.

The table focuses on the concept of "economically active population," which the International Labour Organisation (ILO) defines as persons of all ages who are either employed or looking for work. In general, the economically active population does not include students, persons occupied solely in domestic duties, retired persons, persons living entirely on their own means, and persons wholly dependent on others. Persons engaged in illegal economic activities—smugglers, prostitutes, drug dealers, bootleggers, black marketeers, and others—also fall outside the purview of the ILO definition. Countries differ markedly in their treatment, as part of the labour force, of such groups as members of the armed forces, inmates of institutions, the unemployed (both persons seeking their first job and those previously employed), seasonal and international migrant workers, and persons engaged in informal, subsistence, or part-time economic activities. Some countries include all or most of these groups among the economically active, while others may treat the same groups as inactive.

Three principal structural comparisons of the economically active total are given in the first part of the table: (1) participation rate, or the proportion of the economically active who possess some particular characteristic, is given for women and for those of working age (usually ages 15 to 64), (2) activity rate, the proportion of the total population who *are* economically active, is given for both sexes and as a total, and (3) employment status, usually (and here) grouped as employers, self-employed, employees, family workers (usually unpaid), and others.

Each of these measures indicates certain characteristics in a given national labour market; none should be interpreted in isolation, however, as the meaning of each is influenced by a variety of factors—demographic structure and change, social or religious customs, educational opportunity, sexual differentiation in employment patterns, degree of technological development, and the like. Participation and activity rates, for example, may be high in a particular country because it possesses an older population with few children, hence a higher proportion of working age, or because, despite a young population with many below working age, the economy attracts eligible immigrant workers, themselves almost exclusively of working age. At the same time, low activity and participation rates might be characteristic of a country having a young population with poor employment possibilities or of a country with a good job market distorted by the presence of large numbers of "guest" or contract workers who are not part of the domestic labour force. An illiterate woman in a strongly sex-differentiated labour force is likely to begin and end as a family or

Employment and labour

country	year	economically active population										distribution by economic sector			
		total ('000)	participation rate (%)		activity rate (%)			employment status (%)				agriculture, forestry, fishing		manufacturing; mining, quarrying; public utilities	
			female	ages 15–64	total	male	female	employers, self-employed	employees	unpaid family workers	other	number ('000)	% of econ. active	number ('000)	% of econ. active
Afghanistan	1979	3,941	7.9	49.1	30.3	54.2	4.9	52.2	33.8	14.0	—	2,369	60.1	494	12.5
Albania	1994	1,340	47.0[3]	92.0[3, 4]	57.4[3]	60.8[3]	54.0[3]	…	…	…	…	534	39.9	84[5]	6.3[5]
Algeria	1987	5,341	9.2	44.3	23.6	42.4	4.4	16.8	61.7	2.6	18.9	725	13.6	622	11.6
American Samoa	1990	14.2	41.1	52.6[8]	30.4	34.8	25.7	2.1	92.6	0.2	5.1	0.3	2.3	4.8	33.7
Andorra	1989	25	45.6	74.3	55.1	…	…	…	…	…	…	0.3	1.2	2.7	11.0
Angola	1996	4,581	37.3	65.1[10]	40.0	50.8	29.5	…	…	…	…	3,170	69.2	528	11.5[11]
Antigua and Barbuda	1991	26.8	45.6	69.7	45.1	50.9	39.6	12.1	82.8	0.7	4.4	1.0	3.9	1.9	7.3
Argentina	1995	14,345	36.7	64.5	41.5	53.5	29.9	28.0[13]	60.4[13]	5.0[13]	6.6[13]	1,201[14]	12.0[14]	2,136[14]	21.3[14]
Armenia	1996	1,584	…	75.1[16]	42.1	…	…	…	…	…	…	587	37.1	255	16.1
Aruba	1991	31.1	42.5	67.1	46.7	54.5	39.0	7.0	86.4	0.3	6.3	0.2	0.5	2.3	7.3
Australia	1998[18]	9,343	43.3	73.3[19]	49.8	56.6	43.0	12.7	78.2	0.7	8.4	442	4.7	1,311	14.0
Austria	1998[18]	3,888	43.1	70.7	48.1	56.5	40.3	9.7[20]	87.4[20]	3.0[20]	—	246	6.3	842	21.6
Azerbaijan	1998	3,744	47.8	64.4[16, 20]	47.1	50.1	44.2	…	…	…	…	1,085	29.0	367	9.8
Bahamas, The	1994	139	47.5	77.8	50.7	54.8	46.8	11.6[22]	85.1[22]	0.3[22]	3.0[22]	6.9	5.0	7.3	5.3
Bahrain	1991	226	17.5	66.8	44.6	63.5	18.5	5.1	88.5	0.1	6.3	5	2.3	33	14.6
Bangladesh	1995–96[18]	56,014	38.1	73.7	46.0	55.8	35.7	28.8	12.1	39.1	20.0	34,530	61.6	4,211	7.5
Barbados	1995[18]	137	49.5	79.9	51.8	54.6	49.1	8.8[24]	76.4[24]	0.2[24]	14.6[24]	6.3	4.6	15.6	11.4
Belarus	1999	4,542	52.4	78.2[16]	45.3	46.0	44.7	…	…	…	…	672	14.8	1,258	27.7
Belgium	1992	4,237	42.3	51.5[25]	42.2	49.8	34.9	12.7	72.4	3.4	11.5	95	2.2	788	18.6
Belize	1996	75.5	30.8	58.5[26]	34.1	47.2	21.0	26.2[20]	59.2[20]	4.9[20]	9.8[20]	18.3[13]	31.4[13]	7.0[13]	12.0[13]
Benin	1992	2,085	42.6	73.4	43.0	50.6	35.7	58.4	5.3	30.5	5.8	1,148	55.0	162	7.8
Bermuda	1995	34.1	50.0	63.5[13]	55.8	57.4	54.4	9.7[13]	84.0[13]	0.1[13]	6.2[13]	0.5	1.5	1.4	4.2
Bhutan	…	…	…	…	…	…	…	…	…	…	…	…	…	…	…
Bolivia	1992	2,530	38.2	64.0	39.4	48.7	30.4	41.2	31.5	7.1	20.2	984	38.9	281	11.1
Bosnia and Herzegovina	1990[5]	1,026	36.9	…	22.7	…	…	…	…	…	…	39	3.8	519	50.5
Botswana	1995	440	46.6	65.4	29.9	33.1	27.0	7.9	62.7	7.9	21.5	54	12.2	47	10.8
Brazil	1997	75,213	40.4	66.9	48.2	58.7	38.1	26.3[22]	62.3[22]	7.7[22]	3.7[22]	16,771	22.3	9,281	12.3
Brunei	1991	112	32.9	67.6	43.0	54.6	30.0	3.5	91.4	0.4	4.7	2.2	1.9	11.6	10.4
Bulgaria	1995	3,738	48.4[28]	68.8[28]	46.3[28]	48.7[28]	44.1[28]	8.4	75.9	0.9	14.8	783	20.9	1,003	26.8
Burkina Faso	1995	5,250	45.5	75.8[10]	50.9	56.0	45.9	…	…	…	…	4,397	83.8	298	5.7[11]
Burundi	1990	2,780	52.6	91.4	52.5	51.2	53.8	62.8	5.1	30.3	1.8	2,574	92.6	37	1.3
Cambodia	1993	4,010	55.8	86.2	43.1	39.5	46.4	…	…	…	…	2,454[14]	74.4[14]	220[11, 14]	6.7[11, 14]
Cameroon	1991	4,740	33.2	58.9[10]	40.0	53.9	26.3	60.2[22]	14.6[22]	18.0[22]	7.1[22]	2,856	60.3	628[11]	13.2[11]
Canada	1998[18]	15,631	45.3	75.4	51.0	56.3	45.9	15.8	75.5	0.4	8.3	586	3.7	2,601	16.6
Cape Verde	1990	121	37.1	64.3	35.3	46.9	24.9	24.7	53.7	2.0	19.6	29.9	24.8	6.8	5.7
Central African Republic	1988	1,187	46.8	78.3	48.2	52.2	44.3	75.3	8.0	8.1	8.6	881	74.2	31	2.6
Chad	1991	2,016	18.2	51.6[10]	35.3	56.5	14.7	…	…	…	…	1,489	73.9	149[11]	7.4[11]
Chile	1998[18]	5,852	33.4	59.9	39.3	52.8	26.0	26.4[19]	64.6[19]	3.2[19]	5.8[19]	809	13.8	1,015	17.3
China	1990	657,290	44.9	85.0	57.9	61.8	53.7	…	…	…	…	467,926	71.2	87,275	13.3
Colombia	1985	9,558	32.8	49.4[29]	34.3	46.6	22.3	…	…	…	…	2,412[14]	28.5[14]	1,231[14]	14.5[14]
Comoros	1996	252	38.9	59.2	37.2	44.8	29.3	47.6[14]	25.6[14]	— 26.8[14] —		189	74.7	18[11]	7.1[11]
Congo, Dem. Rep. of the	1996	14,082	35.0	47.9[10]	31.1	40.9	21.6	…	…	…	…	9,124	64.8	2,267[11]	16.1[11]
Congo, Rep. of the	1984	563	45.6	54.0	29.5	33.0	26.2	64.3	31.4	1.2	3.1	294	52.2	50	8.8
Costa Rica	1998	1,377	32.6	59.7[25]	41.2	55.8	26.7	24.0[19]	72.2[19]	3.3[19]	0.6[19]	271	19.7	231	16.8
Côte d'Ivoire	1988	4,263	32.3	66.6	39.4	52.2	26.0	…	…	…	…	2,628	61.6	100	2.3
Croatia	1991	2,040	42.9	65.2	45.3	53.9	37.4	12.7	73.7	2.0	11.6	341	16.7	571	28.0
Cuba	1988	4,570	36.1	56.9[25]	44.2	56.2	32.1	5.7[30]	94.1[30]	0.2[30]	—	791[30]	22.3[30]	668[30]	18.9[30]
Cyprus[31, 32]	1995	303	38.6	71.5	47.0	57.8	36.2	18.7[28]	73.1[28]	6.1[28]	2.1[28]	31	10.1	48	15.9
Czech Republic	1997	5,215	44.1	72.5	50.6	58.2	43.5	12.8	81.6	0.4	5.2	296	5.7	1,617	31.0
Denmark	1998	2,848	46.3	80.3	53.7	58.3	49.2	8.7	85.8	—	5.5	103	3.6	572	20.1
Djibouti	1996	396	41.4	96.3[10]	67.2	79.7	55.0	…	…	…	…	288	72.7	56[11]	14.1[11]
Dominica	1991	26.4	34.5	62.4	38.0	50.0	26.1	29.2[33]	50.6[33]	1.9[33]	18.3[33]	7.3	27.9	2.3	8.8
Dominican Republic	1981	1,915	28.9	53.6	33.9	48.1	19.7	36.5	51.3	3.3	8.9	420	22.0	243	12.7
East Timor	…	…	…	…	…	…	…	…	…	…	…	…	…	…	…
Ecuador	1990	3,360	26.4	55.7	34.8	51.5	18.3	45.7	42.5	4.4	7.4	1,036	30.8	404	12.0
Egypt	1995[18]	17,725	22.0	49.8	29.9	45.9	13.4	24.7[28]	50.0[28]	16.4[28]	9.0[28]	5,221	30.2	2,405	13.9
El Salvador	1997	2,256	36.7	61.4	38.2	50.2	27.0	31.7	48.5	7.4	12.4	607	26.9	373	16.5
Equatorial Guinea	1983	103	35.7	66.7	39.2	52.5	26.9	29.0	16.0	29.9	25.1	59.4	57.9	1.8	1.8
Eritrea	…	…	…	…	…	…	…	…	…	…	…	…	…	…	…
Estonia	1998	711	47.7	71.8[34]	48.9	54.9	43.6	4.8[19]	85.2[19]	0.8[19]	9.2[19]	61	8.6	165	23.2

traditional agricultural worker. Loss of working-age men to war, civil violence, or emigration for job opportunities may also affect the structure of a particular labour market.

The distribution of the economically active population by employment status reveals that a large percentage of economically active persons in some less developed countries falls under the heading "employers, self-employed." This occurs because the countries involved have poor, largely agrarian economies in which the average worker is a farmer who tills his own small plot of land. In countries with well-developed economies, "employees" will usually constitute the largest portion of the economically active.

Caution should be exercised when using the economically active data to make intercountry comparisons, as countries often differ in their choices of classification schemes, definitions, and coverage of groups and in their methods of collection and tabulation of data. The population base containing the economically active population, for example, may range, in developing countries, from age 9 or 10 with no upper limit to, in developed countries, age 18 or 19 upward to a usual retirement age of from 55 to 65, with sometimes a different range for each sex. Data on female labour-force participation, in particular, often lack comparability. In many less developed countries, particularly those dominated by the Islamic faith, a cultural bias favouring traditional roles for women results in the undercounting of economically active women. In other less developed countries, particularly those in which subsistence workers are deemed economically active, the role of women may be overstated.

The second major section of the table provides data on the distribution by economic (also conventionally called industrial) sector of the economically active population. The data usually include such groups as unpaid family workers, members of the armed forces, and the unemployed, the last distributed by industry as far as possible.

The categorization of industrial sectors is based on the divisions listed in the *International Standard Industrial Classification of All Economic Activities*. The "other" category includes persons whose activities were not adequately defined and the unemployed who were not distributable by industrial sector.

A substantial part of the data presented in this table is summarized from various issues of the ILO's *Year Book of Labour Statistics*, which compiles its statistics both from official publications and from information submitted directly by national census and labour authorities. The editors have supplemented and updated ILO statistical data with information from Britannica's holdings of relevant official publications and from direct correspondence with national authorities.

construction		transportation, communications		trade, hotels, restaurants		finance, real estate		public administration, defense		services		other		country
number ('000)	% of econ. active	number ('000)	% of econ. active	number ('000)	% of econ. active	number ('000)	% of econ. active	number ('000)	% of econ. active	number ('000)	% of econ. active	number ('000)	% of econ. active	
51	1.3	66	1.6	138	3.5	[1]	[1]	[1]	[1]	749[1]	19.0[1]	78[2]	2.0[2]	Afghanistan
33[5]	2.5[5]	19[5]	1.4[5]	3[5]	0.2[5]	3[5]	0.2[5]	16[5]	1.2[5]	145[5]	10.8[5]	505[6]	37.7[6]	Albania
690	12.9	216	4.1	391	7.3	143	2.7	[7]	[7]	1,180[7]	22.1[7]	1,374	25.7	Algeria
1.2	8.3	0.8	5.5	1.8	13.0	0.3	2.1	1.4	10.0	2.8	19.8	0.7[9]	5.1[9]	American Samoa
2.9	11.8	...	...	6.0	24.2	1.3	5.4	2.6	10.3	4.1	16.7	0.1	0.5	Andorra
[11]	[11]	[12]	[12]	[12]	[12]	[12]	[12]	[12]	[12]	883[12]	19.3[12]	—	—	Angola
3.1	11.6	2.4	9.0	8.5	31.9	1.5	5.4	[7]	[7]	6.4[7]	23.9[7]	1.9	7.0	Antigua and Barbuda
1,003[14]	10.0[14]	460[14]	4.6[14]	1,702[14]	17.0[14]	396[14]	3.9[14]	[7]	[7]	2,399[7, 14]	23.9[7, 14]	736[14, 15]	7.3[14, 15]	Argentina
68	4.3	24	1.5	110	6.9	[1]	[1]	[1]	[1]	350[1]	22.1[1]	190[17]	12.0[17]	Armenia
3.2	10.4	2.3	7.5	11.0	35.4	2.4	7.0	[7]	[7]	8.6[7]	27.7[7]	1.1[17]	3.5[17]	Aruba
654	7.0	567	6.1	2,279	24.4	1,310	14.0	444	4.7	1,884	20.2	454[17]	4.9[17]	Australia
341	8.8	250	6.4	844	21.7	387	9.9	256	6.6	712	18.3	12[2]	0.3[2]	Austria
150	4.0	167	4.5	772	20.6	10	0.3	[7]	[7]	618[7]	16.5[7]	574[21]	15.3[21]	Azerbaijan
11.6	8.3	11.2	8.1	44.2	31.8	12.9	9.3	10.7	7.7	29.7	21.4	4.5[23]	3.2[23]	Bahamas, The
27	11.8	14	6.1	30	13.2	17	7.6	41	18.1	43	19.0	16[17]	7.3[17]	Bahrain
1,015	1.8	2,308	4.1	6,068	10.8	213	0.4	[7]	[7]	5,092[7]	9.1[7]	2,585[17]	4.6[17]	Bangladesh
12.2	8.9	5.9	4.3	35.3	25.8	8.4	6.1	[7]	[7]	48.8[7]	35.7[7]	4.3[2]	3.1[2]	Barbados
336	7.4	332	7.3	504	11.1	[1]	[1]	[1]	[1]	1,345[1]	29.6[1]	95[9]	2.1[9]	Belarus
245	5.8	257	6.1	634	15.0	342	8.1	7	7	1,393[7]	32.9[7]	484[17]	11.4[17]	Belgium
4.1[13]	7.0[13]	2.9[13]	5.0[13]	10.0[13]	17.2[13]	1.8[13]	3.1[13]	5.4[13]	9.2[13]	6.0[13]	10.3[13]	2.8[13]	4.8[13]	Belize
52	2.5	53	2.5	433	20.7	3	0.1	[7]	[7]	165[7]	7.9[7]	71[21]	3.4[21]	Benin
1.7	5.0	2.2	6.4	10.8	31.6	5.2	15.3	[7]	[7]	12.3[7]	35.9[7]	—	—	Bermuda
...	...	...	...	...	...	...	...	...	...	...	...	...	...	Bhutan
129	5.1	117	4.6	232	9.2	54	2.1	59	2.3	350	13.8	323[15]	12.7[15]	Bolivia
75	7.3	69	6.7	131	12.8	39	3.8	[7]	[7]	155[7]	15.1[7]	—	—	Bosnia and Herzegovina
41	9.3	8	1.8	54	12.3	12	2.7	60	13.6	69	15.7	95[17]	21.6[17]	Botswana
4,583	6.1	2,759	3.7	9,223[27]	12.3[27]	1,287	1.7	[7]	[7]	25,436[7, 27]	33.8[7, 27]	5,882[9]	7.8[9]	Brazil
14.1	12.6	5.4	4.8	15.4	13.8	5.8	5.2	[7]	[7]	52.1[7]	46.6[7]	5.3[17]	4.7[17]	Brunei
188	5.0	251	6.7	357	9.5	51	1.4	76	2.0	532	14.2	497[17]	13.3[17]	Bulgaria
[11]	[11]	[12]	[12]	[12]	[12]	[12]	[12]	[12]	[12]	558[12]	10.6[12]	—	—	Burkina Faso
20	0.7	9	0.3	26	0.9	2.0	0.1	[7]	[7]	85[7]	3.1[7]	27[17]	1.0[17]	Burundi
[11]	[11]	[12]	[12]	[12]	[12]	[12]	[12]	[12]	[12]	625[12, 14]	18.9[12, 14]	—	—	Cambodia
[11]	[11]	[12]	[12]	[12]	[12]	[12]	[12]	[12]	[12]	1,256[12]	26.5[12]	—	—	Cameroon
857	5.5	1,128	7.2	3,585	22.9	2,336	14.9	820	5.2	3,252	20.8	468[2]	3.0[2]	Canada
22.7	18.8	6.1	5.1	12.7	10.6	0.8	0.7	[7]	[7]	17.4[7]	14.4[7]	24.1	20.0	Cape Verde
6	0.5	7	0.6	92	7.8	0.7	0.1	[7]	[7]	70[7]	5.9[7]	100[17]	8.5[17]	Central African Republic
[11]	[11]	[12]	[12]	[12]	[12]	[12]	[12]	[12]	[12]	377[12]	18.7[12]	—	—	Chad
533	9.1	456	7.8	1,075	18.4	437	7.5	[7]	[7]	1,478[7]	25.3[7]	47[15]	0.8[15]	Chile
11,890	1.8	11,814	1.8	25,631	3.9	8,268	1.3	[7]	[7]	34,053[7]	5.2[7]	10,434	1.6	China
242[14]	2.9[14]	353[14]	4.2[14]	1,262[14]	14.9[14]	278[14]	3.3[14]	[7]	[7]	1,998[7, 14]	23.6[7, 14]	691[14, 15]	8.2[14, 15]	Colombia
[11]	[11]	[12]	[12]	[12]	[12]	[12]	[12]	[12]	[12]	46[12]	18.2[12]	—	—	Comoros
[11]	[11]	[12]	[12]	[12]	[12]	[12]	[12]	[12]	[12]	2,691[12]	19.1[12]	—	—	Congo, Dem. Rep. of the
25	4.5	29	5.1	67	11.8	3	0.5	[7]	[7]	85[7]	15.1[7]	10	2.0	Congo, Rep. of the
89	6.5	75	5.5	267	19.4	35	2.6	[7]	[7]	385[7]	27.9[7]	23[23]	1.7[23]	Costa Rica
85	2.0	118	2.8	530	12.4	[1]	[1]	[1]	[1]	591[1]	13.9[1]	210[2]	4.9[2]	Côte d'Ivoire
93	4.5	112	5.5	223	10.9	58	2.8	104	5.1	204	10.0	329[17]	16.1[17]	Croatia
313[30]	8.8[30]	249[30]	7.0[30]	306[30]	8.6[30]	[1]	[1]	[1]	[1]	1,086[1, 30]	30.7[1, 30]	128[30]	3.6[30]	Cuba
26	8.7	19	6.2	77	25.4	23	7.6	[7]	[7]	65[7]	21.6[7]	13	4.4	Cyprus[31, 32]
501	9.6	392	7.5	871	16.7	358	6.9	328	6.3	762	14.6	90[17]	1.7[17]	Czech Republic
185	6.5	191	6.7	467	16.4	321	11.3	175	6.1	821	28.8	18[23]	0.6[23]	Denmark
[11]	[11]	[12]	[12]	[12]	[12]	[12]	[12]	[12]	[12]	52[12]	13.2[12]	—	—	Djibouti
2.8	10.7	1.2	4.6	3.7	13.9	0.8	3.1	1.5	5.8	3.4	13.1	3.2[17]	12.3[17]	Dominica
81	4.3	40	2.1	192	10.0	22	1.2	[7]	[7]	363[7]	18.9[7]	553[15]	28.9[15]	Dominican Republic
...	...	...	...	...	...	...	...	...	...	...	...	...	...	East Timor
197	5.9	131	3.9	477	14.2	81	2.4	[7]	[7]	838[7]	24.9[7]	196[15]	5.8[15]	Ecuador
984	5.7	912	5.3	1,609	9.3	286	1.7	[7]	[7]	4,000[7]	23.2[7]	1,858[23]	10.8[23]	Egypt
159	7.1	103	4.6	462	20.5	32	1.4	[7]	[7]	485[7]	21.5[7]	36[2]	1.6[2]	El Salvador
1.9	1.9	1.8	1.7	3.1	3.0	0.4	0.4	[7]	[7]	8.4[7]	8.2[7]	25.8[17]	25.2[17]	Equatorial Guinea
...	...	...	...	...	...	...	...	...	...	...	...	...	...	Eritrea
48	6.8	60	8.4	105	14.8	44	6.2	37	5.2	122	17.2	68[9]	9.6[9]	Estonia

Employment and labour (continued)

country	year	economically active population										distribution by economic sector			
		total ('000)	participation rate (%)		activity rate (%)			employment status (%)				agriculture, forestry, fishing		manufacturing; mining, quarrying; public utilities	
			female	ages 15–64	total	male	female	employers, self-employed	employees	unpaid family workers	other	number ('000)	% of econ. active	number ('000)	% of econ. active
Ethiopia	1995	24,606	41.1	72.2	43.3	50.3	36.5	58.5[35]	6.5[35]	34.0[35]	1.0[35]	21,605	87.8	419	1.7
Faroe Islands	1977	17.6	27.2	64.0	41.9	58.2	23.9	11.9	86.1	...	2.0	3.3	18.8	3.9	21.9
Fiji	1986	241	21.2	56.0	33.7	52.4	14.5	33.6	42.2	16.3	7.9	106	44.1	22	9.0
Finland	1998	2,532	47.0	73.1	49.1	53.4	45.1	11.9	75.2	0.6	12.3	154	6.1	508	20.1
France	1994[18]	25,871	44.9	67.7	44.8	50.6	39.2	10.2	77.4	—	12.4	1,048	4.1	4,432	17.4
French Guiana	1990	48.8	38.2	67.3	42.5	50.5	33.9	10.6	62.7	2.5	24.2	4.2	8.6	3.1	6.4
French Polynesia	1988	75	37.1	64.8	39.9	48.2	30.9	13.0	55.0	4.0	28.0	7.6	10.0	5.4	7.2
Gabon	1991	504	36.9	56.0[10]	43.9	53.9	30.7	...	...	...	...	338	67.1	71[11]	14.1[11]
Gambia, The	1983	326	46.3	78.2	47.3	51.1	43.6	0.5	78.0	14.3	7.1	240	73.7	9	2.9
Gaza Strip	1996	173	9.0	36.3[25]	18.0	32.0	3.2	15.7	46.8	6.7	30.8	9.0	5.2	17.0[36]	9.8[36]
Georgia	1993	1,920	...	58.1[16, 28]	35.7	...	...	...	...	...	...	562	29.3	303	15.8
Germany	1998	39,709	43.1	70.7	48.4	56.5	40.7	9.1	80.3	1.0	9.6	1,200	3.0	10,019	25.2
Ghana	1984	5,580	51.2	82.5[25]	45.4	44.9	45.8	67.7	15.7	12.2	4.4	3,311	59.3	631	11.3
Greece	1997[18]	4,294	39.2	61.3	4.8	53.0	31.5	29.9	49.2	10.7	10.2	773	18.0	680	15.8
Greenland	1976	21.4	33.4	63.5[25]	43.1	53.0	31.4	12.6	82.5	0.4	4.5	3.2	15.1	3.3	15.3
Grenada	1988	38.9	48.6	72.7[35]	39.9	42.9	37.2	16.0[30]	64.2[30]	0.8[30]	19.0[30]	5.6	14.3	3.3	8.6
Guadeloupe	1990	172	45.5	66.4	44.5	49.6	39.7	13.2	53.7	2.0	31.1	8.4	4.9	9.6	5.6
Guam	1990	66.1	37.4	75.7[8]	49.7	58.4	39.7	2.4	94.4	0.1	3.1	0.5	0.8	3.5	5.3
Guatemala	1999	3,489	22.0	55.0	31.5	48.6	14.0	32.7[33]	47.6[33]	16.2[33]	3.5[33]	1,416[33]	48.9[33]	405[33]	14.0[33]
Guernsey[38]	1996	30.7	44.7	76.4	52.3	60.1	45.1	13.0	87.0	—	—	1.9	6.2	2.5	8.2
Guinea	1983	1,823	39.4	63.5	39.1	48.7	30.1	36.2	15.6	37.6	10.6	1,424	78.1	27	1.5
Guinea-Bissau	1995	491	39.9	65.5[10]	45.8	55.9	36.0	...	...	...	...	373	76.0	20[11]	4.1[11]
Guyana	1992–93	278	34.1	61.8	38.8	51.9	26.0	14.3[14]	63.8[14]	1.9[14]	20.0[14]	50[14]	20.4[14]	41[14]	16.8[14]
Haiti	1990	2,679	40.0	64.8	41.1	50.3	32.3	59.1	16.5	10.4	14.0	1,535	57.3	178	6.6
Honduras	1998[18]	2,135	36.9	61.2[25]	36.9	49.2	25.0	40.6	48.0	11.4	—	738	34.6	380	17.8
Hong Kong	1998[18]	3,359	39.3	70.0	51.1	61.9	40.3	9.9[19]	87.4[19]	0.7[19]	1.9[19]	10	0.3	434	12.9
Hungary	1998[18]	4,011	44.4	58.4	39.3	45.8	33.4	10.6	80.3	0.7	8.4	301	7.5	1,115	27.8
Iceland	1998	152.1	47.1	86.6[8]	55.4	59.2	52.2	17.3	80.3	0.3	2.1	12.8	8.4	27.1	17.8
India	1991	314,131	28.6	60.7[25, 30]	37.5	51.6	22.3	8.8[30]	16.3[30]	3.6[30]	71.3[30]	191,341	60.9	30,423	9.7
Indonesia	1998	92,735	38.8	65.3[25]	45.4	55.8	35.0	42.7[34]	33.0[34]	17.1[34]	7.2[34]	39,415	42.5	10,756	11.6
Iran	1996–97	16,027	12.7	46.8[13]	26.7	45.8	6.9	39.7[13]	45.4[13]	2.3[13]	12.6[13]	3,205[13]	21.8[13]	2,243[13]	15.2[13]
Iraq	1988	4,127	12.0	45.3	24.7	42.3	6.1	25.4[39]	59.5[39]	11.4[39]	3.7[39]	477	11.6	439	10.6
Ireland	1997	1,539	39.1	62.7	42.0	51.6	32.6	17.4	71.1	1.1	10.4	145	9.4	314	20.4
Isle of Man	1991	33.2	42.3	73.2	47.6	56.9	38.9	15.8	80.1	—	4.1	1.2	3.7	3.9	11.6
Israel	1998[18]	2,272	44.3	53.5[25]	40.3	45.2	35.5	13.2	77.7	0.5	8.6	50	2.3	434	19.1
Italy	1994[18]	22,680	36.9	57.4	40.1	52.1	28.8	21.4	62.8	4.0	11.8	1,573	6.9	4,837	21.3
Jamaica	1998	1,129	45.6	69.3[40]	43.9	48.7	39.2	32.3	49.9	1.9	15.9	218[19]	20.0[19]	107[19]	9.8[19]
Japan	1998	67,930	40.7	72.6	53.7	65.1	42.9	11.2	79.0	5.4	4.4	3,440	5.1	14,620	21.5
Jersey	1991	47.5	43.2	66.9[25]	56.5	66.1	47.5	12.6	84.0	...	3.4	2.2	4.7	3.8	8.0
Jordan	1993	859	11.4[42]	43.2[42]	22.2	...	...	22.8[43]	67.2[43]	0.8[43]	9.2[43]	55	6.4	97	11.3
Kazakhstan	1995	6,976	...	71.8[16, 20]	40.8	...	...	...	...	...	...	1,442	20.7	1,372	19.7
Kenya	1996	12,269	38.5	63.6[10]	43.9	53.9	33.8	...	...	...	...	9,100	74.2	1,062[11]	8.7[11]
Kiribati	1990	32.6	46.4	75.6[25]	45.1	48.9	41.4	71.9	25.3	...	2.8	23.1	71.0	0.9	2.8
Korea, North	1985	9,084	46.0	75.3	44.6	48.6	40.6	...	...	...	...	3,726[24]	44.1[24]	2,790[11, 24]	33.0[11, 24]
Korea, South	1998[18]	21,390	39.8	60.7[25]	45.9	54.9	36.8	26.8	57.0	9.3	6.8	2,450	11.5	4,246	19.9
Kuwait	1997	1,217	23.5	61.5[42]	55.1	69.0	33.2	3.9[42]	94.1[42]	0.1[42]	1.9[42]	9[42]	1.3[42]	69[42]	9.4[42]
Kyrgyzstan	1998	1,705	46.1	...	37.2	41.1	33.5	...	...	...	...	831	48.7	104	6.1
Laos	1995	2,166	56.4	83.3	47.3	46.2	52.8	...	...	...	...	1,393[14]	75.7[14]	130[11, 14]	7.1[11, 14]
Latvia	1997	1,186	48.1	70.2	48.0	54.0	42.9	11.1	69.3	5.0	14.6	203	17.1	233	19.6
Lebanon	1997	1,362	21.6	49.3	34.0	55.2	14.2	...	...	...	...	132[44]	19.1[44]	131[44]	18.9[44]
Lesotho	1986	504	27.0	44.0	31.6	47.3	16.7	16.8	55.7	20.5	7.0	131	25.9	142	28.2
Liberia	1984	704	41.0	56.3	33.5	39.1	27.8	59.1	21.6	14.4	5.0	481	68.3	31	4.4
Libya	1991	1,169	9.3	37.1[10]	24.8	42.9	4.9	...	...	...	...	129	11.0	372[11]	31.8[11]
Liechtenstein	1996	16.2	40.3	71.3	52.0	63.7	40.8	6.4	90.8	0.1	2.7	0.3	2.0	4.9	30.2
Lithuania	1998	1,835	47.9	71.7[26]	49.5	54.8	44.9	14.1	69.1	0.2	16.6	317	17.2	411	22.4
Luxembourg	1991[45]	168	36.5	62.5	43.5	56.4	31.2	9.2	85.3	1.1	4.4	5	3.2	26	15.8
Macau	1998[18]	210.7	35.3	70.7[40]	50.2	58.2	43.0	8.0	85.9	1.6	4.5	0.4	0.2	44.5	21.1
Macedonia	1996	789	39.1	60.6	39.6	48.1	31.1	...	...	...	...	103	13.0	165	20.9
Madagascar	1996	5,984	38.2	58.7	39.2	48.9	29.8	...	...	...	...	4,381	73.2	926[11]	15.5[11]
Malawi	1987	3,458	51.0	89.4	43.3	43.9	42.8	4.9	16.2	77.6	1.3	2,968	85.8	114	3.3
Malaysia	1998[18]	8,884	33.5	64.4	40.1	52.0	27.5	21.1[20]	71.4[20]	7.5[20]	—	1,617	18.2	1,986	22.4
Maldives	1990	56.4	19.9	50.2	26.5	41.3	10.8	39.7	49.3	4.5	6.5	14.1	25.0	9.4	16.6
Mali	1987	3,438	37.4	67.4	44.7	57.2	32.7	35.4	5.2	57.6	1.8	2,803	81.5	191	5.6
Malta	1990	132	25.4	47.4[13]	37.2	56.1	18.7	14.1[48]	77.4[48]	...	8.5[48]	3	2.5	38	28.8
Marshall Islands	1988	11.5	30.1	54.1[28]	26.5	37.7	14.8	21.6	58.9	7.1	12.5	2.2	18.7	1.0	9.0
Martinique	1990	165	47.5	68.1	45.9	49.8	42.2	9.5	56.9	1.5	32.1	8.4	5.1	9.7	5.9
Mauritania	1995	704	23.0	44.3[10]	31.0	48.1	14.1	...	...	...	...	437	62.1	84[11]	11.9[11]
Mauritius[49]	1995	484	32.9	63.5	42.9	58.1	28.0	15.1	72.9	2.1	9.9	65	13.5	142	29.4
Mayotte	1991	27.3	29.4	56.4	28.9	39.2	17.7	12.0	42.9	7.3	37.8	3.1	11.4	1.3	4.7
Mexico	1998	39,507	33.7	65.4	41.3	56.1	27.2	30.1[20]	53.8[20]	13.6[20]	2.6[20]	7,842	19.8	7,473	18.9
Micronesia	1990	30.5	29.8[14]	60.6	30.3	...	...	2.7[14]	74.4[14]	0.1[14]	22.7[14]	12.7	41.5	1.6	5.2
Moldova	1996	1,686	...	68.7[16, 19]	39.1	...	...	...	...	...	...	711	42.2	195	11.6
Monaco	1990	12.6	39.7	...	42.0	53.2	31.8	17.4	75.1	0.3	7.2	—	0.3	2.7	21.8
Mongolia	1998	841	48.0	64.3[51]	36.7	38.8	34.6	...	...	...	...	300[20]	35.5[20]	124[20]	14.7[20]
Morocco	1982	5,999	19.7	48.9	29.3	47.1	11.6	27.1	40.5	17.6	14.8	2,352	39.2	1,016	16.9
Mozambique	1996	9,318	46.3	83.2[10]	56.3	61.1	51.5	...	...	...	...	7,360	79.0	987[11]	10.6[11]
Myanmar (Burma)	1997–98[18]	18,337	35.3[48]	64.2[48]	40.2[48]	52.4[48]	28.2[48]	41.4[48]	27.4[48]	30.2[48]	1.0[48]	12,093	65.9	1,831	9.9
Namibia	1991	494	43.6	61.3	35.2	39.9	30.5	17.8	49.1	17.9	15.2	190	38.5	41	8.2
Nauru	1977	2.2	...	...	30.5	...	...	...	...	...	...	...	...	...	...
Nepal	1991	7,340	40.4	57.0[10]	40.0	47.8	32.2	75.8	21.4	2.3	0.4	5,962	81.2	164	2.2
Netherlands, The	1998	7,735	42.5	72.9	49.3	57.2	41.5	10.0	84.8	0.8	4.4	236	3.1	1,162	15.0
Netherlands Antilles	1992	87.8	45.1	68.6	46.3	53.1	40.1	...	...	...	...	0.5	0.6	8.4	9.6
New Caledonia	1989	66	37.5	70.7[53]	40.2	49.1	30.8	16.3	64.3	1.6	17.8	7.8	11.8	6.2	9.3
New Zealand	1998[18]	1,864	45.0	74.0	49.2	54.9	43.6	18.1[20]	73.6[20]	0.8[20]	7.5[20]	161	8.6	326	17.5
Nicaragua	1998	1,630	29.5	61.2	34.1	48.9	19.8	...	...	...	...	457[28]	31.4[28]	183[28]	12.5[28]

construction		transportation, communications		trade, hotels, restaurants		finance, real estate		public administration, defense		services		other		country
number ('000)	% of econ. active	number ('000)	% of econ. active	number ('000)	% of econ. active	number ('000)	% of econ. active	number ('000)	% of econ. active	number ('000)	% of econ. active	number ('000)	% of econ. active	
61	0.2	103	0.4	936	3.8	19	0.1	[7]	[7]	1,252[7]	5.1[7]	210[2]	0.9[2]	Ethiopia
2.0	11.1	1.9	11.1	2.1	11.9	0.3	1.9	[7]	[7]	3.5[7]	20.1[7]	0.6	3.2	Faroe Islands
12	4.9	13	5.5	26	10.8	6	2.5	[7]	[7]	37[7]	15.2[7]	20[17]	8.2[17]	Fiji
163	6.4	178	7.0	366	14.5	269	10.6	148	5.8	653	25.8	95[23]	3.8[23]	Finland
1,443	5.7	1,397	5.5	3,716	14.6	2,340	9.2	[7]	[7]	7,733[7]	30.3[7]	3,376[17]	13.2[17]	France
4.4	9.1	1.9	3.8	4.2	8.5	1.7	3.5	[7]	[7]	17.5[7]	35.9[7]	11.8[9]	24.2[9]	French Guiana
5.5	7.4	2.8	3.7	10.3	13.7	1.2	1.5	[7]	[7]	21.5[7]	28.6[7]	21.1[17]	28.0[17]	French Polynesia
[11]	[11]	[12]	[12]	[12]	[12]	[12]	[12]	[12]	[12]	95[12]	18.8[12]	—	—	Gabon
4	1.3	8	2.5	17	5.1	5	1.4	8	2.5	9	2.9	25	7.7	Gambia, The
17.8	10.3	5.7	3.3	20.8	12.0	[1]	[1]	[1]	[1]	49.3[1, 36]	28.5[1, 36]	53.3[9]	30.8[9]	Gaza Strip
125	6.5	107	5.6	117	6.1	20	1.0	49	2.6	479	24.9	158[17]	8.2[17]	Georgia
3,760	9.5	2,090	5.3	6,924	17.4	4,098	10.3	3,174	8.0	8,182	20.6	262[2]	0.7[2]	Germany
65	1.2	123	2.2	792	14.2	27	0.5	98	1.7	376	6.7	158[9]	2.8[9]	Ghana
262	6.1	264	6.1	933	21.7	268	6.2	285	6.6	593	13.8	235[23]	5.5[23]	Greece
3.1	14.6	1.8	8.6	2.7	12.6	0.3	1.6	[7]	[7]	6.3[7]	29.5[7]	0.6	2.8	Greenland
3.5	9.1	1.7	4.4	5.4	13.9	0.8	2.0	[7]	[7]	5.9[7]	15.3[7]	12.7[17]	32.5[17]	Grenada
14.0	8.1	7.0	4.0	15.0	8.7	2.8	1.6	[7]	[7]	60.8[7]	35.2[7]	54.9[17]	31.8[17]	Guadeloupe
8.0	12.1	4.5	6.8	11.5	17.5	3.9	6.0	17.7	26.7	14.5	21.9	2.0[9]	3.1[9]	Guam
114[33]	3.9[33]	72[33]	2.5[33]	375[33]	12.9[33]	38[33]	1.3[33]	[7]	[7]	417[7]	14.4[7]	60[17]	2.1[17]	Guatemala
2.7	8.7	1.3	4.1	7.0	22.9	8.2	26.6	1.9	6.2	5.0	16.2	0.2	0.8	Guernsey[38]
9	0.5	29	1.6	37	2.0	4	0.2	[7]	[7]	138[7]	7.5[7]	156	8.5	Guinea
[11]	[11]	[12]	[12]	[12]	[12]	[12]	[12]	[12]	[12]	98[12]	20.0[12]	—	—	Guinea-Bissau
7[14]	2.8[14]	9[14]	3.8[14]	15[14]	6.2[14]	3[14]	1.2[14]	30[14]	12.1[14]	29[14]	11.9[14]	61[14, 17]	24.7[14, 17]	Guyana
28	1.0	21	0.8	353	13.2	5	0.2	[7]	[7]	155[7]	5.8[7]	404[17]	15.1[17]	Haiti
111	5.2	55	2.6	440	20.6	52	2.5	[7]	[7]	359[7]	16.8[7]	—	—	Honduras
349	10.4	377	11.2	1,024	30.5	431	12.8	[7]	[7]	718[7]	21.4[7]	16[2]	0.5[2]	Hong Kong
257	6.4	315	7.9	640	16.0	258	6.4	313	7.8	747	18.6	67[23]	1.7[23]	Hungary
11.0	7.2	11.0	7.2	25.7	16.9	14.4	9.5	7.1	4.7	41.4	27.2	1.3[2]	1.1[2]	Iceland
5,543	1.8	8,108	2.6	21,296	6.8	[1]	[1]	[1]	[1]	29,312[1]	9.3[1]	28,199	9.0	India
3,522	3.8	4,154	4.5	16,814	18.1	618	0.7	[7]	[7]	12,394[7]	13.4[7]	5,063[9]	5.5[9]	Indonesia
1,372[13]	9.3[13]	762[13]	5.2[13]	1,238[13]	8.4[13]	195[13]	1.3[13]	[7]	[7]	3,518[7, 13]	23.9[7, 13]	2,203[13, 17]	14.9[13, 17]	Iran
461	11.2	266	6.4	282	6.8	42	1.0	[7]	[7]	2,160[7]	52.3[7]	—	—	Iraq
128	8.3	69	4.5	295	19.2	140	9.1	75	4.8	312	20.3	61[17]	4.0[17]	Ireland
3.4	10.3	2.4	7.3	6.1	18.4	4.4	13.1	[7]	[7]	10.4[7]	31.4[7]	1.4[9]	4.1[9]	Isle of Man
144	6.3	130	5.7	377	16.6	304	13.4	115	5.1	606	26.7	111[17]	4.9[17]	Israel
1,641	7.2	1,000	4.0	1,221	18.6	1,514	6.7	[7]	[7]	5,134[7]	22.6[7]	2,676[9]	11.8[9]	Italy
66[19]	6.1[19]	40[19]	3.7[19]	196[19]	17.9[19]	47[19]	4.3[19]	[7]	[7]	237[7, 19]	21.7[7, 19]	180[17, 19]	16.5[17, 19]	Jamaica
6,670	10.0	4,170	6.1	15,150[41]	22.3[41]	5,930	8.7	[7]	[7]	16,010[7, 41]	23.6[7, 41]	1,810[17]	2.7[17]	Japan
4.4	9.3	2.4	5.0	6.8	14.4	7.4	15.6	3.1	6.5	15.7	33.1	1.6[17]	3.4[17]	Jersey
60	7.0	58	6.7	130	15.1	25	2.9	[7]	[7]	435[7]	50.6[7]	—	—	Jordan
364	5.2	507	7.3	1,035	14.8	334	4.8	[7]	[7]	1,664[7]	23.9[7]	258[17]	3.7[17]	Kazakhstan
[11]	[11]	[12]	[12]	[12]	[12]	[12]	[12]	[12]	[12]	2,107[12]	17.2[12]	—	—	Kenya
0.3	1.0	0.9	2.8	1.3	4.1	0.4	1.4	2.1	6.5	2.3	7.0	1.1[17]	3.4[17]	Kiribati
[11]	[11]	[12]	[12]	[12]	[12]	[12]	[12]	[12]	[12]	1,939[12, 24]	22.9[12, 24]	—	—	Korea, North
1,876	8.8	1,218	5.7	5,911	27.6	1,962	9.2	752	3.5	2,713	12.7	270[15]	1.3[15]	Korea, South
115[42]	15.7[42]	38[42]	5.2[42]	83[42]	11.4[42]	22[42]	3.0[42]	[7]	[7]	384[7, 42]	52.6[7, 42]	11[2, 42]	1.5[2, 42]	Kuwait
51	3.0	75	4.4	178	10.4	15	0.9	61	3.6	258	15.2	132	7.7	Kyrgyzstan
[11]	[11]	[12]	[12]	[12]	[12]	[12]	[12]	[12]	[12]	316[12, 14]	17.2[12, 14]	—	—	Laos
69	5.8	96	8.1	198	16.7	57	4.8	67	5.6	209	17.6	55	4.6	Latvia
43[44]	6.2[44]	48[44]	7.0[44]	115[44]	16.5[44]	24[44]	3.5[44]	[7]	[7]	200[7, 44]	28.8[7, 44]	—	—	Lebanon
28	5.5	8	1.6	24	4.7	2	0.5	[7]	[7]	157[7]	31.1[7]	13	2.6	Lesotho
4	0.6	14	2.0	47	6.7	[1]	[1]	[1]	[1]	63[1]	9.0[1]	64[17]	9.1[17]	Liberia
[11]	[11]	[12]	[12]	[12]	[12]	[12]	[12]	[12]	[12]	668[12]	57.1[12]	—	—	Libya
1.1	7.0	0.5	3.2	2.4	14.8	1.3	7.8	1.0	6.4	4.1	25.4	0.6[17]	3.4[17]	Liechtenstein
128	7.0	119	6.5	302	16.4	70	3.8	82	4.4	347	18.9	61[2]	3.3[2]	Lithuania
14	8.4	11	6.3	29	17.5	15	9.2	21	12.8	31	18.7	14[21]	8.1[21]	Luxembourg
23.0	10.9	14.3	6.8	60.0	28.5	14.4	6.8	16.5	7.8	36.6	17.4	1.0	0.5	Macau
36	4.5	27	3.4	77	9.8	15	1.9	28	3.5	88	11.1	251[46]	31.9[46]	Macedonia
[11]	[11]	[12]	[12]	[12]	[12]	[12]	[12]	[12]	[12]	677[12]	11.3[12]	—	—	Madagascar
46	1.4	25	0.7	94	2.7	6	0.2	[7]	[7]	147[7]	4.3[7]	57	1.7	Malawi
746	8.4	422	4.7	1,616	18.2	426	4.8	[7]	[7]	1,788[7]	20.1[7]	284	3.2	Malaysia
3.2	5.6	5.3	9.4	8.9	15.7	1.1	1.9	[7]	[7]	11.8[7]	21.0[7]	2.7[47]	4.7[47]	Maldives
13	0.4	6	0.2	159	4.6	0.3	—	75	2.2	84	2.4	107	3.1	Mali
6	4.4	9	6.9	13	9.8	5	3.7	[7]	[7]	53[7]	40.0[7]	5[9]	3.8[9]	Malta
1.1	9.4	0.5	4.7	1.4	12.1	0.8	7.3	[7]	[7]	3.1[7]	26.4[7]	1.4[17]	12.5[17]	Marshall Islands
9.3	5.6	6.7	4.0	14.0	8.5	3.0	1.8	[7]	[7]	59.1[7]	35.8[7]	54.8[17]	33.2[17]	Martinique
[11]	[11]	[12]	[12]	[12]	[12]	[12]	[12]	[12]	[12]	183[12]	26.0[12]	—	—	Mauritania
46	9.6	29	5.9	76	15.6	14	2.8	27	5.5	62	12.8	23[2]	4.8[2]	Mauritius[49]
3.1	11.4	1.5	5.4	2.0	7.2	0.1	0.4	[7]	[7]	5.7[7]	21.0[7]	10.5[17]	38.4[17]	Mayotte
2,189	5.5	1,730	4.4	8,777	22.2	1,518	3.8	1,630	4.1	8,051	20.4	298[17]	0.8[17]	Mexico
1.8	6.1	[50]	[50]	[50]	[50]	[50]	[50]	6.3	20.8	3.7[50]	12.1[50]	4.1[9]	13.5[9]	Micronesia
55	3.3	66	3.9	271	16.1	47	2.8	30	1.8	285	16.9	26	1.5	Moldova
0.7	5.3	...	...	2.5	20.2	1.0	8.0	2.8	22.4	1.9	14.9	0.9[21]	7.1[21]	Monaco
33	3.9	38	4.4	62	7.3	[1]	[1]	[1]	[1]	123[1, 20]	14.5[1, 20]	166[20, 21]	19.7[20, 21]	Mongolia
437	7.3	141	2.3	498	8.3	[52]	[52]	533	8.9	474[52]	7.9[52]	548[2]	9.1[2]	Morocco
[11]	[11]	[12]	[12]	[12]	[12]	[12]	[12]	[12]	[12]	971[12]	10.4[12]	—	—	Mozambique
400	2.2	495	2.7	1,781	9.7	...	...	[7]	[7]	1,485[7]	8.1[7]	270	1.5	Myanmar (Burma)
19	3.8	9	1.9	38	7.7	9	1.7	[7]	[7]	6[7]	1.2[7]	183[17]	37.1[17]	Namibia
...	...	...	...	...	...	...	...	...	...	...	...	...	...	Nauru
36	0.5	51	0.7	256	3.5	20	0.3	[7]	[7]	752[7]	10.3[7]	98	1.3	Nepal
451	5.8	442	5.7	1,487	19.2	1,097	14.2	525	6.8	1,833	23.7	498[17]	6.4[17]	Netherlands, The
6.5	7.4	5.0	5.7	20.9	23.8	8.2	9.3	[7]	[7]	24.8[7]	28.2[7]	13.4[9]	15.3[9]	Netherlands Antilles
4.5	6.8	3.1	4.7	9.5	14.3	2.5	3.8	[7]	[7]	22.0[7]	33.4[7]	13.5[9]	16.0[9]	New Caledonia
120	6.5	109	5.8	398	21.3	224	12.0	[7]	[7]	493[7]	26.4[7]	33[17]	1.8[17]	New Zealand
32[28]	2.2[28]	32[28]	2.2[28]	201[28]	13.8[28]	16[28]	1.1[28]	79[28]	5.4[28]	195[28]	13.4[28]	265[9, 28]	18.2[9, 28]	Nicaragua

Employment and labour (continued)

country	year	economically active population										distribution by economic sector			
		total ('000)	participation rate (%)		activity rate (%)			employment status (%)				agriculture, forestry, fishing		manufacturing; mining, quarrying; public utilities	
			female	ages 15–64	total	male	female	employers, self-employed	employees	unpaid family workers	other	number ('000)	% of econ. active	number ('000)	% of econ. active
Niger	1988[54]	2,316	20.4	55.2	31.9	51.1	13.0	51.4	5.0	40.3	3.3	1,764	76.2	73	3.1
Nigeria	1986[18]	30,766	33.3	58.8	31.1	41.1	20.9	64.6	18.8	10.7	5.9	13,259	43.1	1,401	4.6
Northern Mariana Islands	1990	26.6	43.2	83.6[8]	61.3	66.2	55.9	1.4	96.1	0.2	2.3	0.6	2.3	6.0	22.5
Norway	1998	2,317	46.2	80.8	52.3	56.9	47.8	7.4	88.7	0.6	3.2	104	4.5	375	16.2
Oman	1993	705	9.7	60.9	34.9	54.0	8.1	5.2	91.0	0.1	3.7	64	9.1	79	11.3
Pakistan	1996–97[18]	36,407	15.2	51.0	28.7	47.0	9.0	40.6[55]	34.2[55]	19.1[55]	6.1[55]	15,148	41.6	4,222	11.6
Palau	1990	6.1	36.9	64.1[8]	40.2	47.1	32.1	2.5	89.5	0.2	7.8	0.4	7.1	0.2	3.0
Panama	1998	1,049	35.5	66.4	38.4	49.0	27.6	23.9	59.5	2.7	13.9	180	17.2	118	11.3
Papua New Guinea	1980[56]	733	39.8	35.2[10]	24.6	28.3	20.5	72.7	26.4	—	0.9	564	77.0	21	2.9
Paraguay	1982	1,039	19.7	57.5	34.3	54.8	13.6	43.1	37.7	9.2	9.9	446	42.9	129	12.4
Peru	1995	8,906	34.7	60.9	37.8	49.8	26.1	39.8[30]	41.8[30]	8.4[30]	10.0[30]	2,693[20]	32.5[20]	1,091[20]	13.2[20]
Philippines	1998[18]	31,278	37.6	67.9	41.1	51.4	30.8	36.2[19]	41.7[19]	13.7[19]	8.4[19]	11,272	36.0	2,931	9.4
Poland	1998[18]	16,197	45.7	66.1	44.4	49.5	39.5	21.3	69.0	4.5	5.2	3,045	17.7	4,272	24.9
Portugal	1998[18]	5,000	45.0	70.3	50.2	57.3	43.6	24.2	68.0	0.8	7.0	651	13.0	1,243	24.9
Puerto Rico	1998[18]	1,320	42.2	54.5	34.2	41.0	27.9	13.6[34]	85.2[34]	0.7[34]	0.6[34]	35	2.7	203	15.4
Qatar	1988	293	11.2	80.8	53.7	77.3	22.2	1.8[44]	97.7[44]	—	0.5[44]	4.5	1.6	22.0	7.5
Réunion	1990[18]	234	41.1	60.3	39.1	46.8	31.6	8.4	53.1	1.1	37.4	11	4.8	11	4.8
Romania	1998	11,577	45.6	69.0	51.4	57.1	45.9	21.1	55.9	16.7	6.3	4,411	38.1	2,950	25.5
Russia	1996	68,264	46.6	71.9[51]	46.2	52.7	40.5	...	...	...	...	10,079	14.8	15,950	23.4
Rwanda	1996	3,719	47.5	67.5[10]	45.6	48.4	42.8	...	...	...	...	3,375	90.7	133[11]	3.6[11]
St. Kitts and Nevis	1980	17.1	41.0	69.5	39.5	48.4	31.2	9.7	78.5	0.4	11.4	4.5	26.1	3.8	22.3
St. Lucia	1991	53.1	40.3	67.6	39.9	49.1	31.2	21.0[14]	55.8[14]	1.6[14]	21.6[14]	11.6	21.8	7.5	14.0
St. Vincent	1991	41.7	35.9	67.5	39.1	50.3	28.0	18.2	59.6	2.1	20.1	8.4	20.1	3.5	8.4
Samoa	1986	45.6	18.8	48.6[30]	29.0	44.5	11.6	21.1[30]	43.5[30]	35.0[30]	0.4[30]	29.0	63.6	2.4	5.4
San Marino	1998	18.5	39.6	77.9	58.4	66.6	49.2	13.9	79.3	0.2	6.6	0.2	1.4	5.8	31.2
São Tomé and Príncipe	1991	35	33.6	59.1	30.1	40.5	20.0	25.8	68.6	0.7	4.9	13.6	38.4	1.8	5.0
Saudi Arabia	1988	5,369	3.6	59.1	36.3	54.9	3.6	...	...	...	...	192	3.6	595	11.1
Senegal	1995	3,508	38.3	62.1[10]	42.2	52.0	32	...	...	...	...	2,719	77.5	259[11]	7.4[11]
Seychelles	1993[57]	28.1	...	...	38.9	...	...	...	...	...	...	2.2	7.7	4.6[11]	16.4[11]
Sierra Leone	1995	1,648	31.7	54.1[10]	36.5	50.9	22.7	...	...	...	...	964	58.5	319[11]	19.4[11]
Singapore	1998[18]	1,932	41.8	69.0	51.6	60.8	42.6	12.2	83.6	1.0	3.2	4	0.2	429	22.2
Slovakia	1998[18]	2,464	45.6	67.0	45.7	51.1	40.6	6.0	81.9	—	12.1	185	7.5	710	28.8
Slovenia	1998	982	46.3	69.1	49.6	54.5	44.7	11.5	74.7	6.1	7.6	110	11.2	332	33.8
Solomon Islands	1993[58]	29.6	25.6[44]	24.9[44, 59]	13.7[44]	19.7[44]	7.3[44]	29.6[44]	68.6[44]	—	1.8[44]	8.1	27.4	3.1	10.4
Somalia	1996	3,667	39.3	59.9[10]	38.8	47.1	29.9	...	...	...	...	2,446	66.7	417[11]	11.4[11]
South Africa[60]	1991	11,624	39.4	69.3[53]	37.5	45.5	29.5	7.0	74.8	...	18.2	1,224	10.5	2,361	20.3
Spain	1998[18]	16,265	39.2	62.6	41.6	51.9	31.8	11.9	62.4	0.9	24.7	1,286	7.9	2,965	18.2
Sri Lanka	1998	6,693	35.8	58.8[25]	43.4	55.9	30.9	24.9[34]	54.2[34]	7.8[34]	13.1[34]	2,472	36.9	1,028	15.4
Sudan, The	1983[54]	6,343	29.1	57.4	35.1	50.0	20.4	...	...	...	...	4,029	63.5	317	5.0
Suriname	1994[61]	89.8	35.1	52.3	45.2	59.4	31.4	...	...	...	...	4.8	5.3	10.7	11.9
Swaziland	1996	371	37.7	60.5[10]	42.3	55.0	30.6	...	...	...	...	231	62.3	44[11]	11.9[11]
Sweden	1998	4,255	47.5	76.5[8]	48.0	50.9	45.1	9.5	83.6	0.4	6.5	109	2.6	849	20.0
Switzerland	1998[18, 45]	3,975	44.2	67.9[25]	55.9	63.9	48.4	12.8[19]	84.3[19]	2.9[19]	—	179	4.5	715	18.0
Syria	1998[18]	4,411	17.5	51.2	28.3	46.9	9.8	31.0[13]	49.3[13]	13.0[13]	6.7[13]	917[13]	26.3[13]	471[13]	13.5[13]
Taiwan	1996[18]	9,310	39.2	58.4[25]	43.4	51.3	35.0	21.7	67.5	8.1	2.6	918	9.9	2,471	26.5
Tajikistan	1996	1,778	46.5	63.5[16, 20]	30.3	32.5	28.2	...	...	...	...	1,026	57.7	202	11.4
Tanzania	1996	15,170	46.6	74.1[10]	49.7	53.6	45.9	...	...	...	...	11,738	77.4	725[11]	4.8[11]
Thailand	1998[18, 62]	33,352	45.1	73.6[25]	54.5	60.0	49.0	31.2[63]	40.3[63]	19.5[63]	9.1[63]	16,472	49.4	4,449	13.3
Togo	1995	1,575	35.4	57.1[10]	38.1	49.7	26.7	70.3[30]	10.4[30]	11.3[30]	8.0[30]	1,059	67.2	183[11]	11.6[11]
Tonga	1990	32.0	33.0	57.0	33.6	45.2	22.0	33.7	45.4	16.8	4.1	11.7	36.5	5.1	15.8
Trinidad and Tobago	1998	559	38.3	65.4[34]	47.1	57.2	36.6	17.2	69.1	1.6	12.1	41	7.4	88	15.8
Tunisia	1989	2,361	20.9	50.6	29.8	46.5	12.7	20.9	54.9	7.4	16.8	510	21.6	418	17.7
Turkey	1998[18]	23,415	29.0	54.8	36.6	51.4	21.5	27.6[20]	41.5[20]	27.7[20]	3.2[20]	9,601	41.0	3,852	16.5
Turkmenistan	1996	1,680	40.0	71.9[16]	36.1	43.9	28.5	...	...	...	...	746	44.4	165	9.8
Tuvalu	1991	5.9	51.3[43]	85.5	65.3	...	...	0.3[43]	22.2[43]	—77.5[43]—		4.2	68.0	0.1	2.0
Uganda	1996	9,636	39.9	68.9[10]	44.0	53.2	34.8	...	...	...	...	7,440	77.2	637[11]	6.6[11]
Ukraine	1998	25,936	50.9	74.9	51.6	54.6	49.0	...	...	...	...	5,074	19.6	4,227	16.3
United Arab Emirates	1990	690	10.4[42]	69.0[42]	47.0[42]	67.6[42]	12.9[42]	6.8[14]	92.7[14]	0.1[14]	0.5[14]	43	6.3	94	13.6
United Kingdom	1998	28,713	44.3	76.2[20]	49.2	55.7	43.0	11.2[20]	76.7[20]	0.5[20]	11.6[20]	479	1.7	5,592	19.5
United States	1998[18]	137,674	46.3	79.4[53]	50.9	55.9	46.1	7.5	87.9	0.1	4.5	3,724	2.7	23,723	17.2
Uruguay	1998[64]	1,239	44.0	71.3	47.0	55.8	39.1	22.9[28]	72.3[28]	2.3[28]	2.5[28]	47	3.8	215	17.3
Uzbekistan	1998	8,800	...	72.3	36.7	...	...	...	...	...	...	3,467	39.4	1,114	12.7
Vanuatu	1989	67.0	46.3	85.0	47.0	49.0	44.9	...	...	...	...	49.8	74.4	1.0	1.5
Venezuela	1997[18]	9,507	35.9	67.2	41.7	53.2	30.1	30.2[20]	61.8[20]	1.7[20]	6.3[20]	940	9.9	1,430	15.0
Vietnam	1989	30,521	51.7	79.9	47.4	47.0	47.7	...	...	...	...	20,471	67.1	3,390	11.1
Virgin Islands (U.S.)	1990[18]	47.4	47.8	70.3	46.6	50.3	43.1	7.6	85.5	0.2	6.7	0.6	1.2	3.7	7.8
West Bank	1996	356.9	16.1	42.2[25]	22.7	37.7	7.4	24.5	49.0	8.1	18.5	41.3	11.6	51.8[36]	14.5[36]
Western Sahara	...	...	...	...	...	...	...	...	...	...	...	...	...	...	...
Yemen	1988	3,029	31.6	52.6	26.4	36.8	16.4	...	...	...	...	2,152	71.1	129	4.3
Yugoslavia	1996	3,182	43.4[19]	58.7[25, 34]	30.1	...	...	...	...	...	...	104	3.3	903	28.4
Zambia	1996	3,507	30.3	54.5	36.1	50.9	21.7	22.9[14]	42.5[14]	3.6[14]	31.0[14]	2,322	66.2	428[11]	12.2[11]
Zimbabwe	1992	3,601	39.6	63.4	34.6	42.8	26.7	24.1	43.9	9.2	22.8	2,110[66]	64.7[66]	179[66]	5.5[66]

[1]Services includes finance, real estate and public administration, defense. [2]Unemployed, not previously employed only. [3]Includes emigrant workers (352,000). [4]Ages 15–59 (male) and 15–54 (female). [5]State sector only. [6]Includes nonagricultural private sector (241,000) and unemployed (261,000). [7]Services includes public administration, defense. [8]Ages 16–64. [9]Unemployed only. [10]Over age 10. [11]Manufacturing; mining, quarrying; public utilities includes construction. [12]Services includes transportation, communications; trade, hotels, restaurants; finance, real estate; and public administration, defense. [13]1991. [14]1980. [15]Includes unemployed, not previously employed. [16]Ages 16–59 (male) and 16–54 (female). [17]Mostly unemployed. [18]Excludes all or some classes or elements of the military. [19]1994. [20]1993. [21]Includes unemployed. [22]1990. [23]Mostly unemployed, not previously employed. [24]1982. [25]Over age 15. [26]Ages 14–64. [27]Services includes restaurants and hotels. [28]1992. [29]Over age 12. [30]1981. [31]Republic of Cyprus only. [32]1993 population economically active for Turkish Republic of Northern Cyprus is 75,947. [33]1989. [34]1995.

construction		transportation, communications		trade, hotels, restaurants		finance, real estate		public administration, defense		services		other		country
number ('000)	% of econ. active	number ('000)	% of econ. active	number ('000)	% of econ. active	number ('000)	% of econ. active	number ('000)	% of econ. active	number ('000)	% of econ. active	number ('000)	% of econ. active	
14	0.6	15	0.6	209	9.0	2	0.1	[7]	[7]	123[7]	5.3[7]	117[21]	5.0[21]	Niger
546	1.8	1,112	3.6	7,417	24.1	120	0.4	[7]	[7]	4,902[7]	15.9[7]	2,009[17]	6.5[17]	Nigeria
5.8	21.7	1.4	5.3	5.3	19.8	1.0	3.8	1.4	5.3	4.5	16.9	0.6[9]	2.3[9]	Northern Mariana Islands
145	6.3	170	7.3	411	17.7	229	9.9	152	6.6	655	28.3	75	3.2	Norway
108	15.3	25	3.5	104	14.8	17	2.5	166	23.5	111	15.8	30[23]	4.3[23]	Oman
2,330	6.4	1,971	5.4	5,021	13.8	338	0.9	[7]	[7]	5,395[7]	14.8[7]	1,982[23]	5.4[23]	Pakistan
0.9	14.2	0.4	6.6	1.1	18.7	0.2	2.9	0.8	13.7	1.6	26.1	0.5[9]	7.8[9]	Palau
72	6.9	66	6.3	232	22.1	59	5.6	74	7.0	205	19.5	43[23]	4.1[23]	Panama
22	2.9	1.7	2.4	25	3.4	4	0.6	[7]	[7]	77[7]	10.5[7]	2	0.2	Papua New Guinea
70	6.7	31	2.9	86	8.3	18	1.7	[7]	[7]	174[7]	16.8[7]	86[15]	8.3[15]	Paraguay
308[20]	3.7[20]	364[20]	4.4[20]	1,352[20]	16.3[20]	197[20]	2.4[20]	[7]	[7]	2,287[7, 20]	27.6[7, 20]	—	—	Peru
1,511	4.8	1,885	6.0	4,328[27]	13.8[27]	695	2.2	[7]	[7]	5,631[7, 27]	18.0[7, 27]	3,024[17]	9.7[17]	Philippines
1,248	7.3	1,015	5.9	2,641	15.4	866	5.0	844	4.9	2,754	16.0	511[23]	3.0[23]	Poland
539	10.8	184	3.7	953	19.1	277	5.5	309	6.2	798	16.0	45[2]	0.9[2]	Portugal
103	7.8	50	3.8	266[41]	20.2[41]	44	3.3	[7]	[7]	602[7, 41]	45.6[7, 41]	17[23]	1.3[23]	Puerto Rico
64.2	22.0	11.9	4.1	34.2	11.7	6.2	2.1	[7]	[7]	149.6[7]	51.1[7]	—	—	Qatar
17	7.1	7	3.1	18	7.7	3	1.3	[7]	[7]	79[7]	33.9[7]	87[17]	37.4[17]	Réunion
471	4.1	545	4.7	1,134	9.8	245	2.1	522	4.5	1,006	8.7	291[23]	2.5[23]	Romania
5,516	8.1	5,219	7.6	7,165	10.5	5,077	7.4	2,726	4.0	14,229	20.8	2,314	3.4	Russia
[11]	[11]	[12]	[12]	[12]	[12]	[12]	[12]	[12]	[12]	212[12]	5.7[12]	—	—	Rwanda
0.4	2.5	0.3	1.6	1.3	7.3	0.8	4.7	1.0	5.7	2.9	17.0	2.2[17]	12.8[17]	St. Kitts and Nevis
5.0	9.3	2.7	5.0	11.1	20.8	1.9	3.6	[7]	[7]	9.2[7]	17.2[7]	4.3	8.2	St. Lucia
3.5	8.5	2.3	5.5	6.5	15.7	1.4	3.4	[7]	[7]	7.7[7]	18.5[7]	8.3[9]	20.0[9]	St. Vincent
0.1	0.1	1.5	3.3	1.7	3.7	0.8	1.8	[7]	[7]	9.4[7]	20.7[7]	0.6	1.4	Samoa
1.5	8.2	0.4	1.9	2.8	15.2	1.4	7.8	2.3	12.4	2.8	15.2	1.3[21]	6.8[21]	San Marino
2.9	8.1	2.2	6.2	4.5	12.6	0.2	0.5	[7]	[7]	8.0[7]	22.5[7]	2.4	6.7	São Tomé and Príncipe
1,181	22.0	321	6.0	964	18.0	151	2.8	[7]	[7]	1,965[7]	36.6[7]	—	—	Saudi Arabia
[11]	[11]	[12]	[12]	[12]	[12]	[12]	[12]	[12]	[12]	530[12]	15.1[12]	—	—	Senegal
[11]	[11]	3.4	12.2	5.2	18.6	1.0	3.4	2.6	9.1	5.6	20.0	3.6[17]	12.6[17]	Seychelles
[11]	[11]	[12]	[12]	[12]	[12]	[12]	[12]	[12]	[12]	365[12]	22.1[12]	—	—	Sierra Leone
136	7.0	212	11.0	415	21.5	300	15.5	119	6.2	307	15.9	9[2]	0.5[2]	Singapore
222	9.0	176	7.2	368	14.9	127	5.2	162	6.6	400	16.2	113[23]	4.6[23]	Slovakia
56	5.7	53	5.4	163	16.6	68	6.9	42	4.3	134	13.6	2.3[23]	2.4[23]	Slovenia
1.0	3.3	1.7	5.8	3.4	11.5	1.1	3.9	4.3	14.6	6.8	23.1	—	—	Solomon Islands
[11]	[11]	[12]	[12]	[12]	[12]	[12]	[12]	[12]	[12]	804[12]	21.9[12]	—	—	Somalia
526	4.5	497	4.3	1,358	11.7	504	4.3	[7]	[7]	2,641[7]	22.7[7]	2,513[17]	21.6[17]	South Africa[60]
1,546	9.5	828	5.1	3,387	20.8	1,331	8.2	905	5.0	2,004	10.0	1,382[23]	8.5[23]	Spain
309	4.6	268	4.0	594	8.9	117	1.8	[7]	[7]	1,007[7]	15.0[7]	897[17]	13.4[17]	Sri Lanka
139	2.2	215	3.4	294	4.6	21	0.3	[7]	[7]	550[7]	8.7[7]	777[23]	12.3[23]	Sudan, The
4.2	4.6	5.1	5.6	11.4	12.7	3.5	3.9	[7]	[7]	35.7[7]	39.7[7]	14.6[17]	16.3[17]	Suriname
[11]	[11]	[12]	[12]	[12]	[12]	[12]	[12]	[12]	[12]	96[12]	25.9[12]	—	—	Swaziland
244	5.7	285	6.7	663	15.6	519	12.2	218	5.1	1,328	31.2	39[23]	0.9[23]	Sweden
297	7.5	244	6.1	899	22.6	572	14.4	153	3.8	791	19.9	125	3.1	Switzerland
341[13]	9.8[13]	167[13]	4.8[13]	378[13]	10.9[13]	25[13]	0.7[13]	[7]	[7]	951[7, 13]	27.3[7, 13]	235[9, 13]	6.8[9, 13]	Syria
928	10.0	472	5.1	1,976	21.2	567	6.1	324	3.5	1,412	15.2	242[9]	2.6[9]	Taiwan
68	3.8	58	3.3	69	3.9	[1]	[1]	[1]	[1]	309[1]	17.3[1]	46[9]	2.6[9]	Tajikistan
[11]	[11]	[12]	[12]	[12]	[12]	[12]	[12]	[12]	[12]	2,708[12]	17.8[12]	—	—	Tanzania
1,280	3.8	923	2.8	4,464	13.4	[1]	[1]	[1]	[1]	4,584[1]	13.7[1]	1,222[17]	3.7[17]	Thailand
[11]	[11]	[12]	[12]	[12]	[12]	[12]	[12]	[12]	[12]	331[12]	21.0[12]	—	—	Togo
1.3	3.9	1.8	5.7	2.6	8.1	1.2	3.7	[7]	[7]	7.1[7]	22.0[7]	1.3[9]	4.2[9]	Tonga
84	14.9	38	6.8	99	17.6	43	7.7	[7]	[7]	165[7]	29.6[7]	1	0.1	Trinidad and Tobago
248	10.5	96	4.1	217	9.2	15	0.7	[7]	[7]	444[7]	18.8[7]	412[17]	17.5[17]	Tunisia
1,464	6.3	996	4.3	3,075	13.1	536	2.3	[7]	[7]	3,260[7]	13.9[7]	631[2]	2.7[2]	Turkey
155	9.2	83	4.9	107	6.4	55	3.3	25	1.5	300	17.9	44	2.6	Turkmenistan
0.2	4.0	0.1	1.0	0.2	4.0	—	—	[7]	[7]	1.3[7]	22.0[7]	—	—	Tuvalu
[11]	[11]	[12]	[12]	[12]	[12]	[12]	[12]	[12]	[12]	1,559[12]	16.2[12]	—	—	Uganda
1,092	4.2	1,400	5.4	1,514	5.8	213	0.8	[7]	[7]	5,886	22.7	6,509	25.1	Ukraine
119	17.3	72	10.4	101	14.7	19	2.7	[7]	[7]	241[7]	35.0[7]	—	—	United Arab Emirates
2,037	7.1	1,846	6.4	5,695	19.8	4,085	14.2	1,612	5.6	6,857	23.9	509[23]	1.8[23]	United Kingdom
9,094	6.6	8,075	5.9	28,740[41]	20.9[41]	16,151	11.7	[7]	[7]	47,623[7, 41]	34.6[7, 41]	543[23]	0.4[23]	United States
93	7.5	71	5.7	249	20.1	77	6.2	[7]	[7]	465[7]	37.5[7]	23[2]	1.9[2]	Uruguay
841	9.6	362	4.1	715	8.1	284	3.2	[7]	[7]	1,691[7]	19.2[7]	326	3.7	Uzbekistan
1.3	1.9	1.0	1.5	2.7	4.1	0.6	1.0	[7]	[7]	7.9[7]	11.8[7]	2.6	3.8	Vanuatu
841	8.8	578	6.1	2,169	22.8	523	5.5	[7]	[7]	2,616[7]	27.5[7]	410[23]	4.3[23]	Venezuela
581	1.9	576	1.9	1,880	6.2	90	0.3	305	1.0	1,374	4.5	1,854[17]	6.1[17]	Vietnam
5.7	12.0	3.7	7.8	10.3	21.8	3.6	7.7	5.1	10.8	7.8	16.4	6.9	14.6	Virgin Islands (U.S.)
60.8	17.0	15.7	4.4	52.6	14.8	[1]	[1]	[1]	[1]	68.6[1, 36]	19.2[1, 36]	66.0[9]	18.5[9]	West Bank
...	...	...	...	...	...	...	...	...	...	...	...	...	...	Western Sahara
178	5.9	90	3.0	84	2.8	4	0.1	[7]	[7]	391[7]	12.9[7]	—	—	Yemen
130	4.1	142	4.5	557[65]	17.5[65]	77	2.4	92	2.9	356	11.2	819[9]	25.7[9]	Yugoslavia
[11]	[11]	[12]	[12]	[12]	[12]	[12]	[12]	[12]	[12]	757[12]	21.6[12]	—	—	Zambia
51[66]	1.6[66]	76[66]	2.3[66]	128[66]	3.9[66]	24[66]	0.7[66]	[7]	[7]	397[7, 66]	12.2[7, 66]	277[17, 66]	8.5[17, 66]	Zimbabwe

[35]1984. [36]Services includes public utilities. [37]Ages 15–65. [38]Excludes Alderney and Sark. [39]1977. [40]Ages 14–64. [41]Services includes hotels. [42]1988. [43]1979. [44]1986. [45]Excludes foreign border workers. [46]Includes unemployed, emigrant workers, and employees in private nonagricultural sector. [47]Includes unemployed, previously employed. [48]1983. [49]Island of Mauritius only. [50]Services includes transportation, communications; trade, hotels, restaurants; and finance, real estate. [51]Ages 15–59. [52]Services includes finance, real estate. [53]Ages 20–64. [54]Excludes nomadic population. [55]1996–97. [56]Citizens over age 10 involved in money-raising activities only. [57]Excludes domestic workers (private households), self-employed, and family workers. [58]Wage earners only. [59]Over age 14. [60]Excludes the former black independent states of Bophuthatswana, Ciskei, Transkei, and Venda. [61]Districts of Wanica and Paramaribo only. [62]August survey. [63]1994; February survey. [64]Urban areas only. [65]Includes arts and crafts and owners and employees of private shops. [66]1986–87.

Crops and livestock

This table provides comparative data for selected categories of agricultural production for the countries of the world. The data are taken mainly from the United Nations Food and Agriculture Organization's (FAO) annual *Production Yearbook* and the online FAOSTAT statistics database (http://apps.fao.org/default.htm).

The FAO depends largely on questionnaires supplied to each country for its statistics, but, where no official or semiofficial responses are returned, the FAO makes estimates, using incomplete, unofficial, or other similarly limited data. And, although the FAO provides standardized guidelines upon which many nations have organized their data collection systems and methods, persistent, often traditional, variations in standards of coverage, methodology, and reporting periods reduce the comparability of statistics that *can* be supplied on such forms. FAO data are based on calendar-year periods; that is, data for any particular crop refer to the calendar year in which the harvest (or the bulk of the harvest) occurred.

In spite of the often tragic food shortages in a number of countries in recent years, worldwide agricultural production is probably more often underreported than overreported. Many countries do not report complete domestic production. Some countries, for example, report only crops that are sold commercially and ignore subsistence crops produced for family or communal consumption, or barter; others may limit reporting to production for export only, to holdings above a certain size, or represent a sampling only.

Methodological problems attach to much smaller elements of the agricultural whole, however. The FAO's cereals statistics relate, ideally, to weight or volume of crops harvested for dry grain (excluding cereal crops used for grazing, harvested for hay, or harvested green for food, feed, or silage). Some countries, however, collect the basic data they report to the FAO on sown or cultivated areas instead and calculate production statistics from estimates of yield. Millet and sorghum, which in many European and North American countries are used primarily as livestock or poultry feed, may be reportable by such countries as animal fodder only, while elsewhere many nations use the same grains for human consumption and report them as cereals. Statistics for tropical fruits are frequently not compiled by producing countries, and coverage is not uniform, with some countries reporting only commercial fruits and others including those consumed for

Crops and livestock

country	crops															
	grains				roots and tubers[a]				pulses[b]				fruits[c]		vegetables[d]	
	production ('000 metric tons)		yield (kg/hectare)		production ('000 metric tons)		yield (kg/hectare)		production ('000 metric tons)		yield (kg/hectare)		production ('000 metric tons)		production ('000 metric tons)	
	1989–91 average	1999	1989–91 average	1999	1989–91 average	1999	1989–91 average	1999	1989–91 average	1999	1989–91 average	1999	1989–91 average	1999	1989–91 average	1999
Afghanistan	2,754	3,876	1,200	1,388	217	235	16,291	16,786	32	35	913	946	647	615	466	492
Albania	792	512	2,609	2,653	88	162	8,409	14,202	20	28	729	946	154	128	377	640
Algeria	2,482	1,540	823	815	962	996	9,173	15,353	49	37	424	431	1,055	1,478	1,782	2,841
American Samoa	...	...	...	...	2	2	3,721	3,361	...	...	...	...	1	1	—	—
Andorra	...	...	...	...	...	...	...	...	...	...	...	...	...	...	...	...
Angola	313	550	350	619	1,818	3,331	3,914	6,071	35	68	273	356	414	423	250	240
Antigua and Barbuda	—	—	1,921	1,607	—	—	5,171	4,811	...	...	...	...	9	8	2	2
Argentina	19,938	33,426	2,341	3,380	2,296	3,930	18,240	25,941	244	375	1,089	1,194	5,977	7,060	2,798	3,353
Armenia	282[1]	296	1,500[1]	1,705	365[1]	425	12,080[1]	13,690	3[1]	—	1,714[1]	452	237[1]	233	444[1]	457
Aruba	...	...	...	...	...	...	...	...	...	...	...	...	...	...	...	...
Australia	21,390	31,117	1,665	1,945	1,127	1,378	28,301	31,788	1,530	2,232	1,025	1,115	2,361	2,740	1,525	1,809
Austria	5,115	4,756	5,443	5,887	810	660	24,907	28,473	119	86	3,555	3,132	944	1,021	455	607
Azerbaijan	1,130[1]	932	1,733[1]	1,596	153[1]	334	8,179[1]	9,543	...	11	...	2,343	803[1]	390	771[1]	816
Bahamas, The	1	—	1,522	2,168	1	1	6,900	5,585	1	—	1,199	718	12	30	27	22
Bahrain	...	...	...	...	—	—	14,112	16,000	—	—	836	1,091	20	22	10	12
Bangladesh	28,032	31,832	2,530	2,791	1,643	2,100	9,744	11,015	512	513	699	769	1,331	1,405	1,332	1,571
Barbados	2	2	2,656	2,500	6	7	9,271	6,038	1	1	1,261	1,254	3	3	7	12
Belarus	6,749[1]	3,353	2,610[1]	1,556	9,623[1]	8,000	12,975[1]	11,765	235[1]	253	1,335[1]	1,193	561[1]	297	917[1]	1,192
Belgium[2]	2,236	2,378	6,094	7,163	1,838	2,700	37,421	49,091	18	16	4,062	3,926	371	806	1,479	1,719
Belize	28	46	1,640	2,055	4	4	21,838	21,765	3	5	763	956	134	293	5	5
Benin	566	1,047	860	1,170	2,102	4,219	9,354	10,735	60	109	552	719	160	190	211	341
Bermuda	...	...	...	...	1	1	20,985	20,735	...	...	...	...	—	—	3	3
Bhutan	102	112	1,062	1,097	52	56	9,910	10,750	2	2	800	800	64	64	9	10
Bolivia	882	1,164	1,416	1,507	1,219	1,292	6,192	6,950	31	28	1,079	1,010	782	1,042	374	519
Bosnia and Herzegovina	1,176[1]	438	3,230[1]	2,561	230[1]	380	4,672[1]	7,755	19[1]	17	1,086[1]	1,274	130[1]	78	533[1]	609
Botswana	60	20	308	204	7	12	5,385	7,059	17	16	556	500	11	10	16	16
Brazil	37,705	47,635	1,868	2,731	27,247	24,655	12,574	13,382	2,471	2,912	473	680	30,184	37,573	5,590	5,402
Brunei	1	—	1,793	707	1	2	3,344	4,261	...	...	...	...	5	5	8	9
Bulgaria	8,872	4,888	4,121	...	495	478	11,987	9,041	89	39	1,021	709	1,576	992	1,754	1,726
Burkina Faso	1,975	2,662	717	887	79	63	5,830	5,978	60	66	815	825	71	73	229	228
Burundi	283	265	1,299	1,310	1,429	1,479	6,843	6,937	333	262	1,014	922	1,675	1,595	210	210
Cambodia	2,591	3,850	1,431	1,915	105	111	5,366	7,351	13	11	500	420	239	314	472	460
Cameroon	892	1,236	1,182	1,138	2,070	2,449	6,293	5,669	68	101	517	674	1,846	2,188	451	567
Canada	53,016	53,776	2,467	3,083	2,903	4,204	24,683	27,018	628	3,270	1,587	2,183	751	677	1,993	1,689
Cape Verde	10	10	287	313	17	9	9,102	8,000	5	3	380	67	14	15	8	17
Central African Republic	103	157	845	1,006	816	1,019	3,551	3,562	16	29	941	1,000	196	252	60	80
Chad	665	1,400	565	698	648	626	4,812	4,559	36	74	566	650	108	115	74	101
Chile	2,997	2,168	3,862	4,061	858	1,002	14,315	16,297	128	57	1,141	1,039	2,596	4,118	1,943	2,591
China	388,969	457,038	4,208	4,881	141,227	175,627	14,976	18,831	5,589	5,357	1,364	1,881	21,729	59,530	114,949	250,341
Colombia	4,090	3,286	2,471	3,059	4,120	4,931	11,578	12,206	167	141	691	1,007	4,880	6,723	1,598	1,321
Comoros	19	21	1,289	1,338	58	69	5,230	5,818	7	11	838	947	54	62	4	6
Congo, Dem. Rep. of the	1,480	1,550	803	754	19,525	17,272	7,940	7,628	191	176	609	519	3,309	3,038	558	426
Congo, Rep. of the	26	2	885	687	724	884	6,745	7,264	9	17	792	772	168	195	42	46
Costa Rica	262	292	2,775	2,982	152	254	20,865	24,437	34	17	524	422	2,119	3,059	126	257
Côte d'Ivoire	1,239	1,832	884	1,130	4,334	4,996	5,751	5,665	8	8	667	667	1,598	1,952	450	534
Croatia	2,562[1]	2,883	4,128[1]	4,613	517[1]	729	8,085[1]	11,498	22[1]	26	1,914[1]	2,209	539[1]	565	259[1]	505
Cuba	543	551	2,383	2,240	823	684	5,099	4,803	27	16	363	314	1,402	1,265	582	409
Cyprus	107	133	1,901	2,912	187	172	22,328	23,950	2	1	967	1,343	368	283	125	153
Czech Republic	6,622[3]	7,023	4,101[3]	4,405	1,652[3]	1,460	19,261[3]	20,411	175[3]	117	2,371[3]	2,469	496[3]	505	541[3]	567
Denmark	9,211	8,695	5,887	5,887	1,394	1,477	36,010	38,865	481	388	4,303	3,632	88	85	304	308
Djibouti	—	—	1,524	1,625	...	...	...	...	...	...	...	...	...	...	22	23
Dominica	—	—	1,354	1,308	23	26	9,298	9,355	—	1	450	400	85	73	6	6
Dominican Republic	523	601	3,737	3,959	310	261	7,262	6,761	92	69	974	970	1,561	1,355	252	441
East Timor[4]	...	...	...	...	...	...	...	...	...	...	...	...	...	...	...	...
Ecuador	1,422	1,859	1,718	2,102	500	889	6,596	8,176	40	44	489	552	4,446	7,448	357	333
Egypt	12,667	19,590	5,526	7,032	1,904	2,171	21,762	23,030	423	371	2,511	2,255	4,456	6,417	9,249	13,083
El Salvador	785	925	1,840	1,936	38	92	15,090	16,189	55	72	802	956	290	226	146	136
Equatorial Guinea	...	...	...	...	77	81	2,898	2,531	...	...	...	...	16	20	...	...
Eritrea	175[3]	270	740[3]	703	109[3]	125	2,804[3]	3,205	36[3]	44	545[3]	634	4[3]	4	30[3]	28
Estonia	638[1]	485	1,665[1]	1,378	590[1]	340	13,743[1]	10,000	1[1]	11	1,452[1]	1,861	33[1]	20	75[1]	44

subsistence as well. Figures on wild fruits and berries are seldom included in national reports at all. FAO vegetable statistics include vegetables and melons grown for human consumption only. Some countries do not make this distinction in their reports, and some exclude the production of kitchen gardens and small family plots, although in certain countries, such small-scale production may account for 20 to 40 percent of total output.

Livestock statistics may be distorted by the timing of country reports. Ireland, for example, takes a livestock enumeration in December that is reported the following year and that appears low against data for otherwise comparable countries because of the slaughter and export of animals at the close of the grazing season. It balances this, however, with a June enumeration, when numbers tend to be high. Milk production as defined by the FAO includes whole fresh milk, excluding milk sucked by young animals but including amounts fed by farmers or ranchers to livestock, but national practices vary. Certain countries do not distinguish between milk cows and other cattle, so that yield per dairy cow must be estimated. Some countries do not report egg production statistics (here given of metric tons), and external estimates must be based on the numbers of chickens and reported or assumed egg-laying rates. Other countries report egg production by number, and this must be converted to weight, using conversion factors specific to the makeup by species of national poultry flocks.

Metric system units used in the table may be converted to English system units as follow:

metric tons × 1.1023 = short tons
kilograms × 2.2046 = pounds
kilograms per hectare × 0.8922 = pounds per acre.

The notes that follow, keyed by references in the table headings, provide further definitional information.

a. Includes such crops as potatoes and cassava.
b. Includes beans and peas harvested for dry grain only. Does not include green beans and green peas.
c. Excludes melons.
d. Includes melons, green beans, and green peas.
e. From milk cows only.
f. From chickens only.

livestock														country
cattle		sheep		hogs		chickens		milk[e]				eggs[f]		
stock ('000 head)		stock ('000 head)		stock ('000 head)		stock ('000 head)		production ('000 metric tons)		yield (kg/animal)		production (metric tons)		
1989–91 average	1999	1989–91 average	1999	1989–91 average	1999	1989–91 average	1999	1989–91 average	1999	1989–91 average	1999	1989–91 average	1999	
1,500	1,500	14,173	14,300	...	...	7,073	7,200	300	300	395	395	14,300	18,300	Afghanistan
657	720	1,645	1,941	183	81	4,864	4,000	403	761	1,384	1,762	15,033	20,200	Albania
1,366	1,650	17,302	18,200	5	6	73,000	105,000	595	1,040	940	1,300	120,000	120,000	Algeria
—	—	—	—	11	11	34	37	—	—	...	...	30	30	American Samoa
...	...	...	...	...	...	...	...	...	...	...	...	...	...	Andorra
3,117	3,900	240	336	802	800	6,117	6,650	151	191	483	490	3,900	4,200	Angola
16	16	13	12	2	2	87	90	6	6	936	968	173	150	Antigua and Barbuda
52,633	55,000	28,139	14,000	2,633	3,200	42,333	60,000	6,375	9,750	2,621	3,900	298,453	236,170	Argentina
522[1]	512	858[1]	575	130[1]	57	3,209[1]	2,850	394[1]	452	...	1,548	11,242[1]	18,080	Armenia
...	...	1	—	1	—	50	—	...	...	...	...	...	...	Aruba
23,086	26,710	165,046	119,600	2,617	2,680	55,991	85,000	6,514	9,822	3,945	4,906	186,667	200,000	Australia
2,540	2,172	281	384	3,762	3,810	13,738	13,950	3,344	3,256	3,805	4,549	94,284	99,411	Austria
1,726[1]	1,910	4,714[1]	5,132	84[1]	26	21,267[1]	13,200	798[1]	991	...	1,209	37,333[1]	29,400	Azerbaijan
4	1	39	6	12	6	1,733	6,000	1	1	1,000	1,000	500	1,118	Bahamas, The
14	13	21	17	...	...	553	455	19	14	2,602	1,970	2,800	2,968	Bahrain
23,173	23,400	871	1,110	...	...	90,253	138,200	741	751	206	206	56,936	130,100	Bangladesh
28	23	40	41	29	33	3,437	3,600	14	8	1,784	1,688	1,511	980	Barbados
6,216[1]	4,515	332[1]	122	4,397[1]	3,608	47,573[1]	39,000	5,660[1]	4,762	...	2,506	193,200[1]	187,700	Belarus
3,264	3,185	174	155	6,439	7,632	35,000	38,000	3,875	3,294	4,313	4,809	168,171	235,000	Belgium[2]
51	58	4	3	26	23	987	1,400	7	7	1,159	1,045	1,284	1,638	Belize
1,037	1,345	869	634	479	470	23,333	29,000	16	19	130	130	17,940	19,440	Benin
1	...	...	...	1	1	75	45	1	1	2,901	3,857	472	280	Bermuda
402	435	49	59	69	75	250	310	29	29	257	257	317	380	Bhutan
5,542	6,556	7,573	8,575	2,160	2,715	23,697	85,000	113	210	1,399	1,400	47,333	68,000	Bolivia
438[1]	350	518[1]	285	404[1]	80	5,167[1]	3,871	303[1]	210	...	1,273	17,833[1]	8,000	Bosnia and Herzegovina
2,694	2,380	317	250	16	7	2,080	3,500	113	102	350	350	1,860	3,222	Botswana
147,797	163,470	20,061	18,300	33,643	27,425	557,282	950,000	15,004	22,495	780	809	1,244,227	1,500,000	Brazil
2	2	...	...	17	5	2,254	4,929	...	...	...	...	3,083	3,750	Brunei
1,548	671	8,226	2,774	4,219	1,721	34,167	14,626	1,999	1,375	3,370	3,198	129,127	92,680	Bulgaria
3,937	4,550	5,049	6,350	510	590	17,028	21,000	101	160	156	178	15,283	17,000	Burkina Faso
431	329	352	165	92	61	4,000	4,400	33	23	350	350	3,040	3,400	Burundi
2,178	2,821	...	...	1,601	2,438	8,565	12,098	17	20	170	170	8,667	11,000	Cambodia
4,660	5,900	3,407	3,800	1,344	1,430	17,333	25,000	116	125	500	500	11,867	13,600	Cameroon
11,165	12,981	595	656	10,505	12,403	110,000	145,000	7,915	8,340	5,800	6,831	319,848	345,600	Canada
18	22	6	9	115	636	505	417	1	6	447	703	495	2,000	Cape Verde
2,589	2,992	134	201	430	622	2,772	3,900	46	60	224	261	1,314	1,404	Central African Republic
4,298	5,582	1,926	2,432	14	23	3,950	4,800	116	123	270	270	3,555	4,320	Chad
3,402	4,134	4,803	4,116	1,144	2,221	32,000	70,000	1,353	2,050	1,862	1,399	95,761	95,000	Chile
79,282	107,586	112,299	127,163	360,247	429,102	2,120,630	3,420,510	4,410	7,138	1,562	1,541	6,698,453	17,357,890	China
24,383	25,614	2,547	2,196	2,627	2,765	53,333	98,000	3,897	5,600	963	977	236,933	338,700	Colombia
47	50	13	20	...	...	392	440	4	4	500	500	632	720	Comoros
1,535	900	934	930	1,050	1,100	28,623	21,000	8	5	851	825	8,143	7,000	Congo, Dem. Rep. of the
65	75	104	115	49	45	1,650	1,900	1	1	500	500	1,170	1,140	Congo, Rep. of the
2,181	1,617	3	3	270	290	14,000	17,000	431	600	1,308	1,304	18,976	27,150	Costa Rica
1,101	1,330	1,137	1,370	361	275	24,333	29,000	18	24	150	166	12,693	16,000	Côte d'Ivoire
566[1]	439	502[1]	489	1,264[1]	1,362	11,665[1]	10,871	643[1]	635	...	2,347	51,167[1]	49,085	Croatia
4,922	4,650	385	310	2,184	2,400	27,876	13,500	1,100	650	1,866	1,250	109,506	65,700	Cuba
50	63	300	250	281	436	2,625	3,700	98	129	4,746	5,059	7,942	10,130	Cyprus
2,234[3]	1,657	205[3]	94	4,179[3]	4,001	25,574[3]	27,846	3,207[3]	2,754	...	4,173	154,226[3]	183,908	Czech Republic
2,227	1,968	103	156	9,390	11,991	15,808	18,023	4,710	4,530	6,227	6,565	82,800	77,548	Denmark
188	269	433	463	...	...	...	...	7	8	350	350	...	...	Djibouti
9	13	7	8	4	5	129	190	5	6	902	910	155	225	Dominica
2,283	1,904	115	105	543	540	31,227	42,000	345	412	1,701	1,726	38,864	52,853	Dominican Republic
...	...	...	...	...	...	...	...	...	...	...	...	...	...	East Timor[4]
4,351	5,534	1,417	2,180	2,213	2,786	51,901	64,750	1,529	1,994	2,092	2,007	51,471	60,278	Ecuador
2,771	3,150	3,310	4,400	24	29	34,555	87,000	974	1,352	689	1,079	143,817	168,500	Egypt
1,213	1,141	5	5	305	335	5,200	8,000	268	410	999	1,174	45,612	45,000	El Salvador
5	5	35	36	5	5	228	245	...	...	...	...	175	190	Equatorial Guinea
1,290[3]	1,550	1,520[3]	1,570	...	...	4,300[3]	4,600	30[3]	37	...	199	5,934[3]	6,348	Eritrea
595[1]	308	116[1]	31	588[1]	326	3,965[1]	2,636	834[1]	646	...	3,924	22,487[1]	15,160	Estonia

Crops and livestock (continued)

country	crops															
	grains				roots and tubers[a]				pulses[b]				fruits[c]		vegetables[d]	
	production ('000 metric tons)		yield (kg/hectare)		production ('000 metric tons)		yield (kg/hectare)		production ('000 metric tons)		yield (kg/hectare)		production ('000 metric tons)		production ('000 metric tons)	
	1989–91 average	1999	1989–91 average	1999	1989–91 average	1999	1989–91 average	1999	1989–91 average	1999	1989–91 average	1999	1989–91 average	1999	1989–91 average	1999
Ethiopia	7,783[3]	8,406	1,409[3]	1,132	2,000[3]	4,252	3,659[3]	7,370	978[3]	784	890[3]	800	228[3]	231	568[3]	599
Faroe Islands	…	…	…	…	1	2	13,677	13,636	…	…	…	…	…	…	…	…
Fiji	30	19	2,289	2,169	36	67	3,739	9,377	—	—	773	1,000	13	13	9	17
Finland	3,845	3,418	3,360	2,996	845	756	20,656	18,900	14	11	2,549	2,245	90	22	205	215
France	57,683	64,761	6,240	7,248	5,213	6,475	29,853	38,088	3,310	2,707	4,735	5,361	10,560	12,058	7,441	8,150
French Guiana	22	31	4,199	3,376	32	14	10,178	5,906	…	…	…	…	7	13	9	20
French Polynesia	…	…	…	…	13	16	12,273	11,923	…	…	…	…	8	7	7	6
Gabon	22	32	1,563	1,728	376	436	5,409	5,888	—	—	639	667	256	304	30	35
Gambia, The	99	144	1,076	1,112	6	6	3,000	3,000	4	4	267	267	4	4	8	8
Gaza Strip	1	1	510	529	23	35	22,624	21,875	…	…	…	…	168	137	140	158
Georgia	457[1]	766	1,823[1]	1,812	223[1]	433	10,300[1]	12,371	…	…	…	…	745[1]	568	1,205[1]	591
Germany	37,910	44,333	5,534	6,679	14,057	11,420	27,747	38,363	267	797	2,750	3,511	4,652	4,949	3,806	3,219
Ghana	1,155	1,686	1,074	1,292	5,504	12,893	7,000	10,709	18	16	102	100	1,149	2,450	416	729
Greece	5,504	4,554	3,741	3,617	1,065	902	20,131	18,950	51	41	1,511	1,593	3,987	3,614	3,965	4,181
Greenland	…	…	…	…	…	…	…	…	…	…	…	…	…	…	…	…
Grenada	—	—	1,000	1,000	4	4	5,206	5,241	1	1	1,094	1,136	24	17	2	3
Guadeloupe	…	…	…	…	20	17	9,649	10,826	—	—	577	3,833	129	159	24	23
Guam	—	—	2,000	2,000	2	2	14,904	14,903	…	…	…	…	2	2	4	5
Guatemala	1,410	1,199	1,943	1,750	61	74	4,899	5,692	119	129	848	816	838	1,245	380	523
Guernsey	…	…	…	…	…	…	…	…	…	…	…	…	…	…	…	…
Guinea	632	971	1,052	1,309	578	1,065	7,320	6,122	60	60	857	857	856	996	420	476
Guinea-Bissau	165	191	1,556	1,421	67	…	6,953	7,176	2	2	960	600	64	72	20	25
Guyana	213	603	3,115	4,086	31	42	7,045	9,900	1	2	612	593	67	40	12	9
Haiti	405	413	996	914	770	745	3,785	3,882	92	77	634	678	1,005	971	283	218
Honduras	671	562	1,409	1,172	30	36	8,836	8,629	81	53	767	479	1,404	1,350	197	273
Hong Kong	—	—	1,667	—	—	—	22,000	33,333	…	…	…	…	4	4	116	59
Hungary	14,592	11,346	5,173	4,703	1,230	1,035	16,713	18,482	347	141	2,251	2,259	2,184	1,530	2,041	1,733
Iceland	…	…	…	…	9	9	9,553	10,696	…	…	…	…	—	—	2	2
India	195,478	230,042	1,911	2,264	21,280	29,700	15,906	17,533	13,427	16,095	567	634	30,505	38,561	59,320	59,395
Indonesia[4]	51,258	58,668	3,814	3,891	19,150	18,698	11,616	12,299	455	902	1,322	1,601	6,493	7,742	4,558	5,046
Iran	12,973	13,851	1,377	1,861	2,387	3,431	17,383	21,083	398	566	584	590	7,088	11,172	7,630	14,194
Iraq	2,541	1,644	927	545	196	380	15,980	14,615	19	36	995	1,079	1,507	1,492	2,855	2,790
Ireland	1,950	2,022	6,374	7,091	577	500	25,060	27,027	8	19	4,798	4,524	24	23	235	228
Isle of Man	…	…	…	…	…	…	…	…	…	…	…	…	…	…	…	…
Israel	234	90	2,222	1,200	209	341	32,359	41,472	9	9	1,276	1,411	1,711	1,424	1,263	1,675
Italy	17,921	21,005	4,005	5,038	2,340	2,087	19,637	23,680	221	138	1,430	1,722	17,569	19,126	14,436	15,723
Jamaica	3	2	1,232	1,150	225	294	12,534	16,539	6	5	898	1,068	383	416	108	184
Japan	13,946	12,281	5,645	5,998	5,539	4,943	25,459	26,908	145	103	1,670	1,768	4,838	4,169	14,457	13,115
Jersey	…	…	…	…	…	…	…	…	…	…	…	…	…	…	…	…
Jordan	105	29	1,040	257	59	93	23,167	18,525	4	2	740	369	233	268	634	738
Kazakhstan	22,521[1]	14,248	1,040[1]	1,304	2,303[1]	1,695	9,742[1]	10,843	96[1]	16	782[1]	925	160[1]	67	1,096[1]	1,657
Kenya	2,893	2,514	1,567	1,350	1,536	2,000	8,200	7,490	219	240	312	343	888	1,018	624	662
Kiribati	…	…	…	…	7	…	7,449	8,020	…	…	…	…	5	6	4	5
Korea, North	5,955	3,957	3,784	3,127	2,543	901	13,338	8,230	325	270	922	844	1,304	1,300	4,344	3,324
Korea, South	8,412	7,699	5,891	6,554	940	1,506	21,156	22,878	45	31	1,134	1,080	2,027	2,456	9,768	10,832
Kuwait	2	3	4,568	2,535	2	36	19,476	32,458	…	…	…	…	1	10	84	134
Kyrgyzstan	1,339[1]	1,630	2,271[1]	2,629	321[1]	957	12,190[1]	14,948	…	…	…	…	97[1]	109	291[1]	485
Laos	1,433	2,199	2,269	2,890	265	184	8,011	7,931	36	15	1,870	952	130	171	87	150
Latvia	1,072[1]	783	1,739[1]	1,926	1,161[1]	796	13,147[1]	15,878	6[1]	2	1,480[1]	374	73[1]	35	256[1]	131
Lebanon	82	93	1,995	2,396	249	251	18,708	19,096	28	41	1,631	2,062	1,222	1,278	798	1,259
Lesotho	170	174	805	989	45	85	15,319	16,346	9	12	481	792	18	14	24	19
Liberia	225	210	1,032	1,293	432	370	7,327	6,807	3	3	517	500	130	142	73	76
Libya	297	251	676	768	141	209	7,704	7,085	12	19	1,113	1,362	287	376	708	882
Liechtenstein	…	…	…	…	…	…	…	…	…	…	…	…	…	—	…	…
Lithuania	2,319[1]	2,114	1,974[1]	1,990	1,316[1]	1,699	11,213[1]	14,109	30[1]	106	1,239[1]	2,034	145[1]	145	306[1]	437
Luxembourg[2]	…	…	…	…	…	…	…	…	…	…	…	…	…	…	…	…
Macau	…	…	…	…	7	…	13,394	…	1	…	…	…	—	…	1	…
Macedonia	583[1]	760	2,453[1]	3,314	127[1]	180	9,534[1]	13,587	29[1]	28	1,348[1]	2,573	342[1]	356	462[1]	524
Madagascar	2,545	2,829	1,919	1,971	3,155	3,400	6,562	6,489	59	94	876	923	790	860	328	356
Malawi	1,560	2,655	1,104	1,684	506	585	4,294	4,721	268	289	589	600	485	521	252	259
Malaysia	2,014	1,984	2,890	2,826	497	488	9,683	9,513	…	…	…	…	1,115	1,074	334	559
Maldives	—	—	1,125	4,400	7	7	5,108	4,677	—	—	633	750	9	9	20	25
Mali	2,114	2,149	879	1,069	28	41	4,772	4,128	57	120	224	416	15	51	255	351
Malta	9	6	3,517	3,000	17	32	13,181	26,667	1	1	2,341	2,667	12	19	53	59
Marshall Islands	…	…	…	…	…	…	…	…	…	…	…	…	…	…	…	…
Martinique	…	…	…	…	23	18	11,540	10,456	…	1	…	…	273	356	24	28
Mauritania	131	196	831	893	6	6	1,933	2,115	28	34	385	330	19	25	9	12
Mauritius	2	—	3,885	5,200	19	16	18,733	17,612	1	2	708	…	8	12	42	86
Mayotte	…	…	…	…	…	…	…	…	…	…	…	…	…	…	…	…
Mexico	23,553	28,651	2,350	2,843	1,302	1,631	15,957	22,483	1,290	1,396	646	719	9,216	11,498	5,925	9,343
Micronesia	…	…	…	…	…	…	…	…	…	…	…	…	…	…	…	…
Moldova	2,274[1]	2,115	3,019[1]	2,437	504[1]	329	7,989[1]	4,958	107[1]	64	1,537[1]	1,202	1,562[1]	825	689[1]	515
Monaco	…	…	…	…	…	…	…	…	…	…	…	…	…	…	…	…
Mongolia	719	172	1,104	614	128	64	10,613	7,362	3	1	708	800	—	—	41	47
Morocco	7,457	3,860	1,346	746	975	1,148	17,347	18,294	386	214	790	567	2,306	2,589	2,942	3,264
Mozambique	629	1,770	403	869	3,944	5,792	4,136	5,591	87	195	301	484	368	386	197	187
Myanmar (Burma)	14,109	17,632	2,737	2,934	214	356	8,594	9,837	432	1,851	677	865	957	1,223	2,160	3,009
Namibia	103	71	745	236	197	260	8,194	8,966	7	8	1,062	1,096	10	10	8	10
Nauru	…	…	…	…	…	…	…	…	…	…	…	…	—	—	—	—
Nepal	5,685	6,465	1,887	1,987	826	1,236	7,401	8,350	168	213	597	715	457	415	962	1,449
Netherlands, The	1,327	1,345	6,909	7,041	6,947	8,200	40,168	44,809	85	17	4,109	4,000	506	715	3,455	3,560
Netherlands Antilles	…	…	…	…	…	…	…	…	…	…	…	…	…	…	…	…
New Caledonia	1	2	1,837	3,596	21	21	6,023	5,935	—	—	393	600	4	3	4	4
New Zealand	783	910	5,028	5,549	277	553	26,817	34,387	61	58	2,262	2,974	794	988	506	973
Nicaragua	453	522	1,483	1,376	77	83	11,790	10,855	69	94	621	634	304	234	54	59

livestock														country
cattle		sheep		hogs		chickens		milk[e]				eggs[f]		
stock ('000 head)		stock ('000 head)		stock ('000 head)		stock ('000 head)		production ('000 metric tons)		yield (kg/animal)		production (metric tons)		
1989–91 average	1999	1989–91 average	1999	1989–91 average	1999	1989–91 average	1999	1989–91 average	1999	1989–91 average	1999	1989–91 average	1999	
29,575[3]	35,095	21,700[3]	22,000	20[3]	25	54,200[3]	55,400	738[3]	961	...	204	73,370[3]	75,500	Ethiopia
2	2	67	68	...	...	...	...	...	...	...	...	...	...	Faroe Islands
274	345	—	7	88	112	2,600	3,900	58	54	1,705	1,701	2,494	2,700	Fiji
1,352	1,100	59	128	1,322	1,541	5,583	5,507	2,712	2,447	5,666	6,435	72,967	62,000	Finland
21,407	20,214	11,196	10,240	12,233	16,190	198,306	240,972	26,334	24,609	4,797	5,627	903,413	1,044,000	France
15	9	4	3	9	11	202	190	—	—	...	581	250	450	French Guiana
8	7	—	—	33	33	100	150	2	1	2,207	1,905	1,347	1,800	French Polynesia
30	35	161	195	160	212	2,217	3,100	1	2	250	250	1,500	1,980	Gabon
333	360	127	190	11	14	558	680	7	7	175	175	820	585	Gambia, The
3	3	24	24	...	...	2,633	3,600	7	8	4,000	4,000	4,867	8,000	Gaza Strip
1,051[1]	1,051	1,160[1]	550	525[1]	366	15,113[1]	12,500	450[1]	660	...	1,148	12,717[1]	21,670	Georgia
20,048	14,942	3,824	2,298	33,350	26,294	116,263	103,000	30,976	28,300	4,931	5,746	989,467	860,000	Germany
1,159	1,273	2,199	2,516	495	352	9,682	17,467	23	33	130	130	12,278	18,550	Ghana
651	577	8,684	9,290	1,002	933	27,213	28,000	646	770	2,523	4,583	132,343	120,000	Greece
...	...	21	22	...	...	...	...	...	...	...	...	...	...	Greenland
4	4	11	13	3	5	260	220	1	1	...	800	920	920	Grenada
70	80	4	4	28	15	311	200	1	—	506	517	1,412	1,656	Guadeloupe
—	—	...	...	4	4	170	200	...	...	...	...	367	700	Guam
2,052	2,300	432	551	602	825	14,633	24,000	312	320	680	711	66,051	109,000	Guatemala
...	...	...	...	...	...	...	...	...	...	...	...	...	...	Guernsey
1,491	2,368	429	687	24	54	5,800	8,900	42	62	185	185	14,035	7,770	Guinea
412	520	239	280	290	340	807	850	12	13	170	170	580	648	Guinea-Bissau
138	220	129	130	42	20	2,000	11,600	19	13	840	828	8,600	6,800	Guyana
1,067	1,300	86	138	330	800	5,167	5,000	25	38	250	250	3,583	3,750	Haiti
2,412	2,061	10	14	589	700	9,436	18,000	346	674	911	1,070	27,923	45,970	Honduras
2	—	—	—	296	110	5,678	3,000	2	—	...	2,236	1,497	10	Hong Kong
1,619	873	2,050	909	7,996	1,362	50,950	30,557	2,733	2,107	4,977	5,558	253,631	188,207	Hungary
75	75	540	477	18	43	450	180	112	105	3,509	3,570	2,647	2,200	Iceland
191,897	214,877	43,706	57,600	11,193	16,005	400,000	382,500	26,333	36,000	880	1,014	1,229,333	1,732,500	India
10,390	12,239	6,008	8,151	7,231	10,069	560,093	1,000,000	335	384	1,094	1,108	383,000	406,000	Indonesia[4]
7,382	8,047	44,754	53,900	—	—	161,667	230,000	2,480	4,403	1,014	1,243	310,000	538,000	Iran
1,416	1,110	7,804	6,000	...	...	58,500	18,000	297	278	734	750	64,450	23,000	Iraq
5,923	7,093	5,523	5,624	1,125	1,801	8,697	10,991	5,376	5,365	3,849	4,201	32,733	30,000	Ireland
...	...	...	...	...	...	...	...	...	...	...	...	...	...	Isle of Man
340	300	383	340	122	163	22,733	25,340	964	1,186	8,783	8,785	104,663	86,800	Israel
8,541	7,150	11,088	10,770	9,150	8,225	133,000	106,000	10,893	11,236	3,724	5,325	686,867	783,300	Italy
382	400	2	2	192	180	7,107	6,600	51	53	1,000	1,000	25,833	28,000	Jamaica
4,772	4,658	30	16	11,673	9,879	337,667	296,250	8,169	8,480	5,825	6,704	2,446,228	2,526,000	Japan
...	...	...	...	...	...	...	...	...	...	...	...	...	...	Jersey
35	65	1,660	2,000	...	...	52,300	23,300	60	125	2,485	3,205	32,420	48,119	Jordan
9,336[1]	3,960	33,688[1]	9,000	2,610[1]	892	50,400[1]	16,900	5,327[1]	2,400	...	1,733	176,667[1]	83,700	Kazakhstan
13,583	13,392	6,447	5,800	103	110	24,667	30,000	2,297	2,320	497	510	41,440	50,400	Kenya
...	...	...	...	9	10	259	300	...	...	...	...	124	140	Kiribati
1,293	565	385	185	3,215	2,970	20,767	10,371	88	80	2,379	2,286	144,333	75,000	Korea, North
2,149	2,486	3	1	4,792	7,864	70,336	94,587	1,752	2,129	5,944	6,980	398,578	464,901	Korea, South
14	20	197	445	...	...	16,982	29,204	21	42	3,226	606	6,390	17,811	Kuwait
1,124[1]	825	8,261[1]	3,400	257[1]	80	9,867[1]	2,200	918[1]	1,065	...	2,218	22,000[1]	10,730	Kyrgyzstan
853	1,497	...	...	1,397	1,937	8,165	13,882	9	6	200	200	32,500	8,500	Laos
1,068[1]	376	154[1]	27	865[1]	403	5,397[1]	2,700	1,212[1]	797	...	4,308	25,033[1]	27,200	Latvia
65	82	222	355	46	62	21,638	31,000	94	201	2,826	3,295	55,167	42,000	Lebanon
550	510	1,450	720	62	63	967	1,700	24	24	290	290	826	1,428	Lesotho
38	36	222	210	123	120	3,800	3,500	1	1	130	130	3,904	3,600	Liberia
238	142	5,100	6,400	...	...	15,867	24,500	99	135	1,202	1,205	33,917	57,750	Libya
6	6	3	3	3	3	...	...	13	12	4,645	4,444	...	...	Liechtenstein
1,761[1]	928	52[1]	16	1,579[1]	1,168	10,860[1]	6,400	2,128[1]	1,970	...	3,385	41,167[1]	43,960	Lithuania
...	...	...	...	...	...	...	...	...	...	...	...	...	...	Luxembourg[2]
...	...	...	...	...	...	450	500	...	...	...	...	638	650	Macau
282[1]	290	2,425[1]	1,550	176[1]	197	4,458[1]	3,339	127[1]	179	...	1,864	25,653[1]	21,500	Macedonia
10,254	10,353	719	790	1,431	1,700	13,062	17,500	476	530	273	280	15,050	13,800	Madagascar
862	750	179	110	236	230	11,500	14,700	37	34	460	453	11,203	19,100	Malawi
677	713	212	162	2,577	2,961	62,377	118,000	29	38	470	481	287,400	390,000	Malaysia
...	...	...	...	...	...	...	...	...	...	...	...	...	...	Maldives
5,007	6,058	6,072	5,975	59	65	22,000	24,500	123	148	245	245	11,880	11,880	Mali
21	21	6	16	101	69	867	820	24	41	3,851	4,767	6,800	6,550	Malta
...	...	...	...	...	...	...	...	...	...	...	...	...	...	Marshall Islands
37	30	46	42	39	33	347	250	2	2	756	763	1,214	1,500	Martinique
1,350	1,395	5,067	6,200	...	...	3,800	4,100	97	102	350	350	4,250	4,930	Mauritania
34	42	7	7	12	20	2,200	4,300	25	60	2,500	1,714	4,200	5,100	Mauritius
...	...	...	...	...	...	...	...	...	...	...	...	...	...	Mayotte
32,194	30,293	5,862	5,900	15,715	13,855	240,218	420,000	6,336	8,885	992	1,326	1,066,065	1,605,358	Mexico
...	14	...	...	...	...	...	185	...	...	...	...	...	175	Micronesia
962[1]	525	1,300[1]	940	1,468[1]	807	17,767[1]	13,800	998[1]	571	...	1,996	35,833[1]	31,100	Moldova
...	...	...	...	...	...	...	...	...	...	...	...	...	...	Monaco
2,694	3,726	14,266	14,694	166	21	351	72	271	325	352	330	1,669	340	Mongolia
3,284	2,560	13,528	16,576	9	8	71,200	100,000	955	1,130	521	869	170,800	180,000	Morocco
1,373	1,310	120	124	167	178	21,833	27,000	63	60	170	170	11,333	14,000	Mozambique
9,269	10,740	275	378	2,355	3,715	23,989	39,529	422	488	245	392	35,208	69,888	Myanmar (Burma)
2,104	2,000	3,289	2,100	18	14	1,717	2,200	70	75	411	417	1,306	1,580	Namibia
...	...	...	...	3	3	5	5	...	...	...	...	16	16	Nauru
6,274	7,031	903	855	571	825	8,233	17,797	252	329	366	397	16,133	21,270	Nepal
4,918	4,184	1,663	1,465	13,747	13,418	92,050	100,000	11,198	10,895	6,040	6,852	644,480	643,800	Netherlands, The
1	1	6	7	3	2	125	135	—	—	1,278	1,250	432	510	Netherlands Antilles
122	120	3	4	37	38	317	390	4	4	600	600	1,367	2,000	New Caledonia
7,987	8,876	57,861	46,100	404	413	9,067	12,500	7,572	11,372	2,835	3,462	45,507	31,750	New Zealand
1,693	1,693	4	4	565	400	4,533	10,000	162	185	797	789	25,500	30,270	Nicaragua

Crops and livestock (continued)

country	crops: grains production ('000 metric tons)		grains yield (kg/hectare)		roots and tubers[a] production ('000 metric tons)		roots and tubers[a] yield (kg/hectare)		pulses[b] production ('000 metric tons)		pulses[b] yield (kg/hectare)		fruits[c] production ('000 metric tons)		vegetables[d] production ('000 metric tons)	
	1989–91 average	1999	1989–91 average	1999	1989–91 average	1999	1989–91 average	1999	1989–91 average	1999	1989–91 average	1999	1989–91 average	1999	1989–91 average	1999
Niger	1,902	2,822	310	375	248	268	7,689	7,530	330	649	133	170	44	48	274	286
Nigeria	18,100	23,234	1,139	1,194	34,383	63,112	10,031	9,665	1,421	2,149	734	535	6,595	8,768	5,017	6,158
Northern Mariana Islands	...	...	...	...	...	...	...	...	...	...	...	...	...	...	...	...
Norway	1,410	1,299	3,943	3,877	452	453	24,246	25,599	—	—	...	...	122	102	182	138
Oman	5	6	2,124	2,173	5	6	25,208	21,923	...	...	...	...	184	210	155	173
Pakistan	21,038	26,661	1,784	2,129	1,052	1,845	11,467	14,184	719	1,123	483	654	3,931	5,511	3,165	4,460
Palau	...	...	...	...	...	...	...	...	...	...	...	...	...	...	...	...
Panama	336	339	1,884	2,262	66	88	5,901	5,850	9	9	526	479	1,225	838	65	116
Papua New Guinea	3	10	1,761	4,170	1,254	1,202	7,224	6,986	2	2	500	522	1,076	1,178	357	378
Paraguay	859	1,598	1,844	2,394	3,471	3,582	15,074	14,310	49	80	859	843	522	526	264	295
Peru	2,003	3,379	2,492	3,113	2,302	4,443	8,112	10,619	105	193	882	1,059	1,891	3,139	910	1,853
Philippines	14,350	16,031	2,018	2,400	2,716	2,724	6,876	6,662	36	59	792	776	6,250	10,024	4,143	4,960
Poland	27,594	25,750	3,231	2,959	33,247	19,927	18,350	15,717	635	277	1,857	1,948	1,793	2,390	5,797	5,840
Portugal	1,673	1,860	2,012	2,877	1,258	1,174	10,097	13,792	69	32	300	605	2,221	1,419	2,019	2,395
Puerto Rico	—	—	7,462	4,000	28	9	6,499	11,246	2	—	569	609	258	179	43	31
Qatar	3	6	2,910	3,413	—	—	9,611	10,375	...	...	...	...	8	24	30	48
Réunion	12	17	5,590	6,724	15	9	11,006	13,043	1	1	1,429	741	46	49	45	67
Romania	18,286	15,724	3,084	3,051	3,159	3,162	10,517	11,563	149	47	889	1,222	2,295	2,147	3,215	3,745
Russia	92,890[1]	53,783	1,612[1]	1,192	36,603[1]	31,200	10,673[1]	9,600	2,880[1]	877	1,383[1]	845	2,989[1]	2,630	10,411[1]	10,985
Rwanda	299	176	1,234	823	1,631	1,439	6,275	3,841	216	149	777	583	2,912	2,955	131	124
St. Kitts and Nevis	...	...	...	...	1	1	3,688	3,029	—	—	1,000	1,000	1	1	—	1
St. Lucia	—	—	699	...	11	10	4,179	3,945	—	—	2,133	2,000	176	115	1	1
St. Vincent and the Grenadines	1	2	3,348	3,333	21	12	4,917	5,064	—	—	1,000	1,000	78	49	3	4
Samoa	...	...	...	...	41	...	5,002	6,164	...	...	...	...	51	43	1	1
San Marino	...	...	...	...	...	...	...	...	...	...	...	...	...	...	...	...
São Tomé and Príncipe	3	1	2,015	2,124	6	32	7,346	8,886	...	...	...	...	10	40	3	6
Saudi Arabia	4,214	2,440	4,177	4,147	59	331	19,157	17,330	7	8	1,832	1,861	832	1,152	1,987	2,309
Senegal	996	963	823	750	67	49	4,009	2,926	19	35	337	398	105	134	129	392
Seychelles	...	...	...	...	...	...	5,000	5,000	...	...	...	...	2	2	2	2
Sierra Leone	566	280	1,225	1,119	139	262	5,220	4,777	38	42	652	676	163	153	189	180
Singapore	...	...	...	...	—	—	13,933	10,000	...	...	...	...	1	—	8	5
Slovakia	3,494[3]	2,894	4,068[3]	3,916	566[3]	384	13,232[3]	14,329	161[3]	98	2,313[3]	2,238	285[3]	251	528[3]	566
Slovenia	486[1]	469	4,131[1]	5,108	379[1]	194	13,756[1]	19,736	7[1]	5	777[1]	1,590	255[1]	207	77[1]	82
Solomon Islands	...	5	...	...	107	131	17,595	17,023	2	3	1,175	1,296	15	16	6	7
Somalia	497	207	715	489	50	70	10,421	10,000	13	14	312	250	284	211	65	71
South Africa	12,237	9,612	1,956	2,139	1,334	1,700	16,535	22,089	135	114	1,269	1,162	3,903	4,777	1,885	2,216
Spain	19,306	17,943	2,489	2,705	5,337	3,300	19,448	24,452	238	278	755	564	13,490	14,769	10,966	11,659
Sri Lanka	2,370	2,731	2,924	3,156	547	336	8,845	8,174	50	28	780	605	743	833	578	608
Sudan, The	2,755	3,779	505	532	138	170	2,674	2,648	103	178	1,064	1,295	758	964	903	1,120
Suriname	229	181	3,770	3,606	3	5	11,900	12,000	—	—	690	727	75	84	26	24
Swaziland	127	114	1,401	1,803	9	8	1,665	1,930	5	7	569	972	144	69	13	11
Sweden	5,677	5,149	4,594	4,300	1,132	986	32,977	29,000	91	140	2,494	3,180	188	94	261	310
Switzerland	1,331	1,040	6,352	5,628	731	484	37,867	35,073	8	11	4,267	2,523	625	543	308	309
Syria	2,598	3,247	668	1,255	407	250	17,543	12,500	131	113	577	603	1,353	1,699	1,691	1,158
Taiwan	...	...	...	...	...	...	...	...	...	...	...	...	...	...	...	...
Tajikistan	256[1]	521	944[1]	1,806	151[1]	136	12,215[1]	9,067	7[1]	8	742[1]	1,804	248[1]	317	623[1]	526
Tanzania	4,142	3,977	1,390	1,261	8,167	7,947	8,824	7,801	437	423	501	560	2,094	2,066	1,099	1,158
Thailand	23,624	28,105	2,149	2,459	21,776	16,771	14,245	15,471	476	367	794	857	6,164	7,491	2,514	2,774
Togo	505	620	809	887	913	1,293	7,992	6,898	22	39	202	285	48	49	152	160
Tonga	...	...	...	...	99	92	6,551	10,008	...	...	...	...	15	13	20	7
Trinidad and Tobago	17	12	2,816	3,086	10	12	9,645	10,315	3	4	1,458	2,566	62	76	16	24
Tunisia	1,611	1,825	1,115	1,355	205	298	12,592	11,908	73	104	663	913	670	836	1,477	2,053
Turkey	28,283	30,282	2,065	2,255	4,321	5,316	22,388	25,913	1,946	1,661	885	1,006	9,117	10,389	17,963	21,777
Turkmenistan	1,038[1]	1,567	2,870[1]	1,996	32[1]	28	4,750[1]	5,620	...	7	...	1,167	158[1]	194	539[1]	336
Tuvalu	...	...	...	...	...	—	...	...	...	...	...	...	1	1	—	—
Uganda	1,597	1,977	1,483	1,422	5,360	6,369	6,335	6,382	493	448	774	531	8,384	10,050	404	529
Ukraine	37,208[1]	23,764	2,957[1]	1,995	19,129[1]	15,405	12,040[1]	10,182	2,840[1]	605	2,300[1]	1,203	2,597[1]	1,594	5,750[1]	5,746
United Arab Emirates	7	1	5,383	1,455	4	5	19,300	20,909	...	...	...	...	205	358	270	1,055
United Kingdom	22,644	22,045	6,168	7,025	6,333	7,100	35,916	39,978	750	732	3,425	3,883	514	362	3,747	3,055
United States	292,060	336,028	4,582	5,735	18,530	22,246	32,018	38,822	1,621	1,884	1,832	1,989	25,392	28,400	30,808	35,150
Uruguay	1,237	2,212	2,414	3,711	215	212	7,514	11,778	6	6	986	982	391	593	117	158
Uzbekistan	2,281[1]	4,306	1,714[1]	2,480	468[1]	650	10,083[1]	12,492	...	15	...	1,250	985[1]	1,276	3,760[1]	3,201
Vanuatu	1	1	515	539	49	65	10,072	10,000	...	...	...	...	18	20	8	10
Venezuela	1,989	2,097	2,423	3,245	682	1,096	8,686	12,940	57	34	585	719	2,579	2,535	498	1,214
Vietnam	20,013	33,146	3,060	3,977	4,758	3,923	7,432	7,354	187	245	639	686	4,009	3,972	3,625	4,829
Virgin Islands (U.S.)	...	...	...	...	...	...	...	...	...	...	...	...	—	—	...	...
West Bank	...	30	...	...	...	17	...	...	...	2	...	...	...	153	...	228
Western Sahara	...	3	...	794	...	...	...	...	...	...	...	...	...	...	...	...
Yemen	693	635	871	969	153	201	12,223	12,536	64	74	1,424	1,211	314	570	536	591
Yugoslavia	7,613[1]	8,704	3,102[1]	3,852	766[1]	991	6,928[1]	8,543	100[1]	116	1,438[1]	1,850	1,391[1]	1,165	1,045[1]	1,232
Zambia	1,467	1,057	1,569	1,391	573	912	5,388	5,223	15	15	629	500	105	99	274	261
Zimbabwe	2,391	1,987	1,488	1,044	127	202	4,792	4,844	50	49	694	757	170	190	153	145

livestock														country
cattle		sheep		hogs		chickens		milk[e]				eggs[f]		
stock ('000 head)		stock ('000 head)		stock ('000 head)		stock ('000 head)		production ('000 metric tons)		yield (kg/animal)		production (metric tons)		
1989–91 average	1999	1989–91 average	1999	1989–91 average	1999	1989–91 average	1999	1989–91 average	1999	1989–91 average	1999	1989–91 average	1999	
1,712	2,174	3,100	4,312	37	39	17,833	20,000	140	168	393	400	8,500	9,180	Niger
14,650	19,850	12,477	20,500	3,558	12,400	122,120	126,000	350	386	239	244	313,000	628,560	Nigeria
...	...	...	...	...	...	...	...	...	...	...	...	...	...	Northern Mariana Islands
959	1,042	2,202	2,399	696	690	3,663	3,240	1,944	1,833	5,757	5,744	51,046	47,700	Norway
137	148	141	160	...	...	2,500	3,200	18	19	420	420	5,850	6,300	Oman
17,677	18,000	25,703	31,300	...	...	77,767	223,000	3,525	4,708	842	1,078	210,867	285,600	Pakistan
...	...	...	...	...	...	...	...	...	...	...	...	...	...	Palau
1,401	1,400	...	...	228	252	7,668	12,549	129	157	1,162	1,309	11,117	14,000	Panama
103	86	4	6	997	1,500	2,883	3,600	—	—	...	100	2,950	3,900	Papua New Guinea
7,985	9,863	422	395	2,443	2,500	15,065	15,000	224	445	1,904	2,405	34,883	45,000	Paraguay
4,126	4,898	12,484	13,700	2,417	2,784	62,406	79,917	788	1,013	1,323	1,948	103,800	161,300	Peru
1,644	2,395	30	30	7,968	10,390	76,853	137,675	14	10	1,036	1,056	276,000	528,000	Philippines
9,875	6,555	3,934	392	20,056	18,538	58,196	50,017	15,560	12,373	3,260	4,021	410,255	420,158	Poland
1,355	1,270	5,531	5,850	2,531	2,341	19,667	28,000	1,500	1,750	3,734	4,930	85,400	110,000	Portugal
595	388	7	8	204	175	11,241	11,643	396	357	4,233	3,933	16,690	15,143	Puerto Rico
10	14	126	207	...	...	2,932	4,150	3	11	1,490	1,642	3,270	4,050	Qatar
20	27	2	2	88	89	6,916	11,000	7	14	627	964	4,117	5,400	Réunion
6,029	3,143	15,236	8,409	12,675	7,194	120,969	69,480	3,450	4,450	1,867	2,781	354,367	310,000	Romania
51,939[1]	28,637	46,998[1]	13,650	31,820[1]	17,300	582,667[1]	350,000	45,088[1]	31,800	...	2,356	2,233,333[1]	1,853,000	Russia
592	726	387	290	117	160	1,292	1,400	85	86	579	741	1,787	2,000	Rwanda
4	4	14	8	2	3	56	70	...	...	...	...	347	300	St. Kitts and Nevis
12	12	16	13	12	15	223	260	1	1	1,396	1,250	528	516	St. Lucia
6	6	13	13	10	9	205	200	1	1	1,351	1,374	627	640	St. Vincent and the Grenadines
24	26	...	...	186	179	356	350	1	1	1,000	1,000	192	200	Samoa
...	...	...	...	...	...	...	...	...	...	...	...	...	...	San Marino
4	4	2	3	3	2	124	290	—	—	...	170	175	315	São Tomé and Príncipe
195	265	6,370	8,300	...	...	76,000	130,000	274	520	6,254	7,849	113,005	132,000	Saudi Arabia
2,616	2,955	3,500	4,300	295	330	19,667	45,000	98	105	360	360	14,767	33,000	Senegal
2	1	...	...	18	18	293	540	—	—	...	6	1,760	2,100	Seychelles
333	400	271	350	50	52	5,900	6,000	17	17	250	250	6,785	6,900	Sierra Leone
—	—	—	—	300	190	2,500	2,000	...	...	...	...	16,543	16,000	Singapore
1,030[3]	705	412[3]	326	2,162[3]	1,593	13,321[3]	13,117	1,206[3]	1,073	...	4,096	79,549[3]	64,790	Slovakia
488[1]	453	23[1]	72	574[1]	592	10,420[1]	8,550	569[1]	600	...	2,961	19,712[1]	23,648	Slovenia
11	10	...	...	53	58	144	185	1	1	650	650	288	372	Solomon Islands
3,967	5,000	12,117	13,000	9	4	2,833	3,100	435	500	403	385	2,267	2,400	Somalia
12,920	13,565	32,060	28,680	1,480	1,531	46,000	60,000	2,426	2,990	2,637	2,990	213,362	334,000	South Africa
5,125	6,065	23,800	23,751	16,720	21,000	76,000	127,000	6,100	6,300	3,728	4,667	649,413	631,000	Spain
1,690	1,599	25	12	88	76	8,630	9,600	172	217	271	314	46,033	49,657	Sri Lanka
20,593	35,000	20,179	42,500	...	...	32,371	41,000	2,252	2,976	480	480	33,212	43,500	Sudan, The
91	102	9	11	29	25	7,625	2,200	17	16	1,832	2,286	3,033	3,000	Suriname
712	652	24	26	23	31	1,133	980	42	38	274	289	315	340	Swaziland
1,704	1,757	408	420	2,243	2,321	11,433	7,516	3,401	3,303	6,097	7,356	116,333	106,000	Sweden
1,845	1,615	392	490	1,793	1,420	5,912	6,720	3,892	3,827	4,954	5,315	37,833	3,940	Switzerland
786	905	14,571	15,000	1	1	14,405	21,000	782	1,120	2,314	2,635	75,133	125,650	Syria
157	...	...	...	8,813	10,509[5]	80,119	101,838[5]	204	318[5]	4,349	4,802[5]	...	...	Taiwan
1,238[1]	912	2,110[1]	1,620	49[1]	2	4,029[1]	600	472[1]	280	...	509	14,667[1]	615	Tajikistan
13,047	14,350	3,551	4,150	320	345	20,567	28,000	516	680	169	206	41,167	56,160	Tanzania
5,513	5,677	161	41	4,766	7,200	107,858	172,000	137	476	1,659	2,267	430,033	554,188	Thailand
247	223	1,164	740	617	850	6,070	7,500	8	8	225	225	5,558	6,325	Togo
11	9	...	...	94	81	221	266	—	—	...	2	287	28	Tonga
55	34	14	12	53	28	9,500	8,500	11	10	1,593	1,531	9,167	9,000	Trinidad and Tobago
626	780	5,935	6,600	6	6	39,367	37,000	393	800	1,420	1,633	52,250	80,000	Tunisia
12,037	11,185	43,195	30,238	10	5	73,181	166,273	8,183	9,000	1,352	1,597	369,080	820,000	Turkey
962[1]	880	5,793[1]	5,650	203[1]	48	6,900[1]	4,000	565[1]	875	...	1,751	14,933[1]	15,900	Turkmenistan
...	...	...	...	12	13	29	27	...	...	...	...	12	12	Tuvalu
4,777	5,700	1,350	1,970	797	960	18,667	23,000	418	499	350	350	14,933	18,100	Uganda
22,597[1]	11,722	6,658[1]	1,198	16,437[1]	10,083	180,352[1]	105,000	18,363[1]	13,200	...	2,182	664,865[1]	481,500	Ukraine
49	85	255	440	...	...	6,733	14,500	5	9	210	210	9,877	14,000	United Arab Emirates
11,980	11,423	29,241	44,656	7,519	7,284	124,076	154,180	14,976	15,023	5,206	6,157	616,334	583,674	United Kingdom
96,316	98,522	11,384	7,238	54,557	62,206	1,333,000	1,720,000	66,423	73,482	6,672	8,043	4,004,766	4,885,000	United States
9,019	10,700	25,359	15,500	217	360	7,900	13,000	1,006	1,210	1,604	1,780	21,933	37,000	Uruguay
5,273[1]	5,225	8,681[1]	8,000	524[1]	208	26,867[1]	13,935	3,622[1]	3,499	...	1,555	96,833[1]	68,300	Uzbekistan
124	151	...	...	59	62	306	320	2	3	202	203	312	280	Vanuatu
13,311	15,992	551	781	2,801	4,500	59,890	110,000	1,518	1,311	1,285	1,278	118,562	167,900	Venezuela
3,153	4,064	...	...	12,225	18,886	77,228	179,323	38	45	800	800	97,133	164,400	Vietnam
8	8	3	3	3	3	30	35	2	2	2,725	2,703	120	160	Virgin Islands (U.S.)
...	12	...	352	...	...	...	...	...	27	...	35	...	15,000	West Bank
...	...	...	29	...	...	...	...	...	...	...	...	...	...	Western Sahara
1,154	1,289	3,682	4,595	...	...	16,385	27,300	152	172	600	600	17,612	31,200	Yemen
1,925[1]	1,831	2,701[1]	2,392	3,876[1]	4,372	21,920[1]	24,322	1,841[1]	2,197	...	2,093	96,833[1]	90,600	Yugoslavia
2,845	2,273	59	120	296	324	16,033	28,000	77	62	300	300	25,653	44,800	Zambia
6,147	5,500	584	525	300	272	12,000	15,000	609	575	454	439	15,500	19,500	Zimbabwe

[1]1992–94 average. [2]Belgium includes Luxembourg. [3]1993–95 average. [4]Indonesia includes East Timor. [5]1995.

Extractive industries

Extractive industries are generally defined as those exploiting in situ natural resources and include such activities as mining, forestry, fisheries, and agriculture; the definition is often confined, however, to nonrenewable resources only. For the purposes of this table, agriculture is excluded; it is covered in the preceding table.

Extractive industries are divided here into three parts: mining, forestry, and fisheries. These major headings are each divided into two main subheadings, one that treats production and one that treats foreign trade. The production sections are presented in terms of volume except for mining, and the trade sections are presented in terms of U.S. dollars. Volume of production data usually imply output of primary (unprocessed) raw materials only, but, because of the way national statistical information is reported, the data may occasionally include some processed and manufactured materials as well, since these are often indistinguishably associated with the extractive process (sulfur from petroleum extraction, cured or treated lumber, or "processed" fish). This is also the case in the trade sections, where individual national trade nomenclatures may not distinguish some processed and manufactured goods from unprocessed raw materials.

Mining. In the absence of a single international source publication or standard of practice for reporting volume or value of mineral production, single-country sources predominantly have been used to compile mining production figures, supplemented by U.S. Bureau of Mines data, by the United Nations' *National Accounts Statistics* (annual; 2 parts), and by industry sources, especially *Mining Journal's Mining Annual Review*. Each country has its own methods of classifying mining data, which do not always accord with the principal mineral production categories adopted in this table—namely, "metals," "nonmetals," and "energy." The available data have therefore been adjusted to accord better with the definition of each group. Included in the "metal" category are all ferrous and nonferrous metallic ores, concentrates, and scrap; the "nonmetal" group includes all nonmetallic minerals (stone, clay, precious gems, etc.) except the mineral fuels; the last group, "energy," is composed predominantly of the natural hydrocarbon fuels, though it may also include manufactured gas.

The contribution (value) of each national mineral sector to its country's gross domestic product is given, as is the distribution by group of that contribution (to gross domestic product and to foreign trade), although statistics regarding the value of mineral production are less readily available in country sources than those regarding trade or volume of minerals produced. Figures for value added by mineral output, though not always available, were sought first, as they provide the most consistent standard to compare the importance of minerals both within a particular national economy and among national mineral sectors worldwide. Where value added to the gross domestic product was not available, gross value of production or sales was substituted and the exception footnoted. Figures for value of production are reported here in millions of U.S. dollars to permit comparisons to be made from country to country. Comparisons can also be made as to the relative importance of each mineral group within a given country.

Extractive industries

country	mining														
	% of GDP, 1998	mineral production (value added)					trade (value)								
		year	total ('000,000 U.S.$)	by kind (%)			year	exports				imports			
				metals[a]	non-metals[b]	energy[c]		total ('000,000 U.S.$)	by kind (%)			total ('000,000 U.S.$)	by kind (%)		
									metals[a]	non-metals[b]	energy[c]		metals[a]	non-metals[b]	energy[c]
Afghanistan	…	…	…	…	…	…	1997	0.1	—	100.0	—	…	…	…	…
Albania	…	1994[1]	81.4	46.1	0.8	53.1	1997	16.5	93.9	6.1	—	12.9	—	34.9	65.1
Algeria	23.0	1998	10,895.7	—	—	100.0	1996	8,931.6	—	0.2	99.8	22.4	—	—	100.0
American Samoa	…	1998	…	—	100.0	—	…	…	…	…	…	…	…	…	…
Andorra	…	…	…	…	…	…	…	…	…	…	…	…	…	…	…
Angola	60.9[2]	1997	3,935.1	—	7.7	92.3	1997	212.6	—	90.4	9.6	…	…	…	…
Antigua and Barbuda	1.5	1998	9.0[12]	—	100.0	—	…	…	…	…	…	…	…	…	…
Argentina	2.4[2]	1997	7,821.8[3]	…	…	…	1997	2,429.7[4]	—	—	100.0[4]	419.5	65.2	1.6	33.2
Armenia	…	1998	…	—100.0—		—	1997	106.9	—	100.0	—	187.2	50.5	49.5	—
Aruba	…	1998	…	—	100.0	—	1997	1.4	—	100.0	—	…	…	…	…
Australia	4.4	1998	15,105.6	…	…	…	1997	17,083.6	40.1	3.6	56.3	3,181.5	3.4	9.0	87.6
Austria	0.5	1995	819.3	2.5	53.5	44.0	1997	484.0[4]	38.5[4]	61.2[4]	0.3[4]	3,055.2	16.7	10.2	73.1
Azerbaijan	…	…	…	…	…	…	1994	…	…	…	…	224.1	—	—	100.0
Bahamas, The	…	1998	…	—	100.0	—	1997	1.2	100.0	—	—	…	…	…	…
Bahrain	13.6	1998	841.2	—	1.5	98.5	1996	2,471.1[6]	0.6[6]	—	99.3[6]	2,002.2	15.8	0.6	83.7
Bangladesh	1.0	1997–98	417.6	—	47.4	52.6	1996	…	…	…	…	80.0	—	77.5	22.5
Barbados	1.0	1998	4.6[3]	—	—100.0[3]—		1997	0.1	100.0	—	—	8.3	—	43.4	56.6
Belarus	…	1998	…	—	—100.0—		1997	175.2	—	92.5	7.5	39.6	—	100.0	—
Belgium	0.3[2]	1997	617.8	—	—100.0—		1997	13,490.0	8.2	88.6	3.3	21,328.3	12.4	54.9	32.7
Belize	0.5	1998	2.5	—	100.0	—	1997	…	…	…	…	3.4	—	14.7	85.3
Benin	0.7[5]	1995	14.4[8]	—	—100.0[8]—		…	…	…	…	…	…	…	…	…
Bermuda	…	…	…	…	…	…	1997	…	…	…	…	14.0	—	100.0	—
Bhutan	2.3[2]	1997	8.5	—	—100.0—		1994	2.9	—	82.8	17.2	1.7	—	29.4	70.6
Bolivia	11.1	1998	686.1	—49.5—		50.5	1997	377.7	72.9	1.1	26.0	17.7	85.9	14.1	—
Bosnia and Herzegovina	…	…	…	…	…	…	1997	2.9	—	—	100.0	…	…	…	…
Botswana	37.6	1997–98	1,950.6	11.4[9]	88.0[9]	0.7[9]	[10]	…	…	…	…	…	…	…	…
Brazil	0.8[2]	1997	6,760.5	…	…	…	1997	3,454.5	92.4	7.6	—	5,433.9	8.2	4.4	87.4
Brunei	36.7	1998	1,777.6	—8.5—		91.5	1997	1,970.2[6]	—	—	100.0[6]	9.3	—	100.0	—
Bulgaria	1.4	1998	167.4	…	…	…	1997	120.4	37.7	62.3	—	1,166.2	13.4	3.4	83.2
Burkina Faso	…	1998	…	—100.0—		—	…	…	…	…	…	…	…	…	…
Burundi	0.6[2]	1995	6.2	…	…	…	…	…	…	…	…	…	…	…	…
Cambodia	0.3	1998	8.8	—	100.0	—	…	…	…	…	…	…	…	…	…
Cameroon	5.5	1997–98	491.5	—	—	100.0	1996	628.8	—	—	100.0	187.6	16.4	4.0	79.6
Canada	3.7	1998	21,998.8	19.4	12.0	68.6	1997	22,630.2	16.3	3.7	79.9	10,037.9	24.5	6.4	69.1
Cape Verde	0.3[9]	1994	0.9	—	100.0	—	…	…	…	…	…	…	…	…	…
Central African Republic	3.8	1998	39.8[11]	—100.0[11]—		—	1997	104.1	—	100.0	—	0.8[4]	—	100.0[4]	—
Chad	…	…	…	…	…	…	…	…	…	…	…	…	…	…	…
Chile	8.5	1998	3,555.7	—100.0—		—	1997	2,553.3	96.9	3.1	—	1,505.5	4.1	—	95.9
China	…	…	…	…	…	…	1997	5,786.1	2.5	24.5	73.0	10,446.5	32.9	5.6	61.5
Colombia	5.5[4]	1996	4,735.4	…	…	…	1997	3,363.5	0.1	4.2	95.7	86.1	20.0	80.0	—
Comoros	—	1998	…	—	100.0	—	…	…	…	…	…	…	…	…	…
Congo, Dem. Rep. of the	22.8[6]	1995	288.6	—100.0—		—	1995	302.7	—	84.5	15.5	3.4	—	100.0	—
Congo, Rep. of the	40.6[13]	1996[13]	978.8[13]	…	…	…	1995	939.5	—	0.3	99.7	5.2	—	48.1	51.9
Costa Rica	…	…	…	…	…	…	1997	5.1	100.0	—	—	123.1[4]	—	7.0[4]	93.0[4]
Côte d'Ivoire	0.2[13]	1998[13]	28.1[13]	…	…	…	1997	132.0	—	100.0	—	489.9[4]	—	3.2[4]	96.8[4]
Croatia	0.4	1998	96.9	…	…	…	1997	135.0	23.1	14.1	62.8	772.7	—	7.3	92.7
Cuba	…	…	…	…	…	…	1997	…	…	…	…	13.3	—	100.0	—
Cyprus	0.3[14]	1998[14]	25.1	—	100.0	—	1997[14]	20.6	46.6	53.4	—	167.9	—	12.9	87.1
Czech Republic	…	…	…	…	…	…	1997	651.0	23.9	11.0	65.1	2,175.5	13.0	4.1	82.9
Denmark	1.4[2]	1997	2,023.8	—	—100.0—		1997	1,193.7	15.2	6.9	77.8	1,004.3	7.7	18.6	73.7
Djibouti	—	1998	…	—	100.0	—	…	…	…	…	…	…	…	…	…
Dominica	0.9	1998	2.0	—	100.0	—	1996	0.9	—	100.0	—	1.1	—	—	100.0
Dominican Republic	2.0	1998	309.3	—100.0—		—	1994	2.7	—	100.0	—	…	…	…	…
East Timor	…	…	…	…	…	…	…	…	…	…	…	…	…	…	…
Ecuador	7.8	1997	1,560.0	—6.8[15]—		93.2[15]	1997	1,404.8	—	—	100.0	95.0	—	9.4	90.6

Since the data for value of mineral production are obtained mostly from country sources, there is some variation (from a standard calendar year) in the time periods to which the data refer. In addition, the time period for which production data are available does not always correspond with the year for which mineral trade data are available.

The Standard International Trade Classification (SITC), Revision 3, was used to determine the commodity groupings for foreign trade statistics. The actual trade data for these groups is taken largely from the United Nations' *International Trade Statistics Yearbook* (2 vol.) and national sources.

Forestry. Data for the production and trade sections of forestry are based on the Food and Agriculture Organization (FAO) of the United Nations' *Yearbook of Forest Products.* Production of roundwood (all wood obtained in removals from forests) is the principal indicator of the volume of each country's forestry sector; this total is broken down further (as percentages of the roundwood total) into its principal components: fuelwood and charcoal, and industrial roundwood. The latter group was further divided to show its principal component, sawlogs and veneer; lesser categories of industrial roundwood could not be shown for reasons of space. These included pitprops (used in mining, a principal consumer of wood) and pulpwood (used in papermaking and plastics). Value of trade in forest products is given for both imports and exports, although exports alone tend to be the significant indicator for producing countries, while imports of wood are rarely a significant fraction of the trade of most importing countries.

Fisheries. Data for nominal (live weight) catches of fish, crustaceans, mollusks, etc., in all fishing areas (marine areas and inland waters) are taken from the FAO *Yearbook of Fishery Statistics* (*Catches and Landings*). Total catch figures are given in metric tons; the catches in inland waters and marine areas are given as percentages of the total catch, as are the main kinds of catch—fish, crustaceans, and mollusks. The total catch figures exclude marine mammals, such as whales and seals; and such aquatic animal products as corals, sponges, and pearls; but include frogs, turtles, and jellyfish. The subtotals by kind of catch, however, exclude the last group, which do not belong taxonomically to the fish, crustaceans, or mollusks.

Figures for trade in fishery products (including processed products and preparations like oils, meals, and animal feeding stuffs) are taken from the FAO's *Yearbook of Fishery Statistics* (*Commodities*). Value figures for trade in fish products are given for both imports and exports.

The following notes further define the column headings:

a. Includes ferrous and nonferrous metallic ores, concentrates, and scraps, such as iron ore, bauxite and alumina, copper, zinc, gold (except unwrought or semimanufactured), lead, or uranium.

b. Includes natural fertilizers; stone, sand, and aggregate; and pearls, precious and semiprecious stones, worked and unworked.

c. Includes hydrocarbon solids, liquids, and gases.

1 cubic metre = 35.3147 cubic feet

1 metric ton = 1.1023 short tons

forestry						fisheries, 1999									country
production of roundwood, 2000				trade (value, '000 U.S.$), 1999		catch (nominal)							trade (value, '000 U.S.$)		
total ('000 cubic metres)	fuelwood, charcoal (%)	industrial roundwood (%)		exports	imports	total ('000 metric tons)	by source (%)		by kind of catch (%)				exports	imports	
		total	sawlogs, veneer				marine	inland	fish	crustaceans	mollusks				
8,283	78.8	21.2	10.3	…	1,090	1.2	—	100.0	100.0	—	—		…	…	Afghanistan
409	84.5	15.5	15.5	7,063	17,158	2.7	70.3	29.7	90.8	0.7	8.5		4,804	3,965	Albania
2,795	83.9	16.1	2.4	…	375,546	105.7	100.0	—	96.3	3.6	0.1		2,374	13,268	Algeria
…	…	…	…	…	302[2]	0.5	100.0	—	99.6	0.2	0.2		…	…	American Samoa
…	…	…	…	…	6,383	—	—	100.0	100.0	—	—		…	…	Andorra
6,676	83.3	16.7	1.0	1,635	5,124	177.5	96.6	3.4	[illegible]	1.4	0.3		10,043	14,523	Angola
…	…	…	…	…	4,604	3.2	100.0	—	69.3	29.2	1.4		644	2,373	Antigua and Barbuda
5,741	19.2	80.8	—	224,651	755,695	1,024.8	98.8	1.2	63.1	2.9	34.1		807,042	88,368	Argentina
36[5]	100.0[5]	—	—	…	386	0.4	—	100.0	100.0	—	—		494	3,136	Armenia
…	…	…	…	6	7,321	0.2	100.0	—	100.0	—	—		…	17,753	Aruba
22,938	11.8	88.2	43.5	709,553	1,523,192	216.3	98.6	1.4	61.5	25.8	12.7		899,040	485,072	Australia
13,276	21.5	78.5	60.5	4,085,669	2,318,823	0.4	—	100.0	100.0	—	—		10,689	204,997	Austria
…	…	…	…	206	28,116	4.7	—	100.0	100.0	—	—		3,850	846	Azerbaijan
17	—	100.0	100.0	…	30,414	10.5	100.0	—	16.9	78.5	4.5		69,591	4,400	Bahamas, The
—	—	—	—	…	25,821	10.3	100.0	—	65.5	34.1	0.4		6,925	3,203	Bahrain
33,629	98.1	1.9	0.5	14,405	92,529	924.1	37.0	63.0	96.6	3.4	—		297,585	2,050	Bangladesh
5	—	100.0	100.0	…	35,503	0.3	100.0	—	100.0	—	—		951	11,044	Barbados
6,136	15.1	84.9	51.6	73,918	63,254	0.5	—	100.0	88.9	—	11.1		14,028	54,905	Belarus
4,400	12.5	87.5	58.0	3,734,032[7]	4,136,516[7]	29.9	98.2	1.8	92.9	5.0	2.1		447,598[7]	1,063,195[7]	Belgium
188	67.2	32.8	32.8	3,763	4,003	39.9	100.0	—	64.3	5.4	30.3		21,163	1,724	Belize
6,140	94.6	5.4	0.6	931	12,324	38.5	22.2	77.8	80.1	19.9	—		1,928	3,457	Benin
…	…	…	…	…	…	0.5	100.0	—	91.1	8.9	—		…	7,569	Bermuda
1,751	97.4	2.6	1.0	156	2,159	0.3	—	100.0	100.0	—	—		…	…	Bhutan
1,906	72.7	27.3	26.3	25,409	40,384	6.1	—	100.0	100.0	—	—		4	2,938	Bolivia
40	…	100.0	100.0	72,219	23,986	2.5	—	100.0	100.0	—	—		…	9,781	Bosnia and Herzegovina
1,702	93.8	6.2	—	…	15,410	2.0	—	100.0	100.0	—	—		54	5,218	Botswana
197,897	57.6	42.4	23.6	2,579,776	811,923	655.0	73.3	26.7	90.6	8.7	0.6		138,232	289,808	Brazil
296	26.7	73.3	69.6	…	8,426	3.2	99.2	0.8	96.7	2.2	1.1		184	8,881	Brunei
4,766	44.2	55.8	34.1	75,289	77,741	10.6	76.6	23.4	64.0	—	36.0		5,774	13,307	Bulgaria
11,095	95.4	4.6	—	…	14,780	7.6	—	100.0	100.0	—	—		5	1,674	Burkina Faso
1,799	83.9	16.1	12.3	…	1,700	9.2	—	100.0	100.0	—	—		334	8	Burundi
8,157	87.3	12.7	5.0	35,010	8,910	269.1	14.2	85.8	98.0	1.3	0.7		30,525	2,796	Cambodia
15,279	82.0	18.0	11.6	386,415	18,650	95.0	63.2	36.8	99.6	0.4	—		6,152	19,783	Cameroon
185,659	2.6	97.4	78.9	25,469,746	3,777,382	1,021.9	96.0	4.0	62.5	26.2	11.4		2,617,759	1,338,973	Canada
…	…	…	…	2,519	3,760	10.4	100.0	—	99.6	0.4	—		1,852	1,013	Cape Verde
3,548	75.7	24.3	15.6	46,659	…	15.0	—	100.0	100.0	—	—		61	448	Central African Republic
1,969	61.4	38.6	0.7	116	1,650	84.0	—	100.0	100.0	—	—		…	28	Chad
27,972	38.6	61.4	42.1	1,530,190	185,022	5,050.5	100.0	—	97.1	0.8	2.1		1,696,819	54,569	Chile
291,330[12]	65.6[12]	34.4[12]	19.1[12]	6,778,898[12]	25,536,650[12]	17,240.0	98.3	1.7	69.9	17.6	12.5		2,959,530	1,127,412	China
17,845	95.4	4.6	4.5	78,486	316,615	117.9	75.6	24.4	94.8	5.0	0.2		183,668	71,028	Colombia
9	—	100.0	100.0	…	185	12.2	100.0	—	100.0	—	—		1	774	Comoros
50,754	92.7	7.3	0.5	20,754	3,968	208.4	1.9	98.1	99.8	0.2	—		431	41,905	Congo, Dem. Rep. of the
3,243	80.1	19.9	8.5	75,946	1,769	43.7	41.7	58.3	86.0	5.3	8.7		1,720	18,631	Congo, Rep. of the
5,397	69.0	31.0	25.9	20,837	240,616	25.7	90.4	9.6	96.1	3.6	0.3		148,321	25,359	Costa Rica
13,396	76.9	23.1	16.3	225,923	45,038	76.0	82.9	17.1	98.7	1.2	0.1		132,249	162,354	Côte d'Ivoire
3,486	31.4	68.6	54.9	229,147	290,892	19.3	97.9	2.1	93.0	1.5	5.5		34,845	34,825	Croatia
1,593	74.5	25.5	8.0	60	24,509	67.3	93.1	6.9	61.4	22.7	15.9		93,296	22,484	Cuba
25	26.4	73.6	579.7	2,127	37,192	5.3	98.7	1.3	93.8	2.8	3.4		4,343	31,891	Cyprus
14,441	6.5	93.5	55.5	868,057	667,290	4.2	—	100.0	100.0	—	—		25,922	73,795	Czech Republic
3,086	32.4	67.6	42.8	398,653	1,329,135	1,405.0	100.0	—	92.4	0.8	6.9		2,884,334	1,771,500	Denmark
—	—	—	—	…	4,475	0.4	100.0	—	100.0	—	—		130	1,253	Djibouti
…	…	…	…	…	8,358	1.2	100.0	—	100.0	—	—		…	1,595	Dominica
562	98.9	1.1	0.6	578	211,782	8.5	91.6	8.4	74.2	10.4	15.4		700	53,102	Dominican Republic
…	…	…	…	…	…	0.5	100.0	—	98.4	1.4	0.2		…	…	East Timor
11,340	47.8	0.1	45.6	72,103	224,328	497.9	99.9	0.1	99.6	0.4	—		954,471	5,060	Ecuador

Extractive industries (continued)

country	mining														
	% of GDP, 1998	mineral production (value added)					trade (value)								
		year	total ('000,000 U.S.$)	by kind (%)			year	exports				imports			
				metals[a]	non-metals[b]	energy[c]		total ('000,000 U.S.$)	by kind (%) metals[a]	non-metals[b]	energy[c]	total ('000,000 U.S.$)	by kind (%) metals[a]	non-metals[b]	energy[c]
Egypt	9.8[9]	1994	5,151.3	——1.0——		99.0	1997	704.6	—	5.2	94.8	381.9	40.7	19.2	40.1
El Salvador	0.4	1998	47.6	100.0	—	—	1997	…	…	…	…	151.9	—	5.4	94.6
Equatorial Guinea	61.3	1998	279.6	—	—	100.0	…	…	…	…	…	…	…	…	…
Eritrea	0.1	1998	0.5	——100.0——		—	…	…	…	…	…	…	…	…	…
Estonia	1.0	1998	54.2	—	——100.0——		1997	76.5	79.0	—	21.0	113.1	27.9	20.2	52.0
Ethiopia	0.5	1997–98	33.3	——100.0——		—	1995	…	…	…	…	68.4	—	—	100.0
Faroe Islands	0.2[4]	1996	1.7	…	…	…	…	…	…	…	…	…	…	…	…
Fiji	3.4[4]	1996	42.5	——100.0——		—	1994	0.8	100.0	—	—	5.8	—	41.4	58.6
Finland	0.2	1998	307.4	——100.0——		—	1997	295.9	64.2	33.1	2.8	3,383.4	28.5	8.5	63.1
France	0.8[6]	1995	11,521.0	4.8	14.3	81.0	1997	2,335.7	46.6	32.5	20.9	20,162.7	9.2	5.2	85.5
French Guiana	…	1998	…	——100.0——		—	…	…	…	…	…	…	…	…	…
French Polynesia	…	…	…	…	…	…	1997	191.4	—	100.0	—	…	…	…	…
Gabon	41.8[4]	1996	2,382.8	4.0	—	96.0	1996	2,621.1	2.4	—	97.6	6.7	—	50.7	49.3
Gambia, The	—	1998	…	—	100.0	—	1995	…	…	…	…	1.4	—	—	100.0
Gaza Strip	…	…	…	…	…	…	…	…	…	…	…	…	…	…	…
Georgia	…	…	…	…	…	…	…	…	…	…	…	…	…	…	…
Germany	…	…	…	…	…	…	1997	5,631.4	43.6	21.0	35.3	30,568.8	16.3	5.6	78.1
Ghana	5.2	1998	388.6	——100.0——		—	1997	225.2	—	100.0	—	56.5	100.0	—	—
Greece	0.6[2]	1997	707.9	…	…	…	1997	310.3	40.9	35.9	23.2	1,393.2	6.9	7.2	85.9
Greenland	…	…	…	…	…	…	1997	…	…	…	…	1.6	—	100.0	—
Grenada	1.4	1998	1.3	—	100.0	—	1996	…	…	…	…	2.4	—	25.0	75.0
Guadeloupe	…	1998	…	—	100.0	—	…	…	…	…	…	…	…	…	…
Guam	…	1998	…	—	100.0	—	…	…	…	…	…	…	…	…	…
Guatemala	0.6	1998	30.0	…	…	…	1997	102.9	—	6.2	93.8	172.1	—	—	100.0
Guernsey	…	…	…	…	…	…	…	…	…	…	…	…	…	…	…
Guinea	15.7	1998	645.4[17]	——100.0[17]——		—	1997	396.7	80.3	19.7	—	…	…	…	…
Guinea-Bissau	…	1998	…	—	100.0	—	…	…	…	…	…	…	…	…	…
Guyana	13.6	1998	98.0	——100.0——		—	1997	94.3	100.0	—	—	…	…	…	…
Haiti	0.2	1998	1.8	—	100.0	—	…	…	…	…	…	…	…	…	…
Honduras	1.8	1998	82.3	——100.0——		—	1997	30.6	100.0	—	—	10.1	—	—	100.0
Hong Kong	0.02	1998	39.1	—	100.0	—	1997	2,264.8	27.2	72.8	—	4,639.9	12.9	75.8	11.2
Hungary	0.4[2]	1997	181.5	15.6	26.5	57.9	1997	136.5	99.6	—	0.4	1,747.1	1.9	3.5	94.6
Iceland	…	1998	…	—	100.0	—	1997	19.7	34.0	66.0	—	50.7	68.6	21.5	9.9
India	1.0	1996–97	3,268.9	…	…	…	1997	5,168.2	13.3	86.2	0.5	10,499.3[4]	7.8[4]	31.2[4]	61.0[4]
Indonesia	12.9	1998	12,704.4	——34.7——		65.3	1997	13,660.2	12.7	0.9	86.4	2,138.5	16.9	14.5	68.6
Iran	7.2	1998–99	13,441.8	——9.1——		90.9	1995	18,525.9	1.0	0.4	98.6	1,271.4	17.5	7.5	75.0
Iraq	…	…	…	…	…	…	…	…	…	…	…	…	…	…	…
Ireland	…	…	…	…	…	…	1997	538.5	75.1	16.5	8.4	825.7	14.4	12.9	72.7
Isle of Man	…	1998	…	—	100.0	—	…	…	…	…	…	…	…	…	…
Israel	…	…	…	…	…	…	1997	6,948.8	0.5	99.5	—	7,117.3	0.2	73.3	26.5
Italy	…	…	…	…	…	…	1997	851.4	34.6	57.2	8.2	16,573.7	15.0	9.3	75.7
Jamaica	4.5	1998	310.3	97.2	2.8	—	1997	682.4	100.0	—	—	105.8	—	—	100.0
Japan	0.2[4]	1996	9,863.9	…	…	…	1997	1,315.4	44.0	56.0	—	67,595.7	12.8	5.8	81.4
Jersey	…	…	…	…	…	…	…	…	…	…	…	…	…	…	…
Jordan	3.3	1998	239.3	—	100.0	—	1997	353.6	5.0	95.0	—	416.7[6]	0.6[6]	8.8[6]	90.6[6]
Kazakhstan	…	…	…	…	…	…	1996	837.9	18.9	12.8	68.4	170.9	29.9	25.8	44.3
Kenya	0.2[6]	1995	14.1	——100.0——		—	1997	40.4	—	100.0	—	227.3[4]	—	2.6[4]	97.4[4]
Kiribati	…	…	…	…	…	…	1995	…	…	…	…	0.1	—	100.0	—
Korea, North	…	…	…	…	…	…	1997	90.6	30.8	36.9	32.3	52.7[6]	—	36.1[6]	63.9[6]
Korea, South	0.4	1998	1,141.7	…	…	…	1997	238.6	13.9	53.9	32.2	23,311.9[4]	12.8[4]	3.0[4]	84.2[4]
Kuwait	39.5[6]	1995	10,513.4	—	—	100.0	1997	14,130.4[4]	0.2[4]	—	99.8[4]	60.7	—	100.0	—
Kyrgyzstan	…	…	…	…	…	…	1996	15.8	75.9	—	24.1	118.2	2.5	4.8	92.7
Laos	0.4	1998	5.8	——100.0——		—	…	…	…	…	…	…	…	…	…
Latvia	0.5	1998	116.4	—	——100.0——		1997	32.3	85.1	—	14.9	148.9	13.7	8.1	78.2
Lebanon	…	…	…	…	…	…	1997	130.5	31.0	69.0	—	132.8	—	100.0	—
Lesotho	0.01[4]	1996	0.1	—	100.0	—	[10]	…	…	…	…	…	…	…	…
Liberia	2.4	1998	8.6	—	100.0	—	1997	15.7	100.0	—	—	14.8	—	100.0	—
Libya	25.8[4]	1996	8,441.7	—	7.1	92.9	1997	9,451.2[6]	—	—	100.0[6]	51.2	100.0	—	—
Liechtenstein	…	…	…	…	…	…	…	…	…	…	…	…	…	…	…
Lithuania	0.5	1998	49.3	—	33.9[2]	66.1[2]	1997	130.7	48.7	—	51.3	850.6	2.4	7.0	90.6
Luxembourg	0.2	1998	24.8	—	100.0	—	[7]	…	…	…	…	…	…	…	…
Macau	…	…	…	…	…	…	1997	…	…	…	…	17.3	—	20.8	79.2
Macedonia	…	…	…	…	…	…	1995	29.5	68.1	31.9	—	41.8	6.7	39.5	53.8
Madagascar	0.3[9]	1994	5.2	——100.0——		—	1997	26.6	40.6	59.4	—	79.5	—	—	100.0
Malawi	1.0[9]	1994	12.8	…	…	…	1995	…	…	…	…	5.1	—	62.7	37.3
Malaysia	7.9	1998	3,675.2[3]	…	…	…	1996	5,509.7	2.4	2.3	95.3	1,175.0	43.1	32.2	24.7
Maldives	1.6	1998	2.2	—	100.0	—	…	…	…	…	…	…	…	…	…
Mali	5.5	1998	81.7	——100.0——		—	1997	7.0	—	100.0	—	…	…	…	…
Malta	…	1998	…	—	100.0	—	1996	3.5[6]	97.9[6]	2.1[6]	—	10.2	—	100.0	—
Marshall Islands	0.3[6]	1995	0.3	—	100.0	—	…	…	…	…	…	…	…	…	…
Martinique	…	1998	…	—	100.0	—	1995	4.1	19.4	38.3	42.3	102.5	—	—	100.0
Mauritania	9.6[2]	1997	105.9	——100.0——		—	1997	301.6	100.0	—	—	…	…	…	…
Mauritius	0.1	1998	5.6	—	100.0	—	1996	56.2	—	73.8	26.2	56.2	—	73.8	26.2
Mayotte	…	…	…	…	…	…	…	…	…	…	…	…	…	…	…
Mexico	1.2	1998	5,128.4	…	…	…	1997	11,181.6	4.8	2.3	93.0	1,715.3	39.7	25.2	35.1
Micronesia	…	…	…	…	…	…	…	…	…	…	…	…	…	…	…
Moldova	…	1998	…	—	100.0	—	1997	18.7[6]	100.0[6]	—	—	147.5	—	—	100.0
Monaco	…	…	…	…	…	…	…	…	…	…	…	…	…	…	…
Mongolia	…	…	…	…	…	…	1996	254.1	90.9	9.1	—	…	…	…	…
Morocco	2.2[2]	1997	746.5	…	…	…	1997	751.1	23.6	76.4	—	1,449.6	—	11.3	88.7
Mozambique	…	…	…	…	…	…	1996	8.4	72.6	27.4	—	3.3	—	100.0	—
Myanmar (Burma)	0.4	1998–99	1,107.3	…	…	…	1997	39.0	—	100.0	—	…	…	…	…
Namibia	11.7[2]	1997	382.8	——100.0——		—	[10]	…	…	…	…	…	…	…	…
Nauru	…	1998	…	—	100.0	—	1997	151.6	—	100.0	—	…	…	…	…
Nepal	0.5	1998–99	26.8	——100.0——		—	1995	…	…	…	…	9.1	51.6	—	48.4

forestry						fisheries, 1999								country
production of roundwood, 2000				trade (value, '000 U.S.$), 1999		catch (nominal)						trade (value, '000 U.S.$)		
total ('000 cubic metres)	fuelwood, charcoal (%)	industrial roundwood (%)		exports	imports	total ('000 metric tons)	by source (%)		by kind of catch (%)			exports	imports	
		total	sawlogs, veneer				marine	inland	fish	crustaceans	mollusks			
2,883	95.4	4.6	—	11,855	794,951	380.5	40.8	59.2	94.5	4.1	1.4	1,442	153,061	Egypt
5,170	87.4	12.6	12.6	14,360	124,786	15.2	83.9	16.1	24.8	71.1	4.1	33,596	6,640	El Salvador
811	55.1	44.9	44.9	89,885	…	7.0	84.3	15.7	90.8	7.2	2.0	2,565	2,508	Equatorial Guinea
2,285	99.9	0.1	0.1	…	6,833	7.0	100.0	—	98.7	1.1	0.2	973	54	Eritrea
8,910	18.4	81.6	32.0	391,529	112,763	111.8	97.2	2.8	88.9	11.1	—	77,582	30,951	Estonia
89,925	97.3	2.7	—	…	8,894	15.9	—	100.0	100.0	—	—	…	42	Ethiopia
…	…	…	…	221	4,162	358.0	100.0	…	94.1	4.2	1.7	436,000	15,372	Faroe Islands
483	7.7	92.3	40.6	18,189	8,189	36.7	84.7	15.3	56.2	3.4	40.3	22,266	17,294	Fiji
54,263	7.6	92.4	47.9	10,925,450	887,491	160.6	77.1	22.9	99.9	0.1	—	21,493	118,244	Finland
50,170	22.0	78.0	52.8	5,683,978	7,492,308	578.1	99.2	0.8	86.4	3.5	10.1	1,107,169	3,280,940	France
120	49.8	50.2	42.6	2,481	2,424	7.7	100.0	—	45.5	54.5	—	40,495[2]	5,136[2]	French Guiana
…	…	…	…	…	22,201	12.4	99.6	0.4	99.5	0.4	0.1	2,263	6,891	French Polynesia
5,397	48.6	51.4	51.4	380,793	4,799	52.9	84.9	15.1	94.2	5.4	0.4	13,148	6,876	Gabon
618	81.8	18.2	17.2	…	1,416	30.0	91.7	8.3	97.9	1.8	0.3	4,643	848	Gambia, The
…	…	…	…	…	…	3.6	100.0	—	88.1	6.3	5.7	…	…	Gaza Strip
…	…	…	…	11,952	5,749	1.5	93.3	6.7	100.0	—	—	208	2,471	Georgia
37,634	6.8	93.2	62.2	9,923,976	10,776,915	238.9	90.4	9.6	92.0	8.0	—	966,300	2,288,523	Germany
21,907	94.4	5.6	5.2	187,175	24,016	492.8	84.9	15.1	99.1	0.9	—	95,813	20,321	Ghana
2,171	63.3	36.7	31.5	77,993	737,282	136.7	84.5	15.5	78.8	2.5	18.7	278,208	308,553	Greece
—	—	—	—	77	7,179	160.3	100.0	—	48.8	51.2	—	261,255	1,412	Greenland
…	…	…	…	—	5,167	1.6	100.0	—	95.2	4.4	0.4	3,530	2,534	Grenada
15	98.0	2.0	2.0	…	30,639	9.2	100.0	—	92.9	1.6	5.5	266[2]	30,393[2]	Guadeloupe
…	…	…	…	…	…	0.2	100.0	—	98.7	0.4	0.9	…	…	Guam
13,300	96.2	3.8	3.8	17,449	137,727	11.0	36.7	63.3	71.8	28.0	0.2	28,148	6,794	Guatemala
…	…	…	…	…	…	[16]	[16]	[16]	[16]	[16]	[16]	…	…	Guernsey
8,651	92.5	7.5	1.6	6,024	4,542	87.1	95.4	4.6	98.1	0.5	1.5	22,131	14,490	Guinea
592	71.3	28.7	6.8	610	…	5.0	96.0	4.0	81.3	2.4	16.3	6,318	487	Guinea-Bissau
467	2.4	97.6	93.1	36,047	3,239	53.8	98.9	1.1	77.7	22.3	—	34,461	475	Guyana
6,501	96.3	3.7	3.4	…	13,221	5.0	90.0	10.0	86.0	5.0	9.0	9,264	7,990	Haiti
7,413	88.5	11.5	11.5	43,309	59,836	7.2	98.6	1.4	53.7	21.8	24.4	97,207	14,805	Honduras
21[5]	100.0[5]	—	—	2,508,240[5]	3,101,116[5]	127.8	100.0	—	90.4	3.8	5.9	383,398	1,593,661	Hong Kong
5,902	44.0	56.0	23.4	353,145	618,345	7.5	—	100.0	97.6	—	2.4	6,948	39,552	Hungary
—	—	—	—	648	65,695	1,736.3	100.0	—	96.7	2.6	0.7	1,379,379	80,693	Iceland
302,794	92.1	7.9	6.1	54,971	789,321	3,316.8	79.2	20.8	89.3	7.9	2.8	1,019,579	20,188	India
190,601	83.5	16.5	13.0	4,757,769	947,593	4,149.4	92.9	7.1	90.9	6.6	2.6	1,527,092	86,555	Indonesia
1,151	10.5	89.5	26.9	…	201,165	387.2	63.0	37.0	97.3	1.2	1.5	23,945	58,002	Iran
177	66.7	33.3	14.1	…	4,341	24.6	53.2	46.8	100.0		—		1,277	Iraq
2,673	2.7	97.3	59.4	237,008	730,167	285.9	98.9	1.1	90.0	7.4	2.6	343,826	115,853	Ireland
…	…	…	…	…	…	2.6	100.0	—	3.6	9.0	87.3	…	…	Isle of Man
113	11.5	88.5	31.9	34,467	695,578	5.9	63.5	36.5	94.8	3.2	2.0	8,496	129,891	Israel
9,329	60.9	39.1	22.1	2,581,755	7,096,128	294.2	98.2	1.8	59.0	6.0	35.1	356,976	2,728,568	Italy
706	60.0	40.0	18.7	…	71,424	8.5	94.7	5.3	79.1	4.8	16.1	13,905	32,487	Jamaica
19,031	1.4	98.6	70.4	1,729,858	12,348,306	5,176.5	98.6	1.4	77.0	3.7	19.3	719,839	14,748,712	Japan
…	…	…	…	…	…	3.6[16]	100.0[16]	—[16]	25.7[16]	67.3[16]	7.0[16]	…	…	Jersey
11	63.6	36.4	—	5,420	104,204	0.5	31.4	68.6	100.0	—	—	1,231	21,020	Jordan
315[5]	100.0	—	—	598	48,398	25.8	—	100.0	100.0	—	—	12,257	11,903	Kazakhstan
29,908	93.4	6.6	1.5	2,064	38,124	205.3	3.2	96.8	99.5	0.4	0.2	32,415	5,339	Kenya
…	…	…	…	…	769[5]	48.2	100.0	—	97.0	—	3.0	5,611	299	Kiribati
7,000	78.6	21.4	14.3	15,192	8,781	210.0	90.5	9.5	95.2	—	4.8	71,535	2,579	Korea, North
1,722	1.6	98.4	36.1	1,515,287	2,967,578	2,119.7	99.7	0.3	64.0	4.4	31.5	1,393,428	1,140,022	Korea, South
…	…	…	…	13	97,708	6.3	100.0	—	88.5	11.5	—	4,721	22,111	Kuwait
42[5]	74.5[5]	25.5[5]	21.9[5]	225	9,892	—	100.0	100.0	100.0	—	—	…	2,287	Kyrgyzstan
4,869	82.2	17.8	15.1	26,657	1,704	30.0	—	100.0	100.0	—	—	99	1,157	Laos
14,488	11.6	88.4	58.7	600,131	47,946	125.4	99.5	0.5	97.5	2.5	—	51,849	36,097	Latvia
412	98.3	1.7	1.7	4,885	166,234	3.6	99.4	0.6	94.4	3.5	2.1	…	19,863	Lebanon
1,594	100.0	—	—	…	…	0.03	—	100.0	100.0	—	—	[18]	[18]	Lesotho
3,037	88.9	11.1	5.2	24,492	1,635	15.5	74.1	25.9	97.6	0.2	2.2	64	1,412	Liberia
652	82.2	17.8	9.7	…	33,260	32.5	100.0	—	100.0	—	—	32,654	12,561	Libya
13[5]	30.8[5]	69.2[5]	69.2[5]	…	…	—	…	…	…	…	…	…	…	Liechtenstein
5,346	22.4	77.6	52.4	171,231	113,279	33.6	94.9	5.1	87.6	12.4	—	33,560	52,499	Lithuania
259	6.9	93.1	43.6	[7]	[7]	—	…	…	…	…	…	[7]	[7]	Luxembourg
…	…	…	…	1,841	14,022	1.5	100.0	—	68.0	29.3	2.7	2,852	13,236	Macau
1,047	83.6	16.4	15.7	9,093	150,166	0.1	—	100.0	100.0	—	—	129	9,994	Macedonia
10,359	98.9	1.1	0.8	23,784	5,061	131.6	77.2	22.8	89.5	0.9	9.5	101,061	5,661	Madagascar
9,964	94.8	5.2	1.3	688	5,265	45.4	—	100.0	100.0	—	—	302	236	Malawi
29,461	26.2	73.8	68.6	3,114,963	1,000,476	1,251.8	99.7	0.3	78.3	8.5	13.2	299,437	258,747	Malaysia
…	…	…	…	14	4,220	133.5	100.0	—	99.6	—	0.4	38,907	…	Maldives
6,597	93.7	6.3	0.1	1,648	8,731	98.5	—	100.0	100.0	—	—	378	1,211	Mali
…	…	…	…	—	62,831	1.0	100.0	—	95.7	2.3	1.9	6,751	19,442	Malta
…	…	…	…	…	1,923	0.4	100.0	—	100.0	—	—	1,482	120	Marshall Islands
12	83.3	16.7	16.7	110	22,864	5.0	100.0	—	98.0	2.0	—	168[2]	38,658[2]	Martinique
16	62.5	37.5	6.3	…	6,000	47.8	89.5	10.5	64.7	—	35.2	99,348	524	Mauritania
25	48.0	52.0	28.0	3,741	67,773	12.0	100.0	—	97.2	0.3	2.5	38,558	32,642	Mauritius
…	…	…	…	…	…	1.5	100.0	—	100.0	—	—	3[2]	161[2]	Mayotte
24,122	67.1	32.9	27.0	281,218	2,106,097	1,202.2	92.4	7.6	80.6	7.7	11.7	649,787	125,723	Mexico
…	…	…	…	…	2,110	11.9	100.0	—	99.6	0.2	0.2	459	3,280	Micronesia
58	50.6	49.4	7.7	3,303	23,350	0.5	—	100.0	100.0	—	—	1,381	2,763	Moldova
…	…	…	…	…	…	0.004	100.0	—	100.0	—	—	…	…	Monaco
631	29.5	70.5	70.5	6,289	2,944	0.5	—	100.0	100.0	—	—	232	33	Mongolia
1,123	49.2	50.8	15.7	74,985	336,920	745.4	99.7	0.3	83.2	0.1	16.7	750,764	10,509	Morocco
18,043	92.7	7.3	0.7	14,072	10,075	35.6	69.8	30.2	100.0	—	—	76,861	10,341	Mozambique
22,574	85.2	14.8	10.4	239,712	18,874	851.6	84.8	15.2	98.7	1.3	0.1	158,560	559	Myanmar (Burma)
[19]	[19]	[19]	[19]	…	36,449	299.2	99.5	0.5	91.3	8.4	0.3	344,017	…	Namibia
…	…	…	…	23[5]	205[5]	0.3	100.0	—	100.0	—	—	…	…	Nauru
21,962	97.2	2.8	2.8	1,199	2,572	12.8	—	100.0	100.0	—	—	269	261	Nepal

Extractive industries (continued)

country	mining														
	% of GDP, 1998	mineral production (value added)					trade (value)								
		year	total ('000,000 U.S.$)	by kind (%)			year	exports				imports			
				metals[a]	non-metals[b]	energy[c]		total ('000,000 U.S.$)	by kind (%)			total ('000,000 U.S.$)	by kind (%)		
									metals[a]	non-metals[b]	energy[c]		metals[a]	non-metals[b]	energy[c]
Netherlands, The	2.7[6]	1995[3]	9,620.1[3]	...	...	...	1997	6,275.9	19.2	8.5	72.3	12,803.2	12.5	5.9	81.6
Netherlands Antilles	...	1998	...	—	100.0	—	1995	901.5	—	0.1	99.9	900.5	—	—	100.0
New Caledonia	10.7[2]	1997	352.1	100.0	—	—	1997	208.9	100.0	—	—	12.9	—	—	100.0
New Zealand	...	...	...	...	...	...	1996	110.9	31.3	0.4	68.3	854.0	21.1	13.5	65.5
Nicaragua	1.6	1998	34.0	—— 100.0 ——		—	1997	4.0	100.0	—	—	130.0	—	4.6	95.4
Niger	3.5[9]	1994	62.5	—— 100.0 ——		—	...	...	...	...	...	...	...	...	...
Nigeria	26.0	1998	33,716.8	—	0.5	99.5	1995	11,131.5	—	—	100.0	19.9	1.5	98.5	—
Northern Mariana Islands	...	...	...	...	...	...	...	...	...	...	...	...	...	...	...
Norway	10.9	1998	16,068.2	—— 1.8 ——		98.2	1997	24,255.2	0.4	1.0	98.6	1,820.3	73.2	11.3	15.5
Oman	40.6[2]	1997	6,361.2	—	0.7	99.3	1996	5,768.3	—	0.1	99.9	70.7	78.8	21.2	—
Pakistan	0.5	1997–98	301.4	...	...	...	1997	57.3	—	1.4	98.6	338.9	50.5	7.5	42.0
Palau	0.1	1998	0.1	—	100.0	—	...	...	...	...	...	...	...	...	...
Panama	0.2	1998	10.5	—— 100.0 ——		—	1996	6.7	100.0	—	—	324.5	—	—	100.0
Papua New Guinea	26.0	1998	975.2	—— 64.0 ——		36.0	1995	1,123.1	48.0	—	52.0	...	...	...	...
Paraguay	0.3	1998	29.2	—	100.0	—	1996	...	...	...	...	124.9	—	66.9	33.1
Peru	10.9	1998	2,378.8	—— 67.9[6, 20] ——		32.1[6]	1997	1,150.6	79.1	0.1	20.8	564.2	0.4	—	99.6
Philippines	0.7	1998	489.1	57.7[6]	41.3[6]	1.0[6]	1997	567.7	55.4	25.5	19.1	4,078.1	14.2	4.1	81.7
Poland	2.9	1998	4,613.0	...	...	...	1997	1,400.6[4]	7.0[4]	11.6[4]	81.4[4]	3,751.2	11.7	6.5	81.8
Portugal	0.5[6]	1995	529.3	40.2	59.6	0.2	1997	391.8	57.0	35.6	7.5	2,369.2	0.7	7.7	91.6
Puerto Rico	...	...	...	...	...	...	...	...	...	...	...	...	...	...	...
Qatar	38.1[2]	1997	3,502.7[3]	...	...	...	1995	3,000.3	—	0.1	99.9	51.3[9]	75.3[9]	24.7[9]	—
Réunion	...	1998	...	—	100.0	—	1995	0.9	100.0	—	—	15.0	—	—	100.0
Romania	3.3[9]	1994	990.9	—	16.1	83.9	1997	75.6	62.6	37.4	—	1,723.1[9]	9.7[9]	3.7[9]	86.6[9]
Russia	...	...	...	...	...	...	1997	32,522.7	5.6	1.0	93.4	560.0[6]	60.2[6]	16.9[6]	23.0[6]
Rwanda	0.06	1998	1.2	...	...	...	...	...	...	...	...	...	...	...	...
St. Kitts and Nevis	0.3[6]	1995	0.6	—	100.0	—	1997	...	...	...	...	2.1	—	33.3	66.7
St. Lucia	0.5	1998	2.6	—	100.0	—	1996	...	...	...	...	5.1	—	49.0	51.0
St. Vincent	0.3	1998	0.9	—	100.0	—	1997	1.6	—	18.8	81.3	1.6[6]	—	18.8[6]	81.3[6]
Samoa	...	...	...	...	...	...	...	...	...	...	...	...	...	...	...
San Marino	...	...	...	...	...	...	...	...	...	...	...	...	...	...	...
São Tomé and Príncipe	...	1998	—	—	100.0	—	...	...	...	...	...	...	...	...	...
Saudi Arabia	37.2[2]	1997	54,352.5	—— 1.1 ——		98.9	1997	50,116.9[2]	0.1[2]	—	99.9[2]	136.7	88.6	11.4	—
Senegal	0.2	1998	6.3	—	100.0	—	1995	55.8	7.3	92.7	—	102.6	—	13.5	86.5
Seychelles	...	1998	—	—	100.0	—	1996	...	...	...	...	0.5	—	100.0	—
Sierra Leone	16.8[22]	1994–95	117.7	—— 100.0 ——		—	1995	16.7	25.4	74.6	—	0.6	—	100.0	—
Singapore	0.02	1998	14.3	—	100.0	—	1997	787.1	31.0	41.7	27.3	8,895.9	0.7	9.0	90.3
Slovakia	0.9	1998	178.8	...	...	...	1997	68.5	28.0	72.0	—	1,106.3	8.9	4.1	87.0
Slovenia	1.0[2]	1997	182.6	...	...	...	1997	28.6	100.0	—	—	386.4	23.4	17.1	59.4
Solomon Islands	...	1998	...	—— 100.0[23] ——		—	1996	...	...	...	...	2.0	—	—	100.0
Somalia	...	...	...	...	...	...	...	...	...	...	...	...	...	...	...
South Africa	6.5	1998	8,003.2	...	...	...	1997[10]	7,936.4	23.4	51.1	25.4	3,452.8	9.7	14.3	76.0
Spain	...	...	...	...	...	...	1997	771.2	39.7	55.0	5.3	12,200.5[4]	16.5[4]	4.2[4]	79.3[4]
Sri Lanka	1.9	1998	269.4[24]	—— 100.0[24] ——		—	1995	216.5	—	100.0	—	271.1	—	40.0	60.0
Sudan, The	0.3	1998	27.4	...	...	...	1995	...	...	...	...	34.1	—	—	100.0
Suriname	10.9[4]	1996	58.9[25]	...	...	...	1997	594.7	100.0	—	—	15.9[6]	—	31.4[6]	68.6[6]
Swaziland	0.7	1998	8.9	...	...	...	[10]	...	...	...	...	...	...	...	...
Sweden	0.3[6]	1995	634.3	59.2[9]	40.8[9]	—	1997	1,127.6	83.8	11.2	5.0	4,369.9	13.4	6.2	80.4
Switzerland	...	1998	...	—	100.0	—	1997	1,931.1	15.0	85.0	—	4,056.5	3.0	69.0	28.0
Syria	6.6[9]	1994	2,594.1[8]	—	—— 100.0[8] ——		1995	2,675.5	—	1.4	98.6	21.6	—	—	100.0
Taiwan	0.3[6]	1995	791.6	—	79.6	20.4	1995	843.7	...	...	...	8,035.8	—— 35.8 ——		64.2
Tajikistan	...	...	...	...	...	...	1997	1.0	—	100.0	—	228.0[4]	—	100.0[4]	—
Tanzania	1.3	1998	111.9	...	...	...	...	...	...	...	...	...	...	...	...
Thailand	1.8[2]	1997	2,756.6	...	...	...	1997	1,334.0	9.3	74.9	15.7	5,929.7	4.7	14.2	81.1
Togo	5.8	1998	88.3	—	100.0	—	1997	145.3	—	100.0	—	...	...	...	...
Tonga	0.3[6]	1995	0.4	—	100.0	—	1995	0.1	—	100.0	—	1.3	—	46.2	53.6
Trinidad and Tobago	12.2	1998	708.6	—	—	100.0	1996	492.4	—	—	100.0	476.9	12.7	2.1	85.1
Tunisia	5.6	1998	1,456.4	—— 17.1 ——		82.9	1997	438.9	2.7	11.6	85.7	367.1	—	32.4	67.6
Turkey	1.1	1998	2,160.5	...	...	...	1997	325.8	61.7	38.3	—	5,709.8	21.0	3.3	75.7
Turkmenistan	9.7[2]	1997	204.0	—	—	100.0	1997	489.9	—	0.2	99.8	...	...	...	...
Tuvalu	0.9[6]	1995	0.1	—	100.0	—	...	...	...	...	...	...	...	...	...
Uganda	0.3[26]	1995–96	15.8	—— 100.0 ——		—	1996	...	...	...	...	11.2	—	100.0	—
Ukraine	...	...	...	...	...	...	1997	1,421.6	60.4	19.7	19.8	6,790.7	3.4	3.1	93.5
United Arab Emirates	33.4[9]	1994[3]	12,269.1[3]	...	...	...	1996	23,700.1	0.5	0.5	99.0	233.3	17.1	82.9	—
United Kingdom	1.7	1998	21,115.8	—— 8.5 ——		91.5	1997	18,681.6	5.5	32.6	61.8	16,302.2	16.2	38.7	45.1
United States	1.5[2]	1997	120,500.0	4.8	9.5	85.7	1997	13,394.6	35.4	33.2	31.4	80,065.7	5.6	12.8	81.6
Uruguay	0.2	1997	47.6	—	100.0	—	1997	...	...	...	...	229.7	—	6.4	93.6
Uzbekistan	...	...	...	...	...	...	1997	114.5	—	—	100.0	13.9	100.0	—	—
Vanuatu	...	1998	...	—	100.0	—	1994	...	...	...	...	0.5	—	—	100.0
Venezuela	12.1	1998	10,676.5	—— 6.4 ——		93.6	1997	12,510.3	1.8	—	98.2	132.3	41.5	58.5	—
Vietnam	6.2	1998	1,091.3	—— 9.4 ——		90.6	1997	103.2	1.8	—	98.8	32.1	—	100.0	—
Virgin Islands (U.S.)	...	1998	...	—	100.0	—	...	...	...	...	...	...	...	...	...
West Bank	...	...	...	...	...	...	...	...	...	...	...	...	...	...	...
Western Sahara	...	...	...	...	...	...	...	...	...	...	...	...	...	...	...
Yemen	9.8[9]	1994	1,788.2[8]	—	—— 100.0[8] ——		1995	1,424.0	—	—	100.0	208.4	—	—	100.0
Yugoslavia	9.5[9]	1994	981.7	12.0	3.1	84.9	1997	16.8	32.1	—	67.9	708.7	23.6	5.9	70.6
Zambia	6.1	1998	203.0	...	...	...	1995	12.9	—	100.0	—	1.7	100.0	—	—
Zimbabwe	6.9[9]	1994	336.1	...	...	...	1997	95.9	4.9	94.3	0.8	35.3[4]	17.8[4]	37.1[4]	45.0[4]

[1]Gross value of production (output). [2]1997. [3]Mostly crude petroleum and natural gas. [4]1996. [5]1998. [6]1995. [7]Belgium includes Luxembourg. [8]Mostly crude petroleum. [9]1994. [10]South Africa includes Botswana, Lesotho, Namibia, and Swaziland. [11]Mostly diamonds, some gold. [12]China includes Taiwan. [13]Petroleum sector only. [14]Republic of Cyprus only. [15]1993. [16]Jersey includes

forestry						fisheries, 1999								country
production of roundwood, 2000				trade (value, '000 U.S.$), 1999		catch (nominal)						trade (value '000 U.S.$)		
total ('000 cubic metres)	fuelwood, charcoal (%)	industrial roundwood (%)		exports	imports	total ('000 metric tons)	by source (%)		by kind of catch (%)			exports	imports	
		total	sawlogs, veneer				marine	inland	fish	crusta-ceans	mollusks			
1,039	15.4	84.6	55.1	2,706,468	5,705,731	514.6	99.6	0.4	87.2	2.8	9.9	1,744,665	1,304,585	Netherlands, The
...	...	...	...	1,535	19,459	0.9	100.0	—	99.4	—	0.6	1,198	6,380	Netherlands Antilles
5	—	100.0	58.3	...	11,595	3.2	100.0	—	96.1	2.8	1.1	18,766	5,677	New Caledonia
17,953	—	100.0	40.4	1,303,550	310,844	594.1	99.8	0.2	93.4	0.7	5.9	712,256	52,445	New Zealand
4,306	94.7	5.3	5.3	11,725	16,267	20.6	94.6	5.4	46.7	52.3	1.0	78,596	7,843	Nicaragua
6,666	93.8	6.2	—	...	6,334	11.0	—	100.0	100.0	—	—	154	458	Niger
100,637	90.6	9.4	7.1	33,457	172,331	455.6	69.4	30.6	92.0	7.2	0.8	19,662	209,959	Nigeria
...	...	...	...	...	51[5]	0.2	100.0	—	99.5	0.5	—	...	...	Northern Mariana Islands
8,173	8.1	91.9	50.1	1,831,746	1,009,845	2,620.1	100.0	—	97.5	2.5	—	3,764,790	612,469	Norway
...	...	...	...	...	17,179	108.8	100.0	—	92.6	0.5	6.9	38,243	5,077	Oman
33,075	92.7	7.3	5.4	...	137,040	654.5	72.5	27.5	93.6	4.9	1.6	141,476	816	Pakistan
...	...	...	...	...	1,123	1.8	100.0	—	98.0	2.0	—	290	87	Palau
1,052	96.7	3.3	3.3	5,440	67,462	120.5	100.0	—	90.8	7.7	1.5	194,898	15,125	Panama
8,597	64.4	35.6	35.6	168,807	12,439	53.7	74.9	25.1	96.9	3.1	—	25,173	7,819	Papua New Guinea
8,097	52.1	47.9	42.2	88,064	31,132	25.0	—	100.0	100.0	—	—	36	1,592	Paraguay
9,157	80.0	20.0	17.7	71,644	166,328	8,429.3	99.5	0.5	98.4	0.2	1.3	788,411	16,833	Peru
43,399	91.8	8.2	1.1	52,996	606,710	1,870.5	92.3	7.7	88.1	4.2	7.7	372,274	121,492	Philippines
25,652	6.0	94.0	44.1	862,220	1,251,300	235.1	94.1	5.9	89.6	8.3	2.1	282,354	260,653	Poland
9,878	6.1	84.8	32.7	1,185,978	913,640	207.7	100.0	—	90.3	2.3	7.4	278,586	1,017,066	Portugal
...	...	...	...	...	...	2.1	100.0	—	59.2	7.7	33.1	[21]	[21]	Puerto Rico
...	...	...	...	...	15,654	4.2	100.0	—	98.8	1.2	—	28	2,053	Qatar
36	85.9	14.1	11.6	342	69,029	5.8	100.0	—	95.5	4.5	—	19,662	33,053	Réunion
13,148	23.1	76.9	46.7	355,924	172,019	7.8	32.0	68.0	100.0	—	—	7,109	31,911	Romania
158,100	33.1	66.9	30.3	3,190,431	358,552	4,141.2	92.6	7.4	95.9	2.1	2.0	1,247,518	199,065	Russia
7,836	95.7	4.3	1.1	...	2,407	6.4	—	100.0	100.0	—	—	...	61	Rwanda
...	...	...	...	33	1,797	0.4	100.0	—	81.5	5.7	12.8	...	729	St. Kitts and Nevis
...	...	...	...	—	11,692	1.7	100.0	—	96.8	1.7	1.5	6,172	5,186	St. Lucia
...	...	...	...	8	18,545	15.6	100.0	—	100.0	—	—	927	1,537	St. Vincent
131	53.4	46.6	44.3	1,357	2,542	9.8	100.0	—	99.5	0.3	0.2	11,700	5,984	Samoa
...	...	...	...	...	...	—	100.0	—	100.0	—	—	...	...	San Marino
9	—	100.0	100.0	504[5]	196[5]	3.8	100.0	—	99.0	—	1.0	3,836	137	São Tomé and Príncipe
...	...	...	...	19,256	778,185	46.9	100.0	—	87.9	10.4	1.7	10,134	99,412	Saudi Arabia
5,037	84.2	15.8	0.8	...	45,293	418.1	90.4	9.6	87.8	1.5	10.7	301,498	3,784	Senegal
...	...	...	...	99	1,416	37.8	100.0	—	99.7	—	0.2	12,318	12,904	Seychelles
3,419	96.4	3.6	0.1	1,264	2,053	59.4	75.6	24.4	94.9	3.9	1.2	15,654	3,267	Sierra Leone
120[5]	—	—	—	502,202	889,039	5.1	100.0	—	75.4	14.3	10.3	390,062	475,224	Singapore
5,783	5.9	94.1	42.2	431,828	237,213	1.4	—	100.0	100.0	—	—	1,806	32,269	Slovakia
2,253	23.6	76.4	49.7	399,531	296,900	2.0	88.8	11.2	98.6	—	1.4	6,597	29,280	Slovenia
872	15.8	84.2	84.2	51,070	...	82.3	100.0	—	99.9	—	0.1	64,170	75	Solomon Islands
8,329	98.7	1.3	0.3	132[5]	257[5]	20.3	98.8	1.2	95.6	2.0	2.5	4,058	170	Somalia
30,616[19]	39.2[19]	60.8[19]	19.6[19]	827,673	487,114	588.0	99.8	0.2	98.2	0.5	1.3	260,056[18]	55,691[18]	South Africa
14,810	11.1	88.9	38.4	1,626,053	3,813,488	1,167.2	99.3	0.7	86.8	3.1	10.1	1,604,237	3,286,831	Spain
10,344	93.9	6.1	0.6	2,862	81,534	271.6	90.1	9.9	98.7	1.1	0.2	74,120	59,775	Sri Lanka
9,682	77.6	22.4	1.3	1,040	16,928	49.5	11.1	88.9	99.7	—	0.3	88	280	Sudan, The
93	1.1	98.9	96.8	3,249	1,353	13.0	98.5	1.5	98.0	2.0	—	11,640	3,600	Suriname
890	62.9	37.1	29.2	62,000	—	0.1	—	100.0	100.0	—	—	2,242	9,738	Swaziland
61,800	9.5	90.5	49.7	9,720,885	1,615,641	351.3	99.6	0.4	98.9	1.1	—	477,992	715,463	Sweden
10,428	20.1	79.9	73.9	1,937,022	2,393,070	1.8	—	100.0	100.0	—	—	3,031	375,700	Switzerland
50	31.5	68.5	31.7	1,040	141,790	7.9	32.7	67.3	99.1	0.9	—	183	49,546	Syria
...	...	...	...	...	...	1,099.7	99.9	0.1	70.2	2.6	27.2	1,763,572	556,873	Taiwan
...	...	...	...	80	4,131	...	—	100.0	100.0	—	—	54	143	Tajikistan
39,846	94.2	5.8	0.8	5,939	22,531	310.0	16.1	83.9	99.1	—	0.9	60,202	1,975	Tanzania
36,631	92.2	7.9	0.1	758,925	1,006,210	3,004.9	92.5	7.5	86.7	4.3	9.0	4,109,860	840,679	Thailand
1,232	74.5	25.5	5.4	974	4,355	22.9	78.2	21.8	100.0	—	—	1,498	12,222	Togo
2	—	100.0	100.0	...	2,065	3.7	100.0	—	94.3	5.5	0.2	2,625	872	Tonga
44	22.7	77.3	77.3	2,032	65,952	15.0	100.0	—	95.0	5.0	—	12,315	8,009	Trinidad and Tobago
2,842	92.5	7.5	0.7	14,709	151,980	92.1	99.1	0.9	81.6	7.8	10.6	82,118	13,276	Tunisia
17,767	41.3	58.7	29.1	82,545	969,948	575.1	91.3	8.7	97.1	0.4	2.5	98,196	59,207	Turkey
...	...	...	...	501	3,880	8.8	—	100.0	100.0	—	—	316	99	Turkmenistan
...	...	...	...	—	323[5]	0.4	100.0	—	100.0	—	—	326	...	Tuvalu
16,998	81.3	18.7	6.2	...	17,781	226.1	—	100.0	100.0	—	—	24,221	78	Uganda
10,008	17.6	82.4	62.0	132,755	235,646	407.9	98.9	1.1	98.1	1.4	0.6	75,079	96,776	Ukraine
...	...	...	...	7,290	297,934	117.6	100.0	—	99.9	0.1	—	29,436	28,872	United Arab Emirates
7,451	3.1	96.9	57.1	2,192,065	8,983,465	837.8	99.8	0.2	85.3	7.5	7.2	1,427,853	2,276,998	United Kingdom
500,434	14.4	85.6	49.6	14,783,367	23,721,067	4,749.6	99.2	0.8	79.0	8.3	12.7	2,945,014[21]	9,407,307[21]	United States
6,163	70.3	29.7	22.3	77,918	97,102	103.0	97.6	2.4	79.7	3.3	17.0	98,981	13,418	Uruguay
...	...	...	...	240	37,231	2.9	—	100.0	100.0	—	—	44	2,688	Uzbekistan
63	38.0	62.0	62.0	3,074	...	94.6	100.0	—	99.1	0.3	0.6	738	681	Vanuatu
2,713	33.6	66.4	59.7	65,999	297,987	411.9	91.4	8.6	86.2	2.2	11.6	134,120	40,409	Venezuela
36,730	87.6	12.4	6.6	47,277	132,913	1,200.0	93.8	6.3	70.8	22.3	6.9	940,473	13,801	Vietnam
...	...	...	...	...	...	0.8	100.0	—	100.0	—	—	...	...	Virgin Islands (U.S.)
...	...	...	...	...	...	...	...	...	...	...	...	...	...	West Bank
...	...	...	...	...	...	—	—	—	—	—	—	...	...	Western Sahara
—	—	—	—	...	44,915	123.3	100.0	—	96.2	0.4	3.4	19,789	4,636	Yemen
1,140	4.4	95.6	95.6	44,990	166,400	1.3	33.9	66.1	96.6	0.8	2.6	225	43,088	Yugoslavia
8,053	89.6	10.4	4.0	...	8,809	67.3	—	100.0	100.0	—	—	205	1,404	Zambia
9,253	87.7	12.3	10.1	31,415	33,293	12.4	—	100.0	100.0	—	—	1,462	9,925	Zimbabwe

Guernsey. [17]Mostly bauxite and diamonds. [18]South Africa includes Lesotho. [19]South Africa includes Namibia. [20]Includes coal mining. [21]United States includes Puerto Rico. [22]1994–95. [23]Mostly gold. [24]Mostly precious and semiprecious stones. [25]Mostly bauxite. [26]1995–96.

Manufacturing industries

This table provides a summary of manufacturing activity by industrial sector for the countries of the world, providing figures for total manufacturing value added, as well as the percentage contribution of 29 major branches of manufacturing activity to the gross domestic product. U.S. dollar figures for total value added by manufacturing are given but should be used with caution because of uncertainties with respect to national accounting methods; purchasing power parities; preferential price structures and exchange rates; labour costs; and costs for material inputs influenced by " most favored" international trade agreements, barter, and the like.

Manufacturing activity is classified here according to a modification of the International Standard Industrial Classification (ISIC), revision 2, published by the United Nations. A summary of the 2-, 3-, and 4-digit ISIC codes (groups) defining these 29 sectors follows, providing definitional detail beyond that possible in the column headings.

The collection and publication of national manufacturing data is usually carried out by one of three methods: a full census of manufacturing (usually done every 5 to 10 years for a given country), a periodic survey of manufacturing (usually taken at annual or other regular intervals between censuses), and the onetime sample survey (often limited in geographic, sectoral, or size-of-enterprise coverage). The full census is, naturally, the most complete, but, since up to 10 years may elapse between such censuses, it has sometimes been necessary to substitute a survey of more recent date but less complete coverage. In addition to national sources, data published by the United Nations Industrial Development Organization (UNIDO), especially its *International Yearbook of Industrial Statistics* and *Industrial Development Global Report;* occasional publications of the International Monetary Fund (IMF); and other sources have been used.

ISIC code(s)		Products manufactured
31		Food, beverages, and tobacco
	311 + 312	food including prepared animal feeds
	313	alcoholic and nonalcoholic beverages
	314	tobacco manufactures
32		Textiles, wearing apparel, and leather goods
	321	spinning of textile fibres, weaving and finishing of textiles, knitted articles, carpets, rope, etc.
	322	wearing apparel (including leather clothing; excluding knitted articles and footwear)
	323 + 324	leather products (including footwear; excluding wearing apparel), leather substitutes, and fur products

Manufacturing industries

country	year	total manufacturing value added ('000,000 U.S.$)	(31) food (311 + 312)	beverages (313)	tobacco manufactures (314)	(32) textiles (exc. wearing apparel) (321)	wearing apparel (322)	leather and fur products (323 + 324)	(33) wood products (exc. furniture) (331)	wood furniture (332)	(34) paper, paper products (341)	printing and publishing (342)	(35) industrial chemicals (351)	paints, soaps, etc. (352 exc. 3522)	drugs and medicines (3522)
Afghanistan	1988–89[1]	435	18.3	1.9	—	8.0	0.4	16.7	—0.5—		0.9	4.9	4.8	0.2	2.7
Albania	1996[2, 3, 4]	283	34.8	7.5	10.7	—	0.9	1.4	0.5	—	—	0.2	0.1	0.4	—
Algeria	1995	4,147	15.0	3.2	4.1	2.8	2.6	1.2	1.9	0.9	2.2	0.3	0.4	—2.4—	
American Samoa	1993[5, 6]	326	99.5[7]	...	...	...	...	...	...	...	...	...	...	...	...
Andorra	1997[8]	48	1.1	6.1	2.2		—15.7—		0.9	4.4[9]	0.7	10.6	—3.4—		—
Angola	1989	319	20.0	—12.2—			—11.6—		—3.7—		—0.3—		9.1[10]	[10]	[10]
Antigua and Barbuda	1995	8.4	...	...	...	...	...	...	...	...	...	...	...	...	...
Argentina	1993[12]	29,622	16.0	6.0	6.2	4.4	2.4	2.4	1.2	1.2[9]	2.0	5.1	2.2	3.6	3.8
Armenia	1995[2,12]	322	36.8	3.7	1.3	1.9	6.1	1.1	0.4	0.3	0.1	0.8	3.9	—1.3—	
Aruba	1994	89[13]	...	...	...	...	...	...	...	...	...	...	...	...	...
Australia	1995	65,859	15.2	3.4	0.6	2.7	1.9	0.6	2.9	1.8	2.4	8.0	3.2	—4.7—	
Austria	1995[3, 5]	41,735	8.7	2.3	...	3.8	1.3	0.7	4.6	3.8[9]	4.7	4.6	...	...	2.1
Azerbaijan	1996[2, 5]	1,483	1.1	0.2	0.4	13.0	—	—	1.0	...	...	0.2		—3.2—	
Bahamas, The	1992[5]	95	7.4	38.9	—	0.3	3.6	—	—	3.5	...	10.0	...	22.0	...
Bahrain	1992	761	5.0	1.1	—	—	6.5	0.1	0.1	8.4	0.4	4.4	5.6	—	—
Bangladesh	1991–92[12, 14]	1,899	12.7	0.6	12.2	23.5	10.2	3.9	0.7	0.1	2.9	1.2	5.6	4.5	5.8
Barbados	1995	289	18.0	16.9	2.4	0.7	2.1	—	—	1.4	1.0	8.3	5.9	—4.1—	
Belarus	1994[2, 5, 15]	3,006	16.2	...	...	7.0	2.1	2.6	—5.4[16]—		—[16]—		16.3[10]	[10]	[10]
Belgium	1995	53,712	15.4	2.0	0.7	4.3	2.3	0.1	0.6	3.6	2.2	4.6	11.5	—3.8—	
Belize	1992[12]	59	45.9	7.5	3.9		—3.8—		5.5	2.7	1.1	1.5		—14.1—	
Benin	1990	59	20.6	13.1	—	3.2	5.5	6.9	3.6	5.2	—	2.5	—	—9.5—	
Bermuda	1995	170	...	...	...	...	...	...	...	...	...	...	...	...	...
Bhutan	1989[12]	21	6.0	10.1	—		—5.6—		18.1	2.7	0.4	1.0	21.5	—1.7—	
Bolivia	1995[12, 19]	910	20.9	13.5	0.6	2.6	0.6	1.5	2.6	0.5	1.6	1.9	0.5	1.1	1.8
Bosnia and Herzegovina	1991	4,021	9.1	2.6	1.7	5.9	4.5	3.3	6.3	4.2	3.9	1.4	5.5	—4.1—	
Botswana	1995	212	32.5	12.7	—	8.0	5.2	2.8	2.4	1.4	2.8	2.8	1.4	—1.4—	
Brazil	1995	277,242	13.7	1.4	1.2	4.6	2.2	2.6	0.7	0.8	3.6	2.2	8.9	—4.7—	
Brunei	1995	314	...	...	...	...	...	...	...	...	...	...	...	...	...
Bulgaria	1995[20]	5,498	9.3	3.3	3.1	5.9	3.5	3.6	1.6	1.4	1.2	2.0	2.0	—1.9—	
Burkina Faso	1995	162	47.2	15.5	1.2	13.7	1.2	4.4	—	1.2	—	1.2	0.6	—	—
Burundi	1995	117	54.7	21.4	5.1	9.4	—	—	0.9	—	—	0.9	—	—1.7—	
Cambodia	1995[12, 14]	71	—14.2—		5.9	0.7	—21.7—		—10.4[21]—		[21]	0.5		—0.3—	
Cameroon	1995–96[12]	543	19.4	21.0	2.3	10.3	0.3	—	13.0	0.1	1.9	0.5	—	—4.2—	
Canada	1995[12]	126,465	9.6	2.5	1.0	1.6	1.8	0.3	4.9	2.3[9]	10.5	5.6	5.2	3.2	1.9
Cape Verde	1990	14	33.1	0.6	26.8	...	8.0	2.0	...	...	...	9.2	...	...	...
Central African Republic	1995	36	27.0	13.5	21.6	—	—	—	13.5	2.7	...	5.4	2.7	—5.4—	
Chad	1998	200	...	...	...	...	—	—	—	—	—	—	—	...	—
Chile	1995[12, 22]	16,538	20.4	5.0	3.4	2.6	2.2	1.8	3.3	0.8	9.6	3.5	2.9	4.6	2.5
China	1996	174,971	6.9	3.1	5.2	7.1	3.1	1.9	1.6	0.5	2.3	1.2	—9.5—		2.5
Colombia	1995[12, 14]	14,781	19.9	9.6	0.5	6.4	3.3	1.4	0.6	0.5	4.6	3.8	5.9	6.0	4.6
Comoros	1996	11	...	...	—	...	...	...	...	...	—	—	—	—	—
Congo, Dem. Rep. of the	1990	808	86.7	5.4	1.9	0.6	0.2	0.6	0.1	0.2	—	0.1	0.9	—0.1—	
Congo, Rep. of the	1995	86	26.7	24.4	7.0	2.3	1.2	2.3	3.5	2.3	1.2	1.2	3.5	—4.7—	
Costa Rica	1996[5, 12]	1,381	31.6	15.0	2.6	1.8	3.3	0.8	1.3	1.2	3.7	3.4	6.6	3.9	1.6
Côte d'Ivoire	1995	1,395	17.6	4.3	6.0	10.9	2.2	0.9	5.9	0.8	0.2	0.6	5.5	—1.2—	
Croatia	1995	6,539	17.3	3.9	3.6	5.2	5.1	2.1	3.7	2.7	2.0	3.0	3.3	—8.0—	
Cuba	1995	4,077[20]	15.7	5.4	39.9	3.6	1.9	1.2	1.0	0.8	0.2	1.2	1.9	—7.8—	
Cyprus[23]	1996	1,018[12]	17.8	7.9	7.2	3.6	8.0	2.3	6.0	4.3	2.4	5.3	0.5	3.1	1.3
Czech Republic	1998[24]	12,054		—13.5—		—5.8—		0.9	—2.3—		—4.5—			—6.7—	
Denmark	1995	33,560	19.3	3.5	0.9	2.3	1.0	0.4	2.0	2.7	2.7	6.7	5.1	—7.0—	
Djibouti	1992[6]	13		—5.0—			—3.0—		—	—	—0.3—			—1.0—	
Dominica	1997[3, 5]	13	0.1	...	—	—	...	—	...	...	—	—	—	98.1	—
Dominican Republic	1990	1,298	31.9	13.8	5.2	3.5	1.2	3.0	0.2	1.5	2.9	1.7	1.6	—3.4—	
East Timor	...	...	...	...	...	...	...	...	...	...	...	...	...	...	...
Ecuador	1996[12, 14]	2,134	20.1	6.1	0.3	4.5	0.8	1.2	1.3	0.9	3.8	2.3	2.0	2.8	1.7
Egypt	1994–95[3, 27]	6,050	13.6	1.7	2.0	10.0	2.3	0.1	0.8	0.3	1.8	1.4	5.1	3.4	3.8
El Salvador	1996[12, 19, 28]	1,012	16.1	8.5	3.0	6.7	11.4	0.8	0.1	0.7	2.9	4.4	2.6	11.6	4.5
Equatorial Guinea	1990[2]	1.9	27.6	4.1	...	...	2.6	...	...	49.3	...	1.2	...	—13.8—	
Eritrea	1996[12, 14]	53		—65.7—		—2.6—		5.5	...	...	—2.2—			—12.6—	
Estonia	1996[2, 5]	2,134	26.8	6.1	...	8.4	4.3	1.4	8.0	5.8	1.6	4.5	2.5	5.5	0.8

ISIC code(s)		Products manufactured
33		Wood and wood products
	331	sawlogs, wood products (excluding furniture), cane products, and cork products
	332	wood furniture
34		Paper and paper products, printing and publishing
	341	wood pulp, paper, and paper products
	342	printing, publishing, and bookbinding
35		Chemicals and chemical, petroleum, coal, rubber, and plastic products
	351	basic industrial chemicals (including fertilizers, pesticides, and synthetic fibres)
	352 minus 3522	chemical products not elsewhere specified (including paints, varnishes, and soaps and other toiletries)
	3522	drugs and medicines
	353 + 354	refined petroleum and derivatives of petroleum and coal
	355	rubber products
	356	plastic products (excluding synthetic fibres)
36		Glass, ceramic, and nonmetallic mineral products
	361 + 362	pottery, china, glass, and glass products
	369	bricks, tiles, cement, cement products, plaster products, etc.

ISIC code(s)		Products manufactured
37		Basic metals
	371	iron and steel
	372	nonferrous basic metals and processed nickel and cobalt
38		Fabricated metal products, machinery and equipment
	381	fabricated metal products (including cutlery, hand tools, fixtures, and structural metal products)
	382 minus 3825	nonelectrical machinery and apparatus not elsewhere specified
	3825	office, computing, and accounting machinery
	383 minus 3832	electrical machinery and apparatus not elsewhere specified
	3832	radio, television, and communications equipment (including electronic parts)
	384 minus 3843	transport equipment not elsewhere specified
	3843	motor vehicles (excluding motorcycles)
	385	professional and scientific equipment; photographic and optical goods; watches and clocks
39		Other manufactured goods
	390	jewelry, musical instruments, sporting goods, artists' equipment, toys, etc.

			(36)		(37)		(38)								(39)	country
refined petroleum and products	rubber products	plastic products	pottery, china, and glass	bricks, tiles, cement, etc.	iron and steel	non-ferrous metals	fabricated metal products	nonelectrical machinery	office equip., computers	electrical equip.	radio, television	transport equip. exc. motor vehicles	motor vehicles	professional equip.	jewelry, musical instruments	
(353 + 354)	(355)	(356)	(361 + 362)	(369)	(371)	(372)	(381)	(382 exc. 3825)	(3825)	(383 exc. 3832)	(3832)	(384 exc. 3843)	(3843)	(385)	(390)	
—	—	2.1	1.1		0.4	—	—	—	—	—	—	—	0.1	—	37.1	Afghanistan
18.6	0.1	0.3	—	6.8	2.6	13.1	0.6	1.0	—	0.3	—	—	—	—	0.3	Albania
3.8	0.4	0.9	1.3	9.5	15.3	0.9	12.5	1.5		5.8		8.5		1.4	1.3	Algeria
…	…	…	…	…	…	…	…	…	…	…	…	…	…	…	…	American Samoa
—	0.1	2.4	0.2	1.0	0.8		0.7	5.3		19.8		0.1	13.4	3.0	8.0	Andorra
20.0	[10]	[10]	11.3		1.9		5.0					4.7		[11]	0.3[11]	Angola
…	…	…	…	…	…	…	…	…	…	…	…	…	…	…	…	Antigua and Barbuda
9.1	0.9	3.0	1.2	2.4	2.4	0.8	4.6	5.6	0.2	2.2	1.4	0.6	7.6	0.7	0.8	Argentina
0.3	0.8	0.1	0.5	5.0	0.2	2.1	2.2	4.2		6.6		0.6		3.6	16.1	Armenia
…	…	…	…	…	…	…	…	…	…	…	…	…	…	…	…	Aruba
3.5	0.9	3.6	1.1	3.9	3.8	7.2	7.3	6.2		4.6		8.7		0.9	0.8	Australia
…	0.8	3.3	2.4	4.4	5.0	1.6	9.2	10.5	0.1	4.9	6.2	0.9	4.6	1.8	1.6	Austria
47.6	0.6	…	…	…	0.1	—	…	1.1	—	0.8	0.1	0.5	—	0.3	…	Azerbaijan
…	…	…	…	7.0	2.6	—	—	—	—	…	…	—	—	…	…	Bahamas, The
13.7	0.8	—	—	4.5	4.4	33.4	0.3	0.4		3.4	—	3.4	—	—	4.1	Bahrain
0.4	0.5	0.4	1.0	1.7	3.6	0.1	1.2	0.4	—	1.2	0.5	0.8	3.7	—	0.6	Bangladesh
—	6.6	14.9	0.7	2.8	—	—	6.9	3.8		2.4		1.0		—	0.3	Barbados
7.6	[10]	[10]	5.5		3.0		26.8								…	Belarus
1.0	0.6	5.4	2.5	2.1	4.7	1.8	7.1	7.1		7.8		7.0		0.5	1.3	Belgium
—	0.3[17]		[17]	6.2	—	—	2.0	—	—	0.1		4.2		—	1.1	Belize
—	—	—	0.5	24.6	—	—	4.8	—	—	—	—	—	—	—	—	Benin
…	…	…	…	…	…	…	…	…	…	…	…	…	…	…	…	Bermuda
…	0.7	2.2	29.0		…	…	1.0[18]								[18]	Bhutan
36.4	—	1.5	0.7	6.0	—	2.4	1.1	0.3	…	0.4	…	0.1	0.3	0.1	0.8	Bolivia
2.3	0.3	1.3	0.5	3.2	5.5	3.4	10.8	5.0		3.3		8.6		2.6	0.7	Bosnia and Herzegovina
—	0.5	0.5	—	—	—	—	2.4	0.9		0.9		1.4		—	19.8	Botswana
5.0	1.1	2.4	0.8	3.6	5.7	1.5	4.0	7.8		8.4		10.6		0.9	1.5	Brazil
…	…	…	…	…	…	…	…	…	…	…	…	…	…	…	…	Brunei
1.6[20]	0.7	0.6	3.2	2.1	18.6	3.9	5.9	6.6		5.4		5.5		—	7.2	Bulgaria
—	1.2	0.6	—	—	1.2	—	0.6	—	—	0.6		1.2		—	8.1	Burkina Faso
—	—	0.9	—	1.7	—	—	2.6	—	—	—	—	—	—	—	0.9	Burundi
…	17.4		24.6		3.8		0.5	—	—	—	—	—	—	—	0.1	Cambodia
2.4	10.7	0.6	—	2.9	—	7.5	0.6	—	—	1.1		—	—	—	1.0	Cameroon
1.6	1.4	2.2	0.8	1.7	3.5	3.3	5.5	5.3	0.7	2.1	3.9	3.6	12.2	0.5	1.5	Canada
…	…	…	…	…	…	…	…	…	…	…	…	20.1		…	0.2	Cape Verde
—	—	—	—	—	—	—	2.7	…	…	—	—	2.7		—	2.7	Central African Republic
—	—	—	—	—	—	—	—	…	—	—	—	…	—	—	…	Chad
6.0	1.0	2.8	1.0	3.5	2.4	11.5	3.7	2.2	—	1.1	0.2	0.8	0.8	0.2	0.2	Chile
3.8	1.3	2.2	7.3		6.9	2.1	3.4	8.6		5.1	4.6	6.4		1.0	2.5	China
5.2	1.2	3.2	2.3	5.3	2.4	0.4	3.4	1.9	—	2.0	0.6	0.8	2.6	0.5	1.0	Colombia
—	—	—	—	—	—	—	—	—	—	—	—	—	—	—	—	Comoros
0.1	—	—	—	0.2	…	…	0.4	0.3		0.2		0.5		—	1.5	Congo, Dem. Rep. of the
—	2.3	—	—	1.2	—	—	7.0	2.3		3.5		3.5		—	—	Congo, Rep. of the
3.0	1.7	4.3	1.2	2.7	…	0.1	2.2	1.4		1.0	3.8	1.0	0.2	…	0.2	Costa Rica
22.0	1.3	—	0.1	1.9	0.1	0.1	4.9	0.1		0.4		7.6		2.2	3.2	Côte d'Ivoire
3.2	0.3	1.6	1.5	4.0	2.6	0.9	4.5	5.7		6.9		8.2		0.4	0.3	Croatia
…	2.4	2.1	0.5	1.9	0.7	0.9	1.7	1.7		0.9		3.5		0.3	3.0	Cuba
1.2	0.4	3.5	0.4	10.2	—	—	7.3	2.7		1.2	—	0.3	0.8	0.1	2.1	Cyprus[23]
1.4	4.7		8.2		16.7[25]		[25]	11.8		9.2[26]		10.4		[26]	3.9	Czech Republic
1.5	0.4	2.9	0.7	3.6	1.0	0.3	8.1	12.9		4.9		4.7		2.9	2.6	Denmark
			0.1		0.1		13.0								77.5	Djibouti
—	—	—	—	…	—	—	…	—	—	…	—	—	—	—	…	Dominica
16.2	0.8	1.6	0.7	3.5	1.8	0.2	3.7	0.5		0.8		0.1		0.2	0.2	Dominican Republic
…	…	…	…	…	…	…	…	…	…	…	…	…	…	…	…	East Timor
32.7	1.1	3.5	1.2	5.4	1.3	0.4	2.1	1.4	—	1.4	—	0.1	1.3	—	0.4	Ecuador
17.4	0.4	1.1	0.9	10.6	1.8	2.5	3.6	7.3	0.2	3.1	0.6	1.1	2.4	0.4	0.1	Egypt
10.2	0.4	3.1	0.1	5.1	0.8	—	2.2	1.3	—	1.6	0.8	—	0.1	0.1	0.9	El Salvador
…	…	…	…	0.8	…	…	0.6	…	…	…	…	…	…	…	…	Equatorial Guinea
…	2.0		7.1		0.2[25]		[25]	0.5						0.2	1.4	Eritrea
0.3	0.1	1.5	1.4	3.3	—	—	5.4	2.7	0.5	2.4	1.2	2.1	2.0	0.8	0.8	Estonia

Manufacturing industries (continued)

country	year	total manufac-turing value added ('000,000 U.S.$)	(31)			(32)			(33)		(34)		(35)		
			food	bever-ages	tobacco manufac-tures	textiles (exc. wearing apparel)	wearing apparel	leather and fur products	wood products (exc. furniture)	wood furniture	paper, paper products	printing and pub-lishing	industrial chemi-cals	paints, soaps, etc.	drugs and medicines
			(311 + 312)	(313)	(314)	(321)	(322)	(323 + 324)	(331)	(332)	(341)	(342)	(351)	(352 exc. 3522)	(3522)
Ethiopia	1995–96[12, 29]	435	25.3	22.7	4.4	9.8	1.2	7.5	1.7	1.2	1.7	3.6	–0.2	3.2	0.8
Faroe Islands	1997[6]	389	95.8	—	—	—	0.1	0.1	—	—	—	—	—	—	—
Fiji	1994	160	42.6	6.1	—	13.8		1.3	9.7	1.9	3.8	5.1	—	3.1	—
Finland	1995	27,928	8.3	1.4	0.2	1.1	1.1	0.4	4.9	1.5[9]	22.5	6.1	3.9	1.4	1.2
France	1995	297,536	10.5	2.3	1.2	2.4	1.8	0.9	1.7	1.6	2.6	5.6	3.4	5.6	
French Guiana	1991[14]	45	…	…	…	[31]			38.2[31]		…	…	…	…	…
French Polynesia	1993[5]	214	27.2		—	…	…	—	…	…	—	—	—	…	—
Gabon	1995	243	9.1	7.0	6.2	0.8	1.7	—	18.1	2.5	0.8	1.2	4.1	1.7	
Gambia, The	1995[12, 19]	9.2	65.0		—	8.3			6.2[33]		—	4.2	8.8[10]	[10]	[10]
Gaza Strip[34]	…	…	…	…	…	…	…	…	…	…	…	…	…	…	…
Georgia	1997	503	…	…	…	…	…	…	…	…	…	…	…	…	…
Germany	1997[24]	598,758	8.7		2.3	1.4	0.8	0.3	1.3	[35]	2.4	4.6	11.7		
Ghana	1993[12, 24]	610	8.4	9.1	18.1	4.6	0.5		15.2	0.8	1.8	1.3	0.9	8.9	
Greece	1995[3, 14]	10,741	18.3	6.3	2.0	7.0	5.8	1.4	1.6	1.5[9]	3.2	3.7	2.5	8.5	
Greenland	1991	27	…	…	…	…	…	…	…	…	…	…	…	…	…
Grenada	1995[2, 37]	19	29.1	55.2	2.4	—	…	—	…	…	7.0	—	—	6.3	…
Guadeloupe	1995	152	…	…	…	…	…	…	…	…	…	…	…	…	…
Guam	1997[1, 5]	165	14.8			[47]			[47]		—	24.4	[47]		
Guatemala	1995	1,468	28.7	6.2	3.1	5.7	2.5	1.2	0.8	0.5	1.5	4.5	3.5	16.4	
Guernsey	1997[5, 6]	85	…	[38]	…	[38]	…	…	…	7.8[38]	…	18.5	…	…	…
Guinea	1996	143	…	…	…	…	…	…	…	…	…	…	…	…	…
Guinea-Bissau	1995	19	…	…	…	…	…	…	…	…	…	…	…	…	…
Guyana	1998[5, 39]	58	43.2[40]	…	…	…	…	…	…	…	…	…	—	…	…
Haiti	1996[5]	64	35.0	2.9	8.5	19.1			…	…	…	…	11.4		
Honduras	1996[3, 19]	575	28.8	10.4	2.9	2.5	18.8	1.0	4.8	1.5	2.9	2.2	0.4	3.7	1.0
Hong Kong	1996	10,666	7.0	2.2	1.5	11.5	13.3	0.3	0.2	0.1	2.1	13.9	2.7		
Hungary	1998[2, 14]	30,856	16.2	2.1	0.7	1.9	1.8	0.8	1.4	0.9	1.9	2.1	3.2	1.8	3.0
Iceland	1995	933	47.3	2.1	—	2.1	1.5	1.1	0.2	3.6	1.2	9.7	1.0	2.2	—
India	1994–95[3, 41]	29,199	9.8	1.0	1.9	11.3	2.6	0.8	0.3	—	2.0	1.7	10.2	3.6	3.8
Indonesia	1996[3, 24]	39,847	8.4	1.0	9.5	10.3	3.5	3.2	6.3	1.1	3.4	1.8	5.6	2.0	1.5
Iran	1995	9,147	12.8	2.2	0.8	10.8	0.3	0.9	0.7	0.3	1.7	0.9	4.7	5.4	
Iraq	1995	567	9.9	3.4	1.2	3.5	1.2	3.5	—	0.2	3.5	1.4	9.2	1.1	
Ireland	1995[3, 42]	26,040	18.1	4.5	0.8	1.0	1.0	0.2	0.4	0.5[9]	1.4	12.1	13.6	4.8	5.5
Isle of Man	1996–97[3, 5]	120	15.2		…	…	…	…	…	…	…	…	…	…	…
Israel	1995[12, 19]	13,521	10.3	1.7	0.2	3.3	4.5	0.7	1.1	1.6	2.2	5.5	5.6	3.3	
Italy	1995	156,300	7.2	1.5	0.5	6.7	3.9	3.0	1.3	2.4	2.7	3.4	3.5	6.4	
Jamaica	1996[12, 14]	916	25.4	11.5	10.6	6.2		0.6	0.2	2.4	3.9		9.5[10]	[10]	[10]
Japan	1995	1,363,980	8.1	2.0	0.3	2.5	1.1	0.4	1.5	1.0[9]	2.8	5.7	4.1	2.9	3.3
Jersey	1991	45	…	…	…	…	…	…	…	…	…	…	…	…	…
Jordan	1995[12]	1,000	11.3	5.2	13.5	2.9	2.5	1.1	1.0	3.0[9]	2.9	3.1	7.6	2.7	4.8
Kazakhstan	1996[2, 5]	7,167	13.5	1.1	2.0	2.6	0.5	0.1	0.1	0.4	—	0.5	3.4	4.1	0.1
Kenya	1995	814	31.7	9.6	1.5	5.8	1.6	1.4	1.7	0.7	4.4	2.4	1.8	6.6	
Kiribati	1992	0.68	…	…	—	—	—	—	…	—	—	—	—	…	—
Korea, North	…	…	…	…	…	…	…	…	…	…	…	…	…	…	…
Korea, South	1996[19]	216,564	7.1		1.8	5.2	3.0	1.3	0.8	[35]	2.3	2.8	9.2		
Kuwait	1995[12]	3,148	4.3	1.4	—	0.7	3.7	0.1	0.7	1.5	1.0	0.7	4.7	0.7	—
Kyrgyzstan	1996[2]	408	33.9	4.7	2.7	17.3	1.7	1.5	0.3	0.5	—	0.9	—	0.1	0.1
Laos	1990[2]	66	4.5	7.4	16.3	—	5.1	0.3	40.1	5.0	—	1.2	4.0		
Latvia	1996[3, 5]	947	27.6	11.5	…	6.3	4.0	1.2	9.1	2.3[9]	1.0	5.4	0.1	1.5	2.2
Lebanon	1994	1,679	25.2		1.9	3.3	9.6	3.0	3.4		2.4	2.4	2.4	—	—
Lesotho	1995	134	43.3	28.4	…	10.4	3.0	2.2	…	0.7	…	1.5	…	6.7	
Liberia	1995	78	…	…	…	…	…	…	…	…	…	…	…	…	…
Libya	1995	857	4.3	2.2	9.4	3.7	3.3	8.5	0.3	0.2	0.3	1.0	7.0	5.2	
Liechtenstein	1997[5, 6, 45]	1,830	4.2			…	…	…	…	…	…	…	7.8		
Lithuania	1996[2, 5]	3,590	26.9	4.2	…	7.3	6.2	1.4	2.8	2.2[9]	1.5	2.0	…	0.4	0.8
Luxembourg	1995	2,459	4.8	3.1	0.8	7.0	0.6	…	0.3	0.5	3.7	2.1	3.7	4.8	
Macau	1996[5, 12]	425	2.6	0.9	[47]	16.9	59.8	1.1	0.1	0.7	0.3	2.2	—	0.4	0.8
Macedonia	1996	603	19.7	4.8	7.5	5.9	8.0	3.9	0.2	2.1	0.9	4.6	5.5	5.1	
Madagascar	1995	127	15.0	11.8	0.8	35.4	3.1	2.4	0.8	0.8	3.9	1.6	—	6.3	
Malawi	1995	153	35.3	5.9	1.3	7.8	—	…	1.3	—	2.0	5.2	7.8	9.8	
Malaysia	1995[3]	23,810	8.4	0.8	1.2	3.0	2.0	0.2	5.7	1.5	1.8	2.8	5.7	1.9	0.3
Maldives	1997	13[48]	…	…	—	—	…	—	—	…	—	…	—	…	—
Mali	1990	96	18.4	1.2	13.1	36.5	10.3	0.1	0.1	—	0.4	0.8	0.8	0.7	
Malta	1996	700	7.7	7.9	1.4	1.9	9.0	2.7	0.2	4.6	1.2	6.9	0.3	2.5	1.0
Marshall Islands	1997	2.2	…	…	…	…	…	…	…	…	…	…	…	…	…
Martinique	1995	207	…	…	…	…	…	…	…	…	…	…	…	…	…
Mauritania	1993	35	42.9		—	—	—	—	—	—	6.0	—	18.8		
Mauritius	1995[3, 49]	826	17.1	7.7		7.2	43.5	1.2	1.6		1.5		5.2		
Mayotte	1992	…	…	…	—	—	—	—	—	—	—	—	—	—	—
Mexico	1995	54,750	15.4	6.4	1.9	4.9	1.9	1.4	1.2	0.8	2.7	2.6	6.3	7.3	
Micronesia	1992	2.2[6]	[51]	…	…	…	91.0	…	…	…	…	…	…	1.6[51]	…
Moldova	1996[2, 12, 52]	862	46.2	17.9	6.2	2.9	1.9	2.0	0.8	1.9	2.1	0.6	—	0.6	0.5
Monaco	…	…	…	…	…	…	…	…	…	…	…	…	…	…	…
Mongolia	1996[12]	54	34.9	11.3	—	22.2	9.5	4.7	2.5	0.3[9]	—	2.9	—	0.8	1.7
Morocco	1996[5]	5,295	17.1	4.3	13.1	8.9	7.7	1.3	1.1	0.4	2.5	1.2	10.9	2.9	1.9
Mozambique	1996[2]	246	26.9	30.9	1.8	3.8	0.4	0.1	0.4	0.6	1.1	2.5	1.6	5.9	
Myanmar (Burma)	1993	858[53]	14.8	20.4	4.6	26.4	…	…	1.9	0.7	5.7	…	0.2	2.0	1.6
Namibia	1996[5]	327	21.1[54]	…	…	…	…	…	…	…	…	…	…	…	…
Nauru	1989	—	—	—	—	—	—	—	—	—	—	—	—	—	—
Nepal	1996–97[5, 12, 14]	381	13.6	9.1	12.0	25.9	6.3	1.3	1.4	0.9[9]	1.7	1.3	…	3.4	2.4
Netherlands, The	1995	56,417	14.8	4.0	5.2	2.0	0.4	0.2	1.0	0.9	3.5	8.3	8.6	5.5	
Netherlands Antilles	1995	157	…	…	…	…	…	…	…	…	…	…	…	…	…
New Caledonia	1992[5]	341	15.4			…	…	…	…	…	…	…	…	…	
New Zealand	1995	9,878	25.1	3.0	0.6	2.9	2.3	1.1	4.6	1.8	7.7	7.8	3.6	3.1	
Nicaragua	1997[5]	313	39.9	25.6	7.6	1.6	0.1	1.1	2.4	0.5	0.5	1.8	3.1		

			(36)		(37)		(38)								(39)	country
refined petroleum and products	rubber products	plastic products	pottery, china, and glass	bricks, tiles, cement, etc.	iron and steel	non-ferrous metals	fabricated metal products	nonelectrical machinery	office equip., computers	electrical equip.	radio, television	transport equip. exc. motor vehicles	motor vehicles	professional equip.	jewelry, musical instruments	
(353 + 354)	(355)	(356)	(361 + 362)	(369)	(371)	(372)	(381)	(382 exc. 3825)	(3825)	(383 exc. 3832)	(3832)	(384 exc. 3843)	(3843)	(385)	(390)	
—	1.2	1.4	0.5	7.1	3.0	—	1.9	0.2	—	—	—	—	1.8	—	—	Ethiopia
—	—	—	—	—	—	—	—	—	—	—	—	3.4	—	—	0.7	Faroe Islands
—	0.5	2.0	—	3.0[30]	[30]	—	3.2	1.2	—	—	—	0.4	1.0	—	1.2	Fiji
0.8	0.7	2.3	0.7	1.9	6.5		4.0	11.2	0.5	3.8	6.9	3.0	1.2	1.7	0.6	Finland
6.4	1.2	2.7	1.6	2.9	2.8	1.9	8.0	7.8		10.6		11.1		1.6	1.7	France
...	...	...	61.8[32]		[32]		[32]								...	French Guiana
—	...	...	...	...	—	—	35.4								...	French Polynesia
10.3	—	—	0.8	5.8	2.1	2.1	8.7	0.8		5.4		7.0		0.4	3.3	Gabon
—	[10]	[10]	—	—	1.8		4.8	0.8						—	[33]	Gambia, The
...	...	...	...	...	...	...	...	...	...	...	...	...	...	...	...	Gaza Strip[34]
...	...	...	...	...	...	...	...	...	...	...	...	...	...	...	...	Georgia
4.4	4.5		3.8		4.0		6.7	13.2	1.3	7.4	2.1	1.8	12.0	2.7	2.7[35]	Germany
8.1	0.6	2.6	4.4		0.7	8.2	3.4	0.3		1.5		0.6[36]		—	[36]	Ghana
5.2	0.3	3.2	6.3		2.8	3.9	3.6	3.2	0.1	2.2	1.7	4.0	0.6	0.3	0.6	Greece
...	...	...	...	...	...	...	...	...	...	...	...	...	...	...	...	Greenland
—	...	—	—	—	—	—	—	—	—	...	...	—	—	—	...	Grenada
...	...	...	...	...	...	...	...	...	...	...	...	...	...	...	...	Guadeloupe
—	—	—	10.3		—	—	2.6	[47]							0.6	Guam
1.1	2.5	4.0	2.5	4.8	2.7	0.1	2.5	0.8		3.4		0.3		0.2	0.4	Guatemala
...	...	...	...	...	...	...	...	8.8		...	34.3	4.0	...	...	...	Guernsey
...	...	...	...	...	...	...	...	...	...	...	...	...	...	...	...	Guinea
...	...	...	...	...	...	...	...	...	...	...	...	...	...	...	...	Guinea-Bissau
—	—	—	—	—	—	—	—	...	—	...	—	—	—	—	...	Guyana
			...	3.5	...	...	12.1	...	...	...	...	...	...	...	...	Haiti
0.2	1.1	3.3	0.1	7.5	0.5	0.2	3.6	0.7	—	0.9	0.1	—	0.2	0.1	0.7	Honduras
0.1	0.1	2.8	3.0		1.0		4.5	7.0	5.5	0.9	9.7	3.7		3.2	3.7	Hong Kong
5.8	0.8	2.7	1.1	2.1	3.0	2.2	4.1	4.8	7.3	5.1	5.9	0.7	15.0	1.1	0.4	Hungary
—	—	2.9	0.5	3.8	2.2	4.6	7.9	—	—	—	—	2.0	—	—	3.9	Iceland
5.2	1.6	1.0	0.6	3.5	9.0	2.7	2.4	6.1	0.9	5.5	3.1	3.0	4.7	0.7	0.8	India
0.2	1.9	2.0	1.7	2.3	9.3	1.2	4.2	1.4	—	3.9	3.3	5.7	4.3	0.3	0.7	Indonesia
0.7	2.1	1.6	1.7	7.7	15.2	3.6	4.5	4.0		7.8		8.3		0.7	0.4	Iran
25.2	0.5	1.4	0.7	18.2	4.1	—	4.8	2.3		4.4		0.4		—	—	Iraq
[43]	0.7	1.5	2.5		0.1	0.4	1.9	3.2	13.3	3.2	2.1	0.8	0.7	3.8	1.7[43]	Ireland
...	...	...	...	...	...	...	...	...	...	...	...	...	...	...	...	Isle of Man
2.1	0.6	5.4	0.6	3.6	1.2	0.8	12.0	3.3		22.6		5.2		1.4	1.2	Israel
2.5	1.7	2.9	1.5	4.2	3.7	1.3	7.1	13.8		8.1		7.5		2.2	1.0	Italy
9.3	[10]	[10]	5.9		[44]		14.2[44]								0.2	Jamaica
1.3	1.2	3.6	1.4	2.9	4.3	1.2	7.5	10.9	2.4	5.0	8.5	1.2	0.4	1.0	1.7	Japan
...	...	...	...	...	...	...	...	...	...	...	...	...	...	...	...	Jersey
5.4	0.2	3.1	0.1	15.7	3.0	0.9	4.5	1.9	—	1.0	1.0	—	1.2	0.2	0.4	Jordan
8.1	0.2	0.1	0.4	1.2	8.3	17.6	1.5	2.6	...	0.6	...	...	...	0.1	0.1	Kazakhstan
0.7	3.1	3.3	0.5	3.6	1.7	—	6.3	0.6		5.7		3.4		0.1	1.7	Kenya
—	—	—	—	—	—	—	...	—	—	—	—	...	—	—	...	Kiribati
...	...	...	...	...	...	...	...	...	...	...	...	...	...	...	...	Korea, North
2.9	3.8		4.6		6.3		5.5	8.5	1.2	3.7	15.1	3.1	8.6	1.1	2.2[35]	Korea, South
65.4	0.1	1.5	0.5	4.8	0.7	—	3.5	1.5	—	1.3	—	0.6	0.1	—	0.6	Kuwait
—	0.1	0.2	3.6	8.4	—	9.2	0.6	5.8	0.2	5.6	—	0.1	0.9	0.8	0.9	Kyrgyzstan
—	0.5		0.1	3.8	—	—	10.8	0.5		0.2		—	—	—	0.1	Laos
0.1	—	0.8	0.7	1.9	...	0.1	3.1	5.2	0.2	2.3	1.5	5.0	0.4	0.4	1.4	Latvia
1.6	—	3.2	12.0		4.9		8.9	2.2		2.1		1.0		—	10.5	Lebanon
...	...	...	...	0.7	...	...	3.0	...	...	...	...	...	...	...	...	Lesotho
...	...	...	...	...	...	...	...	...	...	...	...	...	...	...	...	Liberia
27.2	0.1	0.8	0.2	21.7	—	—	0.5	—	—	—	—	—	—	—	4.0	Libya
			...	...	1.0		15.3	50.0							...	Liechtenstein
18.0	0.1	0.9	1.0	2.5	0.2	—	1.4	3.3	0.1	1.8	3.3	2.0	0.2	0.6	0.6[46]	Lithuania
0.2	10.6	2.3	3.9	7.5	15.9	3.5	12.2	7.2		3.1		0.7		1.5	0.1	Luxembourg
—	[47]	0.3	—	3.0	—	—	2.0	0.3	—	3.3	—	1.2	—	—	3.7	Macau
0.4	0.1	1.2	0.8	0.6	6.2	—	5.4	1.1		9.5		4.7		0.3	1.7	Macedonia
7.9	0.8	0.8	—	2.4	—	—	3.1	—	—	2.4		0.8		—	—	Madagascar
—	0.7	3.3	—	1.3	—	—	5.9	4.6		1.3		0.7		—	5.9	Malawi
3.2	4.6	3.8	1.2	4.3	1.4	1.0	4.2	4.3	0.7	4.1	24.9	1.7	3.4	1.2	0.8	Malaysia
—	—	...	—	...	—	—	...	—	—	—	—	...	—	—	...	Maldives
0.7	0.3	0.4	—	1.3	—	—	6.2	0.5		1.7		6.5		—	—	Mali
—	3.2	2.4	0.4	3.3	—	—	3.8	1.0	0.3	4.4	23.6	1.1	0.1	3.8	5.3	Malta
...	...	...	...	...	...	...	...	...	...	...	...	...	...	...	...	Marshall Islands
...	...	...	...	...	...	...	...	...	...	...	...	...	...	...	...	Martinique
			—	16.8	—	—	15.5	—	—	—	—	—	—	—	—	Mauritania
—	0.3	1.6	3.9		1.0		1.6	1.6[50]		0.9		[50]		1.7	2.6	Mauritius
—	—	—	—	...	—	—	—	—	—	—	—	—	—	—	—	Mayotte
11.6	1.4	1.8	2.2	1.7	4.1	1.1	3.9	3.1		3.1		9.3		2.0	1.9	Mexico
...	...	...	...	...	...	...	...	...	...	...	...	...	...	...	7.4	Micronesia
—	—	0.3	2.6	3.7	0.1	0.1	0.8	5.0	0.1	0.5	1.3	0.2	—	0.7	0.8	Moldova
...	...	...	...	...	...	...	...	...	...	...	...	...	...	...	...	Monaco
—	—	—	0.1	5.7	–1.5	—	–0.1	0.1	—	0.3	2.0	0.3	0.4	0.7	1.0	Mongolia
...	1.0	1.5	1.4	9.3	1.1	0.3	3.9	0.8	0.5	2.1	0.8	0.3	3.0	0.2	0.1	Morocco
0.2	2.6	1.7	0.3	13.3	0.8	0.5	2.2	0.2		0.7		1.4		—	0.1	Mozambique
...	0.5	0.2	...	0.5	6.1	7.0	0.2	...	...	0.7	—	...	1.5	...	5.0	Myanmar (Burma)
...	...	...	...	...	...	...	...	...	...	...	...	...	...	...	...	Namibia
—	—	—	—	—	—	—	—	—	—	—	—	—	—	—	—	Nauru
0.2	1.3	1.7	0.1	7.2	1.6	0.1	4.8	0.1	—	2.2	0.3	—	—	—	0.5	Nepal
2.4	0.5	3.3	1.7	2.3	2.8	0.1	6.8	8.2		11.4		4.5		0.9	0.3	Netherlands, The
...	...	...	...	...	...	...	...	...	...	...	...	...	...	...	...	Netherlands Antilles
...	...	...	...	...	...	43.2	...	...	...	...	...	...	...	...	...	New Caledonia
1.5	0.7	3.6	1.3	2.1	1.8	2.3	7.7	4.8		4.4		4.4		0.4	1.3	New Zealand
4.5	0.1	...	7.4		...	...	0.7	0.3				0.2		...	...	Nicaragua

Manufacturing industries (continued)

country	year	total manufac-turing value added ('000,000 U.S.$)	(31)			(32)			(33)		(34)		(35)		
			food	bever-ages	tobacco manufac-tures	textiles (exc. wearing apparel)	wearing apparel	leather and fur products	wood products (exc. furniture)	wood furniture	paper, paper products	printing and pub-lishing	industrial chemi-cals	paints, soaps, etc.	drugs and medicines
			(311 + 312)	(313)	(314)	(321)	(322)	(323 + 324)	(331)	(332)	(341)	(342)	(351)	(352 exc. 3522)	(3522)
Niger	1996[12]	9.8	—23.2—			—1.2—			—0.5—		—35.5—		—21.8—		
Nigeria	1995	7,884	17.6	15.3	1.9	10.4	0.1	3.1	0.5	0.9	3.8	3.4	0.3	—11.7—	
Northern Mariana Islands	1997[1, 5]	762	—0.7—			[47]	91.8	—	[47]	[47]	[47]	0.7	—0.3—		
Norway	1995[14]	16,835	—20.7—			1.0	0.4	0.1	3.4	2.1[9]	6.7	9.3	6.7	1.2	2.0
Oman	1995	660	12.1	3.0	—	2.0	6.2	0.1	2.3	2.1[9]	1.3	2.4	0.9	3.5	1.3
Pakistan	1995	7,550	15.2	1.3	7.1	18.7	2.1	1.7	0.3	0.2	1.7	1.8	9.8	—7.9—	
Palau	1998	1.2[56]	…	…	…	…	…	…	…	…	…	…	…	…	…
Panama	1995	694	43.5	10.0	3.6	0.8	2.6	1.1	1.4	1.3	4.0	2.8	1.4	—5.5—	
Papua New Guinea	1989	451	48.4	13.1	4.9	—	0.4	—	11.6	2.0	1.1	2.4	1.1	—1.1—	
Paraguay	1995	904	30.6	10.0	0.7	7.4	0.3	5.3	18.8	1.8	0.1	4.6	0.8	—0.8—	
Peru	1995	7,485	14.8	13.2	0.9	8.7	0.9	0.6	0.6	0.5	1.1	3.2	3.0	—7.7—	
Philippines	1995[12, 14]	15,323	18.9	8.4	4.7	3.1	4.7	0.5	0.7	0.5[9]	2.0	1.4	2.5	5.2	4.0
Poland	1996	27,032	—16.1—		0.8	3.7	4.6	1.7	3.7	4.4[57]	2.0	4.8	—8.4—		
Portugal	1995[12]	20,472	7.5	2.6	4.2	8.5	6.5	3.9	3.5	1.7	4.9	4.3	2.0	1.7	1.6
Puerto Rico	1997[5]	36,427	4.0	5.7	…	0.2	1.9	0.6	…	0.1[9]	0.4	1.2	2.5	2.3	54.0
Qatar	1994	694	3.6	0.2	—	0.3	7.1	0.1	1.0	2.0	0.1	3.4	28.0	0.4	—
Réunion	1994	371	34.5	12.3	—	—0.5—		—	—3.8—		5.0[58]	6.3	…	—3.7—	
Romania	1995[5, 59]	9,387	18.8	8.9	0.7	4.4	6.6	1.7	3.3	3.4[9]	1.3	1.1	3.5	2.4	1.8
Russia	1995	58,394[53]	15.0	1.5	0.3	2.1	1.2	0.7	1.6	0.9	3.1	0.7	6.2	1.5	0.8
Rwanda	1990	178	29.1	18.1	11.2	…	…	…	4.4	0.9	1.0	1.3	9.0	—	—
St. Kitts and Nevis	1995[5]	21	16.0[61]	…	…	…	…	…	…	…	…	…	…	…	…
St. Lucia	1995[2, 37]	46	10.0	—27.6—		2.4	7.2	…	…	…	40.8	…	…	…	…
St. Vincent	1997[3]	19	…	…	…	…	…	…	…	…	…	…	…	…	…
Samoa	1995[5]	25	…	…	…	—	…	—	…	—	—	—	—	…	…
San Marino	…	…	…	…	…	…	…	…	…	…	…	…	…	…	…
São Tomé and Príncipe	1993[2]	4.6	26.3	20.7	—	—	26.3	—	—15.1—		—	1.2	—	6.6	—
Saudi Arabia	1995	7,461	5.8	0.5	0.3	0.4	0.1	0.1	0.1	0.5	2.2	1.0	40.4	—2.3—	
Senegal	1996[12]	309[62]	36.1[62]	3.9	3.9	3.2	—	0.2	0.3	0.1	1.3	1.9	21.1	6.0	3.4
Seychelles	1989	26	—79.6—			—0.6—			—2.1—		—6.0—		—4.1—		
Sierra Leone	1993[12]	92	37.0	21.6	10.5	—	1.0	0.1	0.3	1.2	0.2	2.2	—20.2—		
Singapore	1996[3, 14]	26,157	2.8	0.8	—	0.2	0.7	0.1	0.2	0.6[9]	1.3	4.5	1.6	3.6	4.1
Slovakia	1996	3,277	10.5[53]	2.9	…	2.4[53]	3.3	1.6	1.9	1.6[9]	4.9[53]	2.7	6.7	0.9	2.9
Slovenia	1995[12]	5,857	8.4	2.3	0.6	3.4	4.1	3.3	2.8	3.0	6.1	4.3	7.8	—6.4—	
Solomon Islands	1995	8.2	…	…	…	—	…	—	…	…	—	…	—	—	—
Somalia	1990	36	21.6	6.3	37.5	10.5	0.8	2.0	—	7.3	–0.6	0.3	0.4	—5.1—	
South Africa	1995	29,071	10.4	5.7	0.4	3.2	2.8	1.3	1.3	1.1	5.0	3.4	5.0	—4.9—	
Spain	1996	95,026	11.6	3.9	0.7	3.0	2.3	1.6	2.2	2.5	3.2	5.2	4.3	—6.2—	
Sri Lanka	1993[12, 19]	1,267	14.8	12.4	11.8	8.3	20.1	1.9	0.6	0.2	2.5	1.1	0.9	4.5	0.3
Sudan, The	1990	1,179	40.0	3.0	16.7	11.9	0.4	5.4	0.2	0.2	2.1	6.4	0.7	—2.2—	
Suriname	1992[2, 3, 37]	700	33.4	22.3	12.3	…	1.5	1.6	8.7	1.4	0.7	1.6	…	—8.3—	
Swaziland	1995[3, 5, 14]	335	27.5	42.0	…	0.4	3.0	…	1.2	0.8	17.9	1.1	—	0.2	…
Sweden	1994[3, 14]	35,125	7.2	1.2	0.5	1.0	0.2	0.1	4.9	1.1	9.8	5.8	3.9	1.8	5.4
Switzerland	1994	60,111	8.1	1.4	0.8	1.8	1.0	0.5	4.6	3.0	1.9	7.4	7.4	—5.9—	
Syria	1995	3,805	12.0	5.8	3.8	20.2	1.2	2.1	2.2	0.2	0.4	0.8	0.2	—0.9—	
Taiwan	1997	78,385	—6.6—		1.4	6.3	2.2	0.7	0.5	0.8	1.9	1.1	7.6	—2.1—	
Tajikistan	1996[2, 5]	864	26.1[53]	0.2	0.6	18.9[53]	0.5	0.1[53]	—	0.1	—	0.1[53]	4.7[53]	0.1[53]	…
Tanzania	1995	119	10.7	5.8	10.7	17.4	0.8	1.7	1.7	0.8	3.3	3.3	14.9	—2.5—	
Thailand	1994[12, 14]	38,122	9.3	3.9	2.9	8.0	9.4	0.6	1.3	0.4	1.7	4.6	0.9	0.7	0.7
Togo	1995[5]	59	15.3	40.7	…	16.9	—	6.8	—	—	—	1.7	10.2	…	…
Tonga	1994[2, 12]	13	—45.1—			1.1	1.5	2.0	1.3	[63]	[63]	5.0	—	—24.9—	
Trinidad and Tobago	1995	862	12.0	9.1	3.3	0.2	0.9	0.2	0.4	1.0	2.8	2.5	36.5	1.4	0.1
Tunisia	1996[12]	5,216	9.4	2.9	6.5	7.0	14.9	4.0	—4.8—		—2.2—		4.8	2.8	0.6
Turkey	1997	42,524	8.2	2.5	2.0	11.7	4.3	0.4	0.6	0.4	1.6	1.4	4.5	—7.7—	
Turkmenistan	1992[2, 5, 15]	801	13.3	…	…	18.9	1.2	0.4	—0.3[16]—		—[16]—		3.2[10]	[10]	[10]
Tuvalu	1995[3]	0.35	…	—	—	—	…	—	—	…	—	—	—	…	—
Uganda	1989	155	42.8	11.9	8.9	8.0	1.3	1.5	0.1	4.0	0.9	1.4	0.3	0.7	5.1
Ukraine	1996[3, 5]	27,508	24.1	3.4	0.6	1.4[53]	0.6	0.6	0.7	0.7	0.9	0.4	6.2	1.0[53]	0.8
United Arab Emirates	1993[2]	6,621	—8.7—			—4.7—			—2.8—		—2.8—		—53.8—		
United Kingdom	1996	283,255	10.6	2.7	1.2	2.9	1.7	0.6	1.3	2.2[9]	3.1	9.2	4.6	3.8	3.1
United States	1996	1,749,662	8.2	2.0	1.5	1.9	2.2	0.3	2.4	1.6[9]	4.1	7.5	4.7	3.0	3.4
Uruguay	1996[19]	3,755	24.9	10.9	4.6	5.6	3.0	3.2	0.3	0.4	2.4	4.2	1.6	—8.3—	
Uzbekistan	1992[2, 5, 15]	2,147	12.6	…	…	21.4	3.1	1.9	—1.3[16]—		—[16]—		5.4[10]	[10]	[10]
Vanuatu	1994[5]	11	—37.5—			—6.8—			—24.8—		—7.5—		—6.3[67]—		
Venezuela	1996[12, 19]	15,621	11.3	4.0	12.7	1.8	1.9	0.9	0.4	0.5	1.7	1.5	7.8	3.4	1.3
Vietnam	1997[2, 5]	12,096	—32.7—		4.1	—10.3—		4.9	5.6[68]	…	[68]	1.5	—7.0—		
Virgin Islands (U.S.)	1997[1, 5]	146	—22.0—			[47]	0.8	[47]	1.1	[47]	—	14.5	—[47]—		
West Bank[34]	1994	314	12.9	0.1	0.5	2.8	19.2	4.7	2.5	1.3	2.2	0.5	0.4	2.0	1.0
Western Sahara	…	…	…	…	…	…	…	…	…	…	…	…	…	…	…
Yemen	1996[2, 14]	1,153	—40.4—			—1.5—			—0.4—		—7.9—		—39.0—		
Yugoslavia	1996	4,439	20.0	6.9	1.9	4.2	2.7	2.0	1.8	1.8	1.9	5.2	2.1	—9.4—	
Zambia	1995	450	19.2	17.1	6.7	9.8	1.1	0.7	3.3	1.1	0.9	2.2	4.9	—10.5—	
Zimbabwe	1995–96[3]	1,627	14.9	13.9	4.3	9.0	3.0	2.5	2.6	1.8	2.3	3.0	3.9[77]	2.1	2.9

[1]Gross output in value of sales. [2]Gross output of production. [3]In factor values. [4]State sector only except food and beverages. [5]Complete ISIC detail is not available. [6]Value of manufactured exports. [7]Canned tuna and salmon. [8]Value of manufactured exports (excluding duty-free reexports). [9]Includes metal furniture. [10]351 includes 352, 355, and 356. [11]390 includes 385. [12]In producer's prices. [13]Estimated figure includes agriculture. [14]Establishments employing 10 or more persons. [15]Includes extraction of petroleum, natural gas, metals, and nonmetals. [16]33 includes 34. [17]355 and 356 includes 361 + 362. [18]38 includes 39. [19]Establishments employing five or more persons. [20]Excludes petroleum refining. [21]33 includes 341. [22]Establishments employing 50 or more persons. [23]Republic of Cyprus only. [24]Establishments employing 20 or more persons. [25]37 includes 381. [26]383 includes 385. [27]Private establishments employing 10 or more persons and all public establishments. [28]Excludes establishments processing coffee or cotton. [29]Establishments employing 10 or more persons and using power-driven machines. [30]369 includes 371. [31]33 includes 32. [32]36 includes 37 and 38. [33]34 includes 39. [34]West Bank includes Gaza Strip. [35]390 includes 332. [36]384 includes 390. [37]Selected industries only. [38]332 includes 313 and 321. [39]Includes public

			(36)		(37)		(38)								(39)	country
refined petroleum and products (353 + 354)	rubber products (355)	plastic products (356)	pottery, china, and glass (361+ 362)	bricks, tiles, cement, etc. (369)	iron and steel (371)	non-ferrous metals (372)	fabricated metal products (381)	nonelectrical machinery (382 exc. 3825)	office equip., computers (3825)	electrical equip. (383 exc. 3832)	radio, television (3832)	transport equip. exc. motor vehicles (384 exc. 3843)	motor vehicles (3843)	professional equip. (385)	jewelry, musical instruments (390)	
——			—10.3—		...	...	—7.6—								...	Niger
—	1.9	2.8	0.4	5.8	1.0	1.9	3.7	—1.1—		—2.0—		—9.8—		—	0.5	Nigeria
[47]	[47]	[47]	—2.8—		—	—	—	—	—	—	—	—0.2—		—	[47]	Northern Mariana Islands
0.8	0.2	1.7	0.8	2.4	2.7	6.5	4.3	6.6	0.3	3.4	1.8	11.0[55]	1.3	1.8	0.9	Norway
27.9	—	1.5	1.5	16.5	—	6.0	5.8	1.3	—	1.6	—	0.1	0.1	—	0.4	Oman
3.1	0.9	0.6	1.1	8.3	6.5	—	0.8	—3.0—		—4.6—		—2.8—		0.2	0.3	Pakistan
...	...	...	...	...	...	...	...	...	...	...	...	...	...	...	...	Palau
5.8	0.2	4.1	0.6	4.8	1.2	0.4	2.2	—	—	0.9	—	1.2	0.2	0.1	0.3	Panama
—	—	0.4	0.7	1.6	...	—	6.7	—1.3—		—0.7—		—2.4—		...	...	Papua New Guinea
4.3	—	1.9	0.6	3.0	—	1.3	1.2	—0.2—		—0.1—		—0.7—		0.1	5.5	Paraguay
18.2	0.8	2.4	1.1	4.0	2.0	6.0	3.1	—1.5—		—1.6—		—2.0—		0.3	1.8	Peru
10.5	1.3	1.8	1.3	3.3	3.6	1.6	1.6	0.7	1.3	3.1	7.9	0.8	3.2	0.3	0.9	Philippines
1.9	—4.5—		—6.3—		—5.5—		6.8	9.2	0.3	4.0	1.8	3.1	4.3	1.9	[57]	Poland
13.8	0.6	1.7	3.5	5.1	1.0	0.5	6.1	3.2	0.1	3.3	2.0	1.6	3.1	0.5	1.0	Portugal
2.3	—	1.0	—1.6—		—0.2—		1.1	—7.3—		2.6	5.4	—	0.3	4.2	0.4	Puerto Rico
31.5	—	0.8	—	6.7	11.4	—	2.8	—	—	—0.1—		0.3	—	—	0.2	Qatar
—	—	[58]	...	16.8	—	—	12.2	—5.0—							—	Réunion
2.2	1.4	1.0	—5.3—		5.6	1.3	4.2	8.5	0.2	2.9	2.2	0.9	3.4	1.4	0.9	Romania
7.3	1.4	0.5	1.1	6.0	8.8	9.3	1.8	12.5	0.5	3.2	[47]	2.1[60]	1.5	1.0	1.6	Russia
—	—	—	—	11.7	—	—	10.3	—0.9—		—0.8—		—1.4—		—	...	Rwanda
...	...	...	...	...	...	...	...	...	...	...	...	...	...	...	...	St. Kitts and Nevis
...	...	...	...	...	...	...	...	...	...	—12.0—		...	...	...	...	St. Lucia
...	...	...	...	...	...	...	...	...	...	...	...	...	...	...	...	St. Vincent
—	—	—	—	—	—	—	—	—	—	—	—	—	21.0	—	—	Samoa
...	...	...	...	...	...	...	...	...	...	...	...	...	...	...	...	San Marino
—	—	—	—3.8—		—	—	—	—	—	—	—	—	—	—	—	São Tomé and Príncipe
13.1	0.1	3.0	0.5	12.2	7.5	0.4	5.3	—1.0—		—2.0—		—0.6—		—	0.6	Saudi Arabia
3.7	—	1.6	—	7.4	—	—	4.1	0.5	—	–0.1	—	1.1	0.4	—	—	Senegal
——			—5.2—		—	—	—2.4—								—	Seychelles
——			—3.5—		...	...	2.1	...	...	...	...	...	...	...	0.1	Sierra Leone
5.5	0.3	2.5	0.5	1.5	0.4	0.1	5.9	6.7	25.6	2.9	18.9	5.7	0.3	2.1	0.5	Singapore
5.4	2.4	2.3	3.1	3.2[53]	9.0	3.6[53]	2.3	9.3[53]	0.3	3.0[53]	1.4	2.6[53]	3.6	1.7[53]	0.8[53]	Slovakia
0.4	1.6	2.4	—3.7—		10.2	1.6	7.3	—5.9—		—7.9—		—3.9—		2.0	0.7	Slovenia
—	—	—	—	—	—	—	—	—	—	—	—	...	—	—	—	Solomon Islands
1.6	—	0.5	—	3.0	—	—	1.1	—	—	—	—	—0.9—		—	1.7	Somalia
5.9	1.3	2.6	1.5	3.4	9.3	3.2	6.3	—6.3—		—4.7—		—8.0—		0.9	2.0	South Africa
1.4	1.6	3.1	1.9	5.7	5.3	1.9	8.3	—7.3—		—5.5—		—11.1—		1.0	1.0	Spain
1.4	4.2	1.4	1.8	2.9	1.1	0.2	1.3	0.9	0.2	1.1	0.1	1.6	0.3	—	2.1	Sri Lanka
1.3	0.8	1.2	0.1	0.5	0.1	0.7	2.6	—0.1—		—1.2—		—2.1—		—	0.1	Sudan, The
...	0.7	0.6	—5.3—		...	...	...	...	...	...	...	—0.9—		0.2	0.5	Suriname
...	...	0.2	0.1	0.5	...	...	2.2	2.8	...	...	...	...	0.2	...	—	Swaziland
1.2	0.7	1.4	0.7	1.6	4.8	1.3	7.7	11.9	0.8	3.1	5.6	2.7	10.5	2.8	0.3	Sweden
2.0	0.8	2.3	1.7	2.7	1.2	1.9	6.4	—12.8—		—16.9—		—1.7—		5.4	0.4	Switzerland
17.1	0.3	0.6	4.7	7.1	—	0.6	14.0	—2.4—		—2.4—		—0.5—		—	0.3	Syria
7.7	1.1	5.3	—3.2—		—7.8—		7.0	—4.7—		—21.7—		—7.5—		0.9	2.0	Taiwan
...	—	—	0.3	1.4[53]	...	41.6	...	0.7[53]	...	...	...	...	0.4[53]	...	1.8[53]	Tajikistan
4.1	0.8	1.7	—	5.8	1.7	2.5	4.1	—0.8—		—1.7—		—3.3—		—	—	Tanzania
11.5	1.7	1.2	1.0	3.7	3.0	0.4	3.2	17.4	—	2.4	3.1	1.7	3.7	0.3	1.3	Thailand
...	...	...	—	3.4	3.4	...	—	...	...	...	...	...	...	...	—	Togo
—	—	—	—4.7—		—	—	3.8	—	—	—	—	—4.1—		—	6.4[63]	Tonga
10.5	0.2	0.5	1.2	3.6	8.2	—	1.4	0.3	—	1.4	0.3	0.1	0.1	[11]	1.9[11]	Trinidad and Tobago
16.8	0.8	1.4[64]	2.5	6.9	1.5	3.0[65]	[65]	—0.4—		3.0	[66]	0.2	1.8	[66]	1.8[66]	Tunisia
10.0	1.9	2.9	3.0	4.0	7.2	1.1	2.9	—5.8—		—7.5—		—7.8—		0.4	0.2	Turkey
55.7	[10]	[10]	—4.0—		—0.1—		—0.8—								...	Turkmenistan
—	—	—	—	...	—	—	—	—	—	—	—	—	—	—	...	Tuvalu
—	0.2	—	—	2.5	3.0	—	4.7	0.7	—	1.3	0.5	—	0.1	—	—	Uganda
4.8	2.2	0.1	1.0	4.6	23.6	1.6	5.2	5.6	0.1	—2.1[53]—		2.9[53]	0.8	0.6[53]	0.1[53]	Ukraine
——			—8.3—		—8.2—		—9.2—								1.4	United Arab Emirates
1.9	1.1	3.9	1.6	1.9	—3.7—		6.9	8.5	2.1	3.4	3.5	3.6	6.6	3.0	1.2	United Kingdom
1.8	1.1	3.2	0.9	1.7	2.2	1.8	6.2	8.3	2.3	3.5	7.0	4.0	6.1	5.6	1.5	United States
14.9	0.7	2.5	1.0	2.3	1.6	0.2	2.8	—0.8—		—1.7—		—0.9—		0.6	0.4	Uruguay
12.4	[10]	[10]	—5.4—		—12.2—		—13.2—								...	Uzbekistan
——			—[67]—		—11.4[25]—		[25]	...	...	...	...	...	...	...	...	Vanuatu
15.8	2.2	1.6	2.3	2.9	7.0	6.1	2.7	1.7	—	1.7	0.1	0.3	5.9	0.3	0.3	Venezuela
——	—2.9—		—10.7—		—7.6[25]—		[25]	—1.8—		—5.1—		—3.5—		...	...	Vietnam
——			—15.0—		—	—	2.3	—[47]—		—	—	—3.4—		19.8	1.9	Virgin Islands (U.S.)
—	—	2.1	0.6	26.6	0.1	—	10.6	—1.3—		—0.4—		—	0.5	0.1	7.6	West Bank[34]
...	...	...	...	...	...	...	...	...	...	...	...	...	...	...	...	Western Sahara
——			—7.9—		—2.8—		—	—	—	—	—	—	—	—	—	Yemen
0.9	2.0	1.8	1.4	4.9	1.6	2.6	7.8	—4.5—		—6.3—		—5.6—		0.5	0.4	Yugoslavia
4.2	1.8	1.3	–0.2	3.3	1.3	—	5.3	—1.1—		—3.3—		—0.7—		—	0.2	Zambia
[69]	2.7	1.3	0.4	5.3	8.4	0.8	6.3	—1.2—		3.4	0.2	0.3	2.6	0.2	0.7	Zimbabwe

utilities. [40]Sugar and rice manufacturing only. [41]Establishments with electric power and employing 10 or more workers and all establishments employing 20 or more workers. [42]Establishments employing three or more persons. [43]390 includes 353 + 354. [44]38 includes 37. [45]Excludes exports destined for Switzerland. [46]Includes recycled waste and scrap. [47]Data withheld for reasons of confidentiality. [48]Includes public utilities. [49]Statistical breakdown is based on 89.3% of total manufacturing value added (U.S.$737,000,000); detail for some establishments employing nine or fewer employees is unavailable. [50]382 includes 384. [51]Coconut soap includes coconut oil. [52]Excludes Transdniester area and city of Tighina (Bendery). [53]Sum of available data. [54]Fish and meat processing. [55]Includes petroleum platforms (6.2% of total). [56]Includes mining. [57]332 includes 390. [58]341 includes 356. [59]State enterprises only; state enterprises account for about 80% of all industrial output. [60]Excludes shipbuilding and aircraft. [61]Refined sugar only. [62]Excludes fish processing. [63]39 includes 332 and 341. [64]Includes synthetic fibres. [65]372 includes 381. [66]390 includes 3832 and 385. [67]35 includes 36. [68]331 includes 341. [69]351 includes 353 + 354.

Energy

This table provides data about the commercial energy supplies (reserves, production, consumption, and trade) of the various countries of the world, together with data about oil pipeline networks and traffic. Many of the data and concepts used in this table are adapted from the United Nations' *Energy Statistics Yearbook*.

Electricity. Total installed electrical power capacity comprises the sum of the rated power capacities of all main and auxiliary generators in a country. "Total installed capacity" (kW) is multiplied by 8,760 hours per year to yield "Total production capacity" (kW-hr).

Production of electricity comprises the total gross production of electricity by publicly or privately owned enterprises and also that generated by industrial establishments for their own use, but it usually excludes consumption by the utility itself. Measured in millions of kilowatt-hours (kW-hr), annual production of electricity ranges generally between 50% and 60% of total production capacity. The data are further analyzed by type of generation: fossil fuels, hydroelectric power, and nuclear fuel.

The great majority of the world's electrical and other energy needs are met by the burning of fossil hydrocarbon solids, liquids, and gases, either for thermal generation of electricity or in internal combustion engines. Many renewable and nontraditional sources of energy are being developed worldwide (wood, biogenic gases and liquids, tidal, wave, and wind power, geothermal and photothermal [solar] energy, and so on), but collectively these sources are still negligible in the world's total energy consumption. For this reason only hydroelectric and nuclear generation are considered here separately with fossil fuels.

Trade in electrical energy refers to the transfer of generated electrical output via an international grid. Total electricity consumption (residential and nonresidential) is equal to total electricity requirements less transformation and distribution losses.

Coal. The term coal, as used in the table, comprises all grades of anthracite, bituminous, subbituminous, and lignite that have acquired or may in the future, by reason of new technology or changed market prices, acquire an economic value. These types of coal may be differentiated according to heat content (density) and content of impurities. Most coal reserve data are based on proven recoverable reserves only, of all grades of coal. Exceptions are footnoted, with proven in-place reserves reported only when recoverable reserves are unknown. Production figures include deposits removed from both surface and underground workings as well as quantities used by the producers themselves or issued to the miners. Wastes recovered from mines or nearby preparation plants are excluded from production figures.

Natural gas. This term refers to any combustible gas (usually chiefly methane) of natural origin from underground sources. The data for production cover, to the extent possible, gas obtained from gas fields,

Energy

country	electricity												coal		
	installed capacity, 1997 ('000 kW)	production, 1997		power source, 1997			trade, 1997		consumption				reserves, latest ('000,000 metric tons)	pro-duction, 1997 ('000 metric tons)	con-sump-tion, 1997 ('000 metric tons)
		capacity ('000,000 kW-hr)	amount ('000,000 kW-hr)	fossil fuel (%)	hydro-power (%)	nuclear fuel (%)	exports ('000,000 kW-hr)	imports ('000,000 kW-hr)	amount, 1997 ('000,000 kW-hr)	per capita, 1997 (kW-hr)	resi-dential, 1995 (%)	non-resi-dential, 1995 (%)			
Afghanistan	494	4,327	513	36.6	63.4	—	—	100	613	29	...	...	66	2	2
Albania	1,892	16,574	5,681	5.1	94.9	—	—	200	5,881	1,878	42.9	57.1	15[1]	80	60
Algeria	6,040	52,910	21,489	99.7	0.3	—	312	312	21,489	731	49.5	50.5	40	23	1,193
American Samoa	35	307	130	100.0	—	—	—	—	130	2,131	...	...	—	—	...
Andorra	...	...	...	...	...	...	...	...	...	...	...	...	—	—	...
Angola	617	5,405	1,895	25.9	74.1	—	...	...	1,895	162	29.4	70.6	...	—	—
Antigua and Barbuda	26	228	99	100.0	—	—	—	—	99	1,500	...	...	...	...	...
Argentina	21,791	190,889	73,001	50.5	38.6	10.9	277	5,466	78,190	2,192	30.3	69.7	130	250	1,258
Armenia	3,005	26,324	6,022	50.3	23.1	26.6	—	—	6,022	1,696	...	...	...	...	5
Aruba	90	788	468	100.0	—	—	—	—	468	5,200	...	...	...	...	...
Australia	39,693	347,711	183,069	90.6	9.4	—	—	—	183,069	9,986	...	...	90,400	264,972	115,424
Austria	17,510	153,388	56,850	34.4	65.6	—	9,775	9,007	56,082	6,925	...	...	25	1,130	5,374
Azerbaijan	5,239	45,894	16,966	89.9	10.1	—	803	1,643	17,806	2,330	19.5	80.5	...	...	1
Bahamas, The	401	3,513	1,414	100.0	—	—	—	—	1,414	4,859	...	...	...	—	—
Bahrain	1,100	9,636	5,041	100.0	—	—	—	—	5,041	8,647	53.1	46.9	...	...	...
Bangladesh	3,305	28,952	12,820	94.4	5.6	—	—	—	12,820	105	26.6	73.4	1,756	...	646
Barbados	142	1,244	678	100.0	—	—	—	—	678	2,539	32.7	67.3	...	—	—
Belarus	7,408	64,894	26,057	99.9	0.1	—	2,688	10,308	33,677	3,254	17.1	82.9	...	—	810
Belgium	14,962	131,067	78,939	41.3	1.6	57.1	6,705	9,975	82,209	8,118	...	...	—	427	11,882
Belize	52	456	167	58.7	41.3	—	—	25	192	857	89.4	10.6	...	...	...
Benin	15	131	7	100.0	—	—	—	265	272	48	68.4	31.6	...	...	...
Bermuda	146	1,279	530	100.0	—	—	—	—	530	8,413	...	...	...	—	—
Bhutan	356	3,119	1,838	—	100.0	—	1,430	7	415	213	...	...	...	54	71
Bolivia	971	8,506	3,380	55.6	44.4	—	1	1	3,380	435	38.4	61.6	0.9	—	—
Bosnia and Herzegovina	2,719	23,818	4,984	52.5	47.5	—	550	51	4,485	1,274	...	...	...	1,640	1,640
Botswana	[2]	[2]	[2]	[2]	[2]	[2]	[2]	[2]	[2]	[2]	41.0	59.0	4,313	[2]	[2]
Brazil	63,337	554,832	307,986	8.4	90.6	1.0	8	40,478	348,456	2,129	24.0	76.0	11,950	5,647	17,802
Brunei	477	4,179	1,705	100.0	—	—	—	—	1,705	5,536	47.2	52.8	...	—	—
Bulgaria	12,087	105,882	42,803	51.7	6.8	41.5	4,335	785	39,253	4,677	31.0	69.0	2,711	27,031	31,251
Burkina Faso	78	683	294	60.5	39.5	—	—	—	294	27	...	...	...	...	...
Burundi	43	377	122	1.6	98.4	—	—	30	152	24	73.7	26.3	...	...	...
Cambodia	35	307	208	62.5	37.5	—	—	—	208	20	...	...	...	—	—
Cameroon	627	5,493	2,758	3.3	96.7	—	—	—	2,758	198	...	...	...	1	1
Canada	113,977	998,439	566,782	23.5	62.0	14.5	45,230	9,499	531,051	17,549	...	...	8,623	78,686	56,436
Cape Verde	7	61	41	100.0	—	—	—	—	41	103	...	...	...	—	—
Central African Republic	43	377	104	21.2	78.8	—	—	—	104	30	...	...	3.6	...	...
Chad	29	254	90	100.0	—	—	—	—	90	13	...	...	...	...	...
Chile	7,546	66,103	33,292	43.1	56.9	—	—	—	33,292	2,276	29.2	70.8	1,181	1,080	6,153
China	225,000	1,971,000	1,134,471	82.1	16.7	1.2	7,204	89	1,127,356	922	10.8	89.2	114,500	1,372,820	1,331,589
Colombia	11,736	102,807	46,378	31.6	68.4	—	—	199	46,577	1,163	40.9	59.1	6,749	32,592	5,069
Comoros	5	44	17	88.2	11.8	—	—	—	17	27	...	...	...	...	...
Congo, Dem. Rep. of the	3,197	28,006	5,421	0.4	99.6	—	1,040	50	4,431	90	33.2	66.8	88	95	141
Congo, Rep. of the	118	1,034	441	0.7	99.3	—	—	118	559	206	52.7	47.3	...	...	...
Costa Rica	1,371	12,010	5,589	3.2	85.7	11.1	111	236	5,714	1,525	45.3	54.7	...	...	...
Côte d'Ivoire	1,173	10,275	2,760	38.7	61.3	—	—	—	2,760	196	39.0	61.0	...	...	...
Croatia	3,582	31,378	9,685	45.3	54.7	—	660	4,608	13,633	3,040	43.2	56.8	39	49	419
Cuba	3,988	34,935	14,087	99.2	0.8	—	—	—	14,087	1,273	25.8	74.2	...	—	42
Cyprus	699	6,123	2,711	100.0	—	—	—	—	2,711	3,553	32.2	67.8	...	—	19
Czech Republic	13,852	121,344	64,598	77.4	3.2	19.4	10,201	9,013	63,410	6,156	...	...	6,177	73,515	64,173
Denmark	11,807	103,429	48,384	95.4	0.0	4.6[3]	11,049	3,793	41,128	7,825	...	...	—	23	11,161
Djibouti	85	745	187	100.0	—	—	—	—	187	303	...	...	...	...	...
Dominica	8	70	38	47.4	52.6	—	—	—	38	535	...	...	...	...	...
Dominican Republic	1,450	12,702	7,335	69.6	30.4	—	—	—	7,335	906	24.3	75.7	...	—	139
East Timor	...	...	...	...	...	—	...	...	...	...	...	...	...	...	...
Ecuador	2,762	24,195	9,560	24.1	75.9	—	—	—	9,560	801	36.7	63.3	24	...	...

petroleum fields, or coal mines that is actually collected and marketed. (Much natural gas in Middle Eastern and North African oil fields is flared [burned] because it is often not economical to capture and market it.) Manufactured gas is generally a by-product of industrial operations such as gasworks, coke ovens, and blast furnaces. It is usually burned at the point of production and rarely enters the marketplace. Production of manufactured gas is, therefore, only reported as a percentage of domestic gas consumption.

Crude petroleum. Crude petroleum is the liquid product obtained from oil wells; the term also includes shale oil, tar sand extract, and field or lease condensate. Production and consumption data in the table refer, so far as possible, to the same year so that the relationship between national production and consumption patterns can be clearly seen; both are given in barrels.

Proven reserves are that oil remaining underground in known fields whose existence has been "proved" by the evaluation of nearby producing wells or by seismic tests in sedimentary strata known to contain crude petroleum, and that is judged recoverable within the limits of present technology and economic conditions (prices). The published proven reserve figures do not necessarily reflect the true reserves of a country, because government authorities or corporations often have political or economic motives for withholding or altering such data.

The estimated exhaustion rate of petroleum reserves is an extrapolated ratio of published proven reserves to the current rate of withdrawal/production. Present world published proven reserves will last about 40 to 45 years at the present rate of withdrawal, but there are large country-to-country variations above or below the average.

Data on petroleum and refined product pipelines are provided because of the great importance to both domestic and international energy markets of this means of bringing these energy sources from their production or transportation points to refineries, intermediate consumption and distribution points, and final consumers. Their traffic may represent a very significant fraction of the total movement of goods within a country. Available data for petroleum pipelines are often incomplete and their basis varies internationally, some countries reporting only international shipments, others reporting domestic shipments of 50 kilometres or more, and so on.

For data in the hydrocarbons portions of the table (coal, natural gas, and petroleum), extensive use has been made of a variety of international sources, such as those of the United Nations, the International Energy Agency (of the Organization for Economic Cooperation and Development), the World Energy Council (in its *World Energy Resources* [triennial]); the U.S. Department of Energy (especially its *International Energy Annual*); and of various industry surveys, such as those published by the *International Petroleum Encyclopedia* and *World Oil.*

natural gas						crude petroleum							country
published proven reserves, 2001 ('000,000,000 cu m)	production		consumption			reserves, 2001		produc-tion, 1997 ('000,000 barrels)	consump-tion, 1997 ('000,000 barrels)	refining capacity, 2001 ('000 barrels per day)	pipelines (latest)		
	natural gas, 1997 ('000,000 cu m)	manufac-tured gas, 1997 (% of total gas con-sumption)	amount, 1997 ('000,000 cu m)	resi-dential, 1995 (%)	non-resi-dential, 1995 (%)	published proven ('000,000 barrels)	years to exhaust proven reserves				length (km)	traffic ('000,000 metric ton-km)	
100	147	...	147	...	...	...	...	—	—	—	...	...	Afghanistan
2.8	18	...	18	13.0	87.0	165	68	2.4	2.4	26	189	8	Albania
4,522	74,687	23.7	26,431	11.9	88.1	9,200	31	299	166	503	6,910	...	Algeria
...	...	...	...	...	...	...	...	—	—	—	—	...	American Samoa
...	...	...	...	...	...	...	...	—	—	—	—	—	Andorra
46	187	10.8	187	...	...	5,412	21	256	13	39	179	...	Angola
...	...	...	...	...	...	...	...	—	—	—	—	—	Antigua and Barbuda
748	34,959	9.7	36,717	22.9	77.1	3,071	10	306	191	639	6,990	...	Argentina
...	...	...	1,140	...	...	...	...	—		—	—	—	Armenia
...	...	...	...	...	...	...	...	—	2.4	280	—	—	Aruba
1,264	31,909	18.8	21,116	...	...	2,895	19	153	223	847	3,000	...	Australia
26	1,511	12.7	8,353	...	...	86	12	6.9	66	209	778	8,165	Austria
125	5,758	1.9	5,758	...	...	1,178	18	65	65	442	1,760	1,705	Azerbaijan
...	—	—	...	...	...	...	...	—	—	—	—	—	Bahamas, The
110	7,386	4.5	7,386	...	...	148	11	13	86	249	72	...	Bahrain
301	8,135	0.3	8,135	7.4	92.6	57	...	...	10	33	—	—	Bangladesh
0.1	23	3.5	23	62.6	37.4	3	10	0.3	1.6	4	—	—	Barbados
2.8	243	1.3	16,427	8.1	91.9	198	15	13	86	493	2,570	...	Belarus
—	0.2	17.3	16,469	...	...	...	...	—	240	768	1,328	1,168	Belgium
...	...	...	...	...	...	...	...	—	—	—	—	—	Belize
1.2	...	...	...	...	...	8	20	0.4	...	—	—	—	Benin
...	...	...	...	...	...	...	...	—	—	—	—	—	Bermuda
...	...	...	...	...	...	...	...	—	—	—	—	—	Bhutan
518	3,599	19.0	1,535	0.1	99.9	397	33	12	12	63	2,380	...	Bolivia
...	—	...	116	...	...	...	...	—	...	...	174	—	Bosnia and Herzegovina
...	...	[2]	...	...	...	—	...	—	[2]	—	—	—	Botswana
233	5,462	52.2	5,462	1.1	98.9	8,100	26	307	518	1,918	7,742	...	Brazil
391	9,217	1.5	1,318	3.5	96.5	1,350	23	60	1.4	9	553	...	Brunei
5.9	37	15.5	4,896	...	...	15	75	0.2	48	115	578	244	Bulgaria
...	...	...	...	...	...	...	...	—	—	—	—	—	Burkina Faso
...	...	...	...	...	...	...	...	—	—	—	—	—	Burundi
...	...	...	...	...	...	...	...	—	—	—	—	—	Cambodia
110	—	95.6	...	...	...	400	10	40	4.9	42	—	—	Cameroon
1,728	165,614	23.8	85,938	...	...	4,706	6.5	720	608	1,906	23,564	99,908	Canada
...	...	...	...	...	...	...	...	—	—	—	—	—	Cape Verde
...	...	...	...	...	...	...	...	—	—	—	—	—	Central African Republic
...	...	...	...	...	...	...	...	—	—	—	—	—	Chad
98	2,017	29.3	2,387	12.7	87.3	150	75	2.0	63	205	1,540	...	Chile
1,368	25,203	49.8	22,449	11.2	88.8	24,000	20	1,177	1,281	4,347	11,258	58,050	China
196	5,682	25.5	5,682	6.9	93.1	2,577	11	239	111	286	4,935	...	Colombia
...	...	...	...	...	...	...	...	—	—	—	—	—	Comoros
1.0	—	...	—	—	—	187	22	8.4	0.5	15	390	...	Congo, Dem. Rep. of the
91	3.4	58.1	3.4	...	...	1,506	17	87	0.5	21	25	...	Congo, Rep. of the
...	—	3.9	—	—	—	...	...	—	4.9	15	176	...	Costa Rica
30	—	59.4	—	—	—	100	11	9.3	31	65	—	—	Côte d'Ivoire
35	1,672	19.2	2,679	16.3	83.7	92	8.4	11	37	253	601	951	Croatia
18	22	79.2	22	3.4	96.6	284	29	9.7	21	301	—	—	Cuba
—	—	72.0	—	—	—	...	...	—	7.6	27	—	—	Cyprus
4.0	230	16.6	10,802	...	...	15	14	1.1	48	198	736	2,078	Czech Republic
96	7,479	13.9	3,787	...	...	1,069	12	87	67	176	337	1,385	Denmark
...	...	...	...	...	...	...	...	—	—	—	—	—	Djibouti
...	...	...	...	...	...	—	—	—	—	—	—	—	Dominica
—	—	8.5	...	...	...	...	...	—	17	49	104	...	Dominican Republic
...	...	...	...	...	...	...	...	...	...	...	...	...	East Timor
104	502	25.2	502	—	—	2,115	15	143	52	176	2,158	...	Ecuador

Energy (continued)

country	electricity												coal		
	installed capacity, 1997 ('000 kW)	production, 1997		power source, 1997			trade, 1997		consumption				reserves, latest ('000,000 metric tons)	production, 1997 ('000 metric tons)	consumption, 1997 ('000 metric tons)
		capacity ('000,000 kW-hr)	amount ('000,000 kW-hr)	fossil fuel (%)	hydropower (%)	nuclear fuel (%)	exports ('000,000 kW-hr)	imports ('000,000 kW-hr)	amount, 1997 ('000,000 kW-hr)	per capita, 1997 (kW-hr)	residential, 1995 (%)	nonresidential, 1995 (%)			
Egypt	16,777	146,967	54,924	78.7	21.3	—	—	—	54,924	848	35.4	64.6	22	—	1,880
El Salvador	980	8,585	3,480	32.8	54.3	12.9[3]	18	106	3,568	604	34.2	65.8	…	…	…
Equatorial Guinea	5	44	20	90.0	10.0	—	—	—	20	48	…	…	…	…	…
Eritrea	[4]	[4]	[4]	[4]	[4]	…	…	…	[4]	[4]	…	…	…	…	…
Estonia	2,722	23,845	9,218	99.9	0.1	—	1,184	210	8,244	5,697	17.7	82.3	…	14,383	16,049
Ethiopia	456[4]	3,995[4]	1,662[4]	5.8[4]	94.2[4]	—	—	—	1,662[4]	27[4]	28.8	71.2	61	—	—
Faroe Islands	92	806	181	56.3	43.1	0.6[3]	—	—	181	4,114	…	…	…	—	—
Fiji	200	1,752	545	21.1	78.9	—	—	—	545	693	25.7	74.3	…	—	22
Finland	14,216	124,532	69,175	52.1	17.7	30.2	450	8,103	76,828	14,944	…	…	…	—	6,995
France	112,373[5]	984,387[5]	575,468[5]	9.0[5]	14.3[5]	76.7[5]	69,634[5]	4,238[5]	450,072[5]	7,693[5]	…	…	116	7,316[5]	21,527[5]
French Guiana	139	1,218	450	100.0	—	—	—	—	450	2,813	…	…	…	…	…
French Polynesia	89	780	360	62.8	37.2	—	—	—	360	1,614	…	…	…	…	…
Gabon	378	3,311	1,257	35.6	64.4	—	—	—	1,257	1,106	28.1	71.9	…	…	…
Gambia, The	29	254	77	100.0	—	—	—	—	77	65	…	…	…	…	…
Gaza Strip	…	…	…	…	…	…	…	…	…	…	…	…	…	…	…
Georgia	4,558	39,928	7,172	15.7	84.3	—	462	653	7,363	1,438	…	…	…	5	5
Germany	115,443	1,011,281	546,412	65.0	3.8	31.2	40,361	38,012	544,063	6,630	…	…	67,000	228,371	251,639
Ghana	1,187	10,398	6,652	0.1	99.9	—	230	4	6,426	344	7.0	93.0	…	—	3
Greece	9,575	83,877	48,817	80.7	8.4	10.9[3]	709	3,003	51,111	4,836	…	…	2,874	58,844	59,831
Greenland	106	929	259	100.0	—	—	—	—	259	4,625	…	…	183	…	…
Grenada	15	131	108	100.0	—	—	—	—	108	1,161	88.1	11.9	…	…	…
Guadeloupe	417	3,653	1,211	100.0	—	—	—	—	1,211	2,771	…	…	…	…	…
Guam	302	2,646	825	100.0	—	—	—	—	825	5,222	…	…	…	…	…
Guatemala	938	8,217	4,132	49.1	50.9	—	106	18	4,044	384	34.0	66.0	…	…	…
Guernsey	…	…	…	…	…	…	…	…	…	…	…	…	…	…	…
Guinea	186	1,629	542	65.3	34.7	—	—	—	542	74	…	…	…	…	…
Guinea-Bissau	11	96	53	100.0	—	—	—	—	53	47	…	…	…	…	…
Guyana	114	999	390	98.7	1.3	—	—	14	404	479	…	…	…	…	…
Haiti	153	1,340	633	59.7	40.3	—	—	—	633	81	46.2	53.8	13[1]	…	…
Honduras	615	5,387	3,097	55.5	44.5	—	6	161	3,252	544	54.5	45.5	21[1]	…	…
Hong Kong	10,876	95,274	28,943	100.0	—	—	559	7,876	36,260	5,569	25.2	74.8	…	—	5,711
Hungary	7,012	61,425	35,396	59.9	0.6	39.5	2,261	4,410	37,545	3,697	61.3	38.7	4,460	15,589	17,326
Iceland	1,154	10,109	5,586	0.1	93.2	6.7[3]	—	—	5,586	20,387	…	…	…	—	58
India	101,964	893,205	464,372	81.6	16.0	2.4	85	1,580	465,867	482	15.1	84.9	74,733	319,286	332,988
Indonesia	21,346	186,991	84,096	85.5	11.6	2.9[3]	—	—	84,096	413	32.9	67.1	5,220	52,074	10,330
Iran	29,447	257,956	97,744	92.9	7.1	—	—	—	97,744	1,512	31.6	68.4	193	1,210	1,531
Iraq	9,500	83,220	29,950	98.0	2.0	—	—	—	29,950	1,414	…	…	…	—	—
Ireland	4,412	38,649	20,687	95.1	4.6	0.3[3]	76	64	20,675	5,652	…	…	14	—	2,870
Isle of Man	…	…	…	100.0	—	—	—	—	…	…	…	…	…	…	…
Israel	7,809	68,407	35,065	99.9	0.1	—	1,055	—	34,010	5,804	29.1	70.9	…	—	8,639
Italy	68,239[6]	597,774[6]	250,775[6]	79.8[6]	18.6[6]	1.6[3, 6]	995[6]	39,827[6]	289,607[6]	5,045[6]	…	…	34	102[6]	16,108[6]
Jamaica	1,182	10,354	6,255	97.8	2.2	—	—	—	6,255	2,486	14.4	85.6	…	—	67
Japan	235,482	2,062,822	1,040,108	59.3	9.7	31.0	—	—	1,040,108	8,252	…	…	785	4,291	134,888
Jersey	…	…	…	…	…	…	…	…	…	…	…	…	…	…	…
Jordan	1,276	11,178	6,273	99.6	0.4	—	—	…	6,273	1,024	27.4	72.6	…	…	…
Kazakhstan	18,960	166,090	52,000	87.5	12.5	—	—	6,700	58,700	3,585	10.6	89.4	34,000	72,647	48,717
Kenya	809	7,087	4,223	10.8	79.9	9.3[3]	—	144	4,367	154	30.1	69.9	…	—	114
Kiribati	2	18	7	100.0	—	—	—	—	7	88	…	…	…	—	—
Korea, North	9,500	83,220	33,990	35.3	64.7	—	—	—	33,990	1,479	…	…	600	95,000	96,830
Korea, South	45,334	397,126	248,653	66.8	2.2	31.0	—	—	248,653	5,437	16.2	83.8	82	4,512	53,942
Kuwait	6,992	61,250	27,224	100.0	—	—	—	—	27,224	15,718	93.2	6.8	…	…	…
Kyrgyzstan	3,679	32,228	12,600	11.0	89.0	—	8,700	7,000	10,900	2,360	25.4	…	812	780	2,230
Laos	256	2,243	1,219	3.5	96.5	—	770	46	495	98	…	…	…	1	1
Latvia	2,099	18,387	4,500	34.4	65.6	—	1	1,824	6,323	2,569	23.4	76.6	…	—	196
Lebanon	1,275	11,169	7,082	87.1	12.9	—	—	260	7,342	2,336	54.5	45.5	…	—	200
Lesotho	[2]	[2]	[2]	[2]	[2]	[2]	[2]	[2]	[2]	[2]	…	…	…	[2]	[2]
Liberia	332	2,908	493	63.5	36.5	—	—	—	493	205	…	…	…	…	…
Libya	4,600	40,296	18,300	100.0	—	—	—	—	18,300	3,512	…	…	—	—	5
Liechtenstein	[7]	[7]	[7]	[7]	[7]	[7]	[7]	[7]	[7]	[7]	…	…	…	—	[7]
Lithuania	5,791	50,729	15,630	18.2	4.9	76.9	8,050	4,525	12,105	3,267	16.2	83.8	…	…	256
Luxembourg	1,267	11,099	1,280	26.8	73.2	—	846	6,032	6,466	15,506	…	…	…	—	194
Macau	367	3,215	1,409	100.0	—	—	1	176	1,584	3,520	82.8	17.2	…	—	—
Macedonia	1,494	13,087	6,719	86.6	13.4	—	…	…	6,719	3,381	44.5	55.5	…	6,700	6,800
Madagascar	220	1,927	684	37.8	62.2	—	—	—	684	24	32.2	67.8	1,075[1]	—	14
Malawi	185	1,621	878	2.2	97.8	—	2	—	876	87	65.2	34.8	1.8	—	17
Malaysia	12,840	112,478	58,675	90.8	9.2	—	37	—	58,638	2,795	17.3	82.7	3.6	100	2,636
Maldives	25	219	66	100.0	—	—	—	—	66	251	…	…	…	…	…
Mali	114	999	391	41.4	58.6	—	—	—	391	37	…	…	—	…	…
Malta	250	2,190	1,515	100.0	—	—	—	—	1,515	3,976	29.2	70.8	…	—	310
Marshall Islands	99[8]	867[8]	…	…	…	—	—	—	…	…	…	…	…	…	…
Martinique	396	3,469	1,078	100.0	—	—	—	—	1,078	2,793	…	…	…	…	…
Mauritania	105	920	153	81.7	18.3	—	—	—	153	62	…	…	…	—	6
Mauritius	364	3,189	1,278	91.8	8.2	—	—	—	1,278	1,128	65.2	34.8	…	—	68
Mayotte	…	…	…	…	…	—	—	—	…	…	…	…	…	…	…
Mexico	46,335	405,895	170,751	71.6	18.7	9.7[3]	51	1,512	172,212	1,827	29.7	70.3	1,211	10,337	11,538
Micronesia	…	…	…	…	…	—	…	…	…	…	…	…	…	…	…
Moldova	1,022	8,953	5,274	92.8	7.2	—	27	1,979	7,226	1,651	…	…	…	—	322
Monaco	[5]	[5]	[5]	[5]	[5]	[5]	[5]	[5]	[5]	[5]	…	…	…	[5]	[5]
Mongolia	901	7,893	2,720	100.0	—	—	—	376	3,096	1,220	…	…	24,000[1]	4,924	4,724
Morocco	3,957	34,663	13,092	84.2	15.8	—	—	1,100	14,192	528	28.0	72.0	5.4	376	3,009
Mozambique	2,383	20,875	570	91.2	8.8	—	—	604	1,174	64	33.2	66.8	240	40	60
Myanmar (Burma)	1,458	12,772	4,211	60.0	40.0	—	—	—	4,211	96	43.0	57.0	1.8	59	125
Namibia	[2]	[2]	[2]	[2]	[2]	[2]	[2]	[2]	[2]	[2]	…	…	…	[2]	[2]
Nauru	10	88	32	100.0	—	—	—	—	32	2,909	…	…	…	…	…
Nepal	317	2,777	1,232	5.3	94.7	—	100	130	1,262	57	38.5	61.5	1.8	—	119

natural gas: published proven reserves, 2001 ('000,000,000 cu m)	natural gas: production: natural gas, 1997 ('000,000 cu m)	natural gas: production: manufactured gas, 1997 (% of total gas consumption)	natural gas: consumption: amount, 1997 ('000,000 cu m)	natural gas: consumption: residential, 1995 (%)	natural gas: consumption: nonresidential, 1995 (%)	crude petroleum: reserves, 2001: published proven ('000,000 barrels)	crude petroleum: reserves, 2001: years to exhaust proven reserves	crude petroleum: production, 1997 ('000,000 barrels)	crude petroleum: consumption, 1997 ('000,000 barrels)	crude petroleum: refining capacity, 2001 ('000 barrels per day)	crude petroleum: pipelines (latest): length (km)	crude petroleum: pipelines (latest): traffic ('000,000 metric ton-km)	country
996	14,897	10.1	14,897	5.1	94.9	2,948	10	302	209	726	1,767	...	Egypt
—	—	13.9	—	—	—	...	...	—	5.7	21	—	—	El Salvador
37	...	...	...	...	...	12	0.5	22	1.1	—	—	—	Equatorial Guinea
...	...	[4]	...	...	...	...	...	...	[4]	18	—	—	Eritrea
...	...	...	670	8.2	91.8	—	—	—	...	...	—	—	Estonia
25	—	100.0[4]	—	...	...	0.4	...	—	1.1[4]	—	—	—	Ethiopia
...	...	...	...	...	...	...	...	—	—	—	—	—	Faroe Islands
...	—	...	—	—	—	...	...	—	—	—	—	—	Fiji
—	—	30.6	3,509	...	...	...	...	—	71	200	—	—	Finland
14	2,047	20.1[5]	38,285[5]	32.4[5]	67.6[5]	145	11	13	652[5]	1,895	4,946	24,429	France
...	...	...	...	...	...	...	...	—	—	—	—	—	French Guiana
...	...	...	...	...	...	...	...	—	—	—	—	—	French Polynesia
34	670	1.7	670	19.7	80.3	2,499	18	136	6.2	17	284	...	Gabon
...	...	...	...	...	...	...	...	—	—	—	—	—	Gambia, The
...	...	...	...	...	...	...	...	—	—	—	—	—	Gaza Strip
8.5	2.9	...	915	...	...	35	35	1.0	0.2	106	670	...	Georgia
326	23,925	14.3	108,393	...	...	380	19	20	737	2,259	2,370	37,250	Germany
24	—	94.8	—	—	—	17	...	...	7.3	45	—	—	Ghana
1.0	52	93.3	203	...	...	10	3.2	3.1	130	407	573	...	Greece
...	...	...	...	...	...	...	...	—	—	—	—	—	Greenland
...	...	...	...	...	...	...	...	—	—	—	—	—	Grenada
...	...	...	...	...	...	...	...	—	—	—	—	—	Guadeloupe
...	—	—	—	—	—	...	...	—	—	—	—	—	Guam
3.1	11	3.1	11	...	...	526	75	7.0	6.1	22	275	...	Guatemala
...	...	...	...	...	...	...	...	—	—	—	—	—	Guernsey
...	...	...	...	...	...	...	...	—	—	—	—	—	Guinea
...	...	...	...	...	...	...	...	—	—	—	—	—	Guinea-Bissau
...	...	...	...	...	...	...	...	—	—	—	—	—	Guyana
...	...	...	...	...	...	...	...	—	—	—	—	—	Haiti
—	—	...	—	—	—	...	...	—	...	...	—	—	Honduras
...	—	77.2	—	—	—	...	...	—	—	—	—	—	Hong Kong
81	4,304	7.1	12,438	...	...	110	12	9.1	47	232	2,049	2,470	Hungary
...	...	...	...	...	...	...	...	—	—	—	—	—	Iceland
647	19,430	16.7	19,430	1.3	98.7	4,728	18	257	512	2,113	5,692	...	India
2,046	76,447	10.3	39,818	2.7	97.3	4,980	8.9	560	315	993	2,961	...	Indonesia
23,002	45,012	0.2	44,916	26.8	73.2	89,700	67	1,344	373	1,484	9,800	...	Iran
3,109	3,620	42.5	3,620	...	...	112,500	268	420	215	410	5,070	...	Iraq
20	2,229	3.1	3,242	...	...	—	...	—	21	71	—	—	Ireland
...	—	...	...	...	...	...	...	—	...	—	—	—	Isle of Man
42	13	115.4	13	—	100.0	4	133	0.03	80	220	998	...	Israel
229	19,271	12.7[6]	57,992[6]	...	...	622	15	41	578[6]	2,359	4,329	13,981	Italy
—	—	26.9	—	—	—	...	...	—	8.5	34	10	...	Jamaica
40	2,279	41.8	62,316	...	...	59	16	3.6	1,643	4,962	406	...	Japan
...	...	...	...	...	...	...	...	—	—	—	—	—	Jersey
6.5	—	67.2	—	—	—	0.9	...	...	25	90	209	...	Jordan
1,841	7,839	0.9	7,395	...	...	5,417	31	173	67	427	6,965	15,366	Kazakhstan
—	—	70.6	—	—	—	...	...	—	13	90	483	...	Kenya
...	...	...	...	...	...	...	...	—	—	—	—	—	Kiribati
...	...	...	...	...	...	...	...	—	15	71	217	...	Korea, North
—	—	34.6	15,620	...	...	...	...	—	873	2,560	455	...	Korea, South
1,492	9,063	48.7	9,063	25.0	75.0	96,500	132	731	304	764	917	...	Kuwait
5.7	40	...	610	...	...	40	67	0.6	0.8	10	—	—	Kyrgyzstan
...	...	...	...	...	...	...	...	—	—	—	136	...	Laos
...	—	...	1,143	10.5	89.5	...	...	—	...	...	766	6,569	Latvia
—	—	...	...	...	...	...	...	—	...	38	72	...	Lebanon
—	—	[2]	—	...	...	...	...	—	[2]	—	—	—	Lesotho
—	—	...	—	...	...	...	...	—	—	15	—	—	Liberia
1,314	6,542	18.4	5,442	...	...	29,500	58	509	117	343	4,826	...	Libya
—	—	[7]	[7]	...	...	...	...	—	[7]	—	—	—	Liechtenstein
—	...	13.2	2,148	9.3	90.7	12	7.5	1.6	37	263	399	2,964	Lithuania
...	—	9.0	731	...	...	...	...	—	...	—	48	...	Luxembourg
...	...	...	...	...	...	...	...	—	—	—	—	—	Macau
...	—	18.8	...	...	...	...	...	—	2.9	51	—	—	Macedonia
2.0	—	33.6	—	...	...	...	...	—	1.5	15	—	—	Madagascar
...	—	—	—	—	—	...	...	—	—	—	—	—	Malawi
2,313	39,902	7.4	21,110	2.5	97.5	3,900	15	253	140	514	1,307	...	Malaysia
...	...	...	...	...	...	...	...	—	—	—	—	—	Maldives
...	...	...	...	...	...	...	...	—	—	—	—	—	Mali
—	...	—	...	...	...	...	...	—	—	—	—	—	Malta
...	...	...	...	...	...	...	...	—	—	...	—	—	Marshall Islands
—	—	161.5	...	...	...	...	...	—	5.8	17	—	—	Martinique
...	...	88.4	...	...	...	...	...	—	6.9	—	—	—	Mauritania
...	...	...	...	...	...	...	...	—	—	—	—	—	Mauritius
...	...	...	...	...	...	...	...	—	—	—	—	—	Mayotte
861	29,709	20.0	30,315	...	...	28,260	26	1,099	470	1,525	38,350	...	Mexico
...	...	...	...	...	...	...	...	—	—	...	—	—	Micronesia
...	—	...	3,729	11.6	88.4	...	...	—	...	...	—	—	Moldova
...	...	[5]	[5]	[5]	[5]	...	...	—	[5]	—	—	—	Monaco
...	...	...	...	...	...	...	...	—	—	—	—	—	Mongolia
1.3	30	23.7	30	—	100.0	1.8	...	...	45	157	362	...	Morocco
57	—	—	—	...	...	...	...	—	—	...	595	...	Mozambique
283	1,703	0.7	1,703	—	...	50	18	2.8	7.3	32	1,343	...	Myanmar (Burma)
85	—	[2]	—	...	...	...	...	—	[2]	—	—	—	Namibia
...	...	...	...	...	...	...	...	—	—	—	—	—	Nauru
...	—	—	—	—	—	...	...	—	—	—	—	—	Nepal

Energy (continued)

country	electricity												coal		
	installed capacity, 1997 ('000 kW)	production, 1997		power source, 1997			trade, 1997		consumption				reserves, latest ('000,000 metric tons)	production, 1997 ('000 metric tons)	consumption, 1997 ('000 metric tons)
		capacity ('000,000 kW-hr)	amount ('000,000 kW-hr)	fossil fuel (%)	hydropower (%)	nuclear fuel (%)	exports ('000,000 kW-hr)	imports ('000,000 kW-hr)	amount, 1997 ('000,000 kW-hr)	per capita, 1997 (kW-hr)	residential, 1995 (%)	nonresidential, 1995 (%)			
Netherlands, The	20,065	175,769	86,638	96.6	0.1	3.3	475	13,107	99,270	6,358	…	…	497	—	14,834
Netherlands Antilles	220	1,927	1,485	100.0	—	—	—	—	1,485	7,038	…	…	…	…	…
New Caledonia	253	2,216	1,567	69.6	30.4	—	—	—	1,567	7,757	…	…	1.8	—	168
New Zealand	7,520	65,875	36,219	27.6	67.0	5.4[3]	—	—	36,219	9,630	…	…	571	3,370	2,651
Nicaragua	457	4,003	1,907	49.7	18.9	31.4[3]	—	162	2,069	442	31.5	68.5	…	…	…
Niger	63	552	177	100.0	—	—	—	196	373	38	49.2	50.8	70	174	174
Nigeria	5,881	51,518	14,830	59.5	40.5	—	…	—	14,830	143	50.1	49.9	190	50	50
Northern Mariana Islands	…	…	…	…	…	—	…	…	…	…	…	…	…	…	…
Norway	27,839	243,870	111,551	0.6	99.4	—	4,875	8,693	115,369	26,214	…	…	6.4	386	996
Oman	2,098	18,378	9,662	100.0	—	—	—	—	9,662	4,192	…	…	…	…	…
Pakistan	14,689	128,676	59,119	64.1	35.3	0.6	—	—	59,119	410	37.8	62.2	2,928	3,553	4,393
Palau	62	543	208	85.6	14.4	—	—	—	208	11,556	…	…	—	—	—
Panama	960	8,410	4,185	30.7	69.3	—	170	421	4,436	1,630	74.5	25.5	…	—	57
Papua New Guinea	490	4,292	1,795	72.1	27.9	—	—	—	1,795	399	28.0	72.0	…	…	1
Paraguay	6,529	57,194	50,619	0.1	99.9	—	45,673	—	4,946	972	58.2	41.8	…	…	…
Peru	5,191	45,473	17,951	26.4	73.6	—	—	2	17,953	737	37.7	62.3	1,060	22	310
Philippines	11,149	97,665	39,816	65.2	17.9	16.9[3]	—	—	39,816	557	27.7	72.3	299	1,094	5,182
Poland	29,469	258,148	142,761	97.3	2.7	—	7,542	5,357	140,576	3,633	15.3	84.7	14,309	200,298	167,480
Portugal	9,380	82,169	34,187	61.2	38.5	0.3[3]	2,477	5,376	37,086	3,760	…	…	36	—	5,555
Puerto Rico	4,575	40,077	19,045	98.2	1.8	—	—	—	19,045	5,038	…	…	…	—	173
Qatar	1,475	12,921	6,868	100.0	—	—	—	—	6,868	12,070	83.7	16.3	…	…	…
Réunion	434	3,802	1,133	55.4	44.6	—	—	—	1,133	1,684	…	…	…	…	…
Romania	22,843	200,105	57,148	59.9	30.6	9.5	817	1,038	57,369	2,544	14.4	85.6	3,611	33,807	38,141
Russia	210,957	1,847,983	834,100	68.0	18.9	13.1	26,800	7,100	814,400	5,516	18.3	81.7	157,010	247,800	233,180
Rwanda	34	298	164	2.4	97.6	—	3	14	175	29	…	…	…	…	…
St. Kitts and Nevis	16	140	90	100.0	—	—	—	—	90	2,308	…	…	…	…	…
St. Lucia	22	193	115	100.0	—	—	—	—	115	777	…	…	…	…	…
St. Vincent and the Grenadines	16	140	80	72.5	27.5	—	—	—	80	714	…	…	…	…	…
Samoa	19	166	65	61.5	38.5	—	—	—	65	378	…	…	…	…	…
San Marino	[6]	[6]	[6]	[6]	[6]	[6]	[6]	[6]	[6]	[6]	…	…	…	[6]	[6]
São Tomé and Príncipe	6	53	15	46.7	53.3	—	—	—	15	109	…	…	…	…	…
Saudi Arabia	21,660	189,742	106,979	100.0	—	—	—	—	106,979	5,492	47.2	52.8	…	…	…
Senegal	235	2,059	1,184	100.0	—	—	—	—	1,184	135	21.2	78.8	…	…	…
Seychelles	28	245	148	100.0	—	—	—	—	148	1,973	32.0	68.0	…	…	…
Sierra Leone	126	1,104	242	100.0	—	—	—	—	242	55	…	…	…	—	—
Singapore	5,641	49,415	26,188	100.0	—	—	—	—	26,188	7,642	16.0	84.0	…	—	—
Slovakia	7,863	68,880	24,822	38.9	17.6	43.5	374	4,429	28,877	5,375	20.6	79.4	172	3,915	10,991
Slovenia	2,495	21,856	13,166	38.4	23.5	38.1	2,520	824	11,470	5,749	24.8	75.2	60	4,953	5,386
Solomon Islands	12	105	32	100.0	—	—	—	—	32	79	…	…	…	…	…
Somalia	70	613	276	100.0	—	—	—	—	276	31	…	…	…	…	…
South Africa	35,897[2]	314,458[2]	193,290[2]	93.1[2]	0.8[2]	6.1[2]	5,580[2]	839[2]	188,549[2]	4,203[2]	14.1	85.9	55,333	219,656[2]	149,076[2]
Spain	48,679	426,428	190,201	51.7	18.9	29.4	7,670	4,597	187,128	4,724	…	…	660	26,341	40,745
Sri Lanka	1,699	14,883	5,145	33.0	67.0	—	—	—	5,145	282	22.6	77.4	…	—	—
Sudan, The	500	4,380	1,340	29.3	70.7	—	—	—	1,340	48	18.6	81.4	…	—	—
Suriname	425	3,723	1,626	20.7	79.3	—	—	—	1,626	3,947	…	…	…	—	—
Swaziland	[2]	[2]	[2]	[2]	[2]	[2]	[2]	[2]	[2]	[2]	…	…	116	[2]	[2]
Sweden	35,545	311,374	149,858	7.0	46.1	46.9	12,961	10,253	147,150	16,616	…	…	0.9	…	3,109
Switzerland	16,692[7]	146,222[7]	62,802[7]	3.6[7]	56.0[7]	40.4[7]	27,502[7]	20,748[7]	56,048[7]	7,697[7]	…	…	…	—	133[7]
Syria	4,480	39,245	18,259	85.8	14.2	—	—	—	18,259	1,222	34.6	65.4	…	—	—
Taiwan	25,735	225,439	132,248	66.4	7.2	26.4	—	—	118,299	5,456	21.5	78.5	0.9	98	…
Tajikistan	4,443	38,921	14,005	2.1	97.9	—	4,247	4,345	14,103	2,380	14.6	85.4	…	10	110
Tanzania	543	4,757	1,744	13.7	86.3	—	—	—	1,744	56	36.6	63.4	200	5	5
Thailand	20,359	178,345	97,553	92.6	7.4	—	104	745	98,194	1,644	19.7	80.3	2,000	23,393	25,818
Togo	34	298	94	93.6	6.4	—	—	320	414	97	…	…	…	…	…
Tonga	7	61	34	100.0	—	—	—	—	34	347	…	…	…	…	…
Trinidad and Tobago	1,150	10,074	4,844	100.0	—	—	—	—	4,844	3,793	26.5	73.5	…	—	—
Tunisia	2,016	17,660	8,389	99.5	0.5	—	119	127	8,397	912	26.4	73.6	—	…	2
Turkey	21,889	191,748	105,191	62.1	37.8	0.1[3]	271	2,492	107,412	1,694	…	…	1,075	59,929	72,040
Turkmenistan	3,930	34,427	9,400	100.0	0.0	—	3,600	950	6,750	1,595	…	…	…	…	—
Tuvalu	…	…	…	…	…	…	…	…	…	…	…	…	…	…	…
Uganda	162	1,419	795	0.9	99.1	—	117	—	678	34	…	…	…	…	…
Ukraine	53,868	471,884	178,002	49.7	5.7	44.6	9,873	9,719	177,848	3,483	…	…	34,356	76,947	83,424
United Arab Emirates	5,600	49,056	20,571	100.0	—	—	—	—	20,571	8,917	…	…	…	…	…
United Kingdom	72,589	635,880	344,955	69.7	1.6	28.7	41	16,615	361,529	6,152	…	…	1,500	48,495	63,128
United States	791,659	6,934,933	3,571,654	70.8	10.0	19.2	7,353	45,848	3,610,149	13,284	…	…	249,995	991,236	919,556
Uruguay	2,179	19,088	7,147	9.3	90.7	—	415	271	7,003	2,145	45.4	54.6	…	—	1
Uzbekistan	11,709	102,571	46,055	87.5	12.5	—	11,489	12,418	46,984	2,024	…	…	4,000	2,947	2,792
Vanuatu	11	96	30	100.0	—	—	—	—	30	169	…	…	…	…	…
Venezuela	21,275	186,369	75,300	24.3	75.7	—	155	—	75,145	3,299	21.3	78.7	479	5,552	419
Vietnam	4,642	40,664	19,253	13.8	83.0	3.2[3]	—	—	19,253	252	32.6	67.4	150	11,388	6,984
Virgin Islands (U.S.)	323	2,829	1,079	100.0	—	—	—	—	1,079	11,358	…	…	…	—	252
West Bank	…	…	…	…	…	…	…	…	…	…	…	…	…	…	…
Western Sahara	56	491	87	100.0	—	—	—	—	87	327	…	…	…	…	…
Yemen	810	7,096	2,482	100.0	—	—	—	—	2,482	152	…	…	1[1]	…	…
Yugoslavia	11,779	103,184	40,312	69.8	30.2	—	—	—	40,312	3,793	41.4	…	16,472	40,656	40,708
Zambia	2,436	21,339	7,795	0.5	99.5	—	1,500	20	6,315	736	10.5	89.5	55	360	355
Zimbabwe	2,071	18,142	7,830	72.2	27.8	—	…	3,100	10,930	975	16.5	83.5	734	5,100	5,095

natural gas						crude petroleum							country
published proven reserves, 2001 ('000,000,000 cu m)	production		consumption			reserves, 2001		production, 1997 ('000,000 barrels)	consumption, 1997 ('000,000 barrels)	refining capacity, 2001 ('000 barrels per day)	pipelines (latest)		
	natural gas, 1997 ('000,000 cu m)	manufactured gas, 1997 (% of total gas consumption)	amount, 1997 ('000,000 cu m)	residential, 1995 (%)	non-residential, 1995 (%)	published proven ('000,000 barrels)	years to exhaust proven reserves				length (km)	traffic ('000,000 metric ton-km)	
1,771	88,908	19.0	51,782	...	...	107	7.6	14	393	1,204	391	5,503	Netherlands, The
—	—	118.5	...	...	...	...	...	—	100	320	—	—	Netherlands Antilles
...	...	...	...	...	...	...	...	—	—	—	—	—	New Caledonia
69	5,059	8.1	5,060	...	...	127	6.0	21	38	106	160	...	New Zealand
—	—	60.2	—	—	—	...	...	—	5.5	20	56	...	Nicaragua
...	—	—	—	—	—	...	...	—	—	—	—	—	Niger
3,511	5,500	1.3	5,500	—	100.0	22,500	33	685	41	439	5,042	...	Nigeria
...	...	...	...	...	...	...	...	—	—	...	—	—	Northern Mariana Islands
1,247	47,486	34.1	4,652	...	...	9,447	7.9	1,191	109	305	5,747	3,485	Norway
829	5,368	1.5	5,368	...	...	5,506	17	329	24	85	1,300	...	Oman
612	18,466	1.1	18,466	19.3	80.7	208	9.9	21	47	239	1,135	...	Pakistan
—	—	—	...	...	...	—	—	—	...	...	—	—	Palau
—	—	29.9	61	—	—	...	...	—	17	60	130	...	Panama
224	83	...	83	—	—	360	12	29	0.4	—	—	—	Papua New Guinea
—	—	1.6	...	...	...	...	...	—	1.1	8	—	—	Paraguay
246	142	59.9	142	61.4	38.6	310	7.0	44	57	182	800	...	Peru
79	—	56.3	—	—	—	289	963	0.3	127	420	357	...	Philippines
145	4,752	24.8	13,966	45.0	55.0	115	55	2.1	110	382	2,278	18,448	Poland
—	—	42.8	103	...	...	...	...	—	90	304	80	...	Portugal
—	—	127.8	...	...	...	...	...	—	45	49	—	—	Puerto Rico
11,152	17,900	8.8	17,900	—	100.0	13,157	67	196	23	58	235	...	Qatar
...	...	...	...	...	...	...	...	—	...	—	—	—	Réunion
374	12,511	12.5	16,745	9.6	90.4	1,426	29	49	96	504	4,629	2,257	Romania
48,139	461,660	5.4	308,653	11.2	88.8	48,573	22	2,180	1,312	5,435	63,000	1,899,000	Russia
57	0.2	—	0.2	...	...	...	...	—	—	—	—	—	Rwanda
...	...	...	...	...	...	...	...	—	—	—	—	—	St. Kitts and Nevis
...	...	...	...	...	...	...	...	—	—	—	—	—	St. Lucia
...	...	...	...	...	...	...	...	—	—	—	—	—	St. Vincent and the Grenadines
...	...	...	...	...	...	...	...	...	...	—	—	—	Samoa
...	...	6	6	...	...	...	...	—	6	—	—	—	San Marino
...	...	...	...	...	...	...	...	—	—	—	—	—	São Tomé and Príncipe
6,054	43,399	46.0	43,399	...	...	261,700	90	2,902	604	1,745	6,550	...	Saudi Arabia
—	—	13.1	...	...	...	...	...	—	6.4	27	—	—	Senegal
...	...	...	...	...	...	...	...	—	—	—	—	—	Seychelles
—	...	...	...	...	...	...	...	—	1.7	10	—	—	Sierra Leone
—		341.9	—	—	—	...	...	—	453	1,270	—	—	Singapore
15	241	12.4	6,047	20.9	79.1	9	18	0.5	99	115	...		Slovakia
3.4	11	...	849	7.7	92.3	7	...	...	3.9	14	290	128	Slovenia
...	—	—	—	—	—	...	...	—	—	—	—	—	Solomon Islands
5.7	—	...	...	...	...	...	...	—	...	10	15	...	Somalia
22	1,843	56.6[2]	1,843	...	...	29	0.5	54	159[2]	474	2,679	...	South Africa
0.5	184	25.0	12,999	...	...	21	7.5	2.8	424	1,294	3,693	6,872	Spain
—	—	34.6	—	—	—	...	...	—	13	50	62	...	Sri Lanka
85	—	58.3	...	...	...	262	—	—	7.6	122	815	...	Sudan, The
—	...	...	...	...	...	74	49	1.5	1.2	7	—	—	Suriname
...	...	2	...	...	...	...	...	...	2	—	—	—	Swaziland
—	—	39.7	857	...	...	...	...	...	146	423	—	—	Sweden
—	—	14.5[7]	2,802[7]	...	...	...	...	...	36[7]	132	108	234	Switzerland
241	3,588	7.2	3,588	...	...	2,500	13	192	87	242	1,819	...	Syria
76	929	...	5,290	15.9	84.1	4	4.4	0.9	740	920	3,400	...	Taiwan
5.7	41	...	1,015	...	...	12	60	0.2	0.2	...	—	—	Tajikistan
28	—	100.0	—	...	...	...	...	...	4.4	15	982	...	Tanzania
333	15,046	16.3	15,046	—	100.0	352	38	9.3	257	682	67	...	Thailand
—	...	...	...	...	...	...	...	...	...	—	—	—	Togo
...	...	...	...	...	...	...	...	...	...	—	—	—	Tonga
605	8,137	6.0	8,137	1.8	98.2	686	16	44	38	160	1,051	...	Trinidad and Tobago
78	1,481	4.9	2,107	3.7	96.3	308	11	29	14	34	883	...	Tunisia
8.8	260	20.2	10,420	...	...	296	12	25	193	694	4,059	2,994	Turkey
2,860	16,714	...	10,434	...	...	546	17	33	37	237	464	694	Turkmenistan
...	...	...	...	...	...	...	...	...	...	—	—	—	Tuvalu
...	...	...	...	...	...	...	...	...	...	—	—	—	Uganda
1,121	18,131	0.5	79,081	...	...	395	13	30	96	1,026	8,500	38,402	Ukraine
6,006	35,859	22.0	28,839	...	...	97,800	126	777	86	444	830	...	United Arab Emirates
760	99,216	11.2	97,794	...	...	5,003	5.6	893	642	1,771	3,953	11,666	United Kingdom
4,740	560,635	15.6	640,410	...	...	21,765	9.3	2,334	5,528	16,539	276,000	843,586	United States
—	—	69.7	—	—	—	...	...	...	10	37	—	—	Uruguay
1,875	47,369	0.2	40,592	...	...	594	16	37	35	222	290	200	Uzbekistan
...	...	...	...	...	...	...	...	...	...	—	—	—	Vanuatu
4,157	43,690	11.7	43,690	9.1	90.9	76,862	71	1,084	374	1,282	6,850	...	Venezuela
193	12	...	12	...	...	600	8.5	71	0.3	—	150	...	Vietnam
—	—	102.1	...	...	...	...	...	...	120	525	—	—	Virgin Islands (U.S.)
...	...	...	...	...	...	...	...	...	...	—	—	—	West Bank
...	...	...	...	...	...	...	...	...	...	—	—	—	Western Sahara
479	...	100.0	...	...	...	4,000	30	132	43	130	676	—	Yemen
48	729	2.0	2,915	...	...	78	11	7.3	24	158	545	...	Yugoslavia
—	—	100.0	—	—	—	...	...	...	4.2	24	1,724	...	Zambia
...	—	90.0	—	—	—	...	...	...	...	—	212	...	Zimbabwe

[1]Estimated reserves in place. [2]South Africa includes Botswana, Lesotho, Namibia, and Swaziland. [3]Geothermally generated electricity. [4]Ethiopia includes Eritrea. [5]France includes Monaco. [6]Italy includes San Marino. [7]Switzerland includes Liechtenstein. [8]1993.

Transportation

This table presents data on the transportation infrastructure of the various countries and dependencies of the world and on their commercial passenger and cargo traffic. Most states have roads and airports, with services corresponding to the prevailing level of economic development. A number of states, however, lack railroads or inland waterways because of either geographic constraints or lack of development capital and technical expertise. Pipelines, one of the oldest means of bulk transport if aqueducts are considered, are today among the most narrowly developed transportation modes worldwide for shipment of bulk materials. Because the principal contemporary application of pipeline technology is to facilitate the shipment of hydrocarbon liquids and gases, coverage of pipelines will be found in the "Energy" table. It is, however, also true that pipelines now find increasing application for slurries of coal or other raw materials.

While the United Nations' *Statistical Yearbook, Monthly Bulletin of Statistics,* and *Annual Bulletin of Transport Statistics* provide much data on infrastructure and traffic and have established basic definitions and classifications for transportation statistics, the number of countries covered is limited. Several commercial publications maintain substantial databases and publishing programs for their particular areas of interest: highway and vehicle statistics are provided by the International Road Federation's annual *World Road Statistics;* the International Union of Railway's *International Railway Statistics* and Jane's *World Railways* provide similar data for railways; Lloyd's *Register of Shipping Statistical Tables* summarizes the world's merchant marine; the *Official Airline Guide,* the International Civil Aviation Organization's *Digest of Statistics: Commercial Air Carriers,* and the International Air Transport Association's *World Air Transport Statistics* have also been used to supplement and update data collected by the UN. Because several of these agencies are commercially or insurance-oriented, their data tend to be more complete, accurate, and timely than those of intergovernmental organizations, which depend on periodic responses to questionnaires or publication of results in official sources. All of these international sources have been extensively supplemented by national statistical sources to provide additional data. Such diversity of sources, however, imposes limitations on the comparability of the statistics from country to country because the basis and completeness of data collection and the frequency and timeliness of analysis and publication may vary greatly. Data shown in italic are from 1994 or earlier.

The categories adopted in the table also have special problems of comparability. Total road length is subject to wide international variation of interpretation, as "roads" can mean anything from mere tracks to highly developed highways. Each country also has individual classifications that differ according to climate, availability of road-building materials, traffic patterns, administrative responsibility, and so on. "Paved roads," by contrast, is a much more tightly definable category, but the proportion of paved to total roads may be distorted by the less comparable total road statistics. Automobile and truck and bus fleet statistics, which are usually

Transportation

country	roads and motor vehicles (latest)								railroads (latest)					
	roads			motor vehicles			cargo		track length		traffic			
	length		paved (percent)	automobiles	trucks and buses	persons per vehicle	short ton-mi ('000,000)	metric ton-km ('000,000)	mi	km	passengers		cargo	
	mi	km									passenger-mi ('000,000)	passenger-km ('000,000)	short ton-mi ('000,000)	metric ton-km ('000,000)
Afghanistan	13,000	21,000	13	31,000	25,000	401	*1,993*	*2,910*	16	25	...	...	...	...
Albania	11,000	18,000	30	90,766	34,378	25	550	803	416	670	72	116	0.01	0.02
Algeria	63,643	102,424	69	725,000	780,000	19	*9,589*	*14,000*	2,451[2]	3,945[2]	1,135	1,826	1,465	2,139
American Samoa	*217*	*350*	*43*	*4,672*	*199*	*11*	...	...	—	—	—	—	—	—
Andorra	167	269	74	35,358	4,238	1.6	...	...	—	—	—	—	—	—
Angola	45,128	72,626	25	207,000	25,000	41	...	...	1,834[2]	2,952[2]	*203*	*326*	*1,178*	*1,720*
Antigua and Barbuda	155	250	...	13,588	1,342	4.3	...	...	—	—	—	—	—	—
Argentina	135,630	218,276	29	4,901,608	1,379,044	5.7	...	...	21,100[2]	33,958[2]	5,656	9,102	6,234	9,102
Armenia	5,238	8,431	100	1,300	4,460	655	146	213	516	830	29	46	201	324
Aruba	*236*	*380*	*100*	38,834	990	2.4	...	...	—	—	—	—	—	—
Australia	502,356	808,465	40	9,719,900	2,214,900	1.6	*786,643*	*1,148,480*	22,233[2, 7]	35,780[2, 7]	7,152	11,510	87,262	127,400
Austria	124,000	200,000	100	4,009,604	328,591	1.9	10,773	15,670	3,506	5,643	4,953[7]	7,971[7]	10,617[7]	15,500[7]
Azerbaijan	28,502	45,870	94	281,100	104,300	21	484	706	1,317	2,120	342	550	3,160	4,613
Bahamas, The	1,522	2,450	57	89,263	17,228	2.6	...	...	—	—	—	—	—	—
Bahrain	1,966	3,164	77	149,636	32,213	3.4	...	...	—	—	—	—	—	—
Bangladesh	126,773	204,022	12	54,784	69,394	991	...	...	1,699[2]	2,734[2]	3,094	4,980	567	828
Barbados	1,025	1,650	96	43,711	10,583	4.9	...	...	—	—	—	—	—	—
Belarus	33,186	53,407	99	1,132,843	8,867	8.9	6,323	9,232	3,410	5,488	10,485	16,874	20,911	30,529
Belgium	89,353	143,800	97	4,491,734	453,122	2.1	25,586	37,355	2,100[2]	3,380[2]	4,570	7,354	5,063	7,392
Belize	1,398	2,250	18	9,695	11,698	11	...	...	—	—	—	—	—	—
Benin	4,217	6,787	20	37,772	8,058	123	...	...	359	578	75.7	121.8	193.5	311.4
Bermuda	140	225	100	21,220	4,007	2.4	...	...	—	—	—	—	—	—
Bhutan	2,041	3,285	61	*2,590*	*1,367*	*348*	...	...	—	—	—	—	—	—
Bolivia	30,696	49,400	6	223,829	138,536	21	*1,133*	*1,654*	2,187[2]	3,519[2]	84.9	136.7	359.0	524.2
Bosnia and Herzegovina	13,574	21,846	52	96,182	10,919	30	*2,708*	*3,954*	641	1,031	19.3	31.1	63.6	92.8
Botswana	11,388	18,327	25	30,517	59,710	17	...	...	603	971	60	96	545	795
Brazil	1,030,652	1,658,677	9	21,313,351	3,743,836	6.5	*178,359*	*260,400*	18,458[2]	29,706[2]	8,676	12,667	96,741	141,239
Brunei	1,064	1,712	75	91,047	15,918	2.9	...	...	12[13]	19[13]	—	—	...	...
Bulgaria	23,190	37,320	92	1,730,506	251,382	4.2	4,300	6,278	4,020	6,470	2,341	3,767	3,071	4,484
Burkina Faso	7,519	12,100	16	38,220	17,980	190	...	...	386[2]	622[2]	126	202	31	45
Burundi	8,997	14,480	7	19,200	18,240	145	...	...	—	—	—	—	—	—
Cambodia	22,226	35,769	8	52,919	13,574	171	822	1,200	409	649	37	60	25	36
Cameroon	30,074	48,400	8	98,000	64,350	88	*175*	*255*	625[2]	1,006[2]	197	317	556	812
Canada	560,415	901,903	35	13,887,270	3,694,125	1.7	94,584	138,090	40,639	65,403	906	1,458	205,146	299,508
Cape Verde	680	1,095	78	3,280	820	94	...	...	—	—	—	—	—	—
Central African Republic	14,900	24,000	2	9,500	7,000	195	41	60	—	—	—	—	—	—
Chad	20,800	33,400	1	10,560	14,550	293	580	850	—	—	—	—	—	—
Chile	49,590	79,800	14	1,323,800	687,500	7.5	...	...	5,410[2]	8,707[2]	377	606	1,984	2,896
China	794,405	1,278,474	93	6,548,300	6,278,900	96	375,580	548,338	35,781	57,584	229,657	369,598	843,302	1,236,200
Colombia	71,808	115,564	12	762,000	672,000	27	21	31	*2,007*[2]	*3,230*[2]	*9.6*	*15.5*	504.3	736.2
Comoros	559	900	76	9,100	4,950	36	...	...	—	—	—	—	—	—
Congo, Dem. Rep. of the	95,708	154,027	2	787,000	60,000	55	...	...	3,193	5,138	18[14]	29[14]	121[14]	176[14]
Congo, Rep. of the	7,950	12,800	10	37,240	15,520	49	*46*	*67*	556	894	150	242	92	135
Costa Rica	22,119	35,597	17	294,083	163,428	7.6	2,103	3,070	590[2]	950[2]	3.7	5.9	45.8	66.8
Côte d'Ivoire	31,300	50,400	10	293,000	163,000	32	...	...	397[2]	639[2]	80[17]	129[17]	40[17]	58[17]
Croatia	17,475	28,123	82	1,124,825	117,794	3.4	1,774	2,590	1,694	2,726	619	996	1,321	1,928
Cuba	37,815	60,858	49	172,574	185,495	31	*2,482*	*3,623*	2,987	4,807	1,219	1,962	763	1,075
Cyprus	6,620	10,654	58	234,976	108,452	2.4	...	...	—	—	—	—	—	—
Czech Republic	78,234	125,905	44	3,695,792	426,684	2.5	23,227	33,911	6,469	9,444	4,323	6,957	11,447	16,713
Denmark	44,389	71,663	100	1,854,060	335,690	2.4	14,639	21,372	1,704[2]	2,743[2]	3,304	5,318	1,387	2,025
Djibouti	1,796	2,890	13	9,200	2,040	38	...	...	*66*	*106*	361	762	144	232
Dominica	485	780	50	6,581	2,825	7.8	...	...	—	—	—	—	—	—
Dominican Republic	7,829	12,600	49	224,000	151,550	21	...	...	1,083[2]	1,743[2]	...	...	...	...
East Timor	...	...	...	...	...	...	...	...	...	...	...	...	...	...
Ecuador	26,841	43,197	19	464,902	52,630	23	2,712	3,959	600[2]	966[2]	28	45	686	1,002

based upon registration, are relatively accurate, though some countries round off figures, and unregistered vehicles may cause substantial undercount. There is also inconsistent classification of vehicle types; in some countries a vehicle may serve variously as an automobile, a truck, or a bus, or even as all three on certain occasions. Relatively few countries collect and maintain commercial road traffic statistics.

Data on national railway systems are generally given for railway track length rather than the length of routes, which may be multitracked. Siding tracks usually are not included, but some countries fail to distinguish them. The United States data include only class 1 railways, which account for about 94 percent of total track length. Passenger traffic is usually calculated from tickets sold to fare-paying passengers. Such statistics are subject to distortion if there are large numbers of nonpaying passengers, such as military personnel, or if season tickets are sold and not all the allowed journeys are utilized. Railway cargo traffic is calculated by weight hauled multiplied by the length of the journey. Changes in freight load during the journey should be accounted for but sometimes are not, leading to discrepancies.

Merchant fleet and tonnage statistics collected by Lloyd's registry service for vessels over 100 gross tons are quite accurate. Cargo statistics, however, reflect the port and customs requirements of each country and the reporting rules of each country's merchant marine authority (although these, increasingly, reflect the recommendations of the International Maritime Organization); often, however, they are only estimates based on customs declarations and the count of vessels entered and cleared. Even when these elements are reported consistently, further uncertainties may be introduced because of ballast, bunkers, ships' stores, or transshipped goods included in the data.

Airport data are based on scheduled flights reported in the commercial *Official Airline Guide* and are both reliable and current. The comparability of civil air traffic statistics suffers from differing characteristics of the air transportation systems of different countries; data for an entire country may be two to three years behind those for a single airport.

Outside of Europe, where standardization of data on inland waterways is necessitated by the volume of international traffic, comparability of national data declines markedly. Calculations as to both the length of a country's waterway system (or route length of river, lake, and coastal traffic) and the makeup of its stock of commercially significant vessels (those for which data will be collected) are largely determined by the nature and use of the country's hydrographic net—its seasonality, relief profile, depth, access to potential markets—and inevitably differ widely from country to country. Data for coastal or island states may refer to scheduled coastwise or interisland traffic.

merchant marine (latest)				air					canals and inland waterways (latest)				country
fleet (vessels over 100 gross tons)	total dead-weight tonnage ('000)	international cargo (latest)		airports with sched-uled flights (latest)	traffic (latest)				length		cargo		
		loaded metric tons ('000)	off-loaded metric tons ('000)		passengers		cargo		mi	km	short ton-mi ('000,000)	metric ton-km ('000,000)	
					passenger-mi ('000,000)	passenger-km ('000,000)	short ton-mi ('000,000)	metric ton-km ('000,000)					
—	—	—	—	3	171.5[1]	276.0[1]	26[1]	38[1]	750	1,200	…	…	Afghanistan
24	*81.0*	120	2,040	1	2.2	3.5	0.22	0.32	46	74	*24*	*35*	Albania
149	*1,093.4*	*63,110*	*15,700*	28	1,803[3]	2,901[3]	12.5[3]	18.3[3]	…	…	…	…	Algeria
3	*0.1*	*380*	*581*	3	…	…	…	…	…	…	…	…	American Samoa
—	—	—	—	—	—	—	—	—	—	—	—	—	Andorra
123	73.9	*23,288*	*1,261*	17	385[4]	620[4]	60[4]	97[4]	805	1,295	…	…	Angola
292	*997.4*	*28*	*113*	2	157	252	*0.1*	*0.2*	…	…	…	…	Antigua and Barbuda
423	*1,173.1*	*69,372*	*19,530*	00	7,202[5]	11,735[5]	895[5]	1,307[5]	6,804	10,950	*19,326*	*28,215*	Argentina
…	…	…	…	1	356	572	5.9	9.5	…	…	…	…	Armenia
[6]	[6]	…	…	1	318	511	…	…	…	…	…	…	Aruba
695	*3,857.3*	35,664	43,360	400	46,647	75,071	1,156	1,688	5,200	8,368	*31,891*	*46,560*	Australia
26	*208.5*	1,479	5,766	6	7,742	12,460	247	361	218	351	7,938	11,590	Austria
69	…	…	…	3	1,025	1,650	125	183	…	…	3,112	5,008	Azerbaijan
1,061	*33,081.7*	*5,920*	*5,705*	22	87	140	0.32	0.455	…	…	…	…	Bahamas, The
87	*192.5*	*13,285*	*3,512*	1	1,762[8]	2,836[8]	81.3[8]	118.7[8]	…	…	…	…	Bahrain
301	*566.8*	948	10,404	8	2,154	3,466	95	139	5,000	8,046	…	…	Bangladesh
37	*84.0*	*206*	*538*	1	*93*[9]	*149*[9]	*0.8*[10]	*1.1*[10]	…	…	…	…	Barbados
…	*18,373.0*	…	…	1	864	1,390	7	10	1,092	1,757	71	103	Belarus
232	*218.5*	360,984	367,680	2	12,042	19,379	389	568	957	1,540	3,993	5,830	Belgium
32	*45.7*	255	277	9	…	…	…	…	513	825	…	…	Belize
12	*0.2*	339	1,738	1	160.5[11]	258.3[11]	8.4[11]	13.5[11]	…	…	…	…	Benin
94	*5,206.5*	*130*	*470*	1	…	…	…	…	…	…	…	…	Bermuda
—	—	—	—	1	29	46	…	…	—	—	—	—	Bhutan
1	*15.8*	…	…	14	1,223	1,968	28.7	41.9	6,214	10,000	*90*	*132*	Bolivia
…	…	…	…	1	25.1	40.4	0.29	0.43	…	…	…	…	Bosnia and Herzegovina
—	—	—	—	7	35.3[12]	56.8[12]	0.1[12]	0.2[12]	…	…	…	…	Botswana
635	*9,348.3*	239,932	146,452	139	21,765	35,028	891	1,031	31,069	50,000	*56,030*	*81,803*	Brazil
51	*349.7*	42	1,308	1	1,742	2,803	75.0	109.5	130	209	…	…	Brunei
107	391	*5,290*	*20,080*	3	1,259	2,026	18.9	30.4	292	470	487	711	Bulgaria
—	—	—	—	2	*134.9*	*217.2*	*23.4*	*34.2*	…	…	…	…	Burkina Faso
1	*0.4*	*35*	*188*	1	*1.2*	*2.0*	…	…	…	…	…	…	Burundi
3	*3.8*	*11*	*95*	8	26.1	42.0	0.3	0.4	2,300	3,700	51	75	Cambodia
47	*39.8*	2,385	2,497	5	348	560	57	91	1,299	2,090	…	…	Cameroon
1,185	*2,896.8*	187,716	94,536	269	42,379	68,202	1,224	1,787	1,860	3,000	…	…	Canada
42	*30.9*	*144*	*299*	9	106	171	13.2	19.2	…	…	…	…	Cape Verde
—	—	*53*	*126*	1	139.6[12]	224.7[12]	11.2[12]	16.4[12]	500	800	185	270	Central African Republic
—	—	—	—	1	145	233	25	37	1,240	2,000	…	…	Chad
392	*854.9*	29,532	18,144	23	6,618	10,651	1,443	2,107	450	725	*5,629*	*8,218*	Chile
2,390	*20,658.0*	1,146,084	*101,688*	113	49,725	80,024	2,291	3,345	68,537	110,300	1,329,187	1,940,580	China
101	*403.0*	49,332	15,288	43	3,723	5,991	573	836	11,272	18,140	1.7	2.5	Colombia
6	*3.6*	*12*	*107*	2	1.9	3.0	…	…	…	…	…	…	Comoros
27	*30.7*	*2,395*	*1,453*	22	173[15]	279[15]	29[15]	42[15]	9,300	15,000	*678*	*990*	Congo, Dem. Rep. of the
22	*10.8*	708	533	10	160[11]	258[11]	9.6	14	696	1,120	…	…	Congo, Rep. of the
24	*8.4*	3,017	3,972	14	2,167[16]	3,487[16]	61.9[16]	90.4[16]	454	730	…	…	Costa Rica
51	*98.6*	4,173	7,228	5	191[18]	307[18]	30[18]	44[18]	609	980	…	…	Côte d'Ivoire
203	*140.9*	4,416	7,680	4	474	763	2.0	3.0	580	933	43	63	Croatia
393	*924.6*	*8,092*	*15,440*	14	2,202	3,543	38.5	56.2	149	240	108	158	Cuba
1,416	*36,198.1*	1,344	4,308	2	1,685	2,711	26	38	…	…	…	…	Cyprus
18[19]	*514.1*[19]	759	409	2	2,705	4,354	21	30	413	664	627	915	Czech Republic
456	*7,589.1*	21,060	38,292	13	3,340[20]	5,376[20]	117[20]	171[20]	259	417	*1,100*	*1,600*	Denmark
10	*4.1*	*414*	*958*	1	*42*	*67*	*4*	*6*	…	…	…	…	Djibouti
7	*3.2*	*103*	*181*	2	…	…	…	…	…	…	…	…	Dominica
28	*10.4*	1,668	*4,182*	7	9.8	15.8	7.9	11.6	…	…	…	…	Dominican Republic
…	…	…	…	…	…	…	…	…	…	…	…	…	East Timor
154	*504.1*	*11,783*	*1,958*	14	574	924	79	116	932	1,500	…	…	Ecuador

Transportation (continued)

country	roads and motor vehicles (latest)								railroads (latest)					
	roads			motor vehicles			cargo		track length		traffic			
	length		paved (per-cent)	auto-mobiles	trucks and buses	persons per vehicle	short ton-mi ('000,000)	metric ton-km ('000,000)	mi	km	passengers		cargo	
	mi	km									passen-ger-mi ('000,000)	passen-ger-km ('000,000)	short ton-mi ('000,000)	metric ton-km ('000,000)
Egypt	39,800[21]	64,000[21]	78[21]	1,154,753	510,766	37	21,600	31,500	2,989	4,810	35,211	56,667	2,820	4,117
El Salvador	6,232	10,029	20	177,488	184,859	16	...	...	349[2]	562[2]	4.4	7.1	12	17
Equatorial Guinea	1,740	2,800	13	6,500	4,000	37	...	...	—	—	—	—	—	—
Eritrea	2,491	4,010	22	5,940	...	...	...	...	43	70	...	...	...	...
Estonia	10,209	16,430	51	451,000	86,900	2.7	2,691	3,929	636	1,024	149	238	4,808	7,020
Ethiopia	12,117	19,500	15	52,012	39,936	642	...	...	486[22]	782[22]	98	157	73	106
Faroe Islands	285	458	...	14,608	3,455	2.5	...	...	—	—	—	—	—	—
Fiji	3,200	5,100	20	49,712	33,928	9.4	...	...	370[13]	595[13]	...	...	...	...
Finland	48,340	77,900	65	2,069,055	300,048	2.2	19,884	29,030	3,626[2]	5,836[2]	2,122	3,415	6,680	9,753
France	547,200	893,500	100	27,480,000	5,610,000	1.8	114,382	166,995	19,486[2]	31,821[2]	40,100	64,500	37,000	54,000
French Guiana	*706*	*1,137*	*40*	*29,100*	*10,600*	*3.2*	...	...	—	—	—	—	—	—
French Polynesia	549	884	44	*37,000*	*15,300*	*4.0*	...	...	—	—	—	—	—	—
Gabon	4,760	7,670	8	24,750	16,490	28	...	...	506	814	53	85	345	503
Gambia, The	1,678	2,700	35	8,640	9,000	68	...	...	—	—	—	—	—	—
Gaza Strip	...	...	...	37,061	8,105	23	...	...	—	—	—	—	—	—
Georgia	12,862	20,700	93	427,000	41,510	11	288	420	961	1,546	219	349	2,150	3,139
Germany	143,372	230,735	99	42,323,672	2,550,222	1.8	176,337	257,447	54,188	87,207	41,321	66,500	48,875	71,356
Ghana	24,000	38,700	40	90,000	45,000	133	*873*	*1,275*	*592*[2]	*953*[2]	*731.4*	*1,177*	*93.9*	*137.1*
Greece	72,700	117,000	92	2,675,676	1,013,677	2.9	12,000	17,000	1,555[2]	2,503[2]	1,108	1,783	226	330
Greenland	93	150	60	2,242	1,474	15	...	...	—	—	—	—	—	—
Grenada	646	1,040	61	*4,739*	*3,068*	*12*	...	...	—	—	—	—	—	—
Guadeloupe	2,122	3,415	*80*	*101,600*	*37,500*	*2.9*	...	...	—	—	—	—	—	—
Guam	550	885	76	79,800	34,700	1.3	...	...	—	—	—	—	—	—
Guatemala	8,140	13,100	28	102,000	97,000	51	...	...	549[2]	884[2]	10.3	16.6	58.6	85.6
Guernsey	...	...	...	37,598	7,338	1.4	...	...	—	—	—	—	—	—
Guinea	18,952	30,500	16	14,100	21,000	219	...	...	411[2]	662[2]	25.8	41.5	5.0	7.3
Guinea-Bissau	2,734	4,400	10	7,120	5,640	91	...	...	—	—	—	—	—	—
Guyana	4,952	7,970	7	24,000	9,000	22	...	...	116[13]	187[13]	...	...	...	...
Haiti	2,585	4,160	24	32,000	21,000	121	...	...	—	—	—	—	—	—
Honduras	9,073	14,602	18	81,439	170,006	22	...	...	614	988	*4.8*	*7.7*	*20.7*	*30.2*
Hong Kong	1,183	1,904	100	332,000	133,000	14	...	...	21[2]	34[2]	2,231	3,591	68	99
Hungary	116,944	188,203	43	2,255,526	321,634	4.0	10,950	15,987	4,827[2]	7,768[2]	5,912	9,514	5,297	7,733
Iceland	7,691	12,378	25	151,409	19,428	1.6	*318*	*464*	—	—	—	—	—	—
India	2,062,727	3,319,644	46	4,189,000	2,234,000	148	656	958	39,028[2]	62,809[2]	261,254	420,449	209,259	305,513
Indonesia	212,177	341,467	56	2,734,769	2,189,876	41	*17,000*	*25,000*	4,013[2]	6,458[2]	11,548	18,585	3,449	5,035
Iran	102,976	165,724	50	1,793,000	692,000	24	*46,750*	*68,250*	3,915[2]	6,300[2]	3,792	6,103	9,863	14,400
Iraq	29,453	47,400	86	772,986	323,906	18	...	...	1,263[2]	2,032[2]	973	1,566	1,129	1,649
Ireland	57,477	92,500	94	1,269,245	188,814	2.6	4,041	5,900	1,209[2]	1,945[2]	870	1,400	342	500
Isle of Man	500	805	58	40,168	4,925	1.6	...	...	32[2]	52[2]	...	...	...	...
Israel	9,609	15,464	100	1,316,765	319,581	3.7	*2,993*	*4,370*	379[2]	610[2]	329	529	773	1,128
Italy	191,468	308,139	100	31,370,000	5,127,000	1.6	131,154	191,482	12,133	19,527	25,720	41,392	15,333	22,386
Jamaica	11,800	19,000	71	160,948	55,596	12	...	...	*129*[2]	*208*[2]	*12.1*	*19.5*	*1.7*	*2.5*
Japan	718,300	1,156,000	73	51,222,000	18,425,000	1.8	205,942	300,670	16,937	27,258	241,674	388,938	15,699	22,920
Jersey	346	557	100	58,491	9,922	1.3	...	...	—	—	—	—	—	—
Jordan	4,432	7,133	100	213,874	79,153	15	*19,133*	*27,934*	421[2]	677[2]	*3.7*	*6.0*	915	1,336
Kazakhstan	78,166	125,796	83	973,323	361,920	11	3,176	4,637	8,388[2]	13,500[2]	5,505	8,859	64,987	94,879
Kenya	39,600	63,800	14	278,000	81,200	78	*134*	*196*	1,885[2]	3,034[2]	239	385	813	1,309
Kiribati	416	670	5	222	115	260	...	...	—	—	—	—	—	—
Korea, North	14,526	23,377	8	*248,000*	...	...	...	...	5,302	8,533	*2,100*	*3,400*	*6,200*	*9,100*
Korea, South	55,162	88,775	76	8,084,000	3,938,000	3.9	51,031	74,504	4,165	6,703	18,686	30,072	8,704	12,708
Kuwait	2,765	4,450	81	747,042	140,480	2.3	...	...	—	—	—	—	—	—
Kyrgyzstan	11,495	18,500	91	146,000	...	...	695	1,015	264	424	58	93	323	472
Laos	13,870	22,321	14	16,320	4,200	242	16	23	—	—	—	—	—	—
Latvia	34,761	55,942	38	431,816	95,329	4.7	2,814	4,108	1,499	2,413	611	984	8,363	12,210
Lebanon	3,946	6,350	95	1,299,398	85,242	2.5	...	...	138	222	*5.3*	*8.6*	*29*	*42*
Lesotho	3,079	4,955	18	12,610	25,000	53	...	...	1.6	2.6	...	...	...	...
Liberia	6,600	10,600	6	9,400	25,000	59	...	...	304[2]	490[2]	...	...	534	860
Libya	50,704	81,600	57	809,514	357,528	4.0	...	...	—	—	—	—	—	—
Liechtenstein	201	323	...	21,150	2,684	1.4	...	...	12	19	...	...	...	...
Lithuania	44,350	71,375	91	980,910	105,022	3.4	3,843	5,611	1,241[2]	1,997[2]	463	745	5,376	7,849
Luxembourg	3,209	5,166	100	263,683	20,228	1.5	2,437	3,558	170[2]	274[2]	193	310	410	660
Macau	31	50	100	45,184	6,578	8.2	...	...	—	—	—	—	—	—
Macedonia	7,154	11,513	63	288,678	24,745	6.4	612	894	575	925	93	150	279	408
Madagascar	30,967	49,837	17	62,000	16,460	140	*220*	*321*	*680*[2]	*1,095*[2]	22	35	44	71
Malawi	10,222	16,451	19	27,000	29,700	171	—	—	495[2]	797[2]	16	26	34	49
Malaysia	41,282	66,437	76	3,517,484	644,792	5.1	...	...	1,384[2]	2,227[2]	828[31]	1,332[31]	625[31]	912[31]
Maldives	...	...	...	1,716	586	114	...	...	—	—	—	—	—	—
Mali	9,383	15,100	12	26,190	18,240	213	...	...	398[2]	641[2]	577.6	929.6	371	542.8
Malta	1,219	1,961	94	185,247	49,520	1.6	...	...	—	—	—	—	—	—
Marshall Islands	...	...	...	1,374	262	29	...	...	—	—	—	—	—	—
Martinique	1,299	2,091	*75*	*108,300*	*32,200*	*2.6*	...	...	—	—	—	—	—	—
Mauritania	4,760	7,660	11	18,810	10,450	82	...	...	437[2]	704[2]	...	...	1,603	2,340
Mauritius	1,184	1,905	93	46,300	12,100	20	...	...	—	—	—	—	—	—
Mayotte	145	233	77	——6,553——		20	...	...	—	—	—	—	—	—
Mexico	199,824	321,586	37	8,607,000	4,426,000	7.1	122,663	179,085	16,543[2]	26,623[2]	286	460	32,106	46,874
Micronesia	*140*	*226*	*17*	...	...	...	...	...	—	—	—	—	—	—
Moldova	7,643	12,300	87	166,757	67,638	18	697	1,018	819	1,318	213	343	816	1,191
Monaco	31	50	100	21,120	2,770	1.3	...	...	1	2	...	...	...	...
Mongolia	31,000	50,000	3	39,921	31,061	33	84.4	123.2	1,128	1,815	634	1,020	2,392	3,492
Morocco	35,921	57,810	52	1,018,146	278,075	21	1,429	2,086	1,099[2]	1,768[2]	1,104	1,776	3,258	4,757
Mozambique	18,890	30,400	19	4,900	7,520	1,431	75	110	1,940	3,123	317	510	781	1,140
Myanmar (Burma)	17,523	28,200	12	27,000	42,000	587	*71*	*103.7*	2,458[2]	3,955[2]	2,453	3,948	674	984
Namibia	40,526	65,220	8	74,875	66,500	12	...	...	1,480	2,382	21.6	34.7	738	1,077
Nauru	19	30	79	——*1,448*——		*6.3*	...	...	3[13]	5[13]	...	...	*4.7*	*6.8*
Nepal	4,785	7,700	42	47,541	29,371	306	*984*	*1,437*	37[2]	59[2]	...	...	...	...

merchant marine (latest): fleet (vessels over 100 gross tons)	merchant marine (latest): total dead-weight tonnage ('000)	international cargo (latest): loaded metric tons ('000)	international cargo (latest): off-loaded metric tons ('000)	air: airports with scheduled flights (latest)	air traffic (latest): passengers: passenger-mi ('000,000)	air traffic (latest): passengers: passenger-km ('000,000)	air traffic (latest): cargo: short ton-mi ('000,000)	air traffic (latest): cargo: metric ton-km ('000,000)	canals and inland waterways (latest): length: mi	canals and inland waterways (latest): length: km	canals and inland waterways (latest): cargo: short ton-mi ('000,000)	canals and inland waterways (latest): cargo: metric ton-km ('000,000)	country
444	1,685.2	15,012	22,044	11	5,638	9,074	185	270	2,175	3,500	452	660	Egypt
15	…	221	1,023	1	1,355	2,181	10.9	16.0	…	…	…	…	El Salvador
3	6.7	110	64	1	4	7	0.7	1.0	…	…	…	…	Equatorial Guinea
…	…	…	…	2	…	…	…	…	…	…	…	…	Eritrea
234	680.4	30,024	5,784	1	103.6	166.7	0.6	0.9	199	320	1.4	2.1	Estonia
27	84.3	234	1,242	31	1,190	1,915	225	328	…	…	…	…	Ethiopia
191	59.8	223	443	1	…	…	…	…	…	…	…	…	Faroe Islands
64	60.4	568	625	13	742	1,195	51.6	75.4	126	203	…	…	Fiji
263	989.3	39,312	38,052	27	8,026	12,916	216	316	3,880	6,245	127,945	186,797	Finland
729	4,981.0	64,704	189,504	61	55,344[23]	89,067[23]	3,271[23]	4,775[23]	3,562	5,732	5,436	7,936	France
7	0.7	73	447	8	…	…	…	…	286	460	…	…	French Guiana
41	16.5	15	666	17	…	…	…	…	…	…	…	…	French Polynesia
29	30.2	12,828	212	17	452	728	68	100	994	1,600	…	…	Gabon
11	2.0	185	240	1	31	50	3	5	250	400	…	…	Gambia, The
—	—	…	…	1	…	…	…	…	—	—	…	…	Gaza Strip
54	1,108	…	…	1	78.9	127.1	0.5	0.8	…	…	3,740	5,460	Georgia
1,375	6,832.3	74,568	138,864	35	55,219	88,867	4,520	6,599	4,188	6,740	44,019	64,267	Germany
155	131.0	2,424	2,904	1	407	655	20	30	803	1,293	75	110	Ghana
1,872	45,276.6	16,464	45,024	36	5,160	8,305	71	103	50	80	585	854	Greece
82	17.2	298	288	18	104	167	0.23	0.34	…	…	…	…	Greenland
3	0.5	21	193	2	…	…	…	…	…	…	…	…	Grenada
20	4.4	349	2,285	7	…	…	…	…	…	…	…	…	Guadeloupe
5	0.1	195	1,524	1	…	…	…	…	…	…	…	…	Guam
8	0.4	2,096	3,822	2	311	500	48	70	162	260	…	…	Guatemala
—	—	…	…	2	…	…	…	…	…	…	…	…	Guernsey
23	1.7	16,760	734	1	32	52	3	5	805	1,295	…	…	Guinea
19	1.8	46	283	2	6.2	10.0	0.7	1.0	…	…	…	…	Guinea-Bissau
82	13.5	1,730	673	1	154	248	2.3	3.3	3,660	5,900	…	…	Guyana
4	0.4	170	704	2	…	…	…	…	60	100	…	…	Haiti
966	1,437.3	1,316	1,002	8	212[24]	341[24]	23[24]	33[24]	289	465	…	…	Honduras
387	11,688.6	36,132[25]	80,820[25]	1	…	…	…	…	…	…	…	…	Hong Kong
15	93.2	…	…	1	2,183	3,513	38	56	853	1,373	1,069	1,561	Hungary
394	114.9	1,162	1,733	24	2,273	3,658	50.9	74.4	…	…	58	84	Iceland
888	10,365.9	61,880	102,630	66	11,456	18,436	329	481	10,054	16,180	202,000	295,000	India
2,014	3,130.2	310,246	208,871	81	7,698	12,389	234	341	13,409	21,579	17,000	25,000	Indonesia
403	8,345.3	32,148	37,404	19	3,871	6,229	49	72	562	904	…	…	Iran
131	1,578.8	97,830	8,638	…	970	1,570	37.4	54.6	631	1,015	…	…	Iraq
189	208.6	6,367	17,637	9	4,018	6,466	88.8	129.6	435	700	…	…	Ireland
101	2,836.5	6	203	1	526.1	846.8	0.1	0.2	…	…	…	…	Isle of Man
58	723.4	12,876	20,916	7	8,777[26]	14,125[26]	882[26]	1,288[26]	…	…	…	…	Israel
1,966	7,149.5	48,252	234,120	34	18,312[27]	29,471[27]	835[27]	1,219[27]	918	1,477	85,681	125,092	Italy
12	16.2	8,802	5,285	4	1,038[28]	1,670[28]	20.2[28]	29.5[28]	…	…	…	…	Jamaica
6,140	16,198	124,548	754,464	73	97,745	157,305	4,920	7,183	1,100	1,770	155,468	226,980	Japan
—	—	…	…	1	…	…	…	…	…	…	…	…	Jersey
5	113.6	7,308	5,328	2	2,526	4,065	150.1	219.2	…	…	19,202	28,035	Jordan
…	…	…	…	20	1,509	2,429	162	237	2,425	3,903	97	141	Kazakhstan
29	11.6	1,596	3,228	11	1,062[29]	1,709[29]	126[29]	203[29]	…	…	…	…	Kenya
7	2.7	15	26	9	4.4	7.0	0.6	1.0	3	5	…	…	Kiribati
100	951.2	635	5,520	1	178	286	19	30	1,400	2,253	…	…	Korea, North
2,138	11,724.9	255,888	448,416	14	29,647	47,712	4,987	7,281	1,000	1,609	22,920	33,462	Korea, South
209	3,188.5	51,400	4,522	1	3,813	6,137	151	243	…	…	…	…	Kuwait
…	…	…	…	2	2,739	4,408	44.7	65.2	290	466	41	6.0	Kyrgyzstan
1	1.5	—	—	11	30	48	3	5	2,850	4,587	68	100	Laos
261	1,436.9	45,144	3,888	1	185	298	6	9	66	106	19,241	28,091	Latvia
163	438.2	152	1,150	1	1,315	2,116	218	319	…	…	…	…	Lebanon
—	—	—	—	1	3.9	6.2	0.4	0.6	—	—	—	—	Lesotho
1,672	97,374.0	21,653	1,608	1	4.3	7.0	0.7	1.0	…	…	…	…	Liberia
150	1,223.6	62,491	7,808	12	264[30]	425[30]	23[30]	34[30]	—	—	…	…	Libya
—	—	—	—	—	—	—	—	—	…	…	…	…	Liechtenstein
52	373.9	12,864	2,796	3	190.5	306.6	1.8	2.6	229	369	8.9	13	Lithuania
54	2,603.6	—	—	1	79.5	232	606.9	886.1	23	37	205	300	Luxembourg
6	0.1	755	3,935	—	—	—	—	—	…	…	…	…	Macau
…	…	…	…	2	553.5	890.7	239.2	349.2	…	…	…	…	Macedonia
85	82.1	540	984	44	519	836	20.2	29.5	…	…	1.2	1.8	Madagascar
1	0.3	…	…	5	68	110	10	14	89	144	1,683	2,457	Malawi
552	2,916.3	39,756	54,852	39	20,945	33,708	976	1,425	4,534	7,296	…	…	Malaysia
44	79.0	27	78	5	44	71	…	…	…	…	…	…	Maldives
—	—	—	—	9	150	242	26	38	1,128	1,815	18	27	Mali
889	17,073.2	309	1,781	1	1,173	1,888	7.7	11.2	…	…	…	…	Malta
35	4,182.4	29	123	25	17	28	0.003	0.005	…	…	…	…	Marshall Islands
6	1.1	960	1,584	1	…	…	…	…	…	…	…	…	Martinique
126	23.9	10,400	724	9	160.5	258.3	9.2	13.5	…	…	…	…	Mauritania
35	152.2	966	2,753	1	2,398	3,859	561.2	819.4	…	…	…	…	Mauritius
1	1.1	158	31	1	…	…	…	…	…	…	…	…	Mayotte
635	1,495.3	134,400	67,500	83	14,864	23,922	1,779	2,597	1,800	2,900	14,806	21,616	Mexico
19	9.2	…	…	4	…	…	…	…	…	…	…	…	Micronesia
…	…	…	…	1	0.1	0.2	0.7	1.0	263	424	172	251	Moldova
1	…	…	…	—	—	—	…	…	…	…	…	…	Monaco
—	—	—	—	1	326	525	33	48	247	397	0.1	0.2	Mongolia
492	586.2	24,228	27,972	11	2,789	4,489	260	380	…	…	…	…	Morocco
107	31.6	2,800	3,400	7	239	384	6	9	2,330	3,750	57	83	Mozambique
144	1,354.0	1,788	3,456	19	272	438	2.2	3.2	7,954	12,800	240	351	Myanmar (Burma)
30	5.9	1,132	644	11	470	756	16	23	…	…	…	…	Namibia
2	5.8	1,650	59	1	151[32]	243[32]	15[32]	24[32]	…	…	…	…	Nauru
—	—	—	—	24	532	856	64	93	…	…	…	…	Nepal

Transportation (continued)

country	roads and motor vehicles (latest)								railroads (latest)					
	roads			motor vehicles			cargo		track length		traffic			
	length		paved (percent)	automobiles	trucks and buses	persons per vehicle	short ton-mi ('000,000)	metric ton-km ('000,000)	mi	km	passengers		cargo	
	mi	km									passenger-mi ('000,000)	passenger-km ('000,000)	short ton-mi ('000,000)	metric ton-km ('000,000)
Netherlands, The	77,379	124,530	91	6,343,000	826,000	2.2	98,445	143,727	1,745	2,808	8,904	14,330	2,412	3,521
Netherlands Antilles	367	590	51	75,105	17,753	2.2	...	...	—	—	—	—	—	—
New Caledonia	3,582	5,764	52	56,700	21,200	2.6	...	...	—	—	—	—	—	—
New Zealand	57,213	92,075	62	1,831,118	351,494	1.7	...	...	2,431[2]	3,912[2]	*285*	*458*	2,712	3,960
Nicaragua	11,200	18,000	10	73,000	61,650	33	...	...	—	—	—	—	—	—
Niger	6,276	10,100	8	38,220	15,200	169	*1,044*	*1,524*	—	—	—	—	—	—
Nigeria	38,897	62,598	19	773,000	68,300	131	...	...	2,178	3,505	100	161	74	108
Northern Mariana Islands	225	360	100	12,113	6,479	3.0	...	...	—	—	—	—	—	—
Norway	56,470	90,880	74	1,813,642	447,583	2.0	10,086	14,726	2,489[2]	4,006[2]	1,609	2,589	1,467	2,142
Oman	20,518	33,020	24	229,029	110,717	6.9	...	...	—	—	—	—	—	—
Pakistan	149,679	240,885	55	1,167,635	251,407	95	66,304	96,802	5,452[2]	8,774[2]	11,908	19,164	2,753	4,020
Palau	*40*	*64*	*59*	4,271		3.8	...	...	...	...	...	...	...	...
Panama	7,022	11,301	33	203,760	74,637	9.4	...	...	220[2]	354[2]	242	389	1,096	1,600
Papua New Guinea	*12,263*	*19,736*	*6*	*13,000*	*32,000*	*93*	...	...	—	—	—	—	—	—
Paraguay	18,330	29,500	10	71,000	50,000	41	...	...	274[2]	441[2]	1.9	3.0	3.8	5.5
Peru	45,836	73,766	12	557,042	359,374	26	...	...	1,238[2]	1,992[2]	132	212	0.8	1.1
Philippines	124,243	199,950	39	745,144	263,037	73	...	...	557[2]	897[2]	7.5	12	452	660
Poland	234,286	377,048	66	9,283,000	1,762,000	3.5	47,632	69,542	14,280	22,981	16,279	26,198	37,994	55,471
Portugal	42,708	68,732	88	3,200,000	1,097,000	2.4	16,984	24,796	2,025[2]	3,259[2]	2,860	4,602	1,603	2,340
Puerto Rico	8,948	14,400	100	878,000	190,000	3.5	...	...	—	—	—	—	—	—
Qatar	764	1,230	90	126,000	64,000	2.9	...	...	—	—	—	—	—	—
Réunion	1,711	2,754	*79*	190,300	44,300	3.0	...	...	—	—	—	—	—	—
Romania	95,175	153,170	51	2,408,000	409,550	8.0	14,898	21,750	7,062	11,365	7,658	12,324	10,909	15,927
Russia	354,628	570,719	79	19,717,800	5,021,000	5.9	14,384	21,000	93,800	151,000	88,048	144,700	825	1,205
Rwanda	9,528	14,900	9	13,000	17,100	188	*140*	*200*	—	—	—	—	—	—
St. Kitts and Nevis	199	320	43	5,200	2,300	5.3	...	...	22	36	—	—	—	—
St. Lucia	750	1,210	5	14,783	1,020	9.5	...	...	—	—	—	—	—	—
St. Vincent and the Grenadines	646	1,040	31	6,089	3,670	11	...	...	—	—	—	—	—	—
Samoa	491	790	42	1,068	1,169	74	...	...	—	—	—	—	—	—
San Marino	157	252	...	25,571	2,636	0.9	...	...	—	—	—	—	—	—
São Tomé and Príncipe	199	320	68	4,040	1,540	24	...	...	—	—	—	—	—	—
Saudi Arabia	101,000	162,000	43	1,744,000	1,192,000	6.6	57,859	84,473	864[2]	1,390[2]	138	222	586	856
Senegal	9,134	14,700	29	85,488	36,962	72	*375*	*547*	761	1,225	*128*	*206*	*476*	*695*
Seychelles	263	424	87	7,120	1,980	8.5	...	...	—	—	—	—	—	—
Sierra Leone	7,270	11,700	11	17,640	10,890	163	*36*	*53*	*52*	*84*	...	...	...	...
Singapore	1,875	3,017	97	413,545	147,325	5.8	...	...	73	117	[31]	[31]	[31]	[31]
Slovakia	10,953	17,627	...	1,135,914	100,254	4.4	5,804	8,474	2,282	3,673	1,844	2,968	6,753	9,859
Slovenia	7,771	12,507	81	829,674	67,111	2.2	1,986	2,900	746	1,201	388	625	1,907	2,784
Solomon Islands	845	1,360	3	*2,052*	*2,574*	*75*	...	...	—	—	—	—	—	—
Somalia	13,732	22,100	12	1,020	6,440	866	...	...	—	—	—	—	—	—
South Africa	205,838	331,265	41	3,966,252	2,069,536	7.2	*1,053*	*1,538*	12,626[2]	20,319[2]	1,103	1,775	71,142	103,866
Spain	215,335	346,548	99	16,847,000	3,659,000	2.0	85,801	125,268	8,595[2]	13,832[2]	11,525	18,547	7,959	11,620
Sri Lanka	61,640	99,200	40	107,000	150,160	71	21	30	899[2]	1,447[2]	2,028	3,264	90	132
Sudan, The	7,394	11,900	36	285,000	53,000	93	...	...	2,855[2]	4,595[2]	100	161	1,346	1,965
Suriname	2,815	4,530	26	46,408	19,255	6.4	...	...	187	301	...	...	...	...
Swaziland	2,367	3,810	29	31,882	32,772	17	...	...	187	301	*752*	*1,210*	*1,993*	*2,910*
Sweden	130,500	210,000	74	3,890,159	352,897	2.1	22,798	33,285	6,811	10,961	4,746	7,638	13,074	19,088
Switzerland	44,248	71,211	96	3,467,275	313,646	1.9	9,932	14,500	3,129	5,035	8,764	14,104	5,951	8,688
Syria	25,756	41,451	23	138,900	282,664	37	*1,075*	*1,570*	1,507[2]	2,425[2]	113	182	934	1,364
Taiwan	12,660	20,375	89	4,716,000	833,000	4.0	12,651	18,470	2,410	3,879	7,833	12,606	808	1,179
Tajikistan	8,500	13,700	83	680	8,190	667	34	50	295	474	77	124	1,449	2,115
Tanzania	54,805	88,200	4	23,760	115,700	229	...	...	2,218	3,569	*2,324*	*3,740*	927	1,354
Thailand	40,141	64,600	98	1,661,000	2,855,000	14	...	...	2,873[2]	4,623[2]	6,636	10,680	1,940	2,832
Togo	4,673	7,520	32	79,200	34,240	39	...	...	245[2]	395[2]	10.3	16.5	34	49
Tonga	423	680	27	1,140	780	51	...	...	—	—	—	—	—	—
Trinidad and Tobago	5,170	8,320	51	122,000	24,000	8.7	...	...	—	—	—	—	—	—
Tunisia	14,354	23,100	79	269,000	312,000	16	*678*	*990*	1,348[2]	2,169[2]	743	1,196	1,620	2,365
Turkey	238,380	383,636	25	4,283,080	1,488,016	11	104,255	152,210	5,388	8,671	3,804	6,122	6,871	10,032
Turkmenistan	8,500	13,700	83	220,000	58,200	16	335	489	1,317	2,120	1,307	2,104	4,643	6,779
Tuvalu	5	8	—	...	...	...	...	...	—	—	—	—	—	—
Uganda	16,653	26,800	8	35,361	48,430	249	...	...	771[2]	1,241[2]	17	27	162	236
Ukraine	107,111	172,378	95	4,885,691	...	...	12,534	18,300	14,021	22,564	29,577	47,600	107,081	156,336
United Arab Emirates	2,356	3,791	100	201,000	56,950	9.6	...	...	—	—	—	—	—	—
United Kingdom	231,096	371,914	100	23,393,000	2,368,000	2.3	117,504	171,553	23,518[44]	37,849[44]	23,800	38,300	12,603	18,400
United States	3,906,292	6,286,396	91	131,839,000	79,778,000	1.3	1,051,045	1,534,500	137,900	222,000	14,000	22,500	1,421,000	2,075,000
Uruguay	5,395	8,683	30	516,889	50,264	5.6	*500*	*730*	1,288[2]	2,073[2]	*87.4*	*140.6*	123	180
Uzbekistan	52,444	84,400	87	865,300	14,500	25	1,248	1,822	2,271	3,655	1,553	2,500	11,580	16,907
Vanuatu	665	1,070	24	4,000	2,600	27	...	...	—	—	—	—	—	—
Venezuela	59,443	95,664	36	1,505,000	542,000	11	...	...	390[2]	627[2]	93.1	149.9	37.3	54.5
Vietnam	58,000	93,300	25	*200,000*		*358*	1,462	2,134	1,952[2]	3,142[2]	1,694	2,727	958	1,398
Virgin Islands (U.S.)	532	856	100	*51,000*	*13,300*	1.7	...	...	—	—	—	—	—	—
West Bank	...	...	...	88,056	24,324	18	...	...	...	...	...	...	...	...
Western Sahara	*3,900*	*6,200*	*23*	*6,284*	*424*	*20*	...	...	—	—	—	—	—	—
Yemen	40,218	64,725	8	240,567	291,149	29	...	...	—	—	—	—	—	—
Yugoslavia	31,377	50,497	60	1,400,000	132,000	6.9	852	1,244	2,528	4,069	1,003	1,614	1,760	2,570
Zambia	24,170	38,898	18	157,000	81,000	37	...	...	787	1,266	166	267	316	462
Zimbabwe	11,395	18,338	47	323,000	32,000	31	...	...	1,714[2]	2,759[2]	253.6	408.2	3.2	4.6

[1]Ariana Afghan Airlines only. [2]Route length. [3]Air Algérie International flights only. [4]TAAG airline only. [5]Aerolineas Argentinas only. [6]Included in Netherlands Antilles. [7]Government railways only. [8]Portion of Gulf Air traffic. [9]Caribbean Airways only. [10]Caribbean Air Cargo only. [11]Air Afrique only. [12]Air Botswana only. [13]For industrial purposes only. [14]Zaire National Railways only. [15]Air Zaire only. [16]LASCA only. [17]Traffic between Ouagadougou, Burkina Faso, and Abidjan, Côte d'Ivoire. [18]Air Ivoire only. [19]Data refer to former Czechoslovakia. [20]Including SAS international and domestic traffic. [21]National roads only. [22]Includes 62 mi (100 km) of the Chemin de Fer Djibouti-Ethiopien (CDE) in Djibouti. [23]Air France and UTA only. [24]TAN and SAHSA airlines only. [25]Includes

merchant marine (latest)				air					canals and inland waterways (latest)				country
fleet (vessels over 100 gross tons)	total dead-weight tonnage ('000)	international cargo (latest)		airports with sched-uled flights (latest)	traffic (latest)				length		cargo		
					passengers		cargo						
		loaded metric tons ('000)	off-loaded metric tons ('000)		passenger-mi ('000,000)	passenger-km ('000,000)	short ton-mi ('000,000)	metric ton-km ('000,000)	mi	km	short ton-mi ('000,000)	metric ton-km ('000,000)	
399	2,874	91,920	305,232	6	36,109	58,112	2,679	3,911	3,135	5,046	27,887	40,714	Netherlands, The
154[33]	1,053.6[33]	215	517	6	234[34]	377[34]	1.2[34]	1.8[34]	...	...	...	...	Netherlands Antilles
17	18.1	1,040	930	11	145[35]	233[35]	3.4[35]	4.9[35]	...	...	...	...	New Caledonia
139	279.8	20,640	13,308	36	12,352	19,879	584	852	1,000	1,609	1,503	2,195	New Zealand
25	1.3	320	1,629	10	49	79	6	9	1,379	2,220	...	...	Nicaragua
—	—	—	—	6	160.5	258.3	9.3	13.5	186	300	14	20	Niger
271	733.3	86,993	11,346	12	70	112	1.3	2.1	5,328	8,575	...	...	Nigeria
2	0.9	33	205	2	...	...	...	...	...	...	...	...	Northern Mariana Islands
1,597	20,834	151,116	25,788	50	6,444[20]	10,371[20]	821[20]	1,199[20]	980	1,577	7,640	11,154	Norway
26	11.7	43,525	5,303	6	601[8]	968[8]	11[8]	18[8]	...	...	...	...	Oman
73	513.8	6,408	31,008	35	6,503	10,466	226	330	...	...	...	...	Pakistan
4	...	...	64	1	...	...	...	...	...	...	...	...	Palau
5,217	79,255.6	117,924	76,800	10	853	1,373	14.9	21.8	497	800	...	...	Panama
87	40.9	2,463	1,784	42	457	735	59	86	6,798	10,940	...	...	Papua New Guinea
38	38.5	...	...	5	134	215	13	19	1,900	3,100	...	...	Paraguay
623	615.6	10,197	5,077	27	1,637	2,634	172	251	5,300	8,600	...	...	Peru
1,499	13,807.1	16,980	52,596	21	6,395[36]	10,292[36]	165[36]	241[36]	2,000	3,219	...	...	Philippines
644	4,314.3	33,360	15,864	8	2,878	4,632	55	80	2,369	3,812	753	1,100	Poland
332	1,129.3	7,572	37,740	16	6,278	10,104	159	232	510	820	...	...	Portugal
13	...	...	...	7	...	...	...	...	...	...	...	...	Puerto Rico
64	744	18,145	2,588	1	1,776[8]	2,858[8]	72[8]	105[8]	...	...	...	...	Qatar
7	33.5	454	2,302	2	...	...	...	...	...	...	...	...	Réunion
439	4,845.5	11,676	18,972	12	1,446	2,327	33.8	49.4	1,002	1,613	2,947	4,302	Romania
4,543	16,592.3	7,092	744	75	33,181	53,400	1,575	2,300	55,357	89,089	44,962	65,643	Russia
—	—	—	—	2	1.2	2.0	...	...	...	...	...	...	Rwanda
1	0.6	24	36	2	...	...	...	...	...	...	...	...	St. Kitts and Nevis
7	2.1	138	547	2	...	...	...	...	...	...	...	...	St. Lucia
946	1,253	72	128	5	...	...	...	...	...	...	...	...	St. Vincent and the Grenadines
7	6.5	48	144	3	165	265	18	26	—	—	—	—	Samoa
—	—	—	—	—	—	—	—	—	—	—	—	—	San Marino
4	2.3	16	45	2	6	9	0.7	1.0	...	...	...	...	São Tomé and Príncipe
279	1,278	214,070	46,437	28	11,774	18,949	1,815	2,650	...	...	...	...	Saudi Arabia
183	27.5	1,396	2,894	7	139.6[30]	224.7[30]	11.2[30]	16.4[30]	557	897	...	...	Senegal
9	3.3	47	543	2	389	626	48	70	...	...	...	...	Seychelles
62	18.4	2,310	589	1	68[37]	110[37]	1.4[37]	2.0[37]	500	800	447	652	Sierra Leone
946	14,929.2	326,040	188,234	1	40,096	64,529	3,755	5,482	...	...	...	...	Singapore
...	...	...	...	2	113.8	231.4	0.5	0.7	107	172	1,046	1,527	Slovakia
13	346.5	2,460	5,952	3	517	832	2.8	4.2	...	...	21,900	31,973	Slovenia
33	5.0	278	349	21	29[38]	47[38]	0.9	1.3	...	...	...	...	Solomon Islands
28	18.5	324	1,007	1	81	131	3.0	5.0	...	...	...	...	Somalia
219	282.5	114,331	22,203	24	12,005[39]	19,320[39]	464[39]	677[39]	...	...	...	...	South Africa
2,190	5,077.3	55,752	169,848	25	37,715	60,696	4,388	6,407	649	1,045	21,836[40]	31,880[40]	Spain
66	472.6	9,288	16,632	1	3,204	5,156	459	670	267	430	0.7	1	Sri Lanka
16	62.2	1,543	4,300	3	330[41]	531[41]	14[41]	20[41]	3,300	5,310	...	...	Sudan, The
24	15.7	1,595	1,265	1	549[42]	883[42]	66[42]	106[42]	746	1,200	...	...	Suriname
—	—	—	—	1	30.7	49.4	0.09	0.1	—	—	—	—	Swaziland
430	2,881	61,320	75,528	48	6,997[20]	11,261[20]	196[20]	286[20]	1,275	2,052	5,708	8,334	Sweden
24	602.8	...	...	5	19,739	31,767	1,216	1,776	13	21	34	49	Switzerland
94	210.4	2,136	5,112	5	884	1,422	14	21	541	870	...	...	Syria
649	9,241.3	182,127	301,275	13	24,369	39,218	2,828	4,129	...	...	274	400	Taiwan
...	...	...	...	1	1,386	2,231	140	205	...	...	...	...	Tajikistan
43	48.5	1,249	2,721	11	114	184	2.0	2.9	...	...	...	...	Tanzania
351	1,194.5	42,495	74,579	25	23,826	38,345	1,145	1,671	2,300	3,701	...	...	Thailand
8	20.6	391	1,274	2	139.6	224.7	11.2	16.4	31	50	...	...	Togo
15	13.7	15	104	6	7	11	0.7	1.0	...	...	...	...	Tonga
53	17.5	9,622	10,961	2	1,783	2,869	38	55	...	...	...	...	Trinidad and Tobago
77	443.3	6,792	13,152	5	1,674	2,694	13	21	...	...	...	...	Tunisia
880	7,114.3	24,756	78,168	26	10,248[43]	16,492[43]	260[43]	380[43]	750	1,200	189	276	Turkey
...	...	...	...	1	970	1,562	98	143	240	387	5.5	8.0	Turkmenistan
6	16.0	...	...	1	...	...	...	...	...	...	...	...	Tuvalu
2	8.6	...	...	1	32.4	52.1	3	5	...	...	...	...	Uganda
...	...	77,004	7,116	12	1,225	1,972	18	27	2,734	4,400	3,973	5,800	Ukraine
276	1,491.7	88,153	9,595	6	12,150[8]	19,553[8]	978[8]	1,428[8]	...	...	...	...	United Arab Emirates
1,631	4,355	177,228	178,572	57	99,628	160,336	3,373	4,925	716	1,153	36,302	53,000	United Kingdom
509	18,585	392,076[45]	713,880[45]	834	619,500	997,000	18,116	26,449	25,778	41,485	356,188	520,026	United States
93	172.5	710[46]	1,450[46]	1	398	640	42	62	1,000	1,600	...	...	Uruguay
...	...	...	...	9	2,150	3,460	220	321	684	1,100	...	...	Uzbekistan
280	3,259.6	80	55	29	110.8	178.3	1.3	1.9	...	...	...	...	Vanuatu
271	1,355.4	101,435	17,932	20	3,600	5,800	438	639	4,400	7,100	8.9	13	Venezuela
230	872.8	303	1,510	12	2,380	3,831	67	98	11,000	17,702	1,339	1,955	Vietnam
1	...	105.5	648.3	2	...	...	...	...	...	...	...	...	Virgin Islands (U.S.)
—	—	...	...	—	—	—	—	—	...	...	...	...	West Bank
—	—	40	15	1	...	...	...	...	...	...	...	...	Western Sahara
40	13.7	1,936	7,829	12	978	1,574	22	32	...	...	...	...	Yemen
462[47]	5,173.1[47]	360	972	5	551	887	4,112	6,003	365	587	905	1,322	Yugoslavia
—	—	—	—	4	192	308	6.8	9.9	1,398	2,250	...	...	Zambia
—	—	—	—	7	544	875	24	35	...	...	...	...	Zimbabwe

transshipments. [26]El Al only. [27]Alitalia only. [28]Air Jamaica only. [29]Kenya Airways only. [30]International traffic only. [31]Peninsular Malaysia and Singapore. [32]Air Nauru only. [33]Includes Aruba. [34]Antillean Airlines only. [35]Air Caledonie only. [36]Philippine Air Lines only. [37]Sierra Leone Airlines international traffic only. [38]Solair only. [39]SAA only. [40]Coastal shipping only. [41]Sudan Airways only. [42]Suriname Airways only. [43]Turkish Airlines only. [44]British Railways only; excludes Northern Ireland. [45]Includes Puerto Rico. [46]Port of Montevideo only. [47]Data refer to Yugoslavia as constituted prior to 1991.

Communications

Virtually all the states of the world have a variety of communications media and services available to their citizens: book, periodical, and newspaper publishing (although only daily papers are included in this table); postal services; and telecommunication systems: radio and television broadcasting, telephones (fixed and mobile), facsimile (fax) machines, personal computers (PCs), and access to the Internet. Unfortunately, the availability of information about these services often runs behind the capabilities of the services themselves. Certain countries publish no official information; others publish data analyzed according to a variety of fiscal, calendar, religious, or other years; still others, while they possess such data almost simultaneously with the end of the business or calendar year, may not see them published except in company or parastatal reports of limited distribution. Even when such data are published in national statistical summaries, it may be only after a delay of up to several years.

The data also differ in their completeness and reliability. Figures for book production, for example, generally include all works published in separate bindings except advertising works, timetables, telephone directories, price lists, catalogs of businesses or exhibitions, musical scores, maps, atlases, and the like. The figures include government publications, school texts, theses, offprints, series works, and illustrated works, even those consisting principally of illustrations. Figures refer to works actually published during the year of survey, usually by a registered publisher, and deposited for copyright. A book is defined as a work of 49 or more pages; a work published simultaneously in more than one country is counted as having been published in each. A periodical is a publication issued at regular or stated intervals and, in Unesco's usage, directed to the general public. Newspaper statistics are especially difficult to collect and compare. Newspapers continually are founded, cease publication, merge, or change frequency of publication. Data on circulation are often incomplete, slow to be aggregated at the national level, or regarded as proprietary. In some countries no daily newspaper exists.

Post office statistics are compiled mainly from the Universal Postal Union's annual summary *Statistique des services postaux.* Postal services, unlike the other media discussed earlier, tend most often to be operated by

Communications

country	publishing (latest)							postal services				telecommunications	
	books		periodicals		daily newspapers			post offices, 1998				radio, 1997	
	number of titles	number of copies ('000)	number of titles	number of copies ('000)	number	total circulation ('000)	circulation per 1,000 persons	number	persons per office	pieces of mail handled ('000,000)	pieces handled per person	receivers (all types; '000)	receivers per 1,000 persons
Afghanistan	2,795	3,741	...	...	12	113	6	373	50,400	0.5	—	2,750	132
Albania	381	5,710	143	3,477	5	116	34	698[2]	4,840[2]	3.2	0.6	810	259
Algeria	670	...	48	803	5	1,080	38	3,223[1]	9,140[1]	736[1]	21[1]	7,100	242
American Samoa	...	...	...	...	2	5.0	93	...	...	...	...	57	929
Andorra	57	...	...	...	3	4.0	58	...	...	...	...	16	227
Angola	22	419	...	...	5	128	11	80[1]	145,000[1]	1.2	0.1	630	54
Antigua and Barbuda	...	...	...	...	1	6.0	91	16[4]	4,375[4]	...	...	36	542
Argentina	9,850	39,663	...	...	181	4,320	123	6,678[1]	5,340[1]	472[1]	11[1]	24,300	681
Armenia	396[5]	20,212[5]	44	541	11	85	23	...	...	0.7[6]	0.2[6]	850	239
Aruba	...	...	...	...	13	73	852	4	17,500	10	90	50	557
Australia	10,835	...	...	...	65	5,730	297	3,922	4,780	4,732	225	25,500	1,391
Austria	8,056[7]	...	2,481	...	17	2,382	294	2,436	3,320	3,133[1]	372[1]	6,080	751
Azerbaijan	542	2,643	49	801	6	210	28	1,673[1]	4,560[1]	12[1]	1.3[1]	175	23
Bahamas, The	...	...	...	...	3	28	100	138	2,170	61[8]	51[8]	215	739
Bahrain	40[5]	...	26	73	4	67	117	13	49,200	55	50	338	580
Bangladesh	...	...	...	...	37	1,117	9.0	9,093[1]	13,400[1]	589[1]	4.3[1]	6,150	50
Barbados	...	...	...	...	2	53	199	16	16,900	39	114	237	888
Belarus	3,809	59,073	155	3,765	10	1,899	187	3,852	2,640	709	67	3,020	292
Belgium	13,913	...	13,706	...	30	1,625	160	1,637[4]	6,200[4]	3,713	346	8,075	797
Belize	70	—	...	...	4	23.5	0.5	134[1]	1,720[1]	4.0[1]	12[1]	133	591
Benin	84[5]	42[5]	...	...	1	12	2.2	178	32,500	9.6	1.2	620	110
Bermuda	...	...	...	...	1	17	270	14[2]	4,500[2]	15[2]	240[2]	82	1,296
Bhutan	...	...	...	...	...	...	...	106[1]	17,540[1]	1.8[1]	0.7[1]	37	19
Bolivia	...	...	...	...	18	420	55	171	46,500	9.9	0.7	5,250	675
Bosnia and Herzegovina	...	...	...	...	3	518	146	210	20,050	9.8	1.6	940	267
Botswana	158[5]	...	14	177	1	40	27	180	8,720	54	26	237	154
Brazil	21,574[9]	104,397	...	...	380	6,472	55	11,713	13,800	5,223	32	71,000	434
Brunei	45[5]	56[5]	15	132	1	21	69	18	17,200	20	52	93	302
Bulgaria	4,840	20,317	772	1,740	17	2,145	253	3,303	2,500	156[2]	18[2]	4,510	537
Burkina Faso	12[5]	14[5]	37	24	4	14	1.3	85	130,000	7.3[10]	...	370	34
Burundi	...	...	...	...	1	20	3.2	28	225,000	16	1.3	440	69
Cambodia	...	...	...	...	...	...	...	56	204,000	3.2	0.2	1,340	128
Cameroon	...	...	...	...	2	91	6.7	377[1]	37,000[1]	6.1[1, 11]	0.4[1, 11]	2,270	163
Canada	19,900	...	1,400	37,108	107	4,718	158	18,607[8]	1,570[8]	10,715[10, 12]	370[10, 12]	32,300	1,067
Cape Verde	...	...	...	...	...	...	...	54	7,780	1.6	2.1	73	183
Central African Republic	...	...	...	...	3	6.0	1.8	35	99,710	...	...	283	83
Chad	...	...	...	...	1	2.0	0.2	36	201,900	13	1.0	1,670	236
Chile	2,469	4,095	417	3,450	52	1,411	99	710	20,870	343[11]	23[11]	5,180	354
China	100,951	5,945[13]	6,486	205,060	44	48,000	42	112,204	11,200	6,967[1]	5.5[1]	417,000	335
Colombia	1,481	11,314	...	...	37	1,800	49	1,354	30,200	116[3]	2.2[1]	21,000	524
Comoros	...	...	...	...	...	...	...	37	17,800	0.4	0.3	90	141
Congo, Dem. Rep. of the	64[5]	535[5]	...	...	9	124	2.7	497	98,870	...	...	18,030	376
Congo, Rep. of the	...	...	3	34	6	20	7.8	114[2]	22,720[2]	1.8[2]	0.5[2]	341	126
Costa Rica	963	...	...	...	6	320	88	134	24,900	32[1]	6.9[1]	980	261
Côte d'Ivoire	...	...	...	...	12	231	17	373	38,300	31	1.9	2,260	161
Croatia	1,718	...	352	6,357	10	515	114	1,168	3,910	299	60	1,510	337
Cuba	932	4,610	14	285	17	1,300	118	1,855	5,990	12[11]	1.1[11]	3,900	352
Cyprus	930	1,776	39	338	9	84	111	777	990	64	67	310	406
Czech Republic	10,244	...	1,168	81,387	21	2,620	256	3,369	3,050	803	72	8,270	803
Denmark	12,352	...	157	6,930	37	1,628	311	1,169	4,530	1,828[2]	335[2]	6,020	1,145
Djibouti	...	...	7	6.0	...	...	...	12	51,700	16[2]	12[2]	52	84
Dominica	...	...	...	...	...	...	...	64[8]	1,090[8]	2.9[2]	30[7]	46	647
Dominican Republic	...	...	...	...	12	416	52	239	33,900	9.8[14]	1.3[14]	1,440	178
East Timor	...	...	...	...	...	...	...	...	...	...	...	18	21
Ecuador	12[5]	19[5]	199	...	24	820	70	315	38,600	13	0.4	4,150	348
Egypt	2,215	92,353	258	2,373	17	2,400	38	7,488	8,810	317	3.3	20,500	317
El Salvador	...	...	45	774	5	278	48	289	20,900	18	1.9	2,750	465
Equatorial Guinea	...	...	...	...	1	2.0	4.9	23[8]	17,000[8]	...	...	180	428
Eritrea	106	420	...	...	...	...	...	37[4]	91,900[4]	2.3	0.5	345	100
Estonia	2,628	6,662	517	2,323	15	255	173	560	2,550	75	43	1,010	698

a single national service, to cover a country completely, and to record traffic data according to broadly similar schemes (although the details of *classes* of mail handled may differ). Some countries do not enumerate domestic traffic or may record only international traffic requiring handling charges.

Data for some kinds of telecommunications apparatus are relatively easy to collect; telephones, for example, must be installed, and service recorded so that it may be charged. But in most countries the other types of apparatus mentioned above may be purchased by anyone and used whenever desired. As a result, data on distribution and use of these types of apparatus may be collected in a variety of ways—on the basis of numbers of subscribers, licenses issued, periodic sample surveys, trade data, census or housing surveys, or private consumer surveys. Data on broadcast media refer to receivers; data on telephones to "main lines," or the lines connecting a subscriber's apparatus (fixed or mobile) to the public, switched net. Information on fax machines and PCs is estimated only, as noted above. "Users" refers to the number of people with access to computers connected to the Internet.

The *Statistical Yearbook* of Unesco contains extensive data on book, periodical, and newspaper publishing, and on radio and television broadcasting that have been collected from standardized questionnaires. The quality and recency of its data, however, depend on the completion and timely return of each questionnaire by national authorities. The commercially published annual *World Radio TV Handbook* (Andrew G. Sennitt, editor) is a valuable source of information on broadcast media and has complete and timely coverage. It depends on data received from broadcasters, but, because some do not respond, local correspondents and monitors are used in many countries, and some unconfirmed or unofficial data are included as estimates. The statistics on telecommunication apparatus and computers are derived mainly from the UN-affiliated International Telecommunication Union's *World Telecommunication Development Report* (annual).

... Not available.

— None, nil, or not applicable.

television, 1999		telephones, 1999		cellular phones, 1999		fax, 1999		personal computers, 1999		Internet users, 1999	country
receivers (all types; '000)	receivers per 1,000 persons	main lines ('000)	main lines per 1,000 persons	cellular subscriptions ('000)	subscriptions per 1,000 persons	receivers ('000)	receivers per 1,000 persons	units ('000)	units per 1,000 persons	number ('000)	
270[1]	12[1]	29	1.3	...	...	...	...	...	...	...	Afghanistan
430[3]	112[3]	140	36	11	2.9	18.3	4.8	20	5.2	2.5	Albania
3,300	107	1,600	52	72	2.3	7.0[1]	0.2[1]	180	5.8	20	Algeria
14[1]	212[1]	14	212	2.4	36	...	...	...	...	...	American Samoa
30[3]	400[3]	34	453	21	275	5.0[3]	67[3]	...	...	5.0[3]	Andorra
190	15	96	7.7	24	1.9	...	...	12	1.0	10	Angola
31[3]	413[3]	36	480	8.5	113	...	...	...	...	900	Antigua and Barbuda
10,600	290	7,357	201	4,434	121	87[3]	2.4[3]	1,800	49	...	Argentina
840[3]	238[3]	547	155	8.1	2.3	0.4[4]	0.1[4]	15[3]	4.2[3]	30	Armenia
20[1]	204[1]	36	367	12	122	0.5[2]	6.9[2]	...	...	...	Aruba
13,400	706	9,857	520	6,501	343	900[1]	48[1]	8,900	469	6,000	Australia
4,200[3]	514[3]	3,863	472	4,206	514	285[2]	35[2]	2,100	257	1,840	Austria
1,950[3]	253[3]	730	95	180	23	2.5[2]	0.1[2]	0.4[3]	0.1[3]	8.0[3]	Azerbaijan
67[1]	223[1]	111	369	16	53	0.5[2]	6.9[2]	...	...	...	Bahamas, The
270	406	165	240	133	200	6.9	10	93	140	30	Bahrain
940	7.4	433	3.4	149	1.2	40[2]	0.3[2]	130	1.0	50	Bangladesh
78	290	115	428	30	112	1.8[2]	6.7[2]	21	78	6.0	Barbados
3,300	321	2,638	257	22	2.2	24	2.3	...	...	50[3]	Belarus
5,300	522	5,100	502	3,193	315	190[4]	19[4]	3,200	315	1,400	Belgium
42	179	37	156	6.2	26	0.5[2]	2.6[2]	25	106	12	Belize
65[3]	11[3]	38[3]	6.5[3]	6.3[3]	1.1[3]	1.1[4]	0.2[4]	9	1.5	10	Benin
66[3]	1,031[3]	55	859	13[3]	196[3]	...	...	...	...	...	Bermuda
13	20	12	18	...	...	1.5[3]	2.3[3]	3	4.6	0.5	Bhutan
960	118	502	62	420	52	...	...	100	12	78	Bolivia
385[2]	100[2]	368	96	53	14	...	...	...	...	...	Bosnia and Herzegovina
33	20	124	77	120	74	3.5[1]	2.2[1]	50	31	12	Botswana
56,000	333	24,985	149	15,033	89	500[1]	3.0[1]	6,100	36	3,500	Brazil
205	637	79	246	66	205	2.0[2]	18[2]	20	62	25	Brunei
3,400[3]	411[3]	2,933	354	350	42	1.5[1]	1.8[1]	220	27	235	Bulgaria
120[3]	10[3]	47	4.1	5.0	0.4	0.1	0.0	12	1.0	4.0	Burkina Faso
100	15	19	2.9	0.8	0.1	4.0[4]	0.6[4]	...	...	2.0[3]	Burundi
98	9.0	28	2.5	89	8.1	3.0[1]	0.3[1]	13	1.2	4.0	Cambodia
480[3]	33[3]	95	6.4	4.2	0.3	...	...	40	2.7	20	Cameroon
21,450[1]	703[1]	19,957	655	6,876	226	1,075[1]	36[1]	11,000	361	11,000	Canada
2.0	4.8	47	112	8.1	19	1.0[4]	2.5[4]	...	...	5.0	Cape Verde
20	5.6	10	2.8	4.2	1.2	0.3[1]	0.1[1]	5	1.4	1.0	Central African Republic
10[3]	1.4[3]	10	1.3	...	...	0.2	0.03[1]	10	1.4	1.0	Chad
3,600	240	3,109	207	2,261	151	40[1]	2.7[1]	1,000	67	700	Chile
370,000	292	108,716	86	43,296	34	2,000[1]	1.6[1]	15,500	12	8,900	China
8,273	199	6,665	160	3,134	75	242	5.8	1,400	34	664	Colombia
1.0[1]	1.5[1]	6.0	8.9	...	...	0.2[2]	0.2[2]	...	...	...	Comoros
150[4]	3.0[4]	20	0.4	10[2]	0.2[2]	5.0[2]	0.1[2]	...	...	...	Congo, Dem. Rep. of the
33[1]	12[1]	22	7.7	3.4[3]	1.2[3]	0.1[2]	0.4[2]	...	...	...	Congo, Rep. of the
900	229	803	204	13,807	3,511	8.5[1]	2.2[1]	400	102	150	Costa Rica
1,000[3]	69[3]	219	15	257	18	...	...	80	5.5	20	Côte d'Ivoire
1,250	279	1,634	365	295	66	50[1]	11[1]	300	67	200	Croatia
2,750	246	434	39	5.1	0.5	...	...	110	9.9	35	Cuba
120	178	424	630	152	225	7.0[1]	11[1]	130	193	85	Cyprus
5,000	487	3,806	371	1,945	189	102	9.9	1,100	107	700	Czech Republic
3,300	621	3,638	685	2,629	495	250[2]	48[2]	2,200	414	1,500	Denmark
30	48	8.8	14	0.3	0.4	0.1	0.2	6	9.5	0.8	Djibouti
6.0[1]	79[1]	21	276	0.6[3]	8.6[3]	0.3[2]	4.0[2]	...	...	...	Dominica
770[1]	92[1]	820	98	420	50	2.5[2]	0.3[2]	...	...	...	Dominican Republic
...	...	...	...	...	...	...	...	...	...	...	East Timor
2,500[3]	201[3]	1,129	91	383	31	...	...	250	20	35	Ecuador
11,400	183	4,686	75	481	7.7	34	0.5	750	12	200	Egypt
1,177	191	468	76	383	62	...	...	100	16	40	El Salvador
4.0[1]	9.0[1]	5.6[3]	13[3]	0.3[3]	0.7[3]	0.1[2]	0.3[2]	...	...	...	Equatorial Guinea
60	16	27	7.4	92	25	0.8[2]	0.2[2]	...	...	0.9[3]	Eritrea
800	555	515	357	387	268	13	8.7	195	135	200	Estonia

Communications (continued)

country	publishing (latest): books: number of titles	books: number of copies ('000)	periodicals: number of titles	periodicals: number of copies ('000)	daily newspapers: number	daily newspapers: total circulation ('000)	daily newspapers: circulation per 1,000 persons	postal services: post offices, 1998: number	persons per office	pieces of mail handled ('000,000)	pieces handled per person	telecommunications: radio, 1997: receivers (all types; '000)	receivers per 1,000 persons
Ethiopia	240	674	…	…	4	86	1.5	534	112,000	27	0.3	11,750	202
Faroe Islands	…	…	…	…	1	6.0	136	42[1]	1,190[1]	10[1]	161[1]	26	582
Fiji	401	2,256	…	…	1	40	50	318	2,520	40	35	500	636
Finland	13,104	…	5,711	…	56	2,332	455	1,601	3,220	1,614	305	7,770	1,498
France	34,766	1,041	2,672	120,018	117	12,700	218	17,038	3,450	26,115	436	55,300	946
French Guiana	…	…	…	…	1	2.0	7.0	…	…	…	…	104	650
French Polynesia	…	…	…	…	4	24	108	97	2,370	28	102	128	574
Gabon	…	…	…	…	2	33	30	108	11,000	5.9	2.2	208	183
Gambia, The	14[15]	10[15]	10	885	1	2.0	1.7	…	…	…	…	196	165
Gaza Strip	…	…	…	…	…	…	…	…	…	…	…	…	…
Georgia	58[15]	834[5]	…	…	9	84	111	1,190[1]	4,560[1]	1,025[8, 11]	188[8, 11]	3,020	590
Germany	71,515	…	9,010	395,036	375	25,500	311	14,500	5,650	21,105[1]	249[1]	77,800	948
Ghana	28	648	121	774	4	250	14	1,010	18,800	225	3.4	4,400	236
Greece	4,225	…	…	…	156	1,622	153	1,225	8,590	392[4, 10]	37[4, 10]	5,020	475
Greenland	…	…	…	…	2	1.0	18	75[1]	800[1]	7.8[1]	72[1]	27	483
Grenada	…	…	4	89	1[16]	4.0[16]	45[16]	58[8]	1,550[8]	…	…	57	615
Guadeloupe	…	…	…	…	1	35	81	…	…	…	…	113	258
Guam	…	…	…	…	1	26	180	…	…	…	…	221	1,400
Guatemala	…	…	…	…	7	338	33	540[8]	19,700[8]	79[8]	7.7[8]	835	79
Guernsey	…	…	…	…	…	…	…	18	3,440	10[10]	169[10]	…	…
Guinea	…	…	3	5.0	…	…	…	96	47,400	7.9	0.4	357	49
Guinea-Bissau	…	…	…	…	1	6.0	5.4	10[4]	60,600[4]	311[2, 17]	0.3[2, 17]	49	43
Guyana	42[5]	508[5]	…	…	2	42	50	85[1]	10,000[1]	4.0[1, 11]	4.7[1, 11]	420	498
Haiti	…	…	…	…	4	20	2.5	85	90,000	1.2[17]	0.2[17]	415	53
Honduras	22	80	…	…	7	320	55	435[2]	13,700[2]	35[2]	3.0[2]	2,450	410
Hong Kong	…	…	598	…	52	5,000	800	125	53,500	1,254	175	3,700[4]	586[4]
Hungary	9,193	53,194	1,203	14,927	40	1,895	189	3,236	3,120	1,046	103	7,010	690
Iceland	1,527	…	938	384	5	145	535	94[4]	2,870[4]	73[4]	254[4]	260	950
India	11,903	…	…	…	3,037	22,969	27	153,021	6,240	16,394	16	116,000	120
Indonesia	4,018[15]	8,103[15]	115	4,173	69	4,665	23	20,139	10,200	758	3.4	31,500	155
Iran	15,073	87,861	318	6,166	32	1,651	24	13,715	4,490	274	4.2	17,000	263
Iraq	…	…	…	…	4	407	20	…	…	69	2.1	4,850	229
Ireland	…	…	…	…	6	543	153	1,912	1,940	748	170	2,550	697
Isle of Man	…	…	…	…	…	…	…	36	1,940	21[4, 6]	300[4, 6]	…	…
Israel	2,310[18]	9,368[18]	…	…	34	1,650	291	664	8,990	601	95	3,070	524
Italy	35,236	278,821	9,951	80,469	74	5,985	105	13,967[1]	4,120[1]	5,850[1]	99[1]	50,500	880
Jamaica	…	…	…	…	3	158	63	688	3,690	67	19	1,215	483
Japan	56,221[5]	400,013[5]	2,926	…	122	72,705	580	24,678	5,120	25,731[1]	202[1]	120,500	956
Jersey	…	…	…	…	…	…	…	23[1]	3,650[1]	62[1]	468[1]	…	…
Jordan	511	2,673[5]	31	43	4	250	45	687	9,170	118[1]	17[1]	1,660	271
Kazakhstan	1,226	21,014	…	…	3	500	30	3,580	4,700	201[2, 10]	0.01[2, 10]	6,470	395
Kenya	300[5]	452	…	…	4	263	9.4	1,033	28,100	413	14	3,070	108
Kiribati	…	…	…	…	…	…	…	25[1]	3,200[1]	1.9[1]	1.2[1]	17	212
Korea, North	…	…	…	…	3	4,500	200	…	…	…	…	3,360	146
Korea, South	30,487[5]	142,804[5]	…	…	60	18,000	394	3,610	12,900	3,631	77	47,500	1,039
Kuwait	196[19]	6,107	…	…	8	635	376	51[1]	35,500[1]	99[12]	68[12]	1,175	678
Kyrgyzstan	351	1,980	…	…	3	67	15	914[1]	5,080[1]	39[1, 10]	8.5[1, 10]	520	119
Laos	88[5]	995[5]	…	…	3	18	4.0	106	48,700	5.2	0.9	730	145
Latvia	1,965	7,734	213	1,660	24	616	246	978	2,500	37	12	1,760	715
Lebanon	…	…	…	…	15	435	141	268[1]	11,700[1]	3.9[1]	1.2[1]	2,850	907
Lesotho	…	…	…	…	2	15	7.6	157	13,100	64	16	104	52
Liberia	…	…	…	…	6	35	16	34[4]	8,260[4]	…	…	790	329
Libya	26	2,645	…	…	4	71	14	342	15,600	39	3.5	1,350	259
Liechtenstein	…	…	…	…	2	19	606	12[4]	2,500[4]	17[8]	0.6[8]	21	658
Lithuania	3,645	14,915	269	…	19	344	92	978[1]	3,790[1]	51	11	1,900	513
Luxembourg	681	…	508	…	5	135	327	106	3,960	169	340	285	683
Macau	67	99	16	…	10	197	448	17	25,300	19	30	160	356
Macedonia	892	2,496	74	347	3	41	19	294	6,800	27	11	410	206
Madagascar	119	296	55	108	5	66	4.6	764	19,700	26	1.5	3,050	209
Malawi	117[5, 20]	9,174[5, 20]	…	…	1	25	2.6	314	34,100	44	3.4	2,600	258
Malaysia	5,843	29,040	25	996	42	3,345	163	1,382	7,490	993[6]	96[6]	9,100	434
Maldives	…	…	…	…	2	5.0	18	249[1]	1,080[1]	2.5	5.9	34	129
Mali	14[5]	28[5]	…	…	3	12	1.2	124	86,200	3.4	0.2	570	55
Malta	404	…	359	…	2	48	130	51[11]	7,450[11]	14[11]	34[11]	255	669
Marshall Islands	…	…	…	…	…	…	…	…	…	…	…	…	…
Martinique	…	…	…	…	1	30	78	…	…	…	…	82	213
Mauritania	…	…	…	…	2	1.0	0.5	61	41,500	4.2	0.5	360	146
Mauritius	80	163	62	…	6	85	76	101	11,500	63	47	420	371
Mayotte	…	…	…	…	…	…	…	…	…	…	…	50[4]	427[4]
Mexico	…	…	158	13,097	295	9,030	97	9,432	10,600	1,133	9.4	31,000	329
Micronesia	…	…	…	…	…	…	…	…	…	…	…	70[4]	667[4]
Moldova	921	2,779	76	196	4	261	59	1,276	3,430	41	8.1	3,220	736
Monaco	41	722	3	38	1	8.0	263	…	…	…	…	34	1,039
Mongolia	285[5]	959[5]	45	6,361	4	68	27	339[1]	7,050[1]	1.1[1]	0.3[1]	360	142
Morocco	918	1,836	…	…	22	704	27	1,469	18,900	240	7.7	6,640	247
Mozambique	…	3,490	…	…	2	49	2.7	353	47,900	6.8	0.1	730	40
Myanmar (Burma)	3,660	4,038	…	…	5	449	10	1,238	37,500	88[2]	1.9[2]	4,200	96
Namibia	106	…	…	…	4	30	19	115	14,400	66[10]	4.0[10]	232	143
Nauru	…	…	…	…	…	…	…	1[1]	10,000[1]	…	…	7.0	609
Nepal	…	…	…	…	29	250	11	4,156	5,260	29[4, 6]	1.4[4, 6]	840	38
Netherlands, The	34,067	…	367	19,283	38	4,753	305	2,387	6,580	7,009[21]	447[21]	15,300	980
Netherlands Antilles	…	…	…	…	6	70	334	16	12,625	…	…	217	1,031
New Caledonia	…	…	…	…	3	24	127	54	3,700	21	75	107	527
New Zealand	…	…	126	3,991	23	804	223	…	…	…	…	3,750	997
Nicaragua	…	…	…	…	4	135	30	183	26,300	8.3	1.2	1,240	265

television, 1999		telephones, 1999		cellular phones, 1999		fax, 1999		personal computers, 1999		Internet users, 1999	country
receivers (all types; '000)	receivers per 1,000 persons	main lines ('000)	main lines per 1,000 persons	cellular subscriptions ('000)	subscriptions per 1,000 persons	receivers ('000)	receivers per 1,000 persons	units ('000)	units per 1,000 persons	number ('000)	
350	5.7	195	3.2	6.7	0.1	3.1	0.1	45	0.7	8.0	Ethiopia
15[1]	333	25	556	11	244	...	...	...	...	...	Faroe Islands
89	110	82	102	23	29	2.8	3.5	40	50	7.5	Fiji
3,320	643	2,850	552	3,364	651	198[1]	38[1]	1,860	360	2,143	Finland
36,500	623	34,100	582	21,434	366	2,800[1]	47[1]	13,000	222	5,370	France
30[1]	172[1]	49	282	18	103	...	...	...	...	...	French Guiana
43	186	52	225	22	95	3.0[3]	13[3]	...	...	5.0[3]	French Polynesia
300	251	38	32	8.9	7.4	0.5[1]	0.4[1]	10	8.4	3.0	Gabon
4.0	3.2	29	23	5.3	4.2	1.1[1]	0.9[1]	10	7.9	3.0	Gambia, The
...	...	...	...	...	...	...	...	...	...	...	Gaza Strip
2,580[3]	473[3]	672	123	102	19	0.5[8]	0.1[8]	0.7[3]	0.1[3]	20[3]	Georgia
47,660	580	48,500	590	23,470	286	6,500	79	24,400	297	14,400	Germany
2,266	115	159	8.1	70	3.6	5.0	0.3	50	2.5	20	Ghana
5,100	480	5,611	528	3,904	367	40	3.8	640	60	750	Greece
22[1]	393[1]	26	464	14	250	...	...	...	...	...	Greenland
33	355	29	312	2.0	22	0.3	3.1	...	...	...	Grenada
118	262	201	447	88	196	3.4[2]	8.1[2]	...	...	...	Guadeloupe
106	646	78	476	20	122	3.4	8.1	...	...	...	Guam
660[3]	60[3]	611	55	338	30	10	1.0	110	9.9	65	Guatemala
...	...	51	823	15	242	0.7	11	...	...	...	Guernsey
343	44	46	5.9	25	3.2	3.2	0.4	27	3.5	5.0	Guinea
...	...	8.1[3]	6.8[3]	...	...	0.5[3]	0.4[3]	...	...	1.5[3]	Guinea-Bissau
60	70	64	75	2.8	3.3	...	...	21	25	3.0	Guyana
38	4.7	70	8.7	25	3.1	...	...	...	...	...	Haiti
600	95	379	60	78	12	...	...	60	9.5	20	Honduras
2,884[3]	429[3]	3,869	576	4,275	636	390	58	2,000	298	2,430	Hong Kong
4,500	448	3,726	371	1,628	162	180	18	750	75	600	Hungary
145	520	189	677	173	620	4.1[12]	15[12]	100	358	150	Iceland
75,000	75	26,511	27	1,884	1.9	150[1]	0.2[1]	3,300	3.3	2,800	India
30,000	143	6,080	29	2,221	11	185	0.9	1,900	9.1	900	Indonesia
10,500	157	8,371	125	490	7.3	30	0.5	3,500	52	100	Iran
1,750[1]	78[1]	675	30	...	...	...	...	...	...	...	Iraq
1,505	406	1,770	478	1,655	447	100[1]	27[1]	1,500	405	679	Ireland
...	...	...	...	...	...	...	...	...	...	...	Isle of Man
2,000	328	2,877	471	2,880	472	140	25	1,500	246	800	Israel
28,000[3]	488[3]	26,506	462	30,296	528	1,800	31	11,000	192	7,000	Italy
480[3]	188[3]	510	199	144	56	1.6[12]	0.6[12]	110	43	60	Jamaica
01,000	719	70,530	558	56,846	449	16,000[1]	126[1]	36,300	287	27,060	Japan
...	...	69[3]	742[3]	18[3]	194[3]	0.7	8.0	...		1.0	Jersey
540	83	565	87	118	18	52[3]	8.0[3]	90	14	120	Jordan
3,890[3]	239[3]	1,760	108	50	3.1	2.0	0.1	...	...	70[3]	Kazakhstan
660	22	305	10	24	0.8	3.8	0.1	125	4.2	35	Kenya
10[1]	122[1]	3.5	43	0.2	2.4	0.2	2.5	...	...	...	Kiribati
1,200	51	1,100	46	...	...	3	0.1	...	...	...	Korea, North
16,896	361	20,518	438	23,443	500	400	8.6	8,519	182	10,860	Korea, South
910	480	456	240	300	158	60	32	230	121	100	Kuwait
220[3]	47[3]	356	76	2.6	0.6	...	...	...	...	10[3]	Kyrgyzstan
51	10	34	6.4	9.0	1.7	0.5[8]	0.1[8]	12	2.3	2.0	Laos
1,808	741	731	300	274	112	0.9[2]	0.3[2]	200	82	105	Latvia
1,120[3]	346[3]	650	201	627	194	3.0[12]	1.1[12]	150	46	200	Lebanon
33	16	21[3]	10[3]	10[3]	4.6[3]	0.6[2]	0.3[2]	...	...	1.0	Lesotho
70[1]	24[1]	6.6	2.3	...	...	...	...	...	...	...	Liberia
730[1]	133[1]	550	101	20[3]	3.6[3]	...	...	...	...	...	Libya
12[1]	375[1]	18	563	10	297	...	...	...	...	...	Liechtenstein
1,555	420	1,153	312	332	90	6.2[1]	1.7[1]	220	59	103	Lithuania
165[3]	385[3]	311	725	209	487	30	70	170	396	75	Luxembourg
125	286	178	407	88	201	6.3	14	60	137	40	Macau
500[3]	249[3]	471	234	48	24	3.0	1.5	2	1.1	30	Macedonia
340[3]	22[3]	50	3.2	13[3]	0.8[3]	...	...	30	1.9	8.0	Madagascar
27	2.5	41	3.9	22	2.1	1.3	0.1	10	0.9	10	Malawi
3,800	174	4,431	203	2,990	137	175[3]	8.0[3]	1,500	69	1,500	Malaysia
11	40	22	79	2.9	10	3.5[2]	14[2]	5	18	3.0	Maldives
130[3]	12[3]	27[3]	2.5[3]	4.0[3]	0.4[3]	...	...	11	1.0	10	Mali
212	549	198	513	38	98	6.0[4]	16[4]	70	181	30	Malta
...	...	3.7[3]	60[3]	0.3[3]	4.8[3]	...	...	...	...	...	Marshall Islands
66[1]	168[1]	172	439	102	260	20[2]	52[2]	36[2]	93[2]	...	Martinique
247	96	16	6.2	...	...	3.3	1.3	70	27	13	Mauritania
265	230	257	223	102	89	32	28	110	96	55	Mauritius
3.5[4]	30[4]	10	75	...	...	...	...	...	...	...	Mayotte
26,000	267	10,927	112	7,732	79	285[1]	2.9[1]	4,300	44	1,822	Mexico
2.4	21	9.1[3]	78[3]	...	...	0.5[3]	4.3[3]	...	...	2.0[3]	Micronesia
1,300	297	555	127	18	4.1	0.7	0.2	35	8.0	25	Moldova
25[1]	758[1]	33[3]	1,000[3]	12[3]	364[3]	...	...	...	...	...	Monaco
152[3]	58[3]	103	39	34	13	7.9	3.0	24	9.2	6.0	Mongolia
4,600	165	1,467	53	374	13	18[1]	0.6[1]	300	11	50	Morocco
95	5	78	4.0	12	0.6	7.2[8]	0.4[8]	50	2.6	15	Mozambique
323	7.2	249	5.5	11	0.2	2.5	0.1	50	1.1	0.5	Myanmar (Burma)
65	38	108	64	30	18	...	...	50	29	6.0	Namibia
0.5[1]	0.1[1]	1.7[3]	0.2[3]	0.8[3]	0.1[3]	...	...	...	...	...	Nauru
150	6.7	253	11	5.5	0.2	8.0	0.4	60	2.7	35	Nepal
9,500	600	9,610	607	6,900	436	600[1]	38[1]	5,700	360	3,000	Netherlands, The
69[1]	321[1]	79	367	16[3]	74[3]	...	...	...	...	...	Netherlands Antilles
101	481	51	243	25	119	2.2[8]	12[8]	...	...	5.0[4]	New Caledonia
1,975	518	1,889	496	1,395	366	65[2]	18[2]	1,250	328	700	New Zealand
340	69	150	30	44	8.9	...	...	40	8.1	20	Nicaragua

Communications (continued)

country	publishing (latest)							postal services				telecommunications	
	books		periodicals		daily newspapers			post offices, 1998				radio, 1997	
	number of titles	number of copies ('000)	number of titles	number of copies ('000)	number	total circulation ('000)	circulation per 1,000 persons	number	persons per office	pieces of mail handled ('000,000)	pieces handled per person	receivers (all types; '000)	receivers per 1,000 persons
Niger	5[5]	11[5]	...	...	1	2	0.2	53	190,000	3.4	0.3	680	70
Nigeria	1,314	18,800	...	...	25	2,740	27	3,971	26,800	391	2.0	23,500	226
Northern Mariana Islands	...	...	...	...	...	...	...	...	...	...	...	11[4]	190[4]
Norway	6,900[7, 18]	...	8,017	...	83	2,578	593	1,534[1]	210[1]	2,524[1]	555[1]	4,030	917
Oman	7[5]	21[5]	15	...	4	63	27	90[2]	23,700[2]	43	7.1	1,400	607
Pakistan	124	714	...	...	264	2,840	22	13,294	9,820	413	2.9	13,500	94
Palau	...	...	...	...	...	...	...	...	...	...	...	12	663
Panama	...	...	...	...	7	166	62	176	15,700	18	4.4	815	299
Papua New Guinea	122	...	...	...	2	65	15	108[22]	39,800[22]	39[22]	10[22]	410	91
Paraguay	152	...	...	...	5	213	43	326	16,000	4.6	0.5	925	182
Peru	612	1,836	...	...	74	2,000	85	963	25,800	43	1.3	6,650	273
Philippines	1,507	14,718[5]	1,570	9,468	47	5,700	82	3,023[8]	22,600[8]	3,205[4]	12[4]	11,500	161
Poland	14,104	80,306	5,260	75,358	55	4,351	113	7,836	4,930	2,503	63	20,200	522
Portugal	7,868[9]	26,942	984	10,208	27	740	75	3,712	2,660	1,201	117	3,020	306
Puerto Rico	...	...	...	...	3	475	127	...	...	...	...	2,700	714
Qatar	209[15]	2,205	11	47	5	90	161	26	20,800	20[11]	38[11]	256	450
Réunion	69	...	...	...	3	55	83	...	...	...	...	173	257
Romania	7,199	38,374	987	...	69	6,800	297	6,324	3,560	327	14	7,200	319
Russia	36,237	421,387	2,751	387,832	285	15,517	105	43,900[1]	3,350[1]	5,614[1, 6]	38[1, 6]	61,500	417
Rwanda	...	...	15	101	1	0.5	0.1	39	169,000	3.8	0.4	601	101
St. Kitts and Nevis	...	...	10	44	...	...	...	7	5,710	2.6	46	28	701
St. Lucia	...	...	...	...	...	...	...	63	2,380	2.3[10]	15[10]	111	746
St. Vincent and the Grenadines	...	...	...	...	1	1.0	9.0	41[1]	2,680[1]	...	...	77	690
Samoa	...	...	...	...	...	...	...	38	4,470	0.9	3.0	178	1,035
San Marino	...	...	15	9	3	2.0	72	10[4]	3,000[4]	...	...	16	610
São Tomé and Príncipe	...	...	...	...	...	...	...	18	7,780	0.3	0.6	38	272
Saudi Arabia	3,900[5]	14,493[5, 20]	471	...	13	1,105	59	1,421	14,200	1,246	45	6,250	321
Senegal	...	...	...	...	1	45	5.3	134	69,200	12	0.7	1,240	141
Seychelles	...	...	...	...	1	3.0	46	5	16,000	5.2	49	42	560
Sierra Leone	...	...	...	...	1	20	4.7	54[2]	83,500[2]	1.1[2]	0.1[2]	1,121	253
Singapore	...	...	...	...	8	1,095	324	939	4,120	772[1]	184[1]	2,550	744
Slovakia	3,800	6,139	424	8,725	19	989	185	1,728	3,120	518	90	3,120	581
Slovenia	3,441	6,267	784	...	7	397	206	545	3,630	387	189	805	403
Solomon Islands	...	...	...	...	...	...	...	127	3,150	4.3[2]	11[2]	57	141
Somalia	...	...	...	...	2	10	1.2	...	...	...	...	470	53
South Africa	5,418	31,349	11	2,149	17	1,288	34	2,449	17,200	2,170[6]	52[6]	13,750	355
Spain	46,330	192,019	...	...	94	3,931	99	4,093	9,620	4,565	112	13,100	331
Sri Lanka	4,115	19,650	...	...	9	530	29	4,282	4,380	463	23	3,850	211
Sudan, The	...	...	...	...	5	737	27	491	57,600	4.4[4]	0.1[4]	7,550	272
Suriname	47[5]	21[5]	...	...	4	50	116	33	12,400	...	...	300	728
Swaziland	...	...	...	...	3	24	27	60[1]	15,200[1]	21[1]	18[1]	155	168
Sweden	13,496	...	373	19,242	94	3,933	446	1,720[4]	5,140[4]	4,570[4]	503[4]	8,250	932
Switzerland	15,371	...	60	4,561	88	2,383	330	3,630[4]	1,950[4]	4,230[8]	601[8]	7,100	979
Syria	598	310[5]	30	192	8	287	20	619	25,200	19	1.0	4,150	278
Taiwan	...	...	...	...	...	4,000	188	...	...	...	...	8,620[4]	402[4]
Tajikistan	132[5]	997[5]	11	130	2	120	20	706[1]	8,570[1]	3.0[1]	0.4[1]	850	143
Tanzania	172[5]	364[5]	...	...	3	120	3.9	612	52,400	55	1.3	8,800	280
Thailand	8,142	...	1,522	...	30	3,800	65	4,265	14,300	1,315	21	13,959	234
Togo	...	...	...	...	1	15	3.6	50[1]	86,400[1]	8.3[1]	0.7[1]	940	219
Tonga	...	...	...	...	1	7.0	71	1.8[12]	55,600[12]	4.0[12]	40[12]	61	400
Trinidad and Tobago	26	30	...	...	4	156	121	245	5,220	30[2]	16[2]	680	533
Tunisia	720	6,000[20]	170	1,748	8	280	31	947[2]	9,740[2]	117[2]	12[2]	2,060	224
Turkey	6,546	...	3,554	...	57	6,845	111	16,984	3,740	1,088	16	11,300	178
Turkmenistan	450[5]	5,493[5]	...	...	...	...	...	1,673[4]	2,730[4]	27[4]	6.0[4]	1,225	289
Tuvalu	...	...	...	...	...	...	...	...	...	...	...	4.0	384
Uganda	288	2,229[18]	26	158	2	40	2.1	313	67,200	18[1]	0.5[1]	2,600	130
Ukraine	6,225	68,876	717	2,521	44	2,780	54	15,227	3,320	374	6.3	45,050	882
United Arab Emirates	293[20]	5,117[20]	80	922	7	384	170	243	11,190	182	39	820	355
United Kingdom	107,263	...	...	...	99	19,332	332	18,760	3,130	19,556	325	84,500	1,443
United States	68,175	...	11,593	...	1,520	59,990	212	38,159	7,090	197,688	729	575,000	2,116
Uruguay	934	1,970	...	...	36	950	296	942	3,490	16	6.0	1,970	603
Uzbekistan	1,003	30,914	81	684	3	75	3.0	3,044[1]	7,700[1]	12[1]	0.4[1]	10,800	465
Vanuatu	...	...	...	...	...	...	...	...	...	...	...	62	350
Venezuela	3,468[5]	7,420[5]	...	...	86	4,600	206	407	57,600	141	5.1	10,750	472
Vietnam	5,581	83,000	338	2,710	10	300	4.0	3,075	25,200	...	...	8,200	107
Virgin Islands (U.S.)	...	...	...	...	3	42	326	9[1]	2,000[1]	3.6[8, 11]	0.2[8, 11]	107	1,119
West Bank	...	...	...	...	...	...	...	...	...	...	...	...	...
Western Sahara	...	...	...	...	...	...	...	...	...	...	...	56	211
Yemen	...	...	...	...	3	230	15	265	64,400	5.5	0.1	1,050	64
Yugoslavia	5,367	16,669	395	...	18	1,128	110	1,783	5,940	242	19	3,150	296
Zambia	...	...	...	...	3	114	14	195	45,000	16	0.8	1,030	120
Zimbabwe	232	...	28	680	2	209	19	296	42,800	137	9.4	1,140	102

television, 1999		telephones, 1999		cellular phones, 1999		fax, 1999		personal computers, 1999		Internet users, 1999	country
receivers (all types; '000)	receivers per 1,000 persons	main lines ('000)	main lines per 1,000 persons	cellular subscriptions ('000)	subscriptions per 1,000 persons	receivers ('000)	receivers per 1,000 persons	units ('000)	units per 1,000 persons	number ('000)	
285	27	18[3]	1.7[3]	1.3[3]	0.1[3]	0.3[2]	0.0[2]	4	0.4	3.0	Niger
7,200[3]	66[3]	410	3.8	20[3]	0.2[3]	6.8[2]	0.1[2]	700	6.4	100	Nigeria
...	...	25	481	2.9	56	...	...	...	...	...	Northern Mariana Islands
2,900	648	3,176	709	2,745	613	220[1]	49[1]	2,000	447	2,000	Norway
1,415	575	220	89	121	49	6.4[1]	2.6[1]	65	26	50	Oman
16,000	119	2,986	22	279	2.1	268	2.0	580	4.3	80	Pakistan
...	...	...	...	...	...	...	...	...	...	...	Palau
530[3]	188[3]	462	164	242	86	0.8	0.2	90	32	45	Panama
60	13	60	13	7.1	1.5	0.8[8]	0.2[8]	...	...	2.0	Papua New Guinea
1,100	205	297	55	436	81	1.7[12]	0.4[12]	60	11	20	Paraguay
3,700	147	1,689	67	1,013	40	15[2]	0.6[2]	900	36	400	Peru
8,200	110	2,892	39	2,850	38	50[3]	0.7[3]	1,260	17	500	Philippines
15,000	387	10,175	263	3,957	102	55[2]	1.4[2]	2,400	62	2,100	Poland
5,600	560	4,230	423	4,671	467	70	7.0	930	93	700	Portugal
1,250[3]	321[3]	1,295	333	814	209	543[12]	149[12]	...	...	200[3]	Puerto Rico
490[3]	832[3]	155	263	84	143	10[3]	18[3]	80	136	24	Qatar
127[1]	184[1]	268	388	50[3]	72[3]	1.9[2]	2.9[2]	...	...	...	Réunion
7,000	312	3,740	167	1,356	61	21[2]	0.9[2]	600	27	600	Romania
62,000[3]	421[3]	30,949	210	1,371	9.3	53[3]	0.4[3]	5,500	37	2,700	Russia
10[1]	1.7[1]	13	1.8	11	1.5	0.5[2]	0.1[2]	...	...	...	Rwanda
10[1]	256[1]	20	513	0.7	18	...	...	...	...	...	St. Kitts and Nevis
32[1]	208[1]	44	286	1.9[3]	12[3]	...	...	...	...	...	St. Lucia
18[1]	159[1]	24	212	1.4	12	...	...	...	...	...	St. Vincent and the Grenadines
9.0[3]	51[3]	8.5[3]	48[3]	3.0	17	0.5[3]	2.8[3]	1	5.6	0.5	Samoa
9.0[1]	346[1]	20	769	10	369	...	...	...	...	...	San Marino
23[1]	160[1]	4.5	31	...	...	0.2[2]	15[2]	...	...	...	São Tomé and Príncipe
5,500	263	2,706	129	837	40	150[2]	8.2[2]	1,200	57	300	Saudi Arabia
370[3]	40[3]	166	18	88	9.5	...	...	140	15	30	Senegal
16	200	19	238	16	200	0.6	7.5	10	125	5.0	Seychelles
60[3]	13[3]	17[3]	3.6[3]	511	108	2.5	0.5	0.1	0.02	2.0[3]	Sierra Leone
1,200	308	1,877	482	1,631	419	100[3]	32[3]	1,700	437	950	Singapore
2,250	417	1,655	307	918	170	54[3]	10[3]	590	109	600	Slovakia
710[3]	357[3]	752	378	614	309	21[3]	11[3]	500	251	250	Slovenia
6.0[3]	14[3]	8.1	19	1.1	2.6	0.8	1.9	18	42	2.0	Solomon Islands
135[1]	14[1]	15	1.6	...	...	...	...	...	...	...	Somalia
5,450[3]	124[3]	5,493	125	5,269	120	150[1]	3.4[1]	2,400	55	1,820	South Africa
22,000	547	16,480	410	12,300	306	700[4]	17[4]	4,800	119	4,652	Spain
1,900	102	670	36	228	12	11[8]	0.6[8]	105	5.6	65	Sri Lanka
5,000	173	251	8.7	13	0.5	25	0.9	05	2.0	5.0	Sudan, The
98[3]	236[3]	71	171	18	43	...	...	...	...	10[3]	Suriname
110	112	31	32	14	14	1.2[4]	1.2[4]	1	0.7	5.0	Swaziland
4,700[3]	530[3]	5,889	665	5,165	583	450[4]	51[4]	4	0.5	3,666	Sweden
3,700	518	4,992	699	2,935	411	207[4]	29[4]	3,300	462	1,427	Switzerland
1,070	66	1,600	99	4.0	0.2	22	1.4	230	14	20	Syria
9,220	417	12,044	545	4,727[3]	216[3]	430[8]	20[8]	4,353	197	4,540	Taiwan
2,000	328	212	35	0.6	0.1	2.1	0.3	...	...	2.0	Tajikistan
690	21	150	4.6	51	1.6	2.0[12]	0.1[12]	80	2.4	25	Tanzania
17,600	289	5,216	86	2,339	38	150[1]	2.5[1]	1,382	23	800	Thailand
100	22	38	8.4	17	3.8	18	4.0	80	18	15	Togo
2.0[1]	20[1]	9.1	93	0.1	1.0	0.2[2]	2.0[2]	...	...	...	Tonga
1,430	1,107	279	216	39	30	5.0[3]	3.9[3]	70	54	30	Trinidad and Tobago
1,800	190	850	90	55	5.8	31[1]	3.3[1]	145	15	30	Tunisia
21,500	332	18,054	278	8,122	125	108[1]	1.7[1]	2,200	34	1,500	Turkey
865[3]	197[3]	359	82	4.0	0.9	...	...	...	...	2.0	Turkmenistan
0.1[4]	9.1[4]	0.6	55	...	...	...	...	...	...	...	Tuvalu
580[3]	27[3]	57	2.6	56	2.6	3.0[4]	0.1[4]	55	2.5	25	Uganda
21,000[3]	415[3]	10,074	199	216	4.3	48	0.9	800	16	200	Ukraine
740	252	975	332	832	283	18	6.1	300	102	400	United Arab Emirates
38,800	652	33,750	567	27,185	457	1,992[4]	33[4]	18,000	303	12,500	United Kingdom
233,000	844	183,521	664	86,047	312	21,000[1]	78.0[1]	141,000	510	74,100	United States
1,760	531	897	271	316	95	0.6	3.6	330	100	330	Uruguay
6,700	276	1,599	66	40	1.6	2.2	0.1	...	...	7.5[3]	Uzbekistan
2.0[1]	11[1]	5.5	30	0.3	1.6	0.6[2]	3.6[2]	...	...	...	Vanuatu
4,300[3]	181[3]	2,586	109	3,400	143	70[1]	3.0[1]	1,000	42	525	Venezuela
14,500	184	2,106	27	329	4.2	31	0.4	700	8.9	100	Vietnam
6.8[1]	57[1]	67	562	25[3]	211[3]	...	...	...	...	...	Virgin Islands (U.S.)
...	...	222	72	40[1]	14[1]	...	...	...	...	...	West Bank
6.0[4]	24[4]	...	...	...	...	...	...	...	...	...	Western Sahara
5,000	286	291	17	28	1.6	2.8[2]	0.2[2]	30	1.7	10	Yemen
2,900[3]	273[3]	2,281	214	606	57	20	1.9	220	21	80	Yugoslavia
1,300	145	83	9.2	29	3.2	1.0	0.1	65	7.2	15	Zambia
2,074	180	239	21	174	15	4.1[3]	0.4[3]	150	13	20	Zimbabwe

[1]1997. [2]1995. [3]1998. [4]1996. [5]First editions only. [6]Domestic and foreign-dispatched only. [7]Not including school textbooks. [8]1994. [9]Including reprints. [10]Domestic only. [11]Foreign-dispatched and foreign-received only. [12]1993. [13]Millions of copies. [14]1985. [15]School textbooks and government publications only. [16]1980. [17]Foreign-received only. [18]Not including government publications. [19]Government publications only. [20]School textbooks only. [21]Domestic and foreign-received only.

Trade: external

The following table presents comparative data on the international, or foreign, trade of the countries of the world. The table analyzes data for both imports and exports in two ways: (1) into several major commodity groups defined in accordance with the United Nations system called the Standard International Trade Classification (SITC) and (2) by direction of trade for each country with major world trading blocs and partners. These commodity groupings are defined by the SITC code numbers beneath the column headings. The single-digit numbers represent broad SITC categories (in the SITC, called "sections"); the double-digit numbers represent subcategories ("divisions") of the single-digit categories (27 is a subcategory of 2); the three-digit number is a subcategory ("group") of the double-digit (667 is a subcategory of 66). Where a plus or minus sign is used before one of these SITC numbers, the SITC category or subcategory is being added to or subtracted from the aggregate implied by the total of the preceding sections. The SITC commodity aggregations used here are listed in the table at the end of this headnote. The full SITC commodity breakdown—some 3,118 basic headings—is presented in the 1986 United Nations publication *Standard International Trade Classification, Revision 3.*

The SITC was developed by the United Nations through its Statistical Commission as an outgrowth of the need for a standard system of aggregating commodities of external trade to provide international comparability of foreign trade statistics. The United Nations Statistical Commission has defined external merchandise trade as "all goods whose movement into or out of the customs area of a country compiling the statistics adds to or subtracts from the material resources of the country." Goods passing through a country for transport only are excluded, but goods entering for reexport, or deposited (as in a bonded warehouse, or free trade area) for reimport, are included. Statistics in this table refer only to goods and exclude purely financial transactions that are covered in the "Finance" and "National product and accounts" tables. Gold for fabrication (*e.g.*, as jewelry) is included; monetary and reserve gold are excluded.

For purposes of comparability of data, total value of imports and exports is given in this table in U.S. dollars. Conversions from currencies other than U.S. dollars are determined according to the average market rates for the year for which data are supplied; these are mainly as calculated by the International Monetary Fund (IMF) or other official sources. The commodity categories are given in terms of percentages of the total value of the country's import or export trade (with the exclusions noted above). Value is based on transaction value: for imports, the value at which the goods were purchased by the importer plus the cost of transportation and insurance to the frontier of the importing country (c.i.f. [cost, insurance,

Trade: external

country	year	imports												
		total value ('000,000 U.S.$)	Standard International Trade Classification (SITC) categories (%)							direction of trade (%)				
			food and agricultural raw materials (0 + 1 + 2 – 27 – 28 + 4)	mineral ores and concentrates (27 + 28 + 667)	fuels and other energy (3)	manufactured goods: total[a] (5 + 6 – 667 + 7 + 8 + 9)	of which chemicals and related products (5)	of which machinery and transport equipment (7)	of which other[a] (6 – 667 + 8 + 9)	from European Union (EU)[b]	from United States	from Eastern Europe[c]	from Japan	from all other[d]
Afghanistan	1996[1]	359.0	—19.9[2]—		2.7	77.4[3]	—	15.2	62.2[3]	16.5[4]	1.1[4]	8.3[4]	25.3[4]	48.8[4]
Albania	1997	950.2	28.4	0.5	3.2	68.0	6.9	21.3	39.7	83.4	0.2	4.9	—	11.5
Algeria	1996	9,105.6	34.2	0.2	1.2	64.4	8.7	30.8	24.9	62.5	10.2	2.3	2.6	22.3
American Samoa	1993[6]	427.5	—63.1[2]—		8.1	28.8[3]	0.2	5.5	23.1[3]	0.2[7]	73.4[7]	—[7]	8.5[7]	17.9[7]
Andorra	1998	1,080.5	24.2	3.9	3.5	68.4	10.7	25.8	31.9	88.2	2.3	0.2	3.2	6.1
Angola	1994	1,432.0	—33.6[2, 5]—		0.3[5]	66.1[3, 5]	9.1[5]	30.1[5]	26.9[3, 5]	50.0[4]	15.6[4]	6.2[4]	1.3[4]	26.9[4]
Antigua and Barbuda	1991	245.9	—17.8[2]—		9.9	72.3[3]	6.2	26.8	39.3[3]	41.3[8]	29.5[8]	—[8]	—[8]	29.2[8]
Argentina	1996	23,761.6	6.8	1.4	3.6	88.2	18.5	46.0	23.7	29.0	20.0	1.2	3.1	46.8
Armenia	1997	892.0	32.8	—23.5[2]—		43.7[3]	12.2	13.2	18.3[3]	20.3	13.0	29.9	0.3	36.4
Aruba	1998	832.5[9]	21.7	4.1	—	74.2	10.4	36.9	26.9	12.0	72.0	—	1.9	14.1
Australia	1997	61,832.5	6.2	0.7	6.1	86.9	10.8	46.3	29.8	24.3	22.1	0.3	13.7	39.7
Austria	1996	67,283.8	8.6	1.2	5.3	84.8	10.3	37.9	36.6	70.8	4.5	8.7	2.4	13.6
Azerbaijan	1997	794.0	29.2	—12.3[2]—		58.6[3]	9.9	27.6	21.1[3]	13.3	0.3	34.7	—	51.8
Bahamas, The	1997	1,622.0	—18.4[2]—		9.2	72.4[3]	10.3	28.7	33.3[3]	2.6[10]	93.0[10]	…	…	4.4[10]
Bahrain	1996	4,092.6	12.3	5.3	40.9	41.5	5.2	15.7	20.7	18.9	6.7	0.2	3.7	70.6
Bangladesh	1996[12]	6,225.3	21.3	1.0	7.2	70.5	7.7	19.2	43.6	11.0	4.0	1.0	7.0	77.0
Barbados	1997	995.3	20.4	0.4	8.3	70.9	10.5	29.2	31.3	14.9	45.4	0.1	6.8	32.8
Belarus	1997	8,689.0	15.3	—27.7[2]—		57.0[3]	16.0	19.9	21.2[3]	16.5	1.6	73.9	0.5	7.5
Belgium[13]	1997	152,106.2	12.2	9.4	7.1	71.3	14.6	29.7	26.9	72.2	7.5	2.3	2.4	15.6
Belize	1997	286.1	20.1	0.2	12.9	66.8	10.1	25.6	31.2	9.2	51.7	—	1.7	37.4
Benin	1991	408.0	—32.9[2]—		11.6	55.5[3]	7.5	13.7	34.4[3]	30.6	4.5	0.7	2.4	61.8
Bermuda	1993	588.9	20.5	0.1[2]	5.8	73.6[3]	13.9	23.3	36.3[3]	11.6	70.2	0.2	5.4	12.5
Bhutan	1994	91.5	23.0	0.5	11.5	65.0	8.4	30.2	26.4	9.4	1.3	—	13.9	75.4[17]
Bolivia	1997	1,909.2	9.7	0.9	7.6	81.8	12.2	48.8	20.9	14.7	23.2	0.1	12.4	49.6
Bosnia and Herzegovina	1998	1,193.2	—24.3[2]—		5.7	70.0[3]	10.5	28.2	31.3[3]	40.5	2.3	13.7[4]	1.0[4]	42.6[4]
Botswana	1997	2,261.9	16.6	2.7	5.6	75.0	7.3	37.6	30.2	8.2	…	—	…	91.8[20]
Brazil	1997	65,074.7	11.6	1.1	11.7	75.6	15.1	42.5	18.0	26.2	23.4	1.1	5.9	43.4
Brunei	1994	1,873.7	15.1	1.7	0.4	82.8	4.6	42.3	35.8	17.9	11.3	27.9	10.1	32.8
Bulgaria	1997	4,760.5	13.8	4.1	31.3	50.7	11.3	16.0	23.4	38.3	3.8	38.2	0.8	18.9
Burkina Faso	1997	586.5	—25.6[2, 5]—		11.6[5]	62.8[3, 5]	18.5[5]	20.8[5]	23.5[3, 5]	46.0	4.2	3.4	5.5	40.9
Burundi	1993	204.5	13.0	0.6	12.4	74.0	14.1	21.3	38.6	45.4	1.8	0.4	9.2	43.3
Cambodia	1993	403.9	17.2[22]	…	11.7	…	6.5[22]	17.0[22]	…	9.2[4]	4.5[4]	2.5[4]	12.2[4]	71.6[4]
Cameroon	1996	1,204.3	16.2	3.2	15.7	64.9	14.6	27.6	22.7	53.4	8.5	1.8	5.0	31.3
Canada	1997	196,029.2	6.9	1.6	4.5	87.0	7.9	51.7	27.3	9.9	67.6	0.5	4.6	17.5
Cape Verde	1994	210.1	32.8	—	3.6	63.6	5.1	36.0	22.5	75.0	2.3	0.7	5.0	17.0
Central African Republic	1996	179.9	25.9	0.4	8.1	65.6	7.9	37.4	20.3	48.6	1.7	—	8.7	41.1
Chad	1995	215.2	24.7	0.5	17.9	57.0	7.2	23.8	25.9	51.3	6.5	0.4	2.4	39.5
Chile	1997	18,110.9	7.9	0.6	10.0	81.5	11.2	43.5	26.8	21.9	23.9	0.4	5.8	48.0
China	1997	142,370.4	10.1	2.8	7.3	79.8	13.4	37.0	29.4	13.5	11.5	3.3	20.4	51.4
Colombia	1997	15,378.9	13.2	0.6	3.0	83.2	17.5	38.9	26.7	18.5	35.3	1.0	6.2	39.0
Comoros	1995	62.7	37.8[22]	…	12.4	49.8	1.1[22]	7.2[22]	41.5	49.5[4]	1.6[4]	—[4]	4.8[4]	44.1[4]
Congo, Dem. Rep. of the	1992	420.0	—20.0[8]—		13.8[8]	66.2[8]	4.4[8]	45.5[8]	16.3[8]	57.9[4]	4.9[4]	0.8[4]	2.7[4]	33.7[4]
Congo, Rep. of the	1995	556.0	21.7	0.4	19.6	58.3	13.8	20.3	24.2	45.4	8.0	0.1	2.2	44.3
Costa Rica	1996	3,885.7	12.9	0.2	8.6	78.2	17.3	23.9	37.0	10.1	49.9	0.4	3.8	35.9
Côte d'Ivoire	1996	2,812.0	19.1	0.8	23.1	57.0	15.8	20.9	20.3	49.9	5.9	2.3	4.1	37.8
Croatia	1997	9,122.4	12.3	0.7	9.4	77.7	10.2	33.5	34.0	59.5	3.0	12.3	1.5	23.6
Cuba	1997	3,560.0	—19.8[2]—		33.7	46.5[3]	8.4	19.8	18.3[3]	28.7	0.3	8.9	0.6	61.6
Cyprus	1997	3,698.1	28.0	0.6	8.3	63.0	8.0	21.7	33.3	47.6	19.0	6.7	5.3	21.5
Czech Republic	1997	27,183.6	8.7	1.4	8.7	81.2	11.4	37.8	32.0	61.5	3.8	20.7	1.9	12.1
Denmark	1997	44,492.4	15.8	0.5	3.9	79.8	10.1	33.7	36.1	70.1	5.0	3.4	2.0	19.5
Djibouti	1991	214.4	38.3	0.2	9.1	52.3	6.0	15.5	30.8	46.6	3.7	0.7[4]	7.2	41.8
Dominica	1996	129.9	29.7	0.2	6.5	63.6	13.2	21.7	28.6	18.8	40.9	0.1	5.6	34.6
Dominican Republic	1994	2,626.4	13.7[25]	0.3[25]	35.2[25]	50.7[25]	11.7[25]	23.2[25]	15.9[25]	2.0[4]	37.4[4]	—[4]	1.5[4]	59.1[4]
East Timor[27]	…	…	…	…	…	…	…	…	…	…	…	…	…	…
Ecuador	1997	4,510.7	12.1	0.2	8.5	79.1	18.2	36.0	24.9	16.7	30.5	1.4	5.8	45.5

and freight] valuation); for exports, the value at which the goods were sold by the exporter, including the cost of transportation and insurance to bring the goods onto the transporting vehicle at the frontier of the exporting country (f.o.b. [free-on-board] valuation).

The largest part of the information presented here comes from the United Nations' *Commodity Trade Statistics* (microfiche format) and *International Trade Statistics Yearbook*. These sources, however, cannot always provide the most recent data for all countries listed in this table and must be supplemented by national and regional information. In some cases where the original data were only available for an alternative trade classification, an approximation has been made of the SITC commodity groupings.

The notes that follow further define the column headings.

a. Also includes any unallocated commodities.

b. EU of 15 countries (Austria, Belgium, Denmark, Finland, France, Germany, Greece, Ireland, Italy, Luxembourg, The Netherlands, Portugal, Spain, Sweden, and the United Kingdom).

c. Includes Albania, Bulgaria, Czech Republic, Hungary, Poland, Romania, Slovakia, and European republics of the former U.S.S.R. (Belarus, Estonia, Latvia, Lithuania, Moldova, Russia, and Ukraine).

d. May include value of trade shown as not available (...) in any of the four preceding columns. May include any unspecified areas or countries.

... Not available.

— None, less than 0.05%, or not applicable.

Detail may not add to 100.0 or indicated subtotals because of rounding.

SITC category codes

0		food and live animals
1		beverages and tobacco
2		crude materials, inedible, except fuels
	27	crude fertilizers and crude minerals (excluding coal, petroleum, and precious stones)
	28	metalliferous ores and metal scrap
3		mineral fuels, lubricants, and related materials (including coal, petroleum, natural gas, and electric current)
4		animal and vegetable oils, fats, and waxes
5		chemicals and related products not elsewhere specified
6		manufactured goods classified chiefly by material
	667	pearls, precious and semiprecious stones, unworked or worked
7		machinery and transport equipment
8		miscellaneous manufactured articles
9		commodities and transactions not classified elsewhere

exports													country
total value ('000,000 U.S.$)	Standard International Trade Classification (SITC) categories (%)							direction of trade (%)					
	food and agricultural raw materials (0 + 1 + 2 – 27 – 28 + 4)	mineral ores and concentrates (27 + 28 + 667)	fuels and other energy (3)	manufactured goods				to European Union (EU)[b]	to United States	to Eastern Europe[c]	to Japan	to all other[d]	
				total[a] (5 + 6 – 667 + 7 + 8 + 9)	of which chemicals and related products (5)	of which machinery and transport equipment (7)	of which other[a] (6 – 667 + 8 + 9)						
166.0	—63.0[2, 5]—		...	37.0[3, 5]	...	...	...	19.3[4]	3.0[4]	8.4[4]	0.6[4]	68.7[4]	Afghanistan
210.5	25.2	7.8	1.8	65.3	0.8	5.7	58.8	87.5	1.5	0.6	0.1	10.4	Albania
11,099.2	1.3	0.4	92.9	5.4	2.6	0.4	2.4	60.0	15.3	5.1	0.5	19.0	Algeria
488.2	100.0	—	—	—	—	—	—	—[5]	100.0[5]	—[5]	—[5]	—[5]	American Samoa
57.8	11.9	1.5	—	86.7	6.5	30.7	49.5	87.4	0.2	0.3	8.5	3.6	Andorra
3,002.0	0.3	3.2	96.5	—	—	—	—	22.9[4]	70.2[4]	—[4]	0.3[4]	6.6[4]	Angola
39.8	—4.4[2]—		25.0	70.6[3]	7.1	30.2	33.3[3]	15.0[8]	15.4[8]	—[8]	—[8]	69.5[8]	Antigua and Barbuda
23,809.6	55.8	0.3	13.0	31.0	5.7	10.9	14.4	19.3	8.3	1.3	2.2	69.0	Argentina
233.0	12.6	—7.7[2]—		79.7[3]	5.8	14.7	59.2[3]	28.5	3.0	29.5	—	38.9	Armenia
42.8[9]	23.4	2.8	—	73.7	1.9	44.9	26.9	10.2	55.1	0.1	0.1	34.5	Aruba
62,566.5	29.4	11.9	17.8	40.9	3.6	13.3	24.0	10.2	7.5	0.5	19.9	61.8	Australia
57,830.5	7.3	0.8	1.2	90.6	9.3	40.6	40.6	64.2	3.2	12.3	1.5	18.8	Austria
781.0	7.3	—61.7[2]—		31.0[3]	5.3	5.3	20.4[3]	10.8	2.8	30.1	0.1	56.2	Azerbaijan
181.4	—58.4[2]—		—	41.6[3]	18.9	16.8	5.9[3]	14.6	73.4	...	...	11.9	Bahamas, The
4,602.0	2.1	0.4	66.5	31.0	3.2	1.0	26.7	1.6	2.3	—	4.3	91.8[11]	Bahrain
3,538.5	12.2	—	0.3	87.5	3.0	0.6	84.0	45.3	32.9	0.8	4.2	16.7	Bangladesh
283.0	35.1	0.3	16.1	48.6	13.0	14.0	21.6	20.2	14.7	—	0.4	64.8	Barbados
7,301.0	11.9	—9.5[2]—		78.6[3]	17.5	31.1	30.0[3]	6.7	1.3	80.7	0.1	11.2	Belarus
166,041.0	11.3	7.9	3.1	77.8	16.5	28.3	33.1	73.2	4.9	3.1	1.0	17.8	Belgium[13]
176.2	82.7	—	2.2	15.2	0.5	2.6	12.0	40.0	46.7	—	—	13.2	Belize
43.0	—63.5[2]—		29.0	7.5[3]	1.0	2.8	3.8[3]	18.6	18.7	—	0.4	62.3	Benin
35.3	5.6[14]	3.1[14, 15]	45.6[14]	45.8[14, 16]	9.5[14]	18.5[14]	17.8[14, 16]	27.0[14]	62.3[14]	—[14]	—[14]	10.6[14]	Bermuda
66.8	30.7	3.6	25.6[18]	40.1	20.4	—	19.8	—	—	—	—	100.0[19]	Bhutan
1,272.1	38.2	22.0	8.4	31.4	1.1	1.2	29.1	24.6	20.8	0.1	0.3	54.1	Bolivia
185.3	—37.3[2]—		4.3	58.4[3]	3.9	11.0	43.5[3]	35.8	2.9	1.0[4]	0.1[4]	60.2[4]	Bosnia and Herzegovina
2,923.6	3.3	75.1	—	21.7	1.5	11.9	8.3	56.9	...	—	...	43.1[21]	Botswana
52,985.9	34.5	6.5	0.6	58.3	6.3	22.6	29.4	27.5	17.8	2.4	5.8	46.6	Brazil
2,110.4	—	—	98.7	1.3	—	—	1.3	—	1.1	—	72.3	26.5	Brunei
4,760.4	18.2	2.5	7.9	71.4	18.0	11.6	41.8	44.7	2.7	17.9	0.8	33.8	Bulgaria
228.9	83.5[5]	0.5[5]	—[5]	16.0[5]	0.1[5]	1.0[5]	14.9[5]	32.5	1.5	—	1.0	64.9	Burkina Faso
68.7	85.1	—	—	14.9	1.4	—	13.4	48.4	2.0[4]	—[4]	1.0[4]	47.3[4]	Burundi
219.1[23]	88.9[24]	...	...	...	...	...	...	15.5[4]	0.5[4]	0.5[4]	37.6[4]	45.9[4]	Cambodia
1,757.9	49.5	0.1	36.2	14.3	1.1	1.1	12.1	77.4	2.3	0.2	0.8	19.3	Cameroon
214,333.4	15.4	2.1	10.2	72.2	5.7	39.0	27.4	5.1	82.5	0.3	3.7	8.5	Canada
5.0[24]	50.6	0.6	—	48.9	0.1	2.2	46.6	98.3	0.1	—	—	1.6	Cape Verde
115.1	25.4	60.1	0.2	14.3	—	7.5	6.8	95.1	—	—	—	4.8	Central African Republic
252.0	88.2[14]	—[14]	—[14]	11.9[14]	6.5[14]	3.1[14]	2.3[14]	76.6[4]	2.4[4]	0.8[4]	2.4[4]	17.7[4]	Chad
16,678.3	34.3	15.3	0.3	50.1	4.6	2.6	43.0	24.5	14.6	0.5	16.1	44.3	Chile
182,791.7	8.6	0.9	3.8	86.7	5.5	23.9	57.4	13.1	17.9	2.0	17.4	49.6	China
11,530.2	37.0	1.4	31.4	30.1	9.2	3.8	17.1	22.7	37.8	1.2	3.1	35.2	Colombia
11.4	57.9	—	—	42.1	21.0[22]	—	21.2	44.7[4]	28.1	—	—	27.2[4]	Comoros
506.0	13.1	58.5[2, 15]	11.1	17.3[3, 16]	0.2	1.2	15.9[3, 16]	58.7	15.7[4]	4.5	6.5	14.6[4]	Congo, Dem. Rep. of the
1,089.8	9.3	0.3	87.6	2.7	—	0.4	2.3	41.3	28.5	—	0.3	29.9	Congo, Rep. of the
2,881.6	69.8	0.3	0.8	29.1	6.6	4.0	18.5	29.8	39.0	1.0	1.2	28.9	Costa Rica
4,446.1	68.2[14]	0.3[2, 14, 15]	15.4[14]	16.1[3, 14, 16]	3.3[14]	2.0[14]	10.9[3, 14, 16]	62.8	7.0	3.0	0.2	27.0	Côte d'Ivoire
4,340.9	18.3	1.2	9.8	70.7	12.7	17.3	40.7	51.2	2.2	8.9	0.1	37.5	Croatia
1,850.0	82.2[14]	8.4[2, 14, 15]	4.8[14]	4.6[3, 14, 16]	2.7[14]	0.6[14]	1.3[3, 14, 16]	29.5	0.5	20.4	5.9	43.7	Cuba
1,250.2	59.7	1.6	4.4	34.2	5.4	8.8	20.0	27.1	1.1	31.5	0.1	40.1	Cyprus
22,746.4	8.0	1.0	3.8	87.2	8.2	37.6	41.4	59.9	2.6	26.6	0.4	10.5	Czech Republic
48,800.5	26.5	0.5	3.8	69.2	9.9	26.9	32.4	60.9	4.0	5.4	2.9	26.7	Denmark
17.3	32.5	—	—	67.5	0.4	8.3	58.7	62.6	0.8	—	0.9	35.7	Djibouti
51.2	48.8	1.7	—	49.5	46.3	1.1	2.1	43.5	7.3	—	0.1	49.2	Dominica
2,007.8	20.7	0.1	—	79.2[26]	2.6	11.6	65.1[26]	8.6	83.6	—	0.8	6.9	Dominican Republic
...	...	...	...	...	...	...	...	...	...	...	...	...	East Timor[27]
5,214.2	60.7	0.1	29.7	9.5	1.4	2.0	6.1	19.3	38.2	3.8	3.0	35.7	Ecuador

Trade: external (continued)

country	year	imports												
		total value ('000,000 U.S.$)	Standard International Trade Classification (SITC) categories (%)							direction of trade (%)				
			food and agricultural raw materials (0 + 1 + 2 − 27 − 28 + 4)	mineral ores and concentrates (27 + 28 + 667)	fuels and other energy (3)	manufactured goods				from European Union (EU)[b]	from United States	from Eastern Europe[c]	from Japan	from all other[d]
						total[a] (5 + 6 − 667 + 7 + 8 + 9)	of which chemicals and related products (5)	of which machinery and transport equipment (7)	of which other[a] (6 − 667 + 8 + 9)					
Egypt	1997	13,168.5	32.2	1.7	1.8	64.2	13.1	26.9	24.2	38.2	13.1	7.9	3.4	37.5
El Salvador	1997	2,961.5	19.8	0.4	11.4	68.5	17.0	26.5	25.0	8.9	41.4	0.9	3.1	45.8
Equatorial Guinea	1990	61.6	13.5	3.4	7.7	75.4	3.9	58.2	13.3	31.5	39.9	—	0.3[4]	28.3
Eritrea	1995	423.6	— 21.3[2] —		1.9	76.8[3]	6.0	45.2	25.6[3]	27.2[29]	5.9	…	…	66.9
Estonia	1997	4,438.8	18.6	1.2	8.2	72.0	9.3	34.0	28.7	59.1	3.8	21.5	3.3	12.2
Ethiopia	1993	771.6	17.4	0.1	21.6	60.9	13.8	26.8	20.3	39.3	9.5	—	4.1	47.2
Faroe Islands	1994	238.2	30.7	0.6	11.8	56.8	8.5	19.8	28.5	67.5	1.4	3.6	2.0	25.5
Fiji	1994	830.5	15.9	0.3	11.2	72.5	7.3	30.9	34.3	3.9	14.8	0.1	8.0	73.3
Finland	1997	31,001.1	9.2	4.0	9.7	77.0	11.3	39.3	26.4	57.5	7.3	10.9	5.3	18.9
France[31]	1997	266,575.4	12.1	1.1	8.2	78.6	12.1	36.3	30.2	61.0	8.8	2.9	3.3	24.0
French Guiana	1995	783.3	18.8	0.1	5.3	75.8	8.0	42.2	25.6	76.9	3.3	0.5	1.4	17.9
French Polynesia	1994	880.7	20.4[32]	0.2[32]	5.4[32]	74.1[32]	6.4[32]	35.9[32]	31.8[32]	44.8[29]	13.9	—	4.0	37.3
Gabon	1996	898.1	19.8	0.4	3.4	76.4	10.7	39.3	26.4	68.1	10.4	0.3	6.0	15.2
Gambia, The	1995[12]	141.3	— 35.3[2] —		14.4	50.3[3]	5.6	20.3	24.5[3]	47.3	5.2	0.7	3.5	43.3
Gaza Strip	1994	339.3	…	…	…	…	…	…	…	…	…	…	…	100.0[33]
Georgia	1997	940.0	36.4	— 28.5[2] —		35.1[3]	10.2	16.7	8.2[3]	22.4	7.5	27.9	—	42.2
Germany	1997	436,458.2	11.2	1.5	7.6	79.7	8.5	34.2	37.0	53.1	7.5	8.2	4.8	26.4
Ghana	1992	2,145.4	12.5	3.1	17.4	66.9	11.1	33.6	22.2	43.6	10.2	1.4	6.6	38.2
Greece	1997	25,208.6	17.4	0.8	6.5	75.3	12.9	29.8	32.7	65.0	3.8	6.5	3.8	20.9
Greenland	1997	374.1	16.5	0.4	9.7	73.4	3.6	26.2	43.6	76.0	3.1	0.3	2.9	17.7
Grenada	1996	151.4	29.0	0.3	9.7	60.9	8.1	22.1	30.8	15.1	42.6	0.2	3.7	38.4
Guadeloupe	1995	1,901.3	22.6	0.3	5.8	71.3	9.5	32.0	29.8	77.8	3.3	0.3	2.2	16.5
Guam	1992	450.0	16.9[37]	0.1[37]	46.9[37]	36.2[37]	2.3[37]	19.1[37]	14.8[37]	…	23.4[37]	…	19.9[37]	56.6[37]
Guatemala	1997	3,852.0	15.1	0.3	10.7	73.9	17.8	30.8	25.3	9.5	41.9	1.0	3.4	44.2
Guernsey[38]	…	…	…	…	…	…	…	…	…	…	…	…	…	…
Guinea	1994	687.0	10.8	…	9.9	…	…	22.3	…	54.3[4]	8.0[4]	0.7[4]	3.8[4]	33.2[4]
Guinea-Bissau	1997	88.6	42.7	…	10.7	46.6	…	23.7	…	39.5[4]	3.4[4]	—[4]	7.9[4]	49.2[4]
Guyana	1993	483.8	9.0	…	16.7	74.3	5.1	44.5	24.7	21.9[4]	27.9[4]	0.4[4]	18.2[4]	31.6[4]
Haiti	1993[6]	226.0	— 46.6[2] —		28.4	25.1[3]	6.9	5.4	12.8	18.1[4]	57.9[4]	…	4.8[4]	19.3[4]
Honduras	1997	2,435.1	20.4	0.1	10.4	69.1	13.7	26.1	29.3	4.3	61.2	0.5	2.9	31.1
Hong Kong	1997	213,300.0	6.9	1.7	1.9	89.5	6.3	37.8	45.4	11.2	7.7	0.5	13.5	67.2
Hungary	1997	21,234.1	6.7	0.4	9.2	83.6	10.8	41.3	31.5	62.4	3.7	16.6	3.3	13.9
Iceland	1997	2,019.5	11.8	2.3	7.6	78.3	8.0	37.3	33.0	58.1	9.4	4.1	4.9	23.5
India	1997[1]	39,112.8	7.8	10.5	29.3	52.5	12.7	18.7	21.1	26.5	9.2	2.2	5.6	56.4
Indonesia	1997	41,679.8	13.5	1.6	9.9	74.9	13.8	42.0	19.1	20.0	13.1	1.1	19.8	46.0
Iran	1992	30,712.1	— 11.4[2] —		1.3	87.4[3]	9.8	50.3	27.3[3]	49.8	2.7	2.4[4]	12.0	33.1
Iraq	1990	4,833.9	— 31.5[2] —		0.4	68.1[3]	8.8	30.3	28.9[3]	45.7[4]	10.8[4]	3.0[4]	4.6[4]	35.9[4]
Ireland	1999	46,486.7	8.3	0.6	2.8	88.4	11.4	51.0	26.1	54.1	16.1	1.1	5.7	22.4
Isle of Man[38]	…	…	…	…	…	…	…	…	…	…	…	…	…	…
Israel	1997	29,022.7	8.4	18.0	7.9	65.8	9.1	32.5	24.2	51.0	18.8	1.5	3.6	25.2
Italy[39]	1997	208,317.2	15.3	1.9	8.0	74.8	12.8	30.9	31.1	60.6	5.0	5.7	2.0	26.7
Jamaica	1996	2,916.4	16.2	0.2	15.2	68.4	10.1	26.7	31.7	11.2	52.3	0.5	5.6	30.4
Japan	1997	338,842.4	19.7	3.7	18.6	58.0	6.7	24.6	26.7	13.3	22.4	1.4	—	62.9
Jersey	1980	537.1	23.9	0.4	9.3	66.5	6.5	24.8	35.2	84.9[40]	…	…	…	15.1
Jordan	1995	3,722.7	22.7	1.1	12.9	63.4	12.3	24.5	26.5	33.2	9.3	4.6	3.5	49.4
Kazakhstan	1997	4,275.0	18.1	— 16.2[2] —		65.7[3]	14.3	32.1	19.4[3]	21.6	4.7	54.5	0.7	18.5
Kenya	1998	3,301.8	17.1	0.5	17.5	65.0	15.1	31.2	18.7	32.2	7.9	1.1	7.9	51.0
Kiribati	1995	34.1	40.5	0.3	10.3	49.0	7.0	14.7	27.3	1.1	3.1	—	7.6	88.2
Korea, North	1997	1,444.0[4]	…	…	…	…	…	…	…	17.6[4]	0.2[4]	6.9[4]	13.6[4]	61.7[4]
Korea, South	1996	150,334.3	10.4	2.4	16.2	71.0	8.8	36.4	25.8	14.1	22.2	1.5	20.9	41.3
Kuwait	1996	8,373.7	16.6	0.4	0.6	82.4	7.2	41.6	33.6	32.0	16.7	1.0	12.1	38.3
Kyrgyzstan	1996	837.9	22.4	1.0	28.6	48.0	7.8	26.1	14.0	11.1	4.3	25.1	1.5	58.1
Laos	1995	587.2	— 36.8[2] —		6.1	57.1[3]	…	29.3	27.8[3]	2.0[4]	0.9	0.7[4]	11.8	84.6
Latvia	1997	2,721.0	15.2	1.2	13.6	70.0	11.9	27.3	30.8	53.2	2.3	37.1	0.3	7.1
Lebanon	1994	5,990.0	21.7	— 13.3 —		65.0	10.2	27.0	27.8	49.1[4]	9.3	4.6[4]	4.2	32.8[4]
Lesotho	1992	977.0	23.2[42]	0.4[42]	8.7[42]	67.8[42]	7.4[42]	16.7[42]	43.7[42]	4.8	…	—[4]	—[4]	95.2[43]
Liberia	1992	5,760.0[4]	— 19.8[2, 32] —		20.3[32]	59.9[3, 32]	5.6[32]	30.2[32]	24.1[3, 32]	22.6[4]	0.6[4]	0.8[4]	28.3[4]	47.7[4]
Libya	1991	5,357.5	25.7	0.3	0.4	73.7	7.6	33.8	32.2	62.6	1.3	0.9[4]	3.3	31.9
Liechtenstein	1995	906.4	3.8	0.3[2]	1.1	94.8[3]	4.6	33.9	56.3[3]	…	…	…	…	…
Lithuania	1997	5,469.6	13.7	1.5	14.4	70.4	12.1	30.7	27.6	47.7	2.4	42.7	0.2	7.0
Luxembourg	1998	10,177.5	12.0	— 7.3 —		80.7	13.2	35.3	32.2	89.1	4.4	0.1	1.5	4.9
Macau	1997	2,076.7	14.3	0.2	6.6	78.9	4.1	16.9	57.9	12.3	6.3	—	8.5	72.8
Macedonia	1996	1,626.9	19.6	1.0	9.1	70.3	10.5	22.3	37.5	38.7	4.2	13.0	1.0	43.1
Madagascar	1997	573.1	16.6	0.1	21.1	62.2	12.7	25.6	23.9	37.5	4.5	0.5	6.1	51.5
Malawi	1995	500.5	14.5	0.6	11.1	73.6	22.5	27.6	23.6	31.9	2.6	0.5	5.0	60.0
Malaysia	1996	77,923.4	6.6	1.1	2.7	89.6	6.8	59.9	22.8	14.5	15.6	0.7	24.7	44.5
Maldives	1993	191.4	31.5	2.8	12.8	52.9	7.5	22.2	23.2	7.9	1.0	0.4	3.9	86.9
Mali	1990	601.8	26.2	0.9	19.5	53.5	10.7	22.2	20.6	46.8	4.8	1.3[4]	4.3	42.9
Malta	1996	2,802.3	11.5	0.4	5.4	82.7	7.4	48.4	26.9	68.5	6.9	1.3	3.2	20.1
Marshall Islands	1995	75.1	34.5	1.0[4]	30.0	34.5	2.6	12.8	19.2	…	51.1	…	7.4	41.5
Martinique	1995	1,969.8	20.4	0.2	7.5	71.9	10.3	32.4	29.2	76.8	2.9	0.2	2.2	17.9
Mauritania	1992	600.0[4]	30.6[32]	…	7.0[32]	62.4[32]	…	51.0[32]	11.4[32]	58.4[4]	11.2[4]	1.8[4]	3.8[4]	24.7[4]
Mauritius	1996	2,276.9	19.4	1.8	7.9	70.9	7.7	21.9	41.3	33.0	2.5	0.2	4.4	59.8
Mayotte	1996	144.3	— 23.7 —		4.6	71.7	11.0	35.1	25.6	74.0[14, 46]	…	…	3.3[14]	22.7[14]
Mexico	1997	111,974.2	7.9	1.0	2.7	88.4	9.0	46.2	33.2	9.3	74.3	0.4	4.0	12.0
Micronesia	1994	129.1	— 24.7[2] —		14.3	61.0[3]	4.4	13.5	43.1[3]	…	32.9	…	32.0	35.1
Moldova	1995	840.7	10.7	1.0	45.9	42.4	9.2	15.2	17.9	13.7	1.3	80.2	0.2	4.7
Monaco[31]	…	…	…	…	…	…	…	…	…	…	…	…	…	…
Mongolia	1996	450.9	14.9	0.3	19.3	65.5	5.0	39.7	20.7	14.7	2.3	39.0	11.7	32.2
Morocco	1996	8,253.9	24.1	2.2	15.6	58.1	12.7	23.6	21.8	54.1	7.4	5.4	1.8	31.3
Mozambique	1996	782.6	23.6	0.6	11.5	64.3	8.2	32.3	23.8	27.1	4.2	—	4.0	64.7
Myanmar (Burma)	1996	1,914.0	— 8.7[2] —		4.4	86.9[3]	8.6	27.0	51.3[3]	2.6	4.9	—	22.5	69.9
Namibia	1994	1,374.3	23.8	1.1[2]	4.2	70.9[3]	7.1	31.4	32.5[3]	4.5	0.9	—	1.3	93.3[47]
Nauru	1994	31.8	87.8	…	…	12.2	…	2.8	9.3	…	…	…	…	…
Nepal	1996[12]	1,404.2	13.7	0.5	8.9	77.0	9.1	19.5	48.4	7.9	1.0	0.3	5.5	85.3

exports													country
total value ('000,000 U.S.$)	Standard International Trade Classification (SITC) categories (%)							direction of trade (%)					
	food and agricultural raw materials (0 + 1 + 2 – 27 – 28 + 4)	mineral ores and concen-trates (27 + 28 + 667)	fuels and other energy (3)	manufactured goods				to European Union (EU)[b]	to United States	to Eastern Europe[c]	to Japan	to all other[d]	
				total[a] (5 + 6 – 667 + 7 + 8 + 9)	of which chemicals and related products (5)	of which machinery and transport equipment (7)	of which other[a] (6 – 667 + 8 + 9)						
3,908.0	11.5	1.1	45.4	42.1	5.1	1.2	35.8	41.5	11.4	2.8	2.3	42.0	Egypt
1,354.0	56.0	0.1	3.3	40.6	12.3	3.7	24.6	29.6	19.2	—	1.0	50.2	El Salvador
61.7	48.6	—	—	51.4	0.1	39.8[28]	11.5	47.2	—	—	—	52.8	Equatorial Guinea
86.0	—— 59.8 ——		...	40.2	2.5	3.8	34.0	2.7[29]	...	...	...	97.3[30]	Eritrea
2,926.5	25.5	2.3	6.3	65.8	8.4	24.6	32.8	48.6	1.8	41.1	0.5	7.9	Estonia
201.7	95.3	—	4.0	0.7	0.1	—	0.6	41.6	9.2	0.3	19.0	29.9	Ethiopia
321.3	96.8	—	—	3.2	0.1	2.5	0.6	88.0	2.9	0.1	2.7	6.3	Faroe Islands
544.5	49.3	0.1	7.4	43.2	1.0	8.0	34.3	20.3	17.9	—	6.8	55.0	Fiji
40,980.1	10.2	0.7	2.4	86.8	6.2	38.8	41.8	51.5	6.9	14.9	1.9	24.9	Finland
283,345.8	14.5	0.7	2.6	82.3	12.8	41.6	27.8	62.8	6.5	3.1	1.7	25.9	France[31]
158.2	33.6	0.1	0.2	66.1	1.4	33.0	31.7	77.6	1.0	—	—	21.3	French Guiana
226.2	5.9[32]	31.3[32]	—[32]	62.8[32]	1.6[32]	38.6[32]	22.6[32]	32.7[29]	8.4	—	45.8	13.1	French Polynesia
3,145.6	13.3	2.0	82.7	1.9	0.4	0.4	1.1	11.5	64.1	0.1	2.1	22.3	Gabon
21.5	—— 78.8[2] ——		—	21.2[3]	1.6	2.5	17.1	57.1[4]	3.6[4]	—[4]	—[4]	39.3[4]	Gambia, The
49.4	...	...	...	...	...	...	...	...	...	...	...	100.0[34]	Gaza Strip
240.0	35.7	—— 21.5[2] ——		42.8[3]	10.9	7.3	24.5[3]	9.2	1.7	37.0	—	52.0	Georgia
511,942.1	5.6	0.7	1.3	92.5	12.7	49.5	30.2	54.0	8.4	9.0	2.2	26.4	Germany
1,234.4	37.7	6.2	5.4	50.6	0.2	1.2	49.3[35]	30.3	2.6	1.1	1.8	64.2[36]	Ghana
10,794.6	30.3	2.2	8.7	58.8	5.5	8.3	45.0	47.5	4.5	14.6	0.7	32.8	Greece
285.3	93.2	—	1.1	5.7	—	2.0	3.7	91.3	2.1	—	3.4	3.3	Greenland
19.8	80.5	0.1	—	19.4	2.2	3.3	14.0	38.8	21.4	—	—	39.8	Grenada
162.0	52.3	0.6	—	47.0	1.1	36.5	9.4	77.0	3.4	—	—	19.6	Guadeloupe
86.1	—— 69.5[2] ——		0.7	29.7[3]	0.7	3.8	25.2	2.3[4]	—	—	57.5	40.2	Guam
2,344.1	65.0	0.4	4.2	30.3	11.2	2.2	16.9	13.2	35.9	0.4	2.3	48.2	Guatemala
...	...	...	...	...	...	...	...	...	...	...	...	...	Guernsey[38]
625.9	12.2[22]	66.3	—	21.5	...	...	...	63.4[4]	15.1[4]	8.3[4]	1.3[4]	11.9[4]	Guinea
48.5	97.7	...	—	2.3	...	...	...	14.3[4]	—[4]	—[4]	1.4[4]	84.3[4]	Guinea-Bissau
404.0	43.5[22]	47.3[22]	—	9.2	...	...	...	35.9[4]	22.8[4]	—[4]	2.1[4]	39.2[4]	Guyana
74.3	14.1	—	—	86.0	1.7	14.0	70.3	12.4[4]	78.8[4]	—[4]	0.8[4]	8.0[4]	Haiti
1,033.3	68.3	3.0	0.2	28.6	1.5	1.9	25.2	21.1	68.0	0.2	2.7	8.1	Honduras
188,201.3	4.0	1.2	1.1	93.7	5.6	32.9	55.2	14.8	21.8	0.6	6.1	56.9	Hong Kong
19,099.2	15.5	0.8	2.3	81.5	7.6	44.9	29.0	69.9	3.1	14.4	0.5	12.2	Hungary
1,851.5	74.7	1.1	0.1	24.1	0.4	5.6	18.1	60.6	14.3	2.9	6.6	15.6	Iceland
33,468.6	21.0	15.5	1.5	62.0	9.0	8.2	44.8	25.9	19.6	3.2	6.0	45.3	India
53,443.7	16.0	3.5	24.6	55.9	3.5	8.6	43.7	15.2	13.4	0.5	23.4	47.6	Indonesia
19,868.0	7.8	1.9[2, 15]	80.9	9.3[3, 16]	0.2	0.5	8.6[3, 16]	39.8	0.8	9.9[4]	13.5	36.0	Iran
6,659.0	0.8	0.3[15]	96.8	2.1[16]	1.2	0.2	0.7[16]	26.6[4]	33.6[4]	6.8[4]	9.5[4]	23.5[4]	Iraq
70,525.1	9.9	0.8	0.3	89.0	31.8	39.3	17.9	64.6	15.4	1.5	2.9	15.6	Ireland
...	...	...	...	...	...	...	...	...	...	...	...	...	Isle of Man[38]
22,503.0	6.1	30.8	0.5	62.6	13.6	30.2	18.7	30.1	32.1	3.2	4.6	30.1	Israel
238,265.9	7.0	0.3	1.4	91.2	7.8	37.8	45.6	54.6	7.9	6.2	2.0	29.3	Italy[39]
1,386.9	23.7	49.7	0.4	26.2	3.4	2.3	20.5	31.2	37.1	1.9	2.3	27.5	Jamaica
421,053.0	1.1	0.3	0.5	98.1	6.9	69.0	22.2	15.6	28.1	0.5	—	55.7	Japan
209.2	27.6	4.3[41]	—	68.0	1.2	31.1	35.7	67.3[40]	...	...	...	32.7	Jersey
1,782.0	24.1	19.4	—	56.5	27.0	13.1	16.4	8.0	3.9	1.3	1.1	85.7	Jordan
6,366.0	12.9	—— 37.6[2] ——		49.5[3]	6.9	3.6	39.1[3]	26.8	2.2	42.2	1.7	27.1	Kazakhstan
1,916.6	64.9	2.6	8.6	23.9	6.3	0.9	16.6	31.6	3.6	0.3	0.8	63.7	Kenya
7.2	85.3	—	—	14.7	—	—	14.7	2.2	10.4	—	—	87.4	Kiribati
884.0[4]	...	...	...	...	...	...	...	10.2[4]	—[4]	3.7[4]	30.4[4]	55.7[4]	Korea, North
129,714.6	3.4	0.1	3.0	93.5	7.1	52.1	34.3	11.9	16.9	3.0	12.2	56.0	Korea, South
14,855.7	0.6	0.2	95.2	4.0	1.5	1.3	1.2	12.2[4]	10.9[4]	—[4]	19.4[4]	57.5[4]	Kuwait
507.1	39.7	2.5	15.3	42.4	12.9	9.8	19.8	3.9	3.5	32.1	0.2	60.3	Kyrgyzstan
347.9	—— 35.4[2] ——		7.0	57.5[3]	...	5.1	52.4[3]	9.7[4]	3.2	3.2[4]	0.6	83.3	Laos
1,671.7	38.0	1.9	1.1	59.1	6.7	10.5	41.9	48.9	1.4	42.0	0.3	7.5	Latvia
572.7	19.6	—— 10.5 ——		69.9	9.1	11.5	49.3	17.0[4]	3.7	4.9[4]	0.7	73.7[4]	Lebanon
109.1	14.8	1.3	—	83.9	0.5	10.2	73.2	22.7	23.0[4]	—	—	54.3[44]	Lesotho
389.0	32.4	33.7[2, 15]	2.6	31.3[3, 16]	—	26.0	5.3[3, 16]	66.8	11.4[4]	1.5	—	20.3[4]	Liberia
11,211.7	0.7	—	95.4	3.9	3.4	—	0.5	86.2	—	1.6	—	12.2	Libya
1,817.7	4.4	—[2]	0.1	95.5[3]	8.1	46.9	40.5[3]	45.7[45]	...	...	...	54.3	Liechtenstein
3,343.1	23.4	2.1	4.4	70.1	12.4	23.2	34.6	36.7	1.8	53.0	0.4	8.1	Lithuania
7,921.6	7.9	—— 1.1 ——		91.0	15.5	29.0	46.5	83.2	5.5	0.5	0.4	10.3	Luxembourg
2,282.1	2.5	—	0.4	97.1	0.9	3.9	92.2	31.2	42.5	0.1	1.0	25.2	Macau
1,147.4	24.7	2.3	0.9	72.1	6.1	7.7	58.4	42.8	6.2	8.3	0.2	42.5	Macedonia
277.8	60.7	9.6	2.9	26.9	2.1	0.7	24.0	65.8	3.8	0.5	9.0	20.9	Madagascar
433.4	90.2	—	—	9.8	0.4	2.0	7.4	47.7	13.2	3.5	5.0	30.6	Malawi
78,186.1	13.9	0.4	7.9	77.8	3.2	55.3	19.3	13.7	18.2	0.3	13.4	54.3	Malaysia
34.4	83.7	0.2	—	16.1	0.1	—	16.0	31.3	11.3	—	4.1	53.3	Maldives
330.3	98.4	—	—	1.6	—	0.9	0.8	26.0	0.6[4]	—	0.9[4]	72.5	Mali
1,747.9	3.3	0.2	2.7	93.8	2.9	60.1	30.8	57.1	13.4	1.0	2.0	26.7	Malta
23.1	71.0	—	—	29.0	—	—	29.0	...	80.0[4]	...	...	20.0[4]	Marshall Islands
241.9	62.3	1.0	17.8	18.9	2.1	13.0	3.8	78.0	2.6	—	—	19.3	Martinique
471.0	48.2	48.6[2, 15]	1.9	1.3[3, 16]	—	—	1.3[3, 16]	58.2	4.5	10.8[4]	20.4	6.1	Mauritania
1,699.4	31.8	1.9	—	66.3	0.6	0.4	65.3	77.4	13.4	—	0.6	8.5	Mauritius
8.2	21.3[24]	—[24]	—[24]	78.7[24]	78.7[24]	—[24]	—[24]	70.0[14, 46]	...	...	...	30.0[14]	Mayotte
110,047.0	7.2	0.7	10.0	82.1	3.8	54.0	24.3	3.5	84.5	0.1	0.9	10.9	Mexico
78.2	96.9	—	—	3.1	...	...	...	...	3.5	...	72.7	23.8	Micronesia
745.5	73.5	2.7	0.9	22.9	1.4	7.9	13.7	11.6	1.1	80.5	—	6.8	Moldova
...	...	...	...	...	...	...	...	...	...	...	...	...	Monaco[31]
424.3	29.9	59.9	—	10.2	0.6	7.4	7.8	13.6	0.2	63.1	0.5	22.5	Mongolia
4,741.9	35.4	11.0	1.6	52.0	20.1	2.9	28.9	61.5	3.5	1.8	6.9	26.3	Morocco
226.1	77.9	3.7	1.2	17.2	0.5	11.5	5.3	34.7	11.4	0.3	7.6	46.0	Mozambique
883.1	—— 77.3[2] ——		0.6	22.2[3]	—	1.1	21.1[3]	4.3	4.9	—	7.3	83.5	Myanmar (Burma)
1,321.4	47.0	50.1	—	2.8	...	...	...	...	3.0[4, 5]	...	—[4, 5]	97.0[4, 5]	Namibia
31.2	—	100.0	—	—	—	—	—	...	...	...	...	...	Nauru
363.7	10.8	0.1	—	89.1	1.8	0.1	87.2	42.4	28.3	0.2	0.4	28.7	Nepal

Trade: external (continued)

country	year	imports												
		total value ('000,000 U.S.$)	Standard International Trade Classification (SITC) categories (%)							direction of trade (%)				
			food and agricultural raw materials (0 + 1 + 2 – 27 – 28 + 4)	mineral ores and concentrates (27 + 28 + 667)	fuels and other energy (3)	manufactured goods: total[a] (5 + 6 – 667 + 7 + 8 + 9)	of which chemicals and related products (5)	of which machinery and transport equipment (7)	of which other[a] (6 – 667 + 8 + 9)	from European Union (EU)[b]	from United States	from Eastern Europe[c]	from Japan	from all other[d]
Netherlands, The	1997	162,359.7	13.1	1.5	8.7	76.7	11.2	37.8	27.7	58.8	9.9	3.2	3.9	24.2
Netherlands Antilles	1995	1,832.5	— 12.9[2] —		55.2	31.9[3]	4.5	12.7	14.7[3]	13.1	19.9	—	1.7	65.4
New Caledonia	1997	924.2	— 20.3[2] —		11.7	68.0[3]	7.7	33.3	27.0[3]	41.9	5.3	—	4.3	48.5
New Zealand	1996	14,724.2	8.6	2.0	6.3	83.0	12.6	41.9	28.6	20.2	16.7	0.1	14.3	48.7
Nicaragua	1997	1,469.8	15.2	0.4	12.2	72.2	18.8	26.9	26.6	8.5	37.4	0.5	4.8	48.9
Niger	1991	355.3	25.7	2.1	9.4	62.7	9.6	13.6	39.5	39.6	5.1	0.3	6.6	48.4
Nigeria	1992	8,839.3	7.6	0.9	0.4	91.0	13.9	54.2	22.9	62.8	8.5	0.8[4]	6.3	21.7
Northern Mariana Islands	1991	392.2	19.3	—	20.9	59.8	2.3	22.2	35.3	...	18.2	...	16.6	65.2
Norway	1999	33,810.8	9.3	4.1	3.2	83.3	9.2	41.7	32.4	68.6	7.3	2.7	4.0	15.6
Oman	1996	4,577.8	18.2	1.6	1.0	79.2	6.7	41.5	31.0	25.3	7.5	0.2	17.2	49.8
Pakistan	1998	9,312.5	25.0	1.1	15.9	58.0	20.4	22.8	14.8	18.3	9.8	1.0	8.1	62.8
Palau	1984	25.1[49]	28.9	0.1[2]	0.9[49]	70.0[3]	4.0	24.5	41.5[3]	—	41.8	—	38.2	20.0
Panama	1996	2,779.7	11.8	0.3	15.9	72.0	13.1	30.6	28.3	7.8	37.8	0.1	6.0	48.3
Papua New Guinea	1993	1,298.6	18.8[50]	0.3[50]	6.8[50]	74.1[50]	7.0[50]	38.3[50]	28.8[50]	4.0	3.9	0.9	14.5	76.7
Paraguay	1996	3,107.4	20.9	2.8	8.1	68.2	10.6	36.4	21.2	10.2	11.2	0.2	6.6	71.8
Peru	1997	8,558.4	15.7	0.2	10.4	73.7	12.7	38.3	22.8	15.9	26.5	0.8	5.6	51.2
Philippines	1997	38,581.0	9.2	1.4	8.5	81.0	8.1	38.9	33.9	11.6	19.8	1.5	20.6	46.5
Poland	1996	37,095.0	12.7	1.6	9.2	76.5	13.2	33.0	30.3	64.0	4.4	14.7	1.6	15.2
Portugal	1997	32,964.7	15.6	0.7	8.1	75.7	9.6	35.8	30.2	75.3	3.3	1.4	2.5	17.6
Puerto Rico	1992[12]	15,387.3	17.3	0.3	10.6	71.8	25.4	21.8	24.7	4.8	68.1	0.1	3.7	23.2
Qatar	1994	1,927.4	15.8	2.7	0.6	80.8	7.0	39.7	34.2	33.9	10.6	1.4[4]	13.4	40.8
Réunion	1995	2,711.1	21.5	0.2	4.7	73.6	10.7	29.8	33.1	80.1	0.6	0.1	2.1	17.2
Romania	1997	11,279.8	7.7	2.7	18.9	70.6	9.2	26.4	35.0	52.5	4.1	20.5	1.2	21.7
Russia	1997	67,619.0	19.6	2.4[2]	2.8	75.2[3]	7.3	21.9	46.0[3]	29.0	6.0	20.8	1.5	42.7
Rwanda	1990	291.1	18.2	1.9	15.3	64.6	10.2	16.1	38.3	44.6	1.2	1.4[4]	7.7	45.1
St. Kitts and Nevis	1997	147.2	21.3	0.5	7.5	70.9	7.1	28.9	34.9	12.2	56.0	0.1	4.2	27.6
St. Lucia	1996	313.5	27.7	0.8	8.3	63.3	10.2	21.8	31.3	18.5	39.9	0.1	4.9	36.6
St. Vincent and the Grenadines	1995	134.5	25.1	0.2[2]	6.0	68.6[3]	12.9	17.8	37.9[3]	21.6	36.9	0.1	2.3	39.2
Samoa	1993	130.9	21.6	0.6[2]	8.4	69.4[3]	5.0	37.0	27.4[3]	4.3	8.3	—	15.9	71.5
San Marino[39]	1994	1,652.2	...	...	...	...	...	...	...	...	...	...	...	...
São Tomé and Príncipe	1994	30.4	21.5[22]	...	7.2	71.3	...	40.2	31.1	53.8[29]	25.0[4]	...	5.3	15.9[4]
Saudi Arabia	1996	27,765.0	18.2	0.9	0.2	80.8	9.4	35.5	35.9	34.5	21.9	1.3	7.0	35.2
Senegal	1995	1,224.5	34.7	1.1	10.0	54.2	13.9	18.1	22.2	53.4	5.7	1.8	3.7	35.3
Seychelles	1996	346.7	21.0	0.2	3.3	75.6	4.9	47.9	22.7	31.4	28.9	—	2.4	37.2
Sierra Leone	1995	136.3	— 47.9[2] —		17.4	34.8[3]	7.6	14.7	12.5[3]	48.4[4]	8.1[4]	2.8[4]	0.8[4]	39.8[4]
Singapore	1997	132,441.8	4.9	0.7	9.5	84.9	5.6	57.5	21.8	14.0	16.9	0.5	17.6	51.1
Slovakia	1997	10,264.5	9.4	1.4	11.8	77.4	11.6	32.5	33.3	39.5	3.3	46.5	1.7	8.9
Slovenia	1997	9,365.7	10.9	1.7	8.5	79.0	11.7	33.0	34.4	67.4	3.1	10.6	1.7	17.3
Solomon Islands	1997	184.5	— 17.9[2] —		8.6	73.5[3]	4.9	37.7	30.9[3]	3.4	2.1	—	14.9	79.6
Somalia	1992	228.0[4]	30.3[42]	0.2[42]	4.6[42]	64.9[42]	5.1[42]	37.1[42]	22.7[42]	27.2[4]	10.1[4]	—[4]	0.7[4]	62.0[4]
South Africa[54]	1996	26,872.4	8.4	2.6	9.5	79.5	12.1	38.1	29.3	44.2	12.9	0.4	7.8	34.7
Spain	1996	121,255.4	14.9	2.1	9.1	73.9	11.8	37.3	24.8	66.3	6.2	2.2	2.8	22.5
Sri Lanka	1995	2,833.2	15.0	3.9	7.9	73.2	9.9	19.8	43.5	18.2	3.5	0.9	10.2	67.1
Sudan, The	1996	1,072.9	18.9	0.2	19.4	61.6	15.0	25.7	20.9	25.6	8.5	6.4	5.6	53.8
Suriname	1995	582.9	14.1	0.9	11.8	73.3	14.8	35.6	22.9	24.1	42.4	—	2.1	31.4
Swaziland	1994	962.6	21.8[1]	0.4[1]	10.3[1]	67.4[1]	10.2[1]	26.7[1]	30.6[1]	7.6[1]	0.6[1]	—[1]	0.9[1]	90.9[1, 56]
Sweden	1997	62,864.7	8.9	1.4	7.2	82.5	9.7	42.9	29.8	68.1	6.2	4.1	2.7	18.9
Switzerland[57]	1997	75,900.4	7.8	3.8	4.5	83.8	15.6	31.5	36.7	77.1	8.4	2.0	2.8	9.8
Syria	1995	4,708.8	20.0	0.5	1.1	78.4	10.2	31.6	36.7	34.4	6.8	10.8	4.4	43.7
Taiwan	1999	110,931.0	7.9	1.3	7.4	83.5	11.8	49.3	22.3	13.0	17.8	1.6	27.6	40.0
Tajikistan	1997	750.0	17.4	— 56.8[2] —		25.8[3]	6.9	14.4	4.6[3]	3.6	0.4	20.6	—	75.3
Tanzania	1990	1,021.5	5.4	1.5	10.3	82.8	9.8	45.6	27.4	58.2	1.6	0.8[4]	7.7	31.8
Thailand	1997	62,461.8	7.9	1.8	9.3	80.9	9.6	46.9	24.4	13.9	13.9	1.6	25.6	45.0
Togo	1993	179.5	30.3	0.4	8.0	61.3	16.3	21.8	23.2	66.8	6.8	0.8	4.3	21.2
Tonga	1997	72.9	35.0	0.8	14.1	50.0	7.2	19.2	23.6	0.8	12.3	—	5.7	81.3
Trinidad and Tobago	1996	2,204.5	14.5	3.2	19.2	63.1	10.0	30.7	22.5	17.2	38.1	0.6	4.0	40.1
Tunisia	1997	7,947.1	14.2	1.7	8.0	76.2	8.4	29.6	38.3	72.9	4.3	2.5	2.4	17.8
Turkey	1997	48,585.1	10.1	2.9	10.4	76.7	13.0	38.2	25.4	51.2	8.9	8.9	4.2	26.8
Turkmenistan	1997	1,228.0	26.0	— 8.0[2] —		66.0[3]	12.8	34.7	18.5[3]	11.7	7.2	39.8	0.6	40.7
Tuvalu	1995	15.2	36.1[5]	0.1[2, 5]	14.6[5]	49.2[3, 5]	6.8[5]	13.9[5]	28.5[3, 5]	5.9[29]	2.0	—	1.3	90.8
Uganda	1996	816.1	14.6	1.4[2]	11.2	72.8[3]	14.3	30.5	28.0[3]	27.7	2.7	—	8.1	61.5
Ukraine	1997	17,261.6	8.1	— 47.6[2] —		44.3[3]	11.5	20.2	12.6[3]	19.6	3.8	58.5	0.9	17.3
United Arab Emirates	1992	17,410.0	11.6	0.7	1.7	86.1	5.5	35.1	45.4	33.5	8.9	0.5	16.6	40.5
United Kingdom[38]	1999	320,302.0	10.8	3.2	2.7	83.4	9.7	45.8	27.8	53.0	12.7	2.3	4.8	27.2
United States[59]	1997	898,025.6	6.9	1.6	9.2	82.3	5.7	44.8	31.8	18.1	—	1.0	13.8	67.1
Uruguay	1997	3,715.6	13.2	0.4	9.2	77.2	16.1	35.3	25.7	19.3	11.7	1.6	2.6	64.8
Uzbekistan	1995	2,892.7	19.3	— 2.7 —		78.0	9.0	43.1	25.9	17.7	1.1	36.9	1.5	42.8
Vanuatu	1994	83.3	21.1	0.2	6.8	71.8	6.1	31.8	33.8	9.5	1.4	—	9.5	79.6
Venezuela	1996	8,902.3	18.7	1.3	1.5	78.5	14.8	38.0	25.7	17.9	45.0	0.2	3.4	33.5
Vietnam	1995	8,155.4	— 12.4[2] —		11.1	76.5[3]	15.8	28.7	32.0[3]	8.1	1.6	2.5	11.2	76.5
Virgin Islands (U.S.)	1995	3,200.3	...	...	68.6[60]	...	...	...	...	...	32.7	...	...	...
West Bank[62]	1994	102.5[63]	...	...	...	...	...	...	...	...	...	...	...	...
Western Sahara	...	...	...	...	...	...	...	...	...	...	...	...	...	...
Yemen	1998	2,167.4	36.4	0.1[2]	6.4	57.1[3]	9.7	24.2	23.1[3]	27.4	5.8	0.7	3.4	62.7
Yugoslavia	1997	4,798.8	18.0	4.3	16.1	61.6	12.8	17.8	31.0	41.2	2.8	22.5	1.2	32.2
Zambia	1993	809.0	3.7[50]	1.1[2, 50]	15.2[50]	79.9[3, 50]	12.6[50]	47.0[50]	20.3[3, 50]	24.5	2.8	—	4.3	68.4
Zimbabwe	1997	3,092.3	9.1	1.0	10.2	79.7	14.8	38.8	26.1	22.9	5.5	0.7	5.6	65.4

[1]Year ending March. [2]Excluding precious stones, etc. (667). [3]Including precious stones, etc. (667). [4]Estimate. [5]1991. [6]Year ending September 30. [7]Percentage of the total excluding fish imports or the cannery (52.1% of the overall total), and government purchases (0.1%). [8]1987. [9]Excluding mineral fuels; overall totals on a balance of payments basis, f.o.b.: imports U.S.$1,518,200,000, exports U.S.$1,164,800,000. [10]Percentage of non-oil imports. [11]Includes 66.5% for special categories. [12]Year ending June 30. [13]Figures for Belgium-Luxembourg Economic Union (Luxembourg is also shown separately). [14]1992. [15]Including metals. [16]Excluding metals. [17]Includes 71.5% from India. [18]Mainly electricity. [19]Includes 92.8% to India. [20]Includes 72.2% from South Africa. [21]Includes 19.4% to Switzerland. [22]Main items only. [23]Includes 82.8% for reexports. [24]Domestic exports only. [25]1985. [26]Includes 9.1% for ferronickel. [27]East Timor is included in Indonesia. [28]Includes 38.7% for ships and boats. [29]Main countries only. [30]Includes 63.3% for Ethiopia. [31]Figures for France include Monaco. [32]1988. [33]Includes 82.4% from Israel. [34]Includes 69.2% to Israel and 25.1% to Jordan. [35]Includes 42.5% for nonmonetary gold. [36]Includes 41.5% to Switzerland. [37]1983. [38]Figures for United Kingdom include Guernsey, Isle of Man, and Jersey (data for Jersey is

exports													country
total value ('000,000 U.S.$)	Standard International Trade Classification (SITC) categories (%)							direction of trade (%)					
	food and agricultural raw materials (0 + 1 + 2 – 27 – 28 + 4)	mineral ores and concen-trates (27 + 28 + 667)	fuels and other energy (3)	manufactured goods				to European Union (EU)[b]	to United States	to Eastern Europe[c]	to Japan	to all other[d]	
				total[a] (5 + 6 – 667 + 7 + 8 + 9)	of which chemicals and related products (5)	of which machinery and transport equipment (7)	of which other[a] (6 – 667 + 8 + 9)						
184,433.3	19.1	0.9	7.3	72.6	15.5	32.1	25.0	77.8	3.9	3.4	1.0	13.9	Netherlands, The
1,355.8	6.9	2.0	85.1	6.0	1.0	1.7	3.3	14.3	13.9	—	0.2	71.5	Netherlands Antilles
529.4	—	39.5	—	60.5	—	—	60.5[48]	36.1[4]	11.3[4]	—[4]	29.8[4]	22.7	New Caledonia
14,354.3	61.4	0.4	2.3	36.0	7.2	8.2	20.6	16.1	9.2	1.0	15.4	58.4	New Zealand
666.7	72.2	0.6	1.0	26.2	1.5	7.5	17.2	27.3	45.8	0.9	0.7	25.4	Nicaragua
311.9	22.4	74.8	0.8	2.0	0.1	1.2	0.7	56.4	0.1	—	18.8	24.7	Niger
11,886.5	1.8	—	97.6	0.7	—	—	0.6	46.9	44.1	—	—	9.0	Nigeria
263.0	—	—	—	100.0	—	—	100.0	—	100.0	—	—	—	Northern Mariana Islands
44,917.4	10.6	0.8	51.0	37.6	6.4	12.8	18.4	73.8	7.8	0.7	2.6	13.7	Norway
7,221.9	4.0	0.4	80.4	15.2	0.5	9.4	5.4	0.8	1.0	0.4	15.2	82.5	Oman
8,498.2	15.4	0.2	0.3	84.1	0.7	1.1	82.3	30.8	21.5	0.6	3.4	43.7	Pakistan
0.5	69.1	—	—	30.9	—	—	30.9	—	8.0	—	58.8	33.2	Palau
569.2	71.6	1.2	4.9	22.3	5.1	0.3	16.9	22.9	50.3	0.1	0.8	25.9	Panama
2,624.6	26.8	19.5	30.6	23.1[51]	—	2.5	20.6[51]	12.1	4.0	—	21.4	62.5	Papua New Guinea
1,043.0	82.1	0.2	0.6	17.0	2.2	0.4	14.3	21.7	3.6	—	0.1	74.6	Paraguay
6,759.4	33.9	13.8	5.9	46.4	2.7	0.6	43.0	24.1	23.6	1.0	7.0	44.3	Peru
25,227.7	9.2	0.9	1.2	88.7	1.5	29.9	57.3	18.0	35.1	0.2	16.6	30.0	Philippines
24,393.1	13.1	1.1	6.9	79.0	7.7	23.4	47.9	66.6	2.3	20.0	0.2	10.9	Poland
22,745.7	10.6	1.6	2.3	85.4	4.4	31.6	49.4	80.1	4.8	1.1	0.7	13.3	Portugal
21,051.2	15.8	0.1	2.6	81.5	43.7	21.7	16.2	5.1	87.5	—	0.2	7.2	Puerto Rico
3,212.9	0.5	0.2	73.8	25.4	15.9	1.4	8.1	1.9[4]	2.5[4]	—[4]	55.6[4]	40.0[4]	Qatar
208.7	78.6	0.5	0.2	20.7	1.7	12.7	6.2	79.9	0.6	—	6.1	13.4	Réunion
8,431.1	10.5	0.9	6.1	82.4	7.8	14.0	60.7	56.6	3.8	10.2	0.4	28.9	Romania
87,368.0	4.9	2.5[2]	43.6	49.1[3]	5.2	5.2	38.7[3]	32.3	5.1	18.3	3.4	40.9	Russia
131.9	72.8	3.9	—	23.3[52]	—	—	23.3[52]	64.1[4]	6.1[4]	—[4]	1.9[4]	27.9[4]	Rwanda
41.1	58.2	—	—	41.8	0.2	37.2	4.4	33.7	57.4	—	4.6	4.4	St. Kitts and Nevis
79.5	72.7	—	—	27.3	0.9	5.9	20.4	67.8	14.9	—	0.3	17.0	St. Lucia
59.4	81.2	—[2]	—	18.8[3]	1.0	4.0	13.8[3]	41.0	9.4	—	0.1	49.5	St. Vincent and the Grenadines
17.5	32.7	...	...	67.3	...	...	...	—	3.2	—	—	96.8	Samoa
1,416.3	...	...	...	...	...	...	...	...	...	...	...	...	San Marino[39]
6.5	77.6[22]	...	...	...	...	...	...	88.8[29]	1.9[4]	...	0.5[4]	8.8[4]	São Tomé and Príncipe
56,509.5	0.8	0.2	88.6	10.4	6.9	1.3	2.3	15.6	16.7	—	12.3	55.4[53]	Saudi Arabia
530.8	23.9	10.5	15.1	50.5	39.5	2.5	8.5	23.8	0.6	—	0.4	75.2	Senegal
139.4	29.9	0.1	21.9	48.2	0.2	46.1	1.9	28.6	37.3	—	1.4	32.7	Seychelles
76.1	13.3	77.0	—	9.7	—	—	9.7	65.3[4]	13.3[4]	1.0[4]	1.5[4]	18.9[4]	Sierra Leone
124,988.2	4.2	0.5	7.0	88.2	5.9	65.9	16.4	14.0	18.4	0.8	7.1	59.8	Singapore
8,790.0	7.8	1.0	4.9	86.3	9.3	27.1	49.9	45.0	1.6	45.4	0.1	7.9	Slovakia
8,368.9	5.4	0.4	1.2	93.0	11.0	33.6	48.4	63.6	2.9	11.3	0.2	22.0	Slovenia
156.5	—— 96.5[2] ——		—	3.5[3]	—	—	3.5[3]	24.9	0.1	—	39.7	35.2	Solomon Islands
44.0	95.4	2.3	—	2.3	—	2.3	—	52.3	—	—	—	47.7	Somalia
29,221.0	12.1	15.3	8.7	63.9	7.3	9.0	47.5	28.2	7.7	0.5	6.9	56.7[55]	South Africa[54]
100,955.5	16.9	0.7	2.5	79.9	8.0	42.7	29.2	71.3	4.2	2.2	1.2	21.1	Spain
2,391.4	22.8	7.4	0.9	68.9	0.8	3.2	64.9	31.4	36.3	2.8	5.2	24.3	Sri Lanka
273.2	81.4	0.3	—	18.2	—	0.4	17.8	31.4	1.9	0.1	4.5	62.1	Sudan, The
482.7	18.4	63.6	2.2	15.7	—	1.1	14.7	32.0	22.0	1.2	6.0	38.8	Suriname
751.8	69.1[24]	3.3[24]	0.9[24]	26.7[24]	1.4[24]	8.3[24]	17.1[24]	19.8[24]	3.1[24]	—[24]	0.7[24]	76.4[24]	Swaziland
81,180.3	8.1	1.3	2.2	88.4	6.7	44.9	36.7	54.7	8.5	5.0	3.0	28.8	Sweden
76,150.1	3.4	2.6	0.2	93.8	27.3	31.1	35.4	59.8	10.5	2.9	4.0	22.8	Switzerland[57]
3,969.9	18.6	0.6	62.5	18.2	0.6	0.8	16.8	57.0	0.9	6.1	0.2	35.8	Syria
121,508.9	6.7	0.1	0.8	92.4	8.0	57.0	27.4	15.7	25.4	0.5	9.8	48.6	Taiwan
746.0	4.8	—— 21.5[2] ——		73.7[3]	2.6	2.4	68.8[3]	36.0	0.6	12.7	—	50.7	Tajikistan
416.1	82.0	1.0	2.0	15.1	1.0	2.2	11.8	40.5	6.8	0.7[4]	3.9	48.2	Tanzania
58,282.6	22.3	1.9	2.4	73.4	4.2	38.3	30.9	16.1	19.6	0.8	15.0	48.5	Thailand
136.0	57.7	32.8	0.3	9.2	1.2	3.4	4.6	23.6	0.1	2.9	—	73.3	Togo
10.9	92.0	0.2	—	7.8	0.8	0.1	7.0	1.6	14.6	—	48.8	35.0	Tonga
2,569.2	8.3	0.2	50.3	41.2	22.8	3.8	14.6	9.6	48.8	—	0.2	41.3	Trinidad and Tobago
5,559.4	11.7	1.2	9.1	78.0	12.5	10.8	54.7	78.4	0.7	0.4	0.2	20.3	Tunisia
26,244.8	20.8	1.2	0.7	77.2	4.0	12.7	60.5	46.7	7.7	13.6	0.5	31.5	Turkey
751.0	0.9	—— 77.8[2] ——		21.3[3]	0.6	0.2	20.5[3]	6.5	0.1	37.8	—	55.6	Turkmenistan
2.2	92.2[58]	—[58]	—[58]	7.8[58]	—[58]	—[58]	7.8[58]	9.1[29]	—	—	—	90.9	Tuvalu
665.3	82.4	—	0.6	17.0	5.5	1.5	10.1	62.5	2.3	8.3	1.5	25.5	Uganda
14,231.9	14.1	—— 9.0[2] ——		76.9[3]	13.2	13.4	50.3[3]	12.4	2.1	45.8	0.7	39.0	Ukraine
24,756.0	0.3	0.1	96.6	3.0	0.2	0.2	2.6	7.0[4]	3.2[4]	0.1[4]	35.7[4]	53.9[4]	United Arab Emirates
269,040.3	6.7	2.7	5.5	85.1	13.9	47.7	23.4	58.3	14.7	2.3	2.0	22.8	United Kingdom[38]
687,532.7	11.2	1.3	1.9	85.6	10.0	51.2	24.3	20.6	—	1.0	9.5	68.9	United States[59]
2,729.6	53.2	0.3	0.7	45.8	5.3	5.6	34.9	18.9	6.0	0.8	1.1	73.2	Uruguay
3,109.0	2.5	—— 14.8 ——		82.7	2.8	2.4	77.4	18.6	0.4	24.3	0.1	56.7	Uzbekistan
20.8	87.0	—	—	13.0	—	1.0	12.0	32.4	—	—	23.7	44.0	Vanuatu
22,674.4	2.5	0.5	82.2	14.9	3.1	2.1	9.7	8.3	61.1	0.1	0.6	29.9	Venezuela
5,448.9	—— 45.0[2] ——		22.2	32.8[3]	0.6	1.6	30.6[3]	11.9	3.1	2.5	26.8	55.7	Vietnam
3,026.3	...	...	83.3[60, 61]	...	...	...	...	...	92.7	...	...	...	Virgin Islands (U.S.)
22.6[64]	...	...	...	...	...	...	...	...	...	...	...	...	West Bank[62]
...	...	...	...	...	...	...	...	...	...	...	...	...	Western Sahara
1,497.5	5.4	0.3[2]	91.5	2.8[3]	0.4	1.2	1.2[3]	5.8	2.7	—	3.7	87.8	Yemen
2,367.8	21.0	0.3	2.0	76.7	13.0	9.5	54.1	35.4	0.7	17.0	—	46.9	Yugoslavia
920.6	—— 5.3 ——		1.7	93.0	0.4	0.8	91.8	29.8	0.4	—	13.3	56.6	Zambia
2,127.8	56.5	5.3	1.5	36.8	3.4	3.4	30.0	36.4	5.8	2.7	6.1	49.0	Zimbabwe

also shown separately). [39]Figures for Italy include San Marino. [40]United Kingdom only. [41]Including coins. [42]1986. [43]Includes 83.8% from rest of Customs Union of Southern Africa. [44]Includes 50.8% to rest of Customs Union of Southern Africa. [45]Including also Iceland and Norway. [46]France only. [47]Includes 85.0% from South Africa. [48]Includes 52.5% for ferroalloys. [49]Excluding bulk imports of fuels. [50]1990. [51]Includes 19.7% for nonmonetary gold. [52]Includes 19.8% for nonmonetary gold. [53]Includes 46.0% shown as special categories. [54]Figures for South Africa refer to the Customs Union of Southern Africa (includes South Africa, Botswana, Lesotho, Namibia, and Swaziland, also shown separately). [55]Including unspecified destinations for gold exports of 19.7%. [56]Includes 87.7% from South Africa; these imports may have had their origin from other countries. [57]Figures for Switzerland include Liechtenstein also shown separately. [58]1989. [59]Figures for United States include American Samoa, Guam, Puerto Rico, and Virgin Islands (U.S.), also shown separately. [60]1993. [61]Exports of refined petroleum to United States only. [62]Total external trade for West Bank and Gaza Strip in 1997: imports U.S.$1,860,000,000, exports U.S.$267,000,000. [63]Excluding imports from Israel (90.9% in 1987). [64]Excluding exports to Israel (70.3% in 1987).

Household budgets and consumption

This table provides international data on household income, on the consumption expenditure of households for goods and services, and on the principal object of such expenditure (in most countries), food consumption (by kind). For purposes of this compilation, income comprises pretax monetary payments and payment in kind. The first part of the table provides data on distribution of income by households and by sources of income; the second part analyzes the largest portion of income use—consumption expenditure. Such expenditure is defined as the purchase of goods and services to satisfy current wants and needs. This definition excludes income expended on taxes, debts, savings and investments, and insurance policies. The third and last part of the table focuses on food, which usually, and often by a wide margin, represents the largest share of consumer spending worldwide. The data provided include daily available calories per capita and consumption of major food groups.

For both sources of income and consumption expenditure, the primary basis of analysis for most countries is the household, an economic unit that can be as small as a single person or as large as an extended family. For some of the countries that do not compile information by household, the table provides data on personal income and personal expenditure—*i.e.*, the income and expenditure of all the individuals constituting a society's households. When no expenditure data at all is available, the table reports the weights of each major class of goods and services making up a given country's consumer (or retail) price index (CPI). The weighting of the components of the CPI usually reflects household spending patterns within the country or its principal urban or rural areas.

The data on distribution of income show, collectively for an entire country, the proportion of total income earned (occasionally, expended) by households constituting the lowest quintile and highest decile (poorest 20% and wealthiest 10%) within the country. These figures show the degree to which either group represents a disproportionate share of poverty or wealth.

The data on sources of income illuminate patterns of economic structure in the gaining of an income. They indicate, for example, that in poor, agrarian countries income often derives largely from self-employment (usually farming) or that in industrial countries, with well-developed systems of salaried employment and social welfare, income derives mainly from wages and salaries and secondarily from transfer payments (*see* note a). Because household sizes and numbers of income earners vary so greatly internationally, and because the frequency and methodology of household and CPI surveys do not permit single-year comparisons for more than a few countries at once, no summary of total *household* income or expenditure was possible. Instead, U.S. dollar figures are supplied for *per capita* private final consumption expenditure (for a single, recent year) that are more comparable internationally and refer to the same date. The figures on distribution of consumption expenditure by end use reveal patterns of personal and family use of disposable income and indicate, inter alia, that in developing countries, food may absorb 50% or more of disposable income, while in the larger household budgets of the developed countries, by contrast, food purchases may account for only 20–30% of spending. Each category of expenditure betrays similar complexities of local habit, necessity, and aspiration.

The reader should exercise caution when using these data to make inter-country comparisons. Most of the information comes from single-country surveys, which often differ markedly in their coverage of economically or demographically stratified groups, in sample design, or in the methods

Household budgets and consumption

country	income (latest)						consumption expenditure						
	percent received by		by source (percent)				per capita private final, U.S.$ (1995)	by kind or end use (percent of household or personal budget; latest)					
	lowest 20% of households	highest 10% of households	wages, salaries	self-employment	transfer payments[a]	other[b]		food[c]	housing[d]	clothing[e]	health care	energy, water	education
Afghanistan	…	…	20.7	28.0	8.2	43.1	…	33.9	3.0	…	1.1	0.7	…
Albania	…	…	53.0	4.0	11.5	31.5	680	…	…	…	…	…	…
Algeria	7.0[1]	26.8[1]	43.1	38.3	18.6	1.8	810	52.3	6.7[2]	8.6	2.8	[2]	[3]
American Samoa	…	…	…	…	…	…	1,880[4]	32.9	20.4[5]	5.2	…	…	…
Andorra	…	…	…	…	…	…	…	…	…	…	…	…	…
Angola	…	…	…	…	…	…	370	74.1[6]	10.2[2, 6]	5.5[6]	1.8[6]	[2, 6]	2.7[6]
Antigua and Barbuda	…	…	…	…	…	…	4,050	*42.9*	*23.3*	*7.5*	…	5.5	…
Argentina	*4.4*	*35.2*	53.9	31.5	1.5	12.7	6,620	40.1	9.3	8.0	7.9	9.0	2.6
Armenia	…	…	24.5	13.6[7]	5.5	56.4	360	69.6	…	17.4	…	…	…
Aruba	…	…	…	…	…	…	11,190	26.9	9.9	8.4	2.9	8.5	1.9
Australia	5.9	25.4	72.7	7.5	13.0	6.8	12,040	18.7	18.5	5.6	7.1	2.2	1.6
Austria	*10.4*	*19.3*	55.7	[8]	24.4	19.9[8]	16,020	28.1	14.5	8.5	5.8	4.0	0.4
Azerbaijan	…	…	70.2	10.8[7]	19.0	—	460	42.2	—	13.6	4.8	—	—
Bahamas, The	3.6	32.1	…	…	…	…	3,950[9]	13.8	32.8	5.9	4.4	…	5.3
Bahrain	…	…	…	…	…	…	2,240	32.4	21.2	5.9	2.3	2.2	2.3
Bangladesh	8.7[1]	28.6[1]	18.7	48.3	7.5	25.5	170[10]	63.3	8.8	5.9	1.1	8.4	1.2
Barbados	*7.0*	*44.0*[11]	…	…	…	…	4,860	45.8	16.8	5.1	3.8	5.2	[3]
Belarus	11.4[1]	20.0[1]	47.1	7.3[9]	45.6	—	610	29.0	2.7	…	…	…	…
Belgium	*9.5*[12]	*20.2*[12]	49.6	10.9	20.7	18.8	16,550	18.3	11.4	7.0	10.5	6.2	[3]
Belize	…	…	*84.1*	——*15.9*——			1,780	34.0	9.0	8.8	1.6	9.1	2.3
Benin	*8.0*	*39.0*	26.3	——73.7——			240	37.0	10.0	14.0	5.0	2.0	4.0
Bermuda	7.2	24.7	65.3	9.0	3.3	22.4	12,690[13]	14.6	27.7	4.9	7.6	3.3	3.8
Bhutan	…	…	…	…	…	…	170	*72.3*	…	*21.2*	…	*3.7*	…
Bolivia	5.6[12]	31.7[12]	…	…	…	…	690	46.6	7.8	5.1	2.1	4.7	0.3
Bosnia and Herzegovina	…	…	53.2	12.0	18.2	16.6	1,890[14]	44.7	1.6	8.3	3.4	7.8	[3]
Botswana	3.7	42.9	73.3	15.4	10.8	0.4	1,030	39.5[15]	11.8	5.6	2.3	2.5	4.9
Brazil	2.5[12]	47.6[12]	62.4	14.7	10.9	12.0	4,420	25.3	21.3[2]	12.9	9.1	[2]	…
Brunei	…	…	…	…	…	…	…	*45.1*	*2.6*	*6.1*	…	*2.4*	[3]
Bulgaria	8.5[1]	22.5[1]	34.7	23.6[7]	14.8	—	1,470	47.0	4.1	7.4	3.2	4.3	[3]
Burkina Faso	5.5[1]	39.5[1]	…	…	…	…	220	38.7[6]	5.1[6]	4.4[6]	5.2[6]	13.7[6]	[3]
Burundi	7.9[1]	26.6[1]	…	…	…	…	190	59.6[6]	4.4[6]	11.1[6]	…	5.8[6]	…
Cambodia	6.9[1]	33.8[1]	…	…	…	…	280	…	…	…	…	…	…
Cameroon	…	…	41.4	52.6	3.0	3.0	570	49.1	18.0[2]	7.6	8.6	[2]	…
Canada	7.5[12]	23.8[12]	57.0	13.7	20.7	8.6	11,460	13.4	24.5[2]	5.3	4.7	[2]	3.1
Cape Verde	…	…	…	…	…	…	920	60.0	8.5	2.5	0.5	4.9	[17]
Central African Republic	2.0[1]	47.7[1]	…	…	…	…	350	70.5[6]	0.6[6]	9.5[6]	1.0[6]	6.5[6]	…
Chad	*8.0*	*30.0*	…	…	…	…	170	45.3[6]	…	3.5[6]	11.9[6]	5.8[6]	…
Chile	3.5[12]	46.1[12]	——75.1——		12.0	12.9	2,940	27.9	15.2	22.5	…	…	…
China	5.9[12]	30.4[12]	21.6	72.2	——6.2——		260	49.9[15, 18]	6.8[18]	13.7[18]	2.9[18]	…	2.3[18]
Colombia	3.0[12]	46.1[12]	45.1	35.4	14.2	5.3	1,540	45.0	7.8	4.5	6.4	2.2	1.7
Comoros	…	…	*25.6*	*64.5*	*8.7*	*1.2*	350	67.3	2.3	11.6	3.2	3.8	[3]
Congo, Dem. Rep. of the	…	…	…	…	…	…	190	61.7	11.5[2]	9.7	2.6	[2]	[3]
Congo, Rep. of the	*7.0*	*43.5*	…	…	…	…	870	37.0	6.0	6.0	6.0	3.0	8.0
Costa Rica	4.0[12]	34.7[12]	61.0	22.6	9.6	6.8	1,600	39.1	12.1[2]	9.4	3.7	[2]	[3]
Côte d'Ivoire	7.1[1]	28.8[1]	44.9	49.9	——5.2——		480	48.0	7.8	10.0	0.7	8.5	…
Croatia	9.3[1]	21.6[1]	40.2	40.8	12.1	6.9	3,790	37.8	2.9	8.6	4.3	7.6	[3]
Cuba	…	…	57.3	——42.7——			1,510[9]	26.7	…	…	…	2.5	…
Cyprus	…	…	76.3	5.9	14.4	3.4	8,300	22.7	5.5	10.0	3.1	1.3	1.4
Czech Republic	10.3[12]	22.4[12]	——66.7——		27.6	5.7	2,620	26.7	5.5[2]	7.3	[19]	[2]	…
Denmark	9.6[12]	20.5[12]	63.3	14.6	25.9	−3.8	17,730	17.9	22.9	5.2	2.2	6.1	1.9
Djibouti	…	…	*51.6*	*36.0*	*10.5*	*1.9*	590	50.3	6.4	1.7	2.4	13.1	…
Dominica	…	…	…	…	…	…	2,110	43.1	16.1	6.5	…	5.4	…
Dominican Republic	4.3[12]	37.8[12]	*41.7*	*31.8*	*1.5*	*25.0*	1,150	46.0	10.0	3.0	8.0	5.0	3.0
East Timor	…	…	…	…	…	…	…	…	…	…	…	…	…
Ecuador	5.4[1]	33.8[1]	17.4	76.9	3.6	2.1	1,040	36.1	9.0	10.1	4.2	3.3	[17]

employed for collection, classification, and tabulation of data. Further, the reference period of the data varies greatly; while a significant portion of the data is from 1980 or later, information for some countries dates from the 1970s. This older information is typeset in italic. Finally, intercountry comparisons of annual personal consumption expenditure may be misleading because of the distortions of price and purchasing power present when converting a national currency unit into U.S. dollars.

The table's food consumption data include total daily available calories per capita (food supply), which amounts to domestic production and imports minus exports, animal feed, and nonfood uses, and a percentage breakdown of the major food groups that make up food supply.

The data for daily available calories per capita provide a measure of the nutritional adequacy of each nation's food supply. The following list, based on estimates from the United Nations Food and Agriculture Organization (FAO), indicates the regional variation in recommended daily minimum nutritional requirements, which are defined by factors such as climatic ambience, physical activity, and average body weight: Africa (2,320 calories), formerly Centrally Planned Asia (2,300 calories), Far East (2,240 calories), Latin America (2,360 calories), Near East (2,440 calories).

The breakdown of diet by food groups describes the character of a nation's food supply. A typical breakdown for a low-income country might show a diet with heavy intake of vegetable foods, such as cereals, potatoes, or cassava. In the high-income countries, a relatively larger portion of total calories derives from animal products (meat, eggs, and milk). The reader should note that these data refer to total national *supply* and often do not reflect the differences that may exist within a single country.

In compiling this table, Britannica editors rely on both numerous national reports and principal secondary sources such as the World Bank's *World Development Report* (annual), the International Labour Organisation's *Sources and Methods: Labour Statistics vol. 1 Consumer Price Indices* (3rd ed.), the UN's *Yearbook of National Accounts Statistics* (annual) and *National Accounts Statistics: Compendium of Income Distribution Statistics,* and the FAO's *Food Balance Sheets.*

The following terms further define the column headings:

a. Includes pensions, family allowances, unemployment payments, remittances from abroad, and social security and related benefits.
b. Includes interest and dividends, rents and royalties, and all other income not reported under the three preceding categories.
c. Includes alcoholic and nonalcoholic beverages and meals away from home when identifiable. Excludes tobacco except as noted.
d. Rent, maintenance of dwellings, and taxes only; excludes energy and water (heat, light, power, and water) and household durables (furniture, appliances, utensils, and household operations), shown separately.
e. Includes footwear.
f. Furniture, appliances, and utensils; usually includes expenditure on household operation.
g. Includes expenditure on cultural activities other than education.
h. May include data not shown separately in preceding categories, including meals away from home (*see* note c).
i. Represents pure fats and oils only.
j. Consists mainly of peas, beans, and lentils; spices; stimulants; alcoholic beverages (when combined with "other"); sugars and honey; and nuts and oilseeds.

				food consumption, 1998									country
				daily available calories per capita	percent of total calories derived from:								
transportation, communications	household durable goods[f]	recreation[g]	personal effects, other[h]		cereals	potatoes, cassava	meat, poultry	fish	eggs, milk	fruits, vegetables	fats, oils[i]	other[j]	
…	…	…	61.3	1,716	83.4	1.1	4.1	—	2.4	2.6	3.8	2.6	Afghanistan
…	…	…	…	2,976	51.1	1.8	5.1	0.1	16.9	6.0	9.0	10.0	Albania
12.0	4.5	4.6[3]	8.5	3,020	60.3	2.2	2.7	0.3	6.1	5.1	13.8	9.5	Algeria
17.8	[5]	1.1	22.6	…	…	…	…	…	…	…	…	…	American Samoa
…	…	…	…	3,348	22.6	4.7	13.4	2.4	9.3	6.7	21.6	19.4	Andorra
3.9[6]	…	…	1.8[6]	…	…	…	…	…	…	…	…	…	Angola
10.0	…	…	*10.8*	2,450	25.8	1.0	15.8	1.7	11.3	7.9	16.4	20.2	Antigua and Barbuda
11.6	…	7.5	5.9	3,144	29.5	5.2	16.5	0.5	10.3	4.5	15.4	18.0	Argentina
…	6.6	…	28.7	2,356	52.3	6.7	5.3	0.1	7.0	6.5	11.7	10.4	Armenia
15.5	9.1	3.1	11.9	2,659	28.2	2.3	18.9	1.4	10.8	5.0	13.6	19.7	Aruba
15.1	7.0	7.5	16.7	3,190	22.7	3.2	15.5	0.8	11.8	5.3	17.0	23.5	Australia
16.3	7.8	7.1	7.5	3,531	20.7	3.1	13.8	0.6	11.4	5.5	21.5	23.4	Austria
5.1	6.5	0.7	27.1	2,191	66.6	2.7	4.6	0.1	9.7	5.1	2.8	8.4	Azerbaijan
14.8	8.9	4.9	9.2	2,546	30.1	1.4	18.8	1.1	5.9	8.6	9.3	24.9	Bahamas, The
8.5	9.8	6.4	9.0	…	…	…	…	…	…	…	…	…	Bahrain
0.9	…	…	10.4	2,050	81.6	1.3	0.8	0.9	1.5	1.1	5.6	7.2	Bangladesh
10.5	8.1	4.8[3]	—	2,978	31.6	3.9	12.6	2.3	6.6	3.4	12.8	26.8	Barbados
…	…	…	68.3	3,136	36.2	9.9	10.5	0.1	10.2	2.6	12.0	18.7	Belarus
13.4	10.6	6.8[3]	15.8	3,606	20.4	5.2	8.6	1.1	10.8	6.5	25.7	21.7	Belgium
13.7	8.0	…	9.4	2,922	34.0	1.4	6.3	0.4	7.5	9.6	10.2	30.7	Belize
14.0	5.0	…	9.0	2,571	37.5	36.9	2.2	0.7	0.8	2.6	5.3	14.0	Benin
7.3	16.6	10.8	3.4	2,921	22.8	2.6	15.7	2.7	7.8	12.4	15.2	20.8	Bermuda
…	*0.7*	…	*2.1*	…	…	…	…	…	…	…	…	…	Bhutan
17.7	9.7	2.7	3.3	2,214	40.7	6.6	11.2	0.1	3.7	8.6	11.4	17.7	Bolivia
6.0	4.1	3.5[3]	2.3	2,801	64.6	5.6	4.3	0.1	3.7	4.5	3.7	13.4	Bosnia and Herzegovina
13.1	13.8	3.1	3.4	2,159	46.9	1.8	6.3	0.5	8.9	2.5	11.6	21.6	Botswana
15.0	…	…	16.4	2,926	30.9	4.3	10.8	0.4	8.3	4.5	12.6	28.2	Brazil
17.2	*8.3*	*8.9*[3]	*9.4*	2,851	48.0	1.2	13.0	1.3	6.4	5.0	6.3	18.9	Brunei
6.6	4.0	3.0[3]	21.5	2,740	37.6	2.1	10.7	0.3	12.1	5.4	15.6	16.3	Bulgaria
18.6[6]	3.0[6]	2.3[3, 6]	9.0[6]	2,149	73.2	0.7	2.6	0.1	1.9	0.9	5.2	15.5	Burkina Faso
…	6.0[6]	…	13.1[6, 16]	1,578	16.7	30.0	1.3	0.4	0.8	10.3	1.5	39.0	Burundi
…	…	…	…	2,078	77.9	1.3	6.2	0.8	0.5	2.9	4.7	5.7	Cambodia
13.0	…	2.4	1.3	2,209	41.7	16.3	3.4	0.8	1.4	13.7	9.1	13.6	Cameroon
14.3	8.8	8.0	17.9	3,167	24.9	2.9	11.4	1.1	8.8	6.6	20.5	23.8	Canada
8.8	6.9	[17]	7.9[17]	3,099	40.3	2.5	5.8	1.5	4.9	3.1	17.6	24.2	Cape Verde
4.1[6]	0.8[6]	1.3[6]	5.7[6]	2,056	18.9	35.9	6.4	0.3	1.5	6.2	13.7	17.1	Central African Republic
…	…	…	33.5[6]	2,171	53.8	9.4	2.3	0.5	2.2	1.5	7.1	23.2	Chad
6.4	…	…	28.0	2,844	38.7	3.4	12.5	1.2	6.7	4.8	12.4	20.3	Chile
4.7[18]	5.3[18]	2.4[18]	12.0[18]	2,972	54.7	5.6	13.2	13.2	2.6	5.3	7.3	10.1	China
18.5	5.7	…	8.2	2,559	32.5	7.2	7.2	0.4	8.7	7.9	11.9	24.2	Colombia
2.2	3.0	2.5[3]	4.1	1,858	42.7	15.6	1.8	2.4	1.1	8.0	10.3	18.1	Comoros
5.9	4.8	3.8[3]	—	1,701	19.2	56.3	1.9	0.6	0.1	6.5	6.3	9.1	Congo, Dem. Rep. of the
15.0	4.0	…	15.0	2,241	25.4	37.9	3.1	2.2	1.5	6.2	11.7	11.9	Congo, Rep. of the
11.6	10.9	4.4[3]	8.8	2,781	32.9	1.9	5.3	0.5	9.5	5.0	14.1	30.9	Costa Rica
12.2	3.4	…	9.4	2,695	42.5	24.7	1.9	0.7	0.9	8.7	11.2	9.4	Côte d'Ivoire
9.3	4.5	4.1[3]	1.5	2,479	31.2	8.4	4.2	0.3	10.6	7.5	11.9	25.8	Croatia
5.4	…	…	65.4	2,473	37.3	5.3	5.3	0.8	4.9	5.1	9.6	31.7	Cuba
15.6	10.5	6.3	23.6	3,474	25.6	2.4	14.7	1.0	12.7	8.0	12.7	22.9	Cyprus
3.1	4.5	0.8[19]	52.7	3,292	27.6	4.4	10.1	0.7	9.6	4.3	17.9	25.4	Czech Republic
15.5	6.1	8.3	13.9	3,443	25.4	3.8	11.7	1.4	9.9	4.9	17.6	25.3	Denmark
…	1.5	…	24.6	2,074	51.3	0.2	4.5	0.2	4.8	1.6	17.9	19.4	Djibouti
11.6	6.0	…	11.3	2,996	23.9	9.1	10.6	1.6	8.7	12.5	6.9	26.7	Dominica
4.0	8.0	…	13.0	2,277	28.3	2.8	7.6	0.7	5.2	10.1	19.1	26.4	Dominican Republic
…	…	…	…	…	…	…	…	…	…	…	…	…	East Timor
12.8	5.5	[17]	19.0[17]	2,724	34.5	2.7	5.8	0.6	6.6	4.4	20.6	24.8	Ecuador

Household budgets and consumption (continued)

country	income (latest)						consumption expenditure						
	percent received by		by source (percent)				per capita private final, U.S.$ (1995)	by kind or end use (percent of household or personal budget; latest)					
	lowest 20% of households	highest 10% of households	wages, salaries	self-employment	transfer payments[a]	other[b]		food[c]	housing[d]	clothing[e]	health care	energy, water	education
Egypt	9.8[1]	25.0[1]	…	…	…	…	740	50.2	10.5[2]	10.9	2.7	[2]	[3]
El Salvador	*3.4*[12]	*40.5*[12]	…	…	…	…	1,520	37.0[18]	12.1[18]	6.7[18]	4.2[18]	3.6[18]	3.7[18]
Equatorial Guinea	…	…	57.0[6]	42.0[6]	—	1.0[6]	310	62.0[6]	…	10.0[6]	6.0[6]	…	…
Eritrea	…	…	…	…	…	…	170	…	…	…	…	…	…
Estonia	6.2[12]	26.2[12]	53.0	5.7	12.8	28.5	1,390	41.0	9.6	8.4	[19]	6.5	3.1
Ethiopia	7.1[1]	33.7[1]	0.2	79.5	—	20.3	87	49.0	7.0	6.0	3.0	7.0	4.0
Faroe Islands	…	…	88.3	11.7	—	—	…	40.9	11.0	8.0	…	18.9	…
Fiji	*3.7*	*37.8*	*81.5*	*9.1*	—	*9.4*	1,430[10]	34.7	15.6[2]	9.3	2.4	[2]	[3]
Finland	10.0[12]	21.6[12]	70.3	7.4	9.7	12.6	13,260	22.5	16.9	5.0	4.8	4.6	[3]
France	7.2[12]	25.1[12]	51.1	14.1	27.5	7.3	15,810	17.4	16.2	6.1	9.8	3.8	0.7
French Guiana	…	…	74.6	—— 25.4 ——			…	30.0[15]	16.1[2]	6.7	4.4	[2]	[3]
French Polynesia	…	…	61.9	18.5	16.6	3.0	4,310[20]	39.6	9.7	6.3	1.0	8.1	1.0
Gabon	*3.3*	*54.4*	…	…	…	…	4,060	…	…	…	…	…	…
Gambia, The	…	…	…	…	…	…	330	58.0[21]	5.1[21]	17.5[21]	…	5.4[21]	…
Gaza Strip	…	…	…	…	…	…	910[22]	…	…	…	…	…	…
Georgia	…	…	34.5	21.6[7]	21.7	22.0	430	38.3	…	14.8	…	0.3	…
Germany	8.2[12]	23.7[12]	57.9	[8]	21.3	20.8[8]	16,850	19.0	16.9	7.9	3.5	4.1	[3]
Ghana	8.4[1]	26.1[1]	41.6[23]	47.1[23]	—	11.3[23]	290	*57.4*	*11.5*[2]	*14.3*	*1.3*	[2]	[3]
Greece	7.5[12]	25.3[12]	34.0	22.8	17.0	26.2	8,140	29.9	14.1	6.5	3.1	3.3	0.5
Greenland	…	…	…	…	…	…	11,110	30.1	10.0	7.7	0.3	5.4	…
Grenada	…	…	…	…	…	…	1,650	40.7[15]	11.9	5.2	[24]	3.9	[3]
Guadeloupe	…	…	78.9	13.7	7.4	—	4,080[27]	31.6[15]	11.3[2]	9.3	4.6	[2]	[3]
Guam	…	…	…	…	…	…	…	*24.1*	*28.6*	*10.6*	*4.8*	…	…
Guatemala	2.1[12]	46.6[12]	…	…	…	…	1,180	64.4	16.0[2]	3.1	0.6	[2]	0.3
Guernsey	…	…	…	…	…	…	…	23.7	12.1	7.5	…	8.2	…
Guinea	6.4[1]	32.0[1]	…	…	…	…	510	*61.5*	*7.3*[2]	*7.9*	*11.1*	[2]	…
Guinea-Bissau	2.1[1]	42.4[1]	…	…	…	…	230	…	…	…	…	…	…
Guyana	4.0	40.0[11]	*73.0*	…	*6.3*	*20.7*	…	*42.5*[15]	*21.4*	*8.6*	…	*5.2*	[3]
Haiti	…	…	…	…	…	…	320	51.1[15]	4.3	8.7	2.2	…	[3]
Honduras	3.4[12]	42.1[12]	58.3	[8]	1.8	39.9[8]	450	44.4	22.4[2]	9.1	7.0	[2]	[3]
Hong Kong	…	…	…	…	…	…	13,880	15.1	15.7[2]	21.3	5.0	[2]	0.5
Hungary	8.8[12]	24.8[12]	—— 55.0 ——		19.2	5.8	4,270	38.1	5.7	7.4	1.5	6.1	0.7
Iceland	4.7	27.3	73.1	2.7	10.2	14.0	15,850	31.3	16.0	7.5	2.3	2.9	1.3
India	8.1[1]	33.5[1]	42.2	39.7	—— 18.1 ——		210	52.2	6.1[25]	10.0	2.4	4.7[25]	1.8
Indonesia	8.0[12]	30.3[12]	*42.1*	*41.5*	*2.5*	*13.9*	640	47.5[18]	20.1[2, 18]	5.5[18]	…	[2]	…
Iran	*3.8*	*41.7*	37.4[18]	30.5[18]	—— 32.1[18] ——		1,040	42.6[15]	24.9[2]	11.8	3.9	[2]	[3]
Iraq	…	…	23.9	33.9	23.0	18.6	1,710[13]	50.2	19.9[2]	10.6	1.6	[2]	[3]
Ireland	6.7[12]	27.4[12]	58.6	13.3	19.9	8.2	9,650	30.5	7.1	7.4	3.2	6.1	2.4
Isle of Man	6.4	26.6	64.1	6.6	16.9	12.4	…	31.0	7.9	7.0	…	11.0	…
Israel	6.9[12]	26.9[12]	63.4[18, 26]	14.6[18, 26]	18.9[18, 26]	3.1[18, 26]	9,930	23.8	19.8	5.3	6.2	2.4	2.9
Italy	8.7[12]	21.8[12]	41.7	25.9	20.3	12.1	11,860	19.5	10.0	9.8	6.7	3.8	0.7
Jamaica	7.0[1]	28.9[1]	63.6	13.9	14.0	8.5	1,770	35.7	5.7	4.6	2.8	4.9	0.2
Japan	10.6[12]	21.7[12]	59.3	11.1	19.5	10.1	24,670	22.6	6.7	6.0	2.7	5.6	5.3
Jersey	…	…	…	…	…	…	…	*28.3*	*14.9*	*8.3*	…	*6.5*	…
Jordan	7.6[1]	29.8[1]	51.4	11.1	13.7	23.8	1,020	40.6	15.8	6.7	2.2	5.0	3.5
Kazakhstan	6.7[1]	26.3[1]	67.7	5.8[7]	16.9	9.6	1,290	29.6	2.6	…	…	…	…
Kenya	5.0	34.9	…	…	…	…	220	46.5	10.0	7.7	2.2	2.6	1.0
Kiribati	…	…	*69.7*	*21.4*	*6.0*	*2.9*	370[4]	50.0[15]	7.5[2, 5]	8.0	…	[2]	…
Korea, North	…	…	…	…	…	…	…	46.5[27]	0.6[27]	29.9[27]	…	3.3[27]	…
Korea, South	7.5[1]	24.3[1]	53.8	25.1	13.1	8.0	5,390	29.7	4.1	7.7	5.0	4.0	14.2
Kuwait	…	…	*53.8*	*20.8*	—— *25.4* ——		…	28.1[15]	15.5	8.1	0.7	9.6	[3]
Kyrgyzstan	6.3[12]	31.7[12]	67.3	—— 32.7 ——			670	33.5	2.2	…	…	…	…
Laos	9.6[1]	26.4[1]	…	…	…	…	140[9]	…	…	…	…	…	…
Latvia	7.6[12]	25.9[12]	67.0	5.4[7]	17.4	10.2	2,400	51.6	…	…	…	…	…
Lebanon	*5.0*	*45.0*	*27.9*	…	*3.0*	*69.1*	3,010	*42.8*[6]	*16.8*[6]	*8.6*[6]	*7.2*[6]	*4.5*[6]	*3.9*[6]
Lesotho	2.8[1]	43.4[1]	22.4	27.8	44.7	5.1	530	48.0[15]	10.1	16.4	…	…	…
Liberia	5.0	73.0[11]	…	…	…	…	330[9]	*34.4*[6]	*14.9*[6]	*13.8*[6]	…	*5.0*[6]	…
Libya	…	…	…	…	…	…	2,330[9]	*37.2*[15]	*32.2*[2]	*6.9*	*3.3*	[2]	[3]
Liechtenstein	…	…	…	…	…	…	…	21.3[15]	18.0	6.6	7.7	4.4	[3]
Lithuania	7.8[1]	25.6[1]	66.4	9.7	18.7	5.2	1,910	50.3	…	…	…	…	…
Luxembourg	10.0	34.0[11]	67.1	4.8	28.1	—	15,140[28]	12.8	13.7	5.9	7.3	6.1	[3]
Macau	…	…	65.0	18.1	7.0	9.9	5,480	39.2[15]	17.5	6.8	4.0	5.2	[3]
Macedonia	…	…	57.7	17.2	16.2	9.0	1,010	40.6	1.9	7.8	3.0	7.8	[3]
Madagascar	5.1[1]	36.7[1]	*58.8*[6, 29]	*14.1*[6, 29]	—	*27.1*[6, 29]	220	59.0	6.0	6.0	2.0	6.0	4.0
Malawi	*10.4*	*40.1*	83.3	6.0	—	11.7	109	30.0	4.0	9.0	4.0	5.0	10.0
Malaysia	4.5[12]	37.9[12]	…	…	…	…	2,090	28.7	10.2[2]	4.3	2.5	[2]	0.6
Maldives	…	…	…	…	…	…	270[9]	57.4	1.6	8.0	2.5	…	[3]
Mali	4.6[1]	40.4[1]	…	…	…	…	200	57.0	2.0	6.0	2.0	6.0	4.0
Malta	…	…	63.8	19.3	—	16.9	5,380	31.2	3.5	7.6	3.5	2.0	0.4
Marshall Islands	…	…	…	…	…	…	…	57.7	15.6[2, 5]	12.0	…	[2]	…
Martinique	…	…	80.0	…	…	20.0	4,840[6]	32.1[15]	10.6[2]	8.0	5.2	[2]	[3]
Mauritania	6.2[1]	29.9[1]	…	…	…	…	470	73.1	2.5	8.1	0.9	7.7	0.4
Mauritius	4.0	46.7	51.7	29.0	11.2	8.1	2,290	41.9	8.8	8.4	3.0	6.4	2.9
Mayotte	…	…	…	…	…	…	…	42.2	…	31.5	…	6.8	…
Mexico	3.6[12]	42.8[12]	61.5	29.1	7.8	1.6	2,110	36.6[15]	13.3[2]	8.4	3.4	[2]	[3]
Micronesia	…	…	51.8	23.0	2.1	23.1	…	73.5	…	…	…	…	…
Moldova	6.9[12]	25.8[12]	41.2	10.4	15.3	33.1	220	…	…	…	…	…	…
Monaco	…	…	…	…	…	…	…	…	…	…	…	…	…
Mongolia	7.3[1]	24.5[1]	72.1	9.5[7]	9.7	8.7	230	39.1	5.9[2]	23.4	0.5	[2]	2.9
Morocco	6.5[1]	30.9[1]	…	…	…	…	900	38.0	7.0	11.0	5.0	2.0	8.0
Mozambique	6.5[1]	31.7[1]	51.6	—— 48.4 ——			57	74.6	11.7	3.7	0.8	…	[3]
Myanmar (Burma)	*8.0*	*40.0*[11]	…	…	…	…	750[28]	*49.1*[6]	*10.4*[6]	*15.3*[6]	*2.4*[6]	*4.0*[6]	*5.9*[6]
Namibia	…	…	67.1	27.5	5.4	…	1,050	…	…	…	…	…	…
Nauru	…	…	…	…	…	…	…	…	…	…	…	…	…
Nepal	7.6[1]	29.8[1]	25.1	63.4	—— 11.5 ——		170	61.2	17.3	11.7	3.7	…	[3]

transportation, communications	household durable goods[f]	recreation[g]	personal effects, other[h]	food consumption, 1998: daily available calories per capita	percent of total calories derived from: cereals	potatoes, cassava	meat, poultry	fish	eggs, milk	fruits, vegetables	fats, oils[i]	other[j]	country
4.7	5.0	3.3[3]	12.7	3,282	65.4	1.6	2.9	0.6	2.1	6.9	6.1	14.3	Egypt
10.2[18]	5.7[18]	4.3[18]	12.5[18]	2,522	53.4	1.5	2.6	0.2	6.3	3.5	7.7	24.9	El Salvador
…	…	…	22.0[6]	…	…	…	…	…	…	…	…	…	Equatorial Guinea
…	…	…	…	1,744	73.4	4.4	0.6	0.0	1.9	0.1	0.7	18.8	Eritrea
9.2	2.3	5.0[19]	15.0	3,058	38.5	5.3	8.9	1.6	12.7	4.3	13.3	15.4	Estonia
8.0	2.0	…	14.0	1,805	66.3	13.1	3.2	0.0	1.9	0.6	2.8	12.1	Ethiopia
…	6.6	…	14.6	…	…	…	…	…	…	…	…	…	Faroe Islands
13.8	9.3	4.3[3]	10.6	2,852	42.3	6.9	8.5	1.4	3.0	1.8	18.7	17.3	Fiji
14.8	6.3	9.5[3]	15.6	3,180	33.6	4.2	16.3	2.0	15.7	3.9	12.9	18.6	Finland
16.1	7.7	6.9	15.3	3,541	24.3	3.4	16.5	1.2	12.0	4.7	19.7	18.3	France
17.5	7.9	6.2[3]	11.2	2,818	32.4	7.9	13.2	2.1	7.5	7.0	10.5	19.3	French Guiana
16.4	4.4	4.0	9.5	2,924	33.6	4.0	13.3	4.4	6.1	3.0	13.6	22.1	French Polynesia
…	…	…	…	2,560	29.5	17.9	7.3	3.1	2.4	16.4	7.9	15.5	Gabon
…	…	…	14.0[21]	2,559	54.0	0.7	1.3	1.9	1.4	0.9	17.7	22.1	Gambia, The
…	…	…	…	…	…	…	…	…	…	…	…	…	Gaza Strip
…	5.9	…	40.7	2,252	60.5	4.8	4.9	0.2	7.6	4.8	3.0	14.2	Georgia
17.8	9.4	10.6[3]	10.8	3,402	22.5	4.1	11.7	0.8	10.3	5.7	21.6	23.3	Germany
3.3	*3.8*	*3.9*[3]	*4.5*	2,684	26.2	48.2	1.2	1.8	0.2	9.6	4.6	8.3	Ghana
17.5	6.9	5.2	13.0	3,630	29.1	3.5	8.9	1.2	11.8	8.6	20.0	16.8	Greece
8.0	9.2	15.5	13.8	…	…	…	…	…	…	…	…	…	Greenland
9.1	13.7	4.6[3]	10.9[24]	2,681	25.3	2.5	9.1	1.5	9.5	9.2	13.1	29.8	Grenada
20.5	9.3	4.7[3]	8.7	2,732	37.8	2.6	10.8	2.6	8.5	8.4	13.1	16.1	Guadeloupe
18.0	…	*5.1*	*8.8*	…	…	…	…	…	…	…	…	…	Guam
7.0	5.0	0.9	2.7	2,159	55.3	0.4	3.6	0.1	5.1	3.1	7.0	25.4	Guatemala
15.7	8.3	…	24.7	3,257	22.8	6.1	14.4	1.0	11.6	5.0	19.1	20.0	Guernsey
5.1	*2.9*	*4.1*	*0.1*	2,315	42.9	15.6	0.9	1.2	1.0	13.0	14.7	10.8	Guinea
…	…	…	…	2,411	61.2	7.4	4.6	0.2	1.4	4.2	13.0	8.1	Guinea-Bissau
4.8	*2.9*	*6.4*[3]	*8.2*	2,476	47.3	3.8	4.8	4.2	5.4	2.8	4.1	27.6	Guyana
7.6	9.2	5.3[3]	11.6	1,876	46.7	8.8	3.3	0.3	2.0	7.4	8.8	22.8	Haiti
3.0	8.3	2.4[3]	3.1	2,343	46.7	0.3	3.6	0.3	8.6	6.7	11.9	21.9	Honduras
8.4	17.5	8.1	8.4	3,200	27.1	1.6	20.0	3.3	5.2	4.0	19.7	19.2	Hong Kong
15.2	8.8	5.9	10.6	3,408	25.4	3.6	10.1	0.2	8.4	5.4	22.7	24.1	Hungary
14.5	7.6	9.6	7.0	3,222	20.7	3.2	14.3	3.6	14.6	4.0	13.4	26.2	Iceland
10.6	3.1	1.8	5.7	2,466	62.7	1.6	0.9	0.4	4.5	3.2	8.5	18.3	India
…	2.9[18]	…	24.0	2,850	64.6	5.8	2.2	1.3	0.6	2.3	7.8	15.4	Indonesia
5.0	6.4	1.7[3]	3.7	2,822	51.2	3.2	4.3	0.3	3.8	11.2	10.8	15.1	Iran
6.5	6.7	0.8[3]	3.7	2,419	59.4	1.2	1.4	0.1	1.9	8.0	19.5	8.6	Iraq
14.0	7.2	0.9	13.1	3,622	26.8	6.0	13.1	0.8	11.3	4.0	16.5	21.4	Ireland
14.9	5.7	…	22.5	3,257	22.8	6.1	14.4	1.0	11.6	5.0	10.1	20.0	Isle of Man
12.9	10.8	4.3	11.6	3,466	33.5	2.5	8.2	0.9	7.6	8.6	18.3	20.3	Israel
13.2	9.5	8.4	18.4	3,608	31.8	1.9	11.1	1.1	8.9	7.2	22.0	15.9	Italy
12.4	5.5	2.1	26.1	2,711	30.5	9.3	8.5	0.8	5.3	7.2	13.1	25.3	Jamaica
11.0	3.7	9.5	26.9	2,874	40.7	2.5	5.8	6.3	6.5	4.3	12.0	21.8	Japan
13.9	*7.1*	…	*21.0*	3,257	22.8	6.1	14.4	1.0	11.6	5.0	19.1	20.0	Jersey
11.2	6.1	4.0	4.9	2,791	52.7	1.1	5.1	0.2	5.4	3.9	15.3	16.3	Jordan
…	…	…	67.8	2,517	54.4	4.1	9.1	0.2	12.0	2.1	7.4	10.8	Kazakhstan
8.4	9.4	3.1	9.1	1,968	52.4	8.6	3.7	0.5	7.2	3.2	9.3	15.3	Kenya
8.0	[5]	…	26.5	2,977	34.7	8.3	4.6	4.6	1.6	4.6	7.2	34.4	Kiribati
…	3.8[27]	…	15.9	1,899	64.5	1.1	3.1	1.3	1.0	7.6	5.8	15.5	Korea, North
11.3	5.0	—— 19.0 ——		3,069	49.7	1.1	9.6	3.0	2.2	7.1	9.7	17.7	Korea, South
13.7	11.2	5.2[3]	7.9	3,059	36.8	1.9	11.2	0.5	9.8	8.4	10.2	21.2	Kuwait
…	…	…	64.3	2,535	58.3	6.7	8.7	—	13.0	2.1	3.6	7.6	Kyrgyzstan
…	…	…	…	2,175	77.7	3.8	4.4	0.7	0.5	2.2	2.3	8.5	Laos
…	…	…	54.8	2,994	32.7	8.4	6.0	0.9	12.9	3.8	15.3	20.0	Latvia
5.4[6]	*2.6*[6]	*1.9*[6]	*6.3*[6]	3,285	34.6	3.9	4.9	0.4	5.2	15.9	13.9	21.2	Lebanon
4.7	11.9	…	8.8	2,210	75.5	4.3	3.4	—	1.1	1.4	3.1	11.2	Lesotho
…	*6.1*[6]	…	*25.8*[6]	1,979	41.5	20.4	2.0	0.4	0.5	5.5	19.8	10.0	Liberia
9.4	*4.6*	*8.5*[3]	*2.5*	3,267	46.3	2.0	4.8	0.3	5.7	7.3	17.0	16.7	Libya
13.3	5.8	16.3[3]	6.6	3,222	22.1	2.3	14.8	0.8	12.5	6.1	18.7	22.7	Liechtenstein
…	…	…	49.7	3,104	45.5	7.8	8.9	0.9	6.9	5.3	10.1	14.6	Lithuania
19.1	10.8	4.2[3]	20.1	3,606	20.4	5.2	8.6	1.1	10.8	6.5	25.7	21.7	Luxembourg
8.2	3.0	8.8[3]	7.3	2,471	36.3	0.7	15.7	2.3	4.7	3.7	20.7	15.8	Macau
6.5	4.2	3.3[3]	1.8	2,938	39.7	3.3	7.0	0.3	5.2	6.9	15.7	21.8	Macedonia
4.0	1.0	…	12.0	2,001	53.0	21.1	5.5	0.7	3.1	3.8	4.4	8.3	Madagascar
10.0	3.0	…	25.0	2,226	59.0	15.8	1.3	0.4	0.5	4.2	4.0	14.7	Malawi
20.9	7.7	11.0	14.1	2,901	41.6	2.1	9.2	3.1	5.2	3.4	12.5	22.8	Malaysia
2.6	17.0	5.9[3]	5.0	2,451	43.5	3.2	1.4	13.1	4.3	5.6	5.2	23.7	Maldives
10.0	1.0	…	12.0	2,118	69.9	0.5	4.2	0.8	4.6	1.2	7.4	11.3	Mali
16.4	9.9	7.1	18.4	3,382	30.8	4.0	8.8	1.6	11.3	7.9	11.5	24.0	Malta
…	[5]	…	14.7	…	…	…	…	…	…	…	…	…	Marshall Islands
20.7	9.4	5.4[3]	8.6	2,865	30.0	4.2	12.1	2.9	8.5	11.0	8.7	22.5	Martinique
2.0	1.2	4.0	0.1	2,640	54.8	0.4	4.0	0.9	10.8	1.2	9.9	18.1	Mauritania
10.0	6.4	—	12.2	2,944	44.7	1.3	4.8	1.2	6.3	3.0	16.6	22.2	Mauritius
5.1	8.8	…	5.6	…	…	…	…	…	…	…	…	…	Mayotte
10.0	11.8	5.5[3]	11.0	3,144	46.2	0.8	8.2	0.7	6.0	4.0	11.3	22.8	Mexico
…	…	…	26.5	…	…	…	…	…	…	…	…	…	Micronesia
…	…	…	…	2,763	48.4	4.2	4.0	0.1	8.9	6.6	8.2	19.7	Moldova
…	…	…	…	3,541	24.3	3.4	16.5	1.2	6.3	3.0	16.6	22.2	Monaco
3.5	8.0	0.4	16.2	2,010	47.0	2.2	27.2	—	10.4	1.2	4.7	7.2	Mongolia
8.0	5.0	…	16.0	3,165	59.7	2.0	2.8	0.5	2.0	5.4	10.4	17.3	Morocco
…	…	1.4[3]	7.9	1,911	41.2	37.3	1.4	0.2	0.6	1.4	8.9	9.1	Mozambique
3.8[6]	*0.5*[6]	*1.1*[6]	*7.5*[6]	2,832	76.3	0.5	2.0	1.0	0.9	2.6	7.0	9.6	Myanmar (Burma)
…	…	…	…	2,107	48.6	13.9	5.6	0.6	3.4	1.9	5.1	20.9	Namibia
…	…	…	…	…	…	…	…	…	…	…	…	…	Nauru
1.2	…	2.9[3]	2.0	2,170	76.8	3.4	2.0	0.1	3.8	2.5	4.4	7.0	Nepal

Household budgets and consumption (continued)

country	income (latest)						consumption expenditure						
	percent received by		by source (percent)				per capita private final, U.S.$ (1995)	by kind or end use (percent of household or personal budget; latest)					
	lowest 20% of households	highest 10% of households	wages, salaries	self-employment	transfer payments[a]	other[b]		food[c]	housing[d]	clothing[e]	health care	energy, water	education
Netherlands, The	7.3[1]	25.1[1]	48.2	10.7	29.1	12.0	15,290	13.6	14.9	7.1	12.9	3.1	0.7
Netherlands Antilles	…	…	…	…	…	…	6,050[10]	24.4[30]	10.4[30]	8.7[30]	2.2[30]	8.3[30]	1.2[30]
New Caledonia	…	…	68.2	18.1	13.7	…	5,410[31]	25.9	23.3[2, 5]	3.5	3.2	[2]	…
New Zealand	2.7[12]	29.8[12]	65.8	9.8	15.2	9.1	10,300	20.0	19.4	4.4	2.9	3.2	1.5
Nicaragua	4.2[1]	39.8[1]	…	…	…	…	360	…	…	…	…	…	…
Niger	2.6	35.4	…	…	…	…	210	50.5	19.1[5]	7.3	…	…	…
Nigeria	4.4[1]	40.8[1]	30.2[18]	46.3[18]	0.9[18]	22.6[18]	350[32]	48.0	3.0	5.0	3.0	1.0	4.0
Northern Mariana Islands	…	…	…	…	…	…	…	49.2[15]	19.5[2, 5]	9.1	[19]	[2]	…
Norway	9.7[12]	21.8[12]	58.8	9.9	24.2	7.1	16,570	23.5	13.7	7.0	5.4	6.2	0.6
Oman	…	…	…	…	…	…	3,000	40.6	24.6	5.1	2.4	3.2	[3]
Pakistan	9.5[1]	27.6[1]	22.0	56.0	——22.0——		300	37.0	11.0	6.0	1.0	5.0	1.0
Palau	…	…	63.7	7.4	18.5	10.4	…	…	…	…	…	…	…
Panama	3.6[1]	35.7[1]	60.8[6]	12.8[6]	13.2[6]	13.2[6]	1,570	34.9	12.6[2]	5.1	3.5	[2]	[3]
Papua New Guinea	4.5[1]	40.5[1]	*57.3*	[8]	*1.1*	*41.6*[8]	1,140	40.9	12.5[5]	6.2	…	4.9	…
Paraguay	2.3	46.6	33.9	[8]	2.5	63.6[8]	1,590	48.7	16.4	9.7	3.4	—	1.5
Peru	4.4[12]	35.4[12]	31.2	65.1	3.7	…	1,820	44.1[15]	6.8[2]	10.1	2.7	[2]	[3]
Philippines	5.4[1]	36.6[1]	45.7	42.5	3.4	8.4	800	56.8	4.1[2]	3.9	…	[2]	…
Poland	7.7[12]	26.3[12]	34.0	4.3	20.7	41.0	1,940	41.2	2.8	10.9	8.1	1.0	[3]
Portugal	*7.3*[12]	*28.4*[12]	46.4	[8]	21.8	31.8[8]	6,860	34.8	2.0	10.3	4.5	3.0	1.4
Puerto Rico	*3.2*	*34.7*	56.3	6.4	29.5	7.8	5,640[10]	20.6	11.8[2]	7.4	11.6	[2]	3.1
Qatar	…	…	80.8	5.6	…	13.6	3,600[4]	24.5	35.1[5]	9.1	1.0	1.9	4.3
Réunion	…	…	68.9	[8]	16.0	15.1[8]	4,820[31]	22.4	11.8	7.9	2.2	2.2	[3]
Romania	8.9[12]	22.7[12]	62.6	——37.4——			1,570	51.1	16.4[2, 5]	15.7	1.2	[2]	[3]
Russia	4.4[1]	38.7[1]	68.5	6.4	15.7	12.1	1,180	34.8	2.7	22.3	…	…	…
Rwanda	9.7[1]	24.2[1]	10.4[33]	47.7[33]	13.9[33]	28.0[33]	130	32.1[33]	13.1[33]	9.4[33]	1.3[33]	1.2[33]	[33]
St. Kitts and Nevis	…	…	…	…	…	…	2,480[28]	*55.6*[15]	*7.6*	*7.5*	…	*6.6*	…
St. Lucia	…	…	…	…	…	…	…	49.6[15]	13.5	6.5	2.3	4.5	[3]
St. Vincent and the Grenadines	…	…	…	…	…	…	1,700	59.8	6.3	7.7	…	6.2	…
Samoa	…	…	*49.4*	*22.8*	…	*27.8*	710[1]	58.8	5.1[5]	4.2	…	5.0	…
San Marino	…	…	…	…	…	…	…	22.1	20.9[2]	8.0	2.6	[2]	[3]
São Tomé and Príncipe	…	…	…	…	…	…	270	…	…	…	…	…	…
Saudi Arabia	…	…	…	…	…	…	2,980	52.2[18, 34]	17.2[18, 34]	6.6[18, 34]	2.1[18, 34]	1.8[18, 34]	1.1[18, 34]
Senegal	6.4[1]	33.5[1]	51.6[6]	——48.4[6]——			380	49.0	7.0	11.0	2.0	4.0	6.0
Seychelles	4.1	35.6	*77.2*	*3.8*	*3.2*	*15.8*	3,410[32]	53.9	13.6	4.2	0.4	9.1	…
Sierra Leone	*1.1*[1]	*43.6*[1]	27.9	61.6	——10.5——		190	63.8	5.8[2]	7.3	4.5	[2]	[3]
Singapore	5.1	33.5	81.2	16.8	——2.0——		11,710	18.7	10.2[2]	7.1	4.6	[2]	1.4
Slovakia	11.9[12]	18.2[12]	76.7	[8]	8.7	14.4[8]	1,580	26.8	7.6[2]	8.9	…	[2]	…
Slovenia	8.4[12]	20.7[12]	52.4	13.0	23.4	11.2	5,460	30.8	18.3	8.5	5.0	7.3	[3]
Solomon Islands	…	…	74.1	——25.9——			820[4]	46.8	21.9[2, 5]	5.7	[19]	[2]	…
Somalia	…	…	…	…	…	…	…	62.3[6, 15]	15.3[6]	5.6[6]	…	4.3[6]	…
South Africa	2.9[1]	45.9[1]	73.6	[8]	4.9	21.5[8]	1,970	29.3	12.6[2]	7.5	4.5	[2]	1.4
Spain	7.5[12]	25.2[12]	48.5	27.5	19.5	4.5	8,840	21.6[15]	12.6[2]	8.6	4.7	[2]	[3]
Sri Lanka	8.0[1]	28.0[1]	48.5	[8]	9.7	41.8[8]	520	48.0	1.9	10.1	1.8	3.3	0.8
Sudan, The	*4.0*	*34.6*	…	…	…	…	1,050[35]	63.6	11.5	5.3	4.1	3.8	[3]
Suriname	…	…	*74.6*	…	*3.2*	*22.2*	5,960[10]	*39.9*[6]	*4.4*[6]	*11.0*[6]	*3.6*[6]	*6.9*[6]	*2.6*[6]
Swaziland	*2.8*	*54.5*	44.4	22.2	12.2	21.2	500	33.5[15]	13.4[2]	6.0	1.8	[2]	[3]
Sweden	9.6[12]	20.1[12]	58.9	9.7	25.8	5.6	13,680	21.3	19.9	8.6	3.2	4.9	0.1
Switzerland	6.9[12]	25.2[12]	63.6	[8]	16.5	19.9[8]	26,060	27.0[15]	13.1	4.4	9.9	7.7	[3]
Syria	…	…	40.7	…	25.1	34.2	2,210	58.8[15]	16.0[2]	7.5	…	[2]	[3]
Taiwan	7.1	25.5	64.5	19.7	4.5	11.3	12,230	26.8	22.5	5.6	7.8	3.0	5.6
Tajikistan	…	…	64.3	5.6[7]	30.1	—	340	65.3	…	…	…	…	…
Tanzania	6.8[1]	30.1[1]	28.1	34.2	3.5	34.2	150	66.7	8.3	9.9	1.3	7.6	…
Thailand	6.4[1]	32.4[1]	36.4	45.0	0.9	17.7	1,540	29.0	6.3	11.6	8.0	1.7	0.5
Togo	*8.0*	*30.5*	…	…	…	…	210	42.5[6]	13.4[2, 6]	11.5[6]	5.0[6]	[2, 6]	[3, 6]
Tonga	…	…	…	…	…	…	…	49.3	10.5	5.6	0.3	2.7	…
Trinidad and Tobago	*2.6*	*33.6*	…	…	…	…	2,050	25.5[15]	21.6	10.4	[19]	…	1.5
Tunisia	5.9[1]	30.7[1]	…	…	…	…	1,260	39.0	10.7	6.0	3.0	5.1	1.8
Turkey	5.8[1]	32.3[1]	24.1	51.4	10.8	13.7	1,940	38.5	22.8[2]	9.0	2.6	[2]	1.4
Turkmenistan	6.1[1]	31.7[1]	56.6	26.0[7]	14.4	3.0	570[10]	…	…	…	…	…	…
Tuvalu	…	…	*17.9*	*76.1*	…	*6.0*	…	45.5	11.5[5]	7.5	…	…	…
Uganda	6.6[1]	31.2[1]	…	…	…	…	260	57.1[6, 15]	…	5.5[6]	…	7.3[6]	…
Ukraine	8.6[1]	26.4[1]	66.4	9.3	13.4	10.9	490	41.3	1.7	…	…	…	[3]
United Arab Emirates	…	…	…	…	…	…	7,940	24.1	23.7	9.1	1.1	1.2	3.9
United Kingdom	6.6[12]	27.3[12]	66.2	9.8	13.9	11.0	12,020	17.1	21.7	6.0	…	4.6	…
United States	5.2[12]	30.5[12]	64.4	9.0	19.3	7.3	18,840	15.4	14.9	6.9	17.0	3.5	2.2
Uruguay	5.4[12]	32.7[12]	53.5	17.0	——29.5——		4,140	39.9	17.6[2]	7.0	9.3	[2]	1.3
Uzbekistan	7.4[12]	25.2[12]	59.8	18.5	21.7	…	950	…	…	…	…	…	…
Vanuatu	…	…	59.0	33.7	——7.3——		680	30.5[15]	29.0[2, 5]	4.7	[19]	[2]	…
Venezuela	3.7[12]	37.0[12]	…	…	…	…	2,490	30.4	11.5	10.6	2.9	3.0	0.8
Vietnam	8.0[1]	29.9[1]	17.2	64.6	17.6	0.5	280	62.4	2.5	5.0	…	…	2.9
Virgin Islands (U.S.)	…	…	65.7	2.6	13.0	12.7	…	25.3[36]	*24.9*[36]	*5.4*[36]	…	*6.5*[36]	…
West Bank	…	…	…	…	…	…	1,380[22]	…	…	…	…	…	…
Western Sahara	…	…	…	…	…	…	…	…	…	…	…	…	…
Yemen	6.1[1]	30.8[1]	…	…	…	…	310	61.0[37]	13.2[37]	…	1.1[37]	6.1[37]	…
Yugoslavia	…	…	41.7	15.8	12.7	29.8	2,480[35]	51.6	1.4	7.4	5.2	8.4	[3]
Zambia	4.2[1]	39.2[1]	79.9	17.8	1.3	1.0	220	36.0	7.0	10.0	8.0	4.0	14.0
Zimbabwe	4.0[1]	46.9[1]	92.0	1.0	…	7.0	580	30.1[15]	6.5	10.3	7.1	8.9	6.0

[1]Data refer to consumption shares by fractiles of persons. [2]Housing includes energy, water. [3]Recreation includes education. [4]1988. [5]Housing includes household durable goods. [6]Capital city only. [7]Agricultural self-employment only. [8]Other includes self-employment. [9]1989. [10]1993. [11]Highest 20%. [12]Data refer to income shares by fractiles of persons. [13]1985. [14]1990. [15]Includes tobacco. [16]Includes wage taxes. [17]Personal effects, other includes education and recreation. [18]Urban areas only. [19]Recreation includes health care. [20]1984. [21]Low-income population in Banjul

transportation, communications	household durable goods[f]	recreation[g]	personal effects, other[h]	food consumption, 1998: daily available calories per capita	percent of total calories derived from: cereals	potatoes, cassava	meat, poultry	fish	eggs, milk	fruits, vegetables	fats, oils[i]	other[j]	country
13.3	7.1	9.7	17.6	3,282	17.1	4.5	15.0	1.0	15.0	6.1	16.1	25.1	Netherlands, The
19.5[30]	10.0[30]	4.2[30]	10.1[30]	2,659	28.2	2.3	18.9	1.4	10.8	5.0	13.6	19.7	Netherlands Antilles
16.1	[5]	6.7	21.3	2,812	30.9	6.1	13.1	1.5	8.6	3.9	16.0	19.9	New Caledonia
17.1	10.9	—— 20.6 ——		3,315	22.1	4.1	15.1	1.3	11.1	7.4	16.8	22.3	New Zealand
…	…	…	…	2,208	50.4	1.3	2.4	0.1	4.3	2.7	10.9	27.9	Nicaragua
…	[5]	…	23.1	1,966	70.5	3.2	2.6	0.1	2.2	1.7	4.4	15.2	Niger
3.0	6.0	…	27.0	2,882	45.8	18.6	2.4	0.4	1.0	4.4	14.1	13.3	Nigeria
8.3	[5]	13.9[19]	—	…	…	…	…	…	…	…	…	…	Northern Mariana Islands
12.8	6.9	8.8	15.1	3,425	27.4	4.3	10.7	3.5	12.2	4.9	17.7	19.2	Norway
8.9	7.1	4.1[3]	4.0	…	…	…	…	…	…	…	…	…	Oman
13.0	5.0	…	21.0	2,447	57.0	0.9	3.1	0.2	8.5	2.9	13.2	14.3	Pakistan
…	…	…	…	…	…	…	…	…	…	…	…	…	Palau
15.1	8.4	11.7[3]	8.7	2,476	37.0	2.7	7.5	1.1	7.4	5.7	16.1	22.5	Panama
13.0	[5]	…	22.5	2,168	31.2	25.4	7.7	1.3	0.6	17.6	6.2	9.9	Papua New Guinea
4.5	6.2	2.3	7.3	2,577	27.8	13.9	11.5	0.4	7.3	4.3	16.2	18.7	Paraguay
7.3	7.5	7.6[3]	13.9	2,420	35.7	13.4	4.3	1.8	4.5	6.4	11.6	22.4	Peru
5.0	12.8	…	17.3	2,280	51.7	4.2	8.8	3.0	2.2	8.3	5.9	15.9	Philippines
8.9	8.3	15.0[3]	3.8	3,351	34.4	7.4	10.4	1.0	8.6	4.5	15.6	18.0	Poland
15.4	8.6	4.4	15.6	3,691	28.6	6.3	10.8	2.4	8.3	7.1	17.0	19.6	Portugal
11.8	11.2	7.9	14.7	…	…	…	…	…	…	…	…	…	Puerto Rico
13.0	[5]	—— 11.1 ——		…	…	…	…	…	…	…	…	…	Qatar
24.9	6.0	10.1[3]	12.5	3,308	41.4	1.7	11.9	1.5	5.2	5.0	9.8	23.5	Réunion
6.6	[5]	4.5[3]	4.5	3,263	49.5	4.5	7.4	0.1	11.3	4.5	10.5	12.2	Romania
…	9.4	…	30.8	2,835	41.3	8.0	9.0	1.6	10.3	3.4	9.6	20.6	Russia
1.7[33]	5.3[33]	0.4[33]	35.5[33]	2,035	22.4	23.1	1.1	—	1.4	25.9	5.5	—	Rwanda
4.3	*9.4*	…	*9.0*	2,766	24.9	2.6	13.6	1.9	8.6	4.6	11.6	32.1	St. Kitts and Nevis
6.3	5.8	3.2[3]	8.3	2,842	34.3	4.8	14.0	1.3	6.8	9.3	6.9	22.7	St. Lucia
3.7	6.6	…	9.7	2,554	35.2	4.3	10.4	1.1	6.1	5.2	9.6	28	St. Vincent and the Grenadines
9.0	[5]	…	17.9	…	…	…	…	…	…	…	…	…	Samoa
17.6	7.2	7.1[3]	14.5	3,608	31.8	1.9	11.1	1.1	8.9	7.2	22.0	15.9	San Marino
…	…	…	…	2,201	28.3	15.4	1.4	2.1	0.8	17.0	10.6	24.3	São Tomé and Príncipe
4.5[18, 34]	5.9[18, 34]	…	8.6[18, 34]	2,888	46.6	1.1	7.3	0.4	4.9	10.1	11.4	18.2	Saudi Arabia
5.0	2.0	…	12.0	2,277	57.5	1.0	3.7	2.8	2.4	2.0	18.7	11.9	Senegal
6.4	6.6	1.4	4.4	2,462	37.3	1.2	5.6	5.1	6.5	5.8	11.5	27.1	Seychelles
4.4	3.9	3.8[3]	4.8	2,045	53.4	10.4	1.0	1.4	0.6	2.9	17.6	12.8	Sierra Leone
13.8	8.9	13.1	23.3	…	…	…	…	…	…	…	…	…	Singapore
…	3.9	…	26.2	2,953	27.3	4.3	10.5	0.3	8.9	4.7	20.8	23.2	Slovakia
12.7	3.3	0.1[10]	8.0	2,950	35.4	3.5	11.1	0.4	12.0	5.3	15.2	17.2	Slovenia
9.9	[5]	[19]	15.7	2,130	33.3	36.3	3.1	3.7	0.6	2.7	2.0	17.4	Solomon Islands
…	…	…	12.1[6]	1,531	33.4	1.5	8.7	0.2	28.4	2.8	7.4	17.5	Somalia
16.7	10.0	6.3	11.7	2,909	53.0	2.0	7.0	0.5	4.8	2.8	11.7	18.1	South Africa
15.3	7.1	7.0[3]	23.1	3,348	22.6	4.7	13.4	2.4	9.3	6.7	21.6	19.4	Spain
17.0	3.9	2.4	10.8	2,314	51.3	2.9	0.9	1.9	3.4	4.5	2.9	32.3	Sri Lanka
1.5	5.5	0.7[3]	4.0	2,444	56.5	0.6	5.1	0.1	13.3	2.9	9.5	11.9	Sudan, The
9.5[6]	*12.3*[6]	*5.8*[6]	*4.0*[6]	2,633	41.2	2.3	7.0	1.6	4.8	6.2	12.5	24.5	Suriname
8.8	12.8	3.3[3]	20.4	2,503	48.1	1.3	6.4	—	5.2	1.8	6.2	31.0	Swaziland
15.7	6.6	10.9	8.8	3,114	25.6	3.6	10.2	1.8	14.1	5.2	18.9	20.7	Sweden
12.9	5.1	9.8[3]	10.1	3,222	22.1	2.3	14.8	0.8	12.5	6.1	18.7	22.7	Switzerland
2.4	5.8	2.1[3]	7.4	3,378	53.9	1.2	3.8	0.1	6.6	5.6	12.9	15.9	Syria
10.7	2.2	1.1	4.7	…	…	…	…	…	…	…	…	…	Taiwan
…	…	…	34.7	2,176	67.9	0.1	2.8	—	3.4	4.3	12.2	9.2	Tajikistan
4.1	1.4	0.7	—	1,999	49.0	19.5	2.6	1.1	2.2	5.4	6.8	13.6	Tanzania
12.9	10.9	4.2	14.9	2,462	47.1	1.9	6.6	2.6	2.8	5.7	6.1	27.3	Thailand
9.5[6]	4.4[6]	5.1[3, 6]	8.6[6]	2,513	50.7	29.2	2.3	1.3	0.6	1.3	7.2	7.5	Togo
5.8	10.6	0.5	14.7	…	…	…	…	…	…	…	…	…	Tonga
15.2	14.3	[17]	6.2[17]	2,711	36.8	2.8	4.5	0.9	6.8	3.8	14.6	29.9	Trinidad and Tobago
9.0	11.2	7.1	7.1	3,297	52.9	1.8	3.0	0.5	4.6	6.2	15.8	15.3	Tunisia
8.8	9.0	5.6	2.3	3,554	48.4	3.7	2.5	0.4	6.9	7.9	15.1	15.1	Turkey
…	…	…	…	2,684	57.7	0.5	7.6	0.1	8.2	3.4	16.4	6.1	Turkmenistan
10.5	[5]	…	25.0	…	…	…	…	…	…	…	…	…	Tuvalu
5.9[6]	…	…	24.2[6]	2,216	20.4	23.4	3.2	0.8	1.9	25.8	2.2	22.3	Uganda
…	6.8	6.3[3]	43.9	2,878	44.5	8.8	5.8	0.7	10.3	3.4	10.8	15.7	Ukraine
14.1	11.6	4.7	6.5	3,372	33.8	1.6	11.5	1.4	9.5	14.3	10.3	17.7	United Arab Emirates
15.1	8.0	15.9	11.6	3,257	22.8	6.1	14.4	1.0	11.6	5.0	19.1	20.0	United Kingdom
13.9	1.5	5.8	18.9	3,757	23.6	2.9	11.9	0.8	11.7	5.2	17.9	26.1	United States
10.4	6.3	3.1	5.1	2,866	28.9	3.7	19.1	0.6	12.3	4.0	11.0	20.3	Uruguay
…	…	…	…	2,564	55.8	2.1	6.9	—	9.4	4.1	15.3	6.2	Uzbekistan
13.2	[5]	12.3[19]	10.3	2,737	21.4	30.7	9.2	1.6	1.5	6.4	8.9	20.3	Vanuatu
7.1	4.5	2.7	26.4	2,358	34.9	3.1	6.6	1.7	6.5	7.3	15.2	24.7	Venezuela
…	4.6	…	22.6	2,422	70.9	4.0	7.6	1.3	0.5	3.9	3.2	8.6	Vietnam
11.7[36]	*4.3*[36]	…	*21.9*[36]	…	…	…	…	…	…	…	…	…	Virgin Islands (U.S.)
…	…	…	…	…	…	…	…	…	…	…	…	…	West Bank
…	…	…	…	…	…	…	…	…	…	…	…	…	Western Sahara
1.9[37]	3.0[37]	…	13.7[37]	2,087	68.7	1.0	2.7	0.7	1.8	3.0	8.2	13.9	Yemen
5.7	1.6	2.4[3]	16.3	2,963	29.4	2.3	16.3	0.2	11.4	6.8	17.8	15.8	Yugoslavia
5.0	1.0	…	15.0	1,950	64.9	14.5	2.7	0.8	1.3	1.5	3.4	10.9	Zambia
1.1	12.9	0.6	16.5	2,153	60.5	2.1	2.3	0.3	3.1	1.0	11.9	18.8	Zimbabwe

and Kombo St. Mary only. [22]1986. [23]Urban areas of Eastern region only. [24]Personal effects, other includes health care. [25]Housing includes water. [26]Wage earners only. [27]Workers and clerical workers only. [28]1992. [29]Malagasy households only. [30]Curaçao only. [31]1987. [32]1994. [33]Rural areas only. [34]Middle-income population only. [35]1991. [36]St. Thomas only. [37]Data refer to former Yemen Arab Republic.

Health services

The provision of health services in most countries is both a principal determinant of the quality of life and a large and growing sector of the national economy. This table summarizes the basic indicators of health personnel; hospitals, by kind and utilization; mortality rates that are most indicative of general health services; external controls on health (adequacy of food supply and availability of safe drinking water); and sources and amounts of expenditure on health care. Each datum refers more or less directly to the availability or use of a particular health service in a country, and, while each may be a representative measure at a national level, each may also conceal considerable differences in availability of the particular service to different segments of a population or regions of a country. In the United States, for example, the availability of physicians ranges from about one per 730 persons in the least well-served states to one per 260 in the best-served, with a rate of one per 150 in the national capital. In addition, even when trained personnel exist and facilities have been created, limited financial resources at the national or local level may leave facilities underserved; or lack of good transportation may prevent those most in need from reaching a clinic or hospital that could help them.

Definitions and limits of data have been made as consistent as possible in the compilation of this table. For example, despite wide variation worldwide in the nature of the qualifying or certifying process that permits an individual to represent himself as a physician, organizations such as the World Health Organization (WHO) try to maintain more specific international standards for training and qualification. International statistics presented here for "physicians" refer to persons qualified according to WHO standards and exclude traditional health practitioners, whatever the local custom with regard to the designation "doctor." Statistics for health personnel in this table uniformly include all those actually working in the health service field, whether in the actual provision of services or in teaching, administration, research, or other tasks. One group of practitioners for whom this type of guideline works less well is that of midwives, whose training and qualifications vary enormously from country to country but who must be included, as they represent, after nurses, perhaps the largest and most important category of health auxiliary worldwide. The statistics here refer to those midwives working in some kind of institutional setting (a hospital, clinic, community health-care centre, or the like) and exclude rural noninstitutional midwives and traditional birth attendants.

Hospitals also differ considerably worldwide in terms of staffing and services. In this tabulation, the term hospital refers generally to a permanent facility offering inpatient services and/or nursing care and staffed by at least one physician. Establishments offering only outpatient or custodial care are excluded. These statistics are broken down into data for general hospitals (those providing care in more than one specialty), specialized facilities (with care in only one specialty), local medical centres, and rural health-care centres; the last two generally refer to institutions that provide a more limited range of medical or nursing care, often less than full-time. Hospital data are further analyzed into three categories of administrative classification: public, private nonprofit, and private for profit. Statistics on number of beds refer to beds that are maintained and staffed on a full-time basis for a succession of inpatients to whom care is provided.

Data on hospital utilization refer to institutions defined as above. Admission and discharge, the two principal points at which statistics are normally collected, are the basis for the data on the amount and distribution of care by kind of facility. The data on numbers of patients exclude babies born during a maternal confinement but include persons who die before being discharged. The bed-occupancy and average length-of-stay statistics depend on the concept of a "patient-day," which is the annual total of daily censuses of inpatients. The bed-occupancy rate is the ratio of total patient-days to potential days based on the number of beds; the average length-of-stay rate is the ratio of total patient-days to total admissions. Bed-occu-

Health services

country	health personnel							hospitals									
	year	physicians	dentists	nurses	pharma-cists	midwives	population per physician	year	number	kinds (%)				ownership (%)			hospital beds per 10,000 pop.
										general	specialized	medical centres	rural	government	private nonprofit	private for profit	
Afghanistan	1997	2,556	232	4,182	464	...	9,090	1988–93	...	...	...	...	...	...	...	...	3
Albania	1995	4,848	1,332	14,559	772[2]	9,936[2]	668	1993	40	...	...	...	...	100.0	—	—	31
Algeria	1996	27,650	7,837	...	3,866	...	1,015	1996[3]	186	...	...	...	...	...	...	...	12
American Samoa	1991	26	7[6]	140[6]	2[6]	1[6]	1,885	1990	1	100.0	—	—	—	100.0	—	—	27
Andorra	1998	166	35	188	59	6	434	1996	1	100.0	—	—	—	100.0	—	—	28
Angola	1997	736	...	10,942	...	411	13,228	1990	58	...	...	...	...	...	...	...	12
Antigua and Barbuda	1996	75	12	187	13	31	915	1998	3	50.0	50.0	—	—	100.0	—	—	42
Argentina	1992	88,800	21,900[8]	18,000[6]	...	...	376	1997	1,235	...	...	...	...	56.8	—43.2—		22
Armenia	1998	18,000[9]	[9]	18,258	144	1,750	292[9]	1998	183[10]	...	...	...	...	100.0	...	...	28
Aruba	1997	103	21	515	15	3	874	1999	2	50.0	—	50.0	—	100.0	—	—	32
Australia	1997–98	47,400	8,800	148,300	15,600	...	395	1996–97	1,222	...	...	...	...	61.0	—39.0—		95
Austria	1998	33,698	1,534	35,834	2,137[12]	1,056	240	1998	329	37.7	62.3	—	—	...	...	...	92
Azerbaijan	1998	28,850	2,426	62,213	2,560	10,843	274	1997	762	...	...	...	...	100.0	...	...	92
Bahamas, The	1996	419	72	648	52[4]	...	673	1997	5	60.0	20.0	20.0	—	60.0	—40.0—		38
Bahrain	1997	620	56	1,755	124	...	1,000	1994	12	58.3	42.7	—	—	75.0	16.7	8.3	30[13]
Bangladesh	1997	27,546	938	15,408	7,485[4]	13,211	4,627	1997	976	...	...	...	...	69.3	—30.7—		4
Barbados	1993	330	42	869	138[11]	377[11]	797	1995	9	66.7	33.3	—	—	80.0	—	20.0	74
Belarus	1999	39,007	4,522	47,343	3,152[12]	5,826	261	1999	276	55.4	—44.6—			100.0	...	...	68
Belgium	1998	39,420	7,360	109,187	14,597	6,602	259	1993	363	80.4	19.6	—	—	38.6	61.4	—	76
Belize	1998	155	26	404	30	230	1,542	1998	7	...	...	...	...	100.0	—	—	23
Benin	1995	312	16	1,116	85	432	17,538	1993	...	...	...	...	...	...	...	...	2
Bermuda	1996	96	22	522	29	...	639	1996	2	50.0	50.0	—	—	...	...	...	40
Bhutan	1997	101	9[4]	355[13]	5[4]	326[13]	6,128	1997	28	...	...	...	...	...	...	...	16
Bolivia	1996	4,346	444	2,062	...	...	1,747	1996	336	10.7[13]	8.9[13]	23.5[13]	56.8[13]	...	...	...	11
Bosnia and Herzegovina	1998	4,813	640	15,241	370	1,565[8]	699	1996	...	...	...	...	...	...	...	...	48
Botswana	1994	339	...	3,329	...	...	4,395	1994	30	53.3	3.3	43.3	—	...	...	...	23
Brazil	1997	205,828	137,600	67,760	51,847	...	774	1997	6,410	—100.0—		—	—	35.5	—64.5—		31
Brunei	1996	259	26	1,229	15[13]	278[13]	1,181	1995	10	90.0	—	—	10.0	90.0	—10.0—		33
Bulgaria	1998	28,823	5,324	47,434	1,230	5,923	286	1998	288	—71.2—		28.8	—	...	...	...	104
Burkina Faso	1991[14]	341	19	2,627	113	339	27,158	1993	78	—14.1—		85.9	—	100.0	—	—	5
Burundi	1996	329	9[4]	1,131	55[4]	...	16,507	1996	...	...	...	...	...	...	...	...	0.7
Cambodia	1998	3,464	210	8,608	262[11]	3,359	3,367	1988[3]	188	...	...	...	...	100.0	—	—	16
Cameroon	1996	1,031	56	5,112	206[6]	70	13,510	1988	629	—27.0—		—73.0—		72.3	—27.7—		27
Canada	1996	55,006	15,636	232,869	22,197	...	539	1989	1,079	81.8	16.6	1.6	—	95.8	—	4.2	54[10]
Cape Verde	1996	66	...	213	6	...	5,818	1996	65	8.0	—	92.0	—	100.0	—	—	15[15]
Central African Republic	1995	112	16	282	22[4]	157	28,600	1990	255	—21.1[16]—		—78.9[16]—		79.7[16]	—20.3[16]—		14[8]
Chad	1994	228	14	1,014	10	159	30,260	1994	...	...	...	...	...	...	...	...	13
Chile	1996	13,857	5,817	6,738	1,830[14]	5,369[14]	1,040	1994	198	...	...	...	...	89.4	—10.6—		31
China	1998	1,999,500[9, 17]	[9]	1,218,000	440,000	51,000	621[17]	1998	69,105	11.2	13.4	—75.4—		100.0	—	—	23
Colombia	1997	40,355	22,121	46,187	...	...	1,102	1997	1,657	...	...	...	...	...	...	...	1
Comoros	1997	64	6[4]	180	6[4]	74	7,765	1995	...	...	...	...	...	...	...	...	29
Congo, Dem. Rep. of the	1996	3,224	514	20,652	59[4]	...	14,492	1986	400	...	...	...	...	52.5	—47.5—		21
Congo, Rep. of the	1995	632	35[4]	4,663	175[4]	160	4,083	1990	...	...	...	...	...	...	...	...	33
Costa Rica	1997	5,500	1,420	3,720	1,362	...	641	1997	29	...	...	...	...	87.9	—	12.1	14
Côte d'Ivoire	1996	1,318	219[4]	4,568	135[4]	2,196	11,108	1993	...	...	...	...	...	...	...	...	5
Croatia	1998	9,766	2,802	20,216	1,940	1,407	436	1997	70	52.8	47.2	—	—	...	...	...	63
Cuba	1996	60,129	9,600	76,013	...	...	183	1993	244	...	...	...	...	100.0	—	—	65
Cyprus[18]	1997	1,725	594	2,942	668[13]	120[19]	486	1997[20]	103	71.8	22.1	—	6.1	10.0[19]	0.9[19]	89.1[19]	48
Czech Republic	1999	38,828	6,383	91,213	4,785	4,602	265	1999	365	59.2	40.8	—	—	70.7	—29.3—		67
Denmark	1995	15,175	4,605	36,944	747	1,046	345	1992	163	42.9	57.1	—	—	42.9	57.1	—	35

pancy rates may exceed 100% because stays of partial days are counted as full days.

Two measures that give health planners and policy makers an excellent indication of the level of ordinary health care are those for mortality of children under age five and for maternal mortality. The former reflects the probability of a newborn infant dying before age five. The latter refers to deaths attributable to delivery or complications of pregnancy, childbirth, the puerperium (the period immediately following birth), or abortion. A principal source for the former data was WHO's *The World Health Report* (annual) and for the latter, the UN Development Programme's *Human Development Report* (annual).

Levels of nutrition and access to safe drinking water are two of the most basic limitations imposed by the physical environment in which health-care activities take place. The nutritional data are based on reported levels of food supply (whether or not actually consumed), referred to the recommendations of the United Nations' Food and Agriculture Organization for the necessary daily intake (in calories) for a moderately active person of average size in a climate of a particular kind (fewer calories are needed in a hot climate) to remain in average *good* health. Excess intake in the many developed countries ranges to more than 40% above the minimum required to maintain health (the excess usually being construed to diminish, rather than raise, health). The range of deficiency is less dramatic numerically but far more critical to the countries in which deficiencies are chronic, because the deficiencies lead to overall poor health (raising health service needs and costs), to decreased productivity in nearly every area of national economic life, and to the loss of social and economic potential through early mortality. By "safe" water is meant only water that has no substantial quantities of chemical or biological pollutants—*i.e.*, quantities sufficient to cause "immediate" health problems. Data refer to the proportion of persons having "reasonable access" to an "adequate" supply of water within a "convenient" distance of the person's dwelling, as these concepts are interpreted locally.

The data on health care expenditure were excerpted from a joint effort by the WHO and the World Bank to create better analytical tools by which the interrelations among health policy, health care delivery systems, and human health might be examined against the more general frameworks of government operations, resource allocation, and development process. First published in the World Bank's *World Development Report 1993: Investing in Health* and, the following year, in the World Health Organization's *Global Comparative Assessments in the Health Sector* (edited by C.J.L. Murray and A.D. Lopez), the database and underlying methodology are expected to provide a continuing basis for international comparisons and policy analysis. The first two of ten volumes of the final results appeared in 1996 as *The Global Burden of Disease* and *Global Health Statistics* by the same editors.

Expenditures were tabulated for direct preventative and curative activities and for public health and public education programs having direct impact on health status—family planning, nutrition, and health education—but not more indirect programs like environmental, waste removal, or relief activities. Public, parastatal (semipublic, *e.g.*, social security institutions), international aid, and household expenditure reports and surveys were utilized to build up a comprehensive picture of national, regional, and world patterns of health care expenditures and investment that could not have been assembled from any single type of source. For reasons of space, public and parastatal are combined as the former.

Internet resources for further information:

- Most Recent Values of W.H.O. Global Health-For-All Indicators (for personnel and general indicators) http://www.who.int/htl/countrysup/countrye.htm

No comparable source exists for hospitals.

admissions or discharges					bed occupancy rate (%)	average length of stay (days)	mortality		population with access to safe water 1994–98 (%)	food supply (% of FAO requirement) 1998	total health expenditures, 1990					country
rate per 10,000 pop.	by kinds of hospital (%)						under age 5 per 1,000 live newborn 1997	maternal mortality per 100,000 live births 1990–97			as percent of GDP	per capita (U.S.$)	by source (percent)			
	general	specialized	medical centres	rural									public	private	international aid	
…	…	…	…	…	…	…	257	…	10	73[1]	…	…	…	…	…	Afghanistan
…	…	…	…	…	…	…	40	65	…	124	4.00	26	84.0	16.0	—	Albania
371	…	…	…	…	49.3[4]	5[4]	39	220	90[5]	126	6.95	149	76.9	23.0	0.1	Algeria
965	100.0	—	—	—	38.4	4	…	…	…	…	…	…	…	…	…	American Samoa
…	…	…	…	…	…	…	6	…	…	…	…	…	…	…	…	Andorra
238	…	…	…	…	44.5[7]	16[7]	292	1,500	32	82	…	…	…	…	…	Angola
64[7]	…	…	…	…	50.0[7]	8[7]	21	150	88	99	4.55	241	59.1	37.3	3.6	Antigua and Barbuda
560[3]	…	…	…	…	52.0[3]	7[3]	24	44	81	134	4.21	137	60.1	39.7	0.2	Argentina
…	…	…	…	…	…	…	30	35	…	92	4.17	152	59.8	40.2	—	Armenia
…	…	…	…	…	92.2[11]	…	…	…	…	…	…	…	…	…	…	Aruba
…	…	…	…	…	…	4.5	6	9	95	120	7.67	1,294	69.6	30.4	—	Australia
2,650	…	…	…	…	80.1	10	5	10	100[5]	134	8.38	1,711	66.4	33.6	—	Austria
…	…	…	…	…	…	…	46	37	…	86	4.27	99	61.2	38.8	—	Azerbaijan
837[3]	…	…	…	…	85.4[3]	12[3]	21	…	94	105	…	…	…	…	…	Bahamas, The
…	…	…	…	…	…	…	22	46	100[5]	…	4.62	324	63.0	36.9	0.1	Bahrain
…	…	…	…	…	…	…	109	440	95	89	3.19	6	24.8	56.7	18.5	Bangladesh
810[11]	93.5[11]	6.5[11]	—	—	88.3[11]	32[11]	12	0	100[5]	123	5.04	323	64.3	33.8	1.9	Barbados
…	…	…	…	…	…	…	27	22	100	123	3.19	157	68.7	31.3	—	Belarus
1,963	96.0	4.0	—	—	84.4	12	7	10	100[5]	137	7.50	1,449	82.5	17.5	—	Belgium
…	…	…	…	…	…	…	43	140	83	129	5.88	23	48.4	41.0	10.7	Belize
…	…	…	…	…	…	…	167	500	56	112	4.32	19	26.3	36.4	37.3	Benin
1,313	97.0	3.0	—	—	75.0	8	…	…	…	116	…	…	…	…	…	Bermuda
…	…	…	…	…	…	…	121	380	58	…	5.05	10	41.1	30.4	28.5	Bhutan
250	…	…	…	…	48.0	6	96	390	80	93	4.01	25	39.9	39.6	20.5	Bolivia
529[6, 7]	…	…	…	…	82.4[6, 7]	11[6, 7]	19	10	…	110	…	…	…	…	…	Bosnia and Herzegovina
…	…	…	…	…	93.1[6]	…	49	330	90	93	6.19	139	61.8	21.6	16.5	Botswana
740	…	…	…	…	…	6	44	220	76	122	4.20	146	65.7	33.9	0.4	Brazil
…	…	…	…	…	…	…	10	0	90[5]	127	…	…	…	…	…	Brunei
…	…	…	…	…	…	…	19	15	99[5]	110	5.36	121	81.4	18.6	—	Bulgaria
…	…	…	…	…	…	…	169	930	78[5]	91	8.46	7	9.8	17.9	72.3	Burkina Faso
…	…	…	…	…	…	…	176	1,300	52	68	3.28	30	42.4	48.3	9.3	Burundi
…	…	…	…	…	…	…	167	470	30	94	…	…	…	…	…	Cambodia
…	…	…	…	…	…	…	145	550	54	98	2.62	27	26.4	61.7	11.9	Cameroon
…	…	…	…	…	…	14	7	6	100	119	9.05	1,945	74.1	25.9	—	Canada
…	…	…	…	…	…	…	73	55	65[5]	132	6.32	64	20.7	25.5	53.7	Cape Verde
…	…	…	…	…	…	…	173	1,100	38	91	4.19	18	26.5	37.5	36.0	Central African Republic
…	…	…	…	…	…	…	198	830	54	91	6.22	12	27.6	24.7	47.7	Chad
749[3]	…	…	…	…	69.9[3]	7[3]	13	23	96	117	4.73	100	70.1	29.1	0.7	Chile
418[13]	—60.4[13]—		—39.6[13]—		66.9[13]	15[13]	47	60	67	126	3.51	11	58.5	40.9	0.6	China
614[6]	41.4[6]	16.7[6]	—41.9[6]—		57.2[6]	6[6]	30	80	96	119	3.98	51	44.0	54.4	1.6	Colombia
…	…	…	…	…	…	…	93	500	53[5]	79	5.40	28	46.3	29.2	24.5	Comoros
…	…	…	…	…	…	…	207	870	42	77	2.38	5	8.5	64.8	26.7	Congo, Dem. Rep. of the
…	…	…	…	…	…	…	108	890	34	101	3.99	50	47.1	40.7	12.1	Congo, Rep. of the
958[8]	…	…	…	…	78.2[8]	6[8]	14	29	100	124	6.51	132	73.6	25.2	1.2	Costa Rica
…	…	…	…	…	…	…	150	600	42	117	3.35	28	48.7	47.9	3.4	Côte d'Ivoire
1,578	70.0	30.0	—	—	83.0	13	9	12	96	98	…	…	…	…	…	Croatia
1,376[8]	…	…	…	…	…	…	8	24	93	107	…	…	…	…	…	Cuba
522	…	…	…	…	78.9	6	9	0	100[5]	140	3.96	64	62.9	26.8	10.3	Cyprus[18]
1,982	97.6	2.4	—	—	79.0[13]	9	7	9	100[5]	133	5.94[21]	169[21]	84.9[21]	15.1[21]	—	Czech Republic
1,253	92.9	7.1	—	—	80.4	8	6	10	100	128	6.30	1,588	84.2	15.8	—	Denmark

Health services (continued)

country	health personnel							hospitals									
	year	physicians	dentists	nurses	pharma- cists	midwives	popu- lation per physi- cian	year	number	kinds (%)				ownership (%)			hos- pital beds per 10,000 pop.
										gen- eral	spe- cial- ized	medical centres	rural	govern- ment	private non- profit	private for profit	
Djibouti	1996	60	7	315	8	...	7,100	1993	8	—25.0—		—75.0—		100.0	...	...	27[6]
Dominica	1998	38	10	361	27[10]	...	2,000	1994	53	1.9	—	—	98.1	100.0	—	—	25
Dominican Republic	1997	17,315	1,879	8,600	372	...	464	1992[3]	723	—7.9—		—92.1—		...	...	...	12[10]
East Timor	...	...	...	...	...	...	...	...	...	...	...	...	...	...	...	...	...
Ecuador	1995	15,212	1,788	5,212	906[19]	802	753	1995	474	17.0	8.0	—75.0—		26.0	11.3	62.7	16
Egypt	1998	129,000	15,211	141,770	20,254[12]	...	490	1998	7,411	4.5	—95.5—			87.9	—12.1—		19
El Salvador	1997	6,177	5,604	12,851	...	1,940[8]	936	1993	78	...	...	...	...	61.5	1.3	37.2	17
Equatorial Guinea	1996	105	4	169	...	9	4,086	1988	...	...	...	...	...	...	...	...	29
Eritrea	1996	108	4	574	...	79	33,240	1993	10	...	...	...	...	...	...	...	9
Estonia	1998	4,471	987	9,088[22]	775	[22]	336	1998	78	...	...	...	...	87.2	—12.8—		73
Ethiopia	1988	1,466	...	3,496	364	...	30,195	1986–87	86	...	...	...	...	...	...	...	3
Faroe Islands	1995	85	40	412	10	19	529	1994	3	33.3	—	—	66.7	100.0	—	—	64
Fiji	1997	409	36	1,742	...	...	1,919	1997	25	...	...	...	...	...	...	...	23
Finland	1998	15,407	4,828	111,408	7,472	4,019	334	1994[7]	380	...	...	...	...	...	...	...	98
France	1997	177,585	39,736	291,287	58,609	12,718	330	1997	4,186	—91.6—			8.4	25.4	—74.6—		113
French Guiana	1994	213	38	495	47	40	669	1996	25	...	...	...	...	10	...	15	143
French Polynesia	1999	384	94	599	51	54[19]	599	1999	7	...	...	...	...	...	...	...	37
Gabon	1989	448	32	759	71	240	2,504	1988	27	...	...	...	...	...	...	...	51
Gambia, The	1997	43	...	155	6	102	28,791	1994	13	15.4	—	—84.6—		...	...	...	7
Gaza Strip	1993[23]	...	...	...	...	...	...	1995	6	...	...	...	...	83.3	—16.7—		9
Georgia	1998	22,236	1,800	24,174	469	1,586	229	1997	422[4]	...	...	...	...	100.0	...	...	48
Germany	1998	287,164	62,274	785,190	47,341	9,271	286	1996	2,269	...	...	...	...	49.2[19]	36.0[19]	14.8[19]	72
Ghana	1996[14]	1,117	36	12,970	67[6]	9,583	16,127	1991	121	90.9	9.1	—	—	60.3	—39.7—		16[10]
Greece	1995	40,995	10,667	30,967[10]	8,147[12]	1,837[10]	255	1996	356	49.7	50.3	—	—	...	...	...	50
Greenland	1997	83	28	528	10[8]	11	674	1990	16	6.3	—	—	93.7	100.0	—	—	75
Grenada	1996	96	14	232	47	...	582	1996[7]	3	100.0	—	—	—	100.0	—	—	35
Guadeloupe	1996	690	129	1,640	220	140	597	1995	29	...	...	...	...	44.8	—55.2—		76
Guam	1986	147	...	594[22]	...	[22]	823	1998	1	...	...	...	...	...	...	...	...
Guatemala	1997	9,812	1,367	13,247[19]	...	18,924[19]	1,072	1985	35[13]	...	...	...	...	...	...	...	11[13]
Guernsey	1993	79	...	...	...	...	804	1993	1	100.0	—	—	—	100.0	—	—	...
Guinea	1995	930	22[16]	3,983	197[8]	372	7,688	1991	38	—100.0—		...	...	100.0	—	—	5
Guinea-Bissau	1996	194	11	1,277	12[16]	148	6,015	1993	16	...	...	...	...	62.5	—37.5—		13
Guyana	1996	214	35	504	40	165	3,612	1994	30	...	...	...	...	83.3	—16.7—		30
Haiti	1996	773	95[10]	2,630	...	...	8,418	1994	49	...	...	...	...	...	...	...	10
Honduras	1997	4,896	989	6,152	975[19]	...	1,202	1994	61	...	...	...	...	47.5	—52.5—		9
Hong Kong	1999	9,580	2,052	38,320	1,368	...	714	1995	88	...	...	...	...	78.4	—21.6—		49
Hungary	1998	36,143	5,671	51,965	4,789	2,227	279	1998	167	...	...	...	...	...	...	...	83
Iceland	1998	893	288	2,370	228	235	307	1995	57	89.0	11.0	—	—	...	...	...	147
India	1998[24]	512,352	19,523[19]	449,351[19]	...	...	1,916	1998	15,067[8]	...	...	...	...	55.0[8]	—45.0[8]—		27
Indonesia	1997	31,887[9]	[9]	155,911[22]	5,440[12]	[22]	6,267[9]	1997	1,090	...	...	...	...	...	...	...	6
Iran	1997	50,770	9,427	136,030	6,816	7,387	1,195	1997	685	...	...	...	...	83.5	—16.5—		16
Iraq	1998	11,769	1,220	50,499	2,525	...	1,818	1993	185	...	...	...	...	...	...	...	14
Ireland	1998	8,114	1,712	59,021	2,882	15,228	457	1996	62[3, 7]	100.0	—	—	—	100.0	—	—	33
Isle of Man	1998	117	26	...	25[12]	...	615	1986	3	33.3	33.3	—	33.3	100.0	—	—	...
Israel	1998	22,345	6,733	35,579	3,511	1,080	260	1995	259	18.5	81.5	—	—	12.0	51.7	36.3	61
Italy	1997	318,616	37,039	280,263	58,662	...	180	1997	1,589	91.5	8.5	—	—	59.2	—40.8—		65
Jamaica	1996	421	57	1,241	52	273	5,974	1996	24	75.0	25.0	—	—	75.0	—25.0—		24
Japan	1997	240,908	85,518	960,477	194,300	23,615	525	1997	9,413	88.7	11.3	—	—	73.5	—26.5—		131
Jersey	1995	95	...	...	...	...	895	1990	6	16.7	83.3	—	—	100.0	—	—	88
Jordan	1997	7,250	2,140	12,929	3,363	861[13]	602	1994	63	...	...	...	...	42.9	—57.1—		18[25]
Kazakhstan	1998	53,207	3,783	97,824	9,903	8,456	283	1996	1,518	...	...	...	...	100.0	...	...	123
Kenya	1995	3,606	600	24,610	605[19]	...	7,575	1994	846	—35.1—		—64.9—		...	...	...	14
Kiribati	1998	26	4	208	...	...	3,385	1990	1	...	...	...	...	...	...	...	40
Korea, North	1995	64,006	...	38,792	...	12,931	337	1989	...	...	...	...	...	...	...	...	135
Korea, South	1997	62,609	15,383	133,920	45,820	8,516	735	1997	6,446	70.0	30.0	—	—	...	...	...	47
Kuwait	1997	3,419	470	8,593	633[25]	19[13]	529	1995	24	...	...	...	...	66.7	—	33.3	31
Kyrgyzstan	1998	14,355	1,307	35,768	320	3,472	332	1994	348[13]	89.1	—	10.9	—	100.0	—	—	101[13]
Laos	1996	1,208	214	5,354	...	...	1,603	1995	25	0.7[4]	—99.3[4]—			100.0	—	—	25[4]
Latvia	1998	6,900	1,064	13,445	292[10]	81	355	1998	150	51.2[10]	4.1[10]	28.8[10]	15.9[10]	97.5	2.5	—	94
Lebanon	1997	7,203	2,744	3,430	1,715	...	476	1995	153	...	...	...	...	10.5	—89.5—		22
Lesotho	1995	105	10	1,169	60[14]	914	18,524	1987	22	90.9	9.1	—	—	54.5	45.5	—	15
Liberia	1997	53	2	136	...	99	43,434	1988	92	—37.0—		—63.0—		...	...	...	...
Libya	1997	6,092	619[25]	17,136[25]	1,095[25]	...	781	1991	...	...	...	...	...	...	...	...	41
Liechtenstein	1997	41	18	...	2	...	764	1998	1	...	...	...	...	...	...	...	34
Lithuania	1999	14,578	2,316	37,448	2,143	1,611	254	1999	186	...	...	...	...	100.0	...	...	94
Luxembourg	1998	1,164	282	3,347	297	94	368	1994	34	50.0	50.0	—	—	...	...	...	109
Macau	1998	532	31	706	48	...	800	1994	30	6.7	—	93.3	—	46.7	—53.3—		22
Macedonia	1998	4,110	1,046	9,833	300	1,342	490	1994	58[25]	27.4	24.2	—48.4—		100.0	—	—	52[25]
Madagascar	1996	1,470	137	2,969	19[4]	1,471	9,351	1990	...	...	...	...	...	...	...	...	9
Malawi	1989	186	...	284	5	...	49,118	1987	395	12.2	0.8	—87.0—		59.2	—40.8—		16
Malaysia	1997	14,258	1,865	24,550	...	5,872	1,519	1997	337	...	...	...	...	35.1	—64.9—		20
Maldives	1995	100	...	281	134	461	2,533	1996	5	20.0	—	80.0	—	100.0	—	—	12
Mali	1994	419	9	1,167	57[27]	267	21,269	1987	...	...	...	...	...	...	...	...	4
Malta	1998	987	135	4,158	186	291	383	1996	7	...	...	...	...	71.4	—28.6—		57
Marshall Islands	1997	34	4	141	...	6	1,794	1997	2	100.0	—	—	—	100.0	—	—	21
Martinique	1996	680	130	1,700	230	150	547	1993	8[13]	...	...	...	...	...	...	...	56[13]
Mauritania	1995	323	47	1,461	6[8]	237	7,251	1990	16	...	...	...	...	100.0	—	—	7
Mauritius	1998	1,033	144	2,826[22]	250	[22]	1,117	1998	13	73.9[10]	17.4[10]	8.7[10]	—	60.9[10]	4.3[10]	34.8[10]	33
Mayotte	1985	9	1	51	1	2	7,427	1994	2	100.0	—	—	—	100.0	—	—	9
Mexico	1997	116,047	8,926	161,303	...	...	812	1993	1,888[25]	...	...	...	...	53.9	—46.1—		9[25]
Micronesia	1999	76	16	368	7[19]	...	1,737	1993	4	100.0	—	—	—	100.0	—	—	31
Moldova	1998	14,959	1,761	37,355	2,885	3,723	286	1996	312	...	...	...	...	100.0	...	...	125
Monaco	1997	188	22	500[13]	67[13]	11[13]	170	1997	1	100.0	—	—	—	100.0	—	—	173
Mongolia	1998	5,676	315	7,169	1,113[19]	...	411	1997	407	...	...	...	...	...	...	...	78
Morocco	1997	12,534	1,090	28,610	2,997	874	2,173	1993[28]	201	48.8	—	51.2	—	100.0	—	—	10

admissions or discharges					bed occupancy rate (%)	average length of stay (days)	mortality		population with access to safe water 1994–98 (%)	food supply (% of FAO requirement) 1998	total health expenditures, 1990					country
rate per 10,000 pop.	by kinds of hospital (%)						under age 5 per 1,000 live newborn 1997	maternal mortality per 100,000 live births 1990–97			as percent of GDP	per capita (U.S.$)	by source (percent)			
	general	specialized	medical centres	rural									public	private	international aid	
...	...	...	...	...	...	...	156	...	90[5]	89	...	...	...	...	...	Djibouti
1,026	...	...	...	...	94.6	8	20	65	96[5]	124	8.06	192	65.1	20.4	14.5	Dominica
470	...	...	...	...	...	...	53	230	79	101	3.72	38	52.7	43.3	4.0	Dominican Republic
...	...	...	...	...	...	...	...	...	...	...	...	...	...	...	...	East Timor
508	...	...	...	...	53.1	6	39	160	68	119	4.14	44	55.9	37.3	6.8	Ecuador
317	...	...	...	...	...	...	73	170	87	131	2.61	28	30.3	62.0	7.7	Egypt
...	...	...	...	...	54.9[3, 11]	6[3, 11]	36	160	66	110	5.86	58	29.7	55.6	14.7	El Salvador
...	...	...	...	...	...	...	172	...	95[5]	68	7.60	28	36.6	20.7	42.7	Equatorial Guinea
...	...	...	...	...	...	...	116	1,000	22	75	...	...	...	...	...	Eritrea
1,952	76.7[10]	21.5[10]	—	1.8[10]	75.1	10	23	50	100	120	3.62	228	53.0	47.0	—	Estonia
...	...	...	...	...	...	...	175	1,400	25	78	3.80	4	41.3	39.9	18.8	Ethiopia
...	...	...	...	...	86.4	12	...	...	...	...	...	...	...	...	...	Faroe Islands
...	...	...	...	...	...	...	24	38	77[5]	125	3.76	70	54.9	38.3	6.9	Fiji
2,322	...	...	...	...	70.9	11	4	6	100	117	7.82	2,046	83.3	16.7	—	Finland
2,128	...	...	...	...	...	...	5	10	100	141	9.40	1,869	74.2	25.8	—	France
1,714[19]	...	...	...	...	70.3[19]	8[19]	...	...	84	125	...	...	...	...	...	French Guiana
...	...	...	...	...	...	...	...	...	...	129	...	...	...	...	...	French Polynesia
...	...	...	...	...	...	...	145	500	67	109	4.10	164	52.7	40.9	6.4	Gabon
...	...	...	...	...	...	...	87	1,100	69	108	7.53	22	28.3	20.7	51.0	Gambia, The
752	...	...	...	...	74.9	3	...	...	...	...	...	...	...	...	...	Gaza Strip
...	...	...	...	...	...	...	23	60	...	88	4.45	152	62.5	37.5	—	Georgia
1,812[19]	...	...	...	...	82.8[19]	13[19]	5	8	100[5]	128	8.73	1,511	72.7	27.3	—	Germany
...	...	...	...	...	...	...	107	210	65	117	3.50	15	35.0	51.8	13.2	Ghana
1,370	81.0	19.0	—	—	66.0	9	8	10	99[5]	145	5.39	359	76.0	24.0	—	Greece
2,450	29.2	—	—	70.8	69.4	8	...	...	...	...	...	...	...	...	...	Greenland
774[8]	100.0	—	—	—	59.1[8]	7[8]	29	0	85[5]	111	5.96	133	68.8	27.8	3.5	Grenada
2,154	...	...	...	...	84.0	10	...	...	90	113	...	...	...	...	...	Guadeloupe
...	...	...	...	...	...	...	...	...	...	...	...	...	...	...	...	Guam
284	...	...	...	...	57.7	9	55	190	68	99	3.70	27	44.2	43.2	12.6	Guatemala
1,100	100.0	—	—	—	...	...	...	...	...	...	...	...	...	...	...	Guernsey
...	...	...	...	...	...	...	201	670	46	100	3.90	17	39.7	40.3	20.0	Guinea
...	...	...	...	...	...	...	220	910	43	104	8.15	16	31.3	18.9	49.8	Guinea-Bissau
...	...	...	...	...	...	...	82	180	91[5]	109	10.37	42	40.7	15.1	44.2	Guyana
...	...	...	...	...	...	...	132	1,000	37	83	6.99	27	26.3	54.8	19.0	Haiti
459[19]	...	...	...	...	...	...	45	220	78	104	4.54	52	56.7	35.7	7.7	Honduras
1,811	...	...	...	...	...	...	6	7	100[5]	143	5.69	687	19.5	80.5	0.0	Hong Kong
2,502	...	...	...	...	77.0	10	11	15	100[5]	130	5.95	185	84.4	15.6	—	Hungary
2,828[11]	94.0[11]	6.0[11]	—	—	80.5[11]	12[11]	5	6	100[5]	121	8.34	1,884	87.5	12.5	—	Iceland
...	...	...	...	...	...	...	108	440	81	112	6.00	21	20.0	70.1	1.6	India
...	...	...	...	...	...	...	60	450	74	132	2.01	12	25.6	66.7	7.7	Indonesia
...	...	...	...	...	...	...	35	37	95	117	2.54	244	56.9	43.1	0.0	Iran
645[4]	...	...	...	...	42.4[4]	4[4]	122	310	81	100	...	...	...	...	...	Iraq
1,470	100.0	—	—	—	82.2	7	7	10	100[5]	144	7.22	876	81.1	18.9	—	Ireland
...	...	...	...	...	...	...	...	...	...	...	...	...	...	...	...	Isle of Man
1,979	...	...	...	...	91.2	10	6	5	99	135	4.20	480	49.3	50.6	0.1	Israel
1,743	90.4	9.6	—	—	72.0	9	6	7	100[5]	143	7.54	1,449	77.7	22.3	—	Italy
242[3]	81.7[3]	18.3[3]	—	—	53.7	5	11	120	86	121	5.04	83	57.4	33.2	9.5	Jamaica
...	...	...	...	...	...	...	6	8	97	123	6.45	1.538	74.5	25.5	—	Japan
1,718	84.0	16.0	—	—	...	...	...	...	...	...	...	...	...	...	...	Jersey
478[3]	...	...	...	...	68.1[3]	4[3]	24	41	97	114	3.77	55	36.9	52.3	10.8	Jordan
...	...	...	...	...	...	...	44	70	93	98	4.44	154	62.3	37.7	—	Kazakhstan
...	...	...	...	...	...	...	87	370	44	85	4.33	16	40.0	37.9	22.1	Kenya
...	...	...	...	...	...	...	78[10]	...	99[5]	131	...	...	...	...	...	Kiribati
...	...	...	...	...	...	...	30	110	100	81	...	...	...	...	...	Korea, North
629[13]	97.5[13]	2.5[13]	—	—	65.5[13]	13[13]	6	20	93	131	6.61	365	40.9	58.9	0.2	Korea, South
950[3, 10]	72.2[3, 10]	27.8[3, 10]	—	—	64.9[3, 10]	7[3, 10]	13	5	100[5]	126	4.86	541	64.2	35.6	0.1	Kuwait
1,775	95.5	—	4.5	—	75.6	15	68	65	79	99	4.97	118	66.7	33.3	—	Kyrgyzstan
...	...	...	...	...	...	...	122	650	44	98	2.53	5	17.4	60.7	21.9	Laos
2,210	78.4[10]	4.6[10]	13.8[10]	3.2[10]	76.5	13	22	45	100	117	3.87	220	56.1	43.9	—	Latvia
...	...	...	...	...	...	...	37	100	94	132	...	...	...	...	...	Lebanon
221[7]	...	...	...	...	...	...	137	610	62	97	8.32	26	38.3	26.5	35.2	Lesotho
...	...	...	...	...	...	...	235	...	46	86	8.24	4	19.9	11.8	68.3	Liberia
...	...	...	...	...	...	...	25	75	97	138	...	...	...	...	...	Libya
...	...	...	...	...	...	...	7	...	100[5]	...	...	...	...	...	...	Liechtenstein
2,001[13]	...	...	...	...	74.4[13]	15[13]	24	18	100	121	3.58	159	72.0	28.0	—	Lithuania
1,941	94.6	5.4	—	—	75.0	16	7	0	100[5]	137	6.56	1,662	91.4	8.6	—	Luxembourg
329	...	...	...	...	64.4	16	...	...	...	108	...	...	...	...	...	Macau
995	67.2	6.1	—— 26.7 ——		68.5	14	23	11	...	116	...	...	...	...	...	Macedonia
...	...	...	...	...	...	...	158	490	40	88	2.56	7	29.0	49.6	21.4	Madagascar
...	...	...	...	...	...	...	215	620	47	96	4.98	11	35.0	41.7	23.3	Malawi
717[3, 6]	...	...	...	...	...	...	11	39	70	130	2.96	71	44.0	55.8	0.2	Malaysia
256[19, 26]	...	...	...	...	71.4[19, 26]	4[19, 26]	74	350	60	111	...	...	...	...	...	Maldives
...	...	...	...	...	...	...	239	580	66	90	5.19	15	24.9	46.7	28.4	Mali
...	...	...	...	...	...	...	10	...	100[5]	136	5.38	349	68.3	31.7	0.0	Malta
...	...	...	...	...	...	...	92[10]	...	82	...	...	...	...	...	...	Marshall Islands
2,092	...	...	...	...	73.7	10	...	...	94	118	...	...	...	...	...	Martinique
...	...	...	...	...	...	...	183	550	37	114	3.80	18	28.5	41.5	30.0	Mauritania
1,446[3, 10]	...	...	...	...	74.6[3, 10]	5[3, 10]	23	30	98	130	4.40	100	47.8	39.0	13.3	Mauritius
...	...	...	...	...	...	...	...	...	...	...	...	...	...	...	...	Mayotte
403[3, 8]	...	...	...	...	64.7[3, 8]	5[3, 8]	35	48	85	135	3.17	89	49.3	49.8	0.9	Mexico
...	...	...	...	...	...	...	24	...	100[5]	...	...	...	...	...	...	Micronesia
...	...	...	...	...	...	...	35	42	98	108	3.91	143	74.4	25.6	—	Moldova
...	...	...	...	...	...	...	5	...	100	140	...	...	...	...	...	Monaco
205	...	...	...	...	...	...	150	150	45	83	6.63	58	83.0	15.1	1.9	Mongolia
255	...	...	...	...	63.8	8	72	230	65	131	2.55	26	33.6	63.3	3.1	Morocco

Health services (continued)

country	health personnel							hospitals									
	year	physicians	dentists	nurses	pharmacists	midwives	population per physician	year	number	kinds (%)				ownership (%)			hospital beds per 10,000 pop.
										general	specialized	medical centres	rural	government	private non-profit	private for profit	
Mozambique	1990	387	108	3,533	353	1,139	36,320	1990	238	4.2	0.8	—95.0—		100.0	—	—	8[19]
Myanmar (Burma)	1999	12,313	871	10,820	…	9,162	3,367	1996	737	…	…	…	…	…	…	…	7
Namibia	1997	495	67	2,817	91[8]	1,954	3,388	1992	47	…	…	…	…	91.5	—8.5—		45[8]
Nauru	1995	17	…	62	…	…	624	…	…	…	…	…	…	…	…	…	…
Nepal	1997	874	45[13]	3,845	18[13]	1,621[13]	26,316	1997	74	…	…	…	…	…	…	…	2
Netherlands, The	1997	33,618	7,319	124,000[19]	2,622	1,357	462	1998	222	64.4	35.6	—	—	…	…	…	53
Netherlands Antilles	1998	339	62	1,198	42	11	617	1998	11	38.3	36.3	25.4	—	…	…	…	70
New Caledonia	1996	362	107	852	74	61	549	1996	9	12.5[4]	12.5[4]	75.0[4]	—	62.5[4]	—37.5[4]—		45
New Zealand	1997	12,399	1,467	29,000	3,634	2,114	303	1996	368	…	…	…	…	32.3	—67.7—		59
Nicaragua	1995	4,551	1,099	2,577	…	…	957	1994	56	46.4	7.1	46.4	—	…	…	…	11
Niger	1997	325	19	2,126	29[4]	511	28,560	1987	…	…	…	…	…	…	…	…	5
Nigeria	1993	21,739	1,335	80,186	6,474[11]	62,386	3,707	1985	11,588	6.6	0.5	—92.9—		81.4	—18.6—		7[13]
Northern Mariana Islands	1986	23	4	103	2	2	1,324	1988	1	100.0	—	—	—	100.0	—	—	19
Norway	1998	18,304	5,230	81,548	2,531	2,619	242	1994	…	…	…	…	…	…	…	…	51
Oman	1998	3,061	201	7,453	435	65	773	1998	62	—8.1—		—91.9—		25.8	—74.2—		36
Pakistan	1997	78,470	3,159	28,661	47,618[25]	20,869[13]	1,836	1997	5,118	—7.6[10]—		—92.4[10]—		…	…	…	6
Palau	1998	20	2	26	…	1	900	1998	1	…	…	…	…	…	…	…	37[4]
Panama	1998	3,518	784	3,203	756	…	773	1998	60	…	…	…	…	…	…	…	27
Papua New Guinea	1998	342	127	3,141	…	…	13,708	1993	…	…	…	…	…	…	…	…	34
Paraguay	1995	3,730	1,279	1,875	433	1,547	1,294	1995	…	…	…	…	…	…	…	…	14
Peru	1996	23,249	1,197	16,043	4,789	3,832	1,030	1996	472	…	…	…	…	50.2	—49.8—		13
Philippines	1996	36,375	1,668	5,663	…	13,750	1,923	1996	1,738	96.5	3.1	0.5	—	34.5	—65.5—		12
Poland	1998	91,121	17,869	215,295	20,139	25,014	424	1998	765	93.8	6.2	—	—	100	…	…	54
Portugal	1998	31,097	3,319	37,775	7,505	827	320	1993	335	43.0	18.8	38.2	—	74.3	14.7	11.0	41[13]
Puerto Rico	1989–92	6,269	902	19,666	2,111	120	558	1994	72	83.3	8.3	8.3	—	36.1	30.6	33.3	26
Qatar	1996[14]	703	117	1,612	285	…	793	1995	4	25.0	75.0	—	—	100.0	—	—	18
Réunion	1999	1,346	337	2,906	284	176	520	1998	19	85.5	—14.5—			71.0	—29.0—		39
Romania	1998	41,415	5,379	92,057	1,643	8,913	543	1995	414	…	…	…	…	99.5	—0.5—		77
Russia	1998	618,718	47,322	1,615,000	9,112	91,853	238	1998	11,200	37.4[10]	17.2[10]	—	45.4[10]	99.8	—0.2—		119
Rwanda	1989	272	7	835	25	…	24,697	1985[3]	220	—13.6—		—86.4—		100.0	—	—	9[6]
St. Kitts and Nevis	1998	50	8	274	21	…	846	1998	4	50.0	—50.0—			…	…	…	62
St. Lucia	1997	81	13	312	13	…	1,876	1998	6	25.0[11]	25.0[11]	—	50.0[11]	…	…	…	14
St. Vincent	1998	59	6	267	27[8]	…	2,075	1997	11	…	…	…	…	77.8[11]	—22.2[11]—		19
Samoa	1996	62	7	281	6[11]	65	2,919	1992	36	2.8	—	—	97.2	100.0	—	—	34
San Marino	1998	84	…	…	…	…	309	1998	…	…	…	…	…	…	…	…	58
São Tomé and Príncipe	1996	61	7	167	1[6]	39	2,147	…	…	…	…	…	…	…	…	…	…
Saudi Arabia	1997	33,110	3,191	65,821	4,189	…	602	1996	290	…	…	…	…	74.1	—25.9—		22
Senegal	1996	649	93	1,876	322	588	13,656	1996	17	…	…	…	…	…	…	…	9
Seychelles	1998	93	15	342	7	…	849	1997	7	14.3	14.3	71.4	—	100.0	—	—	54
Sierra Leone	1996	339	19	1,532	…	218	13,696	1998	219	—25.6[16]—		—74.4[16]—		…	…	…	8
Singapore	1998	5,147	914	15,570	858[25]	487[25]	615	1997	23	…	…	…	…	43.5	—56.5—		35
Slovakia	1998	19,030	2,598	38,168	1,822	2,119[13]	283	1991	111	72.1	27.9	—	—	100.0	—	—	92[13]
Slovenia	1998	4,501	1,201	3,125	887	…	440	1998	28	57.7	42.3	—	—	…	…	…	56
Solomon Islands	1997	31	…	464	…	283	13,258	1997	11	100.0	—	—	—	75.0	25.0	—	51
Somalia	1997	265	13	1,327	70	540[15]	25,034	1988	…	…	…	…	…	…	…	…	7
South Africa	1998	29,369	4,387	174,754	9,948	…	1,459	1998	704	…	…	…	…	51.1	—48.9—		34
Spain	1996	165,560	14,877	177,034	43,221	6,314	240	1994	783	57.5	18.5	—24.0—		42.5	—57.5—		40
Sri Lanka	1999	6,881	471	19,362	848	7,899	2,740	1995[3]	407	…	…	…	…	100.0	—	—	26
Sudan, The	1996	2,818	219	18,158	344	…	11,110	1986	…	…	…	…	…	…	…	…	8
Suriname	1996	305	31	631	14	40	1,373	1998	…	…	…	…	…	…	…	…	34
Swaziland	1996	149	7[4]	1,264[4]	13[4]	…	6,617	1986	24	—41.7—		—58.3—		…	…	…	…
Sweden	1997	27,511	13,446	72,625	5,953	6,351	322	1996	…	…	…	…	…	…	…	…	43
Switzerland	1998	22,965	3,470	55,387	4,373	1,884	310	1997	…	…	…	…	…	…	…	…	66
Syria	1998	22,293	11,456	29,259	8,205	6,063[13]	694	1995	294	…	…	…	…	20.5	—79.5—		12
Taiwan	1998	27,168	7,900	71,215	22,761	704	804	1998	700	…	…	…	…	13.7	—86.3—		57
Tajikistan	1998	12,291	1,125	29,597	734	3,999	498	1994	449	…	…	…	…	98.2	—1.8—		88
Tanzania	1995	1,277	218	26,536	…	13,953	24,389	1993	173[8]	…	…	…	…	…	…	…	10
Thailand	1995	14,181	2,920	54,262	5,867	9,713	4,192	1996	1,397	93.6	6.4	—	—	65.8	—34.2—		21
Togo	1995	320	29	1,252	65[8]	438	13,168	1990	…	…	…	…	…	…	…	…	16
Tonga	1997	43	9	309	…	30	2,279	1993	4	…	…	…	…	…	…	…	28
Trinidad and Tobago	1997	949	141	1,378[22]	518	[22]	1,339	1997	77	…	…	…	…	…	…	…	37
Tunisia	1997	6,464	1,200	26,409	1,570	…	1,429	1994[3]	163	—13.5—		—86.5—		100.0	—	—	18
Turkey	1998	77,375	13,428	69,701	21,486	41,181	826	1997	1,078	75.3[10]	8.8[10]	—15.9[10]—		84.3[10]	—15.7[10]—		23
Turkmenistan	1997	14,022	1,010	21,436	1,566	3,664	333	1994	368	…	…	…	…	100.0	…	…	115
Tuvalu	1999	8	1	33	…	10	1,375	1985	8	11.1	—	—	88.9	100.0	—	—	36
Uganda	1996	840[19]	42	3,897	…	2,835	22,399[19]	1989	81	…	…	…	…	…	…	…	12
Ukraine	1998	150,382	19,615	370,171	23,488	29,523	334	1997	3,400	…	…	…	…	100.0	…	…	99
United Arab Emirates	1997	4,749	644[25]	8,450[25]	2,007[25]	…	553	1996	50	…	…	…	…	72.0	—28.0—		29
United Kingdom	1998	82,803	20,216	299,010	33,759[11]	24,801[6]	716	1997	…	…	…	…	…	…	…	…	42
United States	1998	756,700	196,000	2,162,000	184,000[13]	3,000[13]	357	1998	6,097	88.0	12.0	—	—	25.3	49.2	25.5	38
Uruguay	1998	11,964	3,921	2,369	1,009	586	269	1997	118	…	…	…	…	75.4	—24.6—		35
Uzbekistan	1998	74,230	5,869	243,166	746	16,235	324	1995	192	…	…	…	…	100.0	…	…	84
Vanuatu	1997	21	3[13]	259[13]	6[13]	33[13]	8,524	1995	90	5.6	—	21.1	73.3	100.0	—	—	32
Venezuela	1997	53,818	13,000	46,305	8,571	…	423	1997	556	…	…	…	…	37.0	—63.0—		17
Vietnam	1998	36,683	…	42,797	6,500[19]	13,450	2,083	1994	12,500	…	…	…	…	…	…	…	27
Virgin Islands (U.S.)	1985	167	…	…	…	…	622	1985	…	…	…	…	…	…	…	…	49
West Bank	1993[23]	1,344	445	2,279	149	56	1,536	1995	17	…	…	…	…	52.9	—47.1—		9
Western Sahara	1994	100	…	…	24	…	2,504	…	…	…	…	…	…	…	…	…	…
Yemen	1998	3,883	245[25]	7,578[13]	613	385[10]	4,211	1998	81	…	…	…	…	…	…	…	55
Yugoslavia	1997	22,498	4,209	…	2,032	…	471	1997	…	…	…	…	…	…	…	…	55
Zambia	1995	601	26[4]	9,853	24[4]	311[4]	14,496	1987	965	8.2	0.3	19.0	72.5	80.9	19.1	—	29[19]
Zimbabwe	1995	1,522	142	14,095	411[19]	3,078	7,196	1993[3]	1,378	0.9	2.6	83.7	12.7	100.0	—	—	19[13]

[1]1997. [2]1987. [3]Government hospitals only. [4]1990. [5]Data refer to a period other than 1994–95, differ from the standard definition, or refer to only part of the country. [6]1989. [7]General hospitals only. [8]1991. [9]Physicians include dentists. [10]1994. [11]1992. [12]Number of pharmacies. [13]1995. [14]Government-employed personnel only. [15]1987. [16]1988. [17]Includes doctors of traditional Chinese medicine. [18]Republic of Cyprus only. [19]1993. [20]Excludes psychiatric hospitals. [21]Data refer to former Czechoslovakia. [22]Nurses include midwives. [23]West Bank includes Gaza Strip. [24]Registered personnel; all may

admissions or discharges: rate per 10,000 pop.	by kinds of hospital (%): general	by kinds of hospital (%): special-ized	by kinds of hospital (%): medical centres	by kinds of hospital (%): rural	bed occu-pancy rate (%)	aver-age length of stay (days)	mortality: under age 5 per 1,000 live newborn 1997	mortality: maternal mortality per 100,000 live births 1990–97	popu-lation with access to safe water 1994–98 (%)	food supply (% of FAO require-ment) 1998	total health expenditures, 1990: as percent of GDP	total health expenditures, 1990: per capita (U.S.$)	by source (percent): public	by source (percent): private	by source (percent): inter-national aid	country
...	...	...	...	...	...	...	209	1,100	46	82	5.86	5	21.0	25.7	53.3	Mozambique
...	...	...	...	...	...	...	114	230	60	131	...	...	...	...	...	Myanmar (Burma)
...	...	...	...	...	...	...	75	230	83	92	3.92	45	47.8	41.3	10.9	Namibia
...	...	...	...	...	...	...	30	...	...	...	...	...	...	...	...	Nauru
...	...	...	...	...	...	...	104	540	71	99	4.54	7	23.0	51.7	25.4	Nepal
1,028	96.7	3.3	—	—	70.1	10	6	7	100	122	8.03	1,501	72.6	27.4	—	Netherlands, The
...	...	...	...	...	...	...	...	...	...	110	...	...	...	...	...	Netherlands Antilles
1,165[4, 7]	...	...	...	...	84.8[4, 7]	8[4, 7]	...	...	...	123	...	...	...	...	...	New Caledonia
1,332[3]	...	...	...	...	64.0[3]	6[3]	7	15	100[5]	126	7.37	925	81.7	18.3	—	New Zealand
769	—— 76.2 ——		23.8	—	...	...	57	160	78	98	8.61	34	56.9	22.5	20.6	Nicaragua
...	...	...	...	...	...	...	285	590	61	84	4.98	16	24.5	31.3	34.1	Niger
...	...	...	...	...	...	...	187	1,000	49	122	2.72	10	36.5	57.4	6.1	Nigeria
1,550	100.0	—	—	—	54.7	4	...	...	...	...	...	...	...	...	...	Northern Mariana Islands
1,515	96.4	3.6	—	—	83.0	10	4	6	100	128	7.35	1,835	95.7	4.3	—	Norway
911	...	...	...	...	...	...	18	21	85	...	4.22	209	59.5	40.1	0.5	Oman
...	...	...	...	...	...	...	136	340	79	106	3.48	12	47.4	47.1	5.5	Pakistan
1,582	...	...	...	...	48.5	6	34	...	88	...	...	...	...	...	...	Palau
1,239	...	...	...	...	52.5	8	20	85	93	107	7.13	142	72.6	23.1	4.3	Panama
...	...	...	...	...	...	...	112	370	41	95	4.44	37	59.1	36.1	4.8	Papua New Guinea
...	...	...	...	...	...	...	33	190	60	112	2.97	35	35.1	58.2	6.7	Paraguay
...	...	...	...	...	...	...	56	270	67	103	3.21	61	56.1	41.7	2.2	Peru
538	...	...	...	...	62.1	5	46	210	85	101	2.15	16	46.7	46.4	6.9	Philippines
1,288[11]	96.0[11]	4.0[11]	—	—	72.5[11]	14[11]	11	8	100[5]	128	5.07	84	80.3	19.7	—	Poland
1,146	86.3	10.5	3.2	—	74.5	10	8	8	100[5]	151	6.99	383	61.7	38.3	—	Portugal
1,101	94.0	4.3	1.7	—	63.1	5	...	...	...	...	...	...	...	...	...	Puerto Rico
...	...	...	...	...	71.7[11, 29]	7[11, 29]	20	10	100[5]	...	4.73	630	63.0	36.9	0.0	Qatar
1,951[10]	...	...	...	...	79.8[10]	7[10]	...	...	...	146	...	...	...	...	...	Réunion
...	...	...	...	...	...	...	26	41	100[5]	123	3.87	58	61.4	38.6	—	Romania
2,320	...	...	...	...	85.0	14	22	49	...	111	3.02	159	66.8	33.2	—	Russia
85	...	...	...	...	42.8[27]	7[27]	170	1,300	66[5]	88	3.44	10	15.0	45.2	39.8	Rwanda
1,068[7, 11]	...	...	...	...	49.3[7, 11]	9[7, 11]	37	130	100[5]	114	5.99	212	58.1	27.8	14.1	St. Kitts and Nevis
890[11, 27]	...	...	...	...	...	...	29	30	85	117	7.18	169	75.6	23.0	1.4	St. Lucia
728	...	...	...	...	68.2	7	21	43	89	106	5.69	102	68.5	28.8	2.7	St. Vincent
894	70.8	—	—	29.2	32.9	5	27	...	68	...	2.94	20	6.1	54.2	39.7	Samoa
...	...	...	...	...	...	...	6	...	100[5]	...	...	...	...	...	...	San Marino
...	...	...	...	...	...	...	78	...	82	94	9.22	38	28.8	17.0	54.2	São Tomé and Príncipe
...	...	...	...	...	...	...	28	130	95	119	4.76	260	64.3	35.7	0.0	Saudi Arabia
...	...	...	...	...	...	...	124	560	81	96	3.66	29	45.1	38.0	16.9	Senegal
1,744[30]	...	...	...	...	76.4[30]	5[30]	18	...	97[5]	105	6.03	289	50.2	28.0	21.9	Seychelles
...	...	...	...	...	...	...	316	1,800	34[5]	89	2.43	4	19.6	30.9	49.5	Sierra Leone
1,127[25]	...	...	...	...	73.1[10]	8[10]	4	6	100	...	1.87	215	58.3	41.6	0.1	Singapore
1,679[13]	94.9[13]	5.1[13]	—	—	73.2[13]	14[13]	11	9	...	120	...	...	...	...	...	Slovakia
1,643	...	...	...	...	78.4	10	6	11	...	116	...	...	...	...	...	Slovenia
...	...	...	...	...	...	...	28	550	...	93	2.18	117	43.2	50.5	6.3	Solomon Islands
...	...	...	...	...	...	...	211	...	31	66	1.51	8	7.3	41.1	51.6	Somalia
...	...	...	...	...	...	...	82	230	87	119	5.56	77	57.5	42.5	0.0	South Africa
1,053	...	...	...	...	76.7[8]	12[8]	5	6	99	136	6.59	831	78.4	21.6	—	Spain
1,464[4]	...	...	...	...	...	...	19	60	57	104	3.74	18	40.4	51.1	8.6	Sri Lanka
...	...	...	...	...	...	...	115	550	73	104	3.33	34	11.0	84.5	4.5	Sudan, The
766[31]	...	...	...	...	68.8[31]	10[31]	36	110	72[5]	116	2.88	93	37.9	58.0	4.1	Suriname
...	...	...	...	...	...	...	94	230	50	108	7.22	64	43.6	22.2	34.2	Swaziland
1,906[10]	...	...	...	...	82.2[10]	8[10]	4	5	100[5]	116	8.79	2,343	89.3	10.7	—	Sweden
...	...	...	...	...	...	...	5	5	100	120	7.52	2,520	68.5	31.5	—	Switzerland
352[3, 19]	...	...	...	...	75.5[3, 19]	3[3, 19]	33	110	86	136	2.07	41	16.6	79.4	4.0	Syria
...	...	...	...	...	...	...	8	8	90	...	4.30	323	53.0	47.0	0.0	Taiwan
1,492	...	...	...	...	70.2	15	76	85	60	85	5.98	100	72.6	27.4	—	Tajikistan
...	...	...	...	...	...	...	143	530	66	86	4.73	4	14.4	31.6	54.0	Tanzania
...	...	...	...	...	...	...	38	44	81	110	4.98	72	20.4	78.7	0.9	Thailand
...	...	...	...	...	...	...	125	640	55	109	4.10	18	40.4	38.5	21.2	Togo
622[11]	...	...	...	...	56.2[11]	10[11]	23	...	95	...	6.46	63	60.3	25.0	14.8	Tonga
1,114[3, 7]	...	...	...	...	70.7[3, 7]	6[3, 7]	17	90	97	112	4.54	180	62.4	36.9	0.6	Trinidad and Tobago
...	...	...	...	...	...	...	33	70	98	126	4.91	76	63.8	33.3	3.0	Tunisia
709	...	...	...	...	...	...	45	130	92	141	3.94	76	36.2	63.3	0.5	Turkey
...	...	...	...	...	...	...	78	110	74	105	4.99	125	66.4	33.2	0.4	Turkmenistan
1,368	40.9	—	—	59.1	51.5[7]	12.2[7]	56	...	100[5]	...	2.66	472	34.0	66.0	0.1	Tuvalu
...	...	...	...	...	...	...	137	510	46	95	3.40	8	13.3	53.0	33.7	Uganda
...	...	...	...	...	...	...	23	30	97	112	3.30	131	69.7	30.3	—	Ukraine
...	...	...	...	...	...	...	10	3	97	132	2.66	472	34.0	66.0	0.1	United Arab Emirates
...	...	...	...	...	...	...	7	7	100	129	6.11	1,039	84.9	15.1	—	United Kingdom
1,180[32]	...	...	...	...	61.8[32]	6[32]	8	8	90	142	12.71	2,765	44.1	55.9	—	United States
477[3]	...	...	...	...	78.8[3]	9[3]	21	21	93	107	4.62	123	53.8	44.8	1.4	Uruguay
...	...	...	...	...	...	...	58	21	90	100	5.90	116	72.1	27.9	—	Uzbekistan
567	...	...	...	...	41.9	6	50	...	77	120	5.68	67	51.5	25.7	22.8	Vanuatu
601[3]	...	...	...	...	69.7[3]	6[3]	25	65	79	96	3.60	88	54.2	45.6	0.1	Venezuela
...	...	...	...	...	...	...	43	160	45	112	2.11	3	39.3	47.4	13.3	Vietnam
...	...	...	...	...	...	...	...	...	...	...	...	...	...	...	...	Virgin Islands (U.S.)
711	...	...	...	...	80.9	4	...	...	...	...	...	...	...	...	...	West Bank
...	...	...	...	...	...	...	...	...	...	...	...	...	...	...	...	Western Sahara
...	...	...	...	...	...	...	100	1,400	61	86	3.19	20	34.7	54.1	11.3	Yemen
1,154	...	...	...	...	72.0	12	21	10	76	117	5.11[33]	264[33]	80.4[33]	19.6[33]	—	Yugoslavia
1,249	—— 75.7 ——		—— 24.3 ——		68.5	7	202	650	38	84	3.16	17	65.4	30.6	4.1	Zambia
546	...	...	...	...	69.8	7	80	400	79	90	6.23	39	40.3	48.7	11.0	Zimbabwe

not be present and working in the country. [25]1996. [26]Central hospital only. [27]General and specialized hospitals only. [28]Public sector only. [29]Hamad General Hospital only. [30]Victoria Hospital only. [31]Paramaibo hospitals (1,213 beds) only. [32]5,037 community hospitals only. [33]Data refer to the former Socialist Federal Republic of Yugoslavia.

Social protection

This table summarizes three principal areas of social protective activity for the countries of the world: social security, crime and law enforcement, and military affairs. Because the administrative structure, financing, manning, and scope of institutions and programmed tasks in these fields vary so greatly from country to country, no well-accepted or well-documented body of statistical comparisons exists in international convention to permit objective assessment of any of these subjects, either from the perspective of a single country or internationally. The data provided within any single subject area do, however, represent the most consistent approach to problems of international comparison found in the published literature for that field.

The provision of social security programs to answer specific social needs, for example, is summarized simply in terms of the existence or nonexistence of a specific type of benefit program because of the great complexity of national programs in terms of eligibility, coverage, term, age limits, financing, payments, and so on. Activities connected with a particular type of benefit often take place at more than one governmental level, through more than one agency at the same level, or through a mixture of public and private institutions. The data shown here are summarized from the U.S. Social Security Administration's *Social Security Programs Throughout the World* (biennial). A bullet symbol (•) indicates that a country has at least one program within the defined area; in some cases it may have several. A blank space indicates that no program existed providing the benefit shown; ellipses […] indicate that no information was available as to whether a program existed.

Data given for social security expenditure as a percentage of total central governmental expenditure are taken from the International Monetary Fund's *Government Finance Statistics Yearbook,* which provides the most comparable analytic series on the consolidated accounts of central governments, governmentally administered social security funds, and independent national agencies, all usually separate accounting entities, through which these services may be provided in a given country.

Data on the finances of social security programs are taken in large part from the International Labour Office's *The Cost of Social Security* (triennial), supplemented by national data sources.

Figures for criminal offenses known to police, usually excluding civil offenses and minor traffic violations, are taken in part from Interpol's *International Crime Statistics* (annual) and a variety of national sources. Statistics are usually based on the number of offenses reported to police, not the number of offenders apprehended or tried in courts. Attempted offenses are counted as the offense that was attempted. A person identified as having committed multiple offenses is counted only under the most serious offense. Murder refers to all acts involving the voluntary taking of life, including infanticide, but excluding abortion, or involuntary acts such as those normally classified as manslaughter. Assault includes "serious," or aggravated, assault—that involving injury, endangering life, or perpetrated with the use of a dangerous instrument. Burglary involves theft from the premises of another; although Interpol statistics are reported as "breaking and entering," national data may not always distinguish cases of forcible

Social protection

country	social security															
	programs available, 1999					expendi-tures, 1997 (% of total central govt.)[f]	finances									
							year	receipts					expenditures			
	old-age, invalid-ity, death[a]	sickness and mater-nity[b]	work injury[c]	unem-ploy-ment[d]	family allow-ances[e]			total ('000,000 natl. cur.)	insured persons (%)	em-ployers (%)	govern-ment (%)	other (%)	total ('000,000 natl. cur.)	benefits (%)	admin-istration (%)	other (%)
Afghanistan	•	•	•		•	…	…	…	…	…	…	…	…	…	…	…
Albania	•	•	•	•	•	24.4	1990	967.0	—	—	88.8	11.2	1,440.0	99.5	—— 0.5 ——	
Algeria	•	•	•	•	•	…	1990	27,700.0	…	…	…	…	28,748.0	61.8	30.6	7.6
American Samoa	•	…	…	…	…	…	1990	…	…	…	…	…	13.0	100.0	—	—
Andorra	•	•	•			…	1993	11,832.2	…	…	…	…	7,937.2	90.2	4.6	5.2
Angola	…	…	…	…	…	…	…	…	…	…	…	…	…	…	…	…
Antigua and Barbuda	•	•				…	1983	13.0	29.2	48.7	—	22.1	4.2	66.1	33.9	—
Argentina	•	•	•	•	•	52.3	1989	1,015,837.0	28.8	45.0	16.6	9.6	989,009.0	95.0	5.0	—
Armenia	•	•	•	•	•	…	…	…	…	…	…	…	…	…	…	…
Aruba	•	…	•	…	…	[8]	1998	197.1	…	…	…	…	179.0	…	…	…
Australia	•	•	•	•	•	35.3	1998–99	…	…	…	…	1.9	41,825	99.6	0.3	—
Austria	•	•	•	•	•	42.0	1989	425,417.0	30.1	45.9	21.1	2.9	412,134.0	96.5	2.3	1.2
Azerbaijan	•	•	•	•	•	31.9	…	…	…	…	…	…	…	…	…	…
Bahamas, The	•	•	•			5.2	1989	95.9	22.9	38.5	2.1	36.5	43.5	71.1	27.2	1.7
Bahrain	•		•			3.9	1989	39.6	12.3	40.2	—	47.5	9.7	69.8	20.9	9.3
Bangladesh		•	•	•		9.8[9]	1989	73.6	12.4	37.5	2.4	47.7	34.1	94.0	6.0	—
Barbados	•	•	•	•		19.8[5, 10]	1989	191.7	38.0	40.8	1.5	19.7	149.1	93.5	5.8	0.7
Belarus	•	•	•	•	•	32.2	1986	3,199.0	—	—	93.2	6.8	3,199.0	100.0	—	—
Belgium	•	•	•	•	•	42.3[5]	1986	1,347,070.0	24.4	39.7	31.6	4.3	1,322,636.0	94.5	4.3	1.2
Belize	•	•	•			5.9	1989	15.3	8.9	53.2	—	38.0	3.9	56.7	43.3	—
Benin	•		•		•	8.7[13]	1989	3,551.9	16.8	81.4	—	1.8	4,500.9	69.3	28.1	2.6
Bermuda	•		•			…	…	…	…	…	…	…	…	…	…	…
Bhutan	…	…	…	…	…	0.5[14]	1990	…	…	…	…	…	26.0[15]	…	…	…
Bolivia	•	•	•		•	27.7	1989	346.6	29.3	47.7	11.2	11.8	340.2	84.9	14.3	0.8
Bosnia and Herzegovina	•	•	•	•	•	…	…	…	…	…	…	…	…	…	…	…
Botswana	•		•			1.1[11]	1996	—	…	…	…	…	65.0[15]	…	…	…
Brazil	•	•	•	•	•	30.4[17]	1989	71,847.0	24.4	51.0	20.0	4.6	68,957.0	61.9	18.6	19.5
Brunei	•	…	…	…	…	…	1984	…	…	…	…	…	39.5	…	…	…
Bulgaria	•	•	•	•	•	27.1	1989	6,016.8	—	71.4	28.1	0.5	6,000.1	96.6	3.3	0.1
Burkina Faso	•		•		•	0.1[18]	1989	8,816.5	15.6	62.9	—	21.5	4,975.3	69.5	30.4	0.1
Burundi	•		•		•	5.8	1989	1,991.5	31.6	47.6	—	20.8	1,563.9	74.8	16.8	8.4
Cambodia	…	…	•	…	•	…	…	…	…	…	…	…	…	…	…	…
Cameroon	•		•		•	0.7[12]	1989	41,331.8	13.1	64.8	—	22.1	41,332.0	70.6	28.8	0.6
Canada	•	•	•	•	•	42.9[12]	1989	130,306.6	9.9	15.6	64.4	10.1	115,764.2	96.9	2.5	0.6
Cape Verde	•	•	•		•	…	1989	697.7	26.5	58.5	—	15.0	316.7	82.4	16.1	1.5
Central African Republic	•		•		•	6.2[4]	1989	3,604.0	8.4	76.0	—	15.6	3,247.0	64.6	32.9	2.5
Chad	•		•		•	1.9[10, 19]	1989	1,172.8	12.6	77.6	—	9.8	634.5	43.0	51.4	5.6
Chile	•	•	•	•	•	34.5	1989	1,186,056.0	32.8	2.7	37.9	26.6	798,770.0	83.9	14.7	1.4
China	•	•	•	•		0.2	1989	57,446.2	—	99.4	—	0.6	54,654	98.4	0.6	1.0
Colombia	•	•	•		•	8.5	1989	294,438.0	24.8	56.0	0.2	19.0	257,455.0	85.5	11.5	3.0
Comoros	…	…	…	…	…	…	1983	40.7	100.0	—	—	—	54.3	17.4	62.3	20.3
Congo, Dem. Rep. of the	•		•		•	—	1986	1,238.3	28.6	60.2	—	11.2	1,044.2	27.9	72.1	—
Congo, Rep. of the	•		•		•	0.4[10, 22]	1983	15,272.8	12.1	80.2	—	7.7	7,256.7	66.6	21.3	12.1
Costa Rica	•	•	•		•	20.5	1989	36,407.3	33.2	44.4	1.2	21.2	31,049.8	89.0	4.1	6.9
Côte d'Ivoire	•		•		•	3.6[4, 10]	1989	27,288.4	19.3	75.4	—	5.3	20,593.5	100.0	—	—
Croatia	•	•	•	•	•	36.2	…	…	…	…	…	…	…	…	…	…
Cuba	•	•	•			…	1989	2,284.8	—	37.4	62.6	—	2,284.8	96.7	—	3.3
Cyprus[23]	•	•	•	•	•	24.5	1989	217.5	24.7	40.3	17.3	17.7	117.7	98.4	1.6	—
Czech Republic	•	•	•	•	•	36.2	1989[25]	132,748.0	—	3.9	96.1	—	132,748.0	99.7	0.3	—
Denmark	•	•	•	•	•	43.2[12]	1989	225,965.6	4.3	5.0	88.2	2.5	218,258.2	97.0	3.0	—
Djibouti	•	…	…	…	•	6.2[26]	1979	1,352.2	…	…	…	…	1,115.7	…	…	…
Dominica	•	•	•			1.4[10, 13]	1986	12.3	22.6	50.9	—	26.5	4.4	68.0	32.0	—
Dominican Republic	•	•	•			5.6	1986	77.9	20.1	72.9	—	6.8	74.3	75.9	24.1	—
East Timor[28]	…	…	…	…	…	…	…	…	…	…	…	…	…	…	…	…
Ecuador	•	•	•	•		1.9[3]	1988	71,286.0	37.0	50.0	—	13.0	52,032.4	86.0	14.0	—

entry. Automobile theft excludes brief use of a car without the owner's permission, "joyriding," and implies intent to deprive the owner of the vehicle permanently. Criminal offense data for certain countries refer to cases disposed of in court, rather than to complaints. Police manpower figures refer, for the most part, to full-time, paid professional staff, excluding clerical support and volunteer staff. Personnel in military service who perform police functions are presumed to be employed in their principal activity, military service.

The figures for military manpower refer to full-time, active-duty military service and exclude reserve, militia, paramilitary, and similar organizations. Because of the difficulties attached to the analysis of data on military manpower and budgets (including problems such as data withheld on national security grounds, or the publication of budgetary data specifically intended to hide actual expenditure, or the complexity of long-term financing of purchases of military matériel [how much was actually spent as opposed to what was committed, offset by nonmilitary transfers, etc.]), extensive use is made of the principal international analytic tools: publications such as those of the International Institute for Strategic Studies (*The Military Balance*) and the U.S. Arms Control and Disarmament Agency (*World Military Expenditures and Arms Transfers*), both annuals.

The data on military expenditures are from the sources identified above, as well as from the IMF's *Government Finance Statistics Yearbook* and country statistical publications.

The following notes further define the column headings:

a. Programs providing cash payments for *each* of the three types of long-term benefit indicated to persons (1) exceeding a specified working age (usually 50–65, often 5 years earlier for women) who are qualified by a term of covered employment, (2) partially or fully incapacitated for their usual employment by injury or illness, and (3) qualified by their status as spouse, cohabitant, or dependent minor of a qualified person who dies.
b. Programs providing cash payments (jointly, or alternatively, medical services as well) to occupationally qualified persons for *both* of the short-term benefits indicated: (1) illness and (2) maternity.
c. Programs providing cash or medical services to employment-qualified persons who become temporarily or permanently incapacitated (fully or partially) by work-related injury or illness.
d. Programs providing term-limited cash compensation (usually 40–75% of average earnings) to persons qualified by previous employment (of six months minimum, typically) for periods of involuntary unemployment.
e. Programs providing cash payments to families or mothers to mitigate the cost of raising children and to encourage the formation of larger families.
f. Includes welfare.
g. A police officer is a full-time, paid professional, performing domestic security functions. Data include administrative staff but exclude clerical employees, volunteers, and members of paramilitary groups.
h. Includes all active-duty personnel, regular and conscript, performing national security functions. Excludes reserves, paramilitary forces, border patrols, and gendarmeries.

crime and law enforcement (latest)						military protection								country
offenses reported to the police per 100,000 population					population per police officer[g]	manpower, 2001[h]		expenditure, 1997				arms trade, 1997 ('000,000 U.S.$)		
total	personal		property			total ('000)	per 1,000 population	total '000,000	per capita	% of central government expenditure	% of GDP or GNP	imports	exports	
	murder	assault	burglary	automobile theft										
...	...	...	...	...	540[1]	[2]	[2]	408[3]	24[4]	64.4[4]	9.1[4]	5	0	Afghanistan
75	30.3	5.7	9.5	14.0	550	27.0	8.7	157[5]	56[5]	11.3[5]	4.1[5]	10	0	Albania
584	1.5	19.7	11.8	8.5	840	124.0	4.0	1,750	59	12.0	3.9	480	0	Algeria
3,006	8.0	494.0	588.0	6.0	460	—	[6]	—	—	—	—	...	...	American Samoa
2,606	1.6	57.6	648.5	97.0	220	—	—	...	...	...	...	...	...	Andorra
40	10.4	7.1	...	3.7	14[7]	130.5	12.6	1,550	147	36.3	20.5	80	0	Angola
4,977	4.7	475.0	1,984.4	35.9	120	0.2	2.4	...	...		...	...	...	Antigua and Barbuda
606	4.5	86.9	34.7	107.9	1,270	70.1	1.9	3,700	103	6.3	1.2	70	0	Argentina
283	3.8	5.5	18.1	1.1	...	42.1	11.0	342	99	...	3.5	0	0	Armenia
5,461	1.2	180.0	451.3	202.5	...	—	[6]	—	—	—	—	...	...	Aruba
7,001	3.6	713.7	2,338.4	706.2	438	50.7	2.6	8,460	459	8.6	2.2	925	30	Australia
5,940	2.0	2.7	1,008.9	35.8	470	34.6	4.3	1,790	221	1.9	0.9	170	20	Austria
188	5.1	1.1	2.9	0.2	...	72.1	8.9	225	29	10.8	1.9	0	0	Azerbaijan
6,814	21.9	119.6	2,229.1	393.2	125	0.9	2.9	9[4]	40[4]	2.5[4]	0.5[4]	...	...	Bahamas, The
1,390	1.6	0.5	380.1	207.6	180	11.0	17.1	533	883	24.9	10.4	90	0	Bahrain
90	2.8	4.3	4.3	1.1	2,560	137.0	1.0	592	5.0	10.7	1.4	50	0	Bangladesh
3,779	7.5	168.2	966.7	70.8	280	0.6	2.1	14[11]	54[11]	2.0[11]	0.8[11]	5	0	Barbados
1,204	10.2	20.3	173.9	17.5	...	82.9	8.3	841	81	4.8	1.7	0	490	Belarus
8,478	5.3	535.8	2,031.3	376.5	640	37,560	3.7	3,690	363	3.2	1.7	240	110	Belgium
...	12.8	20.0	600.0	4.0	290	1.1	4.3	9[12]	44[12]	5.9[12]	1.6[12]	0	0	Belize
297	5.1	102.0	4.6	0.6	3,250	4.8	0.7	27	5.0	6.8	1.3	0	0	Benin
8,871	5.1	221.7	1,949.2	...	370	—	[6]	—	—	—	—	...	...	Bermuda
...	...	...	...	...	...	4.0[9]	3.1[9]	...	...	...	...	0	0	Bhutan
660	28.6	59.4	0.9	...	...	31.5	3.7	150	20	6.7	1.9	30	0	Bolivia
402	2.5	2.6	...	...	...	[16]	[16]	259	80	14.1	5.9	180	0	Bosnia and Herzegovina
8,281	12.7	431.9	1.9	73.1	750	9.0	5.7	241	168	13.4	5.1	20	0	Botswana
1,404	21.2	255.7	5.2	61.2	...	287.6	1.7	14,100	84	3.9[12]	1.8	430	30	Brazil
849.8	0.6	2.2	67.7	64.6	100	5.9	17.2	374	1,220	13.8	4.6	50	0	Brunei
1,992	7.5	2.3	532.5	97.3	...	66.0	8.3	949	114	9.2	3.0	10	120	Bulgaria
9	0.4	1.7	—	—	...	5.8	0.5	67	6	12.3	2.8	0	0	Burkina Faso
156	9.7	10.8	2.0	0.2	...	40.0	6.4	57	11	25.8	6.1	20	0	Burundi
...	...	...	...	...	1,980	95.0	7.5	126	11	25.8	4.1	10	0	Cambodia
78	0.4	1.2	1.2	5.1	1,170	13.1	0.8	240	16	17.7	3.0	10	0	Cameroon
8,453	4.3	142.3	1,155.7	547.2	8,640	56.8	1.8	7,800	257	7.1[17]	1.3	310	550	Canada
...	...	...	...	...	110	1.2	2.7	4	10	1.7	0.9	5	0	Cape Verde
135	1.6	22.8	2.7	...	2,740[1]	3.2	0.9	39	12	27.7	3.9	0	0	Central African Republic
...	...	...	...	...	990	25.4	2.9	43	6	12.6	2.7	5	0	Chad
1,349	3.5	104.9	464.6	12.9	470	87.5	5.7	2,860	196	17.8	3.9	60	0	Chile
128	0.2	5.2	45.2	6.9	1,360[20]	2,270.0	1.8	74,900	61	17.6	2.3	500	1,100	China
790	56.3	61.8	57.9	75.3	420	158.0	3.7	3,460	91	19.9	3.7	120	0	Colombia
...	...	...	...	...	960	—	[21]	...	...	...	...	...	...	Comoros
...	...	...	...	...	910	81.4	1.5	252	5.0	41.4	5.0	20	0	Congo, Dem. Rep. of the
32	1.5	4.7	0.2	0.2	870	10.0	3.5	74	28	12.3	4.1	10	0	Congo, Rep. of the
868	5.3	11.1	232.4	23.1	480	—	—	58	17	3.1	0.6	5	0	Costa Rica
67	2.5	73.1	19.5	11.9	4,640	8.4	0.5	101	7	4.0	1.1	0	0	Côte d'Ivoire
1,173	6.1	23.2	305.9	20.9	...	58.3	13.3	...	...	...	...	10	0	Croatia
...	...	...	...	...	650	46.0	4.1	720	65	...	2.3	0	0	Cuba
689	1.9	17.7	203.3	3.0	180	10.0[24]	14.8	506	680	16.2	6.1	100	0	Cyprus[23]
4,129	3.0	41.8	892.2	270.4	640[25]	53.6	5.2	1,990	193	5.8	1.9	140	90	Czech Republic
9,428	3.9	17.7	1,925.2	709.5	600	21.4	4.0	2,800	529	3.9	1.7	200	10	Denmark
252	4.2	124.2	45.0	0.5	...	8.4	18.2	20	47	11.4	4.1	0	0	Djibouti
8,846	11.9	125.1	2,019	55.3	300	[27]	[27]	...	...	...	...	...	...	Dominica
...	15.8	28.4	154.0	14.0	580	24.5	2.8	168	21	7.3	1.1	5	0	Dominican Republic
...	...	...	...	...	...	[29]	[29]	...	...	...	...	...	...	East Timor[28]
579	22.2	38.6	125.2	61.2	260	59.5	4.6	746	62	20.3	4.0	160	0	Ecuador

Social protection (continued)

country	social security: programs available, 1999: old-age, invalidity, death[a]	sickness and maternity[b]	work injury[c]	unemployment[d]	family allowances[e]	expenditures, 1997 (% of total central govt.)[f]	finances: year	receipts: total ('000,000 natl. cur.)	insured persons (%)	employers (%)	government (%)	other (%)	expenditures: total ('000,000 natl. cur.)	benefits (%)	administration (%)	other (%)
Egypt	•	•	•	•		0.5	1989	2,443.5	22.8	41.0	2.0	34.2	1,685.6	93.4	6.6	—
El Salvador	•	•	•			5.4	1989	465.3	27.1	51.7	—	21.2	368.3	78.1	21.9	—
Equatorial Guinea	•	•	•		•	…	1989	141.0	7.1	92.9	—	—	134.0	49.3	50.7	—
Eritrea	…	…	…	…	…	…	…	…	…	…	…	…	…	…	…	…
Estonia	•	•	•	•	•	32.0	…	90.1	…	…	…	…	…	…	…	…
Ethiopia	•		•			5.9[12]	1989[30]	190.9	32.8	65.3	—	1.9	153.7	98.3	1.7	—
Faroe Islands	•	…	…	…	•	…	…	…	…	…	…	…	…	…	…	…
Fiji	•		•			4.1[11]	1989	153.5	20.9	33.8	0.8	44.5	75.47	95.3	4.7	—
Finland	•	•	•	•	•	39.2	1989	118,589.0	7.7	41.1	44.0	7.2	106,235	96.3	3.7	—
France	•	•	•	•	•	39.3[31]	1989	1,700,202.0	77.7	—	20.4	1.9	1,669,096.0	95.5	3.7	0.8
French Guiana	•	…	•	…	•	…	1991	1,071.5	…	…	…	…	997.1	…	…	…
French Polynesia	•	…	•	…	•	…	1990	19,268.0	…	…	…	…	17,832.0	…	…	…
Gabon	•		•		•	…	1989	3,415.0	—	44.3	29.3	26.4	2,737.0	55.2	44.8	—
Gambia, The	•		•			3.0[3]	1982	—	…	…	…	…	5.6	…	…	…
Gaza Strip	…	…	…	…	…	—	…	…	…	…	…	…	…	…	…	…
Georgia	•	•	•	•	•	17.6	…	…	…	…	…	…	…	…	…	…
Germany	•	•	•	•	•	50.0[11]	1989[32]	522,172.0	36.9	34.3	26.1	2.7	507,604.0	97.1	2.8	0.1
Ghana	•		•			7.1[31]	1989	17,920.8	21.1	52.9	—	26.0	4,147.7	13.3	64.0	22.7
Greece	•	•	•	•	•	16.8	1989	1,314,421.0	24.9	38.4	30.8	5.9	1,349,693.0	92.5	7.5	—
Greenland	•	…	…	…	•	…	…	…	…	…	…	…	…	…	…	…
Grenada	•	•				8.6[12]	1989	24.1	20.1	60.3	3.2	16.3	13.5	93.1	6.9	—
Guadeloupe	•	…	…	…	•	…	1994	2,607.3	…	…	…	…	5,883.4	…	…	…
Guam	•	…	…	…	•	…	1989	…	…	…	…	…	7.3	…	…	…
Guatemala	•	•	•			5.2[5]	1989	348.5	29.1	54.8	—	16.1	279.7	82.7	14.6	2.7
Guernsey	•	•	•	•	•	…	1999	103,560	—— 45.0 ——		40.7	14.3	85,468	94.8	5.2	…
Guinea	•	•	•		•	…	1989	3,387.0	0.4	90.3	—	9.3	1,108.1	54.9	45.1	—
Guinea-Bissau	…	…	…	…	…	8.8[31]	1986	138.0	22.8	63.4	10.3	3.8	61.9	59.6	40.4	—
Guyana	•	•	•			3.7[10, 33]	1994	1,070.8	…	…	…	…	1,373.7	…	…	…
Haiti	•		•			5.1[10]	1977	60.5	—— 26.6 ——		69.9	3.5	52.4	92.7	7.3	—
Honduras	•	•	•			4.5[10, 13]	1986	166.2	23.9	40.8	3.3	32.0	76.8	84.6	15.4	—
Hong Kong	•	•	•	•	•	…	1998–99	…	…	…	…	…	26,939	…	…	…
Hungary	•	•	•	•	•	33.3	1994	798,000.0	—	—	—	—	737,000.0	—	—	—
Iceland	•	•	•	•	[35]	23.6	1997	14,799	—	—	—	—	96,094	98.2	1.8	—
India	•	•	•			…	1989	43,913.8	23.8	27.7	5.3	43.2	13,775.8	90.0	8.2	1.8
Indonesia	•		•			6.3	1989	239,477.0	50.7	49.3	—	—	181,499.0	12.3	15.8	71.9
Iran	•	•	•	•	•	14.1	1986	346,460.0	83.2	0.1	8.2	8.5	167,879.0	43.4	6.3	50.0
Iraq	•	•	•			…	1977	107.8	9.9	55.6	21.9	12.6	71.0	94.0	2.4	3.6
Ireland	•	•	•	•	•	27.1[11]	1989	4,627.5	16.3	24.8	57.7	1.2	4,612.9	95.2	4.7	0.1
Isle of Man	•	•	•	•	•	37.0[10, 37]	1985	…	…	…	…	…	14.4	…	…	…
Israel	•	•	•	•	•	24.9	1989	13,851.1	31.1	27.7	35.0	6.2	13,593.3	81.7	15.4	2.9
Italy	•	•	•	•	•	38.0[10, 38]	1989	278,383.0	16.5	51.4	30.0	2.1	100,251.0	89.3	2.0	8.7
Jamaica	•		•			…	1989	374.3	11.5	13.6	43.8	31.1	273.6	92.6	7.4	—
Japan	•	•	•	•	•	36.8[31]	1989	59,571,299.0	27.4	31.6	24.4	16.6	46,684,159.0	94.3	1.7	4.0
Jersey	•	•	•	•	•	9.5[10, 31]	1991	60.9	—— 63.8 ——		23.4	12.8	52.8	…	…	…
Jordan	•		•			17.8	1986	53.6	28.7	55.3	—	16.0	9.5	77.4	14.0	8.6
Kazakhstan	•	•	•	•	•	…	…	…	…	…	…	…	…	…	…	…
Kenya	•		•			1.0[17]	1989	4,262.0	18.2	13.7	10.0	58.1	1,857.8	53.8	46.1	0.1
Kiribati	•		•			…	…	…	…	…	…	…	…	…	…	…
Korea, North	…	…	…	…	…	…	…	…	…	…	…	…	…	…	…	…
Korea, South	•		•			10.8	1996	7,425,400.0	—	62.2	—	—	9,656,600.0	…	…	…
Kuwait	•					17.3	1989	445.8	7.1	13.2	54.3	25.4	206.5	97.0	3.0	—
Kyrgyzstan	•	•	•	•	•	15.4	…	…	…	…	…	…	…	…	…	…
Laos	…	…	•	…	…	…	…	…	…	…	…	…	…	…	…	…
Latvia	•	•	•	•	•	42.1	…	…	…	…	…	…	…	…	…	…
Lebanon	•	•	•		•	7.7	…	…	…	…	…	…	…	…	…	…
Lesotho	…	…	…	…	…	1.2[17]	1992	—	…	…	…	…	12.0[15]	…	…	…
Liberia	•		•			1.0[10, 38]	1983	2.9	—	69.0	13.8	17.2	2.6	54.4	45.6	—
Libya	•	•	•			…	1989	314.3	21.6	25.4	50.2	2.8	260.0	77.5	19.5	3.0
Liechtenstein	•	•	•	•	•	…	…	…	…	…	…	…	…	…	…	…
Lithuania	•	•	•	•		32.1	…	…	…	…	…	…	24,981.7	…	…	…
Luxembourg	•	•	•	•	•	52.3[12]	1989	72,471.8	24.2	34.6	34.4	6.8	65,214.4	97.2	2.4	0.4
Macau	•	…	…	…	•	…	1998	223.2	…	…	…	…	207.4	…	…	…
Macedonia	•	•	•	•	•	…	1996	24,482	…	…	…	…	…	…	…	…
Madagascar	•		•		•	0.9[11]	1989	15,229.0	22.2	77.8	—	—	14,542.0	81.2	18.8	—
Malawi			•			0.1[38]	1986	—	…	…	…	…	5.4	…	…	…
Malaysia	•		•			7.2	1989	7,958.7	20.7	40.2	—	39.1	2,826.5	97.0	3.0	—
Maldives	…	…	…	…	…	3.4	1990	—	…	…	…	…	7.1	…	…	…
Mali	•		•		•	3.0[10, 38]	1986	8,128.8	16.6	74.3	—	9.1	7,924.6	63.7	34.7	1.6
Malta	•	•	•	•	•	34.4	1989	82.2	26.1	31.6	42.3	—	110.7	92.5	7.5	—
Marshall Islands	•					…	…	…	…	…	…	…	…	…	…	…
Martinique	•	…	…	…	•	…	1998	3,913.1	…	…	…	…	8,429.6	…	…	…
Mauritania	•		•		•	3.7[10, 13]	1989	808.4	1.5	90.4	—	8.1	735.2	63.5	31.2	5.3
Mauritius	•		•		•	19.4	1989	1,733.5	2.9	47.9	31.7	17.5	1,072.7	95.2	3.0	1.8
Mayotte	…	…	…	…	…	…	…	…	…	…	…	…	…	…	…	…
Mexico	•	•	•			18.1	1989	16,011,795.0	20.9	54.8	12.9	11.4	14,562,293.0	79.9	15.5	4.6
Micronesia	•					…	…	…	…	…	…	…	…	…	…	…
Moldova	•	•	•	•	•	…	…	…	…	…	…	…	…	…	…	…
Monaco	•	•			•	…	…	…	…	…	…	…	…	…	…	…
Mongolia	•	•	…	…	•	23.8	1989	2,431.6	—	—	20.8	79.2	2,304.6	100.0	—	—
Morocco	•	•	•		•	7.0[11]	1989	4,660.5	20.6	47.5	12.9	19.0	3,040.7	94.8	5.0	0.2
Mozambique	•	…	…	…	…	…	1986	228.2	—	86.2	13.7	0.1	145.0	100.0	—	—
Myanmar (Burma)		•	•			2.3	1986	44.3	19.9	59.6	18.5	2.0	35.9	51.5	15.6	32.9
Namibia	•	…	…	…	…	6.8[10, 18]	…	…	…	…	…	…	…	…	…	…
Nauru	•	•	•	…	•	…	…	…	…	…	…	…	…	…	…	…
Nepal	•		•			1.5	1985	—	…	…	…	…	59.3	…	…	…

crime and law enforcement (latest)						military protection								country
offenses reported to the police per 100,000 population					population per police officer[g]	manpower, 2001[h]		expenditure, 1997				arms trade, 1997 ('000,000 U.S.$)		
total	personal		property			total ('000)	per 1,000 population	total '000,000	per capita	% of central government expenditure	% of GDP or GNP	imports	exports	
	murder	assault	burglary	automobile theft										
3,693	1.6	0.7	...	3.1	580	443.0	6.8	2,180	34	11.0	2.8	1,600	5	Egypt
...	38.8	63.7	...	148.5	1,000	16.8	2.7	101	18	6.7	0.9	10	0	El Salvador
...	...	...	...	...	190	1.3	2.7	3[11]	8[11]	5.2[11]	1.5[11]	0	0	Equatorial Guinea
...	...	...	...	...	...	171.9	40.0	65	17	18.1	7.8	90	0	Eritrea
3,145	17.1	27.6	1,468.3	144.9	...	4.5	3.3	111	77	4.5	1.5	10	0	Estonia
319	13.3	87.8	2.2	1.9	1,100[30]	252.5	3.8	117	2	7.9	1.9	0	0	Ethiopia
...	...	...	...	...	...	—	[6]	—	—	—	—	...	...	Faroe Islands
2,784	1.8	418.8	353.5	69.6	407	3.5	4.2	48	61	6.4	2.4	0	0	Fiji
14,405	0.4	35.0	1,757.0	29.5	640	32.3	6.2	1,960	381	4.3[11]	1.7	370	20	Finland
6,096	3.7	148.4	676.9	546.2	630	273.7	4.6	41,500	708	6.4	3.0	260	5,900	France
8,936	27.2	178.7	1,367.3	150.6	...	—	[6]	—	—	—	—	...	...	French Guiana
1,799	0.9	98.9	232.7	...	...	—	[6]	—	—	—	—	...	...	French Polynesia
114	1.4	17.9	2.3	7.5	1,290	4.7	3.8	91	76	7.0	2.0	0	0	Gabon
89	0.4	10.6	5.6	...	3,310	0.8	0.6	15	12	15.0	3.7	30	0	Gambia, The
4,355	...	...	...	...	...	—	—	...	...	...	...	...	...	Gaza Strip
286	4.7	99.5	21.1	0.8	...	16.8	3.4	158	31	9.6	1.4	10	0	Georgia
7,869	3.5	134.4	1,507.1	137.4	...	308.4	3.7	32,900	401	4.7	1.6	750	750	Germany
...	2.2	408.6	1.5	...	620	7.0	0.4	47	3	2.4	0.7	0	0	Ghana
3,759	3.6	67.7	418.7	163.9	380	159.2	14.5	5,530	521	13.8	4.6	850	30	Greece
9,360	18.1	845.0	1,883.5	...	340	—	[6]	—	—	—	—	...	...	Greenland
8,543	7.8	98.9	582.2	...	230	[27]	[27]	...	...	...	...	...	...	Grenada
5,793	13.2	215.2	821.5	453.9	...	—	[6]	—	—	—	—	...	...	Guadeloupe
10,080	7.9	169.3	634.2	333.6	...	—	[6]	—	—	—	—	...	...	Guam
510	27.4	77.1	27.9	58.1	670	31.4	2.7	236[11]	21[11]	15.0[11]	1.4[11]	5	0	Guatemala
...	...	...	...	...	...	—	[6]	—	—	—	—	...	...	Guernsey
18.4	0.5	0.7	0.7	0.1	1,140	9.7	1.3	54	7	8.0	1.5	30	0	Guinea
129	0.5	8.7	4.0	0.2	...	7.3	5.5	8	7	13.0	3.2	0	0	Guinea-Bissau
1,355	17.9	205.1	426.5	32.2	190	1.6	2.0	8	11	2.4	1.1	0	0	Guyana
701	...	...	...	...	400	[34]	[34]	...	...	...	...	5	0	Haiti
392	154.0	44.4	4.3	25.8	1,040	8.3	1.3	52	10	5.6	1.3	10	0	Honduras
1,076	1.0	115.3	146.0	16.8	221	—	[6]	—	—	—	—	...	...	Hong Kong
5,926	4.3	80.4	932.4	46.1	237	33.8	3.3	1,320	129	4.3	1.9	100	5	Hungary
14,727	—	18.2	761.1	112.8	940	—	—	—	—	—	—	10	0	Iceland
594	4.6	...	15.6	...	820	1,263.0	1.2	10,900	11	14.3	2.8	410	90	India
60	0.8	5.1	24.8	8.0	1,119	297.0	1.4	4,810	23	13.1	2.3	410	20	Indonesia
77	0.5	47.7	...	...	...	513.0	8.1	4,730	74	11.6	3.0	850	30	Iran
197	7.1	34.7	...	...	140	424.0	19.2	1,250	59	50.8[36]	4.9	0	0	Iraq
2,279	1.8	19.1	709.6	28.6	310	10.5	2.7	744	206	3.3	1.2	30	0	Ireland
2,867	0.7	12.3	921.4	60.6	...	—	[6]	—	—	—	—	...	...	Isle of Man
5,017	2.4	463.0	1,122.3	694.1	210	163.5	26.1	9,340	1,690	20.9	9.7	1,100	370	Israel
4,214	4.4	46.4	...	537.0	680	230.4	4.0	22,700	395	4.1	2.0	430	700	Italy
1,871	37.2	511.4	135.7	7.2	430	2.8	1.1	53	20	2.4	0.9	5	0	Jamaica
1,671	1.1	15.4	187.9	28.4	480	239.8	1.9	40,800	325	6.6	1.0	2,600	20	Japan
...	...	...	...	...	...	—	[6]	—	—	—	—	...	...	Jersey
1,170	7.9	15.0	11.7	38.2	630	100.2	19.5	626	145	25.0	9.0	130	0	Jordan
815	...	...	...	...	...	64.0	4.3	699	41	4.4	1.9	140	0	Kazakhstan
484	6.4	54.1	76.9	9.7	1,500	24.4	0.8	206	7	7.2	2.1	40	0	Kenya
261	5.1	11.6	38.6	...	330	—	—	...	...	...	...	...	...	Kiribati
...	...	...	...	...	460	1,082.0	49.2	6,000	281	40.7[38]	27.5	30	70	Korea, North
1,348	2.1	54.7	6.8	...	506	683.0	14.3	15,000	327	14.6	3.4	1,100	30	Korea, South
1,346	1.5	36.4	75.9	56.7	80	15.5	6.8	2,760	1,510	26.8	7.5	2,000	0	Kuwait
987	10.4[39]	12.6	482.4	...	...	9.0	1.8	159	34	7.1	1.6	0	0	Kyrgyzstan
...	...	...	...	...	280	29.1	5.2	60	12	17.5	3.4	10	0	Laos
1,492	9.8	17.4	281.0	101.4	...	6.5	2.8	97	40	2.5	0.9	0	0	Latvia
2,713	5.3	152.8	65.9	28.6	530	71.8	19.8	465	135	8.4	3.0	40	0	Lebanon
1,885	33.9	170.6	221.5	...	1,130	2.0	0.9	32	16	6.1	2.5	0	0	Lesotho
...	...	...	...	...	1,570	[40]	[40]	...	...	...	...	0	0	Liberia
966	1.5	5.2	...	...	...	76.0	14.5	1,810	403	19.7	6.1	5	0	Libya
...	...	114.3	614.3	153.6	660	—	[41]	—	—	—	—	...	...	Liechtenstein
2,057	9.4	10.0	601.0	109.6	...	12.2	3.3	127	35	2.8	0.8	5	0	Lithuania
6,409	0.9	251.8	625.2	154.6	829	0.9	2.0	134	319	2.0[11]	0.8	60	0	Luxembourg
1,698	5.4	34.0	250.5	26.6	...	—	[6]	...	...	...	...	...	...	Macau
1,102	5.4	26.9	...	44.7	...	16.0	7.8	83	42	10.2	2.5	0	0	Macedonia
112	0.6	12.0	0.7	0.1	2,900	13.5	0.8	53	4	8.5	1.5	0	0	Madagascar
850	3.1	82.2	13.1	...	1,670	5.3	0.5	26	3	2.9	1.0	0	0	Malawi
604	3.1	25.9	155.6	20.8	760	100.5	4.4	2,090	102	9.9	2.2	725	5	Malaysia
2,353	1.9	3.3	36.1	...	35,710	—	—	...	...	...	...	...	...	Maldives
10.0	0.7	1.5	0.8	0.3	160	7.4	0.7	43	4	7.2	1.7	10	0	Mali
1,841	3.0	35.2	1,079.2	243.9	230	2.1	5.5	31	81	2.0	0.9	0	0	Malta
2,273	...	...	...	...	400	—	[42]	—	—	—	—	...	...	Marshall Islands
6,305	5.8	184.9	641.2	192.8	...	—	[6]	—	—	—	—	...	...	Martinique
225	1.8	38	2.5	9.1	710	15.7	6.0	24	10	9.8	2.3	5	0	Mauritania
3,340	4.4	10.4	109.8	...	240	—	—	12	11	1.2	0.3	10	0	Mauritius
...	...	...	...	...	...	—	[6]	—	—	—	—	...	...	Mayotte
108	7.3	30.2	...	...	...	192.8	1.9	4,290	44	6.2	1.1	130	20	Mexico
...	...	...	...	...	...	—	[42]	—	—	—	—	...	...	Micronesia
957	9.9	11.1	50.4	15.6	...	8.2	2.3	62	14	1.9	1.0	0	0	Moldova
3,337	3.3	33.3	130.0	43.3	...	—	—	...	...	...	...	...	...	Monaco
938	24.6	72.1	425.7	1.3	120	9.1	3.7	19	7	5.1	1.9	0	0	Mongolia
366	1.4	6.7	...	...	840	198.5	6.8	1,390	49	12.9	4.3	180	0	Morocco
166	4.2	9.2	45.9	...	...	[43]	[43]	73	4	9.2	2.8	0	0	Mozambique
350	2.1	18.5	0.1	0.1	650	325.0	7.7	3,960	88	75.5	7.6	280	0	Myanmar (Burma)
4,062	45.2	466.8	562.6	57.7	...	9.0	5.0	90	57	7.3	2.7	5	0	Namibia
...	25.0	400.0	100.0	...	110	—	—	...	...	...	...	...	...	Nauru
9	2.7	1.1	0.8	...	1,000	46.0	1.8	42	2	5.1	0.8	0	0	Nepal

Social protection (continued)

country	social security: programs available, 1999: old-age, invalidity, death[a]	sickness and maternity[b]	work injury[c]	unemployment[d]	family allowances[e]	expenditures, 1997 (% of total central govt.)[f]	finances: year	receipts: total ('000,000 natl. cur.)	insured persons (%)	employers (%)	government (%)	other (%)	expenditures: total ('000,000 natl. cur.)	benefits (%)	administration (%)	other (%)
Netherlands, The	•	•	•	•	•	37.4	1989	154,427.0	37.3	30.3	19.0	13.4	135,609.0	96.9	3.1	—
Netherlands Antilles		…	•	•	…	12.9[8, 12]	1998	317.0	100.0	—	—	—	275.0	…	…	…
New Caledonia	…	…	…	…	•	…	1987	15,834.0	…	…	…	…	14,598.0	…	…	…
New Zealand	•	•	•	•	•	39.9	1989	14,266.0	1.0	4.7	92.5	1.8	14,372.3	95.6	2.8	1.6
Nicaragua	•	•	•		•	14.9[17]	1989	647,454.8	13.5	49.1	7.6	29.8	452,038.6	82.4	17.6	—
Niger	•		•		•	1.7[45]	1989	5,634.9	9.4	90.6	—	—	3,804.2	62.5	—	37.5
Nigeria	•		•			2.5[47]	1989	54.0	50.0	50.0	—	—	22.6	42.5	57.5	—
Northern Mariana Islands	•	…	…	…	…	…	…	…	…	…	…	…	…	…	…	…
Norway	•	•	•	•	•	38.4	1989	158,105.0	18.3	31.4	46.6	3.7	131,578.2	98.7	1.3	—
Oman	•	…	•	…	…	4.3	1995	—	…	…	…	…	62.2[17]	…	…	…
Pakistan	•	•	•			0.2[10, 48]	1989	9,321.4	1.3	8.0	84.3	6.4	8,092.0	97.4	1.2	1.4
Palau	•					…	…	…	…	…	…	…	…	…	…	…
Panama	•	•	•			20.5	1989	496.7	31.0	39.5	7.1	22.4	452.8	94.0	4.8	1.2
Papua New Guinea	•		•			0.7[17]	1983	45.0	40.5	32.1	8.0	19.4	9.4	82.3	9.7	8.0
Paraguay	•	•	•			16.2[31]	1993	42,410[38]	…	…	…	…	253,341	…	…	…
Peru	•	•	•			0.2[10, 33]	1989	1,363,280.6	30.2	65.1	4.7	—	1,435,134.1	78.5	21.5	—
Philippines	•	•	•			2.5	1989	19,213.6	22.2	32.3	—	45.5	7,878.3	87.3	12.3	—
Poland	•	•	•	•	•	50.9	1989	11,572,248.0	2.1	70.2	25.1	2.6	11,452,165.0	98.8	1.2	—
Portugal	•	•	•	•	•	27.3[3]	1989	833,442.5	31.3	50.1	13.4	5.2	756,410.8	94.6	4.2	1.2
Puerto Rico	•	•	•	•	•	…	1980	…	…	…	…	…	1,041.3	100.0	—	—
Qatar	…	…	…	…	…	…	1986	80.0	—	—	100.0	—	80.0	100.0	—	—
Réunion	…	…	…	…	…	…	1998	…	…	…	…	…	13,200.0	…	…	…
Romania	•	•	•	•	•	31.0	1989	90,561.2	—	48.9	51.1	—	90,561.2	100.0	—	—
Russia	•	•	•	•	•	27.7[12]	…	…	…	…	…	…	…	…	…	…
Rwanda	•		•			2.9[36]	1989	2,350.0	23.9	39.8	—	36.3	965.8	60.8	39.2	—
St. Kitts and Nevis	•	•	•			9.4[50]	1989	14.3	…	…	…	…	7.9	…	…	…
St. Lucia	•	•	•			…	1986	14.6	28.6	28.6	—	42.8	3.4	61.4	38.6	—
St. Vincent and the Grenadines	•	•	•			6.4	1989	—	…	…	…	…	—	…	…	…
Samoa	•		•			—	…	—	…	…	…	…	—	…	…	…
San Marino	•	•	•		…	…	1983	51,673.0	12.0	48.7	36.1	3.2	46,179.0	95.7	3.7	0.6
São Tomé and Príncipe	•	•	•			…	1986	46.4	37.7	56.3	—	6.0	23.7	100.0	—	—
Saudi Arabia	•		•			…	1989	1,761.4	26.8	73.2	—	—	4,292.9	100.0	—	—
Senegal	•		•		•	2.6[10, 18]	1989	17,202.0	—	47.6	51.4	1.0	15,371.0	84.6	11.1	4.3
Seychelles	•	•	•			16.0	1983	69.1	30.1	60.2	—	9.7	42.7	69.6	4.9	25.5
Sierra Leone			•			2.3[3]	1990	…	…	…	…	…	153.00	100.00	—	—
Singapore	•	•	•			1.8	1989	7,531.9	49.1	35.3	0.1	15.6	5,045.8	78.0	0.6	21.4
Slovakia	•	•	•	•	•	29.3[53]	1998	74,205	…	…	…	…	87,916	…	…	…
Slovenia	•	•	•	•	•	…	…	…	…	…	…	…	…	…	…	…
Solomon Islands	•		•			0.7[10, 38]	1989	20.9	27.8	41.1	—	31.1	17.4	89.7	10.3	—
Somalia			•			1.7[48]	…	—	…	…	…	…	…	…	…	…
South Africa	•	•	•	•		…	1994	2,034	—	100.0	—	—	2,260.0	…	…	…
Spain	•	•	•	•	•	38.5[11]	1989	8,320,972.0	15.9	53.9	27.9	2.3	8,038,090.0	94.3	2.6	3.1
Sri Lanka	•		•		•	14.0	1989	15,399.9	22.0	24.4	29.1	24.5	5,819.0	98.5	1.3	0.2
Sudan, The	•		•			0.4[5, 10]	1989	62.0	24.9	0.5	—	74.6	14.7	37.5	62.5	—
Suriname	•	…	…	…	•	6.0[10, 48]	1989	73.0	24.7	75.3	—	—	70.6	100.0	—	—
Swaziland	•		•			0.4[31]	1986	10.7	31.4	31.4	—	37.2	3.9	45.8	54.2	—
Sweden	•	•	•	•	•	49.6	1989	446,909.7	2.8	37.9	50.8	8.5	439,997.3	93.7	3.3	3.0
Switzerland	•	•	•	•	•	50.5	1989	45,800.1	45.6	22.6	25.9	5.9	41,745.7	91.5	3.0	5.5
Syria	•		•			2.7	1989	3,147.9	30.4	60.9	…	5.6	1,455.9	95.7	4.2	0.1
Taiwan	•	•	•	•		13.8[3]	…	…	…	…	…	…	…	…	…	…
Tajikistan	•	•	•	•	•	…	…	…	…	…	…	…	…	…	…	…
Tanzania	•		•			0.5[9]	1989	3,275.8	25.9	25.9	—	48.2	2,780.7	5.8	14.1	80.1
Thailand	•	•	•			3.7	1989	654.0	—	60.2	—	39.8	260.0	88.2	11.8	—
Togo	•		•		•	6.5[10, 50]	1989	10,162.0	8.1	61.5	—	30.4	5,844.0	77.5	22.5	—
Tonga	…	…	…	…	…	0.8[18]	…	…	…	…	…	…	…	…	…	…
Trinidad and Tobago	•	•	•		•	14.3[12]	1989	584.9	12.0	24.1	39.7	24.2	438.4	85.6	11.1	3.3
Tunisia	•	•	•	•	•	16.6[11]	1989	325.3	36.9	63.1	—	—	358.3	90.0[56]	6.1[56]	3.9[56]
Turkey	•	•	•			9.0	1989	12,075,809.0	28.5	32.9	22.8	15.8	10,241,427.0	97.2	2.2	0.6
Turkmenistan	•	•	•	•	•	…	…	…	…	…	…	…	…	…	…	…
Tuvalu	•	…	…	…	…	…	1981	…	…	…	…	…	0.1	67.6	32.4	—
Uganda	•		•			2.1[10, 48]	1989	265.9	32.1	64.3	1.1	2.5	145.0	0.3	76.8	22.9
Ukraine	•	•	•	•	•	…	1989	20,350.0	—	—	—	—	20,350.0	100.0	—	—
United Arab Emirates	…	…	…	…	…	3.7	1989	182.2	17.3	6.2	0.5	76.0	182.2	100.0	…	…
United Kingdom	•	•	•	•	•	36.8	1989	92,157.0	18.1	24.9	52.9	4.1	88,294.0	93.8	3.3	2.9
United States	•		•	•		28.8	1989	804,909.0	25.5	33.9	28.8	11.8	627,653.0	95.5	3.3	1.2
Uruguay	•	•	•	•	•	62.0	1989	535,507.0	31.4	37.3	26.0	5.3	548,591.0	93.6	5.4	1.0
Uzbekistan	•	•	•	•	•	…	…	…	…	…	…	…	…	…	…	…
Vanuatu	•					0.9[10, 48]	…	—	…	…	…	…	—	…	…	…
Venezuela	•	•	•	•		6.9[48]	1986	7,457.6	21.3	40.7	12.7	25.3	6,355.7	86.1	14.9	—
Vietnam	•	•	•			…	…	…	…	…	…	…	…	…	…	…
Virgin Islands (U.S.)	•	…	…	•	•	…	…	…	…	…	…	…	…	…	…	…
West Bank	…	…	…	…	…	…	…	…	…	…	…	…	…	…	…	…
Western Sahara	…	…	…	…	…	…	…	…	…	…	…	…	…	…	…	…
Yemen	•	…	•	…	…	—	…	—	…	…	…	…	—	…	…	…
Yugoslavia	•	•	•	•	•	6.0[61]	1986[61]	2,777,651.0	63.3	32.2	3.4	1.1	2,732,679.0	90.3	1.9	7.8
Zambia	•		•			0.8	1986	179.2	28.4	28.4	—	43.2	67.7	40.6	59.4	—
Zimbabwe	•		•			3.4[5]	1983	167.0	25.9	7.6	64.2	2.3	112.2	93.7	6.2	0.1

[1]Rural areas only. [2]No national military from 1992. [3]1990. [4]1984. [5]1989. [6]Political dependency; defense is the responsibility of the administering country. [7]Includes civilian militia. [8]Netherlands Antilles includes Aruba. [9]1985. [10]Social security only. [11]1996. [12]1995. [13]1979. [14]1992. [15]Includes welfare. [16]In 2000 about 20,000 troops of the NATO Commanded Stabilization Forces were stationed in Bosnia and Herzegovina to assure implementation of the Dayton Accords. [17]1994. [18]1991. [19]1976. [20]Local officers only. [21]Military defense is the responsibility of France. [22]1971. [23]Republic of Cyprus only. [24]National Guard only. [25]Data refer to former Czechoslovakia. [26]1981. [27]Paramilitary unit of country participating in the U.S.-sponsored Regional Security System, a defense pact among eastern Caribbean countries. [28]Indonesia includes East Timor, except where noted. [29]UN forces of about 9,600 uniformed personnel are stationed in East Timor. [30]Ethiopia includes Eritrea. [31]1993. [32]Former West Germany. [33]1983. [34]In 1994 the military government of Haiti was replaced by a civilian administration. A national police force of about 5,300 has been formed and all

crime and law enforcement (latest)						military protection								country
offenses reported to the police per 100,000 population					population per police officer[g]	manpower, 2001[h]		expenditure, 1997				arms trade, 1997 ('000,000 U.S.$)		
total	personal		property			total ('000)	per 1,000 population	total '000,000	per capita	% of central government expenditure	% of GDP or GNP	imports	exports	
	murder	assault	burglary	automobile theft										
7,808	10.9	242.8	3,100.4	239.0	510	50.4	3.2	6,840	437	6.4	1.9	460	500	Netherlands, The
5,574[44]	...	396	3,455	...	330	—	[6]	—	—	—	—	...	...	Netherlands Antilles
...	...	...	...	...	...	—	[6]	—	—	—	—	...	...	New Caledonia
13,854	3.9	546.3	2,352.9	788.6	630	9.2	2.4	766	214	3.9	1.3	100	0	New Zealand
1,069	25.6	203.8	110.7	...	90[7]	16.0	3.3	27	6	4.5	1.5	0	0	Nicaragua
99	0.9	16.6	1.0	0.7	2,350[46]	5.3	0.5	20	2	6.9	1.1	5	0	Niger
312	...	...	...	...	1,140	78.5	0.6	2,000	19	12.3	1.4	90	0	Nigeria
245	3.8	92.6	73.7	20.8	...	—	[6]	—	—	—	—	...	...	Northern Mariana Islands
10,048	1.9	59.1	95.0	487.5	660	26.7	5.9	3,250	739	4.8	2.1	250	10	Norway
280	0.8	1.9	...	...	430	43.4	17.4	1,820	795	36.4	26.1	160	0	Oman
331	7.9	21.2	10.6	11.4	720	620.0	4.3	3,380	26	24.2	5.7	600	0	Pakistan
...	...	...	323.0	...	...	—	[42]	—	—	—	—	...	...	Palau
419	2.0	11.8	25.1	77.7	180	—	—	114	42	4.8	1.4	10	0	Panama
766	8.6	66.7	63	22.0	720	4.4	0.8	63	14	4.1	1.3	0	0	Papua New Guinea
456	16.5	56.9	20.4	48.4	310	18.6	3.3	127	25	10.5	1.3	5	0	Paraguay
218	3.2	24.1	7.8	3.6	730	100.0	3.8	1,350	53	13.4	2.1	310	0	Peru
...	13.1	14.9	...	3.3	1,160	107.0	1.4	1,270	17	7.9	1.5	110	0	Philippines
2,775	2.9	84.1	918.6	158.2	370	206.0	5.3	5.600	145	5.6	2.3	150	60	Poland
653	3.1	1.8	110.8	43.8	660	43.6	4.2	2,390	241	5.9	2.4	110	10	Portugal
2,176	16.3	102.4	853.0	389.4	380	—	[6]	—	—	—	—	...	...	Puerto Rico
909	2.4	8.4	39.7	6.1	...	12.3	20.7	975	1,540	27.0	10.5	625	0	Qatar
2,097	7.8	123.1	181.3	137.9	220	—	[6]	—	—	—	—	...	...	Réunion
1,723	2.5	6.2	92.0	17.3	...	103.0	4.6	2,280	102	6.9	2.4	250	10	Romania
1,759	20.1	30.8	549.7	24.5	...	977.1	6.8	41,700	283	30.9	5.8	30	2,300	Russia
14,550	12,500	25.0	12.5	12.5	4,650	[49]	[49]	81	10	22.2	4.4	20	0	Rwanda
5,544	19.5	536.6	2,461.0	...	300	[27]	[27]	...	...	...	...	...	...	St. Kitts and Nevis
4,386	17.0	1,193.0	778.0	...	430	[27]	[27]	...	...	...	...	...	...	St. Lucia
3,977	10.3	986.9	...	...	250	[27]	[27]	...	...	...	...	...	...	St. Vincent and the Grenadines
...	...	...	...	...	...	—	[51]	—	—	—	—	...	...	Samoa
...	4.1	...	...	...	...	—	—	...	...	...	...	...	...	San Marino
558	4.0	...	...	...	400	—	—	—	2	1.2	0.9	0	0	São Tomé and Príncipe
149	0.5	0.2	...	45.4	280	126.5	5.6	21,100	1,050	35.8	14.5	11,600	5	Saudi Arabia
113	1.4	17.1	4.7	...	730	9.4	0.9	69	7	8.5	1.6	0	0	Senegal
4,517	2.7	698.7	1,058.9	...	120	0.2	2.5	8[4]	124[4]	7.4[4]	5.6[4]	...	...	Seychelles
...	...	...	...	...	600	[52]	[52]	48	10	33.0	5.9	0	0	Sierra Leone
991	1.0	10.0	43.6	10.9	230	60.5	18.2	5,660	1,650	19.4	5.7	400	90	Singapore
1,740	2.4	204.6	504.3	142.4	...	33.0	6.1	903	168	8.0	2.1	10	40	Slovakia
2,822	3.4	20.0	677.4	35.1	...	7.6	3.8	1,220	617	12.5	5.2	20	0	Slovenia
...	...	...	...	...	620	—	—	...	...	...	...	0	0	Solomon Islands
144	1.5	8.0	31.2	...	540	[54]	[54]	8[31]	1[31]	30.0[48]	0.9[31]	0	0	Somalia
...	...	...	...	...	870	61.5	1.4	2,320	55	5.6	1.8	20	370	South Africa
2,312	2.6	23.9	570.2	343.1	580	143.5	3.6	7,670	196	6.0	1.5	430	525	Spain
280	8.2	10.8	54.7	...	860	[55]	[55]	762	41	21.2	5.1	90	0	Sri Lanka
...	10.2	46.3	66.6	4.7	740	117.0	3.2	412	13	53.8	4.6	20	0	Sudan, The
17,819	7.6	1,824.4	...	...	...	2.0	4.7	17	41	2.6	1.2	0	0	Suriname
3,987	17.6	474.2	726.7	60.9	610	—	—	32	34	8.2	2.2	0	0	Swaziland
12,982	4.5	42.5	1,615.1	658.9	330	33.9	3.8	5,550	626	5.4	2.5	310	900	Sweden
5,406	2.6	68.5	1,172.5	1,129.9	640	3.6	0.5	3,860	533	5.8[11]	1.4	310	50	Switzerland
89	1.4	7.0	21.2	2.9	1,970	321.0	19.2	3,400	211	26.2[11]	5.6	70	0	Syria
799	8.2	...	...	124.9	720	370.0	16.6	13,100	602	23.8	4.6	9,200	20	Taiwan
317	2.5	4.6	...	...	...	6.0	1.0	113	19	10.6	1.7	0	0	Tajikistan
1,724	6.2	1.8	78.1	0.8	1,330	27.0	0.7	87	3	10.7	1.3	20	0	Tanzania
351	7.7	25.4	9.9	3.3	530	306.0	5.0	3,380	57	12.1	2.3	950	0	Thailand
11	...	...	...	...	1,970	9.5	1.8	29	6	11.6	2.0	5	0	Togo
2,100	...	...	...	...	330	—	[51]	—	—	—	—	...	...	Tonga
1,170	9.7	31.0	452.7	80.6	280	2.7	2.1	83	74	5.4	1.5	5	0	Trinidad and Tobago
1,474	2.1	169.1	72.3	10.3	340	35.0	3.6	359	39	5.3	2.0	20	0	Tunisia
426	2.7	83.6	1.2	30.4	1,570	515.1	7.8	7,790	123	14.7	4.0	1,600	10	Turkey
...	...	...	...	...	...	17.5	3.2	299	71	15.6	4.6	0	0	Turkmenistan
...	...	...	...	—	290	—	—	...	...	...	...	...	...	Tuvalu
172	8.9	35.7	15.5	6.3	1,090	[57]	[57]	268	12	23.9	4.2	30	0	Uganda
1,141	9.1	13.8	240.1	11.1	...	303.8	6.2	4,280	85	8.4	3.7	5	500	Ukraine
360	0.6	1.8	10.1	...	140	65.0	20.9	2,310	1,020	46.5	6.9	1,400	40	United Arab Emirates
9,823[58]	2.8[58]	405.2[58]	1,832.7[58]	752.9[58]	350	211.4	3.5	35,300	600	7.1	2.7	2,100	6,600	United Kingdom
5,374	9.0	430.2	1,041.8	591.2	318	1,367.7	4.8	276,000	1,030	16.3	3.3	1,600	31,800	United States
3,383	8.5	119.5	62.5	137.4	170	23.9	7.2	279	86	4.4	1.4	10	0	Uruguay
300	3.5	3.3	28.7	2.4	...	[59]	[59]	1,440	63	6.1	2.5	5	70	Uzbekistan
...	...	...	...	...	450	—	—	...	...	...	...	...	...	Vanuatu
1,106	22.1	152.2	358.2	239.4	320	82.3	3.3	1,860	83	9.8	2.2	270	0	Venezuela
...	...	...	...	...	...	484.0	6.1	3,390	45	11.1	2.8	120	0	Vietnam
10,441	22.3	1,943.2	3,183.7	954	240	—	[6]	—	—	—	—	...	...	Virgin Islands (U.S.)
2,226	...	...	...	...	...	—	—	...	...	...	...	...	...	West Bank
...	...	...	...	...	...	—	[6]	—	—	—	—	...	...	Western Sahara
170[60]	...	...	...	...	1,940	54.0	3.0	411	26	17.4	8.1	110	0	Yemen
1,268	...	...	...	...	140[62]	105.5	9.9	1,200	114	55.0[3, 61]	4.9	10	0	Yugoslavia
666	9.8	9.5	153.5	9.6	540	21.6	2.2	41	4	3.9	1.1	0	0	Zambia
5,180	9.0	179.9	384.1	13.7	750	39.0	3.4	320	29	11.9	3.8	10	0	Zimbabwe

army equipment destroyed. [35]Coverage is through the tax system. [36]1982. [37]1988–89. [38]1988. [39]Includes attempted murders. [40]As of 2001 there were between 11,000 and 15,000 in all armed forces. West African peacekeepers withdrew in January 1999 and the civil war resumed in some areas. [41]Military defense is the responsibility of Switzerland. [42]Military defense is the responsibility of the United States. [43]Forces are estimated between 10,600 and 11,600. [44]Curaçao only. [45]1980. [46]Includes paramilitary forces. [47]1976. [48]1986. [49]Forces are estimated between 56,000 and 71,000. [50]1987. [51]Military defense is the responsibility of New Zealand. [52]Following the civil war of May–June 1997, the armed forces were reorganized. Estimated strength is 5,000. [53]1998. [54]Following the 1991 revolution, no national armed forces have yet been formed. [55]Forces estimated between 118,000 and 123,000. [56]1977. [57]Forces estimated between 50,000 and 60,000. [58]England and Wales. [59]Forces estimated between 50,000 and 55,000. [60]Former Yemen Arab Republic. [61]Data refer to Yugoslavia as constituted prior to 1991.

Education

This table presents international data on education analyzed to provide maximum comparability among the different educational systems in use among the nations of the world. The principal data are, naturally, numbers of schools, teachers, and students, arranged by four principal levels of education—the first (primary); general second level (secondary); vocational second level; and third level (higher). Whenever possible, data referring to preprimary education programs have been excluded from this compilation. The ratio of students to teachers is calculated for each level. These data are supplemented at each level by a figure for enrollment ratio, an indicator of each country's achieved capability to educate the total number of children potentially educable in the age group usually represented by that level. At the first and second levels this is given as a net enrollment ratio and at the third level as a gross enrollment ratio. Two additional comparative measures are given at the third level: students per 100,000 population and proportion (percentage) of adults age 25 and over who have achieved some level of higher or postsecondary education. Data in this last group are confined as far as possible to those who have completed their educations and are no longer in school. No enrollment ratio is provided for vocational training at the second level because of the great variation worldwide in the academic level at which vocational training takes place, in the need of countries to encourage or direct students into vocational programs (to support national development), and, most particularly, in the age range of students who normally constitute a national vocational system (some will be as young as 14, having just completed a primary cycle; others will be much older).

At each level of education, differences in national statistical practice, in national educational structure, public-private institutional mix, training and deployment of teachers, and timing of cycles of enrollment or completion of particular grades or standards all contribute to the problems of comparability among national educational systems.

Reporting the number of schools in a country is not simply a matter of counting permanent red-brick buildings with classrooms in them. Often the resources of a less developed country are such that temporary or outdoor facilities are all that can be afforded, while in a developed but sparsely settled country students might have to travel 80 km (50 mi) a day to find a classroom with 20 students of the same age, leading to the institution of measures such as traveling teachers, radio or televisual instruction at home under the supervision of parents, or similar systems. According to UNESCO definitions, therefore, a "school" is defined only as "a body of students . . . organized to receive instruction."

Such difficulties also limit the comparability of statistics on numbers of teachers, with the further complications that many at any level must work part-time, or that the institutions in which they work may perform a mixture of functions that do not break down into the tidy categories required by a table of this sort. In certain countries teacher training is confined to higher education, in others as a vocational form of secondary training, and so on. For purposes of this table, teacher training at the secondary level has been treated as vocational education. At the higher level, teacher training is classified as one more specialization in higher education itself.

The number of students may conceal great variation in what each country defines as a particular educational "level." Many countries do, indeed, have a primary system composed of grades 1 through 6 (or 1 through 8) that passes students on to some kind of postprimary education. But the age of intake, the ability of parents to send their children or to permit them to finish that level, or the need to withdraw the children seasonally for agricul-

Education

country	year	first level (primary)					general second level (secondary)					vocational second level[a]	
		schools	teachers[c]	students[d]	student/ teacher ratio	net enroll-ment ratio[b]	schools	teachers[c]	students[d]	student/ teacher ratio	net enroll-ment ratio[b]	schools	teachers[c]
Afghanistan	1995	2,146	21,869	1,312,197	60.0	29	...	19,085	512,815	26.9	14	...	...
Albania	1996	1,782	31,369	558,101	17.8	102	162[1]	4,147	71,391	17.2	...	259[1]	2,174
Algeria	1997	15,426	170,956	4,674,947	27.3	94	3,954	151,948	2,618,242	17.2	56	...	...
American Samoa	1996	32	524[2]	9,971	...	...	9	245[2]	3,624	...	...	1	21[2]
Andorra	1997	12	...	5,424	...	...	6	...	2,655	...	...	...	...
Angola	1992	...	31,062[1]	989,443	...	...	...	5,138[1]	199,099	...	...	...	566[1]
Antigua and Barbuda	1997	58	559	12,229	21.9	...	13	389	4,260	11.0	...	1[3]	16[3]
Argentina	1997	22,437	309,081	5,153,256	16.7	96	7,623[4]	238,791[4]	2,463,608[4]	10.3[4]	42	[4]	[4]
Armenia	1998	1,407	61,965	602,600	9.7	...	...	57,325	365,025	6.4	...	69[5]	...
Aruba	1998	33	397	8,456	21.3	...	15[4]	470[4]	7,157[4]	15.2[4]	[4]	[4]	[4]
Australia	1998	7,709	104,603	1,869,852	17.9	95	2,468	104,477	1,329,000	12.7	89	...	28,900[3]
Austria	1998	3,680	38,491	385,207	10.0	87	1,837[6]	55,337	480,200	8.7	88	981	26,248
Azerbaijan	1998	4,515	36,800	700,900	19.0	...	...	85,300	905,500	10.6	...	78	...
Bahamas, The	1997	113	1,540	34,199	22.2	98	...	1,352	27,970	20.7	86	...	...
Bahrain	1997	124[3, 8]	3,536[3, 8]	72,876	...	98	...	2,305[3, 8]	49,897	...	83	...	820[3, 8]
Bangladesh	1996	75,595	242,252[5]	17,580,000	...	64	12,858	135,217[5]	5,788,000	...	18	156	8,800
Barbados	1996	79	994	18,519	18.6	78	21	1,263	21,455	17.0	74	...	...
Belarus	1998	4,835[9]	115,300[9]	1,580,000[9]	10.9[9]	85	[9]	[9]	[9]	[9]	...	150	...
Belgium	1996	4,401	82,168[10]	742,796	...	98	1,727	115,262	737,823	6.4	88	304[11]	...
Belize	1998	247	2,015	53,118	26.4	99	30	726	11,260	15.5	29	...	...
Benin	1997	3,072	13,957	779,329	55.8	63	145[5]	5,352	146,135	27.3	...	14[5]	283[5]
Bermuda	1997	26	478	5,883	18.3	...	...	355	3,726	10.5	...	...	...
Bhutan	1994	243	1,611	60,089	37.3	...	34	544	7,299	13.4	...	8	95
Bolivia	1995	...	51,763[12]	1,538,454	24.7[12]	91	...	12,434[4, 12]	293,158[4]	17.6[4, 12]	29	...	[4]
Bosnia and Herzegovina	1991	2,205	23,369	539,875	23.1	98	238	9,030	172,063	19.1	...	...	...
Botswana	1997	714	11,454	322,268	28.1	81	274	6,772	116,076	17.1	44	50	2,618
Brazil	1998	187,497	1,460,469	35,845,742	24.5	90	17,602	380,222	6,968,531	18.3	19	...	...
Brunei	1998	184[10]	3,858[10]	58,548[10]	15.2[10]	91	38	2,636	30,956	11.7	68	9	516
Bulgaria	1999	3,011[9]	65,885[9]	887,213[9]	13.5[9]	92	[9]	[9]	[9]	[9]	74	545	20,389
Burkina Faso	1996	3,568	14,037	702,204	50.0	31	252	4,152	137,257	33.0	7	41	731
Burundi	1993	1,418	10,400	651,086	62.6	52	113[12]	2,562	55,713	21.7	5	...	...
Cambodia	1998	5,026	43,282	2,011,772	46.5	100	440[11]	16,820	302,751	18.0	...	65[11]	2,315
Cameroon	1995	6,801	40,970	1,896,722	46.3	67	...	14,917	459,068	30.8	11	...	5,885
Canada	1996	12,685	148,565	2,448,144	16.5	95	3,780	133,275	2,505,389	18.8	91	...	...
Cape Verde	1994	370[12]	2,657	78,173	29.4	100	...	438	11,808	27.0	48	...	94[14]
Central African Republic	1991	930	4,004	308,409	77.0	53	46[4]	845[4]	46,989[4]	55.6[4]	...	[4]	[4]
Chad	1996	2,660	9,395	591,493	63.0	46	153	2,468	90,100	36.5	...	18	216
Chile	1995	8,702	80,155	2,149,501	26.8	89	...	51,042	679,165	13.3	58	...	...
China	1997	628,840	5,794,000	139,954,000	24.2	101	78,642	3,587,000	60,179,000	16.8	...	14,190	598,000
Colombia	1996	48,933	193,911	4,916,934	25.4	85	7,895[4]	165,976[4]	2,323,653	...	46	[4]	[4]
Comoros	1996	327	1,508	78,527	52.1	52	...	591	21,192	35.9	...	...	...
Congo, Dem. Rep. of the	1995	14,885	121,054	5,417,506	44.8	54	4,276[4, 11]	59,325[4, 11]	1,514,323[4]	...	17	[4]	[4]
Congo, Rep. of the	1997	1,612	6,926	489,546	70.7	96	...	5,466	190,409	34.8	...	...	1,746
Costa Rica	1998	3,711	19,235	529,637	27.5	89	353	10,943	202,415	18.5	40	...	...
Côte d'Ivoire	1996	7,401	40,529	1,662,285	41.0	55	147	15,959	489,740	30.7	...	...	1,424[3]
Croatia	1998	2,127	10,365	206,121	19.9	82	1,110	19,776	266,115	13.5	66	442	13,000
Cuba	1997	9,864[16]	78,625	1,028,880	13.0	101	...	71,025	778,028	11.0	59[16]	...	27,267[16]
Cyprus[17]	1997	376	4,159	64,761	15.6	96	125[4]	5,757[4]	61,266[4]	10.6[4]	93	[4]	[4]
Czech Republic	1998	8,067[18]	83,972[18]	1,186,246[18]	14.1[18]	91	367	11,658	83,010	7.1	89	1,776	54,204
Denmark	1996	2,536[3]	33,100	336,690	10.2	99	153[3]	37,000	321,448	8.7	88	237[3]	13,100

tural work all make even even a simple enrollment figure difficult to assess in isolation. All of these difficulties are compounded when a country has instruction in more than one language or when its educational establishment is so small that higher, sometimes even secondary, education cannot take place within the country. Enrollment figures in this table may, therefore, include students enrolled outside the country.

Student-teacher ratio, however, usually provides a good measure of the ratio of trained educators to the enrolled educable. In general, at each level of education both students and teachers have been counted on the basis of full-time enrollment or employment, or full-time equivalent when country statistics permit. At the primary and secondary levels, net enrollment ratio is the ratio of the number of children within the usual age group for a particular level who are actually enrolled to the total number of children in that age group (× 100). This ratio is usually less than (occasionally, equal to) 100 and is the most accurate measure of the completeness of enrollment at that particular level. It is not always, however, the best indication of utilization of teaching staff and facilities. Utilization, provided here for higher education only, is best seen in a gross enrollment ratio, which compares total enrollment (of all ages) to the population within the normal age limits for that level. For a country with substantial adult literacy or general educational programs, the difference may be striking: typically, for a less developed country, even one with a good net enrollment ratio of 90 to 95, the gross enrollment ratio may by 20%, 25%, even 30% higher, indicating the heavy use made by the country of facilities and teachers at that level.

Literacy data provided here have been compiled as far as possible from data for the population age 15 and over for the best comparability internationally. Standards as to what constitutes literacy may also differ markedly; sometimes completion of a certain number of years of school is taken to constitute literacy; elsewhere it may mean only the ability to read or write at a minimal level testable by a census taker; in other countries studies have been undertaken to distinguish among degrees of functional literacy. When a country reports an official 100% (or near) literacy rate, it should usually be viewed with caution, as separate studies of "functional" literacy for such a country may indicate 10%, 20%, or even higher rates of inability to read, or write, effectively. Substantial use has been made of UNESCO literacy estimates, both for some of the least developed countries (where the statistical base is poorest) and for some of the most fully developed, where literacy is no longer perceived as a problem, thus no longer in need of monitoring.

Finally, the data provided for public expenditure on education are complete in that they include all levels of public expenditure (national, state, local) but are incomplete for certain countries in that they do not include data for private expenditure; in some countries this fraction of the educational establishment may be of significant size. Occasionally data for external aid to education may be included in addition to domestic expenditure.

The following notes further define the column headings:

a. Usually includes teacher training at the second level.
b. Latest.
c. Full-time.
d. Full-time; may include students registered in foreign schools.

		third level (higher)							literacy[b]				public expenditure on education (percent of GNP)[b]	country
students[d]	student/ teacher ratio	institutions	teachers[c]	students[d]	student/ teacher ratio	gross enroll- ment ratio[b]	students per 100,000 popula- tion[b]	percent of population age 25 and over with post- secondary education[b]	over age	total (%)	male (%)	female (%)		
…	…	…	…	12,800	…	2.0	165	3.0	15	36.3	51.0	20.8	2.0	Afghanistan
18,601	8.5	10[1]	2,348	34,257	14.6	12.0	1,007	…	10	91.8	95.5	88.0	3.1	Albania
…	…	…	19,910	347,410	17.4	10.9	1,236	…	15	63.3	75.1	51.3	5.1	Algeria
160[2]	7.6[2]	1	…	…	…	…	…	22.6	15	95.0	95.6	96.3	8.2	American Samoa
…	…	—	—	932	—	…	…	…	15	100.0	100.0	100.0	…	Andorra
22,401	…	1	787	6,.331	8.0	0.7	71	…	15	41.7	55.6	28.5	4.9	Angola
46[3]	2.9[3]	1	16	46	2.9	…	…	…	15	90.0	…	…	2.7	Antigua and Barbuda
[4]	[4]	1,831	117,104	936,832	8.0	38.0	3,117	12.0	15	96.9	96.9	96.9	3.5	Argentina
25,200[5]	…	15	4,420	38,500	8.7	12.0	976	…	15	98.8	99.4	98.1	2.0	Armenia
[4]	[4]	2	53	394	7.4	…	…	7.0	15	95.0	…	…	4.9	Aruba
985,000[3]	34.1[3]	92	32,663	671,853	20.6	80.0	5,552	…	15	99.5	…	…	5.5	Australia
307,548	11.7	77	20,356	232,377	11.4	48.0	2,970	6.1	15	100.0	100.0	100.0	5.4	Austria
23,500	…	23	17,900	120,870	6.6	17.0	1,516	…	15	97.3	98.9	95.9	3.0	Azerbaijan
…	…	1[7]	160[7]	3,463[7]	21.6[7]	18.0	…	13.5	15	96.1	95.4	96.8	4.0	Bahamas, The
7,287	…	…	558	7,011	12.6	20.0	1,445	10.3	15	87.6	91.0	82.7	4.4	Bahrain
29,923[5]	16.1[5]	1,268[5]	36,000[5]	1,032,635[5]	28.7[5]	4.0	399	1.3	15	40.8	51.7	29.5	2.2	Bangladesh
…	…	4	…	6,622	…	29.0	2,602	3.3	15	97.4	98.0	96.8	7.2	Barbados
125,600	14.3	59	16,300	224,500	13.8	44.0	3,177	12.5	15	99.4	99.7	99.2	5.9	Belarus
569,041	…	151	38,014	358,214	9.4	56.0	3,494	…	15	100.0	100.0	100.0	3.1	Belgium
…	…	12	228	2,753	12.1	…	…	6.6	14	70.3	…	…	5.0	Belize
4,873[5]	17.2[5]	16[5]	962	14,085	14.6	3.0	253	1.3	15	37.5	47.8	23.6	3.2	Benin
…	…	1	…	543	…	…	…	18.4	15	96.9	96.7	97.0	3.7	Bermuda
1,822[1]	12.2[1]	2[1]	57[1]	2,055	9.1[1]	…	…	…	15	47.3	61.1	33.6	4.1	Bhutan
[4]	[4]	…	4,261[2]	109,503[2]	25.7[2]	21.0	2,154	9.9	15	85.6	92.1	79.4	4.9	Bolivia
…	…	44	2,802	37,541	13.4	…	…	…	10	85.5	96.5	76.6	…	Bosnia and Herzegovina
9,829	3.8	1	1,001	9,660	9.6	6.0	596	1.4	15	77.2	74.4	79.8	8.6	Botswana
…	…	900	173,705[13]	1,948,200[13]	11.2[13]	15.0	1,094	…	15	85.3	85.5	85.4	5.1	Brazil
2,553	4.9	4	370	2,080	5.6	7.0	518	9.4	15	91.6	94.7	88.2	2.5	Brunei
201,736	10.0	86	42,829	258,240	6.0	41.0	3,103	15.0	15	98.5	99.1	98.0	3.2	Bulgaria
9,539	13.0	9	632	9,531	15.1	0.9	83	…	15	23.0	31.2	13.1	3.6	Burkina Faso
…	…	8	556	4,256	7.6	0.8	74	0.6	15	48.1	56.3	40.5	4.0	Burundi
16,350[11]	…	9[11]	784[11]	11,652[11]	14.9[11]	1.0	98	1.0	15	65.3	79.7	53.4	2.9	Cambodia
91,779	15.6	…	1,086[12]	33,177[12]	30.5[12]	3.0	289	…	15	75.4	81.8	69.2	2.9	Cameroon
…	…	265	64,100[5]	980,251[5]	14.4[5]	88.0	5,997	21.4	15	96.6	…	…	6.9	Canada
2,289	…	…	…	…	…	…	…	…	15	73.5	84.3	65.3	4.0	Cape Verde
[4]	[4]	1	136	2,823	20.8	1.0	131	2.0	15	46.5	59.6	34.5	2.3	Central African Republic
2,926	13.5	8	288	3,446	12.0	0.6	54	…	15	53.6	66.9	40.8	1.7	Chad
…	…	…	18,084[11, 15]	367,094	…	31.0	2,546	12.3	15	95.7	95.9	95.5	3.6	Chile
9,773,000	16.3	1,020	405,000	3,174,000	7.8	6.0	473	2.0	15	85.0	92.3	77.4	2.3	China
928,474	…	266	75,568	673,353	8.9	17.0	1,768	10.4	15	91.8	91.8	91.8	4.4	Colombia
…	…	…	…	348	…	0.6	57	…	15	56.2	63.5	49.1	3.9	Comoros
[4]	[4]	…	…	52,501	…	2.0	212	1.3	15	77.3	86.6	67.7	1.0	Congo, Dem. Rep. of the
23,606	13.5	…	1,341[3]	16,602[3]	12.4[3]	7.0	582	3.0	15	80.7	87.5	74.4	6.1	Congo, Rep. of the
…	…	40[13]	…	83,106[13]	…	30.0	2,919	…	15	95.6	95.5	95.7	5.4	Costa Rica
11,037[3]	7.8[3]	…	1,657[3]	43,147[3]	26.0[3]	6.0	396	8.7	15	46.8	54.6	38.5	5.0	Côte d'Ivoire
150,792	11.6	79	6,532	90,021	13.8	28.0	1,905	6.4	15	98.3	99.4	97.3	5.3	Croatia
244,253[16]	9.0[16]	35[1]	22,967[16]	104,595	5.3[16]	12.0	1,013	5.9	15	96.4	96.5	96.4	6.7	Cuba
[4]	[4]	35	812	9,982	12.3	23.0	1,383	17.0	15	96.9	98.7	95.0	4.5	Cyprus[17]
419,843	7.7	272	18,061	203,598	11.3	24.0	1,867	8.5	15	100.0	100.0	100.0	5.1	Czech Republic
123,234	9.4	158[3]	9,600	169,783	17.7	48.0	3,189	19.6	…	100.0	100.0	100.0	8.1	Denmark

Education (continued)

country	year	first level (primary)					general second level (secondary)					vocational second level[a]	
		schools	teachers[c]	students[d]	student/ teacher ratio	net enroll- ment ratio[b]	schools	teachers[c]	students[d]	student/ teacher ratio	net enroll- ment ratio[b]	schools	teachers[c]
Djibouti	1997	81[3]	1,005[3]	33,960	...	32	26[4, 12]	628[3, 4]	11,628[4]	...	12	[4]	[4]
Dominica	1998	63	587	13,636	23.2	...	15	293	5,455	18.6	...	...	...
Dominican Republic	1995	4,001	42,135	1,462,722	34.7	81	...	10,757	240,441	22.4	22	...	1,297
East Timor	...	...	...	...	...	...	...	...	...	...	...	...	...
Ecuador	1997	17,367	74,601	1,888,172	25.3	92	...	62,630[4, 11]	765,073[4]	...	...	...	[4]
Egypt[19]	1997	18,522[16]	310,116	7,499,303	24.2	93	7,307[5, 16]	259,618	4,835,938	18.6	64	1,351[5]	138,277
El Salvador	1996	5,025	34,496	1,130,900	32.8	78	...	9,255	143,588	15.5	22	...	...
Equatorial Guinea	1994	781	1,381	75,751	54.9	...	...	466	14,511	31.1	...	...	122
Eritrea	1996	537	5,828	241,725	41.5	30	86[11]	2,031	78,902	38.8	16	4[11]	174
Estonia	1996	727	...	125,718	...	87	...	9,299	95,342	10.3	83	84	1,793
Ethiopia	1995	9,276	83,113	2,722,192	32.8	32	...	22,779	747,142	32.8	...	...	826
Faroe Islands	1995	62	554[9]	4,898	...	...	6	[9]	3,041	...	...	...	...
Fiji	1997	697[5]	5,011	142,781	28.5	99	147[5]	3,519	70,098	19.9	...	35[5]	625[2]
Finland	1997	4,392	39,966	592,500	14.8	98	454	5,766	131,900	22.9	93	467	15,063
France	1995	41,244	216,962	4,071,599	18.8	100	11,212[4]	473,673[4]	6,003,797[4]	12.7[4]	95	[4]	[4]
French Guiana	1996	78[5]	802	17,006	21.2	...	22[12]	875	13,585	15.5	...	...	210
French Polynesia	1995	278	2,949	48,160	16.3	103	38	1,745	25,541	14.6	61	...	...
Gabon	1996	1,147	4,944	250,606	50.7	...	48	2,683	72,888	27.2	...	11	412
Gambia, The	1995	250[5]	3,158[5]	113,419	33.4[5]	65	32[4, 5]	1,126[4, 5]	31,567	24.1[4, 5]	20	[4]	[4]
Gaza Strip	1997	1,118	15,903	656,353	41.3	...	...	7,634	54,692	7.2	...	...	316
Georgia	1997	3,201	16,542	293,325	17.7	77	3,139	55,817	424,465	7.6	74	...	2,146
Germany	1998	17,829	198,116	3,697,806	18.7	86	19,668	413,993	5,720,092	13.8	88	9,754	110,185
Ghana	1992	11,056	66,068	1,796,490	27.2	...	5,540	43,367	816,578	18.8	...	57[1]	422[1]
Greece	1997	8,651	46,785	652,040	13.9	90	3,044	56,899	682,201	12.0	87	682	13,783
Greenland	1999	88	975	9,341	9.6	...	3	...	1,746	...	...	...	...
Grenada	1997	58	879	23,449	26.7	...	19[3]	381[3]	7,367	19.3	...	...	...
Guadeloupe	1999	348	2,936	38,092[5]	...	...	88[4]	3,392[4]	51,366[4, 5]	13.4[4, 5]	...	[4]	[4]
Guam	1998	24	469	20,248	43.2	...	11	622	17,091	27.5	...	2	370[1]
Guatemala	1995	11,495	43,731	1,470,754	33.6	72	2,308[4]	23,807[4]	372,006[4]	15.6[4]	10	626[12]	[4]
Guernsey	1993	22[2]	236	4,697	19.9	...	8[2]	276	3,642	13.2	...	...	...
Guinea	1998	3,723	13,883	674,732	48.6	42	239	4,958	143,245	28.9	9	55[16]	1,268[16]
Guinea-Bissau	1995	...	...	100,369	...	47	...	...	7,000	...	3	...	...
Guyana	1997	420	3,461	102,000	29.5	87	...	2,150	62,043	29.5	66	...	...
Haiti	1995	10,071	30,205	1,110,398	36.8	26	1,038	...	195,418	...	22	...	...
Honduras	1999	8,768	33,431	1,111,264	33.2	90	661[3, 4]	14,539[4]	189,000[4]	13.0[4]	21	[4]	[4]
Hong Kong	1998	832	20,038	476,682	23.8	90	507	23,077	455,392	19.7	69	9	...
Hungary	1999	3,732	83,404	964,248	11.6	97	1,545	40,130	504,829	12.6	86	1,245	26,344
Iceland	1997	198	3,877	31,100	8.0	98	37	1,454	17,970	12.4	87	...	...
India	1997	598,354	1,789,733	110,393,406	61.7	...	274,944	2,738,205	65,359,339	23.9	...	...	...
Indonesia	1997	173,883	1,327,218	28,236,283	21.3	95	41,847	863,389	12,442,813	14.4	45	3,894	123,505
Iran	1997	63,101	298,755	9,238,393	31.2	90	18,445[1]	280,309	8,776,792	31.3	71	...	20,418[3]
Iraq	1996	8,145	145,455	2,903,923	20.0	76	2,635[3]	49,884	1,075,490	21.6	37	310[3]	9,903
Ireland	1997	3,254	18,968	476,632	25.1	92	440	12,694	375,518	29.6	86	324	8,305
Isle of Man	1999	33	...	6,210	...	...	5	...	4,732	...	...	...	...
Israel	1998	1,651	57,738	532,070	9.2	...	653	62,054	414,405	...	...	338	17,141[11]
Italy	1997	19,890	289,504	2,809,699	9.7	100	16,973	315,920	2,648,535	8.4	67	7,732	305,582
Jamaica	1997	788[2]	9,512	293,863	30.9	95	126[3]	8,377[3]	228,533	...	64[3]	18[3]	950[3]
Japan	1997	24,376	420,901	7,855,387	18.7	103	16,753	546,337	8,852,840	16.2	99	62	4,384
Jersey	1990	32	...	5,794	...	...	14	...	4,405	...	...	1	...
Jordan	1996	2,531	51,721	1,074,877	20.8	89	741[5]	6,309	109,906	17.4	42	54[5]	2,306
Kazakhstan	1997	8,611[16]	262,000[16]	1,342,035	...	...	...	178,900[5]	1,743,623	...	...	239	...
Kenya	1995	15,906	181,975	5,544,998	30.5	91	2,878	41,484	632,388	15.2	11	62	1,147[14]
Kiribati	1997	86	727	17,594	24.2	...	9	215	4,403	20.5	...	...	23
Korea, North	1988	4,810[13]	59,000	1,543,000	26.2	...	4,840[13]	111,000	2,468,000	22.2	...	...	...
Korea, South	1997	5,721	138,670	3,783,986	27.3	93	4,612	202,335	4,517,008	22.3	97	166	13,282
Kuwait	1997	258	9,863	142,265	14.4	62	416	19,402	213,266	11.0	61	38	793
Kyrgyzstan	1996	1,885	24,086	473,077	19.7	95	1,474[5]	38,915	498,849	12.8	...	53[5]	3,371
Laos	1997	7,896	25,831	786,335	30.4	72	750[1]	10,717	180,160	16.8	22	...	1,600[16]
Latvia	1998	638	10,883	146,653	13.5	89	380	24,112	196,148	8.1	79	123	5,470
Lebanon	1997	2,160	...	382,309	...	76	...	...	292,002	...	...	275	7,745
Lesotho	1997	1,249	7,898	374,628	47.4	70	187[3]	2,817	67,454	23.9	18	9[5]	61
Liberia	1987	...	...	...	...	...	...	...	...	...	...	...	...
Libya	1996	2,733[5]	122,020	1,333,679	10.9	96	...	17,668	170,573	9.7	62	480	...
Liechtenstein	1998	14	134	2,021	15.1	...	10[4]	198[4]	4,121[4]	20.8[4]	...	[4]	[4]
Lithuania	1997	2,292	14,093	225,071	16.0	...	...	32,172	325,480	10.1	80	104	5,078
Luxembourg	1997	...	1,844	28,232	15.3	...	...	2,673	9,463	3.5	...	...	2,904[3, 14]
Macau	1998	81	1,744	47,235	27.1	...	47	1,577	28,280	17.9	53	2	47
Macedonia	1998	1,043	13,376	256,275	19.2	94	93[4]	5,226[4]	84,059[4]	16.1[4]	51	[4]	[4]
Madagascar	1996	13,325	44,145	1,638,187	37.1	61	...	16,795	302,036	18.0	...	...	1,150
Malawi	1996	3,706	49,138	2,887,107	58.7	103	...	2,948	139,386	47.2	2	...	475
Malaysia	1997	7,084	150,681	2,870,667	19.1	102	1,460	91,659	1,767,946	19.3	...	101	5,472
Maldives	1998	228	1,992	48,895	24.5	...	...	...	15,933[2]	...	...	...	...
Mali	1998	2,511	10,853	862,875	79.5	31	307[2]	4,549[16]	166,372	...	5	...	21,731
Malta	1998	99	1,457	35,261	24.2	100	75	2,458	27,178	11.1	79	22	626
Marshall Islands	1995	103	669	13,355	20.0	...	12	144	2,400	16.7	...	...	...
Martinique	1997	273	2,603	55,569	21.3	...	76[16]	2,888	36,605	12.7	...	...	896[16]
Mauritania	1997	2,392	6,225	312,671	50.2	57	...	1,865[16]	49,221[16]	26.4[16]	...	...	202
Mauritius	1998	285	5,065	130,505	25.7	98	133	4,820	94,364	19.6	33	13	1,170[13]
Mayotte	1997	88[1]	555[11]	25,805[10]	...	...	8	246[11]	6,190	...	...	2[1]	17[1]
Mexico	1996	94,844	516,051	14,623,400	28.3	101	25,000	467,686	7,589,400	16.2	51	6,571[11]	77,347[11]
Micronesia	1995	174	...	27,281	...	...	24	...	6,898	...	...	...	...
Moldova	1997	1,700[9]	14,097	320,725	22.8	...	[9]	28,615[4]	419,256	...	...	64	[4]
Monaco	1997	8	127	1,917	15.1	...	6	192	2,416	12.6	...	4	89
Mongolia	1997	308	7,587	234,193	30.9	81	337	12,503	184,100	14.7	53	36	668
Morocco	1998	5,730	116,638	3,317,153	28.4	74	1,406	82,589	1,328,789	16.1	20	71[14]	2,951[3, 14]

students[d]	student/teacher ratio	third level (higher): institutions	teachers[c]	students[d]	student/teacher ratio	gross enrollment ratio[b]	students per 100,000 population[b]	percent of population age 25 and over with post-secondary education[b]	literacy[b]: over age	total (%)	male (%)	female (%)	public expenditure on education (percent of GNP)[b]	country
[4]	[4]	1[12]	13[12]	130[18]	...	0.2	26	...	15	51.4	65.0	38.4	3.6	Djibouti
...	...	2[11]	34[11]	484[11]	14.2[11]	...	...	1.7	15	90.0	...	...	5.5	Dominica
22,795	17.6	...	9,041[15]	176,995[15]	19.6[15]	23.0	...	...	15	83.8	84.0	83.7	2.3	Dominican Republic
...	...	...	...	...	...	...	...	...	...	...	...	...	...	East Timor
[4]	...	21	12,856[1]	206,541[1]	16.1[1]	20.0	2,012	12.7	15	91.9	93.6	90.2	3.5	Ecuador
1,912,040	13.8	16[15]	38,828[5, 15]	850,051	...	20.0	1,900	4.6	15	55.3	66.6	43.7	4.8	Egypt[19]
...	...	...	5,919	112,266	19.0	18.0	1,933	6.4	15	78.7	81.6	76.1	2.5	El Salvador
2,105	17.3	...	58	578	10.0	...	164	...	15	83.2	92.5	74.5	1.7	Equatorial Guinea
4,268	24.5	1	136	3,081	22.7	1.0	95	...	...	20.0	...	...	1.8	Eritrea
16,870	9.4	37	...	40,621	...	42.0	2,956	13.7	15	99.7	99.9	99.6	7.2	Estonia
9,103	11.0	...	1,937	32,671	16.9	0.6	62	1.0	15	38.7	43.9	33.4	4.0	Ethiopia
2,090[5]	...	1[12]	20[12]	91[12]	4.6[12]	...	...	...	15	99.0	99.0	99.0	...	Faroe Islands
7,283[2]	11.6[2]	...	277[12]	7,908[12]	28.5[12]	12.0	757	4.5	15	92.9	95.0	90.9	5.4	Fiji
251,600	16.7	29	8,134	168,996	20.8	74.0	4,190	15.4	15	100.0	100.0	100.0	7.5	Finland
[4]	[4]	1,062	52,613	2,083,129	39.6	51.0	3,600	11.4	...	98.8	98.9	98.7	6.0	France
2,404	11.4	1	...	324[11]	...	...	...	6.4	15	83.0	83.6	82.3	...	French Guiana
...	...	...	...	301[2]	...	1.0	...	...	15	95.0	94.9	95.0	9.8	French Polynesia
7,664	18.6	2[2, 15]	299[2, 15]	3,000[2, 15]	10.0[2, 15]	...	650	...	15	70.8	79.8	62.2	2.9	Gabon
[4]	[4]	...	155[5]	1,591[5]	10.3[5]	2.0	148	...	15	36.5	43.8	29.6	4.9	Gambia, The
1,775	5.7	5	2,473	49,599	20.0	...	...	...	...	...	...	...	...	Gaza Strip
19,593	9.1	23	25,549	163,345	6.4	30.0	3,002	...	15	99.5	99.7	99.4	5.2	Georgia
2,838,416	25.8	296	161,383	1,813,348	11.2	47.0	2,628	...	15	100.0	100.0	100.0	4.8	Germany
13,232[1]	31.4[1]	16[1]	700[1]	9,274[1]	13.2[1]	0.6	127	...	15	70.2	79.5	61.2	4.2	Ghana
135,365	9.8	18	16,057	363,180	22.6	47.0	3,149	8.7	15	97.2	98.6	96.0	3.1	Greece
...	...	...	...	...	...	...	...	...	15	100.0	100.0	100.0	...	Greenland
...	...	1[3]	66[3]	651[3]	9.9[3]	...	...	1.5	15	85.0	...	...	4.7	Grenada
[4]	[4]	1[5]	121[5]	4,673[5]	38.6[5]	...	...	5.2	15	90.1	89.7	90.5	...	Guadeloupe
4,369	...	1	192[1]	3,533	...	...	...	39.9	15	99.0	99.0	99.0	8.5	Guam
[4]	[4]	...	...	80,228	...	8.0	755	2.2	15	68.7	76.2	61.1	1.7	Guatemala
...	...	—	—	—	—	...	...	...	15	100.0	100.0	100.0	...	Guernsey
8,151[16]	6.8[16]	2[16]	947[16]	8,151[16]	8.6[16]	1.0	108	...	15	41.1	55.1	27.0	1.9	Guinea
...	...	...	...	...	...	...	...	0.1	15	36.8	53.0	21.4	...	Guinea-Bissau
...	...	...	612	8,965	12.5	11.0	954	1.8	15	98.5	99.0	98.1	5.0	Guyana
...	...	2[20]	817[20]	12,204[20]	14.9[20]	1.0	...	0.7	15	48.6	51.0	46.5	1.5	Haiti
[4]	[4]	8	3,676[3]	56,077	...	10.0	985	3.3	15	72.2	72.5	72.0	3.6	Honduras
42,003	...	18	...	91,748	...	22.0	1,635	14.5	15	93.4	96.5	90.0	2.9	Hong Kong
362,633	13.8	00	21,351	163,164	7.6	24.0	1,926	10.1	15	99.4	99.5	99.3	4.6	Hungary
...	...	10	508	7,972	15.7	37.0	2,787	...	15	100.0	100.0	100.0	5.4	Iceland
...	...	8,407[5]	286,000[5]	5,007,000[5]	17.5[5]	7.0	642	7.3	15	55.8	68.6	42.1	3.2	India
1,767,181	14.3	1,667	180,471	2,703,886	15.0	11.0	1,167	2.3	15	87.0	91.9	82.1	1.4	Indonesia
368,218[3]	18.0[3]	...	40,477	579,070	14.3	18.0	1,599	...	15	76.9	83.7	70.0	4.0	Iran
122,939	12.4	12	11,685	232,896	19.9	12.0	...	4.1	15	58.0	70.7	45.0	4.0	Iraq
96,821	11.7	30	4,872	107,501	22.1	41.0	3,618	13.1	15	100.0	100.0	100.0	6.0	Ireland
...	...	...	...	1,128	...	...	...	...	...	...	...	...	...	Isle of Man
106,393	...	7	9,546	181,038	19.0	41.0	3,598	11.2	15	96.1	97.9	94.3	7.6	Israel
2,597,449	8.5	56[15]	48,891[15]	1,595,642[15]	32.6	47.0	3,103	3.8	15	98.5	98.9	98.1	4.9	Italy
15,898[3]	16.7[3]	15[3]	...	24,200[3]	...	8.0	803	2.7	15	86.7	82.5	90.7	7.5	Jamaica
56,294	12.8	1,243	166,051	3,136,834	18.9	41.0	3,139	20.7	15	100.0	100.0	100.0	3.6	Japan
...	...	...	...	...	...	...	...	...	15	100.0	100.0	100.0	...	Jersey
35,579	15.4	55	4,821	99,020	20.5	27.0	2,542	...	15	89.8	94.9	84.4	7.9	Jordan
177,679	...	69[3]	27,189[3]	260,043[16]	...	33.0	2,806	12.4	15	97.5	99.1	96.1	4.4	Kazakhstan
11,700[14]	10.2[4]	14[11, 15]	4,392[1, 15]	88,180[11]	...	2.0	143	...	15	82.5	89.0	76.0	6.5	Kenya
333	14.5	—	—	—	—	...	...	...	15	90.0	...	...	6.3	Kiribati
220,000	...	519[13]	27,000	390,000	14.4	...	...	...	15	95.0	...	...	...	Korea, North
745,689	56.1	742	53,300	1,469,819	27.6	68.0	5,609	21.1	15	97.8	99.2	96.4	3.7	Korea, South
3,779	4.8	1	1,691	29,509	17.5	19.0	2,247	16.4	15	82.3	84.3	79.9	5.0	Kuwait
32,005	9.5	23	3,691	49,744	13.5	12.0	1,115	...	15	97.0	98.6	95.5	5.3	Kyrgyzstan
9,400[16]	5.9[16]	9[1]	1,369	12,732	9.3	3.0	253	...	15	61.8	73.6	50.5	2.1	Laos
45,672	8.3	28	4,486	56,187	12.5	33.0	2,244	13.4	15	99.7	99.8	99.6	6.3	Latvia
55,848	7.2	20	10,444	81,588	7.8	27.0	2,712	...	15	86.1	92.3	80.4	2.5	Lebanon
678	11.1	1	574	4,614	8.0	2.0	222	...	15	83.9	73.6	93.6	8.4	Lesotho
...	...	...	472	5,095	10.8	2.0	...	...	15	53.4	69.9	36.8	5.7	Liberia
155,483	...	13	...	126,348	...	17.0	1,358	2.7	15	79.8	90.9	67.6	7.1	Libya
[4]	[4]	...	...	...	...	...	...	...	15	100.0	100.0	100.0	...	Liechtenstein
56,400	11.1	15	13,136	83,645	6.4	31.0	2,244	12.6	15	99.5	99.7	99.4	5.5	Lithuania
19,346	...	1	200[3]	957	...	10.0	...	10.8	15	100.0	100.0	100.0	4.0	Luxembourg
699	14.9	7	818	7,682	9.4	28.0	1,700	5.9	15	93.2	96.4	90.1	...	Macau
[4]	[4]	30	1,385	36,167	26.1	20.0	1,415	6.7	10	89.1	94.2	83.8	5.1	Macedonia
8,479	7.3	...	921	18,458	20.0	3.0	174	...	15	80.2	87.7	72.9	1.9	Madagascar
2,228	4.7	6	531[3]	5,561	...	0.6	58	0.4	15	60.3	74.5	46.7	5.4	Malawi
36,573	6.9	48	14,960	210,724	14.1	12.0	971	6.9	15	87.5	91.5	83.6	4.9	Malaysia
452[2]	...	—	—	—	—	...	...	1.7	15	96.3	96.3	96.4	6.4	Maldives
7,200	3.0	7	796	13,847	17.4	1.0	73	...	15	40.3	47.9	33.2	2.2	Mali
4,159	6.6	1	770	7,146	9.3	29.0	1,595	...	15	92.1	91.4	92.8	5.1	Malta
...	...	...	...	...	...	...	...	...	15	91.2	92.4	90.0	...	Marshall Islands
11,101[16]	12.4[16]	1	99[5]	3,079	45.3[5]	...	...	5.6	15	97.4	96.0	97.1	...	Martinique
2,544	12.6	4	270	8,496	31.5	4.0	374	1.3	15	39.9	50.6	29.5	5.1	Mauritania
5,496	...	3	461	6,429	13.9	6.3	594	1.9	15	84.3	87.7	81.0	4.6	Mauritius
839[11]	...	—	—	—	—	...	...	...	15	91.9	...	...	...	Mayotte
1,076,700[11]	13.9[11]	10,341	163,843	1,532,800	9.4	16.0	1,586	9.2	15	91.0	93.1	89.1	4.9	Mexico
...	...	...	...	1,461[5]	...	...	...	...	15	76.7	67.0	87.2	...	Micronesia
26,245	...	20	8,814	93,759	10.6	27.0	2,110	11.3	15	98.9	99.6	98.3	10.6	Moldova
532	6.0	1	...	112	...	...	...	...	...	...	...	...	...	Monaco
11,308	16.9	86	4,471	44,088	9.8	17.0	1,753	23.4	15	99.3	99.2	99.3	5.7	Mongolia
22,415[14]	...	68	9,667	266,507	27.5	11.0	1,132	...	15	48.9	61.9	36.0	5.3	Morocco

Education (continued)

country	year	first level (primary)					general second level (secondary)					vocational second level[a]	
		schools	teachers[c]	students[d]	student/ teacher ratio	net enroll- ment ratio[b]	schools	teachers[c]	students[d]	student/ teacher ratio	net enroll- ment ratio[b]	schools	teachers[c]
Mozambique	1997	6,025	32,670	1,899,531	57.8	40	75	1,555	51,554	33.1	8	25	565
Myanmar (Burma)	1998	35,877	167,134	5,145,400	30.8	...	2,091	56,955	1,545,600	27.1	...	103[3]	2,462[3]
Namibia	1995	933[5]	10,912[2]	368,222	32.0[2]	91	114[5]	3,943[2]	101,838[5]	...	36	17[5]	56[2]
Nauru	1995	10	138	2,207	16.0	...	4	46	...	...	...	1	...
Nepal	1996	22,218	89,378	3,447,607	38.6	...	7,582[4]	36,127[4]	1,121,335[4]	31.0[4]	...	[4]	[4]
Netherlands, The	1999	7,238	99,031[12]	1,534,000	...	100	666	89,370[12]	856,000	...	84	143	18,613[12]
Netherlands Antilles	1998	85[16]	1,111	24,061	21.7	...	21	461[16]	8,372	...	...	33	623[16]
New Caledonia	1996	279	1,622	22,942	14.1	98	46	2,021[4]	20,360	...	72	14	[4]
New Zealand	1998	2,282	23,119	445,868	19.3	100	339	15,228	224,290	14.7	90	29	5,309
Nicaragua	1997	7,224	21,020[16]	783,002	...	77	451[5]	5,990[3]	220,670[3]	36.8[3]	18	...	...
Niger	1998	3,175	11,545	482,065	41.8	24	...	3,579	97,675	27.3	6	...	215
Nigeria	1995	38,649	435,210	16,191,000	37.2	...	6,074	152,596	4,451,000	29.2	...	...	...
Northern Mariana Islands	1993	18	183	4,666	25.5	...	9[4]	152[4]	3,044[4]	20.0[4]	...	[4]	[4]
Norway	1997	3,287	39,385	487,398	12.4	100	714[4]	21,105[4]	208,280[4]	9.9[4]	97	[4]	[4]
Oman	1997	429	11,925[16]	311,955	...	69	128[1]	11,896	205,046	17.2	49	25[1]	342[5]
Pakistan	1998	158,511[10]	346,000[10]	16,642,000[10]	48.0[10]	...	25,913	259,200	5,545,000	21.4	...	673	7,546
Palau	1997	...	172	1,450	8.4	...	...	60	490	8.2	...	...	...
Panama	1997	2,866	15,058	377,898	25.1	91	417	12,450	223,155	17.9	51	...	...
Papua New Guinea	1995	2,790	13,652	525,995	38.5	...	135[1]	2,415[2]	68,818	24.1[2]	...	117[1]	878[2]
Paraguay	1996	5,928	41,713	895,777	21.5	91	804[4]	17,668	293,651[4]	...	38	[4]	...
Peru	1997	33,017	153,951	4,163,180	27.0	91	8,085[3]	106,614	1,969,501	18.5	55	2,425[3]	12,293[3]
Philippines	1997	37,645	341,183	11,902,501	34.9	101	5,880[5]	154,705[4]	4,888,246[4]	31.6[4]	59	1,261[1]	[4]
Poland	1998	19,299	322,600	4,896,400	15.2	95	1,847	39,200	757,500	19.3	85	9,320	89,900
Portugal	1996	12,884	145,462[9]	1,339,744	...	104	664	[9]	477,221	...	78	262	6,895
Puerto Rico	1986	1,542	18,359	427,582	23.3	...	395	13,612	334,661	24.6	...	52	...
Qatar	1996[8]	174	5,864	53,631	9.1	80	123[3]	3,738[3]	36,964[3]	9.9[3]	69	3	120
Réunion	1998	351	...	76,364	...	...	111[4]	6,343	96,811	15.3	...	[4]	1,120[16]
Romania	1997	13,978[18]	175,426[18]	2,546,231[18]	14.5[18]	95	1,295[21]	64,485[21]	792,788[21]	12.3[21]	73	1,692	10,942
Russia	1999	69,613[9]	1,811,000[9]	21,966,900[9]	12.1[9]	93	[9]	[9]	[9]	[9]	...	3,590	...
Rwanda	1992	1,710	18,937	1,104,902	58.3	75	...	3,413[4]	94,586[4]	27.7[4]	8	...	[4]
St. Kitts and Nevis	1998	28	320	5,928	18.5	...	9	341	4,548	13.3	...	...	...
St. Lucia	1998	84	1,160	30,536	26.3	...	17	620	11,405	18.4	...	1[11]	34[11]
St. Vincent and the Grenadines	1998	60	1,007	21,347	21.2	...	21	379	7,775	20.5	...	3	32[16]
Samoa	1995	155	1,475	35,811	24.3	96	...	...	...	...	45	...	...
San Marino	1998	14	225	1,211	5.4	...	3	148	700	4.7	...	...	44[5]
São Tomé and Príncipe	1997	69	638	21,760	34.1	...	10	415	12,280	29.6	...	...	...
Saudi Arabia	1997	11,509	175,458	2,256,185	12.9	61	7,667	115,907	1,505,072	13.0	42	...	6,133
Senegal	1997	3,530	16,567	954,758	57.6	60	359[11]	6,219	206,934	33.3	16	19[11]	182[11]
Seychelles	1999	25	656	9,868	15.0	...	13	545	7,774	14.3	...	12	218
Sierra Leone	1993	1,643	10,595	267,425	25.2	...	167	4,313	70,900	16.4	...	44	709
Singapore	1997	196	11,189	280,108	25.0	93	165	10,673	209,835	19.7	44	10	1,315
Slovakia	1998	2,482	39,535	645,941	16.3	...	198	5,849	80,116	13.7	...	365	10,104
Slovenia	1997	824	7,283	98,866	13.5	95	153	8,665	131,573	15.2	...	...	5,908
Solomon Islands	1994	520	2,514	60,493	24.1	...	23	618	7,981	12.9	...	1	...
Somalia	1990	...	...	377,000	...	10	...	...	44,000	...	3	...	...
South Africa	1996	20,863[9]	224,896	8,159,430	36.3	103	[9]	128,611[5]	3,749,449[5]	29.2[5]	58	187[5]	10,807[5]
Spain	1997	16,540[5]	163,105	2,682,894	16.4	105	25,775[4, 11]	245,118[4]	2,946,191	...	74	[4]	[4]
Sri Lanka	1998	10,947[9]	194,823[9]	4,278,124[9]	22.0[9]	...	[9]	[9]	[9]	[9]	...	36	623
Sudan, The	1997	11,158	102,987	3,000,048	24.1	54	2,578[2]	15,504	405,583	26.2	...	...	761
Suriname	1996	304	3,611	75,585	20.9	...	104	2,286	31,918	13.9	...	1	...
Swaziland	1997	529	6,094	205,829	33.8	91	165[5]	2,954[16]	57,330[16]	19.4[16]	38	5[5]	228[5]
Sweden	1997	4,936	81,800	958,972	11.7	102	641	28,305	310,000	10.9	99	...	...
Switzerland	1998	...	...	462,262	...	100	...	...	421,025	...	79	...	...
Syria	1997	10,783	114,689	2,690,205	23.5	91	2,526[3]	52,182	865,042	16.6	38	292[3]	12,479
Taiwan	1998	2,540	92,104	1,905,690	20.7	...	1,151[4]	99,411[4]	1,874,747[4]	18.9[4]	...	[4]	[4]
Tajikistan	1997	3,432	27,172	638,674	23.5	...	...	112,532	688,150	6.1	...	75[3]	...
Tanzania	1996[22]	10,892[5]	108,874	3,942,888	36.2	48	491[5]	11,689	199,093	17.0	...	40[5]	1,062
Thailand	1997	34,412[11]	445,542[11]	5,909,618	...	...	2,318[11]	107,025[11]	3,267,449	...	...	679[11]	40,116[11]
Togo	1997	3,283[16]	18,535	859,574	46.4	81	314[11]	4,736[16]	169,178	...	18	...	653
Tonga	1994	115	701	16,540	23.6	...	47	809	15,702	19.4	...	9	67[1]
Trinidad and Tobago	1997	478	7,311	181,030	24.8	88	...	5,070[4]	104,349[4]	20.6[4]	65	...	[4]
Tunisia	1997	4,428	60,101	1,450,916	24.1	98	712[3]	45,411	882,730	19.4	...	...	237[16]
Turkey	1997	47,313	217,131	6,389,060	29.4	99	11,144	143,322	3,427,715	23.9	51	4,046	75,507
Turkmenistan	1995	1,900[9]	72,900[9]	940,600[9]	12.9[9]	...	[9]	[9]	[9]	[9]	...	78	...
Tuvalu	1994	12	72[1]	1,906	...	...	2	31	345	...	...	1	10[1]
Uganda	1995[8]	8,531	76,134	2,636,409	34.6	...	...	14,447	255,158	17.7	...	...	1,788
Ukraine	1996	21,900[9]	576,000[3, 9]	7,007,000[9]	12.4[3, 9]	...	[9]	[9]	[9]	[9]	...	782	...
United Arab Emirates	1997	...	16,148	259,509	16.1	78	...	12,388[3]	178,839	12.0	71	9	249[14]
United Kingdom	1997	23,312	283,492	5,328,219	18.5	99	...	312,038	4,435,000	13.2	91	...	152,098
United States	1998	88,223[8, 9]	1,874,000	34,681,000	18.5	95	[9]	1,217,000	17,494,000	14.4	90	...	...
Uruguay	1997	2,410	16,721	348,195	20.8	93	413	19,104	192,399	10.1	...	101	...
Uzbekistan	1996	9,300[9]	413,000[9]	5,090,000[9]	12.3[9]	...	[9]	[9]	[9]	[9]	...	248	22,164[11]
Vanuatu	1992	272	852	26,267	30.8	...	...	220	4,269	19.4	17	...	...
Venezuela	1997	15,894[11]	182,192	4,262,221	23.4	84	1,621[2, 4]	43,369[4]	377,984[4]	8.7[4]	22	[4]	[4]
Vietnam	1998	13,092[5]	324,431	10,431,337	32.2	...	6,298[5]	209,500	6,642,350	31.7	...	451[5]	9,336
Virgin Islands (U.S.)	1993[8]	62	790	14,544	18.4	...	...	541[12]	12,502	17.2[12]	...	—	—
West Bank	1997	1,193[9]	15,912[9]	431,565[9]	27.1[9]	...	[9]	[9]	[9]	[9]	...	...	...
Western Sahara	1995[8]	40	925	32,257	34.9	...	13	1,267	10,541	8.3	...	...	...
Yemen	1997[14]	11,013[5]	90,478	2,699,788	29.8	...	1,224[3]	13,787	286,405	20.8	...	125[3]	369[3]
Yugoslavia	1999	4,431	52,294	864,199	16.5	69	561	27,766	367,587	13.2	62	...	...
Zambia	1996	3,907	38,528[3]	1,670,000	...	75	...	...	255,000	...	16	...	...
Zimbabwe	1996	4,659	63,718	2,493,791	39.1	...	1,536	28,354	751,349	26.5	...	25[2]	1,479[2]

students[d]	student/ teacher ratio	third level (higher) institutions	teachers[c]	students[d]	student/ teacher ratio	gross enroll-ment ratio[b]	students per 100,000 popula-tion[b]	percent of population age 25 and over with post-secondary education[b]	literacy[b] over age	total (%)	male (%)	female (%)	public expenditure on education (percent of GNP)[b]	country
12,001	21.2	3	954	7,158	7.5	0.5	40	0.1	15	43.8	59.9	28.4	4.1	Mozambique
25,374[3]	10.3[3]	51	17,089	385,300	22.5	5.0	564	2.0	15	84.7	89.0	80.6	1.2	Myanmar (Burma)
1,503[5]	...	7[5]	331[12]	11,344	...	8.0	738	4.0	15	82.1	82.9	81.2	9.1	Namibia
...	...	...	...	...	...	...	...	...	15	99.0	...	...	...	Nauru
[4]	[4]	3[2]	4,925[12]	105,694	...	5.0	501	0.6	15	41.4	59.1	21.8	3.2	Nepal
517,000	...	13	...	147,000	...	47.0	3,176	...	15	100.0	100.0	100.0	5.1	Netherlands, The
8,524	...	1	97	686	7.1	...	...	8.8	15	96.6	96.6	96.6	...	Netherlands Antilles
5,916	...	4	79	1,749	22.1	5.0	...	7.5	15	57.9	57.4	58.3	13.5	New Caledonia
105,186	19.8	7	4,973	107,837	21.7	63.0	4,508	39.1	15	100.0	100.0	100.0	7.3	New Zealand
...	...	10[5]	3,840	48,758	12.7	12.0	1,231	...	15	64.3	64.2	64.4	3.9	Nicaragua
2,145	10.0	2	355	5,569	15.7	0.7	55	...	15	15.7	23.5	8.3	2.3	Niger
...	...	31	12,103	228,000	18.8	4.0	367	...	15	64.1	72.3	56.2	0.7	Nigeria
[4]	[4]	...	...	...	...	...	...	...	15	96.3	96.9	95.6	...	Northern Mariana Islands
[4]	[4]	89	11,515	181,741	15.8	54.5	4,164	18.7	15	100.0	100.0	100.0	7.4	Norway
2,350[5]	6.9[5]	5[1]	1,162	13,251	11.4	8.0	532	...	15	71.3	80.4	61.7	4.5	Oman
95,000	12.6	984	34,078	1,052,782	30.9	3.0	291	2.5	15	43.3	57.6	27.8	2.7	Pakistan
...	...	...	...	130	...	...	...	...	15	97.6	98.3	96.6	...	Palau
...	...	14	6,409	95,341	14.9	30.0	3,024	13.2	15	91.9	92.6	91.3	5.1	Panama
9,941	12.9[2]	2[1]	...	13,663	...	3.0	318	...	15	76.0	81.7	67.7	4.7	Papua New Guinea
[4]	...	2	742[11]	42,302	...	10.0	1,049	6.6	15	93.3	94.4	92.2	4.0	Paraguay
270,576[3]	22.0[3]	886	45,443	657,586	14.2	26.0	3,268	20.6	15	89.9	94.7	85.4	2.9	Peru
[4]	[4]	975[5]	56,880[12]	2,022,106[16]	...	29.0	2,981	22.0	15	95.4	95.5	95.2	3.4	Philippines
1,599,900	17.8	246	73,300	1,091,500	14.9	25.0	1,884	7.9	15	99.8	99.8	99.8	7.5	Poland
25,234	3.7	278	16,087	319,525	19.9	39.0	3,060	7.7	15	92.2	94.8	90.0	5.8	Portugal
149,191	...	45	9,045	171,625[16]	...	...	...	28.7	15	93.8	93.7	94.0	8.2	Puerto Rico
670	5.6	1	643	8,475	13.2	27.0	1,518	13.3	15	81.3	80.5	83.2	3.4	Qatar
13,547[16]	12.1[16]	1	286	8,663	30.3	...	...	...	15	87.1	84.8	89.2	...	Réunion
351,900	32.2	102	23,477	354,488	15.1	23.0	1,817	5.6	15	98.2	99.1	97.3	3.6	Romania
1,676,000	...	913	282,400	3,597,900	12.7	43.0	2,998	14.1	15	99.4	99.8	99.2	3.5	Russia
[4]	[4]	...	646[1]	3,389[1]	5.2[1]	0.4	...	...	15	67.0	73.7	60.6	3.8	Rwanda
...	...	1[11]	51[11]	394[11]	7.7[11]	...	...	2.3	15	90.9	90.0	90.0	3.8	St. Kitts and Nevis
808[11]	23.7[11]	1	157[16]	2,760[16]	17.6[16]	...	...	3.4	15	82.0	...	...	9.8	St. Lucia
415	...	...	...	...	...	...	...	1.4	15	96.0	...	...	6.3	St. Vincent and the Grenadines
...	...	...	...	...	...	...	...	5.6	15	100.0	100.0	100.0	4.2	Samoa
455[5]	10.3[5]	...	...	...	...	...	...	...	15	99.1	99.4	98.8	...	San Marino
...	...	...	...	...	...	...	...	0.3	15	54.2	70.2	39.1	3.8	São Tomé and Príncipe
51,916	8.5	68[15]	8,998[13]	105,000[15]	18.4[15]	16.0	1,455	...	15	77.0	84.1	67.2	7.5	Saudi Arabia
7,301[11]	40.1[11]	2	965[15]	24,081[15]	25.0[15]	3.0	297	...	15	37.3	47.0	27.6	3.7	Senegal
2,002	9.2	...	...	...	...	...	...	4.6	15	84.2	82.9	85.7	7.9	Seychelles
7,756	10.9	1	257[12]	2,571[12]	10.0[12]	2.0	119	1.5	15	36.3	50.7	22.6	0.9	Sierra Leone
9,906	7.5	7	7,764	97,392	12.5	39.0	2,722	7.6	15	92.4	96.4	88.5	3.0	Singapore
116,681	11.5	18	8,544	83,942	9.8	22.0	1,903	9.5	15	100.0	100.0	100.0	5.0	Slovakia
80,885	13.7	37	3,907	51,009	13.1	38.0	2,775	10.4	15	100.0	100.0	100.0	5.7	Slovenia
...	...	...	...	...	...	...	...	...	15	54.1	62.4	44.9	3.8	Solomon Islands
10,400	...	1	549[12]	4,640[12]	...	0.5	...	...	15	24.0	36.0	14.0	0.4	Somalia
140,531[5]	13.0[5]	...	27,099[5]	617,897[5]	22.8[5]	19.0	1,664	1.5	15	85.1	85.8	84.5	8.0	South Africa
1,029,606	...	...	88,922	1,741,528	19.6	51.0	4,017	8.4	15	97.7	98.6	96.8	5.0	Spain
11,652	18.7	12	3,050	38,192	12.5	5.0	474	1.1	15	91.6	94.5	88.9	3.4	Sri Lanka
26,421	34.7	6	1,417	52,260	36.9	3.0	272	0.8	15	57.1	68.3	46.0	1.4	Sudan, The
1,462	...	1	155	1,335	8.6	...	1,124	...	15	94.2	95.9	92.6	3.5	Suriname
2,958[5]	13.0[5]	1	467	5,658	12.1	6.0	642	3.3	15	79.8	80.9	78.7	5.7	Swaziland
...	...	64	33,498[13]	275,217[13]	8.2[13]	50.0	2,972	21.0	15	100.0	100.0	100.0	8.3	Sweden
198,452	...	...	7,709[3]	151,021	...	33.0	2,066	11.5	15	100.0	100.0	100.0	5.4	Switzerland
92,622	7.4	...	4,733[3, 15]	215,734[3]	...	16.0	1,559	...	15	74.4	88.3	60.4	3.1	Syria
[4]	[4]	139	38,806	856,186	22.1	...	...	...	15	94.0	97.6	90.2	5.2	Taiwan
29,482[3]	...	10[3]	5,200[3]	76,613	...	20.0	1,864	11.7	15	99.2	99.6	98.9	2.2	Tajikistan
12,571	11.8	...	1,650	12,776	7.7	0.6	43	2.0	15	75.2	84.1	66.6	3.4	Tanzania
658,474	...	102	25,171[16]	481,936[16]	19.1[16]	22.0	2,096	5.1	15	95.6	97.2	94.0	4.6	Thailand
9,076	13.8	1	443	11,639	26.3	4.0	317	1.3	15	57.1	72.2	42.6	4.5	Togo
824	...	1	53	226[2]	...	...	...	2.8	15	92.8	92.9	92.8	4.7	Tonga
[4]	[4]	3	...	6,007	...	7.7	771	3.4	15	98.2	99.0	97.5	4.4	Trinidad and Tobago
3,839[16]	16.2[16]	...	6,641	121,787	18.3	14.0	1,330	2.8	15	70.8	81.4	60.1	7.7	Tunisia
1,333,177	17.6	863	53,805	1,222,362	22.7	21.0	1,960	10.8	15	85.2	93.6	76.7	2.2	Turkey
26,000	...	15	...	29,435[16]	...	22.0	2,072	...	15	97.7	98.8	96.6	3.9	Turkmenistan
58[12]	...	—	—	—	—	...	...	7.0	15	95.0	...	...	...	Tuvalu
36,063	20.2	...	2,006	29,343	14.6	2.0	154	0.5	15	67.3	77.7	57.1	2.6	Uganda
618,000	...	255[15]	...	922,800[15]	...	41.0	2,977	...	15	98.4	99.5	97.4	7.3	Ukraine
1,925[14]	7.7[14]	4	510[11]	17,950	...	12.0	801	...	15	76.5	75.5	79.5	1.8	United Arab Emirates
2,435,321	16.0	...	89,241	1,820,849	20.4	52.0	3,135	...	15	100.0	100.0	100.0	5.3	United Kingdom
...	...	5,758[11]	940,000	14,350,000	15.3	81.0	5,339	46.5	15	95.5	95.7	95.3	5.4	United States
58,246	...	2	7,165	62,026	8.7	30.0	2,487	10.1	15	97.8	97.4	98.2	3.3	Uruguay
240,100[13]	...	55[13]	...	272,300[13]	...	32.0	2,938	...	15	97.2	98.5	96.0	7.7	Uzbekistan
444	...	1	...	124[12]	...	...	...	...	15	52.9	57.3	47.8	4.8	Vanuatu
[4]	[4]	99[12]	36,232	717,192	19.8	28.0	2,820	11.8	15	93.0	93.3	92.7	5.2	Venezuela
179,907	19.3	104[5]	23,522	509,300	21.7	7.0	404	2.6	15	93.3	95.7	91.0	3.0	Vietnam
—	—	1	266	2,924	11.0	...	...	24.4	...	...	...	...	7.5	Virgin Islands (U.S.)
...	...	22	1,598	30,622	19.2	...	...	...	...	...	...	...	...	West Bank
1,222	...	—	...	...	...	...	...	...	...	...	...	...	...	Western Sahara
67,883	...	2	1,991[3]	65,675	...	4.0	419	...	15	46.4	67.4	25.0	7.0	Yemen
...	...	83	10,998	147,981	13.5	22.0	1,674	...	15	93.3	97.6	89.2	...	Yugoslavia
7,982[12]	...	2	640	4,470	7.0	2.0	241	1.5	15	78.0	85.2	71.2	2.2	Zambia
27,431[2]	18.5[2]	28[2]	3,581[3]	43,200[3]	12.1[3]	7.0[3]	638	4.9	15	92.7	95.5	89.9	7.1	Zimbabwe

[1]1990. [2]1992. [3]1995. [4]General second level includes vocational second level. [5]1994. [6]Includes upper primary. [7]College of the Bahamas only. [8]Public schools only. [9]First level includes general second level. [10]Includes preschool. [11]1993. [12]1991. [13]1997. [14]Excludes teacher training. [15]Universities only. [16]1996. [17]Republic of Cyprus only. [18]Includes lower secondary. [19]Data exclude 1,770 primary and 1,449 secondary schools in the Al-Azhar education system. [20]Port-au-Prince universities only. [21]Upper second level only. [22]Mainland Tanzania only.

BIBLIOGRAPHY AND SOURCES

The following list indicates the principal documentary sources used in the compilation of *Britannica World Data.* It is by no means a complete list, either for international or for national sources, but is indicative more of the range of materials to which reference has been made in preparing this compilation.

While *Britannica World Data* has long been based primarily on print sources, many rare in North American library collections, the burgeoning resources of the Internet can be accessed from any appropriately equipped personal computer (PC). At this writing, more than 100 national statistical offices had Internet sites and there were also sites for central banks, national information offices, individual ministries, and the like.

Because of the relative ease of access to these sites for PC users, uniform resource locators (URLs) for mainly official sites have been added to both country statements (at the end, in boldface) and individual Comparative National Statistics tables (at the end of the headnote) when a source providing comparable international data existed. Many sites exist that are narrower in coverage or less official and that may also serve the reader (on-line newspapers; full texts of national constitutions; business and bank sites) but space permitted the listing of only the top national and intergovernmental sites. Sites that are wholly or predominantly in a language other than English are so identified.

International Statistical Sources

Asian Development Bank. *Asian Development Outlook* (annual); *Key Indicators of Developing Member Countries of ADB* (annual).

Billboard Books. *World Radio TV Handbook* (annual).

Caribbean Development Bank. *Annual Report.*

Christian Research. *World Churches Handbook* (1997).

Comité Monétaire de la Zone Franc. *La Zone Franc: Rapport* (annual).

Commonwealth of Independent States. *Demographic Yearbook; Sodruzhestvo Nezavizimykh Gosudarstv v 19** godu; Strany-Chleny SNG: Statistichesky Yezhegodnik (Member States of the CIS: Statistical Yearbook).*

Eastern Caribbean Central Bank. *Report and Statement of Accounts* (annual).

Europa Publications Ltd. *Africa South of the Sahara* (annual); *The Europa Year Book* (2 vol.); *The Far East and Australasia* (annual); *The Middle East and North Africa* (annual).

Food and Agriculture Organization. *Food Balance Sheets; Production Yearbook; Trade Yearbook; World Census of Agriculture* (decennial); *Yearbook of Fishery Statistics* (2 vol.); *Yearbook of Forest Products.*

Her Majesty's Stationery Office. *The Commonwealth Yearbook.*

Instituts d'Émission d'Outre-Mer et des Départements d'Outre-Mer (France). *Bulletin trimestriel* (quarterly); *Rapport annuel.*

Inter-American Development Bank. *Economic and Social Progress in Latin America* (annual).

Inter-Parliamentary Union. *Chronicle of Parliamentary Elections and Developments* (annual); *World Directory of Parliaments* (annual).

International Air Transport Association. *World Air Transport Statistics* (annual).

International Bank for Reconstruction and Development/The World Bank. *Statistical Handbook 19**: States of the Former USSR* (annual); *World Bank Atlas* (annual); *Global Development Finance* (2 vol.; annual); *World Development Report* (annual).

International Civil Aviation Organization. *Civil Aviation Statistics of the World* (annual); *Digest of Statistics.*

International Institute for Strategic Studies. *The Military Balance* (annual).

International Labour Organisation. *Year Book of Labour Statistics; The Cost of Social Security: Basic Tables* (triennial).

International Monetary Fund. *Annual Report on Exchange Arrangements and Exchange Restrictions; Direction of Trade Statistics Yearbook; Government Finance Statistics Yearbook; IMF Staff Country Reports* (irreg.); *International Financial Statistics* (monthly, with yearbook).

International Road Federation. *World Road Statistics* (annual).

International Telecommunication Union. *Yearbook of Statistics: Telecommunication Services* (annual).

Jane's Publishing Co., Ltd. *Jane's World Railways* (annual).

Keesing's Worldwide LLC. *Keesing's Record of World Events* (monthly except August).

Macmillan Press Ltd. *The Statesman's Year-Book.*

Middle East Economic Digest Ltd. *Middle East Economic Digest* (semimonthly).

Mining Journal, Ltd. *Mining Annual Review* (2 vol.).

Organization for Economic Cooperation and Development. *Economic Surveys* (annual); *Financing and External Debt of Developing Countries* (annual).

Organization of Eastern Caribbean States. *Statistical Booklet* (irreg.).

Oxford University Press. *World Christian Encyclopedia* (David B. Barrett, ed. [1982]).

Pan American Health Organization. *Health Conditions in the Americas* (2 vol.; quadrennial).

PennWell Publishing Co. *International Petroleum Encyclopedia* (annual).

René Moreux et Cie. *Marchés tropicaux & Méditerranéens* (weekly).

United Nations (UN). *Demographic Yearbook; Energy Balances and Electricity Profiles* (biennial); *Industrial Commodities Statistics Yearbook; Energy Statistics Yearbook; International Trade Statistics Yearbook* (2 vol.); *Monthly Bulletin of Statistics; Population Studies* (irreg.); *National Accounts Statistics* (2 parts; annual); *Population and Vital Statistics Report* (quarterly); *Statistical Yearbook; World Population Prospects 19*** (biennial).

UN: Economic Commission for Africa. *African Socio-Economic Indicators* (annual); *African Statistical Yearbook* (2 vol. in 4 parts); *Demographic and Related Socio-Economic Data Sheets for ECA Member States* (irreg.); *Economic and Social Survey of Africa* (annual).

UN: Economic Commission for Europe. *Annual Bulletin of Housing and Building Statistics for Europe; Annual Bulletin of Transport Statistics for Europe.*

UN: Economic Commission for Latin America. *Economic Survey of Latin America and the Caribbean* (2 vol.; annual); *Statistical Yearbook for Latin America and the Caribbean.*

UN: Economic and Social Commission for Asia and the Pacific. *Statistical Indicators for Asia and the Pacific* (quarterly); *Statistical Yearbook for Asia and the Pacific.*

UN: Economic and Social Commission for Western Asia. *Demographic and Related Socio-Economic Data Sheets* (irreg.); *National Accounts Studies of the ESCWA Region* (irreg.); *The Population Situation in the ESCWA Region* (irreg.); *Prices and Financial Statistics in the ESCWA Region* (irreg.); *Statistical Abstract of the Region of the Economic and Social Commission for Western Asia* (annual).

UN: Educational, Scientific, and Cultural Organization. *Statistical Yearbook.*

United Nations Industrial Development Organization. *Industrial Development Review Series* (irreg.); *Industrial Development: Global Report* (annual); *International Yearbook of Industrial Statistics.*

United States: Central Intelligence Agency, *The World Factbook* (annual); Dept. of Commerce, *World Population Profile* (biennial); Dept. of Health and Human Services, *Social Security Programs Throughout the World* (biennial); Dept. of Interior, *Minerals Yearbook* (3 vol. in 6 parts); Dept. of State, *Background Notes* (irreg.).

World Health Organization. *World Health Statistics Annual; World Health Statistics Quarterly.*

World Tourism Organization. *Compendium of Tourism Statistics* (annual).

National Statistical Sources

Afghanistan. *Preliminary Results of the First Afghan Population Census (1979).*

Albania. *Albania: Statistical Annex* (IMF Staff Country Report [2001]); *Population and Housing Census 1989; Statistical Yearbook of Albania.*

Algeria. *Annuaire statistique; Recensement général de la population et de l'habitat, 1998; Algeria: Recent Economic Developments* (IMF Country Staff Report [2001]).

American Samoa. *American Samoa Statistical Digest* (annual); *American Samoa Economic Report; Report on the State of the Island* (U.S. Department of the Interior [annual]); *2000 Census of Population and Housing* (U.S.).

Andorra. *Informe Econòmic Anual; Recull Estadístic General de la Població Andorra 90.*

Angola. *Angola—Recent Economic Developments* (IMF Staff Country Report [2000]); *Perfil estatístico de Angola* (annual).

Antigua. *Antigua and Barbuda—Statistical Annex* (IMF Staff Country Report [1999]); *Statistical Yearbook; 1991 Population and Housing Census.*

Argentina. *Anuario estadístico de la República Argentina; Censo nacional de población y vivienda, 1991; Encuesta permanente de hogares* (irreg.).

Armenia. *Recent Economic Development and Selected Issues* (IMF Staff Country Report [1999]); *Statisticheskii Yezhegodnik Armenii* (Statistical Yearbook of Armenia).

Aruba. *Statistical Yearbook; Central Bank of Aruba Bulletin* (quarterly); *Third Population and Housing Census October 6, 1991.*

Australia. *Monthly Summary of Statistics, Australia; Social Indicators* (annual); *Year Book Australia; 1996 Census of Population and Housing.*

Austria. *Grosszählung 1991* (General Census 1991). *Sozialstatistische Daten* (irreg.); *Statistisches Jahrbuch für die Republik Österreich.*

Azerbaijan. *Azerbaijan—Recent Economic Developments* (IMF Staff Country Report [2000]); *Statistical Yearbook of Azerbaijan.*

Bahamas, The. *Census of Population and Housing 1990; Statistical Abstract* (annual); *The Bahamas: Selected Issues and Statistical Appendix* (IMF Staff Country Report [2001]).

Bahrain. *Statistical Abstract* (annual); *The Population, Housing, Buildings and Establishments Census—1991.*

Bangladesh. *Bangladesh Population Census, 1991; Statistical Yearbook of Bangladesh; Bangladesh: Recent Economic Developments* (IMF Staff Country Report [2000]).

Barbados. *Barbados Economic Report* (annual); *Monthly Digest of Statistics; Barbados: Statistical Appendix* (IMF Staff Country Report [2000]).

Belarus. *Narodnoye Khozyaystvo Respubliki Belarus: Statisticheskiy Yezhegodnik* (National Economy of the Republic of Belarus: Statistical Yearbook).

Belgium. *Annuaire statistique de la Belgique; Recensement de la population et des logements au 1er mars 1991.*

Belize. *Abstract of Statistics* (annual); *Belize Economic Survey* (annual); *Belize—Statistical Appendix* (IMF Staff Country Report [2001]); *Labour Force Survey (1993); 1991 Population Census: Major Findings.*

Benin. *Annuaire statistique; Recensement général de la population et de l'habitation* (1992); *Benin—Selected Issues and Statistical Appendix* (IMF Staff Country Report [1998]).

Bermuda. *Bermuda Digest of Statistics* (annual); *Report of the Manpower Survey* (annual); *The 1991 Census of Population and Housing.*

Bhutan. *Bhutan—Statistical Annex* (IMF Staff Country Report [1999]); *Statistical Yearbook of Bhutan.*

Bolivia. *Anuario estadístico; Censo nacional de población y vivienda 1992; Compendio estadístico* (annual); *Estadísticas socio-económicas* (annual); *Resumen estadístico* (annual); *Bolivia: Statistical Annex* (IMF Staff Country Report [2001]).

Bosnia and Herzegovina. *Bosnia and Herzegovina—Selected Issues and Statistical Appendix* (IMF Staff Country Report [2000]).

Botswana. *National Development Plan 7, 1991–1997; 1991 Population and Housing Census; Botswana—Selected Issues and Statistical Appendix* (IMF Staff Country Report [1999]).

Brazil. *Anuário Estatístico do Brasil; Censo Demográfico 2000.*

Brunei. *Brunei Statistical Yearbook; Summary Tables of the Population Census 1991.*

Bulgaria. *Prebroyavaneto na naselenìeto kŭm 4.12.1985 godina* (Census of Population of Dec. 4,

1985); *Naselenie* (Population; annual); *Statisticheskii godishnik na Republika Bŭlgariya* (Statistical Yearbook of the Republic of Bulgaria).

Burkina Faso. *Annuaire Statistique; Burkina Faso—Recent Economic Developments* (IMF Staff Country Report [2000]); *Recensement général de la population du 10 au 20 decembre 1985.*

Burundi. *Annuaire statistique; Recensement général de la population, 1990; Burundi: Statistical Annex* (IMF Staff Country Report [2000]).

Cambodia. *1998 Population Census of Cambodia.*

Cameroon. *Cameroon—Statistical Appendix* (IMF Staff Country Report [2000]); *Recensement général de la population et de l'habitat 1987.*

Canada. *Canada Year Book* (biennial); *Census Canada 1996: Population.*

Cape Verde. *Boletím Anual de Estatística; Cape Verde—Recent Economic Developments* (IMF Staff Country Report [2001]); *I.º Recenseamento Geral da População e Habitação—1990.*

Central African Republic. *Annuaire statistique; Central African Republic—Statistical Annex* (IMF Staff Country Report [2000]); *Recensement général de la population 1988.*

Chad. *Annuaire statistique; Recensement general de la population et de l'habitat 1993; Chad—Recent Economic Developments* (IMF Staff Country Report [1999]).

Chile. *Chile XVI censo nacional de población y V de vivienda, 22 de abril 1992; Compendio estadístico* (annual).

China, People's Republic of. *People's Republic of China Year-Book; Statistical Yearbook of China; 10 Percent Sampling Tabulation on the 1990 Population Census of the People's Republic of China.*

Colombia. *Colombia estadística* (annual); *Censo 93 informacion de vivienda* (1985); *Colombia: Statistical Appendix* (IMF Staff Country Report [2001]).

Comoros. *Comoros—Statistical Annex* (IMF Staff Country Report [2000]); *Recensement général de la population et de l'habitat 15 septembre 1980.*

Congo, Dem. Rep. of the (Zaire). *Annuaire statistique* (irreg.); *Recensement Scientifique de la Population du 1er juillet 1984.*

Congo, Rep. of the. *Annuaire statistique; Recensement général de la population et de l'habitat de 1984.*

Costa Rica. *Anuario estadístico; Costa Rica at a Glance* (annual); *Censo de Población 1984.*

Côte d'Ivoire. *Côte d'Ivoire—Selected Issues and Statistical Appendix* (IMF Staff Country Report [2000]); *Recensement général de la population et de l'habitat 1988.*

Croatia. *Census of Population, Households, Dwellings and Farms 31st March 1991; Statistical Yearbook.*

Cuba. *Anuario estadístico; Censo de población y viviendas, 1981.*

Cyprus. *Census of Industrial Production* (annual); *Census of Population 1992; Economic Report* (annual); *Statistical Abstract* (annual).

Czech Republic. *Statistická ročenka České Republiky* (Statistical Yearbook of the Czech Republic).

Denmark. *Folke-og boligtaellingen, 1981* (Population and Housing Census); *Statistisk årbog* (Statistical Yearbook).

Djibouti. *Annuaire statistique de Djibouti; Djibouti: Statistical Annex* (IMF Staff Country Report [1999]).

Dominica. *Dominica—Statistical Annex* (IMF Staff Country Report [2000]); *Population and Housing Census 1991; Statistical Digest* (irreg.).

Dominican Republic. *Cifras Dominicanas* (irreg.); *VI Censo nacional de población y vivienda, 1981.*

Ecuador. *Serie estadística* (quinquennial); *Censo de población (V) y de vivienda (IV) 1990.*

Egypt. *Population, Housing, and Establishment Census, 1986; Statistical Yearbook.*

El Salvador. *Anuario estadístico* (irreg.); *Censos nacionales: V censo de población y IV de vivienda (1992); El Salvador en cifras* (annual); *Indicadores económicos y sociales* (annual).

Equatorial Guinea. *Censos nacionales, I de población y I de vivienda—4 al 17 de julio de 1983; Equatorial Guinea—Recent Economic Developments* (IMF Staff Country Report [1999]).

Eritrea. *Eritrea—Selected Issues* (IMF Staff Country Report [2000]).

Estonia. *Eesti Statistika Aastaraamat* (Estonia Statistical Yearbook); *Estonian Human Development Report* (annual).

Ethiopia. *1994 Population and Housing Census of Ethiopia; Ethiopia Statistical Abstract* (annual); *Ethiopia—Recent Economic Developments* (IMF Staff Country Report [1999]).

Faroe Islands. *Rigsombudsmanden på Færøerne: Beretning* (annual); *Statistical Bulletin* (annual).

Fiji. *Annual Employment Survey; Census of Industries* (annual); *Current Economic Statistics* (quarterly); *1996 Census of the Population and Housing.*

Finland. *Annual Statistics of Agriculture; Economic Survey* (annual); *Population Census 1990; Statistical Yearbook of Finland.*

France. *Annuaire statistique de la France; Données sociales* (triennial); *Recensement général de la population de 1999; Tableaux de l'Economie Française* (annual).

French Guiana. *Recensement général de la population de 1990: logements-population-emplois, 973: Guyane; Tableaux economiques regionaux: Guyane* (biennial).

French Polynesia. *Résultats du Recensement Général de la Population de la Polynésie Française, du 6 Septembre 1996; Tableaux de l'economie polynesienne* (irreg.); *Te avei'a: Bulletin d'information statistique* (monthly).

Gabon. *Situation économique, financière et sociale de la République Gabonaise* (annual); *Gabon—Statistical Annex* (IMF Staff Country Report [2000]).

Gambia, The. *Statistical Abstract* (annual?); *The Gambia—Selected Issues* (IMF Staff Country Report [2000]).

Gaza Strip. *Judaea, Samaria, and Gaza Area Statistics Quarterly; Palestinian Statistical Abstract* (annual).

Georgia. *Georgia—Recent Economic Developments and Selected Issues* (IMF Staff Country Report [2000]); *Narodnoye Khozyaystvo Gruzinskoy SSR* (National Economy of the Georgian S.S.R. [annual]).

Germany. *Statistisches Jahrbuch für die Bundesrepublik Deutschland; Volkszählung vom 25. Mai 1987* (Census of Population).

Ghana. *Ghana—Statistical Appendix* (IMF Staff Country Report [2000]); *Population Census of Ghana, 1984; Quarterly Digest of Statistics.*

Greece. *Recensement de la population et des habitations, 1991; Statistical Yearbook of Greece.*

Greenland. *Grønland* (annual); *Grønlands befolkning* (Greenland Population [annual]).

Grenada. *Abstract of Statistics* (annual); *Grenada—Statistical Appendix* (IMF Staff Country Report [2000]). *1991 Population and Housing Census.*

Guadeloupe. *Recensement général de la population de 1990: logements-population-emplois, 971: Guadeloupe; Tableaux economiques regionaux: Guadeloupe* (biennial).

Guam. *Guam Annual Economic Review; 2000 Census of Population and Housing (U.S.).*

Guatemala. *Anuario estadística; Censo nacional instituto nacional de estadística 1994: X Nacional de población y V de habitación.*

Guernsey. *Guernsey Census 1996; Statistical Digest* (annual); *Economic and Statistics Review* (annual).

Guinea. *Guinea—Statistical Appendix* (IMF Staff Country Report [2001]).

Guinea-Bissau. *Guinea-Bissau—Statistical Appendix* (IMF Staff Country Report [2001]); *Recenseamento Geral da População e da Habitação, 1994.*

Guyana. *Bank of Guyana: Annual Report and Statement of Accounts; Guyana: Recent Economic Developments* (IMF Staff Country Report [1999]); *Guyana and Belize: Country Studies* (1993).

Haiti. *Banque de la République d'Haiti: Rapport Annuel; Haiti—Statistical Annex* (IMF Staff Country Report [2001]). *Résultats préliminaires du recensement général (Septembre 1982).*

Honduras. *Anuario estadístico; Censo nacional de población y vivienda, 1988; Honduras—Statistical Appendix* (IMF Staff Country Report [2000]); *Honduras en cifras* (annual).

Hong Kong. *Annual Digest of Statistics; Hong Kong* (annual); *Hong Kong 1991 Population Census; Hong Kong Social and Economic Trends* (biennial).

Hungary. *Statisztikai évkönyv* (Statistical Yearbook); *1990, Évi népszámlálás* (Census of Population).

Iceland. *Hagtidhindi* (monthly); *Landshagir* (Statistical Yearbook of Iceland [annual]); *Utanrikisverslun* (External Trade [annual]).

India. *Census of India, 2001; Economic Survey* (annual); *India: A Reference Annual; Statistical Abstract* (annual).

Indonesia. *Indonesia: An Official Handbook* (irreg.); *Hasil Sensus penduduk Indonesia, 1990* (Census of Population); *Statistical Yearbook of Indonesia.*

Iran. *Multi-Round Population Survey 1991; National Census of Population and Housing, October 1996; Iran Statistical Yearbook; Islamic Republic of Iran: Recent Economic Developments* (IMF Staff Country Report [2000]).

Iraq. *Iraq: A Country Study* (1990); *Annual Abstract of Statistics.*

Ireland. *Census of Population of Ireland, 1996; National Income and Expenditure* (annual); *Statistical Yearbook of Ireland* (annual).

Isle of Man. *Census Report 1996; Isle of Man Digest of Economic and Social Statistics* (annual).

Israel. *1995 Census of Population and Housing; Statistical Abstract* (annual).

Italy. *Statistica agrarie; Statistiche demografiche* (4 parts); *Statistiche dell'istruzione; Annuario statistico Italiano; 13º Censimento generale della popolazione e delle Abitazioni 20 Ottobre 1991.*

Jamaica. *Economic and Social Survey* (annual); *Statistical Abstract* (annual); *Statistical Yearbook of Jamaica.*

Japan. *Japan Statistical Yearbook; Statistical Indicators on Social Life* (annual); *1995 Population Census of Japan.*

Jersey. *Report of the Census for 1996; Statistical Digest* (annual); *An Introduction to Jersey* (irreg.).

Jordan. *Population and Housing Census 1994; Jordan—Statistical Appendix* (IMF Staff Country Report [1997]); *National Accounts* (irreg.); *Statistical Yearbook.*

Kazakhstan. *Republic of Kazakhstan: Selected Issues and Statistical Appendix* (IMF Staff Country Report [2000]); *Statistical Yearbook; Statistichesky Yezhegodnik* (Statistical Yearbook).

Kenya. *Economic Survey* (annual); *Population Census 1989; Statistical Abstract* (annual); *Kenya—Selected Issues and Statistical Appendix* (IMF Staff Country Report [1998]).

Kiribati. *Annual Abstract of Statistics; Kiribati Population Census 1990; Kiribati—Statistical Appendix* (IMF Staff Country Report [1997]).

Korea, North. *North Korea: A Country Study* (1994); *The Population of North Korea* (1990).

Korea, South. *Korea Statistical Yearbook; Social Indicators in Korea* (annual); *1995 Population and Housing Census.*

Kuwait. *Annual Statistical Abstract; General Census of Population and Housing and Buildings 1995.*

Kyrgyzstan. *Kyrgyz Republic: Selected Issues and Statistical Appendix* (IMF Staff Country Report [2000]); *Statistichesky Yezhegodnik Kyrgyzstana* (Statistical Yearbook of Kyrgyzstan).

Laos. *Lao People's Democratic Republic—Recent Economic Developments* (IMF Staff Country Report [2000]).

Latvia. *Statistical Yearbook of Latvia.*

Lebanon. *Lebanon: A Country Study* (1989).

Lesotho. *Lesotho—Statistical Annex* (IMF Staff Country Report [2001]); *Statistical Yearbook; 1986 Population Census.*

Liberia. *Economic Survey* (annual); *Liberia: Selected Issues and Statistical Appendix* (IMF Staff Country Report [2000]).

Libya. *Libya Population Census, 1973.*

Liechtenstein. *Statistisches Jahrbuch; Volkszählung, 2 Dezember 1980* (Census of Population); *Liechtenstein in Figures* (annual).

Lithuania. *Lietuvos Statistikos Metraštis* (Lithuanian Statistical Yearbook).

Luxembourg. *Annuaire statistique; Bulletin du STATEC* (monthly); *Recensement général de la population du 31 mars 1991.*

Macau. *Anuário Estatístico; XIII Recenseamento Geral da População, 1991.*

Macedonia. *Former Yugoslav Republic of Macedonia—Recent Economic Developments* (IMF Staff Country Report [2000]); *Statistical Yearbook of the Republic of Macedonia.*

Madagascar. *Madagascar—Statistical Annex* (IMF Staff Country Report [2000]); *Recensement général de la population et de l'habitat, aout 1993; Situation économique* (annual).

Malawi. *1998 Population and Housing Census; Malawi Statistical Yearbook; Malawi Yearbook; Malawi: Selected Issues and Statistical Appendix* (IMF Staff Country Report [2001]).

Malaysia. *Population and Housing Census of Malaysia 1991; Yearbook of Statistics.*

Maldives. *National Development Plan 1991–1993; Population and Housing Census of Maldives 1990; Statistical Year Book of Maldives.*

Mali. *Annuaire statistique du Mali; Recensement general de la population et de l'habitat (du 1er au 14 avril 1987); Mali: Selected Issues and Statistical Annex* (IMF Staff Country Report [2000]).

Malta. *Annual Abstract of Statistics; Quarterly Digest of Statistics.*

Marshall Islands. *Marshall Islands Statistical Abstract* (annual); *Report on the State of the Islands* (U.S. Department of the Interior [annual]).

Martinique. *Recensement de la population de 1990: logements-population-emplois, 972: Martinique; Tableaux economiques regionaux: Martinique* (biennial).

Mauritania. *Annuaire Statistique; Mauritania—Recent Economic Developments* (IMF Staff Country Report [1999]).

Mauritius. *Annual Digest of Statistics; 1990 Housing and Population Census of Mauritius.*
Mayotte. *Bulletin Trimestriel* (quarterly) and *Rapport Annuel* (Institut d'Emission, France); *Recensement de la population de Mayotte: août 1997.*
Mexico. *Anuario estadístico; XII Censo general de población y vivienda, 2000; Anuario estadístico de los Estados Unidos Mexicanos.*
Micronesia. *Micronesia—Recent Economic Developments* (IMF Staff Country Report [1998]); *FSM Statistical Yearbook* (annual).
Moldova. *Republic of Moldova: Recent Economic Developments* (IMF Country Report [2001]); *Republica Moldova in Cifre* (annual).
Monaco. *Recensement general de la population 1990.*
Mongolia. *Mongolian Statistical Yearbook* (annual); *Mongolia—Statistical Annex* (IMF Staff Country Report [2000]).
Morocco. *Annuaire statistique du Maroc; Recensement général de la population et de l'habitat de 1994.*
Mozambique. *Anuário Estatístico; Republic of Mozambique—Selected Issues and Statistical Appendix* (IMF Staff Country Report [2001]); *II Recenseamento Geral da População e habitação, 1997.*
Myanmar (Burma). *Myanmar—Recent Economic Developments* (IMF Staff Country Report [2001]); *Report to the Pyithu Hluttaw on the Financial, Social, and Economic Conditions for 19**** (annual); *Statistical Abstract* (irreg.); *1983 Population Census.*
Namibia. *1991 Population and Housing Census; Statistical/Economic Review* (annual); *Namibia—Statistical Appendix* (IMF Staff Country Report [1999]).
Nauru. *Population Profile* (irreg.).
Nepal. *Economic Survey* (annual); *Population Monograph of Nepal* (1995); *The Seventh Plan (1985–90); Statistical Pocket Book* (irreg.); *Statistical Yearbook of Nepal.*
Netherlands, The. *Statistical Yearbook of the Netherlands; 14e Algemene volkstelling, 28 februari 1971* (14th General Population Census).
Netherlands Antilles. *Netherlands Antilles—Selected Issues* (IMF Staff Country Report [1999]); *Tweede Algemene Volks-en Woningtelling Nederlandse Antillen: toestand per 1 Februari 1992; Statistical Yearbook of the Netherlands Antilles.*
New Caledonia. *Annuaire statistique; Images de la population de la Nouvelle-Calédonie principaux resultats du recensement 1996; Tableaux bilan economique* (annual); *New Caledonia Facts and Figures* (annual).
New Zealand. *2001 New Zealand Census of Population and Dwellings; New Zealand Official Yearbook.*
Nicaragua. *Censos Nacionales 1995; Compendio Estadístico* (annual); *Nicaragua—Recent Economic Developments and Statistical Annex* (IMF Staff Country Report [1999]).
Niger. *Annuaire statistique; Niger—Statistical Annex* (IMF Staff Country Report [2001]); *2ème Recensement général de la population 1988.*
Nigeria. *Annual Abstract of Statistics; Nigeria: A Country Study* (1992); *Nigeria—Statistical Appendix* (IMF Staff Country Report [2001]).
Northern Mariana Islands. *CNMI Population Profile; Report on the State of the Islands* (U.S. Department of the Interior [annual]); *2000 Census of Population and Housing (U.S.).*
Norway. *Folke-og boligtelling 1990* (Population and Housing Census); *Industristatistikk* (annual); *Statistisk årbok* (Statistical Yearbook).
Oman. *General Census of Population, Housing, and Establishments* (1993); *Statistical Year Book.*
Pakistan. *Economic Survey* (annual); *Pakistan Statistical Yearbook; Population Census of Pakistan, 1981.*
Palau. *Statistical Year Book* (annual); *Census '90.*
Panama. *Indicadores económicos y sociales* (annual); *X censo nacional de poblacion y vivienda realizados el 14 de mayo del 2000; Panama en cifras* (annual); *Situación económica: Cuentas nacionales* (annual); *Situación económica: Industria* (annual).
Papua New Guinea. *Papua New Guinea: Recent Economic Developments* (IMF Staff Country Report [2000]); *Summary of Statistics* (annual); *1990 National Population Census.*
Paraguay. *Anuario estadístico del Paraguay; Censo nacional de población y viviendas, 1992.*
Peru. *Censos nacionales; IX de población: IV de vivienda, 11 de julio de 1993; Compendio estadístico* (3 vol.; annual); *Informe estadístico* (annual).
Philippines. *Philippine Statistical Yearbook; Philippine Yearbook; 2000 Census of Population and Housing.*
Poland. *Narodowy spis powszechny 1988* (Census of Population); *Rocznik statystyczny* (Statistical Yearbook).
Portugal. *Anuário Estatístico; XIV Recenseamento Geral da População: IV Recenseamento Geral da Habitação, 2001.*
Puerto Rico. *Estadísticas socioeconomicas* (annual); *Informe económico al gobernador* (Economic Report to the Governor [annual]); *2000 Census of Population and Housing* (U.S.).
Qatar. *Annual Statistical Abstract; Economic Survey of Qatar* (annual); *Qatar Year Book.*
Réunion. *Recensement général de la population de 1990: logements-population-emploi, 974; Réunion; Tableau Economique de la Réunion* (biennial).
Romania. *Anuarul statistic al României; Population and Housing Census January 7, 1992.*
Russia. *Demograficheskiy Yezhegodnik Rossii* (Demographic Yearbook of Russia; [annual]); *Rossiysky Statistichesky Yezhegodnik* (Russian Statistical Yearbook).
Rwanda. *Bulletin de Statistique: Supplement Annuel; Recensement general de la population et de l'habitat 1991; Rwanda: Statistical Appendix* (IMF Staff Country Report [2001]).
St. Kitts and Nevis. *Annual Digest of Statistics; St. Christopher and Nevis—Recent Economic Developments* (IMF Staff Country Report [2000]).
St. Lucia. *Annual Statistical Digest; St. Lucia—Statistical Annex* (IMF Staff Country Report [1999]).
St. Vincent and the Grenadines. *Digest of Statistics* (annual); *Population and Housing Census 1991.*
Samoa (Western Samoa). *Annual Statistical Abstract; Census of Population and Housing, 1981; Seventh Development Plan 1992–1994; Samoa—Statistical Appendix* (IMF Staff Country Report [1999]).
San Marino. *Bollettino di Statistica* (quarterly); *Annuario Statistico Demografico 1992–1996* (irreg.).
São Tomé and Príncipe. *1º Recenseamento Geral da População e da Habitação 1981; Sao Tome—Recent Developments and Selected Issues* (IMF Staff Country Report [1998]).
Saudi Arabia. *Saudi Arabian Monetary Agency: Annual Report* (annual).
Senegal. *Recensement de la population et de l'habitat 1988; Situation économique du Senegal* (annual); *Senegal—Statistical Appendix* (IMF Staff Country Report [1999]).
Seychelles. *Statistical Abstract* (annual); *Seychelles in Figures* (annual); *National Population and Housing Census 1994.*
Sierra Leone. *Sierra Leone—Recent Economic Developments* (IMF Staff Country Report [1997]).
Singapore. *Census of Population, 1990; Singapore Yearbook; Yearbook of Statistics Singapore.*
Slovakia. *Sčítanie Obyvateľov, Domov a Btov 2001* (Population and Housing Census 2001); *Statistical Yearbook of the Slovak Republic.*
Slovenia. *Statistični Letopis Republike Slovenija* (Statistical Yearbook of the Republic of Slovenia).
Solomon Islands. *Solomon Islands 1986 Population Census; Solomon Islands—Statistical Appendix* (IMF Staff Country Report [1998]).
Somalia. *Statistical Abstract* (annual).
South Africa. *The People of South Africa Population Census, 1996; South Africa: Official Yearbook of the Republic of South Africa; Stats in Brief* (annual).
Spain. *Anuario estadístico; Censo de población de 1991.*
Sri Lanka. *Census of Population and Housing, 1981; Sri Lanka Statistical Abstract* (irreg.); *Statistical Pocketbook of the Democratic Socialist Republic of Sri Lanka* (annual).
Sudan, The. *Sudan—Statistical Appendix* (IMF Staff Country Report [2000]); *Third Population Census, 1983.*
Suriname. *General Population Census 1980; Statistisch Jaarboek van Suriname; Suriname—Recent Economic Developments* (IMF Staff Country Report [1997]).
Swaziland. *Annual Statistical Bulletin; Report on the 1986 Swaziland Population Census; Swaziland—Selected Issues and Statistical Appendix* (IMF Staff Country Report [2000]).
Sweden. *Folk-och bostadsräkningen, 1990* (Population and Housing Census); *Statistisk årsbok för Sverige* (Statistical Abstract of Sweden [annual]).
Switzerland. *Recensement fédéral de la population, 1990; Statistisches Jahrbuch* (Statistical Yearbook).
Syria. *General Census of Housing and Inhabitants, 1981; Statistical Abstract* (annual).
Taiwan. *The Republic of China Yearbook; Social Indicators of the Republic of China* (annual); *Statistical Abstract* (annual); *Statistical Yearbook of the Republic of China; Taiwan Statistical Data Book* (annual); *1990 Census of Population and Housing.*
Tajikistan. *Republic of Tajikistan: Statistical Appendix* (IMF Staff Country Report [2001]); *Narodnoye Khozyaystvo Tadzhikskoy SSR* (National Economy of the Tadzhik S.S.R. [annual]).
Tanzania. *Tanzania—Statistical Annex* (IMF Staff Country Report [2000]); *Tanzania in Figures* (annual); *Tanzania Statistical Abstract* (irreg.); *1988 Population Census* (Prelim).
Thailand. *Report of the Industrial Survey, Whole Kingdom* (biennial); *Report of the Labor Force Survey: Whole Kingdom* (three issues annually); *Statistical Handbook of Thailand* (annual); *Statistical Yearbook; Population and Housing Census 2000.*
Togo. *Annuaire statistique du Togo; Eurostat Country Profile: Togo* (1991); *Recensement général de la population et de l'habitat 1981; Togo—Selected Issues* (IMF Staff Country Report [1999]).
Tonga. *Population Census, 1986; Sixth Development Plan 1991–95; Tonga—Statistical Appendix* (IMF Staff Country Report [2001]).
Trinidad and Tobago. *Central Bank of Trinidad and Tobago: Annual Economic Survey; 1990 Population and Housing Census.*
Tunisia. *Annuaire statistique de la Tunisie; Recensement général de la population et des logements, 30 mars 1984; Tunisia: Statistical Appendix* (IMF Staff Country Report [2001]).
Turkey. *1990 Genel Nüfus Sayımı* (1990 Census of Population); *Türkiye İstatistik Yilliği* (Statistical Yearbook of Turkey).
Turkmenistan. *Turkmenistan—Recent Economic Developments* (IMF Staff Country Report [1999]); *Turkmenistan v tsifrakh* (Turkmenistan in figures [annual]).
Tuvalu. *1992–94 Medium-Term Economic Framework Programme.*
Uganda. *Uganda National Household Survey 1999–2000.*
Ukraine. *Statistichniy Shchorichnik Ukraini za 19*** *rik* (Statistical Yearbook of Ukraine for the year 19**); *Ukraine—Recent Economic Developments* (IMF Staff Country Report [1999]).
United Arab Emirates. *Statistical Yearbook* (Abu Dhabi).
United Kingdom. *Annual Abstract of Statistics; Britain: An Official Handbook* (annual); *Census 1991; General Household Survey* series (annual).
United States. *Agricultural Statistics* (annual); *Annual Energy Review; Current Population Reports; Digest of Education Statistics* (annual); *Minerals Yearbook* (3 vol. in 6 parts); *National Transportation Statistics* (annual); *Statistical Abstract* (annual); *U.S. Exports: SIC-Based Products* (annual); *U.S. Imports: SIC-Based Products* (annual); *Vital and Health Statistics* (series 1–20); *1996 Census of Agriculture; 1992 Census of Construction Industries; 1992 Census of Manufacturing; 1992 Census of Retail Trade; 1992 Census of Service Industries; 1992 Census of Wholesale Trade; 2000 Census of Population and Housing.*
Uruguay. *Anuario estadístico; VII Censo general de poblacion III de hogares y V de viviendas, 22 de mayo de 1996; Uruguay—Recent Economic Developments* (IMF Country Report [2001]).
Uzbekistan. *Narodnoye Khozyaystvo Respubliki Uzbekistan v 19*** *g.* (National Economy of Uzbekistan in the Year 19** [annual]); *Republic of Uzbekistan; Uzbekistan—Recent Economic Developments* (IMF Staff Country Report [2000]).
Vanuatu. *National Population Census 1989; Vanuatu Statistical Yearbook.*
Venezuela. *Anuario estadístico; Censo general de la población y vivienda 1990; Encuesta de hogares por muestreo* (annual); *Encuesta industrial* (annual).
Vietnam. *Nien Giam Thong Ke* (Statistical Yearbook); *Tong Dieu Tra Dan So Viet Nam—1989 (Vietnam Population Census—1989); Vietnam—Statistical Appendix and Background Notes* (IMF Staff Country Report [2000]).
Virgin Islands of the United States. *2000 Census of Population and Housing* (U.S.).
West Bank. *Population, Housing and Establishment Census—1997; Palestinian Statistical Abstract* (annual); *West Bank and Gaza Strip; Economic Development in the Five Years Since Oslo* (IMF [irreg.]).
Western Sahara. *Recensement general de la population et de l'habitat* (1994 [Morocco]).
Yemen. *Country Presentation: Republic of Yemen* (1990); *Republic of Yemen: Selected Issues* (IMF Country Staff Report [2001]).
Yugoslavia. *Popis stanovišτva, domaćinstava, stanova i poljoprivrednih gazdinstava 1991 godine* (Census of Population, Households, Housing, and Agricultural Holdings 1991); *Statistički godišnjak Jugoslavije* (Statistical Yearbook of Yugoslavia).
Zambia. *Zambia—Statistical Appendix* (IMF Staff Country Report [1999]); *1990 Census of Population, Housing, Agriculture.*
Zimbabwe. *Population Census 1992; Statistical Yearbook* (irreg.); *Zimbabwe—Statistical Appendix* (IMF Staff Country Report [1999]).

Index

This index covers both *Britannica Book of the Year* (cumulative for 10 years) and *Britannica World Data*.

Entries in dark type are titles of major articles in the *Book of the Year;* **an accompanying year in dark type gives the year the reference appears, and the accompanying page number** in light type **shows where the article appears. References for previous years are preceded by the year in dark type. For example, "Education 02:**206; **01:**204; **00:**191; **99:**209; **98:**201; **97:**203; **96:**191; **95:**174; **94:**154; **93:**153" **indicates that the article "Education" appeared every year from 1993 through 2002. Other references that appear with a page number but without a year refer to references from the current yearbook.**

Indented entries in light type that follow dark-type article titles refer by page number to some other places in the text where the subject of the article is discussed. Light-type entries that are not indented refer by page number to subjects that are not themselves article titles. Names of people covered in biographies and obituaries from previous years are followed by the abbreviation "(biog.)" or "(obit.)" with the year in dark type and a page number in light type, e.g., Bixby, Bill (obit.) **94:**56. Biographies and obituaries for the current year appear as subentries under the main entry. In cases where a person has both a biography and an obituary, the words appear as subentries under the main entry and are alphabetized accordingly, e.g.:
Assad, Hafez, -al 424, 447, 499
  biography **92:**34
  obituary **01:**100
References to illustrations are by page number and are preceded by the abbreviation *il.*

The index uses word-by-word alphabetization (treating a word as one or more characters separated by a space from the next word). Names beginning with "Mc" and "Mac" are alphabetized as "Mac"; "St." is treated as "Saint."

A

B

D

E

F

G

H

I

J

K

L

M

N

O

P

Q

R

S

T

U

V

W

Index of Special Features in *Britannica Book of the Year,* 1993–2002

References giving only a page number in light type are for the current edition.

Special Reports and Spotlights